S0-BFB-881

Almanac of Famous People

ISSN -1040-127X

Almanac of Famous People

A comprehensive reference guide to more than 30,000 famous and infamous newsmakers from Biblical times to the present

SIXTH EDITION

Volume 1
Biographies

Frank V. Castronova
Editor

DETROIT • NEW YORK • TORONTO • LONDON

Staff

Editor: Frank V. Castronova
Contributing Editors: Paula K. Byers, Neil E. Walker
Associate Editor: Katherine H. Nemeh
Assistant Editor: Luann Brennan

Production Manager: Mary Beth Trimper
Production Assistant: Deborah Milliken

Data Entry Manager: Eleanor Allison
Data Entry Coordinator: Gwendolyn S. Tucker
Data Entry Associates: Arlene Kevonian, Nancy Sheridan

Manager, Technical Support Services: Theresa Rocklin
Senior Programmer/Analysts: Piotr Luczycki, Neil Yee

Research Manager: Victoria B. Cariappa
Research Specialists: Barbara McNeil, Michele P. LaMeau
Research Associates: Laura C. Bissey, Julia C. Daniel, Tamara C. Nott, Cheryl L. Warnock
Research Assistants: Alfred A. Gardner, Sean R. Smith, Todd Thirry

∞™ This book is printed on acid-free paper that meets the minimum requirements of American National Standard for Information Sciences—Permanence Paper for Printed Library Materials, ANSI Z39.48-1984.

645 Griswold St.
Detroit, MI 48226-4094

Library of Congress Catalog Card Number
ISBN 0-7876-0044-X (two volume set)
ISBN 0-7876-0045-8 (volume one)
ISBN 0-7876-0046-6 (volume two)
ISSN 1040-127X

Printed in the United States of America

Contents

Volume 1

Volume 2

Introduction

Almanac of Famous People is a biographical dictionary and an index to information about thousands of famous people. It provides immediate, self-contained data on people who have made news, as well as citations to other widely available biographical sources that may be useful to the reader.

Almanac of Famous People includes information on both historical and contemporary famous persons in occupations ranging from abolitionist to zoologist. Fame is broadly defined to include renown resulting from "firsts," controversy or scandal, and awards, etc.

Highlights

Up-to-Date: Most of the more than 30,000 entries in the sixth edition have been updated with some kind of additional information, whether it be a death date, new sources, revised descriptor, or any combination of these things. This edition also contains approximately 2,500 new names, many of which have become well known in the years since the publication of the fifth edition.

Easy-to-Use: Entries are sorted alphabetically by the person's best known name, with information listed in an easy-to-read arrangement. Entries provide immediate concise information to users, while directing them to more detailed information through the listing of additional biographical reference sources.

Special Indexes: Volume 2 contains two chronological indexes, one arranged by year and one by month and day; a geographic index, and an occupation index.

Wide Audience: Information about famous people in this edition will appeal to a wide audience including students, educators, librarians, and researchers. Everyone from the casual reader to the hardcore trivia buff will enjoy these entries.

FORM AND CONTENT OF ENTRIES

[1] **Crawford, Joan**
[2] [Lucille Fay LeSueur]
[3] "Billie Cassin"
[4] American. [5] Actor
[6] Won Oscar for *Mildred Pierce*, 1945; relationship with daughter subject of novel, film *Mommie Dearest*, 1978, 1981.
[7] b. Mar 23, 1908 in San Antonio, Texas
[8] d. May 13, 1977 in New York, New York
[9] Source: *BiDD; IntWW 74, 75, 76, 77; InWom, SUP; LegTOT; MGM; MovMk; OxCFilm; ThFT; TwYS; WhAm 7; WhoAm 74, 76, 78; WhoAmW 58, 61, 64, 66, 68, 70, 74, 75, 77; WhoWest 74, 76; WhoWor 74; WorAl; WorAlBi*

1. Person's name as most popularly known.
2. Pseudonym, real name, married name, or group affiliation in brackets.
3. Nickname in quotation marks.
4. Nationality (current or at time of death).
5. Occupation, career, or best known activity.
6. One-line descriptor.
7. Date and place of birth.
8. Date and place of death.
9. Alphabetically arranged codes for biographical reference sources which provide further information about the individual.

CODES AND LISTS OF TITLES INDEXED

Codes for the biographical reference sources indexed, along with complete bibliographic information on the titles of the volumes referred to by the codes, are given in the Key to Source Codes following the Introduction in Volume 1.

ACKNOWLEDGMENTS

The editors wish to thank Mr. Greg Smith of Graveline Tours, Hollywood, California, for his valuable assistance. We would also like to thank the many other *Almanac of Famous People* users who sent in information about the famous people who appear in this edition.

AVAILABLE IN ELECTRONIC FORMATS

Diskette/Magnetic Tape. The *Almanac of Famous People* is available for licensing on diskette or magnetic tape in a fielded format. Either the complete database or a custom selection of entries may be ordered. The database is available for internal data processing and nonpublishing purposes only. For more information, call 1-800-877-GALE.

Online. The *Almanac of Famous People* database is made available online as part of the Gale Biographies (GALBIO) database accessible through LEXIS-NEXIS.

SUGGESTIONS ARE WELCOME

The editors welcome comments or suggestions for candidates for future editions. We thank the readers who sent in names and corrections for this edition. Please address correspondence to: The Editor, *Almanac of Famous People*, Gale Research, 645 Griswold St., Detroit, MI 48226-4094; Fax 313-961-6741; or call 1-800-347-4253.

Key to Abbreviations

ABA	American Basketball Association
ABC	American Broadcasting Company
ABL	American Basketball League
ACDA	Arms Control and Disarmament Agency
ACLU	American Civil Liberties Union
AFB	Air Force Base
AFC	American Football Conference (of NFL)
AFL	American Federation of Labor, American Football League
AFSCME	American Federation of State, County, and Municipal Employees
AIDS	Acquired Immune Deficiency Syndrome
AIM	American Indian Movement
AK	Alaska
AL	Alabama, American League
AMA	American Medical Association
AP	Associated Press
Apr	April
AR	Arkansas
ASCAP	American Society of Composers, Authors, and Publishers
ASPCA	American Society for the Prevention of Cruelty to Animals
ASPCC	American Society for the Prevention of Cruelty to Children
Assn.	Association
Asst.	Assistant
AT&T	American Telephone and Telegraph
Aug	August
AWCTU	American Women's Christian Temperance Union
AZ	Arizona
b.	Born
BAA	Basketball Association of America
BBC	British Broadcasting Corporation
c.	Century, Circa
CA	California
CAE	Central African Empire
Caldecott	Best Children's Illustrator Award
Capt.	Captain
CBO	Congressional Budget Office
CBS	Columbia Broadcasting System
CEO	Chief Executive Officer
CFL	Canadian Football League
Chm.	Chairman
CIA	Central Intelligence Agency
CIO	Congress of Industrial Organizations
CMA	Country Music Association
CNN	Cable News Network
CO	Colorado
Co.	Company, County
Com.	Committee
Con.	Congressman, Congresswoman
CORE	Committee (or Congress) on Racial Equality
Corp.	Corporation
Coty	Fashion Critics Award
CT	Connecticut
Ctr.	Center
CUNY	City University of New York
d.	Died
DC	District of Columbia
DE	Delaware
Dec	December
Dem.	Democratic
Dept.	Department
Dist.	District
dj	disc jockey
E	East, Eastern
Edgar	Edgar Allan Poe Mystery Writers Award
ERA	Earned Run Average, Equal Rights Amendment
ESP	Extra Sensory Perception
Exec.	Executive
FAA	Federal Aviation Administration
FBI	Federal Bureau of Investigation
FCC	Federal Communications Commission
FDA	Food and Drug Administration
FDR	Franklin Delano Roosevelt
Feb	February
FIBA	International Amateur Basketball Federation
FL	Florida
fl.	flourished
Ft.	Fort
GA	Georgia
GE	General Electric
GM	General Manager, General Motors
GOP	Grand Old Party (Republican)
Govt.	Government
Gr.	Great
HBO	Home Box Office
HEW	Health, Education, and Welfare
HI	Hawaii
hrs.	Hours
Hts.	Heights
HUD	Housing and Urban Development
Hugo	Science Fiction Award
IA	Iowa
IBM	International Business Machines
ID	Idaho
IL	Illinois
ILA	International Longshoremen's Association
ILGWU	International Ladies Garment Workers Union
ILWU	International Longshoremen's and Warehousemen's Union
IN	Indiana
Inc.	Incorporated
INLA	Irish National Liberation Army
Int'l.	International
IOC	International Olympic Committee
IRA	Irish Republic Army
IRS	Internal Revenue Service
Is.	Island

ITT	International Telephone and Telegraph
IWW	Industrial Workers of the World
Jan	January
Jct.	Junction
Jr.	Junior
Jul	July
Jun	June
KC	Kansas City
KO	Knock-out
KS	Kansas
KY	Kentucky
LA	Los Angeles, Louisiana
LC	Library of Congress
LPGA	Ladies Professional Golf Association
Lt.	Lieutenant
Ltd.	Limited
MA	Massachusetts
Mag	Magazine
Mar	March
MCA	Music Corporation of America
MCI	Microwave Communications Inc.
MD	Maryland
ME	Maine
MGM	Metro-Goldwyn-Mayer
Mgr.	Manager
MI	Michigan
min(s).	minute(s)
MIT	Massachusetts Institute of Technology
ML	Major League(s)
MN	Minnesota
MO	Missouri
mo(s).	Month(s)
MP	Member of Parliament, Military Police
mph	miles per hour
MS	Mississippi
MT	Montana
Mt.	Mount, Mountain
Mvmt.	Movement
MVP	Most Valuable Player
N	North, Northern
NAACP	National Association for the Advancement of Colored People
NASL	North American Soccer League
NASA	National Aeronautics and Space Administration
NASCAR	National Association for Stock Car Auto Racing
Nat.	National
NATO	North Atlantic Treaty Organization
NBA	National Basketball Association
NBC	National Broadcasting Company
NC	North Carolina
NCAA	National Collegiate Athletic Association
ND	North Dakota
NE	Nebraska
Newbery	Best Children's Literature Award
NFC	National Football Conference (of NFL)
NFL	National Football League
NH	New Hampshire
NHL	National Hockey League
NJ	New Jersey
NL	National League
NM	New Mexico
Nov	November
NOW	National Organization for Women
NPR	National Public Radio
NRA	National Recovery Administration
NV	Nevada
NY	New York
NYC	New York City
NY Met	New York Metropolitan Opera Company
OAS	Organization of American States
Obie	Off-Broadway Theater Award
Oct	October
OH	Ohio
OK	Oklahoma
OMB	Office of Management and Budget
OR	Oregon
p.	Page
PA	Pennsylvania
Pac	Pacific
PATCO	Professional Air Traffic Controllers Organization
PBA	Professional Bowlers Association
PBS	Public Broadcasting Service
PGA	Professional Golfers Association
PLO	Palestine Liberation Organization
POW	Prisoner of War
PR	Puerto Rico
Pres.	President
Prov.	Province
Pt.	Point, Port
Pte.	Pointe
RBI	Runs Batted In
RCA	Radio Corporation of America
Rep.	Republican, Representative
Repub.	Republic
Rev.	Reverend
RI	Rhode Island
RIF	Reading is Fundamental
Rpds.	Rapids
S	South, Southern
SALT	Strategic Arms Limitation Talks
SC	South Carolina
SCLC	Southern Christian Leadership Conference
SD	South Dakota
sec(s).	second(s)
Sep	September
SI	Sports Illustrated
SLA	Symbionese Liberation Army
SNCC	Student Nonviolent Coordinating Committee
Spingarn	NAACP Award
Sprgs.	Springs
Sq.	Square
Sr.	Senior
St.	Saint, Sainte
Sum.	Summit
SUNY	State University of New York
TB	Tuberculosis
TD	Touchdown
Terr.	Territory
TM	Transcendental Meditation

TN	Tennessee
Tony	Antoinette Perry Broadway Award
tr.	Translated
TV	Television
TWA	Trans World Airlines
Twp.	Township
TX	Texas
U	University
UAW	United Auto Workers
UFO	Unidentified Flying Object
UMW	United Mine Workers
UN	United Nations
UNESCO	United Nations Educational, Scientific, and Cultural Organization
UNICEF	United Nations Children's Fund
UPI	United Press International
US	United States
USC	University of Southern California
USCGA	United States Coast Guard Academy
USFL	United States Football League
USIA	United States Information Agency
USMC	United States Marine Corps
USSR	Union of Soviet Socialist Republics
UT	Utah
VA	Virginia, Veteran's Administration
Vil.	Village
Vol(s).	Volume, Volumes
vp	Vice President
VT	Vermont
W	West, Western
WA	Washington
WASP	White Anglo-Saxon Protestant
WBA	World Boxing Association
WBC	World Boxing Council
WHA	World Hockey Association
WCTU	Women's Christian Temperance Union
WFL	World Football League
WI	Wisconsin
WPBA	Women's Professional Bowlers Association
WV	West Virginia
WW	World War
WY	Wyoming
yds.	Yards
YMCA	Young Men's Christian Association
YWCA	Young Women's Christian Association
yr(s).	Year(s)

Source Codes

Code	*Book Indexed*
ABCMeAm	*The ABC-CLIO Companion to the Media in America.* By Daniel Webster Hollis, III. Santa Barbara, CA: ABC-CLIO, 1995.
AdMenW	*The Ad Men and Women.* A biographical dictionary of advertising. Edited by Edd Applegate. Westport, CT: Greenwood Press, 1994.
AfrA	*African Authors.* A Companion to Black African Writing. Volume I: 1300-1973. By Donald E. Herdeck. Washington, DC: Black Orpheus Press, 1973.
AfrAmAl 6	*The African-American Almanac.* Sixth edition. Detroit: Gale Research, 1994. Formerly published as *The Negro Almanac.* Use the Index to locate biographies.
AfrAmBi	*African American Biographies.* Profiles of ... current men and women. By Walter L. Hawkins. Jefferson, NC: McFarland & Co., 1992-1994. ***AfrAmBi 1*** First edition; 1992. ***AfrAmBi 2*** First edition supplement; 1994.
AfrAmG	*African American Generals and Flag Officers.* Biographies of over 120 blacks in the United States military. By Walter L. Hawkins. Jefferson, NC: McFarland & Co., 1993.
AfrAmOr	*African-American Orators.* A bio-critical sourcebook. Edited by Richard W. Leeman. Westport, CT: Greenwood Press, 1996.
AfrAmPr	*African American History in the Press, 1851-1899.* From the coming of the Civil War to the rise of Jim Crow as reported and illustrated in selected newspapers of the time. Two volumes. Detroit: Gale Research, 1996. Use the Keyword Index to locate biographies.
AfrAmSG	*African-American Sports Greats.* A biographical dictionary. Edited by David L. Porter. Westport, CT: Greenwood Press, 1995.
AfrAmW	*African American Writers.* Edited by Valerie Smith, Lea Baechler, and A. Walton Litz. New York: Charles Scribner's Sons, 1991.

AfroAA *Afro-American Artists.* A bio-bibliographical directory. Compiled and edited by Theresa Dickason Cederholm. Boston: Trustees of the Boston Public Library, 1973.

AfSS *Africa South of the Sahara.* London: Europa Publications, 1978-1982.

AfSS 78 Eighth edition, 1978-1979; 1978.
AfSS 79 Ninth edition, 1979-1980; 1979.
AfSS 80 10th edition, 1980-1981; 1980.
AfSS 81 11th edition, 1981-1982; 1981.
AfSS 82 12th edition, 1982-1983; 1982.

Biographies are located in the ''Who's Who in Africa South of the Sahara'' section.

AgeMat *The Age of Maturity, 1929-1941.* Concise Dictionary of American Literary Biography Series. Detroit: Gale Research, 1989.

ALA *The ALA Yearbook.* A review of library events 1979. Volume 5, 1980. Chicago: American Library Association, 1980.

ALA 80 Biographies begin on page 73.
ALA 80N Obituary section begins on page 227.

Alli *Allibone's Critical Dictionary of English Literature.* British and American authors living and deceased from the earliest accounts to the latter half of the Nineteenth Century. Three volumes. By S. Austin Allibone. Philadelphia: J.B. Lippincott & Co., 1858-1871. Reprint. Detroit: Gale Research, 1965.

Alli SUP *Allibone's Critical Dictionary of English Literature: A Supplement.* British and American authors. Two volumes. By John Foster Kirk. Philadelphia: J.B. Lippincott & Co., 1891. Reprint. Detroit: Gale Research, 1965.

AllMusG *All Music Guide to Jazz.* The experts' guide to the best jazz recordings. Edited by Michael Erlewine. San Francisco, CA: Miller Freeman Books, 1996.

AlmAP *The Almanac of American Politics.* The senators, the representatives, the governors--their records, states, and districts. By Michael Barone, Grant Ujifusa, and Douglas Matthews. New York: E.P. Dutton, 1977-1979.

AlmAP 78 1978 edition; 1977.
AlmAP 80 1980 edition; 1979.

Use the ''Names Index'' to locate biographies.

AlmAP 82 *The Almanac of American Politics.* The president, the senators, the representatives, the governors: their records and election results, their states and districts. 1982 edition. By Michael Barone and Grant Ujifusa. Washington, DC: Barone & Co., 1981.

Use the ''Index of Persons'' to locate biographies.

AlmAP *The Almanac of American Politics.* The senators, the representatives and the governors: their records and election results, their states and districts. By Michael Barone and Grant Ujifusa. Washington, DC: National Journal, 1983-1995.

AlmAP 84 1984 edition; 1983. Use the ''Index of People'' to locate biographies.

AlmAP 88 1988 edition; 1987. Use the "Index of People" to locate biographies.
AlmAP 92 1992 edition; 1991. Use the index to locate biographies.
AlmAP 96 1996 edition; 1995. Use the Index to locate biographies.

AmArch 70 *American Architects Directory.* Third edition. Edited by John F. Gane. New York: R.R. Bowker Co., 1970.

AmArt *American Artists.* An illustrated survey of leading contemporary Americans. Edited by Les Krantz. New York: Facts on File Publications, 1985.

AmAu *American Authors, 1600-1900.* A biographical dictionary of American literature. Edited by Stanley J. Kunitz and Howard Haycraft. Wilson Authors Series. New York: H.W. Wilson Co., 1938.

AmAu&B *American Authors and Books.* 1640 to the present day. Third revised edition. By W.J. Burke and Will D. Howe. Revised by Irving Weiss and Anne Weiss. New York: Crown Publishers, 1972.

AmBench 79 *The American Bench.* Judges of the Nation. Second edition. Edited by Mary Reincke and Nancy Lichterman. Minneapolis: Reginald Bishop Forster & Associates, 1979.
Use the "Name Index" to locate biographies.

AmBi *American Biographies.* By Wheeler Preston. New York: Harper & Brothers Publishers, 1940. Reprint. Detroit: Gale Research, 1974.

AmCath 80 *The American Catholic Who's Who.* Volume 23, 1980-1981. Edited by Joy Anderson. Washington, DC: National Catholic News Service, 1979.

AmComp *American Composers.* A biographical dictionary. By David Ewen. New York: G.P. Putnam's Sons, 1982.

AmCulL *American Cultural Leaders.* From colonial times to the present. By Justin Harmon et al. Santa Barbara, CA: ABC-Clio, 1993.

AmDec *American Decades.* Detroit: Gale Research, 1996.
AmDec 1900 1900-1909. Edited by Vincent Tompkins; 1996.
AmDec 1910 1910-1919. Edited by Vincent Tompkins; 1996.
AmDec 1920 1920-1929. Edited by Judith S. Baughman; 1996.
AmDec 1930 1930-1939. Edited by Victor Bondi; 1995.
AmDec 1940 1940-1949. Edited by Victor Bondi; 1995.
AmDec 1950 1950-1959. Edited by Richard Layman; 1994.
AmDec 1960 1960-1969. Edited by Richard Layman; 1995.
AmDec 1970 1970-1979. Edited by Victor Bondi; 1995.
AmDec 1980 1980-1989. Edited by Victor Bondi; 1996.
Biographies found in "Headline Makers" section of each chapter; use the Index to locate.

AmEA 74 *American Economic Association, Directory of Members, 1974.* Edited by Rendigs Fels. Published as Volume 64, Number 5 (October, 1974) of *The American Economic Review.*

AmEnS *The American Encyclopedia of Soccer.* Edited by Zandler Hollander. New York: Everest House Publishers, 1980.

AmFD *American Film Directors.* Edited by Stanley Hochman. A Library of Film Criticism. New York: Frederick Ungar Publishing Co., 1974.

AmFkP *American Folk Painters of Three Centuries.* Edited by Jean Lipman and Tom Armstrong. New York: Hudson Hills Press, 1980. Distributed by Simon & Schuster, New York. Published in association with the Whitney Museum of American Art.

Use the Index to locate biographies.

AmGrD *American Graphic Designers.* Thirty years of design imagery. By RitaSue Siegel. New York: McGraw-Hill Book Co., 1984.

Use the Table of Contents to locate listings.

AmJust *American Justice.* Two volumes. Edited by Joseph M. Bessette. Pasadena, CA: Salem Press, 1996.

AmLegL *American Legislative Leaders, 1850-1910.* Edited by Charles F. Ritter and Jon L. Wakelyn. New York: Greenwood Press, 1989.

AmLY *The American Literary Yearbook.* A biographical and bibliographical dictionary of living North American authors. Volume 1, 1919. Edited by Hamilton Traub. Henning, MN: Paul Traub, 1919. Reprint. Detroit: Gale Research, 1968.

AmLY ''Biographical and Bibliographical Dictionary of Living North American Authors'' section begins on page 57.
AmLY X ''Pen-names and Pseudonyms'' section begins on page 49.
AmLY XR ''Pen-names and Pseudonyms'' section begins on page 49.

AmMWSc *American Men & Women of Science.* A biographical directory of today's leaders in physical, biological and related sciences. New Providence, NJ: R.R. Bowker Co., 1971-1992.

AmMWSc 73P 12th edition, Physical & Biological Sciences. Seven volumes; 1971.
AmMWSc 73S 12th edition, Social & Behavioral Sciences. Two volumes; 1973.
AmMWSc 76P 13th edition, Physical & Biological Sciences. Seven volumes; 1976.
AmMWSc 78S 13th edition, Social & Behavioral Sciences. One volume; 1978.
AmMWSc 79 14th edition. Eight volumes; 1979.
AmMWSc 82 15th edition. Seven volumes; 1982.
AmMWSc 86 16th edition. Eight volumes; 1986.
AmMWSc 89 17th edition. Eight volumes; 1989.
AmMWSc 92 18th edition, 1992-1993. Eight volumes; 1992.

AmMWSc 95 *American Men & Women of Science™ [Bowker®].* A biographical directory of today's leaders in physical, biological and related sciences. 19th edition. Eight volumes. New Providence, NJ: R.R. Bowker Co., 1994.

AmNov *American Novelists of Today.* By Harry R. Warfel. New York: American Book Co., 1951. Reprint. Westport, Conn.: Greenwood Press, 1976.

AmNov X ''Index of Married Names and Pseudonyms'' begins on page 477.

AmOrN *American Orators before 1900.* Critical studies and sources. Edited by Bernard K. Duffy & Halford R. Ryan. New York: Greenwood Press, 1987.

AmOrTwC *American Orators of the Twentieth Century.* Critical studies and sources. Edited by Bernard K. Duffy & Halford R. Ryan. New York: Greenwood Press, 1987.

AmPB *American Picturebooks from Noah's Ark to The Beast Within.* By Barbara Bader. New York: Macmillan Publishing Co.; London: Collier Macmillan Publishers, 1976.

AmPeW *American Peace Writers, Editors, and Periodicals.* A dictionary. By Nancy L. Roberts. New York: Greenwood Press, 1991.

AmPolLe *American Political Leaders.* From colonial times to the present. By Steven G. O'Brien. Santa Barbara, CA: ABC-Clio, 1991.

AmPolW 80 *American Political Women.* Contemporary and historical profiles. By Esther Stineman. Littleton, CO: Libraries Unlimited, 1980.

AmPolW 80A Appendix I: ''Women of the Congress 1917-1980'' begins on page 191.

AmPolW 80B Appendix II: ''Women Ambassadors of the United States Currently Serving'' begins on page 198.

AmPolW 80C Appendix III: ''Women Chiefs of Mission 1933-1980'' begins on page 199.

AmPolW 80D Appendix IV: ''Women Currently Serving as Federal Judges'' begins on page 202.

AmPolW 80E Appendix V: ''Women Currently Serving in Government in Key Departmental, Agency, and White House Positions'' begins on page 204.

AmPS *American Popular Songs.* From the Revolutionary War to the present. Edited by David Ewen. New York: Random House, 1966.

AmPS A The ''All-Time Best-Selling Popular Recordings'' section begins on page 485.

AmPS B The ''Some American Performers of the Past and Present'' section begins on page 499.

AmRef *American Reformers.* Edited by Alden Whitman. New York: H.W. Wilson Co., 1985.

AmRef&R *American Reform and Reformers.* A biographical dictionary. Edited by Randall M. Miller and Paul A. Cimbala. Westport, CT: Greenwood Press, 1996.

AmRev *The American Revolution, 1775-1783.* An encyclopedia. Two volumes. Edited by Richard L. Blanco. New York: Garland Publishing, 1993.

AmSocL — *American Social Leaders.* By William McGuire and Leslie Wheeler. Santa Barbara, CA: ABC-Clio, 1993.

AmSong — *American Songwriters.* By David Ewen. New York: H.W. Wilson Co., 1987.

AmWom — *American Women.* A revised edition of *Woman of the Century,* 1,500 biographies with over 1,400 portraits; a comprehensive encyclopedia of the lives and achievements of American women during the nineteenth century. Two volumes. Edited by Frances E. Willard and Mary A. Livermore. New York: Mast, Crowell & Kirkpatrick, 1897. Reprint. Detroit: Gale Research, 1973.

AmWomD — *American Women Dramatists of the Twentieth Century.* A bibliography. By Brenda Coven. Metuchen, NJ: Scarecrow Press, 1982.

AmWomHi — *American Women Historians, 1700s-1990s.* A biographical dictionary. By Jennifer Scanlon and Shaaron Cosner. Westport, CT: Greenwood Press, 1996.

AmWomM — *American Women Managers and Administrators.* A selective biographical dictionary of twentieth-century leaders in business, education, and government. By Judith A. Leavitt. Westport, CT: Greenwood Press, 1985.

AmWomPl — *American Women Playwrights, 1900-1930.* A checklist. Compiled by Frances Diodato Bzowski. Bibliographies and Indexes in Women's Studies, no. 15. Westport, CT: Greenwood Press, 1992.

AmWomSc — *American Women in Science.* A biographical dictionary. By Martha J. Bailey. Denver: ABC-CLIO, 1994.

AmWomWr — *American Women Writers.* A critical reference guide from colonial times to the present. Four volumes. Edited by Lina Mainiero. New York: Frederick Ungar Publishing Co., 1979-1982.

AmWomWr 92 — *American Women Writers.* Diverse voices in prose since 1945. Edited by Eileen Barrett and Mary Cullinan. New York: St. Martin's Press, 1992.
Use the Table of Contents to locate biographies.

AmWomWr SUP — *American Women Writers.* A critical reference guide from colonial times to the present. Volume 5: Supplement. Edited by Carol Hurd Green and Mary Grimley Mason. New York: Continuum Publishing Co., 1994.

AmWr — *American Writers.* A collection of literary biographies. New York: Charles Scribner's Sons, 1974-1991.

- ***AmWr*** — Four volumes. Edited by Leonard Unger; 1974.
- ***AmWr S1*** — Supplement I. Two parts. Edited by Leonard Unger; 1979.
- ***AmWr S2*** — Supplement II. Two parts. Edited by A. Walton Litz; 1981.

AmWr S3 Supplement III. Two parts. Edited by Lea Baechler and A. Walton Litz; 1991.

AmWrBE *American Writers before 1800.* A biographical and critical dictionary. Three volumes. Edited by James A. Levernier and Douglas R. Wilmes. Westport, CT: Greenwood Press, 1983.

AnCL *Anthology of Children's Literature.* Fourth edition. Edited by Edna Johnson, Evelyn R. Sickels, and Frances Clarke Sayers. Boston: Houghton Mifflin Co., 1970.
Biographies begin on page 1217.

AncWr *Ancient Writers: Greece and Rome.* Two volumes. Edited by T. James Luce. New York: Charles Scribner's Sons, 1982.

AnMV 1926 *Anthology of Magazine Verse for 1926 and Yearbook of American Poetry.* Edited by William Stanley Braithwaite. New York: G. Sully, 1926. Reprint. Granger Index Reprint Series. Freeport, N.Y.: Books for Libraries Press, 1972.
The ''Biographical Dictionary of Poets in the United States'' section begins on page 3 of part 4.

AnObit *The Annual Obituary.* New York: St. Martin's Press, 1981-1983.
AnObit 1980 *1980.*; 1981.
AnObit 1981 *1981.*; 1982.
AnObit 1982 *1982.*; 1983.
Use the ''Alphabetical Index of Entrants'' to locate biographies.

AnObit *The Annual Obituary.* Detroit: St. James Press, 1984-1994.
AnObit 1983 *1983.*; 1984.
AnObit 1984 *1984.*; 1985.
AnObit 1985 *1985.*; 1988.
AnObit 1986 *1986.*; 1989.
AnObit 1987 *1987.*; 1990.
AnObit 1988 *1988.*; 1990.
AnObit 1989 *1989.*; 1990.
AnObit 1990 *1990.*; 1991.
AnObit 1991 *1991.*; 1992.
AnObit 1992 *1992.*; 1993.
AnObit 1993 *1993.*; 1994.
Use the ''Alphabetical Index of Entrants'' to locate biographies.

AntBDN *The Antique Buyer's Dictionary of Names.* By A.W. Coysh. Newton Abbot, England: David & Charles, 1970.
AntBDN A ''Art Nouveau'' section begins on page 13.
AntBDN B ''Book Illustrations and Prints'' section begins on page 23.
AntBDN C ''Bronzes'' section begins on page 48.
AntBDN D ''Clocks and Barometers'' section begins on page 59.
AntBDN E ''Fashion Plates'' section begins on page 81.
AntBDN F ''Firearms'' section begins on page 86.
AntBDN G ''Furniture'' section begins on page 98.
AntBDN H ''Glass'' section begins on page 123.
AntBDN I ''Maps, Charts, and Globes'' section begins on page 137.
AntBDN J ''Miniatures'' section begins on page 148.

AntBDN K	''Musical Instruments'' section begins on page 170.
AntBDN L	''Netsuke'' section begins on page 179.
AntBDN M	''Pottery and Porcelain'' section begins on page 185.
AntBDN N	''Sheffield Plate'' section begins on page 224.
AntBDN O	''Silhouettes or Profiles'' section begins on page 231.
AntBDN P	''Silk Pictures, Portraits, and Bookmarks'' section begins on page 243.
AntBDN Q	''Silver'' section begins on page 250.

ApCAB *Appleton's Cyclopaedia of American Biography.* New York: D. Appleton & Co., 1888-1901.Reprint. Detroit: Gale Research, 1968.

ApCAB	Six volumes. Edited by James Grant Wilson and John Fiske; 1888.
ApCAB SUP	Volume VII, Supplement. Edited by James Grant Wilson; 1901.

ApCAB X *Appleton's Cyclopaedia of American Biography.* A supplement. Six volumes. Edited by L.E. Dearborn. New York: Press Association Compilers, 1918-1931. Originally published as *The Cyclopaedia of American Biography, Supplementary Edition.*

ArizL *Arizona in Literature.* A collection of the best writings of Arizona authors from early Spanish days to the present time. By Mary G. Boyer. Glendale, CA: Arthur H. Clark Co., 1935. Reprint. Ann Arbor, Mich.: Gryphon Books, 1971.
Use the Index to locate biographies.

ArtclWW 2 *Articles on Women Writers.* Volume 2, 1976-1984: A bibliography. By Narda Lacey Schwartz. Santa Barbara, CA: ABC-Clio, 1986.

ArtCS *The Art of the Comic Strip.* By Judith O'Sullivan. College Park, MD: University of Maryland, Department of Art, 1971.
Biographies begin on page 60.

ArtLatA *Art in Latin America.* The modern era, 1820-1980. By Dawn Ades. New Haven, CT: Yale University Press, 1989.
Biographies begin on page 338.

ArtsAmW *Artists of the American West.* A biographical dictionary. By Doris Ostrander Dawdy. Chicago: Sage Books/Swallow Press, 1974-1981.

ArtsAmW 1	Volume I; 1974.
ArtsAmW 2	Volume II; 1981.

ArtsAmW 3 *Artists of the American West.* A biographical dictionary. Volume III, *Artists Born before 1900.* By Doris Ostrander Dawdy. Athens, OH: Swallow Press/Ohio University Press, 1985.

ArtsCL *Artists of a Certain Line.* A selection of illustrations for children's books. By John Ryder. London: The Bodley Head, 1960.

ArtsEM *Artists of Early Michigan.* A biographical dictionary of artists native to or active in Michigan, 1701-1900. Compiled by Arthur Hopkin Gibson. Detroit: Wayne State University Press, 1975.

ArtsNiC *Artists of the Nineteenth Century and Their Works.* A handbook containing two thousand and fifty biographical sketches. Revised edition. Two volumes. By Clara Erskine Clement and Laurence Hutton. Boston: J.R. Osgood & Co., 1885. Reprint. Two volumes in one. St. Louis: North Point, 1969.

AsAmAlm *The Asian American Almanac.* A reference work on Asians in the United States. Detroit: Gale Research, 1995.
Use the Index to locate biographies.

AsBiEn *Asimov's Biographical Encyclopedia of Science and Technology.* The lives and achievements of 1,195 great scientists from ancient times to the present, chronologically arranged. New revised edition. By Isaac Asimov. New York: Avon, 1976.
Use the "Alphabetic List of Biographical Entries" to locate biographies.

ASCAP 66 *The ASCAP Biographical Dictionary.* Third edition. New York: American Society of Composers, Authors and Publishers, 1966.

ASCAP 80 *ASCAP Biographical Dictionary.* Fourth edition. Compiled for the American Society of Composers, Authors and Publishers by Jaques Cattell Press. New York: R.R. Bowker Co., 1980.

AsERC 80 *Association of Executive Recruiting Consultants, 1980 Directory.* New York: R.R. Bowker Co., 1980.

AstEnc *The Astrology Encyclopedia.* By James R. Lewis. Detroit: Gale Research, 1994.
Use the Index at the back of the book to locate entries.

AtlBL *Atlantic Brief Lives.* A biographical companion to the arts. Edited by Louis Kronenberger. Boston: Little, Brown & Co., 1971.

Au&Arts *Authors & Artists for Young Adults.* Detroit: Gale Research, 1989-1997.

Au&Arts 1 Volume 1; 1989.
Au&Arts 2 Volume 2; 1989.
Au&Arts 3 Volume 3; 1990.
Au&Arts 4 Volume 4; 1990.
Au&Arts 5 Volume 5; 1990.
Au&Arts 6 Volume 6; 1991.
Au&Arts 7 Volume 7; 1991.
Au&Arts 8 Volume 8; 1992.
Au&Arts 9 Volume 9; 1992.
Au&Arts 10 Volume 10; 1993.
Au&Arts 11 Volume 11; 1993.
Au&Arts 12 Volume 12; 1994.
Au&Arts 13 Volume 13; 1994.
Au&Arts 14 Volume 14; 1995.
Au&Arts 15 Volume 15; 1995.
Au&Arts 16 Volume 16; 1995.
Au&Arts 17 Volume 17; 1995.
Au&Arts 18 Volume 18; 1996.
Au&Arts 19 Volume 19; 1997.

Au&ICB *Authors and Illustrators of Children's Books.* Writings on their lives and works. By Miriam Hoffman and Eva Samuels. New York: R.R. Bowker Co., 1972.

Au&Wr 71 *The Author's and Writer's Who's Who.* Sixth edition. Darien, CT: Hafner Publishing Co., 1971.

AuBYP *Authors of Books for Young People.* By Martha E. Ward et al. Metuchen, NJ: Scarecrow Press, 1971-1990.

- ***AuBYP 2*** Second edition; 1971.
- ***AuBYP 2S*** Supplement to the second edition; 1979.
- ***AuBYP 2SA*** Supplement to the second edition; 1979. Addendum to the Supplement begins on page 301.
- ***AuBYP 3*** Third edition; 1990.

AuLitCr *Australian Literary Criticism: 1945-1988.* An annotated bibliography. By Robert L. Ross. Garland Reference Library of the Humanities, vol. 1075. New York: Garland Publishing, 1989.

Biographies are located in the ''Major Writers'' section, which begins on page 155.

AuNews *Authors in the News.* A compilation of news stories and feature articles from American newspapers and magazines covering writers and other members of the communications media. Edited by Barbara Nykoruk. Detroit: Gale Research, 1976.

- ***AuNews 1*** Volume 1.
- ***AuNews 2*** Volume 2.

AuSpks *The Author Speaks.* Selected ''PW'' interviews, 1967-1976. By *Publishers Weekly* editors and contributors. New York: R.R. Bowker Co., 1977.

AutoN 79 *Automotive News.* 1979 Market Data Book Issue, April 25, 1979.

The ''Who's Who in the Auto Industry'' section begins on page 130.

AuWomWr *Australian Women Writers.* A bibliographic guide. By Debra Adelaide. London: Pandora, 1988.

Baker 78 *Baker's Biographical Dictionary of Musicians.* Sixth edition. Revised by Nicolas Slonimsky. New York: Schirmer Books; London: Collier Macmillan Publishers, 1978.

Baker 84 *Baker's Biographical Dictionary of Musicians.* Seventh edition. Revised by Nicolas Slonimsky. New York: Macmillan, Schirmer Books, 1984.

Baker 92 *Baker's Biographical Dictionary of Musicians.* Eighth edition. Revised by Nicolas Slonimsky. New York: Macmillan, 1992.

Ballpl 90 *The Ballplayers.* Baseball's ultimate biographical reference. Edited by Mike Shatzkin. New York: William Morrow and Co., 1990.

BasBi *Basketball Biographies.* 434 U.S. players, coaches and contributors to the game, 1891-1990. By Martin Taragano. Jefferson, NC: McFarland & Co., 1991.

BaseEn 88 *The Baseball Encyclopedia.* The Complete and Official Record of Major League Baseball. Edited by Joseph L. Reichler. New York: Macmillan, 1988.

BaseReg *Official Baseball Register.* Edited by Barry Siegel. St. Louis: The Sporting News, 1985-1988.

BaseReg 85 1985 edition; 1985.
BaseReg 86 1986 edition; 1986.
BaseReg 87 1987 edition; 1987.
BaseReg 88 1988 edition; 1988.

BbD *The Bibliophile Dictionary.* A biographical record of the great authors, with bibliographical notices of their principal works from the beginning of history. Originally published as Volumes 29 and 30 of *The Bibliophile Library of Literature, Art, and Rare Manuscripts.* Compiled and arranged by Nathan Haskell Dole, Forrest Morgan, and Caroline Ticknor. New York: International Bibliophile Society, 1904. Reprint. Detroit: Gale Research, 1966.

BbtC *Bibliotheca Canadensis.* Or, A manual of Canadian literature. By Henry J. Morgan. Ottawa: G.E. Desbarats, 1867. Reprint. Detroit: Gale Research, 1968.

Benet 87 *Benet's Reader's Encyclopedia.* Third edition. New York: Harper & Row, 1987.

Benet 96 *Benet's Reader's Encyclopedia.* Fourth edition. Edited by Bruce Murphy. New York, NY: HarperCollins Publishers, 1996.

BenetAL 91 *Benet's Reader's Encyclopedia of American Literature.* First edition. Edited by George Perkins, Barbara Perkins, and Phillip Leininger. New York: HarperCollins Publishers, 1991.

BestMus *The Best Musicals.* From *Show Boat* to *A Chorus Line*. Revised edition. By Arthur Jackson. New York: Crown Publishers, 1979.

Biographies are found in the "Who's Who of Show and Film Music" section beginning on page 135.

BestSel *Bestsellers.* Books and authors in the news. Detroit: Gale Research, 1989-1991.

BestSel 89-1 89, Issue 1; 1989.
BestSel 89-2 89, Issue 2; 1989.
BestSel 89-3 89, Issue 3; 1989.
BestSel 89-4 89, Issue 4; 1990.
BestSel 90-1 90, Issue 1; 1990.
BestSel 90-2 90, Issue 2; 1990.
BestSel 90-3 90, Issue 3; 1991.
BestSel 90-4 90, Issue 4; 1991.

BgBands 74 *The Big Bands.* Revised edition. By George T. Simon. New York: Macmillan Publishing Co., Collier Books, 1974.

Use the Index to locate biographies.

BgBkCoM *The Big Book of Country Music.* A Biographical Encyclopedia. By Richard Carlin. New York: Penguin Books, 1995.

BiAUS *Biographical Annals of the Civil Government of the United States.* During its first century; from original and official sources. By Charles Lanman. Washington, DC: James Anglim, 1876. Reprint. Detroit: Gale Research, 1976.
- ***BiAUS SUP*** ''Additional Facts'' section begins on page 633.

BiB N *Biographia Britannica Literaria: Anglo-Norman Period.* Biography of literary characters of Great Britain and Ireland, arranged in chronological order. By Thomas Wright. London: John W. Parker, 1846. Reprint. Detroit: Gale Research, 1968.
Use the Index to locate biographies.

BiB S *Biographia Britannica Literaria: Anglo-Saxon Period.* Biography of literary characters of Great Britain and Ireland, arranged in chronological order. By Thomas Wright. London: John W. Parker, 1842. Reprint. Detroit: Gale Research, 1968.
Use the Index to locate biographies.

BibAL *Bibliography of American Literature.* New Haven, CT: Yale University Press, 1955-1990.
- ***BibAL*** Volumes 1-7. Compiled by Jacob Blanck; 1955.
- ***BibAL 8*** Volume 8. Compiled by Jacob Blanck; edited and completed by Michael Winship; 1990.

BiCAW *The Biographical Cyclopaedia of American Women.* Two volumes. Detroit: Gale Research, 1974. Originally published in two volumes. Volume I: Compiled under the supervision of Mabel Ward Cameron, published by Halvord Publishing Co., 1924; Volume II: Compiled under the supervision of Erma Conkling Lee, published by Franklin W
Use the Index in each volume to locate biographies.

BiDAfM *Biographical Dictionary of Afro-American and African Musicians.* By Eileen Southern. Westport, CT: Greenwood Press, 1982.

BiDAmAr *Biographical Dictionary of American Architects, Deceased.* By Henry F. Withey and Elsie Rathburn Withey. Los Angeles: New Age Publishing Co., 1956.

BiDAmBL 83 *Biographical Dictionary of American Business Leaders.* By John N. Ingham. Westport, CT: Greenwood Press, 1983.
Use the Index to locate biographies.

BiDAmCu *Biographical Dictionary of American Cult and Sect Leaders.* By J. Gordon Melton. Garland Reference Library of Social Science, vol. 212. New York: Garland Publishing, 1986.

BiDAmEd *Biographical Dictionary of American Educators.* Three volumes. Edited by John F. Ohles. Westport, CT: Greenwood Press, 1978.

BiDAmJo *Biographical Dictionary of American Journalism.* Edited by Joseph P. McKerns. New York: Greenwood Press, 1989.

BiDAmL *Biographical Dictionary of American Labor.* Edited by Gary M. Fink. Westport, CT: Greenwood Press, 1984.

Biographies begin on page 83.

BiDAmLf *Biographical Dictionary of the American Left.* Edited by Bernard K. Johnpoll and Harvey Klehr. New York: Greenwood Press, 1986.

BiDAmLL *Biographical Dictionary of American Labor Leaders.* Edited by Gary M. Fink. Westport, CT: Greenwood Press, 1974.

BiDAmM *Biographical Dictionary of American Music.* By Charles Eugene Claghorn. West Nyack, NY: Parker Publishing Co., 1973.

BiDAmNC *Biographical Dictionary of American Newspaper Columnists.* By Sam G. Riley. Westport, CT: Greenwood Press, 1995.

BiDAmS *Biographical Dictionary of American Science.* The seventeenth through the nineteenth centuries. By Clark A. Elliott. Westport, CT: Greenwood Press, 1979.

BiDAmSp *Biographical Dictionary of American Sports.* Edited by David L. Porter. Westport, CT: Greenwood Press, 1987-1992.

- ***BiDAmSp BB*** *Baseball.*; 1987.
- ***BiDAmSp BK*** *Basketball and Other Indoor Sports.*; 1989. Use the index to locate biographies.
- ***BiDAmSp FB*** *Football.*; 1987.
- ***BiDAmSp OS*** *Outdoor Sports.*; 1988. Use the Index to locate biographies.
- ***BiDAmSp Sup*** 1989-1992 supplement for baseball, football, basketball, and other sports; 1992. Use the Index to locate biographies.

BiD&SB *Biographical Dictionary and Synopsis of Books Ancient and Modern.* Edited by Charles Dudley Warner. Akron, OH: Werner Co., 1902. Reprint. Detroit: Gale Research, 1965.

BiDBrA *A Biographical Dictionary of British Architects 1600-1840.* By Howard Colvin. New York: Facts on File, 1980.

- ***BiDBrA A*** ''Appendix A'' begins on page 969.

BiDBrF *The Biographical Dictionary of British Feminists.* By Olive Banks. New York: New York University Press, 1985-1990.

- ***BiDBrF 1*** Volume One: 1800-1930; 1985.
- ***BiDBrF 2*** Volume Two: A supplement, 1900-1945; 1990.

BiDConC *Biographical Dictionary of Contemporary Catholic American Writing.* Edited by Daniel J. Tynan. New York: Greenwood Press, 1989.

BiDConf *Biographical Dictionary of the Confederacy.* By Jon L. Wakelyn. Westport, CT: Greenwood Press, 1977.

BiDD *Biographical Dictionary of Dance.* By Barbara Naomi Cohen-Stratyner. New York: Macmillan Publishing Co., Schirmer Books; London: Collier Macmillan Publishers, 1982.

BiDEWW *A Biographical Dictionary of English Women Writers, 1580-1720.* By Maureen Bell, George Parfitt, and Simon Shepherd. Boston: G.K. Hall & Co., 1990.

BiDExR *Biographical Dictionary of the Extreme Right since 1890.* By Philip Rees. New York: Simon & Schuster, 1990.

BiDFedJ *Biographical Dictionary of the Federal Judiciary.* Compiled by Harold Chase, Samuel Krislov, Keith O. Boyum, and Jerry N. Clark. Detroit: Gale Research, 1976.

- ***BiDFedJ A*** Addendum begins on page 319.

BiDFilm *A Biographical Dictionary of Film.* By David Thomson. New York: William Morrow & Co., 1976-1981.

- ***BiDFilm*** First edition; 1976.
- ***BiDFilm 81*** Second edition; 1981.

BiDFilm 94 *A Biographical Dictionary of Film.* By David Thomson. New York: Alfred A. Knopf, 1994.

BiDFrPL *Biographical Dictionary of French Political Leaders since 1870.* Edited by David S. Bell, Douglas Johnson, and Peter Morris. New York: Simon & Schuster, 1990.

BiDHisL *Biographical Dictionary of Hispanic Literature in the United States.* The literature of Puerto Ricans, Cuban Americans, and other Hispanic writers. Edited by Nicolas Kanellos. New York: Greenwood Press, 1989.

BiDInt *Biographical Dictionary of Internationalists.* Edited by Warren F. Kuehl. Westport, CT: Greenwood Press, 1983.

BiDIrW *A Biographical Dictionary of Irish Writers.* By Anne M. Brady and Brian Cleeve. New York: St. Martin's Press, 1985.

- ***BiDIrW*** ''Writers in English'' section begins on page 1.
- ***BiDIrW A*** Addendum begins on page 254.
- ***BiDIrW B*** ''Writers in Irish and Latin'' section begins on page 255.

BiDJaL *Biographical Dictionary of Japanese Literature.* By Sen'ichi Hisamatsu. Tokyo: Kodansha International, 1976. Distributed by Harper & Row, New York.

Use the Index to locate biographies.

BiDJaz *Biographical Dictionary of Jazz.* By Charles Eugene Claghorn. Englewood Cliffs, NJ: Prentice-Hall, 1982.

- ***BiDJaz A*** ''Index of Jazz and Various Small Groups'' section begins on page 327.

BiDLA *A Biographical Dictionary of the Living Authors of Great Britain and Ireland.* Comprising literary memoirs and anecdotes of their lives; and a chronological register of their publications. London: Printed for Henry Colburn, Public Library, Hanover Square, 1816. Reprint. Detroit: Gale Research, 1966.

- ***BiDLA SUP*** ''Supplement of Additions and Corrections'' begins on page 407.

BiDLAmC *Biographical Dictionary of Latin American and Caribbean Political Leaders.* Edited by Robert J. Alexander. New York: Greenwood Press, 1988.

BiDMarx *Biographical Dictionary of Marxism.* Edited by Robert A. Gorman. Westport, CT: Greenwood Press, 1986.

BiDMoER 1 *A Biographical Dictionary of Modern European Radicals and Socialists.* Volume one: 1780-1815. Edited by David Nicholls and Peter Marsh. Sussex, England: The Harvester Press; New York: St. Martin's Press, 1988.

BiDMoPL *Biographical Dictionary of Modern Peace Leaders.* Edited by Harold Josephson. Westport, CT: Greenwood Press, 1985.

BiDNeoM *Biographical Dictionary of Neo-Marxism.* Edited by Robert A. Gorman. Westport, CT: Greenwood Press, 1985.

BiDPara *Biographical Dictionary of Parapsychology, 1964-1966.* Edited by Helene Pleasants. New York: Garrett Publications, Helix Press, 1964.

BiDPsy *Biographical Dictionary of Psychology.* By Leonard Zusne. Westport, CT: Greenwood Press, 1984. A continuation of *Names in the History of Psychology: A Biographical Sourcebook.*

BiDrAC *Biographical Directory of the American Congress, 1774-1971.* The Continental Congress (September 5, 1774 to October 21, 1788) and the Congress of the United States (from the first through the ninety-first Congress March 4, 1789, to January 3, 1971, inclusive). Washington, DC: U.S. Government Printing Office, 1971.

Biographies begin on page 487.

BiDrACP 79 *Biographical Directory of the American College of Physicians.* 1979 edition. New York: R.R. Bowker Co., 1979.

Use the Index, which begins on page 1789, to locate biographies.

BiDrACR *Biographical Directory of American Colonial and Revolutionary Governors, 1607-1789.* By John W. Raimo. Westport, CT: Microform Review, Meckler Books, 1980.

Use the Index to locate biographies.

BiDrAPA 77 *Biographical Directory: Fellows and Members of the American Psychiatric Association.* 1977 edition. New York: R.R. Bowker Co., 1977.

BiDrAPA 89 *Biographical Directory: Fellows and Members of the American Psychiatric Association.* 1989 edition. Washington, DC: American Psychiatric Association, 1989. Distributed by American Psychiatric Press, Washington, DC.

BiDrAPH 79 *Biographical Directory of the American Public Health Association.* 1979 edition. New York: R.R. Bowker Co., 1979.

BiDrATG *Biographical Directory of American Territorial Governors.* By Thomas A. McMullin and David Walker. Westport, CT: Meckler Publishing, 1984.

Use the Index to locate biographies.

BiDrGov *Biographical Directory of the Governors of the United States.* Westport, CT: Meckler, 1978-1989.
- ***BiDrGov 1789*** *1789-1978.* Four volumes. Edited by Robert Sobel and John Raimo; 1978. Use the Index in each volume to locate biographies.
- ***BiDrGov 1978*** *1978-1983.* Edited by John W. Raimo; 1985. Use the Index to locate biographies.
- ***BiDrGov 1983*** *1983-1988.* By Marie Marmo Mullaney; 1989. Use the Index to locate biographies.

BiDrGov 1988 *Biographical Directory of the Governors of the United States. 1988-1994.* By Marie Marmo Mullaney. Westport, CT: Greenwood Press, 1994.
Use the Index to locate biographies.

BiDrLUS 70 *A Biographical Directory of Librarians in the United States and Canada.* Fifth edition. Edited by Lee Ash. Chicago: American Library Association, 1970.

BiDRP&D *A Biographical Dictionary of Renaissance Poets and Dramatists, 1520-1650.* By J.W. Saunders. Sussex, England: Harvester Press, 1983.

BiDrUSC 89 *Biographical Directory of the United States Congress, 1774-1989.* The Continental Congress, September 5, 1774 to October 21, 1788 and the Congress of the United States from the first through the one hundredth Congresses, March 4, 1789, to January 3, 1989, inclusive. Bicentennial Edition. Washington, DC: U.S. Government Printing Office, 1989.
Biographies begin on page 507.

BiDrUSE *Biographical Directory of the United States Executive Branch.* Edited by Robert Sobel. New York: Greenwood Press, 1971-1990.
- ***BiDrUSE 71*** *1774-1971.*; 1971.
- ***BiDrUSE 89*** *1774-1989.*; 1990.

BiDSA *Biographical Dictionary of Southern Authors.* Compiled by Lucian Lamar Knight. Atlanta: Martin & Hoyt Co., 1929. Reprint. Detroit: Gale Research, 1978. Originally published as *Library of Southern Literature, Volume 15, Biographical Dictionary of Authors.*

BiDScF *A Biographical Dictionary of Science Fiction and Fantasy Artists.* By Robert Weinberg. New York: Greenwood Press, 1988.

BiDSocW *Biographical Dictionary of Social Welfare in America.* Edited by Walter I. Trattner. New York: Greenwood Press, 1986.

BiDSovU *A Biographical Dictionary of the Soviet Union, 1917-1988.* By Jeanne Vronskaya with Vladimir Chuguev. London: K.G. Saur, 1989.

BiDTran *Biographical Dictionary of Transcendentalism.* Edited by Wesley T. Mott. Westport, CT: Greenwood Press, 1996.

BiDWomA *A Biographical Dictionary of Women Artists in Europe and America since 1850.* By Penny Dunford. Philadelphia: University of Pennsylvania Press, 1989.

BiDWWGF — *The Biographical Dictionary of World War II Generals and Flag Officers.* The U.S. armed forces. By R. Manning Ancell. Westport, CT: Greenwood Press, 1996.
Use the Index to locate biographies.

BiE&WWA — *The Biographical Encyclopaedia and Who's Who of the American Theatre.* Edited by Walter Rigdon. New York: James H. Heineman, 1966. Revised edition published as *Notable Names in the American Theatre.*
The ''Biographical Who's Who'' section begins on page 227.

BiESc — *A Biographical Encyclopedia of Scientists.* Two volumes. Edited by John Daintith, Sarah Mitchell, and Elizabeth Tootill. New York: Facts on File, 1981.

BiGAW — *A Bio-Bibliography of German-American Writers, 1670-1970.* By Robert E. Ward. White Plains, NY: Kraus International Publications, 1985.

BiHiMed — *A Biographical History of Medicine.* Excerpts and essays on the men and their work. By John H. Talbott. New York: Grune & Stratton, 1970.
Use the ''Name Index,'' which begins on page 1193 to locate biographies.

BiInAmS — *Biographical Index to American Science.* The seventeenth century to 1920. Compiled by Clark A. Elliott. Bibliographies and Indexes in American History, no. 16. New York: Greenwood Press, 1990.

BiNAW — *A Biobibliography of Native American Writers, 1772-1924.* By Daniel F. Littlefield, Jr. and James W. Parins. Native American Bibliography Series, no. 2. Metuchen, NJ: Scarecrow Press, 1981.

BiNAW	Part I: ''A Bibliography of Native American Writers.''
BiNAW A	Part II: ''A Bibliography of Native American Writers Known Only by Pen Names'' begins on page 185.
BiNAW B	Part III: ''Biographical Notes'' begins on page 203.

BiNAW — *A Biobibliography of Native American Writers, 1772-1924: A Supplement.* By Daniel F. Littlefield, Jr. and James W. Parins. Native American Bibliography Series, no. 5. Metuchen, NJ: Scarecrow Press, 1985.

BiNAW Sup	Part I: ''A Bibliography of Native American Writers.''
BiNAW SupA	Part II: ''A Bibliography of Native American Writers Known Only by Pen Names'' begins on page 159.
BiNAW SupB	Part III: ''Biographical Notes'' begins on page 165.

BioAmW — *Biographies of American Women.* An annotated bibliography. By Patricia E. Sweeney. Santa Barbara, CA: ABC-Clio, 1990.

BioIn — *Biography Index.* A cumulative index to biographical material in books and magazines. New York: H.W. Wilson Co., 1949-1996.

BioIn 1	Volume 1: January, 1946-July, 1949; 1949.
BioIn 2	Volume 2: August, 1949-August, 1952; 1953.
BioIn 3	Volume 3: September, 1952-August, 1955; 1956.
BioIn 4	Volume 4: September, 1955-August, 1958; 1960.
BioIn 5	Volume 5: September, 1958-August, 1961; 1962.
BioIn 6	Volume 6: September, 1961-August, 1964; 1965.
BioIn 7	Volume 7: September, 1964-August, 1967; 1968.
BioIn 8	Volume 8: September, 1967-August, 1970; 1971.
BioIn 9	Volume 9: September, 1970-August, 1973; 1974.

BioIn 10 Volume 10: September, 1973-August, 1976; 1977.
BioIn 11 Volume 11: September, 1976-August, 1979; 1980.
BioIn 12 Volume 12: September, 1979-August, 1982; 1983.
BioIn 13 Volume 13: September, 1982-August, 1984; 1984.
BioIn 14 Volume 14: September, 1984-August, 1986; 1986.
BioIn 15 Volume 15: September, 1986-August, 1988; 1988.
BioIn 16 Volume 16: September, 1988-August, 1990; 1990.
BioIn 17 Volume 17: September, 1990-August, 1992; 1992.
BioIn 18 Volume 18: September, 1992-August, 1993; 1993.
BioIn 19 Volume 19: September, 1993-August, 1994; 1994.
BioIn 20 Volume 20: September, 1994-August, 1995; 1995.
BioIn 21 Volume 21: September, 1995-August, 1996; 1996.

BioNews *Biography News.* A compilation of news stories and feature articles from American news media covering personalities of national interest in all fields. Edited by Frank E. Bair. Detroit: Gale Research, 1974-1975.
BioNews 74 Volume 1, Numbers 1-12; 1974.
BioNews 75 Volume 2, Number 1, January-February; 1975.

BkC *The Book of Catholic Authors.* Informal self-portraits of famous modern Catholic writers. Edited by Walter Romig. Detroit: Walter Romig & Co., (n.d.).
BkC 1 First series; 1942.
BkC 2 Second series; 1943.
BkC 3 Third series; 1945.
BkC 4 Fourth series.
BkC 5 Fifth series.
BkC 6 Sixth series.

BkCL *A Book of Children's Literature.* Third edition. Edited by Lillian Hollowell. New York: Holt, Rinehart & Winston, 1966.
Biographies begin on page 553.

BkIE *Book Illustrators in Eighteenth-Century England.* By Hanns Hammelmann. Edited and completed by T.S.R. Boase. New Haven, CT: Yale University Press, 1975.

BkP *Books Are by People.* Interviews with 104 authors and illustrators of books for young children. By Lee Bennett Hopkins. New York: Citation Press, 1969.

BkPepl *The Book of People.* By Christopher P. Anderson. New York: Perigree Books, 1981.

BlkAmP *Black American Playwrights, 1800 to the Present.* A bibliography. By Esther Spring Arata and Nicholas John Rotoli. Metuchen, NJ: Scarecrow Press, 1976.
Updated by *More Black American Playwrights: A Bibliography.*

BlkAmsC *Black Americans in Congress, 1870-1989.* By Bruce A. Ragsdale and Joel D. Treese. Washington, DC: U.S. Government Printing Office, 1990.

BlkAmW *Black American Writers.* Bibliographical essays. Edited by M. Thomas Inge, Maurice Duke, and Jackson R. Bryer. New York: St. Martin's Press, 1978.
BlkAmW 1 Volume 1: The Beginnings through the Harlem Renaissance and Langston Hughes.
BlkAmW 2 Volume 2: Richard Wright, Ralph Ellison, James Baldwin, and Amiri Baraka.
Use the Index to locate biographies.

BlkAmWO *Black American Women in Olympic Track and Field.* A complete illustrated reference. By Michael D. Davis. Jefferson, NC: McFarland & Co., 1992.

BlkAuIl *Black Authors and Illustrators of Children's Books.* By Barbara Rollock. New York: Garland Publishing, 1988-1992.

BlkAuIl First edition. Garland Reference Library of the Humanities, vol. 660; 1988.

BlkAuIl 92 Second edition. Garland Reference Library of the Humanities, vol. 1316; 1992.

BlkAWP *Black American Writers Past and Present.* A biographical and bibliographical dictionary. Two volumes. By Theressa Gunnels Rush, Carol Fairbanks Myers, and Esther Spring Arata. Metuchen, NJ: Scarecrow Press, 1975.

BlkCO *Black Congressional Reconstruction Orators and Their Orations, 1869-1879.* By Annjennette Sophie McFarlin. Metuchen, NJ: Scarecrow Press, 1976.

BlkCond *Black Conductors.* By D. Antoinette Handy. Metuchen, NJ: Scarecrow Press, 1995.

Use the Index to locate biographies.

BlkCS *The Black Composer Speaks.* Edited by David N. Baker, Lida M. Belt, and Herman C. Hudson. Metuchen, NJ: Scarecrow Press, 1978.

BlkLC *Black Literature Criticism.* Excerpts from criticism of the most significant works of Black authors over the past 200 years. Three volumes. Detroit: Gale Research, 1992.

BlkMth *Black Mathematicians and Their Works.* Edited by Virginia K. Newell, Joella H. Gipson, L. Waldo Rich, and Beauregard Stubblefield. Ardmore, PA: Dorrance & Co., 1980.

Biographies are located in the "Biographical Index" which begins on page 277.

BlkOlyM *Black Olympian Medalists.* By James A. Page. Englewood, CO: Libraries Unlimited, 1991.

BlkOpe *Blacks in Opera.* An encyclopedia of people and companies, 1873-1993. By Eric Ledell Smith. Jefferson, NC: McFarland & Co., 1995.

BlksAmF *Blacks in American Films and Television.* An encyclopedia. By Donald Bogle. Garland Reference Library of the Humanities, vol. 604. New York: Garland Publishing, 1988.

Biographies are located in the "Profiles" section which begins on page 353.

BlksB&W *Blacks in Black & White.* A source book on Black films. By Henry T. Sampson. Metuchen, NJ: Scarecrow Press, 1977.

BlksB&W Biographies begin on page 192.

BlksB&W C Appendix C, "Film Credits for Featured Players in Black-cast Films, 1915-1950," begins on page 311.

BlksBF *Blacks in Blackface.* A source book on early Black musical shows. By Henry T. Sampson. Metuchen, NJ: Scarecrow Press, 1980.
Biographies begin on page 330.

BlksCm *Blacks in Communications.* Journalism, public relations, and advertising. By M.L. Stein. New York: Julian Messner, 1972.

BlksScM *Blacks in Science and Medicine.* By Vivian Ovelton Sammons. New York: Hemisphere Publishing, 1990.

BlkWAB *Black Women in American Bands and Orchestras.* By D. Antoinette Handy. Metuchen, NJ: Scarecrow Press, 1981.
Use the ''Index to Profiles'' to locate biographies.

BlkWAm *Black Women in America.* An historical encyclopedia. Two volumes. Edited by Darlene Clark Hine. Brooklyn, NY: Carlson Publishing, 1993.

BlkwCE *The Blackwell Companion to the Enlightenment.* By John W. Yolton, Roy Porter, Pat Rodgers, and Barbara Maria Stafford. Cambridge, MA: Basil Blackwell, 1991.

BlkwEAR *The Blackwell Encyclopedia of the American Revolution.* Edited by Jack P. Greene and J.R. Pole. Cambridge, MA: Basil Blackwell, 1991.
Biographies begin on page 695.

BlkwERR *The Blackwell Encyclopedia of the Russian Revolution.* Edited by Harold Shukman. New York: Basil Blackwell, 1988.
Biographies begin on page 297.

BlkWr *Black Writers.* A selection of sketches from *Contemporary Authors.* Detroit: Gale Research, 1989-1994.
BlkWr 1 First edition; 1989.
BlkWr 2 Second edition; 1994.

BlkWrNE *Black Writers in New England.* A bibliography, with biographical notes, of books by and about Afro-American writers associated with New England in the *Collection of Afro-American Literature.* By Edward Clark. Boston: National Park Service, 1985.
BlkWrNE A Section II, ''Afro-American writers associated with New England not represented with books by or about them in the *Collection of Afro-American Literature,*'' begins on page 70.

BlkWWr *Black Women Writers (1950-1980).* A critical evaluation. Edited by Mari Evans. Garden City, NY: Anchor Press/Doubleday, 1984.

BlmGEL *The Bloomsbury Guide to English Literature.* The new authority on English literature. Edited by Marion Wynne-Davies. New York: Prentice Hall General Reference, 1990. Originally published in hardcover as the *Prentice Hall Guide to English Literature.*
Biographies begin on page 295.

BlmGWL *The Bloomsbury Guide to Women's Literature.* Edited by Claire Buck. New York: Prentice Hall General Reference, 1992.
Biographies begin on page 247.

BlueB 76 *The Blue Book.* Leaders of the English-speaking world. 1976 edition. London: St. James Press; New York: St. Martin's Press, 1976. Reprint. In two volumes by Gale Research, Detroit, 1979.
BlueB 76N Obituary section begins on page 1837.

BluesWW *Blues Who's Who.* A biographical dictionary of blues singers. By Sheldon Harris. New Rochelle, NY: Arlington House Publishers, 1979.

BoxReg *The Boxing Register.* International Boxing Hall of Fame official record book. By James B. Roberts and Alexander G. Skutt. Ithaca, NY: McBooks Press, 1997.
Use the ''Inductees'' list, which begins on page 446, to locate biographies.

BriB *Brilliant Bylines.* A biographical anthology of notable newspaperwomen in America. By Barbara Belford. New York: Columbia University Press, 1986.

BriBkM 80 *Britannica Book of Music.* Edited by Benjamin Hadley. Garden City, NY: Doubleday & Co., 1980.

BriEAA *The Britannica Encyclopedia of American Art.* Chicago: Encyclopaedia Britannica Educational Corp., 1973. Distributed by Simon & Schuster, New York.

BritAS *British and American Sporting Authors: Their Writings and Biographies.* By A. Henry Higginson. London: Hutchinson & Co., 1951.
Use the Index to locate biographies.

BritAu *British Authors before 1800.* A biographical dictionary. Edited by Stanley J. Kunitz and Howard Haycraft. Wilson Authors Series. New York: H.W. Wilson Co., 1952.

BritAu 19 *British Authors of the Nineteenth Century.* Edited by Stanley J. Kunitz. Wilson Authors Series. New York: H.W. Wilson Co., 1936.

BritCA *British Children's Authors.* Interviews at Home. By Cornelia Jones and Olivia R. Way. Chicago: American Library Association, 1976.

BritPl *British Playwrights, 1880-1956.* A research and production sourcebook. Edited by William W. Demastes and Katherine E. Kelly. Westport, CT: Greenwood Press, 1996.

BritWr *British Writers.* New York: Charles Scribner's Sons, 1979-1992.
BritWr 1 Volume I: William Langland to The English Bible; 1979.
BritWr 2 Volume II: Thomas Middleton to George Farquhar; 1979.
BritWr 3 Volume III: Daniel Defoe to The Gothic Novel; 1980.
BritWr 4 Volume IV: William Wordsworth to Robert Browning; 1981.
BritWr 5 Volume V: Elizabeth Gaskell to Francis Thompson; 1982.

BritWr 6 Volume VI: Thomas Hardy to Wilfred Owen; 1983.
BritWr 7 Volume VII: Sean O'Casey to Poets of World War II; 1984.
BritWr S1 Supplement 1; 1987.
BritWr S2 Supplement 2; 1992.
Use the "List of Subjects" to locate biographies.

BroadAu *Broadside Authors and Artists.* An illustrated biographical directory. Compiled and edited by Leaonead Pack Bailey. Detroit: Broadside Press, 1974.

BroV *Broadening Views, 1968-1988.* Concise Dictionary of American Literary Biography Series. Detroit: Gale Research, 1989.

BuCMET *Bud Collins' Modern Encyclopedia of Tennis.* Edited by Bud Collins and Zander Hollander. Detroit: Gale Research, 1994.
Use the Index to locate biographies.

BusPN *Business People in the News.* A compilation of news stories and feature articles from American newspapers and magazines covering people in industry, finance, and labor. Volume 1. Edited by Barbara Nykoruk. Detroit: Gale Research, 1976.

CabMA *The Cabinetmakers of America.* Revised and corrected edition. By Ethel Hall Bjerkoe. Exton, PA: Schiffer, 1978. Originally published by Doubleday & Co., 1957.
Biographies begin on page 19.

Cald 1938 *Caldecott Medal Books: 1938-1957.* With the artist's acceptance papers & related material chiefly from the *Horn Book Magazine.* Edited by Bertha Mahony Miller and Elinor Whitney Field. Horn Book Papers, volume II. Boston: Horn Book, 1957.

CamDcAB *The Cambridge Dictionary of American Biography.* Edited by John S. Bowman. Cambridge: Cambridge University Press, 1995.

CamDcSc *The Cambridge Dictionary of Scientists.* By David Millar, Ian Millar, John Millar, and Margaret Millar. Cambridge: Cambridge University Press, 1996.

CamGEL *The Cambridge Guide to English Literature.* Edited by Michael Stapleton. Cambridge: Cambridge University Press; Middlesex, England: Newnes Books, 1983.

CamGLE *The Cambridge Guide to Literature in English.* Edited by Ian Ousby. Cambridge: Cambridge University Press; London: Hamlyn Publishing Group, 1988.

CamGWoT *The Cambridge Guide to World Theatre.* Edited by Martin Banham. Cambridge: Cambridge University Press, 1988.

CamHAL *The Cambridge Handbook of American Literature.* Edited by Jack Salzman. Cambridge: Cambridge University Press, 1986.

CanNov *Canadian Novelists, 1920-1945.* By Clara Thomas. Toronto: Longmans, Green & Co., 1946. Reprint. Folcroft, Penn.: Folcroft Library Editions, 1970.

CanWr *Canadian Writers.* A biographical dictionary. New edition, revised and enlarged. Edited by Guy Sylvestre, Brandon Conron, and Carl F. Klinck. Toronto: Ryerson Press, 1966.

CanWW 31 *Canadian Who's Who.* Volume 31. Toronto: University of Toronto Press, 1996.

CanWW 70 *Canadian Who's Who.* A biographical dictionary of notable living men and women. Volume 12, 1970-1972. Toronto: Who's Who Canadian Publications, 1972.

CanWW *Canadian Who's Who.* A biographical dictionary of notable living men and women. Edited by Kieran Simpson. Toronto: University of Toronto Press, 1979-1989.

CanWW 79 Volume 14; 1979.
CanWW 80 Volume 15; 1980.
CanWW 81 Volume 16; 1981.
CanWW 83 Volume 18; 1983.
CanWW 89 Volume 24; 1989.

CaP *Canada's Playwrights: A Biographical Guide.* Edited by Don Rubin and Alison Cranmer-Byng. Toronto: Canadian Theatre Review Publications, 1980.

CaribW *Caribbean Writers.* A bio-bibliographical-critical encyclopedia. Edited by Donald E. Herdeck. Washington: Three Continents Press, 1979.

CaribW 1 Volume I: *Anglophone Literature from the Caribbean,* begins on page 17.
CaribW 1A Volume I: *Supplementary List of Writers from Belize,* begins on page 230.
CaribW 2 Volume II: *Francophone Literature from the Caribbean,* begins on page 283.
CaribW 2A Volume II: *Supplementary List of Writers from Haiti,* begins on page 531.
CaribW 3 Volume III: *Literatures of the Netherlands Antilles and Surinam,* begins on page 561.
CaribW 4 Volume IV: *Spanish Language Literature from the Caribbean,* begins on page 629.

CarSB *The Carolyn Sherwin Bailey Historical Collection of Children's Books.* A catalogue. Edited and compiled by Dorothy R. Davis. New Haven, CT: Southern Connecticut State College, 1966.

Not in strict alphabetic sequence.

CasWL *Cassell's Encyclopaedia of World Literature.* Two volumes. Edited by S.H. Steinberg. Revised and enlarged in three volumes by J. Buchanan-Brown. New York: William Morrow & Co., 1973.

Biographies are found in Volumes 2 and 3 of the revised edition.

CathA *Catholic Authors.* Contemporary biographical sketches. Edited by Matthew Hoehn. Newark, NJ: St. Mary's Abbey, 1948-1952.

CathA 1930 First volume: 1930-1947; 1948.
CathA 1952 Second volume; 1952.

CaW *Canada Writes!* The members' book of the Writers' Union of Canada. Edited by K.A. Hamilton. Toronto: Writers' Union of Canada, 1977.

CaW A ''Additional Members'' section begins on page 387.

CelCen *Celebrities of the Century.* Being a dictionary of men and women of the nineteenth century. Two volumes. Edited by Lloyd C. Sanders. London: Cassell & Co., 1887. Reprint. Ann Arbor: Gryphon Books, 1971.

CelR *Celebrity Register.* Third edition. Edited by Earl Blackwell. New York: Simon & Schuster, 1973.

CelR 90 *Celebrity Register, 1990.* Detroit: Gale Research, 1990.

CenC *A Century of Ceramics in the United States, 1878-1978.* A study of its development. By Garth Clark. New York: E.P. Dutton, 1979.
Biographies begin on page 269.

Chambr *Chambers's Cyclopaedia of English Literature.* A history critical and biographical of authors in the English tongue from the earliest times till the present day with specimens of their writings. Edited by David Patrick, revised by J. Liddell Geddie. Philadelphia: J.B. Lippincott, 1938. Reprint. Detroit: Gale Research, 1978.

Chambr 1 Volume I: 7th-17th Century.
Chambr 2 Volume II: 18th Century.
Chambr 3 Volume III: 19th-20th Century.

Use the Index to locate biographies.

ChhPo *Childhood in Poetry.* A catalogue, with biographical and critical annotations, of the books of English and American poets comprising the Shaw Childhood in Poetry Collection in the Library of the Florida State University. By John Mackay Shaw. Detroit: Gale Research, 1967-1980.

ChhPo First edition; 1967.
ChhPo S1 First Supplement; 1972.
ChhPo S2 Second Supplement; 1976.
ChhPo S3 Third Supplement; 1980.

ChiLit *Chicano Literature: A Reference Guide.* Edited by Julio A. Martinez and Francisco A. Lomeli. Westport, CT: Greenwood Press, 1985.

ChiLit A "Appendix A" begins on page 441.

ChiSch *Chicano Scholars and Writers.* A bio-bibliographical directory. Edited and compiled by Julio A. Martinez. Metuchen, NJ: Scarecrow Press, 1979.

ChlBIlD *Children's Book Illustration and Design.* Edited by Julie Cummins. Library of Applied Design. New York: PBC International, 1992. Distributed by Rizzoli International Publications, New York.

ChlBkCr *Children's Books and Their Creators.* Edited by Anita Silvey. Boston: Houghton Mifflin Co., 1995.

ChlFicS *Children's Fiction Sourcebook.* A survey of children's books for 6-13 year olds. By Margaret Hobson, Jennifer Madden, and Ray Prytherch. Brookfield, VT: Ashgate Publishing Co., 1992.

ChlLR *Children's Literature Review.* Excerpts from reviews, criticism, and commentary on books for children and young people. Detroit: Gale Research, 1976-1997.

ChlLR 1	Volume 1; 1976.
ChlLR 2	Volume 2; 1976.
ChlLR 3	Volume 3; 1978.
ChlLR 4	Volume 4; 1982.
ChlLR 5	Volume 5; 1983.
ChlLR 6	Volume 6; 1984.
ChlLR 7	Volume 7; 1984.
ChlLR 8	Volume 8; 1985.
ChlLR 9	Volume 9; 1985.
ChlLR 10	Volume 10; 1986.
ChlLR 11	Volume 11; 1986.
ChlLR 12	Volume 12; 1987.
ChlLR 13	Volume 13; 1987.
ChlLR 14	Volume 14; 1988.
ChlLR 15	Volume 15; 1988.
ChlLR 16	Volume 16; 1989.
ChlLR 17	Volume 17; 1989.
ChlLR 18	Volume 18; 1989.
ChlLR 19	Volume 19; 1990.
ChlLR 20	Volume 20; 1990.
ChlLR 21	Volume 21; 1990.
ChlLR 22	Volume 22; 1991.
ChlLR 23	Volume 23; 1991.
ChlLR 24	Volume 24; 1991.
ChlLR 25	Volume 25; 1991.
ChlLR 26	Volume 26; 1992.
ChlLR 27	Volume 27; 1992.
ChlLR 28	Volume 28; 1992.
ChlLR 29	Volume 29; 1993.
ChlLR 30	Volume 30; 1993.
ChlLR 31	Volume 31; 1994.
ChlLR 32	Volume 32; 1994.
ChlLR 33	Volume 33; 1994.
ChlLR 34	Volume 34; 1995.
ChlLR 35	Volume 35; 1995.
ChlLR 36	Volume 36; 1995.
ChlLR 37	Volume 37; 1996.
ChlLR 38	Volume 38; 1996.
ChlLR 39	Volume 39; 1996.
ChlLR 40	Volume 40; 1996.
ChlLR 41	Volume 41; 1997.
ChlLR 42	Volume 42; 1997.

ChrP *The Children's Poets.* Analyses and appraisals of the greatest English and American poets for children. By Walter Barnes. Yonkers-on-Hudson, NY: World Book Co., 1924.

ChsFB *The Child's First Books.* A critical study of pictures and texts. By Donnarae MacCann and Olga Richard. New York: H.W. Wilson Co., 1973.

ChsFB A	"Author Biographies" begin on page 96.
ChsFB I	"Illustrator Biographies" begin on page 47.

CivR 74 *Civil Rights: A Current Guide to the People, Organizations, and Events.* Second edition. By Joan Martin Burke. New York: R.R. Bowker Co., 1974.

Biographies begin on page 21.

CivRSt *The Civil Rights Struggle: Leaders in Profile.* By John D'Emilio. New York: Facts on File, 1979.

CivWDc *The Civil War Dictionary.* By Mark Mayo Boatner, III. New York: David McKay Co., 1959.

ClaDrA *The Classified Directory of Artists' Signatures, Symbols, & Monograms.* Second edition, enlarged and revised. By H.H. Caplan. London: George Prior Publishers, 1982. Distributed by Gale Research, Detroit.

ClDMEL *Columbia Dictionary of Modern European Literature.* New York: Columbia University Press, 1947-1980.

ClDMEL 47 First edition. Edited by Horatio Smith; 1947.
ClDMEL 80 Second edition. Edited by Jean-Albert Bede and William B. Edgerton; 1980.

ClMLC *Classical and Medieval Literature Criticism.* Excerpts from criticism of the works of world authors from classical antiquity through the fourteenth century, from the first appraisals to current evaluations. Detroit: Gale Research, 1988-1997.

ClMLC 1 Volume 1; 1988.
ClMLC 2 Volume 2; 1988.
ClMLC 3 Volume 3; 1989.
ClMLC 4 Volume 4; 1990.
ClMLC 5 Volume 5; 1991.
ClMLC 6 Volume 6; 1991.
ClMLC 7 Volume 7; 1991.
ClMLC 8 Volume 8; 1992.
ClMLC 9 Volume 9; 1993.
ClMLC 10 Volume 10; 1993.
ClMLC 11 Volume 11; 1993.
ClMLC 12 Volume 12; 1994.
ClMLC 13 Volume 13; 1994.
ClMLC 14 Volume 14; 1995.
ClMLC 15 Volume 15; 1996.
ClMLC 16 Volume 16; 1996.
ClMLC 17 Volume 17; 1996.
ClMLC 18 Volume 18; 1996.
ClMLC 19 Volume 19; 1997.

CmCal *A Companion to California.* By James D. Hart. New York: Oxford University Press, 1978.

CmdGen 1991 *Commanding Generals and Chiefs of Staff, 1775-1991.* Portraits & biographical sketches of the United States Army's Senior Officers. Revised edition, 1775-1991. By William Gardner Bell. Washington, DC: Center of Military History, United States Army, 1992.

Use the Index to locate biographies.

CmFrR *Companion to the French Revolution.* By John Paxton. New York: Facts on File Publications, 1988.

CmMedTh *A Companion to the Medieval Theatre.* Edited by Ronald W. Vince. New York: Greenwood Press, 1989.

CmMov *A Companion to the Movies: From 1903 to the Present Day.* A guide to the leading players, directors, screenwriters, composers, cameramen and other artistes who have worked in the English-speaking cinema over the last 70 years. By Roy Pickard. New York: Hippocrene Books, 1972.
Use the "Who's Who Index" to locate biographies.

CmOp *A Companion to the Opera.* By Robin May. New York: Hippocrene Books, 1977.
Use the "Selective Index: I - People," beginning on page 349, to locate biographies.

CmpBCM *The Complete Book of Classical Music.* By David Ewen. Englewood Cliffs, NJ: Prentice-Hall, 1965.
Use the index at the back of the book to locate biographies.

CmpEPM *The Complete Encyclopedia of Popular Music and Jazz, 1900-1950.* Three volumes. By Roger D. Kinkle. New Rochelle, NY: Arlington House Publishers, 1974.
Biographies are located in Volumes 2 and 3.

CmpGMD *The Complete Guide to Modern Dance.* By Don McDonagh. Garden City, NY: Doubleday & Co., 1976.
Use the Index at the back of the book to locate biographies.

CmScLit *Companion to Scottish Literature.* By Trevor Royle. Detroit: Gale Research, 1983.

CnDAL *Concise Dictionary of American Literature.* Edited by Robert Fulton Richards. New York: Philosophical Library, 1955. Reprint. New York: Greenwood Press, 1969.

CnDBLB *Concise Dictionary of British Literary Biography.* Detroit: Gale Research, 1992.

CnDBLB 1 Volume 1: *Writers of the Middle Ages and Renaissance before 1660.*; 1992.
CnDBLB 2 Volume 2: *Writers of the Restoration and Eighteenth Century, 1660-1789.*; 1992.
CnDBLB 3 Volume 3: *Writers of the Romantic Period, 1789-1832.*; 1992.
CnDBLB 4 Volume 4: *Victorian Writers, 1832-1890.*; 1991.
CnDBLB 5 Volume 5: *Late Victorian and Edwardian Writers, 1890-1914.*; 1991.
CnDBLB 6 Volume 6: *Modern Writers, 1914-1945.*; 1991.
CnDBLB 7 Volume 7: *Writers After World War II, 1945-1960.*; 1991.
CnDBLB 8 Volume 8: *Contemporary Writers, 1960 to the Present.*; 1992.

CnE&AP *The Concise Encyclopedia of English and American Poets and Poetry.* Edited by Stephen Spender and Donald Hall. New York: Hawthorn Books, 1963.

CngDr *Congressional Directory.* Washington, DC: United States Government Printing Office, 1974-1995.

CngDr 74 93rd Congress, 2nd Session; 1974.
CngDr 77 95th Congress, 1st Session; 1977.
CngDr 78 *Supplement,* 95th Congress, 2nd Session; 1978.
CngDr 79 96th Congress, 1st Session; 1979.

CngDr 81	97th Congress; 1981.
CngDr 83	98th Congress, 1983-1984; 1983.
CngDr 85	99th Congress, 1985-1986; 1985.
CngDr 87	100th Congress, 1987-1988; 1987.
CngDr 89	101st Congress, 1989-1990; 1989.
CngDr 91	102d Congress, 1991-1992; 1991.
CngDr 93	103d Congress, 1993-1994; 1993.
CngDr 95	104th Congress, 1995-1996; 1995.

Use the "Name Index" to locate biographies.

CnMD *The Concise Encyclopedia of Modern Drama.* By Siegfried Melchinger. Translated by George Wellwarth. Edited by Henry Popkin. New York: Horizon Press, 1964.

CnMD	Biographies begin on page 159.
CnMD SUP	"Additional Entries" section begins on page 287.

CnMWL *The Concise Encyclopedia of Modern World Literature.* Second edition. Edited by Geoffrey Grigson. London: Hutchinson & Co., 1970.

CnOxB *Concise Oxford Dictionary of Ballet* By Horst Koegler. London: Oxford University Press, 1977.

CnThe *A Concise Encyclopedia of the Theatre.* By Robin May. Reading, England: Osprey Publishing, 1974.
Use the Index to locate biographies.

ColARen *Colonization to the American Renaissance, 1640-1865.* Concise Dictionary of American Literary Biography Series. Detroit: Gale Research, 1988.

ColCR *Columbo's Canadian References.* By John Robert Columbo. New York: Oxford University Press, 1976.

ColdWar *The Cold War, 1945-1991.* Leaders and other important figures in the United States and Western Europe. Edited by Benjamin Frankel. Detroit: Gale Research, 1992.

ColdWar 1	Volume 1.
ColdWar 2	Volume 2.
ColdWar 3	Volume 3. Contains no biographies.

CompSN *Composers since 1900.* A biographical and critical guide. Compiled and edited by David Ewen. New York: H.W. Wilson Co., 1969-1981.

CompSN	First edition; 1969.
CompSN SUP	*First Supplement.*; 1981.

ConAmA *Contemporary American Authors.* A critical survey and 219 bio-bibliographies. By Fred B. Millett. New York: Harcourt, Brace & World, 1940. Reprint. New York: AMS Press, 1970.
Biographies begin on page 207.

ConAmBL *Contemporary American Business Leaders.* A biographical dictionary. By John N. Ingham and Lynne B. Feldman. New York: Greenwood Press, 1990.
Use the Index to locate biographies.

ConAmC *Contemporary American Composers.* A biographical dictionary. Compiled by E. Ruth Anderson. Boston: G.K. Hall & Co., 1976-1982.
- ***ConAmC 76*** First edition; 1976.
- ***ConAmC 76A*** First edition; 1976. Addendum begins on page 495.
- ***ConAmC 82*** Second edition; 1982.

ConAmD *Contemporary American Dramatists.* Edited by K.A. Berney. London: St. James Press, 1994.

ConAmL *Contemporary American Literature.* Bibliographies and study outlines. By John Matthews Manly and Edith Rickert. Revised by Fred B. Millett. New York: Harcourt, 1929. Reprint. New York: Haskell House Publishers, 1974.
Biographies begin on page 101.

ConAmTC *Contemporary American Theater Critics.* A directory and anthology of their works. Compiled by M.E. Comtois and Lynn F. Miller. Metuchen, NJ: Scarecrow Press, 1977.

ConAmWS *Contemporary American Women Sculptors.* By Virginia Watson-Jones. Phoenix, AZ: Oryx Press, 1986.

ConArch 80 *Contemporary Architects.* Edited by Muriel Emanuel. Contemporary Arts Series. New York: St. Martin's Press, 1980.
- ***ConArch 80A*** ''Notes on Advisors and Contributors'' section begins on page 927.

ConArch *Contemporary Architects.* London: St. James Press, 1987-1994.
- ***ConArch 87*** Second edition. Edited by Ann Lee Morgan and Colin Naylor; 1987.
- ***ConArch 94*** Third edition. Edited by Muriel Emanuel; 1994.

ConArt *Contemporary Artists.* Contemporary Arts Series. New York: St. Martin's Press, 1977-1983.
- ***ConArt 77*** First edition. Edited by Colin Naylor and Genesis P-Orridge; 1977.
- ***ConArt 83*** Second edition. Edited by Muriel Emanuel et al; 1983.

ConArt *Contemporary Artists.* Contemporary Arts Series. Detroit: St. James Press, 1989-1996.
- ***ConArt 89*** Third edition. Edited by Colin Naylor; 1989.
- ***ConArt 96*** Fourth edition. Edited by Joann Cerrito; 1996.

ConAu 1AS *Contemporary Authors, Autobiography Series.* Volume 1. Detroit: Gale Research, 1984.

ConAu 1BS *Contemporary Authors, Bibliographical Series.* Volume 1: *American Novelists.* Edited by James J. Martine. Detroit: Gale Research, 1986.

ConAu 1NR *Contemporary Authors, New Revision Series.* A bio-bibliographical guide to current writers in fiction, general nonfiction, poetry, journalism, drama, motion pictures, television, and other fields. Volume 1. Detroit: Gale Research, 1981.

ConAu 1R *Contemporary Authors.* A bio-bibliographical guide to current writers in fiction, general nonfiction, poetry, journalism, drama, motion pictures, television, and other fields. Volumes 1-4, 1st revision. Detroit: Gale Research, 1967.

ConAu 2AS *Contemporary Authors, Autobiography Series.* Volume 2. Detroit: Gale Research, 1985.

ConAu 2BS *Contemporary Authors, Bibliographical Series.* Volume 2: *American Poets.* Edited by Ronald Baughman. Detroit: Gale Research, 1986.

ConAu 2NR *Contemporary Authors, New Revision Series.* A bio-bibliographical guide to current writers in fiction, general nonfiction, poetry, journalism, drama, motion pictures, television, and other fields. Volume 2. Detroit: Gale Research, 1981.

ConAu 3AS *Contemporary Authors, Autobiography Series.* Volume 3. Detroit: Gale Research, 1986.

ConAu 3BS *Contemporary Authors, Bibliographical Series.* Volume 3: *American Dramatists.* Edited by Matthew C. Roudane. Detroit: Gale Research, 1989.

ConAu 3NR *Contemporary Authors, New Revision Series.* A bio-bibliographical guide to current writers in fiction, general nonfiction, poetry, journalism, drama, motion pictures, television, and other fields. Volume 3. Detroit: Gale Research, 1981.

ConAu 4AS *Contemporary Authors, Autobiography Series.* Volume 4. Detroit: Gale Research, 1986.

ConAu 4NR *Contemporary Authors, New Revision Series.* A bio-bibliographical guide to current writers in fiction, general nonfiction, poetry, journalism, drama, motion pictures, television, and other fields. Volume 4. Detroit: Gale Research, 1981.

ConAu 5AS *Contemporary Authors, Autobiography Series.* Volume 5. Detroit: Gale Research, 1987.

ConAu 5NR *Contemporary Authors, New Revision Series.* A bio-bibliographical guide to current writers in fiction, general nonfiction, poetry, journalism, drama, motion pictures, television, and other fields. Volume 5. Detroit: Gale Research, 1982.

ConAu 5R *Contemporary Authors.* A bio-bibliographical guide to current writers in fiction, general nonfiction, poetry, journalism, drama, motion pictures, television, and other fields. Volumes 5-8, 1st revision. Detroit: Gale Research, 1969.

ConAu 6AS *Contemporary Authors, Autobiography Series.* Volume 6. Detroit: Gale Research, 1988.

ConAu 6NR *Contemporary Authors, New Revision Series.* A bio-bibliographical guide to current writers in fiction, general nonfiction, poetry, journalism, drama, motion pictures, television, and other fields. Volume 6. Detroit: Gale Research, 1982.

ConAu 7AS *Contemporary Authors, Autobiography Series.* Volume 7. Detroit: Gale Research, 1988.

ConAu 7NR *Contemporary Authors, New Revision Series.* A bio-bibliographical guide to current writers in fiction, general nonfiction, poetry, journalism, drama, motion pictures, television, and other fields. Volume 7. Detroit: Gale Research, 1982.

ConAu 8AS *Contemporary Authors, Autobiography Series.* Volume 8. Detroit: Gale Research, 1989.

ConAu 8NR *Contemporary Authors, New Revision Series.* A bio-bibliographical guide to current writers in fiction, general nonfiction, poetry, journalism, drama, motion pictures, television, and other fields. Volume 8. Detroit: Gale Research, 1983.

ConAu 9AS *Contemporary Authors, Autobiography Series.* Volume 9. Detroit: Gale Research, 1989.

ConAu 9NR *Contemporary Authors, New Revision Series.* A bio-bibliographical guide to current writers in fiction, general nonfiction, poetry, journalism, drama, motion pictures, television, and other fields. Volume 9. Detroit: Gale Research, 1983.

ConAu 9R *Contemporary Authors.* A bio-bibliographical guide to current writers in fiction, general nonfiction, poetry, journalism, drama, motion pictures, television, and other fields. Volumes 9-12, 1st revision. Detroit: Gale Research, 1974.

ConAu 10AS *Contemporary Authors, Autobiography Series.* Volume 10. Detroit: Gale Research, 1989.

ConAu 10NR *Contemporary Authors, New Revision Series.* A bio-bibliographical guide to current writers in fiction, general nonfiction, poetry, journalism, drama, motion pictures, television, and other fields. Volume 10. Detroit: Gale Research, 1983.

ConAu 11AS *Contemporary Authors, Autobiography Series.* Volume 11. Detroit: Gale Research, 1990.

ConAu 11NR *Contemporary Authors, New Revision Series.* A bio-bibliographical guide to current writers in fiction, general nonfiction, poetry, journalism, drama, motion pictures, television, and other fields. Volume 11. Detroit: Gale Research, 1984.

ConAu 12AS *Contemporary Authors, Autobiography Series.* Volume 12. Detroit: Gale Research, 1990.

ConAu 12NR *Contemporary Authors, New Revision Series.* A bio-bibliographical guide to current writers in fiction, general nonfiction, poetry, journalism, drama, motion pictures, television, and other fields. Volume 12. Detroit: Gale Research, 1984.

ConAu 13AS *Contemporary Authors, Autobiography Series.* Volume 13. Detroit: Gale Research, 1991.

ConAu 13NR *Contemporary Authors, New Revision Series.* A bio-bibliographical guide to current writers in fiction, general nonfiction, poetry, journalism, drama, motion pictures, television, and other fields. Volume 13. Detroit: Gale Research, 1984.

ConAu 13R *Contemporary Authors.* A bio-bibliographical guide to current writers in fiction, general nonfiction, poetry, journalism, drama, motion pictures, television, and other fields. Volumes 13-16, 1st revision. Detroit: Gale Research, 1975.

ConAu 14AS *Contemporary Authors, Autobiography Series.* Volume 14. Detroit: Gale Research, 1991.

ConAu 14NR *Contemporary Authors, New Revision Series.* A bio-bibliographical guide to current writers in fiction, general nonfiction, poetry, journalism, drama, motion pictures, television, and other fields. Volume 14. Detroit: Gale Research, 1985.

ConAu 15AS *Contemporary Authors, Autobiography Series.* Volume 15. Detroit: Gale Research, 1992.

ConAu 15NR *Contemporary Authors, New Revision Series.* A bio-bibliographical guide to current writers in fiction, general nonfiction, poetry, journalism, drama, motion pictures, television, and other fields. Volume 15. Detroit: Gale Research, 1985.

ConAu 16AS *Contemporary Authors, Autobiography Series.* Volume 16. Detroit: Gale Research, 1992.

ConAu 16NR *Contemporary Authors, New Revision Series.* A bio-bibliographical guide to current writers in fiction, general nonfiction, poetry, journalism, drama, motion pictures, television, and other fields. Volume 16. Detroit: Gale Research, 1986.

ConAu 17AS *Contemporary Authors, Autobiography Series.* Volume 17. Detroit: Gale Research, 1993.

ConAu 17NR *Contemporary Authors, New Revision Series.* A bio-bibliographical guide to current writers in fiction, general nonfiction, poetry, journalism, drama, motion pictures, television, and other fields. Volume 17. Detroit: Gale Research, 1986.

ConAu 17R *Contemporary Authors.* A bio-bibliographical guide to current writers in fiction, general nonfiction, poetry, journalism, drama, motion pictures, television, and other fields. Volumes 17-20, 1st revision. Detroit: Gale Research, 1976.

ConAu 18AS *Contemporary Authors, Autobiography Series.* Volume 18. Detroit: Gale Research, 1994.

ConAu 18NR *Contemporary Authors, New Revision Series.* A bio-bibliographical guide to current writers in fiction, general nonfiction, poetry, journalism, drama, motion pictures, television, and other fields. Volume 18. Detroit: Gale Research, 1986.

ConAu 19AS *Contemporary Authors, Autobiography Series.* Volume 19. Detroit: Gale Research, 1994.

ConAu 19NR *Contemporary Authors, New Revision Series.* A bio-bibliographical guide to current writers in fiction, general nonfiction, poetry, journalism, drama, motion pictures, television, and other fields. Volume 19. Detroit: Gale Research, 1987.

ConAu 20AS *Contemporary Authors, Autobiography Series.* Volume 20. Detroit: Gale Research, 1994.

ConAu 20NR *Contemporary Authors, New Revision Series.* A bio-bibliographical guide to current writers in fiction, general nonfiction, poetry, journalism, drama, motion pictures, television, and other fields. Volume 20. Detroit: Gale Research, 1987.

ConAu 21AS *Contemporary Authors, Autobiography Series.* Volume 21. Detroit: Gale Research, 1995.

ConAu 21NR *Contemporary Authors, New Revision Series.* A bio-bibliographical guide to current writers in fiction, general nonfiction, poetry, journalism, drama, motion pictures, television, and other fields. Volume 21. Detroit: Gale Research, 1987.

ConAu 21R *Contemporary Authors.* A bio-bibliographical guide to current writers in fiction, general nonfiction, poetry, journalism, drama, motion pictures, television, and other fields. Volumes 21-24, 1st revision. Detroit: Gale Research, 1977.

ConAu 22AS *Contemporary Authors, Autobiography Series.* Volume 22. Detroit: Gale Research, 1996.

ConAu 22NR *Contemporary Authors, New Revision Series.* A bio-bibliographical guide to current writers in fiction, general nonfiction, poetry, journalism, drama, motion pictures, television, and other fields. Volume 22. Detroit: Gale Research, 1988.

ConAu 23AS *Contemporary Authors, Autobiography Series.* Volume 23. Detroit: Gale Research, 1996.

ConAu 23NR *Contemporary Authors, New Revision Series.* A bio-bibliographical guide to current writers in fiction, general nonfiction, poetry, journalism, drama, motion pictures, television, and other fields. Volume 23. Detroit: Gale Research, 1988.

ConAu 24AS *Contemporary Authors, Autobiography Series.* Volume 24. Detroit: Gale Research, 1996.

ConAu 24NR *Contemporary Authors, New Revision Series.* A bio-bibliographical guide to current writers in fiction, general nonfiction, poetry, journalism, drama, motion pictures, television, and other fields. Volume 24. Detroit: Gale Research, 1988.

ConAu 25AS *Contemporary Authors, Autobiography Series.* Volume 25. Detroit: Gale Research, 1997.

ConAu 25NR *Contemporary Authors, New Revision Series.* A bio-bibliographical guide to current writers in fiction, general nonfiction, poetry, journalism, drama, motion pictures, television, and other fields. Volume 25. Detroit: Gale Research, 1989.

ConAu 25R *Contemporary Authors.* A bio-bibliographical guide to current writers in fiction, general nonfiction, poetry, journalism, drama, motion pictures, television, and other fields. Volumes 25-28, 1st revision. Detroit: Gale Research, 1977.

ConAu *Contemporary Authors, New Revision Series.* A bio-bibliographical guide to current writers in fiction, general nonfiction, poetry, journalism, drama, motion pictures, television, and other fields. Detroit: Gale Research, 1989-1990.
ConAu 26NR Volume 26; 1989.
ConAu 27NR Volume 27; 1989.

ConAu 28NR	Volume 28; 1990.
ConAu 29NR	Volume 29; 1990.

ConAu 29R *Contemporary Authors.* A bio-bibliographical guide to current writers in fiction, general nonfiction, poetry, journalism, drama, motion pictures, television, and other fields. Volumes 29-32, 1st revision. Detroit: Gale Research, 1978.

ConAu *Contemporary Authors, New Revision Series.* A bio-bibliographical guide to current writers in fiction, general nonfiction, poetry, journalism, drama, motion pictures, television, and other fields. Detroit: Gale Research, 1990-1991.

ConAu 30NR	Volume 30; 1990.
ConAu 31NR	Volume 31; 1990.
ConAu 32NR	Volume 32; 1991.
ConAu 33NR	Volume 33; 1991.

ConAu 33R *Contemporary Authors.* A bio-bibliographical guide to current writers in fiction, general nonfiction, poetry, journalism, drama, motion pictures, television, and other fields. Volumes 33-36, 1st revision. Detroit: Gale Research, 1978.

ConAu *Contemporary Authors, New Revision Series.* A bio-bibliographical guide to current writers in fiction, general nonfiction, poetry, journalism, drama, motion pictures, television, and other fields. Detroit: Gale Research, 1991-1992.

ConAu 34NR	Volume 34; 1991.
ConAu 35NR	Volume 35; 1992.
ConAu 36NR	Volume 36; 1992.
ConAu 37NR	Volume 37; 1992.

ConAu 37R *Contemporary Authors.* A bio-bibliographical guide to current writers in fiction, general nonfiction, poetry, journalism, drama, motion pictures, television, and other fields. Volumes 37-40, 1st revision. Detroit: Gale Research, 1979.

ConAu *Contemporary Authors, New Revision Series.* A bio-bibliographical guide to current writers in fiction, general nonfiction, poetry, journalism, drama, motion pictures, television, and other fields. Detroit: Gale Research, 1993-1994.

ConAu 38NR	Volume 38; 1993.
ConAu 39NR	Volume 39; 1992.
ConAu 40NR	Volume 40; 1993.
ConAu 41NR	Volume 41; 1994.

ConAu 41R *Contemporary Authors.* A bio-bibliographical guide to current writers in fiction, general nonfiction, poetry, journalism, drama, motion pictures, television, and other fields. Volumes 41-44, 1st revision. Detroit: Gale Research, 1979.

ConAu *Contemporary Authors, New Revision Series.* A bio-bibliographical guide to current writers in fiction, general nonfiction, poetry, journalism, drama, motion pictures, television, and other fields. Detroit: Gale Research, 1994.

ConAu 42NR	Volume 42.
ConAu 43NR	Volume 43.
ConAu 44NR	Volume 44.

ConAu 45 *Contemporary Authors.* A bio-bibliographical guide to current writers in fiction, general nonfiction, poetry, journalism, drama, motion pictures, television, and other fields. Volumes 45-48. Detroit: Gale Research, 1974.

ConAu *Contemporary Authors, New Revision Series.* A bio-bibliographical guide to current writers in fiction, general nonfiction, poetry, journalism, drama, motion pictures, television, and other fields. Detroit: Gale Research, 1995.

ConAu 45NR	Volume 45.
ConAu 46NR	Volume 46.
ConAu 47NR	Volume 47.
ConAu 48NR	Volume 48.

ConAu 49 *Contemporary Authors.* A bio-bibliographical guide to current writers in fiction, general nonfiction, poetry, journalism, drama, motion pictures, television, and other fields. Volumes 49-52. Detroit: Gale Research, 1975.

ConAu *Contemporary Authors, New Revision Series.* A bio-bibliographic guide to current writers in fiction, general nonfiction, poetry, journalism, drama, motion pictures, television, and other fields. Detroit: Gale Research, 1995-1996.

ConAu 49NR	Volume 49; 1995.
ConAu 50NR	Volume 50; 1996.
ConAu 51NR	Volume 51; 1996.
ConAu 52NR	Volume 52; 1996.

ConAu 53 *Contemporary Authors.* A bio-bibliographical guide to current writers in fiction, general nonfiction, poetry, journalism, drama, motion pictures, television, and other fields. Volumes 53-56. Detroit: Gale Research, 1975.

ConAu *Contemporary Authors, New Revision Series.* A bio-bibliographic guide to current writers in fiction, general nonfiction, poetry, journalism, drama, motion pictures, television, and other fields. Detroit: Gale Research, 1997.

ConAu 53NR	Volume 53.
ConAu 54NR	Volume 54.
ConAu 55NR	Volume 55.

ConAu *Contemporary Authors.* A bio-bibliographic guide to current writers in fiction, general nonfiction, poetry, journalism, drama, motion pictures, television, and other fields. Detroit: Gale Research, 1976-1997.

ConAu 57	Volumes 57-60; 1976.
ConAu 61	Volumes 61-64; 1976.
ConAu 65	Volumes 65-68; 1977.
ConAu 69	Volumes 69-72; 1978.
ConAu 73	Volumes 73-76; 1978.
ConAu 77	Volumes 77-80; 1979.
ConAu 81	Volumes 81-84; 1979.
ConAu 85	Volumes 85-88; 1980.
ConAu 89	Volumes 89-92; 1980.
ConAu 93	Volumes 93-96; 1980.
ConAu 97	Volumes 97-100; 1981.
ConAu 101	Volume 101; 1981.
ConAu 102	Volume 102; 1981.
ConAu 103	Volume 103; 1982.
ConAu 104	Volume 104; 1982.
ConAu 105	Volume 105; 1982.
ConAu 106	Volume 106; 1982.
ConAu 107	Volume 107; 1983.
ConAu 108	Volume 108; 1983.
ConAu 109	Volume 109; 1983.

ConAu 110	Volume 110; 1984.
ConAu 111	Volume 111; 1984.
ConAu 112	Volume 112; 1985.
ConAu 113	Volume 113; 1985.
ConAu 114	Volume 114; 1985.
ConAu 115	Volume 115; 1985.
ConAu 116	Volume 116; 1986.
ConAu 117	Volume 117; 1986.
ConAu 118	Volume 118; 1986.
ConAu 119	Volume 119; 1987.
ConAu 120	Volume 120; 1987.
ConAu 121	Volume 121; 1987.
ConAu 122	Volume 122; 1988.
ConAu 123	Volume 123; 1988.
ConAu 124	Volume 124; 1988.
ConAu 125	Volume 125; 1989.
ConAu 126	Volume 126; 1989.
ConAu 127	Volume 127; 1989.
ConAu 128	Volume 128; 1990.
ConAu 129	Volume 129; 1990.
ConAu 130	Volume 130; 1990.
ConAu 131	Volume 131; 1991.
ConAu 132	Volume 132; 1991.
ConAu 133	Volume 133; 1991.
ConAu 134	Volume 134; 1992.
ConAu 135	Volume 135; 1992.
ConAu 136	Volume 136; 1992.
ConAu 137	Volume 137; 1992.
ConAu 138	Volume 138; 1993.
ConAu 139	Volume 139; 1993.
ConAu 140	Volume 140; 1993.
ConAu 141	Volume 141; 1994.
ConAu 142	Volume 142; 1994.
ConAu 143	Volume 143; 1994.
ConAu 144	Volume 144; 1994.
ConAu 145	Volume 145; 1995.
ConAu 146	Volume 146; 1995.
ConAu 147	Volume 147; 1995.
ConAu 148	Volume 148; 1996.
ConAu 149	Volume 149; 1996.
ConAu 150	Volume 150; 1996.
ConAu 151	Volume 151; 1996.
ConAu 152	Volume 152; 1997.
ConAu 153	Volume 153; 1997.
ConAu 154	Volume 154; 1997.

ConAu *Contemporary Authors, Permanent Series.* A bio-bibliographical guide to current authors and their works. Detroit: Gale Research, 1975-1978.

ConAu P-1	Volume 1; 1975.
ConAu P-1	Volume 1; 1975.
ConAu P-2	Volume 2; 1978.
ConAu P-2	Volume 2; 1978.

ConAu X *Contemporary Authors, Index.* A bio-bibliographical guide to current writers in fiction, general nonfiction, poetry, journalism, drama, motion pictures, television, and other fields. Detroit: Gale Research, (n.d.).
This code refers to Pseudonym Entries which appear only as Cross-References in the Cumulative Index.

ConBlAP 88 *Contemporary Black American Playwrights and Their Plays.* A biographical directory and dramatic index. By Bernard L. Peterson, Jr. New York: Greenwood Press, 1988.

ConBlB *Contemporary Black Biography.* Profiles from the international black community. Detroit: Gale Research, 1992-1997.

ConBlB 1	Volume 1; 1992.
ConBlB 2	Volume 2; 1992.
ConBlB 3	Volume 3; 1993.
ConBlB 4	Volume 4; 1993.
ConBlB 5	Volume 5; 1994.
ConBlB 6	Volume 6; 1994.
ConBlB 7	Volume 7; 1994.
ConBlB 8	Volume 8; 1995.
ConBlB 9	Volume 9; 1995.
ConBlB 10	Volume 10; 1996.
ConBlB 11	Volume 11; 1996.
ConBlB 12	Volume 12; 1996.
ConBlB 13	Volume 13; 1997.

ConBrA 79 *Contemporary British Artists.* Edited by Charlotte Parry-Crooke. New York: St. Martin's Press, 1979.
Biographies are found in the ''Directory'' section.

ConBrDr *Contemporary British Dramatists.* Edited by K.A. Berney. London: St. James Press, 1994.

ConCaAu 1 *Contemporary Canadian Authors.* A bio-bibliographic guide to current Canadian writers in fiction, general nonfiction, poetry, journalism, drama, motion pictures, television, and other fields. Volume 1. Toronto: Gale Canada, 1996.

ConCom 92 *Contemporary Composers.* Edited by Brian Morton and Pamela Collins. Chicago: St. James Press, 1992.

ConDes 84 *Contemporary Designers.* First edition. Edited by Ann Lee Morgan. Contemporary Arts Series. Detroit: Gale Research, 1984.

ConDes *Contemporary Designers.* Contemporary Arts Series. Detroit: St. James Press, 1990-1997.

- ***ConDes 90*** Second edition. Edited by Colin Naylor; 1990.
- ***ConDes 97*** Third edition. Edited by Sara Pendergast; 1997.

ConDr *Contemporary Dramatists.* London: St. James Press, 1973-1993.

- ***ConDr 73*** First edition. Edited by James Vinson; 1973.
- ***ConDr 77*** Second edition. Edited by James Vinson; 1977.
- ***ConDr 77A*** Second edition. Edited by James Vinson; 1977. ''Screen Writers'' section begins on page 893.
- ***ConDr 77B*** Second edition. Edited by James Vinson; 1977. ''Radio Writers'' section begins on page 903.
- ***ConDr 77C*** Second edition. Edited by James Vinson; 1977. ''Television Writers'' section begins on page 915.
- ***ConDr 77D*** Second edition. Edited by James Vinson; 1977. ''Musical Librettists'' section begins on page 925.
- ***ConDr 77E*** Second edition. Edited by James Vinson; 1977. ''The Theatre of the Mixed Means'' section begins on page 941.
- ***ConDr 77F*** Second edition. Edited by James Vinson; 1977. Appendix begins on page 969.
- ***ConDr 82*** Third edition. Edited by James Vinson; 1982.
- ***ConDr 82(A*** Third edition. Edited by James Vinson; 1982. ''Screen Writers'' section begins on page 887.
- ***ConDr 82A*** Third edition. Edited by James Vinson; 1982. ''Screen Writers'' section begins on page 887.
- ***ConDr 82B*** Third edition. Edited by James Vinson; 1982. ''Radio Writers'' section begins on page 899.
- ***ConDr 82C*** Third edition. Edited by James Vinson; 1982. ''Television Writers'' section begins on page 911.
- ***ConDr 82D*** Third edition. Edited by James Vinson; 1982. ''Musical Librettists'' section begins on page 921.
- ***ConDr 82E*** Third edition. Edited by James Vinson; 1982. Appendix begins on page 951.
- ***ConDr 88*** Fourth edition. Edited by D.L. Kirkpatrick; 1988.
- ***ConDr 88A*** Fourth edition. Edited by D.L. Kirkpatrick; 1988. ''Screenwriters'' section begins on page 591.
- ***ConDr 88B*** Fourth edition. Edited by D.L. Kirkpatrick; 1988. ''Radio Writers'' section begins on page 605.
- ***ConDr 88C*** Fourth edition. Edited by D.L. Kirkpatrick; 1988. ''Television Writers'' section begins on page 615.
- ***ConDr 88D*** Fourth edition. Edited by D.L. Kirkpatrick; 1988. ''Musical Librettists'' section begins on page 625.
- ***ConDr 88E*** Fourth edition. Edited by D.L. Kirkpatrick; 1988. Appendix begins on page 651.
- ***ConDr 93*** Fifth edition. Edited by K.A. Berney; 1993.

ConEn *Contemporary Entrepreneurs.* Profiles of entrepreneurs and the businesses they started. Edited by Craig E. Aronoff and John L. Ward. Detroit: Omnigraphics, 1992.

ConFash *Contemporary Fashion.* Edited by Richard Martin. Contemporary Arts Series. Detroit: St. James Press, 1995.

ConFLW 84 *Contemporary Foreign Language Writers.* Edited by James Vinson and Daniel Kirkpatrick. New York: St. Martin's Press, 1984.

ConGAN *Contemporary Gay American Novelists.* A bio-bibliographical critical sourcebook. Edited by Emmanuel S. Nelson. Westport, CT: Greenwood Press, 1993.

ConGrA *Contemporary Graphic Artists.* A biographical, bibliographical, and critical guide to current illustrators, animators, cartoonists, designers, and other graphic artists. Edited by Maurice Horn. Detroit: Gale Research, 1986-1988.

- ***ConGrA 1*** Volume 1; 1986.
- ***ConGrA 2*** Volume 2; 1987.
- ***ConGrA 3*** Volume 3; 1988.

ConHero *Contemporary Heroes and Heroines.* Detroit: Gale Research, 1990-1992.

- ***ConHero 1*** Book I; 1990. Use the Index to locate individuals found in group biographies.
- ***ConHero 2*** Book II; 1992.

ConICB *Contemporary Illustrators of Children's Books.* Compiled by Bertha E. Mahony and Elinor Whitney. Boston: Bookshop for Boys and Girls, 1930. Reprint. Detroit: Gale Research, 1978.

ConIsC *Contemporary Issues Criticism.* Excerpts from criticism of contemporary writings in sociology, economics, politics, psychology, anthropology, education, history, law, theology, and related fields. Detroit: Gale Research, 1982-1984.

- ***ConIsC 1*** Volume 1; 1982.
- ***ConIsC 2*** Volume 2; 1984.

ConLC *Contemporary Literary Criticism.* Excerpts from criticism of the works of today's novelists, poets, playwrights, short story writers, scriptwriters, and other creative writers. Detroit: Gale Research, 1973-1997.

- ***ConLC 1*** Volume 1; 1973.
- ***ConLC 2*** Volume 2; 1974.
- ***ConLC 3*** Volume 3; 1975.
- ***ConLC 4*** Volume 4; 1975.
- ***ConLC 5*** Volume 5; 1976.
- ***ConLC 6*** Volume 6; 1976.
- ***ConLC 7*** Volume 7; 1977.
- ***ConLC 8*** Volume 8; 1978.
- ***ConLC 9*** Volume 9; 1978.
- ***ConLC 10*** Volume 10; 1979.
- ***ConLC 11*** Volume 11; 1979.
- ***ConLC 12*** Volume 12; 1980.
- ***ConLC 13*** Volume 13; 1980.
- ***ConLC 14*** Volume 14; 1980.
- ***ConLC 15*** Volume 15; 1980.
- ***ConLC 16*** Volume 16; 1981.
- ***ConLC 17*** Volume 17; 1981.
- ***ConLC 18*** Volume 18; 1981.
- ***ConLC 19*** Volume 19; 1981.

ConLC 20 Volume 20; 1982.
ConLC 21 Volume 21; 1982.
ConLC 22 Volume 22; 1982.
ConLC 23 Volume 23; 1983.
ConLC 24 Volume 24; 1983.
ConLC 25 Volume 25; 1983.
ConLC 26 Volume 26; 1983.
ConLC 27 Volume 27; 1984.
ConLC 28 Volume 28; 1984.
ConLC 29 Volume 29; 1984.
ConLC 30 Volume 30; 1984.
ConLC 31 Volume 31; 1985.
ConLC 32 Volume 32; 1985.
ConLC 33 Volume 33; 1985.
ConLC 34 Volume 34: Yearbook 1984; 1985. Use the ''Cumulative Author Index'' to locate entries.
ConLC 35 Volume 35; 1985.
ConLC 36 Volume 36; 1986.
ConLC 37 Volume 37; 1986.
ConLC 38 Volume 38; 1986.
ConLC 39 Volume 39: Yearbook 1985; 1986. Use the ''Cumulative Author Index'' to locate entries.
ConLC 40 Volume 40; 1986.
ConLC 41 Volume 41; 1987.
ConLC 42 Volume 42; 1987.
ConLC 43 Volume 43; 1987.
ConLC 44 Volume 44: Yearbook 1986; 1987. Use the ''Cumulative Author Index'' to locate entries.
ConLC 45 Volume 45; 1987.
ConLC 46 Volume 46; 1988.
ConLC 47 Volume 47; 1988.
ConLC 48 Volume 48; 1988.
ConLC 49 Volume 49; 1988.
ConLC 50 Volume 50: Yearbook 1987; 1988. Use the ''Cumulative Author Index'' to locate entries.
ConLC 51 Volume 51; 1989.
ConLC 52 Volume 52; 1989.
ConLC 53 Volume 53; 1989.
ConLC 54 Volume 54; 1989.
ConLC 55 Volume 55: Yearbook 1988; 1989. Use the ''Cumulative Author Index'' to locate entries.
ConLC 56 Volume 56; 1989.
ConLC 57 Volume 57; 1990.
ConLC 58 Volume 58; 1990.
ConLC 59 Volume 59: Yearbook 1989; 1990. Use the ''Cumulative Author Index'' to locate entries.
ConLC 60 Volume 60; 1990.
ConLC 61 Volume 61; 1990.
ConLC 62 Volume 62; 1991.
ConLC 63 Volume 63; 1991.
ConLC 64 Volume 64; 1991.
ConLC 65 Volume 65: Yearbook 1990; 1991. Use the ''Cumulative Author Index'' to locate entries.
ConLC 66 Volume 66; 1991.
ConLC 67 Volume 67; 1992.

ConLC 68	Volume 68; 1992.
ConLC 69	Volume 69; 1992.
ConLC 70	Volume 70: Yearbook 1991; 1992. Use the "Cumulative Author Index" to locate entries.
ConLC 71	Volume 71; 1992.
ConLC 72	Volume 72; 1992.
ConLC 73	Volume 73; 1993.
ConLC 74	Volume 74; 1993.
ConLC 75	Volume 75; 1993.
ConLC 76	Volume 76: Yearbook 1992; 1993. Use the "Cumulative Author Index" to locate entries.
ConLC 77	Volume 77; 1993.
ConLC 78	Volume 78; 1994.
ConLC 79	Volume 79; 1994.
ConLC 80	Volume 80; 1994.
ConLC 81	Volume 81: Yearbook 1993; 1994. Use the "Cumulative Author Index" to locate entries.
ConLC 82	Volume 82; 1994.
ConLC 83	Volume 83; 1994.
ConLC 84	Volume 84; 1995.
ConLC 85	Volume 85; 1995.
ConLC 86	Volume 86: Yearbook 1994; 1995. Use the "Cumulative Author Index" to locate entries.
ConLC 87	Volume 87; 1995.
ConLC 88	Volume 88; 1995.
ConLC 89	Volume 89; 1996.
ConLC 90	Volume 90; 1996.
ConLC 91	Volume 91; 1996.
ConLC 92	Volume 92; 1996.
ConLC 93	Volume 93; 1996.
ConLC 94	Volume 94; 1996.
ConLC 95	Volume 95; 1997.
ConLC 96	Volume 96; 1997.
ConLC 97	Volume 97; 1997.
ConLC 98	Volume 98; 1997.

ConLCrt 77 *Contemporary Literary Critics.* First edition. By Elmer Borklund. London: St. James Press; New York: St. Martin's Press, 1977.

ConLCrt 82 *Contemporary Literary Critics.* Second edition. By Elmer Borklund. Detroit: Gale Research, 1982.

ConMuA *Contemporary Music Almanac, 1980/81.* By Ronald Zalkind. New York: Macmillan Publishing Co., Schirmer Books, 1980.

ConMuA 80A	"Who's Who--Artists" section begins on page 157.
ConMuA 80B	"Music Business Professionals" section begins on page 351.

ConMus *Contemporary Musicians.* Profiles of the people in music. Detroit: Gale Research, 1989-1997.

ConMus 1	Volume 1; 1989.
ConMus 2	Volume 2; 1990.
ConMus 3	Volume 3; 1990.

ConMus 4 Volume 4; 1991.
ConMus 5 Volume 5; 1991.
ConMus 6 Volume 6; 1992.
ConMus 7 Volume 7; 1992.
ConMus 8 Volume 8; 1993.
ConMus 9 Volume 9; 1993.
ConMus 10 Volume 10; 1994.
ConMus 11 Volume 11; 1994.
ConMus 12 Volume 12; 1994.
ConMus 13 Volume 13; 1995.
ConMus 14 Volume 14; 1995.
ConMus 15 Volume 15; 1996.
ConMus 16 Volume 16; 1996.
ConMus 17 Volume 17; 1997.

ConNews *Contemporary Newsmakers.* A biographical guide to people in the news in business, education, technology, social issues, politics, law, economics, international affairs, religion, entertainment, labor, sports, design, psychology, medicine, astronautics, ecology, and other fields. Detroit: Gale Research, 1985-1988.Later editions published as *Newsmakers.*

ConNews 85-1 1985, Issue 1; 1985.
ConNews 85-2 1985, Issue 2; 1985.
ConNews 85-3 1985, Issue 3; 1986.
ConNews 85-4 1985, Issue 4; 1986.
ConNews 86-1 1986, Issue 1; 1986.
ConNews 86-2 1986, Issue 2; 1986.
ConNews 86-3 1986, Issue 3; 1987.
ConNews 86-4 1986, Issue 4; 1987.
ConNews 87-1 1987, Issue 1; 1987.
ConNews 87-2 1987, Issue 2; 1987.
ConNews 87-3 1987, Issue 3; 1988.
ConNews 87-4 1987, Issue 4; 1988.
ConNews 88-1 1988, Issue 1; 1988.

Use the "Cumulative Newsmaker Index" to locate entries in each quarterly edition.

ConNov *Contemporary Novelists.* Detroit: St. James Press, 1972-1996.

ConNov 72 First edition. Edited by James Vinson; 1972.
ConNov 76 Second edition. Edited by James Vinson; 1976.
ConNov 82 Third edition. Edited by James Vinson; 1982.
ConNov 82A Third edition. Edited by James Vinson; 1982. The Appendix is located at the back of this edition.
ConNov 86 Fourth edition. Edited by D.L. Kirkpatrick; 1986.
ConNov 86A Fourth edition. Edited by D.L. Kirkpatrick; 1986. The Appendix is located at the back of this edition.
ConNov 91 Fifth edition. Edited by Lesley Henderson; 1991.
ConNov 96 Sixth edition. Edited by Susan Windisch Brown; 1996.

ConPhot 82 *Contemporary Photographers.* First edition. Edited by George Walsh, Colin Naylor, and Michael Held. Contemporary Arts Series. New York: St. Martin's Press, 1982.

ConPhot *Contemporary Photographers.* Contemporary Arts Series. Detroit: St. James Press, 1988-1995.

ConPhot 88 Second edition. Edited by Colin Naylor; 1988.

ConPhot 95 Third edition. Edited by Martin Marix Evans; 1995.

ConPo *Contemporary Poets.* Detroit: St. James Press, 1970-1996.
- ***ConPo 70*** First edition. Edited by Rosalie Murphy; 1970.
- ***ConPo 75*** Second edition. Edited by James Vinson; 1975.
- ***ConPo 80*** Third edition. Edited by James Vinson; 1980.
- ***ConPo 80A*** Third edition. Edited by James Vinson; 1980. The Appendix is located at the back of this edition.
- ***ConPo 85*** Fourth edition. Edited by James Vinson and D.L. Kirkpatrick; 1985.
- ***ConPo 85A*** Fourth edition. Edited by James Vinson and D.L. Kirkpatrick; 1985. The Appendix is located at the back of this edition.
- ***ConPo 91*** Fifth edition. Edited by Tracy Chevalier; 1991.
- ***ConPo 96*** Sixth edition. Edited by Thomas Riggs; 1996.

ConPopW *Contemporary Popular Writers.* Edited by Dave Mote. Detroit: St. James Press, 1997.

ConSFA *Contemporary Science Fiction Authors.* First edition. Compiled and edited by R. Reginald. New York: Arno Press, 1975. Previously published as *Stella Nova: The Contemporary Science Fiction Authors.* Los Angeles: Unicorn & Son, Publishers, 1970.

ConSFF *Contemporary Science Fiction, Fantasy, and Horror Poetry.* A resource guide and biographical directory. By Scott E. Green. New York: Greenwood Press, 1989. Biographies are found in the ''Biographical Directory of Poets'' section which begins on page 85.

ConSpAP *Contemporary Spanish American Poets.* A bibliography of primary and secondary sources. Compiled by Jacobo Sefami. Bibliographies and Indexes in World Literature, no. 33. New York: Greenwood Press, 1992.

ConSSWr *Contemporary Spanish-Speaking Writers and Illustrators for Children and Young Adults.* A biographical dictionary. Edited by Isabel Schon. Westport, CT: Greenwood Press, 1994.

ContDcW 89 *The Continuum Dictionary of Women's Biography.* Second edition. Edited by Jennifer S. Uglow. New York: Continuum Publishing, 1989. First edition published as *The International Dictionary of Women's Biography.*

ConTFT *Contemporary Theatre, Film, and Television.* A biographical guide featuring performers, directors, writers, producers, designers, managers, choreographers, technicians, composers, executives, dancers, and critics in the United States and Great Britain. Detroit: Gale Research, 1984-1996.Earlier editions published as *Who's Who in the Theatre.*
- ***ConTFT 1*** Volume 1; 1984.
- ***ConTFT 2*** Volume 2; 1986.
- ***ConTFT 3*** Volume 3; 1986.
- ***ConTFT 4*** Volume 4; 1987.
- ***ConTFT 5*** Volume 5; 1988.
- ***ConTFT 6*** Volume 6; 1989.
- ***ConTFT 7*** Volume 7; 1989.
- ***ConTFT 8*** Volume 8; 1990.

ConTFT 9 Volume 9; 1992.
ConTFT 10 Volume 10; 1993.
ConTFT 11 Volume 11; 1994.
ConTFT 12 Volume 12; 1994.
ConTFT 13 Volume 13; 1995.
ConTFT 14 Volume 14; 1996.
ConTFT 15 Volume 15; 1996.

ConTurW *Contemporary Turkish Writers.* A critical bio-bibliography of leading writers in the Turkish Republican Period up to 1980. By Louis Mitler. Uralic and Altaic Series, vol. 146. Bloomington, IN: Indiana University Research Institute for Inner Asian Studies, 1988.

Conv *Conversations.* Conversations series. Detroit: Gale Research, 1977-1978.
Conv 1 Volume 1: *Conversations with Writers.*; 1977.
Conv 2 Volume 2: *Conversations with Jazz Musicians.*; 1977.
Conv 3 Volume 3: *Conversations with Writers II.*; 1978.

ConWomD *Contemporary Women Dramatists.* Edited by K.A. Berney. London: St. James Press, 1994.

ConWomW *Contemporary Women Writers of Spain.* By Janet Perez. Twayne's World Authors Series, no. 798, Spanish Literature. Boston: Twayne Publishers, 1988.
Use the Index to locate biographies.

ConWorW 93 *Contemporary World Writers.* Second edition. Edited by Tracy Chevalier. Contemporary Writers of the English Language Series. Detroit: St. James Press, 1993. First edition published as *Contemporary Foreign-Language Writers.*

CopCroC *Cops, Crooks, and Criminologists.* An international biographical dictionary of law enforcement. By Alan Axelrod and Charles Phillips. New York: Facts on File, 1996.

CorpD *Corpus Delicti of Mystery Fiction.* A guide to the body of the case. By Linda Herman and Beth Stiel. Metuchen, NJ: Scarecrow Press, 1974.
Biographies begin on page 31.

CounME 74 *The Country Music Encyclopedia.* By Melvin Shestack. New York: Thomas Y. Crowell Co., 1974.
CounME 74A The "Discography" begins on page 325.

CpmDNM *Composium Directory of New Music.* Annual index of contemporary compositions. Sedro Woolley, WA: Crystal Musicworks, 1972-1983.
CpmDNM 72 1972 edition; 1972.
CpmDNM 73 1973 edition; 1973.
CpmDNM 74 1974 edition; 1974.
CpmDNM 75 1975 edition; 1975.
CpmDNM 76 1976 edition; 1976.
CpmDNM 77 1977 edition; 1977.
CpmDNM 78 1978 edition; 1978.
CpmDNM 79 1979 edition; 1979.
CpmDNM 80 1980 edition; 1980.
CpmDNM 81 1981 edition; 1981.
CpmDNM 82 1982/83 edition; 1983.

CreCan *Creative Canada.* A biographical dictionary of twentieth-century creative and performing artists. Compiled by the Reference Division, McPherson Library, University of Victoria, British Columbia. Toronto: University of Toronto Press, 1971-1972.

CreCan 1	Volume 1; 1971.
CreCan 2	Volume 2; 1972.

CroCAP *Crowell's Handbook of Contemporary American Poetry.* By Karl Malkoff. New York: Thomas Y. Crowell Co., 1973.
Biographies begin on page 43.

CroCD *Crowell's Handbook of Contemporary Drama.* By Michael Anderson et al. New York: Thomas Y. Crowell Co., 1971.

CroE&S *Crowell's Handbook of Elizabethan & Stuart Literature.* By James E. Ruoff. New York: Thomas Y. Crowell Co., 1975.

CrtSuDr *Critical Survey of Drama.* Revised edition. Seven volumes. Edited by Frank N. Magill. Pasadena, CA: Salem Press, 1994.

CrtSuMy *Critical Survey of Mystery and Detective Fiction.* Four volumes. Edited by Frank N. Magill. Pasadena, CA: Salem Press, 1988.

CrtT *The Critical Temper.* A survey of modern criticism on English and American literature from the beginnings to the twentieth century. Edited by Martin Tucker. A Library of Literary Criticism. New York: Frederick Ungar Publishing Co., 1969-1979.

CrtT 1	Volume I: From Old English to Shakespeare; 1969.
CrtT 2	Volume II: From Milton to Romantic Literature; 1969.
CrtT 3	Volume III: Victorian Literature and American Literature; 1969.
CrtT 4	Volume IV: Supplement; 1979.

CubExWr *Cuban Exile Writers.* A biobibliographic handbook. By Daniel C. Maratos and Marnesba D. Hill. Metuchen, NJ: Scarecrow Press, 1986.
Biographies begin on page 19.

CurBio *Current Biography Yearbook.* New York, NY: H.W. Wilson Co., 1940-1996.

CurBio 40	*1940.*; 1940.
CurBio 41	*1941.*; 1941.
CurBio 42	*1942.*; 1942.
CurBio 43	*1943.*; 1943.
CurBio 44	*1944.*; 1944.
CurBio 45	*1945.*; 1945.
CurBio 46	*1946.*; 1946.
CurBio 47	*1947.*; 1947.
CurBio 48	*1948.*; 1948.
CurBio 49	*1949.*; 1949.
CurBio 50	*1950.*; 1950.
CurBio 51	*1951.*; 1951.
CurBio 52	*1952.*; 1952.

CurBio 53	*1953.*; 1953.
CurBio 54	*1954.*; 1954.
CurBio 55	*1955.*; 1955.
CurBio 56	*1956.*; 1956.
CurBio 57	*1957.*; 1957.
CurBio 58	*1958.*; 1958.
CurBio 59	*1959.*; 1959.
CurBio 60	*1960.*; 1960.
CurBio 61	*1961.*; 1961.
CurBio 62	*1962.*; 1962.
CurBio 63	*1963.*; 1963.
CurBio 64	*1964.*; 1964.
CurBio 65	*1965.*; 1965.
CurBio 66	*1966.*; 1966.
CurBio 67	*1967.*; 1967.
CurBio 68	*1968.*; 1968.
CurBio 69	*1969.*; 1969.
CurBio 70	*1970.*; 1970.
CurBio 71	*1971.*; 1971.
CurBio 71N	*1971.*; 1971. Obituary Section located in the back of the volume.
CurBio 72	*1972.*; 1972.
CurBio 72N	*1972.*; 1972. Obituary Section located in the back of the volume.
CurBio 73	*1973.*; 1973.
CurBio 73N	*1973.*; 1973. Obituary Section located in the back of the volume.
CurBio 74	*1974.*; 1974.
CurBio 74N	*1974.*; 1974. Obituary Section located in the back of the volume.
CurBio 75	*1975.*; 1975.
CurBio 75N	*1975.*; 1975. Obituary Section located in the back of the volume.
CurBio 76	*1976.*; 1976.
CurBio 76N	*1976.*; 1976. Obituary Section located in the back of the volume.
CurBio 77	*1977.*; 1977.
CurBio 77N	*1977.*; 1977. Obituary Section located in the back of the volume.
CurBio 78	*1978.*; 1978.
CurBio 78N	*1978.*; 1978. Obituary Section located in the back of the volume.
CurBio 79	*1979.*; 1979.
CurBio 79N	*1979.*; 1979. Obituary Section located in the back of the volume.
CurBio 80	*1980.*; 1980.
CurBio 80N	*1980.*; 1980. Obituary Section located in the back of the volume.
CurBio 81	*1981.*; 1981.
CurBio 81N	*1981.*; 1981. Obituary Section located in the back of the volume.
CurBio 82	*1982.*; 1982.
CurBio 82N	*1982.*; 1982. Obituary Section located in the back of the volume.
CurBio 83	*1983.*; 1983.

CurBio 83N *1983.*; 1983. Obituary Section located in the back of the volume.
CurBio 84 *1984.*; 1985.
CurBio 84N *1984.*; 1985. Obituary Section located in the back of the volume.
CurBio 85 *1985.*; 1985.
CurBio 85N *1985.*; 1985. Obituary Section located in the back of the volume.
CurBio 86 *1986.*; 1987.
CurBio 86N *1986.*; 1987. Obituary Section located in the back of the volume.
CurBio 87 *1987.*; 1988.
CurBio 87N *1987.*; 1988. Obituary Section located in the back of the volume.
CurBio 88 *1988.*; 1989.
CurBio 88N *1988.*; 1989. Obituary Section located in the back of the volume.
CurBio 89 *1989.*; 1990.
CurBio 89N *1989.*; 1990. Obituary section located in the back of the volume.
CurBio 90 *1990.*; 1990.
CurBio 90N *1990.*; 1990. Obituary section located in the back of the volume.
CurBio 91 *1991.*; 1991.
CurBio 91N *1991.*; 1991. Obituary section located in the back of the volume.
CurBio 92 *1992.*; 1992.
CurBio 92N *1992.*; 1992. Obituary section located in the back of the volume.
CurBio 93 *1993.*; 1993.
CurBio 93N *1993.*; 1993. Obituary section located in the back of the volume.
CurBio 94 *1994.*; 1994.
CurBio 94N *1994.*; 1994. Obituary section located in the back of the volume.
CurBio 95 1995; 1995.
CurBio 95N 1995; 1995. Obituary section located in the back of the volume.
CurBio 96 *1996.*; 1996.
CurBio 96N *1996.*; 1996. Obituary section located in the back of the volume.

CyAG *Cyclopedia of American Government.* Three volumes. Edited by Andrew C. McLaughlin and Albert Bushnell Hart. New York: D. Appleton & Co., 1914. Reprint. Gloucester, Mass.: Peter Smith, 1963.

CyAL *Cyclopaedia of American Literature.* Embracing personal and critical notices of authors, and selections from their writings, from the earliest period to the present day; with portraits, autographs, and other illustrations. By Evert A. Duyckinck and George L. Duyckinck. Philadelphia: William Rutter & Co., 1875. Reprint. Detroit: Gale Research, 1965.
CyAL Two volumes. Use the Index in volume 2 to locate biographies.
CyAL 1 Volume 1. Use the Index in Volume 2 to locate biographies.

CyAL 2 — Volume 2. Use the Index in Volume 2 to locate biographies.

CyEd — *A Cyclopedia of Education.* Five volumes. Edited by Paul Monroe. New York: Macmillan Co., 1911. Reprint. Detroit: Gale Research, 1968.

CyWA 58 — *Cyclopedia of World Authors.* Edited by Frank N. Magill. New York: Harper & Row, Publishers, 1958. Also published as *Masterplots Cyclopedia of World Authors.*

CyWA 89 — *Cyclopedia of World Authors II.* Four volumes. Edited by Frank N. Magill. Pasadena, CA: Salem Press, 1989.

DancEn 78 — *The Dance Encyclopedia.* Revised and enlarged edition. Compiled and edited by Anatole Chujoy and P.W. Manchester. New York: Simon and Schuster, 1978.

DcAfAmP — *Dictionary of Afro-American Performers.* 78 RPM and cylinder recordings of opera, choral music, and songs, c. 1900-1949. By Patricia Turner. Garland Reference Library of the Humanities, vol. 590. New York: Garland Publishing, 1990.

DcAfHiB 86 — *Dictionary of African Historical Biography.* Second edition. By Mark R. Lipschutz and R. Kent Rasmussen. Berkeley, CA and Los Angeles: University of California Press, 1986.

DcAfHiB 86S — "Supplement of Post-1960 Political Leaders" begins on page 258.

DcAfL — *Dictionary of Afro-Latin American Civilization.* By Benjamin Nunez. Westport, CT: Greenwood Press, 1980.

DcAmArt — *Dictionary of American Art.* By Matthew Baigell. New York: Harper & Row, Publishers, 1979.

DcAmAu — *A Dictionary of American Authors.* Fifth edition, revised and enlarged. By Oscar Fay Adams. New York: Houghton Mifflin Co., 1904. Reprint. Detroit: Gale Research, 1969.

Biographies are found in the "Dictionary of American Authors" section which begins on page 1 and in the "Supplement" which begins on page 441.

DcAmB — *Dictionary of American Biography.* New York: Charles Scribner's Sons, 1928-1995.

DcAmB	Volumes 1-20; 1928.
DcAmB S1	Supplement 1; 1944.
DcAmB S2	Supplement 2; 1958.
DcAmB S3	Supplement 3; 1973.
DcAmB S4	Supplement 4; 1974.
DcAmB S5	Supplement 5; 1977.
DcAmB S6	Supplement 6; 1980.
DcAmB S7	Supplement 7; 1981.
DcAmB S8	Supplement 8; 1988.
DcAmB S9	Supplement 9; 1994.
DcAmB S10	Supplement 10; 1995.

DcAmBC — *Dictionary of American Book Collectors.* By Donald C. Dickinson. New York: Greenwood Press, 1986.

DcAmC *Dictionary of American Conservatism.* By Louis Filler. New York: Philosophical Library, 1987.

DcAmChF *Dictionary of American Children's Fiction.* Books of recognized merit. By Alethea K. Helbig and Agnes Regan Perkins. Westport, CT: Greenwood Press, 1986-1993.
- ***DcAmChF 1960*** *1960-1984.*; 1986.
- ***DcAmChF 1985*** *1985-1989.*; 1993.

DcAmDH *Dictionary of American Diplomatic History.* By John E. Findling. New York: Greenwood Press, 1980-1989.
- ***DcAmDH 80*** First edition; 1980.
- ***DcAmDH 89*** Second edition; 1989.

DcAmImH *Dictionary of American Immigration History.* Edited by Francesco Cordasco. Metuchen, NJ: Scarecrow Press, 1990.

DcAmLiB *Dictionary of American Library Biography.* Edited by Bohdan S. Wynar. Littleton, CO: Libraries Unlimited, 1978.

DcAmMeB *Dictionary of American Medical Biography.* Lives of eminent physicians of the United States and Canada, from the earliest times. By Howard A. Kelly and Walter L. Burrage. New York: D. Appleton & Co., 1928. Reprint. Road Town, Tortola, British Virgin Islands: Longwood Press, 1979.

DcAmMeB 84 *Dictionary of American Medical Biography.* Two volumes. Edited by Martin Kaufman, Stuart Galishoff, and Todd L. Savitt. Westport, CT: Greenwood Press, 1984.

DcAmMiB *Dictionary of American Military Biography.* Three volumes. Edited by Roger J. Spiller. Westport, CT: Greenwood Press, 1984.

DcAmNB *Dictionary of American Negro Biography.* Edited by Rayford W. Logan and Michael R. Winston. New York: W.W. Norton & Co., 1982.

DcAmReB *Dictionary of American Religious Biography.* By Henry Warner Bowden. Westport, CT: Greenwood Press, 1977-1993.
- ***DcAmReB 1*** First edition; 1977.
- ***DcAmReB 2*** Second edition; 1993.

DcAmSR *A Dictionary of American Social Reform.* By Louis Filler. New York: Philosophical Library, 1963.

DcAmTB *Dictionary of American Temperance Biography.* From Temperance Reform to Alcohol Research, the 1600s to the 1980s. By Mark Edward Lender. Westport, CT: Greenwood Press, 1984.

DcArts *Dictionary of the Arts.* New York: Facts on File, 1994.

DcBiA *A Dictionary of Biographies of Authors Represented in the Authors Digest Series.* With a supplemental list of later titles and a supplementary biographical

section. Edited by Rossiter Johnson. New York: Authors Press, 1927. Reprint. Detroit: Gale Research, 1974.
"Biographies of Authors" begin on page 3 and "Biographies of Authors Whose Works Are in Volume XVIII" begin on page 437.

DcBiPP *A Dictionary of Biography, Past and Present.* Containing the chief events in the lives of eminent persons of all ages and nations. Edited by Benjamin Vincent. Haydn Series. London: Ward, Lock, & Co., 1877. Reprint. Detroit: Gale Research, 1974.

DcBiPP A	Addenda begin on page 638.

DcBrAmW *A Dictionary of British and American Women Writers, 1660-1800.* Edited by Janet Todd. Totowa, NJ: Rowman & Allanheld, 1985.
Biographies begin on page 27.

DcBrAr *Dictionary of British Artists Working 1900-1950.* By Grant M. Waters. Eastbourne, England: Eastbourne Fine Art Publications, 1975-1976.

DcBrAr 1	Volume I; 1975.
DcBrAr 2	Volume II; 1976.

DcBrazL *Dictionary of Brazilian Literature.* Edited by Irwin Stern. New York: Greenwood Press, 1988.

DcBrBI *The Dictionary of British Book Illustrators and Caricaturists, 1800-1914.* By Simon Houfe. Woodbridge, England: Antique Collectors' Club, 1978.
Biographies begin on page 215.

DcBrECP *The Dictionary of British Eighteenth Century Painters in Oils and Crayons* By Ellis Waterhouse. Woodbridge, England: Antique Collectors' Club, 1981.

DcBrWA *The Dictionary of British Watercolour Artists up to 1920.* By H.L. Mallalieu. Woodbridge, England: Antique Collectors' Club, 1976.

DcCAA *Dictionary of Contemporary American Artists.* By Paul Cummings. New York: St. Martin's Press, 1971-1994.

DcCAA 71	Second edition; 1971.
DcCAA 77	Third edition; 1977.
DcCAA 88	Fifth edition; 1988.
DcCAA 94	Sixth edition; 1994.

DcCanB *Dictionary of Canadian Biography.* Toronto: University of Toronto Press, 1966-1994.

DcCanB 1	*Volume I: 1000 to 1700.* Edited by George W. Brown; 1966.
DcCanB 1A	*Volume I: 1000 to 1700.* Edited by George W. Brown; 1966. Appendix begins on page 675.
DcCanB 2	*Volume II: 1701 to 1740.* Edited by David M. Hayne; 1969.
DcCanB 3	*Volume III: 1741 to 1770.* Edited by Francess G. Halpenny; 1974.
DcCanB 3A	*Volume III: 1741 to 1770.* Edited by Francess G. Halpenny; 1974. Appendix begins on page 675.
DcCanB 4	*Volume IV: 1771 to 1800.* Edited by Francess G. Halpenny; 1979.

DcCanB 4A *Volume IV: 1771 to 1800.* Edited by Francess G. Halpenny; 1979. Appendix begins on page 783.

DcCanB 4S *Volume IV: 1771 to 1800.* Edited by Francess G. Halpenny; 1979. Supplement begins on page 787.

DcCanB 5 *Volume V: 1801 to 1820.* Edited by Francess G. Halpenny; 1983.

DcCanB 5A *Volume V: 1801 to 1820.* Edited by Francess G. Halpenny; 1983. Appendix begins on page 887.

DcCanB 6 *Volume VI: 1821-1835.* Edited by Francess G. Halpenny; 1987.

DcCanB 7 *Volume VII: 1836 to 1850.* Edited by Francess G. Halpenny; 1988.

DcCanB 8 *Volume VIII: 1851-1860.* Edited by Francess G. Halpenny; 1985.

DcCanB 8A *Volume VIII: 1851-1860.* Edited by Francess G. Halpenny; 1985. Appendix begins on page 968.

DcCanB 9 *Volume IX: 1861 to 1870.* Edited by Francess G. Halpenny; 1976.

DcCanB 10 *Volume X: 1871 to 1880.* Edited by Marc La Terreur; 1972.

DcCanB 11 *Volume XI: 1881 to 1890.* Edited by Henri Pilon; 1982.

DcCanB 12 *Volume XII: 1891 to 1900.* Edited by Francess G. Halpenny; 1990.

DcCanB 13 Volume XIII: 1901 to 1910. Edited by Ramsay Cook; 1994.

DcCAr 81 *Dictionary of Contemporary Artists.* Edited by V. Babington Smith. Oxford: Clio Press, 1981.

DcCathB *Dictionary of Catholic Biography.* By John J. Delaney and James Edward Tobin. Garden City, NY: Doubleday & Co., 1961.

DcChlFi *Dictionary of Children's Fiction from Australia, Canada, India, New Zealand, and Selected African Countries.* Books of recognized merit. By Alethea K. Helbig and Agnes Regan Perkins. Westport, CT: Greenwood Press, 1992.

DcCLAA *A Dictionary of Contemporary Latin American Authors.* Compiled by David William Foster. Tempe, AZ: Center for Latin American Studies, Arizona State University, 1975.

DcCM *Dictionary of Contemporary Music.* Edited by John Vinton. New York: E.P. Dutton & Co., 1974.

This book ignores prefixes in filing surnames.

DcCom 77 *The Dictionary of Composers.* Edited by Charles Osborne. London: Bodly Head, 1977.

DcCom&M 79 *The Dictionary of Composers and Their Music.* Every listener's companion. By Eric Gilder and June G. Port. New York: Ballantine Books, 1979.

Entires are found in Part One.

DcCPCAm *The Dictionary of Contemporary Politics of Central America and the Caribbean.* Edited by Phil Gunson and Greg Chamberlain. New York: Simon & Schuster, 1991.

DcCPSAf *The Dictionary of Contemporary Politics of Southern Africa.* By Gwyneth Williams and Brian Hackland. New York: Macmillan Publishing Co., 1989.

DcCPSAm *The Dictionary of Contemporary Politics of South America.* By Phil Gunson, Andrew Thompson, and Greg Chamberlain. New York: Macmillan Publishing Co., 1989.

DcD&D *Dictionary of Design & Decoration.* A Studio Book. New York: Viking Press, 1973.

DcEcMov *Dictionary of the Ecumenical Movement.* Edited by Nicholas Lossky et al. Geneva: WCC Publications; Grand Rapids, MI: William B. Eerdmans Publishing Co., 1991.

DcEnA *A Dictionary of English Authors, Biographical and Bibliographical.* Being a compendious account of the lives and writings of upwards of 800 British and American writers from the year 1400 to the present time. New edition, revised with an appendix. By R. Farquharson Sharp. London: Kegan Paul, Trench, Trubner & Co., 1904. Reprint. Detroit: Gale Research, 1978.

DcEnA A Appendix begins on page 311.

DcEnL *Dictionary of English Literature.* Being a comprehensive guide to English authors and their works. Second edition. By W. Davenport Adams. London: Cassell Petter & Galpin, (n.d.). Reprint. Detroit: Gale Research, 1966.

DcEuL *A Dictionary of European Literature.* Designed as a companion to English studies. Second, revised edition. By Laurie Magnus. London: George Routledge & Sons; New York: E.P. Dutton & Co., 1927. Reprint. Detroit: Gale Research, 1974.

The Appendix begins on page 595.

DcFM *Dictionary of Film Makers.* By Georges Sadoul. Translated, edited, and updated by Peter Morris. Berkeley, CA and Los Angeles: University of California Press, 1972. Originally published as *Dictionnaire des Cineastes,* 1965.

DcHiB *Dictionary of Hispanic Biography.* Detroit: Gale Research, 1996.

DcInB *Dictionary of Indian Biography.* By C.E. Buckland. London: Swan Sonnenschein & Co., 1906. Reprint. Detroit: Gale Research, 1968.

DcInB A Addenda begin on page 467.

DcInv *Dictionary of Inventions & Discoveries.* Edited by E.F. Carter. Stevenage, England: Robin Clark, 1978.

DcIrB 78 *A Dictionary of Irish Biography.* By Henry Boylan. New York: Barnes & Noble Books, 1978.

DcIrB 88 *A Dictionary of Irish Biography.* Second edition. By Henry Boylan. New York: St. Martin's Press, 1988.

DcIrL *Dictionary of Irish Literature.* Edited by Robert Hogan. Westport, CT: Greenwood Press, 1979-1996.

DcIrL ; 1979.

DcIrL 96 Revised and expanded edition. Two volumes; 1996.

DcIrW *Dictionary of Irish Writers.* By Brian Cleeve. Cork, Ireland: Mercier Press, 1967-1971.

- ***DcIrW 1*** Volume 1: Fiction; 1967.
- ***DcIrW 2*** Volume 2: Non-fiction; 1969.
- ***DcIrW 3*** Volume 3: Writers in the Irish Language; 1971.

DcItL *Dictionary of Italian Literature.* Edited by Peter Bondanella and Julia Conaway Bondanella. Westport, CT: Greenwood Press, 1979-1996.

- ***DcItL 1*** First edition; 1979.
- ***DcItL 2*** Second edition; 1996.

DcLB *Dictionary of Literary Biography.* Detroit: Gale Research, 1978-1993.

- ***DcLB 1*** Volume 1: *The American Renaissance in New England.* Edited by Joel Myerson; 1978.
- ***DcLB 2*** Volume 2: *American Novelists since World War II.* Edited by Jeffrey Helterman and Richard Layman; 1978.
- ***DcLB 3*** Volume 3: *Antebellum Writers in New York and the South.* Edited by Joel Myerson; 1979.
- ***DcLB 4*** Volume 4: *American Writers in Paris, 1920-1939.* Edited by Karen Lane Rood; 1980.
- ***DcLB 5*** Volume 5: *American Poets since World War II.* Two parts. Edited by Donald J. Greiner; 1980.
- ***DcLB 6*** Volume 6: *American Novelists since World War II.* Second Series. Edited by James E. Kibler, Jr; 1980.
- ***DcLB 7*** Volume 7: *Twentieth-Century American Dramatists.* Two parts. Edited by John MacNicholas; 1981.
- ***DcLB 8*** Volume 8: *Twentieth-Century American Science-Fiction Writers.* Two parts. Edited by David Cowart and Thomas L. Wymer; 1981.
- ***DcLB 9*** Volume 9: *American Novelists, 1910-1945.* Three parts. Edited by James J. Martine; 1981.
- ***DcLB 10*** Volume 10: *Modern British Dramatists, 1900-1945.* Two parts. Edited by Stanley Weintraub; 1982.
- ***DcLB 11*** Volume 11: *American Humorists, 1800-1950.* Two parts. Edited by Stanley Trachtenberg; 1982.
- ***DcLB 12*** Volume 12: *American Realists and Naturalists.* Edited by Donald Pizer and Earl N. Harbert; 1982.
- ***DcLB 13*** Volume 13: *British Dramatists since World War II.* Two parts. Edited by Stanley Weintraub; 1982.
- ***DcLB 14*** Volume 14: *British Novelists since 1960.* Two parts. Edited by Jay L. Halio; 1983.
- ***DcLB 15*** Volume 15: *British Novelists, 1930-1959.* Two parts. Edited by Bernard Oldsey; 1983.
- ***DcLB 16*** Volume 16: *The Beats: Literary Bohemians in Postwar America.* Two parts. Edited by Ann Charters; 1983.
- ***DcLB 17*** Volume 17: *Twentieth-Century American Historians.* Edited by Clyde N. Wilson; 1983.
- ***DcLB 18*** Volume 18: *Victorian Novelists after 1885.* Edited by Ira B. Nadel and William E. Fredeman; 1983.

DcLB 19 Volume 19: *British Poets, 1880-1914.* Edited by Donald E. Stanford; 1983.

DcLB 20 Volume 20: *British Poets, 1914-1945.* Edited by Donald E. Stanford; 1983.

DcLB 21 Volume 21: *Victorian Novelists before 1885.* Edited by Ira B. Nadel and William E. Fredeman; 1983.

DcLB 22 Volume 22: *American Writers for Children, 1900-1960.* Edited by John Cech; 1983.

DcLB 23 Volume 23: *American Newspaper Journalists, 1873-1900.* Edited by Perry J. Ashley; 1983.

DcLB 24 Volume 24: *American Colonial Writers, 1606-1734.* Edited by Emory Elliott; 1984.

DcLB 25 Volume 25: *American Newspaper Journalists, 1901-1925.* Edited by Perry J. Ashley; 1984.

DcLB 26 Volume 26: *American Screenwriters.* Edited by Robert E. Morsberger, Stephen O. Lesser, and Randall Clark; 1984.

DcLB 27 Volume 27: *Poets of Great Britain and Ireland, 1945-1960.* Edited by Vincent B. Sherry, Jr; 1984.

DcLB 28 Volume 28: *Twentieth-Century American-Jewish Fiction Writers.* Edited by Daniel Walden; 1984.

DcLB 29 Volume 29: *American Newspaper Journalists, 1926-1950.* Edited by Perry J. Ashley; 1984.

DcLB 30 Volume 30: *American Historians, 1607-1865.* Edited by Clyde N. Wilson; 1984.

DcLB 31 Volume 31: *American Colonial Writers, 1735-1781.* Edited by Emory Elliott; 1984.

DcLB 31A Volume 31: *American Colonial Writers, 1735-1781.* Edited by Emory Elliott; 1984. Appendix I: "Eighteenth-Century Philosophical Background." Use the Table of Contents to locate entries.

DcLB 31B Volume 31: *American Colonial Writers, 1735-1781.* Edited by Emory Elliott; 1984. Appendix II: "Eighteenth-Century Aesthetic Theories." Use the Table of Contents to locate entries.

DcLB 32 Volume 32: *Victorian Poets before 1850.* Edited by William E. Fredeman and Ira B. Nadel; 1984.

DcLB 33 Volume 33: *Afro-American Fiction Writers after 1955.* Edited by Thadious M. Davis and Trudier Harris; 1984.

DcLB 34 Volume 34: *British Novelists, 1890-1929: Traditionalists.* Edited by Thomas F. Staley; 1985.

DcLB 35 Volume 35: *Victorian Poets after 1850.* Edited by William E. Fredeman and Ira B. Nadel; 1985.

DcLB 36 Volume 36: *British Novelists, 1890-1929: Modernists.* Edited by Thomas F. Staley; 1985.

DcLB 37 Volume 37: *American Writers of the Early Republic.* Edited by Emory Elliott; 1985.

DcLB 38 Volume 38: *Afro-American Writers after 1955: Dramatists and Prose Writers.* Edited by Thadious M. Davis and Trudier Harris; 1985.

DcLB 39 Volume 39: *British Novelists, 1660-1800.* Two parts. Edited by Martin C. Battestin; 1985.

DcLB 40	Volume 40: *Poets of Great Britain and Ireland since 1960.* Two parts. Edited by Vincent B. Sherry, Jr; 1985.
DcLB 41	Volume 41: *Afro-American Poets since 1955.* Edited by Trudier Harris and Thadious M. Davis; 1985.
DcLB 42	Volume 42: *American Writers for Children before 1900.* Edited by Glenn E. Estes; 1985.
DcLB 43	Volume 43: *American Newspaper Journalists, 1690-1872.* Edited by Perry J. Ashley; 1985.
DcLB 44	Volume 44: *American Screenwriters.* Second Series. Edited by Randall Clark; 1986.
DcLB 45	Volume 45: *American Poets, 1880-1945.* First Series. Edited by Peter Quartermain; 1986.
DcLB 46	Vol. 46: Am Lit Publ. Pt 1; 1986. No bios.
DcLB 47	Volume 47: *American Historians, 1866-1912.* Edited by Clyde N. Wilson; 1986.
DcLB 48	Volume 48: *American Poets, 1880-1945.* Second Series. Edited by Peter Quartermain; 1986.
DcLB 49	Volume 49: *American Literary Publishing Houses, 1638-1899.* Two parts. Edited by Peter Dzwonkoski; 1986. No bios.
DcLB 50	Volume 50: *Afro-American Writers before the Harlem Renaissance.* Edited by Trudier Harris; 1986.
DcLB 51	Volume 51: *Afro-American Writers from the Harlem Renaissance to 1940.* Edited by Trudier Harris; 1987.
DcLB 51A	Volume 51: *Afro-American Writers from the Harlem Renaissance to 1940.* Edited by Trudier Harris; 1987. Appendix. Use the Table of Contents to locate entries.
DcLB 52	Volume 52: *American Writers for Children since 1960: Fiction.* Edited by Glenn E. Estes; 1986.
DcLB 53	Volume 53: *Canadian Writers since 1960.* First Series. Edited by W.H. New; 1986.
DcLB 54	Volume 54: *American Poets, 1880-1945.* Third Series. Two parts. Edited by Peter Quartermain; 1987.
DcLB 55	Volume 55: *Victorian Prose Writers before 1867.* Edited by William B. Thesing; 1987.
DcLB 56	Volume 56: *German Fiction Writers, 1914-1945.* Edited by James Hardin; 1987.
DcLB 57	Volume 57: *Victorian Prose Writers after 1867.* Edited by William B. Thesing; 1987.
DcLB 58	Volume 58: *Jacobean and Caroline Dramatists.* Edited by Fredson Bowers; 1987.
DcLB 59	Volume 59: *American Literary Critics and Scholars, 1800-1850.* Edited by John W. Rathbun; 1987.
DcLB 60	Volume 60: *Canadian Writers since 1960.* Second Series. Edited by W.H. New; 1987.
DcLB 61	Volume 61: *American Writers for Children since 1960: Poets, Illustrators, and Nonfiction Authors.* Edited by Glenn E. Estes; 1987.
DcLB 62	Volume 62: *Elizabethan Dramatists.* Edited by Fredson Bowers; 1987.
DcLB 63	Volume 63: *Modern American Critics, 1920-1955.* Edited by Gregory S. Jay; 1988.

DcLB 64 Volume 64: *American Literary Critics and Scholars, 1850-1880.* Edited by John W. Rathbun and Monica M. Grecu; 1988.

DcLB 65 Volume 65: *French Novelists, 1900-1930.* Edited by Catharine Savage Brosman; 1988.

DcLB 66 Volume 66: *German Fiction Writers, 1885-1913.* Two parts. Edited by James Hardin; 1988.

DcLB 67 Volume 67: *Modern American Critics since 1955.* Edited by Gregory S. Jay; 1988.

DcLB 68 Volume 68: *Canadian Writers, 1920-1959.* First Series. Edited by W.H. New; 1988.

DcLB 69 Volume 69: *Contemporary German Fiction Writers.* First Series. Edited by Wolfgang D. Elfe; 1988.

DcLB 70 Volume 70: *British Mystery Writers, 1860-1919.* Edited by Bernard Benstock; 1988.

DcLB 71 Volume 71: *American Literary Critics and Scholars, 1880-1900.* Edited by John W. Rathbun and Monica M. Grecu; 1988.

DcLB 72 Volume 72: *French Novelists, 1930-1960.* Edited by Catharine Savage Brosman; 1988.

DcLB 73 Volume 73: *American Magazine Journalists, 1741-1850.* Edited by Sam G. Riley; 1988.

DcLB 74 Volume 74: *American Short-Story Writers before 1880.* Edited by Bobby Ellen Kimbel; 1988.

DcLB 75 Volume 75: *Contemporary German Fiction Writers.* Second Series. Edited by Wolfgang D. Elfe and James Hardin; 1988.

DcLB 76 Volume 76: *Afro-American Writers, 1940-1955.* Edited by Trudier Harris; 1988.

DcLB 77 Volume 77: *British Mystery Writers, 1920-1939.* Edited by Bernard Benstock and Thomas F. Staley; 1989.

DcLB 78 Volume 78: *American Short-Story Writers, 1880-1910.* Edited by Bobby Ellen Kimbel; 1989.

DcLB 79 Volume 79: *American Magazine Journalists, 1850-1900.* Edited by Sam G. Riley; 1989.

DcLB 80 Volume 80: *Restoration and Eighteenth-Century Dramatists.* First Series. Edited by Paula R. Backscheider; 1989.

DcLB 81 Volume 81: *Austrian Fiction Writers, 1875-1913.* Edited by James Hardin and Donald G. Daviau; 1989.

DcLB 82 Volume 82: *Chicano Writers.* First Series. Edited by Francisco A. Lomeli and Carl R. Shirley; 1989.

DcLB 83 Volume 83: *French Novelists since 1960.* Edited by Catharine Savage Brosman; 1989.

DcLB 84 Volume 84: *Restoration and Eighteenth-Century Dramatists.* Second Series. Edited by Paula R. Backscheider; 1989.

DcLB 85 Volume 85: *Austrian Fiction Writers after 1914.* Edited by James Hardin and Donald G. Daviau; 1989.

DcLB 86 Volume 86: *American Short-Story Writers, 1910-1945.* First Series. Edited by Bobby Ellen Kimbel; 1989.

DcLB 87 Volume 87: *British Mystery and Thriller Writers since 1940.* First Series. Edited by Bernard Benstock and Thomas F. Staley; 1989.

DcLB 88 Volume 88: *Canadian Writers, 1920-1959.* Second Series. Edited by W.H. New; 1989.

DcLB 89 Volume 89: *Restoration and Eighteenth-Century Dramatists.* Third Series. Edited by Paula R. Backscheider; 1989.

DcLB 90 Volume 90: *German Writers in the Age of Goethe, 1789-1832.* Edited by James Hardin and Christoph E. Schweitzer; 1989.

DcLB 91 Volume 91: *American Magazine Journalists 1900-1960.* First Series. Edited by Sam G. Riley; 1990.

DcLB 92 Volume 92: *Canadian Writers, 1890-1920.* Edited by W.H. New; 1990.

DcLB 93 Volume 93: *British Romantic Poets, 1789-1832.* First Series. Edited by John R. Greenfield; 1990.

DcLB 94 Volume 94: *German Writers in the Age of Goethe: Sturm und Drang to Classicism.* Edited by James Hardin and Christoph Schweitzer; 1990.

DcLB 95 Volume 95: *Eighteenth-Century British Poets.* First Series. Edited by John Sitter; 1990.

DcLB 96 Volume 96: *British Romantic Poets, 1789-1832.* Second Series. Edited by John R. Greenfield; 1990.

DcLB 97 Volume 97: *German Writers from the Enlightenment to Sturm und Drang, 1720-1764.* Edited by James Hardin and Christoph E. Schweitzer; 1990.

DcLB 98 Volume 98: *Modern British Essayists.* First Series. Edited by Robert Beum; 1990.

DcLB 99 Volume 99: *Canadian Writers before 1890.* Edited by W.H. New; 1990.

DcLB 100 Volume 100: *Modern British Essayists.* Second Series. Edited by Robert Beum; 1990.

DcLB 101 Volume 101: *British Prose Writers, 1660-1800.* First Series. Edited by Donald T. Siebert; 1991.

DcLB 102 Volume 102: *American Short-Story Writers, 1910-1945.* Second Series. Edited by Bobby Ellen Kimbel; 1991.

DcLB 103 Volume 103: *American Literary Biographers.* First Series. Edited by Steven Serafin; 1991.

DcLB 104 Volume 104: *British Prose Writers, 1660-1800.* Second Series. Edited by Donald T. Siebert; 1991.

DcLB 105 Volume 105: *American Poets since World War II.* Second Series. Edited by R.S. Gwynn; 1991.

DcLB 106 Volume 106: *British Literary Publishing Houses, 1820-1880.* Edited by Patricia J. Anderson and Jonathan Rose; 1991.

DcLB 107 Volume 107: *British Romantic Prose Writers, 1789-1832.* First Series. Edited by John R. Greenfield; 1991.

DcLB 108 Volume 108: *Twentieth-Century Spanish Poets.* First Series. Edited by Michael L. Perna; 1991.

DcLB 109 Volume 109: *Eighteenth-Century British Poets.* Second Series. Edited by John Sitter; 1991.

DcLB 110 Volume 110: *British Romantic Prose Writers, 1789-1832.* Second Series. Edited by John R. Greenfield; 1991.

DcLB 111 Volume 111: *American Literary Biographers.* Second Series. Edited by Steven Serafin; 1991.

DcLB 112 Volume 112: *British Literary Publishing Houses, 1881-1965.* Edited by Jonathan Rose and Patricia J. Anderson; 1991.

DcLB 113 Volume 113: *Modern Latin-American Fiction Writers.* First Series. Edited by William Luis; 1992.

DcLB 114 Volume 114: *Twentieth-Century Italian Poets.* First Series. Edited by Giovanna Wedel De Stasio, Glauco Cambon, and Antonio Illiano; 1992.

DcLB 115 Volume 115: *Medieval Philosophers.* Edited by Jeremiah Hackett; 1992.

DcLB 116 Volume 116: *British Romantic Novelists, 1789-1832.* Edited by Bradford K. Mudge; 1992.

DcLB 117 Volume 117: *Twentieth-Century Caribbean and Black African Writers.* First Series. Edited by Bernth Lindfors and Reinhard Sander; 1992.

DcLB 118 Volume 118: *Twentieth-Century German Dramatists, 1889-1918.* Edited by Wolfgang D. Elfe and James Hardin; 1992.

DcLB 119 Volume 119: *Nineteenth-Century French Fiction Writers: Romanticism and Realism, 1800-1860.* Edited by Catharine Savage Brosman; 1992.

DcLB 120 Volume 120: *American Poets since World War II.* Third Series. Edited by R.S. Gwynn; 1992.

DcLB 121 Volume 121: *Seventeenth-Century British Nondramatic Poets.* First Series. Edited by M. Thomas Hester; 1992.

DcLB 122 Volume 122: *Chicano Writers.* Second Series. Edited by Francisco A. Lomeli and Carl R. Shirley; 1992.

DcLB 123 Volume 123: *Nineteenth-Century French Fiction Writers: Naturalism and Beyond, 1860-1900.* Edited by Catharine Savage Brosman; 1992.

DcLB 124 Volume 124: *Twentieth-Century German Dramatists, 1919-1992.* Edited by Wolfgang D. Elfe and James Hardin; 1992.

DcLB 125 Volume 125: *Twentieth-Century Caribbean and Black African Writers.* Second Series. Edited by Bernth Lindfors and Reinhard Sander; 1993.

DcLB 126 Volume 126: *Seventeenth-Century British Nondramatic Poets.* Second Series. Edited by M. Thomas Hester; 1993.

DcLB 127 Volume 127: *American Newspaper Publishers, 1950-1990.* Edited by Perry J. Ashley; 1993.

DcLB 128 Volume 128: *Twentieth-Century Italian Poets.* Second Series. Edited by Giovanna Wedel De Stasio, Glauco Cambon, and Antonio Illiano; 1993.

DcLB 129 Volume 129: *Nineteenth-Century German Writers, 1841-1900.* Edited by James Hardin and Siegfried Mews; 1993.

DcLB 130 Volume 130: *American Short-Story Writers since World War II.* Edited by Patrick Meanor; 1993.

DcLB 131 Volume 131: *Seventeenth-Century British Nondramatic Poets.* Third Series. Edited by M. Thomas Hester; 1993.

DcLB 132 Volume 132: *Sixteenth-Century British Nondramatic Writers.* First Series. Edited by David A. Richardson; 1993.

DcLB 133 Volume 133: *Nineteenth-Century German Writers to 1840.* Edited by James Hardin and Siegfried Mews; 1993.

DcLB 134 Volume 134: *Twentieth-Century Spanish Poets.* Second Series. Edited by Jerry Phillips Winfield; 1994.

DcLB 135 Volume 135: *British Short-Fiction Writers, 1880-1914: The Realist Tradition.* Edited by William B. Thesing; 1994.

DcLB 136 Volume 136: *Sixteenth-Century British Nondramatic Writers.* Second Series. Edited by David A. Richardson; 1994.

DcLB 137 Volume 137: *American Magazine Journalists, 1900-1960.* Second Series. Edited by Sam G. Riley; 1994.

DcLB 138 Volume 138: *German Writers and Works of the High Middle Ages: 1170-1280.* Edited by James Hardin and Will Hasty; 1994.

DcLB 139 Volume 139: *British Short-Fiction Writers, 1945-1980.* Edited by Dean Baldwin; 1994.

DcLB 140 Volume 140: *American Book-Collectors and Bibliographers.* First Series. Edited by Joseph Rosenblum; 1994.

DcLB 141 Volume 141: *British Children's Writers, 1880-1914.* Edited by Laura M. Zaidman; 1994.

DcLB 142 Volume 142: *Eighteenth-Century British Literary Biographers.* Edited by Steven Serafin; 1994.

DcLB 143 Volume 143: *American Novelists Since World War II.* Third Series. Edited by James R. Giles and Wanda H. Giles; 1994.

DcLB 144 Volume 144: *Nineteenth-Century British Literary Biographers.* Edited by Steven Serafin; 1994.

DcLB 145 Volume 145: *Modern Latin-American Fiction Writers.* Second Series. Edited by William Luis and Ann Gonzalez; 1994.

DcLB 146 Volume 146: *Old and Middle English Literature.* Edited by Jeffrey Helterman and Jerome Mitchell; 1994.

DcLB 147 Volume 147: *South Slavic Writers Before World War II.* Edited by Vasa D. Mihailovich; 1995.

DcLB 148 Volume 148: *German Writers and Works of the Early Middle Ages: 800-1170.* Edited by Will Hasty and James Hardin; 1995.

DcLB 149 Volume 149: *Late Nineteenth- and Early Twentieth-Century British Literary Biographers.* Edited by Steven Serafin; 1995.

DcLB 150 Volume 150: *Early Modern Russian Writers, Late Seventeenth and Eighteenth Centuries.* Edited by Marcus C. Levitt; 1995.

DcLB 151 Volume 151: *British Prose Writers of the Early Seventeenth Century.* Edited by Clayton D. Lein; 1995.

DcLB 152 Volume 152: *American Novelists Since World War II.* Fourth Series. Edited by James R. Giles and Wanda H. Giles; 1995.

DcLB 153 Volume 153: *Late-Victorian and Edwardian British Novelists.* First Series. Edited by George M. Johnson; 1995.

DcLB 154 Volume 154: *The British Literary Book Trade, 1700-1820.* Edited by James K. Bracken and Joel Silver; 1995.

DcLB 155 Volume 155: *Twentieth-Century British Literary Biographers.* Edited by Steven Serafin; 1995.

DcLB 156 Volume 156: *British Short-Fiction Writers, 1880-1914: The Romantic Tradition.* Edited by William F. Naufftus; 1996.

DcLB 157 Volume 157: *Twentieth-Century Caribbean and Black African Writers.* Third Series. Edited by Bernth Lindfors and Reinhard Sander; 1996.

DcLB 158 Volume 158: *British Reform Writers, 1789-1832.* Edited by Gary Kelly and Edd Applegate; 1996.

DcLB 159 Volume 159: *British Short-Fiction Writers, 1800-1880.* Edited by John R. Greenfield; 1996.

DcLB 160 Volume 160: *British Children's Writers, 1914-1960.* Edited by Donald R. Hettinga and Gary D. Schmidt; 1996.

DcLB 161 Volume 161: *British Children's Writers Since 1960.* First Series. Edited by Caroline C. Hunt; 1996.

DcLB 162 Volume 162: *British Short-Fiction Writers, 1915-1945.* Edited by John H. Rogers; 1996.

DcLB 163 Volume 163: *British Children's Writers, 1800-1880.* Edited by Meena Khorana; 1996.

DcLB 164 Volume 164: *German Baroque Writers, 1580-1660.* Edited by James Hardin; 1996.

DcLB 165 Volume 165: *American Poets Since World War II.* Fourth Series. Edited by Joseph Conte; 1996.

DcLB 166 Volume 166: *British Travel Writers, 1837-1875.* Edited by Barbara Brothers and Julia Gergits; 1996.

DcLB 167 Volume 167: *Sixteenth-Century British Nondramatic Writers.* Third Series. Edited by David A. Richardson; 1996.

DcLB 168 Volume 168: *German Baroque Writers, 1661-1730.* Edited by James Hardin; 1996.

DcLB 169 Volume 169: *American Poets Since World War II.* Fifth Series. Edited by Joseph Conte; 1996.

DcLB 170 Volume 170: *The British Literary Booktrade, 1475-1700.* Edited by James K. Bracken and Joel Silver; 1996.

DcLB 171 Volume 171: *Twentieth-Century American Sportswriters.* Edited by Richard Orodenker; 1996.

DcLB 172 Volume 172: *Sixteenth-Century British Nondramatic Writers.* Fourth Series. Edited by David A. Richardson; 1996.

DcLB 173 Edited by James R. Giles and Wanda H. Giles; 1997.

DcLB 174 Volume 174: *British Travel Writers, 1876-1909.* Edited by Barbara Brothers and Julia Gergits; 1997.

DcLB *Dictionary of Literary Biography, Documentary Series.* An illustrated chronicle. Detroit: Gale Research, 1982-1995.

DcLB DS1 Volume 1. Edited by Margaret A. Van Antwerp; 1982.

DcLB DS2 Volume 2. Edited by Margaret A. Van Antwerp; 1982.

DcLB DS3 Volume 3. Edited by Mary Bruccoli; 1983.

DcLB DS4 Volume 4. Edited by Margaret A. Van Antwerp and Sally Johns; 1984.

DcLB DS5 Volume 5; 1987.
DcLB DS6 Volume 6. Edited by Matthew J. Bruccoli and Richard Layman; 1989.
DcLB DS7 Volume 7. Edited by Karen L. Rood; 1989.
DcLB DS8 Volume 8. Edited by Jeffrey Louis Decker; 1991.
DcLB DS9 Volume 9. Edited by Ronald Baughman; 1991.
DcLB DS10 Volume 10. Edited by Edward L. Bishop; 1992.
DcLB DS11 Volume 11. Edited by Jon Christian Suggs; 1993.
DcLB DS12 Volume 12. Edited by Mary Ann Wimsatt and Karen L. Rood; 1995.
DcLB DS13 Volume 13. Edited by John Delaney; 1995.

Use the Table of Contents to locate entries; multiple essays for the same name are often provided. Volumes 5 and 11 contain no biographies.

DcLB *Dictionary of Literary Biography, Yearbook.* Detroit: Gale Research, 1981-1995.

DcLB Y80A *1980 Yearbook.* Edited by Karen L. Rood, Jean W. Ross, and Richard Ziegfeld; 1981. ''Updated Entries'' section begins on page 3.
DcLB Y80B *1980 Yearbook.* Edited by Karen L. Rood, Jean W. Ross, and Richard Ziegfeld; 1981. ''New Entries'' section begins on page 127.
DcLB Y81A *1981 Yearbook.* Edited by Karen L. Rood, Jean W. Ross, and Richard Ziegfeld; 1982. ''Updated Entries'' section begins on page 21.
DcLB Y81B *1981 Yearbook.* Edited by Karen L. Rood, Jean W. Ross, and Richard Ziegfeld; 1982. ''New Entries'' section begins on page 139.
DcLB Y82A *1982 Yearbook.* Edited by Richard Ziegfeld; 1983. ''Updated Entries'' section begins on page 121.
DcLB Y82B *1982 Yearbook.* Edited by Richard Ziegfeld; 1983. ''New Entries'' section begins on page 203.
DcLB Y83A *1983 Yearbook.* Edited by Mary Bruccoli and Jean W. Ross; 1984. ''Updated Entries'' section begins on page 155.
DcLB Y83B *1983 Yearbook.* Edited by Mary Bruccoli and Jean W. Ross; 1984. ''New Entries'' section begins on page 175.
DcLB Y83N *1983 Yearbook.* Edited by Mary Bruccoli and Jean W. Ross; 1984. Obituaries section begins on page 103.
DcLB Y84A *1984 Yearbook.* Edited by Jean W. Ross; 1985. ''Updated Entry'' section begins on page 219.
DcLB Y84B *1984 Yearbook.* Edited by Jean W. Ross; 1985. ''New Entries'' section begins on page 225.
DcLB Y84N *1984 Yearbook.* Edited by Jean W. Ross; 1985. Obituaries section begins on page 163.
DcLB Y85A *1985 Yearbook.* Edited by Jean W. Ross; 1986. ''Updated Entries'' section begins on page 279.
DcLB Y85B *1985 Yearbook.* Edited by Jean W. Ross; 1986. ''New Entries'' section begins on page 319.
DcLB Y85N *1985 Yearbook.* Edited by Jean W. Ross; 1986. Obituaries section begins on page 253.
DcLB Y86A *1986 Yearbook.* Edited by J.M. Brook; 1987. ''Updated Entries'' section begins on page 247.
DcLB Y86B *1986 Yearbook.* Edited by J.M. Brook; 1987. ''New Entries'' section begins on page 271.

DcLB Y86N *1986 Yearbook.* Edited by J.M. Brook; 1987. Obituaries section begins on page 199.

DcLB Y87A *1987 Yearbook.* Edited by J.M. Brook; 1988. "Updated Entries" section begins on page 241.

DcLB Y87B *1987 Yearbook.* Edited by J.M. Brook; 1988. "New Entries" section begins on page 293.

DcLB Y87N *1987 Yearbook.* Edited by J.M. Brook; 1988. Obituaries section begins on page 219.

DcLB Y88 *1988 Yearbook.* Edited by J.M. Brook; 1989. The Nobel Prize entry begins on page 3.

DcLB Y88N *1988 Yearbook.* Edited by J.M. Brook; 1989. Obituaries section begins on page 199.

DcLB Y89 *1989 Yearbook.* Edited by J.M. Brook; 1990. The Nobel Prize entry begins on page 3.

DcLB Y89N *1989 Yearbook.* Edited by J.M. Brook; 1990. Obituaries section begins on page 170.

DcLB Y90 *1990 Yearbook.* Edited by James W. Hipp; 1991. The Nobel Prize entry begins on page 3.

DcLB Y90N *1990 Yearbook.* Edited by James W. Hipp; 1991. Obituaries section begins on page 206.

DcLB Y91 *1991 Yearbook.* Edited by James W. Hipp; 1992. Use the Table of Contents to locate entries.

DcLB Y91N *1991 Yearbook.* Edited by James W. Hipp; 1992. Obituaries section begins on page 224.

DcLB Y92 *1992 Yearbook.* Edited by James W. Hipp; 1993. Use the Table of Contents to locate entries.

DcLB Y92N *1992 Yearbook.* Edited by James W. Hipp; 1993. Obituaries section begins on page 286.

DcLB Y93 *1993 Yearbook.* Edited by James W. Hipp; 1994. Use the Table of Contents to locate entries.

DcLB Y93N *1993 Yearbook.* Edited by James W. Hipp; 1994. Obituaries section begins on page 261.

DcLB Y94 *1994 Yearbook.* Edited by James W. Hipp; 1995. Use the Table of Contents to locate entries.

DcLB Y94N *1994 Yearbook.* Edited by James W. Hipp; 1995. Obituaries section begins on page 236.

DcLEL *A Dictionary of Literature in the English Language.* Compiled and edited by Robin Myers. Oxford: Pergamon Press, 1970-1978.

DcLEL *From Chaucer to 1940.*; 1970.

DcLEL 1940 *From 1940 to 1970.*; 1978.

DcLP *Dictionary of Literary Pseudonyms.* A selection of popular modern writers in English. Fourth edition. By Frank Atkinson. Chicago: American Library Association; London: Library Association Publishing, 1987.

DcLP 87A Part I: Alphabetical listing by authors' "Real names" begins on page 1.

DcLP 87B Part II: Alphabetical listing by authors' "Pseudonyms" begins on page 140.

DcMexL *Dictionary of Mexican Literature.* Edited by Eladio Cortes. Westport, CT: Greenwood Press, 1992.

DcMidEa *Dictionary of the Middle East.* By Dilip Hiro. New York: St. Martin's Press, 1996.

DcMPSA *Dictionary of the Modern Politics of South-East Asia.* By Michael Leifer. London: Routledge, 1995.

DcNAA *A Dictionary of North American Authors Deceased before 1950.* Compiled by W. Stewart Wallace. Toronto: Ryerson Press, 1951. Reprint. Detroit: Gale Research, 1968.

DcNaB *The Dictionary of National Biography.* London: Oxford University Press, 1953. Contains abstracts of the biographies found in *The Dictionary of National Biography, First Supplement* (Volume 22, New York: Macmillan Co.; London: Smith, Elder & Co., 1909).

DcNaB	The Concise Dictionary. Part 1, From the beginnings to 1900; 1953.
DcNaB 1912	*1912-1921.* Edited by H.W.C. Davis and J.R.H. Weaver; 1927.
DcNaB 1922	*1922-1930.* Edited by J.R.H. Weaver; 1937.
DcNaB 1931	*1931-1940.* Edited by L.G. Wickham Legg; 1949.
DcNaB 1941	*1941-1950.* Edited by L.G. Wickham Legg and E.T. Williams; 1959.
DcNaB 1951	*1951-1960.* Edited by E.T. Williams and Helen M. Palmer; 1971.
DcNaB 1961	*1961-1970.* Edited by E.T. Williams and C.S. Nicholls; 1981.
DcNaB 1971	*1971-1980.* Edited by Lord Blake and C.S. Nicholls; 1986.
DcNaB 1981	*1981-1985.* Edited by Lord Blake and C.S. Nicholls; 1990.
DcNaB 1986	*1986-1990.* Edited by C. S. Nicholls; 1996.
DcNaB C	The Concise Dictionary. Part 1, From the beginnings to 1900; 1953. Corrigenda begins on page 1457.
DcNaB MP	*Missing Persons.* Edited by C. S. Nicholls; 1993.
DcNaB S1	The Concise Dictionary. Part 1, From the beginnings to 1900. First Supplement; 1953.

DcNaB S2 *The Dictionary of National Biography.* Second Supplement. Three volumes. Edited by Sir Sidney Lee. New York: Macmillan Co.; London: Smith, Elder & Co., 1912.

DcNAL *Dictionary of Native American Literature.* Edited by Andrew Wiget. Garland Reference Library of the Humanities, vol. 1815. New York: Garland Publishing, 1994.

Use the Index to locate biographies.

DcNCBi *Dictionary of North Carolina Biography.* Edited by William S. Powell. Chapel Hill, NC: University of North Carolina Press, 1979-1991.

DcNCBi 1	Volume 1, A-C; 1979.
DcNCBi 2	Volume 2, D-G; 1986.
DcNCBi 3	Volume 3, H-K; 1988.
DcNCBi 4	Volume 4, L-O; 1991.

DcNiCA *Dictionary of Ninteenth Century Antiques and Later Objets d'Art.* By George Savage. London: Barrie & Jenkins, 1978.

DcOrL *Dictionary of Oriental Literatures.* New York: Basic Books, 1974.
- ***DcOrL 1*** Volume I: East Asia. Edited by Zbigniew Slupski.
- ***DcOrL 2*** Volume II: South and South-East Asia. Edited by Dusan Zbavitel.
- ***DcOrL 3*** Volume III: West Asia and North Africa. Edited by Jiri Becka.

DcPol *A Dictionary of Politics.* Revised edition. Edited by Walter Laqueur. New York: Macmillan Publishing Co., Free Press, 1974.

DcPup *Dictionary of Puppetry.* By A.R. Philpott. Boston: Plays, 1969.

DcRusL *Dictionary of Russian Literature.* By William E. Harkins. New York: Philosophical Library, 1956. Reprint. Westport, Conn.: Greenwood Press, 1971.

DcRusLS *Dictionary of Russian Literature since 1917.* By Wolfgang Kasack. New York: Columbia University Press, 1988.

DcScanL *Dictionary of Scandinavian Literature.* Edited by Virpi Zuck. New York: Greenwood Press, 1990.

DcScB *Dictionary of Scientific Biography.* New York: Charles Scribner's Sons, 1970-1990.
- ***DcScB*** Volumes I-XIV. Edited by Charles Coulston Gillispie; 1970.
- ***DcScB S1*** Volume XV, Supplement I. Edited by Charles Coulston Gillispie; 1978.
- ***DcScB S2*** Volumes 17-18, Supplement II. Edited by Frederic L. Holmes; 1990.

DcSeaP *Dictionary of Sea Painters.* By E.H.H. Archibald. Woodbridge, England: Antique Collectors' Club, 1980.
Biographies begin on page 59.

DcSoc *A Dictionary of Sociology.* Edited by G. Duncan Mitchell. Chicago: Aldine Publishing Co., 1968.

DcSpL *Dictionary of Spanish Literature.* By Maxim Newmark. New York: Philosophical Library, 1956. Reprint. Totowa, N.J.: Littlefield, Adams & Co., 1970.

DcTwBBL *Dictionary of Twentieth Century British Business Leaders.* By David J. Jeremy and Geoffrey Tweedale. London: Bowker-Saur, 1994.

DcTwCC *A Dictionary of Twentieth-Century Composers, 1911-1971.* By Kenneth Thompson. New York: St. Martin's Press, 1973.
- ***DcTwCC A*** The Addenda begins on page 659.

DcTwCCu *Dictionary of Twentieth Century Culture.* Detroit: Gale Research, 1994-1996.
- ***DcTwCCu 1*** Volume 1: *American Culture After World War II.* Edited by Karen L. Rood; 1994.
- ***DcTwCCu 2*** Volume 2: *French Culture 1900-1975.* Edited by Catharine Savage Brosman; 1995.

DcTwCCu 3 Volume 3: *Hispanic Culture of South America.* Edited by Peter Standish; 1995.

DcTwCCu 4 Volume 4: *Hispanic Culture of Mexico, Central America, and the Caribbean.* Edited by Peter Standish; 1996.

DcTwCCu 5 Volume 5: *African American Culture.* Edited by Sandra Adell; 1996.

DcTwCuL *Dictionary of Twentieth-Century Cuban Literature.* Edited by Julio A. Martinez. New York: Greenwood Press, 1990.
Use the Index to locate individuals found in group biographies.

DcTwDes *Dictionary of Twentieth-Century Design.* By John Pile. New York: Facts on File, 1990.

DcTwHis *Dictionary of Twentieth-Century History, 1914-1990.* By Peter Teed. Oxford: Oxford University Press, 1992.

DcVicP *Dictionary of Victorian Painters.* By Christopher Wood. Suffolk, England: Baron Publishing, 1971.

DcVicP 2 *The Dictionary of Victorian Painters.* Second edition. By Christopher Wood. Woodbridge, England: Antique Collectors' Club, 1978.

DcWomA *Dictionary of Women Artists.* An international dictionary of women artists born before 1900. By Chris Petteys. Boston: G.K. Hall & Co., 1985.

DeafPAS *Deaf Persons in the Arts and Sciences.* A biographical dictionary. By Harry G. Lang and Bonnie Meath-Lang. Westport, CT: Greenwood Press, 1995.

DetWom *Detecting Women 2.* A reader's guide and checklist for mystery series written by women. By Willetta L. Heising. Dearborn, MI: Purple Moon Press, 1996.

DiAASTC *Distinguished African American Scientists of the 20th Century.* By James H. Kessler, J. S. Kidd, Renee A. Kidd, and Katherine A. Morin. Phoenix, AZ: Oryx Press, 1996.

DicTyr *Dictators and Tyrants.* Absolute rulers and would-be rulers in world history. By Alan Axelrod and Charles Phillips. New York: Facts on File, 1995.

DirCG 82 *Directors: A Complete Guide.* Edited by Michael Singer. Beverly Hills: Lone Eagle Productions, Inc., 1982.

Dis&D *Disease and Destiny.* A bibliography of medical references to the famous. By Judson Bennett Gilbert. Additions and introduction by Gordon E. Mestler. London: Dawsons of Pall Mall, 1962.

DivFut *Divining the Future.* Prognostication from astrology to zoomancy. By Eva Shaw. New York: Facts on File, 1995.

DrAF 76 *A Directory of American Fiction Writers.* Names and addresses of more than 800 contemporary fiction writers whose work has been published in the United States. 1976 edition. New York: Poets & Writers, 1976.
Use the Index to locate listings.

Drake *Drake's Dictionary of American Biography.* Including men of the time, containing nearly 10,000 notices of persons of both sexes, of native and foreign birth, who have been remarkable, or prominently connected with the arts, sciences, literature, politics, or history, of the American continent. By Francis S. Drake. Boston: James R. Osgood & Co., 1872. Reprint. Detroit: Gale Research, 1974.

Drake SUP Supplement begins on page 1015.

DramC *Drama Criticism.* Criticism of the most significant and widely studied dramatic works from all the world's literatures. Detroit: Gale Research, 1991-1996.

DramC 1 Volume 1; 1991.
DramC 2 Volume 2; 1992.
DramC 3 Volume 3; 1993.
DramC 4 Volume 4; 1994.
DramC 5 Volume 5; 1995.
DramC 6 Volume 6; 1996.

DrAP 75 *A Directory of American Poets.* Names and addresses of more than 1,500 contemporary poets whose work has been published in the United States. 1975 edition. New York: Poets & Writers, 1974.

Use the Index to locate listings.

DrAPF *A Directory of American Poets and Fiction Writers.* Names and addresses of contemporary poets and fiction writers whose work has been published in the United States. New York: Poets & Writers, 1980-1997.

DrAPF 80 1980-1981 edition; 1980.
DrAPF 83 1983-1984 edition; 1983.
DrAPF 85 1985-1986 edition; 1985.
DrAPF 87 1987-1988 edition; 1987.
DrAPF 89 1989-1990 edition; 1989.
DrAPF 91 1991-1992 edition; 1990.
DrAPF 93 1993-1994 edition; 1992.
DrAPF 97 1997-1998 edition; 1997.

Use the Index to locate listings.

DrAS *Directory of American Scholars.* New York: R.R. Bowker Co., 1974-1982.

DrAS 74E Sixth edition, Volume 2: English, Speech, & Drama; 1974.
DrAS 74F Sixth edition, Volume 3: Foreign Languages, Linguistics, & Philology; 1974.
DrAS 74H Sixth edition, Volume 1: History; 1974.
DrAS 74P Sixth edition, Volume 4: Philosophy, Religion, & Law; 1974.
DrAS 78E Seventh edition, Volume 2: English, Speech, & Drama; 1978.
DrAS 78F Seventh edition, Volume 3: Foreign Languages, Linguistics, & Philology; 1978.
DrAS 78H Seventh edition, Volume 1: History; 1978.
DrAS 78P Seventh edition, Volume 4: Philosophy, Religion, & Law; 1978.
DrAS 82E Eighth edition, Volume 2: English, Speech, & Drama; 1982.
DrAS 82F Eighth edition, Volume 3: Foreign Languages, Linguistics, & Philology; 1982.
DrAS 82H Eighth edition, Volume 1: History; 1982.

DrAS 82P Eighth edition, Volume 4: Philosophy, Religion, & Law; 1982.

DrBlPA *Directory of Blacks in the Performing Arts.* By Edward Mapp. Metuchen, NJ: Scarecrow Press, 1978-1990.
DrBlPA First edition; 1978.
DrBlPA 90 Second edition; 1990.

DrCnP 81 *Directory of Canadian Plays and Playwrights.* Edited by Jane Cunningham. Toronto: Playwrights Canada, 1981.

DrEEuF *Directory of Eastern European Film-Makers and Films, 1945-1991.* By Grzegorz Balski. Westport, CT: Greenwood Press, 1992.

DrIndFM *Directory of Indian Film-Makers and Films.* Compiled and edited by Sanjit Narwekar. Westport, CT: Greenwood Press, 1994.

DrInf *The Directory of Infamy.* The best of the worst: an illustrated compendium of over 600 of the all-time great crooks. By Jonathon Green. London: Mills & Boon, 1980.
Use the Index to locate biographies.

DrLC 69 *Directory of Library Consultants.* Edited by John N. Berry, III. New York: R.R. Bowker Co., 1969.

DrmM *Dream Makers.* The uncommon men & women who write science fiction. Interviews by Charles Platt. New York: Berkley Books, 1980-1983.
DrmM 1 Volume 1; 1980.
DrmM 2 Volume II; 1983.
Use the Table of Contents to locate interviews.

DrRegL 75 *Directory of Registered Lobbyists and Lobbyist Legislation.* Second edition. Chicago: Marquis Academic Media, 1975.
Use the ''Lobbyist Index,'' which begins on page 451, to locate listings.

Dun&B *Dun & Bradstreet Reference Book of Corporate Managements.* Parsippany, NJ: Dun & Bradstreet, 1979-1990.
Dun&B 79 13th edition; 1979.
Dun&B 86 1986 edition; 1985.
Dun&B 88 1988 edition; 1988.
Dun&B 90 1990 edition; 1990.
Use the ''Principal Officers and Directors Index'' in the Cross-Reference volume to locate biographies. The ''Principal Officers and Directors Index'' often alphabetizes by titles of address, such as Dr., Mrs., and Baron. Names with prefixes, such as Mc, De, and De La, may sometimes be located in more than one place in the index.

EarABI *Early American Book Illustrators and Wood Engravers, 1670-1870.* A catalogue of a collection of American books illustrated for the most part with woodcuts and wood engravings in the Princeton University Library. By Sinclair Hamilton. Princeton, NJ: Princeton University Press, 1958-1968.
EarABI Volume I: Main Catalogue; 1958.
EarABI SUP Volume II: Supplement; 1968.

EarBlAP — *Early Black American Playwrights and Dramatic Writers.* A biographical directory and catalog of plays, films, and broadcasting scripts. By Bernard L. Peterson, Jr. New York: Greenwood Press, 1990.

Ebony — *The Ebony Success Library.* By the Editors of *Ebony.* Nashville, TN: Southwestern Co., 1973.

Ebony 1	Volume I: 1,000 Successful Blacks.
Ebony 3	Volume III: Career Guide.

EncAACR — *Encyclopedia of African-American Civil Rights.* From emancipation to the present. Edited by Charles D. Lowery and John F. Marszalek. Westport, CT: Greenwood Press, 1992.

EncAAH — *Encyclopedia of American Agricultural History.* By Edward L. Schapsmeier and Frederick H. Schapsmeier. Westport, CT: Greenwood Press, 1975.

EncAAr 1 — *Encyclopedia of American Architecture.* By William Dudley Hunt, Jr. New York: McGraw-Hill Book Co., 1980.

EncAAr 2 — *Encyclopedia of American Architecture.* Second edition. By Robert T. Packard. New York: McGraw-Hill, 1995.

EncAB-A — *Encyclopedia of American Biography.* New York and West Palm Beach, FL: The American Historical Society, 1934-1970.

EncAB-A 1	New Series. Volume 1; 1934.
EncAB-A 2	New Series. Volume 2; 1934.
EncAB-A 3	New Series. Volume 3; 1935.
EncAB-A 4	New Series. Volume 4; 1935.
EncAB-A 5	New Series. Volume 5; 1936.
EncAB-A 6	New Series. Volume 6; 1936.
EncAB-A 7	New Series. Volume 7; 1937.
EncAB-A 8	New Series. Volume 8; 1938.
EncAB-A 9	New Series. Volume 9; 1938.
EncAB-A 10	New Series. Volume 10; 1939.
EncAB-A 11	New Series. Volume 11; 1940.
EncAB-A 12	New Series. Volume 12; 1941.
EncAB-A 13	New Series. Volume 13; 1941.
EncAB-A 14	New Series. Volume 14; 1942.
EncAB-A 15	New Series. Volume 15; 1942.
EncAB-A 16	New Series. Volume 16; 1943.
EncAB-A 17	New Series. Volume 17; 1944.
EncAB-A 18	New Series. Volume 18; 1945.
EncAB-A 19	New Series. Volume 19; 1947.
EncAB-A 20	New Series. Volume 20; 1948.
EncAB-A 21	New Series. Volume 21; 1949.
EncAB-A 22	New Series. Volume 22; 1950.
EncAB-A 23	New Series. Volume 23; 1952.
EncAB-A 24	New Series. Volume 24; 1954.
EncAB-A 25	New Series. Volume 25; 1955.
EncAB-A 26	New Series. Volume 26; 1957.
EncAB-A 27	New Series. Volume 27; 1957.
EncAB-A 28	New Series. Volume 28; 1958.
EncAB-A 29	New Series. Volume 29; 1959.

EncAB-A 30	New Series. Volume 30; 1960.
EncAB-A 31	New Series. Volume 31; 1961.
EncAB-A 32	New Series. Volume 32; 1963.
EncAB-A 33	New Series. Volume 33; 1965.
EncAB-A 34	New Series. Volume 34; 1965.
EncAB-A 35	New Series. Volume 35; 1966.
EncAB-A 36	New Series. Volume 36; 1967.
EncAB-A 37	New Series. Volume 37; 1968.
EncAB-A 38	New Series. Volume 38; 1968.
EncAB-A 39	New Series. Volume 39; 1969.
EncAB-A 40	New Series. Volume 40; 1970.

Use the Index to locate biographies.

EncAB-H 1974 *Encyclopedia of American Biography.* Edited by John A. Garraty. New York: Harper & Row Publishers, 1974.

EncAB-H 1996 *Encyclopedia of American Biography.* Edited by John A. Garraty and Jerome L. Sternstein. New York: HarperCollins, 1996.

EncABHB *Encyclopedia of American Business History and Biography.* New York: Facts on File, 1988-1994.

EncABHB 1	*Railroads in the Age of Regulation, 1900-1980.* Edited by Keith L. Bryant, Jr; 1988.
EncABHB 2	*Railroads in the Nineteenth Century.* Edited by Robert L. Frey; 1988.
EncABHB 3	*Iron and Steel in the Nineteenth Century.* Edited by Paul F. Paskoff; 1989.
EncABHB 4	*The Automobile Industry, 1896-1920.* Edited by George S. May; 1990. Use the index to locate biographies.
EncABHB 5	*The Automobile Industry, 1920-1980.* Edited by George S. May; 1989. Use the index to locate biographies.
EncABHB 6	*Banking and Finance to 1913.* Edited by Larry Schweikart; 1990.
EncABHB 7	*Banking and Finance, 1913-1989.* Edited by Larry Schweikart; 1990.
EncABHB 8	*The Airline Industry.* Edited by William M. Leary; 1992.
EncABHB 9	*Iron and Steel in the Twentieth Century.* Edited by Bruce E. Seely; 1994.

EncACom *The Encyclopedia of American Comics.* Edited by Ron Goulart. New York: Facts on File, 1990.

EncACr *Encyclopedia of American Crime.* By Carl Sifakis. New York: Facts on File, Inc., 1982.

EncAFC *Encyclopedia of American Film Comedy.* By Larry Langman. Garland Reference Library of the Humanities, vol. 744. New York: Garland Publishing, 1987.

EncAHmr *Encyclopedia of American Humorists.* Edited by Steven H. Gale. New York: Garland Publishing, 1988.

EncAI&E *The Encyclopedia of American Intelligence and Espionage.* From the Revolutionary War to the present. By G.J.A. O'Toole. New York: Facts on File, 1988.

EncAJ *The Encyclopedia of American Journalism.* By Donald Paneth. New York: Facts on File Publications, 1983.

EncAL *Encyclopedia of the American Left.* Edited by Mari Jo Buhle, Paul Buhle, and Dan Georgakas. Garland Reference Library of the Social Sciences, vol. 502. New York: Garland Publishing, 1990.
Cross-references appear before other entries with similar surnames.

EncAmaz 91 *The Encyclopedia of Amazons.* Women warriors from antiquity to the modern era. First edition. By Jessica Amanda Salmonson. New York: Paragon House, 1991.

EncAR *Encyclopedia of the American Revolution.* By Mark Mayo Boatner, III. New York: David McKay Co., 1966.

EncARH *The Encyclopedia of American Religious History.* Two volumes. By Edward L. Queen II, Stephen R. Prothero, and Gardiner H. Shattuck, Jr. New York: Facts on File, 1996.
Use the Index to locate biographies.

EncASM *Encyclopedia of American Silver Manufacturers.* By Dorothy T. Rainwater. New York: Crown Publishers, 1975.

EncBrWW *Encyclopedia of British Women Writers.* Edited by Paul Schlueter and June Schlueter. Garland Reference Library of the Humanities, vol. 818. New York: Garland Publishing, 1988.

EncCoWW *Encyclopedia of Continental Women Writers.* Two volumes. Edited by Katharina M. Wilson. Garland Reference Library of the Humanities, vol. 698. New York: Garland Publishing, 1991.

EncCRAm *The Encyclopedia of Colonial and Revolutionary America.* Edited by John Mack Faragher. New York: Facts on File, 1990.

EncCW *Encyclopedia of the Cold War.* By Thomas S. Arms. New York: Facts on File, 1994.

EncDeaf *The Encyclopedia of Deafness and Hearing Disorders.* By Carol Turkington and Allen E. Sussman. New York: Facts on File, 1992.

EncE 75 *Encyclopedia of Espionage.* New edition. By Ronald Seth. London: New English Library, 1975.

EncEarC *Encyclopedia of Early Christianity.* Edited by Everett Ferguson. Garland Reference Library of the Humanities, vol. 846. New York: Garland Publishing, 1990.

EncEnl *Encyclopedia of the Enlightenment.* By Peter Hanns Reill and Ellen Judy Wilson. New York: Facts on File, 1996.

EncEnv *The Encyclopedia of the Environment.* Edited by Ruth A. Eblen and William R. Eblen. Boston: Houghton Mifflin Co., 1994.

EncEth *Encyclopedia of Ethics.* Two volumes. Edited by Lawrence C. Becker and Charlotte B. Becker. New York: Garland Publishing, 1992.

EncEurC *Encyclopedia of European Cinema.* Edited by Ginette Vincendeau. New York: Facts on File, 1995.

EncFash *The Encyclopaedia of Fashion.* By Georgina O'Hara. New York: Harry N. Abrams, 1986.

EncFCWM *The Encyclopedia of Folk, Country & Western Music.* By Irwin Stambler and Grelun Landon. New York: St. Martin's Press, 1969-1983.
EncFCWM 69 First edition; 1969.
EncFCWM 83 Second edition; 1983.

EncFWF *Encyclopedia of Frontier and Western Fiction.* Edited by Jon Tuska and Vicki Piekarski. New York: McGraw-Hill Book Co., 1983.

EncGRNM *Encyclopedia of German Resistance to the Nazi Movement.* Edited by Wolfgang Benz and Walter H. Pehle. New York, NY: Continuum Publishing, 1997.
The "Biographical Sketches" section begins on page 255.

EncHuEv *Encyclopedia of Human Evolution and Prehistory.* Edited by Ian Tattersall, Eric Delson, and John Van Couvering. Garland Reference Library of the Humanities, vol. 768. New York: Garland Publishing, 1988.

EncJap *Encyclopedia of Japan.* Japanese history and culture, from abacus to zori. By Dorothy Perkins. New York: Facts on File, 1991.

EncJzS *Encyclopedia of Jazz in the Seventies.* By Leonard Feather and Ira Gitler. New York: Horizon Press, 1976.

EncJzS *The Encyclopedia of Jazz in the Seventies.* By Leonard Feather and Ira Gitler. New York: Horizon Press, 1976.

EncLatA *Encyclopedia of Latin America.* Edited by Helen Delpar. New York: McGraw-Hill Book Co., 1974.

EncMA *Encyclopedia of Modern Architecture.* Edited by Wolfgang Pehnt. New York: Harry N. Abrams, 1964.
Biographies begin on page 28.

EncMcCE *Encyclopedia of the McCarthy Era.* By William K. Klingaman. New York: Facts on File, 1996.

EncMot *The Encyclopedia of Motorcycling.* By George Bishop. New York: G.P. Putnam's Sons, 1980.

EncMT *Encyclopaedia of the Musical Theatre.* By Stanley Green. New York: Dodd, Mead & Co., 1976.

EncMys *Encyclopedia of Mystery and Detection.* By Chris Steinbrunner and Otto Penzler. New York: McGraw-Hill Book Co., 1976.

EncNAB *The Encyclopedia of Native American Biography.* Six hundred life stories of important people, from Powhatan to Wilma Mankiller. By Bruce E. Johansen and Donald A. Grinde, Jr. New York: Henry Holt and Co., 1997.

EncNAR *The Encyclopedia of Native American Religions.* By Arlene Hirschfelder and Paulette Molin. New York: Facts on File, 1992.

EncNoAI *Encyclopedia of North American Indians.* Edited by Frederick E. Hoxie. Boston: Houghton Mifflin Co., 1996.

EncO&P *Encyclopedia of Occultism & Parapsychology.* A compendium of information on the occult sciences, magic, demonology, superstitions, spiritism, mysticism, metaphysics, psychical science, and parapsychology, with biographical and bibliographical notes and comprehensive indexes. Edited by Leslie A. Shepard. Detroit: Gale Research, 1978-1991.

EncO&P 1 First edition; 1978.
EncO&P 1S1 First edition, *Occultism Update,* Issue Number 1; 1978.
EncO&P 1S2 First edition, *Occultism Update,* Issue Number 2; 1980.
EncO&P 1S3 First edition, *Occultism Update,* Issue Numbers 3-4; 1981.
EncO&P 2 Second edition; 1984.
EncO&P 2S1 Second edition, *Occultism Update.*; 1987.
EncO&P 3 Third edition. Two volumes; 1991.

EncPaPR 91 *The Encyclopedia of Parapsychology and Psychical Research.* By Arthur S. Berger and Joyce Berger. New York: Paragon House, 1991.

EncPR&S 74 *Encyclopedia of Pop, Rock & Soul.* By Irwin Stambler. New York: St. Martin's Press, 1974.

EncPR&S 89 *The Encyclopedia of Pop, Rock & Soul.* Revised edition. By Irwin Stambler. New York: St. Martin's Press, 1989.

EncRev *The Encyclopedia of Revolutions and Revolutionaries.* From anarchism to Zhou Enlai. By Martin van Creveld. New York: Facts on File, 1996.

EncRk 88 *Encyclopedia of Rock.* By Phil Hardy and Dave Laing. New York: Schirmer Books, 1988.

EncRkSt *Encyclopedia of Rock Stars.* By Dafydd Rees and Luke Crampton. New York: DK Publishing, 1996.

EncSF *The Encyclopedia of Science Fiction.* An Illustrated A to Z. Edited by Peter Nicholls. London: Granada Publishing, 1979.

EncSF 93 *The Encyclopedia of Science Fiction.* Edited by John Clute and Peter Nicholls. New York: St. Martin's Press, 1993.

EncSoA *Encyclopaedia of Southern Africa.* Sixth edition. Compiled and edited by Eric Rosenthal. London: Frederick Warne & Co., 1973.

EncSoB *Encyclopedia of Southern Baptists.* Nashville, TN: Broadman Press, 1958-1971.

EncSoB	Two volumes; 1958.
EncSoB SUP	Volume III, Supplement; 1971.

EncSoH *The Encyclopedia of Southern History.* Edited by David C. Roller and Robert W. Twyman. Baton Rouge, LA: Louisiana State University Press, 1979.

EncSPD *The Encyclopedia of Schizophrenia and the Psychotic Disorders.* By Richard Noll. New York: Facts on File, 1992.

EncSUPP *Encyclopedia of Strange and Unexplained Physical Phenomena.* By Jerome Clark. Detroit: Gale Research, 1993.

EncTR *Encyclopedia of the Third Reich.* By Louis L. Snyder. New York: McGraw-Hill Book Co., 1976.

EncTR 91 *The Encyclopedia of the Third Reich.* Two volumes. Edited by Christian Zentner and Friedemann Bedurftig. Translation edited by Amy Hackett. New York: Macmillan Publishing Co., 1991.

EncTwCJ *Encyclopedia of Twentieth-Century Journalists.* By William H. Taft. Garland Reference Library of the Humanities, vol. 493. New York: Garland Publishing, 1986.

EncUnb *The Encyclopedia of Unbelief.* Two volumes. Edited by Gordon Stein. Buffalo, NY: Prometheus Books, 1985.

EncUrb *Encyclopedia of Urban Planning.* Edited by Arnold Whittick. New York: McGraw-Hill Book Co., 1974.

EncVaud *Encyclopedia of Vaudeville.* By Anthony Slide. Westport, CT: Greenwood Press, 1994.

EncWB *Encyclopedia of World Biography: 20th Century Supplement.* Three volumes. Palatine, IL: Jack Heraty & Associates, 1987-1988. Earlier volumes published as *The McGraw-Hill Encyclopedia of World Biography.*

EncWHA *The Encyclopedia of Women's History in America.* By Kathryn Cullen-DuPont. New York: Facts on File, 1996.

EncWL *Encyclopedia of World Literature in the 20th Century.* New York: Frederick Ungar Publishing Co., 1981- 1967-1981.

EncWL	First edition. Three volumes and supplement. Edited by Wolfgang Bernard Fleischmann; 1967.
EncWL 2	Revised edition. Four volumes. Edited by Leonard S. Klein; 1981.
EncWL 2	Revised edition. Volume 4. Edited by Leonard S. Klein; 1981.
EncWL 2	Revised edition. Volume 2. Edited by Leonard S. Klein; 1981.
EncWL 2	Revised edition. Volume 3. Edited by Leonard S. Klein; 1981.
EncWL 2	Revised edition. Four volumes. Edited by Leonard S. Klein; 1981.

EncWL 2 Revised edition. Volume 1. Edited by Leonard S. Klein; 1981.

EncWL 3 *Encyclopedia of World Literature in the 20th Century.* Revised edition. Five volumes. Edited by Leonard S. Klein. New York: Continuum Publishing Co., 1993. Distributed by Gale Research, Detroit.
Use the index to locate biographies.

EncWL SUP *Encyclopedia of World Literature in the 20th Century.* First edition, Supplement. Three volumes and supplement. Edited by Wolfgang Bernard Fleischmann. New York: Frederick Ungar Publishing Co., 1975. An enlarged and updated edition of the Herder *Lexikon der Weltliteratur im 20. Jahrhundert.*

EncWM *The Encyclopedia of World Methodism.* Two volumes. Edited by Nolan B. Harmon. Nashville, TN: United Methodist Publishing House, 1974.

EncWomS *Encyclopedia of Women and Sports.* By Victoria Sherrow. Santa Barbara, CA: ABC-CLIO, 1996.

EncWT *The Encyclopedia of World Theater.* Translated by Estella Schmid, edited by Martin Esslin. New York: Charles Scribner's Sons, 1977. Based on *Friedrichs Theaterlexikon,* by Karl Groning and Werner Kliess.

EncWW *The Encyclopedia of Witches and Witchcraft.* By Rosemary Ellen Guiley. New York: Facts on File, 1989.

EngPo *English Poetry of the Second World War.* A Biobibliography. By Catherine W. Reilly. Boston: G.K. Hall & Co., 1986.
Biographies begin on page 21.

Ent *The Entertainers.* Edited by Clive Unger-Hamilton. New York: St. Martin's Press, 1980.
Use the ''Index of Entries,'' beginning on page 306, to locate biographies.

Entr *Entrepreneurs.* The men and women behind famous brand names and how they made it. By Joseph J. Fucini and Suzy Fucini. Boston: G.K. Hall & Co., 1985.
Use the Index to locate biographies.

EnvEnc *Environmental Encyclopedia.* First edition. Detroit: Gale Research, 1994.

EnvEnDr *The Environment Encyclopedia and Directory.* London: Europa Publications, 1994.
''Who's Who in the Environment'' section begins on page 329.

EuAu *European Authors, 1000-1900.* A biographical dictionary of European literature. Edited by Stanley J. Kunitz and Vineta Colby. Wilson Authors Series. New York: H.W. Wilson Co., 1967.

EuWr *European Writers.* New York: Charles Scribner's Sons, 1983-1990.

EuWr 1 Volume 1: *The Middle Ages and the Renaissance.* Edited by William T.H. Jackson and George Stade; 1983.

EuWr 2 Volume 2: *The Middle Ages and the Renaissance.* Edited by William T.H. Jackson and George Stade; 1983.

EuWr 3	Volume 3: *The Age of Reason and the Enlightenment.* Edited by George Stade; 1984.
EuWr 4	Volume 4: *The Age of Reason and the Enlightenment.* Edited by George Stade; 1984.
EuWr 5	Volume 5: *The Romantic Century.* Edited by Jacques Barzun and George Stade; 1985.
EuWr 6	Volume 6: *The Romantic Century.* Edited by Jacques Barzun and George Stade; 1985.
EuWr 7	Volume 7: *The Romantic Century.* Edited by Jacques Barzun and George Stade; 1985.
EuWr 8	Volume 8: *The Twentieth Century.* Edited by George Stade; 1989.
EuWr 9	Volume 9: *The Twentieth Century.* Edited by George Stade; 1989.
EuWr 10	Volume 10: *The Twentieth Century.* Edited by George Stade; 1990.
EuWr 11	Volume 11: *The Twentieth Century.* Edited by George Stade; 1990.
EuWr 12	Volume 12: *The Twentieth Century.* Edited by George Stade; 1990.
EuWr 13	Volume 13: *The Twentieth Century.* Edited by George Stade; 1990.

Use the ''List of Subjects'' to locate biographies.

EvEuW *Everyman's Dictionary of European Writers.* By W.N. Hargreaves-Mawdsley. London: J.M. Dent & Sons; New York: E.P. Dutton & Co., 1968.

EvLB *Everyman's Dictionary of Literary Biography, English and American.* Compiled after John W. Cousin by D.C. Browning. Revised edition. London: J.M. Dent & Sons; New York: E.P. Dutton & Co., 1960.

ExpInc *Experience, Inc.* Men and women who founded famous companies after the age of 40. By Joseph J. Fucini and Suzy Fucini. New York: Free Press, 1987.

Use the Index to locate biographies.

Expl 93 *Explorers and Discoverers of the World.* First edition. Edited by Daniel B. Baker. Detroit: Gale Research, 1993.

Use the Table of Contents to locate biographies.

FacFETw *The Facts on File Encyclopedia of the Twentieth Century.* Edited by John Drexel. New York: Facts on File, 1991.

FacPr *Facts about the Presidents.* A compilation of biographical and historical information. By Joseph Nathan Kane. New York: H.W. Wilson Co., 1989-1993.

FacPr 89	Fifth edition; 1989.
FacPr 93	Sixth edition; 1993.

Use the Index to locate biographies of the Presidents. Biographies of the First Ladies appear within the applicable President's biography.

FairDF *Fairchild's Dictionary of Fashion.* By Charlotte Calasibetta. New York: Fairchild Publications, 1975.

FairDF ENG	England section begins on page 548.
FairDF FIN	Finland section begins on page 553.

FairDF FRA	France section begins on page 554.
FairDF IRE	Ireland section begins on page 577.
FairDF ITA	Italy section begins on page 578.
FairDF JAP	Japan section begins on page 583.
FairDF SPA	Spain section begins on page 584.
FairDF US	United States section begins on page 585.

FamA&A — *Famous Actors and Actresses on the American Stage.* Documents of American theater history. Two volumes. By William C. Young. New York: R.R. Bowker Co., 1975.

FamAIYP — *Famous Author-Illustrators for Young People.* By Norah Smaridge. New York: Dodd, Mead & Co., 1973.

FamAYP — *Famous Authors for Young People.* By Ramon P. Coffman and Nathan G. Goodman. New York: Dodd, Mead & Co., 1943.

FamMS — *Famous Modern Storytellers for Young People.* By Norah Smaridge. New York: Dodd, Mead & Co., 1969.

FamPYP — *Famous Poets for Young People.* By Laura Benet. New York: Dodd, Mead & Co., 1964.

FamSYP — *Famous Storytellers for Young People.* By Laura Benet. New York: Dodd, Mead & Co., 1968.

FanAl — *The Fantasy Almanac.* By Jeff Rovin. New York: E.P. Dutton, 1979.

FarE&A — *The Far East and Australasia.* A survey and directory of Asia and the Pacific. London: Europa Publications, 1978-1981.

FarE&A 78	1978-1979 edition; 1978. Biographies are found in the "Who's Who in the Far East and Australasia" section.
FarE&A 79	1979-1980 edition; 1979. Biographies are found in the "Who's Who in the Far East and Australasia" section.
FarE&A 79A	1979-1980 edition; 1979. Wade-Giles/Pinyin spellings of Chinese names begin on page 1155.
FarE&A 80	1980-1981 edition; 1980. Biographies are found in the "Who's Who in the Far East and Australasia" section.
FarE&A 80A	1980-1981 edition; 1980. Wade-Giles/Pinyin spellings of Chinese names begin on page 1174.
FarE&A 81	1981-1982 edition; 1981. Biographies are found in the "Who's Who in the Far East and Australasia" section.

FemiCLE — *The Feminist Companion to Literature in English.* Women writers from the Middle Ages to the present. By Virginia Blain, Patricia Clements, and Isobel Grundy. New Haven, CT: Yale University Press, 1990.

FemiWr — *Feminist Writers.* Edited by Pamela Kester-Shelton. Detroit: St. James Press, 1996.

FemPA — *The Female Poets of America.* With portraits, biographical notices, and specimens of their writings. Seventh edition, revised. By Thomas Buchanan Read. Philadelphia: E.H. Butler & Co., 1857. Reprint. Detroit: Gale Research, 1978.

FifBJA *Fifth Book of Junior Authors & Illustrators.* Edited by Sally Holmes Holtze. New York: H.W. Wilson Co., 1983.

FifCWr *Fifty Caribbean Writers.* A bio-bibliographical critical sourcebook. Edited by Daryl Cumber Dance. New York: Greenwood Press, 1986.

FifIDA *Fifth International Directory of Anthropologists.* Current Anthropology Resource Series, edited by Sol Tax. Chicago: University of Chicago Press, 1975.

FifSWrA *Fifty Southern Writers after 1900.* A bio-bibliographical sourcebook. Edited by Joseph M. Flora and Robert Bain. New York: Greenwood Press, 1987.

FifSWrB *Fifty Southern Writers before 1900.* A bio-bibliographical sourcebook. Edited by Robert Bain and Joseph M. Flora. New York: Greenwood Press, 1987.

FifWWr *Fifty Western Writers.* A bio-bibliographical sourcebook. Edited by Fred Erisman and Richard W. Etulain. Westport, CT: Greenwood Press, 1982.

Film *Filmarama.* Compiled by John Stewart. Metuchen, NJ: Scarecrow Press, 1975-1977.
- ***Film 1*** Volume I: *The Formidable Years, 1893-1919.*; 1975.
- ***Film 2*** Volume II: *The Flaming Years, 1920-1929.*; 1977.

FilmAG WE *Film Actors Guide: Western Europe.* By James Robert Parish. Metuchen, NJ: Scarecrow Press, 1977.

FilmEn *The Film Encyclopedia.* By Ephraim Katz. New York: Thomas Y. Crowell, 1979.

FilmgC *The Filmgoer's Companion.* Fourth edition. By Leslie Halliwell. New York: Hill & Wang, 1974. Later editions published as *Halliwell's Filmgoer's Companion.*

Focus *Focus 101.* An illustrated biography of 101 poets of the 60's and 70's. By LaVerne Harrell Clark. Chico, CA: Heidelberg Graphics, 1979.

FolkA 87 *Folk Artists Biographical Index.* First edition. Edited by George H. Meyer. Detroit: Gale Research, 1987.

FootReg *The Football Register.* St. Louis: The Sporting News, 1981-1985.
- ***FootReg 81*** 1981 edition. Edited by Howard M. Balzar; 1981.
- ***FootReg 85*** 1985 edition. Edited by Howard M. Balzar and Barry Siegel; 1985.

FootReg *Football Register.* Edited by Howard M. Balzar and Barry Siegel. St. Louis: The Sporting News, 1986-1987.
- ***FootReg 86*** 1986 edition; 1986.
- ***FootReg 87*** 1987 edition; 1987.

ForIl *Forty Illustrators and How They Work.* By Ernest W. Watson. Cincinnati: Watson-Guptil Publications, 1946. Reprint. Freeport, New York: Books for Libraries Press, 1970.

ForWC 70 *Foremost Women in Communications.* A biographical reference work on accomplished women in broadcasting, publishing, advertising, public relations, and allied professions. New York: Foremost Americans Publishing Corp., 1970.

ForYSC *Forty Years of Screen Credits, 1929-1969.* Two volumes. Compiled by John T. Weaver. Metuchen, NJ: Scarecrow Press, 1970.
Entries begin on page 57.

FourBJA *Fourth Book of Junior Authors & Illustrators.* Edited by Doris De Montreville and Elizabeth D. Crawford. New York: H.W. Wilson Co., 1978.

FrenWW *French Women Writers.* A bio-bibliographical source book. Edited by Eva Martin Sartori and Dorothy Wynne Zimmerman. New York: Greenwood Press, 1991.

FrThres *From the Threshold. (Desde el umbral.)* Contemporary Peruvian fiction in translation. Bilingual edition. Edited by Luis Ramos-Garcia and Luis Fernando Vidal. Austin, TX: Studia Hispanica Editors, 1987.
Biographies are found in the ''Biographical Notes'' section beginning on page 310.

FunnyW *Funny Women.* American comediennes, 1860-1985. By Mary Unterbrink. Jefferson, NC: McFarland & Co., 1987.
Use the Index to locate biographies.

Funs *The Funsters.* By James Robert Parish and William T. Leonard. New Rochelle, NY: Arlington House Publishers, 1979.

Future *The Future.* A guide to information sources. Second edition. Edited by Edward S. Cornish. Washington: World Future Society, 1979.
Biographies begin on page 125.

GaEncPs *Gale Encyclopedia of Psychology.* Edited by Susan Gall. Detroit: Gale Research, 1996.

GangFlm *Gangster Films.* A comprehensive, illustrated reference to people, films, and terms. By Michael L. Stephens. Jefferson, NC: McFarland & Co., 1996.

GayLesB *Gay & Lesbian Biography.* Detroit: St. James Press, 1997.

GayLL *Gay & Lesbian Literature.* Detroit: St. James Press, 1994.

GayN *The Gay Nineties in America.* A cultural dictionary of the 1890s. By Robert L. Gale. Westport, CT: Greenwood Press, 1992.

GenMudB *Generals in Muddy Boots.* A concise encyclopedia of combat commanders. By Dan Cragg. New York: Berkley Books, 1996.

Geog *Geographers: Biobibliographical Studies.* London: Mansell Publishing, 1977-1986.

Geog 1 Volume 1. Edited by T.W. Freeman, Marguerita Oughton, and Philippe Pinchemel; 1977.

Geog 2 Volume 2. Edited by T.W. Freeman and Philippe Pinchemel; 1978.

Geog 3 Volume 3. Edited by T.W. Freeman and Philippe Pinchemel; 1979.

Geog 4	Volume 4. Edited by T.W. Freeman and Philippe Pinchemel; 1980.
Geog 5	Volume 5. Edited by T.W. Freeman; 1981.
Geog 6	Volume 6. Edited by T.W. Freeman; 1982.
Geog 7	Volume 7. Edited by T.W. Freeman; 1983.
Geog 8	Volume 8. Edited by T.W. Freeman; 1984.
Geog 9	Volume 9. Edited by T.W. Freeman; 1985.
Geog 10	Volume 10. Edited by T.W. Freeman; 1986.

GolEC *Golombek's Encyclopedia of Chess.* Edited by Harry Golombek. New York: Crown Publishers, 1977.

GoodHs *The Good Housekeeping Woman's Almanac.* Edited by Barbara McDowell and Hana Umlauf. New York: Newspaper Enterprise Association, 1977.
Use the Index to locate biographies.

GrAmP *Great American Prints, 1900-1950.* 138 lithographs, etchings and woodcuts. By June Kraeft and Norman Kraeft. New York: Dover Publications, 1984.
Biographies begin on page 139.

GrBIl *The Great Bird Illustrators and Their Art, 1730-1930.* By Peyton Skipwith. New York: Hamlyn Publishing Group, 1979.

GrBr *Great Britons.* Twentieth-century lives. By Harold Oxbury. Oxford: Oxford University Press, 1985.

GrComp *Great Composers 1300-1900.* A biographical and critical guide. Compiled and edited by David Ewen. New York: H.W. Wilson Co., 1966.

GrEconB *Great Economists before Keynes.* An introduction to the lives & works of one hundred great economists of the past. By Mark Blaug. Atlantic Highlands, NJ: Humanities Press International, 1986.

GrEconS *Great Economists since Keynes.* An introduction to the lives & works of one hundred modern economists. By Mark Blaug. Totowa, NJ: Barnes & Noble Books, 1985.

GrFLW *Great Foreign Language Writers.* Edited by James Vinson and Daniel Kirkpatrick. Great Writers Series. New York: St. Martin's Press, 1984.

Grk&L *Greek and Latin Authors, 800 B.C.-A.D. 1000.* By Michael Grant. Wilson Authors Series. New York: H.W. Wilson Co., 1980.

GrLGrT *Great Leaders, Great Tyrants?* Contemporary views of world rulers who made history. Edited by Arnold Blumberg. Westport, CT: Greenwood Press, 1995.

GrLiveH *Great Lives from History.* Five volumes. Edited by Frank N. Magill. American Women Series. Pasadena, CA: Salem Press, 1995.

GrMovC *Great Movie Comedians.* From Charlie Chaplin to Woody Allen. By Leonard Maltin. New York: Crown Publishers, 1978.
Use the Table of Contents to locate biographies.

GrStDi *The Great Stage Directors.* 100 distinguished careers of the theater. By Samuel L. Leiter. New York: Facts on File, 1994.

GrWomMW *Great Women Mystery Writers.* Classic to contemporary. Edited by Kathleen Gregory Klein. Westport, CT: Greenwood Press, 1994.

GrWomW *Great Women Writers.* The lives and works of 135 of the world's most important writers, from antiquity to the present. Edited by Frank N. Magill. New York: Henry Holt & Co., 1994.

GrWrEL *Great Writers of the English Language.* Edited by James Vinson. New York: St. Martin's Press, 1979.
- ***GrWrEL DR*** *Dramatists.*
- ***GrWrEL N*** *Novelists and prose writers.*
- ***GrWrEL P*** *Poets.*

GuBlues *A Guide to the Blues.* History, who's who, research sources. By Austin Sonnier, Jr. Westport, CT: Greenwood Press, 1994.
Biographies begin on page 93.

GuFrLit *Guide to French Literature.* By Anthony Levi. Detroit: St. James Press, 1992-1994.
- ***GuFrLit 1*** 1789 to the present; 1992.
- ***GuFrLit 2*** Beginnings to 1789; 1994.

GuPsyc *A Guide to Psychologists and Their Concepts.* By Vernon J. Nordby and Calvin S. Hall. San Francisco: W.H. Freeman & Co., 1974.

HalFC 80 *Halliwell's Filmgoer's Companion.* Seventh edition. By Leslie Halliwell. New York: Granada Publishing, 1980. Earlier editions published as *The Filmgoer's Companion.*

HalFC *Halliwell's Filmgoer's Companion.* By Leslie Halliwell. New York: Charles Scribner's Sons, 1984-1988.Earlier editions published as *The Filmgoer's Companion.*
- ***HalFC 84*** Eighth edition; 1984.
- ***HalFC 88*** Ninth edition; 1988.

HanAmWH *Handbook of American Women's History.* Edited by Angela Howard Zophy. Garland Reference Library of the Humanities, vol. 696. New York: Garland Publishing, 1990.

HanRL *Handbook of Russian Literature.* Edited by Victor Terras. New Haven, CT: Yale University Press, 1985.

HarEnCM 87 *The Harmony Illustrated Encyclopedia of Country Music.* By Fred Dellar, Allan Cackett, and Roy Thompson. New York: Harmony Books, 1987.
- ***HarEnCM 87A*** Appendix begins on page 197.

HarEnMi *The Harper Encyclopedia of Military Biography.* First edition. By Trevor N. Dupuy, Curt Johnson, and David L. Bongard. New York: HarperCollins Publishers, 1992.

HarEnR 86 *Harmony Illustrated Encyclopedia of Rock.* Seventh edition. New York: Harmony Books, 1986.

HarEnUS *Harper's Encyclopaedia of United States History: From 458 A.D. to 1915.* New edition entirely revised and enlarged. 10 volumes. By Benson John Lossing. New York: Harper & Brothers Publishers, 1915. Reprint. Detroit: Gale Research, 1974.

HarlReB *Harlem Renaissance and Beyond.* Literary biographies of 100 black women writers, 1900-1945. By Lorraine Elena Roses and Ruth Elizabeth Randolph. Boston: G. K. Hall & Co., 1990.

HealPre *The Health of the Presidents.* The 41 United States presidents through 1993 from a physician's point of view. By John R. Bumgarner. Jefferson, NC: McFarland & Co., 1994.
Use Table of Contents to locate biographies.

HeroCon *Heroes of Conscience.* A biographical dictionary. By Kathlyn Gay and Martin K. Gay. Santa Barbara, CA: ABC-CLIO, 1996.

HerW *Her Way.* A guide to biographies of women for young people. Chicago: American Library Association, 1976-1984.
HerW First edition. By Mary-Ellen Kulkin; 1976.
HerW 84 Second edition. By Mary-Ellen Siegel; 1984.

HisDBrE *Historical Dictionary of the British Empire.* Two volumes. Edited by James S. Olson and Robert Shadle. Westport, CT: Greenwood Press, 1996.

HisDcDP *Historical Dictionary of Data Processing: Biographies.* By James W. Cortada. New York: Greenwood Press, 1987.

HisDcKW *Historical Dictionary of the Korean War.* Edited by James I. Matray. New York: Greenwood Press, 1991.

HisDcSE *Historical Dictionary of the Spanish Empire, 1402-1975.* Edited by James S. Olson et al. New York: Greenwood Press, 1992.

HisDcT *Historical Dictionary of Terrorism.* By Sean Anderson and Stephen Sloan. Historical Dictionaries of Religions, Philosophies, and Movements, no. 4. Metuchen, NJ: Scarecrow Press, 1995.

HisDStE *Historical Dictionary of Stuart England, 1603-1689.* Edited by Ronald H. Fritze and William B. Robison. Westport, CT: Greenwood Press, 1996.

HisEAAC *An Historical Encyclopedia of the Arab-Israeli Conflict.* Edited by Bernard Reich. Westport, CT: Greenwood Press, 1996.

HisEWW *The Historical Encyclopedia of World War II.* Edited by Marcel Baudot et al. New York: Facts on File, 1980. Originally published as *Encyclopedie de la Guerre 1939-1945.* Paris: Editions Casterman, 1977.

HispAmA *The Hispanic-American Almanac.* A reference work on Hispanics in the United States. By Nicolas Kanellos. Detroit: Gale Research, 1993.
Use the Index to locate biographies.

HispLC *Hispanic Literature Criticism.* Two volumes. Detroit: Gale Research, 1994.

HispWr *Hispanic Writers.* A selection of sketches from *Contemporary Authors.* Detroit: Gale Research, 1991.

HisWorL *Historic World Leaders.* Five volumes. Edited by Anne Commire. Detroit: Gale Research, 1994.
Use the "Biographies in *Historic World Leaders*" Index at the back of Volume 5 to locate biographies.

HocEn *The Hockey Encyclopedia.* The Complete Record of Professional Ice Hockey. By Stan Fischler and Shirley Walter Fischler. New York: Macmillan Publishing Co., 1983.

HocReg *The Hockey Register.* Edited by Latty Wigge. St. Louis: The Sporting News, 1981-1987.

HocReg 81 1981-82 edition; 1981.
HocReg 85 1985-86 edition; 1985.
HocReg 86 1986-87 edition; 1986.
HocReg 87 1987-88 edition; 1987.

HolBB *Hollywood Baby Boomers.* By James Robert Parish and Don Stanke. New York: Garland Publishing, 1992.

HolCA *Hollywood Character Actors.* By James Robert Parish. Westport, CT: Arlington House Publishers, 1978.

HolP *Hollywood Players.* New Rochelle, NY: Arlington House Publishers, 1976.

HolP 30 *The Thirties.* By James Robert Parish and William T. Leonard.
HolP 40 *The Forties.* By James Robert Parish and Lennard DeCarl.

HorFD *Horror Film Directors, 1931-1990.* By Dennis Fischer. Jefferson, NC: McFarland & Co., 1991.
Use the Table of Contents to locate entries.

HsB&A *The House of Beadle and Adams and Its Dime and Nickel Novels.* The Story of a Vanished Literature. By Albert Johannsen. Norman, OK: University of Oklahoma Press, 1950-1962.

HsB&A Volumes I-II; 1950. Biographies are found in volume II.
HsB&A SUP Volume III, Supplement, Addenda, Corrigenda; 1962.

HumSex *Human Sexuality.* An encyclopedia. Edited by Vern L. Bullough and Bonnie Bullough. Garland Reference Library of Social Science, vol. 685. New York: Garland Publishing, 1994.

ICPEnP *ICP (International Center of Photography) Encyclopedia of Photography.* New York: Crown Publishers, 1984.
- ***ICPEnP A*** "Appendix 1" begins on page 576.

IlBBlP *Illustrated Bio-Bibliography of Black Photographers, 1940-1988.* By Deborah Willis-Thomas. Garland Reference Library of the Humanities, vol. 760. New York: Garland Publishing, 1989.

IlBEAAW *The Illustrated Biographical Encyclopedia of Artists of the American West.* By Peggy Samuels and Harold Samuels. Garden City, NY: Doubleday & Co., 1976.

IlDcG *Illustrated Dictionary of Glass.* 2,442 entries, including definitions of wares, materials, processes, forms, and decorative styles, and entries on principal glass-makers, decorators, and designers, from antiquity to the present. By Harold Newman. London: Thames & Hudson, 1977.

IlEncBM 82 *Illustrated Encyclopedia of Black Music.* Edited by Ray Bonds. New York: Harmony Books, 1982.

IlEncCM *The Illustrated Encyclopedia of Country Music.* By Fred Dellar, Roy Thompson, and Douglas B. Green. New York: Harmony Books, 1977.

IlEncJ *The Illustrated Encyclopedia of Jazz.* By Brian Case and Stan Britt. New York: Harmony Books, 1978.

IlEncMy *Illustrated Encyclopaedia of Mysticism and the Mystery Religions.* By John Ferguson. London: Thames & Hudson, 1976.

IlEncRk *The Illustrated Encyclopedia of Rock.* Revised edition. Compiled by Nick Logan and Bob Woffinden. New York: Harmony Books, 1977.

IlrAm 1880 *The Illustrator in America, 1880-1980.* A century of illustration. By Walt Reed and Roger Reed. New York: Madison Square Press, 1984. Distributed by Robert Silver Associates, New York.
Use the Index to locate biographies.

IlrAm *The Illustrator in America, 1900-1960's.* Compiled and edited by Walt Reed. New York: Reinhold Publishing Corp., 1966.
- ***IlrAm A*** "The Decade: 1900-1910" begins on page 13.
- ***IlrAm B*** "The Decade: 1910-1920" begins on page 43.
- ***IlrAm C*** "The Decade: 1920-1930" begins on page 77.
- ***IlrAm D*** "The Decade: 1930-1940" begins on page 113.
- ***IlrAm E*** "The Decade: 1940-1950" begins on page 167.
- ***IlrAm F*** "The Decade: 1950-1960" begins on page 211.
- ***IlrAm G*** "The Decade: 1960's" begins on page 239.

IlsBYP *Illustrators of Books for Young People.* Second edition. By Martha E. Ward and Dorothy A. Marquardt. Metuchen, NJ: Scarecrow Press, 1975.

IlsCB *Illustrators of Children's Books.* Boston: Horn Book, 1947-1978.

- ***IlsCB 1744*** *1744-1945.* Compiled by Bertha E. Mahony, Louise Payson Latimer, and Beulah Folmsbee; 1947. Biographies begin on page 267.
- ***IlsCB 1946*** *1946-1956.* Compiled by Ruth Hill Viguers, Marcia Dalphin, and Bertha Mahony Miller; 1958. Biographies begin on page 62.
- ***IlsCB 1957*** *1957-1966.* Compiled by Lee Kingman, Joanna Foster, and Ruth Giles Lontoft; 1968. Biographies begin on page 70.
- ***IlsCB 1967*** *1967-1976.* Compiled by Lee Kingman, Grace Allen Hogarth, and Harriet Quimby; 1978. Biographies begin on page 93.

IlWWBF *The Illustrated Who's Who in British Films.* By Denis GGifford. London: Anchor Press, 1978.

- ***IlWWBF A*** The "Biographical Bibliography" section begins on page 317.

IlWWHD *The Illustrated Who's Who of Hollywood Directors.* Volume 1: *The Sound Era.* By Michael Barson. New York: Farrar, Straus & Giroux, 1995.

- ***IlWWHD 1*** Biographies are located in the "Directors" section, beginning on page 1.
- ***IlWWHD 1A*** Biographies are located in the "Short Subjects" section, beginning on page 479.

InB&W *In Black and White.* A guide to magazine articles, newspaper articles, and books concerning Black individuals and groups. Edited by Mary Mace Spradling. Detroit: Gale Research, 1980-1985.

- ***InB&W 80*** Third edition. Two volumes; 1980.
- ***InB&W 85*** Third edition, Supplement; 1985.
- ***InB&W 85A*** Third edition, Supplement; 1985. "Performing Groups" section begins on page 440.
- ***InB&W 85B*** Third edition, Supplement; 1985. "Prominent Duos" section begins on page 451.

IndAu 1816 *Indiana Authors and Their Books, 1816-1916.* Biographical sketches of authors who published during the first century of Indiana statehood with lists of their books. Compiled by R.E. Banta. Crawfordsville, IN: Wabash College, 1949.

IndAu 1917 *Indiana Authors and Their Books, 1917-1966.* A continuation of *Indiana Authors and Their Books, 1816-1916,* and containing additional names from the earlier period. Compiled by Donald E. Thompson. Crawfordsville, IN: Wabash College, 1974.

IndAu 1967 *Indiana Authors and Their Books, 1967-1980.* Biographical sketches of authors who published during the first century of Indiana statehood with lists of their books. Compiled by Donald E. Thompson. Crawfordsville, IN: Wabash College, 1981.

IndCTCL *The Indiana Companion to Traditional Chinese Literature.* Edited and compiled by William H. Nienhauser, Jr. Bloomington, IN: Indiana University Press, 1986. Entries begin on page 195.

InSci *Index to Scientists of the World from Ancient to Modern Times.* Biographies and portraits. By Norma Olin Ireland. Boston: F.W. Faxon Co., 1962.

IntAu&W *The International Authors and Writers Who's Who.* Cambridge: International Biographical Centre, 1976-1993.

IntAu&W 76 Seventh edition. Edited by Ernest Kay; 1976.
IntAu&W 76A Seventh edition. Edited by Ernest Kay; 1976. Addendum begins on page 641.
IntAu&W 76X Seventh edition. Edited by Ernest Kay; 1976. ''Pseudonyms of Included Authors'' section begins on page 645.
IntAu&W 77 Eighth edition. Edited by Adrian Gaster; 1977.
IntAu&W 77X Eighth edition. Edited by Adrian Gaster; 1977. ''Pseudonyms of Included Authors'' section begins on page 1131.
IntAu&W 82 Ninth edition. Edited by Adrian Gaster; 1982.
IntAu&W 82X Ninth edition. Edited by Adrian Gaster; 1982. ''Pseudonyms of Included Authors'' section begins on page 719.
IntAu&W 86 10th edition. Edited by Ernest Kay; 1986.
IntAu&W 86X 10th edition. Edited by Ernest Kay; 1986. ''Pseudonyms of Authors and Writers'' section begins on page 796.
IntAu&W 89 11th edition. Edited by Ernest Kay; 1989.
IntAu&W 91 12th edition. Edited by Ernest Kay; 1991.
IntAu&W 91X 12th edition. Edited by Ernest Kay; 1991. ''Pseudonyms of Authors'' section begins on page 940.
IntAu&W 93 13th edition, 1993-94. Edited by Ernest Kay; 1993.

IntDcAA 90 *International Dictionary of Art and Artists: Artists.*] Edited by James Vinson. Chicago: St. James Press, 1990.

IntDcAn *International Dictionary of Anthropologists.* Edited by Christopher Winters. Garland Reference Library of the Social Sciences, vol. 638. New York: Garland Publishing, 1991.

IntDcAr *International Dictionary of Architects and Architecture.* Volume 1: *Architects.* Edited by Randall J. Van Vynckt. Detroit: St. James Press, 1993.

IntDcB *International Dictionary of Ballet.* Two volumes. Edited by Martha Bremser. Detroit: St. James Press, 1993.

IntDcF *The International Dictionary of Films and Filmmakers.* Detroit: St. James Press, 1984-1993.

IntDcF 1-2 First edition. Volume 2: *Directors/Filmmakers.* Edited by Christopher Lyon; 1984.
IntDcF 1-3 First edition. Volume 3: *Actors and Actresses.* Edited by James Vinson; 1986.
IntDcF 1-4 First edition. Volume 4: *Writers and Production Artists.* Edited by James Vinson; 1987.
IntDcF 2-2 Second edition. Volume 2: *Directors.* Edited by Nicholas Thomas; 1991.
IntDcF 2-3 Second edition. Volume 3: *Actors and Actresses.* Edited by Nicholas Thomas; 1992.
IntDcF 2-4 Second edition. Volume 4: *Writers and Production Artists.* Edited by Samantha Cook; 1993.

IntDcOp *International Dictionary of Opera.* Two volumes. Edited by C. Steven LaRue. Detroit: St. James Press, 1993.

IntDcT *International Dictionary of Theatre.* Detroit: St. James Press, 1994-1996.

IntDcT 2	Volume 2:*Playwrights.* Edited by Mark Hawkins-Dady; 1994.
IntDcT 3	Volume 3: *Actors, Directors and Designers.* Edited by David Pickering; 1996.

IntDcWB *The International Dictionary of Women's Biography.* Compiled and edited by Jennifer S. Uglow. New York: Continuum Publishing Co., 1982. Later edition published as *The Continuum Dictionary of Women's Biography.*

IntEnSS 79 *International Encyclopedia of the Social Sciences.* Volume 18: Biographical Supplement. Edited by David L. Sills. New York: Macmillan Publishing Co., 1979.

IntLitE *International Literature in English.* Essays on the major writers. Edited by Robert L. Ross. New York: Garland Publishing, 1991.
Use the Index to locate biographies.

IntMed 80 *International Medical Who's Who.* A biographical guide in medical research. First edition. Two volumes. Harlow, United Kingdom: Longman Group, 1980.

IntMPA *International Motion Picture Almanac.* New York: Quigley Publishing Co., 1975-1996.

IntMPA 75	1975 edition; 1975.
IntMPA 76	1976 edition; 1976.
IntMPA 77	1977 edition; 1977.
IntMPA 77	1977 edition; 1977.
IntMPA 78	1978 edition; 1978.
IntMPA 79	1979 edition; 1979.
IntMPA 80	1980 edition; 1980.
IntMPA 81	1981 edition; 1981.
IntMPA 82	1982 edition; 1982.
IntMPA 84	1984 edition; 1984.
IntMPA 86	1986 edition; 1986.
IntMPA 88	1988 edition; 1988.
IntMPA 92	1992 edition; 1992.
IntMPA 94	1994 edition; 1994.
IntMPA 94N	1994 edition; 1994. Obituaries section is on page 386.
IntMPA 96	1996 edition; 1996.

IntvLAW *Interviews with Latin American Writers.* By Marie-Lise Gazarian Gautier. Elmwood Park, IL: Dalkey Archive Press, 1989.

IntvSpW *Interviews with Spanish Writers.* By Marie-Lise Gazarian Gautier. Elmwood Park, IL: Dalkey Archive Press, 1991.

IntvTCA 2 *Interviews and Conversations with 20th-Century Authors Writing in English.* An index. Series II. By Stan A. Vrana. Metuchen, NJ: Scarecrow Press, 1986.

IntvWPC *Interviews with Writers of the Post-Colonial World.* Edited by Feroza Jussawalla and Reed Way Dasenbrock. Jackson, MS: University Press of Mississippi, 1992.
Use the Table of Contents to locate biographies.

IntWW *The International Who's Who.* London: Europa Publications, 1974-1993.Distributed by Gale Research, Detroit.

IntWW 74 38th edition, 1974-1975; 1974.
IntWW 75 39th edition, 1975-1976; 1975.
IntWW 75N 39th edition, 1975-1976; 1975. The Obituary section is located at the front of the volume.
IntWW 76 40th edition, 1976-1977; 1976.
IntWW 76N 40th edition, 1976-1977; 1976. The Obituary section is located at the front of the volume.
IntWW 77 41st edition, 1977-1978; 1977.
IntWW 77N 41st edition, 1977-1978; 1977. The Obituary section is located at the front of the volume.
IntWW 78 42nd edition, 1978-1979; 1978.
IntWW 78N 42nd edition, 1978-1979; 1978. The Obituary section is located at the front of the volume.
IntWW 79 43rd edition, 1979-1980; 1979.
IntWW 79N 43rd edition, 1979-1980; 1979. The Obituary section is located at the front of the volume.
IntWW 80 44th edition, 1980-1981; 1980.
IntWW 81 45th edition, 1981-1982; 1981.
IntWW 81N 45th edition, 1981-1982; 1981. The Obituary section is located at the front of the volume.
IntWW 82 46th edition, 1982-1983; 1982.
IntWW 82N 46th edition, 1982-1983; 1982. The Obituary section is located at the front of the volume.
IntWW 83 47th edition, 1983-1984; 1983.
IntWW 83N 47th edition, 1983-1984; 1983. The Obituary section is located at the front of the volume.
IntWW 89 53rd edition, 1989-1990; 1989.
IntWW 89N 53rd edition, 1989-1990; 1989. The Obituary section is located at the front of the volume.
IntWW 91 55th edition, 1991-1992; 1991.
IntWW 91N 55th edition, 1991-1992; 1991. The Obituary section is located at the front of the volume.
IntWW 93 57th edition, 1993-1994; 1993.
IntWW 93N 57th edition, 1993-1994; 1993. The obituary section is located at the front of the volume.

IntWWE *International Who's Who in Energy and Nuclear Sciences.* Harlow, United Kingdom: Longman Group, 1983.

IntWWM *International Who's Who in Music and Musicians' Directory.* Cambridge: International Who's Who in Music, 1977-1990.Distributed by Taylor and Francis International Publication Services, Bristol, Pa.

IntWWM 77 Eighth edition; 1977.
IntWWM 80 Ninth edition. Edited by Adrian Gaster; 1980.
IntWWM 85 10th edition; 1984.
IntWWM 90 12th edition, 1990-1991; 1990.

IntWWM 96 — *International Who's Who in Music and Musicians' Directory.* In the classical and light-classical fields. Fifteenth edition, 1996-1997. Volume one. Cambridge: International Biographical Centre, 1996. Distributed by Taylor and Francis International Publication Services, Bristol, Pa.

IntWWMu 96 — *International Who's Who in Music.* Volume two - popular music. First edition, 1996-1997. Cambridge: International Biographical Centre, 1996. Distributed by Taylor and Francis International Publication Services, Bristol, Pa.

This volume complements *International Who's Who in Music and Musicians' Directory*, fifteenth edition, 1996-1997.

IntWWP — *International Who's Who in Poetry.* Edited by Ernest Kay. Cambridge: International Biographical Centre, 1977-1982.1982 edition is combined with *The International Authors and Writers Who's Who.*

IntWWP 77	Fifth edition; 1977.
IntWWP 77A	Fifth edition; 1977. Addendum begins on page 470.
IntWWP 77X	Fifth edition; 1977. ''Pseudonyms and Pen Names of Included Poets'' section begins on page 702.
IntWWP 82	Sixth edition; 1982. Biographies begin on page 759.
IntWWP 82X	Sixth edition; 1982. ''Pseudonyms of Included Poets'' section begins on page 1035.

IntYB — *The International Year Book and Statesmen's Who's Who.* West Sussex, England: Kelly's Directories, 1978-1981.

IntYB 78	1978 edition; 1978.
IntYB 79	1979 edition; 1979.
IntYB 80	1980 edition; 1980.
IntYB 81	1981 edition; 1981.

Biographies are found in Part 3.

IntYB — *The International Yearbook and Statesmen's Who's Who.* 1982 edition. West Sussex, England: Thomas Skinner Directories, 1982.

IntYB 82	Biographies are found in Part 3.
IntYB 82A	''Late Information'' section begins on page 749 of Part 3.

InWom — *Index to Women of the World from Ancient to Modern Times.* Biographies and portraits. By Norma Olin Ireland. Westwood, MA: F.W. Faxon Co., 1970.

InWom SUP — *Index to Women of the World from Ancient to Modern Times: A Supplement.* By Norma Olin Ireland. Metuchen, NJ: Scarecrow Press, 1988.

IriPla — *Irish Playwrights, 1880-1995.* A research and production sourcebook. Edited by Bernice Schrank and William W. Demastes. Westport, CT: Greenwood Press, 1997.

ItaFilm — *Italian Film.* A who's who. By John Stewart. Jefferson, NC: McFarland & Co., 1994.

JapFilm — *The Japanese Filmography.* A complete reference to 209 filmmakers and the over 1250 films released in the United States, 1900 through 1994. By Stuart Galbraith IV. Jefferson, NC: McFarland & Co., 1996.

JBA *The Junior Book of Authors.* Edited by Stanley J. Kunitz and Howard Haycraft. Wilson Authors Series. New York: H.W. Wilson Co., 1934-1951.
- ***JBA 34*** First edition; 1934.
- ***JBA 51*** Second edition, revised; 1951.

JeAmFiW *Jewish American Fiction Writers.* An annotated bibliography. By Gloria L. Cronin, Blaine H. Hall, and Connie Lamb. Garland Reference Library of the Humanities, vol. 972. New York: Garland Publishing, 1991.

JeAmHC *Jewish-American History and Culture.* An encyclopedia. Edited by Jack Fischel and Sanford Pinkser. Garland Reference Library of the Social Sciences, vol. 429. New York: Garland Publishing, 1992.

JeAmWW *Jewish American Women Writers.* A bio-bibliographical and critical sourcebook. Edited by Ann R. Shapiro. Westport, CT: Greenwood Press, 1994.

JeHun *The Jewish 100.* A ranking of the most influential Jews of all time. By Michael Shapiro. New York: Carol Publishing Group, 1994.
Use the Index to locate biographies.

JoeFr *Joe Franklin's Encyclopedia of Comedians.* Secaucus, NJ: Citadel Press, 1979.

JohnWSW *John Willis' Screen World.* 1981, Volume 32. New York: Crown Publishers, Inc., 1981.

JohnWTW 38 *John Willis' Theatre World.* 1981-82, Volume 38. New York: Crown Publishers, Inc., 1983.

JrnUS *Journalists of the United States.* Biographical sketches of print and broadcast news shapers from the late 17th century to the present. By Robert B. Downs and Jane B. Downs. Jefferson, NC: McFarland & Co., 1991.

LadLa 86 *The Lady Laureates.* Women who have won the Nobel Prize. Second edition. By Olga S. Opfell. Metuchen, NJ: Scarecrow Press, 1986.
Use the Index to locate biographies.

LarDcSc *Larousse Dictionary of Scientists.* Edited by Hazel Muir. New York: Larousse, 1994.

LatAmCC *Latin American Classical Composers.* A biographical dictionary. Compiled and edited by Miguel Ficher, Martha Furman Schleifer, and John M. Furman. Lanham, MD: Scarecrow Press, 1996.

LatAmWr *Latin American Writers.* Three volumes. Edited by Carlos A. Sole and Maria Isabel Abreu. New York: Charles Scribner's Sons, 1989.
Use the Index, which begins on page 1459 of Volume 3, to locate biographies.

Law&B *Law & Business Directory of Corporate Counsel.* New York: Harcourt Brace Jovanovich, 1980-1984.
- ***Law&B 80*** 1980-1981 edition; 1980.
- ***Law&B 84*** 1984-1985 edition; 1984.

Use the "Individual Name Index" to locate listings.

Law&B *Law & Business Directory of Corporate Counsel.* Englewood Cliffs, NJ: Prentice Hall, 1989-1992.
- ***Law&B 89A*** 1989-1990 edition. Volume 1; 1989.
- ***Law&B 89B*** 1989-1990 edition. Volume 2; 1989.
- ***Law&B 92*** 1992-1993 edition; 1992.

Use the ''Individual Name Index'' to locate biographies.

LEduc 74 *Leaders in Education.* Fifth edition. New York: R.R. Bowker Co., 1974.

LegTOT *Legends in Their Own Time.* New York: Prentice Hall General Reference, 1994.

LElec *Leaders in Electronics.* New York: McGraw-Hill Book Co., 1979. Title page reads *McGraw-Hill's Leaders in Electronics.*

LesBEnT *Les Brown's Encyclopedia of Television.* By Les Brown. New York: New York Zoetrope, 1982. Earlier edition published as *The New York Times Encyclopedia of Television.*

LesBEnT 92 *Les Brown's Encyclopedia of Television.* Third edition. By Les Brown. Detroit: Gale Research, 1992.

LibW *Liberty's Women.* Edited by Robert McHenry. Springfield, MA: G. & C. Merriam Co., 1980.

LiExTwC *Literary Exile in the Twentieth Century.* An analysis and biographical dictionary. Edited by Martin Tucker. New York: Greenwood Press, 1991.

Biographies begin on page 47.

LiHiK *A Literary History of Kentucky.* By William S. Ward. Knoxville, TN: University of Tennessee Press, 1988.

Use the Index to locate biographies.

LiJour *Literary Journalists.* A biographical dictionary of writers and editors. By Edd Applegate. Westport, CT: Greenwood Press, 1996.

LinLib *The Lincoln Library of Language Arts.* Third edition. Two volumes. Columbus, OH: Frontier Press Co., 1978.
- ***LinLib L*** Biographies begin on page 345 of Volume 1 and are continued in Volume 2.
- ***LinLib LP*** ''Pen Names'' section begins on page 331.

LinLib S *The Lincoln Library of Social Studies.* Eighth edition. Three volumes. Columbus, OH: Frontier Press Co., 1978.

Biographies begin on page 865 of Volume 3.

LitC *Literature Criticism from 1400 to 1800.* Critical discussion of the works of fifteenth-, sixteenth-, seventeenth-, and eighteenth-century novelists, poets, playwrights, philosophers, and other creative writers. Detroit: Gale Research, 1984-1997.
- ***LitC 1*** Volume 1; 1984.
- ***LitC 2*** Volume 2; 1985.
- ***LitC 3*** Volume 3; 1986.
- ***LitC 4*** Volume 4; 1986.

LitC 5	Volume 5; 1987.
LitC 6	Volume 6; 1987.
LitC 7	Volume 7; 1988.
LitC 8	Volume 8; 1988.
LitC 9	Volume 9; 1989.
LitC 10	Volume 10; 1989.
LitC 11	Volume 11; 1990.
LitC 12	Volume 12; 1990.
LitC 13	Volume 13; 1990.
LitC 14	Volume 14; 1991.
LitC 15	Volume 15; 1991.
LitC 16	Volume 16; 1991.
LitC 17	Volume 17; 1992.
LitC 18	Volume 18; 1992.
LitC 19	Volume 19; 1992.
LitC 20	Volume 20; 1993.
LitC 21	Volume 21; 1993.
LitC 22	Volume 22; 1993.
LitC 23	Volume 23; 1994.
LitC 24	Volume 24; 1994.
LitC 25	Volume 25; 1994.
LitC 26	Volume 26; 1995.
LitC 27	Volume 27; 1995.
LitC 28	Volume 28; 1995.
LitC 29	Volume 29; 1996.
LitC 30	Volume 30; 1996.
LitC 31	Volume 31; 1996.
LitC 32	Volume 32; 1996.
LitC 33	Volume 33; 1996.
LitC 34	Volume 34; 1997. Contains no biographies.
LitC 35	Volume 35; 1997.

LiveLet *Lives and Letters in American Parapsychology.* A biographical history, 1850-1987. By Arthur S. Berger. Jefferson, NC: McFarland & Co., 1988.
Use the Index to locate biographies.

LiveMA *Lives of Mississippi Authors, 1817-1967.* Edited by James B. Lloyd. Jackson, MS: University Press of Mississippi, 1981.

LivgBAA *Living Black American Authors.* A biographical directory. By Ann Allen Shockley and Sue P. Chandler. New York: R.R. Bowker Co., 1973.

LivgFWS *The Living Female Writers of the South.* Edited by Mary T. Tardy. Philadelphia: Claxton, Remsen & Haffelfinger, 1872. Reprint. Detroit: Gale Research, 1978.

LngBDD *Longman Biographical Directory of Decision-Makers in Russia and the Successor States.* Edited by Martin McCauley. Harlow, Essex, England: Longman Current Affairs, 1993. Distributed by Gale Research, Detroit.

LngCEL *Longman Companion to English Literature.* Second edition. By Christopher Gillie. London: Longman Group, 1977. Also published as *A Companion to British Literature.* Detroit: Grand River Books, 1980.

LngCTC *Longman Companion to Twentieth Century Literature.* By A.C. Ward. London: Longman Group, 1970.

LNinSix *Leaders from the 1960's.* A biographical sourcebook of American activism. Edited by David DeLeon. Westport, CT: Greenwood Press, 1994.
Use the Index to locate biographies.

LuthC 75 *Lutheran Cyclopedia.* Revised edition. Edited by Erwin L. Lueker. St. Louis: Concordia Publishing House, 1975.

MacBEP *Macmillan Biographical Encyclopedia of Photographic Artists & Innovators.* By Turner Browne and Elaine Partnow. New York: Macmillan Publishing Co.; London: Collier Macmillan Publishers, 1983.

MacDCB 78 *The Macmillan Dictionary of Canadian Biography.* Fourth edition. Edited by W. Stewart Wallace. Revised, enlarged, and updated by W.A. McKay. Toronto: Macmillan of Canada, 1978.

MacDWB *The Macmillan Dictionary of Women's Biography.* Edited by Jennifer S. Uglow. New York: Macmillan, 1982.

MacEA *Macmillan Encyclopedia of Architects.* Four volumes. Edited by Adolf K. Placzek. New York: Macmillan Publishing Co., Free Press; London: Collier Macmillan Publishers, 1982.
Use the ''Index of Names,'' which begins on page 533 of Volume 4, to locate biographies.

MagIlD *Magic Illustrated Dictionary.* By Geoffrey Lamb. London: Kaye & Ward, 1979.

MagSAmL *Magill's Survey of American Literature.* Six volumes. Edited by Frank N. Magill. North Bellmore, NY: Marshall Cavendish, 1991.

MagSWL *Magill's Survey of World Literature.* Six volumes. Edited by Frank N. Magill. North Bellmore, NY: Marshall Cavendish, 1993.

MajAI *Major Authors and Illustrators for Children and Young Adults.* A selection of sketches from *Something about the Author.* Six volumes. Detroit: Gale Research, 1993.

MajMD *Major Modern Dramatists.* A Library of Literary Criticism. New York: Ungar Publishing Co., 1984-1986.

MajMD 1 Volume I. Compiled and edited by Rita Stein and Friedhelm Rickert; 1984.

MajMD 2 Volume II. Compiled and edited by Blandine M. Rickert, et al; 1986.

Use the ''Dramatists Included'' list on page ix to locate biographies.

MajTwCW *Major Twentieth-Century Writers.* A selection of sketches from *Contemporary Authors.* Four volumes. Detroit: Gale Research, 1991.

MakMC *Makers of Modern Culture.* Edited by Justin Wintle. New York: Facts on File, 1981.

MarqDCG 84 *Marquis Who's Who Directory of Computer Graphics.* First edition. Chicago: Marquis Who's Who, 1984.

McGDA *McGraw-Hill Dictionary of Art.* Five volumes. Edited by Bernard S. Myers. New York: McGraw-Hill Book Co., 1969.

McGEWB *The McGraw-Hill Encyclopedia of World Biography.* New York: McGraw-Hill Book Co., 1973. Supplemental volumes published as *Encyclopedia of World Biography: 20th Century Supplement.*

McGEWD *McGraw-Hill Encyclopedia of World Drama.* New York: McGraw-Hill Book Co., 1972-1984.

McGEWD 72 First edition. Four volumes; 1972.
McGEWD 84 Second edition. Five volumes; 1984.

McGMS 80 *McGraw-Hill Modern Scientists and Engineers.* Three volumes. New York: McGraw-Hill Book Co., 1980.

MedHR *Medal of Honor Recipients, 1863-1978.* 96th Congress, 1st Session, Senate Committee Print No. 3. Prepared by the Committee on Veterans' Affairs, United States Senate. Washington, DC: U.S. Government Printing Office, 1979.
Use the ''Medal of Honor Alphabetical Index,'' which begins on page 1023, to locate biographies.

MedHR 94 *Medal of Honor Recipients, 1863-1994.* Two volumes. Compiled by George Lang, Raymond L. Collins, and Gerard F. White. New York: Facts on File, 1995.
Use the alphabetical Index, which begins on page 865, to locate biographies.

MediFra *Medieval France.* An encyclopedia. Edited by William W. Kibler and Grover A. Zinn. Garland Reference Library of the Humanities, vol. 932. New York: Garland Publishing, 1995.

MediWW *Medieval Women Writers.* Edited by Katharina M. Wilson. Athens, GA: University of Georgia Press, 1984.
Use the Table of Contents to locate biographies.

MedPD *Media Personnel Directory.* An alphabetical guide to names, addresses, and telephone numbers of key editorial and business personnel at over 700 United States and international periodicals. Edited by Alan E. Abrams. Detroit: Gale Research Co., 1979.

MemAm *Memorable Americans, 1750-1950.* By Robert B. Downs, John T. Flanagan, and Harold W. Scott. Littleton, CO: Libraries Unlimited, 1983.

Meth *The Methodists.* By James E. Kirby, Russell E. Richey, and Kenneth E. Rowe. Denominations in America, no. 8. Westport, CT: Greenwood Press, 1996.
Biographies begin on page 257.

MetOEnc *The Metropolitan Opera Encyclopedia.* A comprehensive guide to the world of opera. Edited by David Hamilton. New York: Simon and Schuster, 1987.

MexAmB *Mexican American Biographies.* A historical dictionary, 1836-1987. By Matt S. Meier. New York: Greenwood Press, 1988.

MGM *The MGM Stock Company.* The golden era. By James Robert Parish and Ronald L. Bowers. New Rochelle, NY: Arlington House, 1973.

MGM A ''Capsule Biographies of MGM Executives'' section begins on page 796.

MichAu 80 *Michigan Authors.* Second edition. By the Michigan Association for Media in Education. Ann Arbor, MI: Michigan Association for Media in Education, 1980.

MichAu 80A Addendum begins on page 339.

MidE *The Middle East and North Africa.* London: Europa Publications, 1978-1982.

MidE 78 25th edition, 1978-1979; 1978.
MidE 79 26th edition, 1979-1980; 1979.
MidE 80 27th edition, 1980-1981; 1980.
MidE 81 28th edition, 1981-1982; 1981.
MidE 82 29th edition, 1982-1983; 1982.

Biographies are found in the ''Who's Who in the Middle East and North Africa'' section.

MinnWr *Minnesota Writers.* A collection of autobiographical stories by Minnesota prose writers. Edited and annotated by Carmen Nelson Richards. Minneapolis: T.S. Denison & Co., 1961.

Use the Table of Contents to locate biographies.

MiSFD 9 *Michael Singer's Film Directors.* A complete guide. Ninth international edition. Edited by Michael Singer. Los Angeles: Lone Eagle Publishing Co., 1992.

MiSFD 9N The Obituary section begins on page 318.

MnBBF *The Men behind Boys' Fiction.* By W.O.G. Lofts and D.J. Adley. London: Howard Baker Publishers, 1970.

MnPM *Men of Popular Music.* By David Ewen. Chicago: Ziff-Davis Publishing Co., 1944. Reprint. Freeport, N.Y.: Books for Libraries Press, 1972.

ModAL *Modern American Literature.* A Library of Literary Criticism. New York: Frederick Ungar Publishing Co., 1969-1985.

ModAL Fourth edition. Volumes 1-3. Compiled and edited by Dorothy Nyren Curley, Maurice Kramer, and Elaine Fialka Kramer; 1969.

ModAL S1 Volume 4, Supplement. Compiled and edited by Dorothy Nyren, Maurice Kramer, and Elaine Fialka Kramer; 1976.

ModAL S2 Volume 5, Second Supplement. Compiled and edited by Paul Schlueter and June Schlueter; 1985.

ModArCr *Modern Arts Criticism.* A biographical and critical guide to painters, sculptors, photographers, and architects from the beginning of the modern era to the present. Detroit: Gale Research, 1991-1994.

ModArCr 1	Volume 1; 1991.
ModArCr 2	Volume 2; 1992.
ModArCr 3	Volume 3; 1993.
ModArCr 4	Volume 4; 1994.

ModAWP *Modern American Women Poets.* By Jean Gould. New York: Dodd, Mead & Co., 1984.
Use the Table of Contents to locate biographies.

ModAWWr *Modern American Women Writers.* Edited by Elaine Showalter, Lea Baechler, and A. Walton Litz. New York: Charles Scribner's Sons, 1991.

ModBlW *Modern Black Writers.* Compiled and edited by Michael Popkin. A Library of Literary Criticism. New York: Frederick Ungar Publishing Co., 1978.

ModBrL *Modern British Literature.* A Library of Literary Criticism. New York: Frederick Ungar Publishing Co., 1966-1985.

ModBrL	Volumes 1-3. Compiled and edited by Ruth Z. Temple and Martin Tucker; 1966.
ModBrL S1	Volume 4, Supplement. Compiled and edited by Martin Tucker and Rita Stein; 1975.
ModBrL S2	Volume 5, Second Supplement. Compiled and edited by Denis Lane and Rita Stein; 1985.

ModCmwL *Modern Commonwealth Literature.* Compiled and edited by John H. Ferres and Martin Tucker. A Library of Literary Criticism. New York: Frederick Ungar Publishing Co., 1977.

ModFrL *Modern French Literature.* Two volumes. Compiled and edited by Debra Popkin and Michael Popkin. A Library of Literary Criticism. New York: Frederick Ungar Publishing Co., 1977.

ModGL *Modern German Literature.* Two volumes. Compiled and edited by Agnes Korner Domandi. A Library of Literary Criticism. New York: Frederick Ungar Publishing Co., 1972.

ModIrL *Modern Irish Literature.* Compiled and edited by Denis Lane and Carol McCrory Lane. A Library of Literary Criticism. New York: Ungar Publishing Co., 1988.

ModLAL *Modern Latin American Literature.* Two volumes. Compiled and edited by David William Foster and Virginia Ramos Foster. A Library of Literary Criticism. New York: Frederick Ungar Publishing Co., 1975.

ModRL *Modern Romance Literatures.* Compiled and edited by Dorothy Nyren Curley and Arthur Curley. A Library of Literary Criticism. New York: Frederick Ungar Publishing Co., 1967.

ModSL *Modern Slavic Literatures.* A Library of Literary Criticism. New York: Frederick Ungar Publishing Co., 1972-1976.

ModSL 1 Volume 1: Russian Literature. Compiled and edited by Vasa D. Mihailovich; 1972.

ModSL 2 Volume 2: Bulgarian, Czechoslovak, Polish, Ukrainian and Yugoslav Literatures. Compiled and edited by Vasa D. Mihailovich et al; 1976.

Use the alphabetic listing of authors to locate biographies.

ModSpP *Modern Spanish and Portuguese Literatures.* Compiled and edited by Marshall J. Schneider and Irwin Stern. A Library of Literary Criticism. New York: Continuum, 1988.

ModSpP P Biographies of Portuguese writers are located in the ''Portugal'' section, which begins on page 455.

ModSpP S Biographies of Spanish writers are located in the ''Spain'' section.

ModWD *Modern World Drama.* An encyclopedia. By Myron Matlaw. New York: E.P. Dutton & Co., 1972.

ModWoWr *Modern Women Writers.* Four volumes. Compiled and edited by Lillian S. Robinson. New York, NY: Continuum Publishing Co., 1996.

MorBAP *More Black American Playwrights.* A bibliography. By Esther Spring Arata. Metuchen, NJ: Scarecrow Press, 1978. Updates *Black American Playwrights.*

MorBMP *More Books by More People.* Interviews with sixty-five authors of books for children. By Lee Bennett Hopkins. New York: Citation Press, 1974.

MorJA *More Junior Authors.* Edited by Muriel Fuller. Wilson Authors Series. New York: H.W. Wilson Co., 1963.

MorMA *More Memorable Americans, 1750-1950.* By Robert B. Downs, John T. Flanagan, and Harold W. Scott. Littleton, CO: Libraries Unlimited, 1985.

MotPP *Motion Picture Performers.* A bibliography of magazine and periodical articles, 1900-1969. Compiled by Mel Schuster. Metuchen, NJ: Scarecrow Press, 1971.

MouLC *Moulton's Library of Literary Criticism.* English and American authors through the beginning of the twentieth century. Abridged, revised, and with additions by Martin Tucker. New York: Frederick Ungar Publishing Co., 1966.

MouLC 1 Volume 1: The beginnings to the seventeenth century.

MouLC 2 Volume 2: Neo-Classicism to the Romantic period.

MouLC 3 Volume 3: The Romantic period to the Victorian age.

MouLC 4 Volume 4: The mid-nineteenth century to Edwardianism.

Use the alphabetic listing at the front of the volume to locate biographies.

MovMk *The Movie Makers.* By Sol Chaneles and Albert Wolsky. Secaucus, NJ: Derbibooks, 1974.

The ''Directors'' section begins on page 506.

MugS *Mug Shots.* Who's who in the new Earth. By Jay Acton, Alan Le Mond, and Parker Hodges. New York: World Publishing Co., 1972.

MurCaTw *Murder Cases of the Twentieth Century.* Biographies and bibliographies of 280 convicted or accused killers. By David K. Frasier. Jefferson, NC: McFarland & Co., 1996.

MusmAFA *Museum of American Folk Art Encyclopedia of Twentieth-Century American Folk Art and Artists.* By Chuck and Jan Rosenak. New York: Abbeville Press, 1990.

MusMk *Music Makers.* By Clive Unger-Hamilton. New York: Harry N. Abrams, 1979.
Use the ''Alphabetical List of Entries'' at the front of the book to locate biographies.

MusSN *Musicians since 1900.* Performers in concert and opera. Compiled and edited by David Ewen. New York: H.W. Wilson Co., 1978.

NamesHP *Names in the History of Psychology.* A biographical sourcebook. By Leonard Zusne. Washington, DC: Hemisphere Publishing Corp., 1975. Distributed by John Wiley & Sons, Halstead Press, New York. Continued by *Biographical Dictionary of Psychology.*
Use the ''Alphabetic List of Names,'' which begins on page ix, to locate biographies.

NatCAB *The National Cyclopaedia of American Biography.* New York: James T. White & Co., 1891-1984.

NatCAB 1 Volume 1; 1891. Use the Index to locate biographies.
NatCAB 2 Volume 2; 1891. Use the Index to locate biographies.
NatCAB 3 Volume 3; 1891. Use the Index to locate biographies.
NatCAB 4 Volume 4; 1891. Use the Index to locate biographies.
NatCAB 5 Volume 5; 1891. Use the Index to locate biographies.
NatCAB 6 Volume 6; 1892. Use the Index to locate biographies.
NatCAB 7 Volume 7; 1892. Use the Index to locate biographies.
NatCAB 8 Volume 8; 1898. Use the Index to locate biographies.
NatCAB 9 Volume 9; 1899. Use the Index to locate biographies.
NatCAB 10 Volume 10; 1900. Use the Index to locate biographies.
NatCAB 11 Volume 11; 1901. Use the Index to locate biographies.
NatCAB 12 Volume 12; 1904. Use the Index to locate biographies.
NatCAB 13 Volume 13; 1906. Use the Index to locate biographies.
NatCAB 14 Volume 14; 1910. Use the Index to locate biographies.
NatCAB 15 Volume 15; 1914. Use the Index to locate biographies.
NatCAB 16 Volume 16; 1918. Use the Index to locate biographies.
NatCAB 17 Volume 17; 1921. Use the Index to locate biographies.
NatCAB 18 Volume 18; 1922. Use the Index to locate biographies.
NatCAB 19 Volume 19; 1926. Use the Index to locate biographies.
NatCAB 20 Volume 20; 1929. Use the Index to locate biographies.
NatCAB 21 Volume 21; 1931. Use the Index to locate biographies.
NatCAB 22 Volume 22; 1932. Use the Index to locate biographies.
NatCAB 23 Volume 23; 1933. Use the Index to locate biographies.
NatCAB 24 Volume 24; 1935. Use the Index to locate biographies.
NatCAB 25 Volume 25; 1936. Use the Index to locate biographies.
NatCAB 26 Volume 26; 1937. Use the Index to locate biographies.
NatCAB 27 Volume 27; 1939. Use the Index to locate biographies.
NatCAB 28 Volume 28; 1940. Use the Index to locate biographies.
NatCAB 29 Volume 29; 1941. Use the Index to locate biographies.
NatCAB 30 Volume 30; 1943. Use the Index to locate biographies.
NatCAB 31 Volume 31; 1944. Use the Index to locate biographies.

NatCAB 32	Volume 32; 1945. Use the Index to locate biographies.
NatCAB 33	Volume 33; 1947. Use the Index to locate biographies.
NatCAB 34	Volume 34; 1948. Use the Index to locate biographies.
NatCAB 35	Volume 35; 1949. Use the Index to locate biographies.
NatCAB 36	Volume 36; 1950. Use the Index to locate biographies.
NatCAB 37	Volume 37; 1951. Use the Index to locate biographies.
NatCAB 38	Volume 38; 1953. Use the Index to locate biographies.
NatCAB 39	Volume 39; 1954. Use the Index to locate biographies.
NatCAB 40	Volume 40; 1955. Use the Index to locate biographies.
NatCAB 41	Volume 41; 1956. Use the Index to locate biographies.
NatCAB 42	Volume 42; 1958. Use the Index to locate biographies.
NatCAB 43	Volume 43; 1961. Use the Index to locate biographies.
NatCAB 44	Volume 44; 1962. Use the Index to locate biographies.
NatCAB 45	Volume 45; 1962. Use the Index to locate biographies.
NatCAB 46	Volume 46; 1963. Use the Index to locate biographies.
NatCAB 47	Volume 47; 1965. Use the Index to locate biographies.
NatCAB 48	Volume 48; 1965. Use the Index to locate biographies.
NatCAB 49	Volume 49; 1966. Use the Index to locate biographies.
NatCAB 50	Volume 50; 1968. Use the Index to locate biographies.
NatCAB 51	Volume 51; 1969. Use the Index to locate biographies.
NatCAB 52	Volume 52; 1970. Use the Index to locate biographies.
NatCAB 53	Volume 53; 1972. Use the Index to locate biographies.
NatCAB 54	Volume 54; 1973. Use the Index to locate biographies.
NatCAB 55	Volume 55; 1974. Use the Index to locate biographies.
NatCAB 56	Volume 56; 1975. Use the Index to locate biographies.
NatCAB 57	Volume 57; 1977. Use the Index to locate biographies.
NatCAB 58	Volume 58; 1979. Use the Index to locate biographies.
NatCAB 59	Volume 59; 1980. Use the Index to locate biographies.
NatCAB 60	Volume 60; 1981. Use the Index to locate biographies.
NatCAB 61	Volume 61; 1982. Use the Index to locate biographies.
NatCAB 62	Volume 62; 1984. Use the Index to locate biographies.
NatCAB 63	Volume 63; 1984. Use the Index which begins on page 353 to locate biographies.
NatCAB 63N	Volume 63; 1984. Use the Index which begins on page 349 to locate biographies.

NatLAC *National Leaders of American Conservation.* Edited by Richard H. Stroud. Washington, DC: Smithsonian Institution Press, 1985.

NatNAL *Native North American Literature.* Biographical and critical information on native writers and orators from the United States and Canada from historical times to the present. Detroit: Gale Research, 1994.

Use the Outline of Contents to locate biographies.

NatPD *National Playwrights Directory.* Edited by Phyllis Johnson Kaye. Waterford, CT: The O'Neill Theater Center, 1977-1981.

NatPD 77	First edition; 1977.
NatPD 81	Second edition; 1981.

NegAl 76 *The Negro Almanac.* A reference work on the Afro American. Third edition. Edited by Harry A. Ploski and Warren Marr, II. New York: Bellwether Co., 1976. Later edition published as *The African-American Almanac.*

Use the Index to locate biographies.

NegAl 83 *The Negro Almanac.* A reference work on the Afro-American. Fourth edition. Compiled and edited by Harry A. Ploski and James Williams. New York: John Wiley & Sons, 1983.
Use the Index to locate biographies.

NegAl *The Negro Almanac.* A reference work on the African American. Fifth edition. Detroit: Gale Research, 1989. Later edition published as *The African-American Almanac.*
NegAl 89 Use the Index to locate biographies.
NegAl 89A Unindexed biographies in "The Black Voter and Elected Office Holder" chapter are located on pages 386-468.

NewAgE 90 *New Age Encyclopedia.* A guide to the beliefs, concepts, terms, people, and organizations that make up the New Global Movement toward spritual development, health and healing, higher consciousness, and related subjects. First edition. Detroit: Gale Research, 1990.

NewAgMG *The New Age Music Guide.* Profiles and recordings of 500 top New Age musicians. By Patti Jean Birosik. New York: Colliers Books, Macmillan Publishing Co., 1989.

NewAmDM *The New American Dictionary of Music.* By Philip D. Morehead with Anne MacNeil. New York: Dutton, 1991.

NewbC 1956 *Newbery and Caldecott Medal Books, 1956-1965.* With acceptance papers, biographies and related material chiefly from the *Horn Book Magazine.* Edited by Lee Kingman. Boston: Horn Book, 1965.

NewbC *Newbery and Caldecott Medal Books.* With acceptance papers, biographies and related material chiefly from the *Horn Book Magazine.* Edited by Lee Kingman. Boston: Horn Book, 1965-1975.
NewbC 1956 *1956-1965.*; 1965.
NewbC 1966 *1966-1975.*; 1975.

NewbC 1966 *Newbery and Caldecott Medal Books, 1966-1975.* With acceptance papers, biographies and related material chiefly from the *Horn Book Magazine.* Edited by Lee Kingman. Boston: Horn Book, 1975.

NewbMB 1922 *Newbery Medal Books, 1922-1955.* With their authors' acceptance papers and related material chiefly from the *Horn Book Magazine.* Edited by Bertha Mahony Miller and Elinor Whitney Field. Horn Book Papers, vol. 1. Boston: Horn Book, 1955.

NewC *The New Century Handbook of English Literature.* Revised edition. Edited by Clarence L. Barnhart with the assistance of William D. Halsey. New York: Appleton-Century-Crofts, 1967.

NewCBEL *The New Cambridge Bibliography of English Literature.* Five volumes. Edited by George Watson. Cambridge: Cambridge University Press, 1969-1977.
Use the index in Volume 5 to locate entries.

NewCBMT *New Complete Book of the American Musical Theater.* By David Ewen. New York: Holt, Rinehart & Winston, 1970.
Biographies are found in the "Librettists, Lyricists and Composers" section which begins on page 607.

NewCol 75 *The New Columbia Encyclopedia.* Edited by William H. Harris and Judith S. Levey. New York and London: Columbia University Press, 1975.

NewCon *The New Consciousness, 1941-1968.* Concise Dictionary of American Literary Biography Series. Detroit: Gale Research, 1987.

NewEOp 71 *The New Encyclopedia of the Opera.* By David Ewen. New York: Hill & Wang, 1971.

NewEScF *The New Encyclopedia of Science Fiction.* Edited by James Gunn. New York: Viking, 1988.

NewGrDA 86 *The New Grove Dictionary of American Music.* Four volumes. Edited by H. Wiley Hitchcock and Stanley Sadie. London: Macmillan Press, 1986.

NewGrDJ 88 *The New Grove Dictionary of Jazz.* Two volumes. Edited by Barry Kernfeld. London: Macmillan Press, 1988.

NewGrDJ 94 *The New Grove Dictionary of Jazz.* Edited by Barry Kernfeld. New York: St. Martin's Press, 1994.

NewGrDM 80 *The New Grove Dictionary of Music and Musicians.* 20 volumes. Edited by Stanley Sadie. London: Macmillan Publishers, 1980.

NewGrDO *The New Grove Dictionary of Opera.* Four volumes. Edited by Stanley Sadie. London: Macmillan Press; New York: Grove's Dictionaries of Music, 1992.

NewOrJ *New Orleans Jazz: A Family Album.* Revised edition. By Al Rose and Edmond Souchon. Baton Rouge, LA: Louisiana State University Press, 1978.

NewOrJ	"Who's Who in New Orleans Jazz" begins on page 4.
NewOrJ SUP	"Who's Who in New Orleans Jazz Supplement" begins on page 307.

NewOxM *The New Oxford Companion to Music.* Two volumes. Edited by Denis Arnold. Oxford: Oxford University Press, 1983.

News *Newsmakers.* The people behind today's headlines. Detroit: Gale Research, 1989-1997.Issues prior to 1988, Issue 2, were published as *Contemporary Newsmakers.*

News 88	1988 Cumulation; 1989.
News 89	1989 Cumulation; 1990.
News 90	1990 Cumulation; 1990.
News 91	1991 Cumulation; 1991.
News 92	1992 Cumulation; 1992.
News 93	1993 Cumulation; 1993.

News 94 1994 Cumulation; 1994.
News 95 1995 Cumulation; 1995.
News 96 1996 Cumulation; 1997.
News 88-2 1988, Issue 2; 1988.
News 88-3 1988, Issue 3; 1988.
News 89-1 1989, Issue 1; 1989.
News 89-2 1989, Issue 2; 1989.
News 89-3 1989, Issue 3; 1989.
News 90-1 1990, Issue 1; 1990.
News 90-2 1990, Issue 2; 1990.
News 90-3 1990, Issue 3; 1990.
News 91-1 1991, Issue 1; 1990.
News 91-2 1991, Issue 2; 1991.
News 91-3 1991, Issue 3; 1991.
News 92-1 1992, Issue 1; 1992.
News 92-2 1992, Issue 2; 1992.
News 92-3 1992, Issue 3; 1992.
News 93-1 1993, Issue 1; 1993.
News 93-2 1993, Issue 2; 1993.
News 93-3 1993, Issue 3; 1993.
News 94-1 1994, Issue 1; 1994.
News 94-2 1994, Issue 2; 1994.
News 94-3 1994, Issue 3; 1994.
News 95-1 1995, Issue 1; 1995.
News 95-2 1995, Issue 2; 1995.
News 95-3 1995, Issue 3; 1995.
News 96-1 1996, Issue 1; 1996.
News 96-2 1996, Issue 2; 1996.
News 96-3 1996, Issue 3; 1996.
News 97-1 1997, Issue 1; 1997.

Use the ''Cumulative Newsmaker Index'' to locate entries. Biographies in each quarterly issue can also be located in the annual cumulation.

NewWmR *New Women in Rock.* Edited by Liz Thompson. New York: Delilah Books, 1982.

NewYHSD *The New-York Historical Society's Dictionary of Artists in America, 1564-1860.* By George C. Groce and David H. Wallace. New Haven, CT: Yale University Press, 1957.

NewYTBE *The New York Times Biographical Edition.* A compilation of current biographical information of general interest. New York: Arno Press, 1970-1973.Continued by *The New York Times Biographical Service.*

NewYTBE 70 Volume 1, Numbers 1-12; 1970.
NewYTBE 71 Volume 2, Numbers 1-12; 1971.
NewYTBE 72 Volume 3, Numbers 1-12; 1972.
NewYTBE 73 Volume 4, Numbers 1-12; 1973.

Use the annual Index to locate biographies.

NewYTBS 27 *New York Times Biographical Service.* A compilation of current biographical information of general interest. Volume 27, Numbers 1-12. Ann Arbor, MI: UMI Co., 1996.

Use the annual Index to locate biographies.

NewYTBS *The New York Times Biographical Service.* A compilation of current biographical information of general interest. New York: Arno Press, 1974-1981.A continuation of *The New York Times Biographical Edition.*

NewYTBS 74 Volume 5, Numbers 1-12; 1974.
NewYTBS 75 Volume 6, Numbers 1-12; 1975.
NewYTBS 76 Volume 7, Numbers 1-12; 1976.
NewYTBS 77 Volume 8, Numbers 1-12; 1977.
NewYTBS 78 Volume 9, Numbers 1-12; 1978.
NewYTBS 79 Volume 10, Numbers 1-12; 1979.
NewYTBS 80 Volume 11, Numbers 1-12; 1980.
NewYTBS 81 Volume 12, Numbers 1-12; 1981.
Use the annual Index to locate biographies.

NewYTBS *The New York Times Biographical Service.* A compilation of current biographical information of general interest. Sanford, NC: Microfilming Corp. of America, 1982-1983.

NewYTBS 82 Volume 13, Numbers 1-12; 1982.
NewYTBS 83 Volume 14, Numbers 1-12; 1983.
Use the annual Index to locate biographies.

NewYTBS *The New York Times Biographical Service.* A compilation of current biographical information of general interest. Ann Arbor, MI: University Microfilms International, 1984-1994.

NewYTBS 84 Volume 15, Numbers 1-12; 1984.
NewYTBS 85 Volume 16, Numbers 1-12; 1985.
NewYTBS 86 Volume 17, Numbers 1-12; 1986.
NewYTBS 87 Volume 18, Numbers 1-12; 1987.
NewYTBS 88 Volume 19, Numbers 1-12; 1988.
NewYTBS 89 Volume 20, Numbers 1-12; 1989.
NewYTBS 90 Volume 21, Numbers 1-12; 1990.
NewYTBS 91 Volume 22, Numbers 1-12; 1991.
NewYTBS 92 Volume 23, Numbers 1-12; 1992.
NewYTBS 93 Volume 24, Numbers 1-12; 1993.
NewYTBS 94 Volume 25, Numbers 1-12; 1994.
Use the annual Index to locate biographies.

NewYTBS 95 *The New York Times Biographical Service.* A compilation of current biographical information of general interest. Volume 26, Numbers 1-12. Ann Arbor, MI: UMI Co., 1995.

Use the annual Index to locate biographies.

NewYTET *The New York Times Encyclopedia of Television.* By Les Brown. New York: New York Times Book Co., 1977. Later editions published as *Les Brown's Encyclopedia of Television.*

NinCLC *Nineteenth-Century Literature Criticism.* Criticism of the works of novelists, poets, playwrights, short story writers, philosophers, and other creative writers who died between 1800 and 1899, from the first published critical appraisals to current evaluations. Detroit: Gale Research, 1981-1997.

NinCLC 1 Volume 1; 1981.
NinCLC 2 Volume 2; 1982.

NinCLC 3	Volume 3; 1983.
NinCLC 4	Volume 4; 1983.
NinCLC 5	Volume 5; 1984.
NinCLC 6	Volume 6; 1984.
NinCLC 7	Volume 7; 1984.
NinCLC 8	Volume 8; 1985.
NinCLC 9	Volume 9; 1985.
NinCLC 10	Volume 10; 1985.
NinCLC 11	Volume 11; 1986.
NinCLC 12	Volume 12; 1986.
NinCLC 13	Volume 13; 1986.
NinCLC 14	Volume 14; 1987.
NinCLC 15	Volume 15; 1987.
NinCLC 16	Volume 16; 1987.
NinCLC 17	Volume 17; 1988.
NinCLC 18	Volume 18; 1988.
NinCLC 19	Volume 19; 1988.
NinCLC 20	Volume 20; 1989. Contains no biographies.
NinCLC 21	Volume 21; 1989.
NinCLC 22	Volume 22; 1989.
NinCLC 23	Volume 23; 1989.
NinCLC 24	Volume 24; 1989. Contains no biographies.
NinCLC 25	Volume 25; 1990.
NinCLC 26	Volume 26; 1990.
NinCLC 27	Volume 27; 1990.
NinCLC 28	Volume 28; 1990. Contains no biographies.
NinCLC 29	Volume 29; 1991.
NinCLC 30	Volume 30; 1991.
NinCLC 31	Volume 31; 1991.
NinCLC 32	Volume 32; 1991. Contains no biographies.
NinCLC 33	Volume 33; 1992.
NinCLC 34	Volume 34; 1992.
NinCLC 35	Volume 35; 1992.
NinCLC 36	Volume 36; 1992. Contains no biographies.
NinCLC 37	Volume 37; 1993.
NinCLC 38	Volume 38; 1993.
NinCLC 39	Volume 39; 1993.
NinCLC 40	Volume 40; 1993. Contains no biographies.
NinCLC 41	Volume 41; 1994.
NinCLC 42	Volume 42; 1994.
NinCLC 43	Volume 43; 1994.
NinCLC 44	Volume 44; 1994. Contains no biographies.
NinCLC 45	Volume 45; 1994.
NinCLC 46	Volume 46; 1994.
NinCLC 47	Volume 47; 1995.
NinCLC 48	Volume 48; 1995. Contains no biographies.
NinCLC 49	Volume 49; 1995.
NinCLC 50	Volume 50; 1996.
NinCLC 51	Volume 51; 1996.
NinCLC 52	Volume 52; 1996. Contains no biographies.
NinCLC 53	Volume 53; 1996.
NinCLC 54	Volume 54; 1996.
NinCLC 55	Volume 55; 1997.
NinCLC 56	Volume 56; 1997. Contains no biographies.
NinCLC 57	Volume 57; 1997.

NobelP *Nobel Prize Winners.* New York: H.W. Wilson Co., 1987-1992.

- ***NobelP*** Edited by Tyler Wasson; 1987.
- ***NobelP 91*** Supplement 1987-1991. Edited by Paula McGuire; 1992.
- ***NobelP 91N*** Supplement 1987-1991. Edited by Paula McGuire; 1992. ''Nobel Prize Winners Who Have Died since 1986'' section appears on page 25.

NorAmWA *North American Women Artists of the Twentieth Century.* A biographical dictionary. Edited by Jules Heller and Nancy G. Heller. Garland Reference Library of the Humanities, vol. 1219. New York: Garland Publishing, 1995.

NotAsAm *Notable Asian Americans.* Detroit: Gale Research, 1995.

NotAW *Notable American Women, 1607-1950.* A biographical dictionary. Three volumes. Edited by Edward T. James. Cambridge: Harvard University Press, Belknap Press, 1971.

NotAW MOD *Notable American Women, The Modern Period.* A biographical dictionary. Edited by Barbara Sicherman and Carol Hurd Green. Cambridge: Harvard University Press, Belknap Press, 1980.

NotBlAW *Notable Black American Women.* Edited by Jessie Carney Smith. Detroit: Gale Research, 1992-1996.

- ***NotBlAW 1*** Book I; 1992.
- ***NotBlAW 2*** Book II; 1996.

NotHsAW 93 *Notable Hispanic American Women.* First edition. Detroit: Gale Research, 1993.

NotNaAm *Notable Native Americans.* Detroit: Gale Research, 1995.

NotNAT *Notable Names in the American Theatre.* Clifton, NJ: James T. White & Co., 1976. Earlier edition published as *The Biographical Encyclopaedia and Who's Who of the American Theatre.*

- ***NotNAT*** ''Notable Names in the American Theatre'' section begins on page 489. This book often alphabetizes by titles of address, e.g.: Dr., Mrs., and Sir.
- ***NotNAT A*** ''Biographical Bibliography'' section begins on page 309. This book often alphabetizes by titles of address, e.g.: Dr., Mrs., and Sir.
- ***NotNAT B*** ''Necrology'' section begins on page 343. This book often alphabetizes by titles of address, e.g.: Dr., Mrs., and Sir.

NotTwCP *Notable Twentieth-Century Pianists.* A bio-critical sourcebook. Two volumes. By John Gillespie and Anna Gillespie. Westport, CT: Greenwood Press, 1995.

NotTwCS *Notable Twentieth-Century Scientists.* Four volumes. Detroit: Gale Research, 1995.

NotWoAT *Notable Women in the American Theatre.* A biographical dictionary. Edited by Alice M. Robinson, Vera Mowry Roberts, and Milly S. Barranger. New York: Greenwood Press, 1989.

NotWoLS *Notable Women in the Life Sciences.* A biographical dictionary. Edited by Benjamin F. Shearer and Barbara S. Shearer. Westport, CT: Greenwood Press, 1996.

Novels *Novels and Novelists.* A guide to the world of fiction. Edited by Martin Seymour-Smith. New York: St. Martin's Press, 1980.
Biographies are located in the ''Novelists: An Alphabetical Guide'' section, which begins on page 87.

ObitOF 79 *Obituaries on File.* Two volumes. Compiled by Felice Levy. New York: Facts on File, 1979.

ObitT *Obituaries from the Times.* Compiled by Frank C. Roberts. Reading, England: Newspaper Archive Developments, 1979-1978.

ObitT 1951	*1951-1960.*; 1979.
ObitT 1961	*1961-1970.*; 1975.
ObitT 1971	*1971-1975.*; 1978.

ODwPR *O'Dwyer's Directory of Public Relations Executives.* Edited by Jack O'Dwyer. New York: J.R. O'Dwyer Co., 1979-1990.

ODwPR 79	1979 edition; 1979.
ODwPR 91	1991 edition; 1990.

OfEnT *Official Encyclopedia of Tennis.* United States Tennis Association. Revised and updated. Edited by Bill Shannon. New York: Harper & Row, 1979.

OfNBA *Official NBA Register.* St. Louis: The Sporting News, 1981-1987.

OfNBA 81	1981-1982 edition. Edited by Matt Winick; 1981.
OfNBA 85	1985-1986 edition. Edited by Mike Douchant and Alex Sachare; 1985.
OfNBA 86	1986-1987 edition. Edited by Mike Douchant and Alex Sachare; 1986.
OfNBA 87	1987-1988 edition. Edited by Alex Sachare and Dave Sloan; 1987.

OfPGCP 86 *Official Price Guide to Collector Prints.* Seventh edition. By Ruth M. Pollard. Westminster, MD: House of Collectibles, 1986.

OhA&B *Ohio Authors and Their Books.* Biographical data and selective bibliographies for Ohio authors, native and resident, 1796-1950. Edited by William Coyle. Cleveland: World Publishing Co., 1962.

OlFamFa *Old Familiar Faces.* The great character actors and actresses of Hollywood's golden era. By Robert A. Juran. Sarasota, FL: Movie Memories Publishing, 1995.

OnHuMoP *The One Hundred Most Popular Young Adult Authors.* Biographical sketches and bibliographies. By Bernard A. Drew. Englewood, CO: Libraries Unlimited, 1996.

OnThGG *One Thousand Great Guitarists.* By Hugh Gregory. San Francisco: Miller Freeman Books, 1994; London: Outline Press, 1994. Distributed by Publishers Group West, Emeryville, CA.

OrJudAm *Orthodox Judaism in America.* A biographical dictionary and sourcebook. By Moshe D. Sherman. Westport, CT: Greenwood Press, 1996.

OxCAmH *The Oxford Companion to American History.* By Thomas H. Johnson. New York: Oxford University Press, 1966.

OxCAmL *The Oxford Companion to American Literature.* By James D. Hart. New York: Oxford University Press, 1965-1995.

- ***OxCAmL 65*** Fourth edition; 1965.
- ***OxCAmL 83*** Fifth edition; 1983.
- ***OxCAmL 95*** Sixth edition; 1995.

OxCAmT 84 *The Oxford Companion to American Theatre.* By Gerald Bordman. New York: Oxford University Press, 1984.

OxCArt *The Oxford Companion to Art.* Edited by Harold Osborne. Oxford: Oxford University Press, Clarendon Press, 1970.

OxCAusL *The Oxford Companion to Australian Literature.* By William H. Wilde, Joy Hooton, and Barry Andrews. Melbourne, Australia: Oxford University Press, 1985.

OxCCan *The Oxford Companion to Canadian History and Literature.* Toronto: Oxford University Press, 1967-1973.

- ***OxCCan*** By Norah Story; 1967.
- ***OxCCan SUP*** Supplement. Edited by William Toye; 1973.

OxCCanL *The Oxford Companion to Canadian Literature.* Edited by William Toye. Toronto: Oxford University Press, 1983.

OxCCanT *The Oxford Companion to Canadian Theatre.* Edited by Eugene Benson and L.W. Conolly. Toronto: Oxford University Press, 1989.

OxCChes 84 *The Oxford Companion to Chess.* By David Hooper and Kenneth Whyld. Oxford: Oxford University Press, 1984.

OxCChiL *The Oxford Companion to Children's Literature.* By Humphrey Carpenter and Mari Prichard. Oxford: Oxford University Press, 1984.

OxCClL *The Oxford Companion to Classical Literature.* Oxford: Oxford University Press, 1937-1989.

- ***OxCClL*** First edition. Edited by Sir Paul Harvey; 1937.
- ***OxCClL 89*** Second edition. Edited by M.C. Howatson; 1989.

OxCDecA *The Oxford Companion to the Decorative Arts.* Edited by Harold Osborne. Oxford: Oxford University Press, Clarendon Press, 1975.

OxCEng *The Oxford Companion to English Literature.* Oxford: Oxford University Press, 1967-1995.

OxCEng 67	Fourth edition. Compiled and edited by Sir Paul Harvey, revised by Dorothy Eagle; 1967.
OxCEng 85	Fifth edition. Edited by Margaret Drabble; 1985.
OxCEng 95	Revised fifth edition. Edited by Margaret Drabble; 1995.

OxCFilm *The Oxford Companion to Film.* Edited by Liz-Anne Bawden. New York: Oxford University Press, 1976.

OxCFr *The Oxford Companion to French Literature.* Compiled and edited by Sir Paul Harvey and J.E. Heseltine. Oxford: Oxford University Press, 1959. Reprinted with corrections, 1966.

OxCGer *The Oxford Companion to German Literature.* Oxford: Oxford University Press, 1976-1986.

OxCGer 76	By Henry Garland and Mary Garland; 1976.
OxCGer 86	Second edition. By Mary Garland; 1986.

OxCIri *The Oxford Companion to Irish Literature.* Edited by Robert Welch. Oxford: Oxford University Press, 1996.

OxCLaw *The Oxford Companion to Law.* By David M. Walker. Oxford: Oxford University Press, Clarendon Press, 1980.

OxCLiW 86 *The Oxford Companion to the Literature of Wales.* Compiled and edited by Meic Stephens. Oxford: Oxford University Press, 1986.

OxCMed 86 *The Oxford Companion to Medicine.* Two volumes. Edited by John Walton, Paul B. Beeson, and Ronald Bodley Scott. Oxford: Oxford University Press, 1986.

OxCMus *The Oxford Companion to Music.* 10th edition (corrected). By Percy A. Scholes. Edited by John Owen Ward. London: Oxford University Press, 1974.

OxCPhil *The Oxford Companion to Philosophy.* Edited by Ted Honderich. Oxford: Oxford University Press, 1995.

OxCPMus *The Oxford Companion to Popular Music.* By Peter Gammond. Oxford: Oxford University Press, 1991.

OxCShps *The Oxford Companion to Ships and the Sea.* Edited by Peter Kemp. London: Oxford University Press, 1976.

OxCSpan *The Oxford Companion to Spanish Literature.* Edited by Philip Ward. Oxford: Oxford University Press, Clarendon Press, 1978.

OxCSupC *The Oxford Companion to the Supreme Court of the United States.* Edited by Kermit L. Hall. New York: Oxford University Press, 1992.

OxCThe *The Oxford Companion to the Theatre.* Edited by Phyllis Hartnoll. Oxford: Oxford University Press, 1967-1983.

OxCThe 67	Third edition; 1967.
OxCThe 83	Fourth edition; 1983.

OxCTwCA *The Oxford Companion to Twentieth-Century Art.* Edited by Harold Osborne. Oxford: Oxford University Press, 1981.

OxCTwCP *The Oxford Companion to Twentieth-Century Poetry in English.* Edited by Ian Hamilton. Oxford: Oxford University Press, 1994.

OxCWoWr 95 *The Oxford Companion to Women's Writing in the United States.* Edited by Cathy N. Davidson and Linda Wagner-Martin. New York: Oxford University Press, 1995.

OxDcArt *The Oxford Dictionary of Art.* Edited by Ian Chilvers and Harold Osborne. Oxford: Oxford University Press, 1988.

OxDcByz *The Oxford Dictionary of Byzantium.* Three volumes. Edited by Alexander P. Kazhdan. New York: Oxford University Press, 1991.

OxDcOp *The Oxford Dictionary of Opera.* By John Warrack and Ewan West. Oxford: Oxford University Press, 1992.

OxDcP 86 *The Oxford Dictionary of Popes.* By J.N.D. Kelly. Oxford: Oxford University Press, 1986.

Use the ''Alphabetical List of Popes and Antipopes'' which begins on page 1 to locate biographies.

PenBWP *The Penguin Book of Women Poets.* Edited by Carol Cosman, Joan Keefe, and Kathleen Weaver. New York: Viking Press, 1978.

PenC *The Penguin Companion to World Literature.* New York: McGraw-Hill Book Co., 1971-1969.

- ***PenC AM*** *American Literature.* Edited by Malcolm Bradbury, Eric Mottram, and Jean Franco; 1971. Biographies are found in the ''U.S.A.'' and ''Latin America'' sections.
- ***PenC CL*** *Classical, Oriental and African Literature.* Edited by D.M. Lang and D.R. Dudley; 1969. Biographies are found in the ''Classical,'' ''Byzantine,'' ''Oriental,'' and ''African'' sections.
- ***PenC ENG*** *English Literature.* Edited by David Daiches; 1971.
- ***PenC EUR*** *European Literature.* Edited by Anthony Thorlby; 1969.

PenDiDA 89 *The Penguin Dictionary of Decorative Arts.* Revised edition. By John Fleming and Hugh Honour. London: Viking, 1989.

PenDiMP *The Penguin Dictionary of Musical Performers.* A biographical guide to significant interpreters of classical music - singers, solo instrumentalists, conductors, orchestras and string quartets - ranging from the seventeenth century to the present day. By Arthur Jacobs. London: Viking, 1990.

- ***PenDiMP A*** Biographies located in the ''Index of Composers'' begin on page 239.

PenEncH *The Penguin Encyclopedia of Horror and the Supernatural.* Edited by Jack Sullivan. New York: Viking Penguin, 1986.

PenEncP *The Penguin Encyclopedia of Popular Music.* Edited by Donald Clarke. New York: Viking, 1989.

PenNWW *Pen Names of Women Writers.* From 1600 to the present. A compendium of the literary identities of 2,650 women novelists, playwrights, poets, diarists, journalists and miscellaneous writers. By Alice Kahler Marshall. Camp Hill, PA: Alice Kahler Marshall, 1985.

- ***PenNWW A*** ''Alphabetical Listing by Author's Real Name'' begins on page 1.
- ***PenNWW B*** ''Alphabetical Listing by Author's Pen Name'' begins on page 95.

PeoHis *People in History.* An index to U.S. and Canadian biographies in history journals and dissertations. Two volumes. Edited by Susan K. Kinnell. Santa Barbara, CA: ABC-Clio, 1988.

PhDcTCA 77 *Phaidon Dictionary of Twentieth-Century Art.* Second edition. Oxford: Phaidon Press; New York: E.P. Dutton, 1977.

PiP *The Pied Pipers.* Interviews with the influential creators of children's literature. By Justin Wintle and Emma Fisher. New York: Paddington Press, 1974.
Use the Table of Contents to locate biographies.

PlP&P *Plays, Players, and Playwrights.* An illustrated history of the theatre. By Marion Geisinger. Updated by Peggy Marks. New York: Hart Publishing Co., 1975.

- ***PlP&P*** Use the Index, which begins on page 575, to locate biographies.
- ***PlP&P A*** Use the Supplemental Index to the last chapter, which begins on page 797, to locate biographies.

Po&Wr 77 *The Poets & Writers, Inc. 1977 Supplement.* A complete update to *A Directory of American Poets* (1975) and *A Directory of American Fiction Writers* (1976). New York: Poets & Writers, 1977.
Use the Index to locate listings.

PoChrch *The Poets of the Church.* A series of biographical sketches of hymn-writers with notes on their hymns. By Edwin F. Hatfield. New York: Anson D.F. Randolph & Co., 1884. Reprint. Detroit: Gale Research, 1978.

PoeCrit *Poetry Criticism.* Excerpts from criticism of the works of the most significant and widely studied poets of world literature. Detroit: Gale Research, 1991-1997.

- ***PoeCrit 1*** Volume 1; 1991.
- ***PoeCrit 2*** Volume 2; 1991.
- ***PoeCrit 3*** Volume 3; 1991.
- ***PoeCrit 4*** Volume 4; 1992.
- ***PoeCrit 5*** Volume 5; 1992.
- ***PoeCrit 6*** Volume 6; 1993.
- ***PoeCrit 7*** Volume 7; 1994.
- ***PoeCrit 8*** Volume 8; 1994.
- ***PoeCrit 9*** Volume 9; 1994.
- ***PoeCrit 10*** Volume 10; 1994.
- ***PoeCrit 11*** Volume 11; 1995.
- ***PoeCrit 12*** Volume 12; 1995.

PoeCrit 13	Volume 13; 1995.
PoeCrit 14	Volume 14; 1996.
PoeCrit 15	Volume 15; 1997.
PoeCrit 16	Volume 16; 1997.

PoIre *The Poets of Ireland.* A biographical and bibliographical dictionary of Irish writers of English verse. By D.J. O'Donoghue. Dublin, Ireland: Hodges Figgis & Co.; London: Henry Frowde, Oxford University Press, 1912. Reprint. Detroit: Gale Research, 1968.

''The Poets of Ireland'' begins on page 5. The Appendices begin on page 495.

PolBiDi *Polish Biographical Dictionary.* Profiles of nearly 900 Poles who have made lasting contributions to world civilization. By Stanley S. Sokol and Sharon F. Mrotek Kissane. Wauconda, IL: Bolchazy-Carducci Publishers, 1992.

PoLE *The Poets Laureate of England.* Being a history of the office of poet laureate, biographical notices of its holders, and a collection of the satires, epigrams, and lampoons directed against them. By Walter Hamilton. London: Elliot Stock, 1879. Reprint. Detroit: Gale Research, 1968.

Use the Index to locate biographies.

PolLCME *Political Leaders of the Contemporary Middle East and North Africa.* A biographical dictionary. Edited by Bernard Reich. New York: Greenwood Press, 1990.

PolLCWE *Political Leaders of Contemporary Western Europe.* A biographical dictionary. Edited by David Wilsford. Westport, CT: Greenwood Press, 1995.

PolPar *Political Parties and Elections in the United States.* An encyclopedia. Two volumes. Edited by L. Sandy Maisel. Garland Reference Library of Social Science, vol. 498. New York: Garland Publishing, 1991.

PolProf *Political Profiles.* New York: Facts on File, 1977-1978.

PolProf E	*The Eisenhower Years.* Edited by Eleanora W. Schoenebaum; 1977.
PolProf J	*The Johnson Years.* Edited by Nelson Lichtenstein; 1976.
PolProf K	*The Kennedy Years.* Edited by Nelson Lichtenstein; 1976.
PolProf NF	*The Nixon/Ford Years.* Edited by Eleanora W. Schoenebaum; 1979.
PolProf T	*The Truman Years.* Edited by Eleanora W. Schoenebaum; 1978.

PolsAm 84 *Politics in America.* Members of Congress in Washington and at home. Edited by Alan Ehrenhalt. Washington: Congressional Quarterly, 1983.

Use the Index to locate biographies.

PopAmC *Popular American Composers.* From Revolutionary times to the present. A biographical and critical guide. Compiled and edited by David Ewen. New York: H.W. Wilson Co., 1962-1972.

PopAmC	First edition; 1962.
PopAmC SUP	First Supplement; 1972.

PopAmC SUPN First Supplement; 1972. The "Necrology" section appears on page vi.

PopDcHi *A Popular Dictionary of Hinduism.* By Karel Werner. Richmond, Surrey, England: Curzon Press, 1994.

PorAmW *Portraits of American Women.* From settlement to the present. By G.J. Barker-Benfield and Catherine Clinton. New York: St. Martin's Press, 1991.
Use the Table of Contents to locate biographies.

PorSil *Portraits in Silicon.* By Robert Slater. Cambridge: MIT Press, 1987.
Use the Index to locate biographies.

PostFic *Postmodern Fiction.* A bio-bibliographical guide. Edited by Larry McCaffery. Movements in the Arts, no. 2. New York: Greenwood Press, 1986.
Biographies begin on page 247.

PresAR *Presidential Also-Rans and Running Mates, 1788-1980.* By Leslie H. Southwick. Jefferson, NC: McFarland & Co., 1984.
Use the Index to locate biographies.

PriCCJL 85 *The Princeton Companion to Classical Japanese Literature.* By Earl Miner, Hiroko Odagiri, and Robert E. Morrell. Princeton, NJ: Princeton University Press, 1985.
Biographies begin on page 141.

PrimTiR *Prime-Time Religion.* An encyclopedia of religious broadcasting. By J. Gordon Melton, Philip Charles Lucas, and Jon R. Stone. Phoenix, AZ: Oryx Press, 1997.

PrintW *The Printworld Directory of Contemporary Prints & Prices.* Edited by Selma Smith. Bala Cynwyd, PA: Printworld, 1983-1985.
PrintW 83 *1983/84,* second edition; 1983.
PrintW 85 *1985/86,* third edition; 1985.
Not in strict alphabetical order.

ProFbHF *The Pro Football Hall of Fame.* Players, coaches, team owners and league officials, 1963-1991. By Denis J. Harrington. Jefferson, NC: McFarland & Co., 1991.
Use the Index to locate entries.

Profile *Profiles.* Authors and illustrators, children's literature in Canada. Edited by Irma McDonough. Ottawa: Canadian Library Association, 1975-1982.
Profile 1 Revised edition; 1975.
Profile 2 *Profiles 2.*; 1982.

PseudAu *Pseudonyms of Authors.* Including anonyms and initialisms. By John Edward Haynes. New York: John Edward Haynes, 1882. Reprint. Detroit: Gale Research, 1969.
PseudAu Pseudonyms are given exactly as written by the author and are filed under the first letter of the pseudonym, including the articles "a," "an," and "the."

PseudAu A Addenda begins on page 104. Pseudonyms are given exactly as written by the author and are filed under the first letter of the pseudonym, including the articles "a," "an," and "the."

PseudN 82 *Pseudonyms and Nicknames Dictionary.* Second edition. Edited by Jennifer Mossman. Detroit: Gale Research Inc., 1982.

PueRA *Puerto Rican Authors.* A biobibliographic handbook. By Marnesba D. Hill and Harold B. Schleifer. Translation of entries into Spanish by Daniel Maratos. Metuchen, NJ: Scarecrow Press, 1974.

PupTheA *The Puppet Theatre in America.* A history, 1524-1948. By Paul McPharlin. With a supplement *Puppets in America since 1948.* By Marjorie Batchelder McPharlin. Boston: Plays, Inc., 1969.

PupTheA Biographies are found in Chapter XXI, "A List of Puppeteers, 1524-1948," beginning on page 396.

PupTheA SUP Biographies are found in Chapter V of the Supplement "Some Careers in Puppetry," beginning on page 606.

QDrFCA 92 *Quinlan's Illustrated Directory of Film Comedy Actors.* By David Quinlan. New York: Henry Holt and Co., 1992.

RadHan *The Radicalism Handbook.* Radical activists, groups and movements of the twentieth century. By John Button. Santa Barbara, CA: ABC-CLIO, 1995.
Use the Index to locate biographies.

RadMoSP *Radio's Morning Show Personalities.* Early hour broadcasters and deejays from the 1920s to the 1990s. By Philip A. Lieberman. Jefferson, NC: McFarland & Co., 1996.
Use the Index to locate biographies.

RadStar *Radio Stars.* An illustrated biographical dictionary of 953 performers, 1920 through 1960. By Thomas A. DeLong. Jefferson, NC: McFarland & Co., 1996.

RAdv 1 *The Reader's Adviser.* A layman's guide to literature. 12th edition. Volume 1: *The Best in American and British Fiction, Poetry, Essays, Literary Biography, Bibliography, and Reference..* Edited by Sarah L. Prakken. New York: R.R. Bowker Co., 1974.
Use the "Name Index" to locate biographies.

RAdv 14 *The Reader's Adviser.* 14th edition. Six volumes. Edited by Marion Sader. New Providence, NJ: R.R. Bowker, 1994.
Use the Name Index in Volume 6 to locate entries.

RAdv *The Reader's Adviser.* A layman's guide to literature. New York: R.R. Bowker Co., 1986-1988.

RAdv 13-1 13th edition. Volume 1: *The Best in American and British Fiction, Poetry, Essays, Literary Biography, Bibliography, and Reference.* Edited by Fred Kaplan; 1986.

RAdv 13-2 13th edition. Volume 2: *The Best in American and British Drama and World Literature in English Translation.* Edited by Maurice Charney; 1986.

RAdv 13-3 13th edition. Volume 3: *The Best in General Reference Literature, the Social Sciences, History, and the Arts.* Edited by Paula T. Kaufman; 1986.

RAdv 13-4 13th edition. Volume 4: *The Best in the Literature of Philosophy and World Religions.* Edited by William L. Reese; 1988.

RAdv 13-5 13th edition. Volume 5: *The Best in the Literature of Science, Technology, and Medicine.* Edited by Paul T. Durbin; 1988.

Use the "Name Index" to locate biographies.

RComAH *The Reader's Companion to American History.* Edited by Eric Foner and John A. Garraty. Boston: Houghton Mifflin Co., 1991.

RComWL *The Reader's Companion to World Literature.* Second edition. Revised and updated by Lillian Herlands Hornstein, Leon Edel, and Horst Frenz. New York: New American Library, 1973.

RealN *Realism, Naturalism, and Local Color, 1865-1917.* Concise Dictionary of American Literary Biography Series. Detroit: Gale Research, 1988.

ReelWom *Reel Women.* Pioneers of the cinema, 1896 to the present. By Ally Acker. New York: Continuum, 1991.

Use the Index to locate biographies.

RelLAm 91 *Religious Leaders of America.* A biographical guide to founders and leaders of religious bodies, churches, and spiritual groups in North America. By J. Gordon Melton. Detroit: Gale Research, 1991.

REn *The Reader's Encyclopedia.* Second edition. By William Rose Benet. New York: Thomas Y. Crowell Co., 1965.

REnAL *The Reader's Encyclopedia of American Literature.* By Max J. Herzberg. New York: Thomas Y. Crowell Co., 1962.

REnAW *The Reader's Encyclopedia of the American West.* Edited by Howard R. Lamar. New York: Thomas Y. Crowell Co., 1977.

REnWD *The Reader's Encyclopedia of World Drama.* Edited by John Gassner and Edward Quinn. New York: Thomas Y. Crowell Co., 1969.

RfGAmL *Reference Guide to American Literature.* Detroit: St. James Press, 1987-1994.

RfGAmL 87 Second edition. Edited by D.L. Kirkpatrick; 1987.

RfGAmL 94 Third edition. Edited by Jim Kamp; 1994.

RfGEnL 91 *Reference Guide to English Literature.* Second edition. Three volumes. Edited by D.L. Kirkpatrick. Chicago: St. James Press, 1991.

RfGShF *Reference Guide to Short Fiction.* Edited by Noelle Watson. Detroit: St. James Press, 1994.

RfGWoL 95 *Reference Guide to World Literature.* Second edition. Two volumes. Edited by Lesley Henderson. Detroit: St. James Press, 1995.

RGAfL *A Reader's Guide to African Literature.* Compiled and edited by Hans M. Zell and Helene Silver. New York: Africana Publishing Corp., 1971.
Biographies begin on page 113.

RGFAP *A Reader's Guide to Fifty American Poets.* By Peter Jones. London: Heinemann; Totowa, NJ: Barnes & Noble, 1980.
Use the Index to locate biographies.

RGFBP *A Reader's Guide to Fifty British Poets, 1300-1900.* By Michael Schmidt. London: Heinemann; Totowa, NJ: Barnes & Noble, 1980.
Use the Index to locate biographies.

RGFMBP *A Reader's Guide to Fifty Modern British Poets.* By Michael Schmidt. London: Heinemann; New York: Barnes & Noble, 1979.
Use the Index to locate biographies.

RGFMEP *Reader's Guide to Fifty Modern European Poets.* By John Pilling. London: Heinemann; Totowa, NJ: Barnes & Noble, 1982.
Use the Index to locate biographies.

RGSF *A Reader's Guide to Science Fiction.* By Baird Searles, Martin Last, Beth Meacham, and Michael Franklin. New York: Facts On File, 1979.

RGTwCSF *Reader's Guide to Twentieth-Century Science Fiction.* Edited by Marilyn P. Fletcher. Chicago: American Library Association, 1989.

RGTwCWr *A Reader's Guide to Twentieth-Century Writers.* Edited by Peter Parker. Oxford: Oxford University Press, 1996.

RkOn *Rock On.* The illustrated encyclopedia of rock n' roll. By Norm N. Nite. New York: Thomas Y. Crowell Co., 1974-1978.

RkOn 74 Volume 1: *The Solid Gold Years*; 1974.
RkOn 74 Volume 1: *The Solid Gold Years*; 1974.
RkOn 78 Volume 2: *The Modern Years: 1964-Present*; 1978.
RkOn 78A Volume 2: *The Modern Years: 1964-Present*; 1978.
Appendix begins on page 543.

RkOn *Rock On.* The illustrated encyclopedia of rock n' roll. By Norm N. Nite. New York: Harper & Row, 1982-1985.

RkOn 82 Volume 1: *The Solid Gold Years,* revised 1982; 1982.
RkOn 84 Volume 2: *The Years of Change, 1964-1978,* revised 1984; 1984.
RkOn 85 Volume 3: *The Video Revolution, 1978-Present.*; 1985.
RkOn 85A Volume 3: *The Video Revolution, 1978-Present.*; 1985.
The Appendix begins on page 413.

RkWW 82 *Rock Who's Who.* By Brock Helander. New York: Macmillan, Schirmer Books, 1982.

RolSEnR 83 *The Rolling Stone Encyclopedia of Rock & Roll.* Edited by Jon Pareles and Patricia Romanowski. New York: Rolling Stone Press/Summit Books, 1983.

SaTiSS *Same Time, Same Station.* An a-z guide to radio from Jack Benny to Howard Stern. By Ron Lackmann. New York: Facts on File, 1996.

ScF&FL *Science Fiction and Fantasy Literature.* A checklist, 1700-1974. By R. Reginald. Detroit: Gale Research, 1979.

ScF&FL 1 Volume 1.
ScF&FL 1A Volume 1. Addendum begins on page 581.
ScF&FL 2 Volume 2: *Contemporary Science Fiction Authors II.*

ScF&FL 92 *Science Fiction & Fantasy Literature, 1975-1991.* A bibliography of science fiction, fantasy, and horror fiction books and nonfiction monographs. By Robert Reginald. Detroit: Gale Research, 1992.

ScFEYrs *Science Fiction: The Early Years.* A full description of more than 3,000 science-fiction stories from earliest times to the appearance of the genre magazines in 1930. By Everett F. Bleiler. Kent, OH: Kent State University Press, 1990.

ScFEYrs A First Addenda begins on page 843.
ScFEYrs B Second Addenda begins on page 851.

ScFnry *The Science Fictionary.* An A-Z guide to the world of SF authors, films, and TV shows. Edited by Ed Naha. New York: Seaview Books, 1980.

ScFSB *The Science Fiction Source Book.* Edited by David Wingrove. New York: Van Nostrand Reinhold Co., 1984.
Listings are located in the ''Science Fiction Writers: A Consumers' Guide'' section, which begins on page 87.

ScFWr *Science Fiction Writers.* Critical studies of the major authors from the early nineteenth century to the present day. Edited by E.F. Bleiler. New York: Charles Scribner's Sons, 1982.

SchCGBL *The Schomburg Center Guide to Black Literature.* From the eighteenth century to the present. Detroit: Gale Research, 1996.

SelBAAf *Selected Black American, African, and Caribbean Authors.* A bio-bibliography. Compiled by James A. Page and Jae Min Roh. Littleton, CO: Libraries Unlimited, 1985.

SelBAAu *Selected Black American Authors.* An illustrated bio-bibliography. Compiled by James A. Page. Boston: G.K. Hall & Co., 1977.

SenS *A Sense of Story.* Essays on contemporary writers for children. By John Rowe Townsend. London: Longman Group, 1971.

ShSCr *Short Story Criticism.* Excerpts from criticism of the works of short fiction writers. Detroit: Gale Research, 1988-1996.

ShSCr 1 Volume 1; 1988.
ShSCr 2 Volume 2; 1989.
ShSCr 3 Volume 3; 1989.
ShSCr 4 Volume 4; 1990.
ShSCr 5 Volume 5; 1990.
ShSCr 6 Volume 6; 1990.

ShSCr 7	Volume 7; 1991.
ShSCr 8	Volume 8; 1991.
ShSCr 9	Volume 9; 1992.
ShSCr 10	Volume 10; 1992.
ShSCr 11	Volume 11; 1992.
ShSCr 12	Volume 12; 1993.
ShSCr 13	Volume 13; 1993.
ShSCr 14	Volume 14; 1994.
ShSCr 15	Volume 15; 1994.
ShSCr 16	Volume 16; 1994.
ShSCr 17	Volume 17; 1995.
ShSCr 18	Volume 18; 1995.
ShSCr 19	Volume 19; 1995.
ShSCr 20	Volume 20; 1995.
ShSCr 21	Volume 21; 1996.
ShSCr 22	Volume 22; 1996.
ShSCr 23	Volume 23; 1996.

ShSWr *Short Story Writers & Their Work.* A guide to the best. By Brad Hooper. Chicago: American Library Association, 1988.
Use the ''Author Index'' to locate biographies.

SilFlmP *Silent Film Performers.* An annotated bibliography of published, unpublished, and archival sources for over 350 actors and actresses. By Roy Liebman. Jefferson, NC: McFarland & Co., 1996.

SingR *Singing Roads.* A guide to Australian children's authors and illustrators. Edited by Hugh Anderson. Surry Hills, Australia: Wentworth Books, 1972-1970.

SingR 1	Part 1, Fourth edition; 1972.
SingR 2	Part 2; 1970.

SixAP *Sixty American Poets, 1896-1944.* Revised edition. Selected, with preface and critical notes by Allen Tate. Washington, DC: Library of Congress, 1954. Reprint. Detroit: Gale Research, 1969.

SixBJA *Sixth Book of Junior Authors & Illustrators.* Edited by Sally Holmes Holtze. New York: H.W. Wilson Co., 1989.

SJGFanW *St. James Guide to Fantasy Writers.* Edited by David Pringle. Detroit: St. James Press, 1996.
Foreign-language authors section begins on page 649.

SmATA 1 *Something about the Author.* Facts and pictures about authors and illustrators of books for young people. Volume 1. Detroit: Gale Research, 1971.

SmATA 1AS *Something about the Author, Autobiography Series.* Volume 1. Detroit: Gale Research, 1986.

SmATA 2 *Something about the Author.* Facts and pictures about authors and illustrators of books for young people. Volume 2. Detroit: Gale Research, 1971.

SmATA 2AS *Something about the Author, Autobiography Series.* Volume 2. Detroit: Gale Research, 1986.

SmATA 3 *Something about the Author.* Facts and pictures about authors and illustrators of books for young people. Volume 3. Detroit: Gale Research, 1972.

SmATA 3AS *Something about the Author, Autobiography Series.* Volume 3. Detroit: Gale Research, 1987.

SmATA 4 *Something about the Author.* Facts and pictures about authors and illustrators of books for young people. Volume 4. Detroit: Gale Research, 1973.

SmATA 4AS *Something about the Author, Autobiography Series.* Volume 4. Detroit: Gale Research, 1987.

SmATA 5 *Something about the Author.* Facts and pictures about authors and illustrators of books for young people. Volume 5. Detroit: Gale Research, 1973.

SmATA 5AS *Something about the Author, Autobiography Series.* Volume 5. Detroit: Gale Research, 1988.

SmATA 6 *Something about the Author.* Facts and pictures about authors and illustrators of books for young people. Volume 6. Detroit: Gale Research, 1974.

SmATA 6AS *Something about the Author, Autobiography Series.* Volume 6. Detroit: Gale Research, 1988.

SmATA 7 *Something about the Author.* Facts and pictures about authors and illustrators of books for young people. Volume 7. Detroit: Gale Research, 1975.

SmATA 7AS *Something about the Author, Autobiography Series.* Volume 7. Detroit: Gale Research, 1989.

SmATA 8 *Something about the Author.* Facts and pictures about authors and illustrators of books for young people. Volume 8. Detroit: Gale Research, 1976.

SmATA 8AS *Something about the Author, Autobiography Series.* Volume 8. Detroit: Gale Research, 1989.

SmATA 9 *Something about the Author.* Facts and pictures about authors and illustrators of books for young people. Volume 9. Detroit: Gale Research, 1976.

SmATA 9AS *Something about the Author, Autobiography Series.* Volume 9. Detroit: Gale Research, 1990.

SmATA 10 *Something about the Author.* Facts and pictures about authors and illustrators of books for young people. Volume 10. Detroit: Gale Research, 1976.

SmATA 10AS *Something about the Author, Autobiography Series.* Volume 10. Detroit: Gale Research, 1990.

SmATA 11 *Something about the Author.* Facts and pictures about authors and illustrators of books for young people. Volume 11. Detroit: Gale Research, 1977.

SmATA 11AS *Something about the Author, Autobiography Series.* Volume 11. Detroit: Gale Research, 1991.

SmATA 12 *Something about the Author.* Facts and pictures about authors and illustrators of books for young people. Volume 12. Detroit: Gale Research, 1977.

SmATA 12AS *Something about the Author, Autobiography Series.* Volume 12. Detroit: Gale Research, 1991.

SmATA 13 *Something about the Author.* Facts and pictures about authors and illustrators of books for young people. Volume 13. Detroit: Gale Research, 1978.

SmATA 13AS *Something about the Author, Autobiography Series.* Volume 13. Detroit: Gale Research, 1992.

SmATA 14 *Something about the Author.* Facts and pictures about authors and illustrators of books for young people. Volume 14. Detroit: Gale Research, 1978.

SmATA 14AS *Something about the Author, Autobiography Series.* Volume 14. Detroit: Gale Research, 1992.

SmATA 15 *Something about the Author.* Facts and pictures about authors and illustrators of books for young people. Volume 15. Detroit: Gale Research, 1979.

SmATA 15AS *Something about the Author, Autobiography Series.* Volume 15. Detroit: Gale Research, 1993.

SmATA 16 *Something about the Author.* Facts and pictures about authors and illustrators of books for young people. Volume 16. Detroit: Gale Research, 1979.

SmATA 16AS *Something about the Author, Autobiography Series.* Volume 16. Detroit: Gale Research, 1993.

SmATA 17 *Something about the Author.* Facts and pictures about authors and illustrators of books for young people. Volume 17. Detroit: Gale Research, 1979.

SmATA 17AS *Something about the Author, Autobiography Series.* Volume 17. Detroit: Gale Research, 1994.

SmATA 18 *Something about the Author.* Facts and pictures about authors and illustrators of books for young people. Volume 18. Detroit: Gale Research, 1980.

SmATA 18AS *Something about the Author, Autobiography Series.* Volume 18. Detroit: Gale Research, 1994.

SmATA 19 *Something about the Author.* Facts and pictures about authors and illustrators of books for young people. Volume 19. Detroit: Gale Research, 1980.

SmATA 19AS *Something about the Author, Autobiography Series.* Volume 19. Detroit: Gale Research, 1995.

SmATA 20 *Something about the Author.* Facts and pictures about authors and illustrators of books for young people. Volume 20. Detroit: Gale Research, 1980.

SmATA 20AS *Something about the Author, Autobiography Series.* Volume 20. Detroit: Gale Research, 1995.

SmATA *Something about the Author.* Facts and pictures about authors and illustrators of books for young people. Detroit: Gale Research, 1980.

SmATA 20N Volume 20, Obituary Notice.
SmATA 21 Volume 21.

SmATA 21AS *Something about the Author, Autobiography Series.* Volume 21. Detroit: Gale Research, 1996.

SmATA *Something about the Author.* Facts and pictures about authors and illustrators of books for young people. Detroit: Gale Research, 1980-1981.

SmATA 21N Volume 21, Obituary Notice; 1980.
SmATA 22 Volume 22; 1981.

SmATA 22AS *Something about the Author, Autobiography Series.* Volume 22. Detroit: Gale Research, 1996.

SmATA *Something about the Author.* Facts and pictures about authors and illustrators of books for young people. Detroit: Gale Research, 1981.

SmATA 22N Volume 22, Obituary Notice.
SmATA 23 Volume 23.

SmATA 23AS *Something about the Author, Autobiography Series.* Volume 23. Detroit: Gale Research, 1997.

SmATA *Something about the Author.* Facts and pictures about authors and illustrators of books for young people. Detroit: Gale Research, 1981-1997.

SmATA 23N Volume 23, Obituary Notice; 1981.
SmATA 24 Volume 24; 1981.
SmATA 24N Volume 24, Obituary Notice; 1981.
SmATA 25 Volume 25; 1981.
SmATA 25N Volume 25, Obituary Notice; 1981.
SmATA 26 Volume 26; 1982.
SmATA 26N Volume 26, Obituary Notice; 1982.
SmATA 27 Volume 27; 1982.
SmATA 27N Volume 27, Obituary Notice; 1982.
SmATA 28 Volume 28; 1982.
SmATA 28N Volume 28, Obituary Notice; 1982.
SmATA 29 Volume 29; 1982.
SmATA 29N Volume 29, Obituary Notice; 1982.
SmATA 30 Volume 30; 1983.
SmATA 30N Volume 30, Obituary Notice; 1983.
SmATA 31 Volume 31; 1983.
SmATA 31N Volume 31, Obituary Notice; 1983.
SmATA 32 Volume 32; 1983.

SmATA 32N	Volume 32, Obituary Notice; 1983.
SmATA 33	Volume 33; 1983.
SmATA 33N	Volume 33, Obituary Notice; 1983.
SmATA 34	Volume 34; 1984.
SmATA 34N	Volume 34, Obituary Notice; 1984.
SmATA 35	Volume 35; 1984.
SmATA 35N	Volume 35, Obituary Notice; 1984.
SmATA 36	Volume 36; 1984.
SmATA 36N	Volume 36, Obituary Notice; 1984.
SmATA 37	Volume 37; 1985.
SmATA 37N	Volume 37, Obituary Notice; 1985.
SmATA 38	Volume 38; 1985.
SmATA 38N	Volume 38, Obituary Notice; 1985.
SmATA 39	Volume 39; 1985.
SmATA 39N	Volume 39, Obituary Notice; 1985.
SmATA 40	Volume 40; 1985.
SmATA 40N	Volume 40, Obituary Notice; 1985.
SmATA 41	Volume 41; 1985.
SmATA 41N	Volume 41, Obituary Notice; 1985.
SmATA 42	Volume 42; 1986.
SmATA 42N	Volume 42, Obituary Notice; 1986.
SmATA 43	Volume 43; 1986.
SmATA 43N	Volume 43, Obituary Notice; 1986.
SmATA 44	Volume 44; 1986.
SmATA 44N	Volume 44, Obituary Notice; 1986.
SmATA 45	Volume 45; 1986.
SmATA 45N	Volume 45, Obituary Notice; 1986.
SmATA 46	Volume 46; 1987.
SmATA 46N	Volume 46, Obituary Notice; 1987.
SmATA 47	Volume 47; 1987.
SmATA 47N	Volume 47, Obituary Notice; 1987.
SmATA 48	Volume 48; 1987.
SmATA 48N	Volume 48, Obituary Notice; 1987.
SmATA 49	Volume 49; 1987.
SmATA 49N	Volume 49, Obituary Notice; 1987.
SmATA 50	Volume 50; 1988.
SmATA 50N	Volume 50, Obituary Notice; 1988.
SmATA 51	Volume 51; 1988.
SmATA 51N	Volume 51, Obituary Notice; 1988.
SmATA 52	Volume 52; 1988.
SmATA 52N	Volume 52, Obituary Notice; 1988.
SmATA 53	Volume 53; 1988.
SmATA 53N	Volume 53, Obituary Notice; 1988.
SmATA 54	Volume 54; 1989.
SmATA 54N	Volume 54, Obituary Notice; 1989.
SmATA 55	Volume 55; 1989.
SmATA 55N	Volume 55, Obituary Notice; 1989.
SmATA 56	Volume 56; 1989.
SmATA 56N	Volume 56, Obituary Notice; 1989.
SmATA 57	Volume 57; 1989.
SmATA 58	Volume 58; 1990.
SmATA 59	Volume 59; 1990.
SmATA 60	Volume 60; 1990.
SmATA 61	Volume 61; 1990.
SmATA 62	Volume 62; 1990.

SmATA 63	Volume 63; 1991.
SmATA 64	Volume 64; 1991.
SmATA 65	Volume 65; 1991.
SmATA 66	Volume 66; 1991.
SmATA 67	Volume 67; 1992.
SmATA 68	Volume 68; 1992.
SmATA 69	Volume 69; 1992.
SmATA 70	Volume 70; 1993.
SmATA 71	Volume 71; 1993.
SmATA 72	Volume 72; 1993.
SmATA 73	Volume 73; 1993.
SmATA 74	Volume 74; 1993.
SmATA 75	Volume 75; 1994.
SmATA 76	Volume 76; 1994.
SmATA 77	Volume 77; 1994.
SmATA 78	Volume 78; 1994.
SmATA 79	Volume 79; 1995.
SmATA 80	Volume 80; 1995.
SmATA 81	Volume 81; 1995.
SmATA 82	Volume 82; 1995.
SmATA 83	Volume 83; 1996.
SmATA 84	Volume 84; 1996.
SmATA 85	Volume 85; 1996.
SmATA 86	Volume 86; 1996.
SmATA 87	Volume 87; 1996.
SmATA 88	Volume 88; 1997.
SmATA 89	Volume 89; 1997.
SmATA 90	Volume 90; 1997.
SmATA 91	Volume 91; 1997.

SmATA X *Something about the Author, Index.* Facts and pictures about authors and illustrators of books for young people. Detroit: Gale Research, (n.d.).

This code refers to pseudonym entries which appear only as cross-references in the cumulative index to *Something about the Author.*

SoulM *Soul Music A-Z.* By Hugh Gregory. London: Blandford, 1991. Distributed by Sterling Publishing Co., New York.

SourALJ *A Sourcebook of American Literary Journalism.* Representative writers in an emerging genre. Edited by Thomas B. Connery. New York: Greenwood Press, 1992.

Use the Index to locate biographies.

SouBlCW *Southern Black Creative Writers, 1829-1953.* Biobibliographies. Compiled by M. Marie Booth Foster. Bibliographies and Indexes in Afro-American and African Studies, no. 22. New York: Greenwood Press, 1988.

SouSt *A Sounding of Storytellers.* New and revised essays on contemporary writers for children. By John Rowe Townsend. New York: J.B. Lippincott, 1979.

SouWr *Southern Writers.* A biographical dictionary. Edited by Robert Bain, Joseph M. Flora, and Louis D. Rubin, Jr. Baton Rouge, LA: Louisiana State University Press, 1979.

SovUn *The Soviet Union.* A biographical dictionary. Edited by Archie Brown. New York: Macmillan Publishing Co., 1990.

- ***SovUn A*** Appendix 5: New Politburo Members begins on page 488.

SpAmA *Spanish American Authors.* The twentieth century. By Angel Flores. New York: H.W. Wilson Co., 1992.

SpAmWW *Spanish American Women Writers.* A bio-bibliographical source book. Edited by Diane E. Marting. New York: Greenwood Press, 1990.

SpyCS *Spy/Counterspy: Encyclopedia of Espionage.* By Vincent Buranelli and Nan Buranelli. New York: McGraw-Hill, 1982.

SpyFic *Spy Fiction.* A connoisseur's guide. By Donald McCormick and Katy Fletcher. New York: Facts on File, 1990.

StaCVF *The Stanford Companion to Victorian Fiction.* By John Sutherland. Stanford, CA: Stanford University Press, 1989.

St&PR *Standard & Poor's Register of Corporations, Directors and Executives.* New York: Standard & Poor's Corp., 1975-1997.

- ***St&PR 75*** 1975 edition. Volume 2: *Directors and Executives.*; 1975.
- ***St&PR 84*** 1984 edition. Volume 2: *Directors and Executives.*; 1984.
- ***St&PR 84N*** 1984 edition. Volume 3; 1984. Obituary section begins on page 901.
- ***St&PR 87*** 1987 edition. Volume 2: *Directors and Executives.*; 1987.
- ***St&PR 87N*** 1987 edition. Volume 3; 1987. Obituary section begins on page 901.
- ***St&PR 91*** 1991 edition. Volume 2: *Directors and Executives.*; 1991.
- ***St&PR 91N*** 1991 edition. Volume 3; 1991. Obituary section begins on page 901.
- ***St&PR 93*** 1993 edition. Volume 2: *Directors and Executives.*; 1993.
- ***St&PR 93N*** 1993 edition. Volume 3; 1993. Obituary section begins on page 901.
- ***St&PR 96*** 1996 edition. Volume 2: *Directors and Executives*; 1996.
- ***St&PR 96N*** 1996 edition. Volume 3; 1996. Obituary section begins on page 901.
- ***St&PR 97*** 1997 edition. Volume 2: *Directors and Executives*; 1997.
- ***St&PR 97N*** 1997 edition. Volume 3; 1997. Obituary section begins on page 901.

Str&VC *Story and Verse for Children.* Third edition. By Miriam Blanton Huber. New York: Macmillan Co., 1965.
Biographies begin on page 793.

SupCtJu *The Supreme Court Justices.* A biographical dictionary. Edited by Melvin I. Urofsky. Garland Reference Library of the Humanities, vol. 1851. New York: Garland Publishing, 1994.

SupFW *Supernatural Fiction Writers.* Fantasy and horror. Two volumes. Edited by E.F. Bleiler. New York: Charles Scribner's Sons, 1985.
Use the Index to locate biographies.

Sw&Ld *Sweet and Lowdown.* America's popular song writers. By Warren Craig. Metuchen, NJ: Scarecrow Press, 1978.

Sw&Ld A	Biographies appear in the ''Before Tin Pan Alley'' section, beginning on page 15.
Sw&Ld B	Biographies appear in the ''Tin Pan Alley'' section, beginning on page 23.
Sw&Ld C	Biographies appear in the ''After Tin Pan Alley'' section, beginning on page 91.

SweetSg *Sweethearts of the Sage.* Biographies and filmographies of 258 actresses appearing in Western movies. By Buck Rainey. Jefferson, NC: McFarland & Co., 1992.

SweetSg A	''The Pathfinders'' section begins on page 2.
SweetSg B	''The Trailblazers'' section begins on page 98.
SweetSg C	''The Pioneers'' section begins on page 240.
SweetSg D	''The Homesteaders'' section begins on page 466.

TelT *Tellers of Tales.* British authors of children's books from 1800 to 1964. Revised edition. By Roger Lancelyn Green. New York: Franklin Watts, 1964.

TexWr *Texas Writers of Today.* By Florence Elberta Barns. Dallas: Tardy Publishing Co., 1935. Reprint. Ann Arbor, Mich.: Gryphon Books, 1971.

TheaDir *Theatrical Directors.* A biographical dictionary. Edited by John W. Frick and Stephen M. Vallillo. Westport, CT: Greenwood Press, 1994.

ThFT *They Had Faces Then.* Super stars, stars and starlets of the 1930's. By John Springer and Jack Hamilton. Secaucus, NJ: Citadel Press, 1974.

ThHEIm *The Thames and Hudson Encyclopaedia of Impressionism.* By Bernard Denvir. New York: Thames and Hudson, 1990.

ThrBJA *Third Book of Junior Authors.* Edited by Doris De Montreville and Donna Hill. Wilson Authors Series. New York: H.W. Wilson Co., 1972.

ThrtnMM *Thirteen Mistresses of Murder.* By Elaine Budd. New York: Ungar Publishing Co., 1986.
Use the Table of Contents to locate biographies.

ThTwC 87 *Thinkers of the Twentieth Century.* Second edition. Edited by Roland Turner. Chicago: St. James Press, 1987.

Tw *The Twenties, 1917-1929.* Concise Dictionary of American Literary Biography. Detroit: Gale Research, 1989.

TwCA *Twentieth Century Authors.* A biographical dictionary of modern literature. Wilson Authors Series. New York: H.W. Wilson Co., 1942-1955.

- ***TwCA*** Edited by Stanley J. Kunitz and Howard Haycraft; 1942.
- ***TwCA SUP*** First Supplement. Edited by Stanley J. Kunitz; 1955.

TwCBDA *The Twentieth Century Biographical Dictionary of Notable Americans.* Brief biographies of authors, administrators, clergymen, commanders, editors, engineers, jurists, merchants, officials, philanthropists, scientists, statesmen, and others who are making American history. 10 volumes. Edited by Rossiter Johnson. Boston: The Biographical Society, 1904. Reprint. Detroit: Gale Research, 1968.

TwCBrS *Twentieth-Century Brass Soloists.* By Michael Meckna. Westport, CT: Greenwood Press, 1994.

TwCChW *Twentieth-Century Children's Writers.* Edited by D.L. Kirkpatrick. Twentieth-Century Writers Series. New York: St. Martin's Press, 1978-1983.

- ***TwCChW 78*** First edition; 1978.
- ***TwCChW 78A*** First edition; 1978. Appendix begins on page 1391.
- ***TwCChW 78B*** First edition; 1978. "Children's Books in Translation" section begins on page 1481.
- ***TwCChW 83*** Second edition; 1983.
- ***TwCChW 83A*** Second edition; 1983. Appendix begins on page 859.
- ***TwCChW 83B*** Second edition; 1983. "Foreign-Language Writers" section begins on page 893.

TwCChW *Twentieth-Century Children's Writers.* Detroit: St. James Press, 1989-1995.

- ***TwCChW 89*** Third edition. Edited by Tracy Chevalier; 1989.
- ***TwCChW 89A*** Third edition. Edited by Tracy Chevalier; 1989. Appendix begins on page 1083.
- ***TwCChW 89B*** Third edition. Edited by Tracy Chevalier; 1989. "Foreign-Language Writers" section begins on page 1119.
- ***TwCChW 95*** Fourth edition. Edited by Laura Standley Berger; 1995.
- ***TwCChW 95A*** Fourth edition. Edited by Laura Standley Berger; 1995. Appendix begins on page 1067.
- ***TwCChW 95B*** Fourth edition. Edited by Laura Standley Berger; 1995. "Foreign-Language Writers" section begins on page 1107.

TwCCr&M *Twentieth-Century Crime and Mystery Writers.* Edited by John M. Reilly. Twentieth-Century Writers Series. New York: St. Martin's Press, 1980-1985.

- ***TwCCr&M 80*** First edition; 1980.
- ***TwCCr&M 80A*** First edition; 1980. "Nineteenth-Century Writers" section begins on page 1525.
- ***TwCCr&M 80B*** First edition; 1980. "Foreign-Language Writers" section begins on page 1537.
- ***TwCCr&M 85*** Second edition; 1985.
- ***TwCCr&M 85A*** Second edition; 1985. "Nineteenth-Century Writers" section begins on page 931.

TwCCr&M 85B Second edition; 1985. ''Foreign-Language Writers'' section begins on page 939.

TwCCr&M 91 *Twentieth-Century Crime and Mystery Writers.* Third edition. Edited by Lesley Henderson. Twentieth-Century Writers Series. Chicago: St. James Press, 1991.

TwCCr&M 91A ''Nineteenth-Century Writers'' section begins on page 1121.

TwCCr&M 91B ''Foreign-Language Writers'' section begins on page 1129.

TwCLC *Twentieth-Century Literary Criticism.* Excerpts from criticism of the works of novelists, poets, playwrights, short story writers, and other creative writers who lived between 1900 and 1960, from the first published critical appraisals to current evaluations. Detroit: Gale Research, 1978-1997.

TwCLC 1 Volume 1; 1978.
TwCLC 2 Volume 2; 1979.
TwCLC 3 Volume 3; 1980.
TwCLC 4 Volume 4; 1981.
TwCLC 5 Volume 5; 1981.
TwCLC 6 Volume 6; 1982.
TwCLC 7 Volume 7; 1982.
TwCLC 8 Volume 8; 1982.
TwCLC 9 Volume 9; 1983.
TwCLC 10 Volume 10; 1983.
TwCLC 11 Volume 11; 1983.
TwCLC 12 Volume 12; 1984.
TwCLC 13 Volume 13; 1984.
TwCLC 14 Volume 14; 1984.
TwCLC 15 Volume 15; 1985.
TwCLC 16 Volume 16; 1985.
TwCLC 17 Volume 17; 1985.
TwCLC 18 Volume 18; 1985.
TwCLC 19 Volume 19; 1986.
TwCLC 20 Volume 20; 1986.
TwCLC 21 Volume 21; 1986.
TwCLC 22 Volume 22; 1987.
TwCLC 23 Volume 23; 1987.
TwCLC 24 Volume 24; 1987.
TwCLC 25 Volume 25; 1988.
TwCLC 26 Volume 26; 1988. Contains no biographies.
TwCLC 27 Volume 27; 1988.
TwCLC 28 Volume 28; 1988.
TwCLC 29 Volume 29; 1988.
TwCLC 30 Volume 30; 1989. Contains no biographies.
TwCLC 31 Volume 31; 1989.
TwCLC 32 Volume 32; 1989.
TwCLC 33 Volume 33; 1989.
TwCLC 34 Volume 34; 1990. Contains no biographies.
TwCLC 35 Volume 35; 1990.
TwCLC 36 Volume 36; 1990.
TwCLC 37 Volume 37; 1991.
TwCLC 38 Volume 38; 1991. Contains no biographies.
TwCLC 39 Volume 39; 1991.
TwCLC 40 Volume 40; 1991.
TwCLC 41 Volume 41; 1991.

TwCLC 42 Volume 42; 1992. Contains no biographies.
TwCLC 43 Volume 43; 1992.
TwCLC 44 Volume 44; 1992.
TwCLC 45 Volume 45; 1992.
TwCLC 46 Volume 46; 1992. Contains no biographies.
TwCLC 47 Volume 47; 1993.
TwCLC 48 Volume 48; 1993.
TwCLC 49 Volume 49; 1993.
TwCLC 50 Volume 50; 1993. Contains no biographies.
TwCLC 51 Volume 51; 1994.
TwCLC 52 Volume 52; 1994.
TwCLC 53 Volume 53; 1994.
TwCLC 54 Volume 54; 1994. Contains no biographies.
TwCLC 55 Volume 55; 1995.
TwCLC 56 Volume 56; 1995.
TwCLC 57 Volume 57; 1995.
TwCLC 58 Volume 58; 1995. Contains no biographies.
TwCLC 59 Volume 59; 1995.
TwCLC 60 Volume 60; 1995.
TwCLC 61 Volume 61; 1996.
TwCLC 62 Volume 62; 1996. Contains no biographies.
TwCLC 63 Volume 63; 1996.
TwCLC 64 Volume 64; 1996.
TwCLC 65 Volume 65; 1997.
TwCLC 66 Volume 66; 1997. Contains no biographies.

TwCPaSc *Twentieth Century Painters and Sculptors.* By Frances Spalding. Dictionary of British Art, vol. 6. Suffolk, England: Antique Collectors' Club, 1990.

TwCRGW *Twentieth-Century Romance and Gothic Writers.* Edited by James Vinson. Detroit: Gale Research, 1982.

TwCRHW *Twentieth-Century Romance and Historical Writers.* London: St. James Press, 1990-1994.

TwCRHW 90 Second edition. Edited by Lesley Henderson; 1990.
TwCRHW 94 Third edition. Edited by Aruna Vasudevan; 1994.

TwCSAPR *Twentieth-Century Shapers of American Popular Religion.* Edited by Charles H. Lippy. New York: Greenwood Press, 1989.

TwCSFW *Twentieth-Century Science-Fiction Writers.* Twentieth-Century Writers Series. Chicago: St. James Press, 1981-1991.

TwCSFW 81 Edited by Curtis C. Smith; 1981.
TwCSFW 81A Edited by Curtis C. Smith; 1981. ''Foreign-Language Writers'' section begins on page 613.
TwCSFW 81B Edited by Curtis C. Smith; 1981. ''Major Fantasy Writers'' section begins on page 631.
TwCSFW 86 Second edition. Edited by Curtis C. Smith; 1986.
TwCSFW 86A Second edition. Edited by Curtis C. Smith; 1986. ''Foreign-Language Writers'' section begins on page 837.

TwCSFW 86B Second edition. Edited by Curtis C. Smith; 1986. "Major Fantasy Writers" section begins on page 863.
TwCSFW 91 Third edition. Edited by Noelle Watson and Paul E. Schellinger; 1991.
TwCSFW 91A Third edition. Edited by Noelle Watson and Paul E. Schellinger; 1991. "Foreign-Language Writers" section begins on page 913.

TwCWr *Twentieth Century Writing.* A reader's guide to contemporary literature. Edited by Kenneth Richardson. Levittown, NY: Transatlantic Arts, 1971.

TwCWW 82 *Twentieth-Century Western Writers.* First edition. Edited by James Vinson. Detroit: Gale Research, 1982.

TwCWW 91 *Twentieth-Century Western Writers.* Second edition. Edited by Geoff Sadler. Twentieth-Century Writers Series. Chicago: St. James Press, 1991.

TwCYAW *Twentieth-Century Young Adult Writers.* First edition. Twentieth-Century Writers Series. Detroit: St. James Press, 1994.

TwoTYeD *Two Thousand Years of Disbelief.* By James A. Haught. Amherst, NY: Prometheus Books, 1996.
Use Index or Table of Contents to locate biographies.

TwYS *Twenty Years of Silents, 1908-1928.* Compiled by John T. Weaver. Metuchen, NJ: Scarecrow Press, 1971.
TwYS "The Players" section begins on page 27.
TwYS A "Directors" section begins on page 407.
TwYS B "Producers" section begins on page 502.

UFOEn *The UFO Encyclopedia.* By Margaret Sachs. New York: G.P. Putnam's Sons, 1980.

UlDrSSP *The Ultimate Directory of the Silent Screen Performers.* A necrology of births and deaths and essays on 50 lost players. By Billy H. Doyle. Metuchen, NJ: Scarecrow Press, 1995.
Biographies are found in the "Lost Players" section which begins on page 1.

USBiR 74 *United States. Department of State: The Biographic Register, July, 1974.* Washington, DC: United States Government Printing Office, 1974.

VarWW *Variety Who's Who in Show Business.* Edited by Mike Kaplan. New York: Garland Publishing, 1983-1985.
VarWW 83 1983 edition; 1983.
VarWW 85 Revised edition, 1985; 1985.

Vers *The Versatiles.* A study of supporting character actors and actresses in the American motion picture, 1930-1955. By Alfred E. Twomey and Arthur F. McClure. South Brunswick, NJ: A.S. Barnes & Co.; London: Thomas Yoseloff, 1969.
Vers A "Biographical Section" begins on page 25.
Vers B "Non-Biographical Section" begins on page 249.

VicBrit *Victorian Britain.* An encyclopedia. Edited by Sally Mitchell. Garland Reference Library of Social Sciences, vol. 438. New York: Garland Publishing, 1988.

VicePre *The Vice Presidents.* Biographies of the 45 men who have held the second highest office in the United States. By Carole Chandler Waldrup. Jefferson, NC: McFarland & Co., 1996.
Use the Index to locate biographies.

Ward *Ward's Who's Who among U.S. Motor Vehicle Manufacturers, 1977.* Detroit: Ward's Communications, 1977.

Ward 77	''U.S. Big Four Biographical Section'' begins on page 61.
Ward 77A	''The Independent Truck, Off-Highway and Farm Vehicle Manufacturers'' section begins on page 335.
Ward 77B	''The Importers'' section begins on page 355.
Ward 77C	''United Auto Workers'' section begins on page 371.
Ward 77D	''Government Agencies'' section begins on page 372.
Ward 77E	''Auto Associations'' section begins on page 376.
Ward 77F	''The Automotive Press'' section begins on page 387.
Ward 77G	''Where Are They Now?'' section begins on page 404.
Ward 77H	''Automotive Suppliers' Section'' begins on page 449.

WebAB *Webster's American Biographies.* Edited by Charles Van Doren. Springfield, MA: G. & C. Merriam Co., 1974-1979.

WebAB 74	1974 edition; 1974.
WebAB 79	1979 edition; 1979.

WebAMB *Webster's American Military Biographies.* Springfield, MA: G. & C. Merriam Co., 1978.

WebBD 83 *Webster's Biographical Dictionary.* 1983 edition. Springfield, MA: G. & C. Merriam Co., 1983.

WebE&AL *Webster's New World Companion to English and American Literature.* Edited by Arthur Pollard. New York: World Publishing Co., 1973.

WhAm *Who Was Who in America.* A companion biographical reference work to *Who's Who in America.* Chicago: A.N. Marquis Co., 1943-1963.

WhAm 1	Volume 1, 1897-1942; 1943.
WhAm 1C	Volume 1, 1897-1942; 1943. Corrigenda begins on page x.
WhAm 2	Volume 2, 1943-1950; 1963.
WhAm 2A	Volume 2, 1943-1950; 1963. Addendum begins on page 12.
WhAm 2C	Volume 2, 1943-1950; 1963. Corrigenda begins on page 5.

WhAm *Who Was Who in America.* New Providence, NJ: Marquis Who's Who, 1966-1993.

WhAm 3	Volume 3, 1951-1960; 1966.
WhAm 3A	Volume 3, 1951-1960; 1966. Addendum begins on page 952.
WhAm 4	Volume 4, 1961-1968; 1968.

	WhAm 4A	Volume 4, 1961-1968; 1968. Addendum begins on page 1049.
	WhAm 5	Volume 5, 1969-1973; 1973.
	WhAm 6	Volume 6, 1974-1976; 1976.
	WhAm 7	Volume 7, 1977-1981; 1981.
	WhAm 8	Volume 8, 1982-1985; 1985.
	WhAm 9	Volume 9, 1985-1989; 1989.
	WhAm 10	Volume 10, 1989-1993; 1993.

WhAm 11 *Who Was Who in America® [Marquis™].* Volume 11, 1993-1996. New Providence, NJ: Marquis Who's Who, 1996.

WhAm *Who Was Who in America.* New Providence, NJ: Marquis Who's Who, 1967.

WhAm HS	Historical Volume, 1607-1896. Revised Edition.
WhAm HSA	Historical Volume, 1607-1896. Revised edition. Addendum begins on page 677.

WhAmArt 85 *Who Was Who in American Art.* Compiled from the original thirty-four volumes of *American Art Annual: Who's Who in Art, Biographies of American Artists Active from 1898-1947.* Edited by Peter Hastings Falk. Madison, CT: Sound View Press, 1985.

WhAmArt 85A	The ''European Teachers of American Artists'' section begins on page xxxiii.

WhAmP *Who Was Who in American Politics.* A biographical dictionary of over 4,000 men and women who contributed to the United States political scene from colonial days up to and including the immediate past. By Dan and Inez Morris. New York: Hawthorn Books, 1974.

WhAmRev *Who Was Who in the American Revolution.* New York: Facts on File, 1993.

What *Whatever Became of . . . ?* By Richard Lamparski. New York: Crown Publishers, 1967-1974.Also printed in a paperback edition by Ace Books.

What 1	Volume One; 1967.
What 2	Second Series; 1968.
What 3	Third Series; 1970.
What 4	Fourth Series; 1973.
What 5	Fifth Series; 1974.

WhCiWar *Who Was Who in the Civil War.* By Stewart Sifakis. New York: Facts on File Publications, 1988.

WhDun *Whodunit?* Edited by H.R.F. Keating. New York: Van Nostrand Reinhold Co., 1982.

WhDW *Who Did What.* The lives and achievements of the 5,000 men and women -- leaders of nations, saints and sinners, artists and scientists -- who shaped our world. Edited by Gerald Howat. New York: Crown Publishers, 1974.

WhE&EA *Who Was Who among English and European Authors, 1931-1949.* Based on entries which first appeared in *The Author's and Writer's Who's Who and Reference Guide,* originally compiled by Edward Martell and L.G. Pine, and in *Who's Who among Living Authors of Older Nations,* originally compiled by Alberta Lawrence. Three volumes. Gale Composite Biographical Dictionary Series, Number 2. Detroit: Gale Research, 1978.

WhFla *Who Was Who in Florida.* Written and compiled by Henry S. Marks. Huntsville, AL: Strode Publishers, 1973.

WhJnl *Who Was Who in Journalism, 1925-1928.* A consolidation of all material appearing in the 1928 edition of *Who's Who in Journalism,* with unduplicated biographical entries from the 1925 edition of *Who's Who in Journalism,* originally compiled by M.N. Ask (1925 and 1928 editions) and S. Gershanek (1925 edition). Gale Composite Biographical Dictionary Series, Number 4. Detroit: Gale Research, 1978.

WhJnl SUP The "1925 Supplement" begins on page 639.

WhLit *Who Was Who in Literature, 1906-1934.* Based on entries that first appeared in *Literary Yearbook* (1906-1913), *Literary Yearbook and Author's Who's Who* (1914-1917), *Literary Yearbook* (1920-1922), and *Who's Who in Literature* (1924-1934). Two volumes. Gale Composite Biographical Dictionary Series, Number 5. Detroit: Gale Research, 1979.

WhNAA *Who Was Who among North American Authors, 1921-1939.* Compiled from *Who's Who among North American Authors,* Volumes 1-7, 1921-1939. Two volumes. Gale Composite Biographical Dictionary Series, Number 1. Detroit: Gale Research, 1976.

WhNaAH *Who Was Who in Native American History.* Indians and non-Indians from early contacts through 1900. By Carl Waldman. New York: Facts on File, 1990.

Who *Who's Who.* An annual biographical dictionary. New York: St. Martin's Press, 1974-1994.

Who 74 126th Year of Issue, 1974-1975; 1974.
Who 82 134th Year of Issue, 1982-1983; 1982.
Who 82N 134th Year of Issue, 1982-1983; 1982. Obituary section.
Who 82R 134th Year of Issue, 1982-1983; 1982. The Royal Family section.
Who 82S 134th Year of Issue, 1982-1983; 1982. Supplement.
Who 83 135th Year of Issue, 1983-1984; 1983.
Who 83N 135th Year of Issue, 1983-1984; 1983. Obituary section.
Who 83R 135th Year of Issue, 1983-1984; 1983. The Royal Family section.
Who 83S 135th Year of Issue, 1983-1984; 1983. Supplement.
Who 85 137th Year of Issue, 1985-1986; 1985.
Who 85E 137th Year of Issue, 1985-1986; 1985. Errata section.
Who 85N 137th Year of Issue, 1985-1986; 1985. Obituary section.
Who 85R 137th Year of Issue, 1985-1986; 1985. The Royal Family section.
Who 85S 137th Year of Issue, 1985-1986; 1985. Supplement.
Who 88 140th Year of Issue, 1988; 1988.
Who 88N 140th Year of Issue, 1988; 1988. Obituary section.
Who 88R 140th Year of Issue, 1988; 1988. The Royal Family section.
Who 90 142nd Year of Issue, 1990; 1990.
Who 90N 142nd Year of Issue, 1990; 1990. Obituary section.
Who 90R 142nd Year of Issue, 1990; 1990. The Royal Family section.
Who 92 144th Year of Issue, 1992; 1992.
Who 92N 144th Year of Issue, 1992; 1992. Obituary section.

Who 92R	144th Year of Issue, 1992; 1992. The Royal Family section.
Who 94	146th Year of Issue, 1994; 1994.
Who 94N	146th Year of Issue, 1994; 1994. Obituary section.
Who 94R	146th Year of Issue, 1994; 1994. The Royal Family section.

WhoAdv *Who's Who in Advertising.* Monroe, NY: Redfield Publishing Co., 1972-1980.

WhoAdv 72	Second edition. Edited by Robert S. Morgan; 1972. Biographies are found in "U.S. Advertising Executives," beginning on page 1; "Canadian Advertising Executives," beginning on page 585; and the Addendum beginning on page 637.
WhoAdv 80	Third edition. Edited by Catherine Quinn Serie; 1980.

WhoAdv 90 *Who's Who in Advertising.* First edition, 1990-1991. Wilmette, IL: Marquis Who's Who, 1989.

WhoAfA 96 *Who's Who among African Americans.* Ninth edition, 1996/1997. Detroit: Gale Research, 1996. Eighth edition published as *Who's Who among Black Americans.*

WhoAfr *Who's Who in Africa.* Leaders for the 1990s. By Alan Rake. Metuchen, NJ: Scarecrow Press, 1992.
Use the Index to locate biographies.

WhoAm *Who's Who in America.* New Providence, NJ: Marquis Who's Who, 1974-1993.

WhoAm 74	38th edition, 1974-1975; 1974.
WhoAm 76	39th edition, 1976-1977; 1976.
WhoAm 78	40th edition, 1978-1979; 1978.
WhoAm 80	41st edition, 1980-1981; 1980.
WhoAm 82	42nd edition, 1982-1983; 1982.
WhoAm 84	43rd edition, 1984-1985; 1984.
WhoAm 86	44th edition, 1986-1987; 1986.
WhoAm 88	45th edition, 1988-1989; 1988.
WhoAm 90	46th edition, 1990-1991; 1990.
WhoAm 92	47th edition, 1992-1993; 1992.
WhoAm 94	48th edition, 1994; 1993.

WhoAm *Who's Who in America® [Marquis™].* New Providence, NJ: Marquis Who's Who, 1994-1996.

WhoAm 95	49th edition, 1995; 1994.
WhoAm 96	50th edition, 1996; 1995.
WhoAm 97	51st edition, 1997; 1996.

WhoAmA *Who's Who in American Art.* New Providence, NJ: R.R. Bowker Co., 1973-1993.

WhoAmA 73	11th edition; 1973.
WhoAmA 76	12th edition; 1976.
WhoAmA 76N	12th edition; 1976. The Necrology is located at the back of the volume.
WhoAmA 78	13th edition; 1978.
WhoAmA 78N	13th edition; 1978. The Necrology is located at the back of the volume.
WhoAmA 80	14th edition; 1980.

WhoAmA 80N 14th edition; 1980. The Necrology is located at the back of the volume.
WhoAmA 82 15th edition; 1982.
WhoAmA 82N 15th edition; 1982. The Necrology is located at the back of the volume.
WhoAmA 84 16th edition; 1984.
WhoAmA 84N 16th edition; 1984. The Necrology is located at the back of the volume.
WhoAmA 86 17th edition; 1986.
WhoAmA 86N 17th edition; 1986. The Necrology is located at the back of the volume.
WhoAmA 89 18th edition, 1989-1990; 1989.
WhoAmA 89N 18th edition, 1989-1990; 1989. The Necrology is located at the back of the volume.
WhoAmA 91 19th edition, 1991-1992; 1990.
WhoAmA 91N 19th edition, 1991-1992; 1990. The Necrology begins on page 1387.
WhoAmA 93 20th edition, 1993-1994; 1993.
WhoAmA 93N 20th edition, 1993-1994; 1993. The Necrology begins on page 1455.

WhoAmJ 80 *Who's Who in American Jewry.* Incorporating *The Directory of American Jewish Institutions.*. 1980 edition. Los Angeles: Standard Who's Who, 1980.

WhoAmL *Who's Who in American Law.* New Providence, NJ: Marquis Who's Who, 1978-1994.
WhoAmL 78 First edition; 1978.
WhoAmL 79 Second edition; 1979.
WhoAmL 83 Third edition; 1983.
WhoAmL 85 Fourth edition, 1985-1986; 1985.
WhoAmL 87 Fifth edition, 1987-1988; 1987.
WhoAmL 90 Sixth edition, 1990-1991; 1989.
WhoAmL 92 Seventh edition, 1992-1993; 1991.
WhoAmL 94 Eighth edition, 1994-1995; 1994.

WhoAmL 96 *Who's Who in American Law® [Marquis™].* Ninth edition, 1996-1997. New Providence, NJ: Marquis Who's Who, 1996.

WhoAmM 83 *Who's Who in American Music: Classical.* First edition. New York: R.R. Bowker Co., 1983.

WhoAmP *Who's Who in American Politics.* New Providence, NJ: R.R. Bowker, 1973-1993.
WhoAmP 73 Fourth edition, 1973-1974; 1973.
WhoAmP 75 Fifth edition, 1975-1976; 1975.
WhoAmP 77 Sixth edition, 1977-1978; 1977.
WhoAmP 79 Seventh edition, 1979-1980; 1979.
WhoAmP 81 Eighth edition, 1981-1982; 1981.
WhoAmP 83 Ninth edition, 1983-1984; 1983.
WhoAmP 85 10th edition, 1985-1986; 1985.
WhoAmP 87 11th edition, 1987-1988; 1987.
WhoAmP 89 12th edition, 1989-1990; 1989.
WhoAmP 91 13th edition, 1991-1992; 1991.
WhoAmP 93 14th edition, 1993-1994; 1993.
Use the Index to locate biographies.

WhoAmP 95 *Who's Who in American Politics™ [Bowker®].* 15th edition, 1995-1996. New Providence, NJ: R.R. Bowker, 1995.
Use the Index to locate biographies.

WhoAmW *Who's Who of American Women.* New Providence, NJ: Marquis Who's Who, 1958-1993.

WhoAmW 58	First edition, 1958-1959; 1958.
WhoAmW 58A	First edition, 1958-1959; 1958. Addenda
WhoAmW 61	Second edition, 1961-1962; 1961.
WhoAmW 61A	Second edition, 1961-1962; 1961. Addenda
WhoAmW 64	Third edition, 1964-1965; 1963.
WhoAmW 64A	Third edition, 1964-1965; 1963. Addenda
WhoAmW 66	Fourth edition, 1966-1967; 1965.
WhoAmW 66A	Fourth edition, 1966-1967; 1965. Addenda
WhoAmW 68	Fifth edition, 1968-1969; 1967.
WhoAmW 68A	Fifth edition, 1968-1969; 1967. Addenda
WhoAmW 70	Sixth edition, 1970-1971; 1969.
WhoAmW 70A	Sixth edition, 1970-1971; 1969. Addenda
WhoAmW 72	Seventh edition, 1972-1973; 1971.
WhoAmW 74	Eighth edition, 1974-1975; 1973.
WhoAmW 74	Eighth edition, 1974-1975; 1973.
WhoAmW 75	Ninth edition, 1975-1976; 1975.
WhoAmW 77	10th edition, 1977-1978; 1978.
WhoAmW 79	11th edition, 1979-1980; 1979.
WhoAmW 81	12th edition, 1981-1982; 1981.
WhoAmW 83	13th edition, 1983-1984; 1983.
WhoAmW 85	14th edition, 1985-1986; 1984.
WhoAmW 87	15th edition, 1987-1988; 1986.
WhoAmW 89	16th edition, 1989-1990; 1988.
WhoAmW 91	17th edition, 1991-1992; 1991.
WhoAmW 93	18th edition, 1993-1994; 1993.

WhoAmW *Who's Who of American Women® [Marquis™].* New Providence, NJ: Marquis Who's Who, 1995-1996.

WhoAmW 95	19th edition, 1995-1996; 1995.
WhoAmW 97	20th edition, 1997-1998; 1996.

WhoArab 81 *Who's Who in the Arab World.* Sixth edition, 1981-1982. Edited by Gabriel M. Bustros. Beirut, Lebanon: Publitec Publications, 1981.
Biographies are located in Part III.

WhoArch *Who's Who in Architecture from 1400 to the Present Day.* Edited by J.M. Richards. London: Weidenfeld & Nicolson, 1977.

WhoArt *Who's Who in Art.* Biographies of leading men and women in the world of art today -- artists, designers, craftsmen, critics, writers, teachers and curators, with an appendix of signatures. Havant, England: Art Trade Press, 1980-1996.

WhoArt 80	19th edition; 1980.
WhoArt 80N	19th edition; 1980. The Obituary section is located at the back of the volume.
WhoArt 82	20th edition; 1982.
WhoArt 82N	20th edition; 1982. The Obituary section is located at the back of the volume.
WhoArt 84	21st edition; 1984.

WhoArt 84N 21st edition; 1984. The Obituary section is located at the back of the volume.
WhoArt 96 27th edition; 1996.
WhoArt 96N 27th edition; 1996. The Obituary section is located at the back of the volume.

WhoAsA 94 *Who's Who among Asian Americans.* 1994-1995 edition. Detroit: Gale Research, 1994.
WhoAsA 94N The Obituaries section is located in the back of the volume.

WhoAsAP 91 *Who's Who in Asian and Australasian Politics.* First edition. London: Bowker-Saur, 1991.

WhoAtom 77 *Who's Who in Atoms.* Sixth edition. Edited by Ann Pernet. Guernsey, England: Francis Hodgson, 1977.

WhoBbl 73 *Who's Who in Basketball.* By Ronald L. Mendell. New Rochelle, NY: Arlington House, 1973.

WhoBlA *Who's Who among Black Americans.* Northbrook, IL: Who's Who among Black Americans, 1976-1981.
WhoBlA 75 First edition, 1975-1976; 1976.
WhoBlA 77 Second edition, 1977-1978; 1978.
WhoBlA 80 Third edition, 1980-1981; 1981.

WhoBlA *Who's Who among Black Americans.* Lake Forest, IL: Educational Communications, 1985-1988.
WhoBlA 85 Fourth edition, 1985; 1985.
WhoBlA 88 Fifth edition, 1988; 1988.

WhoBlA *Who's Who among Black Americans.* Detroit: Gale Research, 1990-1994.
WhoBlA 90 Sixth edition, 1990/1991; 1990.
WhoBlA 90N Sixth edition, 1990/1991; 1990. The Obituary section is located in the back of the volume.
WhoBlA 92 Seventh edition, 1992/1993; 1992.
WhoBlA 92N Seventh edition, 1992/1993; 1992. The Obituary section is located in the back of the volume.
WhoBlA 94 Eighth edition, 1994/1995; 1994.
WhoBlA 94N Eighth edition, 1994/1995; 1994. The Obituary section is located in the back of the volume.

WhoBox 74 *Who's Who in Boxing.* By Bob Burrill. New Rochelle, NY: Arlington House, 1974.

WhoCan *Who's Who in Canada.* An illustrated biographical record of men and women of the time in Canada. Toronto: International Press, 1973-1982.
WhoCan 73 1973-1974 edition; 1973.
WhoCan 75 1975-1976 edition; 1975.
WhoCan 77 1977-1978 edition; 1977.

WhoCan 80 1980-1981 edition; 1980.
WhoCan 82 1982-1983 edition; 1982.
Use the Index at the front of the volume to locate biographies.

WhoCan 84 *Who's Who in Canada.* An illustrated biographical record of Canada's leading men and women in business, government and academia. 1984-1985 edition. Agincourt, ON, Canada: Gage Publishing, Global Press, 1984.

WhoCanB 86 *Who's Who in Canadian Business.* Seventh edition, 1986-1987. Edited by Peggy M. Pasternak. Toronto: Trans-Canada Press, 1986.

WhoCanF 86 *Who's Who in Canadian Finance.* Eighth edition, 1986-1987. Edited by Peggy M. Pasternak. Toronto: Trans-Canada Press, 1986.

WhoCanL *Who's Who in Canadian Literature.* By Gordon Ripley and Anne Mercer. Teeswater, ON, Canada: Reference Press, 1985-1992.
WhoCanL 85 1985-1986 edition; 1985.
WhoCanL 87 1987-1988 edition; 1987.
WhoCanL 92 1992-1993 edition; 1992.

WhoChL *The Who's Who of Children's Literature.* Compiled and edited by Brian Doyle. New York: Schocken Books, 1968.
Biographies are found in "The Authors," beginning on page 1, and "The Illustrators," beginning on page 303.

WhoColR *Who's Who of the Colored Race.* A general biographical dictionary of men and women of African descent. Volume one. Edited by Frank Lincoln Mather. Chicago, 1915. Reprint. Detroit: Gale Research, 1976.
WhoColR A Addenda begins on page xxvi.

WhoCom *Who's Who in Comedy.* Comedians, comics, and clowns from vaudeville to today's stand-ups. By Ronald L. Smith. New York: Facts on File, 1992.

WhoCon 73 *Who's Who in Consulting.* A reference guide to professional personnel engaged in consultation for business, industry and government. Second edition. Edited by Paul Wasserman. Detroit: Gale Research, 1973.

WhoCtE 79 *Who's Who in Continuing Education.* Human resources in continuing library-information-media education, 1979. Compiled by CLENE (The Continuing Library Education Network and Exchange). New York and London: K.G. Saur, 1979.

WhoE *Who's Who in the East.* New Providence, NJ: Marquis Who's Who, 1974-1992.
WhoE 74 14th edition, 1974-1975; 1974.
WhoE 75 15th edition, 1975-1976; 1975.
WhoE 77 16th edition, 1977-1978; 1977.
WhoE 79 17th edition, 1979-1980; 1979.
WhoE 81 18th edition, 1981-1982; 1981.
WhoE 83 19th edition, 1983-1984; 1983.
WhoE 85 20th edition, 1985-1986; 1984.
WhoE 85A 20th edition, 1985-1986; 1984. The Addendum is located at the back of the volume.
WhoE 86 21st edition, 1986-1987; 1986.
WhoE 89 22nd edition, 1989-1990; 1988.

WhoE 91 23rd edition, 1991-1992; 1990.
WhoE 93 24th edition, 1993-1994; 1992.

WhoE *Who's Who in the East® [Marquis™].* New Providence, NJ: Marquis Who's Who, 1994-1996.
WhoE 95 25th edition, 1995-1996; 1994.
WhoE 97 26th edition, 1996-1997; 1996.

WhoEc *Who's Who in Economics.* A biographical dictionary of major economists, 1700-1986. Cambridge: MIT Press, 1983-1986.
WhoEc 81 First edition. Edited by Mark Blaug and Paul Sturges; 1983.
WhoEc 86 Second edition. Edited by Mark Blaug; 1986.

WhoEIO 82 *Who's Who in European Institutions and Organizations.* A biographical encyclopedia of the international red series containing some 4,000 biographies of the top administrators, chairmen, politicians and other leading personalities working with European institutions and organizations, and international institutions in Europe. First edition. Edited by Karl Strute and Theodor Doelken. Zurich, Switzerland: Who's Who, 1982.

WhoEmL *Who's Who of Emerging Leaders in America.* New Providence, NJ: Marquis Who's Who, 1987-1992.
WhoEmL 87 First edition, 1987-1988; 1987.
WhoEmL 89 Second edition, 1989-1990; 1988.
WhoEmL 91 Third edition, 1991-1992; 1991.
WhoEmL 93 Fourth edition, 1993-1994; 1992.

WhoEng *Who's Who in Engineering.* Washington, DC: American Association of Engineering Societies, 1980-1988.
WhoEng 80 Fourth edition. Edited by Jean Gregory; 1980.
WhoEng 88 Seventh edition, 1988. Edited by Gordon Davis; 1988.
WhoEng 88A Seventh edition, 1988. Edited by Gordon Davis; 1988. The "Errata" section follows page 852.

WhoEnt 92 *Who's Who in Entertainment.* Second edition, 1992-1993. Wilmette, IL: Marquis Who's Who, 1992.
WhoEnt 92A Addendum follows page 700.

WhoFash *Who's Who in Fashion.* By Anne Stegemeyer. New York: Fairchild Publications, 1980-1988.
WhoFash First edition; 1980.
WhoFash 88 Second edition; 1988.
WhoFash 88A Second edition; 1988. "Names to Know" section begins on page 225.

WhoFI *Who's Who in Finance and Industry.* New Providence, NJ: Marquis Who's Who, 1974-1993.
WhoFI 74 18th edition, 1974-1975; 1974.
WhoFI 75 19th edition, 1975-1976; 1975.
WhoFI 77 20th edition, 1977-1978; 1977.
WhoFI 79 21st edition, 1979-1980; 1979.
WhoFI 81 22nd edition, 1981-1982; 1981.
WhoFI 83 23rd edition, 1983-1984; 1983.

WhoFI 85	24th edition, 1985-1986; 1985.
WhoFI 87	25th edition, 1987-1988; 1987.
WhoFI 89	26th edition, 1989-1990; 1989.
WhoFI 92	27th edition, 1992-1993; 1991.
WhoFI 94	28th edition, 1994-1995; 1993.

WhoFI 96 *Who's Who in Finance and Industry® [Marquis™].* 29th edition, 1996-1997. New Providence, NJ: Marquis Who's Who, 1995.

WhoFla *Who's Who in Florida, 1973/74.* A composite of biographical sketches of outstanding men and women of the State of Florida. First edition. Lexington, KY: Names of Distinction, 1974.

WhoFr *Who's Who in France.* Paris: Editions Jacques Lafitte, 1979-1986.

WhoFr 79	14th edition, 1979-1980; 1979.
WhoFr 79N	14th edition, 1979-1980; 1979. ''Liste des Personnalites Decedees'' begins on page cviii.
WhoFr 86	1986 edition; 1986.

WhoFrS 84 *Who's Who in Frontier Science and Technology.* First edition, 1984-1985. Chicago: Marquis Who's Who, 1984.

WhoFtbl 74 *Who's Who in Football.* By Ronald L. Mendell and Timothy B. Phares. New Rochelle, NY: Arlington House, 1974.

WhoGen 81 *Who's Who in Genealogy & Heraldry.* Volume 1. Edited by Mary Keysor Meyer and P. William Filby. Detroit: Gale Research, 1981.

WhoGen 81A	''Late Additions'' section begins on page 231.

WhoGolf *Who's Who in Golf.* By Len Elliott and Barbara Kelly. New Rochelle, NY: Arlington House Publishers, 1976.

WhoGov *Who's Who in Government.* Chicago: Marquis Who's Who, 1972-1977.

WhoGov 72	First edition, 1972-1973; 1972.
WhoGov 75	Second edition, 1975-1976; 1975.
WhoGov 77	Third edition, 1977; 1977.
WhoGov 77	Third edition, 1977; 1977.

WhoGrA *Who's Who in Graphic Art.* An illustrated book of reference to the world's leading graphic designers, illustrators, typographers and cartoonists. First edition. Edited by Walter Amstutz. Zurich, Switzerland: Amstutz & Herdeg Graphis Press, 1962.

WhoGrA 62	Use the ''Index of Artists' Names,'' which begins on page 576, to locate biographies.
WhoGrA 62	

WhoGrA 82 *Who's Who in Graphic Art.* An illustrated world review of the leading contemporary graphic and typographic designers, illustrators and cartoonists. Volume Two. Edited and designed by Walter Amstutz. Dubendorf, Switzerland: De Clivo Press, 1982.

Use the ''Index of Artists' Names,'' which begins on page 886, to locate biographies.

WhoHcky 73 *Who's Who in Hockey.* By Harry C. Kariher. New Rochelle, NY: Arlington House, 1973.

WhoHisp *Who's Who among Hispanic Americans.* Detroit: Gale Research, 1991-1994.
- ***WhoHisp 91*** First edition, 1991-1992; 1991.
- ***WhoHisp 91N*** First edition, 1991-1992; 1991. The Obituaries section begins on page 423.
- ***WhoHisp 92*** Second edition, 1992-1993; 1992.
- ***WhoHisp 92N*** Second edition, 1992-1993; 1992. The Obituaries section begins on page 743.
- ***WhoHisp 94*** Third edition, 1994-1995; 1994.
- ***WhoHisp 94N*** Third edition, 1994-1995; 1994. The Obituaries section begins on page 887.

WhoHol 92 *Who's Who in Hollywood.* The largest cast of international film personalities ever assembled. Two volumes. By David Ragan. New York: Facts on File, 1992.

WhoHol *Who's Who in Hollywood, 1900-1976.* By David Ragan. New Rochelle, NY: Arlington House, 1976.
- ***WhoHol A*** The "Living Players" section begins on page 11.
- ***WhoHol B*** The "Late Players (1900-1974)" section begins on page 539.
- ***WhoHol C*** The "Players Who Died in 1975 and 1976" section begins on page 845.

WhoHr&F *Who's Who in Horror and Fantasy Fiction.* By Mike Ashley. London: Elm Tree Books, 1977.

WhoHrs 80 *Who's Who of the Horrors and Other Fantasy Films.* The international personality encyclopedia of the fantastic film. First edition. By David J. Hogan San Diego: A.S. Barnes & Co.; London: Tantivy Press, 1980.

WhoIns *Who's Who in Insurance.* Englewood, NJ: Underwriter Printing & Publishing Co., 1975-1997.
- ***WhoIns 75*** 1975 edition; 1975.
- ***WhoIns 76*** 1976 edition; 1976.
- ***WhoIns 76A*** 1976 edition; 1976. The Addenda appear at the back of the volume.
- ***WhoIns 77*** 1977 edition; 1977.
- ***WhoIns 77A*** 1977 edition; 1977. The Addenda appear at the back of the volume.
- ***WhoIns 78*** 1978 edition; 1978.
- ***WhoIns 78A*** 1978 edition; 1978. The Addenda appear at the back of the volume.
- ***WhoIns 79*** 1979 edition; 1979.
- ***WhoIns 79A*** 1979 edition; 1979. The Addenda appear at the back of the volume.
- ***WhoIns 80*** 1980 edition; 1980.
- ***WhoIns 80A*** 1980 edition; 1980. The Addenda appear at the back of the volume.
- ***WhoIns 81*** 1981 edition; 1981.
- ***WhoIns 81A*** 1981 edition; 1981. The Addenda appear at the back of the volume.

WhoIns 82 1982 edition; 1982.
WhoIns 82A 1982 edition; 1982. The Addenda appear at the back of the volume.
WhoIns 84 1984 edition; 1984.
WhoIns 84A 1984 edition; 1984. The Addenda appear at the back of the volume.
WhoIns 86 1986 edition; 1986.
WhoIns 86A 1986 edition; 1986. The Addenda appear at the back of the volume.
WhoIns 88 1988 edition; 1988.
WhoIns 90 1990 edition; 1990.
WhoIns 90A 1990 edition; 1990. The Addenda appear at the back of the volume.
WhoIns 92 1992 edition; 1992.
WhoIns 93 1993 edition; 1993.
WhoIns 94 1994 edition; 1994.
WhoIns 97 1997 edition; 1997.

WhoIntG *Who's Who in International Golf.* Edited by David Emery. New York: Facts on File Publications, 1983.

WhoIntT *Who's Who in International Tennis.* Edited by David Emery. New York: Facts on File Publications, 1983.

WhoJazz 72 *Who's Who of Jazz: Storyville to Swing Street.* By John Chilton. Philadelphia: Chilton Book Co., 1972.

WhoLA *Who's Who among Living Authors of Older Nations.* Covering the literary activities of living authors and writers of all countries of the world except the United States of America, Canada, Mexico, Alaska, Hawaii, Newfoundland, the Philippine Islands, the West Indies, and Central America. Volume 1, 1931-1932. Edited by A. Lawrence. Los Angeles: Golden Syndicate Publishing Co., 1931. Reprint. Detroit: Gale Research, 1966.

WhoLab 76 *Who's Who in Labor.* New York: Arno Press, 1976.

WhoLib 54 *Who's Who in Librarianship.* Edited by Thomas Landau. Cambridge: Bowes & Bowes, 1954.

WhoLib 72 *Who's Who in Librarianship and Information Science.* Second edition. Edited by T. Landau. London: Abelard-Schuman, 1972.

WhoLibI 82 *Who's Who in Library and Information Services.* Edited by Joel M. Lee. Chicago: American Library Association, 1982.

WhoLibS 55 *Who's Who in Library Service.* A biographical directory of professional librarians of the United States and Canada. Third edition. Edited by Dorothy Ethlyn Cole. New York: Grolier Society, 1955.

WhoLibS 66 *Who's Who in Library Service.* A biographical directory of professional librarians in the United States and Canada. Fourth edition. Edited by Lee Ash. Hamden, CT: Shoe String Press, 1966.

WhoMedH *Who's Who in Medicine and Healthcare® [Marquis™].* 1996-1997. New Providence, NJ: Marquis Who's Who, 1997.

WhoMilH 76 *Who's Who in Military History.* From 1453 to the present day. By John Keegan and Andrew Wheatcroft. New York: William Morrow & Co., 1976.

WhoMus 72 *Who's Who in Music and Musicians' International Directory.* Sixth edition. New York: Hafner Publishing Co., 1972. Later editions published as *International Who's Who in Music and Musicians' Directory.*

WhoMW *Who's Who in the Midwest.* New Providence, NJ: Marquis Who's Who, 1974-1994.

WhoMW 74	14th edition, 1974-1975; 1974.
WhoMW 76	15th edition, 1976-1977; 1976.
WhoMW 78	16th edition, 1978-1979; 1978.
WhoMW 80	17th edition, 1980-1981; 1980.
WhoMW 82	18th edition, 1982-1983; 1982.
WhoMW 84	19th edition, 1984-1985; 1984.
WhoMW 86	20th edition, 1986-1987; 1985.
WhoMW 88	21st edition, 1988-1989; 1987.
WhoMW 90	22nd edition, 1990-1991; 1989.
WhoMW 92	23rd edition, 1992-1993; 1992.
WhoMW 93	24th edition, 1994-1995; 1994.

WhoMW 96 *Who's Who in the Midwest® [Marquis™].* New Providence, NJ: Marquis Who's Who, 1996.

WhoNeCM *Who's Who in New Country Music.* By Andrew Vaughan. New York: St. Martin's Press, 1989.

WhoNeCM A	Introduction begins on page 7.
WhoNeCM B	The ''UK Country'' section begins on page 115.
WhoNeCM C	The ''Classic Country'' section begins on page 119.

WhoNob *Who's Who of Nobel Prize Winners.* Edited by Bernard S. Schlessinger and June H. Schlessinger. Phoenix, AZ: Oryx Press, 1986-1991.

WhoNob	First edtion; 1986. Use the ''Name Index,'' which begins on page 195, to locate biographies.
WhoNob 90	Second edition; 1991.

WhoNob 95 *The Who's Who of Nobel Prize Winners.* Third edition. Edited by Bernard S. Schlessinger and June H. Schlessinger. Phoenix, AZ: Oryx Press, 1996.
Use the ''Name Index,'' which begins on page 229, to locate biographies.

WhoOcn 78 *Who's Who in Ocean and Freshwater Science.* First edition. Edited by Allen Varley. Essex, England: Longman Group, Francis Hodgson, 1978.

WhoOp 76 *Who's Who in Opera.* An international biographical directory of singers, conductors, directors, designers, and administrators. Also including profiles of 101 opera companies. Edited by Maria F. Rich. New York: Arno Press, 1976.

WhoPNW *Who's Who among Pacific Northwest Authors.* Second edition. Edited by Frances Valentine Wright. Missoula, MT: Pacific Northwest Library Association, 1969.
Biographies are arranged alphabetically by state. Use the ''Index of Authors'' to locate listings.

WhoPoA 96 *Who's Who in Polish America.* First edition, 1996-1997. New York: Bicentennial Publishing Corp., 1996. Distributed by Hippocrene Books, New York.

WhoPolA *Who's Who in Polish America.* A biographical directory of Polish-American leaders and distinguished Poles resident in the Americas. Third edition. Edited by Francis Bolek. New York: Harbinger House, 1943. Reprint. The American Immigration Collection - Series II. New York: Arno Press and The New York Times, 1970.

WhoPRCh 81 *Who's Who in the People's Republic of China.* By Wolfgang Bartke. Armonk, NY: M.E. Sharpe, 1981.
- ***WhoPRCh 81A*** Wade-Giles/Pinyin Conversion Table begins on page 719.
- ***WhoPRCh 81B*** ''Biographies of Important Deceased and Purged Cadres'' section begins on page 573.

WhoPRCh *Who's Who in the People's Republic of China.* By Wolfgang Bartke. Munich and New York: K.G. Saur, 1987-1991.
- ***WhoPRCh 87*** Second edition; 1987.
- ***WhoPRCh 91*** Third edition. Two volumes; 1991.

WhoProB 73 *Who's Who in Professional Baseball.* By Gene Karst and Martin J. Jones, Jr. New Rochelle, NY: Arlington House, 1973.

WhoPubR *Who's Who in Public Relations (International).* Edited by Adrian A. Paradis. Meriden, NH: PR Publishing Co., 1972-1976.
- ***WhoPubR 72*** Fourth edition; 1972.
- ***WhoPubR 76*** Fifth edition; 1976.

WhoReal 83 *Who's Who in Real Estate.* The directory of the real estate professions. Boston: Warren, Gorham & Lamont, 1983.

WhoRel *Who's Who in Religion.* Wilmette, IL: Marquis Who's Who, 1975-1992.
- ***WhoRel 75*** First edition, 1975-1976; 1975.
- ***WhoRel 77*** Second edition, 1977; 1977.
- ***WhoRel 85*** Third edition, 1985; 1985.
- ***WhoRel 92*** Fourth edition, 1992-1993; 1992.

WhoRock 81 *Who's Who in Rock.* By Michael Bane. New York: Everest House, 1981.

WhoRocM 82 *Who's Who in Rock Music.* By William York. New York: Charles Scribner's Sons, 1982.

WhoRus *Who's Who in Russia and the CIS Republics.* Edited by Vladimir Morozov. New York: Henry Holt & Co., 1995.

WhoSauA *Who's Who in Saudi Arabia.* Jeddah, Saudi Arabia: Tihama; London: Europa Publications, 1977-1978.
- ***WhoSauA 76*** First edition, 1976-1977; 1977.
- ***WhoSauA 78*** Second edition, 1978-1979; 1978.

WhoScEn 94 *Who's Who in Science and Engineering.* Second edition, 1994-1995. New Providence, NJ: Marquis Who's Who, 1994.

WhoScEn 96 *Who's Who in Science and Engineering® [Marquis™].* Third edition, 1996-1997. New Providence, NJ: Marquis Who's Who, 1996.

WhoScEu *Who's Who in Science in Europe.* A biographical guide in science, technology, agriculture, and medicine. Essex, England: Longman Group UK, 1991. Distributed by Gale Research, Detroit.

- ***WhoScEu 91-1*** Seventh edition. Volume 1: *United Kingdom.*
- ***WhoScEu 91-2*** Seventh edition. Volume 2: *EC Countries A to F.*
- ***WhoScEu 91-3*** Seventh edition. Volume 3: *EC Countries G to Z.*
- ***WhoScEu 91-4*** Seventh edition. Volume 4: *Non-EC Countries.*

For volumes covering multiple countries, use the Table of Contents to locate appropriate section. This book often alphabetizes by titles of address, e.g., Dr., Mrs., and Sir.

WhoSciF *Who's Who in Science Fiction.* By Brian Ash. London: Elm Tree Books, 1976.

WhoSecI 86 *Who's Who in the Securities Industry.* The Economist Securities Industry Association Convention editions. Chicago: Economist Publishing Co., 1986.

- ***WhoSecI 86A*** "The Executive Officers and the Principal Staff Members of the Securities Industry Association" section, begins on page 100.

WhoSocC 78 *Who's Who in the Socialist Countries.* A biographical encyclopedia of 10,000 leading personalities in 16 communist countries. First edition. Edited by Borys Lewytzkyj and Juliusz Stroynowski. New York: K.G. Saur Publishing, 1978.

- ***WhoSocC 78A*** The Appendix begins on page 713.

WhoSoCE 89 *Who's Who in the Socialist Countries of Europe.* A biographical encyclopedia of more than 12,600 leading personalities in Albania, Bulgaria, Czechoslovakia, German Democratic Republic, Hungary, Poland, Romania, Yugoslavia. Three volumes. Edited by Juliusz Stroynowski. Munich, Germany: K.G. Saur, 1989.

WhoSpc *Who's Who in Space.* The First 25 Years. By Michael Cassutt. Boston: G.K. Hall & Co., 1987.

Use the Index to locate biographies.

WhoSpor *A Who's Who of Sports Champions.* Their stories and records. By Ralph Hickok. New York, NY: Houghton Mifflin Co., 1995.

WhoSpyF *Who's Who in Spy Fiction.* By Donald McCormick. London: Elm Tree Books, 1977.

WhoSSW *Who's Who in the South and Southwest.* New Providence, NJ: Marquis Who's Who, 1973-1993.

- ***WhoSSW 73*** 13th edition, 1973-1974; 1973.
- ***WhoSSW 75*** 14th edition, 1975-1976; 1975.
- ***WhoSSW 76*** 15th edition, 1976-1977; 1976.
- ***WhoSSW 78*** 16th edition, 1978-1979; 1978.
- ***WhoSSW 80*** 17th edition, 1980-1981; 1980.
- ***WhoSSW 82*** 18th edition, 1982-1983; 1982.
- ***WhoSSW 84*** 19th edition, 1984-1985; 1984.

WhoSSW 86 20th edition, 1986-1987; 1986.
WhoSSW 88 21st edition, 1988-1989; 1988.
WhoSSW 91 22nd edition, 1991-1992; 1990.
WhoSSW 93 23rd edition, 1993-1994; 1993.

WhoSSW *Who's Who in the South and Southwest® [Marquis™].* New Providence, NJ: Marquis Who's Who, 1995-1997.
WhoSSW 95 24th edition, 1995-1996; 1995.
WhoSSW 97 25th edition, 1997-98; 1997.

WhoStg 1906 *Who's Who on the Stage.* The dramatic reference book and biographical dictionary of the theatre. Containing records of the careers of actors, actresses, managers and playwrights of the American stage. 1906 edition. Edited by Walter Browne and F.A. Austin. New York: Walter Browne & F.A. Austin, 1906.
Some entries are not in alphabetic sequence.

WhoStg 1908 *Who's Who on the Stage.* The dramatic reference book and biographical dictionary of the theatre. Containing careers of actors, actresses, managers and playwrights of the American stage. 1908 edition. Edited by Walter Browne and E. De Roy Koch. New York: B.W. Dodge & Co., 1908.
Some entries are not in alphabetic sequence.

WhoTech 82 *Who's Who in Technology Today.* Third edition. Four volumes. Edited by Jan W. Churchwell. Highland Park, IL: J. Dick & Co., 1982.
Use the ''Index of Names,'' which begins on page 667 of Volume 4, to locate biographies.

WhoTech 84 *Who's Who in Technology Today.* Fourth edition. Five volumes. Edited by Barbara A. Tinucci. Lake Bluff, IL: Research Publications, J. Dick Publishing, 1984.
Use the ''Index of Names,'' which begins on page 1125 of Volume 5, to locate biographies.

WhoTech *Who's Who in Technology.* Detroit: Gale Research, 1989-1995.
WhoTech 89 Sixth edition. Two volumes; 1989.
WhoTech 89N Sixth edition. Two volumes; 1989. The ''Obituaries'' section begins on page 1819 of the *Biographies* volume.
WhoTech 95 Seventh edition; 1995.
WhoTech 95N Seventh edition; 1995. The ''Obituaries'' section begins on page 1379.

WhoTelC *Who's Who in Television and Cable.* Edited by Steven H. Scheuer. New York: Facts on File, 1983.

WhoThe *Who's Who in the Theatre.* A biographical record of the contemporary stage. London: Pitman Publishing; Detroit: Gale Research, 1972-1977.Continued as *Contemporary Theatre, Film, and Television.*
WhoThe 72 15th edition. Compiled by John Parker; 1972.
WhoThe 72 15th edition. Compiled by John Parker; 1972.
WhoThe 77 16th edition. Edited by Ian Herbert; 1977.
WhoThe 77 16th edition. Edited by Ian Herbert; 1977.

WhoThe 77A *Who's Who in the Theatre, 16th ed. Appendix*

WhoThe 81 *Who's Who in the Theatre.* A biographical record of the contemporary stage. 17th edition. Edited by Ian Herbert. London: Pitman Publishing; Detroit: Gale Research, 1981. Continued as *Contemporary Theatre, Film, and Television.*
WhoThe 81N Obituary section begins on page 743.

WhoThSc 1996 *Who's Who in Theology and Science.* An international biographical and bibliographical guide to individuals and organizations interested in the interaction of theology and science. New York: Continuum Publishing Co., 1996.

WhoTran *Who's Who in Translating and Interpreting.* Compiled by A. Flegon. London: Flegon Press, 1967.
WhoTran AFR Afrikaans section begins on page 5.
WhoTran ALB Albanian section begins on page 5.
WhoTran ARB Arabic section begins on page 5.
WhoTran BEL Belorussian section begins on page 9.
WhoTran BUL Bulgarian section begins on page 9.
WhoTran CHI Chinese section begins on page 11.
WhoTran CZE Czech section begins on page 12.
WhoTran DAN Danish section begins on page 16.
WhoTran DUT Dutch section begins on page 18.
WhoTran ESP Esperanto section begins on page 29.
WhoTran EST Estonian section begins on page 29.
WhoTran FIN Finnish section begins on page 30.
WhoTran FLE Flemish section begins on page 30.
WhoTran FRE French section begins on page 32.
WhoTran GER German section begins on page 70.
WhoTran GRE Greek section begins on page 110.
WhoTran HEB Hebrew section begins on page 112.
WhoTran HIN Hindi section begins on page 112.
WhoTran HUN Hungarian section begins on page 113.
WhoTran ICE Icelandic section begins on page 116.
WhoTran IND Indonesian section begins on page 116.
WhoTran INT Interlingua section begins on page 116.
WhoTran IRI Irish section begins on page 117.
WhoTran ITA Italian section begins on page 118.
WhoTran JAP Japanese section begins on page 130.
WhoTran LAT Latvian section begins on page 132.
WhoTran LIT Lithuanian section begins on page 133.
WhoTran MLT Maltese section begins on page 134.
WhoTran MLY Malay section begins on page 133.
WhoTran NOR Norwegian section begins on page 136.
WhoTran POL Polish section begins on page 137.
WhoTran POR Portuguese section begins on page 143.
WhoTran RUM Rumanian section begins on page 146.
WhoTran RUS Russian section begins on page 148.
WhoTran SAN Sanskrit section begins on page 162.
WhoTran SCA Scandinavian section begins on page 162.
WhoTran SER Serbo-Croat section begins on page 162.
WhoTran SPA Spanish section begins on page 164.
WhoTran SWA Swahili section begins on page 182.
WhoTran SWE Swedish section begins on page 183.
WhoTran TUR Turkish section begins on page 187.
WhoTran UKR Ukranian section begins on page 188.

WhoTr&F 73 *Who's Who in Track and Field.* By Reid M. Hanley. New Rochelle, NY: Arlington House, 1973.

WhoTwCL *Who's Who in Twentieth Century Literature.* By Martin Seymour-Smith. New York: Holt, Rinehart & Winston, 1976.

WhoUN 75 *Who's Who in the United Nations and Related Agencies.* New York: Arno Press, 1975.

WhoUN 92 *Who's Who in the United Nations and Related Agencies.* Second edition. Edited by Stanley R. Greenfield. Detroit: Omnigraphics, 1992.

WhoUSWr 88 *Who's Who in U.S. Writers, Editors & Poets.* A biographical directory. Second edition. Edited by Curt Johnson. Highland Park, IL: December Press, 1988.

WhoVenC 86 *Who's Who in Venture Capital.* Second edition. By A. David Silver. New York: John Wiley & Sons, 1986.
Biographies begin on page 101.

WhoWest *Who's Who in the West.* New Providence, NJ: Marquis Who's Who, 1974-1993.

WhoWest 74 14th edition, 1974-1975; 1974.
WhoWest 76 15th edition, 1976-1977; 1976.
WhoWest 78 16th edition, 1978-1979; 1978.
WhoWest 80 17th edition, 1980-1981; 1980.
WhoWest 82 18th edition, 1982-1983; 1982.
WhoWest 84 19th edition, 1984-1985; 1983.
WhoWest 87 21st edition, 1987-1988; 1987.
WhoWest 89 22nd edition, 1989-1990; 1989.
WhoWest 92 23rd edition, 1992-1993; 1992.
WhoWest 94 24th edition, 1994-1995; 1993.

WhoWest 96 *Who's Who in the West® [Marquis™].* 25th edition, 1996-1997. New Providence, NJ: Marquis Who's Who, 1995.

WhoWomW 91 *Who's Who of Women in World Politics.* First edition. New York: Bowker-Saur, 1991.

WhoWor *Who's Who in the World.* New Providence, NJ: Marquis Who's Who, 1973-1992.

WhoWor 74 Second edition, 1974-1975; 1973.
WhoWor 76 Third edition, 1976-1977; 1976.
WhoWor 78 Fourth edition, 1978-1979; 1978.
WhoWor 80 Fifth edition, 1980-1981; 1980.
WhoWor 82 Sixth edition, 1982-1983; 1982.
WhoWor 84 Seventh edition, 1984-1985; 1984.
WhoWor 87 Eighth edition, 1987-1988; 1986.
WhoWor 89 Ninth edition, 1989-1990; 1988.
WhoWor 91 10th edition, 1991-1992; 1990.
WhoWor 93 11th edition, 1993-1994; 1992.

WhoWor *Who's Who in the World® [Marquis™].* New Providence, NJ: Marquis Who's Who, 1994-1996.

WhoWor 95 12th edition, 1995-1996; 1994.
WhoWor 96 13th edition, 1996-1997; 1995.

WhoWor 97 14th edition, 1997; 1996.

WhoWorJ 72 *Who's Who in World Jewry.* A biographical dictionary of outstanding Jews. Edited by I.J. Carmin Karpman. New York: Pitman Publishing Corp., 1972.

WhoWorJ 78 *Who's Who in World Jewry.* A biographical dictionary of outstanding Jews. Edited by I.J. Carmin Karpman. Tel-Aviv, Israel: Olive Books of Israel, 1978.

WhoWrEP *Who's Who in Writers, Editors & Poets.* United States & Canada. Edited by Curt Johnson. Highland Park, IL: December Press, 1989-1995.
WhoWrEP 89 Third edition, 1989-1990; 1989.
WhoWrEP 92 Fourth edition, 1992-1993; 1992.
WhoWrEP 95 Fifth edition, 1995-1996; 1995.

WhScrn 74 *Who Was Who on Screen.* First edition. By Evelyn Mack Truitt. New York: R.R. Bowker Co., 1974.
WhScrn 74

WhScrn 77 *Who Was Who on Screen.* Second edition. By Evelyn Mack Truitt. New York: R.R. Bowker, 1977.

WhScrn *Who Was Who on Screen.* By Evelyn Mack Truitt. New York: R.R. Bowker Co., 1977-1983.
WhScrn 77 Second edition; 1977.
WhScrn 83 Third edition; 1983.

WhsNW 85 *Who's New Wave in Music.* An illustrated encyclopedia, 1976-1982 (the first wave). Edited by David Bianco. Ann Arbor, MI: Pierian Press, 1985.

WhThe *Who Was Who in the Theatre: 1912-1976.* A biographical dictionary of actors, actresses, directors, playwrights, and producers of the English-speaking theatre. Compiled from *Who's Who in the Theatre,* Volumes 1-15 (1912-1972). Four volumes. Gale Composite Biographical Dictionary Series, Number 3. Detroit: Gale Research, 1978.

WhWE *Who Was Who in World Exploration.* By Carl Waldman and Alan Wexler. New York: Facts on File, 1992.

WhWW-II *Who Was Who in World War II.* Edited by John Keegan. London: Arms & Armour Press, 1978.

WisWr *Wisconsin Writers.* Sketches and studies. By William A. Titus. Chicago, 1930. Reprint. Detroit: Gale Research, 1974.
Use the Table of Contents to locate biographies.

WomArch *Women in Architecture.* A contemporary perspective. By Clare Lorenz. New York: Rizzoli International Publications, 1990.

WomArt *Women Artists.* An historical, contemporary and feminist bibliography. By Donna G. Bachmann and Sherry Piland. Metuchen, NJ: Scarecrow Press, 1978.
WomArt Use the Table of Contents which begins on page 47 to locate biographies.
WomArt A The Addenda begins on page 322.

WomBeaG *Women of the Beat Generation.* The writers, artists, and muses at the heart of a revolution. By Brenda Knight. Berkeley, CA: Conari Press, 1996.
Use the Index to locate biographies.

WomChHR *Women Champions of Human Rights.* Eleven U.S. leaders of the twentieth century. By Moira Davison Reynolds. Jefferson, NC: McFarland & Co., 1991.
Use the Index to locate biographies.

WomCom *Women Composers, Conductors and Musicians of the Twentieth Century.* Selected biographies. By Jane Weiner LePage. Metuchen, NJ: Scarecrow Press, 1980.

WomComm *Women in Communication.* A biographical sourcebook. Edited by Nancy Signorielli. Westport, CT: Greenwood Press, 1996.

WomCon *Women of Congress.* A twentieth-century odyssey. By Marcy Kaptur. Washington, DC: Congressional Quarterly, 1996.
Use the Index, beginning on page 252, to locate biographies.

WomEdUS *Women Educators in the United States, 1820-1993.* A bio-bibliographical sourcebook. Edited by Maxine Schwartz Seller. Westport, CT: Greenwood Press, 1994.

WomFie *Women in the Field.* America's pioneering women naturalists. By Marcia Myers Bonta. College Station, TX: Texas A & M University Press, 1991.
Use the Index to locate biographies.

WomFir *Women's Firsts.* Edited by Caroline Zilboorg. Detroit: Gale Research, 1997.
Use the Index to locate biographies.

WomLaw *Women in Law.* A bio-bibliographic sourcebook. Edited by Rebecca Mae Salokar and Mary L. Volcansek. Westport, CT: Greenwood Press, 1996.

WomMath *Women of Mathematics.* A biobibliographic sourcebook. Edited by Louise S. Grinstein & Paul J. Campbell. New York: Greenwood Press, 1987.

WomNov *Women Novelists, 1891-1920.* An index to biographical and autobiographical sources. By Doris Robinson. Garland Reference Library of the Humanities, vol. 491. New York: Garland Publishing, 1984.

WomPO 76 *Women in Public Office.* A biographical directory and statistical analysis. Compiled by Center for the American Woman and Politics. New York: R.R. Bowker Co., 1976.
Use the ''Name Index'' to locate listings.

WomPO 78 *Women in Public Office.* A biographical directory and statistical analysis. Second edition. Compiled by Center for the American Woman and Politics. Metuchen, NJ: Scarecrow Press, 1978.
Use the ''Name Index'' to locate listings.

WomPsyc *Women in Psychology.* A bio-bibliographic sourcebook. Edited by Agnes N. O'Connell and Nancy Felipe Russo. New York: Greenwood Press, 1990.

WomPubS 1800 *Women Public Speakers in the United States, 1800-1925.* A bio-critical sourcebook. Edited by Karlyn Kohrs Campbell. Westport, CT: Greenwood Press, 1993.

WomPubS 1925 *Women Public Speakers in the United States, 1925-1993.* A bio-critical sourcebook. Edited by Karlyn Kohrs Campbell. Westport, CT: Greenwood Press, 1994.

WomSc *Women in Science.* Antiquity through the nineteenth century. By Marilyn Bailey Ogilvie. Cambridge: MIT Press, 1986.

WomSc A The Appendix begins on page 181.

WomSoc *Women in Sociology.* A bio-bibliographical sourcebook. Edited by Mary Jo Deegan. New York: Greenwood Press, 1991.

WomStre *Women of Strength.* Biographies of 106 who have excelled in traditionally male fields, A.D. 61 to the present. By Louis Baldwin. Jefferson, NC: McFarland & Co., 1996.

Use the Index to locate biographies.

WomWMM *Women Who Make Movies.* By Sharon Smith. Cinema Study Series. New York: Hopkinson & Blake, 1975.

WomWMM ''Overview'' section. Biographies can be located through the index beginning on page 299.

WomWMM A ''The New Filmmakers'' begin on page 145.

WomWMM B ''Directory'' begins on page 221.

WomWR *Women Who Ruled.* By Guida M. Jackson. Santa Barbara, CA: ABC-Clio, 1990.

WomWrGe *Women Writers of Germany, Austria, and Switzerland.* An annotated bio-bibliographical guide. Edited by Elke Frederiksen. Bibliographies and Indexes in Women's Studies, no. 8. New York: Greenwood Press, 1989.

WomWrRR *Women Writers of the Renaissance and Reformation.* Edited by Katharina M. Wilson. Athens, GA: University of Georgia Press, 1987.

Use the Index to locate biographies.

WomWrS *Women Writers of Spain.* An annotated bio-bibliographical guide. Edited by Carolyn L. Galerstein. Bibliographies and Indexes in Women's Studies, no. 2. New York: Greenwood Press, 1986.

WomWrSA *Women Writers of Spanish America.* An annotated bio-bibliographical guide. Edited by Diane E. Marting. Bibliographies and Indexes in Women's Studies, no. 5. New York: Greenwood Press, 1987.

WomWWA 14 *Woman's Who's Who of America.* A biographical dictionary of contemporary women of the United States and Canada, 1914-1915. Edited by John William Leonard. New York: American Commonwealth Co., 1914. Reprint. Detroit: Gale Research, 1976.

WomWWA 14A ''Addenda and Corrections'' and ''Deaths during Printing'' sections begin on page 29.

WorAl *The World Almanac Book of Who.* Edited by Hana Umlauf Lane. New York: World Almanac Publications, 1980.
Use the "Name Index," which begins on page 326, to locate biographies.

WorAlBi *The World Almanac Biographical Dictionary.* By the editors of *The World Almanac.* New York: World Almanac, 1990.

WorArt 1950 *World Artists, 1950-1980.* Edited by Claude Marks. New York: H.W. Wilson Co., 1984.

WorArt 1980 *World Artists, 1980-1990.* Edited by Claude Marks. New York: H.W. Wilson Co., 1991.

WorAu *World Authors.* Wilson Authors Series. New York: H.W. Wilson Co., 1975-1995.
WorAu 1950 *1950-1970.* Edited by John Wakeman; 1975.
WorAu 1970 *1970-1975.* Edited by John Wakeman; 1980.
WorAu 1975 *1975-1980.* Edited by Vineta Colby; 1985.
WorAu 1980 *1980-1985.* Edited by Vineta Colby; 1991.
WorAu 1985 1985-1990. Edited by Vineta Colby; 1995.

WorDWW *World Defence Who's Who.* Edited by Paul Martell and Grace P. Hayes. London: Macdonald & Jane's, 1974.

WorECar *The World Encyclopedia of Cartoons.* Two volumes. Edited by Maurice Horn. Detroit: Gale Research, 1980. Published in association with Chelsea House Publishers, New York.
WorECar A "Notes on the Contributors" section begins on page 631.

WorECom *The World Encyclopedia of Comics.* Two volumes. Edited by Maurice Horn. New York: Chelsea House Publishers, 1976.
Biographies begin on page 65.

WorEFlm *The World Encyclopedia of the Film.* Edited by John M. Smith and Tim Cawkwell. New York: A. & W. Visual Library, 1972.

WorESoc *The World Encyclopedia of Soccer.* Detroit: Gale Research, 1994.
Biographies are located in the "Who's Who in Soccer" section which begins on page 49.

WorFDir *World Film Directors.* Edited by John Wakeman. New York: H.W. Wilson Co., 1987-1988.
WorFDir 1 Volume 1: 1890-1945; 1987.
WorFDir 2 Volume 2: 1945-1985; 1988.

WorFshn *World of Fashion.* People, places, resources. By Eleanor Lambert. New York: R.R. Bowker Co., 1976.
Use the "Name Index," which begins on page 351, to locate biographies.

WorInv *World of Invention.* History's most significant inventions and the people behind them. Detroit: Gale Research, 1994.

WorLitC *World Literature Criticism.* 1500 to the present. A selection of major authors from Gale's Literary Criticism Series. Six volumes. Detroit: Gale Research, 1992.

WorScD *World of Scientific Discovery.* Scientific milestones and the people who made them possible. Detroit: Gale Research, 1994.

WrChl *Writers for Children.* Critical studies of major authors since the seventeenth century. Edited by Jane M. Bingham. New York: Charles Scribner's Sons, 1988.

WrCNE *Writers of Colonial New England.* By Trentwell Mason White and Paul William Lehmann. Boston: Palmer Company, 1929. Reprint. Detroit: Gale Research, 1971.

Use the Index to locate biographies.

WrDr *The Writers Directory.* London: St. James Press; New York: St. Martin's Press, 1976-1979.

WrDr 76 Third edition, 1976-1978; 1976.
WrDr 80 Fourth edition, 1980-1982; 1979.

WrDr 82 *The Writers Directory.* Fifth edition, 1982-1984. Detroit: Gale Research, 1981.

WrDr *The Writers Directory.* Detroit: St. James Press, 1983-1996.

WrDr 84 Sixth edition, 1984-1986; 1983.
WrDr 86 Seventh edition, 1986-1988; 1986.
WrDr 88 Eighth edition, 1988-1990; 1988.
WrDr 90 Ninth edition, 1990-1992; 1990.
WrDr 92 10th edition, 1992-1994; 1991.
WrDr 94 11th edition, 1994-1996; 1994.
WrDr 94N 11th edition, 1994-1996; 1994. The Obituaries section is located in the back of the volume.
WrDr 96 12th edition, 1996-1998; 1996.

WrPh *Writers and Philosophers.* A sourcebook of philosophical influences on literature. By Edmund J. Thomas and Eugene G. Miller. New York: Greenwood Press, 1990.

WrPh P ''Profiles of Philosophers'' section begins on page 215.

YABC *Yesterday's Authors of Books for Children.* Facts and pictures about authors and illustrators of books for young people, from early times to 1960. Edited by Anne Commire. Detroit: Gale Research, 1977-1978.

YABC 1 Volume 1; 1977.
YABC 2 Volume 2; 1978.

YABC X *Yesterday's Authors of Books for Children, Index.* Facts and pictures about authors and illustrators of books for young people, from early times to 1960. Detroit: Gale Research, 1977-1978.

This code refers to pseudonym entries which appear only as cross-references in the cumulative index to *Yesterday's Authors of Books for Children.*

Almanac of Famous People

Biographies

A

Aadland, Beverly
American. Actor, Dancer, Singer
In film *Cuban Rebel Girls* with Errol Flynn, 1959; their subsequent romance caused scandal.
b. 1944
Source: *BioIn 7, 16; CelR 90; WhoHol A*

Aadlberg, John O.
American. Engineer
Headed sound department, RKO Studios, 1932-57; won three Oscars.
b. Apr 3, 1897 in Chicago, Illinois
d. Aug 30, 1984
Source: *VarWW 85*

Aalto, Alvar Henrik Hugo
Finnish. Architect
Redesigned Finnish cities damaged during WW II.
b. Feb 3, 1898 in Kuortane, Finland
d. May 11, 1976 in Helsinki, Finland
Source: *ConAu 65; CurBio 48, 76; EncMA; IntWW 74, 75, 76, 77; LinLib S; McGDA; McGEWB; NewYTBS 76; OxCDecA; WhAm 7; WhoArch*

Aames, Willie
[William Upton]
American. Actor
Played Tommy Bradford on TV series "Eight Is Enough," 1977-84.
b. Jul 15, 1960 in Newport Beach, California
Source: *BioIn 12, 21; ConTFT 7; IntMPA 88, 92, 94, 96; LegTOT; VarWW 85; WhoHol 92*

Aardema, Verna Norberg
[Verna Norberg Aardema Vugteveen]
American. Author
Known for rewriting African folk tales for children; won Caldecott Medal, 1976, for *Why Mosquitoes Buzz in People's Ears.*
b. Jun 6, 1911 in New Era, Michigan
Source: *AuBYP 2S, 3; BioIn 9, 12; ChlLR 17; ConAu 3NR, 5R, 18NR; FifBJA; IntAu&W 91; MichAu 80; PseudN 82; SmATA 4, 8AS, 68; WhoAmW 68; WrDr 92*

Aaron
Religious Leader, Biblical Figure
Brother of Moses; founded Hebrew priesthood.
Source: *Baker 78, 84, 92; Benet 96; BioIn 2, 4, 5, 8, 17; BlmGEL; DcBiPP; DcCathB; InB&W 80; LegTOT; NewCol 75; OxDcByz*

Aaron, Hank
[Henry Louis Aaron]
"Hammerin' Henry"; "The Hammer"
American. Baseball Player
Outfielder, Milwaukee Braves (later the Atlanta Braves), 1954-76; broke Babe Ruth's all-time home run record, 1974; also holds ML record for RBIs; Hall of Fame, 1982.
b. Feb 5, 1934 in Mobile, Alabama
Source: *AfrAmAl 6; AfrAmBi 1; AfrAmSG; Ballpl 90; BiDAmSp BB; BioIn 10, 11, 12, 13, 14, 15, 16, 17, 18, 19, 20, 21; BioNews 74; BlueB 76; CelR, 90; ConAu 104, 147; ConBlB 5; ConHero 1; CurBio 58; Ebony 1; EncWB; FacFETw; InB&W 80, 85; LegTOT; NegAl 76, 83, 89; NewYTBE 72, 73; NewYTBS 74, 75, 76; PseudN 82; WebAB 74, 79; WhoAfA 96; WhoAm 82, 94, 95; WhoBlA 80, 92, 94; WhoProB 73; WorAl*

Aaron, Tommy
[Thomas D. Aaron]
American. Golfer
Turned pro, 1960; won Masters, 1973.
b. Feb 22, 1937 in Gainesville, Georgia
Source: *BioIn 10; NewYTBE 73; WhoAm 76; WhoGolf*

Aarons, Ruth Hughes
American. Table Tennis Player
Won US national singles table tennis championship, 1934-37.
b. 1910 in Stamford, Connecticut
d. 1980
Source: *WhoSpor*

Abacha, Sani
Nigerian. Military Leader
Took control of Nigeria in a bloodless coup, November 17, 1993.
b. Sep 20, 1943 in Kano, Nigeria
Source: *ConBlB 11; CurBio 96; News 96, 96-3; WhoWor 96, 97*

Abarbanel, Isaac Ben Jehudah
Portuguese. Theologian
Offered Ferdinand 30,000 ducats to prevent expulsion of Jews, 1492; Biblical writings expressed modern views.
b. 1437 in Lisbon, Portugal
d. 1508 in Venice, Italy
Source: *CasWL; DcEuL; EvEuW; PenC EUR*

Abarbanel, Judah
[Leone Ebreo; Leo Judaeus]
Spanish. Philosopher, Poet
Wrote neo-Platonic *Dialoghi d'Amore,* 1502, talks between love and knowledge.
b. 1460 in Lisbon, Portugal
d. 1535 in Naples, Italy
Source: *BioIn 5, 7; CasWL; DcItL 1, 2; EuAu; OxCSpan*

ABBA
[Benny Andersson; Annifrid Lyngstad-Fredriksson; Agetha Ulvaeus; Bjorn Ulvaeus]
Swedish. Music Group
Formed 1973; hit singles "Dancing Queen," 1977; "Take a Chance on Me," 1978.
Source: *BkPepl; ConMuA 80A; ConMus 12; DcArts; EncPR&S 89; EncRk 88; EncRkSt; HarEnR 86; IlEncRk; NewAmDM; OxCPMus; PenEncP; RkOn 74, 78; RolSEnR 83; WhoRock 81; WhoRocM 82*

Abbado, Claudio
Italian. Conductor
Music director, Milan's La Scala, 1968-86; conducted Vienna Philharmonic, 1971; guest conductor, Chicago Symphony, 1982-85.

b. Jun 26, 1933 in Milan, Italy
Source: *Baker 78, 84, 92; BioIn 6, 8, 9, 10, 11, 12, 13, 14, 16; BriBkM 80; CmOp; CurBio 73; DcArts; FacFETw; IntDcOp; IntWW 74, 75, 76, 77, 78, 79, 80, 81, 82, 83, 89, 91, 93; IntWWM 77, 80, 90; LegTOT; MetOEnc; MusMk; MusSN; NewAmDM; NewEOp 71; NewGrDM 80; NewGrDO; NewYTBE 73; OxDcOp; PenDiMP; Who 74, 82, 83, 85, 88, 90, 92, 94; WhoAm 80, 82, 84, 86, 88, 90, 92, 94, 95, 96, 97; WhoAmM 83; WhoEnt 92; WhoMus 72; WhoOp 76; WhoWor 74, 80, 82, 84, 87, 89, 91, 93, 95, 96, 97; WorAlBi*

Abbas, Ferhat
Algerian. Political Leader
Pres. of Algeria's first provisional government, 1958-61; wrote *Manifesto of the Algerian People,* 1943.
b. Oct 24, 1899 in Taher, Algeria
d. Dec 24, 1985 in Algiers, Algeria
Source: *AnObit 1985; BioIn 5, 6, 7, 14, 15, 17, 20; CurBio 61, 86, 86N; DcPol; EncRev; FacFETw; IntWW 79, 80, 81, 82, 83; McGEWB; MidE 78, 79, 80, 81, 82; PolLCME*

Abbas, Khwaja Ahmad
Indian. Author, Filmmaker, Journalist
Writes travel books, biographies, novels, filmscripts on contemporary Indian life.
b. Jul 6, 1914 in Panipat, India
Source: *ConAu 57; DcFM; DcLEL; DcOrL 2; FilmEn; IntAu&W 76, 77; WhE&EA; WorEFlm; WrDr 92, 94, 96*

Abbas I
"Abbas the Great"
Persian. Ruler
Shah of Persia; saved the Safavid Empire by establishing a standing army; encouraged culture, art, and commerce.
b. Jan 27, 1571
d. Jan 19, 1629 in Mazanderan, Persia
Source: *HarEnMi; WhoMilH 76*

Abbe, Cleveland
American. Meteorologist
First official weather forecaster of US government, 1871-1916.
b. Dec 3, 1838 in New York, New York
d. Oct 28, 1916 in Chevy Chase, Maryland
Source: *AmBi; ApCAB, X; AsBiEn; BbD; BiDAmS; BiD&SB; BiESc; BiInAmS; BioIn 4; DcAmAu; DcAmB; DcNAA; DcScB; HarEnUS; InSci; NatCAB 8; OhA&B; OxCAmH; TwCBDA; WebAB 74, 79; WhAm 1; WorAl; WorAlBi; WorInv*

Abbe, Ernst
German. Physicist
Optics research revolutionized microscope design; discovered "Abbe sine condition."
b. Jan 23, 1840 in Eisenach, Germany
d. Jan 14, 1905 in Jena, Germany
Source: *BiESc; BioIn 2, 7, 12, 14, 18; CamDcSc; DcInv; DcScB; ICPEnP; InSci; LarDcSc; MacBEP; WorInv*

Abbey, Edward
American. Author
Writings champion environmental concerns: *Desert Solitaire,* 1968, *The Monkey Wrench Gang,* 1975; called "the Thoreau of the American West," by Larry McMurtry.
b. Jan 29, 1927 in Home, Pennsylvania
d. Mar 14, 1989 in Tucson, Arizona
Source: *AnObit 1989; Benet 96; BenetAL 91; BioIn 10, 11, 12, 14, 15, 16, 17, 20; ConAu 2NR, 41NR, 45, 128; ConLC 36, 59; CyWA 89; DrAF 76; EncFWF; EncSF 93; EnvEnc; FifWWr; IntAu&W 91, 93; LegTOT; LNinSix; MagSAmL; News 89-3; OxCAmL 95; RAdv 14; ScF&FL 92; TwCWW 82, 91; WhoUSWr 88; WhoWrEP 89; WorAu 1980; WrDr 80, 82, 84, 86, 88*

Abbey, Edwin Austin
American. Artist, Illustrator
Best-known work, mural series *The Quest for the Holy Grail* is in Boston Public Library.
b. Apr 1, 1852 in Philadelphia, Pennsylvania
d. Aug 1, 1911 in London, England
Source: *AmBi; AntBDN B; ApCAB, X; Benet 87; BioIn 1, 3, 5, 11, 12, 15, 17; BriEAA; ClaDrA; DcAmArt; DcAmB; DcBrAr 1; DcBrBI; DcBrWA; DcNaB S2; DcVicP, 2; HarEnUS; IlrAm 1880, A; LinLib L, S; McGDA; NatCAB 15; OxCAmL 65; OxDcArt; TwCBDA; TwCPaSc; WebAB 74, 79; WhAm 1; WhAmArt 85; WorECar*

Abbey, Henry Eugene
American. Manager
Introduced Sarah Bernhardt to America, 1880; opened Abbey's Theatre, 1893.
b. Jun 27, 1846 in Akron, Ohio
d. Oct 17, 1896 in New York, New York
Source: *ApCAB X; BiDAmM; BioIn 7, 8, 9, 10; DcAmB; NewEOp 71; OxCThe 67, 83; TwCBDA; WhAm HS*

Abbot, C(harles) G(reeley)
American. Scientist
Solar studies led to weather pattern prediction.
b. May 31, 1872 in Wilton, New Hampshire
d. Dec 17, 1973 in Riverdale, Massachusetts
Source: *AmMWSc 73P; ApCAB X; BioIn 1, 5, 9, 10; ConAu 45; InSci; OxCAmH; WhAm 6; WhNAA; Who 74*

Abbott, Berenice
American. Photographer
Best known for black and white architectural, documentary images of NYC, 1930s.
b. Jul 17, 1898 in Springfield, Ohio
d. Dec 10, 1991 in Monson, Maine
Source: *AmAu&B; AnObit 1991; BioAmW; BioIn 1, 7, 9, 10, 11, 12, 13, 14, 15, 16, 17, 18, 21; BriEAA; ConAu 106, 136; ConPhot 82, 88, 95; ContDcW 89; CurBio 42, 92N; DcArts; DcTwDes; FacFETw; GayLesB; GoodHs; GrLiveH; ICPEnP; IntDcWB; InWom, SUP; LegTOT; MacBEP; ModArCr 2; NewYTBS 80, 91; NorAmWA; WhAm 10; WhAmArt 85; WhoAm 82, 84, 86, 88, 90; WhoAmW 58, 64; WomArt; WorAl; WorAlBi*

Abbott, Bud
[Abbott and Costello; William A. Abbott]
American. Comedian
Starred in over 35 films with partner, Lou Costello, 1940-65.
b. Oct 2, 1900 in Asbury Park, New Jersey
d. Apr 24, 1974 in Woodland Hills, California
Source: *CmMov; CurBio 41, 74; FilmgC; ForYSC; Funs; HalFC 80; JoeFr; MotPP; MovMk; NewYTBS 74; NotNAT B; OxCFilm; PseudN 82; RadStar; WhAm 6; WhDW; WhScrn 77*

Abbott, Diane (Julie)
English. Politician
First black woman to be elected to the British Parliament, 1987.
b. Sep 27, 1953 in London, England
Source: *BioIn 20; ConBlB 9; Who 88, 90, 92, 94; WhoWomW 91*

Abbott, Edith
American. Author, Educator
Wrote books which became classics in social welfare: *Immigration,* 1924.
b. Sep 26, 1876 in Grand Island, Nebraska
d. Jul 28, 1957 in Grand Island, Nebraska
Source: *AmWomWr; BiDSocW; BioIn 3, 4, 12, 15, 16, 17, 21; ContDcW 89; DcAmB S6; DcAmImH; DcAmSR; FemiWr; HanAmWH; InWom, SUP; NotAW MOD; ObitOF 79; OxCWoWr 95; WhAm 3; WhLit; WomFir; WomSoc; WomWWA 14*

Abbott, George (Francis)
American. Director, Dramatist
Outstanding Broadway figure; won many Tonys including one for *The Pajama Game,* 1955.
b. Jun 25, 1887 in Forestville, New York
d. Jan 31, 1995 in Miami Beach, Florida
Source: *AmCulL; Benet 87, 96; BenetAL 91; BestMus; BiDAmM; BiE&WWA; BioIn 7, 10, 11; BlueB 76; CamGWoT; CelR, 90; CnThe; ConAu 93, 147; ConDr 73, 77, 82, 88; ConTFT 5, 14; CurBio 40, 65; DcTwCCu 1; EncMT; EncWT; Ent; FilmEn; FilmgC; GrStDi; HalFC 80, 84, 88; IntAu&W 77, 91; LegTOT; McGEWD 72, 84; MiSFD 9; ModWD; NewCBMT; News 95, 95-3; NewYTBS 86; NotNAT, A; OxCAmL 83, 95; OxCAmT 84; OxCPMus; OxCThe 67, 83; PlP&P; WhoAm 74, 76, 78, 80, 82, 84, 86, 88, 92, 94, 95; WhoE 93; WhoEnt 92; WhoThe 72, 77, 81; WorAl;*

WorAlBi; WorEFlm; WrDr 76, 80, 82, 84, 86, 88, 90

Abbott, Grace
American. Social Reformer
Influential in having child-labor laws declared unconstitutional, 1918.
b. Nov 17, 1878 in Grand Island, Nebraska
d. Jun 19, 1939 in Chicago, Illinois
Source: *AmDec 1920; AmPeW; AmRef; ApCAB X; BiDInt; BiDSocW; BioIn 1, 2, 3, 4, 12, 15, 16, 21; DcAmB S2; DcAmImH; DcAmSR; DcNAA; EncAB-H 1974, 1996; EncWB; FacFETw; GrLiveH; HanAmWH; InWom, SUP; LibW; NatCAB 29; NotAW; WebAB 74, 79; WhAm 1; WhAmP; WhNAA; WomFir; WomWWA 14, 14A; WorAl; WorAlBi*

Abbott, Gregory
American. Singer
Had number one solo debut album *Shake You Down,* 1986.
Source: *BioIn 15; DrBlPA 90; InB&W 80; SoulM; WhoBlA 88, 90, 92, 94; WhoHol 92*

Abbott, Jack
[Rufus Jack Henry Abbott; Jack Eastman]
American. Author, Murderer
Wrote *In the Belly of the Beast: Letters from Prison,* 1981.
b. Jan 21, 1944 in Oscoda, Michigan
Source: *BioIn 12; ConAu 107; PseudN 82*

Abbott, Jacob
American. Children's Author, Educator
Noted for juvenile didactic tales, the *Rollo* series from 1834; father of Lyman.
b. Nov 15, 1803 in Hallowell, Maine
d. Oct 31, 1879 in Farmington, Maine
Source: *Alli, SUP; AmAu; AmAu&B; AmBi; ApCAB; BbD; BenetAL 91; BiDAmEd; BiD&SB; BioIn 1, 3, 13, 15; CarSB; CnDAL; CyAL 2; CyEd; DcAmAu; DcAmB; DcBiPP; DcEnL; DcLB 1, 42; DcNAA; Drake; HarEnUS; JBA 34; LinLib L; NatCAB 6; OxCAmH; OxCAmL 65, 83, 95; OxCChiL; REnAL; SmATA 22; TwCBDA; TwCChW 89A, 95A; WhAm HS*

Abbott, Jim
[James Anthony Abbott]
American. Baseball Player
One-handed pitcher, Angels, 1988-92; Yankees, 1993—;currently plays with the White Sox; Sullivan Award in 1988 Olympics.
b. Sep 19, 1967 in Flint, Michigan
Source: *Ballpl 90; BioIn 14, 15, 16; ConHero 2; CurBio 95; News 88-3; NewYTBS 89; WhoAm 94, 95, 96, 97; WhoE 95; WhoMW 96; WhoSpor*

Abbott, L(enwood) B(allard)
American. Filmmaker
Won four Oscars, numerous Emmys for special effects cinematography.
b. Jun 13, 1908 in Pasadena, California
d. Sep 28, 1985 in Los Angeles, California
Source: *BioIn 15; ConAu 117; VarWW 85*

Abbott, Lyman
"Benauly"; "Laicus"
American. Religious Leader, Editor
Editor, *Illustrated Christian Weekly,* 1870-93; *Outlook,* 1893-1922.
b. Dec 18, 1835 in Roxbury, Massachusetts
d. Oct 22, 1922 in New York, New York
Source: *Alli, SUP; AmAu&B; AmBi; AmDec 1910; AmLY; AmPeW; ApCAB; BbD; BenetAL 91; BiDAmJo; BiD&SB; BiDMoPL; BioIn 2, 3, 6, 9, 11, 16, 17, 19; CyAL 2; DcAmAu; DcAmB; DcAmReB 1, 2; DcEnL; DcLB 79; DcNAA; Drake; EncAJ; EncARH; HarEnUS; LinLib L, S; McGEWB; NatCAB 1; OxCAmH; OxCAmL 65, 83, 95; PseudAu; PseudN 82; RelLAm 91; REn; REnAL; TwCA, SUP; TwCBDA; WebAB 74, 79; WhAm 1; WhAmP; WhLit*

Abbott, Margaret I.
American. Golfer
First American woman to win an Olympic gold medal, 1900.
b. Jun 15, 1878 in Calcutta, India
d. Jun 10, 1955
Source: *WhoSpor*

Abbott, Scott
Canadian. Journalist, Inventor
With Chris and John Haney, invented board game Trivial Pursuit, 1979.
Source: *BioIn 14*

Abbott and Costello
[Bud Abbott; Lou Costello]
American. Comedy Team
Starred in over 35 comedy films, 1940-65; known for baseball comedy routine "Who's on First?"
Source: *Ballpl 90; BioIn 15, 16, 17; CurBio 41, 59; DcArts; EncAFC; EncVaud; FacFETw; FilmEn; ForYSC; Funs; GrMovC; IntDcF 1-3, 2-3; JoeFr; MotPP; NewYTBS 74; ObitOF 79; SaTiSS; WhoCom; WhoHol 92, B*

ABC
[Martin Fry; David Palmer; Stephen Singleton; Mark White]
English. Music Group
Hit albums include *Lexicon of Love,* 1983; *How to be a Zillionaire,* 1985.
Source: *Alli; BioIn 15; ChhPo, S1; ConAu X; DrAPF 85, 87, 89, 91, 93, 97; Dun&B 88, 90; EncRk 88; EncRkSt; HarEnR 86; OxCCan; PenEncP; RkOn 85; WhoAm 96, 97; WhoHol 92; WhoRocM 82*

Abdallah, Ahmed
Sudanese. Political Leader
President of Comoros, 1975, 1978-90.
b. 1919
Source: *AfSS 79, 80, 81, 82; IntWW 79, 80, 81, 82, 83; WhAm 11; WhoWor 80, 82, 84, 87, 89*

Abdnor, James S
American. Politician, Rancher
Conservative Rep. senator from SD who ousted George McGovern, 1980.
b. Feb 13, 1923 in Kennebec, South Dakota
Source: *AlmAP 80; CngDr 79; WhoAm 84; WhoGov 75; WhoMW 78*

Abdul, Paula (Julie)
[Mrs. Brad Beckerman]
American. Singer, Dancer, Choreographer
TV, music, video, and movie choreographer; platinum album *Forever Your Girl,*1988, with hit "Straight Up;" was married to actor Emilio Estevez.
b. Jun 19, 1963 in Los Angeles, California
Source: *WhoAm 94, 95, 96, 97; WhoAmW 95*

Abdul, Raoul
American. Author, Opera Singer
Editorial asst. to Langston Hughes; organized first chamber music concerts in Harlem, 1958.
b. Nov 7, 1929 in Cleveland, Ohio
Source: *BioIn 11, 16; BlkAull, 92; BlkOpe; ChhPo S2; ConAu 29R; DrBlPA, 90; SelBAAf; SelBAAu; SmATA 12; WhoAfA 96; WhoBlA 75, 77, 80, 85, 88, 90, 92, 94; WhoE 77, 79, 81*

Abdu'l-Baha
[Abbas Effendi]
Persian. Religious Leader
Eldest son, successor to Baha'u'llah; wrote first history of Baha'i movement, 1886.
b. May 23, 1844 in Tehran, Persia
d. Nov 28, 1921 in Haifa, Palestine
Source: *BiDAmCu; CasWL; DcAmReB 1*

Abdulhamid II
Turkish. Ruler
Autocratic Ottoman Sultan 1876-1909; deposed 1909.
b. Sep 21, 1842 in Constantinople, Ottoman Empire
d. Feb 10, 1918 in Constantinople, Ottoman Empire

Abdul-Jabbar, Kareem
[Lewis Ferdinand Alcindor, Jr.]
American. Basketball Player, Sportscaster
Center, Milwaukee, 1969-75; LA, 1975-89; held all-time leader records in more than 20 categories during 20 season career; six-time MVP; all-time points leader (38,387).
b. Apr 16, 1947 in New York, New York

Source: *AfrAmAl 6; AfrAmBi 1; AfrAmSG; BasBi; BiDAmSp BK; BioIn 9, 10, 11, 12, 13, 14, 15, 16, 17, 18, 19, 20, 21; BkPepl; BlkWr 2; CelR; ConAu 139; ConBlB 8; ConTFT 13; CurBio 67; Ebony 1; FacFETw; LegTOT; NewYTBS 74, 76, 82, 84, 85; OfNBA 87; WhoAfA 96; WhoAm 74, 76, 78, 80, 82, 84, 86, 88, 90, 92, 94, 95, 96, 97; WhoBbl 73; WhoBlA 80, 85, 88, 90, 92, 94; WhoHol 92; WhoSpor; WhoWest 87, 89, 92, 94; WorAl; WorAlBi*

Abdullah, Mohammad, Sheik
"Lion of Kashmir"
Indian. Political Leader
Struggled to free country from political domination of India.
b. Dec 5, 1905 in Soura, Kashmir
d. Sep 8, 1982 in Srinagar, Kashmir
Source: *BioIn 3, 4, 5, 6, 7, 8, 10, 13, 20; CurBio 52, 83, 83N; FarE&A 80, 81; IntWW 79, 80, 81; NewYTBS 82*

Abdullah Ibn Hussein
Jordanian. Ruler
King of Jordan, 1946-51; supported pro-British policies; assassinated.
b. 1882 in Mecca, Arabia
d. Jul 20, 1951 in Jerusalem, Israel
Source: *CurBio 48, 51; DcTwHis; FacFETw; HisEAAC; NewCol 75; PolLCME*

Abe, Isao
Japanese. Political Leader
Founder, Japanese Socialist Party; introduced baseball to Japan.
b. Feb 4, 1865? in Tokyo, Japan
d. Feb 10, 1949 in Tokyo, Japan
Source: *ObitOF 79*

Abe, Kobo
[Kimifusa Abe]
Japanese. Author
Avant-garde writer whose surrealistic works include *The Woman in the Dunes,* 1964; *The Face of Another,* 1966.
b. Mar 7, 1924 in Tokyo, Japan
d. Jan 22, 1993 in Tokyo, Japan
Source: *AnObit 1993; FacFETw; FarE&A 78, 79, 80, 81; IntAu&W 76, 77, 89; IntWW 74, 75, 76, 77, 78, 79, 80, 81, 82, 83, 89, 91; LegTOT; MajTwCW; MakMC; McGEWD 84; NewEScF; NewYTBS 74, 79, 93; RAdv 13-2; ScF&FL 1, 92; ScFSB; TwCSFW 81A, 86A, 91A; WhAm 11; WhoSciF; WhoWor 74, 76, 78, 82, 84, 87, 89, 91, 93; WorAu 1950*

A'Becket, Thomas, Saint
[Thomas of Canterbury; Thomas of London; Thomas Becket]
English. Religious Leader
Archbishop of Canterbury, 1162-70; conflict with Henry II, martyrdom were subject of T. S. Eliot's *Murder in the Cathedral,* 1935.
b. Dec 21, 1118 in London, England
d. Dec 29, 1170 in Canterbury, England
Source: *Alli; BiD&SB; BlmGEL; DcNaB; HisWorL; McGEWB; NewC; NewCol 75; OxCEng 85, 95; OxCLaw; WebBD 83*

A'Beckett, Gilbert Abbott
English. Editor, Dramatist
Wrote humorous histories of England, Rome, 1848-52.
b. Feb 17, 1811 in London, England
d. Aug 30, 1856 in Boulogne-sur-Mer, France
Source: *Alli; BbD; BiD&SB; BritAu 19; CasWL; Chambr 3; DcEnA; DcEnL; EvLB; NewC; OxCEng 67*

Abel
Biblical Figure
Son of Adam and Eve; killed by brother Cain.
Source: *Benet 96; BioIn 1, 4, 5, 6, 7, 10, 17; DcBiPP; DcCathB; DcNaB; NewCol 75; NewGrDM 80*

Abel, Elie
Canadian. Broadcast Journalist, Educator
Won George Foster Peabody Award for outstanding radio news, 1968.
b. Oct 17, 1920 in Montreal, Quebec, Canada
Source: *BiDAmJo; CanWW 31, 70, 79, 80, 81, 83, 89; ConAu 8NR, 36NR, 61; EncTwCJ; LEduc 74; WhoAm 74, 76, 78, 80, 82, 84, 86, 88, 90, 92, 94, 95, 96, 97; WhoE 74; WhoWor 74, 76; WhoWorJ 72; WrDr 92, 94, 96*

Abel, I(orwith) W(ilbur)
"Abe"
American. Labor Union Official
Co-founder, pres., United Steelworkers of America, 1965-77.
b. Aug 11, 1908 in Magnolia, Ohio
d. Aug 10, 1987 in Malvern, Ohio
Source: *BiDAmLL; BioIn 7, 8, 10, 11, 12, 15, 16; BioNews 74; BlueB 76; BusPN; ConAu 105, 123; CurBio 65, 87; EncABHB 9; IntWW 74, 75; NewYTBE 71; PolProf J, NF; WhoAm 76, 78; WhoFI 75; WhoGov 72, 75; WhoLab 76; WhoWor 74; WorAl*

Abel, John Jacob
American. Scientist, Educator
Pharmacologist noted for endocrine research; isolated adrenalin, insulin in crystal form.
b. May 19, 1857 in Cleveland, Ohio
d. May 26, 1938 in Baltimore, Maryland
Source: *AmBi; BiESc; BioIn 1, 3, 4, 7, 11, 18; CamDcSc; DcAmB S2; DcAmMeB 84; DcScB; FacFETw; InSci; LarDcSc; NatCAB 28; OxCAmH; OxCMed 86; WhAm 1; WhNAA; WorScD*

Abel, Karl Friedrich
German. Musician, Composer
Considered last great viola da gamba virtuoso.
b. Dec 22, 1723 in Cothen, Germany
d. Jun 20, 1787 in London, England
Source: *Baker 84; BioIn 4; BriBkM 80; EncEnl; MusMk; NewGrDM 80; OxCMus*

Abel, Niels Henrik
Norwegian. Mathematician
A major creator of modern math; pioneered in elliptic functions, algebraic geometry.
b. Aug 5, 1802 in Findoe, Norway
d. Apr 6, 1829 in Froland, Norway
Source: *AsBiEn; BiESc; BioIn 4, 8; CelCen; DcBiPP; DcScB; InSci; LarDcSc; LinLib L, S; NewCol 75; WebBD 83; WhDW; WorScD*

Abel, Rudolf Ivanovich
[Mark; Martin Collins; Emil R Goldfus; Andrew Kayotis]
Russian. Spy
Master spy sentenced to 30 years in US prison for espionage; exchanged for Francis Gary Powers, 1962.
b. 1902 in Saint Petersburg, Russia
d. Nov 15, 1971 in Moscow, Union of Soviet Socialist Republics
Source: *BiDSovU; BioIn 4, 5, 6, 8, 9, 10, 12; EncE 75; NewYTBE 71; ObitOF 79; PseudN 82; SpyCS; WhDW; WorAl*

Abel, Sid(ney Gerald)
"Bootnose"
Canadian. Hockey Player, Hockey Coach
Center, 1938-54, mostly with Detroit; on Production Line with Gordie Howe, Ted Lindsay; won Hart Trophy, 1949; coached 16 yrs., mostly with Detroit, 1957-70; Hall of Fame, 1969.
b. Feb 22, 1918 in Melville, Saskatchewan, Canada
Source: *HocEn; LegTOT; WhoHcky 73*

Abel, Taffy
[Clarence J. Abel]
American. Hockey Player
First American to carry the flag in the opening ceremonies of the Winter Olympics; first American Olympic athlete to play with a Stanley Cup winning team, the 1928 New York Rangers.
b. May 28, 1900 in Sault Sainte Marie, Michigan
d. Aug 1, 1964
Source: *WhoSpor*

Abel, Walter Charles
American. Actor
Has appeared in over 80 films including *The Three Musketeers,* 1934; *Man Without a Country,* 1973.
b. Jun 6, 1898 in Saint Paul, Minnesota
d. Mar 26, 1987 in Chester, Connecticut
Source: *BiE&WWA; BlueB 76; ConTFT 5; FilmEn; FilmgC; ForYSC; HalFC 80; HolCA; IntMPA 81; MotPP; MovMk; NotNAT; Vers B; WhoAm 74, 76, 78, 80, 82; WhoHol A; WhoThe 77, 81*

Abelard, Pierre
French. Author, Theologian, Educator
Controversial writings, especially *Sic et Non,* explained theories of logic; best known for tragic love affair with Heloise.
b. 1079 in Pallet, France
d. Apr 21, 1142 in Chalon-sur-Saone, France
Source: *BbD; Benet 87, 96; BiD&SB; BioIn 1, 2, 3, 4, 5, 6, 7, 8, 9, 10, 11, 12; CasWL; ChhPo S2; ClMLC 11; CyWA 58; DcBiPP; DcEuL; DcScB; EuAu; EvEuW; LegTOT; LinLib L, S; LngCEL; McGEWB; MusMk; NewC; OxCEng 67; OxCFr; PenC EUR; RComWL; REn; WebBD 83; WorAl; WorAlBi*

Abell, George O(gden)
American. Astronomer, Author
Discovered the Abell Galaxy; hosted British astronomy TV series.
b. Mar 1, 1927 in Los Angeles, California
d. Oct 7, 1983 in Encino, California
Source: *AmMWSc 73P, 76P, 79, 82; BioIn 13; ConAu 3NR, 9R, 111; WhAm 8; WhoAm 74, 76, 78, 80, 82; WhoWest 82, 84; WhoWor 74; WrDr 76, 80, 82, 84, 86*

Abelson, Philip Hauge
American. Chemist
Co-discoverer of neptunium; uranium-separation process contributed to atomic bomb development; editor, *Science,* 1962-84.
b. Apr 27, 1913 in Tacoma, Washington
Source: *AmMWSc 73P, 76P, 79, 82, 86, 89, 92, 95; AsBiEn; BiESc; BioIn 3, 6, 7, 10, 11, 12; BlueB 76; ConAu 107; FacFETw; IntWW 74, 75, 76, 77, 78, 79, 80, 81, 82, 83, 89, 91, 93; LarDcSc; McGMS 80; NotTwCS; WhoAm 74, 76, 78, 80, 82, 84, 88, 90, 92, 94, 95, 96, 97; WhoE 95; WhoScEn 94, 96; WhoWor 74; WorScD*

Abercrombie, James Smither
American. Businessman, Philanthropist
Invented blow-out valve, nucleus of one of largest oil-tool equipment companies in US.
b. Jul 7, 1891 in Huntsville, Texas
d. Jan 7, 1975 in Houston, Texas
Source: *BioIn 15; NatCAB 59*

Abercrombie, Josephine
"Dragon Lady with a Drawl"; "Mrs. A"
American. Boxing Promoter
Socialite who founded Houston Boxing Association, 1982; daughter of J. S. Abercrombie.
b. 1925 in Kingston, Jamaica
Source: *ConNews 87-2; NewYTBS 86*

Abercrombie, Lascelles
"The Georgian Laureate"
English. Author, Poet, Critic
Writings include *Thomas Hardy: A Critical Study,* 1912.
b. Jan 9, 1881 in Cheshire, England
d. Oct 27, 1938 in London, England
Source: *Benet 87; BioIn 2, 7, 13; CamGEL; CamGLE; Chambr 3; ChhPo, S1; ConAu 112; DcLB 19; DcLEL; DcNaB 1931; EncWL; EvLB; GrWrEL P; LinLib L; LngCTC; ModBrL; NewC; NewCBEL; OxCEng 67, 85, 95; OxCTwCP; PenC ENG; PseudN 82; REn; RfGEnL 91; RGTwCWr; TwCA, SUP; TwCWr; WebE&AL; WhE&EA; WhLit; WhoLA; WhThe*

Abercrombie, Michael
English. Biologist, Educator, Editor
Discovered important factors in cell behavior.
b. Aug 14, 1912 in Ryton, England
d. May 28, 1979 in Cambridge, England
Source: *Au&Wr 71; BioIn 13; BlueB 76; ConAu 115; DcNaB 1971; IntWW 74, 75, 76, 77, 78, 79; WhE&EA; Who 74; WhoWor 74, 76, 78*

Abercromby, Ralph, Sir
Scottish. Military Leader
General; commanded British forces in West Indies, capturing many islands, 1795-97; credited with restoring army's discipline.
b. Oct 7, 1734 in Tullibody, Scotland
d. Mar 21, 1801 in Alexandria, Egypt
Source: *CelCen; CmFrR; DcBiPP; DcNaB; EncAR; HarEnMi; HisDBrE; NewCol 75; WebBD 83; WhAmRev; WhoMilH 76; WorAl; WorAlBi*

Aberhart, William
Canadian. Political Leader
Founded Social Credit Party in Canada; premier of Alberta, 1935-43.
b. Dec 30, 1878 in Hibbard Township, Ontario, Canada
d. May 23, 1943 in Calgary, Alberta, Canada
Source: *BioIn 1, 5, 7, 9, 17; DcNaB 1941; MacDCB 78; McGEWB; OxCCan; RelLAm 91; TwCSAPR*

Abernathy, Ralph David
American. Clergy, Civil Rights Leader
Close friend of Martin Luther King, Jr; succeeded King as pres. of SCLC, 1968-77; wrote controversial autobiography *And the Walls Came Tumbling Down,* 1989.
b. Mar 11, 1926 in Linden, Alabama
d. Apr 17, 1990 in Atlanta, Georgia
Source: *AfrAmBi 1; AmSocL; BlueB 76; CivR 74; ConAu 131, 133; ConBlB 1; CurBio 68, 90; Ebony 1; EncAACR; EncWB; FacFETw; InB&W 80, 85; IntWW 74, 75, 76, 77, 78, 79, 80, 81, 82, 83, 89; LinLib S; NewYTBS 90; PolProf E, J, K, NF; RelLAm 91; WhAm 10; WhoAm 74, 76, 78, 80, 82, 84, 86, 88, 90; WhoBlA 75, 77, 80, 85, 88, 90, 92N; WhoRel 75, 77, 92; WhoSSW 73; WhoWor 74, 78, 80*

Abernethy, Robert Gordon
American. Journalist, Editor
Science editor, NBC News, 1965-66; wrote *Introduction to Tomorrow,* 1966.
b. Nov 5, 1927 in Geneva, Switzerland
Source: *BioIn 10; ConAu 21R; SmATA 5; WhoAm 74, 76, 78, 80, 82*

Abington, Fanny
[Frances Barton]
English. Actor
Street singer, became leading actress of her day; starred at Drury Lane, 1764-82; created Lady Teazle role, 1777.
b. 1737
d. Mar 4, 1815 in London, England
Source: *CnThe; DcNaB; EncWT; LegTOT; NewC; NotNAT A; OxCThe 67; WebBD 83*

Ableman, Paul
English. Dramatist
Plays include *Green Julia,* 1965; *Methuen,* 1966; *Blue Comedy,* 1968.
b. Jun 13, 1927 in Leeds, England
Source: *BioIn 10; ConAu 12NR, 61; ConBrDr; ConDr 73, 77, 82, 88, 93; ConNov 72, 76, 82; ConTFT 11; DcLEL 1940; EncSF, 93; IntAu&W 76, 77, 82, 91, 93; ScF&FL 1, 2; ScFSB; WrDr 76, 80, 82, 84, 86, 88, 90, 92, 94, 96*

Abney, William de Wiveleslie, Sir
English. Chemist
Advanced photographic chemistry; pioneered in color photography.
b. Jul 24, 1843 in Derby, England
d. Dec 3, 1920 in Folkestone, England
Source: *DcScB; WebBD 83; WhLit*

Abourezk, James George
American. Lawyer, Politician
Dem. senator from SD, 1973-78.
b. Feb 24, 1931 in Woods, South Dakota
Source: *AlmAP 78; BiDrUSC 89; CngDr 77; IntWW 83; NewYTBS 77; WhoAm 84; WhoAmL 79; WhoAmP 85; WhoGov 77; WhoMW 78; WhoWor 78*

About, Edmond-Francois-Valentin
French. Author
Wrote satirical, political works; novels include *Le Roi des Montagnes,* 1856.
b. Feb 14, 1828 in Dierize, France
d. Jan 16, 1885 in Paris, France
Source: *BbD; BiD&SB; CasWL; ClDMEL 47; DcBiA; DcEuL; EncSF; OxCFr; ScF&FL 1*

Abplanalp, Robert H
American. Inventor
Invented aerosol valve, 1949.
b. 1923 in New York, New York
Source: *BioIn 12; NewYTBE 73; PolProf NF*

Abraham
[Abram]
"Father of the Faithful"; "Friend of God"
Biblical Figure
Founder, first patriarch of Judaism who was commanded to sacrifice son Isaac as test of faith.

Source: *Benet 96; BioIn 1, 2, 3, 4, 5, 6, 7, 8, 9, 10, 11, 12, 16, 17, 18, 20, 21; DcCanB 9; DcCathB; DcScB; Dis&D; EncEarC; InB&W 80; JeHun; LngCEL; McGDA; PseudAu; REn; WhDW; WhNaAH; WorAl; WorAlBi*

Abraham, F(ahrid) Murray
American. Actor
Won Oscar for *Amadeus*, 1984.
b. Oct 24, 1940 in El Paso, Texas
Source: *ConTFT 1, 4; IntMPA 86; VarWW 85*

Abraham, Spencer
[Edward Spencer Abraham]
American. Politician, Lawyer
Co-chm., Nat. Rep. Congressional Com., 1990—; chm. Michigan Rep. Party, 1983-91; Rep. senator from MI, 1995—.
b. Jun 12, 1952 in Lansing, Michigan
Source: *AlmAP 96; BioIn 20, 21; CngDr 95; News 91; WhoAm 96, 97; WhoAmP 85; WhoMW 96*

Abrahams, Doris Cole
American. Producer
Won Tonys for *Equus*, 1975; *Travesties*, 1976.
b. Jan 29, 1925 in New York, New York
Source: *ConTFT 5; VarWW 85; WhoAm 78, 80, 82; WhoThe 72, 77, 81*

Abrahams, Harold
English. Track Athlete
Long jumper, short distance runner; won gold medal, 1920 Olympics; subject of film *Chariots of Fire*, 1982.
b. Dec 15, 1899 in Bedford, England
d. Jan 14, 1978 in London, England
Source: *BioIn 9, 10; WhoTr&F 73*

Abrahams, Jim
American. Director
Co-creator of hit film *Airplane*, 1980.
b. May 10, 1944 in Milwaukee, Wisconsin
Source: *BioIn 12; ConAu 138; ConTFT 4, 15; DirCG 82; IntMPA 86, 88, 92, 94, 96; MiSFD 9; NewYTBS 80*

Abrahams, Peter Henry
South African. Author
Novel, *Mine Boy*, 1946, first to address oppression of South African blacks; later works include *The Path of Thunder*, 1948, and *Wild Conquest*, 1950.
b. Mar 19, 1919 in Vrededorn, South Africa
Source: *Benet 87; BioIn 14; BlkWr 1; CamGEL; CamGLE; ConAu 26NR; ConNov 91; CyWA 89; DcAfHiB 86; FacFETw; InB&W 85; IntAu&W 91; LiExTwC; MajTwCW; RAdv 13-2; RfGEnL 91; WrDr 92*

Abram, Morris Berthold
American. Civil Rights Leader, Lawyer
First to head Peace Corps legal department, 1961.
b. Jun 19, 1918 in Fitzgerald, Georgia
Source: *BioIn 7, 8; ConAu 108; CurBio 65; JeAmHC; WhoAm 74, 76, 78, 80, 82, 84, 86, 88, 90, 92, 94, 95, 96, 97; WhoAmL 79, 83, 85; WhoAmP 73, 75, 77, 79, 81, 83, 85, 87, 89, 91, 93; WhoE 74; WhoWor 74, 80, 82, 93, 97; WhoWorJ 72*

Abramovitz, Max
American. Architect
Designed US Embassy Bldg., Rio de Janeiro; Philharmonic Hall at Lincoln Center.
b. May 23, 1908 in Chicago, Illinois
Source: *BioIn 5; BlueB 76; ConArch 80, 87, 94; EncMA; IntWW 74, 75, 76, 77, 78, 79, 80, 81, 82, 83, 89, 91, 93; MacEA; McGDA; WhoAm 74, 76, 78, 80, 82, 84, 86, 88, 90, 92, 94, 95, 96, 97; WhoAmA 73, 76, 78, 80; WhoArch; WhoE 74, 75, 77, 79, 81, 83, 85, 86, 89, 91, 93, 95, 97; WhoScEn 96; WhoWor 74, 76, 78, 91; WhoWorJ 72, 78*

Abrams, Creighton Williams
American. Army Officer
Commanding general, US forces in Vietnam, 1968-72.
b. Sep 15, 1914 in Springfield, Massachusetts
d. Sep 4, 1974 in Washington, District of Columbia
Source: *BioIn 6, 7, 8, 9, 10, 11, 12, 16, 18; CurBio 68, 74; DcAmB S9; FacFETw; HarEnMi; IntWW 74; LinLib S; NewCol 75; NewYTBS 74; WebAMB; WhAm 6; WhoAm 74; WorAl; WorDWW*

Abrams, Elliott
American. Government Official
Assistant Secretary of State, 1981-85; was declared *persona non grata* on Capitol Hill when he misrepresented the government's role in the Iran-Contra Affair; senior fellow, Hudson Institute, 1990—.
b. Jan 24, 1948 in New York, New York
Source: *BioIn 12, 13; ConAu 140; ConNews 87-1; CurBio 88; DcAmDH 89; NewYTBS 81, 85, 86, 88; WhoAm 82, 84, 86, 88, 90, 92, 94, 95, 96, 97; WhoAmL 87; WhoAmP 79, 81, 83, 85, 87, 89, 91, 93, 95; WhoEmL 89, 91, 93*

Abrams, George H. J.
[Ha-Doh-Jus]
American. Anthropologist
Involved in the analysis of the remains of the Cornplanter Cemetery, 1965, before it was flooded to create the Kinzua Dam.
b. May 4, 1939 in Salamanca, New York
Source: *BioIn 21*

Abrams, Harry Nathan
English. Publisher
Popularized high-quality art books.
b. Dec 8, 1904 in London, England
d. Nov 25, 1979 in New York, New York
Source: *AmAu&B; BioIn 2, 4, 5, 7, 9, 10, 12; ConAu 93; CurBio 58, 80; NewYTBS 79; WhAm 7; WhoAm 78; WhoAmA 78; WhoWorJ 72*

Abramson, Harold A(lexander)
American. Psychiatrist
One of first US researchers to study medical applications of LSD.
b. Nov 27, 1899 in New York, New York
d. Sep 29, 1980 in Cold Spring Harbor, New York
Source: *AnObit 1980; BiDrAPA 77; BioIn 12; ConAu 102; NewYTBS 84; WhAm 7; WhoAm 74, 76, 78, 80; WhoWor 74, 76, 78, 80*

Abravanel, Maurice
Turkish. Conductor
Conducted Utah Symphony, 1947-79; won 1950 Tony for conducting *Regina*.
b. Jan 6, 1903 in Salonika, Greece
d. Sep 22, 1993 in Salt Lake City, Utah
Source: *AnObit 1993; Baker 78, 84, 92; BiE&WWA; BioIn 2, 4, 10, 11, 12, 16, 19; BriBkM 80; ConTFT 1, 12; IntWWM 85, 90; MetOEnc; NewAmDM; NewGrDA 86; NewGrDM 80; NewYTBS 77, 93; NotNAT; PenDiMP; WhAm 11; WhoAm 74, 76, 78, 80, 82, 84, 86, 88, 90, 92, 94; WhoAmM 83; WhoEnt 92; WhoWest 74, 76, 78, 80, 94; WhoWor 74*

Abruzzi, Luigi Amedeo
[Duke of Abruzzi; Prince of Savoy-Aosta]
Italian. Explorer, Military Leader
Explored N Pole, 1899; commanded Italian fleet, WW I; helped colonize Italian Somaliland.
b. Jan 29, 1873 in Madrid, Spain
d. Mar 18, 1933 in Duca degli Abruzzi, Italian Somaliland
Source: *BioIn 1, 5, 9; LinLib L, S; NewCol 75*

Abruzzo, Ben(jamine Lou)
American. Balloonist, Aviator
Among first to make trans-Atlantic balloon flight, 1978.
b. Jun 9, 1930 in Rockford, Illinois
d. Feb 11, 1985 in Albuquerque, New Mexico
Source: *BioIn 11, 14; ConAu 115; WhoWest 84*

Abs, Hermann J(osef)
German. Banker
Adviser to West German chancellor Adenauer; vice-chairman, Marshall Plan; negotiated settlement of German debt and war reparations, 1952-53.
b. Oct 15, 1901
d. Feb 5, 1994 in Bad Soden, Germany
Source: *CurBio 94N; EncTR 91; WhoFI 74, 75, 77, 79; WhoWor 74*

Abse, Dannie
Welsh. Author
Wrote award-winning play *House of Cowards,* 1960.
b. Sep 22, 1923 in Cardiff, Wales
Source: *Au&Wr 71; Benet 87, 96; BioIn 10, 13; BlmGEL; CamGLE; ChhPo S1; ConAu 1AS, 4NR, 46NR, 53; ConBrDr; ConDr 73, 77, 82, 88, 93; ConLC 7, 29; ConNov 76, 82; ConPo 70, 75, 80, 85, 91, 96; DcLB 27; DcLEL, 1940; DrAP 75; DrAPF 80; IntAu&W 76, 77, 91, 93; IntWW 89, 91, 93; IntWWP 77; ModBrL S1, S2; NewCBEL; OxCEng 85, 95; OxCLiW 86; OxCTwCP; RGTwCWr; WhE&EA; Who 82, 83, 85, 88, 90, 92, 94; WorAu 1950; WrDr 76, 80, 82, 84, 86, 88, 90, 92, 94, 96*

Abu Bakr
Arab. Religious Leader
Father-in-law, first convert, successor of Mohammed; helped make Islam a world religion.
b. 573 in Mecca, Arabia
d. Aug 634
Source: *BioIn 9, 11, 12, 20; HarEnMi; LuthC 75; McGEWB; NewCol 75; WhDW; WorAl; WorAlBi*

Abu Daoud
[Muhamman Daoud Audeh; Tarik Shakir Mahdi]
Palestinian. Terrorist
Most wanted, feared int'l. criminal of 1980s; thought responsible for many terrorist attacks.
b. 1937
Source: *BioIn 11, 12; PseudN 82*

Abu Madi, Iliya
Arab. Poet, Journalist
Publisher, Arabic daily newspaper, *as-Samir,* 1936-57; collections of poetry include, *al-Jadawil.*
b. 1890 in Al-Muhaydithah, Lebanon
d. 1957 in New York, New York

Abu Salma
[Abd al-Karim al-Karmi]
"Father of Peace"; "Palestine Poet"
Palestinian. Poet
Voice of exiled Palestinians; wrote *The Homeless,* 1964.
b. 1906 in Tulkarm City, Palestine
d. Sep 13, 1980 in Washington, District of Columbia
Source: *AnObit 1980*

Abzug, Bella (Savitsky)
"Battling Bella"
American. Lawyer, Politician
First Jewish congresswoman, Dem. from NY; wide-brimmed hats are trademark.
b. Jul 24, 1920 in New York, New York
Source: *AmDec 1970; AmPolW 80; AmWomM; BioIn 9, 10, 11, 12, 13; BioNews 75; BlueB 76; CelR; CngDr 74; ConAu 104; ContDcW 89; CurBio 71; EncWHA; FacFETw; GoodHs; GrLiveH; HanAmWH; HerW 84; IntDcWB; InWom SUP; LegTOT; LibW; LNinSix; NewYTBE 71; PolProf NF; WhoAm 82; WhoAmP 73; WhoAmW 81; WhoE 74; WhoGov 72; WomPO 76, 78; WorAl; WorAlBi*

Accoramboni, Vittoria
Italian. Noblewoman
Noted for her beauty, tragic life; John Webster told tale in play *The White Devil,* 1612.
b. 1557
d. Dec 22, 1585 in Padua, Italy
Source: *InWom; NewC; REn; WebBD 83*

AC-DC
[Mark Evans; Brian Johnson; Phil Rudd; Bon Scott; Cliff Williams; Angus Young; Malcolm Young]
Australian. Music Group
Heavy-metal band formed 1973; had number one album in US *For Those About to Rock,* 1981; hit single "Highway to Hell," 1979; Los Angeles mass-murderer Richard Ramirez (The Night Stalker) cited the album *Fly on the Wall,* as his Satanic inspiration.
Source: *Alli SUP; BiDrAPA 89; BioIn 12; ChhPo S1; ConAu 65; ConMuA 80A; DcLP 87B; Dun&B 86; HarEnR 86; IntAu&W 76X; IntWWM 80, 85, 90; RolSEnR 83; SmATA 19; St&PR 96, 97; Who 85, 88, 90, 92, 94; WhoAmM 83; WhoEnt 92; WhoRock 81; WhoRocM 82; WhoVenC 86; WhoWest 80; WomWMM*

Ace
[Fran Byrne; Parul Carrack; Tex Comer; Phil Harris; Alan King]
English. Music Group
London pop-rock band formed 1973-76; hit single, "How Long," 1973.
Source: *AmPS A, B; BgBands 74; CurBio 70; EncRkSt; ForYSC; IlEncRk; IntAu&W 77X; IntMPA 75, 76, 77, 78, 79, 80, 81, 82; InWom SUP; JoeFr; MotPP; NewYTBS 81, 93, 95; RkOn 78; RolSEnR 83; WhoHol A; WhoRock 81; WhoRocM 82*

Ace, Goodman
American. Radio Performer
Co-starred with wife, Jane, in radio comedy, "Easy Aces," 1928-45.
b. Jan 15, 1899 in Kansas City, Missouri
d. Mar 25, 1982 in New York, New York
Source: *BioIn 1, 3, 4, 5, 6, 10, 12, 13, 19; CelR; ConAu 61, 106; CurBio 48, 82, 82N; JoeFr; LegTOT; NewYTBS 82, 84; NewYTET; RadStar; SaTiSS; WhAm 10; WhoCom*

Ace, Jane Sherwood
[Mrs. Goodman Ace]
American. Actor
Starred with husband in radio comedy, "Easy Aces," 1928-45.
b. Oct 12, 1905 in Kansas City, Missouri
d. Nov 11, 1974 in New York, New York
Source: *BioIn 1, 10; CurBio 48, 75; InWom, SUP; NewYTBS 74; ObitOF 79; WhScrn 77*

Ace, Johnny
[Johnny Marshall Alexander, Jr.]
American. Singer
"Pledging My Love," 1955, became hit after his accidental death while playing Russian Roulette.
b. Jun 9, 1929 in Memphis, Tennessee
d. Dec 25, 1954 in Houston, Texas
Source: *BiDAmM; BioIn 19; EncRk 88; EncRkSt; InB&W 80; LegTOT; NewAmDM; NewGrDA 86; PenEncP; RkOn 74, 78; RolSEnR 83; SoulM; WhoRock 81*

Acevedo Diaz, Eduardo
Uruguayan. Author, Political Activist
Considered founder of the literary movement, "gauchismo."
b. Apr 20, 1851 in Villa de la Union, Uruguay
d. Jun 18, 1924 in Buenos Aires, Argentina
Source: *BioIn 16; CasWL; DcSpL; EncLatA; EncWL; LatAmWr; LinLib L; OxCSpan; PenC AM; REn*

Achab
Ruler
Seventh king of Israel; married to Jezebel.
d. 853
Source: *Chambr 1*

Achard, Franz Karl
German. Chemist
Developed method of crystallizing beet sugar, 1799.
b. Apr 28, 1753 in Berlin, Germany
d. Apr 20, 1821 in Kunern, Silesia
Source: *BioIn 14; CelCen; DcBiPP; DcScB; InSci; LarDcSc; NewCol 75; WebBD 83*

Achard, Marcel
[Marcel Auguste Ferreol]
French. Dramatist, Director
Plays include *I Know My Love,* 1952.
b. Jul 5, 1900 in Foyles Lyon, France
d. Sep 4, 1974 in Paris, France
Source: *BiE&WWA; CasWL; ClDMEL 47; CnMD; ConAu 53, 93; DcFM; EncWL; EvEuW; McGEWD 72; ModWD; NotNAT B; OxCFr; REn; Who 74*

Achebe, Chinua
[Albert Chinualumogu Achebe]
Nigerian. Author
Novels reveal Nigerian life, impact of civilization: *Things Fall Apart,* 1958; *Arrow of God,* 1964.
b. Nov 16, 1930 in Ogidi, Nigeria
Source: *AfrA; AfSS 78, 79, 80, 81, 82; Au&Arts 15; Au&Wr 71; Benet 87, 96; BioIn 7, 8, 9, 10, 12, 13, 14, 15, 16, 17, 18, 19, 20, 21; BlkAull, 92; BlkLC; BlkWr 1; BlmGEL; CamGEL; CamGLE; CasWL; ChlLR 20; ConAu 1R, 6NR, 26NR, X; ConBlB 6; ConLC 1, 3, 5, 7, 11, 26, 51, 75; ConNov 72, 76, 82, 86, 91, 96; ConPo 75, 80, 85, 91, 96; CurBio 92; CyWA 89; DcAfHiB 86; DcArts; DcLB 117; DcLEL 1940;*

DcTwHis; EncWL, 2, 3; FacFETw; GrWrEL N; InB&W 80, 85; IntAu&W 76, 77, 82, 89, 91, 93; IntLitE; IntvWPC; IntWW 74, 75, 76, 77, 78, 79, 80, 81, 82, 83, 89, 91, 93; LegTOT; LinLib L; LngCTC; MagSWL; MajTwCW; McGEWB; ModBlW; ModCmwL; Novels; OxCChiL; OxCEng 85, 95; OxCTwCP; PenC CL, ENG; PseudN 82; RadHan; RAdv 14, 13-2; RfGEnL 91; RfGShF; RGAfL; SchCGBL; SelBAAf; SmATA 38, 40; TwCChW 83, 89, 95; TwCWr; WebE&AL; Who 74, 82, 83, 85, 88, 90, 92, 94; WhoAm 95, 96, 97; WhoTwCL; WhoWor 74, 80, 82, 84, 87, 89, 91, 93, 95, 96, 97; WorAlBi; WorAu 1950; WorLitC; WrDr 76, 80, 82, 84, 86, 88, 90, 92, 94, 96

Acheson, Dean Gooderham
American. Government Official
Truman's secretary of state, 1949-53; primary creator of NATO; won Pulitzer for *Present at the Creation,* 1969.
b. Apr 11, 1893 in Middletown, Connecticut
d. Oct 12, 1971 in Sandy Spring, Maryland
Source: *AmAu&B; AmPolLe; BiDrUSE 71, 89; BioIn 1, 2, 3, 4, 5, 6, 7, 8, 9, 10, 11, 12, 13; ColdWar 1; ConAu 33R, P-2; DcAmB S9; DcAmDH 80, 89; DcPol; DcTwHis; EncAB-H 1974, 1996; McGEWB; NatCAB 56; ObitOF 79; ObitT 1971; OxCAmH; PolProf E, J; REnAL; WebAB 74, 79; WhAm 5; WhDW; WorAl*

Acheson, Edward Goodrich
American. Inventor
Pioneer of electrothermal industry; discovered silicon carbide, 1891.
b. Mar 9, 1856 in Washington, District of Columbia
d. Jul 6, 1931 in New York, New York
Source: *AmBi; AsBiEn; BioIn 3, 4, 7, 9; DcAmB S1; DcNAA; HarEnUS; InSci; LarDcSc; LinLib S; NatCAB 13, 14, 23; WhAm 1; WhDW*

Achtenberg, Roberta
American. Politician
Assistant Secretary for Fair Housing and Equal Opportunity, 1993—.
b. Jul 20, 1950 in Los Angeles, California
Source: *GayLesB; WhoAm 95, 96, 97*

Achterberg, Gerrit
Dutch. Poet
Most prominent Dutch poet of 20th century; won Nat. Prize for Literature, 1949.
b. May 20, 1905 in Neerlangbroek, Netherlands
d. Jan 17, 1962 in Leusden, Netherlands
Source: *CasWL; ClDMEL 80; EncWL, 2, 3; PenC EUR; WhoTwCL; WorAu 1970*

Ackerman, Bettye
American. Actor
Starred in TV series "Ben Casey," 1961-66.
b. Feb 28, 1928 in Cottageville, South Carolina
Source: *ConTFT 1; FilmgC; ForWC 70; IntMPA 75, 76, 77, 78, 79, 80, 81, 82, 84, 86, 88, 92, 94, 96; WhoAm 90; WhoAmW 68; WhoHol 92, A*

Ackerman, Carl William
American. Journalist
Dean, Columbia Graduate Journalism School, 1931-56, who advocated practical newspaper training.
b. Jan 16, 1890 in Richmond, Indiana
d. Oct 9, 1970 in New York, New York
Source: *AmAu&B; AmDec 1940; BioIn 4, 9, 10, 16; ConAu 73; CurBio 45, 70; IndAu 1917; NewYTBE 70; ObitOF 79; WhAm 5*

Ackerman, Diane
American. Writer
Self-described sensuist; wrote *A Natural History of the Senses,* 1990.
b. Oct 7, 1948 in Waukegan, Illinois
Source: *ConAu 20AS, 31NR, 53NR, 54NR, 57; ConPo 85, 96; DcLB 120; DrAP 75; DrAPF 80; DrAS 82E; IntAu&W 89, 91, 93; IntWWP 77, 82; OxCTwCP; RAdv 14; WhoAmW 97; WhoE 83, 85, 86; WhoEmL 87; WhoUSWr 88; WhoWrEP 89, 92, 95; WrDr 86, 88, 90, 92, 94, 96*

Ackerman, Forest J
[Dr. Acula; Jacques DeForest Erman; Alden Lorraine; Hubert George Wells; Weaver Wright]
"World's No. 1 Science Fiction Fan"
American. Author, Editor, Lecturer
Collected over 300,000 items pertaining to science fiction, fantasy; coined abbreviation "sci-fi."
b. Nov 24, 1916 in Los Angeles, California
Source: *ConAu 102; EncSF; FanAl; PseudN 82; ScF&FL 1, 2; WhoSciF*

Ackerman, Harry S
American. Film Executive, Producer
Exec. producer, Screen Gems Pictures Corp., 1958-73; developed several TV shows: "Bachelor Father,""Leave It to Beaver,""Gunsmoke,""I Love Lucy."
b. Nov 17, 1912 in Albany, New York
d. Feb 3, 1991 in Burbank, California
Source: *ConTFT 3; IntMPA 82, 88; NewYTET; St&PR 75; WhoAm 82*

Ackerman, Robert Allan
American. Director
Directed on stage *Bent; Extremities; Slab Boys.*
b. 1945
Source: *BioIn 12; ConTFT 9*

Ackerman, Will
[G. William Ackerman]
American. Musician, Music Executive
Soft rock, soft jazz guitarist; founded Windham Hill Records, 1975.
b. Nov 1949 in Eslingen, Germany (West)
Source: *BioIn 12, 14, 16; ConMus 3; ConNews 87-4; OnThGG; WhoEnt 92*

Ackland, Joss
English. Actor
Character actor typically portraying men of power, especially kings.
b. Feb 29, 1928 in London, England
Source: *BioIn 16, 17; ConTFT 5; FilmEn; FilmgC; HalFC 80, 84, 88; IntMPA 82, 84, 86, 88, 92, 94, 96; IntWW 91, 93; ItaFilm; LegTOT; Who 82, 83, 85, 88, 90, 92, 94; WhoHol 92; WhoThe 72, 77, 81*

Ackroyd, Peter
English. Author
Versatile writer, published books of poetry, novels and biographies; winner of the Somerset Maugham Award, 1984 for *The Last Testament of Oscar Wilde.*
b. Oct 5, 1949 in London, England
Source: *BioIn 15; CamGLE; ConAu 51NR, 123, 127; ConLC 52; ConNov 86, 91, 96; CurBio 93; DcLB 155; EncSF 93; IntAu&W 89, 91, 93; IntWW 89, 91, 93; NewYTBS 91; OxCEng 95; RGTwCWr; ScF&FL 92; TwCRHW 94; Who 88, 90, 92, 94; WhoAm 88; WhoWor 89, 91, 95, 96, 97; WorAu 1980; WrDr 88, 90, 92, 94, 96*

Acton, John Emerich Edward Dalberg-Acton, Baron
English. Historian
Liberal MP who was first editor of *Cambridge Modern History.*
b. Jan 10, 1834 in Naples, Italy
d. Jul 19, 1902 in Tegernsee, Bavaria
Source: *Alli SUP; AtlBL; DcEnA, A; DcEuL; DcLEL; EvLB; OxCEng 67; PenC ENG*

Acuff, Roy (Claxton)
"The King of Country Music"
American. Singer
Country singer who has sold over 30 million records including "Wabash Cannonball;" first living member inducted into Country Music Hall of Fame, 1962.
b. Sep 15, 1903 in Maynardville, Tennessee
d. Nov 23, 1992 in Nashville, Tennessee
Source: *AnObit 1992; Baker 84, 92; BgBkCoM; BiDAmM; BioIn 10, 11, 12, 13, 14, 15, 16, 18, 19, 21; CmpEPM; ConMuA 80A; ConMus 2; CounME 74, 74A; CurBio 76, 93N; DcTwCCu 1; EncFCWM 69, 83; EncRk 88; HarEnCM 87; IlEncCM; LegTOT; NewAmDM; NewGrDA 86; NewGrDM 80; News 93-2; NewYTBS 92; OnThGG; OxCPMus; PenEncP; PseudN 82; RadStar; RolSEnR 83; SaTiSS; WhAm 10; WhoAm 76, 80,*

82, 84, 86, 88, 90, 92; WhoEnt 92; WhoNeCM C; WhoRock 81; WorAl; WorAlBi

Adair, Frank E(arl)
American. Surgeon
Breast cancer specialist who performed over 17,000 operations.
b. Apr 9, 1887 in Beverly, Ohio
d. Dec 31, 1981 in Bedford, New York
Source: *BioIn 1, 12, 13; CurBio 46, 82, 82N; EncAB-A 6; InSci; IntWW 76, 77, 78, 79, 80, 81; WhoAm 74, 76*

Adair, Peter
American. Filmmaker
Produced *The AIDS Show: Artists Involved with Death and Survival,* 1986.
b. 1943
d. Jun 27, 1996
Source: *GayLesB*

Adair, Red
[Paul Neal Adair]
American. Firefighter
Expert at capping runaway oil well fires and blowouts.
b. Jun 18, 1915 in Houston, Texas
Source: *BioIn 16, 17; ConNews 87-3; IntWW 91; PseudN 82; WhoAm 84, 86, 90, 92, 94, 95, 96, 97*

Adam
Biblical Figure
First man; story told in book of Genesis in *Bible;* committed original sin for which Christians are baptized.
Source: *Benet 96; BioIn 2, 4, 5, 6, 7, 8, 9, 10, 17; DcBiPP; DcCathB; DcEnL; EncEarC; EncO&P 2, 3; EncSoB; EuAu; FolkA 87; LngCEL; McGDA; NewCol 75; NewGrDM 80*

Adam, Adolphe Charles
French. Composer
Noted for ballet *Giselle,* 1841.
b. Jul 24, 1803 in Paris, France
d. May 3, 1856 in Paris, France
Source: *Baker 78, 84, 92; BioIn 7, 12; CelCen; DcArts; DcBiPP; LinLib L; NewEOp 71; NewGrDO; OxCMus*

Adam, James
Scottish. Architect
Brother of Robert Adam; work recaptures spirit of antiquity through use of delicate ornaments, mouldings.
b. Jul 21, 1730 in Edinburgh, Scotland
d. Oct 20, 1794 in London, England
Source: *BiDBrA; BioIn 3, 4, 5; DcBrWA; DcNaB; EncEnl; MacEA; McGDA; McGEWB; OxCArt; WhoArch*

Adam, Juliette Lamber
[La Messine; Juliette Lamber; Comte Paul Vasili]
French. Author
Founder, editor, *Nouvelle Revue,* 1879-99.
b. Oct 4, 1836 in Verberie, France
d. Aug 23, 1936 in Callian, France
Source: *BiD&SB; BioIn 1, 5, 11; CelCen; InWom, SUP; OxCFr; PenNWW B; REn*

Adam, Ken
English. Art Director, Designer
Won Oscar for *Barry Lyndon,* 1975; other films include several in James Bond series.
b. Feb 5, 1921 in Berlin, Germany
Source: *BioIn 12; ConDes 84, 90, 97; ConTFT 1, 12; DcFM; FilmEn; FilmgC; HalFC 80, 84, 88; IntDcF 1-4, 2-4; IntMPA 75, 76, 77, 78, 79, 80, 81, 82, 84, 86, 88, 92, 94, 96; IntWW 91, 93; ItaFilm; VarWW 85; WhoHrs 80; WorEFlm*

Adam, Paul
French. Author
Early symbolist; wrote naturalistic novel, *Chair Molle,* 1885.
b. Dec 7, 1862 in Paris, France
d. Jan 2, 1920 in Paris, France
Source: *CasWL; ClDMEL 47; EuAu; EvEuW; LinLib L; OxCFr; REn; WebBD 83*

Adam, Robert
Scottish. Architect, Furniture Designer
Principal work reacts against robustness of Palladian school using lightness, elegance of neoclassicism.
b. Jul 3, 1728 in Kirkcaldy, Scotland
d. Mar 3, 1792 in London, England
Source: *Alli; AntBDN H; AtlBL; BiDBrA; BiDLA; BioIn 1, 2, 3, 4, 5, 6, 7, 9, 11, 12, 13, 14, 15, 17, 20; BlkwCE; BlmGEL; CmScLit; DcArts; DcBiPP; DcBrWA; DcD&D; DcEnL; DcNaB; EncEnl; EncUrb; IlDcG; IntDcAr; LegTOT; LngCEL; MacEA; McGDA; McGEWB; NewC; NewCBEL; OxCArt; OxCDecA; OxDcArt; PenDiDA 89; WhDW; WhoArch; WorAl; WorAlBi*

Adam and the Ants
[Adam Ant; Matthew Ashman; David Barbe; Chris Hughes; Terry Lee Miall; Kevin Mooney; Marco Pirroni; Gary Tibbs; Andrew Warren]
English. Music Group
Fantasy-oriented, new Romantic group, 1977-82; had number one album *Kings of the Wild Frontier,* 1981.
Source: *ConAu X; DcLP 87B; IntAu&W 77X, 91X; RolSEnR 83; WhoRocM 82; WhoScEu 91-1; WhsNW 85; WrDr 76, 80, 82, 84, 86, 88, 90*

Adam Ant
[Adam and the Ants; Stewart Goddard]
English. Singer
Vocalist, guitarist, pianist; had top solo single "Goody Two Shoes," 1982.
b. Nov 3, 1954 in London, England
Source: *BioIn 13; ConMus 13; EncPR&S 89; EncRk 88; HarEnR 86; IlEncRk; PenEncP; RkOn 85; RolSEnR 83; WhoEnt 92*

Adam de la Halle
"Adam le Bossu"; "Adam the Hunchback"
French. Musician, Dramatist
Famed troubadour; wrote *Le Jeu de la Feuillee,* 1262, thought to be earliest French comedy.
b. 1240? in Arras, France
d. 1287? in Naples, Italy
Source: *AtlBL; Baker 84; Benet 96; BiD&SB; BriBkM 80; CasWL; CmMedTh; DcArts; DcEuL; EncWT; EvEuW; LinLib L; McGEWD 72, 84; MediFra; MusMk; NewAmDM; NewCol 75; OxCFr; OxCThe 67; PenC EUR; WebBD 83*

Adamek, Donna
American. Bowler
Woman bowler of the year, 1978-81; WPBA national champion, 1980.
b. Feb 1, 1957 in Duarte, California
Source: *BioIn 21; EncWomS; WhoSpor*

Adamic, Louis
American. Author, Journalist
Social philosophy urged U.S. to embrace unified interracial culture; wrote *Laughing in the Jungle,* 1932; *My America,* 1938.
b. Mar 23, 1899 in Blato, Austria-Hungary
d. Sep 4, 1951 in Riegelsville, New Jersey
Source: *AmAu&B; AmSocL; BenetAL 91; BioIn 1, 2, 3, 4, 9, 11, 12, 19; CnDAL; ConAmA; DcAmB S5; DcAmImH; DcLEL; IntvTCA 2; LinLib L, S; OxCAmH; OxCAmL 65, 83, 95; REn; REnAL; TwCA, SUP; WhAm 3; WhE&EA*

Adamle, Mike
[Michael David Adamle]
American. Broadcast Journalist
Pro football player, 1971-77; host of syndicated TV show, "American Gladiators," 1989—.
b. Oct 4, 1949 in Euclid, Ohio
Source: *WhoAm 82; WhoFtbl 74*

Adamov, Arthur
Russian. Author, Dramatist
Plays range from avant-garde *Ping Pong,* 1955, to social protest *Paolo Paoli,* 1957.
b. Aug 23, 1908 in Kislovodsk, Russia
d. Mar 16, 1970 in Paris, France
Source: *BioIn 8, 9, 10, 12, 17, 20; CamGWoT; CasWL; ClDMEL 80; CnMD; CnThe; ConAu 17R, 25R, P-2; ConLC 4, 25; CroCD; CyWA 89; DcArts; DcTwCCu 2; EncWL, 2, 3; EncWT; Ent; GrFLW; GuFrLit 1; IntDcT 2; LinLib L; MajTwCW; MakMC; McGEWD 72, 84; ModFrL; ModRL; ModWD; NotNAT B; OxCThe 67, 83; PenC EUR; PlP&P; REnWD; RfGWoL 95; WhDW; WorAu 1950*

Adamowski, Timothee
"Idol of the Pops"
Polish. Musician, Conductor
Violin virtuoso; led popular Boston concerts from 1890.
b. Mar 24, 1858 in Warsaw, Poland
d. Apr 18, 1943 in Boston, Massachusetts
Source: *Baker 84; BiDAmM; CurBio 43; NewGrDA 86*

Adams, Abigail Smith
American. First Lady
Only woman to be wife of one pres., John Adams; mother of another, John Quincy Adams.
b. Nov 11, 1744 in Weymouth, Massachusetts
d. Oct 28, 1818 in Quincy, Massachusetts
Source: *AmWom; AmWomWr; ApCAB; Benet 96; BiCAW; DcAmAu; DcAmB; EncWHA; NatCAB 2; NotAW; ObitOF 79; OxCAmL 65; PseudN 82; REn; TwCBDA; WebAB 79; WhAm HS; WhAmP; WorAl*

Adams, Alice
American. Author
Wrote *Beautiful Girl,* 1979; *Second Chances,* 1988.
b. Aug 14, 1926 in Fredericksburg, Virginia
Source: *AmWomWr SUP; BenetAL 91; BiDEWW; BioIn 7, 11, 13, 15, 16, 17, 19; ConAu 26NR, 81; ConLC 6, 13, 46; ConNov 86, 91; CurBio 89; CyWA 89; DcLB Y86B; DrAPF 80, 89; IntAu&W 91, 93; LegTOT; MajTwCW; OxCAmL 83, 95; OxCWoWr 95; WhoAm 80, 82, 84, 86, 88, 90, 92, 94, 95, 96, 97; WhoAmW 89, 91, 93, 95, 97; WhoUSWr 88; WhoWrEP 89, 92, 95; WorAlBi; WorAu 1980; WrDr 84, 86, 88, 90, 92, 94, 96*

Adams, Alvan Leigh
American. Basketball Player
Forward, Phoenix, 1975—; NBA rookie of year, 1976.
b. Jul 29, 1954 in Lawrence, Kansas
Source: *BioIn 10; OfNBA 87*

Adams, Andy
American. Rancher, Author
Wrote *The Log of a Cowboy,* 1903.
b. May 3, 1859 in Whitley County, Indiana
d. Sep 26, 1935
Source: *AmAu&B; AmLY; BenetAL 91; BiDSA; BioIn 2, 7, 8, 11, 15; CamGEL; CamGLE; CamHAL; CnDAL; DcAmAu; DcAmB S1; DcLEL; DcNAA; EncAAH; EncFWF; FifWWr; IndAu 1816; JBA 34, 51; OxCAmH; OxCAmL 65, 83, 95; PeoHis; REnAL; REnAW; TexWr; TwCLC 56; TwCWW 82, 91; WebAB 74, 79; WhAm 2; WhNAA; YABC 1*

Adams, Annette Abbott
American. Politician, Judge
First woman federal prosecutor; ran for Dem. vice presidential spot, 1920.
b. Mar 12, 1877 in Prattville, California
d. Oct 26, 1956 in Sacramento, California
Source: *BiCAW; DcAmB S6; InWom, SUP; NatCAB 43; NotAW MOD; WhAm 3A; WomFir*

Adams, Ansel Easton
American. Photographer
Best known photographer in US, noted for landscape images of western US; helped establish photography as art form.
b. Feb 20, 1902 in San Francisco, California
d. Apr 22, 1984 in Monterey, California
Source: *BioIn 4, 6, 7, 8, 10, 11, 12, 13; BlueB 76; BriEAA; CmCal; ConAu 21R; ConPhot 82; CurBio 84; DcAmArt; DcCAr 81; MacBEP; WebAB 74, 79; WhAm 8; WhoAm 80, 82; WhoAmA 76, 78, 80, 82, 84; WrDr 84*

Adams, Brock(man)
American. Lawyer, Government Official
Secretary of Transportation under Jimmy Carter, 1977-79; Dem. Senator from WA who resigned amid allegations of sexual misconduct, 1987-93.
b. Jan 13, 1927 in Atlanta, Georgia
Source: *AlmAP 88, 92; BiDrAC; BiDrUSC 89; BiDrUSE 89; BioIn 11, 12; CngDr 74, 77, 79, 87, 89, 91; CurBio 77; IntWW 77, 78, 79, 80, 81, 82, 83, 89, 91, 93; IntYB 78, 79, 80, 81, 82; NewYTBS 76; Ward 77D; WhoAm 74, 76, 78, 80, 82, 88, 90, 92; WhoAmL 79; WhoAmP 73, 75, 77, 79, 81, 83, 85, 87, 89, 91, 93, 95; WhoE 77, 79, 81, 83; WhoFI 79; WhoGov 72, 75, 77; WhoWest 74, 76, 78, 82, 84, 87, 89, 92; WhoWor 89, 91*

Adams, Brooke
American. Actor
In film *Invasion of the Body Snatchers,* 1978.
b. Feb 8, 1949 in New York, New York
Source: *BioIn 11, 13, 16; ConTFT 2; HalFC 84, 88; IntMPA 82, 88, 92, 94, 96; LegTOT; WhoAm 82, 84, 86, 90, 92; WhoEnt 92; WhoHol 92*

Adams, Brooks
American. Historian
Known for controversial discussion of world, American history: *The Emancipation of Massachusetts,* 1887; grandson of John Quincy Adams.
b. Jun 24, 1848 in Quincy, Massachusetts
d. Feb 13, 1927 in Boston, Massachusetts
Source: *Alli SUP; AmAu; AmAu&B; AmBi; ApCAB, X; BenetAL 91; BiD&SB; BioIn 1, 2, 4, 5, 6, 8, 9, 10, 12, 15, 16; CamGEL; CamHAL; ConAu 123; DcAmAu; DcAmB; DcAmC; DcAmDH 80, 89; DcAmSR; DcLB 47; DcNAA; EncAB-H 1974, 1996; GayN; HarEnUS; LinLib L; NatCAB 10; OxCAmH; OxCAmL 65, 83, 95; PenC AM; PeoHis; REnAL; TwCBDA; WebAB 74, 79; WhAm 1; WhDW; WorAlBi*

Adams, Bryan Guy
Canadian. Singer, Musician
Hits include album *It Cuts Like a Knife,* 1983; singles "Heaven," 1985; "(Everything I Do) I Do It for You," 1991; featured in the movie *Robin Hood,* 1991.
b. Nov 5, 1959 in Vancouver, British Columbia, Canada
Source: *BioIn 13, 16; ConMus 2; EncRk 88; HarEnR 86; PenEncP; RkOn 85*

Adams, Charles Francis
American. Hockey Executive
Formed, original owner, Boston Bruins, 1924; Hall of Fame, 1960.
b. Oct 18, 1876 in Newport, Vermont
d. Oct 3, 1947
Source: *BioIn 1, 21; WhoHcky 73*

Adams, Charles Francis, Sr.
American. Author, Politician
Vice presidential candidate, 1848; minister to England, 1861-68.
b. Aug 18, 1807 in Boston, Massachusetts
d. Nov 21, 1886 in Boston, Massachusetts
Source: *Alli, SUP; AmAu&B; AmBi; AmPolLe; ApCAB, X; BbD; BenetAL 91; BiAUS; BiD&SB; BiDrAC; BiDrUSC 89; BioIn 1, 3, 4, 5, 7, 8, 9, 10, 15, 16, 21; CelCen; ChhPo S1; CivWDc; CyAG; CyAL 2; DcAmAu; DcAmB; DcAmC; DcAmDH 80, 89; DcBiPP; DcNAA; Drake; EncAB-H 1974, 1996; HarEnUS; LinLib L, S; McGEWB; NatCAB 8; OxCAmH; OxCAmL 65, 83, 95; PolPar; PresAR; RAdv 13-3; TwCBDA; WebAB 74, 79; WhAm HS; WhAmP; WhCiWar*

Adams, Charles Francis, Jr.
American. Historian, Lawyer
Grandson of John Quincy Adams; author of several books on New England history.
b. May 27, 1835 in Boston, Massachusetts
d. Mar 20, 1915 in Washington, District of Columbia
Source: *Alli SUP; AmAu; AmAu&B; ApCAB, X; BbD; Benet 87, 96; BenetAL 91; BiDAmBL 83; BiD&SB; BioIn 1, 5, 7, 8, 9, 15, 16; CivWDc; ConAu 113; DcAmAu; DcAmB; DcAmC; DcAmSR; DcLB 47; DcLEL; DcNAA; EncAB-H 1974, 1996; EncABHB 2; HarEnUS; NatCAB 8; OxCAmH; OxCAmL 65, 83, 95; PeoHis; REn; REnAL; REnAW; TwCBDA; WebAB 74, 79; WhAm 1; WhAmP; WhCiWar; WhLit*

Adams, Cindy
American. Writer
Gossip columnist, New York *Post;* reporter, "A Current Affair," 1989—; married to comedian Joey Adams.
Source: *BioIn 8, 20; CelR 90; ConAu 17NR, 21R; IntAu&W 76*

Adams, Cliff
[Kool and the Gang]
American. Musician
Has played trombone with Kool and the Gang since 1980.
b. Oct 8, 1952 in New Jersey

Adams, Diana
American. Dancer
Performed in *Helen of Troy,* 1944; joined the NY City Ballet, 1950.
b. Mar 29, 1926
d. Jan 10, 1993 in San Andreas, California
Source: *AnObit 1993; BiDD; BioIn 3, 4, 13, 18, 19; CnOxB; CurBio 93N; DancEn 78; IntDcB; InWom; WhoAmW 58*

Adams, Don
[Donald James Yarmy]
American. Actor, Comedian
Played Maxwell Smart on TV series "Get Smart," 1965-70.
b. Apr 19, 1926 in New York, New York
Source: *BioIn 7, 12; ConTFT 3; EncAFC; IntMPA 84, 86, 88, 92, 94, 96; LegTOT; VarWW 85; WhoAm 82; WhoCom; WhoHol 92*

Adams, Douglas Noel
English. Author
Wrote *The Hitchhiker's Guide to the Galaxy,* 1979; made into British TV series shown on PBS.
b. Mar 11, 1952 in Cambridge, England
Source: *BioIn 13, 14; ConAu 106; ConDr 82B; ConLC 27; ScFSB; TwCSFW 86; WrDr 82, 88*

Adams, Edie
[Elizabeth Edith Enke]
American. Singer, Actor
Wife of Ernie Kovacs; appeared in *It's a Mad, Mad, Mad, Mad World,* 1963.
b. Apr 16, 1929 in Kingston, Pennsylvania
Source: *BiE&WWA; BioIn 13, 15, 17; ConTFT 3; EncAFC; FilmgC; ForWC 70; HalFC 80, 84, 88; IntMPA 82; MotPP; MovMk; NotNAT; PseudN 82; WhoAm 74, 76, 78, 80, 82, 84; WhoAmW 66, 68; WhoHol 92, A; WhoThe 77; WorAl; WorAlBi*

Adams, Edwin
American. Actor
Light comedian whose most successful role was Enoch Arden in drama of Tennyson's poem, 1869.
b. Feb 3, 1834 in Medford, Massachusetts
d. Oct 25, 1877 in Philadelphia, Pennsylvania
Source: *ApCAB; CamGWoT; DcAmB; Drake; FamA&A; NatCAB 5; NotNAT, B; OxCAmT 84; OxCThe 67, 83; WhAm HS*

Adams, Eva Bertrand
American. Government Official
Director of US Mint, 1961-69.
b. Sep 10, 1908 in Wonder, Nevada
d. Aug 23, 1991 in Reno, Nevada
Source: *BioIn 6; CurBio 62, 91N; InWom; NewYTBS 91; WhoAm 80, 82, 86; WhoAmP 73; WhoAmW 74*

Adams, Frank Ramsay
American. Author, Songwriter
Wrote lyrics for over 200 songs; scripts for 25 films.
b. Jul 7, 1883 in Morrison, Illinois
d. Oct 8, 1963 in White Lake, Michigan
Source: *BioIn 6; DcAmB S7; TwCWW 91; WhAm 4; WhE&EA*

Adams, Franklin P(ierce)
"F.P.A."
American. Journalist
Best known for columns appearing in *NY Herald-Tribune;* panelist on radio's "Information Please."
b. Nov 15, 1881 in Chicago, Illinois
d. Mar 23, 1960 in New York, New York
Source: *AmAu&B; BiDAmJo; BiDAmM; BiDAmNC; BioIn 1, 4, 5, 8; ChhPo, S1, S2, S3; CnDAL; ConAmA; ConAu 93; CurBio 41, 60; DcAmB S6; EncAHmr; EncTwCJ; JrnUS; LinLib L; NotNAT B; OxCAmL 65, 95; PseudN 82; RadStar; REn; REnAL; TwCA, SUP; WebAB 74, 79; WhAm 3A; WhNAA*

Adams, Gerald
Irish. Political Leader
President of the Sinn Fein political party, 1983—.
b. Oct 6, 1948 in Belfast, Northern Ireland
Source: *CurBio 94; News 94, 94-1*

Adams, Hank
American. Social Reformer
Involved in the struggle for Indian fishing rights in the American Northwest, late 1960s to early 1970s.
b. May 16, 1943 in Wolf Point, Montana
Source: *BioIn 21; NotNaAm; REnAW*

Adams, Hannah
American. Author
Considered first professional American woman writer: *History of New England,* 1799.
b. Oct 2, 1755 in Medford, Massachusetts
d. Dec 15, 1831 in Brookline, Massachusetts
Source: *Alli; AmAu; AmAu&B; AmBi; AmWom; AmWomHi; AmWomWr; AmWrBE; ApCAB; BbD; Benet 87, 96; BenetAL 91; BiD&SB; BioIn 3, 9; BlmGWL; CyAL 1; DcAmAu; DcAmB; DcAmReB 2; DcBrAmW; DcEnL; DcNAA; Drake; FemiCLE; HarEnUS; InWom, SUP; LibW; LinLib L; NatCAB 5; NotAW; OxCAmL 65, 83, 95; OxCWoWr 95; REn; REnAL; TwCBDA; WhAm HS; WomFir*

Adams, Harriet Stratemeyer
[Victor Appleton, II; Franklin W Dixon; Laura Lee Hope; Carolyn Keene]
American. Children's Author
Wrote 200 books for *Hardy Boys; Nancy Drew; Bobbsey Twins* series.
b. Dec 11, 1892? in Newark, New Jersey
d. Mar 27, 1982 in Pottersville, New Jersey
Source: *AmAu&B; AmWomWr; AuNews 2; ConAu 17R, 81, 106; EncMys; EncSF; NewYTBS 82; OnHuMoP; PseudN 82; ScF&FL 92; SmATA 1, 29; WhAm 8; WhoAm 82*

Adams, Henry Brooks
American. Historian, Author
Won Pulitzer Prize for *Education of Henry Adams,* 1919; grandson of John Quincy Adams.
b. Feb 16, 1838 in Boston, Massachusetts
d. Mar 27, 1918 in Washington, District of Columbia
Source: *AmAu; AmBi; ApCAB; AtlBL; Benet 96; DcAmB; DcAmSR; DcBiA; DcLEL; EncAB-H 1996; EvLB; LngCTC; McGEWB; ModAL, S1; OxCAmH; PenC AM; RComWL; REn*

Adams, Herbert Baxter
American. Educator, Historian
First to use seminar method in US higher education; a founder of the American Historical Assn.
b. Apr 16, 1850 in Shutesbury, Massachusetts
d. Jul 30, 1901 in Amherst, Massachusetts
Source: *Alli SUP; AmAu; AmBi; ApCAB; BiDAmEd; BiD&SB; BiDInt; BiDSA; BioIn 1, 13, 14, 15; CyEd; DcAmAu; DcAmB; DcLB 47; DcNAA; EncAB-H 1974, 1996; EncSoH; HarEnUS; McGEWB; NatCAB 8; OxCAmH; OxCAmL 65; PeoHis; TwCBDA; WebAB 74, 79; WhAm 1; WhAmP*

Adams, Herbert Samuel
American. Sculptor
Founder, National Sculpture Society, 1893; known for portrait busts.
b. Jan 28, 1858 in West Concord, Vermont
d. May 21, 1945 in New York, New York
Source: *CurBio 45; DcAmB S3; WhAm 2*

Adams, Jack
[John James Adams]
"Jovial Jawn"
Canadian. Hockey Player, Hockey Coach
Center, 1917-19, 1922-27, mostly with Toronto; coach, Detroit, 1927-47; won three Stanley Cups; Hall of Fame, 1959.
b. Jun 14, 1895 in Fort William, Ontario, Canada
d. May 1, 1968 in Detroit, Michigan
Source: *BioIn 3, 8, 10; HocEn; NatCAB 54; ObitOF 79; WhoHcky 73; WhoSpor*

Adams, James Truslow
American. Historian, Author
Wrote 1922 Pulitzer-winner *Founding of New England and Epic of America,* 1921.
b. Oct 18, 1878 in New York, New York
d. May 18, 1949 in Westport, Connecticut
Source: *AmAu&B; BenetAL 91; BioIn 1, 2, 4, 8, 13; ConAmA; ConAu 115; CurBio 41, 49; DcAmB S4; DcLB 17; DcLEL; DcNAA; EvLB; LinLib L, S; NatCAB 36; ObitOF 79; OxCAmL 65, 83, 95; RAdv 13-3; REn; REnAL; TwCA, SUP; WebAB 74, 79; WhAm 2; WhE&EA; WhNAA*

Adams, Joey
[Joseph Abramowitz]
American. Comedian, Author
Nightclub, film performer who starred in "Joey Adams" TV show, 1956-58; married to gossip columist Cindy Adams.
b. Jan 6, 1911 in New York, New York
Source: *BiE&WWA; BioIn 1, 2, 4, 10; BlueB 76; CelR, 90; ConAu 1NR, 49; JoeFr; LegTOT; NotNAT A; PseudN 82; WhoAm 74, 76, 78, 80, 82, 84, 86, 88, 90, 92, 94, 95, 96, 97; WhoCom; WhoE 74; WhoEnt 92; WhoHol 92, A; WhoWor 74; WhoWorJ 72, 78*

Adams, John
"The Atlas of Independence"
American. US President
Signed Declaration of Independence, 1776; second US pres., 1797-1801; helped negotiate Treaty of Paris, 1793, ending American Revolution.
b. Oct 30, 1735 in Braintree, Massachusetts
d. Jul 4, 1826 in Quincy, Massachusetts
Source: *Alli; AmAu&B; AmBi; AmOrN; AmPolLe; AmRev; AmWrBE; ApCAB; BbD; Benet 87, 96; BenetAL 91; BiAUS; BiD&SB; BiDLA SUP; BiDrAC; BiDrUSC 89; BiDrUSE 71, 89; BioIn 1, 2, 3, 4, 5, 6, 7, 8, 9, 10, 11, 12, 13, 14, 15, 16, 17, 18, 19, 20; BlkwEAR; CelCen; ChhPo S1; CyAG; CyAL 1; CyWA 58; DcAmAu; DcAmB; DcAmBC; DcAmC; DcAmDH 80, 89; DcAmSR; DcBiPP; DcNAA; Dis&D; Drake; EncAAH; EncAB-H 1974, 1996; EncAR; EncCRAm; EncEnl; EncNAB; EncRev; EvLB; FacPr 89, 93; HarEnUS; HealPre; HisDBrE; HisWorL; LegTOT; LinLib L, S; McGEWB; MorMA; NatCAB 2; OxCAmH; OxCAmL 65, 83, 95; PeoHis; PolPar; PresAR; PseudN 82; RAdv 13-3; RComAH; REn; REnAL; TwCBDA; TwoTYeD; VicePre; WebAB 74, 79; WhAm HS; WhAmP; WhAmRev; WhDW; WorAl; WorAlBi*

Adams, John
American. Jockey
Led in winning mounts, 1937, 1942, 1943; member, National Horse Racing Hall of Fame.
b. Sep 1, 1915 in Iola, Kansas
Source: *BiDAmSp OS; WhoSpor*

Adams, John Coolidge
American. Composer
Wrote controversial opera *Nixon in China,* 1986.
b. Feb 15, 1947 in Worcester, Massachusetts
Source: *Baker 92; ConMus 8; CurBio 88; DcArts; NewGrDO; WhoAm 82, 84, 86, 96, 97*

Adams, John Couch
English. Astronomer
Discovered planet Neptune, 1845; official credit given to Leverrier, 1846.
b. Jun 5, 1819 in Laneast, England
d. Jan 21, 1892 in Cambridge, England
Source: *AsBiEn; BiESc; BioIn 1, 5, 11, 14, 21; CamDcSc; DcBiPP; DcInv; DcNaB C, S1; DcScB; InSci; LarDcSc; LinLib S; McGEWB; NewCol 75; WhDW; WorScD*

Adams, John Hanly
American. Author, Editor
Exec. editor, *US News and World Report,* 1970-79; contributing editor, *Nation's Business,* 1980-82.
b. Nov 2, 1918 in Sikeston, Missouri
Source: *EncTwCJ; WhoAm 74, 76, 78, 80, 82, 84, 86, 88, 90, 92, 94; WhoFI 74; WhoSSW 95*

Adams, John Quincy
"Old Man Eloquent"; "Publicola"; "The Accidental President"; "The Second John"
American. US President
Son of John Adams, sixth US president, 1825-29; catalyst behind Monroe Doctrine, 1823.
b. Jul 11, 1767 in Braintree, Massachusetts
d. Feb 23, 1848 in Washington, District of Columbia
Source: *Alli; AmAu&B; AmBi; AmOrN; AmPolLe; ApCAB; BbD; Benet 87, 96; BenetAL 91; BiAUS; BiD&SB; BiDLA; BiDrAC; BiDrUSC 89; BiDrUSE 71, 89; BioIn 1, 2, 3, 4, 5, 6, 7, 8, 9, 10, 11, 12, 13, 14, 15, 16, 17, 18, 19, 20, 21; CelCen; ChhPo, S1; CyAG; CyAL 1; DcAmAu; DcAmB; DcAmDH 80, 89; DcAmSR; DcBiPP; DcEnL; DcLB 37; DcLEL; DcNAA; Drake; EncAAH; EncAB-H 1974, 1996; FacPr 89, 93; HarEnUS; HealPre; HisWorL; LegTOT; LinLib L, S; LuthC 75; McGEWB; MemAm; NatCAB 5; OxCAmH; OxCAmL 65, 83, 95; OxCSupC; PolPar; PresAR; PseudAu; PseudN 82; RAdv 13-3; RComAH; REn; REnAL; REnAW; TwCBDA; WebAB 74, 79; WhAm HS; WhAmP; WhDW; WorAl*

Adams, Julie
[Betty May Adams]
American. Actor
Leading lady in second features; carried off by "Creature from the Black Lagoon," in 1954 film.
b. Oct 17, 1926 in Waterloo, Iowa
Source: *BioIn 18, 21; FilmEn; FilmgC; ForYSC; GangFlm; HalFC 80, 84, 88; IntMPA 75, 76, 77, 78, 79, 80, 81, 82, 92, 94, 96; LegTOT; PseudN 82; SweetSg D; WhoHol 92*

Adams, Leonie Fuller
American. Author
Metaphysical romantic lyricist; verse volumes include *This Measure,* 1933.
b. Dec 9, 1899 in New York, New York
d. Jun 27, 1988 in New Milford, Connecticut
Source: *AmWomWr; Au&Wr 71; BenetAL 91; BioIn 16; CnE&AP; CnMWL; ConAmA; ConAu 125, P-1; ConPo 70, 75, 80, 85; DcLB 48; DcLEL; DrAP 75; DrAPF 87; FemiCLE; IntAu&W 91; IntWW 82, 89, 91N; IntWWP 77; InWom, SUP; ModAL; REn; SixAP; TwCA SUP; WhoAm 88; WhoWor 74; WrDr 82, 88*

Adams, Louisa Catherine
[Mrs. John Quincy Adams]
American. First Lady
Married John Quincy Adams, 1797; Congress adjourned to attend her funeral, making her the first woman so honored.
b. Feb 12, 1775 in London, England
d. May 14, 1852 in Washington, District of Columbia
Source: *AmBi; AmWomWr; BiCAW; BioIn 1, 2, 3, 5, 6, 7, 8, 9, 10, 11, 12, 13, 16, 17; FacPr 89; HerW; InWom; NatCAB 5; NotAW*

Adams, Mason
American. Actor
Played Charlie Hume in TV series "Lou Grant," 1977-82; nominated for three Emmys.
b. Feb 26, 1919 in New York, New York
Source: *ConTFT 4; IntMPA 92, 94, 96; RadStar; SaTiSS; WhoAm 82, 84, 86, 88, 90, 92; WhoEnt 92; WhoWor 96*

Adams, Maud
[Maud Solveig Christina Wikstrom]
Swedish. Actor, Model
Starred with Roger Moore in James Bond films *Man with the Golden Gun,* 1974, *Octopussy,* 1983.
b. Feb 12, 1945 in Lulea, Sweden
Source: *BioIn 10, 12, 15; ConTFT 6; FilmEn; HalFC 88; IntMPA 92, 94, 96; LegTOT; PeoHis; VarWW 85; WhoHol 92, A*

Adams, Maude
[Maude Kiskadden]
American. Actor
Gave more than 1,500 performances in title role of *Peter Pan.*
b. Nov 11, 1872 in Salt Lake City, Utah
d. Jul 17, 1953 in Tannersville, New York
Source: *ApCAB X; BioAmW; BioIn 1, 3, 4, 5, 6, 7, 9, 10, 12, 13, 16, 17; CamGWoT; CnThe; DcAmB S5; EncWT; FacFETw; FamA&A; IntDcT 3; InWom, SUP; LegTOT; LibW; LinLib L, S; NatCAB 13; NotAW MOD; NotNAT A,*

B; NotWoAT; ObitOF 79; OxCAmH; OxCAmL 65; OxCAmT 84; OxCThe 67, 83; PlP&P; REnAL; TwCBDA; WebAB 74, 79; WhAm 3; WhoStg 1906, 1908; WhThe; WomWWA 14; WorAl; WorAlBi

Adams, Nick
[Nicholas Adamschock]
American. Actor
Starred in TV series "The Rebel," 1959-61.
b. Jul 10, 1931 in Nanticoke, Pennsylvania
d. Feb 5, 1968 in Beverly Hills, California
Source: *BioIn 5, 8, 17; FilmEn; FilmgC; GangFlm; HalFC 80, 84, 88; JapFilm; LegTOT; MotPP; MovMk; NotNAT B; ObitOF 79; PseudN 82; WhoHol B; WhScrn 74, 77*

Adams, Oleta
American. Singer
Contributed to British rock group Tears for Fears album *Seeds of Love*, 1987-1989; released debut album, *Circle of One*, 1990, which included hit single "Get Here" and became a platinum album; also released *Evolution*, 1993 and *Moving On*, 1995.
Source: *BioIn 17, 19, 20; ConMus 17; LegTOT; SoulM; WhoAfA 96; WhoBlA 94*

Adams, Richard
English. Author
Wrote best-seller *Watership Down*, 1972.
b. May 9, 1920 in Newbury, England
Source: *Au&Arts 16; AuBYP 2S, 3; AuNews 1, 2; BioIn 10, 11, 12, 14, 15, 17, 18, 19; CamGLE; ChhPo S2; ChlBkCr; ChlFicS; ConAu 3NR, 33R, 35NR, 49; ConLC 4, 5, 18; ConNov 86, 91; CurBio 78; CyWA 89; DcArts; HalFC 84, 88; LegTOT; MajTwCW; Novels; OxCChiL; PiP; ScF&FL 1, 2, 92; ScFSB; SmATA 7, 17, 69; TwCChW 78, 83, 89; WhoAm 82; WorAu 1970; WrDr 76, 80, 82, 84, 86, 88, 90, 92*

Adams, Samuel
"Alfred"; "The American Cato"; "The Cromwell of New England"; "The Father of America"
American. Revolutionary, Statesman
Force behind Boston Tea Party, 1773; signed Declaration of Independence.
b. Sep 27, 1722 in Boston, Massachusetts
d. Oct 2, 1803 in Boston, Massachusetts
Source: *Alli; AmAu; AmAu&B; AmBi; AmOrN; AmPolLe; AmRev; AmWrBE; ApCAB; Benet 87, 96; BenetAL 91; BiAUS; BiDAmJo; BiDrAC; BiDrGov 1789; BiDrUSC 89; BioIn 1, 2, 3, 5, 6, 7, 8, 9, 10, 11, 12, 14, 15, 16, 20; BlkwEAR; CyAG; DcAmAu; DcAmB; DcAmC; DcAmSR; DcBiPP; DcLB 31, 43; DcNAA; Dis&D; Drake; EncAB-H 1974, 1996; EncAJ; EncAR; EncCRAm; EncRev; HarEnUS; HisDBrE; HisWorL; JrnUS; LegTOT; LinLib L, S; McGEWB; MorMA; NatCAB 1; OxCAmH; OxCAmL 65, 83, 95; PeoHis; PolPar; PseudN 82; RComAH; REn; REnAL; TwCBDA; WebAB 74, 79; WhAm HS; WhAmP; WhAmRev; WhDW; WorAl; WorAlBi*

Adams, Samuel Hopkins
[pseud. Warner Fabian]
American. Author, Journalist
Writings included muckraking articles; *Average Jones* detective stories, biographies.
b. Jan 26, 1871 in Dunkirk, New York
d. Nov 15, 1958 in Beaufort, South Carolina
Source: *AmAu&B; AmLY; AmNov; AuBYP 2, 3; BenetAL 91; BiDAmJo; BioIn 1, 2, 3, 4, 5, 6, 8, 16; CnDAL; DcAmB S6; DcAmSR; Dis&D; EncAB-A 28; EncAJ; EncMys; EncSF, 93; JrnUS; LinLib L, S; NatCAB 14, 49; NotNAT B; OxCAmL 65, 83, 95; PseudN 82; REn; REnAL; ScF&FL 1; ScFEYrs; TwCA, SUP; WebAB 74, 79; WhAm 3; WhE&EA; WhLit; WhNAA*

Adams, Scott
American. Cartoonist
Created *Dilbert* comic strip, 1989.
b. Jun 1957 in Windham, New York
Source: *News 96*

Adams, Sherman Llewellyn
American. Government Official
Rep. governor of NH, 1949-53; chief of White House staff, 1953-58; resigned over "gift" scandal, 1958.
b. Jan 8, 1899 in East Dover, Vermont
d. Oct 27, 1986 in Hanover, New Hampshire
Source: *AmAu&B; BiDrAC; CnMWL; CurBio 52, 87; IntWW 82; PolProf E; Who 82; WhoAm 82; WhoAmP 73*

Adams, Stanley
American. Lyricist
Wrote "What a Diff'rence a Day Made," president, American Society of Composers, Authors, and Publishers, 1953-56, 1959-80.
b. Aug 14, 1907
d. Jan 27, 1994 in Manhasset, New York
Source: *ASCAP 66, 80; BiDAmM; BiE&WWA; BioIn 3, 19, 20; CmpEPM; CurBio 94N; NotNAT; WhAm 11; WhoAm 74, 76, 78, 80, 82, 84, 86, 88, 90, 92, 94; WhoEnt 92; WhoMus 72; WhoWor 74; WhoWorJ 72, 78*

Adams, Tom
[John Michael Geoffrey Maningham Adams]
Barbadian. Political Leader
Prime minister of Barbados, 1976-85.
b. Sep 24, 1931, Barbados
d. Mar 12, 1985 in Bridgetown, Barbados
Source: *AnObit 1985; BioIn 14, 16; DcCPCAm; IntWW 82, 83; IntYB 81, 82; NewYTBS 85; Who 83; WhoWor 80, 82*

Adams, Tony
[Anthony Patrick Adams]
Irish. Producer
Films include *10*, 1979; *S.O.B.*, 1981.
b. Feb 15, 1953 in Dublin, Ireland
Source: *BioIn 15; ConTFT 2, 10; IntMPA 88, 92, 94, 96; VarWW 85; WhoEnt 92; WhoWest 92*

Adams, Walter Sydney
American. Astronomer
Pres., American Astronomical Society, 1931-34; focused on stellar spectra, sunspots.
b. Dec 20, 1876 in Antioch, Turkey
d. May 11, 1956 in Pasadena, California
Source: *ApCAB X; AsBiEn; BiESc; BioIn 2, 4, 14, 20; CamDcSc; DcAmB S6; DcScB; FacFETw; InSci; LarDcSc; NotTwCS; WebAB 74, 79; WhAm 3; WhNAA; WorAlBi*

Adams, Weston W, Sir
American. Hockey Executive
Son of Charles; president, Boston Bruins, 1936-51, 1964-69; Hall of Fame, 1972.
b. Aug 9, 1904 in Springfield, Massachusetts
d. Mar 19, 1973 in Brookline, Massachusetts
Source: *WhoHcky 73*

Adams, William
"Anjin Sama"; "Mr. Pilot"
English. Navigator
First Englishman to visit Japan, 1600; remained there until death.
b. 1564? in Kent, England
d. May 16, 1620, Japan
Source: *BioIn 3, 4, 5, 8, 10, 19; EncJap; NewCol 75; WhDW; WhWE; WorAl; WorAlBi*

Adams, William Taylor
[Warren T Ashton; Irving Brown; Brooks McCormick; Oliver Optic]
American. Children's Author
Wrote highly successful boys' adventure tales, many in series; rival of Horatio Alger 1850s; one of his period's best-paid writers.
b. Jul 30, 1822 in Bellingham, Massachusetts
d. Mar 27, 1897 in Dorchester, Massachusetts
Source: *Alli SUP; AmAu; AmAu&B; AmBi; ApCAB; BbD; Benet 87, 96; BenetAL 91; BiD&SB; BioIn 13, 15; CarSB; ChhPo, S2, S3; CnDAL; CyAL 2; CyEd; DcAmAu; DcAmB; DcEnL; DcLB 42; DcNAA; Drake; HarEnUS; HsB&A, SUP; LinLib L, S; NatCAB 1; OxCAmL 65, 83, 95; OxCChiL; REn; REnAL; SmATA 28; TwCBDA; WebAB 74, 79; WebBD 83; WhAm HS*

Adamson, George
Kenyan. Animal Expert
Husband of Joy Adamson; established Kora Reserve wild animal sanctuary, Kenya.
b. 1906, India

d. Aug 20, 1989, Kenya
Source: *AnObit 1989; BioIn 8, 9, 13, 16; ConAu 129; News 90, 90-2; NewYTBS 89; SmATA 63*

Adamson, Joy Friederike Victoria Gessner
[Mrs. George Adamson]
Kenyan. Author, Animal Expert
Best known work, *Born Free,* 1960; filmed, 1966.
b. Jan 20, 1910 in Troppau, Silesia
d. Jan 3, 1980 in Shaba, Kenya
Source: *Au&Wr 71; ConAu 69, 93; ConLC 17; CurBio 72, 80; SmATA 11; Who 74; WhoAm 74*

Addabbo, Joseph Patrick
American. Politician
Dem. congressman from NY, 1961-86; adamant watchdog for military spending.
b. Mar 17, 1925 in New York, New York
d. Apr 10, 1986 in Washington, District of Columbia
Source: *AlmAP 84; AmCath 80; BiDrAC; BiDrUSC 89; BioIn 11; CngDr 74, 77, 79, 81, 83, 85; PolsAm 84; WhAm 9; WhoAm 74, 76, 78, 80, 82, 84; WhoAmL 78, 79; WhoAmP 73, 75, 77, 79, 81, 83, 85; WhoE 74, 75, 77, 79, 81, 83, 85; WhoGov 72, 75, 77*

Addams, Charles Samuel
American. Cartoonist
Known for ghoulish humor published in *New Yorker,* 1935-80s; cartoons basis for "Addams Family" TV series, 1964-66.
b. Jan 7, 1912 in Westfield, New Jersey
d. Sep 29, 1988 in New York, New York
Source: *AmAu&B; BiDScF; BioIn 2, 3, 6, 7, 8, 10; ConAu 61; CurBio 54; EncTwCJ; IntWW 74, 75, 76, 77, 78, 79, 80, 81, 82, 83; WebAB 74, 79; WhAm 9; WhoAm 74, 76, 78, 80, 82, 84, 86, 88; WhoAmA 73, 76, 78, 80, 82, 84, 86; WhoUSWr 88; WhoWor 74, 76, 78, 80, 82, 84, 87; WorAl; WrDr 76*

Addams, Dawn
English. Actor
Best known as Charlie Chaplin's leading lady in *A King in New York,* 1957.
b. Sep 21, 1930 in Felixstowe, England
d. May 7, 1985 in London, England
Source: *AnObit 1985; BioIn 14; ConTFT 2; FilmEn; FilmgC; HalFC 80, 84, 88; IlWWBF; IntMPA 75, 76, 77, 78, 79, 80, 81, 82, 84; InWom; ItaFilm; LegTOT; MotPP; OxCFilm; WhoHol A; WhoHrs 80; WhoThe 72, 77, 81*

Addams, Jane
[Laura Jane Addams]
American. Social Worker, Suffragist
Organized Hull House, Chicago, 1889; first American woman to receive Nobel Peace Prize, 1931.
b. Sep 6, 1860 in Cedarville, Illinois
d. May 21, 1935 in Chicago, Illinois
Source: *AmAu&B; AmBi; AmDec 1900; AmJust; AmLY; AmPeW; AmRef; AmRef&R; AmSocL; AmWomWr; AmWr S1; ApCAB X; ArtclWW 2; Benet 87, 96; BenetAL 91; BiDAmL; BiDMoPL; BiDSocW; BioAmW; BioIn 1, 2, 3, 4, 5, 6, 7, 8, 9, 10, 11, 12, 13, 14, 15, 16, 17, 18, 19, 20, 21; ConHero 2; ContDcW 89; CopCroC; DcAmAu; DcAmB S1; DcAmC; DcAmImH; DcAmReB 2; DcAmSR; DcLEL; DcNAA; DcTwHis; EncAB-H 1974, 1996; EncWHA; FacFETw; FemiWr; GayLesB; GayN; GoodHs; GrLiveH; HanAmWH; HarEnUS; HeroCon; HerW, 84; HisWorL; IntDcWB; InWom, SUP; LadLa 86; LegTOT; LibW; LinLib L, S; McGEWB; MemAm; NatCAB 13, 27; NobelP; NotAW; OxCAmH; OxCAmL 65, 83, 95; OxCWoWr 95; PeoHis; PorAmW; RadHan; RComAH; REn; REnAL; WebAB 74, 79; WebBD 83; WhAm 1; WhAmP; WhE&EA; WhNAA; WhoNob, 90, 95; WomChHR; WomEdUS; WomFir; WomPubS 1800; WomSoc; WomWWA 14; WorAl; WorAlBi*

Adderley, Cannonball
[Julian Edwin Adderley]
American. Musician
Alto-saxophonist who played with Miles Davis in 1950s; had 1960s hit "Mercy, Mercy, Mercy."
b. Sep 9, 1928 in Tampa, Florida
d. Aug 8, 1975 in Gary, Indiana
Source: *AllMusG; Baker 78, 84, 92; BiDAfM; BiDAmM; BiDJaz; BioIn 5, 6, 10, 12, 16; CurBio 61, 75; DcAmB S9; DrBlPA, 90; Ebony 1; EncJzS; IlEncJ; InB&W 80, 85; LegTOT; NewAmDM; NewGrDA 86; NewGrDJ 88, 94; NewYTBS 75; OxCPMus; PenEncP; PseudN 82; RkOn 78; WhAm 6; WhoAm 74; WorAl; WorAlBi*

Adderley, Herb(ert Anthony)
American. Football Player
Five-time all-pro defensive back, 1961-72, mostly with Green Bay; first to play in four Super Bowls, 1966-67, 1971-72; Pro Football Hall of Fame.
b. Jun 8, 1939 in Philadelphia, Pennsylvania
Source: *AfrAmSG; BiDAmSp FB; BioIn 17, 21; InB&W 80; LegTOT; WhoBlA 85, 92; WhoFtbl 74*

Addinsell, Richard
English. Composer
Compositions for films include *Blithe Spirit,* 1945; *Under Capricorn,* 1949; *Macbeth,* 1960.
b. Jan 13, 1904 in Oxford, England
d. Nov 15, 1977 in London, England
Source: *Baker 78, 78; IntWWM 77, 80; MusMk; NewAmDM; NewGrDM 80; NewOxM; NotNAT; OxCFilm; OxCMus; OxCPMus; Who 74; WhoMus 72; WhoThe 77*

Addison, Adele
American. Opera Singer
Soprano; sang role of Bess in *Porgy and Bess,* 1958; made solo debut, 1962.
b. Jul 24, 1925 in New York, New York
Source: *AfrAmAl 6; Baker 84, 92; BiDAfM; BioIn 16; BlkOpe; BlkWAm; DcTwCCu 5; DrBlPA, 90; InB&W 80, 85; IntWWM 90; NegAl 76, 83, 89; NewAmDM; NewGrDA 86; NewGrDM 80; WhoAfA 96; WhoAmW 68, 70, 72, 74; WhoBlA 75, 77, 80, 85, 90, 92, 94; WhoWor 74, 76*

Addison, Christopher, Viscount
English. Politician
MP; served on ministries concerned with public health, social welfare.
b. Jun 19, 1869 in Hogsthorpe, England
d. Dec 11, 1951 in Radnage, England
Source: *BioIn 15; DcNaB 1951; GrBr; OxCMed 86; WhE&EA; WhLit*

Addison, John
English. Composer
Known for film scores including Oscar-winning *Tom Jones,* 1963.
b. Mar 16, 1920 in West Cobham, England
Source: *Baker 78, 84, 92; BiE&WWA; CmMov; ConAmC 76; ConTFT 9; FilmEn; FilmgC; HalFC 80, 84, 88; IntDcF 1-4, 2-4; IntMPA 75, 76, 77, 78, 79, 80, 81, 82, 84, 86, 88, 92, 94, 96; IntWW 89, 91, 93; IntWWM 77, 80; NewGrDM 80; NewOxM; NotNAT, A; OxCFilm; OxCMus; OxCPMus; WhoMus 72*

Addison, Joseph
"Atticus"; "Clio"; "A Literary Machiavel"; "The English Atticus"
English. Essayist
Wrote essays with Sir Richard Steele for the *Tatler,* 1709; *Spectator,* 1711-12.
b. May 1, 1672 in Milston, England
d. Jun 17, 1719 in London, England
Source: *Alli; AtlBL; BbD; Benet 87, 96; BiD&SB; BioIn 1, 2, 3, 4, 5, 6, 8, 10, 11, 12, 13, 17, 18, 21; BlkwCE; BlmGEL; BritAu; BritWr 3; CamGEL; CamGLE; CamGWoT; CasWL; Chambr 2; ChhPo, S1, S2, S3; CnDBLB 2; CrtSuDr; CrtT 2; CyEd; CyWA 58; DcArts; DcBiPP; DcEnA; DcEnL; DcEuL; DcLB 101; DcLEL; DcNaB; DcPup; Dis&D; EncEnl; EncWT; Ent; EvLB; GrWrEL N; LegTOT; LiJour; LinLib L, S; LitC 18; LngCEL; LuthC 75; McGEWB; McGEWD 72, 84; MouLC 2; NewC; NewCBEL; NewGrDM 80; NewGrDO; NotNAT B; OxCArt; OxCEng 67, 85, 95; OxCMus; OxCThe 67, 83; OxDcArt; OxDcOp; PenC ENG; PlP&P; PoChrch; PseudAu; PseudN 82; RAdv 1, 14, 13-1; RComWL; REn; RfGEnL 91; WebE&AL; WhDW; WorAl; WorAlBi*

Addison, Thomas
English. Physician
Identified adrenal disfunction known as Addison's Disease, 1860.

b. Apr 1793 in Long Benton, England
d. Jun 29, 1860 in Brighton, England
Source: *Alli SUP; AsBiEn; BiESc; BiHiMed; BioIn 4, 5, 7, 9, 10, 14; CamDcSc; DcBiPP; DcNaB; DcScB; InSci; LarDcSc; McGEWB; OxCMed 86; WorScD*

Addonizio, Hugh Joseph
American. Politician
Dem. con. from NJ, 1949-61; mayor of Newark, NJ, 1962-70; convicted of extortion, 1970.
b. Jan 31, 1914 in Newark, New Jersey
d. Feb 2, 1981 in Red Bank, New Jersey
Source: *BiDrAC; BiDrUSC 89; BioIn 8, 9, 11, 12; NewYTBE 70; NewYTBS 81; PolProf J, NF; WhAm 7; WhAmP*

Addy, Wesley
American. Actor
Often cast in sinister roles: *Tora! Tora! Tora!*, 1970; *Network*, 1976.
b. Aug 4, 1913 in Omaha, Nebraska
d. Dec 31, 1996 in Danbury, Connecticut
Source: *BiE&WWA; ConTFT 8; FilmEn; FilmgC; HalFC 84; LegTOT; NotNAT; VarWW 85; WhoAm 74, 76, 78; WhoHol 92, A; WhoThe 72, 77, 81*

Ade, George
American. Author, Dramatist
Humorous fables published as *Fables in Slang*, 1900.
b. Feb 9, 1866 in Kentland, Indiana
d. May 16, 1944 in Brookville, Indiana
Source: *AmAu&B; AmLY; ApCAB X; BbD; Benet 87; BenetAL 91; BiDAmJo; BiDAmM; BiDAmNC; BiD&SB; BioIn 1, 2, 4, 5, 6, 7, 10, 11, 12, 13, 14, 15, 16; CamGLE; CamGWoT; CamHAL; CasWL; Chambr 3; ChhPo, S1; CnDAL; ConAmL; ConAu 110; CurBio 44; DcAmAu; DcAmB S3; DcLB 11, 25; DcNAA; EncAHmr; EncAJ; EncWT; EvLB; FacFETw; GayN; GrWrEL N; HarEnUS; IndAu 1816; JrnUS; LegTOT; LiJour; LinLib L, S; McGEWD 72, 84; ModWD; NatCAB 11; NewCBMT; NotNAT A, B; OxCAmL 65, 83, 95; OxCAmT 84; OxCPMus; OxCThe 67, 83; PenC AM; REn; REnAL; RfGAmL 87, 94; TwCA, SUP; TwCBDA; TwCWr; WebAB 74, 79; WhAm 2; WhLit; WhNAA; WhoStg 1906, 1908; WhThe; WorAl; WorAlBi*

Ade, Sunny, King
[Prince Sunday Adeniyi Adegeye]
Nigerian. Musician
Bandleader of groups High Society Band, Green Spots, and King Sunny Ade and his African Beats.
b. Sep 1946 in Ondo, Nigeria
Source: *BioIn 13; CurBio 94*

Adelman, Kenneth Lee
American. Government Official, Journalist
Director, Arms Control and Disarmament Agency, 1983-88; v.p., Institute Contemporary Studies, 1988—.
b. Jun 9, 1946 in Chicago, Illinois
Source: *BioIn 16; CurBio 85; IntWW 89, 91, 93; NewYTBS 83; WhoAm 84, 86, 88, 92, 94, 96*

Adelman, Sybil
Canadian. Writer
TV shows include "The Mary Tyler Moore Show," 1976-83; "Alice," 1970-77.
b. Mar 15, 1942 in Winnipeg, Manitoba, Canada
Source: *ConTFT 3*

Adenauer, Konrad
German. Politician
First Chancellor of Federal German Republic (West Germany), 1949-63.
b. Jan 5, 1876 in Cologne, Germany
d. Apr 19, 1967 in Rhondorf, Germany
Source: *BiDInt; BioIn 2, 3, 4, 5, 6, 7, 8, 9, 10, 11, 12, 13, 14, 17, 18, 19, 20, 21; ColdWar 1; ConAu 112; CurBio 49, 58, 67; DcPol; DcTwHis; EncCW; EncTR, 91; FacFETw; HisWorL; LegTOT; LinLib L, S; McGEWB; ObitT 1961; OxCGer 76, 86; PolLCWE; REn; WhAm 4; WhDW; WorAl; WorAlBi*

Ader, Clement
French. Engineer, Inventor
Steam-powered monoplane proved heavier-than-air machines capable of flight.
b. Feb 4, 1841 in Muret, France
d. Mar 5, 1926 in Toulouse, France
Source: *BioIn 7, 8, 9; LegTOT*

Adjani, Isabelle
French. Actor
Won Cesare Awards for *Possession*, 1981; *Cinematographe*, 1983; *Camille Claudel*, 1988; Super Cesare, 1990 for a decade of best screen performances.
b. Jun 27, 1958 in Paris, France
Source: *BioIn 14, 15; ConTFT 3; CurBio 90; FilmEn; HalFC 84; IntMPA 88; NewYTBS 84; VarWW 85; WhoHol A*

Adler, Alfred
Austrian. Author, Psychoanalyst
Rebelled against Freud's teachings, advocated individual psychology, 1907; originated phrase "inferiority complex."
b. Feb 7, 1870 in Vienna, Austria
d. May 28, 1937 in Aberdeen, Scotland
Source: *AsBiEn; Benet 87, 96; BiDPsy; BiESc; BiGAW; BioIn 1, 2, 4, 5, 6, 7, 9, 10, 11, 12, 13, 14, 15, 20; ConAu 119; FacFETw; GaEncPs; GuPsyc; InSci; LegTOT; LinLib L, S; LngCTC; LuthC 75; MakMC; McGEWB; NamesHP; OxCGer 76, 86; OxCMed 86; RAdv 14, 13-5; REn; ThTwC 87; TwCA, SUP; TwCLC 61; WhAm 4, HSA; WhDW; WhE&EA; WhoLA*

Adler, Buddy
[Maurice Adler]
American. Producer
Won Oscar for *From Here to Eternity*, 1953; succeeded Darryl Zanuck as head of 20th Century Fox.
b. Jun 22, 1909 in New York, New York
d. Jul 12, 1960 in Hollywood, California
Source: *DcFM; FilmEn; FilmgC; NatCAB 47; NotNAT B; ObitOF 79; PseudN 82; WhAm 4; WorEFlm*

Adler, Cyrus
American. Religious Leader, Author
Wrote *Told in the Coffee House*, 1898; edited *American Jewish Yearbook*, 1899-1906.
b. Sep 13, 1863 in Van Buren, Alaska
d. Apr 7, 1940 in Philadelphia, Pennsylvania
Source: *AmAu&B; AmBi; ApCAB SUP, X; BiDAmEd; BioIn 4, 5, 7, 8, 11, 12, 14, 16, 19, 20; ConAu 122; DcAmAu; DcAmB S2; DcAmLiB; DcAmReB 1, 2; DcNAA; EncAB-A 11; EncARH; HarEnUS; JeAmHC; LinLib L; NatCAB 11, 41; TwCBDA; WebAB 74, 79; WhAm 1; WorAl; WorAlBi*

Adler, Dankmar
Prussian. Architect, Engineer
With partner, Louis Sullivan, designed commercial buildings that helped launch modern architectural style.
b. Jul 3, 1844 in Stadtlengsfeld, Prussia
d. Apr 16, 1900 in Chicago, Illinois
Source: *BiDAmAr; BioIn 3, 8, 14, 16, 17, 19; BriEAA; EncMA; MacEA; McGDA; NatCAB 11; WebAB 74, 79; WhAm 1; WhoArch*

Adler, David
American. Architect
Domestic architecture in Chicago, noted for traditional style, conventional form, 1928-49.
b. Jan 3, 1883 in Milwaukee, Wisconsin
d. Sep 27, 1949 in Chicago, Illinois
Source: *BiDAmAr; BioIn 9; WhAm 3*

Adler, Elmer
American. Publisher
Noted bibliophile; founded *Colophon: Book Collectors Quarterly*, 1930-40.
b. Jul 22, 1884 in Rochester, New York
d. Jan 11, 1962 in San Juan, Puerto Rico
Source: *AmAu&B; BioIn 3, 5, 6; ChhPo; ConAu 89; DcAmBC; DcAmB S7; WhAm 4; WhAmArt 85*

Adler, Felix
American. Social Reformer
Ethical Culture Society founder, 1876, aided NY poor.
b. Aug 13, 1851 in Alzey, Germany
d. Apr 24, 1933 in New York, New York
Source: *Alli SUP; AmAu&B; AmBi; AmRef; ApCAB, X; BbD; Benet 87, 96; BenetAL 91; BiDAmCu; BiDAmEd; BiD&SB; BioIn 1, 2, 5, 8, 9, 10, 12, 14, 15, 19; DcAmAu; DcAmB S1; DcAmReB 1, 2; DcAmSR; DcNAA; EncARH;*

EncUnb; HarEnUS; LinLib L, S; LuthC 75; McGEWB; NatCAB 1, 23; OxCAmH; RelLAm 91; REn; REnAL; TwCA, SUP; TwCBDA; WebAB 74, 79; WhAm 1; WhAmP; WhNAA; WorAl; WorAlBi

Adler, Guido
Austrian. Musicologist, Teacher
Pioneer in shaping modern study of musicology; founded musicology research institute, University of Vienna, 1898.
b. Nov 1, 1855 in Eibenschutz, Moravia
d. Feb 15, 1941 in Vienna, Austria
Source: *Baker 78, 84, 92; BioIn 9, 12; CurBio 41; NewGrDM 80; NewGrDO; NewOxM; OxCMus; WhE&EA; WhoLA*

Adler, Irving
[Robert Irving]
American. Author
Scientific books for young people include *The Stars: Decoding Their Messages,* 1980.
b. Apr 27, 1913 in New York, New York
Source: *AmAu&B; AnObit 1991; Au&Wr 71; AuBYP 2, 3; Baker 84; BiDD; BioIn 7, 9, 13, 19; ChlLR 27; CnOxB; ConAu 2NR, 5R, 25R, 47NR, X; DancEn 78; DcLP 87A; IntAu&W 91; MajAI; NewGrDA 86; NewGrDM 80; NewYTBS 91; PenDiMP; PseudN 82; SmATA 1, 15AS, 29; ThrBJA; WhoE 91, 93, 95, 97; WhoFrS 84; WhoWor 93, 95*

Adler, Jacob Pavlovitch
"The Great Eagle"
American. Actor
Star of Yiddish theater; father of Luther, Stella.
b. 1855, Russia
d. Apr 1, 1926 in New York, New York
Source: *BioIn 4, 5, 11; Film 1; NotNAT B; PseudN 82; WhoHol B; WhScrn 77; WhThe*

Adler, Julius Ochs
American. Newspaper Executive
General mgr., *NY Times,* 1935-55; adviser to Dwight D. Eisenhower.
b. Dec 3, 1892 in Chattanooga, Tennessee
d. Oct 3, 1955 in New York, New York
Source: *AmAu&B; BiDWWGF; BioIn 1, 4; CurBio 48, 56; ObitOF 79; ObitT 1951; WhAm 3; WorAl; WorAlBi*

Adler, Kurt
German. Chemist
Won Nobel Prize for chemistry, 1950.
b. Jul 10, 1902 in Koenigshuette, Germany
d. Jun 20, 1958 in Cologne, Germany
Source: *DcScB; McGMS 80; ObitOF 79; WhAm 3; WhoNob; WorAl*

Adler, Kurt Herbert
American. Conductor
General manager, San Francisco Opera, 1956-81; brought it to world-class status.
b. Apr 2, 1905 in Vienna, Austria
d. Feb 9, 1988 in Ross, California
Source: *Baker 78, 84, 92; BioIn 5, 7, 8, 9, 10, 11, 12, 15, 16; BlueB 76; CmCal; CmOp; CurBio 79, 88, 88N; IntWW 74, 75, 76, 77; IntWWM 77, 80; MetOEnc; NewAmDM; NewEOp 71; NewGrDA 86; NewGrDM 80; NewGrDO; NewYTBS 75, 88; OxDcOp; PenDiMP; WhAm 9; WhoAm 74, 76, 78; WhoAmM 83; WhoOp 76; WhoWest 74, 76, 78, 82; WhoWor 74, 76; WhoWorJ 72*

Adler, Larry
[Lawrence Cecil Adler]
American. Musician
Considered world's best harmonica player; performings muscian for children's commercials and stage since 1975.
b. Feb 10, 1914 in Baltimore, Maryland
Source: *AllMusG; Baker 78, 84, 92; BiDAmM; BiE&WWA; BioIn 2, 3, 5, 7, 10, 14; ConTFT 4; DcArts; FilmgC; HalFC 80, 84, 88; IntWW 82, 83, 89, 91, 93; IntWWM 90; NewAmDM; NewGrDA 86; NewGrDJ 88, 94; NewGrDM 80; NotNAT; OxCMus; OxCPMus; PenDiMP; PenEncP; What 1; WhDW; Who 74, 82, 83, 85, 88, 90, 92, 94; WhoEnt 92; WhoHol 92, A; WhoMus 72; WorAl*

Adler, Luther
[Lutha Adler]
American. Actor, Director
Child actor in Yiddish Theater; films include *The Three Sisters,* 1977.
b. May 4, 1903 in New York, New York
d. Dec 8, 1984 in Kutztown, Pennsylvania
Source: *AnObit 1984; BiE&WWA; BioIn 14; ConTFT 2; Ent; FilmEn; FilmgC; ForYSC; GangFlm; HalFC 80, 84, 88; HolCA; IntMPA 77, 78, 79, 80, 81, 82, 84; LegTOT; MotPP; MovMk; NotNAT; OxCAmT 84; PlP&P; PseudN 82; VarWW 85; Vers B; WhAm 8; WhoAm 74, 76, 78, 80; WhoHol A; WhoThe 72, 77, 81; WhoWor 74; WorAl; WorAlBi*

Adler, Mortimer J(erome)
American. Author, Philosopher
Director, Institute for Philosophical Research, 1952—; wrote best-seller, *How to Read a Book,* 1940.
b. Dec 28, 1902 in New York, New York
Source: *AmAu&B; BenetAL 91; BioIn 2, 3, 4, 5, 11, 12, 13, 14, 15, 17, 18; ConAu 33NR, 65; CurBio 40, 52; DrAS 74P, 78P, 82P; FacFETw; IntAu&W 91, 93; MajTwCW; NewYTBS 82; OxCAmL 65, 83, 95; RAdv 13-4; REnAL; TwCA SUP; WebAB 74, 79; WhNAA; WhoAm 76, 78, 80, 82, 84, 86, 88, 90, 92, 94, 95, 96, 97; WhoWor 74, 76, 95, 96, 97; WrDr 86, 92, 94, 96*

Adler, Peter Herman
American. Conductor
Conducted Baltimore Symphony, 1959-67.
b. Dec 2, 1899 in Jablonec, Bohemia
d. Oct 2, 1990 in Ridgefield, Connecticut
Source: *Baker 78, 84, 92; BiDAmM; BioIn 9, 17; CmOp; FacFETw; IntWWM 90; MetOEnc; NewAmDM; NewEOp 71; NewGrDA 86; NewGrDM 80; NewGrDO; NewYTBS 90; OxDcOp; PenDiMP; WhoAm 74, 76, 78, 80, 82, 84; WhoOp 76*

Adler, Polly
[Pearl Adler]
American. Madam
Began career, 1920; wrote *A House Is Not a Home,* 1953.
b. Apr 16, 1900 in Yanow, Poland
d. Jun 9, 1962 in Hollywood, California
Source: *AmAu&B; Au&Wr 71; BioIn 3, 6, 12; DcAmB S7; InWom, SUP; NotAW MOD*

Adler, Richard
American. Composer
Musical film scores include *Damn Yankees,* 1958; *Pajama Game,* 1957; won Tonys for Broadway versions, 1954, 1955.
b. Aug 3, 1921 in New York, New York
Source: *AmSong; ASCAP 66, 80; Baker 84, 92; BestMus; BiDAmM; BiE&WWA; BioIn 3, 5, 6, 9, 10, 12, 14, 15; ConTFT 4, 14; EncMT; HalFC 80, 84, 88; NatCAB 63N; NewAmDM; NewGrDA 86; NewGrDM 80; NotNAT; OxCAmT 84; OxCPMus; PopAmC, SUP; WhoAm 74, 76, 78, 80, 82, 84, 86, 88, 90, 92, 94, 95, 96, 97; WhoAmM 83; WhoEnt 92; WhoGov 72, 75; WhoThe 72, 77, 81; WhoWor 74, 76, 82*

Adler, Stella
American. Actor
Founder, director, Stella Adler Conservatory of Acting, 1949.
b. Feb 10, 1902 in New York, New York
d. Dec 21, 1992 in Los Angeles, California
Source: *BiE&WWA; BioIn 2, 4, 8, 9, 11, 12, 13, 14; ConTFT 3; CurBio 85, 93N; EncWT; FilmgC; InWom SUP; LegTOT; NotNAT; NotWoAT; OxCAmT 84; PlP&P; VarWW 85; WhoHol 92, A; WhoThe 72, 77, 81*

Adler, Victor
Austrian. Political Leader
Leader, leading figure, Social Democratic Party of Austria, 1888-1918; after WW I advocated union of Austria with Germany.
b. Jun 24, 1852 in Prague, Czechoslovakia
d. Nov 11, 1918 in Vienna, Austria
Source: *BioIn 7, 11; EncRev; OxCGer 86*

Adolfo
[Adolfo F Sardina]
American. Fashion Designer
Founded Adolfo, Inc., 1963; designs custom and ready-to-wear; won Cotys, 1955, 1969.

b. Feb 15, 1933 in Cardones, Cuba
Source: *BioIn 8, 9, 10, 16; CelR, 90; ConDes 84, 90, 97; ConFash; CurBio 72; EncFash; IntWW 91, 93; PseudN 82; WhoAm 76, 78, 80, 82, 84, 86, 88, 90, 92, 94, 95, 96; WhoFash 88; WhoHisp 91, 92, 94; WhoWor 91; WorFshn*

Adonias (Aguiar) Filho
Brazilian. Author
Novels include *Os Servos da Morte,* 1946; *Memorias de Lazaro,* 1952; *O Forte,* 1965.
b. Nov 27, 1915 in Itajuipe, Brazil
Source: *DcBrazL*

Adonis, Joe
[Joe Doro]
"Joey A"
Italian. Criminal
Headed Broadway mob that controlled bootleg liquor in Manhattan; deported, 1956.
b. Nov 22, 1902 in Montemarano, Italy
d. Nov 26, 1971 in Aucona, Italy
Source: *BioIn 9; DcAmB S9; EncACr; LegTOT; ObitOF 79; PseudN 82*

Adoree, Renee
[Jeanne de la Fonte]
French. Actor, Circus Performer
Circus dancer; starred in several films, 1920-30.
b. Sep 30, 1898 in Lille, France
d. Oct 5, 1933 in Tujunga, California
Source: *BiDD; BiDFilm, 81; Film 2; FilmEn; FilmgC; HalFC 80, 84, 88; IntDcF 1-3; InWom SUP; LegTOT; MotPP; MovMk; NotNAT B; PseudN 82; TwYS; WhoHol B; WhScrn 74, 77, 83; WorEFlm*

Adorno, Theodor Wiesengrund
German. Philosopher
Prominent in the Frankfurt school during post WWII German intellectual revival; studies based on Freudian-Marxist theory.
b. Sep 11, 1903 in Frankfurt am Main, Germany
d. Aug 6, 1969 in Visa, Switzerland
Source: *Baker 84; BiDNeoM; BioIn 8, 11, 12, 13, 14, 16; CasWL; ConAu 25R, 89; EncWB; EncWL 2; FacFETw; IntEnSS 79; LiExTwC; MakMC; NewOxM; OxCGer 76, 86; OxCPhil; OxDcOp; RAdv 13-4; ThTwC 87; WorAu 1970*

Adrian
[Gilbert Adrain Greenburgh]
American. Fashion Designer
Noted Hollywood designer, 1930-52; clothed Garbo, Harlow, others; wed Janet Gaynor; won Coty, 1944; responsible for giving Joan Crawford the padded shoulders look.
b. Mar 3, 1903 in Naugatuck, Connecticut
d. Sep 13, 1959 in Hollywood, California
Source: *AmDec 1940; BioIn 16, 18; ConDes 84; DcFM; EncFash; FilmEn; FilmgC; HalFC 80, 84, 88; IntDcF 1-4; LegTOT; PseudN 82; WorFshn*

Adrian, Edgar Douglas, Baron
English. Educator
Shared Nobel Prize, 1932, for studies of neuron function.
b. Nov 30, 1889 in London, England
d. Aug 4, 1977 in London, England
Source: *BiESc; BioIn 12, 15, 20; BlueB 76; CamDcSc; ConAu 73; DcLEL; DcNaB 1971; FacFETw; GrBr; InSci; LarDcSc; McGEWB; NotTwCS; OxCMed 86; WhoNob, 90, 95; WorAl; WorAlBi; WorScD*

Adrian II
[Hadrian II]
Italian. Religious Leader
Last pope to be married; approved Slavic liturgy.
b. 792 in Rome, Italy
d. 872
Source: *BioIn 5, 7; WebBD 83*

Ady, Endre
Hungarian. Poet
Regarded as one of the greatest Hungarian lyric poets; wrote *New Poems,* 1906.
b. Nov 22, 1877 in Ermindszent, Hungary
d. Jan 27, 1919 in Budapest, Hungary
Source: *BioIn 1, 3; EuWr 9; EvEuW; FacFETw; LinLib L; PenC EUR; RAdv 14, 13-2; TwCLC 11; TwCWr; WhDW; WhoTwCL*

Adzhubei, Aleksei I(vanovich)
Russian. Journalist
Editor in chief, *Komsomolskaya Pravda,* 1958-59; editor in chief, *Izvestia,* 1959-64.
b. 1924
d. Mar 19, 1993?, Russia
Source: *BioIn 5, 6, 7; CurBio 93N*

Aerosmith
[Tom Hamilton; Joey Kramer; Joe Perry; Steve Tyler; Brad Whitford]
American. Music Group
Heavy metal band formed 1970; known for blues-based, hard-rock style; hits "Dream On," 1975; "Dude (Looks Like a Lady)," 1987.
Source: *AmBench 79; BioIn 10, 20; BkPepl; ConMuA 80A; ConMus 3; EncPR&S 89; EncRk 88; EncRkSt; HarEnR 86; IlEncRk; NewAmDM; NewGrDA 86; PenEncP; ProFbHF; RkOn 78; RolSEnR 83; WhoRock 81; WhoRocM 82*

Aeschbacher, Hans
Swiss. Sculptor
Known for abstract sculptures, including *Explorer I.*
b. Jan 18, 1906 in Zurich, Switzerland
Source: *BioIn 11; PhDcTCA 77*

Aeschylus
"The Father of Greek Drama"; "The Father of Greek Tragedy"; "The Father of Tragedy"; "The Founder of the Greek Drama"
Greek. Dramatist
Wrote *Prometheus Bound;* seven of 90 plays survive.
b. 524?BC in Eleusis
d. 456?BC in Gela, Italy
Source: *AtlBL; BiD&SB; CasWL; ClMLC 11; CyWA 58; DcBiPP; DcEnL; EncWT; Grk&L; LinLib S; LngCEL; McGEWD 72; NewC; OxCThe 67; PenC CL; RComWL; REn; WhDW*

Aesop
Greek. Author
Semi-legendary figure; hundreds of animal fables attributed to him.
b. 620?BC, Phrygia
d. 560?BC, Italy
Source: *AnCL; AtlBL; Benet 87, 96; BiD&SB; CarSB; CasWL; ChhPo, S1, S2; ChlLR 14; CyWA 58; DcEnL; DcPup; Dis&D; LinLib L, S; MajAI; NewC; OxCEng 67; PenC CL; RComWL; REn; SmATA 64; WhoChL; WorAl; WorAlBi*

Aflaq, Michel
Syrian. Politician, Writer
Co-founded Syrian Ba'th Party, 1947.
b. 1910 in Damascus, Syria
d. Jun 23, 1989 in Paris, France
Source: *BioIn 6, 16; ColdWar 2; DcPol; DcTwHis; EncRev; EncWB; FacFETw; IntAu&W 89; IntWW 89; NewYTBS 89; PolLCME; WhoArab 81*

Aga Khan, Sadruddin, Prince
Pakistani. Diplomat, Writer
Consultant to UN secretary-general, 1978; wrote *International Protection of Refugees,* 1976.
b. Jan 17, 1933 in Paris, France
Source: *BioIn 15, 17; IntWW 74, 75, 76, 77, 78, 79, 81, 82, 83, 89, 91, 93; MidE 78, 79, 80, 81, 82; Who 74, 82, 83, 85, 88, 90, 92, 94; WhoEIO 82; WhoUN 75, 92; WhoWor 74, 76, 78, 80, 82, 84, 87, 89, 91, 93, 95*

Aga Khan III
[Aga Sultan Sir Mahomed Shah]
Indian. Religious Leader, Statesman
Descendant of Mohammed; spiritual leader of 80 million Ismaili Moslems, 1885-1957; pres., League of Nations, 1937.
b. Nov 2, 1877 in Karachi, Pakistan
d. Jul 11, 1957 in Versoix, Switzerland
Source: *CurBio 46, 57; McGEWB; NewCol 75; ObitOF 79; PseudN 82; WhAm 3*

Aga Khan IV
[Prince Karim Khan]
Religious Leader
Descendant of Mohammed; grandson of Aga Khan III, whom he succeeded as Imam spiritual leader of Ismaili Moslems, 1957—.

b. Dec 13, 1936 in Geneva, Switzerland
Source: *BioIn 13, 14; CurBio 60; IntWW 83, 91; IntYB 82; NewYTBS 82; Who 85, 92; WhoRel 92; WhoWor 87, 91*

Agam, Yaacov
[Yaacov Gibstein]
Israeli. Artist
Contrapuntal geometric painter; *Jacob's Ladder,* 1964, decorates ceiling of Jerusalem's Convention Center.
b. May 11, 1928 in Rishon Letzion, Palestine
Source: *BioIn 7, 8, 10, 11, 12, 15; ConArt 77, 83, 89, 96; CurBio 81; IntWW 75, 76, 77, 78, 79, 80, 81, 82, 83, 91, 93; McGDA; MidE 78, 79, 80; OxCTwCA; OxDcArt; PhDcTCA 77; PrintW 83, 85; WhoWor 74, 82, 84, 87, 91, 93, 95, 96, 97; WorArt 1950*

Aganbegyan, Abel Gezevich
Russian. Economist
Economic adviser to Mikhail Gorbachev; helped draft plans for perestroika.
b. Nov 8, 1932 in Tbilisi, Union of Soviet Socialist Republics
Source: *BiDSovU; BioIn 15; IntWW 91, 93; LngBDD; NewYTBS 87, 88; WhoRus*

Agar, Herbert Sebastian
American. Author
Won Pulitzer for *The People's Choice, A Time for Greatness,* 1942.
b. Sep 29, 1897 in New Rochelle, New York
d. Nov 24, 1980 in Sussex, England
Source: *AmAu&B; AnObit 1980; Au&Wr 71; BioIn 1, 4; BlueB 76; ConAu 65, 102; CurBio 44, 81; IntAu&W 76, 77; IntWW 74, 80; OxCAmL 83; REnAL; TwCA, SUP; WhAm 7; Who 74; WhoWor 74, 76*

Agar, John
American. Actor
Had roles in action films, but best known as first husband of Shirley Temple, 1946-49.
b. Jan 31, 1921 in Chicago, Illinois
Source: *BioIn 10, 16, 17, 21; ConTFT 8; FilmEn; FilmgC; ForYSC; HalFC 80, 84, 88; IntMPA 75, 76, 77, 78, 79, 80, 81, 82, 84, 86, 88, 92, 94, 96; MotPP; What 4; WhoHol 92, A; WhoHrs 80*

Agase, Alexander A.
American. Football Player
Only player to be named All-American at two different schools, 1943 (Purdue) and 1946 (Illinois); member, College Football Hall of Fame.
b. Mar 27, 1922 in Evanston, Illinois
Source: *WhoSpor*

Agassi, Andre
American. Tennis Player
Number one ranked male player in US, 1988, 1995; won US Open, 1994.
b. Apr 29, 1970 in Las Vegas, Nevada
Source: *BioIn 15, 16, 18; BuCMET; CelR 90; CurBio 89; IntWW 93; LegTOT; News 90, 90-2; WhoSpor*

Agassiz, Alexander Emmanuel Rodolphe
American. Zoologist, Explorer
Used much of fortune to promote scientific research at Harvard; began his own far-ranging oceanographic trips in 1877; son of Louis.
b. Dec 17, 1835 in Neuchatel, Switzerland
d. Mar 27, 1910
Source: *AmAu; ApCAB; BiD&SB; BiInAmS; DcAmB; DcScB; LarDcSc; NewCol 75; TwCBDA; WebAB 74*

Agassiz, Elizabeth Cabot Cary
American. Scientist, Educator
Founder, first pres., Radcliffe College, 1894-1902.
b. Dec 5, 1822 in Boston, Massachusetts
d. Jun 27, 1902 in Arlington, Massachusetts
Source: *Alli SUP; AmAu&B; AmBi; AmRef; AmWom; AmWomM; AmWomSc; AmWomWr; BiCAW; BiDAmEd; BiD&SB; BiInAmS; BioIn 15, 20; DcAmAu; DcAmB; DcNAA; GrLiveH; HarEnUS; IntDcWB; InWom SUP; LibW; NatCAB 12; NotAW; WhAm 1; WomFir*

Agassiz, Louis
[Jean Louis Radolphe Agassiz]
American. Naturalist
Theorized aglacial epoch, epochs of creation; opposed Darwin's theory.
b. May 28, 1807 in Motier, Switzerland
d. Dec 12, 1873 in Cambridge, Massachusetts
Source: *AmAu; AmAu&B; AmBi; BbD; BenetAL 91; BiD&SB; BioIn 1, 2, 3, 4, 5, 6, 8, 9, 11, 12, 13, 14, 15, 16, 17, 19; CamGEL; CamHAL; CyEd; DcAmAu; DcAmB; DcBiPP; DcEnL; EncAB-H 1974; LegTOT; OxCAmH; OxCAmL 65, 83; OxCCan; PenC AM; PeoHis; RAdv 14, 13-5; REn; REnAL; TwCBDA; WebAB 74, 79; WhAm HS; WorAlBi*

Agate, James Evershed
English. Critic, Author
Veteran theater columnist who wrote nine-volume autobiography, *Ego,* 1935.
b. Sep 9, 1877 in Manchester, England
d. Jun 6, 1947 in London, England
Source: *Benet 87; BioIn 1, 2, 4, 5, 11; ChhPo S1; DcArts; DcLEL; DcNaB 1941; EvLB; LngCTC; ModBrL; NewC; NewCBEL; NotNAT A, B; OxCEng 85, 95; OxCThe 67, 83; PenC ENG; REn; TwCA, SUP; TwCWr; WhE&EA; WhLit; WhThe*

Agca, Mehmet Ali
[Faruk Ozgun]
Turkish. Terrorist, Attempted Assassin
Convicted of attempting to assassinate Pope John Paul II, May 1981.
b. Jan 9, 1958 in Malatya, Turkey
Source: *BioIn 13, 14; NewYTBS 81; PseudN 82*

Agee, James Rufus
American. Author, Poet
Won Pulitzer, 1958, for *A Death in the Family.*
b. Nov 27, 1909 in Knoxville, Tennessee
d. May 16, 1955 in New York, New York
Source: *AmAu&B; AmWr; AuNews 1; CasWL; EncWL; FilmgC; ModAL, S1; OxCAmL 65; OxCFilm; PenC AM; RAdv 1; REn; REnAL; SixAP; TwCA SUP; TwCWr; WebAB 74; WebE&AL; WhAm 4; WhoTwCL; WorEFlm*

Agee, Philip
American. Government Official, Author
Former CIA agent who wrote expose *Inside the Company: CIA Diary,* 1975.
b. Jul 19, 1935 in Tacoma Park, Florida
Source: *BioIn 10, 11, 12, 15, 16; ConAu 104, 135; EncAI&E; EncCW; NewYTBS 74; PolProf NF; WrDr 94*

Agee, William McReynolds
American. Business Executive
Chief exec., Bendix Corp., 1977-83; husband of Mary Cunningham.
b. Jan 5, 1938 in Boise, Idaho
Source: *AutoN 79; BioIn 13, 14, 16; Dun&B 79, 90; IntWW 79, 80, 81, 82, 83, 89, 91, 93; NewYTBS 82; St&PR 91; WhoAm 82, 90; WhoFI 74, 75, 77, 79, 81; WhoWest 89; WhoWor 78, 82*

Ager, Milton
American. Composer
Popular balladist; wrote "Ain't She Sweet?," 1927; "Happy Days Are Here Again," 1929.
b. Oct 6, 1893 in Chicago, Illinois
d. May 6, 1979 in Los Angeles, California
Source: *AmPS; AmSong; ASCAP 66, 80; Baker 78, 84, 92; BiDAmM; BioIn 4, 6, 12, 14, 15, 16; CmpEPM; LegTOT; NewAmDM; NewGrDA 86; NewYTBS 79; OxCPMus; PopAmC; Sw&Ld C*

Agle, Nan Hayden
American. Children's Author
Co-writer of popular "Three Boys" series 1951—.
b. Apr 13, 1905 in Baltimore, Maryland
Source: *AuBYP 2, 3; ConAu 1NR, 1R, 3NR; IntAu&W 77, 91; PseudN 82; SmATA 3, 10AS, 13; WhoAmW 58, 61, 72; WrDr 76, 80, 82, 84, 86, 88, 90*

Agnelli, Giovanni
Italian. Auto Manufacturer
A founder and prime mover of Fiat automobile co., 1899; supporter of Benito Mussolini; helped mobilize the war industry in Italy before and during WWII.
b. Aug 13, 1866 in Villar Perosa, Italy
d. Dec 16, 1945 in Turin, Italy

Source: *BioIn 13, 14, 15, 16; EncWB; IntWW 91; News 89; Who 88, 92; WhoWor 91*

Agnelli, Giovanni
Italian. Auto Executive
Chm., FIAT, Italy's largest private business, 1966—.
b. Mar 12, 1921 in Turin, Italy
Source: *BioIn 7, 8, 9, 11, 12, 13, 14, 15, 16; CurBio 72; EncWB; IntWW 74, 75, 76, 77, 78, 79, 80, 81, 82, 83, 89, 91, 93; News 89; Who 74, 82, 83, 85, 88, 90, 92, 94; WhoAm 94, 95, 96, 97; WhoFI 74, 75, 77, 96; WhoWor 74, 76, 78, 80, 82, 84, 87, 89, 91, 93, 95, 96, 97*

Agnes, Saint
Roman. Religious Figure
Well-born virgin martyr; patron saint of young girls.
b. 291? in Rome, Italy
d. 304 in Rome, Italy
Source: *LngCEL; NewC; NewCol 75; WebBD 83*

Agnew, David Hayes
American. Surgeon, Educator
Attended President Garfield when he was shot, 1881; considered fine lecturer.
b. Nov 24, 1818 in Lancaster, Pennsylvania
d. Mar 22, 1892 in Philadelphia, Pennsylvania
Source: *Alli SUP; AmAu; AmBi; ApCAB SUP, X; BiDAmEd; BioIn 1; DcAmAu; DcAmB; DcAmMeB, 84; DcNAA; HarEnUS; InSci; NatCAB 8; TwCBDA; WebAB 74, 79; WhAm HS*

Agnew, Spiro T(heodore)
American. US Vice President
Nixon's vp; resigned, 1973, pleading no contest to income tax evasion charges.
b. Nov 9, 1918 in Baltimore, Maryland
d. Sep 17, 1996 in Berlin, Maryland
Source: *AmOrTwC; AmPolLe; BiDrAC; BiDrUSC 89; BiDrUSE 71, 89; BioIn 8, 9, 10, 11, 12, 14, 16; BioNews 74; ConAu 135, 153; CurBio 68, 96N; DcAmC; EncAB-H 1974, 1996; EncSoH; EncWB; FacFETw; IntAu&W 91; IntWW 74, 75, 76, 77, 78, 79, 80, 81, 82, 83, 89, 91, 93; IntYB 78, 79, 80, 81, 82; LinLib S; News 97-1; PolProf NF; VicePre; WebAB 74, 79; WhAmP; WhDW; Who 74, 82, 83, 85, 88, 90, 92, 94; WhoAm 74, 76, 78, 80, 82, 84, 92, 94, 95, 96, 97; WhoAmP 73, 75, 77, 79, 81, 83; WhoGov 72, 75; WhoSSW 73, 82; WhoWor 74, 78; WorAlBi; WrDr 86, 92, 94*

Agnon, S(hmuel) Y(osef)
[Shmuel Yosef Czaczkes]
Israeli. Author
Wrote *Days of Awe,* 1948; first Israeli to win Nobel Prize for literature, 1966.
b. Jul 17, 1888 in Buczacz, Galicia
d. Feb 17, 1970 in Rehovot, Israel
Source: *Benet 87, 96; BioIn 15, 16, 17; CasWL; ClDMEL 80; ConAu 17R, 25R, P-2; ConLC 4, 8, 14; CurBio 67; CyWA 89; DcArts; EncWL, 2; GrFLW; LiExTwC; LinLib L; MajTwCW; NobelP; Novels; PenC EUR; PseudN 82; RAdv 14; RComWL; WhAm 5; WhoNob, 90, 95; WorAlBi; WorAu 1950*

Agostini, Peter
American. Sculptor
Known for humorous "frozen life" plaster castings.
b. Feb 13, 1913 in New York, New York
d. Mar 27, 1993 in New York, New York
Source: *AnObit 1993; BioIn 6, 7, 18, 19; BriEAA; DcAmArt; DcCAA 71, 77, 88, 94; DcCAr 81; NewYTBS 93; OxCTwCA; PhDcTCA 77; WhoAm 74, 76; WhoAmA 73, 76, 78, 80, 82, 84, 86, 89, 91, 93*

Agostino di Duccio
Italian. Sculptor
Examples of his reliefs are displayed at museums in Rimini, Perugia, Bologna, and Florence.
b. 1418 in Florence, Italy
d. 1481 in Florence, Italy
Source: *BioIn 1; MacEA; McGDA; McGEWB; NewCol 75; OxCArt; OxDcArt; WhDW*

Agoult, Marie Catherine Sophie d'
[Daniel Stern]
French. Author
Wrote romances and political, historical essays; mistress of Franz Liszt, friend of George Sand.
b. Dec 31, 1805 in Frankfurt am Main, Germany
d. Mar 5, 1876 in Paris, France
Source: *Alli; BbD; BiD&SB; BioIn 15, 17; DcNAA; EvEuW; OxCFr; PenNWW B; WebBD 83*

Agpaoa, Tony
[Antonio Agpaoa]
Philippine. Surgeon
Psychic healer; operates with bare hands, without anesthetics.
b. 1939
Source: *BioIn 10; EncO&P 1, 2, 3*

Agramonte y Simoni, Aristides
Cuban. Pathologist, Bacteriologist
Member, Reed Yellow Fever Board, US Army, which discovered role of mosquito in disease's transmission, 1901.
b. Jun 3, 1868 in Camaguey, Cuba
d. Aug 19, 1931 in New Orleans, Louisiana
Source: *DcAmB S1*

Agricola, Georgius
[Georg Bauer]
German. Mineralogist
Father of mineralogy; first to classify minerals scientifically.
b. Apr 20, 1494 in Eisleben, Germany
d. Sep 22, 1566 in Berlin, Germany
Source: *AsBiEn; BiESc; BioIn 14, 20; CamDcSc; DcCathB; DcInv; DcScB; LarDcSc; McGEWB; OxCGer 76; PenC EUR; PseudN 82; WhDW; WorAl; WorAlBi*

Agrippa, Heinrich Cornelius
[Henricus Cornelius von Nettlesheim Agrippa]
"The Omniscious Doctor"
German. Author
Wrote about the occult; *De Occulta Philosophia,* 1529; defended magic.
b. Sep 14, 1486 in Cologne, Germany
d. Feb 18, 1535 in Grenoble, France
Source: *BiD&SB; DcBiPP; DcCathB; DcEnL; DcScB; EncO&P 1; EvEuW; IlEncMy; LuthC 75; OxCEng 67; OxCMed 86*

Agrippa, Marcus Vipsanius
Roman. Statesman, Army Officer
Collected material for map of Roman Empire.
b. 63BC
d. 12BC
Source: *BioIn 13, 14; DcBiPP; LinLib S; OxCShps; PenC CL*

Agrippina
Roman. Ruler
Mother of Nero; murdered by her son.
b. 16
d. 59 in Baige, Italy
Source: *MacDWB; NewCol 75; REn*

Agron, Salvador
American. Murderer
Youngest person, at age 16, to receive death sentence in NY state, 1959; sentence commuted, 1962; paroled, 1979.
b. Apr 24, 1944 in New York
d. Apr 22, 1986 in New York, New York
Source: *NewYTBS 79*

Agronsky, Martin Zama
American. Broadcast Journalist
TV commentator, Washington, DC, 1969-88; won Emmy for TV special, 1969.
b. Jan 12, 1915 in Philadelphia, Pennsylvania
Source: *AuNews 2; BioIn 13; ConAu 109; EncTwCJ; LesBEnT, 92; LinLib L, S; WhoAm 74, 76, 78; WhoSSW 73; WhoWor 74, 76, 78*

Agt, Andries Antonius Maria van
Dutch. Politician
Prime minister, minister of general affairs, 1977-82; minister of foreign affairs, 1982.
b. Feb 2, 1931, Netherlands
Source: *IntWW 91; WhoEIO 82*

Aguilar, Grace
Spanish. Author
Wrote novels, religious works concerning Judaism: *The Jewish Faith,* 1845.

b. Jun 2, 1816 in London, England
d. Sep 16, 1847 in Frankfurt am Main, Germany
Source: *Alli; BbD; BiD&SB; BioIn 16; BlmGWL; BritAu 19; CelCen; Chambr 3; ChhPo S2; ContDcW 89; DcBiA; DcBiPP; DcEnL; DcEuL; DcLEL; DcNaB; EncBrWW; EvLB; FemiCLE; IntDcWB; InWom, SUP; LinLib L, S; MacDWB; NewC; PenNWW A; StaCVF; VicBrit; WomFir*

Aguinaldo, Emilio
Philippine. Army Officer, Political Leader
Pres. of Philippines, 1898-1901; accused of conspiring with Japanese, WW II.
b. Mar 22, 1869 in Cavite, Philippines
d. Feb 6, 1964 in Manila, Philippines
Source: *BioIn 6, 8, 9, 10, 14, 15, 18; DcAmDH 80; DcAmSR; DcTwHis; EncRev; HarEnMi; HisDcSE; LinLib S; McGEWB; OxCAmH; WhAm 4, HSA*

Aguirre, Lope de
Spanish. Adventurer, Revolutionary
Conquistador in S America; noted for plundering, cruelty.
b. 1510?
d. 1561 in Barquisimeto, Venezuela
Source: *ApCAB; Drake; NewCol 75; WebBD 83; WhWE*

Aguirre, Mark (Anthony)
American. Basketball Player
Member US Olympic team, 1980; forward, Dallas, 1981-89, Detroit, 1989-93; LA Clippers, 1993-94; Dallas, 1994—.
b. Dec 10, 1959 in Chicago, Illinois
Source: *BasBi; BiDAmSp Sup; BioIn 13; InB&W 85; NewYTBS 81; OfNBA 87; WhoAfA 96; WhoAm 86, 88, 90, 92; WhoBlA 85, 88, 90, 92, 94; WhoHisp 92, 94; WhoMW 90*

Agus Salim, Hadji
Indonesian. Politician, Religious Leader
Influential moderator during country's political reform of the 1920s; joined Islamic Association, 1915, later becoming highly regarded member.
b. Oct 8, 1884 in Kota Gedang, Dutch East Indies
d. Nov 4, 1954 in Jogjakarta, Indonesia

Agustini, Delmira
Uruguayan. Poet
One of S. America's most influential poets; forerunner of female poets to write with sensual and passionate theme.
b. Oct 24, 1886 in Montevideo, Uruguay
d. Jul 6, 1914 in Montevideo, Uruguay
Source: *Benet 96; BioIn 1, 11, 15, 16, 17; BlmGWL; CasWL; DcSpL; DcTwCCu 3; EncLatA; HispWr; LatAmWr; ModLAL; ModWoWr; PenBWP; PenC AM; SpAmWW; WomWrSA*

Agutter, Jenny
English. Actor
Ballet dancer turned actress; films include *Equus,* 1977.
b. Dec 20, 1952 in Taunton, England
Source: *BioIn 9, 11, 14, 15; ConAu 133; ConTFT 2; FilmEn; FilmgC; HalFC 80, 84, 88; IlWWBF; IntMPA 84, 86, 88, 92, 94, 96; IntWW 89, 91, 93; ItaFilm; LegTOT; Who 92; WhoHol 92; WhoWor 97; WrDr 94*

Agyeman, Jaramogi Abebe
[Albert Buford Cleage]
American. Clergy
Created Pan African Orthodox Christian Church, 1970s.
b. Jun 13, 1911 in Indianapolis, Indiana
Source: *ConBlB 10; RelLAm 91*

Ahearn, Daniel F.
American. Track Athlete
Set triple jump record, 50 feet, 11 inches, 1911; record broken in 1985 by Willie Banks.
b. Apr 2, 1888 in County Limerick, Ireland
d. Jan 10, 1949
Source: *WhoSpor*

Ahearn, Frank
[T. Franklin Ahearn]
Canadian. Hockey Executive
Ottawa Senators owner, 1924, responsible for team becoming NHL power; Hall Fame, 1962.
b. May 10, 1886 in Ottawa, Ontario, Canada
d. Nov 17, 1962
Source: *WhoHcky 73*

Ahern, Thomas Leo, Jr.
American. Hostage
One of 52 held by terrorists, Nov 1979 - Jan 1981.
b. 1932? in Falls Church, Virginia
Source: *BioIn 12; NewYTBS 81*

Aherne, Brian de Lacy
English. Actor
Suave romantic lead; made 37 films including *Sylvia Scarlett,* 1935; *My Sister Eileen,* 1942.
b. May 2, 1902 in King's Norton, England
d. Feb 10, 1986 in Venice, Florida
Source: *BiE&WWA; ConAu 117, 118; CurBio 60, 86; FilmgC; IntMPA 86; MotPP; MovMk; NotNAT; OxCFilm; WhoHol A; WhoThe 77A*

Ahidjo, Ahmadou
Political Leader
Five-term president of Cameroon, 1961-82; died in exile.
b. Aug 24, 1924 in Garoua, Cameroon
d. Nov 30, 1989 in Dakar
Source: *AfSS 78, 79, 80, 81, 82; AnObit 1989; BioIn 5, 13, 16, 18, 20, 21; DcAfHiB 86; DcTwHis; FacFETw; IntWW 74, 75, 76, 77, 78, 79, 80, 81, 82, 83, 89, 91; IntYB 78, 79, 80, 81, 82; McGEWB; NewYTBS 89; WhoGov 72, 75; WhoWor 74, 76, 78, 80, 82*

Ahlin, Lars
Swedish. Author
Influential novelist has received literary awards for works dealing with a secular view of Lutheran theology.
b. Apr 4, 1915 in Sundsvall
Source: *BioIn 12; DcScanL; EncWL 2, 3; WorAu 1975*

Ahmad, Mirza Ghulam Hazat
Pakistani. Religious Leader
Founded Ahmadiyya Muslim Movement, popular in US among blacks.
b. Feb 13, 1835 in Qadian, Pakistan
d. May 26, 1908 in Lahore, Pakistan
Source: *BiDAmCu*

Ahmed, Fakhruddin Ali
Indian. Political Leader
Minister of industrial development, 1967-69; presidential candidate, 1974.
b. May 13, 1905 in Delhi, India
d. Feb 11, 1977 in New Delhi, India
Source: *BioIn 11, 12; IntWW 74, 75, 76; WhoWor 74, 76*

Ahmed Hasim
Turkish. Poet
Symbolist writer of Turkish literature; works include *The Hours of the Lake,* 1921.
b. 1884 in Baghdad, Ottoman Empire
d. Jun 4, 1933 in Istanbul, Turkey
Source: *CasWL; ConTurW*

Aiello, Danny Louis, Jr.
American. Actor
Acts on Broadway; has appeared in *Moonstruck,* 1987; *Do the Right Thing,* 1989.
b. Jun 20, 1933 in New York, New York
Source: *BioIn 12, 16; ConTFT 5; CurBio 92; HalFC 88; IntMPA 92; News 90; NewYTBS 81, 90; WhoEnt 92; WorAlBi*

Aiken, Conrad Potter
[Samuel Jeake, Jr.]
American. Poet, Critic
Won Pulitzer, 1930, for *Selected Poems.*
b. Aug 5, 1889 in Savannah, Georgia
d. Aug 17, 1973 in Savannah, Georgia
Source: *AmAu&B; AmLY; AmWr; AnCL; AuBYP 2; CasWL; Chambr 3; ChhPo S3; CnDAL; CnE&AP; CnMD; CnMWL; ConAmA; ConAmL; ConAu 4NR, 5NR, 45; ConLC 10; ConNov 72; ConPo 70; CurBio 70, 73; DcLEL; EncWL; EvLB; IntAu&W 82; IntWWP 77; LngCTC; ModAL, S1; ModWD; OxCAmL 65; OxCEng 67; PenC AM; PseudN 82; RAdv 1; REn; REnAL; RGFAP; SixAP; SmATA 13; TwCA, SUP; TwCWr; WebAB 74; WebE&AL; WhAm 6; WhE&EA; WhNAA; WhoAm 74; WhoE 74; WhoTwCL; WhoWor 74, 76*

Aiken, George David
American. Politician, Farmer
Rep. senator, 1941-75; active in farm legislation, creation of St. Lawrence Seaway.
b. Aug 20, 1892 in Dummerston, Vermont
d. Nov 19, 1984 in Montpelier, Vermont
Source: *AmAu&B; AnObit 1984; BiDrAC; BiDrUSC 89; BioIn 1, 2, 3, 5, 7, 8, 9, 10, 11, 12; BioNews 74; BlueB 76; CngDr 74; CurBio 47, 85; IntWW 74, 75; PolProf E, J, K, NF, T; WhAm 8; WhE&EA; WhoAm 74, 76; WhoAmP 73, 75, 77, 79; WhoE 74, 75; WhoGov 72, 75; WhoWor 74, 82*

Aiken, Howard Hathaway
American. Educator, Mathematician
Invented world's largest digital calculator—Mark I computer, 1944.
b. Mar 8, 1900 in Hoboken, New Jersey
d. Mar 14, 1973 in Saint Louis, Missouri
Source: *BioIn 1, 7, 9, 10, 12, 15, 20, 21; BlueB 76; CurBio 47, 73; HisDcDP; InSci; LarDcSc; NatCAB 60; NewYTBE 73; WhAm 5; WorAl; WorAlBi*

Aiken, Joan Delano
[Nicholas Dee; Rosie Lee]
English. Author
Popular juvenile, adult mystery writer, who wrote *Night Fall,* 1969.
b. Sep 4, 1924 in Rye, England
Source: *Au&Arts 1; Au&Wr 71; AuBYP 2, 3; BioIn 14, 15, 16; CamGLE; ChlLR 1, 19; ConAu 4NR, 9R, 23NR, 34NR; ConLC 35; FemiCLE; IntAu&W 76, 91; MajTwCW; OxCChiL; PenNWW B; PiP; PseudN 82; ScF&FL 1; SenS; SmATA 1AS, 2; ThrBJA; TwCChW 78, 89; TwCCr&M 91; TwCRHW 90; Who 85, 92; WhoHrs 80; WrDr 86, 92*

Aikens, Willie Mays
American. Baseball Player
Infielder, 1977-85; spent time in prison for cocaine possession, 1983.
b. Oct 14, 1954 in Seneca, South Carolina
Source: *Ballpl 90; BaseReg 85; BioIn 11, 15; NewYTBS 77, 86; WhoAfA 96; WhoBlA 85, 88, 90, 92, 94*

Aikman, Troy (Kenneth)
American. Football Player
Quarterback for the Dallas Cowboys, 1989—; Super Bowl MVP, 1993.
b. Nov 21, 1966 in West Covina, California
Source: *CurBio 95; News 94, 94-2; WhoAm 92, 94, 95, 96, 97; WhoSSW 95; WhoWor 95, 96*

Ailes, Roger Eugene
"Dark Prince of Negative Advertising"
American. Consultant, Producer
Media consultant; founder, pres., Ailes Communications, Inc., 1969—; media strategist for Nixon, Bush presidential campaigns; wrote *You Are the Message,* 1988.
b. May 15, 1940 in Warren, Ohio
Source: *BioIn 8, 15, 16; CurBio 89; LesBEnT 92; News 89-3; WhoAdv 90; WhoAm 76, 78, 80, 82, 84, 86, 88, 90, 92, 94, 95, 96, 97; WhoE 75*

Ailey, Alvin
American. Dancer, Choreographer
Formed Alvin Ailey American Dance Theater, 1958-89; leading figure in establishment of modern dance as popular art form.
b. Jan 5, 1931 in Rogers, Texas
d. Dec 1, 1989 in New York, New York
Source: *AfrAmAl 6; AmCulL; AnObit 1989; BiDD; BiE&WWA; BioIn 5, 6, 7, 8, 9, 10, 11, 12, 13, 14, 16; BlkOpe; CelR, 90; CmpGMD; CnOxB; ConBlB 8; ConTFT 1, 11; CurBio 68, 90, 90N; DancEn 78; DcArts; DcTwCCu 1, 5; DrBlPA, 90; Ebony 1; FacFETw; GayLesB; InB&W 80, 85; LegTOT; NegAl 89; NewGrDA 86; News 90, 89-2, 90-2; NewYTBS 89; NotNAT; PeoHis; RAdv 14; WhAm 10; WhoAm 74, 76, 78, 80, 82, 84, 86, 88; WhoBlA 77, 80, 85, 88, 90, 92N; WhoE 74, 79, 81, 83, 85, 86, 89; WhoHol A; WorAl; WorAlBi*

Aimee, Anouk
[Francoise Dreyfus]
French. Actor
Nominated for Oscar for role in *A Man and a Woman,* 1966.
b. Apr 27, 1934 in Paris, France
Source: *BiDFilm; ConTFT 2, 9; FilmEn; FilmgC; HalFC 88; IntMPA 75, 76, 77, 78, 79, 80, 81, 82, 84, 86, 88, 92; IntWW 91; InWom SUP; MacDWB; MovMk; OxCFilm; PseudN 82; WhoHol A; WorAlBi; WorEFlm*

Ainge, Danny
[Daniel Rae Ainge]
American. Baseball Player, Basketball Player
Infielder, Toronto, 1979-81; guard, Boston Celtics, 1981-89; Sacramento, 1989-90; Portland, 1990-92, Phoenix, 1992-93; won two NBA championships.
b. Mar 17, 1959 in Eugene, Oregon
Source: *Ballpl 90; BasBi; BaseEn 88; BioIn 12, 14, 16; ConNews 87-1; NewYTBS 81; OfNBA 86, 87; WhoSpor*

Ainsworth, W(illiam) H(arrison)
[Cheviot Tichborne]
English. Author, Editor
Prolific historic novelist; works include *Jack Sheppard,* 1839; *Tower of London,* 1840.
b. Feb 4, 1805 in Manchester, England
d. Jan 3, 1882 in Reigate, England
Source: *Alli, SUP; BbD; BiD&SB; BioIn 3, 4, 5, 8, 9, 12, 13, 14, 15, 16; BlmGEL; BritAu 19; CamGEL; CamGLE; CasWL; CelCen; Chambr 3; ChhPo, S1; CyWA 58; DcArts; DcBiA; DcBiPP; DcEnA, A; DcEnL; DcEuL; DcLB 21; DcLEL; DcNaB; EvLB; GrWrEL N; LegTOT; LinLib L; LngCEL; MnBBF; NewC; NewCBEL; NinCLC 13; Novels; OxCEng 67, 85, 95; PenC ENG; PenEncH; PseudN 82; REn; RfGEnL 91; SmATA 24; StaCVF; SupFW; VicBrit; WebE&AL; WhoChL*

Air Supply
[Russell Hitchcock; Graham Russell]
Australian. Music Group
Light pop-rock group, formed 1976; hits include "The One That You Love," 1981.
Source: *EncRk 88; EncRkSt; HarEnR 86; PenEncP; RkOn 85; RolSEnR 83; WhoRocM 82*

Airy, George Biddell, Sir
English. Astronomer
Astronomer royal; directed Greenwich Observatory, 1835-81; discovered cylindrical lens to correct astigmatism.
b. Jul 27, 1801 in Alnwick, England
d. Jan 2, 1892 in Greenwich, England
Source: *Alli, SUP; AntBDN D; AsBiEn; BiD&SB; BiESc; BioIn 1, 7, 14; CamDcSc; CelCen; DcBiPP; DcEnL; DcNaB C, S1; DcScB; InSci; LarDcSc; LinLib L, S; NewCol 75; WhDW*

Aitken, Hugh
American. Composer
Works include chamber music, oratorios, opera, *Felipe,* 1981.
b. Sep 7, 1924 in New York, New York
Source: *AmComp; ASCAP 66, 80; Baker 78, 84, 92; ConAmC 76, 82; IntWWM 77, 80, 85, 90; NewGrDA 86; NewGrDO; WhoAm 90; WhoAmM 83; WrDr 92*

Aitken, Max
[John William Maxwell Aitken]
English. Publisher
Son of Baron Beaverbrook; directed Britain's Beaverbrook Newspapers, 1964-77.
b. Feb 15, 1910 in Montreal, Quebec, Canada
d. Apr 30, 1985 in London, England
Source: *AnObit 1985; BioIn 7, 10; BlueB 76; CanWW 70, 79, 80, 81, 83; ConAu 116; FacFETw; IntWW 74, 75, 76, 77, 78, 79, 80, 81, 82, 83; IntYB 78, 81, 82; WhE&EA; WhoCan 73, 75, 77; WhoWor 74, 76, 78*

Aitken, Robert
American. Sculptor
Works include Hann Memorial, Arlington Cemetery; Pioneer Lumberman Monument, Huron National Forest, MI.
b. May 8, 1878 in San Francisco, California
d. Jan 3, 1949 in New York, New York
Source: *WhAm 2*

Aitkin, Robert Grant
American. Astronomer
Discovered over 3,000 double stars.
b. Dec 31, 1864 in Jackson, California
d. Oct 29, 1951 in Oakland, California
Source: *ApCAB X; DcAmB S5; DcScB; WebBD 83; WhAm 3*

Aitmatov, Chingiz
Russian. Author
Won Lenin Prize, 1963, for *Tales of the Mountains and Steppes;* wrote many of his early works in the Kirghiz language.
b. Dec 12, 1928 in Sheker Village, Union of Soviet Socialist Republics
Source: *Au&Wr 71; Benet 87, 96; BiDSovU; ConAu 103; ConLC 71; FarE&A 78; HanRL; IntAu&W 76, 77; IntWW 74, 75, 76, 77, 78; MajTwCW; RAdv 14, 13-2; ScF&FL 92; WhoSocC 78; WhoWor 74; WorAu 1975*

Akaka, Daniel Kahikina
American. Politician
Dem. senator, HI, 1990—.
b. Sep 11, 1924 in Honolulu, Hawaii
Source: *AlmAP 92; BiDrUSC 89; CngDr 77, 79, 81, 83, 85, 87, 89; IntWW 91, 93; PolsAm 84; WhoAm 78, 80, 82, 84, 86, 88, 90, 92, 94, 95, 96, 97; WhoAmP 77, 79, 81, 83, 85, 87, 89, 91, 93, 95; WhoAsA 94; WhoE 95; WhoGov 77; WhoWest 78, 80, 82, 84, 87, 89, 92, 94, 96*

Akalaitis, JoAnne
American. Director
Off-Broadway productions include *Endgame,* 1984; won three Obies.
b. Jun 29, 1937 in Cicero, Illinois
Source: *BioIn 11, 16; CamGWoT; ConAmD; ConAu 138; ConDr 93; ConTFT 5, 12; ConWomD; CrtSuDr; CurBio 93; CyWA 89; GrLiveH; NotWoAT; TheaDir; WhoAm 92, 94, 95, 96, 97; WhoAmW 93; WhoE 93; WhoEnt 92; WhoThe 81*

Akbar
[Jalalud din Muhammad]
"The Great"
Arab. Ruler
Greatest of Indian Moghul emperors who extended empire to N India; instituted new religion, Din-i-Ilahi.
b. Oct 14, 1542 in Umarkot, Pakistan
d. Oct 15, 1605 in Agra, India
Source: *Benet 87, 96; BioIn 1, 3, 4, 5, 7, 8, 9, 10, 11, 12, 13, 14, 16, 17, 20; DcBiPP; DicTyr; HarEnMi; HisWorL; LinLib L, S; LuthC 75; McGEWB; NewC; PseudN 82; WhDW; WhoMilH 76; WorAl*

Akeley, Carl Ethan
American. Naturalist
Made five trips to Africa, 1896-1926, to study, collect animals; improved taxidermy, museum display methods.
b. May 19, 1864 in Orleans County, New York
d. Nov 17, 1926 in Mount Mikeno, Ruanda-Urundi
Source: *AmAu&B; AmBi; BioIn 3, 4, 5, 6, 8, 14, 17; DcAmB; DcNAA; InSci; LinLib L, S; NatCAB 26; REnAL; WebAB 74, 79; WhAm 1, 1C; WhAmArt 85*

Akeley, Mary Lee Jobe
American. Explorer
Made numerous expeditions to Africa to collect animal and plant specimens, 1920s-30s.
b. Jan 29, 1878 in Tappan, Ohio
d. Jul 19, 1966 in Stonington, Connecticut
Source: *AmAu&B; InWom SUP; NotAW MOD; OhA&B; WhAm 4; WhE&EA; WhNAA*

Akerman, Chantal
Belgian. Filmmaker
Made films *Golden Eighties,* 1986; *Un Divan a New York,* 1996.
b. 1950 in Brussels, Belgium
Source: *ConAu 127; ContDcW 89; EncEurC; GayLesB; IntDcF 1-2, 2-2; IntDcWB; MiSFD 9; WorFDir 2*

Akers, John Fellows
American. Business Executive
Chairman, IBM, 1984-92.
b. Dec 28, 1934 in Boston, Massachusetts
Source: *BioIn 14, 15, 16; CurBio 88; Dun&B 88, 90; IntWW 89, 91, 93; News 88-3; St&PR 91; Who 88, 90, 92, 94; WhoAm 84, 86, 88, 90, 92, 94, 95, 96; WhoE 85, 86, 89, 91, 93; WhoFI 85, 87, 89, 92, 94, 96; WhoWor 89, 91, 93; WorAlBi*

Akers, Michelle
American. Soccer Player
Member, U.S. Women's National Soccer Team, 1985—; became all-time leading scorer, 1995.
b. Feb 1, 1966 in Santa Clara, California
Source: *News 96, 96-1*

Akhmatova, Anna
[Anna Andreyevna Gorenko]
Russian. Author, Poet
Works, which were banned by Soviets until 1959, include *The Willow Tree,* 1940; considered Russia's greatest woman poet.
b. Jun 11, 1888 in Odessa, Russia
d. Mar 5, 1966 in Moscow, Union of Soviet Socialist Republics
Source: *AtlBL; Benet 87, 96; CasWL; ClDMEL 47; ConAu 25R, 35NR, P-1, X; ConLC 11, 25; DcRusL; EncWL; EvEuW; LinLib L; LngCTC; MajTwCW; McGEWB; ModSL 1; PenC EUR; PoeCrit 2; REn; TwCWr; WhDW; WhoTwCL; WorAl; WorAlBi; WorAu 1950*

Akihito
Japanese. Ruler
Succeeded father, Hirohito, to become Japan's 125th emperor, 1989—.
b. Dec 23, 1933 in Tokyo, Japan
Source: *BioIn 2, 3, 5, 10, 13, 14, 16; CurBio 59, 90, 91; DcTwHis; EncJap; FacFETw; IntWW 91, 93; LegTOT; News 90, 90-1; NewYTBS 83, 89, 90; Who 90, 92, 94; WhoAsAP 91; WhoWor 76, 78, 80, 82, 84, 93, 95, 96, 97*

Akimov, Nikolay Pavlovich
Russian. Designer, Producer
Known as diverse and experimental scenic designer; rewrote Shakespeare's *Hamlet,* 1932, which was withdrawn from distribution due to antagonistic reaction.
b. Apr 16, 1901 in Kharkov, Ukraine
d. Sep 6, 1968 in Moscow, Union of Soviet Socialist Republics
Source: *BioIn 8; CamGWoT; ObitOF 79; OxCThe 83; SovUn*

Akins, Claude
American. Actor
Played Sonny Pruitt on TV series "Movin' On," 1974-76, title role in "Sheriff Lobo," 1979-81; in film *From Here to Eternity,* 1953.
b. May 25, 1918 in Nelson, Georgia
d. Jan 27, 1994 in Altadena, California
Source: *BioIn 19; ConTFT 2; FilmEn; FilmgC; HalFC 80, 84, 88; IntMPA 84, 86, 88, 94; ItaFilm; Vers A; WhoAm 78, 80, 82, 84; WhoHol A; WorAl; WorAlBi*

Akins, Virgil B
American. Boxer
Welterweight champ, 1958.
b. Mar 10, 1928 in Saint Louis, Missouri
Source: *BioIn 14; WhoBox 74*

Akins, Zoe
American. Poet, Dramatist
Wrote 1935 Pulitzer winner *The Old Maid.*
b. Oct 30, 1886 in Humansville, Missouri
d. Oct 29, 1958 in Los Angeles, California
Source: *AmAu&B; AmWomD; AmWomPl; AmWomWr; ApCAB X; ArtclWW 2; BenetAL 91; BioIn 4, 5, 14, 16, 20; CamGWoT; ChhPo; CnDAL; CnMD; ConAmA; ConAmL; ConAu 115; DcAmB S6; DcLB 26; DcLEL; FacFETw; FemiCLE; FilmEn; FilmgC; HalFC 80, 84, 88; IntDcF 1-4, 2-4; InWom, SUP; LegTOT; McGEWD 72, 84; ModWD; NotNAT B; NotWoAT; OxCAmL 65, 83, 95; OxCAmT 84; OxCThe 67, 83; OxCWoWr 95; ReelWom; REn; REnAL; TwCA, SUP; WhAm 3; WhLit; WhoAmW 58; WhThe; WomNov; WomWMM; WomWWA 14; WorAl; WorAlBi*

Aksakov, Sergei Timofeyevich
Russian. Author
Known for semi-autobiographical *Family Chronicle,* 1856, describing Russian life.
b. Sep 20, 1791 in Ufa, Russia
d. Apr 30, 1859 in Moscow, Russia
Source: *BbD; Benet 87, 96; BiD&SB; CasWL; DcArts; DcEuL; DcRusL; EuAu; EvEuW; LinLib L; OxCEng 67; PenC EUR; REn*

Aksyonov, Vassily Pavlovich
Russian. Writer
Popular Soviet writer immigrated to US, was divested of Soviet citizenship,

1980, when his work became too controversial; wrote *The Burn,* 1980; *In Search of Melancholy Baby,* 1987.
b. Aug 20, 1932 in Kazan, Union of Soviet Socialist Republics
Source: *Benet 87; BioIn 12, 13, 14, 15, 16; CamGWoT; ConAu 12NR; ConLC 37; CurBio 90; CyWA 89; DcRusLS; EncWL 2; HanRL; IntAu&W 91; IntWW 91; NewYTBS 80, 86; RAdv 13-2; WhoAm 88, 90, 97; WhoUSWr 88; WhoWor 97; WhoWrEP 89*

Akutagawa Ryunosuke
Japanese. Writer
Extensively translated short stories often centered on macabre themes; many made into films including *Rashomon,* 1951.
b. Mar 1, 1892 in Tokyo, Japan
d. Jul 24, 1927 in Tokyo, Japan
Source: *Benet 96; BioIn 15; ConAu 117; CyWA 89; DcArts; EncJap; EncWL 3; FacFETw; RAdv 14, 13-2; TwCLC 16*

Alabama
[Jeff Cook; Teddy Gentry; Mark Herndon; Randy Owen]
American. Music Group
Country-rock group, formed 1969; album *Forty Hour Week,* was number one on country charts, 1985; album sales exceed 10 million; named "country artist of the 1980's," by Academy of Country Music, 1989; won many American Music Awards.
Source: *BgBkCoM; BioIn 16; CelR 90; ConMus 1; EncFCWM 83; EncRk 88; EncRkSt; HarEnCM 87; HarEnR 86; PenEncP; RkOn 85; RolSEnR 83; WhoAm 86, 88, 90, 92, 94, 95, 96, 97; WhoRocM 82*

Alaia, Azzedine
French. Fashion Designer
Designs elegant ready-to-wear for women, characterized as clingy and sexy.
b. 1940 in Tunis, Tunisia
Source: *BioIn 13, 14, 15, 16; ConFash; CurBio 92; DcArts; EncFash*

Alain
[Emil Auguste Chartier]
French. Essayist, Philosopher
Influential writer of articles battering conventional prejudices: *Truth about War,* 1930.
b. Mar 3, 1868 in Montagne, France
d. Jun 2, 1951 in Le Vesinet, France
Source: *AmAu&B; Benet 87, 96; BiDFrPL; BiDMoPL; BioIn 17, 18; CasWL; ClDMEL 47, 80; DcTwCCu 2; EncWL 2, 3; EuAu; EvEuW; GuFrLit 1; IlsBYP; IlsCB 1957; ModFrL; OxCFr; PenC EUR; PseudN 82; REn; TwCLC 41; WhDW; WorAu 1970*

Alain-Fournier
[Henri Alban Fournier]
French. Author
Only completed novel, *Le Grand Meaulnes,* 1913; called outstanding novel of 20th c.
b. Oct 3, 1886 in La Chapelle-d'Angillon, France
d. Sep 22, 1914 in Bois de Saint Remy, France
Source: *AtlBL; Benet 87, 96; BioIn 15, 16; CasWL; ClDMEL 47, 80; CnMWL; ConAu 104; CyWA 58; DcArts; DcLB 65; DcTwCCu 2; EncWL 2, 3; EvEuW; GuFrLit 1; LinLib L; LngCTC; ModFrL; ModRL; Novels; OxCFr; PenC EUR; REn; RfGWoL 95; TwCA, SUP; TwCLC 6; TwCWr; WhoTwCL*

Alajalov, Constantin
American. Artist, Illustrator
Muralist, portrait painter best known for watercolor covers of *New Yorker* magazine.
b. Nov 18, 1900 in Rostov-on-Don, Russia
d. Oct 24, 1987 in Amenia, New York
Source: *BioIn 1, 2, 5, 15, 16, 17; ConAu 123; CurBio 42, 88, 88N; IlrAm 1880, D; IlsBYP; IlsCB 1744, 1946; SmATA 53N; WhAm 9; WhAmArt 85; WhoAm 74, 76, 78, 80, 82, 84, 86; WhoAmA 73, 76, 78, 80, 82, 84, 86; WhoE 86; WorAl; WorECar*

Al-Amin, Jamil Abdullah
[H. Rap Brown; Hubert Gerold Brown]
American. Civil Rights Activist, Writer
Rallied support of angry blacks against the white establishment in the late 1960s by supporting acts of violence; wrote autobiography,*Die Nigger Die!,* 1969.
b. Oct 4, 1943 in Baton Rouge, Louisiana
Source: *BioIn 8, 9, 10, 11, 20; BlkLC; BlkWr 1; CivR 74; CivRSt; ConAu 112, 125; ConBlB 6; DcTwCCu 5; EncAACR; HisWorL; InB&W 85; LegTOT; LNinSix; PolProf J; SchCGBL; WhoAfA 96; WhoAm 74, 76; WhoBlA 77, 80, 85, 88, 90, 92, 94*

Alanbrooke, Alan Francis Brooke, 1st Viscount
Irish. Army Officer
Chief of imperial general staff for Winston Churchill, 1941-46.
b. Jul 23, 1883 in County Fermanagh, Northern Ireland
d. Jun 17, 1963 in Hampshire, England
Source: *BioIn 17; CurBio 41, 63; DcTwHis; HarEnMi; NewCol 75*

Alarcon, Pedro Antonio de
Spanish. Author
Wrote internationally famous novelette, *The Three-Cornered Hat,* 1874.
b. Mar 10, 1833 in Guadix, Spain
d. Jul 20, 1891 in Madrid, Spain
Source: *Benet 87, 96; BiD&SB; BioIn 1, 5, 7, 16; CasWL; ClDMEL 47; CyWA 58; DcArts; DcCathB; EuAu; EvEuW; McGEWB; NinCLC 1; Novels; PenC EUR; RAdv 13-2; REn*

Alarcon y Mendoza, Juan Ruiz de
Spanish. Dramatist
Wrote over 20 heroic tragedies, comedies of character: *Suspicious Truth,* 1634.
b. 1580 in Taxco, Mexico
d. Aug 4, 1639 in Madrid, Spain
Source: *ApCAB; BbD; BiD&SB; CamGWoT; EncWT; Ent; EvEuW; LinLib L; McGEWB; OxCSpan; REn*

Alaric I
Ruler
Visigothic king, 395-410, sacked Rome in 410.
b. 370
d. 410 in Consentia, Italy
Source: *BioIn 4, 5, 9; LinLib L; McGEWB; NewCol 75; OxCGer 76; REn; WhDW*

Albanese, Licia
Italian. Opera Singer
Soprano; with NY Met., 1940s-70s; broadcast with Toscanini.
b. Jul 22, 1913 in Bari, Italy
Source: *Baker 78, 84; BioIn 1, 2, 3, 4, 6, 7, 10, 11, 13; CmOp; CurBio 46; IntDcOp; IntWWM 77, 80, 90; InWom, SUP; LegTOT; MetOEnc; MusSN; NewAmDM; NewEOp 71; NewGrDA 86; NewGrDM 80; NewGrDO; OxDcOp; PenDiMP; RadStar; WhoAm 74, 76, 78, 80, 82, 84, 86, 88, 90, 92, 94, 95, 96, 97; WhoAmW 61, 64, 66, 68, 70, 72, 74, 83, 85; WhoHol 92; WhoMus 72; WhoWor 74, 76; WorAl; WorAlBi*

Albee, Edward
[Edward Franklin Albee, III]
American. Author, Dramatist
Plays critique American society and the loss of contact between individuals: *The Zoo Story,* 1959; won Pulitzers for *A Delicate Balance,* 1967, *Seascape,* 1975; won Tony, 1963, for *Who's Afraid of Virginia Woolf?;* won 1994 Pulitzer for *Three Tall Women,* 1991.
b. Mar 12, 1928 in Washington, District of Columbia
Source: *AmAu&B; AmDec 1960; AmWr; AuNews 1; Benet 87, 96; BenetAL 91; BiE&WWA; BioIn 5, 6, 7, 8, 9, 10, 11, 14, 15, 16, 17, 18, 19, 21; BlueB 76; CamGEL; CamGLE; CamGWoT; CamHAL; CasWL; CelR, 90; CnThe; ConAu 3BS, 5R, 8NR; ConDr 73, 77, 82, 88; ConLC 1, 2, 3, 5, 9, 11, 13, 25, 53, 86; ConTFT 4, 14; CroCD; CrtSuDr; CurBio 63, 96; CyWA 89; DcArts; DcLB 7; DcTwCCu 1; EncAB-H 1996; EncWL 2, 3; EncWT; Ent; FacFETw; FilmgC; GayLesB; GrWrEL DR; HalFC 80, 84, 88; IntAu&W 91; IntvTCA 2; IntWW 91; LegTOT; LinLib L; LngCTC; MagSAmL; MajMD 1; MajTwCW; McGEWD 72, 84; ModAL S1, S2; ModWD; NatPD 77, 81; NewCon; News 97-1; NotNAT, A; OxCAmL 65, 83; OxCAmT 84; OxCThe 67; PenC AM; PlP&P, A; RAdv 14, 13-2; RComWL; REn; REnAL; REnWD;*

RfGAmL 87, 94; RGTwCWr; TwCWr; WebAB 74; WebE&AL; WhDW; Who 74, 82, 83, 85, 88, 90, 92, 94; WhoAm 86, 90, 97; WhoE 91, 97; WhoEnt 92; WhoThe 72, 77, 81; WhoTwCL; WhoWor 87, 91, 97; WhoWrEP 89; WorAlBi; WorAu 1950; WorLitC; WrDr 76, 80, 82, 84, 86, 88, 90, 92; WrPh

Albee, Edward Franklin
American. Theater Owner
Formed Keith-Albee Co., 1885-1920s; controlled almost 400 variety theaters.
b. Oct 8, 1857 in Machias, Maine
d. Mar 11, 1930 in Palm Beach, Florida
Source: *ApCAB X; BioIn 3; DcAmB S1; NatCAB 22; NotNAT B; OxCThe 67, 83; WebBD 83; WhAm 1*

Albeniz, Isaac Manuel Francisco
Spanish. Pianist, Composer
Major works include rhapsody *Catalonia,* 1889; stage composition, *Pepita Jimenez,* 1896.
b. May 29, 1860 in Comprodon, Spain
d. Jun 16, 1909 in Cambo, Spain
Source: *AtlBL*

Alberghetti, Anna Maria
American. Singer, Actor
Operatic soprano who starred in films, Broadway musicals; won Tony for *Carnival,* 1962.
b. May 15, 1936 in Pasaro, Italy
Source: *Baker 78, 84; BiE&WWA; BioIn 2, 3, 4, 5, 6, 10, 15; CurBio 55; FilmEn; FilmgC; ForYSC; HalFC 80, 84, 88; IntMPA 75, 76, 77, 78, 79, 80, 81, 82, 84, 86, 88, 92, 94, 96; InWom SUP; ItaFilm; LegTOT; MotPP; MovMk; NotNAT; WhoAm 74; WhoAmW 61, 64, 66, 68, 70, 72, 74; WhoEnt 92; WhoHol 92, A; WorAl*

Albers, Hans
German. Business Executive
Chairman of German chemical giant, BASF, 1983—.
b. Mar 4, 1925 in Lingen, Germany
Source: *BioIn 15; IntWW 89, 91, 93; Law&B 89A*

Albers, Josef
American. Artist
Known as teacher, color theorist, painted *Homage to the Square,* series of several hundred squares of color.
b. Mar 19, 1888 in Bottrop, Germany
d. Mar 25, 1976 in New Haven, Connecticut
Source: *AmAu&B; BioIn 1, 2, 4, 5, 6, 7, 8, 9, 10, 11, 12, 13, 14, 16, 18, 20; BlueB 76; BriEAA; ConArt 77, 83, 89, 96; ConAu 1R, 3NR, 13NR, 65; CurBio 62, 76, 76N; DcAmArt; DcAmB S10; DcCAA 71, 77, 88, 94; DcTwDes; EncWB; FacFETw; IntDcAA 90; IntWW 74, 75, 76; LegTOT; MacEA; MakMC; McGDA; NewYTBE 71; NewYTBS 76; ObitOF 79; OxCTwCA; OxDcArt; PhDcTCA 77; PrintW 83, 85; REn; WebAB 74, 79; WhAm 7; WhAmArt 85; WhoAm 74, 76; WhoAmA 73, 76, 78N, 80N, 82N, 84N, 86N, 89N, 91N, 93N; WhoE 74; WhoWor 74; WorArt 1950*

Albert, Prince
[Albert Francis Charles Augustus Emmanuel of Saxe]
German. Consort
Married Queen Victoria, Feb 1840; used influence to avert war with US in Trent Affair, 1861.
b. Aug 26, 1819 in Rosenau, Germany
d. Dec 13, 1861 in London, England
Source: *Alli SUP; Baker 78, 84, 92; Benet 87, 96; BioIn 1, 2, 3, 4, 5, 6, 7, 8, 9, 10, 11, 12, 13, 14, 15, 16, 17, 18, 19; ChhPo S1; DcBiPP; Dis&D; LegTOT; LinLib S; LngCEL; McGEWB; NewC; NewCol 75; NewGrDM 80; NewOxM; OxCMus; OxDcArt; REn; VicBrit; WhCiWar; WhDW; WorAlBi*

Albert, Prince
[Albert Alexandre Louis Pierre Grimaldi]
Monacan. Prince
Son of Prince Rainier and Princess Grace; heir to Monacan throne.
b. Mar 14, 1958 in Monte Carlo, Monaco
Source: *BioIn 6, 12, 13, 14, 15, 16, 17, 19, 21; LegTOT*

Albert, II
[Felix Humbert Theodore Christian Eugene Marie]
Belgian. Ruler
King of Belgium, 1993—.
b. Jun 6, 1934 in Brussels, Belgium
Source: *BioIn 5; WhoWor 74, 95, 96, 97*

Albert, Carl Bert
American. Political Leader
Dem. majority leader, 1962-71; Speaker of House, 1971-76.
b. May 10, 1908 in McAlester, Oklahoma
Source: *AmPolLe; BiDrAC; BiDrUSC 89; BioIn 13, 14; BlueB 76; CngDr 74; ConAu 132; CurBio 57; IntWW 74, 75, 76, 77, 78, 79, 80, 81, 82, 83, 89, 91, 93; WebAB 74, 79; Who 85, 92, 94; WhoAmP 73, 75, 77, 79, 81, 83, 85, 87, 89, 91, 93, 95; WhoSSW 73, 75, 76, 86; WhoWor 74; WorAlBi; WrDr 94*

Albert, Eddie
[Edward Albert Heimberger]
American. Actor
Played Oliver Douglas on TV comedy "Green Acres," 1965-71; received Oscar nominations for *Roman Holiday,* 1955, *The Heartbreak Kid,* 1972; father of Edward.
b. Apr 22, 1908 in Rock Island, Illinois
Source: *BiE&WWA; BioIn 3, 6, 10, 11, 14, 17; BkPepl; CelR, 90; CmpEPM; ConTFT 1, 2, 8; CurBio 54; EncAFC; EncMT; FilmEn; FilmgC; ForYSC; HalFC 80, 84, 88; HolP 30; IntMPA 75, 76, 77, 78, 79, 80, 81, 82, 84, 86, 88, 92, 94, 96; LegTOT; LesBEnT 92; MotPP; MovMk; NotNAT; OxCAmT 84; OxCPMus; PlP&P; PseudN 82; RadStar; WhoAm 74, 76, 78, 80, 82, 84, 86, 88, 90, 92, 94, 95, 96, 97; WhoEnt 92; WhoHol 92, A; WhoThe 77, 81; WorAl; WorAlBi*

Albert, Edward Laurence
American. Actor, Photographer
Son of Eddie Albert; starred in *Butterflies Are Free,* 1972, with Goldie Hawn.
b. Feb 20, 1951 in Los Angeles, California
Source: *BkPepl; ConTFT 1, 7; HalFC 88; IntMPA 86, 92; WhoAm 86, 90; WhoEnt 92; WhoHisp 92*

Albert, Frank C.
American. Football Player
First modern T-formation quarterback; All-American with Stanford, 1940, 1941; member, College Football Hall of Fame.
b. Jan 27, 1920 in Chicago, Illinois
Source: *WhoSpor*

Albert, Marv
[Marvin Philip Albert]
American. Sportscaster
Announcer of New York Knicks basketball, 1967—; announcer of New York Rangers hockey, 1967—; sportcaster for NBC, 1977—.
b. Jun 12, 1943
Source: *BioIn 9; ConAu 101; News 94, 94-3; WhoAm 84, 86, 88, 90, 92, 94, 95; WhoEnt 92*

Albert, Stephen Joel
American. Composer
Won Pulitzer, 1985, for music for his *Symphony River Run.*
b. Feb 6, 1941 in New York, New York
d. Dec 27, 1992 in Truro, Massachusetts
Source: *AmComp; AnObit 1992; Baker 78, 84, 92; BioIn 14; ConAmC 76A; ConNews 86-1; IntWWM 85, 90; NewAmDM; NewGrDA 86; WhAm 11; WhoAm 86, 88, 90, 92; WhoAmM 83; WhoE 86, 89; WhoEnt 92*

Albert I
[Albert Leopold Clement Marie Meinrad]
Belgian. Ruler
King who reigned, 1909-34; personally commanded Belgian army during WW I.
b. Apr 8, 1875 in Brussels, Belgium
d. Feb 17, 1934 in Namur, Belgium
Source: *BioIn 12; DcCathB; IntWWM 90; MetOEnc; WhDW*

Alberti, Leon Battista
Italian. Architect, Author
Renaissance humanist; wrote dialogues, *Della Familia,* 1441; essays in fine arts.
b. Feb 14, 1404 in Genoa, Italy
d. Apr 25, 1472 in Rome, Italy
Source: *AtlBL; BiD&SB; BioIn 14, 17, 18; CasWL; DcArts; DcEuL; DcItL 1, 2; Dis&D; EuAu; EvEuW; IntDcAr; LinLib L, S; MacEA; McGDA; McGEWB;*

NewCBEL; OxCEng 67; OxDcArt; PenC EUR; RAdv 14; REn; WorAlBi

Alberti, Rafael
Spanish. Poet
Member of Generation of 1927 poetry group; important 20th c. Spanish poet; wrote *Concerning the Angels,* 1929.
b. Dec 16, 1902 in Puerto de Santa Maria, Spain
Source: *Benet 87, 96; BioIn 1, 4, 11, 12, 17; CasWL; ClDMEL 47, 80; CnMD; CnMWL; ConAu 85; ConFLW 84; ConLC 7; DcLB 108; DcSpL; EncWL 2, 3; EncWT; EvEuW; FacFETw; IntvSpW; LiExTwC; McGEWD 72, 84; ModRL; ModSpP S; ModWD; OxCSpan; OxCThe 83; PenC EUR; RAdv 14, 13-2; REn; TwCA SUP; TwCWr; WhoWor 74*

Albertson, Frank
American. Actor
Character actor whose films include *Psycho,* 1960; *Bye Bye Birdie,* 1963.
b. Feb 2, 1909 in Fergus Falls, Minnesota
d. Feb 29, 1964 in Santa Monica, California
Source: *BioIn 6; EncAFC; Film 2; FilmEn; FilmgC; ForYSC; GangFlm; HalFC 80, 84, 88; HolCA; MotPP; MovMk; NotNAT B; ObitOF 79; Vers A; WhoHol B; WhScrn 74, 77, 83*

Albertson, Jack
American. Actor
Won Oscar, 1968, for *The Subject Was Roses;* Emmy, 1976, for "Chico and the Man."
b. Jun 16, 1910 in Malden, Massachusetts
d. Nov 25, 1981 in Hollywood, California
Source: *BioIn 10, 11, 12, 13; CurBio 76, 82, 82N; FilmEn; FilmgC; IntMPA 77, 81; MovMk; NewYTBE 73; NewYTBS 81; NotNAT; OxCAmT 84; WhAm 8; WhoAm 82; WhoCom; WhoHol A; WhoThe 77; WorAl; WorAlBi*

Albert the Great
[Albertus Magnus; Saint Albert; Albert Count of Bollstadt; Albrecht von Koln]
"Doctor Universalis"; "Le Petit Albert"
German. Philosopher, Religious Figure
Paraphrased Aristotle's works; canonized, 1932.
b. 1193 in Lauingen, Germany
d. Nov 15, 1280 in Cologne, Germany
Source: *AsBiEn; BbD; BiD&SB; BioIn 1, 2, 18, 20; CasWL; ClMLC 16; CyEd; DcBiPP; DcEnL; DcEuL; Dis&D; EncWW; EuAu; EvEuW; InSci; LinLib L, S; LuthC 75; McGEWB; NewC; NewGrDM 80; OxCEng 67, 85, 95; OxCGer 76; PenC EUR; PseudN 82; RAdv 14, 13-4; REn; WorAl; WorAlBi*

Albinoni, Tommaso
Italian. Composer, Violinist
Wrote 53 operas, instrumental music.
b. Jun 14, 1671 in Venice, Italy
d. Jan 17, 1751 in Venice, Italy
Source: *Baker 84; BriBkM 80; DcCom&M 79; MusMk; NewGrDM 80; OxCMus*

Albrand, Martha
[Heide Huberta Freybe; Katrin Holland; Heidi Huberta; Mrs. Sydney J Lamon]
American. Author
Mystery writer; wrote award-winning *Desperate Moment,* 1950.
b. Sep 8, 1914 in Rostock, Germany
d. Jun 24, 1981 in New York, New York
Source: *AmAu&B; WhoE 74; WhoSpyF; WhoWor 78, 80*

Albrecht, Duke
German. Ruler
Second son of Crown Prince Ruprecht of Bavaria; grandson of Ludwig III of Bavaria; pretender to the Bavarian throne.
b. 1905 in Munich, Germany
d. Jul 8, 1996 in Lake Starnberg, Germany

Albright, Ivan Le Lorraine
"The Painter of Horrors"
American. Artist
"Magic realism" painter who emphasized details, emotions.
b. Feb 20, 1897 in Chicago, Illinois
d. Nov 18, 1983 in Woodstock, Vermont
Source: *ConArt 83; DcCAA 94; DcCAr 81; NewYTBS 83; OxCArt; OxCTwCA; PhDcTCA 77; WebAB 79; WhoAm 80, 82; WhoAmA 80, 82, 91N, 93N; WhoWor 78*

Albright, Lola Jean
American. Actor
Appeared in TV series "Peter Gunn," 1958-61; critical acclaim for role in *A Cold Wind in August,* 1961.
b. Jul 20, 1924 in Akron, Ohio
Source: *FilmEn; FilmgC; HalFC 88; IntMPA 82, 92; InWom SUP; MotPP; MovMk; WhoAm 82, 88; WhoEnt 92*

Albright, Madeleine K(orbel)
American. Diplomat, Government Official
US Ambassador to the United Nations, 1993-97; Secretary of State, 1997—.
b. May 15, 1937 in Prague, Czechoslovakia
Source: *BioIn 16, 19, 20, 21; CurBio 95; NewYTBS 88; Who 94; WhoAm 88, 95, 96; WhoAmW 81, 83, 85, 87, 91, 95, 97; WhoE 81, 83, 85; WhoWor 95, 96, 97*

Albright, Malvin Marr
American. Artist, Sculptor
Paintings show great similarity to brother, Ivan, but less emotionally disturbing.
b. Feb 20, 1897 in Chicago, Illinois
d. Sep 14, 1983 in Fort Lauderdale, Florida
Source: *ArtsAmW 3; BioIn 9; McGDA; OxDcArt; WhAm 8; WhAmArt 85; WhoAm 74, 76, 78, 80, 82; WhoAmA 73, 76, 78, 80, 82, 84, 86, 89, 91, 93; WhoWor 76, 78, 80, 82*

Albright, Tenley Emma
American. Skater, Surgeon
Two-time world champion figure skater; won gold medal, 1956 Olympics; currently a surgeon in Boston, 1963— .
b. Jul 18, 1935 in Boston, Massachusetts
Source: *BiDAmSp BK; CurBio 56; InWom SUP; WhoAmW 77; WhoE 89; WorAl*

Albright, William Foxwell
American. Archaeologist
Published over 800 books on archaeology: *From the Stone Age to Christianity,* 1940.
b. May 24, 1891 in Coquimbo, Chile
d. Sep 19, 1971 in Baltimore, Maryland
Source: *AmAu&B; BioIn 1, 4, 5, 6, 9, 10, 11, 12, 19; CurBio 55; DcAmB S9; DcAmReB 2; EncAB-H 1974, 1996; InSci; LuthC 75; NatCAB 56; NewYTBE 72; WebAB 74, 79; WhAm 5*

Albritton, David
American. Track Athlete
High jumper; won silver medal (Cornelius Johnson won gold), 1936 Berlin Olympics.
b. Apr 13, 1913 in Danville, Alabama
d. May 14, 1994
Source: *BlkOlyM; WhoTr&F 73*

Albuquerque, Affonso de
"The Great"; "The Mars of Portugal"; "The Portugese Mars"
Portuguese. Political Leader
Viceroy of India; founded Portuguese empire in the East.
b. 1453 in Alhandra, Portugal
d. Dec 16, 1515 in Goa, India
Source: *BioIn 1, 9; DcBiPP; DcCathB; HarEnMi; McGEWB; OxCShps; WhDW*

Alcala Zamora, Niceto
Spanish. Political Leader
First pres., Second Republic, 1931-36; exiled during Spanish Revolution.
b. Jul 6, 1877 in Priego, Spain
d. Feb 18, 1949 in Buenos Aires, Argentina
Source: *BioIn 1, 16; DcTwHis*

Alcamenes
Greek. Sculptor
Noted for antiquity masterpieces *Aphrodite of the Gardens, Hermes Propylaeus.*
b. fl. 5th cent. BC
Source: *DcBiPP; McGDA; NewCol 75; OxCArt; OxDcArt; WebBD 83*

Alcibiades
Greek. Statesman, Military Leader
Nephew of Pericles who advised Sparta of Athenian weaknesses; blamed for defeat of Athens.
b. 450?BC in Athens, Greece

d. 404?BC, Phrygia
Source: *Benet 87, 96; BioIn 2, 3, 4, 6, 7, 8, 9, 11, 15, 16, 20; DcEnL; DicTyr; HarEnMi; LinLib S; McGEWB; OxCClL, 89; REn; WhDW*

Alcock, John William, Sir
English. Aviator
Piloted plane that made first nonstop transatlantic flight, from Newfoundland to Ireland, Jun 1919.
b. Nov 6, 1892 in Manchester, England
d. Dec 18, 1919 in Cote d'Evrard, France
Source: *BioIn 4, 5, 6, 8, 12; DcNaB 1912; FacFETw*

Alcott, Amos Bronson
American. Educator
Friend of Emerson, Thoreau; founded Concord School of Philosophy, 1879.
b. Nov 29, 1799 in Wolcott, Connecticut
d. Mar 4, 1888 in Boston, Massachusetts
Source: *Alli, SUP; AmAu; AmAu&B; AmBi; AmSocL; ApCAB; BbD; BibAL; BiDAmEd; BiD&SB; BiDTran; BioIn 1, 2, 3, 4, 5, 6, 7, 8, 9, 12, 13, 15, 16, 19; CasWL; Chambr 3; ChhPo, S2; CnDAL; CyAL 2; CyEd; DcAmAu; DcAmB; DcAmSR; DcBiPP; DcLB 1; DcLEL; DcNAA; Drake; EncARH; EvLB; HarEnUS; LinLib L; McGEWB; NatCAB 2; NinCLC 1; OxCAmH; PenC AM; REn; REnAL; TwCBDA; WebAB 74, 79; WhAm HS; WorAl; WorAlBi*

Alcott, Amy Strum
American. Golfer
Turned pro, 1975; won US Women's Open, 1980.
b. Feb 22, 1956 in Kansas City, Missouri
Source: *BiDAmSp Sup; InWom SUP; NewYTBS 80, 86; WhoAm 82, 84, 86, 88, 90, 92, 94, 95, 96, 97; WhoAmW 89, 91, 93; WhoGolf; WhoIntG*

Alcott, John
English. Filmmaker
Best-known films include *A Clockwork Orange*, 1971.
b. 1931? in London, England
d. Jul 28, 1986 in Cannes, France
Source: *FilmgC; IntDcF 2-4; IntMPA 84; NewYTBS 86; WhoAm 84*

Alcott, Louisa May
[A.M. Barnard; Flora Fairchild]
American. Author
Her early life in New England described in *Little Women*, 1868.
b. Nov 29, 1832 in Germantown, Pennsylvania
d. Mar 6, 1888 in Boston, Massachusetts
Source: *Alli SUP; AmAu; AmAu&B; AmBi; AmCulL; AmWom; AmWomWr, 92; AmWr S1; ApCAB; ArtclWW 2; AtlBL; AuBYP 2, 3; BbD; Benet 87, 96; BenetAL 91; BibAL; BiD&SB; BiDTran; BioAmW; BioIn 1, 2, 3, 4, 5, 6, 7, 8, 9, 10, 11, 12, 14, 15, 16, 17, 19, 20, 21; BlmGWL; CamGEL; CamGLE; CamHAL; CarSB; CasWL; Chambr 3; ChhPo, S3; ChlBkCr; ChlLR 1, 38; CivWDc; CnDAL; ContDcW 89; CrtT 3, 4; CyAL 2; CyWA 58; DcAmAu; DcAmB; DcArts; DcBiA; DcEnL; DcLB 1, 42, 79; DcLEL; DcNAA; EncAB-H 1974, 1996; EncWHA; EvLB; FamAYP; FemiCLE; FemiWr; GoodHs; GrLiveH; GrWomW; GrWrEL N; HanAmWH; HarEnUS; HerW, 84; IntDcWB; InWom, SUP; JBA 34; LegTOT; LibW; LinLib L, S; MagSAmL; MajAI; McGEWB; MorMA; MouLC 4; NatCAB 1; NinCLC 6; NotAW; Novels; OnHuMoP; OxCAmH; OxCAmL 65, 83, 95; OxCChiL; OxCEng 67; OxCWoWr 95; PenC AM; PenEncH; PenNWW A; PeoHis; RAdv 14; RComAH; RealN; REn; REnAL; RfGAmL 87, 94; Str&VC; TwCBDA; TwCChW 78A, 83A, 89A, 95A; TwCYAW; WebAB 74, 79; WhAm HS; WhCiWar; WhoChL; WorAl; WorAlBi; WorLitC; WrChl; YABC 1*

Alcuin
[Albinus]
"Ealwhine"; "Flaccus"
English. Theologian, Scholar
Organized scholarly culture of time; wrote 310 letters which reveal history of eighth c.
b. 735 in York, England
d. May 19, 804 in Tours, France
Source: *Alli; BbD; BiB S; BiD&SB; BioIn 1, 2, 3, 4, 6, 7, 8, 10, 16, 21; BritAu; CamGEL; CamGLE; CasWL; Chambr 1; CyEd; DcBiPP; DcCathB; DcEnL; EvLB; LinLib L, S; LuthC 75; MediFra; NewC; NewCBEL; NewGrDM 80; OxCClL; OxCEng 67, 85, 95; OxCFr; OxCGer 76, 86; OxCMus; PenC ENG, EUR; REn; WhDW*

Alda, Alan
[Alphonso d'Abruzzo]
American. Actor, Director
Played Hawkeye on "M*A*S*H," 1972-83; movie roles include *California Suite*, 1978; *The Four Seasons*, 1981; TV Hall of Fame, 1994.
b. Jan 28, 1936 in New York, New York
Source: *BiE&WWA; BioIn 10, 11, 12, 13, 14, 15, 16; BioNews 74; BkPepl; CelR 90; ConAu 103; ConTFT 3, 10; CurBio 77; EncAFC; FilmEn; FilmgC; ForYSC; HalFC 80, 84, 88; IntMPA 77, 78, 79, 80, 81, 82, 84, 86, 88, 92, 94, 96; IntWW 83, 89, 91, 93; LegTOT; LesBEnT 92; MiSFD 9; MotPP; MovMk; NewYTBS 74, 81, 85; NewYTET; NotNAT; PseudN 82; WhoAm 76, 78, 80, 82, 84, 86, 88, 90, 92, 94, 95, 96, 97; WhoCom; WhoEnt 92; WhoHol 92, A; WhoThe 72, 77, 81; WorAl; WorAlBi*

Alda, Frances
[Frances Davis]
American. Opera Singer
Soprano; with NY Met., 1908-29; noted for volatile temperament, law cases.
b. May 31, 1883 in Christchurch, New Zealand
d. Sep 18, 1952 in Venice, Italy
Source: *ApCAB X; Baker 78, 84, 92; BioIn 1, 3, 4, 6, 8, 9, 10, 11, 12, 14; CmOp; InWom, SUP; MetOEnc; MusMk; MusSN; NatCAB 39; NewEOp 71; NewGrDA 86; NewGrDM 80; OxDcOp; PenDiMP*

Alda, Robert
[Alphonso Giovanni Giusseppi Roberto d'Abruzzo]
American. Actor
Father of Alan Alda; best known for playing George Gershwin in *Rhapsody in Blue*, 1945.
b. Feb 26, 1914 in New York, New York
d. May 3, 1986 in Los Angeles, California
Source: *AnObit 1986; BiE&WWA; BioIn 4, 10, 14, 15; CmpEPM; ConNews 86-3; ConTFT 3; FilmEn; FilmgC; ForYSC; HalFC 80, 84, 88; HolP 40; IntMPA 75, 76, 77, 78, 79, 80, 81, 82, 84, 86; ItaFilm; LegTOT; MotPP; MovMk; NewYTBS 86; NotNAT; OxCAmT 84; OxCPMus; PlP&P; PseudN 82; WhoAm 80; WhoHol A; WhoThe 72, 77, 81; WhoWor 80, 82; WorAl; WorAlBi*

Aldecoa, Ignacio
Spanish. Author
Novels include *The Brightness and the Blood*, 1954, *Great Sun*, 1957, and *Part of a Story*, 1967.
b. Jul 11, 1925 in Vitoria, Spain
d. Nov 15, 1969 in Madrid, Spain
Source: *BioIn 12; CIDMEL 80; ModSpP S; OxCSpan*

Alden, Henry M
American. Author, Editor
Dean of American magazine editors; edited *Harper's Monthly*, 1869-1919.
b. Nov 11, 1836 in Mount Tabor, Vermont
d. Oct 7, 1919 in New York, New York
Source: *Alli SUP; AmAu; AmAu&B; AmBi; ApCAB; BbD; BiD&SB; CnDAL; DcAmB; DcNAA; EncAJ; LinLib L; NatCAB 1; OxCAmL 65; REnAL; TwCBDA; WhAm 1*

Alden, Isabella Macdonald
American. Author
Wrote 80 popular religious books for young people.
b. Nov 3, 1841 in Rochester, New York
d. Aug 5, 1930 in Palo Alto, California
Source: *NotAW; OxCAmL 83*

Alden, John
English. Colonial Figure
Founded Duxbury, MA; last surviving signer of *Mayflower* Compact.
b. 1599, England
d. Sep 12, 1687 in Duxbury, Massachusetts
Source: *AmBi; ApCAB; BenetAL 91; BioIn 4, 7, 9, 11, 16; CabMA; DcAmB; Drake; EncCRAm; HarEnUS; LegTOT; LinLib L, S; NatCAB 10; NewCol 75; OxCAmH; OxCAmL 65, 83, 95; REn; REnAL; TwCBDA; WebAB 74, 79; WhAm HS; WorAl; WorAlBi*

Alden, Priscilla Mullens
[Mrs. John Alden]
English. Colonial Figure
Married Alden, 1623; romance subject of Longfellow's poem, "The Courtship of Miles Standish."
b. 1604 in Surrey, England
d. 1680 in Duxbury, Massachusetts
Source: *AmBi; BioIn 2, 4; LibW; NotAW*

Aldington, Richard (Edward Godfree)
English. Author
One of leaders of Imagists poetry movement, 1910-18.
b. Jul 8, 1892 in Portsmouth, England
d. Jul 27, 1962 in Sury-en-Vaux, France
Source: *Benet 87, 96; BioIn 2, 4, 5, 6, 7, 8, 10, 11, 12, 13, 14, 16, 17, 21; CamGLE; CasWL; Chambr 3; ChhPo, S1, S2, S3; ConAu 45NR, 85; ConLC 49; CyWA 58, 89; DcArts; DcLB 20, 36, 100, 149; DcLEL; EncWL; EvLB; FacFETw; GrWrEL N; LinLib L, S; LngCTC; ModBrL; NewC; NewCBEL; NewCol 75; Novels; ObitT 1961; OxCEng 67, 85; OxCTwCP; PenC ENG; REn; RfGEnL 91; RGTwCWr; TwCA, SUP; TwCWr; WebE&AL; WhAm 4; WhDW; WhE&EA; WhLit*

Aldiss, Brian Wilson
[Jael Cracken; Arch Mendicant; Peter Pica; John Runciman; C C Shackleton]
English. Author
Hugo-winning writer who wrote *Moreau's Other Island,* 1980.
b. Aug 18, 1925 in Dereham, England
Source: *Au&Wr 71; Benet 87; BioIn 13; ConAu 2AS, 5NR, 5R, 28NR; ConLC 5, 14, 40; ConNov 72, 76, 91; ConSFF; CyWA 89; FacFETw; IntvTCA 2; IntWW 74; MajTwCW; PseudN 82; ScFSB; SmATA 2; TwCSFW 91; TwCWr; Who 74; WhoWor 74; WorAlBi; WrDr 76, 92*

Aldredge, Theoni (Athanasiou) V(achliotis)
American. Designer
Won Tonys for costumes in *Annie,* 1977; *La Cage Aux Folles,* 1984; Oscar for *The Great Gatsby,* 1974.
b. Aug 22, 1932 in Salonika, Greece
Source: *BioIn 13, 14, 16; CamGWoT; ConDes 90; ConTFT 1, 4; CurBio 94; IntMPA 92; NotWoAT; OxCAmT 84; VarWW 85; WhoAm 90; WhoAmW 91; WhoE 91; WhoEnt 92*

Aldrich, Bess Streeter
[Margaret Dean Stevens]
American. Author
Wrote of midwest pioneer life: *Song of Years,* 1939.
b. Feb 17, 1881 in Cedar Falls, Iowa
d. Aug 3, 1954 in Lincoln, Nebraska
Source: *AmAu&B; AmNov; AmWomWr; ArtclWW 2; BenetAL 91; BioIn 17; BlmGWL; DcAmB S5; EncAB-A 6; InWom; NatCAB 46; OxCAmL 65, 83, 95; PenNWW A, B; PseudN 82; REn; REnAL; TwCA, SUP; TwCWW 91; WhAm 3; WhE&EA; WhLit; WhNAA*

Aldrich, Ki
[Charles C. Aldrich]
American. Football Player
All-American, 1938, with Texas Christian; member, College Football Hall of Fame.
b. Jun 1, 1916 in Temple, Texas
d. Mar 12, 1983
Source: *WhoSpor*

Aldrich, Nelson Wilmarth
American. Statesman
Rep. senator from RI, 1881-1911; expert on tariff, currency legislation.
b. Nov 6, 1841 in Foster, Rhode Island
d. Apr 16, 1915 in New York, New York
Source: *AmBi; AmLegL; AmPolLe; ApCAB, X; BiDrAC; BiDrUSC 89; BioIn 9, 10; CyAG; DcAmB; EncAAH; EncAB-H 1974, 1996; HarEnUS; McGEWB; NatCAB 10, 25; NewCol 75; OxCAmH; TwCBDA; WebAB 74, 79; WhAm 1; WhAmP*

Aldrich, Richard Stoddard
American. Producer, Author
Produced over 30 Broadway plays, including *The Moon Is Blue,* 1951; pioneered growth of summer stock in US.
b. Aug 17, 1902 in Boston, Massachusetts
d. Mar 31, 1986 in Williamsburg, Virginia
Source: *BioIn 1, 3, 4; ConTFT 3; CurBio 55, 86; WhAm 9; WhoAm 74, 76; WhoE 74; WhoWor 74*

Aldrich, Robert
American. Director, Producer
Films include *The Dirty Dozen,* 1967; *The Longest Yard,* 1974.
b. Aug 9, 1918 in Cranston, Rhode Island
d. Dec 5, 1983 in Los Angeles, California
Source: *AnObit 1983; BiDFilm, 81, 94; BioIn 8, 9, 10, 11, 12, 13, 15, 16, 21; CmMov; ConTFT 2; DcFM; FilmEn; FilmgC; GangFlm; HalFC 80, 84, 88; IlWWHD 1; IntDcF 1-2, 2-2; IntMPA 75, 76, 77, 78, 79, 80, 81, 82, 84; IntWW 74, 75, 76, 77, 78, 79, 80, 81, 82, 83; ItaFilm; LegTOT; MiSFD 9N; MovMk; NewYTBS 83; OxCFilm; VarWW 85; WhAm 8; WhoAm 74, 76, 78, 80, 82, 84, 86; WhoHrs 80; WhoWest 78; WhoWor 78; WorEFlm; WorFDir 2*

Aldrich, Thomas Bailey
American. Author
Editor, *Atlantic Monthly,* 1881-90, known for semi-autobiographical novel, *Story of a Bad Boy,* 1870.
b. Nov 11, 1836 in Portsmouth, New Hampshire
d. Mar 19, 1907 in Boston, Massachusetts
Source: *Alli, SUP; AmAu; AmAu&B; AmBi; ApCAB, X; AuBYP 2S; BbD; Benet 87, 96; BenetAL 91; BibAL; BiDAmM; BiD&SB; BioIn 1, 2, 3, 5, 7, 12, 15; CamGEL; CamGLE; CamHAL; CarSB; CasWL; CelCen; Chambr 3; ChhPo, S1, S2, S3; CnDAL; ConAu 111; CrtSuMy; CyAL 2; CyWA 58; DcAmAu; DcAmB; DcBiA; DcEnA A; DcEnL; DcLB 42, 71, 74, 79; DcLEL; DcNAA; Drake; EncAJ; EncMys; EncSF 93; EvLB; GayN; JBA 34; LinLib L, S; MovMk; NatCAB 1; NewGrDA 86; NotNAT B; OxCAmL 65, 83, 95; OxCEng 67, 85, 95; OxCFilm; PenC AM; RAdv 14; REn; REnAL; SmATA 17; TwCBDA; TwCChW 78A, 83A, 89A, 95A; WebAB 74, 79; WhAm 1*

Aldrich, Winthrop Williams
American. Banker
Pres., 1930-33, chm., 1933-53 of Chase National Bank (now Chase Manhattan Bank).
b. Nov 2, 1885 in Providence, Rhode Island
d. Feb 25, 1974 in New York, New York
Source: *BioIn 1, 2, 3, 8, 10, 11, 12, 16, 21; CurBio 40, 53, 74; DcAmDH 80, 89; NatCAB 60; NewYTBS 74; WhAm 6; Who 74; WhoAm 74*

Aldridge, Ira Frederick
"The African Roscius"; "The African Tragedian"
English. Actor
Protege of Edmund Kean; regarded as one of greatest actors of his day.
b. 1805 in New York, New York
d. Aug 10, 1867 in Lodz, Poland
Source: *ApCAB; BioIn 1, 3, 5, 6, 7, 8, 9; DcAmB; Drake; NegAl 76; NotNAT A, B; OxCThe 67; WebAB 74, 79; WhAm HS*

Aldridge, Michael
English. Actor, Director
Active in English theater 1939-86; also made films since 1946.
b. Sep 9, 1920 in Glastonbury, England
d. Jan 10, 1994 in London, England
Source: *BioIn 19; ConTFT 3, 12; Who 92; WhoHol 92; WhoThe 72, 77, 81*

Aldrin, Edwin E(ugene), Jr.
"Buzz"
American. Astronaut, Businessman
Aboard *Apollo 11;* second man to walk on moon, Jul 20, 1969.
b. Jan 20, 1930 in Montclair, New Jersey
Source: *AmMWSc 73P; BioIn 7, 8, 9, 10, 12, 14, 16; BioNews 74; ConAu 89; FacFETw; IntWW 74, 75, 76, 77, 78, 79, 80, 81, 82, 83, 89, 91; LinLib S; PseudN 82; RAdv 14; Who 82, 92; WhoAm 74, 76, 78, 80, 82, 84, 88; WhoSpc; WhoWest 78, 80; WhoWor 74, 76, 78; WorAl; WorAlBi*

Alechinsky, Pierre
Belgian. Artist
Painter in carnival grotesque style; won first Andrew W. Mellon Biennial Prize, 1977; landmark work, *Central Park.*

b. Oct 19, 1927 in Brussels, Belgium
Source: *BioIn 7, 11, 13, 14, 15, 16; ConArt 77, 83, 89, 96; CurBio 88; DcCAr 81; DcTwCCu 2; McGDA; ModArCr 1; NewYTBS 87; OxCTwCA; OxDcArt; PhDcTCA 77; PrintW 83, 85; WorArt 1950*

Alegria, Ciro
Peruvian. Author
Novels deal with Peruvian Indian culture; wrote *The Golden Serpent,* 1935, and *Broad and Alien is the World,* 1941.
b. Nov 4, 1909 in Saltimbanca, Peru
d. Feb 17, 1967 in Lima, Peru
Source: *Benet 87, 96; BenetAL 91; BioIn 1, 4, 5, 7, 16, 18; CasWL; ConAu 131; CyWA 58, 89; DcHiB; DcLB, 113; DcSpL; EncLatA; EncWL 2, 3; HispWr; LatAmWr; LinLib L; ModLAL; OxCSpan; PenC AM; SpAmA; TwCA SUP; TwCWr*

Alegria, Claribel
Salvadoran. Poet
Won Casa de las Americas poetry prize, 1978, for *Sobrevivo.*
b. May 12, 1924 in Esteli, Nicaragua
Source: *Benet 96; BlmGWL; ConAu 15AS, 131; ConLC 75; ConWorW 93; DcLB 145; DcTwCCu 4; EncWL 3; HispWr; LiExTwC; SpAmA; SpAmWW; WomWrSA*

Aleichem, Sholom
[Solomon J Rabinowitz]
"Yiddish Mark Twain"
Russian. Author
Wrote of Jewish Ukranian life; *Tevye* was basis for Broadway's *Fiddler on the Roof,* 1964.
b. Feb 18, 1859 in Pereyaslavl, Russia
d. May 13, 1916 in New York, New York
Source: *AmAu&B; AtlBL; CasWL; CyWA 89; EncWB; EncWL; FacFETw; LegTOT; LinLib L; LngCTC; NotNAT B; OxCThe 67, 83; PseudN 82; REn; REnAL; TwCA, SUP; TwCLC 1; WorAl; WorAlBi*

Aleixandre, Vicente
Spanish. Poet
Surrealist who often used metaphors from nature; won Nobel Prize, 1977.
b. Apr 26, 1898 in Seville, Spain
d. Dec 14, 1984 in Madrid, Spain
Source: *AnObit 1984; Benet 87; BioIn 10, 11, 12, 14, 15, 16, 17; CasWL; ClDMEL 80; ConAu 26NR, 85, 114; ConFLW 84; ConLC 9, 36; CurBio 78, 85, 85N; DcArts; DcHiB; DcLB 108; EncWL, 2, 3; FacFETw; HispWr; IntAu&W 76, 77, 82; IntWW 74, 75, 76, 77, 78, 79, 80, 83; IntWWP 77, 82; MajTwCW; ModSpP S; NobelP; PenC EUR; PoeCrit 15; RAdv 14; REn; Who 82, 83, 85; WhoNob; WhoWor 74, 78, 80, 82, 84; WorAl; WorAu 1950*

Alekhine, Alexander
French. Chess Player
World champion, 1927-35, 1937-46; held world blindfold chess record.
b. Nov 1, 1892 in Moscow, Russia
d. Mar 24, 1946 in Lisbon, Portugal
Source: *BioIn 14, 15, 16, 17; CurBio 46; GolEC; OxCChes 84*

Alekseyev, Vasily Ivanovich
Russian. Weightlifter
Set 79 world records in super-heavy weight category, 1970-78; won Olympic gold medals, 1972, 1976.
b. Jan 7, 1942 in Pokrovo-Shishkino, Union of Soviet Socialist Republics
Source: *NewYTBE 71*

Aleman, Miguel
Mexican. Political Leader
First civilian pres. following 1917 revolution, 1946-52.
b. Sep 29, 1903 in Sayula, Mexico
d. May 14, 1983 in Mexico City, Mexico
Source: *AnObit 1983; ConAu 110; CurBio 46, 83, 83N; IntWW 74; NewYTBS 83*

Alembert, Jean le Rond d'
"Anaxagoras"; "Le Chancelier du Parnasse"; "The Father of French Philosophy"; "The Mazarin of Letters"
French. Mathematician, Philosopher
Known for principle of mechanics, called D'Alembert's Principle; theory of practical elements of music, 1759.
b. Nov 16, 1717 in Paris, France
d. Oct 29, 1783 in Paris, France
Source: *BbD; BiD&SB; BioIn 16, 17; BlkwCE; CamDcSc; CasWL; DcBiPP; DcScB; EncEnl; EuAu; EvEuW; LinLib L; McGEWB; NewCol 75; OxCFr; OxCMus; PenC EUR; REn; WhDW; WorScD*

Alessandri, Jorge
Chilean. Political Leader
Pres. of Chile, 1958-64.
b. May 19, 1896 in Santiago, Chile
d. Sep 1, 1986 in Santiago, Chile
Source: *AnObit 1986; CurBio 86, 86N; DcTwHis; EncLatA; McGEWB*

Alessandri Palma, Arturo
Chilean. Political Leader
Held various governmental posts in Chile, including pres., 1920-25, 1932-38.
b. Dec 20, 1868 in Longavi, Chile
d. Aug 24, 1950 in Santiago, Chile
Source: *BiDLAmC; BiDMoPL; BioIn 2, 6, 16; DcCPSAm*

Alessandro, Victor Nicholas
American. Conductor
Musical director, Oklahoma Symphony, 1931-51; San Antonio Orchestra, 1952-76.
b. Nov 27, 1915 in Waco, Texas
d. Nov 27, 1976 in San Antonio, Texas
Source: *Baker 84; IntWW 74, 75, 76, 77; IntWWM 77; NewEOp 71; NewYTBS 76; WhAm 7; WhoAm 74, 76; WhoMus 72; WhoOp 76; WhoSSW 73, 75, 76*

Alexander, Ben
[Nicholas Benton Alexander]
American. Actor
Popular child star in silent films; Jack Webb's partner on TV series "Dragnet," 1953-59.
b. May 26, 1911 in Garfield, Nevada
d. Jul 5, 1969 in Hollywood, California
Source: *BioIn 3, 9; Film 1, 2; FilmEn; FilmgC; ForYSC; HalFC 80, 84, 88; HolCA; MotPP; MovMk; ObitOF 79; PseudN 82; RadStar; TwYS; WhoHol B; WhScrn 74, 77, 83*

Alexander, Clifford L, Jr.
American. Government Official
Secretary of Army, 1977-80; first black in US history to serve as civilian head of military branch.
b. Sep 21, 1933 in New York, New York
Source: *BioIn 14, 16; BioNews 74; CurBio 77; InB&W 85; IntWW 80, 82, 91; NegAl 89A; PolProf J; WhoAm 90; WhoAmP 81, 89, 91; WhoBlA 80, 90, 92; WhoWor 80*

Alexander, Denise
American. Actor
Played Dr. Leslie Weber on TV soap opera "General Hospital," 1973-84.
b. Nov 11, 1945 in New York, New York
Source: *WhoAm 78, 80, 82, 84*

Alexander, Donald Crichton
American. Government Official
IRS commissioner, 1973-77.
b. May 22, 1921 in Pine Bluff, Arkansas
Source: *BioIn 10*

Alexander, Franz Gabriel
American. Physician, Educator
Founder, director Chicago Institute for Psychoanalysis, 1932-56; started psychosomatic movement.
b. Jan 22, 1891 in Budapest, Austria-Hungary
d. Mar 8, 1964 in Palm Springs, California
Source: *BiDPsy; BioIn 3, 5, 6, 7, 9; DcAmB S7; DcAmMeB 84; NamesHP; WebBD 83*

Alexander, Grover Cleveland
"Alex"; "Alex the Great"; "Buck"; "Dode"; "Old Pete"; "Pete"
American. Baseball Player
Pitcher, 1911-30; 373 victories, third highest in ML history; Hall of Fame, 1938.
b. Feb 26, 1887 in Elba, Nebraska
d. Nov 4, 1950 in Saint Paul, Nebraska
Source: *Ballpl 90; BiDAmSp BB; BioIn 2, 3, 4, 5, 6, 7, 8, 9, 10, 13, 14, 15, 17, 20; DcAmB S4; LegTOT; NewCol 75; WhoProB 73; WhoSpor; WorAl; WorAlBi*

Alexander, Hattie Elizabeth
American. Physician
First woman pres., American Pediatric Society, 1964.
b. Apr 5, 1901 in Baltimore, Maryland
d. Jun 24, 1968 in Port Washington, New York
Source: *BioIn 7, 8, 12, 15, 16, 19, 20; NotAW MOD; NotWoLS; ObitOF 79; WhAm 5; WhoAmW 58, 66, 68, 70; WomFir*

Alexander, James Waddell, II
American. Mathematician
A founder of branch of mathematics known as topology.
b. Sep 19, 1888 in Sea Bright, New Jersey
d. Sep 23, 1971 in Princeton, New Jersey
Source: *WhAm 5, 8*

Alexander, Jane
[Jane Quigley]
American. Actor
Won Tony for *Great White Hope,* 1969; played Eleanor Roosevelt in TV mini-series; chairman National Endowment for Arts, 1993—.
b. Oct 28, 1939 in Boston, Massachusetts
Source: *BioIn 10, 11, 12, 13, 16; BkPepl; CamGWoT; CelR 90; ConTFT 1, 4; CurBio 77; FilmEn; HalFC 80, 84, 88; IntMPA 82, 84, 86, 88, 92, 94, 96; InWom SUP; LegTOT; LesBEnT 92; News 94, 94-2; NotNAT; NotWoAT; PlP&P A; WhoAm 74, 76, 78, 80, 82, 84, 86, 88, 90, 92, 94, 95, 96, 97; WhoAmW 72, 74, 77, 83, 85, 87, 89, 91, 93, 95, 97; WhoE 95; WhoEnt 92; WhoHol 92, A; WhoThe 77, 81; WhoWor 91, 93, 96; WorAl; WorAlBi*

Alexander, Jason
[Jay Scott Greenspan]
American. Actor
Plays George Costanza on TV show "Seinfeld," 1989—; played Conrad Birdie in the 1995 television movie "Bye, Bye Birdie;" won Tony Award, Best Actor, for *Jerome Robbins' Broadway,* 1989.
b. Sep 23, 1959 in Newark, New Jersey
Source: *BioIn 16; ConTFT 1, 8, 15; IntMPA 92, 94, 96; WhoAm 90, 92, 94, 95, 96, 97; WhoEnt 92; WhoHol 92*

Alexander, Katherine
American. Actor
Played refined ladies in 1930s films: *Death Takes a Holiday,* 1934; *The Hunchback of Notre Dame,* 1939.
b. Sep 22, 1901 in Fort Smith, Arkansas
Source: *BiE&WWA; FilmEn; FilmgC; HalFC 80, 84, 88; InWom SUP; MovMk; NotNAT; PlP&P; ThFT; WhThe*

Alexander, Lamar
[Andrew Lamar Alexander, Jr.]
American. Government Official, Politician
U.S. Secretary of Education, 1991-93; Governor, Tennessee, 1979-87; Republican presidential candidate, 1996.
b. Jul 3, 1940 in Knoxville, Tennessee
Source: *AlmAP 80, 82, 84; BiDrGov 1978, 1983; CngDr 91; CurBio 91; IntWW 91, 93; IntYB 82; News 91, 92, 91-2; NewYTBS 95; PolsAm 84; WhoAm 80, 82, 84, 86, 88, 90, 92, 94, 95, 96, 97; WhoAmP 79, 81, 83, 85, 87, 89, 91, 93, 95; WhoE 93; WhoSSW 80, 82, 84, 86, 88, 95, 97; WhoWor 82, 84, 87*

Alexander, Leo
American. Psychiatrist, Educator
Wrote Nuremberg Code used at Nuremberg trials, 1940s; instrumental in solving "Boston Strangler" murders, 1960s.
b. Oct 11, 1905 in Vienna, Austria-Hungary
d. Jul 20, 1985 in Weston, Massachusetts
Source: *AmMWSc 73P, 76P, 79, 82; BiDrAPA 77; BioIn 14; ConAu 116; InSci*

Alexander, Lloyd Chudley
American. Author
Award-winning children's books include *Westmark,* 1981; Newbery Prize for *The High King,* 1969.
b. Jan 30, 1924 in Philadelphia, Pennsylvania
Source: *AnCL; Au&Arts 1; Au&Wr 71; AuBYP 2, 3; BioIn 14, 15, 16; ChlLR 1; ConAu 1NR, 1R, 24NR; ConLC 35; DcLB 52; IntvTCA 2; MajTwCW; OxCChiL; PiP; SmATA 3, 49; SupFW; ThrBJA; TwCChW 89; WhoAm 84, 90; WhoUSWr 88; WhoWrEP 89; WrDr 92*

Alexander, Shana
[Shana Ager]
American. Author, Lecturer
Liberal commentator, "60 Minutes," 1975-79; wrote *Nutcracker: Money, Madness and Murder.*
b. Oct 6, 1925 in New York, New York
Source: *BioIn 6, 8; CelR 90; ConAu 26NR, 61; ConIsC 2; EncTwCJ; ForWC 70; InWom SUP; LegTOT; St&PR 75; WhoAm 74, 76, 78, 80, 82, 84, 86, 90, 92, 94, 95, 96, 97; WhoAmW 72, 74, 77, 79, 81, 83, 85, 87, 89, 91; WhoFI 74; WhoUSWr 88; WhoWor 80; WhoWrEP 89, 92, 95; WorAl; WorAlBi; WrDr 76, 80, 82, 84, 86, 88, 90, 92, 94, 96*

Alexander, Sue
American. Children's Author
Won McKenzie Award for children's literature, 1980; wrote *Witch, Goblin, and Ghost* series.
b. Aug 20, 1933 in Tucson, Arizona
Source: *BioIn 11, 16; ConAu 4NR, 19NR, 53; IntAu&W 91, 93; SixBJA; SmATA 12, 15AS, 89; WrDr 88, 90, 92, 94, 96*

Alexander, William
"Lord Stirling"
American. Army Officer
Revolutionary War hero who commanded troops at Battle of Long Island, 1776; Monmouth, 1778.
b. 1726 in New York, New York
d. Jan 15, 1783 in Albany, New York
Source: *AmBi; AmRev; ApCAB; BilnAmS; BioIn 8, 12, 15; DcAmB; DcNaB; Drake; EncAR; EncCRAm; HarEnMi; HarEnUS; NatCAB 1; NewCol 75; TwCBDA; WebAMB; WhAm HS; WhAmP; WhAmRev*

Alexander I
[Aleksandr Pavlovich]
"The Northern Telemaque"
Russian. Ruler
Grandson of Catherine the Great; czar of Russia, 1801-25; succeeded by brother Nicholas I.
b. Dec 23, 1777 in Saint Petersburg, Russia
d. Dec 1, 1825 in Taganrog, Russia
Source: *NewCol 75; REn; WebBD 83*

Alexander II
[Aleksandr Nikolaevich]
Russian. Ruler
Son of Nicholas I; czar of Russia, 1855-81; freed serfs, 1861; sold Russia, 1867.
b. Apr 29, 1818 in Moscow, Russia
d. Mar 13, 1881 in Saint Petersburg, Russia
Source: *NewCol 75; REn; WebBD 83*

Alexander III
[Aleksandr Aleksandrovich]
Russian. Ruler
Younger son of Alexander II; czar of Russia, 1881-94; reign known for repression of liberal ideas, persecution of Jews.
b. Mar 10, 1845, Russia
d. Nov 1, 1894 in Livadia, Russia
Source: *NewCol 75; REn; WebBD 83*

Alexander of Hales
[Hales Owen]
"Doctor Doctorum"; "The Fountain of Life"; "The Irrefragable Doctor"
English. Philosopher
Wrote *Summa Universae Theologiae,* first systematic writings on Catholic dogma, printed in 1475.
b. 1185 in Hales, England
d. Aug 21, 1245 in Paris, France
Source: *BiD&SB; DcCathB; DcEnL; LinLib L; MediFra; NewC; OxCEng 67; OxCLaw; REn*

Alexander of Tunis
[Harold Rupert Leofric George Alexander]
English. Military Leader, Political Leader
Charismatic commander of Allied forces in WW II Italian invasion, 1943; governor-general of Canada, 1946-52.
b. Dec 10, 1891 in County Tyrone, Ireland
d. Jun 16, 1969 in Slough, England

Source: *BioIn 1, 2, 3, 6, 7, 8, 9, 11, 17; ColCR; CurBio 42, 69; DcIrB 88; DcNaB 1961; DcTwHis; FacFETw; GenMudB; GrBr; McGEWB; NewCol 75; ObitT 1961; WhoMilH 76; WorAl*

Alexanderson, Ernst Frederik Werner
American. Inventor, Engineer
Developed equipment which led to first vocal radio broadcast, 1906; helped develop color TV.
b. Jan 25, 1878 in Uppsala, Sweden
d. May 14, 1975 in Schenectady, New York
Source: *BioIn 1, 3, 4, 10, 11, 13; CurBio 55, 75; InSci; LinLib S; OxCAmH; WebAB 74, 79; WhAm 6; WorInv*

Alexander the Great
[Alexander III]
"Macedonia's Madman"; "The Conqueror of the World"; "The Emathian Conqueror"
Macedonian. Ruler
King who forged largest western empire of ancient world, from Greece to N India.
b. Sep 20, 356BC in Pella, Macedonia
d. Jun 13, 323BC, Babylon
Source: *Benet 87, 96; BioIn 1, 2, 3, 4, 5, 6, 7, 8, 9, 10, 11, 12, 13, 17, 18, 20; BlmGEL; CyEd; DcEuL; Expl 93; FilmgC; GayLesB; GenMudB; HalFC 84, 88; HarEnMi; HisWorL; LegTOT; LinLib L, S; LngCEL; McGEWB; NewC; NewCol 75; OxCClL, 89; OxCEng 85, 95; OxCSpan; OxDcByz; OxDcOp; PenC CL; REn; WhDW; WorAl; WorAlBi*

Alexander VI
[Rodrigo Borgia; Rodrigo de Borja y Doms]
"The Worst Pope"
Spanish. Religious Leader
Pope, 1492-1503, elected by corrupt conclave; father of Cesare and Lucrezia Borgia.
b. Jan 1, 1431 in Xativa, Spain
d. Aug 18, 1503
Source: *Benet 87; McGEWB; NewCol 75; OxCEng 85, 95; REn; WebBD 83*

Alexandra Caroline Mary Charlotte
English. Consort
Queen of Edward VII, remembered for beauty, goodness.
b. Dec 1, 1844 in Copenhagen, Denmark
d. Nov 20, 1925 in Sandringham, England
Source: *DcNaB 1922*

Alexandra Feodorovna
[Alix Victoria Helene Luise Beatrix]
Russian. Consort
Married Nicholas II, last czar of Russia, 1894; slain, with family, by Bolsheviks.
b. 1872 in Hesse-Darmstadt, Germany
d. Jul 16, 1918 in Ekaterinburg, Union of Soviet Socialist Republics
Source: *InWom; NewCol 75; WebBD 83*

Alexandre
[Louis Albert Alexandre Raimon]
French. Hairstylist
Known for reviving the use of false hair; developed extremely short cut called "artichoke."
b. 1922
Source: *BioIn 16, 19; EncFash; WhoFr 79; WorFshn*

Alexandrov, Grigori
[Grigori Mormonenko]
Russian. Director
Worked with Sergei Eisenstein for 10 yrs; films include *Jolly Fellows,* 1934.
b. Feb 23, 1903 in Yekaterinburg, Russia
d. Dec 19, 1983 in Moscow, Union of Soviet Socialist Republics
Source: *BioIn 13; DcFM; Film 2; FilmEn; FilmgC; HalFC 80, 84, 88; IntWW 76; OxCFilm; WorEFlm*

Alexie, Sherman
American. Writer
Published collection of short fiction *The Lone Ranger and Tonto Fistfight in Heaven,* 1993.
b. 1966
Source: *BioIn 18, 21; ConLC 96; NatNAL; NotNaAm*

Alexis, Kim
American. Model
Fashion editor of TV program "Good Morning America," since 1987; has appeared on over 400 magazine covers.
b. Jul 15, 1960 in Lockport, New York
Source: *BioIn 14, 15, 16; CelR 90; LegTOT*

Alexius Comnenus
[Alexius I]
Byzantine. Ruler
Emperor of Eastern Roman Empire, 1081-1118.
b. 1048
d. Aug 15, 1118
Source: *HarEnMi; LinLib S; REn*

Alfieri, Vittorio
Italian. Poet
Called Italy's greatest tragic poet; works are political in nature.
b. Jan 16, 1749 in Asti, Italy
d. Oct 8, 1803 in Florence, Italy
Source: *AtlBL; BbD; Benet 87, 96; BiD&SB; BioIn 1, 2, 3, 4, 6, 7, 10, 14; BlkwCE; CamGWoT; CasWL; CelCen; CnThe; DcArts; DcBiPP; DcCathB; DcEnL; DcEuL; DcItL 1, 2; Dis&D; Ent; EuAu; EuWr 4; EvEuW; GrFLW; IntDcT 2; LinLib L, S; McGEWB; McGEWD 72, 84; NewCBEL; OxCEng 67, 85, 95; OxCThe 67; PenC EUR; RAdv 14, 13-2; RComWL; REn; REnWD; RfGWoL 95*

Alfonsin Foulkes, Raul Ricardo
Argentine. Political Leader
Elected pres., 1983, defeating Peronist Party for first time in 38 yrs; pursued human rights reforms, democratization.
b. Mar 31, 1926 in Chascomus, Argentina
Source: *BiDLAmC; BioIn 13, 14, 15, 16; CurBio 84; DcCPSAm; EncWB; FacFETw; IntWW 91; NewYTBS 83, 85; Who 92; WhoWor 87, 91*

Alfonso XIII
Spanish. Ruler
King of Spain, 1886-1931; reign marked by social unrest, several assassination attempts.
b. May 17, 1886 in Madrid, Spain
d. Feb 28, 1941 in Rome, Italy
Source: *CurBio 41; NewCol 75*

Alfred, William
American. Dramatist, Educator
Harvard U professor, 1963-91; wrote drama, *Hogan's Goat,* 1956.
b. Aug 16, 1922 in New York, New York
Source: *AmCath 80; BioIn 7, 10, 12; ConAmD; ConAu 13R; ConDr 73, 77, 82, 88, 93; CroCD; DrAS 74E, 78E, 82E; McGEWD 72, 84; ModAL; NotNAT; OxCAmL 83, 95; OxCAmT 84; WhoAm 74, 76, 78, 80, 82, 84, 86, 88, 90, 92, 94, 95, 96, 97; WhoUSWr 88; WhoWrEP 89, 92, 95; WorAu 1950; WrDr 76, 80, 82, 84, 86, 88, 90, 92, 94, 96*

Alfred the Great
English. Ruler
King of Wessex, 871-99; revived learning, Old English literary prose.
b. 849 in Wantage, England
d. Oct 28, 901?
Source: *Alli; AsBiEn; BbD; BiD&SB; BioIn 1, 2, 3, 4, 5, 6, 7, 8, 9, 10, 11, 12, 13, 20; CrtT 1, 4; DcBiPP; DcCathB; EncE 75; LegTOT; LinLib L, S; LuthC 75; McGEWB; NewCBEL; NewCol 75; REn; WhDW; WorAl; WorAlBi*

Alfrink, Bernard (Jan), Cardinal
Dutch. Religious Leader
Archbishop of Utrecht, 1955-60; cardinal from 1960; involved in post-Vatican Council II liberalization.
b. Jul 5, 1900 in Nijkerk, Nepal
d. Dec 17, 1987 in Nieuwegein, Nepal
Source: *BioIn 15, 16; CurBio 66, 88, 88N; IntWW 83; NewYTBS 87; WhAm 11; WhoWor 84, 87*

Alfven, Hannes Olof Gosta
Swedish. Scientist
Shared Nobel Prize in physics, 1970, for work in plasma physics; his efforts led to discovery of "Alfven's Waves," expanded understanding of solar system.
b. May 30, 1908 in Norrkoeping, Sweden
d. Apr 2, 1995 in Stockholm, Sweden

Source: *AmMWSc 92, 95; BiESc; BioIn 14, 15; CamDcSc; FacFETw; IntWW 74, 75, 76, 77, 78, 79, 80, 81, 82, 83, 89, 91, 93; LarDcSc; LuthC 75; McGMS 80; NewYTBE 70; NobelP; NotTwCS; WhAm 11; Who 74, 82, 83, 85, 88, 90, 92, 94; WhoAm 82, 84, 88, 90, 92, 94, 95; WhoFrS 84; WhoNob, 90, 95; WhoScEn 94; WhoWest 87, 89, 92, 94; WhoWor 74, 78, 80, 82, 84, 87, 91, 93, 95*

Alger, Horatio
American. Author, Clergy
Wrote over 100 rags-to-riches stories for boys.
b. Jan 13, 1832 in Revere, Massachusetts
d. Jul 18, 1899 in Natick, Massachusetts
Source: *AmAu; AmBi; AmSocL; BbD; Benet 87, 96; BenetAL 91; BiD&SB; BioIn 6, 7, 8, 9, 10, 11, 12, 13, 14, 15, 17, 19; CamGLE; CamHAL; CarSB; CasWL; ChlBkCr; CyAL 2; DcAmB; DcArts; DcLB 42; DcNAA; Drake; EvLB; LegTOT; McGEWB; NatCAB 11; NinCLC 8; OxCAmH; OxCAmL 65, 83, 95; OxCChiL; PenC AM; PeoHis; REn; REnAL; RfGAmL 87, 94; SmATA 16; TwCChW 89A, 95A; WebAB 74, 79; WhAm 1; WorAl; WorAlBi*

Algren, Nelson
[Nelson Algren Abraham]
"Poet of the Chicago Slums"
American. Author
Realistic novels include *The Man with the Golden Arm,* about drug addiction, 1949; made into 1955 film with Frank Sinatra.
b. Mar 28, 1909 in Detroit, Michigan
d. May 9, 1981 in Sag Harbor, New York
Source: *AmAu&B; AmNov; AnObit 1981; Benet 87, 96; BenetAL 91; BioIn 2, 4, 5, 7, 8, 10, 12, 13, 15, 16, 17; BlueB 76; CamGEL; CamGLE; CamHAL; CasWL; CnDAL; CnMWL; ConAu 13R, 20NR, 103; ConLC 4, 10, 33; ConNov 72, 76; CyWA 89; DcArts; DcLB 9, Y81A, Y82A; DcLEL; DcTwCCu 1; DrAF 76; DrAPF 80; EncAL; EncWL 2, 3; FacFETw; FilmgC; GrWrEL N; HalFC 80, 84, 88; IntAu&W 76, 77; LegTOT; LinLib L; MagSAmL; MajTwCW; ModAL, S1, S2; NewCon; NewYTBS 81; Novels; OxCAmL 65, 83, 95; PenC AM; RAdv 1; REn; REnAL; RfGAmL 87, 94; RfGShF; TwCA SUP; TwCWr; WebE&AL; WhAm 7; WhoAm 74, 76, 80; WhoTwCL; WhoWor 74; WorAl; WorAlBi; WrDr 76, 80, 82*

Ali
"The Lion of God"; "The Rugged Lion"
Arab. Religious Leader
Fourth caliph of Arab, Islamic Empire; cousin of Muhammed; division of Islam into Sunni, Shiites began during reign.
b. 600?
d. 661 in Al Kufa, Mesopotamia
Source: *DcBiPP; McGEWB; NewCol 75; PseudN 82; WebBD 83*

Ali, Ahmed
Indian. Author, Diplomat
Founder, Indian Progressive Writers, 1932, wrote *Twilight in Delhi,* 1966.
b. Jul 1, 1908 in Delhi, India
Source: *Au&Wr 71; CamGLE; CasWL; ConAu 15NR, 25R, 34NR; ConLC 69; ConNov 72, 76, 82, 91; IntAu&W 91; WhAm 11; WhE&EA; WrDr 76, 92*

Ali, Muhammad
[Cassius Marcellus Clay]
American. Boxer
First heavyweight boxer ever to hold title three times; Olympic Gold medal winner, 1960.
b. Jan 17, 1942 in Louisville, Kentucky
Source: *AfrAmAl 6; AfrAmBi 1; AfrAmSG; AmDec 1970; BiDAmSp BK; BioIn 5, 8, 9, 10, 11, 12, 13, 14, 15, 16, 17, 18, 19, 20, 21; BioNews 74; BkPepl; BlkOlyM; BlueB 76; BoxReg; CelR 90; ConAu 116; ConBlB 2; CurBio 63, 78; DcTwCCu 1, 5; Ebony 1; EncAB-H 1974, 1996; EncWB; FacFETw; HalFC 88; HeroCon; InB&W 80, 85; IntWW 76, 77, 78, 79, 80, 81, 82, 83, 89, 91, 93; NegAl 89; NewYTBE 73; NewYTBS 80, 84, 85; PolProf J; PseudN 82; RComAH; WebAB 74, 79; WhoAfA 96; WhoAm 74, 76, 78, 80, 82, 84, 86, 88, 90, 92, 94, 95, 96, 97; WhoBlA 75, 77, 80, 85, 88, 90, 92, 94; WhoBox 74; WhoHol 92; WhoSpor; WhoWor 78; WorAl; WorAlBi*

Ali, Salim A
Indian. Ornithologist
Acclaimed ornithologist; best known work *Handbook of the Birds of India and Pakistan.*
b. Nov 12, 1896 in Bombay, India
d. Jun 20, 1987 in Bombay, India
Source: *BioIn 3, 11, 13; ConAu 123*

Alia, Ramiz
Albanian. Political Leader
Communist pres., 1982-91, forced to hold first multi-party elections in 60 years after fall of European Communist bloc, 1991.
b. Oct 18, 1925 in Shkoder, Albania
Source: *BioIn 14, 15, 18; ColdWar 2; CurBio 91; IntWW 83, 89, 91, 93; NewYTBS 85; WhoSocC 78; WhoSoCE 89; WhoWor 84, 87, 89, 91*

Alice
[Countess of Athlone Mary Victoria Augusta Pauline]
English. Princess
Last surviving grandchild of Queen Victoria; great-aunt of Queen Elizabeth II; wrote memoirs: *For My Grandchildren: Some Reminiscences.*
b. Feb 25, 1883 in Windsor, England
d. Jan 3, 1981 in London, England
Source: *AnObit 1981; BioIn 7, 11, 12; ConAu 103; NewYTBS 76, 81; Who 85R*

Ali Mahdi Mohamed
Somali. Political Leader
President of Somalia, 1991—; named president by the United Somali Congress (USC).
b. 1940 in Mogadishu, Somalia
Source: *ConBlB 5*

Alinsky, Saul David
American. Political Activist
Established Industrial Area Foundation, 1940; wrote *Rules for Radicalis,* 1971.
b. Jan 30, 1909 in Chicago, Illinois
d. Jun 12, 1972 in Carmel, California
Source: *AmAu&B; AmRef; AmSocL; BiDSocW; BioIn 6, 7, 8, 9, 10, 11, 13; ConAu 37R; CurBio 68, 72; DcAmB S9; EncAL; EncWB; NewYTBE 72; ObitOF 79; PolProf J; WebAB 74, 79; WhAm 5; WorAl*

Alioto, Joseph Lawrence
American. Politician
Mayor of San Francisco, 1968-76.
b. Feb 12, 1916 in San Francisco, California
Source: *BioIn 8, 9, 10, 11, 12; BlueB 76; CurBio 69; IntWW 75, 76, 77, 78, 79, 80, 81, 82, 83, 89, 91, 93; PolProf J, NF; WhoAm 74, 76, 80; WhoAmP 73, 75; WhoGov 72, 75, 77; WhoWest 74, 76, 84*

Ali Pasha
"The Lion of Yannina"
Turkish. Military Leader
Military governor of Yannina, 1787; rule extended to Albania, Epirus until assassination; Lord Byron wrote of his court.
b. 1741 in Tepeleni, Albania
d. 1822
Source: *BioIn 8; NewCol 75; PseudN 82; WebBD 83*

Alison, Archibald
Scottish. Clergy
Best known for essay *On the Nature and Principle of Taste,* 1790.
b. 1757 in Edinburgh, Scotland
d. May 17, 1839 in Edinburgh, Scotland
Source: *Alli; BiD&SB; BiDLA, SUP; Chambr 2; DcBiPP; DcEnL; DcNaB; EvLB; NewCBEL; OxCArt; OxCEng 85, 95; OxDcArt*

Allain, William A
American. Politician
Dem. governor of Mississippi, 1984—.
b. Feb 14, 1928 in Washington, Mississippi
Source: *AlmAP 88; BiDrGov 1983; WhoAm 80, 82, 84, 86; WhoAmL 85; WhoAmP 85, 87, 89, 91, 93, 95; WhoSSW 80, 82, 84, 86; WhoWor 84, 87*

Allaire, Paul Arthur
American. Business Executive
President of Xerox Corp., 1986-91; chairman and CEO, 1991—.
b. Jul 21, 1938 in Worcester, Massachusetts

Source: *St&PR 87, 91, 93, 96, 97; Who 82, 83, 85, 88, 90, 92, 94; WhoAm 88, 90, 92, 94, 95, 96, 97; WhoE 89, 91, 93, 95, 97; WhoFI 85, 87, 89, 92, 94, 96; WhoScEn 94; WhoWor 89, 95, 96, 97*

Allais, Maurice
French. Economist
Won Nobel Prize in economics, 1988, for influential studies of state monopolies; first French national to win Prize.
b. May 31, 1911 in Paris, France
Source: *BioIn 16, 17, 18; IntAu&W 77, 82; IntWW 74, 75, 76, 77, 78, 79, 80, 81, 82, 83, 89, 91, 93; NewYTBS 88; NobelP 91; Who 92, 94; WhoEc 81, 86; WhoFI 92; WhoFr 79; WhoNob 90, 95; WhoWor 91; WorAlBi*

Allan, Elizabeth
English. Actor
Popular British TV star of 1950s; played ladylike heroines in films: *A Tale of Two Cities,* 1935.
b. Apr 9, 1908 in Skegness, England
Source: *FilmEn; FilmgC; ForYSC; HalFC 80, 84, 88; IlWWBF; InWom SUP; ThFT; WhoHol A; WhoThe 77A*

Allan, Montagu, Sir
Canadian. Hockey Player
Donated Allan Cup, 1908, to Canadian amateur hockey; comparable to Stanley Cup for pros; Hall of Fame, 1945.
b. Oct 13, 1860 in Montreal, Quebec, Canada
d. Sep 26, 1951
Source: *WhoHcky 73*

Allard, Sydney
English. Auto Executive
Founder, chairman, Allard Motor Co., Ltd., 1945-66.
b. Jul 1910 in London, England
d. Apr 12, 1966 in Black Hills, England
Source: *BioIn 7, 12; ObitT 1961*

Allard, Wayne
American. Politician
Rep. senator, CO, 1997—.
b. Dec 2, 1943
Source: *AlmAP 92, 96; CngDr 93; WhoAmP 85, 87, 89, 91, 93, 95*

Allbritton, Louise
[Mrs. Charles Collingwood]
American. Actor
Leading lady of Universal second features: *Egg and I,* 1947; *Sitting Pretty,* 1948.
b. Jul 3, 1920 in Oklahoma City, Oklahoma
d. Feb 16, 1979 in Puerto Vallarta, Mexico
Source: *BioIn 10, 11; EncAFC; FilmEn; FilmgC; ForYSC; HalFC 80, 84, 88; HolP 40; MotPP; NewYTBS 79; WhoHol A; WhScrn 83*

Allegret, Yves
[Yves Champlain]
French. Director
Best known for "noir film" films, 1940s, starring Simone Signoret.
b. Oct 13, 1907 in Paris, France
d. Jan 31, 1986 in Paris, France
Source: *AnObit 1987; BiDFilm, 81, 94; BioIn 15; DcFM; DcTwCCu 2; EncEurC; FacFETw; FilmEn; FilmgC; HalFC 80, 84, 88; IntDcF 1-2, 2-2; ItaFilm; LegTOT; MovMk; OxCFilm; WhoFr 79; WorEFlm*

Allegri, Gregorio
Italian. Composer
His "Miserere" is sung annually in Sistine Chapel on Good Friday.
b. 1582 in Rome, Italy
d. Feb 17, 1652 in Rome, Italy
Source: *Baker 78, 84, 92; BioIn 4, 20; DcArts; DcBiPP; DcCathB; LuthC 75; MusMk; NewGrDM 80; NewOxM; OxCMus; WebBD 83*

Allegro, John Marco
English. Linguist
Helped decipher Dead Sea Scrolls, 1940s-50s; wrote best-seller, *Dead Sea Scrolls,* 1956.
b. Feb 17, 1923 in London, England
d. Feb 17, 1988 in London, England
Source: *Au&Wr 71; BioIn 15, 16; BlueB 76; ConAu 4NR, 9R, 20NR, 124; CurBio 70, 88; DcLEL 1940; IntAu&W 76, 77, 82; IntWW 74, 75, 76, 77, 78, 79, 80, 81, 82, 83; MidE 78, 79, 80, 81, 82; NewYTBS 88; WhAm 9; Who 74, 82, 83, 85, 88; WhoWor 74, 76, 78, 80, 82, 84, 87, 89; WrDr 76, 86*

Allen, Arthur Augustus
American. Ornithologist
Produced 15 records of bird songs; wrote *Book of Bird Life,* 1930.
b. Dec 28, 1885 in Buffalo, New York
d. Jan 17, 1964 in Ithaca, New York
Source: *AmAu&B; BioIn 5, 6, 7; ConAu 1R; CurBio 61, 64; DcAmB S7; InSci; NatLAC; WhAm 4*

Allen, Betty (Lou)
American. Opera Singer, Educator
Opera singer dedicated to musical education of children; exec. director, Harlem School of the Arts, 1979—; faculty, NC School of the Arts, 1978-87.
b. Mar 17, 1930 in Campbell, Ohio
Source: *AfrAmAl 6; AfrAmBi 2; Baker 84, 92; BiDAfM; BiDAmM; BioIn 9, 11, 16, 17; CurBio 90; InB&W 85; IntWWM 77, 80, 90; InWom SUP; MetOEnc; NegAl 76, 83, 89; NewAmDM; NewGrDA 86; NewGrDM 80; NewYTBS 87; OxDcArt; PrintW 85; WhoAm 84, 96, 97; WhoAmW 95, 97; WhoBlA 92; WhoEnt 92; WhoOp 76*

Allen, Byron
[Byron Folks]
American. Comedian
Wrote comedy material for Jimmy Walker, Freddie Prinze; co-host, TV series "Real People," 1979-84; host, "The Byron Allen Show," 1989—.
b. Apr 22, 1961 in Detroit, Michigan
Source: *AfrAmBi 2; BioIn 12, 13, 16; ConBlB 3; ConTFT 11; DrBlPA 90; InB&W 85; LegTOT; VarWW 85; WhoBlA 80, 85, 90, 92, 94; WhoEnt 92*

Allen, Debbie
[Deborah Allen]
American. Actor, Dancer, Director
Starred in TV series "Fame;" won Emmys for choreography, 1982, 1983; producer and director for TV series "A Different World," 1988-92; sister of actress Phylicia Rashad.
b. Jan 16, 1950 in Houston, Texas
Source: *AfrAmAl 6; AfrAmBi 1; BiDD; BioIn 16; BlksAmF; BlkWAm; ConBlB 13; ConMus 8; ConTFT 6, 13; CurBio 87; DcTwCCu 5; DrAPF 91; DrBlPA, 90; IntMPA 92, 94, 96; InWom SUP; LegTOT; NegAl 89; NewYTBS 80; NotBlAW 1; VarWW 85; WhoAfA 96; WhoAm 90; WhoBlA 92, 94; WhoEnt 92*

Allen, Deborah
American. Singer, Songwriter
Country singer who wrote, sang hit single "Baby I Lied," 1983.
b. Sep 30, 1953 in Memphis, Tennessee
Source: *BgBkCoM; InB&W 80, 85; LegTOT; RkOn 85; WhoBlA 90; WhoEnt 92; WorAlBi*

Allen, Duane David
[The Oak Ridge Boys]
American. Singer, Musician
Guitarist, lead singer with country-pop group; hit single "Bobby Sue," 1982; has won several Grammys since 1970.
b. Apr 29, 1943 in Taylortown, Texas
Source: *BioIn 16; WhoAm 80, 82, 84, 86, 88, 90, 92, 94, 95, 96, 97; WhoEnt 92*

Allen, Elizabeth
[Elizabeth Ellen Gillease]
American. Actor, Singer
Nominated for Tony, 1962, for *The Gay Life.*
b. Jan 25, 1934 in Jersey City, New Jersey
Source: *BiE&WWA; ConTFT 8; FilmEn; FilmgC; ForYSC; HalFC 80, 84, 88; LegTOT; NotNAT; PseudN 82; WhoAm 74; WhoAmW 70, 72, 74; WhoHol 92, A; WhoThe 72, 77, 81*

Allen, Elizabeth Ann Chase Akers
American. Poet
Wrote popular verse *Rock Me to Sleep,* 1860.
b. Oct 9, 1832 in Strong, Maine
d. Aug 7, 1911 in Tuckahoe, New York
Source: *AmAu; AmWomWr; ChhPo S3; DcAmB; NotAW*

Allen, Elsie
[Pomo Sage]
American. Artist
Helped to keep the tradition of Pomo basketweaving alive.
b. Sep 22, 1899 in California
d. 1990
Source: *BioIn 21; NotNaAm*

Allen, Ethan
American. Military Leader
Organized Green Mountain Boys, 1770, to harass New Yorkers in land dispute between NY and NH.
b. Jan 21, 1738 in Litchfield, Connecticut
d. Feb 11, 1789 in Burlington, Vermont
Source: *AmBi; AmRev; AmWrBE; ApCAB; BbtC; Benet 87, 96; BenetAL 91; BioIn 1, 2, 3, 4, 5, 6, 7, 8, 9, 10, 11, 12, 13, 14, 19, 20; BlkwEAR; CyAL 1; DcAmB; DcAmMiB; DcAmReB 1, 2; DcLB 31; DcNAA; Drake; EncAR; EncCRAm; EncUnb; GenMudB; HarEnMi; HisWorL; LegTOT; LinLib S; McGEWB; NatCAB 1; OxCAmH; OxCAmL 65, 83, 95; PeoHis; REn; REnAL; TwoTYeD; WebAB 74, 79; WebAMB; WhAm HS; WhAmP; WhAmRev; WhoMilH 76; WorAl; WorAlBi*

Allen, Ethan (Nathan)
American. Baseball Coach, Baseball Player
Led Yale to NCAA Eastern Division titles, 1947, 1948.
b. Jan 1, 1904
d. Sep 15, 1993 in Brookings, Oregon
Source: *Ballpl 90; BioIn 3, 19, 20; CurBio 93N; OhA&B; WhoProB 73*

Allen, Florence Ellinwood
American. Judge
First woman to serve on Ohio Supreme Court, 1922-34.
b. Mar 23, 1884 in Salt Lake City, Utah
d. Sep 12, 1966 in Waite Hill, Ohio
Source: *AmDec 1920; BiDFedJ; BioIn 2, 3, 5, 6, 7, 9, 12, 14, 15; CurBio 41, 63, 66; DcAmB S8; EncAB-A 12; GoodHs; InWom, SUP; LibW; LinLib L, S; NatCAB 52; NotAW MOD; OhA&B; WhAm 4; WhoAmW 58, 64, 66; WomFir; WomLaw*

Allen, Forrest Claire
"Phog"
American. Basketball Coach
Coached three teams simultaneously, 1908-09; helped basketball become Olympic sport, 1936; organized first NCAA tournament, 1939; Hall of Fame.
b. Nov 18, 1885 in Jamesport, Missouri
d. Sep 16, 1974 in Lawrence, Kansas
Source: *BioIn 4, 9, 10; NewYTBS 74; ObitOF 79; WhoBbl 73*

Allen, Fred
[John Florence Sullivan]
American. Comedian
Vaudeville juggler turned comedian who starred in radio show, "Allen's Alley," 1932-49.
b. May 31, 1894 in Cambridge, Massachusetts
d. Mar 17, 1956 in New York, New York
Source: *BenetAL 91; BioIn 1, 2, 3, 4, 5, 7, 12, 14, 15, 16, 17; ChhPo; CurBio 41, 56; DcAmB S6; EncAFC; EncMT; EncVaud; Ent; FacFETw; FilmEn; FilmgC; ForYSC; HalFC 80, 84, 88; JoeFr; LegTOT; NewYTET; NotNAT A, B; OxCAmT 84; OxCFilm; OxCPMus; QDrFCA 92; RadStar; REnAL; SaTiSS; WebAB 74, 79; WhAm 3; WhoCom; WhoHol B; WhScrn 74, 77, 83; WorAl; WorAlBi*

Allen, Frederick Lewis
American. Journalist, Historian
Best known for social histories: *Only Yesterday,* 1931; *Since Yesterday,* 1940.
b. Jul 5, 1890 in Boston, Massachusetts
d. Feb 13, 1954 in New York, New York
Source: *AmAu&B; BenetAL 91; BioIn 1, 3, 4, 5, 6, 10, 12, 20; CnDAL; DcAmB S5; DcLB 137; EncAJ; EncTwCJ; JrnUS; NatCAB 46; OxCAmL 65, 83, 95; REn; REnAL; TwCA, SUP; WebAB 74, 79; WhAm 3*

Allen, George Herbert
"Ice Cream"
American. Football Coach, Football Executive
Coached LA Rams, Washington Redskins in NFL, two USFL teams, 1970s-80s; known for hard-driving work ethic.
b. Apr 29, 1922 in Grosse Pointe Woods, Michigan
d. Dec 31, 1990 in Rancho Palos Verdes, California
Source: *BiDAmSp FB; ConAu 111; CurBio 75, 91N; NewYTBE 72; WhoAm 86*

Allen, Geri
American. Pianist
Received record of the year award for *Etude,* 1989; recipient of SESAE Special Achievement Award, 1991; recorded *The Nurturer,* 1991 and *Maroons,* 1992.
b. 1957 in Pontiac, Michigan
Source: *AllMusG; ConMus 10*

Allen, Gracie Ethel Cecil Rosaline
[Burns and Allen; Mrs. George Burns]
American. Comedian
With husband, starred in "Burns and Allen Show," 1922-58.
b. Jul 26, 1906 in San Francisco, California
d. Aug 27, 1964 in Hollywood, California
Source: *CurBio 40, 51, 64; FilmgC; MotPP; MovMk; ThFT; WhAm 4; WhoHol B; WhScrn 74, 77*

Allen, Henry Tureman
American. Military Leader, Explorer
Army officer; explored, mapped Copper, Tanana, Koyukuk rivers in Alaska, 1885.
b. Apr 13, 1859 in Sharpsburg, Kentucky
d. Aug 30, 1930 in Buena Vista Spring, Pennsylvania
Source: *AmBi; ApCAB X; BioIn 5, 6, 10; DcAmB S1; DcAmMiB; DcNAA; NatCAB 44; REnAW; WebAMB; WhAm 1; WhNAA; WhWE*

Allen, Hervey
[William Hervey Allen]
American. Author, Poet
Wrote best-seller, *Anthony Adverse,* 1933; Poe biography, *Israfel,* 1926.
b. Dec 8, 1889 in Pittsburgh, Pennsylvania
d. Dec 28, 1949 in Miami, Florida
Source: *AmNov; Benet 87; BenetAL 91; BioIn 1, 2, 3, 4, 5, 12, 14, 15; Chambr 3; ConAmA; ConAmL; ConAu 108; CyWA 58; DcAmB S4; DcLB 9, 45; DcLEL; DcNAA; EncWL; EvLB; LegTOT; LinLib L; NatCAB 37; Novels; OxCAmL 65, 83; PenC AM; RAdv 14; REn; REnAL; ScF&FL 92; TwCA, SUP; TwCRGW; TwCRHW 90, 94; WhAm 2; WhE&EA; WhNAA*

Allen, Irwin
"Master of Disaster"
American. Director, Producer
Won Oscar, 1952, for *The Sea Around Us,* based on Rachel Carson's book; produced "disaster" movies including *Towering Inferno* and *The Poseidon Adventure.*
b. Jun 12, 1916 in New York, New York
d. Nov 2, 1991 in Santa Monica, California
Source: *AnObit 1991; BioIn 17, 18; CmMov; ConTFT 12; EncSF, 93; FilmEn; FilmgC; HalFC 80, 84, 88; IntMPA 77, 80, 86, 92; LegTOT; LesBEnT; MiSFD 9N; NewEScF; NewYTBS 74, 91; NewYTET; VarWW 85; WhoAm 86, 90; WhoHrs 80*

Allen, Ivan, Jr.
American. Politician
Mayor of Atlanta, GA, 1961-69.
b. Mar 15, 1911 in Atlanta, Georgia
Source: *BioIn 7, 9, 11; CelR; ConAu 109; Dun&B 86, 88, 90; EncAACR; EncAB-A 27; PolProf J, K; St&PR 75, 84, 87, 91, 93, 96, 97; WhoAm 74, 76, 78, 80, 82, 84, 86, 88, 90, 92, 94, 95, 96, 97; WhoSSW 73; WhoWor 74, 78*

Allen, Jack
American. Author, Educator
Wrote numerous political, historical textbooks: *One Nation Indivisible,* 1979.
b. Jun 18, 1914 in Prestonsburg, Kentucky

Source: *ConAu 4NR, 9R; DrAS 74H, 78H, 82H; LEduc 74; WhoAm 74, 76, 78, 80, 82, 84, 86, 88, 90*

Allen, James Lane
American. Author
Popularized Blue Grass KY life in novels *Kentucky Cardinal,* 1894; *The Choir Invisible,* 1897.
b. Dec 21, 1849 in Lexington, Kentucky
d. Feb 18, 1925 in New York, New York
Source: *AmAu; AmAu&B; AmBi; AmLY; BbD; BenetAL 91; BibAL; BiD&SB; BiDSA; BioIn 1, 7, 8, 12; CamGEL; CamGLE; CamHAL; CarSB; CasWL; ChhPo S1, S3; CnDAL; ConAmL; DcAmAu; DcAmB; DcBiA; DcLB 71; DcLEL; DcNAA; GrWrEL N; HarEnUS; LiHiK; LinLib L, S; LngCTC; NatCAB 8; OxCAmL 65, 83, 95; REn; REnAL; RfGAmL 87, 94; SouWr; TwCBDA; WhAm 1*

Allen, Jay Presson
American. Screenwriter, Author
Noted teleplay, stagewriter who created TV series, "Family," 1976.
b. Mar 3, 1922 in San Angelo, Texas
Source: *BioIn 12, 14, 15; ConAu 45NR, 73; ConDr 88A; ConTFT 1, 7; DcLB 26; HalFC 88; IntDcF 1-4, 2-4; IntMPA 84, 86, 88, 92, 94, 96; InWom SUP; McGEWD 72, 84; NotNAT; ReelWom; WhoAm 82, 84, 86, 88, 90, 92, 94, 95, 96, 97; WhoEnt 92; WomWMM, A*

Allen, Joel Asaph
American. Zoologist
Harvard U's noted curator of birds, mammals, 1860s-80s.
b. Jul 10, 1838 in Springfield, Massachusetts
d. Aug 29, 1921 in Cornwall-on-Hudson, New York
Source: *Alli SUP; AmBi; ApCAB; BiDAmS; BiD&SB; CelCen; DcAmAu; DcAmB; DcNAA; DcScB S2; HarEnUS; InSci; NatCAB 3; TwCBDA; WhAm 1*

Allen, John
American. Dentist, Inventor
Patented false teeth made of porcelain with platium base, 1851.
b. Nov 4, 1810 in Broome County, New York
d. Mar 8, 1892 in Plainfield, New Jersey
Source: *DcAmB; NatCAB 2; News 92; WebAB 74, 79; WhAm HS*

Allen, John Polk
American. Businessman
Founder/leader, Synergia Ranch, 1967-83; director, scientific development for Space Biospheres Venture, 1984—; masterminded Biosphere 2.
b. 1930 in Oklahoma

Allen, Karen Jane
American. Actor
Appeared in movies *Animal House,* 1978, *Raiders of the Lost Ark,* 1981.
b. Oct 5, 1951 in Carrollton, Illinois
Source: *BioIn 16; ConTFT 4; HalFC 88; IntMPA 86, 92; VarWW 85; WhoAm 84, 86, 88, 90, 92, 94, 95, 96, 97; WhoAmW 93, 95, 97; WhoEnt 92*

Allen, Larry
American. Journalist
Called "most shot-at" foreign correspondent; won 1942 Pulitzer for war reporting.
b. Oct 19, 1908 in Mount Savage, Maryland
d. May 12, 1975 in Mexico City, Mexico
Source: *AmEA 74; BioIn 10; CurBio 42; EncTwCJ; NewYTBS 75*

Allen, Leslie
American. Tennis Player
Highest ranking black female tennis player, early 1980s.
b. Mar 12, 1957 in Cleveland, Ohio
Source: *BioIn 12; InB&W 80, 85; NewYTBS 81; WhoAmL 92; WhoIntT*

Allen, Macon B
American. Lawyer, Judge
First licensed black attorney, judge in US; elected to Congress, 1870-72.
b. 1816 in Indiana
d. Oct 10, 1894 in Washington, District of Columbia
Source: *BioIn 10; DcAmNB; InB&W 80, 85; PeoHis*

Allen, Marcus
American. Football Player
Running back, LA Raiders, 1982-92; Kansas City Chiefs, 1993—; has won more major awards than any other football player; won Heisman Trophy, 1981; led NFL in rushing, 1985.
b. Mar 26, 1960 in San Diego, California
Source: *AfrAmSG; BiDAmSp FB; BioIn 12, 13, 16; CelR 90; CurBio 86; FootReg 87; NewAgMG; WhoAfA 96; WhoAm 90, 92, 94, 95, 96, 97; WhoBlA 88, 90, 92, 94; WhoMW 93; WhoSpor; WhoWest 87, 89, 92, 94; WorAlBi*

Allen, Mel
[Melvin Allen Israel]
American. Sportscaster
Versatile sports broadcaster, best known as voice of NY Yankees, 1939-64; hosted TV's "This Week in Baseball," 1977-96.
b. Feb 14, 1913 in Birmingham, Alabama
d. Jun 16, 1996 in Greenwich, Connecticut
Source: *AuBYP 2, 3; Ballpl 90; BioIn 2, 4, 5, 6, 7, 8, 9, 10, 11, 14, 16; ConTFT 15; CurBio 50, 96N; IntMPA 75, 76, 77, 78, 79, 80, 81, 82, 84, 86, 88, 92, 94, 96; LegTOT; LesBEnT, 92; News 96; NewYTBS 27, 78; NewYTET; RadStar; SaTiSS; WhoAm 74, 76, 78; WhoWorJ 72, 78; WorAl; WorAlBi*

Allen, Nancy
American. Actor
Appeared in movies *Blowout,* 1981, *Dressed to Kill,* 1980.
b. Jun 24, 1949 in New York, New York
Source: *ConTFT 5; HalFC 88; IntMPA 82, 92; WhoEnt 92*

Allen, Paul
American. Business Executive
Co-founded, with Bill Gates, Microsoft Corp., 1975; owner, Portland Trail Blazers, 1988—.
Source: *AmMWSc 89; BioIn 10, 17, 18, 19, 20, 21; DrAPF 97; WhoAm 90, 92, 97; WhoWest 89, 92, 94, 96*

Allen, Paula Gunn
American. Poet
Poetry collections include *The Blind Lion,* 1974; *Skins and Bones,* 1988.
b. Oct 24, 1939 in Cubero, New Mexico
Source: *AmWomWr SUP; BenetAL 91; BlmGWL; CamGLE; CamHAL; ConAu 143; ConLC 84; DcNAL; DrAPF 80; FemiCLE; FemiWr; Focus; GayLesB; GayLL; InWom SUP; ModWoWr; NatNAL; NotNaAm; OxCAmL 95; OxCWoWr 95; RAdv 14; RfGAmL 94; TwCWW 91; WrDr 92, 94, 96*

Allen, Peter Woolnough
Australian. Songwriter, Singer
Discovered in Hong Kong by Judy Garland, 1964; wrote songs "I Honestly Love You," recorded by Olivia Newton-John, 1974, "Don't Cry Out Loud," sung by Melissa Manchester, 1978; former husband of Liza Minnelli.
b. Feb 10, 1944 in Tenterfield, Australia
d. Jun 18, 1992 in San Diego, California
Source: *BioIn 13; CelR 90; ConTFT 9; CurBio 83; News 93-1; NewYTBS 77; RkOn 85; RolSEnR 83*

Allen, Red
[Henry James Allen, Jr.]
American. Jazz Musician, Bandleader
Dixieland trumpeter; with Louis Armstrong, 1937-40; led sextet, 1950s.
b. Jan 7, 1908 in New Orleans, Louisiana
d. Apr 17, 1967 in New York, New York
Source: *Baker 84; BiDAfM; BiDJaz; BioIn 16, 20; EncJzS; InB&W 80, 85; PseudN 82; TwCBrS; WhoJazz 72*

Allen, Rex E, Sr.
"Mister Cowboy"
American. Actor, Singer, Songwriter
Star of cowboy films, 1950s; wrote 300 songs including "Crying in the Chapel," 1953.
b. Dec 31, 1924 in Wilcox, Arizona
Source: *BiDAmM; BioIn 14; CmpEPM; EncFCWM 83; FilmEn; FilmgC; HalFC 88; HarEnCM 87; IntMPA 81, 92; NewGrDA 86; RkOn 74; WhoAm 82; WhoHol A; WhoRock 81*

Allen, Richard
American. Religious Leader
First black ordained in Methodist Episcopal Church, 1799; founded African Methodist Church, 1816.
b. Feb 14, 1760 in Philadelphia, Pennsylvania
d. Mar 26, 1831 in Philadelphia, Pennsylvania
Source: *AfrAmAl 6; AmBi; AmRef; AmSocL; AmWrBE; ApCAB; BiDAfM; BiDAmM; BioIn 2, 3, 5, 6, 7, 8, 9, 10, 11, 12, 15, 16, 17, 19, 20; BlkAWP; DcAmB; DcAmNB; DcAmReB 1, 2; EncAB-H 1974, 1996; EncARH; EncWM; InB&W 80, 85; LuthC 75; McGEWB; Meth; NatCAB 13; NegAl 76, 83, 89; NewGrDA 86; RComAH; WebAB 74, 79; WhAm HS*

Allen, Richard Vincent
American. Government Official
Nat. security adviser under Ronald Reagan, 1981-82; resigned amid controversy, replaced by William Clark.
b. Jan 1, 1936 in Collingswood, New Jersey
Source: *BioIn 12, 13, 16; ConAu 21R; DcAmDH 89; IntWW 83, 91; IntYB 82; NewYTBS 80; WhoAm 82, 84, 86, 88, 90, 92, 94, 95, 96, 97; WhoAmP 73, 75, 77, 79; WhoE 97; WhoWor 89, 91, 93, 95, 97*

Allen, Richie
[Richard Anthony Allen]
American. Baseball Player
Controversial infielder, 1963-77; rookie of year, 1964; AL MPV, 1972.
b. Mar 8, 1942 in Wampum, Pennsylvania
Source: *BiDAmSp BB; BioIn 6, 7, 8, 9, 10, 11; InB&W 80, 85; WhoAfA 96; WhoAm 74, 76, 78; WhoBlA 75, 77, 80, 85, 88, 90, 92, 94; WhoMW 74; WhoProB 73*

Allen, Rick
[The Box Tops]
American. Musician
Organist, bassist with Memphis-based soul group, late 1960s.
b. Jan 28, 1946 in Little Rock, Arkansas
Source: *WhoRocM 82*

Allen, Rick
[Def Leppard]
English. Musician
Drummer with British heavy-metal, new wave group; lost arm in car crash, 1984.
b. Nov 1, 1963 in Sheffield, England
Source: *WhoEnt 92; WhoRocM 82*

Allen, Robert Sharon
American. Author, Journalist
Co-columnist, with Drew Pearson, for "Washington Merry Go-Round," 1930s.
b. Jul 14, 1900 in Latonia, Kentucky
d. Feb 23, 1981 in Washington, District of Columbia
Source: *AmAu&B; BiDAmNC; BioIn 1, 12; ConAu 57, 103; CurBio 41, 81; LinLib L; NewYTBS 81; REnAL; WhAm 7; WhoAm 80; WhoWor 74*

Allen, Steve
[Stephen Valentine Patrick William Allen]
American. TV Personality, Songwriter
Versatile entertainer known for ad-libbed witticisms; early host of Tonight Show, "I've Got a Secret."
b. Dec 26, 1921 in New York, New York
Source: *AmAu&B; ASCAP 66, 80; AuBYP 2S, 3; BenetAL 91; BiDAmM; BiDJaz; BiE&WWA; BioIn 2, 3, 4, 5, 6, 8, 10, 12, 13, 16, 17, 18, 20; CelR, 90; CmpEPM; ConAu 25R, 46NR, X; ConTFT 4, 15; CurBio 51, 82; DcLP 87A, 87B; DcTwCCu 1; EncAFC; EncJzS; EncTwCJ; FacFETw; FilmEn; FilmgC; ForYSC; HalFC 80, 84, 88; IntAu&W 76, 91; IntMPA 75, 76, 77, 78, 79, 80, 81, 82, 84, 86, 88, 92, 94, 96; IntvTCA 2; IntWWP 77; JoeFr; LegTOT; NewAmDM; NewGrDA 86; NewGrDJ 88, 94; NewYTET; PenEncP; PseudN 82; RadStar; REnAL; TwoTYeD; WebAB 74, 79; WhoAm 74, 76, 78, 80, 82, 84, 86, 88, 90, 92, 94, 95, 96, 97; WhoCom; WhoEnt 92; WhoHol 92, A; WhoWest 96; WhoWor 74; WorAl; WorAlBi; WrDr 76, 82, 84, 86, 88, 90, 92, 94, 96*

Allen, Tim
[Timothy Allen Dick]
American. Comedian, Actor
Star of popular ABC sitcom "Home Improvement," 1991—.
b. Jun 13, 1953 in Denver, Colorado
Source: *ConTFT 12; CurBio 95; IntMPA 96; LegTOT; News 93-1*

Allen, Verden
[Mott the Hoople]
English. Musician
Organist with hard-rock group, 1969-73.
b. May 26, 1944 in Hereford, England
Source: *WhoRocM 82*

Allen, Viola Emily
American. Actor
Career spanned four decades; known for Shakespearean roles.
b. Oct 27, 1867 in Huntsville, Alabama
d. May 9, 1948 in New York, New York
Source: *DcAmB S4; InWom SUP; LibW; NatCAB 34; NotAW; OxCThe 83; WhAm 2; WomWWA 14*

Allen, Vivian Beaumont
American. Philanthropist
Made $2 million donation to Vivian Beaumont Theatre at Lincoln Center, NYC; opened, 1965.
d. Oct 10, 1962 in New York, New York
Source: *InWom; NotNAT B; ObitOF 79; PlP&P*

Allen, Walter Ernest
English. Author, Critic
Wrote *All in a Lifetime,* 1959; *Short Story in Britain,* 1981.
b. Feb 23, 1911 in Birmingham, England
d. Feb 28, 1995
Source: *Au&Wr 71; BioIn 16; CamGEL; ConAu 6AS, 25NR, 61, 147; ConNov 72, 76, 86; DcLEL; IntAu&W 91; IntWW 91; LngCTC; ModBrL; NewC; PenC ENG; TwCWr; Who 85, 92; WhoTwCL; WorAu 1950; WrDr 76, 88*

Allen, William McPherson
American. Aircraft Manufacturer
Pres., Boeing Co., 1945-72; built Saturn Apollo moon rocket, lunar orbiter.
b. Sep 1, 1900 in Lolo, Montana
d. Oct 29, 1985 in Seattle, Washington
Source: *BiDAmBL 83; BioIn 3, 4, 7, 8, 10, 11; BlueB 76; CurBio 53, 86; InSci; IntWW 74, 75; St&PR 75; WhoAm 82; WhoFI 74; WhoWest 74; WhoWor 74*

Allen, Woody
[Heywood Allen; Allen Stewart Konigsberg]
American. Actor, Director
Won five Oscars, including best picture, director, for *Annie Hall,* 1977.
b. Dec 1, 1935 in New York, New York
Source: *AmAu&B; AmCulL; AmDec 1970; Au&Arts 10; Benet 87, 96; BenetAL 91; BiDFilm 81, 94; BiDJaz; BioIn 7, 8, 9, 10, 11, 12, 13, 14, 15; BkPepl; CelR, 90; ConAu 27NR, 33R, 38NR, X; ConDr 88A; ConLC 16, 52; ConTFT 1, 8, 15; CurBio 66, 79; CyWA 89; DcArts; DcLB 44; DcTwCCu 1; EncAB-H 1996; EncAFC; EncAHmr; FacFETw; FilmEn; FilmgC; ForYSC; Funs; GrMovC; HalFC 80, 84, 88; IlWWHD 1; IntAu&W 89, 91, 93; IntDcF 1-2, 2-2; IntMPA 75, 76, 77, 78, 79, 80, 81, 82, 84, 86, 88, 92, 94, 96; IntWW 79, 80, 81, 82, 83, 89, 91, 93; JeAmHC; JoeFr; LegTOT; MajTwCW; MiSFD 9; MovMk; NatPD 81; News 94, 94-1; NewYTBS 79, 86, 91; NotNAT, A; OxCAmL 83, 95; OxCAmT 84; QDrFCA 92; RAdv 14, 13-1; Who 82, 83, 85, 88, 90, 92, 94; WhoAm 74, 76, 78, 80, 82, 84, 86, 88, 90, 92, 94, 95, 96, 97; WhoAmJ 80; WhoCom; WhoE 91, 93, 95; WhoEnt 92; WhoHol 92, A; WhoHrs 80; WhoThe 77, 81; WhoWor 95, 96, 97; WhoWrEP 92, 95; WorAl; WorAlBi; WorFDir 2; WrDr 76, 80, 82, 84, 86, 88, 90, 92, 94, 96*

Allenby, Edmund Henry Hynman
[1st Viscount]
"The Bull Allenby"
English. Military Leader
WW I field marshal in Middle East; armies captured Jerusalem, defeated Turks, 1917-18.
b. Apr 23, 1861 in Southwell, England
d. May 14, 1936 in London, England
Source: *BioIn 1, 2, 6, 7, 10, 11; DcNaB 1931; DcTwHis; FacFETw; GrBr; HarEnMi; HisDBrE; LinLib S; McGEWB; WhDW; WhoMilH 76; WorAl*

Allende, Isabel
Chilean. Author
Family saga novels include *The House of Spirits,* 1982; *Of Love and Shadows,* 1984; *Eva Luna,* 1987.
b. 1942 in Lima, Peru
Source: *Au&Arts 18; Benet 96; BenetAL 91; BioIn 16; BlmGWL; ConAu 51NR, 125, 130; ConLC 39, 57, 97; ConWorW 93; CurBio 88; DcArts; DcHiB; DcLB 145; EncWL 3; FemiWr; GrWomW; HispLC; HispWr; IntAu&W 91, 93; IntvLAW; IntWW 91, 93; LiExTwC; MajTwCW; ModWoWr; RAdv 14; ScF&FL 92; SpAmWW; WhoHisp 92, 94; WomWrSA; WorAu 1980*

Allende Gossens, Salvador
Chilean. Political Leader
Socialist pres. of Chile, 1970-73; overthrown in violent coup.
b. Jul 26, 1908 in Valparaiso, Chile
d. Sep 11, 1973 in Santiago, Chile
Source: *BiDLAmC; BiDMarx; BioIn 14, 16, 17, 18, 19; ColdWar 2; CurBio 71, 73; DcCPSAm; EncRev; EncWB; FacFETw; LinLib S; NewYTBE 70; WhoGov 75; WhoWor 74; WorAl; WorAlBi*

Allen of Hurtwood, Lady
[Marjory Gill Allen]
English. Author, Architect
Playground consultant whose books include *Space for Play: The Youngest Children,* 1964.
b. May 10, 1897 in London, England
Source: *Au&Wr 71; ConAu P-1; PseudN 82; Who 74*

Allers, Franz
Czech. Conductor
Won Tonys for conducting *My Fair Lady,* 1957; *Camelot,* 1961.
b. Aug 6, 1905 in Karlsbad, Czech Republic
d. Jan 26, 1995 in Las Vegas, Nevada
Source: *Baker 78, 84, 92; BiE&WWA; BioIn 2, 4, 6, 7, 12, 20; CelR; ConTFT 1; IntWWM 77, 80, 85, 90; NewYTBS 80, 95; NotNAT; WhoAm 74, 76, 78, 80, 82, 84, 86, 88, 90, 92, 94, 95; WhoAmM 83; WhoEnt 92; WhoMus 72; WhoOp 76; WhoWor 74, 76*

Alley, Kirstie
American. Actor
Films include *Star Trek II,* 1982; played Rebecca Howe on TV series "Cheers," 1987-93.
b. Jan 12, 1951 in Wichita, Kansas
Source: *BioIn 13, 15, 16; ConTFT 5; CurBio 94; HalFC 88; IntMPA 92; News 90-3; VarWW 85; WhoAm 90; WhoEnt 92; WhoHol 92; WorAlBi*

Alley, Norman William
American. Photojournalist
Documented Spanish Civil War, Ethiopian War, WW I, WW II on film.
b. Jan 22, 1895 in Chicago, Illinois
d. Apr 1, 1981 in Woodland Hills, California
Source: *BioIn 12; ConAu 115; NewYTBS 81; WhAm 7*

Alley, Rewi
New Zealander. Political Activist
Devoted life to promotion of Chinese Communism, during, after 1949 revolution.
b. Dec 2, 1897 in Springfield, New Zealand
d. Dec 27, 1987 in Beijing, China
Source: *BioIn 9, 15, 16; ConAu 13NR, 36NR, 73, 124; ConPo 70, 75, 80; CurBio 43, 88, 88N; DcLEL 1940; IntAu&W 77, 82; IntWWP 77; NewYTBS 87; WhAm 11; WrDr 76, 80, 82, 84, 86*

Allgood, Sara
Irish. Actor
Best known for stage role in *Juno and the Paycock,* 1930.
b. Oct 31, 1883 in Dublin, Ireland
d. Sep 13, 1950 in Woodland Hills, California
Source: *BioIn 2, 7, 17; CnThe; DcIrB 78, 88; EncAFC; EncEurC; EncWT; Film 2; FilmEn; FilmgC; ForYSC; HalFC 80, 84, 88; HolCA; IlWWBF; InWom; MotPP; MovMk; ObitOF 79; OxCIri; OxCThe 67, 83; PlP&P; Vers A; WhoHol B; WhScrn 74, 77, 83; WhThe*

Allingham, Margery
[Margery Louise Allingham Carter]
English. Author
Mystery writer who created sleuth Albert Campion in *Mind Readers,* 1965.
b. May 20, 1904 in London, England
d. Jun 30, 1966 in Colchester, England
Source: *ArtclWW 2; BioIn 1, 2, 4, 7, 9, 12, 14, 16, 17, 18; CamGLE; ConAu 4NR, 5R, 25R; ConLC 19; CrtSuMy; DcLB 77; DcLEL; DetWom; EncBrWW; EncMys; EncSF; EvLB; FemiCLE; GrWomMW; InWom SUP; LegTOT; LngCTC; MajTwCW; MnBBF; Novels; ObitT 1961; PseudN 82; ScF&FL 1, 2; TwCA, SUP; TwCCr&M 80, 85, 91; TwCWr; WhE&EA; WhoSpyF; WorAl; WorAlBi*

Allingham, William
Irish. Poet, Editor
Fraser editor, 1874-79, whose vols. of verse include *The Fairies,* 1883.
b. Mar 19, 1824 in Ballyshannon, Ireland
d. Nov 18, 1889 in Hampstead, England
Source: *Alli SUP; AnCL; BbD; BiD&SB; BiDIrW; BioIn 6, 8, 9, 10, 14, 16, 17, 20; BritAu 19; CamGEL; CamGLE; CasWL; Chambr 3; ChhPo, S1, S2, S3; DcEnL; DcIrB 78, 88; DcIrL, 96; DcIrW 1; DcLB 35; DcLEL; DcNaB S1; EvLB; GrWrEL P; LinLib L; NewC; NewCBEL; NinCLC 25; OxCChiL; OxCEng 85, 95; OxCIri; PenC ENG; PoIre; REn; RfGEnL 91; Str&VC; WebE&AL*

Allison, Bobby
[Robert Arthur Allison]
American. Auto Racer
Stock car racer; won Daytona 500, 1978, 1982; NASCAR grand national champion, 1983.
b. Dec 3, 1937 in Hueytown, Alabama
Source: *BiDAmSp OS; BioIn 10, 11, 12, 13; LegTOT; NewYTBS 81; WhoAm 80, 82, 84, 86, 88, 90, 92, 94, 95, 96, 97; WhoSpor; WhoSSW 95; WorAl; WorAlBi*

Allison, Clay
American. Outlaw
"Fast gun," who killed at least 15 other gunmen in NM area, 1870s.
b. 1840 in Tennessee
d. 1877
Source: *BioIn 6, 8, 9, 11, 13, 15, 17; DrInf; REnAW*

Allison, Dorothy E.
American. Author
Wrote novel *Bastard Out of Carolina,* 1992.
b. Apr 11, 1949 in Greenville County, South Carolina
Source: *ConAu 140; ConLC 78; GayLesB; GayLL*

Allison, Fran(ces)
American. Actor
Best known as the warm-hearted human foil for puppets on the "Kukla, Fran, and Ollie" TV show, 1947-57.
b. Nov 20, 1924 in La Porte City, Iowa
d. Jun 13, 1989 in Van Nuys, California
Source: *IntMPA 86, 88; InWom SUP; VarWW 85; WhoAm 74*

Allison, Mose
[Mose John Allison, Jr.]
American. Pianist, Singer, Songwriter
Piano legend whose works include: *Back Country Suite for Piano, Bass and Drums,* 1957, *Middle Class White Boy,* 1982, *Lessons in Living,* 1983, and *The Earth Wants You,* 1994.
b. Nov 11, 1927 in Tippo, Mississippi
Source: *AllMusG; Baker 92; BiDAmM; BiDJaz; ConMus 17; EncJzS; EncRk 88; IlEncJ; LegTOT; NewAmDM; NewGrDJ 88; OxCPMus; PenEncP; RolSEnR 83; WhoAm 74*

Allison, Samuel King
American. Physicist
Director, Institute for Nuclear Studies, 1946-57; worked on Los Alamos Project, 1944-45.
b. Nov 13, 1900 in Chicago, Illinois
d. Sep 15, 1965 in Chicago, Illinois
Source: *BioIn 7; DcAmB S7; DcScB S2; WhAm 4; WhoAtom 77*

Allison, William Boyd
American. Politician
As senator from IA, 1873-1908, co-sponsored Bland-Allison Act, 1878.
b. Mar 2, 1829 in Ashland, Ohio
d. Aug 4, 1908 in Dubuque, Iowa

Source: *AmBi; ApCAB; BiAUS; BiDrAC; BiDrUSC 89; BioIn 4; CyAG; DcAmB; EncAAH; EncAB-H 1974, 1996; HarEnUS; NatCAB 1; TwCBDA; WebAB 74, 79; WhAm 1; WhAmP*

Allman, Duane
[Allman Brothers Band; Howard Duane Allman]
"Skydog"
American. Singer
Formed band with brother, Gregg, 1968; debut album, *The Alman Brothers Band,* 1969; died in motorcycle accident.
b. Nov 20, 1946 in Nashville, Tennessee
d. Oct 29, 1971 in Macon, Georgia
Source: *BioIn 11, 12; EncPR&S 89; IlEncRk; LegTOT; OnThGG; OxCPMus; PseudN 82; SoulM; WhoRocM 82; WorAl; WorAlBi*

Allman, Gregg
[Allman Brothers Band; Gregory Lenoir Allman]
American. Singer, Musician
Formed "Allman Brothers" band with brother, Duane, 1968; recorded solo album *Laid Back,* 19 74.
b. Nov 8, 1947 in Nashville, Tennessee
Source: *BioIn 11, 14; BkPepl; EncPR&S 89; IlEncRk; LegTOT; OxCPMus; WhoAm 76, 78, 80, 82, 92, 94, 95, 96, 97; WhoEnt 92; WhoRocM 82; WorAl; WorAlBi*

Allman Brothers Band
[Duane Allman; Gregg Allman; Dicky Betts; Jaimoe (Jai Johnny) Johanson; Chuck Leavell; (Raymond) Berry Oakley; Butch (Claude Hudson) Trucks; Lamar Williams]
American. Music Group
Formed in Macon, GA, 1968; *Brothers and Sisters* album contained biggest hit, "Ramblin' Man," 1973.
Source: *BiDJaz A; BioIn 14, 17, 20; ConMuA 80A; ConMus 6; EncPR&S 89; EncRk 88; EncRkSt; HarEnR 86; IlEncRk; NewAmDM; NewGrDA 86; ObitOF 79; OxCPMus; PenEncP; RkOn 74, 78; RolSEnR 83; WhoEnt 92; WhoRock 81; WhoRocM 82; WorAlBi*

Allon, Yigal
[Yigal Paicovich]
Israeli. Army Officer, Statesman
Proposed restoration of heavily populated Arab areas of West Bank to Jordan.
b. Oct 10, 1918 in Kfar Tabor, Palestine
d. Feb 29, 1980 in Afula, Israel
Source: *AnObit 1980; BioIn 8, 9, 10, 12; ConAu 36NR, 73, 97; CurBio 75, 80N; DcMidEa; DcPol; FacFETw; HisEAAC; IntWW 74, 75, 76, 77, 78, 79, 80; IntYB 78, 79, 80; MidE 78, 79; NewYTBE 71; NewYTBS 76; WhoWor 74, 76, 78; WhoWorJ 72, 78*

Allport, Gordon William
American. Psychologist
Best known for theory of personality between Freudianism and Behaviorism.
b. Nov 11, 1897 in Montezuma, Indiana
d. Oct 9, 1967 in Cambridge, Massachusetts
Source: *AmAu&B; ConAu 3NR, 10NR, 25R; CurBio 60, 67; IndAu 1917; LinLib L; REnAL; WebAB 74, 79; WhAm 4, 5; WhoE 74*

Allred, Rulon Clark
American. Religious Leader
Founded Apostolic United Brethren, a Fundamentalist Mormon, polygamy-practicing group.
b. Mar 29, 1906 in Chihuahua, Mexico
d. May 10, 1977 in Murray, Utah
Source: *BiDAmCu; RelLAm 91*

Allsop, Kenneth
English. Author, Journalist, Critic
Popular books include *Bootleggers,* 1961; *Hard Travellin',* 1967.
b. Jan 29, 1920 in Leeds, England
d. May 23, 1973 in West Milton, England
Source: *Au&Wr 71; BioIn 9, 10, 12; ConAu 1R, 6NR; DcLEL 1940; SmATA 17; WhoWor 74; WorAu 1950*

Allston, Washington
American. Artist, Poet
Preeminent Romantic painter known for dramatic subjects; published poetry, a novel, *Monaldi.*
b. Nov 5, 1779 in Georgetown County, South Carolina
d. Jul 9, 1843 in Cambridgeport, Massachusetts
Source: *Alli; AmAu; AmAu&B; AmBi; ApCAB; ArtsNiC; BbD; BenetAL 91; BibAL; BiD&SB; BiDLA; BiDSA; BiDTran; BioIn 1, 3, 4, 5, 6, 7, 8, 9, 10, 12, 13, 14, 19, 21; BriEAA; CasWL; Chambr 3; ChhPo, S1; CnDAL; CyAL 2; DcAmArt; DcAmAu; DcAmB; DcArts; DcBiPP; DcEnL; DcLB 1; DcNAA; DcSeaP; Drake; EncMT; EvLB; HarEnUS; LegTOT; LinLib L; McGDA; McGEWB; NatCAB 5; NewCol 75; NewYHSD; NinCLC 2; OxCAmH; OxCAmL 65, 83, 95; OxCArt; OxCShps; OxDcArt; PenC AM; PeoHis; REnAL; SouWr; TwCBDA; WebAB 74, 79; WebBD 83; WhAm HS; WhDW; WorAl; WorAlBi*

Allyn, Stanley Charles
American. Manufacturer
Chm., chief exec., National Cash Register Co., 1957-62.
b. Jul 20, 1891 in Madison, Wisconsin
d. Oct 31, 1970 in Greenwich, Connecticut
Source: *BioIn 1, 3, 4, 5, 9; CurBio 56, 70; NewYTBE 71; WhAm 5*

Allyson, June
[Ella Geisman]
American. Actor
Movie roles project image of cheerful wholesomeness: *The Sailor Takes a Wife,* 1946; *The Three Musketeers,* 1948.
b. Oct 7, 1917 in Lucerne, New York
Source: *BiDFilm, 81, 94; BioIn 11, 13, 15, 18, 19; CmpEPM; CurBio 52; DcArts; FilmEn; FilmgC; ForYSC; HalFC 80, 84, 88; IntAu&W 86; IntDcF 1-3, 2-3; IntMPA 76, 77, 78, 79, 80, 81, 82, 84, 86, 88, 92, 94, 96; InWom SUP; LegTOT; MGM; MotPP; MovMk; OxCPMus; WhoAm 82; WhoAmW 74; WhoHol 92, A; WorAlBi; WorEFlm*

Alma-Tadema, Lawrence, Sir
English. Artist
Painted vapid scenes of Greek, Roman life.
b. Jan 8, 1836 in Dronrijp, Netherlands
d. Jun 25, 1912 in Wiesbaden, Germany
Source: *BioIn 6, 10, 11, 12, 13, 14, 15, 17, 18; ClaDrA; DcArts; DcBrAr 1; DcNaB 1912; DcVicP, 2; McGDA; NotNAT B; OxCArt; OxCThe 67; OxDcArt; PlP&P; WebBD 83*

Almeida, Laurindo
Brazilian. Musician, Composer
Jazz guitarist featured in Modern Jazz Quartet tours; has won five Grammys.
b. Sep 2, 1917 in Sao Paulo, Brazil
d. Jul 26, 1995 in Los Angeles, California
Source: *AllMusG; ASCAP 66, 80; Baker 84, 92; BiDAmM; BiDJaz; BioIn 13, 21; CmpEPM; EncJzS; IntWWM 77, 80, 90; LatAmCC; NewAmDM; NewGrDJ 88, 94; OnThGG; OxCPMus; PenEncP; WhoAm 74, 76, 78, 80, 82, 84, 86, 88, 90, 92, 94, 95; WhoAmM 83; WhoEnt 92; WhoHol 92; WhoWor 74, 76*

Almendros, Nestor
Spanish. Filmmaker
Award-winning cinematographer whose films include *Sophie's Choice,* 1982; *Places in the Heart,* 1984; won best photography Oscar, 1979, for *Days of Heaven.*
b. Oct 30, 1930 in Barcelona, Spain
d. Mar 4, 1992 in New York, New York
Source: *AnObit 1992; BiDFilm 94; BioIn 12, 14, 15, 16; ConAu 142; ConTFT 5, 10; CubExWr; CurBio 89, 92N; DcHiB; EncEurC; FilmEn; HalFC 80, 84, 88; IntDcF 1-4, 2-4; IntMPA 84, 86, 88, 92; LegTOT; MiSFD 9; OxCFilm; WhAm 10; WhoAm 82, 84, 86, 88, 90; WhoEnt 92; WhoFr 79; WhoHisp 92, 92N*

Almirante, Giorgio
Italian. Politician
Member of Italian Parliament, 1948-87.
b. Jun 27, 1914
d. May 22, 1988 in Rome, Italy
Source: *AnObit 1988; BiDExR; BioIn 9, 10, 15, 16; CurBio 74, 88N; NewYTBE 71; NewYTBS 88; WhoEIO 82*

Almodovar, Pedro
Spanish. Filmmaker
Irreverent films include *Dark Habits,* 1988; *Women on the Verge of a Nervous Breakdown,* 1988; *Tie Me Up! Tie Me Down!* 1990.
b. Sep 25, 1951 in Calzada de Calatrava, Spain
Source: *BiDFilm 94; BioIn 15, 16; ConAu 133; ConTFT 10; CurBio 90; DcHiB; GayLesB; IntDcF 2-2; IntMPA 92, 94, 96; IntWW 91, 93; MiSFD 9; NewYTBS 90*

Almon, John
English. Author, Publisher
Wrote Whig pamphlets; promoted right of printers to publish parliamentary debates; established Parliamentary Register, 1774.
b. Dec 17, 1737 in Liverpool, England
d. Dec 12, 1805
Source: *ApCAB; BioIn 21; DcLB 154; DcNaB; Drake; NewCBEL; OxCLaw; WebBD 83*

Almond, Gabriel Abraham
American. Author, Educator
Stanford professor, 1963-76, whose writings include *Civic Culture Revisited,* 1980.
b. Jan 12, 1911 in Rock Island, Illinois
Source: *AmMWSc 73S, 78S; BioIn 17; BlueB 76; ConAu 18NR, 101; IntAu&W 77; IntWW 74, 75, 76, 77, 78, 79, 80, 81, 82, 83, 89, 91, 93; RAdv 14; WhoAm 74, 76, 78, 80, 82, 84, 86, 88, 90, 92, 94, 95, 96, 97; WrDr 80, 92*

Almond, Paul
Canadian. Producer, Screenwriter
Pres., Quest Films since 1967; films include *Act of the Heart,* 1970; *Journal,* 1972.
b. Apr 26, 1931 in Montreal, Quebec, Canada
Source: *BioIn 10; CanWW 31, 70, 79, 80, 81, 83, 89; ConAu 73; CreCan 2; FilmEn; FilmgC; HalFC 80, 84, 88; IntMPA 75, 76, 77, 78, 79, 80, 81, 82, 84, 86, 88, 92, 94, 96; MiSFD 9; WhoAm 80, 82, 84, 86, 88, 90, 92, 94, 95, 96, 97; WhoAmA 76, 78, 80, 82, 84, 86, 89, 91, 93; WhoE 79, 81; WhoEnt 92; WhoWor 82*

A.L.O.E.
[Charlotte Maria Tucker]
"A Lady of England"
English. Children's Author
Wrote didactic novels for children, 1950s-90s; noted for famous pen name.
b. May 8, 1821 in Barnet, England
d. Dec 2, 1893 in Amritsar, India
Source: *Alli, SUP; BioIn 8, 16; BritAu 19; CarSB; ChhPo S1, S2; DcInB; DcLB 163; DcNaB; FemiCLE; InWom; LuthC 75; NewC; OxCChiL; PenNWW A, B; StaCVF; VicBrit; WhoChL; WomNov*

Alomar, Roberto
American. Baseball Player
Second baseman, San Diego, 1985-91; Toronto, 1991—; won Gold Gloves, 1991-93.
b. Feb 5, 1968 in Salinas, Puerto Rico
Source: *Ballpl 90; BioIn 20; WhoAfA 96; WhoBlA 94; WhoHisp 91, 92, 94*

Alonso, Alicia
[Alicia Ernestina de la Caridad del Cobre Marinez Hoyo]
Cuban. Dancer
First Western dancer invited to dance in USSR, 1957; founded Ballet Nacional de Cuba, 1959.
b. Dec 21, 1921 in Havana, Cuba
Source: *BiDD; BioIn 3, 4, 5, 8, 12; CnOxB; CurBio 55, 77; DancEn 78; DcArts; DcHiB; DcTwCCu 4; FacFETw; HerW 84; IntDcB; InWom, SUP; LegTOT; NewYTBS 76; NotHsAW 93; VarWW 85; WhoEnt 92; WhoWor 82, 84, 87, 89, 91, 97; WorAl; WorAlBi*

Alonso, Damaso
Spanish. Poet, Critic
Member of Generation of 1927 poetry group; wrote *Dark Message,* 1944, and *Children of Wrath,* 1944.
b. Oct 22, 1898 in Madrid, Spain
d. Jan 24, 1990 in Madrid, Spain
Source: *BioIn 1, 3; EvEuW; FacFETw; HispWr; IntAu&W 76, 77; IntWW 74, 75, 76, 77, 78, 79, 80, 81, 82, 83, 89; LinLib L; ModSpP S; NewYTBS 90; OxCSpan; PenC EUR; RAdv 13-2; REn; WhoWor 74, 76, 78; WorAu 1975*

Alou, Felipe Rojas
"Panque"
Dominican. Baseball Player
Outfielder, 1958-74; with two brothers, played in SF Giants outfield at same time, 1963.
b. May 12, 1935 in Santo Domingo, Dominican Republic
Source: *Ballpl 90; BioIn 7; PseudN 82; WhoAm 74, 76, 92, 94, 95, 96, 97; WhoE 95, 97; WhoHisp 91, 92, 94; WhoProB 73*

Alou, Jesus Maria Rojas
"Jay"
Dominican. Baseball Player
Outfielder, 1963-79; had six hits in one game, 1964.
b. Mar 24, 1943 in Haina, Dominican Republic
Source: *Ballpl 90; BioIn 7; PseudN 82; WhoAm 74, 76; WhoHisp 92; WhoProB 73*

Alou, Matty
[Mateo Rojas Alou]
Dominican. Baseball Player
Outfielder, 1960-74; won NL batting title, 1966, with brother Felipe second.
b. Dec 22, 1938 in Haina, Dominican Republic
Source: *Ballpl 90; BioIn 7, 21; PseudN 82; WhoAm 74, 76; WhoHisp 91, 92, 94; WhoProB 73*

Alpert, George
American. Railroad Executive, Lawyer
Pres., board chm., 1956-68, New York, New Haven and Hartford Railroad Co.
b. Mar 24, 1898
d. Sep 11, 1988 in Cohasset, Massachusetts
Source: *BioIn 5, 6, 16; CurBio 88N; NewYTBS 88; WhAm 10*

Alpert, Herb
[Tijuana Brass]
American. Musician, Bandleader
Trumpeter; led Tijuana Brass, 1960s-70s; responsible for new era in instrumental music; hits include "The Lonely Bull," 1962, "Rise," 1979.
b. Mar 31, 1935 in Los Angeles, California
Source: *ASCAP 80; BiDAmM; BioIn 10, 11, 12, 16; BioNews 74; CelR 90; CurBio 67; EncPR&S 89; EncRkSt; HarEnR 86; IntWW 93; LegTOT; NewAmDM; NewGrDA 86; NewYTBS 74; PenEncP; RkOn 74, 78; WhoAm 74, 76, 78, 80, 82, 84, 86, 88, 90, 92, 94, 95, 96, 97; WhoEnt 92; WhoHol 92, A; WhoRock 81; WorAl; WorAlBi*

Alpert, Hollis
American. Critic, Editor
Editor, *American Film* ,1975-83; wrote *The Barrymores,* 1964.
b. Sep 24, 1916 in Herkimer, New York
Source: *AmAu&B; ConAu 1R, 6NR, 23NR, 46NR; HalFC 84, 88; LinLib L; WhoAm 74, 76, 78, 80, 82, 84, 86, 88, 90, 92, 94; WhoEnt 92; WhoUSWr 88; WhoWrEP 89, 92, 95; WrDr 90, 92, 94*

Alphand, Herve
French. Economist, Diplomat
UN ambassador, 1955-56, ambassador to US, 1956-65.
b. May 31, 1907
d. Jan 13, 1994 in Paris, France
Source: *BioIn 1, 2, 4, 7, 19, 20; CurBio 51, 94N; IntWW 74, 75, 76, 77, 78, 79, 80, 81, 82, 83, 89, 91, 93; Who 74, 82, 83, 85, 88, 90, 92, 94; WhoFr 79*

Alsop, Joseph Wright, Jr.
American. Journalist, Author
Noted political columnist, 1935-68; books include *We Accuse,* 1955; brother of Stewart.
b. Oct 11, 1910 in Avon, Connecticut
d. Aug 28, 1989 in Washington, District of Columbia
Source: *AmAu&B; BenetAL 91; BiDAmJo; BiDAmNC; BioIn 1, 2, 3, 4, 5, 6, 7, 8, 9, 10, 11, 13, 16; BlueB 76; ColdWar 1; ConAu 129; CurBio 52, 89, 89N; IntAu&W 76, 77; IntWW 74, 75, 76, 77, 78, 79, 80, 81, 82, 83, 89; LinLib L; NewYTBE 71; NewYTBS 74, 89; REn; REnAL; WhAm 10; WhoAm 74, 76, 78, 80, 82, 84, 86, 88; WhoE 89; WhoSSW 73; WhoWor 74, 78; WorAl; WorAlBi; WorAu 1950; WrDr 88, 90, 92, 94, 96*

Alsop, Stewart Johonnot Oliver
American. Journalist, Author
Editor, *Saturday Evening Post,* 1958-68; co-wrote *Stay of Execution,* 1973.
b. May 17, 1914 in Avon, Connecticut
d. May 26, 1974 in Washington, District of Columbia
Source: *BioIn 2, 3, 4, 10, 11; ConAu 49, 89; CurBio 52, 74; DcAmB S9; EncAI&E; IntWW 74; NewYTBS 74; REn; WhAm 6; WhoAm 74; WhoSSW 73; WhoWor 74; WorAl; WorAu 1950*

Alston, Theodosia Burr
[Mrs. Joseph Alston]
American.
Daughter of Aaron Burr; stood loyally by father through all disasters; lost at sea.
b. Jun 21, 1783 in Albany, New York
d. Jan 1, 1813
Source: *AmBi; BioIn 1, 2, 3, 6, 10; DcAmB; NotAW*

Alston, Walter Emmons
"Smokey"
American. Baseball Manager
Managed Brooklyn/LA Dodgers, 1954-76; four world championships; Hall of Fame, 1983.
b. Dec 1, 1911 in Venice, Ohio
d. Oct 1, 1984 in Oxford, Ohio
Source: *AnObit 1984; BiDAmSp BB; BioIn 3, 4, 5, 6, 7, 9, 10, 11, 12; ConAu 113; CurBio 54, 84; NewYTBS 84; WhAm 8; WhoAm 74, 76, 78, 80, 82; WhoProB 73*

Alt, Carol
[Mrs. Ron Greschner]
American. Model
Has appeared on over 500 magazine covers; made three films in Italy, 1987.
b. Dec 1, 1960 in New York, New York
Source: *BioIn 13, 15, 16; ConTFT 14; LegTOT; WhoHol 92*

Altdorfer, Albrecht
German. Artist, Architect
One of earliest German landscapists; also proficient in woodcutting, engraving; paintings include *Rest on The Flight into Egypt,* 1510.
b. 1480 in Regensburg, Germany
d. Feb 12, 1538 in Regensburg, Germany
Source: *AtlBL; BioIn 1, 2, 4; DcArts; IntDcAA 90; LuthC 75; McGDA; McGEWB; NewCol 75; OxCGer 76, 86; OxDcArt; PenDiDA 89; WebBD 83; WhDW; WorAl; WorAlBi*

Altea, Rosemary
[Rosemary Susan Gail Edwards]
English. Author, Psychic
Founded Rosemary Altea Association of Healers, 1985; wrote *The Eagle and the Rose,* 1995.
b. May 1946 in Leicester, England
Source: *News 96, 96-3*

Alter, Hobie
[Hobart Alter, Jr.]
American. Designer
Designed "Hobie Cat" sailing catamaran.
b. 1934 in Capistrano Beach, California
Source: *BioIn 10, 13, 15; ConNews 85-1*

Altgeld, John Peter
American. Politician
Dem. governor of IL, 1892-96; championed liberal causes, rights of the individual.
b. Dec 30, 1847 in Nassau, Germany
d. Mar 12, 1902 in Joliet, Illinois
Source: *Alli SUP; AmAu&B; AmBi; AmRef; AmSocL; ApCAB SUP; BenetAL 91; BiDrGov 1789; BioIn 1, 4, 5, 6, 9, 10, 15, 19; CopCroC; DcAmAu; DcAmB; DcAmImH; EncAB-H 1974, 1996; GayN; HarEnUS; LinLib S; McGEWB; NatCAB 11; OhA&B; OxCAmH; OxCAmL 65, 83, 95; REnAL; TwCBDA; WebAB 74, 79; WhAm 1; WhAmP*

Althouse, Paul Shearer
American. Opera Singer
Tenor, known for lead roles in *Carmen, Samson et Delilah.*
b. Dec 2, 1889 in Reading, Pennsylvania
d. Feb 6, 1954 in New York, New York
Source: *Baker 84; BiDAmM; MusSN; NewEOp 71; WhAm 3*

Altman, Benjamin
American. Merchant, Art Collector
Founded B Altman & Co., NYC dept. store, 1906.
b. Jul 12, 1840 in New York, New York
d. Oct 7, 1913 in New York, New York
Source: *AmBi; ApCAB X; BioIn 9; DcAmB; LinLib S; NatCAB 15; NewYTBE 70; WebAB 74, 79; WhAm 4; WhAmArt 85; WhAm HSA*

Altman, Dennis
Australian. Writer
Wrote *Homosexual: Oppression and Liberation,* 1971.
b. Aug 16, 1943 in Sydney, Australia
Source: *ConAu 15NR, 33R, 34NR; GayLesB; GayLL; IntAu&W 82, 91, 93; WrDr 76, 80, 82, 84, 86, 88, 90, 92, 94, 96*

Altman, Robert B
American. Director, Producer
Directed *M*A*S*H,* 1970; *A Weddding,* 1978.
b. Feb 20, 1925 in Kansas City, Missouri
Source: *BiDFilm; BioIn 16; BkPepl; CelR 90; ConAu 73; ConLC 16; ConTFT 7; CurBio 74; FilmgC; IntDcF 2-2; IntMPA 86, 92; IntWW 83, 91; MovMk; News 93-2; NewYTBE 71; OxCFilm; Who 92; WhoAm 86, 90; WhoAmJ 80; WhoEnt 92; WorAlBi*

Altman, Sidney
American. Scientist
Won Nobel Prize in chemistry, 1989, for discovering RNA to actively aid chemical reactions in cells.
Source: *AmMWSc 89; BioIn 18, 19, 20; WorAlBi*

Altobelli, Joe
[Joseph Salvatore Altobelli]
American. Baseball Manager
Manager, San Francisco, 1977-79, Baltimore, 1983-85; won World Series, 1983.
b. May 26, 1932 in Detroit, Michigan
Source: *Ballpl 90; BioIn 13; WhoAm 84; WhoE 85*

Altrock, Nick
[Nicholas Altrock]
American. Baseball Player
Had 82 wins in 19-yr. pitching career beginning 1898; known more for clowning antics.
b. Sep 15, 1876 in Cincinnati, Ohio
d. Jan 20, 1965 in Washington, District of Columbia
Source: *Ballpl 90; BioIn 3, 5, 7; WhoProB 73*

Altsheler, Joseph Alexander
American. Children's Author, Journalist
Wrote boys' adventure tales, often in series: *The Young Trailers,* 1907.
b. Apr 29, 1862 in Three Springs, Kentucky
d. Jun 5, 1919 in New York, New York
Source: *AmAu&B; AuBYP 2; BiDSA; BioIn 7, 11; DcAmAu; DcAmB; DcNAA; JBA 34; LiHiK; LinLib L; NatCAB 11; REnAL; TwCA, SUP; TwCBDA; WhAm 1; YABC 1*

al-Turabi, Hassan
Sudanese. Religious Leader
Led Muslin Brotherhood and National Islamic Front; serves as secretary general of Popular Arab and Islamic Conference.
b. c. 1932, Sudan

Aluko, Timothy Mofolorunso
Nigerian. Author
One Man, One Woman was first novel published in English in Nigeria, 1959.
b. Jun 14, 1918 in Ilesha, Nigeria
Source: *AfrA; Au&Wr 71; Benet 87, 96; BioIn 14, 18; BlkWr 1; CamGLE; CasWL; ConAu 10NR, 65; ConNov 72, 76, 82, 91; DcLB 117; DcLEL 1940; IntAu&W 76, 77, 89, 91, 93; IntvTCA 2; PenC CL; RGAfL; TwCWr; WebE&AL; WrDr 76, 92*

Alvarado, Pedro de
Spanish. Conqueror
Helped conquer Mexico, Central America for Spain, 1519-34.
b. 1486 in Badajoz, Spain
d. 1541 in Nochistlan, Mexico

Source: *AmBi; ApCAB; BioIn 3, 4, 8, 9; DcBiPP; DcCathB; Drake; LinLib S; WebBD 83*

Alvardo, Trini(dad)
American. Actor
Star of films *Rich Kids,* 1979; *Times Square,* 1980.
b. 1967 in New York, New York
Source: *ConTFT 7; IntMPA 92; NewYTBS 79; WhoHisp 92*

Alvarez, Alfred
English. Poet, Critic
Influential reviewer-critic who discussed literary suicides in *Savage God,* 1971.
b. Aug 5, 1929 in London, England
Source: *Au&Wr 71; BioIn 10, 12, 13, 14, 15, 18; ConAu 1R, 3NR; ConLC 5, 13; ConNov 86; ConPo 70, 75, 85; DcLEL 1940; IntAu&W 76, 77, 86, 89, 91, 93; IntvTCA 2; IntWWP 82; ModBrL S1; REn; Who 74, 82, 83, 85, 88, 90, 92, 94; WhoWor 74, 78, 80, 95, 96, 97; WorAu 1950; WrDr 76, 86*

Alvarez, Juan
Mexican. Military Leader
Indian general; led revolt which ousted Santa Anna, 1854; temporary president of Mexico, 1855.
b. Jan 27, 1780 in Concepcion de Atayac, Mexico
d. Aug 21, 1867 in Acapulco, Mexico
Source: *ApCAB; Drake; McGEWB; NewCol 75; WebBD 83*

Alvarez, Luis W(alter)
American. Physicist
Won Nobel Prize, 1968, for work, discoveries in nuclear physics.
b. Jun 13, 1911 in San Francisco, California
d. Sep 1, 1988 in Berkeley, California
Source: *AmMWSc 73P, 76P, 79, 82, 86; AsBiEn; BiESc; BioIn 1, 4, 8, 12; BlueB 76; CamDcSc; CmCal; CurBio 47, 88; HispAmA; InSci; IntWW 74, 75, 76, 77, 78, 79, 80, 81, 82, 83; LarDcSc; McGMS 80; NobelP; WebAB 74, 79; Who 74, 82, 83, 85, 88; WhoAm 74, 76, 78, 80, 82, 84, 86, 88; WhoFrS 84; WhoNob, 90, 95; WhoWest 78, 80, 84, 87; WhoWor 74, 76, 78, 80, 82, 84, 87, 89; WorAl; WorInv*

Alvarez, Walter Clement
American. Physician
Authority on digestive tract; had syndicated newspaper column, 1951-78.
b. Jul 22, 1884 in San Francisco, California
d. Jun 18, 1978 in San Francisco, California
Source: *AmAu&B; AmMWSc 73P; BioIn 3, 4, 6, 8, 11; ConAu 61; CurBio 53, 78; DrAP 75; InSci; MinnWr; NewYTBS 78; WhAm 7; WhNAA; WhoAm 74, 76, 78; WhoWor 74*

Alvary, Lorenzo
American. Opera Singer
Bass; with NY Met., 1942-79; host, weekly radio opera program, 1964-86.
b. Feb 20, 1909 in Debrecen, Hungary
d. Dec 13, 1996 in New York, New York
Source: *Baker 84, 92; BioIn 4, 7, 13; IntWWM 90; MetOEnc; NewYTBS 27; WhoAm 74, 76, 78, 80, 82, 84, 86, 88, 90, 92, 94, 95, 96, 97; WhoEnt 92; WhoMus 72; WhoWor 74, 76*

Alvary, Max
[Max Achenbach]
German. Opera Singer
Tenor; with NY Met., 1884-98; first without a beard to sing Wagner.
b. May 3, 1856 in Dusseldorf, Germany
d. Nov 7, 1898 in Gross-Tabarz, Germany
Source: *Baker 78, 84, 92; BioIn 1; CmOp; MetOEnc; NewEOp 71; NewGrDM 80; OxDcOp*

Alvin, Dave
American. Singer, Songwriter, Musician
Formed group the Blasters in 1979 and released first album, *American Music,* 1980; joined group X for one album, *See How We Care,* 1987; released critically acclaimed solo albums *Blue Blvd,* 1991 and *King of California,* 1994.
b. 1955 in Los Angeles, California
Source: *ConMus 17*

Alworth, Lance Dwight
"Bambi"
American. Football Player
Wide receiver, 1962-73; only player to gain over 1,000 yds. receiving in seven consecutive seasons.
b. Aug 3, 1940 in Houston, Texas
Source: *BiDAmSp FB; BioIn 7, 8, 9; WhoFtbl 74; WorAlBi*

Alzado, Lyle Martin
American. Football Player
Defensive end, 1971-86, mostly with Denver; defensive player of year, 1977; blamed his longtime use of steroids for the brain cancer that killed him.
b. Apr 3, 1949 in New York, New York
d. May 14, 1992 in Portland, Oregon
Source: *BioIn 11, 13, 14; ConAu 110; ConTFT 8; FootReg 86; NewYTBS 78; WhAm 10; WhoAm 78, 80, 82, 84, 86, 88, 90*

Alzheimer, Alois
German. Neurologist
First to describe brain-destroying disease that bears his name, 1906.
b. 1864
d. 1915
Source: *BiHiMed; BioIn 9; EncSPD; OxCMed 86*

Amado, Jorge
"Brazilian Boccaccio"
Brazilian. Author
Brazil's greatest living novelist whose social conscious writings have been translated into more than 30 languages.
b. Aug 10, 1912 in Bahia, Brazil
Source: *Benet 87, 96; BenetAL 91; BioIn 5, 10, 12, 14, 15, 16, 17, 18; CasWL; CelR; ConAu 35NR, 77; ConFLW 84; ConLC 13, 40; CurBio 86; CyWA 58, 89; DcBrazL; DcLB 113; EncLatA; EncWL, 2, 3; FacFETw; HispLC; IntAu&W 76, 77, 89, 91, 93; IntWW 74, 75, 76, 77, 78, 79, 80, 81, 82, 83, 89, 91, 93; LatAmWr; LegTOT; LiExTwC; LinLib L; MajTwCW; McGEWB; ModLAL; Novels; PenC AM; RAdv 14, 13-2; REn; ScF&FL 92; TwCWr; WhoAm 84; WhoWor 74, 76, 78, 82, 84, 87, 89, 91, 93, 95, 96; WorAlBi; WorAu 1950*

Amalrik, Andrei Alekseyevich
Russian. Author
Human rights advocate who wrote many anti-Soviet works, spent six years in labor camp.
b. May 12, 1938 in Moscow, Union of Soviet Socialist Republics
d. Nov 11, 1980 in Guadalajara, Spain
Source: *AnObit 1980; BioIn 8, 9, 10, 11; ConAu 102; CurBio 74, 81; FacFETw; NewYTBE 73; NewYTBS 80*

Amanollah Khan
Afghan. Ruler
Afghanistan became independent of Great Britain during his reign, 1919-29.
b. Jun 1, 1892 in Paghman, Afghanistan
d. Apr 25, 1960 in Zurich, Switzerland

Amanpour, Christiane
English. Broadcast Journalist
Reporter for CNN, 1986—; covered Gulf War, 1991.
b. 1958 in London, England
Source: *CurBio 96*

Amara, Lucine
[Lucine Tockqui Armaganian]
American. Opera Singer
Soprano with NY Met. since 1950.
b. Mar 1, 1927 in Hartford, Connecticut
Source: *Baker 78, 84, 92; BioIn 3, 4, 10, 11, 13; IntWWM 90; InWom; MetOEnc; MusSN; NewAmDM; NewEOp 71; NewGrDA 86; NewGrDM 80; NewGrDO; WhoAm 74, 76, 78, 80, 82, 84, 86, 88, 90, 92, 94; WhoAmM 83; WhoAmW 68, 70, 72, 74, 77, 83, 85, 87, 89, 91; WhoEnt 92; WhoMus 72; WhoOp 76; WhoWor 74, 76*

Amati
[Andrea Amati; Antonio Amati; Girolame Amati, II; Girolamo Amati; Nicolo Amati]
Italian. Violin Maker
Family of craftsmen active in Cremona, Italy, 1540-1740; originated forms of violin, viola, cello known today.
Source: *AntBDN K; Baker 78, 84; BioIn 2; NewAmDM; NewGrDM 80; WebAB 74*

Amati, Nicolo
[Nicolaus Amati]
Italian. Violin Maker
Son of Girolamo Amati, considered most refined craftsman of family; teacher of Antonio Stradivari.
b. Dec 3, 1956 in Cremona, Italy
d. Apr 12, 1684 in Cremona, Italy
Source: *AntBDN K; Baker 78; BioIn 2*

Amato, Giuliano
Italian. Politician
Prime minister of Italy, 1992-93.
b. May 13, 1938 in Turin, Italy
Source: *BioIn 18, 19; CurBio 93; IntWW 89, 91, 93*

Amato, Pasquale
Italian. Opera Singer
Baritone, known for performances in *Carmen; Othello.*
b. Mar 21, 1878 in Naples, Italy
d. Aug 12, 1942 in New York, New York
Source: *Baker 78, 84, 92; BiDAmM; BioIn 1, 3, 4, 7, 11; CurBio 42; IntDcOp; MetOEnc; MusSN; NewEOp 71; NewGrDA 86; NewGrDM 80; NewGrDO; OxDcOp; WhAm 2; WhoHol B*

Amaya, Victor
"Big Vic"
American. Tennis Player
Tall lefthander who won French Open doubles with Hank Pfister, 1980.
b. Jul 2, 1954 in Denver, Colorado
Source: *BioIn 12; WhoIntT*

Ambartsumyan, Viktor Amazaspovich
Russian. Astronomer
Established Soviet Union's school of theoretical astrophysics; wrote *Theoretical Astrophysics,* 1958; Pres., International Astronomical Union, 1961-63.
b. Sep 18, 1908 in Tbilisi, Georgia
d. Aug 12, 1996 in Yerevan, Armenia
Source: *BiDSovU; BioIn 13; FacFETw; IntWW 83; Who 92*

Ambers, Lou
[Luigi d'Ambrosio]
"Herkimer Hurricane"
American. Boxer
World lightweight champion, 1936, 1939; Hall of Fame, 1964.
b. Nov 8, 1913 in Herkimer, New York
Source: *BiDAmSp BK; BioIn 10; BoxReg; PseudN 82; WhoBox 74; WhoSpor*

Ambler, Eric
[Eliot Reed]
English. Author, Screenwriter
Famed espionage writer who wrote *Mask of Dimitrios,* 1939; filmed, 1944.
b. Jun 28, 1909 in London, England
Source: *AmAu&B; Au&Wr 71; Benet 87, 96; BioIn 4, 5, 10, 12, 14, 15, 16, 17, 21; BlueB 76; CamGLE; CnMWL; ConAu 7NR, 9R, 38NR; ConLC 4, 6, 9; ConNov 72, 76, 82, 86, 91, 96; CorpD; CrtSuMy; CurBio 75; CyWA 89; DcArts; DcLB 77; DcLEL; DcLP 87A; EncMys; EncWB; FilmEn; FilmgC; GangFlm; HalFC 80, 84, 88; IntAu&W 76, 82, 89, 91, 93; IntWW 83, 89, 91, 93; LegTOT; LinLib L; LngCTC; MajTwCW; NewC; Novels; OxCEng 85, 95; OxCFilm; PseudN 82; REn; RGTwCWr; ScF&FL 1; SpyFic; TwCA SUP; TwCCr&M 85, 91; TwCWr; Who 74, 82, 83, 85, 88, 90, 92, 94; WhoAm 86, 88, 90, 92, 94, 95, 96, 97; WhoSpyF; WhoWor 74, 76, 82, 84, 91; WorAl; WorAlBi; WrDr 76, 80, 82, 84, 86, 88, 90, 92, 94, 96*

Amboy Dukes, The
[Greg Arama; Cliff Davies; Rusty Day; Steve Farmer; Rob Grange; Vic Mastrianni; Ted Nugent; Dave Palmer; Andy Solomon; Derek St. Holmes]
American. Music Group
Formed by Ted Nugent, 1965; had hit "Journey to the Center of Your Mind," 1968.
Source: *ASCAP 80; BiDAmM; BioIn 18; ConMuA 80A, 80B; EncRk 88; WhoRock 81; WhoRocM 82*

Ambrose, Saint
Italian. Religious Leader
Bishop of Milan; first to use hymns extensively as divine praise.
b. 340 in Trier, Germany
d. Apr 4, 397 in Milan, Italy
Source: *BiD&SB; BioIn 1, 2, 3, 4, 5, 6, 7, 8, 10, 12, 13; CasWL; CyEd; DcBiPP; DcCathB; LinLib L, S; LuthC 75; McGDA; McGEWB; NewC; NewGrDM 80; OxCClL, 89; OxCEng 67, 85, 95; OxCMus; PenC CL; PoChrch; RAdv 14, 13-4; REn*

Ambrose, David Edwin
English. Dramatist, Screenwriter
Teleplays include "Alternative 3," controversial drama hoax, 1977.
b. Feb 21, 1943 in Chorley, England
Source: *ConAu 116; ConTFT 1, 5*

Amdahl, Gene M(yron)
American. Engineer, Business Executive
Computer designer, IBM, 1952-70; established Amdahl Corp. to replace IBM mainframes with high-performance emulators, 1970-79.
b. Nov 16, 1922 in Flandreau, South Dakota
Source: *AmMWSc 86, 92; BioIn 13, 14, 15; CurBio 82; HisDcDP; LarDcSc; LElec; PorSil; St&PR 84, 87, 91, 93, 96; WhoAm 78, 80, 82, 84, 86, 88, 90, 92, 94, 95, 96, 97; WhoEng 80, 88; WhoFI 87, 89, 92; WhoFrS 84; WhoTech 84; WhoWest 74, 76, 92, 94*

Ameche, Alan Dante
"The Horse"
American. Football Player
Won Heisman Trophy, 1954; running back, Baltimore, 1955-60; led NFL in rushing, 1955.
b. Jun 1, 1933 in Kenosha, Wisconsin
d. Aug 8, 1988 in Houston, Texas
Source: *BiDAmSp FB; BioIn 3, 4, 7, 11; St&PR 84; WhoFtbl 74*

Ameche, Don
[Dominic Felix Amici]
American. Actor, Radio Performer
Star of over 40 films; won Oscar, 1986, for role in *Cocoon.*
b. May 31, 1908 in Kenosha, Wisconsin
d. Dec 6, 1993 in Scottsdale, Arizona
Source: *AnObit 1993; BiDFilm 94; BiE&WWA; BioIn 3, 4, 7, 9, 10, 14, 16, 19, 20; CmMov; CmpEPM; ConTFT 2, 7, 12; CurBio 65, 94N; EncAFC; EncMT; FilmEn; FilmgC; ForYSC; HalFC 80, 84, 88; IntDcF 1-3, 2-3; IntMPA 77, 78, 79, 80, 81, 82, 84, 86, 88, 92, 94; LegTOT; MotPP; MovMk; News 94, 94-2; NewYTBS 93; OxCFilm; OxCPMus; PseudN 82; RadStar; SaTiSS; WhAm 11; WhoAm 86, 88, 90, 92, 94; WhoHol 92, A; WhoThe 72, 77, 81; WorAl; WorAlBi*

Ameche, Jim
American. Radio Performer
Brother of Don Ameche; portrayed first Jack Armstrong in radio series, 1930s.
b. 1915 in Kenosha, Wisconsin
d. Feb 4, 1983 in Tucson, Arizona
Source: *NewYTBS 83; RadStar; SaTiSS*

Ameling, Elly
Dutch. Opera Singer
Soprano with NY Met., 1950; made numerous recordings.
b. Feb 8, 1938 in Rotterdam, Netherlands
Source: *Baker 84; BioIn 12, 13; BriBkM 80; CurBio 82; IntWW 78, 79, 80, 81, 82, 83, 89, 91, 93; IntWWM 77, 80, 90; MetOEnc; NewAmDM; NewGrDM 80; NewYTBS 74, 79; WhoAm 80, 82, 84, 86, 88, 90, 92, 94; WhoAmM 83; WhoMus 72; WhoWor 74, 84, 87, 89, 91, 93*

Amen, Irving
American. Artist
Designed Peace Medal for end of Vietnam War.
b. Jul 25, 1918 in New York, New York
Source: *BioIn 9; DcCAA 71, 77, 88; WhoAm 74, 76, 78, 80, 82, 84, 86, 88, 90, 92, 94, 95, 96, 97; WhoAmA 73, 76, 78, 80, 82, 84, 86, 89, 91, 93; WhoAmJ 80; WhoWor 76, 78, 80, 82, 84, 87, 89, 91; WhoWorJ 72, 78*

Amerasinghe, Hamilton Shirley
Sri Lankan. Diplomat, Government Official
Pres., UN General Assembly, 1967.
b. Mar 18, 1913 in Colombo, Ceylon
d. Dec 4, 1980 in New York, New York
Source: *AnObit 1981; BiDInt; BioIn 9, 11, 12; CurBio 77, 81, 81N; FarE&A 78, 79, 80; IntWW 74, 75, 76, 77, 78, 79, 80; IntYB 78, 79, 80, 81; NewYTBS 76, 80; WhAm 7; WhoWor 74, 76, 78*

America
[Gerry Beckley; Dewey Bunnell; Daniel Peek]
American. Music Group
First million selling record was "A Horse with No Name," 1972; other hits include "You Can Do Magic," 1982.
Source: *BiDAmM; ConMuA 80A; ConMus 16; EncPR&S 74; EncRk 88; EncRkSt; HarEnR 86; IlEncRk; OxCPMus; PenEncP; RkOn 78; RolSEnR 83; WhoRock 81; WhoRocM 82*

American Horse
[Iron Plume; Iron Shield; Number Two]
American. Native American Leader
Was killed in revenge of the defeat of Gen. Custer at Little Big Horn.
d. 1876
Source: *BioIn 1, 21; NotNaAm*

Amery, Julian
[Baron Amery of LustLeigh; Harold Julian Amery]
English. Politician
MP 1950-66, 1969-92.
b. Mar 27, 1919 in London, England
Source: *Au&Wr 71; BioIn 10; BlueB 76; ConAu 61; IntAu&W 76, 82, 91; IntWW 74, 75, 76, 77, 78, 79, 80, 81, 82, 83, 89, 91; IntYB 78, 79, 80, 81, 82; Who 74, 82, 83, 85, 88, 90, 92; WhoWor 74, 76, 80; WrDr 80, 82, 84, 86, 88, 90, 92*

Ames, Blanche
American. Artist
Botanical illustrator; early champion for birth control, 1916.
b. Feb 18, 1878 in Lowell, Massachusetts
d. Mar 1, 1969 in North Easton, Massachusetts
Source: *BioIn 9, 12, 20; DcWomA; InWom SUP; NatCAB 53; NotAW MOD; ObitOF 79; WhoAmW 58, 61, 64, 66, 68, 70; WomWWA 14*

Ames, Bruce N(athan)
American. Scientist
Proponent of the view that synthetic chemicals are less harmful than many natural carcinogens.
b. Dec 16, 1928 in New York, New York
Source: *AmMWSc 76P, 79, 82, 86, 89, 92, 95; IntWW 77, 78, 79, 80, 81, 82, 83, 89, 91, 93; WhoAm 90, 92, 94, 95, 96, 97; WhoScEn 94, 96; WhoWest 92, 94*

Ames, Ed(mund Dantes)
[The Ames Brothers; Urick Ed]
American. Singer, Actor
Solo recording artist, 1963—; played Mingo in TV series "Daniel Boone," 1963-68.
b. Jul 9, 1927 in Boston, Massachusetts
Source: *BioIn 8; LegTOT; PseudN 82; RkOn 74, 78; WhoAm 82, 86; WorAlBi*

Ames, Jessie Daniel
American. Social Reformer
Founded Assn. of Southern Women for Prevention of Lynching, 1930.
b. Nov 2, 1883 in Palestine, Texas
d. Feb 21, 1972 in Austin, Texas
Source: *AmRef; AmRef&R; AmSocL; BioIn 15, 19, 20, 21; EncSoH; NotAW MOD; RadHan*

Ames, Leon
[Leon Wycoff]
American. Actor
Character actor; appeared in over 100 films since 1932.
b. Jan 20, 1903 in Portland, Indiana
d. Oct 12, 1993 in Laguna Beach, California
Source: *BiE&WWA; BioIn 19; EncAFC; FilmEn; FilmgC; ForYSC; HalFC 80, 84, 88; HolCA; IntMPA 75, 76, 77, 78, 79, 80, 81, 82, 84, 86, 88, 92, 94; LegTOT; MGM; MotPP; MovMk; NotNAT; PseudN 82; Vers B; WhoHol 92, A; WhThe; WorAl; WorAlBi*

Ames, Louise (Bates)
American. Psychologist
Author of several child care books; wrote daily syndicated newspaper column, "Parents Ask."
b. Oct 29, 1908 in Portland, Maine
d. Oct 31, 1996 in Cincinnati, Ohio
Source: *AmAu&B; AmMWSc 73S, 78S; BioIn 4; ConAu 1NR, 1R, 3NR, 18NR, 39NR, 154; CurBio 56; ForWC 70; LEduc 74; WhoAm 74, 76, 78, 80, 82, 84, 86, 88, 90, 92, 94, 95, 96, 97; WhoAmW 58, 64, 66, 68, 70, 72, 74, 77, 85, 87, 89, 91; WhoE 83, 93; WhoMedH; WhoWor 87, 97*

Ames, Nathaniel
American. Publisher
Compiled *Astronomical Diary and Almanack,* 1725-64, model for Benjamin Franklin's *Poor Richard's Almanack.*
b. Jul 22, 1708 in Bridgewater, Massachusetts
d. Jul 11, 1764 in Dedham, Massachusetts
Source: *AmAu; AmAu&B; AmBi; AmWrBE; ApCAB; BenetAL 91; BiD&SB; BiInAmS; BioIn 14; ChhPo S2; CyAL 1; DcAmAu; DcAmB; DcNAA; Drake; NatCAB 8; NewCol 75; OxCAmH; OxCAmL 65, 83, 95; REnAL; WhAm HS; WrCNE*

Ames, Oakes
American. Politician, Manufacturer
Rep. con. from MA, 1863-73; part of scheme to build Union Pacific Railroad, 1865.
b. Jan 10, 1804 in Easton, Massachusetts
d. May 8, 1873 in Easton, Massachusetts
Source: *AmBi; ApCAB; BiAUS; BiDAmBL 83; BiDrAC; BiDrUSC 89; DcAmB; EncABHB 2; HarEnUS; NatCAB 2; REnAW; TwCBDA; WebAB 74, 79; WhAm HS; WhAmP*

Ames, Winthrop
American. Theater Owner, Producer
Built, managed NYC theaters, 1905-15; wrote, produced *Snow White,* 1913, first play especially for children; grandson of Oakes.
b. Nov 25, 1871 in North Easton, Massachusetts
d. Nov 3, 1937 in Boston, Massachusetts
Source: *BioIn 4, 7, 20; CamGWoT; EncWT; NatCAB 15; OxCThe 67, 83; PlP&P; TheaDir; WhAm 1; WhThe*

Ames Brothers, The
[Ed Ames; Gene Ames; Joe Ames; Vic Ames]
American. Music Group
Sang together, 1949-59; had 1953 hit single "You, You, You".
Source: *AmPS A, B; BiDAmM; BioIn 8; CmpEPM; NewAmDM; NewGrDA 86; PenEncP; PseudN 82; RkOn 74, 84; WhoRock 81*

Amfiteatrof, Daniele
American. Conductor
Prolific film composer, credited with 79 film scores including Disney's "Song of the South."
b. Oct 29, 1901 in Saint Petersburg, Russia
d. Jul 7, 1983 in Rome, Italy
Source: *ASCAP 66; Baker 78; BiDAmM; FilmgC; IntMPA 82; OxCFilm; WhoWor 78; WorEFlm*

Amherst, Jeffrey
English. Army Officer
Commander-in-chief, British forces, 1780; Amherst College named for him.
b. Jan 29, 1717 in Riverhead, England
d. Aug 3, 1797 in Kent, England
Source: *AmBi; AmRev; DcNaB; Drake; EncCRAm; EncNAB; HarEnMi; HisDBrE; LegTOT; LinLib S; McGEWB; NewC; OxCAmH; OxCCan; WhAmRev; WhNaAH; WhoMilH 76; WorAlBi*

Amicis, Edmond de
Italian. Author, Essayist
Most famous work *Cuore,* 1876, known for Tuscan style; used in US to teach Italian.
b. Oct 21, 1846 in Oneglia, Italy
d. Mar 12, 1908 in Bordighera, Italy
Source: *CasWL; DcBiA; EuAu; EvEuW; PenC EUR; REn; WhLit*

Amies, Hardy
[Edwin Hardy Aimes]
English. Fashion Designer
Opened boutique, London, 1950, specializing in high fashion ready to wear.
b. Jul 17, 1909 in London, England
Source: *BioIn 3, 6, 14, 16, 17; BlueB 76; CelR, 90; ConAu 129; ConFash; CurBio 62; EncFash; FairDF ENG; IntWW 74, 75, 76, 77, 78, 79, 80, 81, 82, 83, 89, 91; NewYTBE 73; Who 82, 83, 85, 88, 90, 92; WhoFash 88; WhoWor 74, 76, 78; WorFshn*

Amin, Idi
[Idi Amin Dada Oumee]
"Big Daddy"; "The Wild Man of Africa"
Ugandan. Political Leader
Overthrew Milton Obote; president of Uganda, 1971-80; known for torture, murder of dissidents.
b. Jan 1, 1925 in Koboko, Uganda
Source: *BioIn 13, 14, 16, 17, 18, 21; BioNews 74; ColdWar 2; CurBio 73; DcAfHiB 86, 86S; DcPol; EncRev; FacFETw; InB&W 80; IntWW 74; LegTOT; NewYTBE 71, 72; NewYTBS 77; WhoGov 72; WhoWor 74; WorDWW*

Amis, Kingsley (William)
[Robert Markham]
"Angry Young Man"
English. Author
Satirical novelist; several produced as movies, including *Lucky Jim,* 1954.
b. Apr 16, 1922 in London, England
d. Oct 22, 1995 in London, England
Source: *Au&Wr 71; AuNews 2; Benet 87, 96; BioIn 3, 4, 5, 6, 8, 9, 10, 11, 12, 13, 14, 15, 16, 17, 18, 19, 20, 21; BlmGEL; BlueB 76; BritWr S2; CamGEL; CamGLE; CasWL; ChhPo S3; CnDBLB 7; CnMWL; ConAu 8NR, 9R, 28NR, 54NR, 150; ConLC 1, 2, 3, 5, 8, 13, 40, 44; ConNov 72, 76, 82, 86, 91, 96; ConPo 70, 75, 80, 85, 96; ConSFA; CurBio 87, 96N; CyWA 89; DcArts; DcLB 15, 27, 100, 139; DcLEL 1940; DcLP 87A; EncMys; EncSF, 93; EncWL, 2, 3; EngPo; FacFETw; FilmgC; GrWrEL N; HalFC 80, 84, 88; IntAu&W 76, 77, 89, 91, 93; IntvTCA 2; IntWW 74, 75, 76, 77, 78, 79, 80, 81, 82, 83, 89, 91, 93; IntWWP 77; LegTOT; LinLib L; LngCEL; LngCTC; MagSWL; MajTwCW; MakMC; ModBrL, S1, S2; NewC; NewCBEL; NewEScF; News 96-2; Novels; OxCEng 85, 95; OxCTwCP; PenC ENG; PseudN 82; RAdv 1, 14, 13-1; REn; RfGEnL 91; RGTwCWr; ScF&FL 1, 2, 92; ScFSB; SpyFic; TwCCr&M 80; TwCSFW 81, 86, 91; TwCWr; WebE&AL; WhAm 11; WhDW; Who 74, 82, 83, 85, 88, 90, 92, 94; WhoAm 74, 76, 78, 80, 82, 84, 86, 88, 90, 92, 94, 95, 96; WhoSciF; WhoSpyF; WhoTwCL; WhoWor 89, 93, 95, 96; WorAu 1950; WrDr 76, 80, 82, 84, 86, 88, 90, 92, 94, 96*

Amis, Martin (Louis)
English. Author
Works include short stories, *The Moronic Inferno,* 1987; novel *London Fields,* 1989; son of Kingsley.
b. Aug 25, 1949 in Oxford, England
Source: *Benet 96; BestSel 90-3; BioIn 13, 14, 15, 16; BlmGEL; CamGLE; ConAu 8NR, 27NR, 54NR, 65; ConLC 4, 9, 38, 62; ConNov 82, 86, 91, 96; CurBio 90; DcArts; DcLB 14; EncSF 93; FacFETw; IntAu&W 76, 77, 89, 91, 93; IntWW 89, 91, 93; LegTOT; MagSWL; NewYTBS 90; Novels; OxCEng 95; RGTwCWr; ScF&FL 92; Who 85, 88, 90, 92, 94; WhoWor 93, 95, 96; WorAu 1980; WrDr 76, 80, 82, 84, 86, 88, 90, 92, 94, 96*

Ammann, Othmar Hermann
German. Engineer
Master bridge designer, builder: George Washington Bridge, 1927-31; Golden Gate Bridge, 1929-37; Mackinac Bridge, 1958-62.
b. Mar 26, 1876 in Schaffhausen, Switzerland
d. Sep 22, 1965 in Rye, New York
Source: *CurBio 63, 65; EncAB-A 28; McGMS 80; NatCAB 52; ObitOF 79; WhAm 4*

Ammons, Albert C
American. Jazz Musician
Pianist in Chicago clubs, 1929-49.
b. 1907 in Chicago, Illinois
d. Dec 2, 1949 in Chicago, Illinois
Source: *BiDJaz; CmpEPM; WhoJazz 72*

Ammons, Jug
[Eugene Ammons]
American. Musician
Tenor saxist; son of Albert Ammons.
b. Apr 14, 1925 in Chicago, Illinois
d. Aug 6, 1974 in Chicago, Illinois
Source: *BiDAfM; BiDAmM; BiDJaz; BioIn 10; EncJzS; InB&W 80, 85; PseudN 82; WhAm 6*

Amory, Cleveland
American. Author, Historian
Conservationist, pres., The Fund for Animals; wrote *Last Resorts,* 1952.
b. Sep 2, 1917 in Nahant, Massachusetts
Source: *AmAu&B; AuNews 1; BenetAL 91; BiDAmNC; BioIn 2, 4, 5, 7, 10, 11, 12, 13, 15; BkPepl; CelR, 90; ConAu 29NR, 69; ConPopW; EnvEnc; IntAu&W 91; LegTOT; LinLib L, S; REnAL; TwCA SUP; WhoAm 74, 76, 78, 80, 82, 84, 86, 88, 90, 92, 94, 95, 96, 97; WhoE 95; WhoUSWr 88; WhoWor 74; WhoWrEP 89, 92, 95; WrDr 76, 80, 82, 84, 86, 88, 90, 92, 94, 96*

Amos
Prophet, Biblical Figure
Visions recorded in Old Testament book of Amos.
b. 750BC
Source: *BioIn 9; LegTOT; REn*

Amos, John
American. Actor, Director
Played Kunta Kinte in TV mini-series "Roots," 1977; James Evans on TV series "Good Times," 1974-76.
b. Dec 27, 1941 in Newark, New Jersey
Source: *BioIn 20; BioNews 74; ConBlB 8; ConTFT 4, 13; InB&W 80, 85; IntMPA 92, 94, 96; WhoAm 82, 92, 94, 95, 96, 97; WhoEnt 92; WhoHol A*

Amos, Tori
[Myra Ellen Amos]
American. Singer, Songwriter
Known for sex-laden lyrics in songs such as "Leather" and "God."
b. Aug 22, 1964 in Newton, North Carolina

Amos, Wally
[Wallace Amos, Jr.]
"Famous Amos"
American. Business Executive
Best known for "Famous Amos" chocolate chip cookie shops all over US.
b. Jul 1, 1936 in Tallahassee, Florida
Source: *AfrAmBi 2; BioIn 11, 13, 14, 15; BkPepl; ConAmBL; CurBio 95; Entr; InB&W 80, 85; NewYTBS 75; WhoAm 97; WhoBlA 80, 92*

Ampere, Andre Marie
French. Scientist
Made important discoveries in electricity, magnetism, today known as electrodynamics.
b. Jan 22, 1775 in Lyons, France
d. Jun 10, 1836 in Marseilles, France
Source: *AsBiEn; BiESc; BioIn 1, 2, 3, 5, 7, 8, 9, 10, 12, 14, 16; CamDcSc; CelCen; DcBiPP; DcCathB; DcInv; DcScB; Dis&D; LarDcSc; LinLib L, S; McGEWB; OxCFr; REn; WhDW; WorScD*

Amram, David Werner, III
American. Composer, Conductor
Scored films, Broadway plays; won 1959 Obie for works for NY Shakespeare Festival.
b. Nov 17, 1930 in Philadelphia, Pennsylvania
Source: *AmComp; Baker 78, 84; BiDAmM; BiDJaz; BiE&WWA; BioNews 74; ConAu 28NR; CpmDNM 79; CurBio 69; DcCM; EncJzS; HalFC 88; IntWWM 77, 80, 85, 90; NewAmDM; NewEOp 71; NewGrDA 86; NewGrDJ 88; NewGrDM 80; NewGrDO; NotNAT; PenEncP; WhoAm 74, 76, 78, 80, 82, 84, 86, 90, 92, 94, 95, 96, 97; WhoAmM 83; WhoE 85, 86; WhoEnt 92*

Amrouche, Jean
Algerian. Poet
Highly regarded among French-speaking North African poets; wrote *Cinders,* 1934, and *Secret Star,* 1937.
b. Feb 7, 1906 in Ighil Ali, Algeria
d. Apr 16, 1962 in Paris, France

Amsterdam, Birdie
American. Judge
First female New York Supreme Court justice, 1958-75.
b. Mar 25, 1902
d. Jul 8, 1996 in New York, New York
Source: *CurBio 96N; InWom; WhoWorJ 72, 78*

Amsterdam, Jane
American. Editor
First woman to edit major NY daily newspaper, *NY Post,* 1988.
b. Jun 15, 1951? in Philadelphia, Pennsylvania
Source: *BioIn 15, 16; NewYTBS 88, 89; WhoAm 90*

Amsterdam, Morey
American. Actor, Comedian
Cellist, who played Buddy Sorrell in "The Dick Van Dyke Show," 1961-66.
b. Dec 14, 1914 in Chicago, Illinois
d. Oct 28, 1996 in Los Angeles, California
Source: *ASCAP 66, 80; ConAu 111, 148, 154; IntMPA 75, 76, 77, 78, 79, 80, 81, 82, 84, 86, 88, 92, 94, 96; JoeFr; LegTOT; News 97-1; NewYTBS 27; WhoAm 74, 76, 78, 80, 82; WhoHol 92; WorAl; WorAlBi*

Amundsen, Roald Engelbregt
Norwegian. Explorer
First man to reach S Pole, 1911; also proved existence of Northwest Passage, 1903-06.
b. Jul 16, 1872 in Vedsten, Norway
d. Jun 18, 1928 in Spitsbergen, Norway
Source: *AsBiEn; LinLib L, S; MacDCB 78; McGEWB; OxCCan; REn*

Amyot, Jacques
French. Translator, Scholar
Translated classics, especially Plutarch, in clear, colorful style.
b. Oct 30, 1513 in Melun, France
d. Feb 6, 1593 in Auxerre, France
Source: *BiD&SB; BioIn 7, 14; CasWL; DcBiPP; DcCathB; EuAu; EvEuW; LinLib L; NewC; NewCol 75; OxCEng 67, 85, 95; OxCFr; PenC EUR*

Ana-Alicia
[Ana-Alicia Ortiz]
American. Actor
Played Melissa Agretti on TV series "Falcon Crest," 1981-90.
b. Dec 12, 1957 in Mexico City, Mexico
Source: *ConTFT 8; VarWW 85; WhoEnt 92; WhoHisp 92; WhoHol 92*

Anacreon
"The Teian Muse"
Greek. Poet
Lyric poet noted for verse celebrating wine, love.
b. 572?BC in Teos, Asia Minor
d. 488?BC
Source: *AtlBL; BbD; BiD&SB; CasWL; DcBiPP; DcEuL; Dis&D; NewC; OxCEng 67; PenC CL; PseudN 82; RComWL; WorAlBi*

Anand, Mulk Raj
[Narad Muni]
Indian. Author
Wrote on Indian society, politics; novels include *Coolie,* 1913; *Lake Singh* trilogy, 1939-43.
b. Dec 12, 1905 in Peshawar, India
Source: *Au&Wr 71; Benet 96; BioIn 9, 10, 14, 17, 18; CamGLE; CasWL; ConAu 32NR, 65; ConLC 23, 93; ConNov 72, 76, 82, 86, 91, 96; DcOrL 2; EncWL 2, 3; FarE&A 78, 79, 80, 81; GrWrEL N; IntAu&W 76, 77, 86, 89, 91; IntLitE; IntWW 74, 75, 76, 77, 78, 79, 80, 81, 82, 83, 89, 91, 93; MajTwCW; ModCmwL; Novels; OxCEng 85, 95; PenC ENG; PseudN 82; REn; RfGEnL 91; RfGShF; RGTwCWr; WebE&AL; WhoWor 74; WorAu 1950; WrDr 76, 80, 82, 84, 86, 88, 90, 92, 94, 96*

Anastasia, Albert
"Lord High Executioner"; "Mad Hatter"
American. Criminal, Murderer
Joined Louis Buchalter and Murder Inc., 1931; extorted "sweetheart contracts" from unions.
b. Sep 26, 1902 in Tropea, Italy
d. Oct 25, 1957 in New York, New York
Source: *BioIn 4, 11; DrInf; PolProf E; PseudN 82; WhDW*

Anaxagoras
Greek. Philosopher
Taught Pericles, Euripides; disproved doctrine that things may have arisen by chance.
b. 500BC, Asia Minor
d. 428BC in Lampsacus, Greece
Source: *AsBiEn; BbD; Benet 87, 96; BiD&SB; BiDPsy; BioIn 12; CasWL; DcBiPP; DcScB; Dis&D; Grk&L; LarDcSc; LegTOT; LinLib L, S; LuthC 75; McGEWB; OxCClL, 89; OxCPhil; PenC CL; REn; WhDW; WorAl; WorAlBi*

Anaximander
Greek. Astronomer, Philosopher
First to write philosophy in Greek prose; invented sun dial, calculated angle of earth's tilt.
b. 611BC in Miletus, Asia Minor
d. 547BC
Source: *AsBiEn; BbD; BiD&SB; BioIn 12, 13, 14; CamDcSc; CasWL; DcBiPP; DcScB; Dis&D; Grk&L; InSci; LarDcSc; LinLib L, S; LuthC 75; McGEWB; OxCClL 89; PenC CL; REn; WorAl; WorAlBi*

Anaximenes of Miletus
Greek. Philosopher
Student of Anaximander; believed earth was flat, rested on air.
b. 570?BC in Miletus, Asia Minor
d. 500?BC
Source: *DcScB*

Anaya, Toney
American. Politician
Dem, governor of NM, 1983-86; only hispanic governor in US.
b. Apr 29, 1941 in Moriarty, New Mexico
Source: *AlmAP 84; BiDrGov 1983; BioIn 13, 14, 16; HispAmA; MexAmB; PeoHis; PolsAm 84; WhoAm 78, 86; WhoAmL 78; WhoAmP 75, 77, 79, 83, 85, 87, 89, 91, 93, 95; WhoGov 77; WhoHisp 91, 92, 94; WhoReal 83; WhoWest 78, 84, 87; WhoWor 87*

Ancerl, Karel
Czech. Conductor
Conducted Czech Philharmonic, 1950-68; Toronto Symphony, from 1970.
b. Apr 11, 1908 in Tucapy, Czechoslovakia
d. Jul 3, 1973 in Toronto, Ontario, Canada
Source: *Baker 78, 84, 92; BioIn 10; CanWW 70; NewAmDM; NewGrDM 80; NewYTBE 73; PenDiMP; WhAm 6; WhoMus 72; WhoWor 74*

Ancier, Garth
American. TV Executive
Senior vp, Program Development, Fox Broadcasting Co., 1986—.
b. Sep 3, 1957 in Perth Amboy, New Jersey
Source: *BioIn 15, 16; LesBEnT 92; News 89-1*

Anda, Geza
Swiss. Pianist
Known for performing Bela Bartok's concertos.
b. Nov 19, 1921 in Budapest, Hungary
d. Jun 13, 1976 in Zurich, Switzerland
Source: *Baker 78, 84, 92; BioIn 4, 6, 9, 10, 21; BriBkM 80; IntWW 74, 75, 76; NewAmDM; NewGrDM 80; NewYTBS 76; NotTwCP; ObitOF 79; PenDiMP; Who 74; WhoMus 72; WhoWor 74, 76*

Anders, Merry
American. Actor
Co-starred in TV series "How to Marry a Millionaire," 1957-59.
b. 1932
Source: *BioIn 18, 20; FilmEn; FilmgC; ForYSC; HalFC 80, 84, 88; MotPP; SweetSg D; WhoHrs 80*

Anders, William Alison
American. Astronaut
Systems engineer on first lunar flight, Apollo 8, Dec 1968.
b. Oct 17, 1933, Hong Kong
Source: *AmMWSc 92; BioIn 8, 9, 10; BlueB 76; CurBio 69; Dun&B 90; FacFETw; IntWW 74, 75, 76, 77, 78, 79, 80, 81, 82, 83, 89, 91, 93; St&PR 87, 91; WebAMB; WhoAm 74, 86, 88, 90, 92, 94, 95, 96, 97; WhoE 89; WhoFI 85, 87, 89, 92, 94, 96; WhoGov 72, 75, 77; WhoMW 92; WhoScEn 94, 96; WhoSpc; WhoSSW 82; WhoWest 94, 96; WhoWor 74*

Anders, Wladyslaw
Polish. Military Leader
Commander of free Polish forces during WWII; spoke out against Communism in Poland after the war.
b. Aug 11, 1892 in Blonie, Poland
d. May 12, 1970 in London, England
Source: *BiDSovU; BioIn 2, 8; EncTR 91; HisEWW; ObitT 1961; PolBiDi; WhoMilH 76; WhWW-II*

Andersen, Hans Christian
"The Danish Lafontaine"
Danish. Author, Poet
Produced 168 fairy tales, 1835-45; first English translation, 1846.
b. Apr 2, 1805 in Odense, Denmark
d. Aug 4, 1875 in Copenhagen, Denmark
Source: *AnCL; AtlBL; AuBYP 2, 3; BbD; Benet 87, 96; BiD&SB; BioIn 1, 2, 3, 4, 5, 6, 7, 8, 9, 10, 11, 12, 13, 15, 16, 17, 19, 20; BlmGEL; CarSB; CasWL; CelCen; ChhPo, S1, S2; ChlBkCr; ChlLR 6; CnOxB; CyWA 58; DcBiA; DcBiPP; DcEnL; DcEuL; DcPup; DcScanL; Dis&D; EuAu; EuWr 6; EvEuW; FamAYP; FamSYP; FilmgC; GayLesB; GrFLW; HalFC 80, 84, 88; JBA 34, 51; LegTOT; LinLib L, S; LngCEL; MajAI; McGEWB; NewC; NewCBEL; NewEOp 71; NewGrDO; NinCLC 7; NotNAT B; Novels; OxCChiL; OxCEng 67, 85, 95; PenC EUR; PseudN 82; RAdv 14, 13-2; RComWL; REn; RfGShF; RfGWoL 95; ShSCr 6; SJGFanW; Str&VC; WhDW; WhoChL; WorAl; WorAlBi; WorLitC; WrChl; YABC 1*

Andersen, Ib Steen
Danish. Dancer
Royal Danish Ballet, 1973-80, principle dancer NYC Ballet, 1980-94; ballet master, Pittsburgh Ballet Theatre, 1994—.
b. Dec 14, 1954 in Copenhagen, Denmark
Source: *BioIn 11; CurBio 84; WhoAm 82, 84, 86, 88, 90, 92, 96, 97; WhoE 91*

Anderson, Alexander
American. Engraver, Illustrator
Made first wood engravings in US in *Looking Glass of the Mind,* 1794.
b. Apr 21, 1775 in New York, New York
d. Jan 18, 1870 in Jersey City, New Jersey
Source: *AmAu&B; AmBi; AntBDN B; ApCAB; ArtsNiC; BioIn 2, 8, 15; BriEAA; ChhPo, S1; CyAL 1; DcAmArt; DcAmAu; DcAmB; DcAmMeB; DcNAA; EarABI, SUP; HarEnUS; NatCAB 6; NewYHSD; OxCChiL; TwCBDA; WhAm HS*

Anderson, Bill
"Whispering Bill"; "The Pat Boone of Country Music"
American. Singer, Songwriter
Top country music star of 1960s; wrote "Walk Out Backward," 1962; "Strangers," 1965.
b. Nov 1, 1937 in Columbia, South Carolina
Source: *BgBkCoM; BioIn 9, 11, 14, 16, 20; CounME 74, 74A; EncFCWM 69, 83; HarEnCM 87; IlBBlP; IlEncCM; LegTOT; PenEncP; PseudN 82; WhoAm 80; WhoRock 81*

Anderson, Bonnie Marie
American. Broadcast Journalist
Correspondent, NBC News, 1981—.
b. Oct 22, 1955 in Havana, Cuba
Source: *InWom SUP; WhoTelC*

Anderson, C(larence) W(illiam)
American. Children's Author
Wrote, illustrated *Billy and Blaze* series, 1936-70.
b. Apr 12, 1891 in Wahoo, Nebraska
d. Mar 26, 1971 in Boston, Massachusetts
Source: *ArtsAmW 1; AuBYP 2, 3; BioIn 1, 2, 5, 7, 8, 9, 11; BkP; ConAu 29R, 73; IlBEAAW; IlsCB 1744, 1946, 1957; JBA 51; LinLib L; PseudN 82; SmATA 11; Str&VC; ThrBJA; TwCChW 83, 89, 95; WhAmArt 85*

Anderson, Carl David
American. Scientist
Discovered positron, 1932, first meson, 1937; won Nobel Prize in physics, 1936.
b. Sep 3, 1905 in New York, New York
d. Jan 11, 1991 in San Marino, California
Source: *AmMWSc 76P, 79, 82, 86, 89, 92; AsBiEn; BiESc; BioIn 2, 3, 12, 14, 15, 17, 18, 20; BlueB 76; CamDcSc; CurBio 91N; FacFETw; InSci; IntWW 74, 75, 76, 77, 78, 79, 80, 81, 82, 83, 89, 91N; LarDcSc; LinLib S; McGEWB; NewYTBS 91; NobelP; NotTwCS; OxCAmH; WebAB 74, 79; WebBD 83; WhAm 10; WhDW; Who 74, 82, 83, 85, 88, 90, 92N; WhoAm 74, 76, 78, 80, 82, 84, 86, 88, 90; WhoNob, 90, 95; WhoWest 78, 80, 82, 87, 89; WhoWor 74, 82, 84, 87, 89, 91; WorAl; WorAlBi; WorScD*

Anderson, Carl Thomas
American. Cartoonist
Created cartoon, "Henry," 1932, which currently runs in 196 daily newspapers.
b. Feb 14, 1865 in Madison, Wisconsin
d. Nov 4, 1948 in Madison, Wisconsin
Source: *AmAu&B; BioIn 1; WhAm 2; WhE&EA; WhoAmA 89N, 91N, 93N; WorECom*

Anderson, Cat
[William Alonzo Anderson]
American. Composer, Musician
Jazz trumpeter, who recorded "Take the A Train" with Duke Ellington Orchestra, 1940s.
b. Sep 12, 1916 in Greenville, South Carolina
d. Apr 30, 1981 in Norwalk, California
Source: *AllMusG; ASCAP 66, 80; BiDAfM; BiDAmM; BiDJaz; BioIn 12, 13; CmpEPM; EncJzS; InB&W 80, 85; NewAmDM; NewGrDA 86; NewGrDJ 88, 94; NewYTBS 81; OxCPMus; PenEncP; WhoJazz 72*

Anderson, Clint(on Presba)
American. Statesman, Politician
Senator from NM, 1949-73.
b. Oct 23, 1895 in Centerville, South Dakota
d. Nov 11, 1975 in Albuquerque, New Mexico
Source: *BiDrAC; BiDrUSC 89; BiDrUSE 71, 89; BioIn 1, 5, 9, 10, 11; BlueB 76; CurBio 45, 76; DcAmB S9; EncAAH; IntWW 74, 75; St&PR 75; WhAm 6, 7; Who 74; WhoAm 74, 76; WhoAmP 73, 75; WhoGov 72; WhoSSW 73; WhoWor 74*

Anderson, Daryl
American. Actor
Played Animal in TV series "Lou Grant," 1977-82.
b. Jul 1, 1951 in Seattle, Washington
Source: *BioIn 12; VarWW 85; WhoAm 82, 84, 86, 88, 90; WhoEnt 92; WhoSSW 88*

Anderson, Dorothy Hansine
American. Physician
Developed research in cystic fibrosis, 1940s.
b. May 15, 1901 in Asheville, North Carolina
d. Mar 3, 1963 in New York, New York
Source: *NotAW MOD; WomFir*

Anderson, Eddie
American. Actor
Played Jack Benny's manservant Rochester on radio, films, TV.
b. Sep 18, 1905 in Oakland, California
d. Feb 28, 1977 in Los Angeles, California
Source: *BioIn 2, 10, 11, 12; BlksBF; DrBlPA, 90; EncAFC; FilmEn; FilmgC; ForYSC; HalFC 80, 84, 88; IntMPA 75, 76, 78, 79, 80, 81, 82; JoeFr; LegTOT; MotPP; MovMk; NatCAB 60; NegAl 76; ObitOF 79; OxCPMus; QDrFCA 92; RadStar; What 4; WhoCom; WhoHol A; WhoThe 81N; WhScrn 83*

Anderson, Elda Emma
American. Physicist
Leader in study of radiation protection.
b. Apr 5, 1899 in Green Lake, Wisconsin
d. Apr 17, 1961 in Oak Ridge, Tennessee
Source: *BioIn 12, 19; InWom SUP; NatCAB 50; NotAW MOD; WomFir*

Anderson, Elizabeth Garrett
English. Physician
First English woman doctor, 1870s; elected mayor of Aldeburgh, England, 1908; first female mayor in England.
b. 1836 in Aldeburgh, England
d. Dec 17, 1917 in Aldeburgh, England
Source: *Alli SUP; BiDBrF 1; BioIn 14, 15, 16; CelCen; ContDcW 89; GrBr;*

InSci; IntDcWB; InWom, SUP; MacDWB; NotWoLS; OxCMed 86; RadHan; VicBrit; WhDW; WomFir; WomSc

Anderson, Elizabeth Milbank
American. Philanthropist
Founded Milbank Memorial Fund, 1905, to help NY's needy.
b. Dec 20, 1850 in New York, New York
d. Feb 22, 1921 in New York, New York
Source: *AmBi; DcAmB; InWom SUP; NatCAB 23; NotAW*

Anderson, Eugenie M(oore)
American. Diplomat
First female US Ambassador; Ambassador to Denmark, 1949-53; to Bulgaria, 1962-65.
b. May 26, 1909 in Adair, Iowa
d. Mar 31, 1997 in Red Wing, Minnesota
Source: *AmPolW 80, 80C; AmWomM; BlueB 76; IntWW 74, 75, 76, 77, 78, 79, 80, 81, 82, 83, 89; InWom SUP; WhoAm 74, 76, 78, 80, 82; WhoAmP 73, 75, 77, 79, 81, 83, 85; WhoAmW 64, 66, 68, 70, 72, 74; WomFir*

Anderson, George Everett
American. Diplomat, Journalist
Newspaper editorials led to foreign service career, 1904-24; wrote on economic trade conditions.
b. Aug 20, 1869 in Bloomington, Illinois
d. Mar 17, 1940 in Washington, District of Columbia
Source: *BioIn 2; CurBio 40; NatCAB 34; WhAm 1*

Anderson, Gerry
English. Producer
Known for science fiction TV series "Space 1999," 1975.
b. 1929 in Hampstead, England
Source: *EncSF, 93; FanAl; HalFC 80, 84, 88; IntMPA 75, 76, 77, 78, 79, 80, 81, 82, 84, 86, 88, 92, 94, 96; IntWW 89, 91, 93*

Anderson, Gilbert M
[Max Aaronson]
American. Actor
Starred as first cowboy hero, Broncho Billy, in western serial, 1907-14; awarded special Oscar, 1957.
b. Mar 21, 1882 in Little Rock, Arkansas
d. Jan 20, 1971 in South Pasadena, California
Source: *Film 1; MotPP; NewYTBE 71; ObitOF 79; OxCFilm; PseudN 82; WhScrn 74, 77; WorEFlm*

Anderson, Gillian
American. Actor
Plays Dana Scully in TV's "The X-Files," 1993—.
b. Aug 9, 1968 in Chicago, Illinois
Source: *ConTFT 14; News 97-1*

Anderson, Glenn Chris
Canadian. Hockey Player
Right wing, Edmonton, 1980-91; Toronto, 1991—; won five Stanley Cups.
b. Oct 2, 1960 in Vancouver, British Columbia, Canada
Source: *HocReg 87*

Anderson, Harry
American. Actor, Magician, Writer
Played Judge Harry Stone on TV series "Night Court;" was in TV series "Dave's World," 1993-97.
b. Oct 14, 1952 in Newport, Rhode Island
Source: *BioIn 14, 16, 19; ConAu 152; ConTFT 6, 13; IntMPA 92, 94, 96; LegTOT; News 88-2; WhoEnt 92; WorAlBi*

Anderson, Herbert
American. Actor
Best known as the father in TV's "Dennis the Menace."
d. Jun 11, 1994 in Palm Springs, California
Source: *NewYTBS 94*

Anderson, Ian
[Jethro Tull]
Scottish. Musician, Singer
Flute-playing lead vocalist since 1968, known for outlandish stage costumes, antics.
b. Aug 10, 1947 in Dunfermline, Scotland
Source: *BiDAmM; BioIn 11, 14, 16, 19; BkPepl; LegTOT; WhoAm 78, 80, 82, 84; WhoRock 81; WhoRocM 82; WorAl; WorAlBi*

Anderson, Ivie
American. Singer
Jazz vocalist with Duke Ellington Band, 1931-42; hits include "I Got It Bad."
b. Jul 10, 1905 in Gilroy, California
d. Dec 28, 1949 in Los Angeles, California
Source: *AllMusG; AmPS B; IlEncJ; NewGrDJ 88; NotBlAW 2; ObitOF 79; OxCPMus; PenEncP; WhoJazz 72; WhScrn 77*

Anderson, Jack Northman
American. Journalist
Has written syndicated column, "Washington-Merry-Go-Round," since 1969; won Pulitzer, 1972.
b. Oct 19, 1922 in Long Beach, California
Source: *AuNews 1; BioIn 13; BioNews 74; ConAu 57; CurBio 72; EncTwCJ; WhoAm 86, 90, 97; WhoSSW 82; WhoUSWr 88; WhoWor 74; WhoWrEP 89; WrDr 76*

Anderson, Jack Zuinglius
American. Politician
Con., 1939-53; Eisenhower's administrative asst., 1956-61.
b. Mar 22, 1904 in Oakland, California
d. Feb 9, 1981 in Hollister, California
Source: *NewYTBS 81; WhoAmP 73, 75, 77, 79*

Anderson, John
American. Singer, Musician
Country hits include "Swingin'," 1983.
b. Dec 13, 1954 in Apopka, Florida
Source: *OnThGG; PenEncP; RkOn 85*

Anderson, John Bayard
American. Politician
Liberal Rep. con. from IL, 1960-80; Independent Party presidential candidate, 1980.
b. Feb 15, 1922 in Rockford, Illinois
Source: *AmPolLe; BiDrAC; BiDrUSC 89; BioIn 8, 9, 12, 13, 14, 20, 21; ConAu 33R; CurBio 79; IntWW 81, 82, 83, 89, 91, 93; PseudN 82; WhoAm 74, 76, 78, 80, 82, 84, 86, 88, 90, 92, 94, 95, 96, 97; WhoAmL 78, 79, 90, 96; WhoE 83; WhoGov 72, 75, 77; WhoMW 74, 76, 78, 80*

Anderson, John Murray
English. Director
Created, directed first all-color movie musical *The King of Jazz,* 1930.
b. Sep 20, 1886 in Saint John's, Newfoundland, Canada
d. Jan 30, 1954 in New York, New York
Source: *ASCAP 66, 80; BiDAmM; BiDD; BioIn 3, 5; CamGWoT; CmpEPM; EncMT; Ent; NotNAT A, B; ObitOF 79; OxCAmT 84; OxCCanT; OxCPMus; WhAm 3; WhThe*

Anderson, Jon
English. Singer, Musician
Drummer, vocalist who formed Yes, 1968; wrote most of group's lyrics; had three solo albums.
b. Oct 25, 1944 in Lancashire, England
Source: *DrAPF 85, 87; Dun&B 90; LegTOT; WhoRock 81*

Anderson, Judith, Dame
[Frances Margaret Anderson-Anderson]
Australian. Actor
First Australian-born actress invested as Dame Commander, 1960; known for role in film *Rebecca,* 1940; played in soap opera "Santa Barbara," 1984-87.
b. Feb 10, 1898 in Adelaide, Australia
d. Jan 3, 1992 in Santa Barbara, California
Source: *AnObit 1992; BiE&WWA; BioIn 2, 3, 4, 5, 6, 8, 9, 10, 14, 16, 17, 18, 19; BlueB 76; CamGWoT; CelR; CnThe; ContDcW 89; ConTFT 4, 10; CurBio 41, 61, 92N; EncWT; Ent; FamA&A; FarE&A 78, 79, 80, 81; FilmEn; FilmgC; ForYSC; GangFlm; HalFC 80, 84, 88; HolCA; IntDcF 1-3; IntDcWB; IntMPA 75, 76, 77, 78, 79, 80, 81, 82, 84, 86, 88, 92; IntWW 74, 75, 76, 77, 78, 79, 80, 81, 82, 83, 89, 91; InWom, SUP; LegTOT; MotPP; MovMk; News 92; NotNAT; NotWoAT; OxCAmT 84; OxCAusL; OxCFilm; OxCThe 67, 83; PseudN 82; Who 74, 82, 83, 85, 88, 90, 92; WhoAm 74, 76; WhoHol 92, A;*

WhoThe 72, 77, 81; WhoWor 74; WomFir; WorAl; WorAlBi

Anderson, June
American. Singer
Soprano specializing in bel canto roles; career includes performances with every major European and American opera company.
b. Dec 30, 1952 in Boston, Massachusetts
Source: *Baker 92; BioIn 15, 16; CurBio 91; IntWWM 90; MetOEnc; NewGrDO; OxDcOp; PenDiMP; WhoAm 90; WhoAmW 93*

Anderson, Ken(neth Allan)
American. Football Player
Quarterback, Cincinnati, 1971-87; holds several NFL records for passing; played in four Pro Bowls; NFL MVP, 1982.
b. Feb 15, 1949 in Batavia, Illinois
Source: *BiDAmSp FB; BioIn 10, 12, 13; FootReg 87; WhoAm 84, 86; WhoFtbl 74*

Anderson, Laurie
American. Violinist
Avant-garde, multimedia performance artist specializing in the electric violin; recorded works include *United States Live,* 1984; *Home of the Brave,* 1986.
b. 1947 in Wayne, Illinois
Source: *AmArt; Baker 78, 84, 92; BiDWomA; BioIn 13, 14, 15, 17, 21; ConAmC 82; ConArt 83; ConMus 1; ConTFT 8; CurBio 83; DcCAr 81; DcTwCCu 1; EncRk 88; EncRkSt; GrLiveH; IntWW 91, 93; IntWWM 90; InWom SUP; LegTOT; NewAmDM; NewGrDA 86; NewYTBS 83; NorAmWA; OxCWoWr 95; PrintW 85; RolSEnR 83; WhoAm 84, 86, 88, 90, 92, 94, 95, 96, 97; WhoAmA 86, 89, 91, 93; WhoE 86, 89, 91, 93; WhoHol 92; WorArt 1980*

Anderson, Leroy
American. Composer, Conductor
Compositions include "The Typewriter;''''Blue Tango;''''Forgotten Dreams.''
b. Jun 29, 1908 in Cambridge, Massachusetts
d. May 18, 1975 in Woodbury, Connecticut
Source: *AmPS; ASCAP 66, 80; Baker 78, 84, 92; BiDAmM; BiE&WWA; BioIn 3, 5, 6, 10; CmpEPM; ConAmC 76, 82; CurBio 75N; LegTOT; NewAmDM; NewGrDA 86; NewGrDM 80; NewOxM; NotNAT; ObitT 1971; OxCPMus; PenEncP; PopAmC, SUP, SUPN; WhAm 6; WhoAm 74; WhoE 74; WhoMus 72*

Anderson, Lindsay (Gordon)
English. Director, Critic
Co-founder, British documentary movement, Free Cinema, 1956; directed *This Sporting Life,* 1963.
b. Apr 17, 1923 in Bangalore, India
d. Aug 30, 1994 in Dordogne, France
Source: *BiDFilm, 81, 94; BioIn 7, 9, 10, 12, 14, 16, 20; BlueB 76; CamGWoT; ConAu 125, 128, 146; ConLC 20, 86; ConTFT 2, 6, 13; CurBio 75, 94N; DcFM; EncEurC; EncWT; Ent; FacFETw; FilmEn; FilmgC; HalFC 80, 84, 88; IlWWBF, A; IntDcF 1-2, 2-2; IntMPA 75, 76, 77, 78, 79, 80, 81, 82, 84, 86, 88, 92, 94; IntWW 74, 75, 76, 77, 78, 79, 80, 81, 82, 83, 89, 91, 93; LegTOT; MiSFD 9; MovMk; NewYTBE 73; NewYTBS 94; NotNAT; OxCFilm; OxCThe 83; WhAm 11; Who 74, 82, 83, 85, 88, 90, 92, 94; WhoEnt 92; WhoHol 92; WhoThe 72, 77, 81; WhoWor 74, 82, 84, 87, 89, 91, 93; WorEFlm; WorFDir 2*

Anderson, Loni
American. Actor
Played Jennifer on TV series "WKRP in Cincinnati,'' 1978-80.
b. Aug 5, 1946 in Saint Paul, Minnesota
Source: *BioIn 12, 13, 15, 16; CelR 90; ConTFT 9; HalFC 88; IntMPA 88, 92, 94, 96; VarWW 85; WhoAm 82; WhoEnt 92; WorAlBi*

Anderson, Lynn
American. Singer
Country hit "Rose Garden,'' rose to top of country, pop charts, 1970; won Grammy, 1970.
b. Sep 26, 1947 in Grand Forks, North Dakota
Source: *BgBkCoM; BioIn 13, 14; CounME 74, 74A; EncFCWM 83; HarEnCM 87; IlEncCM; InWom SUP; LegTOT; PenEncP; RkOn 78; WhoAm 74, 78, 82, 84, 86, 88, 90, 92, 94, 95, 96, 97; WhoAmW 81, 83; WhoEnt 92; WhoRock 81*

Anderson, Margaret (Carolyn)
American. Editor
Founder, literary magazine *The Little Review,* which published avant-garde writers, 1914-29.
b. Nov 24, 1886 in Indianapolis, Indiana
d. Oct 18, 1973 in Le Cannet, France
Source: *AmAu&B; BioIn 12, 13; ConAu 45; DcAmB S9; DcLB 4, 91; FemiCLE; GayLesB; IndAu 1917; NotAW MOD; ObitOF 79; REnAL; WebAB 74, 79*

Anderson, Marian
American. Singer
Contralto; first black soloist with NY Met., 1955; received Presidential Medal of Freedom, 1963; first black singer to perform at White House.
b. Feb 27, 1897 in South Philadelphia, Pennsylvania
d. Apr 8, 1993 in Portland, Oregon
Source: *AfrAmBi 2; AnObit 1993; Baker 84; BiDAmM; BioAmW; BioIn 13, 14, 15, 16, 18, 19, 20, 21; BlkOpe; BlkWrNE A; ConBlB 2; ConMus 8; ContDcW 89; CurBio 93N; DcAfAmP; DcTwCCu 1, 5; DrBlPA 90; EncAB-H 1974; FacFETw; GrLiveH; HerW, 84; InB&W 85; IntWW 91; IntWWM 90; InWom SUP; MetOEnc; MusMk; NegAl 89; NewAmDM; NewGrDA 86; NewGrDM 80; NewYTBS 93; NotBlAW 1; OxCPMus; PenDiMP; RComAH; REn; SelBAAf; WebAB 74; Who 85, 92; WhoAm 84, 90; WhoAmW 91; WhoBlA 85, 92; WhoMus 72; WorAlBi*

Anderson, Mary
American. Labor Union Official
Director, Women's Trade Union League, 1920-44.
b. Aug 27, 1872 in Lidkoping, Sweden
d. Jan 29, 1964 in Washington, District of Columbia
Source: *AmWomM; BiDAmL; BiDAmLL; BiDSocW; BioIn 1, 2, 6, 7, 12, 17, 21; ContDcW 89; DcAmB S7; EncSF 93; IntDcWB; InWom, SUP; NotAW MOD; ObitOF 79; ScF&FL 92; WhAm 4; WhAmP; WomFir*

Anderson, Mary Antoinette
"Our Mary''
American. Actor
Appeared on stage, 1875-89; wrote *A Few Memories,* 1896.
b. Jul 28, 1859 in Sacramento, California
d. May 29, 1940 in Broadway, England
Source: *BbD; BiD&SB; DcAmAu; DcAmB S2; FamA&A; Film 1, 2; InWom; MacDWB; NotAW; OxCThe 67; PseudN 82; WhAm 4, HSA; WhThe*

Anderson, Max(ie Leroy)
American. Balloonist
Co-pilot of first balloon, *Double Eagle II,* to cross Atlantic, 1978.
b. Sep 10, 1934? in Sayre, Oklahoma
d. Jun 27, 1983 in Bad Brueckenau, Germany (West)
Source: *BioIn 11, 13; ConAu 115; NewYTBS 80, 83; WhoWest 84*

Anderson, Maxwell
American. Dramatist
Plays include *Winterset,* 1935; *Key Largo,* 1939; Pulitzer-winning *Both Your Houses,* 1933.
b. Dec 15, 1888 in Atlantic, Pennsylvania
d. Feb 28, 1959 in Stamford, Connecticut
Source: *AmAu&B; ASCAP 66, 80; Benet 87, 96; BenetAL 91; BiDAmM; BioIn 1, 2, 3, 4, 5, 6, 7, 8, 9, 10, 11, 12, 13, 14, 16, 19, 20; CamGEL; CamGLE; CamGWoT; CamHAL; CasWL; CmpEPM; CnDAL; CnMD; CnThe; ConAmA; ConAmL; ConAu 105, 152; CroCD; CrtSuDr; CurBio 42, 53, 59; CyWA 58, 89; DcAmB S6; DcArts; DcLB 7; DcLEL; EncAB-H 1974, 1996; EncMT; EncWL; EncWT; Ent; EvLB; FacFETw; FilmEn; FilmgC; GangFlm; GrWrEL DR; HalFC 80, 84, 88; IntDcT 2; LegTOT; LinLib L, S; LngCTC; McGEWB; McGEWD 72, 84; ModAL; ModWD; NatCAB 60; NewCBMT; NewGrDA 86; NotNAT A, B; ObitOF 79; ObitT 1951; OxCAmL 65, 83, 95; OxCAmT 84; OxCPMus; OxCThe 67, 83; PenC AM; PlP&P; RAdv 14, 13-2; REn; REnAL; REnWD; RfGAmL 87, 94; RGTwCWr; TwCA, SUP; TwCLC 2; TwCWr; WebAB 74, 79; WebE&AL;*

WhAm 3; WhDW; WhJnl; WhThe; WorAl; WorAlBi; WorEFlm

Anderson, Melissa Sue
American. Actor
Played Mary Ingalls on TV series, "Little House on the Prairie," 1973-81.
b. Sep 26, 1962 in Berkeley, California
Source: *BioIn 10, 11, 12; ConTFT 2, 10; IntMPA 82, 84, 86, 88, 92, 94, 96; LegTOT; VarWW 85; WhoHol 92*

Anderson, Michael
English. Director
Films include *Around the World in 80 Days,* 1956; *Logan's Run,* 1976.
b. Jan 30, 1920 in London, England
Source: *BiDFilm, 78, 79, 80, 81, 82, 84, 86, 88, 92, 94, 96; IntWW 89, 91, 93; LegTOT; MiSFD 9; MovMk; WhoAm 82; WhoHrs 80; WorEFlm*

Anderson, Michael, Jr.
English. Actor
Starred in TV series "The Monroes," 1966-67.
b. Aug 6, 1943 in London, England
Source: *ConTFT 6; FilmgC; ForYSC; HalFC 80, 84, 88; IntMPA 75, 76, 77, 78, 79, 80, 81, 82, 84, 86, 88, 92, 94, 96; VarWW 85; WhoHol 92, A*

Anderson, O(ttis) J(erome)
American. Football Player
Running back, 1976-86, St. Louis Cardinals; NFL player of year, 1979; MVP, 1991 Super Bowl; with NY Giants since 1986.
b. Jan 19, 1957 in West Palm Beach, Florida
Source: *BiDAmSp FB; FootReg 87; WhoBlA 92*

Anderson, Owanah
American. Political Activist
Founded the Ohoyo Resource Center, 1979, assisting Native American women in achieving educational and employment goals.
Source: *BioIn 21; NotNaAm*

Anderson, Peggy
American. Author
Wrote *Nurse,* 1978, adapted into TV series starring Michael Learned.
b. 1938
Source: *ArtclWW 2; BioIn 12; ConAu 93; NewYTBS 79; WrDr 76, 80, 82, 84, 86, 88, 90, 92, 94, 96*

Anderson, Philip Warren
American. Physicist
Researched quantum theory, physics of solids, magnetism; shared Nobel Prize, 1977.
b. Dec 13, 1923 in Indianapolis, Indiana
Source: *AmMWSc 73P, 76P, 79, 86, 89, 92, 95; BiESc; BioIn 10, 11, 14, 15, 20; BlueB 76; CamDcSc; FacFETw; IndAu 1967; IntWW 74, 91; LarDcSc; LElec; McGMS 80; NobelP; NotTwCS; Who 74, 82, 83, 85, 88, 90, 92, 94; WhoAm 78, 80, 82, 84, 86, 88, 90, 92, 94; WhoE 74, 79, 81, 83, 85, 86, 89, 91, 93, 95, 97; WhoFI 92; WhoFrS 84; WhoNob, 90, 95; WhoScEn 94; WhoTech 84; WhoWor 74, 76, 78, 80, 82, 84, 87, 89, 91, 93, 95; WorAl; WorAlBi*

Anderson, Ray
American.
Jazz, funk, and jazz rock fusion trombonist; leads funk band the Slickaphonics with Mark Helias; has recorded with major jazz performers.
b. 1952 in Chicago, Illinois
Source: *AllMusG; BioIn 13, 16; ConMus 7; NewGrDJ 88, 94*

Anderson, Rich
[The Tubes]
American. Musician
Bassist with The Tubes since late 1960s.
b. Aug 1, 1947 in Saint Paul, Minnesota

Anderson, Richard Dean
American. Actor
Played title role in TV action-adventure series "MacGyver," 1986-92.
b. Jan 23, 1950 in Minneapolis, Minnesota
Source: *BioIn 12, 14, 15; CelR 90; ConTFT 8, 15; HolBB; IntMPA 92, 94, 96; LegTOT; WhoAm 94, 95, 96, 97; WhoHol 92; WorAlBi*

Anderson, Richard Norman
American. Actor
Played Oscar Goldman on TV series "Six Million Dollar Man," 1972-77; "Bionic Woman," 1974-77.
b. Aug 8, 1926 in Long Branch, New Jersey
Source: *BiE&WWA; FilmgC; IntMPA 82; MovMk; NotNAT; WhoAm 78, 80, 82, 84, 86, 88, 90, 92, 94, 95, 96, 97; WhoEnt 92; WhoWest 92, 94*

Anderson, Robert
American. Military Leader
General who surrendered Ft. Sumter to Confederates, Apr 13, 1861.
b. Jun 14, 1805 in Louisville, Kentucky
d. Oct 27, 1871 in Nice, France
Source: *Alli SUP; AmBi; ApCAB; BioIn 7; CivWDc; DcAmB; DcNAA; Drake; EncSoH; GenMudB; HarEnMi; HarEnUS; LinLib L, S; NatCAB 4; TwCBDA; WebAMB; WhAm HS; WhCiWar*

Anderson, Robert Orville
American. Business Executive
Pres., Honda Oil & Gas, 1941-63; chief exec., Atlantic Richfield.
b. Apr 13, 1917 in Chicago, Illinois
Source: *BioIn 6, 7, 8, 10, 11, 12, 13, 14, 15, 16; BlueB 76; Dun&B 90; IntWW 74, 75, 76, 77, 78, 79, 80, 81, 82, 83, 89, 91, 93; IntYB 78, 79, 80, 81, 82; NewYTBS 76; St&PR 75, 91; WhoAm 74, 76, 78, 80, 82, 84, 86, 88, 90, 92, 94, 95, 96, 97; WhoAmP 73, 75, 77, 79, 81, 83, 85, 87, 89, 91, 93, 95; WhoFI 74, 75, 77, 79, 81, 83, 85, 92; WhoGov 72, 75; WhoWest 76, 78, 80, 82, 84, 87, 89, 92, 94, 96; WhoWor 82, 84, 87; WorAl*

Anderson, Robert Woodruff
American. Dramatist, Screenwriter
Award-winning plays include *Tea and Sympathy,* 1945.
b. Apr 28, 1917 in New York, New York
Source: *AmAu&B; AuNews 1; Benet 87; BenetAL 91; BiE&WWA; CamGWoT; CnMD; ConAu 21R; IntAu&W 91; Who 74, 90; WhoAm 82, 84, 90, 97; WhoEnt 92; WhoThe 77; WhoWor 74; WorAu 1950; WrDr 76*

Anderson, Roy A(rnold)
American. Business Executive
Chm., CEO, Lockheed Corp., 1977-85; chm. of exec. board, 1985-88; chm. emeritus, Lockheed Corp. since 1989—.
b. Dec 15, 1920 in Ripon, California
Source: *BioIn 11, 13; CurBio 83; Dun&B 79, 90; IntWW 77, 78, 79, 80, 81, 82, 83, 89, 91, 93; St&PR 84, 87, 91, 93; Who 82, 83, 85, 88, 90, 92, 94; WhoAm 74, 76, 78, 80, 82, 84, 86, 88, 90; WhoFI 81, 83, 85; WhoWest 80, 82, 84, 87; WhoWor 82, 84*

Anderson, Sherwood
"America's Most Distinctive Novelist"
American. Author, Poet
Major work *Winesburg, Ohio,* 1919, short stories of small town life.
b. Sep 13, 1876 in Camden, Connecticut
d. Mar 8, 1941 in Colon, Panama
Source: *AmAu&B; AmWr; ApCAB X; AtlBL; Benet 87, 96; BenetAL 91; BioIn 1, 2, 3, 4, 5, 6, 7, 8, 9, 10, 11, 12, 13, 15, 16, 17, 19; CamGLE; CamHAL; CasWL; Chambr 3; CnDAL; CnMWL; ConAmA; ConAmL; ConAu 104, 121; CyWA 58; DcAmB S3; DcArts; DcLB 4, 9, 86, DS1; DcLEL; DcNAA; EncAB-A 14; EncWL, 2, 3; EvLB; FacFETw; GrWrEL N; JrnUS; LegTOT; LinLib L, S; LngCTC; MagSAmL; MajTwCW; MakMC; McGEWB; ModAL, S1; NotNAT B; Novels; OhA&B; OxCAmL 65, 83, 95; OxCEng 67, 85, 95; PenC AM; PeoHis; RAdv 1, 14, 13-1; REn; REnAL; RfGAmL 87; RGTwCWr; ShSCr 1; ShSWr; Tw; TwCA, SUP; TwCLC 1, 10, 24; TwCWr; WebAB 74, 79; WebE&AL; WhAm 1; WhDW; WhJnl; WhLit; WhNAA; WhoTwCL; WorAl; WorAlBi; WorLitC*

Anderson, Sparky
[George Lee Anderson]
American. Baseball Manager
Manager, Cincinnati Reds 1970-78; Detroit Tigers, 1979-95. Only manager to win the World Series in both leagues.
b. Feb 22, 1934 in Bridgewater, South Dakota

Source: *Ballpl 90; BaseReg 87; BiDAmSp BB; BioIn 11, 12, 13, 14, 15, 16; ConAu 111, X; CurBio 77; LegTOT; NewYTBS 89, 95; WhoAm 74, 76, 78, 80, 82, 84, 86, 88, 90, 92, 94, 95, 96, 97; WhoMW 82, 84, 86, 88, 90, 92, 93; WhoProB 73; WhoSpor*

Anderson, Terry A
American. Journalist, Hostage
Chief Middle East correspondent for AP 1983-85; longest-held American hostage in Lebanon, 1985-1991.
b. Oct 27, 1947

Anderson, Vernon Ellsworth
American. Author, Educator
Wrote about education: *Instructors Manual: Principles and Practices of Secondary Education,* 1951.
b. Jun 15, 1908 in Atwater, Minnesota
Source: *ConAu 1NR, 1R, 5NR; IntAu&W 77, 82, 91; LEduc 74; WhoAm 74, 76, 78, 80; WrDr 76, 80, 92*

Anderson, W(illiam) French
American. Biologist
Led a team of scientists that carried out the first gene-therapy experiment on a human, 1990.
b. Dec 31, 1936 in Tulsa, Oklahoma
Source: *CurBio 94*

Anderson, Warner
American. Actor
Noted character performer who appeared in *The Caine Mutiny,* 1954; TV ser ies "The Lineup," 1954-60.
b. Mar 10, 1911 in New York, New York
d. Aug 26, 1976 in Santa Monica, California
Source: *BioIn 3; MotPP; MovMk; WhoHol A; WhoThe 81; WhScrn 83*

Anderson, Wendell Richard
American. Politician
Governor of MN, 1971-76; senator, 1976-79.
b. Feb 1, 1933 in Saint Paul, Minnesota
Source: *AlmAP 78; BiDrGov 1789; BiDrUSC 89; BioIn 10, 11; BioNews 74; BlueB 76; CngDr 77; IntWW 74, 75, 76, 77, 78, 79, 80, 81, 82, 83, 89, 91, 93; IntYB 78, 79, 80, 81, 82; NewYTBS 76; WhoAm 74, 76, 78; WhoAmP 73, 75, 77, 79, 91; WhoGov 72, 75, 77; WhoMW 74, 76, 78; WhoWor 78*

Anderson, William
"Bloody Bill"
American. Murderer
Confederate officer; raided MO-KS border towns during Civil War; killed unarmed men, boys.
d. Oct 1864 in Ray County, Missouri
Source: *Alli, SUP; BiDBrA; BiDLA SUP; BlkAWP; ChhPo S1; ClaDrA; DcAmMeB; DcNaB; DcVicP 2; DcWomA; DrInf; Dun&B 88; EncAR; PoIre; St&PR 96, 97; WhoAm 84, 86; WhoE 74; WhoScEu 91-1*

Anderson, William Robert
American. Naval Officer
Commanded first atomic submarine, the *Nautilus,* 1957-59.
b. Jun 17, 1921 in Bakerville, Tennessee
Source: *BiDrAC; BiDrUSC 89; BioIn 5, 6, 9; BlueB 76; ConAu 5NR, 5R, 7NR; WhoAm 74, 76, 78, 80, 82, 84, 86, 88, 90, 92, 94, 95, 96, 97; WhoAmP 73, 75, 77, 79; WhoGov 72, 75; WhoSSW 73*

Anderson, Willie
Scottish. Golfer
Touring pro, early 1900s; won US Open four times; only player to win it three years in a row; charter member, Hall of Fame, 1940.
b. May 1880 in North Berwick, Scotland
d. 1910
Source: *AmDec 1900; BiDAmSp OS; WhoGolf; WhoSpor*

Anderssen, Adolf
[Karl Ernst Adolf Anderssen]
Polish. Chess Player
Regarded as world's leading player; won international tournaments, 1851, 1862, 1870.
b. Aug 6, 1818 in Breslau, Poland
d. Mar 9, 1878 in Breslau, Poland
Source: *BioIn 5, 10, 17; GolEC; OxCChes 84*

Andersson, Benny
Swedish. Singer, Musician
Part of most successful Swedish singing group, formed 1973; hits include "Fernando," 1976.
b. Dec 16, 1946 in Stockholm, Sweden

Andersson, Bibi
[Birgitta Andersson]
Swedish. Actor
Discovered by Ingmar Bergman, starred in many of his films: *The Seventh Seal,* 19 56; *Brink of Life,* 1958.
b. Nov 11, 1935 in Stockholm, Sweden
Source: *BiDFilm, 81, 94; BioIn 11, 17; CelR; ConTFT 7; CurBio 78; EncEurC; EncWT; Ent; FilmEn; FilmgC; HalFC 80, 84, 88; IntDcF 1-3, 2-3; IntMPA 79, 80, 81, 82, 84, 86, 88, 92, 94, 96; IntWW 74, 75, 76, 77, 78, 79, 80, 81, 82, 83, 89, 91, 93; ItaFilm; LegTOT; MotPP; MovMk; NewYTBS 77; OxCFilm; WhoAmW 74; WhoHol 92, A; WhoWor 74, 82, 84, 87, 91, 93, 95, 96; WorAl; WorAlBi; WorEFlm*

Andersson, Harriet
Swedish. Actor
Starred in Ingmar Bergman's *Monika,* 1952, written especially for her.
b. Jan 14, 1932 in Stockholm, Sweden
Source: *BiDFilm, 81, 94; BioIn 11, 17; ContDcW 89; ConTFT 8; EncEurC; FilmEn; FilmgC; HalFC 80, 84, 88; IntDcF 1-3, 2-3; IntDcWB; IntWW 74, 75, 76, 77, 78, 79, 80, 81, 82, 83, 89, 91, 93; MacDWB; OxCFilm; WhoHol 92, A; WhoWor 74, 82, 84; WorEFlm*

Andersson, Johan Gunnar
Swedish. Geologist, Archaeologist
Helped to discover the remains of ancient civilizations in China; predected the discovery of fossils of homonid Sinanthropus (Peking Man), 1921.
b. Jul 3, 1874 in Knista, Sweden
d. Oct 29, 1960 in Stockholm, Sweden
Source: *BioIn 5*

Andes, Keith
[John Charles Andes]
American. Actor
Co-star of TV series "Glynis," 1963-65.
b. Jul 12, 1920 in Ocean City, New Jersey
Source: *BiE&WWA; FilmEn; FilmgC; ForYSC; HalFC 80, 84, 88; IntMPA 75, 77, 78, 79, 80, 81, 82, 84, 86, 88, 92, 94, 96; MotPP; NotNAT; PseudN 82; WhoHol 92, A*

Andrae, Johann Valentin
German. Clergy
Lutheran pastor, known as originator of Rosicrucian legend.
b. Aug 7, 1586 in Herrenburg, Germany
d. Jan 27, 1654 in Stuttgart, Germany
Source: *BiDAmCu*

Andrassy, Gyula, Count
[Count Julius Andrassy]
Hungarian. Statesman
Prime minister, 1871, of dual monarchy between Germany, Hungary.
b. Mar 3, 1823 in Kassa, Austria-Hungary
d. Feb 18, 1890 in Volosca, Hungary
Source: *BioIn 8; CelCen; DcBiPP; McGEWB*

Andre, Carl
American. Sculptor
Influential minimalist whose work is simple, serenely ordered, quiet.
b. Sep 16, 1935 in Quincy, Massachusetts
Source: *AmArt; BioIn 9, 10, 11, 12, 13, 14, 15, 16, 20; BriEAA; ConArt 77, 83, 89, 96; CurBio 86; DcAmArt; DcArts; DcCAA 71, 77, 88, 94; DcCAr 81; IntWW 89, 91, 93; MurCaTw; OxCTwCA; OxDcArt; WhoAm 74, 76, 78, 80, 82, 84, 86, 88, 90, 92, 94, 95, 96, 97; WhoAmA 73, 76, 78, 80, 82, 84, 86, 89, 91, 93; WhoE 74; WhoWor 84, 87, 89, 91, 93, 95, 96, 97; WorArt 1950*

Andre, John
English. Spy
Benedict Arnold's liaison with the British who was caught, executed as spy.
b. May 2, 1750 in London, England
d. Oct 2, 1780 in Tappan, New York
Source: *Alli; AmBi; AmRev; ApCAB; DcBiPP; Drake; EncAI&E; LinLib S; NatCAB 1; OxCAmH; OxCAmL 65; REn; TwCBDA; WhAm HS; WorAl; WorAlBi*

Andreas, Dwayne Orville
American. Business Executive
CEO, 1970—, chm., 1972—, Archer Daniels Midland (ADM) commodities co.
b. Mar 4, 1918 in Worthington, Minnesota
Source: *BioIn 15, 16; CurBio 92; Dun&B 90; St&PR 91; WhoAm 74, 76, 78, 82, 84, 86, 88, 90, 92, 94, 95, 96, 97; WhoFI 87, 89, 92, 94, 96; WhoMW 88, 90, 92, 93, 96; WhoWor 74, 78, 89, 91, 93, 95, 96, 97*

Andreas-Salome, Lou
[Louise Lelia Andreas]
German. Author
Books were influenced by her interest in psychoanalysis: *Rodninka,* 1923.
b. 1861 in Saint Petersburg, Russia
d. 1937 in Gottingen, Germany
Source: *BiDSovU; BioIn 5, 6, 7, 8, 9, 10, 16, 17, 18, 19; BlmGWL; ClDMEL 80; ContDcW 89; DcLB 66; EncCoWW; IntDcWB; InWom, SUP; OxCGer 76, 86; TwCLC 56; WhE&EA; WhoLA; WomWrGe*

Andree, Salomon August
Swedish. Explorer
First to explore Arctic in air by balloon, 1896, 1897; remains, diaries found, 1930.
b. Oct 18, 1854 in Grenna, Sweden
d. Oct 2, 1897, White Island
Source: *BioIn 1, 3, 8, 11, 13; InSci; McGEWB; NewCol 75; WhWE*

Andreessen, Mark
American. Computer Executive
Co-founded Netscape Communications, Inc., 1994.
b. 1971 in New Lisbon, Wisconsin

Andreotti, Giulio
Italian. Political Leader
Prime minister, 1972-73, 1976-79 (after Aldo Moro), 1989-92.
b. Jan 14, 1919 in Rome, Italy
Source: *BioIn 9, 10, 11, 12, 14; CurBio 77; IntAu&W 89; IntWW 74, 75, 76, 77, 78, 79, 80, 81, 82, 83, 89, 91, 93; IntYB 78, 79, 80, 81, 82; NewYTBE 71, 72; NewYTBS 76, 77; PolLCWE; Who 92, 94; WhoWor 74, 76, 78, 80, 82, 84, 87, 89, 91, 93, 95, 96, 97; WorAl; WorAlBi*

Andresen, Ivar
Norwegian. Opera Singer
Leading Wagnerian bass soloist, 1920s-30s.
b. Jul 17, 1896 in Oslo, Norway
d. Nov 26, 1940 in Stockholm, Sweden
Source: *Baker 84, 92; CmOp; NewEOp 71; NewGrDM 80*

Andress, Ursula
Swiss. Actor
First wife of John Derek; movies include *Dr. No,* 1962.
b. Mar 19, 1936 in Bern, Switzerland
Source: *BiDFilm, 81; BioIn 6, 11, 16; CelR; ConTFT 3; DcArts; EncEurC; FilmAG WE; FilmEn; FilmgC; ForYSC; HalFC 80, 84, 88; IntMPA 75, 76, 77, 78, 79, 80, 81, 82, 84, 86, 88, 92, 94, 96; InWom SUP; ItaFilm; LegTOT; MotPP; MovMk; OxCFilm; VarWW 85; WhoAm 76; WhoHol 92, A; WhoHrs 80; WorAl; WorAlBi; WorEFlm*

Andretti, Mario Gabriel
American. Auto Racer
One of world's wealthiest sports figures; won Indianapolis 500, 1968; World Grand Prix champion, 1978.
b. Feb 28, 1940 in Montona Trieste, Italy
Source: *BiDAmSp OS; BioIn 13, 14, 15, 16; CelR 90; CurBio 68; FacFETw; IntWW 91; WebAB 74, 79; WhoAm 74, 76, 78, 80, 82, 84, 86, 90; WhoWor 82, 87, 91; WorAl*

Andrew
[Andrew Albert Christian Edward; Baron Killyle; Duke of York; Earl of Inverness]
''Randy Andy''
English. Prince
Third child of Queen Elizabeth II and Prince Philip; fought in Falkland Islands War, 1982; currently fourth in line to British throne.
b. Feb 19, 1960 in London, England
Source: *BioIn 5, 6, 7, 10, 11, 12, 13, 14, 15, 16, 17, 18, 19, 20; CurBio 87; LegTOT; Who 82R, 83R, 85, 85R; WhoWor 95, 96, 97*

Andrew, Prince of Russia
[Andrew Romanov]
Russian. Prince
Was oldest surviving relative of Czar Nicholas II.
b. 1897 in Saint Petersburg, Russia
d. May 8, 1981 in Teynham, England
Source: *BioIn 12; NewYTBS 81*

Andrew, Saint
Biblical Figure
One of Twelve Disciples; patron saint of Russia; feast day Nov 30.
d. Nov 30, 70? in Patrae, Greece
Source: *Alli, SUP; Benet 87, 96; BioIn 1, 2, 3, 4, 5, 6, 7, 8, 9, 10, 11, 12, 17; CmScLit; DcBiPP; DcCathB; EncEarC; EngPo; InB&W 80; McGDA; OxDcByz; PoIre; REn*

Andrew, John Albion
American. Politician
Organized 54th MA Regiment, 1863, first black unit during Civil War.
b. May 31, 1818 in Windham, Maine
d. Oct 30, 1867 in Boston, Massachusetts
Source: *Alli SUP; AmBi; ApCAB; BiAUS; BiDrGov 1789; BioIn 2, 6; CivWDc; CyAG; DcAmB; DcNAA; Drake; HarEnUS; McGEWB; NatCAB 1; WebAB 74, 79; WhAm HS; WhAmP; WhCiWar*

Andrews, Anthony Corin Gerald
English. Actor
Starred in TV movies: ''Ivanhoe,'' 1982; ''Sparkling Cyanide,'' 1983; also starred in British mini-series ''Brideshead Revisited,'' 1981.
b. Jan 12, 1948 in London, England
Source: *BioIn 13, 15; ConTFT 7; CurBio 91; HalFC 88; IntMPA 92; IntWW 91; NewYTBS 82; WhoAm 90; WhoEnt 92; WhoFI 87*

Andrews, Bert
American. Journalist
Won Pulitzer, 1947, for Washington reporting; wrote *Washington Witch Hunt,* 1948.
b. Jun 2, 1901 in Colorado Springs, Colorado
d. Aug 21, 1953 in Denver, Colorado
Source: *BioIn 1, 2, 3; CurBio 48, 53; DcAmB S5; ObitOF 79; WhAm 3*

Andrews, Charles McLean
American. Historian
Yale U. professor, 1910-31; won Pulitzer for writings about American history, 1935.
b. Feb 22, 1863 in Wethersfield, Connecticut
d. Sep 9, 1943 in New Haven, Connecticut
Source: *AmAu&B; BiDAmEd; BiD&SB; BioIn 2, 4, 8, 13, 15; ConAu 119; DcAmAu; DcAmB S3; DcNAA; HarEnUS; LinLib L, S; McGEWB; NatCAB 13; OxCAmH; OxCAmL 65; TwCA, SUP; WebAB 74, 79; WhAm 2; WhNAA*

Andrews, (Carver) Dana
American. Actor
Brother of Steve Forrest; starred in *The Ox-Bow Incident,* 1943, *Laura,* 1944.
b. Jan 1, 1909 in Collins, Mississippi
d. Dec 17, 1992 in Los Alamitos, California
Source: *AnObit 1992; BiDFilm, 81, 94; BiE&WWA; BioIn 5, 6, 11, 12, 14, 18, 19; CmMov; ConTFT 4, 11; CurBio 93N; FilmEn; FilmgC; GangFlm; HalFC 80, 84, 88; IntDcF 1-3, 2-3; IntMPA 82, 88, 92; ItaFilm; LegTOT; MotPP; MovMk; NewYTBS 92; OxCFilm; PseudN 82; WhoAm 74, 76, 78, 80, 82; WhoHol 92, A; WhoHrs 80; WorAl; WorAlBi; WorEFlm*

Andrews, Eamonn
Irish. TV Personality
Founded, chaired, Irish Television Authority; wrote, hosted *This is Your Life,* 1952.
b. Dec 19, 1922 in Dublin, Ireland
d. Nov 5, 1987 in London, England
Source: *AnObit 1987; BioIn 15, 17, 18; BlueB 76; ConAu 120, 124; ConTFT 2; DcIrB 88; DcNaB 1986; IntAu&W 82, 89; IntMPA 75, 76, 77, 78, 79, 80, 81, 82, 84, 86, 88; IntWW 74, 75, 76, 77, 78, 79, 80, 81, 82, 83; NewYTET; Who 74, 82, 83, 85, 88; WhoWor 74, 76, 78, 80; WrDr 80, 82, 84, 86, 88*

Andrews, Edward
American. Actor
Character actor on Broadway, in films: *Elmer Gantry,* 1960.
b. Oct 9, 1915 in Griffin, Georgia
d. Mar 8, 1985 in Santa Monica, California
Source: *BioIn 14; FilmEn; FilmgC; HalFC 80, 84; IntMPA 82, 84; MotPP; NewYTBS 85; NotNAT; WhoHol A*

Andrews, Frank M(axwell)
American. Military Leader
General who commanded US forces in Europe, succeeded Eisenhower, 1943.
b. Feb 3, 1884 in Nashville, Tennessee
d. May 3, 1943 in Reykjavik, Iceland
Source: *BiDWWGF; BioIn 1; CurBio 42, 43; DcAmB S3; DcAmMiB; InSci; NatCAB 32; WebAB 74, 79; WebAMB; WhAm 2; WorAl*

Andrews, Harry
English. Actor
Character actor; specialized in playing tough, military officers: *The Battle of Britain,* 1969.
b. Nov 10, 1911 in Tonbridge, England
d. Mar 6, 1989 in Salchurst, England
Source: *AnObit 1989; BioIn 13, 16; BlueB 76; CmMov; CnThe; ConTFT 2, 7; FilmAG WE; FilmEn; FilmgC; ForYSC; HalFC 80, 84, 88; IlWWBF; IntMPA 75, 76, 77, 78, 79, 80, 81, 82, 84, 86, 88; IntWW 82, 83, 89, 89N; ItaFilm; MotPP; MovMk; NewYTBS 89; Who 82, 83, 85, 88; WhoHol A; WhoThe 72, 77, 81*

Andrews, James Frederick
American. Editor, Author
Credited with discovering, launching comic strips "Doonesbury"; "Ziggy."
b. Oct 8, 1936 in Westfield, Massachusetts
d. Oct 19, 1980 in Kansas City, Missouri
Source: *AmCath 80; ConAu 107; EncTwCJ; WhAm 7; WhoAm 78, 80*

Andrews, Jane
American. Children's Author
Wrote *Ten Boys Who Lived on the Road from Long Ago to Now,* 1886.
b. Dec 1, 1833 in Newburyport, Massachusetts
d. Jul 15, 1887 in Newburyport, Massachusetts
Source: *Alli SUP; AmAu&B; AmWomWr; BenetAL 91; BiDAmEd; BiD&SB; CarSB; DcAmAu; DcNAA; InWom, SUP; NotAW; OxCAmL 65, 83, 95; OxCChiL; REnAL*

Andrews, Julie
[Mrs. Blake Edwards; Julia Elizabeth Wells]
English. Singer, Actor, Author
Won Oscar, 1964, for *Mary Poppins;* Oscar nominee, 1965, for *The Sound of Music*; writes children's books as Julie Edwards; appeared on Broadway in *Victor/Victoria.*
b. Oct 1, 1935 in Walton-on-Thames, England
Source: *AuBYP 3; Baker 92; BiDAmM; BiDFilm, 81, 94; BiE&WWA; BioIn 3, 4, 5, 6, 7, 8, 9, 10, 13, 14, 15, 16; BkPepl; BlueB 76; CelR, 90; CmMov; ConAu 37R; ConMus 4, 6; ContDcW 89; ConTFT 1, 7, 14; CurBio 94; DcArts; EncAFC; EncMT; FacFETw; FamA&A; FilmEn; FilmgC; HalFC 88; IntDcF 1-3, 2-3; IntMPA 77, 78, 79, 80, 81, 82, 84, 86, 88, 92, 94, 96; IntWW 74, 75, 76, 77, 78, 79, 80, 81, 82, 83, 89, 91, 93; InWom, SUP; ItaFilm; LegTOT; MotPP; MovMk; NewAmDM; NewGrDA 86; News 96, 96-1; NewYTBS 87; NotNAT, A; OxCAmT 84; OxCFilm; OxCPMus; PenEncP; PlP&P; PseudN 82; SmATA 7; Who 82, 83, 85, 88, 90, 92; WhoAm 74, 76, 78, 80, 82, 84, 86, 88, 90, 92, 94, 95, 96, 97; WhoAmW 64, 66, 68, 70, 72, 74, 83, 85, 87, 89, 91, 93, 95, 97; WhoEnt 92; WhoHol 92, A; WhoThe 72, 77A, 81; WhoWor 74, 78, 84, 87, 89, 91, 93, 95, 96, 97; WhThe; WomFir; WorAl; WorAlBi; WorEFlm; WrDr 76, 80, 82, 84, 86, 88, 90, 92*

Andrews, LaVerne
[Andrews Sisters]
American. Singer
With sisters, popular on radio, in WW II musical movies, 1940s: *Buck Privates,* 1941.
b. Jul 6, 1915 in Minneapolis, Minnesota
d. May 8, 1967 in Brentwood, California
Source: *BiDAmM; BioIn 7, 9; FilmEn; FilmgC; HalFC 84; InWom SUP; MotPP; ObitOF 79; OxCPMus; WhoHol B; WhScrn 74, 77, 83; WorAl; WorAlBi*

Andrews, Mark N
American. Politician
Popular Rep. con. 1963-87.
b. May 19, 1926 in Fargo, North Dakota
Source: *AlmAP 80; BiDrAC; BiDrUSC 89; CngDr 85; IntWW 91; WhoAm 86, 90; WhoAmP 85, 91; WhoMW 78; WhoWor 87*

Andrews, Mary Raymond Shipman
American. Author
Best known works include *Bob and the Guides,* 1906; *Florence Nightingale,* 1929.
b. 1860 in Mobile, Alabama
d. Aug 2, 1936
Source: *AmAu&B; AmWomPl; AmWomWr; ConAmL; InWom SUP; JBA 34; NotAW; REnAL; TwCA; WhAm 1; WhNAA*

Andrews, Maxene
[Andrews Sisters]
"Mackie"
American. Singer
With sisters, popular on radio, in WW II musical movies, 1940s: *Private Buckaroo,* 1942.
b. Jan 3, 1918 in Minneapolis, Minnesota
d. Oct 21, 1995 in Cape Cod, Massachusetts
Source: *BiDAmM; FilmgC; HalFC 84; InWom SUP; OxCPMus; WhoHol 92; WorAlBi*

Andrews, Michael Alford
English. Author
Wrote *The Flight of the Condor,* 1982.
b. Jun 14, 1939 in Bexhill, England
Source: *ConAu 116*

Andrews, Patti
[Andrews Sisters; Patricia Andrews]
American. Singer
With sisters, popular on radio, in WW II musical movies: *Follow the Boys,* 1944.
b. Feb 16, 1920 in Minneapolis, Minnesota
Source: *Baker 92; BioIn 9; FilmEn; ForYSC; HalFC 84; InWom SUP; OxCPMus; WhoHol 92, A; WorAlBi*

Andrews, Raymond
American. Author
First book *Appalachee Red,* 1978 was a critical success and won the first James Baldwin Prize for fiction.
b. Jun 6, 1934 in Morgan City, Georgia
d. Nov 26, 1991 in Athens, Georgia
Source: *AfrAmAl 6; BioIn 19; BlkWr 1, 2; ConAu 15NR, 42NR, 81, 136; ConBlB 4; DrAPF 80, 87, 91; IntAu&W 82; LiExTwC; NegAl 83, 89; SelBAAf; WhoBlA 80, 85, 88, 90, 92, 94N; WhoE 81, 83, 85; WhoUSWr 88; WhoWrEP 89, 92, 95*

Andrews, Roy Chapman
American. Zoologist, Explorer
Discovered fossil fields yielding unknown plant, animal life.
b. Jan 26, 1884 in Beloit, Wisconsin
d. Mar 11, 1960 in Carmel, California
Source: *AmAu&B; ApCAB X; AsBiEn; AuBYP 2, 3; BenetAL 91; BiESc; BioIn 1, 2, 3, 4, 5, 6, 7, 9, 11, 12, 14, 16, 17; CamDcSc; CurBio 41, 53, 60; DcAmB S6; EvLB; FacFETw; InSci; LarDcSc; LinLib L, S; McGEWB; MorMA; NatCAB 44; NewCol 75; ObitT 1951; REnAL; SmATA 19; TwCA, SUP; WebAB 74, 79; WhAm 3A; WhLit; WhNAA; WorAl; WorAlBi*

Andrews, Tige
[Tiger Androwaous]
American. Actor
Played Capt. Adam Greer in TV series "The Mod Squad," 1968-73.
b. Mar 19, 1920? in New York, New York
Source: *ConTFT 3; FilmgC; HalFC 88; PseudN 82; VarWW 85; WhoAm 80, 82, 84; WhoHol A*

Andrews, V(irginia) C(leo)
American. Author
Wrote *Flowers in the Attic,* 1979, filmed 1987; *Petals in the Wind,* 1980.
b. Jun 6, 1924? in Portsmouth, Virginia
d. Dec 19, 1986 in Virginia Beach, Virginia

Source: *ConAu 21NR, 97; NewYTBS 86*

Andrews, Wayne
[Montagu O'Reilly]
American. Author
Wrote historical biographies, architectural surveys: *Architecture of Michigan,* 1967.
b. Sep 5, 1913 in Kenilworth, Illinois
d. Aug 17, 1987 in Paris, France
Source: *AmAu&B; BioIn 15; ConAu 3NR, 9R, 123; DrAS 74H, 78H, 82H; IntAu&W 76; PseudN 82; WhAm 9; WhoAm 74, 76, 78, 80, 82, 84, 86*

Andrews Sisters
[LaVerne Andrews; Maxine Andrews; Patti Andrews]
American. Music Group
Harmony trio of sisters known for 1940s hits: "Boogie Woogie Bugle Boy from Company B."
Source: *AmPS A, B; CmpEPM; ConMus 9; FilmEn; FilmgC; ForYSC; GoodHs; HalFC 80, 84, 88; HolP 40; InWom SUP; MotPP; MovMk; NewAmDM; NewGrDA 86; ObitOF 79; OxCPMus; PenEncP; PlP&P A; RadStar; SaTiSS; What 3; Who 90; WorAl; WorAlBi*

Andreyev, Leonid Nikolayevich
[James Lynch]
"The Edgar Allan Poe of Russian Literature"
Russian. Author
Created macabre, pessimistic short stories: *The Red Laugh,* 1904.
b. Jun 18, 1871 in Orel, Russia
d. Sep 12, 1919 in Helsinki, Finland
Source: *Benet 87, 96; CasWL; ClDMEL 47, 80; CnMD; CnThe; ConAu 104; CyWA 58; DcRusL; Dis&D; EncWL; EncWT; EvEuW; IntDcT 2; LinLib S; LngCTC; McGEWD 72, 84; ModSL 1; NewCol 75; NotNAT B; PenC EUR; PlP&P; REn; REnWD; TwCA, SUP; TwCLC 2; TwCWr; WhDW; WhoHr&F*

Andric, Ivo
Yugoslav. Author
Wrote epic trilogy of Slavic Balkavis *Bridge on the Driva,* 1959; won Nobel Prize for literature, 1961.
b. Oct 10, 1892 in Travnik, Yugoslavia
d. Mar 13, 1975 in Belgrade, Yugoslavia
Source: *Au&Wr 71, 3; EuWr 11; EvEuW; FacFETw; GrFLW; IntAu&W 76, 77; IntWW 74; IntWWP 77; LegTOT; LiExTwC; LinLib L; MajTwCW; ModSL 2; NewYTBS 75; NobelP; Novels; ObitT 1971; PenC EUR; RAdv 14, 13-2; REn; RfGShF; RfGWoL 95; TwCWr; WhAm 6; Who 74; WhoNob, 90, 95; WhoTwCL; WhoWor 74; WorAl; WorAlBi; WorAu 1950*

Androcles
Roman. Slave
Noted for friendship with lion; subject of Shaw's play *Androcles and the Lion,* 1912.
b. fl. 1st cent.
Source: *Benet 96; BioIn 4, 5; DcBiPP; NewC; REn*

Andropov, Yuri Vladimirovich
Russian. Political Leader
General Secretary, Communist Party, after death of Brezhnev, 1982-84; head of KGB, 1967-82.
b. Jun 15, 1914 in Nagutskaia, Russia
d. Feb 9, 1984 in Kuntsevo, Union of Soviet Socialist Republics
Source: *AnObit 1984; BioIn 12, 13; ColdWar 2; CurBio 83, 84; IntWW 74, 75, 76, 82; NewYTBS 82; WhoSocC 78; WhoWor 74, 80*

Andros, Edmund, Sir
English. Colonial Figure
Autocratic governor, New England colonies, 1686-90; arrested by Bostonians; governor of VA, 1692-97.
b. Dec 6, 1637 in London, England
d. Feb 24, 1714 in London, England
Source: *Alli; AmBi; ApCAB; BenetAL 91; BiDrACR; BioIn 10; DcAmB; DcBiPP; DcNaB; Drake; EncAB-H 1974, 1996; EncCRAm; HarEnUS; HisDBrE; LinLib S; McGEWB; NatCAB 6; OxCAmH; OxCAmL 65, 83, 95; TwCBDA; WebAB 74, 79; WhAm HS; WhDW; WhNaAH*

Andrus, Cecil D(ale)
American. Business Executive, Government Official, Academic Administrator
Secretary of Interior under Carter, 1977-81; governor of Idaho, 1971-77, 1987-95.
b. Aug 25, 1931 in Hood River, Oregon
Source: *AlmAP 88, 92; BiDrGov 1789, 1983, 1988; BiDrUSE 89; BioIn 10, 11, 13; BlueB 76; CngDr 77, 79; CurBio 77; IntWW 74, 75, 76, 77, 78, 79, 80, 81, 82, 83, 89, 91, 93; WhoAm 74, 76, 78, 80, 82, 84, 86, 88, 90, 92, 94, 95, 96, 97; WhoAmP 73, 75, 77, 79, 81, 83, 85, 87, 89, 91, 93, 95; WhoE 77, 79, 81; WhoGov 72, 75, 77; WhoWest 74, 76, 78, 87, 89, 92, 94, 96; WhoWor 78, 80, 89, 91; WorAl*

Andrus, Ethel Percy
American. Educator
Founded National Retired Teachers Assn., 1947, American Assn., of Retired Persons, 1958.
b. Sep 21, 1884 in San Francisco, California
d. Jul 13, 1967 in Long Beach, California
Source: *BioIn 3, 8, 12; DcAmB S8; InWom SUP; NotAW MOD; WhoAmW 58, 61*

Andrzejewski, Jerzy
[George Andrzeyevski]
Polish. Author
Best known for novel *Ashes and Diamonds,* 1948.
b. Aug 19, 1909 in Warsaw, Poland
d. Apr 19, 1983 in Warsaw, Poland
Source: *AnObit 1983; BioIn 10, 13; CasWL; ClDMEL 80; ConAu 25R, 29NR, 109, X; CyWA 89; EncWL 2, 3; IntAu&W 76, 77; IntWW 74, 75, 76, 77, 78, 79, 80, 81, 82, 83; ModSL 2; Novels; PenC EUR; PolBiDi; PseudN 82; RfGWoL 95; TwCWr; WhoSocC 78; WhoTwCL; WhoWor 74, 76, 78, 80, 82; WorAu 1950*

Andujar, Joaquin
Dominican. Baseball Player
Pitcher, 1976-88, mostly with Houston.
b. Dec 21, 1952 in San Pedro de Macoris, Dominican Republic
Source: *Ballpl 90; BaseReg 86, 87; BioIn 13, 14, 15; WhoAfA 96; WhoBlA 80, 85, 90, 92, 94; WhoHisp 91, 92, 94*

Anello, John David
American. Conductor
Founded Florentine Opera Co., 1933, Milwaukee Pops Orchestra, 1936, Milwaukee Symphony, 1948; director, UN People to People Concerts, beginning in 1962.
b. 1909 in Milwaukee, Wisconsin
d. Mar 6, 1995 in Milwaukee, Wisconsin
Source: *WhoAm 74, 80; WhoAmM 83*

Anfinsen, Christian Boehmer
American. Chemist
Shared 1972 Nobel Prize in chemistry for research on enzyme ribonuclease.
b. Mar 26, 1916 in Monessen, Pennsylvania
d. May 14, 1995 in Randallstown, Maryland
Source: *AmMWSc 73P, 76P, 79, 82, 86, 89, 92, 95; BiESc; BioIn 9, 10, 15, 19, 20, 21; BlueB 76; CamDcSc; FacFETw; IntMed 80; IntWW 74, 75, 76, 77, 78, 79, 80, 81, 82, 83, 89, 91, 93; LarDcSc; McGMS 80; NobelP; NotTwCS; WebAB 74, 79; WhAm 11; Who 74, 82, 83, 85, 88, 90, 92, 94; WhoAm 74, 76, 78, 80, 82, 84, 88, 90, 92, 94, 95; WhoE 77, 79, 81, 83, 85, 86, 89, 91, 93, 95; WhoFrS 84; WhoGov 72, 75; WhoNob, 90, 95; WhoScEn 94; WhoWor 74, 76, 78, 80, 82, 84, 87, 89, 91, 93, 95; WorAl; WorAlBi*

Angel, Heather Grace
American. Actor
Appeared in TV show "Peyton Place," 1964-69; film *Berkley Square,* 1933.
b. Feb 9, 1909 in Oxford, England
d. Oct 13, 1986 in Santa Barbara, California
Source: *BioIn 10; ConTFT 4; FilmgC; IntMPA 82; InWom; MovMk; ThFT; WhoHol A; WhoThe 77A; WrDr 82*

Angela Merici, Saint
[Angela of Brescia]
Italian. Religious Figure
Founded company of St. Ursula, 1534, first teaching order of women devoted to educating women.
b. Mar 21, 1474? in Desenzano, Italy
d. Jan 27, 1540 in Brescia, Italy

Source: *BioIn 17; ContDcW 89; IntDcWB; InWom, SUP; LuthC 75; MacDWB; WebBD 83; WorAl; WorAlBi*

Angeles, Victoria de los
Spanish. Opera Singer
Soprano, who performed famous title roles in *Madame Butterfly; Carmen,* 1950s.
b. Nov 1, 1923 in Barcelona, Spain
Source: *Baker 84, 92; BioIn 13, 15; CurBio 55; IntWW 74; InWom SUP; NewAmDM; PenDiMP; Who 85, 92; WhoAmW 77; WhoMus 72*

Angeli, Pier
[Anna Maria Pierangeli]
Italian. Actor
Twin sister of Marisa Pavan; most roles were fragile, innocent heroines.
b. Jun 19, 1933, Sardinia
d. Sep 10, 1971 in Beverly Hills, California
Source: *FilmEn; FilmgC; InWom; MGM; MotPP; MovMk; NewYTBE 71; WhAm 5; WhoAmW 64, 66, 68; WhoHol B; WhScrn 74, 77*

Angelico, Fra
[Giovanni da Fiesole; Guido di Pietro]
Italian. Artist
Painter who used strong, pure colors, simple subjects, reflecting new ideas of time.
b. 1387 in Vicchio, Italy
d. Mar 18, 1455 in Rome, Italy
Source: *AtlBL; Benet 87; BioIn 1, 2, 3, 4, 5, 6, 7, 8, 10, 13, 15; DcCathB; IlEncMy; LinLib S; OxCArt; PseudN 82; REn; WhDW; WorAl*

Angell, James Burrill
American. University Administrator, Diplomat
Pres., U of MI, 1871-1909; US Ambassador to China, 1880, Turkey, 1897.
b. Jan 7, 1829 in Scituate, Rhode Island
d. Apr 1, 1916 in Ann Arbor, Michigan
Source: *Alli SUP; AmAu&B; AmBi; ApCAB, X; BbD; BiDAmEd; BiD&SB; BioIn 1, 3, 5, 9, 16; CyAG; CyAL 1, 2; DcAmAu; DcAmB; DcAmDH 80, 89; DcLB 64; DcNAA; EncAB-H 1974; HarEnUS; LinLib L, S; NatCAB 1; TwCBDA; WebAB 74, 79; WhAm 1; WhAmP; WorAl*

Angell, James Rowland
American. University Administrator
Pres., Yale U, 1921-37; educational counselor at NBC, 1937-49.
b. May 8, 1869 in Burlington, Virginia
d. Mar 4, 1949 in Hamden, Connecticut
Source: *AmAu&B; BiDAmEd; BiDPsy; BioIn 1, 2, 4, 8, 16; CurBio 40, 49; DcAmB S4; DcNAA; EncWB; InSci; LinLib L, S; NamesHP; NatCAB 14, 40; WhAm 2; WhNAA*

Angell, Norman
[Sir Ralph Norman Angell]
English. Author, Lecturer
Best known work *The Great Illusion,* 1910, describes futility of war; won Nobel Peace Prize, 1933.
b. Dec 26, 1874 in Holbeach, England
d. Oct 7, 1967 in Surrey, England
Source: *BioIn 1, 2, 4, 5, 7, 8, 9, 10, 11, 12, 14, 15; ConAu P-1; CurBio 48, 67; DcLEL; EvLB; LinLib L, S; LngCTC; NewC; NewCBEL; ObitOF 79; ObitT 1961; OxCEng 67; TwCA, SUP; WhAm 4, 5; WhE&EA; WhLit; WhoLA; WhoNob, 90, 95*

Angell, Robert Cooley
American. Sociologist
Known for work in individual/social group interaction studies; wrote *The Quest for World Order,* 1979.
b. Apr 29, 1899 in Detroit, Michigan
d. May 12, 1984 in Ann Arbor, Michigan
Source: *AmAu&B; AmMWSc 73S, 78S; BioIn 12; ConAu 101; IntEnSS 79; PeoHis; WhAm 8; WhoAm 74, 76, 78, 80; WhoWor 74, 76*

Angell, Roger
American. Author, Editor
Fiction editor, contributor, *The New Yorker,* 1956—; wrote *The Summer Game,* 1972.
b. Sep 19, 1920 in New York, New York
Source: *BiDAmSp Sup; BioIn 13, 15; ConAu 13NR, 44NR, 57; ConLC 26; DcLB 171; DrAF 76; DrAPF 80, 91; WhoAm 74, 76, 78, 80, 82, 84, 86, 88, 90, 92, 94, 95, 96, 97; WhoUSWr 88; WhoWrEP 89, 92, 95; WorAu 1975; WrDr 90, 92, 94, 96*

Angelos, Peter
American. Sports Executive, Lawyer
Principal owner and managing partner of the Baltimore Orioles, 1993—.
b. Jul 4, 1930 in Baltimore, Maryland
Source: *News 95*

Angelou, Maya
American. Actor, Author
Wrote autobiographical best-sellers *I Know Why the Caged Bird Sings,* 1970; *All God's Children Need Traveling Shoes,* 1986.
b. Apr 4, 1928 in Saint Louis, Missouri
Source: *AfrAmAl 6; AfrAmBi 2; AmWomD; AmWomWr, 92; ArtclWW 2; Au&Arts 7; Benet 87, 96; BenetAL 91; BioIn 10, 11, 12, 13, 14, 15, 16, 18; BlkAmP; BlkAWP; BlkLC; BlkWAm; BlkWr 1, 2; BlkWWr; BlmGWL; CamGLE; CamHAL; ConAu 19NR, 42NR, 65; ConBlAP 88; ConBlB 1; ConHero 1; ConLC 12, 35, 64, 77; ConPo 85, 91, 96; ConPopW; ContDcW 89; ConTFT 10; CurBio 74, 94; CyWA 89; DcArts; DcLB 38; DcTwCCu 1, 5; DrAP 75; DrAPF 80; DrBlPA, 90; Ebony 1; EncWB; EncWHA; EncWL 3; FacFETw; FemiCLE; GrLiveH; GrWomW; HanAmWH; HerW, 84; InB&W 80, 85; IntAu&W 91, 93; IntWW 89, 91, 93; InWom SUP; LegTOT; LivgBAA; MajTwCW; ModAL S2; ModAWWr; ModWoWr; MorBAP; NegAl 83, 89; News 93; NewYTBE 72; NewYTBS 93; NotBlAW 1; NotNAT A; NotWoAT; OxCAmL 83, 95; OxCTwCP; OxCWoWr 95; PenNWW B; PeoHis; RAdv 14; ReelWom; RfGAmL 94; RGTwCWr; SchCGBL; SelBAAf; SelBAAu; SmATA 49; TwCYAW; WhoAfA 96; WhoAm 74, 76, 78, 80, 82, 84, 86, 88, 90, 92, 94, 95, 96, 97; WhoAmW 79, 81, 83, 85, 95, 97; WhoBlA 77, 80, 85, 88, 90, 92, 94; WhoUSWr 88; WhoWrEP 89, 92, 95; WomFir; WomWMM; WorAu 1975; WrDr 76, 80, 82, 84, 86, 88, 90, 92, 94, 96*

Anger, Kenneth
American. Director, Author
Avant-garde filmmaker; films reveal obsessions with the occult and fetishism; wrote *Hollywood Babylon,* recounting scandals in film industry, 1959.
b. Feb 3, 1930 in Santa Monica, California
Source: *BioIn 15; ConAu 106; DcFM; EncO&P 1, 2, 3; FilmgC; HalFC 88; IntDcF 1-2, 2-2; MugS; OxCFilm; WhoAm 84, 88; WhoUSWr 88; WhoWrEP 89; WorEFlm*

Angle, Edward Hartley
American. Dentist
Founded modern orthodontia, c. 1886.
b. Jun 1, 1855 in Herrick, Pennsylvania
d. Aug 11, 1930
Source: *DcNAA; InSci; NatCAB 22; WhAm 1; WorAl*

Angleton, James J(esus)
American. Government Official
Head of CIA counter-intelligence, 1954-73.
b. 1917 in Boise, Idaho
d. May 11, 1987 in Washington, District of Columbia
Source: *BioIn 11, 12; EncAI&E; EncCW; FacFETw; NewYTBS 78, 87; PolProf NF*

Anglim, Philip
American. Actor
Played John Merrick in *The Elephant Man* on Broadway, 1979; Dane O'Neill in "The Thorn Birds," 1983.
b. Feb 11, 1953 in San Francisco, California
Source: *ConTFT 4; NewYTBS 79, 80; VarWW 85; WhoAm 84, 86; WhoEnt 92; WhoHol 92; WhoThe 81*

Anglin, Margaret Mary
Canadian. Actor
Stage star from 1894: *Cyrano de Bergerac; Importance of Being Earnest.*
b. Apr 3, 1876 in Ottawa, Ontario, Canada

d. Jan 7, 1958 in Toronto, Ontario, Canada
Source: *BiCAW; DcAmB S6; FamA&A; InWom; LinLib S; MacDCB 78; NotNAT B; ObitOF 79; OxCAmH; OxCThe 67; PlP&P; WhAm 5; WhoStg 1906, 1908; WhThe*

Anglund, Joan Walsh
American. Children's Author, Illustrator
Popular illustrator of mouthless children; wrote *A Friend is Someone Who Likes You,* 1958.
b. Jan 3, 1926 in Hinsdale, Illinois
Source: *AmAu&B; Au&Wr 71; AuBYP 2, 3; ChhPo S1, S2; ChlLR 1; ConAu 5R, 15NR; FamAIYP; IlsCB 1957; IntAu&W 91, 93; InWom SUP; LinLib L; OxCChiL; SmATA 2; ThrBJA; TwCChW 78; WhoAm 74, 76, 78, 80; WhoAmW 61, 64, 66, 68, 70, 74, 83, 85; WrDr 80, 82, 84, 86, 88, 90, 92, 94, 96*

Angoff, Charles
American. Author, Editor
Editor, *American Mercury,* 1934-50; wrote literary histories, novels of Jewish-American life.
b. Apr 22, 1902 in Minsk, Russia
d. May 3, 1979 in New York, New York
Source: *AmAu&B; Au&Wr 71; BenetAL 91; BioIn 1, 3, 4, 11, 12, 15; BlueB 76; ConAu 4NR, 5R, 85; CurBio 55, 79, 79N; DcAmImH; DrAF 76; DrAP 75; DrAS 74E, 78E, 82E; IntAu&W 76, 77; IntWWP 77; JeAmFiW; NewYTBS 79; REnAL; ScF&FL 1, 2, 92; WhAm 7; WhE&EA; WhNAA; WhoAm 74, 76, 78; WhoAmJ 80; WhoWor 74; WhoWorJ 72, 78; WrDr 76, 80*

Angott, Sammy
[Samuel Engotti]
American. Boxer
Won world welterweight title, 1941.
b. Jan 17, 1915 in Washington, Pennsylvania
Source: *WhoBox 74*

Angstrom, Anders Jonas
Swedish. Astronomer, Physicist
Noted for study of light, especially spectrum analysis.
b. Aug 13, 1814 in Logdo, Sweden
d. Jun 21, 1874 in Uppsala, Sweden
Source: *AsBiEn; BiESc; BioIn 3, 7, 14; CelCen; DcInv; DcScB; InSci; LarDcSc; LinLib S; NewCol 75; WebBD 83; WorAl; WorAlBi*

Anhalt, Edward
[Andrew Holt]
American. Screenwriter
Original film writer, story adapter; won Oscar, 1964, for *Becket.*
b. Mar 28, 1914 in New York, New York
Source: *BioIn 7, 9, 14; ConAu 29NR, 85; ConDr 88A; ConTFT 10; DcLB 26; FilmEn; FilmgC; HalFC 80, 84, 88; IntDcF 1-4, 2-4; IntMPA 77, 80, 81, 92, 94, 96; PseudN 82; WomWMM*

Anhava, Tuomas
Finnish. Poet
Wrote *36 Poems,* 1958, and *The Sixth Book,* 1966.
b. Jun 5, 1927 in Helsinki, Finland
Source: *BioIn 11; DcScanL; PenC EUR*

Anielewicz, Mordecai
Polish. Revolutionary
Leader of Jewish resistance against the Nazis during Warsaw Ghetto Uprising, 1943.
b. 1919 in Wyszkow, Poland
d. May 10, 1943 in Warsaw, Poland
Source: *BioIn 16; EncRev*

Animals, The
[Eric Burdon; Bryan Chandler; Barry Jenkins; Alan Price; Dave Rowberry; John Steel; Hilton Valentine]
English. Music Group
Part of British Invasion of early 60s; hit singles: "House of the Rising Sun," 1964; "Don't Let Me Be Misunderstood," 1965.
Source: *Alli; AmPS B; BioIn 16, 21; ConMuA 80A; EncPR&S 74, 89; EncRk 88; EncRkSt; HarEnR 86; IlEncRk; PenEncP; RkOn 74, 78; RolSEnR 83; St&PR 96, 97; WhoHol A; WhoRock 81; WhoRocM 82*

Animuccia, Giovanni
Italian. Composer
Developed oratorio musical form with "Laudi Spirtuali," 1563, 1570.
b. 1500 in Florence, Italy
d. 1571 in Rome, Italy
Source: *Baker 84, 92; BioIn 4; BriBkM 80; DcCathB; NewGrDM 80; NewOxM; WebBD 83*

Aniston, Jennifer
American. Actor
Plays Rachel Green on TV's "Friends," 1994—.
b. Feb 11, 1969 in Sherman Oaks, California
Source: *ConTFT 15*

Anka, Paul
Canadian. Singer, Songwriter
Wrote songs "Diana," 1957; "My Way," 1967; has 15 gold records.
b. Jul 30, 1941 in Ottawa, Ontario, Canada
Source: *AmPS, A, B; Baker 78, 84, 92; BiDAmM; BioIn 5, 6, 7, 9, 10, 12, 13, 14; CanWW 79, 89; CelR, 90; ConMuA 80A; ConMus 2; CreCan 2; CurBio 64; EncPR&S 89; EncRk 88; EncRkSt; FilmEn; FilmgC; ForYSC; HalFC 80, 84, 88; LegTOT; MotPP; OxCPMus; PenEncP; PopAmC SUP; RkOn 74, 78; RolSEnR 83; WhoAm 74, 76, 78, 80, 82, 84, 86, 88, 90, 92, 94, 95, 96, 97; WhoEnt 92; WhoHol 92, A; WhoRock 81; WorAl; WorAlBi*

Ankers, Evelyn
"Queen of the Horror Movies"; "The Screeamer"
English. Actor
Played in Universal B films *Wolf Man; Ghost of Frankenstein,* 1940s.
b. Aug 17, 1918 in Valparaiso, Chile
d. Aug 29, 1985 in Maui, Hawaii
Source: *BioIn 10, 14, 17; FilmEn; FilmgC; ForYSC; HalFC 80, 84, 88; HolP 40; IntMPA 77, 80, 82, 84; LegTOT; MotPP; MovMk; NewYTBS 85; WhoHol A; WhoHrs 80*

Annabella
[Suzanne Georgette Charpentier]
French. Actor
Wife of Tyrone Power, 1939-48; films include *Napoleon,* 1926, *Le Million,* 1931.
b. Jul 14, 1910? in Paris, France
d. Sep 18, 1996 in Neuilly-sur-Seine, France
Source: *BioIn 7; Film 1, 2; FilmgC; ForYSC; HalFC 88; InWom, SUP; MotPP; MovMk; ThFT; What 1; WhoHol A; WhoThe 77A; WorEFlm*

Annabella
[Bow Wow Wow; Myant Myant Aye; Annabella Lwin]
Burmese. Singer
Lead singer with Bow Wow Wow, 1980-83.
b. Oct 31, 1965 in Rangoon, Burma

Annaud, Jean-Jacques
French. Director
Movies include *Quest for Fire,* 1981.
b. Jan 10, 1943 in Draveil, France
Source: *BioIn 13; ConTFT 3, 13; DirCG 82; EncEurC; IntMPA 88, 92, 94, 96; IntWW 91, 93; MiSFD 9; VarWW 85; WhoAm 95, 96, 97; WhoEnt 92; WhoWor 91, 93, 95, 96, 97*

Anne
English. Ruler
Reigned 1702-14; with no heirs, succession passed to Hanoverian line-George I.
b. Feb 6, 1665 in London, England
d. Aug 1, 1714 in Kensington, England
Source: *BiDEWW; BioIn 1, 2, 3, 4, 6, 7, 8, 9, 10, 11, 12, 13, 14, 15, 16; ContDcW 89; DcBiPP; DcNaB; Dis&D; EncAmaz 91; HarEnUS; HerW; HisDBrE; HisDStE; HisWorL; IntDcWB; InWom, SUP; LegTOT; LinLib S; McGEWB; NewC; OxCShps; WhDW; WomFir; WomWR*

Anne
[Anne Elizabeth Alice Louise]
English. Princess
Only daughter of Queen Elizabeth II and Prince Philip, currently eighth in line to British throne; accomplished horsewoman, has represented England in Olympics; children are Peter and Zara Phillips.
b. Aug 15, 1950 in London, England

Source: *BioIn 2, 3, 4, 5, 6, 7, 8, 9, 10, 11, 12, 13, 14, 15, 16, 17, 18; ContDcW 89; CurBio 73; IntWW 75, 76, 77, 78, 79, 80, 81, 82, 83, 91; InWom, SUP; LegTOT; NewCol 75; NewYTBE 70, 73; Who 82R, 83R, 85R; WhoWor 87, 91, 93, 95, 96, 97; WomFir; WrDr 96*

Annenberg, Walter Hubert
American. Publisher, Diplomat
Owns several newspapers, magazines; sold *TV Guide* to Rupert Murdoch, 1988; ambassador to UK, 1969-75.
b. Mar 13, 1908 in Milwaukee, Wisconsin
Source: *BioIn 8, 9, 10, 11, 12, 13, 14, 15, 16; BioNews 74; CelR 90; CurBio 70; DcAmDH 80, 89; Dun&B 90; EncTwCJ; IntWW 83, 91; IntYB 78, 79, 80, 81, 82; LegTOT; LesBEnT 92; News 92; NewYTBS 74; NewYTET; St&PR 84, 87; USBiR 74; Who 85, 92; WhoAm 84, 86, 90; WhoFI 89; WhoGov 72; WhoWorJ 72, 78*

Anne of Bohemia
English. Consort
First queen of Richard II, 1382-94.
b. Mar 11, 1366 in Prague, Bohemia
d. Jun 7, 1394 in Sheen, Bohemia
Source: *BioIn 6, 11; BlmGWL; DcBiPP; DcNaB; InWom, SUP; NewC*

Anne of Cleves
German. Consort
Protestant princess; fourth wife of Henry VIII, Jan-Jul 1540; marriage annulled.
b. Sep 22, 1515 in Cleves, Germany
d. Jul 16, 1557 in London, England
Source: *BioIn 1, 4, 7, 9, 11, 18; DcBiPP; DcNaB; InWom, SUP; LegTOT; LinLib S; NewC; NewCol 75; REn; WhDW*

Annigoni, Pietro
Italian. Artist
Portrait painter of the famous: Elizabeth II, 1955, 1970; John F Kennedy, 1961; Shah of Iran, 1968.
b. Jun 7, 1910 in Milan, Italy
d. Oct 28, 1988 in Florence, Italy
Source: *AnObit 1988; Au&Wr 71; BioIn 4, 5, 6, 9, 11, 16; ClaDrA; ConAu 127; DcArts; DcBrAr 1; IntAu&W 76, 77; IntWW 74, 75, 76, 77, 78, 79, 80, 81, 82, 83, 89N; NewYTBS 88; OxDcArt; WhAm 11; Who 74, 82, 83, 85, 88, 90N; WhoArt 80, 82, 84; WhoWor 74, 76, 78, 82, 84, 87, 89*

Annis, Francesca
English. Actor
Played Lillie Langtry in TV series "Lillie" on PBS, 1979.
b. May 14, 1944 in London, England
Source: *ConTFT 8, 15; FilmEn; FilmgC; HalFC 80, 84, 88; IntWW 91; NewYTBS 79; Who 82, 92; WhoHol 92*

Ann-Margret
[Ann-Margret Olsson; Mrs. Roger Smith]
American. Dancer, Actor
Oscar nominations for *Carnal Knowledge,* 1971; *Tommy,* 1975.
b. Apr 28, 1941 in Valsjobyn, Sweden
Source: *BiDD; BiDFilm, 81, 94; BioIn 6, 7, 9, 10, 11, 13, 14, 15, 16, 17, 19, 20, 21; BioNews 75; BkPepl; CelR, 90; ConTFT 3, 9; CurBio 75; FilmEn; FilmgC; ForYSC; GoodHs; HalFC 80, 84, 88; IntMPA 75, 76, 77, 78, 79, 80, 81, 82, 84, 86, 88, 92, 94, 96; IntWW 89, 91, 93; InWom, SUP; ItaFilm; LegTOT; MotPP; MovMk; OxCFilm; PenEncP; RkOn 74; WhoAm 74, 76, 78, 80, 82, 84, 86, 88, 90, 92, 94, 95, 96, 97; WhoAmW 66, 68, 74; WhoEnt 92; WhoHol 92, A; WhoRock 81; WorAl; WorAlBi*

Anouilh, Jean Marie Lucien Pierre
French. Dramatist
Plays portray human condition with scorn, compassion: *Antigone,* 1944; *Becket,* 1960.
b. Jun 23, 1910 in Bordeaux, France
d. Oct 3, 1987 in Lausanne, Switzerland
Source: *CasWL; CnMWL; ConAu 17R; ConLC 8, 13; ConTFT 5; CurBio 54, 87; CyWA 58; EncWL; FilmgC; IntWW 74, 75, 76, 77, 78, 79, 80, 81, 82, 83; ModFrL; ModRL; NewYTBS 87; OxCFilm; OxCThe 67; REn*

Anquetil, Jacques
French. Cyclist
Cyclist; first to win Tour de France five times, beginning 1957.
b. 1934
d. Nov 18, 1987 in Rouen, France
Source: *AnObit 1987; BioIn 6, 15; WhoFr 79*

Anselm, Saint
Italian. Religious Leader
Archbishop of Canterbury, 1093-1109, called founder of scholasticism; writings characterized by rational argument.
b. 1033 in Aosta, Italy
d. Apr 21, 1109 in Canterbury, England
Source: *Alli; BiB N; BioIn 1, 2, 3, 4, 5, 6, 8, 9, 10, 11, 12, 13, 15, 17, 18; CasWL; CyEd; DcBiPP; DcCathB; DcEnL; DcNaB; EncEth; IlEncMy; LegTOT; LinLib L, S; McGEWB; NewC; OxCEng 67, 85, 95; PenC ENG; WhDW*

Ansermet, Ernest Alexandre
Swiss. Conductor
Founded, conducted Orchestre de la Suisse Romande, Geneva, 1918-67.
b. Nov 11, 1883 in Vevey, Switzerland
d. Feb 20, 1969 in Geneva, Switzerland
Source: *Baker 84; BioIn 1, 2, 3, 4, 6, 7, 8, 11, 12; BriBkM 80; CurBio 49, 69; MusMk; MusSN; WhAm 5; WorAl*

Anslinger, Harry Jacob
American. Statesman
Headed US Bureau of Narcotics, 1930-62; sought uniform drug laws.
b. May 20, 1892 in Altoona, Pennsylvania
d. Nov 14, 1975 in Hollidaysburg, Pennsylvania
Source: *BioIn 1, 5, 7, 8, 10, 11, 15, 17; ConAu 61, P-1; WhAm 6*

Anson, Cap
[Adrian Constantine; Adrian Constantine Anson]
"Pop"
American. Baseball Player, Baseball Manager
Infielder, Chicago Cubs, 1876-97; had 3,041 career hits; credited with starting spring training, 1885; Hall of Fame, 1939.
b. Apr 17, 1851 in Marshalltown, Iowa
d. Apr 14, 1922 in Chicago, Illinois
Source: *Ballpl 90; BioIn 2, 3, 14, 15; DcAmB; NewCol 75; WebAB 74, 79; WhAm 4, HSA; WhoProB 73; WhoSpor*

Anson, George
[Baron Soberton; Lord Anson]
"Father of the Navy"
English. Naval Officer
Circumnavigated globe, 1740-44; adventures described in *Anson's Voyage.*
b. Apr 23, 1697 in Shugborough, England
d. Jun 6, 1762 in Moor Park, England
Source: *Alli; BioIn 20; CamGEL; CamGLE; DcBiPP; DcEnL; DcNaB; GenMudB; HarEnMi; HisDBrE; OxCEng 85, 95; OxCShps; WhDW; WhoMilH 76; WhWE*

Anson, Jay
American. Author
Wrote *The Amityville Horror,* 1977; adapted to film, 1979.
b. Nov 4, 1924 in New York, New York
d. Mar 12, 1980 in Palo Alto, California
Source: *ConAu 81, 97; NewYTBS 80*

Anson, Robert Sam
American. Journalist
Known for feature articles on controversy surrounding assassination of John F Kennedy, published as book, 1975.
b. Mar 12, 1945 in Cleveland, Ohio
Source: *BioIn 9, 16, 17; ConAu 52NR, 115, 125*

Anspach, Susan
[Mrs. Sherwood Ball]
American. Actor
In films *Play It Again Sam,* 1972; *Five Easy Pieces,* 1970.
b. Nov 23, 1945 in New York, New York
Source: *ConTFT 3; HalFC 84; IntMPA 82, 92, 94, 96; InWom SUP; MovMk; VarWW 85; WhoAm 82; WhoHol A*

Anstey, Edgar Harold McFarlane
English. Director
Documentary pioneer; won Oscar for *Wild Wings,* 1966.
b. Feb 16, 1907 in Watford, England
d. Sep 26, 1987 in London, England
Source: *ConAu 69; ConTFT 4, 5; OxCFilm; Who 85*

Antall, Jozsef, Jr.
Hungarian. Political Leader
Prime minister, Hungary, 1990-93; as pres. of Democratic Forum was architect of country's first free, multiparty elections in forty-five years.
b. Apr 8, 1932, Hungary
d. Dec 12, 1993 in Budapest, Hungary
Source: *AnObit 1993; BioIn 19, 20; CurBio 90, 94N; EncRev; IntWW 91, 93; WhoSoCE 89; WhoWor 78, 91*

Antes, Horst
German. Artist
Post-war painter; later works include strange, massive, "gnome" people.
b. Oct 28, 1936 in Heppenheim, Germany
Source: *BioIn 7, 14, 15, 17; ConArt 77, 83, 89, 96; CurBio 86; DcCAr 81; IntWW 76, 77, 78, 79, 80, 81, 82, 83, 89, 91, 93; OxCTwCA; OxDcArt; PhDcTCA 77; WhoWor 82, 84, 87, 89, 91, 93, 95, 97; WorArt 1980*

Antheil, George
American. Composer
Wrote concert music, opera, movie scores; films include *Once in a Blue Moon,* 1935.
b. Jul 8, 1900 in Trenton, New Jersey
d. Feb 12, 1959 in New York, New York
Source: *AmComp; ASCAP 66, 80; Baker 78, 84, 92; BenetAL 91; BiDAmM; BiDD; BioIn 1, 3, 4, 5, 6, 8, 9, 12, 17, 19; BriBkM 80; CnOxB; CompSN, SUP; ConAmC 76, 82; CurBio 54, 59; DancEn 78; DcArts; DcCM; DcCom&M 79; DcFM; FacFETw; FilmEn; HalFC 80, 84, 88; LegTOT; LinLib L; MetOEnc; MusMk; NatCAB 45; NewAmDM; NewEOp 71; NewGrDA 86; NewGrDM 80; NewOxM; NotNAT B; OxCMus; OxDcOp; REnAL; ScF&FL 1; WhAm 3; WorEFlm*

Anthony, Saint
[Saint Anthony the Abbot]
Egyptian. Religious Leader
Founded Christian monasticism, c. 305.
b. 251 in Memphis, Egypt
d. 350 in Mount Kolzim, Egypt
Source: *BioIn 1, 2, 3, 4, 5, 6, 7, 8, 11, 12, 13; Dis&D; EncEarC; LuthC 75; NewCol 75; REn; WebBD 83*

Anthony, Earl
American. Author, Civil Rights Leader
Joined Black Panthers, 1967, wrote *Picking Up the Gun: A Report on the Black Panthers,* 1970.
b. 1941 in Roanoke, Virginia
Source: *BlkAWP; CivR 74; ConBlAP 88; InB&W 80; LivgBAA; NewYTBS 82; WhoAm 80; WorAl*

Anthony, Earl Roderick
American. Bowler
Pro bowler, 1970-84; won 41 PBA; PBA Hall of Fame, 1981.
b. Apr 27, 1938 in Tacoma, Washington
Source: *BiDAmSp BK; BioIn 11, 13; NewYTBS 82; WhoAm 78, 80, 82, 84, 86, 94, 95, 96, 97*

Anthony, Edward
American. Journalist
Publicity director of Herbert Hoover's presidential campaign, 1928; published *Collier's* magazine, 1949.
b. Aug 4, 1895 in New York, New York
d. Aug 16, 1971 in Gloucester, Massachusetts
Source: *AmAu&B; AuBYP 2, 3; BioIn 5, 8, 9, 12; BkCL; ChhPo; ConAu 33R, 73; LinLib L; REnAL; SmATA 21; WhAm 5*

Anthony, Evelyn
[Evelyn Bridget Patricia Stephens Ward-Thomas]
English. Author
Writes historical novels, contemporary thrillers; *The Tamarind Seed,* 1971, adapted to film, 1974.
b. Jul 3, 1928 in London, England
Source: *Au&Wr 71; DcLP 87B; IntAu&W 76, 77, 82, 91; InWom SUP; Novels; PenNWW B; SpyFic; TwCCr&M 80, 85, 91; TwCRGW; TwCRHW 90, 94; Who 82, 83, 85, 88, 90, 92, 94; WhoSpyF; WorAl; WrDr 76, 80, 82, 84, 86, 88, 90, 92, 94, 96*

Anthony, John J(ason)
American. Radio Performer
Best known for radio show "The Good Will Hour," 1930s-57, where he offered advice on marital problems.
b. Sep 1, 1898 in New York, New York
d. Jul 16, 1970 in San Francisco, California
Source: *BioIn 3, 7, 9; CurBio 42, 70; NewYTBE 70; ObitOF 79; WhoHol B*

Anthony, Joseph
[Joseph Deuster]
American. Director, Screenwriter
Best known as director of Broadway plays *The Rainmaker; Under the Yum Yum Tree;* wrote screenplay for *Crime and Punishment,* 1935.
b. May 24, 1912 in Milwaukee, Wisconsin
d. Jan 20, 1993 in Hyannis, Massachusetts
Source: *BiE&WWA; BioIn 18; CamGWoT; FilmEn; FilmgC; HalFC 80, 84, 88; ItaFilm; MiSFD 9; NotNAT; WhoAm 74, 76, 78, 80, 82, 84; WhoE 74; WhoHol 92, A; WhoThe 72, 77, 81; WhoWor 74, 76; WorEFlm*

Anthony, Katharine Susan
American. Biographer
Wrote controversial biography of Charles and Mary Lamb, *The Lambs,* 1945.
b. Nov 27, 1877 in Roseville, Arkansas
d. Nov 20, 1965 in New York, New York
Source: *AmAu&B; AmLY; AmWomHi; BioIn 4, 7; ChhPo S2; DcAmB S7; InWom, SUP; TwCA, SUP; WhAm 4, 5; WhE&EA; WhNAA; WomWWA 14*

Anthony, Michael
English. Actor
Stage performances include *The Dresser;* films include *To Paris with Love,* 1955.
b. Sep 26, 1920 in Saint Helier, Isle of Jers, England
Source: *ConTFT 5*

Anthony, Michael
[Van Halen]
American. Musician
Bassist with group since 1974.
b. Jun 20, 1955 in Chicago, Illinois
Source: *LegTOT*

Anthony, Ray
[Raymond Antonini]
American. Bandleader, Songwriter
Trumpeter; led popular dance band, 1950s; co-wrote "The Bunny Hop," 1952.
b. Jan 20, 1922 in Bentleyville, Pennsylvania
Source: *Baker 84, 92; BgBands 74; BiDAmM; BiDJaz; BioIn 3; CmpEPM; ForYSC; LegTOT; NewGrDJ 88; OxCPMus; PenEncP; RkOn 74; WhoHol 92, A*

Anthony, Susan B(rownell)
American. Social Reformer, Suffragist
Early advocate of women's equality; led women's suffrage movement.
b. Feb 15, 1820 in Adams, Massachusetts
d. Mar 13, 1906 in Rochester, New York
Source: *AmBi; AmRef; AmSocL; AmWom; AmWomWr; ApCAB; BbD; Benet 96; BiDAmJo; BiDMoPL; BioIn 1, 2, 3, 4, 5, 6, 7, 8, 9, 10, 11, 12, 13, 14, 15, 16, 17; BlmGWL; CivWDc; DcAmB; DcAmTB; DcNAA; Drake; EncAB-H 1974, 1996; EncWHA; FemiWr; GayLesB; HarEnUS; HerW, 84; InWom, SUP; LibW; LinLib L, S; McGEWB; NatCAB 4; NewCol 75; NotAW; OxCAmH; OxCAmL 65, 95; OxCWoWr 95; REn; TwCBDA; WebAB 74, 79; WhAm 1; WhAmP; WhCiWar; WorAl*

Anthony, Tony
American. Actor
Hero of "spaghetti Westerns": *A Stranger in Town,* 1967; *The Silent Stranger,* 1975.
b. Oct 16, 1937 in Clarksburg, West Virginia
Source: *FilmEn; FilmgC; ForYSC; HalFC 80, 84, 88; IntMPA 75, 76, 77, 80, 86, 92; ItaFilm; WhoHol 92, A*

Anthony of Padua, Saint
French. Religious Figure
Biblical scholar with reputation as miracle worker; patron saint of lost articles.
b. Aug 15, 1195 in Lisbon, Portugal
d. Jun 13, 1231 in Padua, Italy
Source: *DcCathB; LuthC 75; NewCol 75; REn; WebBD 83*

Antin, Mary
American. Author
Noted for writings on immigrants: *The Promised Land,* 1912.
b. 1881 in Polotsk, Russia
d. May 15, 1949 in Suffern, New York
Source: *AmAu&B; AmWomWr; ArtclWW 2; Benet 96; BenetAL 91; BioIn 1, 2, 3, 4, 7, 12, 14, 17, 20; ConAu 118; DcAmAu; DcAmB S4; DcAmImH; DcLB Y84B; DcNAA; FemiCLE; InWom, SUP; JeAmFiW; JeAmWW; LibW; LinLib L; NatCAB 39; NotAW; OxCAmH; OxCAmL 65, 83, 95; OxCWoWr 95; REn; TwCA, SUP; WebAB 74, 79; WhAm 6; WhNAA*

Antiphon of Rhamnus
Greek. Orator
Argued against conventional law, saying men seek comfort, unlimited pleasure.
b. 480BC
d. 411BC
Source: *CasWL; DcBiPP; DcScB; Grk&L; InB&W 80; LinLib L; PenC CL; REn*

Antisthenes
Greek. Philosopher
Founded Cynic school; urged return to simplicity of nature.
b. 444BC in Athens, Greece
d. 371BC in Athens, Greece
Source: *LinLib L; WebBD 83; WorAl; WorAlBi*

Antoine, Andre
French. Actor, Producer
Founded, directed Paris's Theatre Libre, 1887-94; produced avant-garde plays.
b. 1858 in Limoges, France
d. Oct 23, 1943 in Brestin, France
Source: *BioIn 1, 2, 4, 5, 12, 17, 20; CamGWoT; ClDMEL 47, 80; CnThe; DcArts; DcFM; DcTwCCu 2; EncEurC; EncWT; Ent; FilmEn; GrStDi; IntDcT 3; LngCTC; NewCol 75; OxCFilm; OxCFr; OxCThe 67, 83; REn; WhThe*

Anton, Susan
American. Actor, Singer
Nightclub performer; starred in film *Golden Girl,* 1979.
b. Oct 12, 1950? in Yucaipa, California
Source: *BioIn 11, 12; ConTFT 2, 3; IntMPA 86, 92, 94, 96; LegTOT; WhoAm 86; WhoEnt 92; WhoHol 92*

Antonelli, Giacomo
Italian. Statesman
Held several important government posts, mid-1800s; prominent champion of papal interest.
b. Apr 2, 1806 in Sonnino, Italy
d. Nov 6, 1876 in Rome, Italy
Source: *BioIn 17; CelCen; DcBiPP, A; DcCathB; LuthC 75; WebBD 83*

Antonelli, John(ny August)
American. Baseball Player
Pitcher, 1948-61; led NL in shutouts three yrs.
b. Apr 12, 1930 in Rochester, New York
Source: *Ballpl 90; WhoProB 73*

Antonello da Messina
Italian. Artist
First Italian to master technique of painting with oils.
b. 1430 in Messina, Sicily, Italy
d. Feb 15, 1479 in Messina, Sicily, Italy
Source: *AtlBL; BioIn 1, 2, 10, 13; DcArts; IntDcAA 90; McGDA; McGEWB; OxCArt; OxDcArt; REn*

Antonescu, Ion
Romanian. Political Leader
Dictator, 1940-44; forced abdication of King Carol II, aligned Romania with Nazis; executed by firing squad.
b. Jun 15, 1882 in Pitesti, Romania
d. Jun 1, 1946 in Bucharest, Romania
Source: *BioIn 1, 16; CurBio 40, 46; DcPol; DcTwHis; DicTyr; EncRev; EncTR 91; FacFETw; HisEWW; LegTOT; WhDW; WhWW-II; WorAl; WorAlBi*

Antonini, Joseph
American. Business Executive
Chm. and CEO, K Mart Corp., 1987-1995; pres., 1988-1995; helped K Mart shed "cheap" image by espousing sale of more upscale merchandise.
b. Jul 13, 1941 in Morgantown, West Virginia
Source: *BioIn 16; Dun&B 90; News 91, 91-2; St&PR 91; WhoAm 90; WhoE 89; WhoFI 92; WhoMW 90; WhoWor 89*

Antoninus Pius
[Titus Aurelius Fulvus Boionius Arrius Antoninus]
Roman. Ruler
Emperor of Rome, 138-161; Wall of Antonius built in his honor to protect against British invasion, 142.
b. Sep 19, 86 in Lanurium, France
d. Mar 7, 161 in Lorium, Italy
Source: *BioIn 5, 7, 14; DcBiPP, A; EncEarC; LuthC 75; NewC; OxCClL, 89; WebBD 83; WhDW*

Antonioni, Michelangelo
Italian. Director
First international hit *L'Avventura,* 1960, described modern man's emotional barrenness.
b. Sep 29, 1912 in Ferrara, Italy
Source: *BiDFilm, 81, 94; BioIn 6, 7, 8, 9, 10, 12, 16; CelR; ConAu 45NR, 73; ConLC 20; ConTFT 6, 13; CurBio 64, 93; DcArts; DcFM; EncEurC; FacFETw; FilmEn; FilmgC; HalFC 80, 84, 88; IntDcF 1-2, 2-2; IntMPA 86, 92; IntWW 74, 75, 76, 77, 78, 79, 80, 81, 82, 83, 89, 91, 93; ItaFilm; LegTOT; McGEWB; MiSFD 9; MovMk; OxCFilm; RAdv 14, 13-3; Who 74, 82, 83, 85, 88, 90, 92, 94; WhoAm 95, 96, 97; WhoWor 74, 76, 78, 89, 95, 96, 97; WorAl; WorAlBi; WorEFlm; WorFDir 2*

Antony, Marc
[Marc Anthony; Marcus Antonius]
Roman. Soldier, Political Leader
Prominent soldier, politician under Julius Caesar; defeated by Octavius, 31 BC; committed suicide with Cleopatra.
b. 83?BC
d. 30BC, Egypt
Source: *BioIn 1, 2, 5, 6, 7, 8, 10, 11, 12, 15, 16, 17, 20, 21; DcBiPP; McGEWB; NewCol 75; REn; WebBD 83; WhDW; WorAl*

Antoon, A(lfred) J(oseph)
American. Director
Won Tony for *That Championship Season,* 1973; New York Shakespeare Festival director, 1971-1990.
b. Dec 7, 1944 in Lawrence, Massachusetts
d. Jan 22, 1992 in New York, New York
Source: *BioIn 9, 17, 18; ConTFT 5; NotNAT; PlP&P A; WhAm 10; WhoAm 86; WhoThe 77, 81*

Anuszkiewicz, Richard Joseph
American. Artist
Master of dizzying, optical art.
b. May 23, 1930 in Erie, Pennsylvania
Source: *BriEAA; ConArt 77; CurBio 78; DcAmArt; DcCAA 71, 77; IntWW 91; McGDA; WhoAm 86, 97; WhoAmA 78, 91; WhoPoA 96*

Anville, Jean Baptiste Bourguignon d'
French. Cartographer, Geographer
Produced over 2,000 maps, considered finest of the time.
b. Jul 11, 1697 in Paris, France
d. Jan 1782
Source: *DcBiPP; DcScB; NewCol 75; WebBD 83*

Anza, Juan Bautista de
Spanish. Explorer
Founded San Francisco, 1776; governor of New Mexico, 1777-88.
b. 1735 in Fronteras, Mexico
d. 1788 in Arizpe, Mexico
Source: *AmBi; BenetAL 91; BioIn 1, 2, 4, 7, 8; CmCal; DcAmB; McGEWB; OxCAmH; OxCAmL 65; REnAL; REnAW; WebAB 74, 79; WhAm HS; WhNaAH; WhWE*

Anzaldua, Gloria
American. Writer
Published anthologies *This Bridge Called My Back,* 1981; *Making Face/Making Soul,* 1990.
b. Sep 26, 1942 in Jesus Maria of the Valley,Texas
Source: *AmWomWr SUP; BioIn 19, 20; DcLB 122; GayLesB; ModWoWr; RAdv 14; RfGAmL 94*

Aoki, Hiroaki
"Rocky"
American. Restaurateur
Multimillionaire restaurateur; founded Benihana chain of Japanese steakhouses, 1963.
b. 1940, Japan
Source: *BioIn 9, 10, 11, 13, 14, 15; BusPN; Dun&B 88; NewYTBS 75*

Aoki, Isao
Japanese. Golfer
Turned pro, 1964; first Japanese to win PGA tournament—Hawaiian Open, 1983.
b. Aug 31, 1942 in Abiko, Japan
Source: *BioIn 12, 20; NewYTBS 80; WhoIntG*

Aouita, Said
Moroccan. Track Athlete
Holds current world record in five running events—1,500, 2,000, 3,000, and 5,000 meters, and two-mile; two-time Olympic medalist, 1984, 1988.
b. Nov 2, 1960 in Kenitra, Morocco
Source: *BioIn 16; BlkOlyM; CurBio 90*

Aoun, Michel
Lebanese. Military Leader
Christian general who led unsuccessful six-month war of liberation against Syrian occupiers, 1989; forced to flee by Muslim countrymen after seizing palace.
b. Sep 30, 1935 in Haret Hreik, Lebanon
Source: *BioIn 16; CurBio 90; DcMidEa; IntWW 91, 93*

Apache Kid
American. Criminal
Native American, cavalry scout, convicted of murder, then pardoned by Pres. Cleveland.
b. 1868?
d. 1894? in Tucson, Arizona
Source: *BioIn 1, 3, 4, 5, 13; DrInf*

Aparicio, Luis Ernesto
"Little Looie"
Venezuelan. Baseball Player
Shortstop, 1956-73; had 506 career stolen bases, led AL nine yrs; Hall of Fame, 1984.
b. Apr 29, 1934 in Maracaibo, Venezuela
Source: *BiDAmSp BB; BioIn 5, 6, 13, 14, 15; DcHiB; FacFETw; WhoAm 74; WhoE 74; WhoHisp 92; WhoProB 73*

Apelles
Greek. Artist
Best known work *Aphrodite Anadyomene,* painted for temple of Aesculapius at Cos.
b. fl. 400BC in Ionia, Asia Minor
Source: *BioIn 13; DcBiPP; EncEarC; NewC; OxCArt; OxCClL 89; OxCEng 85; OxDcArt*

Apess, William
American. Clergy
First Native American to publish his autobiography, *A Son in the Forest,* 1829.
b. Jan 31, 1798 in Colrain, Massachusetts
d. Apr 1839 in New York, New York
Source: *EncNAR; EncNoAI; NatNAL; NotNaAm*

Apgar, Virginia
American. Physician
Developed Apgar Test, 1952, given to baby within 60 seconds of birth to determine condition, survival chances.
b. Jul 7, 1909 in Westfield, New Jersey
d. Aug 7, 1974 in New York, New York
Source: *AmMWSc 73P; WhoWor 74; WomFir*

Apollinaire, Guillaume
[Guillaume Kostrowitsky]
French. Author, Critic
Avant-garde writer; coined word "surrealism," promoted early Cubist painters.
b. Aug 26, 1880 in Rome, Italy
d. Nov 10, 1918 in Paris, France
Source: *AtlBL; Benet 87, 96; BioIn 1, 2, 3, 4, 5, 6, 7, 8, 9, 11, 12, 13, 14, 15, 16, 19, 20; CasWL; ClDMEL 47, 80; CnMD; CnMWL; ConAu 152; DcArts; EncWL 2, 3; EncWT; Ent; EuWr 9; EvEuW; FacFETw; GrFLW; GuFrLit 1; IntDcT 2; LegTOT; LinLib L; LngCTC; MakMC; McGEWB; McGEWD 72, 84; ModFrL; ModRL; ModWD; NotNAT B; OxCArt; OxCEng 67, 85, 95; OxCFr; OxCTwCA; OxDcArt; PenC EUR; PhDcTCA 77; PoeCrit 7; RAdv 14, 13-2; RComWL; REn; REnWD; RfGWoL 95; RGFMEP; TwCA, SUP; TwCLC 3, 8, 51; TwCWr; WhDW; WhoTwCL; WorAlBi*

Apollinaris Sidonius, Gaius Sollius
[Saint Sidonius]
French. Religious Figure
Letters describe life during breakup of Roman Empire; feast day Aug 21.
b. Nov 5, 430 in Lyons, France
d. Aug 21, 487 in Clermont, France
Source: *DcBiPP; Dis&D; LinLib L; LuthC 75; McGEWB; ModFrL; NewCol 75; NotNAT B; OxCClL 89; TwCLC 3; WebBD 83*

Aponte-Martinez, Luis, Cardinal
Puerto Rican. Religious Leader
Archbishop of San Juan, 1964—; cardinal since 1973.
b. Aug 4, 1922 in Lajas, Puerto Rico
Source: *IntWW 83; WhoAm 86; WhoHisp 92; WhoRel 85; WhoWor 84, 87*

Apostoli, Fred
American. Boxer
World middleweight champ, 1938-39.
b. Feb 2, 1914
d. Nov 29, 1973 in San Francisco, California
Source: *BioIn 10; ObitOF 79; WhoBox 74*

Appel, James Ziegler
American. Physician
President of AMA, 1966; opposed, then defended Medicare.
b. May 15, 1907 in Lancaster, Pennsylvania
d. Aug 31, 1981 in Lancaster, Pennsylvania
Source: *BioIn 7, 12; CurBio 66, 81; EncAB-A 36; NewYTBS 81; WhAm 8; WhoAm 74, 76, 78, 80*

Appel, Karel Christian
Dutch. Artist
Self-taught abstract expressionist; uses rich, swirling colors.
b. Apr 25, 1921 in Amsterdam, Netherlands
Source: *AmArt; BioIn 13, 14, 15, 16; ConArt 77, 89; CurBio 61; IntDcAA 90; IntWW 74, 75, 76, 77, 78, 79, 80, 81, 82, 83, 89, 91, 93; McGDA; OxDcArt; PrintW 85; Who 74, 82, 83, 85, 88, 90, 92, 94; WhoAm 86, 88, 90, 92, 94; WhoAmA 78, 91; WhoWor 82, 84, 87, 89, 91, 93*

Appert, Nicolas
[Francois Nicolas Appert]
French. Chef
Invented method of preserving food in corked jars, 1809.
b. Nov 17, 1749 in Chalons-sur-Marne, France
d. Jun 2, 1841 in Massy, France
Source: *BioIn 3, 4, 10, 12; NewCol 75*

Appia, Adolphe
Swiss. Designer
Stage designer; theories were highly influential on 20th c. theatrical production; stressed three-dimensional stage settings and specialized lighting.
b. Sep 1, 1862 in Geneva, Switzerland
d. Feb 29, 1928 in Nyon, Switzerland
Source: *BioIn 6, 7, 8, 9, 14, 16, 19; CamGWoT; DcArts; DcTwCCu 2; EncWB; EncWT; Ent; IntDcOp; IntDcT 3; MetOEnc; NewGrDM 80; NotNAT A, B; OxCThe 67, 83; OxDcOp; PlP&P*

Appice, Carmine
[Vqnillq Fudge]
American. Singer
Session drummer; often backs Rod Stewart; inducted into Hollywood Rock Walk, 1991.
b. Dec 15, 1946 in Staten Island, New York

Source: *PenEncP*

Apple, R(aymond) W(alter), Jr.
American. Journalist
Washington, DC, bureau chief of the *NY Times*, 1993—; author of *Europe: An Uncommon Guide*, 1986.
b. Nov 20, 1934 in Akron, Ohio
Source: *BioIn 18, 19, 20; BlueB 76; WhoAm 74, 76, 78, 80, 82, 84, 86, 88, 90, 92, 94, 95, 96, 97; WhoE 89, 91, 95; WhoWor 82*

Appleby, John Francis
American. Inventor
Invented the binding machine, 1878.
b. May 23, 1840 in Westmoreland, New York
d. Nov 8, 1917 in Mazomanie, Wisconsin
Source: *BioIn 5; DcAmB; EncAAH; InSci; NatCAB 11; WebAB 74, 79; WebBD 83*

Appleseed, Johnny
[John Chapman; Jonathan Chapman]
American. Pioneer
Traveled west for 50 years; preaching, distributing apple seeds; immortalized in poetry by Vachel Lindsay.
b. Sep 26, 1774 in Springfield, Massachusetts
d. Mar 11, 1847 in Allen County, Indiana
Source: *AmAu&B; AmBi; Benet 87, 96; BenetAL 91; BioIn 1, 2, 3, 4, 5, 6, 7, 8, 9, 10, 11, 12, 14, 16, 18, 19; DcAmB; DcArts; EncAAH; LegTOT; LinLib S; MorMA; NatCAB 11; OxCAmH; OxCAmL 65, 83, 95; PeoHis; REn; REnAL; WebAB 74, 79; WhAm HS; WorAl; WorAlBi*

Appleton, Daniel
American. Publisher
Founded D Appleton & Co. Publishers, 1838.
b. Dec 10, 1785 in Haverhill, Massachusetts
d. Mar 27, 1849 in New York, New York
Source: *AmAu&B; AmBi; ApCAB; DcAmB; Drake; LinLib L; NatCAB 2; TwCBDA; WhAm HS*

Appleton, Edward Victor, Sir
English. Physicist
Leading figure in ionospheric research; won Nobel Prize in physics, 1947, for discovery of "Appleton Layer."
b. Sep 6, 1892 in Bradford, England
d. Apr 21, 1965 in Edinburgh, Scotland
Source: *AsBiEn; BiESc; BioIn 1, 2, 3, 4, 7, 9, 13, 14, 15, 16, 20; CamDcSc; CurBio 45, 65; DcNaB 1961; DcScB; EncWB; FacFETw; GrBr; InSci; LarDcSc; McGMS 80; ObitOF 79; ObitT 1961; WhAm 4; WhDW; WhE&EA; WhoLA; WhoLab 76; WhoNob, 90, 95; WorAl; WorScD*

Appleton, William Henry
American. Publisher
With father, Daniel, founded D Appleton & Co., 1838.
b. Jan 27, 1814 in Haverhill, Massachusetts
d. Oct 19, 1899 in New York, New York
Source: *AmAu&B; DcAmB; NatCAB 2; TwCBDA; WhAm 1, HS*

Applewhite, Marshall Herff
"Do"
American. Religious Leader
Leader of the Heaven's Gate religious cult; he and 38 other cult members committed mass suicide, the largest in US history.
b. 1930? in Texas
d. Mar 26, 1997 in Rancho Santa Fe, California

Appley, Lawrence A(sa)
American. Business Executive
Pres., American Management Association, 1948-68.
b. Apr 22, 1904
d. Apr 4, 1997 in Hamilton, New York
Source: *BioIn 1, 2, 5; EncAB-A 33*

Appling, Luke
[Lucius Benjamin; Lucius Benjamin Appling]
"Old Aches and Pains"
American. Baseball Player
Shortstop, Chicago White Sox, 1930-50; won two AL batting titles; Hall of Fame, 1964.
b. Apr 2, 1907 in High Point, North Carolina
d. Jan 3, 1991 in Cumming, Georgia
Source: *AnObit 1991; Ballpl 90; BiDAmSp BB; BioIn 13, 14, 15, 17, 18; LegTOT; NewYTBS 91; WhoProB 73; WhoSpor*

Appollonius of Perga
"Great Geometer"
Greek. Mathematician
Influenced development of analytic geometry by developing conic sections, introducing several terms.
b. 262?BC in Perga, Asia Minor
d. 200?BC
Source: *DcScB; LinLib L; McGEWB; WebBD 83*

Apps, Syl
[Charles Joseph Sylvanus Apps]
Canadian. Hockey Player
Center, Toronto, 1936-48; won Calder Trophy, 1937, Lady Byng Trophy, 1942; Hall of Fame, 1961.
b. Jan 8, 1915 in Paris, Ontario, Canada
Source: *BioIn 10, 11; HocEn; WhoHcky 73*

April Wine
[Myles Goodwin; Brian Greenway; Steve Lang; Jerry Mercer; Gary Moffet]
Canadian. Music Group
Earned 10 gold albums in Canada; had platinum album *World's Goin' Crazy*, 1976.
Source: *EncPR&S 89; HarEnR 86; IlEncRk; RkOn 85; RolSEnR 83; WhoRock 81; WhoRocM 82*

Apted, Michael
English. Director
Award-winning films include *Coal Miner's Daughter*, 1980.
b. Feb 10, 1941 in London, England
Source: *BiDFilm 94; BioIn 13, 14; ConTFT 1, 5, 12; FilmEn; HalFC 80, 84, 88; IntMPA 86, 92, 94, 96; IntWW 93; LegTOT; MiSFD 9; WhoEnt 92; WhoHol 92*

Aptheker, Herbert
American. Author, Historian
Edited *Political Affairs*, 1952-63; wrote numerous books on American Negro.
b. Jul 31, 1915 in New York, New York
Source: *AmAu&B; BioIn 10, 14; ConAu 5R, 6NR; DrAS 74H, 78H, 82H; EncAAH; EncAL; IntAu&W 76; WhoAm 74, 76, 78, 80, 82, 84, 86, 88, 90, 92, 94, 95, 96, 97; WhoWor 74; WhoWorJ 72, 78*

Apuleius, Lucius
Roman. Author, Orator
Major work *Metamorphoses* is only Latin novel to survive in its entirety .
b. 125 in Madaura, Byzacium
d. 200
Source: *AtlBL; BbD; BiD&SB; BioIn 5, 8, 11; CasWL; CyWA 58; DcEnL; DcPup; Grk&L; LinLib L, S; NewC; OxCEng 67; PenC CL; RComWL; REn; WorAl*

Apuzzo, Virginia M.
American. Social Reformer
NY governor Cuomo's liaison to the gay/lesbian community, 1986-89; vice-chair of the New York State AIDS Advisory Council, 1985-95.
b. Jun 26, 1941 in New York, New York
Source: *BioIn 19; GayLesB*

Aqqad, Abbas Mahmud al-
Egyptian. Author, Critic
Brought innovations to modern Arabic literature and its criticism; wrote *Sarah*, 1938.
b. Jun 28, 1889 in Aswan, Egypt
d. Mar 12, 1964 in Cairo, Egypt
Source: *CasWL*

Aquash, Anna Mae Pictou
Canadian. Political Activist
Member of the American Indian Movement (AIM); found murdered on the Pine Ridge Reservation.
b. Mar 27, 1945 in Shubenacadie, Nova Scotia, Canada
d. 1976?

Source: *NotNaAm*

Aquino, Benigno Simeon, Jr.
"Ninoy"
Philippine. Politician
Bitter rival of Ferdinand Marcos, assassinated upon return to Manila after three years exile in US.
b. Nov 27, 1932 in Concepcion, Philippines
d. Aug 21, 1983 in Manila, Philippines
Source: *BioIn 11, 12; ConAu 110; FarE&A 81; IntWW 83; NewYTBS 83; ObitOF 79*

Aquino, Corazon (Cojuangco)
"Cory"
Philippine. Political Leader
Widow of Benigno Aquino; opposed Ferdinand Marcos in 1986 elections; served as president, February 1986 to June 30, 1992.
b. Jan 25, 1933 in Manila, Philippines
Source: *BioIn 14, 15, 16; ConHero 1; ConNews 86-2; ContDcW 89; CurBio 86; DcMPSA; EncRev; EncWB; FacFETw; HeroCon; IntWW 89, 91; LegTOT; NewYTBS 85, 86, 90; WhoWor 87, 89, 91, 93, 95, 96, 97; WomFir*

Arafat, Yasir
[Abd al-Rahman Abd al-Raouf Arafat al-Qudwa; Yasser Arafat]
Palestinian. Political Leader
Head of PLO, 1969—; has sought recognition of a Palestinian homeland through both legal and violent means.
b. Aug 24, 1929 in Cairo, Egypt
Source: *BioIn 9, 10, 11, 14, 15, 16, 17, 18, 19, 20, 21; ColdWar 2; CurBio 71, 94; DcMidEa; DcTwHis; DicTyr; EncRev; EncWB; FacFETw; HisDcT; HisEAAC; IntWW 74, 75, 76, 77, 78, 79, 80, 81, 82, 83, 89, 91, 93; LegTOT; MidE 78, 79, 80, 81, 82; News 89-3; NewYTBE 71; NewYTBS 74, 75; PolLCME; WhoArab 81; WhoNob 95; WhoWor 82, 84, 95, 96, 97; WorAl; WorAlBi*

Arago, Dominque Francois Jean
French. Physicist
Noted for contributions to optics, magnetism.
b. Feb 26, 1786 in Perpignan, France
d. Oct 2, 1853 in Paris, France
Source: *AsBiEn; BbD; DcScB*

Aragon, Louis Marie Antoine Alfred
French. Poet
One of founders of French Surrealism, 1924.
b. Oct 3, 1897 in Paris, France
d. Dec 24, 1982 in Paris, France
Source: *ClDMEL 47; ConAu 69; ConLC 3, 22; EncWL 2; IntWW 74; McGEWB; ModFrL; ModRL; NewYTBS 82; PenC EUR; REn; TwCA SUP; WhDW; WorAl*

Araki, Gregg
American. Filmmaker
Released *The Doom Generation,* 1995.
b. 1959 in Los Angeles, California
Source: *GayLesB*

Araki Sadao
Japanese. Army Officer, Government Official
As general and government official, promoted ultranationalism and militarism; after WWII, was convicted of war crimes.
b. May 26, 1877 in Tokyo, Japan
d. Nov 2, 1966 in Totsukawa, Japan

Aramburu, Pedro Eugenio
Argentine. Political Leader
Pres., Argentina, 1955-58; replaced Peron's constitution with original democratic constitution.
b. May 21, 1903 in Buenos Aires, Argentina
d. Jul 16, 1970 in Timote, Argentina
Source: *BiDLAmC; BioIn 4, 9, 16; CurBio 57, 70; DcCPSAm; NewYTBE 70; ObitOF 79; WhAm 5*

Aranason, H. Harvard
American. Art Historian
Former administrator of NYC's Guggenheim Museum; wrote *History of Modern Art,* 1968.
b. 1909
d. May 28, 1986 in New York, New York
Source: *NewYTBS 86*

Araskog, Rand Vincent
American. Business Executive
Pres., CEO, board chm., ITT, 1979—.
b. Oct 30, 1931 in Fergus Falls, Minnesota
Source: *BioIn 12, 16; CurBio 91; Dun&B 90; IntWW 89, 91, 93; St&PR 84, 87, 91, 93, 96, 97; WhoAm 80, 82, 84, 86, 90, 92, 94, 95, 96, 97; WhoE 81, 85, 86, 89, 91, 93, 95, 97; WhoFI 81, 83, 85, 87, 89, 92, 94, 96; WhoWor 80, 82, 84, 87, 89, 91, 93, 95, 96, 97*

Arbatov, Georgi
Russian. Editor, Government Official
Leading Soviet Americanist; director, US, Canadian studies since 1967.
b. May 19, 1923 in Moscow, Union of Soviet Socialist Republics
Source: *BiDSovU; BioIn 13, 14, 16; ConAu 116; EncCW; IntWW 91; WhoWor 91*

Arbenz Guzman, Jacobo
Guatemalan. Political Leader
Pres., Guatemala, 1950-54; overthrown by CIA-organized coup.
b. Sep 14, 1913 in Quetzaltenango, Guatemala
d. Jan 27, 1971 in Mexico City, Mexico
Source: *BiDLAmC; BioIn 9, 10, 16, 18; ColdWar 2; CurBio 71N; DcCPCAm; DcHiB; DcTwHis; EncLatA; EncRev; EncWB; FacFETw*

Arber, Werner
Swiss. Biologist
Shared 1978 Nobel Prize in medicine for research in molecular genetics.
b. Jun 3, 1929 in Granichen, Switzerland
Source: *AmMWSc 89, 92, 95; BiESc; BioIn 12, 15, 20; FacFETw; IntWW 79, 80, 81, 82, 83, 89, 91, 93; LarDcSc; McGMS 80; NobelP; NotTwCS; Who 85, 92; WhoAm 88, 90, 92, 94, 95; WhoMedH; WhoNob, 90, 95; WhoScEn 94, 96; WhoWor 74, 76, 82, 84, 87, 89, 91, 93, 95, 96, 97; WorAl; WorAlBi; WorScD*

Arbib, Robert Simeon, Jr.
American. Ornithologist
Known for books about birds, nature; edited *American Birds* magazine, 1970-84.
b. Mar 17, 1915 in Gloversville, New York
d. Jul 20, 1987 in White Plains, New York
Source: *ConAu 33R, 123*

Arbour, Al(ger Joseph)
Canadian. Hockey Player, Hockey Coach
Defenseman, 1953-71, with four NHL teams; coached NY Islanders, 1973-86, to four straight Stanley Cups, 1980-83.
b. Nov 1, 1932 in Sudbury, Ontario, Canada
Source: *HocEn; WhoAm 84, 86, 90; WhoE 91; WhoHcky 73; WorAlBi*

Arbuckle, Fatty
[Roscoe Conkling Arbuckle; William B Goodrich]
American. Comedian, Director
Involved in famous Hollywood manslaughter scandal, 1921.
b. Mar 24, 1887 in Smith Center, Kansas
d. Jun 29, 1933 in Los Angeles, California
Source: *BiDFilm; BioIn 15, 17, 20; DcArts; FacFETw; Film 1; FilmgC; GrMovC; JoeFr; LegTOT; MotPP; MovMk; OxCFilm; TwYS; WhAm 1; WhoCom; WhoHol B; WhScrn 74, 77; WorAl; WorAlBi; WorEFlm*

Arbus, Diane
American. Photographer
Best known for photographs of "freaks"—midgets, giants, etc.
b. Mar 14, 1923 in New York, New York
d. Jul 26, 1971 in New York, New York
Source: *AmCulL; BioAmW; BioIn 7, 9, 10, 12, 13, 14, 15, 19, 20, 21; BriEAA; ConPhot 82, 88; ContDcW 89; DcAmArt; DcArts; DcTwCCu 1; FacFETw; GoodHs; GrLiveH; ICPEnP; IntDcWB; LegTOT; MacBEP; ModArCr 1; NewYTBE 73; NewYTBS 84; NotAW MOD; WhAm 5; WhoAmW 70, 72; WomArt; WorAl; WorAlBi*

Arbuthnot, John
English. Physician
Wrote five "John Bull" pamphlets, 1712, which popularized idea of John Bull as typical Englishman.
b. 1667 in Arbuthnot, Scotland
d. Feb 27, 1735 in London, England
Source: *Alli; Baker 78, 84, 92; BbD; Benet 87, 96; BiD&SB; BiHiMed; BioIn 3, 7, 8, 9, 17; BlkwCE; BlmGEL; BritAu; CamGEL; CamGLE; CasWL; Chambr 2; ChhPo; DcArts; DcEnA; DcEnL; DcLB 101; DcLEL; DcNaB; DcPup; DcScB; Dis&D; EvLB; InSci; LinLib L; LitC 1; NewC; NewCBEL; OxCEng 67, 85, 95; OxCMed 86; PenC ENG; ScF&FL 1; WebE&AL; WhDW*

Arbuthnot, May Hill
American. Author
Wrote best-selling textbook *Children and Books,* 1947.
b. Aug 27, 1884 in Mason City, Iowa
d. Oct 2, 1969 in Cleveland, Ohio
Source: *AuBYP 2, 3; BiDAmEd; BioIn 15; ChhPo, S2; ConAu 9R; DcAmLiB; InWom SUP; LinLib L; NotAW MOD; OhA&B; SmATA 2; WhAm 5; WhoAmW 70*

Arcand, Denys
Canadian. Filmmaker
Commercial films include *Le Decline De L'Empire Americain,* 1986, which won nine Genies; *Jesus De Montreal,* 1989, won twelve Genies.
b. Jun 25, 1941 in Deschambault, Quebec, Canada
Source: *BioIn 10, 15; CanWW 31, 89; ConAu 133; ConTFT 10; CurBio 90; IntMPA 92, 94, 96; IntWW 91, 93; MiSFD 9; WrDr 94, 96*

Arcaro, Eddie
[George Edward Arcaro]
American. Jockey, Journalist
First jockey to win horse racing's triple crown twice, 1941, 1948.
b. Feb 19, 1916 in Cincinnati, Ohio
Source: *AmDec 1940; BiDAmSp OS; BioIn 2, 3, 4, 5, 6, 7, 10, 12, 15, 16; CelR; CurBio 58; FacFETw; LegTOT; WebAB 74, 79; What 1; WhoAm 76, 78, 80, 82, 84, 86, 94, 95, 96, 97; WhoSpor; WorAl; WorAlBi*

Archambault, JoAllyn
American. Anthropologist
Director of the American Indian Program, National Museum of Natural History, Smithsonian Institution, 1986—.
b. Feb 13, 1942 in Claremore, Oklahoma
Source: *BioIn 21; NotNaAm*

Archer, Anne
[Mrs. Terry Jastrow]
American. Actor
Received Oscar nomination for *Fatal Attraction,* 1987; daughter of Marjorie Lord.
b. Aug 25, 1947? in Los Angeles, California
Source: *BioIn 16; CelR 90; ConTFT 6; HalFC 84, 88; IntMPA 86, 92; LegTOT; WhoHol 92, A*

Archer, Dennis W(ayne)
American. Politician, Lawyer
Justice, Michigan Supreme Court, 1986-90; mayor of Detroit, 1994—.
b. Jan 1, 1942 in Detroit, Michigan
Source: *InB&W 80; WhoAfA 96; WhoAm 82, 88, 90, 92, 94, 95, 96, 97; WhoAmL 78, 83, 85, 87, 90, 92, 94, 96; WhoAmP 87, 89, 91, 93, 95; WhoBlA 85, 88, 90, 92, 94; WhoEmL 87; WhoMW 88, 90, 92, 93, 96*

Archer, George
American. Golfer
On pro tour since 1964; has nine pro wins including Masters, 1969.
b. Oct 1, 1939 in San Francisco, California
Source: *WhoGolf; WhoIntG; WhoWest 92*

Archer, Jeffrey Howard
English. Author, Politician
MP, 1969-74; wrote *Kane and Abel,* 1979; *First Among Equals,* 1984.
b. Apr 15, 1940 in Weston-super-Mare, England
Source: *BioIn 14, 15, 16; ConAu 22NR, 77; ConLC 28; CurBio 88; IntAu&W 82, 91; IntWW 83, 91; NewYTBS 80, 85, 90; Novels; Who 85, 92; WhoWor 80, 91; WorAlBi; WrDr 86, 92*

Archerd, Army
[Armand Archerd]
American. Journalist, Actor
Announcer, "pre-Oscar" show, 1958—; columnist, *Daily Variety,* since 1953.
b. Jan 13, 1919 in New York, New York
Source: *ConAu 115, X; IntMPA 92; LegTOT; VarWW 85*

Archibald, Joe
[Joseph Stopford Archibale]
American. Cartoonist, Author
Wrote *The Fifth Base,* 1973; created first story comic strip "Saga of Steve West," 1928-29.
b. Sep 2, 1898 in Newington, New Hampshire
d. Mar 1, 1986 in Barrington, New Hampshire
Source: *AuBYP 2; ConAu 5NR, 9R, 118, X; SmATA 3*

Archibald, Nate
[Nathaniel Archibald]
"Tiny"
American. Basketball Player
Guard, 1970-84, mostly with Boston; first to lead NBA in scoring and assists in same year, 1973.
b. Apr 18, 1948 in New York, New York
Source: *BasBi; BiDAmSp BK; BioIn 9, 10, 11, 12, 13, 15, 20; CelR; InB&W 80, 85; NewYTBE 72, 73; WhoAfA 96; WhoAm 74, 76, 78, 80, 82, 84; WhoBbl 73; WhoBlA 77, 80, 85, 90, 92, 94; WhoSpor*

Archimedes
Greek. Mathematician
Pioneer in mechanics remembered for saying "Eureka!"; discovered principle of buoyancy.
b. 287?BC in Syracuse, Sicily, Italy
d. 212BC in Syracuse, Sicily, Italy
Source: *AsBiEn; Benet 87, 96; BiESc; BioIn 1, 3, 4, 5, 6, 7, 9, 10, 12, 13, 17, 20; CamDcSc; CasWL; CyEd; DcBiPP; DcEnL; DcScB; Grk&L; InSci; LarDcSc; LegTOT; LinLib L, S; McGEWB; NewC; OxCClL, 89; OxDcByz; PenC CL; RAdv 14, 13-5; REn; WhDW; WorAl; WorAlBi; WorInv; WorScD*

Archipenko, Alexander Porfirievich
American. Artist
Cubist-abstract sculptor; used plastic innovations in modern pieces.
b. May 30, 1887 in Kiev, Ukraine
d. Feb 25, 1964 in New York, New York
Source: *CurBio 53, 64; DcCAA 71; REn; WhAm 4*

Arciniegas, German
Colombian. Diplomat, Writer
Colombian ambassador to several countries, 1959-78; highly regarded modern Spanish-American writer; founder and contributor to *University,* 1928.
b. Dec 6, 1900 in Bogota, Colombia
Source: *BioIn 1, 2, 3, 12, 16; ConAu 10NR, 29NR, 61; CurBio 54; DcCLAA; DcSpL; EncLatA; HispWr; IntAu&W 77, 89; IntWW 74, 75, 76, 77, 78, 79, 80, 81, 82, 83, 89, 91, 93; LatAmWr; ModLAL; OxCSpan; PenC AM; RAdv 14; WhoWor 74, 76, 78*

Arden, Elizabeth
[Florence Nightengale Graham]
American. Cosmetics Executive
Pioneered advertising of beauty aids.
b. Dec 31, 1884 in Woodbridge, Ontario, Canada
d. Oct 18, 1966 in New York, New York
Source: *AmDec 1940; BiDAmBL 83; BioAmW; ContDcW 89; CurBio 57, 66; GayLesB; GoodHs; GrLiveH; IntDcWB; InWom, SUP; LegTOT; LibW; LinLib S; MacDWB; NotAW MOD; ObitOF 79; ObitT 1961; WebAB 74, 79; WhAm 4; WhoAmW 58, 64, 66, 68; WorAl*

Arden, Eve
[Eunice Quedens]
American. Actor
Won Emmy, 1953 for "Our Miss Brooks," radio/TV series, 1948-56; wrote autobiography *The Three Phases of Eve,* 1985.
b. Apr 30, 1912 in Mill Valley, California
d. Nov 12, 1990 in Los Angeles, California

Source: *BiDFilm 94; BiE&WWA; BioIn 3, 4, 10, 11, 14, 15, 17; CmMov; ConTFT 3; CurBio 53, 91N; EncAFC; EncMT; FacFETw; FilmEn; FilmgC; ForYSC; FunnyW; HalFC 80, 84, 88; IntDcF 1-3; IntMPA 77, 78, 79, 80, 81, 82, 84, 86, 88; InWom, SUP; JoeFr; LegTOT; LesBEnT 92; MotPP; MovMk; News 91, 91-2; NewYTBS 90; NotNAT; QDrFCA 92; RadStar; SaTiSS; ThFT; WhAm 10; WhoAm 74, 76, 78, 80, 82, 84; WhoAmW 58, 61, 64, 66, 68, 70, 72, 74; WhoCom; WhoHol A; WhoThe 72, 77, 81; WorAl; WorAlBi*

Arden, John
English. Dramatist
Controversial, innovative playwright whose modernistic plays include *The Workhouse Donkey,* 1963.
b. Oct 26, 1930 in Barnsley, England
Source: *Au&Wr 71; Benet 87, 96; BioIn 7, 8, 9, 10, 12, 13, 15, 16, 17; BlmGEL; BlueB 76; BritWr S2; CamGLE; CamGWoT; CasWL; CnMD; CnThe; ConAu 4AS, 13R, 31NR; ConBrDr; ConDr 73, 77, 82, 88, 93; ConLC 6, 13, 15; CroCD; CrtSuDr; CurBio 88; CyWA 89; DcArts; DcLB 13; DcLEL 1940; EncWL 2, 3; EncWT; Ent; GrWrEL DR; IntAu&W 76, 77, 89, 91, 93; IntDcT 2; IntvTCA 2; IntWW 74, 75, 76, 77, 78, 79, 80, 81, 82, 83, 89, 91, 93; LngCEL; LngCTC; MajTwCW; McGEWD 72, 84; ModBrL S1, S2; ModWD; NewC; NotNAT; OxCEng 85, 95; OxCIri; OxCThe 67, 83; PenC ENG; PlP&P; RAdv 14, 13-2; REnWD; RfGEnL 91; RGTwCWr; TwCWr; WebE&AL; WhDW; Who 74, 82, 83, 85, 88, 90, 92, 94; WhoThe 72, 77, 81; WhoTwCL; WhoWor 74, 84, 87, 89, 91, 93, 95, 96, 97; WorAu 1950; WrDr 76, 80, 82, 84, 86, 88, 90, 92, 94, 96*

Arditi, Luigi
Italian. Composer, Conductor
Operas include *I Briganti,* 1841; *La Spia,* 1856.
b. Jul 22, 1822 in Crescentino, Italy
d. May 1, 1903 in Hove, England
Source: *Baker 78, 84, 92; BioIn 4, 11; CelCen; DcNaB S2; MetOEnc; NewGrDA 86; NewGrDM 80; NewGrDO; NewOxM; OxCMus; OxDcOp; PenDiMP*

Ardizzone, Edward Jeffrey Irving
English. Author, Illustrator
Illustrated over 120 books; official war artist, 1940-45.
b. Oct 16, 1900 in Haiphong, Vietnam
d. Nov 8, 1979 in London, England
Source: *Au&ICB; Au&Wr 71; AuBYP 2; ConAu 5R, 8NR, 89; DcBrAr 1; IlsCB 1946, 1957; IntWW 74; LngCTC; MajAI; MorJA; NewYTBS 79; OxCEng 85, 95; PiP; SmATA 1; TwCChW 95; Who 74; WhoChL; WhoWor 74*

Ardrey, Robert
American. Scientist, Author
Popular scientific works include *African Genesis,* 1961.
b. Oct 16, 1908 in Chicago, Illinois
d. Jan 14, 1980 in Kalk Bay, South Africa
Source: *AmAu&B; AnObit 1980; BiE&WWA; BioIn 4, 9, 10, 12; BlkAWP; CelR; CnMD; ConAmD; ConAu 33R, 93; ConDr 73, 77, 93; CurBio 73, 80N; EncSF, 93; FilmEn; LinLib L; ModWD; NotNAT; OxCThe 83; PlP&P; ScF&FL 1, 2, 92; TwCA SUP; WhAm 7; WhDW; WhoAm 74, 76, 78, 80; WhoWor 74, 76, 78; WhThe; WorEFlm; WrDr 76, 80*

Arenas, Reinaldo
Cuban. Author
Wrote novels *Hallucinations,* 1969; *The Palace of the White Skunks,* 1980; novelist of the Cuban Revolution.
b. Jun 16, 1943, Cuba
d. Dec 7, 1990 in New York, New York
Source: *Benet 96; BenetAL 91; BioIn 12, 13, 16, 17, 18, 19, 20, 21; CaribW 4; ConAu 124, 128, 133; ConLC 41; CubExWr; DcCLAA; DcHiB; DcLB 145; DcTwCCu 4; DcTwCuL; EncWL 3; GayLesB; HispLC; HispWr; LatAmWr; LiExTwC; NewYTBS 90; RAdv 14, 13-2; ScF&FL 92; SpAmA; WhoHisp 91, 92N; WorAu 1985*

Arends, Leslie Cornelius
American. Politician
Rep. congressman, 1934-74; was House Whip for record 30 yrs.
b. Sep 27, 1895 in Melvin, Illinois
d. Jul 16, 1985 in Naples, Florida
Source: *BiDrAC; BiDrUSC 89; BioIn 1, 7, 9, 11, 12, 14; CurBio 48, 85; PolProf E, J, K, NF; WhAm 8; WhoAm 74, 76; WhoAmP 83; WhoGov 72, 75; WhoMW 74*

Arendt, Hannah
American. Author, Historian
Expert on 20th c. communism, nazism; wrote *The Origins of Totalitarianism,* 1951.
b. Oct 14, 1906 in Hannover, Germany
d. Dec 4, 1975 in New York, New York
Source: *AmAu&B; WhoWor 74, 76; WhoWorJ 72; WomFir; WomSoc; WorAl; WorAlBi; WorAu 1950; WrDr 76; WrPh P*

Arens, Moshe
Israeli. Government Official, Diplomat
Ambassador to US, 1982-83; succeeded Ariel Sharon as defense minister, 1983-84; minister without portfolio, 1984-87; foreign minister, 1989-90; defense minister, 1990-92.
b. Dec 27, 1925 in Kaunas, Lithuania
Source: *BioIn 12, 13, 15, 16; ConNews 85-1; CurBio 89; HisEAAC; IntWW 83, 89, 91, 93; MidE 82; NewYTBS 82, 83; WhoWor 84, 93; WhoWorJ 78*

Aretino, Pietro
"The Scourge of Princes"
Italian. Poet, Dramatist
Satirist; works include *Lewd Sonnets,* 1524; comedy *La Cortigiana,* 1525; satirized powerful contemporaries.
b. Apr 20, 1492 in Arezzo, Italy
d. Oct 21, 1556 in Venice, Italy
Source: *AtlBL; Benet 96; BiD&SB; BioIn 4, 5, 7, 8, 9, 11; BlmGEL; CamGWoT; CasWL; CnThe; CyWA 58; DcArts; DcEuL; DcItL 1, 2; EncWT; Ent; EuAu; EvEuW; IntDcT 2; LitC 12; LngCEL; McGEWD 72; NewC; NotNAT B; OxCEng 67, 85, 95; OxCThe 67, 83; PenC EUR; PlP&P; RAdv 14, 13-2; REn; REnWD; RfGWoL 95; WhDW*

Aretsky, Ken
American. Restaurateur
Chm., CEO, "21" Club, 1986—.
b. May 10, 1941 in New York, New York
Source: *ConNews 88-1*

Arevalo, Juan Jose
Guatemalan. Political Leader
Pres., Guatemala, 1945-51; instituted many social reforms during term.
b. Sep 10, 1904 in Taxisco, Guatemala
d. Oct 6, 1990 in Guatemala City, Guatemala
Source: *BioIn 16, 17; EncLatA; FacFETw; McGEWB*

Argelander, Friedrich Wilhelm August
German. Astronomer
Published *Bonn Survey,* 1862; invented modern star-naming system.
b. Mar 22, 1799 in Memel, Prussia
d. Feb 17, 1875 in Bonn, Prussia
Source: *AsBiEn; BiESc; BioIn 12, 14; CelCen; DcBiPP; DcScB; InSci; LarDcSc; NewCol 75; WebBD 83*

Argent
[Rod Argent; Russ Ballard; John Grimaldi; Robert Henrit; Jim Rodford; Jim Verity]
English. Music Group
Group formed, 1969-76; hits include "Hold Your Head Up," 1972.
Source: *ConMuA 80A; EncPR&S 89; EncRk 88; HarEnR 86; IlEncRk; RkOn 78; RolSEnR 83; WhoRock 81; WhoRocM 82*

Argent, Rod(ney Terence)
[Argent; Zombies]
English. Musician, Singer
Keyboardist, vocalist with Zombies, Argent, 1960s-70s.
b. Jun 14, 1945 in Saint Albans, England
Source: *PenEncP; WhoRocM 82*

Argentinita
[Lopez Encarmacion]
Spanish. Dancer
Founded the Ballet de Madrid with Garcia Lorca, 1927.

b. Mar 25, 1905 in Buenos Aires, Argentina
d. Sep 24, 1945 in New York, New York
Source: *BioIn 1, 3; InWom, SUP; NotNAT B; ObitOF 79*

Arghezi, Tudor
[Ion Theo; Ion N. Theodorescu]
Romanian. Author
Wrote *Covinte potrivite,* 1927; once poet laureate of Romania.
b. May 21, 1880 in Bucharest, Romania
d. Jul 14, 1967 in Bucharest, Romania
Source: *CasWL; ClDMEL 80; ConAu 116; ConLC 80; EncWL 2, 3; FacFETw; PenC EUR; RAdv 14, 13-2; WhDW; WhoTwCL; WorAu 1970*

Arguedas, Alcides
Bolivian. Author, Sociologist
Wrote *Race of Bronze,* 1919, a novel about Bolivian Indians, and the text *General History of Bolivia,* 1922.
b. Jul 15, 1879 in La Paz, Bolivia
d. May 8, 1946 in Chulumani, Bolivia
Source: *Benet 87, 3; LinLib L; ModLAL; OxCSpan; PenC AM; REn*

Arguedas, Jose Maria
Peruvian. Author, Ethnologist
Wrote *Bloody Feast,* 1941, and autobiographical novel *Deep Rivers,* 1958; writings show differences between white and Indian cultures.
b. Jan 18, 1911 in Andahuaylas, Peru
d. Nov 28, 1969 in Lima, Peru
Source: *Benet 87, 3; HispWr; LatAmWr; ModLAL; OxCSpan; PenC AM; RAdv 14, 13-2; SpAmA; WorAu 1950*

Arguello, Alexis
Nicaraguan. Boxer
Pro boxer since 1968 who has 76-5 record in three weight divisions.
b. Apr 12, 1952 in Managua, Nicaragua
Source: *BioIn 11, 13, 15; BoxReg; NewYTBS 82, 86; WhoHisp 91, 92, 94; WhoSpor*

Arias, Jimmy
American. Tennis Player
Turned pro, 1981; won 1981 French Open mixed doubles with Andrea Jaeger.
b. Aug 16, 1964 in Grand Island, New York
Source: *BioIn 13, 14; NewYTBS 83; WhoAm 94, 95, 96, 97; WhoE 95; WhoIntT*

Arias, Roberto Emilio
Panamanian. Lawyer, Editor
Diplomat, paralyzed in assassination attempt, 1964; husband of Dame Margot Fontey.
b. 1918
d. Nov 22, 1989 in Panama City, Panama
Source: *BioIn 5, 6, 7, 16; FacFETw; IntWW 74, 75, 76, 77, 78, 79, 80, 81, 82, 83, 89, 91; NewYTBS 89; Who 74, 82, 83, 85, 88, 90; WhoWor 74*

Arias Madrid, Arnulfo
Panamanian. Political Leader
Civilian president of Panama, 1940-41, 1949-51, 1968, each time ousted by military; died in exile.
b. Aug 15, 1901, Panama
d. Aug 10, 1988 in Miami, Florida
Source: *BiDLAmC; DcCPCAm; FacFETw; IntWW 79, 80, 81, 82, 83; NewYTBS 88*

Arias Sanchez, Oscar
Costa Rican. Political Leader
Pres. of Costa Rica, 1986-90; won Nobel Peace Prize for leadership in peace plan involving five Central American countries, 1987.
b. Sep 13, 1941 in Heredia, Costa Rica
Source: *ConHero 1; CurBio 87; DcCPCAm; DcHiB; HispWr; IntWW 89, 91; News 89-3; NewYTBS 87; Who 90, 92; WhoAm 88; WhoWor 87, 89, 91, 93; WorAlBi*

Aries, Philippe
French. Author
Described work as history of non-events; wrote *Centuries of Childhood,* 1960.
b. Jul 21, 1914 in Blois, France
d. Feb 8, 1984 in Toulouse, France
Source: *AnObit 1984; Au&Wr 71; BioIn 10, 14, 17; ConAu 89, 112; IntAu&W 76, 77, 82; NewYTBS 84; ThTwC 87; WhoWor 84; WorAu 1980*

Arieti, Silvano
American. Psychoanalyst, Author
Believed depression treatable with psychotherapy, not drugs; wrote *Interpretation of Schizophrenia,* 1975.
b. Jun 28, 1914 in Pisa, Italy
d. Aug 7, 1981 in New York, New York
Source: *AmMWSc 73S, 76P, 79; AnObit 1981; BiDrAPA 77; BioIn 12; ConAu 10NR, 21R, 104; EncSPD; NewYTBS 81; WhAm 9; WhoAm 76, 78, 80, 82; WhoWor 74, 76*

Ariosto, Ludovico
Italian. Poet
Produced finest Italian romantic epic, *Orlando Furioso,* 1532.
b. Sep 8, 1474 in Reggio Nell'Emilia, Italy
d. Jul 6, 1533 in Ferrara, Italy
Source: *AtlBL; BbD; BiD&SB; BioIn 4, 5, 7, 8, 10, 13; BlmGEL; CamGWoT; CasWL; CyWA 58; DcArts; DcCathB; DcEuL; DcItL 1, 2; EncWT; Ent; EuAu; GrFLW; IntDcT 2; LinLib L, S; LitC 6; LngCEL; McGEWB; McGEWD 72, 84; NewC; NewGrDM 80; NewGrDO; NotNAT B; OxCEng 67, 85, 95; OxCThe 83; PenC EUR; PlP&P; RAdv 14, 13-2; RComWL; REn; RfGWoL 95; WorAlBi*

Arisman, Marshall
American. Artist, Illustrator, Educator
Chaimman, visual journalism program, School of Visual Arts NYC, 1984—.
b. Oct 14, 1938 in Jamestown, New York
Source: *BiDScF; BioIn 16; WhoAm 86; WhoGrA 82*

Arison, Ted
Israeli. Businessman
Founder, chm., Carnival Cruise Lines Inc., 1972—; owner, Miami Heat, 1993—.
b. Feb 24, 1924 in Tel Aviv, Israel
Source: *BioIn 13, 16; News 90, 90-3; WhoAm 84, 86, 88, 90, 92; WhoFI 89; WhoSSW 91; WhoWor 91*

Aristide, Jean-Bertrand
Haitian. Clergy, Political Leader
Roman Catholic priest and Haiti's first democratically elected Pres., 1990-91, 1994-96; popular, aggressive liberation theologist helped undermine Duvalier regime with anti-government sermons; was himself overthrown by military coup.
b. Jul 15, 1953 in Port-Salut, Haiti
Source: *ConAu 147; ConBlB 6; CurBio 91; DcCPCAm; News 91, 91-3; NewYTBS 90; RadHan*

Aristides
"The Just"
Greek. Statesman
Influential in Athenian politics; known for honesty, impartiality.
b. 530?BC in Athens, Greece
d. 468?BC in Athens, Greece
Source: *Benet 87, 96; BiD&SB; DcEnL; DcNAA; LegTOT; LngCEL; NewC; NewCol 75; OxCClL; REn; WhDW*

Aristophanes
Greek. Dramatist
Greatest comic playwright of ancient world; wrote 55 plays, 11 survive today.
b. 448BC
d. 385BC
Source: *AtlBL; BbD; BiD&SB; BioIn 1, 5, 7, 11, 12, 13; BlmGEL; CasWL; CnThe; CyEd; CyWA 58; DcArts; DcEnL; Dis&D; McGEWD 72; NewC; OxCClL; OxCEng 67, 85, 95; OxCThe 67, 83; PenC CL; PlP&P; RComWL; REn; REnWD; WhDW*

Aristotle
Greek. Author, Philosopher
Member Plato's Academy, 367-347 BC; created Logic, the science of reasoning.
b. 384BC in Chalcidice, Greece
d. 322BC in Chalcis, Greece
Source: *AncWr; AsBiEn; AtlBL; Baker 78, 84, 92; BbD; Benet 87, 96; BiD&SB; BiDPsy; BiESc; BioIn 1, 2, 3, 4, 5, 6, 7, 8, 9, 10, 11, 12, 13, 15, 16, 17, 18, 20; BlmGEL; CamDcSc; CamGWoT; CasWL; CnThe; CopCroC; CyEd; CyWA 58; DcAmC; DcArts; DcBiPP; DcEnL;*

DcEuL; DcInv; DcScB; Dis&D; EncDeaf; EncEarC; EncEth; EncPaPR 91; EncUrb; EncWT; Grk&L; IlEncMy; InSci; LarDcSc; LegTOT; LinLib L; LngCEL; LuthC 75; MagSWL; McGEWB; NamesHP; NewC; NewCBEL; NewGrDM 80; NotNAT B; OxCClL, 89; OxCEng 67, 85, 95; OxCLaw; OxCMed 86; OxCPhil; OxCThe 67; OxDcByz; PenC CL; PlP&P; RAdv 14, 13-3, 13-4, 13-5; RComWL; REn; REnWD; RfGWoL 95; WhDW; WorAl; WorAlBi; WorScD; WrPh P

Arius
Alexandrian. Theologian
Priest; believed Christ was created being rather than divine being; his teaching, called Arianism, created rift in church; declared heresy at Council of Nicaea, 325.
b. 256 in Alexandria, Egypt
d. 336 in Alexandria, Egypt
Source: *Benet 87, 96; DcBiPP; LinLib L, S; LuthC 75; REn; WebBD 83; WhDW*

Arizin, Paul Joseph
"Pitchin' Paul"
American. Basketball Player
In NBA with Philadelphia, 1950-51, 1954-62; led league in scoring, 1952, 1957; Hall of Fame, 1977.
b. Apr 9, 1928 in Philadelphia, Pennsylvania
Source: *BiDAmSp BK; BioIn 2, 9; OfNBA 87; WhoBbl 73*

Arkell, Anthony John
English. Abolitionist, Archaeologist
Helped end slave trade between Sudan and Ethiopia; participated in excavations and research dealing with Sudanese prehistory.
b. Jul 29, 1898 in Hinxhill, England
d. Feb 26, 1980 in Chelmsford, England
Source: *Au&Wr 71; BioIn 13; ConAu 97, 102; FifIDA; MidE 78, 79; Who 74*

Arkell, William Joscelyn
English. Paleontologist
Highly regarded for research of Jurassic fossils; wrote *Jurassic Geology of the World,* 1956.
b. Jun 9, 1904 in Highworth, England
d. Apr 18, 1958 in Cambridge, England
Source: *BioIn 4, 5; DcNaB 1951; DcScB; InSci; ObitT 1951; WhE&EA*

Arkin, Alan Wolf
[Roger Short]
American. Actor, Director
Won Tony Award, 1963, for *Enter Laughing.*
b. Mar 26, 1934 in New York, New York
Source: *ASCAP 66; BiE&WWA; BioIn 14, 15, 16; BkPepl; ConTFT 2; CurBio 67; EncAFC; EncFCWM 69; FilmgC; HalFC 88; IntMPA 86, 92; IntWW 79, 80, 81, 82, 83, 89, 91, 93; MotPP; MovMk; NewYTBE 70; NewYTBS 86; NotNAT; SmATA 59; WhoAm 74, 76, 78, 80, 82, 84, 86, 88, 90, 92, 94, 95, 96, 97; WhoEnt 92; WhoHol A; WhoThe 81; WhoWor 74; WorAl; WorAlBi*

Arkoff, Samuel Z
American. Producer, Film Executive
Has produced films since 1961: *Love at First Bite,* 1979; *Dressed to Kill,* 1980.
b. Jun 12, 1918 in Fort Dodge, Iowa
Source: *BioIn 16; ConTFT 3; HalFC 88; IntMPA 92; St&PR 87; WhoAm 90; WhoEnt 92*

Arkwright, Richard, Sir
English. Inventor
Patented spinning frame, 1769, increasing cloth production.
b. Dec 23, 1732 in Preston, England
d. Aug 3, 1792 in Cromford, England
Source: *AsBiEn; BiESc; BioIn 2, 5, 6, 8, 9, 12, 14, 15, 17, 20; DcBiPP; DcInv; DcNaB; EncEnl; InSci; LinLib S; McGEWB; NewCol 75; OxCDecA; WhDW; WorAl; WorAlBi; WorInv*

Arledge, Roone Pinckney, Jr.
American. TV Executive
Currently pres., ABC News; as pres., ABC Sports, changed sports coverage with slow-stop action, split-screens.
b. Jul 8, 1931 in Forest Hills, New York
Source: *BiDAmSp OS; BioIn 8, 10, 11, 12, 13, 14, 15, 16; CelR 90; ConTFT 4; EncTwCJ; FacFETw; IntMPA 92; LesBEnT 92; News 92, 92-2; NewYTBS 79; WhoAdv 90; WhoAm 74, 86, 90; WhoE 91; WhoEnt 92; WhoFI 92*

Arlen, Harold
[Hyman Arluck; Chaim Arluk]
American. Songwriter
Wrote over 500 hits including Oscar winner "Over the Rainbow," 1939; "Stormy Weather," 1933; "Old Black Magic," 1942.
b. Feb 15, 1905 in Buffalo, New York
d. Apr 23, 1986 in New York, New York
Source: *AmCulL; AmPS; AmSong; AnObit 1986; ASCAP 66, 80; Baker 78, 84, 92; BestMus; BiDAmM; BiE&WWA; BioIn 1, 3, 4, 5, 6, 9, 10, 12, 14, 15, 16, 19, 20; CelR; CmpEPM; ConAmC 76, 82; ConNews 86-3; CurBio 55, 86, 86N; EncMT; EncWT; FacFETw; FilmEn; FilmgC; GangFlm; HalFC 80, 84, 88; IntMPA 75, 76, 77, 78, 79, 80, 81, 82, 84, 86; LegTOT; NewAmDM; NewCBMT; NewGrDA 86; NewGrDM 80; NewOxM; NewYTBS 86; NotNAT; OxCAmT 84; OxCFilm; OxCPMus; PenEncP; PlP&P; PopAmC, SUP; Sw&Ld C; WebAB 74, 79; WhAm 9; WhoAm 74, 76; WhoHrs 80; WhoThe 72, 77, 81; WhoWor 74; WorAl; WorAlBi*

Arlen, Michael
English. Author
Melodramatic novelist best known for *The Green Hat,* 1924.
b. Nov 16, 1895 in Roustchouk, Bulgaria
d. Jun 25, 1956 in New York, New York
Source: *Benet 87, 96; BioIn 1, 3, 4, 7, 8, 14, 15; CamGLE; ConAu 120; DcAmB S6; DcArts; DcLB 36, 77, 162; DcLEL; DcNaB 1951; EncMys; EncSF, 93; EvLB; GrWrEL N; HalFC 88; LiExTwC; LngCTC; ModBrL; NewCBEL; NotNAT B; Novels; ObitOF 79; ObitT 1951; OxCEng 85, 95; PenC ENG; PenEncH; REn; RfGEnL 91; RGTwCWr; ScF&FL 1; TwCA, SUP; TwCRGW; TwCRHW 90, 94; TwCWr; WhAm 3; WhLit; WhoHr&F; WhThe*

Arlen, Richard
[Richard Cornelius van Mattimore]
American. Actor
Starred in movies *Wings,* 1927; *The Virginian,* 1929.
b. Sep 1, 1898 in Charlottesville, Virginia
d. Mar 28, 1976 in North Hollywood, California
Source: *BioIn 7, 10; FilmEn; FilmgC; GangFlm; HalFC 80, 84, 88; IntDcF 1-3; IntMPA 75; LegTOT; MovMk; ObitOF 79; SilFlmP; TwYS; WhoHrs 80; WhScrn 83*

Arletty
[Arlette-Leonie Bathiat]
French. Actor
Appeared in films *Children of Paradise,* 1945; *No Exit,* 1954.
b. May 15, 1898 in Courbevoie, France
d. Jul 25, 1992 in Paris, France
Source: *AnObit 1992; BiDFilm, 81, 94; BioIn 11, 13, 14, 18, 19; ContDcW 89; DcTwCCu 2; EncEurC; EncWT; Ent; FilmAG WE; FilmEn; FilmgC; HalFC 80, 84, 88; IntDcF 1-3, 2-3; IntDcWB; IntWW 74, 75, 76, 77, 78, 79, 80, 81, 82, 83, 91; InWom, SUP; ItaFilm; LegTOT; MovMk; NewYTBS 92; OxCFilm; WhoFr 79; WhoHol 92, A; WhoWor 74; WorEFlm*

Arliss, George
[George Augustus Andrews]
English. Actor
Won Oscar for title role in *Disraeli,* 1929.
b. Apr 10, 1868 in London, England
d. Feb 5, 1946 in London, England
Source: *ApCAB X; BioIn 1, 3, 5, 7, 9, 15; CamGWoT; ChhPo; CurBio 46; DcAmB S4; DcNaB 1941; EncWT; FamA&A; Film 2; FilmEn; FilmgC; ForYSC; HalFC 80, 84, 88; IntDcF 1-3, 2-3; LegTOT; LinLib L, S; MotPP; MovMk; NewC; NotNAT A, B; ObitOF 79; OxCAmT 84; OxCFilm; OxCThe 67, 83; PlP&P; SilFlmP; TwYS; WhAm 2; WhoHol B; WhoStg 1908; WhScrn 74, 77, 83; WhThe; WorAl; WorAlBi; WorEFlm*

Arliss, Leslie
[Leslie Andrews]
English. Director
Films included *The Wicked Lady,* 1945; launched careers of James Mason, Stewart Granger.
b. 1901 in London, England

d. Dec 31, 1987? in London, England
Source: *AnObit 1987; ConAu 124; FilmEn; FilmgC; HalFC 80, 84, 88; IlWWBF; WorEFlm*

Armani, Giorgio
Italian. Fashion Designer
Founded Giorgio Armani Co., 1975; developed unconstructed blazer.
b. Jul 11, 1934 in Piacenza, Italy
Source: *BioIn 12, 13, 14, 16; CelR 90; ConDes 84, 90, 97; ConFash; CurBio 83; DcTwDes; EncFash; FacFETw; IntWW 89, 91, 93; LegTOT; News 91, 91-2; WhoAm 82, 84, 86, 90, 92, 94, 95, 96, 97; WhoE 95; WhoFash 88; WhoWor 82, 84, 87, 89, 91, 93, 95, 97*

Armatrading, Joan
British. Singer, Songwriter
Acoustic-based album, *Joan Armatrading,* best-seller in England, 1976; other albums include *Secret Secrets,* 1985.
b. Dec 9, 1950 in Saint Kitts
Source: *Baker 92; BiDJaz; BioIn 11, 12, 13, 17; ConAu 114; ConLC 17; ConMuA 80A; ConMus 4; DrBlPA 90; EncPR&S 89; EncRk 88; EncRkSt; IlEncBM 82; IlEncRk; InB&W 80, 85; IntWW 89, 91, 93; InWom SUP; LegTOT; MacDWB; NewWmR; OnThGG; OxCPMus; PenEncP; RkOn 85; RolSEnR 83; WhoAm 86, 90; WhoEnt 92; WhoRock 81*

Armendariz, Pedro
Mexican. Actor
Top Mexican film star; appeared in over 75 films: *From Russia With Love,* 1963.
b. May 9, 1912 in Mexico City, Mexico
d. Jun 18, 1963 in Los Angeles, California
Source: *BioIn 6; Film 2; FilmEn; FilmgC; ForYSC; HalFC 80, 84, 88; HispAmA; HolCA; IntDcF 1-3, 2-3; ItaFilm; LegTOT; MotPP; MovMk; NotNAT B; WhoHol B; WhScrn 74, 77, 83; WorEFlm*

Armetta, Henry
Italian. Actor
Comedian who played character roles in movies, 1923-46.
b. Jul 4, 1888 in Palermo, Sicily, Italy
d. Oct 21, 1945 in San Diego, California
Source: *BioIn 7; CurBio 45; EncAFC; Film 2; FilmEn; FilmgC; ForYSC; HalFC 80, 84, 88; HolCA; MovMk; NotNAT B; ObitOF 79; TwYS; Vers A; WhoHol B; WhScrn 74, 77, 83*

Armey, Richard K(eith)
American. Politician
Rep. congressman from TX, 1985—; House majority leader, 1995—.
b. Jul 7, 1940 in Cando, North Dakota
Source: *BiDrUSC 89; CngDr 85, 87; CurBio 95; WhoAm 86, 88, 90, 92, 94, 95, 96, 97; WhoAmP 85, 87, 89, 91, 93, 95; WhoE 95; WhoSSW 86, 88, 91, 93, 95, 97; WhoWor 96*

Arminius, Jacobus
[Hermansz; Jacob Harmensen Hermanns]
Dutch. Theologian
Founded, Arminianism, evident today in Methodist theologies.
b. Oct 10, 1560 in Oudewater, Netherlands
d. Oct 19, 1609 in Leiden, Netherlands
Source: *BenetAL 91; BioIn 5, 6, 9, 16; DcBiPP; EncWM; LuthC 75; McGEWB; NewC; WhDW*

Armitage, Kenneth
English. Sculptor
Bronze abstracts noted for suggestions of liberty, movement.
b. Jul 18, 1916 in Leeds, England
Source: *BioIn 4, 6, 8, 10; BlueB 76; ConArt 77, 83, 89, 96; ConBrA 79; CurBio 57; DcBrAr 1; DcCAr 81; IntWW 74, 75, 76, 77, 78, 79, 80, 81, 82, 83, 89, 91, 93; McGDA; OxCArt; OxCTwCA; OxDcArt; PhDcTCA 77; TwCPaSc; Who 74, 82, 83, 85, 88, 90, 92, 94; WhoArt 80, 82, 84, 96; WhoWor 74, 76, 78; WorArt 1950*

Armour, Norman
American. Diplomat
Assistant secretary of state for foreign affairs, 1947-49; negotiated withdrawal of Marines from Haiti, 1933.
b. Oct 4, 1887 in Brighton, England
d. Sep 27, 1982 in New York, New York
Source: *BioIn 1, 3, 11, 13, 16; CurBio 45, 82, 82N; DcAmDH 80, 89; NewYTBS 82; PolProf E, T; WhAm 9*

Armour, Philip Danforth
American. Businessman
Started Armour and Co., major meat packer; estimated worth $50 million at death.
b. May 16, 1832 in Stockbridge, New York
d. Jan 6, 1901 in Chicago, Illinois
Source: *AmBi; ApCAB SUP, X; BiDAmBL 83; BioIn 3, 5, 9, 15; DcAmB; EncAAH; HarEnUS; LinLib S; McGEWB; NatCAB 7; NewCol 75; OxCAmH; TwCBDA; WebAB 74, 79; WhAm 1; WorAl*

Armour, Richard Willard
American. Poet
Whimsical poet known for poking fun at everything; poems usually four lines long ; had syndicated newspaper column "Armour's Armory."
b. Jul 15, 1906 in San Pedro, California
d. Feb 28, 1989 in Claremont, California
Source: *AmAu&B; AnCL; Au&Wr 71; AuBYP 2, 3; BenetAL 91; BioIn 15, 16; ChhPo, S1, S2, S3; ConAu 1R, 4NR, 32NR, 128; CurBio 58, 89, 89N; EncAHmr; FifBJA; IntAu&W 91; NewYTBS 89; REnAL; SmATA 14, 61; WhoAm 74, 76, 82, 84, 88; WhoWor 89; WorAl; WorAlBi; WrDr 76, 90*

Armour, Tommy
[Thomas D Armour]
"Silver Scot"
Scottish. Golfer
International player, joined US tour, 1924; won US Open, 1927, PGA, 1930, British Open, 1931; charter member, Hall of Fame, 1940.
b. Sep 24, 1895 in Edinburgh, Scotland
d. Sep 11, 1968 in Larchmont, New York
Source: *WhoGolf; WhoSpor*

Armstrong, Anne Legendre
[Mrs. Tobin Armstrong]
American. Educator, Government Official
Ambassador to UK, 1976-77.
b. Dec 27, 1927 in New Orleans, Louisiana
Source: *AmMWSc 73S; AmPolW 80; BioIn 14, 16; BioNews 74; ConAu 13R; DcAmDH 80, 89; IntWW 76, 77, 78, 79, 80, 81, 82, 83, 89, 91, 93; InWom SUP; NatCAB 63N; NewYTBE 72; NewYTBS 76; Who 82, 83, 85, 88, 90, 92, 94; WhoAm 74, 76, 78, 80, 82, 84, 86, 88, 90, 92, 94, 95, 96, 97; WhoAmP 73, 75, 77, 79, 81, 83, 85, 87, 89, 91, 93, 95; WhoAmW 66, 68, 70, 72, 74, 83, 85, 87, 89, 91, 93, 95, 97; WhoFI 89; WhoSSW 73; WhoWor 78, 80, 82, 84, 96*

Armstrong, Bess
[Elizabeth Key Armstrong]
American. Actor
Starred on TV in "Lace," 1984; in film in *Four Seasons,* 1981; *High Road to China,* 1983.
b. Dec 11, 1953 in Baltimore, Maryland
Source: *BioIn 11, 12, 17; ConTFT 6; HalFC 88; IntMPA 88, 92, 94, 96; LegTOT; VarWW 85; WhoAmW 97; WhoHol 92*

Armstrong, Billie Joe
American. Singer, Songwriter
In band Green Day; Grammy for Best Alternative Music Performance for *Dookie,* 1994.
b. Feb 17, 1972 in Rodeo, California

Armstrong, Charles B
American. Publisher, Editor
Editor, publisher, Chicago's weekly black-oriented *Metro News,* 1972-85.
b. Jul 22, 1923 in Nashville, Tennessee
d. Mar 25, 1985 in Chicago, Illinois
Source: *ConAu 115; WhoBlA 80*

Armstrong, Charlotte
American. Author
Suspense murder-mystery writer; won Poe award for *A Dram of Poison,* 1956.
b. May 2, 1905 in Vulcan, Michigan
d. Jul 18, 1969 in Glendale, California
Source: *AmAu&B; AmWomWr; ArtclWW 2; BioIn 1, 8, 10, 14; ConAu 1R, 3NR, 25R; CorpD; CrtSuMy; CurBio 46, 69; DetWom; EncMys; FemiCLE; GrWomMW; InWom, SUP; LegTOT; PenNWW A; TwCCr&M 80, 85, 91;*

TwCRGW; TwCRHW 90; WhAm 5; WhoAmW 58, 66, 68, 70; WorAu 1950

Armstrong, Debbie
American. Skier
Won gold medal, women's giant slalom, 1984 Olympics.
b. 1964?
Source: *BiDAmSp OS; BioIn 13*

Armstrong, Edwin Howard
American. Inventor, Engineer
Constructed first FM radio station, 1937, in Alpine, NJ.
b. Dec 18, 1891 in New York, New York
d. Feb 1, 1954 in New York, New York
Source: *CurBio 40, 54; DcAmB S5; DcScB; InSci; McGEWB; NewYTBS 79; NotNAT B; ObitOF 79; OxCAmH; WebAB 74; WhAm 3; WorAl*

Armstrong, Garner Ted
American. Evangelist, Author
Founded Church of God International, 1978; wrote *The Real Jesus,* 1972.
b. 1930 in Eugene, Oregon
Source: *BkPepl; ConAu 113; PrimTiR; RelLAm 91; WhoRel 75*

Armstrong, George Edward
"The Chief"
Canadian. Hockey Player
Center, Toronto, 1949-71; won four Stanley Cups; Hall of Fame, 1975.
b. Jul 6, 1930 in Skead, Ontario, Canada
Source: *HocEn; WhoHcky 73*

Armstrong, Gillian (May)
Australian. Director
Directed *My Brilliant Career,* 1979; *Little Women,* 1994.
b. Dec 18, 1950 in Melbourne, Australia
Source: *ConTFT 7; CurBio 95; IntDcF 2-2; IntMPA 88, 92, 94, 96; LegTOT; MiSFD 9; WhoAm 97*

Armstrong, Hamilton Fish
American. Journalist, Editor
Founder, editor *Foreign Affairs,* 1922-72, who wrote on int'l. politics.
b. Apr 7, 1893 in New York, New York
d. Apr 24, 1973 in New York, New York
Source: *AmAu&B; AmPeW; BiDInt; BioIn 1, 2, 3, 4, 6, 9, 10, 11, 18; ChhPo; ColdWar 1; ConAu 41R, 93; CurBio 48, 73, 73N; DcAmB S9; EncAI&E; EncAJ; LinLib L; TwCA, SUP; WhAm 5; WhE&EA; WhNAA; WhoWor 74*

Armstrong, Henry
"Homicide Hank"
American. Boxer
First boxer to simultaneously hold three official world boxing titles, 1938; Hall of Fame, 1954.
b. Dec 12, 1912 in Columbus, Mississippi
d. Oct 22, 1988 in Los Angeles, California
Source: *AfrAmAl 6; AfrAmSG; AnObit 1988; BiDAmSp BK; BioIn 3, 4, 5, 7, 8, 9, 10, 13, 15, 16, 21; BlksB&W C; BoxReg; CmCal; FacFETw; InB&W 80, 85; LegTOT; NegAl 76, 83, 89; News 89-1; NewYTBS 88; What 5; WhoBox 74; WhoSpor; WorAl; WorAlBi*

Armstrong, Herbert W
American. Evangelist
Founded Worldwide Church of God, 1947; used media to spread fundamentalist beliefs: radio show "The World Tomorrow"; father of Garner Ted.
b. Jul 31, 1892 in Des Moines, Iowa
d. Jan 16, 1986 in Pasadena, California
Source: *BioIn 10, 11; ConAu 116, 118; NewYTBS 86; WhoAm 80, 82, 84; WhoRel 75, 77, 85; WhoWest 80, 82*

Armstrong, Jack Lawrence
American. Air Force Officer
Colonel, whose name was given to "All-American Boy" played by Jim Ameche on radio, 1933-38.
b. 1911 in Winnipeg, Manitoba, Canada
d. Jun 10, 1985 in Laguna Niguel, California

Armstrong, Lil(lian Hardin)
American. Jazz Musician
Ex-wife of Louis Armstrong; pianist, arranger, vocalist, composer, 1920s-60s.
b. Feb 3, 1902 in Memphis, Tennessee
d. Aug 27, 1971 in Chicago, Illinois
Source: *ASCAP 66, 80; BiDAfM; BlkWAB; CmpEPM; EncJzS; GrLiveH; InB&W 80; NegAl 83; WhoJazz 72*

Armstrong, Louis
[Daniel Louis Armstrong]
"Satchmo"
American. Musician, Bandleader
Called world's greatest trumpeter; introduced "scat" singing.
b. Jul 4, 1900 in New Orleans, Louisiana
d. Jul 6, 1971 in New York, New York
Source: *ASCAP 66, 80; Baker 78, 84; BgBands 74; BiDAfM; BiDAmM; BiDJaz; BioIn 1, 2, 3, 4, 5, 6, 7, 8, 9, 10, 11, 12, 13, 14, 15, 16, 17, 18, 19, 20, 21; BriBkM 80; CmpEPM; ConAmC 76, 82; ConAu 29R; ConBlB 2; ConHero 2; ConMus 4; CurBio 44, 66, 71, 71N; DcTwCCu 5; DrBlPA; EncAB-H 1974, 1996; EncJzS; FacFETw; FilmEn; FilmgC; ForYSC; HalFC 80, 84, 88; IlEncJ; InB&W 80, 85; ItaFilm; LegTOT; MakMC; MnPM; MovMk; MusMk; NegAl 76, 83, 89; NewAmDM; NewCol 75; NewGrDM 80; NewOrJ; NewOxM; NewYTBE 70, 71; ObitT 1971; OxCAmH; OxCMus; RAdv 14, 13-3; RComAH; RkOn 74; WebAB 74; WhAm 5; WhDW; WhoHol B; WhoJazz 72; WhScrn 74, 77, 83; WorAl; WorAlBi*

Armstrong, Neil Alden
American. Astronaut
Aboard *Apollo 11;* first man to walk on moon, Jul 20, 1969.
b. Aug 5, 1930 in Wapakoneta, Ohio
Source: *AmMWSc 86, 92; AsBiEn; BioIn 12, 13, 14, 16; ConHero 1; CurBio 69; FacFETw; IntWW 81, 82, 91; LinLib S; McGEWB; NewYTBS 86; PolProf NF; WebAB 74, 79; WebAMB; WhDW; Who 85, 92; WhoAm 84, 86, 90; WhoEng 88; WhoSpc; WhoWor 84, 87, 91; WorAl; WorAlBi*

Armstrong, Otis
American. Football Player
Running back, Denver, 1973-80; led NFL in rushing, 1974.
b. Nov 11, 1950 in Chicago, Illinois
Source: *WhoAm 78, 80; WhoBlA 77, 80; WhoFtbl 74*

Armstrong, R. G
American. Actor
Gruff character actor whose films include *Ride the Wild Country,* 1962; *Heaven Can Wait,* 1978.
b. Apr 7, 1917 in Birmingham, Alabama
Source: *ConTFT 8; FilmEn; FilmgC; HalFC 88; VarWW 85; WhoHol A*

Armstrong, Robb
American. Cartoonist
Created "Jump Start," strip about a young working-class black couple.
Source: *BioIn 17, 21*

Armstrong, Robert
American. Actor
Starred in *King Kong,* 1933, as hunter who brought ape to civilization.
b. Nov 20, 1890 in Saginaw, Michigan
d. Apr 20, 1973 in Santa Monica, California
Source: *BioIn 9, 11; EncAFC; FilmEn; FilmgC; GangFlm; HalFC 80, 84, 88; HolP 30; MovMk; TwYS; Vers B; WhoHol B; WhoHrs 80; WhScrn 77*

Armstrong, Samuel Chapman
American. Military Leader, University Administrator
Commanded Union black soldiers during American Civil War; established Hampton Institute, 1868.
b. Jan 30, 1839 in Maui, Hawaii
d. May 11, 1893 in Hampton, Virginia
Source: *AmBi; AmRef; AmSocL; ApCAB SUP; BiDAmEd; BiDSocW; BioIn 1, 3, 5, 8, 15, 19; CivWDc; DcAmB; DcAmReB 1, 2; DcNAA; EncSoH; HarEnUS; McGEWB; NatCAB 1, 38; PeoHis; TwCBDA; WebAB 74, 79; WhAm HS*

Armstrong, Thomas M
American. Businessman
Cork maker who started linoleum plant, 1908; co. now known for floors, ceilings.
b. 1836 in Pennsylvania
d. 1908
Source: *BioIn 2; Entr*

Armstrong, William Howard
American. Children's Author, Educator
Wrote 1972 Newbery winner, *Sounder.*
b. Sep 14, 1914 in Lexington, Virginia
Source: *AuBYP 2, 3; AuNews 1; BioIn 8, 9, 10, 14, 19; ChlLR 1; ConAu 9NR; DcAmChF 1960; MorBMP; OxCChiL; SmATA, 4; ThrBJA; WhoAm 74, 76, 78, 80, 82, 84, 86, 88, 90; WhoE 74; WrDr 88*

Armstrong, William L
American. Politician
Millionaire Republican senator from CO, 1978-91.
b. Mar 16, 1937 in Fremont, Nebraska
Source: *AlmAP 78, 80, 82, 84, 88; BioIn 9, 12, 13; CngDr 74, 77, 79, 81, 83, 85, 87, 89; PolsAm 84; WhoAm 74, 76, 78, 80, 82, 84, 86, 88, 90; WhoAmP 87, 89, 91, 93, 95; WhoGov 75, 77; WhoWest 74, 76, 78, 80, 82, 84, 87, 89, 92; WhoWor 80, 82, 84, 87, 89, 91*

Armstrong-Jones, Antony Charles Robert
[Earl of Snowden]
English. Photographer, Socialite
Ex-husband of Britain's Princess Margaret; known for celebrity portraits, TV documentaries.
b. Mar 7, 1930 in London, England
Source: *BioIn 5, 6, 7, 8, 9, 10, 11, 13; ConAu 43NR, 118; CurBio 60; MacBEP; Who 82, 92; WhoWor 74, 76, 78, 91, 93, 95, 96, 97; WorFshn*

Arnall, Ellis (Gibbs)
American. Politician
Dem. governor, GA, 1943-47.
b. Mar 20, 1907 in Newnan, Georgia
d. Dec 13, 1992 in Atlanta, Georgia
Source: *BiDrGov 1789; BioIn 1, 2, 11, 12, 18, 19, 21; BlueB 76; CurBio 45, 93N; Dun&B 90; IntMPA 75, 76, 77, 78, 79, 80, 81, 82, 84, 86, 88, 92, 94, 96; IntWW 74, 75, 81, 82, 83, 89, 91; IntYB 78, 79, 80, 81, 82; St&PR 75, 84, 87, 91; WhAm 11; WhoAm 74, 76, 78, 80, 82, 84, 86, 88, 90; WhoAmL 83; WhoAmP 73, 75, 77, 79, 81, 83, 85, 87, 89, 91; WhoFI 89; WhoIns 75, 76, 78, 79, 80, 81, 82, 84, 86, 88, 90*

Arnaz, Desi
[Desiderio Alberto Arnaz de Acha, III]
American. Actor, Singer, Producer
Rumba bandleader; formed Desilu Productions with wife, Lucille Ball, 1950; best known as Ricky Ricardo, 1950-57.
b. Mar 2, 1917 in Santiago de Cuba, Cuba
d. Dec 2, 1986 in Del Mar, California
Source: *AnObit 1986; BioIn 2, 3, 4, 5, 9, 10, 15, 16, 17, 18, 20, 21; CmpEPM; ConAmBL; ConMus 8; ConNews 87-1; ConTFT 3, 4; CurBio 52, 87, 87N; DcHiB; EncAFC; FacFETw; FilmEn; FilmgC; ForYSC; HispAmA; IntMPA 75, 76, 77, 78, 79, 80, 81, 82, 84, 86; LegTOT; NewYTBS 86; PenEncP; VarWW 85; WhAm 9; WhoAm 74; WhoCom; WhoHol A; WorAl; WorAlBi*

Arnaz, Desi(derio Alberto IV), J
American. Actor
Son of Desi Arnaz, Lucille Ball; began career as rock singer; film debut, *Red Sky at Morning,* 1972.
b. Jan 19, 1953 in Los Angeles, California
Source: *BioIn 14, 15; HalFC 88; IntMPA 76, 77, 78, 79, 80, 81, 82, 92; VarWW 85; WhoHisp 92; WhoHol A; WorAlBi*

Arnaz, Lucie Desiree
[Mrs. Lawrence Luckinbill]
American. Actor, Singer
Daughter of Desi Arnaz, Lucille Ball; starred in film *The Jazz Singer,* 1980; *They're Playing Our Song* on Broadway.
b. Jul 17, 1951 in Hollywood, California
Source: *BioIn 9; HalFC 88; IntMPA 92; InWom SUP; VarWW 85; WhoAm 80, 82, 84, 86, 88, 90, 92; WhoEnt 92; WhoHisp 92; WorAlBi*

Arne, Thomas Augustine
English. Composer
His patriotic song "Rule Britannia" is from masque *Alfred,* 1740.
b. Mar 12, 1710 in London, England
d. Mar 5, 1778 in London, England
Source: *Alli; AtlBL; Baker 78, 84, 92; BioIn 4, 5, 11, 12, 20; BriBkM 80; DcBiPP; DcCathB; DcCom 77; DcCom&M 79; DcNaB; IntDcOp; LegTOT; LinLib L, S; McGEWB; MusMk; NewAmDM; NewC; NewEOp 71; NewGrDM 80; NewGrDO; NewOxM; NotNAT B; OxCEng 85, 95; OxCMus; OxDcOp; REn; WhDW*

Arness, James
[James Aurness]
American. Actor
Starred as Matt Dillon in TV series "Gunsmoke," 1955-75; brother of Peter Graves.
b. May 26, 1923 in Minneapolis, Minnesota
Source: *BioIn 4, 9, 10, 11, 12, 15, 16; CelR, 90; ConTFT 3; CurBio 73; FacFETw; FilmEn; FilmgC; ForYSC; HalFC 80, 84, 88; IntMPA 75, 76, 77, 78, 79, 80, 81, 82, 84, 86, 88, 92, 94, 96; LegTOT; LesBEnT 92; MotPP; MovMk; NewYTET; VarWW 85; WhoAm 74, 76, 78, 80, 82, 84; WhoHol 92, A; WhoHrs 80; WorAl; WorAlBi*

Arnett, Peter Gregg
American. Broadcast Journalist
Pulitzer Prize-winning reporter for AP, 1961-81; CNN, 1981—; only American correspondent in Baghdad, Iraq during 1991 Persian Gulf War.
b. Nov 13, 1934 in Riverton, New Zealand
Source: *BioIn 7, 9, 10; CurBio 91; EncTwCJ; IntWW 91; LesBEnT 92; WhoAm 74, 76, 78, 80; WhoWor 74, 80*

Arno, Peter
[Curtis Arnoux Peters, Jr.]
American. Cartoonist
With *New Yorker* as cartoonist, 1925-68; established tone of magazine.
b. Jan 8, 1904 in New York, New York
d. Feb 22, 1968 in Port Chester, New York
Source: *AmAu&B; BioIn 8, 18; ConAu 25R, 73; CurBio 52, 68; DcAmB S8; EncTwCJ; FacFETw; LegTOT; LinLib L; LngCTC; WebAB 74, 79; WhAm 4, 4A; WhAmArt 85; WhoAmA 89N, 91N, 93N; WorAl; WorAlBi; WorECar*

Arnold, Benedict
American. Army Officer, Traitor
Revolutionary patriot; betrayed American cause by offering military information to British, 1779-80.
b. Jan 14, 1741 in Norwich, Connecticut
d. Jun 14, 1801 in London, England
Source: *AmBi; AmRev; AmWrBE; ApCAB; BenetAL 91; BioIn 1, 2, 3, 4, 5, 6, 7, 8, 9, 10, 12, 13, 14, 15, 17, 19, 20; BlkwEAR; DcAmB; DcAmMiB; DcCanB 5; DcNaB; Dis&D; Drake; EncAB-H 1974, 1996; EncAI&E; EncAR; EncCRAm; GenMudB; HarEnMi; HarEnUS; HisDBrE; HisWorL; LegTOT; LinLib S; MacDCB 78; McGEWB; NatCAB 1; OxCAmH; OxCAmL 65, 83, 95; OxCCan; OxCShps; RComAH; REn; REnAL; TwCBDA; WebAB 74, 79; WebAMB; WhAm HS; WhAmRev; WhDW; WhoMilH 76; WorAl; WorAlBi*

Arnold, Danny
[Arnold Rothman]
American. Producer
Produced TV's "Barney Miller," 1973-81.
b. Jan 23, 1925 in New York, New York
d. Aug 19, 1995 in Los Angeles, California
Source: *BioIn 12, 78, 79, 80, 81, 82, 84, 86, 88, 92, 94; LesBEnT 92; NewYTET; VarWW 85; WhoAm 78, 80, 82, 84, 86; WhoHol 92*

Arnold, Eddy
"The Tennessee Plowboy"
American. Singer, Musician
Country singer, guitarist, who made debut, 1936; country Music Hall of Fame, 196 6; recorded *You Don't Miss a Thing,* 1991 and *Last of the Love Song Singers,* 1993.
b. May 15, 1918 in Henderson, Tennessee
Source: *Baker 84, 78, 79, 80, 81, 82, 86, 88, 92, 94, 96; LegTOT; NewAmDM; NewGrDA 86; OxCPMus; PenEncP; RadStar; RkOn 74; VarWW 85; WhoAm 74, 76, 78, 80, 82, 84, 86, 88, 90, 92, 94, 95, 96, 97; WhoEnt 92; WhoHol 92; WorAl; WorAlBi*

Arnold, Edward
[Gunter Edward Arnold Schneider]
American. Actor
Starred in *Diamond Jim,* 1935; *Sutter's Gold,* 1936.

b. Feb 18, 1890 in New York, New York
d. Apr 26, 1956 in San Fernando, California
Source: *BiDFilm 94; BioIn 4, 6, 7, 21; DcAmB S6; EncAFC; Film 1; FilmEn; FilmgC; ForYSC; GangFlm; HalFC 80, 84, 88; HolCA; LegTOT; MGM; MotPP; MovMk; NatCAB 45; NotNAT A, B; OlFamFa; OxCFilm; RadStar; SaTiSS; Vers A; WhAm 3; WhScrn 74, 77, 83; WorAl; WorAlBi*

Arnold, Edwin
English. Author
Wrote blank verse epic *The Light of Asia,* 1879, dealing with life of Buddha.
b. Jul 10, 1832 in Gravesend, England
d. Mar 24, 1904 in London, England
Source: *Alli, SUP; BbD; BiD&SB; BioIn 3, 6, 14; BritAu 19; CamGEL; CelCen; Chambr 3; ChhPo, S1, S2, S3; DcEnA, A; DcEnL; DcEuL; DcInB; DcLB 35; DcLEL; DcNaB S2; EvLB; HisDBrE; LinLib L; LngCTC; NewC; NewCBEL; OxCEng 67, 85, 95; REn*

Arnold, Harold De Forest
American. Physicist
Designed and developed manufacturing methods for thermionic tubes used in transcontinental and intercontinental radio telephony, 1914-15.
b. Sep 3, 1883 in Woodstock, Connecticut
d. Jul 10, 1933 in Summit, New Jersey

Arnold, Henry Harley
''Hap''
American. Military Leader
First general of Air Force, 1949; used air power as weapon during WW II.
b. Jun 25, 1886 in Gladwyne, Pennsylvania
d. Jan 15, 1950 in Sonoma, California
Source: *AmAu&B; BiDWWGF; BioIn 1, 2, 6, 7, 9, 12, 14, 16; CurBio 42, 50; DcAmB S4; DcAmMiB; FacFETw; HarEnMi; InSci; LinLib L, S; McGEWB; NatCAB 45; OxCAmH; WebAB 74, 79; WebAMB; WhAm 2; WhoMilH 76; WhWW-II; WorAl*

Arnold, Leslie Philip
American. Aviator
With others made first around the world flight, flying two planes in 57 hops from Seattle, Apr - Sep 1924.
b. Aug 28, 1893 in New Haven, Connecticut
d. Mar 21, 1961 in Leonia, New Jersey
Source: *BioIn 5; DcAmB S7; WhAm 4*

Arnold, Malcolm, Sir
English. Composer
Film compositions include *Island in the Sun,* 1957; *Trapeze,* 1984.
b. Oct 21, 1921 in Northampton, England
Source: *Baker 78, 84, 92; BiDD; BioIn 6, 8, 17; BlueB 76; CmMov; CnOxB; CompSN, SUP; ConCom 92; CpmDNM 79; DcCM; DcCom&M 79; EncEurC; FilmEn; FilmgC; HalFC 80, 84, 88; IntDcF 1-4, 2-4; IntWW 74, 75, 76, 77, 78, 79, 80, 81, 82, 83, 89, 91, 93; IntWWM 77, 80; MusMk; NewAmDM; NewGrDM 80; NewOxM; OxCFilm; OxCPMus; PenDiMP A; Who 74, 82, 83, 85, 88, 90, 92; WhoMus 72; WhoWor 74, 76, 78; WorEFlm*

Arnold, Matthew
English. Author, Critic
Oxford professor, known for poem ''Dover Beach,'' 1853; social criticism *Culture and Anarchy,* 1869; son of Thomas.
b. Dec 24, 1822 in Laleham, England
d. Apr 15, 1888 in Liverpool, England
Source: *Alli, SUP; AtlBL; BbD; Benet 87, 96; BenetAL 91; BiD&SB; BioIn 1, 2, 3, 4, 5, 6, 7, 8, 9, 10, 11, 12, 13, 14, 15, 16, 18, 20; BlmGEL; BritAu 19; BritWr 5; CamGEL; CamGLE; CasWL; CelCen; ChhPo, S1, S2, S3; CnDBLB 4; CnE&AP; CrtT 3, 4; CyEd; CyWA 58; DcAmC; DcArts; DcBiPP; DcEnA, A; DcEnL; DcEuL; DcLB 32, 57; DcLEL; DcNaB S1; Dis&D; EncUnb; EvLB; GrWrEL P; LegTOT; LinLib L, S; LngCEL; LuthC 75; MagSWL; McGDA; McGEWB; MouLC 4; NewC; NewCBEL; NinCLC 6, 29; NotNAT B; OxCAmL 65, 83, 95; OxCEng 67, 85, 95; OxCIri; OxCLiW 86; OxCMus; OxCThe 67, 83; PenC ENG; PoeCrit 5; RAdv 1, 14, 13-1; RComWL; REn; REnAL; RfGEnL 91; RGFBP; TwoTYeD; VicBrit; WebE&AL; WhDW; WorAl; WorAlBi; WorLitC; WrPh*

Arnold, Oren
American. Children's Author, Editor
Wrote over 2,000 magazine articles, tales of western America: *Wit of the West,* 1980.
b. Jul 20, 1900 in Minden, Texas
Source: *BioIn 3, 9, 10; ConAu 2NR, 5R; SmATA 4*

Arnold, Thomas
''Arnold of Rugby''
English. Educator
Developed modern British schools with introduction of math, modern language.
b. Jun 13, 1795 in Cowes, Isle of Wight, England
d. Jun 12, 1842 in Rugby, England
Source: *Alli; BbD; BiD&SB; BioIn 2, 3, 5, 8, 9, 10, 14, 15, 16; BlmGEL; BritAu 19; CamGEL; CamGLE; CasWL; CelCen; ChhPo; CyEd; DcBiPP; DcEnA; DcEnL; DcEuL; DcLB 55; DcLEL; DcNaB; EvLB; LinLib L, S; LngCEL; LuthC 75; McGEWB; NewC; NewCBEL; News 93-2; NinCLC 18; OxCChiL; OxCClL; OxCEng 67, 85, 95; PenC ENG; REn; VicBrit; WhDW; WorAl; WorAlBi*

Arnold, Thurman Wesley
American. Lawyer
US Asst. Atty. General, Anti-trust division, 1938-43; number one trust-buster of the nation.
b. Jun 2, 1891 in Laramie, Wyoming
d. Nov 7, 1969 in Alexandria, Virginia
Source: *AmAu&B; AmPolLe; BiDFedJ; BioIn 1, 4, 7, 8, 9, 10, 11, 19; ConAu P-1; CurBio 40, 69; DcAmB S8; McGEWB; NatCAB 55; ObitOF 79; REnAL; TwCA SUP; WebAB 74, 79; WhAm 5*

Arnold, Tom
American. Actor, Comedian, Writer
Writer/producer ''Roseanne'' TV Show; star of ''Jackie Thomas'' show, 1992-1993; films include, *True Lies,* 1994; *Nine Months,* 1995.
b. Mar 6, 1959 in Ottumwa, Iowa
Source: *BioIn 16; ConTFT 13; LegTOT; News 93-2*

Arnoldson, Klas Pontus
Swedish. Political Activist
Shared 1908 Nobel Peace Prize for working for peace for 35 yrs.
b. Oct 27, 1844 in Goteborg, Sweden
d. Feb 20, 1916 in Stockholm, Sweden
Source: *BiDMoPL; BioIn 9, 11, 15; LinLib L; WhoNob, 90, 95*

Arnon, Daniel I(srael)
American. Scientist
First person to reproduce photosynthesis outside a living cell, 1954.
b. Nov 14, 1910
d. Dec 20, 1994 in Berkeley, California
Source: *AmMWSc 73P, 76P, 79, 82, 86, 89, 92, 95; BioIn 3, 4; CurBio 95N; InSci; IntWW 74, 75, 76, 77, 78, 79, 80, 81, 82, 83, 89, 91, 93; McGMS 80; WhAm 11; WhoAm 74, 76, 78, 80, 82, 84, 86, 88, 90, 92, 94, 95, 96; WhoFrS 84; WhoWor 74, 76, 78*

Arnoux, Rene Alexandre
French. Auto Racer
One of top drivers on Grand Prix racing circuit, 1980s.
b. Jul 4, 1948 in Grenoble, France
Source: *WhoWor 82*

Arnow, Harriette Louisa Simpson
American. Author
Wrote novels about Appalachian life: *The Dollmaker,* 1954, made into TV movie starring Jane Fonda, 1983.
b. Jul 7, 1908 in Wayne County, Kentucky
d. Mar 22, 1986 in Washtenaw County, Michigan
Source: *AmAu&B; AmNov; AmWomWr; BioIn 14, 15, 16, 17, 20; ConAu 9R, 14NR; ConLC 18; ConNov 82; CurBio 54, 86; MichAu 80; SouWr; WorAu 1950; WrDr 84*

Arnstein, Bobbie
American. Secretary
Hugh Hefner's secretary for 14 yrs; convicted of conspiring to deliver cocaine; committed suicide.
b. 1940
d. Jan 1975 in Chicago, Illinois
Source: *BioIn 10*

Aroldingen, Karin von
[Karin Awny Hannelore Reinbold von Aroldingen und Eltzingen]
German. Dancer
With NYC Ballet, 1962-84.
b. Jul 9, 1941 in Greiz, Germany
Source: *BiDD; BioIn 11, 13; CnOxB; CurBio 83; DcBiPP; InWom SUP; WhoAm 82, 84*

Aron, Raymond Claude Ferdinand
French. Author
Scholar, prominent conservative commentator on world affairs; wrote *In Defense of Decadent Europe,* 1979.
b. Mar 14, 1905 in Paris, France
d. Oct 17, 1983 in Paris, France
Source: *Au&Wr 71; BiDFrPL; CasWL; ClDMEL 80; ConAu 2NR, 49, 111; CurBio 54, 84; IntAu&W 76, 77; IntWW 74, 75, 76, 77, 78, 79, 80, 81, 82, 83; NewYTBS 83; WhAm 8; Who 74, 82, 83; WhoWor 74, 76, 78; WorAu 1950; WrDr 76*

Aronson, Boris
American. Designer
Won five Tonys for stage designing including one for *Cabaret,* 1967.
b. Oct 15, 1900 in Kiev, Russia
d. Nov 16, 1980 in Nyack, New York
Source: *AnObit 1980; BiDD; BiE&WWA; BioIn 7, 10, 12; CelR; CnThe; IntDcT 3; McGDA; MetOEnc; NewYTBS 80; NotNAT; OxCAmT 84; OxCThe 67, 83; PlP&P; WhAm 7; WhAmArt 85; WhoAm 80; WhoAmA 73, 76, 78, 80, 82, 82N, 84N, 86N, 89N, 91N, 93N; WhoAmJ 80; WhoOp 76; WhoThe 72, 77, 77A, 81; WhoWor 74; WhoWorJ 78*

Arp, Hans
[Jean Arp]
French. Author, Sculptor
Founded Dadaist movement; wrote *Dreams and Projects,* 1952.
b. Sep 16, 1887 in Strasbourg, France
d. Jun 7, 1966 in Basel, Switzerland
Source: *AtlBL; Benet 87, 96; BioIn 3, 4, 5, 6, 7, 8, 9, 10, 11, 12, 13, 14, 15, 16; CasWL; ConAu 25R, 42NR, 81; ConLC 5; CurBio 54, 66; DcArts; DcTwCCu 2; DcTwDes; EncWL; FacFETw; IntDcAA 90; LegTOT; MakMC; McGDA; McGEWB; ModArCr 1; ModGL; ObitT 1961; OxCArt; OxCGer 76, 86; OxCTwCA; OxDcArt; PenC EUR; PhDcTCA 77; REn; WhAm 4; WhDW; WhoTwCL; WorAl; WorAlBi; WorArt 1950*

Arquette, Cliff
[Charley Weaver]
American. Actor
Best remembered for appearances on game show "Hollywood Squares."
b. Dec 28, 1905 in Toledo, Ohio
d. Sep 23, 1974 in Burbank, California
Source: *AmAu&B; ASCAP 66, 80; BioIn 3, 5, 6, 10; ConAu 53, X; CurBio 61, 74, 74N; EncAFC; JoeFr; LegTOT; NewYTBS 74; RadStar; WhoCom; WhoHol B; WhScrn 77, 83*

Arquette, Patricia
American. Actor
Sister of actress Rosanna Arquette; performed in movies *Ethan Frome,* 1993; *True Romance,* 1993.
b. Apr 8, 1968 in New York, New York
Source: *BioIn 15; ConTFT 13; IntMPA 94, 96; LegTOT; WhoAm 96, 97; WhoAmW 97; WhoHol 92*

Arquette, Rosanna
[Mrs. James Newton Howard]
American. Actor
Appeared in films *The Executioner's Song,* 1982; *Desperately Seeking Susan,* 1985.
b. Aug 10, 1960 in New York, New York
Source: *BioIn 13, 14, 15, 16; CelR 90; ConNews 85-2; ConTFT 6; HalFC 88; IntMPA 86, 88, 92; VarWW 85; WhoEnt 92*

Arrabal (Teran), Fernando
Spanish. Dramatist
Pioneered in abstract theater; most of his 60 plays published in France.
b. Aug 11, 1932 in Melilla, Spanish Morocco
Source: *Benet 87, 3; EncWT; Ent; IntAu&W 77, 89, 91, 93; IntDcT 2; IntvSpW; IntWW 75, 76, 77, 78, 79, 80, 81, 82, 83, 89, 91, 93; LiExTwC; MakMC; McGEWB; McGEWD 72, 84; ModFrL; ModWD; NewYTBE 72; OxCSpan; OxCThe 83; PenC EUR; TwCWr; WhDW; WhoAm 76; WhoFr 79; WhoThe 72, 77, 81; WhoWor 74, 78, 82, 84, 87, 89, 91, 93, 95, 96, 97; WorAu 1950; WrPh*

Arran, Arthur Kattendyke Strange David Archibald Gore, Earl of
"Boofy"
English. Journalist, Politician
Sponsored 1966 Sexual Offences Bill, legalizing homosexual acts between consenting adults; author *Lord Arran Writes,* 1964.
b. Jul 5, 1910
d. Feb 23, 1983 in Hemel Hempstead, England
Source: *AnObit 1983; BioIn 13; NewYTBS 83; Who 82; WhoAm 82*

Arrau, Claudio
American. Pianist
One of world's great classical pianists and finest interpreters of Beethoven; made international concert debut in Berlin, 1915.
b. Feb 6, 1903 in Chillan, Chile
d. Jun 9, 1991 in Muerzzuschlag, Austria
Source: *AnObit 1991; Baker 78, 84, 92; BiDAmM; BioIn 4, 5, 6, 7, 9, 11, 12, 13, 14, 15, 16, 17, 18, 20, 21; BlueB 76; BriBkM 80; CelR, 90; ConMus 1; CurBio 42, 86, 89, 91N; DcArts; DcHiB; DcTwCCu 3; IntWW 74, 75, 76, 77, 78, 79, 80, 81, 82, 83, 89, 91; IntWWM 77, 80, 85, 90; LegTOT; MusMk; MusSN; NewAmDM; NewGrDA 86; NewGrDM 80; News 92, 92-1; NewYTBS 78, 83, 91; NotTwCP; PenDiMP; WhAm 10; Who 74, 82, 83, 85, 88, 90, 92N; WhoAm 78, 80, 82, 84, 86, 88, 90; WhoAmM 83; WhoHisp 92, 92N; WhoMus 72; WhoWor 74, 76, 78, 80, 82, 84, 87, 89, 91; WorAl; WorAlBi*

Arrested Development
[Baba Oje; Headliner; Montsho Eshe; Rasa Don; Todd "Speech" Thomas]
American. Rap Group
Atlanta-based group known for their casual clothing and positive messages; hit album *3 Years, 5 Months and 2 Days in the Life of,* 1992 had smash single "Tennessee".
Source: *ConMus 14; EncRkSt; News 94, 94-2*

Arrhenius, Svante August
Swedish. Chemist, Physicist
Founded modern physical chemistry, 1884; won Nobel Prize, 1903, for electrolytic dissociation theory.
b. Feb 19, 1859 in Uppsala, Sweden
d. Oct 2, 1927 in Stockholm, Sweden
Source: *AsBiEn; BiESc; BioIn 3, 5, 6, 8, 12, 13, 14, 15, 16, 19, 20; CamDcSc; DcInv; DcScB; FacFETw; InSci; LarDcSc; LinLib L, S; McGEWB; NewCol 75; NotTwCS; WhDW; WhoNob, 90, 95; WorAl; WorScD*

Arrighi, Ludovico degli
Italian. Type Designer
Developed italic lettering; composed first writing manual *La Operina,* 1522.

Arriola, Gus
Mexican. Cartoonist
Created comic strip "Gordo," 1941.
b. Jul 23, 1917 in Florence, Arizona
Source: *BioIn 1, 16; ConAu 127, 129; EncACom; MexAmB; WhoAm 78, 80, 82; WhoHisp 92; WorECom*

Arron, Henck Alphonsus Eugene
Surinamese. Political Leader
Prime minister of Suriname, 1973-80; ousted by a military coup.
b. Apr 25, 1936 in Paramaribo, Dutch Guiana
Source: *BiDLAmC; BioIn 16; DcCPSAm; IntWW 79, 80, 81, 82, 83, 89, 91, 93; WhoWor 89, 91*

Arrow, Kenneth Joseph
American. Economist
Pioneered work on general economic equilibrium theory; won Nobel Prize, 1972.
b. Aug 23, 1921 in New York, New York
Source: *AmMWSc 73S, 78S, 92; BioIn 9, 10, 12, 13, 14, 15, 17; ConAu 13NR; GrEconS; IntWW 83, 91; IntYB 82; NewYTBE 72; NobelP; OxCPhil; RAdv 14, 13-3; ThTwC 87; WebAB 74, 79; Who 74, 82, 83, 85, 88, 90, 92, 94; WhoAm 74, 76, 78, 80, 82, 84, 86, 88, 90, 92, 94, 95, 96, 97; WhoAmJ 80; WhoE 77, 79; WhoEc 81, 86; WhoFI 83, 85, 87, 89, 92, 94, 96; WhoNob, 90, 95; WhoScEn 94, 96; WhoWest 82, 84, 87, 89, 92, 94, 96; WhoWor 74, 76, 78, 80, 82, 84, 87, 89, 91, 93, 95, 96, 97; WrDr 86, 92, 94, 96*

Arroyo, Martina
American. Opera Singer
Leading soprano with NY Met., 1970-74; noted for Verdi, Rossini roles.
b. Feb 2, 1937 in New York, New York
Source: *Baker 84; BioIn 16; BlkWAm; CurBio 71; InB&W 85; IntDcOp; IntWWM 90; InWom SUP; LegTOT; MetOEnc; NegAl 89; NewAmDM; NewGrDA 86; NewGrDM 80; NewYTBE 72; PenDiMP; WhoAm 86, 90; WhoAmW 91; WhoBlA 75, 92; WhoHisp 92; WhoMus 72; WhoWor 74; WorAlBi*

Artaud, Antonin
French. Actor, Director, Poet
Closely identified with "Theater of Cruelty;" died in insane asylum.
b. Sep 4, 1896 in Marseilles, France
d. Mar 4, 1948 in Paris, France
Source: *Benet 87, 96; BioIn 7, 8, 9, 10, 11, 12, 14, 16, 18, 20; BlmGEL; CamGWoT; CasWL; ClDMEL 80; CnThe; ConAu 104; CroCD; CyWA 89; DcArts; DcTwCCu 2; EncWB; EncWL; EncWT; Ent; EuWr 11; EvEuW; FacFETw; FilmEn; FilmgC; GrFLW; GuFrLit 1; HalFC 80, 84, 88; IntDcF 1-3, 2-3; IntDcT 3; LegTOT; LiExTwC; LngCTC; MajMD 2; MakMC; McGEWD 72, 84; ModFrL; ModRL; ModWD; NotNAT A, B; OxCEng 85, 95; OxCFilm; OxCThe 67, 83; PenC EUR; RAdv 14; REn; REnWD; ThTwC 87; TwCLC 3, 36; TwCWr; WhDW; WhoTwCL; WhScrn 77, 83; WorAu 1950; WorEFlm*

Artemisia
Persian. Ruler
Erected one of seven wonders of ancient world, Mausoleum at Halicarnassus, honoring husband Mausolus.
d. 350?BC
Source: *BioIn 4, 16; DcBiPP; EncAmaz 91; InWom, SUP; LinLib L, S; OxCClL, 89; WomWR*

Arthur, Beatrice
[Bernice Frankel]
American. Actor
Starred in TV series "Maude," 1972-78; "The Golden Girls," 1985-92, for which she won Emmy, 1988.
b. May 13, 1926 in New York, New York
Source: *BiE&WWA; BioIn 15; BkPepl; ConTFT 4; CurBio 73; EncAFC; EncMT; HalFC 88; IntMPA 81, 92, 94, 96; InWom SUP; LesBEnT 92; MotPP; NotNAT; WhoAm 78, 80, 82, 84, 86, 88, 90, 92, 94, 95, 96, 97; WhoAmW 79, 95, 97; WhoCom; WhoEnt 92; WhoThe 77, 81; WorAl; WorAlBi*

Arthur, Chester A(lan)
American. US President
Twenty-first pres., succeeded James Garfield, 1881-84; supported civil service reform, 1883.
b. Oct 5, 1830 in Fairfield, Vermont
d. Nov 18, 1886 in New York, New York
Source: *AfrAmPr; AmBi; AmPolLe; ApCAB; BiDrAC; BiDrUSC 89; BiDrUSE 71, 89; BioIn 1, 2, 3, 4, 5, 6, 7, 8, 9, 10, 11, 12, 13, 14, 15, 16, 17, 18, 19, 20; CyAG; DcAmB; EncAAH; HarEnUS; LinLib L, S; McGEWB; NatCAB 4; OxCAmH; OxCAmL 65, 83; REnAL; TwCBDA; VicePre; WebAB 74; WebAMB; WhAm HS; WhAmP; WorAl*

Arthur, Ellen Lewis Herndon
[Mrs. Chester A Arthur]
American.
Soprano soloist; died suddenly year before husband became president.
b. Aug 30, 1837 in Frederick, Virginia
d. Jan 12, 1880 in New York, New York
Source: *BioIn 3, 5, 6, 7, 16, 17; GoodHs; InWom SUP; NotAW*

Arthur, Jean
[Gladys Georgianna Greene]
American. Actor
Squeaky-voiced leading lady of 1930s-40s films; nominated for Oscar for *The More the Merrier,* 1943; last film *Shane,* 1953.
b. Oct 17, 1901 in Plattsburg, New York
d. Jun 19, 1991 in Carmel, California
Source: *BiDFilm; BiE&WWA; BioIn 16; CmMov; CurBio 45, 91N; Film 2; FilmgC; GoodHs; HalFC 88; IntMPA 82; InWom SUP; LegTOT; MotPP; MovMk; News 92, 92-1; NewYTBE 72; NewYTBS 91; NotNAT; TwYS; WhoHol A; WorAl; WorAlBi; WorEFlm*

Arthur, Joseph Charles
American. Botanist
Noted for his work on plant rust and disease.
b. Jan 11, 1850 in Lowville, New York
d. Apr 30, 1942 in Brook, Indiana
Source: *BiDAmS; BioIn 2, 6; CurBio 42; DcAmB S3; DcNAA; IndAu 1816; InSci; NatCAB 12; WhAm 2; WhNAA*

Arthur, King
English. Legendary Figure
Celtic chieftain whose medieval legends began with Monmouth book *History of the Kings of Britain,* 12th c.
Source: *BioIn 10, 15, 21; DcEuL; EncO&P 3; LngCEL; Who 92*

Arthur, Robert
[Robert Arthur Feder]
American. Producer
Films include *Francis,* 1950; *Sweet Charity,* 1969.
b. Nov 1, 1909 in New York, New York
d. Oct 28, 1986 in Beverly Hills, California
Source: *AuBYP 3; BioIn 15; ConAu 110; ConTFT 4; FilmEn; FilmgC; GangFlm; HalFC 80, 84, 88; IntMPA 75, 76, 77, 78, 79, 80, 81, 82, 84, 86; ScF&FL 1; SmATA 35; VarWW 85; WhoHr&F*

Artigas, Jose Gervasio
Uruguayan. Revolutionary
Led Uruguayan struggle for independence.
b. Jun 19, 1764 in Montevideo, Uruguay
d. Sep 23, 1850 in Ibiray, Paraguay
Source: *BiDLAmC; BioIn 16; DcHiB; EncLatA; HarEnMi; HisDcSE; HisWorL; McGEWB*

Artist Formerly Known as Prince, The
[Prince; Prince Roger Nelson]
"His Royal Badness"
American. Musician, Singer, Songwriter
New-wave funk singer whose movie, *Purple Rain,* won Oscar for Best Original Score, 1985; changed name to an unpronouncable symbol, 1993; married Mayte Garcia, 1996.
b. Jun 7, 1958 in Minneapolis, Minnesota
Source: *AfrAmAl 6; Baker 92; BioIn 16; CelR 90; ConLC 35; ConMus 1, 14; ConTFT 12; CurBio 86; DcTwCCu 5; DrBlPA 90; EncPR&S 89; EncRk 88; EncRkSt; HarEnR 86; IlEncBM 82; InB&W 80; IntMPA 92, 94, 96; IntWW 91, 93; LegTOT; NewAmDM; NewGrDA 86; News 95, 95-3; OnThGG; OxCPMus; PenEncP; RkOn 85; RolSEnR 83; SoulM; WhoAfA 96; WhoAm 88, 90, 92, 94, 95, 96, 97; WhoBlA 90, 92, 94; WhoEnt 92; WhoHol 92; WhoMW 90*

Artschwager, Richard (Ernst)
American. Artist
Protophotorealist; uses Celotex and Formica as standard art materials; well-known for *Table with Pink Tablecloth,* 1964.
b. Dec 26, 1923 in Washington, District of Columbia
Source: *AmArt; BioIn 15, 16, 17, 20; ConArt 89, 96; CurBio 90; DcCAA 88, 94; IntWW 89, 91, 93; NewYTBS 88; PrintW 83, 85; WhoAm 84, 92, 94, 95, 96; WhoAmA 80, 82, 84, 86, 89, 91, 93; WorArt 1980*

Artsybashev, Mikhail Petrovich
Russian. Author, Dramatist
Best known for sensational novel *Sanin,* 1907, with frank discussion of sex.
b. Oct 18, 1878 in Kharkov, Russia
d. Mar 3, 1927 in Warsaw, Poland
Source: *BiDSovU; BioIn 1, 5; CasWL; ClDMEL 47, 80; CnMD; CyWA 58; DcRusL; DcRusLS; EncWL; EvEuW; FacFETw; HanRL; ModWD; REn; TwCA, SUP*

Artukovic, Andrija
"Butcher of the Balkans"
German. Government Official
WW II Nazi police minister convicted, 1986, of ordering massacre of villagers, 450 people at Kerestinec camp near Zagreb, 1942.
b. Nov 29, 1899 in Croatia, Austria-Hungary
d. Jan 16, 1988 in Zagreb, Yugoslavia
Source: *BioIn 15, 17; NewYTBS 88*

Artzybasheff, Boris Mikhailovich
American. Author, Illustrator
Designed over 200 *Time* magazine covers; illustrated book jackets, children's books.
b. May 25, 1899 in Kharkov, Russia
d. Jul 16, 1965 in Old Lyme, Connecticut
Source: *AmAu&B; AnCL; AuBYP 2; ChhPo S2; ConICB; CurBio 45, 65; DcAmB S7; IlsCB 1744; JBA 34, 51; SmATA 14; Str&VC; WhAm 4; WhoGrA 62*

Arundel, Honor Morfydd
Welsh. Author
Books deal with emotional problems of adolescence.
b. Aug 15, 1919, Wales
d. Jun 8, 1973 in Hume-by-Kelso, Scotland
Source: *Au&Wr 71; ConAu 21R, 41R, P-2; ConLC 17; SmATA 24*

Arvey, Jacob Meyer
American. Political Leader
Dem. party chief from IL, 1946-53; launched political career of Adlai Stevenson, Jr.
b. Nov 3, 1895 in Chicago, Illinois
d. Aug 25, 1977 in Chicago, Illinois
Source: *BioIn 3, 9, 11; NewYTBS 77; ObitOF 79; WhAm 7; WhoAm 74, 76, 78; WhoWorJ 72, 78*

Arzner, Dorothy
American. Director
First woman director of sound films; credits include *Craig's Wife,* 1935.
b. Jan 3, 1900 in San Francisco, California
d. Oct 1, 1979 in La Quinta, California
Source: *BiDFilm 81, 94; BioIn 3, 10, 11, 12; ContDcW 89; DcFM; FilmEn; FilmgC; GayLesB; HalFC 80, 84, 88; HanAmWH; IlWWHD 1; IntDcF 1-2, 2-2; IntDcWB; IntMPA 75, 76, 77, 78, 79, 80; InWom SUP; LegTOT; MacDWB; MiSFD 9N; NewYTBS 79; OxCFilm; ReelWom; TwYS, A; WhoAmW 61; WomFir; WomWMM*

Asante, Molefi Kete
American. Educator, Author, Scholar
Founder, leading proponent of Afrocentric movement; wrote *The Afrocentric Idea,* 1987.
b. Aug 14, 1942 in Valdosta, Georgia
Source: *AfrAmAl 6; BlkAWP; BlkWr 2; ConBlB 3; IntAu&W 77; LivgBAA; SchCGBL; WhoAfA 96; WhoAm 84, 86, 88; WhoBlA 75, 77, 80, 85, 88, 90, 92, 94; WhoE 83, 85, 86; WhoEmL 87; WrDr 76*

Asbury, Francis
American. Religious Leader
First bishop of Methodist Episcopal Church consecrated in America, 1785.
b. Aug 20, 1745 in Staffordshire, England
d. Mar 31, 1816 in Spotsylvania, Virginia
Source: *AmAu&B; AmBi; AmWrBE; ApCAB; BenetAL 91; BiDSA; BioIn 1, 3, 5, 6, 7, 9, 19; BlkwEAR; DcAmB; DcAmReB 1, 2; DcAmTB; DcNAA; DcNaB; DcNCBi 1; Drake; EncARH; EncCRAm; EncWM; HarEnUS; LinLib S; LuthC 75; McGEWB; Meth; NatCAB 6; OxCAmH; OxCAmL 65, 83, 95; REnAL; TwCBDA; WebAB 74, 79; WhAm HS; WorAl; WorAlBi*

Asbury, Herbert
American. Author
Wrote *The Barbary Coast,* 1933; *The French Quarter,* 1936.
b. Sep 1, 1891 in Farmington, Missouri
d. Feb 24, 1963 in New York, New York
Source: *AmAu&B; BenetAL 91; BioIn 4, 6; ConAu 116; DcAmB S7; EncAJ; REnAL; ScF&FL 1; ScFEYrs; TwCA, SUP; WhAm 4; WhLit; WhNAA*

Ascari, Alberto
Italian. Auto Racer
Won Grand Prix world championships, 1952, 1953.
b. Jul 13, 1918, Italy
d. May 27, 1955 in Monza, Italy
Source: *BioIn 3, 4, 8, 10, 12, 15; ObitT 1951*

Asch, Sholem
American. Author
Biblical novels include best-seller *The Nazarene,* 1939, written in Yiddish.
b. Nov 1, 1880 in Kutno, Poland
d. Jul 10, 1957 in London, England
Source: *AmAu&B; AmNov; Benet 87, 96; BenetAL 91; CasWL; ClDMEL 47, 80; CnDAL; CnMD; CnThe; ConAu 105; CyWA 58, 89; DcAmImH; EncWL 2, 3; EncWT; JeAmFiW; LegTOT; LiExTwC; LinLib L, S; LngCTC; McGEWD 72, 84; ModWD; NatCAB 48; NotNAT B; Novels; OxCAmH; OxCAmL 65, 83, 95; PenC AM; PolBiDi; RAdv 14, 13-2; REn; REnAL; REnWD; TwCA, SUP; TwCLC 3; TwCWr; WhAm 3; WhoLA; WorAl; WorAlBi*

Ascoli, Max
Italian. Editor, Author
Edited *The Reporter,* 1949-68; wrote *Fall of Mussolini,* 1948.
b. Jun 25, 1898 in Ferrara, Italy
d. Jan 1, 1978 in New York, New York
Source: *AmAu&B; BioIn 1, 3, 11, 12; ConAu 77; CurBio 54, 78, 78N; DcAmB S10; EncAJ; EncTwCJ; LegTOT; LinLib L; NatCAB 60; NewYTBS 78; WhAm 7; WhoAm 74, 76, 78; WorAl; WorAlBi*

Asencio, Diego Cortes
American. Diplomat
US ambassador to Colombia; held hostage by terrorists for 61 days, 1980.
b. Jul 15, 1931 in Nijar, Spain
Source: *BioIn 13; NewYTBS 80; USBiR 74; WhoAm 78, 80, 90; WhoGov 72, 75, 77; WhoWor 78, 80, 82*

Ash, Mary Kay
[Mary Kathlyn Wagner]
American. Cosmetics Executive
Founder, chm. of board, Mary Kay Cosmetics, Inc, 1963—.
b. May 12, 1918 in Hot Wells, Texas
Source: *CurBio 95; Dun&B 86, 88, 90*

Ash, Roy Lawrence
"Human Computer"
American. Business Executive
Co-founded Litton Industries, 1953; director, OMB, 1972.
b. Oct 20, 1918 in Los Angeles, California
Source: *BiDAmBL 83; BioIn 8, 9, 10, 11, 12, 13; BlueB 76; CurBio 68; IntWW 74, 75, 76, 77, 78, 79, 80, 81, 82, 83, 89, 91, 93; NewYTBE 71, 72; NewYTBS 74; St&PR 84, 87; WhoAm 74, 76, 78, 80, 82, 84, 86, 88, 90, 92, 94, 95, 96, 97; WhoAmP 73, 91; WhoFI 74, 79, 81, 83; WhoSSW 75; WhoWest 87; WhoWor 74*

Ashbery, John (Lawrence)
[Jonas Berry]
American. Author
Won 1976 Pulitzer for narrative verse, *Self-Portrait in a Convex Mirror.*
b. Jul 28, 1927 in Rochester, New York
Source: *AmAu&B; AmCulL; AmWr S3; Benet 87, 96; BenetAL 91; BioIn 8, 10, 11, 12, 13, 14, 15, 16; BlueB 76; CamGEL; CamGLE; CamHAL; ChhPo S3; ConAu 5R, 9NR, 37NR, 107; ConLC 2, 3, 4, 6, 9, 13, 15, 25, 41, 77; ConPo 70, 75, 80, 85, 91, 96; CroCAP; CurBio 76; DcArts; DcLB 5, 165, Y81A; DcLEL 1940; DrAP 75; DrAPF 80, 89, 91; EncWL 3; FacFETw; GayLL; GrWrEL P; IntAu&W 82, 89; IntvTCA 2; IntWW 89, 91, 93; IntWWP 77; LegTOT; LinLib L; MagSAmL; MajTwCW; ModAL S1, S2; NewYTBS 76; OxCAmL 83, 95; OxCTwCP; PenC AM; RAdv 1, 14, 13-1; RfGAmL 87, 94; RGFAP; RGTwCWr; WebE&AL; WhoAm 74, 76, 78, 80, 82, 84, 86, 88, 90, 92, 94, 95, 96, 97;*

WhoAmA 78, 80, 82, 84, 86, 89, 91, 93; WhoE 77, 79, 81, 83, 85, 86, 89, 91; WhoUSWr 88; WhoWor 80, 82, 84, 87, 89, 91, 93, 95, 96, 97; WhoWrEP 89, 92, 95; WorAu 1950; WrDr 76, 80, 82, 84, 86, 88, 90, 92, 94, 96

Ashbrook, John Milan
American. Businessman, Politician
Rep. senator from OH, 1961-82.
b. Sep 21, 1928 in Johnston, Ohio
d. Apr 24, 1982 in Newark, Ohio
Source: *BiDrAC; WhoMW 74, 76, 78, 80, 82*

Ashbrook, Joseph
American. Astronomer, Editor
Edited *Sky and Telescope* magazine from 1970; asteroid named for him, 1979.
b. Apr 4, 1918 in Philadelphia, Pennsylvania
d. Aug 4, 1980 in Weston, Massachusetts
Source: *AmMWSc 73P, 76P, 79; BioIn 12; ConAu 117, 122; NewYTBS 80; WhAm 7, 8; WhoAm 76, 78, 80*

Ashburn, Richie
[Don Richard Ashburn]
"Whitey"
American. Baseball Player
Outfielder, 1948-62; won two NL batting titles, 1955, 1958.
b. Mar 19, 1927 in Tilden, Nebraska
Source: *Ballpl 90; BioIn 1, 2, 3, 4, 5, 6, 8, 15, 18; WhoProB 73; WhoSpor*

Ashby, Hal
American. Director
Directed *Shampoo,* 1975, *Coming Home,* 1978; as film editor, won Oscar for *In the Heat of the Night,* 1967.
b. 1936 in Ogden, Utah
d. Dec 27, 1988 in Malibu, California
Source: *BiDFilm 81, 94; ConTFT 6; EncAFC; FilmEn; FilmgC; HalFC 80, 84, 88; IlWWHD 1; IntMPA 77, 80, 82; MiSFD 9N; VarWW 85; WhoAm 80, 82, 84, 86; WhoWest 80, 82, 84*

Ashcroft, John David
American. Politician
Rep. governor of MO, 1985-92; Rep. senator from MO, 1995—.
b. May 9, 1942 in Chicago, Illinois
Source: *AlmAP 88, 92; BiDrGov 1983, 1988; BioIn 14, 15; CngDr 95; ConAu 112; ConTFT 4; IntWW 91; NewYTBS 85; WhoAm 86, 90, 92, 96, 97; WhoAmL 78, 79, 83, 85; WhoAmP 73, 75, 77, 79, 81, 83, 85, 87, 89, 91, 93, 95; WhoEmL 87; WhoGov 75; WhoMW 84, 86, 88, 90, 92, 96; WhoWor 91, 93*

Ashcroft, Peggy, Dame
[Edith Margaret Emily Ashcroft]
English. Actor
Best known for role opposite Paul Robeson in *Othello,* 1930; won Oscar for *A Passage to India,* 1984.
b. Dec 22, 1907 in Croydon, England
d. Jun 14, 1991 in London, England
Source: *AnObit 1991; BiE&WWA; BioIn 3, 4, 6, 10, 11, 14, 15, 16, 17, 18; BlueB 76; CamGWoT; CelR 90; CnThe; ContDcW 89; ConTFT 4, 10; CurBio 63, 87, 91N; DcArts; EncEurC; EncWT; Ent; FacFETw; FilmEn; FilmgC; HalFC 80, 84, 88; IlWWBF A; IntDcT 3; IntDcWB; IntWW 74, 75, 76, 77, 78, 79, 80, 81, 82, 83, 89, 91; InWom, SUP; LegTOT; NewC; News 92, 92-1; NewYTBS 85, 91; NotNAT, A; OxCThe 67, 83; PlP&P; VarWW 85; WhAm 10; Who 74, 82, 83, 85, 88, 90, 92N; WhoAmW 70, 72, 74; WhoHol 92, A; WhoThe 72, 77, 81; WhoWor 74, 87, 89, 91*

Ashdown, Paddy
[Jeremy John Durham Ashdown]
English. Politician
Leader, British Liberal Democrats Party, 1988—.
b. Feb 27, 1941 in New Delhi, India
Source: *BioIn 16; CurBio 92; IntWW 89, 91; Who 85, 88, 90, 92, 94; WhoWor 96, 97*

Ashe, Arthur
[Arthur Robert Ashe, Jr.]
American. Tennis Player
First black player to win men's singles at Wimbledon, 1975; Emmy Award for TV adaptation of "Hard Road to Glory;" AIDS spokesman.
b. Jul 10, 1943 in Richmond, Virginia
d. Feb 6, 1993 in New York, New York
Source: *AfrAmAl 6; AfrAmBi 1; AfrAmSG; AnObit 1993; BiDAmSp OS; BioIn 6, 7, 8, 9, 10, 11, 12, 13, 16; BioNews 74; BkPepl; BlueB 76; BuCMET; CelR, 90; ConAu 18NR, 35NR, 65; ConBlB 1; ConHero 2; CurBio 66, 93N; DcTwCCu 5; FacFETw; HeroCon; InB&W 80, 85; IntWW 78, 79, 80, 81, 82, 83, 89, 91; LegTOT; NegAl 76, 83, 89; News 93-3; NewYTBS 93; SchCGBL; SmATA 65; WebAB 74, 79; WhoAm 74, 76, 78, 80, 82, 84, 86, 88, 90, 92; WhoBlA 75, 92; WhoE 89, 91, 93; WhoSSW 75, 76, 82; WorAl; WorAlBi; WrDr 90, 92*

Ashenfelter, Nip
[Horace Ashenfelter]
American. Track Athlete
Only American to win gold medal, 3,000-meter steeplechase, 1952 Olympics.
b. Jan 23, 1923 in Collegeville, Pennsylvania
Source: *BiDAmSp OS; BioIn 9; WhoSpor; WhoTr&F 73*

Asher, Peter
[Peter and Gordon]
English. Singer, Producer
Part of Peter and Gordon duo, 1961-68; has produced albums for James Taylor, Linda Ronstadt.
b. Jun 22, 1944 in London, England
Source: *BioIn 19; HarEnR 86; PenEncP; RolSEnR 83; WhoEnt 92; WhoRocM 82*

Ashford, Daisy
[Margaret Mary Julia Ashford]
English. Author
Wrote *The Young Visitors* at age nine; published with original spelling, 1919.
b. 1881 in Petersham, England
d. Jan 15, 1972 in Norwich, England
Source: *BioIn 9, 10, 11, 16, 19; BlmGWL; CamGLE; CarSB; ContDcW 89; DcArts; DcLEL; DcNaB 1971; EvLB; FemiCLE; InWom SUP; LegTOT; LngCTC; NewCBEL; NewYTBE 72; OxCEng 85, 95; PenC ENG; REn; RGTwCWr; SmATA 10, X; StaCVF; WhoChL; WomFir*

Ashford, Emmett Littleton
American. Baseball Umpire
First black umpire in MLs, 1966-70.
b. Nov 13, 1916 in Los Angeles, California
d. Mar 1, 1980 in Los Angeles, California
Source: *InB&W 80; NewYTBS 80; WhoProB 73*

Ashford, Evelyn
[Mrs. Ray Washington]
American. Track Athlete
Sprinter; won gold medal, 1984 Olympics; held world record in 100 meter dash until broken by Florence Griffith Joyner, 1988.
b. Apr 15, 1957 in Shreveport, Louisiana
Source: *AfrAmBi 2; BiDAmSp OS; BioIn 12, 13, 14, 15, 16; BlkAmWO; BlkOlyM; EncWomS; NewYTBS 83, 85, 88; WhoAfA 96; WhoAm 90; WhoAmW 91; WhoBlA 92, 94; WhoSpor; WorAlBi*

Ashford, Nickolas
[Ashford and Simpson]
American. Singer, Songwriter
Wrote song "Ain't No Mountain High Enough," 1967, recorded by the Supremes.
b. May 4, 1942 in Fairfield, South Carolina
Source: *ASCAP 80; BiDAfM; BioIn 10, 11, 12, 14, 15, 16; BioNews 74; ConAu 130; DrBlPA 90; EncPR&S 89; IlEncBM 82; InB&W 80, 85; LegTOT; NewYTBS 85, 90; RolSEnR 83; WhoAm 82, 86; WhoBlA 80, 90*

Ashford and Simpson
[Nickolas Ashford; Valerie Simpson]
American. Music Group
Husband-wife writers, performers; responsible for some of Motown's biggest hits.
Source: *BioNews 74; CelR; EncPR&S 89; EncRk 88; HarEnR 86; NewYTBS 85; PenEncP; RolSEnR 83; WhoAfA 96; WhoBlA 85, 88, 90, 92, 94; WhoRocM 82*

Ashikaga, Takauji
Japanese. Soldier
Established shoqunate which dominated Japan's govt. 1338-1573.
b. 1305, Japan
d. Jun 7, 1358 in Kyoto, Japan

Source: *HarEnMi; McGEWB; WhDW*

Ashkenazy, Vladimir Davidovich
Russian. Musician
Considered among best of Russian pianists; co-winner of Tchaikovsky piano award, 1962.
b. Jul 6, 1937 in Gorki, Union of Soviet Socialist Republics
Source: *Baker 78, 84, 92; BiDSovU; BioIn 13, 14, 15, 16; BioNews 75; BlueB 76; CelR 90; CurBio 67; FacFETw; IntWW 82, 91; IntWWM 90; MusMk; NewAmDM; NewYTBE 72; PenDiMP; Who 82, 92; WhoAm 82, 84, 86, 88, 90, 92, 94, 95, 96, 97; WhoEnt 92; WhoMus 72; WhoWor 78, 80, 82, 84, 87, 89, 91, 93, 95, 96, 97; WhoWorJ 78; WorAl; WorAlBi*

Ashley, Elizabeth
[Elizabeth Ann Cole]
American. Actor
Won Tony, 1962; films include *The Carpetbaggers,* 1963; played Freida Evans on TV show "Evening Shade," 1990-94.
b. Aug 30, 1941 in Ocala, Florida
Source: *BiE&WWA; ConTFT 8; CurBio 78; FilmgC; HalFC 88; IntMPA 86, 92; InWom SUP; MovMk; NewYTBS 74; NotNAT; WhoAm 74, 78, 80, 82, 84, 86, 88, 90, 92, 94, 95, 96, 97; WhoAmW 83, 85, 89, 95, 97; WhoEnt 92; WhoHol A; WhoThe 81; WorAl; WorAlBi*

Ashley, Laura Mountney
Welsh. Designer, Business Executive
Created int'l fashion empire based on romance of English country gardens.
b. Sep 7, 1925? in Merthyr Tydfil, Wales
d. Sep 17, 1985 in Coventry, England
Source: *WomFir; WorFshn*

Ashley, Merrill
[Linda Merrill]
American. Dancer, Author
Star of NYC Ballet since 1976.
b. Dec 2, 1950 in Saint Paul, Minnesota
Source: *BiDD; BioIn 11, 12, 13, 14, 15; CelR 90; CurBio 81; IntDcB; InWom SUP; NewYTBS 81; WhoAm 82, 90; WhoAmW 91; WhoE 91; WhoEnt 92*

Ashley, Thomas William Ludlow
"Lud"
American. Politician
Ohio Dem. congressman, 1954-80, who headed Energy Committee, 1977.
b. Jan 11, 1923 in Toledo, Ohio
Source: *AlmAP 78, 80; BiDrAC; BiDrUSC 89; BioIn 11, 12, 17; CngDr 79; CurBio 79; NewYTBS 77, 91; PolProf J, NF; WhoAm 74, 76, 78, 80; WhoAmP 77, 91; WhoGov 77; WhoMW 74, 76, 78, 80*

Ashley, William Henry
American. Fur Trader, Politician
Instituted trappers rendezvous, 1824; congressman, 1831-37.
b. Mar 26, 1778 in Powhatan County, Virginia
d. Mar 26, 1838 in Boonville, Missouri
Source: *AmBi; ApCAB; BiAUS; BiDrAC; BiDrUSC 89; BioIn 1, 2, 6, 7, 10, 12, 17, 18; DcAmB; Drake; EncAB-H 1974, 1996; Expl 93; McGEWB; NewCol 75; OxCAmL 65, 83, 95; REnAW; TwCBDA; WebAB 74, 79; WhAm HS, HSA; WhAmP; WhNaAH; WhWE*

Ashman, Howard
American. Lyricist
Won Oscar for song "Under the Sea" in Disney's *The Little Mermaid,* 1989; finished songs for movie *Beauty and the Beast* before his premature death; wrote *Little Shop of Horrors,* 1982.
d. Mar 14, 1991 in New York, New York
Source: *BioIn 15; ConAu 122, 135; ConDr 88D; ConTFT 9; NewYTBS 91*

Ashman, Matthew
[Bow Wow Wow]
English. Musician
One-time back-up to Adam Ant; guitarist with Bow Wow Wow since 1980.
Source: *EncRk 88; PenEncP; RkOn 85; RolSEnR 83; WhsNW 85*

Ashmore, Harry Scott
American. Editor, Author
Pulitzer-winning editorial writer, 1958; books include *Hearts and Minds,* 1982.
b. Jul 27, 1916 in Greenville, South Carolina
Source: *AmAu&B; BioIn 1, 4, 5, 8, 11, 16; CurBio 58; EncAACR; EncTwCJ; EncWB; LinLib L, S; WhoAm 74, 76, 78, 80, 82, 84, 86, 88, 90; WhoWest 74, 76, 78; WhoWor 74, 76, 78*

Ashrawi, Hanan
Palestinian. Political Activist
Voice of the Palestinian people in international news media since late 1980s; official negotiator at peace conferences between Israelis and Palestinians.
b. 1946 in Ramallah, Israel
Source: *CurBio 92; NewYTBS 91; RadHan*

Ashton, Frederick William, Sir
English. Choreographer, Dancer
Created innumerable works for Sadlers Wells, the Royal Ballet director, 1963-70.
b. Sep 17, 1906 in Guayaquil, Ecuador
d. Aug 18, 1988 in Sussex, England
Source: *BiDD; BlueB 76; CurBio 51; IntWW 82; NewYTBE 70; NewYTBS 81; Who 85; WhoMus 72; WhoThe 77A; WhoWor 74*

Ashton, Susan
[Susan Rae Hill]
American. Singer
Contemporary Christian music singer; song "Down on My Knees" became number one Christian single in 1991; released first album, *Wakened by the Wind,* 1991 and later released *So Far,* 1995; received Gospel Music Association female vocalist of the year and contemporary album of the year awards for *Angels of Mercy,* 1993.
b. Jul 17, 1967 in Irving, Texas
Source: *ConMus 17*

Ashton-Warner, Sylvia Constance
New Zealander. Author, Educator
Wrote fiction using experiences as teacher of Maori children in New Zealand as subject matter.
b. Dec 17, 1908 in Stratford, New Zealand
d. Apr 28, 1984 in Tauranga, New Zealand
Source: *AnObit 1984; BlmGWL; BlueB 76; ConAu 69; ConLC 19; ConNov 82; DcLEL, 1940; IntAu&W 76, 77; LngCTC; Novels; PenC ENG; RAdv 1; TwCWr; Who 82; WorAu 1950; WrDr 76*

Ashurbanipal
Assyrian. Ruler
King of Assyria 668 to c. 627 BC; established first collected and cataloged library in ancient Middle East.
Source: *BioIn 4, 8, 15; HarEnMi; LinLib L, S; McGEWB; WhDW*

Asia
[Geoffrey Downes; Steve Howe; Greg Lake; Carl Palmer]
English. Music Group
Hard rock group formed 1981; hit single "Heat of the Moment," 1983.
Source: *BioIn 9, 11, 14, 15, 16, 17, 18; EncPR&S 89; EncRk 88; EncRkSt; HarEnR 86; NewYTBS 85; PenEncP; RkOn 85; RolSEnR 83; St&PR 96, 97; WhoRocM 82*

Asimov, Isaac
[Dr. A; George E. Dale; Paul French]
American. Author, Biochemist
Leading popular scientist; wrote nearly 500 books; coined term "robotics;" wrote *I, Robot,* 1950; *Foundation,* 1951.
b. Jan 2, 1920 in Petrovichi, Union of Soviet Socialist Republics
d. Apr 6, 1992 in New York, New York
Source: *AmAu&B; AmMWSc 73P, 76P, 79, 82, 86, 89, 92; AnObit 1992; AsBiEn; Au&Arts 13; Au&Wr 71; AuBYP 2, 3; Benet 87, 96; BenetAL 91; BestSel 90-2; BioIn 3, 7, 8, 9, 10, 11, 12, 13, 14, 15, 16, 17, 18, 19, 20, 21; BlueB 76; CamGLE; CasWL; CelR, 90; ChlBkCr; ChlLR 12; ConAu 1R, 2NR, 19NR, 36NR, 137; ConLC 1, 3, 9, 19, 26, 76, 92; ConNov 72, 76, 82, 86, 91; ConPopW; ConSFA; ConSFF; CurBio 68, 92N; CyWA 89; DcArts; DcLB 8, Y92N; DcLEL 1940; DcTwCCu 1; DrAF 76; DrAPF 80, 89, 91; DrmM 1; EncMys; EncSF, 93; FacFETw; Future; IntAu&W 76, 77, 82, 86, 89, 91, 93;*

IntWW 77, 78, 79, 80, 81, 82, 83, 89, 91; JeAmHC; LegTOT; LinLib L, S; LngCTC; MajAI; MajTwCW; MakMC; NewCol 75; NewEScF; News 92, 92-3; NewYTBS 92; Novels; OxCAmL 83, 95; PenC AM; RAdv 14, 13-5; REn; REnAL; RfGAmL 94; RGSF; RGTwCSF; RGTwCWr; ScF&FL 1, 2, 92; ScFEYrs, A; ScFSB; ScFWr; SmATA 1, 26, 74; ThrBJA; TwCCr&M 80, 85, 91; TwCSFW 81, 86, 91; TwCWr; TwCYAW; TwoTYeD; WebAB 74, 79; WebE&AL; WhAm 10; Who 82, 83, 85, 88, 90, 92; WhoAm 74, 76, 78, 80, 82, 84, 86, 88, 90; WhoAmJ 80; WhoE 74, 81, 83; WhoEnt 92; WhoSciF; WhoUSWr 88; WhoWor 74, 76, 78, 80, 82, 84, 87, 89, 91; WhoWorJ 72, 78; WhoWrEP 89, 92; WorAl; WorAlBi; WorAu 1950; WrDr 76, 80, 82, 84, 86, 88, 90, 92, 94N

Askew, Reubin O'Donovan
American. Government Official, Politician
Dem. governor of FL, 1971-79; sought Dem. presidential nomination, 1984.
b. Sep 11, 1928 in Muskogee, Oklahoma
Source: *BiDrGov 1789, 1978; BioIn 9, 10, 12, 13; BioNews 74; CurBio 73; IntWW 74, 75, 76, 77, 78, 79, 80, 81, 82, 83, 89, 91, 93; IntYB 78, 79, 80, 81, 82; NewYTBE 72; WhoAm 74, 76, 78, 80, 82, 84, 88, 90, 92, 94; WhoAmL 79; WhoAmP 73, 91; WhoFI 81; WhoGov 75, 77; WhoSSW 75, 76, 78, 80, 82, 88, 91; WhoWor 78, 80*

Asner, Ed(ward)
American. Actor
Six-time Emmy winner best known for role of Lou Grant on ''Mary Tyler Moore Show,'' 1970-77.
b. Nov 15, 1929 in Kansas City, Missouri
Source: *BioIn 11, 12, 13, 16, 17, 20; BkPepl; CelR 90; ConTFT 1, 6, 13; CurBio 78; FilmEn; FilmgC; HalFC 84, 88; IntMPA 84, 86, 88, 92, 94, 96; LegTOT; LesBEnT, 92; NewYTBE 73; WhoAm 74, 76, 78, 80, 82, 84, 86, 88, 90, 92, 94, 95, 96, 97; WhoAmJ 80; WhoEnt 92; WhoHol 92, A; WorAl; WorAlBi*

Asoka the Great
Indian. Ruler
King of Magadha, 273-232 BC; reign marked by prosperous times; made Buddhism a world religion.
b. 300BC
d. 232BC
Source: *BioIn 1; LinLib S; LuthC 75; WhDW; WorAl*

Aspin, Les
[Leslie Aspin, Jr.]
American. Politician, Government Official
Dem. congressman from WI, 1970-93; Secretary of Defense, 1993.
b. Jul 21, 1938 in Milwaukee, Wisconsin
d. May 21, 1995 in Washington, District of Columbia
Source: *AlmAP 78, 80, 82, 84, 88, 92; BiDrUSC 89; BioIn 9, 10, 12, 14, 15; CngDr 74, 77, 79, 81, 83, 85, 87, 89, 91; ConAu 108; CurBio 86; IntWW 93; LegTOT; News 96, 96-1; NewYTBS 85, 92, 95; PolsAm 84; WhoAm 74, 76, 78, 80, 82, 84, 86, 88, 90, 92, 94, 95; WhoAmP 73, 75, 77, 79, 81, 83, 85, 87, 89, 91, 93; WhoGov 72, 75, 77; WhoMW 74, 76, 78, 80, 82, 84, 86, 88, 90, 92; WorAlBi*

Asplund, Erik Gunnar
Swedish. Architect
Major influence in Swedish architecture; best known for designing pavilions at Stockholm Exhibition, 1930.
b. Sep 22, 1885 in Stockholm, Sweden
d. Oct 30, 1940 in Stockholm, Sweden
Source: *BioIn 14; ConArch 80; DcD&D; EncMA; FacFETw; IntDcAr; MacEA; McGDA; NewCol 75; OxCArt; PenDiDA 89; WhDW*

Asquith, Anthony
English. Director
Directed *The Importance of Being Earnest,* 1952.
b. Nov 9, 1902 in London, England
d. Feb 20, 1968 in London, England
Source: *BiDFilm, 81, 94; BioIn 8, 10, 11, 12, 15; CmMov; DcFM; DcNaB 1961; EncEurC; FilmEn; FilmgC; HalFC 80, 84, 88; IlWWBF, A; IntDcF 1-2, 2-2; LegTOT; MiSFD 9N; MovMk; ObitOF 79; ObitT 1961; OxCFilm; WhAm 5; WhScrn 74, 77, 83; WhThe; WorEFlm; WorFDir 1*

Asquith, Emma Alice Margot
[Countess of Oxford and Asquith]
English. Author
Eccentric, outspoken, shrewd; great influence on social, fashionable English life.
b. Feb 2, 1864 in Peebleshire, England
d. Jul 28, 1945 in London, England
Source: *CurBio 45; DcNaB 1941; EvLB; GrBr; LinLib L; LngCTC; WhE&EA*

Asquith, Herbert Henry
[1st Earl of Oxford and Asquith]
English. Political Leader
Liberal prime minister, 1908-16; introduced social welfare programs.
b. Sep 12, 1852 in Morley, England
d. Feb 15, 1928 in Sutton Courtney, England
Source: *Alli SUP; BiDInt; BioIn 14, 15, 17, 18; DcNaB 1922; DcTwHis; FacFETw; GrBr; HisDBrE; McGEWB; OxCLaw; WorAl; WorAlBi*

Assad, Hafez al-
[Hafez Wahsh]
Syrian. Political Leader
Minister of Defense, 1966-70; led coup that made him pres., 1971.
b. Oct 6, 1930 in Qardaha, Syria
Source: *BioIn 13, 14, 15, 16; ColdWar 2; CurBio 75, 92; EncWB; FacFETw; IntWW 80, 83, 91; IntYB 80, 81; MidE 80; NewCol 75; News 92; NewYTBE 70; NewYTBS 77; PolLCME; WhoGov 72; WhoWor 87, 91; WorAlBi*

Assad, Rifaat al-
Syrian. Political Leader
Younger brother of Hafez; one of three VPs of Syria, 1970—.
b. 1937? in Latakia, Syria
Source: *BioIn 13, 15; ConNews 86-3; WhoWor 91*

Assante, Armand
American. Actor
Played Michael Moretti in TV mini-series ''Rage of Angels,'' 1983.
b. Oct 4, 1949 in New York, New York
Source: *BioIn 11, 13, 15; ConTFT 4, 11; HalFC 84, 88; IntMPA 84, 86, 88, 92, 94, 96; LegTOT; VarWW 85; WhoAm 92, 94, 95, 96, 97; WhoEnt 92; WhoHol 92*

Asser, Tobias Michael Carel
Dutch. Educator
Awarded Nobel Peace Prize, 1911, for pioneering field of int'l. legal relations.
b. Apr 29, 1838 in Amsterdam, Netherlands
d. Jul 29, 1913 in The Hague, Netherlands
Source: *BiDInt; BioIn 5, 9, 11, 15; LinLib L, S; OxCLaw; WhoNob, 90, 95*

Association, The
[Gary Alexander; Ted Bluechel; Brian Cole; Russ Giguere; Terry Kirkman; Jim Yester]
American. Music Group
Pop-rock band, 1960s; won gold records for ''Cherish,'' 1966; ''Never My Love,'' 1967.
Source: *BiDAmM; EncPR&S 74, 89; EncRk 88; PenEncP; RkOn 74; RolSEnR 83; WhoAmP 85; WhoRocM 82*

Astaire, Adele
[Adele Austerlitz; Mrs. Kingman Douglas]
American. Dancer
Dancing partner, 1916-32, of brother Fred.
b. Sep 10, 1898 in Omaha, Nebraska
d. Jan 25, 1981 in Scottsdale, Arizona
Source: *AmPS; AnObit 1981; BiDD; BiE&WWA; BioIn 2, 6, 7; CamGWoT; CmpEPM; DancEn 78; EncMT; Film 1; InWom, SUP; LegTOT; NewYTBS 81; NotNAT; OxCAmT 84; OxCPMus; PlP&P; WhScrn 83; WhThe; WorAl; WorAlBi*

Astaire, Fred
[Frederick Austerlitz]
American. Dancer, Actor
Dancing style has influenced all movie musicals; starred in 10 films with best known partner, Ginger Rogers.
b. May 10, 1899 in Omaha, Nebraska
d. Jun 22, 1987 in Los Angeles, California
Source: *AllMusG; AmCulL; AmPS B; AnObit 1987; ASCAP 66, 80; Baker 92;*

BiDD; BiDFilm, 81, 94; BiE&WWA; BioIn 1, 2, 3, 4, 5, 6, 7, 9, 10, 11, 12; BkPepl; BlueB 76; CamGWoT; CelR; CmCal; CmMov; CmpEPM; CnOxB; ConAu 122; ConNews 87-4; ConTFT 3, 5; CurBio 64, 87, 87N; DancEn 78; DcArts; EncAFC; EncMT; EncWB; EncWT; Ent; FacFETw; Film 1; FilmEn; FilmgC; ForYSC; HalFC 80, 84, 88; IntDcF 1-3, 2-3; IntWW 74, 75, 76, 77, 78, 79, 80, 81, 82, 83; LegTOT; LinLib S; MGM; MotPP; MovMk; NewAmDM; NewCol 75; NewGrDA 86; NewGrDJ 88, 94; NewYTBS 79, 87; NewYTET; NotNAT, A; OxCAmT 84; OxCFilm; OxCPMus; PenEncP; PlP&P; RadStar; RAdv 14; RComAH; WebAB 74, 79; WhAm 9; WhDW; Who 74, 82, 83, 85; WhoAm 74, 76, 78, 80, 82, 84, 86; WhoHol A; WhoMus 72; WhoWor 74, 78; WhThe; WorAl; WorAlBi; WorEFlm

Asther, Nils
Swedish. Actor
Leading man in Swedish and German films; in US film *The Bitter Tea of General Yen,* 1933.
b. Jan 17, 1901 in Malmo, Sweden
d. Oct 13, 1981 in Stockholm, Sweden
Source: *Film 2; FilmEn; FilmgC; MotPP; MovMk; NewYTBS 81; TwYS; WhoHol A*

Astin, John Allen
American. Actor
Best known as Gomez Addams on "The Addams Family," 1964-66.
b. Mar 30, 1930 in Baltimore, Maryland
Source: *BioNews 74; ConTFT 6; EncAFC; FilmgC; HalFC 84, 88; IntMPA 86, 92; WhoAm 74, 76, 78, 80, 82, 84, 86, 92, 94, 95, 96, 97; WhoEnt 92; WhoHol A; WorAl; WorAlBi*

Astin, Mackenzie Alexander
"Skeezix"
American. Actor
Played Andy on TV series "Facts of Life"; son of Patty Duke and John Astin.
b. May 12, 1973 in Los Angeles, California
Source: *BioIn 15*

Astley, Rick
[Richard Paul Astley]
English. Singer
Top dance sales artist, 1988; had hit singles "Never Gonna Give You Up,""She Wants to Dance With Me."
b. Jun 2, 1966 in Newton-le-Willows, England
Source: *BioIn 16; CelR 90; ConMus 5; EncRkSt; LegTOT*

Aston, Francis William
English. Scientist
Shared 1922 Nobel Prize in physics; discovered non-radioactive elements.
b. Sep 1, 1877 in Harborne, England
d. Nov 20, 1945 in Cambridge, England
Source: *AsBiEn; BiESc; BioIn 1, 2, 3, 5, 6, 9, 14, 15, 19, 20; CamDcSc; DcNaB 1941; DcScB; FacFETw; InSci; LarDcSc; LinLib L, S; McGEWB; WhE&EA; WhoNob, 90, 95; WorAl; WorScD*

Astor, Brooke Marshall
[Mrs. Vincent Astor; Roberta Brooke Russell]
American. Philanthropist
Pres., trustee, Vincent Astor Foundation, NYC.
b. 1903 in Portsmouth, New Hampshire
Source: *BioIn 13, 14, 15, 16; CelR 90; CurBio 87; NewYTBS 84, 91; WhoAm 90; WhoAmW 72; WhoGov 72; WhoWor 82, 84*

Astor, Gavin
[Lord Astor of Hever]
English. Publisher
Head of Astor dynasty; pres., Times Newspapers Ltd. from 1967.
b. Jun 1, 1918
d. Jun 28, 1984 in Tillypronie, Scotland
Source: *AnObit 1984; ConAu 113; IntWW 82, 83; IntYB 82; Who 82, 83; WhoAm 82; WhoWor 74, 76, 78*

Astor, John Jacob
American. Fur Trader
Chartered American Fur Co; wealthiest man in US at death.
b. Jul 17, 1763 in Heidelberg, Germany
d. Mar 29, 1848 in New York, New York
Source: *AmBi; ApCAB; BenetAL 91; BiDAmBL 83; BioIn 1, 2, 3, 4, 6, 7, 8, 9, 11, 12, 13, 14, 15, 16, 17, 20, 21; CelCen; DcAmB; DcBiPP; Drake; EncAB-H 1974, 1996; EncABHB 6; HarEnUS; LegTOT; LinLib S; MacDCB 78; McGEWB; MemAm; NatCAB 8; NewCol 75; NewGrDA 86; OxCAmH; OxCAmL 65, 83, 95; OxCCan; RComAH; REn; REnAL; REnAW; TwCBDA; WebAB 74, 79; WhAm HS; WhDW; WhNaAH; WhWE; WorAl; WorAlBi*

Astor, Mary
[Lucille Vasconcellos Langhanke]
American. Actor
Made over 100 films in 44-yr. career; best-known role: Brigid O'Shaughnessy in *The Maltese Falcon,* 1941; won Oscar for *The Great Lie,* 1941.
b. May 3, 1906 in Quincy, Illinois
d. Sep 25, 1987 in Los Angeles, California
Source: *AmAu&B; AnObit 1987; BiDFilm, 81, 94; BiE&WWA; BioIn 5, 6, 8, 9, 10, 11, 13, 15, 17; CelR; ConAu 3NR, 5NR, 5R, 123; ConNews 88-1; CurBio 61, 87, 87N; DcArts; EncAFC; Film 2; FilmEn; FilmgC; ForYSC; GangFlm; HalFC 80, 84, 88; IntAu&W 82; IntDcF 1-3, 2-3; IntMPA 75, 76, 77, 78, 79, 80, 81, 82, 84, 86; InWom, SUP; LegTOT; MGM; MotPP; MovMk; NewYTBS 87; NotNAT A; OxCFilm; SilFlmP; ThFT; TwYS; What 4; WhoAmW 64, 66, 68, 70, 72, 74; WhoHol A; WorAl; WorAlBi; WorEFlm*

Astor, Nancy Witcher Langhorne
[Viscountess Astor; Mrs. William Waldorf Astor]
English. Political Leader
First woman to sit in House of Commons, 1919-45; advocated temperance, opposed socialism; wrote *My Two Countries,* 1923.
b. May 19, 1879 in Greenwood, Virginia
d. May 2, 1964 in Lincoln, England
Source: *BioIn 16; CurBio 40, 64; InWom; LinLib L, S; NewCol 75; ObitT 1951, 1961; WhAm 4; WhDW; WhE&EA; WomFir*

Astor, William Vincent
American. Financier
Son of John Jacob Astor IV; left $6 million to Vincent Astor Foundation to "alleviate human misery."
b. Nov 15, 1891 in New York, New York
d. Feb 3, 1959 in New York, New York
Source: *DcAmB S6; NatCAB 47; ObitOF 79; WhAm 3; WhAmP*

Astor, William Waldorf Astor, Viscount
English. Financier
Head of Astor family, 1890; fortune estimated at $100 million.
b. Mar 31, 1848 in New York, New York
d. Jan 18, 1919 in Brighton, England
Source: *AmAu; AmAu&B; AmBi; BbD; BiD&SB; BioIn 6; CyAL 2; DcAmAu; DcAmB; DcBiA; DcNAA; LinLib L, S; NatCAB 8; TwCBDA; WhAm 1*

Astorga, Nora Gadea
Nicaraguan. Revolutionary, Diplomat
Best known for role in assassination of Reynaldo Perez Vegas, 1978; ambassador to US, 1986-87.
b. 1949? in Managua, Nicaragua
d. Feb 14, 1988 in Managua, Nicaragua
Source: *News 88-2; NewYTBS 86*

Asturias, Miguel Angel
Guatemalan. Author, Diplomat
Won Nobel Prize, 1967; wrote *Strong Wind,* 1969; *Le Miroir de Lida Sal,* 1967.
b. Oct 19, 1899 in Guatemala City, Guatemala
d. Jun 9, 1974 in Madrid, Spain
Source: *Benet 87, 96; BenetAL 91; BioIn 7, 8, 9, 10; CasWL; ConAu 32NR, 49, P-2; ConLC 3, 8, 13; CurBio 68, 74, 74N; CyWA 89; DcArts; DcHiB; DcLB 113; DcTwCCu 4; EncLatA; EncWL, 2, 3; FacFETw; HispWr; IntWW 74; IntWWP 77; LatAmWr; LegTOT; LiExTwC; LinLib L; MajTwCW; McGEWB; ModLAL; NewYTBS 74; ObitT 1971; OxCSpan; PenC AM; RAdv 14, 13-2; RfGWoL 95; ScF&FL 1, 2; SpAmA; TwCWr; WhAm 6; Who 74; WhoNob, 90, 95; WhoTwCL; WhoWor 74, 78; WorAl; WorAlBi; WorAu 1950*

Atahualpa
Peruvian. Ruler
Incan emperor, 1532-33, captured by Pizarro; killed in spite of paid ransom.
b. 1500 in Quito, Ecuador
d. Aug 29, 1533 in Cajamarca, Peru
Source: *ApCAB; Benet 87, 96; BioIn 3, 8, 12; DcBiPP; DicTyr; Drake; EncLatA; HisWorL; LinLib S; McGEWB; REn; WhDW; WhoMilH 76*

Ataturk, Kemal
[Mustafa Kemal]
Turkish. Soldier, Political Leader
Founder, first pres., Turkish Republic, 1923-38.
b. Mar 12, 1880 in Salonika, Turkey
d. Nov 10, 1938 in Ankara, Turkey
Source: *BioIn 10; NewCol 75; WebBD 83*

Atchison, David R
American. Politician
As pres. pro tem of senate, served as US pres. for one day, Mar 4, 1849.
b. Aug 11, 1807 in Frogtown, Kentucky
d. Jun 26, 1886 in Gower, Missouri
Source: *ApCAB; BiDrAC; DcAmB; TwCBDA*

Atget, Eugene
[Jean-Eugene-Auguste Atget]
French. Photographer
Documentary photographer, known for photos of Paris.
b. Feb 12, 1857 in Libourne, France
d. Aug 4, 1927 in Paris, France
Source: *BioIn 11; ConPhot 82, 88; DcArts; ICPEnP; MacBEP; ModArCr 3; NewYTBS 81; PrintW 85*

Athanasius, Saint
"Athanasius the Great"; "Father of Orth"
Greek. Religious Leader
Patriarch of Eastern church; constantly opposed Arianism; wrote *Four Orations Against the Arians,* 362.
b. 293?
d. 373
Source: *LuthC 75; McGEWB; NewCol 75; PenC CL; REn; WebBD 83*

Athenagoras I
Greek. Religious Leader
Led Eastern Orthodox Christians, 1948-72; advocated reunion with Roman Catholic Church.
b. Mar 25, 1886 in Vassilikon, Greece
d. Jul 6, 1972 in Istanbul, Turkey
Source: *CurBio 49, 72; CyEd; DcBiPP; DcCathB; LinLib L; LuthC 75; NewYTBE 72; ObitOF 79; ObitT 1971; WhAm 5; WhoWor 74*

Atherton, Alfred LeRoy, Jr.
American. Government Official
Joined foreign service, 1947; ambassador to Egypt, 1979-83.
b. Nov 22, 1921 in Pittsburgh, Pennsylvania
Source: *BioIn 11; WhoWor 80, 82, 84*

Atherton, Gertrude Franklin
American. Author
Novels depict CA society life: *Black Oxen,* 1923.
b. Oct 30, 1857 in San Francisco, California
d. Jun 14, 1948 in San Francisco, California
Source: *AmAu&B; AmWomWr; ApCAB SUP; BbD; CasWL; Chambr 3; CmCal; CnDAL; ConAmA; ConAmL; ConAu 104; CurBio 40, 48; DcAmB S4; DcEnA; DcLEL; DcNAA; EncSF; EvLB; LibW; LngCTC; NatCAB 10, 36; NotAW; Novels; OxCAmL 65; OxCEng 67; PenC AM; RAdv 1; REn; REnAL; REnAW; TwCA; WhAm 2; WhE&EA; WhLit; WhNAA; WhoHr&F; WomWWA 14*

Atherton, William
[William Atherton Knight, II]
American. Actor
Starred in films *Sugarland Express,* 1974; *Looking For Mr. Goodbar,* 1977.
b. Jul 30, 1947 in New Haven, Connecticut
Source: *ConTFT 4; FilmEn; HalFC 80, 84, 88; IntMPA 81, 82, 88, 92, 94, 96; WhoAm 92, 94, 95, 96, 97; WhoE 89; WhoEmL 91, 93; WhoEnt 92; WhoHol 92, A; WhoThe 81*

Atkins, Chet
[Chester B Atkins]
"Mr. Guitar"
American. Musician
Virtuoso guitarist, associated with Grand Ole Opry since 1950.
b. Jun 20, 1924 in Luttrell, Tennessee
Source: *Baker 84, 92; BgBkCoM; BiDAmM; BioIn 10, 12, 14, 15, 16; BioNews 75; CelR, 90; ConAu 113; ConMuA 80A; ConMus 5; CounME 74, 74A; CurBio 75; EncFCWM 69, 83; EncRk 88; HarEnCM 87; HarEnR 86; IlEncCM; IlEncRk; LegTOT; NewAmDM; NewGrDA 86; NewYTBS 74; OnThGG; OxCPMus; PenEncP; RadStar; RolSEnR 83; WhoAm 74, 76, 78, 80, 82, 84, 86, 90; WhoRock 81; WorAl; WorAlBi*

Atkins, Christopher
American. Actor
In films *The Blue Lagoon,* 1980, with Brooke Shields; *The Pirate Movie,* 1982.
b. Feb 21, 1961 in Rye, New York
Source: *BioIn 12, 13; ConTFT 2, 5; HalFC 84, 88; IntMPA 86, 88, 92, 94, 96; LegTOT; NewYTBS 82; WhoHol 92; WhoWor 87*

Atkins, Doug(las L)
American. Football Player
Seven-time all-pro defensive end, 1953-69, mostly with Chicago; Hall of Fame, 1982.
b. May 8, 1930 in Humboldt, Texas
Source: *BiDAmSp FB; LegTOT; WhoFtbl 74*

Atkins, Susan Denise
American. Cultist, Murderer
Convicted, with Charles Manson, of Tate-LaBianca murders, 1969.
b. 1948
Source: *BioIn 8, 9, 10, 11, 12; MurCaTw*

Atkinson, Brooks
[Justin Brooks Atkinson]
American. Critic
One of first supporters of Eugene O'Neill; reviewed over 3,000 opening night performances; won Pulitzer, 1947.
b. Nov 28, 1894 in Melrose, Massachusetts
d. Jan 13, 1984 in Huntsville, Alabama
Source: *AmAu&B; AnObit 1984; BenetAL 91; BiE&WWA; BioIn 1, 4, 5, 6, 7, 10, 13; BlueB 76; CamGWoT; CelR; ConAmTC; ConAu 14NR, 61, 111; CurBio 42, 61, 84, 84N; DcTwCCu 1; EncTwCJ; EncWT; FacFETw; IntAu&W 76, 77, 82; IntWW 74, 75, 76, 77, 78, 79, 80, 81, 82, 83; LegTOT; LinLib L, S; NewYTBE 73; NewYTBS 84; NotNAT; OxCAmL 65, 83; OxCAmT 84; OxCThe 67, 83; REnAL; TwCA, SUP; WebAB 74, 79; WhAm 8; WhJnl; WhLit; WhNAA; Who 74, 82, 83; WhoAm 74, 76, 78, 80, 82; WhoThe 81; WorAl; WorAlBi; WrDr 76, 80, 82*

Atkinson, Henry
American. Army Officer
Led Western expeditions; commanded US volunteers in Black Hawk War, 1832.
b. 1782 in North Carolina
d. Jun 14, 1842 in Jefferson Barracks, Iowa
Source: *ApCAB; BioIn 7; DcAmB; DcAmMiB; DcNCBi 1; Drake; HarEnMi; NatCAB 11; NewCol 75; REnAW; WebAB 74, 79; WebAMB; WhAm HS; WhNaAH; WhWE*

Atkinson, Ted
[Theodore Francis Atkinson]
American. Jockey
First to win $1 million in purses; won national riding championships, 1944, 1946; retired due to illness, 1959.
b. Jun 17, 1916
Source: *BioIn 1, 4, 5, 6, 8, 10; NewYTBE 73; What 2*

Atkinson, Ti-Grace
American. Feminist
Active in women's lib movements; known for helping to pass NY State abortion law, 1970.
b. 1939 in Baton Rouge, Louisiana
Source: *AmOrTwC; BioIn 8, 9, 10, 20, 21; InWom SUP; LNinSix; MugS; WomPubS 1925*

Atkinson, William Walker
American. Religious Leader
New Thought metaphysical writer; first successful popularizer of Hindu thought, practice in US.
b. Dec 5, 1862 in Baltimore, Maryland

d. Nov 22, 1932 in Los Angeles, California
Source: *BiDAmCu; ConAu 120; DcNAA; RelLAm 91; WhAm 1*

Atlanta Rhythm Section
[Barry Bailey; J R Cobb; Dean Daugherty; Paul Goddard; Ronnie Hammond; Robert Nix]
American. Music Group
Had platinum album *Champagne Jam,* 1978; hit singles "So into You," 1977; "Imaginary Lover," 1978.
Source: *ConMuA 80A; IlEncRk; PenEncP; RkOn 74, 78; RolSEnR 83; WhoHol 92; WhoRock 81; WhoRocM 82*

Atlas, Charles
[Angelo Siciliano]
American. Physical Fitness Expert, Bodybuilder
Developed dynamic tension method of bodybuilding.
b. Oct 30, 1894 in Acri, Italy
d. Dec 23, 1972 in Long Beach, New York
Source: *BioIn 1, 4, 5, 6, 7, 8, 10; LegTOT; ObitOF 79; WebAB 74, 79*

Attell, Abe B
American. Boxer
Early featherweight champ, 1901-12; Hall of Fame, 1955.
b. Feb 22, 1884 in San Francisco, California
d. Feb 6, 1970 in Liberty, New York
Source: *BioIn 8; WhoBox 74*

Attenborough, David Frederick
English. Naturalist
CBC travel writer, broadcaster; wrote *Zoo Quest* series, 1956-82.
b. May 8, 1926 in London, England
Source: *Au&Wr 71; BioIn 13, 14, 15; BlueB 76; ConAu 4NR, 6NR, 30NR; CurBio 83; IntAu&W 77, 91; IntMPA 86, 92; IntWW 83, 91; Who 85, 92; WhoWor 84; WrDr 86, 92*

Attenborough, Richard Samuel, Sir
English. Actor, Producer, Director
Won 1983 best director Oscar for *Gandhi;* film took 20 yrs. to make.
b. Aug 29, 1923 in Cambridge, England
Source: *BiDFilm; BioIn 14, 15, 16; BlueB 76; CelR 90; CmMov; ConAu 127; ConTFT 8; CurBio 84; FilmgC; HalFC 84, 88; IntMPA 86, 92; IntWW 76, 77, 78, 79, 80, 81, 82, 83, 89, 91; MotPP; MovMk; OxCFilm; Who 85, 92; WhoAm 78, 84, 86, 88; WhoEnt 92; WhoHol A; WhoThe 77, 81; WhoWor 87, 91; WorAl; WorAlBi; WorEFlm; WorFDir 2*

Atterbury, Grosvenor
American. Architect
Designed earliest practical prefabricated housing, 1907.
b. Jul 7, 1869 in Detroit, Michigan
d. Oct 18, 1956 in Long Island, New York
Source: *BioIn 3, 4; BriEAA; DcAmB S6; MacEA; WhAm 3*

Attila
"Scourge of God"
Ruler
King of the Huns known for attacks on Europe during last stages of Roman Empire.
b. 406
d. 453, Hungary
Source: *BioIn 1, 2, 3, 4, 5, 6, 7, 8, 9, 12; DcBiPP; LinLib L; LngCEL; LuthC 75; McGEWB; NewC; OxCGer 76; REn; WhDW; WorAl; WorAlBi*

Attlee, Clement Richard Attlee, Earl
English. Political Leader
Labour prime minister, 1945-51; directed formulation of welfare state, nationalization of industry; led Labour opposition, 1951-55.
b. Jan 3, 1883 in London, England
d. Oct 8, 1967 in London, England
Source: *BioIn 13; ColdWar 1; CurBio 40, 47, 67; DcPol; HisEWW; LinLib L, S; LngCTC; ObitOF 79; ObitT 1961; WhAm 4; WhDW; WhE&EA; Who 82; WhWW-II; WorAl*

Attles, Al(vin A)
American. Basketball Player, Basketball Coach
Guard, 1960-71; coach, San Francisco/ Golden State, 1969-83; won NBA championship, 1975.
b. Nov 7, 1936 in Newark, New Jersey
Source: *InB&W 85; OfNBA 87; WhoAm 84, 86; WhoBlA 85, 92; WhoWest 87*

Attucks, Crispus
American. Patriot
First colonist killed at Boston Massacre; monument erected on Boston Common, 1880.
b. 1723 in Framingham, Massachusetts
d. Mar 5, 1770 in Boston, Massachusetts
Source: *AfrAmAl 6; ApCAB; BioIn 4, 6, 7, 8, 9, 10, 13; DcAmB; DcAmSR; Drake; EncAR; EncCRAm; InB&W 80, 85; LegTOT; LinLib S; NegAl 76, 83, 89; REn; TwCBDA; WebAB 74, 79; WebAMB; WhAm HS; WhAmRev; WhNaAH; WorAl; WorAlBi*

Attwood, William Hollingsworth
American. Publisher, Journalist, Diplomat
Recounted experiences as ambassador to Guinea, Kenya, 1961-66 in *The Reds and the Blacks: A Personal Adventure,* 1967.
b. Jul 14, 1919 in Paris, France
d. Apr 15, 1989 in New Canaan, Connecticut
Source: *BioIn 16; ConAu 128; CurBio 68, 89, 89N; EncTwCJ; IntWW 74; NewYTBS 89; WhoAdv 90; WhoAm 84, 86, 88; WhoE 89; WhoFI 74*

Atwater, Edith
American. Actor
Played Moriarty to Basil Rathbone's Sherlock Holmes in *The Hound of the Baskervilles,* 1939.
b. Apr 22, 1911 in Chicago, Illinois
d. Mar 19, 1986 in Los Angeles, California
Source: *BiE&WWA; BioIn 14; EncAFC; FilmEn; ForYSC; NotNAT, B; ObitOF 79; WhoHol A; WhoThe 72, 77, 77A; WhThe*

Atwater, Lee
[Harvey Leroy Atwater]
American. Consultant
Chm., Rep. Nat. Com., 1988-91; political campaign consultant infamous for use of negative campaign tactics.
b. Feb 27, 1951 in Atlanta, Georgia
d. Mar 29, 1991 in Washington, District of Columbia
Source: *AnObit 1991; BioIn 14, 15, 16, 17, 18, 19; CurBio 89, 91N; News 89, 91; NewYTBS 88, 91; WhoAm 84; WhoAmP 89; WorAlBi*

Atwill, Lionel
English. Actor
Began career on stage in plays by Shaw, Isben; films include *Son of Frankenstein,* 1939.
b. Mar 1, 1885 in Croydon, England
d. Apr 22, 1946 in Hollywood, California
Source: *BioIn 15, 17, 21; CmMov; CurBio 46; Film 1, 2; FilmEn; FilmgC; HalFC 80, 84, 88; HolCA; LegTOT; MotPP; MovMk; NotNAT B; OlFamFa; OxCAmT 84; PenEncH; REn; Vers A; WhAm 2; WhoHol B; WhoHrs 80; WhScrn 74, 77, 83; WhThe*

Atwood, Angela
[S(ymbionese) L(iberation) A(rmy)]
American. Revolutionary
SLA terrorist involved in Hearst kidnapping, 1974; killed in police shoot-out.
b. 1948?
d. May 24, 1974 in Los Angeles, California
Source: *BioIn 10; InWom SUP; NewYTBS 74*

Atwood, Francis Clarke
American. Inventor
Invented latex paint, technicolor film.
b. May 7, 1893 in Salem, Massachusetts
d. Jul 31, 1982
Source: *AmMWSc 73P, 76P, 79, 82, 86*

Atwood, Margaret (Eleanor)
Canadian. Author, Poet
Wrote best-selling novel *The Handmaid's Tale,* 1986; also wrote *Cat's Eye,* 1990.
b. Nov 18, 1939 in Ottawa, Ontario, Canada
Source: *ArtclWW 2; Au&Arts 12; Au&Wr 71; Benet 87, 96; BenetAL 91; BestSel 89-2; BioIn 14, 15, 16, 17, 18, 20; BlmGEL; BlmGWL; CamGLE;*

CanWW 70, 79, 80, 81, 83, 89; CaW; ConAu 3NR, 24NR, 33NR, 49; ConCaAu 1; ConLC 2, 3, 4, 8, 13, 15, 25, 44, 84; ConNov 76, 82, 86, 91, 96; ConPo 70, 75, 80, 85, 91, 96; ConPopW; ContDcW 89; CurBio 84; CyWA 89; DcArts; DcLB 53; DcLEL 1940; DrAF 76; DrAP 75; DrAPF 80, 91; EncSF 93; EncWL 2, 3; FacFETw; FemiCLE; FemiWr; GrLiveH; GrWomW; GrWrEL P; IntAu&W 76, 77, 82, 86, 89, 91, 93; IntDcWB; IntLitE; IntvTCA 2; IntWW 89, 91, 93; IntWWP 77, 82; InWom SUP; LegTOT; MagSWL; MajTwCW; ModCmwL; ModWoWr; NewYTBS 86; Novels; OxCCan; OxCCanL; OxCCan SUP; OxCEng 85, 95; OxCTwCP; PenBWP; PeoHis; PoeCrit 8; RAdv 14, 13-1; RfGEnL 91; RfGShF; RGTwCWr; ScF&FL 92; ShSCr 2; SmATA 50; TwCYAW; Who 88, 90, 92, 94; WhoAm 74, 76, 78, 80, 84, 86, 88, 90, 92, 94, 95, 96, 97; WhoAmW 81, 83, 85, 87, 89, 91, 93, 95, 97; WhoCanL 85, 87, 92; WhoWor 80, 82, 95, 96, 97; WhoWrEP 89, 92, 95; WorAu 1970; WorLitC; WrDr 76, 80, 82, 84, 86, 88, 90, 92, 94, 96

Auber, Daniel Francois Esprit
French. Composer
Father of French grand opera; greatest work *La Muette de Portici,* 1828.
b. Jan 19, 1782 in Caen, France
d. May 12, 1871 in Paris, France
Source: *AtlBL; Baker 78; BioIn 4, 7, 9, 12, 20; CelCen; DcArts; DcBiPP; Dis&D; LinLib S; NewEOp 71; NewOxM; OxCFr; OxCMus; PenDiMP A; REn*

Auberjonois, Rene Murat
American. Actor
Won Tony for *Coco,* 1969; played Clayton Endicott on TV comedy "Benson," 1980-86.
b. Jun 1, 1940 in New York, New York
Source: *BioIn 13; ConTFT 8; FilmEn; FilmgC; HalFC 88; IntMPA 92; NotNAT; PhDcTCA 77; WhoAm 78, 80, 82, 84, 86, 88, 90, 92, 94, 95, 96, 97; WhoEnt 92; WhoHol A; WhoThe 77, 81; WorAlBi*

Aubrey, James (Thomas), Jr.
American. Business Executive
Head of CBS-TV, 1959; pres. of MGM, 1969-73.
b. Dec 14, 1918 in La Salle, Illinois
d. Sep 3, 1994 in Los Angeles, California
Source: *BioIn 5, 6, 7, 8, 9, 10; CurBio 72, 94N; IntMPA 86, 92; LesBEnT, 92; NewYTET; WhoAm 74, 76; WhoFI 74*

Aubrey, John
English. Author
Wrote *Lives of Eminent Men,* 1813, vivid, intimate portraits of 17th c. personalities.
b. Mar 12, 1626 in Easton Pierce, England
d. Jun 1697 in Oxford, England
Source: *Alli; AtlBL; BioIn 1, 2, 3, 4, 5, 6, 7, 8, 10, 12, 16, 17, 19; BlmGEL; BritAu; CamGEL; CamGLE; CasWL; Chambr 1; CroE&S; DcArts; DcBiPP; DcEnA; DcEnL; DcLEL; DcNaB; Dis&D; EvLB; HisDStE; LinLib L; LngCEL; MouLC 1; NewC; NewCBEL; OxCEng 67, 85, 95; OxCLiW 86; PenC ENG; REn; RfGEnL 91; WebE&AL; WhDW*

Aucherlonie, Laurie
Scottish. Golfer
Touring pro, early 1900s; won US Open, 1902.
b. 1868 in Saint Andrews, Scotland
d. Jan 20, 1948 in Saint Andrews, Scotland
Source: *WhoGolf*

Auchincloss, Hugh D
American.
Stepfather of Jacqueline Onassis.
b. 1897
d. Nov 20, 1976 in Washington, District of Columbia
Source: *BioIn 1; St&PR 75; WhAm 7*

Auchincloss, Louis
[Andrew Lee]
American. Author
Wrote over 30 books, including *The Indifferent Children,* 1947.
b. Sep 27, 1917 in Lawrence, New York
Source: *AmAu&B; Au&Wr 71; Benet 87; BenetAL 91; BioIn 3, 4, 5, 6, 7, 8, 10, 11, 12, 13, 14, 15, 16; BlueB 76; CelR, 90; ConAu 1R, 6NR, 29NR; ConLC 4, 6, 9, 18, 45; ConLCrt 77, 82; ConNov 72, 76, 82, 86, 91; CurBio 78, 84; CyWA 89; DcLB Y80A; DcLP 87A; DrAF 76; DrAPF 80, 91; EncWL 3; GrWrEL N; IntvTCA 2; IntWW 83, 91; LegTOT; LinLib L; MagSAmL; MajTwCW; ModAL, S1, S2; NewYTBS 85; Novels; OxCAmL 65, 83; PenC AM; RAdv 1, 14, 13-1; REn; REnAL; RfGAmL 87; ShSCr 22; TwCWr; WebE&AL; Who 92; WhoAm 90; WhoE 91; WhoWor 87, 91; WhoWrEP 89; WorAlBi; WorAu 1950; WrDr 76, 80, 82, 84, 86, 88, 90, 92*

Auchinleck, Claude, Sir
"The Auk"
English. Military Leader
WW II general, replaced by Montgomery after disobeying Churchill's order to counterattack Rommel outside Cairo.
b. Jun 21, 1884 in Aldershot, England
d. Mar 23, 1981 in Marrakech, Morocco
Source: *AnObit 1981; CurBio 81N; NewYTBS 81; PseudN 82; Who 74; WhoMilH 76; WhoWor 74, 76, 78; WhWW-II*

Auden, W(ystan) H(ugh)
English. Author
Won Pulitzer for verse *Age of Anxiety,* 1948.
b. Feb 21, 1907 in York, England
d. Sep 28, 1973 in Vienna, Austria
Source: *AmAu&B; AmCulL; ASCAP 80; Benet 96; BiDAmM; BioIn 1, 2, 3, 4, 5, 7, 8, 9, 10, 11, 12, 13, 14, 15, 16, 17, 18, 19; ChhPo S3; CmOp; ConDr 93; CurBio 71; DcAmB S9; DcArts; DcNaB 1971; EncWL 3; EncWT; EngPo; Ent; GayLesB; GayLL; GrBr; IntDcOp; IntDcT 2; LngCEL; MakMC; McGEWB; NewCBEL; NewEOp 71; NewGrDO; OxCAmL 95; OxCEng 95; OxCThe 67; OxCTwCP; RAdv 14; RGTwCWr; WebAB 74, 79; WhAm 6; WhDW; WhoAm 74; WhoThe 72; WhoWor 74*

Audiard, Michel
French. Screenwriter
Wrote over 100 French films during 40 yr. career.
b. May 15, 1920 in Paris, France
d. Jul 28, 1985 in Paris, France
Source: *ConAu 116; DcFM; EncEurC; FilmEn; FilmgC; HalFC 80, 84, 88; IntDcF 1-4, 2-4; ItaFilm; WhoFr 79; WorEFlm*

Audiberti, Jacques
French. Author, Poet
Wrote of man, nature: *La Na,* 1944; *Monorail,* 1964.
b. Mar 25, 1899 in Antibes, France
d. Jul 10, 1965 in Paris, France
Source: *CamGWoT; CasWL; ClDMEL 47, 80; CnMD; CnThe; ConLC 38; CroCD; DcTwCCu 2; EncWL 2, 3; EncWT; Ent; EvEuW; IntDcT 2; McGEWD 72, 84; ModFrL; ModWD; OxCFr; OxCThe 67, 83; PenC EUR; REn; WorAu 1950*

Audran, Stephane
[Mrs. Claude Chabrol]
French. Actor
Sophisticated film beauty who starred in *Les Beches,* 1968; *Violette Noziere,* 1978.
b. Nov 8, 1932 in Versailles, France
Source: *BiDFilm, 94; ConTFT 8, 15; EncEurC; FilmEn; FilmgC; HalFC 84; IntDcF 1-3, 2-3; IntMPA 81, 88; IntWW 79, 80, 81, 82, 83; OxCFilm; WhoFr 79*

Audubon, John James
American. Ornithologist
Illustrated wildlife in celebrated folios: *Birds of America,* 1827-38; *Quadrupeds of North America,* 1848.
b. Apr 26, 1785, Haiti
d. Jan 27, 1851 in New York, New York
Source: *AfroAA; Alli; AmAu; AmAu&B; AmBi; AntBDN B; ArtsAmW 1; AsBiEn; AtlBL; BbD; Benet 87, 96; BenetAL 91; BiDAmS; BiD&SB; BiDSA; BiESc; BiInAmS; BioIn 1, 2, 3, 4, 5, 6, 7, 8, 9, 10, 11, 12, 13, 14, 15, 16, 17, 18, 19, 20, 21; BriEAA; CamGEL; CamGLE; CamHAL; CnDAL; CyAL 1; DcAmArt; DcAmAu; DcAmB; DcLEL; DcNAA; DcScB; Dis&D; EncAAH; EncAB-H 1974, 1996; EncSoH; EnvEnc; GrBIl; IlBEAAW; InSci; LarDcSc; LinLib S; McGDA; McGEWB; MemAm; MouLC 3; NatLAC; NegAl 89; NewYHSD; NinCLC 47; OhA&B; OxCAmH; OxCAmL 65, 83, 95; OxCArt; OxCCan; OxCEng 67, 85, 95; OxDcArt; PenC AM; PeoHis; RAdv*

14, 13-5; RComAH; REn; REnAL; REnAW; WebAB 74, 79; WhAm HS; WhFla; WhWE; WorAl; WorAlBi

Auel, Jean Marie
American. Author
Author of Earth's Children series, including, *The Clan of the Cave Bear,* 1980; *The Valley of the Horses,* 1982.
b. Feb 18, 1936 in Chicago, Illinois
Source: *Au&Arts 7; BioIn 12, 14, 15; ConAu 21NR, 103; CurBio 91; DrAPF 91; NewEScF; NewYTBS 80; ScFSB; TwCRHW 90; WhoAm 92, 94, 95, 96, 97; WhoAmW 93, 95, 97; WhoUSWr 88; WhoWor 95, 96, 97; WhoWrEP 89; WorAlBi; WrDr 92*

Auer, Leopold
American. Violinist, Teacher
Soloist for the Czar; taught Zimbalist, Heifetz; wrote manuals on violin playing.
b. Jun 7, 1845 in Vesprem, Hungary
d. Jul 15, 1930 in Loschwitz, Germany
Source: *ASCAP 66, 80; Baker 78, 84, 92; BiDAmM; BioIn 1, 2, 3, 14; BriBkM 80; JeHun; NatCAB 22; NewAmDM; NewGrDA 86; NewGrDM 80; OxCAmH; OxCMus; PenDiMP; WhAm 1*

Auer, Mischa
[Mischa Ounskowski]
Russian. Actor
Appeared in over 60 US films; nominated for Oscar, 1936, for *My Man Godfrey.*
b. Nov 17, 1905 in Saint Petersburg, Russia
d. Mar 5, 1967 in Rome, Italy
Source: *BioIn 2, 7, 21; EncAFC; Film 2; FilmEn; FilmgC; ForYSC; Funs; HalFC 80, 84, 88; HolCA; IntDcF 1-3; ItaFilm; MotPP; MovMk; NotNAT B; ObitOF 79; ObitT 1961; OlFamFa; QDrFCA 92; TwYS; Vers A; What 1; WhoHol B; WhoHrs 80; WhScrn 74, 77, 83*

Auerbach, Red
[Arnold Jacob Auerbach]
American. Basketball Coach
Winningest coach in NBA history, 1946-66, mostly with Boston; won NBA championships, 1958-66; Hall of Fame, 1968.
b. Sep 20, 1917 in New York, New York
Source: *BasBi; BiDAmSp BK; BioIn 14, 15, 16, 17, 18, 20, 21; CelR 90; ConAu 17R, 131; CurBio 69; FacFETw; LegTOT; WhoAm 78, 80, 82, 84, 86, 90, 92, 94, 95; WhoBbl 73; WhoE 74, 89, 91, 93, 95; WhoSpor; WrDr 94, 96*

Auerbach-Levy, William
American. Artist
Magazine caricaturist; satirized theater personalities in *NY World,* 1925-31.
b. Feb 14, 1889 in Brest-Litovsk, Russia
d. Jun 29, 1964 in Ossining, New York
Source: *BioIn 1, 6, 7, 8, 12, 15, 17; CurBio 48, 64; EncAJ; NatCAB 51; WhAm 4; WhAmArt 85; WhoAmA 80, 82, 89N, 91N, 93N; WorECar*

Auermann, Nadja
German. Model
Formerly a waif-like model, she dyed her hair platinum blonde; known for very long legs.
b. 1971 in Berlin, Germany

Auger, Arleen
American. Opera Singer
Soprano; concert performer; Vienna State Opera, 1968-74.
b. Sep 13, 1939 in Los Angeles, California
d. Jun 10, 1993 in Leusden, Netherlands
Source: *AnObit 1993; Baker 84; BioIn 13, 14, 15, 16; CurBio 89, 93N; EncRk 88; IntWW 89, 91, 93; IntWWM 90; MetOEnc; NewGrDA 86; NewGrDO; NewYTBS 84, 93; OxDcOp; PenDiMP; PenEncP; WhAm 11; WhoAm 86, 88, 90, 92; WhoEnt 92; WhoOp 76*

Auger, Brian
English. Musician, Songwriter
Keyboardist who formed Brian Auger's Trinity, 1964; fused jazz-rock hybrids.
b. Jul 18, 1939 in London, England
Source: *BiDJaz; ConMuA 80A; EncJzS; EncRk 88; IlEncRk; PenEncP; RolSEnR 83; WhoRock 81*

August, Jan
[Jan Augustoff]
American. Musician, Bandleader
Self-taught society style pianist, popular 1940s-50s; specialized in Latin American music; hit album *Misirlou,* 1946.
b. 1912? in New York, New York
d. Jan 18, 1976 in New York, New York
Source: *BioIn 10; CmpEPM; NewYTBS 76; PenEncP*

Augustine, Saint
[Saint Augustine of Hippo; Saint Aurelius Augustinus]
Roman. Religious Figure, Philosopher
Early bishop regarded as founder of Christian theology; defended orthodoxy in extensive writings: *City of God,* 413-426.
b. Nov 13, 354 in Agate, Numidia
d. Aug 28, 430 in Hippo, Numidia
Source: *AtlBL; Baker 92; BbD; Benet 87, 96; BiD&SB; BiDPsy; BioIn 1, 2, 3, 4, 5, 6, 7, 8, 10, 11, 12, 13; CasWL; ClMLC 6; CyEd; CyWA 58; DcAmC; DcBiPP; DcCathB; DcLB 115; DcScB; Dis&D; EncEarC; EncEth; EncPaPR 91; EuWr 1; GrFLW; Grk&L; HisWorL; IlEncMy; InSci; LegTOT; LinLib L, S; LuthC 75; McGDA; McGEWB; NamesHP; NewC; NewCBEL; NewGrDM 80; OxCClL, 89; OxCEng 67, 85, 95; OxCLaw; OxCPhil; OxDcByz; PenC CL; RAdv 14, 13-4; RComWL; REn; RfGWoL 95; WebBD 83; WhDW; WorAl; WorAlBi; WrPh P*

Augustine of Canterbury, Saint
"Apostle of the English"
Roman. Religious Leader
First archbishop of Canterbury, 601; feast day May 26.
d. May 26, 604
Source: *Benet 87, 96; BioIn 1, 2, 3, 4, 5, 6, 8, 9, 10, 11, 12; CyEd; EncEarC; LuthC 75; McGDA; McGEWB; NewC; REn; WhDW; WorAlBi*

Augustus
[Augustus Caesar; Octavius Caesar]
Roman. Ruler
Emperor who returned Rome to constitutional rule after death of Caesar, 44 BC.
b. Sep 23, 63BC in Rome, Italy
d. Aug 19, 14AD in Nola, Italy
Source: *AmLY X, XR; Benet 87, 96; BioIn 1, 2, 3, 4, 5, 6, 7, 8, 9, 10, 12, 13, 14, 16, 17, 20; BlmGEL; CopCroC; DcBiPP; Dis&D; EncEarC; Grk&L; HisWorL; LngCEL; LuthC 75; McGEWB; NewC; OxCClL 89; PenC CL; REn; WhDW*

Augustus II
[Augustus the Strong; Frederick Augustine I]
Polish. Ruler
King of Poland, 1697-1733; known for architectural beautification of Dresden.
b. May 12, 1670 in Dresden, Germany
d. Feb 1, 1733 in Warsaw, Poland
Source: *DcBiPP; LuthC 75; NewCol 75; WhDW*

Augustyn, Frank Joseph
Canadian. Dancer
Star of Canada's National Ballet since 1972.
b. Jan 27, 1953 in Hamilton, Ontario, Canada
Source: *BioIn 9; CanWW 31, 83, 89; WhoAm 78, 80, 82, 84, 86, 90, 92, 94, 95, 96, 97; WhoE 81*

Auldridge, Mike
American. Musician
Plays dobro (a modified guitar) for bluegrass band Seldom Scene 1971—; Grammy nomination for Best Male Volcalist in Country Music, 1975.
b. 1938 in Washington, District of Columbia
Source: *ConMus 4*

Auletta, Robert
American. Dramatist
Won Obies for *Stops,* 1972; *Virgins,* 1982.
b. Mar 5, 1940 in New York, New York
Source: *ConAu 48NR, 115, 119; ConTFT 1; NatPD 81*

Aulnoy, Marie-Catherine Jumel de Berneville
French. Author
Wrote fairy tales in manner of Charles Perrault, late 1600s: *Yellow Dwarf, White Cat.*

b. 1650?
d. 1705 in Paris, France
Source: *CasWL; DcEuL; OxCChiL; OxCFr; OxCSpan*

Ault, George Christian
American. Artist
Precisionist who drew nocturnes, cityscapes.
b. Oct 11, 1891 in Cleveland, Ohio
d. Dec 30, 1948 in Woodside, New York
Source: *BioIn 4, 11; DcAmArt; DcCAA 71, 77; IlBEAAW; McGDA; NatCAB 40*

Aumont, Jean-Pierre
[Jean-Pierre Salomons]
French. Author
Brother of Francois Villiers; wrote autobiography *Sun and Shadow,* 1976.
b. Jan 5, 1909 in Paris, France
Source: *BiE&WWA; ConTFT 4; FilmAG WE; FilmEn; FilmgC; ForYSC; HalFC 80, 84, 88; HolP 40; IntAu&W 77; IntDcF 1-3; IntMPA 81, 82, 92; IntWW 91; ItaFilm; LegTOT; MotPP; MovMk; NotNAT; WhoAm 78, 82, 90; WhoEnt 92; WhoHol 92, A; WhoThe 72, 77, 81; WorAlBi*

Aungervyle, Richard
[Richard de Bury]
English. Author, Clergy
Bibliophile; wrote classic tribute to books: *Philobiblon,* 1473.
b. Jan 24, 1281 in Bury Saint Edmunds, England
d. 1345
Source: *Alli; BritAu; DcEnL; DcEuL; DcNaB; EvLB; NewC; OxCEng 67; WebBD 83*

Auque, Roger
French. Hostage
Journalist, captured in Lebanon by terrorists on Jan 13, 1987, held until Nov 27, 1987, 319 days.

Aurangzeb
Indian. Ruler
Last Mogul emperor of India, 1658-1707; contributed to collapse of empire.
b. Oct 24, 1618 in Dohad, India
d. Feb 20, 1707 in Ahmadnagar, India
Source: *BioIn 15, 16, 20; HisDBrE; HisWorL; LinLib S; McGEWB; NewCol 75; WhDW; WorAl; WorAlBi*

Aurell, Tage
Swedish. Author, Translator
Wrote *Skilling Tryck,* 1943.
b. Mar 2, 1895 in Christiania, Norway
d. Feb 20, 1976 in Mansrog, Sweden
Source: *CasWL, 3; WhE&EA*

Auric, Georges
[Les Six]
French. Composer
Scored over 100 films, including *Roman Holiday,* 1953; *Beauty and the Beast,* 1946.
b. Feb 15, 1899 in Lodeve, France
d. Jul 23, 1983 in Paris, France
Source: *AnObit 1983; Baker 78, 84, 92; BiDD; BioIn 3, 4, 6, 8, 12; BriBkM 80; CnOxB; CompSN, SUP; DancEn 78; DcArts; DcCom 77; DcFM; DcTwCCu 2; FacFETw; FilmEn; FilmgC; HalFC 80, 84, 88; IntDcF 1-4, 2-4; IntWW 74, 75, 76, 77, 78, 79, 80, 81, 82, 83; IntWWM 77, 80; ItaFilm; MusMk; NewAmDM; NewEOp 71; NewGrDM 80; NewGrDO; NewOxM; OxCFilm; OxCMus; OxCPMus; PenDiMP A; REn; Who 74, 82, 83; WhoFr 79; WhoWor 74; WorEFlm*

Auriol, Jacqueline Douet
French. Aviator
First woman test pilot; second woman to break sound barrier.
b. Nov 5, 1917 in Challans, France
Source: *BioIn 15; ContDcW 89; CurBio 53; HerW, 84; InSci; IntDcWB; InWom, SUP; WhoAmW 68, 75; WhoWor 74*

Auriol, Vincent
French. Political Leader
Socialist Party leader; first pres. of Fourth Republic, 1947-54.
b. Aug 25, 1884 in Revel, France
d. Jan 1, 1966 in Paris, France
Source: *BioIn 1, 2, 3, 5, 7, 17; CurBio 47, 66; DcPol; DcTwHis; FacFETw; ObitT 1961; WhAm 4*

Auslander, Joseph
American. Author, Poet
Wrote popular history of poetry, *The Winged Horse,* 1927.
b. Oct 11, 1897 in Philadelphia, Pennsylvania
d. Jun 22, 1965 in Coral Gables, Florida
Source: *AmAu&B; BenetAL 91; BioIn 4, 5, 7; ChhPo, S1; CnDAL; ConAu 116; OxCAmL 65, 83, 95; REn; REnAL; TwCA, SUP; WhJnl; WhNAA*

Austen, Jane
English. Author
Her books about family life in rural England and comedies have withstood time in the changing outside world: *Pride and Prejudice,* 1813, *Sense and Sensibility,* 1811.
b. Dec 16, 1775 in Steventon, England
d. Jul 18, 1817 in Winchester, England
Source: *Alli; ArtclWW 2; AtlBL; Au&Arts 19; BbD; Benet 87, 96; BiD&SB; BioIn 1, 2, 3, 4, 5, 6, 7, 8, 9, 10, 11, 12, 13, 14, 15, 16, 17, 18, 20, 21; BlmGEL; BlmGWL; BritAu 19; BritWr 4; CamGEL; CamGLE; CelCen; Chambr 2; CnDBLB 3; ContDcW 89; CrtT 2, 4; CyWA 58; DcArts; DcBiA; DcBiPP; DcEnA; DcEnL; DcEuL; DcLB 116; DcLEL; DcNaB; Dis&D; EncBrWW; EvLB; FemiCLE; GoodHs; GrWomW; GrWrEL N; HalFC 80, 84, 88; HerW, 84; IntDcWB; InWom, SUP; LegTOT; LinLib L, S; LngCEL; MagSWL; McGEWB; MouLC 2; NewC; NewCBEL; NewCol 75; NinCLC 1, 13, 19, 33; Novels; OxCEng 67, 85, 95; PenC ENG; PenNWW A; RAdv 1, 14, 13-1; RComWL; REn; RfGEnL 91; WebBD 83; WebE&AL; WhDW; WomFir; WorAl; WorAlBi; WorLitC*

Auster, Paul
American. Author
Wrote *Moon Palace,* 1989; *Leviathan,* 1992.
b. Feb 3, 1947 in Newark, New Jersey
Source: *Benet 96; BioIn 16, 17, 18, 21; ConAu 23NR, 52NR, 69; ConLC 47; ConNov 91, 96; CurBio 96; DcArts; DrAPF 80; EncSF 93; IntWWP 77, 82; NewYTBS 92; OxCAmL 95; RGTwCWr; ScF&FL 92; TwCCr&M 91; WhoAm 92, 94, 95, 96, 97; WhoWrEP 89, 92, 95; WorAu 1980; WrDr 90, 92, 94, 96*

Austin, Alfred
English. Poet, Critic
Succeeded Tennyson as poet laureate, 1896; wrote *The Human Tragedy,* 1862.
b. May 30, 1835 in Headingley, England
d. Jun 2, 1913 in Ashford, England
Source: *Alli SUP; BbD; BiD&SB; BioIn 3, 10, 14; BritAu 19; CamGLE; CelCen; Chambr 3; ChhPo, S1, S2, S3; DcArts; DcEnA, A; DcEnL; DcEuL; DcLB 35; DcLEL; DcNaB 1912; EvLB; GrWrEL P; LinLib L, S; LngCTC; NewC; NewCBEL; OxCEng 67, 85, 95; OxCTwCP; PenC ENG; RfGEnL 91; StaCVF; TwCWr; WhLit*

Austin, Dallas
American. Producer, Songwriter
Rap musician and producer; wrote and produced most of the songs on Boyz II Men multiplatinum album, *Cooleyhighharmony,* 1991; also produced for artist such as Madonna, TLC, and Lionel Richie; named Producer of the Year by *Billboard* Magazine, 1991; placed first in Top Ten R & B Songwriters of the Year by *Billboard* Magazine.
b. 1971 in Columbus, Georgia
Source: *ConMus 16*

Austin, Gene
American. Actor, Songwriter
Songs include "How Come You Do Me Like You Do?," 1924; "Lonesome Road," 1928.
b. Jun 24, 1900 in Gainesville, Texas
d. Jan 24, 1972 in Palm Springs, California
Source: *AmPS A, B; ASCAP 66, 80; BiDAmM; BioIn 4, 8, 9, 12, 14; CmpEPM; NewYTBE 72; ObitOF 79; OxCPMus; PenEncP; What 2; WhoHol B; WhScrn 77*

Austin, Herbert
English. Auto Manufacturer
Started Austin Motorcars, 1905.
b. Nov 8, 1866 in Missenden, England
d. May 23, 1941 in Bromsgrove, England

Source: *BioIn 12, 15; DcNaB 1941; DcTwBBL; GrBr; LegTOT; WebBD 83; WorAl; WorAlBi*

Austin, John Langshaw
English. Philosopher
Wrote *How to Do Things with Words,* 1962.
b. Mar 26, 1911 in Lancaster, England
d. Feb 8, 1960 in Oxford, England
Source: *BioIn 5, 12, 14, 15; ConAu 112; DcNaB 1951; FacFETw; LngCTC; MakMC; McGEWB; ObitT 1951; OxCEng 67, 85; OxCPhil; RAdv 14, 13-4; WhAm 4; WhDW; WorAu 1970*

Austin, John Paul
American. Business Executive
Coca-Cola exec., 1962-81; added Tab, Sprite, raising sales to $5 billion.
b. Feb 14, 1915 in La Grange, Georgia
d. Dec 26, 1985 in Atlanta, Georgia
Source: *BlueB 76; Dun&B 79; NewYTBS 85; St&PR 75; WhAm 9; WhoAm 74, 76, 78, 80, 82, 84; WhoFI 74, 75; WhoSSW 73, 76, 78, 80, 82, 84*

Austin, Mary Hunter
American. Author
Described Native American life, literature: *Land of Little Rain,* 1903.
b. Sep 9, 1868 in Carlinville, Illinois
d. Aug 13, 1934 in Santa Fe, New Mexico
Source: *AmBi; AnCL; BiCAW; ConAmA; NotAW; OxCAmL 65; Str&VC; TwCA SUP; WebAB 74; WhAm 1*

Austin, Patti
American. Singer
With James Ingram, had hit single "Baby Come to Me," 1982, love theme for soap opera General Hospital.
b. Aug 10, 1948 in New York, New York
Source: *BioIn 16; EncRkSt; InB&W 85; LegTOT; PenEncP; RkOn 85; SoulM; WhoAfA 96; WhoBlA 94; WhoRocM 82*

Austin, Stephen Fuller
American. Colonizer
Established Austin, TX, 1822, first American settlement in TX.
b. Nov 3, 1793 in Austinville, Virginia
d. Dec 27, 1836 in Austin, Texas
Source: *AmAu&B; AmBi; ApCAB; BenetAL 91; BiDAmBL 83; BioIn 1, 2, 3, 4, 5, 7, 8, 9, 12; CopCroC; DcAmB; Drake; EncAAH; EncAB-H 1974, 1996; EncSoH; HarEnUS; McGEWB; NatCAB 6; OxCAmH; REnAL; REnAW; TwCBDA; WebAB 74, 79; WhAm HS; WhAmP; WorAl*

Austin, Tracy Ann
American. Tennis Player
Member of US Federation Cup team, 1978-80; youngest player to crack million dollar prize money barrier.
b. Dec 12, 1962 in Rolling Hills, California
Source: *BiDAmSp OS; BioIn 10, 13, 14, 16; BkPepl; CurBio 81; GoodHs; HerW 84; InWom SUP; NewYTBS 80, 81, 85; WhoAm 82, 84, 86, 88, 92; WhoAmW 81, 83, 85, 87; WorAl; WorAlBi*

Austin, Warren R(obinson)
American. Statesman, Government Official
Rep. senator from VT; first US ambassador to UN, 1946-53.
b. Nov 12, 1877 in Highgate, Vermont
d. Dec 25, 1962 in Burlington, Vermont
Source: *BiDInt; BiDrAC; BiDrUSC 89; BioIn 1, 2, 3, 6, 11, 12, 16; CurBio 44, 63; DcAmB S7; DcAmDH 80, 89; EncAB-A 6; NatCAB 60; WhAm 4; WhAmP*

Austral, Florence Wilson
Australian. Opera Singer
Prominent soprano; touring America, 1920s-30s; noted for Wagner roles.
b. Apr 26, 1894 in Melbourne, Australia
d. May 15, 1968 in Sydney, Australia
Source: *Baker 84; InWom; ObitT 1961*

Autant-Lara, Claude
French. Director
Directed *Devil in the Flesh,* 1947; filmwork known for its leftist and atheistic overtones.
b. Aug 5, 1903 in Luzarches, France
Source: *BiDFilm, 81, 94; BioIn 12, 15; DcFM; DcTwCCu 2; FilmEn; FilmgC; HalFC 80, 84, 88; IntDcF 1-2, 2-2; IntMPA 77, 80; IntWW 91; ItaFilm; MovMk; OxCFilm; WorEFlm; WorFDir 1*

Autori, Franco
Italian. Conductor
Led Tulsa Orchestra, 1961-71; associate conductor, NY Philharmonic, 1949-59.
b. Nov 29, 1903 in Naples, Italy
d. Oct 16, 1990 in Tulsa, Oklahoma
Source: *Baker 78, 84, 92; BioIn 17; NewYTBS 90; WhAm 10; WhoAm 74*

Autry, Gene
"The Singing Cowboy"
American. Actor, Singer, Baseball Executive
Starred in 82 movie Westerns, 1934-54; wrote over 250 songs, including "Here Comes Santa Claus"; owner, CA Angels baseball team.
b. Sep 29, 1907 in Tioga, Texas
Source: *ASCAP 66; BgBkCoM; BioIn 11, 12, 14, 15, 16, 17, 18, 19, 20; CmCal; CmMov; CmpEPM; ConAu 112; ConMus 12; CounME 74, 74A; CurBio 47; EncACom; EncFCWM 69, 83; FacFETw; FilmEn; FilmgC; ForYSC; HalFC 80, 84, 88; HarEnCM 87; IlEncCM; IntDcF 1-3, 2-3; IntMPA 75, 76, 77, 78, 79, 80, 81, 82, 84, 86, 88, 92, 94, 96; LegTOT; LesBEnT 92; MotPP; MovMk; NewAmDM; NewGrDA 86; NewYTET; OxCFilm; OxCPMus; PenEncP; RadStar; SaTiSS; What 1; WhoAm 74, 76, 78, 80, 82, 84, 86, 88, 90, 92, 94, 95, 96, 97; WhoEnt 92; WhoFI 89, 92, 94, 96; WhoHol 92, A; WhoRock 81; WhoWest 80, 82, 84, 87, 89, 92, 94, 96; WorAl; WorAlBi; WorEFlm*

Avakian, Aram A
American. Director
Known for films *The End of the Road,* 1970; *Cops and Robbers,* 1973.
b. 1917 in New York, New York
d. 1987 in New York, New York
Source: *BioIn 8, 15; HalFC 88; IntMPA 88; NewYTBS 87*

Avakian, George
American. Critic
Jazz critic, columnist, 1938-50.
b. Mar 15, 1919 in Amavir, Union of Soviet Socialist Republics
Source: *NewGrDJ 88, 94; WhoWor 74*

Avallone, Michael Angelo, Jr.
American. Author
Wrote over 1,000 paperbacks under dozens of pseuds; created sleuth Ed Noon.
b. Oct 27, 1924 in New York, New York
Source: *Au&Wr 71; BioIn 14; ConAu 4NR, 5R; CrtSuMy; DcLP 87A; EncMys; EncSF 93; IntAu&W 77, 89, 91, 93; SpyFic; TwCCr&M 85, 91; WhoAm 82, 84, 86, 88, 90, 92, 94, 95, 96, 97; WhoE 83; WrDr 76, 80, 86, 92*

Avalon, Frankie
[Francis Thomas Avalone]
American. Actor, Singer, Entertainer
Teen idol, 1960s; starred with Annette Funicello in *Beach* movies; had hit song, "Venus," 1959.
b. Sep 18, 1940 in Philadelphia, Pennsylvania
Source: *BiDAmM; BioIn 11, 15; ConMus 5; ConTFT 3; EncPR&S 89; EncRk 88; FilmgC; HalFC 88; HarEnR 86; IntMPA 75, 76, 77, 78, 79, 80, 81, 82, 84, 86, 88, 92, 94, 96; MotPP; MovMk; OxCPMus; PenEncP; RkOn 74, 82; WhoAm 88, 92, 94, 95, 96, 97; WhoEnt 92; WhoHol A; WhoRock 81; WorAl; WorAlBi*

Avalos, Luis
Cuban. Actor
Stage, film performer; mostly known for TV roles, including "Kojak," 1979.
b. Sep 2, 1946 in Havana, Cuba
Source: *ConTFT 5; WhoEnt 92*

Avedon, Doe
American. Actor
Films include *High and the Mighty,* 1954; *Deep in My Heart,* 1954.
b. 1925 in Old Westbury, New York
Source: *FilmgC; HalFC 84, 88; IntMPA 86, 92; WhoHol A*

Avedon, Richard
American. Photographer
One of world's greatest photographers credited with making fashion photography an art form.
b. May 15, 1923 in New York, New York
Source: *AmArt; BioIn 4, 5, 7, 9, 10, 11, 14, 15, 16; BlueB 76; BriEAA; CelR, 90; ConPhot 82, 88, 95; CurBio 75; DcArts; DcTwCCu 1; DcTwDes; EncFash; EncWB; FacFETw; ICPEnP; IntWW 74, 75, 76, 77, 78, 79, 80, 81, 82, 83, 89, 91, 93; LegTOT; MacBEP; WhoAm 74, 76, 78, 80, 82, 84, 86, 88, 90, 92, 94, 95, 96, 97; WhoAmA 78, 80, 82, 84, 86, 89, 91, 93; WhoE 83, 85, 86, 91, 93; WhoGrA 82; WhoWor 74, 76, 78; WorFshn; WrDr 80, 82, 84, 86, 88, 90, 92, 94, 96*

Average White Band, The
[Roger Ball; Malcolm Duncan; Steven Ferrone; Alan Gorrie; Onnie McIntire; Robbie McIntosh; Michael Rosen; Hamish Stuart]
English. Music Group
Formed 1972; best-selling albums *Cut the Cake,* 1975; *Cupid's in Fashion,* 1982.
Source: *BioIn 15, 16; ConMuA 80A; ConTFT 6; CurBio 42; DcLP 87A; EncPR&S 89; EncRk 88; EncRkSt; HarEnR 86; IlEncBM 82; IlEncRk; IntMPA 92; ObitOF 79; OnThGG; OxCPMus; PenEncP; RkOn 74, 78; RolSEnR 83; SoulM; WhoRock 81; WhoRocM 82*

Averback, Hy
American. Director, Producer
Directed *Where Were You When the Lights Went Out?*; *Suppose They Gave a War a nd Nobody Came?*
b. 1925
Source: *ConTFT 6; FilmEn; FilmgC; HalFC 88; IntMPA 88, 92, 94, 96; LesBEnT; MiSFD 9; NewYTET; VarWW 85*

Averill, Earl
[Howard Earl Averil]
"Earl of Snohomish"
American. Baseball Player
Outfielder, 1929-41; had .318 career batting average; Hall of Fame, 1975.
b. May 21, 1902 in Snohomish, Washington
d. Aug 16, 1983 in Everett, Washington
Source: *Ballpl 90; BioIn 13, 14, 15; LegTOT; NewYTBS 83; WhoSpor*

Averroes
[Ibn Rushd]
Spanish. Philosopher
One of great commentators on Aristotle; provided Christians with first knowledge of him.
b. 1126 in Cordoba, Spain
d. Dec 10, 1198 in Marrakech, Morocco
Source: *AsBiEn; BbD; Benet 96; BiD&SB; BiDPsy; BioIn 7, 8, 17, 18, 20; CasWL; ClMLC 7; DcEuL; DcLB 115; DcOrL 3; DcScB; EncO&P 2S1, 3; EncUnb; EuAu; EvEuW; InSci; LegTOT; LinLib L, S; LuthC 75; McGEWB; OxCEng 67, 85, 95; OxCMed 86; OxCPhil; RAdv 14, 13-4; REn; WebBD 83; WorAl; WorAlBi*

Avery, James
American. Actor
Plays uncle Phil on TV show "The Fresh Prince of Bel Air."
Source: *EncASM; WhoAfA 96; WhoBlA 94; WhoHol 92*

Avery, Milton Clark
American. Artist
Works influenced by Matisse; known as pioneer in American abstractionism.
b. Mar 7, 1893 in Altmar, New York
d. Jan 3, 1965 in New York, New York
Source: *CurBio 58, 65; DcAmB S7; DcCAA 71; WhAm 4*

Avery, Oswald T
Canadian. Scientist
With 2 other scientists, proved that the genetic substance DNA is found in all living cells.
b. Oct 21, 1877 in Halifax, Nova Scotia, Canada
d. Feb 20, 1955 in Nashville, Tennessee
Source: *BioIn 1, 2, 4, 5, 6, 7, 11, 12, 13, 14; DcAmB S5; FacFETw; NatCAB 44; ObitOF 79; OxCMed 86; WhAm 3*

Avery, R. Stanton
American. Businessman
Founder, chm., self-adhesive labels co., 1932; annual sales over $600 million, 1980.
b. 1907 in Oklahoma City, Oklahoma
Source: *Dun&B 79, 86, 88, 90; Entr; St&PR 75, 84, 87*

Avery, Samuel Putnam
American. Artist, Philanthropist
Wood, copper engraver; founded Avery Architectural Library, later housed in Columbia U's Avery Hall, 1912.
b. Mar 8, 1822 in New York, New York
d. Aug 14, 1904 in New York, New York
Source: *AmBi; BioIn 12, 13, 14; DcAmB; DcAmBC; DcNAA; HarEnUS; NatCAB 1; NewYHSD; TwCBDA; WhAm 1; WhAmArt 85*

Avery, Sewell
American. Retailer
Served on board of Montgomery Ward, 1931-56.
b. Nov 4, 1874 in Saginaw, Michigan
d. Oct 31, 1960 in Chicago, Illinois
Source: *BioIn 20; CurBio 44, 61; PolProf E*

Avery, Tex
[Frederick Bean Avery]
American. Cartoonist
Developed Daffy Duck, Bugs Bunny; made animated TV commercials.
b. Feb 26, 1908 in Taylor, Texas
d. Aug 27, 1980 in Burbank, California
Source: *AnObit 1980; BioIn 11; FilmEn; FilmgC; PseudN 82; WorECar; WorEFlm*

Avicenna
[Abu Ali al-Husayn ibn Abd-Allah ibn Sina]
Arab. Physician, Philosopher
Wrote *Canon of Medicine* based on Greek medical works and long used as textbook.
b. 980 in Afshana, Arabia
d. Jun 1037 in Hamadan, Persia
Source: *AsBiEn; Benet 87, 96; BiD&SB; BiDPsy; BiESc; BiHiMed; BioIn 1, 2, 3, 5, 6, 7, 8, 9, 10, 12, 13, 15, 18, 19, 20; CasWL; ClMLC 16; CyEd; DcLB 115; DcOrL 3; DcScB; EncO&P 2, 3; LegTOT; LinLib L, S; LuthC 75; McGEWB; OxCEng 67, 85, 95; OxCMed 86; OxCPhil; PenC CL; RAdv 14, 13-4; REn; WhDW; WorAl; WorAlBi*

Avila, Bobby
[Roberto Gonzalez Avila]
"Beto"
Mexican. Baseball Player
Infielder, Cleveland, 1949-58; won AL batting title, 1954.
b. Apr 2, 1924 in Veracruz, Mexico
Source: *Ballpl 90; BioIn 21; WhoProB 73*

Avogadro, Amedeo
[Conte de Quaregna]
Italian. Physicist
Best known for coining word "molecule"; worked extensively with gases.
b. Jun 9, 1776 in Turin, Italy
d. Jul 9, 1856 in Turin, Italy
Source: *AsBiEn; BioIn 1, 3, 4, 5, 9, 13, 14; DcScB; InSci; McGEWB; NewCol 75; WorScD*

Awdry, W(ilbert Vere)
English. Author, Clergy
Wrote *Thomas the Tank Engine* stories.
b. Jun 15, 1911 in Ampfield
d. Mar 21, 1997 in Stroud, England
Source: *Au&Wr 71; BioIn 8; ConAu 103; DcLB 160; IntAu&W 76, 77, 82, 86, 89; OxCChiL; SmATA 67; Who 90, 92, 94; WhoChL; WhoWor 95, 96, 97; WrDr 76, 80, 82, 84*

Awolowo, Obafemi Awo
Nigerian. Political Leader
A leader in Nigerian independence; prime minister, under British rule, Western Nigeria, 1954-59; ran for president of Nigeria, 1979, 1983.
b. Mar 6, 1909 in Ikenne, Nigeria (Southern)
d. May 9, 1987 in Ikenne, Nigeria
Source: *AfrA; BlkWr 2; ConAu 14NR, 65, 122; CurBio 57, 87; IntWW 83; McGEWB; SchCGBL*

Awoonor, Kofi
Ghanaian. Poet
Poetry has been translated into several languages; work includes *Rediscovery and Other Poems,* 1964.
b. Mar 13, 1935 in Weta, Gold Coast
Source: *AfrA; BioIn 9, 10, 14, 18, 21; BlkWr 1; CamGLE; CasWL; ConAu 13AS, 15NR, 29R; ConPo 70, 75, 80, 85, 91, 96; DcLB 117; DcLEL 1940; DrAF 76; DrAPF 91; EncWL 2, 3; IntAu&W 82, 91; IntvTCA 2; IntWW 91; LiExTwC; ModBlW; ModCmwL; OxCTwCP; RAdv 14, 13-2; RGAfL; SchCGBL; SelBAAf; WhoWor 91; WorAu 1970; WrDr 76, 82, 84, 86, 88, 90, 92, 94, 96*

Ax, Emanuel
Polish. Pianist
Concert pianist, performs often in with Young-Uck Kim, Yo-Yo Ma; won Avery Fisher Prize, 1979.
b. Jun 8, 1949 in Lvov, Poland
Source: *Baker 78, 84, 92; BioIn 9, 12, 13, 17, 21; CelR 90; CurBio 84; EncWB; IntWW 89, 91; IntWWM 90; LegTOT; NewAmDM; NewGrDA 86; NotTwCP; PenDiMP; PolBiDi; WhoAm 86, 90, 92, 94, 95, 96, 97; WhoAmM 83; WhoWor 78, 80, 82, 84, 87, 89, 91, 93, 95*

Axelrod, George
American. Dramatist
Wrote plays *The Seven Year Itch,* 1956; *Breakfast at Tiffany's,* 1962.
b. Jun 9, 1922 in New York, New York
Source: *AmAu&B; BenetAL 91; BiDFilm, 81, 94; BiE&WWA; BioIn 3, 6, 8, 10, 21; CelR; CmMov; CnMD; ConAmD; ConAu 65; ConDr 73, 77, 82, 88, 93; ConTFT 4; EncAFC; FilmEn; FilmgC; HalFC 80, 84, 88; IntDcF 1-4, 2-4; IntMPA 75, 76, 77, 78, 79, 80, 81, 82, 84, 86, 88, 92, 94, 96; LinLib L; McGEWD 72, 84; MiSFD 9; ModAL; NotNAT; OxCAmT 84; OxCFilm; WhoAm 74, 76, 78, 80, 82, 84, 86; WhoEnt 92; WorAu 1950; WorEFlm; WrDr 76, 80, 82, 84, 86, 88, 90, 92, 94, 96*

Axelrod, Julius
American. Scientist
Shared 1970 Nobel Prize in medicine for work with drugs and nerves; co-invented drug Tylenol.
b. May 30, 1912 in New York, New York
Source: *AmMWSc 73P, 76P, 79, 82, 86, 89, 92, 95; BiESc; BioIn 9, 11, 12, 14, 15, 19, 20; BlueB 76; FacFETw; IntWW 74, 75, 76, 77, 78, 79, 80, 81, 82, 83, 89, 91, 93; LarDcSc; LegTOT; McGMS 80; NobelP; NotTwCS; WebAB 74, 79; Who 74, 82, 83, 85, 88, 90, 92, 94; WhoAm 74, 76, 78, 80, 82, 84, 86, 88, 90, 92, 94, 95, 96, 97; WhoE 74, 77, 79, 81, 83, 85, 86, 89, 91, 95, 97; WhoGov 72, 75, 77; WhoMedH; WhoNob, 90, 95; WhoScEn 94, 96; WhoWor 74, 80, 82, 84, 87, 89, 91, 93, 95, 96, 97; WhoWorJ 72, 78; WorAl; WorAlBi*

Axelson, Kenneth Strong
American. Business Executive
Director, JC Penny Life Insurance Co., 1967—.
b. Jul 31, 1922 in Chicago, Illinois
Source: *BioIn 10, 11; News 91, 91-3; NewYTBS 75, 91; St&PR 84; WhoAm 74, 76, 78, 80, 82; WhoE 79, 81, 83, 85, 86, 89, 95, 97; WhoFI 74, 75, 77, 79, 81, 83, 85, 87; WhoUSWr 88; WhoWor 74, 76, 78; WhoWrEP 89*

Axis Sally
[Mildred Elizabeth Gillars]
American. Traitor
Broadcast Nazi propoganda during WW II; imprisoned by Allies for 12 years.
b. Nov 1900 in Portland, Maine
d. Jun 25, 1988 in Columbus, Ohio
Source: *BioIn 6, 8, 9, 16; EncTR; FacFETw*

Axthelm, Pete(r Macrae)
American. Journalist
Sportswriter, *Newsweek,* since 1968; NBC sports commentator, 1980-86.
b. Aug 27, 1943 in New York, New York
d. Feb 2, 1991 in Pittsburgh, Pennsylvania
Source: *ConAu 107; News 91, 91-3; WhAm 10; WhoAm 80, 82, 84, 86; WhoUSWr 88; WhoWrEP 89, 92, 95*

Axton, Hoyt Wayne
American. Singer, Songwriter
Country music singer; has sold over 25 million records in 20-year career.
b. Mar 25, 1938 in Duncan, Oklahoma
Source: *BioIn 14; ConTFT 3; HarEnCM 87; RkOn 78; WhoAm 76, 78, 80, 82, 84, 86, 92, 94, 95, 96, 97; WhoEnt 92*

Ayckbourn, Alan
[Roland Allen; Roland Allen Ayckbourn]
English. Dramatist, Director
One of England's most prolific playwrights; plays include *Joking Apart,* 1978; *A Small Family Business,* 1987.
b. Apr 12, 1939 in London, England
Source: *Benet 87, 96; BioIn 10, 12, 13, 15, 16, 17, 20; BlmGEL; CamGLE; CamGWoT; ConAu 21R, 31NR; ConBrDr; ConDr 73, 77, 82, 88; ConLC 5, 8, 18, 33, 74; ConTFT 4, 12; CrtSuDr; CurBio 80; DcArts; DcLB 13; DcLEL 1940; EncWT; Ent; FacFETw; IntAu&W 76, 77, 82, 86, 89, 91, 93; IntDcT 2; IntvTCA 2; IntWW 76, 77, 78, 79, 80, 81, 82, 83, 89, 91, 93; LegTOT; MajTwCW; McGEWD 84; NewYTBS 74, 79, 90; OxCEng 85, 95; OxCThe 83; RAdv 14; RfGEnL 91; RGTwCWr; Who 82, 83, 85, 88, 90, 92, 94; WhoThe 72, 77, 81; WhoWor 76, 78, 91, 95, 96, 97; WorAl; WorAlBi; WorAu 1970; WrDr 76, 80, 82, 84, 86, 88, 90, 92, 94, 96*

Ayer, Alfred Jules, Sir
English. Author, Philosopher
Advocated logical positivism; wrote *Language, Truth, and Logic,* 1936, which reduced philosophy to empirical logic.
b. Oct 29, 1910 in London, England
d. Jun 27, 1989 in London, England
Source: *Au&Wr 71; Benet 87; BioIn 1, 6, 7, 10, 11, 12, 13, 14, 16, 18; CamGLE; ConAu 5NR, 5R, 34NR, 129; CurBio 64, 89, 89N; DcLEL; DcNaB 1986; EncUnb; EncWB; FacFETw; IntAu&W 77, 89, 91; IntWW 74, 75, 76, 77, 78, 79, 80, 81, 82, 83, 89; LngCTC; MakMC; NewCBEL; NewYTBS 89; OxCEng 67, 85; OxCPhil; RAdv 14, 13-4; REn; ThTwC 87; WhAm 10; Who 88; WhoAm 84, 86, 88; WhoWor 74, 76, 78, 89; WorAu 1950; WrDr 76, 80, 90*

Ayer, Francis Wayland
American. Advertising Executive
Pioneered use of trademarks, slogans in advertising.
b. Feb 4, 1848 in Lee, Massachusetts
d. Mar 5, 1923 in Camden, New Jersey
Source: *AdMenW; AmBi; BiDAmBL 83; BioIn 2, 7, 20; DcAmB; NatCAB 20; WebAB 74, 79; WhAm 1; WorAl*

Ayer, Harriet Hubbard
American. Journalist, Business Executive
Manufactured facial creams, 1886; wrote popular newspaper column on beauty advice.
b. Jun 27, 1849 in Chicago, Illinois
d. Nov 23, 1903 in New York, New York
Source: *AmWomWr; BiDAmBL 83; BioIn 15; ContDcW 89; GoodHs; IntDcWB; InWom SUP; NatCAB 43; NotAW; WhAm 1*

Ayesha
"Mother of the Believers"
Arab.
Daughter of Abu-Bakr; second wife of Mohammad.
b. 614 in Medina, Arabia
d. 678
Source: *DcBiPP; EncAmaz 91; NewC; NewCol 75*

Aykroyd, Dan(iel Edward)
American. Actor, Comedian
Star of "Saturday Night Live," 1975-79; won Emmy, 1976; in films *The Blues Brothers,* 1980; *Ghostbusters,* 1984.
b. Jul 1, 1952 in Ottawa, Ontario, Canada
Source: *BioIn 11, 12, 13, 16; CanWW 31; CelR 90; ConAu 123; ConTFT 6, 13; CurBio 92; EncAFC; HalFC 84, 88; HolBB; IntMPA 84, 86, 88, 92, 94, 96; IntWW 91, 93; LegTOT; LesBEnT 92; MiSFD 9; News 89-3; WhoAm 78, 80, 82, 84, 86, 90, 92, 94, 95, 96, 97; WhoCom; WhoEnt 92; WhoHol 92; WhoRocM 82*

Ayllon, Lucas Vasquez de
Spanish. Explorer
Made unsuccessful attempt to colonize South Carolina, 1526; in Santo Domingo, 1502-20.
b. 1475? in Toledo, Spain

d. 1526 in Winyah Bay, South Carolina
Source: *AmBi; ApCAB; DcAmB; DcCathB; Drake; EncCRAm; NewCol 75; OxCShps; WhWE*

Aylward, Gladys May
"The Small Woman"
English. Missionary
Film *The Inn of Sixth Happiness,* 1958, based on her life in China, 1932-48.
b. 1902 in London, England
d. Jan 3, 1970 in Taipei, Taiwan
Source: *BioIn 8, 9, 10, 11; ConAu 111; DcNaB 1961; GrBr; HalFC 84; IntDcWB; ObitOF 79; ObitT 1961; WhDW*

Aylwin (Azocar), Patricio
Chilean. Political Leader
Succeeded Augusto Pinochet as pres. of Chile, 1990-94, returning country to democracy.
b. Nov 26, 1918 in Vina Del Mar, Chile
Source: *CurBio 90; DcCPSAm; DcHiB; IntWW 91; WhoWor 91, 93*

Ayme, Marcel
French. Author
Wrote *The Hollow Field,* 1933; *The Conscience of Love,* 1962.
b. Mar 28, 1902 in Joigny, France
d. Oct 14, 1967 in Paris, France
Source: *Benet 87; BiE&WWA; BioIn 1, 2, 4, 8, 14; CasWL; ChlLR 25; ClDMEL 47, 80; CnMD; CnThe; ConAu 89; ConLC 11; DcLB 72; DcTwCCu 2; EncSF; EncWL 2, 3; EncWT; Ent; EuWr 12; EvEuW; GuFrLit 1; LinLib L; LngCTC; McGEWD 72, 84; ModFrL; ModRL; ModWD; NotNAT B; Novels; ObitT 1961; OxCFr; PenC EUR; RAdv 14, 13-2; REn; RfGShF; RfGWoL 95; ScF&FL 1; TwCA SUP; TwCWr; WhAm 4A*

Ayres, Agnes
[Agnes Hinkle]
American. Actor
Starred with Rudolph Valentino in *The Sheik,* 1921.
b. Sep 4, 1898 in Carbondale, Illinois
d. Dec 25, 1940 in Los Angeles, California
Source: *BioIn 15; CurBio 41; Film 1; FilmgC; InWom; MotPP; ObitOF 79; SilFlmP; TwYS; WhoHol B; WhScrn 74, 77, 83*

Ayres, Lew
American. Actor
Starred in *All Quiet on the Western Front,* 1930; first actor to register as conscientious objector, WW II.
b. Dec 28, 1908 in Minneapolis, Minnesota
d. Dec 30, 1996 in Los Angeles, California
Source: *BiDFilm, 81, 94; BioIn 1, 4, 8, 9, 10, 11, 18, 19; ConTFT 3, 15; FacFETw; Film 2; FilmEn; FilmgC; ForYSC; GangFlm; HalFC 80, 84, 88; IntDcF 1-3, 2-3; IntMPA 75, 76, 77, 78, 79, 80, 81, 82, 84, 86, 88, 92, 94, 96; LegTOT; MGM; MotPP; MovMk; OxCFilm; What 3; WhoAm 82, 84; WhoHol 92, A; WorAl; WorAlBi; WorEFlm*

Ayres, Mitchell
American. Bandleader
Led band that backed singer Perry Como on radio, TV, 1940s-60s.
b. Dec 24, 1910 in Milwaukee, Wisconsin
d. Sep 5, 1969 in Las Vegas, Nevada
Source: *ASCAP 66, 80; BgBands 74; CmpEPM; RadStar; WhScrn 77*

Ayres, Ruby Mildred
English. Author
Wrote popular romances: *Old-Fashioned Heart,* 1953.
b. Jan 1883
d. Nov 14, 1955 in Weybridge, England
Source: *BioIn 4; ConAu 117; FemiCLE; InWom, SUP; LngCTC; NewC; TwCRGW; TwCWr; WomNov*

Aytoun, William Edmonstoune
Scottish. Author, Educator
Popular *Blackwood* contributor; wrote *Firmilian,* 1854.
b. Jun 21, 1813 in Edinburgh, Scotland
d. Aug 4, 1865 in Elgin, Scotland
Source: *BritAu 19; CamGEL; CelCen; ChhPo S3; CmScLit; DcBiPP; LinLib L; OxCEng 85, 95*

Ayub Khan, Mohammad
Pakistani. Political Leader
Pres. of Pakistan, 1958-69; wrote *Friends Not Masters: A Political Autobiography,* 1967.
b. May 14, 1907 in Hazara, India
d. Apr 19, 1974 in Islamabad, Pakistan
Source: *ConAu P-2; CurBio 59, 74, 74N; NewYTBS 74; Who 74; WhoWor 74*

Azana y Diaz, Manuel
Spanish. Political Leader
Rep. premier, 1931-33, 1936; elected pres., 1936; Franco's victory drove him into exile, 1939.
b. Jan 10, 1880 in Alcala de Henares, Spain
d. Nov 4, 1940 in Montauban, France
Source: *CasWL; ClDMEL 47; CurBio 40; EvEuW; McGEWB; OxCSpan; WebBD 83*

Azcona Hoyo, Jose Simon
Honduran. Political Leader
Pres. of Honduras, 1986-90.
b. Jan 26, 1927 in La Ceiba, Honduras
Source: *BioIn 14, 15, 16; CurBio 88; DcCPCAm; IntWW 91; NewYTBS 86; WhoWor 87, 89, 91*

Azenberg, Emanuel
American. Producer
Credits include dozens of major Broadway hits; won many Tonys: *Ain't Misbehaving,* 1978.
b. Jan 22, 1934 in New York, New York
Source: *BioIn 14; CamGWoT; ConTFT 5; NewYTBS 85; WhoAm 86, 96, 97; WhoThe 81*

Azikiwe, Nnamdi
[Zik Azikiwe]
"Father of Modern Nigerian Nationalism"
Nigerian. Political Leader
First head of independent Nigeria, 1963; overthrown by military coup, 1966.
b. Nov 16, 1904 in Zungeri, Nigeria
d. May 11, 1996 in Lagos, Nigeria
Source: *AfrA; AfSS 78, 79, 80, 81, 82; BioIn 1, 4, 5, 6, 7, 9, 10, 17, 18, 20, 21; ConBlB 13; CurBio 57, 96N; DcAfHiB 86; HisWorL; InB&W 85; IntAu&W 77; IntWW 74, 75, 76, 77, 78, 79, 80, 81, 82, 83, 89, 91, 93; IntWWP 77, 82; IntYB 78, 79, 80, 81, 82; McGEWB; NewYTBS 27; PseudN 82; RadHan; SelBAAf; WhDW; WhE&EA; Who 74, 82, 83, 85, 88, 90, 92, 94; WhoWor 74*

Azinger, Paul
American. Golfer
Turned pro, 1981; PGA Player of the Year, 1987; won Infiniti Tournament of Champions, 1990; left golf for lymphoma treatment, 1993, returned in 1994.
b. Jan 6, 1960 in Holyoke, Massachusetts
Source: *BioIn 15; News 95, 95-2; WhoAm 94, 95, 96, 97; WhoWor 95, 96*

Aziz, Philip John Andrew Ferris
Canadian. Artist
Uses egg tempura technique for portraiture, liturgical themes.
b. Apr 15, 1923 in Saint Thomas, Ontario, Canada
Source: *BlueB 76; CanWW 70, 79, 80, 81, 83, 89; WhoArt 84; WhoWor 74*

Aziz, Tariq Mikhayl
[Mikhail Yuhanna]
Iraqi. Government Official
Deputy prime minister, 1981, 1991—; foreign minister, 1983-91; chief Iraqi negotiator during Persian Gulf Crisis, 1991.
b. 1936 in Mosul, Iraq
Source: *CurBio 91; IntWW 91; NewYTBS 90; WhoWor 87, 89, 91, 93, 95*

Aznavour, Charles
[Shahnour Varenagh Aznavourian]
French. Singer, Actor
Diminutive, foggy-voiced singer who gained fame, 1950s; most memorable film *Shoot the Piano Player,* 1950.
b. May 22, 1924 in Paris, France
Source: *Baker 78, 84, 92; BiDAmM; BioIn 6, 7, 8, 9, 12, 14; CelR; ConAu X; ConTFT 2; CurBio 68; DcTwCCu 2; FilmAG WE; FilmEn; FilmgC; ForYSC; HalFC 80, 84, 88; IntMPA 92, 94, 96; IntWW 74, 75, 76, 77, 78, 79, 80, 81, 82, 83; ItaFilm; LegTOT; MovMk; NewYTBS 92; OxCFilm; OxCPMus; PenEncP; WhoAm 80, 82, 84; WhoFr 79; WhoHol*

92, A; WhoWor 74, 76, 78, 87, 89, 91; WorAl; WorAlBi; WorEFlm

Azuela, Mariano
Mexican. Author
Writings depict Mexican society; *The Underdogs,* 1929, describes 1910 Revolution.
b. Jan 1, 1873 in Logos de Morena, Mexico
d. Mar 1, 1952 in Mexico City, Mexico
Source: *Benet 87, 96; BenetAL 91; BioIn 1, 2, 3, 5, 9, 10, 16, 17, 18; CasWL; ConAu 104, 131; CyWA 58; DcHiB; DcMexL; DcSpL; DcTwCCu 4; EncLatA; EncWL, 2, 3; HispLC; HispWr; LatAmWr; LinLib L; MajTwCW; McGEWB; ModLAL; OxCSpan; PenC AM; RAdv 14, 13-2; REn; SpAmA; TwCLC 3; TwCWr; WhAm 5; WhE&EA; WhNAA; WorAu 1950*

B

B-52's
[Kate Pierson; Fred Schneider; Keith Strickland; Cindy Wilson; Ricky Wilson]
American. Music Group
Formed 1976; known for 50s, 60s vocals, lyrics; hit album *Cosmic Thing,* 1989 with single ''Love Shack.''
Source: *BioIn 16; ConMus 4; EncPR&S 89; EncRk 88; EncRkSt; NewGrDA 86; PenEncP; RkOn 85; RolSEnR 83; St&PR 96, 97; WhoRock 81; WhoRocM 82; WhsNW 85*

Baader, Andreas
[Bernd Andreas Baader]
German. Terrorist, Revolutionary
Co-leader with Ulrike Meinhof, of the Baader-Meinhof Gang, 1968-72; trial lasted two years; convicted, 1977; committed suicide.
b. May 6, 1943 in Munich, Germany
d. Oct 18, 1977 in Stuttgart, Germany (West)
Source: *BioIn 9, 10, 11, 15, 16; LegTOT; NewYTBS 75*

Ba'al Shem Tov, Israel
[Israel ben Eliezer]
Polish. Religious Leader
Founded modern Hasidism, a mystical interpretaion of Judaism.
b. 1700 in Akopy, Poland
d. 1760 in Mezshbozsh, Poland
Source: *CasWL; EncO&P 1; IlEncMy; LinLib L; McGEWB; NewC; WorAl*

Babangida, Ibrahim Badamasi
Nigerian. Political Leader
Military president of Nigeria, brought to power in bloodless coup, 1985-93.
b. Aug 17, 1941 in Minna, Nigeria
Source: *BioIn 14, 15; CurBio 90; IntWW 91; News 92; WhoAfr; WhoWor 91*

Babashoff, Shirley
American. Swimmer
Won gold medals in swimming relay, 1972, 1976 Olympics.
b. Jan 31, 1957 in Whittier, California
Source: *BiDAmSp BK; BioIn 10; EncWomS; GoodHs; InWom SUP; WhoSpor*

Babb, Howard Selden
American. Author
Wrote *Jane Austen's Novels,* 1962; *The Novels of William Golding,* 1970.
b. May 14, 1924 in Portland, Maine
d. Jun 24, 1978
Source: *ConAu 120; DrAS 74E, 78E; WhAm 7; WhoAm 74, 76, 78*

Babbage, Charles
English. Mathematician, Inventor
Tried to perfect mechanical calculating machine, foreshadowing computer, 1830s.
b. Dec 26, 1792 in Totnes, England
d. Oct 18, 1871 in London, England
Source: *Alli SUP; AsBiEn; BiD&SB; BiESc; BioIn 1, 2, 4, 5, 6, 7, 8, 9, 11, 12, 13, 14, 15, 16, 17, 20, 21; BritAu, 19; CelCen; DcBiPP; DcEnL; DcNaB; DcScB; Dis&D; EncAJ; EncSF 93; GrEconB; InSci; LarDcSc; LinLib L; McGEWB; NewCol 75; OxCMus; VicBrit; WhDW; WhoEc 81, 86; WorAl; WorAlBi*

Babbitt, Benjamin Talbot
American. Manufacturer, Inventor
Made one of first baking powders; obtained many patents for soap.
b. 1809 in Westmoreland, New York
d. Oct 20, 1889 in New York, New York
Source: *BiDAmBL 83; DcAmB; NatCAB 8; WhAm HS*

Babbitt, Bruce E(dward)
American. Politician, Author, Government Official
Secretary of Interior, 1993—; Dem. governor of AZ, 1977-87.
b. Jun 27, 1938 in Los Angeles, California
Source: *AlmAP 80, 82, 84; BiDrGov 1789, 1978, 1983; BioIn 11, 12, 13, 14, 15, 16; ConAu 97; CurBio 87; NewYTBS 78, 79; PolsAm 84; WhoAm 80, 82, 84, 86, 88, 90, 92, 94, 95, 96, 97; WhoAmP 79, 81, 85, 87, 89, 91, 93, 95; WhoWest 80, 82, 84, 87, 89, 92; WhoWor 82, 87, 96, 97*

Babbitt, Irving
American. Author, Critic
A leader of new humanism; wrote *Masters of Modern French Criticism,* 1912.
b. Aug 2, 1865 in Dayton, Ohio
d. Jul 15, 1933 in Cambridge, Massachusetts
Source: *AmAu&B; AmBi; AmLY; BenetAL 91; BiDAmEd; BioIn 1, 3, 4, 5, 11, 12, 16; CamGLE; CamHAL; CasWL; CnDAL; ConAmA; ConAmL; DcAmB S1; DcAmC; DcLB 63; DcLEL; DcNAA; EncAB-H 1974, 1996; FacFETw; LngCTC; ModAL; NatCAB 23; OhA&B; OxCAmH; OxCAmL 65, 83, 95; OxCEng 67, 85, 95; PenC AM; REn; REnAL; TwCA, SUP; WebAB 74, 79; WebE&AL; WhAm 1; WhLit; WhoTwCL; WorAl; WorAlBi*

Babbitt, Milton Byron
American. Composer
First composer to work on RCA's Mark II synthesizer; wrote *Composition for Synthesizer,* 1961.
b. May 10, 1916 in Philadelphia, Pennsylvania
Source: *AmComp; Baker 78, 84, 92; BiDAmM; BioIn 13, 14, 15, 16; BlueB 76; BriBkM 80; CompSN; ConCom 92; CpmDNM 78, 81; CurBio 62; DcCM; FacFETw; IntWW 89, 91, 93; IntWWM 77, 80, 90; MakMC; McGEWB; MusMk; NewAmDM; NewGrDA 86; NewGrDM 80; NewOxM; NewYTBS 86; OxCMus; WebAB 74, 79; WhoAm 74, 76, 78, 80, 82, 84, 86, 88, 90, 92, 94, 95; WhoAmM 83; WhoE 85, 86; WhoEnt 92; WhoMus 72; WhoWor 74, 76*

Babcock, Harold Delos
American. Astronomer, Inventor
Helped invent the solar magnetograph, 1951; announced that the Sun reverses its magnetic field periodically, 1959.
b. Jan 24, 1882 in Edgerton, Wisconsin
d. Apr 8, 1968 in Pasadena, California

Source: *BiESc; BioIn 8, 11, 14; FacFETw; InSci; LarDcSc; WhAm 5*

Babcock, Harry
American. Track Athlete
Pole vaulter; won gold medal, 1912 Olympics.
b. Dec 15, 1890 in Pelham Manor, New York
d. Jun 5, 1965 in Norwalk, Connecticut
Source: *WhoTr&F 73*

Babcock, Horace Welcome
American. Astronomer, Inventor
Invented, along with father Harold, the solar magnetograph, which measures the Sun's magnetic field, 1951.
b. Sep 13, 1912 in Pasadena, California
Source: *AmMWSc 76P, 79, 92; BiESc; BlueB 76; CamDcSc; FacFETw; IntWW 91; Who 74, 82, 83, 85, 88, 90, 92, 94; WhoAm 74, 76, 78, 80, 82, 84, 86, 88, 90; WhoWest 74, 76; WhoWor 74, 76, 78*

Babcock, Stephen Moulton
American. Scientist
Agricultural chemist who developed test for butterfat content in milk; pioneered in research which led to discovery of vitamin A.
b. Oct 22, 1843 in Bridgewater, New York
d. Jul 2, 1931 in Madison, Wisconsin
Source: *AmBi; BiDAmS; BiESc; BioIn 1, 2, 3, 5, 6; DcAmB S1; DcNAA; DcScB; EncAAH; FacFETw; InSci; LarDcSc; LinLib S; McGEWB; NatCAB 22; WebAB 74, 79; WhAm 1*

Babe, Thomas
American. Dramatist
Award-winning plays include *Rebel Women,* 1976.
b. Mar 13, 1941 in Buffalo, New York
Source: *ConAmD; ConAu 101; ConDr 82, 88, 93; ConTFT 5; IntAu&W 91, 93; NatPD 77, 81; WhoEnt 92; WhoThe 81; WrDr 84, 86, 88, 90, 92, 94, 96*

Babel, Isaac Emmanuelovich
Russian. Author
Short stories collected in *Jewish Tales,* 1927; disappeared into concentration camp, 1939.
b. Jul 13, 1894 in Odessa, Russia
d. Mar 3, 1941 in Siberia, Union of Soviet Socialist Republics
Source: *AtlBL; CasWL; ClDMEL 47; CnMD; CnMWL; ConAu 104; DcRusL; EvEuW; FacFETw; LngCTC; McGEWB; McGEWD 72; ModSL 1; ModWD; PenC EUR; REn; TwCA; WhoTwCL*

Babeuf, Francois-Noel
[Caius Gracchus]
French. Revolutionary, Journalist
Agitator in French revolution; developed communistic doctrine of Babouvism; conspired to overthrow the Directory, 1796; guillotined.
b. Nov 25, 1760 in Saint-Quentin, France
d. Apr 27, 1797 in Paris, France
Source: *BiD&SB; BlkwCE; EncEnl; McGEWB; OxCFr; REn; WebBD 83*

Babilonia, Tai (Reina)
[Babilonia and Gardner]
American. Skater
With Randy Gardner, won five national, one world championship in pairs figure skating; injury to Gardner prevented competition, 1980 Olympics; co-starred in for three years in ''Ice Capades'' with Randy Gardner after 1980 Oplympics; retired from professional skating in 1988.
b. Sep 22, 1960 in Sherman Oaks, California
Source: *BioIn 12, 16; EncWomS; InB&W 85; LegTOT; NewYTBS 79*

Babin, Victor
[Vronsky and Babin]
American. Pianist
Formed two-piano team with wife Vitya Vronsky, 1933.
b. Dec 12, 1908 in Moscow, Russia
d. Mar 1, 1972 in Cleveland, Ohio
Source: *ASCAP 66, 80; Baker 78, 84, 92; BiDAmM; BioIn 3, 4, 5, 6, 9; ConAmC 76, 82; NewAmDM; NewGrDA 86; NewGrDM 80; NewYTBE 72; PenDiMP; WhAm 5; WhoMus 72; WhoWorJ 72, 78*

Babington, Anthony
English. Conspirator
Planned to murder Elizabeth and install Mary, Queen of Scots on throne; executed.
b. Oct 1561
d. Sep 20, 1586 in London, England
Source: *BioIn 8, 11; DcCathB; DcNaB; NewC; WebBD 83*

Babiuch, Edward
Polish. Political Leader
Deputy chair, State Council, 1976-80.
b. Dec 28, 1927 in Katowice Voivodship, Poland
Source: *BioIn 12; IntWW 74, 75, 76, 77, 78, 79, 80, 81, 82, 83, 89, 91, 93; NewYTBS 80; WhoSocC 78; WhoSoCE 89; WhoWor 74, 76, 78*

Babrius
Greek. Author
Wrote Greek fables similar to Aesop; many of these became known, 1800s.
b. fl. 2nd cent.
Source: *BbD; BiD&SB; CasWL; DcArts; DcBiPP; Grk&L; OxCClL 89; PenC CL; RAdv 13-2; WebBD 83*

Babur
[Zahir un-Din Muhammad]
''Tiger''
Turkish. Military Leader
Descendant of Genghis Khan who was founder, first ruler of Mogul empire.
b. Feb 14, 1483 in Farghana, Turkey
d. Dec 26, 1530 in Agra, India
Source: *BioIn 14, 16, 20, 21; CasWL; DcOrL 3; DicTyr; GenMudB; HarEnMi; LitC 18; McGEWB; PenC CL; WhoMilH 76*

Baby Leroy
[Leroy Winebrenner]
American. Actor
Hollywood toddler who appeared in *Bedtime Story,* 1933; retired at age four.
b. May 12, 1932 in Los Angeles, California
Source: *EncAFC; FilmEn; HalFC 88; MotPP; WhoHol A*

Babys, The
[Tony Brock; Jonathan Cain; Mike Corby; Ricky Phillips; Wally Stocker; John Waite]
English. Music Group
Power pop group, 1976-81; hits include ''Isn't It Time;'' ''Head First.''
Source: *ConMuA 80A; PenEncP; RkOn 78; RolSEnR 83; WhoRock 81; WhoRocM 82; WhScrn 77, 83*

Bacall, Lauren
[Betty Joan Perske]
American. Actor
Won Tonys for *Applause,* 1970; *Woman of the Year,* 1981; once wed to Humphrey Bogart, Jason Robards.
b. Sep 16, 1924 in New York, New York
Source: *BiDFilm, 81, 94; BiE&WWA; BioAmW; BioIn 1, 3, 4, 5, 7, 8, 9, 10, 11, 12, 13, 15, 16, 17, 18, 20; BkPepl; BlueB 76; CelR, 90; CmMov; ConAu 93; ContDcW 89; ConTFT 1, 7, 14; CurBio 70; DcArts; DcLP 87B; EncAFC; EncMT; FacFETw; FilmEn; FilmgC; ForYSC; GangFlm; GoodHs; GrLiveH; HalFC 80, 84, 88; IntDcF 1-3, 2-3; IntDcWB; IntMPA 75, 76, 77, 78, 79, 80, 81, 82, 84, 86, 88, 92, 94, 96; IntWW 74, 75, 76, 77, 78, 79, 80, 81, 82, 83, 89, 91, 93; InWom, SUP; LegTOT; MotPP; MovMk; NewYTBE 70; NewYTBS 80; NotNAT; OxCAmT 84; OxCFilm; WhoAm 74, 76, 78, 80, 82, 84, 86, 88, 90, 92, 94, 95, 96, 97; WhoAmJ 80; WhoAmW 58, 61, 64, 66, 68, 70, 72, 74, 79, 81, 83, 85, 95, 97; WhoEnt 92; WhoHol 92, A; WhoThe 72, 77, 81; WhoWor 74, 78; WorAl; WorAlBi; WorEFlm; WrDr 82, 84, 86, 88, 90, 92, 94, 96*

Bacardi, Don Facundo
Spanish. Merchant
Started world's largest rum co., 1862.
b. 1816
d. 1886
Source: *Entr*

Baccaloni, Salvatore
Italian. Opera Singer
Considered greatest comic bass since Lablanche; with NY Met., 1940-62.
b. Apr 14, 1900 in Rome, Italy
d. Dec 31, 1969 in New York, New York

Source: *Baker 78, 84, 92; BioIn 1, 4, 6, 8, 9, 10, 11; CmOp; CurBio 44, 70, 71; DcAmB S8; FilmEn; FilmgC; HalFC 80, 84, 88; IntDcOp; MetOEnc; MusSN; NewEOp 71; NewGrDA 86; NewGrDM 80; NewGrDO; NewYTBE 70; OxDcOp; PenDiMP; WhAm 5; WhoHol B; WhScrn 74, 77, 83*

Bacchelli, Riccardo
Italian. Author
Best known for historical novels: *Il Mulino del Po,* 1938.
b. Apr 19, 1891 in Bologna, Italy
d. Oct 8, 1985 in Monza, Italy
Source: *AnObit 1985, 3; EvEuW; IntAu&W 76, 77; IntWW 74, 75, 76, 77, 78, 79, 80, 81, 82, 83; ModRL; Novels; PenC EUR; REn; TwCWr; WhoWor 74; WorAu 1950*

Bacchylides
Greek. Poet
Only fragments of work still exist; some discovered in 1800s.
b. 516?BC
d. 450?BC
Source: *CasWL; Grk&L; NewC; OxCEng 67; PenC CL; WebBD 83*

Bach, Barbara
[Barbara Goldbach; Mrs. Ringo Starr]
American. Actor
Married Ringo Starr, 1981, after starring together in movie *Caveman.*
b. Aug 27, 1947 in New York, New York
Source: *BioIn 11; ConTFT 2; HalFC 88; VarWW 85*

Bach, Bert Coates
American. Author
Wrote *Fiction for Composition,* 1968; *Drama for Composition,* 1973.
b. Dec 14, 1936 in Jenkins, Kentucky
Source: *DrAS 74E, 78E, 82E; WhoAm 84, 86; WhoSSW 80, 82*

Bach, Carl Philipp Emanuel
German. Composer
Pioneered sonata-allegro musical form; wrote influential study on clavier playing, 1753; son of Johann Sebastian.
b. Mar 8, 1714 in Weimar, Germany
d. Dec 15, 1788 in Hamburg, Germany
Source: *AtlBL; Baker 78, 84, 92; BioIn 1, 2, 4, 7, 12, 14, 16; BlkwCE; BriBkM 80; CmpBCM; DcBiPP; DcCom 77; EncEnl; GrComp; McGEWB; MusMk; NewAmDM; NewCol 75; NewGrDM 80; NewOxM; PenDiMP A; WhDW; WorAl; WorAlBi*

Bach, Catherine
[Catherine Bachman]
American. Actor
Played Daisy Duke on TV series "The Dukes of Hazzard," 1979-85.
b. Mar 1, 1954 in Warren, Ohio
Source: *BioIn 12, 14, 20; ConTFT 5; IntMPA 92, 94, 96; InWom SUP; LegTOT; VarWW 85; WhoHol 92*

Bach, Johann Christian
"The English Bach"
German. Composer
Wrote operas, taught music to Britain's royalty, 1762-82; eleventh son of Johann Sebastian.
b. Sep 3, 1735 in Leipzig, Germany
d. Jan 1, 1782 in London, England
Source: *AtlBL; Baker 78, 84, 92; BioIn 1, 2, 4, 6, 7, 8, 10, 12, 14, 17, 21; BlkwCE; BriBkM 80; DcArts; DcBiPP; DcCom 77; DcCom&M 79; DcNaB MP; EncEnl; LuthC 75; McGEWB; MetOEnc; MusMk; NewAmDM; NewEOp 71; NewGrDM 80; NewGrDO; NewOxM; OxCMus; OxDcOp; PenDiMP A; WhDW; WorAl; WorAlBi*

Bach, Johann Sebastian
German. Composer, Organist
Master of church music; father of church dynasty; masterpieces include *Brandenburg Concerti,* 1721; *Well-Tempererd Clavier,* 1722-44.
b. Mar 21, 1685 in Eisenach, Germany
d. Jul 28, 1750 in Leipzig, Germany
Source: *AtlBL; Baker 78, 84, 92; Benet 87, 96; BioIn 1, 2, 3, 4, 5, 6, 7, 8, 9, 10, 11, 12, 13, 14, 15, 16, 18, 19, 20, 21; BriBkM 80; CmpBCM; CnOxB; DcArts; DcBiPP; DcCom 77; DcCom&M 79; Dis&D; EncEnl; GrComp; LegTOT; LinLib S; LuthC 75; McGEWB; MusMk; NewAmDM; NewC; NewCol 75; NewGrDM 80; NewOxM; OxCGer 76, 86; OxCMus; OxDcOp; PenDiMP A; RAdv 14, 13-3; REn; WebBD 83; WhDW; WorAl; WorAlBi*

Bach, Richard David
American. Author
Wrote allegorical novel *Jonathan Livingston Seagull;* filmed, 1973.
b. Jun 23, 1936 in Oak Park, Illinois
Source: *AuNews 1; BioNews 74; ConAu 9R; ConLC 14; CurBio 73; EncO&P 1S1, 3; EncPaPR 91; MajTwCW; NewAgE 90; Novels; ScF&FL 1, 2; SmATA 13; WhoAm 80, 90, 94; WorAl; WrDr 76, 86, 92*

Bach, Wilhelm Friedemann
"The Halle Bach"
German. Composer, Organist
Wrote concertos, organ works; eldest son of Johann Sebastian.
b. Nov 22, 1710 in Weimar, Germany
d. Jul 1, 1784 in Berlin, Germany
Source: *Baker 78, 84, 92; BioIn 2, 4, 5, 7; BriBkM 80; CmpBCM; DcArts; DcBiPP; EncEnl; GrComp; LuthC 75; MusMk; NewAmDM; NewGrDM 80; NewOxM; OxCMus; OxDcOp*

Bacharach, Bert(ram Mark)
American. Journalist, Author
Father of Burt Bacharach; had syndicated column, "Now See Here!", 1959-83.
b. Mar 10, 1898 in Philadelphia, Pennsylvania
d. Sep 15, 1983 in New York, New York
Source: *BiDAmNC; BioIn 1, 4, 13; CelR; ConAu 110; CurBio 57, 83; NewYTBS 83*

Bacharach, Burt
American. Composer, Musician, Conductor
Best known for collaborations with Hal David; won Oscar for "Raindrops Keep Falling on My Head," 1970, and numerous other awards.
b. May 12, 1929 in Kansas City, Missouri
Source: *AmPS; AmSong; Baker 78, 84; BiDAmM; BioIn 7, 8, 9, 10, 12, 14, 15; BkPepl; BlueB 76; CelR, 90; ConMus 1; ConTFT 3; CurBio 70; EncMT; EncPR&S 89; EncRk 88; FilmEn; FilmgC; HalFC 80, 84, 88; IntMPA 92; IntWWM 77; ItaFilm; NewAmDM; NewCBMT; NewCol 75; NewGrDA 86; NewOxM; NotNAT; OxCPMus; PenEncP; RolSEnR 83; WebAB 74, 79; WhoAm 74, 76, 78, 80, 82, 84, 86, 88, 90, 92, 94, 95, 96, 97; WhoEnt 92; WorAl; WorAlBi*

Bachauer, Gina
Greek. Pianist
Made US debut, 1950, NYC; repertoire ranged from Mozart to Stravinsky.
b. May 21, 1913 in Athens, Greece
d. Aug 22, 1976 in Athens, Greece
Source: *Baker 78, 84, 92; BioIn 3, 4, 6, 9, 11, 16, 21; BlueB 76; BriBkM 80; CelR; CurBio 54, 77N; FacFETw; IntWW 74, 75, 76; InWom, SUP; MusSN; NewAmDM; NewGrDM 80; NewYTBS 76; NotTwCP; ObitOF 79; PenDiMP; WhAm 7; Who 74; WhoAmW 68, 70, 72, 74; WhoMus 72; WhoWor 74*

Bache, Harold Leopold
American. Businessman, Philanthropist
Broker, chief exec., J S Bache & Co., 1945-68.
b. Jun 17, 1894 in New York, New York
d. Mar 14, 1968 in New York, New York
Source: *BioIn 1, 5, 8, 12; CurBio 59; ObitOF 79; WhAm 5; WorAl*

Bache, Jules Sermon
American. Financier
Head of J S Bache & Co., 1892-1945.
b. Nov 9, 1861 in New York, New York
d. Mar 24, 1944 in Palm Beach, Florida
Source: *CurBio 44; DcAmB S3; ObitOF 79; WhAm 2*

Bacheller, Irving Addison
American. Author
Wrote *Eben Holden,* 1900.
b. Sep 26, 1859 in Pierpont, New York
d. Feb 24, 1950 in White Plains, New York
Source: *AmAu&B; BiD&SB; Chambr 3; ConAmL; DcAmAu; DcAmB S4; DcBiA;*

DcLEL; JBA 34; OxCAmL 65; REn; TwCA SUP; WhAm 2

Bachman, John
American. Naturalist, Clergy
Collaborated with Audubon on *Viviparous Quadrupeds of N America,* 1845-59.
b. Feb 4, 1790 in Rhinebeck, New York
d. Feb 25, 1874 in Columbia, South Carolina
Source: *Alli; AmAu; AmBi; ApCAB; BiDAmS; BiD&SB; BiDSA; BiInAmS; BioIn 2; CelCen; DcAmAu; DcAmB; DcBiPP; DcNAA; Drake; HarEnUS; InSci; LuthC 75; NewCol 75; OxCAmH; TwCBDA; WhAm HS*

Bachman, Randy
[Bachman-Turner Overdrive; Guess Who]
Canadian. Singer, Musician
Guitarist; co-founded Guess Who, 1963; Bachman-Turner Overdrive, 1972.
b. Sep 27, 1943 in Winnipeg, Manitoba, Canada
Source: *OnThGG*

Bachman-Turner Overdrive
[Chad Allen; Randy Bachman; Robin Bachman; Timothy Bachman; Jim Clench; Blair Thornton; C F Turner]
Canadian. Music Group
Heavy-metal group with blue-collar image, 1972-79; hits include "You Ain't Seen Nothin' Yet," 1974.
Source: *BioIn 16; ConMuA 80A; EncPR&S 89; EncRk 88; EncRkSt; HarEnR 86; IlEncRk; OxCMus; OxCPMus; PenEncP; RkOn 78; RolSEnR 83; WhoRock 81; WhoRocM 82*

Back, George, Sir
English. Explorer
With John Franklin on three arctic trips; explored northern Canadian coastline, 1830s; wrote narratives of expeditions.
b. Nov 6, 1796 in Stockport, England
d. Jun 23, 1878 in London, England
Source: *Alli; ApCAB; BiD&SB; BioIn 18, 21; CelCen; DcBiPP; DcBrWA; DcCanB 10; DcNaB; Drake; Expl 93; MacDCB 78; NewCol 75; OxCCan; OxCShps; WebBD 83; WhWE*

Backe, John David
American. TV Executive
Pres., CBS, Inc, 1976-80.
b. Jul 5, 1932 in Akron, Ohio
Source: *BioIn 11, 12; CurBio 78; Dun&B 79; IntMPA 84, 86, 88, 92; IntWW 77, 78, 79, 80, 81, 82, 83, 89, 91, 93; LesBEnT 92; NewYTBS 76, 77; NewYTET; St&PR 75, 91, 93, 96, 97; WhoAdv 90; WhoAm 74, 76, 78, 80, 82, 84, 86, 88, 90, 92, 94, 95, 96, 97; WhoE 74, 79, 81; WhoFI 74, 79*

Backhaus, Wilhelm
German. Pianist
Concert pianist who toured Europe, US, Australia, Japan, S America, 1905-69.
b. Mar 26, 1884 in Leipzig, Germany
d. Jul 5, 1969 in Villach, Austria
Source: *Baker 78, 84, 92; BioIn 4, 5, 8, 9, 11, 12, 21; BriBkM 80; FacFETw; MusMk; MusSN; NewAmDM; NewGrDM 80; NotTwCP; ObitOF 79; ObitT 1961; PenDiMP; WhAm 5; WhDW*

Backus, Isaac
American. Clergy
Baptist minister associated with New Light movement; wrote *History of New England,* 1777-96.
b. Jan 9, 1724 in Norwich, Connecticut
d. Nov 20, 1806 in Middleborough, Connecticut
Source: *Alli; AmBi; AmWrBE; ApCAB; BenetAL 91; BioIn 3, 4, 6, 8, 9, 10, 12, 13, 14, 16, 19; BlkwEAR; DcAmAu; DcAmB; DcAmReB 1, 2; DcNAA; Drake; EncARH; EncCRAm; EncSoB; LuthC 75; McGEWB; NatCAB 7; OxCAmH; OxCAmL 65, 83, 95; PeoHis; TwCBDA; WebAB 74, 79; WhAm HS; WhAmRev*

Backus, Jim
[James Gilmore Backus]
American. Actor
Veteran stage, radio, vaudeville performer; known for voice of Mr. Magoo; role on TV's "Gilligan's Island," 1964-67.
b. Feb 25, 1913 in Cleveland, Ohio
Source: *AnObit 1989; WhAm 10; WhoAm 74, 76, 78; WhoCom; WhoHol A; WorAl; WorAlBi*

Backus, John
American. Computer Scientist
Invented standard computer programming language, Fortran, 1957.
b. Dec 3, 1924 in Philadelphia, Pennsylvania
Source: *AmMWSc 79, 82, 86, 89, 92, 95; BioIn 14, 15, 20; CamDcSc; HisDcDP; IntWW 77, 78, 79, 80, 81, 82, 83, 89, 91, 93; LarDcSc; NotTwCS; PorSil; WhoAm 76, 78, 80, 82, 84, 86, 88, 90, 92, 94, 95, 96, 97; WhoE 89; WhoFrS 84; WhoScEn 94, 96; WhoTech 82, 84, 89; WhoWest 96*

Baclanova, Olga
Russian. Actor
Starred in horror classic about a trapeze artist married to a midget: *Freaks,* 1932.
b. Aug 19, 1899 in Moscow, Russia
d. Sep 6, 1974 in Vevey, Switzerland
Source: *BiDD; BioIn 10, 12, 14; Film 2; FilmEn; FilmgC; ForYSC; HalFC 80, 84, 88; InWom SUP; LegTOT; MotPP; NewYTBS 74; ObitOF 79; ThFT; TwYS; WhoHol B; WhoHrs 80; WhScrn 77, 83; WhThe*

Bacon, Delia Salter
American. Author
Developed theory that Shakespeare's plays were written by Francis Bacon.
b. Feb 2, 1811 in Tallmadge, Ohio
d. Sep 2, 1859 in Hartford, Connecticut
Source: *Alli; AmAu; AmAu&B; AmBi; AmWomWr; ApCAB; BibAL; BiD&SB; BiDTran; BioAmW; BioIn 3, 4, 5, 6, 7, 14; CnDAL; DcAmAu; DcAmB; DcEnL; DcLEL; DcNAA; FemiCLE; LibW; NatCAB 1; NewC; NotAW; OhA&B; OxCAmL 65, 83, 95; REnAL; TwCBDA; WebAB 74, 79; WhAm HS*

Bacon, Francis
English. Artist
Self-taught modern artist whose permanent exhibits are in NYC, other cities.
b. Oct 28, 1909 in Dublin, Ireland
d. Apr 28, 1992 in Madrid, Spain
Source: *AnObit 1992; Benet 96; BioIn 12, 13, 14, 15, 16, 17, 18, 19, 20; BlueB 76; ConArt 77, 83, 89, 96; ConBrA 79; CurBio 85, 92N; DcArts; DcBrAr 1; DcCAr 81; FacFETw; GayLesB; IntDcAA 90; IntWW 74, 79, 80, 81, 82, 83, 89, 91; LegTOT; MakMC; McGEWB; ModArCr 3; NewYTBS 75, 89; OxCArt; OxCTwCA; OxDcArt; PhDcTCA 77; PrintW 85; TwCPaSc; WhAm 10; WhDW; Who 74, 82, 83, 85E, 88, 90, 92; WhoWor 74, 76, 78, 84, 87, 89, 91; WorAl; WorAlBi*

Bacon, Francis, Sir
English. Statesman, Philosopher, Essayist
Advocate of inductive reasoning; wrote famed *Novum Organum,* 1620; *Essayes,* 1597.
b. Jan 22, 1561 in London, England
d. Apr 9, 1626 in Highgate, England
Source: *Alli; AsBiEn; AstEnc; AtlBL; BbD; Benet 87, 96; BiD&SB; BiDPsy; BiESc; BioIn 1, 2, 3, 4, 5, 6, 7, 8, 9, 10, 11, 12, 13, 14, 15, 18, 20, 21; BlkwCE; BlmGEL; BritAu; BritWr 1; CamDcSc; CamGEL; CamGLE; CasWL; Chambr 1; ChhPo, S2; CnDBLB 1; CroE&S; CrtT 1, 4; CyEd; CyWA 58; DcArts; DcBiPP; DcEnA; DcEnL; DcEuL; DcLB 151; DcLEL; DcNaB, C; DcPup; DcScB; Dis&D; EncEnl; EncSF, 93; EnvEnc; EvLB; GrWrEL N; HisDStE; InSci; LarDcSc; LegTOT; LinLib L, S; LitC 18; LngCEL; LuthC 75; McGEWB; MouLC 1; NamesHP; NewC; NewCBEL; NewCol 75; NewEScF; NotNAT B; OxCEng 67, 85, 95; OxCLaw; OxCPhil; PenC ENG; PlP&P; RAdv 1, 14, 13-1, 13-4; RComWL; REn; RfGEnL 91; ScFEYrs; WebE&AL; WhDW; WorAl; WorAlBi; WrPh P*

Bacon, Frank
American. Actor
Star, co-author of long-running play, *Lightin',* 1918.
b. Jan 16, 1864 in Marysville, California
d. Nov 19, 1922 in Chicago, Illinois
Source: *AmAu&B; AmBi; BenetAL 91; BioIn 16; CamGWoT; CmCal; DcAmB; DcNAA; Film 1; ModWD; NatCAB 20; NotNAT B; OxCAmT 84; OxCThe 67, 83; REn; REnAL; WhAm 1; WhoHol B; WhScrn 74, 77, 83; WhThe*

Bacon, Henry
American. Architect
Best known as designer of Lincoln Memorial, completed in 1917.
b. Nov 28, 1866 in Watseka, Illinois
d. Feb 16, 1924 in New York, New York
Source: *AmBi; AmDec 1910; ApCAB X; BiDAmAr; BioIn 11, 13; DcAmB; DcNCBi 1; EncAAr 1, 2; IntDcAr; LegTOT; LinLib S; MacEA; McGDA; NatCAB 20; WhAm 1*

Bacon, Kevin
American. Actor
Starred in films *Footloose,* 1984; *She's Having a Baby,* 1988.
b. Jul 8, 1958 in Philadelphia, Pennsylvania
Source: *BioIn 13, 15; ConTFT 2, 5, 12; HalFC 88; IntMPA 88, 92, 94, 96; LegTOT; News 95, 95-3; WhoAm 90, 92, 94, 95, 96, 97; WhoEnt 92; WhoHol 92*

Bacon, Leonard
American. Poet
Verse volumes include 1940 Pulitzer-winner, *Sunderland Capture and Other Poems.*
b. May 26, 1887 in Solvay, New York
d. Jan 1, 1954 in Peace Dale, Rhode Island
Source: *AmAu&B; BenetAL 91; BioIn 3, 4, 7; ChhPo, S1, S2; CurBio 41, 54; DcAmB S5; DcLEL; NatCAB 49; OxCAmL 65, 83, 95; REn; REnAL; TwCA, SUP; WhAm 3; WhE&EA; WhNAA*

Bacon, Leonard Woolsey
American. Clergy, Editor
Prominent Congregationalist; leader in antislavery, temperance movements; brother of Delia.
b. Feb 19, 1802 in Detroit, Michigan
d. Dec 24, 1881 in New Haven, Connecticut
Source: *Alli; AmBi; ApCAB; BiD&SB; DcAmB; DcAmReB 1; DcEnL; DcNaB; Drake; NatCAB 1; TwCBDA; WhAm HS; WhAmP*

Bacon, Nathaniel
American. Colonial Figure
Leader, Bacon's Rebellion in VA, 1676.
b. Jan 2, 1647 in Suffolk, England
d. Oct 26, 1676 in Gloucester, Virginia
Source: *AmBi; AmWrBE; BenetAL 91; BioIn 1, 3, 4, 8; DcAmB; DcAmMiB; DicTyr; Dis&D; EncAAH; EncAB-A 1; EncAB-H 1974, 1996; HarEnMi; LegTOT; McGEWB; NatCAB 5; REnAL; REnAW; WebAB 74, 79; WebAMB; WhAm HS; WhDW; WhNaAH; WorAl; WorAlBi*

Bacon, Peggy
American. Artist
Wrote, illustrated *The Good American Witch,* 1957; did caricatures of notables, NYC alley cats.
b. May 2, 1895 in Ridgefield, Connecticut
d. Jan 4, 1987 in Kennebunk, Maine
Source: *AmAu&B; BenetAL 91; BiDWomA; BioIn 1, 5, 8, 9, 10, 15, 16, 20; BriEAA; ChhPo, S2; ConAu 121, P-2; ConGrA 3; ConICB; CurBio 40, 87, 87N; DcAmArt; DcWomA; GrAmP; IlsBYP; IlsCB 1744, 1946, 1957; InWom, SUP; LinLib L; McGDA; NewYTBS 87; NorAmWA; OxCAmL 65, 83, 95; REnAL; ScF&FL 1, 92; SmATA 2; Str&VC; WhAm 9; WhAmArt 85; WhoAm 74, 76, 78, 82, 84; WhoAmA 73, 76, 78, 80, 82, 84, 86, 89N, 91N, 93N; WhoAmW 58, 61, 64, 66, 68, 70, 72, 74, 85*

Bacon, Roger
English. Philosopher, Scientist
Wrote on optics, nature of concave and convex lenses; credited with discovery of gunpowder; greatest work *Opus Majus,* 1265.
b. c. 1214 in Ilchester, England
d. 1292 in Oxford, England
Source: *Alli; BbD; Benet 87, 96; BiD&SB; BiDPsy; BiHiMed; BioIn 1, 2, 3, 6, 7, 8, 9, 10, 11, 14, 15, 18; BritAu; CamDcSc; CamGEL; CasWL; Chambr 1; ClMLC 14; CyEd; DcBiPP; DcEnL; DcEuL; DcLB 115; DcNaB; Dis&D; EncO&P 1, 2, 3; EvLB; InSci; LarDcSc; LegTOT; LinLib L, S; LngCEL; McGEWB; NewC; NewGrDM 80; OxCClL; OxCEng 67; OxCMed 86; PenC ENG; RAdv 14, 13-4, 13-5; REn; WorAl; WorAlBi*

Bacon, Selden D(askam)
American. Sociologist
Pioneer in treating alchoholism as an illness; director, Yale U Center of Alcohol Studies, 1942-62.
b. Sep 10, 1909
d. Dec 6, 1992 in Martha's Vineyard, Massachusetts
Source: *AmMWSc 73S, 78S; BioIn 2, 3, 18, 19; CurBio 93N; DcAmTB; WhoWor 74*

Badalamenti, Angelo
Composer, Producer
Worked in partnership with David Lynch to compose music for the film *Blue Velvet,* 1986 as well as Lynch's television show "Twin Peaks," 1990 for which he received a Grammy Award in the pop instrumental category; continued to work with Lynch on films *Wild at Heart,* 1990, and *Twin Peaks: Fire Walk With Me,* 1992 for which he won the Saturn Award for Best Original Score; composed *City of Lost Children,* 1996.
Source: *BioIn 17; ConMus 17; ConTFT 10; WhoAm 96, 97*

Bad Company
[Boz Burrell; Simon Kirke; Michael Ralphs; Paul Rodgers]
English. Music Group
Debut album *Bad Company,* 1974 was number one worldwide; hit singles include "Rock and Roll Fantasy," 1979.
Source: *ConMuA 80A; EncRk 88; EncRkSt; HarEnR 86; IlEncRk; PenEncP; RkOn 78; RolSEnR 83; WhoRock 81; WhoRocM 82*

Baddeley, Angela
[Madeleine Angela Clinton Baddeley]
English. Actor
Played Mrs. Bridges, the cook, in PBS TV series "Upstairs Downstairs."
b. Jul 4, 1900 in London, England
d. Feb 22, 1976 in Essex, England
Source: *BioIn 10; BlueB 76; FilmgC; LegTOT; ObitOF 79; PlP&P; Who 74; WhoThe 77, 81N*

Baddeley, Hermione Clinton
English. Actor, Comedian
Received Oscar nomination, 1959, for *Room at the Top;* played the housekeeper on "Maude," 1974-77.
b. Nov 13, 1906 in Broseley, England
d. Aug 19, 1986 in Los Angeles, California
Source: *BiE&WWA; ConNews 86-4; ConTFT 4; EncMT; FilmEn; IntMPA 82; MovMk; Who 74; WhoAm 82; WhoHol A; WhoThe 81; WorAl*

Baden-Powell, Olave St. Claire, Lady
English. Social Reformer
Founded International Girl Scout Movement, 1909; wrote *Training Girls As Guides,* 1917.
b. Feb 22, 1889 in Chesterfield, England
d. Jun 26, 1977 in Guildford, England
Source: *BioIn 1, 4, 6, 9, 10, 11; BlueB 76; CurBio 46; IntWW 74, 78N; InWom, SUP; Who 74; WhoWor 74, 76*

Baden-Powell, Robert Stephenson Smyth Baden-Powell, Baron
English. Military Leader
Founded English Boy Scouts, 1908; conceived idea when he took some boys camping.
b. Feb 22, 1857 in London, England
d. Jan 8, 1941 in Nyeri, British East Africa
Source: *Alli; CurBio 41; DcBrBI; EncE 75; EncSF; HarEnUS; LinLib L, S; LngCTC; MnBBF; SmATA 16; SpyCS; WhDW; WhLit; WhoChL; WhoLA; WhoMilH 76*

Bader, Douglas Robert Steuart, Sir
"The Chap with the Tin Legs"
English. Air Force Officer
Legless pilot who shot down at least 22 German planes, WW II.
b. Feb 21, 1910 in London, England
d. Sep 5, 1982 in London, England
Source: *ConAu 107; DcNaB 1981; HarEnMi; HisEWW; NewYTBS 82; Who 74, 82; WhWW-II*

Badfinger
[Tom Evans; Mike Gibbons; Ronald Griffiths; Peter Ham; Joey Molland]
English. Music Group
Liverpool quintet formed mid-60s-1975, promoted by Beatles; hit album *Maybe Tomorrow,* 1969.
Source: *ConMuA 80A; EncRk 88; EncRkSt; IlEncRk; ObitOF 79; PenEncP; RkOn 78; RolSEnR 83; WhoRock 81; WhoRocM 82*

Bad Heart Bull, Amos
American. Artist
Called "the Herodotus of his people;" made more than 400 pictographs of the Oglala Sioux people.
b. 1869
d. 1913
Source: *NotNaAm*

Badillo, Herman
American. Politician
Pres., borough of Bronx, 1966-69; deputy mayor for management, NYC, 1978-79.
b. Aug 21, 1929 in Caguas, Puerto Rico
Source: *AlmAP 78; BiDrUSC 89; BioIn 9, 10, 11, 12; BlueB 76; CelR; CivR 74; CngDr 74, 77; ConAu 85; CurBio 71; Dun&B 90; HispAmA; IntWW 74, 75, 76, 77; NewYTBE 73; WhoAm 74, 76, 78, 80, 82, 84; WhoAmP 73, 75, 77, 79, 81, 83, 85, 87, 89, 91, 93, 95; WhoE 74, 75, 77, 79, 81; WhoGov 72, 75, 77; WhoHisp 91, 92, 94; WhoWor 78, 80*

Badings, Henk
Dutch. Composer
One of the pioneers in the use of electronic music and tape recorders; composed radio opera *Orestes,* 1954.
b. Jan 17, 1907 in Bandung, Dutch East Indies
Source: *Baker 78, 84, 92; BiDD; BioIn 3, 8; BriBkM 80; CnOxB; CompSN, SUP; CpmDNM 79, 80, 81; DcCM; IntWW 74, 75, 76, 77, 78, 79, 80, 81, 82, 83, 89, 91, 93; IntWWM 77, 80, 85; MusMk; NewAmDM; NewGrDM 80; NewGrDO; NewOxM; OxCMus; WhoWor 74, 76, 78*

Badoglio, Pietro
Italian. Military Leader
Led forces that defeated Austria, WW I; prime minister, 1943-44.
b. Sep 28, 1871 in Monferrato, Italy
d. Oct 31, 1956 in Monferrato, Italy
Source: *BioIn 1, 2, 4, 16; CurBio 40, 57; DcTwHis; EncTR 91; FacFETw; HarEnMi; HisEWW; LinLib S; McGEWB; ObitOF 79; ObitT 1951; WhDW; WhoMilH 76; WhWW-II*

Badura-Skoda, Paul
Austrian. Pianist
Made concert debut in Vienna, 1948; wrote books on interpreting Mozart.
b. Jan 15, 1927 in Munich, Germany
Source: *Baker 78, 84, 92; BioIn 3, 4, 5, 14, 15; BlueB 76; BriBkM 80; IntWW 74, 75, 76, 77, 78, 79, 80, 81, 82, 83, 89, 91, 93; IntWWM 77, 80, 90; NewAmDM; NewGrDM 80; NotTwCP; PenDiMP; WhoAm 74, 76, 78, 80, 82, 84, 86, 88, 90, 92, 94, 95; WhoMus 72; WhoWor 74, 76, 78*

Baedeker, Karl
German. Publisher
Issued travel handbooks in German, 1820s; later published them in French, English.
b. Nov 3, 1801 in Essen, Germany
d. Oct 4, 1859 in Koblenz, Germany
Source: *Benet 87, 96; BioIn 3, 5, 10, 14; BlmGEL; LegTOT; LinLib L, S; LngCEL; NewC; OxCEng 85, 95; REn; WhDW*

Baekeland, Leo Hendrik
American. Chemist, Inventor
Invented Velox paper for photographic prints, 1893; synthetic plastic Bakelite, 1907.
b. Nov 14, 1863 in Saint Martens-Latem, Belgium
d. Feb 23, 1944 in Beacon, New York
Source: *ApCAB X; AsBiEn; BiESc; BioIn 1, 2, 3, 6, 7, 8, 12, 14, 16; CamDcSc; CurBio 44; DcAmB S3; DcInv; DcScB; LarDcSc; LinLib S; McGEWB; NatCAB 15, 32; OxCAmH; WebAB 74, 79; WhAm 2; WhDW; WorAl*

Baer, Bugs
[Arthur Baer]
American. Journalist, Cartoonist
Staff writer, King Features, NYC, 1930-69; known for comical sayings.
b. 1886 in Philadelphia, Pennsylvania
d. May 17, 1969 in New York, New York
Source: *BiDAmNC; BioIn 5, 8, 9; LegTOT; REnAL; St&PR 75; WebAB 74, 79; WhoHol B; WhScrn 77, 83*

Baer, Karl Ernst von
Russian. Biologist, Educator
Pioneered modern embryology; discovered mammalian ovum, 1827.
b. Feb 19, 1792 in Piep, Russia
d. Nov 28, 1876 in Dorpat, Russia
Source: *AsBiEn; BiD&SB; BiESc; BioIn 1, 4, 9, 10, 12, 14, 15, 17, 19; CamDcSc; CelCen; DcBiPP, A; DcScB; InSci; LinLib S; McGEWB; NewCol 75; WebBD 83; WorScD*

Baer, Max
American. Boxer, Actor
Heavyweight champ, 1934; starred in *The Prizefighter and the Lady,* 1933.
b. Feb 11, 1909 in Omaha, Nebraska
d. Nov 21, 1959 in Hollywood, California
Source: *BioIn 2, 5, 6, 10, 11; BoxReg; CmCal; EncAFC; FilmEn; FilmgC; ForYSC; GangFlm; HalFC 80, 84, 88; LegTOT; NotNAT B; ObitT 1951; WhoBox 74; WhoHol B; WhScrn 74, 77, 83*

Baer, Max, Jr.
American. Actor, Producer, Director
Played Jethro Bodine on "The Beverly Hillbillies," 1962-71.
b. Dec 4, 1937 in Oakland, California
Source: *ConTFT 6; HalFC 80, 84, 88; LegTOT; MiSFD 9; WhoAm 82; WhoEnt 92; WhoHol 92, A*

Baeyer, Adolf Johann Friedrich Wilhelm, von
German. Chemist
Won 1905 Nobel Prize for contributions to organic chemistry.
b. Oct 31, 1835 in Berlin, Germany
d. Aug 20, 1917 in Starnberg, Germany
Source: *AsBiEn; BiESc; DcScB; Dis&D; McGEWB; WhoNob; WorAl*

Baez, Joan
American. Singer, Political Activist
Folk singer, proponent of human rights, 1960s; founded Humanitas/ International Human Rights Committee, 1979.
b. Jan 9, 1941 in New York, New York
Source: *ASCAP 80; Baker 78, 84; BiDAmM; BioIn 6, 7, 8, 9, 10, 11, 12, 13, 14, 15, 16; BioNews 74; BkPepl; BlueB 76; CelR, 90; ChiSch; CivR 74; CmCal; ConAu 21R, 26NR; ConHero 2; ConMuA 80A; ConMus 1; ContDcW 89; CurBio 63; DcArts; DcHiB; DcTwCCu 1; EncFCWM 69, 83; EncRk 88; EncRkSt; EncWB; FacFETw; GoodHs; GrLiveH; HanAmWH; HarEnR 86; HispWr; IlEncRk; IntAu&W 76; IntDcWB; IntWW 76, 77, 78, 79, 80, 81, 82, 83, 89, 91, 93; IntWWM 77, 80, 90; InWom, SUP; ItaFilm; LegTOT; LibW; LNinSix; MexAmB; MugS; NewAmDM; NewGrDA 86; NewYTBS 87; NotHsAW 93; OnThGG; OxCPMus; PenEncP; PolProf J; RadHan; RkOn 78; RolSEnR 83; WebAB 74, 79; WhoAm 74, 76, 78, 80, 82, 84, 86, 88, 90; WhoAmW 66, 68, 70, 72, 74, 91; WhoEnt 92; WhoHisp 92; WhoHol 92; WhoRock 81; WhoWest 74, 76, 78; WhoWor 74, 78, 80, 82, 84; WomFir; WorAl; WorAlBi*

Baffin, William
English. Navigator
Expeditions in search of NW Passage led to discovery of Baffin Bay, 1612-14.
b. 1584?, England
d. Jan 23, 1622 in Qishm, Persia
Source: *Alli; ApCAB; AsBiEn; BiD&SB; BioIn 4, 18; DcBiPP; DcCanB 1; DcEnL; DcNaB, C; Drake; EncCRAm; Expl 93; HarEnUS; HisDBrE; LinLib S; MacDCB 78; McGEWB; NewC; NewCBEL; OxCAmH; OxCCan; OxCEng 85, 95; OxCShps; WhDW; WhWE; WorAl; WorAlBi*

Bagaza, Jean-Baptiste
Burundian. Political Leader
Pres., Republic of Burundi, 1976-87; led coup against former pres., Micombero, Nov. 1976.
b. Aug 29, 1946 in Murambi, Burundi

Source: *AfSS 78, 79, 80, 81, 82; BioIn 12, 21; DcAfHiB 86, 86S; IntWW 78, 79, 80, 81, 82, 83, 89, 91, 93; WhoWor 80, 82, 84, 87, 89, 91*

Bagdikian, Ben Haig
American. Author
Newspaper editor whose writings on poverty include *The Poor In America,* 1964.
b. Jun 30, 1920 in Marash, Turkey
Source: *AmAu&B; BioIn 13, 15; ConAu 6NR, 9R; DrAS 78E, 82E; EncTwCJ; IntAu&W 77, 82; WhoAm 74, 76, 78, 80, 82, 84, 86, 88, 90, 92, 94, 95, 96, 97; WhoSSW 73, 82; WhoUSWr 88; WhoWest 89, 92, 94, 96; WhoWor 74, 82; WhoWrEP 89, 92, 95; WrDr 76, 80, 82, 84, 86, 88, 90, 92, 94, 96*

Bagehot, Walter
English. Economist, Editor
Wrote *English Constitution,* 1867; founded, edited *Economist,* 1860-1877.
b. Feb 3, 1826 in Langport, England
d. Mar 24, 1877 in Langport, England
Source: *Alli SUP; AtlBL; BbD; Benet 87, 96; BiD&SB; BioIn 1, 4, 5, 6, 8, 9, 10, 11, 15, 16, 17; BlmGEL; BritAu 19; CamGEL; CamGLE; CasWL; CelCen; Chambr 3; CrtT 3; DcAmC; DcBiPP, A; DcEnA; DcEnL; DcEuL; DcLB 55; DcLEL; DcNaB; EvLB; GrEconB; LinLib L, S; LngCEL; McGEWB; NewC; NewCBEL; NinCLC 10; OxCEng 67, 85, 95; OxCLaw; PenC ENG; RAdv 13-3; REn; WebE&AL; WhoEc 81, 86; WorAl; WorAlBi*

Bagnold, Enid
[Lady Jones]
English. Author, Dramatist
Noted for novel *National Velvet,* 1935; prize-winning play *The Chalk Garden,* 1956.
b. Oct 27, 1889 in Rochester, England
d. Mar 31, 1981 in London, England
Source: *AnObit 1981; AuBYP 2, 3; Benet 87; BiE&WWA; BioIn 2, 4, 6, 7, 8, 9, 10, 12, 13; BlmGWL; BlueB 76; CamGLE; CamGWoT; ChhPo S2; ChlBkCr; CnMD; ConAu 5NR, 5R, 40NR, 103; ConDr 73, 77; ConLC 25; ConNov 76; CurBio 64, 81, 81N; DcLB 13, 160; DcLEL; DcNaB 1981; EncBrWW; EncWT; EvLB; FemiCLE; FemiWr; FourBJA; IntAu&W 76, 77; IntWW 78, 79, 80, 81, 81N; LegTOT; LinLib L; LngCTC; MajAI; ModWD; NewC; NewCBEL; NotNAT, A; Novels; OxCChiL; OxCEng 67; OxCThe 83; PenNWW A; PlP&P; REn; RfGEnL 91; SmATA 1, 25; TwCA, SUP; TwCChW 83, 89; TwCWr; WhAm 7; WhE&EA; Who 74; WhoAmW 66, 68, 70, 72, 74; WhoChL; WhoThe 72, 77, 81; WhoWor 74, 76, 78; WorAl; WorAlBi; WrDr 76, 80, 82*

Bagramian, Ivan Christofovorich
Russian. Military Leader
Commanded 1st Baltic Army which drove Nazis from Lithuania, 1943-45; given title Hero of Soviet Union twice, Order of Lenin five times.
b. Dec 2, 1897 in Gyandzha, Armenia
d. Sep 21, 1982 in Moscow, Union of Soviet Socialist Republics
Source: *AnObit 1982; ConAu 107; CurBio 44, 83; IntWW 83; NewYTBS 82*

Bagration, Petr Ivanovich
Russian. Military Leader
General who led campaigns against Napoleon; admired for courage at Battle of Friedland, 1807.
b. 1765 in Kizlar, Russia
d. Sep 24, 1812 in Borodino, Russia
Source: *CelCen; DcBiPP; NewCol 75; WhoMilH 76; WorAl*

Baha'u'llah
[Mirza Husayn Ali Nuri]
Persian. Religious Leader
Founded Baha'i faith; writings revealed in over 100 volumes, 1853-92.
b. Nov 12, 1817 in Tehran, Persia
d. May 29, 1892 in Akko, Palestine
Source: *BiDAmCu; BioIn 1, 10, 13; CasWL; LinLib L; LuthC 75; RelLAm 91*

Baikie, William Balfour
Scottish. Explorer, Naturalist
Explored Niger River; built settlements, opened up Niger for navigation.
b. Aug 27, 1825 in Kirkwall, Scotland
d. Dec 12, 1864, Sierra Leone
Source: *Alli SUP; BioIn 9, 18, 21; CelCen; DcAfHiB 86; DcNaB; Expl 93; McGEWB; NewCBEL; WebBD 83; WhWE*

Bailar, Benjamin Franklin
American. Government Official
Postmaster general, 1975-78.
b. Apr 21, 1934 in Champaign, Illinois
Source: *BioIn 10, 11; BlueB 76; IntWW 75, 76, 77, 78, 79, 80, 81, 82, 83, 89, 91, 93; NewYTBS 75; St&PR 75, 84, 87, 91, 93; WhoAm 76, 80, 82, 84, 86, 88, 90, 92, 94, 95, 96, 97; WhoFI 85; WhoGov 75, 77*

Bailey, Ace
[Irvine Wallace Bailey]
Canadian. Hockey Player
Right wing, Toronto, 1926-34; won Art Ross Trophy, 1929; Hall of Fame, 1975.
b. Apr 3, 1903 in Bracebridge, Ontario, Canada
Source: *BioIn 9; HocEn; WhoHcky 73; WhoSpor*

Bailey, Alice A(nne La Trobe-Bateman)
English. Author
Occultist; wrote *Treatise on White Magic,* 1934.
b. 1880 in Manchester, England
d. 1949
Source: *ConAu 116; EncO&P 1*

Bailey, Charles Waldo, II
American. Newspaper Editor, Author
Wrote *No High Ground,* 1960; editor, *Minneapolis Tribune,* 1972-82; radio editor, NPR, Washington, DC, 1984-87.
b. Apr 28, 1929 in Boston, Massachusetts
Source: *BioIn 13; ConAu 1NR, 1R; EncTwCJ; IntAu&W 91, 93; WhoAm 74, 76, 78, 80, 82, 84, 86, 88, 90, 92, 94, 95, 96, 97; WhoE 95, 97; WhoUSWr 88; WhoWrEP 89, 92, 95; WrDr 76, 80, 82, 84, 86, 88, 90, 92, 94, 96*

Bailey, Donald Coleman, Sir
English. Engineer, Inventor
Invented Bailey Bridge to transport troops, tanks across rivers in WW II.
b. Sep 5, 1901 in Yorkshire, England
d. May 5, 1985 in Bournemouth, England
Source: *BioIn 14; CurBio 85, 85N; DcNaB MP; FacFETw; IntYB 78, 79, 80, 81, 82; Who 74, 82, 83, 85*

Bailey, F(rancis) Lee
American. Lawyer
Partner, Bailey & Broder, NYC; defended Patty Hearst, 1976; wrote *The Defense Never Rests,* 1972; defended O.J. Simpson, 1995.
b. Jun 10, 1933 in Waltham, Massachusetts
Source: *BioIn 7, 8, 9, 10, 11, 20; ConAu 89; CopCroC; WhoAm 74, 76, 78, 80, 82, 84, 86, 88, 92, 94, 95, 96, 97; WhoAmL 78, 79, 85, 87, 90, 92, 94, 96; WhoE 74; WrDr 94, 96*

Bailey, Florence Augusta Merriam
American. Ornithologist, Author
Nature books include *Birds of Village and Field,* 1898.
b. Aug 8, 1863 in Locust Grove, New York
d. Sep 22, 1948 in Washington, District of Columbia
Source: *AmAu&B; AmLY; AmWomSc; AmWomWr; BiCAW; DcAmAu; DcAmB S4; InWom, SUP; LibW; NatCAB 13; NotAW; WhAm 2; WomWWA 14*

Bailey, Frederick Marshman
English. Explorer, Naturalist
Expedition mapping course of Tsangpo River in Tibet recounted in *No Passport to Tibet,* 1957.
b. Feb 3, 1882 in Lahore, India
d. Apr 17, 1967 in Stiffkey, England
Source: *BioIn 7, 8, 14; ConAu P-1; DcNaB 1961; GrBr; ObitT 1961*

Bailey, Gamaliel
American. Social Reformer, Editor
Edited antislavery periodicals, including *National Era,* which first serialized *Uncle Tom's Cabin,* 1851-52; died of illness at sea.
b. Dec 3, 1807 in Mount Holly, New Jersey
d. Jun 5, 1859

Source: *AmAu&B; AmBi; ApCAB; BiD&SB; BioIn 15; DcAmB; DcAmSR; Drake; EncAJ; HarEnUS; JrnUS; LegTOT; McGEWB; NatCAB 2; PolPar; TwCBDA; WebAB 74, 79; WhAm HS; WhAmP*

Bailey, H(enry) C(hristopher)
English. Author
Created fictional detectives Reggie Fortune, Joshua Clunk; wrote *Mr. Fortune's Practice,* 1922.
b. Feb 1, 1878 in London, England
d. Mar 24, 1961
Source: *BioIn 4, 14; ConAu 108; EvLB; LngCTC; NewC; NewCBEL; TwCA, SUP; TwCCr&M 85; TwCRHW 94; WhE&EA; WhLit; WhoLA*

Bailey, Jack
American. TV Personality
Emceed for several game shows: "Queen for a Day"; "Truth or Consequences"; "Joker's Wild."
b. Sep 15, 1907 in Hampton, Iowa
d. Feb 1, 1980 in Santa Monica, California
Source: *BioIn 4, 12; NewYTET; RadStar*

Bailey, James Anthony
[Barnum and Bailey]
American. Circus Owner
Merged his Cooper and Bailey Circus with P T Barnum's to form "The Greatest Show on Earth," 1881.
b. Jul 4, 1847 in Detroit, Michigan
d. Apr 11, 1906 in Mount Vernon, New York
Source: *Alli, SUP; BiDAmBL 83; BioIn 4; DcAmB; LegTOT; NatCAB 24; TwCBDA; WhAm 1*

Bailey, Liberty Hyde
American. Botanist
Founded Bailey Hortorium, 1920, world's first botanical institution for studying cultivated plants; wrote many encyclopedias.
b. Mar 15, 1858 in South Haven, Michigan
d. Dec 25, 1954 in Ithaca, New York
Source: *AmAu&B; AmLY; ApCAB X; BiDAmEd; BioIn 1, 2, 3, 4, 5, 6, 7, 8, 10, 13, 16, 17; ChhPo; DcAmAu; DcAmB S5; DcScB; EncAAH; HarEnUS; InSci; LarDcSc; LinLib S; NatCAB 10, 43; NewCol 75; OxCAmH; RAdv 14, 13-5; TwCBDA; WebAB 74, 79; WhAm 3; WhNAA; WorAl; WorAlBi*

Bailey, Martin Jean
American. Author
Wrote *National Income and the Price Level,* 1971; *The Taxation of Income from Capital,* 1968.
b. Oct 17, 1927 in Taft, California
Source: *AmEA 74; AmMWSc 73S, 78S; WhoEc 86; WhoFI 92*

Bailey, Mildred
[Mildred Rinker]
American. Singer
Sang with Paul Whiteman, 1929-33; on radio with Benny Goodman, 1939.
b. Feb 27, 1907 in Tekoa, Washington
d. Dec 12, 1951 in New York, New York
Source: *AllMusG; Baker 84, 92; BiDJaz; BioIn 20; CmpEPM; ConMus 13; DcAmB S5; IlEncJ; NewAmDM; NewGrDA 86; NewGrDJ 88, 94; NewGrDM 80; ObitOF 79; OxCPMus; PenEncP; RadStar; WhoJazz 72*

Bailey, Pearl Mae
American. Singer, Actor
Vaudeville, cabaret performer, best known for starring role in Broadway musical *Hello Dolly,* 1967-69.
b. Mar 29, 1918 in Philadelphia, Pennsylvania
d. Aug 17, 1990 in Philadelphia, Pennsylvania
Source: *ASCAP 66; Baker 84; BiDJaz; BiE&WWA; BioIn 14, 16; BlksAmF; BlkWr 1; CelR 90; ConAu 61, 132; ConMus 5; ConTFT 4, 9; CurBio 55, 69, 90N; DrBlPA 90; EncAFC; EncMT; FacFETw; FilmgC; HalFC 88; HerW, 84; InB&W 85; IntMPA 86, 88; InWom SUP; LivgBAA; MovMk; NegAl 89; NewAmDM; NewGrDA 86; NewGrDJ 88; News 91; NewYTBS 90; NotBlAW 1; NotNAT; OxCAmT 84; OxCPMus; PenEncP; SelBAAf; VarWW 85; WhoAm 86, 90; WhoAmW 85, 89; WhoBlA 85, 90, 92N; WhoHol A; WhoThe 81; WorAlBi; WrDr 86, 90*

Bailey, Philip
[Earth, Wind, and Fire]
American. Singer, Musician
With Phil Collins, sang "Easy Lover," 1984.
b. May 8, 1951 in Denver, Colorado
Source: *EncPR&S 89; LegTOT; RkOn 85; SoulM*

Bailey, Raymond
American. Actor
Played Mr. Drysdale, the banker, in TV series "The Beverly Hillbillies," 1962-69.
b. 1904 in San Francisco, California
d. Apr 15, 1980 in Irvine, California
Source: *FilmgC; HalFC 80, 84, 88; WhoHol A*

Bailey, Xenobia
American. Artist
Artist who entrenches African American aesthetic in American culture, known for chro cheted hats.
b. c. 1955 in Seattle, Washington
Source: *ConBlB 11*

Baillie, Hugh
American. Journalist
Influential war correspondent known for interviews with General MacArthur, Hitler, Mussolini, Emperor Hirohito.
b. Oct 23, 1890 in New York, New York
d. Mar 1, 1966 in La Jolla, California
Source: *BiDAmJo; BioIn 1, 5, 7, 9, 13, 16; ConAu 89; CurBio 46, 66; DcLB 29; EncAJ; EncTwCJ; JrnUS; NatCAB 61, 62; PolProf T; WhAm 4*

Bailly, Jean Sylvain
French. Astronomer, Politician
Calculated Halley's Comet orbit, 1759; briefly pres. of national assembly, mayor of Paris; guillotined.
b. Sep 15, 1736 in Paris, France
d. Nov 12, 1793 in Paris, France
Source: *BiD&SB; BiDMoER 1; BioIn 2, 3, 19; CmFrR; DcBiPP; DcScB; Dis&D; InSci; NewCol 75; OxCFr*

Baily, Francis
English. Astronomer
A founder of Royal Astronomical Society, 1820; described phenomenon called "Baily's Beads," 1836.
b. Apr 28, 1774 in Newberry, England
d. Aug 30, 1844 in London, England
Source: *Alli; AsBiEn; BiD&SB; BiDLA; BiESc; BioIn 14, 21; CamDcSc; CelCen; DcBiPP; DcNaB, C; DcScB; InSci; LarDcSc; WebBD 83*

Bain, Alexander
Scottish. Philosopher
Founded first psychological journal, *Mind,* 1876; writings include *Emotions and the Will,* 1859.
b. Jun 11, 1818 in Aberdeen, Scotland
d. Sep 18, 1903 in Aberdeen, Scotland
Source: *Alli SUP; BbD; BiD&SB; BiDPsy; BioIn 7, 13; BritAu 19; CamGLE; CasWL; CelCen; CmScLit; CyEd; DcBiPP; DcEnA, A; DcEnL; DcNaB S2; DcScB; EvLB; InSci; LinLib L; NamesHP; NewC; NewCBEL; NewCol 75; OxCEng 67, 85, 95; OxCPhil*

Bain, Barbara
American. Actor
Played Cinnamon Carter on TV series "Mission Impossible," 1966-69.
b. Sep 13, 1932 in Chicago, Illinois
Source: *AmMWSc 73P, 76P, 79, 86, 89, 92, 95; BioIn 16; ConTFT 3; HalFC 80, 84, 88; InWom SUP; WhoAm 82, 84; WhoAmW 74; WhoEnt 92*

Bain, Conrad Stafford
Canadian. Actor
Starred in TV series "Maude," 1971-78; founded Actors Federal Credit Union, 1962.
b. Feb 4, 1923 in Lethbridge, Alberta, Canada
Source: *BiE&WWA; ConTFT 4; NotNAT; VarWW 85; WhoAm 78, 80, 82, 84, 86, 88, 90, 92, 94, 95, 96, 97; WhoEnt 92; WhoHol A; WhoThe 77; WhoWest 82, 84, 87; WorAl; WorAlBi*

Bain, Dan
[Donald H Bain]
Canadian. Hockey Player
Multi-talented athlete; played amateur hockey with Winnipeg, 1896, 1899-1902; Hall of Fame, 1945.
b. 1874 in Belleville, Ontario, Canada
d. Aug 15, 1862
Source: *WhoHcky 73*

Bainbridge, Beryl
English. Author
Works include fantasy about Hitler, *Young Adolphe,* 1978; prize-winning novel, *The Bottle Factory Outing,* 1974.
b. Nov 21, 1933 in Liverpool, England
Source: *Benet 87; BioIn 13, 14, 16, 17, 19; BlmGEL; CamGLE; ConAu 21R, 24NR; ConLC 4, 5, 8, 10, 14, 18, 22, 62; ConNov 76, 91; CyWA 89; DcLB 14; EncBrWW; FemiCLE; IntAu&W 76, 77, 91; InWom SUP; MajTwCW; ModBrL S2; OxCEng 85; Who 92; WhoWor 91; WorAu 1970; WrDr 76, 80, 92*

Bainbridge, William
American. Naval Officer
Founded first US naval school at Boston Navy Yard, 1815.
b. May 7, 1774 in Princeton, New Jersey
d. Jul 27, 1833 in Philadelphia, Pennsylvania
Source: *Alli, SUP; AmBi; ApCAB; BioIn 1, 2, 4, 13; DcAmB; DcAmMiB; Drake; HarEnMi; HarEnUS; LinLib S; NatCAB 8; OxCShps; TwCBDA; WebAB 74, 79; WebAMB; WhAm HS*

Baines, Harold Douglass
American. Baseball Player
Outfielder, Chicago White Sox, 1980-89; Texas Rangers, 1989-90, Oakland A's, 1990-92; Baltimore Orioles, 1993—; led AL with 22 game winning RBI's 1989.
b. Mar 15, 1959 in Saint Michaels, Maryland
Source: *Ballpl 90; BaseReg 86, 87; BiDAmSp Sup; BioIn 14; WhoAm 86, 90, 92, 94, 95, 96, 97; WhoBlA 92; WhoE 95; WhoMW 88*

Bainter, Fay Okell
American. Actor
Won Oscar for *Jezebel,* 1938.
b. Dec 7, 1891 in Los Angeles, California
d. Apr 16, 1968 in Hollywood, California
Source: *BiE&WWA; FilmgC; InWom SUP; MGM; MotPP; MovMk; ObitOF 79; ThFT; WhAm 5; WhDW; WhoHol B; WhScrn 74, 77; WorAl*

Bainton, Roland Herbert
English. Scholar, Educator
Professor, Yale U Divinity School, 1920-62; authority on Reformation, Martin Luther; wrote *Here I Stand: A Life of Martin Luther,* 1950, which sold over 1.2 million copies.
b. Mar 30, 1894 in Ilkeston, England
d. Feb 12, 1984 in New Haven, Connecticut
Source: *Au&Wr 71; BioIn 6, 13, 14, 19; ConAu 1R, 5NR, 113; CurBio 62, 84; DcAmReB 2; IntAu&W 76, 77; IntWW 74, 75, 76, 77, 78, 79, 80, 81, 82, 83; NewYTBS 84; WhAm 8; WhE&EA; WhNAA; WhoAm 74, 76, 78, 80, 82; WrDr 76*

Baio, Scott Vincent
American. Actor
Played Chachi on TV series "Happy Days," 1977-82; star of TV series "Charles in Charge," 1984-86.
b. Sep 22, 1961 in New York, New York
Source: *BioIn 12, 13, 14; ConTFT 5; HalFC 88; IntMPA 92; VarWW 85; WhoEnt 92; WorAl; WorAlBi*

Baird, Bil
[William Britton Baird]
American. Puppeteer
Founded Bil and Cora Baird Puppet Theatre, Greenwich Village, 1966.
b. Aug 15, 1904 in Grand Island, Nebraska
d. Mar 18, 1987 in New York, New York
Source: *AmAu&B; AnObit 1987; BiE&WWA; BioIn 1, 3, 5, 10, 14, 15, 16; BioNews 74; CelR; ConAu 106, 122; ConTFT 5; CurBio 54, 87, 87N; DcPup; LegTOT; NotNAT; PupTheA, SUP; SmATA 30, 52N; WhAm 9; WhoAm 74, 76, 78, 80, 82, 84, 86; WhoThe 81; WorAl*

Baird, Bill
[William Ritchie Baird, Jr.]
"Father of the Abortion Movement"
American. Social Reformer
Abortion rights advocate; opened first birth control, abortion clinic in US, 1963.
b. Jun 20, 1932 in New York, New York
Source: *BioIn 12, 14; ConNews 87-2*

Baird, Cora Eisenberg
[Mrs. Bil Baird]
American. Puppeteer
Puppets appeared in movie *The Sound of Music,* 1965.
b. Jan 26, 1912 in New York, New York
d. Dec 7, 1967 in New York, New York
Source: *BiE&WWA; CurBio 54, 68; InWom; WhAm 5; WhScrn 74, 77*

Baird, John Logie
Scottish. Engineer
Developed the flying spot system of scanning for TV picture, 1922, used by BBC for first TV program.
b. Aug 13, 1888 in Helensburgh, Scotland
d. Jun 14, 1946 in Bexhill, England
Source: *BiESc; BioIn 1, 2, 3, 4, 5, 6, 7, 8, 9, 10, 11, 12, 13, 14, 15, 20; CamDcSc; DcNaB 1941; DcPup; EncAJ; FacFETw; GrBr; ICPEnP; InSci; LarDcSc; LegTOT; LngCTC; NewCol 75; NotTwCS; WhDW; WorAl; WorInv*

Baird, Spencer Fullerton
American. Scientist
Developed method of field study of botany, zoology in US; gathered material for Smithsonian Institute.
b. Feb 3, 1823 in Reading, Pennsylvania
d. Aug 19, 1887 in Woods Hole, Massachusetts
Source: *Alli, SUP; AmBi; ApCAB; BiAUS; BiDAmS; BiD&SB; BiESc; BiInAmS; BioIn 1, 3, 6, 15, 18, 19; CelCen; CyAL 2; DcAmAu; DcAmB; DcBiPP; DcEnL; DcNAA; DcScB; Drake; EncAAH; HarEnUS; InSci; LinLib S; NatCAB 3; NatLAC; OxCAmH; PeoHis; TwCBDA; WebAB 74, 79; WhAm HS; WhNaAH*

Bairnsfather, Bruce
English. Cartoonist
Official cartoonist, WW II; war cartoons, *Fragments from France,* published in six volumes.
b. Jul 9, 1888 in Murree, India
d. Sep 29, 1959 in Norton, England
Source: *BioIn 5, 14; ChhPo S1; DcBrAr 1; DcBrBI; GrBr; LinLib L, S; LngCTC; ObitT 1951; WorECar*

Baiul, Oksana
Ukrainian. Skater
Won gold medal in figure skating in 1994 Winter Olympics.
b. Nov 16, 1977 in Dnepropetrovsk, Ukraine
Source: *News 95, 95-3*

Bajer, Fredrik
Danish. Politician
Shared 1908 Nobel Peace Prize; leading proponent of arbitration.
b. Apr 21, 1837 in Vester, Denmark
d. Jan 22, 1922 in Copenhagen, Denmark
Source: *BiDMoPL; LegTOT; NobelP; WhoNob, 90, 95*

Bajor, Gizi
Hungarian. Actor
Versatile, creative performer in Hungarian theatre; honored as an Artist of the People of the Hungarian Republic, 1950.
b. 1893 in Budapest, Hungary
d. Feb 12, 1951 in Budapest, Hungary
Source: *InWom SUP; NotNAT B; WhScrn 83*

Bakeless, John Edwin
American. Author, Editor
His biographies, historical surveys include *Lewis and Clark,* 1947; *Spies of the Revolution,* 1962.
b. Dec 30, 1894 in Carlisle, Pennsylvania
d. Aug 8, 1978 in New Haven, Connecticut
Source: *AmAu&B; Au&Wr 71; AuBYP 2, 3; BioIn 4, 7, 11, 13; ConAu 5NR, 5R; EncAI&E; IntAu&W 76; NatCAB 61; REnAL; SmATA 9; TwCA, SUP; WhAm 7; WhE&EA; WhNAA; WhoAm 76, 78; WrDr 76*

Baker, Anita
American. Singer
Album *Rapture,* 1986, sold over two million copies; won two Grammys, 1987, including best rhythm and blues song for "Sweet Love."
b. Jan 26, 1958 in Toledo, Ohio
Source: *AfrAmAl 6; AfrAmBi 2; BioIn 15, 16; CelR 90; ConMus 9; ConNews 87-4; CurBio 89; DrBlPA 90; EncRkSt; LegTOT; NotBlAW 2; WhoAfA 96; WhoAm 90, 92, 94, 95, 96, 97; WhoAmW 91, 93, 95, 97; WhoBlA 92, 94; WorAlBi*

Baker, Belle
American. Actor
Films include *Song of Love,* 1929; *Atlantic City,* 1944.
b. 1895 in New York, New York
d. Apr 29, 1957 in Los Angeles, California
Source: *BioIn 15; CmpEPM; EncAFC; Film 2; FunnyW; InWom; JoeFr; NotNAT B; OxCAmT 84; OxCPMus; WhoHol B; WhScrn 74, 77, 83*

Baker, Bill
American. Hockey Player
Defenseman; member, US Olympic gold medal-winning team, 1980; in NHL, 1980-84.
b. Nov 29, 1956 in Grand Rapids, Minnesota
Source: *BioIn 13; HocEn; HocReg 81*

Baker, Blanche
American. Actor
Daughter of Carroll Baker; won Emmy for role in TV movie "Holocaust," 1978.
b. Dec 20, 1956 in New York, New York
Source: *ConTFT 1; IntMPA 92, 94, 96; VarWW 85; WhoHol 92*

Baker, Bobby
[Robert Gene Baker]
American. Government Official
Senate Dem. majority secretary who was convicted, 1967, of tax evasion, theft, conspiracy to defraud govt.
b. Nov 12, 1928 in Easley, South Carolina
Source: *BioIn 11; ConAu 85; PolPar; PolProf J, K*

Baker, Bonnie
"Wee Bonnie"
American. Singer
Had number one record: "Oh Johnny, Oh Johnny," 1940.
b. Apr 1, 1917 in Orange, Texas
Source: *BioIn 10; CmpEPM; InWom SUP; SaTiSS; WhoHol 92*

Baker, Carlos Heard
American. Author
Wrote *Ernest Hemingway: A Life Story,* 1969.
b. May 5, 1909 in Biddeford, Maine
d. Apr 18, 1987 in Princeton, New Jersey
Source: *AmAu&B; BioIn 10, 11; BlueB 76; ChhPo, S3; ConAu 3NR, 5R; DcLEL 1940; DrAS 82E; IntAu&W 86; IntWW 83; REnAL; WhAm 9; WhDW; WhNAA; WhoAm 74, 76, 78, 80; WhoWor 74; WorAu 1950; WrDr 76, 86*

Baker, Carroll
American. Actor
Nominated for Oscar, 1956, for *Baby Doll;* groomed in 1960s to replace Marilyn Monroe as screen sex goddess.
b. May 28, 1931 in Johnstown, Pennsylvania
Source: *BiDFilm, 94; BiE&WWA; BioIn 4, 5, 6, 7, 11, 13, 15, 16; ConAu 142; ConTFT 1, 8; FilmEn; FilmgC; HalFC 80, 84, 88; HarEnCM 87; IntAu&W 89, 91; IntDcF 1-3, 2-3; IntMPA 80, 81, 82, 84, 86, 88, 92, 94, 96; IntWW 89, 91, 93; InWom, SUP; ItaFilm; LegTOT; MovMk; OxCFilm; WhoAm 74, 86, 90, 92; WhoEnt 92; WhoHol 92, A; WorAl; WorAlBi; WorEFlm; WrDr 96*

Baker, Charlotte
American. Author
Wrote *A Sombrero for Miss Brown,* 1941; *House on the River,* 1948.
b. Aug 31, 1910 in Nacogdoches, Texas
Source: *AuBYP 2, 3; BioIn 5, 7, 9; ConAu 17R; DcAmChF 1960; IlsCB 1946; SmATA 2; WhoAmW 58, 61, 64, 66*

Baker, Diane
American. Actor
Films include *Diary of Anne Frank,* 1959; *Marnie,* 1969.
b. Feb 25, 1938 in Hollywood, California
Source: *BioIn 7, 16; FilmEn; FilmgC; ForYSC; HalFC 80, 84, 88; IntMPA 92, 94, 96; LegTOT; MotPP; MovMk; WhoAm 80; WhoEnt 92; WhoHol 92, A*

Baker, Dorothy Dodds
American. Author
Writings include *Young Man With a Horn,* 1938; *Cassandra at the Wedding,* 1962.
b. Apr 21, 1907 in Missoula, Montana
d. Jun 18, 1968 in Terra Bella, California
Source: *AmWomWr; BioIn 2, 4, 8, 10; CurBio 43, 68; DcAmB S8; InWom, SUP*

Baker, Dusty
[Johnnie B. Baker, Jr.]
American. Baseball Player, Baseball Manager
Outfielder, Atlanta, 1968-75; Los Angeles, 1976-83; San Francisco, 1984; Oakland, 1985-86; manager, San Francisco, 1993—; won Gold Glove, 1981.
b. Jun 15, 1949 in Riverside, California
Source: *Ballpl 90; BiDAmSp Sup; BioIn 19, 20; ConBlB 8; LegTOT; WhoAfA 96; WhoAm 94, 95, 96, 97; WhoBlA 85, 88, 90, 92, 94; WhoProB 73; WhoWest 94, 96*

Baker, Elbert Hall, II
American. Newspaper Publisher
Pres., publisher, Tribune Publishing Co., Tacoma, WA, 1960—.
b. Jul 18, 1910 in Quincy, Massachusetts
Source: *St&PR 84, 87; WhAm 11; WhoAdv 72; WhoAm 74, 76, 78, 80, 82, 84, 86; WhoFI 74, 75, 77, 79; WhoUSWr 88; WhoWest 74, 84; WhoWrEP 89, 92*

Baker, Ella
American. Social Reformer
Cofounded the Southern Christian Leadership Congress and the Student Nonviolent Coordinating Committee.
b. Dec 13, 1903 in Norfolk, Virginia
d. Dec 13, 1986 in New York, New York
Source: *AnObit 1986; BioIn 14, 15, 16, 17, 18, 19, 20, 21; EncAL; FacFETw; HeroCon; NotBlAW 1; PorAmW; RadHan; RComAH; WomPubS 1925*

Baker, Frank
[John Franklin Baker]
"Home Run Baker"
American. Baseball Player
Third baseman, 1908-22; had .307 lifetime batting average; Hall of Fame, 1955.
b. Mar 13, 1886 in Trappe, Maryland
d. Jun 28, 1963 in Trappe, Maryland
Source: *Ballpl 90; BiDAmSp BB; BioIn 6, 7, 9, 10, 14, 15, 17; DcAmB S7; LegTOT; WhoProB 73; WhoSpor*

Baker, George
American. Cartoonist
Disney animator, 1937-41; staff cartoonist on US Army's newspaper, *Yank,* drawing strip "Sad Sack," 1941-46.
b. May 22, 1915 in Lowell, Massachusetts
d. May 7, 1975 in San Gabriel, California
Source: *AmAu&B; BioIn 2, 10, 13; ConAu 57, 93; CurBio 44, 75, 75N; EncACom; EncTwCJ; LegTOT; LinLib L; NatCAB 62; WebAB 74, 79; WebAMB; WhAm 6; WorECom*

Baker, George Fisher
American. Financier, Philanthropist
A founder, 1863, president from 1877, of First National Bank, NYC; endowed Harvard's Graduate School of Business.
b. Mar 27, 1840 in Troy, New York
d. May 2, 1931 in New York, New York
Source: *AmBi; BiDAmBL 83; BioIn 3, 4, 13, 17, 21; DcAmB S1; LinLib S; NatCAB 23; OxCAmH; WebAB 74, 79; WhAm 1*

Baker, Ginger
[Blind Faith; Cream; Peter Baker]
English. Musician, Singer
Leading British drummer, percussionist, 1960s-70s; formed group Cream, with Eric Clapton, 1967-69; inducted into Hollywood Rock Walk, 1991.
b. Aug 19, 1940 in Lewisham, England

Source: *BiDJaz; BioIn 9, 10, 16; EncJzS; EncPR&S 74, 89; EncRk 88; IlEncRk; PenEncP; RkOn 74; RolSEnR 83; WhoRocM 82; WorAl; WorAlBi*

Baker, Gwendolyn Calvert
American. Educator
President, US Committee for the United Nations Children's Fund (UNICEF), 1993—.
b. Dec 31, 1931 in Ann Arbor, Michigan
Source: *BioIn 13; ConBlB 9; NotBlAW 2; WhoAfA 96; WhoAm 88, 92, 96; WhoAmW 89, 91, 93, 95, 97; WhoBlA 75, 77, 80, 92, 94*

Baker, Hobey
[Hobart Amery Hare Baker]
American. Hockey Player
Rover on US amateur teams, early 1900s; Hall of Fame, 1945; died in air crash, WW I.
b. Jan 1892 in Wissahickon, Pennsylvania
d. Dec 21, 1918, France
Source: *BioIn 7, 13; WhoHcky 73; WhoSpor*

Baker, Houston A(lfred), Jr.
American. Critic, Educator, Writer
President, Modern Language Association of America, 1992; wrote *Workings of the Spirit: The Poetics of Afro-American Women's Writing,* 1991.
b. Mar 22, 1943 in Louisville, Kentucky
Source: *BioIn 13; BlkAWP; IntAu&W 76, 91, 93; LivgBAA; WhoAm 80, 82, 84, 86, 88, 90, 95, 97; WhoE 77, 79, 81; WrDr 76, 80, 82, 84, 86, 88, 90, 92, 94, 96*

Baker, Howard Henry, Jr.
American. Politician, Government Official
Rep. senator from TN, 1966-85; White House Chief of Staff under Reagan, 1987-88.
b. Nov 15, 1925 in Huntsville, Tennessee
Source: *BiDrAC; BiDrUSC 89; BioIn 8, 9, 10, 11, 12, 13, 14, 15, 16; BlueB 76; ConAu 113, 124; CurBio 74, 87; IntWW 74, 75, 76, 77, 78, 79, 80, 81, 82, 83, 89, 91, 93; NewYTBE 73; NewYTBS 77, 79, 87, 88; PolsAm 84; Who 82, 83, 85, 88, 90, 92, 94; WhoAm 74, 76, 78, 80, 82, 84, 86, 88, 92, 94, 96, 97; WhoAmP 91; WhoGov 72, 75, 77; WhoSSW 73, 75, 76, 78, 80, 82, 84; WhoWor 78, 80, 82, 84, 87; WorAl*

Baker, James Addison, III
American. Presidential Aide, Government Official
Secretary of State under Bush, 1989-92; Reagan's Treasury secretary, 1985-88, chief of staff 1981-85.
b. Apr 28, 1930 in Houston, Texas
Source: *AmPolLe; BiDrUSE 89; BioIn 12, 13, 14, 15, 16; CelR 90; CngDr 85, 87, 89, 91; ColdWar 1; CurBio 82; Dun&B 86; EncAB-H 1996; HisEAAC; IntWW 89, 91, 93; News 91-2; NewYTBS 80, 81, 85, 86, 89, 90; Who 88, 92, 94; WhoAm 82, 84, 86, 88, 90, 92, 94, 95, 96, 97; WhoAmL 94; WhoAmP 91; WhoE 86, 89, 91, 93; WhoFI 85, 89, 92; WhoWor 87, 89, 91, 93, 95*

Baker, Janet Abbott, Dame
English. Opera Singer
Mezzo-soprano, English Opera Group, 1961-76; Britten wrote a part for her.
b. Aug 21, 1933 in York, England
Source: *Baker 92; CelR 90; CurBio 71; FacFETw; IntWW 74, 81, 82, 91; IntWWM 77; InWom SUP; NewAmDM; NewGrDO; NewYTBS 82; PenDiMP; Who 74, 85, 92, 94; WhoAm 80, 84, 86; WhoAmM 83; WhoAmW 74, 81, 83, 85; WhoEnt 92; WhoMus 72; WhoOp 76; WhoWor 74, 76, 78, 80, 82, 84, 89, 91, 93, 95*

Baker, Joe Don
American. Actor
Best known for role in movie *Walking Tall,* 1973.
b. Feb 12, 1936 in Groesbeck, Texas
Source: *ConTFT 6; HalFC 84; IntMPA 86, 88, 92, 94, 96; LegTOT; VarWW 85; WhoAm 76, 78, 80, 82, 84, 86, 88, 92, 94, 95, 96, 97; WhoEnt 92; WhoHol 92, A*

Baker, Josephine (Carson)
[Gracie Walker]
French. Singer
Folies-Bergere's "Dark Star," 1920s; noted for banana dance, introduced hot jazz to Paris; recorded *The Josephine Baker Story,* 1926-37; active in Resistance, WWII.
b. Jun 3, 1906 in Saint Louis, Missouri
d. Apr 14, 1975 in Paris, France
Source: *AfrAmAl 6; Baker 92; BiDAfM; BiDAmM; BiDD; BiE&WWA; BioAmW; BioIn 6, 7, 9, 10, 11, 12, 14, 15, 16, 17, 18, 19, 20; BlksB&W C; BlkWAm; CamGWoT; CelR; CnOxB; ConAu 105; ConBlB 3; ConMus 10; ContDcW 89; CurBio 64, 75, 75N; DancEn 78; DcAmB S9; DcTwCCu 2, 5; DrBlPA, 90; EncAB-H 1996; EncEurC; EncFash; EncVaud; Ent; FacFETw; FilmEn; GoodHs; GrLiveH; HanAmWH; InB&W 80, 85; IntDcWB; IntWW 74; InWom, SUP; LegTOT; LibW; NegAl 76, 83, 89; NewAmDM; NewGrDA 86; NewYTBS 75; NotAW MOD; NotBlAW 1; ObitOF 79; ObitT 1971; OxCFilm; OxCPMus; PenEncP; RAdv 14; RComAH; SelBAAf; WebAB 74, 79; WhAm 6; WhoAm 74; WhoAmW 68, 70, 72, 74; WhoHol C; WhoThe 72, 77; WhoWor 74; WhScrn 77, 83; WorAl; WorAlBi*

Baker, Julius
American. Musician
Principal flutist, NY Philharmonic, 1965-83; soloist in concerts throughout US, Europe, Japan.
b. Sep 23, 1915 in Cleveland, Ohio
Source: *Baker 84, 92; BioIn 14; BriBkM 80; IntWWM 77, 80; NewAmDM; NewGrDA 86; WhoAm 74, 76, 78, 80, 82, 84, 86; WhoAmM 83; WhoEnt 92*

Baker, Kathy
American. Actor
Debut in *The Right Stuff,* 1983. Stars in "Picket Fences."
b. Jun 8, 1950 in Midland, Texas
Source: *ConTFT 8, 15; IntMPA 92, 94, 96; LegTOT*

Baker, Kathy
[Kathy Guadaginio]
American. Golfer
Turned pro, 1983; awards include US Women's Open, 1985; San Jose Classic, 1988.
b. Mar 20, 1961 in Albany, New York
Source: *BioIn 14, 15; ConNews 86-1*

Baker, Kenny
[Kenneth Lawrence Baker]
American. Actor, Singer
Nightclub singer who was regular vocalist on Jack Benny's radio show, 1930s.
b. Sep 30, 1912 in Monrovia, California
d. Aug 10, 1985 in Solvang, California
Source: *AmPS B; BiDAmM; BiE&WWA; BioIn 1, 9; CmpEPM; FilmEn; FilmgC; ForYSC; HalFC 80, 84, 88; OxCPMus; RadStar; SaTiSS; What 3; WhoHol A*

Baker, Kenny
English. Actor
Played R2-D2 in *Star Wars* films.
b. Aug 24, 1934 in Birmingham, England
Source: *ConTFT 8*

Baker, Laura Nelson
American. Author
Writings include *The Red Mountain,* 1946; *From Whales to Snails,* 1970.
b. Jan 7, 1911 in Humboldt, Iowa
Source: *Au&Wr 71; AuBYP 2, 3; BioIn 6, 8, 9; ConAu 5NR, 5R; ForWC 70; MinnWr; PenNWW A; SmATA 3, 13; WrDr 76, 80, 84*

Baker, Nicholson
American. Author
Known for his fascination with detail; wrote novels *The Mezzanine,* 1988; *Vox,* 1992.
b. Jan 7, 1957 in Rochester, New York
Source: *ConAu 135; ConLC 61; ConNov 96; ConPopW; CurBio 94; RGTwCWr; WrDr 94, 96*

Baker, Phil
American. Comedian, Composer
Films include *The Goldwyn Follies,* 1938; *The Gang's All Here,* 1943.
b. Aug 24, 1896 in Philadelphia, Pennsylvania
d. Nov 30, 1963 in Copenhagen, Denmark
Source: *ASCAP 66, 80; BiDAmM; CmpEPM; CurBio 46, 64; EncVaud; HalFC 80, 84, 88; NotNAT B; OxCPMus; RadStar; SaTiSS; WhAm 4; WhoHol B; WhScrn 74, 77*

Baker, Rachel
American. Children's Author
Biographies for children include *Sigmund Freud,* 1952; *Maria Mitchell,* 1958.
b. Mar 1, 1904 in Chernigov, Russia
d. Jul 7, 1978
Source: *AuBYP 2; BkCL; ConAu 5R, 103; MorJA; SmATA 2, 12, 26N*

Baker, Ray Stannard
[David Grayson]
American. Author
Won Pulitzer for *Woodrow Wilson: Life and Letters,* 1940.
b. Apr 17, 1870 in Lansing, Michigan
d. Jul 12, 1946 in Amherst, Massachusetts
Source: *AmAu&B; AmLY, XR; AmPeW; AmRef; AmSocL; ApCAB X; BenetAL 91; BiDAmJo; BiDAmNC; BiDInt; BioIn 1, 2, 3, 4, 5, 6, 7, 8, 12, 15, 16, 17, 19; CarSB; ChhPo S2; ConAmL; ConAu 118; CurBio 40, 46; DcAmAu; DcAmB S4; DcAmSR; DcLEL; DcNAA; EncAB-H 1974, 1996; EvLB; JrnUS; LegTOT; LinLib L, S; LngCTC; McGEWB; MichAu 80; NatCAB 14, 49; OxCAmH; OxCAmL 65, 83, 95; REn; REnAL; TwCA, SUP; TwCLC 47; TwCWr; WebAB 74, 79; WhAm 2; WhNAA; WisWr*

Baker, Rick
[Richard A. Baker]
American. Artist, Designer
Make-up artist specializing in horror, science fiction films: *King Kong,* 1976; *Star Wars,* 1977; *The Nutty Professor,* 1996.
b. Dec 8, 1950 in Binghamton, New York
Source: *BioIn 11, 15; ConTFT 6, 15; FanAl; HalFC 84, 88; IntDcF 1-4, 2-4; IntMPA 94, 96; WhoAm 96, 97; WhoHrs 80*

Baker, Russell Wayne
American. Journalist, Author
Columnist, *NY Times;* won Pulitzer, 1982, for autobiography *Growing Up.*
b. Aug 14, 1925 in Morrisonville, Virginia
Source: *AmAu&B; BiDAmNC; BioIn 14, 15; ConAu 11NR, 57; CurBio 80; EncWB; IntvTCA 2; IntWW 91; WhoAm 86, 90, 97; WhoSSW 73; WhoWrEP 89; WrDr 88*

Baker, Samm Sinclair
American. Author
Called America's "leading self-help author"; wrote *The Complete Scarsdale Medical Diet,* 1979, with Herman Tarnower.
b. Jul 29, 1909 in Paterson, New Jersey
d. Mar 5, 1997 in Port Chester, New York
Source: *BioIn 11; ConAu 3NR, 5R, 21NR; IntAu&W 77, 86, 89; NewYTBS 79; SmATA 12; WhoUSWr 88; WhoWrEP 89, 92*

Baker, Samuel White, Sir
English. Explorer
Discovered Lake Albert, the source of the Nile River, 1864.
b. Jun 8, 1821 in London, England
d. Dec 30, 1893 in Sanford Orleigh, England
Source: *Alli SUP; BbD; BiD&SB; BioIn 2, 3, 4, 5, 6, 9, 12, 17, 18, 20, 21; BritAu 19; CelCen; Chambr 3; DcAfHiB 86; DcBiPP; DcBrBI; DcEnL; DcLB 166; DcNaB S1; EvLB; Expl 93; HisDBrE; McGEWB; MnBBF; NewC; NewCBEL; OxCEng 67, 85, 95; WhDW; WhWE; WorAl; WorAlBi*

Baker, Sara Josephine
American. Physician, Feminist
Child health pioneer; first director, Bureau of Child Hygiene, 1909.
b. Nov 15, 1873 in Poughkeepsie, New York
d. Feb 22, 1945 in New York, New York
Source: *AmRef; BiDSocW; BioIn 15, 19, 20; DcAmB S3; GayLesB; GoodHs; InSci; InWom, SUP; LibW; LinLib S; NotAW; NotTwCS; WhAm 2; WomFir; WorInv*

Baker, Shorty
[Harold Baker]
American. Jazz Musician
Trumpeter, 1930-65; played with Duke Ellington, Bud Freeman.
b. May 26, 1914 in Saint Louis, Missouri
d. Nov 8, 1966 in New York, New York
Source: *AllMusG; ASCAP 66, 80; BiDAmM; BiDJaz; CmpEPM; EncJzS; IlEncJ; InB&W 80, 85; NewGrDJ 88, 94; PenEncP; WhoJazz 72*

Baker, Stanley, Sir
Welsh. Actor
Films include *The Guns of Navarone,* 1961; *Accident,* 1967.
b. Feb 28, 1928 in Glamorgan, Wales
d. Jun 28, 1976 in Malaga, Spain
Source: *BiDFilm; BioIn 10, 11, 13, 20; CmMov; FilmAG WE; FilmgC; IlWWBF, A; IntDcF 1-3, 2-3; IntMPA 75, 76; MotPP; MovMk; OxCFilm; Who 74; WhoHol A; WhoThe 81N; WhScrn 83; WorEFlm*

Baker, Terry Wayne
American. Football Player
All-America quarterback, won Heisman Trophy, 1962; first chosen, 1963 NFL draft, with LA Rams, 1963-65.
b. May 5, 1941 in Pine River, Minnesota
Source: *BiDAmSp FB; BioIn 6, 14; WhoFtbl 74*

Baker, Theodore
American. Lexicographer
Music scholar; works include *Dictionary of Musical Terms,* 1895; *Baker's Biographical Dictionary of Musicians,* 1900.
b. Jun 3, 1851 in New York, New York
d. Oct 13, 1934 in Dresden, Germany
Source: *Baker 78, 84, 92; BiDAmM; ChhPo; DcNAA; NewGrDA 86; NewGrDM 80*

Bakewell, William
American. Actor
Films include *All Quiet on the Western Front,* 1930; *Gone With The Wi nd,* 1939.
b. May 2, 1908 in Hollywood, California
Source: *BioIn 17; Film 2; FilmEn; ForYSC; HalFC 80, 84, 88; MovMk; SilFlmP; TwYS; WhoHol 92, A*

Bakhita, Giuseppina
Religious Figure
Beatified, 1992, by Pope John Paul II; former slave who joined Italian religious order after diplomat bought her freedom.
d. 1947

Bakhtiar, Shahpur
Iranian. Political Leader
Leader of Bakhtiaris, Iran's oldest, largest tribe.
b. 1916
d. Aug 8, 1992 in Paris, France
Source: *BioIn 11, 12, 17; IntWW 82, 83, 91; MidE 79, 80, 81, 82; NewYTBS 78, 91*

Bakhtin, Mikhail (Mikhailovich)
Russian. Writer
Credited with introducting several seminal concepts to the field of literary theory; wrote *Marxism and the Philosophy of Language,* 1929.
b. Nov 17, 1895 in Orel, Russia
d. Mar 7, 1975 in Moscow, Union of Soviet Socialist Republics
Source: *Benet 96; BioIn 11, 14, 16, 17, 18, 20; BlmGEL; ConAu 113, 128; ConLC 83; CyWA 89; EncWL 3; FacFETw; HanRL; OxCPhil; ThTwC 87; WorAu 1980*

Bakke, Allan Paul
American. Student
When denied admission to medical school, charged reverse discrimination; won Supreme Court decision, 1978.
b. Feb 4, 1940 in Minneapolis, Minnesota
Source: *BioIn 11; FacFETw; NewYTBS 77, 78*

Bakken, Jim
[James L Bakken]
"Bak"
American. Football Player
Two-time all-pro kicker, St. Louis, 1962-73; led NFL in scoring, 1967; past president, NFL Players Assn.
b. Nov 2, 1940 in Madison, Wisconsin
Source: *BiDAmSp FB; WhoFtbl 74*

Bakker, Jim
[James Orsen Bakker]
American. Evangelist, TV Personality
Spiritual leader, PTL TV ministry; resigned over sex scandal involving Jessica Hahn; sentenced to 45-year jail term, 1989, for defrauding his followers.
b. Jan 2, 1939 in Muskegon, Michigan
Source: *BioIn 11, 12, 13, 15, 16; ConAu 128; LegTOT; NewYTBS 87; RelLAm 91; TwCSAPR; WhoAm 84, 86*

Bakker, Robert T.
American. Paleontologist, Educator
Progenitor of controversial theory that dinosaurs were victims of a series of extinctions, due to the formation of land bridges, and not the victims of one cataclysmic event.
b. c. 1945 in Ridgewood, New Jersey
Source: *CurBio 95; WhoScEn 96*

Bakr, Ahmad Hasan al
Iraqi. Political Leader
Pres., of Iraq, 1968-79.
b. 1914 in Tikrit, Ottoman Empire
d. Oct 4, 1982 in Baghdad, Iraq
Source: *AnObit 1982; IntWW 74, 83N; WhoGov 72; WhoWor 74, 78*

Bakshi, Ralph
American. Cartoonist
Produced, directed animated version of Tolkien's *Lord of the Rings,* 1978.
b. Oct 26, 1938 in Haifa, Palestine
Source: *BioIn 10, 11, 12, 13, 15, 16; ConAu 112, 138; ConLC 26; ConTFT 6, 15; CurBio 79, 81; HalFC 88; IntDcF 1-2, 2-4; IntMPA 92, 94, 96; LegTOT; MiSFD 9; NewYTBS 81; WhoAm 82, 90; WhoEnt 92; WorECar*

Bakula, Scott
American. Actor
Starred as Sam in TV series "Quantum Leap," 1989-1993.
b. Oct 9, 1955 in Saint Louis, Missouri
Source: *ConTFT 7, 14; IntMPA 96; LegTOT; WhoEnt 92*

Bakunin, Mikhail Aleksandrovich
[Jules Elizard]
Russian. Anarchist
A founder of Nihilism; wrote *God and the State,* 1872-74.
b. May 30, 1814 in Premukhine, Russia
d. Jul 1, 1876 in Bern, Switzerland
Source: *Benet 87, 96; BioIn 1, 2, 4, 6, 7, 8, 9, 10, 11, 12, 13, 15, 16, 20; CasWL; DcAmSR; DcRusL; EuAu; HanRL; LinLib S; LuthC 75; McGEWB; REn; WhDW; WorAl*

Balaban, Barney
American. Film Executive
Pres., of Paramount Pictures, 1936-64; introduced primitive air-conditioning to movie theaters, 1917.
b. Jun 8, 1887 in Chicago, Illinois
d. Mar 7, 1971 in Byram, Connecticut
Source: *BioIn 1, 9; CurBio 46, 71, 71N; DcAmB S9; FilmEn; FilmgC; NewYTBE 71; WhAm 5; WorEFlm*

Balaguer, Joaquin
Dominican. Political Leader
Pres., Dominican Republic, 1960, 1966-78, 1986—.
b. Sep 1, 1907 in Villa Bisono, Dominican Republic
Source: *BiDLAmC; BioIn 15, 16, 21; CaribW 4; CurBio 66; DcHiB; DcTwHis; EncLatA; FacFETw; IntWW 74, 75, 76, 77, 78, 79, 80, 81, 82, 83, 89, 91; IntYB 78, 79, 80, 81, 82; McGEWB; NewYTBE 70; NewYTBS 86, 88; WhoGov 72; WhoWor 78, 87, 89, 91, 93, 95*

Balakirev, Mili Alekseyevich
Russian. Composer
Works reflect influence of Liszt, combine Romanticism with Russian, Oriental folk songs.
b. Jan 2, 1837 in Nizhni-Novgorod, Russia
d. May 28, 1910 in Saint Petersburg, Russia
Source: *Baker 78; LinLib S; OxCMus; WhDW*

Balanchine, George
[Georges Malitonovitch Balanchivadze]
"Mr. B"
American. Dancer, Choreographer
Co-founded Ballet Society, now NYC Ballet, 1946; artistic director, 1948-83.
b. Jan 22, 1904 in Saint Petersburg, Russia
d. Apr 30, 1983 in New York, New York
Source: *AmCulL; AnObit 1983; Baker 78, 84, 92; BiDD; BiDSovU; BiE&WWA; BioIn 1, 2, 3, 4, 5, 6, 7, 8, 9, 10, 11, 12, 13, 14, 15, 16, 17, 18, 19, 20, 21; BlueB 76; CelR; CnOxB; ConAu 109, 111; CurBio 42, 54, 83, 83N; DancEn 78; DcArts; DcTwCCu 1, 2; EncAB-H 1974, 1996; EncMT; FacFETw; IntDcB; IntWW 74, 75, 76, 77, 78, 79, 80, 81, 82; LegTOT; LinLib S; McGEWB; MetOEnc; NewGrDA 86; NewGrDM 80; NewOxM; NewYTBE 72; NewYTBS 74, 80, 83; NotNAT, A; OxCAmH; OxCAmT 84; OxCMus; PlP&P; RAdv 14, 13-3; RComAH; SovUn; WebAB 74, 79; WhAm 8; WhDun; WhDW; Who 82; WhoAm 74, 76, 78, 80; WhoE 79, 81, 83; WhoThe 72, 77, 81; WhoWor 74, 78, 80, 82; WorAl; WorAlBi*

Balard, Antoine-Jerome
French. Chemist
Discovered bromine, 1826; teacher of Louis Pasteur.
b. Sep 30, 1802 in Montpellier, France
d. Mar 30, 1876 in Paris, France
Source: *AsBiEn; BiESc; DcScB; WebBD 83*

Balbo, Italo
Italian. Government Official
Governor of Libya, 1936; built up Mussolini's air force; accidentally shot down by own co.
b. Jun 6, 1896 in Ferrara, Italy
d. Jun 28, 1940 in Tobruk, Libya
Source: *BiDExR; BioIn 1, 15; CurBio 40; EncRev; EncTR 91; HarEnMi; InSci; WhWW-II; WorAl; WorAlBi*

Balboa, Vasco Nunez de
Spanish. Explorer
Discovered Pacific Ocean, 1513; beheaded on false charges of treason.
b. 1475 in Jerez Caballeros, Spain
d. Jan 12, 1519 in Acla, Panama
Source: *ApCAB; Benet 87, 96; BioIn 1, 2, 3, 4, 5, 6, 8, 9, 11, 14, 16, 17, 18, 19, 20; DcBiPP; DcCathB; DcHiB; Drake; EncCRAm; EncLatA; Expl 93; HarEnUS; HisDcSE; LegTOT; LinLib S; McGEWB; NatCAB 5; NewC; OxCAmH; OxCEng 85, 95; OxCShps; REn; WhAm HS; WhDW; WhWE; WorAl; WorAlBi*

Balch, Emily G
American. Sociologist
Shared 1946 Nobel Peace Prize with John R Mott; founded Women's International League for Peace, 1919.
b. Jan 8, 1867 in Jamaica Plain, Massachusetts
d. Jan 9, 1961 in Cambridge, Massachusetts
Source: *CurBio 47, 61; NotAW MOD; ObitOF 79; OxCAmH; WebAB 74; WebBD 83; WhAm 4; WhoNob; WomWWA 14; WorAl*

Balchen, Bernt
American. Aviator, Explorer
Piloted first flight over S Pole with Byrd expedition, 1929.
b. Oct 23, 1899 in Tveit Topdal, Norway
d. Oct 17, 1973 in Mount Kisco, New York
Source: *BioIn 1, 2, 3, 4, 5, 10; ConAu 45; CurBio 49, 73, 73N; DcAmB S9; InSci; NewYTBE 73; WebAMB; WhAm 6; WhoAm 74; WhoWor 74; WorAl; WorAlBi*

Balchin, Nigel Marlin
[Mark Spade]
English. Author, Farmer
Wrote novel *Small Back Room,* 1934; thriller *Mine Own Executioner,* 1945.
b. Dec 3, 1908 in Wiltshire, England
d. May 17, 1970 in London, England
Source: *ConAu 29R, 97; DcArts; DcLEL; EncSF 93; EvLB; LngCTC; ModBrL; NewCBEL; PenC ENG; REn; TwCA SUP; TwCWr; WhE&EA*

Balcon, Michael Elias, Sir
English. Producer
Best remembered comedy *The Lavender Hill Mob,* 1951; wrote *A Lifetime of Films,* 1969.
b. May 19, 1896 in Birmingham, England
d. Oct 17, 1977 in Hartfield, England

Source: *BlueB 76; DcNaB 1971; GrBr*

Bald, Kenneth
[K Bruce]
American. Cartoonist
Created "Captain Marvel"; "Doc Savage"; "Captain Battle," 1941-43.
b. 1920 in New York, New York
Source: *WorECom*

Balderston, John Lloyd
American. Dramatist
Writings include *Genius of the Marne,* 1919; *Cleopatra and Caesar,* 1952.
b. Oct 22, 1889 in Philadelphia, Pennsylvania
d. Mar 8, 1954 in Beverly Hills, California
Source: *AmAu&B; BioIn 3, 6; CnMD; ConAu 121; FilmgC; LngCTC; McGEWD 72, 84; ModWD; NatCAB 43; WhAm 3; WhE&EA; WhNAA*

Balderston, William
American. Business Executive
Joined Philco Corp., 1930, chairman, 1954-57; leader in development of car radio.
b. Dec 13, 1896 in Boise, Idaho
d. Jul 25, 1983 in Abington, Pennsylvania
Source: *AnObit 1983; BioIn 1, 2, 13; CurBio 49, 83, 83N; InSci; NewYTBS 83; WhAm 8*

Baldessari, John
American. Artist, Educator
Conceptual artist whose powerful collages juxtapose photographs with text to form "word paintings."
b. Jun 17, 1931 in National City, California
Source: *AmArt; BioIn 14, 16, 17; ConArt 77, 83, 89, 96; ConPhot 82, 88, 95; CurBio 91; DcCAA 77, 88, 94; DcCAr 81; DcTwCCu 1; ICPEnP A; MacBEP; News 91; PrintW 83, 85; WhoAm 90; WhoAmA 91; WorArt 1980*

Baldovinetti, Alesso
Italian. Artist
Mosaicist, decorator at Bapistry in Florence, 1456; painting *Madonna* hangs in Louvre.
b. Oct 14, 1427 in Florence, Italy
d. Aug 29, 1499 in Florence, Italy
Source: *DcBiPP; DcCathB; NewCol 75; OxCArt*

Baldridge, Letitia Katherine
"Tish"
American. Public Relations Executive
Director, Tiffany & Co., 1956-61; White House social secretary, 1961-63; pres., Letitia Baldridge Enterprises, Inc., 1972—.
b. 1927? in Miami Beach, Florida
Source: *BioIn 5, 8, 11, 12; ConAu 17NR; CurBio 88; WhoAm 86; WhoAmW 87*

Baldrige, Malcolm
[Howard Malcolm Baldrise, Jr]
"Mac"
American. Government Official
US secretary of Commerce under Reagan, 1981-87; killed in rodeo accident.
b. Oct 4, 1922 in Omaha, Nebraska
d. Jul 25, 1987 in Walnut Creek, California
Source: *AnObit 1987; BioIn 12, 13; BlueB 76; CngDr 81, 83, 85, 87; ConNews 88-1; CurBio 82, 87, 87N; Dun&B 79; IntWW 83; NatCAB 63N; NewYTBS 80, 81, 87; PseudN 82; St&PR 75, 84, 87; WhAm 9; WhoAm 74, 76, 78, 82, 84, 86; WhoAmP 73, 75, 77, 79, 81, 83, 85, 87; WhoE 74, 81, 85, 86; WhoFI 74, 75, 77, 81, 83; WhoWor 74, 82, 87*

Baldung(-Grien), Hans
[Hans Gruen]
German. Artist, Printmaker
Did portraits, woodcuts, demonic allegories; altar of Freiburg Cathedral, 1512.
b. 1484? in Strassburg, Germany
d. 1545 in Strassburg, Germany
Source: *BioIn 5, 11; IntDcAA 90; McGDA; NewCol 75; OxCArt*

Baldwin, Adam
American. Actor
Films include *My Bodyguard,* 1980; *DC Cab,* 1983.
b. 1962 in Chicago, Illinois
Source: *BioIn 12; ConTFT 7, 14; IntMPA 92, 94, 96; LegTOT; NewYTBS 80; WhoHol 92*

Baldwin, Alec
[Alexander Rae Baldwin, III]
American. Actor
Starred in TV series "Knots Landing," 1984-85; films *Working Girl,* 1988; *The Hunt for Red October,* 1990.
b. Apr 3, 1958 in Massapequa, New York
Source: *BiDFilm 94; BioIn 15, 16; ConTFT 5, 12; CurBio 92; HolBB; IntMPA 92, 94, 96; LegTOT; WhoAm 90, 92, 94, 95, 96, 97; WhoEmL 93; WhoEnt 92; WhoHol 92*

Baldwin, Billy
[William J Baldwin]
American. Designer
Dean of American interior decorators; clients included Jackie Onassis.
b. May 30, 1903 in Roland Park, Maryland
d. Nov 25, 1983 in Nantucket, Massachusetts
Source: *BioIn 13; CelR; ConAu 111; NewYTBS 83; WhAm 8; WhoAm 76*

Baldwin, Faith
American. Author
Romantic novelist; wrote *American Family,* 1935.
b. Oct 1, 1893 in New Rochelle, New York
d. Mar 19, 1978 in Norwalk, Connecticut
Source: *AmAu&B; AmNov; AuNews 1; BenetAL 91; BioIn 1, 2, 4, 5, 10, 11, 14; BioNews 74; ChhPo; ConAu 4NR, 5R, 77; DcAmB S10; FacFETw; FemiCLE; ForWC 70; HalFC 80, 84, 88; InWom; LibW; LinLib L; LngCTC; NewYTBE 73; NewYTBS 78; ObitOF 79; OxCAmL 65, 83, 95; REn; REnAL; TwCA, SUP; TwCRGW; TwCRHW 90, 94; WhAm 7; WhE&EA; WhNAA; WhoAm 74, 76; WhoAmW 58, 64, 66, 68, 70, 72, 74, 77; WorAl; WrDr 76*

Baldwin, Hanson Weightman
American. Journalist
Won Pulitzer, 1942; wrote *The Crucial Years: 1939-1941,* 1976.
b. Mar 22, 1903 in Baltimore, Maryland
d. Nov 13, 1991 in Roxbury, Connecticut
Source: *AmAu&B; Au&Wr 71; BioIn 4, 8, 17, 18; ConAu 61; CurBio 42; LngCTC; NewYTBS 91; REnAL; TwCA SUP; WhAm 10; WhoAm 74, 76*

Baldwin, Horace
American. Physician
Established American Foundation for Allergic Disease.
b. Oct 14, 1895 in Englewood, New Jersey
d. Oct 27, 1983 in Sarasota, Florida
Source: *AnObit 1983; WhoAm 80*

Baldwin, James (Arthur)
American. Author
Described black life in US; best known work *Go Tell It On the Mountain,* 1953.
b. Aug 2, 1924 in New York, New York
d. Nov 30, 1987 in Saint-Paul-de-Vence, France
Source: *AfrAmAl 6; AfrAmW; AmAu&B; AmCulL; AmWr S1; AnObit 1987; Au&Arts 4; Benet 87, 96; BenetAL 91; BioIn 3, 5, 6, 7, 8, 9, 10, 11, 12, 13, 14, 15, 16, 17, 18, 19, 20, 21; BlkAmP; BlkAmW 2; BlkAWP; BlkLC; BlkWr 1; BlueB 76; CamGEL; CamGLE; CamGWoT; CamHAL; CasWL; CelR; CivR 74; ConAmD; ConAu 1BS, 1R, 3NR, 24NR, 124; ConBlB 1; ConDr 73, 77, 82, 88, 93; ConGAN; ConLC 1, 2, 3, 4, 5, 8, 13, 15, 17, 42, 50, 67, 90; ConNov 72, 76, 82, 86; ConPopW; ConTFT 3; CroCD; CrtSuDr; CurBio 64, 88, 88N; CyWA 89; DcArts; DcLB 2, 7, 33, Y87N; DcLEL 1940; DcTwCCu 1, 5; DramC 1; DrAPF 80; DrBlPA 90; Ebony 1; EncAACR; EncAB-H 1974, 1996; EncAJ; EncWL, 2, 3; EncWT; Ent; FacFETw; GayLesB; GayLL; GrWrEL N; InB&W 80, 85; IntAu&W 76, 77; LegTOT; LiExTwC; LiJour; LinLib L, S; LivgBAA; LngCTC; MagSAmL; MajTwCW; MakMC; McGEWB; McGEWD 72, 84; ModAL, S1, S2; ModBlW; ModWD; MorBAP; NatPD 77, 81; NegAl 76, 83, 89; NewCon; News 88-2; NewYTBS 87; NotNAT, A; Novels; OxCAmL 65, 83, 95; OxCEng 85, 95; OxCTwCP; PenC AM; RAdv 1, 14, 13-1; RComAH; REn; REnAL; RfGAmL 87, 94; RfGShF; RGTwCWr; SchCGBL; SelBAAf; SelBAAu; ShSCr 10; SmATA 9,*

54N; TwCWr; TwCYAW; WebAB 74, 79; WebE&AL; WhAm 9; WhDW; Who 74, 82, 83, 85, 88; WhoAm 74, 76, 78, 80, 82, 84, 86; WhoBlA 75, 77, 80, 85, 88, 90N; WhoE 74, 75; WhoTwCL; WhoUSWr 88; WhoWor 74, 78; WorAl; WorAlBi; WorAu 1950; WorLitC; WrDr 76, 80, 82, 84, 86, 88

Baldwin, James Mark
American. Psychologist
Child psychology expert; co-founded, edited *Psychological Review,* 1894-1909.
b. Jan 12, 1861 in Columbia, South Carolina
d. Nov 8, 1934 in Paris, France
Source: *Alli SUP; AmAu&B; AmBi; AmLY; ApCAB X; BiDAmEd; BiDPsy; BiDSA; BioIn 14; DcAmAu; DcAmB S1; DcNAA; InSci; LinLib L, S; NamesHP; NatCAB 10, 25; OxCAmH; TwCBDA; WhAm 1; WhLit*

Baldwin, Matthias William
American. Industrialist, Philanthropist
First to make bookbinder's tools in US.
b. Dec 10, 1795 in Elizabethtown, Pennsylvania
d. Sep 7, 1866 in Philadelphia, Pennsylvania
Source: *AmBi; ApCAB; BioIn 1, 4, 11, 14; DcAmB; Drake; InSci; NatCAB 9; NewCol 75; WebAB 74, 79; WhAm HS*

Baldwin, Robert
Canadian. Statesman
With Lafontaine, formed first Liberal govt., 1842-43; second govt., 1848-51, called "Great Ministry."
b. May 12, 1804 in Toronto, Ontario, Canada
d. Dec 9, 1858 in Spadina, Ontario, Canada
Source: *ApCAB; BioIn 12; DcCanB 8; DcNaB S1; HisDBrE; MacDCB 78; McGEWB; OxCCan*

Baldwin, Roger Nash
American. Social Reformer
Founded ACLU, 1920, with Norman Thomas, Felix Frankfurter; director until 1950.
b. Jan 21, 1884 in Wellesley, Massachusetts
d. Aug 26, 1981 in Ridgewood, New Jersey
Source: *AmMWSc 73S, 78S; AmPeW; AmRef; AmSocL; BiDSocW; BioIn 10, 12, 15, 19, 21; BioNews 74; CopCroC; CurBio 40, 81, 81N; DcAmSR; NewYTBS 81; PolProf T; WhAm 8; WhoAm 74, 76, 78, 80; WhoWor 74; WorAl*

Baldwin, Stanley
[1st Earl Baldwin of Bewdley]
English. Statesman
British prime minister, 1923-29, 1935-37; guided country through Edward VIII's abdication, 1936.
b. Aug 3, 1867 in Bewdley, England
d. Dec 14, 1947 in Astley, England
Source: *BioIn 15; DcNaB 1941; DcPol; DcTwHis; FacFETw; GrBr; HisDBrE; HisWorL; LegTOT; NewC; REn; WhDW; WhE&EA; WhLit*

Baldwin, Stephen
American. Actor
Played Billy Cody on TV series "The Young Riders," 1989-92; starred in *Homeboy,* 1988.
b. May 12, 1966 in Massapequa, New York
Source: *BioIn 15, 16; IntMPA 96; WhoHol 92*

Baldwin, William
American. Actor
Film debut in *Born on the Fourth of July,* 1989; also starred in *Backdraft.*
b. 1963 in Massapequa, New York
Source: *IntMPA 94, 96; WhoHol 92*

Balenciaga, Cristobal
"Prophet of Silhouette"
Spanish. Fashion Designer
Elegant designer of classic soft-shouldered suit, straightline chemise silhouette.
b. Jan 21, 1895 in Guetaria, Spain
d. Mar 23, 1972 in Javea, Spain
Source: *BioIn 5, 7, 8, 9; ConDes 84, 90, 97; ConFash; CurBio 54, 72; DcArts; DcTwDes; EncFash; FacFETw; FairDF FRA; LegTOT; NewYTBE 72; ObitT 1971; WhAm 5; WhoFash 88; WorAl; WorAlBi; WorFshn*

Balewa, Abubakar Tafawa, Sir
Nigerian. Political Leader
Prime minister, Nigeria, 1957-66.
b. Dec 12, 1912 in Bauchi, Nigeria (Northern)
d. Jan 15, 1966 in Lagos, Nigeria
Source: *BioIn 5, 6, 7, 8, 18, 20, 21; DcTwHis; WhAm 4*

Balfe, Michael William
Irish. Composer, Opera Singer
Wrote opera *The Bohemian Girl,* 1843, which included song, "I Dreamt I Dwelt in Marble Halls."
b. May 15, 1808 in Dublin, Ireland
d. Oct 20, 1870 in Rowney Abbey, England
Source: *Baker 78, 84, 92; BioIn 3, 4, 11, 12, 14, 16, 19; CmOp; DcArts; DcBiPP; DcCom 77; DcCom&M 79; DcIrB 78, 88; DcNaB; IntDcOp; LinLib S; MusMk; NewAmDM; NewCol 75; NewEOp 71; NewGrDM 80; NewGrDO; NewOxM; NotNAT B; OxCMus; PenDiMP A; VicBrit*

Balfour, Arthur James
[1st Earl of Balfour]
English. Statesman
Prime minister, 1902-05; wrote *Balfour Declaration,* 1917, approving establishment of Jewish state in Palestine.
b. Jul 25, 1848 in East Lothian, Scotland
d. Mar 19, 1930 in Fisher's Hill, England
Source: *Alli SUP; BbD; BiD&SB; BiDInt; BiDPara; BioIn 12, 16, 17, 20; CamGEL; CamGLE; CelCen; ConAu 120; DcLEL; DcNaB 1922; DcTwHis; Dis&D; EncO&P 1, 2, 3; EncPaPR 91; EvLB; FacFETw; GrBr; HisDBrE; LegTOT; LuthC 75; NewC; OxCEng 67, 85, 95; TwCA, SUP; VicBrit; WhDW; WhLit; WorAl*

Baliles, Gerald L
American. Politician
Dem. governor of Virginia, 1986-90; succeeded by Douglas Wilder.
b. Jul 8, 1940 in Stuart, Virginia
Source: *AlmAP 88; BioIn 15; IntWW 91; WhoAm 86, 90; WhoAmL 85; WhoAmP 85, 87, 91; WhoSSW 86, 91; WhoWor 91*

Balin, Ina
[Ina Rosenberg]
American. Actor
TV movie "Children of An-Lac" detailed own story of airlifting orphans out of Saigon.
b. Nov 12, 1937 in New York, New York
d. Jun 20, 1990 in New Haven, Connecticut
Source: *BiE&WWA; BioIn 13, 17; ConTFT 9; FilmEn; FilmgC; ForYSC; HalFC 80, 84, 88; IntMPA 77, 80, 86; InWom; LegTOT; MotPP; NewYTBS 90; PseudN 82; WhoAmW 72; WhoHol A*

Balin, Marty
[Jefferson Airplane; Martyn Jerel Buchwald]
American. Singer, Songwriter
Founder, Jefferson Airplane/Starship, 1965-71, 75-85; wrote hits "It's No Secret;" "Fantastic Lover."
b. Jan 30, 1943 in Cincinnati, Ohio
Source: *Baker 84; BioIn 9, 13; RkOn 85; WhoAm 86, 90; WhoEnt 92; WhoRock 81; WhoRocM 82*

Ball, Edmund B
American. Manufacturer
With brother, Frank, launched can co., 1880; jars used for canning.
b. Oct 21, 1855 in Greensburg, Ohio
d. Mar 8, 1925 in Muncie, Indiana
Source: *Entr; NatCAB 20*

Ball, Edward
"Mr. Ed"
American. Business Executive
Built empire of banks, railroads, pine land; chief trustee of DuPont Trust, valued at nearly $2 billion.
b. Mar 21, 1888 in Tidewater, Virginia
d. Jun 24, 1981 in New Orleans, Louisiana
Source: *AnObit 1981; BioIn 3, 4, 5, 9, 10, 11, 12; Dun&B 79; NewYTBS 79, 81; St&PR 75; WhoSSW 75, 76*

Ball, Ernest
American. Composer
Compositions include "A Little Bit of Heaven"; "When Irish Eyes Are Smiling."
b. Jul 22, 1878 in Cleveland, Ohio
d. May 3, 1927 in Santa Ana, California
Source: *ASCAP 66; LegTOT; WorAl; WorAlBi*

Ball, Frank
American. Manufacturer
With brother, Edmund, started can co., 1880; jars used for canning.
b. Nov 24, 1857 in Greensburg, Ohio
d. Mar 19, 1943 in Muncie, Indiana
Source: *DcAmB S3; DcNAA; Entr; OhA&B*

Ball, George W(ildman)
American. Government Official
US permanent representative to UN, 1968.
b. Dec 21, 1909 in Des Moines, Iowa
d. May 26, 1994 in New York, New York
Source: *BioIn 13, 16; ColdWar 1; ConAu 73, 145; CurBio 62, 94N; IntWW 74, 91; WhAm 11; WhoAm 80, 82, 90; WhoAmP 91; WhoUSWr 88; WhoWor 74, 84; WhoWrEP 89*

Ball, John Dudley, Jr.
American. Author
Best known for mystery novel *In the Heat of the Night,* 1965, adapted into 1976 Oscar-winning film starring Sidney Poitier.
b. Jul 8, 1911 in Schenectady, New York
d. Oct 15, 1988 in Encino, California
Source: *AmAu&B; BioIn 14, 16; BlueB 76; ConAu 3NR, 7NR, 126; IntAu&W 76, 77, 82, 86; WhAm 9; WhoAm 74, 76, 78, 80, 82, 84, 86, 88; WhoWest 74, 76, 78; WhoWor 76, 80, 82, 89; WorAl; WorAlBi; WrDr 80*

Ball, Joseph H(urst)
American. Politician
Rep. senator, MN, 1940-49.
b. Nov 3, 1905
d. Dec 18, 1993 in Chevy Chase, Maryland
Source: *BiDrAC; BiDrUSC 89; BioIn 1, 10; ConAu 143; CurBio 94N; WhAmP*

Ball, Lucille (Desiree)
[Mrs. Gary Morton]
American. Actor, Comedian
Red-headed actress best known as Lucy Ricardo in TV sitcom "I Love Lucy," 1951-57; show won over 200 awards, including five Emmys.
b. Aug 6, 1911 in Jamestown, New York
d. Apr 26, 1989 in Los Angeles, California
Source: *AnObit 1989; BiDFilm, 81, 94; BiE&WWA; BioAmW; BioIn 2, 3, 4, 5, 6, 8, 9, 10, 11, 12, 13, 14, 15, 16, 17, 18, 20; BkPepl; BlueB 76; CelR; CmMov; ConTFT 3, 8; CurBio 58, 78, 89, 89N; DcArts; EncAFC; EncMcCE; EncMT; FacFETw; Film 2; FilmEn; ForYSC; FunnyW; Funs; GoodHs; GrLiveH; HalFC 84, 88; HerW; IntDcF 1-3, 2-3; IntMPA 84, 86, 88; IntWW 74, 75, 76, 77, 78, 79, 80, 81, 82, 83, 89, 89N; InWom, SUP; JoeFr; LegTOT; LesBEnT, 92; LibW; MGM; MotPP; News 89-3; NewYTBS 86, 89; OxCFilm; OxCPMus; QDrFCA 92; RadStar; ThFT; WebAB 74, 79; WhAm 10; WhoAm 78, 80, 82, 84, 86, 88; WhoAmW 89; WhoCom; WhoWor 78; WorAl; WorAlBi; WorEFlm*

Ball, Thomas
American. Sculptor
Greatest work equestrian statue of Washington, built in Boston Public Garden, 1869.
b. Jun 3, 1819 in Charlestown, Massachusetts
d. Dec 11, 1911 in Montclair, New Jersey
Source: *AmBi; ApCAB, X; ArtsNiC; BioIn 7, 9, 11; BriEAA; DcAmArt; DcAmB; DcNAA; Drake; HarEnUS; McGDA; NatCAB 5; NewYHSD; OxCAmH; OxCArt; OxDcArt; TwCBDA; WhAm 1; WhAmArt 85*

Ball, William
American. Director
Won Obie for *Ivanov,* 1959; received special Tony for contributions to theater, 1979.
b. Apr 29, 1931 in Chicago, Illinois
d. Jul 30, 1991 in Los Angeles, California
Source: *AnObit 1991; BiE&WWA; BioIn 8, 10, 17, 18, 20; BlueB 76; ConTFT 5, 10; CurBio 74, 91N; GrStDi; IntWW 74, 75, 76, 77, 78, 79, 80, 81, 82, 83, 89, 91, 93; NewYTBS 91; NotNAT; OxCAmT 84; PenDiDA 89; TheaDir; VarWW 85; WhAm 10; WhoAm 74, 76, 78, 80, 82, 84, 86; WhoThe 72, 77, 81; WhoWest 74, 76, 78, 80, 84; WhoWor 74*

Balla, Giacomo
Italian. Artist
Member, Italian Futurist Group, 1916-30; art emphasized movement, machines, warfare.
b. Jul 18, 1871 in Turin, Italy
d. Mar 1, 1958 in Rome, Italy
Source: *BioIn 4, 9, 12, 13; ConArt 77, 83; DcArts; FacFETw; IntDcAA 90; MacEA; McGDA; McGEWB; OxCArt; OxCTwCA; OxDcArt; PenDiDA 89; PhDcTCA 77*

Balladur, Edouard
French. Politician
Prime minister of France, 1993-95.
b. May 2, 1929 in Smyrna, Turkey
Source: *BiDFrPL; CurBio 94; IntWW 89, 91, 93; Who 94; WhoFr 79; WhoWor 95, 96, 97*

Ballantine, Ian (Keith)
American. Publisher
One of first to produce hardcover, paperback editions simultaneously; founded Ballantine Books, 1952.
b. Feb 15, 1916 in New York, New York
d. Mar 9, 1995 in Bearsville, New York
Source: *BioIn 3, 11; ConAmBL; CurBio 54, 95N; IntWW 89, 91, 93; LegTOT; NewYTBS 95; WhoAm 74, 76, 78, 80, 82, 84, 86, 88, 90, 92, 94, 95; WhoUSWr 88; WhoWor 74; WhoWrEP 89, 92, 95; WorAl; WorAlBi*

Ballantrae, Lord
[Bernard Edward Fergusson]
English. Author, Government Official
Governor-general, New Zealand, 1962-67; wrote *Beyond the Chindwin,* 1945.
b. May 6, 1911 in London, England
d. Nov 28, 1980 in London, England
Source: *AnObit 1980; ConAu 7NR, 102, 105; DcNaB 1971; HisEWW; IntWW 78, 79; IntYB 78, 79; WhoWor 74, 76*

Ballard, Florence
[The Supremes]
American. Singer
Member of original Supremes; grew up with Diana Ross.
b. Jun 30, 1943 in Detroit, Michigan
d. Feb 22, 1976 in Detroit, Michigan
Source: *BioIn 7, 8, 10; EncPR&S 74; InB&W 80, 85; InWom SUP; LegTOT*

Ballard, Hank
[The Midnighters; John Kendricks]
American. Singer
Had 1960 hit "The Twist," before Chubbie Checker.
b. Nov 18, 1936 in Detroit, Michigan
Source: *AmPS A, B; ConMus 17; EncPR&S 74, 89; EncRk 88; EncRkSt; IlEncBM 82; IlEncRk; InB&W 80, 85; LegTOT; PenEncP; RkOn 74, 84; RolSEnR 83; SoulM*

Ballard, Harold
Canadian. Hockey Executive
Controversial owner, Toronto Maple Leafs, 1961-90, Maple Leaf Gardens, 1961-90; Hall of Fame, 1977.
b. Jul 30, 1905 in Toronto, Ontario, Canada
d. Apr 11, 1990 in Toronto, Ontario, Canada
Source: *BioIn 16; FacFETw; NewYTBS 90*

Ballard, J(ames) G(raham)
English. Author
Wrote best-selling novel *Empire of the Sun,* 1984; most books are surrealistic fiction, with apocalyptic themes.
b. Nov 15, 1930 in Shanghai, China
Source: *Au&Arts 3; BioIn 10, 12, 13, 16; ConAu 15NR, 39NR; ConLC 36; ConNov 86, 91, 96; CurBio 88; CyWA 89; DcArts; DcLB 14; DcLEL 1940; DrAPF 91; EncSF 93; FacFETw; IntAu&W 89, 91, 93; IntWW 89, 91, 93; MajTwCW; OxCEng 85, 95; RfGEnL 91; RfGShF; RGTwCWr; TwCSFW 86, 91; TwCWr; Who 85, 88, 90, 92, 94; WhoAm 94, 95, 96; WhoWor 95, 96; WorAu 1950; WrDr 86, 92, 94, 96*

Ballard, Kaye
[Catherine Gloria Balotta]
American. Actor
Stage, TV comedienne, who starred in TV series, "The Mothers-in-Law," 1967-69.
b. Nov 20, 1926 in Cleveland, Ohio
Source: *BiE&WWA; BioIn 4, 8, 15; CelR; ConTFT 1, 3; CurBio 69; EncAFC; EncMT; FilmEn; FilmgC; FunnyW; HalFC 88; IntMPA 92, 94, 96; InWom SUP; JoeFr; LegTOT; NotNAT; WhoAm 74, 76, 78, 80, 82, 84; WhoAmW 74, 83; WhoEnt 92; WhoHol 92, A; WhoThe 77, 81; WhoWest 82*

Ballard, Louis W.
American. Composer
Compositions include many Native American themes; music curriculum specialist for the U.S Bureau of Indian Affairs.
b. Jul 8, 1931 in Miami, Oklahoma
Source: *Baker 78, 84; BioIn 9, 12; ConAmC 76, 82; NewAmDM; NewGrDA 86; NotNaAm*

Ballard, Robert Duane
American. Geologist, Explorer
Designer of underwater survey sleds that enabled him to locate the *Titanic,* 1985.
b. Jun 30, 1942 in Wichita, Kansas
Source: *AmMWSc 92; BioIn 14, 15; ConAu 112; CurBio 86; RAdv 14; WhoAm 90, 92, 94, 95, 96; WhoE 75, 95; WhoFrS 84; WhoScEn 94, 96*

Ballard, Russ(ell)
English. Singer, Musician
Singer, guitarist with Argent, 1969-74.
b. Oct 31, 1947 in Waltham Cross, England
Source: *RkOn 85*

Ballesteros, Seve(riano)
Spanish. Golfer
Turned pro, 1974; at age 23, youngest ever to win Masters, 1980; won Masters, 1983, British Open, 1979, 1984, 1988.
b. Apr 9, 1957 in Pedrena, Spain
Source: *BioIn 12, 13, 14, 15, 16; CelR 90; CurBio 80; IntWW 81, 82, 83; LegTOT; NewYTBS 80, 82, 83; Who 88, 90, 92, 94; WhoAm 92, 94, 95, 96, 97; WhoIntG; WhoWor 84, 87, 89, 91, 93, 95, 96*

Ballinger, Margaret
[Violet Margaret Livingstone Ballinger; Margaret Hodgson]
South African. Author, Politician
MP, representing black Africans; wrote *From Union to Apartheid, Trek to Isolation,* 1970.
b. Jan 11, 1894 in Glasgow, Scotland
d. Feb 7, 1980 in Cape Province, South Africa
Source: *AfSS 78, 79; AnObit 1980; ConAu 13NR, 61, 105; ContDcW 89; DcAfHiB 86; EncSoA; IntDcWB; IntWW 74, 75, 76, 77, 78, 79, 80; PenNWW A, B; PseudN 82; WhE&EA; WhoWor 74*

Ballou, Maturin Murray
American. Author, Editor
Editor, *Ballou's Pictorial,* 1851-59, early American illustrated paper.
b. Apr 14, 1820 in Boston, Massachusetts
d. Mar 27, 1895 in Cairo, Egypt
Source: *Alli, SUP; AmAu; AmAu&B; ApCAB; BbD; BiD&SB; BioIn 3; DcAmAu; DcAmB; DcLB 79; DcNAA; Drake; HarEnUS; JrnUS; NatCAB 7; OxCAmL 65, 83, 95; WhAm HS*

Balmain, Pierre Alexandre
French. Fashion Designer
Discovered by Gertrude Stein; fashions designed to be timeless, elegant; worn by Sophia Loren, Katherine Hepburn, etc.
b. May 18, 1914 in Saint-Jean-de-Maurienne, France
d. Jun 29, 1982 in Paris, France
Source: *AnObit 1982; CelR; ConAu 107; CurBio 54, 82; FairDF FRA; IntWW 74, 75, 76, 77, 78, 79, 80, 81, 82; NewYTBS 82; WhAm 8; Who 74, 82; WhoAm 82; WhoWor 78; WorAl; WorFshn*

Balopoulos, Michael
Greek. Political Leader
Colonel who led 1967 military coup to overthrow democratic govt.
b. 1920?
d. Mar 3, 1978 in Athens, Greece
Source: *BioIn 11; ObitOF 79*

Balsam, Artur
Polish. Pianist
Accompanist to celebrated artists; has recorded all works of Mozart, Haydn.
b. Feb 8, 1906 in Warsaw, Poland
Source: *ASCAP 80; Baker 78, 84, 92; BioIn 2, 20; IntWWM 77, 80, 85, 90; NewAmDM; NewGrDA 86; NewGrDM 80; NewYTBS 94; PenDiMP; WhAm 11; WhoAm 84, 86, 88; WhoAmM 83; WhoMus 72*

Balsam, Martin Henry
American. Actor
Won 1964 Oscar for *A Thousand Clowns.*
b. Nov 4, 1919 in New York, New York
d. Feb 13, 1996 in Rome, Italy
Source: *BiE&WWA; BioIn 12; CamGWoT; ConTFT 7; FilmgC; HalFC 84, 88; IntMPA 86, 92; IntWW 82, 83, 89, 91, 93; MotPP; MovMk; NotNAT; WhAm 11; WhoAm 74, 76, 78, 80, 82, 84, 86, 88, 90, 92, 94, 95, 96; WhoEnt 92; WhoHol A; WhoThe 81; WorAl; WorAlBi*

Baltard, Victor
French. Architect
Designed Parisian iron, glass structure: Les Halles Centrales, 1854-66.
b. 1805 in Paris, France
d. Jan 13, 1874
Source: *ArtsNiC; DcBiPP; MacEA; McGDA; WhoArch*

Balthus
[Comte Balthazar Klossowski de Rola]
French. Artist
Self-taught painter, noted for doll-like portraits of Miro, Derain, 1936.
b. Feb 29, 1908 in Paris, France
Source: *BioIn 4, 5, 6, 10, 11, 12, 13, 14, 15, 16, 17, 19, 20, 21; ConArt 77, 83, 89, 96; CurBio 79; DcArts; DcCAr 81; EncWB; IntWW 74, 75, 76, 77, 78, 79, 80, 81, 82, 83, 91; McGDA; OxCTwCA; OxDcArt; PhDcTCA 77; PseudN 82; WhoFr 79; WhoWor 74; WorArt 1950*

Baltimore, David
American. Chemist
Shared 1975 Nobel Prize in medicine for cellular research.
b. Mar 7, 1938 in New York, New York
Source: *AmDec 1980; AmMWSc 73P, 76P, 79, 82, 86, 89, 92, 95; BiESc; BioIn 10, 12, 13, 14, 15, 16, 17, 18, 20; CamDcSc; CurBio 83; EncWB; FacFETw; IntWW 76, 77, 78, 79, 80, 81, 82, 83, 89, 91, 93; LarDcSc; McGMS 80; NobelP; NotTwCS; Who 82, 83, 85, 88, 90, 92, 94; WhoAm 76, 78, 80, 82, 84, 86, 88, 90, 92, 94, 95, 96, 97; WhoAmJ 80; WhoE 74, 77, 79, 81, 83, 85, 86, 89, 91, 93, 95, 97; WhoFrS 84; WhoMedH; WhoNob, 90, 95; WhoScEn 94, 96; WhoTech 82, 84, 89, 95; WhoWor 78, 80, 82, 84, 87, 89, 91, 93, 95, 96, 97; WorAl; WorAlBi; WorScD*

Baltimore, George Calvert, Baron
English. Colonizer
Founded Maryland, 1632.
b. 1580 in Kipling, England
d. Apr 15, 1632 in London, England
Source: *Alli, SUP; AmBi; BioIn 1, 3, 5, 7, 8, 12, 13, 19; DcAmB; Drake; HarEnUS; LinLib S; MacDCB 78; OxCCan; TwCBDA; WebAB 74; WhAm HS*

Balukas, Jean
American. Billiards Player
Greatest woman pool player; won seven consecutive US Open Championships, 1976-83.
b. Jun 28, 1959 in New York, New York
Source: *BioIn 11, 12, 15; ConAu 111; GoodHs; InWom SUP; NewYTBS 74, 87; WhoAm 80, 82, 84, 86, 88, 92, 94, 95, 96, 97; WorAl*

Balzac, Honore de
French. Author
Developed the realistic novel; describes French society in masterpiece *Comedie Humaine,* 1841.
b. May 20, 1799 in Tours, France
d. Aug 18, 1850 in Paris, France
Source: *AtlBL; BbD; Benet 87, 96; BiD&SB; BioIn 1, 2, 3, 4, 5, 6, 7, 8, 9, 10, 11, 12, 13, 14, 15, 18, 19, 20, 21; BlmGEL; CasWL; CelCen; ChhPo S2; CrtSuMy; CyWA 58; DcArts; DcBiA; DcBiPP; DcEuL; DcLB 119; Dis&D;*

EncMys; EncSF, 93; EncWT; Ent; EuAu; EuWr 5; EvEuW; GrFLW; GuFrLit 1; LegTOT; LinLib L, S; MagSWL; McGEWB; McGEWD 72, 84; NewC; NewCBEL; NewGrDM 80; NinCLC 5, 35, 53; NotNAT B; Novels; OxCEng 67, 85, 95; OxCFr; OxCThe 67, 83; PenC EUR; PenEncH; RAdv 13-2; RComWL; REn; RfGShF; RfGWoL 95; ScF&FL 1, 92; ScFEYrs; ShSCr 5; SupFW; WhDW; WorAl; WorAlBi; WorLitC

Bambara, Toni Cade
[Miltonia Mirkin Cade]
American. Writer
Author of *Gorilla, My Love,* 1972.
b. Mar 25, 1939 in New York, New York
d. Dec 9, 1995 in Wallingford, Pennsylvania
Source: *AmWomWr 92, SUP; Au&Arts 5; Benet 96; BenetAL 91; BlkAWP; BlkLC; BlkWAm; BlkWr 1, 2; BlmGWL; ConAu 24NR, 49NR, 150; ConBlB 10; ConLC 19, 88; DcLB 38; DcTwCCu 5; DrAPF 80; InB&W 80, 85; LivgBAA; MajTwCW; ModWoWr; OxCAmL 95; OxCWoWr 95; RAdv 14; RfGAmL 94; RfGShF; SchCGBL; SelBAAf; WhoAfA 96; WhoBlA 85, 88, 90, 92, 94; WorAu 1975*

Bamberger, Louis
American. Merchant, Philanthropist
Founded L Bamberger & Co., 1892, one of largest US department stores.
b. May 15, 1855 in Baltimore, Maryland
d. May 11, 1944 in South Orange, New Jersey
Source: *BioIn 1; DcAmB S3; NatCAB 33; WhAm 2; WorAl; WorAlBi*

Bampton, Rose Elizabeth
[Mrs. Wilfred Pelletier]
American. Opera Singer
Contralto turned soprano; with NY Met., 1932-50; regular radio performer.
b. Nov 28, 1909 in Cleveland, Ohio
Source: *Baker 78, 84; BiDAmM; BioIn 13, 16; CurBio 40; IntWWM 90; InWom, SUP; MetOEnc; MusSN; NewAmDM; NewEOp 71; NewGrDA 86; WhoAm 90; WhoE 79; WhoEnt 92*

Bananarama
[Sarah Dallin; Siobhan Fahey; Keren Woodward]
English. Music Group
British invasion pop/rock group; had hit songs "Venus," 1986, "Cruel Summer," 1984.
Source: *DcArts; EncRk 88; EncRkSt; RkOn 85*

Bancroft, Anne
[Mrs. Mel Brooks; Anna Maria Luisa Italiano]
American. Actor
Won Oscar, Tony, 1962, for role of Annie Sullivan in *The Miracle Worker;* played Mrs. Robinson in *The Graduate,* 1967.
b. Sep 17, 1931 in New York, New York
Source: *BiDFilm, 81, 94; BiE&WWA; BioAmW; BioIn 4, 5, 6, 7, 10, 11, 12, 13, 15, 16, 21; BkPepl; BlueB 76; CamGWoT; CelR, 90; CnThe; ConTFT 1, 7; Ent; FilmEn; FilmgC; ForYSC; GangFlm; GrLiveH; HalFC 80, 84, 88; IntDcF 1-3, 2-3; IntMPA 75, 76, 77, 78, 79, 80, 81, 82, 84, 86, 88, 92, 94, 96; IntWW 74, 75, 76, 77, 78, 79, 80, 81, 82, 83, 89, 91, 93; InWom, SUP; ItaFilm; LegTOT; MiSFD 9; MotPP; MovMk; NotNAT; NotWoAT; OxCAmT 84; OxCFilm; OxCFr; WhoAm 74, 76, 78, 80, 82, 84, 86, 88, 90, 92, 94, 95, 96, 97; WhoAmW 58A, 64, 66, 68, 70, 72, 74, 77, 79, 81, 83, 85, 87, 89, 91, 93, 95, 97; WhoEnt 92; WhoHol 92, A; WhoThe 72, 77, 81; WhoWor 74, 78, 95, 96, 97; WorAl; WorAlBi; WorEFlm; WrDr 86*

Bancroft, Dave
[David James Bancroft]
"Banny"; "Beauty Bancroft"
American. Baseball Player
Shortstop, 1915-29, known for defensive play; batted over .300 three times; Hall of Fame, 1971.
b. Apr 20, 1892 in Sioux City, Iowa
d. Oct 9, 1972 in Superior, Wisconsin
Source: *BioIn 9, 10, 14, 15; WhoProB 73*

Bancroft, George
"Father of American History"
American. Author
Wrote 10-vol. *History of the US,* 1834-74.
b. Oct 3, 1800 in Worcester, Massachusetts
d. Jan 17, 1891 in Washington, District of Columbia
Source: *Alli, SUP; AmAu; AmAu&B; AmBi; AmSocL; ApCAB; BbD; BenetAL 91; BiAUS; BibAL; BiD&SB; BiDrUSE 71, 89; BiDTran; BioIn 3, 4, 5, 6, 7, 8, 9, 10, 11, 13, 14, 16, 19; CamGEL; CamGLE; CamHAL; CelCen; ChhPo; CyAL 2; CyEd; DcAmAu; DcAmB; DcAmDH 80, 89; DcAmMiB; DcAmSR; DcBiPP; DcEnA A; DcEnL; DcLB 1, 30, 59; DcLEL; DcNAA; Drake; EncAAH; EncAB-H 1974, 1996; EvLB; Film 2; HarEnUS; LinLib L, S; McGEWB; MorMA; NatCAB 3; OxCAmH; OxCAmL 65, 83, 95; OxCEng 67; OxCShps; PenC AM; PeoHis; RComAH; REn; REnAL; TwCBDA; WebAB 74, 79; WebE&AL; WhAm HS; WhAmP; WhDW; WhoHol B; WorAl; WorAlBi*

Bancroft, George
American. Actor
Known for both hero, villain roles: *Pony Express,* 1925; *The Bugle Sound,* 1942.
b. Sep 30, 1882 in Philadelphia, Pennsylvania
d. Oct 2, 1956 in Santa Monica, California
Source: *BioIn 4, 7, 17; CmMov; Film 2; FilmEn; FilmgC; ForYSC; GangFlm; HalFC 80, 84, 88; HolCA; MotPP; MovMk; NotNAT B; SilFlmP; TwYS; Vers A; WhoHol B; WhScrn 74, 77, 83; WorEFlm*

Band, The
[Rick Danko; Levon Helm; Garth Hudson; Richard Manuel; Robbie Robertson]
American. Music Group
Frequently worked with Bob Dylan; last concert filmed by Martin Scorsese as *The Last Waltz,* 1976.
Source: *BiDAmM; BioIn 8, 15, 16, 17; ConMuA 80A; ConMus 9; DcArts; EncFCWM 83; EncPR&S 74, 89; EncRk 88; EncRkSt; FacFETw; HarEnR 86; IlEncRk; NewAmDM; NewGrDA 86; NewYTBS 86; OxCPMus; PenEncP; RkOn 78; RolSEnR 83; WhoHol 92; WhoRock 81; WhoRocM 82*

Banda, Hastings Kamuzu
"Big Man of Malawi"
Malawian. Political Leader
First prime minister, Nyasaland (which became Malawi, 1964), 1963-66; president of Malawi, 1966-94.
b. Feb 1898 in Chiwengo, Malawi
Source: *BioIn 15; ConBlB 6; CurBio 63; DcAfHiB 86; DcCPSAf; EncSoA; FacFETw; InB&W 80; IntWW 83, 91; McGEWB; NewYTBE 71; WhDW; Who 85, 92; WhoGov 72; WhoWor 74*

Bandaranaike, S(olomon) W(est) R(idgeway) D(ias)
Ceylonese. Political Leader
Prime minister, Ceylon, 1956-59; promoted strong nationalist policies; established Sinhalese as country's official language; assassinated while in office.
b. Jan 8, 1899 in Colombo, Ceylon
d. Sep 26, 1959 in Colombo, Ceylon
Source: *BioIn 4, 5, 16, 20; DcNaB 1951; DcTwHis; FacFETw; WhAm 3*

Bandaranaike, Sirimavo Ratwatte Dias
Sri Lankan. Political Leader
World's first female prime minister, 1959-65, 1970-77.
b. Apr 17, 1916 in Kandy, Ceylon
Source: *BioIn 13, 16; ContDcW 89; CurBio 61; DcPol; DcTwHis; EncWB; FacFETw; FarE&A 78, 79, 80, 81; GoodHs; IntDcWB; IntWW 74, 75, 76, 77, 78, 79, 80, 81, 82, 83, 89, 91, 93; IntYB 80, 81; InWom SUP; NewYTBE 70; NewYTBS 80, 81, 82; Who 85, 92; WhoAmW 64, 66, 68; WhoWor 76, 95, 96, 97; WomWR; WorAl*

Bandeira, Manuel
[Filho Manuel Bandeira]
Brazilian. Poet, Journalist
Wrote verse vols. *Carnaval,* 1919.
b. Apr 19, 1886? in Recife, Brazil
d. Oct 13, 1968 in Rio de Janeiro, Brazil
Source: *Benet 87; BenetAL 91; BioIn 8, 10, 15, 16; ConAu 115; DcBrazL; EncLatA; EncWL 2, 3; LatAmWr;*

ModLAL; PenC AM; RAdv 14; TwCWr; WorAu 1950

Bandelier, Adolph Francis Alphonse
American. Archaeologist
Authority on Native Americans of the Southwest, ancient Mexico, Peru; wrote *The Delight Makers,* 1890.
b. Aug 6, 1840 in Bern, Switzerland
d. Mar 19, 1914 in Seville, Spain
Source: *Alli SUP; AmAu; AmAu&B; AmBi; ApCAB; BenetAL 91; BiD&SB; BilnAmS; BioIn 2, 3, 7, 9, 14, 15; DcAmAu; DcAmB; DcNAA; HarEnUS; InSci; NatCAB 26; NewCol 75; OxCAmH; OxCAmL 65, 83, 95; REnAL; REnAW; WebAB 74, 79; WhAm 1; WhNaAH*

Bandello, Matteo
[Matthew Bandello]
"A Prose Ariosto"
Italian. Author
Short stories imitate Boccaccio, are probable source of Shakespeare's *Romeo and Juliet.*
b. 1485 in Castelnuovo Scrivia, Italy
d. Sep 13, 1562 in Bassens, France
Source: *BbD; Benet 96; BiD&SB; CasWL; CroE&S; DcEuL; DcItL 1, 2; EuAu; EvEuW; LinLib L; NewC; NewCol 75; OxCEng 67, 85, 95; OxCFr; PenC EUR; RAdv 13-2; REn*

Banderas, Antonio
Spanish. Actor
Appeared in *Philadelphia,* 1993; *Four Rooms,* 1995; *Evita,* 1996.
b. Aug 10, 1960 in Malaga, Spain
Source: *BioIn 20, 21; ConTFT 13; DcHiB; EncEurC; IntMPA 94, 96; LegTOT; News 96, 96-2; WhoAm 96, 97; WhoHol 92*

Bando, Sal(vatore Leonard)
American. Baseball Player
Third baseman, 1966-81, known for defensive play; won three World Series with Oakland, 1970s.
b. Feb 13, 1944 in Cleveland, Ohio
Source: *Ballpl 90; BaseEn 88; BiDAmSp Sup; BioIn 9, 11; WhoAm 74, 76, 78, 80, 82, 84; WhoProB 73*

Bandy, Moe
American. Singer
Country singer who had hit "Hank Williams, You Wrote My Life," 1976.
b. 1944? in Meridian, Mississippi
Source: *BgBkCoM; BioIn 14, 15; EncFCWM 83; HarEnCM 87; IlEncCM; LegTOT; NewAmDM; NewGrDA 86; PenEncP; WhoAm 84, 86*

Bandy, Way
American. Designer
One of world's best known make-up artists; created look of 1970s; clients included Elizabeth Taylor, Nancy Reagan; died from AIDS.
b. Aug 9, 1941? in Birmingham, Alabama
d. Aug 13, 1986 in New York, New York
Source: *BioIn 11; ConAu 120, 123; NewYTBS 86*

Bane, Frank B
American. Government Official
First administrator of Social Security system, 1935.
b. 1894? in Smithfield, Virginia
d. Jan 23, 1983 in Alexandria, Virginia
Source: *BioIn 4; NewYTBS 83; WhoAm 80*

Banerjee, Victor
Indian. Actor
First Indian actor since Sabu to win world fame in Hollywood movie: *Passage to India,* 1986.
b. Oct 15, 1946 in Calcutta, India
Source: *BioIn 14; ConTFT 9; HalFC 88; NewYTBS 85*

Bangerter, Norman Howard
American. Politician
Rep. governor of Utah, 1985-93.
b. Jan 4, 1933 in Granger, Utah
Source: *AlmAP 88, 92; BioIn 14; IntWW 89, 91, 93; WhoAm 84, 86, 88, 90, 92, 94, 95, 96; WhoAmP 85, 87, 91; WhoWest 87, 89, 92; WhoWor 87, 89, 91*

Bangles, The
[Susanna Hoffs; Debbi Vicki Peterson; Michael Steele]
American. Music Group
Pop group; had number one hit single "Walk Like an Egyptian," top 10 hit "Manic Monday," from album *Different Light,* 1986.
Source: *BioIn 15, 16, 17; EncPR&S 89; EncRkSt; PenEncP*

Bangor, Edward Henry Harold Ward, Viscount
English. Journalist
BBC foreign correspondent, 1946-60; wrote *Number One Boy,* 1969.
b. Nov 5, 1905, England
Source: *Who 82, 83, 92*

Bangs, Lester
American. Critic, Author
Rock critic *Rolling Stone, Village Voice;* editor *Creem* magazine; recorded album *Juke Savages on the Brazos,* 1981.
b. Dec 1948
d. Apr 30, 1982 in New York, New York
Source: *BioIn 13; ConAu 106; NewGrDA 86; NewYTBS 82*

Bani-Sadr, Abolhassan
Iranian. Political Leader
First pres. elected in Iran's 2,500 year history, 1980; lost power to Khomeini, 1981.
b. Mar 22, 1933 in Hamadan Province, Persia
Source: *BioIn 12, 13, 16; ConAu 143; CurBio 81; IntWW 80, 81, 82, 91; IntYB 81, 82; MidE 80, 81, 82; NewYTBS 79, 80, 88; WhoWor 82, 84; WrDr 96*

Baniszewski, Gertrude Wright
American. Murderer
Known for torture murder of female boarder, 16 yr. old Sylvia Likens, 1965.
b. 1929 in Indiana
Source: *DrInf*

Bankhead, Dan(iel Robert)
American. Baseball Player
With Brooklyn, 1947-51; first black pitcher to appear in ML game—Aug 26, 1947.
b. May 3, 1920 in Empire, Alabama
d. May 2, 1976 in Houston, Texas
Source: *Ballpl 90; BioIn 10, 20; NewYTBS 76; ObitOF 79*

Bankhead, Tallulah Brockman
American. Actor
Flamboyant, husky-voiced actress; best known for Broadway success in *The Little Foxes,* 1939.
b. Jan 31, 1902 in Huntsville, Alabama
d. Dec 12, 1968 in New York, New York
Source: *BiDFilm; BiE&WWA; BioIn 12; CurBio 41, 53, 69; FamA&A; Film 1; FilmgC; InWom; MotPP; MovMk; NotAW MOD; NotWoAT; OxCFilm; OxCThe 83; PlP&P; ThFT; WebAB 74; WhAm 5; WhScrn 74; WorEFlm*

Bankhead, William Brockman
American. Politician
Dem. congressman from AL, 1917-40; Speaker of House, 1936-40; father of Tallulah.
b. Apr 12, 1874 in Moscow, Alabama
d. Sep 15, 1940 in Bethesda, Maryland
Source: *AmPolLe; BiDrAC; BiDrUSC 89; BioIn 1, 2, 4, 7, 14; CurBio 40; DcAmB S2; EncSoH; WebAB 74, 79; WhAm 1; WhAmP*

Banks, Dennis J.
American. Social Reformer
Champion of Native American rights; co-founded American Indian Movement, 1968.
b. Apr 12, 1937 in Leech Lake, Minnesota
Source: *BioIn 13; ConNews 86-4; CurBio 92; NotNaAm*

Banks, Ernie
[Ernest Banks]
American. Baseball Player
Shortstop, Chicago Cubs, 1953-71; had 512 career home runs; Hall of Fame, 1977.
b. Jan 31, 1931 in Dallas, Texas
Source: *AfrAmSG; Ballpl 90; BiDAmSp BB; BioIn 4, 5, 6, 7, 8, 9, 10, 11, 13, 14, 15, 16; BlueB 76; CurBio 59; Ebony 1;*

FacFETw; InB&W 80, 85; LegTOT; WhoAfA 96; WhoAm 74, 76, 78, 80, 82, 84, 86, 92, 94, 95, 96, 97; WhoBlA 75, 77, 80, 85, 88, 90, 92, 94; WhoMW 80, 82; WhoProB 73; WhoSpor; WhoWest 94, 96; WorAl; WorAlBi

Banks, Leslie
English. Actor, Director
Played villain in *The Most Dangerous Game,* 1932.
b. Jun 9, 1890 in Liverpool, England
d. Apr 21, 1952 in London, England
Source: *FilmAG WE; FilmEn; FilmgC; HalFC 80, 84, 88; IlWWBF; MovMk; NotNAT B; ObitT 1951; ODwPR 79; OxCThe 67; WhoHol B; WhoHrs 80; WhScrn 74, 77, 83; WhThe*

Banks, Monty
[Montague Banks; Mario Bianchi]
Italian. Actor, Director
Married to Gracie Fields; appeared in *A Bell for Adano,* 1945.
b. Jul 17, 1897 in Casene, Italy
d. Jan 7, 1950 in Arona, Italy
Source: *BioIn 2; EncAFC; Film 2; FilmEn; FilmgC; ForYSC; HalFC 80, 84, 88; IlWWBF; NotNAT B; ObitOF 79; QDrFCA 92; TwYS; WhoHol B; WhScrn 74, 77, 83*

Banks, Russell
American. Author, Poet
Works include, *Continental Drift,* 1985; *The Sweet Hereafter,* 1991.
b. Mar 28, 1940 in Newton, Massachusetts
Source: *BioIn 13, 14, 16, 17, 18, 19, 20; ConAu 15AS, 19NR, 52NR, 65; ConLC 37, 72; ConNov 86, 91; CurBio 92; DcLB 130; DrAPF 80, 91; IntAu&W 86, 89, 91, 93; IntvTCA 2; LegTOT; NewYTBS 89; OxCAmL 95; RAdv 14; WorAu 1980; WrDr 88, 90, 92*

Banks, Tony
English. Musician
Keyboardist, original member of Genesis.
b. Mar 27, 1950 in East Heathly, England
Source: *LegTOT; Who 92*

Banks, Tyra
American. Actor, Model
Appeared on TV's "The Fresh Prince of Bel Air," 1993-96.
b. Dec 4, 1973 in Inglewood, California
Source: *ConBlB 11; News 96, 96-3*

Banks, William (Venoid)
American. Broadcasting Executive
First black owner of an American television station; president and general manager, WGPR-TV, Detroit, 1975-85.
b. May 6, 1903 in Geneva, Kentucky
d. Aug 24, 1985 in Detroit, Michigan
Source: *BioIn 14; ConBlB 11; WhAm 9; WhoAdv 80; WhoAm 78; WhoBlA 77, 80, 85; WhoMW 80, 82*

Banky, Vilma
[Vilma Lonchit]
"The Hungarian Rhapsody"
American. Actor
Silent film actress who starred with Rudolph Valentino in *The Eagle,* 1925.
b. Jan 9, 1903 in Nagyrodog, Austria-Hungary
d. Mar 18, 1991 in Los Angeles, California
Source: *Film 2; FilmgC; HalFC 88; InWom SUP; MotPP; MovMk; ThFT; TwYS; WhoHol 92, A; WorEFlm*

Banneker, Benjamin
American. Mathematician, Inventor
Accurately calculated an eclipse, 1789; first black appointed to Capital Commission by pres., 1789.
b. Nov 9, 1731 in Ellicott Mills, Maryland
d. Oct 9, 1806 in Baltimore, Maryland
Source: *AfrAmAl 6; AmWrBE; ApCAB; BiDAmS; BiInAmS; BioIn 1, 2, 3, 4, 5, 6, 7, 8, 9, 10, 11, 13, 15, 16, 17, 18, 20, 21; BlkAmW 1; BlkMth; BlksScM; BlkwEAR; DcAmAu; DcAmNB; DcAmSR; Drake; EncAB-H 1974, 1996; EncCRAm; EncSoH; GayLesB; HarEnUS; InB&W 80, 85; LegTOT; McGEWB; NatCAB 5; NegAl 76, 83, 89; OxCAmL 83, 95; RComAH; SchCGBL; SelBAAf; SelBAAu; WebAB 74, 79; WhAm HS; WhAmP; WorAl; WorAlBi; WorInv*

Bannen, Ian
Scottish. Actor
Known for Shakespearean roles including film *Macbeth,* 1959.
b. Jun 29, 1928 in Airdrie, Scotland
Source: *BioIn 13; ConTFT 5; FilmAG WE; FilmEn; FilmgC; ForYSC; HalFC 80, 84, 88; IlWWBF; IntMPA 77, 78, 79, 80, 81, 82, 84, 86, 88, 92, 94, 96; IntWW 91, 93; ItaFilm; LegTOT; MotPP; MovMk; WhoEnt 92; WhoHol 92, A; WhoThe 72, 77, 81*

Banner, Bob
American. Producer, Director
Produced, directed TV series "Solid Gold," 1980-88.
b. Aug 15, 1921 in Ennis, Texas
Source: *BlueB 76; ConTFT 3; IntMPA 75, 76, 77, 78, 79, 80, 81, 82, 84, 86, 88, 92, 94, 96; LesBEnT 92; NewYTET; WhoAm 74, 76, 78, 80, 82, 84, 86, 88, 90, 92, 94, 95, 96, 97; WhoEnt 92; WhoWest 96; WhoWor 74*

Bannerman, Helen
Scottish. Children's Author
Wrote controversial classic *Story of Little Black Sambo,* 1900.
b. Feb 25, 1863? in Edinburgh, Scotland
d. Oct 13, 1946 in Edinburgh, Scotland
Source: *ConAu 111; InWom SUP; NewCBEL; SmATA 19; TwCChW 78*

Banning, Kendall
American. Author
Writings include *The Great Adventure,* 1925; *Our Army Today,* 1943.
b. Sep 20, 1879 in New York, New York
d. Dec 27, 1944
Source: *AmAu&B; AnMV 1926; BioIn 12; ChhPo, S2; CurBio 45; DcNAA; NatCAB 58; WhAm 2; WhE&EA; WhNAA*

Banning, Margaret Culkin
American. Author
Wrote over 30 novels on marriage, parenthood: *Echo Answers,* 1960.
b. Mar 18, 1891 in Buffalo, New York
d. Jan 4, 1982 in Tryon, North Carolina
Source: *AmAu&B; AmCath 80; AmNov; AmWomPl; AmWomWr; AnObit 1982; BenetAL 91; BiCAW; BkC 6; ConAu 4NR, 5R, 105; CurBio 40, 82, 82N; InWom, SUP; MinnWr; NewYTBS 82; OxCAmL 65, 83, 95; REnAL; TwCA, SUP; WhAm 8; WhE&EA; WhLit; WhNAA; WhoAm 74, 76, 78, 80, 82; WhoAmW 58, 61, 64, 66, 68, 70, 72, 74, 77, 79, 81; WhoWor 74; WrDr 80, 82*

Bannister, Constance Gibbs
American. Photographer
Gained worldwide recognition, 1940s-50s, as specialist in photographing babies.
b. Feb 11, 1919 in Ashland, Tennessee
Source: *CurBio 55; NewYTBE 72; WhoAm 78; WhoAmW 74*

Bannister, Edward Mitchell
American. Artist
First black artist to win first place at Philadelphia Centennial Exhibition, 1876.
b. 1833 in Saint Andrew's, New Brunswick, Canada
d. 1901 in Providence, Rhode Island
Source: *AfrA; AfroAA; BioIn 11; DcAmNB; InB&W 80; NegAl 83; NewYHSD; WhAm 4; WhoAmA 82N*

Bannister, Roger, Sir
English. Track Athlete, Physician
First to run mile under four minutes, 1954.
b. Mar 23, 1929 in Harrow, England
Source: *BioIn 3, 4, 5, 6, 7, 8, 9, 10, 12, 16, 21; BlueB 76; CurBio 56; FacFETw; InSci; IntWW 81, 82; LegTOT; NewYTBS 79; WhDW; Who 74, 82, 83, 85, 88, 90, 92; WhoTr&F 73; WhoWor 74, 91; WorAl; WorAlBi; WrDr 76, 80, 82, 84, 86, 88, 90, 92*

Bannon, Ann
American. Author
Wrote novel *I Am a Woman,* 1983.
b. Sep 1932 in Joliet, Illinois
Source: *GayLesB; GayLL*

Bannon, Jim
American. Actor
Fourth actor to star in *Red Ryder* western serials.
b. 1911 in Kansas City, Missouri
Source: *BioIn 4, 8; FilmEn; FilmgC; ForYSC; HalFC 80, 84, 88; LegTOT; WhoHol 92, A*

Banting, Frederick Grant, Sir
Canadian. Physician
With John MacLeod, won 1923 Nobel Prize for discovery of insulin; killed in plane crash.
b. Oct 17, 1891 in Alliston, Ontario, Canada
d. Feb 21, 1941 in Newfoundland, Canada
Source: *AsBiEn; BiESc; BiHiMed; BioIn 1, 3, 4, 5, 6, 7, 8, 9, 10, 11, 13; BkPepl; CurBio 41; DcNaB 1941; DcScB; FacFETw; InSci; LarDcSc; LinLib S; LngCTC; MacDCB 78; McGEWB; OxCMed 86; RAdv 14; WhoNob, 90, 95; WorAl; WorScD*

Bantock, Granville, Sir
English. Composer, Conductor
Music professor, Birmingham U, 1907-34; works often embrace Celtic, Oriental themes.
b. Aug 7, 1868 in London, England
d. Oct 16, 1946 in London, England
Source: *Baker 78, 84, 92; BioIn 1, 3, 4, 5, 8, 9, 10; CompSN, SUP; CurBio 46; DcCom&M 79; LinLib S; MusMk; NewGrDM 80; NewGrDO; NewOxM; ObitOF 79; OxCMus; OxDcOp; PenDiMP, A; WhE&EA*

Banville, John
Irish. Author
Novelist, works include, *Dr. Copernicus*, 1986; *The Book of Evidence*, 1989.
b. Dec 8, 1945 in Wexford, Ireland
Source: *Benet 96; BiDIrW; BioIn 13; ConAu 117, 128; ConLC 46; ConNov 86, 91, 96; CurBio 92; CyWA 89; DcIrL, 96; DcLB 14; IntAu&W 91, 93; IntWW 91; ModIrL; NewYTBS 90; OxCEng 95; OxCIri; RGTwCWr; WhoWor 91, 93, 95, 96, 97; WorAu 1985; WrDr 88, 90, 92, 94, 96*

Banzer-Suarez, Hugo
Bolivian. Political Leader
Pres. of Bolivia, 1971-78; overthrown in coup, Jul, 1978.
b. Jul 10, 1926 in Santa Cruz, Bolivia
Source: *BiDLAmC; BioIn 16; CurBio 73; DcCPSAm; EncWB; IntWW 74, 91; NewYTBE 71; WhoWor 74*

Bara, Theda
[Theodosia Goodman]
American. Actor
Known for silent screen vamp roles, 1914-19, such as Salome, Cleopatra.
b. Jul 20, 1892 in Cincinnati, Ohio
d. Apr 7, 1955 in Los Angeles, California
Source: *BiDFilm; DcAmB S5; Film 1; FilmgC; MotPP; MovMk; OxCFilm; TwYS; WebAB 74; WhAm 3; WhoHol B; WhScrn 74, 77; WorEFlm*

Barabbas
Biblical Figure
Robber who was released by crowd's demand in place of Jesus at crucifixion trial.
Source: *BioIn 1, 2, 3, 5, 11; LngCEL; NewCol 75; WebBD 83*

Barad, Jill E(likann)
American. Business Executive
President and CEO, Mattel, Inc., 1992—.
b. May 23, 1951 in New York, New York
Source: *CurBio 95; St&PR 91, 93, 96, 97; WhoAm 88, 90, 92, 94, 95, 96, 97; WhoAmW 89, 91, 93, 95, 97; WhoFI 89, 92, 94, 96; WhoWest 89, 94, 96*

Baraka, Amiri
[Imamu Amiri Baraka; Everett LeRoy Jones]
American. Poet, Dramatist
Wrote *Black Magic*, 1969; *It's Nation Time*, 1971.
b. Oct 7, 1934 in Newark, New Jersey
Source: *AfrAmAl 6; AfrAmW; AmCulL; AmWr S2; Benet 87, 96; BenetAL 91; BiDAfM; BiDNeoM; BioIn 14, 15, 16, 17, 19, 20; BlkAmP; BlkAmW 2; BlkAWP; BlkLC; BlkWr 1, 2; BroadAu; CamGLE; CamGWoT; CamHAL; CelR; CivR 74; ConAmD; ConAu 3BS, 27NR, 38NR, X; ConBlAP 88; ConBlB 1; ConDr 73, 77, 82, 88, 93; ConLC 1, 2, 3, 5, 10, 14, 33; ConNov 72, 76, 82; ConPo 75, 85, 91, 96; ConPopW; ConTFT 7; CroCAP; CrtSuDr; CurBio 70; CyWA 89; DcLB 5, 7, 16, 38, DS8; DcTwCCu 1, 5; DramC 6; DrAP 75; DrAPF 80; DrBlPA, 90; Ebony 1; EncWL, 2, 3; FacFETw; GrWrEL DR; InB&W 80, 85; IntAu&W 91; LegTOT; LivgBAA; LNinSix; MagSAmL; MajTwCW; McGEWB; McGEWD 72, 84; ModAL S2; ModBlW; MorBAP; NatPD 81; NegAl 76, 83, 89; NewCon; NewGrDJ 88, 94; NotNAT; OxCAmL 65; PenC AM; PlP&P A; PoeCrit 4; RAdv 1, 14, 13-1, 13-2; RComWL; RfGAmL 87, 94; SchCGBL; SelBAAf; SelBAAu; WebAB 74, 79; WebE&AL; WhoAfA 96; WhoAm 74, 84, 86, 90, 92, 94, 95, 96; WhoBlA 75, 77, 80, 90, 92, 94; WhoThe 77, 81; WorAlBi; WorAu 1950; WrDr 76, 86, 94*

Baranski, Christine
American. Actor
Plays Maryann Thorpe in TV's "Cybill," 1995—.
b. May 2, 1952 in Buffalo, New York
Source: *BioIn 13, 20; ConTFT 1, 4, 11; IntMPA 96; WhoAm 90, 92, 96, 97; WhoAmW 91, 93, 95, 97; WhoEnt 92; WhoHol 92*

Barany, Robert
Swedish. Physician, Scientist
Created field of otoneurology—inner ear equilibrium; won 1914 Nobel Prize for studies on the vestibular apparatus.
b. Apr 22, 1876 in Vienna, Austria
d. Apr 8, 1936 in Uppsala, Sweden
Source: *BiESc; BiHiMed; BioIn 3, 5, 9, 15, 20; DcScB; FacFETw; InSci; LarDcSc; NobelP; NotTwCS; OxCMed 86; WhE&EA; WhoLA; WhoNob, 90, 95*

Barbaja, Domenico
"Viceroy of Naples"
Italian. Impresario
Enormously successful mgr. of famed Italian opera houses, 1809-32.
b. 1778 in Milan, Italy
d. Oct 16, 1841 in Posilipo, Italy
Source: *Baker 84; MetOEnc; NewEOp 71*

Barbanell, Maurice
English. Journalist, Psychic
Edited *Psychic News; Two Worlds.*
b. May 3, 1902 in London, England
d. Jul 17, 1981
Source: *BiDPara; BiDPsy; ConAu 113; EncO&P 2, 3; EncPaPR 91; WhE&EA*

Barbarossa, Dave
[Bow Wow Wow]
Mauritian. Musician
Drummer whose tom-tom African ritual beat was key to group's sound.
Source: *EncRk 88; PenEncP; RkOn 85; RolSEnR 83; WhoAmA 91; WhsNW 85*

Barbeau, Adrienne
American. Actor
Starred in TV series "Maude," 1972-78; in movie *The Fog*, 1980.
b. Jun 11, 1945 in Sacramento, California
Source: *BioIn 12; ConTFT 4; HalFC 88; IntMPA 92; ItaFilm; LegTOT; VarWW 85; WhoEnt 92*

Barber, Bernard
American. Author, Educator
Best known for *Science and the Social Order*, 1952.
b. Jan 29, 1918 in Boston, Massachusetts
Source: *AmAu&B; AmMWSc 73S, 78S; ConAu 14NR, 65; WhoAm 74, 76, 78, 80*

Barber, Jerry
[Carl Jerome Barber]
American. Golfer
Turned pro, 1940; won PGA, 1961.
b. Apr 25, 1916 in Woodson, Illinois
d. Sep 23, 1994 in Glendale, California
Source: *BioIn 6, 20; CurBio 62, 94N; WhoGolf*

Barber, Red
[Walter Lanier Barber]
American. Sportscaster
Covered Cincinnati, 1934-38; Brooklyn, 1939-53; NY Yankees, 1953-66; dismissal by Yankees, 1966, raised

issue of sportscaster impartiality; Hall of Fame, 1978.
b. Feb 17, 1908 in Columbus, Mississippi
d. Oct 22, 1992 in Tallahassee, Florida
Source: *AnObit 1992; Ballpl 90; BiDAmSp OS; BioIn 1, 2, 3, 4, 9, 10, 12, 13, 14, 18, 19, 20; BioNews 74; ConAu 113, 141, X; CurBio 43, 93N; LegTOT; LesBEnT; LiveMA; News 93-2; NewYTBS 81, 84, 92; RadStar; SaTiSS; WhAm 10; WhoAm 92; WorAl; WorAlBi*

Barber, Samuel
American. Composer
First composer to win Pulitzer twice; best known for "Adagio on Strings," 1936.
b. Mar 9, 1910 in West Chester, Pennsylvania
d. Jan 23, 1981 in New York, New York
Source: *AmComp; AmCulL; AnObit 1981; ASCAP 66, 80; Baker 78, 84, 92; BiDAmM; BiDD; BioIn 1, 2, 3, 4, 5, 6, 7, 8, 12, 14, 16, 19, 20; BlueB 76; BriBkM 80; CelR; CmOp; CnOxB; CompSN, SUP; ConAmC 76, 82; ConAu 103; CpmDNM 79; CurBio 81N; DancEn 78; DcArts; DcCM; DcCom 77; DcCom&M 79; DcTwCCu 1; FacFETw; IntDcOp; IntWW 74, 75, 76, 77, 78, 79, 80; IntWWM 77, 80; LegTOT; LinLib S; McGEWB; MetOEnc; MusMk; NewAmDM; NewEOp 71; NewGrDA 86; NewGrDM 80; NewGrDO; NewOxM; NewYTBS 81; OxCAmH; OxCAmL 65; OxCMus; OxDcOp; PenDiMP A; RAdv 14; WebAB 74, 79; WhAm 7; WhDW; Who 74; WhoAm 74, 76, 78, 80; WhoMus 72; WhoWor 74; WorAl; WorAlBi*

Barbera, Joseph Roland
[Hanna and Barbera]
American. Cartoonist
With Bill Hanna, created cartoons "Huckleberry Hound"; "The Smurfs"; "The Flintstones."
b. Mar 24, 1911 in New York, New York
Source: *BioIn 16; ConAu 150; ConGrA 1; ConTFT 8; HalFC 88; IntMPA 86, 92; News 88-2; OxCFilm; SmATA 51; WhoAm 86, 90; WhoAmA 91; WhoEnt 92; WhoTelC; WorECar; WorEFlm*

Barbie, Klaus
[Klaus Altmann; Nikolaus Barbie, Jr]
"The Butcher of Lyon"
German. Government Official
Captain of Gestapo, Lyons, France, 1942-44; convicted war criminal, sentenced to life imprisonment, 1987.
b. Oct 25, 1913 in Bad Godesberg, Germany
d. Sep 25, 1991 in Lyon, France
Source: *AnObit 1991; BiDExR; BioIn 9, 13, 14, 15, 16; EncTR 91; EncWB; FacFETw; News 92, 92-2; NewYTBS 87, 91; WorAlBi*

Barbier, Jules
French. Librettist
Co-wrote, with Carre, texts for famous operas including Gounod's *Faust.*
b. Mar 8, 1825 in Paris, France
d. Jan 16, 1901 in Paris, France
Source: *Baker 84; BiD&SB; NewEOp 71; NewGrDO*

Barbieri, Fedora
Italian. Opera Singer
Mezzo-soprano with NY Met., 1950-68; admired as Carmen.
b. Jun 4, 1920 in Trieste, Italy
Source: *Baker 78, 84, 92; CmOp; CurBio 57; IntDcOp; IntWW 82, 91; IntWWM 90; MetOEnc; NewEOp 71; NewGrDM 80; NewGrDO; OxDcOp; PenDiMP; WhoAm 78; WhoMus 72; WhoOp 76; WhoWor 78, 82*

Barbirolli, John, Sir
English. Conductor
Succeeded Toscanini as permanent conductor, NY Philharmonic, 1937-43.
b. Dec 2, 1899 in London, England
d. Jul 28, 1970 in London, England
Source: *Baker 78, 84, 92; BioIn 1, 2, 4, 5, 6, 7, 8, 9, 11, 14; BriBkM 80; CmOp; CurBio 40, 70; DcArts; DcNaB 1961; FacFETw; GrBr; LegTOT; LinLib S; MetOEnc; MusMk; MusSN; NewAmDM; NewEOp 71; NewGrDA 86; NewGrDM 80; NewGrDO; NewYTBE 70; ObitOF 79; ObitT 1961; OxDcOp; PenDiMP; WhAm 5; WhDW; WorAl; WorAlBi*

Barboncito
[Little Bearded One]
American. Native American Leader
Signed the treaty with the US government which granted the Navajos the land on which they live today, 1868.
b. 1820 in Canon de Chelly, Arizona
d. Mar 16, 1871 in Canon de Chelly, Arizona
Source: *EncNAB; NotNaAm*

Barbour, Haley (Reeves)
American. Lawyer
Chairman of the Republican National Committee, 1993—.
b. Oct 22, 1947 in Yazoo City, Mississippi
Source: *CurBio 96; WhoAm 88, 95, 96, 97; WhoAmP 75, 77, 79, 81, 83, 85, 87, 89, 91, 93, 95; WhoWor 95, 96*

Barbour, John
Scottish. Clergy, Poet
Wrote epic poem *The Bruce,* 1375, celebrating Scottish emancipation from England.
b. 1316?
d. Mar 13, 1395 in Aberdeen, Scotland
Source: *Alli; BbD; BiD&SB; BioIn 1, 3, 6, 12, 21; BritAu; CasWL; Chambr 1; ChhPo; CrtT 1; DcBiPP; DcEnL; DcLB 146; DcLEL; DcNaB; EvLB; GrWrEL P; LinLib L, S; LngCEL; MouLC 1; NewC; NewCol 75; OxCEng 67; PenC ENG; REn; RfGEnL 91; WebE&AL*

Barbour, Walworth
American. Diplomat
US ambassador to Israel, 1961-73.
b. Jun 4, 1908 in Cambridge, Massachusetts
d. Jul 21, 1982 in Gloucester, Massachusetts
Source: *AnObit 1982; BioIn 5, 13, 16; BlueB 76; DcAmDH 80, 89; IntWW 74, 75; IntYB 78, 79, 80, 81, 82; NewYTBE 71; NewYTBS 82; WhAm 8; Who 74, 82, 83, 85, 88, 90, 92; WhoAmP 73, 75, 77, 79, 81; WhoGov 72; WhoWor 74*

Barboza, Anthony
American. Photographer
Commercial photographer known for his advertising and fashion photography.
b. May 10, 1944 in New Bedford, Massachusetts
Source: *ConBlB 10; ICPEnP A; IlBBlP; MacBEP; WhoAfA 96; WhoAm 94, 95, 96, 97; WhoAmA 86, 89, 91, 93; WhoE 93, 95, 97*

Barclay, Alexander
English. Poet
Known for *Ship of Fools,* 1509, based on Sebastian Brant's earlier satire.
b. 1475?
d. Jun 10, 1552 in Croydon, England
Source: *Alli; AtlBL; BiD&SB; BioIn 3, 11, 12, 20; BritAu; CamGEL; CamGLE; CasWL; Chambr 1; CroE&S; DcCathB; DcEnL; DcEuL; DcLB 132; DcLEL; DcNaB; EvLB; GrWrEL P; LinLib L; NewC; NewCBEL; NewCol 75; OxCEng 67, 85, 95; PenC ENG; REn; RfGEnL 91*

Barclay, McClelland
American. Artist, Illustrator
Illustrated stories for *Ladies Home Journal; Saturday Evening Post;* designed recruiting posters for both world wars; created "Fisher Body Girl."
b. May 9, 1893 in Saint Louis, Missouri
d. Jul 18, 1943, At Sea
Source: *BioIn 1, 14; CurBio 40, 46; IlrAm D; NatCAB 34; WhAm 2*

Barco Vargas, Virgilio
Colombian. Political Leader
Pres., Columbia, 1986-90, supported by U.S., began assault on country's drug cartel but lost people's mandate with resulting escalation of terrorist violence.
b. Sep 17, 1921 in Cucuta Norte de Santander, Colombia
d. May 20, 1997 in Bogota, Colombia
Source: *BioIn 15, 16; CurBio 90; DcCPSAm; IntWW 89; NewYTBS 86*

Bard, John
American. Physician
NYC's first health officer; established city's first quarantine station on Bedloe's (now Liberty) Island, 1700s.
b. Feb 1, 1716 in Burlington, New Jersey
d. Mar 20, 1799 in Hyde Park, New York

Source: *Alli; AmBi; ApCAB; BiInAmS; BioIn 3; DcAmB; DcAmMeB, 84; Drake; EncCRAm; HarEnUS; InSci; WebAB 74, 79; WhAm HS*

Bardeen, John
American. Physicist
Two-time Nobel Prize winner in physics: 1956, as coinventor of transistor; 1972, as codeveloper of theory of superconductivity.
b. May 23, 1908 in Madison, Wisconsin
d. Jan 30, 1991 in Boston, Massachusetts
Source: *AmMWSc 73P, 76P, 79, 82, 86, 89, 92; AnObit 1991; AsBiEn; BiESc; BioIn 4, 6, 8, 9, 10, 11, 14, 15, 16, 17, 18, 20; BlueB 76; CamDcSc; CurBio 57, 91N; EncWB; FacFETw; InSci; IntWW 74, 75, 76, 77, 78, 79, 80, 81, 82, 83, 89, 91N; LarDcSc; LegTOT; McGMS 80; NobelP; NotTwCS; RAdv 14; WebAB 74, 79; WebBD 83; WhAm 10; Who 74, 82, 83, 85, 88, 90; WhoAm 74, 76, 78, 82, 84, 86, 88, 90; WhoEng 80, 88; WhoFrS 84; WhoMW 74, 76, 78, 80, 82, 84, 86, 88, 90; WhoNob, 90, 95; WhoTech 82, 84, 89; WhoWor 74, 76, 78, 80, 82, 84, 87, 89, 91; WorAl; WorAlBi; WorInv; WorScD*

Barden, Don H.
American. Business Executive
Chairman and president, Barden Communications, Inc. (a Detroit-based cable television company), 1981-95.
b. Dec 20, 1943 in Detroit, Michigan
Source: *ConBlB 9; WhoAfA 96; WhoAm 94, 95, 96; WhoBlA 75, 77, 80, 85, 88, 90, 92, 94; WhoFI 94*

Bardis, Panos Demetrios
Greek. Sociologist, Author
Contributor to numerous journals, newspapers: *Encyclopedia of Campus Unrest,* 1971.
b. Sep 24, 1924 in Lefcohorion, Greece
Source: *AmMWSc 73S; ConAu 10NR; IntAu&W 82, 89, 91, 93; IntWW 91; IntWWP 82; WhoAm 74, 76, 78, 80, 82, 84, 86, 88, 90, 92, 94, 95, 96, 97; WhoMW 84, 90, 93, 96; WhoTech 89; WhoWor 74, 76, 87, 89; WrDr 82, 92*

Bardot, Brigitte
[Camille Javal]
French. Actor
French sex symbol best known for film *And God Created Woman,* 1956; retired from screen to become conservationist.
b. Sep 28, 1934 in Paris, France
Source: *BiDFilm, 81, 94; BioIn 4, 5, 6, 7, 8, 9, 10, 11, 12, 13, 14, 16; BkPepl; CelR; ContDcW 89; ConTFT 3; CurBio 60; DcArts; DcTwCCu 2; EncEurC; EncFash; EnvEnDr; FacFETw; FilmAG WE; FilmEn; FilmgC; ForYSC; GoodHs; HalFC 88; IntDcF 1-3, 2-3; IntDcWB; IntMPA 75, 76, 77, 78, 79, 80, 81, 82, 84, 86, 88, 92, 94, 96; IntWW 74, 75, 76, 77, 78, 79, 80, 81, 82, 83, 89, 91, 93; InWom, SUP; ItaFilm; LegTOT; MotPP; MovMk; OxCFilm; WhDW; WhoAmW 68, 70, 72, 74; WhoFr 79; WhoHol 92, A; WhoWor 74, 78, 80, 82, 87, 89, 91, 93, 95, 96, 97; WorAlBi; WorEFlm*

Barea, Arturo
Spanish. Author
Wrote trilogy *Forging of a Rebel,* 1946.
b. Sep 20, 1897 in Badajoz, Spain
d. Dec 24, 1957 in Faringdon, England
Source: *BioIn 4, 10; CasWL; ClDMEL 80; ConAu 111; EvEuW; LinLib L; LngCTC; ModSpP S; OxCSpan; RAdv 13-2; REn; TwCA SUP; TwCLC 14; TwCWr; WhE&EA*

Barenboim, Daniel
Israeli. Pianist, Conductor
Piano debut, age seven; led international orchestras since 1962; over 100 recordings as pianist, conductor.
b. Nov 15, 1942 in Buenos Aires, Argentina
Source: *Baker 78, 84, 92; BiDAmM; BioIn 6, 7, 8, 9, 10, 11, 12, 14, 15, 16; BriBkM 80; CelR, 90; CurBio 69; DcArts; DcTwCCu 3; EncWB; FacFETw; IntWW 74, 75, 76, 77, 78, 79, 80, 81, 82, 83, 89, 91, 93; IntWWM 77, 80, 90; MidE 78, 79, 80, 81, 82; MusSN; NewAmDM; NewGrDM 80; NewGrDO; NotTwCP; OxDcOp; PenDiMP; Who 74, 82, 83, 85, 88, 90, 92, 94; WhoAm 80, 82, 84, 86, 88, 90, 92, 94, 95, 96, 97; WhoEnt 92; WhoFr 79; WhoMus 72; WhoMW 92, 96; WhoWor 74, 78, 80, 82, 84, 87, 89, 91, 93, 95, 97; WhoWorJ 72, 78*

Barents, Willem
Dutch. Navigator
Searched for northeast passage to eastern Asia through waters later named for him, 1594-96.
b. 1550? in Terschelling, Netherlands
d. Jun 20, 1597
Source: *BioIn 18, 19, 20; Expl 93; HarEnUS; LegTOT; McGEWB; NewCol 75; OxCShps; WebBD 83; WhDW; WorAl; WorAlBi*

Barfield, Jesse Lee
American. Baseball Player
Outfielder, Toronto, 1981-89; NY Yankees 1989—; won AL home run title, 1986; won golden glove, 1987.
b. Oct 29, 1951 in Joliet, Illinois
Source: *BaseReg 86, 87*

Barfield, Velma
American. Criminal
First woman executed in US since 1962.
b. Oct 23, 1932? in Cumberland County, North Carolina
d. Nov 2, 1984 in Raleigh, North Carolina

Bari, Lynn
[Marjorie Schuyler Fisher]
American. Actor
Husky-voiced siren; played the "other woman" in B films, 1930s-40s.
b. Dec 18, 1913 in Roanoke, Virginia
d. Nov 20, 1989 in Goleta, California
Source: *AnObit 1989; BioIn 16; EncAFC; FilmEn; FilmgC; HalFC 88; HolP 30; IntMPA 80, 81, 82, 88; InWom SUP; MotPP; MovMk; NewYTBS 89; ThFT; WhoHol A*

Bar-Ilian, David Jacob
Israeli. Musician
Concert pianist, worldwide recitalist, 1960—.
b. Feb 7, 1930 in Haifa, Palestine
Source: *Baker 84; BioIn 13, 14; IntWWM 90; MusSN; NewAmDM; NewGrDA 86; PenDiMP; WhoAm 86; WhoE 85; WhoEnt 92; WhoMus 72*

Baring, Maurice
English. Author
Wrote autobiography, *Puppet Show of Memory,* 1922.
b. Apr 27, 1874 in London, England
d. Dec 14, 1945 in Inverness-Shire, England
Source: *Benet 87; BioIn 1, 4, 5, 7, 9, 13, 14, 15, 18; BkC 4; CamGLE; CasWL; CathA 1930; ChhPo, S1, S2, S3; ConAu 105; DcCathB; DcLB 34; DcLEL; DcNaB 1941; EncWL; EvLB; GrWrEL N; LngCTC; ModBrL; NewC; NewCBEL; NotNAT B; OxCEng 67, 85, 95; PenEncH; REn; RfGEnL 91; RGTwCWr; ScF&FL 1; ScFEYrs; TwCA, SUP; TwCLC 8; TwCWr; WebE&AL; WhAm 5; WhE&EA; WhLit; WhoHr&F; WhThe*

Baring-Gould, Sabine
English. Clergy
Wrote words to hymns, "Onward Christian Soldiers"; "Now the Day Is Over."
b. Jan 28, 1834 in Exeter, England
d. Jan 2, 1924 in Lew-Trenchard, England
Source: *BbD; BiD&SB; BioIn 4, 8, 9, 11, 12, 19; BritAu 19; CamGLE; CarSB; CathA 1930; CelCen; Chambr 3; ChhPo, S1, S3; DcArts; DcBiA; DcBiPP; DcEnA, A; DcEnL; DcLB 156; DcLEL; DcNaB 1922; EvLB; GrWrEL N; LinLib L, S; LngCTC; LuthC 75; NewC; NewCBEL; NewGrDM 80; Novels; OxCChiL; OxCEng 67, 85, 95; OxCMus; PenC ENG; RfGEnL 91; WebE&AL; WhLit*

Barker, Bernard L
American.
Recruited by E Howard Hunt as one of Watergate burglars, Jan 17, 1972.
b. 1917? in Havana, Cuba
Source: *BioIn 10, 11, 12; NewYTBS 74; PolProf NF*

Barker, Bob
[Robert William Barker]
American. TV Personality
Hosted TV game shows, "Truth or Consequences"; "The Price is Right."
b. Dec 12, 1923? in Darrington, Washington

Source: *BioIn 4, 10, 13; ConTFT 2; LegTOT; WhoAm 80, 82, 84, 86, 88, 90; WhoEnt 92; WhoWest 76, 78, 80; WhoWor 89*

Barker, Cliff
[Fabulous Five]
American. Basketball Player
Won two national championships at U of KY; member US Olympic team, won gold medal, 1948; in NBA, 1950-52.
b. Jan 15, 1921 in Yorktown, Indiana
Source: *BioIn 2; WhoBbl 73*

Barker, Clive
English. Author
Writes horror fiction; works include *The Damnation Game,* 1985, *The Inhuman Condition,* 1986.
b. Oct 5, 1952 in Liverpool, England
Source: *Au&Arts 10; BestSel 90-3; ConAu 121, 129; ConLC 52; ConPopW; ConTFT 13; DcArts; IntAu&W 91; IntMPA 94, 96; LegTOT; MajTwCW; RAdv 14; ScF&FL 92; TwCPaSc; WhoAm 94, 95, 96, 97; WhoWor 95, 96, 97; WorAu 1985; WrDr 92, 94, 96*

Barker, Doc
[Arthur Barker]
American. Criminal
Robber, murderer, kidnapper, captured by Melvin Purvis, 1935, killed in escape attempt, 1939.
b. 1899 in Aurora, Missouri
d. Jun 13, 1939 in Alcatraz, California
Source: *BioIn 1; DrInf*

Barker, Elliott
[Elliott Speer Barker]
American. Firefighter
Sent bear cub that survived forest fire to Washington, DC to represent US Forest Fire Service, 1950; Smokey Bear became national symbol for fire prevention.
b. Dec 25, 1886 in Moran, Texas
d. 1988 in Santa Fe, New Mexico
Source: *BioIn 11, 15, 16; ConAu 89; IntAu&W 76, 77*

Barker, Ernest, Sir
English. Educator, Political Scientist
First political science professor at Cambridge; wrote autobiogarphy *Age and Youth,* 1953.
b. Sep 23, 1874 in Woodley, England
d. Feb 11, 1960 in Cambridge, England
Source: *BioIn 1, 2, 3, 4, 5, 14; ConAu 93, 103; DcNaB 1951; EvLB; GrBr; LinLib L; LngCTC; NewC; NewCBEL; ObitOF 79; ObitT 1951; PenC ENG; TwCA SUP; WhE&EA; WhLit; WhoLA*

Barker, Fred
American. Criminal
Added Alvin Karpis to Barker gang; killed with mother in battle with FBI.
b. 1902 in Aurora, Missouri
d. Jan 16, 1935 in Oklawaha, Florida
Source: *DrInf*

Barker, George Granville
English. Author, Poet
Wrote in neo-romantic style; won Guinness Prize, 1962; Levinson Prize, 1965; wrote *Eros in Dogma,* 1944; *Collected Poems,* 1957.
b. Feb 26, 1913 in Loughton, England
d. Oct 27, 1991 in Itteringham, England
Source: *Au&Wr 71; BlmGEL; CasWL; ChhPo S2; CnE&AP; CnMWL; ConAu 7NR, 9R, 38NR, 135; ConLC 8; ConPo 70, 75; DcLEL; DrAF 76; DrAP 75; DrAPF 80; EncWL; GrWrEL P; IntAu&W 76, 77, 89, 91; IntWW 74, 75, 76, 77, 78, 79, 80, 81, 82, 83, 89, 91; IntWWP 77; LngCTC; MajTwCW; ModBrL, S1; NewC; NewCBEL; OxCEng 67, 85, 95; PenC ENG; REn; RGFMBP; TwCA SUP; TwCWr; WebE&AL; WhAm 10; WhE&EA; Who 74, 82, 83, 85, 88, 90, 92; WhoTwCL; WhoWor 74, 76, 78; WrDr 76, 86, 94N*

Barker, Herman
American. Criminal
Member, Kimes-Terrill Gang, early 1920s, robbed banks; committed suicide.
b. 1894 in Aurora, Missouri
d. Sep 19, 1927 in Newton, Kansas
Source: *DrInf*

Barker, Len
[Leonard Harold Barker, II]
American. Baseball Player
Pitcher, 1976-85; threw perfect game, May 15, 1981.
b. Jul 7, 1955 in Fort Knox, Kentucky
Source: *Ballpl 90; BaseReg 86; BioIn 12, 17*

Barker, Lex
[Alexander Chrichlow Barker, Jr]
American. Actor
Tenth actor to play Tarzan in five films, 1949-53.
b. May 8, 1919 in Rye, New York
d. Apr 11, 1973 in New York, New York
Source: *BioIn 9, 83*

Barker, Lloyd
American. Criminal
Only Barker brother who did not join a gang; jailed for robbing post office, 1922-47.
b. 1896 in Aurora, Missouri
d. 1949 in Colorado
Source: *DrInf*

Barker, Ma
[Arizona Donnie Clark Barker]
"Kate"
American. Criminal
Planned bank robberies with sons; ran hideout in OK for escaped convicts.
b. 1872 in Springfield, Missouri
d. Jan 16, 1935 in Oklawaha, Florida
Source: *WhoFla*

Barker, Ronnie
English. Actor, Comedian
Starred in British TV series "The Two Ronnies"; "Porridge"; "Sorry."
b. Sep 25, 1929 in Bedford, England
Source: *ConTFT 7, 81*

Barker, Sue
English. Tennis Player
Won French Open, 1976; known for devastating forehand shot.
b. Apr 19, 1956 in Paignton, England
Source: *BioIn 11; WhoIntT*

Barkin, Ellen
American. Actor
Supporting film roles include *Down by Law,* 1986; *The Big Easy,* 1987.
b. Apr 16, 1955 in New York, New York
Source: *BioIn 13, 14, 15, 16; ConNews 87-3; ConTFT 6, 13; HolBB; IntMPA 92; IntWW 93; LegTOT; WhoAm 90, 94, 95, 96, 97; WhoAmW 95, 97; WhoEnt 92*

Barkla, Charles Glover
English. Scientist
Studied Roentgen radiation; won 1917 Nobel Prize in physics.
b. Jun 27, 1877 in Widness, England
d. Oct 23, 1944 in Edinburgh, Scotland
Source: *AsBiEn; BiESc; BioIn 3, 4, 5, 7, 14, 15, 20; DcNaB 1941; DcScB; Dis&D; FacFETw; InSci; LarDcSc; NewCol 75; NotTwCS; WhE&EA; WhoNob, 90, 95; WorScD*

Barkley, Alben William
American. US Vice President
Dem. con., 1912-26; Truman's vp, 1949-53.
b. Nov 24, 1877 in Graves County, Kentucky
d. Apr 30, 1956 in Lexington, Virginia
Source: *AmPolLe; BiDrAC; BiDrUSC 89; BiDrUSE 71, 89; BioIn 1, 2, 3, 4, 5, 7, 8, 9, 10, 12, 14, 17; CurBio 41, 49, 56; DcAmB S6; DcAmTB; EncAB-A 6; EncSoH; LinLib S; NatCAB 42; OxCAmH; VicePre; WebAB 74, 79; WhAm 3; WhAmP; WorAl*

Barkley, Charles Wade
American. Basketball Player
Forward, Philadelphia, 1984-92, Phoenix, 1992—; known as outspoken, argumentive player; part of 1992 Olympic Dream Team; NBA MVP, 1993; NBA All-Star MVP, 1991.
b. Feb 20, 1963 in Leeds, Alabama
Source: *AfrAmBi 2; BiDAmSp Sup; BioIn 14, 15, 16; CurBio 91; News 88-2; NewYTBS 84, 91; OfNBA 87; WhoAfA 96; WhoAm 90, 92, 94, 95, 96, 97; WhoBlA 92, 94; WhoWest 94, 96; WhoWor 95, 96; WorAlBi*

Bar Kokhba, Simon
Hebrew. Revolutionary
Led Jewish revolt against Roman domination, 131-135, claiming to be second Messiah.

d. 135
Source: *BioIn 3, 6, 9; WebBD 83*

Barks, Carl
American. Cartoonist
Illustrated Donald Duck, Uncle Scrooge McDuck comic strips.
b. Mar 27, 1901 in Merrill, Oregon
Source: *BioIn 15; ConAu 115; EncACom; SmATA 37; WorECom*

Barlach, Ernst Heinrich
German. Sculptor, Dramatist
Wrote powerful symbolist-realistic plays including *Der Blaue Boll,* 1926; works banned by Nazis.
b. Jan 2, 1870 in Holstein, Germany
d. Jan 24, 1938 in Gustrow, Germany
Source: *AntBDN A; CasWL; ClDMEL 47; EncWL 2; McGDA; McGEWB; McGEWD 84; ModGL; OxCArt; OxCThe 83; OxCTwCA; PenC EUR; PhDcTCA 77; REn; WorECar*

Barlow, Howard
American. Conductor
Noted conductor on several radio shows; led CBS Symphony, 1927-43; Voice of Firestone, 1943-59.
b. May 1, 1892 in Plain City, Ohio
d. Jan 31, 1972 in Portland, Oregon
Source: *ASCAP 66; Baker 78, 84, 92; BiDAmM; BioIn 1, 3, 4, 9, 10; CmpEPM; ConAmC 76, 82; CurBio 40, 54, 72, 72N; NewAmDM; NewGrDA 86; NewYTBE 72; RadStar; SaTiSS; WhAm 5*

Barlow, Joel
American. Diplomat, Journalist
Friend of Thomas Paine; best-known poem *The Hasty-Pudding,* 1793.
b. Mar 24, 1754 in Redding, Connecticut
d. Dec 24, 1812 in Zarnowiec, Poland
Source: *Alli; AmAu; AmAu&B; AmBi; AmWrBE; AmWr S2; ApCAB; Benet 87, 96; BenetAL 91; BibAL; BiD&SB; BioIn 1, 2, 5, 6, 7, 8, 9, 10, 12, 13, 14, 16, 17; BlkwEAR; CamGEL; CamGLE; CamHAL; CasWL; Chambr 3; ChhPo; CnDAL; CyAL 1; DcAmAu; DcAmB; DcAmC; DcAmDH 80, 89; DcAmSR; DcArts; DcEnL; DcLB 37; DcLEL; DcNAA; Dis&D; EncAB-H 1974, 1996; EncEnl; EncUnb; EvLB; GrWrEL P; HarEnUS; LinLib L, S; McGEWB; NatCAB 3; NinCLC 23; OxCAmH; OxCAmL 65, 83, 95; OxCEng 67, 85, 95; PenC AM; PoChrch; RAdv 14, 13-1; REn; REnAL; RfGAmL 87, 94; TwCBDA; WebAB 74, 79; WebE&AL; WhAm HS; WhAmP*

Barnaby, Ralph S
American. Author, Artist
Bronze busts are in US Naval Academy Mariner's Museum; wrote *How to Make and Fly Paper Airplanes,* 1968.
b. Jan 21, 1893 in Meadville, Pennsylvania
Source: *AuBYP 3; BioIn 14, 15; ConAu 61; NewYTBS 86; SmATA 9*

Barnack, Oskar
German. Inventor
Designed the first commercially available precision miniature camera, the Leica 1, 1924.
b. Nov 1, 1879 in Lynow, Germany
d. Jan 16, 1936 in Bad Nauheim, Germany
Source: *DcTwDes; FacFETw; ICPEnP; MacBEP*

Barnard, Chester Irving
American. Business Executive, Government Official
Pres., United Service Organizations (USO), 1942-45.
b. Nov 7, 1886 in Malden, Massachusetts
d. Jun 7, 1961 in New York, New York
Source: *BioIn 5, 6, 7, 18; DcAmB S7; NatCAB 46; WebBD 83; WhAm 4*

Barnard, Christiaan Neethling
South African. Surgeon
Performed first human heart transplant, Dec 3, 1967, on Louis Washkansky.
b. Oct 8, 1922 in Beaufort West, South Africa
Source: *AfSS 78, 79, 80, 81, 82; AsBiEn; BiESc; BioIn 13, 14, 15, 16; CelR, 90; ConAu 14NR, 61; CurBio 68; EncSoA; EncWB; FacFETw; IntAu&W 77, 91; IntWW 74, 75, 76, 77, 78, 79, 80, 81, 82, 83, 89, 91, 93; NotTwCS; WhDW; Who 74, 82, 83, 85, 88, 92, 94; WhoWor 74, 76, 78, 80, 82, 84, 87, 89, 91, 93, 95; WorAl; WorAlBi; WrDr 92*

Barnard, Edward Emerson
American. Astronomer, Educator
Pioneered celestial photography; discovered 16 comets, Jupiter's fifth satellite.
b. Dec 16, 1857 in Nashville, Tennessee
d. Feb 6, 1923 in Williams Bay, Wisconsin
Source: *AmBi; ApCAB; AsBiEn; BiDAmS; BiDSA; BiESc; BioIn 2, 7, 8, 12, 13, 14, 15, 16, 18, 21; CamDcSc; DcAmB; DcNAA; DcScB; HarEnUS; InSci; LarDcSc; LinLib S; McGEWB; NatCAB 7; NewCol 75; TwCBDA; WebAB 74, 79; WhAm 1; WhDW*

Barnard, Frederick Augustus Porter
American. Educator
Pres., Columbia U, 1864-89; founded Barnard College to extend education to women.
b. May 5, 1809 in Sheffield, Massachusetts
d. Apr 27, 1889 in New York, New York
Source: *Alli, SUP; AmAu&B; AmBi; ApCAB; BiDAmEd; BiDAmS; BiDSA; BiInAmS; BioIn 11, 12, 21; CyAL 1; CyEd; DcAmAu; DcAmB; DcBiPP; DcNAA; Drake; HarEnUS; InSci; LinLib S; LiveMA; McGEWB; NatCAB 6; OxCAmH; OxCAmL 65; TwCBDA; WebAB 74, 79; WebBD 83; WhAm HS; WorAl*

Barnard, George Grey
American. Sculptor
His most important works: 31 statues in Pennsylvania Capitol Building.
b. May 24, 1863 in Bellefonte, Pennsylvania
d. Apr 24, 1938 in New York, New York
Source: *AmBi; ApCAB SUP, X; BioIn 2, 4, 5, 6, 8, 11, 15; BriEAA; DcAmArt; DcAmB S2; HarEnUS; LinLib S; OxCAmH; OxCAmL 65, 83, 95; OxCArt; PeoHis; PhDcTCA 77; REnAL; WebAB 74, 79; WhAm 1; WhAmArt 85*

Barnard, Henry
American. Educator
First US Commissioner of Education, 1867-70.
b. Jan 24, 1811 in Hartford, Connecticut
d. Jul 5, 1900 in Hartford, Connecticut
Source: *Alli, SUP; AmAu; AmBi; AmSocL; ApCAB; BbD; BiAUS; BiDAmEd; BiD&SB; BioIn 1, 2, 3, 5, 10, 11, 13, 14, 17, 19; CyAL 1, 2; CyEd; DcAmAu; DcAmB; DcNAA; Drake; EncAB-H 1974, 1996; HarEnUS; LinLib L, S; McGEWB; MemAm; NatCAB 1; OxCAmH; RAdv 14, 13-3; TwCBDA; WebAB 74, 79; WhAm HS*

Barnardo, Thomas John
Irish. Social Reformer
Pioneer in care of destitute children; opened Dr. Barnardo's Homes for Boys, 1870.
b. Jul 4, 1845 in Dublin, Ireland
d. Sep 19, 1905 in Surbiton, Ireland
Source: *BioIn 3, 4, 6, 7, 8, 9, 10, 12, 16, 17; ChhPo S1; DcIrB 78, 88; DcNaB S2; LngCTC; LuthC 75; NewC; NewCol 75; OxCChiL; OxCMed 86*

Barnes, Billy
[William Christopher Barnes]
American. Lyricist, Composer
Wrote songs "Too Long at the Fair," "Make a Little Magic."
b. Jan 27, 1927 in Los Angeles, California
Source: *ASCAP 80; BiE&WWA; NotNAT*

Barnes, Binnie
[Gertrude Maude Barnes]
English. Actor
Starred as Catherine Howard in *The Private Life of Henry VIII,* 1933, with Charles Laughton.
b. Mar 25, 1905 in London, England
Source: *BioIn 8, 11, 17; EncAFC; Film 2; FilmEn; FilmgC; HalFC 80, 84, 88; HolP 30; InWom SUP; ItaFilm; LegTOT; MotPP; MovMk; ThFT; What 2; WhoHol 92, A; WhoThe 77A; WhThe*

Barnes, Clair Cortland
American. Hostage
One of 52 held by terrorists, Nov 1979 - Jan 1981.
Source: *NewYTBS 81*

Barnes, Clive Alexander
English. Journalist, Critic, Author
Well-known dance, drama critic; with *NY Post* since 1978.
b. May 13, 1927 in London, England
Source: *AuNews 2; CamGWoT; CelR 90; ConAu 26NR, 77; ConTFT 3; CurBio 72; IntAu&W 89; IntWW 74, 91; NotNAT; OxCAmT 84; OxCThe 83; Who 85, 92; WhoAm 86, 90, 97; WhoEnt 92; WhoThe 81; WrDr 86, 92*

Barnes, Djuna
[Lydia Steptoe]
American. Author, Journalist
Writings influenced by James Joyce and T S Eliot; wrote novel *Nightwood,* 1933.
b. Jun 12, 1892 in Cornwall-on-Hudson, New York
d. Jun 18, 1982 in New York, New York
Source: *AmAu&B; WhoTwCL; WhoWor 74; WomNov; WorAlBi; WrDr 76, 80, 82*

Barnes, Edward Larrabee
American. Architect
Designed prefabricated aluminum house, 1948.
b. Apr 22, 1915 in Chicago, Illinois
Source: *AmArch 70; BioIn 4, 5, 9, 12, 13; BlueB 76; BriEAA; ConArch 80, 87, 94; IntDcAr; IntWW 74, 75, 76, 77, 78, 79, 80, 81, 82, 83, 89, 91, 93; MacEA; McGDA; WhoAm 74, 76, 78, 80, 82, 84, 86, 88, 90, 92, 94, 95, 96, 97; WhoAmA 80, 82, 84, 86, 89, 91, 93; WhoE 86, 95; WhoTech 89; WhoWor 74*

Barnes, Ernest William
English. Clergy
Bishop of Birmingham, 1924-53; wrote controversial *The Rise of Christianity,* 1947.
b. Apr 1, 1874 in Cheshire, England
d. Nov 29, 1953 in Sussex, England
Source: *BioIn 1, 3, 12, 14; DcNaB 1951; GrBr; LuthC 75; ObitOF 79; ObitT 1951; WhE&EA; WhLit; WhoLA*

Barnes, Jim
[James Barnes]
"Long Jim"
English. Golfer
Touring pro, early 20th c; won PGA, 1916, US Open, 1921, British Open, 1925; charter member, Hall of Fame, 1940.
b. 1887 in Lelant, England
d. May 24, 1966 in East Orange, New Jersey
Source: *BioIn 7; WhoGolf*

Barnes, Joanna
American. Actor, Author
Wrote *Pastora,* 1980; appeared in movie *Spartacus,* 1960.
b. Nov 15, 1934 in Boston, Massachusetts
Source: *ConAu 57; ConTFT 6; FilmEn; FilmgC; ForYSC; HalFC 80, 84, 88; LegTOT; MotPP; WhoAm 74, 76, 78, 80, 82, 90, 92, 94, 95, 96, 97; WhoAmW 95, 97; WhoHol 92, A; WhoWest 94, 96*

Barnes, Julian Patrick
English. Author
Best known for novel *Flaubert's Parrot,* 1984; TV critic, 1977-86.
b. Jan 19, 1946 in Leicester, England
Source: *BioIn 15, 16; CamGLE; ConAu 19NR, 102; ConLC 42; ConNov 86, 91; CurBio 88; CyWA 89; DcLP 87A; IntAu&W 91; IntWW 91; TwCCr&M 91; Who 92; WorAu 1980; WrDr 86, 92*

Barnes, Lee
American. Track Athlete
Pole vaulter; won gold medal, 1924 Olympics.
b. Jul 16, 1906 in Salt Lake City, Utah
Source: *WhoTr&F 73*

Barnes, Leonard John
English. Author
Among his books, *African Renaissance,* 1969; *Africa in Eclipse,* 1971.
b. Jul 21, 1895 in London, England
Source: *ConAu 29R, P-2*

Barnes, Margaret Ayer
American. Author, Dramatist
Wrote Pulitzer novel *Years of Grace,* 1930.
b. Apr 8, 1886 in Chicago, Illinois
d. Oct 26, 1967 in Cambridge, Massachusetts
Source: *AmAu&B; AmWomD; AmWomPl; AmWomWr; ArtclWW 2; BenetAL 91; BioAmW; ConAmA; ConAu 21R, 25R; DcLB 9; DcLEL; InWom, SUP; OxCAmL 65, 83, 95; REnAL; TwCA, SUP; WhAm 4; WhNAA; WhoAmW 58, 64, 66, 68, 70; WomWWA 14*

Barnes, Peter
English. Dramatist
Wrote award-winning play with a "playful nightmare effect," *The Ruling Class,* 1968.
b. Jan 10, 1931 in London, England
Source: *BioIn 10, 12, 13, 17; CamGLE; CamGWoT; ConAu 12AS, 33NR, 34NR, 65; ConBrDr; ConDr 73, 77, 82, 88, 93; ConLC 5, 56; ConTFT 5, 14; CrtSuDr; CyWA 89; DcLB 13; DcLEL 1940; EncWT; IntAu&W 76, 77, 82, 91, 93; IntDcT 2; IntvTCA 2; MajTwCW; RGTwCWr; Who 82, 83, 85, 88, 90, 92, 94; WhoThe 72, 77, 81; WhoWor 76; WrDr 76, 80, 82, 84, 86, 88, 90, 92, 94, 96*

Barnes, Wade
American. Actor, Writer
Films include *Annie Hall,* 1977, *Diner,* 1982; has written plays for TV, radio.
b. May 15, 1917 in Alliance, Ohio
Source: *ASCAP 66, 80; ConTFT 4; IntAu&W 89; WhoEnt 92; WhoUSWr 88; WhoWrEP 89, 92*

Barnes-Taeuber, Irene
American. Sociologist
Work with husband Conrad Taeuber, contributed to founding of demography as a field.
b. Dec 25, 1906 in Meadville, Missouri
d. Feb 24, 1974 in Hyattsville, Maryland

Barnet, Charlie
[Charles Daly Barnet]
"Mad Mab"
American. Bandleader, Jazz Musician
Saxist, vocalist; led big-name band, 1930s-40s; theme song, "Cherokee" by Ray Noble.
b. Oct 26, 1913 in New York, New York
d. Sep 4, 1991 in San Diego, California
Source: *AllMusG; AnObit 1991; Baker 92; BgBands 74; BiDAmM; BiDJaz; BioIn 2, 7, 9, 12, 16, 17, 18, 19; CmpEPM; EncJzS; IlEncJ; LegTOT; NewAmDM; NewGrDA 86; NewGrDJ 88, 94; NewYTBS 91; OxCPMus; PenEncP; WhoHol 92; WhoJazz 72*

Barnet, Sylvan M., Jr.
American. Author, Educator
Chm., English dept., Tufts University, 1954—; wrote *A Dictionary of Litera ry Dramatic & Cinematic Terms,* 1971.
b. Dec 11, 1926 in New York, New York
Source: *ConAu 1R, 4NR; WhoAm 86, 90*

Barnet, Will
American. Artist, Educator
Painter, printmaker who calls style Abstract Reality; professor, Cooper Union Art School, 1945-78.
b. May 25, 1911 in Beverly, Massachusetts
Source: *AmArt; BioIn 1, 2, 6, 7, 8, 9, 10, 13, 14, 15; CurBio 85; DcAmArt; DcCAA 71, 77, 88, 94; PrintW 83, 85; WhAmArt 85; WhoAm 74, 76, 78, 80, 82, 84, 86, 88, 90, 92, 94, 95, 96, 97; WhoAmA 73, 76, 78, 80, 82, 84, 86, 89, 91, 93; WhoE 74*

Barnetson, William Denholm
[Lord Barnetson of Crowborough]
English. Journalist
Chm., Reuters, Ltd., 1968-79.
b. Mar 21, 1917 in Edinburgh, Scotland
d. Mar 12, 1981 in London, England
Source: *AnObit 1981; Au&Wr 71; ConAu 103; DcNaB 1981; DcTwBBL; IntAu&W 76, 77, 82; IntWW 74, 75, 78; IntYB 78; NewYTBS 81; Who 74; WhoFI 74, 75, 77, 79; WhoWor 74, 76, 78, 80, 82*

Barnett, Marvin Robert
American. Business Executive
Has worked in various capacites for visually handicapped organizations since 1944.
b. Oct 31, 1916 in Jacksonville, Florida
Source: *BioIn 2; WhoAm 82; WhoE 74*

Barnett, Ross Robert
American. Politician
Governor of MS, 1960-64; known for racism; attempted to defy US courts; caused riots, 1960-62.
b. Jan 22, 1898 in Standing Pine, Mississippi
d. Nov 6, 1987 in Jackson, Mississippi
Source: *BiDrGov 1789; BioIn 5, 6, 8, 9, 11, 15, 16; CurBio 61, 88; NewYTBS 87; PolProf K; WhoAmP 73, 75, 77, 79, 81*

Barnett, Steve
American. Anthropologist
Studies habits of American consumers for nation's largest corporations.
b. Aug 23, 1942
Source: *BioIn 15; FifIDA; NewYTBS 86*

Barney, Lem(uel Jackson)
American. Football Player
Seven-time all-pro defensive back, Detroit, 1967-77; defensive rookie of year, 1967.
b. Sep 8, 1945 in Gulfport, Mississippi
Source: *BiDAmSp Sup; InB&W 80; WhoAfA 96; WhoAm 78; WhoBlA 77, 80, 94; WhoFtbl 74*

Barney, Natalie Clifford
American. Author
Hostess of celebrated Parisian literary salon, 1920s-30s; wrote risque memoirs.
b. Oct 31, 1876 in Dayton, Ohio
d. Feb 2, 1972 in Paris, France
Source: *ConAu 33R; DcLB 4; GayLesB; IntDcWB; NewYTBE 72; NotAW MOD; ScF&FL 1; WomFir*

Barnhart, Clarence L(ewis)
American. Lexicographer
Co-editor, *The World Book Dictionary,* 1976.
b. Dec 30, 1900 in Plattsburg, Missouri
d. Oct 24, 1993 in Peekskill, New York
Source: *AmAu&B; BioIn 2, 3, 11, 14, 16, 19, 20; ConAu 13R, 143; CurBio 54, 94N; DrAS 74F; NewYTBS 77; SmATA 48, 78; WhoAm 74, 76, 78, 80, 82, 84, 86, 88, 90, 92, 94, 95, 96, 97; WhoUSWr 88; WhoWor 74; WhoWrEP 89, 92, 95; WorAl; WorAlBi*

Barnum, P(hineas) T(aylor)
[Barnum and Bailey]
American. Circus Owner
Opened "The Greatest Show on Earth," 1871, with flashy ads, freak shows; coined expression "There's a sucker born every minute."
b. Jul 5, 1810 in Bethel, Connecticut
d. Apr 7, 1891 in Bridgeport, Connecticut
Source: *Alli, SUP; AmAu&B; AmBi; AmCulL; ApCAB; BbD; BiDAmBL 83; BiD&SB; BioIn 1, 2, 3, 4, 5, 6, 7, 8, 9, 10, 11, 12, 13, 14, 15, 16, 17, 19, 20; BlmGEL; CnThe; DcAmAu; DcAmB; DcAmTB; DcArts; DcNAA; Drake; EncAB-H 1974, 1996; EncWT; Ent; HarEnUS; LinLib L, S; LngCEL; McGEWB; MnBBF; NatCAB 3; NewCol 75; NewYTBS 86; NotNAT A, B; OxCAmH; OxCAmL 65, 95; OxCPMus; OxCThe 67; REn; REnAL; REnAW; TwCBDA; WebAB 74, 79; WebBD 83; WhAm HS; WorAl*

Baron, Samuel
American. Musician, Conductor
Noted flutist; led Bach Aria Group, 1980-97.
b. Apr 27, 1925 in New York, New York
d. May 16, 1997 in New York, New York
Source: *Baker 84, 92; IntWWM 77, 80, 85; NewAmDM; NewGrDA 86; NewGrDM 80; WhoAm 74, 76, 78, 80, 82, 84, 86, 88, 90, 92, 94, 95, 96, 97; WhoAmJ 80; WhoAmM 83; WhoWor 74; WhoWorJ 72, 78*

Barr, Alfred Hamilton, Jr.
"The Pope"
American. Museum Director, Art Historian
First and most influential director, Museum of Modern Art, NYC, 1929-43.
b. Jan 28, 1902 in Detroit, Michigan
d. Aug 15, 1981 in Salisbury, Connecticut
Source: *AmAu&B; AnObit 1981; BioIn 3, 5, 6, 7, 8, 9, 12, 13, 14, 16; BlueB 76; ConAu 49, 105; CurBio 61, 81; FacFETw; IntWW 74, 75, 76, 77, 78, 79, 80, 81, 82; OxCAmH; WhAm 8; WhE&EA; Who 74, 82; WhoAm 74, 76, 78; WhoAmA 73, 76, 78, 80, 82, 82N, 84N, 86N, 89N, 91N, 93N; WhoArt 80, 82*

Barr, Amelia Edith Huddleston
American. Author, Journalist
Wrote historical fiction: *Remember the Alamo,* 1888.
b. Mar 29, 1831 in Lancaster, England
d. Mar 10, 1919 in Richmond Hill, New York
Source: *NotAW; OxCAmL 83*

Barr, Joseph W(alker)
American. Banker, Government Official, Politician
Dem. congressman from IN, 1959-61; Secretary of the Treasury, 1968-69.
b. Jan 17, 1918
d. Feb 23, 1996 in Playa del Carmen, Mexico
Source: *BiDrAC; BiDrUSC 89; BiDrUSE 89; BioIn 5, 6, 7, 8, 10, 11; BlueB 76; CurBio 96N; IntWW 74, 75, 76, 77, 78, 79, 80, 81, 82, 83, 89, 91, 93; WhAm 11; WhoAm 74, 76, 78, 80, 82, 84, 86, 88, 90, 92, 94, 95, 96; WhoFI 74, 75, 77, 79, 81, 83; WhoWor 74, 78, 89, 91, 93*

Barr, Stringfellow
American. Author, Educator
Pres., St. John's College, 1937-46, who initiated great books curriculum.
b. Jan 15, 1897 in Suffolk, Virginia
d. Feb 3, 1982 in Alexandria, Virginia
Source: *AmAu&B; AnObit 1982; BenetAL 91; BioIn 1, 2, 3, 4, 12, 13, 15; ConAu 1NR, 1R, 106; CurBio 40, 82, 82N; DrAS 74H; IntWW 79; IntYB 78, 79, 80, 81; LinLib L, S; NewYTBS 82; OxCAmL 65, 83, 95; REnAL; TwCA SUP; WhAm 10; WhoAm 74, 76, 78, 80; WhoWor 74*

Barr, William Pelham
American. Government Official
US Attorney General, 1991-93, succeeding Richard L. Thornburgh.
b. May 23, 1950 in New York, New York
Source: *CurBio 92; IntWW 93; NewYTBS 90, 91; WhoAm 90, 92, 94, 95, 96; WhoAmL 92, 94, 96; WhoE 93, 95*

Barraclough, Geoffrey
English. Author, Educator
Writings include *The Mediaeval Empire,* 1950.
b. May 10, 1908 in Bradford, England
d. Dec 26, 1984 in Burford, England
Source: *AnObit 1984; BioIn 10, 14, 20; ConAu 101, 114; DcNaB 1981; NewYTBS 85; WhAm 8; Who 74, 82, 83, 85; WhoAm 76, 78; WhoWor 74, 76; WorAu 1950; WrDr 80, 82, 84, 86*

Barragan, Luis
Mexican. Architect
Often considered Mexico's greatest architect; awarded Pritzker Prize, 1980.
b. 1902 in Guadalajara, Mexico
d. Nov 22, 1988 in Mexico City, Mexico
Source: *BioIn 13, 14, 16, 17, 18, 21; ConArch 80, 87, 94; DcArts; DcTwCCu 4; DcTwDes; FacFETw; IntDcAr; MacEA; NewYTBS 86; WhAm 9; WhoAm 82; WhoWor 89*

Barras, Paul Francois Jean Nicolas, Comte de
French. Politician
Helped to overthrow Robespierre, 1794; arranged for marriage between Josephine, Napoleon.
b. Jun 30, 1755 in Fox-Amphoux, France
d. Jan 29, 1829 in Chaillot, France
Source: *DcBiPP; DcInB; Dis&D; LinLib S; McGEWB; OxCFr; WhDW*

Barrasso, Tom
[Thomas Barrasso]
American. Hockey Player
Goalie, Buffalo, 1983-88-; won Calder Trophy, Vezina Trophy, 1984; Goalie, Pittsburgh Penguins, 1988—; has won two Stanley Cups with Penguins, 1991, 1992 .
b. Mar 31, 1965 in Boston, Massachusetts
Source: *BiDAmSp BK; BioIn 13; HocReg 87; NewYTBS 83; WhoSpor*

Barrault, Jean-Louis
French. Actor, Director
Best known for contributions to French theater; director, Theatre de France, 1959-68.
b. Sep 8, 1910 in Vesinet, France
d. Jan 22, 1994 in Paris, France
Source: *BiE&WWA; BioIn 14, 17, 19, 20; CamGWoT; ClDMEL 80; CnThe; ConAu 105, 143; CurBio 94N; DcArts; DcTwCCu 2; EncEurC; EncWT; Ent; FacFETw; FilmAG WE; FilmEn; FilmgC; GrStDi; HalFC 80, 84, 88; IntDcF 1-3, 2-3; IntDcT 3; IntWW 74, 75, 76, 77, 78, 79, 80, 81, 82, 83, 89, 91, 93; LegTOT; LinLib L; MetOEnc; MovMk; NewYTBS 94; NotNAT A; OxCAmT 84; OxCFilm; OxCFr; OxCThe 67, 83; OxDcOp; REn; TheaDir; WhDW; Who 74, 82, 83, 85, 88, 90, 92, 94; WhoFr 79; WhoHol 92, A; WhoOp 76; WhThe; WorEFlm*

Barre, Raymond
French. Government Official
Prime minister of France, 1976-81.
b. Apr 12, 1924 in Saint-Denis, France
Source: *BiDFrPL; BioIn 11, 12, 15, 16; CurBio 77; EncWB; IntWW 74, 75, 76, 77, 78, 79, 80, 81, 82, 83, 89, 91, 93; IntYB 78, 79, 80, 81, 82; NewYTBS 76, 88; Who 82, 83, 85, 88, 90, 92, 94; WhoFr 79; WhoWor 74, 76, 78, 80, 82, 84, 87, 89, 91, 93; WorAl; WorAlBi*

Barrett, Edward Ware
American. Educator, Editor
Editorial director, *Newsweek,* 1933-50.
b. Jul 3, 1910 in Birmingham, Alabama
d. Oct 23, 1989 in Greenwich, Connecticut
Source: *BioIn 1, 2, 4, 8, 13; BlueB 76; ConAu 130; CurBio 47, 90, 91N; DrAS 74E, 78E; IntAu&W 89; IntWW 74, 75, 76, 77, 78, 79, 80, 81, 82, 83, 89; IntYB 78, 79, 80, 81, 82; LEduc 74; St&PR 75, 87; WhAm 10; WhoAm 74, 76, 78; WhoE 74, 75; WrDr 76*

Barrett, John L
American. Radio Performer
Original voice of the Lone Ranger on radio, early 1930s.
b. 1913
d. May 1, 1984 in Buffalo, New York
Source: *BioIn 13*

Barrett, Rona
[Rona Burstein; Mrs. William A Trowbridge]
American. Journalist
Gossip columnist since 1957; fan magazines *Rona Barrett's Hollywood, Rona Barrett's Gossip* sold over one million copies, 1974.
b. Oct 8, 1936 in New York, New York
Source: *AuNews 1; BioIn 8, 10, 12, 13; BioNews 74; BkPepl; ConAu 103; ConTFT 4; GoodHs; HalFC 88; IntMPA 86, 92, 94, 96; InWom SUP; LesBEnT 92; NewYTET; WhoAm 78; WhoAmW 72; WhoEnt 92; WhoHol 92*

Barrett, Stan
American. Stunt Performer
Had fastest ever flat run speed—739.666 mph—in missile-powered vehicle, 1979.
b. 1944 in Saint Louis, Missouri
Source: *BioIn 12*

Barrett, Syd
[Pink Floyd; Roger Keith Barrett]
English. Singer, Songwriter
Founded, named Pink Floyd, 1964; released two solo albums, early 1970s.
b. Jan 4, 1946 in Cambridge, England
Source: *ConMuA 80A; IlEncRk; LegTOT; OnThGG; PenEncP; RolSEnR 83*

Barrett, William Christopher
American. Philosopher
One of best known American philosophers; introduced European existentialism to US after WW II.
b. Dec 30, 1913 in New York, New York
d. Sep 8, 1992
Source: *AnObit 1992; ConAu 11NR, 139; ConLC 27, 76; CurBio 82; WhoAm 84, 86, 90*

Barrett, William Edmund
American. Author
Two of his novels, *The Left Hand of God,* 1951, and *The Lilies of the Field,* 1962, were made into movies.
b. Nov 16, 1900 in New York, New York
d. Sep 17, 1986 in Denver, Colorado
Source: *AmAu&B; AmCath 80; Au&Wr 71; BenetAL 91; BioIn 3, 4; BkC 5; CathA 1952; ConAu 5R; IntAu&W 76; NewYTBS 86; REnAL; WhAm 9; WhoAm 74, 76; WhoWor 74, 76, 78*

Barrie, Barbara
[Barbara Ann Berman]
American. Actor
Films include *Breaking Away,* 1979; *Private Benjamin,* 1980.
b. May 23, 1931 in Chicago, Illinois
Source: *ConTFT 3; ForYSC; HalFC 88; IntMPA 92, 94, 96; LegTOT; NotNAT; WhoAm 82, 88; WhoAmW 81; WhoHol 92, A; WhoThe 77, 81; WorAlBi*

Barrie, James Matthew, Sir
Scottish. Author
Best known for *Little Minister,* 1897; *Peter Pan,* 1904.
b. May 9, 1860 in Kirriemuir, Scotland
d. Jun 19, 1937 in London, England
Source: *Alli SUP; AtlBL; BbD; BiD&SB; BioIn 1, 2, 3, 4, 5, 6, 8, 9, 10, 11, 12, 13, 14, 15, 16, 18, 19, 20; BritPl; CarSB; CasWL; Chambr 3; ChhPo, S1, S2, S3; CnMD; CnThe; CyWA 58; DcBiA; DcEnA, A; DcLEL; DcNaB 1931; Dis&D; EncWL; EncWT; Ent; EvLB; FacFETw; FamAYP; FilmgC; GrBr; JBA 34; LinLib L, S; LngCEL; LngCTC; McGEWB; McGEWD 72, 84; ModBrL; ModWD; NewC; NewCBEL; NewCol 75; NotNAT A, B; OxCEng 67; OxCThe 67, 83; PenC ENG; PlP&P; RAdv 1, 13-2; REn; REnWD; TwCA, SUP; TwCChW 78; TwCWr; WebE&AL; WhDW; WhE&EA; WhLit; WhoChL; WhoStg 1906, 1908; WhoTwCL; WhScrn 77, 83; WhThe; YABC 1*

Barrie, Mona
[Mona Smith]
English. Actor
Starred in 1933 films *Never Give a Sucker an Even Break, Cass Timberlane.*
b. Dec 18, 1909 in London, England
Source: *FilmEn; FilmgC; ForYSC; HalFC 80, 84, 88; IntMPA 75, 76, 77, 78, 79, 80, 81, 82, 84, 86, 88; MovMk*

Barrie, Wendy
[Marguerite Wendy Jenkins]
English. Actor
Radio, TV talk show hostess; films include *Private Life of Henry VIII,* 1933; *Hound of Baskervilles,* 1939.
b. Apr 18, 1912 in London, England
d. Feb 2, 1978 in Englewood, New Jersey
Source: *BioIn 11; DcAmB S10; EncAFC; FilmEn; FilmgC; GangFlm; HalFC 80, 84, 88; IlWWBF; IntMPA 77; InWom SUP; LegTOT; MotPP; MovMk; NewYTBS 78; ObitOF 79; ThFT; WhoHol A; WhoThe 81N; WhScrn 83*

Barrientos, Maria
Spanish. Opera Singer
Soprano; starred at Met. Opera, NYC, 1916-21.
b. Mar 10, 1883 in Barcelona, Spain
d. Aug 8, 1946 in Ciboure, France
Source: *Baker 84; BioIn 14; CmOp; InWom SUP; PenDiMP*

Barrios, Francisco Javier
[Francisco Javier Jimenez]
Mexican. Baseball Player
Pitcher, Chicago White Sox, 1974-81.
b. Jun 10, 1953 in Hermosillo, Mexico
d. Apr 9, 1982 in Hermosillo, Mexico

Barris, Chuck
American. TV Personality, Producer
Created, produced "The Dating Game," 1965-73; "The Newlywed Game," 1966-74; created, starred in "The Gong Show."
b. Jun 2, 1929 in Philadelphia, Pennsylvania
Source: *BioIn 8, 10, 11, 12, 14; BioNews 74; ConAu 109; ConTFT 6; IntAu&W 91; LesBEnT 92; NewYTET; WhoAm 78, 80, 82; WhoHol 92; WrDr 86, 92*

Barron, Blue
American. Bandleader
Led popular, stylized dance band, 1930s-60s.
b. Mar 22, 1911 in Cleveland, Ohio
Source: *AmPS A, B; BgBands 74; CmpEPM; PenEncP*

Barron, Clarence Walker
American. Publisher, Editor
Published *Wall Street Journal,* starting 1901; *Barron's Financial Weekly,* starting 1921.
b. Jul 2, 1855 in Boston, Massachusetts
d. Oct 2, 1928 in Battle Creek, Michigan
Source: *AmBi; ApCAB X; DcAmB S1; DcNAA; EncAJ; EncTwCJ; NatCAB 21; WebAB 74, 79; WhAm 1*

Barros, Joao de
"The Portuguese Livy"
Portuguese. Historian
Considered first great Portuguese historian; wrote *Decadas da Asia,* 1552-1615, about country's explorations.
b. 1496 in Viseu, Portugal
d. Oct 20, 1570 in Ribeira de Litem, Portugal
Source: *BiD&SB; BioIn 13; CasWL; DcAfHiB 86; DcBiPP; DcCathB; EvEuW; NewCol 75; PenC EUR; WebBD 83*

Barrow, Clyde
[Bonnie and Clyde]
"Public Enemy 1 of the Southwest"
American. Outlaw
With Bonnie Parker, accused of 12 murders during two-year crime spree in Southwest.
b. May 24, 1909 in Telice, Texas
d. May 23, 1934 in Gibsland, Louisiana
Source: *BioIn 8, 9, 12; DrInf; EncACr; LegTOT; REnAW; WorAl; WorAlBi*

Barrow, Ed(ward Grant)
American. Baseball Executive
NY Yankees business mgr., 1921-39, pres., 1939-45; Hall of Fame, 1953; known for switching Babe Ruth from pitching to outfield.
b. May 10, 1868 in Springfield, Illinois
d. Dec 15, 1953 in Port Chester, New York
Source: *Ballpl 90; BiDAmSp BB; BioIn 1, 2, 3, 7, 14, 15; DcAmB S5; LegTOT; ObitOF 79; WhoProB 73*

Barrow, Errol Walton
Barbadian. Political Leader
Prime minister, Barbados, 1961-76, 1986-87; led island to independence, Nov, 1966.
b. Jan 21, 1920 in Saint Lucy, Barbados
d. Jun 1, 1987 in Bridgetown, Barbados
Source: *BiDLAmC; BioIn 8; CurBio 68, 87; InB&W 80; IntWW 74, 75, 76, 77, 78, 79, 80, 81, 82, 83; IntYB 78, 79, 80, 81, 82; WhAm 11; Who 74, 82, 83, 85; WhoGov 72; WhoWor 74, 76, 80, 82, 87*

Barrow, Keith E
American. Singer, Songwriter
Popular gospel composer; formed the Soul Shakers.
b. Sep 27, 1954 in Chicago, Illinois
d. Oct 22, 1983 in Chicago, Illinois
Source: *ConAu 111; WhoBlA 80*

Barrow, Ruth Nita, Dame
Barbadian. Nurse, Social Reformer
Promoted worldwide health care; investigated S Africa's apartheid.
b. Nov 15, 1916, Barbados
d. Dec 19, 1995 in Bridgetown, Barbados
Source: *BiDrAPH 79; IntWW 91; WhAm 11; Who 88, 90, 92; WhoAm 94, 95, 96; WhoAmW 95; WhoWor 93, 95, 96; WomFir*

Barrows, Marjorie (Ruth)
[Jack Alden; Noel Ames]
American. Author, Editor
Magazine editor, 1922-66, whose writings include *Little Red Balloon,* 1979.
b. 1902? in Chicago, Illinois
d. Mar 29, 1983 in Evanston, Illinois
Source: *AmAu&B; AuBYP 2; ConAu 109, P-2; WhAm 8; WhoAm 82*

Barry, Charles, Sir
English. Architect
Designed Houses of Parliament, 1840-60.
b. May 23, 1795 in London, England
d. May 12, 1860 in London, England
Source: *BiDBrA; BioIn 2, 3, 5, 10, 14, 16; CelCen; DcArts; DcBiPP; DcBrWA; DcD&D; DcNaB; IntDcAr; MacEA; McGDA; NewCol 75; OxCArt; VicBrit; WhDW; WhoArch*

Barry, Daniel
American. Cartoonist
Drew "Flash Gordon," "Doc Savage," "Commando York" for comic books.
b. Jul 11, 1923 in Long Branch, New Jersey
Source: *EncACom; WorECom*

Barry, Dave
American. Humorist, Journalist
Syndicated columnist, *Miami Herald,* 1983—; won Pulitzer, 1988.
b. 1947 in Armonk, New York
Source: *Au&Arts 14; BiDAmNC; BioIn 16; ConAu 129, 134; ConPopW; LegTOT; News 91, 91-2; NewYTBS 90; WhoAm 90; WhoSSW 91; WrDr 92, 94, 96*

Barry, Donald
[Donald Barry de Acosta]
"Red"
American. Actor
Starred in *Red Ryder* Western film series, 1940s.
b. Jul 11, 1912 in Houston, Texas
d. Jul 17, 1980 in North Hollywood, California
Source: *BioIn 8, 12; FilmEn; IntMPA 82; MotPP; NewYTBS 80; PseudN 82; WhoHol A*

Barry, Gene
[Eugene Klass]
American. Actor
Starred in TV series "Bat Masterson," 1959-61; "Burke's Law," 1963-66; "Name of the Game," 1968-71.
b. Jun 4, 1922 in New York, New York
Source: *BioIn 13; ConTFT 2, 5, 12; FilmgC; HalFC 84; IntMPA 86, 88; MotPP; WhoAm 74, 76, 78, 80, 82, 84, 86; WhoHol A; WorAl; WorAlBi*

Barry, Jack
[Jack Barasch]
American. TV Personality, Producer
Producer of game shows, including "Concentration," 1958-73, longest-running daytime quiz show.
b. Mar 20, 1918 in Lindenhurst, New York
d. May 2, 1984 in New York, New York
Source: *BioIn 3, 5, 12, 13, 14, 16; ConTFT 2; IntMPA 75, 76, 77, 78, 79, 80, 81, 82, 84; NewYTET; RadStar; WhAm 8; WhoAm 82*

Barry, John
American. Naval Officer
First American commodore; first American to capture a British ship, *Edward,* 1775.
b. 1745 in Tacumshane, Ireland
d. Sep 13, 1803 in Philadelphia, Pennsylvania
Source: *AmBi; AmRev; ApCAB; BioIn 1, 2, 3, 4, 5, 6, 7, 11, 17, 20; DcAmB; DcCathB; DcIrB 78, 88; DcNaB; Drake; EncAR; EncCRAm; HarEnMi; HarEnUS; LinLib S; McGEWB; NatCAB 4; OxCAmH; OxCShps; TwCBDA; WebAB 74, 79; WebAMB; WhAm HS; WhAmRev; WorAl; WorAlBi*

Barry, John
English. Composer
Wrote music for several James Bond films; won Oscars for scores of *Lion in Winter,* 1968; *Out of Africa,* 1985.
b. Nov 3, 1933 in York, England
Source: *BioIn 7, 14; CmMov; ConTFT 4, 11; EncEurC; EncMT; EncRk 88; FilmEn; FilmgC; HalFC 80, 84, 88; IntDcF 1-4, 2-4; IntMPA 75, 76, 77, 78, 79, 80, 81, 82, 84, 86, 88, 92, 94, 96; IntWW 93; IntWWM 77; LegTOT; OxCFilm; OxCPMus; VarWW 85; WhAm 7; WhoAm 96, 97; WhoHrs 80; WhoMus 72; WhoWor 74; WorEFlm*

Barry, Leonora Marie Kearney
"Mother Lake"
American. Labor Union Official
Organized women's workers in Knights of Labor, 1886-90.
b. Aug 13, 1849 in Kearney, Ireland
d. Jul 15, 1930 in Minooka, Illinois
Source: *AmRef; BiDAmL; BioIn 15, 19; InWom SUP; LibW; NotAW; WebAB 74, 79; WebBD 83*

Barry, Lynda
American. Cartoonist, Writer
Creator of syndicated strip *Ernie Pook's Comeek;* controversial coloring book *Naked Ladies, Naked Ladies;* authored play, *The Good Times Are Killing Me.*
b. 1956 in Seattle, Washington
Source: *AsAmAlm; Au&Arts 9; BioIn 13, 15, 16; ConTFT 14; CurBio 94; News*

92, 92-1; NotAsAm; WhoEnt 92; WrDr 92, 94

Barry, Marion S(hepilov), Jr.
American. Politician
Democratic mayor of Washington, DC, 1979-90, 1995—; sentenced to six months in prison for cocaine possession, 1990.
b. Mar 6, 1936 in Itta Bena, Mississippi
Source: *BioIn 12, 13, 14, 15, 16; CurBio 87; Ebony 1; InB&W 80, 85; IntWW 89, 91, 93; NegAl 83, 89A; News 91; WhoAfA 96; WhoAm 80, 82, 84, 86, 88, 90, 94, 96, 97; WhoAmP 83, 85, 87, 89, 91, 93, 95; WhoBlA 80, 85, 88, 90, 92, 94; WhoE 81, 83, 85, 86, 89, 91, 97; WhoWor 89, 91*

Barry, Marty
[Martin Barry]
Canadian. Hockey Player
Center, 1927-40, with four NHL teams; won Lady Byng Trophy, 1937; Hall of Fame, 1965.
b. Dec 8, 1905 in Quebec, Quebec, Canada
Source: *HocEn; WhoHcky 73*

Barry, Philip
American. Dramatist
Wrote *The Philadelphia Story;* filmed, 1940, starring Katharine Hepburn, Cary Grant.
b. Jun 18, 1896 in Rochester, New York
d. Dec 3, 1949 in New York, New York
Source: *AmAu&B; Benet 87, 96; BenetAL 91; BioIn 1, 2, 3, 4, 7, 10, 11, 12, 13, 15, 20; CamGLE; CamHAL; CasWL; CathA 1930; CnDAL; CnMD; CnThe; ConAmA; ConAu 109; CrtSuDr; CyWA 89; DcLB 7; DcLEL; DcNAA; EncWT; Ent; EvLB; FacFETw; FilmgC; GrWrEL DR; HalFC 80, 84, 88; IntDcT 2; LegTOT; LinLib L; LngCTC; McGEWD 72, 84; ModAL; ModWD; NewCol 75; NotNAT A, B; OxCAmL 65, 83, 95; OxCAmT 84; OxCThe 67, 83; PenC AM; PlP&P; RAdv 14, 13-2; REn; REnAL; REnWD; RfGAmL 87, 94; TwCA, SUP; TwCLC 11; TwCWr; WebE&AL; WhAm 2; WhThe; WorAl; WorAlBi*

Barry, Rick
[Richard Francis Dennis Barry, III]
American. Basketball Player, Sportscaster
Forward, 1965-80, mostly with Golden State; only player to win scoring title in both NBA, ABA: holds NBA record for field goal percentage; Hall of Fame, 1986.
b. Mar 28, 1944 in Elizabeth, New Jersey
Source: *BasBi; BioIn 7, 8, 9, 10, 11, 12, 13; CelR; CmCal; CurBio 71; Dun&B 88; LegTOT; NewYTBE 72; OfNBA 87; WhoAm 86, 90, 92, 94, 95, 96, 97; WhoBbl 73; WhoEmL 87; WhoSpor; WhoSSW 86, 88; WhoUSWr 88; WhoWest 94, 96; WorAl; WorAlBi*

Barry, Tom
Irish. Military Leader
Leader in Irish War for Independence, 1919-22, who helped develop guerilla warfare.
b. Jul 1, 1897 in Rosscarbery, Ireland
d. Jul 2, 1980 in Cork, Ireland
Source: *AnObit 1980; BioIn 12; DcIrB 88; DcIrW 2; NewYTBS 80*

Barrymore, Diana
[Diana Blanche Blythe]
American. Actor
John Barrymore's daughter; starred in 1940s films; wrote autobiography *Too Much, Too Soon,* 1957.
b. Mar 3, 1921 in New York, New York
d. Jan 25, 1960 in New York, New York
Source: *BioIn 4, 5, 7, 10, 15; EncWT; FilmEn; FilmgC; ForYSC; HalFC 80, 84, 88; HolP 40; InWom; MotPP; NotNAT, A, B; ObitOF 79; WhoHol B; WhScrn 74, 77, 83; WhThe*

Barrymore, Drew
[Andrew Barrymore]
American. Actor
Granddaughter of John Barrymore; played Gertie in *ET,* 1982; starred in *Firestarter,* 1984; *Poison Ivy,* 1992.
b. Feb 22, 1975 in Los Angeles, California
Source: *BioIn 13, 16; ConAu 139; ConTFT 2, 5, 12; HalFC 88; IntMPA 88, 92, 94, 96; LegTOT; News 95, 95-3; VarWW 85; WhoAm 95, 96, 97; WhoAmW 95, 97; WhoHol 92; WorAlBi*

Barrymore, Elaine Jacobs
[Elaine Barrie]
American. Actor
John Barrymore's wife; wrote autobiography *All My Sins Remembered,* 1977.
b. 1914?
Source: *BioIn 11; InWom; NotNAT A*

Barrymore, Ethel Mae Blythe
"First Lady of the American Theatre"
American. Actor
Starred in *Corn Is Green,* 1942, in NYC's Ethel Barrymore Theatre; won Oscar for *None But the Lonely Heart,* 1944; sister of John, Lionel.
b. Aug 15, 1879 in Philadelphia, Pennsylvania
d. Jun 18, 1959 in Hollywood, California
Source: *CurBio 41, 59; FilmEn; MovMk; OxCFilm; OxCThe 83; WebAB 79; WhAm 3; WorEFlm*

Barrymore, Georgiana Emma Drew
[Mrs. Maurice Barrymore]
American. Actor
Starred in *Romeo and Juliet* with husband Maurice, 1883; mother of John, Ethel, Lionel.
b. Jul 11, 1854 in Philadelphia, Pennsylvania
d. Jul 2, 1893 in Santa Barbara, California
Source: *DcAmB; InWom SUP; LibW; NotAW; WhAm HS*

Barrymore, John
[John Sidney Blythe]
American. Actor
Box office attraction due to voice, profile; known for roles as lover, grotesque tortured part in *Dr. Jekyll and Mr. Hyde,* 1920.
b. Feb 15, 1882 in Philadelphia, Pennsylvania
d. May 29, 1942 in Hollywood, California
Source: *AmCulL; BenetAL 91; BiDFilm, 81, 94; BioIn 2, 3, 4, 5, 6, 7, 9, 10, 11, 12, 13, 14, 15, 16, 17, 19, 20, 21; CmMov; CnThe; CurBio 42; DcAmB S3; DcArts; EncAB-H 1974, 1996; EncAFC; EncWT; Ent; FacFETw; FamA&A; Film 1, 2; FilmEn; FilmgC; ForYSC; HalFC 80, 84, 88; IntDcF 1-3, 2-3; LegTOT; LinLib S; LngCTC; McGEWB; MGM; MotPP; MovMk; NatCAB 60; NotNAT A, B; OxCAmH; OxCAmL 83; OxCAmT 84; OxCFilm; OxCThe 67, 83; PlP&P; RadStar; SilFlmP; TwYS; WebAB 74, 79; WhAm 2; WhDW; WhoHol B; WhoHrs 80; WhScrn 74, 77, 83; WhThe; WorAl; WorAlBi; WorEFlm*

Barrymore, John Blythe Drew, Jr.
American. Actor
Appeared in low-budget Italian films; son of John, father of Drew.
b. Jun 4, 1932 in Beverly Hills, California
Source: *BioNews 74; FilmEn; FilmgC; HalFC 88; IntMPA 86, 92; MotPP; WhoHol A*

Barrymore, Lionel Blythe
American. Actor
Brother of Ethel, John; first Barrymore to appear in film; won 1931 Oscar for *Free Soul.*
b. Apr 28, 1878 in Philadelphia, Pennsylvania
d. Nov 15, 1954 in Van Nuys, California
Source: *ASCAP 66; BiDFilm; CurBio 43, 55; DcAmB S5; FamA&A; Film 1; FilmgC; MotPP; MovMk; OxCFilm; TwYS; WebAB 79; WhAm 3; WhScrn 77; WorEFlm*

Barrymore, Maurice
[Herbert Blythe]
English. Actor
Father of Lionel, Ethel, John; made acting debut, 1872; known for supporting roles on stage.
b. Sep 21, 1849 in Agra, India
d. Mar 26, 1905 in Amityville, New York
Source: *AmBi; ApCAB SUP; DcAmB; FamA&A; LngCTC; OxCAmT 84; OxCThe 67; PlP&P; WebAB 74; WhAm 1*

Bart, Jean
French. Naval Officer
Known for heroic exploits during War of Grand Alliance, 1680s-90s.
b. Oct 21, 1651 in Dunkirk, France
d. Apr 27, 1702 in Dunkirk, France
Source: *DcBiPP; NewCol 75; OxCShps; WebBD 83; WhoMilH 76*

Bart, Lionel
[Lionel Begleiter]
English. Composer, Lyricist, Dramatist
Stage musicals include *La Strada,* 1969; Tony award-winning *Oliver,* 1963.
b. Aug 1, 1930 in London, England
Source: *BestMus; BiE&WWA; BioIn 14; BlueB 76; ConAu 65; ConDr 77D, 88D; ConTFT 3; DcArts; EncMT; EncWT; Ent; FilmgC; HalFC 80, 84, 88; IntAu&W 77, 91, 93; IntWW 74, 75, 76, 77, 78, 79, 80, 81, 82, 83, 89, 91, 93; IntWWM 77, 80, 90; NewAmDM; NewGrDM 80; NewOxM; NotNAT; OxCPMus; OxCThe 83; PenEncP; Who 74, 82, 83, 85, 88, 90, 92, 94; WhoAm 94, 95, 96, 97; WhoThe 72, 77, 81; WhoWor 74, 84, 87, 89, 91, 93, 95, 96, 97; WrDr 80, 82, 84, 86, 88, 90, 92, 94, 96*

Barth, Heinrich
German. Explorer
Explored Africa, compiling vocabularies of 40 African languages; crossed Sahara, 1855.
b. Feb 16, 1821 in Hamburg, Germany
d. Dec 25, 1865 in Berlin, Germany
Source: *Alli SUP; BioIn 5, 6, 9, 12; CelCen; DcAfHiB 86; DcBiPP; Expl 93; IntDcAn; LinLib S; McGEWB; WhDW; WhWE*

Barth, John (Simmons)
American. Author
Won National Book Award in Fiction, 1973; books include *The Open Decision,* 1970.
b. May 27, 1930 in Cambridge, Maryland
Source: *AmAu&B; AmCulL; AmWr; Au&Wr 71; AuNews 1, 2; Benet 87, 96; BenetAL 91; BioIn 6, 7, 8, 9, 10, 11, 12, 13, 14, 15, 16; BlueB 76; CamGEL; CamGLE; CamHAL; CasWL; ConAu 1BS, 1R, 5NR, 23NR, 49NR; ConLC 1, 2, 3, 5, 7, 9, 10, 14, 27, 51, 89; ConNov 72, 76, 82, 86, 91, 96; CurBio 69; CyWA 89; DcArts; DcLB 2; DcLEL 1940; DcTwCCu 1; DrAF 76; DrAPF 89, 91; DrAS 74E, 78E, 82E; EncSF, 93; EncWL, 2, 3; FacFETw; FifSWrA; GrWrEL N; IntAu&W 76, 89, 91, 93; IntvTCA 2; IntWW 74, 75, 76, 77, 78, 79, 80, 81, 82, 83, 89, 91, 93; LegTOT; LinLib L, S; MagSAmL; MajTwCW; ModAL, S1, S2; Novels; OxCAmL 65, 83, 95; OxCEng 85, 95; PenC AM; PostFic; RAdv 1, 14, 13-1; RfGAmL 87, 94; RfGShF; RGTwCWr; ScF&FL 1, 2, 92; ScFSB; ShSCr 10; SJGFanW; SouWr; TwCRHW 90, 94; TwCSFW 81; TwCWr; WebAB 74, 79; WebE&AL; WhoAm 74, 76, 78, 80, 82, 84, 86, 88, 90, 92, 94, 95, 96, 97; WhoE 93, 95, 97; WhoTwCL; WhoUSWr 88; WhoWor 74, 78, 80, 82, 84, 87, 89, 91, 93, 95, 96, 97; WhoWrEP 89, 92, 95; WorAl; WorAlBi; WorAu 1950; WrDr 76, 80, 82, 84, 86, 88, 90, 92, 94, 96; WrPh*

Barth, Karl
Swiss. Theologian
Sought to restore belief in fundamental dogmas of Christianity.
b. May 10, 1886 in Basel, Switzerland
d. Dec 9, 1966 in Basel, Switzerland
Source: *BioIn 1, 2, 3, 4, 5, 6, 7, 8, 9, 11, 12, 13, 14, 15, 16; ConAu 25R, 134; CurBio 62, 69; DcEcMov; EncGRNM; EncTR, 91; FacFETw; LegTOT; LinLib L, S; LngCTC; LuthC 75; MakMC; McGEWB; ObitT 1961; OxCGer 76, 86; OxCPhil; RAdv 14, 13-4; ThTwC 87; TwCA SUP; WhAm 5; WhDW; WhE&EA; WorAl; WorAlBi*

Barth, Roland Sawyer
American. Author
Wrote books on education: *Open Education Re-examined,* 1973.
b. May 18, 1937 in Boston, Massachusetts
Source: *ConAu 1NR, 45; WhoE 83*

Barthe, Richmond
American. Sculptor
Known for realistic busts of black historical figures, celebrities.
b. Jan 28, 1901 in Bay Saint Louis, Mississippi
d. Mar 6, 1989 in Pasadena, California
Source: *AfrAmAl 6; AfroAA; BioIn 2, 4, 6, 8, 9, 10, 16, 19; CurBio 40, 89, 89N; DcTwCCu 5; Ebony 1; InB&W 80, 85; NegAl 76, 83, 89; NewYTBS 89; WhAm 11; WhAmArt 85; WhoAm 74, 84, 86; WhoAmA 82, 84, 86, 89, 91N, 93N; WhoBlA 75, 77, 80, 85, 90, 92N; WhoWor 74*

Barthelme, Donald
American. Author
Known for short stories, satires, novels describing absurdity of 20th c. life through use of understatement; gained national fame with novella *Snow White,* 1967, originally published in *New Yorker.*
b. Apr 7, 1931 in Philadelphia, Pennsylvania
d. Jul 23, 1989 in Houston, Texas
Source: *AmAu&B; AnObit 1989; AuBYP 2S, 3; Benet 87, 96; BenetAL 91; BioIn 10, 11, 12, 13, 16; BlueB 76; CamGLE; CamHAL; CelR, 90; ConAu 20NR, 21R, 129; ConLC 1, 2, 3, 5, 6, 8, 13, 23, 46, 59; ConNov 72, 76, 82, 86; CurBio 76, 89, 89N; CyWA 89; DcArts; DcLB 2, Y80A, Y89N; DcLEL 1940; DrAF 76; DrAPF 89; EncAHmr; EncWL 2, 3; FacFETw; GrWrEL N; IntAu&W 76, 77; LegTOT; MagSAmL; MajTwCW; ModAL S1, S2; NewYTBS 89; OxCAmL 83, 95; PenC AM; PostFic; RAdv 1, 14, 13-1; RfGAmL 87, 94; RfGShF; RGTwCWr; ScF&FL 92; ShSCr 2; ShSWr; SJGFanW; SmATA 7, 62; WhAm 10; WhoAm 76, 78, 80, 84, 86, 88; WhoUSWr 88; WhoWrEP 89; WorAl; WorAlBi; WorAu 1950; WrDr 76, 80, 82, 84, 86, 88, 90*

Barthelmess, Richard
American. Actor
Best known roles in DW Griffith movies *Broken Blossoms,* 1919; *Way Down East,* 1920.
b. May 9, 1895 in New York, New York
d. Aug 17, 1963 in Southampton, New York
Source: *BiDFilm, 81, 94; BioIn 13, 14, 17, 18; DcAmB S7; Film 2; FilmEn; FilmgC; ForYSC; GangFlm; HalFC 80, 84, 88; IntDcF 1-3, 2-3; LegTOT; MotPP; MovMk; NotNAT B; ObitOF 79; OxCFilm; SilFlmP; TwYS; WhAm 4; WhoHol B; WhScrn 74, 77; WorEFlm*

Barthes, Roland (Gerard)
French. Critic
Known for contributions to structural linguistics, applications of semiology theories; wrote *Writing Degree Zero,* 1953.
b. Nov 12, 1915 in Cherbourg, France
d. Mar 25, 1980 in Paris, France
Source: *AnObit 1980; Benet 87, 96; BiDNeoM; BioIn 10, 11, 12, 13; BlmGEL; CasWL; ClDMEL 80; ConAu 97, 130; ConLC 24, 83; CurBio 79, 80, 80N; CyWA 89; DcArts; DcTwCCu 2; EncWL 2, 3; EuWr 13; FacFETw; GuFrLit 1; MajTwCW; MakMC; ModFrL; NewYTBS 80; PenC EUR; PostFic; RAdv 14, 13-2; ThTwC 87; WhAm 7; WhoFr 79; WhoTwCL; WhoWor 74; WorAu 1950; WrDr 94, 96*

Bartholdi, Auguste
[Frederic Auguste Bartholdi]
French. Sculptor
Designed Statue of Liberty, France's gift to America, 1886.
b. Apr 2, 1834 in Colmar, France
d. Oct 4, 1904 in Paris, France
Source: *ApCAB; ArtsNiC; BioIn 1, 5, 7, 8, 11, 14, 15; DcArts; HarEnUS; LinLib S; McGDA; NewCol 75; REn; TwCBDA*

Bartholomew, Freddie
[Frederick Llewellyn Bartholomew]
American. Actor
Child actor known for first starring part, in *David Copperfield,* 1935; played in *Little Lord Fauntleroy,* 1936; *Captains Courageous,* 1937.
b. Mar 28, 1924 in Dublin, Ireland
d. Jan 23, 1992 in Sarasota, Florida
Source: *AnObit 1992; BiDFilm, 81, 94; BioIn 7, 9, 15, 17, 19; FilmEn; ForYSC; HalFC 80, 84, 88; IntMPA 75, 76, 77, 78, 79, 80, 81, 82, 84, 86, 88, 92; LegTOT; MGM; MotPP; MovMk; OxCFilm; What 1; WhoHol 92, A; WorAl; WorAlBi; WorEFlm*

Bartholomew, Reginald
American. Diplomat
US ambassador to Lebanon, 1983-86; to Spain, 1986-89; to NATO, 1992-93; to Italy, 1993—.
b. Feb 17, 1936 in Portland, Maine
Source: *BioIn 13, 14; IntWW 93; NewYTBS 83, 84; WhoAm 86, 88, 92, 94, 95, 96, 97; WhoAmP 87, 89, 91, 93, 95; WhoWor 87, 89, 91, 95*

Bartholomew, Saint
Biblical Figure
One of the 12 apostles; feast day Aug 24.
Source: *DcCathB; Dis&D; McGDA; NewC; REn; WebBD 83*

Bartkowski, Steve(n Joseph)
American. Football Player
Quarterback, 1975-86, mostly with Atlanta; led NFL in passing for TDs, 1980.
b. Nov 12, 1952 in Des Moines, Iowa
Source: *BioIn 12; NewYTBS 80; WhoAm 84*

Bartlett, Charles Leffingwell
American. Journalist
Editor, Chicago *Daily News,* 1975-78; Field Syndicate, 1978-81; won a Pulitizer for nat. reporting, 1955.
b. Aug 14, 1921 in Chicago, Illinois
Source: *AmCath 80; BiDAmNC; BioIn 6; BlueB 76; TwCPaSc; Who 92; WhoAm 74, 76, 78, 80, 82, 84, 86, 88, 90, 92, 94, 95, 96, 97; WhoE 89, 95; WhoSSW 73, 75, 76, 82*

Bartlett, Francis Alonzo
American. Business Executive
Founded Bartlett Shade Tree Co., 1910; investigated Dutch elm disease, 1929.
b. Nov 13, 1882 in Belchertown, Massachusetts
d. Nov 21, 1963 in Stamford, Connecticut
Source: *BioIn 2, 6; DcAmB S7; EncAB-A 36*

Bartlett, Jennifer Losch
American. Artist
Realistic painter who paints same image from different perspectives, in different styles: "Graceland Mansion," "At the Lake," series.
b. Mar 14, 1941 in Long Beach, California
Source: *AmArt; BiDWomA; BioIn 13, 16; ConArt 83; CurBio 85; DcCAr 81; IntWW 91; InWom SUP; PrintW 83; WhoAm 84, 90, 97; WhoAmA 91; WhoAmW 91*

Bartlett, John
American. Lexicographer, Publisher
Edited first edition of *Familiar Quotations;* published 1855.
b. Jun 14, 1820 in Plymouth, Massachusetts
d. Dec 3, 1905 in Cambridge, Massachusetts
Source: *Alli, SUP; AmAu; AmAu&B; AmBi; ApCAB; Benet 87, 96; BenetAL 91; BiD&SB; BioIn 3, 4, 10; ChhPo, S3; CnDAL; DcAmAu; DcAmB; DcLB 1; DcNAA; EvLB; HarEnUS; LegTOT; LngCTC; NatCAB 11; OxCAmL 65, 83, 95; REn; REnAL; TwCBDA; WebAB 74, 79; WhAm 1; WorAl; WorAlBi*

Bartlett, John Russell
American. Historian, Bibliographer
NY bookseller, 1836-50, who edited pioneer descriptive bibliography, *John Carter Brown Catalogue,* 1865-82.
b. Oct 23, 1805 in Providence, Rhode Island
d. May 28, 1886 in Providence, Rhode Island
Source: *Alli, SUP; AmAu; AmAu&B; AmBi; ApCAB; ArizL; BiAUS; BiD&SB; BioIn 1, 8, 20; CyAL 2; DcAmAu; DcAmB; DcBiPP; DcEnL; DcNAA; Drake; HarEnUS; IlBEAAW; NatCAB 9; NewYHSD; REnAW; TwCBDA; WebAB 74, 79; WhAm HS; WhAmP; WhNaAH*

Bartlett, John Sherren
American. Newspaper Editor
Established *Albion,* 1822-48, newspaper for British residents of US.
b. 1790 in Dorsetshire, England
d. Aug 23, 1863 in Middletown Point, New Jersey
Source: *ApCAB; DcAmB; DcAmMeB; Drake; NatCAB 22; WhAm HS*

Bartlett, Josiah
American. Continental Congressman, Supreme Court Justice
First to sign Declaration of Independence after president; chief justice of Supreme Court, 1788; first governor of NH, 1793.
b. Nov 21, 1729 in Amesbury, Massachusetts
d. May 19, 1795 in Kingston, Massachusetts
Source: *AmBi; AmRev; ApCAB; BiAUS; BiDrAC; BiDrGov 1789; BiDrUSC 89; BioIn 3, 7, 8, 9, 12; DcAmB; DcAmMeB, 84; Drake; EncAR; EncCRAm; HarEnUS; LegTOT; NatCAB 11; TwCBDA; WhAm HS; WhAmP; WhAmRev; WorAl; WorAlBi*

Bartlett, Paul Wayland
American. Sculptor
Known for portrait statues; Columbus, Michelangelo at Library of Congress, Lafayette at Louvre.
b. Jan 24, 1865 in New Haven, Connecticut
d. Sep 20, 1925 in Paris, France
Source: *AmBi; ApCAB X; BriEAA; DcAmArt; DcAmB; IlBEAAW; LinLib S; McGDA; NatCAB 12, 30; OxCAmH; TwCBDA; WhAm 1*

Bartlett, Robert Abram
American. Explorer
Commanded Robert E Peary's ship on expedition that reached N Pole, 1908-9.
b. Aug 15, 1875 in Brigus, Newfoundland, Canada
d. Apr 28, 1946 in New York, New York
Source: *AmAu&B; ApCAB X; BioIn 1, 4, 5, 7, 11; CurBio 46; DcNAA; EncAB-A 11; InSci; MacDCB 78; NatCAB 41; WebAB 74, 79; WhAm 2; WorAl; WorAlBi*

Bartlett, Vernon
[Peter Oldfield]
English. Author, Politician
Independent MP; favored human rights; wrote *Nazi Germany Explained,* 1933.
b. Apr 30, 1894 in Westbury, England
d. Jan 1983
Source: *Au&Wr 71; BioIn 4, 5, 10; BlueB 76; ConAu 61, 108; DcNaB 1981; IntAu&W 76; IntWW 74, 75, 77, 78, 81, 83N; LngCTC; NewC; ScF&FL 1, 2, 92; TwCA, SUP; WhE&EA; Who 74, 82, 83; WhoLA; WrDr 76, 80, 82, 84*

Bartok, Bela
Hungarian. Composer, Pianist
Works include opera *Bluebeard's Castle,* 1927; *Concerto for Orchestra,* 1943; published over 6,000 folk tunes.
b. May 25, 1881 in Nagyszentmiklos, Austria-Hungary
d. Sep 29, 1945 in New York, New York
Source: *ASCAP 66, 80; AtlBL; Baker 78, 84, 92; Benet 87, 96; BiDAmM; BiDD; BioIn 1, 2, 3, 4, 5, 6, 7, 8, 9, 10, 11, 12, 13, 14, 15, 16, 17, 20, 21; BriBkM 80; CmOp; CnOxB; CompSN, SUP; CurBio 40, 45; DancEn 78; DcArts; DcCM; DcCom 77; DcCom&M 79; DcPup; DcTwCC, A; FacFETw; IntDcB; IntDcOp; LegTOT; LinLib S; MakMC; McGEWB; MetOEnc; MusMk; NewAmDM; NewEOp 71; NewGrDA 86; NewGrDM 80; NewOxM; OxCAmH; OxCMus; OxDcOp; PenDiMP A; PenEncH; RAdv 14, 13-3; REn; WhAm 4, HSA; WhDW; WorAl; WorAlBi*

Bartok, Eva
[Eva Martha Szoke]
English. Actor
Made film debut, 1947; private life love affairs better known; wrote autobiography *Worth Living For,* 1959.
b. Jun 18, 1926 in Kecskemet, Hungary
Source: *FilmEn; FilmgC; HalFC 80, 84, 88; IntWW 74, 75; ItaFilm; LegTOT; WhoHol 92, A*

Bartoli, Cecilia
Italian. Opera Singer
Mezzo-soprano recording artist; repertoire includes Rossini, Mozart recital albums.
b. Jun 4, 1966 in Rome, Italy
Source: *BioIn 17, 18, 19, 20, 21; ConMus 12; CurBio 92; NewGrDO; News 94, 94-1; OxDcOp*

Bartolommeo, Fra
[Bartolommeo di Pagolo del Fatorino; Baccio della Porta]
Italian. Artist
Paintings reflect composition balance, color harmony of High Renaissance; known for "St. Mark," 1517, now in Louvre.
b. Mar 28, 1475 in Florence, Italy
d. Oct 31, 1517 in Florence, Italy
Source: *AtlBL; BioIn 11; DcCathB; IntDcAA 90; LegTOT; LinLib S; LuthC 75; McGDA; NewCol 75; WebBD 83; WorAl; WorAlBi*

Barton, Bruce
American. Author, Advertising Executive
Wrote best-seller *Man Nobody Knows,* 1925, depicting Jesus as prototype of successful businessman.
b. Aug 5, 1886 in Robbins, Tennessee
d. Jul 5, 1967 in New York, New York
Source: *AmAu&B; AmDec 1920; BiDAmBL 83; BiDrAC; BiDrUSC 89; BioIn 2, 3, 5, 6, 8, 11, 12, 16, 17, 18, 19, 20; CurBio 61, 67; EncAB-H 1974, 1996; EncAJ; EncWB; NatCAB 60; ObitOF 79; OhA&B; RelLAm 91; TwCSAPR; WebAB 74, 79; WhAm 4; WhAmP; WhLit; WhNAA; WorAl; WorAlBi*

Barton, Clara Harlowe
"Angel of the Battlefield"
American. Social Reformer
Founded American Red Cross, 1881-82; pres. until 1904.
b. Dec 25, 1821 in Oxford, Massachusetts
d. Apr 12, 1912 in Glen Echo, Maryland
Source: *AmAu&B; AmBi; AmWomWr; BioIn 1, 2, 3, 4, 5, 6, 7, 8, 9, 10, 11, 12, 13; DcAmB; DcNAA; EncAB-H 1974; EncWHA; HerW; InWom, SUP; NewCol 75; NotAW; REn; REnAL; WebAB 74; WhAm 1*

Barton, Derek Harold Richard, Sir
English. Chemist
Shared Nobel Prize in chemistry, 1969; as result of discovery, conformational analysis became part of organic chemistry.
b. Sep 8, 1918 in Gravesend, England
Source: *AmMWSc 92, 95; BiESc; BioIn 1, 3, 4, 6, 8, 9, 13, 14, 15; BlueB 76; CamDcSc; FacFETw; IntWW 74, 75, 76, 77, 78, 79, 80, 81, 82, 83, 89, 91, 93; LarDcSc; McGMS 80; NobelP; Who 74, 82, 83, 85, 88, 90, 92, 94; WhoAm 88, 90, 92, 94, 95; WhoNob, 90, 95; WhoScEn 94, 96; WhoWor 74, 78, 80, 82, 84, 87, 89, 91, 93, 95, 96, 97; WorAl; WorAlBi*

Barton, George
American. Author
Writings include *Angels of the Battlefield,* 1898; *Famous Detective Mysteries,* 1926.
b. Jan 22, 1866 in Philadelphia, Pennsylvania
d. Mar 16, 1940
Source: *AmAu&B; BioIn 1; CathA 1930; CurBio 40; DcCathB; DcNAA; WhAm 1*

Barton, James
American. Actor, Dancer
Starred in Broadway's *The Iceman Cometh,* 1946; *Paint Your Wagon,* 1951.
b. Nov 1, 1890 in Gloucester, New Jersey
d. Feb 19, 1962 in Mineola, New York
Source: *BiDD; BioIn 2, 6, 9, 12; CmpEPM; DcAmB S7; EncAFC; EncMT; EncVaud; FilmEn; FilmgC; ForYSC; HalFC 84, 88; MovMk; NatCAB 60; NotNAT B; ObitOF 79; OxCAmT 84; Vers B; WhoHol B; WhScrn 74, 77, 83; WhThe*

Barton, Robert B(rown) M(orison)
American. Business Executive
Pres., Parker Brothers, a board game company, 1933-58.
b. Aug 19, 1903
d. Feb 14, 1995 in Marblehead, Massachusetts
Source: *BioIn 5; CurBio 95N*

Bartram, John
American. Botanist
Conducted first hybridizing experiments in US; idea basis of modern geology.
b. Mar 23, 1699 in Marple, Pennsylvania
d. Sep 22, 1777 in Kingsessing, Pennsylvania
Source: *Alli; AmAu; AmAu&B; AmBi; AmWrBE; ApCAB; BenetAL 91; BiDAmS; BiD&SB; BiInAmS; BioIn 2, 3, 6, 7, 8, 10, 11, 12, 14, 15, 17, 18, 19; CamGEL; CamGLE; CamHAL; CyAL 1; DcAmAu; DcAmB; DcAmMeB; DcLB 31; DcNAA; DcScB; Drake; EncAAH; EncCRAm; HarEnUS; InSci; LarDcSc; LinLib S; McGEWB; NatCAB 7; NewCBEL; NewYHSD; OxCAmH; OxCAmL 65, 83, 95; OxCCan; PeoHis; REnAL; REnAW; TwCBDA; WebAB 74, 79; WhAm HS; WhWE*

Bartram, William
American. Botanist
Best known for plant and animal descriptions in *Travels through North and South Carolina,* 1791.
b. Feb 9, 1739 in Kingsessing, Pennsylvania
d. Jul 22, 1823 in Philadelphia, Pennsylvania
Source: *Alli; AmAu; AmAu&B; AmBi; AmWrBE; ApCAB; Benet 87, 96; BenetAL 91; BiDAmS; BiDLA; BiDSA; BiInAmS; BioIn 1, 3, 8, 9, 10, 11, 12, 13, 14, 15, 16, 17, 18; CamGEL; CasWL; CyAL 1; DcAmAu; DcAmB; DcLB 37; DcLEL; DcNAA; DcNCBi 1; DcScB; Drake; HarEnUS; InSci; LinLib L; McGEWB; MemAm; NatCAB 7; NewCBEL; NewYHSD; OxCAmH; OxCAmL 65, 83, 95; OxCEng 67, 85, 95; PenC AM; PeoHis; REn; REnAL; TwCBDA; WebAB 74, 79; WhAm HS; WhNaAH; WhWE*

Baruch, Andre
American. Radio Performer
Provided radio voices for "The Shadow," "Your Hit Parade."
d. Sep 15, 1991 in Beverly Hills, California
Source: *IntMPA 75, 76, 77, 78, 79, 80, 81, 82, 84, 86, 88, 92; NewYTBS 91*

Baruch, Bernard Mannes
American. Businessman, Statesman
Adviser to several US presidents; special adviser on war mobilization, WW II.
b. Aug 19, 1870 in Camden, South Carolina
d. Jun 20, 1965 in New York, New York
Source: *AmAu&B; AmPolLe; ApCAB X; BiDAmBL 83; BioIn 1, 2, 3, 4, 5, 7, 8, 9, 10, 12, 13, 14, 16, 17, 18, 21; ColdWar 1; CurBio 41, 50, 65; DcAmB S7; DcAmDH 80, 89; DcPol; DcTwHis; EncAAH; EncAB-H 1974, 1996; EncSoH; LinLib S; McGEWB; NatCAB 60; OxCAmH; REn; REnAL; WebAB 74, 79; WhAm 4; WhAmP; WhWW-II; WorAl*

Baryshnikov, Mikhail
"Misha"
American. Dancer, Director, Choreographer
Artistic director, American Ballet Theatre, 1980-90; films include *The Turning Point,* 1977, *White Nights,* 1985; founder, White Oak Dance Project, 1990—.
b. Jan 28, 1948 in Riga, Latvia
Source: *BiDD; BiDSovU; BioIn 10, 11, 12, 13, 14, 15, 16, 17, 18, 19, 20, 21; BioNews 75; BkPepl; CelR 90; ConAu 113, 133; ConTFT 3, 13; CurBio 75; DcArts; DcTwCCu 1; EncWB; FacFETw; HalFC 84, 88; IntDcB; IntMPA 88, 92, 94, 96; IntWW 77, 78, 79, 80, 81, 82, 83, 89, 91, 93; LegTOT; NewYTBS 74, 89; RAdv 14, 13-3; SovUn; Who 82, 83, 85, 88, 90, 92, 94; WhoAm 76, 78, 80, 82, 84, 86, 88, 90, 92, 94, 95, 96, 97; WhoE 83, 85, 86, 89, 91; WhoEnt 92; WhoHol 92; WhoWor 78, 80, 82, 84, 87, 89, 91, 93, 95; WorAl; WorAlBi*

Barzin, Leon Eugene
American. Conductor
Musical director, Ballet Society, NYC ballet, 1948-58.
b. Nov 27, 1900 in Brussels, Belgium
Source: *Baker 84; CurBio 51; IntWWM 90; NewAmDM; NewGrDA 86; NewYTBE 70; PenDiMP; WhoMus 72; WhoWor 74*

Barzini, Luigi Giorgio, Jr.
Italian. Author
Best known for works about Americans, Italians; *Americans Are Alone in the World; The Italians,* 1964.
b. Dec 21, 1908 in Milan, Italy
d. Mar 30, 1984 in Rome, Italy

Source: *AnObit 1984; BioIn 14; ConAu 13R, 112; CurBio 51, 84; IntWW 74; WhAm 8; WhoWor 74; WorAu 1950*

Barzun, Jacques Martin
American. Educator, Historian
Advocate of liberal arts studies rather than vocational courses.
b. Nov 30, 1907 in Creteil, France
Source: *Baker 84; Benet 87; BenetAL 91; ConAu 22NR, 61; ConLC 51; CurBio 64; FacFETw; IntAu&W 89; IntWW 83, 91; IntWWM 90; NewCol 75; NewGrDA 86; OxCAmL 65; PeoHis; RAdv 13-1; REn; REnAL; TwCA SUP; WebAB 74, 79; Who 85, 92; WhoAm 86, 90; WhoAmA 84, 91; WhoUSWr 88; WhoWor 84; WhoWrEP 89; WrDr 86, 92*

Basehart, Richard
American. Actor
Versatile actor who made film debut, 1947; won 1956 Oscar for *Moby Dick.*
b. Aug 31, 1914 in Zanesville, Ohio
d. Sep 17, 1984 in Los Angeles, California
Source: *AnObit 1984; BiE&WWA; BioIn 14; ConTFT 2; FilmEn; FilmgC; HalFC 88; IntMPA 77, 78, 79, 80, 81, 82, 84; ItaFilm; LegTOT; MovMk; NewYTBS 84; OxCFilm; WhoAm 82; WhoHol A; WhoThe 77, 81; WorAlBi*

Basho
Japanese. Poet
Zen Buddhist haiku master.
b. 1644 in Ueno, Iga, Japan
d. Nov 28, 1694 in Osaka, Japan
Source: *BioIn 3, 5, 9, 16, 19; CasWL; CyWA 58; DcArts; DcOrL 1; EncJap; GrFLW; LegTOT; LinLib L; McGEWB; PenC CL; RAdv 14, 13-2; REn; RfGWoL 95*

Basia
Singer, Songwriter
Pop soloist with Latin, funk and jazz sounds; platinum album *Time and Tide,* 1986; gold album *London Warsaw New York,* 1989.
b. 1959?, Poland
Source: *BioIn 16; ConMus 5*

Basie, Count
[William James Basie, Jr]
American. Jazz Musician, Bandleader
Pianist; revolutionized jazz; one of most influential Big Band leaders, 1930s-50s; hits include "One O'Clock Jump," 1941.
b. Aug 21, 1904 in Red Bank, New Jersey
d. Apr 26, 1984 in Hollywood, Florida
Source: *AllMusG; ASCAP 66; Baker 78, 84, 92; BgBands 74; BioIn 14, 15, 16, 18, 19, 21; BioNews 74; BlkCond; CelR; CmpEPM; ConAu 134; ConMus 2; ConNews 85-1; CurBio 42, 84; DcArts; DcTwCCu 1; DrBlPA, 90; EncJzS; EncWB; IlEncJ; InB&W 85; IntWW 75, 76; LegTOT; MusMk; NewAmDM; NewGrDA 86; NewGrDJ 88, 94; NewGrDM 80; NewOxM; NewYTBS 84; OxCPMus; PenEncP; WebAB 74; WhAm 8; WhoAm 82; WhoBlA 75, 80; WhoWor 74; WorAl; WorAlBi*

Basil, Saint
[Saint (The Great) Basil]
Greek. Religious Leader
Father of Eastern communal monasticism; feast day Jun 14.
b. 330 in Caesarea, Cappadocia
d. Jan 1, 379 in Caesarea, Cappadocia
Source: *CasWL; CyEd; Grk&L; IlEncMy; LuthC 75; McGEWB; PenC CL; WhDW*

Basilio, Carmen
American. Boxer
Won world welterweight title, 1955, 1956, middleweight title, 1957; Hall of Fame, 1969.
b. Apr 2, 1927 in Canastota, New York
Source: *BiDAmSp BK; BioIn 4, 5, 10; BoxReg; LegTOT; WhoBox 74; WhoSpor*

Basinger, Kim
American. Actor, Model
Starred in *The Natural,* 1983; starred in controversial *Nine-and-a-Half Weeks*; co-starred in *Batman* 1989.
b. Dec 8, 1953 in Athens, Georgia
Source: *BioIn 14, 15, 16; CelR 90; ConNews 87-2; ConTFT 6, 13; CurBio 90; HalFC 88; HolBB; IntMPA 92, 94, 96; IntWW 91, 93; LegTOT; VarWW 85; WhoAm 90, 92, 94, 95, 96, 97; WhoAmW 91, 95, 97; WhoEnt 92A; WhoHol 92; WorAlBi*

Baskerville, John
English. Printer, Type Designer
His innovative typeface is still used today; printed *The Bible; The Book of Common Prayer.*
b. Jan 28, 1706 in Wolverley, England
d. Jan 8, 1775 in Birmingham, England
Source: *BioIn 3, 5, 6, 10, 12; BlkwCE; ChhPo S3; DcArts; DcBiPP; DcNaB; Dis&D; LinLib L; NewC; NewCBEL; OxCDecA; OxCEng 85, 95; OxDcArt; PenDiDA 89; WhDW*

Baskin, Burton
American. Businessman
With Irvine Robbins started Baskin-Robbins ice cream stores, 1947.
b. 1913 in Chicago, Illinois
d. 1967 in California
Source: *Entr*

Baskin, Leonard
American. Artist, Illustrator
Sculptor, later print maker; founded Gehanna Press, producer of limited editions, 1952.
b. Aug 15, 1922 in New Brunswick, New Jersey
Source: *AmArt; BioIn 4, 5, 6, 7, 8, 9, 11, 12, 13, 14; BriEAA; ChlBkCr; ConArt 83, 89, 96; ConAu 106; CurBio 64; DcAmArt; DcCAA 71, 77, 88, 94; DcCAr 81; FacFETw; FifBJA; IlsCB 1967; LinLib L, S; McGDA; OxCTwCA; OxDcArt; PhDcTCA 77; PrintW 83, 85; SmATA 27, 30; WebAB 74, 79; WhoAm 74, 76, 78, 80, 86, 88, 90, 92, 94, 95, 96, 97; WhoAmA 73, 76, 78, 80, 82, 84, 86, 89, 91, 93; WhoGrA 62, 82; WhoWor 74; WorArt 1950*

Basov, Nikolai Gennadievich
Russian. Physicist
Shared 1964 Nobel Prize in physics; research in experimental physics led to discovery of maser, laser.
b. Dec 14, 1922 in Usman, Union of Soviet Socialist Republics
Source: *AsBiEn; BioIn 15, 20; IntWW 74, 75, 76, 91, 93; NobelP; Who 74, 82, 83, 85, 88, 90, 92, 94; WhoAtom 77; WhoNob, 90, 95; WhoScEn 94, 96; WhoSocC 78; WhoWor 74, 76, 78, 80, 82, 84, 87, 89, 91, 93, 95, 96, 97; WorAl; WorAlBi*

Basquiat, Jean-Michel
American. Artist
Rose from a homeless graffiti artist to become one of the first black artists to receive international recognition; associated with Andy Warhol.
b. Dec 22, 1960 in New York, New York
d. Aug 12, 1988 in New York, New York
Source: *AfrAmAl 6; AmArt; BioIn 16, 17, 18, 19, 20; ConBlB 5; DcTwCCu 5*

Bass, Alfie
[Alfred Bass]
English. Actor
Character comedian; works include *Help!,* 1965; *Alfie,* 1966.
b. Apr 8, 1921 in London, England
d. Jul 15, 1987 in London, England
Source: *AnObit 1987; BioIn 13; ConTFT 5; FilmEn; FilmgC; IlWWBF; WhoHol A; WhoThe 72, 77, 81*

Bass, Henry
American. Manufacturer
Began making utilitarian shoes, 1876; moccasins became college favorite, 1960s.
b. 1843
d. 1925
Source: *Entr*

Bass, Randy William
American. Baseball Player
Infielder; played 130 games in ML career, 1977-82; most devastating hitter in Ja panese baseball history; won Triple Crown, 1985, 1986, with Honshu Tigers.
b. Mar 13, 1954 in Lawton, Oklahoma
Source: *BaseEn 88; BioIn 14, 15; NewYTBS 85*

Bass, Rick
American. Writer
Published collections of essays *The Deer Pasture,* 1985; *Wild to the Heart,* 1987.
b. 1958 in Fort Worth, Texas

Source: *BioIn 17, 21; ConAu 53NR, 126; ConLC 79; IntAu&W 91*

Bass, Robert M(use)
American. Financier
Aggressive investor; founded Robert M. Bass Group, 1963; took over bankrupt American Savings and Loan Association, 1988.
b. Mar 19, 1948 in Fort Worth, Texas
Source: *CurBio 89; NewYTBS 88; WhoAm 90, 97; WhoFI 89, 92; WhoSSW 93*

Bass, Sam
American. Outlaw
Train robber, ambushed by Texas Rangers, who was hero of Western ballads.
b. Jul 21, 1851 in Mitchell, Indiana
d. Jul 21, 1878 in Round Rock, Texas
Source: *BioIn 4, 5, 8, 11, 13, 15, 17; DcAmB; DrInf; HalFC 84, 88; LinLib S; NewCol 75; OxCAmH; REnAW; WebAB 74, 79; WhAm HS*

Bass, Saul
American. Director, Producer
Revolutionized film credits by animating names; film title designs include *Seven Year Itch,* 1955; *Vertigo,* 1958.
b. May 8, 1920 in New York, New York
d. Apr 25, 1996 in Los Angeles, California
Source: *BioIn 3, 6, 8, 11, 13, 14, 15, 17, 21; ConDes 84, 90, 97; ConGrA 1; DcFM; DcTwDes; FilmEn; FilmgC; HalFC 80, 84, 88; IntDcF 1-4, 2-4; IntMPA 75, 76, 77, 78, 79, 80, 81, 82, 84, 86, 88, 92, 94, 96; McGDA; MiSFD 9; OxCFilm; WhAm 11; WhoAdv 90; WhoAm 74, 76, 78, 84, 86, 92, 94, 95, 96; WhoEnt 92; WhoGrA 62, 82; WhoWor 74, 76; WhoWorJ 72, 78; WorEFlm*

Bassano, Jacopo
[Giacomo da Ponte]
Italian. Artist
One of earliest genre painters; noted for *The Good Samaritan.*
b. 1510? in Bassano, Italy
d. Feb 13, 1592 in Bassano, Italy
Source: *BioIn 1, 2, 4, 11; IntDcAA 90; McGDA; NewCol 75; OxCArt; WhDW*

Bassett, Angela
American. Actor
Winner, Golden Globe Award, Best Actress for *What's Love Got to Do With It,* 1994.
b. Aug 16, 1958 in New York, New York
Source: *ConTFT 13; CurBio 96; DcTwCCu 5; IntMPA 94, 96; WhoAm 94, 95, 96, 97; WhoAmW 95, 97*

Bassett, Ben
American. Journalist
Foreign news editor, Associated Press, 1948-73; supervised coverage of Korean, Vietnam wars.
b. Oct 30, 1909 in Topeka, Kansas
d. Oct 14, 1987 in New Rochelle, New York
Source: *WhAm 9; WhoAm 74, 76; WhoWor 74, 76*

Bassett, John D
American. Businessman
Formed Bassett Furniture Co., 1902, world's largest maker of wooden furniture.
b. 1866 in Bassett, Virginia
d. Feb 26, 1965 in Bassett, Virginia
Source: *Entr; WhAm 4*

Bassey, Shirley
Welsh. Singer
Sang title song from James Bond film *Goldfinger,* 1964.
b. Jan 8, 1937 in Cardiff, Wales
Source: *BiDAfM; BioIn 6; CelR; DrBlPA, 90; EncPR&S 89; FilmgC; HalFC 80, 84, 88; InB&W 85; IntWW 93; InWom SUP; LegTOT; NegAl 83, 89; OxCPMus; PenEncP; RkOn 78; WhoAm 76, 78, 80, 82; WhoRock 81; WorAl; WorAlBi*

Basso, Hamilton
[Joseph Hamilton Basso]
American. Author
Wrote *The View from Pompey's Head,* 1954.
b. Sep 5, 1904 in New Orleans, Louisiana
d. May 13, 1964 in New Haven, Connecticut
Source: *AmAu&B; AmNov; BenetAL 91; BioIn 2, 3, 4, 6, 8, 9, 12; ConAu 89; DcAmB S7; DcLEL; FifSWrA; LinLib L; LngCTC; NatCAB 58; Novels; OxCAmL 65, 83; PenC AM; REn; REnAL; SouWr; TwCA, SUP; WebBD 83; WhAm 4; WhE&EA*

Bastianini, Ettore
Italian. Opera Singer
One of leading Verdi baritones of his day.
b. 1923 in Siena, Italy
d. Jan 25, 1967 in Sirmione, Italy
Source: *BioIn 4, 7; WhAm 4*

Batchelor, Clarence Daniel
American. Cartoonist
Work appeared in *NY Daily News,* 1931-69; won Pulitzer, 1937.
b. Apr 1, 1888 in Osage City, Kansas
d. Sep 5, 1977 in Deep River, Connecticut
Source: *BioIn 7, 11; ConAu 73; WhAm 7; WhoAm 76; WhoAmA 76, 78N, 89N, 91N, 93N; WorECar*

Batchler, Amelia
American. Model
Posed for Columbia Pictures logo—the woman with torch, 1936.
b. 1916?
Source: *BioIn 15*

Bate, Walter Jackson
American. Educator, Author
Won Pulitzers for biographies of John Keats, 1963, Samuel Johnson, 1977.
b. May 23, 1918 in Mankato, Minnesota
Source: *AmAu&B; Benet 87; BioIn 10, 11, 16, 17; BlueB 76; ConAu 5R; ConLCrt 77, 82; DcLB 67, 103; DrAS 74E, 78E, 82E; IntAu&W 77, 82, 91; OxCAmL 65, 83, 95; Who 74, 82, 83, 85, 88, 90, 92, 94; WhoAm 74, 76, 78, 80, 82, 84, 86, 88, 90, 92, 94, 95, 96, 97; WhoE 79, 81, 83, 85, 86; WhoUSWr 88; WhoWrEP 89, 92, 95; WorAu 1950; WrDr 80, 82, 84, 86, 88, 90, 92, 94, 96*

Bateman, Henry Mayo
Welsh. Cartoonist
Most highly paid British cartoonist of his time.
b. Feb 15, 1887 in New South Wales, Australia
d. Feb 11, 1970 in Gozo, Malta
Source: *BioIn 1, 8, 12, 13, 14; DcBrAr 1; DcBrBI; DcNaB 1961; GrBr; IlsCB 1744; WhE&EA; WhLit; WorECom*

Bateman, Jason
American. Actor
Played David Hogan on TV comedy "The Hogan Family," 1986-90; brother of Justine.
b. Jan 14, 1969 in Rye, New York
Source: *BioIn 14, 15, 16; CelR 90; ConTFT 5; IntMPA 92, 94, 96; LegTOT; News 88; WhoAmW 91; WhoHol 92*

Bateman, Justine
American. Actor
Played Mallory Keaton on TV series "Family Ties," 1982-89; sister of Jason.
b. Feb 19, 1966 in Rye, New York
Source: *CelR 90; ConTFT 5; IntMPA 92, 94, 96; LegTOT; News 88; WhoAmW 91, 93; WhoEnt 92; WhoHol 92*

Bateman, Kate Josephine
American. Actor
Starred in play *Leah the Forsaken,* 1863.
b. Oct 7, 1842 in Baltimore, Maryland
d. Apr 8, 1917 in London, England
Source: *AmWom; ApCAB; BioIn 16; CelCen; DcBiPP; Drake; InWom, SUP; NatCAB 10; NotAW; NotNAT B; NotWoAT; OxCThe 83; TwCBDA*

Bateman, Mary
"Yorkshire Witch"
English. Murderer
Pathological criminal who dispensed magical charms to defraud, kill; died on gallows.
b. 1768 in Aisenby, England
d. Mar 20, 1809

Bates, Alan Arthur
English. Actor
Starred in films *King of Hearts,* 1967; *An Unmarried Woman,* 1978.
b. Feb 17, 1934 in Derbyshire, England

Source: *BiE&WWA; BioIn 13; BkPepl; CamGWoT; CelR 90; ConTFT 7; CurBio 69; FilmgC; HalFC 88; IntMPA 86, 92; IntWW 83, 91; MovMk; NotNAT; Who 85, 92; WhoAm 86, 90; WhoEnt 92; WhoHol A; WhoThe 81; WhoWor 74, 91; WorAlBi*

Bates, Arlo
American. Author
Poet, novelist: *Patty's Perversities,* 1881; *The Intoxicated Ghost,* 1908.
b. Dec 16, 1850 in East Machias, Maine
d. Aug 24, 1918 in Boston, Massachusetts
Source: *Alli SUP; AmAu; AmAu&B; AmBi; ApCAB; BbD; BenetAL 91; BiD&SB; CarSB; ChhPo; DcAmAu; DcAmB; DcBiA; DcNAA; NatCAB 8; OxCAmL 65, 83, 95; REnAL; ScF&FL 1; TwCBDA; WhAm 1*

Bates, Blanche Lyon
American. Actor
Starred in David Belasco's *Madame Butterfly,* 1900.
b. Aug 25, 1873 in Portland, Oregon
d. Dec 25, 1941 in San Francisco, California
Source: *DcAmB S3; InWom SUP; LibW; NotAW; OxCThe 83*

Bates, Daisy Lee Gatson
American. Journalist, Civil Rights Leader
Advocate of racial integration, started newspaper *Arkansas State Press,* 1941.
b. 1920 in Huttig, Arkansas
Source: *AfrAmAl 6; BioIn 2, 3, 7, 8, 10, 16; BlkWAm; ConAu 127; HerW 84; IntDcWB; InWom SUP; NegAl 89; NotBlAW 1; PolProf E; WhoBlA 92*

Bates, Florence
[Florence Rabe]
American. Actor
Made film debut at age 50; starred in *Rebecca,* 1940.
b. Apr 15, 1888 in San Antonio, Texas
d. Jan 31, 1954 in Burbank, California
Source: *BioIn 3, 11; EncAFC; FilmEn; FilmgC; HalFC 80, 84, 88; HolCA; MovMk; NotNAT B; ObitOF 79; Vers A; WhoHol B; WhScrn 74, 77, 83*

Bates, H(erbert) E(rnest)
English. Author
Wrote over 50 books including *The Two Sisters,* 1926; books on WW II.
b. May 16, 1905 in Rushden, England
d. Jan 29, 1974 in Canterbury, England
Source: *Au&Wr 71; Benet 96; BioIn 1, 3, 4, 8, 9, 10, 12, 15, 17; CasWL; ChhPo, S1; ConAu 45, 93; CurBio 44, 74; DcLEL; DcNaB 1971; EncWL, 3; EngPo; EvLB; IntAu&W 76, 77; ModBrL; NewCBEL; OxCEng 95; PenC ENG; REn; RfGShF; RGTwCWr; TwCA, SUP; WhAm 6; WhLit; Who 74; WhoWor 74*

Bates, Henry Walter
English. Naturalist, Explorer
His trips revealed over 8,000 new insect species; wrote *The Naturalist on the Amazon,* 1863.
b. Feb 8, 1825 in Leicester, England
d. Feb 16, 1892 in London, England
Source: *Alli SUP; ApCAB; BiESc; BioIn 8, 11, 12, 14, 16, 18; BritAu 19; CelCen; DcNaB S1; DcScB; Expl 93; InSci; LarDcSc; LinLib L, S; McGEWB; NewC; NewCBEL; NewCol 75; OxCEng 67, 85, 95; WhDW; WhWE*

Bates, Katharine Lee
American. Poet, Educator
Best known for writing hymn-patriotic song "America the Beautiful," 1911.
b. Aug 12, 1859 in Falmouth, Massachusetts
d. Mar 28, 1929 in Wellesley, Massachusetts
Source: *Alli SUP; AmAu&B; AmBi; AmLY; AmWom; AmWomPl; AnMV 1926; BiDAmEd; BiD&SB; BioAmW; BioIn 2, 3, 4, 5, 6, 11, 19; CarSB; ChhPo, S1, S2, S3; CnDAL; DcAmAu; DcAmB S1; DcLB 71; DcNAA; EvLB; FemiCLE; GrLiveH; HerW; InWom; JBA 34; LibW; LinLib L, S; NatCAB 9, 42; NotAW; OxCAmL 65; REnAL; TwCA, SUP; TwCBDA; TwCWr; WebAB 74, 79; WhAm 1; WhNAA; WomWWA 14*

Bates, Kathy
[Kathleen Doyle Bates]
American. Actor
Won best actress Oscar for portrayal of psychopath Annie Wilkes in *Misery,* 1991.
b. Jun 28, 1948 in Memphis, Tennessee
Source: *ASCAP 80; ConTFT 1, 10; CurBio 91; IntMPA 92, 94, 96; IntWW 93; LegTOT; News 91; NewYTBS 91; WhoAm 92, 94, 95, 96, 97; WhoAmW 93, 95, 97; WhoEnt 92; WhoHol 92*

Bates, Mary Elizabeth
American. Surgeon, Social Reformer
First female intern at Cook County Hospital, Chicago, 1882; worked to reform child abuse laws, 1905.
b. Feb 25, 1861 in Manitowoc, Wisconsin
d. 1954
Source: *NatCAB 18; WhAm 4; WomWWA 14*

Bates, Peg Leg
[Clayton Bates]
American. Dancer
Amputation of leg forced him to dance with peg leg; in Broadway musical *Blackbirds,* 1925, 1933.
b. Nov 10, 1907 in Fountain Inn, South Carolina
Source: *BiDAfM; BiDD; BioIn 1, 10, 14, 17, 20; BlksBF; DrBlPA, 90; EncVaud; InB&W 80, 85; NewYTBS 85*

Bates, Ted
[Theodore Lewis Bates]
American. Advertising Executive
Founded Ted Bates & Co. advertising agency, 1940; helped develop TV advertising; wrote first Wonder Bread campaign.
b. Sep 11, 1901 in New Haven, Connecticut
d. May 30, 1972
Source: *AdMenW; BioIn 9, 12, 13, 20; DcAmB S9; NatCAB 58; NewYTBE 72; WhAm 5; WhoAdv 72*

Bateson, Gregory
American. Psychologist, Anthropologist
Founded science of cybernetics with first wife, Margaret Mead; formulated "double-bind" theory on cause of schizophrenia.
b. May 9, 1904 in Cambridge, England
d. Jul 4, 1980 in San Francisco, California
Source: *AmAu&B; AmMWSc 73S; AnObit 1980; BioIn 11, 12, 13, 14, 21; ConAu 41R, 101; DcAmB S10; EncSPD; IntDcAn; IntEnSS 79; ThTwC 87; WrDr 76, 80*

Bateson, William
English. Biologist
Coined term "genetics"; known for research in plant inheritance based on work of Mendel.
b. Aug 8, 1861 in Whitby, England
d. Feb 8, 1926 in Merton, England
Source: *AsBiEn; BiESc; BioIn 10, 12, 14, 16, 20; CamDcSc; DcNaB 1922; DcScB; EncWB; FacFETw; InSci; LarDcSc; LegTOT; NotTwCS; WebBD 83; WhDW; WorScD*

Bathgate, Andy
[Andrew James Bathgate]
Canadian. Hockey Player
Right wing, 1952-68, 1970-71, 1974-75, mostly with NY Rangers; won Hart Trophy, 1959; Hall of Fame, 1978.
b. Aug 28, 1932 in Winnipeg, Manitoba, Canada
Source: *BioIn 5, 6, 7, 9; CurBio 64; HocEn; WhoHcky 73; WhoSpor*

Bathory, Elizabeth
[Countess Nadasdy]
"The Blood Countess"
Hungarian. Murderer
Killed 610 servant girls; believed human blood baths essential to retaining youth.
b. 1560
d. 1614
Source: *BioIn 4, 9, 13; FanAl; InWom SUP; MacDWB*

Bathsheba
Biblical Figure
Married King David, who had her first husband killed; mother of Solomon.
b. 1040BC
d. 1015BC
Source: *BioIn 7, 12; InWom, SUP; LegTOT*

Batista y Zaldivar, Fulgencio
Cuban. Political Leader
Dictator who came to power, 1952; overthrown by Fidel Castro, 1959.
b. Jan 16, 1901 in Banes, Cuba
d. Aug 6, 1973 in Marbella, Spain
Source: *BiDLAmC; BioIn 1, 2, 3, 4, 5, 6, 8, 10, 16, 18; ColdWar 2; ConAu 111; CurBio 52, 73; DcCPCAm; DcHiB; FacFETw; McGEWB; NewYTBE 73; WhDW; WorAl; WorAlBi*

Batlle y Ordonez, Jose
Uruguayan. Political Leader
As president of Uruquay 1903-07, 1911-15 established a viable democracy.
b. May 21, 1856 in Montevideo, Uruguay
d. Oct 20, 1929 in Montevideo, Uruguay
Source: *BiDLAmC; BioIn 6, 7, 16; DcCPSAm; DcPol; DcTwHis; McGEWB*

Battelle, Phyllis Marie
American. Journalist
Had a weekly syndicated column, "Assignment: America", 1955-88.
b. Jan 4, 1922 in Dayton, Ohio
Source: *BiDAmNC; ConAu 77; ForWC 70; WhoAm 74, 76, 78, 80; WhoAmW 58, 61, 64, 66, 68, 70, 72, 74*

Batten, Jean Gardner
New Zealander. Aviator
Known for record-breaking flights in one-seater plane, 1930s; autobiography, 1938, reprinted as *Alone in the Sky,* 1979.
b. Sep 15, 1909 in Rotorua, New Zealand
d. Nov 22, 1982 in Majorca, Spain
Source: *BioIn 5, 8; BlueB 76; ConAu 106, 123; ContDcW 89; IntAu&W 82; IntDcWB; IntWW 74, 75, 76, 77, 78, 79, 80, 81, 82, 83; Who 74, 82, 83, 85, 88; WhoWor 74, 76, 78; WomFir; WrDr 76, 80, 82, 84, 86, 88*

Batten, William Milfred
American. Businessman
Chm., chief exec., NY Stock Exchange, 1976-84.
b. Jun 4, 1909 in Reedy, West Virginia
Source: *BioIn 10, 11, 12, 15; BlueB 76; Dun&B 86; IntWW 74, 75, 76, 77, 78, 79, 80, 81, 82, 83, 89, 91, 93; NewYTBS 76; St&PR 75, 84; WhoAm 74, 76, 78, 80, 82, 84, 86, 88, 90, 92, 94, 95, 96, 97; WhoE 74, 75, 77, 85, 89; WhoFI 74, 75, 77, 81, 83*

Battistini, Mattia
Italian. Opera Singer
Was greatest living Italian baritone; had 50-yr. career; never sang in U.S.
b. Feb 27, 1856 in Rome, Italy
d. Nov 7, 1928 in Collebaccaro, Italy
Source: *Baker 78, 84, 92; BioIn 11, 13, 15, 16, 18; CmOp; IntDcOp; MetOEnc; MusSN; NewEOp 71; NewGrDM 80; NewGrDO; OxDcOp; PenDiMP*

Battle, Kathleen Deanne
"The Best Coloratura in the World"
American. Singer
Grammy award winning opera singer; coloratura soprano regular for New York's Metropolitan Opera 1978—.
b. Aug 13, 1948 in Portsmouth, Ohio

Battles, Cliff(ord Franklin)
American. Football Player
Running back, 1932-37; led NFL in rushing, 1933, 1937; Hall of Fame.
b. May 1, 1910 in Akron, Ohio
d. Apr 27, 1981 in Clearwater, Florida
Source: *BiDAmSp FB; BioIn 6, 8, 9, 12, 17; LegTOT; WhoFtbl 74*

Batts, Deborah A.
American. Judge
District court judge, New York, 1994—.
b. Apr 13, 1947 in Philadelphia, Pennsylvania
Source: *GayLesB; WhoAm 97; WhoAmL 96; WhoAmW 95, 97*

Batu Khan
Mongolian. Military Leader
Grandson of Genghis Khan who conquerded Russia, 1240; organized Mogul state Golden Horde.
d. 1255
Source: *HarEnMi; McGEWB; NewCol 75; WhDW*

Baucus, Max Sieben
American. Politician
Dem. senator from MT, 1979—.
b. Dec 11, 1941 in Helena, Montana
Source: *AlmAP 80, 92; BiDrUSC 89; CngDr 87, 89; IntWW 83, 91; PolsAm 84; WhoAm 76, 86, 90; WhoAmP 85, 91; WhoEmL 87; WhoGov 77; WhoWest 78, 92; WhoWor 84, 91*

Baudelaire, Charles Pierre
French. Poet
Best-known poems contained in *Les Fleurs du Mal,* 1857.
b. Apr 9, 1821 in Paris, France
d. Aug 31, 1867 in Paris, France
Source: *AtlBL; BbD; Benet 96; BiD&SB; CasWL; ClDMEL 47; CyWA 58; DcEuL; EuAu; EvEuW; NewC; OxCEng 67; OxCFr; PenC EUR; REn*

Baudouin, I, King
[Albert Charles Baudouin]
Belgian. Ruler
King of Belgium, 1951-93; proclaimed independence of Zaire, 1960.
b. Sep 7, 1930 in Brussels, Belgium
d. Jul 31, 1993 in Motril, Spain
Source: *AnObit 1993; BioIn 2, 3, 5, 6, 12, 16, 19, 21; CurBio 93N; IntWW 74, 75, 76, 77, 78, 79, 80, 81, 82, 83, 89, 91, 93; NewYTBS 93; PolLCWE; WhAm 11; WhoEIO 82; WhoWor 76, 78, 80, 82, 84, 87, 89, 91, 93; WorAl; WorAlBi*

Baudrillard, Jean
French. Sociologist
Views the electronic media as the shaper of the reality of things and events; author of *Amerique,* 1986.
b. 1929 in Reims, France
Source: *Benet 96; BioIn 15, 17, 18, 19, 21; ConLC 60; CurBio 93; DcTwCCu 2; WhoWor 95; WorAu 1985*

Bauer, Eddie
American. Merchant
Pioneered quilted, goose-down insulated jacket; founded mail order sporting goods co., 1921.
b. Oct 19, 1899 in Orcas Island, Washington
d. Apr 18, 1986 in Bellevue, Washington
Source: *BioIn 14, 15, 21; ConNews 86-3; NewYTBS 86*

Bauer, Erwin Adam
American. Photographer, Writer
Noted wildlife photos and essays have appeared in many major publications including *National Geographic, Smithsonian;* has more than 25 books to his credit.
b. Aug 22, 1919 in Cincinnati, Ohio
Source: *ConAu 6NR, 9R; WhoWest 96*

Bauer, Hank
[Henry Albert Bauer]
American. Baseball Player, Baseball Manager
Outfielder, 1948-61; managed Baltimore to world championship, 1966.
b. Jul 31, 1922 in East Saint Louis, Illinois
Source: *Ballpl 90; BioIn 4, 7, 8, 14, 21; CurBio 67; LegTOT; WhoProB 73; WhoSpor*

Bauer, Harold
English. Pianist, Violinist
Celebrated pianist with U.S. orchestras, from 1900; founded NYC's Beethoven Association, 1918.
b. Apr 28, 1873 in London, England
d. Mar 12, 1951 in Miami, Florida
Source: *ASCAP 66; Baker 78, 84, 92; BiDAmM; BioIn 1, 2, 3, 4, 7, 8, 9, 11, 12, 16, 21; BriBkM 80; DcAmB S5; MusSN; NewAmDM; NewGrDA 86; NewGrDM 80; NotTwCP; PenDiMP; WhAm 3*

Bauer, Helen
American. Author
Writings include *California Mission Days,* 1951; *The Avocado Cookbook,* 1967.
b. Aug 14, 1900 in DeQueen, Arkansas
Source: *BioIn 9; ConAu 5R; ForWC 70; SmATA 2; WhoAmW 64*

Bauer, Louis Agricola
American. Scientist, Editor
Expert on terrestrial magnetism; founded journal on magnetism, 1896.
b. Jan 26, 1865 in Cincinnati, Ohio

d. Apr 12, 1932 in Washington, District of Columbia
Source: *AmBi; ApCAB X; BioIn 7; DcAmB S1; DcScB; NatCAB 14, 23; WhAm 1*

Bauer, Peggy
[Grace Margaret Bauer]
American. Photographer
With her husband, has shot thousands of wildlife photos that have appeared in many major publications.
b. Mar 2, 1932 in Riverside, Illinois
Source: *CurBio 93*

Bauersfeld, Walther
German. Inventor, Engineer
Co-inventor of world's first planetarium.
b. 1879
d. Oct 28, 1959 in Heidenheim, Germany (West)
Source: *BioIn 3, 5; ObitOF 79*

Baugh, Albert Croll
American. Author, Educator
Academician, noted for *History of the English Language,* 1935.
b. Feb 26, 1891 in Philadelphia, Pennsylvania
d. Mar 21, 1981 in Philadelphia, Pennsylvania
Source: *AmAu&B; BioIn 3, 12, 13; ConAu 103, 107; DrAS 74E, 78E; NewYTBS 81; WhAm 7; WhE&EA; WhoAm 74, 76, 78, 80; WhoWor 78*

Baugh, Sammy
[Samuel Adrian Baugh]
"Slingin' Sam"
American. Football Player
Quarterback, Washington, 1937-52; led NFL in passing six times; Hall of Fame, 1963.
b. Mar 17, 1914 in Temple, Texas
Source: *BiDAmSp FB; BioIn 1, 3, 5, 6, 7, 8, 9, 10, 12, 17, 20, 21; LegTOT; WebAB 74, 79; WhoFtbl 74; WhoSpor; WorAl; WorAlBi*

Baulieu, Etienne-Emile
French. Physician, Scientist
Endocrinologist, creator of Roussel-Uclaf 38486 (RU 486) birth-control formula (the "abortion pill").
b. Dec 12, 1926 in Strasbourg, France
Source: *BioIn 16; CurBio 95; IntWW 91; News 90, 90-1; WhoFr 79; WhoScEn 94; WhoScEu 91-2; WhoWor 74, 76, 78, 80, 82, 84, 87, 89, 91*

Baum, Kurt
Czech. Opera Singer
Tenor; debut, NY Met., 1941.
b. Mar 15, 1908 in Prague, Bohemia
d. Dec 27, 1989 in New York, New York
Source: *BioIn 2, 4, 5, 13, 16, 17; CurBio 56, 90N; IntWWM 90; MetOEnc; NewEOp 71; NewYTBS 89; WhoWor 74*

Baum, L(yman) Frank
American. Author, Journalist
Wrote *The Wizard of Oz,* 1900.
b. May 15, 1856 in Chittenango, New York
d. May 6, 1919 in Hollywood, California
Source: *AmAu&B; AmBi; ApCAB X; AuBYP 2, 3; Benet 96; BioIn 4, 5, 7, 8, 9, 11, 12, 13, 14, 15, 17, 18, 19, 20; CarSB; ChhPo, S2, S3; CnDAL; DcAmAu; DcAmB; DcArts; DcNAA; DcPup; EncAAH; EncSF 93; FamSYP; FilmgC; GayN; HisDcDP; LngCTC; MajAI; NotNAT B; OxCAmL 65, 95; PenC AM; PIP&P A; RAdv 14; REn; REnAL; RfGAmL 94; SJGFanW; SmATA 18; ThrBJA; TwCA; TwCChW 78, 95; WebAB 74, 79; WhoChL; WhoStg 1906, 1908*

Baum, Vicki
American. Author
Wrote best-seller *Grand Hotel,* 1929, film starred Greta Garbo, 1932.
b. Jan 24, 1888 in Vienna, Austria
d. Aug 29, 1960 in Hollywood, California
Source: *AmAu&B; AmNov; BiGAW; BioIn 2, 3, 4, 5, 6, 9, 14, 21; BlmGWL; CasWL; ConAu 93; CyWA 58; DcLB 85; EncCoWW; EncTR 91; EvEuW; InWom; LegTOT; LiExTwC; LngCTC; NatCAB 52; NotNAT, A, B; Novels; ObitOF 79; ObitT 1951; OxCGer 76, 86; TwCA, SUP; TwCWr; WhAm 4; WhE&EA; WhoLA; WomWrGe; WorAl*

Baum, William Wakefield, Cardinal
American. Religious Leader
Archbishop of Washington DC, 1973-80; prefect in Rome, 1980—.
b. Nov 21, 1926 in Dallas, Texas
Source: *BioIn 9, 11, 12; CurBio 76; IntWW 74, 75, 76, 77, 78, 79, 80, 81, 82, 83, 89, 91, 93; NewYTBE 73; NewYTBS 76, 80; RelLAm 91; WhoAm 74, 76, 86, 90, 95, 96, 97; WhoRel 75, 77, 92; WhoSSW 76; WhoWor 84, 87, 91, 95, 96, 97*

Baumeister, Willi
German. Artist
Abstractionist, who used ideograms, biomorphic shapes; condemned by Nazis, 1937.
b. Jan 22, 1889 in Stuttgart, Germany
d. Aug 31, 1955 in Stuttgart, Germany (West)
Source: *BioIn 2, 4, 7, 17; ConArt 77, 83; FacFETw; McGDA; OxCTwCA; OxDcArt; PhDcTCA 77; WorArt 1950*

Baunsgaard, Hilmar Tormod Ingolf
Danish. Political Leader
Prime minister of Denmark, 1968-71.
b. Feb 26, 1920 in Slagelse, Denmark
d. Jun 30, 1989
Source: *BioIn 8; IntWW 74, 75, 76, 77, 78, 79, 80, 81, 82, 83, 89; WhoWor 74, 76, 78*

Baur, Ferdinand Christian
German. Theologian, Educator
Founded Tubingen school of biblical criticism; doubted authenticity of most New Testament books.
b. Jun 21, 1792 in Schmiden, Germany
d. Dec 2, 1860 in Tubingen, Germany
Source: *BiD&SB; BioIn 10; DcBiPP; EncEarC; LuthC 75; McGEWB; NewCol 75; WebBD 83*

Baur, John I(reland) H(owe)
American. Museum Director
Director, Whitney Museum of American Art, 1968-74; wrote numerous books on subject.
b. Aug 9, 1909 in Woodbridge, Connecticut
d. May 15, 1987 in New York, New York
Source: *BioIn 8, 15; ConAu 122; CurBio 69, 87, 87N; NewYTBS 87; WhAm 9; WhAmArt 85; WhoAm 74, 76, 78, 80, 84, 86; WhoAmA 73, 76, 78, 80, 82, 84, 86; WhoE 75*

Bausch, Edward
American. Inventor
Helped to develop precision optical instruments, particularly the microscope; chm. of Bausch & Lomb Optical Co.
b. Sep 26, 1854 in Rochester, New York
d. Jul 30, 1944 in Rochester, New York
Source: *BiDAmBL 83; CurBio 44; DcAmB S3; DcNAA; ObitOF 79; WhAm 2*

Bausch, James
American. Track Athlete
Won decathlon, 1932 Olympics.
b. Mar 29, 1906 in Marion, South Dakota
Source: *BiDAmSp OS; WhoTr&F 73*

Bausch, John Jacob
American. Inventor
With Henry Lomb began Vulcanite Optical Instrument Co., 1866.
b. Jul 25, 1830 in Suessen, Germany
d. Feb 14, 1925 in Rochester, New York
Source: *BioIn 1; Entr; NatCAB 23; WhAm 1*

Bavier, Frances
American. Actor
Played Aunt Bea in TV series "The Andy Griffith Show," 1960-69.
b. Jan 14, 1905 in New York, New York
d. Dec 6, 1989 in Silver City, North Carolina
Source: *BioIn 16; ForYSC; NewYTBS 89; WhoHol A*

Bawden, Nina Mary Mabey
[Nina Mary Mabey Kark]
English. Author
Writings include *Eyes of Green,* 1953; *Familiar Passions,* 1979.
b. Jan 19, 1925 in London, England
Source: *AuBYP 3; BioIn 13, 16; CamGLE; ChlLR 2; ConAu 18NR,*

29NR; ConNov 86, 91; EncBrWW; FemiCLE; IntAu&W 77, 91; IntWW 91; InWom SUP; MajAI; OxCChiL; OxCEng 95; SmATA 4, 72; TwCChW 78, 89; Who 92; WhoAmW 74, 75; WrDr 86, 92

Bax, Arnold Edward Trevor, Sir
[Dermont O'Byrne]
English. Composer, Author
Master of Music for Elizabeth II, George VI; composed march played at coronation of Queen Elizabeth II.
b. Nov 8, 1883 in Streatham, England
d. Oct 3, 1953 in Cork, Ireland
Source: *BiDIrW; BioIn 1, 3, 4, 8, 9, 10, 12; CurBio 43, 54; DcArts; DcCM; DcIrB 78, 88; DcIrL 96; DcNaB 1951; GrBr; LngCTC; OxCIri; OxCMus; WhE&EA*

Bax, Clifford
English. Dramatist, Critic, Poet
Plays include *Rose Without a Thorn,* 1932.
b. Jul 12, 1886 in Knightsbridge, England
d. Nov 18, 1962
Source: *BioIn 1, 6, 8, 13, 17; CamGWoT; ChhPo, S1, S2; ConAu 113; DcLB 10, 100; DcLEL; GrWrEL DR; LngCTC; McGEWD 72, 84; ModBrL; NewC; NewCBEL; NotNAT B; ObitT 1961; OxCThe 67; REn; RfGEnL 91; WhE&EA; WhLit; WhoLA; WhThe*

Baxley, Barbara
American. Actor
Stage, film, TV performer; won critical acclaim as Sally Field's mother in *Norma Rae,* 1979.
b. Jan 1, 1927 in Stockton, California
d. Jun 7, 1990 in New York, New York
Source: *BiE&WWA; BioIn 16, 17; ConTFT 2; HalFC 88; NewYTBS 90; VarWW 85; WhoThe 72, 77, 81*

Baxter, Anne
American. Actor
Best known for films *The Razor's Edge,* 1946; *All About Eve,* 1950 ; played Victoria Cabot on TV's "Hotel," 1983-85.
b. May 7, 1923 in Michigan City, Indiana
d. Dec 12, 1985 in New York, New York
Source: *AnObit 1985; BiDFilm, 81, 94; BiE&WWA; BioIn 9, 10, 11, 13; CelR; ConAu 111, 114, 118; ConNews 86-1; ConTFT 3; CurBio 72, 86, 86N; FilmEn; FilmgC; ForYSC; HalFC 80, 84, 88; IndAu 1967; IntDcF 1-3, 2-3; IntMPA 75, 76, 77, 78, 79, 80, 81, 82, 84, 86; InWom, SUP; ItaFilm; LegTOT; MotPP; MovMk; NewYTBS 85; NotNAT; OxCAusL; WhAm 9; WhoAm 74, 76, 78, 80, 82, 84; WhoAmW 58, 64, 66, 68, 70, 72, 74, 83; WhoHol A; WhoThe 77, 81; WorAl; WorAlBi; WorEFlm*

Baxter, Charles (Morley)
American. Author
Author of novels *First Light,* 1987; *Shadow Play,* 1993.
b. May 13, 1947 in Minneapolis, Minnesota
Source: *ConAu 40NR, 57; ConLC 45, 78; ConPopW; DcLB 130; DrAPF 80; DrAS 82E; WhoMW 78*

Baxter, Frank Condie
American. Educator
Won seven Emmys for TV show "Shakespeare on TV."
b. May 4, 1896 in Newbold, New Jersey
d. Jan 20, 1982 in San Marino, California
Source: *BioIn 2, 3, 4, 12, 13; CurBio 55; WhAm 8; WhoAm 74, 76, 78*

Baxter, James Phinney, III
American. Educator
Pres., Williams College, 1937-61; won Pulitzer, 1947, for *Scientists Against Time.*
b. Feb 15, 1893 in Portland, Maine
d. Jun 17, 1975 in Williamstown, Massachusetts
Source: *AmAu&B; BioIn 1, 4, 6, 10, 11; ConAu 57, 65; CurBio 47, 75; EncAI&E; NewYTBS 75; OxCAmL 65; PeoHis; TwCA SUP; WhAm 6, 10; WhoWor 74*

Baxter, Keith
[Keith Stanley Baxter Wright]
Welsh. Actor
Starred in London and NY stage production of "Sleuth," 1970.
b. Apr 29, 1935 in Newport, Wales
Source: *BiE&WWA; ConAu 135; ConTFT 4, 13; IntMPA 86, 92; NotNAT; WhoHol A; WhoThe 81*

Baxter, Les
American. Bandleader
Played keyboards for Neil Norman's Cosmic Orchestra, 1975-80.
b. Mar 14, 1922 in Mexia, Texas
d. Jan 15, 1996 in Newport Beach, California
Source: *ASCAP 66; BiDAmM; CmpEPM; HalFC 80, 84, 88; LegTOT; OxCPMus; PenEncP; RkOn 74; WhoHrs 80; WhoRocM 82*

Baxter, Meredith
American. Actor
Starred in TV series "Bridget Loves Bernie," 1971-72; "Family," 1976-80; "Family Ties," 1982-1989.
b. Jun 21, 1947 in Los Angeles, California
Source: *BioIn 9; CelR 90; ConTFT 9; IntMPA 92, 94, 96; InWom SUP; LegTOT; NewYTBE 72; WhoAm 82, 90, 94, 95, 96, 97; WhoAmW 91, 93, 95, 97; WhoEnt 92; WhoHol 92; WorAlBi*

Baxter, Richard
English. Theologian
Nonconformist Puritan preacher; twice imprisoned; writings include *Everlasting Rest,* 1650.
b. Nov 12, 1615 in Rowton, England
d. Dec 8, 1691 in London, England
Source: *Alli; BbD; BiD&SB; BiDRP&D; BioIn 1, 2, 3, 4, 5, 6, 7, 10, 12, 13, 14, 17; BlmGEL; BritAu; CamGEL; CamGLE; CasWL; Chambr 1; ChhPo; CroE&S; DcBiPP; DcEnA; DcEnL; DcNaB; EvLB; HisDStE; LuthC 75; McGEWB; NewC; NewCBEL; OxCEng 67, 85, 95; OxCMus; OxCThe 67; PenC ENG; PoChrch; REn; WebE&AL; WhDW*

Baxter, Warner
American. Actor
Won 1929 Oscar for role of the Cisco Kid in *In Old Arizona.*
b. Mar 29, 1891 in Columbus, Ohio
d. May 7, 1951 in Beverly Hills, California
Source: *BiDFilm, 94; BioIn 2, 3, 4, 7, 8, 9; CmMov; Film 1; FilmEn; FilmgC; IntDcF 1-3; MotPP; MovMk; NatCAB 39; NotNAT B; ObitOF 79; OxCFilm; TwYS; WhAm 3; WhScrn 74, 77, 83; WorEFlm*

Bay, Howard
American. Designer, Director
Won best set design Tonys for *Toys in the Attic,* 1960; *Man of La Mancha,* 1966.
b. May 3, 1912 in Centralia, Washington
d. Nov 21, 1986 in New York, New York
Source: *BiE&WWA; BioIn 13; CamGWoT; ConAu 81, 121; ConDes 84, 90, 97; ConTFT 4; NotNAT; OxCAmT 84; WhAm 9; WhAmArt 85; WhoAm 74, 76, 78, 80, 82, 84, 86; WhoThe 72, 77, 81*

Bayard, Pierre du Terrail
"Chevalier sans Peur et sans Reproche"
French. Soldier
French nat. hero; fought in Italian campaigns, 1520s; noted for knightly character.
b. 1473
d. Apr 30, 1524
Source: *OxCFr; REn*

Bayard, Thomas Francis
American. Diplomat, Politician
First US ambassador to Great Britain, 1893-97.
b. Oct 29, 1828 in Wilmington, Delaware
d. Sep 28, 1898 in Dedham, Massachusetts
Source: *AmBi; AmPolLe; ApCAB, X; BiAUS; BiDrAC; BiDrUSC 89; BiDrUSE 71, 89; BioIn 1, 4, 7, 10, 16; CyAG; DcAmB; DcAmDH 80, 89; EncAB-H 1974; EncSoH; HarEnUS; NatCAB 2; TwCBDA; WebAB 74, 79; WhAm HS; WhAmP*

Bay City Rollers, The
[Eric Faulkner; Alan Longmuir; Derek Longmuir; Leslie McKeown; Stuart "Woody" Wood]
Scottish. Music Group
Group named when manager stuck pin in map hitting Bay City, MI; hit single "Saturday Night," 1976.
Source: *BkPepl; ConMuA 80A; EncRk 88; EncRkSt; HarEnR 86; IlEncRk; OxCPMus; PenEncP; RolSEnR 83; WhoRocM 82*

Bayer, Herbert
American. Architect
One of last surviving teachers of Bauhaus school; believed art should respond to industrial world.
b. Apr 5, 1900 in Haag, Austria
d. Sep 30, 1985 in Montecito, California
Source: *AnObit 1985; BioIn 2, 3, 6, 8, 9, 10, 11, 13, 14, 15, 18; ConArt 77, 83, 89, 96; ConAu 117; ConDes 84, 90, 97; ConPhot 82, 88, 95; DcCAA 71, 77, 88, 94; DcTwDes; FacFETw; ICPEnP; MacBEP; MacEA; McGDA; NewYTBS 85; OxCTwCA; OxDcArt; PhDcTCA 77; PrintW 83, 85; WhAm 9; WhoAm 74, 76, 78, 80, 82, 84; WhoAmA 73, 76, 78, 80, 82, 84, 86N, 89N, 91N, 93N; WhoGrA 62; WhoWor 74*

Bayer, Wolfgang
American. Producer
Produces wildlife films shown on TV's "Nature" series.
b. 1937
Source: *BioIn 14, 15; NewYTBS 86; WhoSoCE 89*

Bayes, Nora
[Dora Goldberg]
American. Singer, Actor
Vaudeville, musical comedy star; co-wrote "Shine On, Harvest Moon," with husband Jack Norwood, 1908.
b. Jan 10, 1880 in Joliet, Illinois
d. Mar 19, 1928 in New York, New York
Source: *ASCAP 80; BiDAmM; BioIn 3, 14, 16, 19; CmpEPM; EncMT; EncVaud; FilmgC; HalFC 80, 84, 88; InWom, SUP; LegTOT; LibW; NewGrDA 86; NotAW; NotNAT B; NotWoAT; OxCAmT 84; OxCPMus; WebAB 74, 79; WhThe*

Bayh, Birch Evans, Jr.
American. Lawyer, Politician
Dem. senator from IN, 1962-81.
b. Jan 22, 1928 in Terre Haute, Indiana
Source: *BiDrAC; WhoMW 74; WhoWor 74, 78, 80, 82; WorAl; WorAlBi*

Bayh, Evan
American. Politician
Dem. governor, IN, 1989—.
b. Dec 26, 1955 in Terre Haute, Indiana
Source: *AlmAP 92, 96; BiDrGov 1988; BioIn 18, 20; IntWW 89, 91, 93; WhoAm 88, 90, 92, 94, 95, 96, 97; WhoAmP 87, 89, 91, 93, 95; WhoMW 88, 90, 92, 93, 96; WhoWor 93, 95*

Bayle, Pierre
French. Philosopher, Critic
Most important work *Historical & Critical Dictionary*, 1697-1706.
b. Nov 18, 1647 in Carlot, France
d. Dec 28, 1706 in Rotterdam, Netherlands
Source: *BbD; Benet 87, 96; BiD&SB; BioIn 3, 5, 7, 8, 13, 14; BlkwCE; CasWL; DcBiPP; DcEnL; DcEuL; Dis&D; EncEnl; EncUnb; EuAu; EvEuW; GuFrLit 2; LinLib L, S; LuthC 75; McGEWB; NewC; NewCBEL; OxCEng 67, 85, 95; OxCFr; OxCPhil; PenC EUR; RAdv 14, 13-4; REn; WhDW*

Bayley, Corrine
American. Educator
Roman Catholic nun; a pioneer in field of bioethics; founded Center for Bioethics.
b. 1941? in Santa Ana, California
Source: *ConNews 86-4*

Baylis, Lilian Mary
English. Manager
Created London's Old Vic Theatre, 1912; Sadler's Wells, 1931.
b. May 9, 1874 in London, England
d. Nov 25, 1937
Source: *InWom SUP; NotNAT A; OxCMus; OxCThe 67; WhDW; WhThe*

Bayliss, William Maddock, Sir
English. Physiologist
Studied digestion, heart action; coined word "hormone."
b. May 2, 1860 in Wednesbury, England
d. Aug 27, 1924 in London, England
Source: *AsBiEn; BiESc; BioIn 5, 14, 20; DcNaB 1922; DcScB; FacFETw; InSci; LarDcSc; NotTwCS; OxCMed 86; WebBD 83; WhLit; WorAl; WorScD*

Baylor, Don(ald) Edward
American. Baseball Player, Baseball Manager
Outfielder, designated hitter, 1970-87; led AL in RBIs, 1978; holds ML record for being hit by pitches; manager, Colorado Rockies, 1993—.
b. Jun 28, 1949 in Austin, Texas
Source: *BaseReg 86, 87; BiDAmSp Sup; BioIn 12; WhoAfA 96; WhoAm 80, 82, 84, 86, 88, 94, 95, 96, 97; WhoBlA 77, 80, 85, 88, 90, 92, 94; WhoWest 82, 89, 96*

Baylor, Elgin Gay
American. Basketball Player
Forward, LA, 1958-72; seventh all-time leading scorer with 23,149 pts; Hall of Fame, 1976.
b. Sep 16, 1934 in Washington, District of Columbia
Source: *BioIn 10; FacFETw; NewYTBE 71; OfNBA 87; WhoAm 88, 90, 92, 94, 95, 96, 97; WhoBbl 73; WhoWest 89, 92, 94, 96*

Baylor, Robert Emmet Bledsoe
American. Judge, Clergy
Helped found first Baptist college in TX, 1845; Baylor U named for him.
b. May 10, 1793 in Lincoln County, Kentucky
d. Dec 30, 1873 in Washington County, Texas
Source: *AmBi; ApCAB; BiDrAC; DcAmB; TwCBDA; WebBD 83; WhAm HS; WhAmP*

Bayne, Beverly Pearl
[Mrs. Francis X Bushman]
American. Actor
Played Juliet in first American film version of *Romeo and Juliet*, 1915.
b. Nov 22, 1894 in Minneapolis, Minnesota
d. Aug 18, 1982 in Scottsdale, Arizona
Source: *Film 1; FilmEn; MotPP; TwYS; WhoHol A*

Bazell, Robert Joseph
American. Broadcast Journalist
Joined NBC News, 1976, science correspondent since 1978.
b. Aug 21, 1946? in Pittsburgh, Pennsylvania
Source: *WhoAm 86; WhoTelC*

Bazelon, David L(ionel)
American. Judge
Redefined the test of criminal insanity, 1954; case decisions also broadened Bill of Rights protections.
b. Sep 3, 1909
d. Feb 19, 1993 in Washington, District of Columbia
Source: *AmBench 79; BiDFedJ; BiDrAPA 77, 89; BioIn 9, 10; BlueB 76; CngDr 74, 77, 79, 81, 83, 85, 87; CurBio 71, 93N; DrAS 74P, 78P, 82P; IntWW 74, 75, 76, 77, 78, 79, 80, 81, 82, 83, 89; IntYB 78, 79, 80, 81, 82; NatCAB 63N; WhAm 11; WhoAm 74, 76, 78, 80, 82, 84, 86, 88, 90, 92; WhoAmL 78, 79, 85; WhoE 79, 81, 83, 85; WhoGov 72, 75, 77; WhoSSW 73, 75, 76; WhoWorJ 72*

Bazin, Andre
French. Critic, Author
Film reviewer who founded *Les Cahiers du Cinema*, 1947.
b. Apr 18, 1918 in Angers, France
d. Nov 11, 1958 in Paris, France
Source: *BioIn 11, 17; ConAu 113; DcTwCCu 2; EncEurC; FilmEn; FilmgC; HalFC 80, 84, 88; LegTOT; OxCFilm; WorAu 1970; WorEFlm*

Bazin, Rene
[Bernard Seigny]
French. Author
Catholic writer of rural family life: *Those of His Own Household*, 1914.
b. Dec 26, 1853 in Angers, France
d. Jul 21, 1932
Source: *BioIn 1; CathA 1930; CIDMEL 47, 80; DcBiA; DcCathB; EvEuW; LinLib L; LngCTC; OxCFr; PenC EUR; REn; TwCA, SUP*

Baziotes, William
American. Artist
Abstract Expressionist; co-founded art school which became meeting place for *avant-garde* artists, "The Club."
b. Jun 11, 1912 in Pittsburgh, Pennsylvania
d. Jun 5, 1963 in New York, New York
Source: *BioIn 14; BriEAA; ConArt 77, 83; DcAmArt; DcAmB S7; DcCAA 71; EncAB-A 34; FacFETw; McGDA; OxCTwCA; OxDcArt; PhDcTCA 77; WhAm 4; WhoAmA 78N, 80N, 82N, 84N, 86N, 89N, 91N, 93N; WorArt 1950*

Bazna, Elyesa
"Cicero"
German. Spy
Photographed notes passing through British Embassy for Germans; arrested WW II.
b. 1904
d. 1970 in Munich, Germany (West)
Source: *BioIn 1, 4, 8, 9, 10, 11, 14; NewYTBE 70; WhDW; WhWW-II*

Beach, Alfred Ely
American. Journalist, Inventor
Built demonstration pneumatic passenger subway under Broadway in NY, 1868.
b. Sep 1, 1826 in Springfield, Massachusetts
d. Jan 1, 1896 in New York, New York
Source: *BiInAmS; BioIn 5; DcAmB; HarEnUS; NatCAB 8; TwCBDA; WebAB 74, 79; WhAm HS*

Beach, H. H A, Mrs.
[Amy Marcy Cheney]
American. Composer
"Gaelic" Symphony, 1896, first symphonic work composed by American woman.
b. Sep 5, 1867 in Henniker, New Hampshire
d. Dec 27, 1944 in New York, New York
Source: *AmWom; ASCAP 66; Baker 84; BiDAmM; CurBio 45; DcAmB S3; NatCAB 15; NotAW; OxCAmH; TwCBDA; WhAm 2*

Beach, Joseph Warren
American. Critic, Author
Writings include *Sonnets of the Head and the Heart,* 1911; *Obsessive Images,* 1958.
b. Jan 14, 1880 in Gloversville, New York
d. Aug 13, 1957 in Minneapolis, Minnesota
Source: *AmAu&B; AmLY; BioIn 4, 7; CnDAL; NatCAB 47; OxCAmL 65, 83, 95; TwCA SUP; WhAm 3*

Beach, Rex Ellingwood
American. Author
Popular adventure tales include *Jungle Gold,* 1935.
b. Dec 1, 1877 in Atwood, Michigan
d. Dec 7, 1949 in Sebring, Florida
Source: *CyWA 58; DcAmB S4; OxCAmL 65; TwCA SUP; WhAm 2; WhE&EA*

Beach, Sylvia
American. Publisher
Printed James Joyce's *Ulysses,* 1919, when no other publisher would.
b. Mar 14, 1887 in Baltimore, Maryland
d. Oct 6, 1962 in Paris, France
Source: *AmWomWr; ArtclWW 2; BenetAL 91; BioIn 5, 6, 7, 8, 9; CamHAL; CasWL; ConAu 108; ContDcW 89; DcLB 4; FacFETw; FemiCLE; IntDcWB; LibW; LngCTC; NatCAB 33, 47; NewCBEL; NotAW MOD; ObitOF 79; ObitT 1961; OxCAmL 95; OxCWoWr 95; PenC AM; REnAL; WhAm 1; WhoAmW 58, 61*

Beacham, Stephanie
English. Actor
Played Sable Colby on TV series "The Colbys" 1985-87.
b. Feb 28, 1947 in Hertfordshire, England
Source: *ConTFT 4, 13; IntMPA 96; ItaFilm; LegTOT; VarWW 85; WhoHol 92; WhoThe 81*

Beach Boys, The
[Al Jardine; Bruce Johnson; Mike Love; Brian Wilson; Carl Wilson; Dennis Wilson]
American. Music Group
Personified CA life-style with mellow songs about surfing, cars, young love: "Surfin' USA," 1963; Hall of Fame, 1988.
Source: *BiDAmM; BioIn 14, 15, 16, 17, 18, 20, 21; BkPepl; CelR 90; CmCal; ConMuA 80A; ConMus 1; DcArts; DcTwCCu 1; EncPR&S 74, 89; EncRk 88; EncRkSt; FacFETw; HarEnR 86; IlEncRk; NewAmDM; NewGrDA 86; NewYTBS 88; OxCPMus; PenEncP; RkOn 74; RolSEnR 83; WhoAm 97; WhoHol 92, A; WhoMW 96; WhoRock 81; WhoRocM 82; WorAl; WorAlBi*

Beadle, Erastus Flavel
American. Publisher, Printer
Originated the dime novel with *Malaeska,* 1860.
b. Sep 11, 1821 in Pierstown, New York
d. Dec 18, 1894 in Cooperstown, New York
Source: *AmAu&B; DcAmB S1; DcNAA; NatCAB 19; OxCAmL 65; REnAL; REnAW; WebAB 74, 79; WebBD 83; WhAm HS; WorAl; WorAlBi*

Beadle, George Wells
American. Biochemist
Shared Nobel Prize in medicine, 1958, for genetics research.
b. Oct 22, 1903 in Wahoo, Nebraska
d. Jun 9, 1989 in Pomona, California
Source: *AmMWSc 76P, 79, 82, 86, 89, 92; AsBiEn; BiESc; BioIn 1, 2, 3, 4, 5, 6, 7, 10, 11; BlueB 76; CamDcSc; CurBio 56, 89; FacFETw; InSci; IntWW 74, 75, 76, 77, 78, 79, 80, 81, 82, 83, 89; LarDcSc; LinLib S; McGEWB; McGMS 80; NotTwCS; RAdv 14; WebAB 74, 79; WhAm 10; WhE&EA; Who 74, 82, 83, 85, 88; WhoAm 74, 76, 78, 80, 82, 84, 86, 88; WhoMW 78, 80, 82; WhoNob, 90, 95; WhoWest 87; WhoWor 74, 89; WorAl; WorScD*

Beadle, William
American. Murderer
Slaughtered his family, then killed himself.
d. Dec 11, 1873 in Wethersfield, Connecticut
Source: *DrInf; EncACr*

Beal, John
[J Alexander Bliedung]
American. Actor
Stage, screen actor since 1930; films include *Madame X,* 1937; *The Sound and the Fury,* 1959.
b. Aug 13, 1909 in Joplin, Missouri
d. Apr 26, 1997 in Santa Cruz, California
Source: *BiE&WWA; BioIn 1, 11, 18; ConTFT 11; FilmEn; FilmgC; ForYSC; HalFC 80, 84, 88; HolP 30; IntMPA 75, 76, 77, 78, 79, 80, 81, 82, 84, 86, 88, 92, 94, 96; LegTOT; MovMk; NotNAT; WhoAm 88, 90, 92, 94, 95, 96, 97; WhoEnt 92; WhoHol 92, A; WhoHrs 80; WhoThe 72, 77, 81*

Beale, Betty
[Mrs. George Graeber]
American. Journalist
Weekly column in News American Syndicate since 1953.
b. 1912 in Washington, District of Columbia
Source: *BioIn 5, 6, 8; ForWC 70; InWom, SUP; WhoAm 86; WhoSSW 82*

Bealer, Alex W(inkler III)
American. Children's Author
Writings include *The Picture-Skin Story,* 1957; *The Log Cabin,* 1978.
b. Mar 6, 1921 in Valdosta, Georgia
d. Mar 17, 1980 in Atlanta, Georgia
Source: *ConAu 2NR, 45, 97; SmATA 8, 22N*

Beall, Lester Thomas
American. Designer, Illustrator
Known for designs in merchandising, layout, packaging; designed magazine *The New Republic.*
b. Mar 14, 1903 in Kansas City, Missouri
d. Jun 20, 1969
Source: *BioIn 1, 2, 3, 8, 10; ConDes 84; CurBio 49, 69; WhAmArt 85; WhoAmA 73, 76, 78N, 80N, 82N; WhoGrA 62*

Beals, Carleton
American. Author
Described Sandinistas' revolt against American occupation of Nicaragua, 1928, in *Banana Gold,* 1932.
b. Nov 13, 1893 in Medicine Lodge, Kansas
d. Jun 26, 1979 in Middletown, Connecticut
Source: *AmAu&B; Au&Wr 71; AuBYP 2, 3; BioIn 1, 4, 5, 7, 11, 12; BlueB 76;*

ConAu 1R, 3NR; CurBio 41, 79, 79N; DcLEL; EncAJ; IntAu&W 76, 77; IntWW 74, 75, 76, 77, 78, 79; LiJour; NewYTBS 79; OxCAmL 65, 83, 95; REnAL; ScF&FL 1, 2, 92; SmATA 12; TwCA, SUP; WhAm 7; WhNAA; WhoAm 74, 76, 78; WhoWor 74; WrDr 76, 80

Beals, Jennifer
American. Actor
Starred in films *Flashdance,* 1983; *The Bride,* 1985.
b. Dec 19, 1963 in Chicago, Illinois
Source: *ConBlB 12; ConTFT 2, 5, 14; DrBlPA 90; IntMPA 92, 94, 96; ItaFilm; LegTOT; VarWW 85; WhoAm 94, 95, 96, 97; WhoEnt 92; WhoHol 92*

Beals, Ralph Leon
American. Anthropologist, Author
Writings include *Ethnology of the Western Mixe Indians,* 1945; *Community in Transition, Nayon Ecuador,* 1966.
b. Jul 19, 1901 in Pasadena, California
Source: *AmAu&B; AmMWSc 73S, 76P; FifIDA; WhoAm 74, 76, 78, 80*

Beals, Vaughn LeRoy, Jr.
American. Business Executive
Chairman, of Harley-Davidson Motor Co., 1981—; CEO, 1981-89.
b. Jan 2, 1928 in Cambridge, Massachusetts
Source: *News 88-2; St&PR 91, 93; WhoAm 82, 84, 86, 88, 90, 92; WhoFI 89, 92; WhoMW 88, 90*

Beam, Jacob D(yneley)
American. Diplomat
Asst. director, Arms Control and Disarmament Agency, 1962-66; ambassador to Czechoslovakia, 1966-69.
b. Mar 24, 1908
d. Aug 16, 1993 in Rockville, Maryland
Source: *AnObit 1993; BioIn 5, 8, 11, 12, 16, 19; BlueB 76; CurBio 93N; DcAmDH 80, 89; WhoAmP 73, 75, 77, 79; WhoGov 72*

Beam, James B
American. Distiller
Headed family business that produced world's first true bourbon.
b. 1864
d. Dec 27, 1947
Source: *Entr*

Beam, Joseph
American. Writer
Edited *In the Life: A Black Gay Anthology,* 1980s.
b. Dec 30, 1954 in Philadelphia, Pennsylvania
Source: *GayLesB*

Beame, Abraham David
American. Politician
First Jewish person to be elected mayor of NYC, 1974-77.
b. Mar 20, 1906 in London, England
Source: *BioIn 7, 9, 10, 11, 12; BlueB 76; CurBio 74; IntWW 77, 78, 79, 80, 81, 82, 83, 89, 91, 93; NewYTBS 74, 85; PolProf NF; WhoAm 74, 76, 78, 80, 82; WhoAmJ 80; WhoAmP 75, 77, 79, 81, 83, 85, 87, 89, 91, 93, 95; WhoE 74, 75, 77; WhoGov 75, 77; WhoWorJ 78*

Beamon, Bob
[Robert Beamon]
American. Track Athlete
Long jumper; won gold medal, set world record in 1968 Olympics; record broken by Mike Powell, 1991.
b. Aug 29, 1946 in Jamaica, New York
Source: *AfrAmSG; BiDAmSp OS; BioIn 8, 13, 21; BlkOlyM; FacFETw; NewYTBE 71; NewYTBS 84; WhoSpor; WhoTr&F 73*

Bean, Alan L
American. Astronaut
Lunar module pilot on Apollo 12 flight to moon, 1969.
b. Mar 15, 1932 in Wheeler, Texas
Source: *ConNews 86-2; NewYTBE 73; WhoAm 86; WhoSSW 82; WhoWor 84*

Bean, Andy
American. Golfer
Turned pro 1975; won Kemper Western Open, 1978.
b. Mar 13, 1953 in Lafayette, Georgia
Source: *NewYTBS 78; WhoIntG*

Bean, Carl
American. Religious Leader
Founded Unity Fellowship Church, Los Angeles, and Minority AIDS Project, both in 1985.
b. 1944
Source: *GayLesB*

Bean, L(eon) L(eonwood)
American. Retailer
With brother Guy, began clothing store, 1912; invented special hunting shoe.
b. 1872 in Greenwood, Maine
d. Feb 5, 1967 in Freeport, Maine
Source: *BioIn 1, 5, 7, 14, 19; Entr; WhAm 4*

Bean, Louis H(yman)
American. Economist
Wrote *Ballot Behavior: A Study of Presidential Elections,* 1940; *How to Predict Elections,* 1948.
b. Apr 15, 1896
d. Aug 5, 1994 in Arlington, Virginia
Source: *AmMWSc 73S, 78S; BioIn 1, 2; CurBio 94N; Future*

Bean, Orson
[Dallas Frederick Burrows]
American. Actor, Comedian
Panelist on TV's "To Tell the Truth," 1964-67.
b. Jul 22, 1928 in Burlington, Vermont
Source: *BiE&WWA; BioIn 3, 4, 7, 8; ConAu 77; ConTFT 3; CurBio 67; IntMPA 84, 86, 88, 92, 94, 96; ItaFilm; JoeFr; LegTOT; MotPP; NotNAT; UFOEn; VarWW 85; WhoAm 74, 76, 78, 80, 82, 84, 86, 88, 90; WhoEnt 92; WhoHol 92, A; WhoThe 72, 77, 81; WhoWor 74*

Bean, Roy
"Law West of the Pecos"
American. Judge
Held court in own saloon; Paul Newman starred in movie *Life and Times of Judge Roy Bean,* 1973.
b. 1825 in Mason County, Kentucky
d. Mar 16, 1903 in Langtry, Texas
Source: *BioIn 8, 9, 10, 17, 18, 20; CopCroC; FilmgC; LegTOT; LinLib S; REnAW; WebAB 74, 79; WorAl; WorAlBi*

Beard, Charles Austin
American. Historian
Controversial writings include *An Economic Interpretation of the Constitution,* 1913; attacked Founding Fathers, many assumptions of U.S. history.
b. Nov 27, 1874 in Knightstown, Indiana
d. Sep 1, 1948 in New Haven, Connecticut
Source: *AmAu&B; AmDec 1910; AmPeW; AmSocL; BiDAmEd; BiDMoPL; BioIn 1, 2, 3, 4, 6, 7, 8, 9, 10, 11, 12, 13, 14, 15, 16, 17, 19; ConAmA; DcAmB S4; DcAmDH 80, 89; DcAmSR; DcLEL; DcNAA; EncAAH; EncAB-H 1974, 1996; EvLB; FacFETw; IndAu 1816; LinLib L, S; LngCTC; McGEWB; MorMA; OxCAmH; OxCAmL 65; OxCSupC; PenC AM; REn; REnAL; SmATA 18; TwCA, SUP; WebAB 74, 79; WebE&AL; WhAm 2, 2C; WorAl*

Beard, Dan(iel Carter)
American. Artist
Founded Boy Scouts of America, 1910; only recipient of Golden Eagle Medal.
b. Jun 21, 1850 in Cincinnati, Ohio
d. Jun 11, 1941 in Suffern, New York
Source: *Alli SUP; AmAu&B; AmLY; ApCAB; AuBYP 2S; BiD&SB; BioIn 1, 2, 3, 4, 6, 9, 10, 13; CarSB; ChhPo; CurBio 41; DcAmAu; DcAmB S3; DcNAA; EncAAH; GayN; IlBEAAW; IlrAm 1880; JBA 34; LinLib L; NatCAB 5, 33; OhA&B; OxCAmL 65; REnAL; ScF&FL 1; SmATA 22; TwCA, SUP; TwCBDA; WebAB 74, 79; WebBD 83; WhAm 1; WhAmArt 85; WhE&EA; WhNAA; WorAl; WorAlBi; WorECar*

Beard, Dita Davis
American. Government Official
Lobbyist involved in ITT attempt to subsidize Rep. National Convention, 1972.
b. Nov 27, 1918 in Fort Riley, Kansas
Source: *InWom SUP; NewYTBE 72; PolProf NF; WhoAmW 68*

Beard, Frank
American. Golfer
Turned pro, 1962; has 11 pro wins; leading money winner, 1969.
b. May 1, 1939 in Dallas, Texas
Source: *BioIn 8, 9, 18; CurBio 70; WhoAm 74, 76, 78; WhoGolf; WhoIntG*

Beard, George Miller
American. Scientist, Physician, Engineer
Researched use of electricity in medicine, 1866; first to determine cause, treatment of seasickness.
b. May 8, 1839 in Montville, Connecticut
d. Jan 23, 1883 in New York, New York
Source: *Alli SUP; AmBi; ApCAB; BbD; BiD&SB; BioIn 13; DcAmAu; DcAmB; DcAmMeB, 84; DcNAA; NatCAB 8; TwCBDA; WhAm HS*

Beard, James Andrews
American. Chef, Author
Popularized American cooking; book *Beard on Bread,* 1973, was definitive text on home baking.
b. May 5, 1903 in Portland, Oregon
d. Jan 23, 1985 in New York, New York
Source: *AmAu&B; BioIn 5, 7, 8, 9, 11, 12, 13; ConAu 15NR, 114; CurBio 64, 85; NewYTBS 85; WhAm 8; WhoAm 74, 76, 78, 80, 82, 84; WhoE 83, 85; WrDr 76*

Beard, Mary Ritter
American. Historian
Works concerning women and labor movements include *Woman as a Force in History,* 1946; often collaborated with husband Charles.
b. Aug 5, 1876 in Indianapolis, Indiana
d. Aug 14, 1958 in Phoenix, Arizona
Source: *AmAu&B; AmRef; AmSocL; AmWomHi; AmWomWr; ArtclWW 2; BioAmW; BioIn 14, 15, 16, 17, 19, 21; ContDcW 89; CurBio 41, 58; DcAmB S4, S6; DcLEL; DcNAA; EncAB-H 1996; EncWB; EncWHA; FemiWr; IndAu 1816; IntDcWB; InWom, SUP; NotAW MOD; ObitOF 79; OxCAmL 65; OxCWoWr 95; PeoHis; RadHan; REnAL; TwCA, SUP; WhAm 3; WhNAA; WhoAmW 58; WomWWA 14*

Beard, Matthew, Jr.
[Our Gang]
"Stymie"
American. Actor
Bald black boy who made 40 "Our Gang" comedies, 1930-35.
b. Jan 1, 1925 in Los Angeles, California
d. Jan 8, 1981 in Los Angeles, California
Source: *BioIn 10; DrBlPA, 90; InB&W 80; PseudN 82; What 5; WhoHol A*

Beard, Myron Gould
"Dan"
American. Aircraft Designer, Pilot
First airplane pilot to fly DC-3, 1935; helped develop Boeing 707.
b. Nov 13, 1896 in Fuzhou, China
d. Dec 25, 1974 in Northport, New York
Source: *BioIn 10; EncAB-A 29, 40; NewYTBS 74*

Beard, Peter Hill
American. Photographer
Known for color photography of dead, decaying animals of Africa.
b. Jan 22, 1938 in New York, New York
Source: *ConPhot 82; MacBEP; NewYTBS 75; WhoAm 78*

Beard, Ralph Milton
[Fabulous Five]
American. Basketball Player
All-America guard, U of KY, 1946-49; won two nat. championships; member US Olympic team, won gold medal, 1948.
b. Dec 1, 1927 in Hardinsburg, Kentucky
Source: *BiDAmSp Sup; BioIn 2, 10; WhoBbl 73*

Bearden, Romare Howard
American. Artist
America's foremost collagist, portraying images common to all cultures; brought recognition to the black American artist.
b. Sep 2, 1914 in Charlotte, North Carolina
d. Mar 11, 1988 in New York, New York
Source: *AfroAA; AmArt; ConArt 77; ConAu 102; CurBio 72, 88; DcAmArt; DcCAA 77; InB&W 85; McGEWB; NewYTBS 88; WhoAm 74, 76, 78, 80, 82, 84, 86; WhoAmA 73, 76, 78, 80, 82, 84, 86; WhoWor 74*

Beardsley, Aubrey Vincent
English. Illustrator
Best known for sensual, often macabre black and white illustrations.
b. Aug 21, 1872 in Brighton, England
d. Mar 16, 1898 in Merton, England
Source: *AtlBL; Benet 87, 96; BioIn 1, 2, 3, 6, 7, 8, 9, 10, 11, 12, 13; BritAu 19; ChhPo, S2; DcArts; DcBrBI; DcBrWA; DcLEL; DcNaB S1; DcNiCA; Dis&D; LinLib L, S; McGDA; McGEWB; NewC; NewCBEL; OxCArt; OxCEng 85, 95; REn; VicBrit; WebE&AL; WorAl*

Bearse, Amanda
American. Actor
Plays Marcy, neighbor to the Bundy's on TV show "Married.With Children," 1987—.
Source: *BioIn 16; ConTFT 8*

Beasley, Allyce
[Allyce Tannenberg]
American. Actor
Played Agnes Dipesto on TV series "Moonlighting," 1985-89.
b. Jul 6, 1954 in New York, New York
Source: *ConTFT 7*

Beastie Boys, The
[Mike Diamond; Adam Horovitz; Adam Yauch]
"Bowery Boys"; "The Three Stooges of Rock-Rap"
American. Rap Group
Formed 1983; album *Licensed to Ill,* with hit single "Fight for Your Right"; sold more copies than any debut album in Columbia Record's history.
Source: *BioIn 16, 21; ConMus 8; EncRkSt; FilmgC; HalFC 84, 88; JoeFr; QDrFCA 92*

Beatles, The
[George Harrison; John Lennon; Paul McCartney; Ringo Starr]
English. Music Group
Most influential music group of all time; hits include "I Want to Hold Your Hand," 1963; Hall of Fame, 1988; series of *Anthology* albums released, 1995, 1996.
Source: *Alli, SUP; AnObit 1981; BiDLA; BioIn 14, 15, 16, 17, 18, 19, 20, 21; BioNews 74; ChhPo S2; ConMuA 80A; ConMus 2; CurBio 65, 66; DcArts; DcNaB; DcTwCCu 1; DcTwHis; DcVicP 2; EncPR&S 74, 89; EncRk 88; EncRkSt; EncSoA; FacFETw; FilmEn; FilmgC; ForYSC; HalFC 80, 84, 88; HarEnR 86; IlEncRk; IlWWBF A; InWom SUP; MakMC; MotPP; MovMk; MugS; NewAmDM; NewCol 75; NewGrDA 86; NewGrDM 80; NewYHSD; NewYTBS 75, 95; OxCFilm; OxCPMus; PenDiMP; PenEncP; RkOn 78; RolSEnR 83; WhoHol 92; WhoRock 81; WhoRocM 82; WorEFlm*

Beaton, Cecil (Walter Hardy), Sir
English. Photographer, Designer
Major 1930s fashion photographer; won Oscars for costume design for *Gigi,* 1959; *My Fair Lady,* 1964.
b. Jan 14, 1904 in London, England
d. Jan 18, 1980 in Salisbury, England
Source: *AnObit 1980; Au&Wr 71; BiDD; BiE&WWA; BioIn 1, 2, 3, 4, 6, 7, 8, 9, 10, 11, 12, 13, 14, 15, 17, 20; BlueB 76; CamGWoT; CelR; CnOxB; CnThe; ConAu 81, 93; ConPhot 82, 88, 95; CurBio 62, 80, 80N; DancEn 78; DcArts; DcNaB 1971; EncFash; EncWT; Ent; FacFETw; FilmEn; GayLesB; GrBr; ICPEnP; IntAu&W 77; IntDcF 1-4, 2-4; IntWW 74, 75, 76, 77, 78, 79; LegTOT; LngCTC; MacBEP; MakMC; MetOEnc; NewC; NewYTBS 80; NotNAT, A; OxCAmT 84; OxCFilm; OxCThe 83; Who 74; WhoArt 80, 82N; WhoFash 88A; WhoThe 72, 77, 81N; WhoWor 74, 76, 78; WorAl; WorAlBi; WorEFlm; WorFshn; WrDr 76, 80*

Beatrice, Princess of York
[Beatrice Elizabeth Mary]
English. Princess
First child of Duke and Duchess of York—Prince Andrew and Sarah Ferguson; currently fifth in line to British throne.
b. Aug 8, 1988 in London, England

Source: *BioIn 16, 17*

Beatrix
[Beatrix Wilhelmina Armgard]
Dutch. Ruler
Daughter of Juliana who was invested as queen, Apr 30, 1980.
b. Jan 31, 1938 in Soestdijk, Netherlands
Source: *BioIn 2, 3, 5, 7, 10, 11, 12, 13, 15, 16; ContDcW 89; CurBio 81; EncWB; IntDcWB; IntWW 82, 83, 89, 91, 93; InWom, SUP; LegTOT; NewCol 75; NewYTBS 80; WhoEIO 82; WhoWomW 91; WhoWor 74, 76, 78, 80, 82, 84, 87, 89, 91, 93, 95, 96, 97*

Beattie, Ann
American. Author
Contributor to *New Yorker;* short stories collected in *Secrets and Surprises,* 1979.
b. Sep 8, 1947 in Washington, District of Columbia
Source: *AmWomWr SUP; ArtclWW 2; Benet 96; BenetAL 91; BestSel 90-2; BioAmW; BioIn 12, 13; BlmGWL; CelR 90; ConAu 53NR, 81; ConLC 8, 13, 18, 40, 63; ConNov 86, 91, 96; ConPopW; CurBio 85; CyWA 89; DcLB Y82B; DrAPF 80; EncWL 3; FacFETw; FemiCLE; GrWomW; InWom SUP; LegTOT; MagSAmL; MajTwCW; ModAL S2; ModWoWr; OxCAmL 83, 95; OxCWoWr 95; PostFic; RAdv 14; RfGShF; ShSCr 11; ShSWr; WhoAm 82, 84, 86, 88, 90, 92, 94, 95, 96, 97; WhoAmW 87, 95, 97; WhoEmL 87; WhoUSWr 88; WhoWrEP 89, 92, 95; WorAlBi; WorAu 1975; WrDr 88, 90, 92, 94, 96*

Beatts, Anne
American. Writer
Won Emmys for "Saturday Night Live," 1976, 1977, 1980.
b. Feb 25, 1947? in Buffalo, New York
Source: *BioIn 20; FunnyW; NewYTBS 83; VarWW 85*

Beatty, Alfred Chester, Sir
American. Engineer, Art Collector
Perfected method of extracting copper from low grade ore; owned largest private collection of Oriental manuscripts.
b. Feb 7, 1815 in New York, New York
d. Jan 20, 1968 in Monte Carlo, Monaco
Source: *DcIrB 78; LuthC 75; NatCAB 14; ObitT 1961*

Beatty, David Beatty, Earl
English. Naval Officer
Commander of successful naval action during WW I; first sea lord of navy, 1919-27.
b. Jan 17, 1871 in Nantwich, England
d. Mar 11, 1936 in London, England
Source: *BioIn 2, 6, 11, 14; NewCol 75; WebBD 83; WhoMilH 76*

Beatty, Jim
[James Tully Beatty]
American. Track Athlete
Long distance runner; first to run less than four-minute mile indoors, 1962.
b. Oct 28, 1934 in New York, New York
Source: *BiDAmSp OS; BioIn 6; CurBio 63; WhoSpor; WhoSSW 75; WhoTr&F 73*

Beatty, Morgan
American. Journalist
With NBC radio, 1941-67; commentator on "News of the World," 1946-67.
b. Sep 6, 1902 in Little Rock, Arkansas
d. Jul 4, 1975 in Saint Johns, Antigua-Barbuda
Source: *BioIn 1, 2, 10, 11; ConAu 61; EncTwCJ; NewYTBS 75; NewYTET; ObitOF 79; RadStar; WhAm 6*

Beatty, Ned
American. Actor
Appeared in films *Deliverance,* 1972; *Superman,* 1978.
b. Jul 6, 1937 in Louisville, Kentucky
Source: *BioIn 12; ConTFT 6, 13; EncAFC; FilmEn; HalFC 84, 88; IntMPA 81, 82, 92, 94, 96; LegTOT; WhoAm 78, 80, 82, 84, 86, 88, 90, 92, 94, 95, 96, 97; WhoEnt 92; WhoHol 92, A; WorAlBi*

Beatty, Robert
Canadian. Actor
Screen debut, 1942; films include *2001: Space Odyssey,* 1968; *Where Eagles Dare,* 1969.
b. Oct 9, 1909 in Hamilton, Ontario, Canada
d. Mar 3, 1992 in London, England
Source: *BioIn 13, 17; CanWW 70, 79; FilmAG WE; FilmEn; FilmgC; ForYSC; HalFC 80, 84, 88; IlWWBF; IntMPA 77, 78, 79, 80, 81, 82, 84, 86, 88, 92; ItaFilm; MovMk; WhoHol 92, A; WhoThe 72, 77, 81*

Beatty, Roger
American. Writer, Director
Won five Emmys for writing "The Carol Burnett Show," 1972-78.
b. Jan 24, 1933 in Los Angeles, California
Source: *VarWW 85*

Beatty, Warren
[Henry Warren Beaty]
American. Actor, Director, Producer
Known for off-screen playboy image; award-winning films include *Heaven Can Wait,* 1978; *Reds,* 1981; brother of Shirley MacLaine, married to Annette Bening.
b. Mar 30, 1937 in Richmond, Virginia
Source: *BiDFilm, 81, 94; BiE&WWA; BioIn 5, 6, 8, 9, 10, 11, 12, 13, 14, 15, 16, 17, 18, 20, 21; BkPepl; CelR, 90; ConTFT 3, 11; CurBio 62, 88; DcArts; DcTwCCu 1; FilmEn; FilmgC; ForYSC; GangFlm; HalFC 80, 84, 88; IntMPA 86, 92, 94, 96; IntWW 79, 80, 81, 82, 83, 89, 91, 93; LegTOT; MiSFD 9; MotPP; MovMk; NewYTBS 74; OxCFilm; WhoAm 86, 88, 90, 92, 94, 95, 96, 97; WhoEnt 92; WhoHol 92, A; WorEFlm*

Beauchamp, Pierre
French. Dancer, Teacher
Developed system of dance notation that raised the technical standards of ballet.
b. 1636 in Versailles, France
d. 1705 in Paris, France
Source: *BiDD; BioIn 10; CnOxB; DancEn 78; NewGrDM 80*

Beaufort, Margaret, Countess of Richmond
English. Noblewoman
Tudor who allied her family with Yorkists through marriage of son Henry who later became Henry VII; patron of education.
b. 1441?
d. Jun 29, 1509
Source: *Alli; BioIn 14, 15; ContDcW 89; DcBiPP; DcCathB; InWom, SUP; WomFir*

Beaumarchais, Pierre Augustin Caron de
French. Author, Courtier, Dramatist
Wrote comedies, *Barber of Seville,* 1775; *Marriage of Figaro,* 1784; both later operatized.
b. Jan 24, 1732 in Paris, France
d. May 18, 1799 in Paris, France
Source: *ApCAB; AtlBL; BbD; BiD&SB; BioIn 1, 2, 5, 6, 7, 9, 10, 11, 14, 16, 21; CasWL; CyWA 58; DcArts; DcBiPP; DcEuL; Dis&D; Drake; DramC 4; EncAI&E; EncWT; EuAu; EvEuW; HarEnUS; LinLib L, S; McGEWD 72; MetOEnc; NewC; NewCBEL; NewEOp 71; OxCEng 67; OxCFr; OxDcOp; PenC EUR; RComWL; REn; REnWD; SpyCS; WhAmRev; WhDW; WorAl*

Beaumont, Francis
English. Dramatist
Collaborated with John Fletcher on about 50 tragicomedies, including *Philaster,* 1610; *A Maid's Tragedy,* 1611.
b. 1584 in Grace-Dieu, England
d. Mar 6, 1616 in London, England
Source: *Alli; BiD&SB; BiDRP&D; BioIn 1, 2, 3, 5, 8, 9, 12, 16, 18; BlmGEL; BritAu; BritWr 2; CamGEL; CamGLE; CamGWoT; CasWL; Chambr 1; ChhPo, S1, S2; CnDBLB 1; CnE&AP; CnThe; CroE&S; CrtSuDr; CrtT 1, 4; DcArts; DcEnA; DcEnL; DcEuL; DcLB 58; DcLEL; DcNaB; DramC 6; EncWT; Ent; EvLB; GrWrEL DR; IntDcT 2; LinLib L, S; LitC 33; LngCEL; McGEWB; McGEWD 72, 84; MouLC 1; NewC; NotNAT A, B; OxCEng 67, 85, 95; OxCMus; OxCThe 67, 83; PenC ENG; PlP&P; RAdv 14, 13-2; REnWD; RfGEnL 91; WebE&AL; WhDW; WorAl; WorAlBi*

Beaumont, Hugh
American. Actor
Played Ward Cleaver in "Leave It to Beaver" TV series, 1957-63.
b. Feb 16, 1909 in Lawrence, Kansas
d. May 14, 1982 in Munich, Germany (West)
Source: *BioIn 12, 13; FilmEn; FilmgC; ForYSC; HalFC 80, 84, 88; IntMPA 75, 76, 77, 78, 79, 80, 81, 82, 84, 86, 88; NewYTBS 82; WhoHol A*

Beaumont, John, Sir
English. Poet
Wrote *Metamorphosis of Tobacco,* 1602, *Bosworth Field,* 1629; introduced heroic couplet; brother of Francis.
b. 1583? in Grace-Dieu, England
d. Apr 19, 1627 in London, England
Source: *Alli; BiDRP&D; BioIn 19; CasWL; DcEnL; DcLB 121; DcLEL; DcNaB, C; EvLB; LinLib L; NewC; NewCBEL*

Beaumont, William
American. Physician
Surgeon who studied gastric digestion, physiology of stomach.
b. Nov 21, 1785 in Lebanon, Connecticut
d. Apr 25, 1853 in Saint Louis, Missouri
Source: *AmBi; AsBiEn; BiDAmS; BiESc; BiHiMed; BiInAmS; BioIn 1, 2, 3, 4, 5, 6, 9, 11, 12, 13, 14, 16, 17; CamDcSc; DcAmB; DcAmMeB, 84; DcAmMiB; DcNAA; DcScB; Drake; EncAB-H 1974, 1996; InSci; LarDcSc; McGEWB; MorMA; NatCAB 18; OxCAmH; OxCMed 86; REnAW; WebAB 74, 79; WebAMB; WhAm HS; WhDW; WorAl; WorAlBi; WorScD*

Beauregard, Pierre Gustav Toutant de
American. Military Leader
Confederate general who directed bombing of Ft. Sumter to start Civil War, 1861.
b. May 28, 1818 in Saint Bernard, Louisiana
d. Feb 20, 1893 in New Orleans, Louisiana
Source: *AmBi; ApCAB; CivWDc; DcAmB; EncAB-H 1974; EncSoH; HarEnUS; McGEWB; NatCAB 4; TwCBDA; WebAB 79; WhAm HS; WhoMilH 76; WorAl*

Beauvoir, Simone de
French. Author
Best known for attack on inferior role of women: *The Second Sex,* 1949.
b. Jan 9, 1908 in Paris, France
d. Apr 14, 1986 in Paris, France
Source: *AnObit 1986; Benet 87, 96; BioIn 1, 3, 4, 5, 6, 7, 8, 9, 10, 11, 12, 13, 14, 15, 17, 18, 19, 20, 21; CasWL; CelR; ClDMEL 80; CnMWL; ConAu 9R, 28NR, 118; ConFLW 84; ConLC 1, 2, 4, 8, 14, 31, 44, 50, 71; CurBio 73, 86, 86N; CyWA 89; DcArts; DcLB 72, Y86N; DcTwCCu 2; EncCoWW; EncUnb; EncWL 2, 3; EvEuW; FemiCLE; FrenWW; GuFrLit 1; IntAu&W 76, 77; InWom; LinLib L; LngCTC; MajTwCW; MakMC; ModFrL; ModRL; ModWoWr; NewYTBS 74, 84; Novels; OxCEng 67, 85, 95; OxCFr; OxCWoWr 95; PenC EUR; RadHan; RAdv 14, 13-2; REn; ScF&FL 1, 2; TwCA SUP; TwCWr; WhDW; Who 74, 82, 83, 85; WhoAmW 66, 68, 70, 72, 74; WhoTwCL; WomSoc; WorAlBi; WorLitC; WrPh*

Beaux, Cecilia
American. Artist
Portrait painter of women and children; first woman instructor, Pennsylvania Academy of Fine Arts, 1895.
b. 1863 in Philadelphia, Pennsylvania
d. Sep 17, 1942 in Gloucester, Massachusetts
Source: *BioIn 2, 4, 7, 8, 10, 11, 15, 16, 20; BriEAA; DcAmB S3; InWom; LinLib S; McGDA; NatCAB 11, 40; NewCol 75; NotAW; ObitOF 79; WhAm 2; WomWWA 14*

Beaverbrook, William Maxwell Aitken, Baron
English. Publisher, Statesman
British newspaper mogul; minister of aircraft production, supply in Churchill's WW II govt., 1940-45.
b. May 25, 1879 in Maple, Ontario, Canada
d. Jun 9, 1964 in Cherkley, England
Source: *ConAu 89, 103; CurBio 40, 64; FacFETw; LinLib L, S; LngCTC; NewCol 75; OxCEng 95; WhE&EA; WhLit; WhWW-II*

Beaver Brown Band
[Michael Antunes; John Cafferty; Robert Cotoia; Gary Gramolino; John Cafferty and the Beaver Brown Band; Pat Lupo; Kenny Jo Silva]
American. Music Group
Rock group from Rhode Island formed during mid-1970's; sold almost 2 million copies of album *Eddie and the Cruisers,* 1983 from movie of the same name, including single "On the Dark Side."
Source: *ConMus 3; RkOn 85*

Beavers, Louise
American. Actor
One of Hollywood's most frequently employed blacks, usually as maid: *Imitation of Life,* 1934.
b. Mar 8, 1902 in Cincinnati, Ohio
d. Oct 26, 1962 in Hollywood, California
Source: *BioIn 6, 11, 18; BlksAmF; DcAmB S7; DcAmNB; DrBlPA, 90; EncAFC; Film 2; FilmEn; FilmgC; ForYSC; HalFC 80, 84, 88; HolP 30; InB&W 80; IntDcF 1-3, 2-3; InWom SUP; LegTOT; MotPP; MovMk; NotBlAW 1; NotNAT B; ObitOF 79; ThFT; Vers A; WhoHol B; WhScrn 74, 77*

Beban, Gary Joseph
American. Football Player
All-American quarterback, won Heisman Trophy, 1967; in NFL, 1968-70.
b. Aug 5, 1946 in San Francisco, California
Source: *BiDAmSp FB; CurBio 70; WhoAm 74, 90, 92, 94, 95, 96, 97; WhoFtbl 74*

Bebel, August
German. Political Leader
Co-founded German Social Democratic Party, 1869; wrote *Women and Socialism,* 1883.
b. Feb 22, 1840 in Deutz, Germany
d. Aug 13, 1913 in Passug, Switzerland
Source: *BbD; BiD&SB; BioIn 10, 12, 16; DcAmSR; Dis&D; EncRev; NewCol 75; OxCGer 76, 86; REn*

Bebey, Francis
Cameroonian. Musician
Guitarist who was influenced by American jazz and by African music; headed UNESCO's department of culture music section, early 1970s.
b. 1929 in Douala, French West Africa
Source: *AfrA; BiDAfM; BioIn 19, 20; BlkWr 1; ConAu 25NR, 69; CurBio 94; LiExTwC; PenEncP; RGAfL; SchCGBL; SelBAAf*

Becaud, Gilbert (Francois Silly)
French. Singer, Songwriter
Wrote, sang many French ballads: "What Now, My Love?"; wrote for films, 1950s-70s.
b. Oct 24, 1927 in Toulon, France
Source: *Baker 84, 92; ItaFilm; NewGrDM 80; OxCPMus; WhoFr 79; WhoHol 92, A; WhoWor 74*

Beccaria, Cesare
Italian. Explorer, Political Leader
Argued against capital punishment of criminals in *Essay on Crimes and Punishment,* 1767.
b. Mar 15, 1738 in Milan, Italy
d. Nov 28, 1794 in Milan, Italy
Source: *Benet 96; CasWL; CopCroC; DcEuL; DcItL 1, 2; EvEuW; McGEWB; NewCol 75; OxCEng 85, 95; OxCFr; PenC EUR; REn; WhDW*

Bech, Joseph
Luxembourg. Diplomat
Foreign minister, 1926-59; instrumental in founding of Benelux, Common Market following WW II.
b. Feb 17, 1887 in Diekirch, Luxembourg
d. Mar 8, 1975, Luxembourg
Source: *BiDInt; BioIn 1, 2, 6, 10; CurBio 50, 75, 75N; IntWW 74; NewYTBS 75; WhAm 6; Who 74; WhoWor 74*

Bechdel, Alison
American. Cartoonist
Published "Dykes to Watch Out For" cartoon, 1983—.

b. Sep 10, 1960 in Lock Haven, Pennsylvania
Source: *BioIn 18; ConAu 138; GayLesB*

Bechet, Sidney
American. Jazz Musician, Bandleader
Clarinetist, early jazz soprano sax innovator; led own bands, 1920s-40s.
b. May 14, 1897 in New Orleans, Louisiana
d. May 14, 1959 in Paris, France
Source: *AfrAmAl 6; AllMusG; Baker 78, 84; BiDAfM; BiDJaz; BioIn 1, 3, 5, 7, 9, 12; CmpEPM; ConMus 17; DcAmB S6; DcAmNB; DcTwCCu 5; DrBlPA, 90; EncAB-H 1974, 1996; IlEncJ; InB&W 80, 85; LegTOT; MusMk; NegAl 76, 83, 89; NewAmDM; NewGrDA 86; NewGrDJ 88; NewGrDM 80; NewOrJ; ObitT 1951; OxCPMus; PenEncP; WhAm 3, 4; WhoJazz 72; WorAl; WorAlBi*

Bechi, Gino
Italian. Opera Singer
Baritone; popular in Italy, 1930s-40s; only US appearance, 1952.
b. 1913 in Florence, Italy
Source: *Baker 84, 92; BioIn 2, 18; IntWWM 90; ItaFilm; NewGrDM 80; NewGrDO; OxDcOp; WhoMus 72*

Bechtel, Stephen Davison
American. Business Executive, Engineer
President, family-owned Bechtel Corp., 1960-73, overseeing growth into one of world's largest construction and engineering firms.
b. Sep 24, 1900 in Aurora, Indiana
d. Mar 14, 1989 in San Francisco, California
Source: *BiDAmBL 83; BioIn 2, 3, 4, 5, 10, 11, 12, 16; CurBio 57, 89; EncWB; FacFETw; IntWW 74, 75, 76, 77, 78, 79, 80, 81, 82, 83, 89; IntYB 78, 79, 80, 81, 82; NewYTBS 89; WhAm 10; WhoAm 74, 76, 78, 80, 82, 84, 86, 88; WhoCan 73, 75, 77, 80, 82; WhoFI 74, 75, 77; WhoWest 74, 76, 78, 80; WhoWor 74, 76, 78*

Bechtel, Stephen Davison, Jr.
American. Business Executive
Chairman of Bechtel Group, Inc., 1980-90; chairman emeritus, 1990—.
b. May 10, 1925 in Oakland, California
Source: *BioIn 13; BlueB 76; CanWW 31, 81, 83, 89; IntWW 82, 83, 89; St&PR 75; WhoAm 74, 76, 78, 80, 82, 84, 86, 88, 90, 92, 94, 95, 96, 97; WhoCan 73, 75, 77, 80, 82, 84; WhoFI 74, 75, 77, 79, 81, 83, 85, 87, 89, 92; WhoFrS 84; WhoScEn 94, 96; WhoWest 74, 76, 78, 84, 87, 89, 92, 94, 96; WhoWor 87, 89, 91*

Beck
[Beck Hansen]
American. Singer, Songwriter
Debuted with album *Mellow Gold,* 1993.
b. 1971 in Los Angeles, California

Beck, C(harles) C(larence)
American. Cartoonist
Created Captain Marvel, the super hero who came to life at the word "shazam," using actor Fred MacMurray as model, 1939.
b. Jun 8, 1910 in Zumbrota, Minnesota
d. Nov 22, 1989 in Gainesville, Florida
Source: *WorAl; WorECom*

Beck, Dave
American. Labor Union Official
Pres., Teamsters Union, 1952-57.
b. 1894 in Stockton, California
d. Dec 26, 1993 in Seattle, Washington
Source: *AnObit 1993; BiDAmL; BiDAmLL; BioIn 1, 2, 3, 4, 5, 6, 8, 11, 12, 19, 20; CurBio 94N; NewYTBS 93; PolProf E; What 2*

Beck, Jeff
[Yardbirds]
English. Musician
Established reputation as guitarist with Yardbirds, 1965; founded Jeff Beck Group, 1967.
b. Jun 24, 1944 in Surrey, England
Source: *BioIn 11, 12, 13; ConMus 4; EncPR&S 74, 89; EncRk 88; EncRkSt; HarEnR 86; IlEncRk; LegTOT; NewGrDJ 88, 94; OnThGG; PenEncP; RolSEnR 83; WhoAm 95, 96, 97; WhoEnt 92; WhoRock 81; WhoRocM 82*

Beck, John
American. Actor
Played Mark Grayson on TV series "Dallas."
b. Jan 28, 1946? in Chicago, Illinois
Source: *IntMPA 82; VarWW 85*

Beck, Julian
American. Dramatist, Actor
Founded Living Theater; used improvisation, superrealistic horror to shock audiences.
b. May 31, 1925 in New York, New York
d. Sep 14, 1985 in New York, New York
Source: *AnObit 1985; BiE&WWA; BioIn 10; CelR; ConAu 102, 117; ConTFT 4; Ent; FacFETw; MugS; NewYTBS 85; NotNAT, A; PlP&P; TheaDir; WhAm 9; WhoAm 78, 80, 82, 84; WhoThe 72, 77, 81; WhoWor 82, 84*

Beck, Marilyn (Mohr)
American. Journalist, Editor
Hollywood columnist who wrote *Marilyn Beck's Hollywood,* 1973.
b. Dec 17, 1928 in Chicago, Illinois
Source: *ConAu 65; ForWC 70; WhoAm 78, 80, 82, 84, 86, 88, 90, 92, 94, 95, 96, 97; WhoAmW 68, 70, 72, 74, 77, 79, 81, 83, 85, 87, 89, 91; WhoEnt 92; WhoWest 94*

Beck, Martin
[Lipto Szent Miklos]
American. Manager
Managed Orpheum Vaudeville Circuit, 1903-23; discovered Harry Houdini.
b. Jul 30, 1867, Austria-Hungary
d. Nov 16, 1940 in New York, New York
Source: *BioIn 4; CurBio 41; DcAmB S2; EncVaud; LegTOT; NotNAT B; ObitOF 79; WhAm 4, HSA*

Beck, Michael
American. Actor
Starred in film *Xanadu,* 1980; TV mini-series "Holocaust," "Mayflower."
b. Feb 4, 1949 in Memphis, Tennessee
Source: *BioIn 12; ConTFT 3; IntMPA 82, 88, 92, 94, 96; VarWW 85*

Becker, B. Jay
American. Bridge Player
Grand master professional player; had syndicated newspaper column "Becker on Bridge," beginning 1956.
b. May 5, 1904 in Philadelphia, Pennsylvania
d. Oct 9, 1987 in Flushing, New York
Source: *ConAu 65, 123*

Becker, Boris
German. Tennis Player
Youngest, and first unseeded, player to win Wimbledon singles, 1985-86, 1989; won US Open, 1989.
b. Nov 22, 1967 in Liemen, Germany (West)
Source: *CelR 90; ConNews 85-3; CurBio 87; FacFETw; IntWW 89, 91, 93; LegTOT; NewYTBS 85, 87; WhoAm 90, 92, 94, 95, 96, 97; WhoSpor; WhoWor 91, 95, 96, 97; WorAlBi*

Becker, Carl Lotus
American. Historian
Known for studies of American Revolutionary War period.
b. Sep 7, 1873 in Waterloo, Iowa
d. Apr 10, 1945 in Ithaca, New York
Source: *AmAu&B; DcAmB S3; DcLEL; DcNAA; OxCAmL 65; REn; REnAL; TwCA SUP; WebAB 74; WhAm 2; WhNAA*

Becker, Gary S(tanley)
American. Economist, Educator
Won Nobel Prize in Economic Science, 1992.
b. Dec 2, 1930 in Pottsville, Pennsylvania
Source: *AmMWSc 95; BioIn 13, 18, 19, 20; BlueB 76; IntAu&W 77; IntWW 89, 91, 93; LEduc 74; RAdv 14; Who 94; WhoAm 74, 76, 78, 80, 82, 84, 88, 90, 92, 94, 95, 96, 97; WhoAmJ 80; WhoEc 81, 86; WhoFI 92, 94, 96; WhoMW 84, 92, 93, 96; WhoNob 95; WhoScEn 94; WhoWor 95, 96, 97*

Becker, Jacques
French. Director
Began career as director in German prisoner-of-war camp, 1942; best known for *Casque d'Or,* 1952.
b. Sep 15, 1906 in Paris, France
d. 1960 in Paris, France
Source: *BiDFilm, 81, 94; BioIn 5, 12, 15; DcFM; DcTwCCu 2; EncEurC; FilmEn; FilmgC; HalFC 80, 84, 88; IntDcF 1-2, 2-2; ItaFilm; OxCFilm; WhScrn 77, 83; WorEFlm; WorFDir 1*

Becker, Ralph E(lihu)
American. Lawyer, Diplomat
US ambassador to Honduras, 1976-77; a founder of the Young Republican National Federation, 1935.
b. Jan 29, 1907
d. Aug 24, 1994 in Washington, District of Columbia
Source: *BioIn 1, 8; CurBio 94N; WhAm 11; WhoAm 76, 78, 80, 82, 84, 86, 88, 90, 92, 94; WhoAmL 78, 79, 83, 85, 87, 90, 92, 94; WhoAmP 73, 75, 77; WhoE 93, 95; WhoFI 74; WhoGov 72, 77; WhoWor 74, 76, 78, 80, 82, 89*

Becker, Stephen David
[Steve Dodge]
American. Author
Writings include *The Season of the Stranger,* 1951; *The Last Mandarin,* 1979.
b. Mar 31, 1927 in Mount Vernon, New York
Source: *AmAu&B; ConAu 3NR, 5R; ConNov 76; DrAF 76; WhoAm 86*

Beckett, Samuel (Barclay)
Irish. Author, Dramatist
Noted for *Waiting for Godot,* 1952; won Obie for *Play,* 1963; won Nobel Prize, 1969.
b. Apr 13, 1906 in Dublin, Ireland
d. Dec 22, 1989 in Paris, France
Source: *AnObit 1989, 3; EncWT; Ent; EvEuW; GrWrEL DR, N; GuFrLit 1; IntAu&W 76, 77, 89, 91; IntDcT 2; IntWW 74, 75, 76, 77, 78, 79, 80, 81, 82, 83, 89; IntWWP 77; IriPla; LegTOT; LiExTwC; LinLib L, S; LngCEL; LngCTC; MagSWL; MajMD 2; MajTwCW; MakMC; McGEWB; McGEWD 72, 84; ModBrL, S1, S2; ModFrL; ModIrL; ModRL; ModWD; NewC; NewCBEL; News 90, 90-2; NewYTBE 72; NewYTBS 86, 89; NobelP; NotNAT, A; Novels; OxCAmT 84; OxCEng 67, 85, 95; OxCIri; OxCThe 67, 83; OxCTwCP; PenC ENG, EUR; PlP&P; RAdv 14, 13-2; RComWL; REn; REnWD; RfGEnL 91; RfGShF; RfGWoL 95; RGTwCWr; ShSCr 16; TwCA SUP; TwCWr; WebE&AL; WhAm 10; WhDW; Who 74, 82, 83, 85, 88, 90; WhoAm 80, 82, 84, 86, 88; WhoFr 79; WhoNob, 90, 95; WhoThe 72, 77, 81; WhoTwCL; WhoWor 74, 78, 80, 82, 84, 87, 89; WorAl; WorAlBi; WorLitC; WrDr 76, 80, 82, 84, 86, 88, 90; WrPh*

Beckford, Tyson
American. Model
First black to sign an exclusive contract with Ralph Lauren, 1995.
b. Dec 19, 1970 in New York, New York
Source: *ConBlB 11*

Beckford, William
English. Author
Best known for *Vathek, An Arabian Tale,* 1786.
b. Sep 29, 1759 in Fonthill, England
d. May 2, 1844 in Bath, England
Source: *Alli; AtlBL; BbD; BiD&SB; BiDLA; BioIn 4, 5, 6, 7, 8, 9, 10, 11, 12, 13; BlmGEL; BritAu 19; CamGEL; CamGLE; CasWL; Chambr 2; CyWA 58; DcBiA; DcEnA; DcEnL; DcLEL; EvLB; GrWrEL N; LinLib L; NewC; OxCEng 67, 85, 95; OxCFr; PenC ENG; REn; WebE&AL; WhDW*

Beckley, Jake
[Jacob Peter Beckley]
"Eagle Eye"
American. Baseball Player
First baseman, 1888-1907; played more games at position than anyone; had .308 lifetime average; Hall of Fame, 1971.
b. Aug 4, 1867 in Hannibal, Missouri
d. Jun 25, 1918 in Kansas City, Missouri
Source: *Ballpl 90; BiDAmSp BB; BioIn 4, 14, 15; WhoProB 73*

Beckman, Johnny
"Becky"; "The Babe Ruth of Basketball"
American. Basketball Player
Guard, one of original Boston Celtics; Hall of Fame.
b. Oct 22, 1895 in New York, New York
d. Jun 22, 1968 in Miami, Florida
Source: *BioIn 8; WhoBbl 73*

Beckmann, Max
German. Artist
Leading German expressionist; works depict social commentaries, grotesque scenes.
b. Feb 12, 1884 in Leipzig, Germany
d. Dec 27, 1950 in New York, New York
Source: *ArtsAmW 3; AtlBL; BiGAW; BioIn 1, 2, 3, 4, 5, 6, 7, 8, 9, 10, 12, 13, 14, 15, 17, 20; ConArt 77, 83; DcArts; EncTR, 91; FacFETw; IlBEAAW; IntDcAA 90; LegTOT; MakMC; McGDA; McGEWB; ModArCr 3; OxCArt; OxCGer 76, 86; OxCTwCA; OxDcArt; PhDcTCA 77; WhAm 4; WhAmArt 85; WhDW; WorAl; WorAlBi; WorArt 1980*

Becknell, William
American. Explorer
Established trading route known as Santa Fe Trail, 1822.
b. 1796 in Amherst County, Virginia
d. Apr 30, 1865 in Texas
Source: *DcAmB; McGEWB; WebAB 74, 79; WhAm HS; WorAl; WorAlBi*

Beckwourth, James Pierson
American. Pioneer
Hunter, whose exploits described in *Life and Adventures of JP Beckwourth,* 1856.
b. Apr 26, 1798 in Virginia
d. 1867 in Denver, Colorado
Source: *AfrAmAl 6; BioIn 3, 4, 5, 6, 7, 8, 9, 10, 11, 12, 17, 18, 20, 21; BlksScM; DcAmB; DcAmNB; InB&W 80, 85; WhAm HS*

Becquerel, Antoine-Cesar
French. Physicist
Known for work with thermoelectricity, voltaic cell.
b. Mar 7, 1788 in Loiret, France
d. Jan 18, 1878 in Paris, France
Source: *DcScB; LinLib S*

Becquerel, Antoine Henri
French. Physicist
Discovered radioactivity, 1896; won Nobel Prize, 1903.
b. Dec 15, 1852 in Paris, France
d. Aug 25, 1908 in Le Croisic, France
Source: *AsBiEn; BiESc; BioIn 2, 3, 4, 5, 9, 12, 14, 15, 20; DcCathB; DcInv; DcScB; Dis&D; FacFETw; InSci; LarDcSc; LinLib S; McGEWB; NewCol 75; OxCMed 86; WhDW; WhoNob, 90, 95; WorAl; WorAlBi; WorScD*

Bedelia, Bonnie
[Bonnie Culkin]
American. Actor, Singer, Dancer
Films include *Heart Like a Wheel,* 1983; *They Shoot Horses Don't They?,* 1969.
b. Mar 25, 1948 in New York, New York
Source: *ConTFT 3; FilmgC; InWom SUP; NotNAT; VarWW 85; WhoAm 78, 80, 82, 84, 88, 90, 92, 94, 95, 96, 97; WhoAmW 74, 79, 81, 95, 97; WhoEnt 92; WhoHol 92, A; WorAl; WorAlBi*

Bedells, Phyllis
English. Dancer
Popular ballet performer. 1906-35.
b. Aug 9, 1893 in Bristol, England
d. May 2, 1985
Source: *BiDD; BioIn 3; CnOxB; ConAu 116; DancEn 78; IntDcB; InWom; WhThe*

Bede the Venerable, Saint
[Baeda; Beda]
English. Scholar, Theologian
His *Ecclesiastical History of the English People,* 731, was crucial to English conversion to Christianity; invented B.C./A.D. dating system.
b. May 26, 673 in Northumbria, England
d. 735 in Jarrow, England
Source: *AtlBL; BbD; BiB S; BiD&SB; BritAu; CasWL; CrtT 1; DcBiPP; DcEnL; DcEuL; DcNaB; EvLB; LinLib S; NewC; OxCEng 67; OxCFr; PenC ENG; RAdv 13-3; REn; UFOEn; WebBD 83; WorAl*

Bedford, Brian
English. Actor
Won Tony, 1971, for *School for Wives.*
b. Feb 16, 1935 in Morley, England
Source: *BiE&WWA; CelR; ConTFT 2, 11; FilmgC; HalFC 80, 84, 88; MotPP; NewYTBE 71; NotNAT; OxCAmT 84; PlP&P; WhoAm 76, 78, 80, 82, 84, 86, 88, 90, 92, 94, 95, 96, 97; WhoEnt 92; WhoHol 92, A; WhoThe 72, 77, 81*

Bedford, Sybille
English. Author
Writings include *A Legacy,* 1956; *A Compass Error,* 1968; *Jigsaw: An Unsentimental Education,* 1989.
b. Mar 16, 1911 in Charlottenburg, Germany
Source: *ArtclWW 2; Au&Wr 71; AuSpks; BioIn 4, 8, 10, 11; BlmGWL; ConAu 9R, 47NR; ConNov 72, 76, 82, 86, 91, 96; CurBio 90; DcLEL 1940; EncBrWW; FemiCLE; IntAu&W 76, 77, 82, 86, 89, 91; InWom SUP; ModBrL, S2; ModWoWr; NewC; Novels; OxCEng 85, 95; RAdv 1; RGTwCWr; ScF&FL 92; Who 82, 83, 85, 88, 90, 92, 94; WhoWor 74, 76; WorAu 1950; WrDr 76, 80, 82, 84, 86, 88, 90, 92, 94, 96*

Bednarik, Chuck
[Charles Philip Bednarik]
American. Football Player
Eight-time all-pro linebacker, Philadelphia, 1949-62; Hall of Fame, 1967; wrote autobiography *Bednarik: Last of the Sixty Minute Men,* 1977.
b. May 1, 1925 in Bethlehem, Pennsylvania
Source: *BiDAmSp FB; BioIn 17, 19; ConAu 77; LegTOT; WhoFtbl 74; WhoSpor*

Bednorz, J(ohannes) Georg
German. Physicist
Shared Nobel Prize in physics, 1987, for research in superconductivity.
b. May 16, 1950?, Germany (West)
Source: *AmMWSc 89, 92, 95; WhoNob 90, 95*

Bedrosian, Steve
[Stephen Wayne Bedrosian]
American. Baseball Player
Relief pitcher, Phillies, 1985-89; Giants, 1989-91; Twins, 1990—; led MLs in saves, won Cy Young Award, 1987.
b. Dec 6, 1957 in Methuen, Massachusetts
Source: *Ballpl 90; BaseEn 88; BaseReg 87, 88; LegTOT; WhoAm 90; WhoWest 89*

Bee, Clair Francis
[Chip Hilton]
"Hillbilly"
American. Basketball Coach
Coached Long Island U, 1931-52; has highest winning percentage in collegiate history; wrote instruction manuals, sports fiction; Hall of Fame, 1967.
b. Mar 2, 1900 in Grafton, West Virginia
d. May 20, 1983 in Cleveland, Ohio
Source: *AnObit 1983; AuBYP 2, 3; BioIn 2, 8, 9, 12; ConAu 1R, 109; NewYTBS 81; WhoBbl 73*

Bee, Molly
[Molly Beachboard]
American. Singer
Country singer; successful singles 1950s-60s include "I Saw Mommy Kissing Santa Claus."
b. Aug 18, 1939 in Oklahoma City, Oklahoma
Source: *BgBkCoM; BiDAmM; BioIn 14; CounME 74, 74A; EncFCWM 69, 83; ForYSC; HarEnCM 87; IlEncCM; InWom SUP; VarWW 85; WhoHol 92, A*

Beebe, Burdetta Faye
[B F Beebe; B F Johnson]
American. Children's Author
Writings include *Run, Light Buck, Run!,* 1962; *African Elephants,* 1968.
b. Feb 4, 1920 in Marshall, Oklahoma
Source: *AuBYP 2S, 3; BioIn 9; ConAu 1R, 3NR; ForWC 70; PenNWW B; SmATA 1; WrDr 76, 80, 82, 84, 86, 88, 90, 92*

Beebe, Lucius Morris
American. Journalist, Author
Writings include *People on Parade,* 1934; *The Trains We Rode, Vol. I,* 1965.
b. Dec 9, 1902 in Wakefield, Massachusetts
d. Feb 4, 1966 in San Mateo, California
Source: *AmAu&B; BiDAmNC; BioIn 4, 6, 7, 8, 10, 12, 16; ChhPo; CurBio 40, 66; EncAB-A 39; EncTwCJ; NatCAB 55; REn; REnAL; WebAB 74, 79; WhAm 4*

Beebe, William
[Charles William Bebbe]
American. Ornithologist, Explorer
Set world deep-sea diving record in bathysphere, 3,028 feet, 1934.
b. Jul 29, 1877 in New York, New York
d. Jun 4, 1962 in San Fernando, Trinidad and Tobago
Source: *AmAu&B; AmLY; BenetAL 91; BioIn 1, 2, 4, 5, 6, 7, 8, 10, 12, 14, 20; ConAmA; ConAmL; ConAu 73; CurBio 41, 62; DcAmB S7; DcLEL; EncAB-A 15; EvLB; LegTOT; LinLib L, S; NatCAB 47; OxCAmH; OxCAmL 65, 83; REnAL; SmATA 19; Str&VC; TwCA, SUP; WebAB 74, 79; WhAm 4; WhE&EA; WhLit; WhNAA; WorAlBi*

Beech, Olive Ann (Mellor)
American. Business Executive
Pres., Beech Aircraft Corp., 1950-68.
b. Sep 25, 1903
d. Jul 6, 1993 in Wichita, Kansas
Source: *AmWomM; AnObit 1993; BiDAmBL 83; BioIn 1, 2, 4, 5, 7, 9, 10, 11, 13, 19, 20, 21; CurBio 93N; Dun&B 79; Entr; InSci; InWom, SUP; LinLib S; St&PR 75, 84, 87, 91; WhoAm 74, 76, 78, 80, 82, 90; WhoAmW 58, 61, 64, 66, 68, 70, 72, 74, 79, 81, 83; WhoFI 74; WhoMW 84; WhoWor 74; WorAl; WorAlBi*

Beech, Walter Herschel
American. Aircraft Manufacturer
Founded Beech Aircraft Co., 1932.
b. Jan 30, 1891 in Pulaski, Tennessee
d. Nov 29, 1950 in Wichita, Kansas
Source: *BioIn 1, 2, 4; NatCAB 39; WhAm 3; WorAl*

Beecham, Thomas, Sir
English. Conductor
Founded British National Opera Co., 1932; London Philharmonic, 1932; Royal Philharmonic, 1946.
b. Apr 29, 1879 in Saint Helens, England
d. Mar 8, 1961 in London, England
Source: *Baker 78, 84, 92; BioIn 1, 2, 3, 4, 5, 6, 7, 8, 10, 11, 12, 14, 17; BriBkM 80; CmOp; ConAu 112; CurBio 41, 51, 61; DancEn 78; DcArts; DcNaB 1961; FacFETw; GrBr; IntDcOp; LegTOT; LinLib S; LngCTC; MetOEnc; MusMk; MusSN; NewAmDM; NewEOp 71; NewGrDM 80; NewGrDO; NotNAT B; ObitOF 79; ObitT 1961; OxCMus; OxDcOp; PenDiMP; REn; WhAm 4; WorAl; WorAlBi*

Beecher, Henry Ward
American. Clergy, Social Reformer
Forceful orator who spoke out on social, political issues, including slavery, Civil War, Reconstruction.
b. Jun 24, 1813 in Litchfield, Connecticut
d. Mar 8, 1887 in New York, New York
Source: *Alli, SUP; AmAu; AmAu&B; AmBi; AmOrN; AmRef; AmSocL; ApCAB; BbD; Benet 87, 96; BenetAL 91; BiDAmJo; BiDAmM; BiD&SB; BioIn 1, 2, 3, 4, 6, 8, 9, 10, 11, 12, 13, 15, 16, 17, 19; CamGLE; CamHAL; CasWL; CelCen; Chambr 3; CivWDc; CyAL 1, 2; DcAmAu; DcAmB; DcAmReB 1, 2; DcAmSR; DcBiA; DcBiPP; DcEnL; DcLB 3, 43; DcNAA; Drake; EncAB-H 1974, 1996; EncARH; EvLB; HarEnUS; JrnUS; LinLib L, S; LuthC 75; McGEWB; MemAm; NatCAB 3; OhA&B; OxCAmH; OxCAmL 65, 83, 95; OxCEng 67; PenC AM; PolPar; RelLAm 91; REn; REnAL; TwCBDA; WebAB 74, 79; WhAm HS; WhAmP; WhCiWar; WorAl; WorAlBi*

Beecher, Janet
[Janet Beecher Meysenburg]
American. Actor
Character actress who usually played society matrons, 1930s.
b. Oct 21, 1884 in Jefferson City, Missouri
d. Aug 6, 1955 in Washington, Connecticut
Source: *BioIn 4; FilmEn; FilmgC; HalFC 80, 84, 88; HolCA; InWom SUP; MotPP; MovMk; NotNAT B; OxCAmT 84; ThFT; WhoHol B; WhScrn 74, 77, 83; WhThe*

Beefheart, Captain
[Don Van Vliet]
American. Songwriter, Musician
Recorded first single, "Diddy Wah Diddy" in 1964 and first album *Safe as Milk* in 1966; released *I May Be Hungary But I Sure Ain't Weird* in 1992; appeared with Frank Zappa and the Mothers of Invention on "Willie the Pimp" in 1969.
b. Jan 15, 1941 in Glendale, California
Source: *IlEncRk*

Bee Gees, The
[Barry Gibb; Maurice Gibb; Robin Gibb]
English. Music Group
Soundtrack album *Saturday Night Fever,* 1977, sold over 15 million copies; was first ever triple platinum album; included hit "How Deep Is Your Love"?.
Source: *BkPepl; ConMuA 80A; ConMus 3; EncPR&S 74, 89; EncRk 88; EncRkSt; HalFC 84, 88; HarEnR 86; IlEncRk; OxCPMus; PenEncP; RkOn 78; RolSEnR 83; WhoHol 92; WhoRock 81; WhoRocM 82; WorAl; WorAlBi*

Beemer, Brace
American. Actor
One of the original radio voices of the Lone Ranger, 1933-54.
b. 1903
d. Mar 1, 1965 in Oxford, Michigan
Source: *BioIn 7; ObitOF 79*

Beene, Geoffrey
American. Fashion Designer
Pres., designer, Geoffrey Beene, Inc., NYC, 1962—.
b. Aug 30, 1927 in Haynesville, Louisiana
Source: *BioIn 10, 11, 13; CelR, 90; ConDes 84, 90, 97; ConFash; CurBio 78; DcTwDes; EncFash; FacFETw; FairDF US; IntWW 91, 93; LegTOT; WhoAm 74, 76, 78, 80, 82, 84, 86, 88, 90, 92, 94, 95, 96, 97; WhoE 74, 95; WhoFash 88; WhoWor 91, 93, 95; WorFshn*

Beer, Thomas
American. Author, Biographer
Wrote *The Mauve Decade,* 1926.
b. Nov 22, 1889 in Council Bluffs, Iowa
d. Apr 18, 1940 in New York, New York
Source: *AmAu&B; BenetAL 91; BioIn 4, 5; ConAmL; DcAmB S2; DcLEL; DcNAA; EvLB; NewCol 75; OxCAmL 65, 83, 95; REn; REnAL; TwCA, SUP; WhAm 1*

Beerbohm, Max
[Sir Henry Maximilian Beerbohm]
"The Incomparable Max"
English. Critic, Author
Writings include essays; wrote novel *Zuleika Dobson,* 1911; vol. of pictorial caricatures: *Rossetti and His Circle,* 1922.
b. Aug 24, 1872 in London, England
d. May 20, 1956 in Rapallo, Italy
Source: *AntBDN B; AtlBL; Benet 87, 96; BioIn 1, 2, 3, 4, 5, 6, 7, 8, 9, 10, 12, 13, 14, 15, 16, 17, 21; BlmGEL; BritPl; BritWr S2; CamGEL; CamGLE; CasWL; Chambr 3; ChhPo S1, S3; ClaDrA; CnMD; CnMWL; CyWA 58; DcArts; DcBrAr 1; DcBrBI; DcLB 34, 100; DcLEL; EncWT; EvLB; FacFETw; GrWrEL N; LegTOT; LinLib L, S; LngCEL; LngCTC; McGDA; ModBrL, S1; ModWD; NewC; NewCBEL; NotNAT A, B; ObitOF 79; ObitT 1951; OxCArt; OxCEng 67, 85; OxCThe 67, 83; OxDcArt; PenC ENG; PhDcTCA 77; RAdv 1, 13-1; REn; RfGEnL 91; ScF&FL 1; TwCA, SUP; TwCLC 1, 24; TwCPaSc; TwCWr; WebE&AL; WhAm 3; WhDW; WhLit; WhThe; WorAl; WorAlBi; WorECar*

Beernaert, Auguste Marie Francois
Belgian. Politician, Lawyer
Awarded 1909 Nobel Peace Prize; member of all peace conferences from 1889.
b. Jul 26, 1829 in Ostend, Belgium
d. Oct 6, 1912 in Lucerne, Switzerland
Source: *BiDMoPL; BioIn 9, 11, 15; WhoNob, 90, 95*

Beers, Clifford Whittingham
American. Social Reformer
Founded National Committee for Mental Hygiene, 1909, to prevent mental disorders, care for mentally ill.
b. Mar 30, 1876 in New Haven, Connecticut
d. Jul 9, 1943 in Providence, Rhode Island
Source: *BiDPsy; BiDSocW; BioIn 1, 2, 3, 6, 12, 19; CurBio 43; DcAmB S3; DcAmMeB 84; DcNAA; EncAB-A 9; LinLib L, S; NamesHP; NatCAB 34; OxCAmH; REnAL; WebAB 74, 79; WhAm 2*

Beery, Noah
American. Actor
Silent screen's most loved villain best known for *Beau Geste,* 1926.
b. Jan 17, 1884 in Kansas City, Missouri
d. Apr 1, 1946 in Beverly Hills, California
Source: *BioIn 17; CmMov; Film 1, 2; FilmEn; FilmgC; ForYSC; GangFlm; HalFC 80, 84, 88; LegTOT; MotPP; MovMk; OxCFilm; TwYS; Vers B; WhoHol B; WhScrn 74, 77, 83*

Beery, Noah, Jr.
American. Actor
Made screen debut with father Noah Beery, 1920; appeared in TV series "The Rockford Files," 1974-80.
b. Aug 10, 1916 in New York, New York
d. Nov 1, 1994
Source: *BioIn 4, 8; ConTFT 3; FilmEn; FilmgC; ForYSC; IntMPA 75, 76, 77, 78, 79, 80, 81, 82, 84, 86, 88, 92; LegTOT; MovMk; Vers B; WhAm 11; WhoAm 80, 82, 84, 86, 88, 92; WhoEnt 92; WorAl; WorAlBi*

Beery, Wallace Fitzgerald
American. Actor
Brother of Noah Beery, known for "lovable slob" roles; won Oscar, 1931, for *The Champ.*
b. Apr 1, 1885 in Kansas City, Missouri
d. Apr 15, 1949 in Los Angeles, California
Source: *BiDFilm; CmMov; DcAmB S4; Film 1; FilmEn; FilmgC; MovMk; OxCFilm; TwYS; WebAB 74; WhAm 2; WhoHol B; WhScrn 74, 77; WorEFlm*

Beesley, H(orace) Brent
"Dr. Doom"
American. Government Official
Director, Federal Savings and Loan Insurance Corp., 1981-83; chairman, CEO, Charter Savings Corp, Jacksonville, FL, 1983-86; pres., CEO, Farm Credit Corp., Denver, 1986-88; chairman, CEO, Heritage Savings Bank, St. George, Utah, 1988—.
b. Jan 30, 1946 in Salt Lake City, Utah
Source: *BioIn 12; WhoAm 84, 86, 88, 90, 92, 94, 95, 96, 97; WhoAmL 79; WhoEmL 89; WhoFI 83; WhoReal 83; WhoWest 87*

Beethoven, Ludwig van
German. Composer
Master of classical music; composed *Ninth Symphony,* 1817-23, when totally deaf.
b. Dec 16, 1770 in Bonn, Germany
d. Mar 26, 1827 in Vienna, Austria
Source: *AtlBL; Baker 78, 84, 92; BbD; Benet 87; BiD&SB; BiDD; BioIn 1, 2, 3, 4, 5, 6, 7, 8, 9, 10, 11, 12, 13, 14, 15, 16, 17, 18, 20, 21; BriBkM 80; CelCen; CmOp; CmpBCM; CnOxB; DancEn 78; DcArts; DcBiPP A; DcCathB; DcCom 77; DcCom&M 79; DeafPAS; Dis&D; EncDeaf; EncEnl; GrComp; HalFC 84, 88; IntDcOp; LegTOT; LinLib L, S; LuthC 75; McGEWB; MetOEnc; MusMk; NewAmDM; NewC; NewCol 75; NewEOp 71; NewGrDM 80; NewGrDO; NewOxM; OxCEng 85, 95; OxCGer 76, 86; OxCMus; OxDcOp; PenDiMP A; RAdv 14, 13-3; REn; WhDW; WorAl; WorAlBi*

Beeton, Isabella Mary Mayson
English. Author
Wrote Victorian text on cookery, domestic economy: *Book of Household Management,* 1861.
b. Mar 14, 1836 in London, England
d. Feb 6, 1865
Source: *Alli SUP; BioIn 15, 16, 19; EncBrWW; EvLB; InWom, SUP; MacDWB; OxCEng 95*

Begay, Fred
American. Physicist
Research focusses on the alternative use for laser, electron, and ion beams to heat thermonuclear plasmas at the Los Alamos National Laboratory, 1971—.

b. 1932 in Towaoc, Colorado
Source: *BioIn 20, 21; NotNaAm; NotTwCS*

Begay, Harrison
American. Artist
Navajo creator of widely collected watercolors and silkscreens.
b. Nov 15, 1917 in White Cone, Arizona
Source: *BioIn 4, 9, 21; IlBEAAW; NotNaAm; WhAmArt 85*

Begelman, David
American. Film Executive
Involved in money scandal that was subject of book *Indecent Exposure,* 1973, by John M Macdonald.
b. Aug 26, 1921 in New York, New York
d. Aug 7, 1995 in Los Angeles, California
Source: *BioIn 11, 12, 13, 21; IntMPA 82; NewYTBS 80; WhoAm 76, 82*

Begiebing, Robert J.
American. Author
Wrote *The Strange Death of Mistress Coffin,* 1991.
b. Nov 18, 1946 in Adams, Massachusetts
Source: *ConAu 122; ConLC 70*

Begin, Menachem (Wolfovitch)
Israeli. Political Leader
Prime minister, 1977-83; shared 1978 Nobel Peace Prize with Anwar Sadat for signing historic Camp David agreement, 1978.
b. Aug 16, 1913 in Brest-Litovsk, Poland
d. Mar 9, 1992 in Tel Aviv, Israel
Source: *AnObit 1992; BioIn 4, 11, 12, 13, 14, 15, 16, 17, 18, 19, 20; BkPepl; ConAu 109; CurBio 77; DcMidEa; DcTwHis; EncWB; FacFETw; HisEAAC; HisWorL; IntWW 74, 75, 76, 77, 78, 79, 80, 81, 82, 83, 89, 91; IntYB 79, 82; JeHun; LegTOT; MidE 78, 79, 80, 81, 82; News 92, 92-3; NewYTBE 70; NewYTBS 77, 92; NobelP; PolBiDi; PolLCME; WhAm 10; Who 82, 83, 85, 88, 90, 92; WhoNob; WhoWor 74, 78, 80, 82, 84, 87, 89, 91; WhoWorJ 72, 78; WorAl; WorAlBi*

Begle, Edward G(riffith)
American. Mathematician, Educator
Stanford U. professor, 1961-78, who studied topology.
b. Nov 27, 1914 in Saginaw, Michigan
d. Mar 2, 1978 in Palo Alto, California
Source: *AmMWSc 73P, 76P; BioIn 11, 12; LEduc 74; WhAm 7; WhoAm 74, 76, 78*

Begley, Ed, Jr.
American. Actor
Played Dr. Victor Ehrlich on TV series "St. Elsewhere," 1982-88.
b. Sep 16, 1949 in Los Angeles, California
Source: *ConTFT 4, 11; IntMPA 92, 94, 96; LegTOT; VarWW 85; WhoAm 86, 88, 90, 92, 94, 95, 96, 97; WhoEnt 92; WhoHol 92, A; WhoWest 89; WorAlBi*

Begley, Ed(ward James)
American. Actor
Began career as radio announcer, 1931; won Oscar, 1964, for *The Unsinkable Molly Brown.*
b. Mar 25, 1901 in Hartford, Connecticut
d. Apr 28, 1970 in Hollywood, California
Source: *BiE&WWA; BioIn 4, 8, 9, 13; CurBio 56, 70; DcAmB S8; FilmEn; FilmgC; ForYSC; HalFC 80, 84, 88; HolCA; LegTOT; MotPP; MovMk; NewYTBE 70; NotNAT B; RadStar; SaTiSS; Vers A; WhAm 5; WhoHol B; WhScrn 74, 77, 83; WhThe; WorAl*

Behan, Brendan (Francis)
Irish. Dramatist, Author
His humorous, vibrant books capture spirit of Irish nationalism; best known for autobiographical *Borstal Boy,* 1958.
b. Feb 9, 1923 in Dublin, Ireland
d. Mar 20, 1964 in Dublin, Ireland
Source: *Benet 87, 96; BiDIrW, B; BiE&WWA; BioIn 5, 6, 7, 8, 9, 10, 11, 12, 13, 17, 18, 21; BlmGEL; BritWr S2; CamGLE; CamGWoT; CasWL; CnDBLB 7; CnMD; CnThe; ConAu 33NR, 73; ConBrDr; ConDr 77F, 82E, 88E; ConLC 1, 8, 11, 15, 79; CroCD; CrtSuDr; CurBio 61, 64; CyWA 89; DcArts; DcIrB 78, 88; DcIrL, 96; DcIrW 1, 2, 3; DcLB 13; DcLEL 1940; EncWL, 2, 3; EncWT; Ent; FacFETw; GrWrEL DR; HalFC 80, 84, 88; IntDcT 2; IriPla; LegTOT; LinLib L; LngCTC; MajMD 1; MajTwCW; MakMC; McGEWD 72, 84; ModBrL, S1, S2; ModWD; NewC; NotNAT A, B; ObitT 1961; OxCEng 85, 95; OxCIri; OxCThe 83; PenC ENG; PlP&P; RAdv 14, 13-2; REn; REnWD; RfGEnL 91; RGTwCWr; TwCWr; WebE&AL; WhAm 4; WhDW; WhoTwCL; WhThe; WorAl; WorAlBi; WorAu 1950*

Beheshti, Mohammad, Ayatollah
Iranian. Political Leader
Founder of Islamic Republican Party, 1979; killed in bomb blast.
b. 1929 in Isfahan, Persia
d. Jun 28, 1981 in Tehran, Iran
Source: *AnObit 1981; BioIn 12*

Behn, Aphra
English. Author, Dramatist
First English woman to support herself by writing; most popular play was *The Rover,* 1677.
b. Jul 10, 1640 in Harbledown, England
d. Apr 16, 1689 in London, England
Source: *Alli; ArtclWW 2; AtlBL; BbD; Benet 87, 96; BiD&SB; BiDEWW; BioIn 1, 2, 3, 5, 6, 8, 11, 12, 13, 14, 15, 16, 17, 19, 20; BlmGEL; BlmGWL; BritAu; CamGEL; CamGLE; CamGWoT; CasWL; Chambr 2; ChhPo; ContDcW 89; CrtSuDr; CyWA 58; DcAfL; DcArts; DcBiA; DcBiPP; DcBrAmW; DcEnA; DcEnL; DcEuL; DcLB 39, 80, 131; DcNaB; DramC 4; EncBrWW; EncEnl; EncWT; Ent; EvLB; FemiCLE; FemiWr; GrWrEL DR; HisDStE; IntDcT 2; IntDcWB; InWom, SUP; LegTOT; LinLib L; LitC 1, 30; McGEWD 72, 84; MouLC 1; NewC; NewCBEL; NotNAT A, B; Novels; OxCEng 67, 85; OxCThe 67, 83; PenBWP; PenC ENG; PenNWW A; PlP&P; PoeCrit 13; RadHan; RAdv 14; REn; RfGEnL 91; WebE&AL; WomFir; WomSc; WorAl; WorAlBi; WorLitC*

Behn, Harry
American. Children's Author
Writings include *Siesta,* 1931; *The Two Uncles of Pablo,* 1959.
b. Sep 24, 1898 in Yavapai County, Arizona
d. Sep 4, 1973
Source: *AnCL; ArizL; ArtsAmW 3; AuBYP 2, 3; BioIn 5, 6, 8, 9, 10; BkCL; ChhPo, S1, S2; ConAu 5NR, 5R, 53; DcAmChF 1960; DcLB 61; IlsCB 1946, 1957; LinLib L; MorBMP; MorJA; OxCChiL; ScF&FL 1, 2; SmATA 2, 34N; Str&VC; TwCChW 78, 83, 89, 95; TwCYAW*

Behn, Noel
American. Author, Producer
Won 1958 Obie for production of *Endgame.*
b. Jan 6, 1928 in Chicago, Illinois
Source: *BiE&WWA; ConAu 116, 129; IntAu&W 91; NotNAT; SpyFic; TwCCr&M 80, 85, 91; WrDr 82, 84, 86, 88, 90, 92, 94*

Behrens, Earl Charles
American. Editor
Noted political journalist; won Medal of Freedom, 1970.
b. Feb 7, 1892 in Shasta, California
d. May 13, 1985 in Menlo Park, California
Source: *ConAu 116; WhoWest 74, 76*

Behrens, Hildegard
German., Opera Singer
Soprano, averages 50 concerts per year; excels in Wagnerian roles.
b. 1940 in Oldenburg, Germany
Source: *CelR 90*

Behring, Emil Adolph von
German. Physiologist
Won Nobel Prize in medicine, 1901, for discovery of serums against tetanus, diphtheria.
b. Mar 15, 1854 in Forsthausen, Prussia
d. Mar 31, 1917 in Marburg, Germany
Source: *AsBiEn; BioIn 3, 6, 9, 10, 15, 20; DcNAA; DcScB; InSci; LinLib S; McGEWB; NewCol 75; WhDW; WhoNob; WorAl*

Behrman, S(amuel) N(athaniel)
American. Author, Dramatist, Screenwriter
The American theater's most accomplished specialist in the comedy

of manners; plays include *No Time for Comedy*, 1939.
b. Jun 9, 1893 in Worcester, Massachusetts
d. Aug 9, 1973 in New York, New York
Source: *Benet 96; BiE&WWA; BioIn 1, 3, 4, 5, 7, 8, 9, 10, 12, 15, 20; CasWL; CmMov; ConAmA; ConAmD; ConAu 45, P-1; ConDr 93; CurBio 43, 73; DcAmB S9; EncWT; Ent; FilmgC; IntAu&W 77; IntDcT 2; McGEWD 84; NewYTBE 72, 73; OxCAmL 95; OxCThe 67, 83; PenC AM; RfGAmL 94; TwCA SUP; WhAm 6; WhoAm 74; WhoThe 72; WhoWor 74; WhoWorJ 72, 78; WhThe*

Beiderbecke, Bix
[Leon Bismark Beiderbecke]
American. Jazz Musician
Legendary coronetist, pianist; wrote "In a Mist"; recognized posthumously as one of jazz greats.
b. Mar 10, 1903 in Davenport, Iowa
d. Aug 7, 1931 in New York, New York
Source: *AllMusG; Baker 78, 84, 92; BiDAmM; BioIn 10, 14, 15, 16, 17, 19, 20; CmpEPM; ConMus 16; DcArts; FacFETw; IlEncJ; LegTOT; MusMk; NewAmDM; NewCol 75; NewGrDA 86; NewGrDJ 88; NewGrDM 80; OxCPMus; PenEncP; WebAB 74; WhAm 4; WhoJazz 72; WorAl; WorAlBi*

Beilenson, Edna Rudolph
[Elisabeth Deane]
American. Publisher
Headed Peter Pauper Press after husband's death.
b. Jun 16, 1909 in New York, New York
d. Feb 28, 1981 in New York, New York
Source: *AmAu&B; ConAu 85, 103; ForWC 70; NewYTBS 81; PenNWW B; WhoAm 78; WhoAmW 74; WhoWor 74*

Bein, Albert
Romanian. Dramatist, Author
Proletarian who wrote social protest drama *Let Freedom Ring*, 1935.
b. May 18, 1902 in Kishinev, Romania
Source: *BiE&WWA; CnMD; ModWD; NotNAT; OxCAmL 65, 83, 95*

Beinum, Eduard van
Dutch. Conductor
Led Amsterdam's famed Concertgebouw Orchestra, 1945-59.
b. Sep 3, 1900 in Arnhem, Netherlands
d. Apr 13, 1959 in Amsterdam, Netherlands
Source: *Baker 78, 84, 92; BioIn 2, 3, 4, 5, 11; CurBio 55, 59*

Bejart, Maurice
French. Choreographer
Avant-garde ballet master of Belgium's nat. dance company, 1959-87.
b. Jan 1, 1927 in Marseilles, France
Source: *BiDD; BioIn 9, 11, 13; CnOxB; ConTFT 11; CurBio 71; DcArts; DcTwCCu 2; EncWT; IntDcB; IntWW 74, 91; LegTOT; NewOxM; Who 82, 83, 85, 88, 90, 92; WhoOp 76; WorAl*

Bekhterev, Vladimir Mikhailovich
Russian. Scientist
Neuropathologist who studied conditioned reflexes; wrote *Nervous System Disease*, 1909.
b. 1857
d. 1927
Source: *BiDPara; BiDPsy; BioIn 11; DcScB; InSci; NamesHP; WebBD 83*

Belafonte, Harry, Jr.
[Harold George Belafonte]
American. Singer, Actor
Helped popularize calypso music; won Tony, 1953, for *John Murray Anderson's Almanac.*
b. Mar 1, 1927 in New York, New York
Source: *AfrAmAl 6; AfrAmBi 1; ASCAP 66, 80; Baker 78, 84, 92; BiDAfM; BiDAmM; BiE&WWA; BioIn 3, 4, 5, 6, 7, 8, 9, 10, 12, 13; BlksAmF; BlueB 76; CelR, 90; CivR 74; CmpEPM; ConBlB 4; ConMus 8; ConTFT 1, 5; CurBio 56; DcTwCCu 1, 5; DrBlPA, 90; Ebony 1, 3; EncFCWM 69, 83; EncRk 88; FacFETw; FilmEn; FilmgC; ForYSC; GangFlm; HalFC 80, 84, 88; InB&W 80, 85; IntMPA 75, 76, 77, 78, 79, 80, 81, 82, 84, 86, 88, 92, 94, 96; IntWW 74, 75, 76, 77, 78, 79, 80, 81, 82, 83, 89, 91, 93; LegTOT; MotPP; MovMk; NegAl 76, 83, 89; NewGrDA 86; NewYTBE 72; OxCFilm; OxCPMus; PenEncP; RkOn 74; WhoAfA 96; WhoAm 74, 76, 78, 80, 82, 84, 86, 88, 90, 92, 94, 95, 96, 97; WhoBlA 75, 77, 80, 85, 88, 90, 92, 94; WhoEnt 92; WhoHol 92, A; WhoWor 74, 78, 80, 82, 84, 87, 89, 91, 93, 95, 96, 97; WorAl; WorAlBi*

Belafonte, Shari
American. Actor, Model
Played Julie Gillette on TV's "Hotel," 1983-88; daughter of Harry.
b. Sep 22, 1954 in New York, New York
Source: *BioIn 11, 12, 13; CelR 90; DrBlPA 90; IntMPA 92, 94, 96; VarWW 85; WhoAfA 96; WhoBlA 94; WhoHol 92*

Belasco, David
American. Dramatist, Producer
Owner, Belasco Theater, NYC, since 1906; noted for realistic stage settings, lighting effects.
b. Jul 25, 1853 in San Francisco, California
d. May 14, 1931 in New York, New York
Source: *AmBi; AmCulL; ApCAB SUP; BiDAmM; BioIn 12, 13, 14, 16, 17, 19, 20; CamGLE; CamGWoT; CamHAL; Chambr 3; CmCal; CnThe; ConAu 104; CrtSuDr; DcAmB S1; DcLB 7; EncAB-H 1974, 1996; EncPaPR 91; EncWT; FacFETw; Film 1; GayN; GrStDi; GrWrEL DR; IntDcT 3; LegTOT; McGEWB; McGEWD 72, 84; MetOEnc; ModAL; MorMA; NatCAB 60; NewGrDA 86; NewGrDO; OxCAmH; OxCAmL 83, 95; OxCThe 67; PlP&P; REn; REnWD; RfGAmL 87, 94; ScF&FL 1; TheaDir; TwCA SUP; TwCBDA; WebAB 74, 79; WhAm 1; WhThe; WorAl; WorAlBi*

Belaunde-Terry, Fernando
Peruvian. Political Leader
Pres. of Peru, 1963-68, 1980-85.
b. Jul 17, 1912 in Lima, Peru
Source: *CurBio 65; DcPol; EncLatA; IntWW 83; NewCol 75; NewYTBS 80; WhoWor 84*

Belbenoit, Rene Lucien
French. Author
Account of conditions on Devil's Island, *My Escape from Devil's Island,* led to abolition of penal colony.
b. Apr 4, 1899 in Paris, France
d. Feb 26, 1959 in Lucerne Valley, California
Source: *ObitOF 79; WhE&EA*

Belcher, Edward, Sir
English. Naval Officer
Led Arctic expedition in search of Sir John Franklin, 1852-54; wrote of voyages.
b. 1799 in Halifax, Nova Scotia, Canada
d. Mar 18, 1877 in London, England
Source: *Alli, SUP; ApCAB; BbtC; CmCal; DcBiPP, A; DcCanB 10; DcNaB; Drake; MacDCB 78; OxCCan; OxCShps; StaCVF; WhWE*

Belew, Adrian
American. Musician
Back-up guitarist to rock stars Frank Zappa, David Bowie, Paul Simon; solo hit single "Oh, Daddy," 1989.
b. 1950?
Source: *BioIn 13, 15; ConMus 5; WhoEnt 92*

Belin, Edouard
French. Engineer, Inventor
Invented first telephoto transmission device, 1907.
b. Mar 5, 1876 in Vesoul, France
d. Mar 4, 1963 in Territet, Switzerland

Belinsky, Bo
[Robert Belinsky]
American. Baseball Player
Pitcher, 1962-70; threw no-hitter May 5, 1962; known for off-field publicity.
b. Dec 7, 1936 in New York, New York
Source: *Ballpl 90; BioIn 6, 9, 10, 20; WhoProB 73*

Belinsky, Vissarion Grigoryevich
Russian. Author
Best-known Russian critic; *Literary Reviews,* 1834, traced Russian literary development.
b. May 30, 1811 in Viapori, Russia
d. May 26, 1848 in Saint Petersburg, Russia
Source: *Benet 87, 96; BiD&SB; BioIn 14, 16, 18; CasWL; DcRusL; EncRev; EuAu; EvEuW; PenC EUR; REn*

Belisarius
Byzantine. Army Officer
One of great military leaders, responsible for much of Justinian I's success.

b. 505 in Germania, Illyria
d. Mar 565
Source: *BioIn 4, 5, 20; DcBiPP; DcInv; GenMudB; HarEnMi; LinLib S; McGEWB; NewC; OxCClL; REn; WhDW; WorAl; WorAlBi*

Beliveau, Jean (Marc A)
"Le Gros Bill"
Canadian. Hockey Player
Center, Montreal, 1950-71; scored 507 goals; won Hart Trophy, 1956, 1964; Hall of Fame, 1972.
b. Aug 31, 1931 in Three Rivers, Quebec, Canada
Source: *CanWW 81, 83; HocEn; LegTOT; WhoHcky 73; WorAl; WorAlBi*

Belk, William E
American. Hostage
One of 52 held by terrorists, Nov 1979 - Jan 1981.
b. 1938? in Winnsboro, South Carolina
Source: *NewYTBS 81*

Belknap, William Worth
American. Army Officer
Grant's secretary of war, 1869-76; resigned after bribery scandal.
b. Sep 22, 1829 in Newburgh, New York
d. Oct 13, 1890 in Washington, District of Columbia
Source: *AmBi; AmPolLe; ApCAB; BiDrUSE 71, 89; BioIn 7, 10; CivWDc; DcAmB; DcNAA; HarEnUS; NatCAB 4, 14; TwCBDA; WhAm HS; WhAmP; WhCiWar*

Bell, Alexander Graham
American. Inventor
Invented telephone, 1876; Bell Telephone Co. organized, 1877.
b. Mar 3, 1847 in Edinburgh, Scotland
d. Aug 2, 1922 in Baddeck, Nova Scotia, Canada
Source: *AmBi; AmLY; ApCAB, X; AsBiEn; BenetAL 91; BiDAmEd; BiDAmS; BiDSocW; BiESc; BioIn 1, 2, 3, 4, 5, 6, 7, 8, 9, 10, 11, 12, 13, 14, 15, 16, 17, 18, 19, 20, 21; CamDcSc; DcAmB; DcInv; DcNAA; DcNaB 1922; DcScB; DcTwDes; Dis&D; EncAB-H 1974, 1996; EncDeaf; FacFETw; GayN; HarEnUS; InSci; LarDcSc; LegTOT; LinLib S; LngCTC; MacDCB 78; McGEWB; MemAm; NatCAB 6; OxCAmH; RComAH; REnAL; TwCBDA; WebAB 74, 79; WhAm 1; WhDW; WorAl; WorAlBi; WorInv*

Bell, Arthur Donald
American. Author, Psychologist, Educator
Wrote *Dimensions of Christian Writing,* 1970; *Marriage Affair,* 1972.
b. Jul 17, 1920 in Vancouver, Washington
Source: *AmMWSc 73S; WhAm 8; WhoAm 74, 76, 78, 80, 82; WhoWor 80, 82*

Bell, Arthur (Irving)
American. Journalist
Writer and columnist, *Village Voice,* 1973-84, covered the gay crime beat.
b. Nov 6, 1939 in New York, New York
d. Jun 2, 1984 in New York, New York
Source: *ConAu 85, 112; GayLesB*

Bell, Bert
[Debenneville Bell]
American. Football Executive
President, Philadelphia Eagles, 1933-40; instituted pro draft, 1936; NFL commissioner, 1946-59, succeeded by Pete Roselle; Hall of Fame, 1963.
b. Feb 25, 1895 in Philadelphia, Pennsylvania
d. Oct 11, 1959 in Philadelphia, Pennsylvania
Source: *CurBio 50, 59; DcAmB S6; WhAm 3; WhoFtbl 74*

Bell, Bobby
[Robert L Bell]
American. Football Player
Three-time all-pro linebacker, Kansas City, 1963-73; Hall of Fame, 1983.
b. Jun 17, 1940 in Shelby, North Carolina
Source: *BioIn 17; LegTOT; WhoFtbl 74; WhoSpor*

Bell, Buddy
[David Gus Bell]
American. Baseball Player
Third baseman; five-time All-Star; Manager, Detroit Tigers, 1996—.
b. Aug 27, 1951 in Pittsburgh, Pennsylvania
Source: *Ballpl 90; BaseReg 86, 87; BiDAmSp BB; BioIn 11, 13; LegTOT; WhoAm 84, 86, 88; WhoProB 73*

Bell, Charles
Scottish. Surgeon
First to describe paralysis of facial nerve—Bell's palsy.
b. Nov 1774 in Edinburgh, Scotland
d. Apr 28, 1842 in Hollow Park, England
Source: *BiDLA; BiDPsy; BiESc; BiHiMed; BioIn 1, 3, 4, 5, 7, 8, 9, 14; CamDcSc; CelCen; DcBiPP; DcBrWA; DcEnL; DcNaB; DcScB; InSci; LarDcSc; NamesHP; OxCMed 86; WhDW; WorScD*

Bell, Clive
English. Critic
Member of the Bloomsbury Group; wrote on art and literature: *Art,* 1914, *Since Cezanne,* 1922.
b. Sep 16, 1881 in East Shefford, England
d. Sep 18, 1964 in London, England
Source: *Benet 87; BioIn 2, 4, 7, 14, 15, 17; CamGLE; ConAu 89, 97; DcLB DS10; DcLEL; DcNaB 1961; FacFETw; LegTOT; LngCTC; MajTwCW; McGDA; ModBrL; NewC; NewCBEL; OxCArt; OxCEng 67, 85; OxCTwCA; OxDcArt; PenC ENG; REn; ThTwC 87; TwCA, SUP; WhLit*

Bell, Cool Papa
[James Thomas Bell]
American. Baseball Player
Outfielder in Negro Leagues, 1922-50, known for his speed; stole 175 bases, 1933. Inducted into Hall of Fame, 1974.
b. May 17, 1903 in Starkville, Mississippi
d. Mar 7, 1991 in Saint Louis, Missouri
Source: *AfrAmSG; Ballpl 90; BiDAmSp BB; BioIn 10, 11, 14, 15, 17; WhoBlA 92N; WhoSpor*

Bell, Daniel
American. Sociologist, Educator
Books include *The Winding Passage,* 1980; labor editor, *Fortune* magazine, 1948-58.
b. May 10, 1919 in New York, New York
Source: *AmAu&B; AmEA 74; AmMWSc 73S, 78S; Au&Wr 71; BioIn 10, 11, 12, 13; ConAu 1R, 4NR; ConIsC 2; CurBio 73; DcLEL 1940; EncWB; Future; NewYTBS 89; PolProf E, K; RAdv 14, 13-3; ThTwC 87; WhoAm 74, 76, 78, 80, 82, 84, 86, 88, 90, 92, 94, 95, 96, 97; WhoAmJ 80; WhoWor 74; WhoWorJ 72, 78; WorAu 1970; WrDr 80, 82, 84, 86, 88, 90, 92, 94, 96*

Bell, Darryl
American. Actor
Played Ron on TV show "A Different World," 1987-93.
b. May 10, in Chicago, Illinois
Source: *WhoEnt 92*

Bell, Derrick Albert, Jr.
American. Educator, Civil Rights Leader, Author
Harvard professor whose tenure was revoked after his protest against the university's alleged racist policies turned into a 2-year unpaid leave of absence; wrote *Faces at the Bottom of the Well.*
b. Nov 6, 1930 in Pittsburgh, Pennsylvania
Source: *AfrAmAl 6; BlkWr 2; ConAu 104; DrAS 74P, 78P; InB&W 85; SchCGBL; WhoAfA 96; WhoAm 76, 78, 80, 82, 84, 86, 88, 90, 92, 94, 95, 96, 97; WhoAmL 83, 85, 87, 90, 92, 96; WhoBlA 75, 77, 80, 85, 88, 90, 92, 94*

Bell, Donald J
American. Businessman
With Albert Howell, formed Bell and Howell Co., 1907, to make, service equipment for film industry.
b. 1869
d. 1934
Source: *Entr*

Bell, Earl
American. Track Athlete
Champion pole-vaulter in 1970s.
b. Aug 25, 1955
Source: *BioIn 12*

Bell, George Antonio
Dominican. Baseball Player
Outfielder, Toronto, 1981, 1983-90; led AL in RBIs, 1987; AL MVP, 1987.
b. Oct 21, 1959 in San Pedro de Macoris, Dominican Republic
Source: *BaseEn 88; BaseReg 87, 88; WhoAfA 96; WhoAm 88, 90, 92, 94, 95; WhoBlA 85, 88, 90, 92, 94; WhoMW 93*

Bell, Gertrude Margaret
English. Archaeologist
Traveled widely in Persia, Arabia; helped start national museum at Baghdad, 1926.
b. Jul 14, 1868 in Durham, England
d. Jul 11, 1926 in Baghdad, Iraq
Source: *DcLEL; DcNaB 1922; EvLB; IntDcWB; LngCTC; PenC ENG; REn; WhWE*

Bell, Greg
American. Track Athlete
Long jumper; won gold medal, 1956 Olympics.
b. Nov 7, 1930 in Terre Haute, Indiana
Source: *BioIn 4; WhoTr&F 73*

Bell, Griffin Boyette
American. Lawyer
US attorney general, Carter administration, 1977-79.
b. Oct 31, 1918 in Americus, Georgia
Source: *BiDFedJ; CngDr 77, 79; CurBio 77; IntWW 77, 78, 79, 80, 81, 82, 83, 89, 91; NewYTBS 76; WhoAm 84; WhoAmL 78, 79, 85; WhoAmP 85; WhoGov 77; WhoSSW 82*

Bell, Herbert A
American. Inventor
Founded firm that eventually became Packard Bell Electronics.
b. 1890 in Rock Valley, Iowa
d. Jan 31, 1970 in New York, New York
Source: *BioIn 8; NewYTBE 70*

Bell, James Ford
American. Business Executive
First pres., General Mills, 1928; chm., 1934.
b. Aug 16, 1879 in Philadelphia, Pennsylvania
d. May 7, 1961 in Minneapolis, Minnesota
Source: *BioIn 1, 5, 6; DcAmBC; DcAmB S7; WhAm 4*

Bell, John
American. Politician
Southern Whig; senator, 1847-59; unsuccessful presidential candidate, 1860, defeated by Lincoln.
b. Feb 15, 1797 in Nashville, Tennessee
d. Sep 10, 1869 in Dover, Tennessee
Source: *AmBi; AmPolLe; ApCAB; BiAUS; BiDrAC; BiDrUSC 89; BiDrUSE 71, 89; BiDSA; BioIn 2, 7, 10, 14; DcAmB; Drake; HarEnUS; NatCAB 3; NewCol 75; OxCAmH; PolPar; PresAR; TwCBDA; WebAB 74; WhAm HS; WhAmP; WhCiWar; WorAl*

Bell, John Kim
American. Conductor
Appointed to conduct with the Toronto Symphony, 1980, making him the first Native North American conductor.
b. Oct 8, 1952 in Quebec, Canada
Source: *BioIn 21; CanWW 31; NotNaAm*

Bell, Joseph
Scottish. Surgeon, Educator
Edited *Edinburg Medical Journal,* 1873-96; thought to be Arthur Conan Doyle's model for Sherlock Holmes.
b. 1837 in Edinburgh, Scotland
d. 1911
Source: *Alli SUP; BioIn 4, 5, 13; DcNaB MP; LngCTC; WhLit*

Bell, Kool
[Kool and the Gang; Robert Bell]
American. Singer, Musician
Leader of rhythm and blues-pop group; number one hit "Celebration," 1980.
b. Oct 8, 1950 in Youngstown, Ohio

Bell, Lawrence Dale
American. Aircraft Manufacturer
Founder of Bell Aircraft, who built fighter planes Airacuda, Airacobra.
b. Apr 5, 1894 in Mentone, Indiana
d. Oct 20, 1956 in Buffalo, New York
Source: *BioIn 1, 4, 5, 8, 12; CurBio 42, 57; DcAmB S6; InSci; ObitOF 79; WhAm 3*

Bell, Marilyn
Canadian. Swimmer
First person to swim Lake Ontario, 1954.
b. Oct 19, 1937 in Toronto, Ontario, Canada
Source: *BioIn 3, 4, 10; CurBio 56; InWom*

Bell, Ralph S.
American. Evangelist
Became associate evangelist of the Billy Graham Crusade, 1965.
b. May 13, 1934 in Saint Catharines, Ontario, Canada
Source: *BioIn 19; ConBlB 5*

Bell, Ricky Lynn
American. Football Player
Running back, 1977-82; number one pick in 1977 NFL draft; set several club records with Tampa Bay; died of cardiac arrest.
b. Apr 8, 1955 in Houston, Texas
d. Nov 28, 1984 in Inglewood, California
Source: *BioIn 10, 11; ConNews 85-1; InB&W 80; NewYTBS 84; WhoBlA 80, 85, 90, 92N*

Bell, Ronald
[Kool and the Gang]
American. Musician
Plays tenor sax with Kool and the Gang.
b. Nov 1, 1951 in Youngstown, Ohio

Bell, Steve
[Stephen Scott Bell]
American. Broadcast Journalist
Correspondent, ABC News since 1967; one of few journalists in Hanoi for release of American POWs.
b. Dec 9, 1935 in Oskaloosa, Iowa
Source: *ConAu 65; EncTwCJ; WhoAm 80, 82, 84, 86, 88, 90, 92, 94, 95, 96, 97; WhoE 79, 81; WhoTelC*

Bell, T(errel) H(oward)
"Ted"
American. Government Official
Secretary of Education, 1981-85.
b. Nov 11, 1921 in Lava Hot Springs, Idaho
d. Jun 22, 1996 in Salt Lake City, Utah
Source: *BiDrUSE 89; BioIn 12, 13; CngDr 83; CurBio 76, 96N; IntWW 81, 82, 83, 89, 91, 93; LEduc 74; NatCAB 63N; NewYTBS 81; PseudN 82; WhAm 11; WhoAm 76, 78, 80, 82, 84, 86, 88, 90, 92, 94, 95, 96; WhoAmP 85; WhoE 81, 83, 85, 86; WhoGov 77; WhoWor 82, 84*

Bell, Tom
English. Actor
In film *The L-Shaped Room,* 1962; PBS series "Sons and Lovers," 1983; "Reilly: Ace of Spies," 1984.
b. 1932 in Liverpool, England
Source: *ConTFT 9; FilmEn; FilmgC; ForYSC; HalFC 84; IntMPA 75, 76, 77, 78, 79, 80, 81, 82, 84, 86, 88, 92, 94, 96; WhoHol 92*

Bell, Vanessa
[Mrs. Clive Bell]
English. Artist
Sister of Virginia Woolf; member of Bloomsburg group of painters.
b. May 30, 1879 in London, England
d. Apr 7, 1961 in East Sussex, England
Source: *BiDWomA; BioIn 11, 13, 14, 16, 17, 19, 20; ConAu 145; ContDcW 89; DcBrAr 1; DcLB DS10; DcNaB 1961; DcWomA; FacFETw; GrBr; IntDcWB; InWom, SUP; LegTOT; LngCTC; NewC; ObitT 1961; OxCEng 85; OxCTwCA; OxDcArt; PhDcTCA 77; TwCPaSc; WomArt*

Bell, William Holden
American. Spy, Engineer
Hughes Aircraft employee, who sold US defense secrets to Polish spy, 1981.
b. 1920?
Source: *BioIn 12*

Bellamy, Edward
American. Author, Social Reformer
Wrote *Looking Backward,* 1888, presenting a method of economic organization guaranteeing material equality.
b. Mar 26, 1850 in Chicopee Falls, Massachusetts
d. May 22, 1898 in Chicopee Falls, Massachusetts
Source: *Alli SUP; AmAu; AmAu&B; AmBi; AmRef; AmSocL; ApCAB SUP;*

BbD; Benet 96; BenetAL 91; BibAL; BiDAmL; BiDAmLf; BiD&SB; BioIn 1, 2, 3, 5, 8, 10, 12, 13, 14, 15, 16, 19, 21; CamGEL; CamGLE; CamHAL; CasWL; CnDAL; CyWA 58; DcAmAu; DcAmB; DcAmC; DcAmSR; DcArts; DcBiA; DcEnA A; DcLB 12; DcLEL; DcNAA; EncAB-H 1974, 1996; EncAL; EncSF, 93; EncUrb; EvLB; GayN; GrWrEL N; HarEnUS; LegTOT; LinLib L, S; LuthC 75; McGEWB; MorMA; MouLC 4; NatCAB 1; NewEScF; NinCLC 4; Novels; OxCAmH; OxCAmL 65, 83, 95; OxCEng 67, 85, 95; PenC AM; RadHan; RAdv 1, 14, 13-1; REn; REnAL; RfGAmL 87, 94; ScF&FL 1, 92; ScFEYrs; ScFSB; TwCBDA; TwCSFW 81, 86, 91; WebAB 74, 79; WebE&AL; WhAm HS; WhAmP; WorAl; WorAlBi

Bellamy, Ralph
American. Actor
Won Tony, 1958, for *Sunrise at Campobello*; original panelist, "To Tell the Truth"; in weekly TV series "Man Against Crime," 1949-54.
b. Jun 17, 1904 in Chicago, Illinois
d. Nov 29, 1991 in Santa Monica, California
Source: *AnObit 1991; BiE&WWA; BioIn 1, 2, 3, 5, 11, 12, 17, 18, 21; CamGWoT; CelR; ConAu 101, 136; ConTFT 1, 6, 10; CurBio 51, 92N; EncAFC; Film 2; FilmEn; FilmgC; GangFlm; HalFC 80, 84, 88; HolP 30; IntDcF 1-3, 2-3; IntMPA 86, 92; LegTOT; MotPP; MovMk; NewYTBS 91; NotNAT; OlFamFa; OxCAmT 84; WhoAm 74, 76, 78, 80, 82, 84, 86, 88; WhoHol 92, A; WhoHrs 80; WhThe; WorAl; WorAlBi*

Bellamy, Walt(er Jones)
American. Basketball Player
In NBA with several teams, 1961-75; ninth all-time scorer with 20,941 pts; member US Olympic team, 1960.
b. Jul 24, 1939 in New Bern, North Carolina
Source: *BasBi; OfNBA 87; WhoAm 76; WhoAmP 85; WhoBbl 73; WhoBlA 85*

Bellamy Brothers, The
[David Bellamy; Howard Bellamy]
American. Music Group
Pop-country duo from FL who had gold record for 1976 hit "Let Your Love Flow."
Source: *BgBkCoM; ConMus 13; EncFCWM 83; HarEnCM 87; PenEncP; RkOn 78; WhoRock 81; WhoRocM 82*

Bellanca, Giuseppe Mario
Italian. Aircraft Manufacturer
Founder of Bellanca Aircraft who built first plane, 1907; invented convertible landing gear.
b. Mar 19, 1886 in Sciacca, Italy
d. Dec 26, 1960 in New York, New York
Source: *BioIn 3, 5, 9, 11, 16; DcAmB S6; EncAB-A 32; InSci; NatCAB 52; ObitOF 79; WhAm 4*

Bellarmine, Robert, Saint
[Roberto Francesco Romolo Bellarmino]
Italian. Theologian
Jesuit cardinal, leading figure in Catholic Reformation; attacked several Protestant theologians; moderated criticisms of his friend, Galileo, 1616.
b. Oct 4, 1542 in Montepulciano, Italy
d. Sep 17, 1621 in Rome, Italy
Source: *DcCathB; DcScB; EvEuW; LinLib L, S; LuthC 75; McGEWB; NewC; NewCBEL; NewCol 75; OxCEng 67; WebBD 83*

Bell Burnell, Jocelyn
[Susan Jocelyn Bell]
English. Astronomer
Discovered pulsars in 1967.
b. Jul 15, 1943 in Belfast, Ireland
Source: *BioIn 18, 19, 20, 21; CurBio 95; Who 92*

Belle, Albert
American. Baseball Player
With the Cleveland Indians, 1989—.
b. Aug 25, 1966 in Shreveport, Louisiana
Source: *BioIn 17, 18, 21; ConBlB 10; News 96*

Belle, Regina
American. Singer
Rhythm and blues singer; albums include *All by Myself,* 1987; *Stay with Me,* 1989.
b. 1963
Source: *ConBlB 1; ConMus 6; WhoAfA 96; WhoAm 95, 96, 97; WhoBlA 92, 94*

Bellecourt, Clyde
American. Social Reformer
One of the cofounders of the American Indian Movement (AIM); opposed to violence.
Source: *BioIn 21; NotNaAm*

Beller, Kathleen
American. Actor
Films include *Godfather II,* 1974; TV shows include "Dynasty," "The Bronx Zoo."
b. Feb 10, 1955 in Westchester, New York
Source: *BioIn 13; HalFC 84, 88; VarWW 85; WhoHol 92*

Belli, Carlos German
Peruvian. Poet
Poems present alienated, dehumanized modern world.
b. Sep 15, 1927 in Lima, Peru
Source: *Benet 87, 96; BenetAL 91; BioIn 18; CasWL; ConAu 131; ConSpAP; DcCLAA; DcTwCCu 3; EncWL 3; HispWr; IntWWP 77, 82; OxCSpan; PenC AM; SpAmA*

Belli, Melvin M(ouron)
"The King of Torts"
American. Lawyer
Has defended such well-known people as Lenny Bruce, Jack Ruby.
b. Jul 29, 1907 in Sonora, California
d. Jul 9, 1996 in San Francisco, California
Source: *BioIn 4, 5, 6, 7, 10, 11, 12; ConAu 104, 152; CurBio 79, 96N; WhoAm 74, 76, 78, 80, 82, 84, 86, 88, 90, 92, 94, 95, 96; WhoAmL 78, 79, 85, 87, 90, 94, 96; WhoWest 74, 76, 78; WhoWor 74; WorAl*

Bellinghausen, Fabian Gottlieb von
[Faddei F Bellinsgauzen]
Russian. Naval Officer, Explorer
First to see Antarctica, 1820; founded Russian Geographic Society, 1845.
b. Aug 30, 1779 in Oesel, Russia
d. Jan 25, 1852 in Kronstadt, Russia
Source: *DcScB; WhDW*

Bellini, Gentile
Italian. Artist
Prominent portraitist, also noted for processions, panoramic views.
b. 1429 in Venice, Italy
d. Feb 23, 1507 in Venice, Italy
Source: *AtlBL; BioIn 1, 5, 6, 12, 14; ClaDrA; DcArts; IntDcAA 90; LegTOT; LinLib S; McGDA; OxCArt; OxDcArt; WebBD 83; WorAl; WorAlBi*

Bellini, Giovanni
Italian. Artist, Architect
Teacher of Giorgione and Titian; founded Venetian school.
b. 1430 in Venice, Italy
d. Nov 29, 1516 in Venice, Italy
Source: *AtlBL; Benet 87, 96; BioIn 1, 2, 4, 5, 6, 8, 9; DcArts; DcBiPP; DcCathB; Dis&D; IntDcAA 90; LinLib S; McGDA; McGEWB; OxCArt; OxDcArt; REn; WhDW; WorAl; WorAlBi*

Bellini, Jacopo
Italian. Artist
Venetian religious painter; father of Gentile, Giovanni Bellini.
b. 1400?
d. 1470?
Source: *BioIn 1, 5, 9, 17; DcArts; IntDcAA 90; McGDA; OxDcArt; WorAlBi*

Bellini, Vincenzo
Italian. Composer
Noted bel canto composer who wrote operas *Il Pirata,* 1827; *Norma,* 1831.
b. Nov 3, 1801 in Catania, Sicily, Italy
d. Sep 23, 1835 in Puteaux, France
Source: *AtlBL; Baker 78, 84, 92; Benet 96; BioIn 1, 3, 4, 5, 6, 7, 8, 9, 12, 20; BriBkM 80; CmOp; CmpBCM; DcArts; DcCom 77; GrComp; IntDcOp; LegTOT; LinLib S; McGEWB; MetOEnc; MusMk; NewAmDM; NewEOp 71; NewGrDM 80; NewGrDO; NewOxM; OxCEng 85, 95; OxCMus; OxDcOp; PenDiMP A; RAdv 14, 13-3; REn; WorAl; WorAlBi*

Bellino, Joe
[Joseph Michael Bellino]
American. Football Player
All-America running back, won Heisman Trophy, 1960; in NFL with Boston, 1965-67.
b. Mar 13, 1938 in Winchester, Massachusetts
Source: *BiDAmSp FB; BioIn 6, 14; WhoFtbl 74*

Bellisario, Donald P
American. Writer, Producer
Created "Magnum P I" TV series, 1980.
b. Aug 8, in Charleroi, Pennsylvania
Source: *LesBEnT; WhoTelC*

Bellison, Simeon
American. Musician
First clarinetist, NY Philharmonic, 1920-48; recorded Hebrew, Russian songs .
b. Dec 4, 1883 in Moscow, Russia
d. May 4, 1953 in New York, New York
Source: *Baker 78, 84; NewGrDA 86; NewGrDM 80; PenDiMP*

Bellman, Carl Michael
Swedish. Poet, Courtier
Composed popular ballads, drinking songs found in *Fredmans Epistlar,* 1790.
b. Feb 4, 1740
d. Feb 11, 1795
Source: *Baker 78, 84, 92; BbD; Benet 96; BiD&SB; BioIn 7, 8, 9; CasWL; ChhPo, S3; DcEuL; DcScanL; EuAu; EvEuW; NewGrDM 80; PenC EUR*

Bellmon, Henry Louis
American. Politician
Rep. governor of Oklahoma, 1963-66, 1987-91, succeeded by David Walters.
b. Sep 3, 1921 in Tonkawa, Oklahoma
Source: *AlmAP 88; BiDrAC; BiDrGov 1789; BiDrUSC 89; CurBio 63; IntWW 83; PolProf J; WhoAm 90; WhoAmP 87; WhoSSW 91; WhoWor 91, 93*

Belloc, Hilaire
[Joseph Hillaire Pierre Belloc]
English. Author
Wrote from Roman Catholic viewpoint; founded *New Witness* newspaper with G K Chesterton.
b. Jul 27, 1870 in La Celle-Saint-Cloud, France
d. Jul 16, 1953 in Guildford, England
Source: *AnCL; AtlBL; AuBYP 2; Benet 87, 96; BioIn 1, 2, 3, 4, 5, 6, 8, 9, 10, 11, 12, 13, 14, 15, 17, 20; BkC 5; BlmGEL; CamGEL; CamGLE; CarSB; CasWL; CathA 1930; Chambr 3; ChhPo, S1, S2, S3; ChlBkCr; CnE&AP; CnMWL; ConAu 106; CyWA 58; DcAmC; DcCathB; DcLB 19, 100, 141, 174; DcLEL; EncSF; EncWL 2, 3; EvLB; FacFETw; GrWrEL P; LngCEL; LngCTC; ModBrL, S1, S2; NewC; NewCBEL; ObitT 1951; OxCEng 67, 85, 95; PenC ENG; RAdv 1, 14, 13-1, 13-3; REn; RfGEnL 91; ScF&FL 1; ScFEYrs; TwCA, SUP; TwCChW 78, 83, 89; TwCLC 7, 18; TwCWr; WebE&AL; WhAm 3; WhDW; WhE&EA; WhLit; WhoChL; WhoLA; WrChl; YABC 1*

Bellotto, Bernardo
Italian. Artist
Court painter for king of Poland, known for paintings of Warsaw.
b. Jan 30, 1720 in Venice, Italy
d. Oct 17, 1780 in Warsaw, Poland
Source: *AtlBL; BioIn 4, 5, 8, 9; EncEnl; McGDA; OxCArt; OxCGer 76, 86; OxDcArt; PolBiDi*

Bellow, Saul
American. Author
Won Pulitzer Prize, 1976, for *Humboldt's Gift;* won Nobel Prize in literature, 1976.
b. Jul 10, 1915 in Lachine, Quebec, Canada
Source: *AmAu&B; AmCulL; AmDec 1970; AmNov; AmWr; AuNews 2; Benet 87, 96; BenetAL 91; BestSel 89-3; BioIn 2, 3, 4, 7, 8, 9, 10, 11, 12, 13; BkPepl; BlueB 76; CamGEL; CamGLE; CamHAL; CasWL; CelR, 90; CnMWL; ConAu 1BS, 5R, 29NR, 53NR; ConDr 73, 77, 82, 93; ConLC 1, 2, 3, 6, 8, 10, 13, 15, 25, 33, 34, 63, 79; ConNov 72, 76, 82, 86, 91, 96; CroCD; CurBio 65, 88; CyWA 89; DcArts; DcLB 2, 28, DS3, Y82A; DcLEL 1940; DcTwCCu 1; DrAF 76; DrAPF 80; DrAS 74E, 78E, 82E; EncAB-H 1974, 1996; EncSF, 93; EncWL, 2, 3; FacFETw; GrWrEL N; IntAu&W 76, 77, 89, 91, 93; IntWW 74, 75, 76, 77, 78, 79, 80, 81, 82, 83, 89, 91, 93; JeAmHC; LegTOT; LinLib L, S; LngCTC; MagSAmL; MajTwCW; MakMC; McGEWB; ModAL, S1, S2; NewCon; NewYTBS 76; NobelP; NotNAT; Novels; OxCAmL 65, 83, 95; OxCEng 85, 95; PenC AM; RAdv 1, 14, 13-1; RComAH; REn; REnAL; RfGAmL 87, 94; RfGShF; RGTwCWr; ShSCr 14; TwCA SUP; TwCWr; WebAB 74, 79; WebE&AL; WhDW; Who 74, 82, 83, 85, 88, 90, 92, 94; WhoAm 74, 76, 78, 80, 82, 84, 86, 88, 90, 92; WhoAmJ 80; WhoMW 78, 80, 82, 84, 86, 88, 90, 92; WhoNob, 90, 95; WhoTwCL; WhoUSWr 88; WhoWor 74, 78, 80, 82, 84, 87, 89, 91, 93; WhoWorJ 72, 78; WhoWrEP 89, 92, 95; WorAl; WorAlBi; WorLitC; WrDr 76, 80, 82, 84, 86, 88, 90, 92, 94, 96; WrPh*

Bellows, George Wesley
American. Artist
Associated with "The Eight"; painted boxing scenes, landscapes: "Stag at Sharkey's," 1907.
b. Aug 12, 1882 in Columbus, Ohio
d. Jan 8, 1925 in New York, New York
Source: *AmBi; ApCAB X; ArtsAmW 1; AtlBL; BioIn 1, 2, 3, 4, 6, 7, 8, 9, 11, 12, 13; BriEAA; DcAmB; DcArts; EncAB-H 1974, 1996; GrAmP; IlBEAAW; McGDA; McGEWB; NatCAB 20; OxCAmH; OxCAmL 65; OxCArt; OxCTwCA; OxDcArt; PhDcTCA 77; REn; WebAB 74, 79; WhAm 1; WorAl; WorAlBi*

Bellshazzar
Babylonian. Ruler, Historical Figure
Co-regent under whose administration Babylon fell to the Persians as predicted by Jewish prophet, Daniel.
d. c. 539BC, Babylon

Belluschi, Pietro
American. Architect
Co-designed NYC's Pan Am Building with Walter Gropius.
b. Aug 18, 1899 in Ancona, Italy
d. Feb 14, 1994 in Portland, Oregon
Source: *AmArch 70; BioIn 1, 2, 4, 5, 9, 12, 13, 19, 20, 21; BlueB 76; BriEAA; ConArch 80, 87, 94; CurBio 59, 94N; EncAAr 1, 2; EncMA; IntDcAr; IntWW 74, 75, 76, 77, 78, 79, 80, 81, 82, 83, 89, 91, 93; MacEA; McGDA; NewYTBS 94; WhAm 11; WhoAm 74, 76, 78, 80, 82, 84, 86, 88, 90, 92, 94; WhoWor 74, 76, 78*

Bellwood, Pamela
American. Actor
In movie *Airport '77;* played Claudia on TV series "Dynasty."
b. Jun 26, 1946 in New York, New York
Source: *VarWW 85*

Belmondo, Jean-Paul
French. Actor
Antihero image established in first feature film *Breathless,* 1960; in *Les Miserables,* 1995.
b. Apr 9, 1933 in Neuilly-sur-Seine, France
Source: *BiDFilm, 81, 94; BioIn 14; CelR, 90; ConTFT 7; CurBio 65; DcTwCCu 2; EncEurC; FacFETw; FilmAG WE; FilmEn; FilmgC; ForYSC; GangFlm; HalFC 80, 84, 88; IntDcF 1-3, 2-3; IntMPA 75, 76, 77, 78, 79, 80, 81, 82, 84, 86, 88, 92, 94, 96; IntWW 74, 75, 76, 77, 78, 79, 80, 81, 82, 83, 89, 91, 93; ItaFilm; LegTOT; MotPP; MovMk; OxCFilm; VarWW 85; WhoFr 79; WhoHol 92, A; WhoWor 74, 82, 84, 87, 89, 91, 93, 95, 96, 97; WorAl; WorAlBi; WorEFlm*

Belmont, Alva Erskine Smith Vanderbilt
American. Socialite, Suffragist
Militant feminist, once wife of William K Vanderbilt.
b. Jan 17, 1853 in Mobile, Alabama
d. Jan 26, 1933 in Paris, France
Source: *AmRef; EncWHA; NotAW*

Belmont, August
[August Shoenberg]
American. Financier
Started August Belmont and Co., 1837, one of largest banking houses in US.
b. Dec 8, 1816 in Alzey, Germany
d. Nov 24, 1890 in New York, New York
Source: *AmBi; ApCAB; BiAUS; BiDAmBL 83; BiDAmSp OS; BioIn 4, 8, 12, 16, 21; DcAmB; DcAmDH 80, 89; DcNAA; EncAB-H 1974; HarEnUS;*

NatCAB 11; OxCAmH; TwCBDA; WebAB 74, 79; WhAm HS; WhAmP

Belmont, August, Jr.
American. Banker
Chief financier, construction of NYC I.R.T. system; owner, Man O'War; Belmont Stakes, racetrack named for family.
b. Feb 18, 1853 in New York, New York
d. Dec 10, 1924
Source: *ApCAB SUP, X; BioIn 3, 4, 8, 10, 12; HarEnUS; NatCAB 11, 37; WhAm 1; WorAl; WorAlBi*

Belmont, Eleanor Robson
[Mrs. August Belmont]
American. Actor, Philanthropist
Associated with Red Cross for over 25 yrs; Shaw wrote play *Major Barbara* based on her life.
b. Dec 13, 1879 in Wigan, England
d. Oct 24, 1979 in New York, New York
Source: *AmWomPl; ConAu 97; CurBio 44, 80, 80N; NewYTBS 79; WhoAmW 68; WomWWA 14*

Belote, Melissa
American. Swimmer
Won three gold medals, 1972 Olympics.
b. Oct 16, 1956 in Washington, District of Columbia
Source: *BioIn 10, 12; EncWomS; InWom SUP; WhoSpor*

Beltrami, Eugenio
Italian. Mathematician, Educator
Noted for research in non-Euclidean geometry.
b. Nov 16, 1835 in Cremona, Austria
d. Feb 18, 1900 in Rome, Italy
Source: *DcScB; InSci; NewCol 75; WebBD 83*

Belushi, Jim
[James Belushi]
American. Actor
Starred on "Saturday Night Live," 1983-85; films include *Trading Places,* 1983; *About Last Night.,* 1986.
b. Jun 15, 1954 in Chicago, Illinois
Source: *BioIn 12; ConNews 86-2; ConTFT 3, 13; CurBio 95; IntMPA 88, 92, 94, 96; ItaFilm; LegTOT; VarWW 85; WhoAm 92, 94, 95, 96, 97; WhoEnt 92; WhoHol 92; WorAlBi*

Belushi, John
"The Black Rhino"
American. Actor, Comedian
Starred in films *Animal House,* 1978; *The Blues Brothers,* 1980; on "Saturday Night Live," 1975-79.
b. Jan 24, 1949 in Chicago, Illinois
d. Mar 5, 1982 in Hollywood, California
Source: *AnObit 1982; BioIn 11, 12, 13, 14, 16, 17; ConAu 106; CurBio 80, 82, 82N; EncAFC; HalFC 84, 88; IntDcF 2-3; IntMPA 82; LegTOT; NewYTBS 82; PseudN 82; QDrFCA 92; RkOn 85; WhAm 8; WhoAm 82; WhoCom; WhoRocM 82; WorAl; WorAlBi*

Bely, Andrey
[Boris Nikolayevich Bugayev]
Russian. Poet
Symbolist; wrote poetic "symphony," *Popal,* 1909; novel, *Petersburg,* 1913.
b. Oct 14, 1880 in Moscow, Russia
d. Jan 8, 1934 in Moscow, Union of Soviet Socialist Republics
Source: *CasWL; ClDMEL 47, 80; CnMWL; ConAu 104; CyWA 89; DcRusL; DcRusLS; EncWL, 2, 3; EuWr 9; EvEuW; GrFLW; ModSL 1; PenC EUR; PoeCrit 11; REn; SovUn; TwCLC 7; WhoTwCL; WorAu 1950; WrPh*

Beman, Deane Randolph
American. Golfer, Golf Executive
Pro golfer, 1967-74; commissioner, Tournament Players Division, PGA, 1974—.
b. Apr 22, 1938 in Washington, District of Columbia
Source: *BioIn 6, 10; WhoAm 76, 78, 80, 82, 84, 86, 88, 90, 92, 94, 95, 96; WhoGolf; WhoSSW 82*

Bemelmans, Ludwig
American. Author
Wrote *Hotel Bemelmans,* 1946; *Madeline* children's stories, 1953-62; won Caldecott for *Madeline's Rescue,* 1954.
b. Apr 27, 1898 in Tirol, Austria
d. Oct 1, 1962 in New York, New York
Source: *AmAu&B; AmNov; Au&ICB; AuBYP 2, 3; Benet 87, 96; BenetAL 91; BioIn 1, 2, 3, 4, 5, 6, 7, 8, 10, 12, 14, 15, 17, 19; Cald 1938; ChhPo, S1, S2, S3; ChlBkCr; ChlLR 6; ChsFB I; CnDAL; ConAu 73; CurBio 41, 62; DcAmB S7; DcLB 22; DcLEL; EncWL; GrWrEL N; IlsBYP; IlsCB 1744, 1946, 1957; LegTOT; LinLib L; LngCTC; MajAI; MorJA; NatCAB 48; Novels; OxCAmL 65, 83, 95; PenC AM; REn; REnAL; RfGAmL 87, 94; SmATA 15; TwCA, SUP; TwCChW 78, 83, 89, 95; TwCWr; WhAm 4; WhoAmA 89N, 91N, 93N; WhoChL; WhoGrA 62; WorAl; WorAlBi; WrChl*

Bemis, Samuel Flagg
American. Historian, Editor
Won Pulitzers for *Pinckney's Treaty,* 1926; *John Quincy Adams and Foundation of American Foreign Policy,* 1949.
b. Oct 20, 1891 in Worcester, Massachusetts
d. Sep 26, 1973 in Bridgeport, Connecticut
Source: *AmAu&B; BenetAL 91; BioIn 2, 4, 8, 10, 13, 16; ConAu 9R, 11NR, 45; CurBio 50, 73, 73N; DcAmB S9; DcAmDH 80, 89; DcLB 17; DcLEL; NewYTBE 73; OxCAmL 65; OxCCan; RAdv 14, 13-3; REnAL; TwCA, SUP; WebAB 74, 79; WhAm 6; WhNAA; WhoWor 74*

Benacerraf, Baruj
American. Scientist, Educator
Shared 1980 Nobel Prize in medicine for researching genetics and the human immune system.
b. Oct 29, 1920 in Caracas, Venezuela
Source: *AmMWSc 73P, 76P, 79, 82, 86, 89, 92, 95; BiESc; BioIn 12, 15, 20; BlueB 76; IntWW 81, 82, 83, 89, 91, 93; LarDcSc; McGMS 80; NewYTBS 80; NobelP; NotTwCS; Who 82, 83, 85, 88, 90, 92, 94; WhoAm 74, 76, 78, 80, 82, 84, 86, 88, 90, 92, 94, 95; WhoE 81, 83, 85, 86, 89, 91, 93, 95, 97; WhoFrS 84; WhoMedH; WhoNob, 90, 95; WhoScEn 94, 96; WhoWor 82, 84, 87, 89, 91, 93, 95, 96, 97; WorAlBi; WorScD*

Benaderet, Bea
American. Actor
Played Kate Bradley on TV series "Petticoat Junction," 1963-68.
b. Apr 4, 1906 in New York, New York
d. Oct 13, 1968 in Los Angeles, California
Source: *LegTOT; NotNAT B; SaTiSS; WhoHol B; WhScrn 74, 77, 83*

Ben & Jerry
American. Manufacturers
Ice cream entrepreneurs known for laid-back corporate style and promotion of social responsibility in business; Ben & Jerry's Homemade, Inc. 1978—; Ben & Jerry's Foundation, 1985—.
Source: *BioIn 14, 17, 19, 20; ConAu X; News 91, 91-3; NewYTBS 94*

Benarde, Melvin Albert
American. Author
Professor, 1967-83; Associate Director, Environmental Studies Institute, Drexel University, Philadelphia, 1983-87; Director, Asbestos/Lead Center, and Professor, Temple University, 1987—; writes on environmental and community problems.
b. Jun 15, 1923 in New York, New York
Source: *AmMWSc 76P, 79, 82, 86, 89, 92, 95; WhoAm 84; WhoE 81; WrDr 86*

Benary-Isbert, Margot
American. Author
Writings include award-winning children's books, *The Ark,* 1953; *Blue Mystery,* 1957.
b. Dec 2, 1899 in Saarbrucken, Germany
Source: *AnCL; AuBYP 2; ConAu 4NR, 7NR, 89; ConLC 12; MorJA; SmATA 2, 21*

Benatar, Pat
[Patricia Andrzejewski; Mrs. Neil Geraldo]
American. Singer
Has two platinum albums: *In the Heat of the Night; Precious Time;* single hit "Love Is a Battlefield," 1985.
b. Jan 10, 1952 in New York, New York
Source: *CelR 90; ConMus 8; ConNews 86-1; IlEncRk; LegTOT; NewWmR; RolSEnR 83; WhoRock 81*

Benavente y Martinez, Jacinto
Spanish. Dramatist
Wrote over 170 plays, including *Bonds of Interest,* 1907; awarded Nobel Prize, 1922.
b. Aug 12, 1866 in Madrid, Spain
d. Jul 14, 1954 in Madrid, Spain
Source: *BioIn 1, 2, 3, 4, 5, 7, 8, 15, 17; CamGWoT; CasWL; CathA 1930; ClDMEL 47; CnMD; CurBio 53, 54; CyWA 58; DcCathB; DcSpL; Dis&D; EncWL; EncWT; EvEuW; FacFETw; HispWr; IntDcT 2; LngCTC; McGEWB; McGEWD 72; ModWD; NewC; NobelP; NotNAT B; OxCEng 67, 85, 95; OxCSpan; OxCThe 83; PenC EUR; REn; TwCA, SUP; WhDW; WhoNob, 90, 95*

Ben Barka, Mehdi
Moroccan. Political Leader
Exiled left-wing revolutionary, murdered in France by Moroccan agents.
b. 1920
d. 1965, France
Source: *BioIn 5, 7, 10; DcPol*

Ben Bella, Ahmed
Algerian. Revolutionary, Political Leader
First premier, pres. of Algeria, 1962-65, and of independent Algeria after ouster of French.
b. Dec 25, 1918 in Marnia, Algeria
Source: *BioIn 7, 8, 11, 17, 18; ColdWar 2; CurBio 63; McGEWB; PolLCME; WhoArab 81*

Bench, Johnny Lee
"Hands"
American. Baseball Player
Catcher, infielder, Cincinnati, 1967-83; led NL in home runs twice, RBIs three times; MVP, NL, 1970, World Series, 1976; Hall of Fame, 1989.
b. Dec 7, 1947 in Oklahoma City, Oklahoma
Source: *BioNews 74; BkPepl; CurBio 71; NewYTBE 70; WhoAm 82, 97; WhoProB 73*

Benchley, Nathaniel Goddard
American. Author
Son of Robert Benchley; writer of humor, historical novels: *Lassiter's Folly,* 1971.
b. Nov 13, 1915 in Newton, Massachusetts
d. Dec 14, 1981 in Boston, Massachusetts
Source: *AmAu&B; Au&Wr 71; AuBYP 2S; BiE&WWA; BlueB 76; ConAu 1R, 2NR; CurBio 53, 82; FourBJA; IntAu&W 82; NewYTBS 81; NotNAT; SmATA 3, 13; WhAm 8; WhoAm 74, 76, 78, 80; WhoWor 74; WorAl; WorAu 1950; WrDr 76*

Benchley, Peter Bradford
American. Author, Journalist
Wrote novels *Jaws,* 1974; *The Deep,* 1976; *The Island,* 1979, all of which were filmed.
b. May 8, 1940 in New York, New York
Source: *AuNews 2; BkPepl; ConAu 12NR, 17R; ConLC 4, 8; ConTFT 5; CurBio 76; IntAu&W 76, 77; NewYTBS 79; SmATA 13; WhoAm 86; WrDr 86*

Benchley, Robert Charles
[Guy Fawkes]
American. Author
Wrote *Chips Off the Old Benchley,* 1949; won Oscar, 1935, for *How to Sleep.*
b. Sep 15, 1889 in Worcester, Massachusetts
d. Nov 21, 1945 in New York, New York
Source: *AmAu&B; ConAmA; CurBio 41, 46; DcAmB S3; DcLEL; DcNAA; EvLB; FilmgC; LngCTC; ModAL; MovMk; ObitOF 79; OxCAmL 65; OxCThe 67; PenC AM; PlP&P; RAdv 1; REn; REnAL; TwCA, SUP; TwCLC 1; TwCWr; WebAB 74; WhAm 2; WhoHol B; WhScrn 74; WorEFlm*

Bender, Ariel
[Mott the Hoople; Luther James Grosvenor]
English. Musician
Guitarist with hard rock group, 1973-74.
b. Dec 23, 1949 in Evesham, England

Bender, Chief
[Charles Albert Bender]
American. Baseball Player
Pitcher, 1903-25; had 210 career wins; Hall of Fame, 1953.
b. May 5, 1884 in Brainerd, Minnesota
d. May 22, 1954 in Philadelphia, Pennsylvania
Source: *LegTOT; WhoProB 73; WhoSpor*

Bender, Hans
German. Psychologist
Wrote *Our Sixth Sense,* 1971; *Hidden Reality,* 1974.
b. Feb 5, 1907 in Freiburg, Germany
Source: *BiDPara; EncO&P 1, 2, 2S1, 3; EncPaPR 91; WhoWor 78, 80, 82*

Bendick, Jeanne
American. Author, Illustrator
Prolific writer, illustrator of children's science books: *Living Things,* 1969.
b. Feb 25, 1919 in New York, New York
Source: *AuBYP 2, 3; BioIn 5, 6, 8, 9, 15, 17, 19; BkP; ChlLR 5; ConAu 2NR, 5R, 48NR; IlsCB 1946, 1957; MajAI; MorJA; SmATA 2, 4AS, 68; WhoAmW 58*

Bendix, Vincent
American. Inventor, Manufacturer
Invented Bendix drive, making self-starting cars practical.
b. Aug 12, 1882 in Moline, Illinois
d. Mar 27, 1945 in New York, New York
Source: *CurBio 45; DcAmB S3; InSci; WebAB 74, 79; WhAm 2; WorAl*

Bendix, William
American. Actor
Played father on radio, TV series, "Life of Riley."
b. Jan 14, 1906 in New York, New York
d. Dec 14, 1964 in Los Angeles, California
Source: *BiE&WWA; BioIn 1, 2, 4, 7, 10, 11; CmMov; CurBio 48, 65; EncAB-A 36; EncAFC; FilmEn; FilmgC; ForYSC; GangFlm; HalFC 80, 84, 88; HolP 40; IntDcF 1-3, 2-3; LegTOT; MotPP; MovMk; NotNAT B; OxCFilm; QDrFCA 92; RadStar; SaTiSS; WhAm 4; WhoCom; WhoHol B; WhScrn 74, 77, 83; WorAl; WorEFlm*

Benedict, Saint
[Benedict of Nursia]
Italian. Religious Figure
Patriarch of Western monks who founded Benedictine monasticism.
b. 480? in Norcia, Italy
d. Mar 21, 547 in Monte Cassino, Italy
Source: *BioIn 1, 2, 3, 4, 5, 6, 7, 8, 9, 10, 12, 13; DcBiPP; DcCathB; DcEuL; EncEarC; Grk&L; HisWorL; LegTOT; LinLib S; LuthC 75; McGDA; McGEWB; NewGrDM 80; OxCMus; RAdv 14; WhDW; WorAl; WorAlBi*

Benedict, Clint(on Stephen)
"Benny"
Canadian. Hockey Player
Goalie, Ottawa, 1917-24, Montreal, 1924-30; led NHL in shutouts seven times; Hall of Fame, 1965.
b. 1894 in Ottawa, Ontario, Canada
d. Nov 13, 1976
Source: *HocEn; WhoHcky 73*

Benedict, Dirk
[Dirk Niewoehner]
American. Actor
Stared in TV series "Battlestar Galactica," 1978-79; "The A-Team," 1983-86.
b. Mar 1, 1945 in Helena, Montana
Source: *BioIn 13, 19; ConTFT 1; HalFC 84, 88; IntMPA 86, 92, 94, 96; VarWW 85; WhoAm 80, 82, 84, 86; WhoEnt 92; WhoHol 92, A*

Benedict, Ruth (Fulton)
American. Anthropologist
Expert on American Indian tribes; wrote classic *Patterns of Culture,* 1934; *Race, Science and Politics,* 1940.
b. Jun 5, 1887 in New York, New York
d. Sep 17, 1948 in New York, New York
Source: *AmAu&B; AmDec 1930; AmSocL; AmWomSc; AmWomWr; ArtclWW 2; BiDAmEd; BiDPsy; BioIn 1, 2, 4, 5, 6, 10, 12, 13, 14, 15, 16, 19, 20, 21; CamDcSc; ContDcW 89; CurBio 41, 48; DcAmB S4; DcNAA; DcSoc; DeafPAS; EncAAH; EncAB-H 1974, 1996; EncWHA; FacFETw; FemiCLE; GayLesB; GoodHs; GrLiveH; HanAmWH; InSci; IntDcAn; IntDcWB; InWom, SUP; LibW; LinLib L; LuthC 75; McGEWB; NamesHP; NatCAB 36;*

NotAW; OxCAmH; PeoHis; RAdv 14, 13-3; REnAL; ThTwC 87; TwCA SUP; TwCLC 60; WebAB 74, 79; WhAm 2; WhDW; WomFir; WorAl; WorAlBi

Benedictos I
[Vassilios Papadopoulos]
Turkish. Religious Leader
Greek Orthodox leader, 1957-80; had historical meeting with Pope Paul VI, 1964.
b. 1892 in Brusa, Ottoman Empire
d. Dec 10, 1980 in Jerusalem, Israel
Source: *AnObit 1980; IntWW 80, 81; MidE 79; WhoWor 74*

Benedictus, David
English. Author
Satiric novels include *Rabbi's Wife,* 1976.
b. Sep 16, 1938 in London, England
Source: *Au&Wr 71; BioIn 6, 13, 16; ConAu 24NR, 73; ConNov 72, 76, 82, 86, 91; DcLB 14; DcLEL 1940; IntAu&W 91; NewC; Novels; WhoThe 72, 77, 81; WrDr 76, 80, 82, 84, 86, 88, 90, 92*

Benedict XV, Pope
[Giacomo della Chiesa]
"The Pope of the Missions"
Italian. Religious Leader
In 1914-22 pontificate, maintained neutrality, urged peace; spurred missionary activity.
b. Nov 21, 1854 in Genoa, Italy
d. Jan 22, 1922 in Rome, Italy
Source: *McGEWB; NewCol 75; WebBD 83*

Benediktsson, Bjarni
Icelandic. Political Leader
b. 1908
d. Jul 10, 1970 in Thingvalla, Iceland
Source: *BioIn 9*

Benediktsson, Einar
Icelandic. Poet
Icelandic nationalist; widely venerated symbolist poetry revealed his interest in mysticism, nature.
b. Oct 31, 1864 in Ellidhavatn, Iceland
d. Jan 14, 1940 in Herdisarvik, Iceland
Source: *BioIn 1, 2; CasWL; ClDMEL 47, 80; DcScanL; EncWL; IntWW 91; REn; Who 92*

Benefield, Barry
[John Barry Benefield]
American. Author
Wrote novel *Valiant Is the Word of Carrie;* made into movie, 1935.
b. 1887 in Jefferson, Texas
d. 1956?
Source: *AmAu&B; AmNov; ConAmL; DcLEL; OxCAmL 83; REnAL; TexWr; TwCA, SUP*

Beneke, Tex
[Gordon Beneke]
American. Singer, Bandleader
Popular saxophonist, vocalist with Glenn Miller; led orchestra after Miller's death, 1946-50.
b. Feb 12, 1914 in Fort Worth, Texas
Source: *Baker 84, 92; BiDJaz; BioIn 2; CmpEPM; EncJzS; LegTOT; NewGrDJ 88, 94; OxCPMus; PenEncP*

Ben-Elissar, Eliahu
Israeli. Diplomat
First Israeli ambassador to Arab country, Egypt, 1980.
b. Aug 2, 1932 in Radom, Poland
Source: *BioIn 11; NewYTBS 77, 80*

Benelli, Giovanni, Cardinal
"The Kissinger"
Italian. Religious Leader
Archbishop of Florence, 1977-82; advisor to Pope Paul VI; his reputed unsuccessful heir apparent.
b. May 21, 1921 in Pistoia, Italy
d. Oct 26, 1982 in Florence, Italy
Source: *AnObit 1982; BioIn 8, 11, 13; CurBio 77, 83N; IntWW 78, 79, 80, 81, 82; NewYTBE 70; NewYTBS 82; WhoWor 78, 80, 82*

Benes, Eduard
Czech. Statesman
Pres. of Czechoslovakia, 1935-38, 1942-48; resigned after communist coup d'etat.
b. May 28, 1884 in Kozlany, Bohemia
d. Sep 3, 1948 in Usti, Czechoslovakia
Source: *BiDInt; CurBio 42, 48; DcAmSR; EncTR; FacFETw; HisEWW; LegTOT; McGEWB; REn; WhAm 2; WhDW; WorAl; WorAlBi*

Benet, Brenda
[Brenda Benet Nelson]
American. Actor
Star of TV soap opera "Days of Our Lives"; married to Bill Bixby; committed suicide.
b. Aug 14, 1945 in Los Angeles, California
d. Apr 7, 1982 in Los Angeles, California
Source: *BioIn 13; NewYTBS 82; WhoHol A*

Benet, Stephen Vincent
American. Author, Poet
Won Pulitzers for poetry volumes *John Browns Body,* 1928; *Western Star,* 1943.
b. Jul 22, 1898 in Bethlehem, Pennsylvania
d. Mar 13, 1943 in New York, New York
Source: *Alli SUP, 3; EvLB; FacFETw; GrWrEL P; HalFC 84, 88; LegTOT; LinLib L, S; LngCTC; McGEWB; ModAL; NatCAB 33; NewEScF; NewGrDA 86; NotNAT B; Novels; OxCAmH; OxCAmL 65, 83; OxCEng 67, 85, 95; OxCTwCP; PenC AM; RAdv 1, 14, 13-1; REn; REnAL; RfGAmL 87, 94; RfGShF; RGTwCWr; ScF&FL 1; ShSCr 10; SixAP; Str&VC; SupFW; TwCA, SUP; TwCLC 7; TwCRHW 90; TwCSFW 81; TwCWr; WebAB 74, 79; WebE&AL; WhAm 2; WhDW; WhLit; WhNAA; WhoHr&F; WhoTwCL; WorAl; WorAlBi; YABC 1*

Benet, William Rose
American. Author, Journalist
Won Pulitzer Prize, 1941, for autobiographical verse *The Dust Which Is God;* brother of Stephen V.
b. Feb 2, 1886 in Fort Hamilton, New York
d. May 4, 1950 in New York, New York
Source: *AmAu&B; ApCAB X; Benet 87, 96; BenetAL 91; BioIn 1, 2, 3, 4, 10, 12, 15; CamGLE; CamHAL; ChhPo, S1, S2, S3; CnDAL; ConAmA; ConAmL; ConAu 118, 152; DcAmB S4; DcLB 45; DcLEL; FacFETw; GrWrEL P; LegTOT; LinLib L; LngCTC; NatCAB 37; OxCAmL 65, 83, 95; OxCEng 67; OxCTwCP; PenC AM; REn; REnAL; RfGAmL 87, 94; TwCA, SUP; TwCLC 28; WebAB 74, 79; WhAm 3; WhE&EA; WhLit; WhNAA; WorAl; WorAlBi*

Benetton, Luciano
Italian. Designer, Businessman
Founder, Benetton clothing stores, with outlets worldwide, 1965—.
b. May 13, 1935 in Treviso, Italy
Source: *ConNews 88-1; Who 94*

Ben-Gal, Avigdor
Israeli. Army Officer
Led Israeli troops into Lebanon, 1978.
b. 1936
Source: *BioIn 11*

Ben-Gurion, David
[David Gruen]
Israeli. Political Leader
Emigrated to Palestine, 1906; Israel's first prime minister, 1948-53, 1955-63.
b. Oct 16, 1886 in Plonsk, Poland
d. Dec 1, 1973 in Tel Aviv, Israel
Source: *Au&Wr 71; BioIn 1, 2, 3, 4, 5, 6, 7, 8, 9, 10, 11, 12, 13, 14, 15, 16, 17, 18, 20; ColdWar 2; ConAu 45, 101; CurBio 47, 57, 74, 74N; DcMidEa; DcTwHis; EncRev; FacFETw; HarEnMi; HisDBrE; HisEAAC; HisWorL; JeHun; LegTOT; LinLib S; McGEWB; NewCol 75; NewYTBE 71, 73; ObitT 1971; PolBiDi; PolLCME; WhAm 6; WhDW; Who 74; WhoWor 74; WhoWorJ 72; WhWW-II; WorAl; WorAlBi*

Bening, Annette
American. Actor
Leading roles in *Regarding Henry,* 1991; *Bugsy,* 1991; wife of Warren Beatty.
b. May 5, 1958 in Topeka, Kansas
Source: *ConTFT 9; GangFlm; IntMPA 92, 94, 96; IntWW 93; LegTOT; News 92, 91-2, 92-1; WhoAm 94, 95, 96, 97; WhoAmW 95, 97; WhoHol 92*

Benirschke, Rolf Joachim
American. Football Player
Placekicker, San Diego, 1977-86; led NFL in extra points made, 1981, 1982.
b. Feb 7, 1955 in Boston, Massachusetts
Source: *BioIn 12, 13; FootReg 87; NewYTBS 82*

Ben-Israel, Ben Ami
[Ben Carter]
American. Religious Leader
Spiritual leader, World African Hebrew Institute Community, 1967—.
b. 1940 in Chicago, Illinois
Source: *BioIn 8; ConBlB 11*

Benjamin, Adam, Jr.
American. Politician
Congressman from IN, 1977-82.
b. Aug 6, 1935 in Gary, Indiana
d. Sep 7, 1982 in Washington, District of Columbia
Source: *AlmAP 78; WhoMW 78, 80, 82*

Benjamin, Arthur
Australian. Composer, Pianist
Wrote operas *Tale of Two Cities,* 1950; *Manana,* 1956; songs of Caribbean influence.
b. Sep 18, 1893 in Sydney, Australia
d. Apr 10, 1960 in London, England
Source: *Baker 78, 84, 92; BioIn 2, 4, 5, 6, 8; CmOp; CompSN, SUP; DcArts; DcCom&M 79; FilmgC; HalFC 80, 84, 88; MusMk; NewAmDM; NewEOp 71; NewGrDM 80; NewGrDO; NewOxM; PenDiMP A*

Benjamin, Asher
American. Architect, Author
Wrote, illustrated architectural guides, promoting good designs, late colonial styles: *American Builder's Companion,* 1806.
b. Jun 15, 1773 in Greenfield, Massachusetts
d. Jul 26, 1845 in Springfield, Massachusetts
Source: *BioIn 1, 2, 3, 12; BriEAA; DcAmB; DcNAA; MacEA; McGDA; McGEWB; OxCAmH; WebAB 74, 79; WhAm HS; WhoArch*

Benjamin, Curtis G
American. Publisher
Pres., chm., McGraw-Hill, 1928-66; excellence in publishing award named for him.
b. Jul 13, 1901 in Providence, Kentucky
d. Nov 5, 1983 in Norwalk, Connecticut
Source: *AmAu&B; BioIn 13, 14; BlueB 76; ConAu 111, 122; IntWW 74, 75, 76, 77, 78, 79, 80, 81, 82, 83; IntYB 78, 79, 80, 81, 82; NewYTBS 83; St&PR 75; WhoAm 74*

Benjamin, Judah Philip
American. Lawyer, Statesman
Confederate secretary of war, 1861-62; of state, 1862-65; unpopular for plan to arm slaves for army duty.
b. Aug 11, 1811 in Saint Thomas, Danish West Indies
d. May 8, 1884 in Paris, France
Source: *Alli SUP; AmBi; AmPolLe; ApCAB; BiAUS; BiD&SB; BiDConf; BiDrAC; BiDrUSC 89; BiDSA; BioIn 1, 2, 3, 4, 5, 6, 8, 9, 10, 12, 14, 15, 16, 17, 20; CelCen; CivWDc; CyAG; DcAmAu; DcAmB; DcAmDH 80, 89; DcNAA; DcNaB; EncSoH; HarEnUS; McGEWB; NatCAB 4; OxCAmH; OxCLaw; REnAW; TwCBDA; WebAB 74, 79; WhAm HS; WhAmP; WhCiWar*

Benjamin, Richard
American. Actor, Director
Husband of Paula Prentiss; starred in film *Goodbye Columbus,* 1969; directed *Little Nikita,* 1987.
b. May 22, 1938 in New York, New York
Source: *BkPepl; CelR, 90; ConTFT 1, 5; EncAFC; FilmEn; FilmgC; HalFC 80, 84, 88; IntMPA 81, 82; LegTOT; MiSFD 9; MovMk; NewYTBE 71; WhoAm 76, 78, 80, 82, 84, 86, 88, 90, 92, 95, 96, 97; WhoEnt 92; WhoHol 92, A; WorAl; WorAlBi*

Benjamin of Tudela
Spanish. Traveler, Author
Jewish traveler said to be first European to reach China.
b. 1130 in Tudela, Spain
d. 1173
Source: *CasWL; DcBiPP; Dis&D; EvEuW; NewC; NewCol 75; OxCEng 67; PenC EUR*

Ben Jelloun, Tahar
Moroccan. Poet, Author
Works focus on human endeavor for freedom; *Les Amandiers Sont Morts De Leurs Blessures,* 1976 won Prix de l'Amitie Franco-Arabe.
b. Dec 21, 1944 in Fez, Morocco
Source: *Benet 96; BioIn 15, 17, 21; ConAu 135; ConWorW 93; EncWL 3; IntAu&W 93; IntWW 89, 91, 93; NewYTBS 87; RAdv 14; ScF&FL 92; WhoFr 79; WorAu 1985*

Benko, Paul Charles
French. Chess Player
Member of US Olympic chess team; US Open chess champion.
b. Jul 15, 1928 in Amiens, France
Source: *WhoAm 74, 76, 78, 80, 82, 84*

Benn, Anthony
English. Business Executive
Director, chm., Price and Pierce Ltd., 1947-72.
b. Oct 7, 1912
Source: *Who 74, 82, 83, 85, 88, 90, 92, 94*

Benn, Ernest John Pickstone, Sir
English. Publisher
Managed family firm, Ernest Benn Ltd; published *Blue Guides* travel books; *Sixpenny Library* of paperback educational books.
b. Jun 25, 1875 in Hackney, England
d. Jan 17, 1954 in Oxted, England
Source: *BioIn 2, 3, 5, 14, 15; DcNaB 1951; GrBr; WhE&EA; WhoLA*

Benn, Tony
[Anthony Wedgwood Benn]
English. Statesman
Member of Parliament in Labour Party since 1950.
b. Apr 3, 1925 in London, England
Source: *BioIn 13, 14, 15, 16, 17, 18, 21; BlueB 76; CurBio 65, 82; DcPol; DcTwHis; EncWB; FacFETw; IntAu&W 89, 91, 93; IntWW 74, 75, 76, 77, 78, 79, 80, 81, 82, 83, 89, 91, 93; IntYB 78, 79, 80, 81, 82; RadHan; Who 74, 83, 85, 88, 90, 92, 94; WhoAtom 77; WhoWor 74, 76, 78; WrDr 80, 82, 84, 86, 88, 90, 92, 94, 96*

Bennett, Alan
English. Dramatist
Wrote plays *Beyond the Fringe,* 1960; *The Madness of George III,* 1991.
b. May 9, 1934 in Leeds, England
Source: *Au&Wr 71; BiDFilm 94; BiE&WWA; BioIn 10, 16, 17, 18, 19, 20, 21; BlueB 76; CamGLE; CamGWoT; CnThe; ConAu 35NR, 55NR, 103; ConBrDr; ConDr 73, 77, 82, 88, 93; ConLC 45, 77; ConTFT 8, 15; DcArts; DcLEL 1940; Ent; FacFETw; IntAu&W 76, 77, 89, 91, 93; IntDcT 2; IntMPA 92, 94, 96; IntWW 81, 82, 83, 89, 91, 93; MajTwCW; NewYTBS 90; NotNAT; OxCEng 85, 95; OxCThe 83; RGTwCWr; Who 74, 82, 83, 85, 88, 90, 92, 94; WhoThe 72, 77, 81; WhoWor 95, 96, 97; WorAu 1985; WrDr 76, 80, 82, 84, 86, 88, 90, 92, 94, 96*

Bennett, Arnold
[Enoch Arnold Bennett]
English. Author
Known for realistic novels: *Old Wives Tales,* 1908; *Five Towns* series.
b. May 27, 1867 in Staffordshire, England
d. Mar 27, 1931 in London, England
Source: *AtlBL, 3; EncWT; EvLB; FacFETw; FilmgC; GrBr; GrWrEL N; HalFC 80, 84, 88; LegTOT; LinLib L, S; LngCEL; LngCTC; MagSWL; MakMC; McGEWB; McGEWD 72, 84; ModBrL, S1, S2; ModWD; NewC; NewCBEL; NewEOp 71; NotNAT B; OxCEng 67, 85; OxCThe 67, 83; PenC ENG; PenEncH; RAdv 1, 14, 13-1; REn; RfGEnL 91; ScF&FL 1; TwCA, SUP; TwCLC 5, 20; TwCWr; WebE&AL; WhDW; WhLit; WhoTwCL; WhThe; WorAl; WorAlBi*

Bennett, Constance Campbell
American. Actor
Starred in sophisticated comedies: *Topper,* 1937; *Topper Takes a Trip,* 1939; daughter of Richard Bennett.
b. Oct 22, 1905 in New York, New York
d. Jul 4, 1965 in Fort Dix, New Jersey

Source: *BiDFilm; BiE&WWA; Film 2; FilmgC; MotPP; ObitOF 79; ObitT 1961; OxCFilm; ThFT; TwYS; WhAm 4; WhoHol B; WhScrn 74, 77; WomWMM; WorAl*

Bennett, Floyd
American. Aviator
National hero; with Richard Byrd, flew three-engine monoplane over N Pole, 1926.
b. Oct 25, 1890 in Warrensburg, New York
d. Apr 25, 1928 in Quebec, Canada
Source: *AmBi; DcAmB; FacFETw; InSci; MedHR, 94; NatCAB 29; OxCAmH; WebAB 74, 79; WebAMB; WhoWest 84*

Bennett, Harry Herbert
American. Auto Executive
Henry Ford's henchman; ran Ford Motor Co., 1930s; fired by Henry II, 1945.
b. Jan 17, 1892 in Ann Arbor, Michigan
d. Jan 4, 1979 in California
Source: *BioIn 2, 6; EncABHB 5*

Bennett, Harve
American. Producer
Won Emmy for "A Woman Called Golda," 1982.
b. Aug 17, 1930 in Chicago, Illinois
Source: *BioIn 8, 16; ConTFT 8; IntMPA 75, 76, 77, 78, 79, 80, 81, 82, 84, 86, 88, 92, 94, 96; NewYTET; VarWW 85; WhoAm 78, 80, 82, 84, 86, 88, 90, 92, 94, 95, 96, 97; WhoEnt 92; WhoWest 76*

Bennett, Hugh Hammond
American. Scientist
First chief of soil conservation service, US Dept. of Agriculture, 1935-52.
b. Apr 15, 1881 in Wadesboro, North Carolina
d. Jul 7, 1960 in Burlington, North Carolina
Source: *BioIn 1, 2, 3, 5, 6, 7, 8, 13, 14, 17; CurBio 46, 60; DcAmB S6; DcNCBi 1; EncAAH; InSci; NatLAC; WhAm 4; WhNAA*

Bennett, James Gordon
American. Newspaper Publisher
Founded *NY Herald* with $500, 1835.
b. Sep 1, 1795 in Newmill, Scotland
d. Jun 1, 1872 in New York, New York
Source: *AmAu&B; AmBi; ApCAB; Benet 87, 96; BenetAL 91; BiDAmJo; BioIn 1, 2, 3, 4, 9, 10, 13, 14, 15, 16; DcAmB; DcLB 43; EncAB-H 1974, 1996; EncAJ; HarEnUS; InSci; JrnUS; LinLib L, S; McGEWB; NatCAB 7; OxCAmH; OxCAmL 65; OxCAmT 84; RComAH; REn; REnAL; TwCBDA; WebAB 74, 79; WhAm HS; WhAmP; WhCiWar*

Bennett, James Gordon, Jr.
American. Author, Publisher
Financed Stanley's expedition to find Livingstone, 1869-72.
b. May 10, 1841 in New York, New York
d. May 14, 1918 in Bealieu, France
Source: *AmAu&B; AmBi; ApCAB; BiDAmJo; BiDAmSp OS; BioIn 2, 3, 4, 6, 9, 10, 11, 13, 16; DcAmB; DcLB 23; EncAB-H 1974, 1996; EncAJ; GayN; InSci; JrnUS; McGEWB; NatCAB 7; OxCAmH; PeoHis; RComAH; TwCBDA; WebAB 74, 79; WhAm 1; WorAlBi*

Bennett, Joan
[Mrs. Walter Wanger]
American. Actor
Her 50-year career took her from innocent blonde roles to sultry temptress parts on TV, stage, screen; appeared in 75 films including *Little Women*, 1933; sister of Constance.
b. Feb 27, 1910 in Palisades, New Jersey
d. Dec 7, 1990 in White Plains, New York
Source: *AnObit 1990; BiDFilm, 81, 94; BiE&WWA; BioIn 1, 8, 9, 10, 11, 17, 18; BlueB 76; CelR; CmMov; ConTFT 4, 9; EncAFC; FacFETw; FilmEn; FilmgC; ForYSC; HalFC 80, 84, 88; IntDcF 1-3, 2-3; IntMPA 75, 76, 77, 78, 79, 80, 81, 82, 84, 86, 88; InWom, SUP; ItaFilm; LegTOT; MotPP; MovMk; News 91, 91-2; NewYTBS 90; NotNAT A; OxCFilm; ThFT; WhAm 10; Who 74, 82, 83, 85, 88, 90; WhoAm 74, 76, 78, 80, 82, 84, 86, 88, 90; WhoAmW 58, 70, 74, 83, 85; WhoE 74; WhoHol A; WhoThe 72, 77, 81; WhoWor 78, 80, 82, 84, 87; WorAl; WorAlBi; WorEFlm*

Bennett, John
American. Author, Illustrator
Wrote children's books, *Master Skylark*, 1877; *Barnaby Lee*, 1902.
b. May 17, 1865 in Chillicothe, Ohio
d. Dec 28, 1956 in Charleston, South Carolina
Source: *AmAu&B; BenetAL 91; BiDLA; BiDSA; BioIn 1, 2, 4, 5, 6, 11, 14, 15, 19; BlkAWP; CarSB; ChhPo, S1; ConICB; DcAmAu; DcLB 42; IlsCB 1744; JBA 34, 51; MnBBF; NatCAB 43; OhA&B; OxCAmL 65, 83, 95; REnAL; ScF&FL 1; WhAm 3; WhAmArt 85; YABC 1*

Bennett, John C(oleman)
American. Clergy
Wrote *Christian Ethics and Social Policy*, 1946.
b. Jul 22, 1902
d. Apr 27, 1995 in Claremont, California
Source: *AmAu&B; AmDec 1960; BioIn 4, 5, 6, 8, 9, 11; CurBio 95N; DrAS 74P, 78P, 82P; IntWW 74, 75, 76, 77, 78, 79, 80, 81, 82, 83, 89; McGEWB; PolProf J; RelLAm 91; WhE&EA; WhoAm 74, 76, 78, 80; WhoRel 75, 77; WhoWor 74*

Bennett, Lerone, Jr.
American. Editor
Senior editor, *Ebony* magazine, 1958-87; executive editor, 1987—; wrote *The Challenge of Blackness*, 1972.
b. Oct 17, 1928 in Clarksdale, Mississippi
Source: *AfrAmBi 2; BioIn 9, 16, 19; BlkAull, 92; BlkAWP; BlksCm; BlkWr 1, 2; CivR 74; ConAu 2NR, 25NR, 45; ConBlB 5; DcTwCCu 5; Ebony 1; EncTwCJ; InB&W 80, 85; LinLib L; LiveMA; LivgBAA; NegAl 76, 83, 89; SchCGBL; SelBAAf; SelBAAu; SouWr; WhoAfA 96; WhoAm 74, 76, 78, 80, 82, 84, 86, 88, 90, 92, 94, 95, 96, 97; WhoBlA 75, 77, 80, 85, 88, 90, 92, 94; WhoMW 74, 76, 78; WhoUSWr 88; WhoWrEP 89, 92, 95*

Bennett, Michael
[Michael Bennett DiFiglia]
American. Choreographer
Won two Tonys, Pulitzer for conceiving, directing, choreographing *A Chorus Line*, 1975; filmed, 1986.
b. Apr 8, 1943 in Buffalo, New York
d. Jul 2, 1987 in Tucson, Arizona
Source: *AnObit 1987; BiDD; BioIn 8, 9, 10, 11, 12, 13; CamGWoT; CnOxB; ConAu 101, 122; ConDr 77D; ConNews 88-1; ConTFT 5; CurBio 81, 87, 87N; DcTwCCu 1; EncMT; FacFETw; GayLesB; GrStDi; NewYTBS 87; NotNAT; OxCAmT 84; TheaDir; WhoAm 76, 78, 80, 82, 84, 86; WhoE 85, 86; WhoThe 77; WhoWor 89; WrDr 80, 82, 84, 86*

Bennett, Ramona
American. Native American Leader
Chairperson, Puyallup tribe, 1971-78; one of the founders of the Survival of American Indians Association, 1964.
b. Apr 28, 1938 in Seattle, Washington
Source: *BioIn 21; NotNaAm*

Bennett, Richard
American. Actor
Leading matinee idol who made stage debut, 1891; father of Joan, Constance.
b. May 21, 1873 in Deacon's Mills, Indiana
d. Oct 22, 1944 in Los Angeles, California
Source: *CamGWoT; CurBio 44; DcAmB S3; EncWT; FamA&A; Film 1, 2; FilmEn; FilmgC; ForYSC; HalFC 80, 84, 88; NatCAB 33; NotNAT B; ObitOF 79; OxCAmT 84; TwYS; Vers A; WhAm 2; WhoHol B; WhoStg 1908; WhScrn 74, 77, 83; WhThe*

Bennett, Richard Bedford
Canadian. Political Leader
Conservative leader, 1927-38; prime minister of Canada, 1930-35.
b. Jul 3, 1870 in Hopewell, New Brunswick, Canada
d. Jun 26, 1947 in Dorking, England
Source: *BioIn 12, 19; DcNaB 1941; DcTwHis; FacFETw; LinLib S; MacDCB 78; McGEWB; OxCCan*

Bennett, Richard Rodney
English. Composer, Musician
Catalogue of works include operas, symphonies, concertos, chamber, vocal, choral music, television and film scores.

b. Mar 29, 1936 in Broadstairs, England
Source: *Baker 78, 84, 92; BioIn 8, 11, 16, 17, 18; BlueB 76; BriBkM 80; CmOp; CompSN, SUP; ConCom 92; ConTFT 12; CpmDNM 75, 81, 82; CurBio 92; DcArts; DcCM; DcCom&M 79; FilmEn; FilmgC; HalFC 80, 84, 88; IntWW 74, 75, 76, 77, 78, 79, 80, 81, 82, 83, 89, 91, 93; IntWWM 77, 80, 90; McGEWB; MusMk; NewAmDM; NewEOp 71; NewGrDM 80; NewGrDO; NewOxM; OxCMus; OxCPMus; OxDcOp; PenDiMP A; Who 74, 82, 83, 85, 88, 90, 92, 94; WhoAm 78, 96, 97; WhoMus 72; WhoWor 74, 76, 78*

Bennett, Robert F.
American. Politician
Rep. senator, UT, 1993—.
b. Sep 18, 1933 in Salt Lake City, Utah
Source: *AlmAP 96; CngDr 93, 95; IntWW 91; WhoAm 90, 95, 96, 97; WhoAmP 91; WhoGov 77; WhoMW 92; WhoWest 96*

Bennett, Robert LaFollette
American. Lawyer
Commissioner, Bureau of Indian Affairs, 1966-69; founded American Indian Athletic Hall of Fame, 1969.
b. Nov 16, 1912 in Wisconsin
Source: *BioIn 7, 8, 9, 11, 21; NotNaAm*

Bennett, Robert Russell
American. Composer
Orchestrated over 300 Broadway musicals including *Show Boat; South Pacific;* won Oscar for *Oklahoma,* 1955.
b. Jun 15, 1894 in Kansas City, Missouri
d. Aug 18, 1981 in New York, New York
Source: *AmComp; AnObit 1981; ASCAP 66, 80; Baker 78, 84, 92; BiDAmM; BiE&WWA; BioIn 1, 2, 3, 6, 8, 9, 12, 17, 19; CelR; CompSN, SUP; ConAmC 76, 82; ConAu 105; CpmDNM 80, 81; CurBio 42, 62, 81, 81N; DcCM; IntWWM 77, 80; NewAmDM; NewGrDA 86; NewGrDM 80; NewGrDO; NewYTBS 81; NotNAT; OxCAmT 84; OxCMus; OxCPMus; WhAm 10; WhoAm 74, 76, 78, 80; WhoMus 72*

Bennett, Tony
[Joe Bari; Anthony Dominick Benedetto]
"The Singer's Singer"
American. Singer
Biggest hit "I Left My Heart in San Francisco," 1963; winner of three Grammy Awards and one Emmy Award.
b. Aug 3, 1926 in New York, New York
Source: *AllMusG; AmPS; Baker 84, 92; BiDAmM; BiDJaz; BioIn 2, 6, 7, 9, 10, 12; BkPepl; BlueB 76; CelR, 90; CmpEPM; ConMus 2, 16; ConTFT 6; CurBio 65, 95; EncJzS; HalFC 88; LegTOT; NewGrDA 86; NewGrDJ 88, 94; News 94; OxCPMus; PenEncP; RkOn 74; WhoAm 74, 76, 78, 80, 82, 84, 86, 88, 90, 92, 94, 95, 96, 97; WhoEnt 92; WhoHol 92, A; WhoWor 80, 82; WorAl; WorAlBi*

Bennett, W(illiam) A(ndrew) C(ecil)
Canadian. Political Leader
Social Credit premier of British Columbia, 1952-72.
b. Sep 6, 1900 in Hastings, New Brunswick, Canada
d. Feb 23, 1979 in Kelowna, British Columbia, Canada
Source: *BioIn 3, 7, 8, 9, 11, 12, 14; BlueB 76; CanWW 70, 79; CurBio 53, 79, 79N; IntWW 74, 75, 76, 77, 78; WhAm 7; WhoCan 73, 75, 77; WhoWest 74*

Bennett, Wallace F(oster)
American. Politician
Rep. senator, UT, 1951-74.
b. Nov 13, 1898
d. Dec 19, 1993 in Salt Lake City, Utah
Source: *BiDrAC; BiDrUSC 89; BioIn 1, 2, 5, 9, 10, 11, 12; BlueB 76; CngDr 74; CurBio 94N; IntWW 74, 75, 76, 77; PolProf E, J, K, NF; St&PR 75, 84, 87; WhoAm 74, 76, 78, 80; WhoAmP 73, 75, 77, 79, 81; WhoFI 85; WhoGov 72, 75; WhoWest 74, 76; WhoWor 74*

Bennett, Willard Harrison
American. Physicist
Discovered pinch effect, a process that may assist controlled nuclear fusion reactions.
b. Jun 13, 1903 in Findlay, Ohio
Source: *AmMWSc 76P, 79, 82, 86; WhAm 9; WhoAm 74, 76, 78, 80, 82, 84, 86, 88, 90; WhoSSW 73; WhoTech 89; WhoWor 74, 76, 78, 80, 82, 84, 87, 89*

Bennett, William
Canadian. Politician
Social Credit Party premier of British Columbia, 1975-86.
b. Apr 14, 1932 in Kelowna, British Columbia, Canada
Source: *BioIn 11; CanWW 83; FacFETw*

Bennett, William John
American. Government Official
Chm., National Endowment for the Humanities, 1981-85; secretary of Education, 1985-88; director, Office of National Drug Control Policy, 1989-90.
b. Jul 31, 1943 in New York, New York
Source: *AmPolLe; BiDrUSE 89; BioIn 12, 13, 14, 15, 16, 17, 19, 20, 21; ConAu 153; CopCroC; CurBio 85, 90; DrAS 74P, 78P, 82P; IntWW 89, 91, 93; NewYTBS 85; WhoAm 84, 86, 88, 90; WhoE 86, 89, 91; WhoWor 87, 89*

Bennett, William Sterndale, Sir
English. Composer, Pianist
Founded London's Bach Society, 1849; wrote a symphony and piano concertos.
b. Apr 13, 1816 in Sheffield, England
d. Feb 1, 1875 in London, England
Source: *Baker 78, 84, 92; BioIn 4, 16; BriBkM 80; CelCen; DcBiPP; DcNaB; LuthC 75; MusMk; NewCol 75; NewGrDM 80; OxCMus; PenDiMP A; VicBrit*

Benny, Jack
[Benjamin Kubelsky]
American. Comedian
Known for stinginess and violin playing; starred in "The Jack Benny Program," on TV, 1950-64.
b. Feb 14, 1894 in Waukegan, Illinois
d. Dec 26, 1974 in Los Angeles, California
Source: *BiDFilm, 81, 94; BioIn 1, 2, 3, 4, 5, 6, 7, 8, 9, 10, 11, 12, 14, 16, 17, 18; BioNews 74, 75; CelR; CmCal; CurBio 41, 63, 75, 75N; DcAmB S9; DcArts; EncAFC; EncVaud; EncWB; Ent; FacFETw; Film 2; FilmEn; FilmgC; ForYSC; Funs; HalFC 80, 84, 88; IntWW 74; JoeFr; LegTOT; MotPP; MovMk; NewYTBE 70; NewYTBS 74; NewYTET; ObitT 1971; OxCFilm; PlP&P; QDrFCA 92; RadStar; SaTiSS; WebAB 74, 79; WhAm 6; WhoAm 74; WhoCom; WhoHol B; WhoWor 74; WhoWorJ 72; WhScrn 77, 83; WorAl; WorAlBi; WorEFlm*

Benoit, Jehane
[Madame Benoit]
"Canada's First Lady of Cuisine"
Canadian. Chef
Star of radio, TV cooking programs, 1960s; wrote over 25 books on cooking.
b. 1904?
d. Nov 24, 1987

Ben-Shalom, Miriam
American. Social Reformer
Founded the Gay, Lesbian, & Bisexual Veterans Association, 1990.
b. May 2, 1948 in Waukesha, Wisconsin
Source: *GayLesB*

Benson, Arthur Christopher
English. Author
Wrote popular essays, wrote words to song "Land of Hope and Glory."
b. Apr 24, 1862 in Wellington, England
d. Jun 17, 1925
Source: *Alli SUP; BioIn 7, 13, 15, 17; Chambr 3; ChhPo, S1, S2, S3; DcEnA A; DcEuL; DcLEL; DcNaB 1922; EvLB; LngCTC; NewC; NewCBEL; PenC ENG; PenEncH; REn; ScF&FL 1; TwCA; WhLit*

Benson, Edward Frederic
English. Author
Prolific writer of satirical novels, historical biographies *Dodo,* 1893; *As We Were,* 1930.
b. Jul 24, 1867 in Berkshire, England
d. Feb 29, 1940
Source: *BbD; BiD&SB; BioIn 2, 4, 17, 18, 20; Chambr 3; CurBio 40; DcEnA A; DcLEL; DcNaB 1931; EvLB; LngCTC; MnBBF; ModBrL; NewC;*

NewCBEL; OxCEng 67; PenC ENG; PenEncH; TwCA; TwCWr

Benson, Ezra Taft
American. Government Official, Religious Leader
Secretary of Agriculture, 1953-61; succeeded Spencer Kimball as leader of Mormon Church, 1985-1994.
b. Sep 3, 1899 in Whitney, Idaho
d. May 30, 1994 in Salt Lake City, Utah
Source: *AmPolLe; BiDrUSE 71, 89; BioIn 3, 4, 5, 9, 10, 11, 12, 13, 19, 20; CurBio 53, 94N; EncAAH; IntWW 74, 75, 76, 77, 78, 79, 80, 81, 82, 83, 89, 91, 93; LinLib S; NewCol 75; News 94; NewYTBS 85, 94; PolProf E; RAdv 14; RelLAm 91; WhAm 11; WhoAm 74, 76, 78, 86, 88, 90, 94; WhoRel 75, 85, 92; WhoWest 87, 89, 92, 94; WhoWor 74*

Benson, Frank Robert, Sir
English. Actor, Manager
Founded touring Shakespearean repertory co., 1880s; only actor to be knighted in a theater, 1916.
b. Nov 4, 1858 in Alresford, England
d. Dec 31, 1939 in London, England
Source: *CnThe; DcNaB 1931; Film 1; NewC; NotNAT A, B; OxCThe 67, 83; PlP&P; WhThe*

Benson, Frank Weston
American. Artist
Impressionist painter, etcher, known for bird prints.
b. Mar 24, 1862 in Salem, Massachusetts
d. Nov 14, 1951 in Salem, Massachusetts
Source: *BioIn 2, 3, 4, 5, 7, 12, 13, 15, 20; BriEAA; ClaDrA; DcAmArt; DcAmB S5; DcBrAr 1; GrAmP; LinLib S; McGDA; NatCAB 13, 41; WhAm 3; WhoAmA 78*

Benson, George
American. Singer, Musician
Jazz guitarist; won three Grammys, including record of the year for "This Masquerade," 1977; album *Breezin'* is largest selling jazz album of all time.
b. Mar 22, 1943 in Pittsburgh, Pennsylvania
Source: *AllMusG; BiDAfM; BiDAmM; BiDJaz; BioIn 11, 12; BkPepl; CelR 90; ConMus 9; DrBlPA, 90; EncJzS; EncJzS; EncPR&S 89; EncRk 88; EncRkSt; HarEnR 86; IlEncBM 82; IlEncJ; InB&W 80, 85; LegTOT; NewGrDA 86; NewGrDJ 88, 94; OnThGG; PenEncP; RkOn 74, 78; RolSEnR 83; WhoAfA 96; WhoAm 78, 80, 82, 84, 86, 88, 90, 92, 94, 95, 96, 97; WhoBlA 85, 88, 90, 92, 94; WhoEnt 92; WhoRock 81*

Benson, Renaldo
[The Four Tops]
American. Musician, Singer
Original member of the Four Tops.
b. 1947 in Detroit, Michigan

Benson, Robby
[Robin Segal]
American. Actor, Director
Starred in movies *One on One,* 1977; *Ice Castles,* 1979; *The Chosen,* 1982.
b. Jan 21, 1956 in Dallas, Texas
Source: *BioIn 10, 11, 12; BkPepl; ConTFT 8; FilmEn; HalFC 80, 84, 88; IntMPA 86, 92, 94, 96; MiSFD 9; NewYTBS 80; WhoAm 94, 95, 96, 97; WhoHol A*

Benson, Sally
American. Author
Wrote best-sellers *Junior Miss,* 1941; *Meet Me In St. Louis,* 1942.
b. Sep 3, 1900 in Saint Louis, Missouri
d. Jul 19, 1972 in Woodland Hills, California
Source: *AmAu&B; AmWomD; AmWomWr; BenetAL 91; BiE&WWA; BioIn 1, 4, 9, 13, 14; CnDAL; ConAu 37R, P-1; ConLC 17; CurBio 41, 72, 72N; DcAmB S9; FemiCLE; FilmEn; HalFC 84, 88; LegTOT; NewYTBE 72; OxCAmL 65, 83, 95; PenNWW B; REn; REnAL; SmATA 1, 27N, 35; TwCA SUP; WhAm 5; WhoAmW 58A; WomWMM; WorAl*

Bentham, George
English. Botanist
Exhaustive taxonony, *Genera Plantarum,* 1862-83, catalogued over 97,000 plant species and is still a standard reference in British Commonwealth.
b. Sep 22, 1800 in Stoke, England
d. Sep 10, 1884 in London, England
Source: *Alli SUP; BiESc; BioIn 11; BritAu 19; CamDcSc; DcNaB; DcScB; InSci; LarDcSc; NewCBEL*

Bentham, Jeremy
English. Philosopher
Originated utilitarianism, equating happiness with pleasure; wrote *Fragment on Government,* 1776.
b. Feb 15, 1748 in London, England
d. Jun 6, 1832 in London, England
Source: *Alli; AmJust; AtlBL; BbD; Benet 87, 96; BiD&SB; BiDInt; BiDLA; BiDPsy; BioIn 1, 2, 3, 4, 6, 7, 8, 9, 10, 11, 12, 13, 14, 16, 17, 18, 20; BlkwCE; BlmGEL; BritAu 19; CamGEL; CamGLE; CasWL; CelCen; Chambr 2; CopCroC; CyAG; CyEd; DcBiPP; DcEnA; DcEnL; DcEuL; DcLB 107; DcLEL; DcNaB, C; EncEth; EncUnb; EvLB; GrEconB; HisDBrE; LegTOT; LinLib L, S; LngCEL; LuthC 75; McGEWB; NamesHP; NewC; NewCBEL; NinCLC 38; OxCEng 67, 85, 95; OxCLaw; OxCPhil; PenC ENG; RAdv 14, 13-3; REn; WebE&AL; WhDW; WhoEc 81, 86; WorAl; WorAlBi*

Bentinck, William Henry Cavendish, Lord
English. Statesman
First governor-general of India, 1833-35; reforms included abolishment of suttee, 1829.
b. Sep 14, 1774 in Bulstrode, England
d. Jun 17, 1839 in Paris, France
Source: *Alli; BiDLA; BioIn 2, 4, 10, 11, 12; CelCen; NewCol 75; WebBD 83*

Bentley, Alvin Morell
American. Diplomat, Politician
Rep. congressman, 1953-60; shot, wounded by Puerto Rican nationalists, 1954.
b. Aug 30, 1918 in Portland, Maine
d. Apr 10, 1969 in Owosso, Michigan
Source: *BiDrAC; BiDrUSC 89; BioIn 8, 10; NatCAB 54; WhAm 5; WhAmP*

Bentley, Charles Edwin
American. Dentist
Known as father of oral hygiene movement; began public school dental examinations.
b. Feb 21, 1859 in Cincinnati, Ohio
d. Oct 13, 1929 in Chicago, Illinois
Source: *InB&W 80; PeoHis; WhAm 1*

Bentley, Doug(las Wagner)
Canadian. Hockey Player
Left wing, Chicago, 1939-52, NY Rangers, 1953-54; won Art Ross Trophy, 1943; Hall of Fame, 1964.
b. Sep 3, 1916 in Delisle, Saskatchewan, Canada
d. Nov 24, 1972 in Saskatoon, Saskatchewan, Canada
Source: *BioIn 9, 10; HocEn; NewYTBE 72; ObitOF 79; WhoHcky 73*

Bentley, Edmund Clerihew
English. Author, Journalist
Wrote detective classic *Trent's Last Case,* 1912.
b. Jul 10, 1875 in London, England
d. Mar 30, 1956 in London, England
Source: *BioIn 4, 6, 14; ChhPo, S2; DcArts; DcLEL; DcNaB 1951; EncMys; EvLB; GrBr; LngCTC; NewC; NewCBEL; OxCEng 67, 85, 95; REn; TwCA, SUP; TwCWr; WhE&EA*

Bentley, Elizabeth Terrill
American. Spy
Spied for USSR in US during WW II.
b. 1908?
d. Dec 3, 1963 in New Haven, Connecticut
Source: *DcAmB S7; ObitOF 79; PolProf T*

Bentley, Eric
American. Critic, Educator
Comparative literature teacher; numerous drama critiques include *Brecht Commentaries,* 1981.
b. Sep 14, 1916 in Bolton, England
Source: *AmAu&B; ASCAP 66; Au&Wr 71; BenetAL 91; BiE&WWA; BioIn 17; CamGWoT; CelR; ConAu 5R, 6NR; ConDr 77, 82, 88; ConLC 24; ConLCrt 77, 82; DcLEL 1940; DrAS 78E, 82E; EncWT; IntAu&W 77, 86, 91; LinLib L; NewC; NotNAT; OxCAmT 84; REnAL; TwCA SUP; WhoAm 74, 76, 78, 80, 82, 84, 86, 88, 90, 92, 94, 95, 96; WhoThe 72, 81; WhoUSWr 88; WhoWor 74;*

WhoWrEP 89, 92, 95; WrDr 76, 80, 82, 84, 86, 88, 90, 92, 94, 96

Bentley, Gladys
American. Singer
Performed in Harlem clubs; recorded blues songs "How Long, How Long Blues" and "How Much Can I Stand?"
b. Aug 12, 1907 in Philadelphia, Pennsylvania
d. 1960
Source: *BioIn 20; BlkWAm; GayLesB*

Bentley, John
English. Actor
Played hero-detective roles, 1950s British films.
b. Dec 2, 1916 in Warwickshire, England
Source: *BiDLA; FilmEn; FilmgC; ForYSC; HalFC 80, 84, 88; IlWWBF; IntMPA 75, 76, 77, 78, 79, 80, 81, 82, 84, 86, 88; WhoHol 92, A*

Bentley, John
English. Musician
Bassist who joined Squeeze, 1979.
b. Apr 16, 1951 in London, England

Bentley, Max(well Herbert Lloyd)
"Dipsy Doodle Dandy of Delisle"
Canadian. Hockey Player
Center, 1940-54, with three NHL teams; won Art Ross Trophy, 1946, 1947, Hart Trophy, 1946; Hall of Fame, 1966.
b. Mar 1, 1920 in Delisle, Saskatchewan, Canada
d. Jan 19, 1984 in Saskatoon, Saskatchewan, Canada
Source: *BioIn 10, 13; HocEn; WhoHcky 73*

Bentley, Richard
English. Author, Clergy, Critic
Proved *Epistles of Phalaris* were spurious, 1669; first to use philology as test of authenticity.
b. Jan 27, 1662 in Oulton, England
d. Jul 14, 1742 in Cambridge, England
Source: *Alli; BiD&SB; BioIn 1, 3, 5, 6, 7, 8, 13, 15; BlkwCE; BlmGEL; BritAu; CamGEL; CamGLE; CasWL; DcBiPP; DcEnA; DcEnL; DcEuL; DcNaB, C; EvLB; LinLib L; LngCEL; LuthC 75; NewC; NewCBEL; OxCClL; OxCEng 67, 85, 95; PenC ENG; REn*

Bentley, Stephen
American. Cartoonist
"Herb & Jamaal" strip depicts adventures of 2 black men who run an ice cream business.
Source: *BioIn 17, 21; WhoSSW 91; WhoWest 92*

Bentley, Walter Owen
English. Auto Manufacturer
Built Bentley automobile; merged with Rolls-Royce, 1931.
b. Sep 16, 1888 in London, England
d. Aug 13, 1971 in Woking, England
Source: *BioIn 5, 6, 8, 9, 10; DcNaB MP; NewYTBE 71; ObitOF 79; ObitT 1971*

Benton, Barbie
[Barbara Klein]
American. Actor, Singer
Longtime girlfriend of Hugh Hefner; appeared in film *Deathstalker.*
b. Jan 28, 1950 in Sacramento, California
Source: *VarWW 85; WhoAmW 83*

Benton, Brook
[Benjamin Franklin Peay]
American. Singer
One of few black singers to write own material; best known hit "Boll Weevil Song," 1961.
b. Sep 19, 1931 in Camden, South Carolina
d. Apr 9, 1988 in New York, New York
Source: *AmPS A; AnObit 1988; BiDAfM; BioIn 6, 11, 12, 15, 16; ConMus 7; DcTwCCu 5; DrBlPA, 90; EncPR&S 74; EncRkSt; InB&W 85; LegTOT; PenEncP; RkOn 74; RolSEnR 83; SoulM; WhoBlA 77, 80, 85, 88, 90N; WhoRock 81*

Benton, Nelson
[Joseph Nelson Benton, Jr]
American. Broadcast Journalist
With CBS News, covered 20 yrs. of events including Vietnam War, civil rights movement.
b. Sep 16, 1924
d. Feb 14, 1988 in New York, New York
Source: *ConAu 110, 112, 124; WhoAm 76, 78, 80, 82, 84, 86, 88; WhoWor 82*

Benton, Robert Douglass
American. Screenwriter, Director
Won Oscars for *Kramer vs. Kramer,* 1979; *Places in the Heart,* 1984.
b. Sep 29, 1932 in Waxahachie, Texas
Source: *ConTFT 3; VarWW 85; WhoE 74*

Benton, Thomas Hart
"Old Bullion"
American. Political Leader
Dem. Senate leader, 1821-51; lost office for opposing extension of slavery.
b. Mar 14, 1782 in Hillsboro, North Carolina
d. Apr 10, 1858 in Washington, District of Columbia
Source: *Alli; AmAu&B; AmBi; AmOrN; AmPolLe; ApCAB; BbD; BenetAL 91; BiAUS; BiD&SB; BiDrAC; BiDrUSC 89; BiDSA; BioIn 1, 3, 4, 5, 7, 8, 9, 10; CyAG; CyAL 1; DcAmAu; DcAmB; DcNAA; DcNCBi 1; Drake; EncAAH; EncAB-H 1974, 1996; EncABHB 6; EncSoH; HarEnUS; LegTOT; LinLib S; McGEWB; NatCAB 4; NewCol 75; OxCAmH; OxCAmL 65, 83, 95; PolPar; REn; REnAL; REnAW; TwCBDA; WebAB 74, 79; WhAm HS; WhAmP; WorAl; WorAlBi*

Benton, Thomas Hart
American. Artist
Regionalist whose paintings depict life in Midwest, South.
b. Apr 15, 1889 in Neosho, Missouri
d. Jan 19, 1975 in Kansas City, Missouri
Source: *AmAu&B; AmCulL; AmDec 1930; ArtsAmW 1, 2; BenetAL 91; BioIn 1, 2, 3, 4, 5, 6, 7, 8, 9, 10, 11, 12, 13, 14, 15, 16, 17, 19; BriEAA; CelR; ConAu 53, 93; CurBio 75N; DcAmArt; DcAmB S9; DcAmSR; DcCAA 71, 77, 88, 94; EncAAH; EncAB-H 1974, 1996; FacFETw; GrAmP; IlBEAAW; IlsCB 1744, 1946; IntDcAA 90; IntWW 74, 75; LegTOT; LinLib S; McGDA; McGEWB; MorMA; NewCol 75; NewYTBS 75; ObitOF 79; OxCAmH; OxCAmL 65, 83, 95; OxCTwCA; OxDcArt; PeoHis; PhDcTCA 77; REn; REnAL; WebAB 74, 79; WhAm 6; WhAmArt 85; WhoAm 74; WhoAmA 73, 76, 76N, 78, 78N, 80N, 82N, 84N, 86N, 89N, 91N, 93N; WhoWor 74; WorAl; WorAlBi; WorArt 1950*

Benton, William
American. Publisher, Politician
Dem. senator from CT, 1949-53; started Voice of America broadcasts; owner, publisher, *Encyclopedia Britannica,* 1942-73.
b. Apr 1, 1900 in Minneapolis, Minnesota
d. Mar 18, 1973 in New York, New York
Source: *AmAu&B; BiDrAC; BiDrUSC 89; BioIn 20; ConAu 41R, P-1; CurBio 73, 73N; EncAJ; PolProf E, T; St&PR 75; WebAB 74, 79; WhAm 5; WhAmP; WhoAmA 73, 76, 78, 80, 82N, 84N, 86N, 89N, 91N, 93N; WhoFI 74*

Bentsen, Lloyd Millard, Jr.
American. Politician, Government Official
Dem. vp candidate, 1988; senator from TX, 1971-93; Secretary of Treasury, 1993-94.
b. Feb 11, 1921 in Mission, Texas
Source: *AlmAP 88; BiDrAC; BiDrUSC 89; BioIn 8, 9, 10, 11, 12; BioNews 75; CngDr 74, 85, 87; CurBio 73; IntWW 74, 75, 76, 77, 78, 79, 80, 81, 82, 83, 89, 91, 93; NewYTBS 88, 92; Who 90, 92, 94; WhoAm 74, 76, 78, 86; WhoAmP 73, 75, 77, 79, 81, 83, 85, 87, 89, 91, 93, 95; WhoGov 72, 75, 77; WhoSSW 75, 80, 82; WhoWor 78, 80, 82; WorAl*

Ben-Yehuda, Eliezer
[Eliezer Perelman]
Israeli. Scholar
Developed spoken Hebrew; wrote *Dictionary of Hebrew Language,* 1908.
b. Jan 7, 1858 in Luzhky, Russia
d. Dec 16, 1922 in Jerusalem, Palestine
Source: *BioIn 15, 17, 19; CasWL; EuAu; McGEWB; PenC CL, EUR*

Benz, Karl Friedrich
German. Auto Manufacturer
Built first car powered by internal combustion engine, 1885; merged with Daimler to form Mercedes Benz, 1926.
b. Nov 25, 1844 in Karlsruhe, Germany
d. Apr 4, 1929 in Ladenburg, Germany
Source: *BiESc; DcInv; InSci; LegTOT; NewCol 75; WebBD 83; WorAl; WorAlBi; WorInv*

Benzell, Mimi
[Miriam Ruth Benzel]
American. Opera Singer, Actor
Popular soprano, light opera singer; star of radio's "Luncheon with Mimi," 1964.
b. Apr 6, 1924 in Bridgeport, Connecticut
d. Dec 23, 1970 in Manhasset, New York
Source: *BiE&WWA; BioIn 4, 9; NewYTBE 70; RadStar*

Beradino, John
American. Actor, Baseball Player
Infielder, 1939-52; played Dr. Hardy on TV soap opera "General Hospital," 1963-96.
b. May 1, 1917 in Los Angeles, California
d. May 19, 1996 in Los Angeles, California
Source: *BioIn 10, 12; VarWW 85; WhoAm 78, 80, 82, 84, 86, 88; WhoHol 92*

Beranger, Pierre-Jean de
French. Poet
Wrote light verse satirizing Bourbons; *Chanson Inedites,* celebrated Napoleon.
b. Aug 19, 1780 in Paris, France
d. Jul 16, 1857 in Paris, France
Source: *BbD; BiD&SB; ChhPo, S1, S2; DcEuL; EuAu; EvEuW; OxCEng 67, 85, 95; OxCFr; PenC EUR; REn; WorAlBi*

Berberian, Cathy
[Mrs. Luciano Berio]
American. Opera Singer, Comedian
Known for singing avant-garde works: John Cage's "Fontana Mix"; Luciana Berio's "Circles."
b. Jul 4, 1928 in Attleboro, Massachusetts
d. Mar 6, 1983 in Rome, Italy
Source: *AnObit 1983; Baker 78; BioIn 7, 13; DcTwCCu 1; IntWW 79, 80, 81, 82; NewGrDM 80; NewYTBS 83; WhoAm 80, 82; WhoAmW 74; WhoMus 72; WhoWor 74*

Berberova, Nina Nikolaevna
American. Author
Wrote autobiography *The Italics Are Mine,* 1969.
b. Aug 8, 1901 in Saint Petersburg, Russia
d. Sep 26, 1993 in Philadelphia, Pennsylvania
Source: *BiDSovU; BlmGWL; ConLC 81; HanRL*

Berbick, Trevor
Canadian. Boxer
WBC world heavyweight champ, 1986; defeated by Mike Tyson, Nov 1986.
b. Aug 1, 1952, Jamaica
Source: *BioIn 12; NewYTBS 81, 86*

Bercovici, Konrad
American. Author
Wrote about NY's East Side, Balkan gypsies in *Peasants,* 1928.
b. Jun 22, 1882 in Braila, Romania
d. Dec 27, 1961 in New York, New York
Source: *AmAu&B; AmNov; BenetAL 91; BioIn 2, 4, 6; CnDAL; ConAmL; DcLEL; NatCAB 46; OxCAmL 65, 83, 95; REnAL; TwCA, SUP; WhAm 4; WhE&EA; WhNAA*

Berdichevsky, Micah Joseph
[Micah Joseph Bin Gorion]
Russian. Author
Chronicled the difficulties that 19th c. Jews experienced when forced to decide between tradition and modern ways.
b. Aug 19, 1865 in Medzhibozh, Russia
d. Nov 18, 1921 in Berlin, Germany
Source: *RAdv 14, 13-2*

Berdyayev, Nikolay Aleksandrovich
Russian. Theologian, Philosopher
Developed Christian existentialism; exiled from Russia, 1922; wrote *Destiny of Man,* 1937.
b. Mar 6, 1874 in Kiev, Russia
d. Mar 23, 1948 in Clamart, France
Source: *BioIn 14, 20; CasWL; ClDMEL 47, 80; DcRusL; EncWL; EvEuW; LngCTC; REn; TwCA, SUP*

Bereano, Nancy K(irp)
American. Publisher
Founded Firebrand Books, 1984, a publisher which focusses on lesbian and feminist issues.
b. Aug 17, 1942 in New York, New York
Source: *GayLesB; IntAu&W 86*

Beregovoi, Georgi
Russian. Cosmonaut
Orbited earth in spaceship *Soyuz 3,* 1964.
b. 1921
d. Jul 5, 1995 in Moscow, Russia
Source: *BioIn 10, 21; WhoSocC 78*

Beregovoy, Pierre (Eugene)
French. Political Leader
French Prime minister, 1992-93, succeeding Edith Cresson.
b. Dec 23, 1925 in Deville-les-Rouen, France
d. May 1, 1993 in Nevers, France
Source: *AnObit 1993; BiDFrPL; BioIn 13, 16; CurBio 93, 93N; IntWW 82, 83, 89, 91, 93; IntYB 82; NewYTBS 88; WhAm 11; Who 90, 92; WhoFr 79; WhoWor 93*

Berendt, John
American. Journalist, Writer
Wrote *Midnight in the Garden of Good and Evil: A Savannah Story,* 1994.
b. Dec 5, 1939 in Syracuse, New York
Source: *ConLC 86*

Berengario da Carpi, Jacopo
Italian. Physician
First person to describe the valves of the heart.
b. 1460 in Carpi, Italy
d. 1530 in Ferrara, Italy

Berengar of Tours
French. Theologian
His *De Sacra Coena* opposing doctrine of transsubstantiation led to church's better formulation of eucharist doctrine.
b. 1000
d. 1088
Source: *MediFra; NewCol 75*

Berenger, Tom
[Thomas Berenger]
American. Actor
Appeared in film *The Big Chill,* 1983; nominated for Oscar for *Platoon,* 1986.
b. May 31, 1950 in Chicago, Illinois
Source: *CelR 90; ConTFT 3, 9; HalFC 84, 88; HolBB; IntMPA 84, 86, 88, 92, 94, 96; IntWW 93; ItaFilm; LegTOT; VarWW 85; WhoAm 94, 95, 96, 97; WhoHol 92; WorAlBi*

Berenice
Roman. Mistress
Mistress of Roman emperor Titus; attempted to stop a Jewish rebellion in Jerusalem.
b. 28AD
Source: *BioIn 2, 5, 7, 10; InWom; NewC; OxCClL 89; OxCEng 85; WomWR*

Berenson, Bernard
American. Art Historian
Italian Renaissance expert; wrote *Drawings of the Florentine Painters,* 1903.
b. Jun 26, 1865 in Vilnius, Lithuania
d. Oct 6, 1959 in Settignano, Italy
Source: *AmAu&B; Benet 87, 96; BenetAL 91; BioIn 2, 3, 4, 5, 6, 7, 9, 10, 11, 12, 13, 14, 15, 16, 17, 19; CamGLE; CasWL; DcAmB S6; DcArts; DcCathB; EncAB-H 1974, 1996; FacFETw; GayN; JeHun; LinLib L; LngCTC; McGDA; NatCAB 48; ObitT 1951; OxCAmH; OxCAmL 65, 83, 95; OxCEng 67, 85, 95; OxDcArt; PenC AM; REn; REnAL; ThTwC 87; TwCA SUP; WebAB 74, 79; WhAm 3; WhoAmA 80N, 82N, 84N, 86N, 89N, 91N, 93N*

Berenson, Marisa
American. Actor
Grandniece of Bernard Berenson; starred in *Barry Lyndon,* 1975.

b. Feb 15, 1948 in New York, New York
Source: *BkPepl; ConTFT 7; FilmEn; MovMk; WhoHol A*

Berenson, Red
[Gordon Arthur Berenson]
"The Red Baron"
Canadian. Hockey Player, Hockey Coach
Center, 1961-78, with four NHL teams; one of only seven NHL players to score six goals in one game (1968).
b. Dec 8, 1941 in Regina, Saskatchewan, Canada
Source: *BioIn 9; HocEn; WhoHcky 73*

Beresford, Bruce
Australian. Filmmaker
Made films *Breaker Morant,* 1979; *Driving Miss Daisy,* 1989.
b. Aug 16, 1940 in Sydney, Australia
Source: *BiDFilm 94; ConTFT 6, 13; CurBio 93; FarE&A 81; HalFC 84, 88; IntDcF 1-2, 2-2; IntMPA 92, 94, 96; IntWW 82, 83, 89, 91, 93; LegTOT; MiSFD 9; WhoAm 86, 88, 90, 92, 94, 95, 96, 97; WhoEnt 92; WhoWor 87, 89, 91, 93, 95, 96; WorFDir 2*

Beresford, Harry
American. Actor, Author
Vaudeville performer; came to US, 1886; toured with own co. for 10 yrs.
b. 1864 in London, England
d. Oct 4, 1944 in Los Angeles, California
Source: *Film 2; ForYSC; HalFC 80, 84, 88; NotNAT B; WhAm 2; WhoHol B; WhScrn 74, 77, 83; WhThe*

Berg, Alban
Austrian. Composer
Wrote opera *Wozzeck,* 1921, in which atonality blends with elements of Viennese tradition.
b. Feb 9, 1885 in Vienna, Austria
d. Dec 24, 1935 in Vienna, Austria
Source: *AtlBL; Baker 78, 84; Benet 87, 96; BioIn 2, 3, 4, 6, 7, 8, 9, 10, 11, 12, 13, 14, 15, 17, 19, 20; BriBkM 80; CmOp; CnOxB; CompSN, SUP; DcArts; DcCM; DcCom 77; DcCom&M 79; DcTwCC; FacFETw; IntDcOp; LegTOT; MakMC; McGEWB; MetOEnc; MusMk; NewAmDM; NewEOp 71; NewGrDM 80; NewOxM; OxCGer 76, 86; OxCMus; OxDcOp; PenDiMP A; PenEncH; RAdv 14, 13-3; WhAm 4; WhDW; WorAl; WorAlBi*

Berg, Gertrude
American. Actor
Starred in "The Goldbergs" on radio, 1929-50, TV, 1949-54.
b. Oct 3, 1899 in New York, New York
d. Sep 14, 1966 in New York, New York
Source: *AmWomD; AmWomWr; BiE&WWA; BioIn 9, 12, 15, 16; CurBio 41, 60, 66; FilmgC; FunnyW; HalFC 80, 84, 88; InWom, SUP; JeAmHC; JoeFr; LegTOT; LibW; NatCAB 52; NewYTET; NotNAT A, B; NotWoAT; OxCAmT 84; RadStar; SaTiSS; WhAm 4; WhoAmW 58, 61, 64, 66; WhoCom; WhoHol B; WhScrn 74, 77; WhThe; WorAl; WorAlBi*

Berg, Matraca
American. Singer, Songwriter
Nashville songwriter who co-wrote hits for Trisha Yearwood, Patty Loveless and Reba McEntire; co-wrote song "Faking Love" which became a number one it for T.G. Sheppard and Karen Brooks; released debut album, *Lying to the Moon,* 1991 and later *The Speed of Grace,* which included songs "Guns In My Head" and "Jolene," 1994.
b. Feb 3, 1963 in Nashville, Tennessee
Source: *ConMus 16*

Berg, Patty
[Patricia Jane Berg]
American. Golfer
Co-founder, first pres., LPGA, 1948; had 83 career wins; leading money winner, 1954, 1955, 1957.
b. Feb 13, 1918 in Minneapolis, Minnesota
Source: *BiDAmSp OS; BioIn 2, 3, 5, 6, 9, 10, 11, 12, 15, 17; CurBio 40; FacFETw; GoodHs; GrLiveH; InWom, SUP; LibW; WhoGolf; WhoSpor; WomFir; WorAl; WorAlBi*

Berg, Paul
American. Biochemist
Author of articles on biochemistry, microbiology; shared Nobel Prize for chemistry, 1980.
b. Jun 30, 1926 in New York, New York
Source: *AmDec 1980; AmMWSc 73P, 76P, 79, 82, 86, 89, 92, 95; BiESc; BioIn 5, 12, 14, 15, 19, 20; BlueB 76; CamDcSc; IntWW 74, 75, 76, 77, 78, 79, 80, 81, 82, 83, 89, 91, 93; LarDcSc; McGMS 80; NewYTBS 80; NobelP; NotTwCS; Who 82, 83, 85, 88, 90, 92, 94; WhoAm 74, 76, 78, 80, 82, 84, 86, 88, 90, 92, 94, 95, 96, 97; WhoFrS 84; WhoNob, 90, 95; WhoScEn 94, 96; WhoWest 82, 84, 87, 89, 92, 94, 96; WhoWor 82, 84, 87, 89, 91, 93, 95, 96, 97; WorAlBi; WorScD*

Bergalis, Kimberly
American. Victim, Social Reformer
Became activist for mandatory AIDS testing of health care workers when she contracted the virus from her dentist, David Acer, during tooth extraction.
b. 1968 in Tamagua, Pennsylvania
d. Dec 8, 1991 in Fort Pierce, Florida
Source: *News 92, 92-3; NewYTBS 91*

Berganza, Teresa
Spanish. Opera Singer
Mezzo-soprano; made NY Met. debut, 1967.
b. Mar 16, 1935 in Madrid, Spain
Source: *Baker 84, 92; CurBio 79; IntDcOp; IntWW 74, 75, 76, 77, 78, 79, 80, 81, 82, 83, 89, 91, 93; IntWWM 77, 80, 90; InWom SUP; NewAmDM; NewGrDM 80; PenDiMP; WhoAm 80, 82, 84, 86, 88, 90, 92; WhoEnt 92; WhoMus 72; WhoOp 76; WhoWor 74, 82, 84, 87, 91*

Berge, Pierre (Vital Georges)
French. Business Executive
Pres., Yves Saint Laurent International, 1971—.
b. Nov 14, 1930 in Ile d'Oleron, France
Source: *BioIn 13, 15, 16; CurBio 90; Dun&B 88; IntWW 89, 91, 93; WhoAm 92, 94; WhoFI 92; WhoFr 79*

Bergen, Candice
[Mrs. Louis Malle]
American. Actor, Photojournalist
Starred in *Starting Over,* 1979; won Golden Globe for TV series "Murphy Brown," 1988—; daughter of Edgar Bergen.
b. May 9, 1946 in Beverly Hills, California
Source: *BiDFilm 94; BioIn 7, 8, 9, 10, 11, 12, 13; BkPepl; CelR, 90; ConAu 142; ConTFT 3, 10; CurBio 76; FilmEn; FilmgC; ForYSC; HalFC 80, 84, 88; HolBB; IntMPA 75, 76, 77, 78, 79, 80, 81, 82, 84, 86, 88, 92, 94, 96; InWom SUP; ItaFilm; LegTOT; MotPP; MovMk; News 90, 90-1; NewYTBE 71; WhoAm 74, 76, 78, 80, 82, 84, 86, 88, 90, 92, 94, 95, 96, 97; WhoAmW 74, 83, 85, 91, 93, 95, 97; WhoEnt 92; WhoHol 92, A; WorAl; WorAlBi; WrDr 88, 90, 92, 94, 96*

Bergen, Edgar John
[Edgar John Bergren]
American. Ventriloquist, Comedian
Vaudeville, film, TV entertainer for 60 yrs; with dummy Charlie McCarthy, starred in radio's "Chase & Sanborn Hour," 1937-47.
b. Feb 16, 1903 in Chicago, Illinois
d. Sep 30, 1978 in Las Vegas, Nevada
Source: *CurBio 45, 78; EncPaPR 91; FilmgC; MotPP; WebAB 74, 79; WhoHol A*

Bergen, John Joseph
American. Financier, Industrialist
Chm., Graham-Page investment firm, involved in building new Madison Square Garden, NYC, 1968.
b. Aug 7, 1896 in Pottsville, Pennsylvania
d. Dec 11, 1980 in Cuernavaca, Mexico
Source: *BioIn 5, 6, 12; CurBio 61, 81*

Bergen, Polly
[Nellie Paulina Burgin]
American. Actor
Radio singer turned actress; won Emmy, 1957, for "The Helen Morgan Story"; played Rhoda Henry on TV miniseries "The Winds of War" and "War and Remembrance."
b. Jul 14, 1930 in Knoxville, Tennessee
Source: *BiE&WWA; BioIn 3, 4, 5, 7, 8, 10, 11, 12, 13; BusPN; CelR, 90; ConAu 57; ConTFT 6, 14; FilmEn; FilmgC; ForYSC; IntMPA 77, 78, 79, 80, 81, 82,*

84, 86, 88, 92, 94, 96; InWom, SUP; NotNAT; VarWW 85; WhoAm 86; WhoAmW 61; WhoHol 92; WorAl; WorAlBi

Berger, Al
[Southside Johnny and the Asbury Jukes]
American. Singer, Musician
Bassist, vocalist with group, 1974-80.
b. Nov 8, 1949

Berger, Arthur
American. Composer, Critic
NYC music reviewer, 1943-53; compositions include "Ideas of Order," 1952.
b. May 15, 1912 in New York, New York
Source: *ASCAP 80; Baker 78, 84; BriBkM 80; CpmDNM 79, 80, 81, 82; DcCM; MusMk; NewAmDM; NewGrDA 86; NewGrDM 80; OxCMus; WhoAm 84, 86; WhoWor 74*

Berger, David
Israeli. Olympic Athlete, Victim
One of 11 members of Israeli Olympic team kidnapped and killed by Arab terrorists during Summer Olympic Games.
b. 1944
d. Sep 5, 1972 in Munich, Germany (West)
Source: *BioIn 9*

Berger, Helmut
[Helmut Steinberger]
Austrian. Actor
Known for sinister roles: *The Damned,* 1969; *Dorian Gray,* 1972.
b. May 29, 1944 in Salzburg, Austria
Source: *FilmAG WE; FilmEn; FilmgC; HalFC 84, 88; IntMPA 86; ItaFilm; LegTOT; WhoHol 92, A*

Berger, John
English. Author
Novels include *The Foot of Clive,* 1962; *Corher's Freedom,* 1964.
b. Nov 5, 1926 in London, England
Source: *BiDNeoM; BioIn 13, 14, 15, 17, 18, 19; BlmGEL; CamGLE; ConAu 81; ConLC 2, 19; ConNov 72, 76, 82, 86, 91; CyWA 89; DcArts; DcLB 14; DcLEL 1940; IntAu&W 76, 77, 89, 91; IntWW 89, 91, 93; ModBrL, S1, S2; Novels; OxCEng 85, 95; RadHan; RfGEnL 91; TwCRHW 90; Who 74, 82, 83, 85, 88, 90, 92, 94; WhoWor 82, 84; WorAu 1970; WrDr 76, 80, 82, 84, 86, 88, 90, 92*

Berger, Marilyn
[Mrs. Don Hewitt]
American. Broadcast Journalist
Chief White House correspondent, NBC-TV, 1976-77; with ABC News, 1982—.
b. Aug 23, 1935 in New York, New York
Source: *BioIn 11; ConAu 101; WhoAm 78, 80, 82; WhoTelC*

Berger, Melvin H
American. Author
Writings include *For Good Measure,* 1969; *Storms,* 1970; *Pollution Lab,* 1973.
b. Aug 23, 1927 in New York, New York
Source: *AuBYP 2; ConAu 4NR, 5NR; ConLC 12; SmATA 5*

Berger, Meyer
American. Journalist, Author
NYC columnist who won Pulitzer for local reporting, 1950; wrote *The Eight Million,* 1942.
b. Sep 1, 1898 in New York, New York
d. Feb 8, 1959 in New York, New York
Source: *AmAu&B; BiDAmNC; BioIn 2, 5, 6; ConAu 120, 154; CopCroC; CurBio 43, 59; DcAmB S6; DcLB 29; EncAJ; JrnUS; LiJour; NatCAB 46; WhAm 3*

Berger, Raoul
American. Author
Wrote books on politics, including *Impeachment: The Constitutional Problems,* 1973.
b. Jan 4, 1901, Russia
Source: *BioIn 10, 11, 13; ConAu 44NR, 93; DcAmC; DrAS 78P, 82P; NewYTBE 73; WhoAm 74, 76, 78, 80, 84, 86, 88, 90, 92, 94, 95, 96, 97; WhoAmL 96; WhoE 95*

Berger, Samuel David
American. Diplomat
US ambassador to S Korea, 1961-64; deputy ambassador to S Vietnam, 1968-72.
b. Dec 6, 1911 in Gloversville, New York
d. Feb 12, 1980 in Washington, District of Columbia
Source: *AnObit 1980; BioIn 12, 16; BlueB 76; DcAmDH 80, 89; IntWW 81; USBiR 74; WhoGov 72, 75*

Berger, Senta
Austrian. Actor
Star of films *Major Dundee,* 1965; *The Glory Guys,* 1965; *Quiller Memorandum,* 1967.
b. May 13, 1941 in Vienna, Austria
Source: *BioIn 16, 17; FilmEn; FilmgC; ForYSC; HalFC 80, 84, 88; IntMPA 96; ItaFilm; MotPP; WhoAmW 72; WhoHol 92, A*

Berger, Terry
American. Author
Juvenile writings include *Black Fairy Tales,* 1969; *I Have Feelings,* 1971.
b. Aug 11, 1933 in New York, New York
Source: *BioIn 11; ConAu 37R; IntAu&W 91, 93; SmATA 8; WrDr 76, 80, 82, 84, 86, 88, 90*

Berger, Thomas Louis
American. Author
Best known for style of dealing with absurdity of American life: *Little Big Man,* 1964, adopted to film, 1970.
b. Jul 20, 1924 in Cincinnati, Ohio
Source: *ConAu 1R, 5NR; ConLC 18, 38; ConNov 86; CurBio 88; DcLEL 1940; ModAL S1; NewYTBS 80; OxCAmL 83; PenC AM; PostFic; RAdv 1; WebE&AL; WhoAm 86; WorAu 1950; WrDr 86*

Berger, Victor Louis
American. Political Leader
First socialist ever elected to Congress, 1911-19.
b. Feb 28, 1860 in Nieder-Rehbach, Romania
d. Aug 7, 1929 in Milwaukee, Wisconsin
Source: *AmBi; AmPolLe; AmRef; BiDMoPL; BiDrAC; BioIn 5, 10, 15; DcAmB S1; DcNAA; EncAB-H 1974, 1996; McGEWB; OxCAmH; WebAB 74, 79; WhAm 1; WhAmP*

Bergerac, Jacques
French. Cosmetics Executive
Pres., Paris branch of Revlon since 1972; appeared in *Gigi,* 1958.
b. May 26, 1927 in Biarritz, France
Source: *FilmEn; FilmgC; ForYSC; HalFC 80, 84, 88; IntMPA 77, 80, 86, 88, 92, 94, 96; ItaFilm; LegTOT; MotPP; WhoFr 79; WhoHol 92, A*

Bergerac, Michel C
American. Cosmetics Executive
Pres., chm., Revlon, Inc., NYC, 1974-85.
b. Feb 13, 1932 in Biarritz, France
Source: *BioIn 12; BusPN; Dun&B 79, 86; WhoAm 78, 80, 82, 84, 86; WhoE 83, 85; WhoFI 74, 77, 79, 81, 83, 85; WhoWor 84*

Bergeron, Victor J
"Trader Vic"
American. Restaurateur
Founder, owner worldwide "Trader Vic" restaurant chain.
b. 1903 in California
d. Oct 11, 1984 in Hillsborough, California
Source: *BioNews 74; BusPN; WhoAm 82; WhoWor 74*

Bergey, David Hendricks
American. Bacteriologist
Principle contributor to taxonomic reference, *Bergey's Manual of Determinative Bacteriology.*
b. Dec 27, 1860 in Skippack, Pennsylvania
d. Sep 5, 1937 in Philadelphia, Pennsylvania
Source: *DcNAA; NatCAB 28; WhAm 1; WhNAA*

Bergh, Henry
American. Social Reformer
Shipbuilder, founder, first pres., ASPCA, 1866; co-founder, ASPCC, 1875.

b. Aug 29, 1811 in New York, New York
d. Mar 12, 1888 in New York, New York
Source: *AmBi; BioIn 1, 3, 4, 8, 12, 13, 17; DcAmAu; DcAmB; NatCAB 3; WebAB 74, 79; WhAm HS*

Bergius, Friedrich Karl Rudolph
German. Chemist
Developed method of making gasoline from coal, oils; produced alcohol, sugar from wood molecules; Nobelist, 1931.
b. Oct 11, 1884 in Goldschmieden, Germany
d. Mar 30, 1949 in Buenos Aires, Argentina
Source: *BiESc; BioIn 14, 15, 16, 19, 20; DcScB; ObitOF 79; WhDW; WhoNob, 90, 95; WorAl*

Bergland, Bob
[Robert Selmer Bergland]
American. Government Official, Farmer
Secretary of Agriculture under Carter, 1977-81; first farmer to fill post since 1945.
b. Jul 22, 1928 in Roseau, Minnesota
Source: *BiDrUSC 89; CngDr 74, 77, 79; CurBio 77; IntWW 77, 78, 79, 80, 81, 82, 83, 89, 91, 93; NewYTBS 76; WhoAm 74; WhoAmP 83, 85; WhoMW 82; WhoWor 80, 82*

Bergman, Alan
American. Lyricist
With wife Marilyn, wrote numerous award-winning songs for stage, screen: *The Way We Were,* 1974.
b. Sep 11, 1925 in New York, New York
Source: *AmSong; ASCAP 66, 80; BioIn 10, 12, 13, 15; IntMPA 84, 86, 88; LegTOT; VarWW 85; WhoAm 74, 76, 78, 80, 82, 84, 86, 88, 96; WhoHol 92*

Bergman, Ingmar (Ernst)
Swedish. Director, Producer
Leading film artist whose works include *The Seventh Seal,* 1957; *Wild Strawberries,* 1957.
b. Jul 14, 1918 in Uppsala, Sweden
Source: *Benet 87, 96; BiDFilm, 81, 94; BioIn 5, 6, 7, 8, 9, 10, 11, 12, 13, 14, 16, 17, 18, 19, 20, 21; BkPepl; CamGWoT; CelR, 90; CnThe; ConAu 33NR, 81; ConLC 16, 72; ConTFT 3; CurBio 60, 81; DcArts; DcFM; EncEurC; EncWT; Ent; FacFETw; FilmEn; FilmgC; GrStDi; HalFC 80, 84, 88; IntDcF 1-2, 2-2; IntDcOp; IntMPA 75, 76, 77, 78, 79, 80, 81, 82, 84, 86, 88, 92, 94, 96; IntWW 74, 75, 76, 77, 78, 79, 80, 81, 82, 83, 89, 91, 93; LegTOT; MakMC; McGEWB; McGEWD 84; MiSFD 9; MovMk; NewYTBE 73; OxCFilm; OxCThe 67, 83; OxDcOp; PlP&P A; RAdv 14, 13-3; REn; TheaDir; WhDW; WhoAm 80, 82, 86, 88, 90, 92, 94, 95, 96, 97; WhoEnt 92; WhoHrs 80; WhoWor 74, 76, 78, 80, 82, 84, 87, 89, 91, 93, 95, 96; WorAl; WorAlBi; WorEFlm; WorFDir 2*

Bergman, Ingrid
Swedish. Actor
Won Oscars for roles in *Gaslight,* 1944; *Anastasia,* 1956; *Murder on the Orient Express,* 1974.
b. Aug 29, 1915 in Stockholm, Sweden
d. Aug 29, 1982 in London, England
Source: *AmCulL, 77, 81; WorAl; WorAlBi; WorEFlm*

Bergman, Jules Verne
American. Broadcast Journalist
Science editor, ABC News, 1961-87; wrote *Anyone Can Fly,* 1965; *Fire,* 1974.
b. Mar 21, 1929 in New York, New York
d. Feb 12, 1987 in New York, New York
Source: *EncTwCJ; WhoAm 80, 82, 84*

Bergman, Marilyn Keith
[Mrs. Alan Bergman]
American. Lyricist
Won Oscars for *Yentl,* 1983; *The Way We Were,* 1974.
b. Nov 10, 1929 in New York, New York
Source: *ASCAP 66, 80; IntMPA 86; VarWW 85; WhoAm 84, 86, 88, 90, 96; WhoAmW 70A*

Bergmann, Carl
German. Conductor
NY Philharmonic conductor, 1855-76, introduced Wagner, Liszt to American audiences.
b. Apr 11, 1821 in Ebersbach, Germany
d. Aug 16, 1876 in New York, New York
Source: *AmBi; ApCAB; Baker 78, 84, 92; DcAmB; NewEOp 71; NewGrDA 86; NewGrDM 80; WhAm HS*

Bergner, Elisabeth
[Elizabeth Ettel]
English. Actor
James Barrie wrote his last play *The Boy David,* for her, 1938; Oscar nominee for *Escape Me Never,* 1935.
b. Aug 22, 1900 in Vienna, Austria
d. May 12, 1986 in London, England
Source: *BiE&WWA; BioIn 14, 15; EncTR; EncWT; Ent; Film 2; FilmEn; FilmgC; ItaFilm; MovMk; NewYTBS 86; NotNAT; OxCAmT 84; OxCFilm; OxCThe 83; ThFT; Who 74, 82, 83, 85; WhoHol A; WhoThe 72, 77, 81; WorEFlm*

Bergonzi, Carlo
Italian. Opera Singer
Lyric tenor; NY Met. debut, 1956; noted for Verdi roles.
b. Jul 13, 1924 in Polesine, Italy
Source: *Baker 78, 84, 92; BioIn 15, 18, 20; CmOp; CurBio 92; FacFETw; IntDcOp; IntWW 74, 75, 76, 77, 78, 79, 80, 81, 82, 83, 89, 91, 93; IntWWM 77, 80, 90; MetOEnc; MusSN; NewAmDM; NewEOp 71; NewGrDM 80; NewGrDO; OxDcOp; PenDiMP; WhoAm 80, 82, 84, 86, 88, 90, 92, 94, 95, 96, 97; WhoMus 72; WhoOp 76; WhoWor 74*

Bergson, Henri Louis
French. Philosopher
Vitalism philosophy asserted importance of pure intuition, duration, liberty; won Nobel Prize, 1927.
b. Oct 18, 1859 in Paris, France
d. Jan 3, 1941 in Paris, France
Source: *AtlBL; BiDPara; BioIn 1, 2, 4, 5, 7, 8, 11, 12; CasWL; ClDMEL 47; CurBio 41; DcScB; Dis&D; EncO&P 1; EncWL; EvEuW; LngCTC; MakMC; NewC; OxCEng 67; OxCFr; PenC EUR; RComWL; REn; TwCA, SUP; TwCWr; WhE&EA; WhoNob, 90, 95; WhoTwCL*

Bergstrom, Sune
Swedish. Scientist
Shared 1982 Nobel Prize in medicine for discoveries in lowering blood pressure.
b. Jan 10, 1916 in Stockholm, Sweden
Source: *BiESc; BioIn 13, 20; NobelP; Who 85, 88, 90, 92, 94; WhoNob, 90, 95; WhoWor 74, 76, 78, 80, 82*

Beria, Lavrenti Pavlovich
Russian. Political Leader
Head of Soviet Intelligence, 1934-53; executed in power struggle after Stalin's death.
b. Mar 29, 1899 in Georgia, Russia
d. Dec 23, 1953 in Moscow, Union of Soviet Socialist Republics
Source: *CopCroC; CurBio 42, 54; DcPol; DcTwHis; EncE 75; HisEWW; LinLib S; McGEWB; ObitT 1951; WhDW; WorAl*

Berigan, Bunny
[Rowland Bernart Berigan]
American. Jazz Musician, Bandleader
Trumpeter, known for theme song "Can't Get Started with You."
b. Nov 2, 1909 in Hilbert, Wisconsin
d. Jun 2, 1942 in New York, New York
Source: *CurBio 42; WhoJazz 72; WorAl; WorAlBi*

Bering, Vitus Jonassen
Danish. Navigator
Member of Russian navy, traveled coast of Asia, discovered Alaska, 1741; sea, island and straits named for him.
b. 1680 in Horsens, Denmark
d. Dec 19, 1741, Bering Island
Source: *ApCAB; HarEnUS; OxCAmH; OxCCan; OxCShps; WhAm HS; WhDW; WorAl*

Berio, Luciano
Italian. Composer, Conductor
Innovative, controversial operas include *Allez-hop,* 1959, *Passagio,* 1963.
b. Oct 24, 1925 in Oneglia, Italy
Source: *Baker 78, 84, 92; BioIn 8, 9, 12; BlueB 76; BriBkM 80; CnOxB; ConAu 146; ConCom 92; CpmDNM 72; CurBio*

71; DcArts; DcCM; DcCom 77; DcCom&M 79; IntDcOp; IntWW 74, 75, 76, 77, 78, 79, 80, 81, 82, 83, 89, 91, 93; IntWWM 77, 80, 90; MakMC; McGEWB; MetOEnc; MusMk; NewAmDM; NewGrDA 86; NewGrDM 80; NewGrDO; NewOxM; OxCMus; OxDcOp; PenDiMP A; RAdv 14, 13-3; WhDW; Who 82, 83, 85, 88, 90, 92; WhoAm 74, 76, 78, 80, 82, 84, 86, 88, 90, 92, 94, 95; WhoEnt 92; WhoFr 79; WhoMus 72; WhoWor 74, 82, 87, 89, 91, 93, 95

Beriosova, Svetlana
Lithuanian. Dancer
Prima ballerina, Sadler's Wells (now Royal) Ballet Co., 1955-75.
b. Sep 24, 1932 in Kaunas, Lithuania
Source: *BiDD; BioIn 3, 4, 5, 6; BlueB 76; CnOxB; ContDcW 89; DancEn 78; DcArts; IntDcB; IntDcWB; IntWW 74, 75, 76, 77, 78, 79, 80, 81, 82, 83, 89, 91, 93; InWom, SUP; Who 88; WhoWor 82; WorAl; WorAlBi*

Berisha, Sali
Albanian. Political Leader
Pres., Albania, 1992—.
b. Aug 1, 1944 in Tropoje, Albania
Source: *EncRev; IntWW 93; WhoWor 95, 96, 97*

Berkeley, Busby
[William Berkeley Enos]
American. Director, Choreographer
Known for choreography, 1930s movies, using dancing girls to form kaleidoscopic patterns; *42nd Street,* 1933; *No No Nanette,* 1971.
b. Nov 29, 1895 in Los Angeles, California
d. Mar 14, 1976 in Palm Springs, California
Source: *BiDD; BiDFilm, 81, 94; BiE&WWA; BioIn 7, 8, 9, 10, 11, 12, 14, 15; CmCal; CmMov; CnOxB; CurBio 71, 76N; DcAmB S10; DcArts; DcFM; EncAFC; EncMT; Ent; FacFETw; FilmEn; FilmgC; HalFC 80, 84, 88; IlWWHD 1; IntDcF 1-2, 2-2; IntMPA 75, 76; IntWW 75, 76; LegTOT; MiSFD 9N; MovMk; NewGrDA 86; NewYTBS 76; NotNAT A; OxCAmT 84; OxCFilm; WebAB 74, 79; WhAm 6, 7; What 3; WhoAm 74, 76; WhoHol C; WhoThe 72, 77; WhScrn 83; WorEFlm; WorFDir 1*

Berkeley, George
Irish. Author, Philosopher
Wrote *Principles of Human Knowledge,* 1710.
b. Mar 12, 1685 in Thomastown, Ireland
d. Jan 14, 1753 in Oxford, England
Source: *Alli; AmWrBE; ApCAB; BbD; Benet 87, 96; BenetAL 91; BiD&SB; BiDIrW; BiDPsy; BioIn 1, 2, 3, 4, 5, 6, 7, 8, 10, 11, 12, 13, 14, 17; BlkwCE; BlmGEL; BritAu; CamGEL; CamGLE; CasWL; ChhPo, S1; CyAL 1; DcAmC; DcEnA; DcEnL; DcEuL; DcIrB 78, 88; DcIrL, 96; DcIrW 2; DcLB 31A, 101; DcLEL; DcNaB; DcScB; Dis&D; Drake; EncCRAm; EncEnl; EvLB; InSci; LinLib L, S; LngCEL; LuthC 75; McGEWB; NamesHP; NewC; NewCBEL; OxCAmH; OxCAmL 65, 83, 95; OxCArt; OxCEng 67, 85, 95; OxCIri; OxCPhil; PenC ENG; PoIre; RAdv 14, 13-4; REn; TwCBDA; WebE&AL; WhDW; WhoEc 81, 86; WorAl; WorAlBi; WrPh P*

Berkeley, William, Sir
English. Colonial figure
Governor of VA, 1641-1652, 1659-1677.
b. 1606 in Somerset, England
d. Jul 9, 1677 in Twickenham, England
Source: *Alli; AmBi; AmWrBE; BenetAL 91; BiDrACR; BiDSA; BioIn 1, 4, 6, 16, 17; CyAL 1; DcAmB; DcAmMiB; DcNaB; EncAB-H 1974, 1996; EncCRAm; HarEnMi; LinLib L, S; McGEWB; NatCAB 13; NewCBEL; OxCAmH; OxCAmL 65, 83, 95; REn; REnAL; WebAB 74, 79; WhAm HS; WhAmP; WhDW; WhNaAH*

Berkman, Alexander
Russian. Anarchist
Believed ideal society based on voluntary anarchist collectivism; wrote *Prison Memoirs of an Anarchist,* 1912.
b. Nov 21, 1870 in Vilna, Russia
d. Jun 28, 1936 in Nice, France
Source: *BiDAmLf; BiDNeoM; BioIn 2, 3, 4, 5, 9, 10, 16; DcAmB S2; DcNAA; EncRev; RadHan; WhAm 4, HSA*

Berkner, Lloyd Viel
American. Physicist, Engineer
First to measure the height and density of the Earth's ionosphere.
b. Feb 1, 1905 in Milwaukee, Wisconsin
d. Jun 4, 1967 in Washington, District of Columbia
Source: *BioIn 1, 2, 3, 4, 5, 7, 8; CurBio 49, 67; DcScB S2; EncAB-A 39; InSci; McGMS 80; WhAm 4A*

Berkow, Ira Harvey
American. Journalist, Author
Writings include *Beyond the Dream,* 1975; *The Man Who Robbed the Pierre,* 1980.
b. Jan 7, 1940 in Chicago, Illinois
Source: *BioIn 10; ConAu 97; IntAu&W 82; WhoAm 84, 86, 88, 90, 92, 94, 95, 96, 97; WhoE 89, 91, 93; WhoUSWr 88; WhoWrEP 89, 92, 95*

Berkowitz, Bob
American. Broadcast Journalist
Correspondent, ABC News since 1982.
b. May 15, 1950 in New York, New York
Source: *WhoTelC*

Berkowitz, David
"Son of Sam"
American. Murderer
Killed six people in NYC, Jul 1976-Aug 1977.
b. Jun 1, 1953 in New York, New York
Source: *BioIn 11; LegTOT; MurCaTw; WorAlBi*

Berlage, Hendrik Petrus
Dutch. Architect
Known for simplicity; most famous work Amsterdam Exchange, the Beurs, 1896-1903.
b. Feb 21, 1856 in Amsterdam, Netherlands
d. Aug 12, 1934 in The Hague, Netherlands
Source: *BioIn 4, 10, 14; ConArch 80; EncMA; EncUrb; IntDcAr; McGDA; NewCol 75; OxCArt; WhoArch*

Berle, Adolf Augustus, Jr.
American. Lawyer, Diplomat
US ambassador to Brazil, 1945-46; chm., task force on Latin America, 1961.
b. Jan 29, 1895 in Boston, Massachusetts
d. Feb 17, 1971 in New York, New York
Source: *AmAu&B; BioIn 5, 6, 8, 9, 11, 15, 16; ConAu P-2; CurBio 40, 61, 71; DcAmB S9; DcAmDH 80, 89; EncAB-A 2; EncAB-H 1974, 1996; EncAI&E; FacFETw; McGEWB; NatCAB 56; NewYTBE 71; WebAB 79; WhAm 5*

Berle, Milton
[Milton Berlinger]
"Mr. Television"; "Uncle Miltie"
American. Actor, Comedian, Radio Performer, TV Personality
Vaudeville, stage performer; dominated early TV with "The Milton Berle Show," 1948-56; known for collecting colleagues' jokes.
b. Jul 12, 1908 in New York, New York
Source: *AmAu&B; AmDec 1950; ASCAP 66, 80; AuNews 1; BiDAmM; BiE&WWA; BioIn 1, 2, 3, 4, 5, 6, 7, 8, 10, 12, 13; BioNews 75; CelR, 90; CmpEPM; ConAu 77; ConTFT 3; DcTwCCu 1; EncAFC; EncMT; EncVaud; Ent; FacFETw; Film 1, 2; FilmEn; FilmgC; ForYSC; Funs; HalFC 80, 84, 88; IntMPA 75, 76, 77, 78, 79, 80, 81, 82, 84, 86, 88, 92, 94, 96; JoeFr; LegTOT; MovMk; NewYTET; NotNAT, A; OxCPMus; PlP&P; QDrFCA 92; RadStar; SaTiSS; TwYS; WebAB 74, 79; WhoAm 74, 76, 78, 80, 82, 84, 86, 88, 90, 92, 94, 95, 96, 97; WhoCom; WhoEnt 92; WhoHol 92, A; WhoThe 72, 77, 81; WhoWor 74; WorAl; WorAlBi*

Berlenbach, Paul
"Astoria Assassin"
American. Boxer
Olympic heavyweight wrestling champ, 1920; world light heavyweight champ, 1925-33.
b. Feb 18, 1901 in New York, New York
Source: *BioIn 12; WhoBox 74; WhoSpor*

Berlichingen, Gotz von
"Gotz with the Iron Hand"
German. Soldier
Known as the German version of Robin Hood.
b. 1480 in Jagsthausen Castle, Germany
d. Jul 23, 1562 in Hornberg Castle, Germany

Source: *BiD&SB; BioIn 4; CasWL; Dis&D; EvEuW; LinLib L; OxCGer 76; REn*

Berlin, Ellin (Mackay)
American. Writer
Roman Catholic whose marriage to Jewish Irving Berlin, 1926, caused sensation; wrote for *New Yorker, Saturday Evening Post* and other popular magazines.
b. Mar 22, 1902
d. Jul 29, 1988 in New York, New York
Source: *BenetAL 91; BioIn 2, 16; ConAu 65, 126; CurBio 44, 88N; NewYTBS 88; WhAm 9*

Berlin, Irving
[Israel Baline]
American. Composer
America's best-loved composer; wrote "God Bless America," 1939, "Easter Parade," 1933, "White Christmas," which won Oscar, 1942.
b. May 11, 1888 in Temun, Russia
d. Sep 22, 1989 in New York, New York
Source: *AmCulL; AmDec 1920; AmPS; AmSong; AnObit 1989; ASCAP 66, 80; Baker 78, 84, 92; Benet 87; BenetAL 91; BestMus; BiDAmM; BiDD; BiE&WWA; BioIn 1, 2, 3, 4, 5, 6, 7, 8, 9, 10, 11, 12, 13, 14, 15, 16, 17, 19, 20, 21; BlueB 76; CamGWoT; CamHAL; CelR, 90; ChhPo S2; CmMov; CmpEPM; ConAmC 76, 82; ConAu 108, 129; ConMus 8; ConTFT 8; CurBio 42, 63, 89N; DcArts; DcFM; EncAB-H 1974, 1996; EncMT; EncVaud; EncWT; Ent; FacFETw; FilmEn; FilmgC; HalFC 80, 84, 88; IntAu&W 89; IntDcF 2-4; IntMPA 75, 76, 77, 78, 80, 81, 82, 84, 86, 88; IntWW 74, 75, 76, 77, 78, 79, 80, 81, 82, 83, 89; IntWWM 77, 80; LegTOT; LinLib S; McGEWB; McGEWD 72, 84; MnPM; MusMk; NewAmDM; NewCBMT; NewGrDA 86; NewGrDM 80; NewGrDO; NewOxM; News 90, 90-1; NewYTBS 87, 88, 89; NotNAT, A; OxCAmH; OxCAmL 65, 83, 95; OxCAmT 84; OxCFilm; OxCPMus; OxDcOp; PenEncP; PlP&P; PopAmC, SUP; RComAH; REn; REnAL; Sw&Ld C; WebAB 74, 79; WhAm 10; WhDW; Who 74, 82, 83, 85, 88, 90; WhoAm 74, 76, 78, 80, 82, 84, 86, 88; WhoMus 72; WhoThe 72, 77, 81; WhoWor 74, 78, 80, 82, 84, 87, 89; WhoWorJ 72, 78; WorAl; WorAlBi*

Berlin, Isaiah, Sir
English. Author, Educator, Philosopher
Breadth of his erudition is suggested in his books on philosophy, political theory, intellectual history, and biography *Historical Inevitability,* 1955, *The Age of Enlightenment,* 1956.
b. Jun 6, 1909 in Riga, Russia
Source: *Au&Wr 71; Benet 87, 96; BioIn 6, 7, 8, 10, 13; BlueB 76; ConAu 85; CurBio 64; CyWA 89; DcLEL 1940; IntWW 74, 75, 76, 77, 78, 79, 80, 81, 82, 83, 89, 91, 93; LegTOT; LinLib L; LngCTC; OxCEng 85, 95; OxCPhil; ThTwC 87; Who 74, 82, 83, 85, 88, 90, 92, 94; WhoWor 74, 76, 78, 82, 84, 87, 89, 91, 93, 95, 96, 97; WhoWorJ 78; WorAu 1950; WrDr 80, 82, 84, 86, 88, 90, 92, 94, 96*

Berlin, Richard E
American. Business Executive
Pres., chief exec., Hearst Corp., 1941-74.
b. Jan 18, 1894 in Omaha, Nebraska
d. Jan 28, 1986 in Rye, New York
Source: *CelR; St&PR 75; WhoAm 74; WhoE 74; WhoFI 74; WhoWest 74*

Berliner, Emile
American. Inventor
Invented microphone, 1877, gramaphone, 1887.
b. May 20, 1851 in Hannover, Germany
d. Aug 3, 1929 in Washington, District of Columbia
Source: *AmBi; ApCAB; AsBiEn; BioIn 1, 2, 3, 4, 5, 8, 10, 12, 13, 14, 17; DcAmB S1; DcNAA; InSci; JeHun; LegTOT; LinLib S; NatCAB 10, 21; OxCAmH; WebAB 74, 79; WhAm 1; WhNAA; WorAl; WorAlBi; WorInv*

Berliner, Ron
American. Actor
In films *The World According to Garp,* 1982; *The Manhattan Project,* 1985.
b. Oct 13, 1958 in Coral Gables, Florida
Source: *ConTFT 3*

Berlinger, Warren
American. Actor
Films include *Blue Denim,* 1959; *World According to Garp,* 1982; also appeared on Broadway, TV.
b. Aug 31, 1937 in New York, New York
Source: *BiE&WWA; ConTFT 5; FilmEn; FilmgC; ForYSC; HalFC 80, 84, 88; IntMPA 75, 76, 77, 78, 79, 80, 81, 82, 84, 86, 88, 92, 94, 96; MotPP; NotNAT; WhoAm 74, 76, 78, 80, 82, 84, 86, 88, 90, 92, 94, 95, 96, 97; WhoEnt 92; WhoHol 92, A; WhoThe 72, 77, 81*

Berlinguer, Enrico
Italian. Political Leader
An architect of Eurocommunism who was general secretary of Italian Communist Party, 1972-84.
b. May 25, 1922 in Sassari, Italy
d. Jun 11, 1984 in Padua, Italy
Source: *AnObit 1984; BiDNeoM; BioIn 8, 10, 11, 12, 14, 21; CurBio 76, 84, 84N; FacFETw; IntWW 74, 75, 76, 77, 78, 79, 80, 81, 82, 83; NewYTBS 78, 84; PolLCWE; WhoEIO 82; WhoWor 80, 82*

Berlioz, Hector
[Louis Hector Berlioz]
French. Composer
Major work *Symphonie Fantastique,* 1830.
b. Dec 11, 1803 in La Cote-Saint-Andre, France
d. Mar 8, 1869 in Paris, France
Source: *AtlBL; Baker 84; BbD; Benet 87; BiD&SB; BioIn 1, 2, 3, 4, 5, 6, 7, 8, 9, 10, 11, 12, 13, 14, 15, 16, 17, 20; BriBkM 80; CelCen; CmOp; CmpBCM; CnOxB; DancEn 78; DcBiPP; DcCathB; DcCom 77; DcCom&M 79; Dis&D; EuWr 6; GrComp; IntDcOp; LegTOT; LinLib S; McGEWB; MetOEnc; MusMk; NewAmDM; NewEOp 71; NewGrDM 80; NewOxM; OxCEng 85, 95; OxCFr; OxCMus; OxDcOp; PenDiMP A; PenEncH; RAdv 14, 13-3; REn; WhDW; WorAl; WorAlBi*

Berlitz, Charles L. Frambach
[Charles Francois Bertin]
American. Author
Wrote controversial *The Bermuda Triangle,* 1974; grandson of Maximilian, founder of Berlitz School of Languages.
b. Nov 22, 1913 in New York, New York
Source: *AmAu&B; ConAu 5R, 7NR; CurBio 57; UFOEn; WhoAm 84*

Berlusconi, Silvio
Italian. Political Leader
Prime Minister of Italy, 1994-96.
b. c. Sep 29, 1938 in Milan, Italy
Source: *CurBio 94*

Berman, Emile Zola
American. Lawyer
Attorney for underdog clients; defended Sirhan Sirhan, 1969.
b. Nov 2, 1903 in New York, New York
d. Jul 3, 1981 in New York, New York
Source: *ConAu 104; CurBio 72, 81, 81N; NewYTBS 81*

Berman, Eugene
American. Artist, Designer
Neo-romantic painter, also known for theater sets, interiors.
b. Nov 4, 1899 in Saint Petersburg, Russia
d. Dec 14, 1972 in Rome, Italy
Source: *ArtsAmW 2; BiDD; BiDSovU; BioIn 1, 2, 5, 6, 7, 9, 10; BriEAA; CamGWoT; CnOxB; ConArt 77; CurBio 65, 73, 73N; DancEn 78; DcCAA 71, 77; EncWT; McGDA; MetOEnc; NewGrDM 80; NewGrDO; OxCTwCA; OxDcArt; PhDcTCA 77; WhAm 5; WhAmArt 85; WhoAmA 78, 78N, 80N, 82N, 84N, 86N, 89N, 91N, 93N; WorArt 1950*

Berman, Lazar
Russian. Pianist
Concert virtuoso, 1957—; made Carnegie Hall debut, 1976.
b. Feb 26, 1930 in Leningrad, Union of Soviet Socialist Republics
Source: *Baker 78, 84; BioIn 10, 11, 16; BriBkM 80; CurBio 77; IntWW 89; IntWWM 90; MusSN; NewGrDM 80; PenDiMP; WhoAm 78, 80, 82, 84, 86, 88, 90, 92, 94, 95, 96, 97; WhoEnt 92; WhoWor 78, 80, 84, 87, 91, 93, 95*

Berman, Pandro Samuel
American. Producer
Producer of several Astaire/Rogers films; won Irving M Thalberg award, 1977.
b. Mar 28, 1905 in Pittsburgh, Pennsylvania
d. Jul 13, 1996 in Beverly Hills, California
Source: *FilmgC; IntMPA 82; WhoAm 78, 80, 82, 84, 86; WhoAmJ 80; WhoEnt 92; WorEFlm*

Berman, Shelley
[Sheldon Leonard Berman]
American. Comedian, Actor
Films include *The Best Man,* 1964; *Divorce American Style,* 1969.
b. Feb 3, 1926 in Chicago, Illinois
Source: *BiE&WWA; BioIn 5, 6, 8, 9; BlueB 76; ConTFT 6; FilmgC; HalFC 80, 84, 88; WhoAm 74, 76; WhoCom; WhoHol 92, A; WhoWor 74; WorAl; WorAlBi*

Bermudez, Juan de
Spanish. Navigator
Discovered Bermuda, 1522, named in his honor.
Source: *ApCAB*

Bern, Paul
[Paul Levy]
American. Director
MGM exec. who supervised all Garbo's films; committed suicide after marriage to Jean Harlow.
b. Dec 3, 1889 in Wandsbek, Germany
d. Sep 4, 1932 in Beverly Hills, California
Source: *BioIn 11, 17; FilmEn; FilmgC; HalFC 80, 84, 88; PseudN 82; TwYS A; WhAm 1; WhScrn 74, 77, 83*

Bernacchi, Antonio Maria
Italian. Opera Singer
Celebrated male soprano, 1700-30s.
b. Jun 23, 1685 in Bologna, Italy
d. Mar 13, 1756 in Bologna, Italy
Source: *Baker 84, 92; IntDcOp; NewEOp 71; NewGrDM 80; NewGrDO; OxDcOp*

Bernadette of Lourdes, Saint
[Soubiroux; Saint Bernadette; Marie Bernarde Soubirous]
French. Religious Figure
Nun who saw 18 visions of Virgin Mary in grotto in Lourdes, 1858; canonized, 1933; subject of 1943 Oscar-winning *Song of Bernadette.*
b. Jan 7, 1844 in Lourdes, France
d. Apr 16, 1879 in Nevers, France
Source: *Benet 87, 96; ContDcW 89; DcCathB; Dis&D; EncPaPR 91; HerW; IntDcWB; InWom, SUP; OxCFr; OxCMed 86; REn; WhDW; WorAl; WorAlBi*

Bernadotte, Folke, Count
Swedish. Diplomat
Intermediary between Heinrich Himmler, Great Britain, US prior to German surrender, 1945.
b. Jan 2, 1895 in Stockholm, Sweden
d. Sep 17, 1948 in Jerusalem, Israel
Source: *BiDInt; BioIn 14, 16, 17, 20; CurBio 45, 48; DcTwHis; EncTR 91; FacFETw; HisEAAC; HisEWW; LinLib S; WhWW-II*

Bernanos, Georges
French. Author
Father of modern theological novel who wrote *The Diary of a Country Priest,* 1937.
b. Feb 20, 1888 in Paris, France
d. Jul 5, 1948 in Paris, France
Source: *Benet 87, 96; BioIn 1, 2, 4, 5, 7, 8, 9, 10, 11, 13, 16, 17; CasWL; CathA 1930; ClDMEL 47, 80; CnMD; ConAu 104, 130; CyWA 58; DcArts; DcCathB; DcLB 72; DcTwCCu 2; EncWL, 2, 3; EncWT; EvEuW; GuFrLit 1; LegTOT; LiExTwC; LinLib L; LngCTC; LuthC 75; McGEWB; ModFrL; ModRL; ModWD; Novels; OxCEng 85, 95; OxCFr; PenC EUR; RAdv 14, 13-2; REn; RfGWoL 95; ScF&FL 1A, 92; TwCA, SUP; TwCLC 3; TwCWr; WhDW; WhoTwCL*

Bernard, Andrew Milroy
[Andrew Milroy Fleming-Bernard]
"Master Bernard, the Blind Poet"
English. Poet
Poet laureate to Henry VII, Henry VIII.
d. 1523?
Source: *Alli; DcEnL; PoLE*

Bernard, Bruno
American. Photographer
Known for shots of film stars including famed photo of Marilyn Monroe in wind-blown skirt.
b. 1912?, France
d. Jun 4, 1987 in Los Angeles, California

Bernard, Claude
French. Physiologist
Called founder of experimental medicine for work on role of pancreas, liver in digestion process.
b. Jul 12, 1813 in Saint-Julien, France
d. Feb 10, 1878 in Paris, France
Source: *AsBiEn; BiDPsy; BiESc; BiHiMed; BioIn 1, 2, 3, 5, 8, 9, 10, 12; CamDcSc; CelCen; DcBiPP, A; DcCathB; DcEuL; DcInv; DcScB; InSci; LarDcSc; McGEWB; NamesHP; OxCFr; OxCMed 86; RAdv 14, 13-5; WhDW; WorScD*

Bernard, Emile
French. Artist
Considered by some to be the founder of Cloisonnism.
b. 1868
d. Apr 16, 1941 in Paris, France
Source: *BioIn 4, 6, 12, 14; CurBio 41; DcTwCCu 2; McGDA; OxCTwCA; OxDcArt; PhDcTCA 77; ThHEIm*

Bernard, Francis, Sir
English.
Governor, MA Bay Colony, 1760; his strict adherence to royal policy hastened American Revolution.
b. Jul 1712, England
d. Jun 16, 1779 in Aylesbury, England
Source: *AmBi; BiDrACR; BioIn 7; BlkwEAR; DcAmB; DcNaB; EncAR; NatCAB 5; OxCAmH; WhAm HS; WhAmP; WhAmRev*

Bernard, Sam
[Samuel Barnet]
English. Actor
Top vaudeville performer; Broadway musicals from 1896.
b. 1863 in Birmingham, England
d. May 16, 1927
Source: *CmpEPM; EncVaud; Film 1; NotNAT B; OxCAmT 84; OxCPMus; WhAm 1; WhoHol B; WhoStg 1906, 1908; WhScrn 74, 77, 83; WhThe*

Bernard De Chartres
French. Philosopher
Leader of French School of Chartres, which attempted to reconcile Platonic and Aristotelian thought.
d. 1130? in Paris, France
Source: *DcLB 115; DcScB*

Bernard De Menthon, Saint
[Bernard of Aosta]
Italian. Religious Figure
Patron saint of mountain climbers; St. Bernard dogs named in honor of him.
d. 1081
Source: *BioIn 2*

Bernardi, Hershel
American. Actor, Singer
Played Tevye on Broadway's *Fiddler on the Roof,* 1970; in TV series "Peter Gunn," 1958-60; "Arnie," 1970-71.
b. Oct 30, 1923 in New York, New York
d. May 9, 1986 in Los Angeles, California
Source: *FilmgC; HalFC 80; NotNAT; WhoAm 82; WhoHol A; WorAl*

Bernardin, Joseph L(ouis), Cardinal
American. Religious Leader
Became archbishop of Chicago after death of Cardinal Cody, 1982-96; archbishop of Cincinnati, 1972-82; named cardinal, 1982.
b. Apr 2, 1928 in Columbia, South Carolina
d. Nov 14, 1996 in Chicago, Illinois
Source: *AmCath 80; BioIn 13; BlueB 76; CurBio 82; NewYTBS 74, 82, 83; RelLAm 91; WhoAm 74, 76, 78, 80, 82, 84, 86, 88, 90, 95, 96, 97; WhoMW 76, 78, 80, 82, 84, 86, 88, 90, 92, 96; WhoRel 77, 85, 92; WhoWor 84, 87, 89, 91, 95, 96, 97*

Bernardine of Siena, Saint
Italian. Religious Figure
Preacher who was leader in Franciscan order; promoted Holy Name of Jesus; feast day May 20.
b. Sep 8, 1380 in Massa di Carrera, Italy
d. May 20, 1444 in Aquila, Italy
Source: *BioIn 1, 3, 4, 5, 6; NewCol 75*

Bernard of Clairvaux, Saint
French. Religious Leader
Monk who preached in Second Crusade, 1146; canonized, 1174.
b. 1090 in Fontaines-les-Dijon, France
d. Aug 20, 1153 in Clairvaux, France
Source: *BbD; BiD&SB; CasWL; EuAu; EvEuW; IlEncMy; LuthC 75; NewC; PenC EUR; PoChrch; REn; WhDW*

Bernard of Cluny
French. Religious Figure
Wrote poem *De Contempu Mundi;* hymn "Jerusalem the Golden" is based on it.
b. 1100
d. 1156
Source: *BiD&SB; CasWL; DcCathB; LinLib L, S; LuthC 75; NewC; PenC EUR; REn*

Bernays, Edward L.
American. Public Relations Executive
Founded Edward L Bernays Foundation, 1946; wrote *Public Relations,* 1945; *The Engineering of Consent,* 1955.
b. Nov 22, 1891 in Vienna, Austria
d. Mar 9, 1995 in Cambridge, Massachusetts
Source: *AmAu&B; BiDAmBL 83; BioIn 2, 4, 5, 7, 11, 13, 14, 15, 16, 17, 20, 21; ConAu 17R, 147; CurBio 42, 60, 95N; EncAJ; EncTwCJ; EncWB; IntAu&W 77; NewYTBS 95; REnAL; WhAm 11; WhE&EA; WhNAA; WhoAdv 90; WhoAm 74, 76, 78, 80, 82, 84, 86, 88, 90, 92, 94, 95; WhoAmJ 80; WhoE 79, 81, 83, 85, 86, 89, 91, 95; WhoPubR 72, 76; WhoWor 74, 76; WhoWorJ 72; WrDr 76, 80, 82, 84, 86, 88, 90, 92, 94, 96*

Bernbach, William
American. Advertising Executive
Founded Doyle Dane Bernbach, tenth largest ad agency in US, 1966.
b. Aug 13, 1911 in New York, New York
d. Oct 1, 1982 in New York, New York
Source: *AdMenW; BioIn 4, 5, 6, 7, 8, 11, 13, 14, 15, 17, 20; ConAmBL; ConAu 108; CurBio 67, 82, 82N; Dun&B 79; NewYTBS 82; St&PR 75; WhAm 8; WhoAm 74, 76, 78, 80, 82; WhoE 77, 79, 81; WhoFI 74, 75, 77, 79; WorAl; WorAlBi*

Berndt, Walter
American. Cartoonist
Best known for syndicated comic strip "Smitty," 1922-73.
b. Nov 22, 1899 in New York, New York
d. Aug 13, 1979 in Port Jefferson, New York
Source: *ConAu 89; EncACom; WorECom*

Berne, Eric Lennard
American. Psychiatrist, Author
Wrote best-seller *Games People Play,* 1964.
b. May 10, 1910 in Montreal, Quebec, Canada
d. Jul 15, 1970 in Monterey, California
Source: *AmAu&B; BioIn 7, 8, 9; ConAu 4NR, 5R; NewYTBE 70; RAdv 14, 13-5; WhAm 5*

Bernhard, Prince
German. Consort
Married Queen Juliana of the Netherlands, Jan 7, 1937.
b. Jun 29, 1911 in Jena, Germany
Source: *BioIn 1, 2, 3, 4, 5, 6, 10, 11; CurBio 50; HisEWW; IntWW 81, 82; NewYTBS 76; WhoWor 76, 78, 80, 82, 84, 87, 89, 91, 93, 95, 96, 97; WhWW-II*

Bernhard, Arnold
American. Publisher
Founded Value Line, Inc., 1930s, largest investment advisory service in the world.
b. Dec 2, 1902 in New York, New York
d. Dec 22, 1987 in New York, New York
Source: *Dun&B 86, 88; NewYTBS 87*

Bernhard, Harvey
American. Producer
Films include *The Omen,* 1976.
b. Mar 5, 1924 in Seattle, Washington
Source: *ConTFT 4; IntMPA 79, 80, 81, 82, 84, 86, 88, 92, 94, 96; VarWW 85; WhoAm 94, 95, 96; WhoEnt 92*

Bernhard, Lucian
American. Type Designer, Artist
Co-founded arts magazine *Das Plakat;* professor of poster art, Royal Art Institute, Berlin.
b. Mar 15, 1883 in Stuttgart, Germany
d. May 29, 1972 in New York, New York
Source: *BioIn 7, 9, 20; ConDes 84, 90, 97; DcTwDes; WhAmArt 85; WhoGrA 62*

Bernhard, Ruth
American. Photographer
Specializes in the female form; photographs collected in *The Eternal Body,* 1986.
b. Oct 14, 1905, Germany
Source: *BioIn 16; ConPhot 82, 88, 95; GayLesB; ICPEnP A; InWom SUP; MacBEP; NorAmWA; WhoAmA 84, 86, 89, 91, 93*

Bernhard, Sandra
American. Comedian
Made film debut in *The King of Comedy,* 1983; had critically acclaimed one-woman Off-Broadway show *Without You I'm Nothing,* 1988.
b. Jun 6, 1955 in Flint, Michigan
Source: *BioIn 13; ConAu 137; ConTFT 6, 10; CurBio 90; FunnyW; IntMPA 92, 94, 96; LegTOT; News 89; WhoAm 94, 95, 96, 97; WhoAmW 95, 97; WhoCom; WhoHol 92; WrDr 96*

Bernhardt, Melvin
[Melvin Bernhard]
American. Director
Won Tony for *Da,* 1978.
b. Feb 26, in Buffalo, New York
Source: *ConTFT 2; VarWW 85; WhoAm 80, 82, 84, 86, 88, 90, 92, 94, 95, 96, 97; WhoEnt 92; WhoThe 72, 77, 81*

Bernhardt, Sarah
[Rosine Bernard]
"The Divine Sarah"
French. Actor
Greatest stage tragedienne of her time; noted for emotional acting, dulcet voice.
b. Oct 22, 1844 in Paris, France
d. Mar 26, 1923 in Paris, France
Source: *BiDWomA; BioIn 1, 2, 3, 4, 5, 6, 7, 8, 9, 10, 11, 12, 13, 14, 15, 16, 17, 18, 20, 21; CamGWoT; CelCen; ContDcW 89; Dis&D; EncVaud; EncWT; Ent; FacFETw; FamA&A; FilmEn; FilmgC; HalFC 80, 84, 88; HerW, 84; IntDcT 3; IntDcWB; InWom, SUP; JeHun; LegTOT; LinLib L; LngCTC; NewC; NewCol 75; NotNAT A, B; OxCEng 85; OxCFilm; OxCFr; OxCThe 83; PlP&P; TwYS; WhAm 1; WhDW; WhoStg 1906, 1908; WhScrn 74, 77, 83; WomFir; WorAl; WorAlBi; WorEFlm*

Bernie, Ben
"The Old Maestro"
American. Comedian, Bandleader
Vaudeville, radio entertainer; led band, 1920s; used phrase "Yowsah, Yowsah."
b. May 30, 1891 in New York, New York
d. Oct 20, 1943 in Beverly Hills, California
Source: *ASCAP 66, 80; BgBands 74; BiDAmM; CmpEPM; CurBio 41, 43; EncVaud; HalFC 80, 84, 88; NotNAT B; OxCPMus; RadStar; SaTiSS; WhAm 2; WhoHol B; WhScrn 74, 77, 83*

Bernier, Rosamond Margaret
American. Lecturer
Offers lively, glamourous information on modern art for major museums; edits, writes for mags., books.
b. 1920? in Germantown, Pennsylvania
Source: *BioIn 11, 13; CurBio 88; NewYTBS 85*

Berning, Susie Maxwell
American. Golfer
Turned pro, 1964; won US Women's Open, 1968, 1972, 1973.
b. Jul 22, 1941 in Pasadena, California
Source: *LegTOT; WhoGolf*

Bernini, Giovanni Lorenzo
Italian. Sculptor, Architect
Created Baroque style in sculpture; noted as famed architect of St. Peter's, from 1629.
b. Dec 7, 1598 in Naples, Italy
d. Nov 28, 1680 in Rome, Italy
Source: *AtlBL; BioIn 1, 4, 6, 7, 8, 9, 10, 12, 13; DcBiPP; DcCathB; Dis&D; EncWT; IntDcAr; LinLib S; MacEA; OxCThe 67, 83; WorAl; WorAlBi*

Bernoulli, Daniel
Swiss. Mathematician
Advanced kinetic theory of gases; published *Hydrodynamica,* 1738.
b. Feb 8, 1700 in Groningen, Netherlands
d. Mar 17, 1782 in Basel, Switzerland
Source: *AsBiEn; BiDPsy; BiESc; BioIn 2, 3, 4, 12, 13, 14, 16; BlkwCE; CamDcSc; DcInv; DcScB; EncEnl; GrEconB; LarDcSc; McGEWB; NewGrDM 80; WhDW; WhoEc 81, 86; WorAl; WorAlBi; WorScD*

Bernsen, Corbin
American. Actor
Played Arnie Becker on TV series "LA Law;"; in film *Hello Again,* 1987.
b. Sep 7, 1955 in North Hollywood, California
Source: *News 90, 90-2*

Bernstein, Alice Frankau
American. Designer
Noted stage, costume designer; pres. Costume Institute from 1944.
b. Dec 22, 1880 in New York, New York
d. Sep 7, 1955 in New York, New York
Source: *NotAW MOD*

Bernstein, Allan
American. Inventor
Invented office intercom adapted as the "squawk box" on WW II warships.
b. 1911?
d. Nov 9, 1987? in Tamarac, Florida

Bernstein, Carl
American. Journalist, Author
With Bob Woodward wrote account of Watergate break-in, cover-up, *All the President's Men,* 1974.
b. Feb 14, 1944 in Washington, District of Columbia
Source: *AmDec 1970; AuNews 1; BioIn 10, 11, 12, 13; BioNews 74; BkPepl; ConAu 81; CurBio 76; EncAJ; EncTwCJ; IntWW 93; JrnUS; LegTOT; LiJour; PolProf NF; WhoAm 74, 76, 78, 80, 82, 84, 86, 88, 90, 92, 94, 95, 96, 97; WhoUSWr 88; WhoWrEP 89, 92, 95; WorAl; WorAlBi; WrDr 80, 82, 84, 86, 88, 90, 92, 94, 96*

Bernstein, Eduard
German. Political Leader
Critic of Marxism who became leader of revisionism, 1901; wrote *Evolutionary Socialism,* 1899.
b. Jan 6, 1850 in Berlin, Germany
d. Dec 18, 1932 in Berlin, Germany
Source: *BiDMoPL; BiDNeoM; BioIn 11, 13, 17; DcAmSR; DcTwHis; EncRev; GrEconB; McGEWB; REn; WhoEc 81, 86*

Bernstein, Elmer
American. Composer, Conductor
Won Oscar for original score of *Thoroughly Modern Millie,* 1967.
b. Apr 4, 1922 in New York, New York
Source: *ASCAP 66, 80; Baker 78, 84, 92; BiDAmM; BioIn 9, 18, 19; CelR; CmMov; CmpEPM; ConAmC 76, 82; ConTFT 4, 11; DcFM; FilmEn; FilmgC; HalFC 80, 84, 88; IntDcF 1-4, 2-4; IntMPA 75, 76, 77, 78, 79, 80, 81, 82, 84, 86, 88, 92, 94, 96; IntWWM 90; LegTOT; NewAmDM; NewGrDA 86; NewGrDM 80; NewOxM; OxCFilm; OxCPMus; PenEncP; PopAmC SUP; WhoAm 74, 76, 78, 80, 82, 84, 86, 88, 90, 92, 94, 95, 96, 97; WhoHol 92; WhoWest 74, 76, 78, 80, 82, 84, 87, 89, 92; WhoWor 74; WorAl; WorAlBi; WorEFlm*

Bernstein, Felicia Montealegre
[Mrs. Leonard Bernstein]
American. Actor
Narrated concerts for NY Philharmonic.
b. 1921, Costa Rica
d. Jun 16, 1978 in East Hampton, New York
Source: *BioIn 10, 11; NewYTBS 78*

Bernstein, Jay
American. Agent
Hollywood talent agent whose protegees include Farrah Fawcett, Suzanne Somers.
b. Jun 7, 1937 in Oklahoma City, Oklahoma
Source: *BioIn 12; ConTFT 5; IntMPA 84, 86, 88, 92, 94, 96*

Bernstein, Leonard
American. Composer, Conductor, Musician, Author
First American-born conductor of NY Philharmonic, 1957; best known work was *West Side Story,* 1957; also composed theater and chamber music, symphonies, ballets.
b. Aug 25, 1918 in Lawrence, Massachusetts
d. Oct 14, 1990 in New York, New York
Source: *AmAu&B; AmComp; AmCulL; AmDec 1950; AmPS; AmSong; AnObit 1990; ASCAP 66, 80; Baker 78, 84, 92; BenetAL 91; BestMus; BiDAmM; BiE&WWA; BioIn 1, 2, 3, 4, 5, 6, 7, 8, 9, 10, 11, 12, 13, 14, 15, 16, 17, 18, 19, 20, 21; BlueB 76; BriBkM 80; CamGWoT; CelR, 90; CmOp; CmpEPM; CnOxB; CompSN, SUP; ConAmC 76, 82; ConAu 1R, 2NR, 21NR, 132; ConCom 92; ConHero 2; ConMus 2; ConTFT 3, 11; CpmDNM 79, 82; CurBio 60, 90N; DancEn 78; DcArts; DcCM; DcCom 77; DcCom&M 79; DcTwCCu 1; EncAB-H 1974, 1996; EncMT; EncWT; FacFETw; FilmEn; FilmgC; GangFlm; GayLesB; HalFC 80, 84, 88; IntAu&W 77, 82; IntDcB; IntDcOp; IntWW 74, 75, 76, 77, 78, 79, 80, 81, 82, 83, 89; IntWWM 77, 80, 85, 90; JeAmHC; JeHun; LegTOT; LinLib L, S; McGEWB; McGEWD 72, 84; MetOEnc; MusMk; MusSN; NewAmDM; NewCBMT; NewEOp 71; NewGrDA 86; NewGrDM 80; NewGrDO; NewOxM; News 91, 91-1; NewYTBS 86, 87, 90; NewYTET; NotNAT; OxCAmH; OxCAmL 65, 83, 95; OxCAmT 84; OxCFilm; OxCMus; OxCPMus; OxDcOp; PenDiMP, A; PenEncP; PlP&P, A; PopAmC, SUP; RAdv 14, 13-3; RComAH; REn; REnAL; WebAB 74, 79; WhAm 10; WhDW; Who 74, 82, 83, 85, 88, 90; WhoAm 74, 76, 78, 80, 82, 84, 86, 88, 90; WhoAmJ 80; WhoAmM 83; WhoE 74, 79, 81, 83, 85, 86, 89, 91; WhoMus 72; WhoOp 76; WhoThe 72, 77, 81; WhoWor 74, 76, 78, 80, 82, 84, 87, 89, 91; WhoWorJ 72, 78; WorAl; WorAlBi; WorEFlm; WrDr 80, 82, 84, 86, 88, 90*

Bernstein, Robert L(ouis)
American. Publisher
President, Random House, 1966-67; CEO, 1967-75; chairman, 1975; chairman, president, CEO, 1975-89; publisher-at-large, John Wiley & Sons, 1991—.
b. Jan 5, 1923 in New York, New York
Source: *BlueB 76; CurBio 87; IntWW 74, 75, 76, 77, 78, 79, 80, 81, 82, 83, 89, 91, 93; WhoAm 74, 76, 78, 80, 82, 84, 86, 88, 90, 92, 94, 95, 96, 97; WhoFI 79, 81; WhoUSWr 88; WhoWor 95, 96, 97; WhoWrEP 89, 92, 95*

Bernstein, Sid(ney Ralph)
American. Editor, Business Executive
Chm., exec. committee, Crain Communications, 1973-93; pres., 1964-73.
b. Jan 29, 1907 in Chicago, Illinois
d. May 29, 1993 in Chicago, Illinois
Source: *WhAm 11; WhoAdv 72, 90; WhoAm 74, 76, 78, 80, 82, 84, 86, 88, 90, 92; WhoFI 74; WhoMW 90, 92; WhoUSWr 88; WhoWrEP 89, 92*

Bernstein, Theodore Menline
American. Journalist
With *NY Times* since 1925; wrote *The Careful Writer,* 1965.
b. Nov 17, 1904 in New York, New York
d. Jun 27, 1979 in New York, New York
Source: *BiDAmNC; BioIn 6, 11, 12, 13; ConAu 1R, 3NR; DcAmB S10; EncTwCJ; NewYTBS 79; SmATA 12; WhAm 7; WhNAA; WhoAm 74, 76, 78; WhoWorJ 72, 78*

Beroff, Michel
French. Pianist
Toured as concert pianist, from age 16, often performing modernistic French composers.
b. May 9, 1950 in Espinal, France

Source: *Baker 84, 92; IntWWM 77, 80, 90; NewGrDM 80; PenDiMP; WhoMus 72*

Berosus
Babylonian. Clergy
His books about the history and culture of ancient Babylon provided the ancient Greeks with information that otherwise would have been lost forever.
b. 290BC
Source: *OxCClL*

Berra, Yogi
[Lawrence Peter Berra]
American. Baseball Player, Baseball Manager
Catcher, NY Yankees, 1946-63; known for "Berraisms," including "It ain't over till it's over"; Hall of Fame, 1972.
b. May 12, 1925 in Saint Louis, Missouri
Source: *Ballpl 90; BiDAmSp BB; BioIn 2, 3, 4, 5, 6, 7, 8, 9, 10, 11, 13, 14, 15, 16, 17; BioNews 74; BlueB 76; CelR, 90; CurBio 52; FacFETw; LegTOT; NewYTBE 72, 73; NewYTBS 75; WebAB 74, 79; WhoAm 74, 76, 78, 80, 82, 84, 86, 88, 92, 94, 95, 96, 97; WhoE 74; WhoProB 73; WhoSpor; WorAl; WorAlBi*

Berri, Nabih
Lebanese. Government Official
Leader of Shiite Muslims-Amal-in Lebanon since 1980, known for role in Beirut TWA hostage crisis, 1985.
b. 1938 in Freetown, Sierra Leone
Source: *BioIn 13; ConNews 85-2; CurBio 85; DcMidEa*

Berrigan, Daniel J
American. Poet, Political Activist, Clergy
Convicted of destroying draft records with brother Philip, 1968.
b. May 9, 1921 in Virginia, Minnesota
Source: *AmAu&B; AuSpks; ConAu 33R; ConLC 4; ConPo 85; CurBio 70; DrAP 75; EncWB; IntWWP 77; MugS; NewYTBE 70; PolProf J, NF; WhoAm 80, 82, 84; WrDr 80, 86*

Berrigan, Elizabeth McAlister
[Mrs. Philip Berrigan]
American. Political Activist
Former nun, member of Catholic anti-war movement, who was indicted for plotting to kidnap Henry Kissinger, 1971.
b. 1939
Source: *BioIn 10, 11; NewYTBE 71*

Berrigan, Philip Francis
American. Political Activist
With brother Daniel, was first Catholic priest imprisoned for peace agitation in US, 1968.
b. Oct 5, 1923 in Minneapolis, Minnesota
Source: *AmAu&B; BenetAL 91; BioNews 74; ConAu 11NR, 13R; CurBio 76; WhoAm 74, 76, 78, 80, 82, 84, 86; WhoUSWr 88*

Berrill, Jack
American. Cartoonist
Created "Gil Thorp," 1958; character named for Jim Thorpe and Gil Hodges.
b. 1924? in New York, New York
d. Mar 14, 1996 in Brookfield, Connecticut

Berry, Bertice
American. TV Personality
Host of "The Bertice Berry Show," 1993-94.
b. 1960 in Wilmington, Delaware

Berry, Chu
[Leon Berry]
American. Jazz Musician
Tenor saxophonist with Cab Calloway, 1937-41.
b. Sep 13, 1910 in Wheeling, West Virginia
d. Oct 31, 1941 in Conneaut, Ohio
Source: *AllMusG; BiDAfM; BiDAmM; BiDJaz; CmpEPM; IlEncJ; InB&W 80, 85; PenEncP; WhoJazz 72*

Berry, Chuck
[Charles Edward Anderson Berry]
American. Singer, Songwriter
Influential figure in development of rock music, 1950s-60s; wrote songs "Roll Over Beethoven," 1956; "Johnny B Goode," 1958.
b. Jan 15, 1926 in San Jose, California
Source: *AfrAmAl 6; AmCulL; AmSong; Baker 78, 84, 92; BiDAfM; BiDAmM; BioIn 8, 9, 11, 12, 13, 15, 16, 19, 21; BluesWW; ConLC 17; ConMus 1; CurBio 77; DcArts; DcTwCCu 1, 5; DrBlPA, 90; EncPR&S 89; EncRkSt; FacFETw; GuBlues; HarEnR 86; InB&W 85; IntWW 89, 91, 93; LegTOT; NegAl 89; NewAmDM; NewGrDA 86; NewGrDM 80; OnThGG; OxCPMus; PenEncP; RComAH; RkOn 74; RolSEnR 83; SoulM; VarWW 85; WebAB 74, 79; WhoAfA 96; WhoAm 74, 76, 78, 80, 82, 84, 86, 88, 90, 92, 94, 95, 96, 97; WhoBlA 75, 77, 80, 85, 88, 90, 92, 94; WhoHol 92; WhoRock 81; WhoRocM 82; WorAl; WorAlBi*

Berry, Halle
American. Actor
Appeared in *Jungle Fever,* 1991; *Boomerang,* 1992; *Losing Isaiah,* 1995.
b. Aug 14, 1968 in Cleveland, Ohio
Source: *ConTFT 11; IntMPA 96; News 96, 96-2; WhoAm 95, 96, 97; WhoAmW 95, 97*

Berry, James Gomer
[Viscount Kemsley]
Welsh. Publisher
Largest newspaper proprietor in Britain; sold holdings to Roy H Thomson, 1959.
b. May 7, 1883 in Merthyr Tydfil, Wales
d. Feb 6, 1968 in Monte Carlo, Monaco
Source: *BioIn 14, 15; ConAu 89; CurBio 51, 68; DcNaB 1961; DcTwBBL; GrBr; ObitOF 79; ObitT 1961; WhAm 5*

Berry, Jan
[Jan and Dean]
American. Singer
Co-wrote duo's hit single "Surf City," 1963; suffered brain damage in car crash, 1966.
b. Apr 3, 1941 in Los Angeles, California
Source: *Baker 84, 92; LegTOT; WhoRocM 82*

Berry, Jim
American. Cartoonist
Editorial cartoonist who draws "Berry's World," 1963—.
b. Jan 16, 1932 in Chicago, Illinois
Source: *ConAu 107; WorECar; WorECom*

Berry, John
American. Singer, Musician
Country music singer who contributed to the "New Country" movement with his southern soul, soft rock, and country style; released album *John Berry,* 1993 which includes number one hit song "Your Love Amazes Me," and became a platinum record; released *Standing on the Edge,* 1995 and *Faces,* 1996.
b. Sep 14, 1959 in Aiken, South Carolina
Source: *ConMus 17*

Berry, Ken
American. Actor
Dancer on stage; best known for roles in TV comedies "F-Troop," 1965-67, "Mayberry RFD," 1968-71.
b. Nov 3, 1933 in Moline, Illinois
Source: *BiDD; ConTFT 8; FilmgC; HalFC 84, 88; IntMPA 86, 92, 94, 96; LegTOT; VarWW 85; WhoAm 82, 84; WorAlBi*

Berry, Martha McChesney
"The Sunday Lady"
American. Educator
Founded the Berry Schools for GA mountaineers, 1902.
b. 1866 in Rome, Georgia
d. Feb 27, 1942 in Mount Berry, Georgia
Source: *AmWomM; BiDAmEd; BioIn 3, 4, 5, 7, 8, 9, 10, 11; CurBio 40, 42; DcAmB S3; EncAB-A 2; EncSoH; HerW; InWom, SUP; LibW; LinLib S; NotAW; WhAm 2; WomFir; WomWWA 14*

Berry, Mary Frances
American. Government Official, Author
Chief educational officer of United States, 1977-80; Civil Rights commissioner, 1980—; author of *Black Resistance/White Law,* 1971.
b. Feb 17, 1938 in Nashville, Tennessee
Source: *AfrAmAl 6; AfrAmBi 2; AmWomHi; AmWomM; BioIn 11, 12, 13,*

14, 15; BlkWAm; BlkWr 1; ConAu 14NR, 33R; ConBlB 7; DrAS 74H; EncAACR; InWom SUP; LNinSix; NegAl 89, 89A; NotBlAW 1; SchCGBL; SelBAAf; WhoAfA 96; WhoAm 76, 78, 80, 82, 84, 86, 88, 90, 95, 96, 97; WhoAmL 87; WhoAmW 79, 83, 95, 97; WhoBlA 77, 80, 85, 88, 90, 92, 94; WhoGov 77

Berry, Raymond Emmett
American. Football Player, Football Coach
Wide receiver, Baltimore Colts, 1955-67; led NFL in receptions, 1958-60; Hall of Fame, 1973; coach, New England, 1984-89.
b. Feb 27, 1933 in Corpus Christi, Texas
Source: *BiDAmSp FB; BioIn 6, 7, 8, 9, 10, 11; FootReg 87; WhoAm 86, 88; WhoE 89; WhoFtbl 74*

Berry, Richard
American. Songwriter
Wrote "Louie Louie," 1956.
b. 1935 in Extension, Louisiana
d. Jan 23, 1997 in Los Angeles, California
Source: *EncRk 88*

Berry, Walter
Austrian. Opera Singer
Bass-baritone; NY Met. debut, 1966; known for Wagnerian roles; often sang with wife, Christa Ludwig.
b. Apr 8, 1929 in Vienna, Austria
Source: *Baker 84, 92; BioIn 9, 10; IntDcOp; IntWW 74, 75, 76, 77, 78, 79, 80, 81, 82, 83, 89, 91, 93; IntWWM 90; MetOEnc; NewGrDM 80; NewGrDO; OxDcOp; PenDiMP; WhoAm 86, 88, 90, 92, 94, 95, 96, 97; WhoEnt 92; WhoWor 74, 78*

Berry, Wendell
American. Poet
Wrote *Gift of Good Land,* 1981.
b. Aug 5, 1934 in Henry County, Kentucky
Source: *AuNews 1; Benet 96; BenetAL 91; BioIn 10, 11, 12, 14, 15, 17, 18, 19, 20; ConAu 73; ConLC 4, 6, 8, 27, 46; ConPo 70, 75, 80, 85, 91; CurBio 86; CyWA 89; DcLB 5, 6; DrAF 76; DrAP 75; DrAPF 80; EnvEnc; FacFETw; IntWW 89, 91, 93; LegTOT; LiHiK; MagSAmL; Novels; OxCAmL 83, 95; OxCTwCP; PenC AM; RadHan; RAdv 1, 14; RGTwCWr; SouWr; WhoAm 74, 76, 78, 80, 82, 84, 86, 88, 90, 92, 94, 95, 96; WhoSSW 73, 82; WhoUSWr 88; WhoWrEP 89, 92, 95; WorAu 1975; WrDr 76, 80, 82, 84, 86, 88, 90, 92*

Berryman, Clifford Kennedy
American. Cartoonist
Editorial cartoonist, Washington *Star,* 1907-49; created "Teddy Bear" after Theodore Roosevelt's bear-hunting trip, 1902.
b. Apr 2, 1869 in Versailles, Kentucky
d. Dec 11, 1949 in Washington, District of Columbia
Source: *BiDAmJo; BioIn 1, 2, 4, 12; DcAmB S4; EncAB-A 3; NatCAB 39; ObitOF 79; WhAm 2; WhAmArt 85; WhoAmA 78, 80, 82, 89N, 91N, 93N; WorECar*

Berryman, John
American. Author, Poet
Won Pulitzer Prize, 1964, for *77 Dream Songs.*
b. Oct 25, 1914 in McAlester, Oklahoma
d. Jan 7, 1972 in Minneapolis, Minnesota
Source: *AmAu&B; AmCulL; AmWr; Au&Wr 71; Benet 87, 96; BenetAL 91; BiDConC; BioIn 4, 8, 9, 10, 11, 12, 13, 15, 16, 17, 19, 20, 21; CamGEL; CamGLE; CamHAL; CasWL; CnE&AP; ConAu 2BS, 33R, 35NR, P-1; ConLC 1, 2, 3, 4, 6, 8, 10, 13, 25, 62; ConPo 70, 75, 80A, 85A; CroCAP; CurBio 69, 72, 72N; DcAmB S9; DcArts; DcLB 48; DcLEL 1940; DcTwCCu 1; EncWL 2, 3; FacFETw; GrWrEL P; LegTOT; LinLib L; MagSAmL; MajTwCW; MakMC; ModAL, S1, S2; NewCon; NewYTBE 72; OxCAmL 65, 83, 95; OxCEng 85, 95; OxCTwCP; PenC AM; RAdv 1, 14, 13-1; REn; REnAL; RfGAmL 87, 94; RGFAP; RGTwCWr; TwCA SUP; WebAB 74, 79; WebE&AL; WhAm 5; WhoTwCL; WorAl; WorAlBi*

Bertelli, Angelo B
"Accurate Angelo"
American. Football Player
Two-time All-America quarterback; first player from Notre Dame to win Heisman Trophy, 1942.
b. 1922 in West Springfield, Massachusetts
Source: *WhoFtbl 74*

Berthelot, Marcellin
[Pierre Eugene Marcellin Berthelot]
French. Chemist
Had a great impact on chemistry during the 19th century.
b. Oct 27, 1827 in Paris, France
d. Mar 18, 1907 in Paris, France
Source: *BiESc; BioIn 2, 3, 6, 7, 13, 14; DcScB; LinLib S; OxCFr; WorAlBi; WorInv*

Berthollet, Claude Louis, Comte
French. Chemist
Discovered bleaching properties of chlorine; wrote *Essay on Chemical Statics,* 1803.
b. Dec 9, 1749 in Talloires, France
d. Nov 6, 1822 in Arcueil, France
Source: *BioIn 1, 6; LarDcSc; NewCol 75*

Bertillon, Alphonse
French. Criminologist
Invented first scientific method to identify criminals, using body measurements, eye, hair, skin color.
b. Apr 24, 1853 in Paris, France
d. Feb 13, 1914 in Paris, France
Source: *BioIn 2, 4, 7, 8, 9, 12, 13; CopCroC; HarEnUS; LinLib S; LngCTC; McGEWB; OxCFr; OxCLaw; WhDW*

Bertinelli, Valerie
[Mrs. Eddie Van Halen]
American. Actor
Played Barbara on TV series "One Day at a Time," 1975-84.
b. Apr 23, 1960 in Wilmington, Delaware
Source: *BioIn 11, 12, 13, 14, 15, 16, 17, 19, 20; ConTFT 3, 13; IntMPA 86, 88, 92, 94, 96; InWom SUP; LegTOT; VarWW 85; WhoAm 94, 95, 96, 97; WhoEnt 92; WhoHol 92; WorAlBi*

Bertini, Gary
Israeli. Conductor, Composer
Musical director, Jerusalem Symphony, 1978-81.
b. May 1, 1927 in Bessarabia, Union of Soviet Socialist Republics
Source: *Baker 78, 84, 92; IntWWM 77, 80, 90; MidE 78, 79, 80, 81, 82; NewGrDM 80; NewGrDO; PenDiMP; WhoAmM 83; WhoEnt 92; WhoMus 72; WhoOp 76; WhoWor 74, 76, 82, 84, 87, 89, 91, 93, 95; WhoWorJ 72, 78*

Bertinoro, Obadiah ben Abraham Yare
Italian. Clergy, Author
His commentary on the Mishnah is a well respected work in Jewish literature.
b. 1450 in Bertinoro, Papal States
d. 1515

Bertoia, Harry
American. Artist, Designer
Noted for abstract, metal sculptures; prize-winning wire shell chairs.
b. Mar 10, 1915 in San Lorenzo, Italy
d. Nov 6, 1978 in Barto, Pennsylvania
Source: *BioIn 4, 5, 7, 9, 11, 12, 14, 15; ConArt 77, 83, 89; ConDes 84, 90, 97; DcAmArt; DcCAA 71, 77, 88, 94; DcD&D; DcTwDes; FacFETw; McGDA; NewYTBS 78; OxCTwCA; PenDiDA 89; PhDcTCA 77; WhAm 7; WhAmArt 85; WhoAm 74, 76, 78; WhoAmA 73, 76, 78, 80N, 82N, 84N, 86N, 89N, 91N, 93N; WhoWor 74; WorArt 1950*

Bertoldo di Giovanni
Italian. Sculptor
Studied under Donatello and taught Michelangelo; work is characterized by precise anatomic details.
b. 1420
d. 1491 in Poggio a Caiano, Italy
Source: *BioIn 15; McGDA; McGEWB; OxCArt; OxDcArt*

Bertolucci, Bernardo
Italian. Director
Directed *Last Tango in Paris,* 1972; won Oscar for *The Last Emperor,* 1988.
b. Mar 16, 1941 in Parma, Italy
Source: *BiDFilm; CelR; ConLC 16; ConTFT 4; CurBio 74; DcFM; EncEurC; IntMPA 79, 80, 81, 82, 84, 86, 88; MovMk; OxCFilm; WhoAm 86, 90, 92, 94, 95, 96, 97; WhoEnt 92; WhoWor 80, 91, 93, 95, 96, 97; WorAl; WorEFlm*

Berton, Pierre
Canadian. Author, TV Personality
Host, weekly TV show "My Country"; wrote 30 books including *Klondike Quest,* 1983; Canada's most popular historian.
b. Jul 12, 1920 in Whitehorse, Yukon Territory, Canada
Source: *Au&Wr 71; BioIn 5, 10, 15, 17, 21; BlueB 76; CanWr; CanWW 31, 70, 79, 80, 81, 83, 89; CaW; ConAu 1NR, 1R, 2NR; ConPopW; CurBio 91; DcLB 68; OxCCan; OxCCanL; OxCCan SUP; ScF&FL 1, 2; WhoAm 78, 80, 82, 84, 86, 88, 90, 92, 94, 95, 96, 97; WhoCanL 85, 87, 92; WhoE 74, 75, 77; WhoWrEP 89, 92; WorAu 1975; WrDr 76, 80, 82, 84, 86, 88, 90, 92, 94, 96*

Bertrand, Joseph Louis Francois
French. Mathematician
Known for contributions to thermodynamics.
b. Mar 11, 1822 in Paris, France
d. Apr 5, 1900 in Paris, France
Source: *DcBiPP; DcScB; WhoEc 81, 86*

Berwanger, J. Jay
American. Football Player
Two-time All-America quarterback-running back; first winner of Heisman Trophy, 1935; first player drafted in first pro draft, 1936, but never played in NFL.
b. Mar 19, 1914 in Dubuque, Iowa
Source: *WhoFtbl 74*

Berwind, Charles G
American. Industrialist
Founded Big Brothers of America, 1947, to help fatherless boys.
b. 1894?
d. Nov 9, 1972 in Bryn Mawr, Pennsylvania
Source: *BioIn 9; St&PR 75*

Berzelius, Jons Jacob, Baron
Swedish. Chemist
Developed symbols, formulas used in chemistry; coined words protein, isomerism.
b. Aug 29, 1779 in Vaversunda, Sweden
d. Aug 7, 1848 in Stockholm, Sweden
Source: *BiESc; BiHiMed; BioIn 1, 3, 6, 7, 8, 9, 10, 11; CamDcSc; CelCen; DcBiPP; DcScB; InSci; LarDcSc; McGEWB; NewCol 75; WorScD*

Besant, Annie Wood
English. Social Reformer, Author
Pres., Theosophical Society, 1907-33; organized India Home Rule League, 1916; disciple of Madame Blavatsky.
b. Oct 1, 1847 in London, England
d. Sep 20, 1933 in Adyar, India
Source: *Alli SUP; ArtclWW 2; BiDAmCu; Chambr 3; DcAmReB 1, 2; DcLEL; Dis&D; EvLB; InWom, SUP; LngCTC; McGEWB; NewC; OxCEng 95; PopDcHi; RelLAm 91; REn; TwCA, SUP; VicBrit; WhoLA*

Besant, Walter, Sir
English. Author
Wrote *All Sorts and Conditions of Men,* 1882; founded Society of Authors, 1884.
b. Aug 14, 1836 in Portsmouth, England
d. Jun 9, 1901 in London, England
Source: *Alli SUP; BbD; BiD&SB; BioIn 3, 9, 12, 20; BritAu 19; CamGEL; CamGLE; CasWL; Chambr 3; CyEd; DcArts; DcBiA; DcEnA, A; DcEuL; DcLB 135; DcLEL; DcNaB S2; EncSF, 93; EvLB; GrWrEL N; HsB&A; MouLC 4; NewC; NewCBEL; OxCEng 67, 85, 95; PenC ENG; REn; RfGEnL 91; ScF&FL 1; ScFEYrs; StaCVF; WebE&AL; WhoHr&F*

Besse, Georges Noel
French. Auto Executive
President, Renault, France's largest auto maker; assassinated.
b. Dec 25, 1927 in Clermont-Ferrand, France
d. Nov 17, 1986 in Paris, France
Source: *ConNews 87-1; NewYTBS 86; WhoAtom 77; WhoWor 80, 82*

Bessel, Friedrich Wilhelm
German. Astronomer
Made first authentic measurement of a star from earth, 1838.
b. Jul 22, 1784 in Minden, Germany
d. Mar 17, 1846 in Konigsberg, Germany
Source: *AsBiEn; BiDPsy; BiESc; BioIn 1, 14; CamDcSc; CelCen; DcBiPP; DcScB; Dis&D; InSci; LarDcSc; LinLib S; McGEWB; NamesHP; NewCol 75; WorAl; WorAlBi*

Bessell, Ted
American. Actor
Played Donald Hollinger on TV series "That Girl," 1966-71.
b. May 20, 1935 in Flushing, New York
d. Oct 6, 1996 in Los Angeles, California
Source: *LegTOT; VarWW 85; WhoHol 92, A*

Bessemer, Henry, Sir
English. Engineer, Inventor
Invented industrial process for manufacturing steel from molten pig iron.
b. Jan 19, 1813 in Charlton, England
d. Mar 15, 1898 in London, England
Source: *AsBiEn; BiESc; BioIn 1, 2, 3, 4, 5, 6, 7, 11, 12, 13, 14, 15, 21; CamDcSc; CelCen; DcBiPP; DcInv; DcNaB S1; DcScB S1; InSci; LarDcSc; LegTOT; LinLib S; McGEWB; NewCol 75; OxCShps; WhDW; WorAl; WorAlBi; WorInv*

Besser, Joe
[The Three Stooges]
American. Comedian
One of the members of The Three Stooges, 1956-58, replacing Shemp Howard.
b. Aug 12, 1907? in Saint Louis, Missouri
d. Mar 1, 1988 in Los Angeles, California
Source: *BioIn 2, 14, 15, 16; ConAu 124; EncAFC; HalFC 84; WhoCom*

Bessie, Alvah
[Hollywood Ten]
American. Screenwriter
Book *Inquisition of Eden,* 1965 tells of Hollywood Ten blacklisting.
b. Jun 4, 1904 in New York, New York
d. Jul 21, 1985 in Terra Linda, California
Source: *AmAu&B; AmNov; AnObit 1985; ConAmA; ConAu 2NR, 5R, 116; ConLC 23; DcLB 26; DrAPF 80; EncMcCE; FilmEn; FilmgC; HalFC 84, 88; NewYTBS 85; PlP&P; TwCA, SUP; WhNAA; WrDr 76, 80, 82, 84, 86*

Bessmertnova, Natalya (Igorevna)
Russian. Dancer
Prima ballerina of Bolshoi Ballet; won Lenin Award, 1970, for performance in *Spartacus.*
b. Jul 19, 1941 in Moscow, Union of Soviet Socialist Republics
Source: *BiDD; CurBio 88; IntWW 74, 75, 76, 77, 78, 79, 80, 81, 82, 83, 89, 91, 93; SovUn; WhoWor 74, 82, 84, 87, 89, 91, 93, 95*

Bessmertnykh, Aleksandr Aleksandrovich
Russian. Diplomat
Foreign minister dismissed after failed attempt to overthrow Mikhail Gorbachev, 1991.
b. Nov 10, 1933 in Biysk, Union of Soviet Socialist Republics
Source: *BiDSovU; CurBio 91; IntWW 91, 93; NewYTBS 90, 91; SovUn; WhoRus*

Best, Charles Herbert
Canadian. Physiologist
With F G Banting, discovered use of insulin in treatment of diabetes, 1921.
b. Feb 27, 1899 in West Pembroke, Maine
d. Mar 31, 1978 in Toronto, Ontario, Canada
Source: *AmMWSc 73P, 76P; AsBiEn; Au&Wr 71; BiESc; BioIn 1, 2, 3, 4, 5, 7, 10, 11, 12, 13, 20; BlueB 76; CanWW 70; ConAu 45; CurBio 57, 78; DcScB S2; InSci; IntAu&W 76; IntWW 74, 75, 76, 77, 78; IntYB 78; LarDcSc; LegTOT; McGEWB; McGMS 80; NewCol 75; NewYTBS 78; NotTwCS; OxCMed 86; Who 74; WhoAm 74; WhoCan 73, 75; WhoWor 74, 76, 78; WrDr 76*

Best, Edna
American. Actor
Made stage debut, 1917; greatest success in "The Constant Nymph," 1926.
b. Mar 3, 1900 in Hove, England
d. Sep 18, 1974 in Geneva, Switzerland
Source: *BiE&WWA; BioIn 3, 10; CurBio 54, 74, 74N; Film 2; FilmEn; FilmgC; ForYSC; HalFC 80, 84, 88; IlWWBF; InWom, SUP; LegTOT; NewYTBS 74; NotNAT B; ObitOF 79; ObitT 1971;*

OxCAmT 84; ThFT; Who 74; WhoHol B; WhScrn 77, 83; WhThe

Best, George
"Georgie"
Irish. Soccer Player
British superstar, 1960s; player-coach, San Jose Earthquakes, 1980.
b. May 22, 1946 in Belfast, Northern Ireland
Source: *BioIn 8, 9, 10, 11, 12; WorESoc*

Best, Oswald Herbert
English. Children's Author
Educational books include *Carolina Gold,* 1961.
b. Mar 25, 1894 in Chester, England
Source: *AmAu&B; AmNov; AuBYP 2; ConAu P-2; JBA 34, 51; NewCBEL; SmATA 2*

Best, Peter
English. Musician
Replaced by Ringo Starr as drummer for The Beatles, 1962.
b. Nov 24, 1941? in Liverpool, England
Source: *WhoRocM 82*

Bester, Alfred
American. Author
Science fiction novelist; won first Hugo for *The Demolished Man,* 1953; best known work *Tiger! Tiger!,* later published as *The Stars My Destination,* 1974.
b. Dec 18, 1913 in New York, New York
d. Sep 20, 1987 in Doylestown, Pennsylvania
Source: *AmAu&B; AnObit 1987; Benet 87, 96; BioIn 11, 12, 13, 15, 16, 17; ConAu 12NR, 13R, 36NR, 123; ConSFA; DcLB 8; DcLEL 1940; DrmM 1; EncSF, 93; IntAu&W 91; LegTOT; MajTwCW; NewEScF; Novels; RGSF; RGTwCSF; ScF&FL 1, 2, 92; ScFSB; ScFWr; TwCSFW 81, 86, 91; WhoSciF; WorAu 1980; WrDr 76, 80, 82, 84, 86, 88*

Bestor, Arthur Eugene
American. Educator
Director, pres., NY's Chautauqua Institution, beginning in 1907.
b. May 19, 1879 in Dixon, Illinois
d. Feb 3, 1944 in New York, New York
Source: *BiDAmEd; BioIn 1; CurBio 44; DcAmB S3; NatCAB 33; WhAm 2*

Bestor, Arthur (Eugene)
American. Historian
Author of *Backwoods Utopias,* 1950.
b. Sep 20, 1908
d. Dec 13, 1994 in Seattle, Washington
Source: *AmAu&B; Au&Wr 71; BioIn 3, 5, 14, 20, 21; BlueB 76; ConAu 1R, 6NR; CurBio 95N; DrAS 74H, 78H, 82H; IntWW 74, 75, 76, 77, 78, 79, 80, 81, 82, 83, 89, 91, 93; Who 74, 82, 83, 85, 88, 90, 92, 94; WhoAm 74, 76, 78; WrDr 76, 80*

Betancourt, Romulo
Venezuelan. Statesman
Pres., 1945-48, 1959-64; founded nation's first modern political party, advanced economic reform.
b. Feb 22, 1908 in Guatire, Venezuela
d. Sep 28, 1981 in New York, New York
Source: *AnObit 1981; BiDLAmC; BioIn 1, 5, 6, 12, 16, 17; ConAu 104; CurBio 81, 81N; DcCPSAm; DcPol; DcTwHis; EncLatA; EncRev; FacFETw; IntWW 74, 75, 76, 77, 78, 79, 80, 81; McGEWB; NewCol 75; NewYTBS 81; WhDW; WhoWor 74; WorAl; WorAlBi*

Betancur, Belisario
[Belisario Betancur Cuartas]
Colombian. Political Leader
Conservative party leader elected pres. of Colombia, 1982.
b. Feb 4, 1923 in Amaga, Colombia
Source: *CurBio 85; IntWW 79, 80, 81, 82, 83; WhoWor 82, 84, 87, 89, 91*

Bethe, Hans Albrecht
German. Physicist
Cornell U professor, 1937-75; won 1967 Nobel prize in physics for advancing nuclear reaction theory.
b. Jul 2, 1906 in Strassburg, Germany
Source: *AmMWSc 76P, 79, 82, 86, 89, 92, 95; AsBiEn; BiESc; BioIn 2, 4, 5, 6, 8, 11, 12, 13, 14, 15, 18, 19, 20, 21; BlueB 76; CamDcSc; ConAu 115; CurBio 40, 50; EncCW; InSci; IntWW 74, 75, 76, 77, 78, 79, 80, 81, 82, 83, 89, 91, 93; LarDcSc; McGEWB; McGMS 80; OxCAmH; RAdv 14, 13-5; WebAB 74, 79; Who 74, 82, 83, 85, 88, 90, 92, 94; WhoAm 74, 76, 78, 80, 82, 84, 86, 88, 90, 92, 94, 95, 96, 97; WhoE 74, 77, 79, 81, 83, 85, 86, 89, 91, 95, 97; WhoFrS 84; WhoNob, 90, 95; WhoScEn 94, 96; WhoWor 74, 80, 82, 84, 87, 89, 91, 93, 95, 96, 97; WorAl; WorScD*

Bethune, Louise Blanchard
[Jennie Louise Blanchard Bethune]
American. Architect
First woman in the US to work as a professional architect.
b. Jul 21, 1856 in Waterloo, New York
d. Dec 18, 1913 in Buffalo, New York
Source: *AmWom; BiDAmAr; BioIn 5, 6, 10; ContDcW 89; IntDcWB; InWom SUP; LibW; NatCAB 12; NotAW; WhAm 1; WomArt; WomFir; WomWWA 14*

Bethune, Mary McLeod
American. Educator, Social Reformer
Founder, pres., National Council of Negro Women, 1935-49; adviser to FDR, Truman.
b. Jul 10, 1875 in Mayesville, South Carolina
d. May 18, 1955 in Daytona Beach, Florida
Source: *AfrAmAl 6; AfrAmOr; AmDec 1930, 1940; AmWomM; AmWomWr; Au&Wr 71; BiDAmEd; BiDSocW; BioAmW; BlkWAm; ConBlB 4; ConHero 2; CurBio 42, 55; DcAmB S5; DcAmReB 1, 2; DcTwCCu 5; EncAACR; EncAB-H 1974, 1996; EncSoH; EncWHA; EncWM; FacFETw; GoodHs; GrLiveH; HanAmWH; HeroCon; HerW, 84; InWom, SUP; LegTOT; LibW; LinLib L, S; McGEWB; NatCAB 49; NegAl 76, 83, 89; NotAW MOD; NotBlAW 1; PeoHis; RComAH; RelLAm 91; WebAB 74, 79; WhAm 3; WhAmP; WhoColR; WomChHR; WomEdUS; WomFir; WomStre; WorAl; WorAlBi*

Bethune, Norman
Canadian. Surgeon
Served as front-line physician during WW I, Spanish Civil War, Chinese Revolution.
b. Mar 3, 1890 in Gravenhurst, Ontario, Canada
d. Nov 12, 1939, China
Source: *BioIn 3, 10, 11, 12; ColCR; MacDCB 78; OxCMed 86*

Bethune, Thomas Greene
"Blind Tom"
American. Musician
Mentally challenged black who toured US, 1850s demonstrating uncanny musical memory.
b. May 25, 1849 in Columbus, Georgia
d. Jun 13, 1908 in Hoboken, New Jersey
Source: *Baker 78, 84, 92; BiDAmM; BioIn 4, 8, 9, 10, 15, 16; DcAmNB; InB&W 80; NewGrDM 80; OxCMus*

Beti, Mongo
Cameroonian. Writer
His novels reflected his dislike of colonialism; *Rape of Cameroun* was banned in France and Africa.
b. Jun 30, 1932 in Mbalmayo, Cameroon
Source: *AfrA, 3; LiExTwC; MajTwCW; McGEWB; ModBlW; ModFrL; Novels; PenC CL; RAdv 14, 13-2; RGAfL; SchCGBL; SelBAAf; TwCWr*

Betjeman, John, Sir
English. Poet
Poet laureate, 1972-84; style of simple words in easy swinging rhythm sold more copies than any poet since Kipling.
b. Aug 28, 1906 in Highgate, England
d. May 19, 1984 in Trebetherick, England
Source: *AnObit 1984; Au&Wr 71; Benet 87, 96; BioIn 3, 4, 5, 6, 8, 9, 10, 11, 12, 13, 14, 16, 17, 18; BlmGEL; BlueB 76; BritWr 7; CamGEL; CamGLE; CasWL; ChhPo, S1, S2, S3; CnDBLB 7; CnE&AP; CnMWL; ConAu 9R, 11NR, 33NR, 112; ConLC 2, 6, 10, 34, 43; ConPo 70, 75, 80; CurBio 73, 84N; DcArts; DcLB 20, Y84N; DcLEL; DcNaB 1981; EncWB; EncWL 3; EngPo; EvLB; FacFETw; GrWrEL P; IntAu&W 76, 77; IntWW 74, 75, 76, 77, 78, 79, 80, 81, 82, 83; IntWWP 77; LegTOT; LinLib L; LngCEL; LngCTC; MagSWL; MajTwCW; MakMC; ModBrL, S1, S2; NewC; NewCBEL; NewCol 75; NewYTBS 84; OxCEng 67, 85, 95;*

OxCTwCP; PenC ENG; RAdv 1, 14, 13-1; REn; RfGEnL 91; RGFMBP; RGTwCWr; TwCA SUP; TwCWr; WebE&AL; WhAm 8; WhDW; Who 74, 82, 83; WhoTwCL; WhoWor 74, 82; WorAl; WorAlBi; WrDr 76, 80, 82, 84

Bettelheim, Bruno
American. Psychologist
Child psychologist; author of books on the psychology of fairy tales, child rearing.
b. Aug 28, 1903 in Vienna, Austria
d. Mar 13, 1990 in Silver Spring, Maryland
Source: *AmAu&B; AmMWSc 73S, 78S; AmSocL; AnObit 1990; Benet 87, 96; BenetAL 91; BiDAmEd; BioIn 5, 6, 8, 12, 13; BlueB 76; CelR, 90; ConAu 23NR, 81, 131; ConLC 79; CurBio 61, 90, 90N; FacFETw; IntAu&W 91; IntEnSS 79; IntWW 74, 75, 76, 77, 78, 79, 80, 81, 82, 83, 89; JeAmHC; LEduc 74; LegTOT; MajTwCW; McGEWB; News 90, 90-3; NewYTBS 90; OxCChiL; RAdv 14, 13-5; ScF&FL 92; ThTwC 87; WebAB 74, 79; WhAm 10; WhoAm 74, 76, 78, 80, 82, 84, 86, 88; WhoWor 74, 78, 80, 82, 84, 87, 89; WhoWorJ 72, 78; WorAu 1970; WrDr 80, 82, 84, 86, 88, 90*

Betterton, Thomas
English. Actor
Opened London Theatre, 1695.
b. Aug 1635 in London, England
d. Apr 27, 1710 in London, England
Source: *Alli; BioIn 2, 3, 4, 9, 10, 12; BlmGEL; BritAu; CamGWoT; CasWL; CnThe; DcArts; DcBiPP; DcEnL; DcLEL; DcNaB, C; EncWT; Ent; IntDcT 3; NewC; NewCBEL; NewGrDO; NotNAT A, B; OxCEng 67, 85, 95; OxCMus; OxCThe 67, 83; PlP&P; REn*

Bettger, Lyle
American. Actor
Since 1950, usually typecast as villain in films: *The Lone Ranger,* 1956.
b. Feb 13, 1915 in Philadelphia, Pennsylvania
Source: *ConTFT 1; FilmEn; FilmgC; ForYSC; HalFC 80, 84, 88; IntMPA 75, 76, 77, 78, 79, 80, 81, 82, 84, 86, 88, 92, 94, 96; LegTOT; WhoHol 92, A*

Betti, Ugo
Italian. Dramatist, Poet
Wrote symbolist plays: *The Landlady,* 1927; *The Inquiry,* 1942; won Italian drama award, 1949.
b. Feb 4, 1892 in Camerino, Italy
d. Jun 9, 1953 in Rome, Italy
Source: *Benet 87, 3; EncWT; Ent; EvEuW; IntDcT 2; ItaFilm; LinLib L; LngCTC; MajMD 2; McGEWB; McGEWD 72, 84; ModRL; ModWD; NotNAT B; OxCEng 67; OxCThe 67, 83; PenC EUR; RAdv 14; REnWD; RfGWoL 95; TwCLC 5; TwCWr; WhAm 4; WhDW; WorAu 1950*

Bettis, Valerie
American. Choreographer
With Virginia Sampler, first to choregraph a modern dance for ballet co., 1947.
b. Dec 20, 1919 in Houston, Texas
d. Sep 26, 1982 in New York, New York
Source: *AnObit 1982; BiE&WWA; BioIn 1, 3, 10, 11, 13; CurBio 53, 82, 82N; NewYTBS 82; NotNAT; WhAm 8; WhoAm 82; WhoAmW 58, 61, 74; WhoHol A; WhoThe 81*

Bettmann, Otto Ludwig
American. Historian
Founded Bettmann Archive, Inc., 1941; picture library on history of civilization.
b. Oct 15, 1903 in Leipzig, Germany
Source: *BiDAmJo; BioIn 1, 5, 6, 10, 12, 15, 16, 19, 20; ConAu 17R; CurBio 61; NewYTBS 81; SmATA 46; WhoAm 74, 76, 78, 80, 82, 84, 86, 88, 90, 92, 94, 95, 96, 97; WhoAmA 73, 76, 78, 80, 82, 84, 86, 89, 91, 93; WhoWor 74, 76*

Betz, Carl
American. Actor
Played husband in "The Donna Reed Show," 1958-66; had own series "Judd for the Defense," 1967-69.
b. Mar 9, 1920 in Pittsburgh, Pennsylvania
d. Jan 18, 1978 in Los Angeles, California
Source: *FilmEn; LegTOT; NewYTBS 78; WhoHol A*

Betz, Pauline
American. Tennis Player
Four-time US women's singles champ, 1942-44, 1946.
b. Aug 6, 1919
Source: *BioIn 1, 2, 9, 14; BuCMET; CmCal; EncWomS; InWom; LegTOT; WhoSpor*

Beutel, Bill
[William Charles Beutel]
American. Broadcast Journalist
Anchorman, WABC TV, 1970—; host "AM America," 1975.
b. Dec 12, 1930 in Cleveland, Ohio
Source: *ConAu 101; WhoAm 76, 78, 80, 82, 84*

Beuve-Mery, Hubert
French. Publisher, Editor
Found internationally respected *Le Monde* newspaper, 1944 which he managed until 1969.
b. Jan 5, 1902 in Paris, France
d. Aug 6, 1989 in Fontainebleau, France
Source: *AnObit 1989; BiDFrPL; BioIn 8, 16, 17; ConAu 129; FacFETw; IntAu&W 77, 89, 91; IntWW 74, 75, 76, 77, 78, 79, 80, 81, 82, 83, 89; NewYTBS 89; WhAm 10; WhoFr 79; WhoWor 74, 76, 78*

Beuys, Joseph
German. Artist
Sculptor, political activist who saw art as means of reshaping society.
b. May 12, 1921 in Krefeld, Germany
d. Jan 23, 1986 in Dusseldorf, Germany (West)
Source: *AnObit 1986; Benet 96; BioIn 8, 9, 10, 12, 13, 14, 15, 16, 17, 18, 19; ConArt 77, 83, 89, 96; ConNews 86-3; CurBio 80, 86, 86N; DcArts; DcCAr 81; EncWB; FacFETw; IntWW 74, 75, 76, 77, 78, 79, 80, 81, 82, 83; MakMC; NewYTBS 79, 86; OxCTwCA; OxDcArt; PhDcTCA 77; PrintW 85; WhoWor 82, 84; WorArt 1950*

Bevan, Aneurin
English. Political Leader, Orator
Labor party leader; introduced British socialized medicine system, 1948.
b. Nov 15, 1897 in Tredagar, Wales
d. Jul 6, 1960 in Chesham, England
Source: *BioIn 1, 2, 3, 4, 5, 6, 8, 10, 12, 14, 15, 16, 18, 19; ColdWar 1; ConAu 106; CurBio 43, 60; DcNaB 1951; DcPol; DcTwHis; EncWB; FacFETw; GrBr; HisDcKW; HisEWW; LinLib L, S; ObitT 1951; OxCLiW 86; OxCMed 86; WhDW; WorAl*

Bevan, Brian
Australian. Rugby Player
Rugby player, Warrington, 1946-62; Blackpool, 1962-64; once held try scoring record with career total of 796.
b. Apr 24, 1924 in Sydney, Australia
Source: *AnObit 1991; BioIn 18*

Beveridge, Albert Jeremiah
American. Politician, Historian
IN senator, 1899-1911, wrote 1920 Pulitzer-winning *Life of John Marshall.*
b. Oct 6, 1862 in Highland County, Ohio
d. Apr 27, 1927 in Indianapolis, Indiana
Source: *AmAu&B; AmBi; AmOrTwC; AmPolLe; ApCAB SUP, X; BiDrAC; BiDrUSC 89; BioIn 1, 2, 3, 4, 6, 9, 10, 13, 16; DcAmAu; DcAmB; DcAmDH 80, 89; DcNAA; EncAB-H 1974, 1996; HarEnUS; IndAu 1816; LinLib S; NatCAB 13; OhA&B; OxCAmH; OxCAmL 65; REn; REnAL; TwCA, SUP; TwCBDA; WebAB 74, 79; WhAm 1; WhAmP*

Beveridge, William Henry, Lord
English. Economist
Wrote "Beveridge Report," 1942, which became basis for British welfare legislation.
b. Mar 5, 1879 in Rangpur, British India
d. Mar 16, 1963 in Oxford, England
Source: *BioIn 12, 13, 15, 18; CurBio 43, 63; DcNaB 1961; DcTwHis; FacFETw; GrBr; HisEWW; LinLib L, S; McGEWB; NewCBEL; ObitOF 79; WhAm 4; WhE&EA; WhLit; WhoEc 81, 86; WhWW-II*

Bevilacqua, Anthony Joseph, Cardinal
American. Religious Leader
Replaced Cardinal John Krol as archbishop of Philadelphia, 1988—.
b. Jun 17, 1923 in New York, New York
Source: *WhoAm 84, 86, 95, 96, 97; WhoE 93, 95; WhoRel 77, 85, 92; WhoWor 95, 96, 97*

Bevin, Ernest
English. Labor Union Official, Government Official
Labor party leader who helped found NATO, 1940s.
b. Mar 9, 1881 in Winsford, England
d. Apr 14, 1951 in London, England
Source: *BioIn 1, 2, 3, 4, 5, 7, 8, 10, 12, 13, 19; ColdWar 1; CurBio 40, 49, 51; DcNaB 1951; DcPol; DcTwHis; EncCW; EncTR 91; GrBr; HisDcKW; HisEAAC; HisEWW; McGEWB; ObitT 1951; WhAm 3; WhDW; WhWW-II; WorAl; WorAlBi*

Bewick, Thomas
English. Illustrator, Engraver
Pioneered revival of wood engraving; noted for animal vignettes; illustrated *General History of Quadrupeds,* 1790.
b. Aug 12, 1753 in Cherryburn, England
d. Nov 8, 1828 in Gateshead, England
Source: *Alli; AntBDN B; BioIn 1, 2, 3, 4, 6, 8, 9, 10, 11, 12; BkIE; CamGLE; CarSB; CelCen; ChhPo, S1, S2, S3; DcArts; DcBiPP; DcBrBI; DcBrWA; DcLEL; DcNaB; LinLib L, S; McGDA; NewC; NewCBEL; OxCChiL; OxCEng 85, 95; OxDcArt; SmATA 16; Str&VC; WhDW; WhoChL*

Bey, Turhan
[Turhan Gilbert Selahettin Saultavey]
Turkish. Actor
Starred in Arabian Nights adventure films of 1940s.
b. Mar 30, 1920 in Vienna, Austria
Source: *BioIn 10, 21; FilmEn; FilmgC; ForYSC; HalFC 80, 84, 88; HolP 40; IntMPA 77, 80, 86, 92; LegTOT; MotPP; MovMk; WhoHol 92, A; WhoHrs 80*

Beymer, Richard
[George Richard Beymer]
American. Actor
Films include *The Diary of Anne Frank,* 1959; *West Side Story,* 1961.
b. Feb 21, 1939 in Avoca, Iowa
Source: *BioIn 10; ConTFT 9; FilmEn; FilmgC; ForYSC; HalFC 80, 84, 88; IntMPA 75, 76, 77, 78, 79, 80, 81, 82, 84, 86, 88, 92, 94, 96; ItaFilm; MotPP; What 4; WhoHol 92, A*

Bhaktivedanta, A(bhay) C(haranaravinda)
Indian. Religious Leader, Author
Founder, International Society for Krishna Consciousness (Hare Krishna), 1965; wrote over fifty books about Vedic culture.
b. Sep 1, 1896 in Calcutta, India
d. Nov 14, 1977 in Vrindavan, India
Source: *BioIn 11, 13; ConAu X; EncO&P 3; EncWB; WhAm 7; WhoAm 76; WorAlBi*

Bhave, Acharya Vinoba
[Vinayak Narahari Bhave]
Indian. Revolutionary
Disciple of Gandhi; crusaded for social reforms.
b. Sep 11, 1895 in Gagoda, India
d. Nov 15, 1982 in Paunar, India
Source: *AnObit 1982; BiDMoPL; CurBio 83; FarE&A 78, 79, 80, 81; IntWW 74, 75, 76, 77, 78, 79, 80, 81, 82; McGEWB; NewYTBS 82; WhDW; WhoWor 74*

Bhumibol, Adulyadej
[King Rama IX]
Thai. Ruler
King of Thailand, 1946—.
b. Dec 5, 1927 in Cambridge, Massachusetts
Source: *CurBio 50; DcTwHis; IntWW 83; WhoWor 84, 87*

Bhutto, Benazir
[Asif Zardari, Mrs.]
Pakistani. Political Leader
Prime minister of Pakistan, 1988-90, 1993-97; first female head of Moslem nation; daughter of Zulfikar Ali Bhutto.
b. Jun 21, 1953 in Karachi, Pakistan
Source: *BioIn 12; ConAu 131; ContDcW 89; CurBio 86; DcTwHis; FacFETw; IntDcWB; IntWW 89, 91, 93; LegTOT; News 89; NewYTBS 86, 88; Who 92, 94; WhoAsAP 91; WhoWomW 91; WhoWor 91, 93, 95, 96, 97; WomFir; WomStre; WomWR; WorAlBi; WrDr 94, 96*

Bhutto, Zulfikar Ali
Pakistani. Political Leader
Served as pres., prime minister, 1970s; overthrown, 1977, executed.
b. Jan 5, 1928 in Larkana, Pakistan
d. Apr 4, 1979 in Rawalpindi, Pakistan
Source: *BioIn 8, 9, 10, 16, 17, 18, 19, 20; ColdWar 2; ConAu 11NR, 53; CurBio 72, 79, 79N; DcNaB 1971; DcPol; DcTwHis; DicTyr; EncWB; FacFETw; IntWW 74, 75; NewYTBE 71, 72; NewYTBS 77, 79; Who 74; WhoAm 74, 76; WhoGov 72; WhoWor 74, 76; WorDWW*

Biafra, Jello
[Eric Boucher]
American. Singer
Formed, recorded and toured with the Dead Kennedys punk rock group, 1978-1986; founded record label Alternative Tentacles, 1980; recorded *Prairie Home Invasion,* 1994.
b. 1959 in Boulder, Colorado

Biaggi, Mario
American. Politician
Dem. representative from NY, 1969-88; resigned following racketeering conviction.
b. Oct 26, 1917 in New York, New York
Source: *AlmAP 78, 80, 82, 84, 88; AmCath 80; BiDrAC; BiDrUSC 89; BioIn 9, 14, 15, 16; CngDr 74, 77, 79, 81, 83, 85, 87; CopCroC; CurBio 86; IntWW 89, 91, 93; NewYTBE 71; NewYTBS 88; PolsAm 84; WhoAm 74, 76, 78, 80, 82, 84, 86, 88; WhoAmL 78, 79; WhoAmP 73, 75, 77, 79, 81, 83, 85, 87; WhoE 74, 75, 77, 79, 81, 83, 85, 86; WhoGov 72, 75, 77*

Bialik, Chaim Nachman
Israeli. Author, Poet
Greatest modern Hebrew poet; first work *In the City of Slaughter,* 1903.
b. Jan 9, 1873 in Rady, Russia
d. Jul 4, 1934 in Tel Aviv, Palestine
Source: *CasWL; EncWL 2; PenC CL; TwCLC 25; WorAu 1950*

Bialik, Mayim
American. Actor
Star of TV show "Blossom."
b. Dec 12, 1975
Source: *LegTOT; News 93-3*

Bianco, Margery Williams
American. Children's Author
Wrote popular "toy" stories for children: *Velveteen Rabbit,* 1922; *Poor Cecco,* 1925.
b. Jul 22, 1881 in London, England
d. Sep 4, 1944 in New York, New York
Source: *AmAu&B; AmWomWr; AnCL; AuBYP 2; BkCL; ChlLR 19; ConAu 109; DcLB 160; DcNAA; InWom SUP; JBA 34, 51; LinLib L; MajAI; NewC; NotAW; OxCChiL; SmATA 15; Str&VC; TwCChW 78, 83, 89; WhAm 6; WhoChL; WrChl*

Bias, Len
American. Basketball Player
First draft choice of Boston, 1986; died of cocaine overdose.
b. Nov 18, 1963 in Hyattsville, Maryland
d. Jun 19, 1986 in College Park, Maryland
Source: *AnObit 1986; BioIn 15, 16, 18; ConNews 86-3; NewYTBS 86*

Biba
[Barbara Hulanicki]
English. Designer
Founded British fashion business for men, women, 1970.
b. 1936, Poland
Source: *ConFash; EncFash; WorFshn*

Bibaud, Michel
Canadian. Historian
Wrote first major history of French Canada, *Histoire du Canada,* 1837; advocate of Anglo-French cooperation.
b. Jan 20, 1782 in Cote des Neiges, Quebec, Canada
d. Jul 3, 1857 in Montreal, Quebec, Canada
Source: *Alli; ApCAB; BbtC; BioIn 17; CanWr; DcCanB 8; DcLB 99; DcNAA;*

Drake; MacDCB 78; OxCCan, SUP; WebBD 83

Bibby, Thomas Geoffrey
English. Archaeologist
Developed carbon dating used in archaeology; wrote *4000 Years Ago,* 1961.
b. Oct 14, 1917 in Heversham, England
Source: *Au&Wr 71; ConAu 1R, 4NR; IntAu&W 77, 82; WhoWor 76*

Biberman, Herbert
[The Hollywood Ten]
American. Screenwriter, Producer, Director
Blacklisted by Hollywood studios when convicted of contempt of Congress, 1950; on his own, directed *Salt of the Earth,* 1954.
b. Mar 4, 1900 in Philadelphia, Pennsylvania
d. Jun 30, 1971 in New York, New York
Source: *ConAu 33R, P-1; DcFM; EncMcCE; FilmgC; NewYTBE 71; OxCFilm; WhAm 5; WorEFlm*

Bible, Alan
American. Politician
US Dem. senator, Nevada, 1954-74; helped create eighty-six national parks, monuments, historic sites.
b. Nov 20, 1909
d. Sep 12, 1988 in Auburn, California
Source: *BiDrUSC 89; BioIn 5, 9, 10, 11, 12, 16; BlueB 76; CngDr 74; CurBio 57, 88N; IntWW 74, 75; NewYTBS 88; PolProf E, J, K, NF; WhAm 9; WhoAm 74, 76; WhoAmP 73, 75, 77, 79; WhoGov 72, 75; WhoWest 74*

Bible, Frances Lillian
American. Opera Singer
Mezzo-soprano, soloist with major symphonies.
b. Jan 26, in Sackets Harbor, New York
Source: *NewEOp 71; WhoAm 80, 82, 84, 86, 88, 94, 95, 96, 97; WhoAmM 83; WhoAmW 85, 87, 89, 95, 97; WhoSSW 82, 84; WhoWest 94, 96; WhoWor 84, 87, 89, 95*

Bich, Marcel
French. Manufacturer
Invented first disposable pen, Bic, 1953; later introduced disposable cigarette lighters, razors.
b. Jul 29, 1914 in Turin, Italy
Source: *BioIn 9, 11, 12, 19, 20; Entr; IntWW 89, 91; NewYTBS 94; WhoAm 78, 80, 82, 84, 86; WhoFr 79; WhoWor 74, 76; WorAl; WorAlBi*

Bichat, Marie Francois Xavier
French. Scientist
Founded science of histology, the study of tissue.
b. Nov 11, 1771 in Thoirette, France
d. Jul 22, 1802 in Paris, France
Source: *AsBiEn; BiDPsy; BiESc; BiHiMed; BioIn 5, 9, 12; CelCen; DcBiPP; DcScB; InSci; LarDcSc; McGEWB; NamesHP; OxCMed 86; WhDW*

Bichler, Joyce
American. Victim, Author
Sued Eli Lilly & Co., major producer of drug, DES, 1979; awarded $500,000; wrote *DES Daughter,* 1981.
b. Jan 19, 1954 in New York, New York
Source: *ConAu 107*

Bickerdyke, Mary Ann Ball
"Mother Bickerdyke"
American. Nurse
Volunteer nurse; established hospitals for Union soldiers, Civil War.
b. Jul 19, 1817 in Knox County, Ohio
d. Nov 8, 1901 in Bunker Hill, Kansas
Source: *AmWom; BioIn 16, 18; CivWDc; DcAmB; InWom SUP; LibW; NatCAB 21; NotAW; WebAMB; WhAm HS; WhCiWar*

Bickerman, Elias Joseph
American. Historian
Award-winning expert on Greek, Middle-East history: *Chronology of Ancient World,* 1968.
b. Jul 1, 1897, Russia
d. 1981 in Tel Aviv, Israel
Source: *BioIn 12; ConAu 104; DrAS 74H, 78H; WhAm 8; WhoAm 74, 76, 78, 80, 82; WhoAmJ 80; WhoWorJ 72; WrDr 76*

Bickford, Charles Ambrose
American. Actor
Three-time Oscar nominee; starred in TV's "The Virginian," 1966-67.
b. Jan 1, 1889 in Cambridge, Massachusetts
d. Nov 9, 1967 in Boston, Massachusetts
Source: *BiDFilm; BiE&WWA; FilmgC; HolP 30; MotPP; MovMk; ObitOF 79; OxCFilm; WhoHol B; WhScrn 74, 77; WhThe; WorAl; WorEFlm*

Bickmore, Lee Smith
American. Business Executive
Chairman, National Biscuit Co. (Nabisco brands), 1968.
b. Jun 5, 1908 in Paradise, Utah
d. Jun 7, 1986 in Vero Beach, Florida
Source: *BioIn 7, 8, 11, 15; BlueB 76; IntWW 74, 75, 76, 77, 78, 79, 80, 81, 82, 83; St&PR 84; WhAm 9; WhoAm 74, 76, 78; WhoE 74; WhoFI 75; WhoWor 74*

Bidault, Georges
French. Politician
Held various posts in French govt. after WW II; known as skilled negotiator.
b. Oct 5, 1899 in Moulins, France
d. Jan 27, 1983 in Cambo-les-Bains, France
Source: *AnObit 1983; BioIn 1, 3, 6, 7, 8, 13, 17; ConAu 109; CurBio 45, 83, 83N; DcPol; DcTwHis; EncCW; FacFETw; HisEWW; IntWW 74, 75, 76, 77, 78, 79, 80, 81, 82; LinLib S; NewYTBS 83; Who 74, 82, 83; WhoFr 79*

Biddle, Anthony Joseph
American. Statesman
US ambassador to European governments in exile during WW II.
b. Dec 17, 1896 in Philadelphia, Pennsylvania
d. Nov 13, 1961 in Washington, District of Columbia
Source: *CurBio 41, 62*

Biddle, Francis Beverley
American. Lawyer, Government Official
First chair of National Labor Relations Board, 1934; attorney general, 1941-45; judge at Nuremberg trials.
b. May 9, 1886 in Paris, France
d. Oct 4, 1968 in Hyannis, Massachusetts
Source: *AmAu&B; BiDFedJ; BiDrUSE 71, 89; ConAu 5R, 103; CurBio 41, 68; DcAmB S8; PolProf T; WhAm 5, 7*

Biddle, George
American. Artist, Author
Leader of Federal Arts Project during Depression; known for portraits, murals.
b. Jan 24, 1885 in Philadelphia, Pennsylvania
d. Nov 6, 1973 in Croton-on-Hudson, New York
Source: *AmAu&B; ArtsAmW 1, 3; BioIn 1, 2, 5, 6, 8, 10, 12, 20; BriEAA; ConAu 45; CurBio 42, 74, 74N; DcAmArt; DcAmB S9; DcCAA 71, 77, 88, 94; IlBEAAW; McGDA; NatCAB 58; NewYTBE 73; WhAm 6; WhAmArt 85; WhE&EA; WhNAA; WhoAm 74; WhoAmA 73, 76N, 78N, 80N, 82N, 84N, 86N, 89N, 91N, 93N*

Biddle, John
English. Philosopher
Founded English Unitarianism; imprisoned for disputing Trinity in *Twelve Arguments,* tract, 1645.
b. 1615 in Wotton-under-Edge, England
d. Sep 22, 1662 in London, England
Source: *Alli; DcBiPP; DcEnL; DcNaB; LinLib S; LuthC 75; NewCol 75; WhDW; WorAl; WorAlBi*

Biddle, Nicholas
American. Scholar, Banker
Pres., Bank of US, 1823-39; edited literary periodical *Portfolio.*
b. Jan 8, 1786 in Philadelphia, Pennsylvania
d. Feb 27, 1844 in Philadelphia, Pennsylvania
Source: *Alli; AmAu; AmAu&B; AmBi; AmPolLe; ApCAB; BiAUS; BiDAmBL 83; BiD&SB; BioIn 3, 5, 7, 9, 10, 11, 14, 19, 21; CyAL 1; DcAmAu; DcAmB; DcNAA; Drake; EncAB-H 1974, 1996; EncABHB 6; HarEnUS; LegTOT; McGEWB; NatCAB 6; OxCAmH; OxCAmL 65, 83, 95; REn; TwCBDA; WebAB 74, 79; WhAm HS; WhAmP; WorAl; WorAlBi*

Biden, Joe
[Joseph Robinette Biden, Jr]
American. Politician
Dem. senator from DE, 1973—; early presidential candidate, 1988.
b. Nov 20, 1942 in Scranton, Pennsylvania
Source: *AlmAP 84; BiDrUSC 89; BlueB 76; CngDr 74, 77, 79, 81, 83, 85, 87; ConNews 86-3; CurBio 87; IntWW 74, 75, 76, 77, 78, 79, 80, 81, 82, 83, 89, 91, 93; WhoAm 74, 76, 78, 80, 82, 84, 86, 88, 90, 92, 94, 95, 96, 97; WhoAmP 73, 75, 77, 79, 81, 83, 85, 87, 89, 91, 93, 95; WhoE 77, 79, 81, 83, 85, 86, 89, 91, 93, 95, 97; WhoEmL 87; WhoGov 75, 77; WhoWor 80, 82, 84, 87, 89, 91*

Bidwell, Charles W
American. Football Executive
Owner-president, Chicago Cardinals pro team, 1933-47; Hall of Fame, 1967.
b. Sep 16, 1895 in Chicago, Illinois
d. Apr 19, 1947 in Chicago, Illinois
Source: *WhoFtbl 74*

Bieber, Owen Frederick
American. Labor Union Official
President of UAW, 1983—.
b. Dec 28, 1929 in North Dorr, Michigan
Source: *BiDAmL; BusPN; ConNews 86-1; CurBio 86; EncABHB 5; NewYTBS 83; WhoAm 84, 86*

Biebuyck, Daniel Prosper
Belgian. Anthropologist
Wrote on African tribes: *African Agrarian Systems,* 1965.
b. Oct 1, 1925 in Deinze, Belgium
Source: *AmMWSc 73S; ConAu 11NR; WhoAm 74, 76, 78, 80, 82, 84, 86, 88, 90, 92, 94, 95, 96, 97; WhoSSW 95; WrDr 86*

Biellmann, Denise
Swiss. Skater
World champion figure skater, 1981.
b. 1964?
Source: *BioIn 12*

Bierce, Ambrose Gwinett
[Dod Grile]
American. Journalist
Newspaper, fiction writer; disappeared in Mexico covering revolution led by Pancho Villa.
b. Jun 24, 1842 in Meigs County, Ohio
d. 1914?, Mexico
Source: *AmAu; AmBi; AmWr; ApCAB SUP; AtlBL; CasWL; Chambr 3; CnDAL; CrtT 3; CyWA 58; DcAmB; DcLEL; DcNAA; EncAB-H 1974; EncMys; EvLB; ModAL, S1; OhA&B; OxCAmL 65; OxCEng 67; PenC AM; RAdv 1; REn; REnAL; WebAB 74; WebE&AL; WhAm 4, HSA*

Bierstadt, Albert
American. Artist
Landscape painter; best known works depict Far West.
b. Jan 7, 1830 in Dusseldorf, Germany
d. Feb 18, 1902 in New York, New York
Source: *AmBi; AmCulL; ApCAB; ArtsAmW 1; BioIn 1, 3, 4, 5, 7, 9, 10, 12, 13, 14, 15, 16, 17, 18, 19; BriEAA; CelCen; CmCal; DcAmArt; DcAmB; DcArts; DcSeaP; Drake; EarABI; EncAAH; EncAB-H 1974, 1996; HarEnUS; IlBEAAW; IntDcAA 90; McGDA; McGEWB; NatCAB 11; NewYHSD; OxCAmH; OxCAmL 65; OxCShps; OxDcArt; REnAW; TwCBDA; WebAB 74, 79; WhAm 1; WhAmArt 85; WhCiWar; WhNaAH; WorAlBi*

Bierut, Boleslaw
Polish. Political Leader
Prime minister, Poland, 1952-53; chm., Polish United Workers Party, 1948-1952.
b. Apr 18, 1892 in Rury Jezuickie, Poland
d. Mar 12, 1956 in Moscow, Union of Soviet Socialist Republics
Source: *BioIn 1, 2, 4, 18; ColdWar 2; CurBio 56; DcTwHis; EncRev; EncTR 91; ObitOF 79; PolBiDi*

Bigard, Albany Barney Leon
American. Jazz Musician
Jazz clarinetist; played with King Oliver, Louis Armstrong, Duke Ellington; co-wrote "Mood Indigo," 1931.
b. Mar 3, 1906 in New Orleans, Louisiana
d. Jun 27, 1980 in Culver City, California
Source: *BioIn 10; CmpEPM; EncJzS; IlEncJ; WhAm 7; WhoAm 74, 76, 78, 80; WhoBlA 75, 77, 80; WhoJazz 72*

Big Bopper, The
[J P Richardson]
American. Radio Performer, Singer
Disc jockey/pop star; had rockabilly hit, "Chantilly Lace," 1958; killed with Buddy Holly, Richie Valens in plane crash.
b. Oct 24, 1930 in Sabine Pass, Texas
d. Feb 3, 1959 in Clear Lake, Iowa
Source: *BiDAmM; ConMuA 80A; EncRkSt; LegTOT; PenEncP; RkOn 74; RolSEnR 83*

Big Brother and the Holding Company
[Peter Albin; Sam Andrew; David Getz; James Gurley; Janis Joplin]
American. Music Group
Blues band featuring vocals by Janis Joplin; album *Cheap Thrills* had hit single "Piece of My Heart," 1968.
Source: *BiDAmM; BiDJaz A; BioNews 74; ConMuA 80A; CurBio 70; EncPR&S 74, 89; EncRk 88; IlEncRk; NewGrDA 86; NewYTBE 70; ObitOF 79; RkOn 78; RolSEnR 83; WhAm 5; WhoHol 92; WhoRock 81; WhoRocM 82*

Big Country
[Stuart Adamson; Mark Brzezick; Tony Butler; Bruce Watson]
English. Music Group
Scottish band; debut album, *The Crossing,* had hit single "In a Big Country," 1983.
Source: *BioIn 8, 13, 15; EncRk 88; EncRkSt; HarEnR 86; PenEncP; RkOn 85; WhoRocM 82*

Bigelow, Erastus Brigham
American. Inventor, Manufacturer
Invented power loom, 1837; founded Clinton Co., 1838, to build looms.
b. Apr 2, 1814 in West Boylston, Massachusetts
d. Dec 6, 1879 in Boston, Massachusetts
Source: *Alli SUP; ApCAB; DcAmAu; DcAmB; DcBiPP; DcNAA; Drake; InSci; NatCAB 3; TwCBDA; WebAB 74, 79; WhAm HS; WorAl; WorInv*

Bigelow, Henry Bryant
American. Zoologist
Harvard U zoology professor, 1905-50; wrote on oceanography.
b. Oct 3, 1879 in Boston, Massachusetts
d. Dec 11, 1967 in Concord, Massachusetts
Source: *BioIn 5, 8, 11; DcAmB S8; InSci; WhAm 4A; WhNAA*

Bigelow, Kathryn
American. Director
Works include cult classic *Near Dark,* 1987; thriller *Blue Steel,* 1989.
b. 1952
Source: *ConAu 139; News 90; WrDr 96*

Big Foot
[Si Tanka; Spotted Elk]
American. Native American Leader
Chief of the Minniconjou, 1874-1890.
b. 1825?
d. Dec 29, 1890
Source: *NotNaAm; WhNaAH*

Biggers, Earl Derr
American. Author
Created Chinese fictional detective Charlie Chan; first appeared in *House Without a Key,* 1925.
b. Aug 26, 1884 in Warren, Ohio
d. Apr 5, 1933 in Pasadena, California
Source: *AmAu&B; BenetAL 91; BioIn 11, 14; ChhPo S1; CmCal; ConAu 108, 153; CorpD; CrtSuMy; DcAmB S1; DcNAA; EncMys; EvLB; FilmgC; HalFC 80, 84, 88; LegTOT; MnBBF; NotNAT B; Novels; OhA&B; OxCAmL 65, 83, 95; PenC AM; REn; REnAL; TwCA; TwCCr&M 80, 85, 91; TwCLC 65; TwCWr; WhAm 1; WhFla; WhLit; WhNAA; WhThe; WorAl; WorAlBi*

Biggs, Edward George Power
American. Organist
Concert, recording artist; noted for weekly radio organ recitals, 1942-58.
b. Mar 29, 1906 in Westcliff, England

d. Mar 10, 1977 in Boston, Massachusetts
Source: *Baker 84; BioIn 1, 2, 3, 4, 5, 11; DcAmB S10; IntWW 74, 75, 76, 77; IntWWM 77, 80; WhAm 7; WhoAm 74, 76; WhoMus 72*

Biggs, Ronald Arthur
"The Great Train Robber"
English. Criminal
With 14 others, stole $7.3 million from mail train, 1963; escaped prison, 1965.
b. Aug 8, 1929? in Brixton, England
Source: *BioIn 8, 9, 10, 12*

Bignone, Reynaldo Benito Antonio
Argentine. Political Leader
Mild-mannered general thrust into presidency, 1981, to lead Argentine civilian government.
b. Jan 21, 1928 in Moron, Argentina
Source: *BioIn 13; IntWW 83; NewYTBS 82; WhoWor 82*

Bijan
Iranian. Fashion Designer
Designs exceptionally expensive men's apparel and perfumes.
b. Apr 4, 1940 in Tehran, Iran
Source: *BioIn 13, 14, 15; CelR 90; NewYTBS 85*

Bijedic, Dzemal
Yugoslav. Political Leader
Prime minister, 1971-77; killed in plane crash.
b. Apr 12, 1917 in Mostar, Yugoslavia
d. Jan 18, 1977, Yugoslavia
Source: *BioIn 11; IntWW 74, 75, 76, 77N; NewYTBS 77; WhoSocC 78; WhoSoCE 89*

Bikel, Theodore Meir
American. Actor, Singer
Made film debut in *African Queen,* 1952; Oscar nominee for *The Defiant Ones,* 1958.
b. May 2, 1924 in Vienna, Austria
Source: *BioNews 74; ConAu 1NR, 1R; ConTFT 5; CurBio 60; EncFCWM 83; FilmEn; FilmgC; MotPP; MovMk; NotNAT; WhoAm 86; WhoHol A; WhoThe 81; WhoWor 74*

Biko, Steven
South African. Political Activist
A leader of Black Consciousness Movement; died while in custody of S African security police; subject of 1987 film *Cry Freedom.*
b. Dec 18, 1946 in King William's Town, South Africa
d. Sep 12, 1977 in Port Elizabeth, South Africa
Source: *BioIn 11, 13; ConBlB 4; HeroCon*

Bikoff, James L
American. Businessman, Lawyer
Founded International Anticounterfeiting Coalition (IACC), 1978; pres., 1982-86, estimates counterfeiting is $60 million business.
b. May 26, 1940 in New York, New York
Source: *ConNews 86-2*

Bilandic, Michael Anthony
American. Lawyer, Politician
Succeeded Richard Daley as mayor of Chicago, 1976; lost re-election to Jane Byrne, 1979.
b. Feb 13, 1923 in Chicago, Illinois
Source: *BioIn 11, 12; CurBio 79; NewYTBS 77; WhoAm 80, 82; WhoAmL 79; WhoGov 77*

Bilbo, Theodore Gilmore
American. Politician
Dem. senator from MS, 1934-47; investigated by Senate, 1946, for anti-Negro campaigns.
b. Oct 13, 1877 in Poplarville, Mississippi
d. Aug 21, 1947 in New Orleans, Louisiana
Source: *BiDrAC; BiDrGov 1789; BiDrUSC 89; BioIn 1, 2, 3, 6; CurBio 43, 47; DcAmB S4; EncSoH; LiveMA; WebAB 74, 79; WhAm 2; WhAmP*

Bildt, Carl
Swedish. Political Leader
Prime minister, 1991-94; moderate whose election upset 59-year rule of Social Democratic party.
b. Jul 15, 1949 in Halmstad, Sweden
Source: *CurBio 93; IntWW 89, 91, 93; WhoWor 93, 95*

Biletnikoff, Fred(erick)
American. Football Player
End, Oakland, 1965-73; led NFL in receptions, 1968; MVP, 1977 Super Bowl; Hall of Fame, 1988.
b. Feb 23, 1943 in Erie, Pennsylvania
Source: *BiDAmSp FB; BioIn 9, 11, 12; LegTOT; WhoAm 74; WhoFtbl 74; WhoSpor*

Bilibin, Ivan Iakolevich
Russian. Illustrator
Leading Russian artist of children's books.
b. Aug 16, 1876 in Tarkhovka, Russia
d. Feb 7, 1942 in Leningrad, Union of Soviet Socialist Republics
Source: *BioIn 13; WorECar*

Bill, Max
Swiss. Artist, Architect
Known for his advertisement designs.
b. Dec 22, 1908 in Winterthur, Switzerland
Source: *BioIn 5, 10, 11, 14, 15, 16, 18, 20, 21; ClaDrA; ConArch 80, 87, 94; ConArt 77, 83, 89, 96; ConDes 84, 90, 97; DcCAr 81; DcTwDes; EncMA; FacFETw; IntAu&W 77, 89; IntWW 74, 75, 76, 77, 78, 79, 80, 81, 82, 83, 89, 91, 93; MacEA; McGDA; NewYTBS 94; OxCTwCA; OxDcArt; PenDiDA 89; PhDcTCA 77; PrintW 85; WhAm 11; WhoArt 80, 82, 84; WhoGrA 62; WhoWor 74, 82, 84, 87, 89, 91, 93, 95; WorArt 1950*

Bill, Tony
American. Actor, Director, Producer
Directed *My Bodyguard,* 1980; won Oscar, 1973, for co-producing *The Sting.*
b. Aug 23, 1940 in San Diego, California
Source: *ConTFT 6; FilmEn; FilmgC; HalFC 80, 84, 88; IntMPA 77, 86, 92, 94, 96; LegTOT; MiSFD 9; VarWW 85; WhoAm 78, 80, 82, 84, 86, 88, 90, 92, 94, 95, 96, 97; WhoEnt 92; WhoHol 92, A*

Biller, Moe
[Morris Biller]
American. Labor Union Official
Irascible president of American Postal Workers Union, 1980—.
b. Nov 5, 1915 in New York, New York
Source: *BioIn 15; CurBio 87; WhoAm 84, 86, 88, 90, 92, 94, 95, 96, 97; WhoE 86, 91; WhoFI 83, 85, 87, 89*

Billings, Grace Bedell
American. Student
Wrote letter to Abraham Lincoln suggesting he grow beard; Lincoln grew one, wore it from then on.
Source: *GoodHs; InWom SUP*

Billings, John Shaw
American. Editor
Editorial director, Time Inc., 1944-54.
b. May 11, 1898 in Beech Island, South Carolina
d. Aug 25, 1975 in Augusta, Georgia
Source: *BioIn 3, 10, 20; ConAu 104; DcLB 137; WhAm 6*

Billings, Josh
[Henry Wheeler Shaw]
American. Author
Wrote bucolic aphorisms phrased in grotesque misspellings: *Josh Billings' Farmer's Allminax,* 1869-80.
b. Apr 21, 1818 in Lanesboro, Massachusetts
d. Oct 14, 1885 in Monterey, California
Source: *Alli, SUP; AmAu; AmAu&B; AmBi; ApCAB; BbD; Benet 87, 96; BenetAL 91; BibAL; BiDAmNC; BiD&SB; BioIn 3, 10, 11, 12, 13; CamGEL; CamGLE; CamHAL; CasWL; Chambr 3; ChhPo S1; CnDAL; DcAmAu; DcAmB; DcEnL; DcLB 11; DcLEL; DcNAA; Drake; EncAAH; EvLB; GrWrEL N; HarEnUS; LegTOT; LinLib L, S; NatCAB 6; NinCLC 15; OhA&B; OxCAmL 65, 83, 95; OxCEng 67, 85, 95; PenC AM; REn; REnAL; RfGAmL 87, 94; TwCBDA; WebAB 74, 79; WhAm HS*

Billingsley, Barbara
American. Actor
Played June Cleaver on TV series "Leave It to Beaver," 1957-63.
b. Dec 22, 1922 in Los Angeles, California
Source: *LegTOT*

Billingsley, Ray
American. Cartoonist
Nationally syndicated strip "Curtis," depicts inner-city life of African-American boy.
b. Jul 25, 1957 in Wake Forest, North Carolina
Source: *BioIn 16; DcTwCCu 5; WhoBlA 92*

Billingsley, Sherman
American. Business Executive
Owned Stork Club, 1929-65; hosted "The Stork Club" TV show, 1950-53.
b. Mar 10, 1900 in Enid, Oklahoma
d. Oct 4, 1966 in New York, New York
Source: *BioIn 1, 7, 9; CurBio 46, 66; ObitOF 79; WhAm 4*

Billington, Elizabeth
English. Opera Singer
Star soprano at Covent Garden, Drury Lane, 1790-1801; favorite of Prince of Wales.
b. 1768? in London, England
d. Aug 25, 1818 in Venice, Italy
Source: *Baker 84; BioIn 3, 7, 14, 15; DcNaB*

Billington, James H(adley)
American. Historian, Librarian
Librarian of Congress, 1987—; director Woodrow Wilson Int'l. Center for Scholars at the Smithsonian Institution, 1973-87; Russian Scholar who wrote *The Icon and the Axe.*
b. Jun 1, 1929 in Bryn Mawr, Pennsylvania
Source: *BioIn 11, 15, 16; ConAu 117, 132; CurBio 89; DrAS 82H; IntWW 89, 91, 93; NewYTBS 87; Who 92, 94; WhoAm 74, 76, 78, 88, 90, 92, 94, 95, 96, 97; WhoE 89, 91, 93, 95, 97; WhoWor 74, 76, 91, 93, 95, 96, 97; WorAlBi; WrDr 94, 96*

Billington, John
American. Murderer
One of pilgrims who arrived on the Mayflower; first murderer in US.
d. 1630
Source: *BiDBrA; ConAu X; DrInf; NotNAT B*

Billington, Ray Allen
American. Historian, Educator
Authority on American West; wrote prize-winning *Frederick Jackson Turner,* 1974.
b. Sep 28, 1903 in Bay City, Michigan
d. Mar 7, 1981 in San Marino, California
Source: *AmAu&B; Au&Wr 71; BioIn 12, 13; BlueB 76; CmCal; ConAu 1R, 5NR, 103; DrAS 74H, 78H, 82H; EncAAH; IntAu&W 76, 77, 82; PeoHis; REnAW; WhAm 7; Who 74; WhoAm 74, 76, 78, 80; WhoWor 74, 76; WrDr 84*

Billroth, Theodore
[Christian Albert Theodore Billroth]
German. Surgeon
Introduced procedure for total laryngectomy, 1873.
b. Apr 26, 1829 in Bergen, Prussia
d. Feb 6, 1894 in Abbazia, Austria
Source: *Baker 78; BiHiMed; DcScB*

Billy the Kid
[William H Bonney]
American. Outlaw
Had career of killing and cattle rustling; fatally shot by Sheriff Pat Garrett.
b. Nov 23, 1859 in New York, New York
d. Jul 14, 1881 in Fort Sumner, New Mexico
Source: *BenetAL 91; BioIn 1, 2, 3, 4, 5, 6, 7, 8, 9, 10, 11, 12, 13; DcAmB; DrInf; LegTOT; McGEWB; NewCol 75; OxCAmH; OxCAmL 83; OxCChiL; OxCFilm; REnAL; REnAW; WebAB 74, 79; WhAm HS; WhDW; WorAl; WorAlBi*

Bilon, Michael Patrick
American. Actor
Played title role in *ET,* 1982; was 2 feet, 10 inches tall.
b. 1947? in Youngstown, Ohio
d. Jan 27, 1983 in Youngstown, Ohio
Source: *BioIn 13*

Binchy, Maeve
Irish. Author
Wrote *Circle of Friends,* 1990; became a film in 1995.
b. May 28, 1940 in Dublin, Ireland
Source: *BestSel 90-1; BiDIrW; BlmGWL; ConAu 50NR, 127, 134; ConNov 91, 96; ConPopW; CurBio 95; DcIrL 96; FemiCLE; IntWW 93; OxCIri; TwCRHW 90, 94; Who 94; WhoWor 95, 96; WorAu 1985; WrDr 90, 92, 94, 96*

Binet, Alfred
French. Psychologist
Developed early standard tests for intelligence, 1905.
b. Jul 8, 1857 in Nice, France
d. Oct 8, 1911 in Paris, France
Source: *AsBiEn; BiDPsy; BioIn 4, 7, 10, 13, 14, 18; DcAmImH; DcScB; FacFETw; GaEncPs; InSci; LegTOT; LinLib L, S; McGEWB; NamesHP; OxCMed 86; RAdv 14, 13-3; ThTwC 87; WhDW; WorAl; WorAlBi*

Bing, Dave
[David Bing]
American. Basketball Player, Businessman
Guard, 1966-78, mostly with Detroit; inducted into Basketball Hall of Fame, 1990; owner, pres., Bing Steel, Inc., 1980—.
b. Nov 29, 1943 in Washington, District of Columbia
Source: *AfrAmAl 6; BasBi; BiDAmSp BK; BioIn 10, 11; ConBlB 3; ConEn; InB&W 80, 85; LegTOT; OfNBA 87; WhoAfA 96; WhoBbl 73; WhoBlA 75, 77, 80, 85, 88, 90, 92, 94; WhoSpor; WorAl; WorAlBi*

Bing, Rudolf (Franz Josef), Sir
Austrian. Manager
General manager, NY Met., 1950-72; noted for controversial dealings with prima donnas.
b. Jan 9, 1902 in Vienna, Austria
Source: *Baker 78, 84; BioIn 2, 3, 4, 5, 6, 7, 8, 9, 10, 13, 15, 16, 17, 19; BlueB 76; CelR; ConAu 89; CurBio 50; IntWW 74, 75, 76, 77, 78, 79, 80, 81, 82, 83, 89, 91, 93; IntWWM 77, 80, 85; LegTOT; LinLib S; MetOEnc; NewAmDM; NewEOp 71; NewGrDA 86; NewGrDM 80; NewGrDO; NewYTBE 71, 72, 73; NewYTBS 90; OxDcOp; REn; Who 74, 82, 83, 85, 88, 90, 92; WhoAm 74, 76, 78, 80, 82, 84; WhoMus 72; WhoOp 76; WhoWor 74, 78, 80, 82, 84*

Bingaman, Jeff
American. Politician
Dem. senator from NM, 1983—.
b. Oct 3, 1943 in El Paso, Texas
Source: *AlmAP 84, 88, 92, 96; BioIn 13; CngDr 83, 85, 87, 89, 91, 93, 95; IntWW 83, 89, 91, 93; PolsAm 84; WhoAm 80, 82, 84, 86, 88, 90, 92, 94, 95, 96, 97; WhoAmL 79; WhoAmP 83, 85, 87, 89, 91, 93, 95; WhoWest 80, 82, 84, 87, 89, 92, 94, 96; WhoWor 84, 87, 89, 91*

Bingham, Barry
[George Barry Bingham]
American. Newspaper Publisher, Editor
Louisville, KY, *Courier-Journal, Times.*
b. Feb 10, 1906
d. Aug 15, 1988 in Louisville, Kentucky
Source: *BiDAmJo; BioIn 2, 4, 7, 15, 16, 17, 19; BlueB 76; ConAu 126; CurBio 88N; Dun&B 88; IntMPA 75, 76; IntWW 74; IntYB 78, 79, 80, 81, 82; NewYTBS 88; WhAm 9; WhoAm 74, 76, 78, 80, 82, 84, 86; WhoSSW 73, 75, 76, 78, 80, 82, 86; WhoWor 74*

Bingham, George Caleb
American. Artist
Portrait, genre painter of old-time Missouri life: *Jolly Flatboatman,* 1846.
b. Mar 20, 1811 in Augusta County, Virginia
d. Jul 7, 1879 in Kansas City, Missouri
Source: *AmCulL; ArtsAmW 1; AtlBL; BenetAL 91; BioIn 1, 3, 4, 5, 6, 7, 8, 9, 10, 11, 12, 14, 19; BriEAA; DcAmArt; DcAmB; DcArts; EncAAH; EncAB-H 1974, 1996; IlBEAAW; IntDcAA 90; McGDA; McGEWB; NewYHSD; OxCAmH; OxCAmL 65; OxCArt; OxDcArt; REn; REnAW; WebAB 74, 79; WhAm HS; WhAmP; WorAl; WorAlBi*

Bingham, Hiram
American. Explorer, Statesman
Discovered ruins of last Inca capital, Machu Picchu, Peru, 1911.

b. Nov 19, 1875 in Honolulu, Hawaii
d. Jun 6, 1956 in Washington, District of Columbia
Source: *Alli SUP; AmAu&B; AmLY; ApCAB X; BenetAL 91; BiDrAC; BiDrGov 1789; BiDrUSC 89; BioIn 1, 2, 4, 8, 18, 19, 20; CurBio 51, 56; DcAmB S6; Expl 93; FacFETw; InSci; OxCAmH; REnAL; WhAm 3; WhAmP; WhDW; WhLit; WhNAA; WorAlBi*

Bingham, Jonathan Brewster
American. Politician
Member US mission to UN, 1961-64; Dem. con. from NY, 1965-83.
b. Apr 24, 1914 in New Haven, Connecticut
d. Jul 3, 1986 in New York, New York
Source: *BiDrAC; BiDrUSC 89; BioIn 3, 5; CngDr 81; ConAu 33R, 119; CurBio 54, 86; IntWW 74, 75, 76, 77, 78, 79, 80, 81, 82; IntWWM 77; NewYTBS 86; WhAm 9; WhoAm 74, 76, 78, 80, 82, 84, 86; WhoAmP 85; WhoE 74; WhoGov 72, 75, 77*

Binnig, Gerd
German. Physicist
Shared Nobel Prize for Physics, 1986; with Rahrer, designed and built the first scanning tunneling microscope.
b. Jul 20, 1947 in Frankfurt am Main, Germany (West)
Source: *AmMWSc 89, 92, 95; IntWW 89, 91, 93; NobelP; NotTwCS; RAdv 14; Who 92; WhoAm 90; WhoNob 90; WhoScEu 91-4; WhoWor 91; WorAlBi*

Binns, Archie Fred
American. Author
Publishing company editor; wrote *Sea Pup, Again,* 1965.
b. Jul 30, 1899 in Port Ludlow, Washington
d. Jun 28, 1971
Source: *AmAu&B; ConAu 73; OxCAmL 65; REnAL; TwCA, SUP; WhAm 5; WhoPNW*

Binns, Joseph Patterson
American. Hotel Executive
VP, Hilton Hotels, 1946-62; managed Waldorf-Astoria, NYC, 1949-61.
b. Jun 28, 1905 in Winona, Ohio
d. Nov 23, 1980 in Indian Creek Island, Florida
Source: *BioIn 3, 6; CurBio 54, 81, 81N; WhAm 7*

Binswanger, Ludwig
Swiss. Psychiatrist
Proponent of Daseinsanalysis, psychotherapeutic technique based on existentialism.
b. Apr 13, 1881 in Kreuzlingen, Switzerland
d. Feb 5, 1966 in Kreuzlingen, Switzerland
Source: *BiDPsy; ConAu 107; NamesHP; RAdv 14, 13-5; WhoWor 74*

Binyon, Laurence
English. Poet, Critic, Orientalist
Wrote blank verse drama, Dante translations, works about oriental art.
b. Aug 10, 1869 in Lancaster, England
d. Mar 10, 1943 in Streatley, England
Source: *BioIn 1, 4, 5, 13, 14; CamGEL; CamGLE; CasWL; Chambr 3; ChhPo, S1, S2, S3; CnE&AP; ConAu 115; DcArts; DcLB 19; DcNaB 1941; EngPo; GrWrEL P; LngCTC; ModBrL; NewC; OxCEng 67, 85; OxCThe 67; REn; RfGEnL 91; TwCA, SUP; TwCWr; WebE&AL; WhE&EA; WhLit; WhoLA; WhThe*

Biondi, Frank J., Jr.
American. TV Executive
Pres. of Home Box Office (HBO) 1983; chm. and CEO 1984-7; pres. and CEO, Viacom International Inc., NYC, 1987-96.
b. Jan 9, 1945 in Livingston, New Jersey
Source: *IntMPA 84, 86, 88, 92, 94, 96; St&PR 93, 96, 97; WhoAm 84, 88, 90, 92, 94, 95, 96, 97; WhoE 91, 95, 97; WhoEnt 92; WhoFI 89, 92, 94, 96; WhoTelC*

Biondi, Matt
American. Swimmer
Winner of 9 medals, including 6 gold, 2 silver, 1 bronze, in 1988, 1992 Olympics.
b. Oct 8, 1965 in Palo Alto, California
Source: *BioIn 14, 15, 16; CelR 90; LegTOT; NewYTBS 86; WorAlBi*

Biossat, Bruce
American. Journalist
Political reporter for Newspaper Enterprise Associates; articles published in 400 newpapers.
b. 1910
d. May 27, 1974 in Washington, District of Columbia
Source: *BioIn 10; ConAu 104; WhAm 6*

Bioy Casares, Adolfo
[Javier Miranda; Martin Sacastru]
Argentine. Author
Writes metaphysical narratives: *Prologo,* 1929; *La Invencion de Morel,* 1940.
b. Sep 15, 1914 in Buenos Aires, Argentina
Source: *Benet 96; BioIn 12, 16, 17, 18, 20; ConAu 19NR, 29R, 43NR; ConLC 4, 8, 13, 88; ConWorW 93; CyWA 89; DcCLAA; DcHiB; DcLB 113; DcTwCCu 3; EncLatA; EncSF, 93; EncWL 2, 3; HispLC; HispWr; IntAu&W 77, 82; IntWW 91, 93; LatAmWr; MajTwCW; ModLAL; OxCSpan; PenC AM; RAdv 14, 13-2; RfGShF; ScF&FL 1, 2, 92; ShSCr 17; SpAmA; WhoWor 74, 76; WorAu 1975*

Birch, John
American. Spy
US intelligence officer killed by Communist Chinese; name adopted by ultraconservative anticommunist group, The John Birch Society.
b. May 28, 1918 in Landour, India
d. Aug 25, 1945 in Shuzhou, China
Source: *BioIn 5; EncAI&E; LegTOT; WorAl*

Birch, Stephen
American. Business Executive
President of Kennecott Copper Corp., 1915-33.
b. Mar 24, 1872 in New York, New York
d. Dec 29, 1940
Source: *BiDAmBL 83; BioIn 4; EncAB-A 14; NatCAB 15, 41; ObitOF 79; WhAm 1; WorAl; WorAlBi*

Bird, Junius Bouton
American. Anthropologist
Authority on pre-Columbian cultures, textiles; archaeology curator, American Museum of Natural History, 1957-73.
b. Sep 21, 1907 in Rye, New York
d. Apr 2, 1982 in New York, New York
Source: *AmMWSc 73S, 76P; BioIn 12, 13, 14, 16; ConAu 106; IntDcAn; NewYTBS 82*

Bird, Larry (Joe)
American. Basketball Player, Basketball Coach
Forward, Boston, 1980-92; three-time NBA MVP, 1984-86; played on 1992 Olympic Dream Team; coach, Indiana Pacers, 1997—.
b. Dec 7, 1956 in West Baden, Indiana
Source: *BasBi; BiDAmSp BK; BioIn 11, 12, 13, 18; ConAu 139; CurBio 82; LegTOT; News 90, 90-3; NewYTBS 79, 82, 85; OfNBA 87; WhoAm 84, 86, 88, 90, 92, 94, 95, 96, 97; WhoE 85, 86, 89, 91, 93, 95, 97; WorAlBi*

Birdseye, Clarence Frank
American. Inventor
Developed method for quick-freezing food, 1924; method for dehydrating food, 1949.
b. Dec 9, 1886 in New York, New York
d. Oct 7, 1956 in New York, New York
Source: *CurBio 46, 56; WhAm 3*

Birdwell, Russell Juarez
American. Public Relations Executive
Publicized MGM's search for actress to play Scarlett O'Hara in *Gone With the Wind,* 1939.
b. Oct 17, 1903 in Coleman, Texas
d. Dec 15, 1977 in Oxnard, California
Source: *ConAu 107; CurBio 46, 78; ScF&FL 1; WhoWest 74*

Birendra Bir Bikram, Shah Dev
Nepalese. Ruler
One of few remaining monarchs with absolute power; inherited throne from father, Mahendra Bir Bikram Shah Dev, 1972, crowned, 1975.
b. Dec 28, 1945 in Kathmandu, Nepal
Source: *CurBio 75; IntWW 83; NewYTBS 75; WhoWor 84*

Birkhoff, George David
American. Mathematician
Researched dynamics, differential equations; developed ergodic theorem; wrote *Dynamical Systems,* 1928.
b. Mar 21, 1884 in Overisel, Michigan
d. Nov 12, 1944 in Cambridge, Massachusetts
Source: *BiDAmEd; BiESc; BioIn 1, 2, 3, 13, 20; DcAmB S3; DcNAA; DcScB; InSci; LarDcSc; NewCol 75; NotTwCS; ThTwC 87; WebAB 74, 79; WhAm 2; WhNAA*

Birley, Oswald Hornby Joseph, Sir
English. Artist
Commissioned by Royal Naval College to paint portraits of George VI, his admirals, Winston Churchill, WW II.
b. Mar 31, 1880 in Auckland, New Zealand
d. May 6, 1952 in London, England
Source: *BioIn 2; DcBrAr 1; DcNaB 1951; ObitOF 79; ObitT 1951; OxCShps*

Birmingham, Stephen
American. Author
Writes histories of the rich: *Jacqueline Bouvier Kennedy Onassis,* 1978; *Duchess,* 1981.
b. May 28, 1931 in Hartford, Connecticut
Source: *AmAu&B; Au&Wr 71; AuNews 1; CelR, 90; ConAu 2NR, 49; CurBio 74; WhoAm 74, 76, 78, 80, 82, 84, 86, 88, 90, 92, 94, 95, 96, 97; WhoE 95, 97; WhoUSWr 88; WhoWor 80, 82, 84, 87, 89; WhoWrEP 89, 92, 95; WrDr 80, 82, 84, 86, 88, 90, 92, 94, 96*

Birney, David Edwin
American. Actor
Star of TV series "Bridget Loves Bernie," 1972-73, "St. Elsewhere," 1982.
b. Apr 23, 1940 in Washington, District of Columbia
Source: *ConTFT 5; IntMPA 86; NewYTBE 72; NotNAT; VarWW 85; WhoAm 86; WhoHol A; WhoThe 81*

Birney, Earle
[Alfred Earle Birney]
Canadian. Poet, Author, Critic
Wrote *David and Other Poems,* 1942; *Turvey,* 1949; *Trial of a City,* 1952.
b. May 13, 1904 in Calgary, Alberta, Canada
Source: *Au&Wr 71; Benet 87; BenetAL 91; BioIn 1, 3, 5, 8, 9, 10, 17, 21; BlueB 76; CamGEL; CamGLE; CanWr; CanWW 70, 79, 80, 81, 83, 89; CasWL; ChhPo S1; ConAu 1R, 5NR, 20NR; ConLC 1, 4, 6, 11; ConNov 72, 76, 82, 86; ConPo 70, 75, 80, 85, 91; CreCan 1; CyWA 89; DcLB 88; DcLEL; DrAP 75; DrAPF 80; DrAS 74E, 78E, 82E; GrWrEL P; IntAu&W 76, 77, 82, 86, 89, 91; IntWW 74, 75, 76, 77, 78, 79, 80, 81, 82, 83, 89, 91, 93; IntWWP 77, 82; LngCTC; MajTwCW; ModCmwL; OxCCan; OxCCanL; OxCCan SUP; OxCCanT; PenC ENG; RAdv 14, 13-1; REnAL; RfGEnL 91; TwCWr; WebE&AL; WhDW; WhE&EA; WhoAm 76, 78, 80, 82, 84, 86, 88; WhoCanL 85, 87, 92; WhoWor 82, 89; WhoWrEP 89; WorAu 1970; WrDr 76, 80, 82, 84, 86, 88, 90, 92, 94, 96*

Birney, James Gillespie
American. Abolitionist
Formed KY Anti-Slavery Society, 1835; Liberty Party's presidential candidate, 1840, 1844.
b. Feb 4, 1792 in Danville, Kentucky
d. Nov 25, 1857 in Perth Amboy, New Jersey
Source: *AmBi; AmPolLe; AmRef; ApCAB; BbD; BiD&SB; BiDSA; BioIn 4, 8, 15, 19; CivWDc; CyAG; DcAmAu; DcAmB; DcAmReB 2; DcAmSR; DcNAA; Drake; EncAAH; EncAB-H 1974, 1996; EncSoH; HarEnUS; McGEWB; NatCAB 2; OxCAmH; OxCAmL 65, 83, 95; TwCBDA; WebAB 74, 79; WhAm HS; WhAmP; WhCiWar; WorAl*

Birnie, William Alfred Hart
American. Editor, Journalist
Editor, *Reader's Digest,* 1960-67; editor, publisher *Woman's Home Companion,* 1943-57.
b. Aug 4, 1910 in Springfield, Massachusetts
d. Sep 19, 1979 in Rockport, Massachusetts
Source: *BioIn 3, 12; CurBio 52, 79; EncTwCJ; WhoAm 74, 76, 78, 80*

Biro, Val
[Balint Stephen Biro]
English. Illustrator
Books include *Dicovering Chesham,* 1968; *Gumdrop: The Adventures of a Vintage Car,* 1966.
b. Oct 6, 1921 in Budapest, Hungary
Source: *Au&Wr 71; BioIn 14, 17, 19; ChlLR 28; ConAu 25R; IlsBYP; IlsCB 1957; IntAu&W 89, 91, 93; OxCChiL; SmATA 1, 13AS; TwCChW 78, 83, 89, 95; WhoArt 80, 82, 84, 96; WhoWor 80; WrDr 80, 82, 84, 86, 88, 90, 92, 94, 96*

Birrell, Augustine
English. Author, Statesman
Wrote literary biographies, essays: *Obiter Dicta* series, 1884-1924.
b. Jan 19, 1850 in Wavertree, England
d. Nov 20, 1933 in London, England
Source: *Alli SUP; Benet 87, 96; BiD&SB; BioIn 2, 8, 11, 17, 21; CamGEL; CamGLE; Chambr 3; ChhPo, S1, S3; DcEnA A; DcLB 98; DcLEL; DcNaB 1931; EvLB; LngCTC; NewC; NewCBEL; OxCEng 67, 85, 95; PenC ENG; REn; TwCA, SUP; TwCWr; WhE&EA*

Bishop, Billy
[William Avery Bishop]
"Hell's Handmaiden"
Canadian. Military Leader
WW I ace who shot down 72 enemy aircraft; wrote *Winged Warfare,* 1918.
b. Feb 8, 1894 in Owen Sound, Ontario, Canada
d. Sep 11, 1956 in Palm Beach, Florida
Source: *BioIn 4, 5, 7, 8, 12, 15, 16; CurBio 41; FacFETw; InSci; MacDCB 78; ObitOF 79; WhLit; WhoMilH 76*

Bishop, Elizabeth
American. Poet
Won Pulitzer for *North and South: A Gold Spring,* 1955.
b. Feb 8, 1911 in Worcester, Massachusetts
d. Oct 6, 1979 in Boston, Massachusetts
Source: *AmAu&B; AmCulL; AmWomWr; AmWr S1; ArtclWW 2; Au&Wr 71; AuBYP 2S, 3; Benet 87, 96; BenetAL 91; BioAmW; BioIn 4, 7, 8, 10, 11, 12, 13, 14, 15, 16, 17, 18, 19, 20, 21; BlmGWL; BlueB 76; BroV; CamGLE; CamHAL; CelR; ChhPo, S1, S3; CnE&AP; ConAu 2BS, 5R, 7NR, 26NR, 89; ConLC 1, 4, 9, 13, 15, 32; ConPo 70, 75, 80; ContDcW 89; CroCAP; CurBio 77, 79, 79N; DcAmB S10; DcLB 5, 169; DcLEL 1940; DrAP 75; EncWB; EncWHA; EncWL 2, 3; FacFETw; FemiCLE; FourBJA; GayLesB; GrLiveH; GrWomW; GrWrEL P; IntAu&W 77; IntDcWB; IntWW 74, 75, 76, 77, 78, 79; IntWWP 77; InWom SUP; LegTOT; LibW; LiExTwC; LinLib L; MagSAmL; MajTwCW; MakMC; ModAL, S1, S2; ModAWP; ModAWWr; ModWoWr; NewCol 75; NewYTBS 79; OxCAmL 65, 83, 95; OxCEng 85, 95; OxCTwCP; OxCWoWr 95; PenC AM; PoeCrit 3; RAdv 1, 14, 13-1; REn; REnAL; RfGAmL 87, 94; RGFAP; RGTwCWr; SmATA 24N; TwCA SUP; TwCWr; WebE&AL; WhAm 7; WhoAm 74, 76, 78; WhoAmW 58, 64, 66, 68, 70, 72, 74; WhoE 74; WhoWor 74; WrDr 76, 80*

Bishop, Elvin
American. Musician
Hit single "Fooled Around and Fell in Love," 1976, from eighth solo album *Struttin' My Stuff.*
b. Oct 21, 1942 in Tulsa, Oklahoma
Source: *ASCAP 80; EncPR&S 74, 89; EncRk 88; GuBlues; IlEncRk; LegTOT; OnThGG; PenEncP; RkOn 74, 78; RolSEnR 83; WhoRock 81*

Bishop, Hazel
American. Cosmetics Executive, Scientist
Chemist who introduced first non-smear, long-lasting lipstick, 1950.
b. Aug 17, 1906 in Hoboken, New Jersey
Source: *BioIn 4, 12; CurBio 57; InSci; InWom; LibW; WhoAm 86, 88; WhoAmW 58; WorAl*

Bishop, Isabel
American. Artist
Known for representational paintings, drawings of women in everyday settings.
b. Mar 3, 1902 in Cincinnati, Ohio
d. Feb 19, 1988 in New York, New York

Source: *AmArt; BiDWomA; BioIn 1, 2, 5, 6, 10, 11, 12, 13, 14, 15, 16, 18, 20; BriEAA; ConArt 83, 89; CurBio 77, 88, 88N; DcAmArt; DcCAA 71, 77, 88, 94; GrAmP; InWom SUP; McGDA; NewYTBS 88; NorAmWA; OxCTwCA; PhDcTCA 77; WhAm 9; WhAmArt 85; WhoAm 74, 76, 78, 80, 82, 84, 86; WhoAmA 73, 76, 78, 80, 82, 84, 86; WhoAmW 58, 61, 64, 66, 68, 70, 72, 74, 77, 81, 83, 85, 87; WomArt; WorArt 1950*

Bishop, Isabella Lucy Bird
English. Traveler, Author
First woman member, Royal Geographic Society, 1892; wrote *Unbeaten Tracks in Japan,* 1880.
b. Oct 15, 1831 in Yorkshire, England
d. Oct 4, 1904 in Edinburgh, Scotland
Source: *Alli SUP; BioIn 14, 15, 16, 18, 19, 20; BritAu 19; Chambr 3; DcNaB S2; EncBrWW; IntDcWB; InWom, SUP; NewC; WhWE*

Bishop, J(ohn) Michael
American. Biochemist
Shared Nobel Prize for Physiology or Medicine, 1989; with Varmus, performed important research regarding the origins of cancer.
b. Feb 22, 1936 in York, Pennsylvania
Source: *AmMWSc 73P, 76P, 79, 82, 86, 89, 92, 95; IntWW 93; RAdv 14; WhAm 8; Who 92; WhoAm 80, 90, 92, 94, 95, 96, 97; WhoFrS 84; WhoMedH; WhoNob 90, 95; WhoScEn 94, 96; WhoWest 92, 94, 96; WhoWor 91, 93, 95, 96, 97*

Bishop, Jim
[James Alonzo Bishop]
American. Author, Journalist
Syndicated newspaper columnist for 27 yrs; wrote many historical books: *The Day Lincoln Was Shot,* 1955, sold over three million copies.
b. Nov 21, 1907 in Jersey City, New Jersey
d. Jul 26, 1987 in Delray Beach, Florida
Source: *AmAu&B; AnObit 1987; AuNews 1, 2; BiDAmNC; BioIn 3, 4, 8, 10, 11, 12, 15; CelR; ConAu 17R, 19NR, 123, X; CurBio 69, 87, 87N; DrAP 75; DrAPF 80; EncTwCJ; LegTOT; LiJour; LinLib L; NewYTBS 87; REnAL; WhAm 9; WhoAm 74, 76, 78, 80, 82, 84, 86; WhoSSW 73, 75, 76, 82; WhoWor 74, 76, 78; WorAl; WorAlBi*

Bishop, Joey
[Joseph Abraham Gottlieb]
American. Comedian
Nightclub entertainer, member of Frank Sinatra's "rat pack," 1950s; popular TV personality, 1960s.
b. Feb 3, 1918 in New York, New York
Source: *BioIn 8; BlueB 76; CelR; ConTFT 7; CurBio 62; EncAFC; FilmEn; FilmgC; ForYSC; HalFC 80, 84, 88; LegTOT; WhoAm 74, 76, 78, 80, 82, 90, 92, 94, 95, 96, 97; WhoCom; WhoHol 92, A; WhoWor 74; WorAl; WorAlBi*

Bishop, Julie
[Jacqueline Brown; Jacqueline Wells]
American. Actor
Child star in silent films, leading lady in second features under name Jacqueline Wells, 1923-39; used name Julie Bishop from 1941-57.
b. Aug 30, 1914 in Denver, Colorado
Source: *BioIn 18; EncAFC; FilmEn; FilmgC; ForYSC; HalFC 84, 88; IntMPA 86; LegTOT; MotPP; MovMk; SweetSg C; WhoAmW 81; WhoHol 92, A; WhoWest 78*

Bishop, Kelly
[Carole Bishop]
American. Actor
Won Tony for role of Sheila in *A Chorus Line,* 1976.
b. Feb 28, 1944 in Colorado Springs, Colorado
Source: *BiDD; BioIn 11; ConTFT 5; VarWW 85; WhoHol 92; WhoThe 81*

Bishop, Maurice Rupert
Grenadian. Political Leader
Marxist who became prime minister in 1979 coup; killed 1983 coup.
b. May 29, 1944, Aruba
d. Oct 19, 1983 in Saint George's, Grenada
Source: *BiDLAmC; ColdWar 2; ConAu 111; InB&W 80; IntWW 83; NewYTBS 83; WhoWor 82*

Bishop, Stephen
American. Singer, Songwriter
Hit songs include "Save It for a Rainy Day," 1976; theme from *Tootsie,* "It Might Be You," 1983.
b. Nov 14, 1951 in San Diego, California
Source: *BioIn 11; LegTOT; RkOn 78, 84; VarWW 85; WhoAm 86*

Bismarck, Otto Edward Leopold von
"The Iron Chancellor"
German. Statesman
Founder, first chancellor of German Empire, 1870-90; unified German states into one empire under Prussian leadership.
b. Apr 1, 1815 in Schonhausen, Germany
d. Jul 30, 1898 in Friedrichsruh, Germany
Source: *BbD; BiD&SB; McGEWB; NewC; OxCGer 76; REn; WebBD 83*

Bissell, Anna
[Mrs. Melville Bissell]
American. Business Executive
With husband, formed Bissell Carpet Sweeper Co., 1876.
b. 1846
d. 1934
Source: *Entr*

Bissell, Melville Reuben
American. Inventor
Patented carpet sweeper, 1876.
b. Sep 25, 1843 in Hartwick, New York
d. Mar 15, 1889 in Grand Rapids, Michigan
Source: *NatCAB 7*

Bissell, Patrick
[Walter Patrick Bissel]
American. Dancer
At time of death from drug overdose, was principal dancer, American Ballet Theater, NY.
b. Dec 1, 1957 in Corpus Christi, Texas
d. Dec 29, 1987 in Hoboken, New Jersey
Source: *AnObit 1987; BiDD; BioIn 11, 13; IntDcB; News 88-2; WhoAm 84*

Bissell, Richard Pike
American. Dramatist
Co-wrote Tony winner *The Pajama Game,* 1954.
b. Jun 27, 1913 in Dubuque, Iowa
d. May 4, 1977 in Dubuque, Iowa
Source: *BioIn 2, 3, 4, 5, 6, 10, 11; ConAu 1R, 69; NotNAT; REnAL; WhoAm 74; WorAu 1950; WrDr 76*

Bisset, Jacqueline Fraser
English. Actor
Starred in movies *The Deep,* 1977; *Rich and Famous,* 1981.
b. Sep 13, 1946 in Weybridge, England
Source: *BioNews 74; BkPepl; CurBio 77; FilmEn; FilmgC; IntMPA 86; MovMk; VarWW 85; WhoAm 86; WhoHol A*

Bissett, Josie
American. Actor
Plays Jane Mancini on TV's "Melrose Place," 1992—.
b. Oct 5, 1969 in Seattle, Washington

Bittan, Roy
[E Street Band]
"Professor"
American. Musician, Singer
Keyboardist, accordion player with Bruce Springsteen, 1974-89.
b. Jul 2, 1949 in Rockaway Beach, New York
Source: *WhoRocM 82*

Bitter, Francis
American. Inventor, Educator
Magnetism expert who invented the Bitter magnet.
b. Jul 22, 1902 in Weehawken, New Jersey
d. Jul 26, 1967 in Cambridge, Massachusetts
Source: *BioIn 4, 8; ConAu 113; WhAm 4*

Bitter, Karl Theodore Francis
American. Sculptor
Last work "Abundance" is the figure which stands at the Grand Army Plaza, NYC.
b. Dec 6, 1867 in Vienna, Austria
d. Apr 10, 1915 in New York, New York
Source: *AmBi; ApCAB X; BioIn 1, 8, 15; BriEAA; DcAmB; LinLib S; NatCAB 5, 24; TwCBDA; WebAB 74, 79; WhAm 1*

Bitzer, George William
"Billy"
American. Filmmaker, Photographer
Pioneer cameraman; filmed D W Griffith's *Birth of a Nation,* 1914.
b. Apr 21, 1872 in Boston, Massachusetts
d. Apr 29, 1944 in Hollywood, California
Source: *DcAmB S3; WebBD 83*

Bixby, Bill
American. Actor
Starred in TV series "My Favorite Martian"; "The Courtship of Eddie's Father"; "The Incredible Hulk."
b. Jan 22, 1934 in San Francisco, California
d. Nov 21, 1993 in Century City, California
Source: *AnObit 1993; BioIn 19, 20; ConTFT 3, 9, 12; FilmEn; FilmgC; ForYSC; HalFC 80, 84, 88; IntMPA 77, 80, 84, 86, 88, 92, 94; LegTOT; MiSFD 9; News 94, 94-2; WhAm 11; WhoAm 82, 88, 92, 94; WhoHol 92, A; WorAl; WorAlBi*

Biyidi, Alexandre
[Mongo Beti; Eza Boto]
French. Author
Novels on life in French West Africa include *The Poor Christ of Bomba,* 1971.
b. Jun 30, 1932 in Mbalmayo, Cameroon
Source: *AfrA; Benet 87, 96; BioIn 14, 17, 21; BlkLC; BlkWr 1; CasWL; ConAu 114, 124; ConLC 27; CyWA 89; DcAfHiB 86; EncWL 2, 3; LiExTwC; MajTwCW; McGEWB; ModBlW; ModFrL; Novels; PenC CL; RAdv 14, 13-2; RGAfL; SchCGBL; SelBAAf; TwCWr*

Bizet, Georges (Alexandre Cesar Leopold)
French. Composer
Known for his operatic masterpiece *Carmen,* 1875.
b. Oct 25, 1838 in Paris, France
d. Jun 3, 1875 in Bougival, France
Source: *AtlBL; Baker 78, 84, 92; BioIn 1, 2, 3, 4, 5, 6, 7, 8, 9, 10, 11, 12, 20; BriBkM 80; CmOp; CmpBCM; CnOxB; DancEn 78; DcArts; DcCom 77; DcCom&M 79; DcLP 87B; GrComp; IntDcOp; LegTOT; LinLib S; McGEWB; MetOEnc; MusMk; NewAmDM; NewEOp 71; NewGrDM 80; NewGrDO; NewOxM; NotNAT B; OxCEng 85, 95; OxCMus; OxDcOp; PenDiMP, A; WhDW; WorAl; WorAlBi*

Bjoerling, Jussi
[Stora Tuna Dalarna]
Swedish. Opera Singer
Tenor; made NY Met. debut, 1938; starred in over 50 operas, noted for French, Italian roles.
b. Feb 2, 1911 in Stora Tuna, Sweden
d. Sep 9, 1960 in Siar Oe, Sweden
Source: *CurBio 47, 60; LegTOT; MetOEnc; NewGrDA 86; WhAm 4*

Bjork
[Bjork Gundmundsdottir]
Icelandic. Singer
Formed the Sugarcubes, 1986; released first International solo LP, *Debut,* 1993.
b. Nov 21, 1965 in Reykjavik, Iceland
Source: *ConMus 16; EncRkSt; News 96, 96-1*

Bjorn-Larsen, Knut
American. Inventor
Developed garterless girdle.
b. 1923, Norway
Source: *BioIn 12*

Bjornson, Bjornstjerne Martinius
Norwegian. Poet, Political Leader
Nat. poet of Norway; shared Nobel Prize for literature, 1902.
b. Dec 8, 1832 in Kvikne, Norway
d. Apr 26, 1910 in Paris, France
Source: *AtlBL; ClDMEL 47; CyWA 58; DcBiA; DcEuL; McGEWB; McGEWD 84; OxCThe 83; PenC EUR; REn; WhoNob, 95; WorAl*

Blab, Uwe Konstantine
American. Basketball Player
Forward, Dallas, 1985-89; member W German Olympic team, 1984.
b. Mar 26, 1962 in Munich, Germany (West)
Source: *OfNBA 87*

Black, Clint
American. Singer, Musician, Songwriter
Country star with platinum debut album *Killin' Time,* 1989; had five no. 1 singles including "A Better Man."
b. Feb 4, 1962 in Houston, Texas
Source: *BgBkCoM; ConMus 5; CurBio 94; LegTOT; WhoAm 94, 95, 96, 97*

Black, Conrad Moffat
Canadian. Business Executive
Chm. of board, exec. committee, Argus Corp. Ltd., 1979—.
b. Aug 25, 1944 in Montreal, Quebec, Canada
Source: *ConNews 86-2; CurBio 92; St&PR 84, 87, 91, 93, 96, 97; Who 88, 90, 92, 94; WhoAm 80, 82, 84, 86, 88, 90, 92, 94, 95, 96, 97; WhoE 83, 85, 86, 89; WhoEmL 87; WhoFI 79, 81, 83, 85, 87, 89, 92, 94, 96*

Black, David (Jay)
[Jay and the Americans]
American. Singer
Lead singer, group's second "Jay," 1962-70.
b. Nov 2, 1941 in New York, New York
Source: *ConAu 25R; ConPo 80, 85, 91; DcLB 40; IntAu&W 91; WrDr 82, 84, 86, 88, 90, 92*

Black, Eli M
American. Businessman
First chairman, United Brands; ordained rabbi.
b. 1922?
d. Feb 3, 1975 in New York, New York
Source: *NewYTBS 75; WhAm 6*

Black, Frank J.
American. Composer, Musician
Organized music dept., NBC, 1928; general music director, NBC, 1932-48.
b. Nov 28, 1896 in Philadelphia, Pennsylvania
d. Jan 29, 1968 in Atlanta, Georgia
Source: *ASCAP 66; Baker 84; ConAmC 82*

Black, Hugo LaFayette
American. Supreme Court Justice
Member of Ku Klux Klan, mid-1920s; served on Supreme Court 34 yrs.
b. Feb 27, 1886 in Harlan, Alabama
d. Sep 25, 1971 in Bethesda, Maryland
Source: *AmPolLe; BiDFedJ; BiDrAC; BiDrUSC 89; BioIn 1, 2, 4, 5, 6, 7, 8, 9, 10, 11, 12, 13, 14, 15, 16, 17, 18, 20; ConAu 33R; CurBio 64, 71; DcAmB S9; EncAB-H 1974; EncSoH; LinLib L, S; McGEWB; NewYTBE 71; OxCAmH; OxCSupC; SupCtJu; WebAB 74, 79; WhAm 5; WhAmP; WorAl*

Black, James Whyte, Sir
Scottish. Physician
Co-winner Nobel Prize for physiology or Medicine, 1988; developed pain killers called beta-blockers.
b. Jun 14, 1924 in Uddingston, Scotland
Source: *BioIn 16, 17, 18, 20; IntWW 93; LarDcSc; Who 82, 83, 85, 88, 92, 94; WhoNob 90; WhoScEn 94, 96; WhoWor 78, 82, 93, 95, 96; WorAlBi*

Black, Joseph
Scottish. Chemist, Physicist
Formulated concept of latent heat, the heat absorbed by a substance changing state without a temperature rise.
b. Apr 16, 1728 in Bordeaux, France
d. Nov 10, 1799 in Edinburgh, Scotland
Source: *Alli; AsBiEn; BiESc; BiHiMed; BioIn 2, 3, 4, 6, 7, 9, 11, 12, 14; BlkwCE; CamDcSc; DcBiPP; DcInv; DcNaB; DcScB; Dis&D; EncEnl; InSci; LarDcSc; McGEWB; NewCBEL; OxCMed 86; WhDW; WorScD*

Black, Karen
[Karen Blanche Ziegler]
American. Actor
Appeared in films *Easy Rider,* 1969; *Five Easy Pieces,* 1970; *The Great Gatsby,* 1975.
b. Jul 1, 1942 in Park Ridge, Illinois
Source: *BioIn 9, 10, 11, 16; BkPepl; CelR, 90; ConTFT 4; CurBio 76; FilmEn; HalFC 84, 88; IntDcF 1-3, 2-3; IntMPA 86, 88, 92, 94, 96; ItaFilm; LegTOT; MovMk; WhoAm 74, 76, 78, 80, 82, 84, 86, 88, 92; WhoAmW 83, 85; WhoEnt 92; WhoHol 92, A; WorAl; WorAlBi*

Black, Samuel Duncan
American. Businessman
Formed business, 1907, with Alonzo Decker; produced first electric drill, 1914.
b. Aug 2, 1883 in White Hall, Maryland
d. 1953
Source: *BioIn 18; Entr; WhAm 3*

Black, Shirley Temple
[Mrs. Charles A Black]
American. Actor, Diplomat
Child actress who was number one Hollywood attraction, 1938; US ambassador to Ghana, 1974-76.
b. Apr 23, 1928 in Santa Monica, California
Source: *AmPolW 80; AmWomM; BestSel 89-2; BiDFilm; BioIn 14, 15, 16, 17, 19; BkPepl; CelR, 90; CmMov; CurBio 70; DcAmDH 80, 89; FilmEn; FilmgC; GrLiveH; IntWW 74, 75, 76, 77, 78, 79, 80, 81, 82, 83, 89, 91, 93; InWom SUP; MotPP; MovMk; NewYTBS 76; OxCFilm; ThFT; WhoAm 76, 78, 80, 82, 84, 86, 88, 90, 92, 94, 95, 96, 97; WhoAmP 73, 75, 77, 79, 81, 83, 85, 87, 89, 91, 93, 95; WhoAmW 74, 77, 83, 85, 91, 93, 95, 97; WhoEnt 92; WhoHol A; WhoWor 80, 82, 84, 87, 91, 93; WomFir*

Black, Walter J
American. Publisher
Pres., Walter J Black, Inc., 1928-58.
b. May 12, 1893 in New York, New York
d. Apr 16, 1958 in Roslyn, New York
Source: *NatCAB 44; WhAm 3*

Black, William
American. Business Executive, Philanthropist
Made Chock Full O'Nuts Co. multimillion dollar empire; founded Parkinson's Disease Foundation, 1957.
b. 1904? in New York, New York
d. Mar 7, 1983 in New York, New York
Source: *AnObit 1983; CurBio 64, 83, 83N; NewYTBS 83*

Black, Winifred Sweet
[Annie Laurie]
American. Journalist
One of original women reporters; often wrote in first person; inaugurated many reforms.
b. Oct 14, 1863 in Chilton, Wisconsin
d. May 26, 1936 in San Francisco, California
Source: *BioIn 14, 15, 16; BriB; CmCal; DcLB 25; EncWomS; InWom SUP; JrnUS; LibW; NotAW; PenNWW B; WhAm 1; WomFir*

Blackbeard
[Edward Teach]
English. Pirate
Privateer during War of Spanish Succession, 1701-14; became pirate at end of war.
b. 1680 in Bristol, England
d. Nov 22, 1718 in Ocracoke Island, North Carolina
Source: *BioIn 3, 4, 5, 6, 7, 10, 15, 18; NewCol 75; OxCAmL 65; REn; REnAL; WhAm HS*

Blackburn, Jack
[Charles Henry Blackburn]
"Chappie"
American. Boxer, Boxing Trainer
Lightweight boxer, 1900-23; trainer of Joe Louis.
b. 1883 in Versailles, Kentucky
d. Apr 24, 1942 in Chicago, Illinois
Source: *BioIn 1, 17; BoxReg; InB&W 80; ObitOF 79; WhoBox 74*

Black Crowes, The
[Jeff Cease; Johnny Colt; Marc Ford; Steve Gorman; Chris Robinson; Rich Robinson]
American. Music Group
Blues-influenced rock band; double platinum debut album *Shake Your Money Maker,* 1990.
Source: *BioIn 14, 15, 17, 20; ConMus 7; EncRkSt; WhoHol A; WhoRocM 82*

Black Elk
American. Religious Leader
Spiritual leader of the Ogala Lakota Sioux; converted to Catholicism, 1904.
b. 1863?
d. Aug 17, 1950
Source: *BenetAL 91; BioIn 9, 10, 13, 14, 17, 19, 21; CamGLE; CamHAL; ConAu 144; DcNAL; EncNAB; EncNAR; EncNoAI; NatNAL; NotNaAm; RelLAm 91; REnAW; TwCLC 33; WhNaAH*

Blackett, Patrick Maynard Stuart
English. Physicist, Educator
Nobel Laureate for physics, 1948; wrote *Lectures on Rock Magnetism,* 1956.
b. Nov 18, 1897 in London, England
d. Jul 13, 1974 in London, England
Source: *AsBiEn; BiESc; BioIn 1, 2, 3, 4, 10, 11; CamDcSc; ConAu 49; DcNaB 1971; GrBr; InSci; IntWW 74; LarDcSc; McGMS 80; NotTwCS; ObitOF 79; WhAm 6; Who 74; WhoNob, 90, 95; WhoWor 74; WorAl; WorScD*

Black Hawk
[Black Sparrow Hawk]
American. Native American Chief
Sauk chief during Black Hawk War of 1832; served under Tecumseh in War of 1812.
b. 1767 in Sauk Village, Illinois
d. Oct 3, 1838 in Keokuk, Iowa
Source: *AmBi; ApCAB; BenetAL 91; BioIn 2, 4, 5, 6, 7, 8, 9, 10, 12, 20; DcAmB; DcAmMiB; DcNAA; Drake; EncAAH; EncNoAI; HarEnMi; HarEnUS; LegTOT; LinLib S; McGEWB; NatCAB 9; NatNAL; NotNaAm; OxCAmH; OxCAmL 65, 83, 95; RComAH; REnAW; TwCBDA; WebAB 74, 79; WebAMB; WhAm HS; WhNaAH; WorAl; WorAlBi*

Black Kettle
American. Native American Chief
Principal chief of the Cheyenne, 1860-1868.
b. 1803?
d. Nov 26, 1868
Source: *BioIn 8, 12; NatCAB 19; NotNaAm; WhAm HS; WhNaAH*

Blackman, Honor
English. Actor
Played Pussy Galore in Bond film *Goldfinger,* 1964.
b. Aug 22, 1926 in London, England
Source: *BioIn 16; ConTFT 4; FilmAG WE; FilmEn; FilmgC; ForYSC; HalFC 80, 84, 88; IlWWBF; IntMPA 77, 80, 82, 94, 96; ItaFilm; LegTOT; MotPP; WhoAmW 74; WhoHol 92, A; WhoHrs 80; WhoThe 77, 81; WhoWor 74*

Blackmer, Sidney Alderman
American. Actor
Made Broadway debut, 1917; portrayed Teddy Roosevelt more than a dozen times in films, plays.
b. Jul 13, 1895 in Salisbury, North Carolina
d. Oct 5, 1973 in New York, New York
Source: *BiE&WWA; DcNCBi 1; FilmgC; MovMk; NewYTBE 73; ObitOF 79; Vers A; WhoAm 74; WhoHol B; WhScrn 77; WhThe; WorAl*

Blackmore, Richard Doddridge
English. Author
Romantic novels include classic *Lorna Doone,* 1869.
b. Jun 7, 1825 in Longworth, England
d. Jan 20, 1900 in Teddington, England
Source: *Alli SUP; BbD; Benet 87, 96; BiD&SB; BioIn 1, 2, 3, 4, 5, 10, 11, 12, 13, 16; BritAu 19; CelCen; Chambr 3; ChhPo, S1, S2, S3; CyWA 58; DcBiA; DcEnA, A; DcEnL; DcEuL; DcLEL; DcNaB S1; EvLB; JBA 34; LinLib L, S; MouLC 4; NewC; NewCBEL; OxCEng 67; OxCLiW 86; PenC ENG; REn; VicBrit; WebE&AL*

Blackmore, Ritchie
[Deep Purple; Ritchie Blackmore's Rainbow]
English. Musician
Co-founded Deep Purple, 1968; had hit "Stone Cold."
b. Apr 14, 1945 in Weston-super-Mare, England
Source: *BioIn 12, 13; ConMuA 80A; IlEncRk; LegTOT; OnThGG; PenEncP; RolSEnR 83; WhoRock 81; WhoRocM 82*

Blackmun, Harry Andrew
American. Supreme Court Justice
Moderate/conservative justice appointed by Richard Nixon, 1970.
b. Nov 12, 1908 in Nashville, Illinois
Source: *BiDFedJ, A; BioIn 8, 9, 10, 11, 12, 13; BlueB 76; CngDr 83; CurBio 70; DrAS 74P, 78P, 82P; IntWW 83; LinLib L, S; NatCAB 63N; NewYTBE 70; NewYTBS 83; OxCSupC; PolProf NF; SupCtJu; WebAB 74, 79; Who 85;*

WhoAm 74, 76, 78, 80, 82, 84, 86, 88, 90, 92, 94, 95, 96, 97; WhoAmL 78, 79, 83, 85, 87, 90, 92, 94, 96; WhoAmP 73, 75, 77, 79, 81, 83, 85, 87, 89, 91, 93, 95; WhoE 79, 81, 83, 85, 86, 89, 91, 93, 95, 97; WhoSSW 73, 75, 76, 82; WhoWor 78, 80, 82, 84, 87, 89, 91, 93, 95; WorAl

Blackmur, Richard Palmer
American. Poet, Educator, Critic
Writings include *Double Agent,* 1935; *Language As Gesture: Essays in Poetry.*
b. Jan 21, 1904 in Springfield, Massachusetts
d. Feb 2, 1965 in Princeton, New Jersey
Source: *AmAu&B; BioIn 1, 4, 7, 10, 11, 12, 13; CasWL; CnDAL; ConAu P-1; ConLC 2, 24; DcAmB S7; DcLEL; EncWL 2; EvLB; LngCTC; ModAL, S1; OxCAmL 65; PenC AM; PeoHis; RAdv 1; REn; REnAL; SixAP; TwCA, SUP; TwCWr; WebE&AL; WhAm 4*

Black Oak Arkansas
[Pat Daugherty; Wayne Evans; Jimmy Henderson; Stan "Goober" Knight; Jim "Dandy" Mangrum; Ricky Reynolds]
American. Music Group
Southern band named after group's hometown, 1969; number one hit "Jim Dandy to the Rescue," 1973.
Source: *ConMuA 80A; EncRk 88; IlEncRk; PenEncP; RkOn 78, 84; RolSEnR 83; WhoRock 81; WhoRocM 82*

Black Panther Party
American. Political Activists
Marxist revolutionary group; founded 1966 by Huey Newton, Bobby Seale; history marked by numerous conflicts with police prompting Congressional investigations.

Black Sabbath
[Terry "Geezer" Butler; Ronnie Dio; Jan Gillan; Anthony Iommi; John "Ozzie" Osbourne; William Ward]
English. Music Group
Heavy-metal band formed, 1969, under name Earth; changed name when material became mystical; hit album *Paranoid,* 1970.
Source: *Alli, SUP; BiDLA; ConMuA 80A; ConMus 9; DcCathB; DcVicP, 2; EncPR&S 89; EncRk 88; EncRkSt; HarEnR 86; IlEncRk; InB&W 80; NewCBEL; NewYHSD; PenEncP; RkOn 78; RolSEnR 83; WhoRock 81; WhoRocM 82*

Blackstone, Harry
[Henri Bouton]
American. Magician
Oldtime vaudeville act, became internationally famous; entertained Pres. Coolidge in White House, troops during WW II.
b. Sep 27, 1885 in Chicago, Illinois
d. Nov 17, 1965 in Hollywood, California
Source: *BioIn 2, 5, 7, 16; DcAmB S7; LegTOT; MagIlD*

Blackstone, Harry, Jr.
American. Magician
Son of "The Great Blackstone;" took magic act to Broadway.
b. Jun 30, 1934 in Colon, Michigan
d. May 14, 1997 in Loma Linda, California
Source: *BioIn 11, 12, 16, 18; ConAu 114; LegTOT*

Blackstone, William, Sir
English. Judge, Author
Wrote *Commentaries on the Laws of England,* 1765-69, in four vols.
b. Jul 10, 1723 in London, England
d. Feb 14, 1780 in London, England
Source: *Alli; AmJust; AtlBL; Benet 87, 96; BiD&SB; BioIn 1, 3, 4, 6, 9, 11, 13; BlkwCE; BlkwEAR; BritAu; CamGLE; CasWL; Chambr 2; ChhPo; CopCroC; CyEd; DcBiPP; DcEnA; DcEnL; DcNaB; EncEnl; EvLB; LinLib L, S; McGEWB; NewC; OxCEng 67, 85, 95; OxCLaw; REn; WhDW; WorAl; WorAlBi*

Blackton, James Stuart
American. Filmmaker
Founder, Vitagraph Films, 1896; first to produce film plays.
b. Jan 5, 1875 in Sheffield, England
d. Aug 13, 1941 in Los Angeles, California
Source: *BioIn 17; CurBio 41; DcAmB S3; DcFM; OxCFilm; WebBD 83; WhAm 1*

Blackton, Jay S
American. Conductor
Musical director of *Oklahoma!,* 1943 (for which he won an Oscar);*Hello Dolly,* 1965; *The King and I,* 1972.
b. Mar 25, 1909 in New York, New York
d. Jan 8, 1994 in Granada Hills, California
Source: *ASCAP 66; BiE&WWA; NotNAT*

Blackwell, Antoinette Louisa Brown
American. Abolitionist, Feminist, Clergy
First woman ordained minister in US, 1853; wrote *The Making of the Universe,* 1914.
b. May 20, 1825 in Henrietta, New York
d. Nov 5, 1921 in Elizabeth, New Jersey
Source: *AmBi; AmRef; AmSocL; AmWom; ApCAB; BbD; BiD&SB; BioIn 14, 15, 17, 19, 21; DcAmB; DcAmReB 2; EncWHA; HarEnUS; LibW; NatCAB 9, 29; NewCol 75; NotAW; TwCBDA; WebAB 74, 79; WhAm 1; WhAmP; WomWWA 14*

Blackwell, Basil Henry, Sir
English. Publisher
BH Blackwell, Ltd., founder, chmn., 1922-69; pres., 1969-84.
b. May 29, 1889 in Oxford, England
d. Apr 9, 1984 in Oxford, England
Source: *BioIn 9; BlueB 76; ConAu 112; DcNaB 1981; IntWW 74, 75, 76, 77, 78, 79, 80; IntYB 78, 79, 80, 81, 82; NewYTBS 84; Who 74, 82, 83; WhoWor 74, 78*

Blackwell, Betsy Talbot
American. Editor
Editor-in-chief, *Mademoiselle* magazine, 1937-71; raised literary standards of women's magazines.
b. 1905 in New York, New York
d. Feb 4, 1985 in Norwalk, Connecticut
Source: *BioIn 14; ConAu 115; CurBio 54, 85, 85N; ForWC 70; InWom SUP; NewYTBE 70; NewYTBS 85; WhAm 8; WhoAm 74; WorFshn*

Blackwell, (Samuel) Earl, Jr.
American. Author, Publisher, Impresario
Founder, Celebrity Service in the early 1940s; noted for organization of celebrity events.
b. May 3, 1913 in Atlanta, Georgia
d. Mar 1, 1995 in New York, New York
Source: *BiE&WWA; BioIn 3, 5, 6, 10, 20, 21; BlueB 76; CelR, 90; ConAu 81, 148; CurBio 60, 95N; LegTOT; NotNAT; WhAm 11; WhoAm 74, 76, 78, 80, 82, 84, 86, 88, 90, 92, 94, 95; WhoHol 92; WhoUSWr 88; WhoWor 74, 84, 87, 89, 91, 93; WhoWrEP 89, 92, 95; WorAl*

Blackwell, Elizabeth
American. Physician, Author
First woman to receive MD in modern times, 1849; practiced in NY, 1850-67.
b. Feb 3, 1821 in Bristol, England
d. May 31, 1910 in Hastings, England
Source: *Alli, SUP; AmBi; AmRef; AmSocL; AmWom; AmWomWr; ApCAB; ArtclWW 2; BiD&SB; BiDSocW; BiHiMed; BiInAmS; BioAmW; BioIn 1, 2, 3, 4, 5, 6, 7, 8, 9, 10, 11, 12, 13, 14, 15, 16, 17, 18, 19, 21; CamDcSc; CelCen; CivWDc; ContDcW 89; DcAmAu; DcAmB; DcAmMeB, 84; DcBiPP; DcNAA; DcNaB S2; Drake; EncAB-H 1974, 1996; EncWHA; GoodHs; GrLiveH; HanAmWH; HarEnUS; HerW, 84; HisWorL; InSci; IntDcWB; InWom, SUP; LibW; LinLib S; McGEWB; NatCAB 9; NotAW; NotWoLS; OhA&B; OxCAmH; OxCMed 86; OxCWoWr 95; PeoHis; RComAH; TwCBDA; VicBrit; WebAB 74, 79; WhAm 1; WhCiWar; WhDW; WhLit; WomFir; WomSc; WorAl; WorAlBi*

Blackwell, Emily
American. Physician
Founder, faculty member, Women's Medical College, 1868-1899, one of the first medical schools to require four years of study.
b. 1826 in Bristol, England
d. Sep 7, 1910
Source: *AmRef; AmSocL; AmWom; BioIn 8, 10, 15, 19, 21; ContDcW 89; DcAmMeB, 84; GayLesB; InSci; IntDcWB; InWom, SUP; LibW; NatCAB 9; NotAW; WhAm 1, 1C; WomFir*

Blackwell, Mr. (Richard)
[Richard Blackwell]
American. Fashion Designer, Critic
Famous for yearly list of "worst dressed" women in world.
Source: *BioIn 14, 21; WhoRocM 82; WorFshn*

Blackwood, Algernon Henry
English. Author
Writings on the supernatural include *Jimbo, a Fantasy,* 1909; *Full Circle,* 1927.
b. Mar 14, 1869 in Kent, England
d. Dec 10, 1951 in London, England
Source: *Chambr 3; DcLB 153; DcNaB 1951; PenC ENG; REn; TwCA SUP; TwCWr*

Blacque, Taurean
American. Actor
Played Neal Washington on TV series "Hill Street Blues," 1981-87.
b. May 10, 1946? in Newark, New Jersey
Source: *WhoTelC*

Blades, Ruben, Jr.
Panamanian. Singer, Songwriter
Revolutionized salsa music, universalized appeal; first salsa singer to write own songs.
b. Jul 16, 1948 in Panama City, Panama
Source: *ASCAP 80; Baker 92; ConAu 131; ConMus 2; ConTFT 5, 12; CurBio 86; DcHiB; HispAmA; HispWr; IntMPA 92, 94, 96; LegTOT; NewGrDA 86; PenEncP; WhoAm 88, 90, 92, 94, 95, 96, 97; WhoE 86; WhoHisp 91, 92, 94; WhoHol 92*

Blaga, Lucien
Romanian. Poet, Philosopher
Published collection of poems *Poems of Light,* 1919 (*Poemele luminii*); founded journal *Gindirea* (*Thought*).
b. May 9, 1895 in Lancram, Transylvania
d. May 6, 1961 in Cluj, Romania
Source: *ConLC 75*

Blaiberg, Philip
South African. Dentist, Transplant Patient
Received second heart transplanted by Dr. Christiaan Barnard, Jan 2, 1968; wrote *Looking at My Heart,* 1968.
b. May 24, 1909 in Uniondale, South Africa
d. Aug 17, 1969 in Cape Town, South Africa
Source: *BioIn 8, 9; LinLib S*

Blaik, Red
[Earl Henry Blaik]
American. Football Coach
Coach, US Military Academy, 1941-58; won three national championships.
b. Feb 15, 1897 in Detroit, Michigan
d. May 6, 1989 in Colorado Springs, Colorado
Source: *BiDAmSp FB; BioIn 16; CurBio 45; St&PR 75; WhAm 10; WhoAm 74, 76, 78, 80, 82, 84, 86, 88; WhoFtbl 74; WhoSpor*

Blaikie, William
American. Athlete
Held amateur long distance outdoor walking record for 10 years; walked from Boston to NYC, 225 miles in 4 1/2 days.
b. May 24, 1843 in New York, New York
d. Dec 6, 1904 in New York, New York
Source: *Alli SUP; ApCAB; BiD&SB; BioIn 11; DcAmAu; DcAmB; DcNAA; TwCBDA; WhAm 1*

Blaine, James Gillespie
American. Statesman
Co-founder Republican Party, 1856; nominated for pres., 1884, lost election to Grover Cleveland.
b. Jan 31, 1830 in West Brownsville, Pennsylvania
d. Jan 27, 1893 in Washington, District of Columbia
Source: *Alli SUP; AmAu&B; AmBi; AmLegL; AmPolLe; ApCAB; BbD; BiAUS; BiD&SB; BiDrAC; BiDrUSC 89; BiDrUSE 71, 89; BioIn 3, 4, 5, 6, 7, 8, 10, 11, 12, 13, 14, 16, 19; CyAG; DcAmAu; DcAmB; DcAmDH 80, 89; DcNAA; DcSpL; Drake; EncAB-H 1974, 1996; HarEnUS; LinLib L, S; McGEWB; NatCAB 1; OxCAmH; OxCAmL 65, 83; REn; REnAL; TwCBDA; WebAB 74, 79; WhAm 5, HS; WhAmP; WorAl; WrDr 76*

Blaine, Vivian
[Vivian S Stapleton]
American. Actor
Star of stage, 1950, film version, 1955, of *Guys and Dolls.*
b. Nov 21, 1924? in Newark, New Jersey
d. Dec 9, 1995 in New York, New York
Source: *AmPS B; BiE&WWA; CmpEPM; ConTFT 5; EncMT; FilmEn; FilmgC; ForYSC; HalFC 84; HolP 40; IntMPA 75, 76, 77, 78, 79, 80, 81, 82, 84, 86, 88; InWom; MotPP; NotNAT; WhoAm 74, 82; WhoAmW 58, 70, 72, 74; WhoHol A; WhoThe 81*

Blair, Betsy
[Betsy Roger]
American. Actor
Best known as Oscar nominee for role in *Marty,* 1955.
b. Dec 11, 1923 in Cliffside Park, New Jersey
Source: *BiE&WWA; BioIn 13; FilmEn; FilmgC; ForYSC; HalFC 80, 84, 88; IntMPA 77, 80, 82, 88, 92, 94, 96; ItaFilm; LegTOT; MotPP; OxCFilm; WhoAmW 58A; WhoEnt 92; WhoHol 92, A*

Blair, Bonnie Kathleen
[Mrs. David Cruikshank]
American. Skater
Speed skater; first woman in US history to win three gold medals in consecutive Winter Olympics, 1988, 1992.
b. Mar 18, 1964 in Cornwall, New York
Source: *BioIn 13; CurBio 92; EncWomS; News 92*

Blair, Clay, Jr.
American. Author, Editor
Writings include *Beyond Courage,* 1955; *Survive!,* 1973.
b. May 1, 1925 in Lexington, Virginia
Source: *AmAu&B; AuNews 2; ConAu 77; IntWW 74; WhoAm 82*

Blair, David
English. Dancer
Best known for title role in *The Prince of the Pagodas,* 1957.
b. Jul 27, 1932 in Halifax, England
d. Apr 1, 1976 in London, England
Source: *Alli SUP; BiDD; BioIn 4, 5, 6, 10, 11; CnOxB; CurBio 76, 76N; DancEn 78; DcNaB 1971; IntDcB; NewYTBS 76, 77; WhAm 7; Who 74; WhoWor 74; WhScrn 83; WhWW-II; WorAl*

Blair, Francis Preston, Jr.
American. Soldier, Statesman
Fought with General Sherman, member of Congress, 1856, US senator, 1871; member of one of the most influential families in 19th c. American politics.
b. Feb 19, 1821 in Lexington, Kentucky
d. Jul 8, 1875 in Saint Louis, Missouri
Source: *AmBi; ApCAB; BiAUS; BiDrAC; BiDrUSC 89; BiDSA; BioIn 1, 3, 7; CivWDc; DcAmB; Drake; HarEnUS; NatCAB 4; OxCAmH; REnAW; TwCBDA; WebAB 74, 79; WhAm HS; WhAmP; WhCiWar*

Blair, Frank
American. Broadcast Journalist
First newscaster on TV's "Today Show," 1952-75; autobiography *Let's Be Frank About It,* 1979.
b. May 30, 1915 in Yemassee, South Carolina
d. Mar 14, 1995 in Hilton Head Island, South Carolina
Source: *BioIn 4, 10, 12, 20; CelR; ConAu 93, 97, 148; NewYTET; Ward 77; WhoAm 74, 76*

Blair, James
Scottish. Clergy, Educator
Founder, first pres., College of William and Mary, 1693.
b. 1655 in Edinburgh, Scotland
d. Apr 18, 1743 in Williamsburg, Virginia
Source: *Alli; AmAu; AmAu&B; AmBi; AmWrBE; BenetAL 91; BiDrACR; BiDSA; BioIn 9, 14, 19; CyAL 1; DcAmAu; DcAmB; DcAmReB 1, 2; DcLB 24; EncCRAm; EncSoH; LuthC 75; McGEWB; NatCAB 3; OxCAmH; OxCAmL 65, 83, 95; REnAL; SouWr; WebAB 74, 79; WhAm HS; WorAl; WorAlBi*

Blair, Janet
[Martha Janet Lafferty]
American. Actor
Appeared in *Three Girls about Town,* 1941; *My Sister Eileen,* 1942.
b. Apr 23, 1921 in Altoona, Pennsylvania
Source: *BiDAmM; BiE&WWA; BioIn 3, 4, 10; CmpEPM; EncAFC; FilmEn; FilmgC; ForYSC; HalFC 80, 84, 88; HolP 40; IntMPA 77, 78, 79, 80, 81, 82, 84, 86, 88, 92, 94, 96; InWom, SUP; MotPP; MovMk; WhoAm 74; WhoAmW 64, 66, 68, 70, 72, 74; WhoHol 92, A*

Blair, Linda Denise
American. Actor
Played the possessed girl in *The Exorcist,* 1973.
b. Jan 22, 1959 in Saint Louis, Missouri
Source: *BkPepl; ConTFT 3; HalFC 84; IntMPA 86; WhoAm 78, 80, 82, 84, 86, 88; WhoEnt 92; WhoHol A; WorAl*

Blair, Montgomery
American. Statesman, Lawyer
Counsel for Dred Scott before Supreme Court, 1857; postmaster under Lincoln, 1861-64.
b. May 10, 1813 in Franklin County, Kentucky
d. Jul 27, 1883 in Silver Spring, Maryland
Source: *AmBi; ApCAB; BiAUS; BiDrUSE 71, 89; BioIn 15; CivWDc; CyAG; DcAmB; Drake; EncSoH; HarEnUS; NatCAB 2, 44; OxCAmH; TwCBDA; WebAB 74, 79; WhAm HS; WhAmP; WhCiWar*

Blair, Tony
[Anthony Charles Lynton Blair]
English. Politician
Leader of British Labour Party, 1994—; prime minister, 1997—.
b. May 6, 1953 in Edinburgh, Scotland
Source: *CurBio 96; IntWW 91, 93; News 96, 96-3; NewYTBS 94; Who 85, 88, 90, 92, 94; WhoWor 91*

Blair, William Richards
American. Physicist, Inventor
Claimed to invent pulse-echo radar, 1926; considered father of radar by US Army.
b. Nov 7, 1874 in Coleraine, Ireland
d. Sep 2, 1962 in Fair Haven, New Jersey
Source: *BioIn 6, 9; DcAmB S7; NatCAB 53; WhAm 6*

Blaisdell, George G
"Mr. Zippo"
American. Businessman
Founded cigarette lighter co., marketing inexpensive windproof product with lifetime guarantee.
b. 1895
d. 1978 in Miami Beach, Florida
Source: *BioIn 7, 11; PseudN 82; St&PR 75*

Blaise, Saint
Religious Figure
Patron of throat ailments; bishop of Sebastea, Armenia; commemorated, Feb 2.
d. 316?
Source: *DcBiPP; DcCathB; Dis&D*

Blake, Amanda
[Beverly Louise Neill]
American. Actor
Played Miss Kitty on TV series "Gunsmoke," 1955-75.
b. Feb 20, 1931 in Buffalo, New York
d. Aug 16, 1989 in Los Angeles, California
Source: *BioIn 12; FilmEn; FilmgC; HalFC 84; IntMPA 84, 86, 88; InWom SUP; WhAm 10; WhoAm 74; WhoHol A; WorAl*

Blake, Eubie
[James Hubert Blake]
American. Pianist, Composer
Ragtime pioneer, whose best known songs include "I'm Just Wild About Harry," 1921; "Memories of You," 1930.
b. Feb 7, 1883 in Baltimore, Maryland
d. Feb 12, 1983 in New York, New York
Source: *AfrAmAl 6; AllMusG; AmSong; AnObit 1983; ASCAP 66, 80; Baker 84, 92; BiDAfM; BiDAmM; BiDJaz; BioIn 8, 9, 10, 11, 12, 13, 14, 15, 16; BlkAmP; BlksB&W C; BlksBF; BluesWW; CmpEPM; ConAmC 76, 82; ConAu 109; CurBio 74, 83N; DcTwCCu 5; DrBlPA, 90; Ebony 1; EncJzS; EncMT; FacFETw; IlEncJ; InB&W 80, 85; LegTOT; MorBAP; NegAl 83, 89; NewAmDM; NewGrDA 86; NewGrDJ 88, 94; NewGrDM 80; NewYTBS 83; OxCAmT 84; OxCPMus; PenEncP; WhAm 7, 8; WhoAm 74, 76, 78, 80, 82; WhoBlA 75, 77, 80; WhoJazz 72*

Blake, Eugene Carson
American. Clergy
Leader in American Protestantism; was secretary-general of World Council of Churches, 1966-72.
b. Nov 7, 1906 in Saint Louis, Missouri
d. Jul 31, 1985 in Stamford, Connecticut
Source: *AmDec 1960; BioIn 3, 4, 5, 6, 7, 8, 9, 11, 12, 14, 15, 18, 19; BlueB 76; CelR; ConAu 116; CurBio 55, 85, 85N; DcAmReB 2; DcEcMov; DrAS 74P; EncAACR; IntWW 74, 75, 76, 77, 78, 79, 80, 81, 82, 83; LinLib S; NewYTBS 85; PolProf E, J, K; RelLAm 91; WhAm 9; Who 74, 82, 83, 85; WhoAm 74, 76, 78, 80; WhoE 74; WhoRel 75, 77; WhoWor 74, 76, 78; WorAl; WorAlBi*

Blake, Quentin
English. Children's Author, Illustrator
Writings include *Jack and Nancy,* 1969; *The Bear's Water Picnic,* 1970.
b. Dec 16, 1932 in Sidcup, England
Source: *BioIn 6, 8, 11, 14, 15, 16, 17, 19; ChhPo S1; ChlBIID; ChlBkCr; ChlLR 31; ConAu 11NR, 25R; DcArts; FifBJA; IlsBYP; IlsCB 1957; OxCChiL; SmATA 9, 52; WhoArt 96; WrDr 90, 92, 94, 96*

Blake, Robert
English. Naval Officer
Captured the Scilly Islands, 1651; sank the Spanish Fleet at Santa Cruz, 1657.
b. Aug 1599 in Bridgwater, England
d. Aug 7, 1657
Source: *BioIn 2, 3, 4, 9; DcBiPP; DcNaB; GenMudB; HarEnMi; LinLib S; NewCol 75; OxCShps; WhDW; WhoMilH 76*

Blake, Robert
[Our Gang; Michael Gubitosi]
American. Actor
Starred in TV series "Baretta," 1974-78; won Emmy, 1975.
b. Sep 18, 1934 in Nutley, New Jersey
Source: *BioIn 7, 10, 11; BkPepl; ConTFT 3; CurBio 75; FilmgC; HalFC 80, 84; IntMPA 86; MovMk; WhoAm 74; WhoHol A*

Blake, Toe
[Hector Blake]
Canadian. Hockey Player, Hockey Coach
Left wing, Montreal, 1932-48; won Hart, Art Ross trophies, 1939; coached Montreal, 1955-68, to eight Stanley Cups, Hall of Fame, 1966.
b. Aug 21, 1912 in Victoria Mines, Ontario, Canada
d. May 17, 1995 in Montreal, Quebec, Canada
Source: *BioIn 7, 9, 20, 21; HocEn; LegTOT; WhoHcky 73; WhoSpor*

Blake, William
English. Poet, Artist
Wrote *Songs of Innocence,* 1789; engraved, published own poetry.
b. Nov 28, 1757 in London, England
d. Aug 12, 1827 in London, England
Source: *Alli; AnCL; AntBDN B; AtlBL; AuBYP 2S, 3; BbD; Benet 87, 96; BiD&SB; BiDLA; BioIn 1, 2, 3, 4, 5, 6, 7, 8, 9, 10, 11, 12, 13, 14, 15, 16, 17, 18, 19, 20, 21; BkIE; BlkwCE; BlmGEL; BritAu 19; BritWr 3; CamGEL; CamGLE; CarSB; CasWL; CelCen; Chambr 2; ChhPo, S1, S2, S3; ChrP; ClaDrA; CmFrR; CnDBLB 3; CnE&AP; CrtT 2, 4; CyWA 58; DcArts; DcBiPP; DcBrBI; DcBrWA; DcEnA, A; DcEnL; DcEuL; DcLB 93, 154, 163; DcLEL; DcNaB; DcNiCA; Dis&D; EncEnl; EncO&P 1, 2, 3; EncPaPR 91; EvLB; GrWrEL P; IlEncMy; IntDcAA 90; LegTOT; LinLib L, S; LngCEL; LuthC 75; MagSWL; MajAI; McGDA; McGEWB; MouLC 3; NewC; NewCBEL; NinCLC 13, 37, 57; OxCArt; OxCChiL; OxCEng 67, 85, 95; OxDcArt; PenC ENG; PenEncH; PoeCrit 12; RadHan; RAdv 1, 14, 13-1; RComWL; REn; RfGEnL 91; RGFBP; SmATA 30; Str&VC; WebE&AL; WhDW; WorAl; WorAlBi; WorLitC; WrChl; WrPh*

Blakeley, Ronee
American. Actor, Singer
Screen debut in *Nashville,* 1975; received Oscar nomination.
b. 1946 in Stanley, Idaho
Source: *BioIn 13; FilmEn; VarWW 85*

Blakelock, Ralph Albert
American. Artist
Original self-taught landscapist who did moody scenes, often with Native Americans.
b. Oct 15, 1847 in New York, New York
d. Aug 9, 1919 in Elizabethtown, New York
Source: *AmBi; ApCAB, X; ArtsAmW 1; BioIn 1, 3, 4, 6, 7, 8, 9, 15, 16; BriEAA; DcAmArt; DcAmB; GayN; IlBEAAW; LinLib S; McGDA; McGEWB; NatCAB 15; OxCAmH; OxCAmL 65; WebAB 74, 79; WhAm 1; WhNaAH*

Blakely, Colin (George Edward)
Irish. Actor
Played Dr. Watson in film *The Private Life of Sherlock Holmes,* 1970.
b. Sep 23, 1930 in Bangor, Northern Ireland
d. May 7, 1987 in London, England
Source: *AnObit 1987; BioIn 15; CamGWoT; CnThe; ConTFT 4; FacFETw; FilmEn; FilmgC; HalFC 80, 84, 88; LegTOT; OxCThe 83; PiP; PlP&P; Who 82, 83, 85; WhoHol A; WhoThe 72, 77, 81*

Blakely, Susan
American. Actor
Played in TV miniseries "Rich Man, Poor Man"; movies *The Way We Were,* 1973 ; *Towering Inferno,* 1974.
b. Sep 7, 1948 in Frankfurt, Germany
Source: *ConTFT 6; HalFC 84; IntMPA 86; LegTOT; VarWW 85; WhoAm 80, 82; WhoHol A*

Blakey, Art
American. Jazz Musician
Drummer, major innovator of modern jazz; best known for leading Jazz Messengers, 1954-90, and turning group into jazz training ground; created "hard bop" school that added blues, gospel rhythms to music.
b. Oct 11, 1919 in Pittsburgh, Pennsylvania
d. Oct 16, 1990 in New York, New York
Source: *AfrAmAl 6; AllMusG; AnObit 1990; Baker 84, 92; BiDAmM; BiDJaz; BioIn 5, 7, 11, 12; CmpEPM; ConMus 11; CurBio 88, 91N; DcArts; DcTwCCu 5; DrBlPA, 90; EncJzS; FacFETw; IlEncJ; InB&W 80; LegTOT; NegAl 89; NewAmDM; NewGrDA 86; NewGrDJ 88, 94; NewGrDM 80; News 91, 91-1; OxCPMus; PenEncP; WhAm 10; WhoAm 74, 84, 86, 88, 90; WhoBlA 75, 77, 80, 85, 88, 90, 92N; WorAl; WorAlBi*

Blalock, Alfred
American. Surgeon
Developed artery bypass operation, 1944, that saved "blue babies."
b. Apr 5, 1899 in Culloden, Georgia
d. Sep 15, 1964 in Baltimore, Maryland
Source: *AmDec 1940; BioIn 1, 2, 3, 5, 7, 11, 13, 16, 21; CurBio 46, 64; DcAmB S7; DcAmMeB 84; FacFETw; InSci; LarDcSc; McGMS 80; ObitT 1961; OxCAmH; OxCMed 86; WebAB 74, 79; WhAm 4*

Blalock, Jane
American. Golfer
Turned pro, 1969; has over 30 tour wins; wrote autobiography *The Guts to Win,* 1977.
b. Sep 19, 1945 in Portsmouth, New Hampshire
Source: *BiDAmSp Sup; ConAu 112; EncWomS; GoodHs; InWom SUP; NewYTBE 72; NewYTBS 77; WhoAm 78, 80, 82; WhoGolf; WhoSpor; WorAl*

Blanc, Louis
[Jean Joseph Charles Louis Blanc]
French. Political Leader, Author
Considered father of state socialism; wrote *History of French Revolution,* 1847-62.
b. Oct 29, 1811 in Madrid, Spain
d. Dec 6, 1882 in Cannes, France
Source: *BioIn 5, 12, 17; Dis&D; EncRev; McGEWB; OxCFr; REn; WorAl; WorAlBi*

Blanc, Mel(vin Jerome)
American. Actor
Voice of many cartoon characters: Bugs Bunny, Porky Pig, Daffy Duck.
b. May 30, 1908 in San Francisco, California
d. Jul 10, 1989 in Los Angeles, California
Source: *AnObit 1989; ASCAP 66, 80; BioIn 1, 10, 11, 12, 17; ConTFT 8; CurBio 76, 89N, 90; EncAFC; FacFETw; FilmEn; FilmgC; HalFC 80, 84, 88; IntDcF 2-4; IntMPA 75, 76, 77, 78, 79, 80, 81, 82, 84, 86, 88; JoeFr; LegTOT; News 89; NewYTBS 89; RadStar; SaTiSS; SmATA 64; WhoAm 74; WhoCom; WhoHol A; WorAl; WorAlBi*

Blanchard, Doc
[Felix Anthony Blanchard]
"Mr. Inside"
American. Football Player, Football Coach
Fullback at West Point, 1944-46; won Heisman Trophy, 1945; became nat. figure even though he never played pro football.
b. Dec 11, 1924 in Bishopville, South Carolina
Source: *BiDAmSp FB; BioIn 1, 3, 4, 5, 6, 7, 8, 10, 14, 16; CurBio 46; WhoFtbl 74; WhoSpor*

Blanchard, Francois
[Jean Pierre Francois Blanchard]
French. Balloonist
Credited with first balloon crossing of English Channel, first ascents in US.
b. Jul 4, 1753 in Les Andelys, France
d. Mar 7, 1809 in Paris, France
Source: *AsBiEn; InSci; NewCol 75*

Blanchard, Jim
[James Johnston Blanchard]
American. Politician
Democratic governor of MI, 1983-91, defeated in upset by John Engler.
b. Aug 8, 1942 in Detroit, Michigan
Source: *AlmAP 88; BiDrGov 1983, 1988; BiDrUSC 89; BioIn 13; CngDr 81; IntWW 83; WhoAm 86, 95, 96, 97; WhoAmP 75, 77, 79, 81, 83, 85, 87, 89, 91, 93, 95; WhoGov 77; WhoMW 80, 82; WhoWor 84, 95*

Blanchard, Thomas
American. Inventor
Developed principle for turning irregular forms from a pattern; patented stem carriage, 1825.
b. Jun 24, 1788 in Sutton, Massachusetts
d. Apr 16, 1864 in Boston, Massachusetts
Source: *AmBi; ApCAB; BioIn 3, 14, 17; DcAmB; Drake; HarEnUS; InSci; NatCAB 6; TwCBDA; WebAB 74, 79; WhAm HS; WorInv*

Bland, Bobby Blue
[Robert Calvin Bland]
American. Singer
Blues albums include *Blues in the Night,* 1985.
b. Jan 27, 1930 in Rosemark, Tennessee
Source: *BiDAfM; BiDAmM; BioIn 18; BluesWW; DrBlPA; GuBlues; HarEnR 86; IlEncRk; InB&W 85; RkOn 74, 82; WhoAfA 96; WhoRocM 82*

Bland, Richard Parks
American. Statesman
Dem. congressman; leader of Free Silver movement, 1875-77; defeated by Bryan for presidential nomination, 1896.
b. Aug 19, 1835 in Hartford, Kentucky
d. 1899
Source: *AmBi; AmPolLe; ApCAB; BiAUS; BiDrAC; BiDrUSC 89; BiDSA; DcAmB; EncAAH; HarEnUS; NatCAB 10; REnAW; TwCBDA; WhAm 1; WhAmP*

Blanda, George Frederick
American. Football Player
Quarterback, placekicker, 1949-75, mostly with Oakland; scored NFL record 2,002 pts; Hall of Fame, 1981.
b. Sep 17, 1927 in Youngwood, Pennsylvania
Source: *BiDAmSp FB; CmCal; ConAu 114; CurBio 72; WebAB 74, 79; WhoAm 74; WhoFtbl 74; WorAl*

Blanding, Don
American. Author, Illustrator
Wrote, illustrated books on FL, HI: *Vagabond's House,* 1928; *Hula Moon,* 1930.
b. Nov 7, 1894 in Kingfisher, Oklahoma
d. Jun 9, 1957 in Los Angeles, California

Source: *BioIn 1, 4, 6; CurBio 57; NatCAB 46; ObitOF 79; WhAm 3; WhoAmA 89N, 91N, 93N*

Blanding, Sarah Gibson
American. Educator
First woman pres. of Vassar College, 1946-64.
b. Nov 22, 1898 in Lexington, Kentucky
d. Mar 3, 1985 in Newton, Pennsylvania
Source: *AmWomM*

Blane, Sally
[Elizabeth Jane Young]
American. Actor
Sister of Loretta Young; played in B movies in the 1930s.
b. Jul 11, 1910 in Salida, Colorado
Source: *BioIn 9, 18; EncAFC; Film 2; FilmEn; FilmgC; ForYSC; HalFC 80, 84, 88; InWom SUP; LegTOT; MovMk; SilFlmP; SweetSg B; ThFT; TwYS; What 3; WhoHol 92, A*

Blankers-Koen, Fanny
Dutch. Track Athlete
Won four gold medals, 1948 Olympics.
b. Apr 7, 1946 in Amsterdam, Netherlands
Source: *WhoTr&F 73*

Blanqui, Auguste
[Louis Auguste Blanqui]
French. Revolutionary
Active in French Revolution from 1825; strongly influenced Karl Marx.
b. Feb 1, 1805 in Ruget, France
d. Jan 1, 1881 in Paris, France
Source: *BiDFrPL; BioIn 7, 9, 12, 13, 17; CelCen; DcBiPP; EncRev; McGEWB; McGEWD 72; OxCFr; REn; WhDW*

Blanton, Jimmy
American. Jazz Musician
Bass player with Duke Ellington, 1939-42.
b. 1918 in Chattanooga, Tennessee
d. Jul 30, 1942 in Los Angeles, California
Source: *AfrAmAl 6; AllMusG; Baker 92; BioIn 16; CmpEPM; LegTOT; NegAl 89; NewAmDM; NewGrDA 86; NewGrDJ 88, 94; OxCPMus; PenEncP; WhoJazz 72*

Blanton, (Leonard) Ray
American. Politician
Governor of TN 1975-79; congressman, 1966-72.
b. Apr 10, 1930 in Hardin County, Tennessee
d. Nov 22, 1996 in Jackson, Tennessee
Source: *BiDrAC; BiDrGov 1789, 1978; BiDrUSC 89; BioIn 10, 11, 12; BlueB 76; IntWW 75, 76, 77, 78, 79, 80, 81, 82, 83, 89, 91, 93; WhoAm 76, 78; WhoAmP 81; WhoGov 72, 75, 77; WhoSSW 73, 76, 78; WhoWor 78*

Blasco-Ibanez, Vicente
Spanish. Author
Wrote realistic novels *Blood and Sand*, 1913; *Four Horsemen of the Apocalypse*, 1918.
b. Jan 29, 1867 in Valencia, Spain
d. Jan 28, 1928 in Menton, France
Source: *CasWL; ClDMEL 47; CyWA 58; DcSpL; EncWL 2; EvEuW; LngCTC; ModRL; OxCEng 67; PenC EUR; REn; TwCA, SUP; TwCWr; WhDW*

Blashfield, Edwin Howland
American. Artist
Mural, genre painter; did murals for congressional library, 1895.
b. Dec 15, 1848 in New York, New York
d. Oct 12, 1936
Source: *AmAu&B; AmBi; ApCAB, X; ArtsAmW 2; BioIn 4; BriEAA; ChhPo; DcAmArt; DcAmAu; DcAmB S2; DcNAA; EncAB-A 8; LinLib S; McGDA; NatCAB 9, 27; TwCBDA; WhAm 1*

Blass, Bill
[William Ralph Blass]
American. Fashion Designer
Known for apparel, home furnishings, cars, designs.
b. Jun 22, 1922 in Fort Wayne, Indiana
Source: *AmDec 1970; BioIn 7, 8, 9, 10, 12; CelR, 90; ConDes 84, 90, 97; ConFash; CurBio 66; DcTwDes; EncFash; Entr; FacFETw; FairDF US; LegTOT; NewYTBS 80; WhoAm 74, 76, 78, 80, 82, 84, 86, 88, 90, 92, 94, 95, 96, 97; WhoE 74, 75, 77, 85, 86, 93, 95; WhoFash 88; WhoFI 74; WorAl; WorAlBi; WorFshn*

Blassingale, Wyatt Rainey
American. Author
Children's non-fiction books include *French Foreign Legion*, 1955.
b. Feb 6, 1909 in Demopolis, Alabama
Source: *AuBYP 2; ConAu 1R; SmATA 1; WrDr 76*

Blatch, Harriot Eaton Stanton
American. Feminist, Lecturer
Daughter of Elizabeth Cady Stanton; founded Women's Political Union, 1908; leader in women's suffrage movement.
b. Jan 20, 1856 in Seneca Falls, New York
d. Nov 20, 1940 in Greenwich, Connecticut
Source: *AmRef; AmWomWr; BiCAW; BioIn 15, 21; CurBio 41; DcAmB S2; DcNAA; EncWHA; InWom SUP; LibW; NotAW; OxCAmL 65; WhAm 1; WhAmP; WhNAA; WomWWA 14*

Blatchford, Joseph Hoffer
American. Government Official
Director of Peace Corps, 1969-71.
b. Jun 7, 1934 in Milwaukee, Wisconsin
Source: *BioIn 8, 9, 10; CurBio 71; IntWW 74, 75, 76, 77, 78; NewYTBE 71; WhoAm 74, 76; WhoAmL 83, 85, 87, 94; WhoAmP 73; WhoGov 72, 75; WhoWor 76, 78, 80, 82*

Blatchford, Samuel
American. Supreme Court Justice
Respected Supreme Court Justice, 1882-93; expert on maritime, patent law.
b. Mar 9, 1820 in New York, New York
d. Jul 7, 1893 in Newport, Rhode Island
Source: *Alli SUP; ApCAB; BiAUS; BiDFedJ; BioIn 2, 5, 15; DcAmB; DcNAA; HarEnUS; NatCAB 1; OxCSupC; TwCBDA; WebAB 74, 79; WhAm HS*

Blatty, William Peter
American. Author
Wrote *The Exorcist*, 1971; sold over 10 million copies; on best-seller list 55 weeks.
b. Jan 7, 1928 in New York, New York
Source: *ConAu 5R, 9NR; ConLC 2; ConTFT 4; CurBio 74; FilmgC; HalFC 84; IntAu&W 86; IntMPA 82, 96; WhoAm 86; WrDr 86*

Blavatsky, Helena Petrovna
"Madame"
Russian. Religious Leader
Founded Theosophical Society, 1875; combines Buddhist, Brahmanic theories of evolution, reincarnation.
b. Jul 30, 1831 in Ekaterinoslav, Russia
d. May 8, 1891 in London, England
Source: *Alli SUP; AmAu&B; AmBi; AmWom; ApCAB; BbD; Benet 87, 96; BenetAL 91; BiD&SB; DcAmAu; DcAmB; DcAmReB 2; DcInB; EncARH; EncPaPR 91; LinLib L, S; NatCAB 15; NewAgE 90; NewC; NewCBEL; NotAW; OxCAmH; OxCAmL 65; OxCEng 85, 95; PopDcHi; RelLAm 91; REn; TwCBDA; WhAm HS; WomFir; WorAl*

Blech, Leo
German. Conductor, Composer
Conducted Berlin Operas, 1906-37; wrote opera *Versiegelt*, 1908.
b. Apr 21, 1871 in Aachen, Prussia
d. Aug 24, 1958 in Berlin, Germany (West)
Source: *Baker 78, 84, 92; BioIn 2, 4, 5; CmOp; IntDcOp; MetOEnc; NewEOp 71; NewGrDM 80; NewGrDO; ObitT 1951; OxDcOp; PenDiMP*

Bleckner, Jeff
American. Director
Won Tony for *Sticks and Bones*, 1971.
Source: *BioIn 9; ConTFT 4; WhoThe 77, 81*

Bledsoe, Drew
American. Football Player
Quarterback for the New England Patriots, 1993—.
b. Feb 14, 1972 in Ellensburg, Washington
Source: *BioIn 20, 21; News 95, 95-1; WhoAm 97*

Bledsoe, Jules
American. Actor, Singer
Sang "Ol' Man River" in *Show Boat,* 1927 stage, 1929 film.
b. Dec 29, 1898
d. Jul 14, 1943 in Hollywood, California
Source: *AmPS B; Baker 78, 84, 92; BiDAmM; BioIn 17, 18; BlkOpe; ConAmC 82; CurBio 43; DrBlPA, 90; NewAmDM; NewGrDA 86; NewGrDO; NotNAT B; OxCAmT 84; OxCPMus; WhScrn 74, 77*

Bledsoe, Tempestt Kenieth
American. Actor
Played Vanessa Huxtable on "The Cosby Show," 1984-92.
b. Aug 1, 1973 in Chicago, Illinois

Bleeker, Sonia
[Sonia Bleeker Zim]
Russian. Children's Author, Editor
Books on Native Americans, African tribes include *The Crow Indians,* 1953.
b. Nov 28, 1909 in Starchevicvhi, Russia
d. Nov 13, 1971
Source: *BkP; ConAu 1R, 3NR, 4NR, 33R, X; ForWC 70; MorJA; SmATA 2, 26N*

Bleeth, Yasmine
American. Actor
Plays Lee Ann Demarest on soap opera *One Life to Live.*
b. 1968? in New York, New York

Blegen, Carl William
American. Archaeologist
Discovered one of the earliest known samples of European writing; using archaeological techniques, was able to prove the date of the sack of Troy.
b. Jan 27, 1887 in Minneapolis, Minnesota
d. Aug 24, 1971 in Athens, Greece
Source: *BioIn 9, 10; ConAu 33R; NewYTBE 71; ObitOF 79; WhAm 5*

Blegen, Judith Eyer
American. Opera Singer
Lyric coloratura soprano; soloist with US, European opera companies.
b. Apr 27, 1941 in Missoula, Montana
Source: *Baker 84; CurBio 77; IntWW 83; MusSN; NewYTBS 74; WhoAm 76, 78, 80, 82, 84, 86; WhoAmM 83; WhoAmW 83, 85; WhoOp 76*

Bleiberg, Robert Marvin
American. Publisher, Editor
Publisher, editorial director, *Barron's National Business and Financial Weekly.*
b. Jun 21, 1924 in New York, New York
Source: *BlueB 76; ConAu 103; EncTwCJ; WhoAm 74, 76, 78, 80, 82, 84, 86, 88, 90, 92, 94, 95, 96, 97; WhoFI 74, 83, 85, 87, 89, 92, 94; WhoUSWr 88; WhoWrEP 89, 92, 95*

Bleier, Rocky
[Robert Patrick Bleier]
American. Football Player
Lost part of right foot in Vietnam, 1969; running back, Pittsburgh, 1968, 1971-80; wrote *Fighting Back,* 1976.
b. Mar 5, 1946 in Appleton, Wisconsin
Source: *BiDAmSp Sup; BioIn 11, 12; ConAu 85; NewYTBS 74, 75, 80; WhoAm 78, 80*

Bleriot, Louis
French. Aviator, Engineer
First to fly plane across English Channel, 1909.
b. Jul 1, 1872 in Cambrai, France
d. Aug 2, 1936 in Paris, France
Source: *BioIn 4, 6, 7, 8, 9, 13; DcTwDes; FacFETw; InSci; LinLib S; WebBD 83; WhDW; WorAl; WorAlBi; WorInv*

Blessington, Marguerite Gardiner, Countess
English. Socialite, Writer
Renowned beauty; headed intellectual circle; wrote memoir of Byron, 1834.
b. Sep 1, 1789 in Knockbrit, Ireland
d. Jun 4, 1849 in Paris, France
Source: *Alli; BbD; BiD&SB; BritAu 19; CasWL; DcEnL; DcLEL; EvLB; NewC; PoIre; REn*

Bley, Carla
American. Composer, Bandleader, Pianist
Began composing in 50s; unique style of composing and arranging considered one of most eclectic of all jazz artists; founded recording label, WAH, 1973; formed Carla Bley Band, 1977.
b. May 11, 1938 in Oakland, California
Source: *AllMusG; BioIn 10, 11, 12, 15, 16; ConAmC 76, 82; ConMus 8; EncJzS; IntWW 91; InWom SUP; NewAmDM; NewGrDA 86; NewGrDJ 88, 94; NewYTBS 74; PenEncP; RolSEnR 83; WhoAm 88; WhoAmW 85; WhoE 74; WhoEnt 92*

Bleyer, Archie
American. Musician
Head of Cadence records, 1952; had hit single "Mr. Sandman," 1954.
b. Jun 12, 1909 in Corona, New York
Source: *BgBands 74; BioIn 16; CmpEPM; LegTOT; RkOn 74*

Blier, Bertrand
French. Filmmaker, Author
Known for outrageously farcical films including *Femmes Fatales* and *Get Out Your Hankerchiefs;* wrote novel *Les Valseuses.*
b. Mar 14, 1939 in Boulogne-Billancourt, France
Source: *BiDFilm 94; BioIn 16; ConAu 143; ConTFT 8; CurBio 88; EncEurC; FilmEn; HalFC 84, 88; IntDcF 1-2, 2-2; IntMPA 92, 94, 96; IntWW 91, 93; LegTOT; MiSFD 9; WhoFr 79; WhoWor 95, 96, 97; WorFDir 2; WrDr 96*

Blige, Mary J(ane)
American. Singer, Songwriter
Rhythm and blues singer; winner of the Soul Train Music Award, 1993.
b. Jan 11, 1971 in New York, New York
Source: *WhoAmW 97*

Bligh, William, Captain
English. Naval Officer
Captain, HMS *Bounty* when mutiny occurred; cast adrift for 4,000 miles.
b. Sep 9, 1754 in Plymouth, England
d. Dec 7, 1817 in London, England
Source: *Alli; Benet 87, 96; BiDLA; BioIn 2, 3, 4, 6, 7, 8, 9, 10, 11, 16, 17; CelCen; DcBiPP; DcNaB; HarEnMi; HisDBrE; HisWorL; LegTOT; McGEWB; NewC; NewCBEL; OxCAusL; OxCShps; REn; WhDW; WhWE; WorAl; WorAlBi*

Blind Faith
["Ginger" Baker; Eric Clapton; Rick Grech; Stevie Winwood]
English. Music Group
Only album *Blind Faith,* 1969, with hits "Can't Find My Way Home"; "Presence of the Lord."
Source: *BiDJaz A; BioIn 14, 15, 16, 17, 18, 19, 20, 21; ConMuA 80A; EncPR&S 89; EncRk 88; EncRkSt; HarEnR 86; IlEncRk; PenEncP; RolSEnR 83; WhoAm 74, 76, 78; WhoRock 81; WhoRocM 82; WhoWor 78*

Blind Willie McTell
[Blind Sammie; Georgia Bill; William Samuel McTell]
American. Singer, Musician
Guitarist and singer who played blues, ragtime, gospel, pop, and country material; recorded with Curly Weaver, Buddy Moss, and Ruth Day, 1927-1956; recorded songs "Kill It, Kid" and "Broke Down Engine Blues;" posthumously inducted into the Georgia Music Hall of Fame, 1990.
b. May 5, 1901 in Thomson, Georgia
d. Aug 19, 1959 in Georgia

Blinn, Holbrook
American. Actor, Producer
Silent film star who appeared opposite Marion Davies in *Janice Meredith,* 1924; *Zander the Great,* 1925.
b. 1872 in San Francisco, California
d. Jun 24, 1928 in Croton-on-Hudson, New York
Source: *BioIn 3; CamGWoT; CmCal; DcAmB; Film 1, 2; HalFC 80, 84, 88; MotPP; NatCAB 21; NotNAT B; OxCAmT 84; TwYS; WhAm 1; WhoHol B; WhoStg 1906, 1908; WhScrn 74, 77, 83; WhThe*

Blish, James Benjamin
American. Author
Science fiction writer; won Hugo for *A Case of Conscience,* 1958.
b. May 23, 1921 in East Orange, New Jersey
d. Jul 30, 1975 in Henley-on-Thames, England

Source: *AmAu&B; Au&Wr 71; ConAu 1R, 3NR, 57; ConLC 14; ConNov 76; DcLEL 1940; LinLib L; WorAu 1950; WrDr 76*

Bliss, Arthur, Sir
English. Composer
Master of the Queen's Music, 1953-75; wrote ballet *Lady of Shallott,* 1958.
b. Aug 2, 1891 in London, England
d. Mar 27, 1975 in London, England
Source: *Baker 78, 84; BiDD; BioIn 1, 3, 4, 8, 9, 10, 11, 12, 14, 16; BriBkM 80; CnOxB; CompSN, SUP; CpmDNM 74, 75; DancEn 78; DcCM; DcCom 77; DcCom&M 79; FilmgC; HalFC 80, 84, 88; IntDcB; IntWW 74; LegTOT; MusMk; NewAmDM; NewEOp 71; NewGrDM 80; NewOxM; ObitT 1971; OxCEng 85, 95; OxCMus; OxDcOp; PenDiMP A; WhAm 6; WhDW; Who 74; WhoMus 72; WhoWor 74*

Bliss, Ray C(harles)
American. Political Leader
Chm., GOP, 1966-68; credited with rebuilding party after defeat of Goldwater, 1964.
b. Dec 16, 1907 in Akron, Ohio
d. Aug 6, 1981 in Akron, Ohio
Source: *BioIn 6, 7, 8, 11, 12; BlueB 76; CurBio 81; IntWW 74, 75, 76, 77, 78, 79, 80, 81; NewYTBS 81; PolProf J; WhAm 8; WhoAm 74, 76, 78, 80, 82; WhoAmP 73, 75, 77, 79; WhoWor 74, 76, 78, 80*

Bliss, Tasker Howard
American. Military Leader
As chief of staff, WW I, transformed army from small peacetime organization to huge war machine.
b. Dec 31, 1853 in Lewisburg, Pennsylvania
d. Nov 9, 1930 in Washington, District of Columbia
Source: *AmBi; AmPeW; ApCAB X; BiDInt; BioIn 7, 9, 16; CmdGen 1991; DcAmB S1; DcAmDH 80, 89; DcAmMiB; HarEnMi; LinLib S; NatCAB 21; OxCAmH; WebAB 74, 79; WebAMB; WhAm 1*

Blitch, Iris F(aircloth)
American. Politician
Dem. representative from GA, 1955-63.
b. Apr 25, 1912
d. Aug 19, 1993 in San Diego, California
Source: *BiDrAC; BiDrUSC 89; BioIn 17, 19; CurBio 93N; InWom, SUP; WhAmP; WhoAmW 58, 61, 64*

Blitzstein, Marc
American. Composer, Author
Wrote *The Cradle Will Rock,* libretto for American version of *Three Penny Opera,* 1952.
b. Mar 2, 1905 in Philadelphia, Pennsylvania
d. Jan 22, 1964
Source: *AmAu&B; AmComp; ASCAP 66, 80; Baker 78, 84, 92; BenetAL 91; BestMus; BiDAmM; BiDD; BiE&WWA; BioIn 1, 2, 3, 4, 5, 6, 7, 8, 9, 10, 12; BriBkM 80; CamGLE; CamHAL; CmOp; CnMD; CompSN, SUP; ConAmC 76, 82; ConAu 110; CurBio 40, 64; DcAmB S7; DcArts; DcCM; DcTwCCu 1; EncAL; EncMT; FacFETw; GayLesB; HalFC 88; IntDcOp; IntWWM 77, 80; LegTOT; McGEWD 72, 84; MetOEnc; ModWD; MusMk; NatCAB 52; NewAmDM; NewCBMT; NewEOp 71; NewGrDA 86; NewGrDM 80; NewGrDO; NewOxM; NotNAT B; OxCAmH; OxCAmL 65, 83, 95; OxCAmT 84; OxCMus; OxCPMus; OxDcOp; PlP&P; REn; REnAL; WebAB 74, 79; WhAm 4*

Bliven, Bruce
American. Author, Editor
Editor, pres., of *New Republic,* 1923-53.
b. Jul 27, 1889 in Emmetsburg, Iowa
d. May 27, 1977 in Palo Alto, California
Source: *AmAu&B; Au&Wr 71; AuBYP 2, 3; BioIn 4, 8, 11, 13, 20; BlueB 76; ConAu 37R, 69; CurBio 41, 77N; DcLB 137; EncAJ; IntWW 74, 75, 76, 77; NatCAB 62; TwCA, SUP; WhAm 7; WhJnl; Who 74; WhoAm 74, 76; WhoWest 74, 76; WrDr 76*

Blixen, Karen Christentze, Baroness
[Pierre Andrezel; Isak Dinesen]
Danish. Author
Known for memoirs of life in Kenya, *Out of Africa,* 1937; film version won best picture Oscar, 1985.
b. Apr 17, 1885 in Rungsted, Denmark
d. Sep 7, 1962 in Rungsted, Denmark
Source: *ArtclWW 2; AtlBL; Benet 87, 96; BioIn 14, 15, 16, 17, 19, 20, 21; CamGLE; CasWL; ClDMEL 80; ConAu P-2, X; ConLC 10, 29, 95; CyWA 58, 89; DcAfHiB 86; DcArts; DcScanL; EncCoWW; EncWL 2, 3; EuWr 10; EvEuW; FacFETw; FemiCLE; GrFLW; GrWomW; InWom, SUP; LiExTwC; LinLib L; LngCTC; McGEWB; ModWoWr; Novels; ObitT 1961; OxCEng 85; PenC ENG, EUR; PenEncH; PenNWW B; RAdv 14, 13-2; REn; RfGShF; RfGWoL 95; RGTwCWr; ScF&FL 1, 2; ShSCr 7; ShSWr; TwCA, SUP; TwCWr; WhoTwCL; WomWMM; WorAl; WorAlBi; WrPh*

Bloch, Bertram
American. Dramatist
Co-wrote play *Dark Victory,* 1934; filmed, 1939.
b. May 5, 1892 in New York, New York
d. Jun 21, 1987 in New York, New York
Source: *BiE&WWA; BioIn 3, 4, 15; ConAu 122; NotNAT; ScF&FL 1, 92*

Bloch, Claude Charles
American. Military Leader
Admiral at Pearl Harbor during Japanese attack, 1941.
b. Jul 12, 1878 in Woodbury, Kentucky
d. Oct 6, 1967 in Washington, District of Columbia
Source: *BiDWWGF; BioIn 1, 8, 9; CurBio 42, 67; DcAmB S8; NatCAB 53; WhAm 4A*

Bloch, Eric
American. Government Official
Director, Nat. Science Foundation, 1984-90; advocates research, developed to maintain American economic competitiveness.
b. Jan 9, 1925 in Salzburg, Germany
Source: *AmMWSc 82; ConNews 87-4; WhoAm 86*

Bloch, Ernest
American. Composer
Noted for tone poem, "Israel Symphony"; "America," 1926; Bloch Society founded in London, 1937.
b. Jul 24, 1880 in Geneva, Switzerland
d. Jul 15, 1959 in Portland, Oregon
Source: *AmComp; ASCAP 66, 80; AtlBL; Baker 78, 84, 92; Benet 87; BiDAmM; BioIn 1, 2, 3, 4, 5, 6, 8, 11, 12, 13, 14; BriBkM 80; CmCal; CompSN, SUP; ConAmC 76, 82; ConPhot 82, 88; CurBio 53, 59; DcAmB S6; DcArts; DcCM; DcCom 77; DcCom&M 79; DcTwCC; FacFETw; ICPEnP A; IntDcOp; LegTOT; MacBEP; McGEWB; MetOEnc; MusMk; NatCAB 44; NewAmDM; NewGrDA 86; NewGrDM 80; NewGrDO; NewOxM; ObitT 1951; OxCAmH; OxCAmL 65; OxCMus; OxDcOp; PenDiMP A; REn; WebAB 74, 79; WhAm 3*

Bloch, Felix
Swiss. Physicist, Educator
Shared Nobel Prize in Physics with Edward Purcell for study of NMR (nuclear magnetic resonance).
b. Oct 23, 1905 in Zurich, Switzerland
d. Sep 10, 1983 in Zurich, Switzerland
Source: *AmMWSc 76P, 79, 82; AnObit 1983; AsBiEn; BiESc; BioIn 3, 5, 11, 13, 14, 15, 16, 20; BlueB 76; CamDcSc; CurBio 83N; InSci; IntWW 74, 75, 76, 77, 78, 79, 80, 81, 82, 83; LarDcSc; LegTOT; McGMS 80; NewYTBS 83; NobelP; NotTwCS; PeoHis; RAdv 14, 13-5; WebAB 74, 79; WhAm 8; Who 74, 82, 83; WhoAm 74, 76, 78, 80, 82; WhoAmJ 80; WhoNob, 90, 95; WhoWest 78, 80, 82, 84; WhoWor 74, 82, 84; WhoWorJ 72, 78; WorAl; WorAlBi; WorScD*

Bloch, Henry W(ollman)
American. Businessman
Co-founder, pres., CEO, H&R Block, Inc., 1955—.
b. Jul 30, 1922 in Kansas City, Missouri
Source: *BioIn 12, 15, 16, 17, 21; ConAmBL; Dun&B 88; St&PR 75, 84, 87, 91, 93; WhoAm 74, 76, 78, 80, 82, 84, 86, 88, 92, 94, 95, 96, 97; WhoAmJ 80; WhoFI 74, 75, 77, 79, 87, 89, 94, 96; WhoMW 74, 76, 78, 88, 90, 92; WhoWor 76, 93*

Bloch, Ivan Sol
American. Producer, Restaurateur
Co-owner, Sardi's, NYC; Broadway productions include *The Real Thing;* won two Tonys.
b. Nov 16, 1940 in Detroit, Michigan
Source: *ConNews 86-3; WhoFI 77, 81, 83; WhoMW 76, 78, 82; WhoWor 82*

Bloch, Konrad Emil
American. Scientist, Educator
Shared Nobel Prize in medicine, 1964, for research about cholesterol.
b. Jan 21, 1912 in Neisse, Germany
Source: *AmMWSc 76P, 79, 82, 86, 89, 92, 95; AsBiEn; BiESc; BioIn 7, 14, 15, 20; LarDcSc; McGMS 80; WebAB 74; Who 85; WhoAm 90, 92, 94, 95, 96, 97; WhoE 89, 91, 95, 97; WhoMedH; WhoNob; WhoScEn 94, 96; WhoWor 74, 89, 91, 93, 95, 96, 97; WorAl*

Bloch, Raymond A
American. Bandleader, Conductor
Best known as TV conductor on Jackie Gleason, Ed Sullivan shows, 1950-60.
b. Aug 3, 1902 in Alsace-Lorraine, Germany
d. Mar 29, 1982 in Miami, Florida
Source: *ASCAP 66, 80; BiDAmM; CmpEPM; NewYTBS 82; WorAl*

Bloch, Robert Albert
[Tarleton Fiske; Nathan Hindin; Collier Young]
American. Author, Screenwriter
Mystery writer who wrote film version of his novel *Psycho,* 1959, sequel *Psycho II,* 1982.
b. Apr 5, 1917 in Chicago, Illinois
d. Sep 23, 1994
Source: *AmAu&B; ConAu 5NR, 5R; ConLC 33, 86; EncMys; EncSF; FanAl; IntMPA 81; LinLib L; PseudN 82; SmATA 12; WhAm 11; WhoAm 82, 84, 86, 88, 90, 92, 94; WhoEnt 92; WhoSciF; WhoUSWr 88; WhoWrEP 89, 92, 95*

Block, John Rusling
American. Government Official
Millionaire farmer who was secretary of Agriculture under Ronald Reagan, 1981-86.
b. Feb 15, 1935 in Galesburg, Illinois
Source: *BiDrUSE 89; BioIn 12, 13; CngDr 81; CurBio 82; IntWW 89, 91, 93; IntYB 82; NatCAB 63N; NewYTBS 80, 84; WhoAm 82, 84, 86, 88, 90, 92, 94, 95, 96, 97; WhoE 81, 83, 85; WhoFI 83, 85; WhoWor 82, 84, 87*

Block, Joseph L(eopold)
American. Business Executive
Island Steel exec., 1928-71; succeeded Randall as pres., 1953.
b. Oct 6, 1902 in Chicago, Illinois
d. Nov 17, 1992 in Chicago, Illinois
Source: *BioIn 2, 5, 6, 8, 11; BlueB 76; CurBio 61, 93N; IntWW 74, 75, 76, 77, 78, 79, 80, 81, 82, 83; St&PR 75; WhoAm 74, 76, 78; WhoAmJ 80; WhoWor 74; WhoWorJ 72, 78*

Block, Martin
Radio Performer
Radio host of "Make Believe Ballroom," 1934-54.
b. 1903
d. Sep 19, 1967 in Englewood, New Jersey
Source: *BioIn 1, 4, 8; CmpEPM; ObitOF 79; RadStar*

Block, Rory
[Aurora Block]
American. Musician, Singer
Blues guitarist whose works include: *How to Play Blues Guitar,* 1966, *You're the One,* 1978, *High Heeled Blues,* 1981, *Blue Horizon,* 1982, *Angel of Mercey,* 1994, and *Tornado,* 1996.
Source: *WhoRocM 82*

Blocker, Dan
American. Actor
Played Hoss Cartwright on TV series "Bonanza," 1959-72.
b. Dec 12, 1927 in Bowie, Texas
d. May 13, 1972 in Inglewood, California
Source: *FilmgC; LegTOT; NewYTBE 72; WhAm 5; WhoHol B; WhScrn 77*

Blodgett, Katherine Burr
American. Physicist
Developed non-reflecting glass, used on almost all camera, optical lenses.
b. Jan 10, 1898 in Schenectady, New York
d. Dec 10, 1979 in Schenectady, New York
Source: *NewYTBS 79; WhAm 7; WhoAmW 58; WomFir; WorInv*

Bloembergen, Nicolaas
American. Physicist
Shared 1981 Nobel Prize in physics for work with laser spectroscopy; studied nonlinear optics.
b. Mar 11, 1920 in Dordrecht, Netherlands
Source: *AmMWSc 76P, 79, 82, 86, 89, 92, 95; AsBiEn; BiESc; BioIn 12, 13, 14, 15, 20; BlueB 76; IntWW 74, 75, 76, 77, 78, 79, 80, 81, 82, 83, 89, 91, 93; LarDcSc; LElec; McGMS 80; NobelP; NotTwCS; Who 83, 85, 88, 90, 92, 94; WhoAm 74, 76, 78, 80, 82, 84, 86, 88, 90, 92, 94, 95, 96, 97; WhoE 83, 85, 86, 89, 91, 93, 95, 97; WhoFrS 84; WhoNob, 90, 95; WhoScEn 94, 96; WhoTech 89, 95; WhoWor 82, 84, 87, 89, 91, 93, 95, 96, 97; WorAlBi; WrDr 76, 82, 84, 86, 88, 90, 92, 94, 96*

Blofeld, John
American. Author
Books on China include *Taoism: Road to Immortality,* 1978.
b. Apr 2, 1913 in London, England
Source: *Au&Wr 71; ConAu 4NR, 19NR, 53, 123; EncO&P 1S1, 2, 3*

Blok, Aleksandr Aleksandrovich
Russian. Author, Poet
Symbolist; wrote *The Twelve,* 1920.
b. Nov 28, 1880 in Saint Petersburg, Russia
d. Aug 7, 1921 in Petrograd, Union of Soviet Socialist Republics
Source: *AtlBL; Benet 87, 96; BiDSovU; BioIn 1, 2, 3, 6, 8, 9, 12, 13; CamGWoT; CasWL; ChhPo S1; ClDMEL 47; CnMD; CnMWL; DcRusL; DcRusLS; EncWL; Ent; EvEuW; HanRL; LngCTC; McGEWB; McGEWD 72, 84; ModSL 1; ModWD; OxCEng 67, 85, 95; PenC EUR; REn; SovUn; TwCA, SUP; TwCWr; WhDW; WhoTwCL; WorAl*

Blomberg, Ron(ald Mark)
American. Baseball Player
Had eight-yr. ML career, mostly with NY Yankees; first player ever to bat as designated hitter, 1973.
b. Aug 23, 1948 in Atlanta, Georgia
Source: *Ballpl 90; BaseEn 88; BioIn 9, 16; WhoAm 76*

Blomfield, Reginald Theodore, Sir
English. Architect
Designs noted for elaborate style include Menin Gate Memorial at Ypres, Belgium, dedicated to WW I dead, 1926.
b. Dec 20, 1856 in Devon, England
d. Dec 28, 1942 in Frognal, England
Source: *BioIn 5, 14, 15; DcNaB 1941; MacEA; McGDA; WhE&EA; WhoArch*

Blondell, Joan
American. Actor
Appeared in over 80 films; best known role Aunt Sissy in *A Tree Grows in Brooklyn,* 1945.
b. Aug 30, 1912 in New York, New York
d. Dec 25, 1979 in Santa Monica, California
Source: *BiDFilm, 78, 79, 80; MotPP; MovMk; NewYTBE 72; NotNAT; OxCFilm; ThFT; WhAm 7; WhoAm 74, 76, 78; WhoAmW 74, 77; WhoHol A; WhoThe 72; WorEFlm*

Blondie
[Clem Burke; Jimmy Destri; Nigel Harrison; Deborah Harry; Frank Infante; Chris Stein]
American. Music Group
Forerunner of original punk rock, formed 1976-82; had four number-one hits including "Rapture," 1981.
Source: *BioIn 15, 17, 20; ConMuA 80A; ConMus 14; EncPR&S 89; EncRk 88; EncRkSt; HarEnR 86; InWom SUP; LegTOT; NewGrDA 86; NewYTBS 79; PenEncP; RkOn 85; RolSEnR 83; WhoRock 81; WhoRocM 82; WhsNW 85*

Blondin, Jean Francois Gravelet
French. Entertainer
Crossed Niagara Falls on a tightrope, 1859, repeated act blindfolded.
b. Feb 28, 1824 in Saint-Omer, France
d. Feb 19, 1897 in London, England

Source: *BioIn 1, 3, 4, 5, 6, 9*

Blondin-Andrew, Ethel
Canadian. Politician
First aboriginal woman to sit in Canada's House of Commons, 1988-93.
b. Mar 25, 1951 in Fort Norman, Northwest Territories, Canada
Source: *BioIn 21; NotNaAm; WhoAm 95, 96, 97*

Blood, Ernest
"Gray Thatched Wizard"; "Prof"
American. Basketball Coach
Coached Passaic, NJ high school team that won 159 straight games, 1920s; overall coaching record 1296-165; Hall of Fame.
b. Oct 4, 1872 in Manchester, New Hampshire
d. Feb 5, 1955 in New Smyrna, Florida
Source: *BioIn 3, 9; ObitOF 79; WhoBbl 73*

Blood, Thomas
"Colonel Blood"
Irish. Adventurer
Stole English crown jewels, 1671; pardoned by Charles II, who admired his audacity.
b. 1618, Ireland
d. Aug 24, 1680
Source: *BioIn 1, 2, 3, 4, 8, 16; DcIrB 78, 88; DcNaB; NewC; OxCEng 85, 95; WhDW*

Blood, Sweat and Tears
[Dave Bargeron; David Clayton-Thomas; Bobby Colomby; Steve Fieldeer; Jerry Fisher; Dick Halligan; Jeff Hyman; Steve Katz; Al Kooper; Fred Lipsiu; Tom Malone; Lou Marini, Jr; Jaco Pastorius; Lew Soloff; Georg Wadenius]
American. Music Group
Group formed 1968; hit singles "Spinning Wheel"; "And When I Die."
Source: *BiDAmM; BiDJaz A; BioIn 12, 14, 15, 16, 21; ConMuA 80A; ConMus 7; DrAF 76; DrAP 75; DrAPF 83, 85, 87, 89, 91, 93, 97; EncJzS; EncPR&S 74, 89; EncRk 88; HarEnR 86; IlEncRk; NewAmDM; NewGrDA 86; NewGrDJ 88, 94; NewYTBS 87; OxCPMus; PenEncP; RkOn 74, 78; RolSEnR 83; WhoAm 95; WhoHol 92; WhoRock 81; WhoRocM 82; WorAl; WorAlBi*

Bloodworth-Thomason, Linda Joyce
American. Producer, Writer
Creator, TV series, "Designing Women," "Evening Shade," "Hearts Afire"; head, with husband, Harry Thomason, of Mozark Productions.
b. Apr 15, 1948 in Poplar Bluff, Missouri

Bloom, Allan David
American. Educator, Author
Wrote best-selling *Closing of the American Mind,* 1987, damning critique of American higher education.
b. Sep 14, 1930 in Indianapolis, Indiana
d. Oct 7, 1992 in Chicago, Illinois
Source: *ConAu 139; ConLC 76; CurBio 88, 92N; NewYTBS 88; WorAu 1985; WrDr 94N*

Bloom, Claire
English. Actor
Best known for Chaplin film *Limelight,* 1952; former wife of Rod Steiger.
b. Feb 15, 1931 in London, England
Source: *BiDFilm, 81, 94; BiE&WWA; BioIn 3, 4, 6, 7, 8, 9, 11, 12, 13, 14; BlueB 76; CamGWoT; CelR, 90; CnThe; ConAu 114; ContDcW 89; ConTFT 4, 11; CurBio 56; DcArts; FilmAG WE; FilmEn; FilmgC; ForYSC; HalFC 80, 84, 88; IlWWBF; IntDcF 1-3, 2-3; IntDcT 3; IntMPA 75, 76, 77, 78, 79, 80, 81, 82, 84, 86, 88, 92, 94, 96; IntWW 74, 75, 76, 77, 78, 79, 80, 81, 82, 83, 89, 91, 93; InWom, SUP; ItaFilm; LegTOT; MotPP; MovMk; NotNAT; OxCFilm; OxCThe 83; Who 74, 82, 83, 85, 88, 90, 92, 94; WhoAm 74, 76, 78, 80, 82, 84, 86, 88, 92, 94, 95, 96, 97; WhoAmW 83, 85, 87, 91; WhoEnt 92; WhoHol 92; WhoHrs 80; WhoThe 72, 77, 81; WhoWor 78, 89; WorAl; WorAlBi; WorEFlm*

Bloom, Eric
[Blue Oyster Cult]
American. Singer, Musician
Guitarist, vocalist with hard rock group since 1969.
b. Dec 1, 1944 in Long Island, New York
Source: *ASCAP 80*

Bloom, Harold
American. Critic
Books of literary criticism include *A Map of Misreading,* 1975; *Agon,* 1982.
b. Jul 11, 1930 in New York, New York
Source: *AmAu&B; Benet 96; BenetAL 91; BioIn 13, 14, 15, 16, 17, 18, 20, 21; BlmGEL; BlueB 76; ChhPo; ConAu 13R, 39NR; ConLC 24; ConLCrt 77, 82; CurBio 87; CyWA 89; DcLB 67; DcLEL 1940; DrAS 74E, 78E, 82E; EncSF 93; EncWL 3; IntAu&W 77, 82; IntWW 89, 91, 93; JeAmHC; NewYTBS 94; PostFic; RAdv 14, 13-1; ScF&FL 92; WhoAm 74, 76, 78, 80, 82, 84, 86, 88, 90, 92, 94, 95, 96, 97; WhoAmJ 80; WhoE 83; WhoRel 92; WhoUSWr 88; WhoWorJ 72, 78; WhoWrEP 89, 92, 95; WorAu 1970; WrDr 76, 80, 82, 84, 86, 88, 90, 92, 94, 96*

Bloom, Harry
South African. Author, Lawyer
Imprisoned for writing award-winning, anti-apartheid novel *Episode,* 1956.
b. 1913?, South Africa
d. Jul 28, 1981 in Canterbury, England
Source: *BioIn 12; ConAu 104; TwCWr*

Bloom, Julius
American. Director
Exec., director, Carnegie Hall, 1960-77; founded Brooklyn Symphony Orchestra, 1939.
b. Sep 23, 1912 in New York, New York
d. Jul 5, 1984 in New York, New York
Source: *BioIn 9, 14; IntWWM 80, 85; NewYTBS 84; WhAm 8; WhoAm 76, 78, 80, 82, 84; WhoAmJ 80; WhoAmM 83; WhoE 77; WhoWor 82, 84*

Bloom, Mickey
[Milton Bloom]
American. Musician, Composer
Trumpeter with Hal Kemp, 1935-39.
b. Aug 26, 1906 in New York, New York
Source: *ASCAP 66; BiDAmM; BiDJaz; WhoJazz 72*

Bloom, Murray Teigh
American. Journalist
Reporter, *NY Post,* 1939; free-lance writer for mags., 1940—.
b. May 19, 1916 in New York, New York
Source: *AuSpks; ConAu 17R; IntAu&W 86, 89; WhoAm 74, 76, 80, 82, 84, 86, 88, 90, 92, 94, 95, 96, 97; WhoE 74; WrDr 76, 80, 82, 84, 86, 88, 90, 92, 94, 96*

Bloom, Ursula
[Shiela Burns; Mary Essex; Rachel Harvey; Deborah Mann; Lozania Prole; Sara Sloane]
English. Author
Prolific literary figure who wrote more than 500 novels, 1924-79, including *Secret Lover,* 1930.
b. Dec 11, 1892? in Chelmsford, England
d. Oct 29, 1984 in London, England
Source: *AnObit 1984; ConAu 25R, 114; IntAu&W 82; NewC; Novels; ScF&FL 1; Who 82; WrDr 82*

Bloomberg, Michael (R.)
American. Business Executive
Founder, president, Bloomberg Financial Markets, 1982—.
b. Feb 14, 1942 in Boston, Massachusetts
Source: *CurBio 96; News 97-1; WhoAm 97*

Bloomer, Amelia Jenks
American. Social Reformer
Advocate of women's rights, dress reform; led to costume called "bloomers."
b. May 27, 1818 in Homer, New York
d. Dec 30, 1894 in Council Bluffs, Iowa
Source: *AmBi; AmRef; AmSocL; AmWom; AmWomWr; ApCAB; BioAmW; BioIn 15, 19, 20, 21; DcAmAu; DcAmB; DcAmTB; EncFash; EncWomS; FemiCLE; GrLiveH; HanAmWH; HarEnUS; InWom, SUP; LibW; McGEWB; NatCAB 8; NotAW; OxCAmH; OxCAmL 65, 83, 95; PeoHis;*

REnAL; TwCBDA; WebAB 74, 79; WhAm HS; WhAmP; WomFir

Bloomfield, Leonard
American. Linguist
Famous for his behavioristic approach to linguistics; *Language*, 1933, is standard text.
b. Apr 1, 1887 in Chicago, Illinois
d. Apr 18, 1949 in New Haven, Connecticut
Source: *AmAu&B; BiDAmEd; BioIn 1, 7, 14; DcAmB S4; DcNAA; IntDcAn; LinLib L, S; McGEWB; NewCol 75; OxCAmH; OxCCan; OxCEng 85, 95; RAdv 14, 13-3; ThTwC 87; WebAB 74, 79; WebBD 83; WhAm 2; WhDW; WhNAA*

Bloomfield, Mike
[Michael Bloomfield]
American. Musician, Singer
Blues guitarist; formed supergroup Electric Flag, 1967-68; album *My Labors*, 1971.
b. Jul 28, 1944 in Chicago, Illinois
d. Feb 15, 1981 in San Francisco, California
Source: *AnObit 1981; BluesWW; EncPR&S 74; EncRk 88; EncRkSt; GuBlues; HarEnR 86; LegTOT; OnThGG; PenEncP; RolSEnR 83; WhoAm 74*

Bloomfield, Robert
English. Poet
Known for poem "The Farmer's Boy," 1800, describing rural simplicity.
b. Dec 3, 1766 in Honington, England
d. Aug 19, 1823 in Shefford, England
Source: *Alli; BbD; BiD&SB; BiDLA; BioIn 1, 2, 8, 9, 12, 17, 19; BritAu, 19; CamGEL; CamGLE; CarSB; CasWL; Chambr 2; ChhPo, S1, S2; DcBiPP; DcEnL; DcLB 93; DcLEL; DcNaB; EvLB; GrWrEL P; NewC; NewCBEL; OxCChiL; OxCEng 67, 85, 95; OxCLiW 86; RfGEnL 91; WebE&AL*

Bloomgarden, Kermit
American. Producer
Produced *Diary of Anne Frank*, 1959.
b. Dec 15, 1904 in New York, New York
d. Sep 20, 1976 in New York, New York
Source: *BiE&WWA; BioIn 4, 5, 11, 13; BlueB 76; CamGWoT; CurBio 76N; DcAmB S10; NatCAB 61; NewYTBS 76; NotNAT B; ObitOF 79; OxCAmT 84; PlP&P; WhAm 7; WhoAm 74, 76; WhoThe 72, 77, 81N; WhoWor 74*

Bloomingdale, Alfred S
American. Business Executive
Launched Diners' Club credit card co., 1950.
b. Apr 15, 1916 in New York, New York
d. Aug 20, 1982 in Santa Monica, California
Source: *AmCath 80; AnObit 1982; BioIn 8, 13, 14; CelR; IntYB 78, 79, 80, 81, 82; NewYTBS 82; WhAm 8; WhoAm 74, 76, 78, 80, 82; WhoFI 74*

Bloomingdale, Betsy
American. Socialite
Wife of late Alfred Bloomingdale; best friend of Nancy Reagan.
b. Aug 2, 1926 in Los Angeles, California
Source: *BioIn 11; CelR 90*

Bloomingdale, Joseph Bernard
American. Merchant
Co-founded Bloomingdale's Dept. Store, 1872.
b. Dec 22, 1842 in New York, New York
d. Nov 21, 1904 in New York, New York
Source: *NatCAB 2, 30; WorAl*

Bloomingdale, Samuel
American. Retailer
Director of Federated Dept. Stores, 1930-62.
b. Jun 17, 1873 in New York, New York
d. May 10, 1968 in New York
Source: *BioIn 7, 8; ObitOF 79; WhAm 5*

Bloor, Mother
[Ella Reeve Bloor]
American. Feminist
Leading US female communist, 1930s-40s; helped organize Communist Labor Party, 1919.
b. Jul 8, 1862 in Staten Island, New York
d. Aug 10, 1951 in Richlandtown, Pennsylvania
Source: *AmDec 1930; BiDAmL; BiDAmLf; BiDAmLL; BioIn 2, 3, 12, 15, 17, 19; DcAmB S5; EncAL; InWom SUP; LibW; NotAW MOD*

Blore, Eric
American. Actor
Best known for roles as butler in films, 1926-59.
b. Dec 23, 1887 in London, England
d. Mar 2, 1959 in Hollywood, California
Source: *BioIn 5, 21; EncAFC; Film 2; FilmEn; FilmgC; HalFC 80, 84, 88; HolCA; MotPP; MovMk; NotNAT B; OlFamFa; QDrFCA 92; Vers A; WhScrn 74, 77, 83; WhThe*

Blotta, Anthony
Italian. Fashion Designer
Opened NYC boutique, 1919; designed pant suits for Marlene Dietrich in early, 1930s.
d. Sep 11, 1971 in New York
Source: *NewYTBE 71*

Blough, Glenn Orlando
American. Author
Science books for young people include *Discovering Insects*, 1967.
b. Sep 5, 1907 in Edmore, Michigan
Source: *AmAu&B; AuBYP 2, 3; ConAu P-1; LEduc 74; MorJA; SmATA 1; WhoAm 74, 76, 78, 80, 82, 84, 86, 88, 90; WhoUSWr 88; WhoWrEP 89, 92*

Blough, Roger Miles
American. Lawyer, Businessman
Chm., CEO, US Steel, 1955-69, during its domination of steel market.
b. Jan 19, 1904 in Riverside, Pennsylvania
d. Oct 8, 1985 in Hawley, Pennsylvania
Source: *BioIn 3, 4, 5, 6, 7, 8, 11; CurBio 55, 86; IntWW 74; WhoAm 82; WhoWor 74*

Blount, Charles
English. Author
Deist, known for *The Two First Books of Philostratus, Concerning Life of Apollonius Tyaneus*, 1680.
b. Apr 27, 1654 in Upper Holloway, England
d. Aug 1693
Source: *Alli; BioIn 3; BritAu; CasWL; DcBiPP; DcEnL; DcNaB; LuthC 75; NewC; NewCBEL*

Blount, Mel(vin Cornell)
American. Football Player
Defensive back, Pittsburgh, 1970-83; led NFL in interceptions with 11, 1975.
b. Apr 10, 1948 in Vidalia, Georgia
Source: *BioIn 11, 13; WhoAfA 96; WhoAm 78, 80, 82, 84; WhoBlA 77, 80, 85, 88, 90, 92, 94; WhoE 86; WhoEmL 87*

Blount, Winton Malcolm
American. Businessman, Government Official
Postmaster General, 1979-71; chairman, CEO, Blount, Inc., 1974-90, 1991-93; chairman, 1990-91, 1993—.
b. Feb 1, 1921 in Union Springs, Alabama
Source: *BiDrUSE 71, 89; BioIn 8, 9, 10, 11, 12, 15, 16; BlueB 76; CurBio 69; IntWW 83, 89, 91; NewYTBE 71; St&PR 75, 84, 87, 91, 93, 96, 97; WhoAm 74, 76, 78, 80, 82, 84, 86, 88, 90, 92, 94, 95, 96, 97; WhoAmP 73; WhoFI 85, 87, 89, 94, 96; WhoSSW 73, 82, 84, 86, 88, 91, 93, 95; WhoWor 80, 82*

Bloustein, Edward J.
American. University Administrator
Pres., Rutgers Univ., 1971-89; pres., Bennington College, VT, 1965-71.
b. Jan 20, 1925 in New York, New York
d. Dec 9, 1989 in Weston, Connecticut
Source: *BioIn 7, 16; ConAu 41R; CurBio 65, 90N; DrAS 74P, 78P, 82P; LEduc 74; NewYTBE 71; NewYTBS 89; WhAm 10; WhoAm 74, 76, 78, 80, 82, 84, 86, 88; WhoAmJ 80; WhoAmL 90; WhoE 74, 75, 77, 79, 81, 83, 85, 86, 89; WhoWor 89; WhoWorJ 72, 78*

Blow, John
English. Composer
Wrote over 100 anthems; his *Venus and Adonis*, 1685, considered first true English opera.

b. Feb 23, 1649? in Newark-on-Trent, England
d. Oct 1, 1708 in London, England
Source: *Alli; AtlBL; Baker 84, 92; BriBkM 80; DcCom&M 79; GrComp; MetOEnc; MusMk; NewAmDM; NewCol 75; NewGrDM 80; NewGrDO; NewOxM; OxCEng 85, 95; OxCMus; OxDcOp*

Blow, Susan Elizabeth
American. Educator
Opened first kindergarten in US, in NY, 1871.
b. Jun 7, 1843 in Saint Louis, Missouri
d. Mar 26, 1916 in New York, New York
Source: *Alli SUP; AmAu&B; AmBi; BiDAmEd; BioIn 10, 13; ChhPo S1; DcAmB; DcNAA; HanAmWH; IntDcWB; InWom SUP; LibW; NotAW*

Bloy, Leon Marie
French. Author
Wrote autobiographical novels, *Le Desespere,* 1886; *La Femme Pauvre,* 1897.
b. Jul 11, 1846 in Perigueux, France
d. Nov 3, 1917 in Bourg-la-Reine, France
Source: *CasWL; ClDMEL 47, 80; EncWL; EuAu; EvEuW; OxCFr; PenC EUR; REn*

Blucher, Gebhard Leberecht von
Russian. Military Leader
Led Prussian army in Napoleon's defeat at Laon; entered Paris, 1814; aided British at Waterloo.
b. Dec 16, 1742 in Rostock, Germany
d. Sep 12, 1819 in Schlesian, Germany
Source: *CelCen; DcBiPP; Dis&D; GenMudB; HarEnMi; LinLib S; McGEWB; OxCGer 76, 86; WhoMilH 76*

Blucker, Robert Olof
American. Hostage
One of 52 held by terrorists, Nov 1979-Jan 1981.
b. Oct 21, 1927 in North Little Rock, Arkansas
Source: *BioIn 12; NewYTBS 81; USBiR 74*

Blue, Ben
[Benjamin Bernstein]
Canadian. Comedian, Dancer
Vaudeville star 1916; appeared in film *It's a Mad, Mad, Mad, Mad World,* 1963.
b. Sep 12, 1901 in Montreal, Quebec, Canada
d. Mar 7, 1975 in Los Angeles, California
Source: *DcAmB S9; EncVaud; Film 2; FilmEn; FilmgC; ForYSC; HalFC 84, 88; IntMPA 75; LegTOT; MovMk; QDrFCA 92; WhScrn 77, 83; WorAl; WorAlBi*

Blue, Monte
American. Actor
Appeared in 200 films, 1915-54; playing romantic leads, 1920s: *Orphans of the Storm,* 1922.
b. Jan 11, 1890 in Indianapolis, Indiana
d. Feb 18, 1963 in Milwaukee, Wisconsin
Source: *BioIn 12, 17; EncAFC; Film 1, 2; FilmEn; FilmgC; ForYSC; GangFlm; HalFC 80, 84, 88; HarEnR 86; MotPP; MovMk; NotNAT B; TwYS; Vers A; WhoHol B; WhScrn 74, 77, 83*

Blue, Vida Rochelle
American. Baseball Player
Pitcher, 1969-83; fifth pitcher to win Cy Young Award, MVP in same year, 1971.
b. Jul 28, 1949 in Mansfield, Louisiana
Source: *BiDAmSp BB; CurBio 72; InB&W 85; NewYTBE 71; NewYTBS 74; WhoAm 78, 80, 82; WhoBlA 75; WorAl*

Blue Oyster Cult
[Eric Bloom; Albert Bouchard; Joe Bouchard; Rick Downey; Allen Lanier; Donald "Buck Dharma" Roeser]
American. Music Group
Major heavy metal band; hit single "Don't Fear the Reaper," 1976.
Source: *ConMuA 80A; ConMus 16; EncPR&S 89; EncRk 88; EncRkSt; IlEncRk; NewGrDA 86; PenEncP; RkOn 85; RolSEnR 83; WhoRock 81; WhoRocM 82*

Blues Brothers, The
American. Music Group
Blues duo started as a warmup to TV's "Saturday Night Live" in 1978; four albums, including the double-platium *Briefcase Full of Blues,* 1978; dissolved with death of John Belushi in 1982.
Source: *BioIn 11, 12, 13; ConAu 106; ConMus 3; CurBio 80, 82N; HalFC 84; IntMPA 81, 82; NewYTBS 82; RkOn 85; RolSEnR 83; WhAm 8; WhoAm 78, 80, 82; WhoHol 92; WhoRocM 82; WorAl*

Bluford, Guy
[Guion Stewart Bluford, Jr]
American. Astronaut
First black American to fly in space aboard space shuttle *Challenger,* 1983.
b. Nov 22, 1942 in Philadelphia, Pennsylvania
Source: *AfrAmAl 6; AfrAmBi 1; AmMWSc 79, 82, 86, 89, 92, 95; BlksScM; ConBlB 2; CurBio 84; InB&W 80; NewYTBS 83; WhoAfA 96; WhoAm 84, 86, 88, 90, 92, 94, 95, 96, 97; WhoBlA 80, 88, 90, 92, 94; WhoEmL 87; WhoScEn 96; WhoSSW 84, 86, 88*

Bluhdorn, Charles G
American. Business Executive
Founder, chm., Gulf & Western Industries, Inc., 1958-83.
b. Sep 20, 1926 in Vienna, Austria
d. Feb 19, 1983
Source: *AnObit 1983; BiDAmBL 83; BioIn 7, 8, 9, 11, 12, 13; BlueB 76; Dun&B 79; IntWW 74, 75, 76, 77, 78, 79, 80, 81, 82, 83, 83N; NewYTBS 83; St&PR 75; WhAm 8; WhoAm 74, 76, 78, 80, 82; WhoE 74; WhoFI 74, 75, 77, 79, 81, 83; WhoWor 74*

Blum, Leon
French. Statesman
Socialist premier of France, 1936-38; imprisoned by Vichy govt., 1940-45.
b. Apr 9, 1872 in Paris, France
d. Mar 30, 1950 in Versailles, France
Source: *BiDFrPL; BiDInt; BiDNeoM; BioIn 1, 2, 5, 6, 7, 9, 10, 11, 12, 13, 15, 16, 17; ClDMEL 47, 80; ConAu 119; CurBio 40, 50; DcPol; DcTwCCu 2; DcTwHis; EncRev; EncTR 91; FacFETw; HisWorL; LinLib S; McGEWB; OxCFr; REn; WhAm 2, 2A; WhDW; WhWW-II*

Blum, Stella
American. Museum Director
First costume curator at Costume Institute of Metropolitan Museum of Art, 1970-82.
b. Oct 19, 1916 in Schenectady, New York
d. Jul 31, 1985 in Ravenna, Ohio
Source: *AmWomHi; AnObit 1985; BioIn 14; ConAu 97, 116; WhAm 8; WhoAm 84*

Blumberg, Baruch Samuel
American. Scientist, Physician
Shared Nobel Prize in medicine, 1976, for career work on infectious diseases.
b. Jul 28, 1925 in New York, New York
Source: *AmMWSc 76P, 79, 82, 86, 89, 92, 95; BiESc; BioIn 10, 11; CurBio 77; FacFETw; IntWW 77, 78, 79, 80, 81, 82, 83, 89, 91, 93; LarDcSc; McGMS 80; NotTwCS; Who 82, 83, 85, 88, 90, 92, 94; WhoAm 76, 78, 80, 82, 84, 86, 88, 90, 92, 94, 95, 96, 97; WhoAmJ 80; WhoE 75, 77, 79, 81, 83, 85, 86, 89, 91, 93, 95, 97; WhoMedH; WhoNob, 90, 95; WhoScEn 94, 96; WhoWor 78, 80, 82, 84, 87, 89, 91, 93, 95, 96, 97*

Blumberg, Judy
[Blumberg and Seibert]
American. Skater
With Michael Seibert, won bronze medal in ice dancing, 1983 world championships.
b. 1957? in Santa Monica, California
Source: *BioIn 12, 13; NewYTBS 83, 84*

Blume, Judy Sussman
American. Author
Wrote *Are You There God? It's Me Margaret,* 1970; *Wifey,* 1978; books for children noted for sexual frankness.
b. Feb 12, 1938 in Elizabeth, New Jersey
Source: *ChlLR 2; ConAu 13NR, 37NR; ConLC 30; CurBio 80; FourBJA; InWom SUP; MajAI; NewYTBS 82; OxCChiL; SmATA 31, 79; TwCChW 83; WhoAm 76, 78, 80, 82, 84, 86, 88, 90, 92, 94,*

95, 96; WhoAmW 74, 81, 83, 85, 87, 89, 91, 93, 95; WhoEnt 92; WhoUSWr 88; WhoWor 96; WhoWrEP 89, 92, 95; WrDr 86

Blume, Peter
American. Artist
Surrealist painter with meticulous style: "The Eternal City," 1937.
b. Oct 27, 1906 in Smorgon, Russia
d. Nov 30, 1992 in New Milford, Connecticut
Source: *BioIn 1, 2, 4, 5, 6, 14, 15, 16, 17, 18, 19, 20; BlueB 76; BriEAA; ConArt 83, 89, 96; CurBio 56, 93N; DcAmArt; DcCAA 71, 77, 88, 94; DcCAr 81; IntWW 74, 75, 76, 77, 78, 79, 80, 81, 82, 83, 89, 91; McGDA; NewYTBS 92; OxCAmH; OxCTwCA; PhDcTCA 77; WhAm 10; WhAmArt 85; WhoAm 74, 76, 78, 80, 82, 84, 86, 88, 90, 92; WhoAmA 73, 76, 78, 80, 82, 84, 86, 89, 91, 93N; WhoE 74, 91*

Blumenbach, Johann Friedrich
German. Physiologist
Founder of modern anthropology; wrote *Handbook of Natural History,* 1779.
b. May 11, 1752 in Gotha, Germany
d. Jan 22, 1840 in Gottingen, Germany
Source: *BiESc; BlkwCE; CelCen; DcBiPP; DcScB, S1; Dis&D; EncEnl; InSci; LinLib L, S*

Blumenfeld, Isadore
"Kid Cann"
American. Criminal
Bootlegger acquitted in kidnapping, murder, fraud charges; finally convicted, jailed for jury tampering, 1961-67.
b. 1901 in Minneapolis, Minnesota
d. 1981 in New York, New York
Source: *BioIn 12*

Blumenthal, Monica David
American. Psychiatrist, Educator
Expert on violence, geriatric psychiatry; won Emmy for "What Shall We Do About Mother?" 1980.
b. Sep 1, 1930 in Tubingen, Germany
d. Mar 16, 1981 in Pittsburgh, Pennsylvania
Source: *AmMWSc 76P, 79, 82, 86; BiDrAPA 77; ConAu 73, 103; NewYTBS 81; WhoAmW 74*

Blumenthal, W. Michael
American. Business Executive, Government Official
Secretary of Treasury under Jimmy Carter, 1977-79; chm. of Burroughs Corp., 1981-90.
b. Jan 3, 1926 in Berlin, Germany
Source: *AmEA 74; BlueB 76; BusPN; CngDr 77, 79; ConAmBL; CurBio 77; Dun&B 86, 88, 90; IntWW 74, 75, 76, 77, 78, 79, 80, 81, 82, 83, 89, 91; NewYTBE 72; St&PR 75, 84, 87, 91, 93; Who 82, 83, 85, 88, 90, 92; WhoAm 76, 78, 80, 82, 84, 86, 88, 90; WhoAmP 77, 79, 81, 83, 85, 87, 89, 91, 93, 95; WhoE 77, 79, 91; WhoFI 74, 75, 77, 79, 81, 83, 85, 87, 89; WhoGov 77; WhoMW 82, 84, 86, 88, 90; WhoWor 78, 84, 89; WorAl*

Blunden, Edmund Charles
English. Poet, Critic
Named to Oxford's poetry chair, 1966; wrote *War Poets, 1914-18,* 1962.
b. Nov 1, 1896 in London, England
d. Jan 20, 1974 in Sudbury, England
Source: *Au&Wr 71; BioIn 1, 2, 4, 7, 8, 10, 11, 12, 13; CasWL; Chambr 3; ChhPo, S1, S2, S3; CnE&AP; ConAu 45, P-2; ConLC 2; ConPo 70, 75; DcLEL; DcNaB 1971; EncWL; EvLB; GrBr; GrWrEL P; LngCTC; ModBrL, S1; NewC; NewCBEL; NewYTBS 74; OxCEng 67, 85, 95; OxCTwCP; PenC ENG; REn; RGFMBP; TwCA, SUP; TwCWr; WebE&AL; Who 74; WhoTwCL*

Blunstone, Colin
[The Zombies]
English. Musician
Rock singer; founded the Zombies, 1962; solo album *Journey,* 1974.
b. Jun 24, 1945 in Hatfield, England
Source: *EncRk 88; IlEncRk; PenEncP; WhoRock 81; WhoRocM 82*

Blunt, Anthony Frederick
English. Art Historian, Spy
Queen Elizabeth's art curator, 1945-79, who was fourth man in Burgess-Philby-Maclean spy ring.
b. Sep 26, 1907 in Bournemouth, England
d. Mar 26, 1983 in London, England
Source: *Au&Wr 71; BioIn 10, 12, 13; ColdWar 1; ConAu 109; DcNaB 1981; IntAu&W 76, 77, 82; IntWW 83; IntYB 78, 79, 80, 81, 82; NewYTBS 79, 83; Who 74, 82, 83; WhoArt 80; WhoWest 80; WrDr 84*

Blunt, Wilfrid Scawen
English. Poet, Politician, Traveler
Colorful Victorian, whose writings include lyric verse, *Love Sonnets of Proteus,* 1881.
b. Aug 17, 1840 in Petworth, England
d. Sep 10, 1922 in Newbuildings, England
Source: *Alli SUP; BbD; Benet 87, 96; BiD&SB; BioIn 1, 3, 6, 11, 13, 14, 15, 18, 20; BritAu 19; CamGEL; CamGLE; Chambr 3; DcArts; DcEnA, A; DcLB 19, 174; DcNaB 1922; EvLB; GrBr; GrWrEL P; HisDBrE; ModBrL; NewC; NewCBEL; OxCEng 67, 85, 95; OxCIri; PenC ENG; REn; RfGEnL 91; WebE&AL; WhLit; WhWE*

Bly, Nellie
[Elizabeth Cochrane Seaman]
American. Journalist
Wrote muckraking articles on prisons, asylums; author *Around the World in 72 Days,* 1890.
b. May 5, 1867 in Cochrane's Mill, Pennsylvania
d. Jan 27, 1922 in New York, New York
Source: *AmAu; AmAu&B; Benet 87, 96; BenetAL 91; BiDAmNC; BioIn 14, 15, 16, 17, 18, 19, 21; BlmGWL; CnDAL; DcAmB; DcNAA; EncAJ; EncSPD; GayN; HerW, 84; InWom, SUP; LegTOT; LibW; NotAW; OxCAmL 65, 83, 95; PenNWW B; REn; REnAL; WebAB 74, 79; WhAm 4, HSA; WomStre; WorAl; WorAlBi*

Bly, Robert Elwood
American. Poet
Won National Book Award for *The Light Around the Body,* 1968.
b. Dec 23, 1926 in Madison, Minnesota
Source: *ConAu 5R; ConLC 15; ConPo 85; CurBio 84; News 92; RAdv 1; WhoAm 86; WhoWor 74; WorAu 1950; WrDr 86*

Blyden, Larry
[Ivan Lawrence Blieden]
American. Actor, TV Personality
Made stage debut in *Mr. Roberts,* 1948; in film *On a Clear Day You Can See Forever,* 1969; hosted TV's "What's My Line?"
b. Jun 23, 1925 in Houston, Texas
d. Jun 6, 1975 in Agadir, Morocco
Source: *BiE&WWA; BioIn 10; FilmgC; HalFC 80, 84, 88; IntMPA 75; NewYTBS 75, 84; NotNAT, B; WhAm 6; WhoAm 74; WhoHol C; WhoThe 72, 77; WhScrn 77, 83*

Blyleven, Bert
[Rik Albert Blyleven]
American. Baseball Player
Pitcher, 1970-93; 11th in ML history to record 3,000 strikeouts, 1986.
b. Apr 6, 1951 in Zeist, Netherlands
Source: *Ballpl 90; BaseReg 86, 87; BioIn 12; LegTOT; NewYTBS 81; PseudN 82; WhoSpor; WorAlBi*

Blyth, Ann Marie
American. Actor
Received Oscar nomination for *Mildred Pierce,* 1945.
b. Aug 16, 1928 in Mount Kisco, New York
Source: *CmpEPM; FilmgC; HolP 40; IntMPA 86; MotPP; MovMk; WhoAm 74; WhoAmW 70, 72, 74; WomWMM; WorAl; WorEFlm*

Blyth, Chay
English. Author, Adventurer
Circumnavigated globe alone in yacht, 1970-71; wrote *The Impossible Voyage,* 1972.
b. 1940 in Hawick, England
Source: *BioIn 8, 9; ConAu 110; IntAu&W 76, 91, 93; OxCShps; WrDr 76, 80, 82, 84, 86, 88, 90, 92, 94, 96*

Blythe, Betty
[Elizabeth Blythe Slaughter]
American. Actor
Popular Vitagraph silent star; title role in *Queen of Sheba,* 1921.

b. Sep 1, 1893 in Los Angeles, California
d. Apr 7, 1972 in Woodland Hills, California
Source: *BioIn 9, 11; EncAFC; Film 1, 2; FilmEn; FilmgC; ForYSC; HalFC 80, 84, 88; MotPP; MovMk; SilFlmP; TwYS; WhoHol B; WhScrn 77, 83*

Blythe, David Gilmour
American. Artist
Self-taught, satiric, genre painter, who drew mostly PA, Civil War scenes.
b. May 9, 1815 in East Liverpool, Ohio
d. May 15, 1865 in East Liverpool, Ohio
Source: *BioIn 1, 2, 6, 10, 13; BriEAA; DcAmArt; FolkA 87; McGDA; NewYHSD; WhAm HS*

Blyton, Carey
English. Author, Composer
Composer for documentary films, TV commercials and plays; author of children's nonsense poems and books.
b. Mar 14, 1932 in Beckenham, England
Source: *BioIn 11, 12; ChhPo S2; ConAu 49; IntWWM 77, 80, 85, 90; NewGrDM 80; SmATA 9; WhoMus 72; WhoWor 76*

Blyton, Enid Mary
[Mary Pollock]
English. Author
Wrote over 400 children's stories, 1922-68, including *The Secret Seven* adventure series, 1949-54.
b. Aug 11, 1897 in East Dulwich, England
d. Nov 28, 1968 in London, England
Source: *AuBYP 2; ConAu 77; LngCTC; ObitT 1961; PenNWW B; SmATA 25; TwCChW 78; WhFla; WhoChL*

Boadicea
Ruler
Queen of Iceni, AD 60, who raised rebellion against Romans in Britain.
d. 62
Source: *Benet 96; BioIn 4, 5, 6, 8, 9, 10, 11, 12; BlmGEL; ContDcW 89; DcAmB; DcBiPP; DcNaB; EncAmaz 91; GoodHs; IntDcWB; InWom, SUP; LngCEL; NewC; OxCClL, 89; OxCEng 85, 95; OxCLiW 86; WhDW; WomStre*

Boardman, Eleanor
American. Model, Actor
"Kodak Girl" model; silent movie star; films include *Tell It to the Marines.*
b. 1898 in Philadelphia, Pennsylvania
d. Dec 12, 1991 in Santa Barbara, California
Source: *BioIn 10, 16, 17, 19; Film 2; FilmEn; FilmgC; HalFC 80, 84, 88; InWom SUP; MotPP; MovMk; NewYTBS 91; SilFlmP; ThFT; TwYS; WhoHol 92, A*

Boas, Franz
American. Anthropologist
Authority on primitive art, Native Americans; wrote *Primitive Art,* 1927.
b. Jul 9, 1858 in Minden, Germany
d. Dec 21, 1942 in New York, New York
Source: *AmAu&B; AmDec 1930; AmLY; AmSocL; ApCAB X; Benet 87, 96; BiDAmEd; BiDPsy; BioIn 1, 2, 3, 4, 5, 6, 7, 12, 13, 14, 17, 19, 21; ConAu 115; CurBio 40, 43; DcAmAu; DcAmB S3; DcNAA; DcScB; EncAB-H 1974, 1996; FacFETw; InSci; IntDcAn; LegTOT; LinLib L, S; MakMC; McGEWB; MorMA; NamesHP; NatCAB 12; NewGrDA 86; NewGrDM 80; OxCAmH; OxCAmL 65; OxCCan, SUP; RAdv 14, 13-3; REnAL; REnAW; ThTwC 87; TwCA SUP; TwCLC 56; WebAB 74, 79; WebBD 83; WhAm 2; WhDW; WhNAA; WhNaAH; WorAl; WorAlBi*

Bobbs, William Conrad
American. Publisher
Worked for Merrill, Meigs & Co., booksellers, 1879.
b. Jan 25, 1861 in Montgomery, Ohio
d. Feb 11, 1926 in Indianapolis, Indiana
Source: *LinLib L; WhAm 1*

Bobst, Elmer Holmes
"The Vitamin King"
American. Business Executive
Pres., chm., Warner-Lambert Pharmaceutical Co., 1945-67.
b. Dec 16, 1884 in Clear Springs, Maryland
d. Aug 2, 1978 in New York, New York
Source: *BioIn 2, 3, 4, 9, 10, 11; ConAu 113; CurBio 73, 78*

Bocca, Julio
Argentine. Dancer
Ballet dancer; won gold medal in Fifth International Ballet Competition, Moscow, 1985; toured with Teatro Colon, American Ballet Theatre, Ballet Argentino.
b. Mar 7, 1967 in Munro, Argentina
Source: *IntDcB; News 95, 95-3*

Boccaccio, Giovanni
Italian. Author
Father of classical Italian prose; wrote *The Decameron,* 1353.
b. 1313 in Paris, France
d. Dec 21, 1375 in Certaldo, Italy
Source: *AtlBL; BbD; Benet 87, 96; BiD&SB; BioIn 1, 4, 5, 6, 7, 8, 9, 11, 12, 13, 17, 18, 20; BlmGEL; CasWL; ClMLC 13; CyWA 58; DcArts; DcBiA; DcBiPP; DcCathB; DcEnL; DcEuL; DcItL 1, 2; DcPup; Dis&D; EuAu; EuWr 2; EvEuW; GrFLW; LegTOT; LinLib L, S; LngCEL; LuthC 75; MagSWL; McGEWB; NewC; NewCBEL; NewEOp 71; NewGrDM 80; Novels; OxCClL; OxCEng 67, 85, 95; PenC EUR; RAdv 14, 13-2; RComWL; REn; RfGWoL 95; ShSCr 10; WhDW; WorAl; WorAlBi*

Boccherini, Luigi
Italian. Composer, Violinist
Prolific composer of chamber music; created the string quintet.
b. Feb 19, 1743 in Lucca, Italy
d. May 28, 1805 in Madrid, Spain
Source: *AtlBL; Baker 78, 84; BioIn 4, 7, 13, 19, 20, 21; BriBkM 80; CmpBCM; DcCom&M 79; GrComp; MusMk; NewAmDM; NewGrDM 80; NewOxM; OxCMus; WhDW*

Boccioni, Umberto
Italian. Artist
Futurist painter, sculptor; helped draft "Futurist Manifests," 1910.
b. Oct 19, 1882 in Reggio di Calabria, Italy
d. Aug 16, 1916 in Verona, Italy
Source: *BioIn 4, 5, 6, 10, 12, 14; ConArt 77, 83; DcArts; IntDcAA 90; McGDA; McGEWB; OxCArt; OxCTwCA; OxDcArt; PhDcTCA 77; WhDW*

Bochco, Steven Ronald
American. Writer, Producer
Writer, producer, MTM Enterprises, 1978-85; Twentieth-Century Fox, 1985-87; with Steven Bochco Productions, 1987—; Emmy-winning co-creator of TV series "Hill Street Blues" and "LA Law."
b. Dec 16, 1943 in New York, New York
Source: *LesBEnT; NewYTET; WhoTelC*

Bochner, Hart
Canadian. Actor
Star of film *Breaking Away,* 1979; TV film "East of Eden," 1981.
b. Dec 3, 1956 in Toronto, Ontario, Canada
Source: *BioIn 11; ConTFT 2; IntMPA 86, 88, 92, 94, 96; JohnWSW; LegTOT; NewYTBS 77; VarWW 85; WhoAm 92, 94, 95, 96, 97; WhoEnt 92*

Bochner, Lloyd
Canadian. Actor
Played Cecil Colby on TV's "Dynasty," 1981-83.
b. Jul 29, 1924 in Toronto, Ontario, Canada
Source: *ConTFT 7; FilmgC; ForYSC; HalFC 80, 84, 88; IntMPA 88, 92, 94, 96; LegTOT; WhoAm 92; WhoEnt 92; WhoHol 92, A*

Bochner, Salomon
American. Mathematician
Authored the Bochner theorem of positive-definite functions.
b. Aug 20, 1899 in Krakow, Austria-Hungary
d. May 2, 1982 in Houston, Texas
Source: *AmMWSc 76P, 79, 82; BioIn 12, 13, 14; BlueB 76; ConAu 41R; DcScB S2; IntWW 74, 75, 76, 77, 78, 79, 80, 81, 82, 83; McGMS 80; WhAm 8; WhoAm 74, 76, 78, 80, 82; WhoAmJ 80; WhoWor 74; WhoWorJ 72, 78; WrDr 80, 82, 84, 86, 88, 90*

Bock, Jerry
[Jerrold Lewis Bock]
American. Composer
Broadway scores include Pulitzer-winning *Fiorello,* 1959.
b. Nov 23, 1928 in New Haven, Connecticut
Source: *AmPS; AmSong; Baker 84, 92; BestMus; BiDAmM; BiE&WWA; BioIn 6, 9, 10, 12, 15; BlueB 76; CelR; EncMT; HalFC 80, 84, 88; IntWW 74, 75, 76, 77, 78, 79, 80, 81, 82, 83, 89, 91, 93; IntWWM 77; LegTOT; NewAmDM; NewCBMT; NewGrDA 86; NewGrDM 80; NotNAT; OxCAmT 84; OxCPMus; PlP&P; PopAmC, SUP; WhoAm 74, 76, 78, 80, 82, 84, 86, 88, 90, 92, 94, 95, 96, 97; WhoEnt 92; WhoThe 72, 77, 81; WhoWor 74; WorAl; WorAlBi*

Bocklin, Arnold
Swiss. Artist
Moody landscapes, fantastic creatures presaged Surrealist art.
b. Oct 16, 1827 in Basel, Switzerland
d. Jan 16, 1901 in Domenico, Italy
Source: *ArtsNiC; AtlBL; BioIn 6, 9, 10, 15; CelCen; DcArts; IntDcAA 90; McGDA; McGEWB; OxCGer 76, 86; OxDcArt; PenEncH; WhDW*

Bocuse, Paul
French. Chef, Restaurateur
Wrote *Paul Bocuse's French Cooking;* associated with "novelle cuisine."
b. Feb 11, 1926 in Collonges, France
Source: *BioIn 7, 8, 9, 10, 15, 16; BioNews 74; CurBio 88; IntWW 91, 93; NewYTBE 72; WhoFr 79; WhoWor 91; WorAl; WorAlBi*

Bodanzky, Artur
American. Conductor
Led German repertoire at NY Met., 1915-29.
b. Dec 16, 1887 in Vienna, Austria
d. Nov 23, 1939 in New York, New York
Source: *CurBio 40; DcAmB S2; WhAm 1*

Bodard, Lucien Albert
French. Journalist, Author
Wrote award-winning novel *Annie-Marie,* 1981.
b. Jan 3, 1914 in Chongqing, China
Source: *ConAu 116*

Boddicker, Mike
[Michael James Boddicker]
American. Baseball Player
Pitcher, Baltimore, 1980-88; Boston Red Sox 1988-90; Kansas City Royals, 1990-9 3; Milwaukee Brewers, 1993— ; led AL in wins, ERA, 1984.
b. Aug 23, 1957 in Cedar Rapids, Iowa
Source: *Ballpl 90; BaseReg 86, 87; BioIn 13; LegTOT; WhoSpor*

Bode, Carl
American. Author, Educator
Works on American literature include *Portable Thoreau,* 1947; *Portable Emerson,* 1981.
b. Mar 14, 1911 in Milwaukee, Wisconsin
d. Jan 5, 1993 in Chestertown, Maryland
Source: *AmAu&B; Au&Wr 71; BiDAmNC; BioIn 18, 19; ConAu 1NR, 1R, 3NR, 20NR, 140; DrAP 75; DrAPF 80; DrAS 74E, 78E, 82E; IntAu&W 76, 77, 82, 86, 89; IntWWP 77, 82; WhAm 11; WhoAm 74, 76, 78, 80, 82, 84, 86, 88, 90, 92; WhoUSWr 88; WhoWor 74, 76, 78, 80, 82, 84, 87, 89; WhoWrEP 89, 92; WrDr 76, 80, 82, 84, 86, 88, 90, 92, 94N*

Bode, Vaughn
American. Cartoonist
Underground comic artist; strips show worlds of beauty, cruelty; best known for lizards.
b. Jul 22, 1941 in Syracuse, New York
Source: *BioIn 10; MugS; ScF&FL 92*

BoDeans
American. Music Group
Rock group from Waukesha, WI, formed in 1984; style alternately called cowpunk, rockabilly, rootsrock, or revivalist rock; first album *Love & Hope & Sex & Dreams,* 1986 sold 100,000 copies.
Source: *ConMus 3; CreCan 1; WhoRocM 82*

Bodenheim, Maxwell
American. Author, Poet
Sardonic writings include poem *Bringing Jazz,* 1930; novel *Crazy Man,* 1924; murdered with wife in Greenwich Village.
b. May 23, 1893 in Hermanville, Mississippi
d. Feb 6, 1954 in New York, New York
Source: *AmAu&B; Benet 87, 96; BenetAL 91; BioIn 2, 3, 4, 5, 6, 7, 8; CnDAL; ConAmL; DcLEL; LegTOT; ModAL; NotNAT B; Novels; OxCAmL 65, 83, 95; PenC AM; REn; REnAL; TwCA, SUP; WebAB 74, 79; WhAm 3*

Bodley, Thomas, Sir
English. Diplomat, Scholar
Organized Oxford University's famed Bodley Library, opened 1602.
b. 1545 in Exeter, England
d. Jan 28, 1613 in London, England
Source: *Alli; BioIn 1, 8, 11, 13, 14, 15; CamGLE; CasWL; ChhPo; CroE&S; DcEuL; DcLEL; DcNaB; EvLB; LinLib L, S; NewC; OxCEng 85, 95; WhDW*

Bodmer, Johann Jakob
Swiss. Critic, Poet, Translator
Noted for editions of medieval German literature.
b. Jul 19, 1698 in Greifensee, Switzerland
d. Jan 2, 1783 in Zurich, Switzerland
Source: *BiD&SB; BioIn 6, 7, 17; BlkwCE; CasWL; DcEuL; DcLB 97; EncEnl; EuAu; EvEuW; LinLib L; NewCBEL; OxCGer 76, 86; PenC EUR; REn*

Bodmer, Karl
Swiss. Artist, Explorer
Toured America, 1832-34, painting landscapes, Great Plains Indians.
b. Feb 6, 1809 in Riesbach, Switzerland
d. Oct 30, 1893 in Barbizon, France
Source: *ApCAB; ArtsAmW 1; BioIn 1, 3, 6, 7, 9, 11, 13, 14, 15, 17, 18; BriEAA; ClaDrA; DcAmArt; IlBEAAW; NewYHSD; REnAW; WhAm HS; WhNaAH; WhWE*

Bodoni, Giambattista
Italian. Type Designer
Among first to use modern typefaces; designed Bodoni type, 1790.
b. Feb 16, 1740 in Saluzzo, Italy
d. Nov 20, 1813 in Parma, Italy
Source: *BlkwCE; DcArts; DcBiPP; EncAJ; LinLib L; OxCDecA; WebBD 83; WhDW*

Bodsworth, Charles Frederick
Canadian. Author
Naturalist; books include *Wilderness Canada,* 1970.
b. Oct 11, 1918 in Port Burwell, Quebec, Canada
Source: *BioIn 13; CanWW 83; ConAu 1R, 3NR; WhoAm 74, 76, 78, 80, 82, 84, 86, 88, 90, 92; WhoE 83*

Boehm, Edward M
American. Sculptor
Founded fine porcelain sculpture co., Trenton, NJ, 1950.
b. Aug 21, 1913 in Baltimore, Maryland
d. Jan 29, 1969 in Trenton, New Jersey
Source: *WhAm 5*

Boehm, Eric Hartzell
American. Publisher, Author
Consultant on books on bibliographies, computer use, information systems; editor *Historical Abstracts,* 1955-83.
b. Jul 15, 1918 in Hof, Germany
Source: *BlueB 76; ConAu 13R; DrAS 82H; WhoAm 74, 76, 78, 80, 82, 84, 86, 88, 90, 92, 94, 95, 96, 97; WhoWor 76, 78, 80, 82, 91, 93*

Boehm, Helen
[Mrs. Edward Marshall Boehm; Helen Francesca Stefanie Franzolin]
American. Business Executive
Widow of porcelain sculptor Edward Boehm; owner of Boehm Co; race horse breeder.
b. 1922? in New York, New York
Source: *BioIn 12, 14, 15; NewYTBS 76, 77; WhoAmW 85*

Boehme, Jakob
German. Mystic, Religious Leader
Claimed divine revelation; wrote *Mysterium Magnum,* 1623.
b. Apr 24, 1575 in Alt-Seidenberg, Prussia
d. Nov 17, 1624 in Gorlitz, Prussia
Source: *DcBiPP; EncO&P 1, 2, 3; EncPaPR 91; IlEncMy; LinLib L, S; REn; WhDW; WorAl; WorAlBi*

Boeing, William Edward
American. Aircraft Manufacturer
Founded Boeing Aircraft, 1916; United Aircraft and Transport, 1928.
b. Oct 1, 1881 in Detroit, Michigan
d. Sep 28, 1956 in Seattle, Washington
Source: *AmDec 1940; BiDAmBL 83; BioIn 4, 7, 8, 10, 11, 13, 14; DcAmB S6; FacFETw; InSci; ObitOF 79; WhAm 3*

Boerhaave, Hermann
Dutch. Physician
Founded modern system of clinical medical instruction, 1708.
b. Dec 31, 1668 in Voorhout, Netherlands
d. Sep 23, 1738 in Leiden, Netherlands
Source: *AsBiEn; BiESc; BiHiMed; BioIn 4, 5, 6, 8, 9, 10, 14, 16; BlkwCE; DcBiPP; DcScB; EncEnl; EncSPD; InSci; LarDcSc; LinLib S; McGEWB; OxCMed 86; WhDW*

Boesak, Allan Aubrey
South African. Clergy, Social Reformer
President, World Alliance of Reformed Churches, 1982-89; founded Foundation for Peace and Justice, 1986—.
b. Feb 23, 1945 in Kakamas, South Africa
Source: *CurBio 86; NewYTBS 85*

Boesky, Ivan Frederick
American. Banker
Powerful Wall Street speculator involved in 1986 insider trading scandal; sentenced to prison for conspiracy, 1987.
b. Mar 6, 1937 in Detroit, Michigan
Source: *NewYTBS 84; St&PR 75, 84, 87; WhoAm 78, 80, 82, 84, 86; WhoAmJ 80; WhoE 77; WhoFI 75, 77, 79, 81, 83*

Boethius
[Anicius Manlius Severinus Boethius]
Roman. Philosopher, Translator
Credited with introducing Aristotle to western world.
b. c. 480
d. c. 524
Source: *AsBiEn; AtlBL; Benet 87, 96; BiD&SB; BioIn 1, 2, 5, 7, 12; CasWL; ClMLC 15; CyWA 58; DcEnL; DcEuL; DcLB 115; DcScB; EncEarC; GrFLW; Grk&L; InSci; McGEWB; NewC; NewCol 75; NewGrDM 80; OxCClL; OxCEng 67, 85; OxDcByz; PenC CL, EUR; RAdv 14, 13-4; RComWL; REn; RfGWoL 95; WebBD 83; WhDW; WrPh P*

Boettiger, John
American. Publisher
Son-in-law of Franklin Roosevelt; publisher, Seattle *Post-Intelligencer,* 1936-45.
b. Mar 25, 1900 in Chicago, Illinois
d. Oct 31, 1950 in New York, New York
Source: *BioIn 1, 2, 11; ObitOF 79; WhAm 3*

Boeynants, Paul Vanden
Belgian. Political Leader
Minister of Defense, 1972-79; of Brussels Affairs, 1974-77.
b. May 22, 1919
Source: *BioIn 7; IntWW 74, 75, 76, 77, 78, 79, 80, 81, 82, 83*

Boff, Leonardo
Brazilian. Theologian, Clergy
Roman Catholic priest silenced by Vatican for controversial writngs on liberation theology, 1985-86.
b. Dec 14, 1938 in Concordia, Brazil
Source: *CurBio 88; HispLC*

Bofill, Angela
American. Singer, Songwriter
Album *Something About You* was in top five on jazz charts.
b. May 2, 1954? in New York, New York
Source: *BioIn 12; InB&W 80, 85; LegTOT; RolSEnR 83; WhoAfA 96; WhoBlA 80, 92, 94*

Bogan, Louise
American. Poet, Critic
Wrote *Body of This Death,* 1923; *A Poet's Alphabet,* 1970.
b. Aug 11, 1897 in Livermore Falls, Maine
d. Feb 4, 1970 in New York, New York
Source: *AmAu&B; AmWomWr; AmWr S3; ArtclWW 2; AuBYP 2, 3; Benet 87, 96; BenetAL 91; BioAmW; BioIn 4, 8, 10, 12, 13, 14, 15, 17, 19; BlmGWL; CamGLE; CamHAL; ChhPo, S3; CnDAL; CnE&AP; ConAmA; ConAu 25R, 33NR, 73; ConLC 4, 46, 93; ConPo 70; DcLB 45, 169; DcLEL; EncWL 2, 3; FacFETw; FemiCLE; Focus; GrLiveH; GrWrEL P; InWom, SUP; LegTOT; LibW; LinLib L; MajTwCW; ModAL, S1, S2; ModAWWr; ModWoWr; NewYTBE 70; NotAW MOD; OxCAmL 65, 83, 95; OxCTwCP; PenBWP; PenC AM; PoeCrit 12; RAdv 1, 14, 13-1; REn; REnAL; RfGAmL 87, 94; RGTwCWr; SixAP; TwCA, SUP; TwCWr; WhAm 5; WhE&EA; WhoAmW 58, 64, 66, 68, 70, 72; WomFir*

Bogarde, Dirk
[Derek Niven van den Bogaerde]
English. Actor, Author
Won British Academy Award for *The Servant,* 1963; *Darling,* 1965.
b. Mar 28, 1921 in London, England
Source: *BiDFilm, 81, 94; BioIn 6, 7, 8, 9, 10, 11, 12, 13, 14, 15, 17, 19; BlueB 76; CelR, 90; CmMov; ConAu 77; ConLC 19; ConTFT 9; CurBio 67; DcArts; DcLB 14; EncEurC; FilmAG WE; FilmgC; HalFC 84, 88; IntAu&W 91, 93; IntDcF 1-3, 2-3; IntMPA 75, 76, 77, 78, 79, 80, 81, 82, 84, 86, 88, 92, 94, 96; IntWW 82, 83, 89, 91, 93; MotPP; MovMk; NewYTBS 80; OxCFilm; Who 85; WhoHol 92, A; WhoThe 77A; WhoWor 74, 82, 84, 87, 89; WorAl; WorAu 1975; WorEFlm; WrDr 82, 84, 86, 88, 90, 92, 94, 96*

Bogardus, James
American. Architect, Inventor
Noted for constructing cast-iron building exteriors; built first cast-iron building, NYC, 1848.
b. Mar 14, 1800 in Catskill, New York
d. Apr 13, 1874 in New York, New York
Source: *AmBi; ApCAB; BioIn 4; BriEAA; CelCen; DcAmB; DcBiPP; Drake; EncAAr 1, 2; EncMA; HarEnUS; InSci; IntDcAr; LinLib S; MacEA; McGDA; NatCAB 8; NewCol 75; NewYHSD; WhAm HS; WorInv*

Bogart, Humphrey de Forest
"Bogey"
American. Actor
Starred in *Casablanca,* 1942; won Oscar for *The African Queen,* 1951; a leading cult figure, played quintessential tough guy.
b. Jan 23, 1899 in New York, New York
d. Jan 14, 1957 in Los Angeles, California
Source: *BiDFilm; CmMov; CurBio 42, 57; FilmgC; McGEWB; MotPP; MovMk; OxCFilm; WebAB 79; WhAm 3; WhoHol B; WhScrn 77; WorEFlm*

Bogart, Leo
American. Author, Sociologist
Public opinion researcher who wrote *Silent Politics,* 1972.
b. Sep 23, 1921
Source: *AmMWSc 73S, 78S; ConAu 14NR, 41R; WhoE 74, 95, 97*

Bogart, Neil
[Neil Bogatz]
American. Business Executive, Producer
Founder, 1974, pres., Casablanca Record and Film Works.
b. Feb 3, 1943 in New York, New York
d. May 8, 1982 in Los Angeles, California
Source: *AnObit 1982; BioIn 12, 13, 17; IntMPA 82; WhAm 8; WhoAm 78, 80, 82; WhoWest 80, 82*

Bogatja, Vinto
Yugoslav. Skier
Epitomizes "agony of defeat" for ABC's "Wide World of Sports."

Bogdanovich, Peter
American. Director, Producer
Won NY Film Critics Award, best screenplay for *The Last Picture Show,* 1971.
b. Jul 30, 1939 in Kingston, New York

Source: *BiDFilm, 81, 94; BioIn 9, 10, 11, 12, 13, 14, 15, 16, 17, 19; BioNews 74; CelR, 90; ConAu 5R, 21NR; ConTFT 1, 4, 12; CurBio 72; DcArts; FilmEn; HalFC 80, 84, 88; IlWWHD 1; IntAu&W 82, 89, 91, 93; IntDcF 1-2, 2-2; IntMPA 75, 76, 77, 78, 79, 80, 81, 82, 84, 86, 88, 92, 94, 96; IntWW 75, 76, 77, 78, 79, 80, 81, 82, 83, 89, 91, 93; LegTOT; MiSFD 9; MovMk; NewYTBS 77; Who 90, 92, 94; WhoAm 74, 76, 78, 80, 82, 84, 86, 88, 90, 92, 94, 95, 96, 97; WhoEnt 92; WhoHol 92; WhoHrs 80; WhoWest 78; WhoWor 76, 78, 91; WorAl; WorAlBi; WorFDir 2; WrDr 76, 86, 88, 90, 92, 94, 96*

Bogert, Tim
[Vanilla Fudge]
American. Singer, Musician
Bassist, vocalist with group formed 1966.
b. Aug 27, 1944 in New York, New York

Boggs, Hale
[Thomas Hale Boggs]
American. Politician
Dem. con. from LA, 1941-43, 1947-72; lost in Alaska plane crash.
b. Feb 15, 1914 in Long Beach, Mississippi
d. Oct 1972 in Alaska
Source: *BiDrAC; BiDrUSC 89; BioIn 4, 5, 7, 8, 9, 10, 11, 12; CurBio 58, 73N; DcAmB S9; NatCAB 57; NewYTBE 71; PolProf J, K, NF; WhAm 5; WhAmP; WhoGov 72, 75; WhoSSW 73, 82*

Boggs, Lindy
[Mrs. Hale Boggs]
American. Politician
Entered Congress as widow, replacing husband; chairwoman of Democratic National Convention, 1976.
b. Mar 13, 1916 in Brunswick, Louisiana
Source: *AlmAP 78, 80, 82, 84, 88; BioIn 20; NewYTBE 71; PolsAm 84; WhoAm 84; WomFir; WomPO 78*

Boggs, Tom
[The Box Tops; Thomas Boggs]
American. Musician
Drummer with Memphis-based, blue-eyed soul group, 1966-70.
b. Jul 16, 1947 in Wynne, Arkansas

Boggs, Wade (Anthony)
American. Baseball Player
Infielder, Boston, 1982-92; NY Yankees, 1992—; won AL batting title, 1983, 1985-88.
b. Jun 15, 1958 in Omaha, Nebraska
Source: *Ballpl 90; BaseReg 86, 87; BioIn 13; CelR 90; CurBio 90; LegTOT; News 89-3; WhoAm 90, 92, 94, 95, 96, 97; WhoE 89, 93, 95, 97; WorAlBi*

Bogner, Willi
German. Designer, Director, Producer
Several times German ski champion; directs documentaries, sports films; special cameraman for James Bond films since 1960.
b. Jan 23, 1942 in Munich, Germany
Source: *WorFshn*

Bogosian, Eric
American. Actor, Dramatist
Won Obie, Drama Desk awards for one-man show *Drinking in America,* 1986.
b. Apr 24, 1953 in Boston, Massachusetts
Source: *BioIn 13; ConAmD; ConAu 138; ConDr 93; ConLC 45; ConTFT 7, 14; CurBio 87; IntMPA 92, 94, 96; IntWW 93; LegTOT; News 90; NewYTBS 83; WhoAm 92, 94, 95, 96, 97; WhoAmA 84; WhoE 89, 93; WhoEnt 92; WhoHol 92; WrDr 96*

Bogues, Mugsy
[Tyrone Curtis Bogues]
American. Basketball Player
Guard, Washington, 1987-88; Charlotte Hornets, 1988—; shortest player (five foot, three inches) in NBA today.
b. Jan 9, 1965 in Baltimore, Maryland
Source: *OfNBA 87; WhoAm 97*

Boguslawski, Wojciech
Polish. Director, Dramatist
Considered father of Polish theater; director, National Theater, 1783-1814; wrote over 80 plays.
b. Apr 9, 1757 in Glinno, Poland
d. Jul 23, 1829 in Warsaw, Poland
Source: *CamGWoT; CasWL; EncWL; Ent; NewGrDM 80; NewGrDO; NotNAT B; OxCThe 83; WebBD 83*

Bohannon, Judy
[Judith Layton Bohannon; Judy Fields]
American. Actor
Starred in TV soap opera "Capitol," 1982-83.
b. Jun 30, in Louisville, Kentucky
Source: *ConTFT 2*

Bohay, Heidi
American. Actor
Played Megan Kendal on TV series "Hotel," 1983-88.
b. Dec 15, 1959 in Bound Brook, New Jersey
Source: *ConTFT 3; LegTOT; WhoHol 92*

Bohlem, Arndt von
German.
Last heir to Krupp industrial fortune.
b. 1938
d. May 13, 1986 in Essen, Germany (West)
Source: *NewYTBS 86*

Bohlen, Charles Eustis
American. Diplomat
Expert on Russian affairs for US foriegn service, 1930s-70s.
b. Aug 30, 1904 in Clayton, New York
d. Jan 2, 1974 in Washington, District of Columbia
Source: *BioIn 1, 2, 3, 4, 5, 6, 8, 9, 10, 11; ColdWar 1; ConAu 111; CurBio 48, 60, 74; DcAmB S9; DcAmDH 80, 89; EncAB-H 1974; LinLib S; NewYTBS 74; WhAm 6; Who 74; WhoAm 74; WhoAmP 73*

Bohm, Karl
[Karl Boehm]
Austrian. Conductor
Noted for interpretations of Mozart, Wagner, Strauss; usually associated with Vienna Philharmonic, Salzburg Festival.
b. Aug 28, 1894 in Graz, Austria
d. Aug 14, 1981 in Salzburg, Austria
Source: *AnObit 1981; Baker 78, 84, 92; BiDAmM; BioIn 4, 6, 7, 8, 9, 10, 11, 12, 13; BriBkM 80; CelR; CmOp; ConAu 105; CurBio 68, 81, 81N; DcArts; FacFETw; IntDcOp; IntWW 74, 75, 76, 77, 78, 79, 80, 81; IntWWM 77, 80; MetOEnc; MusSN; NewAmDM; NewEOp 71; NewGrDM 80; NewGrDO; NewYTBE 72; NewYTBS 81; OxDcOp; PenDiMP; WhAm 8; WhoAm 76, 78, 80, 82; WhoMus 72; WhoOp 76; WhoWor 74, 80, 84; WorAl; WorAlBi*

Bohm von Bawerk, Eugene
Austrian. Economist, Politician
Introduced theory of interest; wrote *Kapital and Kapitalzins,* 1884-89.
b. Feb 12, 1851 in Brunn, Austria-Hungary
d. Aug 27, 1914 in Kramsach, Austria
Source: *BioIn 2, 8*

Bohr, Aage Niels
Danish. Scientist
Shared Nobel Prize in physics, 1975, for work with atomic nucleus.
b. Jun 19, 1922 in Copenhagen, Denmark
Source: *BiESc; BioIn 14, 15, 20; FacFETw; IntWW 74, 75, 76, 77, 78, 79, 80, 81, 82, 83, 89, 91, 93; LarDcSc; Who 82, 83, 85, 88, 90, 92, 94; WhoAm 88, 90, 92, 94, 95; WhoNob, 90, 95; WhoScEn 94, 96; WhoWor 78, 80, 82, 84, 87, 89, 91, 93, 95, 96, 97; WorAl; WorAlBi*

Bohr, Niels Henrik David
Danish. Physicist
Helped develop atom bomb in Los Alamos, NM, 1943-45; shared 1922 Nobel Prize.
b. Oct 7, 1885 in Copenhagen, Denmark
d. Nov 18, 1962 in Copenhagen, Denmark
Source: *AsBiEn; BioIn 2, 3, 4, 5, 6, 7, 8, 10, 11, 12, 13, 14, 15, 16, 17, 20, 21; CamDcSc; CurBio 45, 63; DcScB; HisEWW; InSci; LarDcSc; LinLib L, S; MakMC; McGEWB; McGMS 80; OxCEng 67; RAdv 13-5; WhAm 4; WhoNob, 90, 95; WorAl; WorScD*

Bohrod, Aaron
American. Artist
Realistic painter, commissioned by *Life* to record WW II; did outstanding examples of *Trompe-l'-o eil.*
b. Nov 21, 1907 in Chicago, Illinois
d. Apr 3, 1992 in Madison, Wisconsin
Source: *AmArt; BioIn 1, 3, 4, 8, 10, 17, 18; BriEAA; ConAu 21R; CurBio 55, 92N; DcAmArt; DcCAA 71, 77, 88, 94; DcCAr 81; GrAmP; McGDA; WhAm 10; WhAmArt 85; WhoAm 74, 76, 78, 80, 82, 84, 86, 88, 90; WhoAmA 73, 76, 78, 80, 82, 84, 86, 89, 91, 93N; WhoWor 74; WhoWorJ 72, 78*

Boiardi, Hector
American. Chef, Manufacturer
Founded Chef Boy-ar-dee Foods, 1928, pres. until 1946.
b. 1897 in Piacenza, Italy
d. Jun 21, 1985 in Parma, Ohio
Source: *ConNews 85-3; Entr*

Boiardo, Matteo Maria
Italian. Poet
Famous for unfinished epic poem on Charlemagne, *Orlando Innamorato,* 1487.
b. 1441 in Scandiano, Italy
d. 1494 in Reggio Nell'Emilia, Italy
Source: *Benet 87, 96; CasWL; CyWA 58; DcEnL; DcEuL; DcItL 1, 2; EuAu; EvEuW; LinLib L; LitC 6; McGEWB; OxCEng 67; PenC EUR; RComWL; REn; WhDW*

Boieldieu, Francois Adrien
French. Composer
Wrote piano music, scores of comic operas including *Jean de Paris,* 1812.
b. Dec 16, 1775 in Rouen, France
d. Oct 8, 1834 in Jarcy, France
Source: *BioIn 4, 7, 12; BriBkM 80; CelCen; DcCom 77; Dis&D; MusMk; NewEOp 71; OxCFr; OxCMus*

Boileau(-Despreaux), Nicolas
"Legislator of Parnassus"
French. Author, Poet, Critic
Wrote *Satires,* 1666; *Art Poetique,* 1674, which defined principles of classic French verse.
b. Nov 1, 1636 in Paris, France
d. Mar 13, 1711 in Paris, France
Source: *AtlBL; BbD; BiD&SB; BioIn 5, 7, 9, 14; BlmGEL; CamGWoT; CasWL; CyWA 58; DcArts; DcBiPP; DcCathB; DcEuL; EncWT; EuAu; EuWr 3; EvEuW; GrFLW; GuFrLit 2; LinLib L, S; LitC 3; LngCEL; LuthC 75; NewCBEL; OxCEng 67; OxCFr; OxCThe 67, 83; PenC EUR; RComWL; REn; RfGWoL 95; WhDW; WorAlBi*

Boitano, Brian
American. Skater
Four-time US champion, two-time world champion figure skater; won gold medal, 1988 Olympics.
b. Oct 22, 1963 in Mountain View, California
Source: *BiDAmSp BK; CelR 90; CurBio 89; LegTOT; News 88-3; WhoSpor; WorAlBi*

Boito, Arrigo
Italian. Composer, Librettist
Wrote play *Mefistofele,* 1868, based on Goethe's *Faust.*
b. Feb 24, 1842 in Padua, Italy
d. Jun 10, 1918 in Milan, Italy
Source: *AtlBL; Baker 78, 84, 92; Benet 87, 96; BiD&SB; BioIn 1, 3, 7, 8, 9, 10, 12, 16, 20; BriBkM 80; CasWL; ClDMEL 47; CmOp; CmpBCM; DcCom 77; DcItL 1, 2; EuAu; EvEuW; GrComp; IntDcOp; LegTOT; LinLib L, S; MetOEnc; MusMk; NewAmDM; NewEOp 71; NewGrDM 80; NewGrDO; NewOxM; NotNAT B; OxCEng 85, 95; OxCMus; OxCThe 67; OxDcOp; PenC EUR; PenDiMP A; REn; WorAl; WorAlBi*

Boivin, Leo Joseph
Canadian. Hockey Player
Defenseman, 1951-70, with five NHL teams; Hall of Fame, 1986.
b. Aug 2, 1932 in Prescott, Ontario, Canada
Source: *BioIn 8; HocEn; WhoHcky 73*

Bojer, Johan
Norwegian. Author
Best-known work is *The Great Hunger,* 1916.
b. Mar 6, 1872 in Orkesdalsoren, Norway
d. Jul 3, 1959 in Oslo, Norway
Source: *Benet 87, 3; EvEuW; LinLib L; LngCTC; OxCAmL 65, 83, 95; PenC EUR; REn; REnAL; TwCA, SUP; TwCLC 64; WhAm 3; WhE&EA; WhLit; WhoLA*

Bok, Bart J(an)
American. Astronomer
Leading authority on Milky Way; wrote *The Milky Way,* definitive source of information on galaxy, 1941.
b. Apr 28, 1906 in Hoorn, Netherlands
d. Aug 5, 1983 in Tucson, Arizona
Source: *AmMWSc 73P, 76P, 79, 82; AnObit 1983; BiESc; BioIn 1, 2, 4, 11, 13, 14, 18, 19; BlueB 76; ConAu 30NR, 49, 110; FacFETw; InSci; IntWW 74, 75, 76, 77, 78, 79, 80, 81, 82, 83; LarDcSc; NewYTBS 83; RAdv 14, 13-5; WhAm 8; WhoAm 74, 76, 78, 80, 82; WrDr 80, 82, 84*

Bok, Derek Curtis
American. Educator, University Administrator
Pres. of Harvard U, 1971-91; Professor Emeritus, Harvard U, 1991—.
b. Mar 22, 1930 in Bryn Mawr, Pennsylvania
Source: *BioIn 9, 10, 13; BlueB 76; CelR; ConAu 106; CurBio 71; DrAS 74P, 78P, 82P; EncWB; IntWW 74, 75, 76, 77, 78, 79, 80, 81, 82, 83; LEduc 74; NewYTBE 71; Who 74, 82, 83, 85; WhoAm 74, 76, 78, 80, 82, 86; WhoAmL 79; WhoE 74, 77, 79, 81; WorAl; WrDr 86*

Bok, Edward William
American. Editor, Author
Editor *Ladies Home Journal,* 1889-1919; won Pulitzer for *The Americanization of Edward Bok,* 1920.
b. Oct 9, 1863 in Den Helder, Netherlands
d. Jan 9, 1930 in Lake Wales, Florida
Source: *Alli SUP; AmAu&B; AmBi; AmRef; ApCAB X; BiDAmJo; BiD&SB; BioIn 1, 5, 6, 7, 8, 9, 12, 14, 15, 16, 17; DcAmAu; DcAmB S1; DcAmTB; DcLEL; DcNAA; Dis&D; EncAB-H 1974, 1996; LinLib L, S; MorMA; NatCAB 10, 23; OxCAmL 65, 83, 95; REn; REnAL; TwCA, SUP; TwCBDA; WebAB 74, 79; WhAm 1; WhAmP; WhJnl; WhLit; WhNAA*

Bok, Hannes Vajn
American. Artist, Author
Famed fantasy illustrator who drew woodcut-like scenes for *Weird Tales.*
b. Jul 2, 1914 in Minnesota
d. Apr 11, 1964 in New York
Source: *EncSF; FanAl; PseudN 82; ScF&FL 1; WhoHr&F; WhoSciF*

Bok, Sissela
Swedish. Philosopher
Wrote *Lying: Moral Choice in Public and Private Life,* 1978; *Common Values,* 1995.
b. Dec 2, 1934 in Stockholm, Sweden
Source: *CurBio 96; IntAu&W 89; LegTOT; WhoAm 88, 90, 92, 94, 95, 96, 97; WhoAmW 85, 87, 89, 91, 93, 95, 97; WorAu 1980; WrDr 90, 92, 94, 96*

Bokassa, Jean-Bedel
African. Political Leader
Self-proclaimed emperor of the Central African Republic, 1966-79.
b. Feb 22, 1921 in Boubangui, Central African Republic
d. Nov 3, 1996 in Bangui, Central African Republic
Source: *FacFETw; InB&W 85; NewYTBS 27*

Bokassa I
[Jean Bedel Bokassa]
African. Political Leader
Took control of Central African Empire, 1966; named pres., for life, 1972; crowned emperor, 1977.
b. Feb 21, 1921 in Boubangui, Africa
Source: *AfSS 78, 79, 80, 81, 82; BioIn 7, 9, 10, 11; CurBio 78; DcTwHis; IntWW 74, 75, 76, 77, 78, 79, 80, 81, 82, 83, 89, 91, 93; IntYB 78, 79; NewYTBS 77; WhoAfr; WhoGov 72; WhoWor 74, 76, 78; WomFir; WorDWW*

Bol, Manute
Sudanese. Basketball Player
Dinka tribesman who stands seven foot, six inches; center, Washington, 1986-88; Golden State, 1989-90;

Philadelphia, 1990—; ranked 2nd in NBA in blocked shots, 1986.
b. Oct 16, 1962 in Gogrial, Sudan
Source: *BasBi; OfNBA 87*

Bolan, Marc
[T. Rex; Mark Feld]
English. Musician
Co-founder, lead vocalist, T. Rex; died in car crash; recorded 16 albums including *Slider,* 1972.
b. May 8, 1948? in London, England
d. Sep 16, 1977 in London, England
Source: *BioIn 9, 11, 12; HarEnR 86; LegTOT; ObitOF 79; PseudN 82; RolSEnR 83; WhoRock 81*

Boland, Edward P(atrick)
American. Politician
Dem. congressman from MA, 1953-89; sponsored Boland amendments, 1983-86, which restricted US covert aid to Nicaraguan Contras.
b. Oct 1, 1911 in Springfield, Massachusetts
Source: *AlmAP 78, 80, 82, 84, 88; AmCath 80; BiDrAC; BiDrUSC 89; CngDr 87; ColdWar 1; CurBio 87; PolsAm 84; WhoAm 74, 76, 78, 80, 82, 84, 86, 88; WhoAmP 73, 75, 77, 79, 81, 83, 85, 87, 89, 91, 93, 95; WhoE 74, 75, 77, 79, 81, 83, 85, 86, 89, 91; WhoGov 72, 75, 77*

Boland, Mary
American. Actor
Played opposite Charles Ruggles in many 1930s films including *Ruggles of Red Gap,* 1935.
b. Jan 28, 1880 in Philadelphia, Pennsylvania
d. Jun 23, 1965 in New York, New York
Source: *BiE&WWA; EncAFC; EncMT; Film 1; FilmEn; FilmgC; Funs; HalFC 80, 84, 88; InWom SUP; MotPP; MovMk; NotNAT B; NotWoAT; OlFamFa; QDrFCA 92; ThFT; TwYS; Vers A; WhAm 4; WhoHol A; WhScrn 74, 77, 83*

Bolcom, William Elden
American. Composer, Pianist
Renowned for compositions which synthesize serious and popular music; composed *Songs of Innocence and Songs of Experience,* 1982; won Pulitzer, "Twelve New Etudes for Piano," 1987.
b. May 26, 1938 in Seattle, Washington
Source: *AmComp; Baker 84, 92; BioIn 9, 11, 12; BlueB 76; ConAmC 82; ConAu 93; DcCM; IntWWM 77, 90; NewGrDO; WhoAm 74, 76, 78, 80, 82, 84, 86, 88, 90, 92, 94, 95, 96, 97; WhoAmM 83; WhoE 74; WhoEnt 92; WhoMW 90, 92, 93, 96*

Bolden, Buddy
[Charles Bolden]
American. Jazz Musician
Cornettist who is credited with originating jazz, 1890s.
b. Sep 6, 1868 in New Orleans, Louisiana
d. Nov 4, 1931 in New Orleans, Louisiana
Source: *AfrAmAl 6; Baker 84; BiDAmM; CmpEPM; DrBlPA 90; InB&W 80; LegTOT; NegAl 76, 83, 89; NewAmDM; NewGrDM 80; WebAB 74, 79; WhAm 4, HSA; WhoJazz 72; WorAl; WorAlBi*

Bolden, Charles F(rank), Jr.
American. Astronaut
Astronaut, NASA, 1981—; assistant deputy administrator of NASA headquarters, 1992—.
b. Aug 19, 1946 in Columbia, South Carolina
Source: *AfrAmAl 6; WhoAfA 96; WhoBlA 88, 90, 92, 94*

Boles, John
American. Actor
Leading man of 30s-40s; films include *Curly Top,* 1935; *The Littlest Rebel,* 1935; *Stella Dallas,* 1937.
b. Oct 28, 1895 in Greenville, Texas
d. Feb 27, 1969 in San Angelo, Texas
Source: *BiE&WWA; BioIn 11; EncMT; Film 2; FilmEn; FilmgC; HalFC 80, 84, 88; HolP 30; MovMk; ObitOF 79; SilFlmP; TwYS; WhAm 5; WhoHol B; WhScrn 74, 77, 83*

Boles, Paul Darcy
American. Author
Wrote of small-town American life in novels *The Beggars in the Sun,* 1954; *Glenport, Illinois,* 1956.
b. Mar 5, 1919 in Auburn, Idaho
d. May 4, 1984 in Atlanta, Georgia
Source: *Au&Wr 71; BioIn 3, 4, 11; ConAu 4NR, 9R; CurBio 56, 84, 84N; IndAu 1917; SmATA 9; WhoSSW 73, 75*

Bolet, Jorge
Cuban. Pianist
Romantic concert pianist; recorded piano soundtrack for *Song Without End,* 1960, film about life of Franz Liszt.
b. Nov 15, 1914 in Havana, Cuba
d. Oct 16, 1990 in Mountain View, California
Source: *AnObit 1990; Baker 78, 84, 92; BioIn 3, 4, 10, 11, 16, 17, 19, 21; BriBkM 80; DcTwCCu 4; FacFETw; IntWW 91; IntWWM 77, 80, 90; MusSN; NewAmDM; NewGrDA 86; NewGrDM 80; NewYTBE 73; NewYTBS 90; NotTwCP; PenDiMP; WhAm 10; WhoAm 76, 78; WhoAmM 83; WhoE 83, 85; WhoHisp 91, 92N; WhoMus 72*

Boley, Forrest Irving
American. Educator, Physicist, Author
Dartmouth physics professor, 1964—; editor *Cemenial Journal of Physics,* 1966-73.
b. Nov 27, 1925 in Fort Madison, Iowa
Source: *AmMWSc 73P, 76P, 79, 82, 86, 89, 92, 95; BioIn 9, 10; WhoAm 74, 76, 78, 80, 82, 84, 86, 88, 90*

Boleyn, Anne
English. Consort
Second wife of Henry VIII, whose marriage was voided by church, May 17, 1536; mother of Elizabeth I.
b. 1507
d. May 19, 1536 in London, England
Source: *Benet 87, 96; BioIn 14, 15, 17, 18, 19, 20; BlmGWL; ContDcW 89; DcBiPP; DcNaB; Dis&D; IntDcWB; InWom, SUP; LegTOT; LinLib S; LuthC 75; NewC; NewCol 75; REn; WomFir; WorAl; WorAlBi*

Bolger, Jim
[James Brendan Bolger]
New Zealander. Political Leader
Prime minister of New Zealand, 1990—.
b. May 31, 1935 in Taranaki, New Zealand
Source: *IntWW 89, 91, 93; WhoAsAP 91; WhoWor 89, 91, 93, 95, 96, 97*

Bolger, Ray(mond Wallace)
American. Actor, Dancer
Show business veteran best known for playing the Scarecrow in *The Wizard of Oz,* 1939.
b. Jan 10, 1904 in Dorchester, Massachusetts
d. Jan 15, 1987 in Los Angeles, California
Source: *AnObit 1987; BiDD; BiE&WWA; BioIn 1, 2, 3, 4, 5, 6, 8, 10, 11, 15, 16; CamGWoT; CmMov; CmpEPM; CnOxB; ConNews 87-2; ConTFT 3; CurBio 87, 87N; DancEn 78; EncAFC; EncMT; EncVaud; Ent; FilmEn; FilmgC; ForYSC; HalFC 80, 84, 88; IntMPA 82; LegTOT; MovMk; NewYTBS 87; NotNAT; OxCAmT 84; OxCPMus; VarWW 85; WhAm 9; WhoAm 74, 76, 78, 80, 82, 84, 86; WhoHrs 80; WhoThe 72, 77, 81; WhoWor 74, 76, 82, 84, 87; WorAl; WorAlBi*

Bolger, William Frederick
American. Government Official
First career postal employee to rise through the ranks to become Postmaster General, 1978.
b. Mar 13, 1923 in Waterbury, Connecticut
d. Aug 21, 1989 in Arlington, Virginia
Source: *CurBio 79; IntWW 82; NewYTBS 78; WhAm 10; WhoAm 80, 82, 84, 88; WhoE 85*

Bolingbroke, Henry St. John, Viscount
English. Statesman, Author
Prominent political leader, reign of Queen Anne, 1702-14; secretary of state, 1710-14.
b. Oct 1, 1678 in London, England
d. Dec 12, 1751 in Battersea, England
Source: *Alli; BbD; BiD&SB; BiDLA; BioIn 14, 19; BlkwCE; BlmGEL; BritAu; CamGEL; CamGLE; CasWL; Chambr 2; DcBiPP; DcEnA; DcEnL; DcEuL; DcLB 101; DcLEL; EvLB; LinLib L, S; LngCEL; LuthC 75; McGEWB; NewC;*

NewCBEL; OxCEng 67, 85, 95; PenC ENG; REn; WebE&AL; WorAl; WorAlBi

Bolinger, Dwight Lemerton
American. Linguist, Author, Educator
Expert on English and Spanish languages; wrote *Aspects of Language,* 1968 and *Language: The Loaded Weapon.*
b. Aug 18, 1907 in Topeka, Kansas
d. Feb 23, 1992 in Palo Alto, California
Source: *AnObit 1992; ConAu 13R; DcSpL; DrAS 74F, 78F, 82F; IntAu&W 77, 82; WhAm 10; WhoAm 74, 76, 78, 80; WhoWor 89; WrDr 76, 80, 82, 84, 86, 88, 90, 92, 94N*

Bolitho, Henry Hector
New Zealander. Author, Lecturer
Wrote *Reign of Queen Victoria,* 1948; *No. 10 Downing Street,* 1957.
b. May 28, 1897, New Zealand
d. 1974
Source: *Au&Wr 71; ConAu 53, P-1; DcLEL; EvLB; IntWW 74; LngCTC; NewC; PenC ENG; TwCA, SUP; Who 74; WhoWor 74*

Bolitho, William
[William Bolitho Ryall]
Author, Journalist
Works include *Leviathan,* 1924; *Twelve Against the Gods,* 1929.
b. 1890 in Cape Town, South Africa
d. Jun 2, 1930 in Avignon, France
Source: *DcLEL; EncAJ; LngCTC; NewC; TwCA; WhLit*

Bolivar, Simon
"El Libertador"
Venezuelan. Revolutionary, Statesman
Led armies against Spanish in S America; resulted in creation of six nations.
b. Jul 24, 1783 in Caracas, Venezuela
d. Dec 17, 1830 in Santa Marta, Colombia
Source: *ApCAB; Benet 87, 96; BiDInt; BiDLAmC; BioIn 1, 2, 3, 4, 5, 6, 7, 8, 9, 10, 11, 12, 13, 14, 16, 17, 18, 19, 20; CasWL; CelCen; DcAmSR; DcHiB; DcSpL; Dis&D; Drake; EncLatA; EncRev; GenMudB; HarEnMi; HisDcSE; HisWorL; LegTOT; LinLib S; McGEWB; NewCol 75; PenC AM; REn; WebBD 83; WhAm HS; WhDW; WhoMilH 76; WorAl; WorAlBi*

Bolkiah, Muda Hassanal, Sir
Bruneian. Ruler
Sultan of Brunei (29th); richest man in the world; alleged to be, involved in Iran-Contra scandal, 1987.
b. Jul 15, 1946 in Bandar Seri Begawan, Brunei Darussalam
Source: *BioIn 15, 16, 17, 19; ConNews 85-4; CurBio 89; IntWW 91*

Boll, Heinrich (Theodor)
German. Author
Won Nobel Prize, 1972, for works dealing with drift of German society during Nazi, post-war periods.
b. Dec 21, 1917 in Cologne, Germany
d. Jul 16, 1985 in Hurtgenwald, Germany (West)
Source: *AnObit 1985; Benet 87, 96; BioIn 5, 9, 10, 12, 13, 14, 15, 16, 17; CasWL; CelR; ClDMEL 80; ConAu 116; ConFLW 84; ConLC 2, 3, 6, 9, 11, 15, 27, 39, 72; CurBio 72, 85, 85N; CyWA 89; DcArts; DcLB 69, Y85N; EncWL 2, 3; EuWr 13; EvEuW; FacFETw; GrFLW; IntAu&W 76, 77; IntWW 74, 75, 76, 77, 78, 79, 80, 81, 82, 83; LegTOT; LinLib L, S; MagSWL; MakMC; ModGL; NewYTBE 72; NewYTBS 74, 85; NobelP; Novels; OxCEng 85, 95; OxCGer 76, 86; PenC EUR; RadHan; RAdv 14, 13-2; REn; RfGShF; RfGWoL 95; ShSCr 23; TwCWr; WhAm 8; WhDW; Who 74, 82, 83, 85; WhoAm 76, 78, 80, 82, 84; WhoNob, 90, 95; WhoTwCL; WhoWor 74, 78, 80, 82, 84; WorAl; WorAlBi; WorAu 1950; WorLitC*

Boller, Paul Franklin, Jr.
American. Author, Educator
Books on American thought include *This Is Our Nation,* 1961; *Presidential Campaigns,* 1984.
b. Dec 31, 1916 in Spring Lake, New Jersey
Source: *ConAu 1R, 3NR, 19NR, 41NR; DrAS 74H, 78H, 82H; WrDr 86*

Bolles, Don F
American. Journalist
Investigative reporter for *Arizona Republic;* killed in car bomb explosion.
b. 1928 in Milwaukee, Wisconsin
d. Jun 13, 1976 in Phoenix, Arizona
Source: *BioIn 10; ConAu 65, 73; NewYTBS 76; ObitOF 79*

Bologna, Joseph
American. Actor
Films include *My Favorite Year,* 1982; *Blame It on Rio,* 1984.
b. Dec 30, 1938 in New York, New York
Source: *ConAu 77; ConTFT 3, 9; HalFC 80, 84, 88; IntMPA 80, 86, 92, 94, 96; WhoAm 78, 80, 82, 84, 86, 88, 90, 92; WhoEnt 92*

Bolotowsky, Ilya
American. Artist, Sculptor
Painter, known for diamond-shaped canvases; co-founder, American Abstract Artists, 1936.
b. Jul 1, 1907 in Saint Petersburg, Russia
d. Nov 21, 1981 in New York, New York
Source: *AnObit 1981; BioIn 8, 9, 10, 11, 12, 13, 14, 17; BriEAA; ConArt 77, 83, 89, 96; ConAu 108; CurBio 75, 82, 82N; DcAmArt; DcCAA 71, 77, 88, 94; DcCAr 81; FacFETw; NewYTBS 81; OxCTwCA; OxDcArt; PhDcTCA 77; PrintW 85; WhAm 8; WhAmArt 85; WhoAm 74, 76, 78, 80; WhoAmA 73, 76, 78, 80, 82N, 84N, 86N, 89N, 91N, 93N; WhoWorJ 72, 78; WorArt 1950*

Bolt, Carol
Canadian. Dramatist
Plays include *Cyclone Jack,* 1972.
b. Aug 25, 1941 in Winnipeg, Manitoba, Canada
Source: *ArtclWW 2; BioIn 16; BlmGWL; CaP; ConAu 101; ConDr 77, 82, 88, 93; ConWomD; DcLB 60; DrCnP 81; FemiCLE; OxCCanL; OxCCan SUP; OxCCanT; WhoCanL 85, 87, 92; WrDr 80, 82, 84, 86, 88, 90*

Bolt, Robert (Oxton)
English. Author
Plays include award-winning *Man for All Seasons,* 1960; won Oscar for *Dr. Zhivago* screenplay, 1965.
b. Aug 15, 1924 in Manchester, England
d. Feb 20, 1995 in Petersfield, England
Source: *Benet 87, 96; BiE&WWA; BioIn 6, 7, 8, 9, 10, 11, 12, 13; BlmGEL; BlueB 76; CamGLE; CamGWoT; CasWL; CelR; CnThe; ConAu 17R, 35NR, 147; ConBrDr; ConDr 73, 77, 82, 88, 93; ConLC 14; ConTFT 4, 12; CroCD; CrtSuDr; CurBio 95N; CyWA 89; DcArts; DcLB 13; DcLEL 1940; EncWL 2, 3; EncWT; Ent; FacFETw; FilmEn; FilmgC; HalFC 80, 84, 88; IntAu&W 76, 77, 82, 91, 93; IntDcT 2; IntMPA 77, 78, 79, 80, 81, 82, 84, 86, 88, 92, 94, 96; IntWW 74, 75, 76, 77, 78, 79, 80, 81, 82, 83, 89, 91, 93; LegTOT; LinLib L; MajTwCW; McGEWD 72, 84; MiSFD 9; ModWD; NewC; NewYTBS 95; NotNAT; OxCEng 85, 95; OxCThe 67, 83; PenC ENG; RAdv 14, 13-2; REnWD; RGTwCWr; TwCWr; WebE&AL; WhAm 11; Who 74, 82, 83, 85, 88, 90, 92; WhoThe 72, 77, 81; WhoWor 74, 76, 78, 82, 84, 87, 89, 91, 93, 95; WorAu 1950; WorEFlm; WrDr 76, 80, 82, 84, 86, 88, 90, 92, 94, 96*

Bolt, Tommy
[Thomas Bolt]
American. Golfer
Turned pro, 1946; won 13 pro tournaments including US Open, 1958; known for explosive temper.
b. Mar 31, 1918 in Haworth, Oklahoma
Source: *BioIn 5, 6, 11, 21; LegTOT; NewYTBS 77; WhoGolf*

Bolte, Charles G(uy)
American. Publishing Executive
Officer of Viking Press until 1966; wrote *The Price of Peace: A Plan for Disarmament,* 1956.
b. Jan 19, 1920
d. Mar 7, 1994 in Augusta, Maine
Source: *AmAu&B; BioIn 1, 2, 4; CurBio 94N; WhoAm 74, 76, 78, 80, 82, 84, 86, 88; WhoUSWr 88; WhoWrEP 89, 92, 95*

Bolton, Frances Payne
American. Politician
Held 28-yr. term in Congress as Rep. representative; her grandfather, husband and son have also served.
b. Mar 29, 1885 in Cleveland, Ohio
d. Mar 9, 1977 in Lyndhurst, Ohio
Source: *AmPolW 80; WomCon*

Bolton, Guy Reginald
English. Dramatist
Wrote over 50 musicals including *Lady be Good; Anything Goes.*
b. Nov 23, 1884 in Brozbourne, England
d. Sep 5, 1979 in Goring, England
Source: *AmAu&B; ASCAP 66; BiDAmM; BioIn 3, 5, 7, 11, 12; ConAu 5NR, 5R, 89; ConDr 73, 77; IntAu&W 76, 77; LngCTC; ModWD; Who 74; WhoThe 72, 81*

Bolton, Isabel
[Mary Britten Miller]
American. Author
Wrote *The Christmas Tree,* 1949; *Many Mansions,* 1952.
b. Aug 6, 1883 in New London, Connecticut
d. Apr 13, 1975 in New York, New York
Source: *AmAu&B; AmNov; AuSpks; ConAu 1R, 16NR, 57; LngCTC; ObitOF 79; PenNWW B; TwCA SUP*

Bolton, Michael
[Michael Bolotin]
American. Singer
Albums include, *Time, Love and Tenderness; Timeless (The Classics),* 1992.
b. Feb 26, 1953 in New Haven, Connecticut
Source: *BioIn 16; ConMus 6; CurBio 93; EncRkSt; News 93-2; RkOn 85; WhoEnt 92*

Bolton, Sarah Tittle Barrett
American. Poet
Wrote verse *Paddle Your Own Canoe,* 1851.
b. Dec 18, 1814 in Newport, Kentucky
d. Aug 4, 1893 in Indianapolis, Indiana
Source: *Alli; AmAu; AmAu&B; AmWomWr; BiD&SB; BiDSA; ChhPo, S2; DcAmAu; DcAmB; DcNAA; IndAu 1816; NotAW; WhAm HS*

Bolz, Lothar
German. Government Official
Deputy prime minister of East Germany, 1950-67.
b. Sep 3, 1903 in Gleiwitz, Germany
d. Dec 29, 1986 in Berlin, German Democratic Republic
Source: *BioIn 5, 15; CurBio 59, 87, 87N; EncGRNM; IntWW 74, 75, 76, 77, 78, 79, 80, 81, 82, 83; NewYTBS 86; WhoSocC 78; WhoSoCE 89*

Bombeck, Erma (Louise)
American. Journalist, Author, Humorist
Syndicated columnist, 1965-96; books include, *If Life Is a Bowl of Cherries, What Am I Doing in the Pits?,* 1971.
b. Feb 21, 1927 in Dayton, Ohio
d. Apr 22, 1996 in San Francisco, California
Source: *AmCath 80; AmWomWr SUP; ArtclWW 2; AuNews 1; BenetAL 91; BestSel 89-4; BiDAmNC; BioIn 10, 11, 12, 13; CelR 90; ConAu 12NR, 21R, 39NR, 151; ConPopW; CurBio 79, 96N; EncAHmr; EncTwCJ; ForWC 70; FunnyW; IntAu&W 89, 91, 93; InWom SUP; LegTOT; LibW; MajTwCW; News 96; NewYTBS 27; WhAm 11; WhoAm 76, 78, 80, 82, 84, 86, 88, 90, 92, 94, 95, 96, 97; WhoAmW 72, 74, 79, 81, 83, 85, 87, 89, 91, 93, 95; WhoEnt 92; WhoUSWr 88; WhoWrEP 89, 92, 95; WorAl; WorAlBi; WrDr 80, 82, 84, 86, 88, 90, 92, 94, 96*

Bomberg, Dave
[David Bomberg]
English. Artist
Original member of the "London Group," 1914; landscape paintings have a documentary character.
b. Dec 5, 1890 in Birmingham, England
d. Aug 19, 1951 in London, England
Source: *BioIn 1, 5, 8, 11, 15, 16, 17, 18, 21; ConArt 77, 83; DcArts; DcBrAr 1; DcNaB MP; McGDA; ObitT 1951; OxCTwCA; PhDcTCA 77; TwCPaSc*

Bonaly, Surya
French. Skater
Won European championship, 1991, 1992, 1993, 1994; skated in 1992 and 1994 Winter Olympics.
b. 1973 in Nice, France
Source: *BioIn 20, 21; ConBlB 7*

Bonanno, Joseph
"Joe Bananas"
American. Criminal
Sought to increase power against other Mafia families in Banana crime war, 1964-69.
b. Jan 18, 1905 in Castellammare del Golfo, Italy
Source: *BioIn 9, 20; EncACr*

Bonaparte, Elizabeth Patterson
American. Socialite
Married Napoleon's youngest brother, Jerome, 1803; annulled, 1805.
b. Feb 6, 1785 in Baltimore, Maryland
d. Apr 4, 1879 in Baltimore, Maryland
Source: *AmAu&B; AmBi; AmWom; ApCAB; BioIn 1, 2, 4, 6, 11, 15; DcAmB; HerW; LibW; TwCBDA; WebAB 74, 79; WhAm HS*

Bonaparte, Francois Charles Joseph
[Napoleon II]
French. Political Leader
Son of Napoleon Bonaparte; titular king of Rome, 1811-14; prince of Parma, 1814-18.
b. Mar 20, 1811 in Paris, France
d. Jul 22, 1832 in Schonbrunn, Austria
Source: *BioIn 1, 2, 5, 6; NewCol 75; WebBD 83*

Bonaparte, Jerome
French. Ruler
Youngest brother of Napoleon; king of Westphalia, 1807-13.
b. Nov 15, 1784 in Ajaccio, Corsica, France
d. Jun 24, 1860 in Paris, France
Source: *AmBi; ApCAB; BioIn 15; CelCen; DcBiPP; HarEnMi; HarEnUS; LinLib S*

Bonaparte, Joseph
French. Ruler
Older brother of Napoleon; king of Naples, 1806-08; king of Spain, 1808-13.
b. Jan 7, 1768 in Corte, Corsica, France
d. Jul 28, 1844 in Florence, Italy
Source: *ApCAB; BioIn 16; CelCen; DcBiPP; DicTyr; HarEnMi; HarEnUS; LinLib S; McGEWB*

Bonaparte, Letizia
[Maria Letizia Bonaparte]
"Madame Mother"
French.
Mother of Napoleon I.
b. Aug 24, 1750 in Ajaccio, Corsica, France
d. Feb 2, 1836 in Rome, Italy
Source: *BioIn 6, 8, 10, 11; DcBiPP; Dis&D*

Bonaparte, Louis Lucien
French. Scholar
Philologist who was made prince by Napoleon III, 1863.
b. Jan 4, 1813 in Thorngrove, England
d. Nov 3, 1891 in Fano, Italy
Source: *Alli SUP; CelCen; DcBiPP*

Bonaparte, Lucien
French. Statesman
Exiled for opposing brother, Napoleon's polices, 1810.
b. May 21, 1775 in Ajaccio, Corsica, France
d. Jun 30, 1840 in Viterbo, Italy
Source: *BioIn 2, 4, 5; CelCen; DcBiPP; Dis&D; LinLib S; WebBD 83*

Bonatti, Walter
Italian. Author
Travel books include *On the Heights,* 1964; *The Great Days,* 1974.
b. Jun 22, 1930 in Bergamo, Italy
Source: *BioIn 19; ConAu 23NR, 48NR, 106; WrDr 76, 80*

Bonavena, Oscar
Argentine. Boxer
South American heavyweight champ; KO'd by Muhammed Ali, 1970.
b. Sep 25, 1942 in Buenos Aires, Argentina
d. May 22, 1976

Source: *BioIn 7, 9, 10; NewYTBE 72; NewYTBS 76; WhoBox 74*

Bonaventure, Saint
[Giovanni DeFidenza]
"Seraphic Doctor"
Italian. Religious Figure
Developed scholasticism in medieval thought.
b. 1221 in Bagnoregio, Italy
d. Jul 15, 1274 in Lyons, France
Source: *Benet 87, 96; BiD&SB; BioIn 2, 3, 4, 5, 6, 7, 9; CasWL; CyEd; DcCathB; DcEuL; EuAu; EvEuW; IlEncMy; LinLib S; LuthC 75; OxCPhil; PenC EUR; REn*

Bonci, Alessandro
Italian. Opera Singer
Tenor who is often ranked second to Caruso.
b. Feb 10, 1870 in Cesena, Italy
d. Aug 8, 1940 in Vitterbo, Italy
Source: *Baker 78, 84, 92; BioIn 11, 14; CmOp; CurBio 40; IntDcOp; MetOEnc; MusSN; NewEOp 71; NewGrDM 80; NewGrDO; OxDcOp; PenDiMP; WhAm 5*

Bond, Alan
Australian. Business Executive
Founder/Chm. of the Board, Bond Corp; executive of yacht-racing syndicate that won 1983 America's Cup with *Australia II.*
b. Apr 22, 1938 in London, England
Source: *BioIn 10, 13, 15, 16; IntWW 89, 91, 93; LesBEnT 92; News 89-2; NewYTBS 74, 83; Who 85, 88, 90, 92, 94; WhoFI 92; WhoWor 89, 91*

Bond, Carrie Jacobs
American. Composer
Wrote hits "End of a Perfect Day"; "I Love You Truly."
b. Aug 11, 1862 in Janesville, Wisconsin
d. Dec 28, 1946 in Los Angeles, California
Source: *AmAu&B; ASCAP 66; ChhPo; DcAmB S4; DcNAA; NotAW; REnAL; WhAm 2; WhNAA; WisWr; WomWWA 14*

Bond, Christopher Samuel
"Kit"
American. Politician
Rep. senator, MO, 1987—.
b. Mar 6, 1939 in Saint Louis, Missouri
Source: *AlmAP 88; BiDrGov 1978, 1983; BiDrUSC 89; BioIn 9, 10, 11, 15; BlueB 76; CngDr 87; IntWW 74, 75, 76, 77, 78, 79, 80, 81, 82, 83, 89, 91, 93; IntYB 78, 79, 80, 81, 82; PolsAm 84; WhoAm 74, 76, 78, 80, 82, 84, 86, 88, 90, 92, 94, 95, 96, 97; WhoAmP 73, 75, 77, 79, 81, 83, 85, 87, 89, 91, 93, 95; WhoGov 77; WhoMW 74, 76, 78, 82, 84, 88, 90, 92, 93, 96; WhoWor 82, 89, 91*

Bond, Edward
English. Dramatist
Controversial plays include *Saved,* 1965; *Lear,* 1971.
b. Jul 18, 1934 in London, England
Source: *Benet 87, 96; BioIn 9, 10, 11, 12, 13; BlmGEL; BlueB 76; BritWr S1; CamGLE; CamGWoT; CnThe; ConAu 25R, 38NR; ConBrDr; ConDr 73, 77, 82, 88, 93; ConLC 4, 6, 13, 23; ConTFT 4; CroCD; CrtSuDr; CurBio 78; CyWA 89; DcLB 13; DcLEL 1940; EncWL 2, 3; EncWT; EngPo; FacFETw; GrWrEL DR; IntAu&W 76, 77, 82, 86, 89, 91, 93; IntWW 79, 80, 81, 82, 83, 89, 91, 93; LinLib L; MajMD 1; MajTwCW; MakMC; McGEWD 84; ModBrL S1, S2; NewGrDO; NotNAT; OxCEng 85; RAdv 14; RfGEnL 91; RGTwCWr; Who 74, 82, 83, 85, 88, 90, 92, 94; WhoThe 81; WhoTwCL; WhoWor 84, 87, 89, 91; WorAu 1970; WrDr 76, 80, 82, 84, 86, 88, 90, 92, 94, 96*

Bond, George Foote
"Papa Topside"
American. Physician
Medical officer, Sealab missions, 1964-69; tested human endurance undersea.
b. 1915
d. Jan 3, 1983 in Charlotte, North Carolina
Source: *BioIn 3, 8, 13; NewYTBS 83*

Bond, James
American. Ornithologist
His name was adopted by author Ian Fleming for his fictional secret agent after he read one of his books *Birds of the West Indies.*
b. Jan 4, 1900 in Philadelphia, Pennsylvania
d. Feb 14, 1989 in Philadelphia, Pennsylvania
Source: *AmMWSc 73P, 76P, 79, 82, 86; AnObit 1989; BioIn 12, 16, 17, 19; ConAu 127; Dun&B 88; NewYTBS 89*

Bond, Julian
American. Politician, Civil Rights Leader
First black to be nominated for vp, 1968; member, GA senate, 1975-87; hosted "America's Black Forum"; narrated TV documentary "Eyes on the Prize," 1987, 1990, history of civil rights movements.
b. Jan 14, 1940 in Nashville, Tennessee
Source: *AfrAmAl 6; AfrAmBi 2; AmSocL; BioIn 7, 8, 9, 10, 11, 12, 13; BlkWr 1; CelR; CivR 74; CivRSt; ConAu 49; ConBlB 2; CurBio 69; DcTwCCu 5; Ebony 1; EncWB; FacFETw; HisWorL; IntWW 77, 78, 79, 80, 81, 82, 83, 89, 91, 93; LegTOT; LinLib L; LivgBAA; LNinSix; NegAl 76, 83; NewYTBE 70; PolPar; PolProf J; SchCGBL; WebAB 74, 79; WhoAfA 96; WhoAm 74, 76, 78, 80, 82, 84, 86, 88, 90, 92, 94, 95, 96, 97; WhoAmP 73, 75, 77, 79, 81, 83, 85, 87, 89, 91, 93, 95; WhoBlA 75, 90, 92, 94; WhoEmL 87; WhoGov 75, 77; WhoSSW 73, 75, 76, 78, 80, 82, 84, 86, 88, 93, 95, 97; WhoWor 74; WorAl; WorAlBi*

Bond, Sudie
American. Actor
Played Flo on TV's "Alice," 1980-82.
b. Jul 13, 1928 in Louisville, Kentucky
d. Nov 10, 1984 in New York, New York
Source: *BiE&WWA; BioIn 14; ConTFT 1; NewYTBS 84; NotNAT; WhoAm 82; WhoHol A; WhoThe 72, 77, 81*

Bond, Tommy
[Our Gang]
American. Actor
Played Butch in 1930s "Our Gang" serial.
b. Sep 16, 1927 in Dallas, Texas
Source: *EncAFC; FilmEn; WhoHol 92, A*

Bond, Victoria
American. Conductor
First woman to co-conduct major US symphony; assisted Previn in leading Pittsburgh Orchestra, 1978-80.
b. May 6, 1950 in Los Angeles, California
Source: *IntWWM 80, 85; NewAmDM; WhoAm 80, 82, 84, 86, 88; WhoAmM 83*

Bond, Ward
American. Actor
Appeared in over 200 films; starred in TV series "Wagon Train," 1957-61.
b. Apr 9, 1903 in Denver, Colorado
d. Nov 5, 1960 in Dallas, Texas
Source: *CmMov; EncAFC; FilmEn; FilmgC; GangFlm; HalFC 80, 84, 88; LegTOT; MotPP; MovMk; OxCFilm; WhoHol B; WhScrn 74, 77, 83; WorAl; WorAlBi*

Bondarchuk, Sergei (Fedorovich)
Russian. Director, Actor
Played lead roles in Russian films *Destiny of a Man,* 1961; *War and Peace,* 1966.
b. Sep 25, 1922 in Byelozerka, Union of Soviet Socialist Republics
Source: *DcFM; IntWW 83; MovMk; OxCFilm; WhoHol A; WorEFlm*

Bondfield, Margaret Grace
English. Government Official
First British woman cabinet minister: minister of labor, 1929-31.
b. Mar 17, 1873 in Furnham, England
d. Jun 16, 1953 in Sanderstead, England
Source: *BiDBrF 1; BioIn 1, 2, 3, 14; ContDcW 89; DcNaB 1951; GrBr; IntDcWB; InWom, SUP; LinLib S; ObitOF 79; ObitT 1951; WhDW; WhE&EA; WomFir*

Bondi, Beulah
American. Actor
Oscar nominee for *Gorgeous Hussy; Of Human Hearts;* won 1977 Emmy for "The Waltons."
b. May 3, 1892 in Chicago, Illinois
d. Jan 12, 1981 in Hollywood, California
Source: *BiE&WWA; BioIn 10; FilmEn; FilmgC; ForYSC; HalFC 80, 84; HolCA; IntDcF 1-3, 2-3; IntMPA 75, 76, 77, 78,*

79, 80, 81; InWom SUP; MotPP; MovMk; NewYTBS 81; NotNAT; OlFamFa; ThFT; Vers A; What 4; WhoHol A; WhoThe 77A, 81; WhScrn 83; WhThe

Bondi, Hermann, Sir
English. Mathematician
Most important work done in applied mathematics, cosmology; wrote *Cosmology,* 1952.
b. Nov 1, 1919 in Vienna, Austria
Source: *BiESc; BioIn 3, 12, 13, 14, 17, 20; BlueB 76; CamDcSc; FacFETw; InSci; IntAu&W 77, 82, 86, 89; IntWW 74, 75, 76, 77, 78, 79, 80, 81, 82, 83, 89, 91, 93; IntWWE; LarDcSc; NotTwCS; Who 74, 82, 83, 85, 88, 90, 92, 94; WhoWor 74, 76, 78, 82, 84, 87, 89, 91, 93, 95, 96, 97*

Bonds, Barry (Lamar)
American. Baseball Player
Outfielder, Pittsburgh, 1985-92; San Francisco, 1993—; NL MVP, 1990, 1992, 1993; son of Bobby.
b. Jul 24, 1964 in Riverside, California
Source: *AfrAmSG; Ballpl 90; BaseEn 88; BaseReg 88; ConBlB 6; CurBio 94; News 93-3; WhoAfA 96; WhoAm 92, 94, 95, 96, 97; WhoBlA 92, 94; WhoWest 94, 96; WhoWor 95, 96, 97*

Bonds, Bobby (Lee)
American. Baseball Player
Outfielder, 1968-81; only player ever to hit grand slam home run in first at-bat.
b. Mar 15, 1946 in Riverside, California
Source: *Ballpl 90; BiDAmSp BB; BioIn 9, 10, 11, 14, 15, 19; InB&W 80, 85; NewYTBS 75; WhoAfA 96; WhoBlA 77, 80, 85, 88, 90, 92, 94; WhoProB 73*

Bonds, Gary U. S
[Gary Anderson]
American. Singer, Songwriter
Had hit single "Quarter to Three," 1961 teamed with Bruce Springsteen on *Dedication* album, 1981.
b. Jun 6, 1939 in Jacksonville, Florida
Source: *BioIn 12; EncPR&S 74; HarEnR 86; IlEncBM 82; PseudN 82; RkOn 74; RolSEnR 83; WhoRock 81*

Bone, Muirhead, Sir
Scottish. Artist
An official artist in WW I, WW II; known for drypoint city scenes.
b. Mar 23, 1876 in Glasgow, Scotland
d. Oct 23, 1953 in Oxford, England
Source: *BioIn 3, 6, 14, 15; DcBrBI; DcNaB 1951; DcSeaP; LinLib S; LngCTC; McGDA; ObitT 1951; OxCArt; OxCShps; OxDcArt; TwCPaSc*

Bonelli, Richard
[Richard Bunn]
American. Opera Singer
Light, grand opera baritone, 1920s-50s; NY Met. star, 1932-45.
b. Feb 6, 1894 in Port Byron, New York
d. Jun 7, 1980 in Los Angeles, California
Source: *AnObit 1980; Baker 84; BioIn 4, 9, 10, 11, 12; MusSN; NewEOp 71; NewYTBS 80; PseudN 82; WhScrn 83*

Bonerz, Peter
American. Actor, Director
TV actor, director of episodes of "Bob Newhart Show," 1972-78; director *It's Your Move,* 1984.
b. Aug 6, 1938 in Portsmouth, New Hampshire
Source: *ConTFT 1, 11; LegTOT; MiSFD 9; WhoAm 74, 76, 78, 80, 82, 84, 86, 88, 90, 92, 94, 95, 96, 97; WhoEnt 92; WhoHol 92, A*

Bonestell, Chesley
American. Illustrator
Outer space specialist best known for mural "A Trip to the Moon," 1957.
b. 1888 in San Francisco, California
d. Jun 11, 1986 in Carmel, California
Source: *ArtsAmW 2; BiDScF; BioIn 11; ConAu 119; EncSF, 93; FacFETw; FanAl; NewEScF; ScF&FL 92; SmATA 48N; WhoHrs 80*

Bonet, Lisa
American. Actor
Played Denise Huxtable on "The Cosby Show," 1984-87, "A Different World."
b. Nov 16, 1967 in Los Angeles, California
Source: *ConTFT 4, 10; DrBlPA 90; IntMPA 92, 94, 96; LegTOT; News 89-2; WhoAfA 96; WhoBlA 88, 90, 92, 94; WhoHol 92; WorAlBi*

Boney M.
[Marcia Barrett; Bobby Farrell; Liz Mitchell; Marzie Williams]
German. Music Group
Became int'l. success with singles "River of Bablyon"; "Mary's Boy Child," 1978.
Source: *RkOn 85*

Bonfanti, Jim Alexander
[The Raspberries]
American. Musician
Drummer with power pop group, 1970-73.
b. Dec 17, 1948 in Windber, Pennsylvania

Bonfanti, Marie
American. Dancer
Popular dancer, 1860s-90s; starred in *The Black Crook,* 1868.
b. 1847? in Milan, Italy
d. Jan 25, 1921 in New York, New York
Source: *InWom SUP; NotAW*

Bong, Richard Ira
American. Aviator
Leading American ace, WW II; shot down 40 enemy planes in three hours; killed in jet test flight.
b. Sep 24, 1920 in Superior, Wisconsin
d. Aug 6, 1945 in Los Angeles, California
Source: *BioIn 2, 5, 9; MedHR 94; NatCAB 34; WebAB 74; WebAMB; WhWW-II*

Bongo, Albert-Bernard (Omar)
Gabonese. Political Leader
Pres. of Gabon, 1967—; prime minister, 1967-75.
b. Dec 30, 1935 in Franceville, Gabon
Source: *DcAfHiB 86S; IntWW 76, 77, 78, 79, 80, 81, 82, 83, 89, 91, 93; WhoFr 79; WhoWor 78, 82, 84, 87, 89, 91, 93, 95*

Bonham, Frank
American. Author, Dramatist
Adventure tales for young people include *Devilhorn,* 1978.
b. Feb 25, 1914 in Los Angeles, California
Source: *Au&Arts 1; AuBYP 2, 3; BioIn 8, 9, 10; ConAu 4NR, 9R, 36NR; ConLC 12; DcAmChF 1960; EncFWF; EncSF 93; IntAu&W 91, 93; MajAI; MorBMP; OxCChiL; ScF&FL 92; SmATA 1, 3AS, 49, 62; ThrBJA; TwCChW 78, 83, 89; TwCWW 82, 91; TwCYAW; WrDr 80, 82, 84, 86, 88*

Bonham, John Henry
[Led Zeppelin]
"Bonzo"
English. Musician
Led Zeppelin drummer; group disbanded after his death.
b. May 31, 1949 in Redditch, England
d. Sep 25, 1980 in Windsor, England
Source: *AnObit 1980; NewYTBS 80; WhAm 7; WhoAm 80*

Bonham Carter, Violet
[Baroness Asquith of Yarnbury; Helen Violet Bonham Carter]
English. Biographer
Wrote *Winston Churchill as I Knew Him,* 1965.
b. Apr 15, 1887 in London, England
d. Feb 19, 1969 in London, England
Source: *BioIn 3, 14; ConAu P-2; DcNaB 1961; GrBr; LngCTC; ObitT 1961*

Bonheur, Rosa
[Marie Rosalie Bonheur]
French. Artist
Specialized in paintings, sculptures of animals.
b. Mar 16, 1822 in Bordeaux, France
d. May 25, 1899 in Melun, France
Source: *AntBDN C; BiDWomA; BioIn 1, 2, 3, 4, 5, 9, 10, 11, 12, 13, 15, 16, 17, 19, 20, 21; CelCen; ClaDrA; ContDcW 89; DcArts; DcNiCA; DcWomA; Dis&D; GayLesB; GoodHs; HerW, 84; IlBEAAW; IntDcAA 90; IntDcWB; InWom, SUP; LegTOT; LinLib S; McGDA; OxCArt; OxDcArt; WomArt; WorAlBi*

Bonhoeffer, Dietrich
German. Theologian
Member of anti-Nazi resistance movement; killed by Gestapo in concentration camp.
b. Feb 4, 1906 in Breslau, Germany
d. Apr 9, 1945 in Flossenberg, Germany
Source: *BiDMoPL; BioIn 1, 3, 5, 6, 7, 8, 9, 10, 11, 12, 13, 14, 15, 16, 17, 18, 19, 20, 21; ConAu 122, 148; ConHero 1; CyWA 89; DcEcMov; DcTwHis; EncGRNM; EncTR, 91; FacFETw; HeroCon; HisEWW; HisWorL; LegTOT; LinLib L; LuthC 75; MakMC; McGEWB; OxCGer 76, 86; RadHan; RAdv 14, 13-4; ThTwC 87; WebBD 83; WhDW; WorAu 1950*

Boni, Albert
American. Publisher
Founder, Boni & Liveright, 1917; started Modern Library series, 1917.
b. Oct 21, 1892 in New York, New York
d. Jul 31, 1981 in Ormond Beach, Florida
Source: *AmAu&B; AnObit 1981; BioIn 12, 13; ConAu 65, 104; LinLib L; NewYTBS 81; St&PR 75; WhAm 8; WhoAm 74, 76, 78, 80; WhoWor 76; WhoWorJ 72*

Boniface, Saint
English. Missionary, Religious Figure
Advanced Christianity; founded monasteries in Germany; martyred.
b. 675? in Wessex, England
d. Jun 5, 754 in Dokkum, Frisia
Source: *Alli; BiD&SB; CasWL; CyEd; DcEnL; LegTOT; NewC; OxCGer 76*

Bonilla, Bobby
[Roberto Martin Antonio Bonilla]
American. Baseball Player
With Pittsburgh Pirates, 1986-91; New York Mets, 1991-95; Baltimore Orioles, 1996—; has played on several NL All-Star teams.
b. Feb 23, 1963 in New York, New York
Source: *Ballpl 90; BioIn 16, 17, 18, 19, 20, 21; DcHiB; News 92, 92-2; WhoAfA 96; WhoAm 92, 94, 95, 96, 97; WhoBlA 92, 94; WhoE 95; WhoHisp 91, 92, 94*

Bonington, Richard Parkes
English. Artist
Subjects for paintings include landscapes, historical figures.
b. Oct 25, 1802 in Arnold, England
d. Sep 23, 1828 in London, England
Source: *AtlBL; DcAmB; DcArts; DcBrWA; DcSeaP; IntDcAA 90; McGDA; McGEWB; OxCArt; OxDcArt*

Bonivard, Francois
Swiss. Patriot
Led Genevese revolt against Charles III, 1528; imprisoned, 1530-36; subject of Lord Byron's "Prisoner of Chillon."
b. 1494?
d. 1570
Source: *NewC; NewCol 75; WebBD 83*

Bon Jovi
[Jon Bon Jovi; Dave Bryan; Alec Johnsuch; Richie Sambora; Tico Torres]
American. Music Group
Rock band formed, 1980s; had number one album *Slippery When Wet,* 1987.
Source: *BioIn 15, 16, 17, 20, 21; CelR 90; ConMus 10; EncPR&S 89; EncRkSt; RkOn 85*

Bon Jovi, Jon
[John Bongiovi]
American. Singer, Bandleader
Founder, lead singer of rock group Bon Jovi, 1984—; had number-one hit album, *Slippery When Wet,* 1987.
b. May 2, 1962 in Sayreville, New Jersey
Source: *CelR 90; ConNews 87-4; CurBio 90; WhoAm 90, 92, 94, 95, 96, 97; WhoEnt 92*

Bonnard, Pierre
French. Artist
Subjects for paintings include still lifes, women bathing, self-portraits.
b. Oct 30, 1867 in Fontenay, France
d. Jan 23, 1947 in Le Cannet, France
Source: *AntBDN A; AtlBL; BioIn 1, 2, 3, 4, 5, 6, 7, 8, 10, 12, 14, 16, 17, 20, 21; ClaDrA; DcArts; DcTwCCu 2; FacFETw; IntDcAA 90; LegTOT; MakMC; McGDA; McGEWB; ObitOF 79; OxCArt; OxCTwCA; OxDcArt; PhDcTCA 77; WhDW; WorAl; WorAlBi*

Bonner, Frank
[Frank Boers, Jr.]
American. Actor
Played Herb Tarlek on TV series "WKRP in Cincinnati," 1978-82.
b. Feb 28, 1942 in Little Rock, Arkansas
Source: *BioIn 13; ConTFT 7; WhoAm 80, 82; WhoHol 92*

Bonner, Yelena
[Mrs. Andrei Sakharov]
Russian. Social Reformer
Accepted husband's Nobel Peace Prize, 1975; formed group of dissidents, 1976; internally exiled, 1984-86.
b. Feb 15, 1923 in Moscow, Union of Soviet Socialist Republics
Source: *BioIn 13; ContDcW 89; CurBio 87; RadHan*

Bonnet, Georges Etienne
French. Politician
Foreign minister, 1938-39; main architect of 1938 Munich agreements.
b. Jul 23, 1889 in Bassillac, France
d. Jun 18, 1973 in Paris, France
Source: *NewYTBS 74; ObitT 1971*

Bonneville, Benjamin Louie Eulalie de
American. Army Officer
Explored Northwest, 1832-35; subject of Irving's *Adventures of Captain Bonneville,* 1837.
b. Apr 14, 1796 in Paris, France
d. Jun 12, 1878 in Fort Smith, Arkansas
Source: *OxCAmL 65; WebAB 74; WebBD 83*

Bonnin, Gertrude Simmons
[Red Bird; Zitkala-Sa]
American. Writer
Published *Old Indian Legends,* 1902; *American Indian Stories,* 1921.
b. Feb 22, 1876 in Yankton Reservation, South Dakota
d. Jan 26, 1938 in Washington, District of Columbia
Source: *AmRef; AmSocL; AmWomWr 92; ArtclWW 2; BioIn 15, 16, 19, 21; DcNAL; EncWHA; HanAmWH; NotAW; NotNaAm; OxCWoWr 95*

Bonny, Anne
[Anne Bonney]
Irish. Pirate
With a series of husbands operated in vicinity of West Indies; captured, 1720; released, then disappeared.
b. 1700
d. 1720
Source: *BioIn 4, 5, 6, 7, 10, 11, 15, 20; DrInf; EncAmaz 91; GayLesB; GoodHs; InWom, SUP; OxCShps*

Bono
[U2; Paul Hewson]
Irish. Singer, Songwriter
Lead singer, U2, 1976—; won Grammys for *The Joshua Tree,* "I Still Haven't Found What I'm Looking For," 1987.
b. May 10, 1960 in Dublin, Ireland
Source: *BioIn 14, 15, 16; CurBio 93; IntWW 91, 93; LegTOT; News 88; WhoAm 94, 95, 96, 97; WhoWor 95; WorAlBi*

Bono, Chastity
American.
Daughter of Sonny and Cher.
b. Mar 4, 1969 in Los Angeles, California
Source: *LegTOT*

Bono, Sonny
[Sonny and Cher; Salvatore Phillip Bono]
American. Actor, Politician, Singer
Best known for hits while married to Cher: "The Beat Goes On," 1966; mayor of Palm Springs, CA, 1988-92; member of U.S. House of Representatives, 1995—.
b. Feb 16, 1935 in Detroit, Michigan
Source: *AlmAP 96; BioIn 10, 11, 13; BioNews 74; CelR 90; CngDr 95; ConTFT 7; CurBio 74; IntMPA 88, 92, 94, 96; LegTOT; News 92, 92-2; WhoAm 86; WhoAmP 95; WhoHol 92, A; WhoRock 81; WhoRocM 82; WorAlBi*

Bonoff, Karla
[Mrs. Robby Benson]
American. Singer, Songwriter
Writer of Linda Ronstadt's "Someone to Lay Down Beside Me," 1976; solo

albums include *Wild Heart of the Young,* 1981.
b. Dec 27, 1952 in Los Angeles, California
Source: *BioIn 11, 12, 13, 14; EncFCWM 83; LegTOT; PenEncP; RkOn 85; RolSEnR 83*

Bononcini, Giovanni Battista
Italian. Composer
Operas include *Astarto,* 1715; *Griselda,* 1722.
b. Jul 18, 1670 in Modena, Italy
d. Jul 9, 1747 in Vienna, Austria
Source: *BioIn 4, 7, 10; NewEOp 71; OxCMus*

Bonsal, Philip Wilson
American. Diplomat
Ambassador to Cuba, 1959-60, when Fidel Castro had overthrown the government.
b. May 22, 1903
d. Jun 28, 1995 in Washington, District of Columbia
Source: *BioIn 5, 16, 21; ConAu 85; CurBio 95N; DcAmDH 80, 89; WhoAm 74, 76, 78, 80*

Bonsal, Stephen
American. Journalist
Foreign affairs writer; won 1944 Pulitzer for *Unfinished Business.*
b. Mar 29, 1865 in Baltimore, Maryland
d. Jun 8, 1951 in Washington, District of Columbia
Source: *AmAu&B; BiD&SB; BiDSA; BioIn 1, 2, 3, 4; CurBio 45, 51; DcAmAu; DcAmB S5; EncAJ; HarEnUS; NatCAB 14; OxCAmL 65; REnAL; TwCA SUP; WhAm 3*

Bonsall, Joe
[The Oak Ridge Boys]
American. Singer
Tenor with country-pop group; hit single "So Fine," 1982.
b. May 18, 1948 in Philadelphia, Pennsylvania

Bonstelle, Jessie
American. Director, Actor
Tutored Broadway stars; founded civic theatre in Detroit, 1925.
b. Nov 18, 1871 in Greece, New York
d. Oct 14, 1932 in Detroit, Michigan
Source: *InWom SUP; LibW; NatCAB 25; NotAW; NotWoAT*

Bontemps, Arna Wendell
American. Author
Leader, "Harlem Renaissance" movement, 1920s; wrote *Black Thunder,* 1936.
b. Oct 13, 1902 in Alexandria, Louisiana
d. Jun 4, 1973 in Nashville, Tennessee
Source: *AmAu&B; AmNov; AnMV 1926; Au&Wr 71; AuBYP 2, 3; BioIn 1, 2, 7, 8, 9, 10, 12, 13, 14, 15, 16, 17, 19, 20; BkCL; BlkAmP; BlkAmW 1; BlkAuII, 92; BlkAWP; BroadAu; ChhPo S1; ConAu 1R, 4NR, 41R; ConLC 1, 18; ConPo 70; CurBio 46, 73; DcAmB S9; DcAmLiB; Ebony 1; EncAACR; InB&W 80, 85; JBA 34, 51; MorBAP; MorBMP; NewYTBE 70; OxCAmL 65, 95; REnAL; SelBAAf; SelBAAu; SmATA 2; SouBlCW; SouWr; Str&VC; WebE&AL; WhAm 5; WhoAm 74; WhoBlA 75; WhoLibS 55; WhoWor 74*

Bonynge, Richard
Australian. Conductor
Musical director, Australian Opera, 1975-85.
b. Sep 29, 1930 in Sydney, Australia
Source: *Baker 84; BioIn 7, 8, 10, 12, 13; CnOxB; CurBio 81; FarE&A 78, 80, 81; IntWW 75, 76, 77, 78, 79, 80, 81, 82, 83, 89, 91, 93; IntWWM 77, 80, 90; MetOEnc; NewAmDM; NewGrDM 80; OxDcOp; PenDiMP; Who 82, 83, 85, 88, 90, 92, 94; WhoAm 88, 90, 92, 94, 95, 96, 97; WhoEnt 92; WhoMus 72; WhoOp 76; WhoWor 74, 87, 89, 91, 93, 95, 96, 97*

Booke, Sorrell
American. Actor
Best known for role of Boss Hogg in TV series "The Dukes of Hazzard," 1979-86.
b. Jan 4, 1930 in Buffalo, New York
d. Feb 11, 1994 in Sherman Oaks, California
Source: *BioIn 19; ConTFT 4, 13; FilmEn; HalFC 84; IntMPA 86, 88, 92, 94; NotNAT; WhoAm 84; WhoThe 77, 81*

Booker T. and the MG's
[Steve Cropper; Donald Dunn; Al Jackson, Jr; Booker T Jones; Bobby Manuel; Carson Whitsett]
American. Music Group
First hit single "Green Onions," 1962; group disbanded, 1972.
Source: *AmPS A; BiDAmM; EncPR&S 74; HarEnR 86; IlEncBM 82; IlEncRk; RolSEnR 83; SoulM; WhAm 6; WhoRocM 82*

Bookout, John Frank, Jr.
American. Businessman
Geologist, Shell Oil Co., 1950-76; pres., CEO, 1976-87.
b. Dec 31, 1922 in Shreveport, Louisiana
Source: *BioIn 12; CanWW 70; Dun&B 79; IntWW 79, 80, 81, 82, 83, 89, 91, 93; NewYTBS 76; St&PR 84; WhoAm 74, 76, 78, 80, 82, 84, 86, 88, 90, 92, 94, 95, 96, 97; WhoCan 73; WhoFI 79, 81, 83, 85, 87, 89; WhoSSW 78, 80, 82, 88; WhoWor 82, 84, 87, 89, 91*

Bookspan, Martin
American. Critic
TV commentator, "Live from Lincoln Center," 1976—; "Great Performances," 1977—.
b. Jul 30, 1926 in Boston, Massachusetts
Source: *Baker 84, 92; ConAu 41R; IntAu&W 76; IntWWM 80, 85, 90; WhoAmJ 80; WhoAmM 83; WhoE 74; WhoEnt 92; WhoWorJ 72, 78*

Boole, Ella Alexander
American. Social Reformer
Pres., of World WCTU, 1931-47; wrote *Give Prohibition Its Chance,* 1929.
b. Jul 26, 1858 in Van Wert, Ohio
d. Mar 13, 1952 in New York, New York
Source: *DcAmB S5; DcAmTB; InWom, SUP; NatCAB 38; NotAW MOD; OhA&B; WhAm 3; WomWWA 14*

Boole, George
English. Mathematician
Helped establish Boolean algebra, which is essential in the design of digital computer circuits.
b. Nov 2, 1815 in Lincoln, England
d. Dec 8, 1864 in Ballintemple, Ireland
Source: *Alli, SUP; AsBiEn; BiDPsy; BiESc; BioIn 2, 11, 13, 15, 16, 21; BritAu 19; CamDcSc; DcBiPP; DcNaB; DcScB; HisDcDP; InSci; LarDcSc; LinLib L, S; McGEWB; NewCBEL; OxCPhil; RAdv 14; VicBrit; WhDW; WorAl; WorAlBi*

Boolootian, Richard Andrew
American. Scientist
Pres., Scientific Software Systems, Inc., 1969—; has written three college zoology textbooks.
b. Oct 17, 1927 in Fresno, California
Source: *AmMWSc 73P, 76P, 79, 82, 86, 89, 92, 95; WhoWest 82, 89, 92, 94*

Boomtown Rats
[Pete Briquette; Gerry Cott; Johnny Fingers; Bob Geldof; Simon Grove; Garry Roberts]
Irish. Music Group
Punk band, formed late 1970s; albums include *Boomtown Rats,* 1978.
Source: *BioIn 14, 15, 16, 17; ConMuA 80A; EncPR&S 89; EncRk 88; EncRkSt; HarEnR 86; IlEncRk; IntWW 89; OnThGG; PenEncP; RkOn 85; RolSEnR 83; WhoRock 81; WhoRocM 82; WhsNW 85*

Boon, Dickie
[Richard R Boon]
Canadian. Hockey Player
Defenseman on amateur Montreal teams, 1900-05; Hall of Fame, 1952.
b. Feb 14, 1874 in Belleville, Ontario, Canada
d. May 3, 1961
Source: *WhoHcky 73*

Boone, Bob
[Robert Raymond Boone]
American. Baseball Player
Catcher, 1972-93, mostly with the Philadelphia Phillies; first to catch 2,000 ML games, 1988.
b. Nov 19, 1947 in San Diego, California
Source: *Ballpl 90; BaseEn 88; BaseReg 87, 88; BiDAmSp Sup; BioIn 12, 13; WhoAm 78, 96, 97*

Boone, Daniel
American. Pioneer
Legendary frontiersman blazed the Wilderness Road; established Boonesboro, first settlement in KY, 1775.
b. Nov 2, 1734 in Reading, Pennsylvania
d. Sep 26, 1820 in Saint Charles County, Missouri
Source: *Alli; AmAu&B; AmBi; AmRev; ApCAB; Benet 87, 96; BenetAL 91; BiDSA; BioIn 1, 2, 3, 4, 5, 6, 7, 8, 9, 10, 11, 12, 13, 14, 15, 16, 17, 18, 19, 20; DcAmB; DcNCBi 1; Drake; EncAAH; EncAB-H 1974, 1996; EncAR; EncCRAm; EncSoH; Expl 93; FilmgC; HalFC 80, 84, 88; HarEnMi; HisWorL; LegTOT; LinLib S; McGEWB; MemAm; OxCAmH; OxCAmL 83, 95; RComAH; REn; REnAL; REnAW; TwCBDA; WebAB 74, 79; WebBD 83; WhAm HS; WhAmP; WhAmRev; WhDW; WhNaAH; WhWE*

Boone, Debby
[Deborah Ann Boone; Mrs. Gabriel Ferrer]
American. Singer
Daughter of Pat Boone; best known for "You Light Up My Life," 1977.
b. Sep 22, 1956 in Hackensack, New Jersey
Source: *Baker 92; BkPepl; CelR 90; ConAu 110; ConTFT 1; EncFCWM 83; HarEnCM 87; HerW 84; LegTOT; PenEncP; RkOn 78; RolSEnR 83; WhoAm 80, 82, 84, 86, 88, 90; WhoAmW 79, 81, 83, 85, 87, 89, 91; WhoEmL 87; WhoEnt 92; WhoRock 81*

Boone, Pat
[Charles Eugene Boone]
American. Singer
Noted for clean cut image, white buck shoes; starred in *April Love,* 1957.
b. Jun 1, 1934 in Jacksonville, Florida
Source: *AmAu&B; ASCAP 66, 80; Baker 84; BiDAmM; BioIn 4, 5, 9, 10, 11, 12, 13, 14, 15, 16, 17; BkPepl; CelR, 90; ConAu 1R, 2NR; ConMuA 80A; ConMus 13; CurBio 79; DcTwCCu 1; EncFCWM 83; EncRk 88; EncRkSt; FilmEn; FilmgC; ForYSC; HalFC 80, 84, 88; IntMPA 75, 76, 77, 78, 79, 80, 81, 82, 84, 86, 88, 92, 94, 96; LegTOT; MotPP; MovMk; NewGrDA 86; OxCPMus; PenEncP; PrimTiR; RkOn 74; RolSEnR 83; SmATA 7; WhoAm 74, 76, 78, 80, 82, 84, 86, 88, 92, 94, 95, 96, 97; WhoEnt 92; WhoHol 92, A; WhoRel 75, 77; WhoRock 81; WorAl; WorAlBi; WrDr 76, 80, 82, 84, 86, 88, 90, 92, 94, 96*

Boone, Rebecca B
American.
Wife of Daniel Boone.
b. 1739
d. 1813
Source: *BioIn 7; HerW; InWom SUP*

Boone, Richard
American. Actor
Starred in TV series "Medic," 1954-56, "Have Gun Will Travel," 1957-63.
b. Jun 18, 1917 in Los Angeles, California
d. Jan 10, 1981 in Saint Augustine, Florida
Source: *AnObit 1981; BiE&WWA; BioIn 12; CelR; CmMov; CurBio 64, 81N; FilmgC; HalFC 80, 84, 88; IntDcF 1-3; IntMPA 77, 78, 79, 80, 81; ItaFilm; MotPP; MovMk; NewYTBE 72; NewYTBS 81; WhoHol A; WhScrn 83; WorAlBi*

Boone, Ron(ald Bruce)
American. Basketball Player
Guard, 1968-81, mostly with Utah; played in NBA record 1,041 consecutive games.
b. Sep 6, 1946 in Oklahoma City, Oklahoma
Source: *BasBi; BioIn 11, 21; InB&W 80; OfNBA 87; WhoAfA 96; WhoBlA 92, 94*

Boorman, John
English. Director
Films include *Deliverance,* 1970; *Exorcist II,* 1977.
b. Jan 18, 1933 in Shepperton, England
Source: *Au&Arts 3; BiDFilm 94; BioIn 12, 13; ConAu 112, 121; ConTFT 6, 15; CurBio 88; DcArts; DcFM; EncEurC; EncSF; FilmEn; FilmgC; HalFC 80, 84, 88; IIWWHD 1; IntDcF 1-2, 2-2; IntMPA 77, 86, 92, 94, 96; IntWW 79, 80, 81, 82, 83, 89, 91, 93; LegTOT; MiSFD 9; OxCFilm; ScF&FL 1; WhoAm 74, 76, 82, 84, 86, 88, 90, 92, 94, 95, 96, 97; WhoHrs 80; WhoWor 89, 95, 96, 97; WorEFlm; WorFDir 2*

Boorstin, Daniel J(oseph)
American. Government Official
Librarian of Congress, 1975-87; Emeritus, 1987—; wrote *The Democratic Experience,* 1973; Pulitzer Prize, 1974.
b. Oct 1, 1914 in Atlanta, Georgia
Source: *AmAu&B; BioIn 6, 7, 8, 10, 11, 12, 13; ConAu 1NR; CurBio 68, 84; DcLEL 1940; DrAS 74H, 78H, 82H; EncAAH; IntAu&W 89, 91, 93; IntWW 83; RAdv 14; Who 85; WhoAm 86, 97; WhoAmJ 80; WhoAmP 85, 87, 89, 91, 93, 95; WhoE 81, 83, 85, 86, 97; WhoGov 77; WhoSSW 73; WhoWor 84, 87, 97; WhoWorJ 78; WorAl; WorAu 1950; WrDr 86*

Boosler, Elayne
American. Comedian
Stand-up comedian with 4 Showtime specials; noted for her sound delivery style.
b. Aug 18, 1952 in New York, New York
Source: *BioIn 11, 15, 16, 18, 19; ConTFT 11; LegTOT*

Booth, Albie
[Albert James Booth, Jr]
"Little Boy Blue"; "Mighty Atom"
American. Football Player
Called one of Yale's greatest halfbacks, all-around athletes; earned eight varsity letters, 1929-32.
b. Feb 1, 1908 in New Haven, Connecticut
d. Mar 1, 1959 in New York, New York
Source: *BiDAmSp FB; BioIn 3, 5, 8; DcAmB S6; ObitOF 79; WhoFtbl 74; WhoSpor*

Booth, Ballington
American. Social Reformer
Son of William, Catherine Booth; withdrew from Salvation Army to found Volunteers of America, 1896.
b. Jul 28, 1859 in Brighouse, England
d. Oct 5, 1940 in Blue Point, New York
Source: *CurBio 40; DcAmB S2; HarEnUS; LuthC 75; NatCAB 14; TwCBDA; WhAm 1, 2; WorAl; WorAlBi*

Booth, Catherine Mumford
[Mrs. William Booth]
English. Social Reformer
Played leading role in founding, developing Salvation Army.
b. Jan 17, 1829 in Derbyshire, England
d. Oct 4, 1890 in Clacton, England
Source: *Alli, SUP; Benet 87; BiDAmCu; BioIn 1, 2, 3, 5, 6, 7, 8, 10, 11, 12, 13, 14, 19, 21; CelCen; DcAmB S1; DcNaB 1912; Dis&D; EncWM; HarEnUS; IntDcWB; InWom, SUP; LinLib L, S; LngCTC; LuthC 75; McGEWB; NewC; OxCEng 85, 95; OxCMus; RelLAm 91; REn; WhDW; WomFir; WorAl; WorAlBi*

Booth, Charles Brandon
American. Social Reformer
Head of Volunteers of America, 1949-58; grandson of Salvation Army founder William Booth.
b. Dec 26, 1887 in New York, New York
d. Apr 14, 1975 in La Mesa, California
Source: *BioIn 10; NewYTBS 75; WhAm 6*

Booth, Edwin Thomas
American. Actor
Brother of John Wilkes Booth; noted Shakespearean actor; founded Players Club, 1888.
b. Nov 13, 1833 in Bel Air, Maryland
d. Jun 7, 1893 in New York, New York
Source: *CnThe; DcAmB; EncWT; LinLib S; OxCAmL 65; OxCThe 67; REn; REnAL; TwCBDA; WebAB 74; WhAm HS*

Booth, Evangeline Cory
"White Angel"
American. Social Reformer
Daughter of William, Catherine Booth; with Salvation Army, beginning 1895, general, 1934-39.
b. Dec 25, 1865 in London, England
d. Jul 17, 1950 in Hartsdale, New York

Source: *AmDec 1900; ApCAB X; BiCAW; BioIn 1, 2, 3, 4, 6, 7, 8, 11, 12, 13; CurBio 41, 50; DcAmB S4; DcAmReB 1, 2; DcAmTB; HerW; InWom, SUP; LibW; LinLib L, S; NotAW; OxCAmH; RelLAm 91; WhAm 3; WomWWA 14; WorAl; WorAlBi*

Booth, George
American. Cartoonist
With *New Yorker* mag; known for unique sketches of dogs, cats, people.
b. Jun 28, 1926 in Cainsville, Missouri
Source: *WhoAm 82, 84, 86, 88, 90, 92, 94, 95, 96, 97; WorECar*

Booth, George Gough
American. Editor
Founded Booth newspaper syndicate, Cranbrook Foundation; published *Detroit News,* 1888-1949.
b. Sep 24, 1864 in Toronto, Ontario, Canada
d. Apr 11, 1949 in Detroit, Michigan
Source: *ApCAB X; BiDAmJo; BioIn 7, 16; ObitOF 79; WhAm 2; WhJnl*

Booth, Hubert Cecil
English. Inventor
Invented the vacuum cleaner, 1901.
b. 1871
d. Jan 14, 1955 in Croydon, England
Source: *BioIn 3; DcNaB 1951; InSci; ObitOF 79; ObitT 1951*

Booth, John Wilkes
American. Assassin
Shakespearean actor; shot, killed Lincoln at Ford's Theatre, Apr 14, 1865.
b. May 10, 1838 in Harford County, Maryland
d. Apr 26, 1865 in Port Royal, Virginia
Source: *AmBi; Benet 87, 96; BenetAL 91; BioIn 1, 2, 3, 4, 5, 6, 7, 8, 9, 10, 11, 12, 13, 14, 16, 17, 18, 20; CivWDc; DcAmB; Dis&D; Drake; EncAB-H 1974, 1996; EncSoH; FamA&A; LegTOT; McGEWB; NatCAB 3; OxCAmH; OxCAmL 65, 83, 95; OxCThe 67; PeoHis; PlP&P; REn; REnAL; TwCBDA; WebAB 74, 79; WhAm HS; WhAmP; WhCiWar; WhDW; WorAl; WorAlBi*

Booth, Junius Brutus
English. Actor
Father of Edwin and John Wilkes; dominated stage for 30 yrs.
b. May 1, 1796 in London, England
d. Nov 30, 1852
Source: *AmBi; ApCAB; BioIn 8, 9, 10, 18; CamGWoT; CelCen; DcAmB; DcBiPP; DcNaB; Drake; EncWT; FamA&A; IntDcT 3; NatCAB 3; NotNAT A, B; OxCAmH; OxCAmL 65, 83, 95; OxCAmT 84; OxCThe 67, 83; PlP&P; REn; REnAL; TwCBDA; WebAB 74, 79; WhAm HS*

Booth, Shirley
[Thelma Booth Ford]
American. Actor
Won Oscar for *Come Back, Little Sheba,* 1953; starred on "Hazel," 1961-66; won Emmy, 1963.
b. Aug 30, 1907 in New York, New York
d. Nov 16, 1992 in North Chatham, Massachusetts
Source: *BiE&WWA; BioIn 3, 4, 5, 6, 7, 9, 11, 16; CamGWoT; CelR; ConTFT 4; CurBio 42, 53, 93N; EncMT; FilmEn; FilmgC; ForYSC; HalFC 80, 84, 88; IntMPA 75, 76, 77, 78, 79, 80, 81, 82, 84, 86, 88; InWom, SUP; LegTOT; MotPP; MovMk; News 93-2; NotNAT; NotWoAT; OxCAmT 84; OxCThe 83; PlP&P; RadStar; SaTiSS; WhoAm 82; WhoHol 92, A; WhoThe 72, 77, 81; WorAl; WorAlBi; WorEFlm*

Booth, William
English. Religious Leader, Social Reformer
Started Christian Mission in E London, 1865, became Salvation Army, 1878.
b. Apr 10, 1829 in Nottinghamshire, England
d. Aug 20, 1912 in London, England
Source: *Alli SUP; Benet 87; BiDAmCu; BioIn 1, 2, 3, 5, 6, 7, 8, 10, 11, 12, 13, 14, 19, 21; CelCen; DcNaB 1912; Dis&D; EncWM; HarEnUS; LinLib L, S; LngCTC; LuthC 75; McGEWB; NewC; OxCEng 85, 95; OxCMus; RelLAm 91; REn; WhDW; WorAl; WorAlBi*

Boothby, Robert John Graham, Lord
Scottish. Politician
British conservative who served in Parliament 62 yrs; private secretary to Winston Churchill, 1926-29.
b. Feb 12, 1900 in Edinburgh, Scotland
d. Jul 16, 1986 in London, England
Source: *BioIn 1, 3, 4, 7, 11, 15, 17, 18; ConAu 117, 120; DcNaB 1986; IntWW 74; NewYTBS 86*

Boothe, Powers
American. Actor
Portrayed Rev. Jim Jones in TV movie *Guyana Tragedy: The Story of Jim Jones,* 1980; won Emmy, 1980.
b. Jun 1, 1949 in Snyder, Texas
Source: *ConTFT 4; IntMPA 84, 86, 88, 94, 96; LegTOT; NewYTBS 79; VarWW 85; WhoHol 92*

Boothroyd, Betty
English. Politician
Labor Party member; first woman Speaker of British Parliament, 1992—.
Source: *InWom SUP*

Boothroyd, John Basil
English. Writer
Contributor to *Punch* mag., 1938-88; TV series writer; wrote *Philip (Duke of Edinburgh),* 1971.
b. Mar 4, 1910 in Worksop, England
d. Feb 27, 1988
Source: *AuBYP 2; DcLEL 1940; IntAu&W 76; WhE&EA; Who 74, 82, 83, 85, 88; WrDr 84*

Borah, William Edgar
American. Politician
Isolationist Rep. senator from ID, 1907-40; opposed US entry into World Court, League of Nations.
b. Jun 29, 1865 in Fairfield, Illinois
d. Jan 19, 1940 in Washington, District of Columbia
Source: *AmBi; AmOrTwC; AmPolLe; ApCAB X; BiDrAC; BiDrUSC 89; BioIn 1, 3, 4, 5, 6, 7, 8, 9, 11, 16, 19; DcAmB S2; DcAmDH 80, 89; DcNAA; EncAAH; EncAB-H 1974, 1996; FacFETw; LinLib S; McGEWB; NatCAB 14; OxCAmH; REn; REnAW; WebAB 74, 79; WebBD 83; WhAm 1; WhAmP; WorAl*

Borch, Fred J.
American. Businessman
Pres., General Electric Co., 1963-68; chm., CEO, 1968-72.
b. Apr 28, 1910 in New York, New York
d. Mar 1, 1995 in Naples, Florida
Source: *BioIn 20; BlueB 76; CurBio 71; IntWW 74; NewYTBS 95; St&PR 75; WhoAm 74; WhoE 74; WhoFI 74; WhoWor 74*

Bordeaux, Henry
French. Author
His 50 novels of provincial life were widely read: *The Gardens of Omar,* 1923; *Footprints Beneath the Snow,* 1912.
b. Jan 29, 1870 in Thonon-les-Bains, France
d. Mar 27, 1964 in Paris, France
Source: *BioIn 1, 4, 6; CasWL; CathA 1930; ClDMEL 47, 80; EncWL; EvEuW; LngCTC; OxCFr; REn; TwCA, SUP*

Bordeaux, Lionel R.
American. University Administrator
President, Sinte Gleska University, 1973, a Native American institution.
b. Feb 9, 1940 in Rosebud Reservation, South Dakota
Source: *BioIn 21; LEduc 74; NotNaAm*

Borden, Barry
[Molly Hatchet]
American. Musician
Drummer with heavy metal band since 1982.
b. May 12, 1954 in Atlanta, Georgia

Borden, Gail
American. Inventor
Patented evaporated milk, 1856.
b. Nov 9, 1801 in Norwich, New York
d. Jan 11, 1874 in Borden, Texas
Source: *AmBi; ApCAB, X; AsBiEn; BiDAmBL 83; BiInAmS; BioIn 2, 3, 4, 6, 7, 9, 18; DcAmB; EncAAH; EncSoB; Entr; HarEnUS; LegTOT; LinLib S; McGEWB; NatCAB 7; NewCol 75;*

TwCBDA; WebAB 74, 79; WhAm HS; WhFla; WorAl; WorAlBi; WorInv

Borden, Lizzie Andrew
American. Murderer
Arrested for murdering father, stepmother, Aug 4, 1892; acquitted, 1893.
b. Jul 19, 1860 in Fall River, Massachusetts
d. Jun 1, 1927 in Fall River, Massachusetts
Source: *BioIn 1, 5, 6, 8, 9, 10, 13; DcAmB S1; EncACr; GoodHs; InWom SUP; LibW; NotAW; OxCAmL 65; REn; REnAL; WebAB 74, 79; WhAm 4, HSA; WorAl*

Borden, Robert Laird, Sir
Canadian. Political Leader
Twice prime minister; headed Conservative govt., 1911-17; Union govt., 1917-20.
b. Jun 26, 1854 in Grand Pre, Nova Scotia, Canada
d. Jun 10, 1937 in Ottawa, Ontario, Canada
Source: *BiDInt; BioIn 2, 7, 8, 9, 10, 11, 12, 13; DcNAA; DcNaB 1931; DcTwHis; FacFETw; HisDBrE; LinLib S; MacDCB 78; McGEWB; OxCCan; WhNAA; WhoPubR 72*

Borders, James
[James Buchanan Borders, IV]
American. Art Director
Managing Director, National Black Arts Festival, Atlanta, 1993—.
b. Apr 5, 1949 in New Orleans, Louisiana
Source: *ConBlB 9*

Bordes, Francois
[Francois Carsac]
French. Archaeologist
Authority on Stone Age tools; manufactured over 100,000 replicas.
b. 1919
d. Apr 30, 1981 in Tucson, Arizona
Source: *BioIn 12, 13; ConAu 103; EncHuEv; NewYTBS 81; WhoFr 79*

Bordet, Jules Jean Baptiste Vincent
Belgian. Scientist
Developed vaccine against whooping cough bacillus, 1906; won Nobel Prize for medicine, 1919.
b. Jun 13, 1870 in Soighies, Belgium
d. Apr 6, 1961 in Brussels, Belgium
Source: *BiESc; BioIn 15, 20; CamDcSc; DcScB; FacFETw; LarDcSc; OxCMed 86; WhAm 4; WhDW; WhoNob, 90, 95; WorAl*

Bordoni, Faustina
[Faustina Bordoni Hasse]
"The New Siren"
Italian. Opera Singer
Noted Dresden Opera prima donna, 1730s-40s; starred in husband's compositions.
b. 1700
d. Nov 4, 1781 in Venice, Italy
Source: *Baker 84; BriBkM 80; IntDcOp; InWom; MetOEnc; NewEOp 71; NewGrDM 80; OxDcOp; PenDiMP*

Bordoni, Irene
American. Actor
Musical comedy star, 1920s; films include *Paris,* 1929.
b. Jan 16, 1893 in Ajaccio, Corsica, France
d. Mar 19, 1953 in New York, New York
Source: *AmPS B; BioIn 3; CmpEPM; InWom; NotNAT B; ObitOF 79; WhoHol B; WhScrn 74, 77; WhThe*

Borduas, Paul-Emile
Canadian. Artist
Leader of "Montreal Automatistes," exponents of objective painting.
b. Nov 1, 1905 in Saint Hilaire, Quebec, Canada
d. Feb 22, 1960 in Paris, France
Source: *ConArt 77, 83; CreCan 1; MacDCB 78; McGDA; OxCCan, SUP; OxCTwCA; OxDcArt; PhDcTCA 77*

Borel d'Hauterive, Petrus
French. Poet, Author
Led group of Romantics called *Bousingos;* translated *Robinson Crusoe* into French.
b. Jun 28, 1809 in Lyons, France
d. Jul 14, 1859 in Mostaganem, Algeria
Source: *BiD&SB; CasWL; EuAu; EvEuW; OxCFr; PenC EUR*

Boren, David (Lyle)
American. Politician, University Administrator
Governor of OK, 1975-79; OK senator, 1979-94; president, Univ. of Oklahoma, 1994—.
b. Apr 21, 1941 in Washington, District of Columbia
Source: *AlmAP 78, 82, 84, 88, 92; BiDrGov 1789, 1978; BiDrUSC 89; BioIn 10, 12; BlueB 76; CngDr 79, 81, 83, 85, 87; IntYB 81, 82; WhoAm 76, 78, 80, 82, 84, 86, 88, 90, 92, 94, 95, 96, 97; WhoAmL 79; WhoAmP 73, 75, 77, 79, 81, 83, 85, 87, 89, 91, 93, 95; WhoEmL 87; WhoGov 75, 77; WhoSSW 73, 75, 76, 78, 80, 82, 86, 88, 91, 93, 95, 97; WhoWor 80, 82, 84, 87, 89, 91, 96, 97*

Borg, Bjorn Rune
Swedish. Tennis Player
Won Wimbledon championships, 1976-80; retired, 1983.
b. Jun 6, 1956 in Sodertalje, Sweden
Source: *BkPepl; ConAu 114; CurBio 74; IntWW 81, 82, 83, 89, 91, 93; Who 82, 83, 85E, 88, 90, 92, 94; WhoAm 84, 86; WhoWor 84, 87*

Borg, Kim
Finnish. Opera Singer
Bass; one of few non-Russian artists to sing lead in *Boris Godunov* at Bolshoi Ballet.
b. Aug 7, 1919 in Helsinki, Finland
Source: *Baker 84, 92; IntWW 74, 75, 76, 77, 78, 79, 80, 81, 82, 83, 89, 91, 93; IntWWM 77, 80, 90; MetOEnc; NewGrDM 80; NewGrDO; PenDiMP; WhoMus 72; WhoWor 74, 76, 78, 82, 84, 87, 89, 91, 93, 95, 96, 97*

Borg, Veda Ann
American. Actor
Played tough blonde in many 1940s films; face was reconstructed in 10 operations after car crash.
b. Jan 15, 1915 in Boston, Massachusetts
d. Aug 16, 1973 in Hollywood, California
Source: *BioIn 18; EncAFC; FilmEn; FilmgC; ForYSC; HalFC 80, 84, 88; HolCA; InWom SUP; LegTOT; MotPP; MovMk; ThFT; Vers A; WhoHol B; WhoHrs 80; WhScrn 77, 83*

Borge, Victor
[Borge Rosenbaum]
American. Pianist, Comedian
Combines music with humor to create musical satire.
b. Jan 3, 1909 in Copenhagen, Denmark
Source: *ASCAP 66, 80; Baker 78, 84, 92; BiDAmM; BiE&WWA; BioIn 1, 3, 4, 5, 6, 9, 10, 11, 12, 16, 18, 19; BioNews 74; BlueB 76; CelR 90; CurBio 46, 93; IntMPA 80, 84, 86, 88, 92, 94, 96; IntWW 74, 75, 76, 77, 78, 79, 80, 81, 82, 83, 89, 91, 93; JoeFr; LegTOT; NewAmDM; NewGrDA 86; NewYTBS 89; NotNAT; OxCAmT 84; PenDiMP; RadStar; WhoAm 74, 76, 78, 80, 82, 84, 86, 88, 90, 92, 94, 95, 96, 97; WhoCom; WhoEnt 92; WhoHol 92, A; WhoMus 72; WhoWor 74, 76, 78; WorAl; WorAlBi; WrDr 76, 80, 82, 84*

Borge Martinez, Tomas
Nicaraguan. Revolutionary, Government Official
Helped found the Sandinista National Liberation Front, which overthrew Anastasio Somoza Garcia in 1979.
b. Aug 12, 1930 in Matagalpa, Nicaragua
Source: *BiDMarx; BioIn 18; ColdWar 2; DcCPCAm; IntWW 82, 83, 89, 91, 93*

Borges, Jorge Luis
Argentine. Author
Leader, "Ultraismo" literary movement, combining surrealism, imagism.
b. Aug 24, 1899 in Buenos Aires, Argentina
d. Jun 14, 1986 in Geneva, Switzerland
Source: *AnObit 1986; Benet 87, 96; BenetAL 91; BioIn 12, 13, 14, 15, 16, 17, 18, 19, 21; CasWL; CelR; ConAu 19NR, 21R, 33NR; ConFLW 84; ConLC 1, 2, 3, 4, 6, 8, 9, 10, 13, 19, 44, 48, 83; CrtSuMy; CurBio 70, 86, 86N; CyWA 89; DcArts; DcCLAA; DcHiB; DcLB 113, Y86N; DcSpL; DcTwCCu 3;*

DcTwHis; EncLatA; EncSF, 93; EncWL, 2, 3; FacFETw; GrFLW; HispLC; HispWr; IntAu&W 77, 89, 91; IntWW 74, 75, 76, 77, 78, 79, 80, 81, 82, 83; IntWWP 77; LatAmWr; LinLib L, S; MagSWL; MajTwCW; MakMC; McGEWB; ModLAL; NewEScF; NewYTBE 71; NewYTBS 86; Novels; OxCEng 85, 95; OxCSpan; PenC AM; PenEncH; RAdv 14, 13-2; REn; RfGShF; RfGWoL 95; RGFMEP; ScF&FL 92; ScFSB; ShSCr 4; ShSWr; SJGFanW; SpAmA; TwCCr&M 80B, 85B, 91B; TwCSFW 81A, 86A, 91A; TwCWr; WhDW; Who 74, 82, 83, 85; WhoTwCL; WhoWor 74, 78, 80, 82, 84; WorAl; WorAlBi; WorAu 1950; WorLitC; WrPh

Borghese, Maria Paolina
French.
Sister of Napoleon I.
b. Sep 20, 1780 in Ajaccio, Corsica, France
d. Jun 9, 1825 in Florence, Italy
Source: *BioIn 1, 2, 7, 9, 10, 11, 12*

Borgia, Cesare
Italian. Military Leader
Said to be prototype for Machiavelli's *The Prince.*
b. 1475 in Rome, Italy
d. Mar 12, 1507 in Navarre, France
Source: *DicTyr; Dis&D; HarEnMi; LegTOT; LinLib S; McGEWB; NewC; WhDW; WorAl; WorAlBi*

Borgia, Lucrezia
[Duchess of Ferrara]
Italian. Noblewoman
Daughter of Pope Alexander VI; unfairly known as poisoner and participant in family plots.
b. Apr 18, 1480 in Rome, Italy
d. Mar 12, 1519
Source: *Benet 87; BioIn 1, 2, 3, 4, 7, 8, 10, 11, 12, 14, 20; ContDcW 89; DcBiPP; Dis&D; HisWorL; IntDcWB; InWom, SUP; LegTOT; LinLib S; NewC; OxCEng 85, 95; OxCMed 86; WhDW; WorAl; WorAlBi*

Borglum, James Lincoln Delamothe
American. Sculptor
Completed statues on Mt. Rushmore after death of father, Gutzon, 1941.
b. Apr 9, 1912 in Stamford, Connecticut
d. Jan 27, 1986 in Corpus Christi, Texas
Source: *IlBEAAW; NewYTBS 86; WhoAm 74, 76, 78, 80, 82, 84; WhoAmA 76, 78, 80, 82, 84, 86, 89N*

Borglum, John Gutzon de la Mothe
American. Sculptor
Best known as sculptor of US presidents on Mt. Rushmore, 1927-41.
b. Mar 25, 1867 in Bear Lake, Idaho
d. Mar 6, 1941 in Chicago, Illinois
Source: *ArtsAmW 1; CmCal; CurBio 41; FacFETw; OxCAmH; OxCAmL 65; REn; REnAL; WebAB 74; WhAm 1*

Borglum, Solon Hannibal
American. Sculptor
Brother of Gutzon Borglum; known for sculptures of horses, cowboys, and Indians.
b. Dec 22, 1868 in Ogden, Utah
d. Jan 31, 1922
Source: *ArtsAmW 1; BioIn 14; BriEAA; DcAmArt; DcAmB; IlBEAAW; LinLib S; McGDA; NatCAB 13; OxDcArt; REnAW; WhAm 1*

Borgmann, Benny
[Bernhard Borgmann]
American. Basketball Player
Top-scoring guard in early days of basketball; Hall of Fame.
b. Nov 21, 1899 in Haledon, New Jersey
d. Nov 11, 1978
Source: *WhoBbl 73; WhoSpor*

Borgnine, Ernest
[Ermes Effron Borgnino]
American. Actor
Starred in TV series "McHale's Navy," 1962-66; won Oscar for *Marty,* 1955.
b. Jan 24, 1917 in Hamden, Connecticut
Source: *BiDFilm, 94; BioIn 4, 5, 6, 7, 10, 11, 12; BlueB 76; ConTFT 2, 7; CurBio 56; FilmEn; FilmgC; GangFlm; HalFC 84; IntDcF 2-3; IntMPA 86, 94, 96; IntWW 74, 75, 76, 77, 78, 79, 80, 81, 82, 83, 89, 91, 93; ItaFilm; LegTOT; MotPP; MovMk; NewYTBE 73; OxCFilm; WhoAm 74, 76, 78, 80, 82, 84, 86, 88, 90, 92, 94, 95, 96, 97; WhoEnt 92; WhoHol A; WhoWor 74, 78; WorAl; WorAlBi; WorEFlm*

Borja Cevallos, Rodrigo
Ecuadorean. Political Leader
Founded Dem. Left Party, 1970; succeeded Leon Febres Cordero as pres. of Ecuador, 1988—.
b. Jun 19, 1935 in Quito, Ecuador
Source: *BioIn 16; DcCPSAm; IntWW 91; NewYTBS 88; WhoWor 89, 91, 93*

Bork, Robert Heron
American. Judge
Controversial Reagan nominee for Supreme Court; overwhelmingly rejected by Senate, 1987.
b. Mar 1, 1927 in Pittsburgh, Pennsylvania
Source: *BioIn 10*

Borland, Hal
[Harold Glenn Borland; Ward West]
American. Author
Books on nature include *Hill Country Harvest,* 1967; wrote outdoor editorials for *NY Times,* beginning in 1942.
b. May 14, 1900 in Sterling, Nebraska
d. Feb 22, 1978 in Sharon, Connecticut
Source: *AmAu&B; Au&Wr 71; BenetAL 91; BioIn 17; ChhPo; ConAu 1R, 77; NewYTBS 78; REnAL; SmATA 5, 24N; TwCWW 82, 91; WhAm 7; WhoAm 74, 76, 78; WhoWor 74; WorAu 1950; WrDr 84, 86*

Borlaug, Norman Ernest
American. Agriculturist, Scientist
Known for experiments in crop breeding, specifically with wheat; won Nobel Peace Prize, 1970.
b. Mar 25, 1914 in Cresco, Iowa
Source: *AmMWSc 73P, 76P, 79, 82, 86, 89, 92, 95; BiESc; BioIn 8, 9, 11, 13; BlueB 76; CurBio 71; EncAB-H 1974, 1996; EncWB; FacFETw; IntWW 74, 75, 76, 77, 78, 79, 80, 81, 82, 83, 89, 91, 93; NewYTBE 70; WebAB 74, 79; Who 74, 82, 83, 85, 88, 90, 92, 94; WhoAm 74, 76, 78, 80, 82, 84, 86, 88, 90, 92, 94, 95, 96, 97; WhoFrS 84; WhoNob, 90, 95; WhoSSW 78, 80, 82, 84, 86, 88, 91, 93, 95, 97; WhoWor 74, 76, 78, 84, 87, 89, 91, 93, 95, 96, 97*

Borman, Frank
American. Astronaut, Airline Executive
Made first flight around moon, 1968, on Apollo 8; pres. of Eastern Airlines, 1975-85.
b. Mar 14, 1928 in Gary, Indiana
Source: *BioIn 7, 8, 9, 10, 11, 12, 13, 14, 15, 16; BlueB 76; CelR 90; CurBio 80; Dun&B 79, 86, 90; EncABHB 8; FacFETw; IntWW 74, 75, 76, 77, 78, 79, 80, 81, 82, 83, 89, 91, 93; LegTOT; NatCAB 63N; NewYTBS 75, 76; PolProf NF; St&PR 84, 87, 91, 93, 96, 97; WebAMB; WhoAm 74, 76, 78, 80, 82, 84, 86, 88, 90, 92, 94, 95, 96, 97; WhoFI 77, 79, 81, 83, 85, 89, 96; WhoSpc; WhoSSW 73, 82, 84, 86, 88; WhoWor 74, 78, 80, 82, 84, 87, 89, 91, 93, 95, 96, 97; WorAl; WorAlBi*

Bormann, Martin Ludwig
German. Government Official
Chief of staff to Rudolf Hess, 1933-41; pronounced dead, 1973, when skeleton was found near Hitler's bunker.
b. Jun 17, 1900 in Halberstadt, Germany
d. May 2, 1945 in Berlin, Germany
Source: *BioNews 75; NewYTBE 73*

Born, Ernest Alexander
American. Architect
Noted CA designer, who wrote plans for Fisherman's Wharf, 1961.
b. 1898 in San Francisco, California
Source: *ArtsAmW 2; ConAu 102; WhoAm 74*

Born, Max
British. Physicist, Educator
Co-winner, Nobel Prize in physics, 1954, for statistical interpretation of the quantum theory.
b. Dec 11, 1882 in Breslau, Germany
d. Jan 5, 1970 in Gottingen, Germany (West)
Source: *AsBiEn; BiESc; BioIn 2, 3, 4, 5, 7, 8, 9, 13, 14, 15, 20; CamDcSc; ConAu 2NR, 5R, 25R; DcScB S1; EncTR; FacFETw; InSci; LarDcSc; LinLib L; McGEWB; McGMS 80; NewYTBE 70; NobelP; NotTwCS; ObitOF 79; RAdv 14, 13-5; ThTwC 87; WebBD 83; WhAm 5, 7; WhE&EA; WhoNob, 90, 95; WorScD*

Bornstein, Kate
[Albert Herman Bornstein]
American. Writer, Transsexual
Wrote play *Hidden: A Gender,* 1989.
b. Mar 15, 1948 in Neptune, New Jersey
Source: *GayLesB*

Borodin, Alexander Profirevich
Russian. Composer
Physician, chemist by vocation, known for unfinished opera *Prince Igor.*
b. Nov 12, 1833 in Saint Petersburg, Russia
d. Feb 27, 1887 in Saint Petersburg, Russia
Source: *AtlBL; REn*

Borofsky, Jonathan
American. Artist
Post-modernist artist known for figurative work in all media.
b. 1942 in Boston, Massachusetts
Source: *BioIn 12, 13; ConArt 83; CurBio 85; DcCAA 88, 94; DcCAr 81; PrintW 83, 85; WhoAm 84, 86, 88, 92, 94, 95, 96; WhoAmA 84; WhoE 83; WorArt 1980*

Boros, Julius (Nicholas)
American. Golfer
Turned pro, 1950; won US Open, 1952, 1963, PGA, 1968; leading money winner, 1952, 1955.
b. Mar 3, 1920 in Fairfield, Connecticut
d. May 28, 1994 in Fort Lauderdale, Florida
Source: *BiDAmSp OS; BioIn 2, 6, 8, 13, 19, 20; CurBio 94N; NewYTBS 82; WhoGolf; WorAl; WorAlBi*

Borotra, Jean Robert
[The Four Musketeers]
"Bounding Basque"
French. Tennis Player
Won six Wimbledon Championships, member of French Davis Cup Team, 1920s-40s; awarded Legion of Honor, Croix de Guerre.
b. Aug 13, 1898 in Barritz, France
Source: *IntWW 83; WhoWor 74*

Borromeo, Charles, Saint
Italian. Religious Leader
Archbishop of Milan, 1560s; noted for ecclesiastical reforms; canonized, 1610.
b. Oct 2, 1538 in Rocca d'Arona, Italy
d. Nov 3, 1584 in Milan, Italy
Source: *BioIn 11; DcBiPP; DcCathB; McGDA; McGEWB; NewCol 75; WebBD 83*

Borromini, Francesco
[Francesco Castelli]
Italian. Architect
Baroque designs for churches, palaces had great impact throughout Europe: Sant' Ivo della Sapienza, Rome, 1642.
b. Sep 25, 1559 in Bissone, Italy
d. Aug 3, 1677 in Rome, Italy
Source: *AtlBL; NewCol 75; WebBD 83; WhoArch*

Borrow, George Henry
English. Author
Wrote part autobiographical, part fantasy volumes *The Bible In Spain; Lavengro; The Romany Rye,* 1857.
b. Jul 5, 1803 in East Dereham, England
d. Jul 26, 1881 in Oulton, England
Source: *Alli, SUP; AtlBL; BbD; BiD&SB; BioIn 10, 12, 13; BlmGEL; BritAu 19; CasWL; CelCen; Chambr 3; ChhPo S3; CyWA 58; DcArts; DcBiA; DcEnA; DcEnL; DcEuL; DcLEL; DcNaB, C; EvLB; GrWrEL N; LinLib L; MouLC 3; NewC; NewCBEL; OxCEng 67, 85, 95; PenC AM, ENG; REn; WebE&AL; WhDW*

Bortoluzzi, Paolo
Italian. Dancer
Ballet director, Grand Theatre, Bordeaux, France, 1990-93; artistic adviser, choreographer for La Scala, Milan in 1970s-80s.
b. May 17, 1938 in Genoa, Italy
d. Oct 16, 1993 in Brussels, Belgium
Source: *BiDD; BioIn 9, 11, 19; CnOxB; DancEn 78; IntDcB; IntWW 74, 75, 76, 77, 78, 79, 80, 81, 82, 83, 89, 91, 93; WhAm 11; WhoWor 87, 89, 91, 93*

Borysenko, Joan
American. Psychologist
Studied mind/body phenomena; wrote *Mind to Heal,* 1994.
b. Oct 25, 1945 in Boston, Massachusetts
Source: *CurBio 96*

Borzage, Frank
American. Director
Pioneered use of soft focus for his sentimental love stories; won Oscars for *Seventh Heaven,* 1927; *Bad Girl,* 1931.
b. Apr 23, 1893 in Salt Lake City, Utah
d. Jun 19, 1962 in Hollywood, California
Source: *AmFD; BiDFilm, 81, 94; BioIn 1, 6, 11, 12, 15; CmMov; DcAmB S7; DcFM; EncAFC; Film 1; FilmEn; FilmgC; GangFlm; HalFC 80, 84, 88; IlWWHD 1; IntDcF 1-2, 2-2; LegTOT; MiSFD 9N; MovMk; ObitOF 79; ObitT 1961; OxCFilm; TwYS, A; WhAm 4; WhoHol B; WhScrn 74, 77, 83; WorAl; WorEFlm; WorFDir 1*

Bosanquet, Bernard
English. Philosopher
Idealist who reacted against empiricism; wrote *The Philosophical Theory of the State,* 1899.
b. Jun 14, 1848 in Alnwick, England
d. Feb 8, 1923 in London, England
Source: *Alli SUP; BioIn 11; DcNaB 1922; LinLib L; LngCTC; LuthC 75; McGEWB; NewCBEL; OxCPhil; RAdv 13-4*

Bosch, Carl
German. Chemist
Won Nobel Prize, 1931, for discovery and development of chemical high-pressure methods.
b. Aug 27, 1874 in Cologne, Germany
d. Apr 26, 1940 in Heidelberg, Germany
Source: *BiESc; BioIn 3, 6; DcScB; FacFETw; InSci; LarDcSc; NobelP; WhoNob, 90, 95; WorInv*

Bosch, Hieronymous
[Hieronymous VanAeken]
Dutch. Artist
Allegorical painter who depicted evil with fantastic images: "Seven Deadly Sins"; influenced Pieter the Elder, considered forerunner of surrealism.
b. 1450 in Hertogenbosch, Netherlands
d. Aug 9, 1516 in Hertogenbosch, Netherlands
Source: *AtlBL; McGDA; NewCol 75; OxCArt; REn; WebBD 83*

Bosch, Robert August
German. Inventor
Invented the Bosch magneto, to generate current in internal-combustion engines; founder of Bosch manufacturing, which introduced the spark plug.
b. Sep 23, 1861 in Albeck, Wurttemberg
d. Mar 9, 1942 in Stuttgart, Germany
Source: *BioIn 14, 20; CurBio 42; InSci; ObitOF 79; WorInv*

Bosch Gavino, Juan
Dominican. Author, Politician
Pres., Dominican Republic, 1963; ousted same year, exiled to Puerto Rico.
b. Jun 30, 1909 in La Vega, Dominican Republic
Source: *ColdWar 2; CurBio 63; DcCLAA; DcPol; EncLatA; IntWW 74, 83; NewYTBE 70; WorAl*

Boschwitz, Rudy
[Rudolf E Boschwitz]
American. Politician
Moderate Republican senator from MN, 1979-91.
b. 1930 in Berlin, Germany
Source: *AlmAP 80, 82, 84, 88; BioIn 11, 12; CngDr 79, 81, 83, 85, 87, 89; IntWW 89, 91, 93; PolsAm 84; WhoAm 80, 82, 84, 86, 88, 90, 92; WhoAmJ 80; WhoAmP 73, 75, 77, 79, 81, 83, 85, 87, 89, 91, 93, 95; WhoMW 80, 82, 84, 86, 88, 90; WhoWor 80, 82, 87, 89, 91*

Boscovich, Ruggiero Giuseppe
Italian. Mathematician, Physicist
Developed ways of calculating rotations of celestial objects, improved geodetic surveys.
b. May 18, 1711 in Ragusa, Dalmatia
d. Feb 13, 1787 in Milan, Italy
Source: *BioIn 5, 8; DcBiPP; DcCathB; EncEnl; WebBD 83*

Bose, Amar Gopal
American. Business Executive
Founder, chairman, Bose Corp., 1964—; manufacturers of high-fidelity stereo speakers.
b. Nov 2, 1929 in Philadelphia, Pennsylvania
Source: *ConNews 86-4; LElec; St&PR 75, 84, 87, 91, 93, 96, 97; WhoAm 74,*

76, 78, 80, 82, 84, 86, 88, 90, 92, 94, 95, 96, 97; WhoE 89; WhoFI 94; WhoScEn 94, 96; WhoTech 82

Bose, Jagadis Chandra, Sir
Indian. Physicist, Biologist
Invented instruments for the detection of very slight plant movements that may demonstrate feelings in plants.
b. Nov 30, 1858 in Mymensingh, India
d. Nov 23, 1937 in Giridih, India
Source: *BiESc; BioIn 2, 4, 5, 12; EncO&P 3; FacFETw; InSci; LarDcSc; McGEWB*

Bose, Subhas Chandra
Indian. Politician
Headed puppet regime planned for India by Japan, 1943.
b. Jan 23, 1897 in Cuttack, India
d. Aug 19, 1945 in Taipei, Taiwan
Source: *BioIn 1, 2, 3, 5, 7, 8, 9, 11, 12, 13, 15, 16, 17, 18, 20, 21; DcTwHis; DicTyr; HisDBrE; HisEWW; McGEWB; ObitOF 79; WhDW; WhoMilH 76; WhWW-II*

Bosin, Blackbear
American. Artist, Designer
Award-winning painter, who draws birds, animals, Native American lore in flat, two-dimens ional style.
b. Jun 5, 1921 in Anadarko, Oklahoma
Source: *WhoAmA 73, 76, 78, 80, 82N, 84N, 86N, 89N, 91N, 93N*

Boskin, Michael J(ay)
American. Economist, Government Official
Chm., Council of Economic Advisers for the Bush administration, 1989-93; authored ''Flexible-freeze'' economic plan, wrote *Too Many Promises: The Uncertain Future of Social Security,* 1986.
b. Sep 23, 1945 in New York, New York
Source: *AmEA 74; CurBio 89; IntWW 89, 91, 93; NewYTBS 88; WhoAm 88, 90, 92, 94, 95, 96, 97; WhoAmP 89, 91, 93, 95; WhoEc 86; WhoFI 89, 92; WhoWest 96*

Bosley, Freeman (Robertson), Jr.
American. Lawyer, Politician
Mayor of St. Louis, 1993—.
b. Jul 20, 1954 in Saint Louis, Missouri
Source: *AfrAmBi 2; BioIn 19, 20; ConBlB 7; WhoAfA 96; WhoAm 95, 96, 97; WhoBlA 85, 88, 90, 92, 94*

Bosley, Harold A
American. Clergy, Author
Among his works were *The Deeds of Christ,* 1969; *Men Who Build Churches,* 1972.
b. Feb 19, 1907 in Burchard, Nebraska
d. Jan 21, 1975 in Beach Haven Terrace, New Jersey
Source: *AmAu&B; ConAu 49, 53; DrAS 74P; EncWM; WhoAm 74; WhoRel 75*

Bosley, Tom
American. Actor
Played Mr. C on TV series ''Happy Days'' 1974-1980; star of ''Father Dowling Mysteries,'' 1989-91.
b. Oct 1, 1927 in Chicago, Illinois
Source: *BiE&WWA; BioIn 5, 6, 11; ConTFT 4, 14; EncAFC; FilmEn; FilmgC; HalFC 80, 84, 88; IntMPA 79, 80, 81, 82, 84, 86, 88, 92, 94, 96; ItaFilm; LegTOT; NotNAT; OxCAmT 84; WhoAm 74, 76, 78, 80, 82, 84, 86, 88, 92, 94, 95, 96, 97; WhoEnt 92; WhoHol 92, A; WhoThe 72, 77, 81; WhoWor 74, 82, 84, 87; WorAl; WorAlBi*

Bosson, Barbara
[Mrs. Steven Bochco]
American. Actor
Played Fay Furillo on TV drama ''Hill Street Blues,'' 1981-85.
b. Nov 1, 1939 in Charleroi, Pennsylvania
Source: *ConTFT 7; LegTOT; WhoTelC*

Bossuet, Jacques Benigne
French. Author, Orator
Wrote *Discourse on Universal History,* 1681, treatise in history from Christian viewpoint.
b. Sep 27, 1627 in Dijon, France
d. Apr 12, 1704 in Paris, France
Source: *AtlBL; BbD; Benet 96; BiD&SB; BioIn 6, 7, 9, 11, 14; CasWL; CyEd; DcBiPP; DcCathB; DcEuL; Dis&D; EuAu; EuWr 3; EvEuW; IlEncMy; LinLib L, S; LuthC 75; McGEWB; NewCBEL; OxCEng 67, 85, 95; OxCFr; PenC EUR; REn*

Bossy, Mike
[Michael Bossy]
''Boss''
Canadian. Hockey Player
Right wing, NY Islanders, 1977-87; first player to score 50 or more goals in nine consecutive seasons.
b. Jan 22, 1957 in Montreal, Quebec, Canada
Source: *BioIn 11, 12, 13; CurBio 81; HocReg 87; LegTOT; NewYTBS 81, 84; WhoAm 80, 82, 84, 86, 88, 92, 94, 95, 96, 97; WhoE 85, 86, 95; WhoSpor; WorAl; WorAlBi*

Bostock, Lyman Wesley
American. Baseball Player
Promising outfielder, 1975-78; shot to death by husband of friend.
b. Nov 22, 1950 in Birmingham, Alabama
d. Sep 24, 1978 in Gary, Indiana
Source: *BioIn 11; InB&W 80; WhoBlA 77, 80*

Boston
[Brad Delp; Barry Goudreau; Sib Hashian; Tom Scholz; Fran Sheehan]
American. Music Group
Debut album *Boston,* 1976, sold 6.5 million copies.
Source: *BioIn 11, 15, 16; ConMuA 80A, 80B; ConMus 11; EncPR&S 89; EncRk 88; EncRkSt; HarEnR 86; IlEncRk; PenEncP; RkOn 74, 78; RolSEnR 83; Who 82, 83, 85, 88, 90, 92, 94; WhoRock 81; WhoRocM 82*

Boston, Ralph
American. Track Athlete
Long jumper; won gold medal, 1960 Olympics, broke Jesse Owens' record.
b. May 9, 1939 in Laurel, Mississippi
Source: *AfrAmSG; BioIn 5, 6, 8, 9, 21; WhoAfA 96; WhoBlA 77, 80, 85, 88, 90, 92, 94; WhoTr&F 73*

Bostwick, Barry
American. Actor
Won 1977 Tony for *The Robber Bridegroom;* plays the mayor on ABC's ''Spin City,'' 1996—.
b. Feb 24, 1945 in San Mateo, California
Source: *BioIn 12, 13; ConTFT 5, 12; IntMPA 88, 92, 94, 96; LegTOT; VarWW 85; WhoAm 90, 92, 94, 95, 96, 97; WhoEnt 92*

Bosustow, Stephen
Canadian. Producer
Co-founded United Productions of America, animation co; won three Oscars.
b. Nov 6, 1911 in Victoria, British Columbia, Canada
d. 1981
Source: *BioIn 3, 4, 5; CurBio 58; DcFM; FilmEn; FilmgC; HalFC 80, 84, 88; IntDcF 2-4; IntMPA 75, 76, 77, 78, 79, 80, 81; NewYTET; OxCFilm; WhAm 8; WhoAm 80, 82; WhoWest 74, 76, 78; WorECar; WorEFlm*

Boswell, Charles Albert
American. Golfer
Blind as result of WW II wounds; took up golf, had 13 wins in US Blind Golfers Assn.
b. Dec 22, 1916 in Birmingham, Alabama
d. Oct 22, 1995 in Birmingham, Alabama
Source: *BioIn 1, 3, 11, 12; WhoGolf*

Boswell, Connee
[Boswell Sisters]
American. Singer, Actor
Enjoyed long career after trio disbanded in 1935; performed in wheelchair.
b. Dec 3, 1907 in New Orleans, Louisiana
d. Oct 10, 1962 in New York, New York
Source: *ASCAP 66, 80; Baker 92; BiDJaz; CmpEPM; FilmEn; HalFC 84, 88; InWom SUP; LegTOT; NewGrDA 86; NewGrDJ 88, 94; OxCPMus; RadStar; WhoHol A; WhoJazz 72; WhScrn 83*

Boswell, James
Scottish. Lawyer, Biographer
Wrote *Life of Johnson,* 1791, best-known biography in English language.
b. Oct 18, 1740 in Edinburgh, Scotland
d. May 19, 1795 in London, England

Source: *Alli; AtlBL; BbD; Benet 87, 96; BiD&SB; BioIn 1, 2, 3, 4, 5, 6, 7, 8, 9, 10, 11, 12, 13, 14, 15, 16, 17, 18, 19, 20, 21; BlkwCE; BlmGEL; BritAu; BritWr 3; CamGEL; CamGLE; CasWL; Chambr 2; ChhPo S2, S3; CmScLit; CnDBLB 2; CrtT 2, 4; CyWA 58; DcArts; DcBiPP; DcEnA; DcEnL; DcEuL; DcLB 104, 142; DcLEL; DcNaB; DcPup; Dis&D; EncEnl; EvLB; GrWrEL N; IlsCB 1957; LegTOT; LinLib L, S; LitC 4; LngCEL; LngCTC; McGEWB; MnBBF; MouLC 2; NewC; NewCBEL; OxCEng 67, 85, 95; OxCLaw; OxCMus; PenC ENG; RAdv 1, 14, 13-1; RComWL; REn; RfGEnL 91; WebE&AL; WhDW; WorAl; WorAlBi; WorLitC*

Boswell, John (Eastburn)
American. Historian
Wrote *Christianity, Social Tolerance and Homosexuality,* 1980.
b. Mar 20, 1947 in Boston, Massachusetts
d. Dec 24, 1994
Source: *ConAu 121, 147; GayLesB; GayLL; WrDr 90, 92, 94, 96*

Boswell, Martha
[Boswell Sisters]
American. Singer
Member of singing group trio with sisters.
b. 1905 in New Orleans, Louisiana
d. Jul 2, 1958 in Peekskill, New York
Source: *LegTOT; ObitOF 79; WhoHol B; WhScrn 74, 77, 83*

Boswell, Vet
[Boswell Sisters; Helvetia Boswell]
American. Singer
In films with sisters *Big Broadcast,* 1932; *Moulin Rouge,* 1934.
b. 1911 in New Orleans, Louisiana
d. Nov 12, 1988 in Peekskill, New York
Source: *AnObit 1988; LegTOT; WhoHol A*

Boswell Sisters
[Connee Boswell; Martha Boswell; Vet Boswell]
American. Music Group
Three Southern girls who blended voices in a way never heard before; made three movies, 1930s.
Source: *AllMusG; AmWomPl; ASCAP 66; BiDAmM; BioIn 4, 7, 11, 17; CmpEPM; InWom, SUP; NewYTBS 76; ObitOF 79; OxCPMus; SaTiSS; ThFT; WhoAmW 61; WhoHol 92, A; WhoThe 81N*

Bosworth, Brian Keith
"Boz"
American. Football Player
Linebacker, Seattle, 1987-89; controversial autobiography *The Boz* led to Barry Switzer's downfall as coach at Oklahoma U; starred in movie *Stone Cold,* 1991.
b. Mar 9, 1965 in Irving, Texas
Source: *CelR 90; News 89-1; NewYTBS 86*

Bosworth, Hobart van Zandt
American. Actor
Began film career, 1909, in *In the Sultan's Power,* first dramatic film shot on West Coast.
b. Aug 11, 1867 in Marietta, Ohio
d. Dec 30, 1943 in Glendale, California
Source: *CurBio 44; Film 1; FilmgC; MotPP; MovMk; NotNAT B; ObitOF 79; TwYS; WhAm 2; WhoHol B; WhScrn 74, 77*

Botero, Fernando
[Fernando Botero Angulo]
Colombian. Artist
Figurative painter; exhibits in Europe, North, South America.
b. Apr 19, 1932 in Medellin, Colombia
Source: *ArtLatA; BioIn 10, 11, 12, 13, 15, 16, 19, 20; ConArt 77, 83, 89, 96; CurBio 80; DcArts; DcCAr 81; DcHiB; DcTwCCu 3; EncLatA; FacFETw; ModArCr 1; News 94, 94-3; OxCTwCA; OxDcArt; PhDcTCA 77; WhoAm 84, 86, 88, 92, 94, 95, 96; WhoAmA 78, 80, 82, 84, 86, 89, 91, 93; WhoE 89; WhoWor 84, 87, 89, 91, 93, 95; WorArt 1950*

Botha, Louis
South African. Military Leader, Political Leader
Boer military leader, who helped form Union of S Africa; became first premier, 1910-19.
b. Sep 27, 1862 in Honigfontein, South Africa
d. Aug 27, 1919 in Pretoria, South Africa
Source: *BioIn 1, 20, 21; DcAfHiB 86; DcNaB 1912; DcTwHis; EncSoA; FacFETw; GenMudB; HarEnMi; HisDBrE; HisWorL; LinLib S; McGEWB; WhDW; WhoMilH 76; WorAl*

Botha, Pieter Willem
South African. Political Leader
Eighth prime minister of S Africa, elected 1978.
b. Jan 12, 1916 in Paul Roux, South Africa
Source: *AfSS 78, 79, 80, 81, 82; BioIn 7, 11, 12, 13; CurBio 79; DcAfHiB 86S; DcCPSAf; DcTwHis; EncWB; IntWW 74, 75, 76, 77, 78, 79, 80, 81, 82, 83, 89, 91, 93; NewYTBS 78, 84; Who 82, 83, 85, 88, 90, 92, 94; WhoAfr; WhoWor 74, 76, 78, 82, 84, 87, 89, 91, 93, 95*

Botha, Roelof Frederik
South African. Political Leader
Minister of Foreign Affairs, 1977-94; minister of mineral and energy affairs, 1994—.
b. Apr 27, 1932 in Rustenburg, South Africa
Source: *AfSS 78, 79, 80, 81, 82; BioIn 14, 15, 17; CurBio 84; DcCPSAf; IntWW 75, 76, 77, 78, 79, 80, 81, 82, 83, 89, 91; IntYB 78, 79, 80, 81, 82; Who 82, 83, 85E, 88, 90, 92, 94; WhoAfr; WhoUN 75; WhoWor 82, 84, 87, 91, 93, 95, 96, 97*

Bothe, Walter Wilhelm Georg
German. Physicist
Won 1954 Nobel Prize for method of studying cosmic rays.
b. Jun 8, 1891 in Oranienburg, Germany
d. Feb 8, 1957 in Heidelberg, Germany (West)
Source: *McGMS 80; ObitOF 79; WhoNob; WorAl*

Bothwell, James Hepburn, Earl of
Scottish. Nobleman
Engineered murder of Lord Darnley, became Mary, Queen of Scots' third husband.
b. 1536
d. 1578
Source: *BioIn 1, 7, 9, 10, 11; DcBiPP; OxCEng 85, 95; WebAB 74*

Bothwell, Jean
American. Children's Author
Wrote award-winning *The Thirteenth Stone,* 1946.
d. Mar 2, 1977 in Missouri
Source: *AuBYP 2, 3; BioIn 1, 2, 7, 9; ConAu 1R, 3NR; CurBio 46; InWom; JBA 51; SmATA 2*

Botstein, Leon
American. Educator
President, Bard College, Annandale-on-Hudson, NY, 1975—.
b. Dec 14, 1946 in Zurich, Switzerland
Source: *BioIn 15, 16, 17, 18; ConNews 85-3; CurBio 96; LEduc 74; WhoAm 74, 76, 78, 80, 82, 84, 86, 88, 90, 94, 96, 97; WhoE 74, 75, 97*

Bottel, Helen Alfea
American. Journalist
Syndicated columnist with King Features; writes on human relations, youth and parental problems.
b. Mar 13, 1914 in Beaumont, California
Source: *ForWC 70; WhoAm 86; WhoAmW 77; WhoWest 84; WrDr 84*

Bottger, Johann Friedrich
German. Chemist
Originated Dresden china; established porcelain works, Meissen, Germany.
b. Feb 4, 1682
d. Mar 13, 1719
Source: *AntBDN M; BioIn 1, 3, 4, 11; EncEnl; LinLib S; PenDiDA 89; WhDW*

Botticelli, Sandro
[Alessandrodi Mariano dei Filipipi]
Italian. Artist
Favorite artist, protege of Medici family; best known work "The Birth of Venus."
b. 1444 in Florence, Italy
d. May 17, 1510 in Florence, Italy
Source: *AtlBL; Benet 87, 96; BioIn 16, 17, 19; ClaDrA; DcCathB; Dis&D; LuthC 75; McGDA; McGEWB; NewC;*

NewCol 75; OxCArt; REn; WhDW; WorAl

Bottome, Phyllis
[Mrs. Ernan Forbes-Dennis]
English. Author
A prolific writer, best known for anti-Nazi novel *The Mortal Storm,* 1937; *Private Worlds,* 1937.
b. May 31, 1884 in Rochester, England
d. Aug 23, 1963 in Hampstead, England
Source: *BioIn 1, 3, 4, 6, 8, 16; ConAu 93; DcLEL; EncBrWW; EvLB; FemiCLE; InWom, SUP; LngCTC; ModBrL; ModWoWr; NewC; NewCBEL; ObitT 1961; PenC ENG; PenNWW B; REn; TwCA, SUP; TwCWr; WhAm 4; WhE&EA; WhLit; WhoAmW 64; WhoSpyF; WomNov*

Bottomley, Gordon
English. Dramatist, Poet
Associated with the Georgians, revived English verse drama: *King Lear's Wife,* 1915.
b. Feb 20, 1874 in Keighley, England
d. Aug 25, 1948 in Oare, England
Source: *BioIn 3, 4, 5, 7, 13; BritPl; CamGEL; CamGLE; CamGWoT; CasWL; Chambr 3; ChhPo, S1, S2; ConAu 120; CrtSuDr; DcLB 10; DcLEL; DcNaB 1941; EvLB; GrWrEL DR; LngCTC; ModBrL; NewC; NewCBEL; OxCEng 85, 95; OxCThe 67, 83; OxCTwCP; PenC ENG; PlP&P; REn; RfGEnL 91; TwCA, SUP; TwCWr; WebE&AL; WhE&EA; WhLit; WhoLA; WhThe*

Bottomley, Jim
[James Leroy Bottomley]
"Sunny Jim"
American. Baseball Player
First baseman, 1922-37; holds ML record for RBIs in one game, 12, on Sep 16, 1924; Hall of Fame, 1974.
b. Apr 23, 1900 in Oglesby, Illinois
d. Dec 11, 1959 in Saint Louis, Missouri
Source: *Ballpl 90; BiDAmSp BB; BioIn 4, 5, 8, 15; WhoProB 73; WhoSpor*

Bottoms, Joseph
American. Actor
Film debut, 1974, in *The Dove.*
b. Apr 22, 1954 in Santa Barbara, California
Source: *BioIn 12; ConTFT 4; HalFC 80, 84, 88; IntMPA 75, 76, 77, 78, 79, 80, 81, 82, 84, 86, 88, 92, 94, 96; LegTOT; WhoHol 92, A*

Bottoms, Sam
American. Actor
Brother of Joseph and Timothy; films include *Apocalyse Now,* 1979; TV film "East of Eden," 1981.
b. Oct 17, 1955 in Santa Barbara, California
Source: *ConTFT 4; IntMPA 84, 86, 88, 92, 94, 96; LegTOT; VarWW 85; WhoEnt 92; WhoHol 92, A*

Bottoms, Timothy
American. Actor
In movie *The Last Picture Show,* 1971.
b. Aug 30, 1951 in Santa Barbara, California
Source: *BioIn 9; ConTFT 3; FilmgC; IntMPA 75, 76, 77, 78, 79, 80, 81, 82, 84, 86, 88, 92, 94, 96; LegTOT; MovMk; WhoAm 80, 82, 84, 86, 88, 92; WhoEnt 92; WhoHol 92, A; WorAl; WorAlBi*

Botvinnik, Mikhail (Moisseyevich)
Russian. Chess Player
World chess champion, 1948-63; books include *Championship Chess,* 1951.
b. Aug 17, 1911 in Saint Petersburg, Russia
d. May 5, 1995 in Moscow, Russia
Source: *CurBio 65, 95N; IntWW 74; Who 74, 82, 83, 85E, 88, 90, 92, 94; WhoWor 74, 76, 78*

Bouchard, Butch
[Emile Joseph Bouchard]
Canadian. Hockey Player
Defenseman, Montreal, 1941-56; won four Stanley Cups; Hall of Fame, 1966.
b. Sep 11, 1920 in Montreal, Quebec, Canada
Source: *HocEn; WhoHcky 73*

Bouchard, Joe
[Blue Oyster Cult]
American. Singer, Musician
Bassist, vocalist with hard-rock group since 1969.
b. Nov 9, 1948 in Long Island, New York

Bouche, Rene Robert
American. Illustrator
Fashion, advertising illustrator with *Vogue,* 1938-63.
b. Sep 20, 1905 in Prague, Austria-Hungary
d. Jul 3, 1963 in East Grinstead, England
Source: *BioIn 5, 6; DcAmB S7*

Boucher, Buck
[George Boucher]
Canadian. Hockey Player
Forward, 1917-32, mostly with Ottawa; won four Stanley Cups; Hall of Fame, 1960; brother of Frank.
b. 1896 in Ottawa, Ontario, Canada
d. Oct 17, 1960
Source: *HocEn; WhoHcky 73*

Boucher, Francois
French. Artist
Chief court painter, 1765; tapestry, porcelain designer, favorite of Mme. de Pompadour.
b. Sep 29, 1703 in Paris, France
d. May 30, 1770 in Paris, France
Source: *AtlBL; Benet 87; BioIn 1, 6, 7, 9, 10, 11, 12, 13, 15; BlkwCE; ClaDrA; DcArts; DcBiPP; Dis&D; EncEnl; EncWT; Ent; IntDcAA 90; LegTOT; McGDA; McGEWB; NotNAT B; OxCArt; OxCDecA; OxCFr; OxCThe 67; OxDcArt; PenDiDA 89; REn; WhDW; WorAl; WorAlBi*

Boucher, Frank
"Raffles"
Canadian. Hockey Player, Hockey Coach
Center, one of original NY Rangers, 1926-38; won Lady Byng Trophy seven times; coached Rangers, 1939-54; Hall of Fame, 1958.
b. Oct 7, 1901 in Ottawa, Ontario, Canada
d. Dec 12, 1977 in Ottawa, Ontario, Canada
Source: *BioIn 4, 10, 11; ConAu 110, 122; HocEn; NewYTBS 77; WhoHcky 73; WhoSpor*

Boucher, Gaetan
Canadian. Skater
Speed skater; won two gold medals, one bronze medal, 1984 Olympics.
b. May 10, 1958 in Charlesbourg, Quebec, Canada
Source: *BioIn 12, 13; WhoSpor*

Bouchet, Edward Alexander
American. Educator
First US black to earn doctorate from an American university, 1876; teacher, school administrator, 1874-1918.
b. Sep 15, 1852 in New Haven, Connecticut
d. Oct 28, 1918 in New Haven, Connecticut
Source: *BioIn 8; BlksScM; DcAmNB; InB&W 80, 85; WhoColR*

Boucicault, Dion Lardner
American. Actor, Dramatist
Leading figure on New York stage, 1853-62.
b. Dec 26, 1820 in Dublin, Ireland
d. Sep 18, 1890 in New York, New York
Source: *BritAu 19; CasWL; Chambr 3; DcAmB; DcIrB 78, 88; DcIrL; McGEWB; McGEWD 84; MouLC 4; OxCAmL 65; OxCEng 85; OxCThe 83; PenC ENG; REn; REnAL; WebAB 79; WhAm HS; WhDW*

Boudin, Eugene Louis
French. Artist
His seascapes strongly influenced the impressionist painters.
b. Jul 12, 1824 in Honfleur, France
d. Aug 8, 1898 in Deauville, France
Source: *AtlBL; BioIn 3, 4, 5, 6, 7, 8, 9, 11; ClaDrA; DcSeaP; McGDA; OxCFr; OxCShps*

Boudin, Kathy
[Katherine Boudin]
American. Revolutionary
Involved in bomb factory explosion, 1970; captured after armored car robbery, 1981.
b. May 13, 1942 in New York, New York
Source: *BioAmW; BioIn 11*

Boudinot, Elias
American. Editor
Editor, *Cherokee Phoenix*, 1828-32.
b. 1803? in Georgia
d. Jun 22, 1839
Source: *AmAu; AmAu&B; BenetAL 91; BiDAmJo; BioIn 11, 13; DcAmB; EncNAB; NotNaAm; REnAL; REnAW; WhAm HS; WhNaAH*

Boudjedra, Rachid
Algerian. Writer
His first novel, *The Repudiation*, 1969 was controversial due to its attack on Muslim Traditionalism in Algeria.
b. Sep 5, 1941 in Ain Beida, Algeria
Source: *EncWL 3; RAdv 14*

Boudreau, Lou(is)
American. Baseball Player, Baseball Manager
Shortstop, Cleveland, 1938-50, Boston, 1951-52; won AL batting title, 1944; Hall of Fame, 1970.
b. Jul 17, 1917 in Harvey, Illinois
Source: *Ballpl 90; BiDAmSp BB; BioIn 1, 2, 3, 4, 5, 6, 14, 15, 18; CurBio 42; FacFETw; LegTOT; WhoEnt 92; WhoProB 73; WhoSpor; WorAl*

Bougainville, Louis-Antoine de
French. Navigator
Established settlement in Falkland Islands, 1763; colorful climbing plant is named for him.
b. Nov 11, 1729 in Paris, France
d. Aug 31, 1811 in Paris, France
Source: *ApCAB; BbtC; DcBiPP; DcCanB 5; Drake; EncEnl; McGEWB; NewCBEL; OxCCan; OxCFr; OxCShps*

Boulanger, Georges Ernest Jean Marie
French. Soldier, Politician
Popular minister of war, 1886; plotted to overthrow Third Republic, condemned for treason.
b. Apr 29, 1837 in Rennes, France
d. Sep 30, 1891 in Brussels, Belgium
Source: *BioIn 4, 6, 9; CelCen; Dis&D; OxCFr; REn; WhDW*

Boulanger, Nadia Juliette
French. Composer, Conductor, Teacher
Influential teacher; first female instructor at the Paris Conservatory; first woman to conduct the Boston Symphony.
b. Sep 16, 1887 in Paris, France
d. Oct 22, 1979 in Paris, France
Source: *CurBio 80; DcCM; GoodHs; IntWW 78; NewYTBS 79; REn; WhAm 7; WhDW; Who 74; WhoAmW 74; WhoMus 72; WhoWor 74; WorAl*

Boulding, Kenneth E(wart)
American. Economist, Author, Educator
Professor of economics, author of numerous books, articles in field.
b. Jan 18, 1910 in Liverpool, England
d. Mar 19, 1993 in Boulder, Colorado
Source: *AmAu&B; AmEA 74; AmMWSc 73S, 78S; AmPeW; BioIn 7, 9, 10, 11, 14, 17, 18, 19, 20, 21; BlueB 76; ConAu 5NR, 5R, 7NR, 26NR, 140; CurBio 65, 93N; Future; GrEconS; IntAu&W 77, 91; IntWW 74, 75, 76, 77, 78, 79, 80, 81, 82, 83, 89, 91, 93; LinLib L; WhAm 11; WhoAm 74, 76, 78, 80, 82, 84, 90, 92; WhoEc 81, 86; WhoFI 92; WhoWest 74; WrDr 88, 90, 92, 94, 96*

Boule, Marcellin
[Pierre Marcellin Boule]
French. Geologist
The first to completely reconstruct a Neanderthal skeleton, 1908; wrote *Fossil Men*, 1957.
b. Jan 1, 1861 in Montsalvy, France
d. Jul 4, 1942 in Montsalvy, France
Source: *DcScB; EncHuEv; ObitOF 79*

Boulez, Pierre
French. Composer, Conductor
Influential figure in avant-garde French music; music director, New York Philharmonic, 1971-77.
b. Mar 26, 1925 in Montbrison, France
Source: *Baker 78, 84, 92; Benet 87, 96; BioIn 7, 8, 9, 10, 11, 12, 13, 14, 15, 17, 19, 20, 21; BlueB 76; BriBkM 80; CelR, 90; CmOp; CnOxB; CompSN, SUP; ConAu 148; ConCom 92; CurBio 69; DcArts; DcCM; DcCom&M 79; DcTwCCu 2; FacFETw; IntDcOp; IntWW 74, 75, 76, 77, 78, 79, 80, 81, 82, 83, 89, 91, 93; IntWWM 77, 80, 90; LegTOT; MakMC; McGEWB; MetOEnc; MusMk; MusSN; NewAmDM; NewEOp 71; NewGrDA 86; NewGrDM 80; NewGrDO; NewOxM; NewYTBE 71, 73; OxCMus; OxDcOp; PenDiMP, A; RAdv 14; REn; WhDW; Who 74, 82, 83, 85, 88, 90, 92, 94; WhoAm 74, 76, 78, 80, 82, 84, 86, 88, 90, 92, 94, 95, 96, 97; WhoE 77; WhoEnt 92; WhoFr 79; WhoMus 72; WhoWor 74, 76, 78, 80, 82, 84, 87, 89, 91, 93, 95, 96, 97; WorAl; WorAlBi*

Boulle, Andre Charles
[Andre Charles Buhl]
French. Designer
Cabinetmaker to Louis XIV; known for elaborate inlaid furniture.
b. Nov 11, 1642 in Paris, France
d. Feb 29, 1732 in Paris, France
Source: *BioIn 2; DcD&D; McGDA; NewCol 75; OxCFr; WebBD 83*

Boulle, Pierre Francois Marie-Louis
French. Author
Popular novels include *Bridge On River Kwai*, 1952; *Planet of the Apes*, 1963.
b. Feb 20, 1912 in Avignon, France
d. Jan 30, 1994 in Paris, France
Source: *Au&Wr 71; CasWL; ConAu 9R; REn; TwCSFW 81A; TwCWr; WorAl; WorAu 1950*

Boullioun, E(rnest) H(erman Jr.)
"Tex"
American. Aircraft Manufacturer
With Boeing since 1940; pres. 1972-84.
b. Nov 3, 1918 in Little Rock, Arkansas
Source: *Dun&B 79, 86; NewYTBS 81; WhoAm 78; WhoFI 77*

Boult, Adrian Cedric, Sir
English. Musician, Conductor
Conducted at coronations of King George VI, Queen Elizabeth II.
b. Apr 8, 1889 in Chester, England
d. Feb 23, 1983 in Kent, England
Source: *Au&Wr 71; Baker 78; BioIn 1, 2, 3, 4, 8, 10, 11, 15; CurBio 83, 83N; IntAu&W 76, 77, 82; IntWW 81; IntWWM 77, 80; OxCMus; WhAm 8; Who 82; WhoMus 72; WhoWor 74, 76, 78; WorAl*

Boulting, John
English. Director
Films poked fun at British institutions, featured recurring cast of comic actors including Peter Sellers: *Heavens Above!* 1963.
b. Nov 21, 1913 in Bray, England
d. Jun 19, 1985 in Warfield Dale, England
Source: *AnObit 1985; BiDFilm, 81, 94; BioIn 14, 15; CmMov; ConAu 116; DcArts; DcFM; DcNaB 1981; EncEurC; FacFETw; FilmEn; FilmgC; HalFC 80, 84, 88; IlWWBF; IntDcF 1-2, 2-2; IntMPA 75, 76, 77, 78, 79, 80, 81, 82, 84; IntWW 83; MiSFD 9N; MovMk; NewYTBS 85; OxCFilm; Who 83; WhoWor 78; WorEFlm; WorFDir 1*

Boulting, Roy
English. Producer
Founded Charter Films, 1937, with twin brother, John; films include *There's a Girl in My Soup*, 1970.
b. Nov 21, 1913 in Bray, England
Source: *BiDFilm, 81, 94; BioIn 15, 19; BlueB 76; CmMov; DcArts; DcFM; EncEurC; FacFETw; FilmEn; FilmgC; HalFC 80, 84, 88; IlWWBF; IntDcF 1-2, 2-2; IntMPA 75, 76, 77, 78, 79, 80, 81, 82, 84, 86, 88, 92, 94, 96; IntWW 75, 76, 77, 78, 79, 80, 81, 82, 83, 89, 91, 93; MiSFD 9; OxCFilm; Who 74, 82, 83, 85, 88, 90, 92, 94; WhoWor 74, 76, 78; WorEFlm; WorFDir 1*

Boulton, Matthew
English. Manufacturer, Engineer
Built steam engines with James Watt; invented steel inlay process.
b. Sep 3, 1728 in Birmingham, England
d. Aug 17, 1809 in Birmingham, England
Source: *AntBDN C, G, N, Q; BiESc; BioIn 2, 3, 4, 8, 9, 10, 13; DcBiPP; DcD&D; DcInv; DcNaB; EncEnl; InSci; MacEA; OxCDecA; PenDiDA 89; WebBD 83; WhDW; WorInv*

Boumedienne, Houari
Algerian. Political Leader
Pres. of Algeria, 1965-78; helped country gain independence from France, 1962; major Third World spokesman.
b. Aug 23, 1927 in Clauzel, Algeria
d. Dec 27, 1978 in Algiers, Algeria

Source: *BioIn 7, 8, 9, 11, 12, 17, 18; ColdWar 2; CurBio 71, 79, 79N; DcTwHis; EncRev; IntWW 74, 75, 76, 77, 78; IntYB 78, 79; McGEWB; MidE 78; WhAm 7; WhDW; WhoGov 75; WorDWW*

Bouquet, Henry
English. Army Officer
Fought in French and Indian wars, defeating Indians in Pontiac's Rebellion, 1763.
b. 1719 in Rolle, Switzerland
d. Sep 2, 1765 in Pensacola, Florida
Source: *AmBi; ApCAB; BioIn 5, 9, 10, 14; DcAmB; DcAmMiB; DcNaB; Drake; EncAR; EncCRAm; GenMudB; HarEnUS; MacDCB 78; NatCAB 20; NewCol 75; PeoHis; REnAW; WebAMB; WhAm HS; WhNaAH; WhoMilH 76*

Bourassa, Henri
Canadian. Author, Politician
Founded Montreal newspaper *Le Devoir,* 1910.
b. Sep 1, 1868 in Montreal, Quebec, Canada
d. Aug 31, 1952 in Montreal, Quebec, Canada
Source: *AmLY; BiDMoPL; BioIn 3, 8, 9, 10, 12, 13; CanWr; HisWorL; MacDCB 78; ObitOF 79; OxCCan; PeoHis*

Bourassa, (Jean) Robert
Canadian. Politician
Liberal Party premier of Quebec, 1970-76, 1985-94.
b. Jul 13, 1933 in Montreal, Quebec, Canada
d. Oct 2, 1996 in Montreal, Quebec, Canada
Source: *BioIn 9, 11, 13, 14, 15, 17, 19; BlueB 76; CanWW 31, 70, 79, 80, 81, 83, 89; CurBio 76; IntWW 74, 75, 76, 77, 78, 79, 80, 81, 82, 83, 89, 91, 93; IntYB 78, 79, 80, 81, 82; News 97-1; NewYTBS 27, 85; Who 82, 83, 85, 88, 90, 92, 94; WhoAm 74, 76, 78, 88, 90, 92, 94, 95, 96; WhoCan 73, 75; WhoE 74, 75, 77, 86, 89, 91, 93; WhoWor 74, 76*

Bourdonnais, Louis Charles de la
French. Chess Player
Most famous player in the world, 1818-1838.
b. 1795 in Ile Bourbon, France
d. 1840

Bourgeois, Leon-Victor Auguste
French. Politician
Won 1920 Nobel Peace Prize for pioneering the League of Nations.
b. May 29, 1851 in Paris, France
d. Sep 29, 1925 in Epernay, France
Source: *LinLib L; McGEWB; OxCLaw; WhoNob, 90, 95*

Bourgeois, Louise
American. Artist
Had first show, 1945; first retrospective, 1982; shows include Venice Biennale.
b. 1911 in Paris, France
Source: *AmArt; Benet 96; BiDWomA; BioIn 13; BriEAA; ConAmWS; ConArt 77, 83, 89, 96; CurBio 83; DcAmArt; DcCAA 71, 77, 88, 94; GrLiveH; InWom SUP; McGDA; News 94, 94-1; NewYTBS 82; NorAmWA; OxCTwCA; OxDcArt; PhDcTCA 77; WhAmArt 85; WhoAm 74, 78, 80, 82, 84, 86, 88, 90, 94, 95, 96; WhoAmA 80, 82, 84, 86, 89, 91, 93; WhoAmW 68, 70, 72, 74, 85, 89, 91, 93, 95; WhoE 86; WhoWor 84, 87, 89, 91, 93, 95, 96, 97; WomArt; WorArt 1950*

Bourget, Paul (Charles Joseph)
French. Author, Critic
Wrote psychological, critical novels: *Le Disciple,* 1889.
b. Sep 2, 1852 in Amiens, France
d. Dec 25, 1935 in Paris, France
Source: *BbD; Benet 87, 96; BiD&SB; BioIn 1, 4, 5, 11, 19; CasWL; CathA 1930; ClDMEL 47, 80; ConAu 107; CyWA 58; DcBiA; DcCathB; DcLB 123; EncWL; EncWT; EvEuW; GuFrLit 1; LinLib L, S; LngCTC; NotNAT B; OxCAmH; OxCEng 67; OxCFr; PenC EUR; REn; TwCA, SUP; TwCLC 12; WhLit; WhThe*

Bourgholtzer, Frank
American. Broadcast Journalist
With NBC News since 1946.
b. Oct 26, 1919 in New York, New York
Source: *ConAu 25R; WhoAm 82, 84; WhoTelC; WhoWest 74, 76, 78*

Bourguiba, Habib Ben Ali
"Father of Tunisian Independence"
Tunisian. Political Leader
Tunisia's first pres., 1957-87; Pro-West, liberal leader gave up day-to-day control of govt. due to illness, 1969; named pres. for life in 1975.
b. Aug 3, 1903 in Monastir, Tunisia
Source: *ColdWar 2; CurBio 55; IntWW 75, 76, 77, 78, 80, 81, 82, 83, 89, 91, 93; McGEWB; WhoWor 76, 78, 80, 82, 84, 87, 89, 91*

Bourjaily, Vance
American. Author
Gained prominence in generation of young writers after WW II; novels include *Brill Among the Ruins,* 1970.
b. Sep 17, 1922 in Cleveland, Ohio
Source: *AmAu&B; Au&Wr 71; AuSpks; Benet 87; BenetAL 91; BioIn 14, 15, 21; BlueB 76; ConAu 1AS, 1R, 2NR; ConLC 8, 62; ConNov 72, 76, 82, 86, 91; Conv 1; DcLB 2, 143; DcLEL 1940; DrAF 76; DrAPF 80; IntAu&W 76, 77; IntWW 77, 78, 79, 80, 81, 82, 83, 89, 91, 93; LinLib L; ModAL; Novels; OhA&B; OxCAmL 65, 83; PenC AM; REn; REnAL; WhoAm 74, 76, 78, 80, 82, 84, 86, 88, 90, 92, 94, 95, 96, 97; WhoSSW 95, 97; WhoUSWr 88; WhoWor 74, 76; WhoWrEP 89, 92, 95; WorAu 1950; WrDr 76, 80, 82, 84, 86, 88, 90, 92*

Bourke-White, Margaret
American. Photojournalist
Life photographer, 1936-69; first official woman photojournalist of WW II: *You Have Seen Their Faces,* 1937.
b. Jun 14, 1904 in New York, New York
d. Aug 27, 1971 in Stamford, Connecticut
Source: *ABCMeAm; AmAu&B; AmWomWr; ArtclWW 2; Benet 87; BiDAmJo; BioAmW; BioIn 14, 15, 16, 17, 18, 19, 20, 21; ConAu 29R; ConHero 1; ConPhot 82, 88; ContDcW 89; CurBio 71; DcAmB S9; EncWB; GrLiveH; HerW; ICPEnP; IntDcWB; MacDWB; NewYTBE 71; NorAmWA; NotAW MOD; RComAH; REn; REnAL; WebAB 74; WhAm 5; WhAmArt 85; WomArt; WomChHR; WomComm; WomFir; WomStre*

Bourque, Ray(mond Jean)
Canadian. Hockey Player
Defenseman, Boston, 1979—; won Calder Trophy, 1980, Norris Trophy, 1987, 1988, 1990, 1991, 1994.
b. Dec 28, 1960 in Montreal, Quebec, Canada
Source: *BioIn 14, 15; HocEn; HocReg 87; NewYTBS 86; WhoAm 88, 92, 94, 95, 96, 97; WorAlBi*

Boussac, Marcel
"Cotton King of France"
French. Manufacturer
Made cotton airplane fabric during WW I; later used as fashion fabric.
b. Apr 17, 1889 in Chateauroux, France
d. Mar 31, 1980 in Montargis, France
Source: *AnObit 1980; BioIn 2, 3, 5, 11, 12; FacFETw; NewYTBE 71; NewYTBS 80; Who 74; WhoFr 79; WhoWor 74*

Boussingault, Jean Baptiste
French. Chemist
Contributed to research on nitrogen cycle, composition of plant tissues, nutritive value of forages.
b. Feb 2, 1802 in Paris, France
d. May 12, 1887 in Paris, France
Source: *BiESc; BioIn 1, 2, 3, 5, 6, 7; DcBiPP; NewCol 75*

Bouton, Jim
[James Alan Mouton]
"Bulldog"
American. Baseball Player, Author
Pitcher, 1962-68; wrote best-selling baseball expose, *Ball Four,* 1970.
b. Mar 8, 1939 in Newark, New Jersey
Source: *Ballpl 90; BioIn 12, 13; CelR; ConAu 89; CurBio 71; LegTOT; NewYTBE 70; WhoAm 82; WhoHol 92; WhoProB 73; WorAl*

Boutros-Ghali, Boutros
Egyptian. Diplomat
UN Secretary General, 1991-97; first Arab, African to head organization.
b. Nov 14, 1922 in Cairo, Egypt
Source: *BioIn 17, 18, 19, 21; CurBio 92; DcMidEa; IntWW 81, 82, 83, 89, 91, 93; LegTOT; MidE 81, 82; NewYTBS 94;*

Who 94; WhoAm 95, 96, 97; WhoArab 81; WhoUN 92; WhoWor 76, 78, 95, 96, 97

Bouts, Dierick C
Dutch. Artist
Painted austere religious works: "The Last Supper," 1464; "Last Judgment," 1468.
b. 1420 in Haarlem, Netherlands
d. 1475 in Louvain, Belgium
Source: *McGDA; OxCArt; WhDW; WorAl*

Boutte, Alvin J
American. Banker
CEO, Independence Bank, 1970—; second largest black bank in US.
b. Oct 10, 1929 in Lake Charles, Louisiana
Source: *InB&W 85; WhoBlA 85, 88*

Boutwell, George Sewall
American. Politician
Secretary of treasury under US Grant, 1869; prepared new edition of *United States Revised Statutes* for Pres. Hayes, 1878.
b. Jan 23, 1818 in Brookline, Massachusetts
d. Feb 27, 1905 in Groton, Massachusetts
Source: *Alli SUP; AmBi; ApCAB; BiD&SB; BiDrGov 1789; BiDrUSE 71, 89; BioIn 8, 10, 11; CivWDc; DcAmAu; DcAmB; DcNAA; Drake; HarEnUS; NatCAB 1, 4; OxCAmH; PeoHis; TwCBDA; WebAB 74, 79; WhAm 1; WhCiWar*

Bova, Ben(jamin William)
American. Author, Editor
Writer of science, science fiction books: *Kinsman,* 1979; *The Exiles Trilogy,* 1980.
b. Nov 8, 1932 in Philadelphia, Pennsylvania
Source: *Au&Arts 16; AuBYP 2S, 3; BioIn 10, 13, 16, 17, 19; ChlLR 3; ConAu 7NR, 11NR, 18AS; ConLC 45; ConSFA; DcLB Y81B; EncSF, 93; FifBJA; IntAu&W 89, 91, 93; LegTOT; MajAI; MajTwCW; NewEScF; Novels; RGSF; RGTwCSF; ScF&FL 1, 2, 92; ScFSB; SmATA 6, 68; TwCSFW 81, 86, 91; WhoAm 74, 76, 78, 82, 84, 90, 92, 94, 95, 96, 97; WhoE 74, 75, 77, 89; WhoSciF; WhoWor 82; WrDr 80, 82, 84, 86, 88, 90, 92, 94, 96*

Bovet, Daniele
Italian. Chemist
Won Nobel Prize, 1957, for developing drugs to relieve allergies.
b. Mar 23, 1907 in Neuchatel, Switzerland
d. Apr 8, 1992 in Rome, Italy
Source: *AsBiEn; BiESc; BioIn 4, 5, 6; CurBio 58, 92N; InSci; NewYTBS 92; WhoNob; WorAl; WorAlBi; WorScD*

Bow, Clara Gordon
[The It Girl]
American. Actor
Starred in Roaring 20s silent films; symbol of flapper age.
b. Aug 25, 1905 in New York, New York
d. Sep 27, 1965 in Los Angeles, California
Source: *BiDFilm; BioAmW; CmCal; DcAmB S7; Film 2; FilmgC; InWom SUP; LibW; MotPP; MovMk; NotAW MOD; OxCFilm; ThFT; TwYS; WebAB 74; WhoHol B; WhScrn 77; WomWMM; WorEFlm*

Bowa, Larry
[Lawrence Robert Bowa]
American. Baseball Player, Baseball Manager
Shortstop, 1970-85, known for defensive play; manager, San Diego, 1987-88.
b. Dec 6, 1945 in Sacramento, California
Source: *Ballpl 90; BaseReg 87; BiDAmSp BB; BioIn 11; LegTOT; WhoAm 88; WhoProB 73; WhoWest 87; WorAl*

Bowden, Bobby
American. Football Coach
Coach, Florida State University Seminoles, 1975—; Alabama Sports Hall of Fame, 1986.
b. Nov 8, 1929 in Birmingham, Alabama
Source: *CurBio 96; WhoAm 95, 96, 97; WhoSpor; WhoSSW 95*

Bowden, Don
American. Track Athlete
First American to run an under four-minute mile, 1957.
b. Aug 8, 1936 in San Jose, California
Source: *BioIn 7; WhoTr&F 73*

Bowditch, Nathaniel
American. Astronomer, Mathematician
Published first usable navigation guide, *New Practical Navigator,* 1802.
b. Mar 26, 1773 in Salem, Massachusetts
d. Mar 16, 1838 in Boston, Massachusetts
Source: *Alli; AmAu; AmBi; ApCAB; BenetAL 91; BiDAmS; BiInAmS; BioIn 1, 2, 3, 4, 5, 6, 7, 8, 13, 15, 17; CyAL 1; DcAmAu; DcAmB; DcNAA; DcScB; Drake; EncAB-H 1974, 1996; HarEnUS; InSci; LinLib S; McGEWB; MemAm; NatCAB 6, 16; OxCAmH; OxCAmL 65, 83, 95; OxCShps; PeoHis; REnAL; TwCBDA; WebAB 74, 79; WhAm HS*

Bowdler, Thomas
English. Editor
His expurgated editions of Shakespeare's works and Gibbon's *Decline & Fall* resulted in term "bowdlerize."
b. Jul 11, 1754 in Ashley, England
d. Feb 24, 1825 in Rhyddings, England
Source: *Alli; BiDLA, SUP; BioIn 3, 6, 13; BlmGEL; BritAu; CamGLE; CasWL; Chambr 2; DcArts; DcBiPP; DcEnL; DcLEL; DcNaB; EvLB; LinLib L; LngCEL; NewC; NewCBEL; NotNAT B; OxCChiL; OxCEng 67, 85, 95; OxCMed 86*

Bowdoin, James
American. Merchant, Colonial Figure
Governor of MA, 1785-87; Bowdoin College founded in his honor, 1794.
b. Aug 7, 1726 in Boston, Massachusetts
d. Nov 6, 1790 in Boston, Massachusetts
Source: *Alli; AmAu&B; AmBi; AmWrBE; ApCAB; BiAUS; BiDAmS; BiDrACR; BiInAmS; BioIn 2, 5; BlkwEAR; CyAL 1; DcAmB; Drake; EncCRAm; McGEWB; OxCAmH; TwCBDA; WebAB 74, 79; WhAm HS; WhAmP; WhAmRev*

Bowe, Riddick (Lamont)
American. Boxer
Defeated Evander Holyfield to become heavyweight champion, 1992-93; defeated Evander Holyfield to retain title, 1995.
b. Aug 10, 1967 in New York, New York
Source: *BlkOlyM; ConBlB 6; CurBio 96; LegTOT; News 93-2; WhoAfA 96; WhoAm 94, 95, 96, 97; WhoBlA 94; WhoWor 95, 96, 97*

Bowell, Mackenzie, Sir
Canadian. Statesman, Journalist
Conservative prime minister, 1894-96; owned, edited Belleville *Intelligencer.*
b. Dec 27, 1823 in Rickinghall, England
d. Dec 10, 1917 in Belleville, Ontario, Canada
Source: *ApCAB; BioIn 7; MacDCB 78; OxCCan; WebBD 83*

Bowen, Billy
[Ink Spots]
American. Singer
One of first black groups to break color barrier over airwaves.
b. 1909 in Birmingham, Alabama
d. Sep 27, 1982 in New York, New York
Source: *DrBlPA 90*

Bowen, Catherine Drinker
American. Author
Wrote best-selling *John Adams and the American Revolution,* 1950; biographies on Francis Bacon, Sir Edward Coke.
b. Jan 1, 1897 in Haverford, Pennsylvania
d. Nov 1, 1973 in Haverford, Pennsylvania
Source: *AmAu&B; WhoGov 72; WhoWor 74*

Bowen, Elizabeth Dorthea Cole
Irish. Author
Wrote *The Heat of the Day,* 1949; noted for sensitive use of language, character.
b. Jun 7, 1899 in Dublin, Ireland
d. Feb 22, 1973 in London, England
Source: *CasWL; ConAu P-2; ConLC 22; ConNov 72; CyWA 58; EncWL;*

McGEWB; NewYTBE 73; OxCEng 85; PenC ENG; TwCA SUP; WhAm 5

Bowen, Otis Ray
American. Physician, Politician
Secretary of Health and Human Services, 1985-89.
b. Feb 26, 1918 in Rochester, Indiana
Source: *BiDrUSE 89; BioIn 9, 12; CurBio 86; IntWW 74, 75, 76, 77, 78, 79, 80, 81, 82, 83, 89, 91, 93; IntYB 78, 79, 80, 81, 82; NewYTBS 85; WhoAm 74, 76, 78, 80, 82, 84, 86, 88; WhoE 86, 89; WhoGov 72, 75, 77; WhoMW 74, 76, 78, 80; WhoWor 78, 80, 87, 89*

Bowen, Roger
American. Actor
Played Henry Blake in movie *M*A*S*H,* 1970.
b. May 25, 1932 in Attleboro, Massachusetts
d. Feb 16, 1996 in Marathon, Florida
Source: *ConTFT 7; WhoHol A*

Bower, Johnny
[John William Bower]
"China Wall"
Canadian. Hockey Player
Goalie, 1953-70, mostly with Toronto; won Vezina Trophy, 1961, 1965; Hall of Fame, 1976.
b. Nov 8, 1924 in Prince Albert, Saskatchewan, Canada
Source: *BioIn 6, 8, 10; HocEn; WhoHcky 73; WhoSpor*

Bowers, Claude Gernade
American. Historian, Diplomat
His historical works include *Jefferson and Hamilton,* 1925; *The Tragic Era: The Revolution After Lincoln,* 1929.
b. Nov 20, 1878? in Hamilton County, Indiana
d. Jan 21, 1958 in New York, New York
Source: *AmAu&B; BioIn 4, 5, 6, 13, 16; CurBio 41, 58; DcAmB S6; DcAmDH 80, 89; EncAB-A 1; EncAB-H 1974, 1996; EncSoH; IndAu 1816; McGEWB; NatCAB 44; OxCAmL 65; REn; REnAL; TwCA, SUP; WhAm 3*

Bowes, Major
[Edward Bowes]
American. Broadcaster
Best known for radio program "Major Bowes' Amateur Hour," 1934-46.
b. Jun 13, 1874 in San Francisco, California
d. Jun 13, 1946 in Rumson, New Jersey
Source: *BiDAmM; BioIn 1; CurBio 41, 46; DcAmB S4; LegTOT; NotNAT B; ObitOF 79; RadStar; SaTiSS; WhAm 2; WhScrn 77; WorAl; WorAlBi*

Bowes, Walter
American. Businessman
With Arthur Pitney, formed Pitney Bowes Co.
b. 1882, England
d. Jun 24, 1957 in Washington, District of Columbia
Source: *Entr; ObitOF 79*

Bowie, David
[David Robert Hayward-Jones]
English. Singer, Songwriter, Actor
Pop-rock singer, 1970s-80s; starred in film *The Man Who Fell to Earth,* 1976; songs include "Let's Dance," 1983, "Loving the Alien," 1985; Grammy award winner for best short-form video, 1984.
b. Jan 8, 1947 in London, England
Source: *Baker 84, 92; BioIn 9, 10, 11, 12, 13; BioNews 74; BkPepl; CelR 90; ConLC 17; ConMuA 80A; ConMus 1; ConTFT 3; CurBio 76, 94; DcArts; EncPR&S 89; EncRk 88; EncRkSt; FacFETw; HalFC 80, 84, 88; HarEnR 86; IlEncRk; IntMPA 86, 88, 92, 94, 96; IntWW 89, 91, 93; LegTOT; NewAmDM; OxCPMus; PenEncP; RkOn 74, 78; RolSEnR 83; Who 83, 85, 88, 90, 92, 94; WhoAm 78, 80, 82, 84, 86, 88, 90, 92, 94, 95, 96, 97; WhoEnt 92; WhoHol 92, A; WhoRock 81; WorAl; WorAlBi*

Bowie, Jim
[James Bowie]
American. Soldier, Inventor
Reputed inventor of Bowie knife; killed at the Alamo.
b. 1796 in Burke County, Georgia
d. Mar 6, 1836 in San Antonio, Texas
Source: *AmBi; ApCAB; BioIn 1, 2; DcAmB; EncSoH; FilmgC; HalFC 80, 84, 88; HarEnMi; LegTOT; LinLib S; TwCBDA; WebAB 74, 79; WebAMB; WhAm HS; WorAl; WorAlBi*

Bowie, Norman Ernest
American. Author
Business Ethics, 1982; *Ethical Issues in Government,* 1981, are among his works.
b. Jun 6, 1942 in Biddeford, Maine
Source: *ConAu 13NR; DrAS 74P, 78P, 82F, 82P; WhoAm 74, 76, 78, 80, 82, 84, 86, 88, 90, 92, 94, 95, 96, 97; WhoE 74, 83; WhoFI 87; WrDr 76*

Bowie, Russell
"Dubbie"
Canadian. Hockey Player
Center on amateur Winnipeg team, 1899-1908, averaging three goals per game throughout career; Hall of Fame, 1945.
b. Aug 24, 1880 in Montreal, Quebec, Canada
d. Apr 8, 1959
Source: *WhoHcky 73*

Bowie, Walter
"Wat Bowie"
American. Lawyer, Spy
Spy for Confederacy, 1861-64.
b. 1837 in Maryland
d. 1864 in Annapolis, Maryland
Source: *BioIn 3, 6; SpyCS*

Bowker, Albert Hosmer
American. Educator
Chancellor, City University of NY, 1963-71; U of CA, Berkeley, 1971-80; exec. vp, U of MD, 1983-86; vp for City Univ., NY, 1986—.
b. Sep 8, 1919 in Winchendon, Massachusetts
Source: *AmMWSc 76P, 79, 82, 86, 89, 92, 95; BioIn 7, 9; BlueB 76; CurBio 66; LEduc 74; NewYTBE 71; WhoAm 74, 76, 78, 80, 82, 84, 86, 88, 90, 92, 94, 95, 96, 97; WhoWest 74, 76, 78, 80*

Bowker, R(ichard) R(ogers)
American. Publisher, Editor, Author
Founded R R Bowker Co., 1872; co-founder *Library Journal,* 1876.
b. Sep 4, 1848 in Salem, Massachusetts
d. Nov 12, 1933 in Stockbridge, Massachusetts
Source: *Alli SUP; AmAu&B; AmBi; ApCAB X; BbD; BiD&SB; BioIn 2, 3, 10, 15; DcAmAu; DcAmB S1; DcAmLiB; DcNAA; LinLib L; NatCAB 12, 24; WebAB 74, 79; WhAm 1; WhLit; WhNAA*

Bowlegs, Billy
American. Native American Chief
Seminole Chief during the Second and Third Seminole Wars.
b. 1810
d. 1859?
Source: *BioIn 21; EncNAB; NotNaAm; WhFla; WhNaAH*

Bowlen, Patrick Dennis
American. Business Executive, Football Executive
President, Bowlen Holdings, 1979—; owner, Denver Broncos football team, 1984—.
b. Feb 18, 1944 in Prairie du Chien, Wisconsin
Source: *CanWW 79, 80, 81, 83, 89; WhoAm 86, 88, 92; WhoCan 80, 82, 84; WhoWest 87, 89, 92, 94, 96*

Bowles, Chester Bliss
American. Diplomat, Businessman, Author
Liberal Dem. who was presidential adviser, governor, congressman during 25-yr. public career.
b. Apr 5, 1901 in Springfield, Massachusetts
d. May 26, 1986 in Essex, Connecticut
Source: *AdMenW; AmAu&B; AmPolLe; Au&Wr 71; BiDrAC; BiDrGov 1789; BiDrUSC 89; ConAu 69; CurBio 43, 57, 86; DcAmDH 80, 89; IntWW 74; REnAL; Who 74; WhoAm 74; WhoWor 74*

Bowles, Erskine B.
American. Government Official
Chief of Staff to Pres. Clinton, 1997—.
b. Aug 8, 1945

Bowles, Jane Sydney
[Mrs. Paul Bowles]
American. Author
Noted "writer's writer," who wrote stories about women and their attempts at independence.
b. Feb 22, 1917 in New York, New York
d. May 4, 1973 in Malaga, Spain
Source: *AmWomWr; Au&Wr 71; BiE&WWA; ConAu 41R, P-2; ConLC 3; ConNov 72; DcLEL 1940; InWom SUP; ModAL; NewYTBE 73; PenC AM; WhoTwCL; WorAu 1950*

Bowles, Paul (Frederick)
American. Composer, Author
Composed music for theater, motion pictures, opera; writes dark novels with exotic settings including, *Call at Corzon,* 1988.
b. Dec 30, 1910 in New York, New York
Source: *AmAu&B; ASCAP 66, 80; Au&Wr 71; Benet 96; BenetAL 91; BiE&WWA; BioIn 4, 8, 9, 10, 12, 13, 14, 16, 17, 19, 20, 21; BlueB 76; CamGEL; CamGLE; CamHAL; ConAmC 76, 82; ConAu 1AS, 1NR, 1R, 19NR, 50NR; ConLC 1, 2, 19, 53; ConNov 72, 76, 82, 86, 91, 96; ConTFT 1; CurBio 90; CyWA 89; DcArts; DcLB 5, 6; DrAF 76; EncWL 2, 3; FacFETw; GayLL; GrWrEL N; IntAu&W 82, 86, 89, 91, 93; IntWW 74, 75, 76, 77, 78, 79, 80, 81, 82, 83, 89, 91, 93; IntWWM 77, 80, 85, 90; LegTOT; LiExTwC; LinLib L; MagSAmL; MajTwCW; ModAL, S1, S2; NewGrDA 86; NewGrDM 80; NewGrDO; NewYTBS 95; NotNAT; Novels; OxCAmL 65, 83, 95; PenC AM; RAdv 1; REnAL; RfGAmL 87, 94; RGTwCWr; ShSCr 3; TwCA SUP; TwCWr; WhoAm 74, 76, 78, 80, 82, 84, 86, 88, 90, 92, 94, 95, 96, 97; WhoAmM 83; WhoE 74; WhoEnt 92; WhoTwCL; WhoUSWr 88; WhoWor 74, 76, 78, 82, 84, 87, 93; WhoWrEP 89, 92; WrDr 76, 80, 82, 84, 86, 88, 90, 92, 94, 96*

Bowles, Samuel, II
American. Journalist
Edited notable *Springfield Republican,* 1848-78.
b. Feb 9, 1826 in Springfield, Massachusetts
d. Jan 16, 1878 in Springfield, Massachusetts
Source: *Alli SUP; AmAu&B; AmBi; BbD; BbtC; BenetAL 91; BiDAmJo; BiD&SB; BioIn 3, 6, 8, 15, 16; DcAmAu; DcAmB; DcLB 43; DcNAA; Drake; EncAB-H 1974, 1996; EncAJ; HarEnUS; JrnUS; LinLib L, S; McGEWB; NatCAB 1; OxCAmH; OxCAmL 65, 83, 95; REnAL; TwCBDA; WebAB 74, 79; WhAm HS*

Bowles, William Augustus
American. Adventurer
With Maryland Loyalist regiment in Florida during American Revolution; became director general of Creek Nation.
b. 1763
d. 1802
Source: *ApCAB; BioIn 7, 8, 9; DcAmB; Drake; NatCAB 9; WhAm HS; WhFla; WhNaAH; WhoFla*

Bowling, Roger
American. Songwriter
Wrote songs "Lucille" and "Coward of the County."
b. 1944?
d. Dec 25, 1982 in Clayton, Georgia
Source: *BioIn 13*

Bowman, Isaiah
American. Geographer, University Administrator
Directed American Geographical Society, 1915-35; president, Johns Hopkins U, 1935-48.
b. Dec 26, 1878 in Waterloo, Ontario, Canada
d. Jan 6, 1950 in Baltimore, Maryland
Source: *AmAu&B; AmLY; AmPeW; BiDAmEd; BiDInt; BioIn 1, 2, 3, 4, 5, 12, 15, 18; CurBio 45, 50; DcAmB S4; DcScB; Geog 1; InSci; McGEWB; NatCAB 40; RAdv 14; WebAB 74, 79; WhAm 2, 2A; WhDW*

Bowman, Lee
[Lucien Lee Bowman, Sr]
American. Actor
Played opposite Susan Hayward in film *Smash-Up,* 1947.
b. Dec 28, 1914 in Cincinnati, Ohio
Source: *BiE&WWA, 78, 79, 80; MotPP; MovMk; NewYTBS 79; What 5; WhoHol A; WhScrn 83*

Bowman, Scotty
[William Scott Bowman]
Canadian. Hockey Player, Hockey Coach
Coached Montreal, 1971-79, to five Stanley Cups (1973, 1976-79); coach, Buffalo, 1982-86; coach, Pittsburgh, 1991-93, Stanley Cup, 1992; coach, Detroit, 1993—, Stanley Cup, 1997; winningest coach in NHL history; first coach to lead three different teams to the Stanley Cup.
b. Sep 18, 1933 in Montreal, Quebec, Canada
Source: *BioIn 12, 14, 19; HocEn; NewYTBS 79, 84; WhoAm 74, 76, 78, 80, 82, 84, 86, 88, 90, 92, 94, 95, 96, 97; WhoE 83, 85, 86, 89, 95; WhoHcky 73; WhoMW 93, 96; WhoSpor; WhoWor 96, 97*

Bowra, Maurice, Sir
English. Educator, Critic
Considered among leading classical scholars, critics of time.
b. Apr 8, 1898 in Jiujiang, China
d. Jul 4, 1971 in Oxford, England
Source: *Au&Wr 71; BioIn 9, 10, 12; CamGLE; ConAu 2NR, 29R; DcNaB 1971; EvLB; GrBr; ModBrL; ObitT 1971; OxCEng 85*

Bowser, Betty Ann
American. Broadcast Journalist
Co-editor, "30 Minutes," 1980—; with CBS news, 1974—.
b. 1944 in Norfolk, Virginia
Source: *ForWC 70; WhoAm 82; WhoAmW 72, 74*

Bow Wow Wow
[Matthew Ashman; Dave Barbarossa; Leroy Gorman]
English. Music Group
New Wave band, 1980-83; combined African rhythms, chants, surf instrumentals, pop melodies.
Source: *BlmGWL; EncRk 88; HarEnR 86; IlEncRk; NewWmR; NewYTBS 27; PenEncP; RkOn 85; RolSEnR 83; WhsNW 85*

Box, John
English. Filmmaker
Art director who won Oscars for *Doctor Zhivago,* 1965; *Oliver,* 1968.
b. Jan 27, 1920 in Kent, England
Source: *ConDes 84, 90, 97; ConTFT 10; FilmEn; FilmgC; HalFC 80, 84, 88; IntDcF 1-4, 2-4; VarWW 85*

Boxer, Barbara Levy
American. Politician
Dem. senator, CA, 1993—.
b. Nov 11, 1940 in New York, New York
Source: *AlmAP 92; CngDr 89; CurBio 94; WhoAm 90; WhoAmP 91; WhoAmW 91; WhoEmL 87; WhoWest 92*

Boxleitner, Bruce
American. Actor
Co-star of TV series "Scarecrow and Mrs. King," 1983-87.
b. May 12, 1951? in Elgin, Illinois
Source: *BioIn 11; ConTFT 3*

Box Tops, The
[Rick Allen; Thomas Boggs; Alex Chilton; Harold Cloud; William Cunningham; John Evans; Swain Scharfer; Daniel Smythe; Gary Talley]
American. Music Group
Memphis-based blue-eyed soul band, 1965-70; hit single "The Letter," 1967.
Source: *AfrAmBi 1; Alli, SUP; ApCAB; BiAUS; BiDAmM; BiD&SB; BiDLA; BiDrAC; BiDrUSC 89; BioIn 19; ConAu 73, X; ConMuA 80A; DcAmB; DcLP 87B; DcNaB, C; DcVicP 2; Drake; Dun&B 86; EncMys; EncRk 88; EncRkSt; FolkA 87; HarEnUS; IntAu&W 91X; IntvTCA 2; Law&B 84, 89A; NewCBEL; NewYHSD; PenEncP; RkOn 78; RolSEnR 83; St&PR 96; TwCCr&M 85, 91; WhAm HS; WhAmRev; Who 82, 83, 85, 88, 90, 92, 94; WhoReal 83; WhoRock 81; WhoRocM 82; WhoScEu 91-1; WrDr 96*

Boyce, Christopher John
[Anthony Lester]
"Falcon"
American. Spy
Former CIA clerk, sentenced to 40 yrs. imprisonment for selling classified documents to Soviets.
b. 1953 in Palos Verdes, California
Source: *BioIn 11; NewYTBS 77; PseudN 82; SpyCS*

Boyce, Westray Battle
American. Government Official
Director of Women's Army Corps (WACs), 1945, as it demobilized after WW II.
b. Aug 1901 in Rocky Mount, North Carolina
d. Jan 31, 1972 in Washington, District of Columbia
Source: *BioIn 9; CurBio 45, 72, 72N; InWom*

Boyce, William
English. Organist, Composer
Master of King's Band of Music, 1755; organist to Chapel Royal, 1758; published collection of *Cathedral Music*. 1760-73.
b. 1710 in London, England
d. Feb 7, 1779 in Kensington, England
Source: *Alli; BioIn 3, 4, 5, 7, 9, 10, 12; BriBkM 80; DcBiPP; DcCom&M 79; DcNaB; GrComp; LuthC 75; MusMk; OxCMus; WebBD 83; WhDW*

Boycott, Charles Cunningham
English. Manager
Land agent ostracized for collecting excessive rents; name used for tactic of isolating one's opponents.
b. Mar 12, 1832 in Norfolk, England
d. Jul 19, 1897 in Flixton, England
Source: *BioIn 1, 7, 10; CelCen; DcNaB C, S1; WebBD 83; WorAl*

Boyd, Belle
[Isabelle Boyd]
American. Spy, Actor
Confederate spy, 1861-62.
b. May 8, 1843 in Martinsburg, Virginia
d. Jun 11, 1900 in Kilbourne, Wisconsin
Source: *Alli SUP; AmAu&B; AmBi; BioAmW; BioIn 3, 4, 6, 8, 9, 11, 12; CivWDc; DcAmB; DcNAA; EncAI&E; HarEnUS; HerW; NatCAB 23; NotAW; OxCAmH; WhAm HS; WhCiWar*

Boyd, Bill
"Cowboy Rambler"
American. Singer
Popular Dallas dj for over 35 years; songs include "Under the Double Eagle"; "Ridin' on a Humpback Mule."
b. Sep 29, 1910 in Fannin County, Texas
Source: *BgBkCoM; BioIn 14; EncFCWM 69, 83; HarEnCM 87; IlEncCM; PenEncP; WhScrn 83*

Boyd, James
American. Author
Historical novels include *Drums*, 1925.
b. Jul 2, 1888 in Harrisburg, Pennsylvania
d. Feb 25, 1944 in Princeton, New Jersey
Source: *AmAu&B; BenetAL 91; BioIn 2, 3, 4, 5, 9, 11, 12; CnDAL; ConAmA; ConAmL; CyWA 58; DcAmB S3; DcLB 9; DcLEL; DcNAA; DcNCBi 1; GrWrEL N; LinLib L; LngCTC; NatCAB 35; Novels; OxCAmL 65, 83, 95; PenC AM; REnAL; RfGAmL 87, 94; SouWr; TwCA, SUP; TwCRHW 90, 94; WhAm 2; WhLit; WhNAA*

Boyd, Julian Parks
American. Historian, Editor
Edited *The Papers of Thomas Jefferson*, 1950-76; complete written record of Thomas Jefferson.
b. Nov 3, 1903 in Converse, South Carolina
d. May 21, 1980 in Princeton, New Jersey
Source: *AmAu&B; BioIn 2, 10, 11, 12; ConAu 65, 97; CurBio 76, 80; DcAmB S10; DrAS 74H, 78H; NewYTBS 80; PeoHis; REnAL; WhAm 7; WhoAm 74, 76, 78, 80; WhoE 74*

Boyd, Liona Maria
"First Lady of Classical Guitar"
Canadian. Musician
Won Canadian instrumentalist awards, 1982, 1985.
b. Jul 11, 1949 in London, Ontario, Canada
Source: *CanWW 83; WhoAm 86*

Boyd, Louise Arner
American. Explorer
First woman to successfully fly over N Pole, 1955.
b. Sep 16, 1887 in San Rafael, California
d. Sep 14, 1972 in San Francisco, California
Source: *AmAu&B; AmWomSc; BioAmW; BioIn 1, 5, 7, 9, 14, 18, 20; CurBio 60, 72; DcAmB S9; Expl 93; InSci; InWom, SUP; WhAm 5; WhoAmW 58, 61, 64, 66, 68, 70, 72, 74; WhWE*

Boyd, Malcolm
American. Author, Clergy
Episcopalian priest whose books deal with spirituality, human rights: *Are You Running with Me, Jesus?*, 1965.
b. Jun 8, 1923 in Buffalo, New York
Source: *AmAu&B; AmDec 1960; AmMWSc 73P; Au&Wr 71; AuSpks; BioIn 6, 7, 8, 10, 11, 15; BlueB 76; CelR; ConAu 4NR, 5NR, 5R, 11AS, 26NR, 51NR; GayLL; IntAu&W 76, 77, 82, 86, 89; RelLAm 91; ScF&FL 1, 2; WhoAm 74, 76, 78, 80, 82, 84, 86, 88, 90, 92, 94, 95, 96, 97; WhoE 74; WhoRel 75, 77, 85, 92; WhoUSWr 88; WhoWest 96; WhoWor 74, 76; WhoWrEP 89, 92, 95; WorAl; WorAlBi; WrDr 76, 80, 82, 84, 86, 88, 90, 92, 94, 96*

Boyd, Stephen
American. Actor
Played Messala in *Ben Hur*, 1959.
b. Jul 4, 1928 in Belfast, Northern Ireland
d. Jun 2, 1977 in Los Angeles, California
Source: *BioIn 5; ItaFilm; MotPP; MovMk; WhoAm 74; WhoHol A; WhScrn 83; WorAl; WorAlBi; WorEFlm*

Boyd, T(heophilus) B(artholomew), III
American. Clergy
President and CEO, National Baptist Publishing Board, 1979—.
b. May 15, 1947 in Nashville, Tennessee
Source: *WhoAm 90, 95, 96, 97; WhoSSW 88, 91, 95; WhoWor 91, 93, 95, 97*

Boyd, William
"Bill Boyd"; "Hopalong Cassidy"
American. Actor
Best known as Hopalong Cassidy, character he played 66 times, 1935-48.
b. Jun 5, 1898 in Cambridge, Ohio
d. Sep 12, 1972 in South Laguna, California
Source: *BioIn 1, 2, 9, 12; CmMov; CurBio 50, 72, 72N; DcAmB S9; Film 1, 2; FilmEn; FilmgC; ForYSC; IntDcF 1-3; LegTOT; MovMk; OxCFilm; RadStar; WhAm 5; WhoHol B; WhScrn 77*

Boyd, William
English. Author
Won James Tait Black Memorial Book Prize for *Brazzaville Beach*, 1990.
b. Mar 7, 1952 in Accra, Ghana
Source: *BioIn 13, 15, 17; ConAu 51NR, 114, 120; ConLC 28, 53, 70; ConNov 86, 91, 96; IntAu&W 91, 93; WorAu 1980; WrDr 86, 88, 90, 92, 94, 96*

Boyd, William Clouser
American. Physician
Founder of modern immunology, 1945; discovered 13 blood types.
b. Mar 4, 1903 in Dearborn, Missouri
d. Feb 19, 1983 in Falmouth, Massachusetts
Source: *AmMWSc 76P, 79; AnObit 1983; AsBiEn; BiESc; BioIn 1, 13; ConAu 109; FacFETw; LarDcSc; McGMS 80; NewYTBS 83; WhAm 8; WhoAm 74, 76, 78, 80, 82*

Boyd-Orr, John, Baron
Scottish. Nutritionist
Helped avert famine in Europe after WW II; won Nobel Peace Prize, 1949.
b. Sep 23, 1880 in Kilmaurs, Scotland
d. Jun 25, 1971 in Brechin, Scotland
Source: *Au&Wr 71; ConAu 113; CurBio 46, 71; ObitT 1971; WhoNob; WorAl*

Boyer, Charles
French. Actor
Romantic lead starred in films *Algiers*, 1938; *Gaslight*, 1944.
b. Aug 28, 1899 in Figeac, France
d. Aug 26, 1978 in Phoenix, Arizona

Source: *BiDFilm, 78; LegTOT; MotPP; MovMk; OxCAmT 84; OxCFilm; WhAm 7; WhoAm 74, 76, 78; WhoHol A; WhoThe 72, 77A; WhoWor 74; WhScrn 83; WhThe; WorAl; WorAlBi; WorEFlm*

Boyer, Ernest L(eroy)
American. Educator
Chancellor, SUNY, 1970-77; US commissioner of education, 1977-79; president, Carnegie Foundation, 1979-95.
b. Sep 13, 1928 in Dayton, Ohio
d. Dec 8, 1995 in Princeton, New Jersey
Source: *AmMWSc 73S, 78S; BioIn 11, 12, 13; ConAu 110, 150; CurBio 88; LEduc 74; NewYTBS 77; WhAm 11; WhoAm 74, 76, 78, 80, 82, 84, 86, 88, 90, 92, 94, 95, 96; WhoAmP 77, 79, 81, 83, 85, 87, 89, 91, 93, 95; WhoE 75, 77, 91, 95; WhoGov 77*

Boyer, Herbert Wayne
American. Biochemist
Director, Genetech, Inc., who patented procedure of gene splicing, 1970s.
b. Jul 10, 1936 in Pittsburgh, Pennsylvania
Source: *AmMWSc 76P, 79, 82, 86, 89, 92, 95; BiESc; BioIn 12, 15, 20; CamDcSc; ConNews 85-1; FacFETw; LarDcSc; WhoAm 78, 80, 82, 84, 92, 94, 95, 96; WhoFrS 84; WhoScEn 94; WhoWest 89; WorScD*

Boyer, Ken(ton Lloyd)
American. Baseball Player
Third baseman, 1955-69, known for defensive play; NL MVP, 1964.
b. May 20, 1931 in Liberty, Missouri
d. Sep 7, 1982 in Saint Louis, Missouri
Source: *Ballpl 90; BiDAmSp BB; BioIn 6, 7, 8, 13, 15; CurBio 66, 82, 82N; NewYTBS 82; WhoMW 80; WhoProB 73*

Boy George
[Culture Club; George Alan O'Dowd]
English. Singer
Flamboyant lead singer, known for avant-garde dress, make-up; had number-one hit, "Karma Chameleon," 1983.
b. Jun 14, 1961 in Bexleyheath, England
Source: *Baker 92; BioIn 13; CurBio 85; EncRkSt; LegTOT; OxCPMus; PenEncP*

Boyington, Pappy
[Gregory Boyington]
American. Pilot
Led Black Sheep Squadron, made up of those rejected from other squadrons, WW II; shot down 28 enemy planes; received Medal of Honor.
b. Dec 4, 1912 in Coeur d'Alene, Idaho
d. Jan 11, 1988 in Fresno, California
Source: *AmAu&B; BioIn 5, 10, 12, 15, 16, 17; ConAu 124; FacFETw; LegTOT; MedHR, 94; News 88-2; NewYTBS 88; WebAMB; What 5*

Boykin, Otis Frank
American. Inventor
Invented guided missile device, artificial heart stimulator control unit.
b. Aug 29, 1920 in Dallas, Texas
d. Apr 1982
Source: *InB&W 80; NegAl 83; WhoMW 78, 80*

Boyle, Gertrude
American. Businesswoman
President and CEO of Columbia Sportswear, 1970-88; CEO, 1988-94; Chairman, 1994—.
b. 1924 in Augsberg, Germany
Source: *News 95, 95-3; WhoAmW 97*

Boyle, Harold Vincent
American. Journalist
Awarded Pulitzer for correspondence, WW II; called "The American Infantryman's Boswell."
b. Feb 21, 1911 in Kansas City, Missouri
d. Apr 1, 1974 in New York, New York
Source: *BioIn 4, 8, 10; ConAu 89, 101; CurBio 45, 74; DcAmB S9; EncTwCJ; WhAm 6; WhoAm 74; WhoWor 74*

Boyle, Jack
"Boston Blackie"
American. Author
Wrote mystery, *Boston Blackie,* 1919; title character became subject of films, TV series, radio shows, 1920s-50s; Boyle himself remains a mystery.
Source: *ConMuA 80B; EncMys; TwCCr&M 80*

Boyle, Kay
American. Author
Writings include *Wedding Day,* 1931; *Generation without Farewell,* 1959.
b. Feb 19, 1902 in Saint Paul, Minnesota
d. Dec 27, 1992 in Mill Valley, California
Source: *AmNov; AnObit 1992; BioIn 12, 13, 15, 16, 17, 18, 19, 20; BlmGWL; CasWL; ConAmA; ConAu 1AS, 29NR, 140; ConLC 1, 5, 19, 58, 76; ConNov 82, 86, 91; ConPo 80, 85, 91; DcLB 4, 9, 48, 86, Y93N; EncWL; FemiCLE; IntAu&W 89, 91; InWom SUP; LiExTwC; LinLib L; MajTwCW; ModAL; NewYTBS 92; OxCAmL 83; OxCWoWr 95; PenC AM; REn; RfGAmL 87, 94; RfGShF; TwCA SUP; WhAm 11; Who 82, 83, 85, 88, 90, 92; WhoAm 80, 82, 84, 86, 88, 90, 92; WhoAmW 85, 87, 89, 91, 93; WhoTwCL; WhoWrEP 89, 92; WrDr 84, 86, 88, 90, 92, 94, 96*

Boyle, Peter
American. Actor
Films include *Taxi Driver,* 1976; *Joe,* 1970.
b. Oct 18, 1935 in Philadelphia, Pennsylvania
Source: *ConTFT 3; FilmgC; IntMPA 82; MovMk; NewYTBE 71; VarWW 85; WhoAm 82; WhoHol A*

Boyle, Robert
Irish. Scientist
First to isolate, collect a gas; formulated physics law that bears name.
b. Jan 25, 1627 in Lismore, Ireland
d. Dec 30, 1691 in London, England
Source: *Alli; AsBiEn; BiDIrW; BiESc; BiHiMed; BioIn 1, 2, 3, 4, 5, 6, 7, 8, 9, 12, 13, 14, 15, 17, 18, 19, 20, 21; BlkwCE; CamDcSc; CamGLE; CasWL; CyAL 1; CyEd; DcBiPP; DcEnL; DcInv; DcIrB 78, 88; DcIrW 2; DcNaB; DcScB; Dis&D; EvLB; InSci; LarDcSc; LinLib S; LuthC 75; McGEWB; NewCBEL; OxCEng 85, 95; OxCIri; OxCMed 86; OxCPhil; RAdv 14, 13-5; REn; WhDW; WorAl; WorAlBi; WorInv; WorScD*

Boyle, T. Coraghessan
[Thomas John Boyle]
American. Author
Satiric fiction writer's work include *World's End,* 1987; *East Is East,* 1990.
b. Dec 2, 1948 in Peekskill, New York
Source: *BenetAL 91; BestSel 90-4; BioIn 15; ConAu 120; ConLC 36, 55, 90; ConNov 96; CurBio 91; CyWA 89; DcLB Y86B; DrAPF 80, 87; IntAu&W 93; MagSAmL; OxCAmL 95; RAdv 14; ScF&FL 92; ShSCr 16; WorAu 1980*

Boyle, Tony
[William Anthony Boyle]
American. Labor Union Official
Pres., UMW, 1963-72; convicted of 1969 murders of rival Joseph Yablonski and family.
b. Dec 1, 1904 in Bald Butte, Montana
Source: *BiDAmL; BiDAmLL; BioIn 9, 10, 11, 12; FacFETw; NewYTBE 72; NewYTBS 85; PolProf J; WhAm 8; WhoSSW 73*

Boylston, Helen Dore
American. Author
Used experience as nurse to write *Sue Barton* novels for girls, 1936-52.
b. Apr 4, 1895 in Portsmouth, New Hampshire
d. Sep 30, 1984 in Trumbull, Connecticut
Source: *AmWomWr; AuBYP 2; BioIn 13, 14, 15, 19; ChlBkCr; ConAu 21NR, 73, 113; CurBio 42, 84, 84N; FemiCLE; InWom, SUP; JBA 51; MajAI; NewYTBS 84; OxCChiL; SmATA 23; TwCChW 78, 83, 89, 95; WhoChL; WrDr 80, 82, 84*

Boylston, Zabdiel
American. Physician
Despite objections, he was the first to use the smallpox vaccination in the American colonies.
b. Mar 9, 1676 in Muddy River, Massachusetts
d. Mar 1, 1766 in Muddy River, Massachusetts
Source: *AmWrBE; BioIn 11; DcAmB; EncCRAm; McGEWB; NatCAB 7; OxCAmH; OxCMed 86; WebAB 79; WhAm HS*

Boyz II Men
American. Music Group
Grammy award winning rhythm and blues group from Pittsburg; hit song "It's So Hard to Say Goodbye to Yesterday."
Source: *BioIn 9; ConMus 15; EncRkSt; News 95, 95-1*

Bozeman, John M
American. Pioneer
Blazed trail across Rockies, Bozeman Pass, 1863; founded town of Bozeman, MT.
b. 1835 in Georgia
d. Apr 20, 1867 in Yellowstone National Park,Montana
Source: *AmBi; WebAB 74; WhAm HS*

Brabham, Jack
[John Arthur Brabham]
Australian. Auto Racer
Won Grand Prix races, 1959, 1960, 1966.
b. Apr 2, 1926 in Sydney, Australia
Source: *BioIn 7, 8, 9, 10, 12, 15; FarE&A 81; IntWW 76, 77, 78, 79, 80, 81, 82, 83, 89, 91, 93; Who 74, 82, 83, 85, 88, 92, 94; WorAl; WorAlBi*

Brace, Charles Loring
American. Social Reformer
Cofounded Children's Aid Society, 1853; concerned himself with immigration problems, stressed self-reliance.
b. Jun 19, 1826 in Litchfield, Connecticut
d. Aug 11, 1890 in Campfer, Switzerland
Source: *Alli, SUP; AmAu&B; AmBi; AmRef; AmRef&R; AmSocL; ApCAB; BbD; BiD&SB; BiDSocW; BioIn 6, 15, 19, 21; CyAL 2; DcAmAu; DcAmB; DcAmC; DcAmImH; DcBiPP; DcEnL; DcNAA; Drake; NatCAB 10; TwCBDA; WebAB 74, 79; WhAm HS*

Brace, Gerald Warner
American. Author, Educator
Described New England life in his 11 novels including *Bell's Landing*, 1955.
b. Sep 23, 1901 in Islip, New York
d. Jul 20, 1978 in Blue Hill, Maine
Source: *AmAu&B; AmNov; Au&Wr 71; BenetAL 91; BioIn 1, 2, 4, 11; ConAu 13R, 81; CurBio 47, 78, 78N; DrAS 74E, 78E; NewYTBS 78; OxCAmL 65, 83, 95; REnAL; TwCA SUP; WhAm 7; WhoAm 74, 76, 78; WrDr 76*

Bracegirdle, Anne
English. Actor
Starred in Congreve's comedies, which were written for her, 1690s; favorite of Colley Cibber.
b. 1674?
d. Sep 15, 1748 in London, England
Source: *CnThe; EncWL; EncWT; Ent; NewC; NewCol 75; OxCThe 67; PlP&P; REn*

Braceland, Francis J(ames)
American. Psychiatrist, Editor
With Institute of Living, 1951-68; editor, *American Journal of Psychiatry*, 1965-78.
b. Jul 22, 1900 in Philadelphia, Pennsylvania
d. Feb 23, 1985 in Sarasota, Florida
Source: *AmCath 80; AmMWSc 73P, 76P, 79; BiDrACP 79; BiDrAPA 77; BioIn 11, 14, 15; ConAu 115; WhAm 9; WhoAm 74, 76, 78, 80, 82*

Bracey, John H(enry Jr.)
American. Author
Subject of books, articles is Afro-American culture.
b. Jul 17, 1941 in Chicago, Illinois
Source: *ConAu 29R; LivgBAA; WhoBlA 85*

Brach, Emil J
American. Candy Manufacturer
Opened candy store/factory in Chicago, 1904.
b. 1859 in Schoenwald, Germany
d. Oct 29, 1947 in Chicago, Illinois
Source: *Entr; WhAm 2*

Bracken, Brendan Rendall, Viscount
Irish. Publisher
Churchill's Parliamentary private secretary; chm., *Financial Times; Financial News.*
b. Feb 15, 1901 in Tipperary, Ireland
d. Aug 8, 1958 in London, England
Source: *CurBio 41, 58; DcIrB 78, 88; DcNaB 1951; GrBr; ObitOF 79; WhE&EA; WhWW-II*

Bracken, Eddie
[Edward Vincent Bracken]
American. Actor
Stage, film performer, 1940s-60s; started career in *Our Gang* series, 1920s.
b. Feb 7, 1920 in New York, New York
Source: *BiE&WWA; BioIn 2, 4, 10, 11, 18; BioNews 74; BusPN; ConTFT 3; CurBio 44; EncAFC; FilmEn; FilmgC; ForYSC; HalFC 80, 84, 88; HolP 40; IntMPA 75, 76, 77, 78, 79, 80, 81, 82, 84, 86, 88, 92, 94, 96; ItaFilm; LegTOT; MotPP; MovMk; NewYTBE 71; NotNAT; QDrFCA 92; RadStar; WhoAm 74, 76, 78, 80, 82, 84, 86, 88, 90, 92, 94, 95, 96, 97; WhoCom; WhoEnt 92; WhoHol A; WhoThe 72, 77, 81; WorAl; WorAlBi*

Brackett, Charles
American. Producer
Produced five Oscar-winners; often collaborated with Billy Wilder.
b. Nov 26, 1892 in Saratoga Springs, New York
d. Mar 9, 1969 in Beverly Hills, California
Source: *AmAu&B; BenetAL 91; BioIn 2, 8, 13, 14; CmMov; ConAu 113; CurBio 51; DcLB 26; EncAFC; FilmEn; FilmgC; HalFC 80, 84, 88; IntDcF 1-4, 2-4; NotNAT B; REnAL; WhNAA; WorEFlm*

Brackman, Robert
American. Artist
Still life painter, portraitist of notable Americans including the Rockefellers.
b. Sep 25, 1898 in Odessa, Russia
d. Jul 16, 1980 in New London, Connecticut
Source: *AnObit 1980; BioIn 1, 2, 3, 6, 10, 12; CurBio 53, 80, 80N; DcCAA 71, 77, 88; McGDA; WhAmArt 85; WhoAm 80; WhoAmA 73, 76, 78, 80, 82N, 84N, 86N, 89N, 91N, 93N; WhoE 74*

Bracton, Henry de
English. Judge
Wrote *De Legibus et Consuetudinibus Angliae*, first systematic treatise about laws of England.
d. 1268
Source: *Alli; BioIn 3, 6; BritAu; Chambr 1; DcBiPP; DcCathB; DcEnL; DcNaB; LinLib L, S; NewC; NewCBEL; NewCol 75; OxCEng 67, 85, 95; OxCLaw; WhDW*

Bradbury, Malcolm Stanley
English. Author
Novels reflect changes in university life in past 30 years: *Eating People is Wrong*, 1959, *The History of Man*, 1975.
b. Sep 7, 1932 in Sheffield, England
Source: *Au&Wr 71; BlueB 76; ConAu 1NR, 1R; ConLC 32; ConNov 86; ConPo 70; DcLB 14; IntAu&W 82; IntWW 83; IntWWP 82; ModBrL; NewC; Novels; Who 85, 90; WhoWor 87; WrDr 86*

Bradbury, Ray Douglas
American. Author
Has written over 1,000 science fiction stories, including *The Martian Chronicles*, 1950, *Fahrenheit 451*, 1954.
b. Aug 22, 1920 in Waukegan, Illinois
Source: *AmAu&B; Au&Wr 71; AuNews 1, 2; BioNews 74; CasWL; CmMov; CnMWL; ConAu 1R, 2NR; ConLC 15; ConNov 76; CurBio 53, 82; FilmgC; HalFC 84; LngCTC; OxCAmL 83; PenC AM; REn; REnAL; SmATA 11; TwCWr; WebAB 74; Who 85; WhoAm 86; WhoWor 74; WorEFlm; WrDr 86*

Braddock, Edward
English. Military Leader
Commanded British in French and Indian War, 1755; killed in expedition on Ft. Duquesne.
b. 1695 in Perthshire, Scotland
d. Jul 13, 1755 in Fort Duquesne, Pennsylvania
Source: *AmBi; ApCAB; BioIn 3, 4, 11, 15; DcAmB; DcNaB; Drake; EncAR; EncCRAm; HarEnMi; HarEnUS; LinLib S; MacDCB 78; McGEWB; NatCAB 2; OxCAmH; OxCCan; REn; TwCBDA; WhAm HS; WhNaAH; WorAl; WorAlBi*

Braddock, Jim
[James J Braddock]
"Cinderella Man"
American. Boxer
Defeated Max Baer for heavyweight crown in boxing's greatest upset, 1935; Joe Louis defeated him to become heavyweight champ, 1937.
b. Dec 6, 1905 in New York, New York
d. Nov 29, 1974 in North Bergen, New Jersey
Source: *BioNews 75; LegTOT; NewYTBS 74; WhoBox 74*

Brademas, John
American. Politician, University Administrator
US representative, 1959-78; pres., NYU, 1981-92.
b. Mar 2, 1927 in Mishawaka, Indiana
Source: *AlmAP 78; WhoMW 74, 76, 78, 80; WhoWor 78, 80, 84, 87, 89, 91; WorAl; WorAlBi*

Braden, Spruille
American. Diplomat
Asst. secretary of State under Truman, 1945.
b. Mar 13, 1894 in Elkhorn, Montana
d. Jan 10, 1978 in Los Angeles, California
Source: *BioIn 1, 7, 9, 11, 13, 14, 16; BlueB 76; ConAu 115; CurBio 45, 78, 78N; DcAmB S10; DcAmDH 80, 89; EncLatA; NewYTBS 78; PolProf E, T; WhAm 7; WhoAm 74, 76, 78; WhoWor 74, 76*

Bradford, Barbara Taylor
English. Author
Popular works include *A Woman of Substance,* 1979; *Hold the Dream,* 1985, both of which became TV miniseries.
b. 1933 in Leeds, England
Source: *ArtclWW 2; BestSel 89-1; BioIn 12, 17, 18; BlmGWL; ConAu 32NR, 89; ConPopW; CurBio 91; EncTwCJ; ForWC 70; IntWW 89, 91, 93; LegTOT; MajTwCW; NewYTBS 79; SmATA 66; TwCRHW 90, 94; WhoAm 78, 80, 82, 84, 86, 88; WhoAmW 77, 79, 81, 83, 85, 87, 89; WhoE 83, 85, 86, 89; WorAlBi; WrDr 90, 92, 94, 96*

Bradford, Gamaliel
American. Author
Known for psychological biographies of literary, historical figures: *Damaged Souls,* 1923.
b. Oct 9, 1863 in Boston, Massachusetts
d. Apr 11, 1932
Source: *AmAu&B; AmBi; AmLY; AnMV 1926; Benet 87; BenetAL 91; BioIn 1, 3, 5, 8, 12, 13; CasWL; ChhPo S3; CnDAL; ConAmA; ConAmL; DcAmB S1; DcLB 17; DcLEL; DcNAA; LinLib L, S; NatCAB 23; OxCAmH; OxCAmL 65, 83, 95; PeoHis; REn; REnAL; TwCA, SUP; TwCLC 36; WhAm 1; WhLit; WhNAA*

Bradford, Roark Whitney Wickliffe
American. Author, Dramatist
Wrote about blacks, Bible; play *Green Pastures,* 1940, was dramatization of *John Henry,* 1931.
b. Aug 21, 1896 in Lauderdale County, Tennessee
d. Nov 13, 1948 in New Orleans, Louisiana
Source: *AmAu&B; ASCAP 66; CnDAL; DcAmB S4; DcNAA; LngCTC; ObitOF 79; OxCAmL 65; REn; REnAL; TwCA, SUP; WhAm 2*

Bradford, William
American. Colonial Figure
Landed at Plymouth Rock, Dec, 1620; reelected governor of Plymouth Colony 30 times.
b. 1590 in Austerfield, England
d. May 9, 1657 in Plymouth, Massachusetts
Source: *Alli; AmAu; AmAu&B; AmBi; AmPolLe; AmWrBE; ApCAB; BbD; Benet 87, 96; BenetAL 91; BiD&SB; BiDLA; BiDrACR; BioIn 1, 2, 3, 4, 5, 6, 7, 8, 10, 11; CamGEL; CamGLE; CamHAL; CasWL; CyAL 1; DcAmAu; DcAmB; DcAmReB 1, 2; DcLB 24, 30; DcLEL; DcNAA; DcNaB; EncAAH; EncAB-H 1974, 1996; EncARH; EncCRAm; EvLB; HisDBrE; HisWorL; LegTOT; LinLib L, S; LuthC 75; McGEWB; MouLC 1; NewCBEL; OxCAmH; OxCAmL 65, 83, 95; PenC AM; RAdv 14; RComAH; REn; REnAL; TwCBDA; WebAB 74, 79; WebE&AL; WhAm HS; WhAmP; WhDW; WhNaAH; WorAl; WorAlBi; WrCNE*

Bradford, William
American. Artist
Marine painter; first American to portray Arctic regions.
b. Apr 30, 1823 in Fairhaven, Massachusetts
d. Apr 25, 1892 in New York, New York
Source: *AmBi; ArtsAmW 1; BioIn 13, 17; BriEAA; DcAmArt; DcAmB; DcCanB 12; Drake; FolkA 87; NewYHSD; TwCBDA; WhAm HS*

Bradham, Caleb D
American. Inventor
Invented Pepsi-Cola, 1890s to rival Coke.

Bradlee, Ben(jamin Crowninshield)
American. Journalist, Editor
VP, exec. editor, *Washington Post,* 1968-91.
b. Aug 26, 1921 in Boston, Massachusetts
Source: *AuNews 2; BioIn 3, 10, 11, 12, 13; CelR 90; ConAu 61; EncTwCJ; IntWW 93; LegTOT; WhoAm 74, 76, 78, 80, 82, 84, 86, 88, 90, 92, 94, 95, 96, 97; WhoE 83, 85, 86, 89, 91, 93, 95, 97; WhoSSW 73, 82; WhoUSWr 88; WhoWor 74, 76; WhoWrEP 89, 92, 95; WrDr 80, 82, 84, 86, 88, 90, 92, 94, 96*

Bradley, Andrew Cecil
English. Critic
Accepted chair of poetry at Oxford, 1901; wrote masterpiece *Shakespearean Tragedy,* 1904.
b. Mar 26, 1851 in Cheltenham, England
d. Sep 2, 1935 in London, England
Source: *BioIn 2, 9, 14; Chambr 3; DcLEL; DcNaB 1931; EvLB; GrBr; LngCTC; NewC; NewCBEL; OxCEng 67; PenC ENG; TwCA, SUP; WhLit*

Bradley, Bill
[William Warren Bradley]
American. Basketball Player, Politician
Forward, NY Knicks, 1967-77; Hall of Fame, 1982; Dem. senator from NJ, 1979-96.
b. Jul 28, 1943 in Crystal City, Missouri
Source: *AlmAP 80, 82, 84, 88, 92, 96; BasBi; BiDAmSp BK; BiDrUSC 89; BioIn 6, 7, 8, 9, 10, 11, 12, 13; CelR, 90; CngDr 79, 81, 83, 85, 87, 89, 91, 93, 95; ConAu 55NR, 101; ConHero 1; CurBio 65, 82; IntWW 89, 91, 93; LegTOT; NewYTBS 83; PolsAm 84; WhoAm 80, 82, 84, 86, 88, 90, 92, 94, 95, 96, 97; WhoAmL 94; WhoAmP 79, 81, 83, 85, 87, 89, 91, 93, 95; WhoBbl 73; WhoE 79, 81, 83, 85, 86, 89, 91, 93, 95, 97; WhoSpor; WhoWor 80, 82, 84, 87, 89, 91, 93, 95, 96, 97; WorAl; WorAlBi*

Bradley, David Henry, Jr.
American. Author
Relates tragedy of black history in novel *Chaneysville Incident,* 1981.
b. Sep 7, 1950 in Bedford, Pennsylvania
Source: *BioIn 10, 11; ConAu 104; InB&W 85; NewYTBS 81; SelBAAf; WhoAfA 96; WhoAm 92, 94; WhoBlA 77, 80, 85, 88, 90, 92, 94; WhoUSWr 88; WhoWrEP 89, 92, 95*

Bradley, Ed(ward R.)
American. Broadcast Journalist
Correspondent, "60 Minutes," replacing Dan Rather, 1981—; with CBS since 1971.
b. Jun 22, 1941 in Philadelphia, Pennsylvania
Source: *AfrAmAl 6; BlkWr 1; CelR 90; ConAu 108, 113; ConBlB 2; CurBio 88; DcTwCCu 5; InB&W 85; IntMPA 92, 94, 96; LegTOT; LesBEnT; SchCGBL; WhoAfA 96; WhoAm 84, 86, 88, 90, 92, 94, 95, 96, 97; WhoBlA 94; WhoE 91*

Bradley, Francis Herbert
English. Philosopher
Wrote *Appearance and Reality,* 1893; attacked utilitarianism.
b. Jan 30, 1846 in Clapham, England
d. Sep 18, 1924 in Oxford, England
Source: *Alli SUP; BioIn 2, 5, 18; BritAu 19; CamGEL; CasWL; Chambr 3; DcEuL; DcLEL; DcNaB, 1922; EvLB; IlEncMy; LngCTC; LuthC 75; McGEWB;*

NewC; NewCBEL; NewCol 75; OxCEng 67; OxCPhil; RAdv 14; WhDW; WhLit

Bradley, Henry
English. Lexicographer
Editor, *Oxford English Dictionary*, 1915.
b. Dec 3, 1845 in Manchester, England
d. May 23, 1923 in Oxford, England
Source: *Alli, SUP; BioIn 10; DcLEL; DcNaB 1922; EvLB; LngCTC; NewC; NewCBEL; OxCEng 67, 85, 95; WhLit*

Bradley, James
English. Astronomer
First to calculate speed of light, discovered "nutation," 1728.
b. Mar 1693 in Shireborn, England
d. Jul 13, 1762 in Chalford, England
Source: *Alli; AsBiEn; BiAUS; BiESc; BioIn 2, 6, 14; BlkwCE; CamDcSc; DcBiPP; DcNaB; DcScB; EncEnl; InSci; LarDcSc; LinLib S; McGEWB; NewCBEL; WhDW; WorAl; WorAlBi; WorScD*

Bradley, Joseph P
American. Supreme Court Justice
Appointed to Supreme Court by Grant, 1870.
b. Mar 14, 1813 in Berne, New York
d. Jan 22, 1892 in Washington, District of Columbia
Source: *ApCAB; BiAUS; DcAmB; DcNAA; Drake; HarEnUS; TwCBDA; WebAB 74; WhAm HS*

Bradley, Milton
American. Manufacturer, Publisher
First game, "The Checkered Game of Life," led to success of Milton Bradley Co.
b. Nov 8, 1836 in Vienna, Maine
d. May 30, 1911 in Springfield, Massachusetts
Source: *AmAu&B; BiDAmBL 83; BioIn 5; DcAmB; DcNAA; Entr; NatCAB 11; WebAB 74, 79; WhAm 1*

Bradley, Omar Nelson
"The GI's General"
American. Army Officer
Last five-star general; first permanent chm., Joint Chiefs of Staff, 1949-53.
b. Feb 12, 1893 in Clark, Missouri
d. Apr 8, 1981 in New York, New York
Source: *AnObit 1981; BiDWWGF; BioIn 1, 2, 3, 4, 6, 8, 9, 10, 11, 12, 13, 15, 19, 20; CmdGen 1991; ConAu 103; CurBio 43, 81; DcAmMiB; DcTwHis; EncAB-H 1974, 1996; FacFETw; HarEnMi; HisEWW; IntWW 74, 75, 76, 77, 78, 79, 80, 81; LinLib S; McGEWB; NewYTBS 81; OxCAmH; PseudN 82; St&PR 75; WebAB 74, 79; WebAMB; WhAm 7; Who 74; WhoAm 74, 76, 78, 80; WhoWor 74, 78; WhWW-II; WorAl; WorDWW*

Bradley, Pat(ricia Ellen)
American. Golfer
Turned pro, 1974; won US Women's Open, 1981; first woman golfer to win $2 million; LPGA Hall of Fame, 1992.
b. Mar 24, 1951 in Westford, Massachusetts
Source: *BioIn 11; CurBio 94; WhoAm 78, 80, 82, 84, 86, 88, 94, 95, 96, 97; WhoAmW 93, 97; WhoGolf; WhoIntG; WhoSpor; WorAlBi*

Bradley, Tom
[Thomas J Bradley]
"Long Tom"
American. Politician
First black mayor of predominantly white city, Los Angeles, 1973-92; served an unprecedented five terms.
b. Dec 29, 1917 in Calvert, Texas
Source: *AfrAmBi 1; BioIn 16, 17, 18; CelR 90; CopCroC; CurBio 73, 92; EncWB; InB&W 80, 85; LegTOT; NewYTBE 73; NewYTBS 83, 84; WhoAfA 96; WhoAm 86; WhoAmP 85; WhoBlA 75, 77, 85; WhoGov 77*

Bradley, Will
[Wilbur Schwichtenberg]
American. Jazz Musician, Bandleader
Trombonist; led swing band that featured boogie woogie, 1940s.
b. Jul 12, 1912 in Newton, New Jersey
d. Jul 15, 1989 in Flemington, New Jersey
Source: *AllMusG; BgBands 74; BiDJaz; BioIn 9, 12, 16; CmpEPM; NewGrDJ 88, 94; OxCPMus; PenEncP; WhoJazz 72*

Bradshaw, George
English. Printer
Originated *Bradshaw's Railway Guide*, 1841.
b. 1801
d. 1853
Source: *BioIn 1; DcBiPP; DcNaB; NewC*

Bradshaw, John Elliot
American. Lecturer, Author, Philosopher
Author of *Homecoming: Reclaiming and Championing Your Inner Child*, 1990; conducts seminars, sells tapes on "healing the inner child."
b. Jun 29, 1933 in Houston, Texas
Source: *News 92, 92-1*

Bradshaw, Terry Paxton
American. Football Player, Sportscaster
Quarterback, Pittsburgh, 1970-84; won four Super Bowls; sportscaster *NFL To day*, 1987-94; sportscaster on *Fox Sports*, 1995—.
b. Sep 2, 1948 in Shreveport, Louisiana
Source: *BiDAmSp FB; BioIn 10, 11, 12; ConAu 111; CurBio 79; NewYTBS 75; WhoAm 86; WhoFtbl 74*

Bradstreet, Anne
American. Poet
Verse, published 1650, considered first significant literary work in Colonial America.
b. 1612? in Northampton, England
d. Sep 16, 1672 in Andover, Massachusetts
Source: *Alli; AmAu; AmAu&B; AmBi; AmWrBE; AmWr S1; ApCAB; ArtclWW 2; Benet 87, 96; BenetAL 91; BiD&SB; BioAmW; BioIn 1, 2, 4, 7, 8, 9, 10, 11, 12, 13, 14, 16, 17, 20, 21; CamGEL; CamGLE; CamHAL; CasWL; ChhPo, S2; CnDAL; CnE&AP; ColARen; ContDcW 89; CyAL 1; DcAmAu; DcAmB; DcEnL; DcLB 24; DcLEL; DcNAA; DcNaB; Drake; EncAB-H 1996; EvLB; FemiCLE; GrLiveH; GrWomW; GrWrEL P; HanAmWH; IntDcWB; InWom; LegTOT; LibW; LinLib L, S; LitC 4, 30; MagSAmL; NewCBEL; OxCAmL 65, 83; OxCEng 67, 85, 95; OxCWoWr 95; PenBWP; PenC AM; PeoHis; PoeCrit 10; RAdv 1, 14, 13-1; REn; REnAL; RfGAmL 87, 94; RGFAP; WebAB 79; WebE&AL; WhAm HS; WhDW; WomFir; WorAlBi; WrCNE*

Brady, Alice
American. Actor
Won Oscar for *In Old Chicago*, 1938.
b. Nov 2, 1893 in New York, New York
d. Oct 28, 1939 in New York, New York
Source: *AmBi; DcAmB S2; Film 1, 2; FilmgC; ForYSC; LibW; MotPP; MovMk; NotAW; OxCThe 67; ThFT; TwYS; Vers A; WebAB 74, 79; WhAm 1; WhoHol A; WhScrn 74*

Brady, Diamond Jim
[James Buchanan Brady]
American. Financier
Famous for great weight, extravagant lifestyle; jewelry valued at $2 million.
b. Aug 12, 1856 in New York, New York
d. Apr 13, 1917 in Atlantic City, New Jersey
Source: *AmBi; BiDAmBL 83; BioIn 3, 7, 9, 15, 18, 21; LegTOT; NatCAB 19; OxCAmH; WebAB 74, 79; WhAm 4, HSA; WorAl*

Brady, James Scott
"The Bear"
American. Presidential Aide
Reagan Presidential Press Secretary, 1981-89; shot during Reagan assassination attempt, 1981; handgun control advocate; awarded Presidential Medal of Freedom, 1996.
b. Aug 29, 1940 in Centralia, Illinois
Source: *BioIn 12; NewYTBS 81; PseudN 82*

Brady, James Winston
American. Editor, Publisher
Publisher, *Women's Wear Daily*, 1964-71; editor, *Harper's Bazaar*, 1971-72; news commentator, WCBS-TV, New York, 1981-87; editor-at-large, *Advertising Age*, 1977—.
b. Nov 15, 1928 in New York, New York
Source: *BiDAmNC; BiDConC; ConAu 21NR, 101; IntAu&W 89, 91, 93; WhoAm 78, 84, 86, 88, 90, 92, 94, 95, 96; WhoE 74, 75, 77; WhoFI 74*

Brady, Joan
American. Author
Won 1994 Whitbread Award for *Theory of War,* 1993.
b. Dec 4, 1939 in San Francisco, California
Source: *ConAu 141; ConLC 86; RGTwCWr; WhoWor 95, 96, 97; WrDr 96*

Brady, Mathew B
"Mr. Lincoln's Cameraman"
American. Photographer
Accompanied Union army, 1861-65; photographed all aspects of Civil War.
b. Jan 15, 1823? in Warren County, New York
d. Jan 15, 1896 in New York, New York
Source: *AmAu&B; AmBi; BriEAA; DcAmB; EncAB-H 1974; OxCAmL 65; REn; REnAL; WebAB 74, 79; WhAm HS*

Brady, Nicholas Frederick
American. Government Official
Succeeded James Brady as Treasury secretary, 1988-93.
b. Apr 11, 1930 in New York, New York
Source: *BiDrUSC 89; BiDrUSE 89; BioIn 13; NewYTBS 87; Who 90, 92, 94; WhoAm 76, 78, 82, 84, 86, 88, 90, 92, 94, 95, 96; WhoAmP 89, 91, 93, 95; WhoE 86, 89, 91, 93; WhoFI 74, 75, 89, 92; WhoWor 91, 93*

Brady, Pat
[Sons of the Pioneers; Robert Patrick Brady]
American. Actor, Singer
Played Roy Rogers sidekick in films, TV.
b. Dec 31, 1914 in Toledo, Ohio
d. Feb 27, 1972 in Green Mountain Falls, Colorado
Source: *BiDAmM; BioIn 9; EncAFC; FilmEn; NewYTBE 72; ObitOF 79; WhoHol B; WhScrn 77, 83*

Brady, Paul Joseph
Irish. Singer, Songwriter
Famous traditional Irish folk singer until he changed to rock music in 1981; album *Trick or Treat,* 1991.
b. May 19, 1947 in Tyrone, Ireland
Source: *ConMus 8; PenEncP*

Brady, Sarah Jane
"Raccoon"
American. Social Reformer
Began advocating for gun control after her husband, Presidential Press Secretary, James Brady, was shot during Reagan assassination attempt, 1981.
b. Feb 6, 1942 in Missouri
Source: *BioIn 14, 15, 16; CurBio 96; News 91; NewYTBS 90*

Brady, Scott
[Gerard Kenneth Tierney]
American. Actor
Played in TV series "Shotgun Slade," 1959-62.
b. Sep 13, 1924 in New York, New York
d. Apr 17, 1985 in Woodland Hills, California
Source: *BioIn 5, 10, 11, 14, 15, 17; ConTFT 2; FilmEn; FilmgC; ForYSC; GangFlm; HalFC 80, 84, 88; HolP 40; IntMPA 75, 76, 77, 78, 79, 80, 81, 82, 84; MotPP; NewYTBS 85; WhAm 8; WhoAm 74, 76, 78, 80, 82, 84; WhoHol A; WhoHrs 80*

Brady, William Aloysius
American. Actor, Producer
Built Playhouse Theatre, 1910; Fourty-eighth Street Theatre, 1912, NYC; produced over 250 plays.
b. Jun 19, 1863 in San Francisco, California
d. Jan 6, 1950 in New York, New York
Source: *BioIn 2, 12; CamGWoT; DcAmB S4; ObitOF 79; OxCThe 67, 83; WebAB 74, 79; WhAm 2*

Braestrup, Carl Bjorn
American. Scientist, Inventor
Invented the Theratron, cobalt radiation machine used for cancer treatment; one of first to warn of danger of radiation.
b. Apr 13, 1897 in Copenhagen, Denmark
d. Aug 8, 1982 in Middletown, Connecticut
Source: *AmMWSc 76P, 79, 82; AnObit 1982; BioIn 13; ConAu 107; NewYTBS 82*

Braff, Ruby
American. Jazz Musician
Trumpeter of Dixieland, mainstream jazz, 1940s-50s.
b. Mar 16, 1927 in Boston, Massachusetts
Source: *AllMusG; BioIn 10, 11; CmpEPM; EncJzS; IlEncJ; MusMk; NewGrDJ 88, 94; PenEncP*

Braga, Sonia
"Brazilian Bombshell"
Brazilian. Actor
Films include *The Milagro Beanfield War,* 1988.
b. 1951?
Source: *BioIn 12, 13; ConTFT 7; IntMPA 92; LegTOT*

Bragg, Billy
[Steven William Bragg]
English. Singer, Songwriter
Sings combination of folk and punk rock with political lyrics; album *Don't Try This at Home,* 1991; with hit single "Sexuality"; co-founded activist group Red Wedge.
b. Dec 20, 1957 in London, England
Source: *BioIn 14, 16; ConMus 7; EncRk 88; EncRkSt; PenEncP*

Bragg, Braxton
American. Army Officer
Commander-in-chief, Confederate Army, 1864-65.
b. Mar 22, 1817 in Warrenton, North Carolina
d. Sep 27, 1876 in Galveston, Texas
Source: *AmBi; ApCAB; BiDConf; BioIn 1, 3, 5, 7, 8, 9, 17; CivWDc; DcAmB; DcAmMiB; DcNCBi 1; Drake; EncSoH; HarEnMi; HarEnUS; LegTOT; LinLib S; NatCAB 11; OxCAmH; TwCBDA; WebAB 74, 79; WebAMB; WhAm HS; WhCiWar; WhFla; WhoMilH 76; WorAl; WorAlBi*

Bragg, Don(ald)
"Tarzan"
American. Track Athlete
Pole vaulter, one of last to use metal pole; won gold medal, 1960 Olympics.
b. May 15, 1935 in Penns Grove, New Jersey
Source: *BioIn 6, 9, 10, 12; What 4; WhoTr&F 73*

Bragg, Mabel Caroline
American. Children's Author
Wrote *The Little Engine That Could,* 1930; numerous children's picture anthologies.
b. Sep 15, 1870 in Milford, Massachusetts
d. Apr 25, 1945 in Massachusetts
Source: *BioIn 13; FourBJA; InWom; SmATA 24*

Bragg, Melvyn
English. Author
Wrote film script for *Jesus Christ Superstar,* 1973.
b. Oct 6, 1939 in Carlisle, England
Source: *Benet 87, 96; BestSel 89-3; BioIn 11, 13, 14, 16, 17; ConAu 10NR, 48NR, 57; ConLC 10; ConNov 72, 76, 82, 86, 91, 96; ConTFT 11; DcLB 14; DcLEL 1940; IntAu&W 76, 77, 82, 89; IntWW 89, 91, 93; Novels; OxCEng 85, 95; RAdv 13-1; RGTwCWr; TwCRHW 94; Who 74, 82, 83, 85, 88, 90, 92, 94; WorAu 1970; WrDr 76, 80, 82, 84, 86, 88, 90, 92, 94, 96*

Bragg, William Henry, Sir
English. Physicist
With son, founded modern science of crystallography; won Nobel Prize, 1915.
b. Jul 2, 1862 in Westward, England
d. Mar 12, 1942 in London, England
Source: *AsBiEn; BiESc; BioIn 2, 3, 4, 5, 6, 11, 12, 13, 14, 15, 20; CamDcSc; ConAu 123; DcLEL; DcNaB 1941; DcScB; Dis&D; FacFETw; GrBr; InSci; LarDcSc; McGEWB; NewCBEL; NotTwCS; ObitOF 79; WhDW; WhLit; WhoNob, 90, 95; WorAl; WorInv*

Bragg, William Lawrence, Sir
English. Physicist
Youngest man ever to win Nobel Prize, 1915, for research in X-rays.
b. Mar 31, 1890 in Adelaide, Australia

d. Jul 1, 1971 in London, England
Source: *AsBiEn; BiESc; BioIn 1, 14, 15, 20; ConAu 115; DcScB, S1; FacFETw; GrBr; InSci; LinLib S; NotTwCS; WhE&EA; WhLit; WhoNob, 90, 95; WorAl; WorInv*

Brahe, Tycho
Danish. Astronomer
Considered the earth to be motionless; discovered "new star" in Cassiopeia, 1572; wrote many treatises.
b. Dec 14, 1546 in Skane, Denmark
d. Oct 24, 1601 in Prague, Bohemia
Source: *AsBiEn; AstEnc; BiESc; BioIn 11, 12, 13, 14, 16, 17, 19, 20; CamDcSc; DcBiPP; DcScB; Dis&D; InSci; LarDcSc; LegTOT; LinLib S; McGEWB; RAdv 14, 13-5; REn; WhDW; WorAl; WorAlBi; WorScD*

Brahms, Johannes
German. Composer, Pianist
Combined romanticism, classicism in works; best known "Brahms' Lullaby" officially called Opus 49, no. 4.
b. May 7, 1833 in Hamburg, Germany
d. Apr 3, 1897 in Vienna, Austria
Source: *AtlBL; Baker 78, 84, 92; Benet 87, 96; BioIn 1, 2, 3, 4, 5, 6, 7, 8, 9, 10, 11, 12, 13, 14, 15, 16, 17, 19, 20; BriBkM 80; CelCen; CmpBCM; CnOxB; DancEn 78; DcArts; DcCom 77; DcCom&M 79; Dis&D; GrComp; LegTOT; LinLib S; LuthC 75; McGEWB; MusMk; NewAmDM; NewC; NewGrDM 80; NewOxM; OxCEng 85, 95; OxCGer 76, 86; OxCMus; PenDiMP A; RAdv 14, 13-3; REn; WhDW; WorAl; WorAlBi*

Braid, James
"Big Jim"; "Great Triumvirate"
Scottish. Golfer
With JH Taylor, Harry Vardon, dominated game, late 19th, early 20th c; first to win British Open five times.
b. Feb 6, 1870 in Earlsferry Fife, Scotland
d. Nov 27, 1950 in London, England
Source: *BioIn 2, 3, 5, 13; DcNaB 1941; ObitOF 79; WhoGolf*

Braille, Louis
French. Teacher
Blinded at age 3; devised system of raised-point writing.
b. Jan 4, 1809 in Coupvray, France
d. Mar 28, 1852
Source: *BioIn 1, 2, 3, 4, 5, 6, 7, 8, 9, 11, 12, 14, 15, 16, 17, 20; DcCathB; InSci; LegTOT; LinLib L, S; OxCEng 85, 95; OxCFr; REn; WhDW; WorAl; WorAlBi; WorInv*

Brailowsky, Alexander
American. Pianist
Performed complete cycle of Chopin's works, 1930s.
b. Feb 16, 1896 in Kiev, Russia
d. Apr 25, 1976 in New York, New York
Source: *Baker 78, 84, 92; BioIn 1, 2, 4, 10, 11; BriBkM 80; CurBio 56, 76N; MusSN; NewGrDA 86; NewGrDM 80; NewYTBS 76; PenDiMP; WhAm 7; WhoAm 74, 76; WhoMus 72; WhoWor 74*

Brain, Aubrey
English. Musician
French horn player, who starred with BBC symphony orchestra.
b. Jul 12, 1893 in London, England
d. Sep 21, 1955 in London, England
Source: *Baker 78, 84; NewGrDM 80; PenDiMP*

Brain, Dennis
English. Musician
Renowned French horn player, son of Aubrey Brain; Britten's "Serenade" written for him.
b. May 17, 1921 in London, England
d. Sep 1, 1957 in Hatfield, England
Source: *Baker 78, 84, 92; BioIn 11, 20; BriBkM 80; DcNaB 1951; FacFETw; MusMk; NewAmDM; NewGrDM 80; ObitT 1951; PenDiMP; TwCBrS; WhDW*

Braine, John Gerard
English. Author
One of the "angry young men"; wrote *Room at the Top,* 1957; filmed, 1958.
b. Apr 13, 1922 in Yorkshire, England
d. Oct 28, 1986 in London, England
Source: *Au&Wr 71; Benet 96; BioIn 4, 5, 6, 8, 10, 13; CasWL; ConNov 86; DcLEL 1940; DcNaB 1986; IntAu&W 76, 77, 89, 91; IntWW 74, 75, 76, 77, 78, 79, 80, 81, 82, 83; LngCTC; NewC; OxCEng 85, 95; PenC ENG; RAdv 1; REn; RGTwCWr; TwCWr; WebE&AL; Who 85; WhoLib 54; WhoWor 74; WorAu 1950; WrDr 86*

Brainerd, David
American. Missionary
Preached to American Indians in Hudson Valley, 1744-47; his diary long considered a guide for missionaries.
b. Apr 20, 1718 in Haddam, Connecticut
d. Oct 9, 1747 in Northampton, Massachusetts
Source: *Alli; AmAu; AmAu&B; AmBi; AmWrBE; ApCAB; BenetAL 91; BioIn 1, 2, 3, 4, 6, 7, 8, 9, 10, 11, 16, 17, 19, 20; CyAL 1; DcAmAu; DcAmB; DcAmReB 1, 2; DcNAA; Drake; EncNAR; LuthC 75; NatCAB 2; NewCBEL; OxCAmL 65, 83, 95; PeoHis; REnAL; TwCBDA; WebBD 83; WhAm HS; WhNaAH*

Braithwaite, William Stanley Beaumont
American. Critic, Poet
Originated, edited *Anthology of American Verse; Year Book of American Poetry.*
b. Dec 6, 1878 in Boston, Massachusetts
d. Jun 8, 1962
Source: *AmAu&B; BioIn 1, 2, 4, 6, 7, 8; BlkAWP; ChhPo, S1, S2; DcAmNB; EncAACR; InB&W 80, 85; LinLib L; NegAl 83; OxCAmL 65, 83, 95; REn; REnAL; SouBlCW; TwCA, SUP; WhAm 4; WhoColR*

Brakhage, Stan
American. Author, Producer
Freelance, avant-garde, filmmaker since 1953.
b. Jan 14, 1933 in Kansas City, Missouri
Source: *AmAu&B; BioIn 10, 12; BlueB 76; ConAu 15NR, 41R; DcFM; FilmEn; HalFC 80, 84, 88; IntDcF 1-2, 2-2; MakMC; MugS; OxCFilm; RAdv 14; WhoAm 74, 76, 78; WhoHrs 80; WorEFlm; WorFDir 2; WrDr 76, 80, 82, 84, 86, 88, 90, 92*

Braly, Malcolm
American. Author
Wrote novel, screenplay *On the Yard;* filmed, 1979.
b. Jul 16, 1925 in Portland, Oregon
d. Apr 7, 1980 in Baltimore, Maryland
Source: *AuSpks; BioIn 8, 10, 11, 12; ConAu 12NR, 17R, 97; DrAPF 80; NewYTBS 80*

Bramah, Joseph
English. Inventor
Patented hydraulic press, called Bramah press, 1795.
b. Apr 13, 1748 in Stainborough, England
d. Dec 9, 1814 in London, England
Source: *BiESc; BioIn 2, 7, 8, 12, 14; DcNaB; EncEnl; InSci; WhDW; WorInv*

Bramante, Donata d'Agnolo
Italian. Architect
Known for Roman buildings in High Renaissance style; drafted original plans for St. Peters.
b. 1444 in Urbino, Italy
d. Mar 11, 1514 in Rome, Italy
Source: *MacEA; McGDA; McGEWB; NewCol 75; OxCArt; REn; WhoArch*

Brambell, Wilfrid
Irish. Actor
Star of British TV show "Steptoe and Son," which was basis for "Sanford and Son" in US.
b. Mar 22, 1912 in Dublin, Ireland
d. Jan 18, 1985 in London, England
Source: *AnObit 1985; BioIn 11; ConAu 113; FilmgC; HalFC 80, 84, 88; IntMPA 75, 76, 77, 78, 79, 80, 81, 82, 84; QDrFCA 92; WhoThe 72, 77, 81*

Brameld, Theodore
American. Educator
Professor of educational psychology, 1947-69; wrote *The Use of Explosive Ideas in Education,* 1965.
b. Jan 20, 1904 in Neillsville, Wisconsin
d. Oct 18, 1987 in Durham, North Carolina
Source: *BioIn 7, 8, 16; ConAu 17R, 123; CurBio 67, 88, 88N; DrAS 74P; LEduc 74; NewYTBS 87; WhAm 9; WhNAA; WhoAm 74, 76, 78, 80; WhoWor 74; WrDr 76, 80, 82, 84, 86, 88*

Branagh, Kenneth (Charles)
Irish. Actor, Director, Writer
Co-founder Renaissance Theater Co., 1987; directed, played two roles *Dead Again,* 1991; directed, starred in *Hamlet,* 1997.
b. Dec 10, 1960 in Belfast, Northern Ireland
Source: *BiDFilm 94; BioIn 15, 16; ConTFT 9; DcArts; EncEurC; HalFC 88; IntMPA 92, 94, 96; IntWW 89, 91, 93; LegTOT; MiSFD 9; News 92, 92-2; Who 90, 92, 94; WhoAm 92, 94, 95, 96, 97; WhoEnt 92; WhoWor 95, 96, 97*

Branca, Ralph Theodore Joseph
"Hawk"
American. Baseball Player
Pitcher, 1944-54; best known as pitcher who gave up home run to Bobby Thomson in playoff game, 1951.
b. Jan 6, 1926 in Mount Vernon, New York
Source: *WhoProB 73*

Branch, Anna Hempstead
American. Poet
Metaphysical verse collected in *Sonnets From a Lock Box,* 1929.
b. Mar 18, 1875 in New London, Connecticut
d. Sep 8, 1937 in New London, Connecticut
Source: *AmAu&B; AmWomPl; AmWomWr; BenetAL 91; BiDSocW; BioIn 5; ChhPo, S1; DcAmAu; DcNAA; InWom, SUP; NotAW; OxCAmL 65, 83, 95; REn; REnAL; TwCA, SUP; WhAm 1; WhNAA; WomWWA 14*

Branch, Cliff(ord)
American. Football Player
Wide receiver, Oakland/LA Raiders, 1972-85; led NFL in receiving TDs, 1974, 1976.
b. Aug 1, 1948 in Houston, Texas
Source: *BiDAmSp FB; NewYTBS 74; WhoAm 78, 80, 82, 84; WhoBlA 77, 80, 85, 90, 92, 94*

Brancusi, Constantin
Romanian. Sculptor
Leader in growth of modern sculpture famous for simple, abstract style: "Bird in Space," 1919.
b. Feb 21, 1876 in Pestisanigorj, Romania
d. Mar 16, 1957 in Paris, France
Source: *AtlBL; Benet 87, 96; BioIn 1, 2, 4, 5, 6, 7, 8, 10, 11, 12, 14, 15, 16, 17, 20, 21; ConArt 77, 83; CurBio 55, 57; DcArts; DcTwDes; FacFETw; IlEncMy; IntDcAA 90; LegTOT; MacBEP; MakMC; McGDA; McGEWB; OxCArt; OxCTwCA; OxDcArt; PhDcTCA 77; REn; WebBD 83; WhAm 3; WhDW; WorAl; WorAlBi; WorArt 1950*

Brand, Jack
Canadian. Soccer Player
Goalie, NY Cosmos, 1978-79; had career goals against average of under two per game.
b. Aug 4, 1953 in Braunschweig, Germany (West)
Source: *AmEnS; BioIn 12*

Brand, Max
[Frederick Schiller Faust]
"King of the Pulps"
American. Author, Journalist
Popular Westerns include *Destry Rides Again,* 1930; wrote Dr. Kildare films.
b. May 29, 1892 in Seattle, Washington
d. May 12, 1944, Italy
Source: *AmAu&B; BioIn 14, 15, 16; CurBio 44; DcAmB S3; DcLEL; DcNAA; EncMys; EncSF 93; FifWWr; FilmgC; HalFC 80, 84, 88; LegTOT; LngCTC; MnBBF; NewEScF; OxCAmL 83, 95; RAdv 14; REn; REnAL; REnAW; ScF&FL 1, 92; TwCA, SUP; TwCCr&M 80; TwCWW 82, 91; WebAB 74, 79; WorAl; WorAlBi*

Brand, Neville
American. Actor
Played on TV's "Laredo," 1965-67; films include *The Birdman of Alcatraz,* 1962.
b. Aug 13, 1921 in Kewanee, Illinois
d. 1992 in Sacramento, California
Source: *FilmEn; FilmgC; ForYSC; GangFlm; HalFC 84, 88; IntMPA 75, 76, 77, 78, 79, 80, 81, 82, 84, 86, 88, 92; LegTOT; MotPP; WhAm 10; WhoAm 74, 76, 78, 80, 82, 84; WhoHol A; WorAl*

Brand, Oscar
Canadian. Singer, Composer
Prolific country performer; won many awards.
b. Feb 7, 1920 in Winnipeg, Manitoba, Canada
Source: *AmAu&B; AuBYP 2, 3; Baker 84, 92; BiDAmM; BioIn 6, 8, 14; BlueB 76; CanWW 31, 70, 79, 80, 81, 83, 89; ConAu 1NR, 1R, 4NR; ConTFT 1; CurBio 62; EncFCWM 69, 83; IntAu&W 77, 91, 93; IntWWM 90; NatPD 77, 81; NotNAT; PenEncP; WhoAm 74, 76, 78, 80, 82, 84, 86, 88, 90, 92, 94, 95, 96, 97; WhoEnt 92; WhoWor 74, 76, 96, 97; WhoWorJ 72, 78; WrDr 76, 80, 82, 84, 86, 88, 90, 92, 94, 96*

Brand, Stewart
American. Publisher
Editor, publisher, *CoEvolution Quarterly,* 1974-85; publishes *The Last Whole Earth Catalog.*
b. Dec 14, 1938 in Rockford, Illinois
Source: *AuNews 1; BioIn 8, 10, 11, 13; ConAu 44NR, 81; EncTwCJ; Future; MugS; NewYTBS 84; WhoAm 74, 76, 78, 80, 82, 84, 86, 88, 90, 92, 94, 95, 96, 97; WhoUSWr 88; WhoWor 78; WhoWrEP 89, 92, 95*

Brand, Vance DeVoe
American. Astronaut
Crew member, joint US/USSR space mission, 1973-75.
b. May 9, 1931 in Longmont, Colorado
Source: *BioIn 10, 13, 14; BlueB 76; IntWW 74; NewYTBS 75, 82, 84; WhoAm 76, 78, 80, 82, 84, 86, 88, 90, 92, 94, 95, 96, 97; WhoFI 74; WhoGov 77; WhoScEn 94, 96; WhoSSW 73, 75, 76, 82; WorDWW*

Brandauer, Klaus Maria
Austrian. Actor
Stage actor in European theater since 1963; films include *Never Say Never Again,* 1983, *Out of Africa,* 1985.
b. Jun 22, 1944 in Altaussee, Austria
Source: *ConNews 87-3; ConTFT 6; CurBio 90; EncEurC; IntMPA 92, 94, 96; IntWW 89, 91, 93; LegTOT; MiSFD 9; WhoAm 92, 94, 95, 96, 97; WhoEnt 92; WhoHol 92*

Brandeis, Louis Dembitz
"The People's Attorney"
American. Supreme Court Justice
First Jewish associate justice, US Supreme Court, 1916-39; noted for devotion to free speech.
b. Nov 13, 1856 in Louisville, Kentucky
d. Oct 5, 1941 in Washington, District of Columbia
Source: *AmPolLe; AmRef; AmSocL; BiDFedJ; BioIn 1, 2, 3, 4, 5, 6, 7, 8, 9, 10, 11, 12, 13, 14, 15, 16, 17, 18, 19, 20; ConAu 118; CopCroC; CurBio 41; DcAmB S3; DcAmC; DcNAA; DcPol; EncAB-H 1974, 1996; EncSoH; HarEnUS; JeAmHC; LinLib L, S; McGEWB; MorMA; NatCAB 14, 36; OxCAmH; OxCAmL 65; OxCLaw; OxCSupC; REn; REnAL; SupCtJu; WebAB 74, 79; WhAm 1; WhNAA; WorAl*

Brandel, Fernand Paul
French. Historian
Influential member of Annales school of historiography; wrote *The Mediterranean and the Mediterranean World in the Age of Philip II,* 1949.
b. Aug 24, 1902 in Lumeville, France
d. Nov 28, 1985 in Paris, France
Source: *ConAu 14NR, 93; CurBio 85; IntEnSS 79; IntWW 83; MakMC; WhoAm 84*

Brandes, Georg Morris Cohen
Danish. Critic, Historian
Leading Scandinavian literary authority; biographies include *Goethe,* 1924.
b. Feb 4, 1842 in Copenhagen, Denmark
d. Feb 19, 1927 in Berlin, Germany
Source: *BbD; Benet 87, 96; BiD&SB; BioIn 1, 4, 6, 9, 11, 13, 18; CasWL; ClDMEL 47, 80; DcEuL; EncWL; EvEuW; LngCTC; NotNAT B; OxCGer 76; OxCThe 67, 83; PenC EUR; REn; TwCA, SUP; TwCWr*

Brando, Cheyenne
American. Model
Daughter of actor Marlon Brando.
b. Feb 20, 1970 in Tahiti
d. Apr 16, 1995 in Tahiti
Source: *News 95*

Brando, Marlon, Jr.
"Buddy"
American. Actor
Controversial, acclaimed actor; won Oscars for *On the Waterfront,* 1954; *The Godfather,* 1972.
b. Apr 3, 1924 in Omaha, Nebraska
Source: *AmCulL; AmDec 1950; BiDFilm, 81, 94; BiE&WWA; BioIn 1, 2, 3, 4, 5, 6, 7, 8, 9, 10, 11, 12, 14, 15, 16, 17, 18, 19, 20, 21; BkPepl; BlueB 76; CamGWoT; CelR, 90; CivR 74; CmCal; ConAu 148; ConTFT 3, 10; CurBio 74; DcArts; DcTwCCu 1; EncNAB; Ent; FacFETw; FilmEn; FilmgC; ForYSC; GangFlm; HalFC 80, 84, 88; IntDcF 1-3, 2-3; IntMPA 75, 76, 77, 78, 79, 80, 81, 82, 84, 86, 88, 92, 94, 96; IntWW 74, 75, 76, 77, 78, 79, 80, 81, 82, 83, 89, 91, 93; ItaFilm; LegTOT; MiSFD 9; MotPP; MovMk; NotNAT A; OxCFilm; PlP&P; WebAB 74, 79; WhDW; Who 74, 82, 83, 85, 88, 90, 92, 94; WhoAm 74, 76, 78, 80, 82, 84, 86, 88, 90, 92, 94, 95, 96, 97; WhoEnt 92; WhoHol 92, A; WhoHrs 80; WhoWor 74, 76, 78, 95, 96, 97; WorAl; WorAlBi; WorEFlm*

Brandon, Barbara
American. Cartoonist
First nationally syndicated African-American female cartoonist; weekly comic, "Where I'm Coming From," addresses women's issues from a black perspective.
b. 1960 in New York, New York
Source: *ConBlB 3*

Brandon, Brumsic, Jr.
American. Artist, Author
Best known for syndicated comic strip "Luther," 1970—; first major strip to highlight a black character.
b. Apr 10, 1927 in Washington, District of Columbia
Source: *AfroAA; BioIn 11; ConAu 61; DcTwCCu 5; EncTwCJ; InB&W 80, 85; SmATA 9; WhoAm 78, 80, 82, 84, 86, 88; WhoAmA 82; WhoBlA 75, 77, 80, 85, 88, 90, 92*

Brandon, Henry Oscar
American. Author, Editor
Chief American Correspondent, *Sunday Times of London,* 1949-83; international correspondent, 1982-93; wrote *The Retreat of American Power,* 1973.
b. Mar 9, 1916 in Liberec, Czech Republic
d. Apr 20, 1993
Source: *BlueB 76; ConAu 49; IntWW 83; WhAm 11; Who 85; WhoAm 82; WrDr 86*

Brandt, Bill
[William Brandt]
English. Photographer
Landscape, portrait photographer known for series of distorted female nudes: *Perspectives of Nudes,* 1961.
b. May 3, 1904 in London, England
d. Dec 20, 1983 in London, England
Source: *AnObit 1983; BioIn 12, 13, 14, 15, 20; ConAu 111; ConPhot 82, 88, 95; CurBio 81, 84, 84N; DcCAr 81; ICPEnP; NewYTBS 83; PrintW 85; WhAm 11; Who 82, 83; WhoWor 82, 84, 87*

Brandt, Willy
[Herbert Ernst Karl Frahm]
German. Political Leader
Chancellor of W Germany, 1969-74; won Nobel Peace Prize, 1971; mayor of W Berlin, 1957-66.
b. Dec 18, 1913 in Lubeck, Germany
d. Oct 8, 1992 in Unkel, Germany
Source: *AnObit 1992; BioIn 4, 5, 6, 7, 8, 9, 10, 11, 12, 13, 14, 15, 16, 17, 18, 19, 21; CelR; ColdWar 1; ConAu 85; CurBio 58, 73, 92N; DcPol; DcTwHis; EncCW; EncGRNM; EncTR; FacFETw; HeroCon; HisWorL; IntAu&W 77, 82; IntWW 74, 75, 76, 77, 78, 79, 80, 81, 82, 83, 89, 91; IntYB 78, 79, 80, 81, 82; LegTOT; LinLib L, S; McGEWB; News 93-2; NewYTBE 71; NewYTBS 92; NobelP; PolLCWE; WhAm 10; WhDW; Who 74, 82, 83, 85, 88, 90, 92; WhoEIO 82; WhoGov 72; WhoNob, 90, 95; WhoWor 74, 78, 82, 84, 87, 89, 91, 93; WorAl; WorAlBi*

Brandy
[Brandy Norwood]
American. Actor, Singer
Star of TV's "Moesha," 1995—; won Favorite New Artist at 1996 American Music Awards.
b. Feb 11, 1979 in McComb, Mississippi
Source: *News 96; WhoAfA 96*

Brangwyn, Frank, Sir
English. Artist
Official war artist during WW I; best known for marine paintings; murals hang in RCA Building, NYC, British House of Lords.
b. May 13, 1867 in Bruges, Belgium
d. Jun 11, 1956 in Ditchling, England
Source: *AntBDN B; BioIn 1, 2, 3, 4, 5, 7, 12, 14, 15; DcArts; DcBrBI; DcNaB 1951; DcNiCA; DcSeaP; DcVicP, 2; LinLib L, S; McGDA; ObitOF 79; ObitT 1951; OxCArt; OxCLiW 86; OxCShps; OxCTwCA; OxDcArt; PenDiDA 89; PhDcTCA 77; TwCPaSc; WhAm 3; WhAmArt 85A*

Braniff, Thomas Elmer
American. Airline Executive
Founded Braniff International Airways; became Braniff, 1952.
b. Dec 6, 1883 in Salina, Kansas
d. Jan 9, 1954
Source: *BiDAmBL 83; BioIn 2, 3, 4; CurBio 52, 54; DcAmB S5; InSci; WhAm 3*

Branigan, Laura
American. Singer
Hit singles include "Gloria," 1982; "Solitaire," 1983; "Self Control," 1984.
b. Jul 3, 1957 in Brewster, New York
Source: *LegTOT; PenEncP; RkOn 85; WhoHol 92*

Branley, Franklyn Mansfield
American. Educator, Author
Scientific children's books include *Dinosaurs, Asteroids & Superstars,* 1982.
b. Jun 5, 1915 in New Rochelle, New York
Source: *AmMWSc 82; Au&Wr 71; AuBYP 2, 3; BioIn 6, 7, 9, 17, 19; BkP; BlueB 76; ConAu 14NR; MorJA; SmATA 4; WhoAm 74, 76, 78, 80*

Brann, William Cowper
American. Journalist, Editor
Wrote vituperative articles against frauds, humbugs; founded monthly *The Iconoclast,* 1891.
b. Jan 4, 1855 in Humboldt, Illinois
d. Apr 2, 1898 in Waco, Texas
Source: *AmAu; AmAu&B; BenetAL 91; BiDAmJo; BioIn 4, 5, 11, 12, 14, 16; DcAmB S1; DcNAA; EncAJ; EncUnb; GayN; OxCAmL 65, 83, 95; REnAL; WhAm HS*

Brannan, Samuel
American. Publisher
Published San Francisco's first newspaper, *California Star,* 1847.
b. Mar 2, 1819 in Saco, Maine
d. May 5, 1889 in Escondido, California
Source: *AmBi; ApCAB; BioIn 1, 2, 3, 5, 8, 11; CmCal; DcAmB; NewCol 75; REnAW; TwCBDA; WebAB 74, 79; WhAm HS; WhAmP*

Branner, Martin Michael
American. Cartoonist
Comic strips include "Louie, the Lawyer"; "Pete & Pinto"; "Winnie Winkle," 1920s.
b. Dec 28, 1888 in New York, New York
d. May 19, 1970 in New London, Connecticut
Source: *BioIn 8, 10; NatCAB 55; NewYTBE 70; WhAm 5*

Brannigan, Bill
American. Journalist
UPI bureau chief, Nairobi, 1973-76; Cairo, 1976—.
b. Jan 12, 1936 in Long Island, New York
Source: *ConAu 65*

Brannigan, Owen
English. Actor, Singer
Bass with Sadler's Wells Opera, 1943-48, 1952-58.
b. 1909 in Annitsford, England
d. May 9, 1973 in Newcastle-upon-Tyne, England
Source: *ObitT 1971; WhoMus 72; WhScrn 77, 83*

Brannum, Hugh
American. Entertainer
Played Mr. Green Jeans on children's morning TV program, "Captain Kangaroo," for 29 yrs.
b. Jan 5, 1910 in Sandwich, Illinois
d. Apr 19, 1987 in East Stroudsburg, Pennsylvania
Source: *ASCAP 80; BioIn 15; IntMPA 75, 76, 77, 78, 79, 80, 81, 82; NewYTBS 87*

Bransfield, Edward
English. Naval Officer
Believed to be the first to discover Antarctica and chart a portion of the Antarctic mainland.
b. 1795
d. 1852
Source: *DcIrB 88*

Branson, Richard
English. Airline Executive, Music Executive
Founder, president, Virgin Records, Virgin Atlantic Airways.
b. Jul 18, 1950 in Surrey, England
Source: *ConNews 87-1; CurBio 95; IntWW 89, 91, 93; NewYTBS 84; Who 88, 90; WhoAm 92, 96, 97; WhoFI 94; WhoWor 97*

Branstad, Terry Edward
American. Politician
Rep. governor of Iowa, 1983—.
b. Nov 17, 1946 in Leland, Iowa
Source: *AlmAP 88; IntWW 83, 89, 91, 93; WhoAm 80, 82, 84, 86, 88, 90, 92, 94, 95, 96, 97; WhoAmP 73, 75, 77, 79, 81, 83, 85, 87, 89, 91, 93, 95; WhoEmL 87; WhoMW 88, 90, 92, 93, 96; WhoWor 84, 87, 89, 91, 93, 95, 96, 97*

Brant, Beth
American. Writer
Wrote *Mohawk Trail,* 1985; *Food and Spirits,* 1991.
b. May 6, 1941 in Detroit, Michigan
Source: *BioIn 19, 21; GayLesB; NatNAL; NotNaAm; OxCWoWr 95*

Brant, Joseph
American. Missionary, Soldier
Son of Mohawk Indian chief; loyal to British during Revolutionary War.
b. 1742 in Ohio
d. Nov 24, 1807 in Wellington Square, Ontario, Canada
Source: *Alli; AmBi; AmRev; ApCAB; BbtC; Benet 87; BenetAL 91; BioIn 3, 4, 5, 6, 7, 8, 9, 10, 11, 12, 13, 15, 18, 20, 21; BlkwEAR; DcAmB; DcAmMiB; EncAAH; EncAR; EncCRAm; EncNAB; GenMudB; HarEnMi; HarEnUS; HisWorL; LinLib L, S; MacDCB 78; McGEWB; NotNaAm; OxCAmH; OxCAmL 65, 83, 95; OxCCan; OxCCanL; PeoHis; REn; REnAL; REnAW; TwCBDA; WebAB 74, 79; WebAMB; WhAm HS; WhAmRev; WhNaAH*

Brant, Molly
American. Native American Leader
Involved in spy activities during the American Revolution; member of the Mohawk tribe.
b. 1736
d. 1796
Source: *AmRev; BioIn 21; ContDcW 89; IntDcWB; NotNaAm*

Brant, Sebastian
German. Poet
His allegorical *Ship of Fools,* 1494, became big hit with several editions; basis for 1960s novel, film.
b. 1457? in Strassburg, Germany
d. May 10, 1521 in Strassburg, Germany
Source: *CasWL; DcEuL; Dis&D; LinLib L; McGEWB; NewCol 75; OxCGer 76, 86; RAdv 14, 13-2; REn; RfGWoL 95*

Branting, Karl Hjalmar
Swedish. Astronomer, Political Leader
Shared Nobel Peace Prize, 1921; prime minister of Sweden, 1889-1925.
b. Nov 23, 1860 in Stockholm, Sweden
d. Feb 24, 1925 in Stockholm, Sweden
Source: *BiDInt; BioIn 9, 11, 15; LinLib L, S; WhoNob, 90, 95*

Branzell, Karin
Swedish. Opera Singer
Contralto with NY Met., 1924-44; noted for Wagner, Italian roles.
b. Sep 24, 1891 in Stockholm, Sweden
d. Dec 15, 1974 in Altadena, California
Source: *Baker 84; BioIn 1, 4, 7, 10, 11, 14, 19; CmOp; CurBio 46, 75, 75N; MetOEnc; MusSN; NewEOp 71; NewGrDA 86; NewGrDM 80; NewYTBS 74; OxDcOp; PenDiMP; WhAm 6*

Braque, Georges
French. Artist
Founded Cubism with Picasso, 1907; developed the collage, 1911.
b. May 13, 1882 in Argenteuil, France
d. Aug 31, 1963 in Paris, France
Source: *Benet 87, 96; BioIn 1, 2, 3, 4, 5, 6, 8, 9, 10, 12, 13, 14, 16, 17, 19; ClaDrA; CnOxB; ConArt 77, 83; ConAu 112; CurBio 49, 63; DancEn 78; DcArts; DcTwCCu 2; EncFash; EncWT; FacFETw; IntDcAA 90; LegTOT; LinLib S; MakMC; McGDA; McGEWB; ModArCr 4; ObitT 1961; OxCArt; OxCTwCA; OxDcArt; PhDcTCA 77; REn; WhAm 4; WhDW; WhoGrA 62; WorAl; WorAlBi; WorArt 1950*

Brasch, Rudolph
German. Religious Leader, Author
Wrote *There's a Reason for Everything,* 1982; *The Supernatural & You,* 1976.
b. Nov 6, 1912 in Berlin, Germany
Source: *Au&Wr 71; ConAu 8NR, 21R, 27NR, 51NR; IntAu&W 76, 91; WhoRel 92; WhoWor 74, 76; WhoWorJ 72, 78; WrDr 76, 80, 82, 84, 86, 88, 90, 92, 94, 96*

Brasher, Rex
American. Ornithologist, Artist, Author
Wrote 12-volumed *Birds and Trees of North America,* 1934.
b. Jul 31, 1869 in New York, New York
d. Feb 29, 1960 in Kent, Connecticut
Source: *ArtsAmW 2; BioIn 3, 5, 6; ObitOF 79; WhAm 3; WhAmArt 85; WhNAA*

Braslau, Sophie
American. Opera Singer
Contralto; member, NY Met., 1914-21.
b. Aug 16, 1892 in New York, New York
d. Dec 22, 1935 in New York, New York
Source: *Baker 78, 84, 92; BiDAmM; BioIn 1, 2, 11; DcAmB S1; MusSN; NewEOp 71; NotAW; WhAm 1*

Brassai
[Gyula Halasz]
French. Photographer
Best known for pictures of the night people of Paris, 1930s; reproduced in *The Secret Paris of the 30s,* 1976.
b. Sep 9, 1899 in Brasso, Austria-Hungary
d. Jul 8, 1984 in Nice, France
Source: *AnObit 1984; BioIn 8, 10, 11, 13, 14; ConAu 113, 126; ConPhot 82, 88, 95; DcArts; DcCAr 81; FacFETw; ICPEnP; MacBEP; ModArCr 1; NewYTBS 84; WhoFr 79*

Brasselle, Keefe
[John J Brasselli]
American. Actor, Producer
Best known for title role in *Eddie Cantor Story,* 1953.
b. Feb 7, 1923 in Lorain, Ohio
d. Jul 7, 1981 in Downey, California
Source: *ASCAP 66; BioIn 8, 12; ConAu 104; FilmEn; FilmgC; ForYSC; HalFC 80, 84, 88; IntMPA 75, 76, 77, 78, 79, 80, 81; LegTOT; MotPP; NewYTET; PseudN 82; WhoHol A; WhScrn 83*

Brassens, Georges
French. Singer, Poet
Wrote over 140 songs describing lives of everyday people; best known was anti-war song "The Two Uncles."
b. Oct 22, 1921 in Sete, France
d. Oct 30, 1981 in Sete, France
Source: *AnObit 1982; Baker 84, 92; BioIn 7, 8, 9, 12; CamGWoT; ConAu 105; DcTwCCu 2; IntWW 74, 75, 76, 77, 78, 79, 80, 81; IntWWM 77, 80; OxCPMus; WhoFr 79; WhoMus 72; WhScrn 83*

Brassey, Thomas
English. Surveyor, Businessman
British railway contractor who built railway lines in many parts of the world.
b. Nov 7, 1805 in Buerton, England
d. Dec 8, 1870 in Hastings, England
Source: *BioIn 8, 10, 12; DcBiPP; DcNaB; LinLib S*

Brattain, Walter Houser
American. Physicist
One of three to receive Nobel Prize in physics, 1956, for developing transistor.
b. Feb 10, 1902 in Xiamen, China
d. Oct 13, 1987 in Seattle, Washington
Source: *AmMWSc 73P, 76P, 79, 82, 86; AsBiEn; BiESc; BioIn 4, 5, 9, 12, 14, 15, 16, 20; CamDcSc; CurBio 57, 87; FacFETw; InSci; IntWW 74; LarDcSc; McGMS 80; NotTwCS; WebAB 74, 79; WhAm 9; Who 74; WhoAm 74, 76, 78, 80, 82, 86; WhoNob, 90, 95; WhoWest 78, 80, 82, 84, 87; WhoWor 74, 82, 84, 87; WorAl; WorInv*

Bratteli, Trygve Martin
Norwegian. Journalist, Political Leader
Former prime minister of Norway.
b. Jan 11, 1910 in Notteroy, Norway
d. Nov 20, 1984 in Oslo, Norway
Source: *IntWW 74, 75, 76, 77, 78, 79, 80, 81, 82, 83; IntYB 78, 79, 80, 81, 82; NewYTBE 71; WhoWor 74, 76, 78*

Brattle, Thomas
American. University Administrator
Treasurer, Harvard U, 1693-1713; opposed Salem witchcraft proceedings, 1692.
b. Jun 20, 1658 in Boston, Massachusetts
d. May 18, 1713 in Boston, Massachusetts
Source: *Alli; AmWrBE; ApCAB; BenetAL 91; BiDAmM; BiDAmS; BiInAmS; BioIn 17; DcAmB; EncCRAm; InSci; OxCAmH; REnAL; WebAB 74, 79; WhAm HS*

Brauchitsch, Heinrich Alfred
German. Military Leader
Commander-in-chief of German Army, 1938-41; made scapegoat for failure to capture Moscow, removed from command, 1941.
b. Oct 4, 1881 in Berlin, Germany
d. Oct 18, 1948 in Hamburg, Germany
Source: *CurBio 40, 48; WorAl*

Brauer, Jerald C(arl)
American. Educator, Historian
Lutheran minister whose books include *Protestantism in America,* 1953.
b. Sep 16, 1921 in Fond du Lac, Wisconsin
Source: *AmAu&B; BlueB 76; ConAu 13NR, 33R; DrAS 74P; IntAu&W 82; IntWW 74, 75, 76, 77, 78, 79, 80, 81, 82, 83, 89, 91, 93; WhoAm 74, 76, 78, 80, 82, 84, 86, 88, 90; WhoRel 75, 77, 85; WhoWor 74, 76, 78; WrDr 76, 80, 82, 84, 86, 88, 90, 92, 94, 96*

Brauer, Max Julius Friedrich
German. Politician
Relinquished US citizenship to rebuild Hamburg after WW II.
b. 1887
d. Feb 1, 1973 in Bonn, Germany (West)
Source: *BioIn 1, 2, 4, 9; NewYTBE 73; ObitOF 79*

Braun, Eva
[Mrs. Adolf Hilter]
German.
Married Hitler a few days before their suicides.
b. Feb 6, 1912 in Simbach am Inn, Germany
d. Apr 30, 1945 in Berlin, Germany
Source: *BioIn 2, 4, 5, 8, 9, 10, 14; ContDcW 89; EncTR, 91; IntDcWB; InWom SUP; LegTOT; ObitOF 79; WhWW-II; WorAl; WorAlBi*

Braun, Karl Ferdinand
German. Physicist
Invented the oscillograph, 1897; shared Nobel Prize in physics, 1909.
b. Jun 6, 1850 in Fulda, Germany
d. Apr 20, 1918 in New York, New York
Source: *AsBiEn; BiESc; BioIn 14, 15, 16, 20; CamDcSc; FacFETw; InSci; LinLib S; NotTwCS; WhoNob, 90, 95; WorAl; WorInv*

Braun, Lily von Kretschman
German. Feminist, Writer
In *The Women's Question, Its Historical Development and Its Economic Aspect,* 1901, she wrote that capitalism destroys the family by taking women out of the home and putting them into industry.
b. Jul 2, 1865 in Halberstadt, Prussia
d. Aug 9, 1916 in Zehlendorf, Germany
Source: *BioIn 15; ContDcW 89; OxCGer 86; WomWrGe*

Braun, Otto
German. Political Leader
Military adviser to Chinese Communists, 1933-39.
b. 1901
d. Aug 15, 1974 in Berlin, Germany (West)
Source: *BioIn 10; NewYTBS 74; ObitOF 79*

Brautigan, Richard
American. Author, Poet
Became campus hero, 1960s, with whimsical novel *Trout Fishing in America,* 1967.
b. Jan 30, 1933 in Tacoma, Washington
d. Oct 25, 1984 in Bolinas, California
Source: *AmAu&B; AnObit 1984; Benet 87; ConAu 53; ConLC 12; ConNov 76, 82; ConPo 80, 85; DcLEL 1940; DrAF 76; DrAP 75; IntAu&W 76, 77; LegTOT; ModAL S1; OxCTwCP; PenC AM; ScF&FL 92; SJGFanW; WhAm 8; WhoAm 78, 84; WorAu 1970; WrDr 80, 82, 84*

Bravais, Auguste
French. Physicist
Known for his work on the lattice theory of crystals.
b. Aug 23, 1811 in Annonay, France
d. Mar 30, 1863 in Le Chesnay, France
Source: *DcBiPP; DcScB; WhDW*

Brawley, Benjamin Griffith
American. Clergy, Educator
Books include *A Short History of the American Negro; Negro Builders & Heroes,* 1937.
b. Apr 22, 1882 in Columbia, South Carolina
d. Feb 1, 1939 in Washington, District of Columbia
Source: *AmAu&B; AmBi; AmLY; BiDAmEd; BioIn 2, 3, 4, 5, 9, 16; BlkAWP; DcAmNB; DcNAA; InB&W 80, 85; NatCAB 37; NegAl 83; REnAL; SelBAAf; SelBAAu; SouWr; TwCA, SUP; WhAm 1; WhNAA; WhoColR*

Braxton, Carter
American. Continental Congressman
Planter; most conservative member of VA delegation; signed Declaration of Independence, 1776.
b. Sep 10, 1736 in Newington, Virginia
d. Oct 10, 1797 in Richmond, Virginia
Source: *AmBi; ApCAB; BiAUS; BiDrAC; BiDrUSC 89; BioIn 7, 8, 9, 14; DcAmB; Drake; EncAR; EncCRAm; HarEnUS; NatCAB 7; NewYTBS 81; TwCBDA; WhAm HS; WhAmP; WhAmRev*

Braxton, Toni
American. Singer
Grammy Award, Best New Artist, 1993; Best R&B Vocal-Female, "Another Sad Love Song," 1993.
b. 1968 in Severn, Maryland
Source: *EncRkSt; LegTOT; WhoAfA 96*

Bray, Charles William, III
American. Government Official
Deputy director, US Information Agency, 1977-81; ambassador to Senegal, 1981-85 .
b. Oct 24, 1933 in New York, New York
Source: *NewYTBE 70; USBiR 74; WhoAm 80, 82, 84, 90, 92, 94, 95, 96, 97; WhoAmP 85, 87, 89; WhoWor 82*

Brayman, Harold
American. Educator, Journalist
Accompanied both Alfred E Smith, FDR on presidential campaigns; wrote public relations books.
b. Mar 10, 1900 in Middleburg, New York
d. Jan 3, 1988 in Wilmington, Delaware
Source: *BioIn 15; BlueB 76; ConAu 73, 124; IntYB 78, 79, 80, 81, 82; WhAm 9; WhoAm 74, 76, 78, 80, 82, 84, 86; WhoE 74, 75, 77, 79, 81, 83, 85, 86; WhoFI 74, 75, 77, 79, 81, 83, 85, 87; WhoPubR 72, 76; WhoWor 76, 78, 80, 82, 84, 87, 89, 91*

Brazelton, T(homas) Berry
American. Physician, Author
Researcher in child development; wrote *On Becoming a Family,* 1981; *Working and Caring,* 1985.
b. May 10, 1918 in Waco, Texas
Source: *BioIn 11, 12, 13; ConAu 97; WhoAm 74, 76, 78, 80, 82, 86, 88, 90, 92, 94, 95, 96, 97*

Brazza, Pierre Paul Francois Camille Savorgnan de
French. Explorer, Colonizer
Founded the French (Middle) Congo and the city of Brazaville; explored Gabon.
b. Jan 26, 1852 in Rome, Italy
d. Sep 14, 1905 in Dakar, Senegal
Source: *BioIn 2, 5; DcAfHiB 86; McGEWB*

Brazzi, Rossano
Italian. Actor
Starred in *The Barefoot Contessa,* 1954; *South Pacific,* 1958.
b. Sep 18, 1916 in Bologna, Italy
d. Dec 24, 1994 in Rome, Italy
Source: *BioIn 5, 6, 20, 21; CmMov; ConTFT 10, 15; CurBio 61, 95N; EncEurC; FilmEn; FilmgC; HalFC 80, 84, 88; IntDcF 1-3, 2-3; IntMPA 75, 76, 77, 78, 79, 80, 81, 82, 84, 86, 88, 92, 94; ItaFilm; LegTOT; MotPP; MovMk; NewYTBS 94; WhoHol 92, A; WorAl; WorAlBi*

Bread
[Mike Botts; David Gates; James Gordon; James Grifin; Larry Knechtel; Robb Royer]
American. Music Group
Soft-rock hit songs include "Lost Without Your Love," 1976; "Make It with You," 1970.
Source: *Alli, SUP; BiDLA; BiDSA; DcNaB; EncPR&S 89; EncRk 88; EncRkSt; EngPo; IlEncRk; NewGrDA 86; PenEncP; RkOn 78; RolSEnR 83; WhoHol 92; WhoRock 81; WhoRocM 82; WorAl*

Bream, Julian Alexander
English. Musician
Guitarist, lutenist; known for Elizabethan lute music.
b. Jul 15, 1933 in London, England
Source: *Baker 84; BlueB 76; ConMus 9; IntWW 74, 83; Who 83; WhoAm 84; WhoAmM 83; WhoMus 72; WhoWor 74, 82; WorAl*

Breasted, James Henry
American. Archaeologist, Historian
Wrote standard texts: *History of Egypt,* 1905; *Ancient Times,* 1916.
b. Aug 27, 1865 in Rockford, Illinois
d. Dec 2, 1933 in New York, New York
Source: *AmAu&B; AmBi; AmLY; BiDAmEd; BioIn 2, 6, 11, 15, 21; DcAmB S1; DcLB 47; DcLEL; DcNAA; EncAB-A 9; EvLB; InSci; IntDcAn; LinLib L, S; LngCTC; McGEWB; NatCAB 29; OxCAmH; OxCAmL 65; REn; REnAL; TwCA, SUP; WebAB 74, 79; WhAm 1; WhNAA; WorAlBi*

Breathed, Berke
American. Cartoonist
Pulitzer-winning creator of comic strip, "Bloom County," 1980-89; has written books based on comic strip.
b. Jun 21, 1957 in Encino, California
Source: *Au&Arts 5; BioIn 18; ConAu 27NR, 110; EncACom; LegTOT*

Breaux, John B.
American. Politician
Dem. senator, LA, 1987—.
b. Mar 1, 1944 in Crowley, Louisiana
Source: *AlmAP 78, 80, 82, 84, 88, 92, 96; AmCath 80; BioIn 15, 16, 20; CngDr 74, 77, 79, 81, 83, 85, 87, 89; IntWW 89, 91, 93; PolsAm 84; WhoAm 74, 76, 78, 80, 82, 84, 86, 88, 90, 92, 94, 95, 96, 97; WhoAmP 73, 75, 77, 79, 81, 83, 85, 87, 89, 91, 93, 95; WhoSSW 75, 76, 78, 88, 91, 93, 95, 97; WhoWor 89, 91*

Brecheen, Harry David
"The Cat"
American. Baseball Player
Pitcher, 1940-53; first left-hander to win three World Series games, 1946.
b. Oct 14, 1914 in Broken Bow, Oklahoma
Source: *BiDAmSp Sup; BioIn 1, 2; WhoProB 73*

Brecht, Bertolt (Eugen Friedrich)
German. Poet, Dramatist
Best known for collaboration with Kurt Weill on *Threepenny Opera,* 1928.
b. Feb 10, 1898 in Augsburg, Germany
d. Aug 14, 1956 in Berlin, German Democratic Republic
Source: *AtlBL; Benet 87, 96; BiDMarx; BiGAW; BioIn 1, 2, 3, 4, 5, 6, 7, 8, 9, 10, 11, 12, 13, 14, 15, 16, 17, 18, 19, 20, 21; BlmGEL; CamGWoT; CasWL; ClDMEL 47, 80; CnMD; CnMWL; CnThe; ConAu 104, 133; CroCD; CyWA 58, 89; DcArts; DcFM; DcLB 56, 124; DcPup; DcTwHis; DramC 3; EncMcCE; EncRev; EncTR, 91; EncWL, 2, 3; EncWT; Ent; EuWr 11; EvEuW; FilmEn; FilmgC; GrFLW; GrStDi; HalFC 80, 84, 88; IntDcOp; IntDcT 2; LegTOT; LiExTwC; LinLib L, S; LngCTC; MagSWL; MajMD 1; MajTwCW; MakMC; McGEWB; McGEWD 72, 84; MetOEnc; ModGL; ModWD; NewEOp 71; NewGrDM 80; NewGrDO; NotNAT A, B; OxCAmT 84; OxCEng 67, 85, 95; OxCFilm; OxCGer 76, 86; OxCMed 86; OxCPMus; OxCThe 67, 83; OxDcOp; PenC EUR; RadHan; RAdv 14, 13-2; RComWL; REn; REnWD; RfGWoL 95; RGFMEP; TheaDir; ThTwC 87; TwCA, SUP; TwCLC 1, 6, 13, 35; TwCWr; WhAm 4, HSA; WhDW; WhoTwCL; WorAl; WorAlBi; WorEFlm; WorLitC; WrPh*

Breck, John Henry
American. Businessman
Founded Breck, Inc., hair care firm, 1929.
b. Jun 5, 1877 in Holyoke, Massachusetts
d. Feb 16, 1965 in Springfield, Massachusetts
Source: *BioIn 7, 9; Entr; NatCAB 52; WhAm 4; WorAl*

Breckinridge, John
American. Statesman
Attorney-general under Jefferson, 1805.
b. Dec 2, 1760 in Augusta County, Virginia
d. Dec 14, 1806 in Lexington, Kentucky
Source: *AmBi; BiAUS; BiDrAC; BiDrUSC 89; BiDrUSE 71, 89; BiDSA; BioIn 3, 8, 10, 17; DcAmB; Drake; EncSoH; TwCBDA; WhAmP*

Breckinridge, John Cabell
American. US Vice President
Vp under James Buchanan, 1857-61.
b. Jan 21, 1821 in Lexington, Kentucky
d. May 17, 1875 in Lexington, Kentucky
Source: *AmBi; AmPolLe; ApCAB; BiAUS; BiDConf; BiDrAC; BiDrUSC 89; BiDrUSE 71, 89; BiDSA; BioIn 1, 4, 5, 7, 8, 9, 10, 11, 13, 14, 15, 17, 18; CivWDc; DcAmB; Drake; EncAB-H 1974, 1996; EncSoH; LinLib S; NatCAB 5; OxCAmH; TwCBDA; VicePre; WebAB 74, 79; WebAMB; WhAmP; WhCiWar; WhoMilH 76; WorAlBi*

Breckinridge, Mary
American. Nurse
Brought health care services to KY mountaineers; founded, Frontier Nursing Service, 1928.
b. Feb 17, 1881 in Memphis, Tennessee
d. May 16, 1965 in Hyden, Kentucky
Source: *BioIn 2, 3, 7, 8, 9, 11, 12, 16; ConAu 114; EncWHA; NotAW MOD; WhAm 4; WhoAmW 61, 64, 66; WomFir*

Breckinridge, Sophonisba Preston
American. Social Reformer
First woman admitted to Bar in KY, 1897.
b. Apr 1, 1866 in Lexington, Kentucky
d. Jul 30, 1948 in Chicago, Illinois
Source: *AmRef; AmWomWr; BiDAmEd; BioIn 1, 2, 3, 11, 15, 16, 17, 20, 21; DcAmB S4; DcNAA; EncAB-H 1974, 1996; InWom SUP; LibW; NatCAB 37; NotAW; WhAm 2; WomFir; WomWWA 14; WorAl; WorAlBi*

Breech, Ernest Robert
American. Industrialist
First board chm. of Ford Motor Co., 1955.
b. Feb 24, 1897 in Lebanon, Missouri
d. Jul 3, 1978 in Royal Oak, Michigan
Source: *BioIn 1, 2, 3, 4, 5, 7, 8, 11; CurBio 55; NewYTBS 78; WhAm 7; Who 74; WhoAm 74, 76, 78; WhoFI 74*

Breedlove, Craig
[Norman Craig Breedlove]
"Fastest Man on Wheels"
American. Auto Racer
Set world land speed record, 1965, averaging over 600 mph in jet-powered machine driven on Bonneville Salt Flats, Utah.
b. Mar 23, 1938 in Los Angeles, California
Source: *BioIn 6, 7, 8, 9, 10, 18; CurBio 66; NewYTBS 76; WhoSpor*

Breen, Joseph Ignatius
American. Critic
Powerful 1930s-40s Hollywood film censor; won special Oscar, 1953.
b. Oct 4, 1890 in Philadelphia, Pennsylvania
d. Dec 7, 1965 in Hollywood, California
Source: *BioIn 2, 7; CurBio 50, 66; DcAmB S7; WhAm 4*

Breese, Edmund
American. Actor
Screen character actor, 1915-35; worked with James O'Neill on stage *Count of Monte Cristo,* 1892.
b. Jun 18, 1871 in New York, New York
d. Apr 6, 1936 in New York, New York
Source: *Film 1, 2; ForYSC; MovMk; NotNAT B; OxCAmT 84; TwYS; WhAm 1; WhoHol B; WhoStg 1906, 1908; WhScrn 74, 77, 83; WhThe*

Breeskin, Adelyn Dohme
American. Museum Director
Director, Baltimore Museum of Art, 1947-62; first woman director of museum in US.
b. Jul 19, 1896 in Baltimore, Maryland
d. Jul 24, 1986 in Lake Garda, Italy
Source: *BioIn 15; ConAu 33R, 119; NewYTBS 86; WhAm 9; WhoAm 74, 76, 78, 80, 82; WhoAmA 73, 76, 78, 80, 82, 84, 86N, 89N, 91N, 93N; WhoAmW 58, 64, 66, 68, 70, 72, 74, 85; WhoGov 72; WhoSSW 73*

Breger, Dave
American. Cartoonist, Illustrator
Originated term "G I Joe" with WW II cartoon series.
b. 1908 in Chicago, Illinois
d. Jan 16, 1970 in South Nyack, New York
Source: *BioIn 8; EncACom; NewYTBE 70; ObitOF 79; WhoAmA 78N, 80N, 82N, 84N, 86N, 89N, 91N, 93N*

Breguet, Abraham Louis
French. Inventor, Jeweler
One of the greatest and most influential watchmakers in the world.
b. Jan 10, 1747 in Neuchatel, Switzerland
d. Sep 17, 1823 in Paris, France
Source: *AntBDN D; BioIn 2, 4, 10, 11, 14; DcBiPP; OxCDecA; PenDiDA 89*

Breguet, Louis Charles
French. Aircraft Manufacturer
Founded Air France, 1919; his planes set many world records.
b. Jan 2, 1880 in Paris, France
d. May 4, 1955 in Paris, France
Source: *BioIn 3, 12; InSci; ObitOF 79*

Breitenstein, Ted
[Theodore P Breitenstein]
American. Baseball Player
Pitcher, 1891-1901, mostly with St. Louis; one of only three to throw no-hitter in first ML game.
b. Jun 1, 1869 in Saint Louis, Missouri
d. May 3, 1935 in Saint Louis, Missouri
Source: *Ballpl 90; BaseEn 88; BioIn 3; WhoProB 73*

Breitschwerdt, Werner
German. Auto Executive
Chairman of Daimler-Benz, West Germany's biggest conglomerate, 1982-87.
b. Sep 23, 1927 in Stuttgart, Germany
Source: *BioIn 13; IntWW 89, 91, 93; News 88; WhoWor 84*

Brel, Jacques
Belgian. Songwriter
Known for popular revue containing 25 songs: *Jacques Brel Is Alive and Well and Living in Paris.*
b. Apr 8, 1929 in Brussels, Belgium
d. Oct 9, 1978 in Bobigny, France
Source: *Baker 84, 92; BioIn 8, 9, 11; CamGWoT; CelR; CurBio 71, 78N; DcArts; DcTwCCu 2; EncEurC; FacFETw; LegTOT; NewGrDM 80; OxCPMus; PenEncP; WhAm 7; WhoE 74; WhoHol A; WhoWor 74; WhScrn 83; WorAl; WorAlBi*

Bremer, Arthur Herman
American. Attempted Assassin
Shot George Wallace, May 5, 1972 in Lowell, MD.
b. Aug 21, 1950 in Milwaukee, Wisconsin
Source: *BioIn 9, 10, 12, 13; NewYTBE 72*

Brenan, Gerald
[Edward Fitz-Gerald Brenan]
English. Author
Definitive interpreter of Spanish literature, culture: *The Spanish Labyrinth,* 1943.
b. Apr 7, 1894, Malta
d. Jan 16, 1987 in Malaga, Spain
Source: *AnObit 1987; BioIn 4, 6, 10, 11, 12, 15, 18, 19; BlueB 76; ConAu 1R, 3NR, 121; CurBio 86, 87, 87N; IntAu&W 89, 91; LinLib L; LngCTC; NewCBEL; NewYTBS 87; OxCEng 85, 95; OxCSpan; TwCA SUP; Who 74, 82, 83, 85; WrDr 76, 80, 82, 84, 86*

Brendan of Clonfert, Saint
Irish. Religious Figure
Subject of 10th c. tale *Brendan's Voyage,* recounting adventures; feast day May 16.
b. 484 in Tralee, Ireland
d. 577 in Annaghdown, Ireland
Source: *BioIn 4, 5, 6, 7, 8, 10; DcCathB; LuthC 75; NewC; OxCFr; OxCShps*

Brendel, Alfred
Austrian. Pianist
Gives recitals, appears with major orchestras world wide; interpreter of Vienna classics.
b. Jan 5, 1931 in Wisenberg, Austria
Source: *Baker 78, 84, 92; BiDAmM; BioIn 9, 10, 11, 12, 13; BriBkM 80; CurBio 77; DcArts; IntAu&W 89; IntWW 74, 75, 76, 77, 78, 79, 80, 81, 82, 83, 89, 91, 93; IntWWM 77, 80, 85, 90; NewAmDM; NewGrDM 80; NewYTBS 84; NotTwCP; PenDiMP; Who 74, 82, 83, 85, 88, 90, 92, 94; WhoAm 84, 86, 88, 90, 92, 94, 95, 96, 97; WhoMus 72; WhoWor 74, 76, 78, 82, 84, 87, 89, 91, 93, 95, 96, 97*

Brendel, El(mer)
American. Actor, Comedian
Vaudeville, comic film roles, 1926-56.
b. Mar 25, 1890 in Philadelphia, Pennsylvania
d. Apr 9, 1964 in Hollywood, California
Source: *EncAFC; Film 2; FilmEn; FilmgC; HalFC 84, 88; LegTOT; MovMk; NotNAT B; ObitOF 79; QDrFCA 92; TwYS; Vers A; WhoHol B; WhScrn 74, 77, 83*

Breneman, Tom
American. Actor
Radio emcee of "Breakfast in Hollywood."
b. 1902
d. Apr 28, 1948 in Encino, California
Source: *ObitOF 79; RadStar; SaTiSS; WhoHol B; WhScrn 74, 77, 83*

Brenly, Bob
[Robert Earl Brenly]
American. Baseball Player
Catcher, San Francisco, 1981-89; Toronto, 1989—; tied ML record with four errors in one inning playing third base, 1986.
b. Feb 25, 1954 in Coshocton, Ohio
Source: *Ballpl 90; BaseReg 86, 87; LegTOT*

Brennan, Edward A.
"Captain Marvel of Merchandising"
American. Business Executive
Chairman, CEO of Sears, Roebuck and Co., the world's largest retail organization, 1985-95.
b. Jan 16, 1934 in Chicago, Illinois
Source: *CurBio 90; Dun&B 79; IntWW 89, 91, 93; News 89-1; St&PR 84, 87, 91, 93, 96, 97; Who 88, 90, 92, 94; WhoAm 82, 84, 86, 88, 90, 92, 94, 95, 96, 97; WhoFI 81, 83, 85, 87, 89, 92, 94, 96; WhoMW 82, 88, 90, 92, 93, 96; WhoWor 87, 91, 93, 95, 96, 97*

Brennan, Eileen Regina
American. Actor
Nominated for Oscar for role of Capt. Doreen Lewis in *Private Benjamin,* 1980; won Emmy for same role in TV comedy "Private Benjamin," 1982.
b. Sep 3, 1935? in Los Angeles, California
Source: *BiE&WWA; ConTFT 8; IntMPA 86; NotNAT; WhoAm 80, 82, 84, 86, 88, 92, 94, 95, 96, 97; WhoAmW 87, 89; WhoEnt 92; WhoHol A*

Brennan, Peter J(oseph)
American. Government Official
Secretary of Labor, 1973-74.
b. May 24, 1918 in New York, New York
d. Oct 2, 1996 in Massapequa, New York
Source: *BiDAmL; BiDAmLL; BiDrUSE 89; BioIn 9, 10, 11, 12; BioNews 74; BusPN; CelR; CngDr 74; CurBio 73; IntWW 74, 75, 76, 77, 78, 79, 80, 81, 82, 83; NewYTBE 72; PolProf NF; WhoAm 74, 76; WhoAmP 73, 75, 77, 79*

Brennan, Robert E
American. Businessman
Founder, CEO, First Jersey Securities, 1974-87; heads International Thoroughbred Breeders, Inc; built Due Process Stable, 1980.
b. 1943 in Newark, New Jersey
Source: *BioIn 12, 13, 14, 15; ConNews 88-1; Dun&B 90*

Brennan, Walter Andrew
American. Actor
First actor to win three Oscars, 1936, 1938, 1940; known for character roles, TV series "The Real McCoys," 1957-63.
b. Jul 25, 1894 in Lynn, Massachusetts
d. Sep 22, 1974 in Oxnard, California
Source: *CmMov; CurBio 41, 74; FilmgC; IntMPA 75; MotPP; MovMk; NewYTBS 74; OxCFilm; TwYS; Vers A; WhAm 6; WhoAm 74; WhoWor 74; WhScrn 77; WorEFlm*

Brennan, William Joseph, Jr.
American. Supreme Court Justice
Leading liberal justice appointed by Dwight Eisenhower, 1956-90.
b. Apr 25, 1906 in Newark, New Jersey
d. Jul 24, 1997 in Washington, District of Columbia
Source: *AmCath 80; BiDFedJ; BioIn 4, 5, 6, 7, 8, 9, 10, 11, 12, 13; CngDr 74; CurBio 57; DrAS 74P; EncAB-H 1996; IntWW 74, 75, 76, 77, 78, 79, 80, 81, 82, 83, 89, 91, 93; IntYB 78, 79, 80, 81, 82; LinLib L, S; OxCSupC; SupCtJu; WebAB 74, 79; Who 74, 82, 83, 85, 88, 90, 92, 94; WhoAm 74, 76, 78, 80, 82, 84, 86, 88, 90, 92, 94, 95, 96, 97; WhoAmL 78, 79, 83, 85, 87, 90, 92, 94, 96; WhoAmP 73, 93, 95; WhoE 79, 81, 83, 85, 86, 89, 91, 93, 95, 97; WhoGov 72, 75, 77; WhoSSW 75; WorAl*

Brenner, Barbara Johnes
American. Author
Free-lance writer of children's books: *Barto Takes the Subway,* 1960; *A Snake-Lover's Diary,* 1970.
b. Jun 26, 1925 in New York, New York
Source: *AuBYP 2; ConAu 9NR, 9R, 12NR; DcAmChF 1985; ForWC 70; MajAI; SmATA 4, 76; WhoUSWr 88; WhoWrEP 89, 92, 95*

Brenner, David
American. Comedian
Nightclub performer; named Las Vegas entertainer of year, 1977; host of syndicated TV show "Nightlife", 1986-87.
b. Feb 4, 1945 in Philadelphia, Pennsylvania
Source: *BioIn 10, 13, 15, 17, 18; ConAu 133; ConTFT 2; CurBio 87; LegTOT; VarWW 85; WhoAm 78, 80, 82, 84, 86, 88, 90, 92, 94, 95; WhoCom; WhoEnt 92; WhoHol 92; WorAl; WorAlBi; WrDr 94, 96*

Brenner, Eleanor P
American. Fashion Designer
Founded, Eleanor P. Brenner Ltd. label, 1983; a versatile, stylish sportswear line.
Source: *CelR 90; InWom SUP*

Brent, Evelyn
[Mary Elizabeth Riggs]
American. Actor
Played lead opposite John Barrymore in *Raffles the Amateur Cracksman,* 1917.
b. Oct 20, 1899 in Tampa, Florida
d. Jun 7, 1975 in Los Angeles, California
Source: *BioIn 9, 10, 11, 14, 18; Film 1, 2; FilmEn; FilmgC; ForYSC; GangFlm; HalFC 80, 84, 88; IlWWBF; InWom SUP; MotPP; MovMk; NewYTBS 75; SilFlmP; SweetSg B; ThFT; TwYS; What 3; WhoHol C; WhScrn 77, 83*

Brent, George
[George B Nolan]
American. Actor
Played in 11 films with Bette Davis including *Dark Victory,* 1939; *Jezebel,* 1938.
b. Mar 15, 1904 in Dublin, Ireland
d. May 26, 1979 in Solana Beach, California
Source: *BiDFilm 94, 78, 79; LegTOT; MotPP; MovMk; What 4; WhoHol A; WhoThe 81N; WhScrn 83; WorAl; WorAlBi*

Brent, Margaret
American. Feminist
First woman landowner in MD.
b. 1600 in Gloucester, England
d. 1671 in Virginia
Source: *AmBi; BiCAW; BioIn 6; DcAmB; GoodHs; InWom, SUP; LibW; WebAB 74, 79; WhAm HS; WhAmP; WorAl; WorAlBi*

Brent, Romney
[Romulo Larralde]
Actor, Dramatist, Director
Collaborated with Cole Porter on musical *Nymph Errant* which starred Gertrude Lawrence.
b. Jan 26, 1902 in Saltillo, Mexico
d. Sep 24, 1976
Source: *BiE&WWA; BioIn 10, 11; FilmEn; FilmgC; ForYSC; HalFC 80, 84, 88; NotNAT; PlP&P; WhoHol A; WhoThe 72, 81, 81N; WhScrn 83; WhThe*

Brentano, Clemens Maria
German. Dramatist, Author, Poet
Romantic poet; co-published *Des Knaben Wunderhorn* (Boy's Magic Horn), a collection of German folksongs.
b. Sep 8, 1778 in Ehrenbrehstein, Germany
d. Jul 28, 1842 in Aschaffenburg, Bavaria
Source: *BbD; Benet 87, 96; BiD&SB; BioIn 7, 10; CasWL; CelCen; ChhPo S1; DcEuL; EuAu; EvEuW; LegTOT; LinLib L; McGEWB; NewCBEL; OxCGer 76; PenC EUR; REn*

Bresler, Jerry
American. Producer
Won Oscars for *Heavenly Music; Stairway to Light;* known for Our Gang comedies, Gidget series.
b. Apr 13, 1908 in Denver, Colorado
Source: *FilmEn; FilmgC; IntMPA 75, 76, 77; WorEFlm*

Breslin, Jimmy
American. Author, Journalist
Pulitzer-winning NYC columnist who wrote *Table Money,* 1983.
b. Oct 17, 1930 in Jamaica, New York
Source: *AmAu&B; AuNews 1; BiDConC; BioIn 8, 10, 11, 13; CelR, 90; ConLC 4, 43; CurBio 73; EncAJ; EncTwCJ; LegTOT; LiJour; LinLib L; WhoAm 74, 76, 78, 80, 82, 86; WhoE 74; WhoHol 92; WhoWor 74; WorAl; WrDr 76, 80, 82, 84, 86, 88, 90, 92, 94, 96*

Bresnaham, Roger Philip
"The Duke of Tralee"
American. Baseball Player
Catcher, 1897-1915; invented shin guards for catchers, 1908; Hall of Fame, 1945.
b. Jun 11, 1879 in Toledo, Ohio
d. Dec 4, 1944 in Toledo, Ohio
Source: *BioIn 3, 7, 8, 10; WhoProB 73*

Bresson, Robert
French. Director
Stylist who does not use professional actors; films, often character studies, include *Pickpocket,* 1959.
b. Sep 25, 1907 in Bromont-Lamothe, France
Source: *Benet 87, 96; BiDFilm, 81, 94; BioIn 5, 8, 9, 11, 12, 13; ConAu 110; ConLC 16; ConTFT 8; CurBio 71; DcFM; DcTwCCu 2; EncEurC; FacFETw; FilmEn; FilmgC; HalFC 80, 84, 88; IntDcF 1-2, 2-2; IntMPA 88, 92, 94, 96; IntWW 82; MiSFD 9; MovMk; OxCFilm; Who 74, 82, 83, 85, 88, 90; WorEFlm; WorFDir 1*

Breton, Andre
French. Poet
Founded Surrealist movement, 1924; wrote *Surrealist of Manifesto.*
b. Feb 18, 1896 in Tinchebray, France
d. Sep 28, 1966 in Paris, France
Source: *AtlBL; Benet 87, 96; BiDMoPL; BioIn 1, 4, 7, 8, 9, 10, 12, 14, 16, 17, 21; BlmGEL; CasWL; ClDMEL 47, 80;*

ConAu 25R, 40NR, P-2; ConLC 2, 9, 15, 54; DcArts; DcLB 65; DcTwCCu 2; EncWL, 2, 3; EuWr 11; EvEuW; FacFETw; GrFLW; GuFrLit 1; LegTOT; LiExTwC; LinLib L; LngCTC; MajTwCW; MakMC; McGEWB; ModFrL; ModRL; ModWD; ObitT 1961; OxCArt; OxCEng 85, 95; OxCFr; OxCTwCA; OxDcArt; PenC EUR; PoeCrit 15; RAdv 14, 13-2; RComWL; REn; REnWD; TwCA SUP; TwCWr; WhAm 4; WhDW; WhoTwCL; WorAl; WorAlBi

Breton, Jules Adolphe
French. Artist, Author
Harmonizes landscapes, human nature in paintings: "A Gleaner," 1877; "The Weed-Gathers," 1861.
b. May 1, 1827 in Calais, France
d. Jul 5, 1906 in Paris, France
Source: *ArtsNiC; BioIn 13; LinLib L, S*

Bretonneau, Pierre Fidele
French. Physician
Sought cause of several diseases, including smallpox, typhoid fever, diphtheria; performed first successful tracheotomy, 1825.
b. Apr 3, 1778 in Saint-Georges-sur-Cher, France
d. Feb 18, 1862 in Passy, France
Source: *BiESc; BiHiMed; DcScB; InSci*

Brett, George (Howard)
"Mulletthead"
American. Baseball Player
Infielder, KC, 1974-93; has established many AL hitting records; hit .390, 1980, highest average in ML in 39 yrs; won AL batting titles, 1976, 1980, 1990, becoming first in ML history to win titles in three decades.
b. May 15, 1953 in Glendale, West Virginia
Source: *Ballpl 90; BaseReg 87; BiDAmSp BB; BioIn 10, 11, 12, 13; CelR 90; CurBio 81; LegTOT; WhoAm 78, 80, 82, 84, 86, 88, 92, 94, 95, 96, 97; WhoMW 88, 90, 92, 93, 96; WorAl; WorAlBi*

Brett, George Platt, Jr.
American. Publisher
Pres., Macmillan, 1931-58; published Mitchell's *Gone With the Wind,* 1936.
b. Dec 9, 1893 in Darien, Connecticut
d. Feb 11, 1984 in Southport, Connecticut
Source: *AmAu&B; BioIn 1, 13, 14; ConAu 112; CurBio 48, 84; NewYTBS 84; Who 82, 83*

Brett, Jan Churchill
American. Children's Author, Illustrator
Self-illustrated children's books include *Good Luck Sneakers,* 1981.
b. Dec 1, 1949 in Hingham, Massachusetts
Source: *ConAu 41NR, 116; IntAu&W 89, 91, 93; MajAI; SmATA 71; WhoAm 94, 95, 96, 97; WhoAmW 95, 97*

Brett, Jeremy
[Jeremy Huggins]
English. Actor
Played on PBS "Rebecca"; "The Good Soldier." Portrayed Sherlock Holmes 1984-95.
b. Nov 3, 1935 in Berkswell, England
d. Sep 12, 1995 in London, England
Source: *BioIn 21; ConTFT 15; FilmgC; HalFC 80, 84, 88; LegTOT; NewYTBS 95; Who 82, 83, 85, 88, 90, 92, 94; WhoAm 92; WhoHol 92, A; WhoThe 72, 77, 81; WhoWor 74, 76, 89*

Brett, Simon Anthony Lee
English. Author
Wrote mystery novels, plays *So Much Blood,* 1977; created detective Charles Paris.
b. Oct 28, 1945 in Worcester, England
Source: *ConAu 69; TwCCr&M 80*

Breuer, Josef
Austrian. Physician
The forerunner of psychoanalysis; wrote *Studien uber Hysterie* 1895, with Sigmund Freud.
b. Jan 15, 1842 in Vienna, Austria
d. Jun 20, 1925 in Vienna, Austria
Source: *BiDPsy; BioIn 17; DcScB; InSci; NamesHP; OxCMed 86*

Breuer, Lee
American. Dramatist
Won Obies for *Shaggy Dog Animation,* 1978; *A Prelude to Death in Venice,* 1980.
b. Feb 6, 1937 in Philadelphia, Pennsylvania
Source: *CamGWoT; ConAmD; ConAu 110; ConDr 88, 93; ConTFT 5; GrStDi; IntDcT 3; TheaDir; WhoAm 96, 97; WhoThe 81; WrDr 88, 90, 92*

Breuer, Marcel Lajos
American. Designer, Architect
Designed NYC's Whitney Museum, 1963-66; designed tubular chair ("Wassily") while studying at Gropius' Bauhaus, 1920s.
b. May 22, 1902 in Pecs, Austria-Hungary
d. Jul 1, 1981 in New York, New York
Source: *AmArch 70; BioIn 1; BriEAA; ConArch 87, 94; ConAu 5NR, 104; CurBio 41, 60, 81; DcNiCA; EncAAr 1, 2; IntAu&W 76; IntWW 74, 75, 76, 77, 78, 79, 80, 81; McGDA; McGEWB; NewYTBS 81; PenDiDA 89; PlP&P; WhAm 8; WhoAm 80; WhoArch; WhoWor 74; WorAl*

Breuil, Henri Abbe
French. Archaeologist
One of first to record, interpret Paleolithic art; showed how cultures flourished simultaneously.
b. Feb 28, 1877 in Mortain, France
d. Aug 14, 1961 in L'Isle-Adam, France
Source: *DcScB; InSci; LngCTC; McGEWB*

Brewer, David Josiah
American. Supreme Court Justice
Conservative served 1889-1910.
b. Jun 20, 1837 in Smyrna, Turkey
d. Mar 28, 1910 in Washington, District of Columbia
Source: *AmBi; ApCAB; BiDFedJ; BioIn 2, 5, 7, 15, 19; DcAmAu; DcAmB; DcNAA; HarEnUS; NatCAB 1; OxCSupC; SupCtJu; TwCBDA; WebAB 74, 79; WhAm 1*

Brewer, Ebenezer Cobham
English. Clergy, Educator
Wrote *A Guide to Scientific Knowledge of Things Familiar,* 1850.
b. May 2, 1810 in London, England
d. Mar 6, 1897
Source: *Alli, SUP; BiD&SB; ChhPo; DcEnL; DcNaB C, S1; EvLB; NewC*

Brewer, Gay, Jr.
American. Golfer
Turned pro, 1956; won Masters, 1967.
b. Mar 19, 1932 in Middletown, Ohio
Source: *BioIn 7; LegTOT; WhoGolf; WhoIntG*

Brewer, Teresa
[Theresa Brewer]
American. Singer, Actor
1950s pop hits had upbeat tone: "Music! Music! Music!," 1950; started singing at age two, still performing in clubs.
b. May 7, 1931 in Toledo, Ohio
Source: *AllMusG; ASCAP 66, 80; BiDAmM; BiDJaz; BioIn 15; CmpEPM; EncJzS; InWom, SUP; LegTOT; NewGrDJ 88, 94; OxCPMus; PenEncP; RkOn 74, 82; VarWW 85; WhoHol 92, A; WhoRock 81; WorAl; WorAlBi*

Brewer and Shipley
[Michael Brewer; Thomas Shipley]
American. Music Group
Folk-rock duo formed, 1968; hit "One Toke Over the Line," 1971.
Source: *EncFCWM 83; EncRk 88; PenEncP; RkOn 74, 78; RolSEnR 83; WhoRock 81; WhoRocM 82*

Brewster, David, Sir
Scottish. Philosopher, Scientist
Invented kaleidoscope, 1816; brought stereoscope into scientific use; introduced the Bude light.
b. Dec 11, 1781 in Jedburgh, Scotland
d. Feb 10, 1868 in Allerby, Scotland
Source: *Alli; AsBiEn; BiDLA; BiESc; BioIn 1, 4, 8, 13, 14; BritAu 19; CamDcSc; CasWL; CelCen; Chambr 3; CmScLit; DcBiPP; DcEnA; DcEnL; DcInv; DcNaB, C; DcScB; EncO&P 1, 2, 3; EvLB; ICPEnP; InSci; LarDcSc; LinLib L, S; MacBEP; MagIlD; NewCBEL; WorInv; WorScD*

Brewster, Kingman, Jr.
American. University Administrator, Diplomat
President, Yale U, 1963-77; ambassador to UK, 1977-81.

b. Jun 17, 1919 in Longmeadow, Massachusetts
d. Nov 8, 1988 in Oxford, England
Source: *AnObit 1988; BioIn 6, 7, 8, 9, 11, 12, 16; BlueB 76; CelR; CurBio 64, 79, 89N; DcAmDH 80, 89; DrAS 74P, 78P; EncAB-H 1974; EncWB; IntWW 74, 75, 76, 77, 78, 79, 80, 81, 82, 83; IntYB 82; LEduc 74; NewYTBE 70; NewYTBS 88; WhAm 9; Who 74, 82, 83, 85, 88; WhoAm 74, 76, 78, 80, 82, 84, 86, 88; WhoAmL 85; WhoAmP 77, 79, 81, 83, 85, 87; WhoE 74, 77; WhoGov 77; WhoWor 74, 78, 80, 82, 84; WorAl; WorAlBi*

Brewster, (Ralph) Owen
American. Politician
Governor of ME, 1924-29; Rep. senator, 1946-52.
b. Feb 22, 1888 in Dexter, Maine
d. Dec 25, 1961 in Brookline, Massachusetts
Source: *BiDrAC; BiDrGov 1789; BiDrUSC 89; BioIn 1, 3, 6; CurBio 47, 62; DcAmB S7; ObitOF 79; PolProf T; WhAm 4*

Brewster, William
English. Colonial Figure
Influential unordained leader of Plymouth Colony, 1620-29.
b. 1566 in Nottinghamshire, England
d. Apr 10, 1644 in Plymouth, Massachusetts
Source: *Alli; AmBi; ApCAB; BiDLA; BioIn 5, 9, 13, 17, 19; DcAmB; DcNaB C; Drake; HarEnUS; LuthC 75; McGEWB; NewCol 75; OxCAmH; TwCBDA; WebAB 79; WebBD 83; WhAm HS; WhAmP; WorAl*

Breyer, Stephen Gerald
American. Supreme Court Justice
Associate Justice, US Supreme Court, 1994—.
b. Aug 15, 1938 in San Francisco, California
Source: *ConAu 107; CurBio 96; DrAS 74P, 78P, 82P; WhoAm 80, 82, 84, 86, 88, 90, 92, 94, 95, 96, 97; WhoAmL 79, 83, 85, 87, 90, 92, 94, 96; WhoE 83, 85, 86, 89, 97; WhoWor 96, 97*

Breytenbach, Breyten
South African. Poet, Artist, Political Activist
Wrote *True Confessions of an Albino Terrorist,* 1985, describing imprisonment, 1975-82, for anti-apartheid activities.
b. Sep 16, 1939 in Bonnievale, South Africa
Source: *CasWL; ConAu 113, 129; ConLC 23, 37; ConWorW 93; CurBio 86; CyWA 89; EncWL 3; FacFETw; LiExTwC; WorAu 1975*

Brezhnev, Leonid Ilyich
Russian. Political Leader
Leader of the Soviet Union, head of the Soviet Communist Party, 1964-82.
b. Dec 19, 1906 in Kamenskoye, Russia
d. Nov 10, 1982 in Moscow, Union of Soviet Socialist Republics
Source: *BiDMarx; BioNews 74; ColdWar 2; CurBio 78, 83; DcPol; DcRusLS; DcTwHis; EncCW; FacFETw; IntWW 74, 75, 76, 77, 78, 79, 80, 81, 82; IntYB 78, 79, 80, 81, 82; McGEWB; NewYTBE 71, 72, 73; NewYTBS 82; WhDW; Who 74, 82, 83; WhoWor 74, 76, 78, 80, 82; WorAl*

Brian, David
American. Actor
Film debut in *Flamingo Road,* 1949; TV series "Mr. District Attorney."
b. Aug 5, 1914 in New York, New York
d. Jul 15, 1993 in Sherman Oaks, California
Source: *BioIn 4, 78, 79, 80, 81, 82, 84, 86, 88, 92; MotPP; WhoHol 92, A*

Brian, Donald
American. Actor, Singer
Starred on broadway *Chocolate Soldier; Merry Widow; No, No, Nanette.*
b. Feb 17, 1875 in Saint John's, Newfoundland, Canada
d. Dec 22, 1948 in Great Neck, New York
Source: *CmpEPM; EncMT; Film 1; NatCAB 36; NotNAT B; WhAm 2; WhoHol B; WhoStg 1908; WhScrn 74, 77*

Brian Boru
Irish. Ruler
High king of Ireland through conquest, 1002-1014; defeated Norse in battle, broke Norse power in Ireland.
b. 926
d. Apr 23, 1014 in Clontarf, Ireland
Source: *BioIn 8, 13; LinLib S; NewC; NewCol 75; REn*

Briand, Aristide
French. Statesman
Nobel Peace Prize-winning foreign minister; co-authored Kellogg-Briand Pact, 1928, to abolish war.
b. Mar 28, 1862 in Nantes, France
d. Mar 7, 1932 in Paris, France
Source: *BiDFrPL; BioIn 1, 4, 6, 9, 11, 15, 17; DcTwCCu 2; DcTwHis; EncTR 91; FacFETw; LegTOT; LinLib S; McGEWB; NobelP; WebBD 83; WhDW; WhoNob, 90, 95; WorAl; WorAlBi*

Briand, Rena
Canadian. Journalist, Author
Writer of non-fiction, memories, documentaries.
b. Nov 12, 1935
Source: *ConAu 29R; WrDr 76, 80, 82, 84*

Brice, Fanny
[Fanny Borach]
"Baby Snooks"
American. Actor, Singer
Ziegfeld Follies star, noted for torch song "My Man"; created radio character, "Baby Snooks"; life portrayed in *Funny Girl,* 1968.
b. Oct 29, 1891 in New York, New York
d. May 29, 1951 in Beverly Hills, California
Source: *Baker 92; BiDAmM; BiDD; BioAmW; BioIn 1, 2, 3, 4, 5, 6, 11, 12, 13, 14, 15, 16, 17, 18; CamGWoT; CmpEPM; ContDcW 89; CurBio 46, 51; DcAmB S5; EncAFC; EncMT; EncVaud; EncWB; EncWT; Ent; FacFETw; FamA&A; Film 2; FilmEn; FilmgC; ForYSC; FunnyW; Funs; GoodHs; GrLiveH; HalFC 80, 84, 88; IntDcWB; JoeFr; LegTOT; LibW; MovMk; NewAmDM; NewGrDA 86; NotAW MOD; NotNAT A, B; NotWoAT; OxCAmT 84; OxCFilm; OxCPMus; PenEncP; PlP&P; QDrFCA 92; RadStar; SaTiSS; ThFT; WhAm 3; WhoCom; WhoHol B; WhScrn 74, 77, 83; WhThe; WorAl; WorAlBi*

Brickell, Edie
American. Music Group
Lead singer, pop-rock band; musical genre varies from funk, disco, reggae, neo-rockabilly, and psychedelia; hit singles "What I Am," "Little Miss S," 1988; married to Paul Simon.
b. 1966 in Oak Cliff, Texas
Source: *BioIn 16; ConMus 3; LegTOT*

Bricker, John William
American. Politician, Lawyer
Three-term Rep. governor of OH, 1939-45; lost 1944 presidential nomination to Thomas Dewey.
b. Sep 6, 1893 in Madison County, Ohio
d. Mar 22, 1986 in Columbus, Ohio
Source: *BiDrAC; BiDrGov 1789; BiDrUSC 89; BioIn 1, 3, 4, 5, 6, 7, 8, 11, 14, 15, 19; CurBio 43, 56, 86; LinLib S; St&PR 75; WhAm 9; Who 74, 82, 83, 85; WhoAm 74, 76, 78, 80, 82; WhoAmP 73, 75, 77, 79*

Bricklin, Malcolm N
American. Business Executive
Founded Bricklin Motor Co., 1971.
b. Mar 9, 1939 in Philadelphia, Pennsylvania
Source: *BioIn 10, 11, 12, 13; BusPN; WhoAm 76, 78, 80; WhoFI 74, 75*

Brickman, Morrie
American. Cartoonist
Wrote *This Little Pigeon Went to Market,* 1965; syndicated cartoonist, 1954—.
b. Jul 24, 1917 in Chicago, Illinois
Source: *BioIn 6; WhoAm 74, 76, 78, 80, 82, 84, 86, 88*

Bricktop
[Ada Beatrice Queen Victoria Louise Virginia Smith]
American. Singer, Restaurateur
Had famous pre-WW II nightclub in Paris; Cole Porter wrote "Miss Otis Regrets" for her.
b. Aug 14, 1894 in Iderson, West Virginia

d. Jan 31, 1984 in New York, New York
Source: *AnObit 1984; BiDAfM; BioIn 14, 18; BioNews 74; BlkWAm; ConAu 111; DrBlPA, 90; FacFETw; NewYTBS 84; PseudAu*

Brico, Antonia
American. Conductor
First woman to conduct LA Philharmonic Orchestra, several other major symphony orchestras; subject of film documentary *Portrait of Antonia,* 1975.
b. Jun 26, 1902 in Rotterdam, Netherlands
d. Aug 3, 1989 in Denver, Colorado
Source: *Baker 78, 84, 92; BioIn 1, 4, 10, 12, 16; CurBio 48, 89, 89N; FacFETw; GrLiveH; InWom, SUP; LibW; NewAmDM; NewGrDA 86; NewYTBS 89; WhoAm 80, 82, 84; WhoAmW 66, 68, 70, 72, 74; WomCom; WorAl*

Bricusse, Leslie
English. Lyricist, Composer
Won Grammy for "What Kind of Fool Am I?," 1962; Oscar for "Talk to the Animals," 1967.
b. Jan 29, 1931 in London, England
Source: *BioIn 14; ConTFT 9; EncMT; FilmEn; FilmgC; HalFC 80, 84, 88; IntMPA 94, 96; IntWWM 77; NotNAT; OxCPMus; VarWW 85; WhoThe 81*

Bridge, Frank
English. Composer
Composed chamber music; one of his pupils was Benjamin Britten.
b. Feb 26, 1879 in Brighton, England
d. Jan 11, 1941 in London, England
Source: *Baker 78, 84, 92; BioIn 4, 5, 9, 11, 14, 17; BriBkM 80; CurBio 41; DcArts; DcCM; DcCom&M 79; DcNaB 1941; FacFETw; MusMk; NewAmDM; NewGrDM 80; NewGrDO; NewOxM; OxCMus; PenDiMP A*

Bridger, James
American. Fur Trader, Pioneer
First white man to see Great Salt Lake, 1824; dominated western fur trade, 1830-34.
b. Mar 17, 1804 in Richmond, Virginia
d. Jul 17, 1881 in Kansas City, Missouri
Source: *AmBi; BenetAL 91; BioIn 1, 2, 3, 4, 5, 6, 7, 8, 9, 10, 15; DcAmB; EncAAH; McGEWB; NatCAB 13; OxCAmH; OxCAmL 65, 83, 95; REnAL; REnAW; WebAB 74, 79; WhAm HS; WhNaAH; WhWE*

Bridges, Beau
[Lloyd Vernet Bridges, III]
American. Actor
Films include *The Other Side of the Mountain,* 1975; *Norma Rae,* 1979; son of actor Lloyd.
b. Dec 9, 1941 in Los Angeles, California
Source: *BioIn 8, 9, 10; BkPepl; CelR; ConTFT 3, 10; FilmEn; FilmgC; ForYSC; HalFC 80, 84, 88; IntMPA 75, 76, 77, 78, 79, 80, 81, 82, 84, 86, 88, 92, 94, 96; LegTOT; MiSFD 9; MovMk; NewYTBE 70; WhoAm 76, 78, 80, 82, 84, 86, 88, 90, 92, 94, 95, 96, 97; WhoEnt 92; WhoHol 92, A; WorAl; WorAlBi*

Bridges, Bill
American. Basketball Player
Guard, 1961-63, with KC, ABL, 1962-75, with several NBA teams; led ABL in scoring, 1963.
b. Apr 4, 1939 in Hobbs, New Mexico
Source: *BasBi; BiDAmSp BK; OfNBA 87; WhoAfA 96; WhoBbl 73; WhoBlA 92, 94*

Bridges, Calvin Blackman
American. Geneticist
Developed chromosome theory of heredity.
b. Jan 11, 1889 in Schuyler Falls, New York
d. Dec 27, 1938 in Los Angeles, California
Source: *BioIn 4; DcAmB S2; DcNAA; DcScB; InSci; NatCAB 30; WebBD 83; WhAm 1*

Bridges, Harry Renton
American. Labor Union Official
Founder, president, ILWU, 1937-77; known for alleged communist ideology.
b. Jul 29, 1901 in Melbourne, Australia
d. Mar 30, 1990 in San Francisco, California
Source: *CurBio 40, 50, 90; EncAB-H 1974, 1996; NewYTBE 72; NewYTBS 90; REnAW; WebAB 74; WhoAm 74; WhoWest 74; WhoWor 74*

Bridges, James
American. Director, Screenwriter
Author, director of prize-winning films *China Syndrome,* 1979; *Urban Cowboy,* 1980.
b. Feb 3, 1936 in Little Rock, Arkansas
d. Jun 6, 1993 in Los Angeles, California
Source: *AnObit 1993; ConAu 116, 127, 141; ConLC 81; ConTFT 4, 12; FilmEn; IlWWHD 1A; IntMPA 81, 92; LegTOT; MiSFD 9; VarWW 85; WhAm 11; WhoAm 86; WhoEnt 92; WhoHol 92*

Bridges, Jeff
American. Actor
Nominated for Oscars for roles in *The Last Picture Show,* 1971; *Thunderbolt & Lightfoot,* 1974; *Tron,* 1982; in *The Mirror Has Two Faces,* 1996, with Barbra Streisand.
b. Dec 4, 1949 in Los Angeles, California
Source: *BiDFilm 94; BkPepl; CelR 90; ConTFT 3, 10; FilmEn; FilmgC; GangFlm; HalFC 84, 88; HolBB; IntDcF 1-3, 2-3; IntMPA 86, 92, 94, 96; IntWW 91, 93; LegTOT; MovMk; NewYTBS 75; WhoAm 95, 96, 97; WhoHol 92, A; WorAlBi*

Bridges, Lloyd
[Lloyd Vernet Bridges, Jr]
American. Actor
Starred in TV series "Sea Hunt," 1958; films include *High Noon,* 1952; *Airplane!,* 1980; *Airplane II,* 1982; father of actors Jeff, Beau.
b. Jan 15, 1913 in San Leandro, California
Source: *BioIn 5, 8, 10, 17, 19, 20, 21; CelR, 90; ConTFT 3, 11; CurBio 90; FilmEn; FilmgC; ForYSC; GangFlm; HalFC 80, 84, 88; IntMPA 75, 76, 77, 78, 79, 80, 81, 82, 84, 86, 88, 92, 94, 96; ItaFilm; LegTOT; MotPP; MovMk; WhoAm 86, 95, 96, 97; WhoHol 92, A; WhoHrs 80; WorAl; WorAlBi*

Bridges, Robert Seymour
English. Author, Poet
Poet laureate, 1913-30, who wrote philosophical poem "Testament of Beauty," 1929.
b. Oct 23, 1844 in Walmer, England
d. Apr 21, 1930 in Chilswell, England
Source: *AtlBL; CasWL; EncWL; ModBrL; OxCEng 85; PenC ENG; REn; TwCA SUP*

Bridges, Styles
[Henry Styles Bridges]
American. Politician
Governor, NH, 1935-37; leading Rep. senator, 1937-54.
b. Sep 9, 1898 in West Pembroke, Maine
d. Nov 26, 1961 in Concord, New Hampshire
Source: *BiDrAC; BiDrGov 1789; BiDrUSC 89; BioIn 1, 2, 3, 5, 6, 11; DcAmB S7; EncCW; EncMcCE; InSci; ObitOF 79; ObitT 1961; PolProf E, K, T; WhAm 4; WhAmP*

Bridges, Todd
American. Actor
Played Willis on TV series "Diff'rent Strokes."
b. May 27, 1965 in San Francisco, California
Source: *BioIn 12, 13; DrBlPA 90; InB&W 80; LegTOT; WhoHol 92*

Bridges, Tommy
[Thomas Jefferson Davis Bridges]
American. Baseball Player
Pitcher, Detroit, 1930-46; three-time 20-game winner.
b. Dec 28, 1906 in Gordonsville, Tennessee
d. Apr 19, 1968 in Nashville, Tennessee
Source: *Ballpl 90; BiDAmSp BB; BioIn 3, 8, 15; DcAmB S8; WhoProB 73*

Bridgewater, Dee Dee
American. Singer, Actor
Won Tony for *The Wiz,* 1975.
b. May 27, 1950 in Memphis, Tennessee
Source: *AllMusG; DrBlPA, 90; EncJzS; NewGrDJ 88, 94; NewYTBS 75; PenEncP; WhoAm 82; WhoAmW 81; WhoBlA 80*

Bridgman, Frederic Arthur
American. Artist
Painted figure, oriental, archeological pictures.
b. Nov 10, 1847 in Tuskegee, Alabama
d. Jan 13, 1927 in Rouen, France
Source: *AmBi; BiDSA; DcAmAu; DcAmB; DcNAA; TwCBDA; WhAm 1*

Bridgman, Laura Dewey
American. Student
First blind, deaf-mute to be successfully educated; taught by Samuel G Howe, 1837.
b. Dec 21, 1829 in Hanover, New Hampshire
d. May 24, 1889 in Boston, Massachusetts
Source: *AmBi; AmWom; ApCAB; BioIn 2, 4, 6, 9, 10, 11, 20; DcAmB; Dis&D; Drake; EncDeaf; InWom, SUP; LibW; NatCAB 2; NotAW; OxCAmH; TwCBDA; WebAB 74, 79; WhAm HS; WomFir*

Bridgman, Percy Williams
American. Scientist, Physician, Engineer
Known for work with substances under high pressures; won Nobel Prize in physics, 1946, for development of high-pressure chamber.
b. Apr 21, 1882 in Cambridge, Massachusetts
d. Aug 20, 1961 in Randolph, New Hampshire
Source: *AmAu&B; AsBiEn; BiDPsy; BiESc; BioIn 1, 2, 3, 4, 6, 7, 8, 14, 15, 17, 20; CamDcSc; DcAmB S7; DcScB; FacFETw; InSci; LarDcSc; McGEWB; McGMS 80; NamesHP; NatCAB 48; NotTwCS; OxCAmH; RAdv 14, 13-5; WebAB 74, 79; WhAm 4; WhNAA; WhoNob, 90, 95; WorAl; WorAlBi*

Bridie, James
[Osborne Henry Mavor]
Scottish. Dramatist
Witty, fanciful plays include *The Sleeping Clergyman,* 1933; *Storm in a Teacup,* 1936.
b. Jan 3, 1888 in Glasgow, Scotland
d. Jan 29, 1951 in Edinburgh, Scotland
Source: *BioIn 1, 3; EncWT; Ent; EvLB; GrBr; GrWrEL DR; HalFC 80, 84, 88; IntDcT 2; LngCTC; McGEWD 72, 84; ModBrL; ModWD; NewCBEL; NotNAT A, B; ObitT 1951; OxCEng 67, 85, 95; OxCMed 86; OxCThe 67, 83; PenC ENG; PlP&P; REn; REnWD; RfGEnL 91; RGTwCWr; TwCLC 3; TwCWr; WebE&AL; WhDW; WhE&EA; WhLit; WhoLA; WhoTwCL; WhThe; WorAu 1950; WorEFlm*

Brieux, Eugene
French. Dramatist
Wrote on moral, social themes: *Blanchette,* 1892; *La Robe Rouge,* 1900.
b. Jan 19, 1858 in Paris, France
d. Dec 7, 1932 in Nice, France
Source: *BioIn 1; CamGWoT; CasWL; ClDMEL 47, 80; CnMD; CnThe; DcArts; EvEuW; IntDcT 2; LinLib L, S; LngCTC; McGEWD 72, 84; ModFrL; ModWD; NewC; NotNAT B; OxCEng 67, 85, 95; OxCFr; OxCThe 67, 83; PenC EUR; REn; REnWD; TwCA, SUP; WhThe*

Brigati, Eddie
[The Rascals]
American. Singer
Vocalist with blue-eyed soul group, 1965-71; composed most of groups songs with Frank Cavaliere.
b. Oct 22, 1946 in New York, New York

Briggs, Austin Eugene
American. Artist, Illustrator
Illustrated Henry Ford's *Dearborn Independent,* 1925-27; cofounder, member, Famous Artists School, 1950-73.
b. Sep 8, 1908 in Humboldt, Minnesota
d. Oct 13, 1973 in Paris, France
Source: *NewYTBE 73; WhAm 6; WhoAm 74; WhoAmA 73*

Briggs, Clare A
American. Cartoonist
Created cartoon character "Skin-nay."
b. Aug 5, 1875 in Reedsburgh, Wisconsin
d. Jan 3, 1930 in New York, New York
Source: *DcAmB S1; WhAm 1*

Briggs, Ellis O(rmsbee)
American. Diplomat
US Ambassador to seven countries, 1944-62; wrote *Shots Heard Round the World,* 1957.
b. Dec 1, 1899 in Watertown, Massachusetts
d. Feb 21, 1976 in Gainesville, Georgia
Source: *BioIn 4, 7, 10, 11, 16; BlueB 76; CurBio 65, 76; DcAmDH 80, 89; IntWW 74, 75; WhAm 7; WhoAm 74, 76; WhoE 74; WhoWor 74*

Briggs, Fred
American. Broadcast Journalist
With NBC News 1966-95.
b. May 31, 1932 in Chicago, Illinois
d. Feb 7, 1995 in Boston, Massachusetts
Source: *ConAu 73, 147; WhoAm 80, 82, 84; WhoTelC*

Briggs, Walter Owen
American. Business Executive, Baseball Executive
Established Briggs Manufacturing Co., 1909, known for developing auto mass production methods; owner, Detroit Tigers, 1920-52; move to obtain Mickey Cochrane, 1934, credited with AL pennant, World Series win, 1935.
b. Feb 27, 1877 in Ypsilanti, Michigan
d. Jan 17, 1952 in Miami Beach, Florida
Source: *BiDAmSp BB; BioIn 2, 3, 8, 15; NatCAB 51; ObitOF 79; WhAm 3*

Bright, John
English. Government Official, Author
Founded Anti-Corn Law League, 1839; supported Northern cause in American Civil War.
b. Nov 16, 1811 in Greenbank, England
d. Mar 27, 1889 in Greenbank, England
Source: *Alli SUP; BbD; BiD&SB; BiDMoPL; BioIn 1, 3, 4, 7, 8, 9, 10, 12, 14, 16, 20; CelCen; Chambr 3; DcAmSR; DcBiPP; DcInB; DcNaB S1; HarEnUS; HisDBrE; HisWorL; LinLib S; McGEWB; NewC; OxCEng 85, 95; REn; VicBrit; WhDW; WorAl*

Bright, Richard
English. Physician
Studied disease by morbid anatomy; discovered Bright's Disease; invented modern shorthand writing.
b. Sep 28, 1789 in Bristol, England
d. Dec 16, 1858 in London, England
Source: *Alli, SUP; BiESc; BiHiMed; BioIn 4, 5, 7, 9, 13, 14; CamDcSc; CelCen; DcNaB; DcScB; InSci; LarDcSc; LinLib S; McGEWB; OxCMed 86; WhDW*

Bright, Susie
American. Writer
Wrote *Herotica,* 1987; *Susie Sexpert's Lesbian Sex World,* 1990.
b. Mar 25, 1958 in Arlington, Virginia
Source: *GayLesB*

Brigid of Kildare
Irish. Religious Figure
Founded first religious community for women in Ireland; revered only less than St. Patrick.
b. 453? in Faughart, Ireland
d. 523? in Kildare, Ireland
Source: *DcCathB; DcIrB 78; IlEncMy; InWom; LuthC 75; NewC*

Briles, Judith Joyce
American. Author
Writes on women's issues, ethics, finance: *Woman to Woman: From Sabotage to Support,* 1988.
b. Feb 20, 1946 in Pasadena, California
Source: *ConAu 106; WhoAmW 87; WhoFI 85, 87*

Briley, John Richard
American. Screenwriter
Won 1983 best original screenplay Oscar for *Gandhi.*
b. Jun 25, 1925 in Kalamazoo, Michigan
Source: *Au&Wr 71; ConAu 44NR, 101; HalFC 84; IntAu&W 76, 77, 82; WhoAm 95, 96, 97; WhoEnt 92; WhoWor 76, 78; WrDr 76, 84, 86*

Brill, Abraham Arden
American. Psychiatrist
Chief of psychiatry clinic, Columbia U; lecturer, NYU; wrote *The Basic Writings of Sigmund Freud,* 1938.
b. Oct 12, 1874 in Kanczuga, Austria
d. Mar 2, 1948 in New York, New York

Source: *AmAu&B; BiDPsy; BioIn 1, 4, 7, 8; DcAmB S4; DcAmMeB 84; DcNAA; LinLib L; NamesHP; REnAL; TwCA SUP; WhAm 2; WhNAA*

Brillat-Savarin, Jean Anthelme
French. Author, Chef
Wrote gastronomic classic *Physiology of Taste,* 1884.
b. Apr 1, 1755 in Bellay, France
d. Feb 2, 1826 in Paris, France
Source: *ApCAB; AtlBL; BbD; BiD&SB; BioIn 3, 4, 7, 9, 14, 18; CasWL; DcBiPP; EuAu; EvEuW; LinLib S; NewC; OxCEng 67; OxCFr; OxCPhil; REn*

Brimley, Wilford
American. Actor
Star of TV series "Our House," 1986-88; had supporting role in film *The Natural,* 1984.
b. Sep 27, 1934 in Salt Lake City, Utah
Source: *ConTFT 6, 13; IntMPA 92, 94, 96; LegTOT; WhoAm 88, 90, 92, 94, 95, 96, 97; WhoEnt 92; WhoHol 92*

Brimmer, Andrew Felton
American. Economist, Government Official
First black man to serve on Federal Reserve Board, 1966.
b. Sep 13, 1926 in Newellton, Louisiana
Source: *AmEA 74; AmMWSc 73S; BioIn 7, 8, 9, 13; BlueB 76; CurBio 68; InB&W 80, 85; IntWW 74, 75, 76, 77, 78, 79, 80, 81, 82, 83, 89, 91, 93; NegAl 76, 83, 89A; NewYTBE 73; SelBAAf; SelBAAu; St&PR 84, 87, 91, 93, 96; WhoAm 74, 76, 78, 80, 82, 84, 86, 88, 90; WhoAmP 73, 75, 77, 79; WhoBlA 85; WhoGov 72, 75; WhoSSW 73, 75*

Brimsek, Frankie
[Francis Charles Brimsek]
"Mr. Zero"
American. Hockey Player
Goalie, 1938-43, 1945-50, mostly with Boston; won Calder Trophy, 1939; won Vezina Trophy, 1939, 1942; Hall of Fame, 1966.
b. Sep 26, 1915 in Eveleth, Minnesota
Source: *BiDAmSp BK; BioIn 2, 8; HocEn; WhoHcky 73; WhoSpor*

Brindley, James
English. Engineer
Known for civil engineering; constructed over 365 canals; remained illiterate, did most of work in head.
b. 1716 in Tunstead, England
d. Sep 30, 1772 in Turnhurst, England
Source: *Alli; BioIn 2, 4, 5, 6, 7, 8, 9, 10, 14; DcBiPP; DcNaB; InSci; RAdv 14; WhDW*

Brinegar, Claude Stout
American. Government Official
Secretary of Transportation under Nixon, Ford, 1973-75.
b. Dec 16, 1926 in Rockport, California
Source: *AmMWSc 73S; BiDrUSE 89; BioIn 10, 12; BlueB 76; CngDr 74; NewYTBE 72; St&PR 87, 91, 93, 96; WhoAm 74, 76, 78, 80, 82, 90, 92, 94, 95, 96, 97; WhoAmP 75; WhoFI 74, 89, 92, 94, 96; WhoScEn 94; WhoSSW 75; WhoWest 89, 92, 94; WhoWor 74, 91, 93, 95, 97*

Brinig, Myron
American. Author
Writings include *No Marriage in Paradise,* 1949; *Wide Open Town,* 1929.
b. Dec 22, 1900 in Minneapolis, Minnesota
d. May 13, 1991 in New York, New York
Source: *AmAu&B; AmNov; BioIn 2, 4; OxCAmL 65, 83, 95; REnAL; ScF&FL 1; TwCA, SUP; TwCWW 91*

Brink, Andre Philippus
South African. Author
Works reveal apartheid's destruction of human values; wrote *An Instant in the Wind,* 1975, *A Dry White Season,* 1979.
b. May 29, 1935 in Vrede, South Africa
Source: *BioIn 21; RGTwCWr; Who 90; WhoWor 97*

Brink, Carol Ryrie
American. Author
Prolific adult, children's writer; won Newbery for *Caddie Woodlawn,* 1936.
b. Dec 28, 1895 in Moscow, Idaho
d. Aug 15, 1981 in La Jolla, California
Source: *AmAu&B; AmWomPl; AmWomWr; AmWr; AnCL; AnObit 1981; Au&Wr 71; AuBYP 2, 3; BioIn 14, 18, 19; ChhPo S1; ChlBkCr; ChlLR 30; ConAu 1R, 3NR, 104; CurBio 46, 81; IntAu&W 76, 77, 82; InWom, SUP; JBA 51; LinLib L; MajAI; MinnWr; MorBMP; NewbMB 1922; OxCChiL; REnAL; ScF&FL 2; SmATA 1, 27N, 31; Str&VC; TwCChW 78, 83, 89, 95; TwCWW 91; WhAm 8; WhE&EA; WhoAm 74, 76, 78, 80; WhoAmW 58, 66, 68, 70, 72, 74; WhoPNW; WrChl; WrDr 76, 80, 82*

Brinkley, Christie
[Mrs. Peter Cook]
American. Model
Super model credited with several cover pgs, commercials.
b. Feb 2, 1954 in Malibu, California
Source: *BioIn 12, 13; CelR 90; CurBio 94; InWom SUP; WhoHol 92*

Brinkley, David McClure
American. Broadcast Journalist
NBC News co-anchor with Chet Huntley, 1958-70; host of ABC's "This Week With David Brinkley," 1981-96.
b. Jul 10, 1920 in Wilmington, North Carolina
Source: *BkPepl; ConAu 97; CurBio 60, 87; EncTwCJ; IntMPA 86; LesBEnT; WhoAm 86, 96, 97; WhoE 97; WhoSSW 75; WhoWor 74, 96, 97; WorAl*

Brinkley, John Romulus
American. Surgeon
Alleged charlatan, who became rich by rejuvenating men with goat gland transplants.
b. Jul 8, 1885 in Jackson County, North Carolina
d. May 26, 1942 in San Antonio, Texas
Source: *BioIn 5, 8, 11; CurBio 42; DcAmB S3; DcNCBi 1; InSci; ObitOF 79; WorAl*

Brinkley, Nell
American. Illustrator
Self-taught artist; pen-and-ink drawings of boys, girls were syndicated throughout US.
b. 1888
d. Oct 21, 1944
Source: *ArtsAmW 3; BioIn 1; CurBio 44; DcWomA; InWom; NatCAB 33*

Brinsmead, Hesba Fay
[Pixie Hungerford]
Australian. Author
Writings include *Pastures of the Blue Crane,* 1964; *Isle of the Sea Horse,* 1969.
b. Mar 15, 1922 in New South Wales, Australia
Source: *BioIn 12, 16, 19, 20; ChlFicS; ConAu 10NR; ConLC 21; FourBJA; OxCChiL; SenS; SmATA 18; TwCChW 83, 95; WrDr 76, 80, 86*

Brinton, Clarence Crane
American. Historian
Specialized in the history of ideas, the pattern of revolution; history professor at Harvard U; wrote 15 books.
b. Feb 2, 1898 in Winsted, Connecticut
d. Sep 7, 1968
Source: *AmAu&B; BioIn 4, 5, 8; ConAu 5R; CurBio 58, 68; DcAmB S8; REn; REnAL; TwCA, SUP*

Brinton, Daniel Garrison
American. Author
Books on ethnology include *American Hero Myths,* 1882.
b. May 13, 1837 in Thornbury, Pennsylvania
d. Jul 31, 1899
Source: *Alli SUP; AmAu; AmAu&B; AmBi; ApCAB; BenetAL 91; BiD&SB; BiInAmS; CyAL 2; DcAmAu; DcAmB; DcNAA; HarEnUS; InSci; IntDcAn; LinLib L; NatCAB 9; OxCAmH; OxCAmL 65, 83, 95; TwCBDA; WebAB 74, 79; WhAm 1; WhFla; WhNaAH*

Brioni, Gaetano Savini, Marquis
Italian. Fashion Designer
Founded Brioni Menswear, 1944; known for traditional Italian tailoring since 1930s.
b. Sep 10, 1909 in Termi, Italy
Source: *WhoAm 84, 86; WorFshn*

Brisbane, Albert
American. Social Reformer, Author
Wrote *Social Destiny of Man,* 1840; promoted Fourierism in *NY Tribune* columns; father of Arthur.
b. Aug 22, 1809 in Batavia, New York
d. May 1, 1890 in Richmond, Virginia
Source: *AmAu; AmAu&B; AmBi; AmRef; BenetAL 91; BiDTran; BioIn 1, 3, 5, 8, 12, 15; DcAmB; DcAmSR; DcLB 3; DcNAA; McGEWB; NatCAB 4; OxCAmH; OxCAmL 65, 83, 95; REnAL; WebAB 74, 79; WhAm HS*

Brisbane, Arthur
American. Journalist
Articles swayed public opinion to contribute to outbreak of Spanish-American War, 1898.
b. Dec 12, 1864 in Buffalo, New York
d. Dec 25, 1936 in New York, New York
Source: *AmAu&B; AmBi; ApCAB X; BiDAmJo; BiDAmNC; BioIn 1, 3, 4, 9, 14, 16; DcAmB S2; DcLB 25; DcNAA; EncAB-A 8; EncAJ; GayN; HarEnUS; JrnUS; LinLib L, S; NatCAB 14, 27; OxCAmH; OxCAmL 65, 83, 95; REnAL; TwCA; WebAB 74, 79; WhAm 1; WhJnl*

Briscoe, Dolph
American. Politician
Dem. governor of TX, 1973-79.
b. Apr 23, 1923 in Uvalde, Texas
Source: *AlmAP 78; BiDrGov 1789, 1978; BioIn 9, 10, 11; WhoAm 74, 76, 78; WhoAmP 75; WhoGov 77; WhoSSW 78*

Briscoe, Robert
Irish. Government Official
First Jewish Lord Mayor of Dublin, 1956; a founder of the Fianna Fail Party, 1926.
b. Sep 25, 1894 in Dublin, Ireland
d. May 30, 1969 in Dublin, Ireland
Source: *BiDIrW; BioIn 4, 5, 8; CurBio 57, 69; DcIrB 78, 88; DcIrW 2; ObitOF 79*

Brisebois, Danielle
American. Actor
Appeared in TV series ''Archie Bunker's Place,'' 1981; ''Knots Landing,'' 1983-84.
b. Jun 28, 1969 in New York, New York
Source: *BioIn 12; LegTOT; VarWW 85; WhoHol 92*

Brissie, Lou
[Leland Victor Brissie, Jr]
American. Baseball Player
WW II paratrooper wounded in action; pitcher, 1947-53, playing with leg brace, artificial leg.
b. Jun 5, 1924 in Anderson, South Carolina
Source: *Ballpl 90; BioIn 1, 8, 14; WhoProB 73*

Brisson, Frederick
Danish. Producer
Stage, film productions include *Damn Yankees,* 1955.
b. Mar 17, 1917 in Copenhagen, Denmark
d. Oct 8, 1984 in New York, New York
Source: *AnObit 1984; BiE&WWA; CelR; FilmgC; IntMPA 82; NotNAT; WhoAm 74, 76, 78, 80, 82; WhoThe 81*

Bristow, Lonnie
American. Physician
President, American Medical Association, 1995—.
b. Apr 6, 1930 in New York, New York
Source: *ConBlB 12; News 96, 96-1*

Britain, Radie
American. Composer
Wrote choral compositions, string quartets, song cycles including ''Translunar Cycle,'' 1967.
b. Mar 17, 1903 in Amarillo, Texas
Source: *AmComp; ASCAP 66; Baker 78, 84, 92; BiDAmM; BioIn 1, 3, 12, 16; ConAmC 76, 82; InWom, SUP; WhoAm 74, 76, 86; WhoAmM 83; WhoAmW 58, 70, 72, 74, 77; WhoMus 72; WomCom*

Britt, May
[Maybritt Wilkens]
Swedish. Actor
Starred in *The Blue Angel,* 1959; former wife of Sammy Davis, Jr.
b. Mar 22, 1933 in Lidingo, Sweden
Source: *FilmEn; FilmgC; ForYSC; HalFC 80, 84, 88; LegTOT; MotPP; WhoHol A*

Britt, Steuart Henderson
American. Psychologist, Author
Published nearly 200 articles on marketing, law, psychology; wrote *The Spenders,* 1960.
b. Jun 17, 1907 in Fulton, Missouri
d. Mar 15, 1979 in Evanston, Illinois
Source: *AmMWSc 78S; BioIn 12; BlueB 76; ConAu 1R, 2NR, 85; WhAm 7; WhoAm 78; WhoCan 73; WhoFI 79; WhoMW 78; WhoWor 78*

Brittain, Harry Ernest, Sir
English. Newspaper Publisher
Founder, Commonwealth Press Union, 1909; Pilgrim's Club, 1902.
b. Dec 24, 1873
d. Jul 9, 1974
Source: *Au&Wr 71; BioIn 1, 2, 10; NewYTBS 74; ObitT 1971; Who 74*

Brittain, Vera Mary
English. Author
Wrote of WW I experiences in *Testament of Youth,* 1933; made into English series shown on PBS.
b. 1896 in Newcastle-upon-Tyne, England
d. Mar 29, 1970
Source: *ChhPo; ConAu P-1; DcLEL; EvLB; LngCTC; NewC; NewYTBE 73; ObitT 1961; PenC ENG; REn; TwCA, SUP; TwCWr; WhE&EA*

Brittan, Leon
English. Politician
Vice president, Commission of European Communities, 1989—.
b. Sep 25, 1939 in London, England
Source: *CurBio 94; IntWW 81, 82, 83, 89, 91, 93; IntYB 78, 79, 80, 81, 82; Who 82, 83, 85, 88, 90, 92, 94; WhoEIO 82; WhoWor 82, 84, 87, 89, 91, 93, 95, 96, 97; WhoWorJ 78*

Brittany, Morgan
[Suzanne Cupito; Mrs. Jack Gill]
American. Actor
Played Katherine Wentworth on TV drama ''Dallas,'' 1981-84.
b. Dec 5, 1951 in Hollywood, California
Source: *ConTFT 7; IntMPA 88, 92, 94, 96; LegTOT; VarWW 85; WhoHol 92*

Britten, (Edward) Benjamin
English. Composer
Best known for modern operas, including *Gloriana,* 1953, written for coronation of Elizabeth II.
b. Nov 22, 1913 in Lowestoft, England
d. Dec 4, 1976 in Aldeburgh, England
Source: *Baker 78, 84, 92; Benet 87, 96; BiDMoPL; BioIn 1, 2, 3, 4, 5, 6, 7, 8, 9, 10, 11, 12, 13, 14, 15, 16, 17, 18, 19, 20, 21; BlueB 76; BriBkM 80; CelR; ChhPo S2; CmOp; CnOxB; CompSN, SUP; ConMus 15; CurBio 42, 61, 77N; DancEn 78; DcArts; DcCM; DcCom 77; DcCom&M 79; DcNaB 1971; FacFETw; GayLesB; GrBr; IntDcOp; IntWW 74, 75, 76; IntWWM 77; LegTOT; LinLib L, S; MakMC; McGEWB; MetOEnc; MusMk; NewAmDM; NewEOp 71; NewGrDM 80; NewGrDO; NewOxM; NewYTBS 76; OxCEng 85, 95; OxCFilm; OxCMus; OxDcOp; PenDiMP A; PenEncH; RAdv 14, 13-3; WhAm 7; WhDW; Who 74; WhoMus 72; WhoWor 74, 78; WorAl; WorAlBi*

Britton, Barbara
[Barbara Brantingham]
American. Actor
Spokesperson for Revlon cosmetics, 12 yrs.
b. Sep 26, 1919 in Long Beach, California
d. Jan 18, 1980 in New York, New York
Source: *BioIn 3, 10, 12; FilmEn; FilmgC; ForWC 70; HolP 40; IntMPA 77; MotPP; MovMk; NewYTBS 80; WhoAmW 79; WhoHol A*

Britton, Jack
[William J Breslin]
American. Boxer
Welterweight champ, 1924; fought Ted Lewis in record-long series, 1915-21.
b. Oct 10, 1885 in Clinton, New York
d. Mar 27, 1962 in Miami, Florida
Source: *BiDAmSp BK; BioIn 6; BoxReg; ObitOF 79; WhoBox 74; WhoSpor*

Britton, Nathaniel, Lord
American. Botanist
First director, NY Botanical Garden, 1896-1929; co-wrote *Illustrated Flora of the Northern United States, Canada, and the British Possessions,* 1896-98.
b. Jan 15, 1859 in Staten Island, New York
d. Jun 15, 1934 in New York, New York
Source: *DcAmB S1; DcScB; NatCAB 12, 25; NewCol 75; WhAm 1*

Britz, Jerilyn
American. Golfer
Member LPGA; won US Women's Open, 1979.
b. Jan 1, 1943 in Minneapolis, Minnesota
Source: *BioIn 12; LegTOT*

Broadbent, Ed
[John Edward Broadbent]
Canadian. Government Official
Leader, New Democratic Party, 1975-89; MP, 1968-89; wrote *The Liberal Rip-off,* 1970.
b. Mar 21, 1936 in Oshawa, Ontario, Canada
Source: *AmMWSc 73S; BioIn 11; CanWW 83; CurBio 88; IntWW 76, 77, 78, 79, 80, 81, 82, 83, 89, 91, 93; WhoAm 78, 80, 82, 84, 86, 88; WhoCan 77, 80, 82, 84; WhoWor 78, 80, 82, 84*

Broadbent, Punch
[Harry Broadbent]
Canadian. Hockey Player
Right wing, 1918-29, mostly with Ottawa; won Art Ross Trophy, 1922; holds NHL record, scoring goals in 16 consecutive games; Hall of Fame, 1962.
b. Jul 13, 1892 in Ottawa, Ontario, Canada
d. Mar 6, 1971
Source: *HocEn; WhoHcky 73; WhoSpor*

Broadhurst, Kent
American. Actor
Films include *The Verdict,* 1982; *Silkwood,* 1983.
b. Feb 4, 1940 in Saint Louis, Missouri
Source: *ConAu 137; ConTFT 2; WrDr 96*

Brock, Alice May
American. Author, Restaurateur
Owner, Alice's Restaurant; Arlo Guthrie's song of same name was written about her.
b. Feb 28, 1941 in New York, New York
Source: *BioIn 8, 9, 10, 11, 14, 15; ConAu 41R; NewYTBE 71; WhoAm 74, 76, 78, 80, 82, 84, 86, 88, 90, 92, 94, 95, 96, 97; WhoAmW 74*

Brock, Bill
[William Emerson Brock]
American. Politician
Reagan's secretary of Labor, 1985-87; Rep. representative, 1970s.
b. Nov 23, 1930 in Chattanooga, Tennessee
Source: *BiDrAC; BiDrUSC 89; BiDrUSE 89; BioIn 9, 10, 11, 12, 13, 14, 15, 18; BlueB 76; CngDr 74, 85, 87; CurBio 71; IntWW 81, 82, 83, 89, 91, 93; NewYTBS 81, 85; WhoAm 86, 88, 90, 92, 94, 95, 96; WhoAmP 73, 75, 77, 79, 81, 83, 85, 87, 89, 91, 93, 95; WhoE 86, 89; WhoGov 72, 75, 77; WhoSSW 73, 75, 76; WhoWor 87, 89, 91*

Brock, Isaac, Sir
English. Soldier
Major-general, Upper Canada, 1811; forced victory over General Hull at Detroit, 1812.
b. Oct 6, 1769 in Saint Peter Port, England
d. Oct 13, 1812 in Queenston, Ontario, Canada
Source: *AmBi; ApCAB; BbtC; BioIn 4, 7, 8; DcCanB 5; DcNaB; Drake; HarEnMi; HarEnUS; LinLib S; MacDCB 78; McGEWB; OxCCan; WhNaAH*

Brock, Lou(is Clark)
American. Baseball Player
Outfielder, 1961-79; held ML record for stolen bases, 938, for 12 years, until surpassed by Rickey Henderson, 1991; Hall of Fame, 1985.
b. Jun 18, 1939 in El Dorado, Arkansas
Source: *AfrAmSG; Ballpl 90; BiDAmSp BB; BioIn 10, 11, 12; ConAu 113; CurBio 75; FacFETw; InB&W 85; LegTOT; NewYTBE 72, 73; WhoAfA 96; WhoAm 74, 76, 78, 86, 88, 90, 92, 94, 95, 96; WhoBlA 75, 77, 80, 85, 88, 90, 92, 94; WhoProB 73; WorAl; WorAlBi*

Brock, Tony
[The Babys]
English. Singer, Musician
Drummer, vocalist with power pop group, 1976-81.
b. Mar 31, 1954 in Bournemouth, England

Brockington, John Stanley
American. Football Player
Three-time all-pro running back, 1971-77, mostly with Green Bay; rookie of year, 1971.
b. Sep 7, 1948 in New York, New York
Source: *CelR; WhoAm 74, 76; WhoFtbl 74*

Brod, Max
Israeli. Author
Writings deal mainly with Jewish themes: *Franz Kafka,* 1937.
b. May 27, 1884 in Prague, Bohemia
d. Dec 20, 1968 in Tel Aviv, Israel
Source: *Baker 78, 3; EvEuW; FacFETw; LiExTwC; LngCTC; McGEWD 72, 84; ModGL; NewEOp 71; NewGrDM 80; NewGrDO; ObitT 1961; OxCGer 76, 86; PenC EUR; REn; TwCA, SUP; WhE&EA; WhoLA*

Broda, Turk
[Walter Broda]
Canadian. Hockey Player
Goalie, Toronto, 1936-52; won Vezina Trophy, 1941, 1948; Hall of Fame, 1967.
b. May 15, 1914 in Brandon, Manitoba, Canada
d. Oct 17, 1972 in Toronto, Ontario, Canada
Source: *BioIn 1, 2, 9, 10; HocEn; NewYTBE 72; WhoHcky 73; WhoSpor*

Broder, David S
American. Journalist
National political correspondent for the *Washington Post*; Pulitzer Prize, 1973.
b. Sep 11, 1929 in Chicago, Illinois
Source: *BioIn 8, 16; CelR 90; ConAu 97; WhoAm 90; WhoE 91; WhoWrEP 89*

Broderick, Elisabeth Bisceglia
American. Murderer
California housewife who gunned down her millionairre lawyer ex-husband and his 28 year old second wife when they were sleeping; story made into a TV movie.

Broderick, Helen
American. Actor
Star of first Ziegfeld Follies,1907; mother of actor Broderick Crawford.
b. Aug 11, 1891 in Philadelphia, Pennsylvania
d. Sep 25, 1959 in Beverly Hills, California
Source: *BioIn 5; EncAFC; EncMT; Film 2; FilmEn; FilmgC; ForYSC; HolCA; InWom SUP; MotPP; MovMk; NotNAT B; ObitOF 79; OxCAmT 84; OxCPMus; ThFT; Vers A; WhoHol B; WhScrn 74, 77, 83; WhThe; WorAl*

Broderick, James Joseph
American. Actor
Played father, Doug Lawrence, in TV series "Family," 1976-81.
b. Mar 7, 1927 in Charlestown, New Hampshire
d. Nov 1, 1982 in New Haven, Connecticut
Source: *HalFC 84; IntMPA 82; NewYTBS 82; NotNAT; WhAm 8; WhoAm 78, 80, 82; WhoHol A*

Broderick, Matthew
American. Actor
Won 1983 Tony for *Brighton Beach Memoirs;* in films *Ferris Bueller's Day Off,* 1986; *War Games,* 1983.
b. Mar 21, 1962 in New York, New York
Source: *BioIn 13; CelR 90; ConTFT 4, 11; CurBio 87; IntMPA 86, 92, 94, 96; IntWW 91, 93; JohnWTW 38; LegTOT; NewYTBS 83; VarWW 85; WhoAm 90, 92, 94, 95, 96, 97; WhoEnt 92; WhoHol 92; WorAlBi*

Brodie, Fawn McKay
American. Author
Wrote biographies of Sir Richard Burton, Joseph Smith, Thomas Jefferson; won Knopf biography award, 1943.
b. Sep 15, 1915 in Ogden, Utah
d. Jan 10, 1981 in Santa Monica, California
Source: *Au&Wr 71; BioIn 16, 17, 19; ConAu 17R, 102; DrAS 74H, 78H; ForWC 70; NewYTBS 81; WhAm 7; WhoAm 78, 80; WhoAmW 70, 72, 74, 77*

Brodie, John Riley
American. Football Player, Sportscaster
Quarterback, San Francisco, 1957-73; with NBC Sports, 1974—.
b. Aug 14, 1935 in San Francisco, California
Source: *BiDAmSp FB; BioIn 7, 8, 9, 10; ConAu 115; NewYTBE 71; WhoAm 74, 76, 82, 84, 86; WhoFtbl 74*

Brodie, Steve
[John Stevens]
American. Actor
Films include *Thirty Seconds Over Tokyo,* 1944; *Winchester '73,* 1950.
b. Nov 25, 1919 in El Dorado, Kansas
Source: *FilmEn; FilmgC; ForYSC; HalFC 80, 84, 88; WhoHol 92, A; WrDr 94*

Brodkey, Harold
[Aaron Roy Weintraub]
American. Writer
Wrote *First Love and Other Stories,* 1958; *Stories in an Almost Classical Mode,* 1988; staff writer for *The New Yorker.*
b. Oct 25, 1930 in Alton, Illinois
d. Jan 26, 1996 in New York, New York
Source: *Benet 96; BenetAL 91; BioIn 16; ConAu 111; ConLC 56; ConNov 86, 91; CurBio 89, 96N; CyWA 89; DcLB 130; DrAPF 80, 91; IntAu&W 91, 93; IntWW 91; MagSAmL; NewYTBS 27; OxCAmL 95; RGTwCWr; WhoAm 90; WorAu 1980; WrDr 88, 90, 92, 94, 96*

Brodovitch, Alexey
American. Photographer, Designer
Award-winning works exhibited throughout US; art director, *Harper's Bazaar* mag., 1934-58.
b. 1898, Russia
d. Apr 15, 1971 in Lethor, France
Source: *BioIn 3, 6, 8, 9, 10, 16, 17; ConDes 84, 90, 97; ConPhot 82, 88; DcTwDes; EncFash; FacFETw; ICPEnP; NewYTBE 71; WhAmArt 85*

Brodsky, Joseph (Alexandrovich)
[Iosif Alexandrovich Brodsky]
American. Author, Poet
Accused, sentenced to hard labor in USSR for dissent for his vocation, poetry, 1964; won Nobel Prize in literature, 1987; fifth and first foreign-born US poet laureate, 1991.
b. May 24, 1940 in Leningrad, Union of Soviet Socialist Republics
d. Jan 28, 1996 in New York, New York
Source: *AuNews 1; Benet 87; BenetAL 91; BioIn 14, 15, 16, 17, 18, 20, 21; ClDMEL 80; ConAu 37NR, 41R, 151, X; ConFLW 84; ConLC 4, 6, 13, 36, 50; CurBio 82, 96N; CyWA 89; DcArts; EncWL 2, 3; FacFETw; LegTOT; LiExTwC; MajTwCW; News 96, 96-3; NewYTBE 72; NewYTBS 27, 87, 91; NobelP 91; OxCTwCP; PoeCrit 9; RAdv 14, 13-2; RGFMEP; WhAm 11; Who 90, 92, 94; WhoAm 82, 84, 86, 88, 90, 92, 94, 95, 96; WhoE 89, 91, 93, 95; WhoNob 90, 95; WhoUSWr 88; WhoWor 89, 91, 93, 95, 96; WhoWrEP 89, 92, 95; WorAlBi; WorAu 1950; WrDr 90, 92, 96*

Brody, Jane Ellen
American. Author, Journalist
Syndicated columnist writing on nutrition, health: *Jane Brody's Nutrition Book,* 1981.
b. May 19, 1941 in New York, New York
Source: *ConAu 102; CurBio 86; WhoAm 84, 86, 97; WhoAmW 97; WhoE 97*

Brogan, Denis William, Sir
Scottish. Author, Political Scientist
Writings include *American Character,* 1944; *America in the Modern World,* 1960.
b. Aug 11, 1900 in Glasgow, Scotland
d. Jan 5, 1974 in Cambridge, England
Source: *Au&Wr 71; BioIn 1, 4, 10, 14; ConAu 45, 97; DcLEL; DcNaB 1971; EvLB; GrBr; IntEnSS 79; LngCTC; NewC; NewCBEL; NewYTBS 74; ObitOF 79; ObitT 1961; TwCA SUP; WhAm 6; Who 74*

Broglie, Louis Prince De
[Victor Pierre Raymong Broglie]
French. Physicist
Won 1929 Nobel Prize for contributions to quantum wave mechanics; discovered wave nature of the electron.
b. Aug 15, 1892 in Dieppe, France
d. Mar 19, 1987 in Paris, France
Source: *BiESc; CurBio 55, 87; IntWW 83; McGMS 80; WhDW; WhoNob; WhoWor 84*

Brokaw, Tom
[Thomas John Brokaw]
American. Broadcast Journalist
Host, "Today" show, 1976-81; anchor, "NBC Nightly News," 1981—.
b. Feb 6, 1940 in Yankton, South Dakota
Source: *BioIn 10, 11, 12, 13; BkPepl; CelR 90; ConAu 108; ConTFT 6; CurBio 81; EncAJ; EncTwCJ; IntMPA 86, 88, 92, 94, 96; IntWW 91, 93; JrnUS; LegTOT; LesBEnT; NewYTET; WhoAm 78, 80, 82, 84, 86, 88, 90, 92, 94, 95, 96, 97; WhoE 91, 93; WorAlBi*

Brokenshire, Norman
Canadian. Radio Performer
Pioneer announcer; programs include "Inner Sanctum;" "Theater Guild of the Air."
b. Jun 10, 1898 in Murcheson, Ontario, Canada
d. May 4, 1965 in Hauppauge, New York
Source: *BioIn 2, 3, 7; CurBio 50, 65; EncAJ; ObitOF 79; RadStar; SaTiSS; WhAm 4; WhScrn 83*

Brolin, James
American. Actor
Won Emmy for "Marcus Welby, MD," 1969; played Peter McDermott in TV series "Hotel," 1983-88.
b. Jul 18, 1940 in Los Angeles, California
Source: *CelR 90; ConTFT 14; FilmEn; FilmgC; HalFC 80, 84, 88; IntMPA 86, 88, 92, 94, 96; LegTOT; MovMk; WhoAm 86, 95, 96, 97; WhoHol 92, A; WhoHrs 80; WorAl*

Bromberg, David
American. Singer, Musician
Played backing guitar for Phoenix Singers in the early 1960s; worked frequently with Jerry Jeff Walker in the 1960s; recorded first album, *David Bromberg,* 1971; formed David Bromberg Big Band, 1980; released *Sideman Serenade,* 1990.
b. Sep 19, 1945 in Philadelphia, Pennsylvania
Source: *ASCAP 80; BioIn 14; ConMuA 80A; EncFCWM 83; IlEncRk; IntWWM 77; OnThGG; PenEncP; RolSEnR 83; WhoRock 81*

Bromberg, J. Edward
American. Actor
Character actor in films, 1936-50.
b. Dec 25, 1903 in Temesvar, Austria-Hungary
d. Dec 6, 1951 in London, England
Source: *FilmgC; MotPP; MovMk; PlP&P*

Bromfield, John
[Farron Bromfield]
American. Actor
TV series include "The Sheriff of Cochise," 1956-60.
b. Jun 11, 1922 in South Bend, Indiana
Source: *BioIn 4; FilmEn; FilmgC; ForYSC; HalFC 80, 84, 88; IntMPA 75, 76, 77, 78, 79, 80, 81, 82, 84, 86, 88; MotPP; WhoHol 92, A*

Bromfield, Louis Brucker
American. Author
Developed experimental farming community; won Pulitzer for *Early Autumn,* 1926.
b. Dec 27, 1896 in Mansfield, Ohio
d. Mar 18, 1956 in Columbus, Ohio
Source: *AmAu&B; AmNov; CnDAL; ConAmA; ConAmL; ConAu 107; CurBio 44, 56; CyWA 58; DcBiA; DcLEL; EncWL; EvLB; LiExTwC; LngCTC; Novels; WhAm 3; WorAl*

Bron, Eleanor
English. Actor
Light character player, stage, screen, TV; films include *Women in Love,* 1969.
b. 1934 in Stanmore, England
Source: *FilmEn; FilmgC; HalFC 80, 84, 88; IntMPA 77, 86, 92, 94, 96; Who 85; WhoHol 92, A; WhoThe 77, 81; WhoWor 74*

Bronfman, Edgar Miles
Canadian. Distiller
CEO, chm., Seagram Co., Ltd., 1976-86.
b. Jun 20, 1929 in Montreal, Quebec, Canada
Source: *BioIn 7, 8, 9, 10, 12, 13; BlueB 76; CanWW 83; CurBio 74; Dun&B 79; IntWW 83; St&PR 75, 84, 87, 91, 93; Who 82, 83, 85, 88, 90, 92, 94; WhoAm 74, 76, 78, 80, 82, 84, 86, 88, 90, 92, 94, 95, 96, 97; WhoAmJ 80; WhoCan 77; WhoCanB 86; WhoCanF 86; WhoE 83, 85, 86, 89, 91, 95; WhoFI 74, 81, 83, 85, 87, 89, 92, 94, 96; WhoGov 72; WhoSSW 86; WhoWor 74, 76, 78, 80, 82, 84, 87, 89, 95, 96*

Bronfman, Edgar Miles, Jr.
American. Distiller, Business Executive
President and CEO, Seagram Co., Ltd., 1986—.
b. May 16, 1955 in New York, New York
Source: *CurBio 94*

Bronfman, Samuel
Canadian. Distiller
At death, Seagram's world's largest distiller; sales exceeded $1.3 billion.
b. Mar 4, 1891 in Brandon, Manitoba, Canada
d. Jul 10, 1971 in Montreal, Quebec, Canada
Source: *BioIn 9, 10, 11, 18; MacDCB 78; NatCAB 56; NewYTBE 71; NewYTBS 74; ObitOF 79; WhAm 5; WhoWorJ 72*

Bronfman, Samuel
Canadian. Kidnap Victim
Heir to Seagram's fortune; kidnapped, 1975.
b. 1954
Source: *BioIn 10, 11*

Bronfman, Yefim
American. Pianist
Professional debut as pianist with the Israel Philharmonic, 1974; soloist with orchestras in North America, Europe, Israel.
b. Apr 10, 1958 in Tashkent, Union of Soviet Socialist Republics
Source: *Baker 92; BioIn 16, 17; ConMus 6; IntWWM 90; WhoAmM 83*

Bronk, Detlev Wulf
American. Biologist
Founded biophysics; pioneered use of electro-microscopy to monitor human nerve network.
b. Aug 13, 1897 in New York, New York
d. Nov 17, 1975 in New York, New York
Source: *AmMWSc 73P, 76P; BiESc; BioIn 1, 2, 3, 4, 10, 11, 20; BlueB 76; CurBio 76; DcAmB S9; DcAmMeB 84; FacFETw; InSci; IntWW 74, 75, 76; McGMS 80; NewYTBS 75; NotTwCS; OxCMed 86; WebAB 74, 79; WhAm 6; Who 74; WhoAm 76; WhoAtom 77; WhoWor 74, 76; WorAl*

Bronowski, Jacob
English. Mathematician, Author
Wrote TV series for BBC: "The Ascent of Man," 1974.
b. Jan 18, 1908, Poland
d. Aug 22, 1974 in East Hampton, New York
Source: *AmAu&B; AnCL; AuBYP 2S, 3; Benet 87, 96; BioIn 2, 4, 5, 7, 10, 11, 12, 13, 14, 15, 16; BlueB 76; ConAu 1R, 3NR, 53; DcLEL; DcNaB 1971; EngPo; FacFETw; InSci; IntAu&W 76; IntWW 74; LegTOT; LinLib L, S; NewCBEL; NewYTBS 74; ObitOF 79; ObitT 1971; RAdv 14, 13-5; SmATA 55; ThTwC 87; WhAm 6; Who 74; WhoAm 74; WhoWor 74; WorAl; WorAlBi; WorAu 1950*

Bronson, Betty
[Elizabeth Ada Bronson]
American. Actor
Starred in first film version of *Peter Pan,* 1924.
b. Nov 17, 1906 in Trenton, New Jersey
d. Oct 21, 1971 in Pasadena, California
Source: *EncAFC; Film 2; FilmEn; FilmgC; ForYSC; HalFC 80, 84, 88; InWom SUP; MotPP; MovMk; NewYTBE 71; SilFlmP; ThFT; TwYS; WhoAmW 64, 68, 70, 72; WhoHol B; WhScrn 74, 77*

Bronson, Charles
[Charles Buchinsky]
American. Actor
Known for tough-guy roles: *Death Wish,* 1974.
b. Nov 3, 1921? in Ehrenfeld, Pennsylvania
Source: *BiDFilm 94; BioNews 74; BkPepl; CelR 90; ConTFT 3; CurBio 75; DcArts; FilmEn; IntMPA 86, 94, 96; LegTOT; MovMk; NewYTBS 74; WhoAm 86, 95, 96, 97*

Bronte, Anne
[pseud. Acton Bell]
English. Author
Sister of Charlotte and Emily; wrote *Agnes Grey,* 1847.
b. Jan 17, 1820 in Thornton, England
d. May 28, 1849 in Scarborough, England
Source: *ArtclWW 2; BbD; BiD&SB; BioIn 1, 2, 3, 4, 5, 6, 7, 8, 9, 10, 11, 12, 13, 14, 15, 16, 17, 18, 19, 20, 21; BlmGEL; BlmGWL; BritAu 19; BritWr 5; CamGEL; CamGLE; CasWL; Chambr 3; ChhPo, S1; ContDcW 89; CyWA 58; DcArts; DcBiA; DcEnA, A; DcEnL; DcEuL; DcLB 21; DcLEL; DcNaB; Dis&D; EncBrWW; EvLB; FemiCLE; GoodHs; GrWrEL N; HerW, 84; IntDcWB; InWom, SUP; LegTOT; LinLib L; LngCEL; NewCBEL; NinCLC 4; Novels; OxCEng 67, 85, 95; PenC ENG; PenEncH; PenNWW A, B; RAdv 1, 14, 13-1; RfGEnL 91; StaCVF; VicBrit; WebE&AL; WhDW; WorAl; WorAlBi*

Bronte, Charlotte
[Currer Bell; Mrs. Arthur Bell Nicholls]
English. Author
Most successful of sisters; wrote *Jane Eyre,* 1847.
b. Apr 21, 1816 in Thornton, England
d. Mar 31, 1855 in Haworth, England
Source: *Alli; ArtclWW 2; AtlBL; Au&Arts 17; BbD; BiD&SB; BioIn 1, 2, 3, 4, 5, 6, 7, 8, 9, 10, 11, 12, 13, 14, 15, 16, 17, 18, 19, 20, 21; BlmGEL; BlmGWL; BritAu 19; BritWr 5; CamGEL; CamGLE; CasWL; Chambr 3; ChhPo, S1, S2, S3; CnDBLB 4; ContDcW 89; CrtT 3, 4; CyWA 58; DcArts; DcBiA; DcBiPP; DcEnA, A; DcEnL; DcEuL; DcLB 21, 159; DcLEL; DcNaB; DcWomA; Dis&D; EncBrWW; EvLB; FemiCLE; FilmgC; GoodHs; GrWomW; GrWrEL N; HalFC 80, 84, 88; HerW, 84; HsB&A; IntDcWB; InWom, SUP; LegTOT; LinLib L, S; LngCEL; MagSWL; McGEWB; MouLC 3; NewC; NewCBEL; NinCLC 3, 8, 33; NotNAT B; Novels; OxCEng 67, 85, 95; PenC ENG; PenEncH; PenNWW A, B; RAdv 1, 14, 13-1; RComWL; RfGEnL 91; ScF&FL 1; StaCVF; VicBrit; WebE&AL; WhDW; WorAl; WorAlBi; WorLitC*

Bronte, Emily Jane
[Ellis Bell]
English. Author
Wrote *Wuthering Heights,* 1848.
b. Jul 30, 1818 in Thornton, England
d. Dec 19, 1848 in Haworth, England
Source: *AtlBL; BbD; BiD&SB; BioIn 1, 2, 3, 4, 5, 6, 7, 8, 9, 10, 11, 12, 13, 15, 16, 17, 18, 19, 20; BritAu 19; CasWL; Chambr 3; ChhPo, S1, S2; CnE&AP; CrtT 3; CyWA 58; DcBiA; DcEnA, A; DcEnL; DcEuL; DcLEL; DcNaB; DcWomA; Dis&D; EvLB; FilmgC; GrWrEL N, P; InWom, SUP; MouLC 3; NewCBEL; OxCEng 67, 85, 95; PenBWP; PenC ENG; PenEncH; PenNWW B; RAdv 1, 14, 13-1; RComWL; VicBrit; WebE&AL; WorAl*

Bronte, Patrick Branwell
English. Poet
Dissolute brother of the Bronte sisters.
b. Jun 26, 1817 in Thornton, England
d. Sep 26, 1848 in Haworth, England
Source: *BioIn 1, 2, 5, 6, 9, 10, 11, 16, 17, 21; ChhPo S1; DcEuL; DcNaB, C; PoIre*

Bronzino, Il
[Agnoli di Cosimo Allori]
Italian. Artist
Florentine portraitist whose best-known work was *Eleanora of Toledo with Her Son,* c. 1545.
b. Nov 17, 1503 in Montecelli, Italy
d. Nov 23, 1572 in Florence, Italy
Source: *AtlBL; DcCathB; Dis&D; McGEWB; REn; WorAl; WorAlBi*

Brook, Alexander
American. Artist
Portraitist, landscape painter called the "unstruggling artist;" best known for 1940 portrait of Katherine Hepburn.
b. Jul 14, 1898 in New York, New York
d. Feb 26, 1980 in Sag Harbor, New York
Source: *AnObit 1980; ArtsAmW 3; BioIn 1, 2, 4, 6, 12; BlueB 76; BriEAA; CurBio 41, 80, 80N; DcCAA 71, 77, 88, 94; IntWW 74, 75, 76, 77, 78, 79, 80; McGDA; NewYTBS 80; PhDcTCA 77; WhAm 7; WhAmArt 85; WhoAm 74, 76, 78, 80; WhoAmA 73, 76, 78, 80N, 82N, 84N, 86N, 89N, 91N, 93N*

Brook, Clive
[Clifford Brook]
English. Actor
Played leads, supporting roles for over 40 yrs; model of British suavity, elegance.
b. Jun 1, 1887 in London, England
d. Nov 18, 1974 in London, England
Source: *BiDFilm, 94; BioIn 10, 14; BlueB 76N; FilmAG WE; FilmEn; FilmgC; GangFlm; HalFC 80, 84, 88; IlWWBF; IntDcF 1-3; LegTOT; MotPP; MovMk; NewYTBS 74; ObitOF 79; ObitT 1971; TwYS; WhAm 6; Who 74; WhoHol B; WhoThe 72; WhScrn 77, 83; WhThe; WorEFlm*

Brook, Peter Stephen Paul
English. Director, Producer
Films include *Lord of the Flies,* 1962; producing started on stage in 1943.
b. Mar 21, 1925 in London, England
Source: *BiDFilm; CurBio 61; DcFM; FilmgC; IntWW 83; MovMk; NewYTBE 71; NotNAT; OxCThe 83; WhDW; Who 85; WhoThe 81; WorAl; WorEFlm*

Brooke, Edward William, III
American. Politician
Rep. senator, MA, 1967-79; first black man elected to Senate since reconstruction.
b. Oct 26, 1919 in Washington, District of Columbia
Source: *AmPolLe; WhoWor 74, 76, 78, 80, 82, 84; WorAl; WorAlBi*

Brooke, Hillary
[Beatrice Sofia Mathilda Peterson]
American. Actor
Played "bad girl" roles, films, 1940-50.
b. Sep 8, 1914 in Astoria, New York
Source: *EncAFC; FilmEn; FilmgC; HalFC 84, 88; IntMPA 75; InWom SUP; MovMk; What 5; WhoHol 92, A*

Brooke, James, Sir
English. Political Leader
First rajah, (Borneo), 1841.
b. Apr 29, 1803 in Benares, India
d. Jun 11, 1868 in Bath, England
Source: *Alli, SUP; BioIn 3, 4, 8, 9; CelCen; DcBiPP; DcInB; DcNaB; HarEnMi; HisDBrE; McGEWB; NewCBEL*

Brooke, L. Leslie
English. Author, Illustrator
Wrote, illustrated children's *Johnny Crow* series.
b. Sep 24, 1862 in Birkenhead, England
d. May 1, 1940 in London, England
Source: *TwCChW 83*

Brooke, Rupert Chawner
English. Poet
Wrote romantic, patriotic poetry, WW I.
b. Aug 3, 1887 in Rugby, England
d. Apr 23, 1915 in Scyros, Greece
Source: *AtlBL; CasWL; Chambr 3; CnMWL; DcArts; EncWL; EvLB; GrBr; GrWrEL P; MakMC; ModBrL S1; NewCBEL; OxCEng 85, 95; OxCTwCP; PenC ENG; REn*

Brookings, Robert Somers
American. Merchant, Philanthropist
Founded Brookings Institution, Washington, DC, 1927; devoted to social sciences, public service research.
b. Jan 22, 1850 in Cecil County, Maryland
d. Nov 15, 1932 in Washington, District of Columbia
Source: *AmBi; ApCAB X; BiDAmBL 83; BioIn 1, 6, 14; DcAmB S1; DcNAA; NatCAB 7, 33; WebAB 74, 79; WhAm 1; WorAl*

Brookner, Anita
English. Writer, Art Historian
Has written biographical studies of eighteenth-century French painters, including *Jacques-Louis David,* 1981; novels include *Hotel du Lac,* 1984, *A Misalliance,* 1986.
b. Jul 16, 1928 in London, England
Source: *Benet 96; BioIn 14, 16; BlmGEL; CamGLE; ConAu 37NR, 114, 120; ConLC 51; ConNov 86, 91, 96; ConPopW; CurBio 89; CyWA 89; DcArts; DcLB Y87B; EncBrWW; EncWL 3; FacFETw; FemiCLE; IntAu&W 91, 93; IntWW 93; MajTwCW; ModWoWr; OxCEng 95; RAdv 14; RGTwCWr; Who 74, 85, 92; WhoAm 90; WhoWor 91; WomFir; WorAu 1975; WrDr 86, 88, 90, 92, 94, 96*

Brooks, Albert (Lawrence Einstein)
American. Comedian, Actor, Writer
Roles in *Private Benjamin,* 1980; *Twilight Zone,* 1983; *Broadcast News,* 1988; *Mother,* 1996.
b. Jul 22, 1947 in Los Angeles, California
Source: *BioIn 10; ConAu X; ConTFT 6, 14; EncAFC; IntMPA 88, 92, 94, 96; LegTOT; MiSFD 9; WhoAm 82, 84, 86, 88, 90, 92, 94, 95, 96, 97; WhoCom; WhoEnt 92; WhoHol 92; WorAlBi*

Brooks, Angie Elizabeth
Liberian. Diplomat
Member, UN General Assembly 1954—; first African woman pres., 1969.
b. Aug 24, 1928 in Virginia, Liberia
Source: *BioIn 6, 8, 9, 11; CurBio 70; InB&W 80; IntWW 74, 75; InWom SUP; WhoAmW 72, 74; WhoUN 75*

Brooks, Avery
American. Actor
Appeared on "Spencer for Hire," 1985-89; "Star Trek: Deep Space Nine," 1993—.
b. 1949 in Evansville, Indiana
Source: *ConBlB 9; ConTFT 9; DcTwCCu 5; WhoBlA 90, 92*

Brooks, Charlie, Jr.
American. Murderer
First US felon executed by injection.
b. 1942?
d. Dec 7, 1982 in Huntsville, Texas

Brooks, Cleanth
American. Author, Critic
Wrote college textbooks which were major influence on contemporary methods of teaching literature; wrote *Modern Rhetoric,* 1949, with Robert Penn Warren.
b. Oct 16, 1906 in Murray, Kentucky
d. May 10, 1994
Source: *AmAu&B, 3; FacFETw; IntAu&W 82; IntWW 74, 75, 76, 77, 78, 79, 80, 81, 82, 83, 89, 91, 93; LinLib L; LngCTC; MajTwCW; ModAL; OxCAmL 65, 83; PenC AM; RAdv 1, 14; REn; REnAL; SouWr; ThTwC 87; TwCA SUP; WhAm 11; Who 74, 82, 83, 85, 88, 90, 92, 94; WhoAm 74, 76, 78, 80, 86, 88, 90, 92, 94; WhoTwCL; WhoWor 74; WrDr 76, 80, 82, 84, 86, 88, 90, 92, 94, 96*

Brooks, David Owen
American. Murderer
Killed 27 young boys, TX, 1973.
b. 1955
Source: *BioIn 10*

Brooks, Diana D
American. Business Executive
Pres. and CEO, Sotheby's, Inc., 1990—; first woman to head major art auction house.
b. 1950 in Glen Cove, New York
Source: *BioIn 15; News 90, 90-1; NewYTBS 87; St&PR 91; WhoAm 90; WhoAmW 91*

Brooks, Donald Marc
American. Fashion Designer
Designed costumes for movie *The Bell Jar,* 1979.

b. Jan 10, 1928 in New York, New York
Source: *BiE&WWA; CurBio 72; NotNAT; WhoAm 74, 76, 78, 80, 82; WhoFash; WorFshn*

Brooks, Foster Murrell
American. Comedian, Actor
Known for "drunk" skits in nightclubs, TV shows.
b. May 11, 1912 in Louisville, Kentucky

Brooks, Garth
[Troyal Garth Brooks]
American. Singer, Songwriter
First country music singer to win six Academy of Country Music Awards, 1991; album *Ropin' the Wind,* 1991, first to enter *Billboard's* pop and country charts at No. 1.
b. Feb 7, 1962 in Tulsa, Oklahoma
Source: *BgBkCoM; BioIn 18; ConMus 8; CurBio 92; EncRkSt; LegTOT; News 92, 92-1; WhoAm 94, 95, 96, 97; WhoEnt 92*

Brooks, Geraldine
[Geraldine Stroock]
American. Actor
Published book of her bird photographs *Swan Watch,* 1975.
b. Oct 29, 1925 in New York, New York
d. Jun 19, 1977 in Riverhead, New York
Source: *BiE&WWA; InWom; ItaFilm; LegTOT; NatCAB 59; NotNAT A; WhoHol A; WhScrn 83*

Brooks, Gwendolyn Elizabeth
American. Author, Poet
First black woman to win Pulitzer for poetry, 1950, for *Annie Allen.*
b. Jun 7, 1917 in Topeka, Kansas
Source: *AuNews 1; BlkWWr; BroadAu; CasWL; ConAu 1NR, 1R; ConLC 15; ConPo 75; CurBio 50; IntWW 83; LibW; ModAL S1; NotBlAW 1; PenC AM; SelBAAu; SmATA 6; TwCA SUP; WebAB 79; WhoAm 86; WhoAmW 85; WhoBlA 88, 90, 92; WorAl; WrDr 86*

Brooks, Henry Sands
American. Businessman
Founded Brooks Brothers, America's oldest clothier, in Manhattan, 1817.
b. 1770 in Connecticut
d. 1833
Source: *Entr*

Brooks, Herb(ert Paul)
American. Hockey Coach
Coach, US Olympic gold medal-winning team, 1980; in NHL, NY Rangers, 1981-85, Minnesota North Stars, 1987-88; New Jersey Devils 1992-93.
b. Aug 5, 1937 in Saint Paul, Minnesota
Source: *BiDAmSp BK; BioIn 12; HocEn; WhoAm 80, 82, 84, 88, 92; WhoE 83, 85, 93; WhoMW 88; WorAlBi*

Brooks, Jack Bascom
American. Politician
Dem. congressman from TX, 1953-94.
b. Dec 18, 1922 in Crowley, Louisiana
Source: *BiDrAC; WhoSSW 80, 82, 84, 86, 88, 91, 93, 95, 97*

Brooks, James L.
American. Producer, Director, Actor, Screenwriter
One of TV's best story minds who co-created "The Mary Tyler Moore Show."
b. May 9, 1940 in North Bergen, New Jersey
Source: *Au&Arts 17; BiDFilm 94; BioIn 10, 12, 13, 14, 16, 19; ConAu 32NR, 54NR, 73; ConTFT 3, 10; IntMPA 92, 94, 96; LegTOT; MiSFD 9; NewYTBS 84; WhoAm 74, 76, 78, 80, 82, 84, 86, 88, 90, 92, 94, 95, 96, 97; WhoEnt 92; WhoTelC*

Brooks, Louise
American. Actor
Film performances include *Pandora's Box,* 1929; *Overland Stage Raiders,* 1938.
b. Nov 14, 1906 in Cherryvale, Kansas
d. Aug 8, 1985 in Rochester, New York
Source: *Alli SUP; AnObit 1985; BiDD; BiDFilm, 81, 94; BioAmW; BioIn 7, 9, 10, 11, 12, 13, 14, 15, 16, 17; ConAu 117, 134; CurBio 84, 85N; DcArts; EncAFC; EncEurC; FacFETw; FilmEn; FilmgC; HalFC 80, 84, 88; IntDcF 1-3, 2-3; InWom SUP; MotPP; MovMk; OxCFilm; SilFlmP; ThFT; TwYS; What 3; WhoAmA 82; WhoHol A; WorEFlm*

Brooks, Maria Gowen
[Maria del Occidente]
American. Poet
Wrote epic poem *Zophiel,* 1833.
b. 1794? in Medford, Massachusetts
d. Nov 11, 1845, Cuba
Source: *AmBi; AmWomWr; BibAL; BlmGWL; DcAmB; InWom SUP; LibW; NotAW; OxCAmL 83, 95; PenNWW A, B; WhAm HS*

Brooks, Mel
[Melvin Kaminski]
American. Producer, Director
Writer, director *Blazing Saddles,* 1974, *Young Frankenstein,* 1975.
b. Jun 28, 1926 in New York, New York
Source: *Au&Arts 13; BiDFilm 81, 94; BiE&WWA; BioIn 7, 8; BkPepl; CelR 90; ConLC 12; ConTFT 1, 6, 13; CurBio 74; DcArts; DcLB 26; DcTwCCu 1; EncAFC; FacFETw; FilmEn; FilmgC; HalFC 84, 88; IlWWHD 1; IntAu&W 89, 91, 93; IntDcF 1-2, 2-2; IntMPA 77, 78, 79, 80, 81, 82, 84, 86, 88, 92, 94, 96; IntWW 82, 83, 89, 91, 93; JoeFr; LegTOT; LesBEnT; MiSFD 9; MovMk; NewYTBS 75; QDrFCA 92; Who 82, 83, 85, 88, 90, 92, 94; WhoAm 86, 90, 92, 94, 95, 96, 97; WhoCom; WhoEnt 92; WhoHol 92; WorAl; WorAlBi; WorFDir 2*

Brooks, Phillips
American. Religious Leader
Episcopal minister who said sermon over Abraham Lincoln's body, 1865; wrote "O Little Town of Bethlehem."
b. Dec 13, 1835 in Boston, Massachusetts
d. Jan 23, 1893 in Boston, Massachusetts
Source: *Alli SUP; AmAu&B; AmBi; AmOrN; AnCL; ApCAB, X; BbD; BenetAL 91; BiDAmM; BiD&SB; BioIn 2, 3, 5, 6, 9, 10, 11, 19; Chambr 3; ChhPo, S1, S2; CyEd; DcAmAu; DcAmB; DcAmReB 1, 2; DcNAA; Drake; EncARH; HarEnUS; LinLib L, S; LuthC 75; McGEWB; NatCAB 2; OxCAmH; OxCAmL 65, 83, 95; RelLAm 91; REnAL; TwCBDA; WebAB 74, 79; WhAm HS*

Brooks, Richard
American. Director, Screenwriter
Won award, screenplay *Elmer Gantry,* 1960; writer-director *Looking for Mr. Goodbar,* 1977; wrote *The Producer,* 1951.
b. May 18, 1912 in Philadelphia, Pennsylvania
d. Mar 11, 1992 in Beverly Hills, California
Source: *AmAu&B; AmFD; AmNov; AnObit 1992; BiDFilm, 81, 94; BioIn 2, 11, 13, 15, 16, 17, 19; CelR; ConAu 73, 137; ConDr 73, 77A; ConTFT 10; DcFM; DcLB 44; FilmEn; FilmgC; GangFlm; HalFC 80, 84, 88; IlWWHD 1; IntAu&W 76, 77, 89, 91, 93; IntDcF 1-2, 2-2; IntMPA 75, 76, 77, 78, 79, 80, 81, 82, 84, 86, 88, 92; IntWW 74, 75, 76, 77, 78, 79, 80, 81, 82, 83, 89, 91; LegTOT; MiSFD 9; MovMk; OxCFilm; WhAm 10; WhoAm 74, 76, 78, 80, 82, 84, 86, 88, 90; WhoEnt 92; WhoWor 74; WorEFlm; WorFDir 2; WrDr 88, 90, 92, 94N*

Brooks, Romaine
American. Painter
Noted for her ghoulish drawings and paintings.
b. May 1, 1874 in Rome, Italy
d. 1970
Source: *BiDWomA; BioAmW; BioIn 9, 10, 11, 12, 20; ContDcW 89; DcWomA; GayLesB; GayLL; GoodHs; GrLiveH; HanAmWH; IntDcWB; InWom SUP; NotAW MOD; WomArt*

Brooks, Van Wyck
American. Author
First to write of American cultural, literary development; won Pulitzer, 1936: *The Flowering of New England, 1815-1865.*
b. Feb 16, 1886 in Plainfield, New Jersey
d. May 2, 1963 in Bridgewater, Connecticut
Source: *AmAu&B; AmLY; AmWr; AtlBL; Benet 87, 96; BenetAL 91; BioIn 1, 2, 3, 4, 5, 6, 7, 8, 9, 11, 12, 14, 15, 16, 17; CasWL; Chambr 3; CnDAL; ConAmA; ConAmL; ConAu 1R, 4NR, 6NR; ConLC 29; ConLCrt 77, 82; CurBio 41, 60, 63; DcAmB S7; DcArts; DcLB 45, 63, 103;*

DcLEL; EncAB-A 15; EvLB; FacFETw; LegTOT; LinLib L, S; LngCTC; ModAL; MorMA; OxCAmH; OxCAmL 65, 83, 95; PenC AM; RAdv 1; REn; REnAL; ScF&FL 92; TwCA, SUP; TwCWr; WebAB 74, 79; WebE&AL; WhAm 4; WhLit; WhNAA; WorAl; WorAlBi

Brooks, Walter R(ollin)
American. Editor, Author
Children's books include *Freddy the Detective,* 1932.
b. Jan 9, 1886 in Rome, New York
d. Aug 17, 1958 in Roxbury, New York
Source: *AmAu&B; BioIn 2, 3, 5, 7, 12; ChhPo; ConAu 111; JBA 51; NatCAB 47; TwCChW 95; WhAm 3; WhE&EA; WhNAA*

Brooks, William Keith
American. Zoologist
Professor, Johns Hopkins U, 1876-1908; wrote *The Law of Heredity,* 1883.
b. Mar 25, 1848 in Cleveland, Ohio
d. Nov 12, 1908 in Baltimore, Maryland
Source: *Alli SUP; AmBi; ApCAB; BiDAmS; BiInAmS; DcAmAu; DcAmB; DcNAA; DcScB; InSci; NatCAB 23; OhA&B; PeoHis; TwCBDA; WhAm 1*

Broonzy, Big Bill
American. Singer, Musician
One of the greatest country blues singers of all time.
b. Jun 26, 1893 in Scott, Mississippi
d. Aug 14, 1958 in Chicago, Illinois
Source: *Baker 84, 92; BiDAmM; BiDJaz; CmpEPM; EncFCWM 83; EncRk 88; IlEncJ; LegTOT; NewAmDM; NewGrDA 86; NewGrDM 80; OnThGG; OxCPMus; PenEncP; WhoRock 81; WhoRocM 82; WorAl; WorAlBi*

Brophy, Brigid Antonia
English. Author, Dramatist
Writes fiction, non-fiction: *Hackenfeller's Ape,* 1953; *Mozart the Dramatist,* 1964.
b. Jun 12, 1929 in London, England
d. Aug 7, 1995 in Louth, England
Source: *CasWL; ConAu 5R; ConLC 29; ConNov 86; EncWL 2; IntWW 83; ModBrL S1; NewC; Novels; TwCWr; Who 83, 85; WhoTwCL; WhoWor 74; WorAu 1950; WrDr 82, 86*

Brophy, John
English. Labor Union Official
Exponent of public ownership of mines; wrote *A Miner's Life,* 1964.
b. Nov 6, 1883 in Lancaster, England
d. Feb 19, 1963
Source: *BiDAmL; BiDAmLL; BioIn 7; DcAmB S7; ObitOF 79; WhAm 7*

Brosio, Manilo Giovanni
Italian. Diplomat
Leader of Liberal party, ambassador to US, 1955-61; NATO secretary-general, 1964-71.
b. Jul 10, 1897 in Turin, Italy
d. Mar 14, 1980 in Turin, Italy
Source: *AnObit 1980; CurBio 55; IntWW 79; NewYTBS 80; WhAm 7; Who 74; WhoWor 74*

Brosnan, Jim
[James Patrick Brosnan]
"Professor"
American. Baseball Player, Author
Pitcher, 1954-63; wrote one of first exposes on baseball, *The Long Season,* 1960.
b. Oct 24, 1929 in Cincinnati, Ohio
Source: *AuBYP 2S, 3; Ballpl 90; BioIn 5, 6, 7, 8, 10, 12; ConAu 1R, 3NR; CurBio 64; SmATA 14; WhoMW 74, 76; WhoProB 73*

Brosnan, Pierce
Irish. Actor
Star of TV series "Remington Steele," 1982-86; in James Bond movie *Goldeneye,* 1995.
b. May 16, 1953 in Navan, Ireland
Source: *ConTFT 6; IntMPA 88, 92, 94, 96; VarWW 85; WhoAm 92, 94, 95, 96, 97; WhoEnt 92*

Brosten, Harve
American. Writer, Director, Producer
Won Emmy for comedy writing for "All in the Family," 1978.
b. May 15, 1943 in Chicago, Illinois
Source: *ConTFT 2; VarWW 85; WhoE 83*

Broten, Neal LaMoy
American. Hockey Player
Center, Minnesota, 1980—; first American-born player to score 100 pts. in one season, 1985-86; member, 1980 US Olympic gold medal-winning team.
b. Nov 29, 1959 in Roseau, Minnesota
Source: *BiDAmSp BK; HocEn; HocReg 87*

Brothers, Joyce Diane Bauer
[Mrs. Milton Brothers]
American. Psychologist, Author
Syndicated columnist, radio, TV show hostess; books include *What Every Woman Ought to Know About Love and Marriage,* 1984.
b. Oct 20, 1928 in New York, New York
Source: *AuNews 1; BioNews 74; BkPepl; ConAu 13NR; CurBio 71; ForWC 70; LesBEnT; WhoAm 86; WhoAmW 85; WrDr 86*

Brothers Johnson, The
[George Johnson; Louis Johnson]
American. Music Group
Hit singles include "Strawberry Letter 23," 1977; "I'll Be Good to You," 1976.
Source: *Alli SUP; BioIn 4; BlkOpe; DancEn 78; EncRk 88; IlEncBM 82; InB&W 80, 85; IntvTCA 2; NewYTBS 84; PenEncP; RkOn 74, 78; RolSEnR 83; SoulM; WhoAdv 80; WhoAmP 79, 81, 83; WhoBlA 77; WhoRocM 82*

Brough, Louise Althea
American. Tennis Player
US women's singles champion, 1947; won three titles, Wimbledon, 1948, 1950.
b. Mar 11, 1923 in Oklahoma City, Oklahoma
Source: *Alli SUP; CurBio 48; InWom; MacDWB*

Broumas, Olga
American. Poet
Won Yale Younger Poets Award, 1977, for *Beginning with O,*; also wrote *Perpetua,* 1989.
b. May 6, 1949 in Syros, Greece
Source: *AmWomWr; ArtclWW 2; BioIn 19; BlmGWL; ConAu 20NR, 85; ConLC 10, 73; ConPo 91, 96; DrAPF 80; FemiCLE; OxCWoWr 95; WhoUSWr 88; WhoWrEP 89, 92, 95; WrDr 88, 90, 92, 94, 96*

Broun, Heywood Hale
American. Author, Actor, Broadcast Journalist
Stage debut, 1949, in *I Remember Mama*; sports, news correspondent, CBS News; son of Heywood.
b. Mar 10, 1918 in New York, New York
Source: *BiE&WWA; BioIn 1, 3, 7, 8, 10, 13, 15, 16; BioNews 74; ConAu 12NR, 17R; ConTFT 1; DcAmSR; NotNAT, A; OxCAmH; PlP&P; WebAB 79; WhoAm 80, 82, 84, 86, 88, 92, 94, 95; WhoE 95; WhoHol 92*

Broun, (Matthew) Heywood (Campbell)
American. Journalist, Author
Helped found "The Newspaper Guild," 1934, which presents annual reporting awards in his name; noted NYC newsman, 1908-40.
b. Dec 7, 1888 in New York, New York
d. Dec 18, 1939 in New York, New York
Source: *AmBi; AmDec 1920; AmRef; ApCAB X; Benet 87; BenetAL 91; BioIn 15, 16; CathA 1930; ConAmA; CurBio 40; DcAmB S2; DcAmSR; DcLB 29, 171; EncAJ; EncTwCJ; JrnUS; LegTOT; LinLib L, S; NatCAB 30; NotNAT B; OxCAmH; OxCAmL 83; OxCAmT 84; PlP&P; REn; ScF&FL 1; TwCA SUP; WebAB 74, 79; WhAm 1; WhJnl; WhThe; WorAlBi*

Brousse, Amy Elizabeth Thorpe
"Cynthia"
American. Spy
Worked for British intelligence, Washington, DC, before America entered WW II.
b. 1910 in Minneapolis, Minnesota
d. 1963 in Castelnov, France
Source: *BioIn 7, 19; SpyCS*

Brouthers, Dan
[Dennis Joseph Brouthers]
"Big Dan"
American. Baseball Player
First baseman, 1879-96; had lifetime .343 batting average; Hall of Fame, 1945.
b. May 8, 1858 in Sylvan Lake, New York
d. Aug 3, 1932 in East Orange, New Jersey
Source: *Ballpl 90; BiDAmSp BB; BioIn 14, 15; LegTOT; WhoProB 73; WhoSpor*

Brouwer, Adriaen C
Flemish. Artist
Pupil of Frans Hals, genre painter whose landscapes were among greatest of his age.
b. 1606 in Oudenaarde, Belgium
d. Jan 1638 in Antwerp, Belgium
Source: *AtlBL; Dis&D; OxCArt; WhDW*

Browder, Earl Russell
American. Political Leader
Editor, *Daily Worker,* 1944; secretary-general, US Communist party, 1930-45.
b. May 20, 1891 in Wichita, Kansas
d. Jun 27, 1973 in Princeton, New Jersey
Source: *AmPolLe; BioIn 1, 2, 9, 10, 11; ConAu 45; CurBio 44, 73; DcAmB S9; EncAB-H 1974, 1996; McGEWB; NewYTBE 73; OxCAmH; WebAB 74, 79; WhAm 5; WhAmP; WorAl*

Brower, David Ross
"The Archdruid"
American. Naturalist, Social Reformer
Environmental activist; pres., Friends of the Earth Foundation, 1972-84; founder, Earth Island Action Group, 1989; founder biennial, Fate and Hope of the Earth Conferences, 1982-89; founder, League of Conservation Voters.
b. Jul 1, 1912 in Berkeley, California
Source: *BioIn 7, 8, 9, 10, 11, 12, 13, 16, 17, 19, 20; EnvEnc; EnvEnDr; NatLAC; WhoAm 74, 76, 78, 80, 82, 84, 86, 88, 90, 92, 94, 95, 96, 97; WhoScEn 96; WhoWest 82, 84, 94, 96; WhoWor 74, 93, 95; WrDr 92, 94, 96*

Browles, William Dodson, Jr.
American. Editor
Editor-in-chief, *Newsweek,* 1981-83.
b. Oct 8, 1944 in Houston, Texas
Source: *ConAu 73; IntWW 83; WhoAm 84; WhoWor 78*

Brown, A. Roy
Canadian. Pilot
Shot down the "Red Baron" in WW I, 1918.
b. 1893 in Carleton Place, Ontario, Canada
d. Mar 9, 1944 in Stouffville, Ontario, Canada
Source: *ColCR; ObitOF 79*

Brown, Alice
American. Author
Wrote stories of New England; play *Children of Earth,* 1914.
b. Dec 5, 1856 in Hampton Falls, New Hampshire
d. Jun 21, 1948 in Boston, Massachusetts
Source: *BioAmW; DcLB 78; InWom SUP; LibW; NotAW; OxCAmL 83*

Brown, Arthur Whitten, Sir
Scottish. Aviator
Was navigator for the first nonstop airplane flight across the Atlantic (with pilot John Alcock), 1919.
b. Jul 23, 1886 in Glasgow, Scotland
d. Oct 4, 1948 in Swansea, Wales
Source: *BioIn 1, 4, 5, 6, 8, 12; DcNaB 1941; FacFETw; InSci*

Brown, Blair
American. Actor
Played Jackie Kennedy in TV miniseries "Kennedy," 1983; in film *Continental Divide,* 1981; star of TV show "The Days and Nights of Molly Dodd," 1987—.
b. 1948 in Washington, District of Columbia
Source: *BioIn 12, 13; ConTFT 6, 14; HalFC 84, 88; IntMPA 86, 88, 92, 94, 96; LegTOT; NewYTBS 81; VarWW 85; WhoHol 92; WorAlBi*

Brown, Bobby
[Robert William Brown]
"Golden Boy"
American. Baseball Player, Baseball Executive, Physician
Infielder, NY Yankees, 1946-54, retired to become cardiologist; pres. of AL, 1984—.
b. Oct 25, 1924 in Seattle, Washington
Source: *Ballpl 90; BiDAmSp BB; BioIn 1, 3, 4, 14, 15, 16, 20; WhoAm 86, 88, 92, 94, 95, 96, 97; WhoProB 73*

Brown, Bobby
American. Singer, Dancer, Songwriter
Innovator of hip-hop; works include multiplatinum *Don't Be Cruel,* 1989.
b. Feb 5, 1969 in Boston, Massachusetts
Source: *BioIn 16; ConMus 4; CurBio 91; EncRkSt; InB&W 85; LegTOT; WhoBlA 92; WhoEnt 92*

Brown, Bryan
Australian. Actor
Played Luke O'Neill in TV mini-series "The Thorn Birds," 1983.
b. Jun 23, 1947 in Panania, Austria
Source: *BioIn 12; ConTFT 7, 14; HalFC 84, 88; IntMPA 88, 92, 94, 96; LegTOT; VarWW 83; WhoHol 92*

Brown, Carter
[Alan Geoffrey Yates]
English. Author
Wrote 270 detective novels.
b. Aug 1, 1923 in London, England
d. May 5, 1985 in Sydney, Australia
Source: *AnObit 1985; Au&Wr 71; BioIn 14; ConAu 1R; LinLib L; NewYTBS 85; Novels; OxCAusL; TwCCr&M 80, 85, 91; WhoAm 82; WrDr 82, 84*

Brown, Cecil B
American. Broadcaster, Journalist
Newspaper reporter, WW II correspondent known for dramatic style; with CBS, 1940-43; NBC, 1960s.
b. Sep 14, 1907 in New Brighton, Pennsylvania
d. Oct 25, 1987 in Los Angeles, California
Source: *CurBio 42, 88; WhoAm 84*

Brown, Charles Brockden
American. Author, Editor
First American professional author; introduced Native Americans to US fiction; wrote six gothic romances.
b. Jan 17, 1771 in Philadelphia, Pennsylvania
d. Feb 22, 1810 in Philadelphia, Pennsylvania
Source: *Alli; AmAu; AmAu&B; AmBi; AmWrBE; AmWr S1; ApCAB; AtlBL; BbD; Benet 87, 96; BenetAL 91; BibAL; BiD&SB; BioIn 1, 2, 3, 4, 5, 6, 7, 9, 10, 11, 12, 14, 15, 16, 20; CamGEL; CamGLE; CamHAL; CasWL; Chambr 3; CnDAL; ColARen; CrtT 3, 4; CyAL 1; CyWA 58; DcAmAu; DcAmB; DcArts; DcBiPP; DcEnL; DcLB 37, 59, 73; DcLEL; DcNAA; Drake; EncAJ; EncMys; EvLB; FemiWr; GrWrEL N; HarEnUS; LinLib L, S; McGEWB; MouLC 2; NatCAB 7; NinCLC 22; Novels; OxCAmL 65, 83, 95; OxCEng 67, 85, 95; PenC AM; PenEncH; RAdv 1, 14, 13-1; REn; REnAL; RfGAmL 87, 94; TwCBDA; WebAB 74, 79; WebE&AL; WhAm HS; WhoHr&F*

Brown, Charles Lee
American. Business Executive
With AT&T since 1946; president, 1977-79; chairman, 1979—.
b. Aug 23, 1921 in Richmond, Virginia
Source: *BioIn 12, 13; CurBio 81; IntWW 83; NewYTBS 78, 82; St&PR 84; WhoAm 74, 76, 78, 80, 82, 84, 86; WhoE 79, 81, 83, 85; WhoFI 74, 75, 77, 79, 81, 83, 85, 87*

Brown, Charlie
American. Teacher
Boyhood friend of Charles Schulz who supplied name, demeanor for comic strip character.
b. 1926?
d. Dec 5, 1983 in Minneapolis, Minnesota
Source: *BioIn 13*

Brown, Christy
Irish. Author, Poet
Born with crippling cerebral palsy and only usable limb was left foot; wrote best-seller *Down All the Days,* 1970; film *My Left Foot,* 1989, was his life story.

b. Jun 5, 1932 in Dublin, Ireland
d. Sep 6, 1981 in Parbrook, England
Source: *AnObit 1981; BiDIrW; BioIn 8, 9, 10, 12, 13, 17, 18; ConAu 104, 105; ConHero 2; ConLC 63; DcIrB 88; DcIrL 96; DcIrW 2; DcLB 14; FacFETw; NewYTBE 70, 71; Novels; OxCIri; WrDr 76, 80, 82, 84*

Brown, Clarence
American. Director
Directed 52 films; received six Oscar nominations; launched Garbo's career, 1927, in *Flesh and the Devil.*
b. May 10, 1890 in Clinton, Massachusetts
d. Aug 17, 1987 in Santa Monica, California
Source: *AmFD; AnObit 1987; BiDFilm, 81, 94; BioIn 10, 11, 15, 17; CmMov; DcFM; FacFETw; FilmEn; FilmgC; HalFC 80, 84, 88; IlWWHD 1; IntDcF 1-2, 2-2; IntMPA 75, 76, 77, 78, 79, 80, 81, 82, 84, 86; LegTOT; MiSFD 9N; MovMk; OxCFilm; TwYS, A; VarWW 85; WorEFlm; WorFDir 1*

Brown, David
American. Producer
Produced films *The Sting,* 1973; *Jaws,* 1975; *Cocoon,* 1985; husband of Helen Gurley Brown.
b. Jul 28, 1916 in New York, New York
Source: *BioIn 13, 14, 16, 17, 20; CelR 90; ConAu 13R; ConTFT 3; FilmEn; HalFC 84, 88; IntMPA 75, 76, 77, 78, 79, 80, 81, 82, 84, 86, 88, 92, 94, 96; WhE&EA; WhoAm 74, 76, 78, 80, 82, 84, 86, 88, 90, 92, 94, 95, 96, 97; WhoE 74, 89, 91, 95, 97; WhoFI 74, 75, 77, 79, 81, 83, 85, 87, 89; WhoUSWr 88; WhoWor 74, 76, 78, 80, 82, 84, 87, 89; WhoWrEP 89, 92, 95*

Brown, Dean
American. Photographer
Free-lance photographer for several magazines; known chiefly for color landscapes.
b. 1936
d. Jul 10, 1973 in New Hampshire
Source: *BioIn 10; ConPhot 82, 88; ICPEnP A; MacBEP*

Brown, Dee (Alexander)
American. Author, Historian
Has written on American West, conquest of Native Americans; *Bury My Heart At Wounded Knee,* 1971.
b. Feb 28, 1908 in Louisiana
Source: *ArtclWW 2; AuBYP 2S, 3; BiDrLUS 70; BioIn 10, 11, 12; ConAu 6AS, 11NR, 13R, 45NR; ConLC 18, 47; ConPopW; CurBio 79; DcLB Y80B; DrAS 78H, 82H; EncFWF; LegTOT; MajTwCW; PeoHis; REnAW; SmATA 5; TwCWW 82, 91; WhoAm 74, 76, 78, 80, 82, 84, 86, 88, 90, 92, 94, 95, 96, 97; WhoLibS 66; WhoMW 74; WhoSSW 97; WhoUSWr 88; WhoWest 94, 96; WhoWrEP 89, 92, 95; WorAu 1975; WrDr 76, 80, 82, 84, 86, 88, 90, 92, 94, 96*

Brown, Dorothy Lavinia
American. Surgeon
First black woman chief of surgery, Riverside Hospital, Nashville, 1960-83.
b. Jan 7, 1919 in Philadelphia, Pennsylvania
Source: *BioIn 11; BlksScM; BlkWAm; Ebony 1; InB&W 80, 85; NegAl 76, 83; WhoAm 76, 78, 80, 82, 84; WhoAmW 61, 64, 66, 68, 70, 72, 74, 77; WhoBlA 85, 88; WhoSSW 73, 75, 76*

Brown, Earle
American. Composer
One of America's foremost avant-garde composers; created open-form system of composition and a radical graphic notation technique widely used in his work.
b. Dec 26, 1926 in Lunenburg, Massachusetts
Source: *AmComp; Baker 78, 84; BiDD; BioIn 4, 7, 8, 13; BriBkM 80; CompSN SUP; ConAmC 76, 82; ConCom 92; CpmDNM 81; DcArts; DcCM; DcCom&M 79; IntWWM 77, 80, 85, 90; NewAmDM; NewGrDA 86; NewGrDM 80; NewOxM; NewYTBE 70; WhoAm 74, 76, 78, 80, 82, 84, 86, 88, 90, 92, 94, 95, 96, 97; WhoEnt 92; WhoMus 72; WhoWor 74, 96*

Brown, Eddie Lee
American. Football Player
Wide receiver, Cincinnati, 1985—; rookie of year, 1985.
b. Dec 17, 1962 in Miami, Florida
Source: *FootReg 86, 87*

Brown, Edmund G.
[Edmund Gerald Brown, Sr; Pat Brown]
American. Lawyer, Politician
Dem. governor of CA, 1959-67; lost to Ronald Reagan; father of Jerry.
b. Apr 21, 1905 in San Francisco, California
d. Feb 16, 1996 in Beverly Hills, California
Source: *AmCath 80; BiDrGov 1789; BioIn 21; CmCal; ConAu 132; CurBio 60; IntWW 74, 75, 76, 77, 78, 79, 80, 81, 82, 83, 89, 91; News 96, 96-3; NewYTBS 27; PolPar; PolProf E; WhAm 11; WhoAm 74, 76, 78, 80, 82, 84, 86, 88, 90, 92, 94, 95, 96; WhoAmP 73, 75, 77, 79, 81, 83, 85; WorAl; WorAlBi*

Brown, Elaine
American. Political Activist
Chairperson and minister of defense, Black Panther Party, 1974-77; wrote *A Taste of Power: A Black Woman's Story,* 1992.
b. Mar 2, 1943 in Philadelphia, Pennsylvania
Source: *BioIn 10; BlkWAm; BlkWr 2; ConAu 142; ConBlB 8; NotBlAW 2; SchCGBL; WomFir*

Brown, Frank Arthur, Jr.
American. Biologist, Educator
Wrote *Comparative Animal Physiology,* 1950; *Biological Clocks,* 1970.
b. Aug 30, 1908 in Beverly, Massachusetts
Source: *AmMWSc 76P, 79, 82; WhAm 8; WhoAm 74, 76, 78, 80, 82; WhoE 81, 83; WhoWor 76, 78, 80, 82*

Brown, George
[Kool and the Gang]
"Funky"
American. Musician
Drummer with Kool and the Gang.
b. Jan 5, 1949 in Jersey City, New Jersey
Source: *InB&W 85*

Brown, George Alfred
English. Government Official
Controversial MP, 1945-70; deputy leader of Labour Party, 1960-70.
b. Sep 2, 1914 in London, England
d. Jun 2, 1985 in Truro, England
Source: *BioIn 6, 7, 8, 18; ColdWar 1; CurBio 85; DcNaB 1981*

Brown, George Mackay
Scottish. Poet, Author
Wrote *Pictures in the Cave,* 1977; *Selected Poems,* 1977.
b. Oct 17, 1921 in Stromness, Scotland
d. Apr 13, 1996 in Kirkwall, Scotland
Source: *BioIn 13; BlueB 76; CamGLE; CasWL; ChhPo S2, S3; CmScLit; ConAu 6AS, 12NR, 21R, 37NR, 151; ConLC 5, 48; ConNov 72, 76, 82, 86, 91, 96; ConPo 70, 75, 80, 85, 91, 96; DcLB 14, 27, 139; IntAu&W 76, 77, 82, 86, 89; IntWWP 77, 82; LinLib L; MajTwCW; OxCEng 85, 95; OxCTwCP; RfGEnL 91; RfGShF; RGTwCWr; ScF&FL 92; SmATA 35; WhAm 11; Who 82, 83, 85, 88, 90, 92, 94; WhoWor 76, 80, 95, 96; WorAu 1970; WrDr 76, 80, 82, 84, 86, 88, 90, 92, 94, 96*

Brown, George Scratchley
American. Military Leader, Government Official
Commanded Seventh Air Force, Vietnam, 1968-70; controversial chm., Joint Chiefs of Staff, 1974-78.
b. Aug 17, 1918 in Montclair, New Jersey
d. Dec 5, 1978 in Washington, District of Columbia
Source: *BioIn 10, 11, 12; BlueB 76; DcAmB S10; HarEnMi; IntWW 74, 75, 76, 77, 78; ObitOF 79; WebAMB; WhAm 7; WhoAm 74, 76, 78; WhoGov 72, 75, 77; WhoWor 78; WorAl; WorDWW*

Brown, Georgia
English. Actor
Stage works include London, Broadway productions of *Threepenny Opera; Oliver .*
b. Oct 21, 1933 in London, England
d. Jul 5, 1992 in London, England

Source: *AnObit 1992; BiE&WWA; BioIn 6, 15, 18, 19; ConTFT 9; FilmEn; FilmgC; HalFC 80, 84, 88; InB&W 80; LegTOT; NotNAT; OxCPMus; WhoHol 92, A; WhoThe 72, 77, 81*

Brown, H(ubert) Rap
[Jamiel Abdul Al-Amin]
American. Civil Rights Leader
Chairman, SNCC, 1967; converted to Islam while serving prison term.
b. Oct 4, 1943 in Baton Rouge, Louisiana
Source: *AmAu&B; CivRSt; LivgBAA; WhoBlA 80*

Brown, Hank
American. Politician
Rep. senator from CO, 1991-96.
b. Feb 12, 1940 in Denver, Colorado
Source: *AlmAP 82, 84, 88, 92, 96; BioIn 17; CngDr 81, 83, 85, 87, 89, 91, 93, 95; IntWW 91, 93; PolsAm 84; WhoAm 82, 84, 86, 88, 90, 92, 94, 95, 96, 97; WhoAmL 87; WhoAmP 83, 85, 87, 89, 91, 93, 95; WhoE 95; WhoEmL 87; WhoWest 82, 84, 87, 89, 92, 94, 96*

Brown, Harold
American. Businessman, Government Official
Secretary of Defense under Jimmy Carter, 1977-81.
b. Sep 19, 1927 in New York, New York
Source: *AmMWSc 73P, 76P, 79, 82, 86, 89, 92, 95; BiDrUSE 89; BioIn 5, 6, 7, 8, 11, 12, 13, 18; BlueB 76; CngDr 77, 79; ColdWar 1; CurBio 61, 77; InSci; IntWW 74, 75, 76, 77, 78, 79, 80, 81, 82, 83, 89, 91, 93; IntYB 78, 79, 80, 81, 82; LEduc 74; PolProf J, K; Who 82, 83, 85, 88, 90, 92, 94; WhoAm 74, 76, 78, 80, 82, 84, 86, 88, 90, 92, 94, 95, 96, 97; WhoAmP 77, 79, 81, 83, 85, 87, 89, 91, 93, 95; WhoE 77, 79, 81; WhoEng 80, 88; WhoFI 89; WhoFrS 84; WhoGov 77; WhoScEn 94, 96; WhoWest 74, 76; WhoWor 74, 76, 78, 80, 82, 84; WorAl*

Brown, Helen Gurley
American. Author, Editor
Cosmopolitan magazine editor, 1965-97; wrote best-selling novel *Sex & the Single Girl*, 1962.
b. Feb 18, 1922 in Green Forest, Arkansas
Source: *AmAu&B; AmDec 1970; AmSocL; ArtclWW 2; BenetAL 91; BlueB 76; CelR, 90; ConAu 5NR, 5R; CurBio 69; EncTwCJ; FacFETw; ForWC 70; GoodHs; GrLiveH; IntAu&W 76, 93; IntWW 83; InWom, SUP; LegTOT; LibW; NewYTBS 82; WhoAm 74, 76, 78, 80, 82, 84, 86, 88, 90, 92, 94, 95, 96, 97; WhoAmW 64, 68, 70, 72, 74, 77, 79, 81, 83, 85, 87, 89, 91, 93, 95, 97; WhoE 74, 83, 85, 93; WhoUSWr 88; WhoWor 74, 76, 78, 80, 82, 84, 87, 89, 91, 93, 95, 96, 97; WhoWrEP 89, 92, 95; WomComm; WorAl; WorAlBi; WrDr 76, 80, 82, 84, 86, 88, 90, 92, 94, 96*

Brown, Henry Billings
American. Jurist
US district judge, 1875-90; associate justice, US Supreme Court, 1890-1906.
b. Mar 2, 1836 in South Lee, Massachusetts
d. Sep 4, 1913 in Bronxville, New York
Source: *Alli SUP; ApCAB; BiDFedJ; BioIn 2, 5, 15; DcAmAu; DcAmB; DcNAA; HarEnUS; NatCAB 1; OxCSupC; SupCtJu; TwCBDA; WebAB 74, 79; WhAm 1*

Brown, Herbert Charles
[Herbert Charles Brovarnik]
English. Chemist
Won 1979 Nobel Prize in chemistry; proposed new class of compounds.
b. May 22, 1912 in London, England
Source: *AmMWSc 76P, 79, 82, 86, 89, 92, 95; BiESc; BioIn 3, 5, 9, 12, 13, 15, 19, 20; CamDcSc; FacFETw; IntAu&W 77; IntWW 74, 75, 76, 77, 78, 79, 80, 81, 82, 83, 89, 91, 93; LarDcSc; McGMS 80; Who 82, 83, 85, 88, 90, 92, 94; WhoAm 74, 76, 78, 80, 82, 84, 86, 88, 90, 92, 94, 95, 96, 97; WhoAmJ 80; WhoFrS 84; WhoMW 80, 82, 84, 86, 88, 90, 92, 93, 96; WhoNob, 90, 95; WhoScEn 94, 96; WhoWor 74, 76, 78, 80, 82, 84, 87, 89, 91, 93, 95, 96, 97; WhoWorJ 72, 78*

Brown, Hubie
[Hubert Jude Brown]
American. Basketball Coach
Coach, Atlanta, 1976-81, NY Knicks, 1982-87; NBA coach of year, 1978.
b. Sep 25, 1933 in Elizabeth, New Jersey
Source: *BasBi; BioIn 12, 13; NewYTBS 80, 82; WhoAm 78, 80, 84, 86; WhoE 85, 86*

Brown, Jacob Jennings
American. Military Leader
Commanded Battle of Niagara, War of 1812; commanding general of US Army, 1821-28.
b. May 9, 1775 in Bucks County, Pennsylvania
d. Feb 24, 1828 in Washington, District of Columbia
Source: *AmBi; ApCAB; BiAUS; BioIn 1, 9, 12; CmdGen 1991; DcAmB; DcAmMiB; Drake; HarEnMi; NatCAB 5; NewCol 75; TwCBDA; WebAB 74, 79; WebAMB; WhAm HS*

Brown, James
American. Publisher
With Charles Little, formed Little, Brown and Co., 1837.
b. May 19, 1800 in Acton, Massachusetts
d. Mar 10, 1855 in Watertown, Massachusetts
Source: *AmAu&B; ApCAB; BioIn 3; DcAmB; NatCAB 5; TwCBDA; WhAm HS*

Brown, James
"Godfather of Soul"; "Mister Dynamite"; "Soul Brother Number"
American. Singer
Has 38 gold records in 20 yrs; won Grammys, 1965, 1986; inducted into Rock and Roll Hall of Fame, 1986; songs include "Living in America."
b. May 3, 1928 in Augusta, Georgia
Source: *Baker 84, 92; BiDAfM; BiDAmM; BioIn 12, 14; ConMus 2; CurBio 92; DcArts; DcTwCCu 1, 5; EncPR&S 89; EncRk 88; FacFETw; HarEnR 86; IlEncBM 82; InB&W 85; IntWW 89, 91, 93; LegTOT; News 91; OxCPMus; PenEncP; RkOn 74; RolSEnR 83; WebAB 74; Who 83, 85, 88, 90, 92, 94; WhoAm 78, 80, 82, 84, 86, 88, 92, 94, 95, 96, 97; WhoBlA 75, 80, 88, 90; WhoE 74; WhoEnt 92; WorAl; WorAlBi*

Brown, Jerry
[Edmund Gerald Brown, Jr.]
American. Politician
Dem. governor of CA, 1975-83; succeeded by George Deukmejian; son of Pat Brown.
b. Apr 7, 1938 in San Francisco, California
Source: *BiDrGov 1978; BioIn 10, 11, 12, 13, 14, 15, 16, 17, 18, 21; BioNews 74; BkPepl; CurBio 75; IntWW 89, 91, 93; LegTOT; News 92; NewYTBS 91; Who 82, 83, 85, 88, 90, 92, 94; WhoAm 76, 78, 80, 82, 84, 86, 88, 92, 94, 95; WhoAmL 79; WhoAmP 73, 75, 77, 79, 81, 83, 85, 87, 89, 91, 93, 95; WhoGov 72, 75, 77; WhoWest 92, 94; WhoWor 78, 80, 82, 84*

Brown, Jesse
American. Government Official
Secretary, Veterans Affairs, 1993—.
b. Mar 27, 1944 in Detroit, Michigan
Source: *AfrAmBi 2; BioIn 19, 20; CngDr 93, 95; ConBlB 6; CurBio 93; WhoAm 95, 96, 97; WhoAmP 93, 95; WhoWor 96, 97*

Brown, Jim
[James Nathaniel Brown]
American. Actor, Football Player
Running back, Cleveland, 1956-65; held NFL record for career rushing yds. until broken by Walter Payton, 1984; Hall of Fame.
b. Feb 17, 1936 in Saint Simons Island, Georgia
Source: *AfrAmAl 6; AfrAmSG; BiDAmSp FB; BioIn 5, 6, 7, 8, 9, 10, 11, 14, 15, 16, 17, 18, 19, 20, 21; BioNews 74; CelR 90; CivR 74; ConBlB 11; ConTFT 9; FacFETw; FilmgC; HalFC 80, 84, 88; InB&W 80, 85; IntMPA 77, 78, 79, 80, 81, 82, 84, 86, 88, 92, 94, 96; ItaFilm; LegTOT; MotPP; MovMk; NegAl 83, 89; News 93-2; NewYTBE 73; WhoAfA 96; WhoAm 74, 76, 78, 80, 82, 84, 86, 88, 92, 94, 95, 96, 97; WhoBlA 75, 77, 80, 85, 88, 90, 92, 94; WhoEnt 92; WhoHol A; WhoSpor; WorAl; WorAlBi*

Brown, Jim Ed
[James Edward Brown]
American. Singer
Country music singer popular in 1950s, 60s.
b. Apr 1, 1934 in Sparkman, Arkansas
Source: *BioIn 12, 14, 15; CounME 74, 74A; EncFCWM 83; IlEncCM; LegTOT; WhoAm 80, 82, 84*

Brown, Joe E(van)
American. Comedian, Actor
Known for comical, wide-mouthed expressions in musical comedies of stage, films including *Some Like It Hot,* 1959.
b. Jul 28, 1892 in Holgate, Ohio
d. Jul 6, 1973 in Brentwood, California
Source: *BiE&WWA; BioIn 1, 2, 3, 4, 5, 8, 10, 11; CurBio 45, 73; EncMT; FilmgC; MotPP; MovMk; NewYTBE 73; OhA&B; OxCFilm; WhAm 5; WhoAm 74; WhoThe 72; WhScrn 77*

Brown, John
"Old Brown of Osawatomie"
American. Abolitionist
Led raid at Harper's Ferry, VA, 1859; his conviction, hanging for treason made him a hero to antislavery cause.
b. May 9, 1800 in Torrington, Connecticut
d. Dec 2, 1859 in Charles Town, West Virginia
Source: *AmBi; AmRef; AmSocL; ApCAB; Benet 87, 96; BenetAL 91; BiDTran; BioIn 1, 2, 3, 4, 5, 6, 7, 8, 9, 10, 11, 12, 13, 14, 15, 16, 17, 19, 20, 21; CamGEL; CamHAL; CelCen; CivWDc; CmCal; CyAG; DcAmB; DcAmSR; Drake; EncAAH; EncAB-H 1974, 1996; EncRev; HarEnUS; HisWorL; LegTOT; LinLib L, S; McGEWB; NatCAB 2; OxCAmH; OxCAmL 65, 83, 95; OxCEng 67, 85, 95; PolPar; RComAH; REn; REnAL; REnAW; TwCBDA; WebAB 74, 79; WhAm HS; WhAmP; WhCiWar; WhDW; WorAl; WorAlBi*

Brown, John Carter
American. Museum Director
Director, National Gallery of Art, Washington, DC, 1969-92.
b. Oct 8, 1934 in Providence, Rhode Island
Source: *BioIn 10; WhoSSW 73, 76; WhoWor 84, 91*

Brown, John Mason
American. Critic, Lecturer
Wrote *Morning Faces,* 1949; *Through These Men,* 1956.
b. Jul 3, 1900 in Louisville, Kentucky
d. Mar 16, 1969 in New York, New York
Source: *AmAu&B; BenetAL 91; BiE&WWA; BioIn 1, 2, 3, 4, 5, 8, 9, 10; CamGWoT; CnDAL; ConAu 9R, 25R; DcAmB S8; EncAJ; LiHiK; LinLib L, S; LngCTC; NotNAT A, B; OxCAmL 65, 83, 95; OxCAmT 84; OxCThe 67; PenC AM; PlP&P; REnAL; TwCA, SUP*

Brown, John Young, Jr.
American. Businessman, Politician
Bought Kentucky Fried Chicken from Colonel Sanders, 1964, for $2 million; governor of KY, 1980-83.
b. Dec 28, 1933 in Lexington, Kentucky
Source: *AlmAP 82, 84; BiDrGov 1978, 1983; BioIn 10, 11, 12, 13; WhoAm 82; WhoAmP 81; WhoE 81; WhoFI 74; WhoSSW 73, 82*

Brown, Johnny Mack
American. Football Player, Actor
Collegiate running back, 1923-25; as actor, known for cowboy roles.
b. Sep 1, 1904 in Dothan, Alabama
d. Nov 14, 1974 in Woodland Hills, California
Source: *BioIn 8, 9, 10, 12, 21; CmMov; DcAmB S9; Film 2; FilmEn; ForYSC; NewYTBS 74; TwYS; What 3; WhoFtbl 74; WhoHol A, B; WhScrn 77, 83*

Brown, Judie
American. Social Reformer
Founder, pres., American Life League, American Life Lobby, 1979—; goal to amend Constitution to prohibit abortion.
b. Mar 4, 1944 in Los Angeles, California
Source: *ConNews 86-2*

Brown, Kelly
[Elford Cornelious Kelly Kingman Brown]
American. Actor, Dancer
Soloist, American Ballet Theater; films include *Daddy Long Legs,* 1955; father of dancer Leslie Browne.
b. Sep 24, 1928 in Maysville, Kentucky
d. Mar 13, 1981 in Phoenix, Arizona
Source: *BiDD; BiE&WWA; BioIn 12; CnOxB; DancEn 78; NewYTBS 81; NotNAT*

Brown, Kenneth H
American. Dramatist
Wrote *The Brig,* 1963.
b. Mar 9, 1936 in New York, New York
Source: *ConTFT 2*

Brown, Lancelot
"Capability"
English. Architect
Founded modern "English style" landscapes.
b. 1715 in Harle-Kirk, England
d. Feb 6, 1783 in London, England
Source: *AtlBL; BiDBrA; BioIn 2, 4, 9, 10, 11; DcBiPP; DcD&D; DcNaB; EncUrb; LegTOT; NewC; WhDW; WorAl; WorAlBi*

Brown, Larry
[Lawrence Harvey Brown]
American. Basketball Coach
Head coach of several college, pro teams, including U of Kansas, 1983-88, winning NCAA championship, 1988; with San Antonio Spurs, 1988-92; LA Clippers, 1992-93; Indiana Pacers, 1993-97; Philadelphia 76ers, 1997—.
b. Sep 14, 1940 in New York, New York
Source: *Ballpl 90; BasBi; BiDAmSp BK; BioIn 11, 13; CurBio 96; WhoAm 84, 86, 88, 94, 95, 96, 97; WhoMW 93; WhoSpor; WhoSSW 88, 91, 93; WorAlBi*

Brown, Larry
[Lawrence Brown, Jr]
American. Football Player
Running back, 1969-71, tight end, 1971-84; MVP, 1973; wrote *I'll Always Get Up,* 1973.
b. Sep 19, 1947 in Clairton, Pennsylvania
Source: *BiDAmSp Sup; BioIn 9, 10; CelR; ConAu 114; CurBio 73; InB&W 80, 85; NewYTBE 70; WhoAm 74, 76, 78; WhoBlA 77, 80, 85, 90; WhoFtbl 74; WhoSpor*

Brown, Larry
American. Author
Wrote novels *Dirty Work,* 1989; *Joe,* 1991.
b. Jul 9, 1951 in Oxford, Mississippi
Source: *BioIn 17, 19, 20, 21; ConAu 130, 134; ConLC 73*

Brown, Lee Patrick
American. Criminologist, Government Official
NYC police commissioner, 1990-92; noted for implementation of Community Patrol Operations Program (CPOC) which stresses neighborhood beat patrols for officers; dir. National Drug control Policy, 1993-96; Cabinet member 1993-96; professor, rice University, 1996—.
b. Oct 4, 1937 in Wewoka, Oklahoma
Source: *AfrAmBi 2; BioIn 12, 13, 14; CopCroC; WhoAfA 96; WhoAm 80, 82, 84, 88, 90, 92, 94, 95, 96, 97; WhoBlA 85, 88, 90, 92, 94; WhoE 91, 93, 95, 97; WhoSSW 88; WhoWest 74*

Brown, Les(lie Calvin)
American. Author
Motivational speaker, 1986—; founder of Les Brown Unlimited, Inc.
b. Feb 17, 1945 in Miami, Florida
Source: *ConBlB 5; News 94, 94-3*

Brown, Les(ter Louis)
American. Journalist, Author
Editor-in-chief, *Channels* magazine, 1980-87; editorial director at New York's Center for Communication; numerous books, including *Les Brown's Encyclopedia of Television, 3rd ed.* 1992.
b. Dec 20, 1928 in Indiana Harbor, Indiana
Source: *BioIn 9; ConAu 13NR, 33R, 132; IndAu 1967; IntAu&W 89; WhoAm 74, 76, 78, 80, 82, 84, 86, 88, 90, 92, 94, 95, 96, 97; WhoAmJ 80; WhoEnt 92; WhoWrEP 89*

Brown, Les(ter Raymond)
"Les Brown and His Band of Renown"
American. Bandleader
Often played with Bob Hope; wrote "Sentimental Journey."
b. Mar 12, 1912 in Reinerton, Pennsylvania
Source: *AllMusG; ASCAP 66, 80; Baker 84, 92; BgBands 74; BiDAmM; BiDJaz; BioIn 9, 12, 16, 17; CmpEPM; EncJzS; LegTOT; NewGrDA 86; NewGrDJ 88, 94; OxCPMus; PenEncP; RadStar; WhoEnt 92; WhoHol 92; WorAl; WorAlBi*

Brown, Lester Russell
American. Agriculturist
Founder, pres., Worldwatch Institute, 1974—; publishes *State of the World* yearbooks and other ecology-minded publications, 1984-95; editor *Watch,* 1988—.
b. Mar 28, 1934 in Bridgeton, New Jersey
Source: *AmMWSc 92; BioIn 7, 10, 12, 15, 18, 19, 20, 21; ConAu 132; NatLAC; RAdv 14; WhoAm 74, 76, 78, 80, 82, 84, 86, 88, 90, 92, 94, 95, 96, 97; WhoScEn 96; WhoWor 74, 97*

Brown, Lew
American. Songwriter
Songs include "Button Up Your Overcoat"; "Beer Barrel Polka."
b. Dec 10, 1893 in Odessa, Russia
d. Feb 5, 1958 in New York, New York
Source: *AmPS; AmSong; ASCAP 66, 80; BiDAmM; BioIn 4, 5, 6, 9, 10, 12, 14, 15; CmpEPM; EncMT; NatCAB 43; NewCBMT; NewGrDA 86; NotNAT B; OxCAmT 84; OxCPMus; Sw&Ld C; WhAm 3; WhoHol A*

Brown, Louise Joy
English. Test Tube Baby
First test tube baby; procedure developed by Drs. Patrick Steptoe, Robert Edwards.
b. Jul 25, 1978 in Oldham, England
Source: *BioIn 11, 12; BkPepl*

Brown, Marcia
American. Children's Author, Illustrator
Self-illustrated books include *Stone Soup,* 1947; *Skipper John's Cook,* 1951; three-time Caldecott winner.
b. Jul 13, 1918 in Rochester, New York
Source: *AmAu&B; AnCL; ArtclWW 2; AuBYP 2; BioIn 3, 4, 5, 6, 7, 8, 10, 11, 12, 13, 15, 16, 18, 19; BkP; Cald 1938; ChhPo, S2; ChlBkCr; ChlLR 12; ChsFB I; ConAu 41R, 46NR; DcLB 61; FamAIYP; IlsBYP; IlsCB 1946, 1957; InWom SUP; LinLib L; MorJA; NewbC 1956; OxCChiL; SmATA 7, 47; TwCChW 89, 95; WhoAm 74, 76, 78, 80, 82, 84, 86, 88; WhoAmW 58, 61, 64, 66, 68, 70, 72, 74, 89; WrDr 90, 92, 94, 96*

Brown, Margaret Wise
American. Children's Author
Wrote popular *Noisy Book* series, 1939-51.
b. May 23, 1910 in New York, New York
d. Nov 13, 1952 in Nice, France
Source: *AmWomWr; ASCAP 66, 80; Au&ICB; AuBYP 2, 3; BenetAL 91; BioIn 1, 2, 3, 4, 7, 9, 11, 12, 13, 14, 16, 17, 18, 19, 20; ChhPo, S1; ChlBkCr; ChlLR 10; ConAu 108, 136; DcAmB S5; DcLB 22; GrLiveH; InWom SUP; JBA 51; MajAI; NotAW MOD; OxCChiL; PenNWW A, B; REnAL; TwCChW 78, 83, 89, 95; WhAm 3; YABC 2*

Brown, Michael Stuart
American. Geneticist
With Joseph L Goldstein, won Nobel Prize, 1985, for research into role of cholesterol in cardiovascular disease.
b. Apr 13, 1941 in New York, New York
Source: *BioIn 14, 15, 20; IntWW 89, 91, 93; LarDcSc; Who 90, 92, 94; WhoAm 82, 84, 86, 88, 90, 92, 94, 95, 96, 97; WhoFrS 84; WhoMedH; WhoNob, 90, 95; WhoScEn 94, 96; WhoSSW 86, 88, 91, 93, 95, 97; WhoWor 87, 89, 91, 93, 95, 96, 97*

Brown, Mordecai Peter Centennial
"Miner"; "Three Finger Brown"
American. Baseball Player
Pitcher, 1903-16; farm accident injured fingers, helped make curve ball more effective; Hall of Fame, 1949.
b. Oct 19, 1876 in Byesville, Indiana
d. Feb 14, 1948 in Terre Haute, Indiana
Source: *BiDAmSp BB; BioIn 1, 3, 7, 8, 10; WhoProB 73; WorAl*

Brown, Nacio Herb
American. Songwriter
Composed scores, songs, for MGM: "You Were Meant for Me"; "Singin' in the Rain."
b. Feb 22, 1896 in Deming, New Mexico
d. Sep 28, 1964 in San Francisco, California
Source: *AmPS; AmSong; ASCAP 66, 80; Baker 78, 84; BestMus; BiDAmM; BioIn 4, 6, 7, 14, 15, 16; CmpEPM; Film 2; FilmEn; FilmgC; HalFC 80, 84, 88; IntDcF 1-4, 2-4; LegTOT; NewAmDM; NewGrDA 86; NewGrDM 80; NotNAT B; OxCPMus; PenEncP; PopAmC, SUP; Sw&Ld C*

Brown, Oscar, Jr.
American. Actor, Composer
Wrote "Brown Baby," 1960, sung by Mahalia Jackson.
b. Oct 10, 1926 in Chicago, Illinois
Source: *AllMusG; BiDAfM; BiDAmM; BiDJaz; BioIn 5, 6; BlkAmP; ConBlAP 88; DrBlPA, 90; InB&W 85; MorBAP; NegAl 76, 83, 89; NewGrDJ 88, 94; PenEncP; WhoAm 74, 76, 78, 80, 82, 84, 86, 88, 92, 94, 95, 96, 97; WhoBlA 75, 77, 80; WhoWor 74*

Brown, Pamela
English. Actor
Broadway debut, 1947, opposite John Gielgud in *Importance of Being Earnest;* won 1961 Emmy for "Victoria Regina."
b. Jul 8, 1917 in London, England
d. Sep 18, 1975 in London, England
Source: *BiE&WWA; BioIn 10; FilmEn; FilmgC; ForYSC; HalFC 80, 84, 88; InWom; NotNAT B; ObitOF 79; ObitT 1971; OxCFilm; OxCThe 83; PlP&P; WhoHol C; WhScrn 77, 83*

Brown, Pamela Beatrice
English. Author, Actor
Writes novels for young people: *A Little Universe,* 1970; *Summer Is a Festival,* 1972.
b. Dec 31, 1924 in Colchester, England
Source: *Au&Wr 71; AuBYP 2, 3; BioIn 7, 8, 10; ConAu 13R; IntMPA 75; NewCBEL; SmATA 5; WhoChL*

Brown, Paul
American. Football Coach
With Cleveland, 1946-62, Cincinnati, 1968-76; vp and General Manager, Bengals, known for calling plays from sidelines; Hall of Fame, 1967.
b. Jul 9, 1908 in Norwalk, Ohio
d. Aug 5, 1991 in Cincinnati, Ohio
Source: *AnObit 1991; BioIn 8, 10, 12, 13, 15, 16, 17, 18, 21; CelR; LegTOT; News 92, 92-1; WhAm 10; WhoAm 74, 76, 78, 82, 84, 86, 88; WhoFtbl 74; WhoMW 80, 82, 84, 86, 88, 90; WorAl; WorAlBi*

Brown, Peter
English. Singer, Songwriter
Best known for songwriting with Jack Bruce; songs for group Cream include "Sunshine of Your Love," 1968.
b. Dec 25, 1940 in London, England
Source: *IlEncRk; RkOn 85; St&PR 84*

Brown, Rita Mae
American. Author
Wrote *Rubyfruit Jungle,* 1973; *Bingo,* 1988.
b. Nov 28, 1944 in Hanover, Pennsylvania
Source: *AmWomWr; ArtclWW 2; Benet 96; BenetAL 91; BioIn 10, 11, 13; BlmGWL; CamGLE; CamHAL; ConAu 2NR, 11NR, 35NR, 45; ConLC 18, 43, 79; ConNov 91, 96; ConPopW; CurBio 86; CyWA 89; DrAF 76; DrAP 75; DrAPF 80; FemiCLE; FemiWr; ForWC 70; GayLesB; GayLL; GrLiveH; HanAmWH; IntAu&W 77, 89, 91, 93; IntWWP 77; LegTOT; MajTwCW; OxCAmL 95; OxCWoWr 95; RadHan; RfGAmL 94; ScF&FL 92; WhoAm 84, 86, 88, 90, 92, 94, 95, 96, 97; WhoAmW 81, 83, 85, 87, 91; WhoEmL 87; WhoUSWr 88; WhoWrEP 89, 92, 95; WorAu 1985; WrDr 88, 90, 92, 94, 96*

Brown, Robert
English. Botanist
Observed Brownian Movement, 1827; discovered cell nucleus, 1831.
b. Dec 21, 1773 in Montrose, Scotland
d. Jun 10, 1858 in London, England
Source: *Alli; AsBiEn; BiESc; BioIn 2, 3, 4, 5, 14; BritAu 19; CamDcSc; CelCen; DcBiPP; DcNaB; DcScB; InSci; LarDcSc; LinLib S; NewCol 75; WhWE; WorScD*

Brown, Ron(ald Harmon)
American. Lawyer, Government Official
Chm., Dem. Nat. Com., 1989-93; first black to chair any major American political party; Secretary of Commerce, 1993-96;first cabinet secretary to die on a mission overseas and first in 152 years to be killed in the line of duty.
b. Aug 1, 1941 in Washington, District of Columbia
d. Apr 3, 1996 in Dubrovnik, Croatia
Source: *ConBlB 5; CurBio 89, 96N; IntWW 91; News 90, 90-3; NewYTBS 89; WhAm 11; WhoAm 90, 92, 94, 95, 96; WhoAmL 90, 92, 94; WhoAmP 91; WhoBlA 85, 88, 90, 92; WhoE 95; WhoFI 94, 96; WhoWor 96*

Brown, Ron(ald James)
American. Football Player
Won gold medal in relay, 1984 Olympics; wide receiver, LA Rams, 1984—; tied NFL record by returning two kickoffs for TDs in same game, 1985.
b. Mar 31, 1961 in Los Angeles, California
Source: *BlkOlyM; FootReg 87; WhoBlA 85, 92*

Brown, Roosevelt
American. Football Player
Ten-time all-pro offensive tackle, NY Giants, 1953-65; Hall of Fame, 1975.
b. Oct 20, 1932 in Charlottesville, Virginia
Source: *BiDAmSp FB; BioIn 7, 8, 17; InB&W 80; LegTOT; NewYTBS 75; WhoBlA 75, 77, 80, 85*

Brown, Rosemary
English. Psychic
Wrote *Unfinished Symphonies: Voices from the Beyond,* 1971.
b. 1917
Source: *Baker 84, 92; CanWW 80, 81; ContDcW 89; EncO&P 1S2; IntDcWB; MacDWB; NewGrDM 80*

Brown, Sterling (Allen)
American. Folklorist, Writer
Produced some of the most outstanding works by a black American during the Depression era; wrote poem "When de Saints Go Ma'ching Home," 1927.
b. May 1, 1901 in Washington, District of Columbia
Source: *AfrAmW; AmAu&B; AnObit 1989; BioIn 2, 10, 11, 12, 13, 15, 16, 17, 20; BlkAWP; BlkLC; BlkWr 1; ChhPo S3; ConAu 26NR, 85, 127; ConBlB 10; ConLC 1, 59; ConPo 80; CurBio 82, 89N; DcLB 48; DrAP 75; DrAPF 80; FacFETw; GrWrEL P; InB&W 80; LivgBAA; MajTwCW; NegAl 76, 83, 89; RAdv 14; REnAL; SelBAAf; SelBAAu; SouBlCW; WorAu 1970; WrDr 82, 84, 86*

Brown, Tim
American. Football Player
Wide receiver, Notre Dame; won 1987 Heisman Trophy; with NFL LA Raiders, 1988—; among NFL receiving leaders, 1995-96.
b. Jul 22, 1966 in Dallas, Texas

Brown, Tina
[Christina Hambley Brown]
English. Editor, Journalist
Editor-in-chief, *Vanity Fair,* 1984-92; *New Yorker,* NYC 1992—.
b. Nov 21, 1953 in Maidenhead, England
Source: *AmDec 1980; BioIn 12, 13; CelR 90; ConAu 116, 118; CurBio 90; IntWW 91, 93; News 92, 92-1; Who 88, 90, 92, 94; WhoAm 86, 88, 90, 92, 94, 95, 96, 97; WhoAmW 89, 91, 93, 95, 97; WhoE 89, 91, 93, 95, 97; WhoFI 92; WhoWor 91; WorAlBi*

Brown, Tom
[Thomas Edward Brown]
American. Actor
Played boy-next-door roles, 1930s films; TV soap opera "General Hospital."
b. Jan 6, 1913 in New York, New York
Source: *BioIn 10, 15, 17; Film 2; FilmEn; FilmgC; ForYSC; HalFC 80, 84, 88; IntMPA 75, 76, 77, 78, 79, 80, 81, 82, 84, 86, 88; MovMk; TwYS; Vers B; What 5; WhoHol A*

Brown, Tony
[William Anthony Brown]
American. TV Personality, Lecturer
Host, PBS's *Black Journal,* 1968-77; *Tony Brown's Journal,* 1982—; commentator, National Public Radio Network program, "All Things Considered."
b. Apr 11, 1933 in Charleston, West Virginia
Source: *AfrAmAl 6; AfrAmBi 1; BioIn 12; BlkWr 1; CelR 90; ConAu 125, 153; ConBlB 3; DcTwCCu 5; DrBlPA, 90; Ebony 1; InB&W 80, 85; SchCGBL; WhoAfA 96; WhoAm 76, 78; WhoBlA 75, 77, 80, 85, 88, 90, 92, 94; WhoWor 78*

Brown, Trisha
American. Choreographer
Choreographed Lina Wertmuller's production of *Carmen,* 1986; *M. O.,* 1995, set to Bach's *Musical Offering;* won the Samuel H. Scripps Amercian Dance Festival Award, 1994.
b. Nov 25, 1936 in Aberdeen, Washington
Source: *BiDD; DcArts; NewGrDA 86; RAdv 14; WhoAm 94, 95, 96, 97; WhoAmW 95, 97; WhoE 95, 97*

Brown, Vanessa
[Smylla Brind]
American. Actor, Author, Artist
Free-lance correspondent for "Voice of America"; films include *Late George Apley; Foxes of Harrow; Ghost and Mrs. Muir.*
b. Mar 24, 1928 in Vienna, Austria
Source: *BioIn 1, 4, 18; FilmEn; FilmgC; ForYSC; HalFC 80, 84, 88; InWom; MotPP; RadStar; WhoAmW 61, 77, 79, 95; WhoHol 92, A*

Brown, Walter Augustine
American. Basketball Executive, Hockey Executive
One of founders of BAA, 1946, forerunner of NBA; organized Boston Marathon; pres., Boston Bruins; member of basketball, hockey Halls of Fame.
b. Feb 10, 1905 in Hopkinton, Massachusetts
d. Sep 7, 1964 in Boston, Massachusetts
Source: *BioIn 7, 9; EncAB-A 37; WhoBbl 73; WhoHcky 73*

Brown, William Hill
American. Author
Wrote "first American novel," *The Power of Sympathy,* 1789.
b. Dec 1, 1765 in Boston, Massachusetts
d. Sep 2, 1793 in Murfreesboro, North Carolina
Source: *Alli; AmAu; AmAu&B; AmWrBE; Benet 87, 96; BenetAL 91; BiDSA; BioIn 3, 9, 13, 14; CamGLE; CamHAL; CnDAL; DcAmB S1, S3; DcLB 37; DcLEL; DcNAA; DcNCBi 1; OxCAmL 65, 83, 95; REn; REnAL; WhAm HS*

Brown, William Melvin, Jr.
American. Business Executive
Founded defense manufacturing co., 1972; director, SC State Ports Authority, 1980—.
b. Feb 19, 1934 in Charleston, South Carolina
Source: *WhoAfA 96; WhoBlA 85, 88, 90, 92, 94; WhoFI 75, 77*

Brown, William Wells
American. Author, Social Reformer
First black American to publish novel.
b. Mar 15, 1815 in Lexington, Kentucky
d. Nov 6, 1884 in Chelsea, Massachusetts
Source: *AfrAmAl 6; AmAu; AmAu&B; BioIn 1, 3, 5, 8, 9, 11, 12, 13, 15, 18, 19, 21; BlkAWP; DcAmB; DcNAA; EarBlAP; EncAB-H 1974, 1996; InB&W 80; LegTOT; McGEWB; NegAl 76, 83, 89; REnAL; SouWr; WhAm HS; WhAmP*

Brown, Willie
[Willie Lewis Brown, Jr.]
American. Lawyer, Politician
Member of the California State Assembly, 1965-96; mayor of San Francisco, 1996—.
b. Mar 20, 1934 in Mineola, Texas

Source: *BioIn 12, 13; News 96; WhoAm 84, 86, 88, 90, 92, 94, 95, 96, 97; WhoGov 75; WhoWest 84, 89, 92, 96*

Brown, Willie
[William F Brown]
American. Football Player
Four-time all-pro defensive back, 1963-73, mostly with Oakland; Hall of Fame, 1984.
b. Dec 2, 1940 in Yazoo City, Mississippi
Source: *LegTOT; WhoFtbl 74; WhoSpor*

Brownback, Sam
American. Politician
Rep. senator, KS, 1996—.
b. Sep 12, 1956
Source: *AlmAP 96; BioIn 21*

Browne, Coral Edith
[Mrs. Vincent Price]
Australian. Actor
Sophisticated character roles in *Ruling Class; Theater of Blood; Drowning Pool,* 1970s; met husband when they co-starred in *Theater of Blood,* 1971.
b. Jul 23, 1913 in Melbourne, Australia
d. May 29, 1991 in Los Angeles, California
Source: *BiE&WWA; BlueB 76; CurBio 59; FilmgC; InWom; MotPP; MovMk; NotNAT; Who 82; WhoHol A; WhoThe 81*

Browne, Dik
American. Cartoonist
Created "Hi and Lois," 1954; "Hagar the Horrible," 1973.
b. Aug 11, 1917 in New York, New York
d. Jun 3, 1989 in Sarasota, Florida
Source: *AnObit 1989; AuNews 1; BioIn 10, 11, 15, 16, 17; EncACom; EncTwCJ; LegTOT; WhAm 10; WhoAm 76, 78, 80, 82, 84, 86, 88*

Browne, Jackson
American. Singer, Songwriter
Hit single "Doctor My Eyes," 1971; gold album *The Pretender,* 1976; *World in Motion,* 1989.
b. Oct 9, 1948 in Heidelberg, Germany
Source: *ASCAP 80; Baker 84, 92; BkPepl; CelR 90; ConAu 120; ConMus 3; CurBio 89; EncFCWM 83; EncPR&S 74, 89; EncRk 88; EncRkSt; HarEnR 86; IlEncRk; LegTOT; OxCPMus; PenEncP; RkOn 74; RolSEnR 83; WhoAm 86; WhoRock 81; WhoRocM 82; WorAl; WorAlBi*

Browne, Leslie
American. Dancer, Actor
Soloist, American Ballet Theater, 1976-86; principle dancer, 1986-92; starred in *The Turning Point,* 1977; *Nijinsky,* 1980.
b. Jun 29, 1957 in New York, New York
Source: *BioIn 11, 14; NewYTBS 77; WhoAm 80, 82, 84, 86, 88, 92, 94, 95; WhoAmW 81, 83, 85, 89, 91; WhoE 83; WhoEnt 92*

Browne, Phiz
[Hablot Knight Browne]
English. Artist, Illustrator
Remembered as Dickens' chief illustrator; depicted *Pickwick Papers,* 1837; *David Copperfield,* 1850.
b. Jun 15, 1815 in Kensington, England
d. Jul 8, 1882 in West Brighton, England
Source: *AntBDN B; BioIn 1, 9, 11, 12; ChhPo, S1, S2; DcArts; DcBrBI; DcBrWA; DcNaB; DcVicP, 2; HsB&A; NewC; NewCBEL; OxCArt; OxCEng 85, 95; OxDcArt; SmATA 21; VicBrit*

Browne, Roscoe Lee
American. Actor, Director
TV, stage, screen performances include film *The Cowboys,* with John Wayne, 1972.
b. May 2, 1925 in Woodbury, New Jersey
Source: *BiE&WWA; ConBlAP 88; ConTFT 4, 11; DcTwCCu 5; DrBlPA, 90; FilmgC; HalFC 80, 84, 88; InB&W 80, 85; IntMPA 77, 80, 86, 88, 92, 94, 96; LegTOT; NotNAT; VarWW 85; WhoAfA 96; WhoAm 86; WhoBlA 92, 94; WhoHol 92, A; WhoThe 72, 77, 81*

Browne, Walter Shawn
American. Chess Player, Journalist
US grandmaster, champion, 1974-75.
b. Jan 21, 1949 in Sydney, Australia
Source: *BioNews 74; GolEC; OxCChes 84; WhoAm 76, 78, 80, 82, 84, 86, 88, 90, 92, 94, 95, 96, 97; WhoWest 94*

Brownell, Herbert, Jr.
American. Lawyer, Government Official
Managed Thomas Dewey's presidential campaigns; attorney general, under Dwight Eisebhower, 1953-57.
b. Feb 20, 1904 in Peru, Nebraska
d. May 1, 1996 in New York, New York
Source: *BiDrUSE 71, 89; BioIn 1, 3, 4, 5, 6, 10, 11, 17, 19, 21; BlueB 76; CurBio 44, 54, 96N; EncAB-A 9; IntWW 74, 75, 76, 77, 78, 79, 80, 81, 82, 83, 89, 91, 93; IntYB 78, 79, 80, 81, 82; NewYTBS 27; PolPar; PolProf E; WhAm 11; WhoAm 74, 76, 78, 80, 82, 84, 86, 88, 90; WhoAmL 78, 79, 83, 85, 90; WhoAmP 73, 75, 77, 79, 81, 83, 85, 87, 89, 91, 93, 95; WhoWor 74, 76, 78*

Brownell, Samuel Miller
American. Government Official
US Commissioner of Education, 1953-56; wrote *Progress in Educational Administration,* 1935.
b. Apr 3, 1900 in Peru, Nebraska
d. Oct 12, 1990 in New Haven, Connecticut
Source: *BioIn 3, 4, 5, 6, 7, 17; BlueB 76; CurBio 54, 91N; IntWW 74, 75, 76, 77, 78, 79, 80, 81, 82, 83, 89; LEduc 74; WhAm 10; WhoAm 74, 76, 78, 80*

Browner, Carol M.
American. Government Official
Head of US Environmental Protection Agency, 1993—.
b. Dec 16, 1955 in Miami, Florida
Source: *BioIn 19, 20; CurBio 94; News 94, 94-1*

Browner, Ross
American. Football Player
Defensive end, Cincinnati, 1978-84, 1986; suspended for several games for violating NFL drug policy, 1983.
b. Mar 22, 1954 in Warren, Ohio
Source: *BiDAmSp Sup; FootReg 87; InB&W 85; WhoAfA 96; WhoBlA 80, 85, 88, 90, 92, 94; WhoSpor*

Browning, Alice Crolley
American. Educator, Editor
Wrote *Negro Story,* 1944; founded International Black Writers Conference, 1970.
b. Nov 5, 1907 in Chicago, Illinois
d. Oct 15, 1985 in Chicago, Illinois
Source: *ConAu 117; WhoAmW 79; WhoBlA 80*

Browning, Edmond Lee
American. Religious Leader
Bishop of HI, 1976-86; head of Episcopal Church of America, 1986—.
b. Mar 11, 1929 in Corpus Christi, Texas
Source: *NewYTBS 85; Who 82, 83, 85, 88, 90, 92, 94; WhoAm 84; WhoRel 85; WhoWest 74*

Browning, Elizabeth Barrett
[Mrs. Robert Browning]
English. Poet
Wrote *Sonnets from the Portuguese,* 1850, her own love story in verse.
b. Mar 6, 1806 in Durham, England
d. Jun 29, 1861 in Florence, Italy
Source: *Alli, SUP; ArtclWW 2; AtlBL; BbD; Benet 87, 96; BiD&SB; BioIn 14, 15, 16, 17, 18, 20, 21; BlmGEL; BlmGWL; BritAu 19; BritWr 4; CamGEL; CamGLE; CasWL; Chambr 3; ChhPo, S1, S2, S3; CnDBLB 4; CnE&AP; ContDcW 89; CrtT 3; CyWA 58; DcEnA A; DcEnL; DcEuL; DcLB 32; DcLEL; DcNaB; EncBrWW; EncPaPR 91; EvLB; GoodHs; GrWomW; GrWrEL P; IntDcWB; InWom, SUP; LegTOT; LinLib L, S; LngCEL; LuthC 75; MagSWL; McGEWB; MouLC 3; NewC; NewCBEL; NinCLC 1, 16; OxCEng 67, 85, 95; PenBWP; PenC ENG; PoeCrit 6; RAdv 1, 14, 13-1; RComWL; REn; RfGEnL 91; VicBrit; WebE&AL; WhDW; WomFir; WorAl; WorAlBi; WorLitC*

Browning, Frederick A(rthur) M(ontague), Sir
"Boy"
English. Army Officer
Organized Red Devils Airborne Division, WW II; husband of author Daphne DuMaurier.
b. Dec 20, 1896 in London, England

d. Mar 14, 1965 in Cornwall, England
Source: *BioIn 7; CurBio 43, 65; DcNaB 1961; ObitOF 79; PseudN 82; WhWW-II*

Browning, John
American. Pianist
Child prodigy, international concertizer; had Carnegie Hall debut, 1956.
b. May 23, 1933 in Denver, Colorado
Source: *Baker 78, 84, 92; BioIn 8, 11, 12, 14, 19, 21; BriBkM 80; CelR, 90; CurBio 69; IntWWM 77, 80, 90; MusSN; NewAmDM; NewGrDA 86; NewGrDM 80; NotTwCP; PenDiMP; WhoAm 78, 80, 82, 84, 86, 88, 90, 92, 94, 95, 96, 97; WhoAmM 83; WhoMus 72*

Browning, John Moses
American. Inventor
Developed automatic rifle, pistol, machine gun.
b. Jan 21, 1855 in Ogden, Utah
d. Nov 26, 1926 in Liege, Belgium
Source: *AmBi; BioIn 3, 5, 7, 11, 17, 18; DcAmB; Entr; FacFETw; InSci; LinLib S; NatCAB 20; PeoHis; REnAW; WebAB 74, 79; WebAMB; WhAm 1*

Browning, Oscar
English. Author
Fellow, King's College, Cambridge, 1856-1923; wrote *A General History of the World,* 1913.
b. Jan 17, 1837 in London, England
d. Oct 6, 1923 in Rome, Italy
Source: *Alli SUP; BioIn 3, 4, 5, 11, 14, 15; BritAu 19; CamGLE; Chambr 3; DcNaB 1922; EvLB; GrBr; LinLib L, S; LngCTC; NewC; OxCEng 67, 85, 95; WhLit*

Browning, Robert
English. Poet
Married Elizabeth Barrett, 1846; wrote *Pippa Passes,* 1841.
b. May 7, 1812 in London, England
d. Dec 12, 1889 in Venice, Italy
Source: *Alli, SUP; AnCL; AtlBL; Benet 87, 96; BiD&SB; BioIn 1, 2, 3, 4, 5, 6, 7, 8, 9, 10, 11, 12, 13, 14, 15, 16, 17, 18, 20, 21; BlmGEL; BritAu 19; BritWr 4; CamGEL; CamGLE; CasWL; CelCen; Chambr 3; ChhPo, S1, S2, S3; CnDBLB 4; CnE&AP; CnThe; CrtSuDr; CrtT 3, 4; CyWA 58; DcArts; DcBiPP; DcEnA, A; DcEnL; DcEuL; DcLB 32, 163; DcLEL; DcNaB C, S1; DcPup; Dis&D; EncO&P 1, 2, 3; EncPaPR 91; EncWT; EvLB; GrWrEL P; IlEncMy; LegTOT; LinLib L, S; LngCEL; LuthC 75; MagSWL; McGEWB; McGEWD 72, 84; MouLC 4; NewC; NewCBEL; NinCLC 19; OxCEng 67, 85, 95; OxCMus; OxCThe 67, 83; OxDcOp; PenC ENG; PlP&P; PoeCrit 2; RAdv 1, 14, 13-1; RComWL; REn; REnWD; RfGEnL 91; RGFBP; Str&VC; VicBrit; WebE&AL; WhDW; WorAl; WorAlBi; YABC 1*

Browning, Tod
American. Director
Made macabre horror films starring Lon Chaney, Bela Lugosi: *Dracula,* 1931; *Freaks,* 1932.
b. Jul 12, 1882 in Louisville, Kentucky
d. Oct 6, 1962 in Santa Monica, California
Source: *AmFD; BiDFilm, 81, 94; BioIn 6, 11, 12, 15, 18; CmMov; ConAu 117, 141; ConLC 16; DcFM; FacFETw; Film 1; FilmEn; FilmgC; HalFC 80, 84, 88; HorFD; IlWWHD 1; LegTOT; MiSFD 9N; MovMk; ObitOF 79; OxCFilm; PenEncH; WhoHrs 80; WhScrn 74, 77, 83; WorEFlm*

Browning, Tom
[Thomas Leo Browning]
American. Baseball Player
Pitcher, Cincinnati, 1985—; first rookie in 31 yrs. to win 20 games, 1985; 14th in ML history to throw perfect game, 1988.
b. Apr 28, 1960 in Casper, Wyoming
Source: *Ballpl 90; BaseReg 86, 87; LegTOT*

Brownlee, John
Australian. Opera Singer
Baritone; protege of Melba's; NY Met., 1937-56.
b. Jan 7, 1901 in Geelong, Australia
d. Jan 10, 1969 in New York, New York
Source: *Baker 84; BiDAmM; BiE&WWA; BioIn 4, 8, 9, 10; MetOEnc; NewEOp 71; NewGrDA 86; NewGrDM 80; ObitT 1961; OxDcOp*

Brownlow, Kevin
English. Filmmaker
Restored Abel Gance's silent film *Napoleon* and brought it accompanied by a live orchestra, to Radio City Music Hall in the mid-1980s.
b. Jun 2, 1938 in Crowborough, England
Source: *Au&Wr 71; BioIn 15, 16; ConAu 12NR, 25R; ConTFT 5; CurBio 92; FilmgC; HalFC 80, 84, 88; IlWWBF; IntAu&W 76, 89, 91, 93; IntMPA 92, 94, 96; IntWW 89, 91, 93; OxCFilm; SmATA 65; Who 82, 83, 85, 88, 90, 92, 94; WhoWor 76; WorFDir 2; WrDr 76, 80, 82, 84, 86, 88, 90, 92, 94, 96*

Brownmiller, Susan
American. Author, Feminist
Wrote best-selling *Against Our Will,* 1975.
b. Feb 15, 1935 in New York, New York
Source: *AmSocL; BioIn 10, 11, 12, 13; CelR 90; ConAu 35NR, 103; CurBio 78; FemiWr; GoodHs; InWom SUP; MajTwCW; RadHan; WhoAm 78, 80, 84; WhoAmW 79, 81, 83, 85, 91, 93, 95; WhoUSWr 88; WhoWrEP 89, 92, 95; WorAl; WorAlBi; WrDr 86, 88, 90, 92, 94, 96*

Brownscombe, Jennie Augusta
American. Artist
Painted genre, American historical scenes.
b. Dec 10, 1850 in Honesdale, Pennsylvania
d. Aug 5, 1936 in New York, New York
Source: *AmWom; ChhPo; DcWomA; InWom SUP; NatCAB 16; NorAmWA; NotAW; WhAm 1; WomWWA 14*

Brownson, Orestes Augustus
American. Author, Editor
Established *Brownson's Quarterly Review,* 1844-75; wrote *The Convert,* an autobiography, 1857.
b. Sep 16, 1803 in Stockbridge, Vermont
d. Apr 17, 1876 in Detroit, Michigan
Source: *Alli, SUP; AmAu; AmAu&B; AmBi; AmRef; ApCAB; BbD; BenetAL 91; BiD&SB; BiDTran; BioIn 1, 2, 3, 4, 6, 7, 8, 9, 11, 12, 15, 16, 19; CasWL; CyAL 2; DcAmAu; DcAmB; DcAmReB 1, 2; DcCathB; DcEnL; DcLB 1; DcLEL; DcNAA; Drake; EncARH; HarEnUS; LinLib L; LuthC 75; McGEWB; NatCAB 7; OxCAmH; OxCAmL 65, 83, 95; OxCPhil; PenC AM; REn; REnAL; TwCBDA; WebAB 74, 79; WebE&AL; WhAm HS*

Broyhill, James E
American. Businessman
Started furniture business, 1926; first to use assembly line to make furniture.
b. 1892 in Wilkes County, North Carolina
Source: *Entr; St&PR 75, 84, 87; WhoAm 74, 78; WhoAmP 81, 83; WhoSSW 73*

Broyhill, Joel Thomas
American. Politician
Conservative Rep. congressman from VA, 1953-75.
b. Nov 4, 1919 in Hopewell, Georgia
Source: *AlmAP 82; BiDrAC; BiDrUSC 89; BioIn 10; BioNews 74; CngDr 74; CurBio 74; WhoAm 74, 76; WhoAmP 75; WhoGov 72, 75; WhoSSW 73, 75, 76*

Brubeck, Dave
[David Warren Brubeck]
American. Jazz Musician
Avant-garde pianist, noted for modernistic chords; led popular jazz quartet, 1951-67.
b. Dec 6, 1920 in Concord, California
Source: *AllMusG; AmComp; AmDec 1960; Baker 78, 84, 92; BiDJaz; BioIn 3, 4, 5, 8, 10, 12, 13, 15, 16, 17, 18, 19, 20; BlueB 76; CelR, 90; CmCal; CmpEPM; ConAmC 76, 82; ConMus 8; CpmDNM 81; CurBio 56, 93; DcArts; DcTwCCu 1; EncJzS; FacFETw; IntWW 74, 75, 76, 77, 78, 79, 80, 81, 82, 83, 89, 91, 93; IntWWM 77, 80, 90; LegTOT; MusMk; NewAmDM; NewGrDA 86; NewGrDJ 88, 94; NewGrDM 80; OxCPMus; PenDiMP A; PenEncP; RkOn 74; WebAB 74, 79; Who 74, 82, 83, 85, 88, 90, 92, 94; WhoAm 74, 76, 78, 80, 82, 84, 86, 88, 90, 92, 94, 95, 96, 97; WhoE 74, 75; WhoEnt*

92; WhoWor 74, 76, 78, 80, 82, 84, 87, 89, 91, 93, 95; WorAl; WorAlBi

Bruce, Ailsa Mellon
American. Philanthropist
Daughter of Andrew Mellon; considered richest woman in US.
b. Jun 28, 1901 in Pittsburgh, Pennsylvania
d. Aug 25, 1969 in New York, New York
Source: *BioIn 8, 10; InWom SUP; NatCAB 55*

Bruce, Carol
American. Actor, Singer
Performed on stage in *Do I Hear a Waltz; Show Boat; Pal Joey.*
b. Nov 15, 1919 in Great Neck, New York
Source: *BiE&WWA; CmpEPM; ConTFT 15; EncMT; NotNAT; OxCPMus; RadStar; WhoAmW 70, 72, 74; WhoHol 92, A; WhoThe 72, 77, 81*

Bruce, David, Sir
English. Physician
Discovered causes of Malta fever, sleeping sickness.
b. May 29, 1855 in Melbourne, Australia
d. Nov 27, 1931 in London, England
Source: *BiESc; BioIn 2, 4, 6, 14; CamDcSc; DcNaB 1931; DcScB; FacFETw; GrBr; HisDBrE; InSci; LarDcSc; McGEWB; OxCMed 86; WorScD*

Bruce, David Kirkpatrick Estes
American. Diplomat
Head of US diplomatic office in Peking, China, 1973-74; US Ambassador to NATO, 1974-76.
b. Feb 12, 1898 in Baltimore, Maryland
d. Dec 4, 1978 in Washington, District of Columbia
Source: *CurBio 49, 61; IntWW 74; NewYTBE 70, 73; USBiR 74; WhoAm 74; WhoWor 74*

Bruce, Jack
[Cream; John Bruce]
Scottish. Musician
Vocalist/bassist with Cream, 1966-69; solo albums include *I've Always Wanted To Do This,* 1980.
b. May 14, 1943 in Glasgow, Scotland
Source: *BioIn 8, 11, 19; EncJzS; EncPR&S 74; EncRk 88; HarEnR 86; IlEncRk; NewGrDJ 88, 94; RolSEnR 83; WhoRock 81; WhoRocM 82*

Bruce, Lenny
[Leonard Alfred Schneider]
American. Author, Comedian
Charged with obscenity for using four-letter words in act; Dustin Hoffman starred in *Lenny,* 1974.
b. Oct 13, 1925 in Mineola, New York
d. Aug 3, 1966 in Hollywood, California
Source: *AmAu&B; BioIn 5, 6, 7, 8, 9, 10, 11, 13, 15, 16, 17, 19; ConAu 25R, 89; ConLC 21; DcAmB S8; DcTwCCu 1; EncAHmr; Ent; FacFETw; NewYTBE 71; WhAm 4; WhoCom; WhScrn 77*

Bruce, Louis R., Jr.
American. Government Official
Commissioner, Bureau of Indian Afairs, 1969-72; worked to "Indianize" the BIA.
b. Dec 30, 1906 in Pine Ridge, South Dakota
d. 1989
Source: *CurBio 89N; EncNAB; NotNaAm*

Bruce, Nigel
American. Actor
Played Dr. Watson to Basil Rathbone's Sherlock Holmes in a dozen 1940s films.
b. Feb 4, 1895 in Ensenada, Mexico
d. Oct 8, 1953 in Santa Monica, California
Source: *BioIn 3, 21; CmMov; EncAFC; Film 2; FilmEn; FilmgC; ForYSC; HalFC 80, 84, 88; HolCA; IntDcF 1-3; LegTOT; MotPP; MovMk; NotNAT B; ObitOF 79; OlFamFa; RadStar; Vers A; WhoHol B; WhoHrs 80; WhScrn 74, 77, 83; WorAl; WorAlBi*

Bruce, Virginia
[Helen Virginia Briggs]
American. Actor
Leading lady in almost 50 films, 1930s-40s: *Great Ziegfeld,* 1934.
b. Sep 29, 1910 in Minneapolis, Minnesota
d. Feb 24, 1982 in Woodland Hills, California
Source: *BioIn 8, 12, 13; EncAFC; Film 2; FilmEn; FilmgC; ForYSC; GangFlm; HalFC 80, 84, 88; InWom SUP; LegTOT; MGM; MotPP; MovMk; NewYTBS 82; PseudN 82; ThFT; What 2; WhoHol A; WorAl*

Bruce Lockhart, Robert Hamilton, Sir
Scottish. Diplomat, Author
Wrote of experiences in foreign office during WW II: *Comes the Reckoning,* 1947.
b. Sep 2, 1887 in Anstruther, Scotland
d. Feb 27, 1970 in Hore, England
Source: *Au&Wr 71; DcNaB 1961; GrBr; LngCTC*

Bruch, Max
German. Conductor, Composer
Wrote concertos, operas, including *Hermione,* 1872.
b. Jan 6, 1838 in Cologne, Germany
d. Oct 2, 1920 in Friedenau, Germany
Source: *Baker 78, 84; BioIn 2, 4, 6, 7, 12, 16; BriBkM 80; CmpBCM; DcArts; DcCom 77; DcCom&M 79; GrComp; LegTOT; LinLib S; MusMk; NewAmDM; NewEOp 71; NewGrDM 80; NewOxM; OxCMus; OxDcOp; PenDiMP A*

Bruchac, Joseph, III
American. Author
Wrote *Keepers of the Earth,* 1988.
b. Oct 16, 1942 in Saratoga Springs, New York
Source: *Au&Arts 19; BioIn 15, 19, 21; ChlBkCr; ConAu 13NR, 33R, 47NR; DcNAL; DrAF 76; DrAP 75; DrAPF 80; IntAu&W 91, 93; NatNAL; NotNaAm; SmATA 42, 89; WrDr 76, 80, 82, 84, 86, 88, 90, 92, 94, 96*

Bruckner, Anton
Austrian. Composer, Organist
Virtuoso organist influenced by Wagner; music includes nine symphonies, three masses.
b. Sep 4, 1824 in Ausfelden, Austria
d. Oct 11, 1896 in Vienna, Austria
Source: *AtlBL; Baker 78, 84; Benet 87, 96; BioIn 1, 2, 3, 4, 5, 6, 7, 8, 9, 10, 11, 12, 13, 14, 15, 16, 20; BriBkM 80; CmpBCM; DcCathB; DcCom 77; DcCom&M 79; Dis&D; GrComp; LegTOT; LinLib S; LuthC 75; MusMk; NewAmDM; NewGrDM 80; NewOxM; OxCGer 76, 86; OxCMus; PenDiMP A; RAdv 14, 13-3; REn; WhDW; WorAl; WorAlBi*

Bruegel, Jan
"Flower Brughel"; "Velvet Brughel"
Flemish. Artist
Noted for painting landscapes, flowers; did backgrounds for figure painters, especially Rubens; son of Pieter.
b. 1568 in Brussels, Belgium
d. 1625
Source: *DcArts; IntDcAA 90; McGDA; NewCol 75; OxCArt; WebBD 83*

Brugnon, Jacques
[The Four Musketeers]
"Toto"
French. Tennis Player
Doubles champion with several international titles, 1920s; with Suzanne Lenglen, won French mixed doubles, 1921-26.
b. May 11, 1895 in Paris, France
d. Mar 20, 1978 in Paris, France
Source: *BioIn 11, 12; BuCMET; NewYTBS 78*

Bruhn, Erik Belton Evers
Danish. Dancer, Producer
One of greatest classical dancers, 1953-72; appeared with American Ballet Theater.
b. Oct 3, 1928 in Copenhagen, Denmark
d. Apr 1, 1986 in Toronto, Ontario, Canada
Source: *CurBio 86; IntWW 74, 75, 76, 77, 78, 79, 80, 81, 82, 83; NewYTBE 73; NewYTBS 86; WhAm 9; Who 74, 82, 83, 85; WhoAm 82, 84; WhoE 85; WhoWor 74, 78, 80, 82, 84*

Brule, Etienne
Canadian. Explorer
Apparently the first European to explore the Canadian province of Ontario.
b. 1592? in Champigny-sur-Marne, France
d. Jun 1633, Canada

Source: *BioIn 2, 6, 10; DcAmB; DcCanB 1; EncCRAm; Expl 93; MacDCB 78; McGEWB; OxCCan; WebAB 74, 79; WhAm HS; WhDW; WhNaAH; WhWE; WorAl; WorAlBi*

Brumidi, Constantino
Italian. Artist
Painted portrait of Pope Pius IX, frescoes in Capitol building, 1855-80.
b. Jul 26, 1805 in Rome, Italy
d. Feb 19, 1880 in Washington, District of Columbia
Source: *BioIn 2, 3, 4, 7, 8; DcAmArt; DcAmB; DcAmImH; DcCathB; NewYHSD; WhAm HS*

Brummell, Beau
[George Bryan Brummell]
English. Dandy, Gambler
Set fashion standards for English society: trousers instead of breeches.
b. Jun 7, 1778 in London, England
d. Mar 30, 1840 in Caen, France
Source: *BioIn 1, 2, 5, 7, 11, 13; DcNaB; Dis&D; FilmgC; HalFC 80, 84, 88; LegTOT; LinLib L, S; NewC; NewCol 75; OxCEng 85, 95; WorAl*

Brundage, Avery
American. Olympic Official
Pres., IOC, 1952-72.
b. Sep 28, 1887 in Detroit, Michigan
d. May 8, 1975 in Garmisch, Germany (West)
Source: *BiDAmSp OS; BioIn 1, 2, 4, 5, 7, 8, 9, 10, 12, 13, 21; CelR; CmCal; CurBio 48, 75N; DcAmB S9; EncAB-A 33; IntWW 74, 75; LegTOT; NatCAB 60; NewYTBE 72; NewYTBS 75; ObitT 1971; St&PR 75; WebAB 74, 79; WhAm 6; Who 74; WhoAm 74; WhoAmA 73, 89N, 91N, 93N; WhoSpor; WhoTr&F 73; WhoWor 74; WorAl; WorAlBi*

Brundtland, Gro Harlem
"The Green Goddess"
Norwegian. Political Leader
Prime minister, Feb-Oct, 1981, 1986; youngest woman to run modern govt.
b. Apr 20, 1939 in Oslo, Norway
Source: *BioIn 12; ContDcW 89; CurBio 81; DcTwHis; EnvEnc; EnvEnDr; HeroCon; IntWW 75, 76, 77, 78, 79, 80, 81, 82, 83, 89, 91, 93; IntYB 80, 81, 82; InWom SUP; NewYTBS 81; PolLCWE; PseudN 82; RadHan; Who 94; WhoWomW 91; WhoWor 78, 87, 89, 91, 93, 95, 96, 97; WomFir*

Brunel, Isambard Kingdom
English. Engineer, Inventor
Constructed London's Thames Tunnel, 1825-43; knighted, 1841.
b. Apr 9, 1806 in Portsmouth, England
d. Sep 15, 1859 in London, England
Source: *BioIn 1, 2, 3, 4, 5, 6, 7, 8, 9, 10, 11, 12, 16, 20; CamDcSc; CelCen; DcBiPP; DcD&D; DcNaB; InSci; LarDcSc; McGDA; McGEWB; NewCol 75; OxCShps; RAdv 14; VicBrit; WhDW; WhoArch; WorInv*

Brunel, Marc Isambard, Sir
English. Inventor, Engineer
Invented tunneling shield; built Thames Tunnel, 1825-43.
b. Apr 25, 1769 in Hacqueville, France
d. Dec 12, 1849 in London, England
Source: *BioIn 2, 14; CelCen; DcBiPP; DcD&D; DcNaB; InSci; NewCol 75; OxCShps; WhoArch; WorInv*

Brunelleschi, Filippo
Italian. Architect, Sculptor
Considered greatest architect, engineer of time; designed dome for Florence cathedral.
b. 1377 in Florence, Italy
d. Apr 16, 1446 in Florence, Italy
Source: *AtlBL; Benet 87, 96; BioIn 1, 4, 5, 9, 10, 12, 13, 14, 15, 18; CmMedTh; DcArts; DcBiPP; DcD&D; DcScB; IntDcAr; LegTOT; LinLib S; LuthC 75; MacEA; McGDA; McGEWB; OxCThe 67; OxDcArt; REn; WhDW; WhoArch; WorAl; WorAlBi*

Bruner, Jerome Seymour
American. Psychologist
Major contributor to cognitive psychology; founded Center for Cognitive Studies, Harvard U, 1960.
b. Oct 1, 1915 in New York, New York
Source: *AmMWSc 73S, 78S; BioIn 6, 7, 9, 12, 13; BlueB 76; ConAu 45; CurBio 84; EncWB; IntWW 89, 91, 93; LEduc 74; Who 74, 82, 83, 85, 88, 90, 92, 94; WhoAm 74, 78; WhoE 74; WhoWor 74, 76*

Brunhoff, Jean de
French. Children's Author, Illustrator
Creator of the *Babar* series, 1931.
b. 1899, France
d. Oct 16, 1937, Switzerland
Source: *AuBYP 2, 3; BioIn 1, 2, 5, 6, 7, 8, 13, 19; ChlLR 4; ChsFB A; ConAu 118, 137; IlsCB 1946; JBA 51; LegTOT; LinLib L; MajAI; SmATA 24; WhoChL; WorAl; WorAlBi; WorECar; WrChl*

Brunhoff, Laurent de
French. Author, Illustrator
Continues "Barbar" children's books his father originated.
b. Aug 30, 1925 in Paris, France
Source: *AuBYP 2, 3; BioIn 5, 6, 7, 8, 10, 12, 13, 16, 18, 19; ChlLR 4; ConAu 45NR, 73; IlsCB 1946, 1957; IntAu&W 82; LinLib L; MajAI; MorJA; NewYTBE 72; PiP; SmATA 24, 71; WhoChL; WorECar*

Brunis, George
"King of the Tailgate Trombone"
American. Jazz Musician
Member, New Orleans Rhythm Kings, founded in Chicago, 1921, an early northern Dixieland.
b. Feb 6, 1902 in New Orleans, Louisiana
d. Nov 19, 1974 in Chicago, Illinois
Source: *BiDAmM; BioIn 10; WhoAm 74*

Brunner, Emil
[Heinrich Emil Brunner]
Swiss. Theologian, Author
Advocated Protestant ecumenism; wrote *Gott und sein Rebell*, 1958.
b. Dec 23, 1889 in Winterthur, Switzerland
d. Apr 6, 1966 in Zurich, Switzerland
Source: *BioIn 1, 3, 4, 6, 11, 16; EncWB; FacFETw; LinLib L; LuthC 75; ObitOF 79; ObitT 1961; TwCA, SUP; WorAl; WorAlBi*

Bruno, Giordano
Italian. Philosopher, Author
Wrote metaphysical *On the Infinite Universe and Its Worlds*, 1582; challenged dogma; burned at stake.
b. 1548 in Nola, Italy
d. Feb 17, 1600 in Rome, Italy
Source: *AsBiEn; Benet 96; BiD&SB; BiESc; BioIn 1, 2, 4, 5, 6, 7, 8, 9, 10, 11, 13, 14, 15, 17, 19, 20; CamDcSc; CamGWoT; CasWL; DcEuL; DcItL 1, 2; DcScB; Dis&D; EuAu; EvEuW; IlEncMy; InSci; LinLib L, S; LitC 27; McGEWB; McGEWD 72, 84; NewCBEL; OxCEng 85, 95; OxCPhil; OxCThe 67, 83; PenC EUR; RAdv 14, 13-2, 13-4; RComWL; REn; REnWD; RfGWoL 95; WhDW; WrPh P*

Brunson, Dorothy
American. Broadcasting Executive
Owner, pres., WBMS-Radio, Wilmington, NC, 1984—; WIGO-Radio, Atlanta, 1981—; WEBB-Radio, Baltimore, 1979—; owner,WGTW-TV, Philadelphia, 19 79-95.
b. Mar 13, 1938 in Glensville, Georgia
Source: *BioIn 15, 17; ConBlB 1; IntAu&W 86; WhoAm 90; WhoAmW 91; WhoBlA 85, 92; WhoEnt 92*

Brush, Charles Francis
American. Inventor, Industrialist
Invented an electric arc lamp and a generator that was more efficient than previous devices.
b. Mar 17, 1849 in Euclid, Ohio
d. Jun 15, 1929 in Cleveland, Ohio
Source: *AmBi; ApCAB; BiDAmS; BioIn 5, 10, 19; DcAmB S1; DcInv; HarEnUS; NatCAB 4, 21; OxCAmH; TwCBDA; WhAm 1; WhDW; WorAl; WorAlBi*

Brush, George
American. Artist
Prize-winning portraitist of Native Americans, family groups.
b. Sep 28, 1855 in Shelbyville, Tennessee
d. Apr 24, 1941 in Hanover, New Hampshire
Source: *BioIn 3, 9; CurBio 41*

Brustein, Robert Sanford
American. Educator, Author
Drama critic, *New Republic*, 1959-67, 1978—; founder, director, American Repertory Theater.
b. Apr 21, 1927 in New York, New York

Source: *AmAu&B; Au&Wr 71; BiE&WWA; BioIn 12, 13; ConAu 9NR; CurBio 75; LEduc 74; NewYTBS 83; NotNAT; WhoAm 74, 76, 78, 80, 82, 84, 86, 88, 90, 92, 94, 95, 96, 97; WhoE 74, 75, 95; WhoEnt 92; WhoThe 77; WhoUSWr 88; WhoWor 74, 76; WhoWrEP 89, 92, 95; WorAu 1950*

Bruton, John (Gerard)
Irish. Political Leader
Prime minister of Ireland, 1994—.
b. May 18, 1947 in Dublin, Ireland
Source: *BlueB 76; CurBio 96; IntWW 82, 83, 89, 91, 93; IntYB 82, 82A; Who 82, 83, 85, 88, 90, 92, 94; WhoWor 96, 97*

Brutus, Dennis Vincent
Rhodesian. Poet, Educator
Verse volumes include *Salutes and Censures,* 1982; imprisoned for opposing apartheid, 1964-65.
b. Nov 28, 1924 in Salisbury, Rhodesia
Source: *CasWL; ConAu 2NR, 49; ConPo 70, 75; IntWW 83; PenC CL; RGAfL; TwCWr; WhoAm 82, 84; WrDr 86*

Brutus, Marcus Junius
Roman. Politician
Principal assassin, with Cassius, of Julius Caesar, 44BC.
b. 85BC
d. Oct 24, 42BC
Source: *Benet 87; BioIn 2, 11, 12; DcBiPP; Dis&D; HarEnMi; LegTOT; LinLib L, S; McGEWB; NewC; OxCClL 89; REn; WhDW; WorAl; WorAlBi*

Brutus Albinus, Decimus Junius
Roman. Military Leader
General who helped assassinate Julius Caesar.
d. 43BC
Source: *Benet 87; CmFrR; OxCClL 89*

Bryan, Dora
[Mrs. William Lawton]
English. Actor
Won British Academy Award for *A Taste of Honey,* 1961; appears mostly on stage.
b. Feb 7, 1924 in Southport, England
Source: *ConTFT 5; EncMT; FilmEn; FilmgC; HalFC 84; IlWWBF; IntMPA 86, 92, 94, 96; OxCPMus; OxCThe 83; Who 74, 82, 83, 85, 88, 90, 92, 94; WhoThe 72, 77, 81; WhoWor 80*

Bryan, Richard H.
American. Politician
Governor of Nevada, 1983-89; Dem senator from NV, 1989—.
b. Jul 16, 1937 in Washington, District of Columbia
Source: *AlmAP 84, 88, 92, 96; BiDrGov 1983, 1988; CngDr 89, 91, 93, 95; IntWW 83, 89, 91, 93; PolsAm 84; WhoAm 80, 82, 84, 86, 88, 90, 92, 94, 95, 96, 97; WhoAmL 79; WhoAmP 73, 75, 77, 79, 81, 83, 85, 87, 89, 91, 93, 95; WhoWest 80, 82, 87, 89, 92, 94, 96; WhoWor 84, 87, 89, 91*

Bryan, William Jennings
"The Great Commoner"
American. Lawyer, Political Leader
Three-time populist Dem. presidential candidate; secretary of State, 1913-15.
b. Mar 18, 1860 in Salem, Illinois
d. Jul 26, 1925 in Dayton, Tennessee
Source: *AmAu&B; AmBi; AmDec 1900; AmJust; AmOrTwC; AmPeW; AmPolLe; AmRef; ApCAB SUP; Benet 87, 96; BenetAL 91; BiDMoPL; BiDrAC; BiDrUSC 89; BiDrUSE 71, 89; BioIn 1, 2, 3, 4, 5, 6, 7, 8, 9, 10, 11, 12, 13, 14, 15, 16, 17, 18, 19, 20; CyAG; DcAmAu; DcAmB; DcAmDH 80, 89; DcAmReB 1, 2; DcAmSR; DcAmTB; DcNAA; DcTwHis; EncAAH; EncAB-H 1974, 1996; EncARH; FacFETw; GayN; HarEnUS; HisWorL; LegTOT; LinLib L, S; LuthC 75; McGEWB; MorMA; NatCAB 9, 19; OxCAmH; OxCAmL 65, 83, 95; PolPar; PresAR; RComAH; RelLAm 91; REn; REnAL; REnAW; TwCBDA; TwCSAPR; WebAB 74, 79; WhAm 1; WhAmP; WhFla; WhLit; WorAl; WorAlBi*

Bryant, Anita Jane
American. Singer
Lost contract promoting orange juice due to views on homosexuals.
b. Mar 25, 1940 in Barnsdall, Oklahoma
Source: *AmWomWr; BkPepl; ConAu 85; CurBio 75; InWom SUP; NewYTBS 78; WhoAm 74, 76, 78, 80, 82, 84, 86; WhoAmW 74, 79, 81, 83; WorAl*

Bryant, Arthur W. M, Sir
English. Author
Historian and biographer of King Charles II and Samuel Pepys.
b. Feb 18, 1899 in Norfolk, England
d. Jan 22, 1985 in Salisbury, England
Source: *ConAu 104, 114; IntWW 83; Who 83, 85; WrDr 84*

Bryant, Bear
[Paul William Bryant]
"The Titan of Tuscaloosa"
American. Football Coach
Coach, U. of AL, 1958-83; compiled 323 wins, six national championships.
b. Sep 11, 1913 in Kingsland, Arkansas
d. Jan 26, 1983 in Tuscaloosa, Alabama
Source: *AnObit 1983; BiDAmSp FB; BioIn 2, 6, 7, 9, 10, 11, 12, 13; BioNews 75; ConAu 111; CurBio 80, 83; LegTOT; NewYTBS 79, 81, 83; WhAm 8; WhoAm 74, 76, 78, 80, 82; WhoFtbl 74; WhoSpor; WhoSSW 73*

Bryant, Boudleaux
American. Songwriter
With wife Felice, wrote over 1,500 songs including early rock hit "Bye Bye Love," 27 for Everly Brothers: "Wake Up Little Susie," "All I Have to Do Is Dream."
b. Feb 13, 1920 in Shellman, Georgia
d. Jun 26, 1987 in Knoxville, Tennessee
Source: *AmSong; BiDAmM; BioIn 9, 14, 15; EncFCWM 69, 83; EncRk 88; HarEnCM 87; IlEncCM; NewGrDA 86; OxCPMus; PenEncP; PopAmC SUP; RolSEnR 83; WhoAm 80*

Bryant, Felice
American. Songwriter
Songs include "Wake Up Little Susie"; "Bye, Bye Love"; "Raining in My Heart."
b. Aug 7, 1925 in Milwaukee, Wisconsin
Source: *AmSong; BgBkCoM; BioIn 9, 19; EncFCWM 69; EncRk 88; HarEnCM 87; IlEncCM; InWom; OxCPMus; PenEncP; RolSEnR 83; WhoAm 80; WhoAmW 61*

Bryant, Hugh
[Delta Rhythm Boys]
American. Singer
Member, Delta Rhythm Boys, 1962; died singing at Lee Gaines' funeral.
b. 1929?
d. Jul 23, 1987 in Helsinki, Finland
Source: *NewYTBS 87*

Bryant, Lane
[Lena Himmelstein]
American. Retailer
Founded Lane Bryant clothing stores, circa 1904.
b. Dec 1, 1879, Lithuania
d. Sep 26, 1951
Source: *BioIn 1, 2, 3, 7; Entr; NatCAB 47; WorAl; WorAlBi*

Bryant, Wayne R(ichard)
American. Politician
Member, New Jersey General Assembly, 1982—; introduced Family Development Act, calling for significant welfare reform in New Jersey, 1991.
b. Nov 7, 1947 in Lawnside, New Jersey
Source: *WhoAmP 83, 85, 87, 89, 91, 93, 95; WhoE 97*

Bryant, William Cullen
American. Poet, Editor
Best known poem *Thanatopsis,* 1811; edited, *NY Evening Post,* 1829-78.
b. Nov 3, 1794 in Cummington, Massachusetts
d. Jun 12, 1878 in New York, New York
Source: *ABCMeAm; Alli, SUP; AmAu; AmAu&B; AmBi; AmSocL; AmWr S1; ApCAB; AtlBL; BbD; Benet 87, 96; BenetAL 91; BibAL; BiDAmJo; BiDAmM; BiD&SB; BiDTran; BioIn 1, 2, 3, 4, 5, 6, 7, 8, 9, 10, 11, 12, 14, 15, 16, 19; CamGEL; CamGLE; CamHAL; CarSB; CasWL; CelCen; Chambr 3; ChhPo, S1, S2, S3; CnDAL; CnE&AP; ColARen; CrtT 3, 4; CyAL 1; CyWA 58; DcAmAu; DcAmB; DcAmC; DcAmSR; DcArts; DcBiPP; DcEnL; DcLB 3, 43, 59; DcLEL; DcNAA; Drake; EncAAH; EncAB-H 1974, 1996; EncAJ; EvLB; GrWrEL P; HarEnUS; JrnUS; LegTOT; LinLib L, S; LuthC 75; McGEWB; MouLC 3; NatCAB 4; NewGrDA 86; NinCLC 6, 46; OxCAmH; OxCAmL 65,*

83, 95; OxCEng 67, 85, 95; PenC AM; PoChrch; RAdv 1, 14, 13-1; REn; REnAL; RfGAmL 87, 94; RGFAP; Str&VC; TwCBDA; WebAB 74, 79; WebE&AL; WhAm HS; WhFla; WorAl; WorAlBi

Bryce, James Bryce, Viscount
English. Diplomat, Author
Ambassador to US, 1907-13; wrote classics *Holy Roman Empire,* 1864; *American Commonwealth,* 1888.
b. May 10, 1838 in Belfast, Northern Ireland
d. Jan 22, 1922 in Sidmouth, England
Source: *BbD; BiD&SB; BioIn 1, 5, 8, 11, 12, 13, 14; BritAu 19; DcEnA, A; EvLB; LngCTC; NewC; OxCAmL 65; OxCEng 67; PenC AM, ENG; REn; WhAm 1*

Brymer, Jack
English. Musician
Clarinetist with Royal Philharmonic Orchestra; autobiography, *From Where I Sit,* 1979.
b. Jan 27, 1915 in South Shields, England
Source: *Baker 84, 92; BlueB 76; ConAu 110; IntWW 74, 75, 76, 77, 78, 79, 80, 81, 82, 83, 89, 91, 93; IntWWM 77, 80, 85, 90; NewGrDM 80; PenDiMP; Who 74, 82, 83, 85, 88, 90, 92, 94; WhoMus 72; WhoWor 74, 76, 78*

Brynner, Yul
[Taidje Khan]
American. Actor
Won Tony, 1951, Oscar, 1956, for role in *The King and I.*
b. Jul 12, 1915 in Sakhalin, Russia
d. Oct 10, 1985 in New York, New York
Source: *BiDFilm, 81, 94; BioIn 2; CelR; CmMov; ConNews 85-4; ConTFT 3; CurBio 85; DcArts; EncMT; FacFETw; FilmEn; FilmgC; ForYSC; HalFC 80, 84, 88; IntDcF 1-3, 2-3; IntMPA 82; IntWW 74; ItaFilm; LegTOT; MotPP; MovMk; OxCFilm; OxCPMus; PlP&P; WhoAm 84; WhoHol A; WhoHrs 80; WhoThe 81; WhoWor 74; WorEFlm*

Bryson, Peabo
[Robert Peabo Bryson]
American. Singer
Rhythm, blues balladeer; had hit single with Roberta Flack: "Lookin' Like Love," 1984.
b. Apr 13, 1951 in Greenville, South Carolina
Source: *BioIn 12; ConMus 11; LegTOT; PenEncP; RkOn 85; RolSEnR 83; SoulM; WhoAfA 96; WhoBlA 94*

Bryson, Wally Carter
[The Raspberries]
American. Musician
Guitarist with power pop group.
b. Jul 18, 1949 in Gastonia, North Carolina

Brzezinski, Zbigniew Kazimierz
American. Author, Educator, Businessman
Advisor to Jimmy Carter on national security affairs, 1977-81.
b. Mar 28, 1928 in Warsaw, Poland
Source: *AmAu&B; AmMWSc 73S; AmPolLe; BioIn 6, 7, 8, 9, 10, 11, 12; ColdWar 1; ConAu 1R, 5NR; CurBio 70; WhoAm 82; WhoWor 74*

Buatta, Mario
American. Interior Decorator
Known for creating a sophisticated yet comfortable environment in the English country-house style; clients include Barbara Walters, Nelson Doubleday.
b. Oct 20, 1935 in Staten Island, New York
Source: *BioIn 13, 14, 15, 16, 17; CurBio 91; NewYTBS 86; WhoAm 95, 96, 97; WhoE 83, 85, 86, 89, 95*

Bubbles, John
American. Dancer
Created rhythm tap dancing; starred in *Porgy and Bess,* 1935; first black to appear on "The Tonight Show."
b. Feb 19, 1902 in Louisville, Kentucky
d. May 18, 1986 in Baldwin Hills, California
Source: *AfrAmAl 6; AmPS B; AnObit 1986; BiDAfM; BioIn 7, 8, 9, 10, 14, 15; BlkOpe; DrBlPA, 90; LegTOT; NegAl 76, 83, 89; NewGrDJ 88; NewYTBS 86; PlP&P; What 5; WhoBlA 85; WorAl*

Buber, Martin
Israeli. Philosopher, Author
Hasidic scholar whose philosophy of religious existentialism is described in book *I and Thou,* 1922.
b. Feb 8, 1878 in Vienna, Austria
d. Jun 13, 1965 in Jerusalem, Israel
Source: *Benet 87, 96; BioIn 2, 3, 4, 5, 6, 7, 8, 9, 10, 11, 12, 13, 14, 17, 18, 21; ConAu 25R, 125; ConIsC 2; CurBio 53, 65; EncWL, 2, 3; FacFETw; HisEAAC; JeHun; LegTOT; LiExTwC; LinLib L, S; LuthC 75; MajTwCW; MakMC; McGEWB; ModGL; ObitT 1961; OxCGer 76, 86; OxCPhil; RadHan; RAdv 14, 13-4; REn; ThTwC 87; TwCA SUP; WhAm 4; WhDW; WhE&EA; WhoTwCL; WorAl; WorAlBi; WrPh P*

Bubka, Sergei (Nazarovich)
Ukrainian. Track Athlete
First pole vaulter to clear 6 meters; won gold medal at 1988 Olympics.
b. Dec 4, 1963 in Voroshilovgrad, Union of Soviet Socialist Republics
Source: *BioIn 13, 14, 16; CurBio 96; IntWW 91; NewYTBS 84*

Buchalter, Lepke
[Louis Buchalter]
American. Criminal
Number one labor racketeer; founded Murder Inc. "hit" squad, 1930s; died in the electric chair.
b. 1897 in New York, New York
d. Mar 4, 1944 in Ossining, New York
Source: *CopCroC; DrInf; LegTOT; WorAl; WorAlBi*

Buchan, John, Sir
[Baron Tweedsmuir]
Scottish. Author, Government Official
Canadian governor-general, 1935-40; adventure novels include classic *Thirty-Nine Steps,* 1915.
b. Aug 26, 1875 in Perth, Scotland
d. Feb 11, 1940 in Montreal, Quebec, Canada
Source: *Benet 87, 96; BioIn 1, 2, 3, 4, 5, 6, 7, 10, 11, 13, 14, 15, 17, 18, 21; CamGLE; CasWL; ChhPo S3; CmScLit; CnMWL; ConAu 108, 145; CorpD; CrtSuMy; CurBio 40; CyWA 58; DcArts; DcLB 34, 70, 156; DcLEL; DcNaB 1931; EncMys; EncSoA; EvLB; FacFETw; FilmgC; GrBr; HalFC 80, 84, 88; JBA 51; LegTOT; LinLib S; LngCTC; MnBBF; ModBrL; NewC; Novels; OxCChiL; OxCEng 85, 95; REn; RfGEnL 91; RGTwCWr; ScF&FL 1, 92; SpyFic; StaCVF; TwCCr&M 80, 85, 91; TwCLC 41; TwCRHW 90, 94; TwCWr; WebE&AL; WhDW; WhE&EA; WhLit; WhoHr&F; WhoSpyF; YABC 2*

Buchanan, Angela Marie
"Bay"
American. Government Official
Headed US Treasury Dept., 1981-83; sister of Pat Buchanan.
b. 1948 in Washington, District of Columbia
Source: *BioIn 12; WhoAm 82; WhoAmP 81, 83, 85, 87, 89, 91, 93; WhoAmW 85; WhoFI 83*

Buchanan, Buck
[Junius Buchanan]
American. Football Player
Defensive tackle, KC, 1963-73; Hall of Fame, 1990.
b. Sep 10, 1940 in Birmingham, Alabama
d. Jul 16, 1992 in Kansas City, Missouri
Source: *BiDAmSp FB; BioIn 17, 18; NewYTBS 92; WhoSpor*

Buchanan, Edgar
[J J Jackson]
American. Actor
Played Uncle Joe on TV series "Petticoat Junction," 1963-70; was originally a dentist; head of oral surgery at Eugene OR Hospital, 1929-37.
b. Mar 20, 1903 in Humansville, Missouri
d. Apr 4, 1979 in Palm Desert, California
Source: *CmMov; DcAmB S10; FilmEn; FilmgC; ForYSC; HolCA; IntMPA 75, 76, 77; MotPP; MovMk; NewYTBS 79; WhoHol A; WhScrn 83; WorAl*

Buchanan, George
Scottish. Author
Wrote *De Juri Regni,* 1579, stating that kings rule by popular will; had great impact on 16th-c. political thought.
b. Feb 1, 1506 in Killearn, Scotland
d. Sep 28, 1582 in Edinburgh, Scotland
Source: *Alli; BioIn 3, 4, 10, 11, 13, 14, 20; BlmGEL; BritAu; CamGEL; CamGLE; CasWL; Chambr 1; CmScLit; CroE&S; CyEd; DcBiPP; DcEnA; DcEnL; DcEuL; DcLB 132; DcNaB; Dis&D; EvLB; LinLib L; LitC 4; LuthC 75; NewC; NewCBEL; NewCol 75; OxCEng 67, 85, 95; OxCFr; PenC ENG; WhDW*

Buchanan, Jack
Scottish. Comedian, Actor
Debonair musical comedy actor since 1915; made comeback in *The Band Wagon,* 1953.
b. Apr 2, 1891 in Glasgow, Scotland
d. Oct 20, 1957 in London, England
Source: *BiDD; BioIn 9, 11; CmpEPM; DcArts; EncEurC; EncMT; Film 1, 2; FilmAG WE; FilmEn; FilmgC; ForYSC; HalFC 80, 84, 88; IlWWBF, A; LegTOT; MotPP; NotNAT B; OxCAmT 84; OxCFilm; OxCPMus; PenEncP; WhoHol B; WhScrn 74, 77, 83; WorAl*

Buchanan, James McGill
American. US President
Fifteenth pres., 1857-61; opposed slavery in principle, but defended it under Constitution.
b. Apr 23, 1791 in Mercersburg, Pennsylvania
d. Jun 1, 1868 in Lancaster, Pennsylvania
Source: *Alli SUP; AmAu&B; AmBi; ApCAB; BiAUS; BiDrAC; BiDrUSE 71; CelCen; CyAG; DcAmAu; DcAmB; Drake; EncAB-H 1974; HarEnUS; OxCAmL 65; REnAL; WhAm HS*

Buchanan, James McGill
American. Economist
Won Nobel Prize in economics, 1986, for advocating firm rules to keep national budgets balanced.
b. Oct 2, 1919 in Murfreesboro, Tennessee
Source: *AmMWSc 73S, 78S; ConAu 3NR, 5R, 22NR; IntWW 89, 91, 93; NewYTBS 86; Who 90, 92, 94; WhoAm 74, 76, 78, 80, 82, 84, 86, 88, 90, 92, 94, 95, 96, 97; WhoEc 81; WhoFI 89, 92, 94, 96; WhoNob 90, 95; WhoSSW 73, 75, 76, 88, 91, 93, 95, 97; WhoWor 89, 91, 93, 95, 96, 97; WhoWrEP 89, 92, 95; WrDr 76, 84, 86*

Buchanan, John
Canadian. Politician
Progressive-Conservative Party premier of Nova Scotia, 1978-90.
b. Apr 22, 1931 in Sydney, Nova Scotia, Canada
Source: *BiDrLUS 70; CanWW 83; WhoLibS 66*

Buchanan, Patrick Joseph
American. Presidential Aide, Politician
Director of communications, under Reagan, 1985-87; presidential candidate, 1992, 1996.
b. Nov 2, 1938 in Washington, District of Columbia
Source: *BiDAmNC; BioIn 10, 12; CurBio 85; EncTwCJ; IntWW 89, 91, 93; NewYTBS 92; WhoAm 74, 76, 78, 80, 82, 84, 86, 88, 90, 92, 94, 95, 96, 97; WhoAmP 73, 75, 77, 79, 81, 91, 93, 95; WhoE 93; WhoGov 72; WhoSSW 73*

Bucher, Lloyd Mark
American. Naval Officer
Commander, USS *Pueblo,* seized by N Korea, 1968.
b. Sep 1, 1927 in Pocatello, Idaho
Source: *BioIn 8, 9, 11, 12; PolProf NF*

Buchholz, Horst
German. Actor
Films include *Tiger Bay,* 1959; *Fanny,* 1961.
b. Dec 4, 1933 in Berlin, Germany
Source: *BiE&WWA; BioIn 5, 6; ConTFT 1; CurBio 60; EncEurC; FilmgC; ForYSC; HalFC 80, 84, 88; IntMPA 75, 76, 77, 78, 79, 80, 81, 82, 84, 86, 88, 92, 94, 96; LegTOT; MotPP; MovMk; WhoHol 92, A; WorAl; WorAlBi; WorEFlm*

Buchman, Frank Nathan Daniel
American. Religious Leader
Founded religious sect, Oxford Group, 1921; Moral Re-Armament, 1938, to prevent war.
b. Jun 4, 1878 in Pennsburg, Pennsylvania
d. Aug 7, 1961 in Freudenstadt, Germany
Source: *AmAu&B; BiDAmCu; BioIn 1, 2, 4, 5, 6, 9, 10, 11, 18, 19; CurBio 40, 61; DcAmB S7; DcAmReB 1, 2; EncARH; LinLib S; LngCTC; LuthC 75; RelLAm 91; WebAB 74, 79; WhAm 4; WhDW*

Buchner, Eduard
German. Chemist
Won 1907 Nobel Prize for discovery of cell-free fermentation.
b. May 20, 1860 in Munich, Germany
d. Aug 13, 1917 in Focsani, Romania
Source: *AsBiEn; BiESc; BioIn 3, 5, 6, 7, 14, 15, 19, 20; CamDcSc; DcScB; Dis&D; FacFETw; LarDcSc; LinLib S; NobelP; NotTwCS; WhoNob, 90, 95; WorAl; WorAlBi; WorScD*

Buchner, Georg
German. Dramatist
Considered one of Germany's greatest playwrights; best known for *Danton's Death,* 1835; unfinished *Wozzeck,* 1836.
b. Oct 17, 1813 in Goddelan-bei-Darmst, Prussia
d. Feb 19, 1837 in Zurich, Switzerland
Source: *AtlBL; Benet 87, 96; BiD&SB; BioIn 2, 3, 5, 7, 10, 12, 14, 15, 20; CamGWoT; CnThe; CyWA 58; DcArts; DcLB 133; Dis&D; EncWT; Ent; EuAu; EuWr 6; GrFLW; IntDcT 2; LinLib L; McGEWD 72, 84; NewEOp 71; NewGrDO; NinCLC 26; NotNAT B; OxCGer 76, 86; OxCThe 67, 83; OxDcOp; PenC EUR; PlP&P; RAdv 14, 13-2; REn; REnWD; RfGShF; RfGWoL 95; WhDW*

Buchwald, Art(hur)
American. Journalist
Column syndicated in over 550 newspapers; wrote *The Buchwald Stops Here,* 1978.
b. Oct 20, 1925 in Mount Vernon, New York
Source: *AmAu&B; AuBYP 2S, 3; AuNews 1; BiDAmNC; BioIn 3, 4, 5, 6, 7, 8, 9, 10, 11, 12, 13; BioNews 74; BlueB 76; CelR, 90; ConAu 5R, 21NR; ConLC 33; CurBio 60; DcLEL 1940; EncAHmr; EncAJ; EncTwCJ; IntAu&W 76, 77, 82, 89, 91, 93; IntWW 74, 75, 76, 77, 78, 79, 80, 81, 82, 83, 89, 91, 93; JrnUS; LegTOT; MajTwCW; NewYTBE 72; PenC AM; SmATA 10; Who 74, 82, 83, 85, 88, 90, 92, 94; WhoAm 74, 76, 78, 80, 82, 84, 86, 88, 90, 92, 94, 95, 96, 97; WhoE 91, 93; WhoSSW 73, 75, 76; WhoUSWr 88; WhoWor 74, 76, 78, 80, 82, 84, 87, 89, 91, 93, 95, 96, 97; WhoWrEP 89, 92, 95; WorAl; WorAlBi; WorAu 1950; WrDr 76, 80, 82, 84, 86, 88, 90, 92, 94, 96*

Buck, Dudley
American. Composer, Organist
Known for church music, cantatas; wrote opera *Deseret,* 1880.
b. Mar 10, 1839 in Hartford, Connecticut
d. Oct 6, 1909 in Orange, New Jersey
Source: *Alli SUP; AmBi; ApCAB; Baker 78, 84, 92; BbD; BiDAmM; BiD&SB; BioIn 1; DcAmAu; DcAmB; DcNAA; LinLib S; LuthC 75; NatCAB 7; NewAmDM; NewGrDA 86; NewGrDM 80; NewGrDO; OxCMus; WhAm 1*

Buck, Frank
American. Animal Dealer
Supplied everything from birds to elephants to zoos, circuses; wrote *Bring 'Em Back Alive,* 1930.
b. Mar 17, 1884 in Gainesville, Texas
d. Mar 25, 1950 in Houston, Texas
Source: *AmAu&B; BenetAL 91; BioIn 1, 2, 4; CurBio 43, 50; FilmgC; LinLib L, S; MnBBF; ObitOF 79; REnAL; WebAB 74, 79; WhAm 2A; WhoHol B; WhScrn 74, 77*

Buck, Gene
American. Songwriter
Co-founder ASCAP, 1914, pres., 1924-41; composed Ziegfeld Follies hits.
b. Aug 8, 1886 in Detroit, Michigan
d. Feb 24, 1957 in Manhasset, New York
Source: *AmAu&B; CurBio 41, 57; EncMT; NewCBMT; REnAL*

Buck, Paul Herman
American. Author, Educator
Head of Harvard U Libraries; won Pulitzer for *Road to Reunion,* 1937.
b. Sep 25, 1899 in Columbus, Ohio
d. Dec 23, 1978 in Cambridge, Massachusetts
Source: *AmAu&B; BioIn 3, 4, 5, 12, 16; ConAu 81; CurBio 55, 79; DrAS 74H, 78H; EncSoH; OhA&B; OxCAmL 65; PeoHis; TwCA, SUP; WhAm 7; WhoAm 74, 76; WhoWor 74, 76*

Buck, Pearl S(ydenstricker)
American. Author
Won Pulitzer, 1932, Nobel Prize, 1938; wrote *The Good Earth,* 1930.
b. Jun 26, 1892 in Hillsboro, West Virginia
d. Mar 6, 1973 in Danby, Vermont
Source: *AmAu&B; Au&Wr 71; AuNews 1; Benet 96; CasWL; ConAmA; ConAu 1NR, 1R; ConLC 18; ConNov 72; CurBio 56, 73; DcArts; DcLEL; EvLB; FilmgC; InWom; LngCTC; ModAL; NewYTBE 73; OxCAmL 65; PenC AM; REn; REnAL; RfGAmL 94; SmATA 1; TwCA, SUP; TwCRHW 94; TwCWr; WebAB 74; WhAm 5; WhNAA; WhoAmW 58, 61, 64, 66, 68, 70, 72, 74; WomFir*

Buckingham, Lindsey
[Fleetwood Mac]
American. Musician
Joined Fleetwood Mac, 1975; solo LP *Law and Order,* 1981.
b. Oct 3, 1947 in Palo Alto, California
Source: *BioIn 13; ConMus 8; LegTOT; RkOn 85; WhoAm 80, 82, 84*

Buckinghams, The
[Nick Fortune; Carl Giamarese; Marty Grebb; Jon Paulos; Denny Tufano]
American. Music Group
Chicago area band popular 1966-68; had number one hit "Kind of a Drag," 1966.
Source: *BiDAmM; EncRkSt; RkOn 78; RolSEnR 83; WhoRock 81; WhoRocM 82*

Buckland, William
English. Geologist
Denied evolution; tried to reconcile geology with Bible; wrote *Reliquiae Diluvianae,* 1823.
b. Mar 12, 1784 in Axminster, England
d. Aug 14, 1856 in Islip, England
Source: *Alli; BioIn 1, 4, 9; CelCen; DcBiPP; DcEnL; DcNaB; DcScB; InSci; LarDcSc; WorScD*

Buckley, Betty Lynn
American. Actor
Won Tony for *Cats,* 1983; starred in TV's "Eight Is Enough," 1977-81.
b. Jul 3, 1947 in Big Spring, Texas
Source: *BioIn 12; ConTFT 1, 4; VarWW 85; WhoAm 94, 95, 96, 97; WhoAmW 95*

Buckley, Charles Anthony
American. Politician
Dem. congressman from NY, 1935-64.
b. Jun 23, 1890 in New York, New York
d. Jan 22, 1967 in New York, New York
Source: *BiDrAC; BiDrUSC 89; BioIn 6, 7, 11; WhAm 4; WhAmP*

Buckley, Christopher (Taylor)
American. Writer
Wrote humorous novels *The White House Mess,* 1986; *Thank You for Smoking,* 1994.
b. 1952 in New York, New York
Source: *BioIn 12, 13, 15, 17, 20; ConAu 139; ScF&FL 92; WhoAm 97; WhoE 95*

Buckley, Emerson
American. Conductor
Director, Tulsa, Seattle, Miami Opera cos; won John Jay achievement award, 1984.
b. Apr 14, 1916 in New York, New York
d. Nov 18, 1989 in North Miami Beach, Florida
Source: *Baker 84, 92; BioIn 9, 11, 12, 16, 17; IntWWM 77, 80, 85, 90; NewEOp 71; NewGrDA 86; WhAm 10; WhoAm 74, 76, 78, 80, 82, 84, 86, 88; WhoAmM 83; WhoOp 76; WhoSSW 73, 75, 76, 78, 80, 82, 84; WhoWor 78*

Buckley, James Lane
American. Politician, Author
Conservative, Rep. senator from NY, 1971-77; wrote *If Men were Angels,* 1975.
b. Mar 9, 1923 in New York, New York
Source: *BiDrUSC 89; BioIn 9, 10, 11, 12; CngDr 74, 87, 89, 91, 93, 95; ConAu 61; CurBio 71; IntWW 74, 75, 76, 77, 78, 79, 80, 81, 82, 83, 89, 91, 93; WhoAm 74, 76, 82, 84, 86, 88, 90, 92, 94, 95, 96, 97; WhoAmL 90, 92, 94, 96; WhoAmP 85; WhoE 74, 75, 89, 91, 93; WhoGov 72, 75, 77*

Buckley, Tim
American. Singer, Songwriter
Pop singer-guitarist, 1960s; albums include *Goodbye and Hello,* 1967.
b. Feb 17, 1947 in Washington, District of Columbia
d. Jun 29, 1975 in Santa Monica, California
Source: *BioIn 10, 14; ConMuA 80A; ConMus 14; EncFCWM 83; EncPR&S 74; EncRk 88; EncRkSt; HarEnR 86; IlEncRk; PenEncP; RolSEnR 83; WhAm 6; WhoAm 74; WhoRock 81*

Buckley, William F
American. Hostage
Former CIA Bureau Chief, Beirut, taken hostage by Islamic Jihad, Mar 16, 1984, reported dead Oct 4, 1985.
d. Oct 4, 1985, Lebanon
Source: *BioNews 74; CurBio 62; DcAmSR; NewYTBE 70; NewYTBS 80, 88*

Buckley, William Frank, Jr.
"Scourge of American Liberalism"
American. Editor
Editor, *National Review* mag., 1955-88; wrote *Atlantic High,* 1982.
b. Nov 24, 1925 in New York, New York
Source: *AmAu&B; AmCath 80; AmSocL; AuNews 1; BiDAmNC; BioIn 3, 5, 6, 7, 8, 9, 10, 11, 12, 13; ConAu 1NR; ConLC 18, 37; CurBio 82; DcLEL 1940; EncAI&E; IntAu&W 76, 77, 82, 89; IntWW 74, 75, 76, 77, 78, 79, 80, 81, 82, 83, 89, 91, 93; LinLib S; SpyFic; St&PR 75; WebAB 74, 79; WhoAm 74, 76, 78, 80, 82, 84, 86, 88, 90, 92, 94, 95, 96, 97; WhoAmP 73, 75, 77, 79, 81, 83, 85, 87, 89, 91, 93; WhoE 74, 75, 77, 91; WhoFI 74; WhoGov 72, 75, 77; WhoUSWr 88; WhoWor 74, 76, 78, 80, 82, 84, 87, 89; WhoWrEP 89, 92, 95; WorAl; WrDr 80, 86*

Buckmaster, Henrietta
[Henrietta Henkle; H H Stephens]
American. Author, Journalist
Best known for historical novels *Let My People Go,* 1941; *Deep River,* 1944.
b. 1909 in Cleveland, Ohio
d. Apr 26, 1983 in Chestnut Hill, Massachusetts
Source: *AmAu&B; AmNov; AmWomWr; BioIn 1, 2, 10, 13; ConAu 9R, 69; CurBio 46, 83N; FemiCLE; InWom, SUP; OhA&B; ScF&FL 92; SmATA 6; WhoAmW 77; WorAu 1950*

Buckmire, Ron
American. Mathematician
Founder of the Queer Resources Directory, the largest repository of homosexual and AIDS information on the Internet, 1991.
b. May 21, 1968 in Grenville, Grenada
Source: *GayLesB*

Buckner, Bill
[William Joseph Buckner]
"Buck"
American. Baseball Player
Outfielder-first baseman, 1969-90; won NL Battling title, 1980.
b. Dec 14, 1949 in Vallejo, California
Source: *Ballpl 90; BaseReg 86, 87; BiDAmSp BB; BioIn 15, 16, 17, 20; NewYTBS 81; PseudN 82; WhoAm 82, 84; WhoProB 73*

Buckner, Simon Bolivar
American. Military Leader
Confederate general, 1864; governor of KY, 1887-91.
b. Apr 1, 1823 in Hart County, Kentucky
d. Jan 8, 1914 in Mundfordville, Kentucky
Source: *AmBi; ApCAB; BiDConf; BiDrGov 1789; BioIn 4, 5; CivWDc; DcAmB; EncSoH; HarEnUS; NatCAB 13, 16; PeoHis; TwCBDA; WebAB 74, 79; WebAMB; WhAm 1; WhCiWar; WhoMilH 76; WorAl; WorAlBi*

Buckner, Simon Bolivar, Jr.
American. Military Leader, Politician
Commanded American 10th Army, Pacific Theater; killed few days before Okinawa conquest.
b. Jul 18, 1886 in Munfordville, Kentucky
d. Jun 18, 1945 in Okinawa, Japan
Source: *BiDWWGF; BioIn 1, 3; CurBio 42, 45; DcAmB S3; HisEWW; NatCAB 37; WebAB 74, 79; WebAMB; WhAm 2; WhWW-II; WorAl; WorAlBi*

Buckstone, John Baldwin
English. Dramatist, Actor
Wrote over 150 plays, including *Luke the Labourer,* 1826; *Married Life,* 1834.
b. Sep 14, 1802 in London, England
d. Oct 31, 1879 in London, England
Source: *BbD; BiD&SB; BioIn 10; BritAu 19; CamGLE; CamGWoT; CelCen; DcBiPP; DcEnL; DcNaB; GrWrEL DR; NewC; NewCBEL; NotNAT B; OxCThe 67, 83; RfGEnL 91*

Buckwheat Zydeco
[Stanley Dural, Jr.]
American. Musician
Zydeco musician (mixture of black dance and Cajun French music); album *On a Night Like This,* 1987 first Zydeco act recruited by a major label.
b. 1947? in Lafayette, Louisiana
Source: *BioIn 15; ConMus 6; GuBlues; WhoRocM 82*

Bucyk, John Paul
"The Chief"
Canadian. Hockey Player
Left wing, 1955-78, mostly with Boston; won Lady Byng Trophy, 1971, 1974; Hall of Fame, 1981.
b. May 12, 1935 in Edmonton, Alberta, Canada
Source: *BioIn 9, 10; HocEn; WhoHcky 73*

Budd, Ralph
American. Railroad Executive
Youngest railway pres. in US, 1919; pres., Chicago, Burlington, Quincy Railroad, 1932-49.
b. Aug 20, 1879 in Waterloo, Iowa
d. Feb 2, 1962 in Chicago, Illinois
Source: *BiDAmBL 83; BioIn 1, 2, 3, 6; DcAmB S7; EncABHB 1; REnAW; WhAm 4; WorAl; WorAlBi*

Buddha
[Siddhartha Gautama]
"Bhagavat"; "Sugata"; "Tathagata"
Indian. Religious Leader, Philosopher
Renounced world at age 29 to search for solution to human suffering; founded Buddhism, c. 528 BC.
b. Apr 8, 563BC in Kapilavastu, India
d. Feb 25, 483BC in Kusinagara, India
Source: *Benet 87; BioIn 1, 3, 4, 5, 6, 7, 8, 9, 10, 11, 12, 13; Dis&D; LegTOT; LuthC 75; NewC; NewCol 75; PopDcHi; RComWL; WorAl*

Budding, Edwin
English. Inventor
Invented the lawnmower, 1830.
b. 1795
d. 1846
Source: *WhDW*

Budenz, Louis Francis
American. Educator, Author
Former Communist, wrote autobiographical account of his spiritual, political experiences: *This Is My Story,* 1941.
b. Jul 17, 1891 in Indianapolis, Indiana
d. Apr 27, 1972
Source: *AmAu&B; BioIn 1, 2, 3, 9; BkC 6; CathA 1952; CurBio 51, 72; DcAmB S9; IndAu 1917; WhAm 5*

Budge, Don
[John Donald Budge]
American. Tennis Player
First to win "grand slam" of tennis, 1938; known for graceful, powerful backhand shot.
b. Jun 13, 1915 in Oakland, California
Source: *BiDAmSp OS; BioIn 14, 15; CurBio 41; FacFETw; IntWW 83; LegTOT; WebAB 74, 79; WhoSpor; WorAl; WorAlBi*

Budge, Ernest Alfred Thompson Wallis, Sir
English. Egyptologist, Author
Conducted excavations in Egypt, Mesopotamia; author *Babylonian Life and History.*
b. Jul 27, 1857 in Cornwall, England
d. Nov 23, 1934 in London, England
Source: *Alli SUP; BiD&SB; LinLib L*

Buechner, Frederick
American. Author, Clergy
Prize-winning writer of psychological novels: *Long Days Dying,* 1950; *Return of Ansel Gibbs,* 1959.
b. Jul 11, 1926 in New York, New York
Source: *AmAu&B; BenetAL 91; BioIn 2, 5, 9, 10, 12, 13, 14, 16, 17, 18; ConAu 11NR, 13R; ConLC 2, 4, 6, 9; ConNov 72, 76, 82, 86, 91; CurBio 59; CyWA 89; DcLB Y80B; DrAF 76; DrAPF 80; EncWB; IntAu&W 76, 77, 82; LinLib L; MajTwCW; ModAL S1; OxCAmL 65, 83; TwCWr; WhoAm 82; WorAu 1950; WrDr 76, 80, 82, 84, 86, 88, 90, 92*

Buehrig, Gordon
American. Designer
Revolutionized auto design with Duesenberg Model J, Cord 810, Auburn Boattail Speedster, 1930s.
b. Jun 18, 1904 in Mason City, Illinois
d. Jan 22, 1990 in Grosse Pointe Woods, Michigan
Source: *BioIn 11, 12, 15, 16; ConAu 101; DcTwDes; NewYTBS 90*

Buell, Don Carlos
American. Army Officer
Civil War major general, 1862; failed to pursue Confederates in KY; resigned, 1864.
b. Mar 23, 1818 in Marietta, Ohio
d. Nov 19, 1898 in Rockport, Kentucky
Source: *AmBi; ApCAB; BioIn 1, 7, 21; CivWDc; DcAmB; DcAmMiB; Drake; NatCAB 4; NewCol 75; OxCAmH; TwCBDA; WebAB 74, 79; WebAMB; WhAm HS; WhCiWar; WhoMilH 76*

Bueno, Maria Ester Audion
Brazilian. Tennis Player
Won women's singles title at Wimbledon, US Forest Hills tournaments, 1959.
b. Oct 11, 1939 in Sao Paulo, Brazil
Source: *CurBio 65*

Buero Vallejo, Antonio
Spanish. Dramatist
Leading Spanish playwright in the years following WWII.
b. Sep 29, 1916 in Guadalajara, Spain
Source: *Benet 96, 3; HispWr; IntAu&W 76, 77, 82, 86, 89, 91, 93; IntDcT 2; IntvSpW; IntWW 74, 75, 76, 77, 78, 79, 80, 81, 82, 83, 89, 91, 93; MajMD 2; MajTwCW; McGEWD 72, 84; ModSpP S; ModWD; ObitOF 79; OxCSpan; OxCThe 83; PenC EUR; RAdv 14; TwCWr; WhoWor 74, 76, 78, 82, 84, 87, 89, 91, 93, 95, 96, 97*

Bufalino, Gesualdo
Italian. Author
Won the Campiello Prize for *The Plague Sower,* 1981 (*Diceria dell'untore*); also wrote *Lies of the Night,* 1988 (*La menzogne della notte*).
b. Nov 15, 1920 in Comiso, Italy
d. 1990
Source: *ConLC 74; ConWorW 93; WorAu 1985*

Buffalo Springfield
[Richie Furay; Dewey Martin; Jim Messina; Bruce Palmer; Stephen Stills; Neil Young]
American. Music Group
W coast folk rockers, 1966-68; hit single, "For What It's Worth," 1966.
Source: *BiDAmM; BioIn 14, 16, 17, 18, 19, 21; ConMuA 80A; DrAPF 97; EncPR&S 89; EncRk 88; EncRkSt; HarEnR 86; IlEncRk; IntMPA 75, 76, 78, 79, 81, 82, 84, 86, 88; NewGrDA 86; PenEncP; RkOn 78; RolSEnR 83; ScF&FL 92; Who 92, 94; WhoHol A; WhoRock 81; WhoRocM 82*

Buffet, Bernard
French. Artist
One of the leading artists of the 20th c; paintings in genre of post-war France.
b. Jul 10, 1928 in Paris, France
Source: *BioIn 2, 3, 4, 5, 7, 14, 21; CurBio 59; DcArts; DcTwCCu 2; FacFETw; IntWW 74, 75, 76, 77, 78, 79, 80, 81, 82, 83, 89, 91, 93; McGDA; OxCTwCA; OxDcArt; PhDcTCA 77;*

Who 74, 82, 83, 85, 88, 90, 92, 94; WhoArt 80, 82, 84, 96; WhoFr 79; WhoGrA 62; WhoWor 76, 78, 84, 87, 89, 91, 93, 95, 96, 97; WorArt 1950

Buffett, Jimmy
American. Singer, Songwriter
Had hit single "Margaritaville," 1977.
b. Dec 25, 1946 in Pascagoula, Mississippi
Source: *BestSel 90-2; BioIn 11, 12, 14, 19, 20; ConAu 141; ConMus 4; ConPopW; EncFCWM 83; EncRkSt; IlEncRk; LegTOT; PenEncP; RkOn 74, 78; RolSEnR 83; SmATA 76; WhoAm 80, 82, 84, 88, 90, 92, 94, 95, 96, 97; WhoEnt 92; WhoRock 81; WrDr 96*

Buffett, Warren Edward
American. Business Executive
Chairman, Berkshire, Hathaway, Inc., investment firm, 1969—; only man to make $1 billion in stock market.
b. Aug 30, 1930 in Omaha, Nebraska
Source: *BioIn 12, 13; ConAmBL; CurBio 87; EncTwCJ; NewYTBS 85; St&PR 84; WhoAm 74, 76, 78, 80, 82, 84, 86, 88, 90, 92, 94, 95, 96, 97; WhoFI 89, 92, 94, 96; WhoMW 88, 90, 92; WhoWor 91, 96, 97*

Buffon, Georges Louis Leclerc
French. Author
Naturalist; best known for 36-volume *Histoire Naturelle,* 1749-88.
b. Sep 7, 1707 in Montbard, France
d. Apr 16, 1788 in Paris, France
Source: *AsBiEn; AtlBL; BbD; BiD&SB; BiESc; BioIn 2, 4, 7, 8, 9, 11, 12, 13, 14, 16; CasWL; DcBiPP; DcEuL; DcScB; Dis&D; EuAu; EvEuW; InSci; LinLib L, S; McGEWB; OxCEng 67; OxCFr; PenC EUR; REn; WorScD*

Bufman, Zev
Israeli. Producer
American productions include *Little Foxes; Your Own Thing; Peter Pan.*
b. Oct 11, 1930 in Tel Aviv, Palestine
Source: *BiE&WWA; BioIn 13; ConTFT 4; OxCAmT 84; WhoAm 82, 84, 86, 88, 90, 92, 94, 95, 96, 97; WhoHol 92; WhoThe 72, 77, 81*

Buford, John
American. Military Leader
Major-general; took part in Sioux Expedition, 1855; chief of cavalry, Army of Potomac, 1862.
b. Mar 4, 1826 in Woodford County, Kentucky
d. Dec 16, 1863 in Washington, District of Columbia
Source: *AmBi; ApCAB; BioIn 1, 7; CivWDc; DcAmB; Drake; EncSoH; GenMudB; TwCBDA; WebAMB; WhAm HS; WhCiWar; WorAl; WorAlBi*

Bugas, John Stephen
American. Business Executive, Lawyer
Helped to reorganize Ford Motor Co., 1945, after Henry II became pres.
b. Apr 26, 1908 in Rock Springs, Wyoming
d. Dec 2, 1982 in Ypsilanti, Michigan
Source: *BioIn 1, 4, 5, 13; CurBio 47, 83; NewYTBS 82; WhAm 8*

Bugatti, Ettore Arco Isidoro
Italian. Engineer, Auto Manufacturer
Established factory, 1909, in Olsace; noted for racing, luxury cars.
b. Sep 15, 1881 in Milan, Italy
d. Aug 21, 1947 in Paris, France
Source: *BioIn 10*

Bugbee, Emma
American. Journalist, Suffragist
With *NY Herald Tribune,* 1911-66; broke barrier excluding women from newspaper city rooms.
b. 1888? in Shippensburg, Pennsylvania
d. Oct 6, 1981 in Warwick, Rhode Island
Source: *AuBYP 2, 3; BioIn 12, 13, 15; BriB; ConAu 105; EncAJ; InWom SUP; NewYTBS 81; SmATA 29N*

Bugliosi, Vincent T
American. Lawyer, Author
Prosecutor in Manson family murder trials; wrote *Helter-Skelter,* 1974.
b. Aug 18, 1934 in Hibbing, Minnesota
Source: *ConAu 13NR, 73; WhoAm 84*

Buick, David Dunbar
American. Auto Manufacturer
Formed Buick Co., 1902; built first car, 1903.
b. Sep 17, 1854 in Arbroth, Scotland
d. Mar 6, 1929 in Detroit, Michigan
Source: *BioIn 2, 18; EncABHB 4; FacFETw; NatCAB 34; WebBD 83*

Buisson, Ferdinand Edouard
French. Educator, Government Official
Won Nobel Peace Prize, 1927.
b. Dec 20, 1841 in Paris, France
d. Feb 16, 1932 in Thieuloy-Saint-Antoine, France
Source: *BiDMoPL; WhoNob, 90, 95*

Buitoni, Giovanni
Italian. Business Executive, Manufacturer
Chm., Buitoni Foods Corp., specializing in Italian food.
b. Nov 6, 1891 in Perugia, Italy
d. Jan 13, 1979 in Rome, Italy
Source: *BioIn 6, 9, 11, 12; CurBio 62, 79, 79N; NewYTBS 79; St&PR 75*

Bujold, Genevieve
Canadian. Actor
Golden Globe Award for *Anne of a Thousand Days,* 1972; films include *Coma,* 1978.
b. Jul 1, 1942 in Montreal, Quebec, Canada
Source: *BiDFilm 94; BioIn 8, 10, 11, 16; CanWW 31, 70, 79, 80, 81, 83, 89; CelR, 90; ConTFT 3, 11; CreCan 1; FilmEn; FilmgC; ForYSC; HalFC 80, 84, 88; IntDcF 1-3, 2-3; IntMPA 76, 77, 78, 79, 80, 81, 82, 84, 86, 88, 92, 94, 96; IntWW 93; InWom SUP; LegTOT; WhoAm 86; WhoHol A; WhoHrs 80; WorAl; WorAlBi*

Bujones, Fernando
American. Dancer
Principal, American Ballet Theatre, 1974-85.
b. Mar 9, 1955 in Miami, Florida
Source: *BiDD; BioIn 10, 11, 12, 13, 14; CelR 90; CnOxB; CurBio 76; DcArts; IntDcB; IntWW 79, 80, 81, 82, 83, 89, 91, 93; NewYTBS 86; WhoAm 88; WhoE 85; WhoEnt 92; WhoHisp 91, 92, 94*

Buketoff, Igor
American. Conductor
Led St. Paul Opera, 1968-74; founded World Music Bank, 1959.
b. May 29, 1915 in Hartford, Connecticut
Source: *ASCAP 80; Baker 78, 84, 92; IntWWM 77, 80, 90; NewGrDA 86; WhoAm 74, 76, 78, 80, 82, 84, 86; WhoAmM 83; WhoEnt 92; WhoMus 72; WhoWor 74*

Bukharin, Nikolai Ivanovich
Russian. Political Leader
Co-edited Communist Party organ *Pravda* with Lenin; executed in purges of 1938.
b. Oct 9, 1888 in Moscow, Russia
d. Mar 14, 1938 in Moscow, Union of Soviet Socialist Republics
Source: *BiDSovU; BioIn 1, 8, 10, 11, 12, 15, 16, 17, 18, 19; BlkwERR; DcTwHis; EncRev; FacFETw; McGEWB; REn; WhDW; WhoEc 81, 86; WorAl*

Bukovsky, Vladimir
Russian. Political Activist
Released from Soviet labor camp in exchange for Chilean Communist Party leader, Luis Corvalan.
b. Dec 30, 1942 in Moscow, Union of Soviet Socialist Republics
Source: *BioIn 9, 11; CurBio 78; DcPol; IntAu&W 82, 89; IntWW 78, 79, 80, 81, 82, 83, 89, 91; LiExTwC; NewYTBS 76, 77; WhoWor 84, 87, 89, 91, 93, 95*

Bukowski, Charles
[Henry Charles Bukowski, Jr.]
American. Author
Wrote *Post Office,* 1971; *Hollywood,* 1989.
b. Aug 16, 1920 in Andermach, Germany
d. Mar 9, 1994 in San Pedro, California
Source: *AmAu&B; Benet 96; BenetAL 91; BioIn 8, 9, 10, 12, 13; CamGLE; CamHAL; ConAu 17R, 40NR, 144; ConLC 2, 5, 9, 41, 82, 86; ConNov 86, 91; ConPo 70, 75, 80, 85, 91; ConPopW; CurBio 94, 94N; DcArts; DcLB 5, 130, 169; DcLEL 1940; DrAF 76; DrAP 75; DrAPF 80; FacFETw; IntAu&W 77, 82, 91, 93; LegTOT; MagSAmL; MajTwCW; ModAL S1; MugS; OxCAmL 83, 95; OxCTwCP; PenC AM; RAdv 1, 13-1; WhAm 11; WhoAm 76, 78, 80, 82, 84, 86, 88, 90,*

92, 94; WhoTwCL; WhoUSWr 88; WhoWrEP 89, 92; WorAu 1970; WrDr 76, 80, 82, 84, 86, 88, 90, 92, 94, 96

Bulfinch, Charles
American. Architect
First professional architect in US; made nat. capital architect, 1817.
b. Aug 8, 1763 in Boston, Massachusetts
d. Apr 15, 1844 in Boston, Massachusetts
Source: *AmBi; ApCAB; AtlBL; BenetAL 91; BiAUS; BiDAmAr; BioIn 1, 3, 6, 7, 8, 9, 10; BriEAA; DcAmB; DcArts; DcD&D; Drake; EncAAr 1, 2; EncAB-H 1974, 1996; IntDcAr; LegTOT; LinLib S; MacEA; McGDA; McGEWB; NatCAB 13; NewYHSD; NotNAT B; OxCAmH; OxCAmL 65, 83, 95; OxCArt; REnAL; TwCBDA; WebAB 74, 79; WhAm HS; WhoArch; WorAl; WorAlBi*

Bulfinch, Thomas
American. Author
Published *The Age of Fable,* 1855, later called *Bulfinch's Mythology;* has become standard reference work.
b. Jul 15, 1796 in Newton, Massachusetts
d. May 27, 1867 in Boston, Massachusetts
Source: *Alli, SUP; AmAu; AmAu&B; AmBi; ApCAB; Benet 87, 96; BenetAL 91; BiD&SB; BioIn 3, 14; CarSB; ChhPo, S3; DcAmAu; DcAmB; DcNAA; Drake; LegTOT; OxCAmL 65, 83, 95; REn; REnAL; SmATA 35; WebAB 74, 79; WhAm HS*

Bulgakov, Mikhail Afanasyevich
Russian. Author, Dramatist
Noted for play *Days of the Turbins,* 1935; novel *Master and Margarita* published posthumously.
b. May 15, 1891 in Kiev, Russia
d. Mar 10, 1940 in Moscow, Union of Soviet Socialist Republics
Source: *Benet 87, 96; CasWL; ClDMEL 47, 80; CnMD; CnThe; CurBio 40; DcArts; DcRusL; DcRusLS; EncWL; EncWT; EvEuW; FacFETw; McGEWD 72, 84; ModSL 1; ModWD; NewGrDO; PenC EUR; REn; REnWD; TwCWr; WhDW; WhoTwCL; WorAl; WorAu 1950*

Bulganin, Nikolai Aleksandrovich
Russian. Political Leader
Premier, 1955-58; defense minister, 1947-49, 1953-55.
b. Jun 11, 1895 in Nizhni-Novgorod, Russia
d. Feb 24, 1975 in Moscow, Union of Soviet Socialist Republics
Source: *BiDSovU; BioIn 1, 3, 4, 5, 10, 16, 18; ColdWar 2; CurBio 55, 75N; IntWW 74; NewYTBS 75; WhAm 6; Who 74; WhoWor 74; WorAl*

Bulgari, Constantine
Italian. Jeweler
Jewelry house first to introduce ornate chains, pendants as fashion accessories, 1960.
d. 1973
Source: *WorFshn*

Bulgari, Giorgio
Italian. Jeweler
Co-founded with brother Constantine, Rome's deluxe jewelry house, early 1900s.
Source: *WorFshn*

Bulkeley, Morgan G
American. Baseball Executive, Politician
Held various political posts including governor of CT, 1888-93; first pres. of NL, 1876; Hall of Fame, 1937.
b. Dec 26, 1837 in East Haddam, Connecticut
d. Nov 6, 1922 in Hartford, Connecticut
Source: *ApCAB; BiDrAC; BiDrGov 1789; BioIn 3, 7, 9; DcAmB; NatCAB 10; TwCBDA; WhAm 1; WhAmP; WhoProB 73*

Bull, John
English. Organist, Composer
Supposedly wrote early form of melody "God Save the King," 1619.
b. 1562 in Somerset, England
d. Dec 13, 1628 in Antwerp, Belgium
Source: *Alli; Baker 78, 84, 92; BioIn 8; BriBkM 80; CmpBCM; DcArts; GrComp; LuthC 75; MusMk; NewAmDM; NewGrDM 80; NewOxM; OxCEng 85, 95; OxCMus; WebBD 83*

Bull, Odd
Norwegian. Statesman
Chief of staff, UN truce supervision, Palestine, 1963-70.
b. Jun 28, 1907 in Oslo, Norway
Source: *BioIn 8; ConAu 81; CurBio 68; HisEAAC; IntWW 74, 75, 76, 77, 78, 79, 80, 81, 82, 83, 89, 91, 93; WhoUN 75; WhoWor 74, 76, 78*

Bull, Ole Bornemann
Norwegian. Musician, Composer
Internationally known violinist who attempted to found Norwegian settlement in PA, 1852.
b. Feb 5, 1810 in Bergen, Norway
d. Aug 17, 1880 in Lysoe, Norway
Source: *ApCAB; DcBiPP; Drake; OxCAmL 65; OxCThe 67; REnAL; TwCBDA*

Bull, Peter
English. Actor
Journalist-turned actor, films include *African Queen,* 1952; *Dr. Strangelove,* 1963.
b. Mar 21, 1912 in London, England
d. May 20, 1984 in London, England
Source: *AnObit 1984; BiE&WWA; BioIn 5, 7, 10, 13, 14, 15; ConAu 11NR, 25R, 112; ConTFT 1; FilmEn; FilmgC; ForYSC; HalFC 80, 84, 88; IlWWBF A; MotPP; NotNAT, A; PlP&P; SmATA 39N; WhoHol A; WhoThe 72; WhoWor 76; WrDr 80, 82, 84*

Bullard, Dexter Means
American. Psychiatrist
Pioneer in psychoanalytic treatment, whose hospital was setting for novel *I Never Promised You a Rose Garden,* 1964.
b. Aug 14, 1898 in Waukesha, Wisconsin
d. Oct 5, 1981 in Rockville, Maryland
Source: *AmMWSc 73P; BiDrAPA 77; BioIn 14; BlueB 76; NewYTBS 81*

Bullard, Edward Crisp, Sir
English. Physicist
Advocate of continental drift theory, who conducted research on gravity, heat flow, terrestrial magnetism.
b. Sep 21, 1907 in Norwich, England
d. Apr 3, 1980 in La Jolla, California
Source: *AmMWSc 73P, 76P, 79, 82; BiESc; BioIn 2, 3, 6, 12, 14, 20; CurBio 54, 80; DcNaB 1971; DcScB S2; FacFETw; InSci; LarDcSc; WhAm 7; WhoAm 74, 76, 78, 80; WhoWor 74*

Bullard, Robert Lee
American. Military Leader
WW I Commander of Second Army; wrote famous message at Battle of the Marne, turning point of the war, 1918.
b. Jan 15, 1861 in Youngsboro, Alabama
d. Sep 11, 1947 in New York, New York
Source: *BioIn 1, 11; DcAmB S4; DcAmMiB; DcNAA; HarEnMi; ObitOF 79; WebAMB; WhAm 2; WhNAA*

Bullins, Ed
[Kingsley B. Bass, Jr.]
American. Author, Dramatist, Producer
Writers unit coordinator, NY Shakespeare Festival, 1975-82; plays include the award winning *The Talking of Miss Janie,* 1974.
b. Jul 25, 1935 in Philadelphia, Pennsylvania
Source: *AfrAmAl 6; Benet 87, 96; BenetAL 91; BioIn 9, 10, 11, 12, 13, 14, 17; BlkAmP; BlkAWP; BlkLC; BlkWr 1, 2; CamGLE; CamGWoT; CamHAL; ConAmD; ConAu 16AS, 24NR, 46NR, 49; ConDr 73, 77, 82, 88, 93; ConLC 1, 5, 7; ConTFT 7; CroCD; CrtSuDr; CurBio 77; CyWA 89; DcLB 7, 38; DcLEL 1940; DcTwCCu 5; DramC 6; DrBlPA, 90; Ebony 1; EncWL 2, 3; EncWT; Ent; GrWrEL DR; InB&W 80, 85; IntAu&W 76, 77, 82; IntDcT 2; LinLib L; LivgBAA; MajTwCW; McGEWD 84; ModAL S1; ModBlW; NatPD 81; NegAl 83, 89; NotNAT; OxCAmL 95; PlP&P A; RAdv 14; RfGAmL 87, 94; SchCGBL; SelBAAf; SelBAAu; WhoAfA 96; WhoAm 74, 76, 78, 80, 82, 84, 86, 88, 90, 92, 94, 95, 96, 97; WhoBlA 75, 77, 80, 90, 92, 94; WhoE 74; WhoThe 77, 81; WorAu 1970; WrDr 76, 80, 82, 84, 86, 88, 90, 92, 94, 96*

Bullitt, William Christian
American. Statesman, Author
First US ambassador to USSR, 1933-36; warned of Soviet threat after WW II.
b. Jan 25, 1891 in Philadelphia, Pennsylvania
d. Feb 15, 1967 in Neuilly, France
Source: *BioIn 3, 4, 5, 7, 8; ConAu 89; CurBio 40, 67; DcAmB S8; DcAmDH 80, 89; DcPol; ObitT 1961; REn; REnAL; WhAm 4; WorAl*

Bullock, Alan Louis Charles
English. Author, Educator
Joint editor, *Oxford History of Modern Europe;* editor, *The Doubleday Pictorial Library of World History,* 1962.
b. Dec 13, 1914 in Trowbridge, England
Source: *BlueB 76; ConAu 1R; DcLEL 1940; IntAu&W 82; IntWW 74, 75, 81; LngCTC; WhoWor 84*

Bullock, Sandra
American. Actor
In *Speed* and *While You Were Sleeping.*
b. 1967 in Arlington, Virginia
Source: *LegTOT; News 95*

Bulova, Joseph
American. Jeweler, Businessman
Jewelry manufacturer known for watches; his co. was first sponsor of radio ad, "Bulova Watch Time," 1926; first to sponsor TV commercial, 1941.
b. 1851, Czechoslovakia
d. Nov 18, 1935 in New York, New York
Source: *Entr*

Bulow, Bernhard H. M
German. Political Leader
Chancellor, 1900-09; isolated Germany in foreign policy which led to French-British-Russian alliance.
b. May 3, 1849 in Altona, Germany
d. Oct 28, 1929 in Rome, Italy
Source: *OxCGer 76; WorAl*

Bulow, Hans Guido von
German. Conductor, Pianist
Directed Wagner premieres, Munich Opera, 1860s; wed Liszt's daughter, Cosima, who later married Wagner.
b. Jan 8, 1830 in Dresden, Germany
d. Feb 12, 1894 in Cairo, Egypt
Source: *Baker 78, 84; BioIn 4, 7, 8, 9, 12; CelCen; Dis&D; NewEOp 71; NewOxM; OxCMus; WhDW; WorAl*

Bultmann, Rudolf
German. Theologian
One of most influential Protestant theologians of 20th c; theology professor, U of Marburg, 1921-51.
b. Aug 20, 1884 in Wiefelstede, Germany
d. Jul 30, 1976 in Marburg, Germany (West)
Source: *ConAu 5NR, 65; CurBio 72, 76N; FacFETw; IntWW 74; LinLib L; LuthC 75; MakMC; OxCGer 76; OxCPhil; RAdv 14; ThTwC 87; WhoWor 74; WorAu 1950*

Bumbry, Grace Ann Jaeckel
American. Opera Singer
Noted mezzo-soprano; first black to star in role of goddess, 1961; NY Met. debut, 1965; 1979 Grammy winner.
b. Jan 4, 1937 in Saint Louis, Missouri
Source: *Baker 84; CurBio 64; InB&W 85; NewGrDM 80; WhoAm 86; WhoBlA 75; WhoMus 72; WhoWor 74*

Bumpers, Dale Leon
American. Politician
Governor of AR, 1970-74; Dem. senator from AR, 1975—.
b. Aug 12, 1925 in Charleston, Arkansas
Source: *AlmAP 80, 84; BiDrGov 1789; BioIn 12, 13; CngDr 85, 87; CurBio 79; IntWW 83, 89, 91, 93; WhoAm 74, 76, 78, 80, 82, 86; WhoAmP 85; WhoGov 75, 77; WhoSSW 80, 82, 84, 86; WhoWor 78, 80, 82, 84; WorAl*

Bunch, Charlotte
American. Educator, Writer
Founded *Quest: A Feminist Quarterly,* 1970s.
b. 1944 in West Jefferson, North Carolina
Source: *BioIn 21; ConAu 126; FemiWr; GayLesB; IntAu&W 91, 93*

Bunche, Ralph Johnson
American. Statesman
First black American to receive Nobel Peace Prize, 1950, for UN work.
b. Aug 7, 1904 in Detroit, Michigan
d. Dec 9, 1971 in New York, New York
Source: *AmPeW; AmSocL; BiDInt; BioIn 1, 2, 3, 4, 5, 6, 7, 8, 9, 10, 11; ConAu 33R; CurBio 72; DcAmB S9; DcAmDH 80, 89; EncAACR; EncAB-H 1974, 1996; EncAI&E; HisEAAC; HisWorL; InB&W 80, 85; LinLib S; McGEWB; NatCAB 57; NewYTBE 71; ObitT 1971; OxCAmH; PolProf E, J, K, T; REnAL; SelBAAf; SelBAAu; WebAB 74, 79; WhAm 5; WhoNob, 90, 95; WorAl*

Bundy, McGeorge
American. Educator, Presidential Aide
Foreign policy adviser to Presidents Kennedy and Johnson; president of the Ford Foundation, 1965-79.
b. Mar 30, 1919 in Boston, Massachusetts
d. Sep 16, 1996 in Boston, Massachusetts
Source: *AmMWSc 73S, 78S; AmPolLe; BioIn 2, 5, 6, 7, 8, 9, 11, 12; BlueB 76; CelR; ColdWar 1; CurBio 62; DcAmDH 80, 89; EncAB-H 1974, 1996; EncCW; EncWB; FacFETw; IntWW 74, 75, 76, 77, 78, 79, 80, 81, 82, 83, 89, 91, 93; LEduc 74; LinLib L, S; News 97-1; NewYTBS 27, 79; PolProf J, K, NF; Who 74, 82, 83, 85, 88, 90, 92, 94; WhoAm 74, 76, 78, 80, 82, 84, 86, 88, 90, 92, 94, 95, 96, 97; WhoE 74; WhoWor 74, 78, 80, 82, 84, 87, 89, 91*

Bundy, Ted
[Theodore Robert Bundy]
American. Murderer
Serial killer; convicted of three murders, confessed to killing over 20 women, 1970s, before death by electrocution.
b. Nov 24, 1946 in Burlington, Vermont
d. Jan 24, 1989 in Starke, Florida
Source: *BioIn 11, 12, 13; LegTOT; MurCaTw; NewYTBS 78; WorAlBi*

Bundy, William Putnam
American. Government Official, Editor
Asst. secretary of State, Far Eastern Affairs, 1964-69; editor, *Foreign Affairs Quarterly* mag., 1972-84.
b. Sep 24, 1917 in Washington, District of Columbia
Source: *BioIn 5, 6, 7, 9, 11; BlueB 76; CurBio 64; EncAI&E; IntWW 74, 75, 76, 77, 78, 79, 80, 81, 82, 83, 89, 91; WhoAm 74, 76, 78, 80, 82, 84; WhoAmP 85; WhoE 74; WorAl*

Bunin, Ivan Alekseevich
Russian. Author, Translator
First Russian to win Nobel Prize for literature, 1933; wrote novel *Derevnya,* 1910.
b. Oct 22, 1870 in Voronezh, Russia
d. Nov 8, 1953 in Paris, France
Source: *BiDSovU; BioIn 12, 13, 14, 15, 18, 19, 21; CasWL; CnMWL; ConAu 104; CyWA 58; EncWL; HanRL; LngCTC; McGEWB; ModSL 1; ObitT 1951; OxCEng 85, 95; PenC EUR; RfGWoL 95; TwCA, SUP; TwCLC 6; TwCWr; WhAm 3; WhDW; WhoNob; WorAl*

Bunker, Ellsworth
American. Diplomat
Ambassador to Vietnam, 1967-73; chief negotiator, Panama Canal Treaties, 1973-78.
b. May 11, 1894 in Yonkers, New York
d. Sep 27, 1984 in Brattleboro, Vermont
Source: *AnObit 1984; BioIn 2, 3, 6, 7, 9, 10, 11, 12, 14, 16; BlueB 76; CurBio 78, 84N; DcAmDH 80, 89; EncAB-A 12; EncCW; IntWW 74, 75, 76, 77, 78, 79, 80, 81, 82, 83; NewYTBS 84; PolProf J, NF; USBiR 74; WhAm 8; WhoAm 74, 76, 78, 80; WhoAmP 73, 75, 77, 79, 81, 83; WhoGov 72, 75, 77; WhoWor 74, 76, 78, 80, 82; WorAl; WorAlBi*

Bunner, Henry Cuyler
American. Journalist
Best remembered for short stories; editor, *Puck,* weekly humor mag., 1878-96.
b. Aug 3, 1855 in Oswego, New York
d. May 11, 1896 in Nutley, New Jersey
Source: *Alli SUP; AmAu; AmAu&B; AmBi; ApCAB SUP; BbD; BibAL; BiD&SB; Chambr 3; ChhPo, S1, S2, S3; CnDAL; DcAmAu; DcAmB; DcLEL; DcNAA; EvLB; LinLib S; NatCAB 7; OxCAmL 65; REn; REnAL; TwCBDA; WhAm HS*

Bunning, Jim
[James Paul David Bunning]
American. Baseball Player, Politician
Pitcher, 1955-71; threw perfect game, 1964; Rep. congressman from Kentucky, 1987—; admitted to Baseball Hall of Fame, 1996.
b. Oct 23, 1931 in Southgate, Kentucky
Source: *AlmAP 88, 92, 96; Ballpl 90; BiDAmSp BB; BiDrUSC 89; CngDr 87, 89, 91, 93, 95; LegTOT; WhoAm 88, 90, 92, 94, 95, 96, 97; WhoAmP 85; WhoE 95; WhoProB 73; WhoSSW 88, 91, 93, 95; WorAl; WorAlBi*

Bunny, John
American. Actor
First comic film star; joined Vitagraph, 1910; made over 200 shorts in five years.
b. Sep 21, 1863 in New York, New York
d. Apr 26, 1915 in New York, New York
Source: *BioIn 2, 21; EncAFC; Film 1; FilmEn; FilmgC; HalFC 80, 84, 88; IntDcF 1-3, 2-3; JoeFr; MotPP; NotNAT B; QDrFCA 92; SilFlmP; TwYS; WhoHol B; WhScrn 77, 83*

Bunsen, Robert Wilhelm Eberhard
German. Chemist, Inventor
Developed, improved laboratory equipment, including Bunsen burner.
b. Mar 31, 1811 in Gottingen, Germany
d. Aug 16, 1899 in Heidelberg, Germany
Source: *AsBiEn; BioIn 2, 3, 4, 5, 6, 9; DcInv; DcScB; Dis&D; InSci; LinLib S; McGEWB; NewCol 75; OxCGer 76; REn; WorScD*

Bunshaft, Gordon
American. Architect
Modernist, noted for corporate buildings in NYC: Lever House, 1952; won 1988 Pritzger.
b. May 9, 1909 in Buffalo, New York
d. Aug 6, 1990 in New York, New York
Source: *AmArch 70; AmCulL; AnObit 1990; BioIn 4, 5, 9, 11, 14, 16, 17, 19; BlueB 76; BriEAA; ConArch 80, 87, 94; CurBio 89, 90N; DcArts; DcD&D; DcTwDes; EncMA; EncWB; FacFETw; IntWW 74, 75, 76, 77, 78, 79, 80, 81, 82, 83, 89; MacEA; News 91, 89-3, 91-1; NewYTBE 72; NewYTBS 90; St&PR 75; WhAm 10; WhoAm 74, 76, 78, 80, 82, 84, 86, 88, 90; WhoAmA 73, 76, 78, 80, 82, 84, 86, 89; WhoArch; WhoGov 72; WhoWor 74*

Bunting, Basil
English. Poet
Greatest popularity in 1960s as leader of British literary avant-garde.
b. Mar 1, 1900 in Scotswood, England
d. Apr 17, 1985 in Hexham, England
Source: *AnObit 1985; Benet 87, 96; BioIn 10, 11, 12, 13; BlmGEL; BlueB 76; CamGLE; ConAu 7NR, 53, 115; ConLC 10, 39, 47; ConPo 70, 75, 80, 85; DcLB 20; DcNaB 1981; EncWL 2, 3; FacFETw; GrWrEL P; IntAu&W 91; IntWWP 77; ModBrL S1, S2; NewCBEL; OxCEng 85, 95; OxCTwCP; RAdv 14, 13-1; RfGEnL 91; RGFMBP; RGTwCWr; Who 74, 82, 83, 85; WhoTwCL; WhoWor 74; WorAu 1950; WrDr 76, 80, 82, 84, 86*

Bunting, Mary Ingraham
American. University Administrator
Pres. of Radcliffe College, 1960-72.
b. Jul 10, 1910 in New York, New York
Source: *AmMWSc 76P, 79, 82; AmWomSc; BlueB 76; CurBio 67; InWom, SUP; WhoAm 74, 76, 78, 80; WhoAmW 58, 61A, 64, 66, 68, 70, 72, 74, 77, 79; WhoE 74; WhoWor 74*

Bunuel, Luis
Mexican. Director
Started career by working with Salvador Dali on surrealist film *An Andalusian Dog,* 1928.
b. Feb 22, 1900 in Calanda, Spain
d. Jul 29, 1983 in Mexico City, Mexico
Source: *AnObit 1983; Benet 87, 96; BiDFilm, 81, 94; BioIn 5, 6, 7, 8, 9, 10, 11, 12, 13, 14, 15, 19, 21; CelR; ConAu 32NR, 101, 110; ConLC 16, 80; CurBio 65, 83N; DcArts; DcFM; DcHiB; DcTwCCu 2; EncEurC; FacFETw; FilmEn; FilmgC; HalFC 80, 84, 88; HispLC; HispWr; IntDcF 1-2, 2-2; IntMPA 75, 76, 77, 78, 79, 80, 81, 82; IntWW 74, 75, 76, 77, 78, 79, 80, 81, 82, 83; ItaFilm; LegTOT; MakMC; McGEWB; MiSFD 9N; MovMk; NewYTBS 83; OxCFilm; OxCSpan; RAdv 14, 13-3; WhDW; Who 74, 82, 83; WhoFr 79; WhoHrs 80; WhoSSW 73, 75; WhoWor 74, 78, 82; WorAl; WorAlBi; WorEFlm; WorFDir 1*

Bunyan, John
English. Clergy, Author
Wrote religious allegory *Pilgrim's Progress,* 1678, while in prison.
b. Nov 28, 1628 in Elstow, England
d. Aug 31, 1688 in London, England
Source: *Alli; AtlBL; BbD; Benet 87, 96; BiD&SB; BioIn 1, 2, 3, 4, 5, 6, 7, 8, 9, 10, 11, 12, 13, 14, 15, 16, 18; BlmGEL; BritAu; BritWr 2; CamGEL; CamGLE; CarSB; CasWL; Chambr 1; ChhPo, S1, S2, S3; CnDBLB 2; CroE&S; CrtT 2; CyWA 58; DcArts; DcBiPP; DcEnA; DcEnL; DcEuL; DcLB 39; DcLEL; DcNaB; DcPup; Dis&D; EncSoB; EvLB; GrWrEL N; HisDStE; LegTOT; LinLib L, S; LitC 4; LngCEL; LuthC 75; MagSWL; McGEWB; MouLC 1; NewC; NewCBEL; NewEOp 71; Novels; OxCChiL; OxCEng 67, 85, 95; OxCMus; PenC ENG; RAdv 1, 14, 13-1; RComWL; REn; RfGEnL 91; WebE&AL; WhDW; WorAlBi; WorLitC; WrChl*

Buoniconti, Nick
[Nicholas Buontconti]
"Skip"
American. Football Player
Linebacker, 1969-73; won two Super Bowls with Miami, 1973, 1974.
b. Dec 15, 1940 in Springfield, Massachusetts
Source: *BioIn 10; NewYTBE 72; WhoFtbl 74*

Buono, Victor
[Charles Victor Buono]
American. Actor
Oscar nominee for first film *Whatever Happened to Baby Jane?,* 1962.
b. Feb 3, 1938 in San Diego, California
d. Jan 1, 1982 in Apple Valley, California
Source: *ConTFT 2; EncAFC; FilmEn; FilmgC; ForYSC; HalFC 80, 84, 88; HolCA; IntMPA 82; ItaFilm; LegTOT; MotPP; MovMk; NewYTBS 82; WhoAm 80; WhoHol A; WhoHrs 80; WorAl; WorAlBi*

Burbage, James
English. Actor
Built first English playhouse, 1576, called The Theatre.
b. 1530
d. 1597
Source: *BioIn 11; CamGWoT; EncWT; Ent; NotNAT B; OxCEng 85, 95; OxCThe 67, 83; PlP&P*

Burbage, Richard
English. Actor
Original player of Shakespeare's Hamlet, Lear, Othello; son of James; name synonymous with highest quality acting.
b. 1567 in London, England
d. Mar 1619 in London, England
Source: *Benet 87, 96; BioIn 2, 4, 11; BlmGEL; CnThe; DcArts; DcNaB; EncWT; Ent; IntDcT 3; LngCEL; NewC; NotNAT A, B; OxCEng 85, 95; OxCThe 67, 83; PlP&P; REn; WhDW*

Burbank, Luther
American. Horticulturist
Known for developing new varieties of vegetables, fruits, flowers.
b. Mar 7, 1849 in Lancaster, Massachusetts
d. Apr 11, 1926 in Santa Rosa, California
Source: *AmBi; AmDec 1900; AmSocL; ApCAB X; AsBiEn; BiESc; BioIn 1, 2, 3, 4, 5, 6, 7, 8, 9, 10, 11, 12, 14, 15, 17, 19, 20, 21; CmCal; DcAmB; DcNAA; Dis&D; EncAAH; EncAB-H 1974, 1996; EncPaPR 91; FacFETw; GayN; HarEnUS; InSci; LinLib L, S; McGEWB; MorMA; NatCAB 11, 33; OxCAmH; REn; TwoTYeD; WebAB 74, 79; WhAm 1; WorAl; WorAlBi; WorScD*

Burberry, Thomas
English. Fashion Designer
Founded rain, sportswear co., 1856; raincoat became generic term, because of usage by King Edward VII.
b. 1835
d. 1889
Source: *EncFash; WorFshn*

Burbidge, Margaret
[Eleanor Margaret Peachey Burbidge]
English. Astronomer
Made valuable contributions to astronomical theory; served as first woman director, Royal Greenwich Observatory, 1972-73.
b. 1925 in Davenport, England
Source: *AmMWSc 92; BioIn 9, 13, 14; FacFETw; IntDcWB; IntWW 91; InWom SUP; Who 92; WhoAm 90; WhoAmW 91; WhoTech 89*

Burch, Billy
[William Burch]
American. Hockey Player
Center, 1922-33, mostly with NY Americans; won Hart Trophy, 1925; won Lady Byng Trophy, 1927; Hall of Fame, 1974.
b. Nov 20, 1900 in Yonkers, New York
d. Dec 1950
Source: *HocEn*

Burch, Dean
American. Lawyer, Government Official
Chm., FCC, 1969-74; senior adviser, Reagan-Bush campaign, 1980.
b. Dec 20, 1927 in Enid, Oklahoma
d. Aug 4, 1991 in Potomac, Maryland
Source: *AnObit 1991; BioIn 7, 8, 9, 10, 11, 12, 17, 18, 19; BioNews 74; BlueB 76; CelR; EncAJ; IntWW 74, 75, 76, 77, 78, 79, 80, 81, 82, 83, 89, 91; LesBEnT; NewYTBS 91; NewYTET; PolPar; PolProf J, NF; WhAm 10; WhoAm 74, 76, 78, 80, 82, 84, 86, 88, 90; WhoAmL 85; WhoAmP 73, 75, 77, 79, 81, 83, 85, 87, 89, 91; WhoGov 72; WhoSSW 73*

Burch, Robert Joseph
American. Author
Juvenile fiction writer: *Ida Early Comes Over the Mountain,* 1980, Juvenile Literary Guild selection.
b. Jun 26, 1925 in Inman, Georgia
Source: *AuBYP 2, 3; ConAu 2NR, 5NR, 5R; MorBMP; SmATA 1; ThrBJA; WhoAm 84, 86, 88, 90, 92, 94, 95; WrDr 76*

Burcham, Lester Arthur
American. Business Executive
Pres., FW Woolworth Co., 1964-70; chairman, CEO, 1970-77.
b. Apr 26, 1913 in Lancaster, Ohio
d. Jan 24, 1987 in Winston-Salem, North Carolina
Source: *BlueB 76; IntWW 74, 75, 76, 77, 78, 79, 80, 81; St&PR 84; WhAm 9; WhoAm 74, 76, 78; WhoE 74, 77; WhoFI 74, 75, 77*

Burchard, John Ely
American. Author, Historian
Wrote articles on housing, library planning, urbanism: *Architecture of America,* 1961.
b. Dec 8, 1898 in Marshall, Minnesota
d. Dec 25, 1975 in Boston, Massachusetts
Source: *AmAu&B; BioIn 4, 5, 10, 11; ConAu 1R, 6NR, 61; DrAS 74H; InSci; NewYTBS 75; ObitOF 79; WhAm 6, 7; WhoAm 74, 76; WhoWor 74*

Burchenal, Elizabeth
American. Dancer, Teacher
Leading authority on American folk dances, folk art, 1920s-30s.
b. 1876? in Richmond, Indiana
d. Nov 21, 1956 in New York, New York
Source: *BioIn 20; EncWomS; InWom SUP; NotAW MOD*

Burchfield, Charles Ephraim
American. Artist
Watercolorist, painted urban scenes, landscapes; won 1960 Gold medal for painting.
b. Apr 9, 1893 in Ashtabula, Ohio
d. Jan 10, 1967 in Gardenville, New York
Source: *BioIn 1, 2, 3, 4, 5, 6, 7, 8, 12, 13, 14, 15, 18, 19; BriEAA; CurBio 42, 61, 67; DcAmB S8; DcCAA 71; Dis&D; GrAmP; LinLib S; McGEWB; WebAB 74, 79; WhAm 4*

Burck, Jacob
American. Cartoonist
Created daily editorial cartoon in *Chicago Sun Times;* won Pulitzer, 1941.
b. Jan 10, 1904, Poland
d. May 11, 1982 in Chicago, Illinois
Source: *BioIn 12; ConAu 106; WhAm 8; WhoAm 74, 76, 78, 80, 82; WhoAmA 76, 78, 80, 82, 84N, 86N, 89N, 91N, 93N; WorECar*

Burckhardt, Carl Jacob
Swiss. Diplomat, Historian
League of Nations Commissioner for Danzig, 1937-39; pres., International Red Cross, 1944-48.
b. Sep 10, 1891 in Basel, Switzerland
d. Mar 3, 1974 in Geneva, Switzerland
Source: *BiDInt; BioIn 9, 10; ConAu 49, 93; EncTR 91; EncWL; NewYTBS 74; ObitOF 79; OxCGer 76, 86*

Burden, Carter
[Shirley Carter Burden, Jr.]
American. Lawyer, Publisher
Founder, Studio Museum in Harlem, collector of American abstract art.
b. Aug 25, 1941 in Los Angeles, California
d. Jan 23, 1996 in New York, New York
Source: *BioIn 21; CelR; NewYTBS 27; WhoAm 76, 78, 80, 82; WhoAmA 73, 76, 78, 80, 82, 84, 86, 89, 91, 93*

Burdett, Winston M.
American. Journalist
Joined CBS in 1943; Rome correspondent beginning in 1956.
b. Dec 12, 1913
d. May 19, 1993 in Rome, Italy
Source: *CurBio 93N*

Burdette, Lew
[Selva Lewis Burdette, Jr]
American. Baseball Player
Pitcher, 1950-67; often accused of throwing spitball; had 203 career wins.
b. Nov 22, 1926 in Nitro, West Virginia
Source: *Ballpl 90; BiDAmSp BB; BioIn 4, 5, 7, 15, 17; LegTOT; WhoProB 73*

Burdick, Eugene Leonard
American. Author
Wrote controversial, political theory best sellers, *Ninth Wave,* 1956; *Ugly American,* 1958; *Fail Safe,* 1962.
b. Dec 12, 1918 in Sheldon, Louisiana
d. Jul 26, 1965 in San Diego, California
Source: *AmAu&B; BioIn 5, 6, 7, 10, 13; ConAu 5R, 25R; DcAmB S7; EncSF; SmATA 22; TwCWr; WhAm 4; WhoSciF; WorAu 1950*

Burdick, Quentin Northrop
American. Politician
Dem. senator from ND, 1960—.
b. Jun 19, 1908 in Munich, North Dakota
d. Sep 8, 1992 in Fargo, North Dakota
Source: *AlmAP 80; BiDrAC; BiDrUSC 89; BioIn 5, 6, 9, 10, 11; CngDr 87; CurBio 63; EncAAH; IntWW 74, 75, 76, 77, 78, 79, 80, 81, 82, 83, 89, 91; PolProf J, K; WhAm 10; WhoAm 74, 76, 78, 80, 82, 84, 86, 88, 90, 92; WhoAmP 73, 75, 77, 79, 85; WhoGov 72, 75, 77; WhoMW 74, 76, 78, 80, 82, 84, 86, 88, 90, 92; WhoWor 80, 82, 87, 89, 91*

Burdon, Eric
[The Animals]
English. Singer
Vocalist for the Animals, War; solo albums include hit singles, Sky Pilot; San Franciscan Nights.
b. Apr 5, 1941 in Walker-on-Tyne, England
Source: *BioIn 13; ConMus 14; EncPR&S 74, 89; EncRk 88; HarEnR 86; IlEncRk; LegTOT; OxCPMus; PenEncP; RolSEnR 83; WhoRock 81; WhoRocM 82; WorAl; WorAlBi*

Burford, Anne McGill Gorsuch
"Ice Queen"
American. Lawyer, Government Official
EPA adminstrator under Reagan, 1981-83; resigned following "Superfund" management controversy.
b. Apr 21, 1942 in Casper, Wyoming
Source: *CurBio 82; Law&B 80; NewYTBS 82; WhoAmP 85; WhoAmW 85; WhoWest 80; WomPO 78*

Burger, Carl Victor
American. Author, Illustrator
Illustrated nature, children's books; wrote and illustrated popular "All About series."
b. Jun 18, 1888 in Maryville, Tennessee
d. Dec 30, 1967 in Mount Kisco, New York
Source: *BioIn 8, 11; ConAu P-2; IlsCB 1957, 1967; SmATA 9*

Burger, Warren E(arl)
American. Supreme Court Justice
Appointed chief justice by Richard Nixon, 1969; retired, 1986; advocated judicial reforms.
b. Sep 17, 1907 in Saint Paul, Minnesota
d. Jun 25, 1995 in Washington, District of Columbia
Source: *AmBench 79; AmPolLe; BiDFedJ A; BioIn 3, 8, 9, 10, 11, 12, 13; BlueB 76; CngDr 74, 77, 79, 81, 83, 85; CurBio 69, 95N; DrAS 74P, 78P, 82P; EncAB-H 1996; IntWW 93; IntYB 78, 79, 80, 81, 82; NatCAB 63N; NewYTBE 70; OxCLaw; OxCSupC; PolProf NF; SupCtJu; WebAB 74, 79; WhAm 11; Who 74, 82, 83, 85, 88, 90, 92, 94; WhoAm 74, 76, 78, 80, 82, 84, 86, 88, 90, 92, 94, 95, 96; WhoAmL 78, 79, 83, 85, 87, 90, 92, 94; WhoAmP 89; WhoE 77, 79, 81, 83, 85, 86, 89, 93; WhoGov 72, 75, 77; WhoWor 87; WorAl*

Burgess, Anthony
[Joseph Kell; John Anthony Burgess Wilson; John Burgess Wilson]
English. Author, Journalist
His inventive, sophisticated novels include *Clockwork Orange,* 1962; *Napoleon Symphony,* 1974.
b. Feb 25, 1917 in Manchester, England
d. Nov 25, 1993 in London, England
Source: *AnObit 1993; Au&Wr 71; AuNews 1; Baker 78, 84, 92; Benet 87, 96; BioIn 7, 8, 9, 10, 12, 13, 15, 16, 17, 18, 19, 20; BlmGEL; BlueB 76; BritWr S1; CamGEL; CamGLE; CasWL; CelR, 90; CnDBLB 8; ConAu 1R, 2NR; ConCom 92; ConLC 1, 2, 4, 5, 8, 10, 13, 15, 22, 40, 62, 81, 94; ConNov 72, 76, 82, 86, 91; ConSFA; CurBio 72, 94N; CyWA 89; DcArts; DcLB 14; DcLEL 1940; DrAF 76; DrAPF 80; EncSF, 93; EncWB; EncWL, 2, 3; FacFETw; HalFC 84, 88; IntAu&W 76, 77, 86, 89, 91, 93; IntWW 74, 75, 76, 77, 78, 79, 80, 81, 82, 83, 89, 91, 93; IntWWM 90; ItaFilm; LegTOT; LiExTwC; LinLib L; LngCTC; MagSWL; MajTwCW; MakMC; ModBrL, S1, S2; NewC; NewEScF; NewGrDO; News 94, 94-2; NewYTBS 93; Novels; OxCEng 85, 95; PenC ENG; RAdv 1, 14, 13-1; RfGEnL 91; RGTwCSF; ScF&FL 1, 2, 92; ScFSB; TwCRHW 90, 94; TwCSFW 81, 86, 91; TwCWr; TwCYAW; WebE&AL; WhAm 11; Who 74, 82, 83, 85, 88, 90, 92, 94; WhoAm 76, 78, 80, 82, 84, 86, 88, 94; WhoFr 79; WhoSciF; WhoTwCL; WhoWor 74, 76, 80, 82, 84, 87, 89, 91, 93; WorAl; WorAlBi; WorAu 1950; WrDr 76, 80, 82, 84, 86, 88, 90, 92, 94, 96*

Burgess, Gelett
[Frank Gelett Burgess]
American. Author
Humorist whose best-known poem was "The Purple Cow."
b. Jan 30, 1866 in Boston, Massachusetts
d. Sep 18, 1951 in Carmel, California
Source: *AmAu&B; AmLY; AnMV 1926; BenetAL 91; BiD&SB; BioIn 1, 2, 3, 4, 5; ChhPo, S1, S3; ChlBkCr; CmCal; CnDAL; ConAmL; ConAu 113; ConICB; DcAmAu; DcAmB S5; DcLB 11; EncAHmr; EncAJ; EncMys; EvLB; IlsCB 1744, 1946; LinLib L, S; LngCTC; NatCAB 14; OxCAmL 65, 83; REn; REnAL; ScF&FL 1; ScFEYrs, A; SmATA 30, 32; TwCA, SUP; TwCCr&M 80; TwCWr; WebAB 74, 79; WhAm 3; WhLit; WhNAA*

Burgess, Guy Francis de Moncy
English. Spy
Member of notorious British Foreign Office trio that passed classified data to Soviets, 1950s.
b. 1911 in London, England
d. 1963 in Moscow, Union of Soviet Socialist Republics
Source: *BioIn 9, 11, 17, 18, 21; ColdWar 1; DcNaB MP; EncCW; EncE 75*

Burgess, John Lawrie, Sir
English. Journalist, Broadcasting Executive
Chairman of Border Television, Great Britain, 1960-81.
b. Nov 17, 1912 in Carlisle, England
d. Feb 10, 1987
Source: *IntWW 83; Who 85; WhoWor 84*

Burgess, Smoky
[Forrest Harrill Burgess]
American. Baseball Player
Catcher, 1949-67; once held ML record for pinch hits in career, 145.
b. Feb 6, 1927 in Caroleen, North Carolina
d. Sep 15, 1991 in Asheville, North Carolina
Source: *Ballpl 90; BiDAmSp Sup; BioIn 8, 10, 17; WhoProB 73*

Burgess, Thornton Waldo
American. Author, Journalist
Wrote syndicated series of animal stories for children *Bedtime Stories.*
b. Jan 14, 1874 in Sandwich, Massachusetts
d. Jun 7, 1965 in Hampden, Massachusetts
Source: *AmAu&B; AuBYP 2, 3; BioIn 1, 2, 4, 5, 7, 8, 12, 13; CarSB; ChhPo; ConAu 41NR, 73; DcAmB S7; JBA 34, 51; LegTOT; MajAI; ObitOF 79; OxCAmL 65; REn; REnAL; SmATA 17; TwCChW 83, 89, 95; WhAm 4; WhNAA; WhoChL*

Burghley, William Cecil, Baron
English. Statesman
Queen Elizabeth I's most trusted minister; implemented execution of Mary Queen of Scots.
b. 1520
d. 1598
Source: *BioIn 2, 3, 4, 5, 8, 9, 11, 13, 17, 19; DcNaB; NewC; NewCBEL; REn; WhDW*

Burghoff, Gary
American. Actor
Played Radar O'Reilly in film *M*A*S*H,* 1970, and on TV series, 1972-79; only actor to play same character in film, on TV; won Emmy, 1977.
b. May 24, 1943 in Bristol, Connecticut
Source: *ASCAP 80; ConTFT 8; IntMPA 92, 94, 96; WhoAm 82; WhoHol 92*

Burgoyne, John, Sir
"Gentleman Johnny"
English. Army Officer, Dramatist
Defeated by Americans, surrendered at Saratoga, 1777.
b. Feb 24, 1722 in Sutton, England
d. Jun 4, 1792 in London, England
Source: *Alli; AmBi; AmRev; BbtC; BenetAL 91; BioIn 3, 4, 6, 7, 8, 9, 10, 11, 12, 17; BlkwEAR; BritAu; CamGEL; CamGLE; ChhPo; DcArts; DcCanB 4; DcEnL; DcInB; DcLEL; DcNaB, C; Dis&D; EncAR; EncCRAm; GrWrEL DR; HarEnMi; HisDBrE; LegTOT; LinLib L, S; NewC; NewCBEL; NotNAT B; OxCAmH; OxCAmL 65, 83, 95; OxCEng 67, 85, 95; PlP&P; REn; REnAL; RfGEnL 91; WhAm HS; WhDW; WhNaAH; WhoMilH 76; WorAl; WorAlBi*

Burke, Arleigh A(lbert)
"31 Knot Burke"
American. Naval Officer
Chief of staff, Atlantic Fleet, 1945-47; chief, US naval operations, 1955-61.
b. Oct 19, 1901 in Boulder, Colorado
d. Jan 1, 1996 in Bethesda, Maryland
Source: *BiDWWGF; BioIn 2, 3, 4, 5, 6, 8, 10, 11; BlueB 76; CurBio 55, 96N; DcAmMiB; HarEnMi; IntWW 74; OxCShps; St&PR 75; WebAMB; Who 74, 82, 83, 85, 88, 90, 92, 94; WhoAm 74, 76; WhoWor 74; WhWW-II*

Burke, Billie
[Mrs. Flo Ziegfeld]
American. Actor
Played Glinda, the Good Witch, in *The Wizard of Oz,* 1939.
b. Aug 7, 1886 in Washington, District of Columbia
d. May 14, 1970 in Verdugo City, California
Source: *BiE&WWA; DcAmB S8; Film 1, 2; FilmgC; MotPP; MovMk; NewYTBE 70; NotNAT B; RadStar; Vers B; WhAm 5; WhoStg 1906, 1908; WhScrn 77; WomWWA 14*

Burke, Billy
[William Burke]
American. Golfer
Touring pro, 1930s; won US Open, 1931; Hall of Fame, 1966.
b. Dec 14, 1902 in Naugatuck, Connecticut
d. Apr 19, 1972 in Clearwater, Florida
Source: *WhoGolf*

Burke, Christopher
American. Actor
First person with Down's Syndrome to star in TV series; plays Corky Thatcher on TV show "Life Goes On," 1989—.

b. Aug 26, 1965 in New York, New York

Burke, Delta
[Mrs. Gerald McRaney]
American. Actor
Played Suzanne Sugarbaker in TV comedy "Designing Women," 1986-91; star of TV series "Delta" 1992-93.
b. Jul 30, 1956 in Orlando, Florida
Source: *ConTFT 7, 15; IntMPA 92, 94, 96; LegTOT; VarWW 85; WhoAm 96, 97; WhoEnt 92; WorAlBi*

Burke, Edmund
English. Statesman, Orator
Leading parliamentarian, 1760s-90s; his views of government, tradition were admired by many American conservatives.
b. Jan 12, 1729 in Dublin, Ireland
d. Jul 9, 1797 in Beaconsfield, England
Source: *Alli; AmRev; AtlBL; BbD; Benet 87, 96; BiD&SB; BiDIrW; BioIn 1, 2, 3, 4, 5, 6, 7, 8, 9, 10, 11, 12, 13, 14, 16, 17, 18, 20; BlkwCE; BlkwEAR; BlmGEL; BritAu; BritWr 3; CamGEL; CamGLE; CasWL; Chambr 2; CmFrR; CyEd; CyWA 58; DcAmC; DcBiPP; DcEnA; DcEnL; DcEuL; DcInB; DcIrB 78, 88; DcIrL, 96; DcIrW 2; DcLB 104; DcLEL; DcNaB; Dis&D; EncAR; EncEnl; EncEth; EvLB; GrWrEL N; HisDBrE; LinLib L, S; LitC 7; LngCEL; McGEWB; MouLC 2; NewC; NewCBEL; OxCAmH; OxCAmL 65, 83, 95; OxCArt; OxCEng 67, 85, 95; OxCIri; OxCLaw; OxCPhil; OxDcArt; PenC ENG; PoIre; RAdv 14, 13-3; REn; RfGEnL 91; WebBD 83; WebE&AL; WhAm HS; WhAmRev; WhDW; WorAl; WorAlBi; WorLitC*

Burke, Glenn
American. Baseball Player
With Los Angeles, 1976-78; Oakland, 1978-79; first openly gay baseball player.
b. 1952
d. Jun 1995
Source: *Ballpl 90; BioIn 20, 21; GayLesB*

Burke, Jack, Jr.
American. Golfer
Turned pro, 1950; won PGA, Masters, 1956.
b. Jan 29, 1923 in Fort Worth, Texas
Source: *BioIn 2, 4, 5, 10, 15; WhoGolf*

Burke, James Edward
American. Business Executive
President, Johnson & Johnson Products, 1966-70; chairman, 1970-71; CEO, Johnson & Johnson, 1976-89.
b. Feb 28, 1925 in Rutland, Vermont
Source: *BioIn 12; NewYTBS 86; St&PR 84, 87; WhoAm 74, 78, 80, 88, 92, 94, 95, 96, 97; WhoE 83, 85, 86, 91; WhoFI 79, 81, 83, 85, 87, 89, 96; WhoWor 82, 84, 89, 91, 93, 95, 96, 97*

Burke, John
Irish. Author
Burke's Peerage published annually since 1847, first systematic genealogical compilation.
b. Nov 12, 1787 in Tipperary, Ireland
d. Mar 27, 1848 in Aachen, Prussia
Source: *Alli, SUP; BiDIrW; DcEnL; DcIrB 78, 88; DcIrW 2; DcNaB; NewC; PoIre*

Burke, Johnny
American. Songwriter
Lyricist for many Bing Crosby films, 1930s-50s; songs include "Pennies from Heaven."
b. Oct 3, 1908 in Antioch, California
d. Feb 25, 1964 in New York, New York
Source: *AmPS; AmSong; ASCAP 66, 80; BiDAmM; BiE&WWA; BioIn 4, 6, 9, 15; CmpEPM; ConAmC 76A, 82; EncAB-A 37; Film 2; FilmEn; FilmgC; HalFC 80, 84, 88; LegTOT; NatCAB 52; NotNAT B; OxCPMus; WorAl; WorAlBi*

Burke, Kenneth
American. Critic, Author
Among his writings are *A Grammar of Motives,* 1945; *Rhetoric of Motives,* 1950.
b. May 5, 1897 in Pittsburgh, Pennsylvania
d. Nov 19, 1993 in Andover, New Jersey
Source: *AmAu&B; AmWr; Au&Wr 71; Benet 87; BenetAL 91; BioIn 1, 4, 6, 8, 9, 11, 12, 13, 14, 15, 16, 17, 19, 20; BlueB 76; CamGLE; CamHAL; CasWL; CnDAL; ConAmA; ConAu 5R; ConLC 2, 24; ConLCrt 77, 82; ConNov 72, 76; ConPo 70, 75, 80, 85, 91; CyWA 89; DcLB 45, 63; DcLEL; DrAS 74E; EncWB; EncWL 3; EvLB; IntAu&W 89, 91; IntEnSS 79; IntWW 74, 75, 76, 77, 78, 79, 80, 81, 82, 83, 89, 91, 93; LinLib L; MajTwCW; ModAL, S1; NewYTBS 81; OxCAmL 65, 83; OxCTwCP; PenC AM; RAdv 1, 14, 13-1; REn; REnAL; RfGAmL 87; ThTwC 87; TwCA, SUP; WebE&AL; WhoAm 74, 76, 78, 80, 82, 84, 86, 88; WhoTwCL; WrDr 76, 80, 82, 84, 86, 88, 90*

Burke, Mike
[Michael Burke]
American. Baseball Executive
Chief executive, NY Yankees, 1966-73; president, Madison Square Garden, NYC, 1973-81.
b. Aug 6, 1916 in Enfield, Connecticut
d. Feb 5, 1987, Ireland
Source: *BioIn 9, 11, 13, 15; CurBio 72, 87, 87N; NewYTBS 82*

Burke, Paul
American. Actor
Played in TV series "Naked City," 1960-63; "Twelve O'Clock High," 1964-67.
b. Jul 21, 1926 in New Orleans, Louisiana
Source: *FilmEn; FilmgC; ForYSC; HalFC 80, 84, 88; IntMPA 75, 76, 77, 78, 79, 80, 81, 82, 84, 86, 88, 92, 94, 96; WhoHol 92, A*

Burke, Thomas
English. Author
Books on English life include *Limehouse Nights,* 1916.
b. Nov 1886 in London, England
d. Sep 22, 1945 in London, England
Source: *BioIn 4, 14; ChhPo, S1, S2; ConAu 113; EncMys; EngPo; EvLB; LngCTC; NewC; NewCBEL; REn; TwCA, SUP; TwCCr&M 80, 85, 91; TwCLC 63; WhE&EA; WhoHr&F*

Burke, William
[Burke and Hare]
Irish. Murderer
With William Hare, killed 15 people, sold bodies to surgeons for dissection; hanged.
b. 1792 in Orrery, Ireland
d. Jan 28, 1829 in Edinburgh, Scotland
Source: *BioIn 1, 4, 8, 10; CmScLit; DcIrB 78, 88; DcNaB; NewC; OxCLaw; OxCMed 86; WhDW*

Burke, Yvonne Watson Brathwaite
[Mrs. William A Burke]
American. Lawyer, Politician
First black woman elected to CA General Assembly, 1966; Dem. congresswoman, 1973-79.
b. Oct 5, 1932 in Los Angeles, California
Source: *BioNews 74; WhoWest 82, 87, 89, 92, 94*

Burkemo, Walter
"Sarge"
American. Golfer
Touring pro, 1950s; won PGA, 1953.
b. Oct 9, 1918 in Detroit, Michigan
Source: *WhoGolf*

Burkett, Jesse Cail
"The Crab"
American. Baseball Player
Outfielder, 1890-1905; won three batting titles; had lifetime .341 average; Hall of Fame, 1946.
b. Feb 12, 1870 in Wheeling, West Virginia
d. May 27, 1953 in Worcester, Massachusetts
Source: *BioIn 3, 7; WhoProB 73*

Burleigh, Harry Thacker
American. Singer, Songwriter
Collected, arranged black spirituals including "Swing Low, Sweet Chariot"; "Go Down Moses."
b. Dec 2, 1866 in Erie, Pennsylvania
d. Sep 12, 1949 in Stamford, Connecticut
Source: *ASCAP 66; BioIn 1, 2, 5, 6, 8, 9, 13; CurBio 41, 49; FacFETw; InB&W 80; ObitOF 79; WebAB 74, 79; WhAm 2*

Burlingame, Anson
American. Diplomat
Minister to China, 1861-67; negotiated Burlingame Treaty with US, 1868, promoting friendship, int'l. law.
b. Nov 14, 1820 in New Berlin, New York
d. Feb 23, 1870 in Saint Petersburg, Russia
Source: *AmBi; ApCAB; BiDrAC; BiDrUSC 89; BioIn 3, 9, 12; DcAmB; HarEnUS; McGEWB; NatCAB 8; NewCol 75; TwCBDA; WebAB 74, 79; WhAm HS; WhAmP; WhCiWar*

Burlington, Richard Boyle, Earl
English. Architect, Art Patron
Most influential art patron of time; promoted English Palladian architecture.
b. Apr 25, 1694 in London, England
d. Dec 3, 1753 in London, England
Source: *BioIn 14, 16, 21; DcArts; DcD&D; OxCArt; OxDcArt; WhoArch*

Burman, Ben Lucien
American. Journalist, Author
Last of his 22 books was *Thunderbolt at Catfish Bend,* 1984.
b. Dec 12, 1895 in Covington, Kentucky
d. Nov 12, 1984 in New York, New York
Source: *AmAu&B; AmNov; Au&Wr 71; BioIn 2, 3, 4, 10, 14, 15; ConAu 5R, 8NR; IntAu&W 82; LiHiK; NewYTBS 84; OxCAmL 65, 83, 95; REnAL; ScF&FL 92; SmATA 6; TwCA, SUP; TwCChW 83; WhAm 8; WhE&EA; WhNAA; WhoAm 74, 76, 78, 84; WhoWor 74, 76; WrDr 76, 80, 82, 84*

Burnaby, Frederick Gustavus
English. Traveler, Soldier
Journey across Russia on horseback described in *Ride to Khiva,* 1876; killed in battle.
b. Mar 3, 1842 in Bedford, England
d. Jan 17, 1885 in Abu Klea, Egypt
Source: *Alli SUP; BiD&SB; BioIn 1, 4; CelCen; DcNaB; HisDBrE; NewC; OxCEng 67, 85, 95*

Burne-Jones, Edward Coley, Sir
English. Artist, Designer
Late Pre-Raphaelite painter; joined with William Morris in Arts & Crafts movement to design furniture, books, tapestries.
b. Aug 23, 1833 in Birmingham, England
d. Jun 17, 1898 in London, England
Source: *AtlBL; Benet 87, 96; BioIn 1, 3, 4, 6, 7, 8, 9, 10, 11, 12, 13, 14, 16, 18; ChhPo, S2; ClaDrA; DcArts; DcBrBI; DcNaB S1; DcNiCA; DcVicP, 2; LegTOT; McGDA; McGEWB; NewC; NewCBEL; OxCArt; OxCEng 85, 95; OxDcArt; REn; WebBD 83; WorAl*

Burnet, F(rank) MacFarlane, Sir
Australian. Biologist
Pioneered work on human immune systems; shared Nobel Prize for immunology research, 1960.
b. Sep 3, 1899 in Traralgon, Australia
d. Aug 31, 1985 in Melbourne, Australia
Source: *AsBiEn; Au&Wr 71; BiESc; BioIn 1, 3, 4, 5, 6, 8, 9, 14, 15, 19, 20; ConAu 117; CurBio 54, 85; FarE&A 78, 79, 80, 81; InSci; IntWW 74, 75, 76, 77, 78, 79, 80, 81, 82, 83; McGEWB; NotTwCS; WhAm 9; WhDW; Who 74, 82, 83, 85; WhoNob, 90, 95; WhoWor 74, 78, 80, 82, 84; WorAl; WorAlBi; WorScD; WrDr 76, 80, 82, 84, 86*

Burnet, Gilbert
Scottish. Theologian
Influential bishop offered confidential advice to William and Mary; wrote *History of His Time,* 1734.
b. Sep 8, 1643 in Edinburgh, Scotland
d. Mar 17, 1715 in London, England
Source: *Alli; BioIn 1, 3, 11, 12, 15, 17; BritAu; CamGEL; CamGLE; CasWL; Chambr 2; CmScLit; DcBiPP; DcEnA; DcEnL; DcLB 101; DcLEL; DcNaB; EvLB; HisDStE; LuthC 75; McGEWB; NewC; NewCBEL; OxCEng 67, 85, 95; PenC ENG; REn; WebE&AL*

Burnett, Carol
American. Actor, Comedian
Best known as host of "The Carol Burnett Show," 1966-77; won many performance awards.
b. Apr 26, 1933 in San Antonio, Texas
Source: *BiE&WWA; BioIn 5; BioNews 74; BkPepl; CelR, 90; ConAu 127; ConTFT 1, 8; CurBio 62, 90; EncAFC; EncMT; FilmEn; FilmgC; ForWC 70; HalFC 84, 88; IntMPA 86, 92, 94, 96; InWom SUP; JoeFr; LegTOT; NewYTBE 73; WhoAm 86, 94, 95, 96, 97; WhoAmW 85, 95, 97; WhoCom; WhoHol 92, A; WhoThe 77, 81; WorAlBi*

Burnett, Charles
American. Filmmaker
Made films *To Sleep With Anger,* 1990; *The Glass Shield,* 1995.
b. 1944 in Vicksburg, Mississippi
Source: *CurBio 95; DcTwCCu 5; IntMPA 96; MiSFD 9; WhoAm 97*

Burnett, Frances Eliza Hodgson
American. Author
Wrote *Little Lord Fauntleroy,* 1886; *The Little Princess,* 1905; *The Secret Garden,* 1911.
b. Nov 24, 1849 in Manchester, England
d. Oct 29, 1924 in Plandome, New York
Source: *Alli SUP; AmAu&B; AmBi; AmWom; AmWomPl; AmWomWr; ApCAB, X; AuBYP 2; BbD; BibAL; BiD&SB; BiDSA; BlmGWL; CamGEL; CarSB; Chambr 3; ChhPo, S2; ConAmL; DcAmAu; DcAmB; DcBiA; DcLEL; DcNAA; DcNaB MP; EvLB; FacFETw; FamSYP; GrWrEL N; InWom, SUP; JBA 34; LibW; LngCTC; NatCAB 1, 20; NewCBEL; NotAW; NotWoAT; OxCAmL 65, 83; OxCEng 67, 85; PenC AM, ENG; REn; REnAL; SouWr; TwCA, SUP; TwCBDA; WhAm 1; WhoChL; WomWWA 14; WorAl; WorAlBi; YABC 2*

Burnett, Leo
American. Advertising Executive
Founder, chm., Leo Burnett Co., world's fifth largest advertising agency, 1935-71.
b. Oct 21, 1891 in Saint John's, Michigan
d. Jun 7, 1971 in Lake Zurich, Illinois
Source: *BioIn 2, 3, 4, 5, 6, 9, 13; ConAmBL; ConAu 116; DcAmB S9; EncAB-A 32; NewYTBE 71; WhAm 5, 6; WhoMW 74*

Burnett, W(illiam) R(iley)
[James Updyke]
American. Author
Wrote gangster story *Little Caesar,* 1929; film script of *Asphalt Jungle,* 1949.
b. Nov 25, 1899 in Springfield, Ohio
d. Apr 25, 1982 in Santa Monica, California
Source: *AmAu&B; AmNov; BioIn 1, 2, 4, 12, 13, 14, 15; CmMov; CnDAL; ConAmA; ConAu 5NR, 5R, 106; DcLB 9; DcLEL; EncMys; FilmEn; FilmgC; HalFC 80; IntMPA 75, 76, 77, 78, 79, 80, 81, 82, 84, 86, 88; LngCTC; NewYTBS 82; Novels; OhA&B; OxCAmL 65, 83, 95; PenC AM; REn; REnAL; TwCA, SUP; TwCCr&M 80, 85; TwCWr; WhAm 8; WhE&EA; WhNAA; WhoAm 74, 76, 78, 80, 82; WhoWor 74; WorEFlm; WrDr 82*

Burnett, Whit
American. Author, Editor
Co-founder of *Story* magazine, 1931; edited numerous anthologies.
b. Aug 14, 1899 in Salt Lake City, Utah
d. Apr 22, 1973 in Norwalk, Connecticut
Source: *AmAu&B; BenetAL 91; BioIn 4, 9, 10, 13, 20; ConAu 41R, P-2; CurBio 41, 73, 73N; DcLB 137; EncAJ; ObitOF 79; REnAL; ScF&FL 1; TwCA, SUP; WhAm 5; WhE&EA; WhoAm 74*

Burnette, Johnny
American. Singer, Composer
Guitarist; hits include "You're Sixteen," 1961.
b. Mar 25, 1934 in Memphis, Tennessee
d. Aug 14, 1964 in Clear Lake, California
Source: *BioIn 13, 21; EncRk 88; EncRkSt; HarEnR 86; LegTOT; OxCPMus; PenEncP; RkOn 74, 82; RolSEnR 83; WhoRock 81*

Burnette, Smiley
[Lester Alvin Burnette]
American. Actor
Gene Autry's sidekick in 81 films, 1935-42.
b. Mar 18, 1911 in Summun, Illinois
d. Feb 16, 1967 in Los Angeles, California
Source: *BiDAmM; BioIn 1, 7, 8; EncAFC; FilmEn; FilmgC; HalFC 80,*

84, 88; MotPP; ObitOF 79; QDrFCA 92; WhoHol B; WhScrn 74, 77, 83

Burney, Charles
English. Organist, Musicologist
Wrote four-vol. *A General History of Music,* 1776-89.
b. Apr 7, 1726 in Shrewsbury, England
d. Apr 12, 1814 in Chelsea, England
Source: *Alli, SUP; Baker 78, 84, 92; BiD&SB; BiDLA, SUP; BioIn 1, 2, 4, 5, 6, 7, 8, 9, 10, 19; BlkwCE; BlmGEL; BriBkM 80; CasWL; DcBiPP; DcEnA; DcEnL; DcEuL; DcLEL; DcNaB; EncEnl; MusMk; NewAmDM; NewGrDM 80; NewGrDO; NewOxM; OxCEng 67, 85, 95; OxCMus; OxDcOp; WhDW*

Burney, Fanny
[Madame d'Arblay; Frances Burney]
English. Author
Best-known work *Diaries and Letters,* 1778-1840.
b. Jun 13, 1752 in King's Lynn, England
d. Jan 6, 1840 in London, England
Source: *Alli; ArtclWW 2; AtlBL; BbD; Benet 87, 96; BiD&SB; BiDLA; BioIn 14, 15, 16, 17, 18, 19, 20; BlkwCE; BlmGEL; BlmGWL; BritAu 19; CamGEL; CamGLE; CasWL; Chambr 2; ContDcW 89; CyWA 58; DcArts; DcBiA; DcBiPP; DcBrAmW; DcEnA, A; DcEnL; DcEuL; DcLB 39; DcLEL; DcNaB; EncBrWW; EncEnl; EvLB; FemiCLE; GrWomW; GrWrEL N; IntDcWB; InWom, SUP; LegTOT; LinLib L; LngCEL; MacDWB; McGEWB; MouLC 3; NewC; NewCBEL; NinCLC 12, 54; OxCEng 67, 85, 95; PenC ENG; RAdv 1, 14, 13-1; REn; RfGEnL 91; WebE&AL; WhDW; WorAlBi*

Burnford, Sheila
[Philip Cochrane Every Burnford]
Scottish. Author
Wrote *The Incredible Journey,* 1961.
b. May 11, 1918, Scotland
d. Apr 20, 1984 in Bucklers Hard, England
Source: *ArtclWW 2; Au&Wr 71; AuBYP 2, 3; BioIn 7, 9, 10, 11, 15, 19; BkCL; BlmGWL; ChlBkCr; ChlLR 2; ConAu 1NR, 1R, 112; DcChlFi; FemiCLE; FourBJA; OxCCan; PenNWW A; Profile 1; ScF&FL 1, 2, 92; SmATA 3, 38N; TwCChW 78, 83, 89; WhoCanL 85, 87, 92; WrDr 76, 82, 84*

Burnham, Daniel H(udson)
American. Architect
Designed first fireproof skyscrapers; Union Station, Washington, DC, 1909.
b. Sep 4, 1846 in Henderson, New York
d. Jun 1, 1912 in Heidelberg, Germany
Source: *AmBi; AmCulL; ApCAB SUP; BiDAmAr; BioIn 6, 8, 9, 10, 12, 14, 19; BriEAA; CmCal; DcAmB; EncAAr 1; EncAB-H 1974, 1996; EncMA; GayN; LinLib S; McGDA; McGEWB; NatCAB 9; OxCAmH; TwCBDA; WebAB 74, 79; WebBD 83; WhAm 1, 4; WhoArch; WorAl*

Burnham, Forbes
[Linden Forbes Sampson Burnham]
Guinean. Political Leader
First prime minister of newly independent Guyana, 1966-70, of Co-operative Republic of Guyana, 1970-80.
b. Feb 20, 1923 in Kitty, British Guiana
d. Aug 6, 1985 in Georgetown, Guyana
Source: *BiDLAmC; BioIn 7, 8, 9, 12, 14, 16; ConAu 117; CurBio 66, 85, 85N; DcCPSAm; DcPol; DcTwHis; EncWB; InB&W 80; IntWW 74, 75, 76; IntYB 78, 79, 80, 81, 82; Who 85; WhoGov 72; WhoWor 74, 76, 78, 80, 82, 84*

Burnham, James
American. Editor, Author
A founding editor of *National Review* mag., 1955-78; wrote books warning of communist threat: *The Struggle for the World,* 1947.
b. Nov 22, 1905 in Chicago, Illinois
d. Jul 28, 1987 in Kent, Connecticut
Source: *AmAu&B; AnObit 1987; BiDAmLf; BioIn 2, 4, 11, 12, 13, 15, 16, 17, 18; ConAu 123; CurBio 41, 88, 88N; DcAmC; EncAI&E; EncMcCE; FacFETw; NewYTBS 87; PenC AM; PolProf E; ThTwC 87; TwCA SUP; WhAm 9; Who 74, 82, 83, 85; WhoAm 74, 76, 78; WhoWor 74, 76; WrDr 86*

Burnison, Chantal Simone
Belgian. Lawyer, Manufacturer
Pres., CEO, Chantal Pharmaceutical Corp., 1982—, a health and beauty products manufacturer.
b. 1950, Belgium
Source: *BioIn 14; News 88-3*

Burnley, James H, IV
American. Government Official
Succeeded Elizabeth Dole as Reagan's third transportation secretary, 1987.
b. Jul 30, 1948 in High Point, North Carolina
Source: *WhoAm 86*

Burns, Arthur Frank
American. Economist, Educator, Diplomat
Helped shape American economic policy; chm., Federal Reserve Board, 1970-78; ambassador to W. Germany, 1980-85.
b. Apr 27, 1904 in Stanislau, Austria
d. Jun 26, 1987 in Baltimore, Maryland
Source: *AmAu&B; AmEA 74; AmMWSc 73S; AmSocL; BioIn 3, 4, 8, 9, 10, 11, 12, 13; ConAu 13R; CurBio 53, 87; IntWW 74; NewYTBS 87; WebAB 74, 79; Who 74; WhoAm 74, 76, 78, 80; WhoAmP 73, 75, 77, 79, 81, 83, 85; WhoGov 72, 75, 77; WhoSSW 75; WhoWor 78, 80, 82, 84, 87; WhoWorJ 72; WrDr 76*

Burns, Bob
"Bazooka"; "The Arkansas Philosopher"
American. Actor
Nicknamed "Bazooka" after wind instrument he invented and played.
b. Aug 2, 1893 in Van Buren, Alaska
d. Feb 2, 1956 in San Fernando, California
Source: *DcAmB S6; EncAFC; FilmEn; FilmgC; HalFC 80, 84, 88; NatCAB 42; ObitOF 79; SaTiSS; WhAm 3; WhoCom; WhoHol B; WhScrn 74, 77*

Burns, Charles R
American. Clergy
Popular Roman Catholic priest dismissed in 1987 due to criticism of Church's stand on women, homosexuality and birth control.
b. 1939
Source: *ConNews 88-1; WhoMW 86*

Burns, Conrad Ray
American. Politician
Dem. senator, MT, 1989—.
b. Jan 25, 1935 in Gallatin, Missouri
Source: *BioIn 17, 21; CngDr 89; WhoAm 90, 92, 94, 95, 96, 97; WhoAmP 91; WhoWest 89, 92, 94, 96; WhoWor 91*

Burns, David
American. Actor
Won Tony for *The Music Man.*
b. Jun 22, 1902 in New York, New York
d. Mar 12, 1971 in Philadelphia, Pennsylvania
Source: *BiE&WWA; EncAFC; EncMT; FilmEn; FilmgC; HalFC 80, 84, 88; NewYTBE 73; NotNAT B; ObitOF 79; OxCAmT 84; OxCPMus; WhAm 5; WhoHol B; WhoThe 72; WhScrn 74, 77*

Burns, Diane M.
American. Poet
Publsihed first volume of poetry, *Riding the One-Eyed Ford,* 1981.
b. 1957 in California
Source: *BioIn 21; NotNaAm*

Burns, Edward
American. Filmmaker
Won Sundance Film Festival Grand Jury Prize for *The Brothers McMullen,* 1995.
b. 1968 in New York
Source: *News 97-1*

Burns, Eveline Mabel
American. Economist
Helped design Social Security Act, 1935; author *Toward Social Security,* 1936, explaining system to layman.
b. Mar 16, 1900 in London, England
d. Sep 2, 1985 in Newton, Pennsylvania
Source: *AmEA 74; BioIn 5; ConAu 117; CurBio 60, 86; InWom; NewYTBS 85; WhoAm 74, 76; WhoAmW 58*

Burns, George
[Burns and Allen; Nathan Birnbaum]
American. Comedian, Actor
Comedian whose career spanned vaudeville, TV, stage, film, concerts; won Oscar, 1976, for *The Sunshine*

Boys; comedy team with wife Gracie Allen, 1923-64.
b. Jan 20, 1896 in New York, New York
d. Mar 9, 1996 in Beverly Hills, California
Source: *BestSel 89-2; BioIn 2, 3, 4, 5, 7, 8, 10, 11, 12, 13, 14, 15, 16, 17, 21; CamGWoT; CelR, 90; ConAu 112, 151; ConTFT 3, 9; CurBio 51, 76, 96N; EncVaud; Ent; FacFETw; Film 2; FilmEn; FilmgC; ForYSC; Funs; HalFC 80, 84, 88; IntAu&W 91, 93; IntMPA 77, 80, 84, 86, 88, 92, 94, 96; IntWW 79, 80, 81, 82, 83, 89, 91, 93; JoeFr; LegTOT; MotPP; MovMk; News 96, 96-3; NewYTBS 27; NotNAT A; QDrFCA 92; RadStar; RkOn 85; WhAm 11; WhoAm 74, 76, 78, 80, 82, 84, 86, 88, 90, 92, 94, 95, 96; WhoCom; WhoEnt 92; WhoHol 92, A; WhoHrs 80; WhoWor 74; WorAl; WorAlBi; WrDr 88, 90, 92, 94, 96*

Burns, Jack
[Burns and Schrieber]
American. Comedian
Played straight man to Avery Schrieber in "Burns and Schrieber Comedy Hour," 1973.
b. Nov 15, 1933 in Boston, Massachusetts
Source: *BioIn 10; EncAFC*

Burns, James MacGregor
American. Author
Writes political biographies, particularly those of presidents; won Pulitzer, 1971, for Roosevelt biographies.
b. Aug 3, 1918
Source: *AmAu&B; AmMWSc 73S, 78S; Au&Wr 71; BioIn 4, 5, 6, 10, 11, 12; CelR, 90; ConAu 5R, 19NR, 43NR; DcLEL 1940; DrAS 74H; IntAu&W 91, 93; LinLib L; PolProf K; RAdv 14; WhoAm 74, 76, 78, 80, 82, 84, 86, 88, 90, 92, 96, 97; WhoE 95; WhoGov 72; WhoWor 74; WorAu 1950; WrDr 82, 84, 86, 88, 90, 92, 94, 96*

Burns, Jerry
[Jerome Monahan Burns]
American. Football Coach
Replaced Bud Grant as head coach, Minnesota Vikings, 1986-91.
b. Jan 24, 1927 in Detroit, Michigan
Source: *FootReg 86, 87; WhoAm 90; WhoMW 88, 90, 92*

Burns, John Horne
American. Author
The Gallery, 1947, best example of his colorful, forceful expression.
b. Oct 7, 1916 in Andover, Massachusetts
d. Aug 10, 1953 in Leghorn, Italy
Source: *AmAu&B; AmNov; BenetAL 91; BioIn 1, 2, 3, 4, 10, 15; ConAu 115; DcArts; DcLB Y85B; EvLB; LinLib L; ModAL; Novels; OxCAmL 65, 83, 95; PenC AM; REn; REnAL; RGTwCWr; TwCA SUP; TwCWr; WebE&AL; WhAm 4*

Burns, John L(awrence)
American. Business Executive
President, RCA, 1957-62; president, Boys Club of America, 1968-81.
b. Nov 16, 1908
d. Sep 8, 1996 in Greenwich, Connecticut
Source: *BioIn 5, 8; CurBio 96N; IntYB 78, 79, 80, 81, 82; NewYTBS 27; St&PR 75, 84, 87, 91; WhAm 10; WhoAm 78, 80, 82, 84, 86, 88, 90*

Burns, Ken(neth Lauren)
American. Filmmaker
Creator of historical documentaries including Emmy-Award winning, eleven-hour "The Civil War," 1990, and "Baseball," 1994.
b. Jul 29, 1953 in New York, New York
Source: *BiDFilm 94; ConAu 141; ConTFT 11; CurBio 92; IntMPA 96; LesBEnT 92; News 95, 95-2; WhoAm 94, 95, 96, 97; WrDr 96*

Burns, Pat
Canadian. Hockey Coach
Coach, Montreal, 1988-89, 1991-92; won Adams Trophy, 1989.
Source: *BioIn 16*

Burns, Robert
[Robert Burnes]
"Bard of Ayrshire"
Scottish. Poet
Beloved nat. poet; wrote songs "Auld Lang Syne" and "Comin' thro' the Rye"; most work in vernacular, praised lowland life.
b. Jan 25, 1759 in Alloway, Scotland
d. Jul 21, 1796 in Dumfries, Scotland
Source: *Alli; AtlBL; Benet 87, 96; BiD&SB; BioIn 1, 2, 3, 4, 5, 6, 7, 8, 9, 10, 11, 12, 13, 14, 15, 16, 17, 18, 19, 20; BlmGEL; BritAu; BritWr 3; CamGEL; CamGLE; CasWL; Chambr 2; ChhPo, S1, S2, S3; CmScLit; CnDBLB 3; CnE&AP; CrtT 2, 4; CyWA 58; DcArts; DcBiPP; DcEnA, A; DcEnL; DcEuL; DcLB 109; DcLEL; DcNaB; Dis&D; EvLB; FamAYP; GrWrEL P; LegTOT; LinLib L, S; LitC 3, 29; LngCEL; MagSWL; McGEWB; MouLC 2; NewC; NewCBEL; NewGrDM 80; OxCEng 67, 85, 95; OxCMus; PenC ENG; PoeCrit 6; RAdv 1, 14, 13-1; RComWL; REn; RfGEnL 91; RGFBP; WebBD 83; WebE&AL; WhDW; WorAl; WorAlBi; WorLitC*

Burns, Robin
American. Business Executive
Pres., CEO, Estee Lauder, 1990—.
b. 1953 in Colorado
Source: *BioIn 15; News 91, 91-2; NewYTBS 87; WhoAmW 91; WhoFI 92*

Burns, Tommy
[Noah Brusso]
Canadian. Boxer
Lost world heavyweight crown to Jack Johnson, 1908; Hall of Fame, 1960.
b. Jun 17, 1881 in Hanover, Ontario, Canada
d. May 10, 1955 in Vancouver, British Columbia, Canada
Source: *BioIn 1, 2, 3, 4, 10; BoxReg; ObitT 1951; WhoBox 74*

Burns, William John
American. Detective
With son, Raymond, founded William J Burns National Detective Agency, 1909.
b. Oct 19, 1861 in Baltimore, Maryland
d. Apr 14, 1932
Source: *ApCAB X; BiDAmBL 83; BioIn 8; DcAmB S1; DcNAA; NatCAB 15, 24; OhA&B; WhAm 1; WhScrn 77, 83; WorAl*

Burnshaw, Stanley
American. Author, Poet, Editor
Pres., editor-in-chief, Holt, Rinehart & Winston, 1939-58; wrote first anthology of modern Hebrew poetry, *The Modern Hebrew Poem Itself,* 1965.
b. Jun 20, 1906 in New York, New York
Source: *AmAu&B; AnMV 1926; BioIn 10, 15, 20; ConAu 9R; ConLC 3, 13; ConPo 70, 75, 80, 85, 91, 96; DcLB 48; DrAP 75; DrAPF 80; IntAu&W 76, 89, 91, 93; IntWWP 77; IntYB 78, 79, 80, 81, 82; OxCTwCP; REnAL; WhoAm 74, 76, 78, 80, 82, 84, 86, 88, 90, 92, 94, 95, 96, 97; WorAu 1950; WrDr 76, 80, 82, 84, 86, 88, 90, 92, 94, 96*

Burnside, Ambrose Everett
American. Army Officer
As general, commanded Army of the Potomac, 1862; governor of RI, senator; term "sideburns" named for him.
b. May 23, 1824 in Liberty, Indiana
d. Sep 13, 1881 in Bristol, Rhode Island
Source: *AmBi; ApCAB; BiAUS; BiDrAC; BiDrGov 1789; BiDrUSC 89; BioIn 1, 3, 6, 7, 17; CelCen; CivWDc; DcAmB; DcAmMiB; DcBiPP; Drake; EncSoH; HarEnMi; HarEnUS; IndAu 1917; LinLib S; NatCAB 4, 9; OxCAmH; TwCBDA; WebAB 74, 79; WebAMB; WhAm HS; WhAmP; WhCiWar; WhoMilH 76; WorAl*

Burpee, David
American. Horticulturist
Plant breeder who created, introduced new flowers and vegetables.
b. Apr 5, 1893 in Philadelphia, Pennsylvania
d. Jun 24, 1980 in Doylestown, Pennsylvania
Source: *AnObit 1980; BiDAmBL 83; BioIn 1, 3, 4, 5, 6, 10, 12; CurBio 55, 80N; DcAmB S10; FacFETw; NatCAB 16; St&PR 75; WhAm 7, 8; WhoAm 74, 76, 78, 80; WhoWor 78; WorAl; WorAlBi*

Burpee, W(ashington) Atlee
American. Horticulturist
Started world's largest mail-order seed house, 1876.

b. Apr 5, 1858 in Sheffield, New Brunswick, Canada
d. Nov 26, 1915 in Doylestown, Pennsylvania
Source: *BiDAmBL 83; BioIn 5; Entr; NatCAB 6; WebBD 83; WhAm 1; WorAl*

Burr, Aaron
American. US Vice President
VP under Thomas Jefferson who shot, killed Alexander Hamilton in duel, 1804.
b. Feb 6, 1756 in Newark, New Jersey
d. Sep 14, 1836 in New York, New York
Source: *Alli; AmAu&B; AmBi; AmPolLe; AmRev; AmWrBE; ApCAB; Benet 87, 96; BenetAL 91; BiAUS; BiDrAC; BiDrUSC 89; BiDrUSE 71, 89; BioIn 1, 2, 3, 4, 5, 6, 7, 8, 9, 10, 11, 12, 13, 14, 15, 21; CelCen; CyAG; DcAmB; DcBiPP; DcNAA; Dis&D; Drake; EncAAH; EncAB-H 1974, 1996; EncAR; EncCRAm; HarEnUS; LegTOT; LinLib S; McGEWB; NatCAB 3; OxCAmH; OxCAmL 65, 83, 95; OxCSupC; PeoHis; PolPar; PresAR; RComAH; REn; REnAL; TwCBDA; VicePre; WebAB 74, 79; WhAm HS; WhAmP; WhAmRev; WorAl; WorAlBi*

Burr, Henry
[Harry H McClaskey]
"Dean of Ballad Singers"
American. Singer
Known through radio, concerts, recordings; song "Goodnight Little Girl, Goodnight" sold over 3,000,000 copies.
b. Jan 15, 1885 in Saint Stephen, New Brunswick, Canada
d. Apr 6, 1941 in Chicago, Illinois
Source: *CurBio 41; ObitOF 79*

Burr, Raymond (William Stacy)
American. Actor
Starred in TV series "Perry Mason," 1957-66; "Ironside," 1967-75.
b. May 21, 1917 in New Westminster, British Columbia, Canada
d. Sep 12, 1993 in Dry Creek Valley, California
Source: *AnObit 1993; BiDFilm, 81, 94; BioIn 5, 6, 10, 19, 20, 21; BioNews 75; CelR; ConTFT 3, 9, 12; CurBio 61, 93N; DcArts; FilmEn; FilmgC; ForYSC; GangFlm; HalFC 80, 84, 88; HolCA; IntMPA 75, 76, 77, 78, 79, 80, 81, 82, 84, 86, 88, 92, 94; LegTOT; MotPP; MovMk; News 94, 94-1; NewYTET; WhAm 11; WhoAm 74, 76, 78, 80, 82, 84, 86, 88, 90, 92, 94; WhoEnt 92; WhoHol 92, A; WhoHrs 80; WhoWor 74; WorAl; WorAlBi; WorEFlm*

Burrell, Thomas Jason
American. Advertising Executive
Co-owner, largest black-owned advertising agency, Burrell Advertising 1971-74; owner, Burrell Communications Group, 1974—.
b. Mar 18, 1939 in Chicago, Illinois
Source: *AdMenW; WhoAm 84; WhoBlA 77, 85, 88*

Burrenchobay, Dayendranath
Mauritian. Political Leader
Governor-general of Mauritius 1978-84.
b. Mar 24, 1919
Source: *AfSS 79, 80, 81, 82; IntWW 78, 79, 80, 81, 82, 83, 89, 91, 93; Who 82, 83, 85, 88, 90, 92, 94; WhoWor 80, 82*

Burritt, Elihu
"The Learned Blacksmith"
American. Social Reformer, Author
Self-taught lecturer on pacifist causes; traveled, wrote extensively for world peace: *Sparks from the Anvil,* 1846.
b. Dec 8, 1812 in New Britain, Connecticut
d. Mar 6, 1879 in New Britain, Connecticut
Source: *Alli; AmBi; ApCAB; BiD&SB; DcAmB; Drake; OxCAmL 83; REnAL; WebAB 79; WhAm HS*

Burroughs, Edgar Rice
American. Author, Cartoonist
Wrote *Tarzan* series; more than 35 million copies sold.
b. Sep 1, 1875 in Chicago, Illinois
d. Mar 19, 1950 in Encino, California
Source: *AmAu&B; AmCulL; AmLY; ApCAB X; Au&Arts 11; BenetAL 91; BioIn 1, 2, 4, 6, 7, 8, 10, 12, 14, 15, 17, 19; CamGLE; CmCal; ConAu 104, 132; DcAmB S4; DcArts; DcLB 8; EncFWF; EncSF, 93; EvLB; FacFETw; FilmgC; GrWrEL N; HalFC 80, 84, 88; LegTOT; LinLib L; LngCTC; MajTwCW; MnBBF; NewEScF; Novels; OxCAmL 65, 83, 95; OxCChiL; OxCEng 85, 95; PenC AM; RAdv 14; REn; REnAL; RfGAmL 87, 94; RGSF; RGTwCSF; ScF&FL 1, 2, 92; ScFEYrs; ScFSB; ScFWr; SJGFanW; SmATA 41; TwCA, SUP; TwCLC 2, 32; TwCSFW 81, 86, 91; TwCWr; TwCWW 82, 91; TwCYAW; WebAB 74, 79; WhAm 2, 2A; WhE&EA; WhLit; WhoHr&F; WhoHrs 80; WhoSciF; WorAl; WorAlBi*

Burroughs, John
American. Author, Naturalist
Popular nature volumes include *Wake Robin,* 1871; *Birds and Poets,* 1877.
b. Apr 3, 1837 in Roxbury, New York
d. Mar 25, 1921
Source: *Alli SUP; AmAu; AmAu&B; AmBi; AmLY; AnCL; ApCAB, X; BbD; Benet 87, 96; BenetAL 91; BibAL; BiD&SB; BiDTran; BioIn 1, 2, 3, 4, 5, 6, 7, 8, 9, 10, 11, 12, 13, 15, 16, 17, 18, 20, 21; CarSB; Chambr 3; ChhPo; ConAmL; ConAu 109; DcAmAu; DcAmB; DcEnA A; DcLB 64; DcLEL; DcNAA; EncAAH; EvLB; GayN; InSci; JBA 34; LinLib L, S; McGEWB; NatCAB 1; NatLAC; OxCAmH; OxCAmL 65, 83, 95; PenC AM; REn; REnAL; TwCBDA; TwoTYeD; WebAB 74, 79; WhAm 1*

Burroughs, Margaret Taylor
American. Artist
Works in various mediums, art reflects social vision.
b. Nov 1, 1917 in Saint Rose Parish, Louisiana
Source: *AuBYP 3; BioIn 2, 8, 16; BlkWr 1; ConAu 21R, 25NR; ConBlB 9; NegAl 89; NotBlAW 1; SchCGBL; WhoAfA 96; WhoAmA 91; WhoBlA 75, 77, 80, 85, 88, 90, 92, 94*

Burroughs, William S(eward)
American. Author
A chief spokesman for the "beat movement," 1950s; wrote *Naked Lunch,* 1959.
b. Feb 5, 1914 in Saint Louis, Missouri
Source: *AuNews 2; Benet 96; BioIn 7, 8, 9, 10, 11, 12, 13; ConAu 9R, 20NR, 52NR; ConGAN; ConLC 1, 2, 5, 15, 22, 42, 75; ConNov 86, 96; ConPopW; CurBio 71; DcArts; DcLB 2, 8, 16; DcLEL 1940; EncSF 93; EncWL; GayLL; IntAu&W 76, 77, 82, 93; IntWW 77, 78, 79, 80, 81, 82, 83, 89, 91, 93; MakMC; ModAL S1; OxCAmL 65, 95; OxCEng 85, 95; PenC AM; REn; RfGAmL 94; WebAB 74, 79; WhoAm 74, 76, 78, 80, 82, 84, 86, 88, 92, 94, 95, 96; WhoUSWr 88; WhoWor 74, 95, 96, 97; WhoWrEP 89, 92, 95; WorAu 1950; WrDr 94, 96*

Burroughs, William Seward
American. Inventor
Developed practical calculator, 1891.
b. Jan 28, 1855 in Auburn, New York
d. Sep 14, 1898 in Citronelle, Alabama
Source: *BiDAmBL 83; BiInAmS; BioIn 8; DcAmB S1; HisDcDP; WebAB 74, 79; WhAm HS; WhDW; WorInv*

Burrows, Abe
[Abram Solman Burrows]
American. Dramatist, Author
Won Pulitzer, 1961, for *How to Succeed in Business Without Really Trying.*
b. Dec 18, 1910 in New York, New York
d. May 17, 1985 in New York, New York
Source: *AmAu&B; AnObit 1985; ASCAP 66, 80; BestMus; BiE&WWA; BioIn 1, 2, 3, 4, 5, 7, 10, 12, 14; CamGWoT; CelR; ChhPo S1; ConAu 110, 116; ConDr 73, 77, 82, 93; ConTFT 2; CurBio 51, 85N; EncMT; Ent; FilmgC; HalFC 80, 84, 88; LegTOT; ModWD; NatPD 81; NewCBMT; NewYTBS 85; NotNAT; OxCAmL 65, 83; OxCAmT 84; OxCPMus; WhAm 8; WhoAm 74, 76, 78, 80, 82, 84; WhoThe 72, 77, 81; WhoWor 74, 76; WhoWorJ 72, 78; WorAl; WorAlBi; WrDr 76, 80, 82, 84*

Burrows, Darren E
American. Actor
Plays Ed on TV show "Northern Exposure," 1990—.

Burrows, James
American. Producer, Director
Has directed "The Mary Tyler Moore Show," other comedies; co-creator, "Cheers," 1982. Other shows include "Frasier," "Friends," and "Caroline in the City," all NBC.
b. Dec 30, 1940 in Los Angeles, California
Source: *ConTFT 10; IntMPA 88, 92, 94, 96; MiSFD 9; WhoAm 92, 94, 95, 96, 97; WhoEnt 92; WhoTelC; WhoWest 96*

Burstyn, Ellen
[Edna Rae Gillooly]
American. Actor
Won Oscar, 1974, for *Alice Doesn't Live Here Anymore.*
b. Dec 7, 1932 in Detroit, Michigan
Source: *BiDFilm 81, 94; BioIn 10, 11, 12, 13, 16; BkPepl; CelR 90; ConTFT 1, 6, 13; CurBio 75; EncAFC; FacFETw; FilmEn; HalFC 80, 84, 88; IntDcF 1-3, 2-3; IntMPA 76, 77, 78, 79, 80, 81, 82, 84, 86, 88, 92, 94, 96; IntWW 78, 79, 80, 81, 82, 83, 89, 91, 93; InWom SUP; LegTOT; MovMk; NewYTBE 72; NewYTBS 75; NotWoAT; OxCAmT 84; WhoAm 76, 78, 80, 82, 84, 86, 88, 90, 92, 94, 95, 96, 97; WhoAmW 79, 81, 83, 85, 87, 89, 91, 93, 95, 97; WhoEnt 92; WhoHol 92, A; WomWMM; WorAl; WorAlBi*

Burt, Cyril Lodowic, Sir
English. Psychologist
A pioneer in field of educational psychology.
b. Mar 23, 1883 in London, England
d. Oct 10, 1971 in London, England
Source: *BiDPara; BiDPsy; BioIn 2, 8, 9, 10, 11, 12, 13, 14, 15, 20; ConAu 33R, P-1; DcNaB 1971; EncO&P 1; GrBr; InSci; NamesHP; NewCBEL; NewYTBE 71; WhE&EA; WhLit; WhNAA; WhoLA*

Burt, Maxwell Struthers
American. Author
Wrote *Powder River,* 1939; *Along These Streets,* 1942.
b. Oct 18, 1882 in Baltimore, Maryland
d. Aug 28, 1954 in Jackson, Wyoming
Source: *BioIn 1, 2, 3, 4; ChhPo, S2; DcLB 86; TwCA, SUP; WhJnl; WhLit*

Burtin, Will
American. Designer
Art director, *Fortune,* 1945-49; designer for govt., industry, NYC, 1949-72.
b. Jan 27, 1908 in Cologne, Germany
d. Jan 18, 1972 in New York, New York
Source: *BioIn 7, 9, 16; ConDes 84; DcTwDes; NewYTBE 72; WhAm 5; WhoGrA 62*

Burton, Gary
American. Musician
Jazz musician who received Grammy awards for *Alone at Last* in 1971 and *Duet* in 1979; inducted in Percussive Arts Society Hall of Fame, 1989; recorded *Six Pack* and *Benny Rides Again* in 1992.
b. Jan 23, 1943 in Anderson, Indiana
Source: *AllMusG; BiDAmM; BiDJaz; BioIn 7, 8, 11, 12; ConMus 10; EncJzS; IlEncJ; NewAmDM; NewGrDA 86; NewGrDJ 88, 94; PenEncP; WhoAm 74, 80, 82, 84, 86, 88; WhoWor 96*

Burton, Isabel Arundel
English. Traveler, Author
Wrote books about her travels with husband Sir Richard Burton.
b. Mar 20, 1831 in London, England
d. Mar 21, 1896 in London, England
Source: *Alli SUP; BioIn 10; DcEuL; InWom; NewC*

Burton, James
American. Musician
Guitarist; played with Rick Nelson, Everly Brothers.
b. Aug 21, 1939 in Shreveport, Louisiana
Source: *BgBkCoM; BioIn 13; EncRk 88; HarEnR 86; IlEncRk; OnThGG; PenEncP; WhoRocM 82*

Burton, John Hill, Sir
Scottish. Historian
Wrote *History of Scotland,* 1853-70.
b. Aug 22, 1809 in Aberdeen, Scotland
d. Aug 10, 1881 in Edinburgh, Scotland
Source: *Alli, SUP; BiD&SB; BritAu 19; CasWL; CelCen; Chambr 3; CmScLit; DcBiPP; DcEnL; DcLEL; DcNaB; EvLB; NewC; OxCEng 67; OxCLaw; PenC ENG*

Burton, Kate
[Katherine Burton]
Actor
Starred in CBS mini-series "Ellis Island," 1984; daughter of actor Richard.
b. Sep 10, 1957 in Geneva, Switzerland
Source: *BioIn 13; ConTFT 2; IntMPA 92, 94, 96*

Burton, LeVar(dis Robert Martyn Jr.)
American. Actor
Played young Kunta Kinte in TV series "Roots," 1977.
b. Feb 16, 1957 in Landstuhl, Germany (West)
Source: *BioIn 11, 20; ConBlB 8; ConTFT 7; DrBlPA 90; InB&W 80, 85; IntMPA 82, 84, 86, 88, 92, 94, 96; LegTOT; WhoAfA 96; WhoAm 86, 96, 97; WhoBlA 85, 94; WhoHol 92*

Burton, Michael
American. Swimmer
Only swimmer to win gold medal in 1,500 meters freestyle in two succesive Olympics, 1968, 1972.
b. Jul 3, 1947 in Des Moines, Iowa
Source: *WorDWW*

Burton, Montague Maurice, Sir
English. Merchant
A pioneer in field of industrial welfare.
b. Aug 15, 1885, Lithuania
d. Sep 21, 1952 in Leeds, England
Source: *DcNaB 1951; DcTwBBL; GrBr; ObitOF 79; ObitT 1951; WhE&EA*

Burton, Nelson, Jr.
American. Bowler, Sportscaster
Pro bowler since 1960; with ABC Sports since 1975; bowler of year, 1970; PBA Hall of Fame.
b. Jun 5, 1942 in Saint Louis, Missouri
Source: *BiDAmSp BK; BioIn 11; ConAu 57; WhoSpor*

Burton, Phillip
American. Politician
Dem. con. from CA, 1964-83; lost bid for House leadership by one vote, 1976.
b. Jun 1, 1926 in Cincinnati, Ohio
d. Apr 10, 1983 in San Francisco, California
Source: *AlmAP 78, 80, 82; AnObit 1983; BiDrAC; BiDrUSC 89; BioIn 10, 11, 12, 13, 21; CngDr 74, 77, 79, 81, 83; FacFETw; NewYTBS 75, 83; PolProf J, NF; WhAm 8; WhoAm 74, 76, 78, 80, 82; WhoAmP 73, 75, 77, 79, 81, 83, 85, 87; WhoGov 72, 75, 77; WorAl; WorAlBi*

Burton, Richard
[Richard Jenkins]
Welsh. Actor
Won Tony, 1961, for *Camelot;* nominated for seven Oscars.
b. Nov 10, 1925 in Pontrhydfen, Wales
d. Aug 5, 1984 in Geneva, Switzerland
Source: *AnObit 1984; BiDFilm, 81, 94; BiE&WWA; BioIn 3, 5, 6, 7, 8, 9, 10, 11, 12, 13, 14, 15, 16, 17, 18, 19, 20; BlueB 76; CamGWoT; CelR; CmMov; CnThe; ConAu 113; ConTFT 2; CurBio 60, 84N; DcArts; DcNaB 1981; DcTwCCu 1; EncEurC; EncMT; EncWB; EncWT; Ent; FacFETw; FilmAG WE; FilmEn; FilmgC; ForYSC; HalFC 80, 84, 88; IlWWBF, A; IntDcF 1-3, 2-3; IntMPA 75, 76, 77, 78, 79, 80, 81, 82, 84; IntWW 74, 75, 76, 77, 78, 79, 80, 81, 82, 83; ItaFilm; LegTOT; MotPP; MovMk; NewC; NewYTBE 73; NewYTBS 84; NotNAT, A; OxCAmT 84; OxCFilm; OxCLiW 86; WhAm 8; Who 74, 82, 83; WhoAm 74, 76, 78, 80, 82, 84; WhoHol A; WhoThe 72, 77, 81; WhoWor 74, 76, 78, 82; WorAl; WorAlBi; WorEFlm*

Burton, Richard Francis, Sir
English. Author, Explorer, Orientalist
Discovered Lake Tanganyika, 1858; noted for 16-vol. translation of *Arabian Nights,* 1885-88.
b. Mar 19, 1821 in Hertfordshire, England
d. Oct 20, 1890 in Trieste, Italy
Source: *Alli, SUP; AtlBL; BbD; Benet 87, 96; BiD&SB; BioIn 3, 4, 5, 6, 7, 8, 9, 10, 11, 12, 14, 15, 16, 17, 18, 19, 20, 21; BlmGEL; BritAu 19; CamGEL; CasWL; CelCen; Chambr 3; ChhPo, S2, S3; DcAfHiB 86; DcArts; DcBiPP; DcBrBI; DcEnA, A; DcEnL; DcEuL; DcInB; DcLB 166; DcLEL; DcNaB S1;*

Dis&D; EvLB; HisDBrE; IntDcAn; LegTOT; LinLib L, S; LngCEL; McGEWB; MouLC 4; NewC; NewCBEL; OxCEng 67, 85, 95; OxCIri; PenC ENG; PoIre; REn; VicBrit; WebE&AL; WhDW; WhWE; WorAl; WorAlBi

Burton, Robert
English. Author
Left one major work *The Anatomy of Melancholy,* 1621.
b. Feb 8, 1577 in Lindley, England
d. Jan 25, 1640 in Oxford, England
Source: *Alli; AtlBL; BbD; Benet 87, 96; BiD&SB; BioIn 2, 3, 5, 9, 11, 12, 14, 21; BlmGEL; BritAu; CamGEL; CamGLE; CasWL; Chambr 1; CroE&S; CrtT 1, 4; CyEd; CyWA 58; DcArts; DcEnA; DcEnL; DcEuL; DcLB 151; DcLEL; DcNaB; Dis&D; EvLB; GrWrEL N; LinLib L; LngCEL; LuthC 75; McGEWB; MouLC 1; NewC; NewCBEL; OxCEng 67, 85, 95; PenC ENG; RAdv 1, 13-1; REn; RfGEnL 91; WebE&AL; WhDW*

Burton, Tim
American. Director
Director of offbeat movies such as *Pee-Wee's Big Adventure,* 1985; *Beetlejuice,* 1988; *Batman,* 1989; *Edward Scissorhands,* 1990.
b. 1958 in Burbank, California
Source: *Au&Arts 14; BioIn 16; ConAu 148; ConTFT 9; CurBio 91; IntMPA 92, 94, 96; News 93-1; NewYTBS 89; WhoAm 90; WhoEnt 92*

Burton, Virginia Lee
American. Children's Author, Illustrator
Won 1943 Caldecott for *Little House;* wrote *Mike Mulligan and His Steam Shovel,* 1939.
b. Aug 30, 1909 in Newton Centre, Massachusetts
d. Oct 15, 1968 in Boston, Massachusetts
Source: *AmAu&B; AmWomWr; AnCL; ArtclWW 2; Au&ICB; AuBYP 2, 3; BioIn 1, 2, 4, 5, 7, 8, 9, 14, 19; Cald 1938; ChlBkCr; ChlLR 11; ChsFB A; ConAu 25R, P-1; CurBio 43, 68; DcLB 22; IlsBYP; IlsCB 1744, 1946, 1957; InWom, SUP; JBA 51; LibW; LinLib L; MajAI; OxCChiL; SmATA 2; TwCChW 78, 83, 89, 95; WrChl*

Burum, Stephen H
American. Filmmaker
Cinematographer whose abstract style of camera work was prominent in *8 Million Ways to Die,* 1986; *Rumble Fish,* 1983.
b. 1940? in California
Source: *ConNews 87-2*

Bury, John Bagnell
Irish. Historian
Wrote books on ancient history: *History of Freedom of Thought,* 1914.
b. Oct 16, 1861 in Monaghan, Ireland
d. Jun 1, 1927 in Rome, Italy
Source: *BiDIrW; BioIn 11, 14; CamGEL; Chambr 3; DcEnA A; DcIrB 78, 88; DcIrW 2; DcNaB 1922; EvLB; GrBr; LinLib L; LngCTC; NewCBEL; PenC ENG; PoIre; TwCA*

Busbee, George Dekle
American. Politician
Dem. governor of GA, 1975-82; succeeded Jimmy Carter.
b. Aug 7, 1927 in Vienna, Georgia
Source: *BiDrGov 1789, 1978; BioNews 74; BlueB 76; WhoAm 76, 78, 80, 82, 90, 92; WhoAmL 79; WhoAmP 85; WhoGov 77; WhoSSW 80, 82; WhoWor 82*

Busby, Jheryl
American. Business Executive
Pres., CEO, Motown Records, 1988—.
b. 1949 in Los Angeles, California
Source: *ConBlB 3; ConMus 9; WhoAm 90, 94, 95, 96; WhoBlA 92; WhoEnt 92*

Busby, Matthew, Sir
English. Soccer Executive
Manchester United Football Club, manager, 1945-69; director, 1971-80, pres., 1980—.
b. May 26, 1909
d. Jan 22, 1994 in Manchester, England
Source: *BioIn 8, 9, 10; Who 74, 82, 83, 85, 88, 90, 92, 94*

Buscaglia, Leo
[Felice Leonardo Buscaglia]
"Dr. Hug"; "Dr. Love"
American. Educator, Author
Lecturer on interpersonal relationships who wrote *Living, Loving, Learning,* 1982.
b. Mar 31, 1925 in Los Angeles, California
Source: *ConAu 110, 112; CurBio 83; LegTOT; WrDr 86*

Busch, Adolphus
German. Brewer
Developed process of bottling beers to withstand all temperatures, 1873; pres., Anheuser-Busch, 1880-1913.
b. Jul 10, 1839 in Kastel, Germany
d. Oct 10, 1913 in Langenschwalbach, Germany
Source: *BioIn 15; DcAmB S1; Entr; NatCAB 12; WebAB 74, 79; WhAm 1; WorAl; WorAlBi*

Busch, August Adolphus, III
American. Brewer, Business Executive
CEO, Anheuser-Busch, Inc., 1979—.
b. Jun 16, 1937 in Saint Louis, Missouri
Source: *BioIn 11, 12; Dun&B 86; News 88-2; NewYTBS 80; St&PR 84; WhoAm 74, 76, 78, 80, 82, 84, 86, 88, 90, 92, 94, 95, 96, 97; WhoFI 74, 75, 77, 79, 81, 83, 85, 87, 89, 92, 94, 96; WhoMW 80, 82, 84, 86, 88, 90, 92, 93, 96; WhoWor 84, 87, 89, 91, 95, 96, 97*

Busch, August Anheuser, Jr.
"Gussie"
American. Brewer, Baseball Executive
President, Anheuser-Busch, Inc., 1946-72; owner, St. Louis Cardinals, 1953-89.
b. Mar 28, 1899 in Saint Louis, Missouri
d. Sep 29, 1989 in Affton, Missouri
Source: *BioIn 4, 9, 10; CurBio 73; FacFETw; IntWW 74; News 90, 90-2; St&PR 75; WhoAm 82; WhoFI 75; WhoProB 73*

Busch, Charles
American. Actor, Dramatist
Played a two thousand-year old lesbian vampire in *The Vampire Lesbians of Sodom,* 1987.
b. Aug 23, 1954 in New York, New York
Source: *ConAu 145; ConTFT 10; CurBio 95; GayLesB; WhoAm 97*

Busch, Fritz
German. Conductor
Guest conductor with NY Met., 1945-49; renowned for performances of Mozart's works.
b. Mar 13, 1890 in Siegen, Germany
d. Sep 14, 1951 in London, England
Source: *Baker 78, 84, 92; BioIn 1, 2, 4, 9, 11, 14; BriBkM 80; CmOp; CurBio 46, 51; IntDcOp; MetOEnc; MusMk; MusSN; NewAmDM; NewEOp 71; NewGrDA 86; NewGrDM 80; NewGrDO; ObitT 1951; OxCMus; OxDcOp; PenDiMP; WhAm 3*

Busch, Niven
American. Screenwriter, Author
Novel *Duel in the Sun,* 1944 made into classic western film; wrote screenplay *The Postman Always Rings Twice,* 1946.
b. 1903 in New York, New York
d. Aug 25, 1991 in San Francisco, California
Source: *AmAu&B; AmNov; AnObit 1991; Au&Wr 71; BenetAL 91; BioIn 2, 4, 14, 15, 17, 18; CmMov; ConAu 7NR, 13R, 135; ConLC 70; DcLB 44; EncFWF; FilmEn; FilmgC; HalFC 80, 84, 88; IntMPA 75, 76, 77, 78, 79, 80, 81, 82, 84, 86, 88; LegTOT; NewYTBS 91; REn; REnAL; TwCA SUP; TwCWW 82, 91; WhAm 10; WhoAm 74, 76, 78, 80, 82, 84, 86, 88, 90; WhoEnt 92; WhoWor 74; WorEFlm; WrDr 84, 86, 88, 90, 92, 94N*

Busch, Wilhelm
German. Poet, Illustrator
Illustrated, wrote book of verses *Max and Moritz,* 1865.
b. Apr 15, 1832 in Hannover, Germany
d. Jan 9, 1908 in Mechtshausen, Germany
Source: *Benet 87, 96; BiD&SB; BioIn 1, 2, 3, 7, 12, 13, 14; CasWL; ChhPo, S1, S2, S3; ClDMEL 47; ConGrA 3; Dis&D; EuAu; EvEuW; LinLib L; McGDA; OxCGer 76, 86; PenC EUR; RAdv 14; REn; WhDW; WorECom*

Busching, Anton Friedrich
German. Geographer
Wrote *Neue Erdbeschreibung,* 1792, which laid foundation of modern statistical geography.
b. Sep 27, 1724 in Stadthagen, Germany
d. May 28, 1793 in Berlin, Prussia
Source: *BioIn 18; DcBiPP; Geog 6; InSci; NewCol 75; WebBD 83*

Buse, Don(ald R)
American. Basketball Player
Guard, 1973-85, mostly with Indiana; led NBA in assists and steals, 1977.
b. Aug 10, 1950 in Holland, Indiana
Source: *BasBi; BioIn 11; OfNBA 85; WhoBbl 73*

Busey, Gary
[Teddy Jack Eddy]
American. Actor, Musician
Starred in *The Buddy Holly Story,* 1978; *The Last American Hero,* 1973; *A Star is Born,* 1976.
b. Jun 29, 1944 in Goose Creek, Texas
Source: *BioIn 21; ConTFT 1, 6, 14; HalFC 84, 88; IntMPA 84, 86, 88, 92, 94, 96; LegTOT; NewYTBS 78; WhoAm 80, 82, 84, 86, 88, 90, 92, 94, 95, 96, 97; WhoEnt 92; WhoHol 92; WhoRocM 82; WorAlBi*

Busfield, Timothy
American. Actor
Emmy, Best Supporting Actor in a Drama, "Thirtysomething," 1991.
b. Jun 12, 1957 in Lansing, Michigan
Source: *ConTFT 15; IntMPA 92, 94, 96; LegTOT; WhoAm 92, 94, 95, 96, 97; WhoEnt 92; WhoHol 92*

Bush, Alan (Dudley)
English. Composer, Conductor
Traveled to USSR, wrote many operas about social rebellion; organizer, pres., Worker's Music Association, London, 1941-81.
b. Dec 22, 1900 in Dulwich, England
d. Oct 31, 1995 in Watford, England
Source: *Baker 78, 84, 92; BioIn 3, 6, 7, 21; BlueB 76; CmOp; CompSN, SUP; ConAu 110, 150; ConCom 92; DcArts; DcCM; IntAu&W 86; IntWW 74, 75, 76, 77, 78, 79, 80, 81, 82, 83, 89, 91, 93; IntWWM 77, 80, 85, 90; MusMk; NewGrDM 80; NewGrDO; NewOxM; OxCMus; OxDcOp; PenDiMP A; WebAB 79; Who 74, 82, 83, 85, 88, 90, 92, 94; WhoMus 72; WhoWor 74, 76, 78*

Bush, Barbara Pierce
[Mrs. George Bush]
American. First Lady
Established Barbara Bush Foundation for Family Literacy, 1989; wrote *C. Fred's Story: A Dog's Life,* 1984 as a contribution to literacy campaign; promotes voluntarism.
b. Jun 8, 1925 in New York, New York
Source: *ConAu 141; FacPr 89; IntWW 91, 93; MichAu 80; NewYTBS 81; WhoAm 82, 84, 86, 88, 90, 92, 94, 95, 96, 97; WhoAmW 83, 85, 87, 89, 91, 93, 95, 97; WhoE 81, 83, 85, 86, 89, 91, 93; WhoMW 96; WhoSSW 95, 97; WhoWomW 91; WhoWor 91, 93, 95, 96, 97*

Bush, Barney Furman
American. Poet
Awarded grant from the National Endowment for the Arts, 1981; published *Longhouse of the Blackberry Moon,* 1975.
b. 1945
Source: *NotNaAm*

Bush, George (Herbert Walker)
American. US President
41st US pres., 1989-93; vp under Reagan, 1981-89; CIA director under Ford, 1976-77.
b. Jun 12, 1924 in Milton, Massachusetts
Source: *AlmAP 88; WhoMW 96; WhoSSW 95, 97; WhoWor 80, 82, 84, 87, 89, 91, 93, 95, 96, 97; WorAl; WorAlBi*

Bush, George W(alker)
American. Politician, Baseball Executive
Partner, Texas Rangers baseball team, 1989—; Governor of Texas, 1994—.
b. Jul 6, 1946 in New Haven, Connecticut
Source: *St&PR 87, 91*

Bush, Guy Terrell
"The Mississippi Mudcat"
American. Baseball Player
Pitcher, 1923-45; best known for giving up Babe Ruth's last home run, May 25, 1935.
b. Aug 23, 1901 in Aberdeen, Mississippi
d. Jul 2, 1985 in Shannon, Mississippi

Bush, Kate
[Catherine Bush]
English. Singer, Songwriter
Hit singles include "Wuthering Heights," 1978; "Running Up That Hill," 1985.
b. Jul 30, 1958 in Bexleyheath, England
Source: *Baker 92; CurBio 95; EncRk 88; EncRkSt; HarEnR 86; IlEncRk; LegTOT; News 94, 94-3; NewWmR; OxCPMus; PenEncP; RkOn 85; RolSEnR 83; WhoAm 94, 95, 96, 97; WhoAmW 95*

Bush, Melinda
American. Publisher
Senior vp, publisher, *Hotel & Travel Index,* 1976—.
b. Jun 14, 1942 in Champaign, Illinois
Source: *CelR 90; WhoAmW 85; WhoE 91; WhoEmL 87; WhoWor 91*

Bush, Vannevar
American. Engineer
Built differential analyzer, the first analogue computer; pres., Carnegie Institute of Washington, 1939-55.
b. Mar 11, 1890 in Everett, Massachusetts
d. Jun 28, 1974 in Belmont, Massachusetts
Source: *AmAu&B; AmDec 1940; AsBiEn; BioIn 1, 2, 3, 4, 5, 7, 9, 10, 11, 15, 16, 18, 19, 20, 21; CelR; ConAu 53, 97; CurBio 40, 47, 74N; DcAmB S9; DcScB S2; EncAB-A 29; EncAB-H 1974, 1996; EncCW; EncWB; FacFETw; HisDcDP; InSci; IntWW 74; LarDcSc; LegTOT; LinLib S; McGMS 80; NewYTBS 74; NotTwCS; OxCAmH; PolProf E, T; RAdv 13-5; REnAL; St&PR 75; WebAB 74, 79; WebAMB; WhAm 6; WhNAA; Who 74; WhoAm 74; WhWW-II; WorAl; WorAlBi; WorInv*

Bush-Brown, Albert
American. Author, University Administrator
Chancellor, Long Island U, 1971-85; wrote *Architecture in America,* 1961.
b. Jan 2, 1926 in West Hartford, Connecticut
Source: *BioIn 6, 20; BlueB 76; ConAu 128; DrAS 74H, 78H, 82H; Dun&B 90; ODwPR 91; St&PR 84, 87, 91, 93; WhAm 11; WhoAm 74, 76, 78, 80, 84, 86, 88, 90, 92, 94; WhoAmA 73, 76, 78, 80, 82, 84, 86, 89, 91, 93; WhoE 86, 89, 93; WhoFI 83; WhoWor 74*

Bushell, Anthony
English. Actor
Was associate producer of Laurence Oliver's film *Hamlet,* 1949.
b. May 19, 1904 in Kent, England
Source: *Film 2; FilmEn; FilmgC; ForYSC; HalFC 80, 84, 88; IIWWBF; WhoHol 92, A; WhoThe 77A*

Bushkin, Joe
[Joseph Bushkin]
American. Jazz Musician, Bandleader
Pianist, trumpeter; led own quartet, 1950s-60s; accompanied Bing Crosby, late 1970s.
b. Nov 6, 1916 in New York, New York
Source: *AllMusG; ASCAP 66, 80; BiDAmM; BiDJaz; BioIn 2, 13; CmpEPM; EncJzS; NewGrDJ 88, 94; PenEncP; WhoAm 74; WhoHol 92; WhoJazz 72*

Bushman, Francis X(avier)
American. Actor
Romantic hero of silent films, 1911-28; played Messala in *Ben-Hur,* 1926.
b. Jan 10, 1883 in Baltimore, Maryland
d. Aug 23, 1966 in Pacific Palisades, California
Source: *DcAmB S8; Film 1, 2; FilmgC; MotPP; MovMk; ObitOF 79; OxCFilm; TwYS; WebAB 74, 79; WhAm 4; WhoHol B; WhScrn 74, 77; WorAl*

Bushmiller, Ernie
[Ernest Paul Bushmiller]
American. Cartoonist
Created comic strip Nancy.
b. Aug 23, 1905 in New York, New York
d. Aug 15, 1982 in Stamford, Connecticut

Source: *AnObit 1982; AuNews 1; BioIn 1, 10, 11, 13, 14; ConAu 29R, 107; EncACom; EncTwCJ; LegTOT; NewYTBS 82; SmATA 31N; WhAm 8; WhAmArt 85; WhoAm 74, 76, 78, 80, 82; WhoAmA 84; WorECom*

Bushnell, David
American. Inventor
Built man-propelled submarine boat, 1775; originated submarine warfare.
b. 1742 in Saybrook, Connecticut
d. 1824 in Warrenton, Georgia
Source: *ApCAB; BiInAmS; BioIn 5, 6, 10, 11, 14, 17; DcAmB; EncAR; EncCRAm; InSci; NatCAB 9; OxCShps; TwCBDA; WebAB 74, 79; WebAMB; WhAm HS; WhAmRev; WorAl; WorAlBi; WorInv*

Bushnell, Horace
''Father of American Religious Liberalism''
American. Religious Leader
Wrote *Forgiveness and Law,* 1874.
b. Apr 14, 1802 in Bantam, Connecticut
d. Feb 17, 1876 in Hartford, Connecticut
Source: *Alli, SUP; AmAu&B; AmBi; ApCAB; BbD; BenetAL 91; BiD&SB; BioIn 1, 2, 4, 5, 7, 9, 10, 12, 14, 17, 18, 19; CyAL 2; DcAmAu; DcAmB; DcAmC; DcAmReB 1, 2; DcBiPP; DcEnL; DcLB DS13; DcLEL; DcNAA; Drake; EncARH; LinLib L, S; LuthC 75; McGEWB; NatCAB 8; OxCAmH; OxCAmL 65, 83, 95; TwCBDA; WebAB 74, 79; WhAm HS*

Bushnell, Nolan Kay
''King Pong''
American. Computer Executive
Founder, chm., Atari, 1972-79, Pizza Time Theatres, 1979-83; chm. Octus Corp. 1991—; created video game ''Pong,'' 1972.
b. Feb 5, 1943 in Ogden, Utah
Source: *ConNews 85-1; LElec; WhoAm 84, 86, 88; WhoAmP 81, 83, 85; WhoFI 87; WhoWest 78*

Busia, Kofi A(brefa)
Ghanaian. Political Leader
Prime minister of Ghana, 1969-72; prominent intellectual, promoted African self-respect.
b. Jul 11, 1913 in Wenchi, Gold Coast
d. Aug 28, 1978 in Oxford, England
Source: *AfrA; AfSS 78; BioIn 8, 9, 11, 20, 21; BlkWr 2; ConAu 46NR, 69, 126; InB&W 80; IntDcAn; IntWW 74, 75, 76, 77, 78; McGEWB; SchCGBL; Who 74; WhoGov 72, 75; WhoWor 74*

Busoni, Ferruccio Benvenuto
Italian. Pianist, Composer
Acclaimed concert pianist; his opera *Dokter Faust,* produced 1925, seldom performed today.
b. Apr 1, 1866 in Empoli, Italy
d. Jul 27, 1924 in Berlin, Germany
Source: *AtlBL; Baker 84; BioIn 1, 2, 3, 4, 7, 8, 9, 10, 12; DcCM; MakMC; McGEWB; OxCMus*

Busoni, Rafaello
American. Artist
Illustrated books for Heritage, Limited Editions Press.
b. Feb 1, 1900 in Berlin, Germany
d. Mar 17, 1962 in New York, New York
Source: *AmAu&B; AuBYP 2, 3; BioIn 1, 2, 3, 5, 6, 7, 8, 12; ConAu 117; IlsCB 1744, 1946, 1957; JBA 51; SmATA 16; WhAmArt 85*

Buss, Jerry Hatten
American. Businessman, Sports Executive
Self-made multi-millionaire; owner, LA Lakers basketball team; former owner, LA Kings hockey team.
b. Jan 27, 1933 in Salt Lake City, Utah
Source: *BioIn 12; NewYTBS 79; WhoAm 80, 82, 84, 86; WhoFI 81; WhoWest 82, 84*

Busse, Henry
American. Jazz Musician, Bandleader
Trumpeter for Paul Whiteman, 1918-28; noted for exaggerated vibrato; led own bands, 1930s-40s.
b. May 19, 1894 in Magdeburg, Germany
d. Apr 23, 1955 in Memphis, Tennessee
Source: *ASCAP 66, 80; BgBands 74; BioIn 2, 3; CmpEPM; OxCPMus; PenEncP*

Bustamante, John H
American. Banker
Co-founder, pres. of First Bank National in Cleveland, 1974—.
b. Aug 11, 1929 in Santiago de Cuba, Cuba
Source: *BioIn 10, 13; WhoBlA 85, 88*

Bustamante, William Alexander Clarke, Sir
Jamaican. Political Leader
Prime minister, 1962-77; led Labour Party, 1943-77.
b. Feb 24, 1884 in Blenheim, Jamaica
d. Aug 6, 1977 in Kingston, Jamaica
Source: *BioIn 1, 2, 6, 7, 10, 11, 12; IntWW 74; WhAm 7*

Busta Rhymes
[Trevor Smith]
American. Rapper
Co-founded rap group Leaders of the New School and released debut album, *A Future Without A Past. . .,* 1991, and later produced *T.I.M.E,* 1993; recorded solo album, *The Coming,* 1996
b. 1972 in New York, New York

Butala, Tony
[The Letterman]
American. Singer
Member of trio who rejuvenated group, expanded touring, 1970s-80s.
b. Nov 20, 1940 in Sharon, Pennsylvania
Source: *WhoRocM 82*

Butcher, Susan
American. Athlete
Four-time winner of Iditarod Trail Sled Dog Race, 1986-88, 1990.
b. Dec 26, 1954 in Boston, Massachusetts
Source: *BioIn 13, 15; CurBio 91; EncWomS; News 90, 91, 91-1, 91-2; WhoAmW 91; WhoSpor; WomStre*

Butcher, Willard C(arlisle)
American. Banker
President, Chase Manhattan Bank, 1972-81; CEO, 1980-90; chm., 1981-90.
b. Oct 25, 1926 in Bronxville, New York
Source: *BioIn 12, 13; CurBio 80; IntWW 74, 75, 76, 77, 78, 79, 80, 81, 82, 83, 89, 91, 93; NewYTBS 79; Who 82, 83, 85, 88, 90, 92, 94; WhoAm 74, 76, 78, 80, 82, 84, 86, 88, 90, 92, 94, 95, 96; WhoE 74, 77, 79, 81, 83, 85, 86, 89, 91, 95; WhoFI 74, 75, 79, 81, 83, 85, 87; WhoWor 82, 84, 91, 93, 97*

Butenandt, Adolf Fredrick Johann
German. Chemist
Isolated and analyzed sex hormones; won Nobel Prize, 1939; Nazi govt. forced him to refuse it; received in 1949.
b. Mar 24, 1903 in Bremerhaven-Lebe, Germany
d. Jan 18, 1995 in Munich, Germany
Source: *BiESc; IntWW 83; McGMS 80; Who 83; WhoNob; WhoWor 82; WorAl*

Buthelezi, Gatsha Mangosuthu
South African. Political Leader
Descendant of Zulu royalty; has served as head of Kwazulu, semi-autonomous Zulu homeland within S Africa since 1970.
b. Aug 27, 1928 in Mahlabatini, South Africa
Source: *BioIn 15, 16; CurBio 86; DcTwHis; WhoAfr*

Butkus, Dick
[Richard J Butkus]
''Animal''; ''Maestro of Mayhem''; ''Paddles''; ''The Enforcer''
American. Football Player, Actor
Seven-time all-pro linebacker, Chicago, 1965-73; Hall of Fame, 1979; sportscast er, CBS *NFL Today,* 1988-89.
b. Dec 9, 1942 in Chicago, Illinois
Source: *BioIn 8, 9, 10; CelR; ConTFT 7; ItaFilm; LegTOT; NewYTBS 74; WhoAm 74, 76, 78, 80, 82, 84, 86, 88, 92, 94, 95, 96, 97; WhoEnt 92; WhoFtbl 74; WhoSpor; WhoWor 78; WorAl; WorAlBi*

Butler, Alban
English. Author, Clergy
Catholic priest; author of two important works: *The Lives of the Fathers, Martyrs, and other Principal Saints* and *Lives of the Saints.*
b. Oct 24, 1710 in Northampton, England
d. May 15, 1773 in Saint-Omer, France

Source: *Alli; DcBiPP; DcCathB; DcEnL; DcNaB; NewC; OxCEng 67*

Butler, Benjamin Franklin
American. Army Officer, Politician
Commanded Ft. Monroe, VA during Civil War; managed impeachment trial of Andrew Johnson in Congress.
b. Nov 5, 1818 in Deerfield, New Hampshire
d. Jan 11, 1893 in Washington, District of Columbia
Source: *AmBi; AmPolLe; ApCAB; BiAUS; BiDrAC; BiDrGov 1789; BiDrUSC 89; BioIn 1, 2, 3, 4, 5, 6, 7, 8, 10, 13, 14, 16, 17; CelCen; CivWDc; CyAG; DcAmAu; DcAmB; DcAmMiB; DcAmTB; DcBiPP; DcNAA; Drake; EncAACR; EncAB-H 1974, 1996; HarEnMi; HarEnUS; LinLib S; NatCAB 1; OxCAmH; TwCBDA; WebAB 74, 79; WebAMB; WhAm HS; WhAmP; WhCiWar; WorAl; WorAlBi*

Butler, Brett
American. Baseball Player
Outfielder, Atlanta, 1981-83; Cleveland, 1984-88; San Francisco, 1988-91; Los Angeles, 1991—; led AL in triples, 1986.
b. Jun 15, 1957 in Los Angeles, California
Source: *Ballpl 90; LegTOT*

Butler, Brett
American. Actor
Star of TV's "Grace Under Fire," 1993—.
b. Jan 30, 1958 in Montgomery, Alabama
Source: *LegTOT; News 95, 95-1; WhoAmW 95, 97*

Butler, Daws
[Charles Dawson Butler]
American. Entertainer
Voice of many cartoon characters including Yogi Bear, Huckleberry Hound, Quick Draw McGraw.
b. Nov 16, 1916 in Toledo, Ohio
d. May 18, 1988 in Los Angeles, California
Source: *IntMPA 75, 76, 77, 78, 79, 80, 81, 82, 84, 86, 88*

Butler, Eleanor, Lady
[Ladies of Llangollen]
Irish. Writer
Eloped with fellow noblewoman Sarah Ponsonby.
b. 1739
d. 1829
Source: *GayLesB; OxCLiW 86*

Butler, John
American. Choreographer, Dancer
Student of Martha Graham; prolific opera choreographer.
b. Sep 29, 1920 in Memphis, Tennessee
d. Sep 11, 1993 in New York, New York
Source: *BiDD; BiE&WWA; BioIn 3, 4, 7, 9; CmpGMD; CnOxB; CurBio 93N; DancEn 78; IntDcB; WhoAm 74; WhoMus 72; WhoWor 74*

Butler, Joseph
English. Philosopher, Theologian
Wrote *The Analogy of Religion,* 1736; manuscripts destroyed on his death at his request.
b. May 18, 1692 in Wantage, England
d. Jun 16, 1752 in Bath, England
Source: *Alli; BiD&SB; BioIn 1, 3, 8, 9, 13; BlkwCE; BritAu; CamGEL; CamGLE; CasWL; Chambr 2; DcBiPP; DcEnA; DcEnL; DcEuL; DcNaB, C; EncEnl; EncEth; EncWM; EvLB; LinLib L, S; LuthC 75; McGEWB; NewC; NewCBEL; OxCEng 67, 85, 95; OxCPhil; PenC ENG; RAdv 14; REn; WebE&AL; WhDW*

Butler, Matthew Calbraith
American. Soldier, Statesman
Major-general, Confederate Army; US senator, 1877-95.
b. Mar 8, 1836 in Greenville, South Carolina
d. Apr 14, 1909 in Columbia, South Carolina
Source: *AmBi; ApCAB; BiDConf; BiDrAC; BiDrUSC 89; BiDSA; BioIn 5; CivWDc; DcAmB; EncSoH; HarEnUS; NatCAB 1; TwCBDA; WhAm 1; WhAmP; WhCiWar*

Butler, Michael
American. Businessman, Financier
Adviser to senator John F Kennedy for Indian, Middle East affairs; produced musical *Hair.*
b. Nov 26, 1926 in Chicago, Illinois
Source: *BioIn 8, 9; BlueB 76; CelR; IntWW 74, 75, 79, 80, 81, 82, 83, 89; IntYB 78, 79, 80, 81, 82; WhoAm 74, 76, 78, 80, 82, 84, 86; WhoWor 74*

Butler, Nicholas Murray
American. Educator
Pres., Columbia U, 1902-45; shared 1931 Nobel Peace Prize for support of world peace, Kellogg-Briand pact.
b. Apr 2, 1862 in Elizabeth, New Jersey
d. Dec 4, 1947 in New York, New York
Source: *Alli SUP; AmAu&B; AmDec 1920; AmPeW; AmSocL; ApCAB X; BenetAL 91; BiDAmEd; BiDInt; BioIn 1, 2, 3, 5, 9, 10, 11; ChhPo S2; CurBio 40, 47; DcAmAu; DcAmB S4; DcAmDH 80, 89; DcAmSR; DcNAA; EncAB-H 1974, 1996; HarEnUS; LinLib L, S; McGEWB; MorMA; NatCAB 9, 34; NobelP; OxCAmH; OxCAmL 65, 83, 95; PolPar; REnAL; TwCBDA; WebAB 74, 79; WebBD 83; WhAm 2; WhE&EA; WhLit; WhNAA; WhoNob, 90, 95; WorAl; WorAlBi*

Butler, Octavia E(stelle)
American. Author
Wrote *Patternmaster,* 1976; *Imago,* 1989; winner of two Hugo Awards and one Nebula Award.
b. Jun 22, 1947 in Pasadena, California
Source: *AmWomWr SUP; BlkWr 2; ConAu 38NR; ConPopW; EncSF 93; OxCAmL 95; RfGAmL 94; SmATA 84; TwCYAW; WhoAm 96, 97; WhoAmW 89, 91; WhoEmL 89, 91, 93; WhoWest 87*

Butler, Paul
American. Industrialist
Founded Butler Aviation Co., 1946, providing fuel, service for private aircraft.
b. Jun 23, 1892 in Chicago, Illinois
d. Jun 24, 1981 in Oak Brook, Illinois
Source: *BioIn 6, 12; NewYTBS 81; WhAm 8; WhoFI 74, 75*

Butler, Robert
American. Director
Won Emmy for direction of "Hill Street Blues," 1981.
b. Nov 16, 1927 in Los Angeles, California
Source: *ConTFT 12; MiSFD 9; VarWW 85*

Butler, Robert N(eil)
American. Physician, Psychiatrist
An authority on the aging process; won Pulitzer for *Why Survive?,* 1975.
b. Jan 21, 1927 in New York, New York
Source: *AmMWSc 73P, 76P, 79, 82, 86, 89, 92, 95; BiDrAPA 77, 89; BioIn 10, 11, 13; ConAu 41R; IntMed 80; WhoAm 78, 80, 82, 84, 86, 88, 90, 92, 94, 95, 96, 97; WhoAmP 73, 75, 77; WhoE 79, 81, 83, 85, 86, 91; WhoFrS 84; WhoMedH; WhoScEn 96; WhoSSW 73, 75, 76*

Butler, Robert Olen
American. Author
Author of *A Good Scent from a Strange Mountain,* 1993; won 1993 Pulitzer Prize for Fiction.
b. Jan 20, 1945 in Granite City, Illinois
Source: *BiDConC; ConAu 112; ConLC 81; DcLB 173; IntAu&W 89; WhoAm 94, 95, 96, 97; WhoSSW 95, 97; WhoUSWr 88; WhoWrEP 89, 92, 95*

Butler, Samuel
English. Poet
Famous for mock epic *Hudibras,* ridiculing the Puritans.
b. Feb 14, 1612 in Langar, England
d. Sep 25, 1680 in London, England
Source: *Alli; AtlBL; BbD; Benet 87, 96; BiD&SB; BioIn 2, 3, 5, 7, 9, 10, 11, 17, 19; BlmGEL; BritAu; CamGEL; CamGLE; CasWL; ChhPo, S1; CnE&AP; CrtT 2, 4; CyWA 58; DcArts; DcBiPP; DcEnA; DcEnL; DcEuL; DcLB 126; DcLEL; DcNaB, C; Dis&D; EvLB; LegTOT; LinLib L, S; LitC 16; LngCEL; MouLC 1; NewC; OxCEng 67, 85; PenC ENG; REn; WebE&AL; WhDW*

Butler, Samuel
English. Author
Wrote realistic novel *Way of All Flesh,* 1903; satire *Erewhon,* 1872.

b. Dec 4, 1835 in Nottinghamshire, England
d. Jun 18, 1902 in London, England
Source: *Alli SUP; AtlBL; BbD; Benet 87, 96; BioIn 1, 2, 3, 4, 5, 6, 7, 8, 9, 10, 11, 12, 13, 14, 16, 17, 18; BlmGEL; BritAu 19; BritWr S2; CamGEL; CamGLE; CasWL; CnDBLB 5; CnMWL; ConAu 104, 143; CrtT 3; CyWA 58; DcArts; DcBrAr 2; DcEnA, A; DcEuL; DcLB 18, 57, 174; DcLEL; DcNaB S2; EncSF, 93; EvLB; GrWrEL N; LegTOT; LinLib L, S; LngCEL; LngCTC; McGEWB; ModBrL; NewC; NewCBEL; NewGrDM 80; Novels; OxCEng 67, 85, 95; OxCMus; OxCPhil; PenC ENG; RAdv 1, 14, 13-1; REn; RfGEnL 91; ScF&FL 1; ScFEYrs; ScFSB; StaCVF; TwCLC 1, 33; TwCSFW 81, 86, 91; VicBrit; WebE&AL; WhDW; WorAl; WorAlBi; WorLitC*

Butler of Saffron Walden, Richard Austen, Baron
"Rab"
English. Statesman
Conservative MP, 1929-65.
b. Dec 9, 1902 in Attock Serai, India
d. Mar 9, 1982 in Great Yeldham, England
Source: *AnObit 1982; BioIn 18; CurBio 44, 82; IntWW 78, 79; Who 82; WhoWor 78; WrDr 82*

Butlin, William Heygate Edmund, Sir
English. Businessman
Pioneer of holiday camps; were national institution by 1960.
b. Sep 29, 1899 in Cape Town, South Africa
d. Jun 12, 1980 in Isle of Jersey, England
Source: *BlueB 76; IntWW 81; Who 74*

Butor, Michel
French. Author
Wrote *Passing Time,* 1957; *Second Thoughts,* 1957; *Degrees,* 1960.
b. Sep 14, 1926 in Mans-en-Baroeul, France
Source: *Au&Wr 71, 3; EuWr 13; EvEuW; FacFETw; GuFrLit 1; IntAu&W 89; IntWW 74, 75, 76, 77, 78, 79, 80, 81, 82, 83, 89, 91, 93; LinLib L; MajTwCW; ModFrL; ModRL; NewEScF; NewGrDM 80; Novels; OxCEng 85, 95; PenC EUR; RAdv 14, 13-2; REn; TwCCr&M 80B, 85B; TwCWr; WhoFr 79; WhoTwCL; WhoWor 74, 84, 87, 89, 91, 93, 95, 96, 97; WorAlBi; WorAu 1950*

Buttafuoco, Joey
[Joseph Buttafuoco]
American. Actor
Convicted of having an affair with teenager, Amy Fisher, who gunned his wife down in a murder attempt; pursued an acting career beginning in 1996.
b. 1956 in Massapequa, New York

Buttafuoco, Mary Jo
American. Victim
Victim of murder attempt by husband's alleged teenage lover, Amy Fisher.
Source: *BioIn 17, 18, 19, 20*

Buttenheim, Edgar Joseph
American. Publisher
Pres., American City Magazine Corp., 1911-64; chm., Buttenheim Publishing Corp.
b. Oct 16, 1882 in Jersey City, New Jersey
d. Nov 23, 1964
Source: *BioIn 7, 9; NatCAB 53; WhAm 4*

Butterfield, Alexander Porter
American. Government Official
Asst. to Richard Nixon, 1969-73; FAA administrator, 1973-75.
b. Apr 6, 1926 in Pensacola, Florida
Source: *BioIn 10, 11, 12; BlueB 76; NewYTBE 73; WhoAm 74, 76, 78, 80, 82, 84, 90, 95, 96, 97; WhoAmP 73, 75, 77, 79, 81, 83, 85, 87; WhoSSW 73, 75; WhoWor 78*

Butterfield, Billy
American. Jazz Musician
Bib Band trumpeter, recorder; with World's Greatest Jazzband, 1968-73; introduced song "What's New?," 1930s.
b. Jan 14, 1917 in Middletown, Ohio
d. Mar 18, 1988 in North Palm Beach, Florida
Source: *AllMusG; AnObit 1988; BgBands 74; BiDAmM; BiDJaz; CmpEPM; EncJzS; IlEncJ; LegTOT; NewAmDM; NewGrDJ 88, 94; OxCPMus; PenEncP; WhoJazz 72*

Butterfield, Herbert, Sir
English. Author
Vice-chancellor, Cambridge U, 1959-61; wrote *International Conflict in the 20th Century,* 1960.
b. Oct 7, 1900 in Oxenhope, England
Source: *Au&Wr 71; BioIn 4, 5, 12, 14; BlueB 76; ConAu 1NR, 1R, 46NR; DcLEL; DcNaB 1971; EncWM; IntAu&W 76, 77; IntEnSS 79; IntWW 74, 75, 76, 77, 78, 79; LngCTC; NewCBEL; ThTwC 87; TwCA SUP; WhE&EA; WhLit; Who 74; WhoWor 74, 78; WrDr 80*

Butterfield, John
American. Businessman
Merged express companies to form American Express, 1850; Wells Fargo, 1852.
b. Nov 18, 1801 in Berne, New York
d. Nov 14, 1869 in Utica, New York
Source: *AmBi; ApCAB; BiDAmBL 83; BioIn 4, 6; CmCal; DcAmB; McGEWB; NatCAB 22; NewCol 75; REnAW; TwCBDA; WebAB 74, 79; WhAm HS*

Butterfield, Lyman Henry
American. Historian
Edited the 20-volume *Adams Papers.*
b. Aug 8, 1909 in Lyndonville, New York
d. Apr 25, 1982 in Boston, Massachusetts
Source: *AmAu&B; AnObit 1982; BioIn 8, 12, 13; ConAu 106; DrAS 74H, 78H, 82H; NewYTBS 82; WhAm 8; WhoAm 74, 76, 78, 80*

Butterfield, Paul
American. Singer
Albums include *An Offer You Can't Refuse,* 1982.
b. Dec 17, 1942 in Chicago, Illinois
Source: *AnObit 1987; BiDAmM; BioIn 15, 16; BluesWW; ConMuA 80A; ConNews 87-3; EncPR&S 89; EncRk 88; EncRkSt; GuBlues; HarEnR 86; IlEncRk; LegTOT; NewGrDA 86; PenEncP; RolSEnR 83; WhoRock 81; WhoRocM 82*

Butterfield, Roger Place
American. Historian, Journalist
Wrote Americana series *The American Past,* 1947-66.
b. Jul 29, 1907 in Lyndonville, New York
d. Jan 31, 1981 in Hartwick, New York
Source: *AmAu&B; BioIn 1, 12, 13, 17; ConAu P-1; CurBio 48, 81; REnAL*

Butterfield, William
English. Architect
Leading gothic revival architect, best known for All Saints Church, London, 1850.
b. Sep 7, 1814 in London, England
d. Feb 23, 1900 in London, England
Source: *BioIn 9, 14; CelCen; DcArts; DcBiPP; DcD&D; DcNaB S1; DcNiCA; IntDcAr; MacEA; McGDA; OxCArt; WhDW; WhoArch*

Butterford, Daniel
American. Soldier
Much-decorated Union Civil War fighter; chief of staff for Generals Hooker, Meade.
b. Oct 31, 1831 in Utica, New York
d. Jul 17, 1901 in Cold Spring, New York
Source: *Alli SUP; ApCAB; DcAmB; NatCAB 4; TwCBDA; WhAm HS*

Butterick, Ebenezer
American. Inventor
Invented standardized paper patterns for clothes; first marketed, 1863.
b. May 29, 1826 in Sterling, Massachusetts
d. Mar 31, 1903 in New York, New York
Source: *AmBi; BiDAmBL 83; DcAmB; NatCAB 13; WhAm HS; WhDW*

Butterworth, Charles
American. Actor
Supporting actor in films, 1930-46.
b. Jul 26, 1897 in South Bend, Indiana
d. Jun 14, 1946 in Los Angeles, California

Source: *CurBio 46; Film 2; FilmgC; MotPP; MovMk; ObitOF 79; Vers A; WhoHol B; WhScrn 74, 77; WorAl*

Buttigieg, Anton
Maltese. Political Leader, Editor
Pres. of Malta, 1976-81; edited *The Voice of Malta,* 1959-70; wrote much light poetry.
b. Feb 19, 1912 in Gozo, Malta
d. May 5, 1983
Source: *ConAu 109; IntAu&W 82; IntWW 74, 75, 76, 77, 78, 79, 80, 81, 82, 83; IntYB 78, 79, 80, 81, 82; Who 82, 83; WhoWor 74, 78, 80, 82*

Button, Dick
[Richard Totten Button]
American. Skater
US, world champion figure skater; won gold medals, 1948, 1952 Olympics.
b. Jul 18, 1929 in Englewood, New Jersey
Source: *BiDAmSp BK; BiE&WWA; BioIn 12; CelR; ConAu 9R; CurBio 49; FacFETw; LegTOT; WebAB 74, 79; What 4; WhoAm 76, 78, 80, 82, 84, 86, 88, 90, 92, 94, 95, 96, 97; WhoE 93, 97; WhoEnt 92; WhoHol 92, A; WhoSpor; WorAl; WorAlBi*

Buttons, Red
[Aaron Chwatt]
American. Comedian, Actor
Won Oscar, 1957, for *Sayonara.*
b. Feb 5, 1919 in New York, New York
Source: *ASCAP 66, 80; BioIn 3, 4, 5, 16; ConTFT 6, 13; CurBio 58; EncAFC; FilmEn; FilmgC; ForYSC; IntMPA 75, 76, 77, 78, 79, 80, 81, 82, 84, 86, 88, 92, 94, 96; JoeFr; LegTOT; MotPP; MovMk; RkOn 74; WhoAm 74, 76, 78, 80, 82; WhoAmJ 80; WhoCom; WhoHol 92, A; WhoWor 74; WorAl; WorAlBi*

Buttram, Pat
[Maxwell E Buttram]
American. Actor
Played in TV series "Green Acres," 1965-71.
b. Jun 19, 1917 in Winston County, Alabama
d. Jan 8, 1994 in Los Angeles, California
Source: *ConTFT 9; LegTOT; WhoHol A*

Buttrick, George Arthur
American. Clergy, Author
Prominent Protestant theologian known for eloquence; wrote several books, including *God, Pain, and Evil,* 1966.
b. Mar 23, 1892 in Seaham Harbour, England
d. Jan 23, 1980 in Louisville, Kentucky
Source: *AmAu&B; Au&Wr 71; BioIn 2, 3, 12; ConAu 61, 93; DcAmB S10; IntAu&W 76; NewYTBS 80; RelLAm 91; WhAm 7; WhoAm 74, 76, 78*

Butts, Alfred M(osher)
American. Architect
Invented word game Scrabble, 1933.
b. Apr 13, 1899 in Poughkeepsie, New York
d. Apr 4, 1993 in Rhinebeck, New York
Source: *BioIn 3; CurBio 54, 93N; InSci; WhAmArt 85*

Butts, Calvin O(tis), III
American. Clergy
Pastor, Abyssinian Baptist Chruch, Harlem, 1989—.
b. 1949 in New York, New York

Butz, Earl Lauer
American. Government Official
Secretary of Agriculture, 1971-76; sentenced to five years in prison for tax evasion, 1981.
b. Jul 3, 1909 in Noble County, Indiana
Source: *AmMWSc 73S, 78S; BiDrUSE 89; BioIn 9, 10, 11, 12; CngDr 74; CurBio 72; EncAAH; IndAu 1917; IntWW 74; NewYTBE 71, 72; USBiR 74; WhoAm 74, 76, 78; WhoAmP 73, 75, 77, 79, 81, 83, 85, 87, 89, 91, 93, 95; WhoGov 72, 75, 77; WhoSSW 75, 76*

Buxtehude, Dietrich
Danish. Organist, Composer
Organ virtuoso; Bach walked 200 miles to hear his famed music series.
b. 1637 in Elsinore, Denmark
d. May 9, 1707 in Lubeck, Germany
Source: *AtlBL; Baker 78, 84, 92; BioIn 1, 4, 7, 12, 16; BriBkM 80; CmpBCM; DcCom&M 79; GrComp; LinLib S; LuthC 75; McGEWB; MusMk; NewAmDM; NewCol 75; NewGrDM 80; NewOxM; OxCMus; WebBD 83*

Buzhardt, J(oseph) Fred, Jr.
American. Lawyer
Special counsel to Richard Nixon on Watergate matters, 1973-74.
b. Feb 21, 1924 in Greenwood, South Carolina
d. Dec 16, 1978 in Hilton Head Island, South Carolina
Source: *BioIn 9, 10, 11, 12, 13; NatCAB 62; NewYTBS 78; PolProf NF; WhoAmP 73, 75, 77*

Buzzell, Eddie
[Edward Buzzel]
American. Actor, Director
Star of Broadway musical comedies who became director, 1932.
b. Nov 13, 1907 in New York, New York
d. Jan 11, 1985 in Los Angeles, California
Source: *CmpEPM; Film 2; FilmgC; WhoHol A*

Buzzi, Ruth Ann
American. Actor, Comedian
Best known for appearances in TV series "Laugh-In," 1968-73.
b. Jul 24, 1936 in Westerly, Rhode Island
Source: *ConTFT 3; IntMPA 82; WhoAm 76, 78, 80, 82, 84; WhoAmW 70, 72, 74*

Buzzocks, The
English. Music Group
One of the most influential punk rock bands, 1977-81, 1990—.
Source: *Alli; BioIn 14, 15, 16, 17, 19; ConAu 69, X; ConMus 9; DcIrL 96; DcLP 87B; EncRk 88; NewYTBS 75, 84, 88; OnThGG; PenEncP; WhoAdv 80; WhoRocM 82; WhsNW 85*

Byars, Betsy
American. Children's Author
Won Newberry Medal for *Summer of the Swans,* 1971.
b. Aug 7, 1928 in Charlotte, North Carolina
Source: *Au&Arts 19; AuBYP 2, 3; BioIn 8, 9, 10, 12, 13; CamGLE; ChlBkCr; ChlFicS; ChlLR 1, 16; ConAu 18NR, 33R, 36NR; ConLC 35; DcLB 52; IntAu&W 91; InWom SUP; MajTwCW; MorBMP; NewbC 1966; OnHuMoP; OxCChiL; ScF&FL 92; SmATA 1AS, 4, 46; ThrBJA; TwCChW 78, 83, 89; TwCYAW; WrDr 80, 82, 84, 86, 88, 90, 92*

Byatt, A. S
English. Author
Works include novel, *The Virgin in the Garden,* 1978; short stories, *Sugar and Other Stories,* 1987; sister of Margaret Drabble.
b. Aug 24, 1936 in Sheffield, England
Source: *BioIn 13, 14, 15, 16; ConAu 13NR, 13R; ConLC 19; ConNov 86, 91; CurBio 91; DcLB 14; IntAu&W 91; IntWW 91; OxCEng 85; Who 92; WorAu 1975; WrDr 92*

Byers, Walter
American. Sports Executive
Executive director, NCAA, 1951-88.
b. Mar 13, 1922 in Kansas City, Missouri
Source: *BioIn 14, 15, 21; WhoAm 76, 78, 80, 82, 84, 86, 88, 90, 92, 94, 95, 96, 97; WhoMW 88, 92*

Byers, William Newton
American. Editor
Issued first newspaper in Denver, CO, "Rocky Mountain News," 1859-1878.
b. Feb 22, 1831 in Madison County, Ohio
d. Mar 25, 1903 in Denver, Colorado
Source: *Alli SUP; BioIn 8; DcNAA; NatCAB 13; OhA&B; REnAW; WhAm 1*

Byington, Spring
American. Actor
Star of TV series "December Bride," 1954-59.
b. Oct 17, 1893 in Colorado Springs, Colorado
d. Sep 7, 1971 in Hollywood, California
Source: *BiE&WWA; BioIn 3, 4, 9, 21; CurBio 56, 71, 71N; DcAmB S9; EncAFC; FilmEn; FilmgC; ForYSC; HalFC 80, 84, 88; InWom, SUP; MGM; MotPP; MovMk; NewYTBE 71; NewYTET; OlFamFa; ThFT; Vers A;*

WhAm 5; What 3; WhoHol B; WhScrn 74, 77, 83; WorAl; WorAlBi

Bykovsky, Valery Fyodorovich
Russian. Cosmonaut
Orbited Earth in the space ship Vostok 5, June, 1963.
b. Aug 2, 1934 in Pavlovsky-Posad, Union of Soviet Socialist Republics
Source: *BioIn 6, 7; CurBio 65; FacFETw; IntWW 74, 75, 76; WhoSpc; WorDWW*

Byng, George Torrington, Viscount
British. Explorer
First Lord of Admiralty, 1727-33.
b. 1663
d. Jan 17, 1733
Source: *Alli; DcBiPP; OxCShps*

Byng, Julian Hedworth George, Viscount
English. Political Leader
Governor-general of Canada, 1921-26.
b. Sep 11, 1862 in Barnet, England
d. Jun 6, 1935 in Thorpe-le-Soken, England
Source: *DcNaB 1931; GrBr; HarEnMi; LinLib S; MacDCB 78; WhoMilH 76*

Bynner, Harold Witter
American. Author
Wrote *The Jade Mountain,* 1929, translation of Chinese poetry; *Indian Earth,* 1929.
b. Aug 10, 1881 in New York, New York
d. Jun 1, 1968 in Santa Fe, New Mexico
Source: *ChhPo, S1, S3; CnDAL; ConAmA; ConAu 4NR; DcLEL*

Byrd, Charlie
[Charles Lee Byrd]
American. Jazz Musician
Guitarist who promoted bossa nova craze, 1960s; headed own trio.
b. Sep 16, 1925 in Chuckatuck, Virginia
Source: *AllMusG; ASCAP 80; BiDJaz; BioIn 15; BioNews 74; CmpEPM; CurBio 67; EncJzS; IlEncJ; LegTOT; NewGrDJ 88, 94; OnThGG; OxCPMus; PenEncP; WhoAm 74, 76, 78, 80; WorAl; WorAlBi*

Byrd, Donald
American. Jazz Musician
Trumpet, fluegelhorn player; albums include *Ethiopian Knights,* 1972; *Black Byrd,* 1975.
b. Dec 9, 1932 in Detroit, Michigan
Source: *AllMusG; BiDAmM; BiDJaz; DrBlPA 90; Ebony 1; EncJzS; IlEncJ; InB&W 80; NewAmDM; NewGrDA 86; NewGrDJ 88; PenEncP; WhoAm 74; WhoWor 74*

Byrd, Donald
American. Choreographer
Unique style incorporates many styles, from classical ballet to modern dance.
b. Jul 21, 1949 in New London, North Carolina
Source: *ConBlB 10*

Byrd, Harry Flood
American. Politician, Editor
Dem. governor of VA, 1926-30; US senator, 1933-65.
b. Jun 10, 1887 in Martinsburg, West Virginia
d. Oct 20, 1966 in Berryville, Virginia
Source: *BiDrAC; BiDrGov 1789; BiDrUSC 89; BioIn 1, 2, 3, 4, 5, 6, 7, 8, 9, 11, 13, 15, 17, 21; CurBio 66; DcAmB S8; EncAB-A 2; EncSoH; LinLib L, S; ObitOF 79; WhAm 4; WhAmP*

Byrd, Harry Flood, Jr.
American. Politician
Dem. senator from VA, 1965-83; son of Harry Flood.
b. Dec 20, 1914 in Winchester, Virginia
Source: *AlmAP 82; WhoSSW 73, 75, 76, 78, 80, 82, 84; WhoWor 80, 82, 84; WorAl*

Byrd, Henry
"Professor Longhair"
American. Composer, Musician
New Orleans rock-n-roll pianist, songwriter, who wrote "Go to the Mardi Gras," "Big Chief."
b. Dec 19, 1918 in Bogalusa, Louisiana
d. Jan 30, 1980 in New Orleans, Louisiana
Source: *AnObit 1980; BioIn 18; ConMus 6; DcTwCCu 5; NewAmDM; NewGrDA 86; NewYTBS 80; PenEncP; RolSEnR 83; SoulM*

Byrd, Richard Evelyn, Admiral
American. Explorer
First man to fly over N Pole, 1925, S Pole, 1929; led 1930 expedition to Antarctica; wrote *Discovery,* 1935.
b. Oct 25, 1888 in Winchester, Virginia
d. Mar 11, 1957 in Boston, Massachusetts
Source: *AmAu&B; AsBiEn; BiDWWGF; BiESc; BioIn 1, 2, 3, 4, 5, 6, 7, 8, 9, 11, 12, 13, 16, 17, 18, 20, 21; ConAu 57; CurBio 42, 56, 57; DcAmB S6; DcAmMiB; EncAB-H 1974, 1996; Expl 93; FacFETw; InSci; LinLib L, S; McGEWB; MedHR, 94; NatCAB 46; ObitOF 79; OxCAmH; OxCAmL 65, 83, 95; REn; REnAL; TwCA, SUP; WebAB 74, 79; WebAMB; WhAm 3; WhDW; WhNAA; WhWE; WorAl*

Byrd, Robert
[Robert Oliver Daniel Byrd, III]
American. Producer, Director
Made several documentary films including *Legacy of Tears, A Red Star in Minnesota,* and *Understanding Hate.*
b. Mar 30, 1952 in Pensacola, Florida
Source: *ConBlB 11*

Byrd, Robert C(arlyle)
American. Politician
Dem. senator from WV, 1959—; majority leader, 1977-81, 1987-89.
b. Jan 15, 1918 in North Wilkesboro, North Carolina
Source: *AlmAP 78*

Byrd, William
English. Organist, Composer, Songwriter
Wrote anthems, Roman Masses, first English madrigals, during reign of Elizabeth I.
b. 1542 in London, England
d. Jul 4, 1623 in London, England
Source: *Alli; AtlBL; Baker 84; BiDSA; BioIn 1, 2, 3; BritAu; Chambr 3; CroE&S; DcCathB; DcNaB; LuthC 75; McGEWB; OxCEng 85; OxCMus; REn; WhDW*

Byrd, William
American. Colonial Figure
Cultured Virginia planter; managed Westover estate; designed city of Richmond, 1737.
b. Mar 28, 1674 in Virginia
d. Aug 26, 1744 in Westover, Virginia
Source: *AmAu; AmAu&B; AmBi; AmWrBE; ApCAB; Benet 87, 96; BenetAL 91; BiDAmBL 83; BiInAmS; BioIn 1, 2, 3, 4, 5, 6, 8, 9, 10, 11, 13, 14, 15, 16, 20; CamGEL; CamGLE; CamHAL; CasWL; CnDAL; CyAL 1; DcAmAu; DcAmB; DcAmBC; DcLB 24, 140; DcLEL; DcNAA; Drake; EncAAH; EncAB-H 1974, 1996; EncCRAm; EncSoH; EvLB; FifSWrB; HarEnUS; LegTOT; LinLib L; McGEWB; NatCAB 7; OxCAmH; OxCAmL 65, 83, 95; PenC AM; PeoHis; REn; REnAL; RfGAmL 87, 94; SouWr; TwCBDA; WebAB 74, 79; WebE&AL; WhAm HS*

Byrds, The
[Skip Battin; Michael Clark; Gene Clarke; David Crosby; Chris Hillman; Kevin Kelly; Roger McGuinn; Gram Parsons]
American. Music Group
Pioneer folk-rock band, 1964-73; hits include "Mr. Tambourine Man," "Turn! Turn! Turn!," 1965.
Source: *BgBkCoM; BiDAmM; BioIn 14, 15, 16, 17, 20, 21; ConMuA 80A; ConMus 8; DcArts; DrAPF 83, 85, 87, 89, 91, 93, 97; EncPR&S 74, 89; EncRk 88; EncRkSt; FacFETw; HarEnCM 87; HarEnR 86; IlEncCM; IlEncRk; NewGrDA 86; NewYTBS 94; OxCPMus; PenEncP; RkOn 78; RolSEnR 83; ScF&FL 92; WhoAmP 87, 89; WhoEnt 92; WhoNeCM A; WhoRock 81; WhoRocM 82; WorAl; WorAlBi*

Byrne, Brendan Thomas
American. Politician
Dem. governor of NJ, 1974-82.
b. Apr 1, 1924 in West Orange, New Jersey
Source: *AlmAP 80; AmCath 80; BiDrGov 1789, 1978; BioIn 12; CurBio 74; IntWW 79, 80, 81, 82, 83; NewYTBE*

73; NewYTBS 77; PolProf NF; WhoAm 76, 78, 80, 82; WhoAmL 79; WhoAmP 79, 81, 83, 85, 87, 89, 91, 93, 95; WhoE 75, 77, 79, 81; WhoGov 75, 77

Byrne, David
[The Talking Heads]
Scottish. Musician, Composer
Leader of Talking Heads; composed music for Broadway's *The Catherine Wheel,* 1981; Grammy for best original score *The Last Emperor,* 1987.
b. May 14, 1952 in Dumbarton, Scotland
Source: *ASCAP 80; Baker 84, 92; BioIn 13; CelR 90; ConAu 127; ConMus 8; ConTFT 6, 15; CurBio 85; IntMPA 92, 94, 96; IntWW 91, 93; LegTOT; MiSFD 9; OnThGG; OxCPMus; WhoAm 84, 86, 88, 90, 92, 94, 95, 96, 97; WhoEnt 92; WhoHol 92*

Byrne, Jane Margaret Burke
[Mrs. Jay McMullen]
American. Politician
Dem. mayor of Chicago, 1979-83.
b. May 24, 1934 in Chicago, Illinois
Source: *AmWomM; BioIn 11, 12; CurBio 80; InWom SUP; WhoAm 80, 82; WhoAmP 77; WhoAmW 81, 83, 85; WhoGov 77*

Byrnes, Edd
[Edward Breitenberger]
American. Actor
Played Kookie on TV series "77 Sunset Strip," 1958-63; his combing on show led to fad, song.
b. Jul 30, 1933 in New York, New York
Source: *FilmEn; FilmgC; ForYSC; HalFC 80, 84, 88; IntMPA 86, 92, 94, 96; ItaFilm; LegTOT; MotPP; WhoHol 92, A*

Byrnes, James Francis
American. Government Official
Appointed to Supreme Court by FDR, 1941-42; secretary of State under Truman, 1945-47; governor of SC, 1951-55.
b. May 2, 1879 in Charleston, South Carolina
d. Apr 9, 1972 in Columbia, South Carolina
Source: *AmAu&B; AmPolLe; BiDFedJ; BiDrAC; BiDrGov 1789; BiDrUSC 89; BiDrUSE 71, 89; BioIn 1, 2, 3, 4, 5, 6, 7, 8, 9, 10, 11, 12, 15, 16, 18, 20, 21; ColdWar 1; ConAu 112; CurBio 41, 51, 72; DcAmB S9; DcAmDH 80; DcPol; DcTwHis; EncAB-H 1974, 1996; EncSoH; HisEWW; LinLib L, S; McGEWB; NewYTBE 73; ObitT 1971; OxCAmH; OxCSupC; SupCtJu; WebAB 74, 79; WhAm 5; WhAmP; WhWW-II; WorAl*

Byroade, Henry A(lfred)
American. Diplomat
Director, Bureau of German Affairs, 1949-51; asst. secretary of state, Near Eastern, South Asian, and African affairs, 1952-55.
b. Jul 24, 1913
d. Dec 31, 1993 in Bethesda, Maryland
Source: *BioIn 2, 3, 16, 19, 20; CurBio 94N; DcAmDH 89; Dun&B 79; InSci; USBiR 74; WhoAm 74, 76, 78; WhoAmP 73, 75, 77; WhoGov 72, 75, 77; WhoWor 74, 76*

Byron, George Gordon, Baron
[Lord Byron]
English. Poet
Writer of Romantic narrative poems: "Childe Harold's Pilgrimage," 1812.
b. Jan 22, 1788 in London, England
d. Apr 19, 1824 in Missolonghi, Greece
Source: *AtlBL; Benet 87; BioIn 15, 16, 17, 18, 20; BlmGEL; BritAu 19; BritWr 4; CamGEL; CamGLE; CamGWoT; CasWL; Chambr 3; ChhPo S3; CnDBLB 3; CnThe; CrtSuDr; CyWA 58; DcArts; DcBiPP; DcLB 96; DcNaB; Dis&D; EncEnl; EncUnb; EncWT; LngCEL; McGEWD 72, 84; MetOEnc; NewCBEL; NewGrDM 80; NinCLC 2, 12; NotNAT B; OxCEng 85, 95; OxCThe 67, 83; OxDcOp; PenC ENG; PenEncH; RComWL; REn; REnWD; WebBD 83; WhDW; WorAlBi*

C

Caan, James
"The Jewish Cowboy"
American. Actor
Starred in *The Godfather,* 1972; TV movie "Brian's Song," 1971.
b. Mar 26, 1940 in New York, New York
Source: *BkPepl; CelR; ConTFT 7; CurBio 76; FilmgC; HalFC 84; IntMPA 86, 88, 92, 96; IntWW 83; MovMk; NewYTBE 73; WhoAm 84, 86, 88, 90, 92, 94, 95, 96, 97; WhoEnt 92; WhoHol A; WorAl*

Caballe, Montserrat Folch
Spanish. Opera Singer
Soprano; sang, recorded over 120 roles; noted for Mozart, bel canto parts.
b. Apr 12, 1933 in Barcelona, Spain
Source: *Baker 84; CurBio 67; IntWW 83; NewYTBE 73; Who 85; WhoAm 86; WhoAmM 83; WhoMus 72; WhoOp 76; WhoWor 84*

Caballero, Fernan
[Cecilia Francesca Bohl de Faber]
Spanish. Author
Realistic novels include *La Gaviota,* 1849.
b. Dec 25, 1796 in Morges, Switzerland
d. Apr 7, 1877 in Seville, Spain
Source: *BbD; BiD&SB; Bioln 2, 7, 10; CasWL; ContDcW 89; ConWomW; EncCoWW; EuAu; EvEuW; IntDcWB; LinLib L; NewCol 75; NinCLC 10; OxCSpan; PenC EUR; REn*

Cabell, James Branch
American. Author
Writings include autobiographical *These Restless Years,* 1932.
b. Apr 14, 1879 in Richmond, Virginia
d. May 5, 1958 in Richmond, Virginia
Source: *AmAu&B; AmLY; AmNov; ApCAB X; Benet 87, 96; BenetAL 91; BiDSA; Bioln 1, 2, 3, 4, 5, 6, 7, 8, 10, 12, 14, 19; CamGEL; CamGLE; CamHAL; CasWL; Chambr 3; CnDAL; CnMWL; ConAmA; ConAmL; ConAu 105, 152; CyWA 58; DcAmAu; DcAmB S6; DcAmC; DcBiA; DcLB 9, 78; DcLEL; EncAB-A 1; EncSF, 93; EncSoH; EncWL; EvLB; FacFETw; FifSWrA; LegTOT; LinLib L, S; LngCTC; McGEWB; ModAL; NatCAB 48; Novels; ObitT 1951; OxCAmL 65, 83, 95; OxCEng 67; PenC AM; RAdv 1; REn; REnAL; RfGAmL 87, 94; ScF&FL 1, 92; ScFSB; SJGFanW; SupFW; TwCA, SUP; TwCLC 6; TwCRHW 90; TwCWr; WebAB 74, 79; WebE&AL; WhAm 3; WhE&EA; WhLit; WhNAA; WhoHr&F; WhoSciF*

Cabeza de Vaca, Alvar Nunez
Spanish. Explorer
Went on Narvaez expedition to FL, 1528; shipwrecked, imprisoned by Indians.
b. 1490, Spain
d. 1557, Spain
Source: *BenetAL 91; BiDSA; DcHiB; Drake; EncCRAm; EncLatA; EncSoH; EuAu; Expl 93; HarEnUS; HisDcSE; McGEWB; NatCAB 25; OxCAmL 65, 95; REn; REnAW; WhNaAH; WhWE; WorAl; WorAlBi*

Cable, George Washington
American. Author
Depicted local color, charm of New Orleans society: *Bylow Hill,* 1902.
b. Oct 12, 1844 in New Orleans, Louisiana
d. Jan 31, 1925 in Saint Petersburg, Florida
Source: *Alli; AmAu; AmAu&B; AmBi; AmLY; AmSocL; ApCAB, X; AtlBL; BbD; Benet 87, 96; BenetAL 91; BiD&SB; BiDSA; Bioln 1, 2, 3, 4, 5, 6, 8, 11, 12, 13, 19; CamGEL; CamGLE; CamHAL; CasWL; Chambr 3; ChhPo, S1; CnDAL; ConAu 104; CrtT 3, 4; CyWA 58; DcAmAu; DcAmB; DcAmC; DcBiA; DcEnA A; DcLB 12, 74, DS13; DcLEL; DcNAA; EncAACR; EncAAH; EncSoH; EvLB; FifSWrB; GayN; HarEnUS; LegTOT; LinLib L, S; McGEWB; NatCAB 1, 45; Novels; OxCAmH; OxCAmL 65, 83, 95; OxCEng 67, 85, 95; PenC AM; PeoHis; RAdv 1, 14, 13-1; REn; REnAL; RfGAmL 87, 94; ShSCr 4; TwCBDA; TwCLC 3, 4; WebAB 74, 79; WebE&AL; WhAm 1; WhLit; WhNAA*

Cabot, Bruce
[Jacques Etienne de Bujac]
American. Actor
Best known as hero who saved Fay Wray in *King Kong,* 1933.
b. Apr 20, 1904 in Carlsbad, New Mexico
d. May 3, 1972 in Woodland Hills, California
Source: *Bioln 9, 11; FilmgC; GangFlm; HalFC 84, 88; HolP 30; ItaFilm; LegTOT; MotPP; MovMk; NewYTBE 72; ObitOF 79; WhoHol B; WhScrn 77, 83; WorAl*

Cabot, George
American. Merchant, Politician
Influential New England shipowner; introduced Fugitive Slave Act in US Senate, 1793.
b. Dec 16, 1751 in Salem, Massachusetts
d. Apr 18, 1825 in Boston, Massachusetts
Source: *AmBi; ApCAB; BiDrAC; CyAG; Drake; HarEnUS; NatCAB 2; NewCol 75; PolPar; TwCBDA; WhAm HS; WhAmP*

Cabot, John
[Giovanni Caboto]
Italian. Navigator, Explorer
Conceived notion of sailing westward to Orient; credited with discovery of N America.
b. Jun 24, 1450 in Genoa, Italy
d. 1498
Source: *AmBi; Benet 87, 96; BenetAL 91; Bioln 1, 4, 6, 7, 8, 9, 10, 11, 12, 15, 16, 18, 20; DcCathB; HisDBrE; LegTOT; LinLib S; NewC; OxCAmH; OxCCan; OxCShps; REn; REnAL; WebAB 74, 79; WhAm HS; WhNaAH; WhWE; WorAl; WorAlBi*

Cabot, John Moors
American. Diplomat
US ambassador to five countries, 1954-65; wrote *Towards Our Common American Destiny,* 1955.
b. Dec 11, 1901 in Cambridge, Massachusetts

d. Feb 23, 1981 in Washington, District of Columbia
Source: *AmAu&B; AnObit 1981; BioIn 3, 5, 11, 12; BlueB 76; ConAu 103; CurBio 53, 81; DcAmDH 89; IntWW 74, 75, 76, 77, 78, 79, 80, 81, 81N; IntYB 78, 79, 80, 81, 82; NewYTBS 81; PolProf E, K; WhAm 7; WhoAm 76*

Cabot, Richard C
American. Scientist
Pioneer in medical social work.
b. May 21, 1868 in Brookline, Massachusetts
d. May 8, 1939
Source: *AmAu&B; BioIn 15; DcAmB S2; DcNAA; WhAm 1*

Cabot, Sebastian
Italian. Explorer
Son of John Cabot; reached Hudson Bay in attempt to find Northwest Passage, 1509.
b. 1476 in Venice, Italy
d. 1557 in London, England
Source: *Alli; ApCAB; Benet 87, 96; BioIn 3, 4, 8, 9, 10, 11; Drake; HisDBrE; LegTOT; NewC; OxCCan; OxCShps; REn; TwCBDA; WhAm HS; WhDW; WhWE; WorAl*

Cabot, Sebastian
English. Actor
Played Mr. French on TV series "Family Affair," 1966-71.
b. Jul 6, 1918 in London, England
d. Aug 23, 1977 in Victoria, British Columbia, Canada
Source: *BioIn 11; CelR; FilmgC; HalFC 84, 88; ItaFilm; LegTOT; MotPP; MovMk; WhoAm 76; WhoHol A; WhScrn 83; WorAl*

Cabot, Susan
[Susan Cabot-Roman; Harriet Shapiro]
American. Actor
Starred in 1950s B action films: *The Wasp Woman,* 1959.
b. Jul 6, 1927 in Boston, Massachusetts
d. Dec 10, 1986 in Encino, California
Source: *BioIn 15, 16; FilmEn; FilmgC; GangFlm; HalFC 84, 88; WhoHol A*

Cabot, Thomas D(udley)
American. Business Executive
With Cabot Corp., 1922-60; named first director of the Office of International Security Affairs, 1950.
b. May 1, 1897
d. Jun 8, 1995 in Weston, Massachusetts
Source: *BioIn 2, 3; ConAu 93; CurBio 95N; St&PR 75, 84, 87; WhAm 11; WhoAm 74, 76, 78, 80, 82, 84, 86, 88, 90, 92, 94, 95; WhoWor 80, 82*

Cabral, Amilcar Lopes
Guinean. Revolutionary
Co-founder, African Party for the Liberation of Guinea and Cape Verde, 1956.
b. Sep 12, 1924 in Bafata
d. Jan 20, 1973 in Conakry
Source: *BiDMarx; BioIn 9, 10, 13, 14, 16; ColdWar 2; DcAfHiB 86; EncWB; ObitOF 79*

Cabral, Luis de Almeida
Guinean. Political Leader
Pres., Guinea-Bisseau, 1974-80; deposed in coup; fled to Cuba.
b. 1931 in Bissau, Portuguese Guinea
Source: *BioIn 21; IntWW 89, 91, 93; NewYTBS 74*

Cabral, Pedro Alvarez
Portuguese. Explorer
Credited with discovery of Brazil, Apr 24, 1500.
b. 1460?, Guinea-Bissau
d. 1526
Source: *ApCAB; DcCathB; Drake; HarEnUS*

Cabral de Melo Neto, Joao
Brazilian. Poet
The most influential Brazilian poet of the "Generation of '45;" won Neustadt International Prize for Literature, 1992.
b. Jan 6, 1920 in Recife, Brazil
Source: *BioIn 10, 18; CasWL; ConAu 151; ConLC 76; DcBrazL; LatAmWr; PenC AM*

Cabrera Infante, Guillermo
Cuban. Writer
Most noted work, *Tres Tristes Tigres,* 1967 is a chronicle of the end of the Batista regime.
b. Apr 22, 1929 in Gibara, Cuba
Source: *Benet 87, 96; BenetAL 91; BioIn 9, 11, 13, 16, 17, 18; CasWL; ConAu 29NR; ConFLW 84; ConLC 5; CubExWr; CyWA 89; DcCLAA; DcHiB; DcLB 113; DcTwCCu 4; DcTwCuL; EncLatA; EncWL, 3; HispLC; HispWr; IntvLAW; IntWW 91, 93; LatAmWr; LiExTwC; MajTwCW; ModLAL; OxCSpan; PenC AM; RAdv 14, 13-2; WorAu 1970*

Cabrillo, Juan Rodriguez
Portuguese. Explorer
Explored CA coast, 1542; discovered San Diego Bay.
b. 1520, Portugal
d. Jan 3, 1543 in San Miguel Island, California
Source: *AmBi; ApCAB; DcAmB; McGEWB; REnAW; WhAm HS*

Cabrini, Frances Xavier, Saint
[Mother Cabrini]
American. Religious Figure
First American saint; founded convents, orphanages, hospitals in Europe, US; canonized, 1946.
b. Jul 15, 1850 in Saint Angelo, Italy
d. Dec 22, 1917 in Chicago, Illinois
Source: *AmSocL; BioIn 1, 2, 3, 4, 5, 6, 7, 8, 9, 10, 11, 12, 15, 16, 17, 19, 21; DcAmImH; DcAmReB 1, 2; DcCathB; GoodHs; GrLiveH; HanAmWH; HisWorL; InWom, SUP; LibW; McGEWB; NotAW; RelLAm 91; WebAB 74, 79; WhAm 4, HS, HSA; WomFir*

Caccini, Giulio
Italian. Composer, Musician
His *Euridice,* 1601, was first published opera.
b. 1546 in Rome, Italy
d. Dec 10, 1618 in Florence, Italy
Source: *Baker 84; NewCol 75; OxCMus; REn*

Cacers, Ernest
American. Jazz Musician
Clarinetist, saxist; with Glen Miller, early 1940s; recorded with Eddie Condon, 1940s-50s.
b. Nov 22, 1911 in Rockport, Texas
d. Jan 10, 1971 in Texas
Source: *BiDAmM; CmpEPM; EncJzS; WhoJazz 72*

Cacoyannis, Michael
Greek. Director
Films include *Zorba the Greek,* 1964; *The Trojan Women,* 1971.
b. Jun 11, 1922 in Limassol, Cyprus
Source: *BiDFilm, 94; BioIn 7, 9, 16; CelR; ConAu 101; ConTFT 11; CurBio 66; DcArts; DcFM; EncEurC; FilmgC; HalFC 84, 88; IntMPA 75, 76, 77, 78, 79, 81, 82, 84, 86, 88, 92, 94, 96; IntWW 74, 75, 76, 77, 78, 79, 80, 81, 82, 83, 89, 91, 93; ItaFilm; MiSFD 9; MovMk; NotNAT; OxCFilm; Who 74, 82, 83, 85, 88, 90, 92, 94; WhoFr 79; WhoWor 74, 78, 80, 82, 84, 87, 89, 91, 93, 95, 96; WorEFlm; WorFDir 2*

Cadamosto, Alvise Luigi da
Italian. Explorer
Explored west coast of Africa for Portuguese; credited with discovery of Cape Verde Islands, 1456.
b. 1432? in Venice, Italy
d. Jul 18, 1488 in Venice, Italy
Source: *McGEWB; NewCol 75; WebBD 83*

Cadbury, George Adrian Hayhurst, Sir
English. Manufacturer
Chm., Cadbury Schweppes, Ltd. 1975—.
b. Apr 15, 1929 in Birmingham, England
Source: *BioIn 7; IntWW 74, 75, 76, 78; IntYB 79; St&PR 84, 87; Who 85; WhoWor 74, 76, 78*

Cadbury, John
English. Candy Manufacturer
Opened small shop, 1824; had 15 varieties of chocolates, 1841.
b. 1801
d. 1889
Source: *BioIn 1; DcNaB MP; Entr*

Caddell, Pat(rick Hayward)
American. Pollster
Pres., Cambridge Survey Research, 1971—; consultant to presidential campaigns of George McGovern,

Jimmy Carter, Walter Mondale, and Gary Hart.
b. May 19, 1950 in Rock Hill, South Carolina
Source: *CurBio 79; NewYTBS 76; WhoAm 80, 82, 84, 86, 88*

Cadieux, Marcel (Joseph David Romeo)
Canadian. Diplomat
First French-Canadian to hold post of ambassdor to US, 1969-74; Canada's first ambassador to European Economic Community, 1975.
b. Jun 17, 1915 in Montreal, Quebec, Canada
d. Mar 19, 1981 in Pompano Beach, Florida
Source: *AnObit 1981; BioIn 12; BlueB 76; CanWW 70, 79, 80, 81, 83; ConAu 108; IntWW 74, 75, 76, 77, 78, 79, 80, 81; WhAm 7; WhoAm 74, 76; WhoGov 72; WhoWor 74, 76, 78*

Cadillac, Antoine de la Mothe
French. Explorer
Founded Detroit, Jul 24, 1701.
b. Mar 5, 1658 in Les Laumets, France
d. Oct 15, 1730 in Castelsarrasen, France
Source: *AmBi; ApCAB; BenetAL 91; DcAmB; DcCanB 2; DcCathB; EncCRAm; HarEnUS; MacDCB 78; NatCAB 5; OxCAmH; OxCCan; REnAL; TwCBDA; WebAB 74, 79; WhAmP; WorAl; WorAlBi*

Cadman, Charles Wakefield
American. Composer
Used Native American melodies; wrote opera *The Sunset Trail,* 1925; song, "From the Land of Sky-Blue Water," 1908.
b. Dec 4, 1881 in Johnstown, Pennsylvania
d. Dec 30, 1946 in Los Angeles, California
Source: *AmComp; ApCAB X; ASCAP 66; Baker 78, 84, 92; BenetAL 91; BiDAmM; BioIn 1, 8, 10; CmCal; CmpEPM; CompSN SUP; ConAmC 76, 82; DcAmB S4; MetOEnc; NewCol 75; NewEOp 71; NewGrDA 86; NewGrDO; OxCAmL 65; OxCMus; OxDcOp; REnAL; WhAm 2*

Cadmus, Paul
American. Artist
Best known during WW II for his tempera portraits of realism.
b. Dec 17, 1904 in New York, New York
Source: *AmArt; BioIn 1, 2, 6; BlueB 76; BriEAA; CelR, 90; ConArt 77, 83, 89, 96; CurBio 42; DcAmArt; DcCAA 71, 77, 88, 94; GayLesB; GrAmP; McGDA; OxCTwCA; OxDcArt; PhDcTCA 77; WhAmArt 85; WhoAm 74, 76, 78, 80, 82, 84, 86, 88, 90, 92, 94, 95, 96, 97; WhoAmA 73, 76, 78, 80, 82, 84, 86, 89, 91, 93; WhoE 74*

Cadogan, Alexander George Montague, Sir
English. Statesman
Permanent under secretary of state for foreign affairs, 1938-46; wartime adviser to Churchill.
b. Nov 25, 1884, England
d. Jul 9, 1968 in London, England
Source: *ConAu 106; CurBio 44, 68; ObitOF 79; ObitT 1961; WhAm 7*

Cadogan, William, Earl
British. Army Officer, Diplomat
Faithful supporter of First Duke of Marlborough during War of Spanish Succession, 1702-11.
b. 1676 in Dublin, Ireland
d. Jul 17, 1726 in Kensington Gravel Pits, England
Source: *DcNaB; NewCol 75*

Cady, (Walter) Harrison
American. Cartoonist, Illustrator
Created works for periodicals; best known for illustrations of *Bedtime Stories of Peter Rabbit,* 1913.
b. Jun 17, 1877 in Gardner, Massachusetts
d. Dec 9, 1970 in New York, New York
Source: *BioIn 1, 2, 3, 9, 12; ChhPo, S1; ConAu 116; IlsCB 1744; NewYTBE 70; OxCChiL; SmATA 19; WhAmArt 85; WhNAA; WorECar*

Caedmon, Saint
Anglo-Saxon. Poet
Monk; wrote scripture history.
b. 650, England
d. 680, England
Source: *Alli; BbD; BiB S; BiD&SB; BritAu; CasWL; Chambr 1; CrtT 1; DcBiPP; DcCathB; DcEnL; DcNaB; EvLB; MouLC 1; NewC; OxCEng 67; WebE&AL*

Caen, Herb
American. Journalist, Author
Had column in *San Francisco Chronicle,* 1936-50, 1958-97; *San Francisco Examiner,* 1950-58; wrote *One Man's San Francisco,* 1976; won Pulitzer Prize, 1996.
b. Apr 3, 1916 in Sacramento, California
d. Feb 1, 1997 in San Francisco, California
Source: *AmCath 80; AuBYP 2S, 3; AuNews 1; BiDrGov 1789; BioIn 2, 4, 8, 10; BlueB 76; CelR, 90; CmCal; ConAu 1NR, 1R; EncTwCJ; JrnUS; LegTOT; WhoAm 74, 76, 78, 80, 82, 84, 86, 88, 92, 94, 95, 96, 97; WhoWest 89, 92, 96; WhoWor 74*

Caesar, Adolph
American. Actor
Nominated for Oscar for *A Soldier's Story,* 1984; appeared in *The Color Purple,* 1985.
b. 1934 in New York, New York
d. Mar 6, 1986 in Los Angeles, California
Source: *BlksAmF; ConBlAP 88; ConNews 86-3; ConTFT 3; DrBlPA 90; InB&W 85; NewYTBS 86; VarWW 85*

Caesar, Irving
American. Songwriter
Popular during 1920s-30s; wrote "Tea for Two," 1925.
b. Jul 4, 1895 in New York, New York
d. Dec 17, 1996 in New York, New York
Source: *AmPS; AmSong; ASCAP 66; Au&Wr 71; BiDAmM; BiE&WWA; BioIn 1, 4; ChhPo; CmpEPM; EncMT; HalFC 84, 88; IntAu&W 89; IntMPA 75, 76, 77, 78, 79, 81, 82, 84, 86, 88, 92, 94, 96; NewCBMT; NewYTBS 27; NotNAT; OxCAmT 84; OxCPMus; REnAL; Who 74, 82, 83, 85, 88, 90, 92, 94; WhoAm 78; WhoThe 77, 81*

Caesar, Julius
[Caius Julius Caesar]
Roman. Army Officer, Statesman
Conquered all Gaul, Britain, 58-49 BC; Roman dictator, 49-44 BC, known for reforms; wrote on Gallic wars; assassinated by Brutus; month of July named for him.
b. Jul 12, 100BC in Rome, Italy
d. Mar 15, 44BC in Rome, Italy
Source: *BbD; Benet 87; BiD&SB; BioIn 1, 2, 3, 4, 5, 6, 7, 8, 9, 10, 11, 15, 16, 17, 18, 19, 20; DcBiPP; LegTOT; LinLib L; NewCol 75; RAdv 14, 13-3; REn; WebBD 83; WorAl*

Caesar, Sid
American. Comedian, Actor
Accomplished mimic, sketch comic; teamed with Imogene Coca in TV's "Caesar's Hour," 1950s; won Emmy, 1956.
b. Sep 8, 1922 in Yonkers, New York
Source: *ASCAP 66; BiE&WWA; BioIn 2, 3, 4, 6, 8, 9, 11, 13; CelR, 90; ConTFT 1, 9; CurBio 51; DcTwCCu 1; EncAFC; EncMT; FacFETw; FilmgC; HalFC 84, 88; IntMPA 75, 76, 77, 78, 79, 81, 82, 84, 86, 88, 92, 94, 96; LegTOT; MovMk; NewYTET; OxCAmT 84; QDrFCA 92; WhoAm 74, 76, 78, 80, 82, 84, 86, 88, 90, 92, 94, 95, 96, 97; WhoCom; WhoEnt 92; WhoHol 92, A; WhoTelC; WhoThe 72, 77, 81; WhoWor 74; WorAl; WorAlBi*

Caetano, Marcello
Portuguese. Political Leader
Premier of Portugal, 1968-74, who was ousted by military.
b. Aug 17, 1906 in Lisbon, Portugal
d. Oct 26, 1980 in Rio de Janeiro, Brazil
Source: *AnObit 1980; BioIn 8, 9, 10, 12; CurBio 70, 81, 81N; DcPol; FacFETw; IntWW 74, 81; IntYB 80; NewYTBS 80; WhoGov 72; WhoWor 74*

Caffieri, Jacques
French. Artist
Bronze founder; member of respected family of artists; executed rococo decorations for Versailles.

b. 1678
d. 1755
Source: *AntBDN C, G; McGDA; NewCol 75; OxCArt; OxCDecA; OxDcArt*

Cage, John
[John Milton Cage, Jr.]
American. Composer, Author
Composed scores for choreography by Merce Cunningham; writes essays, books on music, dance; noted for prepared "piano procedure."
b. Sep 5, 1912 in Los Angeles, California
d. Aug 12, 1992 in New York, New York
Source: *AmAu&B; AmComp; AmCulL; AnObit 1992; ASCAP 66; Baker 78, 84; Benet 96; BenetAL 91; BiDAmM; BiDD; BioIn 6, 7, 8, 9, 11, 12, 13; BlueB 76; CelR; CmCal; CompSN SUP; ConAmC 76, 82; ConArt 83, 89, 96; ConAu 9NR, 13R; ConCom 92; ConDr 73, 77E; ConLC 41; ConMus 8; CpmDNM 81; CurBio 61; DcArts; DcCAr 81; DcCM; DcLEL 1940; DcTwCCu 1; EncAB-H 1974, 1996; FacFETw; GayLesB; IntAu&W 89; IntWW 74, 75, 76, 77, 78, 79, 80, 81, 82, 83, 89, 91; IntWWM 77, 90; LegTOT; LinLib L; MakMC; McGEWB; NewAmDM; NewGrDA 86; NewOxM; News 93-1; NewYTBE 73; NewYTBS 92; OxCMus; PenC AM; PenDiMP A; PenEncP; PeoHis; PrintW 83, 85; RAdv 14, 13-3; RComAH; ThTwC 87; WebAB 74, 79; WhAm 10; WhDW; WhoAm 74, 76, 78, 80, 82, 84, 86, 88, 90, 92; WhoAmA 80, 82, 84, 86, 89, 91, 93N; WhoAmM 83; WhoE 74; WhoEnt 92; WhoMus 72; WhoWor 74; WorAl; WorAlBi; WorAu 1970; WrDr 76, 80, 82, 84, 86, 88, 90, 92, 94, 96*

Cage, Nicolas
[Nicholas Coppola]
American. Actor
Films include *The Cotton Club,* 1984, *Moonstruck,* 1987, *Leaving Las Vegas,* 1995, *The Rock,* 1996.
b. Jan 7, 1964 in Long Beach, California
Source: *CelR 90; ConTFT 5; CurBio 94; IntMPA 86, 92, 94, 96; IntWW 91, 93; LegTOT; News 91, 91-1; VarWW 85; WhoAm 94, 95, 96, 97; WhoHol 92*

Cagle, Red
[Christian Kenner Cagle]
American. Football Player
All-American running back, Army, 1926-29; played pro ball with NY Giants.
b. May 1, 1905 in De Ridder, Louisiana
d. Dec 23, 1942 in New York, New York
Source: *ObitOF 79; WhoFtbl 74*

Cagliostro, Alessandro, Conte di
[Giuseppe Balsamo]
Italian. Magician
Traveled throughout Europe posing as an alchemist; condemned to death in Rome as a heretic.
b. Jun 2, 1743 in Palermo, Sicily, Italy
d. Aug 26, 1795 in Rome, Italy
Source: *BioIn 1, 4, 5, 8, 10, 19; DcBiPP; Dis&D; EncWW; NewC; OxCGer 76; REn; WhDW; WorAl; WorAlBi*

Cagney, James
[James Francis Cagney, Jr]
American. Actor
Best known for tough-guy roles; won Oscar for *Yankee Doodle Dandy,* 1942.
b. Jul 17, 1899 in New York, New York
d. Mar 30, 1986 in Stanfordville, New York
Source: *AnObit 1986; BiDD; BiDFilm, 94; BiE&WWA; BioIn 12, 13, 14, 15, 17, 18; BioNews 74; CmMov; ConAu 118; ConNews 86-2; ConTFT 3; CurBio 86; DcArts; EncAFC; FacFETw; FilmgC; GangFlm; HalFC 84, 88; IntDcF 1-3, 2-3; IntMPA 82; IntWW 75, 76, 77, 78, 79, 80, 81, 82, 83; LegTOT; MotPP; MovMk; NewYTBS 81, 86; OxCFilm; OxCPMus; WhAm 9; WhoAm 82, 84; WhoHol A; WorAl; WorAlBi; WorEFlm*

Cagney, Jeanne
American. Actor
Films include *Town Tamer,* 1965; sister of James Cagney.
b. Mar 25, 1919 in New York, New York
Source: *BiE&WWA; BioIn 1, 14; FilmgC; HalFC 84; IntMPA 77, 82; MotPP; NotNAT; WhoHol A; WhoThe 77A; WhThe*

Cahan, Abraham
Russian. Editor
Established newspaper *Jewish Daily Forward,* 1897; wrote five vol. autobiography, 1916-36.
b. Jul 7, 1860 in Vilna, Russia
d. Aug 31, 1951 in New York, New York
Source: *AmAu&B; AmDec 1900; BbD; BenetAL 91; BiDAmJo; BiDAmL; BiDAmLf; BiDAmLL; BiD&SB; BioIn 1, 2, 3, 4, 8, 11, 12, 14, 16, 20; CamGLE; CamHAL; CasWL; ConAmL; ConAu 108, 154; DcAmAu; DcAmB S5; DcAmImH; DcAmSR; DcLB 9, 25, 28; EncAJ; EncAL; EncWL; GayN; JeAmFiW; JeAmHC; JrnUS; LiJour; McGEWB; ModAL; NatCAB 11; Novels; OxCAmH; OxCAmL 65, 83, 95; PenC AM; RAdv 14, 13-2; REn; REnAL; RfGAmL 87, 94; TwCA, SUP; WebAB 74, 79; WebBD 83; WhAm 3; WhJnl; WhNAA*

Cahill, Marie
American. Actor
Starred in vaudeville musical *Nancy Brown,* 1903.
b. Dec 20, 1870 in New York, New York
d. Aug 23, 1933 in New York, New York
Source: *BiDAmM; BioIn 3; CmpEPM; EncMT; EncVaud; NewGrDA 86; NotAW; NotNAT B; OxCAmT 84; OxCPMus; WhAm 1; WhoStg 1906, 1908; WomWWA 14*

Cahill, William T(homas)
American. Politician
Governor of New Jersey, 1970-74.
b. Jun 25, 1912 in Philadelphia, Pennsylvania
d. Jul 1, 1996 in Haddonfield, New Jersey
Source: *BiDrAC; BiDrGov 1789; BiDrUSC 89; BioIn 8, 9, 10, 12; BioNews 74; BlueB 76; CurBio 70, 96N; IntWW 74, 75, 76, 77; NewYTBE 72; PolProf NF; WhoAm 74, 76; WhoAmP 73, 75, 77, 79; WhoE 74, 75; WhoGov 72, 75, 77*

Cahn, Sammy
[Samuel Cohen]
American. Lyricist
Won Oscars for title songs "Three Coins in the Fountain," 1954; "All the Way," 1957.
b. Jun 18, 1913 in New York, New York
d. Jan 15, 1993 in Los Angeles, California
Source: *AmPS; AmSong; AnObit 1993; ASCAP 66; AuSpks; Baker 78, 84, 92; BiDAmM; BioIn 1, 5, 9, 10, 11; CelR, 90; CmpEPM; ConAu 85, 140; ConMus 11; ConTFT 12; CurBio 74, 93N; Dun&B 90; EncMT; FacFETw; FilmgC; HalFC 84, 88; IntDcF 1-4, 2-4; IntMPA 75, 76, 77, 78, 79, 81, 82, 84, 86, 88, 92, 94; LegTOT; NewCBMT; NewGrDA 86; NewYTBS 74; NotNAT, A; OxCPMus; PenEncP; WhAm 11; Who 90, 92; WhoAm 74, 76, 78, 80, 82, 84, 86, 88, 90, 92; WhoEnt 92; WhoThe 77, 81; WhoWor 74; WhoWorJ 72, 78*

Cahners, Norman Lee
American. Publisher
Founder, CEO, Cahners Publishing Co., publishers of trade magazines, 1946-86.
b. Jun 5, 1914 in Bangor, Maine
d. Mar 14, 1986 in Boston, Massachusetts
Source: *St&PR 84, 87N; WhAm 9; WhoFI 77*

Caidin, Martin
American. Author
Novels, short stories are of fantasy, space: *Man Into Space,* 1961.
b. Sep 14, 1927 in New York, New York
d. Mar 24, 1997 in Tallahassee, Florida
Source: *AmAu&B; AuNews 2; BioIn 6, 10, 11, 12; ConAu 1R, 2NR; ConSFA; EncSF, 93; LinLib L; NewEScF; ScF&FL 1, 2, 92; ScFSB; TwCSFW 86, 91; WhoSciF; WrDr 84, 86, 88, 90, 92, 94, 96*

Caillaux, Joseph Marie Auguste
French. Political Leader
Premier, 1911-12; imprisoned, 1920-23, for corresponding with Germany in WW I.
b. Mar 30, 1863 in Le Mans, France

d. Nov 21, 1944 in Paris, France
Source: *CurBio 45; WebBD 83*

Caillie, Rene Auguste
French. Explorer
First European to visit, return from Timbuktu, 1820s.
b. Nov 19, 1799 in Mauze, France
d. 1838 in La Badere, France
Source: *NewCol 75; WhDW*

Cain
Biblical Figure
Son of Adam and Eve; killed brother Abel out of jealousy.
Source: *Benet 96; BioIn 10; BlkAWP; LngCEL; NewCol 75; NewYHSD; Who 82*

Cain, Dean
American. Actor
Star of TV's "Lois & Clark: The New Adventures of Superman," 1993-97.
b. Jul 31, 1966 in Mount Clemens, Michigan
Source: *BioIn 21; LegTOT*

Cain, James M(allahan)
American. Author
Wrote *The Postman Always Rings Twice,* 1934; filmed, 1946; *Mildred Pierce,* 1941; filmed, 1945.
b. Jul 1, 1892 in Annapolis, Maryland
d. Oct 27, 1977 in Hyattsville, Maryland
Source: *AmAu&B; AmNov; AuNews 1; Benet 96; BiDAmNC; BiE&WWA; BioIn 1, 2, 4, 5, 6, 7, 8, 9, 10, 11, 12, 13; BlueB 76; CelR; CmCal; CnDAL; CnMWL; ConAu 17R, 73; ConLC 3, 11; ConNov 72, 76; CorpD; DcAmB S10; DcArts; DcLEL; EncMys; FilmgC; IntAu&W 76, 77; LngCTC; ModAL; NatCAB 62; NotNAT; Novels; ObitOF 79; OxCAmL 65, 95; PenC AM; REn; REnAL; RfGAmL 94; RGTwCWr; TwCA, SUP; TwCCr&M 80; TwCWr; WebE&AL; WhAm 1, 7; WhNAA; WhoAm 74, 76, 78; WhoWor 74; WorAl; WrDr 76*

Cain, Richard H
American. Politician
A founder, second pres., Paul Quinn College, Waco, TX; African Methodist Episcopal bishop of New England states, 1880-87.
b. 1825
d. 1887
Source: *BlkCO; DcAmNB; EncWM; NegAl 83*

Caine, Hall
[Thomas Henry Hall Caine]
English. Author
Wrote popular novels of biblical themes *The Eternal City,* 1901; *The Prodigal Son,* 1904.
b. May 14, 1853 in Runcorn, England
d. Aug 31, 1931 in Greeba Castle, Isle of Man, England
Source: *Alli SUP; BbD; BiD&SB; BioIn 1, 2, 3, 4, 10; CamGEL; CamGLE; Chambr 3; ConAu 122; DcBiA; DcEnA, A; DcLEL; DcNaB 1931; EncSF; EvLB; LinLib L, S; LngCTC; ModBrL; NewC; NotNAT B; OxCAmT 84; OxCEng 67, 85; REn; ScF&FL 1; StaCVF; TwCA, SUP; TwCWr; WhLit; WhoStg 1908; WhThe*

Caine, Michael
[Maurice Joseph Micklewhite]
English. Actor
Films include *Educating Rita,* 1983; won 1986 Oscar for *Hannah and Her Sisters.*
b. Mar 14, 1933 in London, England
Source: *BiDFilm, 94; BioIn 7, 8, 9, 11, 12, 13, 14, 15, 16, 17, 18; BkPepl; CelR, 90; CmMov; ConAu 146; ConTFT 6, 13; CurBio 68, 88; DcArts; EncEurC; FilmgC; GangFlm; HalFC 84, 88; IntDcF 1-3, 2-3; IntMPA 75, 76, 77, 78, 79, 81, 82, 84, 86, 88, 92, 94, 96; IntWW 77, 78, 79, 80, 81, 82, 83, 89, 91, 93; ItaFilm; LegTOT; MotPP; MovMk; NewYTBS 81; OxCFilm; VarWW 85; Who 74, 82, 83, 85, 88, 90, 92, 94; WhoAm 80, 82, 84, 86, 88, 90, 92, 94, 95, 96, 97; WhoEnt 92; WhoHol 92, A; WhoWor 74, 82, 84, 87, 91, 93, 95, 96, 97; WorAl; WorAlBi; WorEFlm*

Cairncross, Alexander Kirkland, Sir
Scottish. Author
Wrote *The Managed Economy,* 1969.
b. Feb 11, 1911 in Lesmahagow, Scotland
Source: *BlueB 76; ConAu 8NR, 61; DcNaB; IntWW 83; Who 85; WhoAm 86, 97; WhoE 83, 86; WhoWor 87, 97; WrDr 86*

Cairnes, John Elliott
Irish. Economist
Often regarded as last of classical economists; wrote *Slave Power,* 1862, a defense of North in American Civil War.
b. Dec 26, 1823 in Louth, Ireland
d. Jul 8, 1875 in London, England
Source: *Alli SUP; BiDIrW; BioIn 5, 8, 9; BritAu 19; DcIrB 78, 88; GrEconB; NewC; NewCol 75; WhoEc 81, 86*

Caius, John
English. Physician
Royal physician to Edward VI; founded Cambridge Gonville and Caius College, 1557.
b. Oct 6, 1510 in Norwich, England
d. Jul 29, 1573 in London, England
Source: *Alli; BioIn 1, 2, 3, 7, 9; CyEd; DcBiPP; DcCathB; DcNaB, C; DcScB; InSci; MacEA; OxCMed 86*

Cakobau, Ratu George, Sir
Fijian. Politician
Governor-general of Fiji, 1973-83.
b. Nov 6, 1912 in Suva, Fiji
d. Nov 25, 1989 in Suva, Fiji
Source: *FarE&A 81; IntWW 83; IntYB 82; WhoWor 84*

Calamity Jane
[Martha Jane Canary Burke]
American. Pioneer
Friend of Wild Bill Hickok who scouted for General Custer.
b. 1852 in Princeton, Missouri
d. Aug 1, 1903 in Terry, South Dakota
Source: *AmBi; BenetAL 91; BioIn 14, 18, 20; ContDcW 89; FilmgC; GoodHs; IntDcWB; InWom SUP; LegTOT; LibW; McGEWB; NotAW; OxCAmH; OxCFilm; REnAW; WebAB 74, 79; WhDW; WomFir*

Calas, Jean
French. Merchant
Calvanist condemned to death by torture for strangling son who turned Catholic; case was made famous by Voltaire; conviction overturned, 1765.
b. Mar 19, 1698 in Lacabarede, France
d. Mar 10, 1762 in Toulouse, France
Source: *BioIn 4, 5, 6; DcBiPP; EncEnl; LuthC 75; OxCAmL 65; OxCFr; OxCLaw*

Calasso, Robert
Italian. Author
Author of *The Marriage of Cadmus and Harmony,* 1993.
b. May 30, 1941 in Florence, Italy
Source: *ConLC 81*

Calcavecchia, Mark
American. Golfer
Won British Open, 1989.
b. Jun 12, 1960 in Laurel, Nebraska
Source: *BioIn 16*

Caldecott, Randolph
English. Artist
Caldecott Medal given annually to outstanding children's book illustrator established, 1938.
b. Mar 22, 1846 in Chester, England
d. Feb 12, 1886 in Saint Augustine, Florida
Source: *AnCL; AntBDN B; BenetAL 91; BioIn 1, 2, 3, 4, 5, 8, 11, 12, 16, 19; CamGLE; CarSB; CelCen; ChhPo, S1, S2, S3; ChlBkCr; ChlLR 14; DcArts; DcBrBI; DcBrWA; DcLB 163; DcNaB; DcVicP, 2; IlsBYP; JBA 34, 51; LinLib L; McGDA; OxCArt; OxCChiL; OxDcArt; RAdv 14; SmATA 17; StaCVF; Str&VC; VicBrit; WhoChL*

Calder, Alexander
American. Artist
Best known for abstract sculptures of metal, bent wire called "mobiles."
b. Jul 22, 1898 in Philadelphia, Pennsylvania
d. Nov 11, 1976 in New York, New York
Source: *Alli SUP; Benet 87, 96; BioIn 1, 2, 3, 4, 5, 6, 7, 8, 9, 10, 11, 12, 13, 14, 15, 16, 19, 20; BioNews 74; BlueB 76; BriEAA; CelR; ChhPo; ConArt 77, 83, 89, 96; ConAu 111; CurBio 46, 66, 77N; DcAmArt; DcAmB S10; DcArts; DcCAA 71, 77, 88, 94; DcTwCCu 1; DcTwDes; EncAB-H 1974, 1996; FacFETw;*

IntDcAA 90; IntWW 74, 75, 76; LinLib S; MakMC; McGDA; McGEWB; ModArCr 2; NatCAB 61; NewYTBE 73; NewYTBS 76; OxCAmH; OxCArt; OxCTwCA; OxDcArt; PeoHis; PhDcTCA 77; PrintW 83, 85; RComAH; REn; WebAB 74, 79; WhAm 7; WhAmArt 85; WhDW; Who 74; WhoAm 74, 76, 78; WhoAmA 73, 76, 78N, 80N, 82N, 84N, 86N, 89N, 91N, 93N; WhoWor 74; WorAl; WorAlBi; WorArt 1950

Calder, Frank
Canadian. Hockey Executive
First president of NHL, 1917-43; Calder Trophy named in his honor; Hall of Fame, 1945.
b. 1877, Scotland
d. Feb 4, 1942 in Montreal, Quebec, Canada
Source: *ObitOF 79; WhoHcky 73*

Calder, Nigel David Ritchie
English. Author
Writer of popular science books: *The Restless Earth,* 1972; *The Comet Is Coming!* 1981.
b. Dec 2, 1931 in London, England
Source: *Au&Wr 71; ConAu 21R; CurBio 86; DcLEL 1940; Who 85; WrDr 86*

Calder, Peter Ritchie
[Lord Ritchie-Calder of Balmashannar]
Scottish. Journalist
Newspaper, mag. articles bridged gap between scientist, layman, 1922-50s.
b. Jul 1, 1906 in Forfar, Scotland
d. Jan 31, 1982 in Edinburgh, Scotland
Source: *CurBio 63, 86; DcNaB 1981; IntAu&W 76, 77; NewYTBS 82; WhoWor 78; WrDr 80*

Calder-Marshall, Anna Lucia
English. Actor
TV, stage performer since 1967; starred in numerous Shakesperean roles; won 1970 Emmy.
b. Jan 11, 1947 in London, England
Source: *FilmgC; WhoThe 81; WhoWor 74, 76, 78*

Calderon de la Barca, Pedro
Spanish. Dramatist, Poet
Popular during Spain's Golden Age; wrote over 120 plays: *Mayor of Zalamea,* 1638.
b. Jan 17, 1600 in Madrid, Spain
d. May 25, 1681 in Madrid, Spain
Source: *AtlBL; BbD; Benet 87; BiD&SB; BioIn 1, 5, 6, 7, 8, 10, 13, 14; CamGWoT; CasWL; CnThe; CyWA 58; DcArts; DcBiPP; DcCathB; DcEuL; DcHiB; DcSpL; Dis&D; DramC 3; EncWT; EuAu; EuWr 2; EvEuW; GrFLW; LinLib L, S; LitC 23; MagSWL; McGEWD 72, 84; NewC; NewEOp 71; NewGrDO; NotNAT B; OxCEng 67, 85, 95; OxCSpan; OxCThe 67, 83; PenC EUR; RAdv 14, 13-2; RComWL; REn; REnWD; RfGWoL 95; WhDW; WorAl; WorAlBi*

Calderone, Frank Anthony
American. Physician
Developed, headed World Health Organization, 1951-54.
b. Mar 10, 1901 in New York, New York
d. Feb 10, 1987 in New York, New York
Source: *BiDrAPH 79; BioIn 2, 3; CurBio 52, 87; InSci; WhAm 9; WhoAm 74, 76, 80, 82; WhoWor 80, 82*

Calderone, Mary Steichen
American. Physician
Co-wrote *The Family Book About Sexuality,* 1981; won numerous achievement awards.
b. Jul 1, 1904 in New York, New York
Source: *AmSocL; AuNews 1; BiDAmEd; BioNews 74; ConAu 104; CurBio 67; InWom, SUP; LibW; WhoAm 74, 76, 78, 80, 82, 84, 86, 88, 90, 92; WhoAmW 58, 61, 66, 68, 70, 72, 74, 75, 79, 81, 83, 85, 87, 89, 91, 93; WhoWor 74, 93; WomEdUS*

Caldicott, Helen Broinowski
Australian. Social Reformer
Leader, Physicians for Social Responsibility, an antinuclear coalition, 1978-83 ; pres. emeritus 1983—.
b. Aug 7, 1938 in Melbourne, Australia
Source: *AmPeW; ConAu 114; CurBio 83; NewYTBS 79; WomFir*

Caldwell, Erskine Preston
American. Author
Known for earthy depictions of rural poor: *God's Little Acre,* 1933; filmed, 1958; *Tobacco Road,* 1932; filmed, 1941.
b. Dec 17, 1903 in Moreland, Georgia
d. Apr 11, 1987 in Paradise Valley, Arizona
Source: *AmAu&B; AmNov; AmWr; Au&Wr 71; AuNews 1; BioNews 74; CasWL; CnDAL; ConAmA; ConAu 1R, 2NR; ConLC 14; ConNov 86; CurBio 40, 87; EncAAH; IntWW 83; LinLib S; LngCTC; McGEWB; ModAL, S1; OxCAmL 65; PenC AM; PlP&P; RAdv 1; REn; REnAL; TwCA, SUP; WebAB 74, 79; Who 85; WhoAm 84; WhoSSW 75; WhoTwCL; WhoWor 84; WrDr 86*

Caldwell, John Charles
Australian. Educator
Writings on reproduction, population control: *Population Growth and Family Change in Africa,* 1968.
b. Dec 8, 1928 in Sydney, Australia
Source: *WhoWor 74, 76*

Caldwell, Sarah
American. Conductor, Director
Founded Opera Co. of Boston, 1957; first woman to conduct at NY Met., 1976.
b. Mar 6, 1924 in Maryville, Missouri
Source: *Baker 78, 84, 92; BioIn 12, 13, 19; BioNews 74; CelR 90; ContDcW 89; CurBio 73; DcTwCCu 1; GoodHs; GrLiveH; IntDcOp; IntWWM 90; LegTOT; LibW; MusSN; NewAmDM; NewGrDA 86; NewGrDO; NewYTBE 72; OxDcOp; PenDiMP; WhoAm 80, 82, 84, 86, 88, 92, 94, 95, 96, 97; WhoAmM 83; WhoAmW 81, 89, 91, 93, 95, 97; WhoE 83, 86, 89, 91, 95; WhoEnt 92; WhoMW 96; WhoOp 76; WhoWor 74; WorAl; WorAlBi*

Caldwell, Taylor
[Janet Miriam Taylor Caldwell; Mrs. William Robert Prestie]
English. Author
Wrote *Testimony of Two Men,* 1968; *The Captains and the Kings,* 1972.
b. Sep 7, 1900 in Manchester, England
d. Aug 30, 1985 in Greenwich, Connecticut
Source: *AmAu&B; AmNov; AmWomWr; AnObit 1985; Au&Wr 71; Benet 87; BenetAL 91; BioAmW; BioIn 14, 16; BlmGWL; BlueB 76; CelR; ConAu 5NR, 5R, 116; ConLC 2, 28, 39; CurBio 40, 85, 85N; EncBrWW; EncPaPR 91; EncSF; FacFETw; ForWC 70; IntAu&W 77; InWom, SUP; LegTOT; LibW; LngCTC; NewYTBS 85; Novels; OxCAmL 65, 83; OxCWoWr 95; PenNWW A; REn; REnAL; ScF&FL 1, 2, 92; ScFSB; TwCRHW 90; WhAm 9; Who 74, 82, 83, 85; WhoAm 80, 82; WhoAmW 58, 64, 66, 68, 70, 72, 81; WhoWor 80, 82; WorAl; WrDr 76, 80, 82, 84, 86*

Caldwell, Zoe
Australian. Actor
Best known for the title role on stage, TV of "Medea."
b. Sep 14, 1933 in Melbourne, Australia
Source: *BioIn 8, 9, 10; CelR, 90; ConTFT 1, 10; CurBio 70; IntDcT 3; InWom SUP; LegTOT; NotNAT; OxCAmT 84; OxCCanT; PlP&P, A; WhoAm 74, 94, 95, 96, 97; WhoAmW 74, 87, 91, 93, 95, 97; WhoEnt 92; WhoHol 92; WhoThe 81; WhoWor 74; WorAl*

Cale, J. J
American. Singer, Songwriter
Guitarist, composer, who wrote Eric Clapton's hit single, "After Midnight," 1970.
b. Dec 5, 1938 in Oklahoma City, Oklahoma
Source: *ConMuA 80A; HarEnR 86; IlEncRk; RolSEnR 83; WhoRock 81*

Cale, John
English. Singer, Musician
Formerly with Velvet Underground; solo hits include "Black Rose," 1985.
b. Dec 5, 1942 in Garnant, England
Source: *ASCAP 80; ConMus 9; EncRk 88; HarEnR 86; IlEncRk; RolSEnR 83*

Caleb
Biblical Figure
Sent to gather information about the land of Canaan for the Hebrews under Moses.

Source: *Benet 96; BioIn 4, 5*

Calero (Portocarrero), Adolfo
Nicaraguan. Political Activist
Supported by US, led rebels in attempt to overthrow Sandinista regime in Nicaragua, 1988.
b. 1932?, Nicaragua
Source: *CurBio 87*

Calhern, Louis
[Carl Henry Vogt]
American. Actor
Stage, screen star, who won many awards for portraying Oliver Wendell Holmes in *Magnificent Yankee,* 1946.
b. Feb 19, 1895 in New York, New York
d. May 12, 1956 in Nara, Japan
Source: *BiDFilm, 83; WhThe; WorAl; WorAlBi*

Calhoun, John Caldwell
American. US Vice President
Secretary of War 1817-25; vp under Adams, 1824-32; promoted southern unity, state's rights.
b. Mar 18, 1782 in Calhoun Mills, South Carolina
d. Mar 31, 1850 in Washington, District of Columbia
Source: *Alli; AmAu; AmAu&B; AmBi; AmPolLe; ApCAB; BbD; BiAUS; BiD&SB; BiDrAC; BiDrUSC 89; BiDrUSE 71; BiDSA; BioIn 1, 2, 3, 4, 5, 7, 8, 9, 10, 11, 12, 13; CelCen; CivWDc; CyAG; CyAL 1; DcAmAu; DcAmB; DcAmDH 80, 89; DcAmMiB; DcBiPP; DcLB 3; Drake; EncAAH; EncAB-H 1974, 1996; EncSoH; HarEnUS; LinLib L, S; McGEWB; NatCAB 6; NinCLC 15; OxCAmH; OxCAmL 65; RAdv 13-3; REn; REnAL; REnAW; TwCBDA; VicePre; WebAB 74, 79; WhAm HS; WhAmP; WhCiWar; WhNaAH; WorAl*

Calhoun, Lee
American. Track Athlete
Only man to win gold medal in 110-meter hurdles twice, 1956, 1960 Olympics.
b. Feb 23, 1933 in Laurel, Mississippi
Source: *AfrAmSG; BioIn 16, 21; InB&W 80; WhoBlA 77, 80; WhoTr&F 73*

Calhoun, Rory
[Francis Timothy Durgin]
American. Actor
Western films include *Ticket to Tomahawk; River of No Return; Treasure of Pancho Villa.*
b. Aug 8, 1923 in Los Angeles, California
Source: *FilmgC; HalFC 84; InB&W 85; IntMPA 75, 76, 77, 78, 79, 81, 82, 84, 86, 88; MotPP; MovMk; WhoAm 86, 88; WhoHol A; WorAl; WorAlBi*

Califano, Joseph Anthony, Jr.
American. Lawyer
Secretary, HEW, 1977-81; wrote *The Media and the Law,* 1976.
b. May 15, 1931 in New York, New York
Source: *BiDrUSE 89; BioIn 7, 8, 10, 11, 12, 13; ConAu 2NR, 45; CurBio 77; IntWW 74, 75, 76, 77, 78, 79, 80, 81, 82, 83, 89, 91, 93; NewYTBS 76; WhoAm 74, 76, 78, 80, 82, 84, 86, 88, 90, 92, 94, 95, 96, 97; WhoAmL 78, 79, 87, 90, 92, 94; WhoAmP 85; WhoE 77, 79, 81, 89, 95; WhoFI 75; WhoGov 77; WhoSSW 73, 75; WhoWor 78; WorAl; WrDr 86*

Califia, Pat
American. Writer
Wrote *Sapphistry,* 1980; *Public Sex,* 1994.
b. 1954
Source: *BioIn 19; ConAu 133; GayLesB; GayLL; OxCWoWr 95; ScF&FL 92; WrDr 94, 96*

Caliguiri, Richard
American. Politician
Dem. mayor of Pittsburgh, 1977-88.
b. Oct 20, 1931 in Pittsburgh, Pennsylvania
d. May 6, 1988 in Pittsburgh, Pennsylvania
Source: *BioIn 12; WhoAm 84, 86; WhoAmP 85*

Caligula
[Gaius Caesar Germanicus]
Roman. Ruler
Succeeded Tiberius as Roman emperor, 37-41; main character in Camus' play *Caligula,* 1944.
b. Aug 31, 12 in Antium, Italy
d. Jan 24, 41 in Rome, Italy
Source: *Benet 87, 96; BioIn 1, 3, 4, 5, 9, 10, 11, 12, 14, 17, 18, 20; DcBiPP; DicTyr; HisWorL; LegTOT; McGEWB; NewC; REn; WorAlBi*

Calisher, Hortense
[Mrs. Curtis Harnack]
American. Author
Novels include *The Bobby-Soxer,* 1986; *Eagle Eye,* 1972.
b. Dec 20, 1911 in New York, New York
Source: *AmAu&B; AmWomWr, 92; Au&Wr 71; AuSpks; Benet 87, 96; BenetAL 91; BioIn 2, 6, 7, 8, 9, 10, 11, 12; BlueB 76; CamGLE; CamHAL; CelR; ConAu 1NR, 1R, 22NR; ConLC 2, 4, 8, 38; ConNov 72, 76, 82, 86, 91, 96; CurBio 73; CyWA 89; DcLB 2; DcLEL 1940; DrAF 76; EncSF, 93; FemiCLE; IntAu&W 76, 77; IntDcWB; IntWW 89, 91, 93; InWom SUP; JeAmFiW; JeAmWW; LegTOT; LinLib L; MajTwCW; ModAL S1; ModWoWr; NewYTBE 72; Novels; OxCAmL 65, 83, 95; OxCWoWr 95; PenC AM; RfGAmL 87, 94; RfGShF; RGTwCWr; ScF&FL 1, 2; ScFSB; ShSCr 15; ShSWr; TwCWr; WhoAm 74, 76, 78, 80, 82, 84, 86, 88, 90, 92, 94, 95, 96, 97; WhoAmW 66, 68, 70, 72, 74, 75, 83, 85, 91, 93, 95, 97; WhoE 95; WhoUSWr 88; WhoWor 74, 91; WhoWrEP 89, 92; WorAlBi; WorAu 1950; WrDr 76, 80, 82, 84, 86, 88, 90, 92, 94, 96*

Calkins, Dick
American. Cartoonist
Drew science-fiction comic strip "Buck Rogers," 1929-47; wrote stories for Red Ryder comic books, 1950s.
b. 1895 in Grand Rapids, Michigan
d. May 13, 1962 in Tucson, Arizona
Source: *EncSF 93; WorECom*

Calkins, Earnest Elmo
American. Advertising Executive
Deaf from age six; founded Calkins and Holden, first modern ad agency.
b. Mar 25, 1868 in Geneseo, Illinois
d. Oct 4, 1964
Source: *AdMenW; AmAu&B; BioIn 1, 3, 5, 7, 20, 21; ChhPo; DcAmB S7; DeafPAS; EncAB-A 5; LinLib S; REnAL; WhAm 4; WhLit; WhNAA*

Callaghan, James
[Leonard James Callaghan]
English. Government Official
Labor Party leader; prime minister, 1976-79.
b. Mar 27, 1912 in Portsmouth, England
Source: *BioIn 6, 7, 8, 9, 10, 11, 12; BlueB 76; ColdWar 1; CurBio 68; DcPol; DcTwHis; EncCW; EncWB; FacFETw; IntWW 74, 75, 76, 77, 78, 79, 80, 81, 82, 83; IntYB 78, 79, 80, 81, 82; NewYTBS 76; Who 74, 82, 83, 85, 88; WhoWor 74, 76, 78, 80, 82, 84, 87, 91, 93, 95, 96, 97; WorAl; WorAlBi*

Callaghan, Morley Edward
Canadian. Author
Best known for allegorical fiction written in 1930s: *Such Is My Beloved,* 1934; autobiographical memoir *That Summer in Paris,* 1963, describes friendship with Hemingway and Fitzgerald.
b. Sep 22, 1903 in Toronto, Ontario, Canada
d. Aug 25, 1990 in Toronto, Ontario, Canada
Source: *CamGEL; CanNov; CanWr; CasWL; CathA 1930; ConAu 9R, 33NR, 132; ConCaAu 1; ConLC 3, 41; ConNov 72, 76, 86; CreCan 2; DcLEL; EncWL; FacFETw; IntWW 83; LngCTC; MajTwCW; NewC; OxCAmL 65; OxCCan, SUP; PenC ENG; REn; REnAL; RfGShF; RGTwCWr; TwCA, SUP; TwCWr; WebE&AL; WhAm 10; Who 85; WhoAm 74; WhoTwCL; WhoWor 84, 87, 89; WrDr 76, 86*

Callahan, Daniel John
American. Editor, Philosopher
Founded Institute of Social Ethics and Life Sciences, 1969; editor *The Commonweal,* 1961-68.
b. Jul 19, 1930 in Washington, District of Columbia
Source: *AmCath 80; AmMWSc 86; BioIn 10, 11; WhoAm 74, 76, 78, 80, 82, 84, 86, 88, 90, 92, 94, 95, 96, 97; WhoE 74; WhoFI 92; WhoMedH; WhoScEn 96; WhoWor 74, 76, 80, 82, 84, 87, 89*

Callahan, Harry Morey
American. Photographer
Known for his abstract photographs of everyday scenes.
b. Oct 22, 1912 in Detroit, Michigan
Source: *AmArt; BioIn 12, 13, 14; CurBio 84; WhoAm 78, 80, 84, 86, 88, 90, 92, 94, 95, 96, 97; WhoWor 84, 87, 89, 91, 93, 95, 96, 97*

Callan, Michael
American. Actor
Films include *Gidget Goes Hawaiian,* 1961; *Cat Ballou,* 1965.
b. Nov 22, 1935 in Philadelphia, Pennsylvania
Source: *FilmgC; HalFC 84, 88; IntMPA 77, 84, 86, 88, 92, 94, 96; MotPP; WhoHol 92, A*

Callas, Charlie
American. Comedian
Night club performer, 1962—; films include *Pete's Dragon,* 1977.
b. Dec 20, in New York, New York
Source: *EncAFC; WhoAm 80, 82, 84; WhoHol A; WorAl; WorAlBi*

Callas, Maria
[Maria Kalogeropoulou; Maria Meneghini]
American. Opera Singer
Soprano, 1938-60; romantically involved with Aristotle Onassis, 1960s.
b. Dec 3, 1923 in New York, New York
d. Sep 16, 1977 in Paris, France
Source: *AmCulL; Baker 78, 84, 92; BiDAmM; BioAmW; BioIn 10, 12, 13, 14, 15, 16, 17, 18, 19, 20, 21; BioNews 74; BlueB 76; CelR; ConMus 11; ContDcW 89; CurBio 56, 77, 77N; DcAmB S10; DcArts; DcTwCCu 1; GoodHs; HalFC 84, 88; IntDcOp; IntDcWB; IntWW 74, 75, 76, 77; IntWWM 77; ItaFilm; LegTOT; LibW; LinLib S; MetOEnc; NewAmDM; NewEOp 71; NewGrDA 86; NewYTBE 71; NewYTBS 77; OxDcOp; PenDiMP; RAdv 14, 13-3; WebAB 74, 79; WhDW; Who 74; WhoAm 74, 76, 78; WhoAmW 64, 66, 68, 70, 72, 74, 75; WhoHol A; WhoMus 72; WhoWor 74, 76; WhScrn 83; WomFir; WorAl; WorAlBi*

Callaway, Howard Hollis
American. Business Executive, Government Official
Secretary of Army, 1973-75.
b. Apr 2, 1927 in La Grange, Georgia
Source: *BiDrAC; BiDrUSC 89; BioIn 8, 10, 11, 12; CngDr 74; IntWW 83; PolProf NF; St&PR 84, 87; WhoAm 74, 76, 78, 80, 82, 90, 92, 94, 95, 96, 97; WhoAmP 73, 75, 77, 79, 81, 83, 85, 87, 89, 91, 93, 95; WhoSSW 75; WhoWest 92, 94; WhoWor 74, 76, 78*

Callen, Michael
American. AIDS Activist, Songwriter
Wrote autobiography *Surviving AIDS,* 1990.
b. 1955 in Rising Sun, Indiana
d. Dec 27, 1993
Source: *BioIn 19, 20; GayLesB*

Callender, Clive O(rville)
American. Surgeon
One of the foremost transplant surgeons; only top-rated black surgeon in US.
b. Nov 16, 1936 in New York, New York
Source: *AfrAmBi 2; BlksScM; WhoAfA 96; WhoAm 86, 88, 90, 92, 94, 95, 96, 97; WhoBlA 77, 80, 85, 88, 90, 92, 94; WhoE 77, 79, 81, 83, 85, 86, 89, 95; WhoMedH; WhoScEn 94; WhoWor 91, 93, 95*

Callender, John Hancock
American. Architect
Wrote *Before You Buy a House,* 1953; consultant to housing agencies.
b. Jan 18, 1908
d. Mar 30, 1995 in Worcester, Pennsylvania
Source: *BioIn 4; CurBio 95N; WhAm 11; WhoAm 74, 76, 78, 80, 82, 84, 86, 88, 90, 92, 94, 95, 96*

Calles, Plutarco Elias
Mexican. Statesman, Army Officer
Pres., of Mexico, 1924-28; sponsored agrarian reforms; exiled in US, 1936-41.
b. Sep 25, 1877 in Guaymas, Mexico
d. Oct 19, 1945 in Mexico City, Mexico
Source: *BiDLAmC; BioIn 1, 8, 16, 17; CurBio 45; DcCPCAm; EncRev; FacFETw; LinLib S; McGEWB; WhAm 2*

Calley, William Laws, Jr.
American. Army Officer
Convicted of mass murder of Vietnamese civilians at My Lai, 1974.
b. Jun 8, 1943 in Miami, Florida
Source: *BioIn 8, 9, 10, 11, 12; NewYTBS 74*

Callimachus
Greek. Critic, Poet
Chief librarian for royalty; noted for wit; supposedly wrote 80 works.
b. c. 305BC in Cyrene, Greece
d. c. 240BC
Source: *AtlBL; BbD; BiD&SB; BioIn 12, 15; CasWL; ClMLC 18; OxCEng 67; PenC CL; RAdv 14, 13-2; REn*

Callistus II, Pope
[Calixtus II; Guido di Borgogne]
French. Religious Leader
Signed Concordat of Worms, 1122; called first Lateran Council, 1123.
b. 1050?
d. Dec 14, 1124
Source: *DcCathB; NewCol 75; WebBD 83*

Callot, Jacques
French. Artist
First to make engraving an independent art; produced over 1,600 caricatures, engravings.
b. 1592? in Nancy, France
d. Mar 24, 1635 in Nancy, France
Source: *AtlBL; BioIn 2, 3, 4, 5, 8, 9, 10, 11; ClaDrA; DcArts; DcCathB; Dis&D; EncWT; IntDcAA 90; McGDA; NewCol 75; NotNAT B; OxCArt; OxCFr; OxDcArt; PenDiDA 89*

Calloway, Cab
[Cabell Calloway, III]
"King of Hi De Ho"
American. Bandleader, Singer
Acclaimed scat singer; noted for song "Minnie the Moocher"; role in *Porgy and Bess,* 1953.
b. Dec 25, 1907 in Rochester, New York
d. Nov 18, 1994 in Hosckessin, Delaware
Source: *AllMusG; ASCAP 66; Baker 78, 84; BiDAfM; BiDAmM; BiDJaz; BioIn 2, 9, 10, 11, 12, 13, 14, 15, 16, 17, 20, 21; BioNews 74; BlkCond; CelR, 90; CmpEPM; ConAu 113; ConMus 6; CurBio 45, 95N; DcTwCCu 5; DrBlPA, 90; FacFETw; FilmgC; HalFC 84, 88; IlEncJ; InB&W 80, 85; LegTOT; MovMk; NegAl 76, 83, 89; NewAmDM; NewGrDA 86; NewGrDJ 88; NewYTBS 88, 94; OxCPMus; PenEncP; RadStar; WhoAfA 96; WhoAm 74; WhoBlA 75, 77, 80, 85, 88, 90, 92, 94; WhoHol 92, A; WhoJazz 72; WhoThe 77, 81; WorAl; WorAlBi*

Calloway, D(avid) Wayne
American. Business Executive
Chairman, CEO, Pepsico Inc., 1986—.
b. Sep 12, 1935 in Elkin, North Carolina
Source: *CanWW 79, 80; ConNews 87-3; WhoAm 74, 76, 78, 80*

Calment, Jean
French. Centenarian
Listed by Guinness as the world's oldest person, turned 121 in 1996.
b. Feb 21, 1875, France

Calmer, Ned
[Edgar Calmer]
American. Journalist
News editor, broadcaster, CBS, 1940-67.
b. Jul 16, 1907 in Chicago, Illinois
d. Mar 9, 1986 in New York, New York
Source: *BioIn 12, 14; ConAu 20NR, 69, 118; DcLB 4; RadStar; WhAm 9; WhoAm 74, 76, 78, 80, 82, 84; WhoWor 74*

Calmette, Albert Leon Charles
French. Bacteriologist
Student of Louis Pasteur; co-developed tuberculosis vaccine, BCG; diagnostic test.
b. Jul 12, 1863 in Nice, France
d. Oct 29, 1933 in Paris, France

Calpurnia
Roman.
Third wife of Julius Caesar; had prophetic dream of Caesar's assassination.
b. 59BC
Source: *REn*

Calve, Emma
[Rosa Calvet]
French. Opera Singer
Famed soprano; with NY Met., 1893-98; noted for roles in *Sapho; Carmen.*
b. Aug 15, 1858 in Decazeville, France
d. Jan 6, 1942 in Millau, France
Source: *Baker 78, 84, 92; BiDAmM; BioIn 3, 4, 7, 9, 11, 13, 14, 15; CurBio 42; IntDcOp; InWom, SUP; LegTOT; MetOEnc; MusSN; NewAmDM; NewEOp 71; NewGrDA 86; OxDcOp; PenDiMP; WhAm 1, 2; WhoStg 1906, 1908*

Calvert, Catherine
[Catherine Cassidy]
American. Actor
Notable films include *Behind the Mask,* 1917; *Marriage,* 1918; *That Woman,* 1922.
b. 1891 in Baltimore, Maryland
d. Jan 18, 1971 in Uniondale, New York
Source: *Film 2; MotPP; SilFlmP; TwYS; WhoHol B; WhScrn 74, 77, 83; WhThe*

Calvert, Edward
English. Artist
Engraved wood, copper; painted with oils.
b. 1799 in Appledore, England
d. 1883
Source: *BioIn 1, 4, 6, 13; DcBrWA; DcNaB; DcVicP, 2; McGDA; OxCArt; OxDcArt*

Calvert, Louis
English. Actor
London stage actor; formed, managed own company; wrote *Problems of the Actor,* 1918.
b. 1859 in Manchester, England
d. Jul 2, 1923, England
Source: *BioIn 10; EncWT; Film 1; NotNAT B; OxCThe 67, 83; WhScrn 77, 83; WhThe*

Calvert, Phyllis
[Phyllis Bickle]
English. Actor
Popular star of 1940s: *Young Mr. Pitt,* 1942; *Fanny by Gaslight,* 1944.
b. Feb 18, 1915 in London, England
Source: *BioIn 1, 19; CmMov; EncEurC; FilmgC; HalFC 84, 88; IntMPA 86; ItaFilm; MovMk; OxCFilm; Who 85, 88, 90, 92, 94; WhoHol 92, A; WhoThe 72, 77, 81*

Calvet, Corinne
[Corinne Dibos]
French. Actor
Film star of 1950s: *What Price Glory?,* 1952; *Flight to Tangiers,* 1953.
b. Apr 30, 1925 in Paris, France
Source: *BioIn 2, 9, 13; FilmgC; HalFC 84, 88; IntMPA 86, 92, 94, 96; InWom, SUP; ItaFilm; MotPP; MovMk; WhoAmW 91; WhoEnt 92; WhoHol 92, A*

Calvet, Jacques
French. Auto Executive
Vice-president, Automobiles Peugeot 1984-90; pres., 1990—.
b. Sep 19, 1931 in Boulogne-sur-Seine, France
Source: *IntWW 81, 82, 83, 89, 91, 93; Who 88, 90, 92, 94; WhoFr 79; WhoWor 78, 80, 82*

Calvin, John
[Jean Chauvin]
French. Theologian, Social Reformer
Established Calvinism; recognized Bible as only source of knowledge.
b. Jul 10, 1509 in Noyon, France
d. May 27, 1564 in Geneva, Switzerland
Source: *BbD; Benet 87, 96; BiD&SB; BioIn 1, 2, 3, 4, 5, 6, 7, 8, 9, 10, 11, 12, 13, 14, 15, 16, 17, 18, 19, 20; BlmGEL; CyEd; Dis&D; EncEth; EncPaPR 91; EncRev; EncWM; HisWorL; LegTOT; LinLib L, S; LuthC 75; McGEWB; NewC; OxCMus; RAdv 14, 13-4; RComWL; REn; WhAm 1; WhDW; WorAl; WorAlBi; WrPh P*

Calvin, Melvin
American. Chemist
Received Nobel Prize in chemistry, 1961, for researching carbon-dioxide assimilation in plants.
b. Apr 8, 1911 in Saint Paul, Minnesota
d. Jan 8, 1997 in Berkeley, California
Source: *AmMWSc 73P, 76P, 79, 82, 86, 89, 92, 95; AsBiEn; BiESc; BioIn 3, 4, 5, 6, 8, 12, 14, 15, 17, 19, 20; BlueB 76; CamDcSc; CurBio 62; FacFETw; IntWW 74, 75, 76, 77, 78, 79, 80, 81, 82, 83, 89, 91, 93; LarDcSc; LegTOT; McGEWB; McGMS 80; NobelP; NotTwCS; RAdv 14; WebAB 74, 79; Who 74, 82, 83, 85, 88, 90, 92, 94; WhoAm 74, 76, 78, 80, 82, 84, 86, 88, 90, 92, 94, 95, 96, 97; WhoFrS 84; WhoNob, 90, 95; WhoScEn 94, 96; WhoWest 78, 80, 82, 84, 87, 89, 92, 94, 96; WhoWor 74, 80, 82, 84, 87, 89, 91, 93, 95, 96, 97; WorAl; WorAlBi; WorScD; WrDr 80, 82, 84, 86, 88, 90, 92, 94, 96*

Calvino, Italo
Italian. Author
Writings include allegorical fantasy *If on a Winter's Night a Traveler,* 1979.
b. Oct 15, 1923 in Santiago de Las Vegas, Cuba
d. Sep 19, 1985 in Siena, Italy
Source: *AnObit 1985; Benet 87, 96; BioIn 10, 12, 13; CasWL; ConAu 23NR, 85, 116; ConFLW 84; ConLC 5, 8, 11, 22, 33, 39, 72, 73; CurBio 84, 85, 85N; CyWA 89; DcItL 1, 2; EncSF, 93; EncWL, 2, 3; EuWr 13; FacFETw; IntAu&W 76, 77, 82; IntWW 74, 75, 76, 77, 78, 79, 80, 81, 82, 83; LegTOT; LiExTwC; MagSWL; MajTwCW; ModRL; NewEScF; NewYTBS 81, 85; Novels; OxCEng 85, 95; PenC EUR; PostFic; RAdv 14, 13-2; RfGShF; RfGWoL 95; ScF&FL 1, 92; ScFSB; ShSCr 3; SJGFanW; TwCSFW 86A, 91A; TwCWr; Who 83, 85; WhoTwCL; WhoWor 74, 76, 78, 82, 84; WorAlBi; WorAu 1950*

Calvo, Paul McDonald
American. Politician
Governor of Guam, 1978-82.
b. Jul 25, 1934 in Agana, Guam
Source: *FarE&A 79, 80, 81; WhoAm 80, 82, 84, 86; WhoAmP 85; WhoWest 82; WhoWor 80, 82*

Calvo Sotelo (y Bustelo), Leopoldo
Spanish. Businessman, Politician
Prime minister of Spain, 1981-82.
b. Apr 14, 1926 in Madrid, Spain
Source: *BioIn 12; CurBio 81; IntWW 83; IntYB 82; NewYTBS 81; WhoWor 82, 84, 87, 89, 91, 93, 95, 96, 97*

Camargo, Marie Anne de Cupis de
French. Dancer
Paris Opera ballerina, 1726-35, 1741-51; introduced shortened ballet skirt, heelless slippers.
b. Apr 15, 1710 in Brussels, Belgium
d. Apr 28, 1770 in Paris, France
Source: *BiDD; OxCFr; WebBD 83*

Cambaceres, Jean Jacques Regis de
[Duke of Parma]
French. Statesman
Napoleon's chief legal adviser.
b. Oct 18, 1753 in Montpellier, France
d. Mar 8, 1824 in Paris, France
Source: *DcBiPP; LinLib S; OxCFr; OxCLaw*

Cambert, Robert
French. Composer
Wrote first French operas, including *Pomone,* 1671; co-founded first French opera company, 1669.
b. 1628 in Paris, France
d. 1677 in London, England
Source: *Baker 78, 84, 92; BioIn 10, 21; NewCol 75; NewEOp 71; NewGrDO; OxCMus*

Cambon, Pierre Paul
French. Diplomat
Ambassador to Great Britain, 1898-1920; helped create Entente Cordiale, 1904; encouraged Britain to enter WW I.
b. Jan 20, 1843 in Paris, France
d. May 29, 1924 in Paris, France
Source: *NewCol 75; WebBD 83*

Cambridge, Godfrey
American. Actor, Comedian
Films include *Purlie Victorious,* 1963; *Cotton Comes to Harlem,* 1970.
b. Feb 26, 1933 in New York, New York
d. Nov 29, 1976 in Hollywood, California
Source: *AfrAmAl 6; MotPP; MovMk; NegAl 76, 83, 89; NewYTBS 76; NotNAT; ObitOF 79; OxCFilm; WhAm*

7; WhoAm 74, 76; WhoBlA 75; WhoCom; WhoHol A; WhoThe 81N; WhoWor 78; WorAl; WorAlBi

Cambyses, II
Persian. Ruler
Son, successor of Cyrus the Great, 529-522 BC; added Eygpt to Persian empire, 525 BC.
d. 522BC
Source: *BioIn 20; DcBiPP; Dis&D; LinLib S; OxCClL 89; REn; WebBD 83; WhDW*

Camerarius, Rudolf Jakob
German. Botanist, Educator
First to prove sexuality in plants, c. 1694.
b. Feb 17, 1665 in Tubingen, Germany
d. Sep 11, 1721 in Tubingen, Germany
Source: *CamDcSc; DcScB; NewCol 75*

Camerini, Mario
Italian. Director
Directed Vittorio DeSica in various film comedies, 1932-39.
b. Feb 6, 1895 in Rome, Italy
d. Feb 6, 1981
Source: *AnObit 1981; BioIn 15; ConAu 103; DcFM; EncEurC; FilmgC; HalFC 84, 88; IntDcF 2-2; ItaFilm; OxCFilm; WorEFlm; WorFDir 1*

Cameron, Candace
[Mrs. Valeri Bure]
American. Actor
PlayED D.J. Tanner on TV series, "Full House;" sister of Kirk.
b. 1976?
Source: *BioIn 20, 21; WhoHol 92*

Cameron, David
American. Fashion Designer
Eclectic designer; 1st winner, Perry Ellis Award.
b. Feb 1961 in Santa Barbara, California
Source: *BioIn 15; ConNews 88-1; WhoFash 88*

Cameron, Eleanor Frances
Canadian. Author
Wrote prize-winning children's stories *Court of the Stone Children,* 1973; *Julia Redfern,* 1982.
b. Mar 23, 1912 in Winnipeg, Manitoba, Canada
d. Oct 11, 1996 in Monterey, California
Source: *AuBYP 2; ChlLR 1; ConAu 1R, 2NR; MajAI; SmATA 1; ThrBJA; TwCYAW; WhoAm 76, 78, 80, 82, 84, 86, 88, 90, 92, 94; WhoAmW 81, 83; WhoUSWr 88; WhoWrEP 89, 92, 95*

Cameron, Harry
[Harold Hugh Cameron]
Canadian. Hockey Player
Defenseman, 1917-23, mostly with Toronto; Hall of Fame, 1962.
b. Feb 6, 1890 in Pembroke, Ontario, Canada
d. Oct 20, 1953 in Vancouver, British Columbia, Canada
Source: *HocEn; WhoHcky 73*

Cameron, James
Canadian. Director
Co-wrote with Sylvester Stallone *Rambo: First Blood, Part II;* directed *Aliens II,* 1986.
b. Aug 16, 1954 in Kapuskasing, Ontario, Canada
Source: *Au&Arts 9; BiDFilm 94; ConAu 137; ConCaAu 1; ConTFT 3, 10; IntMPA 92, 94, 96; LegTOT; MiSFD 9; ScF&FL 92; WhoAm 95, 96, 97; WhoWor 95, 96, 97*

Cameron, Kirk
American. Actor
Played Mike Seaver in TV show "Growing Pains," 1986-92.
b. Oct 12, 1970 in Canoga Park, California
Source: *CelR 90; ConTFT 5, 10; IntMPA 92, 94, 96; LegTOT; WhoHol 92; WorAlBi*

Cameron, Rod
[Rod Cox]
American. Actor
Played leads in Westerns: *The Bounty Killer,* 1965; *Jessie's Girl,* 1976.
b. Dec 7, 1912 in Calgary, Alberta, Canada
d. Dec 21, 1983 in Gainesville, Georgia
Source: *BioIn 8; CmMov; FilmgC; HolP 40; IntMPA 75, 76, 77, 78, 79, 81, 82, 84; MotPP; WhoHol A*

Cameron, Roderick W
American. Author
Wrote books on history, travel.
b. Nov 15, 1913 in New York, New York
d. Sep 18, 1985 in Menerbes, France
Source: *Au&Wr 71; IntAu&W 77; NewYTBS 84; WhoWor 78; WrDr 82, 84*

Cameron, Simon
American. Politician, Government Official
Controlled PA Republican politics, 1857-77; US Secretary of War, 1861; censured by Congress, 1862, for questionable awarding of army contracts.
b. Mar 8, 1799 in Lancaster County, Pennsylvania
d. Jun 26, 1889 in Donegal Springs, Pennsylvania
Source: *AmBi; AmPolLe; ApCAB; BiAUS; BiDrAC; BiDrUSC 89; BiDrUSE 71, 89; BioIn 2, 3, 7, 9, 10, 11, 16; CivWDc; DcAmB; DcAmDH 80, 89; DcBiPP; Drake; EncAB-H 1974, 1996; HarEnUS; McGEWB; NatCAB 2; OxCAmH; PolPar; TwCBDA; WebAB 74, 79; WebBD 83; WhAm HS; WhAmP; WhCiWar*

Cameron, Verney Lovett
English. Explorer
First European to cross equatorial Africa from sea to sea, 1875.
b. Jul 1, 1844 in Radipole, England
d. Mar 27, 1894 in Leighton Buzzard, England
Source: *Alli SUP; BbD; BiD&SB; BioIn 10, 18; CelCen; DcAfHiB 86; DcBiPP; DcNaB S1; Expl 93; HisDBrE; ScF&FL 1; WhWE*

Camilli, Dolf
[Adolf Louis Camilli]
American. Baseball Player
First baseman, 1933-45; led NL in home runs, RBIs, 1941; NL MVP, 1941.
b. Apr 23, 1908 in San Francisco, California
Source: *LegTOT; WhoProB 73*

Cammermeyer, Margarethe
American. Nurse
Won Veterans Administration Nurse of the Year Award, 1985; dismissed from the military in 1992 because she admitted that she was a lesbian.
b. Mar 24, 1942 in Oslo, Norway
Source: *ConAu 152; GayLesB; News 95, 95-2; WhoAmW 91, 93, 95, 97; WhoMedH; WhoWest 96*

Camoes, Luis de
[Luis de Camoens]
Portuguese. Poet
Best known work, epic poem *Os Lusiadas,* 1572.
b. 1524 in Lisbon, Portugal
d. 1580 in Lisbon, Portugal
Source: *AtlBL; BbD; BiD&SB; BioIn 1, 5, 6, 7, 9, 10, 13; CasWL; ChhPo S1, S2; CyWA 58; DcBiA; DcBiPP; DcCathB; DcEuL; Dis&D; EuAu; EvEuW; GrFLW; OxCEng 67, 85, 95; OxCThe 67; PenC EUR; RAdv 13-2; RComWL; REn; WhDW; WorAl*

Camp, Walter Chauncey
"Father of American Football"
American. Football Executive
Developed rules, scoring system for modern-day football, late 1800s; innovations included set scrimmage, signal calling.
b. Apr 7, 1859 in New Haven, Connecticut
d. Mar 14, 1925 in New York, New York
Source: *AmAu&B; AmBi; AmLY; BiDAmSp FB; BiD&SB; BioIn 2, 3, 5, 6, 9, 11, 12; ChhPo; DcAmAu; DcAmB; DcNAA; JBA 34, 51; LegTOT; NatCAB 21; OxCAmH; REnAL; WebAB 74, 79; WhAm 1; WhNAA; WhoFtbl 74; WorAl; YABC 1*

Campagnolo, Gitullio
"Campy"
Italian. Manufacturer
Patented 182 mechanical devices; founded Campagnolo Co., 1933, most respected name in cycledom.
b. 1901?, Italy

d. Feb 1982 in Monselice, Italy
Source: *BioIn 12, 13*

Campana, Dino
Italian. Poet
Only verse published during lifetime *Orphic Songs,* 1914.
b. Aug 20, 1885 in Marradi, Italy
d. Mar 11, 1932 in Florence, Italy
Source: *BioIn 1, 10, 14, 18; CasWL; ClDMEL 47; CnMWL; ConAu 117; DcItL 1, 2; DcLB 114; EncWL 3; FacFETw; ModRL; PenC EUR; TwCLC 20; WhoTwCL; WorAu 1950*

Campanella, Joseph Mario
American. Actor
Star of TV series "The Lawyers," 1969-72.
b. Nov 21, 1927 in New York, New York
Source: *BiE&WWA; FilmgC; HalFC 84; NotNAT; WhoAm 78, 80, 82, 84, 86; WhoHol A*

Campanella, Roy
American. Baseball Player
Catcher, Brooklyn, 1948-57; led NL in RBIs, 1953; paralyzed in car accident, 1958; Hall of Fame, 1969.
b. Nov 19, 1921 in Homestead, Pennsylvania
d. Jun 26, 1993 in Woodland Hills, California
Source: *AfrAmAl 6; AfrAmSG; AnObit 1993; Ballpl 90; BiDAmSp BB; BioIn 1, 2, 3, 4, 5, 6, 7, 8, 9, 10, 11, 13, 14, 15, 17, 19, 20, 21; CelR; CurBio 53, 93N; FacFETw; InB&W 80, 85; LegTOT; NegAl 76, 83, 89; News 94, 94-1; NewYTBS 93; WhoAm 74, 76, 78; WhoBlA 75, 77, 80, 85, 88, 90, 92, 94N; WhoProB 73; WhoSpor; WorAl; WorAlBi*

Campanella, Tommaso
[Domenico Giovanni]
Italian. Philosopher, Poet, Author
Wrote *Civitas Solis,* 1623, his idea of Utopian society.
b. Sep 5, 1568 in Stilo, Italy
d. May 21, 1639 in Paris, France
Source: *BbD; Benet 96; BiD&SB; BioIn 1, 3, 4, 7, 8, 9, 13; CasWL; DcAmSR; DcBiPP; DcCathB; DcEuL; DcItL 1, 2; DcScB, S1; Dis&D; EncSF, 93; EuAu; EvEuW; LinLib L, S; LuthC 75; McGEWB; OxCPhil; PenC EUR; RAdv 14, 13-4; REn; RfGWoL 95; ScFEYrs*

Campaneris, Bert
[Dagoberto Blanco Campaneris]
"Campy"
Cuban. Baseball Player
Shortstop, 1964-81, 1983; led AL in stolen bases six times.
b. Mar 9, 1942 in Pueblo Nuevo, Cuba
Source: *Ballpl 90; BioIn 13, 21; LegTOT; WhoAm 74; WhoBlA 77, 80, 85, 90; WhoHisp 91, 92, 94; WhoProB 73*

Campbell, Bebe Moore
American. Author
Author of *Your Blues Ain't Like Mine,* 1992; *Brothers and Sisters,* 1994.
b. 1950 in Philadelphia, Pennsylvania
Source: *BlkWr 2; ConAu 139; ConBlB 6; News 96, 96-2; SchCGBL; WrDr 96*

Campbell, Ben Nighthorse
American. Politician
Rep. senator, CO, 1993—.
b. Apr 13, 1933 in Auburn, California
Source: *AlmAP 88, 92, 96; BiDrUSC 89; BioIn 15; CngDr 87, 89, 91, 93, 95; CurBio 94; EncNAB; IntWW 93; NewYTBS 91; NotNaAm; WhoAm 88, 90, 92, 94, 95, 96, 97; WhoAmP 83, 85, 87, 89, 91, 93, 95; WhoE 95; WhoWest 87, 89, 92, 94, 96*

Campbell, Bill
American. Politician
Mayor of Atlanta, 1994—.
b. 1953 in Raleigh, North Carolina
Source: *CurBio 96; News 97-1*

Campbell, Carroll Ashmore, Jr.
American. Politician
Rep. congressman from SC, 1979-87; governor of SC, 1987—.
b. Jul 24, 1940 in Greenville, South Carolina
Source: *AlmAP 88; BiDrUSC 89; BioIn 13; CngDr 79, 81, 83, 85; IntWW 89, 91, 93; WhoAm 80, 82, 84, 86, 88, 90, 92, 94, 95; WhoAmP 73, 75, 77, 79, 81, 83, 85, 87, 89, 91, 93, 95; WhoEmL 87; WhoSSW 80, 82, 86, 88, 91, 93, 95; WhoWor 91, 93, 95*

Campbell, Clarence Sutherland
Canadian. Hockey Executive
Succeeded "Red" Dutton as president of NHL, 1946-77; best known for league expansion, 1967, suspension of Maurice Richard before 1955 playoffs; Hall of Fame, 1966.
b. Jul 9, 1905 in Fleming, Saskatchewan, Canada
d. Jun 24, 1984 in Montreal, Quebec, Canada
Source: *BioIn 14; BlueB 76; CanWW 70, 79, 80, 81, 83; NewYTBS 84; WhAm 8; WhoAm 74, 76, 78, 80, 82, 84; WhoHcky 73*

Campbell, Clifford, Sir
English. Government Official
Governor-general of Jamaica, 1962-73.
b. Jun 28, 1892 in Petersfield, England
Source: *InB&W 80; IntYB 82; Who 74, 82, 83, 85, 88, 90, 92; WhoGov 72; WhoWor 74*

Campbell, Donald Fraser
English. Engineer
Pres., U. College of Cape Breton, 1974—.
b. 1881
d. 1966
Source: *BioIn 7; CanWW 83*

Campbell, Donald Guy
American. Journalist, Author
Wrote *Understanding Stocks,* 1965; *The Handbook of Real Estate Investment,* 1968.
b. Jun 27, 1922 in Brownsburg, Idaho
Source: *ConAu 19NR; IndAu 1917; WhoAm 74, 76, 78, 80, 82, 84, 86, 88, 90*

Campbell, Donald Malcolm
English. Auto Racer, Boat Racer
Son of Malcolm; killed while attempting to break the water speed record.
b. Mar 23, 1921 in Reigate, England
d. Jan 4, 1967 in Coniston, England
Source: *DcNaB MP; FacFETw; ObitT 1961; Who 74; WhoGov 72; WhoWor 74*

Campbell, Douglas
Scottish. Actor
Starred in London's Old Vic, Canada's Stratford theaters; organized Canadian Players.
b. Jun 11, 1922 in Glasgow, Scotland
Source: *BiE&WWA; BioIn 1, 5; CnThe; ConTFT 6; CreCan 1; NotNAT; OxCCanT; WhoAm 74, 76, 78; WhoHol 92; WhoThe 72, 77, 81*

Campbell, E. Simms
American. Cartoonist
First black artist to work for nat. publications; cartoonist for *Esquire,* other leading periodicals, 1933-71.
b. Jan 2, 1906 in Saint Louis, Missouri
d. Jan 27, 1971 in White Plains, New York
Source: *BioIn 6, 7, 8, 9; ConAu 93; CurBio 41, 71, 71N; EncAJ*

Campbell, Earl Christian
American. Football Player
Running back, 1978-86, mostly with Houston; led NFL in rushing three times; won Heisman Trophy, 1977; NFL Hall of Fame, 1991.
b. Mar 29, 1955 in Tyler, Texas
Source: *BiDAmSp FB; CurBio 83; FootReg 86; InB&W 85; NewYTBS 79, 84; WhoAfA 96; WhoAm 82, 84, 86; WhoBlA 85, 92, 94; WorAl*

Campbell, Glen Travis
American. Singer, Musician
Country-pop singer with 12 gold, 7 platinum albums; number one singles "Rhinestone Cowboy," 1975; "Southern Nights," 1977; hosted several music-themed TV shows; five time Grammy award winner.
b. Apr 22, 1936 in Delight, Arkansas
Source: *Baker 84; BioNews 74; BkPepl; CurBio 69; EncFCWM 83; FilmgC; HarEnR 86; IntMPA 86; WhoAm 86; WhoHol A; WhoWest 76; WorAl*

Campbell, James
American. Baseball Executive
With the Detroit Tigers 1949-92; promoted to general manager, 1962; became team president, 1978.

d. Oct 31, 1995 in Lakeland, Florida
Source: *Alli, SUP; BiDLA; BiNAW Sup, SupB; CabMA; CmpEPM; DcCanB 5; FolkA 87; NatCAB 12; NewYTBS 77; ObitOF 79; StaCVF; WrDr 80, 82*

Campbell, John W
American. Author, Editor
Science fiction books include *Invaders from the Infinite,* 1961.
b. Jun 8, 1910 in Newark, New Jersey
d. Jul 11, 1971 in Mountainside, New Jersey
Source: *ConAu 21R, 29R, P-2; ConSFA; ScF&FL 2; WorAu 1950*

Campbell, Joseph
American. Manufacturer, Businessman
Started canning business, 1869; introduced condensed soup, 1898.
b. 1817
d. 1900
Source: *Entr*

Campbell, Joseph
American. Author
Best known book *The Hero of a Thousand Faces,* 1949; his mythological writings were inspiration for *Star Wars* film trilogy.
b. Mar 26, 1904 in New York, New York
d. Oct 31, 1987 in Honolulu, Hawaii
Source: *AmAu&B; AnObit 1987; Au&Arts 3; BenetAL 91; BestSel 89-2; BioIn 4, 11, 12, 13, 14, 15, 16, 17, 18; ConAu 1R, 3NR, 28NR, 124; ConLC 69; CurBio 84, 88, 88N; CyWA 89; DrAS 74P, 78P; EncO&P 3; FacFETw; LegTOT; LinLib L; MajTwCW; NewYTBS 87; OxCAmL 95; RAdv 14; REnAL; TwCA SUP; WhAm 9; WhoAm 74, 76, 78, 80, 82, 84, 86; WhoE 74; WrDr 88*

Campbell, Kim
Canadian. Political Leader
Progressive Conservative party member; first woman prime minister of Canada, 1993.
b. Mar 10, 1947 in Port Alberni, British Columbia, Canada
Source: *GrLiveH; IntWW 93; News 93; Who 94; WomFir*

Campbell, Luther
[2 Live Crew]
American. Singer
Rap singer; former member of controversial rap group 2 Live Crew which released *As Nasty as They Want to Be,* 1988; solo albums include *I Got Shit on My Mind,* 1992 and *In the Nude,* 1993.
b. 1961 in Miami, Florida
Source: *ConMus 10*

Campbell, Malcolm, Sir
English. Auto Racer, Boat Racer
First to attain speed of 150 mph on land, 1925.
b. Mar 11, 1885 in Chislehurst, England
d. Jan 1, 1949
Source: *BioIn 1, 2, 5, 8, 9, 12, 13, 14; CurBio 47, 49; DcNaB 1941; EncSoA; FacFETw; GrBr; WhDW; WhE&EA*

Campbell, Maria
[June Stifle]
Canadian. Writer
Wrote autobiography *Halfbreed,* 1973, which relates her struggle as a Metis woman.
b. Apr 1940 in Park Valley, Saskatchewan, Canada
Source: *ArtclWW 2; BioIn 13; BlmGWL; CaW; ConAu 54NR, 102; ConCaAu 1; ConLC 85; FemiCLE; NatNAL; WhoCanL 85, 92*

Campbell, Naomi
English. Model, Actor
First ethnic woman to appear on the cover of French *Vogue,*; played Julia on "The Cosby Show."
b. May 22, 1970 in London, England
Source: *BioIn 16; ConBlB 1; DcTwCCu 5; IntWW 93; LegTOT*

Campbell, Patrick, Mrs.
[Beatrice Stella Tanner]
English. Actor
G B Shaw wrote Eliza Doolittle role in *Pygmalion* especially for her.
b. Feb 9, 1865 in London, England
d. Apr 9, 1940 in Pau, France
Source: *BioIn 2, 3, 4, 5, 6, 8, 9, 10, 11, 13, 14, 16, 17; CamGWoT; CnThe; ContDcW 89; CurBio 40; DcArts; EncBrWW; EncVaud; EncWT; FamA&A; FilmgC; HalFC 84, 88; IntDcT 3; IntDcWB; InWom; LegTOT; LngCTC; NewC; NotNAT A, B; OxCAmT 84; OxCCan; OxCFilm; OxCThe 67, 83; PlP&P; REn; ThFT; VicBrit; WhAm 1; WhoHol B; WhScrn 74, 77, 83; WhThe; WorAl; WorAlBi*

Campbell, Roy
English. Author, Journalist
War correspondent, who wrote autobiography *Light on a Dark Horse,* 1951.
b. Oct 2, 1901 in Durban, South Africa
d. Apr 22, 1957 in Setubal, Portugal
Source: *BioIn 2, 3, 4, 6, 8, 12, 13, 14, 15; CathA 1930; ChhPo, S3; CnE&AP; CnMWL; ConAu 104; DcArts; DcCathB; DcLB 20; EncSoA; EncWL 2, 3; EngPo; FacFETw; LiExTwC; LinLib L; LngCEL; LngCTC; ModBrL, S1; ModCmwL; ObitT 1951; OxCEng 67, 85; PenC ENG; REn; RfGEnL 91; TwCA, SUP; TwCLC 5; TwCWr; WebE&AL; WhDW; WhoTwCL*

Campbell, Tevin
American. Singer
Rhythm and blues singer signed by Quincy Jones at age 12; topped R & B charts with single "Tomorrow (A Better You, Better Me)."
b. Nov 12, 1976 in Waxahachie, Texas

Campbell, Thomas
Scottish. Poet
Known for patriotic war song, "Ye Mariners of England," 1800; wrote *Pleasures of Hope,* 1799.
b. Aug 27, 1777 in Glasgow, Scotland
d. Jun 15, 1844 in Boulogne-sur-Mer, France
Source: *Alli; BbD; Benet 87, 96; BiD&SB; BiDLA; BioIn 10, 12, 17, 21; BlmGEL; BritAu 19; CamGEL; CamGLE; CasWL; CelCen; ChhPo, S1, S2, S3; CmScLit; CrtT 2; DcArts; DcBiPP; DcEnA, A; DcEnL; DcEuL; DcLB 93, 144; DcLEL; DcNaB; EvLB; LinLib L, S; MouLC 3; NewC; NinCLC 19; OxCAmL 65, 83, 95; OxCEng 67, 85, 95; PenC ENG; PoChrch; REn; RfGEnL 91; WebE&AL*

Campbell, Tisha
American. Actor, Singer
Appeared in *Little Shop of Horrors,* 1987; *House Party,* 1990.
b. c. 1969 in Oklahoma
Source: *ConBlB 8*

Campbell, Walter Stanley
[Stanley Vestal]
American. Author
Books on southwestern frontier include *Sitting Bull,* 1928.
b. Aug 15, 1887 in Severy, Kansas
d. Dec 25, 1957 in Oklahoma City, Oklahoma
Source: *AmAu&B; BenetAL 91; BioIn 4; CnDAL; OxCAmL 65, 83; REn; REnAL; REnAW; TwCA, SUP; WhAm 3; WhE&EA; WhNAA*

Campbell, William Edward March
[William March]
American. Author
Wrote *The Bad Seed,* 1954; dramatized by Maxwell Anderson, 1955.
b. Sep 18, 1893 in Mobile, Alabama
d. May 15, 1954 in New Orleans, Louisiana
Source: *AmAu&B; AmNov X; BenetAL 91; CnDAL; ConAmA; ConAu 108; DcAmB S5; DcLB 9, 86; LngCTC; ModAL; OxCAmL 65, 83, 95; REn; REnAL; SouWr; TwCA SUP*

Campbell, William Wallace
American. Astronomer
Director, Lick Observatory, 1901-30; made seven eclipse expeditions.
b. Apr 11, 1862 in Hancock County, Ohio
d. Jun 14, 1938 in San Francisco, California
Source: *BioIn 2, 4, 14, 18; DcAmB S2; DcNAA; DcScB; InSci; LarDcSc; LinLib S; NatCAB 11; WebAB 74, 79; WhAm 1; WhNAA*

Campbell-Bannerman, Henry, Sir
English. Political Leader
Prime minister, 1905-08, after Balfour's resignation; furthered liberal measures, criticized British methods in S Africa.

b. Sep 7, 1836 in Glasgow, Scotland
d. Apr 22, 1908 in London, England
Source: *BioIn 4, 8, 9, 10, 11, 12, 14, 17, 21; DcNaB S2; FacFETw; HisDBrE; NewCol 75; WebBD 83; WhDW*

Campeau, Robert Joseph
Canadian. Real Estate Executive
Developer; founder, Campeau Construction Co., Inc., 1953; executed hostile takeovers of Allied Stores Corp., 1986 and Federated Dept. Stores, 1988.
b. Aug 3, 1924 in Sudbury, Ontario, Canada
Source: *BioIn 13, 14, 15, 16; CurBio 89; Dun&B 90; News 90, 90-1; NewYTBS 88; St&PR 91; WhoAm 90; WhoCanB 86; WhoE 85; WhoFI 89, 92; WhoWor 89*

Campin, Robert
"Master of Flemalle"; "Master of Merode"
Flemish. Artist
Considered founder, with Van Eyck, of Netherlandish school; did Merode Altarpiece, c. 1428.
b. 1375?
d. 1444
Source: *AtlBL; BioIn 10; DcCathB; McGDA; McGEWB; NewCol 75; OxCArt*

Campion, Jane
New Zealander. Director
Won Cannes' Palm d'Or for Best Short Film for *Peel,* 1982, Best Film, *The Piano,* 1993; seven prizes at Venice Film Festival for *An Angel at My Table,* 1991.
b. 1954? in Wellington, New Zealand
Source: *BiDFilm 94; CurBio 94; DcArts; LegTOT; News 91*

Campion, Thomas
English. Poet, Composer
Wrote graceful songs for the lute and lyric poems set to music for court presentations.
b. Feb 12, 1567 in London, England
d. Mar 1, 1620 in London, England
Source: *Alli; AtlBL; Baker 78, 84, 92; BbD; Benet 87, 96; BiD&SB; BioIn 2, 3, 4, 5, 7, 9, 12, 16, 18; BlmGEL; BritAu; CamGEL; CamGLE; CamGWoT; CasWL; Chambr 1; ChhPo, S1, S2; CnDBLB 1; CnE&AP; CroE&S; CrtT 1, 4; DcArts; DcEnL; DcEuL; DcLB 58, 172; DcLEL; DcNaB, C; Dis&D; EvLB; LegTOT; LinLib L; LngCEL; NewAmDM; NewC; NewOxM; OxCEng 67, 85, 95; OxCMed 86; OxCMus; OxCThe 67, 83; PenC ENG; RAdv 1, 14, 13-1; REn; RfGEnL 91; WebE&AL; WhDW*

Campo, John(ny)
"The Fat Man"
American. Horse Trainer
Colorful trainer of 1981 Derby, Preakness winner "Pleasant Colony."
b. 1938? in New York, New York
Source: *BioIn 9, 11, 12; NewYTBS 81; PseudN 82*

Campora, Hector Jose
Argentine. Political Leader
Peronist, who resigned presidency after seven wks. allowing Peron's return to power, 1973.
b. Mar 26, 1909 in Mercedes, Argentina
d. Dec 19, 1980 in Mexico City, Mexico
Source: *BiDLAmC; BioIn 11, 12, 16; CurBio 73, 81, 81N; DcCPSAm; EncLatA; NewYTBE 73; NewYTBS 80; WhoWor 74*

Camus, Albert
[Bauchart; Saetone; Albert Mathe]
French. Author, Philosopher
Proponent of absurdism philosophy; major novel *L'Etranger,* 1942; won Nobel Prize in literature, 1957. *The First Man* published posthumously in 1995.
b. Nov 7, 1913 in Mondovi, Algeria
d. Jan 4, 1960 in Sens, France
Source: *AtlBL; Benet 87, 96; BiDFrPL; BioIn 1, 3, 4, 5, 6, 7, 8, 9, 10, 11, 12, 13, 14, 15, 16, 17, 20, 21; CamGWoT; CasWL; ClDMEL 47; CnMD; CnMWL; CnThe; ConAu 89; ConLC 1, 2, 4, 9, 11, 14, 32, 63, 69; CroCD; CyWA 58, 89; DcArts; DcLB 72; DcTwCCu 2; DramC 2; EncEth; EncUnb; EncWL 2, 3; EncWT; EuWr 13; EvEuW; FacFETw; GrFLW; GuFrLit 1; IntDcT 2; LegTOT; LinLib L, S; LngCTC; MagSWL; MajMD 2; MajTwCW; MakMC; McGEWB; McGEWD 72, 84; ModFrL; ModRL; ModWD; NobelP; NotNAT A, B; Novels; ObitT 1951; OxCEng 67, 85, 95; OxCFr; OxCPhil; OxCThe 67, 83; PenC EUR; RAdv 14, 13-2; RComWL; REn; REnWD; RfGShF; RfGWoL 95; ShSCr 9; ThTwC 87; TwCA SUP; TwCWr; WhAm 3; WhDW; WhoNob, 90, 95; WhoTwCL; WorAl; WorAlBi; WorLitC; WrPh*

Camus, Marcel
French. Director
Won Oscar, 1958, for *Black Orpheus.*
b. Apr 21, 1912 in Chappes, France
d. Jan 13, 1982 in Paris, France
Source: *AnObit 1982; BioIn 13; DcFM; FilmgC; HalFC 84, 88; LegTOT; OxCFilm; WhoFr 79; WorEFlm*

Canaday, John (Edwin John)
[Matthew Head]
American. Critic, Author
Controversial *NY Times* art news editor, 1959-77; wrote classic text *Mainstreams of Modern Art,* 1959.
b. Feb 1, 1907 in Fort Scott, Kansas
d. Jul 19, 1985 in New York, New York
Source: *AmAu&B; BioIn 14; CelR; ConAu 13R, X; CurBio 62, 85; DrAS 74H; EncMys; LinLib L; NewYTBE 72; NewYTBS 85; St&PR 75; TwCCr&M 80, 85, 91; WhAm 8; WhoAm 74; WhoAmA 73; WhoE 74; WhoWest 74; WorAu 1950; WrDr 82, 84, 86*

Canadeo, Tony
[Anthony]
"Gray Ghost of Gonzaga"
American. Football Player
Two-time all-pro running back, Green Bay, 1941-44, 1946-52; Hall of Fame, 1974.
b. 1919
Source: *BioIn 17; LegTOT; WhoFtbl 74; WhoSpor*

Canadian Brass, The
[Charles Daellenbach; Fred Mills; David Ohanian; Ronald Romm; Eugene Watts]
"The Court Jesters of Chamber Music"; "The Marx Brothers of Brass"
Canadian. Music Group
First self-supporting professional brass quintet group, formed in early 70s; known for comical onstage antics; hit album *Basin Street.*
Source: *ConMus 4*

Canaletto, Antonio
[Giovanni Canal]
Italian. Artist
Widely imitated painter of atmospheric Venetian scenes.
b. Oct 18, 1697 in Venice, Italy
d. Apr 20, 1768 in Venice, Italy
Source: *AtlBL; Benet 87, 96; ClaDrA; DcArts; IntDcAA 90; REn; WhDW*

Canaris, Wilhelm
German. Naval Officer, Spy
Director of German military intelligence; killed in plot against Hitler.
b. Jan 1, 1887 in Aplerbeck, Germany
d. Apr 9, 1945 in Flossenberg, Germany
Source: *BioIn 2, 3, 4, 8, 10, 12, 14, 16; DcTwHis; EncE 75; EncGRNM; EncTR, 91; FacFETw; HarEnMi; HisEWW; NewCol 75; ObitOF 79; OxCShps; WhoMilH 76; WorAlBi*

Canary, David
American. Actor
Played Candy on TV series "Bonanza," 1967-70; 1972-73; won Emmy for role as Adam/Stuart Chandler on "All My Children," 1986.
b. Aug 25, 1939 in Elwood, Indiana
Source: *HalFC 84; WhoHol A*

Canby, Henry Seidel
American. Editor, Critic, Educator
Edited *Saturday Review of Literature,* 1924-36; wrote *Walt Whitman,* 1943.
b. Sep 6, 1878 in Wilmington, Delaware
d. Apr 5, 1961 in Ossining, New York
Source: *AmAu&B; AmLY; ApCAB X; BenetAL 91; BioIn 1, 2, 4, 5, 6, 7, 8, 17; ChhPo S1; CnDAL; ConAmA; ConAmL; ConAu 89; CurBio 42, 61; DcAmB S7; DcLB 91; DcLEL; EncAJ; JrnUS; LinLib L, S; LngCTC; NatCAB 48; OxCAmL 65, 83, 95; REn; REnAL; TwCA, SUP; WhAm 4; WhE&EA; WhLit; WhNAA*

Canby, Vincent
American. Journalist, Critic
NY Times film critic, 1969-93; Sunday drama critic, 1993—.
b. Jul 27, 1924 in Chicago, Illinois
Source: *BioIn 8, 13; ConAu 81; ConLC 13; ConTFT 4; DcTwCCu 1; IntMPA 75, 76, 77, 78, 79, 81, 82, 84, 86, 88, 92, 94, 96; LegTOT; WhoAm 78, 80, 82, 84, 86, 88, 92, 94, 95, 96, 97; WhoEnt 92*

Candela, Felix
[Outerino Felix Candela]
Spanish. Architect, Engineer
Well known for curved shell design of the Cosmic Ray Pavilion, Mexico City U., 1950-51.
b. Jan 27, 1910 in Madrid, Spain
Source: *BioIn 5, 6, 10; ConArch 80, 87; DcArts; DcD&D; DcTwCCu 4; EncMA; IntDcAr; IntWW 74, 75, 76, 77, 78, 79, 80, 81, 82, 83, 89, 91; MacEA; McGDA; Who 74, 82, 83, 85, 88, 90, 92, 94; WhoAm 74, 76, 78; WhoArch; WhoSSW 73, 75; WhoWor 74, 76, 78*

Candler, Asa Griggs
American. Philanthropist, Manufacturer
Bought Coca-Cola formula, 1887; retired as Coke pres., 1916.
b. Dec 30, 1851 in Villa Rica, Georgia
d. Mar 12, 1929 in Atlanta, Georgia
Source: *BiDAmBL 83; BioIn 2, 3; DcAmB; EncSoH; EncWM; FacFETw; GayN; NatCAB 7, 31; WebAB 74, 79; WhAm 1; WorAl*

Candler, Charles Howard
American. Business Executive
Pres., original Coca-Cola Co., 1916-19.
b. Dec 2, 1878 in Atlanta, Georgia
d. Oct 1, 1957 in Atlanta, Georgia
Source: *BioIn 4, 6; NatCAB 46; ObitOF 79; WhAm 3*

Candolle, Augustin Pyrame de
Swiss. Botanist
Developed new method of classifying plants by structure; coined term "taxonomy."
b. Feb 4, 1778 in Geneva, Switzerland
d. Sep 9, 1841 in Geneva, Switzerland
Source: *AsBiEn; BiESc; DcScB; InSci; LarDcSc; WebBD 83*

Candy, John (Franklin)
Canadian. Actor, Comedian
Films include *Splash,* 1984; *Summer Rental,* 1985; *Brewster's Millions,* 1985; *Wagons East,* 1994.
b. Oct 31, 1950 in Toronto, Ontario, Canada
d. Mar 4, 1994 in Chupederos, Mexico
Source: *BioIn 12, 19, 20, 21; ConTFT 5, 12; CurBio 90, 94N; EncAFC; IntMPA 92, 94; LegTOT; News 94, 88-2, 94-3; NewYTBS 94; QDrFCA 92; VarWW 85; WhAm 11; WhoAm 86, 88, 90, 92, 94; WhoCom; WhoEnt 92; WorAlBi*

Canetti, Elias
Swiss. Author
Works include novel *Auto-da-Fe,* 1935; nonfiction *Crowds and Power,* 1960; won Nobel Prize, 1981.
b. Jul 25, 1905 in Ruschuk, Bulgaria
d. Aug 13, 1994 in Zurich, Switzerland
Source: *Benet 87, 96; BioIn 10, 11, 12, 13, 14, 15, 17, 19, 20; CasWL; CnMD; CnMWL; ConAu 21R, 23NR, 146; ConFLW 84; ConLC 3, 14, 25, 75, 86; ConWorW 93; CroCD; CurBio 83, 94N; CyWA 89; DcArts; DcLB 85, 124; EncWL 3; EncWT; EuWr 12; FacFETw; GrFLW; IntWW 82, 83, 89, 91, 93; LegTOT; LiExTwC; MajTwCW; ModGL; NewYTBS 81; NobelP; Novels; OxCEng 85, 95; OxCGer 76, 86; PenC EUR; RAdv 14, 13-2; RfGWoL 95; TwCWr; WhAm 11; Who 85, 88, 90, 92, 94; WhoNob, 90, 95; WhoWor 74, 82, 84, 87, 89, 91, 93; WorAlBi; WorAu 1950*

Canfield, Cass
American. Publisher
Spent entire career at Harper & Row, 1929-86; wrote biographies of Pierpont Morgan, Jefferson Davis.
b. Apr 26, 1897 in New York, New York
d. Mar 27, 1986 in New York, New York
Source: *AmAu&B; AnObit 1986; BiE&WWA; BioIn 1, 3, 9, 10, 13, 14, 15; ConAu 41R, 118; CurBio 54, 86, 86N; IntAu&W 77, 82; IntWW 78, 79, 80, 81, 82, 83; LegTOT; NewYTBE 71; NewYTBS 86; WhAm 9; Who 74, 82, 83, 85; WhoAm 74, 76, 78, 80, 82, 84; WorAl; WorAlBi; WrDr 76, 80, 82, 84, 86*

Canfield, Francis X(avier)
American. Clergy, Educator, Editor
Pres., American Friends of the Vatican Library, 1981—; wrote *With Eyes of Faith,* 1984.
b. Dec 3, 1920 in Detroit, Michigan
Source: *AmCath 80; DrAS 74E, 78E; WhoAm 74, 76, 78, 80, 82, 84, 86, 88, 90, 92, 94, 95, 96, 97; WhoLibS 55; WhoMW 88; WhoRel 75, 77, 85, 92*

Canham, Erwin Dain
American. Newspaper Editor, Journalist
Edited *Christian Science Monitor,* 1945-79.
b. Feb 3, 1904 in Auburn, Maine
d. Jan 3, 1982 in Agana, Guam
Source: *AmAu&B; BiDAmJo; BiDAmNC; BioIn 1, 2, 3, 5, 7, 9, 12, 13, 16, 19; BlueB 76; CelR; ConAu P-1; CurBio 45, 60, 82; EncAB-A 23; IntWW 74, 75, 76, 77, 78, 79, 80, 81; IntYB 78, 79, 80, 81, 82; NewYTBS 82; WhAm 8; Who 74, 82; WhoAm 74, 76, 78, 80; WhoWor 74*

Caniff, Milt(on Arthur)
American. Cartoonist
Created comic strips "Terry and the Pirates," "Steve Canyon," 1934.
b. Feb 28, 1907 in Hillsboro, Ohio
d. Apr 3, 1988 in New York, New York
Source: *AuNews 1; BioIn 1, 2, 3, 4, 5, 8, 9, 10, 12; ConAu 85; CurBio 44, 88; EncTwCJ; OhA&B; REnAL; WebAB 74, 79; WebAMB; WhoAm 74, 76, 78, 80, 82, 84, 86; WhoAmA 73, 76, 78, 80, 82, 84, 86; WhoE 74; WhoWor 74*

Caniglia, Maria
Italian. Opera Singer
Leading Italian dramatic soprano of 1930s; admired as Tosca.
b. May 5, 1905 in Naples, Italy
d. Apr 15, 1979 in Rome, Italy
Source: *Baker 84, 92; IntDcOp; MetOEnc; NewGrDO; OxDcOp; PenDiMP; WhoMus 72*

Canned Heat
[Ronnie Baron; Bob Hite; Chris Morgan; Adolfo "Fito" de la Palma; Mark Skyer]
American. Music Group
Blues-styled group, 1966-70; songs include "Let's Work Together," 1970.
Source: *BiDAmM; BiDJaz A; ConMuA 80A; EncRk 88; EncRkSt; HarEnR 86; IlEncRk; OxCPMus; PenEncP; RkOn 78, 84; RolSEnR 83; WhoRock 81; WhoRocM 82*

Cannell, Stephen Joseph
American. Producer, Writer
Creator, producer of many TV shows: "Rockford Files"; "A-Team."
b. Feb 5, 1943 in Los Angeles, California
Source: *LesBEnT; WhoAm 80, 82, 84; WhoWest 82, 84; WhoWor 80, 82, 84*

Canning, Charles John, Earl
"Clemency Canning"
English. Political Leader
Governor-general of India during Sepoy Mutiny, 1857; first viceroy, 1858-62; son of George.
b. Dec 14, 1812 in London, England
d. Jun 17, 1862 in London, England
Source: *CelCen; DcBiPP; DcInB; DcNaB; HisDBrE; NewCol 75; WebBD 83*

Canning, George
English. Statesman, Orator
Prime minister, Apr, 1827, foreign secretary, 1807-09, 1822; founded *Anti-Jacobin* journal, 1791.
b. Apr 11, 1770 in London, England
d. Aug 8, 1827 in London, England
Source: *Alli; BiD&SB; BioIn 1, 2, 3, 5, 7, 8, 9, 10, 11, 12, 13, 14, 16, 17, 18, 19, 21; BritAu 19; CamGLE; CasWL; CelCen; ChhPo; DcBiPP; DcEnL; DcEuL; DcInB; DcLB 158; DcLEL; DcNaB; EvLB; HarEnUS; HisDBrE; LinLib S; McGEWB; NewC; OxCEng 67, 85, 95; PoIre; WhAm HS; WhDW*

Cannizzaro, Stanislao
Italian. Chemist
Devised method of deducing atomic weights of elements based on molecular weight.

b. Jul 13, 1826 in Palermo, Sicily, Italy
d. May 10, 1910 in Rome, Italy
Source: *AsBiEn; BiESc; BioIn 4, 6, 9, 14; CamDcSc; DcScB; InSci; LarDcSc; LinLib S; NewCol 75; RAdv 14; WhDW; WorScD*

Cannon, Annie Jump
American. Astronomer
Developed system of spectral classification at Harvard Observatory.
b. Dec 11, 1863 in Dover, Delaware
d. Apr 13, 1941 in Cambridge, Massachusetts
Source: *AmWomSc; BiCAW; BiESc; BioIn 1, 4, 11, 14, 15, 16, 17, 19, 20, 21; CamDcSc; ContDcW 89; CurBio 41; DcAmB S3; DcScB; DeafPAS; EncWB; FacFETw; GrLiveH; InSci; IntDcWB; InWom, SUP; LarDcSc; LegTOT; LibW; LinLib S; NotAW; NotTwCS; ObitOF 79; OxCAmH; WebAB 74, 79; WhAm 1, 1C; WomFir; WomSc; WomWWA 14; WorAl; WorAlBi; WorScD*

Cannon, Billy
[William A Cannon]
American. Football Player
All-America halfback, LA State, 1957-59; won Heisman Trophy, 1959; in NFL, 1960-70, mostly with Houston; led AFL in rushing, 1961.
b. Aug 2, 1937 in Philadelphia, Mississippi
Source: *BioIn 13, 14; WhoFtbl 74; WhoSpor*

Cannon, Dyan
[Samille Diane Friesen]
''Frosty''
American. Actor
Former wife of Cary Grant, mother of his only child, Jennifer; films include *Bob & Carol & Ted & Alice,* 1969.
b. Jan 4, 1937 in Tacoma, Washington
Source: *CelR 90; ConTFT 3, 12; FilmgC; IntMPA 77, 78, 79, 81, 82, 84, 86, 88, 92, 94, 96; ItaFilm; LegTOT; MiSFD 9; MovMk; WhoAm 86, 90, 92, 94, 95, 96, 97; WhoEnt 92; WhoHol A; WorAl; WorAlBi*

Cannon, Howard Walter
American. Politician
Conservative Dem. senator from NV, 1958-82.
b. Jan 26, 1912 in Saint George, Utah
Source: *AlmAP 82; WhoSSW 95; WhoWest 74, 76, 78, 80, 82; WhoWor 80, 82, 96*

Cannon, James W
American. Merchant
First towel manufacturer to put name on product, 1894.
b. Apr 25, 1852 in Mecklenburg County, North Carolina
d. Dec 19, 1921 in Concord, North Carolina
Source: *BiDAmBL 83; Entr; NatCAB 33*

Cannon, Jimmy
[James J Cannon]
American. Journalist
Syndicated sports columnist, 1946—.
b. Apr 10, 1909 in New York, New York
d. Dec 5, 1973 in New York, New York
Source: *BioIn 2, 3, 5, 10, 16, 21; ConAu 104; EncAJ; LiJour; ObitOF 79; REnAL; WhAm 6*

Cannon, Joseph Gurney
''Uncle Joe''
American. Politician
Conservative Rep. congressman from IL, 1870s-1920s; House speaker, 1903-11; autocratic rule led to loss of much of speaker's power.
b. May 7, 1836 in New Garden, North Carolina
d. Nov 12, 1926 in Danville, North Carolina
Source: *AmBi; AmPolLe; ApCAB X; BiAUS; BiDrAC; BiDrUSC 89; BioIn 2, 5, 6, 7, 9, 10, 13, 14; DcAmB; DcNCBi 1; EncAAH; EncAB-A 1, 5; EncAB-H 1974, 1996; FacFETw; LinLib S; McGEWB; NatCAB 13, 22; NewCol 75; OxCAmH; TwCBDA; WebAB 74, 79; WebBD 83; WhAm 1; WhAmP; WorAl*

Cannon, Katie
American. Clergy
First black woman to be ordained a Presbyterian minister.
b. Jan 3, 1950 in Kannapolis, North Carolina
Source: *ConBlB 10*

Cannon, Poppy
[Mrs. Walter White]
American. Journalist, Author
Food editor for magazines including *Ladies Home Journal; Mademoiselle* ; author of cookbooks including *The Fast Gourmet Cookbook,* 1964.
b. 1907 in Cape Town, South Africa
d. Apr 2, 1975 in New York, New York
Source: *BioIn 4, 10; ConAu 57, 65; ForWC 70; WhoAmW 58A, 70*

Cannon, Walter Bradford
American. Physiologist
Researched digestive tract, autonomic nervous system; discovered ''sympathin,'' 1931.
b. Oct 19, 1871 in Prairie du Chien, Wisconsin
d. Oct 1, 1945 in Franklin, New Hampshire
Source: *AsBiEn; BiDPsy; BiESc; BiHiMed; BioIn 1, 2, 7, 9, 10, 13, 14, 15, 16, 18, 21; CamDcSc; CurBio 45; DcAmB S3; DcAmMeB 84; DcNAA; DcScB, S1; EncAB-H 1974, 1996; FacFETw; InSci; LarDcSc; NamesHP; NatCAB 15, 34; ObitOF 79; OxCMed 86; WebAB 74, 79; WhAm 2; WhNAA*

Canova, Antonio
Italian. Artist
Neo-classic sculptor: ''Cupid and Psyche,'' 1793; ''Tomb of Maria Christina,'' 1798.
b. Nov 1, 1757 in Passagno, Italy
d. Oct 13, 1822 in Venice, Italy
Source: *AtlBL; BioIn 4, 5, 6, 8, 9, 11, 12, 15, 17; BlkwCE; CelCen; DcArts; DcBiPP; DcCathB; DcNiCA; Dis&D; EncEnl; IntDcAA 90; LegTOT; LinLib S; McGDA; McGEWB; OxCArt; OxDcArt; WhDW*

Canova, Diana
[Diana Canova Rivero]
American. Actor
Star of TV comedy series ''Soap'' 1977-81.
b. Jun 2, 1953 in West Palm Beach, Florida
Source: *BioIn 11, 12; ConTFT 1; HalFC 84, 88; LegTOT; VarWW 85; WhoHol 92*

Canova, Judy
American. Singer, Actor, Comedian
Popular hillbilly-type entertainer; radio program ''Judy Canova Show,'' 1930s-40s; mother of Diana.
b. Nov 20, 1916 in Jacksonville, Florida
d. Aug 5, 1983 in Hollywood, California
Source: *AnObit 1983; BgBkCoM; BiDAmM; BioIn 2, 7, 9, 13, 15; CmpEPM; EncAFC; FilmgC; ForWC 70; FunnyW; HalFC 84, 88; HarEnCM 87; IntMPA 75, 76, 77, 78, 79, 81, 82; InWom, SUP; LegTOT; MotPP; MovMk; NewYTBS 83; OxCPMus; QDrFCA 92; RadStar; SaTiSS; WhAm 8; WhoAm 76, 78, 80, 82; WhoAmW 64, 75; WhoCom; WhoHol A*

Canseco, Jose
Cuban. Baseball Player
Outfielder, Oakland, 1985-92; Texas, 1992-94; Boston, 1994-96; Oakland, 1997—; AL rookie of year, 1986, led AL in home runs, RBIs, 1988; first player to have 40 home runs, 40 stolen bases in one year, 1988, AL MVP, 1988.
b. Jul 2, 1964 in Havana, Cuba
Source: *Ballpl 90; BaseReg 86, 87; CelR 90; CurBio 91; DcHiB; LegTOT; News 90, 90-2; WhoAm 90, 92, 94, 95, 96, 97; WhoE 97; WhoHisp 91, 92, 94; WhoSpor; WhoWest 89, 92, 94; WorAlBi*

Cantacuzene, Princess
[Julia Dent Grant]
American. Author
Granddaughter of U S Grant; author of *Revolutionary Days; Russian People; My Life - Here and There.*
b. Jun 7, 1876 in Washington, District of Columbia
d. Oct 5, 1975 in Washington, District of Columbia
Source: *AmAu&B; ConAu 61; WhAm 6; WhNAA; WhoAmW 58*

Cantinflas
[Mario Moreno]
Mexican. Actor, Comedian
Won Oscar, 1957, for *Around the World in 80 Days*.
b. Aug 12, 1911 in Mexico City, Mexico
d. Apr 20, 1993 in Mexico City, Mexico
Source: *AnObit 1993; BioIn 1, 3, 4, 5, 6, 7, 18, 19; CurBio 53, 93N; DcHiB; DcTwCCu 3, 4; EncLatA; FilmgC; HalFC 84, 88; LegTOT; MotPP; MovMk; NewYTBS 93; OxCFilm; WhoHol 92, A; WhoWor 74*

Cantor, Eddie
[Edward Israel Itskowitz]
"Izzie"
American. Comedian, Singer
Starred on Broadway in *The Ziegfield Follies;* won special Oscar, 1956.
b. Jan 31, 1892 in New York, New York
d. Oct 10, 1964 in Beverly Hills, California
Source: *ASCAP 66; Baker 92; BiDAmM; BiDD; BiE&WWA; BioIn 1, 2, 3, 4, 5, 6, 7, 8, 9, 12, 13, 14, 16, 21; CamGWoT; CmpEPM; CurBio 41, 54, 65; DcAmB S7; EncAB-A 36; EncAFC; EncMT; EncVaud; EncWB; FacFETw; Film 2; FilmgC; HalFC 84, 88; JeAmHC; LegTOT; MotPP; MovMk; NatCAB 52; NewAmDM; NewGrDA 86; NotNAT B; ObitT 1961; OxCAmT 84; OxCFilm; OxCPMus; PenEncP; PlP&P; QDrFCA 92; RadStar; SaTiSS; TwYS; WebAB 74, 79; WhAm 4; WhoCom; WhScrn 74, 77, 83; WhThe; WorAlBi; WorEFlm*

Cantor, Georg Ferdinand Ludwig Philipp
German. Mathematician
Advanced irrational numbers theory; pioneered set theory.
b. Mar 3, 1845 in Saint Petersburg, Russia
d. Jan 6, 1918 in Halle, Germany
Source: *NewCol 75; WebBD 83; WhDW*

Cantrell, Lana
Australian. Singer, Actor
Popular recording star; won Grammy Award, 1967.
b. Aug 7, 1943 in Sydney, Australia
Source: *BioIn 7; WhoAm 76, 78, 80, 82, 84, 86, 88, 90, 92, 94, 95, 96, 97; WhoAmW 95, 97; WhoEnt 92*

Cantrick, Robert
American. Educator, Composer
Wrote chamber works for flute, orchestra; wrote *The Development of the Modern Flute,* 1979.
b. Dec 8, 1917 in Monroe, Michigan
Source: *ConAmC 82; WhoAm 74; WhoAmM 83; WhoE 74*

Cantu, Cesare
Italian. Historian
Wrote 35-vol. *Storia Universale,* 1838-46; novel *Margherita Pusterla,* 1838, written with toothpick as pen, candle smoke for ink.
b. Dec 5, 1804 in Brivio, Italy
d. Mar 11, 1895 in Milan, Italy
Source: *BiD&SB; CasWL; DcBiA; DcCathB; DcItL 2; EuAu; EvEuW; LinLib L; WebBD 83*

Cantwell, Robert Emmett
American. Author, Editor
Novelist, magazine contributor; on editorial staff of *Newsweek, Sports Illustrated,* 1956-73.
b. Jan 31, 1908 in Little Falls, Washington
d. Dec 8, 1978 in New York, New York
Source: *AmAu&B; Au&Wr 71; ConAmA; ConAu 4NR, 5R, 81; ConNov 72, 76; NewYTBS 78; OxCAmL 65; REnAL; TwCA, SUP; TwCWr; WhAm 7; WhE&EA; WhoAm 74, 76, 78; WhoE 74; WrDr 76*

Canute
[Canute of Denmark; Canute the Great]
English. Ruler
Conquered England, ruled, 1016-35; Denmark, 1018-35; Norway, 1028-35.
b. 995
d. Nov 12, 1035 in Shaftesbury, England
Source: *BioIn 5, 6, 8, 9, 12, 15, 18, 20; DcBiPP; HisWorL; LinLib S; NewC; OxCShps; REn; WebBD 83*

Canutt, Yakima
[Enos Edward Canutt]
American. Stunt Performer, Actor
Cowboy film star, 1920s, who did own stunts, later doubled for other stars; won special Oscar, 1966, for creating profession of stuntman.
b. Nov 29, 1895 in Colfax, Washington
d. May 24, 1986 in Los Angeles, California
Source: *AnObit 1986; BioIn 7, 8, 12; CmMov; ConAu 114, 119; Film 2; FilmEn; FilmgC; HalFC 84, 88; IntDcF 1-4, 2-4; IntMPA 75, 76, 77, 78, 79, 81, 82, 84, 86, 88; ItaFilm; OxCFilm; TwYS; WhoHol A; WorEFlm*

Canzoneri, Tony
American. Boxer, Actor
Won world featherweight, lightweight, junior welter titles, 1930s; Hall of Fame, 1956.
b. Nov 6, 1908 in Slidell, Louisiana
d. Dec 9, 1959 in New York, New York
Source: *BiDAmSp BK; BioIn 5; BoxReg; WhoBox 74; WhoSpor; WhScrn 83*

Capa, Cornell
American. Journalist, Photographer
Gives a visual history of our century with his documentary scenes.
b. Apr 19, 1918 in Budapest, Hungary
Source: *BioIn 4, 10, 14, 15, 16, 19; ConPhot 82, 88, 95; EncTwCJ; FacFETw; MacBEP; WhoAm 82, 84, 86, 90, 94, 96; WhoAmA 78, 80, 82, 84, 86, 89, 91, 93; WhoE 85, 86, 91*

Capa, Robert
[Andrei Friedmann]
American. Photographer
First war photographer to get dramatic close-ups of action; photographs in *Images of War,* 1964.
b. Oct 22, 1913 in Budapest, Austria-Hungary
d. May 25, 1954 in Hanoi, Vietnam
Source: *BiDAmJo; BioIn 1, 3, 4, 6, 8, 10, 12, 13, 14, 15, 16; ConPhot 82, 88; DcArts; EncAJ; EncWB; FacFETw; ICPEnP; MacBEP; WhAm 4; WhDW; WorAlBi*

Capablanca, Jose Raoul
Cuban. Chess Player
Chess champion at age 12; world title, 1921-27.
b. Nov 19, 1888 in Havana, Cuba
d. Mar 8, 1942 in New York, New York
Source: *BioIn 1; NewCol 75; ObitOF 79*

Capaldi, Jim
English. Singer, Musician
Drummer for Traffic, 1967-71; had solo hit single "Living on the Edge," 1983.
b. Aug 24, 1944 in Evesham, England
Source: *BioIn 19; EncRk 88; LegTOT; RkOn 78; WhoRock 81; WhoRocM 82*

Cape, Herbert Jonathan
English. Publisher
Founded Jonathan Cape, Inc., 1921.
b. Nov 15, 1879 in London, England
d. Feb 10, 1960 in London, England
Source: *BioIn 5; DcNaB 1951; WhE&EA*

Capehart, Homer Earl
American. Politician
Rep. senator, 1945-63.
b. Jun 6, 1897 in Algiers, Indiana
d. Sep 3, 1979 in Indianapolis, Indiana
Source: *BiDrAC; BiDrUSC 89; BioIn 1, 3, 6, 9, 11, 12; BlueB 76; CurBio 47, 79; DcAmB S10; IntWW 74; NewYTBS 79; PolProf E, K, T; WhAm 7; WhoAm 84*

Capek, Karel
Czech. Author, Essayist
His play *R.U.R.,* 1920, introduced word "robot."
b. Jan 9, 1890 in Male Svatonovice, Bohemia
d. Dec 24, 1938 in Prague, Czechoslovakia
Source: *Benet 87, 96; BioIn 1, 5, 6, 7, 12, 16, 17; CamGWoT; CasWL; ClDMEL 47; CnMD; CnThe; ConAu 104, 140; CyWA 58; DcArts; DramC 1; EncSF, 93; EncWL, 2, 3; EncWT; EuWr 10; EvEuW; FacFETw; GrFLW; IntDcT 2; LegTOT; LinLib L; LngCTC; MajMD 2; MakMC; McGEWB; McGEWD 72, 84; ModSL 2; ModWD; NewEScF; NewGrDO; NotNAT B; OxCEng 85, 95; OxCThe 67, 83; OxDcOp; PenC EUR; RAdv 14, 13-2; REn; REnWD; RfGShF; RfGWoL 95; RGTwCSF; ScF&FL 1, 92; ScFEYrs; ScFSB; TwCA, SUP; TwCLC 6, 37; TwCSFW 86A, 91A; TwCWr;*

WhDW; WhE&EA; WhoSciF; WhoTwCL; WhThe; WorAl; WorAlBi; WorLitC

Capero, Virginia
American. Actor
Films include *Lady Sings the Blues,* 1972; won Tony for *Raisin,* 1974.
b. Sep 22, in Sumter, South Carolina
Source: *VarWW 85*

Caperton, Gaston
American. Politician
Dem. governor, WV, 1989—.
b. Feb 21, 1940 in West Virginia
Source: *AlmAP 92, 96; BiDrGov 1988; BioIn 16, 20; WhoAm 90, 92; WhoAmP 89, 91, 93, 95; WhoSSW 91; WhoWor 93*

Capezio, Salvatore
American. Designer
Designer of ballet slippers, 1887.
Source: *WorFshn*

Caples, John
American. Advertising Executive, Author
Wrote *How to Make Your Advertising Make Money,* 1981.
b. May 1, 1900 in New York, New York
Source: *AdMenW; AmAu&B; BioIn 1, 5, 10, 11, 16, 17, 20; ConAu 21R, 131; WhAm 10; WhoAdv 72, 90; WhoAm 74, 76, 78, 80, 82, 84, 86, 88*

Capone, Al(phonse)
"Big Al"; "Scarface Al"
American. Criminal
Dominated Chicago crime scene, gang warfare, 1920s; implicated in St. Valentine's Day massacre, 1929.
b. Jan 17, 1899 in New York, New York
d. Jan 25, 1947 in Miami Beach, Florida
Source: *AmDec 1920; AmJust; BiDAmBL 83; BioIn 1, 2, 3, 4, 6, 7, 9, 10, 11, 12, 13, 14, 15, 16, 18, 19, 20, 21; CopCroC; DcAmB S4; DrInf; FacFETw; FilmgC; GangFlm; HalFC 84, 88; LegTOT; McGEWB; OxCAmH; OxCFilm; WebAB 74, 79; WhFla; WorAl; WorAlBi*

Capone, Teresa
Italian.
Mother of Al Capone.
b. 1867?, Italy
d. Nov 29, 1952 in Chicago, Illinois
Source: *BioIn 10; InWom SUP; ObitOF 79*

Caponi, Donna
American. Golfer
Turned pro, 1965; won US Women's Open, 1969, 1970; third woman to win over $1 million on tour.
b. Jan 29, 1945 in Detroit, Michigan
Source: *NewYTBS 81; WhoGolf; WhoIntG*

Capote, Truman
American. Author
Wrote *Breakfast at Tiffany's* filmed, 1961; *In Cold Blood* filmed, 1968.
b. Sep 30, 1924 in New Orleans, Louisiana
d. Aug 25, 1984 in Los Angeles, California
Source: *AmAu&B; AmCulL; AmNov; AmWr S3; AnObit 1984; ASCAP 66; Au&Wr 71; Benet 87, 96; BenetAL 91; BiE&WWA; BioIn 2, 3, 4, 7, 8, 9, 10, 11, 12, 13, 14, 15, 16, 17, 18, 19, 21; BlueB 76; CamGEL; CamGLE; CamHAL; CasWL; CelR; CnDAL; CnMD; ConAu 5NR, 5R, 18NR, 113; ConDr 73, 82; ConGAN; ConLC 1, 3, 8, 13, 19, 34, 38, 58; ConNov 72, 76, 82, 86A; ConPopW; CurBio 51, 68, 84N; CyWA 89; DcArts; DcLB 2, Y80A, Y84N; DcLEL 1940; DcTwCCu 1; DrAF 76; EncWL 3; FacFETw; FifSWrA; FilmgC; GayLesB; GayLL; IntAu&W 76, 77, 82; IntWW 74, 75, 76, 77, 78, 79, 80, 81, 82, 83; ItaFilm; LegTOT; LiJour; LinLib L; LngCTC; MagSAmL; MajTwCW; MakMC; ModAL S1, S2; ModWD; NewCon; NewYTBS 84, 88; NotNAT; Novels; OxCAmL 65, 83, 95; OxCEng 85, 95; PenC AM; RAdv 1, 14, 13-1; REn; REnAL; RfGAmL 87, 94; RfGShF; RGTwCWr; ShSCr 2; SmATA 91; SourALJ; TwCA SUP; TwCWr; WebAB 74, 79; WebE&AL; WhAm 9; WhDW; Who 74, 82, 83; WhoAm 74, 76, 78, 80, 82, 84; WhoTwCL; WhoWor 74, 78; WorAl; WorAlBi; WorLitC; WrDr 76, 80, 82, 84*

Capp, Al
[Alfred Gerald Caplin]
American. Cartoonist
Created "Li'l Abner," 1934-77; syndicated in over 900 newspapers.
b. Sep 28, 1909 in New Haven, Connecticut
d. Nov 5, 1979 in Cambridge, Massachusetts
Source: *AmAu&B; AmDec 1930; BenetAL 91; BioIn 1, 2, 3, 4, 5, 6, 8, 9, 11, 12, 15, 17, 20; BlueB 76; CelR; ConAu 57, 89; CurBio 47, 80, 80N; DcAmB S10; DcAmC; EncACom; EncAJ; FacFETw; IntAu&W 77; IntWW 79; LegTOT; LinLib L; NewYTBS 79; REnAL; SmATA 21N, 61; WebAB 74, 79; WhAm 7; WhAmArt 85; WhDW; WhoAm 74, 76, 78; WhoAmA 73, 76, 78, 80N, 82N, 89N, 91N, 93N; WhoWor 74; WhScrn 83; WorAl; WorAlBi; WorECom*

Cappeletti, Gino
"Cappy"; "Duke"
American. Football Player
Kicker, Boston, 1960-70; led AFL in scoring, 1963-66.
b. Mar 26, 1934 in Keewatin, Minnesota
Source: *WhoFtbl 74*

Cappelletti, John Raymond
American. Football Player
Running back, 1974-83; won Heisman Trophy, 1973; TV movie *Something for Joey,* 1977, about his relationship with his cancer-stricken brother.
b. Aug 9, 1952 in Philadelphia, Pennsylvania
Source: *BiDAmSp FB; WhoAm 78, 80, 82; WhoFtbl 74*

Capper, Arthur
American. Editor, Publisher, Politician
World's largest publisher of farm journals; appointed DD Eisenhower to West Point.
b. Jul 14, 1865 in Garnett, Kansas
d. Dec 19, 1951 in Topeka, Kansas
Source: *AmAu&B; ApCAB X; BiDrAC; BiDrGov 1789; BiDrUSC 89; BioIn 1, 2, 3, 4, 6, 10, 12, 17; CurBio 46, 52; DcAmB S5; DcAmTB; EncAAH; EncAB-A 2; EncAJ; LinLib L, S; NatCAB 15, 41; ObitOF 79; REnAW; WhAm 3; WhAmP; WhJnl; WhNAA*

Capra, Frank
Italian. Director, Producer
Won Oscars for *It Happened One Night, Mr. Deeds Goes to Town;* known for folksy, sentimental style.
b. May 18, 1897 in Palermo, Sicily, Italy
d. Sep 3, 1991 in La Quinta, California
Source: *AmCulL; AnObit 1991; BenetAL 91; BiDFilm, 94; BioIn 1, 2, 6, 9, 10, 11, 12, 13, 14, 15, 16, 17, 18, 19, 21; BlueB 76; CelR; CmCal; CmMov; ConAu 61, 135; ConLC 16; ConTFT 9; CurBio 48, 91N; DcArts; DcFM; EncAB-H 1996; EncAFC; FacFETw; FilmgC; HalFC 84, 88; IlWWHD 1; IntDcF 1-2, 2-2; IntMPA 75, 76, 77, 78, 79, 81, 82, 84, 86, 88; IntWW 74, 75; LegTOT; MiSFD 9N; MovMk; News 92, 92-2; NewYTBE 71; NewYTBS 91; OxCFilm; RAdv 14; REnAL; TwYS A; WebAB 74, 79; WhAm 10; Who 74, 82, 83, 85, 88, 90; WhoAm 74, 76, 78, 80, 82, 84, 86, 88, 90; WhoWest 74; WhoWor 74, 76, 78; WorAl; WorAlBi; WorEFlm; WorFDir 1*

Capriati, Jennifer
American. Tennis Player
Joined pro circuit at 13, youngest tennis player to do so, 1990; won Olympic gold medal, 1992.
b. Mar 29, 1976 in Long Island, New York
Source: *BioIn 16; BuCMET; EncWomS; IntWW 93; LegTOT; News 91, 91-1; NewYTBS 90; WhoSpor*

Capshaw, Kate
[Kathy Sue Nail]
American. Actor
Starred in *Indiana Jones and the Temple of Doom,* 1984.
Source: *BioIn 14, 16, 21; ConTFT 2, 5; IntMPA 86; VarWW 85; WhoEnt 92*

Captain and Tennile, The
[Daryl Dragon; Toni Tennille]
American. Music Group
Pop-rock husband and wife team; won 1975 Grammy for "Love Will Keep Us Together."
Source: *BioIn 11; BkPepl; RkOn 84; WhoRocM 82*

Captain Beefheart
[Captain Beefheart and the Magic Band; Don Van Vliet]
American. Singer, Musician
Music combines blues, jazz, classic, rock; is more influential than popular; album *Ice Cream for Crow,* 1982.
b. Jan 15, 1941 in Glendale, California
Source: *BiDAmM; ConMuA 80A; ConMus 10; HarEnR 86; LegTOT; NewAmDM; NewGrDA 86; OxCPMus; RolSEnR 83; WhoRock 81*

Captain Jack
American. Native American Leader
Major figure in the Modoc War, 1872-73; executed for shooting a man during negotiations.
b. 1837?
d. Oct 3, 1873
Source: *BioIn 7, 8, 13; DcAmB; EncNAB; NotNaAm; WebAMB; WhAm HS*

Capucci, Roberto
Italian. Fashion Designer
Called a genius when he started fashion house in Rome, 1950; asked by Indian govt. to study their textiles, 1970.
b. 1930?
Source: *ConFash; WorFshn*

Capucine
[Germaine Lefebvre]
French. Actor
Best known among her American films was *What's New, Pussycat?,* 1965; suicide victim.
b. Jan 6, 1935 in Toulon, France
d. Mar 17, 1990 in Lausanne, Switzerland
Source: *ConTFT 9; FilmEn; FilmgC; IntMPA 86, 88; MotPP; MovMk; WhoAmW 72; WhoHol A*

Caputo, Philip Joseph
American. Author, Journalist
Wrote *Rumor of War,* memoir of Vietnam; won Pulitzer, 1972.
b. Jan 10, 1941 in Chicago, Illinois
Source: *ConAu 73; CurBio 96; IntAu&W 89, 91, 93; NewYTBS 81; WhoAm 74, 76, 78, 80, 82, 84, 86, 88, 90, 92, 94, 95, 96, 97; WhoE 97; WhoUSWr 88; WhoWor 80, 82, 84, 87, 91; WhoWrEP 89, 92, 95*

Cara, Irene (Escalera)
American. Actor, Singer
Starred in movie *Fame,* 1980; sang Oscar-winning song, theme from *Flashdance,* 1983; won Obie for *The Me Nobody Knows,* 1970.
b. Mar 18, 1959 in New York, New York
Source: *BioIn 10; ConTFT 5; DrBlPA, 90; EncPR&S 89; InB&W 85; IntMPA 88, 92, 94, 96; LegTOT; NewGrDA 86; RkOn 85; WhoEnt 92*

Caracalla, Marcus Aurelius Antonius
Roman. Ruler
Ruled, 211-217; murdered brother to gain control of throne.
b. Apr 4, 186 in Lugdunum, France
d. Apr 8, 217 in Carrhae, Mesopotamia
Source: *DcBiPP; Dis&D; NewCol 75; WebBD 83*

Caras, Roger Andrew
American. Journalist
Authority on nature, environment; ABC News animal, wildlife correspondent since 1975; wrote *The Forest,* 1979.
b. May 24, 1928 in Methuen, Massachusetts
Source: *BioIn 11; ConAu 5NR; CurBio 88; IntAu&W 76, 77, 82, 86, 89, 91, 93; SmATA 12; WhoAm 74, 76, 78, 80, 82, 84, 86, 88, 90, 92, 94, 95, 96, 97; WhoE 74; WhoWor 74; WhoWorJ 72, 78; WhoWrEP 89, 92, 95; WrDr 86*

Caravaggio, Michelangelo da
[Michelangelo Merisi]
Italian. Artist
Interpreted religious figures, scenes as contemporary events, people; early exponent of "chiaroscuro."
b. Sep 8, 1573 in Caravaggio, Italy
d. Jul 18, 1610 in Port'Ercole, Italy
Source: *AtlBL; DcBiPP; DcCathB; GayLesB; McGEWB; NewCol 75; OxCArt; REn; WebBD 83; WhDW*

Caraway, Hattie Wyatt
American. Politician
First woman elected to Senate, 1932; Dem. represented AR, 1932-45.
b. Feb 1, 1878 in Bakerville, Tennessee
d. Dec 21, 1950 in Falls Church, Virginia
Source: *AmWomM; BiDrAC; BiDrUSC 89; BioIn 17, 20; CurBio 45, 51; DcAmB S4; InWom; NotAW; WhAm 3; WhAmP; WomFir; WorAl*

Caray, Harry
[Harry Christopher Carabina]
American. Sportscaster
Play-by-play announcer, Chicago Cubs, 1982—; National Assoc. of Broadcasters Hall of Fame, 1994; Baseball Hall of Fame, 1988.
b. Mar 1, 1919 in Saint Louis, Missouri
Source: *Ballpl 90; BioIn 8, 9, 10, 11, 15, 16; News 88-3; NewYTBS 87; WhoAm 88; WhoMW 92*

Carazo (Odio), Rodrigo
Costa Rican. Statesman, Economist
President, 1978-82, who ousted long-ruling National Liberation Party.
b. Dec 27, 1926 in Cartago, Costa Rica
Source: *BiDLAmC; BioIn 12, 16; DcCPCAm; IntWW 78, 79, 80, 81, 82, 83, 89, 91, 93; IntYB 79, 80, 81, 82; WhoWor 80, 82; WorAl*

Carberry, John J, Cardinal
American. Religious Leader
Archbishop of St. Louis, 1968-79.
b. Jul 31, 1904 in New York, New York
Source: *BioIn 11; IntWW 74, 75, 76, 77, 78, 79, 80, 81, 82, 83; WhoAm 84, 86, 88; WhoWor 84, 89*

Carbine, Patricia Theresa
American. Journalist
Publisher, editor-in-chief, *Ms* magazine, 1972-79; pres. Ms. Foundation for Education and Communication 1979—
b. Jan 31, 1931 in Villanova, Pennsylvania
Source: *CelR; ConAu 107; EncTwCJ; ForWC 70; WhoAm 74, 76, 78, 80, 82, 84, 86; WhoAmW 61, 64, 66, 68, 72, 74, 75, 79, 81, 83, 85, 87*

Carbonneau, Guy
Canadian. Hockey Player
Center, Montreal, 1980—; won Selke Trophy, 1988, 1989, 1992.
b. Mar 18, 1960 in Sept Iles, Quebec, Canada
Source: *HocReg 87; WhoAm 94, 95, 96, 97; WhoSpor; WhoWor 96*

Carcaterra, Lorenzo
American. Author
Wrote *Sleepers,* 1995.
b. Oct 16, 1954 in New York, New York
Source: *BioIn 17, 18; ConAu 140; News 96, 96-1; WhoWrEP 92, 95; WrDr 96*

Cardano, Geronimo
Italian. Philosopher, Mathematician
First to publish solutions to cubic and quartic equations, calculations of theory of probability; wrote *Rules of Algebra,* 1545.
b. Sep 24, 1501 in Pavia, Italy
d. Sep 21, 1576 in Rome, Italy
Source: *BiESc; BioIn 8; DcBiPP; DcCathB; Dis&D; McGEWB; REn; WhDW*

Cardenal, Ernesto
Nicaraguan. Poet, Clergy
Roman Catholic priest; protest poetry denounces tyranny, imperialism; advocates revolutionary politics.
b. Jan 20, 1925 in Granada, Nicaragua
Source: *Benet 96; BioIn 8, 12, 15, 16, 17, 18; CasWL; ConAu 2NR, 32NR, 49; ConFLW 84; ConHero 1; ConLC 31; ConSpAP; ConWorW 93; DcCLAA; DcHiB; DcTwCCu 4; EncWL 3; HispLC; HispWr; MajTwCW; OxCSpan; PenC AM; RAdv 14, 13-2; RfGWoL 95; SpAmA; WhoTwCL; WorAu 1970*

Cardenas, Lazaro
Mexican. Political Leader
Inaugurated 6-yr. program of agrarian reform and industrialization, 1934-40.
b. May 21, 1895 in Jiquilpan, Mexico
d. Oct 19, 1970 in Mexico City, Mexico
Source: *BiDLAmC; BioIn 1, 2, 3, 4, 6, 7, 8, 9, 10, 12, 15, 16; DcCPCAm; DcPol;*

DcTwHis; EncLatA; EncRev; HisWorL; LinLib S; McGEWB; NewYTBE 70; ObitOF 79; ObitT 1961; WhAm 5

Carder, Frederick
English. Manufacturer
Steuben Glass Works founder, 1903; authority on 19th, 20th c, art glass.
b. 1863 in Brockmoor, England
d. 1963 in Corning, New York
Source: *BioIn 6, 9; BriEAA; DcNiCA; IlDcG; ObitOF 79; OxCDecA*

Cardiff, Gladys
American. Poet
Published *To Frighten a Storm,* 1976, winner of the Governor's Writer's Award for a first book.
b. 1942 in Browning, Montana
Source: *BioIn 21; NotNaAm*

Cardigan, James Thomas Brudenell, Earl of
English. Army Officer
Led disastrous charge immortalized in "The Charge of the Light Brigade," 1854; cardigan sweater named for him.
b. Oct 16, 1797 in Hambleden, England
d. Mar 27, 1868 in Deene Park, England
Source: *Alli SUP; BioIn 16; CelCen; DcBiPP; DcNaB; HarEnMi; ObitT 1971*

Cardin, Pierre
French. Fashion Designer
Founded fashion house, 1949; purchased Paris restaurant, Maxim's, 1981.
b. Jul 7, 1922 in Venice, Italy
Source: *BioIn 7, 8, 9, 12, 13; BkPepl; CelR 90; ConDes 84, 90, 97; ConFash; CurBio 65; DcArts; DcTwDes; EncFash; Entr; FacFETw; FairDF FRA; IntWW 74, 75, 76, 77, 78, 79, 80, 81, 82, 83, 89, 91, 93; LegTOT; NewYTBS 81; Who 90, 92, 94; WhoAm 74, 76, 78, 80, 82, 84, 86, 88; WhoFash 88; WhoFr 79; WhoWor 74, 78, 80, 82, 84, 87, 89, 91, 93, 95, 97; WorAl; WorAlBi; WorFshn*

Cardinal, Douglas
Canadian. Architect
Firm designed the National Museum of the American Indian, Washington, DC.
b. 1934 in Red Deer, Alberta, Canada
Source: *BioIn 21; ConArch 80; NotNaAm*

Cardinal, Harold
Canadian. Native American Leader
Elected chief of the Sucker Creek band, 1983; wrote *The Unjust Society: The Tragedy of Canada's Indians,* 1969.
b. Jan 27, 1945, Canada
Source: *BioIn 8, 21; NotNaAm*

Cardinal, Tantoo
Canadian. Actor
Had a leading role in *Legends of the Fall,* 1993.
b. 1950 in Anzac, Alberta, Canada
Source: *BioIn 21; CanWW 31, 89; NotNaAm*

Cardinale, Claudia
Italian. Actor
Appeared in over 40 films, including *The Pink Panther,* 1963.
b. Apr 15, 1938 in Tunis, Tunisia
Source: *BiDFilm; ConTFT 4; FilmgC; IntMPA 82; IntWW 74, 75, 76, 77, 78, 79, 80, 81, 82, 83, 89, 91, 93; LegTOT; MovMk; OxCFilm; WhoHol A; WhoWor 74, 95, 96; WorEFlm*

Cardoso, Fernando Henrique
Brazilian. Political Leader
Pres., Brazil, 1995—.
b. Jun 18, 1931 in Rio de Janeiro, Brazil
Source: *BiDNeoM; CurBio 96; News 96; WhoWor 95, 96, 97*

Cardozo, Benjamin Nathan
American. Supreme Court Justice
Appointed by Hoover, served 1932-38; wrote *Nature of the Judicial Process,* 1921.
b. May 24, 1870 in New York, New York
d. Jul 9, 1938 in Port Chester, New York
Source: *AmAu&B; AmBi; AmJust; AmPolLe; Benet 87; BenetAL 91; BiDFedJ; BioIn 1, 2, 3, 4, 5, 7, 8, 9, 11; DcAmB S2; DcLEL; DcNAA; EncAB-H 1974, 1996; JeAmHC; LinLib L, S; McGEWB; MorMA; NatCAB 27; OxCAmH; OxCAmL 65; OxCLaw; OxCSupC; REn; REnAL; SupCtJu; TwCLC 65; WebAB 74, 79; WebBD 83; WhAm 1; WhNAA; WorAl*

Cardozo, Francis Louis
American. Educator, Politician
Established, administered normal school for black youths, 1865.
b. 1837 in Charleston, South Carolina
d. 1903 in Washington, District of Columbia
Source: *BioIn 12; DcAmNB; EncSoH; InB&W 85*

Carducci, Giosue Alessandro Guiseppe
Italian. Poet, Critic
Won Nobel Prize for literature, 1906; notable poems include "Barbaric Odes," "Hymn to Satan," "Rime."
b. Jul 27, 1835 in Val di Castello, Italy
d. Feb 16, 1907 in Bologna, Italy
Source: *CasWL; ClDMEL 47; CyWA 58; DcItL 1; McGEWB; OxCEng 85; PenC EUR; RComWL; REn; WhDW; WhoNob, 90, 95; WorAl*

Cardus, Neville, Sir
English. Author
Music critic for *Manchester Guardian,* 1927-74; authority on cricket.
b. Apr 2, 1889 in Manchester, England
d. Feb 28, 1975 in London, England
Source: *Au&Wr 71; Baker 78, 84; BioIn 1, 2, 8, 9, 10, 11, 14; ConAu 11NR, 57, 61; DcLEL; DcNaB 1971; GrBr; LngCTC; NewYTBS 75; ObitT 1971; OxCMus; WhLit; Who 74; WhoMus 72; WhoWor 74*

Carew, Rod(ney Cline)
American. Baseball Player
Infielder, Minnesota, 1967-78; California 1979-85; currently batting coach with California; won seven batting titles; had .328 career batting average, 3,053 hits; Hall of Fame, 1991.
b. Oct 1, 1945 in Gatun, Panama
Source: *AfrAmSG; Ballpl 90; BaseReg 86; BiDAmSp BB; BioIn 9, 10, 11, 12, 13; ConAu 104; CurBio 78; DcHiB; HispAmA; InB&W 80, 85; LegTOT; NewYTBS 74; WhoAfA 96; WhoAm 74, 76, 78, 80, 82, 84, 86, 92, 94, 95, 96, 97; WhoBlA 77, 80, 85, 88, 90, 92, 94; WhoE 95; WhoProB 73; WorAl; WorAlBi*

Carew, Thomas
English. Poet
First of Cavalier poets; influenced by Donne and Jonson.
b. 1595 in West Wickham, England
d. Mar 22, 1639 in London, England
Source: *Alli; AtlBL; BbD; Benet 87, 96; BiD&SB; BiDRP&D; BioIn 12, 17, 19; BritAu; BritWr 2; CamGLE; CasWL; Chambr 1; ChhPo; CnE&AP; CroE&S; CrtT 1; DcArts; DcEnA A; DcEnL; DcEuL; DcLB 126; DcLEL; DcNaB; EvLB; LegTOT; LinLib L; LitC 13; LngCEL; MouLC 1; NewC; OxCEng 67, 85; PenC ENG; REn; WebE&AL*

Carey, Clare
American. Actor
Plays Hayden Fox's daughter, Kelly, on TV show "Coach" 1989—.

Carey, Ernestine Moller Gilbreth
[Mrs. Charles E Carey]
American. Author, Lecturer
With brother, Frank, wrote reminiscences of their childhood, *Cheaper by the Dozen,* 1948.
b. Apr 5, 1908 in New York, New York
Source: *BioIn 1, 2; ConAu 5R; ConLC 17; CurBio 49; InWom, SUP; SmATA 2; WhoAm 86; WhoAmW 87; WhoWor 87; WorAl; WrDr 86*

Carey, George Leonard, Archbishop
English. Religious Leader
Anglican, Archbishop of Canterbury, 1991—.
b. Nov 13, 1935 in London, England
Source: *CurBio 91; FacFETw; IntWW 91, 93; News 92; NewYTBS 90; Who 83, 85, 92; WhoRel 92; WhoWor 93, 95, 96, 97*

Carey, Harry
[Henry Dewitt Carey, II]
American. Actor
Appeared in 26 westerns for John Ford as "Cheyenne Harry."
b. Jan 16, 1878 in New York, New York
d. Sep 21, 1947 in Brentwood, California
Source: *BioIn 1, 8, 12, 17; CmMov; EncAFC; Film 2; FilmEn; FilmgC; HalFC 84, 88; IntDcF 1-3, 2-3; LegTOT; MotPP; MovMk; NotNAT B;*

ObitOF 79; TwYS; Vers A; WhoHol B; WhScrn 74, 77, 83; WorEFlm

Carey, Henry
English. Composer, Poet
Alleged author of "God Save the King"; most remembered song, "Sally in Our Alley."
b. 1687? in Yorkshire, England
d. Oct 5, 1743 in London, England
Source: *Alli; Baker 78, 84, 92; BiD&SB; BioIn 3, 12, 17; BritAu; CamGEL; CamGLE; CamGWoT; CasWL; ChhPo, S1; DcBiPP; DcEnL; DcLB 84; DcLEL; EvLB; LinLib L; NewC; NewGrDO; OxCEng 67, 85, 95; PenC ENG; REn; RfGEnL 91*

Carey, Henry Charles
American. Economist, Sociologist
Wrote *Principles of Political Economy,* 1837-40; *Principles of Social Science,* 1858-59; among first American works in their field.
b. Dec 15, 1793 in Philadelphia, Pennsylvania
d. Oct 13, 1879 in Philadelphia, Pennsylvania
Source: *Alli, SUP; AmAu; AmAu&B; AmBi; ApCAB; BbD; BiD&SB; BioIn 2, 15, 16; CelCen; Chambr 3; CyAL 1; DcAmAu; DcAmB; DcEnL; DcNAA; Drake; EncAB-H 1974; EncABHB 3, 6; Geog 10; HarEnUS; McGEWB; NatCAB 5; OxCAmH; OxCAmL 65, 83; REnAL; TwCBDA; WebAB 74, 79; WhAm HS; WhoEc 81, 86*

Carey, Hugh Leo
American. Politician
Dem. governor of NY, 1974-81; prevented default by selling bonds.
b. Apr 11, 1919 in New York, New York
Source: *BiDrAC; BiDrUSC 89; BioIn 7, 10, 11, 12, 13; CngDr 74; CurBio 65; NewYTBS 74; Who 82, 83, 85, 88, 90, 92, 94; WhoAm 78, 80, 82; WhoAmP 75; WhoE 74, 79, 81, 83; WhoGov 75; WhoWor 78, 80, 82; WorAl*

Carey, Macdonald
[Edward MacDonald Carey]
American. Actor
Plays Dr. Tom Horton in TV soap opera "Days of our Lives."
b. Mar 15, 1913 in Sioux City, Iowa
Source: *BiE&WWA; BioIn 17, 18, 19, 20; ConTFT 8, 13; FilmgC; HalFC 84, 88; HolP 40; IntMPA 75, 76, 77, 78, 79, 81, 82, 84, 86, 88, 92, 94; ItaFilm; LegTOT; MotPP; MovMk; NewYTBS 94; RadStar; SaTiSS; WhAm 11; WhoAm 78, 80, 82, 84, 86, 88, 92; WhoEnt 92; WhoHol 92, A; WorAl; WorAlBi*

Carey, Mariah
American. Singer, Songwriter
Pop vocalist; won Grammy for best new artist, 1990; debut album, *Mariah Carey,* includes hit "Vision of Love."
b. Mar 27, 1970 in New York, New York
Source: *ConMus 6; CurBio 92; DcHiB; EncRkSt; LegTOT; News 91, 91-3; SoulM; WhoAfA 96; WhoEnt 92; WhoHisp 92*

Carey, Mathew
American. Publisher
Published *Pennsylvania Herald,* 1785-87; *American Museum,* 1787-92; father of Henry Charles.
b. Jan 28, 1760 in Dublin, Ireland
d. Sep 16, 1839 in Philadelphia, Pennsylvania
Source: *Alli; AmAu; AmBi; AmWrBE; AntBDN I; ApCAB; BenetAL 91; BiD&SB; BiDSocW; BioIn 5, 9, 14, 17, 19; BlkwEAR; CyAL 1; DcAmB; DcLB 37, 73; DcLEL; EncAB-H 1974, 1996; NatCAB 6; OxCAmH; OxCAmL 65, 83, 95; PoIre; REn; REnAL; TwCBDA; WebAB 74, 79; WhAm HS*

Carey, Max George
[Maximilian Carnarius]
"Scoops"
American. Baseball Player
Outfielder, 1910-29; led NL in stolen bases 10 times; Hall of Fame, 1961.
b. Jan 11, 1890 in Terre Haute, Indiana
d. May 30, 1976 in Miami Beach, Florida
Source: *BiDAmSp BB; BioIn 1, 3, 6, 7, 10; DcAmB S10; WhoProB 73*

Carey, Phil(ip)
American. Actor
Starred in TV series "Laredo," 1965-67; "Philip Marlowe," 1959-60; plays Asa Buchanan on series "One Life to Live," 1982—.
b. Jul 15, 1925 in Hackensack, New Jersey
Source: *BioIn 4; FilmgC; HalFC 84, 88; IntMPA 75, 76, 77, 78, 79, 81, 82, 84, 86, 88, 92, 94, 96; MotPP; WhoHol 92, A*

Carey, Ron(ald Robert)
American. Labor Union Official
Pres., International Brotherhood of Teamsters, 1991—; won first direct election since Unions founding in 1903 over two old-guard candidates.
b. Mar 22, 1936
Source: *CurBio 92; News 93-3; NewYTBS 27, 91; WhoAm 86*

Carey, William
English. Missionary, Educator
Missionary work in India became the model for later missionaries.
b. Aug 17, 1761 in Paulerspury, England
d. Jun 9, 1834 in Frederiksnagar, India
Source: *Alli; BioIn 1, 2, 3, 4, 5, 6, 7, 8, 10, 12, 13, 16, 17, 18, 19; CelCen; DcBiPP; DcInB; DcNaB, C; EncSoB; LinLib L; LuthC 75; McGEWB*

Carey, William F
American. Boxing Promoter
Pres., Madison Square Garden, 1930-33; promoted over 90 headline bouts.
b. Sep 14, 1878 in Hoosick Falls, New York
d. Feb 24, 1951 in Indio, California
Source: *NatCAB 41; WhAm 3; WhoBox 74*

Carfagno, Edward
American. Designer
Production designs include *Pale Rider,* 1985; won Oscar for *Ben Hur,* 1959.
d. Dec 28, 1996 in Los Angeles, California
Source: *VarWW 85*

Cariou, Len
[Leonard Cariou]
Canadian. Actor, Singer, Director
Won Tony, 1979, for *Sweeney Todd.*
b. Sep 30, 1939 in Saint Boniface, Manitoba, Canada
Source: *BioIn 12; CamGWoT; ConTFT 1, 3; IntMPA 92, 94, 96; NotNAT; OxCAmT 84; OxCCanT; WhoAm 80, 82, 84, 86, 88; WhoHol 92; WhoThe 72, 77, 81; WorAlBi*

Carle, Eric
American. Artist, Illustrator
On *New York Times* 10 Best list for his self-illustrated *The Very Hungry Caterpillar,* 1969.
b. Jun 25, 1929 in Syracuse, New York
Source: *BioIn 9, 12, 13; ChhPo S2; ChlBkCr; ChlLR 10; ConAu 10NR, 25NR, 25R; FourBJA; IlsBYP; IlsCB 1967; IntAu&W 77, 82, 91; MajAI; OxCChiL; SmATA 4, 6AS, 65; TwCChW 89, 95; WhoE 74, 75, 77, 79, 81, 83, 85, 86, 89; WrDr 90, 92, 94, 96*

Carle, Frankie
American. Pianist, Composer, Conductor
Unique style pianist, 1930s; bandleader, 1940s-50s; wrote "Sunrise Serenade," 1939.
b. Mar 25, 1903 in Providence, Rhode Island
Source: *ASCAP 66; BiDAmM; BioIn 2, 9, 12, 13; CmpEPM; NewGrDA 86; OxCPMus; PenEncP; RadStar; WhoHol 92, A*

Carle, Richard
American. Actor
Broadway musical comedian, 1900-20s; character actor in over 80 films, 1928-41.
b. Jul 7, 1871 in Somerville, Massachusetts
d. Jun 28, 1941 in North Hollywood, California
Source: *AmAu&B; CamGWoT; CmpEPM; CurBio 41; EncAFC; Film 2; FilmEn; FilmgC; HalFC 84, 88; MovMk; NotNAT B; OxCAmT 84; TwYS; Vers A; WhAm 1; WhoHol B; WhoStg 1906, 1908; WhScrn 74, 77, 83; WhThe*

Carleton, Will
American. Poet, Journalist, Lecturer
Best known for poems on rural life, including "Farm Legends," 1875.

b. Oct 21, 1845 in Hudson, Michigan
d. Dec 18, 1912 in New York, New York
Source: *Alli SUP; AmAu; AmAu&B; AmBi; ApCAB; BbD; BenetAL 91; BiD&SB; BioIn 5; ChhPo, S1, S2, S3; ConAu 115; CyAL 2; DcAmB; DcNAA; EvLB; HarEnUS; LinLib L; MichAu 80; NatCAB 2; OxCAmL 65, 83, 95; REnAL; TwCBDA; WhAm 1*

Carl Gustaf XVI
[Carl Gustaf Folke Hubertus]
Swedish. Ruler
Became king, Sep 19, 1973, as world's youngest reigning monarch.
b. Apr 30, 1946 in Stockholm, Sweden
Source: *BioIn 10; CurBio 74; NewYTBE 73; NewYTBS 76, 81; WhoWor 87*

Carlile, Richard
English. Journalist, Social Reformer
Disciple of Thomas Paine; imprisoned for publishing free-thought papers, 1819-25, and refusing to pay church rates, 1830s.
b. Dec 8, 1790 in Ashburton, England
d. Feb 10, 1843 in London, England
Source: *BioIn 11, 14, 17; BritAu, 19; DcLB 110, 158; DcNaB; EncUnb; LinLib L; NewC; NewCol 75; WebBD 83*

Carlin, George Dennis
American. Comedian
Created characters Biff Burns, sportscaster; Al Sleet, weatherman; broadcast of explicit record led to landmark "Seven Dirty Words" Supreme Court decision.
b. May 12, 1937 in New York, New York
Source: *BioIn 7, 10, 11; BioNews 75; BkPepl; CurBio 76; WhoHol A*

Carlino, Lewis John
American. Dramatist, Filmmaker
Film adaptation of *I Never Promised You a Rose Garden* won Academy Award nomination, 1977.
b. Jan 1, 1932 in New York, New York
Source: *BioIn 9, 10, 13; ConAmD; ConAu 77; ConDr 73, 77, 82, 88, 93; CurBio 83; HalFC 84, 88; IntAu&W 91, 93; IntMPA 75, 76, 77, 78, 79, 81, 82, 84, 86, 88, 92, 94, 96; MiSFD 9; NewYTET; NotNAT; WrDr 76, 80, 82, 84, 86, 88, 90, 92, 94, 96*

Carlisle, Belinda
[The Go-Go's]
American. Singer
Lead singer for Go-Go's, 1978-85; solo hits include "Mad About You," 1986; "Heaven on Earth," 1987; "Circle in the Sand," 1988.
b. Aug 17, 1958 in Hollywood, California
Source: *ConMus 8; EncRkSt; LegTOT; News 89-3*

Carlisle, John Griffin
American. Government Official
Dem. senator, 1890-93; secretary of treasury, 1893-97; promoted sound-money policy.
b. Sep 5, 1835 in Kenton County, Kentucky
d. Jul 31, 1910 in New York, New York
Source: *AmBi; AmPolLe; ApCAB; BiDrAC; BiDrUSC 89; BiDrUSE 71, 89; BiDSA; BioIn 7, 10, 14; CyAG; DcAmB; HarEnUS; NatCAB 1; OxCAmH; TwCBDA; WebAB 74, 79; WebBD 83; WhAm 1; WhAmP*

Carlisle, Kevin
American. Director, Producer, Choreographer
Int'l. concert, TV, stage work includes several Barry Manilow specials.
b. Dec 24, 1935 in New York, New York
Source: *BiDD; ConTFT 2*

Carlisle, Kitty
[Katherine Conn; Mrs. Moss Hart]
American. Actor, Singer
Panelist, TV series "To Tell the Truth," 1956-67.
b. Sep 3, 1915 in New Orleans, Louisiana
Source: *BiE&WWA; BioIn 7, 10; CelR; ConTFT 3; CurBio 82; EncMT; FilmgC; HalFC 84, 88; NewYTBS 76; NotNAT; OxCAmT 84; ThFT; WhoAmW 58, 61, 68, 70, 72, 74; WhoEnt 92; WhoHol 92, A; WhoThe 81; WorAl*

Carlisle, Mary
American. Actor
Brief screen career, retired in early 1940s.
b. Feb 3, 1912 in Boston, Massachusetts
Source: *BioIn 9; EncAFC; FilmEn; FilmgC; GangFlm; HalFC 84, 88; InWom SUP; MotPP; MovMk; ThFT; WhoHol 92, A*

Carlos, John
American. Track Athlete
Won bronze medal in 200-meters, 1968 Olympics; on winner's stand with Tommie Smith, protested treatment of blacks in US by raising clenched fists; expelled from games.
b. Jun 5, 1945 in New York, New York
Source: *BioIn 10, 11; WhoBlA 77, 80, 85, 88, 90, 92; WhoTr&F 73*

Carlota
Belgian. Ruler
Wife of Maximilian, empress of Mexico, 1864-67; went insane after realizing failure of husband's cause, 1866.
b. Jun 7, 1840 in Laeken, Belgium
d. Jan 19, 1927 in Brussels, Belgium
Source: *LegTOT; REn; WebBD 83*

Carlson, Arne Helge
American. Politician
Rep. governor, MN, 1991—.
b. Sep 24, 1934 in New York, New York
Source: *AlmAP 92; WhoAm 92, 94, 95, 96, 97; WhoAmP 87, 91; WhoMW 90, 92, 93, 96*

Carlson, Chester Floyd
American. Inventor, Physicist
Invented photocopying process called xerography, 1940; Xerox made first machine, 1959.
b. Feb 8, 1906 in Seattle, Washington
d. Sep 19, 1968 in New York, New York
Source: *DcAmB S8; EncAB-H 1974; LarDcSc; WebAB 74, 79; WhAm 5; WorInv*

Carlson, Curtis L.
American. Businessman
Founded Gold Bond Stamp Co., 1938; became Carlson Companies, 1973.
b. Jul 9, 1914 in Minneapolis, Minnesota
Source: *Dun&B 86, 88, 90; St&PR 75, 84, 87, 91, 93, 96, 97*

Carlson, Doc
[Harold Clifford Carlson]
American. Basketball Coach
Coach, U of Pittsburgh, 1922-53, with 367-250 career record; one of original 15 inducted into Hall of Fame, 1959.
b. Jul 4, 1894 in Murray City, Ohio
d. Nov 1, 1964
Source: *BasBi; BioIn 7, 9; WhoBbl 73; WhoSpor*

Carlson, Edward Elmer
American. Businessman
Chm. of board, United Airlines, 1979-90.
b. Jun 4, 1911 in Tacoma, Washington
d. Apr 3, 1990 in Seattle, Washington
Source: *BioIn 12, 14, 15, 16, 17; IntWW 74, 75, 76, 77, 78, 79, 80, 81, 82, 83, 89; NatCAB 63N; St&PR 75; WhAm 10; WhoAm 74, 76, 78, 80, 82, 84; WhoFI 74, 75, 77, 79, 81, 83; WhoMW 74, 76, 78, 80*

Carlson, Evans Fordyce
American. Soldier
Led commando force "Carlson's Raiders"; battle cry was "Gung Ho," during WW II.
b. Feb 26, 1896 in Sidney, New York
d. May 27, 1947 in Plymouth, Connecticut
Source: *BioIn 1, 6, 8, 13; CurBio 43, 47; DcAmB S4; DcAmMiB; DcNAA; GenMudB; HarEnMi; WebAMB; WhAm 2; WhWW-II; WorAl; WorAlBi*

Carlson, Frank
American. Politician
Rep. governor, KS, 1947-51; congressman, 1935-45.
b. Jan 23, 1893 in Concordia, Kansas
d. May 30, 1987 in Concordia, Kansas
Source: *BiDrAC; BiDrGov 1789; BiDrUSC 89; BioIn 1, 2, 3, 8, 11, 15, 17; CurBio 49, 87, 87N; NewYTBS 87;*

PolProf E, J; WhAm 9; WhoAmP 73, 75, 77, 79, 81, 83, 85

Carlson, Richard
American. Actor
In TV series "I Led Three Lives," 1953; "Mackenzie's Raiders," 1958.
b. Apr 29, 1912 in Albert Lea, Minnesota
d. Nov 25, 1977 in Encino, California
Source: *BioIn 11; ConAu 73; FilmgC; HalFC 84, 88; IntMPA 77; MotPP; MovMk; NewEScF; WhScrn 83*

Carlson, Wally
[Wallace A. Carlson]
American. Cartoonist
Drew comic strip "The Nebbs," 1923-46.
b. Mar 28, 1894 in Saint Louis, Missouri
d. 1969
Source: *WhAm 4; WorECom*

Carlson, William Hugh
American. Author, Librarian
Wrote on library planning: *In a Grand and Awful Time,* 1967.
b. Sep 5, 1898 in Waverly, Nebraska
Source: *BiDrLUS 70; BioIn 17; ConAu P-2; WhAm 10; WhoCon 73; WhoLibS 55, 66; WhoPNW*

Carlson, William S(amuel)
American. University Administrator
Pres., Univ. of Delaware, 1946-50; Univ. of Vermont, 1950-52; State Univ. of New York, 1952-58; Univ. of Toledo, 1958-72.
b. Nov 18, 1905
d. May 8, 1994 in Belleair Bluffs, Florida
Source: *AmMWSc 73P, 76P; BioIn 2, 3, 5; ConAu 1R, 145; CurBio 94N; LEduc 74; MichAu 80; WhoAm 74, 76, 78, 80*

Carlsson, Ingvar Gosta
Swedish. Political Leader
Prime minister of Sweden, 1986-91; 1994-96.
b. Nov 9, 1934 in Boras, Sweden
Source: *CurBio 88; IntWW 74, 75, 76, 77, 78, 79, 80, 81, 82, 83, 89, 91, 93; WhoWor 74, 76, 78, 87, 89, 91, 93, 95, 96, 97*

Carlton, Larry
[The Crusaders; Lawrence Eugene Carlton]
American. Musician
Guitarist with Crusaders 1973-76; solo albums include *Sleepwalk,* 1982; *Friends,* 1983.
b. 1948 in Torrance, California
Source: *EncJzS; HarEnR 86; IlEncBM 82; NewGrDJ 88; OnThGG; SoulM*

Carlton, Steve(n Norman)
"Lefty"
American. Baseball Player
Pitcher, 1965-87; only ML pitcher to win Cy Young Award four times; second to Nolan Ryan in career strikeouts.
b. Dec 22, 1944 in Miami, Florida
Source: *Ballpl 90; BaseReg 86, 87; BiDAmSp BB; BioIn 9, 10, 11, 12, 13; CelR; LegTOT; WhoAm 74, 76, 78, 80, 82, 84, 86, 88, 92, 94, 95, 96, 97; WhoProB 73; WorAl; WorAlBi*

Carlucci, Frank Charles, III
American. Government Official
Govt. service veteran; succeeded Caspar Weinberger as defense secretary under Reagan, 1987.
b. Oct 18, 1930 in Scranton, Pennsylvania
Source: *BiDrUSE 89; BioIn 9, 11, 12, 13; CngDr 81; ColdWar 1; CurBio 81; DcAmDH 89; EncAI&E; IntWW 75, 76, 77, 78, 79, 80, 81, 82, 83, 89, 91, 93; NewYTBE 70; USBiR 74; WhoAm 76, 78, 80, 82, 84, 86, 88, 90, 92, 94, 95, 96, 97; WhoE 89, 93; WhoFI 87, 89; WhoGov 72, 75, 77; WhoSSW 73; WhoWor 78, 89, 91*

Carlyle, Randy
Canadian. Hockey Player
Defenseman, 1976—, mostly with Pittsburgh, currently with Winnipeg; won Norris Trophy, 1981.
b. Apr 19, 1956 in Sudbury, Ontario, Canada
Source: *HocReg 87*

Carlyle, Thomas
Scottish. Critic, Historian
His *The French Revolution,* 1837, made him a prominent man of letters; considered one of era's great sages.
b. Dec 4, 1795 in Ecclefechan, Scotland
d. Feb 4, 1881 in London, England
Source: *Alli, SUP; AtlBL; BbD; Benet 87, 96; BiD&SB; BiDTran; BioIn 1, 2, 3, 4, 5, 6, 7, 8, 9, 10, 11, 12, 13, 14, 15, 16, 17, 18, 20, 21; BlmGEL; BritAu 19; BritWr 4; CamGEL; CamGLE; CasWL; CelCen; ChhPo, S1, S2, S3; CmScLit; CnDBLB 3; CrtT 3, 4; CyEd; CyWA 58; DcAmC; DcAmSR; DcArts; DcBiPP; DcEnA; DcEnL; DcEuL; DcLB 55, 144; DcLEL; DcNaB; Dis&D; EvLB; FamAYP; LegTOT; LinLib L, S; LngCEL; LuthC 75; McGEWB; MouLC 3; NewC; NinCLC 22; OxCEng 67, 85, 95; OxCIri; PenC ENG; RadHan; RAdv 1, 14, 13-1, 13-3; RComWL; REn; RfGEnL 91; VicBrit; WebBD 83; WebE&AL; WhDW; WorAl; WorAlBi; WrPh*

Carman, Bliss
[William Bliss Carman]
Canadian. Author, Poet
Popular verse vols. include *Sappho,* 1902; *Songs from Vagabondia,* 1894.
b. Apr 15, 1861 in Fredericton, New Brunswick, Canada
d. Jun 8, 1929 in New Canaan, Connecticut
Source: *ApCAB SUP, X; BbD; Benet 87; BenetAL 91; BiD&SB; BioIn 1, 5, 7, 17; CamGLE; CanWr; CasWL; Chambr 3; ChhPo, S1, S2; CnDAL; ConAmL; ConAu 104; CreCan 1; DcAmAu; DcEnA A; DcLB 92; DcLEL; DcNAA; DcNaB 1922; EvLB; GayN; LinLib L, S; LngCTC; MacDCB 78; NatCAB 18, 21; OxCAmL 65, 83; OxCCan; OxCCanL; OxCEng 67, 85, 95; PenC AM, ENG; RAdv 14, 13-1; REn; REnAL; RfGEnL 91; TwCA, SUP; TwCBDA; TwCLC 7; WebE&AL; WhAm 1; WhDW; WhNAA*

Carmel, Roger C
American. Actor
Episodic TV actor; voice of Smokey the Bear in commercials.
b. 1932 in New York, New York
d. Nov 11, 1986 in Hollywood, California
Source: *ConTFT 4; EncAFC; HalFC 84*

Carmen, Eric
[The Raspberries]
American. Singer, Musician
Had hit singles "All By Myself," 1975, "Make Me Lose Control," 1988.
b. Aug 11, 1949 in Cleveland, Ohio
Source: *EncRkSt; HarEnR 86; LegTOT; RkOn 74, 78; RolSEnR 83; WhoRock 81*

Carmer, Carl Lamson
American. Author, Educator
Wrote about history, folklore of upstate NY: *Listen for a Lonesome Drum,* 19 36.
b. Oct 16, 1893 in Cortland, New York
d. Sep 11, 1976 in Bronxville, New York
Source: *AmAu&B; Au&Wr 71; AuBYP 2; ChhPo, S1, S2, S3; ConAu 4NR, 5R, 69; NewYTBS 76; OxCAmL 65; REn; REnAL; ScF&FL 2; SmATA 30; Str&VC; TwCA, SUP; WhAm 7; WhoAm 76*

Carmichael, Franklin
[Group of Seven]
Canadian. Artist
Oil landscape painter; original Group of Seven member, 1919.
b. May 4, 1890 in Orillia, Ontario, Canada
d. Oct 24, 1945 in Toronto, Ontario, Canada
Source: *CreCan 2; MacDCB 78; McGDA*

Carmichael, Harold
[Lee Harold Carmichael]
American. Football Player
End, 1971-84, mostly with Philadelphia; set NFL record for most consecutive games with a pass reception, 127, since broken by Steve Largent.
b. Sep 22, 1949 in Jacksonville, Florida
Source: *BiDAmSp FB; BioIn 11, 12, 14; FootReg 85; NewYTBS 84; WhoBlA 77, 80, 85, 90, 92, 94; WhoFtbl 74*

Carmichael, Hoagy
[Hoagland Howard Carmichael]
American. Songwriter
Music characterized by slow, dreamy melodies; wrote "Stardust," 1927, "Georgia On My Mind," 1930.
b. Nov 22, 1899 in Bloomington, Indiana
d. Dec 27, 1981 in Rancho Mirage, California
Source: *AllMusG; AmPS; AmSong; AnObit 1981; ASCAP 66, 80; Baker 78, 84, 92; BiDAmM; BiDJaz; BioIn 1, 3, 4, 6, 7, 8, 9, 12, 13, 14, 15, 16, 20; CelR; CmpEPM; ConAmC 82; ConAu 108; CurBio 41, 82, 82N; DcArts; FacFETw; FilmgC; HalFC 84, 88; IndAu 1917; IntDcF 1-4, 2-4; IntMPA 75, 76, 77, 78, 79, 81, 82; LegTOT; MotPP; MovMk; NewAmDM; NewGrDA 86; NewGrDJ 88, 94; NewOxM; NewYTBS 81; OxCFilm; OxCPMus; PenEncP; WebAB 74, 79; WhAm 8; WhoAm 74, 76, 80; WhoHol A; WhoMus 72; WhoWor 74; WhScrn 83; WorAl; WorAlBi; WorEFlm*

Carmichael, Ian
English. Actor
Played Lord Peter Wimsey in Dorothy Sayers mysteries on PBS.
b. Jun 18, 1920 in Hull, England
Source: *BioIn 12, 13, 19; CmMov; ConAu 129; ConTFT 6; EncMT; FilmgC; HalFC 84, 88; IntMPA 75, 76, 77, 78, 79, 81, 82, 84, 86, 88, 92, 94, 96; LegTOT; OxCPMus; QDrFCA 92; Who 74, 82, 83, 85, 88, 90, 92; WhoHol 92, A; WhoThe 72, 77, 81; WorAl; WorAlBi*

Carmichael, James Vinson
American. Business Executive, Politician
Led Scripto, Inc., 1947-72; won Dem. primary for Georgia governor, 1946, but county unit system elected Talmadge.
b. Oct 2, 1910 in Smyrna, Georgia
d. Nov 28, 1972 in Marietta, Georgia
Source: *BioIn 7, 9; EncAB-A 36; NewYTBE 72; ObitOF 79; St&PR 75; WhAm 6; WhoSSW 73*

Carmichael, John P
American. Journalist
Sportswriter, *Chicago Daily News;* known for syndicated column "Barber Shop."
b. 1903?
d. Jun 6, 1986 in Chicago, Illinois
Source: *ConAu 119*

Carmichael, Stokely
[Kwame Toure]
American. Civil Rights Leader
Responsible for Black Power concept, 1960s.
b. Jun 29, 1941 in Port of Spain, Trinidad and Tobago
Source: *AfrAmAl 6; AmAu&B; AmSocL; BiDAmLf; BioIn 7, 8, 9, 11, 13, 16, 17, 19; BlkWr 1; CivR 74; CivRSt; ConAu 25NR, 57; ConBlB 5; CurBio 70; DcTwCCu 5; EncAACR; EncWB; FacFETw; HisWorL; InB&W 85; LegTOT; NegAl 76, 83, 89; PolPar; PolProf J; SchCGBL; SelBAAf; SelBAAu; WhoAfA 96; WhoBlA 90, 92, 94; WhoSSW 73, 82; WhoWor 74, 76; WorAl; WorAlBi*

Carmines, Al(vin Allison Jr.)
American. Composer
Prolific songwriter in non-Broadway musical theater; wrote music, lyrics, book for "A Look at the Fifties," 1972.
b. Jul 25, 1937 in Hampton, Virginia
Source: *ConAmC 82; ConAu 103; CurBio 72; NotNAT; WhoThe 77, 81*

Carnahan, Mel Eugene
American. Politician
Dem. governor, MO, 1993—.
b. Feb 11, 1934 in Birch Tree, Missouri
Source: *IntWW 93; WhoAm 90, 92; WhoAmP 91; WhoMW 92*

Carnap, Rudolf
German. Philosopher, Educator
Noted logician; member, Vienna school of logical positivists, 1920s; wrote *Unity of Science,* 1934.
b. May 18, 1891 in Ronsdorf, Germany
d. Sep 14, 1970 in Santa Monica, California
Source: *AmAu&B; BiESc; BioIn 7, 8, 9, 10, 12, 13, 14, 15, 17; ConAu P-1; DcAmB S8; FacFETw; IntEnSS 79; MakMC; McGEWB; NewYTBE 70; OxCPhil; RAdv 14, 13-5; ThTwC 87; WebAB 74, 79; WhAm 5; WorAu 1950*

Carne, Judy
[Joyce A Botterill]
English. Comedian
Appeared in TV series "Laugh In," 1968-70; first wife of Burt Reynolds.
b. Apr 27, 1939 in Northampton, England
Source: *ConTFT 3; FilmgC; HalFC 84, 88; InWom SUP; LegTOT; WhoHol 92, A; WorAl*

Carne, Marcel Albert
French. Director
Worked with screenwriter Jacques Prevert on *Children of Paradise,* 1945; *Port of Shadows,* 1939.
b. Aug 18, 1909 in Paris, France
d. Oct 31, 1996 in Clamart, France
Source: *BiDFilm; DcFM; FilmEn; FilmgC; HalFC 84; IntWW 83; MovMk; OxCFilm; REn; WhoWor 87; WorEFlm*

Carnegie, Andrew
American. Industrialist
Steel producer; endowed 1,700 libraries; built Carnegie Hall, NYC, 1891.
b. Nov 25, 1835 in Dunfermline, Scotland
d. Aug 11, 1919 in Lenox, Massachusetts
Source: *Alli SUP; AmAu&B; AmBi; AmDec 1900; AmPeW; AmSocL; ApCAB, X; BbD; Benet 87, 96; BenetAL 91; BiD&SB; BiDMoPL; BioIn 1, 2, 3, 4, 5, 6, 7, 8, 9, 10, 11, 12, 13, 14, 15, 16, 17, 18, 19, 20, 21; ChhPo S3; CivWDc; CmScLit; CyAG; DcAmAu; DcAmB; DcAmC; DcAmDH 80; DcAmLiB; DcAmSR; DcNAA; DcNaB 1912; Dis&D; EncAB-H 1974, 1996; EncABHB 3; GayN; HarEnUS; InSci; LegTOT; LinLib L, S; LngCTC; McGEWB; MemAm; NewGrDA 86; OxCAmH; OxCAmL 65, 83, 95; OxCEng 85, 95; OxCMed 86; PenC AM; RComAH; REn; REnAL; TwCBDA; WebAB 74, 79; WhAm 1; WhAmP; WhCiWar; WhDW; WorAl; WorAlBi*

Carnegie, Dale
American. Author
Wrote *How to Win Friends and Influence People,* 1936; has sold over five million copies.
b. Nov 24, 1888 in Maryville, Missouri
d. Nov 1, 1955 in Forest Hills, New York
Source: *AmSocL; BenetAL 91; BioIn 1, 4, 11, 15, 16, 19; CurBio 41, 55; DcAmB S5; DcArts; FacFETw; LegTOT; LngCTC; PenC AM; REnAL; TwCLC 53; WebAB 74, 79; WhAm 3; WorAl; WorAlBi*

Carnegie, Hattie
[Henriette Kannengiser; H C Zanft]
American. Fashion Designer
First internationally famed American couturiere; introduced first fashion collection, 1918.
b. 1889 in Vienna, Austria
d. Feb 22, 1956 in New York, New York
Source: *AmDec 1930; BioIn 1, 4, 12; ConFash; CurBio 42, 56; EncFash; InWom; LegTOT; WhAm 3; WhoFash 88; WorFshn*

Carnegie, Mary Elizabeth Lancaster
American. Nurse, Editor
Influential in lowering segregation barriers in nursing.
b. Apr 19, 1916 in Baltimore, Maryland
Source: *BioIn 3; BlksScM; BlkWAm; DcWomA; InB&W 80; NotBlAW 1*

Carner, Joanne Gunderson
"The Great Gundy"
American. Golfer
Turned pro, 1970; has over 40 tour wins, including US Women's Open, 1971, 1976; is LPGA's all-time leading money winner; 1980.
b. Mar 4, 1939 in Kirkland, Washington
Source: *BiDAmSp OS; EncWomS; GoodHs; InWom SUP; LegTOT; WhoAm 82, 84, 86, 88; WhoGolf; WorAl*

Carnera, Primo
"Ambling Alp"
American. Boxer
Heavyweight champ, 1933; lost to Max Baer, 1934.
b. Oct 26, 1906 in Sequals, Italy
d. Jun 29, 1967 in Sequals, Italy

Source: *BioIn 1, 2, 5, 6, 7, 8, 9, 10; ItaFilm; LegTOT; ObitT 1961; WhoBox 74; WhoHol B; WhScrn 77, 83*

Carnes, Kim
American. Singer, Songwriter
Known for deep, raw voice; won Grammy for "Bette Davis Eyes," 1981.
b. Jul 20, 1946 in Hollywood, California
Source: *EncRkSt; HarEnR 86; NewWmR; RkOn 85*

Carnesseca, Lou
American. Basketball Coach
College coach, St. John's University, 1965-70, 1973-92; Basketball Hall of Fame, 1992.
b. Jan 25, 1925 in New York, New York
Source: *BioIn 16; NewYTBS 83, 85; WhoAm 88*

Carnevale, Ben
[Bernard L Carnevale]
American. Basketball Coach
Coach, NC State, 1945-46, US Naval Academy, 1947-67; Hall of Fame.
b. Oct 30, 1915 in Raritan, New Jersey
Source: *BasBi; BiDAmSp BK; WhoBbl 73; WhoSpor*

Carney, Art
[Arthur William Matthew Carney]
American. Actor
Won Oscar, 1974, for *Harry and Tonto;* played Ed Norton in TV series "The Honeymooners"; won three Emmys.
b. Nov 4, 1918 in Mount Vernon, New York
Source: *BiE&WWA; BioIn 2, 3, 4, 5, 6, 7, 10, 11, 12; BioNews 74; CelR, 90; ConTFT 4; CurBio 58; EncAFC; FilmgC; HalFC 84, 88; IntMPA 75, 76, 77, 78, 79, 81, 82, 84, 86, 88, 92, 94, 96; LegTOT; NewYTET; NotNAT; OxCAmT 84; SaTiSS; WhoAm 74, 76, 78, 80, 82, 84, 86, 88, 90, 92, 94, 95, 96, 97; WhoCom; WhoEnt 92; WhoHol 92, A; WhoThe 72, 77, 81; WhoWor 74; WorAl; WorAlBi*

Carney, Don
"Uncle Don"
American. Actor
Star of 1930s children's radio show.
b. 1897
d. Jan 14, 1954 in Miami, Florida
Source: *BioIn 3; ObitOF 79; WhScrn 74, 77, 83*

Carney, Harry Howell
American. Jazz Musician
Baritone saxophonist with Duke Ellington since 1927.
b. Apr 1, 1910 in Boston, Massachusetts
d. Oct 8, 1974 in New York, New York
Source: *BiDAmM; BiDJaz; NewYTBS 74; WhAm 6; WhoAm 74; WhoJazz 72; WhScrn 77*

Carney, Robert Bostwick
American. Naval Officer
Appointed NATO commander-in-chief of Allied Forces in Mediterranean by Eisenhower, 1951; planned key Pacific naval battles, WW II.
b. Mar 26, 1895 in Vallejo, California
d. Jun 25, 1990 in Washington, District of Columbia
Source: *BiDWWGF; BioIn 2, 3, 4, 17; CurBio 51, 90; FacFETw; WebAMB; WhAm 10; Who 74, 82, 83, 85, 88, 90; WhoSSW 73, 82*

Carnot, Hippolyte
[Lazare Hippolyte Carnot]
French. Revolutionary, Statesman
Involved in radical agitation leading to 1848 revolution; son of Lazare Carnot.
b. Apr 13, 1801 in Saint-Omer, France
d. Mar 16, 1888 in Paris, France
Source: *DcBiPP; NewCol 75*

Carnot, Lazare
[Nicolas Marguerite Carnot]
"Le Grand Carnot"
French. Revolutionary
Military genius of French revolutionary wars; wrote classic text on fortification, 1810.
b. May 13, 1753 in Nolay, France
d. Aug 2, 1823 in Magdeburg, Prussia
Source: *DcBiPP; DcInv; DcScB; Dis&D; EncRev; LinLib S; McGEWB; NewCol 75; WhoMilH 76*

Carnovsky, Morris
American. Actor
Stage, film actor, 1937-51; victim of Hollywood blacklisting, 1951.
b. Sep 5, 1897 in Saint Louis, Missouri
d. Sep 1, 1992 in Easton, Connecticut
Source: *AnObit 1992; BiE&WWA; BioIn 17, 18, 19; CamGWoT; CnThe; CurBio 91, 92N; FacFETw; FamA&A; FilmgC; HalFC 84, 88; IntDcT 3; LegTOT; MotPP; MovMk; NewYTBS 92; NotNAT; OxCAmT 84; OxCThe 83; PlP&P; WhAm 10; WhoAm 74; WhoHol 92, A; WhoThe 72, 77, 81*

Caro, Anthony, Sir
English. Sculptor
Known for abstract, complex steel, aluminum sculptures; often painted in primary colors.
b. Mar 8, 1924 in London, England
Source: *BioIn 7, 8, 10, 12, 13, 14, 16, 19, 20; BlueB 76; CenC; ConArt 77, 83, 89; ConBrA 79; CurBio 81; DcArts; DcBrAr 2; DcCAr 81; IntWW 74, 75, 76, 77, 78, 79, 80, 81, 82, 83, 89, 91, 93; McGDA; McGEWB; OxCTwCA; OxDcArt; PhDcTCA 77; TwCPaSc; Who 74, 82, 83, 85, 88, 90, 92; WhoAm 82, 84, 86, 88; WhoArt 80, 82, 84, 96; WhoWor 74, 76, 78, 82, 84, 87, 89, 91, 93, 95; WhoWorJ 78; WorArt 1950*

Caro, Joseph
Spanish. Scholar
Wrote *Shulhan'Arukh,* 1565, outlining legal code for Orthodox Jewery.
b. 1488 in Toledo, Spain
d. Mar 24, 1575
Source: *BioIn 2, 3, 6, 7, 11; CasWL; EuAu; LuthC 75; McGEWB; OxCLaw*

Caro, Robert A
American. Author
Wrote best-sellers about power: *The Power Broker: Robert Moses and the Fall of New York,* 1974; *The Path to Power* (about Lyndon Johnson), 1982.
b. Oct 30, 1936 in New York, New York
Source: *BioIn 13; ConAu 101; CurBio 84; WorAu 1970; WrDr 86*

Carol, Martine
[Maryse Mourer]
French. Actor
French sex symbol of early 1950s; films include *Beauties of the Night,* 1952; *Lola Montes,* 1955.
b. May 16, 1922 in Biarritz, France
d. Feb 6, 1967 in Monte Carlo, Monaco
Source: *BiDFilm, 94; BioIn 4, 7; FilmgC; HalFC 84, 88; ItaFilm; MotPP; MovMk; OxCFilm; WhoHol B; WhScrn 74, 77; WorEFlm*

Carol II
Romanian. Ruler
Reigned, 1930-40; noted for abolishing political parties, founding Front of National Rebirth; ousted by Germans.
b. Oct 16, 1893 in Sinaia, Romania
d. Apr 4, 1953 in Estoril, Portugal
Source: *NewCol 75; WebBD 83*

Caroline, Princess
[Caroline Louise Marguerite Grimaldi]
Monacan. Princess
Daughter of Princess Grace and Prince Rainier of Monaco; has taken on many of mother's official duties.
b. Jan 23, 1957 in Monte Carlo, Monaco
Source: *BioIn 4, 10, 11, 12, 13; BkPepl; CurBio 89; LegTOT; NewYTBS 75*

Carols
[Ilitch Ramirez Sanchez]
"The Jackel"
Venezuelan. Terrorist, Murderer
Most-wanted man in world, 1981; linked to Red Brigade, Khadafi, etc.
b. 1947?, Venezuela
Source: *BioIn 10, 11; PseudN 82*

Caron, Leslie Clare Margaret
French. Actor, Dancer
Starred in MGM musicals: *An American in Paris,* 1951; *Gigi,* 1958.
b. Jul 1, 1931 in Paris, France
Source: *BiDFilm; CmMov; CurBio 54; FilmgC; HalFC 84; IntMPA 86; IntWW 83; MotPP; MovMk; OxCFilm; Who 85; WhoAm 86, 92; WhoHol A; WhoThe 77A; WorEFlm*

Carothers, Wallace Hume
American. Chemist
Work in organic chemistry resulted in discovery of synthetic rubber, nylon.

b. Apr 27, 1896 in Burlington, Iowa
d. Apr 29, 1937 in Philadelphia, Pennsylvania
Source: *AsBiEn; BiESc; BioIn 1, 2, 3, 4, 6, 9, 11, 12; CamDcSc; DcAmB S2; DcScB; EncAB-H 1974, 1996; FacFETw; InSci; LarDcSc; LegTOT; McGEWB; NatCAB 38; NotTwCS; OxCAmH; WebAB 74, 79; WhAm 1; WorAl; WorInv*

Carpaccio, Vittore
Italian. Artist
Painted colorful, detailed narrative scenes; noted for St. Ursula series.
b. 1455? in Venice, Italy
d. 1525? in Venice, Italy
Source: *AtlBL; DcCathB; LinLib S; REn*

Carpenter, Bobby
[Robert Carpenter]
American. Hockey Player
Center, Capitals, 1981-87; LA, 1987—; first American-born player to score 50 goals in a season (1984-85).
b. Jul 13, 1963 in Beverly, Massachusetts
Source: *BiDAmSp BK; BioIn 12; HocEn; HocReg 87; NewYTBS 81*

Carpenter, Edward
English. Author, Clergy
Socialist views caused him to give up church; wrote *Love's Coming of Age,* 1896.
b. Aug 29, 1844 in Brighton, England
d. Jun 28, 1929 in Guildford, England
Source: *Alli SUP; BiDBrF 2; BioIn 2, 9, 10, 12, 13, 14, 15, 16, 17, 18, 20; BritAu 19; CamGLE; Chambr 3; ChhPo, S3; DcAmSR; DcArts; DcNaB 1922; EvLB; GayLesB; GayLL; LinLib L; LngCTC; ModBrL; NewC; OxCEng 85, 95; PenC ENG; RadHan; REn; RGTwCWr; VicBrit; WhLit; WhoTwCL*

Carpenter, Francis Bicknell
American. Artist
Best known for paintings of Abraham Lincoln; wrote *Six Months in the White House,* 1866.
b. Aug 6, 1830 in Homer, New York
d. May 23, 1900 in New York, New York
Source: *Alli SUP; AmBi; ApCAB; ArtsNiC; BioIn 1; DcAmAu; DcAmB, S2; DcNAA; Drake; HarEnUS; NatCAB 11; NewYHSD; TwCBDA; WhAm 1*

Carpenter, John Alden
American. Composer
Used jazz motifs in ballets, orchestral suites: *Adventures in a Perambulator,* 1915.
b. Feb 28, 1876 in Park Ridge, Illinois
d. Apr 26, 1951 in Chicago, Illinois
Source: *AmComp; ApCAB X; ASCAP 66; Baker 78, 84, 92; BiDAmM; BioIn 1, 2, 3, 4, 8, 20; ChhPo S1; ConAmC 76, 82; CurBio 47, 51; DcAmB S5; EncAB-A 24; FacFETw; LegTOT; LinLib S; NatCAB 40; NewAmDM; NewGrDA 86; OxCAmL 65; OxCMus; WhAm 3*

Carpenter, John Howard
American. Director
Known for horror films; directed *Halloween,* 1978, which became the highest grossing independently made movie of all time.
b. Jan 16, 1948 in Carthage, New York
Source: *ConTFT 8; DcBrWA; HalFC 84; IntMPA 86; NewYTBS 81; WhoAm 82, 97; WhoHol A*

Carpenter, Karen (Anne)
[The Carpenters; Mrs. Thomas J. Burris]
American. Singer
With brother, Richard, sold over 80 million records; first hit "Close to You," 1970.
b. Mar 2, 1950 in New Haven, Connecticut
d. Feb 4, 1983 in Downey, California
Source: *AnObit 1983; Baker 84, 92; BioIn 12, 13, 14, 16, 20; BkPepl; EncPR&S 74, 89; GoodHs; InWom SUP; LegTOT; NewYTBS 83; OxCPMus; WhAm 8; WhoAm 76, 78, 80, 82; WhoAmW 81; WorAl; WorAlBi*

Carpenter, Ken(neth)
American. Track Athlete
Discus thrower; won gold medal, 1936 Olympics.
b. Apr 19, 1913 in Compton, California
Source: *WhoTr&F 73*

Carpenter, Leslie
American. Journalist
Syndicated Washington correspondent, 1944-74.
b. Feb 20, 1922 in Austin, Texas
d. Jul 24, 1974 in Washington, District of Columbia
Source: *BioIn 10; ObitOF 79; WhAm 6; WhoAm 74*

Carpenter, Liz
[Elizabeth Sutherland Carpenter]
American. Journalist
Press secretary, staff director for Lady Bird Johnson, 1963-69.
b. Sep 1, 1920 in Salado, Texas
Source: *ChhPo; ConAu 41R; EncTwCJ; InWom SUP; NewYTBS 87; WhoAdv 90; WhoAm 74, 76, 78, 80, 82, 84, 86, 88, 90, 92, 94, 95, 96, 97; WhoAmP 75; WhoAmW 58, 61, 72, 74, 75, 79, 81, 83, 85, 87, 89, 91; WhoWrEP 89, 92, 95*

Carpenter, Mary Chapin
American. Singer, Songwriter
Labeled a contemporary country singer; hit singles "Quittin' Time" and "You Never Had It So Good," 1989.
b. Feb 21, 1958 in Princeton, New Jersey
Source: *BgBkCoM; ConMus 6; CurBio 94; WhoAm 96, 97; WhoAmW 97; WhoNeCM*

Carpenter, Richard Lynn
[The Carpenters]
American. Singer, Musician, Songwriter
With sister, Karen, had several hits including "We've Only Just Begun," 1970; three time Grammy winner.
b. Oct 15, 1946 in New Haven, Connecticut
Source: *BkPepl; EncPR&S 74; WhoAm 76, 78, 80, 82, 84; WhoEmL 93; WhoEnt 92; WhoWor 82; WorAl*

Carpenter, Scott
[Malcolm Scott Carpenter]
American. Astronaut
One of seven original astronauts; orbited Earth three times in *Mercury* spacecraft, May 1962.
b. May 1, 1925 in Boulder, Colorado
Source: *BioIn 6, 7, 9, 10, 13; BlueB 76; CurBio 62; FacFETw; IntWW 74, 75, 76, 77; LegTOT; ScF&FL 92; WhoAm 74, 76, 78, 80, 82, 84, 86, 88, 92, 94, 95, 96; WhoScEn 94; WhoSpc; WhoWor 74; WorAl; WorAlBi*

Carpenters, The
[Karen Carpenter; Richard Carpenter]
American. Music Group
Pop brother-sister team with many hits, 1970s: "For All We Know," 1971; "Top of the World," 1973.
Source: *Alli; BiDAmM; BioIn 15, 20; BkPepl; DcNaB, C; HarEnR 86; NewYTBS 27; RkOn 78*

Carpentier, Georges
French. Boxer, Entertainer
Fought in flyweight thru heavyweight divisions; lost heavyweight title to Dempsey, 1921.
b. Jan 12, 1894 in Lens, France
d. Oct 27, 1975 in Paris, France
Source: *BioIn 1, 2, 4, 7, 10; BoxReg; Dis&D; Film 2; ObitT 1971; WhoBox 74; WhoHol C; WhScrn 77, 83*

Carper, Thomas Richard
American. Politician
Dem. governor, DE, 1993—.
b. Jan 23, 1947 in Beckley, West Virginia
Source: *AlmAP 92; BiDrUSC 89; CngDr 83, 85, 87, 89; IntWW 93; PolsAm 84; WhoAm 80, 86, 88, 90, 92, 94, 95, 96, 97; WhoAmP 91; WhoE 83, 85, 86, 89, 91, 93, 95, 97*

Carpini, Giovanni de Piano
Italian. Religious Figure, Traveler
Wrote first account of court of Great Khan in Mongolia, 1246.
b. 1180 in Pian di Carpine, Italy
d. 1252
Source: *DcCathB; NewCol 75; WhDW*

Carr, Alexander
American. Actor
Best known for role of Perlmutter in *Potash and Perlmutter* silent comedies, 1920s.
b. 1878 in Rumni, Russia

d. Sep 19, 1946 in Los Angeles, California
Source: *BioIn 1; CurBio 46; EncAFC; Film 2; NotNAT, B; ObitOF 79; WhoHol B; WhScrn 74, 77, 83; WhThe*

Carr, Allan
[Allan Solomon]
American. Producer
Co-produced *Grease* on Broadway, 1977.
b. May 27, 1941 in Highland Park, Illinois
Source: *BioIn 12, 13; CelR 90; ConTFT 3; HalFC 88; IntMPA 86; WhoAm 76, 78, 80, 82, 84, 86, 88, 96, 97; WhoFI 96; WhoWest 80, 82, 84, 87*

Carr, Caleb
American. Author
Author of *The Alienist,* 1994.
b. Aug 2, 1955 in New York, New York
Source: *BioIn 20, 21; ConAu 147; ConLC 86*

Carr, Elizabeth Jordan
American. Test Tube Baby
First test tube baby born in US.
b. Dec 28, 1981 in Norfolk, Virginia

Carr, Emily
Canadian. Artist, Author
Painted, wrote about British Columbia Indians: *Heart of a Peacock,* 1953.
b. Dec 12, 1871 in Victoria, British Columbia, Canada
d. Mar 2, 1945 in Victoria, British Columbia, Canada
Source: *ArtclWW 2; ArtsAmW 2; BenetAL 91; BioIn 1, 2, 3, 5, 7, 8, 9, 10, 11, 12, 13, 14, 15, 16, 17, 18, 20, 21; BlmGWL; CamGLE; ContDcW 89; CreCan 1; DcLB 68; DcLEL 1940; DcNAA; DcWomA; FemiCLE; FemiWr; IntDcWB; InWom, SUP; LngCTC; MacDCB 78; McGDA; McGEWB; NorAmWA; OxCArt; OxCCan; OxCCanL; OxDcArt; PhDcTCA 77; REnAL; TwCLC 32; WomArt, A*

Carr, Gerald Paul
American. Astronaut
Commanded third *Skylab* manned mission, 1973-74.
b. Aug 22, 1932 in Denver, Colorado
Source: *AmMWSc 92, 95; BlueB 76; IntWW 74, 75, 76, 77, 78, 79, 80, 81, 82, 83, 89, 91, 93; NewYTBE 73; WhoAm 76, 78, 80, 82, 84, 86, 88, 90, 92, 94, 95, 96, 97; WhoScEn 94, 96; WhoSSW 73, 75, 76, 95, 97; WorDWW*

Carr, Harold Noflet
American. Businessman
Chairman, Republic Airlines, 1979-84.
b. Mar 14, 1921 in Kansas City, Kansas
Source: *AmEA 74; St&PR 75; WhoAm 74, 76, 78, 80, 82, 84, 86, 88, 90, 92, 94, 95, 96, 97; WhoFI 77, 79, 81, 83, 85, 87, 89, 92, 94, 96; WhoMW 78, 80, 82, 84, 86; WhoSSW 76, 78, 80, 82, 84, 86, 88, 91, 93, 95; WhoWor 97*

Carr, Henry
American. Track Athlete
Sprinter; won gold medal in 200 meters, in team relay, 1964 Olympics.
b. Nov 27, 1942 in Montgomery, Alabama
Source: *BiDAmSp OS; BlkOlyM; WhoTr&F 73*

Carr, Joe
[Joseph F Carr]
American. Football Executive
One of founders of NFL, 1919; president, NFL, 1921-39, succeeding Jim Thorpe; Hall of Fame, 1963.
b. Oct 22, 1880 in Columbus, Ohio
d. May 20, 1939
Source: *BiDAmSp FB; BioIn 6, 8; WhoFtbl 74*

Carr, Joe
"Fingers"
American. Musician
Ragtime, honky tonk pianist, popular in 1950s.
b. 1910 in Louisville, Kentucky
Source: *ASCAP 80; CmpEPM; RkOn 82; WhScrn 83*

Carr, John Dickson
American. Author
Detective, mystery writer; created character of Dr. Gideon Fell, corpulent sleuth.
b. Nov 30, 1906 in Uniontown, Pennsylvania
d. Feb 27, 1977 in Greenville, South Carolina
Source: *AmAu&B; Au&Wr 71; BenetAL 91; BioIn 14, 17, 20; ConAu 3NR, 33NR, 49, 69; ConLC 3; CorpD; CrtSuMy; DcAmB S10; DcLEL; EncMys; EncSF, 93; EvLB; FacFETw; IntAu&W 77; LngCTC; MajTwCW; NewC; NewYTBS 77; Novels; ObitOF 79; PenC ENG; REn; REnAL; ScF&FL 1, 2; ScFSB; TwCCr&M 80, 85, 91; WhAm 7; WhoAm 74, 76; WhoWor 74; WorAl; WorAlBi*

Carr, Martin
[Martin Douglas Conovitz]
American. Producer
TV documentaries include "Smithsonian World," 1981-85.
b. Jan 20, 1932 in Flushing, New York
d. 1987
Source: *ConTFT 2; IntMPA 75, 76, 77, 78, 79, 81, 82, 84, 86, 88, 92, 94, 96; NewYTET; VarWW 85*

Carr, Sabin
American. Track Athlete
Pole vaulter; won gold medal, 1928 Olympics; first to vault 14 feet, 1928.
b. Sep 4, 1904 in Dubuque, Iowa
d. Sep 1983 in Ventura, California
Source: *WhoTr&F 73*

Carr, Vikki
[Florencia Bisenta de Casillas]
American. Singer
Multilingual pop songstess; records include *It Must Be Him;* Grammy awar d winner.
b. Jul 19, 1941 in El Paso, Texas
Source: *BioIn 10; EncPR&S 74; InWom SUP; LegTOT; PenEncP; RkOn 78; WhoAm 86; WhoAmW 83; WorAl; WorAlBi*

Carr, William G(eorge)
American. Educator
Executive Secretary, National Education Association, 1952-67.
b. Jun 1, 1901
d. Mar 1, 1996 in Denver, Colorado
Source: *AmAu&B; BiDAmEd; BioIn 2, 3, 5, 7, 9, 12; BlueB 76; ConAu 53, 151; CurBio 96N; IntAu&W 77, 89; LEduc 74; WhE&EA; WhoAm 74, 76, 78, 80; WrDr 76, 80, 82, 84, 86, 88, 90, 92, 94, 96*

Carra, Carlo
Italian. Artist
Founded Italian metaphysical school, futurist movement, 1910; paintings include *Lot's Daughters.*
b. Feb 11, 1881 in Quargnento, Italy
d. Apr 13, 1966 in Milan, Italy
Source: *BioIn 4, 7, 17; DcArts; FacFETw; IntDcAA 90; McGDA; ObitOF 79; OxCArt; OxCTwCA; OxDcArt; PhDcTCA 77; WebBD 83*

Carracci, Annibale
Italian. Artist
Did first of great baroque ceilings, frescoes of Farness Palace, 1597-1604; a work, once bought for $22, brought $1.52 million, 1987.
b. Nov 3, 1560 in Bologna, Italy
d. Jul 15, 1609 in Rome, Italy
Source: *AtlBL; BioIn 4, 9, 14, 19; ClaDrA; DcArts; DcCathB; IntDcAA 90; LinLib S; McGDA; McGEWB; OxCArt; OxCEng 85, 95; OxDcArt; REn; WhDW; WorAl; WorAlBi*

Carracci, Lodovico
Italian. Artist
Founded, with cousins Agostino and Annibale, famed art academy, Accademia degli Incamminati, 1582.
b. Apr 21, 1555 in Bologna, Italy
d. Nov 13, 1619 in Bologna, Italy
Source: *AtlBL; BioIn 4, 6, 19; ClaDrA; DcCathB; LinLib S; McGDA*

Carrack, Paul
[Ace; Squeeze]
English. Singer, Musician
Original member of Ace, who joined Squeeze, 1981-82.
b. Apr 22, 1951 in Sheffield, England
Source: *BioIn 13; LegTOT; RkOn 85*

Carradine, David
[John Arthur Carradine]
American. Actor
Son of John Carradine; starred in TV shows "Shane," 1966; "Kung Fu," 1972-75; in films since 1965.
b. Dec 8, 1936 in Hollywood, California
Source: *BkPepl; ConTFT 4, 11; FilmgC; GangFlm; HalFC 84, 88; IntMPA 86, 88, 92, 94, 96; LegTOT; MiSFD 9; MotPP; NewYTBE 73; WhoAm 86, 90, 92, 94, 95, 96, 97; WhoEnt 92; WhoHol 92, A; WorAlBi*

Carradine, John
[Richmond Reed Carradine]
American. Actor
Father of David, Keith, Robert; starred in over 500 films.
b. Feb 5, 1906 in New York, New York
d. Nov 27, 1988 in Milan, Italy
Source: *AnObit 1988; BiE&WWA; BioIn 1, 11, 15, 16, 17, 21; CmMov; ConTFT 4, 7; EncAFC; FilmgC; GangFlm; HalFC 84, 88; IntDcF 1-3, 2-3; IntMPA 86; LegTOT; MotPP; MovMk; News 89-2; NewYTBS 88; OlFamFa; OxCFilm; PenEncH; Vers A; WhoAm 86; WhoHol A; WhoThe 72, 77, 81; WorAl; WorAlBi; WorEFlm*

Carradine, Keith Ian
American. Actor, Singer
Won Oscar for writing, singing "I'm Easy," 1976.
b. Aug 8, 1949 in San Mateo, California
Source: *BkPepl; HalFC 84; IntMPA 86; WhoAm 80, 82, 84, 86, 88, 90, 92, 94, 95, 96, 97; WhoEnt 92; WhoHol A*

Carradine, Robert Reed
American. Actor
Youngest son of John Carradine, half brother of David, who starred in *The Big Red One*, 1979.
b. Mar 24, 1954 in Los Angeles, California
Source: *ConTFT 3; FilmEn; HalFC 84; IntMPA 86; VarWW 85; WhoHol A*

Carranza, Venustiano
Mexican. Political Leader
Pres. of Mexico, 1917-20.
b. Dec 29, 1859 in Cuatroa Cienegas, Mexico
d. May 21, 1920 in Tlaxcalantongo, Mexico
Source: *BiDLAmC; BioIn 4, 8, 9, 11, 16; DcTwHis; EncLatA; EncRev; HarEnMi; LinLib S; McGEWB; REn; WorAl; WorAlBi*

Carre, Mathilde
"Mata Hari of WW II"
German. Spy
Double agent for Germans; imprisoned 1949-54.
b. 1910?
Source: *BioIn 5, 8, 10, 11; EncE 75; InWom SUP; WhWW-II*

Carrel, Alexis
American. Biologist, Surgeon
With Charles Lindbergh, invented perfusion pump called artificial heart, 1936; Nobelist, 1912.
b. Jun 28, 1873 in Sainte-Foy-les-Lyon, France
d. Nov 5, 1944 in Paris, France
Source: *AmDec 1930; ApCAB X; AsBiEn; BiESc; BioIn 1, 3, 4, 6, 7, 9, 10, 12, 15, 18, 20; CamDcSc; CathA 1930; ConAu 120; CurBio 40, 44; DcAmB S3; DcAmMeB 84; DcCathB; DcScB; EncO&P 1, 2, 3; EncPaPR 91; FacFETw; InSci; LarDcSc; LinLib L, S; McGEWB; NatCAB 15; NobelP; NotTwCS; OxCAmH; OxCMed 86; TwCA SUP; WhAm 2; WhNAA; WhoNob, 90, 95; WorAl; WorAlBi; WorInv*

Carrera, Barbara
American. Actor
Portrayed Fatima Blush in *Never Say Never Again*, 1983; starred in TV series "Dallas," 1985-91.
b. Dec 31, 1945? in Managua, Nicaragua
Source: *BioIn 11, 12; ConTFT 6; FilmEn; IntMPA 92; LegTOT; NewYTBS 77; WhoHol A*

Carrera, Jose Miguel
Chilean. Revolutionary
Overthrew Conservative junta with brothers, 1811; military dictator of Chile, 1811-13; executed.
b. Oct 15, 1785 in Santiago, Chile
d. Sep 4, 1821 in Mendoza, Argentina
Source: *DicTyr; Drake; McGEWB; NewCol 75; WebBD 83*

Carreras, Jose
[Jose Maria Carreras-Coll]
Spanish. Opera Singer
Lyric tenor; NY Met. debut, 1974; TV, film roles; Grammy for *Carreras, Domingo, Pavrotti*, 1990.
b. Dec 5, 1946 in Barcelona, Spain
Source: *Baker 84; BioIn 9, 11, 12, 15, 16, 17, 18, 19, 21; CelR 90; ConAu 141; ConMus 8; CurBio 79; DcHiB; FacFETw; IntDcOp; IntWWM 90; MetOEnc; NewAmDM; NewGrDO; News 95, 95-2; NewYTBS 78; OxDcOp; PenDiMP; RAdv 14; WhoAm 86; WhoAmM 83; WhoOp 76*

Carrere, Emmanuel
French. Author
Work has been compared to that of Kafka and Poe; wrote *The Mustache*, 1986.
b. 1957
Source: *ConLC 89; ScF&FL 92*

Carrere, Tia
[Althea Janairo]
American. Actor, Singer
Played singer Cassandra in movie *Wayne's World*, 1992.
b. 1967 in Honolulu, Hawaii
Source: *ConTFT 11; IntMPA 96; LegTOT; WhoAmW 97*

Carrey, Jim
[James Eugene Carrey]
Canadian. Actor
Cast member on TV show "In Living Color;" Films include *Dumb and Dumber, 1994; Ace Ventura*, 1994; and *Batman Forver*, 1995.
b. Jan 17, 1962 in Newmarket, Ontario, Canada
Source: *ConTFT 13; CurBio 96; IntMPA 96; LegTOT; News 95, 95-1; WhoAm 95, 96, 97*

Carrier, Roch
Canadian. Author
Wrote novels *La guerre, Yes Sir!*, 1970; *They Won't Demolish Me!*, 1973 (*Le deux-millieme etage*)
b. May 13, 1937 in Sainte-Justine-de-Dorchest Quebec, Canada
Source: *Benet 96; BioIn 15, 17, 21; ConAu 130; ConCaAu 1; ConLC 13, 78; DcLB 53; ModCmwL; OxCCanL; OxCCan SUP; OxCCanT; WhoCanL 85, 87, 92; WrDr 94, 96*

Carrier, Willis Haviland
American. Inventor
Developed first practical air-conditioning process, 1911.
b. Nov 26, 1876 in Angola, New York
d. Oct 7, 1950 in New York, New York
Source: *BiDAmBL 83; BioIn 2, 3, 6, 7, 9, 12, 16, 20; DcAmB S4; InSci; WhAm 3; WhDW; WhE&EA*

Carriera, Rosalba Giovanna
Italian. Artist
Miniature painter, specialist in pastel portraits.
b. Oct 7, 1675 in Venice, Italy
d. Apr 15, 1757 in Venice, Italy
Source: *BioIn 3, 5, 10, 11, 16; GoodHs; IntDcWB; McGDA; OxCArt; WomArt*

Carrier-Belleuse, Albert Ernest
French. Sculptor
Works include *Bacchante;* taught Rodin, 1864-70.
b. Jun 12, 1824 in Anizy-le-Chateau, France
d. Jun 3, 1887 in Sevres, France
Source: *BioIn 11*

Carriere, Eugene
French. Artist
Known for religious themes, portraits: *Verlaine; Alphonse Daudet and his Daughter.*
b. Jan 17, 1849 in Gournay, France
d. Mar 27, 1906 in Paris, France
Source: *BioIn 2, 4, 8, 9, 11; ClaDrA; Dis&D; McGDA; OxCArt; OxCFr; OxDcArt*

Carriere, Jean-Claude
French. Screenwriter
France's leading scriptwriter, 1960s-70s: *The Discreet Charm of the Bourgeoise*, 1972; *The Tin Drum*, 1978.
b. Aug 6, 1932 in Colombieres, France

Source: *FilmEn; HalFC 80; NewYTBS 83; OxCFilm*

Carrillo, Leo
American. Actor
Played Pancho in *Cisco Kid,* 1951.
b. Aug 6, 1880 in Los Angeles, California
d. Sep 10, 1961 in Santa Monica, California
Source: *BioIn 6, 8, 16, 21; CmCal; Film 2; FilmgC; HalFC 84, 88; HispAmA; LegTOT; MotPP; MovMk; NotNAT B; ObitOF 79; WhoHol B; WhScrn 77; WorAl; WorAlBi*

Carrington, Peter Alexander Rupert, Baron
English. Politician
NATO secretary-general, 1984-88; foreign secretary, 1979-82; awarded Presidential Medal of Freedom, 1988.
b. Jun 6, 1919 in London, England
Source: *IntWW 74, 93; NewYTBS 79; Who 85; WhoWor 74, 80, 82, 84, 87, 89, 91, 93, 95, 96, 97*

Carritt, David Graham
[Hugh David Graham Carritt]
English. Art Historian
Discovered various lost Old Master paintings including Caravaggio's *The Musicians.*
b. Apr 15, 1927, England
d. Aug 3, 1982 in London, England
Source: *BioIn 10; NewYTBS 82; Who 82*

Carroll, Anna Ella
American. Author, Pamphleteer
Political writings include *The Great American Battle,* 1856.
b. Aug 29, 1815 in Kingston Hall, Maryland
d. Feb 19, 1893 in Washington, District of Columbia
Source: *Alli SUP; AmWom; ApCAB SUP; BiD&SB; BiDSA; BioIn 1, 2, 3, 4, 6, 15, 16, 17, 18, 20; DcAmAu; DcNAA; InWom, SUP; LibW; NatCAB 5; NotAW; PolPar; TwCBDA; WhAm HS; WhCiWar*

Carroll, Charles
American. Patriot, Lawyer, Continental Congressman
Called wealthiest man in the colonies; only Catholic to sign Declaration of Independence, 1776; outlived all other signers.
b. Sep 19, 1737 in Annapolis, Maryland
d. Nov 14, 1832 in Baltimore, Maryland
Source: *AmBi; AmWrBE; ApCAB; BiAUS; BiDAmBL 83; BiDrAC; BiDrUSC 89; BiDSA; BioIn 1, 3, 4, 5, 6, 7, 8, 9, 10, 12, 15, 16, 19; BlkwEAR; DcAmB; DcCathB; Drake; EncAR; EncCRAm; EncSoH; HarEnUS; LinLib S; NatCAB 7; OxCAmH; TwCBDA; WebAB 74, 79; WhAm HS; WhAmP; WorAl; WorAlBi*

Carroll, Diahann
[Mrs. Vic Damone; Carol Diahann Johnson]
American. Actor, Singer
Won Tony, 1962, for performance in Broadway musical *No Strings,* which Richard Rodgers wrote for her; starred in TV comedy, "Julia," 1968-71; became first black performer to star on TV in non-stereotypical role; "Dynasty," 1984-85.
b. Jul 17, 1935 in New York, New York
Source: *AfrAmAl 6; BiDAfM; BiDAmM; BiE&WWA; BioIn 5, 6, 8, 9, 10, 11, 12, 13; BioNews 74; BkPepl; BlksAmF; BlkWAm; CelR, 90; ConBlB 9; ConTFT 3; CurBio 62; DcTwCCu 5; DrBlPA, 90; EncMT; FilmgC; HalFC 84, 88; InB&W 80, 85; IntMPA 88, 92, 94, 96; InWom; LegTOT; MotPP; NotBlAW 1; NotNAT; WhoAfA 96; WhoAm 74, 76, 78, 80, 82, 84, 86, 88, 92; WhoAmW 83, 87, 89, 91; WhoBlA 80, 85, 88, 90, 92, 94; WhoEnt 92; WhoHol 92, A; WhoWor 74; WomWMM; WorAl; WorAlBi*

Carroll, Earl
American. Producer
Lyricist of over 400 songs; produced Earl Carroll Vanities, 1923-36.
b. Sep 16, 1893 in Pittsburgh, Pennsylvania
d. Jun 17, 1948 in Mount Carmel, Pennsylvania
Source: *AmAu&B; ASCAP 66; BiDD; BioIn 1, 5, 11; CmpEPM; DcAmB S4; EncMT; NotNAT B; OxCAmT 84; OxCPMus; OxCThe 67; PlP&P; WhAm 2; WhScrn 77, 83; WhThe*

Carroll, Gladys Hasty
American. Author
Regional novel *As the Earth Turns,* 1933, translated into 60 languages.
b. Jun 26, 1904 in Rochester, New Hampshire
Source: *AmAu&B; AmNov; AmWomWr; ArtclWW 2; Au&Wr 71; BenetAL 91; BlueB 76; ConAu 1R, 5NR; DcLB 9; ForWC 70; IntAu&W 89; InWom, SUP; LinLib L; OxCAmL 65, 83, 95; REnAL; ScF&FL 1, 2; TwCA, SUP; WhE&EA; WhNAA; WhoAm 74, 76, 78, 80, 82, 84, 86, 88, 90, 92, 94, 95, 96, 97; WhoAmW 58, 61, 64, 66, 68, 70, 72, 74; WhoE 74; WhoWor 74; WrDr 76, 80, 82, 84, 86, 88, 90, 92, 94, 96*

Carroll, James
American. Author
Won a National Book Award for *An American Requiem,* 1996.
b. Jan 22, 1943 in Chicago, Illinois
Source: *BiDConC; BioIn 11, 12; ConLC 38; WhoAm 82, 84, 86, 88, 90, 92, 94, 95, 96, 97; WrDr 80, 82, 84, 86, 88, 90, 92, 94, 96*

Carroll, Jim
[James Dennis Carroll]
American. Poet, Singer
Rock composer who depicts NYC brutality; wrote Pulitzer nominee book of verse *Living at the Movies,* 1973.
b. Aug 1, 1951 in New York, New York
Source: *Au&Arts 17; BiDConC; BioIn 12; ConAu 42NR, 45; ConLC 35; CurBio 95; DrAP 75; WhoAm 97*

Carroll, Joe Barry
[Joseph Barry Carrol]
American. Basketball Player
Center, Golden State, 1980-88; member NBA all-rookie team, 1981; New Jersey Denvers 1989-90; Phoenix 1990-91.
b. Jul 24, 1958 in Denver, Colorado
Source: *BasBi; BioIn 12; NewYTBS 80; OfNBA 87; WhoAfA 96; WhoBlA 85, 88, 90, 92, 94*

Carroll, John
American. Religious Leader
First Roman Catholic bishop in US; founded Georgetown, 1789.
b. Jan 8, 1735 in Upper Marlboro, Maryland
d. Dec 3, 1815 in Baltimore, Maryland
Source: *AmAu&B; AmBi; AmWrBE; ApCAB; BenetAL 91; BiDSA; BioIn 2, 3, 4, 5, 10, 11, 14, 15, 17, 19; DcAmB; DcAmReB 1, 2; DcCathB; DcLB 37; DcNAA; Drake; EncARH; EncCRAm; EncSoH; HarEnUS; LuthC 75; McGEWB; NatCAB 1; OxCAmH; TwCBDA; WebAB 74, 79; WhAm HS; WhAmRev; WorAl; WorAlBi*

Carroll, Leo G
English. Actor
Played Cosmo Topper in TV series "Topper," 1953-56; Mr. Waverly in "Man from Uncle," 1964-68.
b. Oct 18, 1892 in Weedon, England
d. Oct 16, 1972 in Hollywood, California
Source: *BiE&WWA; CmMov; FilmgC; MotPP; MovMk; NewYTBE 72; NotNAT B; ObitOF 79; Vers A; WhAm 5; WhoHol B; WhScrn 77; WhThe*

Carroll, Lewis
[Charles Lutwidge Dodgson]
English. Author
Wrote *Alice's Adventures in Wonderland,* 1865; *Through the Looking Glass,* 1872.
b. Jan 27, 1832 in Cheshire, England
d. Jan 14, 1898 in Guildford, England
Source: *Alli SUP; AnCL; AtlBL; AuBYP 2, 3; BbD; Benet 87, 96; BiD&SB; BioIn 1, 2, 3, 4, 5, 6, 7, 8, 9, 10, 11, 12, 13, 14, 15, 16, 17, 18, 19, 21; BlmGEL; BritAu 19; BritWr 5; CamGEL; CamGLE; CarSB; CasWL; Chambr 3; ChhPo, S1, S2, S3; ChlBkCr; ChlLR 2, 18; ChrP; CnDBLB 4; CnE&AP; CrtT 3, 4; CyWA 58; DcArts; DcBrBI; DcEnA, A; DcEnL; DcEuL; DcLB 18, 163; DcLEL; DcNaB S1; DcScB; Dis&D; EncSF, 93; EvLB; FamAYP; FilmgC; GrWrEL N; HalFC 84, 88; ICPEnP A;*

InSci; JBA 34; LegTOT; LinLib L, S; LngCEL; MacBEP; MagSWL; MajAI; McGEWB; MouLC 4; NewC; NewCBEL; NewEScF; NinCLC 2, 53; Novels; OxCChiL; OxCEng 67, 85, 95; OxCPhil; PenC ENG; RAdv 1, 14, 13-1; RComWL; REn; RfGEnL 91; ScF&FL 1; ScFSB; SJGFanW; StaCVF; Str&VC; SupFW; TwCChW 78A, 83A, 89A, 95A; VicBrit; WebE&AL; WhDW; WhoChL; WorAl; WorAlBi; WorLitC; WorScD; WrChl; YABC 2

Carroll, Madeleine

[Marie-Madeline Bernadette O'Carroll]
English. Actor
Appeared in over 36 films, including Hitchcock thrillers *The 39 Steps*, 1935; *Secret Agent*, 1936.
b. Feb 26, 1909 in West Bronwich, England
d. Oct 2, 1987 in Marbella, Spain
Source: *BiDFilm; BiE&WWA; BioIn 1, 2, 8, 9; CurBio 49, 87; Film 2; FilmgC; IntMPA 82; MotPP; MovMk; NewYTBS 87; OxCFilm; ThFT; Who 82; WhoHol A; WhThe; WorAl; WorEFlm*

Carroll, Nancy

[Ann Veronica Lattiff]
American. Actor
Oscar nominee for *The Devil's Holiday*, 1930.
b. Nov 19, 1906 in New York, New York
d. Aug 6, 1965 in New York, New York
Source: *CmpEPM; Film 2; FilmEn; FilmgC; InWom; MotPP; MovMk; NotNAT B; ObitOF 79; ThFT; TwYS; WhoHol B; WhScrn 74, 77, 83; WhThe; WomWMM; WorAl*

Carroll, Pat(ricia Ann Angela Bridgit)

American. Actor, Comedian
Won Emmy for "Caesar's Hour," 1956-57; Tony for *Catch a Star*, 1955.
b. May 5, 1927 in Shreveport, Louisiana
Source: *BiE&WWA; BioIn 12; ConTFT 3; CurBio 80; IntMPA 75, 76, 77, 78, 79, 81, 82, 84, 86, 88, 92, 94, 96; InWom SUP; NotNAT, B; WhoAm 80, 82, 84, 86, 88, 90, 94, 95, 96, 97; WhoAmW 66, 68, 70, 81, 83, 95; WhoHol 92; WhoWest 94, 96; WhThe*

Carroll, Vinnette

[Justine Carrol]
American. Actor, Producer
Collaborated on musical revues: *Don't Bother Me, I Can't Cope*, 1970; *Your Arms Too Short to Box with God*, 1975.
b. Mar 11, 1922 in New York, New York
Source: *AmWomD; BiE&WWA; BioIn 13, 16, 20; BlkAmW 1; BlkWAm; ConAu 114; ConBlAP 88; ConTFT 5; CurBio 83; DcTwCCu 5; DrBlPA, 90; ForWC 70; InB&W 80, 85; InWom SUP; NegAl 83; NotNAT; NotWoAT; TheaDir; WhoAm 86; WhoAmW 77; WhoBlA 85; WhoE 77; WhoHol 92; WhoThe 72, 77, 81*

Carruth, Hayden

American. Poet, Writer
Prolific, prizewinning poet; works include *Nothing for Tigers*, 1965; *For You*, 1971; *The Sleeping Beauty*, 1982.
b. Aug 3, 1921 in Waterbury, Connecticut
Source: *AmAu&B; Benet 96; BenetAL 91; BioIn 12, 13, 16, 17, 18, 19, 20; ConAu 4NR, 9NR, 9R, 38NR; ConLC 4, 7, 10, 18, 84; ConPo 70, 75, 80, 85, 91, 96; CurBio 92; DcLB 5, 165; DcLEL 1940; DrAP 75; DrAPF 91; IntAu&W 77, 82; IntWWP 77; LegTOT; LinLib L; MajTwCW; OxCAmL 83, 95; OxCTwCP; PoeCrit 10; RAdv 1, 13-1; REnAL; SmATA 47; WhoAm 74, 76, 78, 80, 82, 84, 86, 88, 90, 92, 94, 95, 96, 97; WhoE 74; WhoUSWr 88; WhoWor 74, 76; WhoWrEP 89, 92, 95; WorAu 1950; WrDr 76, 80, 82, 84, 86, 88, 90, 92, 94, 96*

Carruthers, Garrey E

American. Politician
Republican governor of New Mexico, 1987-91, succeeded by Bruce King.
b. Aug 29, 1939 in Alamosa, Colorado
Source: *AlmAP 88; WhoAm 82, 84; WhoAmP 85, 87, 89, 91, 93, 95; WhoWest 87*

Carruthers, George Robert, Dr.

American. Physicist
Developed lunar surface ultraviolet camera used by Apollo 16, 1972; received NASA achievement award.
b. Oct 1, 1939 in Cincinnati, Ohio
Source: *AmMWSc 73P; BioIn 9, 11; NegAl 83; WhoAfA 96; WhoBlA 85, 88, 90, 92, 94*

Carruthers, John(ny)

Australian. Boxer
Won world bantam title, 1952; last fight, 1962.
b. Jul 5, 1929 in Paddington, Australia
Source: *WhoBox 74*

Carruthers, Kitty

[Caitlin Carruthers]
American. Skater
With brother Peter, won silver medal in pairs figure skating, 1984 Olympics; first US pairs skaters to win Olympic medal since, 1952.
b. 1962
Source: *BioIn 12, 13; LegTOT; NewYTBS 80, 81*

Carruthers, Peter

American. Skater
With sister Kitty, won silver medal in pairs figure skating, 1984 Olympics; first US pairs skaters to win Olympic medal since 1952.
b. 1960
Source: *BioIn 12, 13; NewYTBS 80, 81*

Cars, The

[Elliot Easton; Greg Hawkes; Ric Ocasek; Ben Orr; David Robinson]
American. Music Group
Pop music quintet, formed, 1976; platinum albums *The Cars*, 1978; *Panarama*, 1980.
Source: *Alli; BioIn 12, 14, 15, 16, 17, 18, 19, 20, 21; ConMuA 80A, 80B; EncPR&S 89; EncRk 88; EncRkSt; Law&B 80, 84; NewAmDM; NewGrDA 86; NewYTBS 85, 87; PenEncP; RkOn 85, 85A; RolSEnR 83; Who 85S, 88N; WhoAm 92; WhoHol A; WhoRock 81; WhoRocM 82; WhoScEu 91-1; WhsNW 85*

Carsey, Marcy

American. Producer
Senior vp, all prime time series, ABC, 1978-81; executive producer, "The Cosby Show," 1984-92; "A Different World," 1987-1993; "Roseanne," 1988—; "Cybill," 1995—.
b. Nov 21, 1944 in South Weymouth, Massachusetts
Source: *ConTFT 13; IntMPA 96; VarWW 85*

Carson, Benjamin S.

[Benjamin Solomon Carson, Sr.]
American. Surgeon
Director, pediatric neurosurgery at Johns Hopkins; successfully separated Siamese twins joined at the back of their heads, 1987.
b. Sep 18, 1951 in Detroit, Michigan
Source: *BioIn 16; BlksScM; ConBlB 1; DiAASTC; NotTwCS; WhoAfA 96; WhoAm 90; WhoBlA 90, 92, 94*

Carson, Edward Henry

English. Judge, Politician
Defended Marquis of Queensberry in Oscar Wilde's libel suit, 1895.
b. Feb 9, 1854 in Dublin, Ireland
d. Oct 22, 1935 in Minster, England
Source: *BioIn 2, 3, 10, 13, 17; DcIrB 78, 88; DcNaB 1931; DcTwHis; FacFETw; GrBr; HisDBrE; OxCLaw*

Carson, Jack

American. Actor
Teamed with Dennis Morgan in series of 1940s musicals.
b. Oct 27, 1910 in Carman, Manitoba, Canada
d. Jan 2, 1963 in Encino, California
Source: *BioIn 2, 6, 7, 10, 11, 19; CmpEPM; DcAmB S7; EncAFC; FilmgC; HalFC 84, 88; HolP 40; LegTOT; MotPP; MovMk; NotNAT B; OxCFilm; QDrFCA 92; RadStar; SaTiSS; WhoCom; WhoHol B; WhScrn 74, 77, 83; WorAl; WorAlBi*

Carson, Jimmy

[James Carson]
American. Hockey Player
Center, LA, 1986-88, chosen second overall in NHL entry draft; traded to Edmonton for Wayne Gretzky, Aug 1988.

b. Jul 20, 1968 in Southfield, Michigan
Source: *BiDAmSp Sup; HocReg 86, 87; WhoSpor*

Carson, Johnny
American. Comedian, TV Personality
Host of "The Tonight Show," 1962-92.
b. Oct 23, 1925 in Corning, Iowa
Source: *AmDec 1960; BiDFilm 94; BioIn 4, 6, 7, 8, 9, 10, 11, 12, 13, 14, 15, 16, 17, 18, 19, 20; BkPepl; BlueB 76; CelR, 90; ConTFT 3; CurBio 82; EncAB-H 1996; FacFETw; HalFC 88; IntMPA 75, 76, 77, 78, 79, 81, 82, 84, 86, 88, 92, 94, 96; IntWW 82, 83, 89, 91, 93; LegTOT; NewYTET; WhoAm 74, 76, 78, 80, 82, 84, 86, 88, 90, 92, 94, 95, 96, 97; WhoCom; WhoE 74; WhoEnt 92; WhoHol 92; WhoWor 74; WorAl; WorAlBi*

Carson, Kit
[Christopher Carson]
American. Pioneer
Brigadier general during Civil War; commanded Ft. Garland, Colorado, 1866-67.
b. Dec 24, 1809 in Madison County, Kentucky
d. May 23, 1868 in Fort Lyon, Colorado
Source: *AmBi; ApCAB; Benet 87, 96; BenetAL 91; BioIn 1, 2, 3, 4, 5, 6, 7, 8, 9, 10, 12, 14, 15, 16, 17, 18, 20, 21; CivWDc; CmCal; DcAmB; DcCathB; Drake; EncAAH; EncNAB; FilmgC; HalFC 84, 88; HarEnUS; LegTOT; LinLib S; LngCTC; McGEWB; MnBBF; MorMA; NatCAB 3; OxCAmH; OxCAmL 65, 83, 95; OxCFilm; REn; REnAL; REnAW; TwCBDA; WebAB 74, 79; WebAMB; WhAm HS; WhDW; WorAl; WorAlBi*

Carson, Mindy
American. Actor, Singer
Popular radio vocalist, late 1940s; hosted own TV show, 1950s; sang "Wake the Town and Tell the People," 1954.
b. Jul 16, 1926 in New York, New York
Source: *AmPS B; BiE&WWA; CmpEPM; RkOn 74; WhoAmW 70*

Carson, Rachel (Louise)
American. Biologist, Author
Writings combine scientific accuracy with lyrical prose: *The Sea Around Us*, 1951, *Silent Spring*, 1962.
b. May 27, 1907 in Springdale, Pennsylvania
d. Apr 14, 1964 in Silver Spring, Maryland
Source: *AmAu&B; AmDec 1960; AmRef; AmSocL; AmWomSc; AmWomWr; AnCL; BioAmW; BioIn 2, 3, 4, 5, 6, 7, 8, 9, 10, 11, 12, 13, 14, 15, 16, 17, 18, 19, 20, 21; CamDcSc; ConAu 35NR, 77; ConHero 1; ConLC 71; ContDcW 89; CurBio 51, 64; DcAmB S7; DcScB S2; EncAAH; EncAB-H 1974, 1996; EncEnv; EncWHA; EnvEnc; EvLB; FacFETw; FemiCLE; FemiWr; GoodHs; GrLiveH; HeroCon; HerW, 84; InSci; IntDcWB; InWom, SUP; LegTOT; LibW; LinLib L, S; LngCTC; MajTwCW; McGEWB; NatCAB 51; NatLAC; NewYTBS 82; NotAW, MOD; NotTwCS; NotWoLS; OxCAmL 65, 83, 95; OxCEng 85, 95; OxCWoWr 95; RadHan; RAdv 14; RComAH; REn; SmATA 23; TwCA SUP; TwCWr; WebAB 74, 79; WhAm 4; WomChHR; WomFie; WomFir; WomPubS 1925; WomStre; WorScD*

Carson, Robert
American. Author
Won Oscar for screenplay for *A Star Is Born*, 1937.
b. Oct 6, 1909 in Clayton, Washington
d. Jan 19, 1983 in Los Angeles, California
Source: *AmAu&B; AnObit 1983; Au&Wr 71; BioIn 3, 13; ConAu 21R, 108; WhAm 8; WhoAm 74, 76, 78, 80, 82*

Carstens, Karl Walter
German. Political Leader
President, Federal Republic of Germany, 1979-84.
b. Dec 14, 1914 in Bremen, Germany
d. May 30, 1992 in Meckenheim, Germany
Source: *CurBio 80, 92N; IntYB 82; WhAm 10; Who 85; WhoEIO 82; WhoWor 74, 76, 78, 80, 82, 84*

Carte, Richard d'Oyly
English. Opera Singer
Responsible for bringing composer Arthur Sullivan, librettist William Gilbert together, 1871.
b. May 3, 1844 in London, England
d. Apr 3, 1901 in London, England
Source: *Baker 78, 84, 92; BioIn 3, 9, 14, 16, 17; DcNaB S2; LngCTC; NewAmDM; NewCol 75; NewGrDO; NotNAT B; OxCPMus; OxCThe 67; OxDcOp; VicBrit*

Carter, Amy Lynn
[Mrs. Jim Wentzel]
American.
Only daughter of Jimmy, Rosalynn Carter; involved in various forms of political activism in college.
b. Oct 19, 1967 in Plains, Georgia
Source: *BioIn 12, 13; ConNews 87-4; GoodHs; NewYTBS 76*

Carter, Angela (Olive)
English. Author
Wrote *The Bloody Chamber, and Other Stories*, 1979.
b. May 7, 1940 in Eastbourne, England
d. Feb 16, 1992 in London, England
Source: *AnObit 1992; ArtclWW 2; BioIn 13, 14, 16, 17, 18, 19, 20; BlmGEL; BlmGWL; CamGLE; ConAu 12NR, 36NR, 53, 136; ConIsC 1; ConLC 5, 41, 76; ConNov 82, 86, 91; ContDcW 89; DcArts; DcLB 14; DcLEL 1940; EncBrWW; EncSF; FacFETw; FemiCLE; FemiWr; GrWomW; IntAu&W 77, 89, 91, 93; IntWW 89, 91; InWom SUP; LegTOT; MajTwCW; ModWoWr; NewYTBS 92; Novels; RAdv 14, 13-1; RfGShF; RGTwCWr; ScF&FL 1, 2, 92; ScFSB; ShSCr 13; SJGFanW; SmATA 66, 70; TwCRHW 90; TwCSFW 86, 91; Who 88, 90, 92; WhoHr&F; WorAu 1980; WrDr 84, 86, 88, 90, 92*

Carter, Anthony Calvin
American. Football Player
Wide receiver in USFL, 1983-85, with NFL Minnesota, 1985-93; Detroit, 1994—.
b. Sep 17, 1960 in Riviera Beach, Florida
Source: *FootReg 86, 87; WhoBlA 85, 88, 90*

Carter, Benny
[Bennett Lester Carter]
American. Jazz Musician
Helped shape jazz music; known for alto sax playing; wrote "Melancholy Lullaby," 1939; Grammy for arrangement of "Busted," 1963 by Ray Charles.
b. Aug 8, 1907 in New York, New York
Source: *AfrAmAl 6; AllMusG; ASCAP 66; Baker 84, 92; BiDAfM; BiDAmM; BiDJaz; BioIn 9, 10, 11, 12, 13; BlkCond; CmpEPM; ConMus 3; CurBio 87; DcTwCCu 5; DrBlPA, 90; EncJzS; IlEncJ; InB&W 80, 85; LegTOT; NegAl 89; NewAmDM; NewGrDA 86; NewGrDJ 88, 94; OxCPMus; PenEncP; RAdv 14; WhoAm 78, 80, 88, 92, 94, 95, 96, 97; WhoEnt 92; WhoHol 92; WhoJazz 72; WorAl; WorAlBi*

Carter, Betty
[Lillie Mae Jones]
American. Singer
Jazz vocalist little known until appearence in show *Don't Call Me Man*, 1975.
b. May 16, 1930 in Flint, Michigan
Source: *AllMusG; Baker 84, 92; BiDAfM; BiDAmM; BiDJaz; BioIn 11, 12; BlkWAm; ConMus 6; CurBio 82; DrBlPA, 90; EncJzS; InB&W 80, 85; LegTOT; NewAmDM; NewGrDA 86; NewGrDJ 88, 94; PenEncP; WhoAfA 96; WhoAm 84; WhoBlA 85, 94*

Carter, Billy
American.
Brother of Jimmy Carter.
b. Mar 29, 1937 in Plains, Georgia
d. Sep 25, 1988 in Plains, Georgia
Source: *BioIn 11, 12; BkPepl; LegTOT; News 89-1; NewYTBS 88*

Carter, Boake
American. Radio Performer
Syndicated columnist, radio broadcaster, 1930s; noted for distinctive voice, tirades against New Deal, unionism.
b. Sep 28, 1898 in Baku, Russia
d. Nov 16, 1947 in Hollywood, California
Source: *BiDAmJo; BiDAmNC; BioIn 1, 2, 11, 16; CurBio 42, 47; DcAmB S3; DcNAA; EncAJ; LegTOT; WhAm 2; WhScrn 77*

Carter, Carlene
[Mrs. Nick Lowe]
American. Singer, Songwriter
Daughter of June Carter; stepdaughter of Johnny Cash; country hit ''I Fell in Love,'' 1990.
b. Sep 26, 1955 in Madisonville, Tennessee
Source: *BgBkCoM; BioIn 11, 12, 17, 19; ConMus 8; LegTOT; NewWmR; PenEncP; WhoRock 81*

Carter, Caroline Louise Dudley
American. Actor
Starred in Belasco plays: *DuBarry,* 1901.
b. Jun 10, 1862 in Lexington, Kentucky
d. Nov 13, 1937 in Los Angeles, California
Source: *DcAmB S2; InWom SUP; LibW; NotAW*

Carter, Chip
[James Earl Carter, III]
American.
Second son of Jimmy and Rosalynn Carter.
b. Apr 12, 1950 in Honolulu, Hawaii
Source: *BioIn 11, 12, 14, 21; PseudN 82; WhoAmP 77, 79, 81*

Carter, Dixie
American. Actor
Played Julia Sugarbaker on TV series ''Designing Women,'' 1987-93.
b. May 25, 1939 in McLemoresville, Tennessee
Source: *BioIn 13; ConTFT 5; IntMPA 92, 94, 96; LegTOT; VarWW 85; WhoHol 92; WorAlBi*

Carter, Don(ald James)
''Mr. Bowling''
American. Bowler
Dominated pro bowling, 1950s-60s; first president of PBA; Hall of Fame.
b. Jul 29, 1926 in Saint Louis, Missouri
Source: *AmMWSc 73P, 79, 82; BiDAmSp BK; BioIn 4, 6, 10; CurBio 63*

Carter, Dorothy Sharp
American. Children's Author
Wrote *Enchanted Orchard and Other Folktales of Central America,* 1973.
b. Mar 22, 1921 in Chicago, Illinois
Source: *BiDrLUS 70; ConAu 49; IntAu&W 77; SmATA 8; WhoAmW 77, 79*

Carter, Elliott Cook, Jr.
American. Composer
Won Pulitzer in music, 1960, 1973; works include ''Concerto for Orchestra,'' 1969.
b. Dec 11, 1908 in New York, New York
Source: *AmComp; Baker 78, 84; BiDAmM; ConAmC 82; ConAu 89; CurBio 60; DcCM; IntWW 75, 76, 77, 78, 79, 80, 81, 82, 83, 89, 91, 93; IntWWM 77, 85; McGEWB; Who 85; WhoAm 74, 76, 78, 80, 82, 84, 86, 88, 90, 92, 94, 95, 96, 97; WhoAmM 83; WhoEnt 92; WhoWor 74*

Carter, Ernestine Marie
American. Author, Journalist
With London *Times,* 1955-72; books include *Flash in the Pan,* 1953.
d. Aug 1, 1983
Source: *Au&Wr 71; BlueB 76; ConAu 110; Who 74, 82, 83; WrDr 76, 80, 82*

Carter, Gary Edmund
American. Baseball Player
Catcher, 1974-92, mostly with Montreal; 10-time All-Star.
b. Apr 8, 1954 in Culver City, California
Source: *BaseEn 88; BaseReg 87, 88; BiDAmSp BB; BioIn 11, 12; ConNews 87-1; WhoAm 86, 88; WhoE 86, 89*

Carter, Hodding
[William Hodding Carter, III]
American. Broadcast Journalist
Anchorman, Inside Story, PBS, 1981-84; State Dept. spokesman, 1977-80; presiden t, MainStreet TV productions, 1985-95.
b. Apr 7, 1935 in New Orleans, Louisiana
Source: *BiDAmNC; BioIn 11, 12; CelR 90; CurBio 81; EncTwCJ; JrnUS; WhoAm 78, 80, 82, 84, 86, 88, 90, 92, 94, 95, 96, 97; WhoAmP 77, 79, 81, 83, 85, 87, 89, 91, 93, 95; WhoEnt 92; WhoSSW 75, 76*

Carter, Howard
English. Archaeologist
Discovered tomb of Tutankhamen, 1922; author of numerous works on Egyptology.
b. May 9, 1874 in Brompton, England
d. Mar 2, 1939 in London, England
Source: *BioIn 2, 4, 6, 8, 9, 11, 12, 14, 17, 19, 21; DcBrAr 1; DcNaB 1931; GrBr; InSci; LngCTC; WhDW*

Carter, Hurricane
[Rubin Carter]
American. Boxer
Former middleweight contender, jailed for shooting three people, 1967; conviction overturned, 1985.
b. 1937
Source: *BioIn 6, 7, 10, 11, 12; ConAu 113; InB&W 80, 85; NewYTBE 72; NewYTBS 74*

Carter, Jack
[Jack Chakrin]
American. Comedian
Performer in major nightclubs; films include *Viva Las Vegas,* 1964.
b. Jun 24, 1923 in New York, New York
Source: *BiDD; BioIn 16; ConTFT 11; EncAFC; HalFC 84; IntDcB; IntMPA 75, 76, 77, 78, 79, 81, 82, 84, 86, 88, 92, 94, 96; LegTOT; WhoCom; WhoHol 92, A; WorAl; WorAlBi*

Carter, Jack
[John William Carter]
American.
First child of Jimmy and Rosalynn Carter.
b. Jul 3, 1947 in Portsmouth, Virginia
Source: *BioIn 14, 21; WhoAmP 75*

Carter, James
American. Musician
Saxophonist; released albums *Jurassic CLassics,* 1996; *Conversin' with the Elders,* 1996.
b. Jan 3, 1969 in Detroit, Michigan

Carter, Jeff
[Donnel Jeffrey Carter]
American.
Third son of Jimmy and Rosalynn Carter.
b. Aug 18, 1952 in New London, Connecticut
Source: *BioIn 12, 14, 21; NewYTBS 81*

Carter, Jimmy
[James W Carter]
American. Boxer
Held world lightweight title three times, 1950s.
b. Dec 15, 1923 in Aiken, South Carolina
Source: *InB&W 80; WhoBox 74*

Carter, Jimmy
[James Earl Carter, Jr.]
American. US President
Dem. 39th president, 1977-81; first elected from deep South; Iran hostage crisis contributed to defeat, 1980.
b. Oct 1, 1924 in Plains, Georgia
Source: *AlmAP 82; AmDec 1970; AmJust; AmOrTwC; AmPolLe; Benet 87, 96; BenetAL 91; BiDrGov 1789; BiDrUSE 89; BioIn 9, 10, 11, 12, 13, 14, 15, 16, 17, 18, 19, 20, 21; BlueB 76; CelR 90; CngDr 77, 78, 79; ColdWar 1; ConAu 32NR, 69; ConHero 2; CurBio 71, 77; DcAmC; DcTwHis; DrRegL 75; EncAB-H 1996; EncCW; EncSoH; EncWB; EnvEnDr; FacFETw; FacPr 89, 93; HealPre; HeroCon; HisEAAC; IntWW 74, 75, 76, 77, 78, 79, 80, 81, 82, 83, 89, 91, 93; IntYB 78, 79, 80, 81, 82; LegTOT; LinLib L, S; MajTwCW; News 95, 95-1; NewYTBS 76; OxCAmL 83; PolPar; PolProf NF; PresAR; RComAH; SmATA 79; WebAB 79; Who 82, 83, 85, 88, 90, 92, 94; WhoAm 74, 76, 78, 80, 82, 84, 86, 88, 90, 92, 94, 95, 96, 97; WhoAmP 73, 75, 85, 87, 89, 91, 93, 95; WhoE 77, 79, 81; WhoEng 80, 88; WhoGov 75, 77; WhoSSW 73, 75, 76, 78, 80, 82, 84, 86, 88, 91, 93, 95, 97; WhoWor 78, 80, 82, 84, 87, 89, 91, 93, 95, 96, 97; WorAl; WorAlBi; WrDr 94, 96*

Carter, Joe
[Joseph Chris Carter]
American. Baseball Player
Outfielder, infielder, Chicago Cubs, 1983-84; Cleveland, 1984-89; San

Diego, 1989-90; Toronto, 1990—; led AL in RBIs, 1986.
b. Mar 7, 1960 in Oklahoma City, Oklahoma
Source: *Ballpl 90; BaseEn 88; BaseReg 87, 88; News 94, 94-2; WhoAm 88, 90, 92, 94, 95, 96, 97; WhoE 95; WhoSpor; WhoWor 95, 96*

Carter, John Garnet
American. Businessman
Invented miniature golf, 1928.
b. Feb 9, 1883 in Sweetwater, Tennessee
d. Jul 21, 1954 in Lookout Mountain, Tennessee
Source: *BioIn 3, 9; NatCAB 52*

Carter, June
[The Carter Family]
American. Singer
Country singer; songs include "He Don't Love Me Anymore"; married Johnny Cash, 1968.
b. Jun 23, 1929 in Maces Spring, Virginia
Source: *BiDAmM; EncFCWM 69; InWom SUP; LegTOT; WhoAm 82; WhoHol 92, A; WorAl*

Carter, Katherine Jones
American. Children's Author
Books include *Hoppy Long Legs,* 1963.
b. Feb 25, 1905 in Greenbackville, Virginia
Source: *ConAu 5R; SmATA 2*

Carter, Leslie, Mrs.
[Caroline Louise Dudley]
American. Actor
Widely acclaimed "emotional" actress; first success in *The Heart of Maryland,* 1895.
b. Jun 10, 1862 in Lexington, Kentucky
d. Nov 12, 1937 in Los Angeles, California
Source: *AmBi; BioIn 3, 4, 13, 16; CamGWoT; DcAmB S2; FamA&A; Film 1; FilmgC; HalFC 84, 88; NotAW; NotNAT B; NotWoAT; OxCAmT 84; OxCThe 67, 83; PlP&P; TwYS; WhAm 1; WhoHol B; WhoStg 1906, 1908; WhScrn 74, 77, 83; WhThe; WorAl*

Carter, Lillian
[Bessie Lillian Gordy Carter]
"Miss Lillian"
American. Nurse
Mother of Jimmy Carter; joined Peace Corps serving in India at age 68.
b. Aug 15, 1898 in Richmond, Georgia
d. Oct 30, 1983 in Americus, Georgia
Source: *AnObit 1983; BioIn 11, 12, 13, 14; ConAu 105, 111, 118; CurBio 78, 84, 84N; GoodHs; InWom SUP; NewYTBS 83; WhoAmW 79, 81*

Carter, Lynda Jean
American. Actor, Singer
Starred in TV series "Wonder Woman," 1977-79; spokeswoman for Max Factor Cosmetics.
b. Jul 24, 1951 in Phoenix, Arizona
Source: *ConTFT 5; IntMPA 86; WhoAm 86*

Carter, Mandy
American. Civil Rights Activist
Founding member of Our Own Place, a lesbian center, and the black gay and lesbian organization UMOJA.
b. Nov 2, 1946 in Albany, New York
Source: *ConBlB 11*

Carter, Mother Maybelle
[The Carter Family; Maybelle Carter]
American. Singer, Songwriter
Grand Ole Opry star 1950-67; formed Carter Family, 1927; mother of June.
b. May 10, 1909 in Nickelsville, Virginia
d. Oct 23, 1978 in Nashville, Tennessee
Source: *Baker 84, 92; BiDAmM; BioIn 9, 11, 14, 15, 19, 21; DcArts; EncFCWM 69, 83; FacFETw; GoodHs; OnThGG; WhAm 7; WhoAm 74, 76, 78*

Carter, Nell
[Nell Hardy]
American. Actor, Singer
Appeared on stage in *Ain't Misbehavin';* played Nell Harper on TV series "Gimme a Break," 1981-86.
b. Sep 13, 1948 in Birmingham, Alabama
Source: *CelR 90; ConMus 7; ConTFT 3, 13; DrBlPA 90; IntMPA 88, 92, 94, 96; LegTOT; WhoAfA 96; WhoAm 80, 82, 84, 86, 88, 92, 95, 96, 97; WhoBlA 85, 88, 90, 92, 94; WhoEnt 92; WhoHol 92*

Carter, Rosalynn
[Mrs. Jimmy Carter; Eleanor Rosalynn Smith]
American. First Lady
Married Jimmy Carter, 1946; wrote memoirs: *First Lady from Plains,* 1984.
b. Aug 18, 1927 in Plains, Georgia
Source: *BioIn 11, 12, 13; BkPepl; ConAu 113; CurBio 78; FacPr 89; GoodHs; LegTOT; NewYTBS 79; WhoAm 86; WhoAmW 87; WhoSSW 86; WhoWor 84; WorAl; WorAlBi; WrDr 92*

Carter, Stephen L(isle)
American. Educator, Lawyer
Professor of law, Yale University, 1985—; wrote *Reflections of an Affirmative Action Baby,* 1991.
b. 1954
Source: *ConAu 147*

Carter, Wilf
"Montana Slim"
Canadian. Singer, Songwriter
Pioneer western singer; known for plaintive ballads, yodels; wrote over 500 songs.
b. Dec 12, 1904 in Port Hilford, Nova Scotia, Canada
Source: *BgBkCoM; BiDAmM; BioIn 14; CmpEPM; EncFCWM 69, 83; HarEnCM 87; NewAmDM; PenEncP*

Carter, William
American. Manufacturer
Manufactured infant wear, knit underwear, beginning 1878.
b. Feb 25, 1830 in Alfreton, England
d. Jul 16, 1918 in Needham Heights, Massachusetts
Source: *ApCAB X; Entr; NatCAB 15, 31*

Carter Family, The
[A P Carter; Anita Carter; Helen Carter; June Carter; Maybelle Carter]
American. Music Group
Recorded over 250 hits, 1927-43, including "Wildwood Flower," 1928; first group honored in Country Music Hall of Fame, 1970.
Source: *BioIn 9, 10, 11, 12; ConMus 3; EncFCWM 69, 83; HarEnCM 87; NewAmDM; ObitOF 79; OxCPMus; RolSEnR 83; WhoAmW 68, 70, 72, 74; WhoEc 81; WhoHol A; WhoNeCM C; WhoRock 81; WomPO 78*

Carteris, Gabrielle
American. Actor
Plays Andrea on TV show "Beverly Hills 90210."
Source: *BioIn 18, 20*

Cartier, Claude
American. Jeweler
President, chairman of Cartier, Inc., 1948-62.
b. 1925
d. Nov 28, 1975 in New York, New York
Source: *BioIn 10; NewYTBS 75*

Cartier, Georges Etienne, Sir
Canadian. Statesman
Joint prime minister of Canada with John MacDonald, 1858-62.
b. Sep 6, 1814 in Saint Antoine, Quebec, Canada
d. May 21, 1873 in London, England
Source: *BioIn 9, 11; DcCathB*

Cartier, Jacques
French. Navigator, Explorer
Founded St. Lawrence River, city of Montreal, 1535.
b. Dec 31, 1491 in Saint-Malo, France
d. Sep 1, 1557 in Saint-Malo, France
Source: *ApCAB; Benet 87, 96; BioIn 1, 2, 4, 5, 6, 8, 9, 11, 15, 16, 18, 19, 20; DcCanB 1; DcCathB; Drake; EncCRAm; Expl 93; LegTOT; LinLib S; MacDCB 78; McGEWB; OxCAmH; OxCCan; OxCFr; OxCShps; REn; REnAL; WhAm HS; WhDW; WhNaAH; WhWE; WorAl; WorAlBi*

Cartier, Louis J
French. Jeweler
Founded world famous jewelry house in Paris, 1847.

Cartier, Pierre C
American. Jeweler
Opened internationally known fine jewelry store in NYC, 1908; the Hope Diamond was among jewels sold.
b. 1878, France
d. Oct 27, 1964 in Geneva, Switzerland
Source: *BioIn 7*

Cartier-Bresson, Henri
French. Photographer
Black and white photographer known for brilliant clarity; published *The Decisive Moment,* 1952.
b. Aug 22, 1908 in Chanteloup, France
Source: *Benet 87, 96; BioIn 1, 3, 4, 6, 7, 8, 9, 10, 11, 12, 13, 14, 15, 16, 17, 18, 20, 21; ConPhot 82, 88, 95; CurBio 47, 76; DcArts; DcCAr 81; DcFM; DcTwDes; FacFETw; ICPEnP; IntAu&W 77; IntWW 74, 75, 76, 77, 78, 79, 80, 81, 82, 83, 89, 91, 93; LegTOT; MacBEP; ModArCr 2; NewYTBS 95; OxCFilm; Who 74, 82, 83, 85, 88, 90, 92, 94; WhoFr 79; WhoWor 74, 76, 78, 82, 84, 87, 89, 91, 93, 95, 96, 97; WorAl; WorAlBi; WorEFlm*

Cartland, Barbara Hamilton
"The Queen of Romance"
English. Author
World's top-selling romance novelist; step-grandmother of Princess Diana.
b. Jul 9, 1901 in Hatfield, England
Source: *Au&Wr 71; ConAu 6NR, 9R; CurBio 79; LngCTC; NewYTBE 73; NewYTBS 81; TwCWr; Who 85; WhoWor 84; WrDr 86*

Carton, Marcel
French. Hostage
Diplomat in Lebanon seized by Islamic Jihad Mar 22, 1985 and held captive 1,139 days; released May 4, 1988.

Cartouche, Louis Dominique
[Louis Dominique Bourguignon]
French. Criminal
Legendary figure; leader of bank robbers.
b. 1693
d. Nov 28, 1721
Source: *BioIn 8; DcBiPP; OxCFr*

Cartwright, Alexander Joy, Jr.
"Father of Modern Baseball"
American. Baseball Pioneer
Devised rules that made baseball playable; organized first recorded baseball game, 1846; Hall of Fame, 1938.
b. Apr 17, 1820 in New York, New York
d. Jul 12, 1892 in Honolulu, Hawaii
Source: *BiDAmSp BB; BioIn 3, 5, 7, 9, 10; WhAm HS; WhoProB 73*

Cartwright, Angela
American. Actor
In TV series "Lost in Space," 1965-68; "Danny Thomas Show," 1957-64.
b. Sep 9, 1952 in Cheshire, England
Source: *ForWC 70; LegTOT; VarWW 85; WhoHol 92, A*

Cartwright, Bill
[James William Cartwright]
American. Basketball Player
Center, NY Knicks, 1980-84, 1986-88; Chicago Bulls 1989—; member NBA all rookie team 1981.
b. Jul 30, 1957 in Lodi, California
Source: *BioIn 10, 12, 13; InB&W 80; NewYTBS 83; OfNBA 87; WhoAfA 96; WhoBlA 85, 92, 94*

Cartwright, Edmund
English. Clergy, Inventor
Developed first power loom, 1785-87; assisted Robt Fulton in steamboat experiments.
b. Apr 24, 1743 in Marnham, England
d. Oct 30, 1823 in Hastings, England
Source: *Alli; BiDLA; BiESc; BioIn 9, 14; DcEnL; DcNaB; EncEnl; InSci; LinLib S; OxCDecA; WhDW; WorInv*

Cartwright, Nancy
American. Actor
Plays voice of Bart Simpson on animated TV show "The Simpsons," 1990—.

Cartwright, Veronica
American. Actor
Films include *The Birds,* 1963; *The Right Stuff,* 1983; sister of Angela.
b. 1950 in Bristol, England
Source: *ConTFT 2, 6; VarWW 85; WhoHol 92*

Carty, Rico
[Ricardo Adolfo Jacobo Carty]
Dominican. Baseball Player
Outfielder, designated hitter, 1963-79; won NL batting title, 1970.
b. Sep 1, 1939 in San Pedro de Macoris, Dominican Republic
Source: *BioIn 8, 21; WhoAm 74, 76, 78; WhoProB 73*

Carusi, Ugo
American. Government Official
Exec. secretary to US Attorney General, 1930-45; commissioner, immigration and naturalization, 1945-48.
b. Mar 17, 1902
d. Jul 21, 1994 in Washington, District of Columbia
Source: *BioIn 1, 20; CurBio 94N*

Caruso, David
American. Actor
Appeared on TV's "NYPD Blue," 1993-94.
b. Jan 17, 1956 in New York, New York
Source: *ConTFT 13; IntMPA 94, 96; LegTOT; News 94, 94-3; WhoAm 95, 96, 97*

Caruso, Enrico
Italian. Opera Singer
Legendary tenor, chief attraction of NY Met., 1903-20.
b. Feb 25, 1873 in Naples, Italy
d. Aug 2, 1921 in Naples, Italy
Source: *AmBi; ApCAB X; Baker 78, 84, 92; BiDAmM; BioIn 1, 2, 3, 4, 5, 6, 7, 8, 9, 10, 11, 12, 13, 14, 15, 16, 17, 19, 20, 21; ChhPo S1; ConAu 115; ConMus 10; DcAmB; DcArts; DcCathB; Dis&D; FacFETw; Film 1; FilmgC; HalFC 84, 88; IntDcOp; LegTOT; LinLib S; McGEWB; MetOEnc; MusSN; NewAmDM; NewC; NewEOp 71; NewGrDA 86; NewGrDO; NewYTBE 73; OxCAmH; OxCMus; OxDcOp; PenDiMP; RAdv 14; REn; TwYS; WhAm 1; WhDW; WhoHol B; WhScrn 74, 77, 83; WorAl; WorAlBi; WorECar*

Carvel, Thomas A
Canadian. Businessman
Founded Carvel Corp., 1934; which had over 700 franchises at his death; invented frozen-custard machine.
b. 1906
d. Oct 21, 1990 in Pine Plains, New York
Source: *BusPN; NewYTBE 73; NewYTBS 79*

Carver, George Washington
American. Chemist, Educator
Agricultural researcher, 1896-1903; discovered industrial uses for peanut, sweet potato, soybean.
b. Jan 5, 1864 in Diamond, Missouri
d. Jan 5, 1943 in Tuskegee, Alabama
Source: *AfrAmAl 6; AfroAA; AmSocL; AsBiEn; BiESc; BioIn 1, 2, 3, 4, 5, 6, 7, 8, 9, 10, 11, 12, 13, 14, 15, 16, 17, 18, 19, 20, 21; BlksScM; ConHero 2; CurBio 40, 43; DcAmB S3; DcAmC; EncAAH; EncAB-H 1974; FacFETw; HeroCon; InSci; LarDcSc; LinLib S; McGEWB; MemAm; NatCAB 33; NegAl 76, 83, 89; OxCAmH; RComAH; WebAB 74, 79; WhAm 2, 4A, HSA; WorAl; WorAlBi; WorInv*

Carver, John
English. Colonial Figure
First governor of Plymouth Colony, 1620-21.
b. 1576 in Nottinghamshire, England
d. Apr 5, 1621 in Plymouth, Massachusetts
Source: *AmBi; ApCAB; BiDBrA; BiDrACR; DcAmB; DcBiPP; Drake; HarEnUS; LegTOT; LinLib S; NatCAB 7; OxCAmH; REn; TwCBDA; WhAm HS; WhDW*

Carver, Raymond Clevie, Jr.
American. Author
One of best known short-story writers in US: *Will You Please Be Quiet, Please?* 1976; *Cathedral,* 1983.
b. May 25, 1938 in Clatskanie, Oregon
d. Aug 2, 1988 in Port Angeles, Washington

Source: *ConAu 17NR; ConLC 22, 36; ConNov 86; CurBio 84, 88; DcLB Y84B; IntAu&W 86; ModAL S2; PostFic; WhoAm 84, 86; WorAu 1975*

Carvey, Dana
American. Comedian, Actor
Played Church Lady on "Saturday Night Live," 1986-93; starred in *"Wayne's World,"* 1992 and *Wayne's World 2,* 1993.
b. Apr 2, 1955 in Missoula, Montana
Source: *BioIn 18; ConTFT 10; CurBio 92; IntMPA 92, 94, 96; LegTOT; News 94, 94-1; WhoAm 94, 95, 96, 97; WhoCom; WhoHol 92*

Carville, James
[Chester James Carville, Jr.]
American. Consultant
Political strategist for Bill Clinton's successful 1992 presidential campaign.
b. Oct 25, 1944 in Fort Benning, Georgia
Source: *CurBio 93; LegTOT; NewYTBS 92; WhoAm 94, 95*

Cary, Alice
American. Author, Poet
First president of first women's club, Sorosis; writings include *A Book for Young Folks,* 1867.
b. Apr 26, 1820 in Cincinnati, Ohio
d. Feb 12, 1871 in New York, New York
Source: *Alli SUP; AmAu; AmAu&B; AmBi; AmWom; AmWomWr, 92; ApCAB; ArtclWW 2; BbD; BenetAL 91; BiDAmM; BiD&SB; BioAmW; BioIn 5, 21; BlmGWL; CarSB; Chambr 3; ChhPo, S1, S3; CyAL 2; DcAmAu; DcAmB; DcNAA; Drake; EvLB; FemiCLE; InWom, SUP; LibW; LinLib L, S; NatCAB 1; NotAW; OhA&B; OxCAmL 65, 83, 95; OxCWoWr 95; PenNWW A; TwCBDA; WebAB 74, 79; WhAm HS; WomFir*

Cary, Anne Louise
American. Opera Singer
Contralto; first American woman to sing Wagnerian role in US, 1877.
b. Oct 22, 1842 in Wayne, Maine
d. Apr 3, 1921 in Norwalk, Connecticut
Source: *AmBi; ApCAB; Baker 84; DcAmB; NatCAB 1; NewEOp 71; NotAW; TwCBDA; WhAm 1; WomWWA 14*

Cary, Elizabeth Tanfield
[Viscountess Falkland]
English. Dramatist
First woman to publish a full-length original play in English—*The Tragedie of Mariam, Faire Queene of Jewry,* 1613.
b. 1585?
d. 1639
Source: *BlmGWL*

Cary, Frank Taylor
American. Businessman
IBM, pres. 1971-3; chm., 1973-83; chm. of exec. committee, 1979-85; board of directors, 1971-91; advisory board, 1991—.
b. Dec 14, 1920 in Gooding, Idaho
Source: *BioIn 12, 13, 14, 15; BlueB 76; CurBio 80; HisDcDP; IntWW 83; LElec; WhoAm 76, 78, 80, 82, 84, 86, 88, 90, 92; WhoE 77, 79, 81, 83, 85; WhoFI 74, 75, 77, 79, 81, 83, 85; WhoWor 80, 82, 84*

Cary, Joyce
[Arthur Joyce Lunel Cary]
English. Author
Wrote trilogies *The Horse's Mouth,* 1944; *Prisoner of Grace,* 1952.
b. Dec 7, 1888 in Londonderry, Northern Ireland
d. Mar 29, 1957 in Oxford, England
Source: *Benet 87; BiDIrW; BioIn 1, 2, 3, 4, 5, 6, 7, 8, 10, 11, 13, 14, 16, 17, 18; BlmGEL; BritWr 7; CamGEL; CasWL; CnDBLB 6; CnMWL; ConAu 104; ConNov 76; CurBio 49, 57; CyWA 58, 89; DcIrB 78; DcIrL; DcIrW 1; DcLB 1, 15, 100; DcLEL; DcNaB 1951; EncWL 2, 3; EngPo; EvLB; FacFETw; HisDBrE; LegTOT; LinLib L; LngCEL; LngCTC; ModBrL, S1, S2; NewC; Novels; ObitT 1951; OxCEng 67, 85; PenC ENG; RAdv 1, 14, 13-1; REn; RfGEnL 91; TwCA SUP; TwCLC 1, 29; TwCWr; WebE&AL; WhAm 3; WhE&EA; WhoTwCL; WorAlBi; WrPh*

Cary, Lorene
American. Writer
Contributing editor, *Newsweek,* 1991—; wrote *Black Ice,* 1991.
b. Nov 29, 1956 in Philadelphia, Pennsylvania
Source: *BlkWr 2; ConAu 135; ConBlB 3; SchCGBL; WhoAfA 96; WhoBlA 94; WrDr 94, 96*

Cary, Phoebe
American. Poet
Collaborated with sister, Alice, on hymns, verse vols.
b. Sep 4, 1824 in Cincinnati, Ohio
d. Jul 31, 1871 in Newport, Rhode Island
Source: *Alli SUP; AmAu; AmAu&B; AmBi; AmWom; AmWomWr; ApCAB; BbD; BenetAL 91; BiDAmM; BiD&SB; BioAmW; BioIn 5; Chambr 3; ChhPo, S1; CyAL 2; DcAmAu; DcAmB; DcNAA; EvLB; FemiCLE; InWom, SUP; LegTOT; LibW; LinLib L, S; LuthC 75; NatCAB 1; NotAW; OhA&B; OxCAmL 65, 83; PenC AM; PenNWW A; TwCBDA; WebAB 74, 79; WhAm HS*

Carzou, Jean
French. Artist
Landscape, still-life painter, who uses linear style, rich colors.
b. Jan 1, 1907 in Alep, Syria
Source: *OxCTwCA; WhoFr 79; WhoWor 74*

Casablancas, John(ny)
American. Business Executive
Opened Manhattan modeling agency, 1977, challenging Ford, world's major firm.
b. Dec 12, 1942 in New York, New York

Casadesus, Gaby Lhote
French. Musician
Wife of Robert, performed with him in his two piano concertos.
b. Aug 9, 1901 in Marseilles, France
Source: *WhoAmW 66, 75*

Casadesus, Jean
French. Musician
Pianist son of Robert, performed with his parents in three piano concertos.
b. Jul 7, 1927 in Paris, France
d. Jan 20, 1972 in Renfrew, Ontario, Canada
Source: *Baker 78, 84, 92; BiDAmM; BioIn 3, 9; NewAmDM; ObitOF 79; PenDiMP*

Casadesus, Robert
French. Musician, Composer
Noted interpreter of Mozart; wrote neo-classic style symphonies.
b. Apr 7, 1899 in Paris, France
d. Sep 19, 1972 in Paris, France
Source: *Baker 78, 84, 92; BioIn 3, 4, 9, 11, 21; CurBio 45, 72, 72N; FacFETw; MusSN; NewAmDM; NewYTBE 72; NotTwCP; PenDiMP; WhAm 5; WhoMus 72; WorAl; WorAlBi*

Casady, Jack
[Jefferson Airplane]
American. Musician, Singer
One of original members of group, 1965-70; with Hot Tuna, 1970-77.
b. Apr 13, 1944 in Washington, District of Columbia
Source: *LegTOT; WhoRocM 82*

Casals, Pablo (Pau Carlos Salvador)
Spanish. Musician
Modernized playing techniques of cello, elevating status to serious solo orchestral instrument.
b. Dec 29, 1876 in Vendrell, Spain
d. Oct 22, 1973 in Rio Piedras, Puerto Rico
Source: *ASCAP 66; Baker 78, 84; BiDAmM; BioIn 1, 2, 3, 4, 5, 6, 7, 8, 9, 10, 11, 12, 13, 14, 16, 17, 18, 19, 20; CelR; ConAu 45, 93, X; ConMus 9; CurBio 50, 64, 73, 73N; DcAmB S9; DcArts; DcHiB; DcTwCCu 4; FacFETw; LegTOT; LinLib S; MusSN; NewAmDM; NewGrDA 86; NewYTBE 73; ObitOF 79; ObitT 1971; OxCMus; PenDiMP, A; REn; WhAm 6; WhDW; Who 74; WhoMus 72; WhoWor 74; WhScrn 77, 83; WorAl; WorAlBi*

Casals, Rosemary
American. Tennis Player
Won first Virginia Slims Tournament, 1970; US Open doubles champ, 1967, 71, 74, with Bille Jean King.
b. Sep 16, 1948 in San Francisco, California
Source: *BiDAmSp OS; BioIn 7, 10, 11, 12, 13; BioNews 74; CurBio 74; GoodHs; HerW, 84; HispAmA; InWom SUP; LegTOT; NotHsAW 93; WhoAm 78, 80, 82, 84, 86, 88, 90, 92, 94, 95, 96, 97; WhoAmW 79, 81, 83; WhoWest 94, 96*

Casanova (de Seingalt), Giovanni Giacomo
Italian. Author, Adventurer
His bawdy accounts of career as charlatan, gambler, lover, *Memories,* 1826-38, were published, 1960.
b. Apr 5, 1725 in Venice, Italy
d. Jun 4, 1798 in Dux, Bohemia
Source: *DcBiPP; DcItL 1; Dis&D; EncEnl; RAdv 1; REn; ScFEYrs; WhDW; WorAlBi*

Casaubon, Isaac
Theologian, Scholar
Regarded as one of greatest 16th c. classical scholars; appointed prebendary of Canterbury and Westminster by James I.
b. Feb 8, 1559 in Geneva, Switzerland
d. Jul 1, 1614 in London, England
Source: *BbD; CyEd; DcBiPP; DcEuL; DcNaB; LinLib L; LuthC 75; NewC; OxCEng 67, 85, 95; OxCFr*

Case, Anna
American. Opera Singer, Actor
Metropolitan Opera soprano who sang lead in first US production of *Der Rosenkavalier,* 1913.
b. 1889 in Clinton, New Jersey
d. Jan 7, 1984 in New York, New York
Source: *BiDAmM; Film 1; InWom, SUP; NewGrDO; WhAm 8; WhoHol A*

Case, Clifford Philip
American. Lawyer, Politician
Moderate Rep. senator from NJ, 1955-79, who sponsored social legislation, civil rights bills.
b. Apr 16, 1904 in Franklin Park, New Jersey
d. Mar 5, 1982 in Washington, District of Columbia
Source: *AlmAP 78; WhoWor 74, 78, 80*

Case, Steve
[Stephen M. Case]
American. Business Executive
President and CEO of America Online, 1991—.
b. Aug 21, 1958 in Honolulu, Hawaii
Source: *CurBio 96; News 95*

Casella, Max
American. Actor
Played Vinnie on TV show "Doogie Howser, M.D.," 1989-1993.
b. 1967 in Cambridge, Massachusetts

Caselotti, Adriana
American. Entertainer
Original voice of Snow White in films.
b. 1916?
d. Jan 19, 1997 in Los Angeles, California

Casement, Roger David
Irish. Diplomat
Irish Nationalist, opposed Irish participation in WW I; hanged for treason by British.
b. Sep 1, 1864 in Dun Laoghaire, Ireland
d. Aug 3, 1916 in London, England
Source: *BioIn 1, 3, 4, 5, 6, 7, 9, 10, 11, 12, 13; DcIrB 78; DcIrW 2; DcNaB 1912; DcTwHis; GrBr; HisDBrE; WhDW; WorAl*

Casewit, Curtis
American. Author
Contributor of short stories, articles to mags; books include *How to Get a Job Overseas.*
b. Mar 21, 1922 in Mannheim, Germany
Source: *BioIn 9; ConAu 6NR, 13R; SmATA 4; WhoWest 76, 78*

Casey, Dan(iel Maurice)
American. Baseball Player
Pitcher, 1884-90; probable inspiration for Ernest Thayer's poem, "Casey at the Bat."
b. Oct 2, 1865 in Binghamton, New York
d. Feb 8, 1943 in Washington, District of Columbia
Source: *WhoProB 73*

Casey, Edward Pearce
American. Architect
Designed memorial bridge across Potomac at Washington, 1900; Grant monument, Washington, 1902.
b. Jun 18, 1864 in Portland, Maine
d. Jan 2, 1940
Source: *BiDAmAr; BioIn 2; NatCAB 36; WhAm 1*

Casey, H(arry) W(ayne)
[K C and the Sunshine Band]
American. Singer, Musician
Lead singer, keyboardist who co-founded band, 1973; hit single "Shake Your Booty," 1975.
b. Jan 31, 1951 in Hialeah, Florida
Source: *WhoAm 82, 84, 86, 88*

Casey, Hugh Thomas
American. Baseball Player
Relief pitching specialist, Brooklyn Dodgers, 1939-49.
b. Oct 14, 1913 in Buckhead, Georgia
d. Jul 3, 1951 in Atlanta, Georgia
Source: *BioIn 3, 7; WhoProB 73*

Casey, James E
American. Business Executive
Founded United Parcel Service, 1909; name changed to UPS, 1917.
b. Mar 29, 1888 in Candelaria, Nevada
d. Jun 6, 1983 in Seattle, Washington
Source: *BioIn 1, 3, 4; NewYTBS 83*

Casey, Robert P
American. Politician
Dem. governor of Pennsylvania, 1987—.
b. Jan 9, 1932 in Jackson Heights, New York
Source: *AlmAP 88, 92; BiDrGov 1983, 1988; IntWW 89, 91, 93; WhoAm 88, 90, 92, 94, 95; WhoAmP 73, 77, 87, 89, 91, 93, 95; WhoE 74, 89, 91, 95; WhoGov 72, 75; WhoWor 89, 91, 93, 95*

Casey, William Joseph
American. Government Official, Lawyer
CIA director under Reagan, 1981-87; name figured prominently in Iran-Contra hearings, 1987.
b. Mar 13, 1913 in Elmhurst, New York
d. May 6, 1987 in Glen Cove, New York
Source: *AmPolLe; BioIn 9, 10, 12, 13; ColdWar 1; ConNews 87-3; CurBio 72; EncAI&E; IntWW 74, 75, 76, 77, 78, 79, 80, 81, 82, 83; NatCAB 63N; NewYTBS 80, 84; WhAm 9; WhoAm 74, 76, 82, 84, 86; WhoGov 75, 77*

Cash, Jim
American. Educator, Screenwriter
With Jack Epps, wrote screenplays for 1986 films *Top Gun, Legal Eagles.*
b. 1941?

Cash, Johnny
[Tennessee Three; J.R. Cash]
"The Man in Black"
American. Singer, Songwriter
Country-western hit songs include "I Walk the Line," 1964, "A Boy Named Sue," 1969.
b. Feb 26, 1932 in Kingsland, Arkansas
Source: *AmDec 1960; AmSong; Baker 78, 84, 92; BgBkCoM; BioIn 8, 9, 10, 12, 13; CelR, 90; ConAu 110, 142; ConMus 1, 17; CurBio 69; DcArts; DcTwCCu 1; EncFCWM 69, 83; EncPR&S 89; EncRk 88; EncRkSt; FilmgC; HalFC 84, 88; HarEnCM 87; HarEnR 86; LegTOT; NewAmDM; NewGrDA 86; News 95, 95-3; NewYTBE 73; OxCPMus; PenEncP; RkOn 74; RolSEnR 83; WebAB 74, 79; WhoAm 74, 76, 78, 80, 82, 84, 86, 88, 90, 92, 94, 95, 96, 97; WhoEnt 92; WhoHol 92, A; WhoNeCM C; WhoRock 81; WhoSSW 73, 75; WorAl; WorAlBi; WrDr 96*

Cash, Norm(an Dalton)
"Stormin' Norman"
American. Baseball Player
First baseman, Detroit, 1960-74; won AL batting title, 1961.
b. Nov 10, 1934 in Justiceburg, Texas
d. Oct 11, 1986 in Charlevoix, Michigan
Source: *Ballpl 90; BiDAmSp BB; BioIn 5, 6, 8, 15; LegTOT; WhoAm 74; WhoProB 73*

Cash, Pat(rick)
Australian. Tennis Player
Won Wimbledon singles, 1987, becoming first Australian champ since 1971.
b. May 27, 1965 in Melbourne, Australia
Source: *CelR 90; IntWW 89, 91, 93; LegTOT; NewYTBS 84, 87*

Cash, Roseanne
[Mrs. Rodney Crowell]
American. Singer
Country-rock singer, who is daughter of Johnny Cash; albums include *Seven-Year Ache,* 1981.
b. May 24, 1955 in Memphis, Tennessee
Source: *BioIn 12, 13; EncFCWM 83; RkOn 85*

Cashen, Frank
American. Baseball Executive
GM, NY Mets; known for wearing bow tie to all games.
Source: *NewYTBS 84, 86*

Cashin, Bonnie
American. Fashion Designer
Award-winning sportswear designer; started Bonnie Cashin Designs, 1952.
b. 1915 in Oakland, California
Source: *BioIn 4, 8, 9, 12; ConFash; CurBio 70; DcTwDes; EncFash; FairDF US; InWom, SUP; WhoAm 74, 76, 78, 80, 82, 84, 86, 88, 92; WhoAmW 58A, 64, 66, 68, 74, 79, 81, 83, 91, 93; WhoFash 88; WhoWor 74; WorFshn*

Casimir, Saint
Polish.
Imprisoned at age 15 for refusing to obey orders of his father, King Casimir IV.
b. Oct 5, 1458 in Kracow, Poland
d. Mar 4, 1484 in Grodno, Poland
Source: *DcBiPP; DcCathB*

Casiraghi, Stefano
Italian.
Second husband of Princess Caroline of Monaco, married Dec 29, 1983; killed in power boating accident.
b. Sep 8, 1960, Italy
d. Oct 3, 1990 in Monte Carlo, Monaco
Source: *BioIn 13*

Caslavska, Vera
Czech. Gymnast
Gymnast; winner of 6 gold medals in the 1964, 1968 Olympics.
b. May 3, 1942 in Prague, Czechoslovakia
Source: *ContDcW 89; GoodHs; IntDcWB; IntWW 81, 82, 83, 89, 91, 93; InWom SUP; WhoWor 91; WorAl*

Caslon, William
English. Type Designer
Designed English Arabic, 1720, and Caslon typeface, 1726.
b. Jan 23, 1692 in Cradley, England
d. Jan 23, 1766 in London, England
Source: *BioIn 3, 10; BlkwCE; DcBiPP; DcNaB; EncAJ; NewC; OxCDecA; OxCEng 85, 95; OxDcArt; WhDW*

Caspary, Vera
American. Author, Screenwriter
Wrote mystery novel *Laura,* 1942; made into film, 1944.
b. Nov 13, 1904 in Chicago, Illinois
d. Jun 13, 1987 in New York, New York
Source: *AmAu&B; AmWomD; AmWomPl; AmWomWr; AnObit 1987; Au&Wr 71; BenetAL 91; BiE&WWA; BioIn 1, 4; ConAu 13R; CrtSuMy; CurBio 47, 87, 87N; EncMys; FilmgC; GrWomMW; InWom SUP; LngCTC; NotNAT; Novels; REnAL; TwCA SUP; TwCCr&M 80, 85, 91; WorEFlm; WrDr 76, 86*

Casper, Billy
[William Earl Casper]
American. Golfer
Turned pro, 1954; won US Open, 1959, 1966, Masters, 1970; second player (Arnold Palmer first) to win $1 million on tour.
b. Jun 24, 1931 in San Diego, California
Source: *BiDAmSp OS; BioIn 4, 5, 7, 8, 9, 10, 13; CelR; CmCal; ConAu 121; CurBio 66; IntWW 91, 93; LegTOT; WhoAm 74, 76, 78, 80, 82, 84; WhoGolf; WhoIntG; WhoSSW 93; WorAl; WorAlBi*

Cass, Lewis
American. Statesman
Governor of MI Territory, 1813-31; unsuccessful Dem. presidential candidate, 1848; secretary of state, 1857-60.
b. Oct 9, 1782 in Exeter, New Hampshire
d. Jun 17, 1866 in Detroit, Michigan
Source: *Alli; AmAu&B; AmBi; AmPolLe; ApCAB, X; BiAUS; BiD&SB; BiDrAC; BiDrATG; BiDrUSC 89; BiDrUSE 71, 89; BioIn 1, 2, 3, 4, 7, 8, 9, 10, 12, 15, 16; CyAG; CyAL 1; DcAmAu; DcAmB; DcAmDH 80, 89; DcAmTB; DcBiPP; DcNAA; Drake; EncAAH; EncAB-H 1974, 1996; HarEnUS; LinLib S; McGEWB; NatCAB 5; OhA&B; OxCAmH; PeoHis; PolPar; PresAR; REnAW; TwCBDA; WebAB 74, 79; WhAm HS; WhAmP; WhNaAH*

Cass, Peggy
[Mary Margaret Cass]
American. Actor
Won Tony for *Auntie Mame,* 1956; regular panelist on TV game show "To Tell the Truth," 1964-67.
b. May 21, 1925 in Boston, Massachusetts
Source: *BiE&WWA; CelR; ConTFT 3; IntMPA 86; InWom; MotPP; NotNAT; WhoHol 92, A*

Cassady, Howard
"Hopalong"
American. Football Player
All-America halfback, Ohio State U., 1952-55; won Heisman Trophy, 1955; in NFL, 1956-63, mostly with Detroit.
b. Mar 2, 1934 in Columbus, Ohio
Source: *BiDAmSp FB; BioIn 4, 10, 14; WhoFtbl 74; WhoSpor*

Cassady, Neal
American. Author
One of people most responsible for Beat Generation; writings consisted chiefly of letters to friends.
b. Feb 8, 1926? in Salt Lake City, Utah
d. Feb 4, 1968 in San Miguel de Allende, Mexico
Source: *BenetAL 91; BioIn 11, 13; ConAu 141; DcLB 16*

Cassandre, A(dolphe) M(ouron)
French. Artist, Type Designer
Noted for posters, modern typefaces.
b. Jan 24, 1909 in Kharkov, Russia
d. 1968
Source: *WhoGrA 62*

Cassatt, Mary Stevenson
American. Artist
Impressionist noted for paintings of mother and child; friend of Degas.
b. May 22, 1844 in Allegheny City, Pennsylvania
d. Jun 14, 1926 in Chateau de Beaufresne, France
Source: *AmBi; AmCulL; ArtsNiC; AtlBL; BiDWomA; BriEAA; DcAmB; DcWomA; EncAB-H 1974; EncWHA; GoodHs; HanAmWH; HerW; InWom SUP; LibW; McGEWB; NotAW; OxCAmH; OxCAmL 65; OxCArt; REn; WebAB 79; WebBD 83; WhAm 1; WomArt*

Cassavetes, John
American. Actor, Director
Known for free-wheeling, improvisational directing style in *Faces,* 1968, *A Woman Under the Influence,* 1974; husband of Gena Rowlands.
b. Dec 9, 1929 in New York, New York
d. Feb 3, 1989 in Los Angeles, California
Source: *AnObit 1989; BenetAL 91; BiDFilm, 94; BioIn 4, 6, 8, 9, 10, 11, 12; CelR; ConAu 85, 127; ConDr 77A; ConLC 20; ConTFT 3, 7; CurBio 69, 89N; DcArts; DcFM; FacFETw; FilmgC; GangFlm; HalFC 84, 88; IlWWHD 1; IntDcF 1-2, 2-2; IntMPA 75, 76, 77, 78, 79, 81, 82, 84, 86, 88; IntWW 74, 75, 76, 77, 78, 79, 80, 81, 82, 83; ItaFilm; LegTOT; MiSFD 9N; MotPP; MovMk; News 89-2; NewYTBS 89; OxCFilm; WhAm 9; WhoAm 74, 76, 78, 80, 82, 84, 86, 88; WhoHol A; WhoWor 78; WorAl; WorAlBi; WorEFlm; WorFDir 2*

CasSelle, Malcolm
American. Computer Executive
Founded NetNoir Inc. with E. David Ellington, 1995.
b. Mar 22, 1970 in Allentown, Pennsylvania
Source: *ConBlB 11*

Cassidy, Butch
[Robert Leroy Parker]
American. Outlaw
Train robber whose life was subject of hit film *Butch Cassidy and the Sundance Kid,* 1969; fled to S America with partner, fate uncertain.
b. Apr 6, 1866 in Beaver, Utah
d. 1937?
Source: *BioIn 10, 15, 16, 17, 20, 21; DrInf; EncACr; REnAW; WhDW*

Cassidy, Claudia
American. Critic
Chicago performing arts critic; wrote monthly "On the Aisle" column, 1974-87.
b. 1900 in Shawneetown, Illinois
d. Jul 21, 1996 in Chicago, Illinois
Source: *AmAu&B; BiE&WWA; BioIn 2, 4, 7, 9; CelR; ConAmTC; CurBio 55, 96N; NotNAT; WhoAm 84; WhoAmW 85*

Cassidy, David Bruce
American. Singer, Actor
Played Keith Partridge on TV series "The Partridge Family," 1970-74; son of Jack Cassidy.
b. Apr 12, 1950 in New York, New York
Source: *ConTFT 8; IntMPA 86; WhoAm 80, 82, 84, 86; WhoEnt 92*

Cassidy, Harold Gomes
American. Chemist, Educator, Author
Invented concept of polymers capable of oxidation, reduction; wrote *Principles of Organic Chemistry,* 1949.
b. Oct 17, 1906 in Havana, Cuba
Source: *AmMWSc 76P, 79, 82, 86, 89, 92, 95; ConAu 25R; WhoAm 74, 76, 78, 80, 82, 84, 86, 88, 90*

Cassidy, Jack
American. Actor, Singer, Dancer
Won Tony for *She Loves Me,* 1964; Shirley Jones was second wife.
b. Mar 5, 1927 in New York, New York
d. Dec 12, 1976 in West Hollywood, California
Source: *BiE&WWA; BioNews 74; DcAmB S10; EncMT; FilmgC; LegTOT; NewYTBS 76; NotNAT; ObitOF 79; WhoHol A; WhoThe 72, 77, 81N; WhScrn 83; WorAl; WorAlBi*

Cassidy, Joanna
[Joanna Virginia Caskey]
American. Actor
Movies include *Blade Runner; Under Fire* ; TV series "Buffalo Bill."
b. Aug 2, 1944 in Camden, New Jersey
Source: *BioIn 13; ConTFT 6; HalFC 84, 88; IntMPA 86, 88, 92, 94, 96; ItaFilm; LegTOT; VarWW 85; WhoHol 92, A*

Cassidy, Marshall
American. Horse Racing Official
Invented stall starting gates, perfected photo-finish camera system; director of racing, New York Racing Association, 1963-68.
b. 1892
d. Oct 23, 1968 in Glen Cove, New York
Source: *BioIn 8; ObitOF 79*

Cassidy, Shaun Paul
American. Singer, Actor
Starred in TV series "Hardy Boys Mysteries," 1977-79.
b. Sep 27, 1958 in Los Angeles, California
Source: *BkPepl; ConTFT 3; VarWW 85; WhoAm 82*

Cassill, R(onald) V(erlin)
American. Author
Award-winning short stories include *The Prize,* 1968.
b. May 17, 1919 in Cedar Falls, Iowa
Source: *BioIn 5, 8, 9, 10, 14; ConAu 7NR, 9NR, 45NR; ConLC 23; ConNov 86, 96; DcLEL 1940; OxCAmL 83, 95; WhoAm 74, 76, 78, 80, 82, 84, 86, 88, 90, 92, 94, 95, 96, 97; WhoUSWr 88; WhoWrEP 89; WrDr 86, 94, 96*

Cassin, Rene-Samuel
French. Judge
Awarded Nobel Peace Prize, 1969; pres., UN Human Rights commission, 1946-68.
b. Oct 5, 1887 in Bayonne, France
d. Feb 20, 1976 in Paris, France
Source: *BiDInt; ConAu 65; IntWW 76N; NewYTBS 76; WhAm 6; Who 74; WhoNob, 90, 95; WhoWor 78; WhoWorJ 72; WorAl*

Cassini, Igor Loiewski
American. Journalist
Gossip columnist under the name "Cholly Knickerbocker;" brother of Oleg.
b. Sep 15, 1915 in Sevastopol, Russia
Source: *BioIn 6*

Cassini, Oleg Loiewski
American. Fashion Designer
Official White House designer for Jacqueline Kennedy, 1961-63.
b. Apr 11, 1913 in Paris, France
Source: *BioIn 5, 6, 13; CurBio 61; WhoAm 82; WhoWor 74, 76; WorFshn*

Cassirer, Ernst
German. Philosopher
Wrote neo-Kantian texts of cultural, scientific value: *Myth of the State,* 1946.
b. Jul 28, 1874 in Breslau, Prussia
d. Apr 13, 1945 in New York, New York
Source: *BioIn 1, 2, 4, 7, 9, 11, 12, 13, 14, 17; DcNAA; EncTR, 91; FacFETw; LiExTwC; LinLib L; LuthC 75; OxCPhil; PenC EUR; RAdv 14, 13-4; ThTwC 87; TwCA SUP; TwCLC 61; WhAm 4; WhE&EA; WhoLA*

Cassius
[Caius Cassius Longinus]
"The Last of the Romans"
Roman. Army Officer, Politician
Led conspiracy to murder Caesar, 44 BC.
d. 42BC
Source: *Benet 87, 96; DcCathB; DcLP 87B; IntAu&W 91X; LegTOT; LinLib S; NewCol 75; OxCLaw; PseudN 82; REn; ScF&FL 1*

Cassou, Jean
[Jean Noir]
French. Author, Critic
Wrote *33 Sonnets Composes au Secret,* 1944, while imprisoned during German occupation.
b. Jul 9, 1897 in Deusto, France
Source: *CasWL; EncWL; EvEuW; IntAu&W 76, 77, 89; IntWW 74, 75, 76, 77, 78, 79, 80, 81, 82, 83; IntWWP 77; WhoFr 79; WhoWor 74, 76*

Castagna, Bruna
Italian. Opera Singer
Contralto with NY Met., 1935-45; noted for Verdi roles.
b. Oct 15, 1908 in Bari, Italy
d. Jul 10, 1983 in Pinamar, Argentina
Source: *Baker 84; BioIn 1, 4, 11; InWom; MusSN; NewEOp 71*

Castagno, Andrea del
[Andrea di Bartolo de Bargilla]
Italian. Artist
Influenced by Masaccio; frescoes include portraits of noted Italians and "Last Supper."
b. 1421 in San Martino a Corella, Italy
d. Aug 19, 1457 in Florence, Italy
Source: *AtlBL; DcArts; McGDA; OxCArt; WebBD 83; WorAl; WorAlBi*

Castaneda, Carlos
American. Anthropologist, Author
Wrote *Teachings of Don Juan: The Yaqui Way of Knowledge,* 1968.
b. Dec 25, 1931 in Sao Paulo, Brazil
Source: *BenetAL 91; BioIn 12, 14; ConAu 25R, 32NR; ConLC 12; HispWr; LegTOT; MajTwCW; NewYTBE 72; ThTwC 87; WhoAm 74, 76, 78, 80, 82, 84, 86, 88, 94, 95, 96, 97; WhoUSWr 88; WhoWest 96; WorAl; WorAlBi; WrDr 76, 80, 82, 84, 86, 88, 90, 92, 94, 96*

Castel, Frederic
French. Designer
Fur designer known for using mink and sable in sports coats.
Source: *WorFshn*

Castellaneta, Dan
American. Actor
Plays voice of Homer on animated TV show "The Simpsons," 1990—.
Source: *ConTFT 6, 13*

Castellano, Richard
American. Actor
Appeared in *The Godfather,* 1972; nominated for Oscar, 1970, for *Lovers and Other Strangers.*
b. Sep 4, 1933 in New York, New York
d. Dec 10, 1988 in North Bergen, New Jersey
Source: *BioIn 16; CelR; ConTFT 7; FilmgC; IntMPA 86; LegTOT; NewYTBS 88; WhoAm 86; WhoHol A; WorAl*

Castello Branco, Humberto
Brazilian. Political Leader
Pres. of Brazil, 1964-67; developed new constitution increasing presidential power.
b. Sep 20, 1900 in Fortaleza, Brazil
d. Jul 18, 1967
Source: *BioIn 6, 7, 8, 12; CurBio 65, 67; EncLatA*

Castelnuovo-Tedesco, Mario
American. Composer
Wrote piano music, film scores, overtures to 12 Shakespearean plays; composed opera *La Mandragola,* 1923.
b. Apr 3, 1895 in Florence, Italy
d. Mar 15, 1968 in Hollywood, California
Source: *AmComp; ASCAP 66; Baker 78, 84, 92; BiDAmM; BioIn 1, 2, 4, 5, 6, 8, 10, 17; CompSN SUP; ConAmC 76, 82; DcCM; FacFETw; HalFC 84, 88; NatCAB 54; NewAmDM; NewEOp 71; NewGrDA 86; NewGrDO; NewOxM; OxCEng 85, 95; OxCMus; PenDiMP A; WhAm 5*

Castiglione, Baldassare, Conte
Italian. Diplomat, Writer, Courtier
Writer of Renaissance Europe; chief work *The Courtier,* 1518.
b. Dec 3, 1478 in Casatico, Italy
d. Feb 2, 1529 in Toledo, Spain
Source: *AtlBL; BbD; Benet 87, 96; BiD&SB; BioIn 1, 5, 7, 10, 11, 15; BlmGEL; CasWL; CroE&S; CyEd; DcArts; DcEuL; EuAu; EvEuW; LinLib L, S; LitC 12; LngCEL; McGEWB; NewC; OxCEng 67, 85, 95; PenC EUR; RAdv 14, 13-2; RComWL; REn*

Castil-Blaze, Francois-Joseph
French. Musicologist
Writer on music, *De l'opera en France* (2 vols.), 1820-26.
b. Dec 1, 1784 in Cavaillon, France
d. Dec 11, 1857 in Paris, France
Source: *Baker 84; NewEOp 71*

Castillo, Antonio Canovas del
French. Fashion Designer
Designer for House of Lanvin, 1950-64; founded own couture house, 1964.
b. 1908 in Madrid, Spain
Source: *WorFshn*

Castillo, Edward (Daniel)
American. Educator
Wrote several papers on Native American topics including *Lost River: The Modoc Indian War of 1872-1873,* 1990.
b. Aug 25, 1947 in California
Source: *NotNaAm*

Castle, Barbara Anne Betts
English. Politician
Labour member, House of Commons, 1945-79; wrote *The Castle Diaries,* 1980.
b. Oct 6, 1911 in Chesterfield, England
Source: *BlueB 76; CurBio 67; DcPol; IntDcWB; IntWW 82; IntYB 82; InWom; NewYTBE 72; Who 85; WhoWor 82*

Castle, Frederick W
American. Army Officer, Aviator
Medal of Honor recipient, 1944; Air Commander, leader of 2,000 heavy bombers against German airfields; killed in action.
b. Oct 14, 1908 in Manila, Philippines
d. Dec 24, 1944 in Liege, Belgium
Source: *BioIn 7; MedHR; ObitOF 79*

Castle, Irene Foote
[Mrs. Vernon Castle]
American. Dancer
Rogers and Astaire portrayed her and husband in film *Story of Vernon and Irene Castle,* 1939; credited with starting bobbed hair fad.
b. Apr 7, 1893 in New Rochelle, New York
d. Jan 25, 1969 in Eureka Springs, Arkansas
Source: *CmpEPM; DcAmB S8; EncMT; Film 2; FilmgC; HalFC 88; InWom; NotAW MOD; OxCFilm; PlP&P; TwYS; WebAB 79; WhScrn 77; WorAl*

Castle, John
English. Actor
Films include *Blow-up; The Lion in Winter;* PBS series "I Claudius;" "Lillie."
b. Jan 14, 1940 in Croydon, England
Source: *HalFC 84, 88; ItaFilm; WhoHol 92; WhoThe 72, 77, 81*

Castle, Michael Newbold
American. Politician
Rep. governor of Delaware, 1985-93.
b. Jul 2, 1939 in Wilmington, Delaware
Source: *AlmAP 88; BiDrGov 1983, 1988; WhoAm 86; WhoAmP 73, 75, 81, 83, 85, 87, 89, 91, 93, 95; WhoWor 87*

Castle, Peggie
American. Actor
Films include *I the Jury; Jesse James' Women.*
b. Dec 22, 1927 in Appalachia, Virginia
d. Aug 11, 1973 in Hollywood, California
Source: *BioIn 18; FilmEn; FilmgC; HalFC 84, 88; LegTOT; SweetSg D; WhoHol B; WhScrn 77*

Castle, Vernon
[Vernon Blythe]
American. Dancer, Aviator
Dance innovator, 1910s; originated one-step, turkey trot, castle walk; husband of Irene, portrayed by Fred Astaire in 1939 film.
b. May 2, 1887 in Norwich, England
d. Feb 15, 1918 in Fort Worth, Texas
Source: *AmDec 1910; BioIn 5, 12, 16; CmpEPM; DcAmB; DcNAA; EncMT; EncVaud; EncWB; FacFETw; Film 1; FilmgC; LegTOT; NewGrDA 86; NotNAT B; OxCAmH; OxCAmT 84; OxCFilm; OxCPMus; PlP&P; WebAB 74, 79; WhAm 4; WhScrn 77, 83; WorAl; WorAlBi*

Castle, Wendell Keith
American. Artist, Sculptor
Noted for non-traditional furniture forms; unique creations in wood.
b. Nov 6, 1932 in Emporia, Kansas
Source: *DcTwDes; PenDiDA 89; WhoAm 78, 80, 82, 84, 86, 88, 90, 94; WhoAmA 73, 76, 78, 80, 82, 84, 86, 89, 91, 93; WhoE 91*

Castle, William
[William Schloss]
American. Director, Producer
Made over 100 horror films, including *Rosemary's Baby,* 1968.
b. Apr 24, 1914 in New York, New York
d. May 31, 1977 in Beverly Hills, California
Source: *BioIn 5; MiSFD 9N; NewYTET; PenEncH; PseudN 82; WhAm 7; WhoAm 74, 76, 78; WhoWest 74, 76; WhScrn 83; WorEFlm*

Castlemon, Harry
[Charles Austin Fosdick]
American. Children's Author
Noted for boys adventure series: *Gunboat,* 1864-68; *Rocky Mountain,* 1868-71.
b. Sep 16, 1842 in Randolph, New York
d. Aug 22, 1915
Source: *Alli SUP; AmAu; AmAu&B; BbD; BenetAL 91; BiD&SB; BioIn 1, 15; CarSB; ConAu 119; DcAmAu; DcAmB; DcLB 42; DcNAA; NatCAB 33; OxCAmL 65, 83, 95; OxCChiL; REnAL; WhAm 1*

Castlereagh, Robert Stewart, Viscount
English. Statesman, Politician
Foreign secretary, 1812-22; led coalition against Napoleon, having him confined to St. Helena; suicide victim.
b. Jun 18, 1769 in Dublin, Ireland
d. Aug 12, 1822 in London, England
Source: *Alli; BiDIrW; BioIn 16, 19, 20; CelCen; DcInB; DcIrW 2; LinLib S; McGEWB; OxCEng 85, 95; WebBD 83; WhDW*

Caston, Saul
American. Conductor
Conductor, Denver Symphony Orchestra, 1945-64.
b. Aug 22, 1901 in New York, New York
d. Jul 28, 1970 in Winston-Salem, North Carolina
Source: *Baker 78, 84, 92; BioIn 4, 11; NatCAB 56; NewGrDA 86; WhAm 5*

Castro, Raul
Cuban. Political Leader
First vice premier; younger brother of Fidel Castro.
b. May 13, 1927 in Mayari, Cuba
Source: *ColdWar 2; CurBio 77*

Castro (Ruz), Fidel
Cuban. Political Leader
Led campaign to overthrow Batista regime, 1959; prime minister, Cuba, 1959-76; pres., 1976—.
b. Aug 13, 1927 in Mayari, Cuba
Source: *Ballpl 90; BioIn 4, 5, 6, 7, 8, 9, 10, 11, 12, 13; ColdWar 2; ConAu 110, 129; CurBio 58, 70; DcAmSR; DcHiB; DcPol; DicTyr; EncCW; EncLatA; EncRev; FacFETw; GrLGrT; LinLib S; MakMC; McGEWB; News 91; WhDW; WhoHol 92, A; WhoWor 87; WorAl*

Castroviejo, Ramon
Spanish. Surgeon
One of first to perform successful cornea transplants; pioneered eyebanks.
b. Aug 24, 1904 in Logrono, Spain
d. Jan 1, 1987 in Madrid, Spain
Source: *BioIn 15; FacFETw; WhAm 9; WhoAm 74, 76*

Caswell, Richard
American. Politician, Army Officer
First governor of NC, 1777-79.
b. Aug 3, 1729 in Cecil County, Maryland
d. Nov 10, 1789 in Fayetteville, North Carolina
Source: *AmRev; ApCAB; BiAUS; BiDrAC; BiDrACR; BiDrUSC 89; BioIn 1, 5; DcAmB, S2; DcNCBi 1; Drake; EncAR; HarEnMi; HarEnUS; NatCAB 4; TwCBDA; WebAB 74; WebAMB; WhAm HS; WhAmRev*

Catalani, Alfredo
Italian. Composer
Operas included *La Wally,* 1852; work admired by Toscanini.
b. Jun 19, 1854 in Lucca, Italy
d. Aug 7, 1893 in Milan, Italy
Source: *Baker 78, 84, 92; BioIn 3, 5, 7, 20; IntDcOp; MetOEnc; NewAmDM; NewEOp 71; NewGrDO; NewOxM; OxCMus; OxDcOp; PenDiMP A*

Cater, Douglass
[Silas Douglass Cater, Jr.]
American. Author, Editor, Educator
Political analyst, wrote *Power in Washington,* 1964; *The Evolution & Fate of the Surgeon General's Report,* 1975.
b. Aug 24, 1923 in Montgomery, Alabama
d. Sep 15, 1995 in Chestertown, Maryland
Source: *AmAu&B; BioIn 8, 11, 21; BlueB 76; ConAu 1NR, 1R; EncTwCJ; IntAu&W 76, 82, 89; IntWW 74, 75, 76, 77, 78, 79, 80, 81, 82, 83, 89, 91, 93; PolProf J; WhAm 11; Who 82, 83, 85, 88, 90, 92, 94; WhoAm 74, 76, 78, 80, 82, 84, 86, 88, 90, 92, 94, 95, 96; WhoE 86; WhoWor 74; WhoWrEP 89, 92, 95; WrDr 76, 80, 82, 84, 86, 88, 90, 92*

Cates, Clifton Bledsoe
American. Military Leader
US Marine, 1917-54; distinguished veteran of WW I and II.
b. Aug 31, 1884 in Tiptonville, Tennessee
d. Jun 6, 1970 in Annapolis, Maryland
Source: *CurBio 50, 70; NewYTBE 70; WhAm 5*

Cates, Gilbert
American. Producer
Producer, Academy Awards telecast, 1989—.
b. Jun 6, 1934 in New York, New York
Source: *BiE&WWA; ConTFT 10; HalFC 84, 88; IntMPA 75, 76, 77, 78, 79, 81, 82, 84, 86, 88, 92, 94, 96; MiSFD 9; NewYTET; NotNAT; WhoAm 78, 80, 82, 84, 86, 88, 90, 92, 94, 95, 96, 97; WhoE 74, 75, 77; WhoEnt 92; WhoWest 80, 82, 84, 87*

Cates, Joseph
Producer, Director
Won Emmy for "Annie: The Woman in the Life of a Man," 1970; films include *Last Married Couple in America.*
b. 1924
Source: *BiE&WWA; IntMPA 84, 86, 88, 92, 94, 96; MiSFD 9; NewYTET; NotNAT; VarWW 85; WhoEnt 92*

Cates, Phoebe
[Phoebe Katz]
American. Actor
In TV movie "Lace," 1984; "Lace II," 1985; in film *Gremlins,* 1984; married to actor Kevin Kline.
b. Jun 16, 1964 in New York, New York
Source: *BioIn 13; ConTFT 5, 10; IntMPA 88; VarWW 85; WhoAm 92, 94, 95, 96, 97; WhoEnt 92; WhoHol 92*

Catesby, Mark
English. Naturalist
Documented the flora and fauna of early US; wrote *The Natural History of Carolina, Florida and the Bahama Islands,* 1731-1747.
b. 1683 in Castle Hedingham, England
d. 1749
Source: *AmWrBE; BenetAL 91; BiDAmS; BiInAmS; BioIn 2, 3, 15; DcAmB; DcNaB; DcNCBi 1; DcScB; EncCRAm; GrBIl; OxCAmL 83; REnAL; WhAm HS*

Cather, Willa (Sibert)
American. Author
Won Pulitzer for novel *One of Ours,* 1923; wrote *Death Comes for the Archbishop,* 1927.
b. Dec 7, 1873 in Winchester, Virginia
d. Apr 24, 1947 in New York, New York
Source: *ABCMeAm; AmAu&B; AmCulL; AmDec 1910; AmWomWr, 92; AmWr; ArtclWW 2; AtlBL; BenetAL 91; BiDAmJo; BioIn 12, 13, 14, 15, 16, 17, 18, 19, 20, 21; BlmGWL; CamGEL; CamGLE; CamHAL; CasWL; Chambr 3; ChhPo, S1, S3; CnDAL; ConAmA; ConAmL; ConAu 104, 128; ContDcW 89; CyWA 58, 89; DcAmB S4; DcArts; DcBiA; DcLB 9, 54, 78, DS1; DcLEL; DcNAA; EncAAH; EncAB-H 1974, 1996; EncFWF; EncWHA; EncWL, 3; EvLB; FemiCLE; GayLesB; GayLL; GoodHs; GrLiveH; GrWomW; HanAmWH; HerW, 84; IntDcWB; InWom, SUP; JBA 34; LegTOT; LibW; LinLib L, S; LngCTC; MagSAmL; MajTwCW; McGEWB; ModAL, S1; ModAWWr; ModWoWr; MorMA; NatCAB 44; NotAW; Novels; OxCAmH; OxCAmL 65, 83, 95; OxCCan; OxCEng 67, 85; OxCWoWr 95; PenC AM; PenNWW B; PeoHis; RAdv 1; RComAH; RComWL; RealN; REn; REnAL; REnAW; RfGAmL 87, 94; RfGShF; ShSCr 2; ShSWr; SmATA 30; TwCA, SUP; TwCLC 1, 11, 31; TwCRHW 94; TwCWr; TwCWW 91; WebAB 74, 79; WebE&AL; WhDW; WhNAA; WhoTwCL; WomNov; WorAlBi; WorLitC; WrPh*

Catherall, Arthur
[A R Channel; Dan Corby; Peter Hallard]
English. Author
Wrote dozens of boys' adventure stories: *Rod o' the Rail,* 1936.
b. Feb 6, 1906 in Bolton, England
d. 1980
Source: *Au&Wr 71; AuBYP 2, 3; BioIn 8, 9, 19; ConAu 5R, 38NR; IntAu&W 76, 77, 82; MajAI; MnBBF; OxCChiL; SmATA 3, 74; TwCChW 78, 83, 89, 95; WrDr 76, 80*

Catherine de Medici
Italian. Consort
Daughter of Lorenzo de Medici who married Henry II, 1533, adviser to son Charles IX, 1560-74.
b. Apr 13, 1519 in Florence, Italy
d. Jan 5, 1589 in Blois, France
Source: *BioIn 10; BlmGWL; DicTyr; Dis&D; LinLib S; LuthC 75; McGEWB; NewCol 75; OxCFr; OxCMus; REn; WebBD 83; WorAl*

Catherine of Alexandria, Saint
Religious Figure
Condemned to torture on a spiked wheel, later named "Catherine wheel"; later beheaded.
d. 307?
Source: *BioIn 2, 3, 4, 5, 6, 7, 8, 9; LuthC 75; NewC*

Catherine of Aragon
English. Consort
Mother of Mary I; marriage voided, 1533, so Henry could marry Anne Boleyn.
b. Dec 16, 1485 in Alcala de Henares, Spain
d. Jan 7, 1536 in Kimbolton, England
Source: *BioIn 4, 5, 6, 7, 8, 9, 10, 11, 12, 15, 18, 20; BlmGWL; ContDcW 89; DcCathB; Dis&D; HerW, 84; IntDcWB; InWom, SUP; LegTOT; LinLib S; NewCol 75; WomFir; WomWR; WorAl; WorAlBi*

Catherine of Genoa, Saint
[Caterina Fieschi]
Italian. Religious Figure
Converted from pleasure-loving Genoese society to spiritual life, 1473; doctrine contained in *Vita e dottrinea,* 1551.
b. 1447 in Genoa, Italy
d. Sep 14, 1510 in Genoa, Italy
Source: *BioIn 1, 2, 4, 5, 6, 7, 12; ContDcW 89; DcCathB; EncPaPR 91; IlEncMy; IntDcWB; InWom, SUP; LuthC 75; OxCEng 85, 95; WomWrRR*

Catherine of Siena, Saint
[Caterina Benincasa]
Italian. Religious Leader
Influenced Pope Gregory XI to return papacy to Rome from Avignon, 1376; canonized, 1461.
b. Mar 25, 1347 in Siena, Italy
d. Apr 29, 1380 in Rome, Italy
Source: *Benet 96; BioIn 1, 2, 3, 4, 5, 6, 7, 8, 10, 11, 12, 17, 20; CasWL; ContDcW 89; DcCathB; DcItL 1, 2; Dis&D; DivFut; IlEncMy; IntDcWB; InWom, SUP; LuthC 75; McGDA; McGEWB; MediWW; OxCEng 85, 95; RAdv 14; WomFir*

Catherine of Valois
French. Consort
Lived in obscurity after death of husband, Henry V, due to unpopular remarriage to poor commoner.
b. Oct 27, 1401 in Paris, France
d. Jan 3, 1437 in Bermondsey Abbey, England
Source: *BioIn 3, 4, 6, 11; DcNaB; InWom, SUP; NewCol 75*

Catherine the Great
[Catherine II; Sophia Augusta Frederike of Anhaltzerbst]
Russian. Ruler
Empress, 1762-96; worked toward westernization, expansion; made St. Petersburg cultural rival with Paris.
b. May 2, 1729 in Stettin, Germany
d. Nov 6, 1796 in Saint Petersburg, Russia
Source: *AmRev; Benet 87, 96; BlkwCE; CasWL; DcEuL; DcRusL; Dis&D; EncAmaz 91; EvEuW; GrLGrT; HalFC 84, 88; HanRL; HerW, 84; HisWorL; McGEWB; NewCol 75; OxCFr; OxDcOp; REn; WebBD 83; WhDW; WomWR; WorAl*

Catherwood, Frederick
English. Artist, Architect
Made archaeological recordings of antiquities of Nile Valley, Palestine, Arabia, later in the Mayan cities of Central America.
b. 1799 in London, England
d. 1854
Source: *AntBDN B; ArtLatA; ArtsAmW 1, 3; BiDBrA; BioIn 1, 2, 5, 6, 7, 8, 10, 14; DcArts; DcBrBI; DcBrWA; IlBEAAW; IntDcAn; NewYHSD*

Catiline, Lucius
Roman. Statesman
Governor of Africa, 67-66; conspired to assassinate consuls who voted his defeat; foiled by Cicero, his orations.
b. 108BC
d. 62BC
Source: *BioIn 7, 8; DcBiPP; NewCol 75*

Catledge, Turner
American. Journalist, Editor
Managing editor, *NY Times,* 1951-64; exec. editor, 1964-68.
b. Mar 17, 1901 in Ackerman, Mississippi
d. Apr 27, 1983 in New Orleans, Louisiana
Source: *AmAu&B; AnObit 1983; AuNews 1; BiDAmJo; BioIn 2, 5, 7, 8, 9, 10, 13, 14, 16, 19; BlueB 76; ConAu 57, 109; CurBio 75, 83N; DcLB 127; EncTwCJ; IntWW 74, 75, 76, 77, 78, 79, 80, 81, 82, 83, 83N; JrnUS; NewYTBE 70; NewYTBS 83; WhAm 8; Who 74, 82, 83; WhoAm 74, 76; WhoWor 74*

Catlett, Big Sid
[Sidney Catlett]
American. Jazz Musician
A leading Big Band drummer, 1930s-40s.
b. Jan 17, 1910 in Evansville, Idaho
d. Mar 25, 1951 in Chicago, Illinois
Source: *Baker 84, 92; BiDAfM; BiDAmM; BiDJaz; BioIn 10; DcAmB S5; IlEncJ; InB&W 80, 85; OxCPMus; PenEncP; WhoJazz 72; WorAl; WorAlBi*

Catlett, Elizabeth
Mexican. Sculptor, Printmaker
Artistic theme depicts the lives of black women.
b. Apr 15, 1919 in Washington, District of Columbia
Source: *BiDWomA; BioIn 14; BlkWAm; ConAmWS; ConBlB 2; DcTwCCu 5; InWom SUP; NegAl 83, 89; NorAmWA; NotBlAW 1; SmATA 82; WhoAfA 96; WhoAm 94, 95, 96, 97; WhoAmA 76, 78, 80, 82, 86, 89, 91, 93; WhoAmW 95; WhoBlA 75, 77, 80, 90, 92, 94; WhoWor 96*

Catlett, Walter
American. Actor
Comical performer of hundreds of cameo roles.
b. Feb 4, 1889 in San Francisco, California
d. Nov 14, 1960 in Woodland Hills, California
Source: *BioIn 5; EncAFC; EncMT; Film 2; FilmgC; HalFC 84, 88; MotPP; MovMk; NotNAT B; ObitOF 79; OxCAmT 84; OxCPMus; QDrFCA 92; Vers A; WhoHol B; WhScrn 74, 77, 83; WhThe*

Catlin, George
American. Explorer, Artist
Best known for paintings of Native Americans, tribal life, 1829-38.
b. Jul 26, 1796 in Wilkes-Barre, Pennsylvania
d. Dec 23, 1872 in Jersey City, New Jersey
Source: *Alli SUP; AmAu; AmAu&B; AmBi; AntBDN B; ApCAB; ArtsAmW 1; ArtsNiC; AtlBL; BbD; Benet 87, 96; BenetAL 91; BiD&SB; BiInAmS; BioIn 1, 3, 4, 5, 6, 7, 9, 10, 11, 12, 13, 14, 15, 17, 20, 21; BriEAA; CasWL; DcAmArt; DcAmAu; DcAmB; DcArts; DcEnL; DcLEL; DcNAA; DeafPAS; Drake; EncAAH; EncAB-H 1974, 1996; EncNAB; EvLB; HarEnUS; IlBEAAW; InSci; IntDcAn; LegTOT; McGDA; McGEWB; MemAm; NatCAB 3; NewYHSD; OxCAmH; OxCAmL 65, 83, 95; OxDcArt; PeoHis; REn; REnAL; REnAW; TwCBDA; WebAB 74, 79; WhAm HS; WhNaAH; WhWE; WorAl; WorAlBi*

Catlin, George Edward Gordon, Sir
English. Political Scientist, Educator
Co-founder, English Speaking Union, who wrote *Story of the Political Philosophies,* 1939.
b. Jul 29, 1896 in Liverpool, England
d. Feb 8, 1979
Source: *Au&Wr 71; ConAu 13R; IntAu&W 77; IntWW 74, 75, 76, 77, 78; IntYB 78, 79; WhAm 7; WhE&EA; WhNAA; Who 74; WhoAm 74, 76, 78; WrDr 76*

Cato, Marcus Porcius Censorius
[Cato the Censor; Cato the Elder]
Roman. Statesman, Historian
First Latin prose writer of importance: *On Farming,* 160 B.C.
b. 234BC in Tusculum, Italy
d. 149BC
Source: *BiD&SB; BlmGEL; CasWL; CyEd; DcBiPP; NewC; PenC CL; REn; WebBD 83; WhDW; WorAl*

Cato, Marcus Porcius Uticensis
[Cato the Younger]
Roman. Philosopher
Leading politician, head of an aristocratic faction; sided with Pompey against Caesar, defeated, committed suicide.
b. 95BC
d. 46BC
Source: *DcAmSR; DcBiPP; HarEnMi; WebBD 83*

Caton-Thompson, Gertrude
English. Archaeologist, Author
African researcher; wrote *Zimbabwe Culture.*
b. Feb 1, 1888 in London, England
d. Apr 18, 1985 in Worcestershire, England
Source: *AnObit 1985; ConAu 116, 122; DcNaB 1981; IntAu&W 77; IntWW 74, 75, 76, 77, 78, 79, 80, 81, 82, 83; Who 83; WhoWor 74, 76; WrDr 76*

Catt, Carrie Chapman
American. Feminist
Organized League of Women Voters, 1920; helped win women's suffrage.
b. Jan 9, 1859 in Ripon, Wisconsin
d. Mar 9, 1947 in New Rochelle, New York
Source: *AmDec 1910; AmPeW; AmWom; BiCAW; BiDMoPL; BioAmW; BioIn 1, 2, 3, 4, 5, 6, 8, 10, 11, 14, 15, 17, 19, 20, 21; CurBio 40, 47; DcAmB S4; DcAmSR; EncAB-H 1974; GoodHs; GrLiveH; HanAmWH; LinLib L, S; MorMA; NotAW; OxCAmH; OxCWoWr 95; PolPar; RComAH; WebAB 79; WhAm 2; WhAmP; WomChHR; WomWWA 14; WorAl; WorAlBi*

Cattani, Richard J
American. Journalist
Editor, *Christian Science Monitor,* 1988—.
b. Jun 17, 1936 in Detroit, Michigan
Source: *WhoAm 90*

Cattell, James McKeen
American. Psychologist, Editor
Founder, Psychological Corp., 1921; editor, *Science* from 1894.
b. May 25, 1860 in Easton, Pennsylvania
d. Jan 20, 1944 in Lancaster, Pennsylvania
Source: *AmAu&B; BiDAmEd; BiDPsy; BioIn 2, 6, 7, 9, 12, 13, 15, 16; CurBio 44; DcAmB S3; DcNAA; DcScB; EncWB; GaEncPs; HarEnUS; InSci; JrnUS; LinLib S; NamesHP; NatCAB 13; OxCAmH; TwCBDA; WebAB 74, 79; WebBD 83*

Catto, Thomas Sivewright, Baron
English. Financier
Governor of Bank of England, 1944-49; oversaw transition of Bank from private to public ownership, 1946.
b. Mar 15, 1879 in Newcastle-upon-Tyne, England
d. Aug 23, 1959 in Holmbury Saint Mary, England
Source: *BioIn 15; CurBio 44; DcNaB 1951; GrBr; WhAm 6*

Catton, Bruce
[Charles Bruce Catton]
American. Author, Journalist
Historical works on the Civil War include 1953 Pulitzer winner, *A Stillness at Appomattox.*
b. Oct 9, 1899 in Petoskey, Michigan
d. Aug 28, 1978 in Frankfort, Michigan
Source: *Alli SUP; AmAu&B; AuNews 1; Benet 87; BenetAL 91; BioIn 3, 4, 5, 6, 7, 8, 9, 10, 11, 12, 13, 15, 17; BlueB 76; CelR; ConAu 5R, 7NR, 81; ConLC 35; CurBio 54, 78N; DcAmB S10; DcLB 17; DcLEL 1940; EncSoH; FacFETw; IntAu&W 76, 77; IntWW 74, 75, 76, 77, 78; JrnUS; LinLib L, S; MichAu 80; OxCAmL 65, 83, 95; PenC AM; PeoHis; RAdv 14, 13-3; REn; REnAL; SmATA 2, 24N; TwCA SUP; WebAB 74, 79; WhAm 7; Who 74; WhoAm 74, 76, 78; WhoWor 74, 78; WorAl; WorAlBi; WrDr 76*

Cattrall, Kim
American. Actor
Played Judy McCoy in movie *Bonfire of the Vanities*; played Valeris, a Vulcan, in movie *Star Trek VI: The Undiscovered Country.*
b. Aug 21, 1956 in Liverpool, England
Source: *ConTFT 8, 15; IntMPA 88, 92, 94, 96; LegTOT; WhoHol 92*

Catullus, Gaius Valerius
Roman. Poet
Wrote over 100 lyric poems.
b. c. 84BC in Verona, Gaul
d. c. 54BC in Rome, Italy
Source: *AtlBL; BioIn 1, 3, 4, 5, 14, 18; BlmGEL; CasWL; ClMLC 18; CyWA 58; DcArts; Grk&L; LegTOT; LngCEL; McGEWB; NewC; OxCClL 89; OxCEng 67, 85, 95; PenC CL; RComWL; REn; WebBD 83; WhDW; WorAl; WorAlBi*

Cauchon, Pierre
French. Religious Leader
Bishop responsible for the execution of Joan of Arc, 1430.
b. 1371 in Reims, France
d. Dec 18, 1442 in Roven, France
Source: *MediFra*

Caudill, Rebecca
[Mrs. James Ayars]
American. Children's Author
Wrote of childhood in KY, TN; runner-up, Newbery Award, 1964, for *A Pocket Full of Cricket.*
b. Feb 2, 1899 in Poor Fork, Kentucky
d. Oct 2, 1985 in Urbana, Illinois
Source: *AmAu&B; AuBYP 2, 3; BioIn 2, 6, 7, 9, 10, 14, 15, 19; ChhPo S1; ChlBkCr; ConAu 2NR, 5R, 44NR, 117; CurBio 50, 86N; DcAmChF 1960; ForWC 70; InWom; LiHiK; MajAI; MorJA; SmATA 1, 44N; TwCChW 78, 83, 89; TwCYAW; WhAm 9; WhoAm 74, 76, 78, 80, 82, 84; WhoAmW 58, 61, 64, 66, 68, 70, 72, 74; WrDr 76, 80, 82, 84, 86*

Caulfield, Joan
[Beatrice Joan Caulfield]
American. Actor
Ex-model, Broadway, movie star, turned to TV, 1953; starred in "My Favorite Husband," 1953-57.
b. Jun 1, 1922 in West Orange, New Jersey
d. Jun 18, 1991 in Los Angeles, California
Source: *AnObit 1991; BioIn 1, 3, 17, 18; CurBio 54, 91N; FilmgC; HalFC 84, 88; IntMPA 77, 84, 86, 88; InWom; LegTOT; MotPP; News 92, 92-1; WhAm 10; WhoAmW 58; WhoHol 92, A*

Caulfield, Maxwell
English. Actor
Played Miles Colby on TV series "The Colbys," 1985-87; married to Juliet Mills.
b. Nov 23, 1959 in Derbyshire, England
Source: *BioIn 21; ConTFT 3, 10; IntMPA 88, 92, 94, 96; LegTOT; NewYTBS 81; WhoHol 92*

Caulkins, Tracy
American. Swimmer
Won gold medal, 1984 LA Olympics; invented "Caulkins flutter" style of breaststroke swimming.
b. Jan 11, 1963 in Nashville, Tennessee
Source: *BiDAmSp BK; BioIn 11; EncWomS; InWom SUP; LegTOT; WhoSpor; WorAl; WorAlBi*

Causley, Charles Stanley
English. Author
Folk poetry is based on his Cornish childhood, later yrs. in the navy, as a teacher.
b. Aug 24, 1917 in Launceston, England
Source: *ConAu 5NR, 9R; ConLC 7; ConPo 85; DcLB 27; OxCEng 85; SmATA 3; WhDW; Who 85; WorAu 1950; WrDr 86*

Cauthen, Steve
American. Jockey, Sportscaster
First jockey to win both US Triple Crown, 1978, British Epsom Derby, 1985; Hall of Fame, 1994.
b. May 1, 1960 in Covington, Kentucky
Source: *BioIn 11, 12, 13, 14, 15, 18, 19, 20; BkPepl; CurBio 77; FacFETw; LegTOT; NewYTBS 81; WhoAm 78, 80, 82, 84, 86, 90, 92, 94, 95, 96, 97; WhoSpor; WhoWor 91; WorAl*

Cavaco Silva, Anibal Antonio
Portuguese. Political Leader
Prime minister, Portugal, 1985-96.
b. Jul 15, 1939 in Boliqueime, Portugal
Source: *BioIn 14; CurBio 91; IntWW 91; WhoWor 91*

Cavalcanti, Alberto
Brazilian. Director
Produced documentary, commercial films in Brazil; exiled to Europe on suspicion of being a communist.
b. Feb 6, 1897 in Rio de Janeiro, Brazil
d. Aug 23, 1982 in Paris, France
Source: *AnObit 1982; BiDFilm, 94; BioIn 9, 10, 12, 13, 15; ConAu 107; DcFM; EncEurC; FilmgC; HalFC 84, 88; IntDcF 1-2, 2-2; IntMPA 75, 76, 77, 78, 79, 81, 82; ItaFilm; MovMk; OxCFilm; Who 82; WorEFlm; WorFDir 1*

Cavalier, Jean
French. Revolutionary
Led Camisards Calvinist insurgents, against King Louis XIV, 1703; fled to England.
b. Nov 28, 1681 in Mas Roux, France
d. May 17, 1740 in London, England
Source: *DcNaB; LuthC 75; NewCol 75; OxCFr; WebBD 83*

Cavaliere, Felix
[The Rascals]
American. Singer, Musician
Keyboardist, vocalist with blue-eyed soul group; has recorded several solo albums.
b. Nov 29, 1944 in Pelham, New York
Source: *WhoRocM 82*

Cavalieri, Lina
[Natalina Cavalieri]
Italian. Opera Singer
Dramatic soprano noted for her beauty; Gina Lollobrigida starred in film of her life, 1957.
b. Dec 25, 1874 in Viterbo, Italy
d. Feb 8, 1944 in Florence, Italy
Source: *Baker 78, 84, 92; BioIn 11, 14, 15; Film 1, 2; IntDcOp; InWom, SUP; ItaFilm; MetOEnc; MusSN; NewEOp 71; NewGrDO; OxDcOp; PenDiMP; TwYS; WhAm 5; WhoHol B; WhScrn 77, 83*

Cavallaro, Carmen
American. Bandleader, Composer
Big Band pianist, noted for chording technique; played soundtrack *Eddy Duchin Story*, 1956.
b. May 6, 1913 in New York, New York
Source: *ASCAP 66; BgBands 74; BiDAmM; CmpEPM; LegTOT; OxCPMus; PenEncP; RadStar*

Cavalli, Francesco
Italian. Composer
Developed modern opera; wrote over 40 operas, some revived in 1970s.
b. Feb 14, 1602 in Crema, Italy
d. Jan 14, 1676 in Venice, Italy
Source: *Baker 84; BioIn 4, 7, 8, 11, 12; IntDcOp; LinLib S; MetOEnc; NewEOp 71; NewOxM; OxCMus; OxDcOp*

Cavallini, Pietro
Italian. Artist
Mosaicist, frescoist; an innovator of naturalism who broke with Byzantine style.
b. 1250 in Rome, Italy
d. 1330
Source: *AtlBL; BioIn 5; McGDA; NewCol 75; WhDW*

Cavanagh, Jerome Patrick
American. Lawyer, Politician
Mayor of Detroit, 1962-70.
b. Jun 11, 1928 in Detroit, Michigan
d. Nov 27, 1979 in Lexington, Kentucky
Source: *AmCath 80; BioIn 6, 7, 8, 11, 12; DcAmB S10; WhAm 7; WhoAm 74, 76, 78*

Cavanaugh, Hobart
American. Actor
Character actor; played assortment of meek, henpecked, nervous little men, sometimes villain.
b. 1887 in Virginia City, Nevada
d. Apr 27, 1950 in Woodland Hills, California
Source: *FilmgC; MovMk; ObitOF 79; Vers A; WhoHol B; WhScrn 74, 77, 83*

Cavanna, Betty
[Betsy Allen; Elizabeth Allen Cavanna; Elizabeth Headley]
American. Children's Author
Has written books for girls for 30 yrs., including *Going on Sixteen.*
b. Jun 24, 1909 in Camden, New Jersey
Source: *Au&Wr 71; AuBYP 2, 3; BioIn 2, 6, 7, 9, 14, 15, 19; ChlBkCr; ConAu 6NR, 9R, X; ConLC 12; CurBio 50; DcAmChF 1960; IntAu&W 76, 77, 82, 89, 91; InWom; MajAI; MorJA; PenNWW B; SmATA 1, 4AS, 30; TwCChW 78, 83, 89; TwCYAW; WhoAmW 58, 61; WrDr 76, 82, 84, 86, 88, 90, 92, 94, 96*

Cavarretta, Phil(ip Joseph)
American. Baseball Player
Outfielder, first baseman, Chicago, 1934-55; won NL batting title, 1945.
b. Jul 19, 1916 in Chicago, Illinois
Source: *Ballpl 90; BioIn 3, 4, 15; WhoProB 73*

Cavazos, Lauro F(red, Jr.)
American. Educator, Government Official
US Secretary of Education, 1988-90; first Hispanic-American cabinet officer in US history.
b. Jan 4, 1927 in King Ranch, Texas
Source: *AmMWSc 92; BiDrUSE 89; BioIn 16; CngDr 89; CurBio 89; IntWW 91; MexAmB; News 89-2; NewYTBS 88; WhoAm 90; WhoAmP 91; WhoE 91; WhoHisp 92; WhoSSW 88; WhoWor 91*

Cave, Nicholas Edward
[Nick Cave]
Australian. Singer, Songwriter
Formed band, Boys Next Door, in mid-1970s, band changed name to The Birthday Party in 1980 and energized the Gothic or "goth" rock movement; formed new band in 1984 called Nick Cave and the Bad Seeds and released *From Her to Eternity*, 1984; released *Henry's Dream* in 1992.
b. 1957 in Warracknabeal, Australia
Source: *BioIn 17, 20; ConMus 10; EncRkSt*

Cavell, Edith Louisa
English. Nurse
Executed by Germans for helping allied soldiers in WW I.
b. Dec 4, 1865 in Swardeston, England
d. Oct 12, 1915 in Brussels, Belgium
Source: *BioIn 10, 11; GoodHs; HerW; InWom, SUP; LngCTC; WhDW; WomFir*

Cavendish, Henry
English. Chemist, Physicist
Discovered nitric acid; devised Cavendish experiment, which determined gravitational constant, density of Earth, late 1790s.
b. Oct 10, 1731 in Nice, France
d. Feb 24, 1810 in London, England
Source: *Alli; AsBiEn; BiESc; BioIn 1, 2, 3, 4, 5, 6, 8, 9, 10, 12, 14, 15; CamDcSc; CelCen; DcBiPP; DcInv; DcNaB; DcScB; EncEnl; InSci; LarDcSc; LinLib S; McGEWB; NewC; NewCol 75; WebBD 83; WhDW; WorAl; WorAlBi; WorScD*

Cavendish, Margaret
English. Poet, Dramatist
Known for her contribution to the genre of biographical writing; author of *A True Relation of the Birth, Breeding, and Life of Margaret Cavendish, Duchess of Newcastle,* 1656.
b. 1623 in Colchester, England
d. 1673
Source: *BiDEWW; BlmGWL; ContDcW 89; EncBrWW; LitC 30; RfGEnL 91; WomSc*

Cavendish, Thomas
English. Navigator
Third to circumnavigate globe, 1586.
b. 1555? in Suffolk, England
d. Jun 1592
Source: *Alli; BioIn 1, 2, 3, 4, 10; NewC; NewCol 75; OxCShps; WebBD 83*

Cavendish, William, Duke of Newcastle
English. Statesman, Author
Governor to Prince of Wales, 1638-41; wrote several works on horsemanship, plays, poems.
b. 1592
d. Dec 25, 1676 in London, England
Source: *Alli; BritAu; CasWL; CroE&S; DcEnL; DcNaB; WebBD 83*

Cavett, Dick
[Richard Alva Cavett]
American. Entertainer
Won 3 Emmys for ABC's "Dick Cavett Show," 1968-72; hosted PBS's "The Dick Cavett Show," for 5 years; wrote *Cavett,* 1974.
b. Nov 19, 1936 in Gibbon, Nebraska
Source: *BioIn 7, 8, 9, 10, 11, 12, 13; BioNews 74; BkPepl; CelR, 90; ConTFT 1, 8, 15; CurBio 70; IntMPA 86, 96; LegTOT; NewYTBS 77, 81; WhoAm 74, 76, 78, 80, 82, 84, 86, 88, 90, 92, 94, 95, 96, 97; WhoCom; WhoEnt 92; WhoHol 92; WorAl; WorAlBi*

Cavour, Camillo Benso, Conte di
Italian. Statesman
Instrumental in uniting Italy under House of Savoy, early 1860s.
b. Aug 10, 1810 in Turin, Italy
d. Jun 6, 1861 in Turin, Italy
Source: *BiD&SB; BioIn 1, 3, 5, 6, 8, 9, 10, 11, 14, 19, 20, 21; DcBiPP; Dis&D;*

McGEWB; NewC; NewCol 75; REn; WebBD 83; WhDW; WorAl; WorAlBi

Cawein, Madison Julius
American. Poet
Wrote numerous poems on his native Kentucky.
b. Mar 23, 1865 in Louisville, Kentucky
d. Dec 7, 1914 in Louisville, Kentucky
Source: *AmAu&B; BbD; BiDSA; DcEnL; OxCAmL 83; REn; REnAL*

Caxton, William
English. Translator, Printer
First English printer, 1476; published first book printed in English, 1475.
b. Aug 13, 1422 in Weald, England
d. 1491 in Westminster, England
Source: *Alli; BbD; Benet 87, 96; BiD&SB; BioIn 1, 2, 3, 4, 5, 6, 7, 9, 10, 11, 14; BlmGEL; BritAu; CasWL; Chambr 1; CrtT 1; DcArts; DcCathB; DcEnA; DcEnL; DcEuL; DcLB 170; DcLEL; DcNaB; EvLB; InSci; LegTOT; LinLib L, S; LngCEL; LuthC 75; McGEWB; MouLC 1; NewC; OxCDecA; OxCEng 67, 85, 95; OxCMus; PenC ENG; REn; WebE&AL; WhDW; WorAl; WorAlBi*

Cayatte, Andre
French. Director
Films on social, legal problems include *Le Dossier Noir,* 1955.
b. Feb 3, 1909 in Carcassonne, France
Source: *BiDFilm, 94; BioIn 15, 16; DcFM; FilmgC; HalFC 84, 88; IntDcF 1-2, 2-2; ItaFilm; OxCFilm; WhoFr 79; WorEFlm; WorFDir 1*

Cayce, Edgar
American. Psychic
Worked from trances to yield diagnoses, prescriptions for patients.
b. Mar 18, 1877 in Hopkinsville, Kentucky
d. Jan 3, 1945 in Virginia Beach, Virginia
Source: *BiDAmCu; BiDPara; BioIn 5, 6, 7, 8, 9, 10, 11, 13, 16, 17, 19, 21; DcAmReB 2; DivFut; EncO&P 1, 2, 3; EncPaPR 91; LegTOT; NewAgE 90; RelLAm 91; WhAm 4; WorAl; WorAlBi*

Cayley, Arthur
English. Mathematician
Developed algebraic matrices, invariants.
b. Aug 16, 1821 in Richmond, England
d. Jan 26, 1895 in Cambridge, England
Source: *Alli, SUP; BiDLA; BiESc; BioIn 21; CamDcSc; CelCen; DcBiPP; DcNaB S1; DcScB; InSci; LarDcSc; NewCol 75; WhDW; WorScD*

Cayley, George, Sir
English. Engineer, Scientist
Founder of aerodynamics, who built first glider, 1853; developed some elements of modern airplane.
b. Dec 27, 1773 in Yorkshire, England
d. Dec 15, 1857 in Yorkshire, England
Source: *Alli; BiESc; BioIn 2, 3, 4, 5, 6, 7, 8, 9, 12, 14; CamDcSc; DcInv; DcNaB MP; InSci; LarDcSc; NewCol 75; WhDW; WorAl; WorAlBi; WorInv*

Cazenove, Christopher
English. Actor
Films include *Heat and Dust,* 1983; played Ben Carrington on TV series "Dynasty," 1985-87.
b. Dec 17, 1945 in Winchester, England
Source: *ConTFT 4; HalFC 88; IntMPA 92, 94, 96; WhoHol 92; WhoThe 81*

Ceasar, Shirley
"Queen of Gospel"
American. Singer
Received Grammy Awards for the popular song "Put Your Hand in the Hand of the Man from Galilee," 1971, and the albums *Rejoice,* 1980, *Sailin',* 1984 *He's Working It Out For You,* 1992 and *Stand Still,* 1994; inducted into Gospel Hall of Fame, 1982; recipient of NAACP Achievement Award, 1987.
b. Oct 13, 1938 in Durham, North Carolina
Source: *AfrAmAl 6*

Ceausescu, Nicolae
Romanian. Political Leader
Pres. of Romania, 1974-89.
b. Jan 26, 1918 in Scornicesti-Olt, Romania
d. Dec 25, 1989 in Bucharest, Romania
Source: *AnObit 1989; BioIn 7, 8, 9, 10, 11, 12, 13; ColdWar 2; CurBio 67, 90, 90N; DcPol; DcTwHis; DicTyr; EncCW; EncRev; FacFETw; HisWorL; IntWW 74, 75, 76, 77, 78, 79, 80, 81, 82, 83, 89; IntYB 78, 79, 80, 81, 82; LegTOT; McGEWB; News 90, 90-2; NewYTBE 70; NewYTBS 78, 79, 89; WhAm 11; WhoGov 72; WhoSocC 78; WhoSoCE 89; WhoWor 74, 76, 78, 80, 84, 87, 89; WorAlBi*

Cebotari, Maria
Russian. Opera Singer
Soprano with Berlin State Opera, 1935-44; noted for Mozart, R Strauss roles.
b. Feb 10, 1910 in Kishinev, Russia
d. Jun 9, 1949 in Vienna, Austria
Source: *Baker 78, 84, 92; BioIn 2, 10; IntDcOp; InWom; ItaFilm; MetOEnc; NewEOp 71; NewGrDO; OxDcOp; PenDiMP*

Cecchetti, Enrico
Italian. Dancer
Taught Pavlova, Nijinsky, Fokine technique of progressive exercises.
b. Jun 21, 1850 in Rome, Papal States
d. Nov 16, 1928 in Milan, Italy
Source: *BiDD; BioIn 3, 4, 5, 8, 9; DcArts; IntDcB; NotNAT B; WhDW; WhThe*

Cecchi, Emilio
[Il Tarlo]
Italian. Essayist, Critic
Credited with the introduction into Italy of the essay as a literary genre.
b. Jul 14, 1884 in Florence, Italy
d. Sep 5, 1966 in Rome, Italy
Source: *BioIn 1, 7; CasWL; ClDMEL 47; DcFM; DcItL 1, 2; EncEurC; EncWL; EvEuW; ItaFilm; PenC EUR*

Cecelia, Saint
Religious Figure
Martyr, regarded as patroness of musicians; feast day Nov 22.
d. 230 in Rome, Italy
Source: *BioIn 1, 2, 3, 4, 5, 6, 7, 8; NewC; REn*

Cech, Thomas Robert
American. Biologist, Biochemist, Scientist
Won Nobel Prize in Chemistry, 1989, for discovering RNA to actively aid chemical reactions in cells.
b. Dec 8, 1947 in Chicago, Illinois
Source: *AmMWSc 79, 82, 86, 89, 92, 95; IntWW 91, 93; WhoAm 88, 90, 92, 94, 95, 96, 97; WhoFrS 84; WhoNob 90, 95; WhoScEn 94, 96; WhoTech 89; WhoWest 89, 92, 94, 96; WhoWor 91, 93, 95, 96, 97; WorAlBi*

Cecil, Edgar Algernon Robert
English. Statesman, Author
Won Nobel Peace Prize, 1937; among architects of League of Nations.
b. Sep 14, 1864 in London, England
d. Nov 24, 1958 in Tunbridge Wells, England
Source: *DcNaB 1951; McGEWB; WebBD 83; WhoNob*

Cecil, Edward Christian David Gascoyne
English. Educator, Biographer
Oxford English literature professor, 1948-69; wrote *Hardy, the Novelist,* 1943; *A Portrait of Jane Austen,* 1978.
b. Apr 9, 1902 in London, England
d. Jan 1, 1986 in Cranborne, England
Source: *Benet 87; BioIn 14, 16; CamGLE; ConAu 34NR, 118; EvLB; FacFETw; NewYTBS 86; OxCEng 85; RAdv 13-1; TwCA, SUP; Who 83, 85*

Cedras, Raoul
Haitian. Military Leader
Military commander to Haitian President Jean-Bertrand Aristide.
b. 1950, Haiti
Source: *CurBio 95; News 94*

Cefalo, Jimmy
[James Carmen Cefalo]
American. Football Player, Sportscaster
Wide receiver, Miami, 1978-84; analyst with NBC Sports.
b. Oct 6, 1956 in Pittston, Pennsylvania
Source: *FootReg 85; NewYTBS 75, 78*

Cela (Trulock), Camilo Jose
Spanish. Writer
Won Nobel Prize for literature, 1989; most popular novel *La Familia de Pascual Duarte.*
b. May 11, 1916 in Iria Flavia, Spain
Source: *Benet 87, 96; BestSel 90-2; BioIn 2, 3, 7, 8, 10, 12, 16, 17, 18, 21; CasWL; CnMWL; ConAu 10AS, 21NR, 21R, 32NR; ConFLW 84; ConLC 4, 13, 59; ConSSWr; CurBio 90; DcArts; DcHiB; DcLB Y89; EncWL 3; EuWr 13; EvEuW; HispLC; HispWr; IntAu&W 76, 77, 89, 91; IntvSpW; IntWW 74, 75, 76, 77, 78, 79, 80, 81, 82, 83, 89, 91, 93; MajTwCW; ModRL; ModSpP S; NobelP 91; Novels; OxCSpan; RAdv 14, 13-2; REn; RfGWoL 95; TwCWr; Who 94; WhoNob 90, 95; WhoTwCL; WhoWor 74, 76, 78, 80, 82, 84, 87, 89, 91, 93, 95, 96, 97; WorAu 1950*

Celan, Paul
[Paul Antschel]
Romanian. Poet
Surrealistic writings deal with his experience as a Jew under Nazi opression; works include *Poppy and Memory,* 1952.
b. Nov 23, 1920 in Cernauti, Romania
d. May 1, 1970 in Paris, France
Source: *Benet 96; BioIn 10, 12, 14; CasWL; ConAu 33NR, 85, X; ConLC 10, 19, 53, 82; DcLB 69; EncWL 2, 3; FacFETw; GrFLW; LiExTwC; LinLib L; MajTwCW; MakMC; ModGL; OxCEng 85, 95; OxCGer 76, 86; PenC EUR; PoeCrit 10; RAdv 14; RfGWoL 95; TwCWr; WhoTwCL; WorAlBi; WorAu 1950*

Celebrezze, Anthony Joseph
American. Politician, Judge
Secretary of HEW, 1962-65.
b. Sep 4, 1910 in Anzi, Italy
Source: *BiDrUSE 71, 89; BioIn 6, 7, 10, 11; BlueB 76; CurBio 63; IntWW 83; PolProf J, K; WhoAm 74; WhoAmL 78, 79; WhoAmP 73; WhoGov 72, 75, 77; WhoMW 74, 80, 82, 84*

Celeste, Richard F
American. Politician
Democratic governor of OH, 1983-91, succeeded by George Voinovich.
b. Nov 11, 1937 in Cleveland, Ohio
Source: *AlmAP 84; WhoMW 78, 84, 86, 88, 90; WhoWor 84, 87, 89, 91*

Celestine V, Saint
[Pietro da Morrone]
Italian. Religious Leader
Only pope to voluntarily resign, 1294; five-month pontificate marked by chaos.
b. 1210? in Isernia, Italy
d. May 19, 1296 in Rome, Italy
Source: *DcCathB; NewCol 75; WebBD 83*

Celibidache, Sergiu
Romanian. Conductor
Led European orchestras from 1940s; US debut, 1984.
b. Jun 28, 1912 in Roman, Romania
d. Aug 14, 1996 in Paris, France
Source: *Baker 78, 84, 92; BioIn 7, 10, 13, 14; FacFETw; IntWW 74, 75, 76, 77, 78, 79, 80, 81, 82, 83, 89, 91, 93; IntWWM 90; NewAmDM; NewGrDM 80; NewYTBS 27; PenDiMP; Who 74, 82, 83, 85, 88, 90, 92, 94; WhoEnt 92; WhoWor 74, 84, 87, 91*

Celine, Louis-Ferdinand
[Louis-Ferdinand Destouches]
French. Author
Misanthropic views expressed in *Journey to the End of Night,* 1932, *Death on the Installment Plan,* 1936.
b. May 27, 1894 in Courbevoie, France
d. Jul 4, 1961 in Meudon, France
Source: *AtlBL; Benet 87, 96; BiDExR; BioIn 17, 18, 20, 21; CasWL; ClDMEL 47; ConAu 28NR, 85; ConLC 1, 3, 4, 7, 9, 15, 47; CyWA 58, 89; DcLB 72; DcTwCCu 2; EncWL 3; EuWr 11; EvEuW; FacFETw; GrFLW; GuFrLit 1; LiExTwC; LinLib L; LngCTC; MajTwCW; MakMC; ModFrL; ModRL; Novels; OxCEng 85, 95; OxCFr; PenC EUR; RAdv 14, 13-2; REn; RfGWoL 95; TwCA, SUP; TwCWr; WhAm 4; WhoTwCL*

Celler, Emanuel
American. Politician
Liberal Dem. congressman from NY, 1923-72; wrote, fought for Civil Rights Acts of 1957, 1960, 1964.
b. May 6, 1888 in New York, New York
d. Jan 15, 1981 in New York, New York
Source: *AnObit 1981; BiDrAC; BiDrUSC 89; BioIn 2, 3, 4, 5, 7, 9, 11, 12; CelR; ConAu 108; CurBio 49, 66, 81, 81N; DcAmImH; FacFETw; IntWW 74, 75, 76, 77, 78, 79, 80; JeAmHC; NewYTBE 72; NewYTBS 81; PolProf E, J, K, NF, T; St&PR 75; WhAm 7; WhoAm 74, 76, 78; WhoAmP 73, 75, 77, 79; WhoE 74; WhoGov 72; WorAl; WorAlBi*

Cellini, Benvenuto
Italian. Sculptor
Goldsmith; designed intricate metalwork; noted for *Autobiography,* first printed, 1728.
b. Nov 1, 1500 in Florence, Italy
d. Feb 14, 1571 in Florence, Italy
Source: *AtlBL; BbD; Benet 87, 96; BiD&SB; BioIn 1, 2, 3, 4, 5, 6, 7, 8, 9, 11, 12, 13, 14, 15; CasWL; CyWA 58; DcArts; DcBiPP; DcCathB; DcEuL; DcItL 1, 2; DcNiCA; Dis&D; EncO&P 2, 3; EuAu; EvEuW; InSci; IntDcAA 90; LegTOT; LinLib L, S; LitC 7; McGDA; McGEWB; NewC; NewEOp 71; OxCArt; OxCDecA; OxCEng 67, 85, 95; OxCFr; OxDcArt; PenC EUR; PenDiDA 89; RAdv 14, 13-3; RComWL; REn; WhDW; WorAl; WorAlBi*

Celsius, Anders
Swedish. Astronomer
Invented centigrade temperature scale, 1742.
b. Nov 27, 1701 in Uppsala, Sweden
d. Apr 25, 1744 in Uppsala, Sweden
Source: *AsBiEn; BiESc; BioIn 3, 11, 12, 13, 14; BlkwCE; CamDcSc; DcBiPP; DcInv; DcScB; InSci; LarDcSc; LegTOT; LinLib S; OxCMed 86; WhDW; WorAl; WorAlBi; WorInv*

Celsus, Aulus Cornelius
Roman. Writer
Classic medical text, *De Medicina,* provided historical insight into ancient medical practices.
Source: *BioIn 1, 5, 9, 12; CasWL; DcBiPP; DcScB; Grk&L; LarDcSc; LinLib L; LuthC 75; OxCMed 86; PenC CL*

Cenci, Beatrice
"Beautiful Parricide"
Italian. Noblewoman
Beheaded for plotting father's death; subject of Shelley's tragedy *The Cenci,* 1819.
b. Feb 6, 1577 in Rome, Italy
d. Sep 11, 1599 in Rome, Italy
Source: *Benet 87, 96; BioIn 4, 7, 8, 9, 11, 12, 17; InWom, SUP; NewCol 75; REn; WebBD 83*

Cepeda, Orlando Manuel
"Cha-Cha"; "The Baby Bull"
Puerto Rican. Baseball Player
First baseman, 1958-74; led NL in home runs, RBIs, 1961; MVP, 1967.
b. Sep 17, 1937 in Ponce, Puerto Rico
Source: *BaseEn 88; BiDAmSp BB; BioIn 4, 5, 6, 8, 11; CurBio 68; InB&W 80; WhoAm 74; WhoProB 73*

Cerdan, Marcel B
French. Boxer
World middleweight champ, 1948; killed in plane crash; Hall of Fame, 1962.
b. Jul 22, 1916 in Sidi Bel-Abbes, Algeria
d. Oct 27, 1949, Azores
Source: *BioIn 1, 2, 8; WhoBox 74*

Cerezo (Arevalo), Vinicio
[Marco Vinicio Cerezo]
Guatemalan. Political Leader
President of Guatemala, 1986—; first elected civilian since 1970.
b. Dec 26, 1942 in Guatemala City, Guatemala
Source: *BioIn 13; CurBio 87; WhoWor 87, 89, 91*

Cerf, Bennett Alfred
American. Publisher, Journalist
Co-founded Random House Publishers, 1927; panelist on TVs "What's My Line?," 1952-68.
b. May 25, 1898 in New York, New York
d. Aug 27, 1971 in Mount Kisco, New York

Source: *AmAu&B; Au&Wr 71; AuBYP 2; BiE&WWA; BioIn 1, 2, 3, 4, 5, 6, 7, 8, 9, 10, 11, 12, 13; ConAu P-2; CurBio 41, 58, 71; DcAmB S9; EncAHmr; NewYTBE 71; PlP&P; REn; REnAL; SmATA 7; WebAB 74, 79; WhAm 5; WorAl*

Cermak, Anton Joseph
American. Politician
Mayor of Chicago, 1931-33; killed by bullet intended for FDR.
b. May 9, 1873 in Prague, Bohemia
d. Mar 6, 1933 in Miami, Florida
Source: *BioIn 3, 6, 11, 15, 21; DcAmB S1; WebBD 83; WhAm 1; WhAmP*

Cernan, Eugene Andrew
American. Astronaut
On board *Gemini* 9, *Apollo* 10, 17; last American to walk on moon, 1972.
b. Mar 14, 1934 in Chicago, Illinois
Source: *BlueB 76; CurBio 73; IntWW 74; NewYTBE 72; WhoAm 86; WhoSSW 82*

Cerovsek, Corey
Canadian. Violinist
Prodigy compared to Yehudi Menuhin, Mozart in talent; has performed with over 12 Canadian, American orchestras.
b. 1972 in Vancouver, British Columbia, Canada
Source: *ConNews 87-4*

Cervantes, Alfonso Juan
American. Politician
Mayor of St. Louis, 1965-73.
b. Aug 27, 1929 in Saint Louis, Missouri
d. Jun 23, 1983 in Saint Louis, Missouri
Source: *WhoAm 74; WhoAmP 73; WhoGov 75*

Cervantes (Saavedra), Miguel (de)
Spanish. Poet, Dramatist
Began writing *Don Quixote* in prison, 1605; forerunner of modern novel; considered Spain's equivalent of Shakespeare.
b. Sep 29, 1547 in Alcala de Henares, Spain
d. Apr 23, 1616 in Madrid, Spain
Source: *AtlBL; BbD; BiD&SB; BioIn 1, 2, 3, 4, 5, 6, 7, 8, 9, 10, 11, 12, 13, 14, 16, 18, 19, 20; CasWL; CyWA 58; DcArts; DcBiA; DcBiPP; DcCathB; DcEuL; DcSpL; Dis&D; EncUnb; EncWT; EuAu; EvEuW; HarEnMi; LinLib L, S; LngCEL; McGEWB; McGEWD 72; NewCol 75; NotNAT B; OxCEng 67, 85, 95; OxCSpan; OxCThe 67, 83; OxDcOp; PenC EUR; RAdv 14, 13-2; RComWL; REn; WebBD 83; WorAl; WorAlBi*

Cervi, Al
American. Basketball Player, Basketball Coach
One of NBA's most successful player-coaches, with Syracuse-Philadelphia, 1949-56, 1958; Hall of Fame.
b. Feb 12, 1917 in Buffalo, New York
Source: *BasBi; BioIn 4; WhoBbl 73*

Cesaire, Aime Fernand
African. Poet, Dramatist, Political Activist
Cofounder of Negritude, a political movement to re-establish cultural identity for black Africans; supported decolonization of Africa's French colonies.
b. Jun 25, 1913 in Basse-Pointe, Martinique
Source: *Benet 87; BiDLAmC; BioIn 1, 2, 10, 11, 13, 16; BlkWr 1; ConAu 24NR; ConFLW 84; ConLC 32; CroCD; GuFrLit 1; IntAu&W 89; LiExTwC; SelBAAf*

Cesnola, Luigi Palma di
Italian. Archaeologist
Excavated sites on Cyprus, 1865-76; director Metropolitan Museum of Art, 1879-1904.
b. Jul 29, 1832 in Rivarola, Italy
d. Nov 20, 1904 in New York, New York
Source: *Alli SUP; AmBi; ApCAB; BbD; BiD&SB; BioIn 7, 9; CelCen; DcAmAu; DcAmB; DcNAA; HarEnUS; InSci; LinLib S; NatCAB 1; TwCBDA; WhAm 1*

Cessna, Clyde Vernon
American. Aircraft Manufacturer
Organized Cessna Aircraft Co; built cantilever monoplanes, 1928.
b. Dec 5, 1879 in Hawthorne, Iowa
d. Nov 20, 1954 in Rago, Kansas
Source: *BioIn 3, 4; Entr; FacFETw; NatCAB 41; ObitOF 79; WorAl; WorAlBi*

Cetera, Peter
American. Singer, Musician
Lead singer with Chicago; had solo hit "Glory of Love," 1986.
b. Sep 13, 1944 in Chicago, Illinois
Source: *LegTOT; WhoRocM 82; WorAlBi*

Cey, Ron(ald Charles)
"The Penguin"
American. Baseball Player
Third baseman, Los Angeles 1972-82; Chicago 1983—; shares several records for hitting in playoff series.
b. Feb 15, 1948 in Tacoma, Washington
Source: *Ballpl 90; BaseReg 86, 87; BiDAmSp Sup; BioIn 11, 15, 16; PseudN 82; WhoAm 78, 80, 82, 84, 86, 88, 90*

Cezanne, Paul
French. Artist
Post-impressionist painter; his geometric forms influenced cubism.
b. Jan 19, 1839 in Aix-en-Provence, France
d. Oct 22, 1906 in Aix-en-Provence, France
Source: *AtlBL; Benet 87, 96; BioIn 1, 2, 3, 4, 5, 6, 7, 8, 9, 10, 11, 12, 13, 14, 15, 16, 17, 18, 19, 20, 21; ClaDrA; DcArts; DcCathB; DcTwCCu 2; IntDcAA 90; LegTOT; LinLib S; McGDA; McGEWB; NewYTBS 95; OxCArt; OxCEng 85, 95; OxCFr; OxDcArt; PhDcTCA 77; RAdv 14, 13-3; REn; ThHElm; WhDW; WorAl; WorAlBi*

Chaban-Delmas, Jacques Pierre Michel
French. Political Leader
Prime minister of France, 1969-72; pres., Nat Assembly, 1958-69; 1978-81.
b. Mar 7, 1915 in Paris, France
Source: *CurBio 58; DcPol; IntWW 74, 83; Who 82, 83, 85, 88, 90, 92, 94; WhoWor 74*

Chabrier, Emmanuel
[Alexis Emmanuel Chabrier]
French. Composer
Wrote operas, vocal works; best known for piano pieces, "Espana," 1883, and "Habanera," 1885.
b. Jan 18, 1841 in Ambert, France
d. Sep 13, 1894 in Paris, France
Source: *AtlBL; Baker 78, 84; BioIn 1, 4, 5, 6, 7, 8, 9, 10, 12, 13; IntDcOp; MetOEnc; NewAmDM; NewEOp 71; NewOxM; OxCFr; OxCMus; OxDcOp; PenDiMP A; WhDW*

Chabrol, Claude
French. Director
Influenced by Hitchcock-style thrillers: *The Champagne Murders*, 1967; *Blood Relatives*, 1981.
b. Jun 24, 1930 in Paris, France
Source: *BiDFilm, 94; BioIn 9, 10, 12, 16, 17; CelR; ConAu 110; ConLC 16; ConTFT 8; CurBio 75; DcArts; DcFM; DcTwCCu 2; EncEurC; FacFETw; FilmgC; HalFC 84, 88; IntDcF 1-2, 2-2; IntMPA 75, 76, 77, 78, 79, 81, 82, 84, 86, 88, 92, 94, 96; IntWW 75, 76, 77, 78, 79, 80, 81, 82, 83, 89, 91, 93; ItaFilm; LegTOT; MiSFD 9; MovMk; NewYTBE 70; OxCFilm; WhoFr 79; WhoHol 92; WhoWor 82, 84, 93, 95, 96; WorAl; WorAlBi; WorEFlm; WorFDir 2*

Chace, Marian
American. Dancer
Created dance therapy for mentally ill; founded American Dance Therapy Assn., 1965.
b. Oct 31, 1896 in Providence, Rhode Island
d. Jul 20, 1970 in Washington, District of Columbia
Source: *BioIn 9, 11, 12; InWom SUP; NotAW MOD*

Chad and Jeremy
[Jeremy Clyde; Chad Stuart]
English. Music Group
Soft-rock group, 1964-66; hits include "Yesterday's Gone," "A Summer Song," "Distant Shores."

Source: *BiDAmM; ConMuA 80A; EncPR&S 89; EncRk 88; LegTOT; NewYTBE 70; RkOn 78, 84; RolSEnR 83; WhoRock 81; WhoRocM 82*

Chadli, Bendjedid
Algerian. Political Leader
National pres., 1979—; secretary-general, National Liberation Front, 1979—.
b. Apr 14, 1929 in Bouteldja, Algeria
Source: *BioIn 16; CurBio 91; EncWB; IntWW 79, 80, 81, 82, 83, 89, 91, 93; IntYB 82; MidE 79, 80, 81, 82*

Chadwick, Cassie L
[Elizabeth Bigley]
"Queen of Ohio"
Canadian. Criminal
Notorious swindler; masqueraded as Andrew Carnegie's illegitimate daughter.
b. 1859 in Strathroy, Ontario, Canada
d. 1907
Source: *BioIn 2, 5, 10*

Chadwick, Florence (May)
American. Swimmer
Set record for women swimming the English Channel, 13 hrs., 20 mins., 1950.
b. Nov 9, 1918 in San Diego, California
d. Mar 15, 1995 in San Diego, California
Source: *BiDAmSp BK; BioIn 2, 3, 4, 5, 17, 20, 21; CurBio 50, 95N; EncWomS; GoodHs; InWom, SUP; LegTOT; WhoSpor; WorAl; WorAlBi*

Chadwick, French Ensor
American. Naval Officer
Rear admiral, 1903; commander-in-chief, S Atlantic Squadron, 1904-06.
b. Feb 29, 1844 in Morgantown, West Virginia
d. Jan 27, 1919 in Newport, Rhode Island
Source: *AmBi; ApCAB SUP, X; BioIn 11, 12; DcAmB, S2; DcNAA; EncAI&E; NatCAB 9; WhAm 1*

Chadwick, George Whitefield
American. Composer
Wrote symphonies, choral pieces; orchestral works include *Rip Van Winkle,* 1879.
b. Nov 13, 1854 in Lowell, Massachusetts
d. Apr 7, 1931 in Boston, Massachusetts
Source: *AmBi; AmComp; ApCAB; Baker 78, 84; BioIn 1, 3, 4, 8, 10; DcAmB S1; LinLib S; NewGrDA 86; OxCAmL 65; OxCMus; TwCBDA; WebBD 83; WhAm 1*

Chadwick, Henry
American. Journalist
Authored baseball's first book of rules, about 1860; edited Spaulding's *Official Baseball Guide.*
b. Oct 5, 1824 in Exeter, England
d. Apr 20, 1908 in New York, New York
Source: *Alli SUP; AmAu&B; Ballpl 90; BiDAmSp BB; BioIn 3, 7, 14, 15, 21; DcAmAu; DcAmB; DcNAA; EncAJ; HsB&A; WebAB 74, 79; WhoProB 73*

Chadwick, James, Sir
English. Scientist
Won Nobel Prize in physics, 1932, for discovery of neutron which made uranium fission possible.
b. Oct 22, 1891 in Manchester, England
d. Jul 24, 1974 in Cambridge, England
Source: *AsBiEn; BiESc; BioIn 1, 2, 3, 5, 10, 11, 12, 13; CamDcSc; ConAu 49; CurBio 45, 74, 74N; DcInv; DcNaB 1971; DcScB S2; FacFETw; GrBr; InSci; IntWW 74; LarDcSc; McGEWB; McGMS 80; NewYTBS 74; NobelP; NotTwCS; ObitT 1971; WhAm 6; WhDW; Who 74; WhoAm 74; WhoNob, 90, 95; WhoWor 74; WorAl; WorAlBi; WorScD*

Chadwick, William Owen
English. Historian
Professor of modern history, Cambridge U., 1968-83; wrote *Catholicism and History,* 1978.
b. May 20, 1916 in Bromley, England
Source: *Au&Wr 71; ConAu 1NR, 1R; DcLEL 1940; IntWW 74, 75, 76, 77, 78, 79, 83; Who 74, 82, 83, 85, 88, 90, 92; WhoWor 74, 76, 78*

Chafee, John H(ubbard)
American. Politician
Rep. senator from RI, 1977—; first Rep. elected from RI in 46 yrs.
b. Oct 22, 1922 in Providence, Rhode Island
Source: *BiDrGov 1789; BiDrUSC 89; BioIn 7, 8, 9, 11, 12; CngDr 77, 79, 81, 83, 85, 87; CurBio 69; PolsAm 84; WhoAm 74, 76, 78, 80, 82, 84, 86, 88, 90, 92, 94, 95, 96, 97; WhoAmP 73, 75, 77, 79, 81, 83, 85, 87, 89, 91, 93, 95; WhoE 74, 75, 77, 79, 81, 83, 85, 86, 89, 91, 93, 95, 97; WhoWor 80, 82, 84, 87, 89, 91*

Chaffee, Adna Romanza
American. Army Officer
Led US troops in capture of Peking, Boxer Rebellion, 1900; military governor of Philippines, 1901-02.
b. Apr 14, 1842 in Orwell, Ohio
d. Nov 14, 1914 in Los Angeles, California
Source: *AmBi; ApCAB SUP; CmdGen 1991; DcAmB; GenMudB; HarEnMi; HarEnUS; NatCAB 10, 30; TwCBDA; WebAB 74, 79; WebAMB; WhAm 1; WorAl; WorAlBi*

Chaffee, Adna Romanza
"Father of the Armored Forces"
American. Army Officer
Organized first US mechanized brigade, 1934; headed Armored Force, 1940; son of Adna R.
b. Sep 23, 1884 in Junction City, Kansas
d. Aug 22, 1941 in Boston, Massachusetts
Source: *DcAmB S3; DcAmMiB; HarEnMi; NatCAB 30; WebAB 74, 79; WebAMB; WhAm 1; WorAl; WorAlBi*

Chaffee, Roger Bruce
American. Astronaut
Killed in fire with Gus Grissom, Ed White, aboard spacecraft during simulation of *Apollo* flight.
b. Feb 15, 1935 in Grand Rapids, Michigan
d. Jan 27, 1967 in Cape Canaveral, Florida
Source: *BioIn 7, 8, 9, 10; DcAmB S8; WhAm 4*

Chaffee, Suzy
American. Skier
Captain, US Olympic ski team, 1968; world free-style champ, 1971-73.
b. Nov 29, 1946
Source: *BioIn 9; LegTOT; WhoAm 80, 82*

Chagall, Marc
Russian. Artist
Influenced by cubism; paintings depict Russian village life.
b. Jul 7, 1887 in Vitebsk, Russia
d. Mar 28, 1985 in Saint-Paul-de-Vence, France
Source: *AnObit 1985; BiDD; BioIn 1, 2, 3, 4, 5, 6, 7, 8, 9, 10, 11, 12, 14, 15, 16, 17, 18, 20, 21; CelR; ClaDrA; ConArt 77, 83, 89; ConAu 114, 122; ConNews 85-2; CurBio 43, 60, 85N; DcArts; Dis&D; EncWT; FacFETw; IntDcAA 90; IntWW 74, 75, 76, 77, 78, 79, 80, 81, 82, 83; JeHun; LegTOT; LinLib S; MakMC; McGDA; McGEWB; MetOEnc; ModArCr 2; NewYTBE 73; NewYTBS 85; OxCTwCA; OxDcArt; PrintW 83, 85; REn; SovUn; WhAm 8; WhDW; Who 82, 83, 85; WhoFr 79; WhoGrA 62, 82; WhoWor 74, 76, 78, 80, 82, 84; WhoWorJ 78; WorAl; WorAlBi; WorArt 1950*

Chaikin, Joseph
American. Actor, Director
Founder, director, Open Theater, NYC, 1963-73.
b. Sep 16, 1935 in New York, New York
Source: *BioIn 9, 10, 11, 12, 13, 14, 17, 18, 20; CamGWoT; ConTFT 7; CurBio 81; EncWT; GrStDi; NotNAT; TheaDir; WhoHol 92; WhoThe 77, 81; WhoWorJ 72, 78*

Chaikin, Sol Chick
American. Labor Union Official
Pres., International Ladies Garment Workers Union, 1975-86; led fight to eliminate sweatshops.
b. Jan 9, 1918 in New York, New York
d. Apr 1, 1991 in New York, New York
Source: *CurBio 79; NewYTBS 75; WhAm 10; WhoAm 78, 80, 82, 84, 86; WhoE 77, 79, 81, 83; WhoLab 76*

Chai Ling
Chinese. Political Activist
Leader of Chinese pro-democracy movement; former Beijing U student who led student demonstration in Tiananmen Square that resulted in government intervention and a number of student deaths on Jun 3, 1989.
b. 1966 in Shandong, China
Source: *ConHero 2; RadHan*

Chailly, Riccardo
Italian. Conductor
Chief conductor, music director, Royal Concertgebouw Orchestra since 1988, its first non-Dutch conductor.
b. Feb 20, 1953 in Milan, Italy
Source: *Baker 84, 92; BioIn 13, 17; CurBio 91; IntDcOp; IntWW 89, 91, 93; IntWWM 85, 90; MetOEnc; NewGrDO; NewYTBS 82; OxDcOp; PenDiMP; Who 94; WhoEnt 92; WhoOp 76; WhoWor 78, 80, 82, 84, 87, 89, 95, 96, 97*

Chain, Ernest Boris, Sir
British. Biochemist, Educator
Developed penicillin, 1928, with Alexander Fleming, Howard Florey; shared 1945 Nobel Prize.
b. Jun 19, 1906 in Berlin, Germany
d. Aug 12, 1979 in Mulranny, Ireland
Source: *AsBiEn; BioIn 7; CurBio 65, 79; InSci; IntWW 78; Who 74; WhoNob; WhoWor 78; WhoWorJ 72*

Chaka
African. Political Leader
Founded Zulu Empire, mid-1820s; ruled 50,000 people.
b. 1773
d. Sep 1828
Source: *BioIn 1, 4, 6, 7, 8, 9, 10; InB&W 80; WhDW*

Chakiris, George
American. Dancer, Actor
Won Oscar for role of Bernardo in *West Side Story,* 1961.
b. Sep 16, 1934 in Norwood, Ohio
Source: *BiDD; BioIn 6; ConTFT 12; FilmgC; IntMPA 75, 76, 77, 78, 79, 81, 82, 84, 86, 88, 92; MotPP; MovMk; WhoAm 74, 76, 78, 80, 82; WhoHol A*

Chalgrin, Francois
[Jean Francois Therese Chalgrin]
French. Architect
Neo-classicist; designed Arc de Triomphe; begun, 1806, completed after his death.
b. 1739 in Paris, France
d. Jan 20, 1811 in Paris, France
Source: *MacEA; McGDA; WhoArch*

Chaliapin, Feodor Ivanovitch, Jr.
[Feodor Ivanovich Shaliapin; Fyodor Shalyapin]
Russian. Opera Singer
Bass, unrivalled as singing actor; known for role in *Boris Gudunov,* 1890-1930s.
b. Feb 13, 1873 in Kazan, Russia
d. Sep 17, 1992 in Rome, Italy
Source: *Baker 84; BioIn 1, 2, 3, 4, 7, 8, 9, 10, 11, 12, 13; FilmgC; OxCFilm; OxDcOp; REn; WhAm 1; WhScrn 77*

Chalk, O(scar) Roy
American. Entrepreneur
Founder of several businesses, including Trans Caribbean Airlines, which he sold to American Airlines in 1970.
b. Jun 7, 1907
d. Dec 1, 1995 in New York, New York
Source: *BioIn 5, 6, 7, 8, 9; BlueB 76; CurBio 71, 96N; St&PR 75; WhoAm 76, 78*

Chalmers, William James
American. Manufacturer
Founding partner of Allis-Chalmers Corp., 1901.
b. Jul 10, 1852 in Chicago, Illinois
d. Dec 10, 1938 in Chicago, Illinois
Source: *BioIn 4; DcAmB S2; WhAm 1*

Chamberlain, Austen, Sir
[Joseph Austen Chamberlain]
English. Statesman
Conservative Party leader, 1921-29; won Nobel Peace Prize, 1925; half-brother of Neville.
b. Oct 16, 1863 in Birmingham, England
d. Mar 16, 1937 in London, England
Source: *BioIn 2, 7, 9, 11, 14, 15, 16, 21; DcNaB 1931; DcTwHis; EncTR 91; FacFETw; GrBr; LinLib S; McGEWB; WebBD 83; WhE&EA; WhoNob, 90, 95; WorAl*

Chamberlain, John Rensselaer
American. Journalist
Wrote *The Enterprising Americans,* 1962, a business history of US.
b. Oct 28, 1903 in New Haven, Connecticut
d. Apr 9, 1995 in New Haven, Connecticut
Source: *AmAu&B; BiDAmNC; BioIn 4, 10, 13; ConAu 57; CurBio 40; OxCAmL 65; REnAL; TwCA, SUP; WhAm 11; WhoAm 74, 76, 78, 80, 82, 84, 86, 88, 90, 92, 94, 95; WhoWor 74*

Chamberlain, Joseph
English. Statesman
Involved in Parliamentary politics for 40 yrs; favored social reform at home, expansion abroad; father of Austen and Neville.
b. Jul 8, 1836 in London, England
d. Jul 2, 1914 in Birmingham, England
Source: *Alli SUP; BioIn 2, 3, 4, 6, 7, 9, 10, 11, 12, 14, 15, 16, 17, 20; CelCen; DcNaB 1912; HarEnUS; HisDBrE; LinLib S; McGEWB; VicBrit; WhDW*

Chamberlain, Neville
[Arthur Neville Chamberlain]
English. Political Leader
Conservative prime minister, 1937-40; sought "peace in our time" through appeasement of Hitler.
b. Mar 18, 1869 in Edgbaston, England
d. Nov 9, 1940 in Heckfield, England
Source: *Benet 87; BioIn 1, 2, 3, 6, 7, 8, 9, 11, 12, 13, 14, 15, 16, 19, 21; ConAu 113; CurBio 40; DcNaB 1931; DcPol; DcTwHis; EncTR, 91; FacFETw; GrBr; HisDBrE; HisEWW; HisWorL; LegTOT; LinLib S; McGEWB; REn; WhDW; WhWW-II; WorAl; WorAlBi*

Chamberlain, Owen
American. Physicist, Educator
Shared Nobel Prize in physics, 1959, for confirmation of existence of antiproton.
b. Jul 10, 1920 in San Francisco, California
Source: *AmMWSc 73P, 76P, 79, 82, 86, 89, 92, 95; AsBiEn; BiESc; BioIn 5, 15, 20; BlueB 76; CamDcSc; CmCal; FacFETw; InSci; IntWW 74, 75, 76, 77, 78, 79, 80, 81, 82, 83, 89, 91, 93; LarDcSc; LegTOT; McGMS 80; NobelP; NotTwCS; WebAB 74, 79; Who 74, 82, 83, 85, 88, 90, 92, 94; WhoAm 78, 80, 82, 84, 86, 88, 90, 92, 94, 95, 96, 97; WhoFrS 84; WhoNob, 90, 95; WhoScEn 94, 96; WhoWest 74, 78, 80, 84, 87, 89, 92, 94, 96; WhoWor 74, 82, 84, 87, 89, 91, 93, 95, 96, 97; WorAl; WorAlBi*

Chamberlain, Richard
[George Richard Chamberlain]
American. Actor
Starred in TV series "Dr. Kildare," 1961-65; mini-series "Shogun," 1980; "The Thorn Birds," 1983.
b. Mar 31, 1935 in Los Angeles, California
Source: *BioIn 6, 9, 10, 12, 13; BioNews 75; BkPepl; CelR, 90; ConTFT 1, 5; CurBio 63, 87; FilmgC; HalFC 84, 88; IntMPA 75, 76, 77, 78, 79, 81, 82, 84, 86, 88, 92, 94, 96; IntWW 89, 91; LegTOT; MotPP; MovMk; RkOn 74; WhoAm 74, 76, 78, 80, 82, 84, 86, 88, 90, 92, 94, 95, 96, 97; WhoEnt 92; WhoHol 92, A; WhoThe 77, 81; WhoWor 82, 84; WorAl; WorAlBi*

Chamberlain, Samuel
American. Author, Photographer
Produced etchings, photographs of European, American landscapes; co-wrote popular books about foreign cuisine.
b. Oct 28, 1895 in Cresco, Iowa
d. Jan 10, 1975 in Marblehead, Massachusetts
Source: *AmAu&B; Au&Wr 71; BioIn 1, 3, 5, 7, 8, 10, 13; ConAu 53, P-2; CurBio 54, 75, 75N; GrAmP; MacBEP; WhAm 6; WhAmArt 85; WhNAA; WhoAm 74; WhoAmA 73, 76N, 78N, 80N, 82N, 84N, 86N, 89N, 91N, 93N*

Chamberlain, Wilt(on Norman)
"Wilt the Stilt"
American. Basketball Player
Center, Harlem globetrotters, 1958-59; Philadelphia Warriors, 1959-65; Philadelphis 76ers, 1965-68; LA Lakers, 1968-73; four-time MVP; Hall of Fame, 1978.

b. Aug 21, 1936 in West Philadelphia, Pennsylvania
Source: *AfrAmAl 6; AfrAmSG; BasBi; BiDAmSp BK; BioIn 12, 13, 14, 15, 16, 17, 20, 21; BkPepl; CelR, 90; CmCal; ConAu 103; ConHero 1; CurBio 60; Ebony 1; FacFETw; InB&W 80, 85; LegTOT; NegAl 76, 83, 89; NewYTBE 72, 73; NewYTBS 75; OfNBA 87; WebAB 79; WhoAm 88, 90, 92, 94, 95, 96, 97; WhoBbl 73; WhoBlA 75, 77, 80, 85; WhoHol 92; WhoWest 94, 96; WorAl; WorAlBi*

Chamberlin, B. Guy
American. Football Player, Football Coach
All-America end-running back; played in pros, 1920-27; player-coach, 1922-26; Hall of Fame.
b. Jan 16, 1894 in Blue Springs, Nebraska
d. Apr 4, 1967
Source: *BioIn 3, 6, 8; WhoFtbl 74*

Chamberlin, Thomas Chrowder
American. Geologist
Studied glacial deposits; founded *Journal of Geology,* 1893.
b. Sep 25, 1843 in Mattoon, Illinois
d. Nov 15, 1928 in Chicago, Illinois
Source: *Alli SUP; AmAu&B; AmBi; ApCAB, X; AsBiEn; BiDAmS; BiESc; BioIn 4, 5, 9, 20; DcAmAu; DcAmB; DcNAA; DcScB; FacFETw; InSci; LarDcSc; LinLib S; McGEWB; NatCAB 11, 19; NewCol 75; NotTwCS; TwCBDA; WhAm 1*

Chamberlin, William Henry
American. Author, Critic
Correspondent in USSR for *The Christian Science Monitor,* 1922-34; wrote *Evolution of a Conservative,* 1959.
b. Feb 17, 1897 in New York, New York
d. Sep 12, 1969
Source: *AmAu&B; BioIn 2, 4, 5, 8; ConAu 5R; DcAmC; DcLB 29; JrnUS; OxCAmL 65; OxCCan; REnAL; TwCA, SUP; WhAm 5; WhE&EA*

Chambers, Anne Cox
American. Diplomat, Business Executive
US Ambassador to Belgium, 1977-81; chm., Atlanta Newspapers, director, Cox Broadcasting Corp; one of 10 richest women in US.
b. Dec 1, 1919 in Dayton, Ohio
Source: *BioIn 11, 20; CelR 90; InWom SUP; WhoAm 78, 80, 82, 84, 90; WhoAmW 79, 81, 83, 85; WhoGov 77; WhoSSW 78, 88; WhoWor 78, 80*

Chambers, Edmund Kerchever, Sir
English. Essayist, Critic
Literary scholar; works considered standards: *The Elizabethan Stage,* 1923; *William Shakespeare,* 1930.
b. Mar 16, 1866 in Berkshire, England
d. Jan 21, 1954 in Beer, England
Source: *BioIn 3, 4; CasWL; DcLEL; DcNaB 1951; EvLB; LngCEL; LngCTC; NewC; OxCEng 67; PenC ENG; REn; TwCA, SUP; WhLit*

Chambers, Julius LeVonne
American. Lawyer, Civil Rights Leader
NAACP Legal Defense Fund, director-counsel, 1984-92.
b. Oct 6, 1936 in Montgomery Co., North Carolina
Source: *BioIn 14; ConBlB 3; NewYTBS 84; WhoAfA 96; WhoAm 90, 92, 94, 95, 96, 97; WhoAmL 83, 85, 94, 96; WhoBlA 80, 85, 88, 90, 92, 94; WhoSSW 73, 95, 97*

Chambers, Paul
[Paul Lawrence Dunbar Chambers, Jr.]
American. Musician
Jazz bassist who performed in the Detroit jazz scene during the early 1950s; performed with the band of George Wallington and the Miles Davis Quintet, 1955; received *Down Beat* New Star Award, 1956.
b. Apr 22, 1935 in Pittsburgh, Pennsylvania
d. Jan 4, 1969 in New York, New York
Source: *AllMusG; BioIn 16; DcTwCCu 5; NewGrDA 86; NewGrDJ 88; PenEncP*

Chambers, Robert
Scottish. Publisher, Author
Wrote *Vestiges of Creation,* 1844; *Chambers' Encyclopedia,* 1850-75.
b. Jul 10, 1802 in Peebles, Scotland
d. Mar 17, 1871 in Saint Andrews, Scotland
Source: *Alli, SUP; BbD; BiD&SB; BioIn 2, 5, 10, 12, 14, 16, 17; BritAu 19; CasWL; CelCen; ChhPo, S1, S2, S3; CmScLit; DcBiPP; DcEnA; DcEnL; DcEuL; DcLEL; DcNaB; DcScB; EncO&P 1, 2, 3; EncUnb; EvLB; InSci; LinLib L; NewC; OxCEng 67, 85, 95; PenC ENG; VicBrit*

Chambers, Robert W
American. Author
Wrote series of pseudo-historical novels: *The Drums of Aulone,* 1927.
b. May 26, 1865 in New York, New York
d. Dec 16, 1933
Source: *AmAu&B; AmBi; ApCAB SUP, X; BbD; BiD&SB; CarSB; Chambr 3; DcAmB S1; REnAL; WhAm 1; WhAmArt 85; WhLit*

Chambers, Tom
[Thomas Doane Chambers]
American. Basketball Player
Center, San Diego Clippers, 1981-83; Seattle SuperSonics, 1983-88; Phoenix Suns, 1988-93; Utah Jazz, 1993-94; MVP, All-Star Game, 1987; first unrestricted free agent to go to another team, signing with Phoenix, 1988.
b. Jun 21, 1959 in Ogden, Vermont
Source: *BasBi; OfNBA 86, 87; WhoAm 90, 94; WhoWest 87, 89, 92, 94*

Chambers, Whittaker
[Jay David Chambers]
American. Editor, Journalist
Principal witness in Alger Hiss espionage case, 1948-50.
b. Apr 1, 1901 in Philadelphia, Pennsylvania
d. Jun 9, 1961 in Carroll County, Maryland
Source: *AmAu&B; BioIn 1, 2, 3, 4, 5, 6, 7, 8, 9, 10, 11, 12, 13; ColdWar 1; ConAu 89; DcAmB S7; DcAmC; DcAmSR; EncAI&E; EncAJ; EncCW; EncMcCE; EncWB; LegTOT; LngCTC; ObitOF 79; PolPar; PolProf E, T; WorAl; WorAlBi; WorAu 1950*

Chambers, William, Sir
"W C"
British. Architect
Designed Somerset House, London; Kew Palace buildings, 1757.
b. 1723 in Gothenburg, Sweden
d. Mar 8, 1796 in London, England
Source: *AtlBL; BiDBrA; BioIn 2, 3, 7, 8, 9, 17; BlkwCE; DcD&D; IntDcAr; MacEA; McGDA; OxCArt; PenDiDA 89; PseudN 82; WhDW; WhoArch*

Chaminade, Cecile
[Louise Stephanie Chaminade]
French. Composer, Pianist
Wrote over 500 enormously popular piano pieces.
b. Aug 8, 1861 in Paris, France
d. Apr 18, 1944 in Monte Carlo, Monaco
Source: *Baker 84; CurBio 44; OxCMus*

Chamorro, Violeta Barrios de
Nicaraguan. Political Leader
Pres. of Nicaragua, 1990—; election upset leftist Sandinistas.
b. Oct 18, 1929 in Rivas, Nicaragua
Source: *ColdWar 2; CurBio 90; WomWR; WorAlBi*

Chamoun, Camille N(imer)
Lebanese. Political Leader
Maronite Christian leader; pres. of Lebanon, 1952-58; founded National Liberal party, 1958; followers called "Chamounists."
b. Apr 3, 1900 in Deir el-Kamar, Lebanon
d. Aug 7, 1987 in Beirut, Lebanon
Source: *BioIn 1, 3, 4, 5, 15, 17; CurBio 56, 87, 87N; FacFETw; IntWW 83*

Champagne, Duane (Willard)
American. Educator, Sociologist
Director, UCLA American Indian Studies Center, 1991—.
b. May 18, 1951 in Belcourt, North Dakota
Source: *EncNAB; NotNaAm; WhoAm 96, 97; WhoWest 96*

Champion, Gower
American. Choreographer, Dancer
Won Tonys for *Bye Bye Birdie,* 1961; *Hello, Dolly,* 1964; *42nd Street,* 1981.
b. Jun 22, 1921 in Geneva, Illinois

d. Aug 25, 1980 in New York, New York
Source: *AnObit 1980; BiDD; BiE&WWA; BioIn 3, 4, 6, 7, 8; CamGWoT; CelR; CmMov; CurBio 80N; EncMT; FilmgC; IntMPA 77, 78, 79, 81; MGM; MotPP; MovMk; NewYTBS 80; NotNAT; WhoAm 74, 76, 78, 80; WhoHol A; WhoThe 77; WhoWor 74; WorAl; WorAlBi; WorEFlm*

Champion, Marge Celeste
[Marjorie Celeste Belcher; Mrs. Gower Champion]
American. Dancer, Actor
Teamed with husband, Gower, in film musicals; won Emmy for "Queen of the Stardust Ballroom," 1975.
b. Sep 2, 1923 in Los Angeles, California
Source: *BiDD; BiE&WWA; CmMov; ConTFT 1; CurBio 53; FilmgC; IntMPA 86; InWom SUP; MovMk; NotNAT; WhoAm 86; WhoAmW 85; WhoHol A*

Champlain, Samuel de
French. Explorer
Founded Quebec, 1608; discovered Lake Champlain, 1609.
b. Jul 3, 1567 in Rochefort, France
d. Dec 25, 1635 in Quebec, Canada
Source: *AmBi; ApCAB; Benet 87, 96; BenetAL 91; BioIn 1, 2, 3, 4, 5, 6, 7, 8, 9, 10, 12, 16, 18, 19, 20; DcAmB; DcCanB 1; DcCathB; Dis&D; Drake; EncCRAm; HarEnMi; HarEnUS; LegTOT; LinLib L, S; MacDCB 78; NewYHSD; OxCAmH; OxCAmL 65; OxCCan; OxCFr; OxCShps; REn; REnAL; WebAB 74, 79; WhAm HS; WhDW; WhNaAH; WhWE; WorAl; WorAlBi*

Champollin-Figeac, Jacques-Joseph
French. Librarian, Author
Paleographer; wrote books on French and ancient Egyptian history, French dialects and idioms.
b. Oct 5, 1778 in Figeac, France
d. May 9, 1867 in Fontainebleau, France

Champollion, Jean Francois
French. Egyptologist
Deciphered Rosetta stone found in Egypt by French troops, 1799.
b. Dec 23, 1790 in Figeac, France
d. Mar 4, 1832 in Paris, France
Source: *BbD; Benet 87, 96; BioIn 3, 4, 6, 10, 16, 17, 19, 21; CelCen; DcBiPP; DcCathB; LinLib L, S; McGEWB; NewCol 75; OxCFr; REn; WhDW; WorAl*

Chan, Jackie
[Chan Kwong-Sang]
Chinese. Actor, Director
Film roles include *Operation Condor,* 1991; *Thunderbolt,* 1995.
b. Apr 7, 1954, Hong Kong
Source: *BioIn 16, 20, 21; IntDcF 2-3; MiSFD 9; News 96, 96-1; WhoHol 92*

Chan, June
American. Biologist
Founder of the Asian Lesbians of the East Coast, 1983; researcher at Cornell Medical College.
b. Jun 6, 1956 in New York, New York
Source: *AsAmAlm; BioIn 20; GayLesB; NotAsAm*

Chance, Dean
[Wilmer Dean Chance]
American. Baseball Player
Pitcher, 1961-71; set ML record by winning six 1-0 games, 1964.
b. Jun 1, 1941 in Wayne, Ohio
Source: *Ballpl 90; BioIn 7, 8, 21; CurBio 69; WhoProB 73; WhoSpor*

Chance, Frank Leroy
"Husk"; "Peerless Leader"
American. Baseball Player, Baseball Manager
Infielder, 1898-1914; first baseman in "Tinker to Evers to Chance" double play combination, 1906-10; Hall of Fame, 1946.
b. Sep 9, 1877 in Fresno, California
d. Sep 14, 1924 in Los Angeles, California
Source: *BiDAmSp BB; BioIn 2, 3, 4, 5, 7, 10; CmCal; WhoProB 73*

Chancellor, John (William)
American. Broadcast Journalist
Correspondent for NBC News, 1957-61, 1962-70; host of "Today," 1961-62; anchor, "NBC Nightly News," 1970-82; senior commentator, "NBC Nightly News," 1982-93.
b. Jul 14, 1927 in Chicago, Illinois
d. Jul 12, 1996 in Princeton, New Jersey
Source: *AuNews 1; BestSel 90-4; BioIn 5, 6, 7, 9, 10, 11, 16, 21; BioNews 74; CelR, 90; ConAu 109, 152; ConTFT 7; CurBio 62, 88, 96N; EncAJ; EncTwCJ; IntAu&W 89, 91; IntMPA 76, 77, 78, 79, 81, 82, 84, 86, 88, 92, 94, 96; IntWW 74, 75, 76, 77, 78, 79, 80, 81, 82, 83, 89, 91, 93; JrnUS; LegTOT; News 97-1; NewYTET; PolProf J; WhAm 11; WhoAm 74, 76, 78, 80, 82, 84, 86, 88, 90, 92, 94, 95, 96, 97; WhoE 91, 93; WhoWor 78, 80, 82, 84, 87, 89; WorAl; WrDr 92, 94, 96*

Chancellor, Richard
English. Explorer
Negotiated trade agreements between Russia, England; organized Muscovy Co., 1554.
d. Nov 10, 1556 in Pitsligo Bay, Scotland
Source: *BioIn 4, 7, 18; DcBiPP; DcNaB; Expl 93; HisDBrE; IntAu&W 77X; McGEWB; NewC; OxCShps; WhDW; WhWE*

Chandler, Colby H
American. Business Executive
Pres., Eastman Kodak Co., 1977-93; chief exec., 1983-93.
b. 1925
Source: *Dun&B 79; IntWW 83; WhoAm 86; WhoFI 83*

Chandler, Don(ald G)
"Babe"
American. Football Player
End-kicker, NY Giants, Green Bay, 1956-68; led NFL in punting, 1957, in scoring, 1963.
b. Sep 9, 1934 in Council Bluffs, Iowa
Source: *BiDAmSp FB; BioIn 8; WhoFtbl 74*

Chandler, Dorothy (Buffum)
[Mrs. Norman Chandler]
American. Art Patron, Newspaper Executive
Assisted husband in publishing *LA Times,* 1945-60; active in civic affairs; Dorothy Chandler Pavilion in LA named for her.
b. May 19, 1901 in Lafayette, Illinois
d. Jul 7, 1997 in Hollywood, California
Source: *BioIn 4, 5, 7, 8, 9, 11, 12; CelR; CurBio 57; InWom, SUP; WhoAm 80; WhoWest 82*

Chandler, Happy
[Albert Benjamin Chandler]
American. Politician, Baseball Executive
Dem. governor of KY, 1935-39, 1955-59; US senator, 1939-45; baseball commissioner, 1945-51; known for allowing Jackie Robinson to play with Brooklyn, 1947, becoming first black in MLs.
b. Jul 14, 1898 in Corydon, Kentucky
d. Jun 15, 1991 in Versailles, Kentucky
Source: *BiDAmSp BB; BiDrAC; BiDrGov 1789; BiDrUSC 89; BioIn 1, 2, 3, 4, 6, 9, 10, 11, 12, 14, 15, 17, 18; CmCal; EncAB-A 18; FacFETw; LegTOT; WebAB 74, 79; WebBD 83; WhAm 10; WhoAm 74, 76, 78, 80, 82, 84, 86, 88; WhoAmP 73, 75, 77, 79; WhoProB 73; WhoSSW 73*

Chandler, Jeff
[Ira Grossel]
American. Actor, Author
Played in action films: *The Spoilers,* 1955; *Ten Seconds to Hell,* 1960.
b. Dec 15, 1918 in New York, New York
d. Jun 17, 1961 in Culver City, California
Source: *ASCAP 66; BiDFilm; BioIn 5, 7, 11, 18; CmMov; FilmgC; HalFC 84, 88; IntDcF 1-3; ItaFilm; MotPP; MovMk; NotNAT B; OxCFilm; RadStar; SaTiSS; WhoHol B; WhScrn 74, 77, 83; WorEFlm*

Chandler, Kyle
American. Actor
Played Jeff Metcalf on TV show "Homefront," 1992-93.
Source: *WhoHol 92*

Chandler, Norman
American. Newspaper Publisher, Business Executive
Third-generation publisher of *LA Times,* 1945-60; credited with paper's growth, phenomenal success; CEO of parent co., Times Mirror, 1961-68.
b. Sep 14, 1899 in Chicago, Illinois
d. Oct 20, 1973 in Los Angeles, California
Source: *BiDAmJo; BioIn 2, 4, 5, 10, 12, 13, 16, 19; BlueB 76; ConAu 89; CurBio 57, 73, 73N; DcAmB S9; DcLB 127; EncAJ; NatCAB 58; WhAm 6; WhoFI 74; WhoWest 74; WhoWor 74*

Chandler, Otis
American. Newspaper Publisher, Business Executive
Son of Norman and Dorothy; succeeded father as publisher, *LA Times,* 1960 - 80; editor in chief, Times Mirror Co., 1980-86; chmn. exec. comm., Times Mirror co., 1986—.
b. Nov 23, 1927 in Los Angeles, California
Source: *BioIn 5, 7, 8, 9, 11, 12, 13, 19; BlueB 76; CelR, 90; ConAu 111; CurBio 68; DcLB 127; Dun&B 79, 86, 90; EncAJ; IntAu&W 89, 91, 93; IntWW 74, 75, 76, 77, 78, 79, 80, 81, 82, 83, 89, 91, 93; JrnUS; LegTOT; PolProf J; St&PR 75, 84, 87, 91, 93; WhoAm 74, 76, 78, 80, 82, 84, 88, 92, 94, 95; WhoFI 74, 75, 77, 79, 81, 83, 85, 87; WhoWest 74, 76, 78, 80, 82, 84, 87, 89, 92; WhoWor 74; WorAl*

Chandler, Raymond Thornton
American. Author
Created private detective Philip Marlowe; wrote novel *The Big Sleep,* 1939.
b. Jul 23, 1888 in Chicago, Illinois
d. Mar 26, 1959 in La Jolla, California
Source: *CnMWL; CurBio 46, 59; DcAmB S6; FilmgC; ModAL S1; NewYTBE 73; OxCAmL 83; OxCEng 85; PenC AM; REn; REnAL; TwCA SUP; WebAB 79; WhAm 3; WorEFlm*

Chandler, Spud
[Spurgeon Ferdinand Chandler]
American. Baseball Player
Pitcher, 1937-47; AL MVP, 1943.
b. Sep 12, 1909 in Commerce, Georgia
d. Jan 9, 1990
Source: *BioIn 1, 10; WhoProB 73*

Chandler, Zachariah
American. Politician, Abolitionist
A founder of Rep. party, 1854; senator from MI, 1850s-70s; secretary of Interior, 1875-77.
b. Dec 10, 1813 in Bedford, New Hampshire
d. Nov 1, 1879 in Chicago, Illinois
Source: *AmBi; ApCAB; BiAUS; BiDrAC; BiDrUSC 89; BiDrUSE 71, 89; BioIn 3, 8, 10, 17; CivWDc; DcAmB; HarEnUS; McGEWB; NatCAB 4; NewCol 75; OxCAmH; PolPar; TwCBDA; WhAm HS; WhAmP; WhCiWar*

Chandra, Sheila
English. Singer
Performed with acoustic band Monsoon which released such British chart hits as "Ever So Lonely" and "Shakti," 1982; later recorded *Out On My Own,* 1984, *Weaving My Ancestors' Voices,* 1993 and *The Zen Kiss,* 1994.
b. 1965 in London, England
Source: *ConMus 16*

Chandrasekhar, Subrahmanyan
American. Physicist
Shared Nobel Prize in physics, 1983; best known for study of structure of white dwarf stars, 1940.
b. Oct 19, 1910 in Lahore, India
d. Aug 21, 1995 in Chicago, Illinois
Source: *AmMWSc 76P, 79, 82, 86, 89, 92, 95; AsAmAlm; AsBiEn; BiESc; BioIn 1, 3, 4, 6, 9, 13, 15, 17, 20, 21; BlueB 76; CamDcSc; CurBio 86, 95N; FacFETw; InSci; IntWW 74, 75, 76, 77, 78, 79, 80, 81, 82, 83, 89, 91, 93; LarDcSc; McGMS 80; NewYTBS 83, 95; NobelP; NotAsAm; NotTwCS; RAdv 14; WhAm 11; WhE&EA; Who 74, 82, 83, 85, 88, 90, 92, 94; WhoAm 74, 76, 78, 80, 82, 84, 86, 88, 90, 92, 94, 95; WhoAsA 94; WhoFrS 84; WhoMW 84, 86, 88, 90, 92, 93; WhoNob, 90, 95; WhoScEn 94; WhoWor 74, 84, 87, 89, 91, 93, 95; WorAlBi; WrDr 80, 82, 84, 86, 88, 90, 92, 94, 96*

Chanel, Coco
[Gabrielle]
French. Fashion Designer
Created Chanel No. 5 perfume, 1924; subject of Broadway musical *Coco.*
b. Aug 19, 1882 in Saumur, France
d. Jan 10, 1971 in Paris, France
Source: *CurBio 54, 71; NewYTBE 71; WhAm 5; WorFshn*

Chaney, John
American. Basketball Coach
Head coach, Temple University, 1982—.
b. Jan 21, 1932 in Jacksonville, Florida
Source: *BiDAmSp Sup; BioIn 15, 16; News 89-1; NewYTBS 88; WhoBlA 90; WhoSpor*

Chaney, Lon
[Alonso Chaney]
"Man of a Thousand Faces"
American. Actor
Starred in *The Hunchback of Notre Dame,* 1923; *The Phantom of the Opera,* 1925.
b. Apr 1, 1883 in Colorado Springs, Colorado
d. Aug 26, 1930 in Los Angeles, California
Source: *BiDFilm, 94; BioIn 4, 6, 7, 9, 11, 15, 17, 19, 21; CmCal; CmMov; DcAmB S1; DcArts; FacFETw; Film 1, 2; FilmgC; GangFlm; HalFC 84, 88; IntDcF 1-3, 2-3; LegTOT; MotPP; MovMk; NotNAT B; OxCFilm; PenEncH; SilFlmP; TwYS; WebAB 74, 79; WhAm 4, HSA; WhoHol B; WhScrn 74, 77, 83; WorAl; WorAlBi; WorEFlm*

Chaney, Lon, Jr.
[Creighton Chaney]
American. Actor
Starred in over 100 films, mostly horror; played Lenny in *Of Mice and Men,* 1940.
b. Feb 10, 1905 in Oklahoma City, Oklahoma
d. Jul 12, 1973 in San Clemente, California
Source: *CmMov; FilmgC; LegTOT; MovMk; OxCFilm; WhoHol B; WhScrn 77, 83*

Chaney, Norman
[Our Gang]
"Chubby"
American. Actor
Played Joe Cobb, "Our Gang," 1926-34.
b. Jan 18, 1918 in Baltimore, Maryland
d. May 30, 1936 in Baltimore, Maryland
Source: *EncAFC; Film 2; PseudN 82; WhScrn 74, 77, 83*

Chang, Jung
Chinese. Author
Wrote memoir *Wild Swans: Three Daughters of China.*
b. Mar 25, 1952 in Yibin, China
Source: *ConAu 142; ConLC 71*

Chang, M(in) C(heuh), Dr.
American. Biologist
Pioneered in-vitro fertilization; co-developed birth control pill.
b. Oct 10, 1908 in Taiyuan, China
d. Jun 5, 1991 in Worcester, Massachusetts
Source: *AmMWSc 89; BioIn 7; NewYTBS 91; WhoAm 88; WhoTech 82, 84, 89*

Chang, Michael
American. Tennis Player
Won French Open, 1989; first American male to win in 34 years (since 1955).
b. Feb 22, 1972 in Hoboken, New Jersey
Source: *AsAmAlm; BioIn 15, 16; BuCMET; NewYTBS 87, 89; NotAsAm; WhoAm 92, 94, 95, 96, 97; WhoAsA 94; WhoWor 97*

Chang, Sarah Yong-chu
American. Violinist
Child prodigy; solo appearances with New York Philharmonic Orchestra, Montreal Symphony, Philadelphia Orchestra, and Milan, Italy's La Scala Orchestra.
b. 1980 in Philadelphia, Pennsylvania
Source: *ConMus 7*

Chang and Eng
[Chang and Eng Bunker]
American. Siamese Twins
Toured carnivals in US, Europe, 1829-54; Chang died first, Eng died of fright two hrs. later.
b. May 11, 1811 in Meklong, Thailand
d. Jan 17, 1874 in Mount Airy, North Carolina

Source: *ApCAB; BioIn 6, 11, 12, 13; DcAmB; Dis&D; WebAB 74, 79; WhAm HS*

Chang Tso-Lin
"Old Marshall"
Chinese. Military Leader
Manchurian leader from 1918; his army driven from Peking by Nationalists, 1928.
b. 1873 in Shenyang, China
d. Jun 4, 1928 in Manchuria, China
Source: *HarEnMi; NewCol 75; WebBD 83*

Channing, Carol
[Carol Channing Lowe]
American. Actor
Vivacious, husky-voiced blonde best-known for Tony-winning role in *Hello Dolly,* 1964.
b. Jan 31, 1923 in Seattle, Washington
Source: *BiDAmM; BiE&WWA; BkPepl; ConMus 6; ConTFT 3; CurBio 64; EncMT; FamA&A; FilmgC; IntMPA 82, 84, 86, 88; IntWW 75, 76; LibW; MotPP; NewYTBE 70; NotNAT; WhoAm 74, 76, 78, 80, 82, 84, 86, 88, 92, 94, 95, 96, 97; WhoAmW 64, 66, 68, 70, 72, 74, 83, 91, 93, 95, 97; WhoEnt 92; WhoHol A; WhoWor 74, 78; WorAl; WorAlBi*

Channing, Edward Perkins
American. Historian
Wrote *History of the United States* (six vols.), 1905-25; won Pulitzer for sixth vol., *War for Southern Independence.*
b. Jun 15, 1856 in Dorchester, Massachusetts
d. Jan 7, 1931 in Cambridge, Massachusetts
Source: *AmBi; ApCAB; DcAmB; DcLB 17; HarEnUS; McGEWB; NatCAB 13; OxCAmH; TwCBDA; WebBD 83; WhAm 1*

Channing, Stockard
[Susan Williams Antonia Stockard Channing Schmidt]
American. Actor
Comic actress; played Rizzo in *Grease,* 1978; won Tony for *A Day in the Death of Joe Egg,* 1985; Desk Award for *Woman in Mind,* 1988.
b. Feb 13, 1944 in New York, New York
Source: *BiDFilm 94; ConTFT 1, 7; CurBio 91; EncAFC; HalFC 84, 88; IntMPA 86, 88, 92, 94, 96; InWom SUP; LegTOT; VarWW 85; WhoAm 86, 95, 96, 97; WhoAmW 81; WhoHol 92, A; WhoThe 81*

Channing, Walter
American. Physician
First to use ether in childbirth cases, 1847.
b. Apr 15, 1786 in Newport, Rhode Island
d. Jul 27, 1876 in Boston, Massachusetts
Source: *Alli, SUP; ApCAB; BioIn 3; DcAmAu; DcAmB; DcAmMeB, 84; DcNAA; Drake; TwCBDA; WhAm HS*

Channing, William Ellery
American. Clergy, Abolitionist
Apostle of Unitarian movement; contributed to development of Transcendentalism.
b. Apr 7, 1780 in Newport, Rhode Island
d. Oct 2, 1842 in Bennington, Vermont
Source: *Alli; AmAu; AmAu&B; AmBi; AmOrN; AmPeW; AmRef; AmSocL; ApCAB; BbD; Benet 87, 96; BenetAL 91; BiD&SB; BiDMoPL; BiDTran; BioIn 1, 2, 3, 4, 5, 6, 9, 12, 15, 16, 19; CamGEL; CamGLE; CamHAL; CasWL; CelCen; Chambr 3; CnDAL; CyAL 1; DcAmAu; DcAmB; DcAmC; DcAmReB 1, 2; DcAmSR; DcAmTB; DcBiPP; DcEnL; DcLB 1, 59; DcNAA; Drake; EncAB-H 1974, 1996; EncARH; EvLB; HarEnUS; LinLib L, S; LuthC 75; McGEWB; NatCAB 5; NinCLC 17; OxCAmH; OxCAmL 65, 83, 95; OxCEng 67, 85, 95; PenC AM; REn; REnAL; TwCBDA; WebAB 74, 79; WhAm HS; WhCiWar*

Chantrey, Francis Legatt, Sir
English. Artist
Famous sculptures include equestrians of Wellington, George IV, London.
b. Apr 7, 1781 in Jordanthorpe, England
d. Nov 25, 1841 in London, England
Source: *BioIn 4, 13, 14, 16; CelCen; DcArts; DcNaB, C; NewC; NewCol 75*

Chanute, Octave
American. Engineer, Aviator
Built railroads, bridges, c. 1853; improved glider designs contributed to successful flights of Orville, Wilbur Wright.
b. Feb 18, 1832 in Paris, France
d. Nov 23, 1910 in Chicago, Illinois
Source: *AmBi; BiInAmS; BioIn 1, 3, 6, 7, 9, 12; DcAmB; DcNAA; InSci; NatCAB 10; TwCBDA; WebAB 74, 79; WhAm 1*

Chao, Yuen Ren
Chinese. Poet
Best known for creating a phonetic alphabet to translate Chinese to English.
b. Nov 3, 1892 in Tientsin
d. Feb 24, 1982 in Cambridge, Massachusetts
Source: *AmAu&B; BioIn 12, 13, 14; ConAu 106, P-2; DrAS 74F, 78F; FifIDA; IntAu&W 76, 82; NewYTBS 84; WhAm 8; WhoAm 74; WhoLA; WhoWest 78, 80, 82; WhoWor 76, 78, 80, 82; WrDr 76, 80, 82*

Chapais, Thomas, Sir
Canadian. Journalist, Statesman
Leader in Quebec Legislative Council, 1946.
b. Mar 23, 1858 in Saint Denis, Quebec, Canada
d. Jul 15, 1948? in Saint Denis, Quebec, Canada
Source: *AmLY; BioIn 1; CanWr; DcNAA; MacDCB 78; ObitOF 79; OxCCan, SUP*

Chapelle, Dickey
American. Photojournalist
Combat photojournalist; killed in Vietnam mine blast.
b. Mar 14, 1918 in Shorewood, Wisconsin
d. Nov 4, 1965 in Chulai, Vietnam
Source: *BioIn 6, 7, 10; DcAmB S7; EncAJ*

Chapin, Dwight Lee
American. Criminal
Organized "dirty tricks" unit to harass Democrats; convicted of perjury, 1974.
b. Dec 2, 1940 in Wichita, Kansas
Source: *PolProf NF; WhoAm 80, 82, 84; WhoAmP 73, 75, 77, 79; WhoMW 82*

Chapin, Harry Foster
American. Singer, Songwriter
Popular 1960s ballader, whose story songs include "Taxi," 1972.
b. Dec 7, 1942 in New York, New York
d. Jul 16, 1981 in Jericho, New York
Source: *ConAu 104; HarEnR 86; IlEncRk; NewYTBS 81; RkOn 78; WhoAm 78, 80; WhoRock 81*

Chapin, James Ormsbee
American. Artist
Americana painter of "environmental realism"; subjects range from "Barn in Snow" to portraits of Robert Frost.
b. Jul 9, 1887 in West Orange, New Jersey
d. Jul 12, 1975 in Toronto, Ontario, Canada
Source: *CurBio 40, 75; McGDA; WhAm 6*

Chapin, Roy Dikeman
American. Manufacturer, Government Official
With J L Hudson, H E Coffin, R B Jackson, organized Hudson Motor Car Co., 1900; secretary of Commerce, 1932-34.
b. Feb 23, 1880 in Lansing, Michigan
d. Feb 16, 1936 in Detroit, Michigan
Source: *BiDAmBL 83; BiDrUSE 71, 89; BioIn 2, 4, 10; DcAmB S2; EncABHB 4; NatCAB 34; WhAm 1*

Chapin, Roy Dikeman, Jr.
American. Auto Executive
Director, Hudson Motor Car Co., 1946-54; chairman, American Motors, 1967-78.
b. Sep 21, 1915 in Detroit, Michigan
Source: *BioIn 10, 11; BlueB 76; EncABHB 5; IntWW 74, 75, 76, 77, 78, 79, 80, 81, 82, 83; NewYTBS 74; St&PR 84; Ward 77; WhoAm 74, 76, 78, 80, 82, 84, 86, 88, 90, 92, 94, 95, 96, 97; WhoFI 74, 75, 77, 79, 81; WhoMW 80, 82; WhoWor 74, 76, 78*

Chapin, Schuyler Garrison
American. Manager, Impresario
Manager, Metropolitan Opera Association, 1972-75; wrote autobiography, *Musical Chairs,* 1977.
b. Feb 13, 1923 in New York, New York
Source: *BioIn 6, 9, 10, 11; BlueB 76; ConAu 77; CurBio 74; IntWW 74, 75, 76, 77, 78, 79, 80, 81, 82, 83, 89, 91, 93; IntWWM 77, 85, 90; WhoAm 74, 76, 78, 80, 82, 84, 86, 88, 90, 92, 94, 95, 96, 97; WhoAmM 83; WhoE 74, 75, 77; WhoEnt 92; WhoOp 76*

Chaplin, Charlie
[Sir Charles Spencer]
English. Actor, Author, Composer
Known for character created in *The Tramp,* 1915; won special Oscar, 1972; considered greatest comic actor of silents; much imitated style.
b. Apr 16, 1889 in London, England
d. Dec 25, 1977 in Vevey, Switzerland
Source: *AmDec 1920; Benet 87, 96; BenetAL 91; BioIn 14, 15, 16, 17, 18, 19, 20, 21; CelR; CmCal; ConAu 73, 81; ConDr 73, 77A; CurBio 40, 61; DcArts; DcFM; DcLB 44; EncAB-H 1974; EncAFC; EncTR 91; FacFETw; Film 1, 2; IlWWHD 1; IntDcF 1-2; IntMPA 77; IntWW 74; LegTOT; LiExTwC; NewYTBS 77; OxCAmL 65; OxCPMus; QDrFCA 92; RAdv 14; RComAH; REn; REnAL; TwYS, A; WebAB 79; Who 74; WhoAm 74; WhoThe 77A; WhScrn 83*

Chaplin, Geraldine
American. Actor
Daughter of Charlie Chaplin; films include *Doctor Zhivago,* 1965; *Nashville,* 1975.
b. Jul 31, 1944 in Santa Monica, California
Source: *BiDFilm 94; BioIn 6, 7, 8, 9, 11, 12; ConTFT 3, 9; CurBio 79; EncEurC; FilmgC; HalFC 84, 88; IntDcF 1-3, 2-3; IntMPA 81, 82, 84, 86, 88, 92, 94, 96; IntWW 91, 93; InWom SUP; ItaFilm; LegTOT; MotPP; NewYTBS 77; WhoAm 74, 76, 78, 80, 82, 84, 86, 88, 90, 92, 94, 95, 96, 97; WhoAmW 83, 85, 95, 97; WhoEnt 92; WhoHol 92, A; WorAl; WorAlBi*

Chaplin, Saul
American. Songwriter, Producer
Often collaborated with Sammy Cahn; scored films *Kiss Me Kate,* 1953; *West Side Story,* 1961; wrote "Anniversary Song."
b. Feb 19, 1912 in New York, New York
Source: *ASCAP 66; BiDAmM; BioIn 10, 20; CmMov; CmpEPM; FilmgC; HalFC 84, 88; IntMPA 75, 76, 77, 78, 79, 81, 82, 84, 86, 88, 92, 94, 96; ItaFilm; OxCFilm; OxCPMus*

Chaplin, Sydney
American.
Broadway musicals include *Funny Girl;* son of Charlie Chaplin, Lita Grey.
b. Mar 30, 1926 in Los Angeles, California
Source: *BiE&WWA; EncMT; FilmEn; FilmgC; HalFC 84, 88; ItaFilm; MotPP; NotNAT; WhoHol 92, A*

Chaplin, Sydney Dryden
English. Actor, Comedian
Half-brother, manager of Charlie Chaplin, who appeared in comedies, 1920s.
b. Mar 17, 1885 in Cape Town, South Africa
d. Apr 16, 1956 in Nice, France
Source: *FilmEn; FilmgC; MotPP; ObitOF 79; TwYS*

Chapman, Ceil
[Cecilia Mitchell Chapman]
American. Fashion Designer
Known for designing seductive evening gowns with Chapman Inc., 1940-65.
b. Feb 19, 1912 in New York, New York
d. Jul 13, 1979 in New York, New York
Source: *BioIn 12; WorFshn*

Chapman, Christian Addison
American. Diplomat
Veteran US foreign service official; survived assassination attempt while ambassador to France, 1981.
b. Sep 19, 1921 in Paris, France
Source: *USBiR 74*

Chapman, (Anthony) Colin (Bruce)
English. Auto Manufacturer
Founded Lotus Cars Co., Ltd., 1955; involved in development of DeLorean sports car.
b. May 19, 1928 in Richmond, England
d. Dec 16, 1982 in Norfolk, England
Source: *AnObit 1982; BioIn 7, 8, 13, 15, 16; DcNaB 1981; IntWW 82; NewYTBS 82; Who 82; WhoWor 80, 82*

Chapman, Frank Michler
American. Ornithologist
Founder, *Bird Lore* mag., later *Audubon,* 1899; edited until 1935; wrote *Handbook of Birds* series.
b. Jun 12, 1864 in Englewood, New Jersey
d. Nov 15, 1945 in New York, New York
Source: *AmAu&B; BioIn 1, 2, 3, 4, 7, 12; CurBio 46; DcAmAu; DcAmB S3; DcNAA; DcScB S2; InSci; JBA 34; LinLib S; NatCAB 9, 36; NatLAC; REnAL; TwCA, SUP; WebAB 74, 79; WhAm 2*

Chapman, George
English. Poet, Dramatist
Best known for poetic translation of Homer works, 1598-1624.
b. 1560 in Hitchin, England
d. May 12, 1634 in London, England
Source: *AtlBL; BritAu; BritWr 1; CamGLE; CamGWoT; CasWL; Chambr 1; CrtT 1; CyWA 58; McGEWB; McGEWD 72, 84; MouLC 1; OxCEng 85; OxCThe 67, 83; PenC ENG; PlP&P; REn*

Chapman, Gilbert Whipple
American. Business Executive
Pres., NY Public Library, 1959-71; one of original directors of Lincoln Center for Performing Arts.
b. May 24, 1902 in Woodmere, New York
d. Dec 16, 1979 in New York, New York
Source: *BiE&WWA; BioIn 4, 12; CurBio 57, 80; NewYTBS 79; WhAm 7*

Chapman, Graham
[Monty Python's Flying Circus]
English. Actor, Comedian
Founding member, Monty Python's Flying Circus comedy troupe; TV program broadcast by BBC, 1969-74.
b. Jan 8, 1941 in Leicester, England
d. Oct 4, 1989 in Maidstone, England
Source: *AnObit 1989; BioIn 10; ConAu 35NR, 116, 129; ConLC 21; ConTFT 8; HalFC 88; ItaFilm; WhAm 10; WhoAm 82, 84, 86, 88*

Chapman, John (Arthur)
American. Critic
Editor, *Broadway's Best,* 1957-60; with *NY News,* 1920-72.
b. Jun 25, 1900 in Denver, Colorado
d. Jan 19, 1972 in Westport, Connecticut
Source: *AmAu&B; BiE&WWA; BioIn 6, 9; ConAu 33R; DcAmB S9; IntAu&W 77; NotNAT B; OxCAmT 84; WhAm 5; WhoThe 72*

Chapman, Leonard F, Jr.
American. Army Officer
With USMC, 1935-72; commander, Immigration and Naturalization Service, 1973-77.
b. Nov 3, 1913 in Key West, Florida
Source: *BlueB 76; WebAMB; WhoAm 80; WhoGov 72*

Chapman, Mark David
American. Murderer
Shot, killed John Lennon, Dec 8, 1980.
b. May 10, 1955 in Fort Worth, Texas
Source: *BioIn 12, 13; LegTOT; MurCaTw; WorAlBi*

Chapman, Tracy
American. Singer, Songwriter
Folksinger; won several Grammys, 1989, for hit single "Fast Car."
b. Mar 30, 1964 in Cleveland, Ohio
Source: *ConMus 4; CurBio 89; DcTwCCu 5; DrBlPA 90; EncRkSt; LegTOT; News 89-2; NotBlAW 2; WhoAfA 96; WhoAm 92, 94, 95, 96, 97; WhoAmW 91, 93; WhoBlA 90, 92, 94; WhoEnt 92*

Chappell, Fred (Davis)
American. Author
Novels include *I Am One of You Forever,* 1985; *Brighten the Corner Where You Are,* 1989.
b. May 28, 1936 in Canton, North Carolina
Source: *AmAu&B; Au&Wr 71; BioIn 9, 13, 14, 15, 17, 19, 20; ConAu 4AS, 5R, 8NR, 33NR; ConLC 40, 78; ConNov 96; ConPo 96; DcLB 6, 105; DrAF 76; DrAP 75; DrAS 74E, 78E, 82E; EncAHmr; IntAu&W 76, 93; IntWWP 82; OxCAmL 95; OxCTwCP; PenEncH; ScF&FL 92; WhoAm 82, 84, 86, 88, 90, 92, 94, 95, 96, 97; WhoSSW 73, 75, 76, 91, 93; WhoUSWr 88; WhoWrEP 89, 92, 95; WorAu 1980*

Chappell, Tom
[Thomas Matthew Chappell]
American. Entrepreneur
Founded Tom's of Maine, 1970, a manufacturer of personal-care products.
b. Feb 17, 1943 in Pittsfield, Massachusetts
Source: *CurBio 94*

Chappell, William
English. Dancer, Designer
Designed scenery, costumes for Sadler's Well, 1937—; Covent Garden, 1947—.
b. Sep 27, 1908 in Wolverhampton, England
Source: *BiDD; BioIn 3, 4, 11; ConAu 106; EncMT; IntDcB; Who 74, 82, 83, 85, 88, 90, 92, 94; WhoThe 72, 77, 81*

Chaptal, Jean Antoine, Comte de Chanteloup
French. Chemist
Produced gunpowder, acids during Revolution; minister of Agriculture, Commerce, and Industry, 1815.
b. Jun 4, 1756 in Lozere, France
d. Jul 30, 1832 in Paris, France
Source: *AsBiEn; BlkwCE; DcBiPP; DcCathB; DcScB; Dis&D; NewCol 75; WebBD 83*

Char, Rene (Emile)
French. Poet
Outspoken poet of the Resistance; wrote short, brillant pieces including "Hammer without a Master," 1934.
b. Jun 14, 1907 in L'Isle Sorgue, France
d. Feb 19, 1988 in Paris, France
Source: *AnObit 1988; Benet 87, 96; BioIn 15, 16, 17; CasWL; CnMWL; ConAu 13R, 32NR, 124; ConFLW 84; ConLC 9, 11, 14, 55; DcTwCCu 2; EncWL 3; EvEuW; FacFETw; GuFrLit 1; IntAu&W 77, 89; IntWW 74, 75, 76, 77, 78, 79, 80, 81, 82, 83; IntWWP 77; LinLib L; MajTwCW; ModFrL; ModRL; NewYTBS 88; OxCFr; PenC EUR; RAdv 14, 13-2; REn; TwCWr; WhoAm 74, 76; WhoFr 79; WhoTwCL; WhoWor 74, 76, 78; WorAu 1950*

Charcot, Jean Baptiste Etienne Auguste
French. Explorer
Did oceanographic studies during seven Greenland voyages; drowned in shipwreck; son of Jean Martin.
b. Jul 15, 1867 in Neuilly-sur-Seine, France
d. Sep 16, 1936, Iceland
Source: *DcScB; InSci; NewCol 75; OxCShps*

Charcot, Jean Martin
French. Physician
Neurologist; his work on hysteria, hypnotism influenced his pupil, Sigmund Freud.
b. Nov 29, 1825 in Paris, France
d. Aug 16, 1893 in Morvan, France
Source: *BiESc; BioIn 5, 6, 7, 9; DcBiPP; EncO&P 2, 3; InSci; LarDcSc; McGEWB; NamesHP; OxCMed 86; WebBD 83; WorAl*

Chardin, Jean Baptiste Simeon
French. Artist
Wholesome still lifes include "Le Benedicte," 1740.
b. Nov 2, 1699 in Paris, France
d. Dec 6, 1779 in Paris, France
Source: *AtlBL; BioIn 1, 3, 4, 5, 6, 7, 8, 10, 11, 12, 13; BlkwCE; ClaDrA; Dis&D; McGEWB; OxCArt; OxCFr; REn; WebBD 83; WhDW; WorAl*

Chardonnet, Louis Marie Hilaire Bernigaud
French. Chemist, Inventor
Patented rayon, 1884, first artificial fiber commonly used.
b. May 1, 1839 in Besancon, France
d. Mar 12, 1924 in Paris, France
Source: *AsBiEn*

Chares
Greek. Sculptor
Carved Colossus of Rhodes, one of the seven wonders of the ancient world.
b. 320BC
Source: *NewCol 75; WebBD 83*

Charisse, Cyd
[Tula Ellice Finklea; Mrs. Tony Martin]
American. Dancer, Actor
Renowned for long, shapely legs; films include *Silk Stockings,* 1957; Fred Astaire's last dancing partner.
b. Mar 8, 1923 in Amarillo, Texas
Source: *BiDD; BiDFilm; BioIn 3, 4, 5, 10, 11; CmMov; CurBio 54; FilmgC; GoodHs; IntMPA 75, 76, 77, 78, 79, 81, 82, 84, 86, 88; InWom; LegTOT; MotPP; MovMk; OxCFilm; VarWW 85; WhoAm 74, 76, 78, 80, 82, 90, 92; WhoAmW 58, 66, 68, 70, 72, 74, 83; WhoEnt 92; WhoHol A; WorAl; WorAlBi; WorEFlm*

Charlemagne
[Charles the Great]
French. Ruler
Conquered, ruled almost all Christian lands of Europe, 768-814.
b. Apr 2, 742 in Aix-la-Chapelle, France
d. Jan 28, 814 in Aix-la-Chapelle, Austrasia
Source: *AsBiEn; Benet 87, 96; BioIn 1, 2, 3, 4, 5, 6, 7, 8, 9, 10, 11, 12, 14, 15, 16, 17, 18, 19, 20; BlmGEL; DcCathB; DcEuL; DcSpL; DicTyr; Dis&D; EncO&P 1, 2, 3; GenMudB; HarEnMi; HisWorL; LegTOT; LinLib L, S; LuthC 75; McGEWB; MediFra; NewC; OxCEng 85, 95; OxCFr; OxCGer 76; OxCLaw; OxDcByz; REn; WebBD 83; WhDW; WorAl; WorAlBi*

Charlemagne, Manno
[Emmanuel Charlemagne]
Haitian. Politician, Singer
Mayor of Port-au-Prince, 1995—.
b. 1948 in Port-au-Prince, Haiti
Source: *ConBlB 11*

Charles, Prince of Wales
[Charles Philip Arthur George]
English. Prince
First child of Queen Elizabeth II and Prince Philip; currently heir to British throne; divorced Diana, Princess of Wales, 1996.
b. Nov 14, 1948 in London, England
Source: *BioIn 1, 2, 3, 4, 5, 6, 7, 8, 9, 10, 11, 12, 13, 14, 15, 16, 17, 18, 19, 20, 21; BkPepl; CurBio 69; EncWB; FacFETw; LegTOT; News 95, 95-3; NewYTBS 77, 81, 88; WhoWor 76, 78, 80, 82, 84, 87, 89, 91, 93, 95, 96, 97; WorAlBi*

Charles, Bob
[Robert Charles]
New Zealander. Golfer
Joined US tour, 1963; won British Open, 1963; considered golf's best left-handed player.
b. Mar 14, 1936 in Cartenton, New Zealand
Source: *BioIn 6, 13, 20; WhoGolf*

Charles, Ezzard
[The Hawk]
American. Boxer
Heavyweight champ, 1949-51; lost to Walcott; Hall of Fame, 1970.
b. Jul 7, 1921 in Lawrenceville, Georgia
d. May 28, 1975 in Chicago, Illinois
Source: *BioIn 1, 2, 3, 5, 8, 9, 10; BioNews 74; BoxReg; CurBio 49, 75, 75N; InB&W 80; LegTOT; NewYTBS 75; ObitT 1971; WhoBox 74*

Charles, Glen
American. Writer, Producer
Won Emmys, 1979, 1980, 1981, for "Taxi"; 1983, 1984 for "Cheers."
Source: *BioIn 16, 21; VarWW 85; WhoAm 92, 94, 95, 96, 97; WhoEnt 92*

Charles, Jacques-Alexandre-Cesar
French. Physicist, Mathematician
Constructed first hydrogen balloon, 1783.
b. Nov 12, 1746 in Beaugency, France
d. Apr 7, 1823 in Paris, France
Source: *AsBiEn; BiESc; BioIn 1, 7; DcScB; LarDcSc; WhDW; WorAl; WorScD*

Charles, Lee
American. Writer, Producer
Wrote award-winning scripts for several TV shows, including "Taxi"; "Cheers"; "MASH."
Source: *VarWW 85*

Charles, Mary Eugenia
Dominican. Political Leader
Prime minister of Dominica, 1980—; requested US invasion of Grenada, 1983.
b. May 15, 1919 in Pointe Michel, Dominica
Source: *BiDLAmC; BioIn 12, 13; ConBlB 10; CurBio 86; Who 85, 88, 90, 92; WhoWor 82, 84, 87, 89, 91, 93, 95, 96, 97; WomFir; WomWR*

Charles, Ray
[Charles Raymond Offenberg]
American. Composer
Won Emmys for "The First Nine Months Are the Hardest," 1971; "The Funny Side of Marriage," 1972.
b. Sep 13, 1918 in Chicago, Illinois
Source: *ASCAP 66; BiDAmM; PenEncP; VarWW 85; WhoEnt 92*

Charles, Ray
[Ray Charles Robinson]
"The Genius of Soul"
American. Singer, Songwriter, Musician
Blind 10-time Grammy winner; signature song is his 1960 version of "Georgia on My Mind."
b. Sep 23, 1930 in Albany, Georgia
Source: *Baker 78, 84, 92; BgBkCoM; BiDAfM; BiDAmM; BkPepl; BlueB 76; BluesWW; CelR 90; ConMus 1; CurBio 65, 92; DcArts; DcTwCCu 1, 5; DrBlPA, 90; Ebony 1; EncAB-H 1974; EncFCWM 83; EncJzS; EncPR&S 89; EncRk 88; EncRkSt; FacFETw; HarEnCM 87; HarEnR 86; IlEncJ; InB&W 80, 85; IntWW 75, 76, 77, 78, 79, 80, 81, 82, 83, 89, 91, 93; LegTOT; NewAmDM; NewGrDA 86; NewGrDJ 88, 94; OxCPMus; RAdv 14, 13-3; RkOn 74, 82; RolSEnR 83; SoulM; WhoAfA 96; WhoAm 74, 76, 78, 80, 82, 84, 86, 88, 90, 92, 94, 95, 96, 97; WhoBlA 75, 77, 80, 85, 92, 94; WhoEnt 92; WhoHol 92; WhoRock 81; WhoWor 74, 76, 78; WorAl; WorAlBi*

Charles, Suzette
[Suzette DeGaetano]
American. Beauty Contest Winner
First runner-up in Miss America pageant, 1983; succeed Vanessa Williams, Jul 1983 when she was forced to give up crown.
b. 1963 in Philadelphia, Pennsylvania

Charles I
English. Ruler
King of Great Britain, Ireland, 1625-49; need for money, power led to English Civil Wars.
b. Nov 19, 1600 in Dunfermline, Scotland
d. Jan 30, 1649 in London, England
Source: *BioIn 10; DcBiPP; WebBD 83; WhDW*

Charles II
[Charles the Bald]
French. Ruler
Holy Roman emperor, 875-77; successfully invaded Italy, 875; failed to take over German kingdom.
b. Jun 13, 823 in Frankfurt am Main, Germany
d. Oct 6, 877 in Mont Cenis, France
Source: *HarEnMi; NewCol 75; WebBD 83*

CharlesII
"Merry Monarch"
English. Ruler
King of Great Britain, Ireland, 1660-85; wanted to strengthen monarchy, reduce financial power of Parliament.
b. May 29, 1630 in London, England
d. Feb 6, 1685 in London, England
Source: *DcBiPP; WebBD 83; WhDW*

Charles Martel
[Charles the Hammer]
Ruler
Head of Frankish empire later ruled by grandson Charlemagne.
b. 689
d. 741
Source: *DcBiPP; DcCathB; LinLib S; OxCFr; REn; WhDW; WorAl*

Charleson, Ian
Scottish. Actor
Starred in Oscar-winning *Chariots of Fire,* 1981; died of AIDS.
b. Aug 11, 1949 in Edinburgh, Scotland
d. Jan 6, 1990 in London, England
Source: *AnObit 1990; BioIn 12, 16, 17; ConTFT 1, 4, 11; IntMPA 86, 88; ItaFilm; LegTOT; NewYTBS 81; Who 90; WhoThe 81*

Charleston, Oscar McKinley
"Charlie"
American. Baseball Player, Baseball Manager
Player/mgr. for Pittsburgh Crawfords, great team in Negro leagues, 1932-38; Hall of Fame, 1976.
b. Oct 12, 1896 in Indianapolis, Indiana
d. Oct 5, 1954 in Philadelphia, Pennsylvania
Source: *BiDAmSp BB*

Charles V
Ruler
Hapsburg King of Spain, 1516-50; Holy Roman emperor, 1519; signed the Treaty of Crecy, 1544; Peace of Augsburg, 1555.
b. Feb 24, 1500 in Ghent, Flanders
d. Sep 21, 1558 in Placiencia, Spain
Source: *DcBiPP; DcCathB; McGEWB; WhDW*

Charles VII
[Charles Albert; Charles of Bavaria]
Ruler
Holy Roman emperor, 1742-45; in War of Austrian Succession, 1740-48.
b. Aug 6, 1697 in Brussels, Belgium
d. Jan 20, 1745 in Munich, Germany
Source: *DcBiPP; NewCol 75; WebBD 83*

Charles XII
Swedish. Ruler
King of Sweden, 1697-1718; lost battle of Poltava, 1709, which ended Swedish Supremacy.
b. Jun 17, 1682 in Stockholm, Sweden
d. Nov 30, 1718 in Fredrikshald, Norway
Source: *NewCol 75; WebBD 83; WhDW*

Charlevoix, Pierre Francis Xavier de
French. Traveler, Author
Jesuit; wrote detailed accounts of travels across North America: *Journal Historique,* 1744.
b. Oct 29, 1682 in Saint-Quentin, France
d. Feb 1, 1761 in La Fleche, France
Source: *BiDSA; DcBiPP; DcCanB 3; DcCathB; HarEnUS; OxCAmH; OxCCan*

Charlie Daniels Band, The
[Tom "Bigfoot" Crain; Charlie Daniels; Joe "Taz" DiGregorio; Fred Edwards; Charlie Hatward; Don Murray]
American. Music Group
Country-rock band, formed 1973; biggest hit, "The Devil Went Down to Georgia," 1979, popularized in film *Urban Cowboy.*
Source: *ConMuA 80A; CurBio 59; EncFCWM 83; HarEnR 86; IlEncRk; RolSEnR 83; WhoRocM 82*

Charlip, Remy
American. Dancer, Author, Actor
Member of Cunningham dance co., 1950-62; designed sets, costumes for concert, theater works, 1951—.
b. Jan 10, 1929 in New York, New York
Source: *AuBYP 2, 3; BiDD; BioIn 5, 7, 8, 9, 13; ChhPo S1; ChlBkCr; ChlLR 8; ConAu 33R, 44NR; IlsCB 1946, 1957; IntAu&W 91, 93; MajAI; SmATA 4, 68; ThrBJA; WrDr 76, 80, 82, 84, 86, 88, 90, 92, 94, 96*

Charlot, Jean
French. Artist, Illustrator
Muralist; known for his frescoes with a Mayan influence; book illustrator.
b. Feb 7, 1898 in Paris, France
d. Mar 20, 1979 in Honolulu, Hawaii

Source: *ArtsAmW 1; BioIn 1, 2, 3, 4, 5, 6, 8, 9, 10, 11, 12, 14; BriEAA; CathA 1952; ChlBkCr; ConAu 4NR, 5R; CurBio 84N; DcTwCCu 4; GrAmP; IlsBYP; IlsCB 1744, 1946, 1957; IntWW 91; McGDA; MorJA; SmATA 8, 31N; WhAm 7; WhAmArt 85; WhoAm 74, 76, 78, 80; WhoAmA 73, 76, 78, 80N, 82N, 84N, 86N, 89N, 91N, 93N; WhoWest 74, 76, 78; WrDr 76, 80*

Charlotte Aldegonde E. M. Wilhelmine
Luxembourg. Ruler
Grand Duchess of Luxembourg, 1919-64; helped to found European Common Market.
b. Jan 23, 1896 in Chateau de Berg, Luxembourg
d. Jul 9, 1985, Luxembourg
Source: *CurBio 49, 85N; IntWW 83; WhoWor 84*

Charlotte Sophia
English. Consort
Queen of George III.
b. 1744
d. Nov 17, 1818 in Kew, England
Source: *BioIn 1, 2, 4, 8, 10, 11, 12, 15; DcNaB; Dis&D; InWom*

Charlton, Bobby
[Robert Charlton]
British. Soccer Player
With Manchester United, 1954-73; scored 245 career goals; won World Cup, 1966; author of books on soccer.
b. Oct 11, 1937
Source: *BioIn 7, 9; FacFETw; IntWW 82, 83, 89, 91, 93; Who 74, 82, 83, 85, 88, 90, 92, 94; WorESoc; WrDr 80, 82, 84, 86, 88, 90, 92, 94, 96*

Charmoli, Tony
American. Choreographer
Most successful presentation was *Your Hit Parade,* 1950-58.
b. Jun 11, 1922 in Mountain Iron, Montana
Source: *BiDD; LesBEnT; WhoAm 80*

Charney, Nicolas Herman
American. Publisher
Publisher, *Book Digest,* 1973-75; founded *Videofashion Monthly,* 1980.
b. May 11, 1941 in Saint Paul, Minnesota
Source: *BioIn 12; WhoAm 74, 76, 78, 80, 82; WhoEnt 92*

Charnin, Martin
American. Director, Producer, Lyricist
Won Tony, best score, 1977, for *Annie* which he also directed.
b. Nov 24, 1934 in New York, New York
Source: *ASCAP 66; BiE&WWA; BioIn 12; CelR 90; ConAu 103; ConTFT 2, 10; LesBEnT 92; NewYTET; NotNAT; OxCAmT 84; WhoAm 86, 88, 90, 92, 94, 95, 96, 97; WhoE 95, 97; WhoEnt 92; WhoThe 72, 77, 81; WhoWor 96, 97*

Charnley, John, Sir
English. Surgeon
Orthopedic surgeon who perfected total prosthetic hip replacement.
b. Aug 29, 1911 in Burg, England
d. Aug 12, 1982 in Knutsford, England
Source: *AnObit 1982; BioIn 10, 11, 13, 14, 17; CamDcSc; ConAu 107; DcNaB 1981; LarDcSc; OxCMed 86; Who 74, 82; WhoWor 82; WorInv*

Charo
[Maria Rosario Pilar Martinez]
Spanish. Actor, Singer
Recorded several albums; appeared on TV shows including "Love Boat."
b. Jan 15, 1951 in Murcia, Spain
Source: *LegTOT; VarWW 85; WhoHol 92*

Charoux, Siegfried
English. Sculptor
Best known for works in London: *The Judge; The Cellist; The Motor Cyclist.*
b. Oct 15, 1896 in Vienna, Austria
d. Apr 26, 1967 in London, England
Source: *DcNaB 1961; ObitOF 79; OxCTwCA; TwCPaSc; WhoArt 80, 82, 84*

Charpak, George
French. Physicist
Won Nobel Prize in Physics, 1992 for inventions that aid in high-energy physics research.

Charpentier, Gustave
French. Composer
Wrote realist opera *Louise,* 1900, which depicted working class.
b. Jun 25, 1860 in Dieuze, France
d. Feb 18, 1956 in Paris, France
Source: *Baker 78, 84, 92; BioIn 1, 2, 3, 4, 8, 9, 12; DcArts; DcTwCCu 2; IntDcOp; LinLib S; MetOEnc; NewAmDM; NewEOp 71; NewGrDO; NewOxM; NotNAT B; OxCFr; OxCMus; OxDcOp; PenDiMP A; REn*

Charpentier, Johann von
German. Scientist
Glaciologist; pioneered theory that the movement of glaciers over great distances created various geologic phenomena.
b. Dec 8, 1786 in Freiberg, Saxony
d. Dec 12, 1855 in Bex, Switzerland
Source: *DcScB*

Charpentier, Marc-Antoine
French. Composer
Seventeen operas include *Medee,* 1693.
b. 1634 in Paris, France
d. Feb 24, 1704 in Paris, France
Source: *Baker 84; IntDcOp; NewEOp 71*

Charriere, Henri
"Papillon"
French. Author, Murderer
Escaped from Devil's Island, 1941; book *Papillion* sold over five million copies; Steve McQueen starred in movie, 1973.
b. Nov 6, 1906 in Ardeche, France
d. Jul 29, 1973 in Madrid, Spain
Source: *AuSpks; BioIn 8, 9, 10, 11; ConAu 45, 101; NewYTBE 73; ObitOF 79; ObitT 1971; WhScrn 77*

Charron, Pierre
French. Theologian, Philosopher
Contributed to 17th century theological thought.
b. 1541 in Paris, France
d. Nov 16, 1603 in Paris, France
Source: *BioIn 6, 13, 14; CasWL; DcBiPP; DcCathB; DcEuL; EncUnb; GuFrLit 2; McGEWB; OxCFr; PenC EUR*

Charteris, Leslie
[Leslie Charles Bowyer Yin]
American. Author
Best known for creating Simon Templar in *The Saint* series; films, TV shows have been based on the stories.
b. May 12, 1907, Singapore
d. Apr 15, 1993 in Windsor, England
Source: *AmAu&B; AnObit 1993; Au&Wr 71; BioIn 1, 4, 9, 14, 18, 19; BlueB 76; ConAu 5R, 10NR, 141; ConLC 81; CorpD; CrtSuMy; DcArts; DcLB 77; EncMys; EncSF 93; EvLB; FilmgC; HalFC 84, 88; IntAu&W 76, 77, 82, 86, 89, 91, 93; IntMPA 75, 76, 77, 78, 79, 81, 82, 84, 86, 88; IntWW 74, 75, 76, 77, 78, 79, 80, 81, 82, 83, 89, 91, 93; LegTOT; LngCTC; MnBBF; NewC; Novels; REn; REnAL; ScF&FL 1, 2, 92; TwCA, SUP; TwCCr&M 80, 85, 91; TwCWr; WhAm 11; WhE&EA; WhLit; Who 74, 82, 83, 85, 88, 90, 92; WhoAm 74, 76, 78, 80, 82, 84, 86, 88, 90, 92; WhoSpyF; WhoSSW 73; WrDr 76, 80, 82, 84, 86, 88, 90, 92, 94N*

Chartier, Alain
"Father of French Eloquence"; "Seneca of France"
French. Author, Poet
Best-known prose, *Le Quadrilogue Invectif,* 1422, symbolized emerging European nationalism; poem, "La Belle Dame sans Merci," 1424, provided title for Keats.
b. 1392? in Bayeux, France
d. 1430? in Avignon, France
Source: *DcEuL; EuAu; EvEuW; NewCol 75; OxCFr*

Chartoff, Robert
American. Producer
Films include *Rocky III; Right Stuff;* won Oscar for *Rocky,* 1976.
b. Aug 26, 1933 in New York, New York
Source: *ConTFT 12; IntMPA 92, 94, 96; VarWW 85*

Chase, Charley
American. Comedian
Started acting career in Max Sennett's "Keystone Kop" series; wrote,

produced, acted in slapstick-type comedy "shorts."
b. Oct 20, 1893 in Baltimore, Maryland
d. Jun 20, 1940 in Hollywood, California
Source: *BioIn 21; CurBio 40; EncAFC; MiSFD 9N; MotPP; OxCFilm; QDrFCA 92; SilFlmP; TwYS; WhoCom; WhoHol B; WhScrn 74, 77, 83; WorEFlm*

Chase, Chevy
[Cornelius Crane Chase]
American. Actor, Comedian
Starred on "Saturday Night Live," 1975-1976; has won several Emmys for acting and writing; films include *Caddyshack* and *National Lampoon* series.
b. Oct 8, 1943 in Woodstock, New York
Source: *BioIn 10, 11, 12, 13; CelR 90; ConTFT 3, 9; CurBio 79; EncAFC; HalFC 84, 88; IntMPA 86, 94, 96; IntWW 91, 93; LegTOT; News 90, 90-1; NewYTBS 77; WhoAm 78, 80, 82, 84, 86, 88, 90, 92, 94, 95, 96, 97; WhoCom; WhoEnt 92; WhoHol 92; WorAl; WorAlBi*

Chase, David
Writer, Producer
Winner of four Emmys who produced "Rockford Files;" "Off the Minnesota Strip."
b. Aug 22, 1945
Source: *VarWW 85*

Chase, Edna Woolman
American. Editor
Editor-in-chief, *Vogue* mag., 1914-55; organized first US fashion show, 1944.
b. Mar 14, 1877 in Asbury Park, New Jersey
d. Mar 20, 1957 in Sarasota, Florida
Source: *AmDec 1910; BenetAL 91; BioIn 3, 4, 12, 17; CurBio 40, 57; DcAmB S6; DcLB 91; EncAB-A 28; EncAJ; EncFash; InWom, SUP; NotAW MOD; ObitOF 79; REnAL; WhAm 3; WhoFash 88A; WorFshn*

Chase, Ilka
American. Actor
One of her best stage roles was as Sylvia Flowers in *The Women,* 1937; wrote memoirs, *Past Imperfect,* 1942.
b. Apr 8, 1905 in New York, New York
d. Feb 15, 1978 in Mexico City, Mexico
Source: *AmAu&B, 78, 79; InWom; MovMk; NewYTBS 78; NotNAT, A; ObitOF 79; REnAL; ThFT; WhAm 7; WhoAm 74; WhoHol A; WhoThe 72, 77, 81N; WhScrn 83*

Chase, Lucia
American. Dancer
Principal dancer, American Ballet Theatre, 1940-60; co-director, 1945-80.
b. Mar 27, 1907 in Waterbury, Connecticut
d. Jan 9, 1986 in New York, New York
Source: *AnObit 1986; BiDD; BioIn 4, 5, 9, 10, 12; CelR; ContDcW 89; CurBio 47, 75, 86, 86N; IntDcB; InWom, SUP; WhoAm 74, 84; WhoAmW 58, 64, 66, 68, 70, 72, 74, 75; WhoE 79, 81; WhoWor 74, 78, 80, 82*

Chase, Mary Agnes
American. Botanist
Expert on grasses; wrote popular manual *First Book of Grasses,* 1922.
b. Apr 20, 1869 in Iroquois County, Illinois
d. Sep 24, 1963 in Washington, District of Columbia
Source: *InWom SUP; NotAW MOD*

Chase, Mary Coyle
American. Dramatist
Best known for Pulitzer-winning play *Harvey,* 1944.
b. Feb 25, 1907 in Denver, Colorado
d. Oct 20, 1981 in Denver, Colorado
Source: *AmAu&B; AmWomWr; AuBYP 2; BenetAL 91; CnDAL; ConAu 73, 77; ConDr 73, 93; DcLEL; EncWT; InWom, SUP; LegTOT; LngCTC; McGEWB; McGEWD 84; ModWD; NewYTBS 81; NotWoAT; OxCAmL 65, 83, 95; OxCAmT 84; REn; REnAL; SmATA 29N; TwCA SUP; WhAm 8; WhoAm 74, 76, 78; WhoAmW 58, 64, 66, 68, 70, 72, 74; WorAl; WrDr 76*

Chase, Mary Ellen
American. Children's Author, Educator
English professor, Smith College, 1926-73; author of novels, biographies with Maine seacoast setting.
b. Feb 24, 1887 in Blue Hill, Maine
d. Jul 28, 1973 in Northampton, Massachusetts
Source: *AmAu&B; AmNov; AmWomWr; ArtclWW 2; AuBYP 2, 3; Benet 87, 96; BenetAL 91; BioAmW; BioIn 1, 2, 3, 4, 5, 7, 8, 10, 11, 21; BlueB 76; ChhPo; ConAmA; ConAu 41R, P-1; ConLC 2; CurBio 40, 73, 73N; DcAmB S9; DcLEL; FemiCLE; FourBJA; InWom, SUP; LibW; LinLib L; LngCTC; Novels; ObitOF 79; OxCAmL 65, 83, 95; PenC AM; REn; REnAL; SmATA 10; TwCA, SUP; WhAm 5; WhLit; WhNAA; Who 74; WhoAmW 58, 64, 66, 68, 70, 72, 74*

Chase, Philander
American. Clergy
Episcopal priest who founded Kenyon College, 1824.
b. Dec 14, 1775 in Cornish, New Hampshire
d. Sep 20, 1852 in Robin's Nest, Illinois
Source: *Alli; AmBi; ApCAB; BioIn 19; CyAL 1; DcAmAu; DcAmB; DcAmReB 1, 2; DcNAA; Drake; McGEWB; NatCAB 7; OhA&B; TwCBDA; WebAB 74, 79; WhAm HS*

Chase, Richard Volney
American. Critic, Educator
With English Dept., Columbia U, 1949-62; wrote *Herman Melville: A Critical Study,* 1949.
b. Oct 12, 1914 in Lakeport, New Hampshire
d. Aug 26, 1962 in Plymouth, Massachusetts
Source: *AmAu&B; BioIn 4, 6, 9, 13; NatCAB 52; PenC AM; REnAL; TwCA SUP*

Chase, Salmon Portland
American. Supreme Court Justice
Devoted life to ending slavery; co-founded Rep. Party; portrait on $10,000 bill.
b. Jan 13, 1808 in Cornish, New Hampshire
d. May 7, 1873 in New York, New York
Source: *AmAu&B; AmBi; AmPolLe; ApCAB; BbD; BiAUS; BiD&SB; BiDFedJ; BiDrAC; BiDrGov 1789; BiDrUSC 89; BiDrUSE 71, 89; BioIn 2, 3, 4, 5, 6, 7, 8, 9, 10, 11, 12, 15, 19, 21; CelCen; CivWDc; CyAG; DcAmB; DcBiPP; DcNAA; Drake; EncAB-H 1974, 1996; HarEnUS; LinLib L, S; McGEWB; NatCAB 1; OhA&B; OxCAmH; OxCLaw; OxCSupC; SupCtJu; TwCBDA; WebAB 74, 79; WhAm HS; WhAmP; WhCiWar; WorAl*

Chase, Samuel
American. Supreme Court Justice, Continental Congressman
Signed Declaration of Independence, 1776; appointed to Supreme Court by Washington, 1796; only justice ever impeached, 1804; found not guilty in Senate trial, 1805.
b. Apr 17, 1741 in Somerset County, Missouri
d. Jun 19, 1811 in Baltimore, Maryland
Source: *AmBi; AmJust; AmPolLe; AmWrBE; ApCAB; BiAUS; BiDFedJ; BiDrAC; BiDrUSC 89; BioIn 2, 3, 5, 7, 8, 9, 10, 12; BlkwEAR; CyAG; DcAmB; Drake; EncAR; EncCRAm; EncSoH; HarEnUS; HisWorL; LegTOT; McGEWB; NatCAB 1; OxCAmH; OxCLaw; OxCSupC; SupCtJu; TwCBDA; WebAB 74, 79; WhAm HS; WhAmP; WhAmRev; WorAl; WorAlBi*

Chase, Stuart
American. Author, Economist
Member of FDR's brain trust; coined phrase "New Deal."
b. Mar 8, 1888 in Somersworth, New Hampshire
d. Nov 17, 1985 in Redding, Connecticut
Source: *AmAu&B; AnObit 1985; BenetAL 91; BioIn 2, 3, 4, 14, 15; BlueB 76; ChhPo S2; ConAmA; ConAu 65, 117; CurBio 40, 86N; DcAmSR; DcLEL; FacFETw; Future; IntAu&W 77, 82; IntWW 74, 75, 76, 77, 78, 79, 80, 81, 82, 83; LinLib L, S; LngCTC; NewYTBS 85; OxCAmH; OxCAmL 65, 83; REn; REnAL; TwCA, SUP; WebAB 74, 79; WhAm 9; WhNAA; Who 74, 82, 83, 85; WhoAm 74, 76, 78; WhoWor 74*

Chase, Sylvia B
American. Broadcast Journalist
Correspondent, ABC News "20/20," 1978-86; correspondent, "Primeime

Live,'' 1990—; won Emmys, 1978, 1980, 1986, 1987.
b. Feb 23, 1938 in Northfield, Minnesota
Source: *ConAu 110, 115; WhoAm 84, 86*

Chase, William Curtis
American. Army Officer
Major general; led first American troops to enter Tokyo, 1945; advocate of Nationalist China.
b. Mar 9, 1895 in Providence, Rhode Island
d. Aug 21, 1986 in Houston, Texas
Source: *BiDWWGF; BioIn 3, 4, 10; WebAMB*

Chase, William Merritt
American. Artist
With florid, colorful style painted American life in landscapes, portraits, still lifes.
b. Nov 1, 1849 in Williamsburg, Indiana
d. Oct 25, 1916 in New York, New York
Source: *AmBi; ApCAB; ArtsAmW 3; ArtsNiC; BiDAmEd; BioIn 2, 6, 7, 9, 10, 12, 13, 14, 15, 16, 17, 19, 20; BriEAA; DcAmArt; DcAmB; LinLib S; McGDA; McGEWB; NatCAB 13; OxCAmL 65; OxDcArt; TwCBDA; WhAm 1; WorAlBi*

Chase-Riboud, Barbara
American. Sculptor, Writer
Artistic style influenced by Albers; author of novel *Sally Hemings.*
b. Jun 26, 1939 in Philadelphia, Pennsylvania
Source: *AfroAA; BiDWomA; BioIn 12, 13, 18; BlkWr 1; ConAmWS; ConArt 77; ConAu 113; DcLB 33; DcTwCCu 5; InWom SUP; LiExTwC; NegAl 89; NotBlAW 1; SchCGBL; WhoAm 90; WhoAmA 84, 86, 89, 91, 93; WhoAmW 91; WhoBlA 77, 80, 92*

Chasins, Abram
American. Pianist, Composer
His over 100 compositions include piano work ''Three Chinese Pieces''; directed classical music broadcasts, 1941-65.
b. Aug 17, 1903 in New York, New York
d. Jun 21, 1987 in New York, New York
Source: *AmAu&B; ASCAP 66; AuBYP 2S, 3; Baker 78, 84, 92; BiDAmM; BioIn 1, 2, 4, 5, 9, 15; ConAmC 76, 82; ConAu 14NR, 37R, 122; CurBio 60, 87, 87N; IntWWM 77, 85, 90; NewAmDM; NewGrDA 86; OxCMus; WhAm 9; WhoAm 74, 76; WhoAmJ 80; WhoAmM 83; WhoMus 72; WhoWorJ 72, 78*

Chasnoff, Debra
American. Filmmaker
Won Academy Award for Best Documentary, 1992, for *Deadly Decpetion.*
b. Oct 12, 1957 in Philadelphia, Pennsylvania
Source: *GayLesB*

Chataway, Christopher John
English. Government Official
Held various political posts including Deputy chm., United City Merchants, 1981-83.
b. Jan 31, 1931
Source: *BioIn 7; BlueB 76; IntWW 74, 75, 76, 77, 78, 79, 80, 81, 82, 83, 89, 91, 93; IntYB 78, 79, 80, 81, 82; Who 74, 82, 83, 85, 88, 90, 92, 94; WhoWor 74, 76, 78, 87*

Chateaubriand, Francois Rene de
French. Author
Pioneer of romantic movement; wrote *Memories from Beyond the Tomb,* 1850.
b. Sep 4, 1768 in Saint-Malo, France
d. Jul 4, 1848 in Paris, France
Source: *ApCAB; AtlBL; BbD; Benet 87, 96; BiD&SB; BiDLA SUP; CasWL; CelCen; CyWA 58; DcBiA; DcEuL; EuAu; EuWr 5; EvEuW; LuthC 75; NewC; NinCLC 3; OxCAmL 65; OxCEng 67; OxCFr; RComWL; REnAL; WhDW*

Chatfield, Alfred E. Montacute, Baron
English. Naval Officer
Autobiographies include *The Navy & Defense,* 1942; *It Might Happen Again,* 1947.
b. Sep 27, 1873 in Southsea, England
d. Nov 15, 1967 in London, England
Source: *DcNaB 1961; HisEWW; ObitOF 79; ObitT 1961; OxCShps*

Chatham, Russell
American. Artist
Painter, known for Western landscapes.
b. Oct 27, 1939 in San Francisco, California
Source: *BioIn 12; ConAu 69; News 90, 90-1; WhoWest 92*

Chato, Alfred
American. Native American Leader
Subchief of the Chiracahua Apaches; US Army scout.
b. 1860?
d. Mar 1934
Source: *NotNaAm*

Chatterton, Ruth
American. Actor
Wrote several novels in 1950s; Oscar nominee for *Madame X,* 1929; *Sarah and Son,* 1930.
b. Dec 24, 1893 in New York, New York
d. Nov 24, 1961 in Norwalk, Connecticut
Source: *AmAu&B, 83; WhThe; WomWMM; WorAl*

Chatterton, Thomas
English. Poet
Claimed his ''Rowley Poems'' were copies of 15th c. manuscripts.
b. Nov 20, 1752 in Bristol, England
d. Aug 25, 1770 in Bristol, England
Source: *Alli; AtlBL; BbD; Benet 87, 96; BiD&SB; BioIn 1, 2, 3, 4, 5, 8, 9, 10, 11, 12, 13, 15, 17; BlkwCE; BlmGEL; BritAu; CamGEL; CamGLE; CasWL; Chambr 2; ChhPo, S1, S3; CnE&AP; CrtT 2, 4; DcArts; DcBiPP; DcEnA; DcEnL; DcEuL; DcLB 109; DcLEL; DcNaB; Dis&D; DrInf; EvLB; LegTOT; LinLib L; LitC 3; LngCEL; McGEWB; MouLC 2; NewC; OxCEng 67, 85, 95; PenC ENG; RAdv 14, 13-1; RComWL; REn; RfGEnL 91; WebE&AL*

Chatwin, Bruce
[Charles Bruce Chatwin]
English. Author
Known for distinctive travel books, novels; wrote *The Songlines,* 1987.
b. May 13, 1940 in Yorkshire, England
d. Jan 18, 1989 in Nice, France
Source: *AnObit 1989; Au&Arts 4; Benet 96; BestSel 90-1; BioIn 12, 13; ConAu 85, 127; ConLC 28, 57, 59; CurBio 88, 89N; CyWA 89; DcArts; FacFETw; IntAu&W 82; MagSWL; News 89-2; NewYTBS 83, 89; WorAu 1975*

Chaucer, Geoffrey
English. Poet
Wrote *The Canterbury Tales,* ca. 1387, never completed.
b. 1340 in London, England
d. Oct 25, 1400 in London, England
Source: *Alli; AnCL; AtlBL; BbD; BiD&SB; BioIn 1, 2, 3, 4, 5, 6, 7, 8, 9, 10, 11, 12, 13; BlmGEL; BritAu; BritWr 1; CamGEL; CasWL; Chambr 1; ChhPo, S1, S2, S3; CnDBLB 1; CnE&AP; CrtT 1, 4; CyWA 58; DcArts; DcCathB; DcEnA; DcEnL; DcEuL; DcLB 146; DcLEL; DcNaB; Dis&D; EncUnb; EvLB; LegTOT; LitC 17; LngCEL; LuthC 75; MouLC 1; NewC; NewEOp 71; OxCChiL; OxCEng 67; OxCMus; OxDcOp; PenC ENG; PoLE; RAdv 1, 13-1; RComWL; REn; RfGEnL 91; WebE&AL; WhDW; WorAl; WorAlBi*

Chaudhari, Praveen
Indian. Physicist, Business Executive
Director, Dept. of Physical Science, IBM, 1980—; vp for Science, 1982—; heads team that created ''superconductors'' (ceramic crystal conductors), 1987.
b. Nov 30, 1937 in Ludhiana, India
Source: *AmMWSc 73P, 79, 82, 86, 89, 92, 95; BioIn 20; News 89; NotTwCS; WhoAm 90, 92; WhoAsA 94; WhoScEn 96; WhoTech 89*

Chaudhuri, Haridas
Indian. Author
Books include *The Rhythm of Truth,* 1958; *Mastering the Problems of Living,* 1968.
b. May 24, 1913 in Calcutta, India
d. Jun 20, 1975 in San Francisco, California
Source: *BioIn 12; ConAu 4NR, 5R; IntAu&W 76; NatCAB 59; RelLAm 91; WhoWest 74*

Chauncey, George
American. Historian
Wrote *Gay New York: Gender, Urban Culture, and the Making of the Gay Male World 1890-1940,* 1995.
b. 1954 in Brownsville, Tennessee
Source: *GayLesB*

Chauncey, Isaac
American. Military Leader
Served with US Navy, 1798-1840; commander of naval forces on lakes Ontario, Erie during War of 1812.
b. Feb 20, 1772 in Black Rock, Connecticut
d. Jan 27, 1840 in Washington, District of Columbia
Source: *AmBi; ApCAB; BioIn 2; DcAmB; DcAmMiB; DcNaB; Drake; HarEnMi; HarEnUS; NatCAB 8; OxCAmH; TwCBDA; WebAMB; WhAm HS*

Chausson, Ernest
[Amedee-Ernest Chausson]
French. Composer
Wrote chamber music, opera *Le Roi Arthus,* performed 1903.
b. Jun 21, 1855 in Paris, France
d. Jun 10, 1899 in Limay, France
Source: *AtlBL; Baker 78, 84; BioIn 1, 3, 4, 6, 7, 10, 12; IntDcOp; MetOEnc; NewAmDM; NewCol 75; NewOxM; OxCMus; OxDcOp; PenDiMP A; WebBD 83*

Chautemps, Camille
French. Political Leader
Prime minister of France, 1930-38.
b. Feb 1, 1885 in Paris, France
d. Jul 1, 1963 in Washington, District of Columbia
Source: *BioIn 1, 6, 17; ObitOF 79; WhAm 4*

Chauvin, Nicholas
French. Soldier
His complete devotion to Napoleon and military life led to coining of term "chauvinism."
Source: *NewC; OxCFr; WorAl*

Chauvire, Yvette
French. Dancer
Roles include those of Giselle, Petrouchka, Sylvia; with Paris Opera Ballet, 1930—.
b. Apr 22, 1917 in Paris, France
Source: *BiDD; BioIn 3, 4, 5; ContDcW 89; DcTwCCu 2; IntDcB; IntDcWB; IntWW 74, 75, 76, 77, 78, 79, 80, 81, 82, 83, 89, 91, 93; InWom; ItaFilm; Who 74, 82, 83, 85, 88, 90, 92, 94; WhoFr 79; WhoWor 74, 76, 78*

Chavers, Dean
American. Educator
President, Native American Scholarship Fund, 1970-78.
b. Feb 4, 1941 in Pembroke, North Carolina
Source: *BioIn 21; NotNaAm; WhoEmL 87; WhoSSW 78, 80, 82, 84, 86*

Chavez, Cesar (Estrada)
American. Labor Union Official
Organized National Farm Workers Assn., 1962.
b. Mar 31, 1927 in Yuma, Arizona
d. Apr 23, 1993 in San Luis, Arizona
Source: *AmCath 80; AmDec 1960, 1970; AmJust; AmOrTwC; AmRef&R; AmSocL; AnObit 1993; BiDAmL; BiDAmLL; BioIn 8, 9, 10, 11, 12, 14, 15, 16, 17, 18, 19, 20, 21; BioNews 74; BkPepl; BlueB 76; BusPN; CelR; ChiSch; CmCal; ConHero 1; CurBio 69, 93N; DcHiB; DcTwHis; EncAAH; EncAB-H 1974, 1996; FacFETw; HeroCon; HispAmA; LegTOT; LNinSix; McGEWB; MexAmB; MugS; News 93; NewYTBS 93; PolPar; PolProf J; RComAH; REnAW; WebAB 74, 79; WhAm 11; WhoAm 76, 78, 80, 82, 84, 86, 88, 90, 92; WhoFI 83, 85, 87; WhoHisp 91, 92, 94N; WhoWest 78, 80, 82, 84, 87, 89, 92; WhoWor 74, 76; WorAl; WorAlBi*

Chavez (y Ramirez), Carlos Antonio de Pauda
Mexican. Composer, Conductor
Founder, director, Mexico's Orquestra Sinfonica, 1928-48; early compositions used Mexican rhythms.
b. Jun 13, 1899 in Mexico City, Mexico
d. Aug 2, 1978 in Mexico City, Mexico
Source: *ASCAP 66; Baker 84; CurBio 49, 78; DcCM; IntWW 74; REn; WhoMus 72; WhoSSW 82; WhoWor 74*

Chavis, Benjamin Franklin, Jr.
[Wilmington 10]
American. Civil Rights Leader
Central figure of Wilmington 10; imprisoned, 1972, released, 1980; executive director, NAACP, 1993-94; joined Nation of Islam, 1997.
b. Jan 22, 1948 in Oxford, North Carolina
Source: *AfrAmAl 6; BioIn 10, 11, 12, 13; CurBio 94; InB&W 80; NewYTBS 93; WhoAfA 96; WhoAm 94, 95, 96; WhoBlA 77, 80, 92, 94*

Chavis, John
American. Clergy, Educator
First black minister in Presbyterian church, missionary to slaves, 1802-32; opposed Nat Turner's rebellion, caused him to lose ministry, 1833.
b. 1763
d. Jun 13, 1838
Source: *AmBi; BioIn 1, 2, 7, 9, 18; DcAmB; DcAmNB; DcNCBi 1; EncSoH; InB&W 80, 85; NatCAB 7; WhAm HS*

Chayefsky, Paddy
[Sidney Chayefsky]
American. Dramatist
Best known for screenplays *Marty,* 1953; won Oscar, 1976, for *Network.*
b. Jan 29, 1923 in New York, New York
d. Aug 1, 1981 in New York, New York
Source: *AmAu&B; AnObit 1981; ASCAP 66, 80; Benet 87; BenetAL 91; BiDFilm 94; BiE&WWA; BioIn 3, 4, 10, 11, 12, 13, 15, 20; BlueB 76; CamGWoT; CelR; CnMD; CnThe; ConAmD; ConAu 9NR, 9R, 18NR, 104; ConDr 73, 77, 93; ConLC 23; ConTFT 1; CroCD; CurBio 57, 81, 81N; DcFM; DcLB 7, 44, Y81A; DcLEL 1940; EncSF, 93; EncWT; FilmgC; IntAu&W 76, 77, 82; IntDcF 1-4, 2-4; IntDcT 2; IntMPA 75, 76, 77, 78, 79, 81; IntWW 74, 75, 76, 77, 78, 79, 80, 81; LegTOT; LinLib L; McGEWD 72, 84; ModWD; NewYTBS 81; NewYTET; NotNAT; OxCAmL 65, 83, 95; OxCAmT 84; OxCFilm; PenC AM; PlP&P; REnAL; RfGAmL 87, 94; ScF&FL 92; ScFSB; WebAB 74, 79; WhAm 8; WhoAm 74, 76, 78, 80; WhoE 74; WhoThe 72, 77, 81; WhoTwCL; WhoWor 74, 78, 80; WorAl; WorAlBi; WorAu 1950; WorEFlm; WrDr 76, 80, 82*

Chayes, Abram J(oseph)
American. Lawyer, Educator
Co-author, *The International Legal Process,* 1968, two volumes.
b. Jul 18, 1922 in Chicago, Illinois
Source: *BioIn 5, 11; BlueB 76; ConAu 14NR, 65; DrAS 74P, 78P, 82P; IntWW 74, 75, 76, 77, 78, 79, 80, 83; NewYTBS 84; WhoAm 84; WhoAmL 83; WhoWorJ 78*

Cheap Trick
[Bun E Carlos; Rick Nielsen; Tom Petesson; Robin Zander]
American. Music Group
IL-based foursome started 1972, known for weird antics.
Source: *BioIn 11, 12; ConMuA 80A; ConMus 12; EncPR&S 89; EncRk 88; EncRkSt; HarEnR 86; NewAmDM; PenEncP; RkOn 85; RolSEnR 83; WhoRock 81; WhoRocM 82*

Checker, Chubby
[Ernest Evans]
American. Singer
Had hit "The Twist," 1960; created dance sensation of early 1960s.
b. Oct 3, 1941 in South Philadelphia, Pennsylvania
Source: *ASCAP 66, 80; Baker 92; BiDAfM; BiDAmM; BiDD; BioIn 5, 12, 15, 17; ConMus 7; DcTwCCu 5; DrBlPA, 90; EncPR&S 89; EncRk 88; EncRkSt; FilmgC; HalFC 84, 88; IlEncBM 82; InB&W 80, 85; LegTOT; NewAmDM; NewGrDA 86; OxCPMus; PenEncP; RkOn 74; RolSEnR 83; SoulM; WhoAfA 96; WhoAm 74, 76, 95, 96, 97; WhoBlA 75, 77, 80, 85, 90, 92, 94; WhoHol 92, A; WhoRock 81; WhoRocM 82; WorAl; WorAlBi*

Cheech and Chong
[Tommy Chong; Cheech Marin]
American. Comedy Team
First of the rock-culture comedians, 1970s; films include *Up In Smoke,* 1978.
Source: *BioIn 16, 17; ConAu 148, X; EncAFC; EncPR&S 74, 89; HalFC 84, 88; IntMPA 82, 84; QDrFCA 92; RkOn 78, 84; WhoAm 84, 86; WhoCom;*

WhoHol 92; WhoRock 81; WorAl; WorAlBi

Cheek, James Edward
American. University Administrator
Pres., Howard University, Washington, DC, 1969-90.
b. Dec 4, 1932 in Roanoke Rapids, North Carolina
Source: *BioIn 8, 16; BlueB 76; ConNews 87-1; InB&W 80, 85; IntWW 74, 75, 76, 77, 78, 79, 80, 81, 82, 83, 89, 91, 93; LEduc 74; WhoAfA 96; WhoAm 74, 76, 78, 80, 82, 84, 86, 88, 90, 92, 94, 95, 96, 97; WhoBlA 85, 92, 94; WhoE 83, 85, 86, 89; WhoGov 72, 75; WhoSSW 73; WhoWor 78, 93, 95*

Cheever, John
American. Author
Won Pulitzer, 1979; noted for subtle, comic style; short story collections include *World of Apples,* 1973.
b. May 27, 1912 in Quincy, Massachusetts
d. Jun 18, 1982 in Ossining, New York
Source: *AmAu&B; AmWr S1; AnObit 1982; Benet 87, 96; BenetAL 91; BioIn 3, 4, 5, 6, 8, 10, 11, 12, 13, 14, 15, 16, 17, 18, 19; BlueB 76; CamGEL; CamGLE; CamHAL; CasWL; CelR; ConAu 1BS, 5NR, 5R, 27NR, 106; ConLC 3, 7, 8, 11, 15, 25, 64; ConNov 72, 76, 82, 86A; ConPopW; CurBio 75, 82, 82N; CyWA 89; DcArts; DcLB 2, 102, Y80A, Y82A; DcLEL 1940; DrAF 76; EncAB-H 1996; EncWB; EncWL 3; FacFETw; IntAu&W 76, 77; IntWW 74, 75, 76, 77, 78, 79, 80, 81, 82; LegTOT; LinLib L; MagSAmL; MajTwCW; ModAL, S1, S2; NewCon; NewYTBS 79, 82; Novels; OxCAmL 65, 83, 95; OxCEng 85, 95; PenC AM; RAdv 1, 14, 13-1; REn; REnAL; RfGAmL 87; RGTwCWr; ShSCr 1; ShSWr; TwCWr; WebE&AL; WhAm 8; Who 74, 82; WhoAm 74, 76, 78, 80, 82; WhoTwCL; WhoWor 74, 76, 78; WorAl; WorAlBi; WorAu 1950; WorLitC; WrDr 76, 80, 82*

Cheevers, Gerry
[Gerald Michael Cheevers]
"Cheesey"
Canadian. Hockey Player
Goalie, 1961-62, 1965-80, mostly with Boston; Hall of Fame, 1985.
b. Dec 7, 1940 in Saint Catharines, Ontario, Canada
Source: *BioIn 9, 10, 11; HocEn; WhoAm 84; WhoHcky 73; WhoSpor*

Chekhov, Anton Pavlovich
Russian. Author, Dramatist
Wrote *Three Sisters,* 1901; *The Cherry Orchard,* 1904.
b. Jan 17, 1860 in Teganrog, Russia
d. Jul 2, 1904 in Badenweiler, Germany
Source: *AtlBL; Benet 87, 96; BioIn 1, 2, 3, 4, 5, 6, 7, 8, 9, 10, 11, 12, 14, 15, 16, 17, 20, 21; BlmGEL; CamGWoT; CasWL; ClDMEL 47; CnMD; CnThe; CyWA 58; DcArts; DcEuL; DcRusL; Dis&D; EncUnb; EncWL 3; EncWT; EuAu; EvEuW; HanRL; IntDcT 2; LngCEL; McGEWB; McGEWD 72, 84; ModSL 1; ModWD; NewC; NewGrDO; NotNAT A, B; OxCEng 67, 85, 95; OxCMed 86; OxCThe 67, 83; PenC EUR; PlP&P, A; RComWL; REn; REnWD; RfGShF; RfGWoL 95; SmATA 90; WorAl*

Chekhov, Michael
Russian. Director
Nephew of Anton Chekov; founded drama schools in England, US; nominated for Oscar, 1945, for *Spellbound.*
b. Aug 28, 1891 in Saint Petersburg, Russia
d. Sep 30, 1955 in Beverly Hills, California
Source: *BioIn 4, 14, 15, 20; CamGWoT; FilmgC; HalFC 84, 88; IntDcT 3; MotPP; NotNAT B; OxCThe 67; TheaDir; WhoHol B; WhScrn 74, 77, 83; WhThe*

Chelios, Chris
American. Hockey Player
Defenseman, Montreal, 1983-90; Chicago, 1990—; won Norris Trophy, 1989, 1993, 1996.
b. Jan 25, 1962 in Chicago, Illinois
Source: *BioIn 21; WorAlBi*

Chenault, Kenneth I
American. Business Executive
Pres., American Express Consumer Card Group USA, 1990-93; pres., American Express Travel Related Services, 1993-95; vice chm. American Express Co., 1995—.
b. Jun 2, 1951 in New York, New York
Source: *BioIn 14, 16; WhoAm 90; WhoBlA 92*

Cheney, Dick
[Richard Bruce Cheney]
American. Government Official
Secretary of Defense, 1989-93.
b. Jan 30, 1941 in Lincoln, Nebraska
Source: *AlmAP 80, 82, 84, 88; BiDrUSC 89; BiDrUSE 89; BioIn 10, 13; CngDr 79, 81, 83, 85, 87, 89; ColdWar 1; CurBio 89; EncCW; News 91, 91-3; NewYTBS 75, 91; PolsAm 84; Who 90, 92, 94; WhoAm 76, 78, 80, 82, 84, 86, 88, 90, 92, 94, 95, 96, 97; WhoAmP 79, 81, 83, 85, 87, 89, 91, 93, 95; WhoE 91, 93; WhoGov 72, 77; WhoWest 80, 82, 87, 89, 92, 94; WhoWor 91, 93, 95*

Cheney, John Vance
American. Poet
Lyric poems include "Wood Blooms," 1888.
b. Dec 29, 1848 in Groveland, New York
d. May 1, 1922 in San Diego, California
Source: *Alli SUP; AmAu; AmAu&B; AmBi; AmLY; BbD; BenetAL 91; BiD&SB; ChhPo, S1, S3; CmCal; DcAmAu; DcAmB; DcNAA; NatCAB 6; OxCAmL 65, 83, 95; REnAL; TwCBDA; WhAm 1*

Cheney, Lynne V
[Lynne Ann Vincent Cheney]
American.
Chm., National Endowment for the Humanities, 1986-93; wife of former Sec. of Defense, Dick Cheney.
b. Aug 14, 1941 in Casper, Wyoming
Source: *BioIn 13, 15; CurBio 92; News 90; NewYTBS 86; WhoAm 90; WhoAmP 91; WhoAmW 91; WhoWor 89*

Cheney, Sheldon Warren
American. Critic
Wrote classic surveys: *The Theater,* 1929; *World History of Art,* 1937.
b. Jun 29, 1886 in Berkeley, California
d. Oct 10, 1980 in Berkeley, California
Source: *AmAu&B; BiE&WWA; BioIn 12; ConAu 102; IntAu&W 76; NewYTBS 80; NotNAT; REnAL; TwCA, SUP; WhAm 7; WhE&EA; WhoAm 74, 76, 78; WhoAmA 78; WhoWor 74, 76; WhThe*

Chenier, Andre Marie de
b. 1762
d. 1794
Source: *AtlBL; Benet 87, 96; BiD&SB; BioIn 1, 2, 4, 7, 9, 11, 13; CasWL; DcBiPP; DcEuL; Dis&D; EuAu; EvEuW; LinLib L; OxCEng 67; OxCFr; PenC EUR; REn; WhDW*

Chenier, Clifton
American. Singer, Musician
Known for contribution to resurgence of Zydeco (combination of black dance and Cajun French) music in 70s; Grammy for album *I'm Here,* 1984.
b. Jun 25, 1925 in Opelousas, Louisiana
d. Dec 12, 1987 in Lafayette, Louisiana
Source: *AnObit 1987; BioIn 12; BluesWW; ConMus 6; EncRk 88; GuBlues; InB&W 80, 85; NewGrDA 86; NewYTBS 87; PenEncP; RolSEnR 83*

Chenier, Marie-Andre de
French. Author, Poet
Early French Romanticist whose verse volumes include *La Jeune Captive,* 1795.
b. Oct 30, 1762 in Constantinople, Ottoman Empire
d. Jul 25, 1794 in Paris, France
Source: *AtlBL; BbD; BiD&SB; CasWL; DcEuL; EuAu; EvEuW; OxCEng 67; OxCFr; PenC EUR; REn*

Chennault, Anna Chan
[Mrs. Claire Lee Chennault]
Chinese. Journalist, Author
US correspondent *Hsin Shen Daily News,* Taipei, 1958—; wrote best seller *Chennault and the Flying Tigers,* 1963; vp, Int'l. Affairs, Flying Tiger Line, Washington 1968-76; pres., TAC Int'l., 1976—.
b. Jun 23, 1925 in Beijing, China
Source: *AmAu&B; BlueB 76; ConAu 61; ForWC 70; IntAu&W 76, 89; WhoAm 74, 76, 78, 80, 82, 84, 86, 88, 90; WhoAmP 73, 75, 77, 79, 81, 83, 85, 87, 89, 91, 93, 95; WhoAmW 70, 72, 74, 75, 77, 79, 81, 83, 85, 87, 89, 91; WhoEnt*

92; WhoSSW 73, 75, 76; WhoWor 80, 82, 84, 87, 89, 91

Chennault, Claire Lee
American. Aviator
Commanding general, US Air Forces, China, WW II; created, led the "Flying Tigers."
b. Sep 6, 1890 in Commerce, Texas
d. Jul 27, 1958 in New Orleans, Louisiana
Source: *AmAu&B; BiDWWGF; BioIn 1, 3, 4, 5, 6, 7, 12, 14, 15; CurBio 42, 58; HarEnMi; InSci; ObitOF 79; WebAMB; WhAm 3; WhWW-II; WorAl*

Chenoweth, Dean
"Comeback Kid"
American. Boat Racer
Four-time national champion.
b. 1934? in Xenia, Ohio
d. Jul 31, 1982 in Pasco, Washington

Chen Yi
Chinese. Military Leader, Politician
Communist military leader during 1930s-1940s; China's foreign minister 1958-1966.
b. 1901 in Lo-chih, China
d. Jan 6, 1972 in Beijing, China

Cheops
Egyptian. Ruler
Builder of the Great Pyramid at Giza.
Source: *BioIn 2, 3, 7, 8, 10, 14, 16; LegTOT; LinLib S; WebBD 83; WhDW; WorAl; WorAlBi*

Cher
[Sonny and Cher; Cherylynn LaPiere; Cherilyn Sarkisian]
American. Singer, Actor
Part of pop duo with ex-husband, Sonny Bono, 1960s-70s; won Oscar, 1988, for *Moonstruck.*
b. May 20, 1946 in El Centro, California
Source: *BiDFilm 94; BioIn 10, 11, 12, 13, 14, 15, 16, 17, 18, 19, 20, 21; BkPepl; CelR 90; ConMus 1; ConTFT 2, 3, 9; CurBio 74, 91; EncRk 88; EncRkSt; GrLiveH; HalFC 84, 88; HerW; HolBB; IntDcF 2-3; IntMPA 75, 76, 77, 78, 79, 81, 82, 84, 86, 88, 92, 94, 96; InWom SUP; LegTOT; News 93-1; NewYTBS 87; NewYTET; WhoAm 78, 80, 82, 84, 86, 88, 90, 92, 94, 95, 96, 97; WhoAmW 81, 83, 85, 87, 89, 91, 93, 95; WhoEnt 92; WhoHol 92, A; WhoRock 81; WhoWor 95; WorAl; WorAlBi*

Cherberg, John A(ndrew)
American. Government Official
Lt. governor of WA, 1957-1988; has served longer in position than anyone in US.
b. Oct 17, 1910 in Pensacola, Florida
d. Apr 8, 1992 in Seattle, Washington
Source: *BioIn 15; NewYTBS 86; PolsAm 84; WhAm 10; WhoAm 74, 76, 78, 80, 82, 84, 86, 88, 90; WhoAmP 73, 75, 77, 79, 81, 83, 85, 87, 89, 91; WhoGov 72, 75, 77; WhoWest 74, 76, 78, 80, 82, 84, 87, 89*

Chereau, Patrice
French. Director
Theater, opera, film; controversial for non-traditional interpretations of classics.
b. Nov 2, 1944 in Lezigne, France
Source: *Baker 92; BioIn 11, 13, 16, 20; CamGWoT; CurBio 90; IntDcOp; IntWW 89, 91, 93; IntWWM 90; MetOEnc; NewGrDO; OxDcOp; TheaDir; WhoWor 87, 89, 91, 93, 95, 96, 97*

Cherenkov, Pavel Alekseyevich
Russian. Physicist
Shared Nobel Prize, 1958, for discovery, interpretation of Cherenkov effect.
b. Nov 28, 1904 in Novaya Chigla, Russia
d. Jan 6, 1990
Source: *AsBiEn; BiESc; CamDcSc; FacFETw; IntWW 77, 78, 79, 80, 81, 82, 83; LarDcSc; Who 83; WhoNob, 90, 95; WhoWor 82; WorAl*

Cherkassky, Shura
Ukrainian. Pianist
Internationally renowned classic concert performer for over 70 years.
b. Oct 11, 1911 in Odessa, Russia
d. Dec 27, 1995 in London, England
Source: *Baker 78, 84; BioIn 2, 5, 11, 21; BlueB 76; CurBio 90, 96N; IntWW 74, 75, 76, 77, 78, 79, 80, 81, 82, 83, 89, 91, 93; IntWWM 77, 85, 90; NewAmDM; NewGrDA 86; NewYTBS 78, 95; NotTwCP; PenDiMP; Who 74, 83, 85, 88, 90, 92, 94; WhoAmM 83; WhoMus 72; WhoWor 76, 78*

Chermayeff, Ivan
American. Artist
Work involves industrial, graphic designs, children's books; wrote *Observation on American Literature,* 1973.
b. Jun 6, 1932 in London, England
Source: *AmGrD; BioIn 8, 9, 10, 16, 18; ChhPo; ConAu 97; ConDes 90, 97; ConGrA 3; DcTwDes; IlsCB 1957; SmATA 47; WhoAdv 90; WhoAm 74, 76, 78, 80, 82, 84, 86, 88, 92, 94, 95, 96, 97; WhoAmA 73, 76, 78, 80, 82, 84, 86, 89, 91, 93; WhoE 74, 75, 77; WhoEnt 92; WhoGrA 82*

Chermayeff, Serge (Ivan)
[Sergei Ivanovitch Issakovitch]
American. Author, Architect, Educator
Most important architectural works are in England; professor, Harvard U., 1953-71; wrote *Shape of Community,* 1970.
b. Oct 8, 1900 in Caucasia, Colombia
d. May 8, 1996 in Wellfleet, Massachusetts
Source: *BioIn 9, 21; ConArch 80, 87, 94; ConAu 21R, 152; ConDes 84, 90, 97; DcTwDes; IntDcAr; IntWW 77, 78, 79, 80, 81, 82, 83, 89, 91, 93; MacEA; McGDA; Who 82, 83, 85, 88, 90, 92, 94; WhoArch*

Chern, Shiing-shen
American. Mathematician, Educator
Developed the Chern characteristic classes in fibre spaces through his studies in differential geometry.
b. Oct 26, 1911 in Jiaxing, China
Source: *AmMWSc 76P, 82, 86, 89, 92, 95; BioIn 13; BlueB 76; IntWW 74, 75, 76, 77, 78, 79, 80, 81, 82, 83, 89, 91, 93; McGMS 80; WhoAm 76, 78, 80, 82, 86, 88, 90, 92, 94, 95, 96, 97; WhoScEn 94, 96; WhoWest 94, 96; WhoWor 74, 76, 78*

Cherne, Leo
American. Economist, Political Scientist, Sculptor
"Guiding Light" of International Rescue Committee, 1951—; does bronze sculptures of famous statesmen, among them Lincoln, Churchill, John F. Kennedy; awarded Medal of Freedom, 1984.
b. Sep 8, 1912 in New York, New York
Source: *BioIn 5, 15; CelR, 90; CurBio 40; St&PR 75, 84, 87; WhoAm 74, 76, 78, 80, 82, 84, 86; WhoAmL 78, 79; WhoE 74; WhoWor 78*

Chernenko, Konstantin Ustinovich
Russian. Political Leader
Called first Siberian, first peasant to lead USSR; oldest man elected general secretary of USSR's Communist Party; succeeded Andropov, Feb 13, 1984.
b. Sep 24, 1911 in Bolshaya Tes, Russia
d. Mar 10, 1985 in Moscow, Union of Soviet Socialist Republics
Source: *AnObit 1985; BiDSovU; BioIn 11, 12, 13, 14, 15, 16, 18; ColdWar 2; ConAu 115; ConNews 85-1; CurBio 84, 85; EncWB; IntWW 78, 79, 80, 81, 82, 83; NewYTBS 78, 84; SovUn; WhoSocC 78, 78A; WhoWor 80, 82, 84*

Chernov, Viktor Mikhailovich
[Boris Olenin]
Russian. Journalist
Founded Social Revolutionary party, 1902; pres., All-Russian Constituent Assembly, 1918.
b. Dec 1, 1873 in Kamyshin, Russia
d. Apr 15, 1952 in New York, New York
Source: *BioIn 2, 3, 11, 16; BlkwERR; ObitOF 79; WebBD 83*

Cherrington, Ben Mark
American. Statesman, Educator
One of founding fathers of UNESCO, 1945; member, US commission on UNESCO matters, 1946-51.
b. Nov 1, 1885 in Gibbon, Nebraska
d. May 4, 1980 in Denver, Colorado
Source: *AmAu&B; AmMWSc 73S; BiDInt; BioIn 6, 12; NewYTBS 80; WhAm 7; WhoAm 74; WhoWest 74, 76*

Cherry, Don
American. Musician
Played in Samuel Brown's jazz band, 1951; co-founded NY Contemporary

Five band, 1962; quartet member of Old and New Dreams Band; recorded *MultiKulti*, 1991, for which he received the Bay Area Music award for outstanding jazz album.
b. Nov 18, 1936 in Oklahoma City, Oklahoma
Source: *AllMusG; Baker 84; BioIn 13, 21; ConMus 10; DrBlPA, 90; EncJzS; IlEncJ; NewAmDM; NewGrDA 86; NewGrDJ 88; PenEncP*

Cherry, Don(ald Stewart)
"Grapes"
Canadian. Hockey Coach, Sportscaster
Colorful coach, Boston, 1974-79, Colorado, 1979-80; commentator on CBC's "Hockey Night in Canada."
b. Feb 5, 1934 in Kingston, Ontario, Canada
Source: *BioIn 11; HocEn; News 93; WhoAm 78, 80, 82; WhoE 79; WhoWest 82*

Cherry, Neneh
Singer
Combines rap and pop music; hit single "Buffalo Stance," 1989 topped charts in United States and England.
b. Aug 10, 1964 in Stockholm, Sweden
Source: *ConMus 4; EncRkSt; LegTOT*

Cherubini, Luigi Carlo Zenobio Salvadore Maria
Italian. Composer
A founder of Romantic opera; master of counterpoint; wrote opera *Medee*, 1797.
b. Sep 14, 1760 in Florence, Italy
d. Mar 15, 1842 in Paris, France
Source: *Baker 84; NewEOp 71; OxCMus; WebBD 83*

Chervenkov, Vulko
Bulgarian. Political Leader
Prime Minister, Bulgaria, 1949-56; General Secretary, Bulgarian Communist Party, 1949-1956.
b. Aug 24, 1900 in Zlatitsa, Bulgaria
d. Oct 21, 1980 in Sofia, Bulgaria
Source: *AnObit 1980; BioIn 4, 12, 18; ColdWar 2; DicTyr; FacFETw; NewYTBS 80*

Cherwell, Frederick Alexander L, Viscount
English. Scientist, Government Official
Supervised Britain's atomic energy program, 1942; privy counselor, wartime assistant to Churchill, 1943.
b. 1886 in Sidmouth, England
d. Jul 2, 1957 in Oxford, England
Source: *CurBio 52, 57*

Chesbro, Jack
[John Dwight Chesbro]
"Happy Jack"
American. Baseball Player
Pitcher, 1899-1909; won 41 games, 1904; Hall of Fame, 1946.
b. Jun 5, 1874 in North Adams, Massachusetts
d. Nov 6, 1931 in Conway, Massachusetts
Source: *Ballpl 90; BiDAmSp BB; BioIn 3, 7, 14, 15; LegTOT; WhoProB 73; WhoSpor*

Chesebrough, Robert Augustus
American. Chemist
Began manufacturing petroleum products, 1858; patented Vaseline, 1870.
b. Jan 9, 1837 in London, England
d. Sep 8, 1933 in Spring Lake, New Jersey
Source: *BiDAmBL 83; BioIn 3, 18; NatCAB 3, 25; TwCBDA; WhAm 1*

Cheshire, Maxine
[Mrs. Bert W Cheshire]
American. Journalist
Reporter, Washington *Post*, 1954-65; columnist LA Times Syndicate since 1965.
b. Apr 5, 1930 in Harlan, Kentucky
Source: *BiDAmNC; BioIn 8, 9, 11; CelR; ConAu 108; InWom SUP; WhoAm 74, 76, 78, 80, 82, 84; WhoAmW 72, 74, 75, 79, 83, 85*

Chesney, Charles Cornwallis
Irish. Historian
Military history expert; *Waterloo Lectures*, 1868, criticized Wellington's tactics; nephew of Francis R.
b. Sep 29, 1826 in Kilkeel, Ireland
d. Mar 19, 1876 in London, England
Source: *Alli SUP; ApCAB; BiDIrW; CelCen; DcIrB 78, 88; DcIrW 2; DcNaB; HarEnUS*

Chesney, Francis Rawdon
British. Soldier, Explorer
Surveyed the Isthmus of Suez, 1829, Euphrates valley, 1829; mapped railway from Antioch to Euphrates, 1856.
b. Mar 16, 1789 in Annalong, Ireland
d. Jan 30, 1872 in Mourne, Ireland
Source: *Alli, SUP; BiDIrW; BioIn 2, 7, 17; CelCen; DcBiPP; DcIrB 78, 88; DcIrW 2; DcNaB; HisDBrE; NewCol 75; WebBD 83*

Chesney, Marion
[M C Beaton; Ann Fairfax; Jennie Tremaine]
Scottish. Author
Historical novels include *Sally*, 1982.
b. Jun 10, 1936 in Glasgow, Scotland
Source: *ConAu 53NR, 111, 115; ScF&FL 92; TwCRHW 90, 94; WhoAm 92; WrDr 90, 92, 94, 96*

Chesnutt, Charles Waddell
American. Author, Lawyer
Works depicting struggle of American blacks include *The Conjure Woman*, 1899; awarded Spingarn Medal.
b. Jun 20, 1858 in Cleveland, Ohio
d. Nov 15, 1932 in Cleveland, Ohio
Source: *AfrAmAl 6; AmAu&B; AmBi; AmLY; BioIn 2, 3, 4, 5, 6, 8, 9, 10, 11, 12, 13, 17, 18, 19, 21; BlkAuII, 92; BlkAWP; CasWL; CnDAL; ConAu 106; CyWA 58; DcAmAu; DcAmNB; DcLB 12, 50, 78; DcNAA; DcNCBi 1; EncAACR; EncSoH; EncWL 2; FifSWrB; InB&W 80, 85; LinLib L; NatCAB 12; NegAl 76, 83, 89; OhA&B; OxCAmL 65, 83; PenC AM; REn; REnAL; RfGAmL 87, 94; RfGShF; SelBAAf; SelBAAu; ShSCr 7; TwCA, SUP; TwCLC 5, 39; WebAB 74, 79; WebBD 83; WhAm 1; WhNAA; WhoColR*

Chessman, Caryl Whittier
American. Criminal, Author
Lived on Death Row 12 years; Alan Alda starred in movie of his life, 1977.
b. May 27, 1921 in Saint Joseph, Michigan
d. May 2, 1960 in San Quentin, California
Source: *AmAu&B; ConAu 73; DcAmB S6; WebAB 74, 79; WorAl*

Chesterfield, Philip Dormer, Earl
[Philip Dormer Stanhope]
English. Author, Statesman
Letters to His Son, 1774, classic portrait of 18th-c. gentleman.
b. Sep 22, 1694 in London, England
d. Mar 24, 1773 in London, England
Source: *Alli; AtlBL; BiD&SB; BioIn 14, 15, 17, 19; BritAu; CasWL; Chambr 3; CyWA 58; DcEnL; DcEuL; DcLEL; DcNaB, C; Dis&D; EvLB; LngCEL; MouLC 2; NewC; NewCBEL; OxCEng 85; PenC ENG; REn*

Chesterton, G(ilbert) K(eith)
English. Poet, Critic, Essayist
Wrote *Father Brown* detective stories, 1911-45; literary criticism.
b. May 29, 1874 in Kensington, England
d. Jun 14, 1936 in Chiltern Hills, England
Source: *AnCL; AtlBL; Benet 96; BioIn 1, 2, 3, 4, 5, 6, 7, 8, 9, 10, 11, 12, 13, 14, 15, 16, 17, 18; BkC 6; CasWL; CathA 1930; Chambr 3; ChhPo, S1, S2, S3; CnMWL; ConAu 104; CorpD; CyWA 58; DcArts; DcBrBI; DcCathB; DcLEL; DcNaB 1931; EncSF 93; EncWL 3; EvLB; GrBr; LinLib L, S; LngCEL; LuthC 75; MakMC; McGEWB; NotNAT B; OxCEng 67, 85, 95; OxCTwCP; PenC ENG; RAdv 14; REn; RfGShF; RGTwCWr; ScFEYrs; SJGFanW; SpyFic; TwCA, SUP; TwCWr; WhDW; WhE&EA; WhLit; WhoLA*

Chevalier, Jules
French. Clergy, Author
Catholic priest; founded the Missionaries of the Sacred Heart of Jesus congregation, 1854; cofounded the Daughters of Our Lady of the Sacred Heart, 1882.
b. Mar 15, 1824 in Richelieu, France
d. Oct 21, 1907 in Issoudun, France

Chevalier, Maurice Auguste
French. Actor, Singer
Most popular French entertainer of century; starred in film *Gigi,* 1958; won special Oscar, 1958.
b. Sep 12, 1888 in Paris, France
d. Jan 1, 1972 in Paris, France
Source: *Baker 84; BiDFilm; BiE&WWA; CmMov; CurBio 48, 69, 72; Film 1; FilmgC; MovMk; OxCFilm; OxCThe 67; WhAm 5; WhScrn 77; WorEFlm*

Chevallier, Gabriel
French. Author
Best known for comic satire *Clochemerle,* 1934.
b. May 1895 in Lyons, France
d. 1969
Source: *BioIn 8; CasWL; ConAu 113; EvEuW; HalFC 84, 88; Novels; ObitT 1961; REn; TwCWr*

Chevreul, Michel Eugene
"Father of Fatty Acids"
French. Chemist
Discovered olein, stearin; appointed director of Gobelin's dyeing dept. by Louis XVIII, 1824.
b. Aug 31, 1786 in Angers, France
d. Apr 9, 1889 in Paris, France
Source: *AsBiEn; BiESc; BioIn 1, 3, 5, 6, 10, 14, 15, 16; CamDcSc; CelCen; DcBiPP; DcCathB; DcInv; DcScB; Dis&D; EncO&P 1, 2, 3; ICPEnP; InSci; LarDcSc; LinLib S; NewCol 75; WorScD*

Chevrier, Lionel
Canadian. Politician
Known as father of St. Lawrence Seaway; Seaway president, 1945-57.
b. Apr 2, 1903 in Cornwall, Ontario, Canada
d. Jul 8, 1987 in Montreal, Quebec, Canada
Source: *AnObit 1987; BioIn 2, 3, 4, 6; BlueB 76; CanWW 70, 83; CurBio 52; FacFETw; IntWW 83; OxCCan; Who 74, 85; WhoWor 74*

Chevrolet, Louis Joseph
American. Auto Racer
Defeated Barney Oldfield in auto race, 1905; designed six-cylinder car, Chevrolet, 1910.
b. Dec 25, 1878 in La Chaux-de-Fonds, Switzerland
d. Jun 6, 1941 in Detroit, Michigan
Source: *BioIn 9, 21; CurBio 41; Entr; NatCAB 53*

Chew, Peter
American. Journalist, Author
Newspaper, magazine reporter who wrote *The Kentucky Derby: The First One Hundred Years,* 1974.
b. Apr 5, 1924 in New Rochelle, New York
Source: *ConAu 57*

Cheyne, William Watson, Sir
British. Surgeon, Bacteriologist
Early advocate of the use of antiseptic methods in surgery.
b. Dec 14, 1852, At Sea
d. Apr 19, 1932 in Fetlar, Scotland
Source: *BioIn 2, 3; DcNaB 1931; InSci*

Cheyney, Peter
[Harold Brust; Reginald E Cheyney]
English. Author
Suspense novels include *Lemmy Caution* series, 1930s.
b. 1896 in London, England
d. Jun 26, 1951
Source: *BiDIrW; BioIn 2, 3, 14; ConAu 113; CrtSuMy; DcIrB 78, 88; DcIrW 1; DcLEL; EncMys; EvLB; FilmgC; HalFC 84, 88; MnBBF; Novels; ObitT 1951; OxCIri; REn; TwCCr&M 80, 85, 91; TwCWr; WhoSpyF*

Chia, Sandro
Italian. Artist
Among most successful of neoexpressionists: *The Idleness of Sisyphus;* painter, printmaker, sculptor with exhibits in US, Europe.
b. Apr 20, 1946 in Florence, Italy
Source: *BioIn 14, 16, 17; ConArt 89, 96; ConNews 87-2; CurBio 90; DcCAr 81; PrintW 83, 85; WhoAm 97; WhoAmA 86, 89, 91, 93; WorArt 1980*

Chiang, Ching
[Ping Lan; Chiang Ching Mao]
Chinese. Actor, Political Leader
Wife of Mao Tse-tung, sentenced to death as member of "gang of four," 1981, later commuted to life imprisonment.
b. 1913 in Chucheng, China
d. May 14, 1991 in Beijing, China
Source: *BioIn 7, 8, 9; CurBio 75; DcOrL 1; DcPol; FarE&A 78; GoodHs; WhoAmW 75; WomWMM*

Chiang, Yee
American. Author, Educator
Columbia U professor, 1968-71; wrote, illustrated *Silent Traveller* series, 1937-56.
b. May 19, 1903 in Kiukiang
d. Oct 17, 1977 in Peking
Source: *BioIn 1, 2, 3, 4, 5, 11; ConAu 15NR, 65, 73; DrAS 74F; IlsCB 1744, 1946; IntAu&W 77; IntWW 75, 76, 77, 78N; LinLib L; LngCTC; NewYTBS 77; TwCA SUP; WhAm 7; Who 74; WhoAm 74, 76, 78; WhoE 75*

Chiang Ching-Kuo
Chinese. Political Leader
President, Republic of China (Taiwan), 1978-88; liberalized policies, dropped martial law; son of Chiang Kai-Shek.
b. Mar 18, 1906 in Fenghua, China
d. Jan 13, 1988 in Taipei, Taiwan
Source: *CurBio 54, 88; NewYTBE 70, 72; NewYTBS 88; WhoWor 84, 87*

Chiang Kai-Shek
Chinese. Statesman
Head of state, 1928-49; exiled by communists to Taiwan, 1949-75.
b. Oct 31, 1886 in Fenghua, China
d. Apr 5, 1975 in Taipei, Taiwan
Source: *ColdWar 2; CurBio 40, 53; DcPol; EncWM; HisEWW; IntWW 75N; LinLib S; McGEWB; REn; WhAm 6; Who 74*

Chiang K'ang-Hu
Chinese. Social Reformer, Scholar
As early 20th c. advocate of Chinese socialism, he helped establish what became the Social Democratic Party; accused of collaboration with deposed Emperor, fled country and eventually abandoned socialism to embrace traditional Chinese ideology.
b. Jul 18, 1883 in Shangrao, China
d. 1945?, China

Chiang Mei-Ling
[Madame Chiang Kai-Shek; Mayling Soong]
Chinese. Sociologist
American educated, she exerted strong influence on policies of her husband, Chiang Kai-Shek; introduced Western methods into China.
b. Jun 5, 1897
Source: *CurBio 40; REn; Who 85*

Chic
[Claire Beth; Bernard Edwards; Norma Jean; Kenny Lehman; Nile Rodgers; Andy Schwartz; Tony Thompson]
American. Music Group
Disco group, formed 1977; hits include "Dance Dance Dance," 1977; "Good Times," 1979.
Source: *BioIn 14, 15, 16; ConMuA 80B; EncRk 88; EncRkSt; HarEnR 86; InB&W 80, 85A; NewGrDA 86; NewYTBS 27; PenEncP; RkOn 78, 84; RolSEnR 83; SoulM; WhoAfA 96; WhoBlA 94; WhoRock 81*

Chicago
[Peter Cetera; Donnie Dacus; Laudir DeOliveira; Terry Kath; Robert Lamm; Lee Loughnane; James Pankow Walter Parazaider; Walt Perry; Daniel Serphine]
American. Music Group
Jazz-oriented rock band, formed 1967; first called Chicago Transit Authority; hits include "Saturday in the Park," 1972; Grammy for "If You Leave Me Now," 1976.
Source: *BiDAmM; BiDJaz A; BioIn 15; BioNews 74; CelR 90; ConMus 3; EncJzS; EncPR&S 89; EncRk 88; EncRkSt; HarEnR 86; IlEncRk; NewAmDM; NewGrDA 86; PenEncP; RkOn 78, 84; RolSEnR 83; WhoRock 81; WhoRocM 82*

Chicago, Judy
[Judy Cohen]
American. Artist, Feminist
Most well-known work is "The Dinner Party," a monumental work conveying the social history of women.
b. Jul 20, 1939 in Chicago, Illinois
Source: *AmArt; BiDWomA; BioIn 9, 10, 12, 13, 16, 17, 21; CelR 90; ConArt 77, 83, 89, 96; ConAu 21NR, 85; ContDcW 89; CurBio 81; DcCAr 81; EncWB; GrLiveH; HanAmWH; IntDcWB; InWom SUP; LegTOT; NewYTBS 79; PenNWW B; PrintW 83, 85; RadHan; WhoAm 76, 78, 80, 82, 84, 86, 88, 90, 92, 94, 95, 96; WhoAmA 73, 76, 78, 80, 82, 84, 86, 89, 91, 93; WhoAmW 75, 77, 79, 81, 83, 85, 87, 89, 91, 93, 95; WhoUSWr 88; WhoWrEP 89, 92, 95; WomFir; WomWMM B; WorArt 1980*

Chicago Seven, The
[Rennie Davis; David Dellinger; John Radford Froines; Tom Hayden; Abbie Hoffman; Jerry Rubin; Lee Weiner]
American. Political Activists
Disrupted 1968 Democratic National Convention, Chicago, with antiwar demonstrations; courtroom proceedings described in Hayden's book *Trial,* 1970.
Source: *AmAu&B; BioIn 14, 15, 16, 17, 18, 19, 20, 21; BioNews 74; ConAu 41NR, X; DcAmC; EncAL; IntvTCA 2; NewYTBE 70; NewYTBS 76, 87; PeoHis; RComAH; WhoHol 92*

Chichester, Francis Charles, Sir
English. Adventurer, Yachtsman
Yachtsman who made solo trip around world in yacht *Gipsy Moth,* 1966-67.
b. Sep 17, 1901 in Shirwell, England
d. Aug 26, 1972 in Plymouth, England
Source: *Au&Wr 71; CurBio 67, 72, 72N; DcNaB 1971; GrBr; LinLib L; NewYTBE 72; ObitT 1971; OxCShps; WhAm 5; WhDW*

Chickering, Jonas
American. Manufacturer
Built first grand piano with full iron frame in single casting, 1837.
b. Apr 5, 1798 in Mason Village, New Hampshire
d. Dec 8, 1853 in Boston, Massachusetts
Source: *AmBi; ApCAB; Baker 78, 84, 92; BiDAmM; BioIn 2, 3, 10; DcAmB; Drake; NatCAB 6; TwCBDA; WhAm HS*

Chidsey, Donald Barr
American. Author, Historian
Writer, historical novels, biographies, magazine articles: *Valley Forge,* 1959.
b. May 14, 1902 in Elizabeth, New Jersey
d. 1981 in New London, Connecticut
Source: *AmAu&B; AmNov; Au&Wr 71; BioIn 2, 4, 9, 13; ConAu 2NR, 5R, 103; REnAL; SmATA 3, 27N; TwCA SUP*

Chieftains, The
[David Fallon; Martin Fay; Paddy Maloney; Sean Potts; Michael Tubridy]
Irish. Music Group
Irish folk ensemble formed in 1963 (original members listed above); soundtrack to *The Gray Fox,* 1983; often record with pop singers.
Source: *ConMus 7; EncRkSt; FacFETw; PenEncP; WhoRocM 82*

Ch'ien Lung
Chinese. Ruler
Fourth ruler of Manchu dynasty, 1735-99.
b. Sep 25, 1711 in Beijing, China
d. Feb 7, 1799 in Beijing, China
Source: *McGEWB*

Chihuly, Dale (Patrick)
American. Sculptor
Glass sculptor; co-founded Pilchuck Glass Center in Stanwood, WA, 1971.
b. Sep 20, 1941 in Tacoma, Washington
Source: *AmArt; BioIn 18, 19, 20, 21; CurBio 95; DcCAr 81; News 95, 95-2; WhoAm 80, 82, 86, 88, 90, 92, 94, 95, 96; WhoAmA 78, 80, 82, 84, 86, 89, 91, 93*

Chikamatsu, Monzaemon
[Sugimori Mobumori]
Japanese. Dramatist
Prominent author of Joruri, Kabuki plays, based on myths, legends.
b. 1653 in Eichizen Province, Japan
d. Jan 6, 1725
Source: *Benet 87, 96; BiDJaL; EncWT; McGEWB; NewCol 75; PriCCJL 85; RAdv 13-2; WhDW*

Chikatilo, Andrei
Russian. Murderer
Mass murderer believed to have tortured, killed 53 women and children in Russia, the Ukraine, Uzbekistan from 1978-90.
b. 1934

Child, Julia McWilliams
[Mrs. Paul Child]
American. Chef, Author, TV Personality
Star of "The French Chef," 1962-83; wrote *Mastering the Art of French Cooking,* 1961.
b. Aug 15, 1912 in Pasadena, California
Source: *AmAu&B; BkPepl; CurBio 67; EncAI&E; ForWC 70; GoodHs; InWom, SUP; LibW; WhoAm 74, 76, 78, 80, 82, 84, 86, 88, 90, 92, 95, 96, 97; WhoAmW 66, 68, 70, 72, 74, 75, 79, 81, 83, 85, 87, 89, 91, 93, 95, 97; WhoEnt 92; WhoWor 74, 78, 80, 82; WrDr 86*

Child, Lydia Maria Francis
American. Author, Feminist
Founded, edited *Juvenile Miscellany,* 1826-34, first children's monthly in US; wrote novel *Philothea,* 1836.
b. Feb 11, 1802 in Medford, Massachusetts
d. Oct 22, 1880 in Wayland, Massachusetts
Source: *AmAu; AmPeW; AmRef; AmSocL; AmWomWr; BiDMoPL; BioIn 15, 17, 18, 19, 20, 21; BlmGWL; CasWL; Chambr 3; CyAL 2; Drake; EncAB-H 1996; EncNAB; HanAmWH; InWom; LibW; OxCAmL 65; REnAL; WebAB 79; WebBD 83; WhAm HS; WhCiWar; WomEdUS*

Childe, Vere Gordon
Australian. Archaeologist
Influenced by Darwin's *Origin of Species.*
b. Apr 14, 1892 in Sydney, Australia
d. Sep 19, 1957 in Mount Victoria, Australia
Source: *BioIn 1, 4, 5, 12, 13; DcNaB 1951; InSci; MakMC; McGEWB; ObitOF 79; OxCAusL; TwCA SUP; WhDW*

Childers, Erskine
[Robert Erskine Childers]
Irish. Author, Social Reformer
Wrote *The Riddle of the Sands,* 1903.
b. Jun 25, 1870 in London, England
d. Nov 24, 1922 in Dublin, Ireland
Source: *Benet 96; BiDIrW; BioIn 10, 11, 14, 16, 20; CamGLE; ConAu 113; CrtSuMy; DcIrB 78, 88; DcIrL; DcIrW 1, 2; DcLB 70; DcLEL; DcNaB 1922; EncMys; EncSF; EvLB; GrBr; LngCTC; Novels; OxCEng 85; OxCShps; REn; SpyFic; TwCA; TwCCr&M 80, 85, 91; TwCLC 65; TwCWr; WhDW; WhoSpyF*

Childers, Erskine Hamilton
Irish. Political Leader
Protestant elected to the presidency of the Irish Republic, 1973-74, after nearly 30 years of Catholic presidents; son of Robert Erskine Childers.
b. Dec 11, 1905 in London, England
d. Nov 17, 1974 in Dublin, Ireland
Source: *BioIn 10, 11; DcIrB 78, 88; IntWW 74; NewYTBE 73; WhoWor 74*

Childress, Alice
American. Author, Dramatist
Wrote plays dealing with controversial topics such as miscegenation and racism; with *Gold through the Trees,* 1952, she became the first black woman to have a drama professionally produced on the American stage.
b. Oct 12, 1920 in Charleston, South Carolina
d. Aug 14, 1994
Source: *AfrAmAl 6; AmWomD; AmWomWr SUP; ArtclWW 2; Au&Arts 8; AuBYP 2S, 3; BioIn 10, 12, 14, 15, 16, 17, 18, 19, 20, 21; BlkAull, 92; BlkAWP; BlkLC; BlkWAm; BlkWr 1, 2; BlkWrNE; BlmGWL; CamGWoT; ChlBkCr; ChlLR 14; ConAmD; ConAu 3NR, 27NR, 45, 50NR, 146; ConBlAP 88; ConDr 77, 82, 88, 93; ConLC 12, 15, 86, 96; ConTFT 10, 13; ConWomD; DcAmChF 1960; DcLB 7, 38; DcTwCCu 5; DramC 4; DrBlPA, 90; FemiCLE; FifBJA; InB&W 80, 85; IntAu&W 91;*

IntDcT 2; LivgBAA; MajAI; MajTwCW; McGEWD 84; NegAl 83, 89; NotBlAW 1; NotNAT; NotWoAT; OxCWoWr 95; PlP&P A; RfGAmL 94; SchCGBL; SelBAAf; SelBAAu; SmATA 7, 48, 81; TwCChW 89; TwCYAW; WhAm 11; WhoAfA 96; WhoAm 82, 84, 86, 88, 90, 92, 94; WhoBlA 90, 92, 94; WhoEnt 92; WorAu 1975; WrDr 80, 82, 84, 86, 88, 90, 92, 94, 96

Childress, Alvin
American. Actor
Played Amos Jones in TV series "Amos 'n Andy," 1950-53.
b. 1908 in Meridian, Mississippi
d. Apr 19, 1986 in Inglewood, California
Source: *AnObit 1986; BioIn 14, 15; BlksAmF; DrBlPA; EarBlAP; InB&W 80; NotNAT*

Childs, George William
American. Publisher
Established the *Public Ledger* in Philadelphia, 1864.
b. May 12, 1829 in Baltimore, Maryland
d. Feb 3, 1894 in Philadelphia, Pennsylvania
Source: *AmAu&B; AmBi; ApCAB, X; BbD; BiD&SB; BioIn 4, 8; ChhPo S1; DcAmAu; DcAmB; DcLB 23; DcNAA; HarEnUS; JrnUS; LinLib L, S; NatCAB 2; TwCBDA; WhAm HS*

Childs, Marquis William
American. Journalist, Author
Pulitzer-winning political columnist, 1969: *Ethics in a Business Society.*
b. Mar 17, 1903 in Clinton, Iowa
d. Jun 30, 1990 in San Francisco, California
Source: *AmAu&B; BiDAmJo; BiDAmNC; BioIn 3, 4, 6, 16, 17; ConAu 61; CurBio 43, 90; IntAu&W 77, 89; IntWW 74, 75, 76, 77, 78, 79, 80, 81, 82, 83, 89; OxCAmL 65; REn; REnAL; TwCA SUP; WhAm 10; WhoAm 74, 76, 78, 80, 82, 84, 86, 88; WhoSSW 75; WhoWor 78, 80, 84, 89, 91; WorAl*

Childs, Toni
American. Singer
Folk singer with African accents in album, *Union,* 1988.
b. 1957 in California
Source: *BioIn 15, 16; ConMus 2*

Chiles, Lawton Mainor, Jr.
American. Politician
Democratic governor of FL, 1991—, defeated incumbent Bob Martinez; US senator, 1971-89.
b. Apr 3, 1930 in Lakeland, Florida
Source: *AlmAP 84; BiDrUSC 89; BioNews 74; CngDr 74, 77, 79, 81, 83, 87; CurBio 71; IntWW 74, 75, 76, 77, 78, 79, 80, 81, 82, 83, 89, 91, 93; NewYTBS 83; WhoAm 74, 76, 78, 80, 82, 84, 86, 88, 90, 92, 94, 95, 96, 97; WhoAmP 73, 75, 77, 79, 81, 83, 85, 87, 89, 91, 93, 95; WhoGov 72, 75, 77; WhoSSW 80, 82, 84, 86, 88, 91, 95, 97; WhoWor 80, 82, 87, 89*

Chillida, Eduard
Spanish. Artist
Abstract sculptor whose works are on display in Germany, Switzerland, US.
b. Jan 10, 1924 in San Sebastian, Spain
Source: *ConArt 83; CurBio 75; DcCAr 81; McGDA; OxCTwCA; PhDcTCA 77; PrintW 83*

Chilton, Alex
[The Box Tops]
American. Singer
Lead singer with Memphis-based blue-eyed soul group, late 1960s.
b. Dec 28, 1950 in Memphis, Tennessee
Source: *ConMus 10; NewGrDA 86; OnThGG; WhoRocM 82*

Chiluba, Frederick Jacob Titus
Zimbabwean. Political Leader
Pres., Republic of Zambia, 1991—; won landslide victory over 27 year old, one-party regime of Kenneth Kaunda.
b. Apr 30, 1943 in Kitwe, Zimbabwe
Source: *CurBio 92; DcCPSAf; EncRev; News 92; WhoWor 93, 95, 96, 97*

Chinaglia, Giorgio
Italian. Soccer Player
Star of NY Cosmos, 1976-83; leading scorer of North American Soccer League, 1976, 1978-79, 1982.
b. Jan 24, 1947 in Carrara, Italy
Source: *NewYTBS 81, 84; WorAl*

Chinard, Gilbert
French. Educator
Biographies include *Thomas Jefferson; Benjamin Franklin; John Adams.*
b. Oct 17, 1881 in Chatellerault, France
d. Feb 8, 1972 in Princeton, New Jersey
Source: *AmAu&B; BioIn 4, 9, 11; ConAu 104; NewYTBE 72; OxCAmL 65; WhAm 5; WhNAA*

Chinh, Truong
Vietnamese. Political Leader
Pres., Council of State, Vietnam, 1981-86.
b. 1906?
d. Sep 30, 1988 in Hanoi, Vietnam
Source: *BioIn 8; WhoWor 78*

Ch'i Pai-Shih
[Ch'i Huang]
Chinese. Artist
Influenced by traditional school of Chinese art, became one of their greatest painters.
b. Nov 22, 1863 in Xiangtan, China
d. Sep 16, 1957 in Beijing, China
Source: *BioIn 1, 4, 6, 10, 11; McGDA; McGEWB; ObitOF 79*

Chippendale, Thomas
English. Cabinetmaker, Furniture Designer
Catalog *Gentleman and Cabinet-Maker's Director,* 1754, influenced 18th-c. designs.
b. Jun 5, 1718 in Otley, England
d. Nov 1779 in London, England
Source: *Alli; AntBDN G; BioIn 2, 3, 6, 8, 9, 10, 12; BlmGEL; DcArts; DcD&D; LegTOT; LinLib S; McGDA; McGEWB; NewC; NewCol 75; OxCDecA; PenDiDA 89; WorAl; WorAlBi*

Chipperfield, Joseph Eugene
English. Author
Books in wildlife, geology genres include *Sabre of Storm Valley,* 1963.
b. Apr 20, 1912 in Saint Austell, England
Source: *Au&Wr 71; AuBYP 2, 3; ConAu 6NR, 9R; IntAu&W 76; MorJA; SmATA 2; TwCChW 83*

Chirac, Jacques (Rene)
French. Politician
Mayor of Paris, 1977-83, 1989-95; prime minister of France, 1974-76, 1986-88; pres., France, 1995—.
b. Nov 29, 1932 in Paris, France
Source: *BiDFrPL; BioIn 10, 11, 13, 14, 15, 16, 17, 18, 19, 21; CurBio 75, 93; EncWB; FacFETw; IntWW 74, 75, 76, 77, 78, 79, 80, 81, 82, 83, 89, 91, 93; IntYB 78, 79, 80, 81, 82; News 95; NewYTBS 77, 86; PolLCWE; Who 82, 83, 85, 88, 90, 92, 94; WhoFr 79; WhoWor 74, 76, 78, 82, 84, 87, 91, 93, 95, 96, 97; WorAlBi*

Chirico, Giorgio de
Italian. Artist
Founded Italian school of metaphysical painting.
b. Jul 10, 1888 in Volos, Greece
d. Nov 20, 1978 in Rome, Italy
Source: *Benet 87, 96; BioIn 1, 2, 3, 4, 5, 6, 8, 9, 11, 12, 13; ClaDrA; ConArt 77, 83; ConAu 81, 89; CurBio 56, 72, 79, 79N; DcArts; EncWT; FacFETw; IntDcAA 90; IntDcB; LegTOT; LinLib S; MakMC; McGDA; McGEWB; ModArCr 2; NewYTBE 70, 72; NewYTBS 78; ObitOF 79; OxCArt; OxCTwCA; OxDcArt; PhDcTCA 77; REn; WhDW; Who 74; WorAlBi*

Chirol, Valentine, Sir
English. Author, Journalist
Headed foreign dept. of London *Times;* wrote *India Old and New,* 1921.
b. May 23, 1852
d. Oct 22, 1929 in Chelsea, England
Source: *BioIn 7, 14; DcNaB 1922; GrBr; LngCTC; NewC; WhLit*

Chisholm, Caroline
English. Social Reformer
Pioneer in Australian social reform.
b. May 1808? in Northampton, England
d. Mar 25, 1877 in London, England
Source: *BioIn 2, 5, 7, 9, 10; ContDcW 89; DcNaB; FemiCLE; HisDBrE; HisWorL; IntDcWB; OxCAusL*

Chisholm, Jesse
American. Pioneer
Frontier tradesman; Chisholm Trail, cattle highway from TX to KS, named after him.
b. 1805 in Tennessee
d. Mar 4, 1868 in Blaine City, Oklahoma
Source: *BioIn 5; EncNAB; NatCAB 19; REnAW; WebAB 79; WhNaAH; WhWE*

Chisholm, Shirley Anita St. Hill
American. Politician, Author
First black woman elected to Congress, 1968; Dem. from NY, 1969-83; wrote *Good Fight,* 1973.
b. Nov 30, 1924 in New York, New York
Source: *AfrAmOr; AmAu&B; AmPolLe; BiDrAC; CngDr 81; CurBio 69; EncAACR; EncWB; EncWHA; HerW; InB&W 80, 85; LibW; LivgBAA; NotBlAW 1; PolProf NF; WhoAm 74, 76, 78, 80, 82, 84, 86, 88, 90, 92, 94, 95, 96; WhoAmP 85; WhoAmW 68, 70, 72, 74, 75, 77, 79, 81, 83, 85, 95, 97; WhoBlA 75, 77, 80, 85; WhoE 74, 75, 77, 79, 81, 83; WhoGov 77*

Chissano, Joaquim Alberto
Mozambican. Political Leader
Succeeded Samora Machel as president of Mozambique, Nov. 1986.
b. Oct 22, 1939 in Malehice, Mozambique
Source: *BioIn 15, 16, 17, 20, 21; ConNews 87-4; IntWW 93; NewYTBS 86; WhoAfr; WhoWor 78, 82, 84, 87, 89, 91, 93, 95, 96, 97*

Chisum, John Simpson
American. Rancher
Largest cattle owner in country who was instrumental in death of Billy the Kid.
b. Aug 15, 1824 in Hardeman County, Tennessee
d. Dec 23, 1884 in Eureka Springs, Arkansas
Source: *AmBi; BiDAmBL 83; BioIn 4, 7, 11, 13, 15; DcAmB; EncAAH; McGEWB; NatCAB 22; REnAW; WebAB 74, 79; WhAm HS*

Chittenden, Thomas
American. Politician
First governor of VT, from independence to statehood, 1778-1797.
b. Jan 6, 1730 in East Guilford, Connecticut
d. Aug 25, 1797 in Williston, Vermont
Source: *Alli; AmBi; ApCAB; BiAUS; BiDrGov 1789; BioIn 1, 6; DcAmB; Drake; EncAB-A 31; HarEnUS; NatCAB 8; TwCBDA; WhAm HS; WhAmP; WhAmRev*

Cho, Margaret
[Moran Cho]
American. Actor, Comedian
Star of TV's "All American Girl," 1994-95.
b. 1970 in San Francisco, California
Source: *News 95, 95-2; WhoAmW 97*

Choate, Joseph Hodges
American. Lawyer, Diplomat
Legal victories included Tweed Ring expose, 1871; ambassador to Britain, 1899-1905.
b. Jan 24, 1832 in Salem, Massachusetts
d. May 14, 1917 in New York, New York
Source: *AmAu&B; AmBi; ApCAB, X; BioIn 10, 15, 16; CyAG; DcAmB; DcAmDH 80, 89; DcNAA; HarEnUS; LinLib L, S; NatCAB 9; NewCol 75; OxCAmH; OxCSupC; REnAL; TwCBDA; WebAB 74, 79; WhAm 1; WhAmP*

Choate, Rufus
American. Lawyer, Politician
Succeeded Daniel Webster in Senate, 1841-45.
b. Oct 1, 1799 in Ipswich, Massachusetts
d. Jul 15, 1859 in Halifax, Nova Scotia, Canada
Source: *Alli, SUP; AmAu; AmAu&B; AmBi; ApCAB; BbD; BiAUS; BiD&SB; BiDrAC; BiDrUSC 89; BioIn 3, 6, 9, 12; CyAL 2; DcAmAu; DcAmB; DcNAA; Drake; HarEnUS; LinLib L, S; NatCAB 6; OxCAmH; REnAL; TwCBDA; WebAB 74, 79; WebBD 83; WhAm HS; WhAmP*

Chodorov, Edward
American. Author, Director, Producer
Wrote plays, films, TV series, "The Billy Rose Show"; plays include *Wonder Boy* , 1932; *Kind Lady,* 1935.
b. Apr 17, 1904 in New York, New York
d. Oct 9, 1988 in New York, New York
Source: *AmAu&B; BiE&WWA; CnMD; ConAu 102, 126; ConTFT 7; CurBio 44, 88N; FilmgC; HalFC 84, 88; IntMPA 84; ModWD; NotNAT; OxCAmL 65, 83; OxCAmT 84; REnAL; WhoThe 81*

Chodorov, Jerome
American. Dramatist, Director
Collaborated with Joseph Field in plays: *My Sister Eileen,* 1940; *Anniversary Waltz,* 1954.
b. Aug 10, 1911 in New York, New York
Source: *AmAu&B; BiE&WWA; BioIn 10; ConAu 15NR, 65; ConDr 73, 77D, 82D; FilmgC; HalFC 84, 88; IntAu&W 77; McGEWD 72, 84; ModWD; NatPD 77, 81; NewCBMT; NotNAT; OxCAmL 83; OxCAmT 84; OxCThe 83; REnAL; WhoThe 72, 77, 81; WhoWor 74; WrDr 76, 80, 82, 84, 86, 88, 90*

Choiseul, Cesar, Comte Du Plessis-Praslin, duc de
French. Soldier
Marshal of France; credited with making confection "pralines."
b. 1598
d. 1675
Source: *DcBiPP; HarEnMi; NewCol 75*

Chomsky, Marvin
American. Director
TV credits include "Star Trek:" "Roots;" "Gunsmoke."
b. May 23, 1929 in New York, New York
Source: *HalFC 84, 88; IntMPA 86; LegTOT; LesBEnT; NewYTET; WhoAm 82, 84, 86*

Chomsky, Noam Avram
American. Linguist, Political Activist
Developed Cartesian theory, influenced development of modern linguistics.
b. Dec 7, 1928 in Philadelphia, Pennsylvania
Source: *AmAu&B; ConAu 17R; CurBio 70, 95; IntWW 83; OxCEng 85; PenC AM; WebAB 79; Who 85; WhoWorJ 72; WrDr 86*

Chona, Maria
American. Historian
Oral autobiography *Papago Woman,* published 1979.
b. 1858? in Mesquite Root, Arizona
d. 1936
Source: *BioIn 21; NotNaAm*

Chong, Tommy
[Cheech and Chong; Thomas Chong]
Canadian. Actor, Comedian
Teamed with Richard Marin in counterculture records, nightclub acts, film series: *Up in Smoke,* 1978; *Still Smokin',* 1983.
b. May 24, 1938 in Edmonton, Alberta, Canada
Source: *BioIn 13; ConAu 112; ConTFT 2, 5; IntMPA 86, 88, 92, 94, 96; LegTOT; MiSFD 9; RkOn 84; VarWW 85; WhoAm 80, 82, 84, 86, 88, 90, 92, 94, 95, 96, 97; WhoAsA 94; WhoEnt 92; WhoWest 82, 84, 87*

Chopin, Frederic Francois
[Fryderyk Franciszek Chopin]
Polish. Pianist, Composer
Legendary virtuoso; piano compositions include concertos, etudes; good friend of George Sand.
b. Feb 22, 1810 in Zelazowa Wola, Poland
d. Oct 17, 1849 in Paris, France
Source: *AtlBL; Baker 84; McGEWB; NewC; OxCEng 85, 95; OxCFr; REn; WebBD 83*

Chopin, Kate
[Katherine O'Flaherty]
American. Author
Novels of Cajun, Creole life include *Bayou Folk,* 1894.
b. Feb 8, 1851 in Saint Louis, Missouri
d. Aug 22, 1904 in Saint Louis, Missouri
Source: *AmAu; AmAu&B; AmWomWr; AmWr S1; ArtclWW 2; BbD; Benet 87; BenetAL 91; BiDSA; BioIn 8, 10, 12, 13, 16, 17, 19, 20, 21; CamGEL; CamGLE; CamHAL; CasWL; CnDAL; ConAu 104; CrtT 4; CyWA 89; DcAmAu; DcArts; DcLB 12; DcLEL; DcNAA; EncSoH; FifSWrB; GayN; GoodHs; GrLiveH; GrWomW; LegTOT; MagSAmL; ModAL, S1; ModWoWr; Novels; OxCAmL 65, 83; PenC AM; RadHan; RAdv 14, 13-1; REn; REnAL; RfGAmL 87, 94; RfGShF;*

ShSCr 8; ShSWr; TwCLC 5, 14; WomNov; WorAlBi

Chopra, Deepak
Indian. Author, Physician
Practices form of medicine known as Maharishi Ayur-Veda; executive director, Chopra Center for Well Being, 1996—.
b. 1949 in New Delhi, India
Source: *CurBio 95*

Choquette, Robert Guy
Canadian. Author, Poet
Highly influential French-Canadian writer.
b. Apr 22, 1905 in Manchester, New Hampshire
Source: *Benet 87; BenetAL 91; BioIn 15; CanWW 89; DcLB 68; OxCCanL; REn; REnAL; WhoCanL 87*

Chorell, Walentin
Finnish. Dramatist
Wrote *Kattorna,* 1961.
b. Apr 4, 1912 in Turku, Finland
d. Jan 1984
Source: *ConAu 111; CroCD; DcScanL; EncWL, 2, 3; McGEWD 84; PenC EUR; REnWD*

Chorzempa, Daniel Walter
American. Musician, Composer
Has given int'l. piano, organ recitals, 1968—; won Leipzig Bach prize, 1968.
b. Dec 7, 1944 in Minneapolis, Minnesota
Source: *Baker 84, 92; BlueB 76; IntWW 74, 75, 76, 77, 78, 79, 80, 81, 82, 83, 89, 91, 93; IntWWM 90; WhoMus 72*

Chotzinoff, Samuel
American. Writer, Critic
NY Post music critic, 1930s; NBC music director, consultant.
b. Jul 4, 1889 in Vitebsk, Russia
d. Feb 9, 1964
Source: *Baker 78, 84, 92; BiDAmM; BioIn 3, 6, 7, 14; ConAu 93; CurBio 40, 64; DcAmB S7; EncAJ; NewGrDA 86; WhAm 4*

Chou En-Lai
Chinese. Government Official
With Mao Tse-Tung, founded Chinese Communist Party; premier, 1949-76.
b. 1898 in Shaoxing, China
d. Jan 8, 1976 in Beijing, China
Source: *BioIn 19; ConAu 112; CurBio 46, 57, 76N; DcPol; DicTyr; EncCW; FacFETw; HisDcKW; HisEWW; IntWW 74; LegTOT; McGEWB; NewYTBE 72; NewYTBS 76; REn; WhAm 6; Who 74; WhoWor 74; WorAlBi*

Chouteau, Yvonne
American. Dancer
Ballerina with Ballet Russe de Monte Carlo, 1943-57.
b. Mar 7, 1929 in Vinita, Oklahoma
Source: *BiDD; BioIn 3, 4, 5; InWom; WhoAmW 68, 70*

Chou Tso-Jen
Chinese. Essayist, Translator
Urged use of vernacular in China through his writings and translations of the literary works of foreign writers.
b. Jan 16, 1885 in Shaoxing, China
d. Nov 1966 in Beijing, China
Source: *BioIn 9; CasWL*

Chraibi, Driss
Moroccan. Author
Writings deal with social and political criticisms of various European and Third World civilizations; wrote *Simple Past,* 1954, and *A Friend Is Coming to See You,* 1966.
b. Jul 15, 1926 in Mazagan, Morocco
Source: *ConAu 151; ConWorW 93; DcOrL 3; EncWL 3; IntWW 89, 91, 93; RAdv 14*

Chretien, Henri
French. Inventor
Invented anamorphic lens used in cinemascope films.
b. Feb 1, 1879 in Paris, France
d. Feb 6, 1956 in Washington, District of Columbia
Source: *BioIn 4; DcFM; FilmEn; FilmgC; HalFC 84, 88; ObitOF 79; OxCFilm; WorEFlm*

Chretien, Jean (Joseph-Jacques)
Canadian. Government Official, Politician
Succeeded John Turner as leader of Canada's Liberal Party, 1990—; member, Parliament, 1963-86; prime minister, 1993—.
b. Jan 11, 1934 in Shawinigan, Quebec, Canada
Source: *BioIn 13, 14, 15, 16; BlueB 76; CanWW 89; CurBio 90; IntWW 74, 75, 76, 77, 78, 79, 80, 81, 82, 83, 91; IntYB 82; News 90; NewYTBS 93; Who 82, 83, 85, 88, 90, 92, 94; WhoAm 74, 76, 78, 80, 82, 84, 90, 95, 96, 97; WhoCan 82, 84; WhoE 81, 83, 85, 86; WhoWor 82, 84, 95, 96, 97*

Chretien de Troyes
French. Poet, Author
Wrote earliest known Arthurian legends, first known version of Grail legend, *Perceval, ou Le Conte de Graal.*
b. 1130?
d. 1183
Source: *AtlBL; BbD; BiD&SB; CasWL; ClMLC 10; CyWA 58; DcEuL; EuAu; EvEuW; NewC; OxCEng 67; OxCFr; OxCGer 76; PenC EUR; RComWL; REn*

Christaller, Walter
German. Geographer
Best known as father of theoretical geography.
b. Apr 21, 1893 in Berneck, Germany
d. Mar 9, 1969 in Koenigstein, German Democratic Republic
Source: *BioIn 18; ConAu 115, 116; Geog 7; WhoEc 81, 86*

Christen, Emanuel
Swiss. Hostage
Swiss relief worker held in captivity 306 days by Lebanese terrorist group, Oct 6, 1989-Aug 8, 1990.

Christensen, Harold
American. Dancer
Performed with several ballet companies, including Metropolitan Opera Ballet, 1934; San Francisco Ballet Company, 1941-46; director, San Francisco Ballet School, 1946-75.
b. Dec 25, 1904 in Brigham City, Utah
d. Feb 20, 1989 in San Anselmo, California
Source: *BiDD; BioIn 16*

Christensen, Lew Farr
American. Dancer, Choreographer
Highly influential in promoting ballet in western US; choreographic work brought fame to San Francisco Ballet Co., which he directed/co-directed, 1952-84.
b. May 6, 1909 in Brigham City, Utah
d. Oct 9, 1984 in Burlingame, California
Source: *BioIn 12, 13, 14; WhAm 8; WhoAm 76, 78, 80, 82, 84; WhoWest 82, 84*

Christensen, William
[William Farr Christensen]
American. Dancer, Choreographer
Founder, San Francisco Ballet Co., 1937; choreographed works to music of Bach, Mendelssohn, and Beethoven.
b. Aug 27, 1902 in Brigham City, Utah
Source: *BiDD; BioIn 6; IntDcB; WhoAm 80, 82; WhoWest 76, 78, 80, 82*

Christian, Charlie
[Charles Christian]
American. Jazz Musician
Guitarist who pioneered use of electrical amplification; with Benny Goodman sextet, 1940s.
b. Jul 29, 1916 in Dallas, Texas
d. Mar 2, 1942 in New York, New York
Source: *AfrAmAl 6; AllMusG; Baker 84, 92; BiDAfM; BiDJaz; BioIn 12, 13, 15, 16, 17; CmpEPM; ConMus 11; InB&W 85; NewGrDA 86; NewGrDJ 88, 94; OnThGG; OxCPMus; PenEncP; WhoJazz 72*

Christian, Dave
[David Christian]
American. Hockey Player
Center, Winnipeg, 1980-83, Washington Capitals 1983-89; Chicago Blackhawks 1992—; member US Olympic gold medal-winning team, 1980.
b. May 12, 1959 in Warroad, Minnesota
Source: *HocEn; HocReg 87*

Christian, Fletcher
English. Revolutionary
Led mutiny on *Bounty*, Apr 1784, in protest against alleged brutality of Capt. William Bligh.
b. 1764, England
d. 1793
Source: *BioIn 6, 9, 10, 17; NewC*

Christian, Linda
[Blanca Rosa Welter]
American. Actor
Married to Tyrone Power, 1949-55.
b. Nov 13, 1923 in Tampico, Mexico
Source: *BioIn 18; FilmgC; HalFC 84, 88; IntMPA 86; InWom, SUP; ItaFilm; LegTOT; MotPP; NotHsAW 93; WhoHol 92, A*

Christian, Mary Blount
American. Children's Author
Fiction writings include *Sebastian: Super Sleuth*, 1973; *The Doggone Mystery*, 1980.
b. Feb 20, 1933 in Houston, Texas
Source: *ArtclWW 2; AuBYP 3; ConAu 1NR, 17NR, 45; IntAu&W 77, 91, 93; SmATA 9; WhoAmW 83; WrDr 76, 80, 82, 84, 86, 88, 90, 92, 94, 96*

Christian, Meg
American. Singer, Songwriter
Released albums *I KNow You Know*, 1975; *Face the Music*, 1977.
b. 1946 in Lynchburg, Virginia
Source: *GayLesB*

Christian IV
Danish. Ruler
Reigned 1588-1648; city of Christiania, now Oslo, named after him.
b. Apr 12, 1577 in Hillerod, Denmark
d. Feb 28, 1648 in Copenhagen, Denmark
Source: *DcBiPP A; LinLib S; NewCol 75; WebBD 83*

Christian-Jacque
French. Director
Won best director award, Cannes, 1952: *Fanfan la Tulipe*.
b. Sep 4, 1904 in Paris, France
Source: *BiDFilm; DcFM; FilmgC; OxCFilm; WorEFlm*

Christians, Mady
[Marguerite Maria]
American. Actor
Known for performance as Mama in popular play *I Remember Mama*, 1944.
b. Jan 19, 1900 in Vienna, Austria
d. Oct 28, 1951 in Norwalk, Connecticut
Source: *BioIn 1, 2, 3; CurBio 45, 51; EncMcCE; Film 2; FilmgC; HalFC 84, 88; InWom, SUP; MotPP; MovMk; NotNAT B; OxCAmT 84; ThFT; WhoHol B; WhScrn 74, 77, 83; WhThe*

Christiansen, Arthur
English. Editor
Editor, *London Daily Express*, 1933-57.
b. Jul 27, 1904 in Wallasey, England
d. Sep 27, 1963 in Norwich, England
Source: *BioIn 1, 5, 6; ConAu 1NR, 1R; DcNaB 1961; LngCTC; ObitOF 79; WhAm 4; WhE&EA*

Christiansen, Jack L
"Chris"
American. Football Player, Football Coach
Defensive back, Detroit, 1951-58, known for punt returns; coach, San Francisco, 1963-67; Hall of Fame, 1969.
b. Dec 20, 1928 in Sublette, Kansas
d. Jun 30, 1986 in Palo Alto, California
Source: *NewYTBS 86; WhoFtbl 74*

Christian X
Danish. Ruler
King from 1912; enfranchised women, 1915; granted independence to Iceland, 1918; symbolized resistance to Nazis during 1943-45 imprisonment.
b. Sep 26, 1870 in Copenhagen, Denmark
d. Apr 20, 1947 in Copenhagen, Denmark
Source: *CurBio 43, 47; NewCol 75; WebBD 83*

Christie, Agatha Mary Clarissa Miller, Dame
"Queen of Crime"
English. Author, Dramatist
Play *Mousetrap* longest running in British history; created detectives Miss Marple, Hercule Poirot; mysteries sold over 100 million copies.
b. Sep 15, 1890 in Torquay, England
d. Jan 12, 1976 in Wallingford, England
Source: *AuNews 2; CasWL; ConAu 17R, 61; ConDr 73; ConLC 12; ConNov 76; CorpD; CurBio 40, 64, 76; OxCEng 85; PenC ENG; REn; TwCA SUP; WhAm 6; WhoThe 77; WrDr 76*

Christie, Audrey
American. Actor
Had career on stage, films, TV, 1927-78, including film *Harper Valley PTA*, 1978.
b. Jun 27, 1912 in Chicago, Illinois
Source: *BiE&WWA; ForWC 70; HalFC 84, 88; NotNAT; WhoAmW 61; WhoHol A; WhoThe 72, 77, 81; WhThe*

Christie, James
English. Auctioneer
Founded Christie's Auction Gallery in London, 1766.
b. 1730, England
d. Nov 8, 1803 in London, England
Source: *BioIn 7; DcNaB; NewC*

Christie, John
English. Philanthropist
Founded Glyndebourne Festival, for opera performances on grounds of estate, 1934.
b. Dec 14, 1882 in Glyndebourne, England
d. Jul 4, 1962 in Glyndebourne, England
Source: *BioIn 6, 8, 12, 14; DcNaB 1961; GrBr; LngCTC; MetOEnc; NewEOp 71; NewGrDO; NotNAT B; ObitT 1961; OxCMus; OxDcOp*

Christie, John Reginald Halliday
"The Strangler of Notting Hill"
English. Murderer
Strangled at least six women, including wife, 1943-53; hanged.
b. Apr 8, 1899? in Boothstown, England
d. Jul 15, 1953 in Pentonville, England
Source: *BioIn 4, 5, 6; DcNaB MP*

Christie, John Walter
American. Inventor, Engineer
Developed world's first amphibian tank, 1920s.
b. May 6, 1865 in River Edge, New Jersey
d. Jan 11, 1944 in Falls Church, Virginia
Source: *CurBio 44; DcAmB S3*

Christie, Julie
English. Actor
Won Oscar, 1965, for *Darling;* starred in *Doctor Zhivago*, 1965.
b. Apr 14, 1940 in Chukua, India
Source: *BiDFilm; BioIn 11, 14, 15, 16, 17; BkPepl; BlueB 76; CelR 90; ConTFT 9; CurBio 66; DcArts; FacFETw; FilmgC; HalFC 84, 88; IntMPA 86; IntWW 83; ItaFilm; LegTOT; MotPP; MovMk; NewYTBS 85; OxCFilm; Who 74, 82, 83, 85, 88, 90, 92; WhoAm 80, 82, 84, 86, 88, 90, 92, 94, 95, 96, 97; WhoEnt 92; WhoHol 92, A; WhoWor 82, 84, 87, 89, 91, 93, 95, 96, 97; WorAlBi; WorEFlm*

Christie, Linford
Jamaican. Track Athlete
Won Gold Medal, 100-meter dash, 1992 Olympics, oldest man to win that event.
b. Apr 2, 1960 in Saint Andrews, Jamaica
Source: *BlkOlyM; ConBlB 8; IntWW 91, 93; Who 94*

Christie, William Lincoln
American. Musician, Conductor
Harpsichordist, founded Les Arts Florissants, 1978, group which performs French, Italian repertoire.
b. Dec 19, 1944 in Buffalo, New York
Source: *CurBio 92; IntWWM 90; NewAmDM; NewGrDA 86; PenDiMP*

Christina
Swedish. Ruler
Daughter of Gustav II Adolphus; ruled, 1632-54; abdicated throne to cousin Charles X Gustav.
b. Dec 8, 1626 in Stockholm, Sweden
d. Apr 19, 1689 in Rome, Italy
Source: *BioIn 1, 4, 5, 6, 7, 8, 9, 10, 11, 12, 14, 15, 16, 17, 20; DcBiPP; DcEuL; DcWomA; Dis&D; EncAmaz 91;*

GayLesB; InWom, SUP; LegTOT; LinLib L, S; LuthC 75; NewGrDO; REn; WebBD 83; WomWR

Christina
Dutch. Princess
Daughter of Queen Juliana, Prince Bernhard; sister of Irene.
b. Feb 18, 1947 in Soestdijk, Netherlands
Source: *WhoWor 74, 76, 78*

Christine, Virginia
[Virginia Kraft]
American. Actor
Portrayed Mrs. Olson in Folger's coffee commercials for 21 years; made movie debut in 1943's *Edge of Darkness.*
b. 1920 in Stanton, Iowa
d. Jul 24, 1996 in Los Angeles, California
Source: *ConTFT 1; IntMPA 92, 94, 96; NewYTBS 27; WhoHol A*

Christison, (Alexander Frank) Philip
Scottish. Military Leader
Commanded first British force to defeat the Japanese in WWII, Bay of Bengal, 1944.
b. Nov 17, 1893
d. Dec 21, 1993 in Melrose, Scotland
Source: *BioIn 19, 20; CurBio 94N; Who 82, 83, 85, 88, 90, 92, 94*

Christ-Janer, Albert
American. Artist, Author, Educator
Watercolorist, graphic designer, who wrote numerous biographies of artists.
b. Jun 13, 1910 in Appleton, Wisconsin
d. Dec 12, 1973 in Como, Italy
Source: *AmAu&B; BioIn 7, 10, 12; ConAu 45; NatCAB 58; NewYTBE 73; WhAm 6; WhoAm 74; WhoAmA 73, 76N, 78N; WhoWor 74*

Christo
[Christo Javacheff]
Bulgarian. Artist
Created 24-mile long fabric fence in Sonoma, Marin Counties, CA, 1972-76; project *The Umbrellas: Joint Project for Japan and USA,* 1991 shut down after high winds toppled one, crushing bystander; wrapped the Reichstag, Berlli n, Germany, with Jeanne Claude, 1995.
b. Jun 13, 1935 in Gabrovo, Bulgaria
Source: *AmArt; Benet 87, 96; BioIn 8, 9, 10, 11, 12, 13, 14, 15, 16, 18, 19; BlueB 76; CelR; ConArt 77, 83, 89, 96; CurBio 77; DcAmArt; DcArts; DcCAA 77, 88, 94; DcCAr 81; DcTwCCu 1; EncWB; FacFETw; IntWW 74, 75, 76, 77, 78, 79, 80, 81, 82, 83, 89, 91, 93; LegTOT; News 92, 92-3; OxCTwCA; OxDcArt; PrintW 83, 85; WhoAm 84, 86, 88, 90, 92, 94, 95, 96, 97; WhoAmA 73, 76, 78, 80, 82, 84, 86, 89, 91, 93; WhoE 91, 95; WhoWor 78, 80, 82, 84, 87, 89; WorAlBi; WorArt 1950*

Christoff, Boris
Bulgarian. Opera Singer
Bass, Chicago Opera, 1958-63; noted for *Boris Godunov.*
b. May 18, 1918 in Sofia, Bulgaria
d. Jun 28, 1993 in Rome, Italy
Source: *Baker 84; BioIn 11, 12, 13; DcArts; IntWW 74; NewAmDM; NewEOp 71; Who 74; WhoMus 72; WhoWor 74*

Christoff, Steve
American. Hockey Player
Center, member US Olympic gold medal-winning team, 1980; in NHL, 1980-83.
b. Jan 23, 1958 in Springfield, Illinois
Source: *HocEn; HocReg 81*

Christophe, Henri
Haitian. Ruler
Revolutionary who ruled, 1811-20; shot himself after having a stroke.
b. Oct 6, 1767, Grenada
d. Oct 8, 1820 in Cap Haitien, Haiti
Source: *ApCAB; Benet 87, 96; BiDLAmC; BioIn 1, 2, 3, 4, 6, 7, 8, 9, 11, 15, 16, 20; CelCen; DcAfL; DicTyr; Drake; EncRev; HisWorL; LinLib S; McGEWB; REn; WebBD 83; WhAmRev*

Christopher, Saint
Religious Figure
Martyr, patron saint of travelers, until dropped from liturgical calendar, 1969.
b. fl. 3rd cent.
Source: *Benet 87; BioIn 1, 2, 3, 4, 5, 6, 7, 8, 9, 11, 15; DcBiPP; DcCathB; NewC; OxDcByz; OxDcP 86; REn; WhoRel 85*

Christopher, Dennis
[Dennis Carelli]
American. Actor
In films *Breaking Away,* 1979; *Chariots of Fire,* 1981.
b. Dec 2, 1955 in Philadelphia, Pennsylvania
Source: *BioIn 12; ConTFT 3; HalFC 84, 88; IntMPA 92, 94, 96; ItaFilm; NewYTBS 79; WhoHol 92*

Christopher, Matthew F
American. Children's Author
Writes children's sports novels: *Wild Pitch; Run Billy Run,* 1980.
b. Aug 16, 1917 in Bath, Pennsylvania
Source: *AuBYP 2; ConAu 1R, 5NR; IntAu&W 82; MorBMP; SmATA 2; WrDr 86*

Christopher, Sybil Williams Burton
[Mrs. Jordan Christopher; Sybil Williams]
Welsh. Actor
First wife of Richard Burton, 1949-63; Burton divorced her to marry Elizabeth Taylor.
b. 1928 in Taylorstown, Wales
Source: *BioIn 6, 7*

Christopher, Warren M(inor)
American. Lawyer, Government Official
Secretary of State, 1993-97; negotiator for release of American hostages in Iran, 1980-81.
b. Oct 27, 1925 in Scranton, North Dakota
Source: *BioIn 11, 12; CngDr 77, 79; CurBio 81, 95; DcAmDH 89; NewYTBS 78, 80, 81, 92; WhoAm 74, 76, 78, 80, 82, 84; WhoAmL 87; WhoAmP 73; WhoGov 77*

Christopher, William
American. Actor
Played Father Mulcahy on TV series "M*A*S*H," 1972-83.
b. Oct 20, 1932 in Evanston, Illinois
Source: *VarWW 85; WhoAm 86*

Christophers, S(amuel) Rickard, Sir
English. Zoologist
Discovered the cause of blackwater fever; noted for studies on malaria.
b. Nov 27, 1873 in Liverpool, England
d. Feb 19, 1978 in Broadstone, England
Source: *Au&Wr 71; BioIn 3, 12; McGMS 80; WhE&EA; Who 74*

Christy, Howard Chandler
American. Artist
Created the "Christy Girl"; paintings include "Signing the Constitution," 1940, in the Capitol building, Washington, DC.
b. Jan 10, 1873 in Morgan County, Ohio
d. Mar 4, 1952 in New York, New York
Source: *AmAu&B; BioIn 1, 2, 3, 5, 11, 12; ChhPo, S2; DcAmB S5; EncAB-A 25; EncAJ; IlBEAAW; IlrAm 1880, B; IlsCB 1744; LinLib L, S; NatCAB 11; SmATA 21; WhAm 3; WhoAmA 82*

Christy, Marian
American. Journalist
Syndicated fashion, style columnist, 1952—; won several awards, honors.
b. Nov 9, 1932 in Ridgefield, Connecticut
Source: *CelR 90; ConAu 65; ForWC 70; WhoAm 78, 80, 82, 86; WhoAmW 70, 75, 77, 79*

Chrysander, Karl Franz Friedrich
German. Musicologist
Instrumental in publishing a complete edition of the musical works of G.F. Handel; highly regarded as a 19th c. musicologist.
b. Jul 8, 1826 in Lubtheen, Germany
d. Sep 1, 1901 in Hamburg, Germany
Source: *Baker 78, 84; NewOxM; OxCMus*

Chrysler, Walter Percy
American. Auto Manufacturer
Pres., Buick Motor Co., 1916-19; founded Chrysler Corp., 1925.
b. Apr 2, 1875 in Wamego, Kansas

d. Aug 18, 1940 in Great Neck, New York
Source: *BiDAmBL 83; BioIn 2, 3, 4, 5, 16, 19; CurBio 40; DcAmB S2; EncAB-A 21; EncABHB 5; InSci; LinLib S; McGEWB; WebAB 74, 79; WhAm 1; WorAl*

Chrysostom, John, Saint
"The Golden-Mouthed"
Syrian. Religious Leader
Doctor of the church; beloved for his preaching, charity; archbishop of Constantinople, 398-404, banished due to controversy over sermons.
b. 345? in Antioch, Syria
d. Sep 14, 407 in Comana, Cappadocia
Source: *Grk&L; LuthC 75; NewCol 75; OxCEng 85, 95; REn; WebBD 83*

Chrystos
American. Writer
Self-described as an "Urban Indian;" published collection of poems, *Deam On,* 1991.
b. Nov 7, 1946 in San Francisco, California
Source: *BioIn 19; EncNAB; GayLesB*

Chu, Paul C. W
American. Physicist
As head of U of Houston's superconductivity research team, discovered a method that may make commercial applications possible for superconductors.
b. Dec 2, 1941, China
Source: *News 88-2*

Chubak, Sadeq-i
Iranian. Writer
One of the foremost modern Iranian writers; writes short stories, novels, and dramatic works.
b. Aug 5, 1916 in Bushire, Iran
Source: *CasWL; EncWL 2*

Chuck D
[Public Enemy; Carlton Ridenhour]
American. Rapper
Recorded *It Takes a Nation of Millions to Hold Us Back,* 1988; active in anti-drug movement.
b. 1960 in New York

Chuikov, Vasili Ivanovitch
Russian. Military Leader
Fought in Red Army during Russian Revolution, 1918-21; defended Stalingrad against Hitler, 1942.
b. Feb 12, 1900 in Serebryanye Prudy, Russia
d. Mar 18, 1982 in Moscow, Union of Soviet Socialist Republics
Source: *CurBio 43, 82N; HisEWW; IntWW 74, 75; NewYTBS 82; WhoMilH 76; WhoSocC 78; WhWW-II*

Chukarin, Viktor Ivanovich
Russian. Gymnast
Premier Soviet gymnast; won several gold medals in 1952, 1956 Olympics.
b. Nov 9, 1921 in Krasnoarmeyskoye, Union of Soviet Socialist Republics
d. Aug 1984 in Moscow, Union of Soviet Socialist Republics
Source: *BiDSovU; SovUn*

Chukovsky, Korney Ivanovich
[Nikolai Ivanovich Korneichuk]
Russian. Scholar, Children's Author
One of first to translate English works into Russian; censors largely ignored children's books, due to his immense popularity.
b. Mar 31, 1882 in Saint Petersburg, Russia
d. Oct 28, 1969 in Moscow, Union of Soviet Socialist Republics
Source: *AuBYP 2; CasWL; ChhPo S1, S2; ConAu 4NR, 5R; DcRusLS; PenC EUR; SmATA 5; SovUn; WorAu 1950*

Chukrai, Grigori
Russian. Director
Important in Soviet cinema; known for films about war: *Forty-First,* 1956; *Ballad of a Soldier,* 1959.
b. May 23, 1921 in Melitopol, Union of Soviet Socialist Republics
Source: *DcFM; FilmEn; FilmgC; IntWW 82; OxCFilm; WhoWor 80; WorEFlm*

Chun Doo Hwan
Korean. Government Official
Pres. of Republic of Korea, 1980-88; convicted of mutiny and treason for the 1979 coup that brought him to power; sentenced to death, 1996.
b. Jan 23, 1931 in Naechonri, Korea
Source: *CurBio 81; FarE&A 81; IntWW 91; NewYTBS 81; WhoWor 87, 91, 93*

Chung, Arthur
[Raymond Arthur Chung]
Guyanese. Government Official
First pres. of Republic of Guyana, 1970-80.
b. Jan 10, 1918 in Demerara, British Guiana
Source: *IntWW 74, 75, 76, 77, 78, 79, 80, 81, 82, 83, 89, 91; IntYB 78, 79, 80, 81, 82; WhoGov 72, 75; WhoWor 74, 76, 78, 80*

Chung, Connie
[Constance Yu-Hwa Chung; Mrs. Maury Povich]
American. Broadcast Journalist
NBC News anchor, 1983-86; with CBS News, 1989-95.
b. Aug 20, 1946 in Washington, District of Columbia
Source: *AsAmAlm; BioIn 10, 13; CelR 90; ConAu 119, 132; ConTFT 9; CurBio 89; EncTwCJ; GrLiveH; IntMPA 88, 92, 94, 96; InWom SUP; LegTOT; News 88; NotAsAm; WhoAm 76, 78, 80, 82, 84, 86, 88, 90, 92, 94, 95, 96, 97; WhoAmW 77, 91, 93, 95, 97; WhoAsA 94; WhoE 91, 93; WomComm; WomStre; WorAlBi*

Chung, Il-Kwon
Korean. Diplomat, Politician
Prime minister, 1964-70; adviser to pres. of Democratic Republic, 1979-80.
b. Nov 21, 1917
Source: *FarE&A 81; IntWW 81; WhoGov 72; WhoWor 78*

Chung, Myung-Whun
Korean. Director, Conductor, Pianist
Prizewinning musician, conductor; director, Bastille Opera, 1989—.
b. Jan 22, 1953 in Seoul, Korea (South)
Source: *Baker 84, 92; BioIn 12, 17, 20; CanWW 83; CurBio 90; IntWW 91, 93; IntWWM 77, 90; MetOEnc; NewGrDA 86; OxDcOp; PenDiMP*

Church, Frank
American. Lawyer, Politician
Four-term Dem. senator; instrumental in getting Panama Canal treaty through Senate, 1978.
b. Jul 25, 1924 in Boise, Idaho
d. Apr 7, 1984 in Bethesda, Maryland
Source: *AlmAP 78, 80; AmDec 1970; AmOrTwC; AnObit 1984; BiDrAC; BioIn 4, 5, 7, 8, 9, 10, 11, 12, 13, 14, 15, 18, 20; BlueB 76; CelR; CngDr 74, 77, 79; ColdWar 1; CurBio 78, 84N; FacFETw; IntWW 74, 75, 76, 77, 78, 79, 80, 81, 82, 83; NewYTBS 84; PolProf E, J, K, NF; WhAm 8; WhoAm 74, 76, 78, 80, 82; WhoAmP 73, 75, 77, 79, 81, 83; WhoGov 72, 75, 77; WhoWest 74, 76, 78, 80; WhoWor 74, 78, 80; WorAl; WorAlBi*

Church, Frederick Edwin
American. Artist
Of the Hudson River School genre, with flair for dramatic in rainbows, mists, clouds, sunsets.
b. May 4, 1826 in Hartford, Connecticut
d. Apr 2, 1900 in Hudson, New York
Source: *AmBi; AmCulL; ApCAB; BioIn 1, 4, 7, 14; BriEAA; CelCen; DcAmArt; DcAmB; DcBiPP; DcSeaP; Drake; EarABI; EncAAH; HarEnUS; LinLib S; McGDA; McGEWB; NatCAB 20; OxCAmH; OxCAmL 65; OxDcArt; WebAB 74, 79; WhAm 1; WorAl; WorAlBi*

Church, George W
American. Restaurateur
Opened first Church's Fried Chicken to Go, 1952, in San Antonio, TX.
b. 1887 in Texas
d. 1956
Source: *Entr*

Church, Sam(uel Morgan Jr.)
American. Labor Union Official
Pres., UMW, 1979-82.
b. Sep 20, 1936 in Matewan, West Virginia
Source: *BioIn 12, 13; CurBio 81; NewYTBS 79, 81; WhoAm 82, 84*

Church, Sandra
American. Actor
Won Tony for performance in *Gypsy,* 1960; stage, film, TV appearances.
b. Jan 13, 1943 in San Francisco, California
Source: *BiE&WWA; InWom; NotNAT; WhoHol A*

Churchill, Caryl
English. Dramatist
Explores male-dominated society in Obie-winning plays *Cloud Nine,* 1978; *Top Girls,* 1981.
b. Sep 3, 1938 in London, England
Source: *BioIn 12, 13; BlmGEL; BlmGWL; CamGLE; CamGWoT; ConAu 22NR, 46NR, 102; ConBrDr; ConDr 77, 82, 88, 93; ConLC 31, 55; ContDcW 89; ConTFT 3, 10; ConWomD; CrtSuDr; CurBio 85; DcArts; DcLB 13, Y82A; DramC 5; EncBrWW; FemiCLE; FemiWr; IntAu&W 82; IntDcT 2; IntWW 91, 93; InWom SUP; MajTwCW; ModWoWr; NewYTBS 83; OxCEng 85, 95; RAdv 14, 13-2; RfGEnL 91; RGTwCWr; Who 94; WhoThe 81; WorAu 1980; WrDr 80, 82, 84, 86, 88, 90, 92, 94, 96*

Churchill, Charles
English. Poet, Satirist
Wrote biting verse: *The Rosciad,* 1761; *The Ghost,* 1762.
b. Feb 1731 in London, England
d. Nov 4, 1764 in Boulogne-sur-Mer, France
Source: *Alli; Benet 87, 96; BiD&SB; BioIn 1, 3, 4, 5, 6, 11, 17; BlmGEL; BritAu; CamGEL; CamGLE; CasWL; ChhPo, S1, S2, S3; CnE&AP; CrtT 2; DcArts; DcBiPP; DcEnA; DcEnL; DcEuL; DcLB 109; DcLEL; DcNaB; EvLB; LitC 3; MouLC 2; NewC; OxCEng 67, 85; PenC ENG; REn; WebE&AL*

Churchill, Clementine Ogilvy (Hozier) Spencer, Baroness
"Clemmie"
English.
Wife of Winston Churchill.
b. Apr 1, 1885 in London, England
d. Dec 12, 1977 in London, England
Source: *CurBio 53, 78*

Churchill, Diana Josephine
English. Actor
Leading lady on stage, screen; films include *The Winter's Tale,* 1968.
b. Aug 21, 1913 in Wembley, England
Source: *FilmgC; Who 83; WhoHol A; WhoThe 77A*

Churchill, Jennie Jerome
American. Socialite
Vivacious society leader, mother of Winston Churchill.
b. Jan 9, 1854 in New York, New York
d. Jun 29, 1921 in London, England
Source: *AmWom; ApCAB SUP; GoodHs; LibW; NotAW; WhAm 1*

Churchill, May
[Beatrice Desmond Chuchill; May Lambert]
"Chicago May"; "Queen of the Badgers"
Criminal
Red-headed beauty who blackmailed lovers; planned robbery, Parisian American Ex press 1901.
b. 1876 in Sligo, Ireland
d. 1929 in Philadelphia, Pennsylvania
Source: *BioIn 10*

Churchill, Randolph Frederick Edward Spencer
English.
Son of Winston Churchill.
b. May 28, 1911 in London, England
d. Jun 6, 1968 in East Bergholt, England
Source: *ConAu 89; CurBio 47, 68; LngCTC*

Churchill, Randolph Henry Spencer, Lord
English. Statesman
Chancellor of the Exchequer, 1886; leader of House of Commons; father of Winston, son of Duke of Marlborough.
b. Feb 13, 1849 in Woodstock, England
d. Jan 24, 1895 in London, England
Source: *Alli SUP; BioIn 1, 2, 4, 5, 6, 9, 12, 13, 14, 16; CelCen; DcInB; DcNaB C, S1; VicBrit; WhDW; WorAl*

Churchill, Sarah
[Lady Audley]
"Mule"
English. Singer, Actor
Second daughter of Winston Churchill; wrote *A Thread in the Tapestry,* memoir of father.
b. Oct 7, 1914 in London, England
d. Sep 24, 1982 in London, England
Source: *AnObit 1982; BioIn 1, 2, 3, 4, 12, 13, 15; ConAu 107, 129; CurBio 55, 83, 83N; EngPo; FilmgC; HalFC 84, 88; IntMPA 82; InWom, SUP; ItaFilm; NewYTBS 82; REn; WhoAmW 70; WhoHol A; WhoThe 72, 77, 81*

Churchill, Winston
American. Author
Wrote novels on political, historical subjects: *The Crisis,* 1901; *The Crossing,* 1904.
b. Nov 10, 1871 in Saint Louis, Missouri
d. Mar 12, 1947 in Winter Park, Florida
Source: *AmAu&B; ApCAB SUP, X; BbD; Benet 87; BenetAL 91; BiD&SB; BiDSA; BioIn 1, 2, 4, 5, 10, 12; CamGEL; CarSB; CasWL; CnDAL; ConAmA; ConAmL; CyWA 58; DcAmAu; DcAmB S4; DcAmSR; DcBiA; DcLEL; DcNAA; EvLB; FacFETw; GayN; LinLib L, S; LngCTC; McGEWB; NatCAB 10; NotNAT B; Novels; OxCAmL 65, 83, 95; OxCEng 67, 85, 95; PenC AM; PeoHis; PolPar; REn; REnAL; RfGAmL 87, 94; TwCA SUP; TwCBDA; TwCRHW 90, 94; TwCWr; WebE&AL; WhAm 2; WhE&EA; WhLit; WhNAA; WhThe*

Churchill, Winston Leonard Spencer, Sir
English. Statesman, Author
Conservative WW II prime minister, 1940-55; rallied English, Americans to confront Hitler; won 1953 Nobel in literature, wrote *The Second War,* 1948-53, in six vols.
b. Nov 30, 1874 in Woodstock, England
d. Jan 24, 1965 in London, England
Source: *ApCAB SUP; BioIn 1, 2, 3, 4, 5, 6, 7, 8, 9, 10, 11, 12, 13; CasWL; Chambr 3; ColdWar 1; CurBio 53, 65; CyWA 58; DcBrAr 1; DcLEL; DcNaB 1961; DcPol; DcTwHis; EvLB; FacFETw; GrBr; HarEnMi; HisDBrE; HisEAAC; LinLib L; LngCTC; McGEWB; NewC; OxCAmH; OxCEng 67, 85, 95; OxCShps; PenC ENG; REn; TwCA, SUP; TwCWr; WebBD 83; WebE&AL; WhAm 4; WhDW; WhoNob, 90, 95; WhWW-II*

Chu Te
Chinese. Army Officer
Became commander, military forces, under Mao Tse-tung, 1927.
b. Dec 18, 1886 in Sichuan, China
d. Aug 6, 1976 in Beijing, China
Source: *CurBio 42; IntWW 74, 77; McGEWB; NewYTBS 76; WhWW-II*

Chute, Beatrice Joy
American. Author
Best known for novel *Greenwillow,* 1956; made into Broadway musical, 1960.
b. Jan 3, 1913 in Minneapolis, Minnesota
d. Sep 6, 1987 in New York, New York
Source: *AmWomWr; BioIn 2, 6, 9, 15, 16; ConAu 4NR; CurBio 50, 87; IntAu&W 77, 82; InWom; NewYTBS 87; PenNWW A; SmATA 2; WhoAm 82*

Chute, Marchette (Gaylord)
American. Author
Award-winning writer of children's verse, literary biographies; *Geoffrey Chaucer of England,* 1946.
b. Aug 16, 1909 in Minneapolis, Minnesota
d. May 6, 1994 in Montclair, New Jersey
Source: *AmAu&B; AmWomWr; Au&Wr 71; AuBYP 2, 3; BiE&WWA; BioIn 2, 3, 4, 5, 6, 7, 9, 17, 19, 20; BkCL; ChhPo, S1, S2; ChlBkCr; ConAu 1R, 5NR, 145; CurBio 50, 94N; DcLB 103; DrAS 74H, 78H, 82H; EvLB; IntAu&W 76, 77, 82, 89; IntWWP 77; InWom; LinLib L; MinnWr; MorJA; NotNAT; RAdv 1; REnAL; SmATA 1; TwCA SUP; TwCChW 78, 83, 89, 95; TwCYAW; WhAm 11; Who 74, 82, 83, 85, 88, 90, 92, 94; WhoAm 74, 76, 78, 80, 82, 84, 86, 88, 90, 92, 94; WhoAmW 58, 64, 66, 68, 70, 72, 74, 83, 85, 87, 89, 93; WhoUSWr 88; WhoWrEP 89, 92; WrDr 76, 80, 82, 84, 86, 88, 90, 92, 94, 96*

Chuvalo, George
Canadian. Boxer
Canadian heavyweight champ, 1958-60s; lost world title to Ali, 1966.

b. Sep 12, 1937 in Toronto, Ontario, Canada
Source: *BioIn 7, 8; WhoBox 74*

Chwast, Seymour
American. Designer, Illustrator
Originated Push Pin style; *Sara's Granny and the Groodle* chosen best illustrated book, 1969, by *NY Times.*
b. Aug 18, 1931 in New York, New York
Source: *AmGrD; BioIn 9, 12; ConDes 84, 90, 97; CurBio 95; DcTwDes; FourBJA; IlrAm 1880; IlsBYP; IlsCB 1967; SmATA 18; WhoAdv 90; WhoAm 86, 88, 90, 92, 94, 95, 96, 97; WhoAmA 78, 80, 82, 84, 86, 89, 91, 93; WhoEnt 92; WhoGrA 82*

Chylak, Nester
American. Baseball Umpire
AL umpire, 1954-77.
b. May 11, 1922 in Olyphant, Pennsylvania
d. Feb 17, 1982 in Dunmore, Pennsylvania
Source: *NewYTBS 82; WhoProB 73*

Ciano (di Cortellazzo), Galeazzo
Italian. Government Official
Fascist foreign minister, 1936-43; chiefly responsible for Rome-Berlin Axis; executed by father-in-law, Mussolini.
b. Mar 8, 1903 in Livorno, Italy
d. Jan 11, 1944 in Verona, Italy
Source: *BiDExR; BioIn 1, 3, 10, 21; CurBio 40, 44; DcTwHis; EncTR 91; FacFETw; HisEWW; LinLib L; WhDW; WhWW-II*

Ciardi, John Anthony
American. Poet, Author
Award-winning writer known for English translation of Dante's *Inferno,* 1954.
b. Jun 24, 1916 in Boston, Massachusetts
d. Apr 1, 1986 in Metuchen, New Jersey
Source: *BkP; CasWL; ConAu 5NR, 5R; ConLC 10; ConPo 75; CurBio 67, 86; DcLEL 1940; DrAS 78E, 82E; IntWWP 77; ModAL; OxCAmL 65; PenC AM; REn; REnAL; SmATA 1; WebAB 74, 79; WhoAm 86*

Cibber, Colley
English. Author, Actor, Dramatist
Poet laureate, 1730; ridiculed in Alexander Pope's *The Dunciad.*
b. Nov 6, 1671 in London, England
d. Dec 12, 1757 in London, England
Source: *Alli; BbD; Benet 87, 96; BiD&SB; BioIn 2, 3, 4, 5, 6, 8, 10, 12, 15, 17; BlmGEL; BritAu; CamGEL; CamGLE; CamGWoT; CasWL; Chambr 2; ChhPo; CnThe; CrtSuDr; CrtT 2; CyWA 58; DcBiPP; DcEnA; DcEnL; DcEuL; DcLB 84; DcLEL; DcNaB; EncWT; EvLB; IntDcT 2; LinLib L, S; LngCEL; McGEWD 72, 84; NewC; NotNAT A, B; OxCEng 67, 85, 95; OxCMus; OxCThe 67, 83; PenC ENG; PlP&P; PoLE; REn; REnWD; RfGEnL 91; WebE&AL; WhDW*

Cicciolina
[Ilona Staller]
Italian. Actor, Politician
Hard-core porn star elected to Italian parliament, 1987; wrote autobiography, *Confessions,* 1988.
Source: *BioIn 15, 17; LegTOT*

Cicero
[Elyesa Bazna]
German. Spy
Served Nazi Germany, 1943-44, while working as valet at the British Embassy in Turkey.
b. 1904, Albania
d. Dec 21, 1970 in Munich, Germany
Source: *BioIn 4, 8, 9, 10, 11, 14; WhDW*

Cicero, Marcus Tullius
Roman. Philosopher, Statesman
Introduced Greek philosophy to ancient Rome through his treatises based on Plato, Aristotle, etc.
b. Jan 3, 106BC in Arpinum, Latinum
d. Dec 7, 43BC in Formiae, Latinum
Source: *AtlBL; BbD; Benet 87, 96; BiD&SB; BioIn 1, 2, 3, 4, 5, 6, 7, 8, 9, 10, 11, 12, 13, 16, 17, 18, 20; BlmGEL; CasWL; ClMLC 3; CyWA 58; DcArts; DcBiPP; DcEuL; Dis&D; EncEth; Grk&L; LinLib L, S; LngCEL; LuthC 75; McGEWB; NewC; OxCClL 89; OxCEng 67, 85, 95; OxCLaw; OxCPhil; PenC CL; RAdv 13-3; RComWL; REn; WhDW; WorAl; WorAlBi; WrPh P*

Cicippio, Joseph
American. Hostage
Former comptroller, American University of Beirut, taken hostage and kept in captivity for 1,907 days, Sept 12, 1986-Dec 2, 1991.
Source: *BioIn 16, 19*

Cicotte, Eddie
[Edward Victor Cicotte]
"Knuckles"
American. Baseball Player
Pitcher, 1905-20; part of "Black Sox" plot to throw 1919 World Series; blacklisted for life.
b. Jun 19, 1894 in Detroit, Michigan
d. May 5, 1969 in Detroit, Michigan
Source: *WhoProB 73*

Cid, El
[Rodrigo Diaz de Bivar]
Spanish. Soldier
Conquered, ruled kingdom of Valencia, 1094-99.
b. 1040 in Burgos, Spain
d. Jul 10, 1099 in Valencia, Spain
Source: *DcSpL; LinLib L, S; NewC; NewCol 75; RComWL; REn; WebBD 83*

Cierva, Juan de la
Spanish. Aeronautical Engineer
Invented helicopter, 1923.
b. 1895
d. 1936
Source: *BioIn 1, 4, 8; NewCol 75*

Cigna, Gina
French. Opera Singer
Leading IT dramatic soprano, 1930s; repertory of 70 operas.
b. Mar 6, 1900 in Paris, France
Source: *Baker 78, 84, 92; BioIn 13, 14; IntDcOp; IntWWM 90; MetOEnc; NewEOp 71; NewGrDO; OxDcOp; PenDiMP*

Cilea, Francesco
Italian. Composer
Operas include *Adriana Lecouvreur,* 1902; *Gloria,* 1907.
b. Jul 26, 1866 in Palmi, Italy
d. Nov 20, 1950 in Verazza, Italy
Source: *Baker 78, 84, 92; BioIn 2, 6, 12; IntDcOp; MetOEnc; NewAmDM; NewEOp 71; NewGrDO; NewOxM; OxCMus; OxDcOp*

Cilento, Diane
Australian. Actor
Wife of Sean Connery, 1962-73; Oscar nominee for *Tom Jones,* 1963.
b. Oct 5, 1933 in Brisbane, Australia
Source: *BiE&WWA; ConTFT 5; FilmgC; HalFC 84, 88; IntMPA 86; ItaFilm; LegTOT; MotPP; MovMk; NotNAT; WhoHol 92, A; WhoThe 81*

Ciller, Tansu
Turkish. Political Leader
Prime minister of Turkey, 1993-96.
b. 1946 in Istanbul, Turkey
Source: *BioIn 19, 20; CurBio 94; WhoWor 95, 96, 97*

Cimabue, Giovanni
[Cenni de Pepo]
"Father of Italian Painting"
Italian. Artist
Considered first modern painter; developed space, figure modelling; noted for Assisi church frescoes.
b. 1240 in Florence, Italy
d. 1302 in Florence, Italy
Source: *AtlBL; Benet 87, 96; LegTOT; McGDA; McGEWB; NewC; NewCol 75; OxCArt; REn; WhDW; WorAl; WorAlBi*

Cimarosa, Domenico
Italian. Composer
Wrote opera *Il Matrimonio Segreto,* 1792; noted for opera buffa.
b. Dec 17, 1749 in Aversa, Italy
d. Jan 11, 1801 in Venice, Italy
Source: *AtlBL; Baker 78, 84, 92; BioIn 1, 4, 5, 6, 7, 12; BlkwCE; DcArts; DcBiPP; Dis&D; IntDcOp; McGEWB; MetOEnc; NewAmDM; NewEOp 71; NewGrDO; NewOxM; OxCMus; OxDcOp; PenDiMP A; WhDW*

Cimino, Michael
American. Director
Won Oscar for directing *The Deer Hunter,* 1978.
b. 1948 in New York, New York
Source: *ConAu 105; ConTFT 2; CurBio 81; IntMPA 86; IntWW 83; WhoAm 84,*

86, 88, 90, 92, 94, 95, 96, 97; WhoEnt 92; WorAlBi

Cinque, Joseph
African. Slave, Revolutionary
Led slave mutiny aboard ship, 1839; Supreme Court ruled that escaped slaves should be treated as free men.
b. 1811
d. 1852
Source: *BioIn 6, 8, 10; InB&W 80; NegAl 76, 83, 89*

Cipriani, Amilcare
Italian. Revolutionary
Fought with Garibaldi, Mazzini for Italian liberation, 1834.
b. 1845 in Rimini, Italy
d. 1918

Cipullo, Aldo Massimo Fabrizio
American. Designer
Designed gold Love Bracelet for Cartier, 1969; became status symbol of many celebrities; won Coty for jewelry, 1974.
b. Nov 18, 1938 in Naples, Italy
d. Jan 31, 1984 in New York, New York
Source: *NewYTBS 84; WhoAm 80, 82, 84; WorFshn*

Cisler, Walker (Lee)
American. Business Executive
Pres., Detroit Edison, 1951-64; chairman, 1964-75.
b. Oct 8, 1897 in Marietta, Ohio
d. Oct 18, 1994 in Grosse Pointe, Michigan
Source: *AmMWSc 73P; BioIn 2, 4, 5, 6, 7, 10, 11, 20, 21; BioNews 74; BlueB 76; BusPN; CurBio 55, 95N; IntWW 74, 75, 76, 77, 78, 79, 80, 81, 82, 83; St&PR 75; WhAm 10; WhoAm 74, 76, 78, 80, 82, 84; WhoFI 74, 75, 81; WhoMW 74, 76; WhoWor 74, 78*

Cisneros, Eleanora
[Eleanor Broadfoot]
American. Opera Singer
Principal contralto, Manhattan Opera, 1906-11.
b. Nov 1, 1878 in New York, New York
d. Feb 3, 1934 in New York, New York
Source: *Baker 84; NewEOp 71; NotAW*

Cisneros, Henry G(abriel)
"Official Hispanic"
American. Politician, Government Official
Mayor, San Antonio, TX, 1981-89; first Mexican-American to head major US city; Secretary of HUD, 1993-97.
b. Jun 11, 1947 in San Antonio, Texas
Source: *ConNews 87-2; CurBio 87; WhoAm 86; WhoAmP 83, 85, 87, 89, 91, 93, 95; WhoHisp 91, 92, 94; WhoSSW 78, 86*

Citroen, Andre Gustave
French. Auto Manufacturer
Introduced American mass-production methods into his auto plant, 1920s.
b. Feb 5, 1878 in Paris, France
d. Jul 3, 1935 in Paris, France
Source: *WebBD 83*

Ciulei, Liviu
Romanian. Actor, Director
Art Director, Minneapolis Theater, 1980—; won Cannes director award for *Forest of the Hanged,* 1965.
b. Jul 7, 1923 in Bucharest, Romania
Source: *BioIn 20; CamGWoT; DcFM; DrEEuF; GrStDi; IntWW 74, 75, 76, 77, 78, 79, 80, 81, 82, 83, 89, 91, 93; TheaDir; WhoSocC 78; WhoSoCE 89; WhoWor 82, 84*

Civiletti, Benjamin Richard
American. Government Official
Jimmy Carter's second US Attorney General, 1979-81.
b. Jul 17, 1935 in Peekskill, New York
Source: *BiDrUSE 89; BioIn 11, 12; CurBio 80; IntWW 83; NewYTBS 77, 79; WhoAm 86; WhoAmL 78, 79*

Claflin, Tennessee Celeste
American. Social Reformer
With sister, Victoria Woodhull, founded *Woodhull and Claflin's Weekly,* 1870, which advocated equal rights for women.
b. Oct 26, 1846 in Homer, Ohio
d. Jan 18, 1923 in London, England
Source: *DcAmB; EncO&P 2, 3; IntDcWB; NotAW; OxCAmL 83*

Claiborne, Craig
American. Author, Editor
Food editor, *NY Times;* wrote *The New New York Times Cook Book,* 1979.
b. Sep 4, 1920 in Sunflower, Mississippi
Source: *AmAu&B; BioIn 6, 7, 8, 9, 10, 11, 12, 13; CelR 90; ConAu 1R, 5NR; CurBio 69; EncTwCJ; LegTOT; NewYTBS 80; WhoAm 74, 76, 78, 80, 82, 84, 86, 88, 94, 95, 96; WhoE 74; WhoUSWr 88; WhoWrEP 89, 92, 95; WorAl; WorAlBi; WrDr 86, 88, 90, 92, 94, 96*

Claiborne, Liz
[Elisabeth Claiborne; Mrs. Arthur Ortenberg]
American. Fashion Designer
Specialist in moderate-priced sportswear; founded Liz Claiborne, Inc., 1976.
b. Mar 31, 1929 in Brussels, Belgium
Source: *BioIn 12, 13; ConAmBL; ConFash; ConNews 86-3; CurBio 89; EncFash; GrLiveH; LegTOT; WhoAm 80, 82, 84, 86, 88, 90, 92, 94, 95, 96, 97; WhoAmA 80; WhoAmW 85, 89, 91, 93, 95, 97; WhoE 85, 86, 89, 91, 93, 95; WhoFash 88; WhoFI 89, 92; WhoWor 91*

Claiborne, Loretta (Lynn)
American. Track Athlete
Special Olympics Female Athlete of the Year, 1988.
b. Aug 14, 1953 in York, Pennsylvania
Source: *CurBio 96*

Clair, Rene
French. Filmmaker
Films satirized human behavior; *Sous les Toits de Paris,* 1930.
b. Nov 11, 1898 in Paris, France
d. Mar 15, 1981 in Neuilly-sur-Seine, France
Source: *AnObit 1981; Benet 87, 96; BiDFilm, 94; BioIn 1, 5, 9, 12, 13, 15; ConAu 103; ConLC 20; CurBio 41, 81; DcArts; DcFM; DcTwCCu 2; EncEurC; FacFETw; Film 2; FilmgC; HalFC 84, 88; IntAu&W 77, 82; IntDcF 1-2, 2-2; IntMPA 77; IntWW 74, 75, 76, 77, 78, 79, 80, 81, 81N; ItaFilm; LegTOT; MovMk; NewYTBS 81; OxCFilm; REn; WhAm 7; Who 74, 82N; WhoFr 79; WhoWor 74; WhScrn 83; WorEFlm; WorFDir 1*

Clairborne, William Charles Coles
American. Politician
Youngest sworn into House of Representatives, 1797; first governor of Louisiana Territory, 1803-16.
b. 1775 in Sussex County, Virginia
d. Nov 23, 1817 in New Orleans, Louisiana
Source: *AmBi; ApCAB; BiAUS; DcAmNB; Drake; NatCAB 13; WhAm HS*

Claire, Ina
[Ina Fagan]
American. Actor
Vaudeville performer, later with Ziegfield Follies; portrayed witty, chic sophisticates on stage and screen.
b. Oct 15, 1895 in Washington, District of Columbia
d. Feb 21, 1985 in San Francisco, California
Source: *AnObit 1985; BiE&WWA; CmpEPM; CurBio 54, 85; EncMT; EncWT; FamA&A; Film 2; FilmgC; MotPP; NotNAT; OxCAmT 84; ThFT; WhoHol A; WhoThe 77A; WhThe*

Clairmont, Claire
[Clara Mary Jane Clairmont]
English.
Stepdaughter of William Godwin; friend of Percy, Mary Shelley; mother of Lord Byron's daughter, Allegra.
b. Apr 27, 1798 in Clifton, England
d. Mar 19, 1879 in Florence, Italy
Source: *BioIn 2, 4, 8, 10, 18, 19; DcNaB; InWom SUP; NewC; OxCEng 85, 95; REn*

Clampett, Bob
[Robert Clampett]
American. Cartoonist, Filmmaker
Animator; worked at Warner Brothers, 1930s-40s; created "Looney Tune," "Merry Melodie cartoons."
b. May 8, 1913 in San Diego, California
d. May 2, 1984 in Detroit, Michigan
Source: *AuNews 1; WhoAm 82*

Clampitt, Amy
American. Poet
Works include, *The Kingfisher,* 1983; often compared to Gerard Manley Hopkins, Marianne Moore, Elizabeth Bishop.
b. Jun 15, 1920 in New Providence, Iowa
d. Sep 10, 1994 in Lenox, Massachusetts
Source: *Benet 96; BenetAL 91; ConAu 29NR, 146; ConLC 32, 86; ConPo 85, 91; CurBio 92, 94N; DcLB 105; DrAPF 91; FemiCLE; OxCAmL 95; OxCTwCP; RAdv 14; RGTwCWr; WhoAmW 91; WhoWrEP 89; WorAu 1980; WrDr 86, 88, 90, 92, 94, 96*

Clancy, King
[Francis Michael Clancy]
Canadian. Hockey Player, Hockey Executive
Defenseman, 1921-37; coach, vp, Toronto, 1950s-70s; Hall of Fame, 1958.
b. Feb 25, 1903 in Ottawa, Ontario, Canada
d. Nov 10, 1986 in Toronto, Ontario, Canada
Source: *BioIn 8, 10, 15, 16; ConAu 121; HocEn; WhoHcky 73; WhoSpor*

Clancy, Thomas L., Jr.
American. Author
Had surprise hit with first novel, *The Hunt for Red October,* 1984; other military thrillers include *Patriot Games,* 1987.
b. 1947 in Baltimore, Maryland
Source: *ConAu 125, 131; CurBio 88; IntAu&W 91; MajTwCW; NewYTBS 86; SpyFic; WhoAm 92, 94, 95, 96, 97; WorAu 1985*

Clapp, Margaret Antoinette
American. Educator
Pres., Wellesley College, 1949-66; won Pulitzer for *Forgotten First Citizen: John Bigelow,* 1947.
b. Apr 11, 1910 in East Orange, New Jersey
d. May 3, 1974 in Tyringham, Massachusetts
Source: *AmAu&B; AmWomHi; AmWomM; AmWomWr; BiDAmEd; ConAu 49; CurBio 48, 74; DcAmB S9; EncWB; IntWW 74; InWom, SUP; NewYTBS 74; NotAW MOD; ObitOF 79; OxCAmL 65; REnAL; TwCA SUP; WhAm 6; WhoGov 75*

Clapp, Patricia
American. Author
Writes plays, novels mostly for juveniles: *Constance: A Story of Early Plymouth,* 1969, *Witches' Children,* 1982.
b. Jun 9, 1912 in Boston, Massachusetts
Source: *BioIn 9, 15, 19; ConAu 10NR, 25R, 37NR; DcAmChF 1960; FifBJA; IntAu&W 82, 91; MajAI; OxCChiL; ScF&FL 1, 2; SmATA 4, 4AS, 74; TwCChW 78, 83, 89; TwCYAW; WhoE 83; WrDr 76, 80, 82, 84, 86, 88, 90, 92, 94, 96*

Clapper, Dit
[Aubrey Victor Clapper]
Canadian. Hockey Player
Right wing, Boston, 1927-47; Hall of Fame, 1945.
b. Feb 9, 1907 in Newmarket, Ontario, Canada
d. Jan 20, 1978
Source: *BioIn 11; HocEn; WhoHcky 73; WhoSpor*

Clapper, Raymond Lewis
American. Journalist
Newspaper correspondent, commentator, Scripps-Howard chain, 1936-44; read by millions, he died in plane crash.
b. Apr 30, 1892 in La Cygne, Kansas
d. Feb 1, 1944? in Eniwetok Atoll, Marshall Islands
Source: *AmAu&B; BiDAmNC; CurBio 40, 44; DcAmB S3; NatCAB 35; WhAm 2; WhNAA*

Clapperton, Hugh
Scottish. Explorer
First European to discover Nigeria's Lake Chad, 1823; died trying to find source of Niger River.
b. May 8, 1788 in Annan, Scotland
d. Apr 13, 1827 in Sokoto, Fulah Empire
Source: *Alli; BioIn 6, 9, 18; CelCen; DcAfHiB 86; DcBiPP; DcNaB; Expl 93; HisDBrE; McGEWB; NewCol 75; WhWE*

Clapton, Eric
[Blind Faith; Cream; Yardbirds; Eric Clap; Eric Patrick Clapp]
English. Musician
Top guitarist in British rock, 1960s; appeared in film of rock opera, *Tommy,* 1975.
b. Mar 30, 1945 in Ripley, England
Source: *Baker 84; BioIn 8, 9, 10, 11, 12, 13; BkPepl; CelR, 90; ConMus 1, 11; CurBio 87; DcArts; EncPR&S 89; EncRk 88; EncRkSt; FacFETw; IntWW 89, 91, 93; LegTOT; NewAmDM; News 93-3; OnThGG; OxCPMus; PenEncP; RkOn 78, 84; RolSEnR 83; WhoAm 80, 82, 84, 86, 88, 90, 92, 94, 95, 96, 97; WhoEnt 92; WhoRock 81; WhoRocM 82; WhoWor 95, 96, 97; WorAl; WorAlBi*

Clare, John
"Northamptonshire Peasant Poet"
English. Poet
Romantic nature writer; wrote *Rural Muse,* 1835; declared insane, 1837.
b. Jul 13, 1793 in Helpstone, England
d. May 20, 1864 in Northampton, England
Source: *Alli; AtlBL; BbD; Benet 87, 96; BiD&SB; BioIn 2, 4, 5, 6, 7, 8, 9, 10, 12, 13, 15, 16, 17, 18; BlmGEL; BritAu 19; CamGEL; CamGLE; CasWL; Chambr 3; ChhPo, S1, S2, S3; CnE&AP; CrtT 4; DcArts; DcBiPP; DcEnL; DcLB 55, 96; DcLEL; DcNaB; EvLB; LinLib L; LngCEL; NewC; NinCLC 9; OxCEng 67, 85, 95; PenC ENG; RAdv 14; REn; RfGEnL 91; WebE&AL; WhDW*

Clarendon, Edward Hyde, Earl of
English. Statesman
Adviser to Charles I, lord chancellor under Charles II; falsely accused of treason, banished to France, 1661.
b. Feb 18, 1609 in Wiltshire, England
d. Dec 9, 1674 in Rouen, France
Source: *Alli; AtlBL; Benet 87, 96; BiD&SB; BioIn 2, 3, 4, 6, 8, 10, 11, 13, 14, 16, 18; BlmGEL; BritAu; CamGEL; CamGLE; CasWL; Chambr 1; DcBiPP; DcEnA; DcEnL; DcLB 101; DcLEL; EvLB; HarEnUS; LngCEL; McGEWB; NewC; OxCEng 67, 85, 95; PenC ENG; RAdv 13-3; REn; WebE&AL*

Clare of Assisi, Saint
Italian. Religious Figure
Influenced by St. Francis to become nun; founded Poor Clares order; feast day Aug 12.
b. Jul 16, 1194 in Assisi, Italy
d. Aug 11, 1253 in Assisi, Italy
Source: *ContDcW 89; IntDcWB; LuthC 75; NewCol 75; WhDW; WomFir*

Clark, Abraham
"The Poor Man's Counselor"
American. Lawyer, Continental Congressman
Surveyer; member, first and second Colonial Congresses, US Congress, 1791-94; signed Declaration of Independence, 1776.
b. Feb 15, 1726 in Elizabethtown, New Jersey
d. Sep 15, 1794 in Rahway, New Jersey
Source: *AmBi; ApCAB; BiAUS; BiDrAC; BiDrUSC 89; BioIn 7, 8, 9; DcAmB; Drake; EncAR; EncCRAm; HarEnUS; NatCAB 3; NewCol 75; TwCBDA; WhAm HS; WhAmP; WhAmRev*

Clark, Alvin Graham
American. Astronomer
Directed the manufacturing of the world's largest telescope lens at Yerkes Observatory, Williams Bay, WI.
b. Jul 10, 1832 in Fall River, Massachusetts
d. Jun 9, 1897 in Cambridge, Massachusetts
Source: *BiInAmS; BioIn 3, 8; DcAmB; DcScB; NatCAB 5; WebAB 79; WhAm HS*

Clark, Barney Bailey
American. Dentist, Transplant Patient
First recipient of permanent, completely artificial heart, Dec, 1982; lived 112 days.
b. Jan 21, 1921 in Provo, Utah
d. Mar 24, 1983 in Salt Lake City, Utah
Source: *AnObit 1983; NewYTBS 82*

Clark, Barrett H
American. Author
Works include *Oedipus and Pollyanna,* 1927; *America's Lost Plays,* 1940-41, in 20 volumes.
b. Aug 26, 1890 in Toronto, Ontario, Canada
d. Aug 5, 1953 in Briarcliff, New York
Source: *AmAu&B; NotNAT B; ObitOF 79; OxCAmL 65, 83; OxCAmT 84; REnAL; TwCA, SUP; WhAm 3; WhE&EA; WhLit; WhNAA; WhThe*

Clark, Bennett Champ
American. Politician
Senator from MO, 1933-45.
b. Jan 8, 1890 in Bowling Green, Missouri
d. Jul 13, 1954 in Gloucester, Massachusetts
Source: *AmAu&B; BiDFedJ; BioIn 3; CurBio 41, 54; DcAmB S5; ObitOF 79; WhAm 3*

Clark, Bobby
American. Comedian
Known as the "world's funniest clown"; worked in films, vaudeville, circuses, minstrel shows.
b. Jun 16, 1888 in Springfield, Ohio
d. Feb 12, 1960 in New York, New York
Source: *BioIn 1, 2, 3, 5; CamGWoT; CmpEPM; CurBio 49, 60; DcAmB S6; EncMT; EncVaud; Film 2; FilmgC; HalFC 84, 88; NotNAT A, B; ObitOF 79; OxCAmT 84; OxCPMus; QDrFCA 92; WhAm 3; WhoHol B; WhScrn 74, 77, 83; WhThe*

Clark, C(arter) Blue
American. Historian
Professor of American Indian Studies, California State University, Long Beach, 1984-93; Executive Vice President, Oklahoma City University, 1993—.
b. 1946
Source: *BioIn 21; ConAu 150; WhoSSW 97*

Clark, Champ
[James Beauchamp Clark]
American. Politician
Democratic leader, 1909-11; House Speaker, 1911-19.
b. Mar 7, 1850 in Lawrenceburg, Kentucky
d. Mar 2, 1921 in Washington, District of Columbia
Source: *AmBi; AmPolLe; ApCAB X; BiDrAC; BiDrUSC 89; BiDSA; BioIn 6, 7, 14; DcAmB; DcNAA; EncSoH; FacFETw; HarEnUS; LinLib L, S; NatCAB 14; OxCAmH; REnAW; TwCBDA; WebAB 74, 79; WhAm 1; WhAmP; WhoAm 74; WorAl; WorAlBi*

Clark, Charles Badger
American. Poet
Specialized in western lore, cowboy life: "Sky Lines and Wood Smoke," 1935.
b. Jan 1, 1883 in Albia, Iowa
d. Sep 26, 1957
Source: *AmAu&B; ChhPo, S1; DcLEL; REnAL*

Clark, Colin Grant
English. Economist
Writings on economics include *Poverty before Politics,* 1977.
b. Nov 2, 1905 in Westminster, England
Source: *BlueB 76; ConAu 8NR, 61; DcNaB 1986; FarE&A 78, 79, 80, 81; IntAu&W 77; IntEnSS 79; IntWW 74, 75, 76, 77, 78, 79, 80, 81, 82, 83, 89; Who 74, 82, 83, 85, 88; WhoAm 84; WhoEc 81, 86; WhoWor 74, 78, 80, 82, 84*

Clark, Dane
[Bernard Zanville]
American. Actor
Tough guy leading man in action films, 1940s; on TV, 1950s-60s.
b. Feb 18, 1913 in New York, New York
Source: *BioIn 10; FilmgC; HalFC 84, 88; HolP 40; IntMPA 86; MotPP; MovMk; ObitOF 79; WhoAm 74; WhoHol A*

Clark, Dave
[Dave Clark Five]
English. Musician, Singer
Formed Dave Clark Five, 1964-73.
b. Dec 15, 1942 in London, England
Source: *BioIn 12; EncPR&S 74, 89; EncRk 88; LegTOT; PenEncP; RkOn 84; WorAl; WorAlBi*

Clark, David L
American. Candy Manufacturer
Made Clark Bar to distribute to US Army, WW II.
b. 1864
d. 1939
Source: *Entr*

Clark, Dick
[Richard Wagstaff Clark]
American. Entertainer, Business Executive, Producer
Host, American Bandstand, 1952-1988.
b. Nov 30, 1929 in Mount Vernon, New York
Source: *AlmAP 78; Baker 84; BiDD; BioIn 5, 11, 14, 15, 16, 17, 18, 19, 21; BkPepl; CelR 90; CngDr 77; ConAu 113, 130; ConMus 2; ConTFT 3; CurBio 59, 87; EncPR&S 89; EncRk 88; FacFETw; HarEnR 86; IntMPA 75, 76, 77, 78, 79, 81, 82, 84, 86, 88, 92, 94, 96; IntWW 74, 75, 76, 77, 78; LegTOT; NewYTET; PenEncP; RolSEnR 83; WhoAm 74, 76, 78, 80, 82, 84, 86, 88, 90, 92, 94, 95, 96, 97; WhoEnt 92; WhoHol 92, A; WhoRock 81; WrDr 94, 96*

Clark, Dutch
[Earl Harry Clark]
American. Football Player, Football Coach
Six-time all-pro quarterback, 1931-38, mostly with Detroit; led NFL in scoring twice; charter member, Hall of Fame.
b. Oct 11, 1906 in Fowler, Colorado
d. Aug 5, 1978 in Canon City, Colorado
Source: *BiDAmSp FB; BioIn 6, 8, 9, 17; LegTOT; WhoFtbl 74; WhoSpor*

Clark, Eleanor
American. Author
Wrote *Rome and a Villa,* 1952.
b. Jul 6, 1913 in Los Angeles, California
d. Feb 16, 1996 in Boston, Massachusetts
Source: *AmAu&B; AmWomWr; ArtclWW 2; BenetAL 91; BioIn 2, 4, 11, 21; ConAu 9R, 41NR, 151; ConLC 5, 19; ConNov 72, 76, 82, 86, 91, 96; CurBio 78, 96N; DcLB 6; DcLEL 1940; DrAF 76; FemiCLE; IntAu&W 76, 77, 82, 91, 93; InWom SUP; OxCAmL 83, 95; REnAL; TwCA SUP; WhAm 11; WhoAm 96; WhoAmW 58, 68; WrDr 76, 80, 82, 84, 86, 88, 90, 92, 94, 96*

Clark, Fred
American. Actor
Character parts include Burns and Allen's TV shows, 1950s.
b. Mar 9, 1914 in Lincoln, California
d. Dec 5, 1968 in Santa Monica, California
Source: *BiE&WWA; BioIn 8; EncAFC; FilmgC; HalFC 84, 88; ItaFilm; MotPP; MovMk; NotNAT B; ObitOF 79; Vers A; WhAm 5; WhoHol B; WhScrn 74, 77, 83; WhThe*

Clark, George Rogers
American. Soldier
Assured colonial control of KY, IL, 1778-79.
b. Nov 19, 1752 in Charlottesville, Virginia
d. Feb 13, 1818 in Louisville, Kentucky
Source: *AmBi; AmRev; AmWrBE; ApCAB; BenetAL 91; BioIn 1, 2, 3, 4, 5, 6, 7, 8, 9, 10, 11, 12, 14, 15, 16, 19; BlkwEAR; CyAG; DcAmAu; DcAmB; DcAmMiB; EncAAH; EncAB-H 1974, 1996; EncAR; EncCRAm; EncSoH; GenMudB; HarEnMi; HarEnUS; HisWorL; LinLib L, S; McGEWB; MorMA; NatCAB 1; OxCAmH; OxCAmL 65, 83, 95; PeoHis; REn; REnAL; REnAW; TwCBDA; WebAB 74, 79; WebAMB; WhAm HS; WhAmRev; WhNaAH; WorAl*

Clark, Georgia Neese
[Georgia Neese Clark Gray]
American. Government Official
First female Treasurer of the United States, 1949-53.
b. Jan 27, 1900 in Richland, Kansas

d. Oct 26, 1995 in Topeka, Kansas
Source: *AmWomM; BioIn 21; CurBio 96N; InWom, SUP; LibW; WomFir*

Clark, Guy
American. Singer, Songwriter
Country music singer and songwriter; released first album, *Old No. 1,* 1975; later released *South Coast of Texas,* 1981, *Better Days,* 1983, *Old Days,* 1989 and *Dublin Blues,* 1995.
b. Nov 6, 1941 in Monahans, Texas
Source: *BgBkCoM; ConMus 17; EncFCWM 83; HarEnCM 87; PenEncP*

Clark, Jack Anthony
American. Baseball Player
Outfielder-infielder, SF Giants, 1976-84; ST. Louis Cardinals, 1985-87; NY Yankees, 1988; San diego Padres, 1989-93; Montreal Expos 1993—; three-time NL All-Star.
b. Nov 10, 1955 in New Brighton, Pennsylvania
Source: *BaseReg 86, 87; BiDAmSp Sup; BioIn 11; WhoAm 86, 88, 92; WhoMW 88*

Clark, James
Scottish. Auto Racer
World champion, youngest Grand Prix winner in history, 1963, 1965.
b. Mar 4, 1936 in Kilmany, Scotland
d. Apr 7, 1968 in Hochheim, Germany (West)
Source: *BioIn 6, 7, 8, 10, 12, 15; CurBio 65, 68; DcNaB 1961*

Clark, James H.
American. Computer Executive
Cofounder, Netscape Communications, Inc., 1994.
b. 1944? in Plainview, Texas
Source: *BioIn 21; ConEn; News 97-1; St&PR 91, 93; WhoAm 94, 95, 96; WhoFI 94; WhoWest 94*

Clark, Joe
American. Educator
Baseball bat-toting NJ principal, 1982-89; strict disciplinary measures resulted in the expulsion of 60 students and brought insubordination proceedings against him.
b. May 7, 1939 in Newark, New Jersey
Source: *AfrAmAl 6; BioIn 10, 11, 13, 14, 15, 17, 19; ConBlB 1; CurBio 76, 86; FacFETw; NewYTBS 88; Who 88; WhoAm 78, 80, 82, 84, 88, 92, 94; WhoBlA 92; WhoE 83, 85, 89, 93; WhoWest 92; WhoWor 93*

Clark, Joe
[Charles Joseph Clark]
Canadian. Politician
Prime minister, 1979-80.
b. Jun 5, 1939 in High River, Alberta, Canada
Source: *AfrAmAl 6; AmCath 80; BioIn 10, 11, 12, 13, 15, 17, 19; CanWW 31, 79, 80, 81, 83, 89; ConBlB 1; CurBio 76; DcTwHis; FacFETw; IntWW 76, 77, 78, 79, 80, 81, 82, 83, 89, 91; IntYB 82; NewYTBS 79; Who 82, 83, 85, 88, 90, 92, 94; WhoAm 78, 80, 82, 84, 86, 88, 90, 92, 94, 95, 96; WhoCan 77, 80, 82; WhoE 83, 85, 86, 89, 91, 93, 95; WhoWest 87, 89, 92; WhoWor 80, 82, 84, 93, 95, 96, 97*

Clark, John Bates
American. Economist
Developed marginal-productivity theory; wrote *Distribution of Wealth,* 1899.
b. Jan 26, 1847 in Providence, Rhode Island
d. Mar 21, 1938 in New York, New York
Source: *Alli SUP; AmAu&B; AmBi; AmLY; AmPeW; BioIn 1, 4, 8, 14, 16, 21; DcAmAu; DcAmB S2; DcNAA; EncAB-H 1974, 1996; GrEconB; HarEnUS; McGEWB; NatCAB 13; RAdv 14, 13-3; TwCBDA; WebAB 74, 79; WebBD 83; WhAm 1; WhNAA; WhoEc 81, 86*

Clark, John Pepper
Nigerian. Dramatist
Playwright known for uniting Western literary techniques with themes, images, and speech patterns of traditional African theatre; wrote *Song of a Goat,* 1961.
b. 1935, Nigeria
Source: *AfrA; BioIn 10, 13, 14, 21; BlkLC; BlkWr 1; CasWL; ChhPo S2; ConAu 16NR, 65; ConDr 73, 77, 82, 88, 93; ConLC 38; ConPo 75, 80, 85, 91, 96; CyWA 89; DcLEL 1940; DramC 5; EncWL, 3; IntAu&W 91, 93; IntDcT 2; IntWWP 77; LngCTC; McGEWD 84; ModBlW; ModCmwL; ModWD; OxCThe 83; PenC CL; REnWD; RfGEnL 91; RGAfL; SelBAAf; TwCWr; WebE&AL; WhoThe 81; WhoWor 80; WorAu 1970; WrDr 76, 80, 82, 84, 86, 88, 90, 92, 94, 96*

Clark, Joseph Sill
American. Politician
First dem. mayor of Philadelphia in 67 yrs., 1952-56; senator from PA, 1956-68.
b. Oct 21, 1901 in Philadelphia, Pennsylvania
d. Jan 12, 1990 in Philadelphia, Pennsylvania
Source: *BiDrAC; BiDrUSC 89; BioIn 2, 3, 4, 5, 6, 8, 10, 11; BlueB 76; CurBio 52, 90; IntWW 74, 75, 76, 77, 78, 79, 80, 81, 82, 83; NewYTBS 90; PolProf E; WhoAm 84; WhoAmP 77, 79*

Clark, Kenneth Bancroft
American. Educator, Psychologist
Early advocate of non-segregated schools; first black member of NY State Board of Regents, 1966—; 1974 Spingarn winner.
b. Jul 24, 1914, Panama Canal Zone
Source: *AmAu&B; AmMWSc 73S, 78S; AmSocL; BioIn 7, 8, 9, 11, 12, 13; BlksScM; CurBio 64; Ebony 1; EncAACR; InB&W 80, 85; IntWW 89, 91, 93; LEduc 74; LivgBAA; NegAl 76, 83, 89; SelBAAf; SelBAAu; WebAB 74, 79; WhoAfA 96; WhoAm 74, 76, 78, 80, 82, 84, 86, 88, 90, 92, 94, 95, 96, 97; WhoBlA 75, 77, 80, 85, 88, 90, 92, 94; WhoE 74, 93; WhoGov 72, 75, 77; WhoWor 74, 76; WrDr 80, 82, 84, 86, 88, 90, 92, 94, 96*

Clark, Kenneth MacKenzie, Sir
English. Art Historian, Author
Preeminent supporter of British arts; created, narrated acclaimed TV series "Civilization," 1969.
b. Jul 13, 1903 in London, England
d. May 21, 1983 in Hythe, England
Source: *BioIn 12, 13; BlueB 76; CamGLE; ConAu 93; CurBio 63, 83; DcNaB 1981; IntAu&W 77; IntMPA 75; IntWW 74, 79, 81; NewYTBS 83; OxCEng 85, 95; Who 74; WhoWor 82; WrDr 82*

Clark, Marcia
American. Lawyer
Prosecutor in O.J. Simpson murder trial, 1994-95; wrote *Without a Doubt,* 1997.
b. 1954? in Berkeley, California
Source: *News 95, 95-1*

Clark, Marguerite
American. Actor
Rivaled Mary Pickford as silent screen star, 1914-21; best known for *Wildflowers,* 1914; *Uncle Tom's Cabin,* 1919.
b. Feb 22, 1887 in Avondale, Ohio
d. Sep 25, 1940 in New York, New York
Source: *BioAmW; BioIn 13; CmpEPM; FilmEn; InWom; LibW; MotPP; NatCAB 30; NotAW; NotNAT B; OxCAmT 84; TwYS; WhAm 1; WhScrn 74, 77, 83; WhThe*

Clark, Mark Wayne
American. Army Officer
Led Allied invasion of Italy during WW II; commanded UN forces in Korea, 1952-53; signed Korean armistice July 27, 1953.
b. May 1, 1896 in Madison Barracks, New York
d. Apr 17, 1984 in Charleston, South Carolina
Source: *AnObit 1984; BiDWWGF; BioIn 1, 2, 3, 4, 7, 9, 11, 13; BlueB 76; CurBio 42, 84; DcAmMiB; HarEnMi; HisEWW; IntWW 74; LinLib S; McGEWB; OxCAmH; WebAB 74, 79; WebAMB; WhAm 8; Who 74, 82, 83; WhoAm 74, 76; WhoGov 72, 75, 77; WhoMilH 76; WhoWor 74; WhWW-II; WorAl*

Clark, Mary Higgins
[Mrs. John Conheeney]
American. Author
"A mistress of high fiction," wrote bestsellers *Where Are the Children,*; *The Cradle Will Fall,* 1980.

b. Dec 24, 1929 in New York, New York
Source: *Au&Arts 10; BioIn 5, 11, 12, 14, 16; CelR 90; ConAu 16NR, 36NR, 51NR, 81; ConPopW; CurBio 94; GrWomMW; IntAu&W 82, 89, 91, 93; MajTwCW; SmATA 46; ThrtnMM; TwCCr&M 85, 91; TwCYAW; WhoAm 82, 84, 86, 90; WhoAmW 91; WhoUSWr 88; WhoWrEP 89, 92, 95; WorAu 1985; WrDr 86, 88, 90, 92, 94, 96*

Clark, Monte Dale
American. Football Player, Football Coach
Player in NFL, 1959-69; head coach, Detroit, 1978-83.
b. Jan 24, 1937 in Fillmore, California
Source: *BioIn 11; WhoMW 82, 84*

Clark, Peggy
American. Designer
Worked with costumes on Broadway, 1938-51; did lighting, scenery for musicals, ballets, 1949-80.
b. Sep 30, 1915 in Baltimore, Maryland
Source: *BiE&WWA; BioIn 16; NotNAT; NotWoAT; OxCAmT 84; WhoAm 74, 76, 78, 80, 82, 84, 86, 88, 90, 92, 94, 95, 96; WhoAmW 58, 64, 66, 68, 70, 72, 74, 75, 77, 79, 89; WhoE 74, 79, 81, 83, 85, 86, 89; WhoEnt 92; WhoThe 81*

Clark, Petula
English. Singer
Won Grammys for "Downtown," 1964; "I Know a Place," 1965.
b. Nov 15, 1932 in Epsom, England
Source: *BioIn 4, 7, 8, 9, 10, 11; BkPepl; CelR; CurBio 70; EncRkSt; FilmgC; HalFC 84, 88; IntMPA 75, 76, 77, 78, 79, 81, 82, 84, 86, 88, 92, 94, 96; IntWW 83; InWom SUP; ItaFilm; LegTOT; MotPP; MovMk; OxCPMus; PenEncP; RolSEnR 83; Who 85; WhoAm 82; WhoHol 92, A; WhoRock 81; WhoRocM 82; WorAlBi*

Clark, Ramsey
[William Ramsey Clark]
American. Government Official
Attorney general under Lyndon Johnson, 1967-69.
b. Dec 18, 1927 in Dallas, Texas
Source: *AmAu&B; BiDrUSE 71, 89; BioIn 5, 7, 8, 9, 10, 11, 12, 17; BioNews 74; BlueB 76; CelR; ConAu 29R; CopCroC; CurBio 67; FacFETw; IntWW 74, 75, 76, 77, 78, 79, 80, 81, 82, 83, 89, 91, 93; LegTOT; NewYTBS 80; PolProf J, NF; Who 74, 82, 83, 85, 88, 90, 92, 94; WhoAm 74, 76, 78, 80, 82, 84, 86, 88, 90, 92, 94, 95, 96; WhoAmL 78, 79, 83, 85, 87, 90; WhoAmP 73, 75, 77, 79, 81, 83, 85, 87, 89, 91, 93, 95; WhoWor 74, 78, 80; WorAl; WorAlBi*

Clark, Richard Clarence
American. Politician
Dem. senator from IA, 1973-79; ambassador-at-large, 1979-84.
b. Sep 14, 1929 in Paris, Iowa
Source: *WhoAmP 73, 75, 77, 79, 81, 83; WhoGov 72*

Clark, Robert Edward
American. Journalist
Washington, DC correspondent, 1981—.
b. May 14, 1922 in Omaha, Nebraska
Source: *WhoAm 74, 76, 78, 80, 82, 84; WhoWest 84*

Clark, Roy Linwood
American. Singer, Songwriter
Named Entertainer of the Year by CMA, 1973; banjo-playing host of TV's "Hee Haw," 1969—; longest continuously-running program in TV history; Grammy award winner, 1983.
b. Apr 15, 1933 in Meherrin, Virginia
Source: *BioNews 74; CurBio 78; EncFCWM 69; RkOn 84; WhoAm 86; WhoPubR 72; WorAl*

Clark, Septima
American. Civil Rights Activist, Educator
Fired as a Charleston (SC) schoolteacher, 1956, because of her NAACP membership; first black female member of the Charleston School Board, 1974-82.
b. May 3, 1898 in Charleston, South Carolina
d. Dec 15, 1987 in Charleston, South Carolina
Source: *AnObit 1987; BioIn 6, 10, 11; ConBlB 7; NotBlAW 1*

Clark, Steve
[Def Leppard; Stephen Maynard Clark]
"Steamin'"
English. Musician
Guitarist with heavy-metal band since 1978.
b. Apr 23, 1960 in Sheffield, England
d. Jan 8, 1991 in London, England
Source: *AnObit 1991; BioIn 17, 18; OnThGG*

Clark, Susan Nora Goulding
[Mrs. Alex Karras]
Canadian. Actor
Starred with husband in movies *Babe; Jimmy B and Andre; Maid in America.*
b. Mar 8, 1944 in Sarnia, Ontario, Canada
Source: *FilmEn; FilmgC; HalFC 84; IntMPA 86; WhoAm 84, 86; WhoAmW 87; WhoHol A*

Clark, Sydney
American. Author, Traveler
Popular travel writer known for *All the Best* series, 1939-72.
b. Aug 18, 1890 in Auburndale, Massachusetts
d. Apr 20, 1975
Source: *AmAu&B; Au&Wr 71; ConAu 4NR, 5R, 57; CurBio 56*

Clark, Thomas Dionysius
American. Author
Prolific writer of southern, western history; wrote *The South Since Appomattox,* 1967.
b. Jul 14, 1903 in Louisville, Mississippi
Source: *AmAu&B; BioIn 21; BlueB 76; ConAu 4NR, 5R; DrAS 74H, 78H, 82H; EncAAH; EncSoH; REnAW; WhNAA; WhoAm 86, 88, 90; WhoWor 74*

Clark, Tom
[Thomas Campbell Clark]
American. Supreme Court Justice
US Attorney General, 1945-49; justice, 1949-67.
b. Sep 23, 1899 in Dallas, Texas
d. Jun 13, 1977 in New York, New York
Source: *BiDrUSE 71; BioIn 1, 2, 3, 4, 5, 6, 7, 10, 11, 15; CngDr 74; CurBio 45; DrAS 74P; IntWW 74, 75, 76, 77; WebAB 74; Who 74; WhoAm 74; WhoAmP 73; WhoGov 75; WorAl*

Clark, Walter van Tilburg
American. Author
Best known for book *The Ox-Bow Incident,* 1940; filmed, 1942.
b. Aug 3, 1909 in East Oreland, Maine
d. Nov 10, 1971 in Reno, Nevada
Source: *AmAu&B; AmNov; BenetAL 91; CmCal; CnDAL; ConAu 9R; ConLC 28; ConNov 82A; CyWA 58, 89; DcAmB S9; DcLB 9; ModAL; NewYTBE 71; Novels; ObitOF 79; OxCAmL 65, 95; PenC AM; RAdv 1; REn; REnAL; RfGAmL 94; SmATA 8; TwCA SUP; TwCWW 91; WhAm 5; WorAl; WorAlBi*

Clark, Wendel
Canadian. Hockey Player
Defenseman-left wing, Toronto, 1996—.
b. Oct 25, 1966 in Kelvington, Saskatchewan, Canada
Source: *BioIn 20, 21; HocReg 87*

Clark, Will(iam Nuschler, Jr.)
American. Baseball Player
First baseman, Giants, 1986-93; Rangers, 1993—; led NL in RBIs, 1988.
b. Mar 13, 1964 in New Orleans, Louisiana
Source: *Ballpl 90; BaseEn 88; BaseReg 88; LegTOT; WhoAm 90, 92, 94, 95, 96, 97; WhoSpor; WhoSSW 95; WhoWest 92, 94, 96; WorAlBi*

Clark, William
[Lewis and Clark]
American. Explorer
With Meriwether Lewis, went on overland expedition to Pacific, 1803.
b. Aug 1, 1770 in Caroline County, Virginia
d. Sep 1, 1838 in Saint Louis, Missouri
Source: *Alli, SUP; AmBi; ApCAB; BenetAL 91; BiDrAC; BiDrATG; BioIn 1, 2, 3, 4, 5, 6, 7, 8, 9, 10, 11, 12, 13, 14, 15, 16, 17, 18, 19, 20, 21; CamGEL; CamHAL; DcAmB; DcAmMiB; Dis&D; EncAAH; EncSoH; HarEnMi; HarEnUS; LegTOT; LinLib L, S; McGEWB; NatCAB 12; OxCAmH; OxCAmL 65, 83,*

95; RAdv 14, 13-3; REnAL; REnAW; TwCBDA; WebAB 74, 79; WebAMB; WhAm HS; WhAmP; WhDW; WhNaAH; WhWE; WorAl; WorAlBi

Clark, William P(atrick Jr.)
American. Government Official
Deputy secretary, Dept. of State, 1981-82; Asst. to Pres. for Nation al Security Affairs, 1982-83; Secretary of the Interior, 1983-85.
b. Oct 23, 1931 in Oxnard, California
Source: *CngDr 81; CurBio 82; IntWW 83; NewYTBS 83; Who 85; WhoAm 84; WhoWor 87*

Clarke, Alexander Ross
English. Scientist
Calculated first acceptable measurements on shape and size of the Earth; wrote *Geodesy,* 1880; remains a primary sourcebook in the field.
b. Dec 16, 1828 in Reading, England
d. Feb 11, 1914 in Reigate, England
Source: *DcNaB MP; InSci*

Clarke, Allan
[The Hollies]
English. Singer
Formed Hollies with childhood friend Graham Nash, 1962.
b. Apr 15, 1942 in Salford, England
Source: *RkOn 85; WhoRocM 82*

Clarke, Arthur C(harles)
English. Author, Scientist
With Stanley Kubrick, wrote novel, screenplay *2001: A Space Odyssey,* 196 8.
b. Dec 16, 1917 in Minehead, England
Source: *Alli; AmMWSc 73P; Au&Wr 71; AuBYP 2, 3; Benet 96; BioIn 3, 4, 6, 7, 8, 10, 11, 12, 13, 14; CamDcSc; ConAu 1R, 2NR, 55NR; ConLC 1, 4, 18; ConNov 72, 76, 86, 96; ConPopW; CurBio 66; DcArts; DcLEL 1940; EncSF 93; EvLB; Future; HalFC 84; IntAu&W 76, 77; IntWW 74, 75, 76, 77, 78, 79, 80, 81, 82, 83, 89, 91, 93; LngCTC; MajAI; NewC; OxCEng 95; RAdv 14, 13-5; RGTwCWr; SmATA 70; TwCA SUP; TwCWr; TwCYAW; WebE&AL; Who 74, 82, 83, 85, 88, 90, 92, 94; WhoAm 86, 88, 92, 94, 95, 96, 97; WhoWor 74, 76, 78, 82, 84, 87, 89, 91, 93, 95, 96, 97; WorAl; WrDr 76, 86, 94, 96*

Clarke, Austin
Irish. Poet
Wrote verse plays, novels inspired by the Irish countryside, history, legends.
b. May 9, 1896 in Dublin, Ireland
d. Mar 20, 1974 in Dublin, Ireland
Source: *Au&Wr 71; BiDIrW; BioIn 4, 8, 9, 10, 12, 13, 20; CamGEL; CamGLE; CamGWoT; CasWL; ChhPo S1, S3; CnMD SUP; ConAu 49, P-2; ConLC 6, 9; ConPo 70, 75; CrtSuDr; DcIrB 78, 88; DcIrL; DcIrW 1; DcLB 10, 20; EncWL 3; EngPo; FacFETw; IntWWP 77; IriPla; LngCTC; ModBrL S1, S2; ModIrL; NewC; ObitOF 79; OxCEng 85, 95; OxCThe 83; OxCTwCP; RAdv 1, 14, 13-1; REn; RfGEnL 91; TwCA SUP; TwCWr; WhLit; Who 74*

Clarke, Bobby
[Robert Earl Clarke]
Canadian. Hockey Player, Hockey Executive
Center, Philadelphia, 1969-84, known for leadership; won Hart Trophy three times ; general manager, 1984-90; general manager, Minnesota 1990-92; now president, Philadelphia; Hall of Fame, 1987.
b. Aug 13, 1949 in Flin Flon, Manitoba, Canada
Source: *BioIn 13, 14, 21; HocEn; LegTOT; NewYTBS 75, 84; WhoAm 84, 86, 92, 94, 95, 96, 97; WhoHcky 73; WhoMW 92; WhoSpor; WorAl; WorAlBi*

Clarke, Ellis Emmanuel Innocent, Sir
Trinidadian. Political Leader
Pres. of Trinidad and Tobago, 1976-86.
b. Dec 28, 1917 in Port of Spain, Trinidad and Tobago
Source: *IntWW 74, 75, 76, 77, 78, 79, 80, 81, 82, 83, 89, 91, 93; IntYB 82; Who 85, 94; WhoGov 72, 75; WhoWor 74, 76, 78, 80, 82, 84, 87, 89, 91*

Clarke, Fred Clifford
"Cap"
American. Baseball Player, Baseball Manager
Player/mgr., 1900-15; had .315 career batting average; Hall of Fame, 1945.
b. Oct 3, 1872 in Winterset, Iowa
d. Aug 14, 1960 in Winfield, Kansas
Source: *BiDAmSp BB; WhoProB 73*

Clarke, Gilmore David
American. Architect
Chm., National Commission of Fine Arts, 1937-50.
b. Jul 12, 1892 in New York, New York
d. Aug 6, 1982
Source: *BioIn 9, 13; EncAB-A 11; NewYTBS 82; WhAm 8; WhoAm 74, 76, 78, 80, 82*

Clarke, Harry
Irish. Illustrator
Did macabre, bizarre book illustrations: Poe's *Tales of Mystery and Imagination,* 1919.
b. Mar 17, 1890 in Dublin, Ireland
d. 1931 in Corre, Switzerland
Source: *ConICB; DcBrAr 1; DcBrBI; DcIrB 78*

Clarke, James Freeman
American. Clergy
Influential liberal preacher, reformer; writings include *Ten Great Religions,* 1883.
b. Apr 4, 1810 in Hanover, New Hampshire
d. Jun 8, 1888 in Jamaica Plain, Massachusetts
Source: *Alli, SUP; AmAu; AmAu&B; AmBi; ApCAB; BbD; BbtC; BenetAL 91; BiDAmM; BiD&SB; BiDTran; BioIn 2, 3, 4, 5, 6, 15, 16, 19; ChhPo S1, S2; CyAL 2; DcAmAu; DcAmB; DcAmReB 1, 2; DcLB 1, 59; DcLEL; DcNAA; Drake; EncARH; HarEnUS; LinLib L, S; LuthC 75; NatCAB 2; OxCAmH; OxCAmL 65, 83, 95; RelLAm 91; REnAL; TwCBDA; WebAB 74, 79; WhAm HS*

Clarke, Jeremiah
English. Composer
Organist, St. Paul's Cathedral, 1695, who composed church harpsichord pieces.
b. 1673 in London, England
d. Dec 1, 1701 in London, England
Source: *Alli; Baker 78, 84, 92; OxCMus*

Clarke, John
English. Colonial Figure
Co-founder of RI, 1638.
b. Oct 8, 1609 in Westhorpe, England
d. Apr 28, 1676 in Newport, Rhode Island
Source: *AmBi; AmWrBE; ApCAB; BenetAL 91; BioIn 1, 6, 11, 16, 19; CyAL 1; DcAmB; DcAmReB 1, 2; DcNaB; Drake; EncSoB; HarEnUS; LuthC 75; NatCAB 7; NewCol 75; OxCAmH; OxCAmL 65, 83, 95; REnAL; TwCBDA; WhAm HS*

Clarke, John Henrik
American. Author
Co-founder, *Harlem Quarterly,* 1950.
b. Jan 1, 1915 in Union Springs, Alabama
Source: *AmAu&B; AuNews 1; BioIn 4, 5, 10, 18, 19; BlkAWP; BlkWr 1, 2; CivR 74; ConAu 24NR, 43NR, 53; Ebony 1; InB&W 80, 85; LinLib L; LivgBAA; NegAl 76, 83, 89; SchCGBL; SelBAAf; SelBAAu; SouBlCW; WhoAfA 96; WhoAm 74, 76; WhoBlA 90, 92, 94; WhoE 74, 75*

Clarke, Kenny
[Kenneth Spearman Clarke]
"Klook"
American. Musician
Revolutionary drummer during the modern jazz movement in the 1940s; founding member of the Modern Jazz Quartet.
b. Jan 9, 1914 in Pittsburgh, Pennsylvania
d. Jan 25, 1985 in Montreuil-sous-Bois, France
Source: *AfrAmAl 6; AllMusG; AnObit 1985; Baker 84, 92; BiDAfM; BiDAmM; BioIn 5, 8, 11, 14, 16; CmpEPM; EncJzS; FacFETw; InB&W 80, 85; NegAl 83, 89; NewAmDM; NewGrDA 86; NewGrDJ 88, 94; NewYTBS 85; OxCPMus; PenEncP; WhoAm 74, 76*

Clarke, Mae
[Mary Klotz]
American. Actor
Starred in *The Public Enemy,* 1931, with James Cagney, when he mashed grapefruit in her face.

b. Aug 16, 1907 in Philadelphia, Pennsylvania
d. Apr 29, 1992 in Woodland Hills, California
Source: *BiDD; EncAFC; FilmEn; HalFC 84; HolP 30; MovMk; SweetSg C; ThFT; VarWW 85; WhoHol 92, A; WhThe*

Clarke, Martha
American. Choreographer, Dancer
Known for her choreographed interpretations of the works of famous painters; "The Garden of Earthy Delights," 1984, won high praise; Pilobolus, 1972-79; Crowsnest, 1979—.
b. Jun 3, 1944 in Baltimore, Maryland
Source: *BiDD; BioIn 15, 16, 17, 20; CrtSuDr; CurBio 89; GrStDi; LegTOT; NewYTBS 87; TheaDir; WhoAm 92; WhoAmW 91; WhoEnt 92*

Clarke, Rebecca Sophia
[Sophie May]
American. Children's Author
Wrote *Little Prudy,* 1863-65; *Dotty Dimple* series, 1867-69.
b. Feb 22, 1833 in Norridgewock, Maine
d. Aug 10, 1906 in Norridgewock, Maine
Source: *Alli SUP; AmAu; AmAu&B; AmWom; AmWomWr; ApCAB SUP; BiD&SB; BioIn 15; CarSB; ConAu 119; DcAmAu; DcAmB; DcLB 42; DcNAA; InWom, SUP; LibW; NatCAB 8; NotAW; OxCChiL; PenNWW B; TwCBDA; WhAm 1; WomNov*

Clarke, Ron
Australian. Track Athlete
Long-distance runner; set 19 records, 1960s; won bronze medal in 10,000 meters, 1964 Olympics.
b. Feb 21, 1937 in Melbourne, Australia
Source: *BioIn 9, 10, 12; ConAu 107; CurBio 71; WhoTr&F 73*

Clarke, Shirley
American. Director
Cinema-verite films include *Portrait of Jason,* 1967.
b. Oct 2, 1927 in New York, New York
Source: *ConLC 16; DcFM; FilmgC; HalFC 84; InB&W 80; IntDcWB; InWom SUP; OxCFilm; WhoAm 74; WhoAmW 66A, 68A, 70, 72, 74; WhoWor 74; WomWMM*

Clarke, Stanley Marvin
American. Musician, Composer
Known for jazz-funk style; hit albums include *Find Out,* 1985; often teamed with George Duke.
b. Jun 30, 1951 in Philadelphia, Pennsylvania
Source: *ConNews 85-4; EncJzS; HarEnR 86; RolSEnR 83; WhoAfA 96; WhoAm 78, 80, 82, 84, 86, 88, 96, 97; WhoBlA 92, 94; WhoWor 80, 82, 84, 87*

Clarke, Thomas Ernest Bennett
English. Screenwriter, Writer
Wrote many of the classic English comedies; received Academy Award for film script *The Lavender Hill Mob,* 1952.
b. Jun 7, 1907 in Watford, England
d. Feb 11, 1989 in London, England
Source: *Au&Wr 71; BioIn 10, 16; ConAu 19NR, 103, 127; DcNaB 1986; IntAu&W 76, 77, 82, 86, 89, 91; WhE&EA; Who 74, 82, 83, 85, 88, 90N*

Clarkson, Ewan
English. Author
Works include *The Wake of the Storm,* 1983; *The Many Forked Branch,* 1980.
b. Jan 23, 1929, England
Source: *BioIn 11; ConAu 17NR, 25R; IntAu&W 91, 93; SmATA 9; TwCChW 78; WhoWor 76, 78; WrDr 76, 80, 82, 84, 86, 88, 90, 92, 94, 96*

Clarkson, John Gibson
American. Baseball Player
Pitcher-outfielder, 1882-94; won 53 games, 1885; had 326 career victories; Hall of Fame, 1963.
b. Jul 1, 1861 in Cambridge, Massachusetts
d. Feb 4, 1909 in Cambridge, Massachusetts
Source: *BiDAmSp BB; BioIn 7; DcAmB; WhoProB 73*

Clarkson, Thomas
English. Abolitionist
Led fight abolishing African slave trade from 1785; tried to persuade French, Russians to abandon traffic.
b. Mar 28, 1760 in Wisbech, England
d. Sep 26, 1846 in Ipswich, England
Source: *Alli; BiDLA; BiDMoPL; BioIn 1, 2, 4, 9, 17; BritAu 19; CelCen; DcAfL; DcBiPP; DcEnL; DcLB 158; DcNaB; HarEnUS; HisDBrE; NewCol 75; WebBD 83*

Clary, Robert
American. Actor
Played LaBeau in TV series "Hogan's Heroes," 1965-71.
b. Mar 1, 1926 in Paris, France
Source: *BiE&WWA; BioIn 3; ConTFT 1; WhoAm 74, 76, 78, 80, 82, 90, 92; WhoEnt 92; WhoHol 92, A*

Clash, The
[Topper Headon; Mick Jones; Paul Simonon; Joe Strummer]
English. Music Group
London-based band started, 1976; hit album *Combat Rock,* 1982.
Source: *BioIn 15; ConLC 30; ConMuA 80A; ConMus 4; DcArts; EncPR&S 89; EncRk 88; EncRkSt; HarEnR 86; NewAmDM; PenEncP; RkOn 85; RolSEnR 83; WhoRock 81; WhoRocM 82; WhsNW 85*

Classen, Willie
American. Boxer
Puerto Rican middleweight who died of brain damage incurred during fight.
b. Sep 16, 1950 in Santurce, Puerto Rico
d. Nov 28, 1979 in New York, New York
Source: *BioIn 12; NewYTBS 79*

Claude, Albert
American. Scientist
Founder of modern cell biology who won Nobel Prize in medicine, 1974; first to isolate cancer virus.
b. Aug 23, 1898 in Luxembourg, Belgium
d. May 20, 1983 in Brussels, Belgium
Source: *AnObit 1983; BiESc; BioIn 13, 15, 20; FacFETw; IntWW 80, 81, 82, 83; McGMS 80; NewYTBS 74, 83; NotTwCS; WhAm 8; Who 82, 83; WhoAm 78, 80, 82; WhoNob, 90, 95; WhoWor 80, 82, 84; WorAl; WorAlBi*

Claude, Georges
French. Chemist, Physicist
Research in liquefying gases led to invention of neon lights.
b. Sep 24, 1870 in Paris, France
d. May 23, 1960 in Saint-Cloud, France
Source: *AsBiEn; BiESc; BioIn 5, 20; DcScB; FacFETw; InSci; LarDcSc; LinLib S; NotTwCS; WebBD 83; WhDW; WorInv*

Claudel, Paul Louis Charles
French. Author, Diplomat, Poet
Foremost Catholic writer of his era; wrote poetic dramas, *The Hostage,* 1909; *Satin Slipper,* 1931.
b. Aug 6, 1868 in Villeneuve, France
d. Feb 23, 1955 in Paris, France
Source: *AtlBL; CasWL; CathA 1930; ClDMEL 47; CnMWL; EncWL; McGEWB; McGEWD 84; ModRL; OxCEng 85; PenC EUR; REn; TwCA SUP; WhAm 3*

Claudian
Alexandrian. Poet
Considered the last great classical Latin poet; wrote unfinished epic *Rape of Proserpine.*
b. 365 in Alexandria, Egypt
d. 408 in Rome, Italy
Source: *CasWL; DcCathB; Grk&L; LinLib L; NewC; OxCEng 67; PenC CL; WhDW*

Claudius, Matthias
German. Poet
Wrote the "Rhine Wine Song."
b. Aug 15, 1740 in Reinfeld, Germany
d. Jan 21, 1815 in Hamburg, Germany
Source: *BiD&SB; BioIn 7, 11, 17; CasWL; ChhPo S1; DcBiPP; DcEnL; DcEuL; DcLB 97; Dis&D; EuAu; EvEuW; LinLib L; LuthC 75; OxCGer 76, 86; PenC EUR; REn*

Claudius I
[Tiberius Claudius Nero Germanicus]
Roman. Ruler
Ruled, AD 41-54, began Roman occupation of Britain, AD 43; adopted son Nero became emperor upon his death, by poison.
b. Aug 1, 10BC in Lugdunum, Gaul
d. Oct 13, 54AD in Rome, Italy
Source: *Dis&D; LuthC 75; McGEWB; NewCol 75; WebBD 83; WhDW; WorAl*

Claus, Hugo
Belgian. Poet, Dramatist
Leading representative of 1950s surrealistic Flemish poets.
b. Apr 5, 1929
Source: *CamGWoT; CasWL; CnMD; ConAu 116; ConFLW 84; EncEurC; EncWL, 3; EncWT; McGEWD 84; ModWD; OxCThe 83; RAdv 14; WorAu 1970*

Clausen, A(lden) W(inship)
American. Banker
Pres., World Bank, 1981-86.
b. Feb 17, 1923 in Hamilton, Illinois
Source: *BioIn 8, 11, 12, 13; BlueB 76; CurBio 81; Dun&B 79; IntWW 74, 75, 76, 77, 78, 79, 80, 81, 82, 83, 89, 91; NewYTBS 86; PolProf NF; St&PR 75; Who 82, 83, 85, 88, 90, 92, 94; WhoAm 74, 76, 78, 80, 82, 84, 86, 88, 90, 92; WhoE 85; WhoFI 74, 75, 77, 79, 81, 87, 89; WhoWest 76, 78, 80, 82, 87, 89, 92; WhoWor 74, 82, 84, 89*

Clausewitz, Karl (Philipp Gottlieb) von
Prussian. Author, Military Leader
Book *On War* expounded philosophy of war; had enormous effect on military strategy, tactics, in World Wars.
b. Jun 1, 1780 in Burg, Prussia
d. Nov 16, 1831 in Breslau, Silesia
Source: *CelCen; OxCGer 76; WhoMilH 76; WorAl*

Clausius, Rudolf Julius Emmanuel
German. Physicist, Mathematician
Pioneer in thermodynamics, 1850s; developed kinetic theory of gases.
b. Jan 2, 1822 in Koslin, Pomerania
d. Aug 24, 1888 in Bonn, Germany
Source: *AsBiEn; BiESc; BioIn 14; DcScB; LarDcSc; McGEWB; NewCol 75; WorAl; WorScD*

Clave, Antoni
French. Artist, Illustrator
Noted lithographer, book illustrator: *Gargantua,* 1951.
b. Apr 5, 1913 in Barcelona, Spain
Source: *BioIn 2, 3, 4, 5, 11, 16; DcCAr 81; IntWW 76, 77, 78, 79, 80, 81, 82, 83, 89, 91, 93; McGDA; OxCTwCA; PhDcTCA 77; WhoFr 79; WhoGrA 62*

Clavell, James (Edmund Du Maresq)
English. Author
Wrote *Taipan,* 1966; *Shogun,* 1975; *Noble House,* 1981.
b. Oct 10, 1924 in Sydney, Australia
d. Sep 6, 1994 in Vevey, Switzerland
Source: *AuBYP 3; Benet 87; BioIn 12, 13; CelR 90; ConAu 25R; ConLC 6, 25, 86, 87; CurBio 81, 94N; IntWW 89, 91, 93; LegTOT; MiSFD 9; News 95, 95-1; NewYTBS 81; WhAm 11; Who 85; WhoAm 74, 76, 78, 80, 82, 84, 86, 88, 90, 92, 94; WhoEnt 92; WhoWor 74; WorAlBi; WorAu 1975; WorEFlm; WrDr 80, 82, 84, 86, 88, 90, 92, 94, 96*

Clay, Andrew Dice
[Andrew Clay Silverstein]
American. Comedian
Comedy Store regular, 1980-88; controversial routine includes profanity and disparagement of women, gays, immigrants, etc; his was first act banned from MTV.
b. 1958 in New York, New York
Source: *BioIn 16; ConTFT 11; News 91, 91-1; WhoAm 94, 95, 96, 97; WhoCom*

Clay, Cassius Marcellus
American. Government Official, Abolitionist
Assisted in purchase of AK, 1867; close friend of Lincoln.
b. Oct 19, 1810 in Madison County, Kentucky
d. Jul 22, 1903 in Whitehall, Kentucky
Source: *Alli, SUP; AmBi; AmRef; AmSocL; ApCAB; BiAUS; BiDAmJo; BiD&SB; BiDSA; BioIn 4, 5, 6, 7, 8, 9, 10, 11, 15, 16, 17, 19; BlueB 76; CivWDc; ConAu 120; DcAmAu; DcAmB; DcAmDH 80, 89; DcAmSR; DcBiPP; DcLB 43; DcNAA; Drake; EncSoH; HarEnUS; JrnUS; NatCAB 2; TwCBDA; WebAB 74, 79; WebBD 83; WhAm 1; WhAmP; WhCiWar*

Clay, Henry
"The Great Compromiser"
American. Lawyer, Statesman
Secured MO Compromise; Compromise Tariff of 1833; Compromise of 1850, which sought to avoid Civil War; US senator, representative, speaker.
b. Apr 12, 1777 in Hanover County, Virginia
d. Jun 29, 1852 in Washington, District of Columbia
Source: *Alli; AmAu; AmAu&B; AmBi; AmJust; AmOrN; AmPolLe; ApCAB; BbD; Benet 87, 96; BenetAL 91; BiAUS; BiD&SB; BiDrAC; BiDrUSC 89; BiDrUSE 71, 89; BioIn 1, 2, 3, 4, 5, 6, 7, 8, 9, 10, 11, 12, 13, 14, 15, 16, 17, 18, 19; CelCen; CyAG; CyAL 1; DcAmAu; DcAmB; DcAmC; DcAmDH 80, 89; DcBiPP; DcNAA; Drake; EncAAH; EncAB-H 1974, 1996; EncABHB 6; EncSoH; HarEnUS; HisWorL; LegTOT; LinLib L, S; McGEWB; MemAm; NatCAB 5; OxCAmH; OxCAmL 65, 83; PolPar; PresAR; RAdv 13-3; RComAH; REn; REnAL; REnAW; TwCBDA; WebAB 74, 79; WebBD 83; WhAm HS; WhAmP; WorAl; WorAlBi*

Clay, Lucius du Bignon
American. Army Officer
Leader of Berlin Airlift, 1948-49; commander-in-chief, US forces in Europe, 1947-49.
b. Apr 23, 1897 in Marietta, Georgia
d. Apr 16, 1978 in Chatham, Massachusetts
Source: *BiDWWGF; BlueB 76; ConAu 77, 81; CurBio 45, 63; IntWW 74; NatCAB 61; ObitOF 79; WhAm 7; Who 74; WhoAm 74; WhoAmP 73, 81; WhoWor 74; WorAl*

Clay, William Lacy
American. Politician
Dem. congressman from MO, 1969—.
b. Apr 30, 1931 in Saint Louis, Missouri
Source: *BiDrUSC 89; BioIn 8, 9, 10; BlkAmsC; CngDr 87; ConBlB 8; Ebony 1; InB&W 80; WhoAm 74, 76, 78, 80, 82, 84, 86, 88, 90, 92, 94, 95, 96, 97; WhoAmP 73, 75, 77, 79, 81, 83, 85, 87, 89, 91, 93, 95; WhoBlA 85; WhoGov 72, 75, 77; WhoMW 74, 76, 78, 80, 86, 88, 90, 92, 93, 96*

Claybrook, Joan B
American. Government Official, Social Reformer
Headed National Highway Traffic Safety Administration, 1977-81; pres. of consumer group, Public Citizen, 1982—.
b. Jun 12, 1937 in Baltimore, Maryland
Source: *BioIn 11, 12; WhoAm 78, 80; WhoAmW 79, 81, 83, 85*

Clayburgh, Jill
[Mrs. David Rabe]
American. Actor
Best known for role in *An Unmarried Woman,* 1978, nominated for Oscar.
b. Apr 30, 1944 in New York, New York
Source: *BioIn 10, 11, 12, 13, 16; CelR 90; ConTFT 2, 5; CurBio 79; IntMPA 86, 88, 92, 94, 96; IntWW 89, 91, 93; InWom SUP; ItaFilm; LegTOT; NewYTBS 76, 79, 82; WhoAm 80, 82, 84, 86, 88, 90, 92, 94, 95, 96, 97; WhoAmW 95, 97; WhoEnt 92; WhoHol 92, A; WhoWor 95, 96, 97; WorAlBi*

Clayderman, Richard
"The Prince of Romance"
French. Musician
Popular pianist who has sold over 40 million records, including 177 gold, 42 platinum.
b. Dec 28, 1953 in Paris, France
Source: *LegTOT*

Clayton, Buck
American. Jazz Musician
Trumpeter; with Count Basie, 1936-43; led own sextet, bands, 1950s; *The Benny Goodman Story.*

b. Nov 12, 1911 in Parsons, Kansas
d. Dec 8, 1991 in New York, New York
Source: *AllMusG; AnObit 1991; ASCAP 66; BiDJaz; BioIn 16, 17, 18; CmpEPM; DrBlPA, 90; EncJzS; IlEncJ; NewAmDM; NewGrDA 86; NewGrDJ 88, 94; OxCPMus; PenEncP; WhoJazz 72*

Clayton, Constance Elaine
American. Educator
Superintendent, Philadelphia Public Schools, 1982—.
b. 1937 in Philadelphia, Pennsylvania
Source: *ConBlB 1; NewYTBS 91; WhoAmW 85; WhoBlA 85, 92*

Clayton, Jack
English. Director
His first feature film, *Room at the Top,* 1958, started a new trend in British films.
b. Mar 1, 1921 in Brighton, England
d. Feb 25, 1995 in Slough, England
Source: *BiDFilm, 94; BioIn 10, 12; BlueB 76; ConTFT 5, 14; DcArts; DcFM; FilmgC; HalFC 84, 88; HorFD; IntDcF 1-2, 2-2; IntMPA 75, 76, 77, 78, 79, 81, 82, 84, 86, 88, 92, 94, 96; IntWW 74, 75, 76, 77, 78, 79, 80, 81, 82, 83, 89, 91, 93; MiSFD 9; MovMk; OxCFilm; WhAm 11; Who 74, 82, 83, 85, 88, 90, 92, 94; WhoWor 74, 84, 87, 89, 91, 93, 95; WorEFlm; WorFDir 2*

Clayton, Jan(e Byral)
American. Actor
Played mother in TV series "Lassie," 1954-57.
b. Aug 26, 1925 in Alamogordo, New Mexico
d. Aug 28, 1983 in Los Angeles, California
Source: *BiE&WWA; EncMT; IntMPA 82, 84; WhoAmW 61; WhoHol A; WorAl*

Clayton, John Middleton
American. Politician
Secretary of State, 1849-50; negotiated Clayton-Bulwer treaty with Britain that set stage for Panama Canal, 1850.
b. Jul 24, 1796 in Dagsboro, Delaware
d. Nov 9, 1856 in Dover, Delaware
Source: *AmBi; AmPolLe; ApCAB; BiAUS; BiDrAC; BiDrUSC 89; BiDrUSE 71, 89; BioIn 3, 4, 7, 10, 16; CelCen; CyAG; DcAmB; DcAmDH 80, 89; Drake; HarEnUS; LinLib S; McGEWB; NatCAB 4, 6; TwCBDA; WebAB 74, 79; WhAm HS; WhAmP*

Clayton, Lou
[Louis Finkelstein]
American. Actor
Starred with Jimmy Durante in vaudeville; featured in *Show Girl,* 1929.
b. 1887 in New York, New York
d. Sep 12, 1950 in Santa Monica, California
Source: *BioIn 2; NotNAT B; ObitOF 79; WhoHol B; WhScrn 74, 77, 83*

Clayton, Xernona
American. Broadcasting Executive
Assistant corporate vp of urban affairs, Turner Broadcasting System, Inc., 1988—; creator of "Moments in History" which celebrate Black History Month.
b. Aug 30, 1930 in Muskogee, Oklahoma
Source: *AfrAmBi 1; ConBlB 3; Ebony 1; NotBlAW 2; WhoAfA 96; WhoAm 76, 78; WhoAmW 93, 95; WhoBlA 75, 77, 80, 85, 88, 90, 92, 94; WhoEnt 92*

Claytor, W(illiam) Graham, Jr.
American. Government Official, Railroad Executive
Pres., Southern Railway, 1963-76; chm., 1976-77; held posts under Pres. Carter, 1977-81; pres., National Railroad Passenger Corp., 1982-93.
b. Mar 14, 1912
d. May 14, 1994 in Bradenton, Florida
Source: *BioIn 9, 11, 12, 13; CngDr 77, 79; CurBio 94N; NewYTBS 79; WhAm 11; WhoAm 74, 76, 78, 80, 82, 84, 86, 88, 90, 94; WhoE 85, 86, 89; WhoFI 74, 75, 77, 83, 85, 87, 89, 92; WhoGov 77; WhoWor 80, 82, 84*

Cleary, Beverly (Atlee Bunn)
American. Children's Author
Won 1984 Newbery Award for *Dear Mr. Henshaw;* wrote *Henry Higgins, Ramona* series.
b. Apr 12, 1916 in McMinnville, Oregon
Source: *AmAu&B; AmWomWr; Au&Arts 6; Au&ICB; AuBYP 2, 3; BioIn 6, 7, 8, 9, 10, 12, 13; ChlBkCr; ChlFicS; ChlLR 2, 8; ConAu 1R, 2NR, 19NR, 36NR; DcLB 52; LegTOT; MajAI; MajTwCW; MorBMP; MorJA; OxCChiL; SmATA 2, 20AS, 43, 79; TwCChW 78, 83, 89, 95; WhoAm 86; WhoAmW 87; WorAlBi; WrDr 76, 86, 88, 90, 92, 94, 96*

Cleaveland, Moses
American. Soldier, Lawyer
Founded Cleaveland, Ohio, 1796; spelling later changed to Cleveland.
b. Jan 29, 1754 in Canterbury, Connecticut
d. Nov 16, 1806 in Canterbury, Connecticut
Source: *AmBi; ApCAB; DcAmB; HarEnUS; OhA&B; TwCBDA; WhAm HS; WhAmRev*

Cleaver, Eldridge
American. Political Activist, Author
Civil rights radical; wrote *Soul on Ice,* 1968; *Soul on Fire,* 1978.
b. Aug 31, 1935 in Little Rock, Arkansas
Source: *AmAu&B; AmDec 1960; BenetAL 91; BioIn 8, 9, 10, 11, 12, 14, 15, 16, 17, 19, 20; BlkAWP; BlkLC; BlkWr 1; CelR; CivR 74; CmCal; ConAu 16NR, 21R; ConBlB 5; ConLC 30; CurBio 70; DcLEL 1940; DcTwCCu 5; EncAACR; FacFETw; HisWorL; LegTOT; LiExTwC; LinLib L; LivgBAA; LNinSix; MugS; NegAl 76, 83, 89; NewYTBS 77; PenC AM; PolPar; PolProf NF; SchCGBL; SelBAAf; WebE&AL; WhoAfA 96; WhoBlA 85, 88, 90, 92, 94; WrDr 76, 80, 82, 84, 86, 88, 90, 92, 94, 96*

Cleaver, Emanuel, II
American. Politician
First black mayor of Kansas City, MO, 1991—.
b. Oct 26, 1944 in Waxahachie, Texas
Source: *ConBlB 4; WhoAfA 96; WhoAm 92, 94, 97; WhoAmP 95; WhoBlA 85, 88, 90, 92, 94; WhoMW 92, 93, 96*

Cleaver, Vera Allen
[Mrs. William Joseph Cleaver]
American. Children's Author
With husband, co-wrote popular children's books: *Queen of Hearts,* 1978.
b. Jan 6, 1919 in Virgil, South Dakota
Source: *ChlLR 6; ConAu 73; FourBJA; SmATA 22; WhAm 11; WhoAm 78, 80, 82, 84, 86, 88, 90, 92; WhoUSWr 88; WhoWrEP 89, 92, 95; WrDr 86*

Cleaver, William Joseph
"Bill Cleaver"
American. Author
With wife Vera, co-wrote numerous children's books: *Trial Valley,* 1977.
b. Mar 20, 1920 in Hugo, Oklahoma
d. Aug 20, 1981 in Winter Haven, Florida
Source: *AuBYP 3; BioIn 12, 13; ChlBkCr; ChlLR 6; ConAu 73, 104; DcAmChF 1960; DcLB 52; FourBJA; SmATA 27N; TwCChW 83, 89; TwCYAW; WhAm 8; WhoAm 78, 80, 82*

Cleese, John Marwood
[Monty Python's Flying Circus]
English. Actor, Writer
Created Monty Python, 1969; humor based on conviction of senselessness of life; won 1987 Emmy.
b. Oct 27, 1939 in Weston-super-Mare, England
Source: *ConTFT 4; CurBio 84; IntWW 82; Who 85; WhoAm 97; WhoWor 97*

Clegg, Johnny
South African. Singer, Songwriter
Known in South Africa and Europe for hit albums *African Litany,* 1981; *Third World Child,* 1987; *Shadow Man,* 1988.
b. Oct 31, 1953 in Rochdale, England
Source: *BioIn 16; ConMus 8; HeroCon; PenEncP*

Cleghorn, Sarah Norcliffe
American. Author
Poems collected in *Poems and Protests,* 1917.
b. Feb 4, 1876 in Norfolk, Virginia
d. Apr 4, 1959 in Philadelphia, Pennsylvania
Source: *AmAu&B; AmPeW; AmWomWr; BioIn 4, 5, 6, 12; ChhPo, S1, S2, S3; DcAmB S6; InWom; NatCAB 45; REnAL; TwCA, SUP; WhAm 3; WhNAA; WomNov; WomWWA 14*

Cleghorn, Sprague
Canadian. Hockey Player
Defenseman, 1918-28, with four NHL teams; Hall of Fame, 1958.
b. 1890 in Montreal, Quebec, Canada
d. Jul 11, 1956 in Montreal, Quebec, Canada
Source: *BioIn 10; HocEn; WhoHcky 73*

Cleghorne, Ellen
American. Actor
Regular cast member on TV show "Saturday Night Live," 1992—; plays Queen Shenequa.

Cleisthenes
Greek. Statesman
Founder of Athenian democracy who established a dem. constitution.
b. 570?BC
d. 500?BC
Source: *BioIn 5; DcBiPP; McGEWB*

Cleland, John
English. Author, Dramatist
Wrote erotic classic, *Fanny Hill or Memories of a Woman of Pleasure,* 1749.
b. 1709 in London, England
d. Jan 23, 1789 in London, England
Source: *Alli, SUP; BiDSA; BioIn 10, 12, 15; BlmGEL; CamGEL; CamGLE; CasWL; DcArts; DcBiPP; DcNaB; EncEnl; LegTOT; LitC 2; NewC; Novels; OxCEng 67, 85, 95; WorAl; WorAlBi*

Cleland, Max
[Joseph Maxwell Cleland]
American. Government Official, Politician
Lost legs, forearm in Vietnam; VA head, 1977-80; Dem. senator, GA, 1997—.
b. Aug 24, 1942 in Atlanta, Georgia
Source: *BioIn 11, 12, 15; ConAu 113, 129; CurBio 78; NewYTBS 77; WhoAm 78, 80, 82, 84, 86, 88, 90, 92, 94, 95, 96, 97; WhoAmP 73, 77, 79, 81, 83, 85, 87, 89, 91, 93, 95; WhoGov 77; WhoSSW 84, 86, 88, 91, 93, 95*

Cleland, Thomas Maitland
American. Illustrator
Award-winning typographer, graphic designer known for illustrating deluxe books.
b. Aug 18, 1880 in New York, New York
d. Nov 9, 1964
Source: *BioIn 1, 3, 7, 9, 10, 21; IlrAm 1880, C; WhAm 4; WhoAmA 78N, 89N, 91N, 93N*

Clemenceau, Georges Eugene Benjamin
French. Statesman
Forceful wartime premier, 1917-20; opposed leniency toward Germany after Allied victory, WW I.
b. Sep 28, 1841 in Mouilleron-en-Pareds, France
d. Nov 24, 1929 in Paris, France
Source: *BiDFrPL; BioIn 1, 2, 4, 5, 6, 9, 10, 11, 12; ClDMEL 47; ConAu 114; McGEWB; REn; WebBD 83*

Clemens, (William) Roger
"Rocket Man"
American. Baseball Player
Pitcher, Boston, 1984-96, Toronto, 1997—; A.L. MVP, 1986; Cy Young Award, 1986-87, 1991; holds M.L. record for strikeouts in one game, 20, 4/29/86.
b. Aug 4, 1962 in Dayton, Ohio
Source: *Ballpl 90; BaseEn 88; BaseReg 87, 88; BioIn 16; CelR 90; CurBio 88; LegTOT; News 91; NewYTBS 86; WhoAm 88, 90, 92, 94, 95, 96, 97; WhoE 89; WhoSpor; WorAlBi*

Clement, Rene
French. Director
Won Oscars for best foreign films *Forbidden Games; The Walls of Malapaga,* 1952.
b. Mar 18, 1913 in Bordeaux, France
d. Mar 17, 1996, France
Source: *BiDFilm, 94; BioIn 12, 15, 21; DcFM; DcTwCCu 2; EncEurC; FilmgC; HalFC 84, 88; IntDcF 1-2, 2-2; IntWW 74, 75, 76, 77, 78, 79, 80, 81, 82, 83, 89, 91, 93; ItaFilm; LegTOT; MiSFD 9; MovMk; OxCFilm; Who 74, 82, 83, 85, 88, 90, 92, 94; WhoFr 79; WhoWor 74; WorEFlm; WorFDir 1*

Clemente, Francesco
Italian. Artist
Avante-garde artist known for enigmatic self-portraits, photographs, paintings, drawings, collages.
b. Mar 1952 in Naples, Italy
Source: *BioIn 12, 13, 14, 15; ConArt 83, 89, 96; DcArts; DcCAr 81; News 92, 92-2; PrintW 83, 85; WhoAm 97; WhoAmA 86, 89, 91, 93; WorAlBi; WorArt 1980*

Clemente, Roberto Walker
Puerto Rican. Baseball Player
Outfielder, Pittsburgh, 1955-72; won three NL batting titles; Hall of Fame, 1973; killed in plane crash.
b. Aug 18, 1934 in Carolina, Puerto Rico
d. Dec 31, 1972 in San Juan, Puerto Rico
Source: *BioIn 6, 7, 8, 9, 10, 11, 12; CurBio 73; HeroCon; InB&W 85; NewYTBE 71, 72, 73; WhAm 5; WhoProB 73*

Clement I, Saint
[Clemens Romanus]
Religious Leader
Fourth pope; known for *First Epistle of Clement,* c. 96, which asserted authority of Roman church; feast day Nov 23.
b. fl. 1st cent. in Rome, Italy
d. 100 in Rome, Italy
Source: *DcCathB; McGDA; NewCol 75; OxCEng 67; WebBD 83*

Clementi, Muzio
Italian. Pianist, Composer
Leader in modern piano technique; noted London music publisher, 1799.
b. Jan 24, 1752 in Rome, Italy
d. Mar 10, 1832 in Evesham, England
Source: *Baker 78, 84, 92; BioIn 1, 4, 7, 8, 11, 12, 16, 20; CelCen; DcArts; DcBiPP; DcNaB MP; NewAmDM; NewCol 75; NewOxM; OxCMus; WebBD 83*

Clements, George Harold
American. Clergy, Civil Rights Leader
Black priest known for adopting son, 1981; heads largest black Catholic school in US, emphasizing discipline, rigorous academics.
b. Jan 26, 1932 in Chicago, Illinois
Source: *AmCath 80; ConNews 85-1; WhoAm 76, 78; WhoBlA 80*

Clements, Vassar
American. Singer, Songwriter, Violinist
World reknown fiddler of a wide range of musical genres, including bluegrass, country, pop, rock, swing, and jazz; performed on legendary *Will the Circle Be Broken* album, 1972; received the MRL Living Legend Award, 1991, the RCA Honors Award, and the British Fiddlers Award.
b. Apr 25, 1928 in Kinard, South Carolina
Source: *BgBkCoM; HarEnCM 87; NewGrDA 86; PenEncP; WhoRock 81*

Clements, William Perry, Jr.
American. Politician
Rep. governor of Texas, 1979-83, 1987-91.
b. Apr 3, 1917 in Dallas, Texas
Source: *AlmAP 88; BioIn 11, 12, 13; CngDr 74; IntWW 80, 81, 82, 83, 89, 91, 93; WhoAm 80, 82, 84, 86, 88, 90, 92, 94, 95; WhoAmP 85, 87; WhoSSW 88, 91; WhoWor 82, 91, 93, 95, 97*

Clement VII
[Giulio DeMedici]
Florentine. Religious Leader
Pope, 1523-34; Henry VIII attempted to divorce Catherine of Aragon during his reign.
b. May 26, 1478 in Florence, Italy
d. Sep 25, 1534 in Rome, Italy
Source: *DcCathB; NewCol 75; REn; WorAl*

Clement VIII
[Gil Sanchez Munoz]
Spanish. Religious Leader
Last of the antipopes, 1423-29; voluntarily renounced rank, was reconciled with church.
b. 1360? in Teruel, Spain
d. Dec 28, 1446

Clement XIV, Pope
[Giovanni Vincenzo Antonio Ganganelli]
Italian. Religious Leader
Pope, 1769-74; his suppression of Jesuits, 1773, weakened church for years.
b. Oct 31, 1705 in Sant'Arcangelo, Italy
d. Sep 22, 1774 in Rome, Italy
Source: *DcCathB; NewCol 75; WebBD 83*

Clemo, Jack
[Reginald John Clemo]
English. Poet
Writing highly reflected by personal life, including his blindness and deafness.
b. Mar 11, 1916 in Saint Austell, England
Source: *Au&Wr 71; ConPo 70, 75, 80, 85, 91; DcLB 27; DcLEL 1940; DcLP 87B; IntAu&W 76, 77, 82, 86, 89, 91, 93; IntWWP 77, 82; LngCTC; OxCEng 85, 95; OxCTwCP; TwCWr; WrDr 76, 80, 82, 84, 86, 88, 90, 92, 94, 96*

Clemons, Clarence
[E Street Band]
"King of the World"; "Master of the Universe"; "The Big Man"
American. Musician, Singer
Tenor saxophonist with Bruce Springsteen; solo album *Rescue,* 1983.
b. Jan 11, 1942 in Norfolk, Virginia
Source: *BioIn 14; ConMus 7; LegTOT; WhoRocM 82*

Cleopatra VII
Macedonian. Ruler
Mistress of Julius Caesar, Marc Antony; killed herself with asp.
b. 69BC in Alexandria, Egypt
d. Aug 30, 30BC in Alexandria, Egypt
Source: *FilmgC; GoodHs; HerW; LngCEL; McGEWB; NewC; NewCol 75; REn*

Clerc, Jose-Luis
"Batata"
Argentine. Tennis Player
Won Italian Open, 1981.
b. Aug 16, 1958 in Buenos Aires, Argentina
Source: *BioIn 12; WhoIntT*

Cleva, Fausto
American. Conductor
Member, conducting staff, NY Met. for 50 yrs.
b. May 17, 1902 in Trieste, Italy
d. Aug 6, 1971 in Athens, Greece
Source: *Baker 78, 84; BiDAmM; BioIn 2, 3, 4, 7, 9, 11; MetOEnc; MusSN; NewAmDM; NewEOp 71; NewGrDA 86; NewYTBE 71; PenDiMP; WhAm 5; WhoMus 72*

Cleve, Joos van
Flemish. Artist
Royalty portraitist, religious painter; works include *Lamentation,* c. 1530.
b. 1485
d. 1540 in Antwerp, Belgium
Source: *McGDA*

Cleve, Per Teodor
Swedish. Chemist
Discovered the chemical elements holmium and thulium, 1879.
b. Feb 10, 1840 in Stockholm, Sweden
d. Jun 18, 1905 in Uppsala, Sweden
Source: *AsBiEn; BiESc; DcScB*

Cleveland, Frances Folsom
[Mrs. Grover Cleveland]
American. First Lady
Youngest first lady, first White House bride, 1886.
b. Jul 21, 1864 in Buffalo, New York
d. Oct 29, 1947 in Baltimore, Maryland
Source: *AmWom; ApCAB SUP; FacPr 89; GoodHs; InWom, SUP; NatCAB 2; NotAW; TwCBDA; WomFir*

Cleveland, Grover
[Stephen Grover Cleveland]
American. US President
Dem. 22nd, 24th president, 1885-89, 1893-97; worked to stablilize currency.
b. Mar 18, 1837 in Caldwell, New Jersey
d. Jun 24, 1908 in Princeton, New Jersey
Source: *AmAu&B; AmBi; AmPolLe; ApCAB, SUP; Benet 87; BenetAL 91; BiD&SB; BiDrAC; BiDrUSE 71, 89; BioIn 1, 2, 3, 4, 5, 6, 7, 8, 9, 10, 11, 12, 13, 14, 15, 16, 17, 18, 19, 20; CelCen; CyAG; DcAmAu; DcAmB; DcAmC; DcAmSR; Dis&D; EncAAH; EncAB-H 1974, 1996; FacPr 89, 93; GayN; HarEnUS; HealPre; HisWorL; LegTOT; LinLib L, S; McGEWB; MorMA; NatCAB 2; NewCol 75; OxCAmH; OxCAmL 65, 83; PolPar; PresAR; RComAH; REn; REnAL; TwCBDA; WebAB 74, 79; WhAm 1; WhAmP; WhDW; WorAl; WorAlBi*

Cleveland, James
"Crown Prince of Gospel"; "King of Gospel Music"
American. Clergy, Singer
Founded Gospel Music Workshop of America, 1968; hits include "Peace Be Still," 1963.
b. Dec 5, 1931 in Chicago, Illinois
d. Feb 9, 1991 in Los Angeles, California
Source: *AnObit 1991; Baker 92; BiDAfM; ConMus 1; CurBio 85, 91N; DcTwCCu 5; DrBlPA, 90; Ebony 1; InB&W 80, 85; LegTOT; News 91; NewYTBS 91; PenEncP; WhAm 10; WhoAm 84, 86, 88; WhoBlA 75, 77, 80, 85, 90, 92N*

Cleveland, James Harlan
American. Political Scientist
US ambassador to NATO, 1965-69; wrote *The Third Try at World Order,* 1977; *Humangrowth,* 1978.
b. Jan 19, 1918 in New York, New York
Source: *AmMWSc 73S; ConAu 1R; CurBio 61; IntWW 74; LEduc 74; Who 74; WhoAm 76, 78, 84, 86; WhoAmP 73; WhoWor 84; WrDr 82, 88*

Clevenger, Shobal Vail
American. Sculptor
His bust of Daniel Webster was selected by Post Office for 15 cent stamp.
b. Oct 22, 1812 in Middletown, Ohio
d. Sep 23, 1843
Source: *AmBi; ApCAB; BioIn 6, 7, 8; BriEAA; DcAmArt; DcAmB; Drake; McGDA; NatCAB 8; NewYHSD; TwCBDA; WhAm HS*

Cliburn, Van
[Harvey Lavan Cliburn, Jr.]
American. Pianist
Classical concert pianist; won International Tchaikovsky Piano Competition, Moscow, 1958.
b. Jul 12, 1934 in Shreveport, Louisiana
Source: *Baker 78, 84, 92; BiDAmM; BioIn 4, 5, 6, 7, 8, 9, 10, 11, 12, 14, 15, 16, 17, 18, 20, 21; BlueB 76; CelR, 90; ConMus 13; CurBio 58; DcTwCCu 1; FacFETw; IntWW 74, 75, 76, 77, 78, 79, 80, 81, 82, 83, 89, 91, 93; IntWWM 77, 90; LegTOT; LinLib S; MusSN; NewAmDM; NewGrDA 86; News 95, 95-1; NewYTBS 85, 86, 89, 91; NotTwCP; PenDiMP; Who 74, 82, 83, 85, 88, 90, 92, 94; WhoAm 74, 76, 78, 80, 82, 84, 86, 88, 90, 92, 94, 95, 96, 97; WhoAmM 83; WhoEnt 92; WhoMus 72; WhoWor 74, 78, 80, 82, 84, 87, 89, 91; WorAl; WorAlBi*

Cliff, Jimmy
[James Chambers]
Jamaican. Singer, Songwriter
Helped popularize reggae outside Jamaica; albums include *The Power and the Glory,* 1983.
b. 1948 in Saint Catherine, Jamaica
Source: *BioIn 13, 14, 15; ConAu 124, X; ConLC 21; ConMuA 80A; ConMus 8; DcTwCCu 5; DrBlPA; EncPR&S 89; EncRk 88; EncRkSt; HarEnR 86; IlEncRk; LegTOT; RkOn 78; RolSEnR 83; WhoAm 94, 95, 96, 97; WhoEnt 92; WhoRock 81*

Clifford, Clark McAdams
American. Government Official
Special adviser to presidents Truman, Kennedy, Johnson; defense secretary under Johnson, 1968-69.
b. Dec 25, 1906 in Fort Scott, Kansas
Source: *AmPolLe; BiDrUSE 71, 89; BioIn 14; ColdWar 1; CurBio 47, 68; Dun&B 88; EncAB-H 1974; IntWW 83, 91; NewYTBE 71; NewYTBS 77, 88, 91; PolProf J, K, T; St&PR 91; Who 85, 92; WhoAm 86, 90, 97; WhoAmL 87; WhoAmP 85, 91; WhoE 97; WhoWor 84, 91, 97*

Clifford, Nathan
American. Supreme Court Justice
Helped negotiate Mexican Treaty of Guadaloupe Hidalgo, 1848; Supreme Court Justice, 1858-81.
b. Aug 18, 1803 in Rumney, New Hampshire
d. Jul 25, 1881 in Cornish, Maine

Source: *Alli SUP; AmBi; ApCAB; BiAUS; BiDFedJ; BiDrAC; BiDrUSC 89; BiDrUSE 71, 89; BioIn 2, 5, 10, 15; DcAmAu; DcAmB; Drake; HarEnUS; NatCAB 2; OxCSupC; SupCtJu; TwCBDA; WebAB 74, 79; WhAm HS; WhAmP; WhCiWar*

Clift, Montgomery
[Edward Montgomery Clift]
American. Actor
Known for playing troubled heroes: *From Here to Eternity*, 1953; *The Misfits*, 1961.
b. Oct 17, 1920 in Omaha, Nebraska
d. Jul 23, 1966 in New York, New York
Source: *BiDFilm, 94; BiE&WWA; BioIn 1, 2, 3, 4, 5, 6, 7, 11, 12, 14, 16, 17, 18, 19, 20, 21; CmMov; CurBio 54, 66; DcAmB S8; DcTwCCu 1; FacFETw; FilmgC; HalFC 84, 88; IntDcF 2-3; ItaFilm; LegTOT; MotPP; MovMk; NotNAT B; OxCAmT 84; OxCFilm; WhAm 4; WhoHol B; WhScrn 74, 77, 83; WhThe; WorAl; WorAlBi; WorEFlm*

Climax Blues Band, The
[Colin Cooper; John Cuffley; Peter Haycock; Derek Holt; Richard Jones; George Newsome; Arthur Wood]
English. Music Group
Founded 1969; first US hit single "Couldn't Get It Right," 1977.
Source: *Alli, SUP; BiDLA; BioIn 9; ConMuA 80A; DcEnL; DcNaB; DcVicP 2; DrAPF 85, 87, 89, 91, 93, 97; EncRk 88; IlEncRk; NewGrDM 80; NotNAT B; ODwPR 91; OhA&B; OxCMus; OxCThe 67, 83; PenEncP; RkOn 78, 84; RolSEnR 83; St&PR 96, 97; TwYS A; WhE&EA; WhoRock 81; WhoRocM 82*

Clinchy, Everett Ross
American. Clergy
Co-founded National Conference of Christians and Jews, 1929, World Brotherhood of Christians and Jews, 1950.
b. Dec 16, 1896 in New York, New York
d. Jan 22, 1986 in Guilford, Connecticut
Source: *AmAu&B; BlueB 76; CurBio 41, 86; IntWW 74, 75, 76, 77, 78, 79, 80, 81, 82, 83; WhAm 9; WhoAm 74, 76, 78, 80, 82, 84*

Cline, Genevieve Rose
American. Judge, Government Official
First woman federal judge, appointed by Coolidge, 1928.
b. Jul 27, 1878? in Warren, Ohio
d. Oct 25, 1959 in Cleveland, Ohio
Source: *BioIn 12; DcAmB S6; InWom SUP; NotAW MOD*

Cline, Maggie
American. Singer
Vaudeville performer, first woman Irish comedy singer.
b. Jan 1, 1857 in Haverhill, Massachusetts
d. Jun 11, 1934 in Fair Haven, New Jersey
Source: *BioIn 16; EncVaud; InWom SUP; LibW; NotAW; NotNAT B; OxCAmT 84; WomFir*

Cline, Patsy
[Virginia Patterson Hensley]
American. Singer
Country singer; had hits "Crazy," "I Fall to Pieces," 1961; killed in plane crash; Jessica Lange played her in film *Sweet Dreams*, 1985.
b. Sep 8, 1932 in Winchester, Virginia
d. Mar 5, 1963 in Camden, Tennessee
Source: *Baker 84, 92; BgBkCoM; BiDAmM; BioIn 14, 15, 17, 18, 19, 20, 21; ConMus 5; EncFCWM 69, 83; EncRkSt; GrLiveH; HarEnCM 87; InWom SUP; LegTOT; NewAmDM; NewGrDA 86; OxCPMus; PenEncP; RkOn 74; RolSEnR 83*

Clinton, Bill
[William Jefferson Blythe, IV; William Jefferson Clinton]
American. US President
42nd pres., Dem. 1993—; governor of AR, 1979-81, 1983-92.
b. Aug 19, 1946 in Hope, Arkansas
Source: *AlmAP 80, 84, 88, 92; BiDrGov 1978, 1983, 1988; BioIn 13, 14, 15, 16, 17, 18, 19, 20, 21; CngDr 95; CurBio 88, 94; FacPr 93; HisEAAC; IntWW 79, 80, 81, 82, 83, 89, 91; LegTOT; News 92, 92-1; NewYTBS 78, 92; PolsAm 84; Who 94; WhoAm 86, 88, 90, 92, 94, 95, 96, 97; WhoAmL 78, 79, 92; WhoAmP 79, 81, 83, 85, 87, 89, 91, 93, 95; WhoEmL 87, 93; WhoSSW 78, 80, 88, 91, 93; WhoWor 84, 89, 91, 93, 95, 96, 97*

Clinton, Chelsea Victoria
American.
Only child of Bill, Hillary Clinton.
b. Feb 27, 1980 in Arkansas

Clinton, DeWitt
American. Lawyer, Statesman
NY governor, 1817-23, 1825-28; promoted Erie Canal; unsuccessful pres. candidate, 1812.
b. Mar 2, 1769 in Little Britain, New York
d. Feb 11, 1828 in Albany, New York
Source: *Alli; AmAu&B; AmBi; AmPolLe; ApCAB; BiAUS; BiDAmEd; BiD&SB; BiDrAC; BiDrGov 1789; BiInAmS; BioIn 3, 4, 5, 6, 7, 8, 9, 15; CelCen; CyAG; CyAL 1; CyEd; DcAmAu; DcAmB; DcAmSR; DcNAA; Drake; EncAB-H 1974, 1996; EncABHB 6; HarEnUS; LinLib L, S; McGEWB; NatCAB 3; OxCAmH; PolPar; PresAR; REnAL; TwCBDA; WebAB 74, 79; WhAm HS; WhAmP; WorAl; WorAlBi*

Clinton, George
American. US Vice President
VP under Jefferson, 1805-12; NY governor, 1777-95, 1801-04; opposed adoption of US Constitution.
b. Jul 26, 1739 in Little Britain, New York
d. Apr 20, 1812 in Washington, District of Columbia
Source: *AmBi; AmPolLe; AmWrBE; ApCAB; BenetAL 91; BiAUS; BiDrAC; BiDrACR; BiDrGov 1789; BiDrUSC 89; BiDrUSE 71, 89; BioIn 1, 3, 4, 6, 7, 8, 9, 10, 11, 12, 14; BlkwEAR; CyAG; DcAmB; DcNAA; Drake; EncAB-H 1974, 1996; EncAR; EncCRAm; HarEnUS; LegTOT; LinLib S; McGEWB; NatCAB 3; OxCAmH; OxCAmL 65; PolPar; PresAR; REnAL; TwCBDA; VicePre; WebAB 74, 79; WebAMB; WhAm HS; WhAmP; WhAmRev; WhNaAH; WorAl; WorAlBi*

Clinton, George
American. Composer, Producer, Singer
Best known for producing groups Parliament, Funkadelic; hits include "One Nation Under a Groove," 1978.
b. Jul 22, 1941 in Kannapolis, North Carolina
Source: *BioIn 11, 13; ConBlB 9; ConMuA 80A; ConMus 7; CurBio 93; EncPR&S 89; EncRk 88; HarEnR 86; NewAmDM; NewGrDA 86; WhoRocM 82*

Clinton, Henry, Sir
British. Military Leader
Commander-in-chief of British troops in American Revolution, 1778-81, succeeding Howe.
b. 1738 in Newfoundland, Canada
d. Dec 23, 1795, Gibraltar
Source: *Alli; AmBi; ApCAB; BenetAL 91; BioIn 5, 6, 7, 8, 9, 16; DcBiPP; DcNaB; Drake; EncAR; EncCRAm; HarEnMi; HarEnUS; HisDBrE; LinLib S; McGEWB; OxCAmH; OxCAmL 65; REn; REnAL; WhAm HS; WhoMilH 76; WorAl; WorAlBi*

Clinton, Hillary Rodham
American. First Lady
Married Bill Clinton, 1975; partner, Rose Law Firm, 1977-92.
b. Oct 26, 1947 in Chicago, Illinois
Source: *BioIn 18, 19, 20, 21; ConAu 153; CurBio 93; EncWHA; GrLiveH; IntWW 93; News 93-2; NewYTBS 93; WhoAm 94, 95, 96, 97; WhoAmL 85, 90, 92, 94; WhoAmP 93, 95; WhoAmW 93, 95, 97; WhoEmL 87, 91, 93; WhoWor 95, 96, 97; WomStre*

Clinton, James
American. Army Officer
Continental Army general known for futile defense of Fort Clinton, 1777; brother of George.
b. Aug 9, 1733 in Little Britain, New York
d. Dec 22, 1812 in Orange County, New York
Source: *AmBi; AmRev; DcAmB; Drake; EncAR; HarEnMi; NatCAB 1; NewCol 75; TwCBDA; WebAMB; WebBD 83; WhAm HS; WhAmRev; WhNaAH*

Clinton, Larry
American. Bandleader
Composer, arranger during big band era; tune The Dipsy Doodle was one of top hits, late 1930s.
b. Aug 17, 1909 in New York, New York
d. May 2, 1985 in Tucson, Arizona
Source: *ASCAP 66; BiDJaz; BioIn 2, 9, 12, 14, 16; CmpEPM; NewGrDJ 88, 94; NewYTBS 85; OxCPMus; PenEncP; WhoJazz 72*

Clive, Colin
[Clive Greig]
British. Actor
Played title role in *Dr. Frankenstein,* 1931; Mr. Rochester in *Jane Eyre,* 1934.
b. Jan 20, 1900 in Saint-Malo, France
d. Jun 25, 1937 in Hollywood, California
Source: *CmMov; FilmgC; MovMk; NotNAT B; PlP&P; WhoHol B; WhScrn 74, 77, 83; WhThe*

Clive, Robert
[Baron Clive of Plassey]
English. Statesman, Soldier
Founded empire of British India; recovered Calcutta, 1757.
b. Sep 29, 1725 in Styche, England
d. Nov 22, 1774 in London, England
Source: *Benet 87, 96; BioIn 12, 16, 20; DcBiPP; DcInB; DcNaB; Dis&D; GenMudB; HarEnMi; HisDBrE; HisWorL; McGEWB; NewC; OxCEng 85, 95; REn; WhDW; WhoMilH 76; WorAl; WorAlBi*

Clodagh
[Clodagh Aubry]
Irish. Designer
Designs one-of-a-kind "collector's pieces" for private customers in NY, Dublin.
b. Oct 8, 1937 in Galway, Ireland
Source: *BioIn 16; FairDF IRE; WorFshn*

Cloete, Stuart
South African. Author
Novels of S Africa include *The Turning Wheels,* 1937; *Mamba,* 1956.
b. Jul 23, 1897 in Paris, France
d. Mar 19, 1976 in Cape Town, South Africa
Source: *AmAu&B; Benet 87; BioIn 1, 3, 4, 5, 9, 10; CamGLE; CasWL; ConAu 1R, 3NR, 65; ConNov 72, 76; EncSoA; EncWL; EngPo; IntAu&W 77, 82; IntWW 74, 75, 76; IntWWP 77; LngCTC; NewYTBS 76; Novels; REn; TwCA, SUP; TwCWr; WhAm 7; WhNAA; WhoWor 74, 76; WrDr 76, 80*

Clokey, Art
American. Illustrator
Created cartoon character Gumby, 1956.
b. 1922?
Source: *BioIn 4, 16; SmATA 59*

Clooney, George
American. Actor
On television's *ER,* 1994—; in *One Fine Day,* 1996.
b. May 5, 1961 in Lexington, Kentucky
Source: *ConTFT 15; News 96; WhoHol 92*

Clooney, Rosemary
American. Actor, Singer
Had million-selling single "Come On-a My House," 1951; autobiography *This for Remembrance,* 1979.
b. May 23, 1928 in Maysville, Kentucky
Source: *AllMusG; Baker 92; BiDAmM; BioIn 2, 3, 4, 5, 6, 10, 11, 12, 13, 14; CelR 90; CmpEPM; ConMus 9; CurBio 57; FilmgC; HalFC 84, 88; IntMPA 96; InWom, SUP; LegTOT; NewGrDA 86; NewGrDJ 88, 94; OxCPMus; PenEncP; RadStar; RkOn 74; WhoAm 74, 94, 95, 96, 97; WhoAmW 58, 61, 64, 66, 68, 70, 72, 74, 95; WhoHol 92, A; WhoMus 72*

Close, Glenn
American. Actor
Received Oscar nominations for *The World According to Garp,* 1982; *The Big Chill,* 1983; *Fatal Attraction,* 1988; received Emmy for *Serving in Silence: The Margarethe Cammermeyer Story,* 1995.
b. Mar 19, 1947 in Greenwich, Connecticut
Source: *BiDFilm 94; BioIn 13, 14, 15, 16; CamGWoT; CelR 90; ConTFT 3, 5, 9; CurBio 83, 84; GrLiveH; HalFC 88; HolBB; IntDcF 2-3; IntMPA 88, 92, 94, 96; IntWW 89, 91, 93; InWom SUP; News 88-3; NewYTBS 82, 85; VarWW 85; WhoAm 86, 88, 90, 92, 94, 95, 96, 97; WhoAmW 89, 91, 93, 95, 97; WhoEnt 92; WhoHol 92; WorAlBi*

Close, Upton
[Josef Washington Hall]
American. Author, Radio Performer
Works, radio lectures dealt with Asian and Pacific Basin people: *Behind the Face of Japan,* 1942.
b. Feb 27, 1894 in Kelso, Washington
d. Nov 13, 1960 in Guadalajara, Mexico
Source: *AmAu&B; AnMV 1926; BiDAmJo; BioIn 4, 5, 6, 11, 16; ConAu 89; CurBio 44, 61; EvLB; TwCA, SUP; WhLit; WhNAA*

Cloud, Henry Roe
American. Educator
First Native American to graduate from Yale University, 1910; established the Roe Indian Institute (later the American Indian Institute), 1915.
b. Dec 28, 1886 in Winnebago, Nebraska
d. Feb 9, 1950 in Siletz, Oregon
Source: *AmSocL; BiDAmEd; BioIn 19, 21; DcAmB S4; NotNaAm; WhAm 2A*

Clouet, Francois
French. Artist
Chief painter to Francis I, 1523; portraitist of royalty; son of Jean.
b. 1510 in Tours, France
d. 1572 in Paris, France
Source: *AtlBL; BioIn 11; DcCathB; McGDA; OxCArt; OxDcArt; REn*

Clouet, Jean
French. Artist
Painter to four French kings; did portraits, genre scenes.
b. 1485, Netherlands
d. 1540 in Paris, France
Source: *AtlBL; BioIn 1, 8; DcCathB; IntDcAA 90; McGEWB; OxCArt*

Clough, Arthur Hugh
English. Poet
Wrote pastoral verse "Bothie of Toper-na-Vuolich," 1848; subject of Matthew Arnold's elegy, "Thyrsis."
b. Jan 1, 1819 in Liverpool, England
d. Nov 13, 1861 in Florence, Italy
Source: *Alli, SUP; AtlBL; BiD&SB; BiDTran; BioIn 1, 3, 4, 5, 6, 7, 8, 9, 11, 12, 13, 14, 16, 17, 18; BlmGEL; BritAu 19; BritWr 5; CamGEL; CamGLE; CasWL; CelCen; Chambr 3; ChhPo, S1, S2, S3; CnE&AP; CrtT 3, 4; DcArts; DcBiPP; DcEnA; DcEnL; DcEuL; DcLB 32; DcLEL; DcNaB, C; EvLB; LinLib L; LngCEL; McGEWB; MouLC 3; NewC; NewCol 75; NinCLC 27; OxCEng 67, 85, 95; PenC ENG; RAdv 14, 13-1; RfGEnL 91; VicBrit; WebE&AL*

Clouzot, Henri-George
French. Director
Noted for suspense films *The Wage of Fear,* 1953; *The Diaboliques,* 1954.
b. Nov 20, 1907 in Niort, France
d. Jan 12, 1977 in Paris, France
Source: *BiDFilm; DcFM; FilmgC; IntMPA 75; IntWW 74, 75; MovMk; NewYTBS 77; ObitOF 79; OxCFilm; WhoWor 74; WorAl; WorEFlm*

Clovis I
German. Ruler
Barbarian king who conquered northern Gaul, 481; first barbarian ruler to convert to Catholicism.
b. 466
d. Nov 27, 511 in Paris, Gaul
Source: *EncEarC; OxCFr; REn*

Club Nouveau
[Denzil Foster; Jay King; Thomas McElroy; Samuelle Prater; Valerie Watson]
American. Music Group
Dance band, formed 1980s; their hit "Lean on Me," 1987, sold over six million copies.
Source: *BioIn 15; Dun&B 88, 90*

Clurman, Harold Edgar
American. Author, Director
Best known for award-winning film *A Member of the Wedding,* 1950.
b. Sep 18, 1901 in New York, New York
d. Sep 9, 1980 in New York, New York
Source: *AmAu&B; BiE&WWA; BioIn 2, 5, 8, 9, 10, 11; ConAu 1R, 2NR, 101;*

CurBio 59, 80N; EncWT; IntWW 74, 75, 76, 77, 78, 79, 80; NewYTBS 79; NotNAT, A; OxCThe 67; PenC AM; PlP&P; REnAL; WhAm 7; WhoAm 78, 80; WhoAmJ 80; WhoWor 74, 76, 78; WorEFlm

Cluytens, Andre
Belgian. Conductor
First French conductor to perform at Bayreuth, 1955; led Belgium Orchestra, 1960-67.
b. Mar 26, 1905 in Antwerp, Belgium
d. Jun 3, 1967 in Paris, France
Source: *Baker 78, 84, 92; BioIn 4, 7, 8, 11; IntDcOp; MusSN; NewAmDM; NewEOp 71; NewGrDO; OxDcOp; PenDiMP; WhAm 4*

Clyde, Andy
American. Actor, Comedian
Played in Mack Sennett two-reel comedies, later as Hopalong Cassidy's sidekick; TV series "No Time for Sergeants," 1960s.
b. Mar 25, 1892 in Blairgowrie, Scotland
d. May 18, 1967 in Los Angeles, California
Source: *BioIn 7, 8; EncAFC; Film 2; FilmgC; HalFC 84, 88; LegTOT; MotPP; ObitOF 79; QDrFCA 92; TwYS; Vers A; WhoHol B; WhScrn 74, 77, 83*

Clyde, Colin Campbell, Baron
English. Army Officer
Victorious general at Balaklava, Crimean War, 1854; suppressed Indian mutiny, 1857.
b. Oct 20, 1792 in Glasgow, Scotland
d. Aug 14, 1863 in London, England
Source: *ApCAB; BioIn 3; CelCen; DcBiPP; DcInB; LinLib S; NewCol 75; WebBD 83*

Clymer, George
American. Merchant, Politician
Signed US Constitution, 1787, Declaration of Independence; member, first Congress, 1789-91.
b. Mar 16, 1739 in Philadelphia, Pennsylvania
d. Jan 24, 1813 in Morrisville, Pennsylvania
Source: *AmBi; ApCAB; BiAUS; BiDrAC; BiDrUSC 89; BioIn 7, 8, 9, 15, 16; DcAmB; Drake; EncAR; EncCRAm; HarEnUS; NatCAB 3; TwCBDA; WhAm HS; WhAmP; WhAmRev*

Coachman, Alice
American. Track Athlete
First black woman to win an Olympic gold medal in track and field, 1948.
b. Nov 9, 1923 in Albany, Georgia
Source: *BlkOlyM; EncWomS; NotBlAW 1; WhoSpor; WhoTr&F 73*

Coanda, Henri Marie
French. Engineer, Inventor
Designed rudimentary jet plane, 1910.
b. Jun 6, 1885 in Bucharest, Romania
d. Nov 25, 1972
Source: *CurBio 56, 73; NewYTBE 72*

Coasters, The
[Carl Gardner; Cornelius Gunter; Billy Guy; Adolph Jacobs]
American. Music Group
Rock 'n' roll band known for humorous, off-beat songs: "Yakety-Yak," 1958; "Charlie Brown," 1959; "Love Potion No. 9," 1971.
Source: *AmPS A; BiDAmM; ConMus 5; DcTwCCu 5; EncPR&S 74, 89; EncRk 88; EncRkSt; HarEnR 86; IlEncRk; NewAmDM; NewGrDA 86; OxCPMus; PenEncP; RkOn 74, 84; RolSEnR 83; SoulM; WhoHol 92; WhoRock 81*

Coates, Albert
English. Conductor, Composer
Led Russian Imperial Opera, from 1911; American debut, 1920; operas include *Pickwick,* 1936.
b. Apr 23, 1882 in Saint Petersburg, Russia
d. Dec 11, 1953 in Cape Town, South Africa
Source: *Baker 78, 84, 92; BioIn 1, 3, 4, 11; IntDcOp; MusSN; NewAmDM; NewEOp 71; NewGrDO; ObitT 1951; OxCMus; OxDcOp; PenDiMP*

Coates, Edith
English. Singer
Founding member of Covent Garden Opera Co., 1937.
b. May 31, 1908 in Lincoln, England
d. Jan 7, 1983 in Worthing, England
Source: *AnObit 1983; Baker 84; BioIn 2, 3, 5, 13; IntWWM 77; InWom; NewYTBS 83; OxDcOp; PenDiMP; Who 74, 82, 83; WhoMus 72*

Coates, Robert Myron
American. Author, Critic
Novels include *Eater of Darkness,* 1929; *Wisteria Cottage,* 1948.
b. Apr 6, 1897 in New Haven, Connecticut
d. Feb 8, 1973 in New York, New York
Source: *AmAu&B; AmNov; Au&Wr 71; BioIn 2, 4, 5, 9, 12; CnDAL; ConAu 5R; ConNov 72; DcLEL; IntAu&W 76, 77; NewYTBE 73; OxCAmL 65; PenC AM; REn; REnAL; TwCA, SUP; WhAm 5, 10*

Coats, Dan(iel R)
American. Politician
Rep. senator from IN, 1989—.
b. May 16, 1943 in Jackson, Michigan
Source: *AlmAP 92; BioIn 16; CngDr 89, 91, 93, 95; PolsAm 84; WhoAm 90; WhoAmL 85; WhoAmP 91; WhoMW 92; WhoWor 91*

Coats, James
Scottish. Manufacturer
Organized factory to make thread, 1826; became J P Coats, Ltd., 1890.
b. 1774
d. 1857

Coatsworth, Elizabeth Jane
American. Poet, Children's Author
Won Newbery Award for *The Cat Who Went to Heaven,* 1930.
b. May 31, 1893 in Buffalo, New York
d. Aug 31, 1986 in Nobleboro, Maine
Source: *AmAu&B; AmNov; AnCL; Au&ICB; AuBYP 2, 3; BioIn 14, 15, 16, 19, 20; BkCL; ConAu 4NR, 5R; MajAI; MorBMP; OxCAmL 65, 95; REnAL; SmATA 2; TwCA SUP; TwCChW 95; TwCYAW; WhoAm 86*

Cobain, Kurt
[Nirvana]
American. Musician
Founded musical group Nirvana, 1987.
b. Feb 20, 1967 in Hoquiam, Washington
d. Apr 8, 1994 in Seattle, Washington
Source: *BioIn 19, 20, 21; News 94, 94-3; OnThGG*

Cobb, Arnett Cleophus
American. Jazz Musician, Composer
Noted tenor sax star of 1940s-50s; with Lionel Hampton, 1943-47.
b. Aug 10, 1918 in Houston, Texas
d. Mar 24, 1989 in Houston, Texas
Source: *BiDJaz; BioIn 10, 12, 15, 16; CmpEPM; DrBlPA, 90; FacFETw; InB&W 85; NewGrDJ 88; PenEncP; WhoJazz 72*

Cobb, Irvin Shrewsbury
American. Journalist, Author
Noted humor columnist, after-dinner speaker; wrote *Speaking of Operations,* 1915; *Old Judge Priest,* 1916.
b. Jun 23, 1876 in Paducah, Kentucky
d. Mar 10, 1944 in New York, New York
Source: *AmAu&B; ApCAB X; BiDAmJo; BiDAmNC; BioIn 1, 2, 3, 4, 6, 9, 10; CnDAL; ConAmL; CurBio 44; DcAmB S3; EncAB-A 15; EncMys; EvLB; Film 1; JrnUS; LiHiK; LinLib S; NatCAB 18; NotNAT B; ObitOF 79; OxCAmL 65; REn; REnAL; TwCA SUP; WhAm 2; WhScrn 77*

Cobb, Jerrie
American. Pilot
First woman chosen for astronaut program, 1960; Woman of the Year in Aviation, 1959.
b. Mar 5, 1931 in Norman, Oklahoma
Source: *BioIn 7, 17; CurBio 61; InWom, SUP; WhoAmW 74; WhoSSW 73*

Cobb, Jewel Plummer
American. Biologist, University Administrator
Pres., CA State U, Fullerton, 1981-90; research interest, cancer cell biology.
b. Jan 17, 1924 in Chicago, Illinois
Source: *AfrAmBi 1; AmMWSc 73P, 76P, 79, 82, 86, 89, 92, 95; BioIn 13, 20; BlksScM; Ebony 1; InB&W 85; LEduc 74; NotBlAW 1; NotTwCS; NotWoLS; WhoAfA 96; WhoAm 74, 76, 78, 82, 84, 86, 88, 92, 95, 96, 97; WhoAmW 70, 72, 74, 79, 81, 85, 91, 93; WhoBlA 90, 92,*

94; WhoMedH; WhoWest 84, 87, 89, 92, 94

Cobb, Joe
[Our Gang]
"Fat Joe"; "Wheezer"
American. Actor
First fat boy of Our Gang comedies, 1922.
b. Nov 7, 1917 in Shawnee, Oklahoma
Source: *EncAFC; Film 2; TwYS; WhoHol 92, A*

Cobb, John Rhodes
Scottish. Auto Racer, Boat Racer
First to achieve 400 mph on land, 1947; killed in speedboat accident on Loch Ness.
b. Dec 2, 1899 in Esher, England
d. Sep 29, 1952 in Inverness, Scotland
Source: *BioIn 3, 8; DcNaB 1951*

Cobb, Lee J
[Leo Jacob Cobb]
American. Actor
Created role of Willy Loman in *Death of a Salesman* on Broadway, 1949.
b. Dec 9, 1911 in New York, New York
d. Feb 11, 1976 in Los Angeles, California
Source: *BiDFilm; BiE&WWA; CmMov; CurBio 60; FamA&A; FilmgC; IntMPA 75, 76; MotPP; MovMk; OxCFilm; WhAm 6, 7; WhoAm 74, 76; WorAl; WorEFlm*

Cobb, Ty(rus Raymond)
"The Georgia Peach"
American. Baseball Player
Outfielder, Detroit, 1905-26; considered greatest offensive player of all time; won 12 batting titles; Hall of Fame, 1936.
b. Dec 18, 1886 in Narrows, Georgia
d. Jul 17, 1961 in Atlanta, Georgia
Source: *AmDec 1920; Ballpl 90; BiDAmSp BB; BioIn 1, 2, 3, 4, 5, 6, 7, 8, 9, 10, 11, 12, 13, 14, 15, 16, 17, 18, 19, 20, 21; CurBio 51, 61; DcAmB S7; EncAB-H 1996; FacFETw; LegTOT; LinLib S; OxCAmH; WebAB 74, 79; WhAm 4, HSA; WhoProB 73; WhScrn 77, 83; WorAl; WorAlBi*

Cobb, Vicki
American. Children's Author, Scientist
Wrote award-winning children's TV series, "The Science Game," 1972.
b. Aug 19, 1938 in New York, New York
Source: *AuBYP 2S, 3; BioIn 11, 18, 19; ChlBkCr; ChlLR 2; ConAu 14NR, 33R; FifBJA; IntAu&W 89, 91, 93; MajAI; SmATA 6AS, 8, 69; WrDr 76, 80, 82, 84, 86, 88, 90, 92, 94, 96*

Cobb, Will D
American. Songwriter
Often collaborated with Gus Edwards; hits include "School Days"; "Sunbonnet Sue."
b. Jul 6, 1876 in Philadelphia, Pennsylvania
d. Jan 20, 1930 in New York, New York
Source: *ASCAP 66; BioIn 4*

Cobb, William Montague
American. Civil Rights Leader, Educator
President, NAACP, 1976-82; editor, *Journal of National Medical Assn.*, 1949-77.
b. Oct 12, 1904 in Washington, District of Columbia
d. Nov 20, 1990 in Washington, District of Columbia
Source: *AmMWSc 73P, 73S, 76P, 79, 82, 86, 89, 92; BioIn 2, 7, 11, 13, 16, 17, 18, 20; BlksScM; BlueB 76; InB&W 80; NotTwCS; WhAm 10; WhoAm 74, 76, 78, 80, 82, 84, 86, 88, 90; WhoBlA 75, 77, 80, 85, 88; WhoWor 80, 89, 91*

Cobbett, William
[Peter Porcupine]
English. Journalist, Author
Wrote *Rural Rides*, 1860, pro-British pamphlets while in US.
b. Mar 19, 1762 in Farnham, England
d. Jun 18, 1835 in London, England
Source: *Alli; ApCAB; AtlBL; BbD; BbtC; BiD&SB; BiDLA, SUP; BlmGEL; BritAu 19; CamGEL; CarSB; CasWL; CelCen; Chambr 2; CnDAL; DcAmB; DcAmC; DcAmSR; DcBiPP; DcEnA; DcEnL; DcEuL; DcLB 43; DcLEL; Drake; EvLB; HarEnUS; LngCEL; MouLC 3; NewC; OxCAmL 65; OxCEng 67, 85; PenC ENG; REn; WebE&AL; WhAm HS; WhDW*

Cobbs, Price M(ashaw)
American. Psychiatrist
Co-authored, with William H. Grier, *Black Rage*, 1968, a portrayal of the anger and frustration plaguing black people in the United States.
b. Nov 2, 1928 in Los Angeles, California
Source: *BiDrAPA 77; BlksScM; InB&W 85; WhoAfA 96; WhoAm 76, 78, 80, 86, 88, 90, 92, 94, 95, 97; WhoBlA 85, 88, 90, 92, 94; WhoWest 74, 76, 78, 80, 82, 84*

Cobden, Richard
English. Political Leader, Economist
Free trade advocate, opposed Crimean War; leader of Anti-Cow-Law League, 1839-46.
b. Jun 3, 1804 in Sussex, England
d. Apr 2, 1865 in London, England
Source: *Alli, SUP; BiD&SB; BiDMoPL; BioIn 2, 3, 4, 7, 8, 10, 15, 16, 17, 20; BritAu 19; CelCen; DcAmSR; DcBiPP; DcNaB; HisDBrE; HisWorL; LinLib L, S; McGEWB; NewC; OxCEng 85, 95; REn; VicBrit; WhDW; WhoEc 81, 86*

Cobden-Sanderson, Thomas James
English. Printer
Master bookbinder; operated Doves Press with Emery Walker, 1900-16.
b. Dec 2, 1840 in Alnwick, England
d. Sep 7, 1922 in Hammersmith, England
Source: *AntBDN B; BioIn 1, 18; DcArts; DcNaB 1922; LngCTC; PenDiDA 89*

Cobham, Alan John, Sir
English. Aviator
Early supporter of long-distance air travel; developed a system of aerial refueling of aircraft.
b. May 6, 1894 in London, England
d. Oct 21, 1973 in Bournemouth, England
Source: *BioIn 4, 10, 12, 15; ConAu X; DcNaB 1971; InSci; ObitOF 79; SmATA X; WhE&EA; WhoLA*

Cobham, Billy
American. Jazz Musician, Composer
Albums include *Flight Time*, 1981.
b. May 16, 1944, Panama
Source: *BioIn 14, 15, 16; ConMuA 80A; DrBlPA, 90; EncJzS; EncJzS; HarEnR 86; IlEncRk; InB&W 80; LegTOT; NewGrDA 86; NewGrDJ 88, 94; PenEncP; RolSEnR 83; WhoRocM 82*

Cobleigh, Ira Underwood
American. Author, Economist
Has written many books on money and investment.
b. Dec 25, 1903 in Derby, Connecticut
Source: *ConAu 81; WhoE 74*

Coburn, Charles Douville
American. Actor, Manager
Won Oscar for *The More the Merrier*, 1943.
b. Jun 19, 1877 in Savannah, Georgia
d. Aug 30, 1961 in New York, New York
Source: *BiDFilm; CamGWoT; CurBio 44, 61; FilmgC; MotPP; MovMk; ObitOF 79; OxCFilm; OxCThe 67, 83; Vers A; WhAm 4; WhScrn 77, 83; WorAl; WorEFlm*

Coburn, D(onald) L(ee)
American. Dramatist
Won Pulitzer, 1978, for *The Gin Game*.
b. Aug 4, 1938 in Baltimore, Maryland
Source: *ConAu 89; ConTFT 1; NatPD 81; OxCAmL 83, 95; VarWW 85; WhoAm 80, 82, 84, 86, 88, 90, 92, 94, 95, 96, 97; WhoEnt 92*

Coburn, James
American. Actor
Starred in *Our Man Flint*, 1966; *In Like Flint*, 1967.
b. Aug 31, 1928 in Laurel, Nebraska
Source: *BiDFilm, 94; BioIn 7, 8, 11, 17; BkPepl; CelR; ConTFT 3; DcArts; FilmgC; HalFC 84, 88; IntDcF 1-3, 2-3; IntMPA 75, 76, 77, 78, 79, 81, 82, 84, 86, 88, 92, 94, 96; IntWW 79, 80, 81, 82, 83, 89, 91, 93; ItaFilm; LegTOT; MotPP; MovMk; OxCFilm; WhoAm 74, 76, 78, 80, 82, 84, 86, 88, 90, 92, 94, 95, 96, 97; WhoEnt 92A; WhoHol 92, A; WorAl; WorAlBi; WorEFlm*

Coburn, Julia
American. Fashion Editor
Fashion editor, *Ladies Home Journal*, 1932-37.
Source: *WhoAm 78; WhoAmW 72, 74*

Coca, Imogene Fernandez y
American. Comedian, Actor
Appeared with Sid Caesar in "Your Show of Shows," 1950-52; had own show, "Grindl," 1963-64.
b. Nov 19, 1908 in Philadelphia, Pennsylvania
Source: *BiE&WWA; BioIn 15, 16; BioNews 74; ConTFT 2, 9; CurBio 51; EncAFC; EncMT; FilmgC; FunnyW; HalFC 88; IntMPA 86, 92; InWom SUP; LesBEnT, 92; NotNAT; WhoAm 84; WhoHol A; WhoThe 81; WhoWor 74*

Cochet, Henri
[The Four Musketeers]
French. Tennis Player
Won five French singles, two Wimbledons as part of famed Four Musketeers who dominated French tennis, 1922-32.
b. Dec 14, 1901 in Lyons, France
d. Apr 1, 1987 in Saint-Germain-en-Laye, France
Source: *AnObit 1987; BioIn 11, 15; BuCMET; WhoFr 79*

Cochin, Charles Nicholas
"The Son"; "The Younger"
French. Type Designer
His 1500 works include book illustrations, pencil, crayon portraits, engraved f rontispieces.
b. Feb 22, 1715 in Paris, France
d. Apr 29, 1790 in Paris, France
Source: *NewCol 75; WebBD 83*

Cochise
American. Native American Chief
Waged war against US Army, 1861-72.
b. 1815 in Arizona
d. Jun 9, 1874 in Arizona
Source: *BioIn 2, 3, 5, 9, 11; FilmgC; McGEWB; NewCol 75; OxCAmH; REnAW; WebAB 74; WhAm HS*

Cochran, Barbara Ann
American. Skier
Won gold medal in women's slalom, 1972 Olympics.
b. Jan 4, 1951 in Claremont, New Hampshire
Source: *BiDAmSp OS; BioIn 10, 11; EncWomS; InWom SUP; WhoSpor*

Cochran, C(harles) B(lake)
"Britain's Greatest Showman"
English. Impresario
Prolific producer of musical revues, 1920s-30s; agent for Sarah Bernhardt, Harry Houdini.
b. Sep 25, 1872 in Lindfield, England
d. Jan 31, 1951 in London, England
Source: *BiDD; BioIn 2, 8, 14, 15; CamGWoT; CurBio 40, 51; DcArts; DcNaB 1951; EncMT; GrBr; LinLib S; NotNAT B; ObitOF 79; OxCThe 67, 83; WhE&EA; WhLit; WhThe*

Cochran, Eddie
American. Singer, Songwriter
Had British hit single "Three Steps to Heaven," 1960; albums include *Words and Music*, 1982.
b. Oct 3, 1938 in Oklahoma City, Oklahoma
d. Apr 17, 1960 in London, England
Source: *BiDAmM; BioIn 11, 13, 21; DcArts; EncPR&S 89; EncRk 88; EncRkSt; HarEnR 86; LegTOT; NewAmDM; NewGrDA 86; OnThGG; OxCPMus; PenEncP; RkOn 74, 84; RolSEnR 83; WhoRock 81; WhScrn 77*

Cochran, Jacqueline
[Mrs. Floyd B Odlum]
American. Aviator, Journalist
Organized Women's Air Force Service (WASP), 1943; first woman to break sonic barrier, 1953.
b. May 11, 1910 in Pensacola, Florida
d. Aug 9, 1980 in Indio, California
Source: *AmAu&B; BioIn 2, 3, 4, 5, 6, 7, 10, 11, 12, 15, 17, 21; ConAu 101; ContDcW 89; CurBio 40, 63, 80, 80N; DcAmB S10; GoodHs; GrLiveH; HerW, 84; IntWW 78; InWom SUP; LibW; NewYTBS 80; WebAB 74, 79; WebAMB; WhoAm 78; WhoAmW 75; WhoSpor; WomFir; WomStre; WorAl; WorAlBi*

Cochran, Johnnie
American. Lawyer
Defended former football star O. J. Simpson in a murder trial, 1995.
b. Oct 2, 1937 in Shreveport, Louisiana
Source: *ConBlB 11; News 96, 96-1*

Cochran, Roy
American. Track Athlete
Hurdler; won gold medals, 400-meter hurdles, 1,600-meter relay, 1948 Olympics.
b. Jan 16, 1919 in Richton, Mississippi
Source: *WhoTr&F 73*

Cochran, Steve
American. Actor
Discovered by Mae West; appeared with her in film *Diamond Lil*, 1949.
b. May 25, 1917 in Eureka, California
d. Jun 15, 1965, Guatemala
Source: *BiE&WWA; BioIn 10; FilmgC; GangFlm; HalFC 84, 88; HolP 40; ItaFilm; MotPP; MovMk; WhoHol B; WhScrn 74, 77, 83; WorEFlm*

Cochran, Thad
American. Politician
Rep. senator from MS, 1978—.
b. Dec 7, 1937 in Pontotoc, Mississippi
Source: *AlmAP 78, 80, 82, 84, 88, 92, 96; BioIn 11, 14; CngDr 77, 79, 81, 83, 85, 87, 89, 91, 93, 95; IntWW 79, 80, 81, 82, 83, 89, 91, 93; NewYTBS 84; PolsAm 84; WhoAm 74, 76, 78, 80, 82, 84, 86, 88, 90, 92, 94, 95, 96, 97; WhoAmP 83, 85, 87, 89, 91, 93, 95; WhoGov 77; WhoSSW 75, 76, 78, 80, 82, 84, 86, 88, 91, 93, 95, 97; WhoWor 80, 82, 87, 89, 91*

Cochrane, Edward Lull
American. Government Official, Naval Officer
Vice-admiral; chm., Federal Maritime Board, 1950-52.
b. Mar 18, 1892 in Mare Island, California
d. Nov 14, 1959 in New Haven, Connecticut
Source: *BiDWWGF; BioIn 1, 2, 3, 5, 6; CurBio 51, 60; InSci; NatCAB 46; WhAm 3*

Cochrane, Mickey
[Gordon Stanley Cochrane]
"Black Mike"
American. Baseball Player, Baseball Manager
Catcher, 1925-37; player/mgr., Detroit, 1934-37; won two pennants; Hall of Fame, 1947.
b. Apr 6, 1903 in Bridgewater, Massachusetts
d. Jun 28, 1962 in Lake Forest, Illinois
Source: *Ballpl 90; BiDAmSp BB; BioIn 1, 2, 3, 4, 5, 6, 7, 8, 9, 10, 13, 14, 15, 17; DcAmB S7; LegTOT; WhoProB 73; WhoSpor*

Cockburn, Alexander James Edmund, Sir
English. Lawyer
Lord Chief Justice of England, 1859-80.
b. Dec 24, 1802 in Langton, England
d. Nov 21, 1880 in London, England
Source: *Alli SUP; CelCen; DcNaB; HarEnUS; OxCLaw*

Cockburn, Claud
[Francis Claud Cockburn; James Helvick; Frank Pitcairn]
British. Journalist
Published *The Week* newssheet, 1933-46.
b. Apr 12, 1904 in Peking
d. Dec 15, 1981 in Cork, Ireland
Source: *AnObit 1981; Au&Wr 71; BioIn 4, 5, 6, 8, 10, 12, 13; ConAu 102, 105; DcNaB 1981; NewYTBS 81; ScF&FL 1, 92; Who 74, 82; WorAu 1950*

Cockcroft, John Douglas, Sir
English. Physicist
Directed Great Britain's atomic energy research establishment at Harwell; shared Nobel Prize in physics, 1951, with ETS Walton.
b. May 27, 1897 in Todmoor, England
d. Sep 18, 1967 in Cambridge, England
Source: *AsBiEn; BiESc; BioIn 1, 2, 3, 4, 5, 6, 8, 12; CamDcSc; DcNaB 1961; FacFETw; GrBr; InSci; LarDcSc; LinLib S; McGEWB; McGMS 80; ObitOF 79; ObitT 1961; WhAm 4; WhDW; WhoNob, 90, 95; WhWW-II; WorAl; WorInv*

Cocker, Joe
[Robert John Cocker]
English. Musician, Singer
Recorded "Up Where We Belong" from *An Officer and a Gentleman,* with Jennifer Warnes, 1983.
b. May 20, 1944 in Sheffield, England
Source: *Baker 84, 92; BkPepl; ConMus 4; EncPR&S 74, 89; EncRk 88; EncRkSt; HarEnR 86; IlEncRk; LegTOT; OxCPMus; PenEncP; RkOn 78, 84; RolSEnR 83; WhoAm 94, 95, 96, 97; WhoEnt 92; WhoRock 81; WhoRocM 82; WorAl; WorAlBi*

Cockerell, Christopher Sydney, Sir
English. Engineer
Invented the hovercraft, 1954; formed Hovercraft Ltd, 1957.
b. Jun 1910 in Cambridge, England
Source: *BlueB 76; CamDcSc; IntWW 74, 83, 91, 93; IntYB 82; LarDcSc; WhDW; Who 83, 92, 94; WhoWor 74, 91*

Cockrell, Ewing
American. Judge
Founder, first pres., US Federation of Justice, 1929; devoted to world peace.
b. May 28, 1874 in Warrensburg, Missouri
d. Jan 21, 1962 in Washington, District of Columbia
Source: *BioIn 2, 6; CurBio 51, 62; WhAm 4*

Coco, James Emil
American. Actor
Oscar nomination for *Only When I Laugh,* 1981.
b. Mar 21, 1929 in New York, New York
d. Feb 25, 1987 in New York, New York
Source: *ConNews 87-2; ConTFT 3; CurBio 74, 87; FilmgC; IntMPA 82; NewYTBE 70; NotNAT; WhoAm 86; WhoE 74; WhoHol A; WhoThe 77*

Cocteau, Jean
French. Author, Director, Poet
Wrote *Les Enfants Terribles,* 1924; *Thomas L'Imposteur,* 1923.
b. Jul 5, 1889 in Maisons-Lafitte, France
d. Oct 12, 1963 in Paris, France
Source: *AtlBL; Benet 87, 96; BiDD; BiDFilm, 94; BioIn 12, 13, 14, 15, 16, 17, 19, 20, 21; CamGWoT; CasWL; ClDMEL 47; CnMD; CnMWL; CnThe; ConAu P-2; ConLC 1, 8, 15, 16, 43; CyWA 58, 89; DcArts; DcFM; DcLB 65; DcTwCCu 2; EncFash; EncPaPR 91; EncWL 2, 3; EncWT; EuWr 10; EvEuW; FilmgC; GrFLW; GuFrLit 1; HalFC 84, 88; IntDcB; IntDcF 1-2, 2-2; ItaFilm; LegTOT; LinLib L, S; LngCTC; MagSWL; MajMD 2; MajTwCW; MakMC; McGEWB; McGEWD 72, 84; MetOEnc; MiSFD 9N; ModFrL; ModRL; ModWD; MovMk; NotNAT B; Novels; ObitT 1961; OxCEng 67, 85, 95; OxCFilm; OxCFr; OxCThe 67; OxDcArt; OxDcOp; PenC EUR; PhDcTCA 77; RAdv 14, 13-2, 13-3; REn; REnWD; TwCA, SUP; TwCWr; WhAm 4; WhDW; WhoGrA 62; WhoTwCL; WhScrn 77, 83; WhThe; WorAl; WorAlBi; WorEFlm; WorFDir 1; WorLitC*

Coddington, William
American. Colonial Figure
A founder of Rhode Island; defended Anne Hutchinson; founded Newport, 1639.
b. 1601 in Boston, England
d. Nov 1, 1678 in Newport, Rhode Island
Source: *Alli; AmBi; ApCAB; BiDrACR; DcAmAu; DcAmB; DcNAA; DcNaB; Drake; EncCRAm; HarEnUS; NatCAB 7, 10; OxCAmH; TwCBDA; WhAm HS*

Codrington, Edward, Sir
British. Naval Officer
Commanded British, Russian ships in destroying Turkish fleet at *Navarino,* 1827.
b. 1770
d. 1851
Source: *CelCen; DcBiPP; DcNaB; HarEnMi; NewCol 75; OxCShps; WhoMilH 76*

Codron, Michael
English. Producer
Won Tony, 1984, for *The Real Thing.*
b. Jun 8, 1930 in London, England
Source: *CamGWoT; ConTFT 2; VarWW 85; Who 92; WhoThe 72, 77, 81; WhoWor 91*

Cody, Buffalo Bill
[William Frederick Cody]
American. Entertainer, Pioneer
Buffalo hunter who organized Buffalo Bill's Wild West Show, touring US, Europe, 1883-1901.
b. Feb 26, 1846 in Scout County, Iowa
d. Jan 10, 1917 in Denver, Colorado
Source: *AmAu&B; AmBi; ApCAB; BenetAL 91; BioIn 1, 2, 3, 4, 5, 6, 7, 8, 9, 10, 11, 12, 13, 14, 15, 16, 17, 18, 20; DcAmB; DcCathB; DcNAA; EncAAH; EncAB-H 1974, 1996; EncNAB; FilmgC; HalFC 84, 88; HarEnUS; HsB&A; LinLib L, S; MedHR 94; MorMA; NotNAT B; OxCAmH; OxCAmL 65, 83, 95; OxCAmT 84; OxCFilm; OxCThe 67, 83; RComAH; REn; REnAL; REnAW; TwCBDA; WebAB 74, 79; WebAMB; WhAm 1; WhDW; WhNaAH; WhoHol B; WhScrn 77; WorAl*

Cody, Iron Eyes
American. Actor
Cherokee who wept in TV ecology ads; films include *Grayeagle,* 1977.
b. Apr 3, 1915 in Oklahoma
Source: *ConTFT 1; FilmEn; HalFC 88; MotPP; WhoAm 76, 78, 80, 82, 84, 86, 88, 92; WhoEnt 92; WhoHol A; WhoWor 82, 84, 87*

Cody, John Patrick
American. Religious Leader
Archbishop of Chicago, 1965-82; involved in scandal concerning misuse of church funds, 1981.
b. Dec 24, 1907 in Saint Louis, Missouri
d. Apr 25, 1982 in Chicago, Illinois
Source: *AmCath 80; AnObit 1982; BioIn 7, 10, 11, 12, 13, 19; BlueB 76; CurBio 65, 82, 82N; DcAmReB 2; IntWW 78; NewYTBS 82; RelLAm 91; WhoAm 82; WhoMW 82; WhoRel 77; WhoWor 74*

Cody, Lew
[Louis Joseph Cote]
American. Comedian
Played leading, supporting roles in films: *Adam and Evil,* 1927; *Wine, Women, and Song,* 1934.
b. Feb 22, 1887 in Waterville, Maine
d. May 31, 1934 in Beverly Hills, California
Source: *Film 1; FilmgC; MotPP; MovMk; NotNAT B; TwYS; WhoHol B; WhScrn 74, 77, 83*

Coe, David Allan
American. Songwriter, Singer
Wrote "Take This Job and Shove It," 1978 sung by Johnny Paycheck.
b. Sep 6, 1939 in Akron, Ohio
Source: *BioIn 11, 14, 16; ConMus 4; EncFCWM 83; HarEnCM 87; LegTOT; NewGrDA 86; PenEncP; RolSEnR 83*

Coe, Frederick H
American. Producer, Director
Pioneer TV producer; launched over 500 hour-long teleplays, 1940s-50s; directed Broadway hits *Two for the Seesaw; Miracle Worker.*
b. Dec 23, 1914 in Alligator, Mississippi
d. Apr 29, 1979 in Los Angeles, California
Source: *BiE&WWA; ConAu 85; CurBio 59, 79; FilmgC; IntMPA 79; NewYTBS 79; NewYTET; NotNAT; WhoAm 74; WhoThe 77*

Coe, Sebastian Newbold
English. Track Athlete
First to hold world records in mile, 800-meter, and 1,500-meters, 1979; only man to win two Olympic gold medals in 1,500-meters, 1980, 1984.
b. Sep 29, 1956 in Sheffield, England
Source: *BioIn 13, 14; CurBio 80; IntWW 81, 82, 83, 89, 91, 93; NewYTBS 79, 80, 81; Who 88, 90, 92, 94; WorAlBi*

Coen, Ethan
American. Filmmaker
With brother, Joel, produced box office success *Raising Arizona,* 1987; won 1991 Palme D'Or for *Barton Fink.*
b. 1958 in Minneapolis, Minnesota
Source: *BiDFilm 94; BioIn 14, 15; ConAu 126; ConTFT 7, 15; CurBio 94; IntAu&W 91, 93; IntMPA 88, 92, 94; LegTOT; News 92, 92-1; WhoAm 92, 94, 95, 96, 97; WhoEnt 92; WhoWor 95, 96, 97*

Coen, Jan Pieterszoon
Dutch. Statesman
Governor-general of Dutch East India Co., 1617-29.
b. Jan 8, 1587 in Hoorn, Netherlands
d. Sep 21, 1629 in Batavia, Dutch East Indies
Source: *BioIn 4, 12; McGEWB*

Coen, Joel
American. Filmmaker
With brother, Ethan, produced box office success *Raising Arizona,* 1987; won 1991 Palme D'Or for *Barton Fink.*
b. 1955 in Minneapolis, Minnesota
Source: *BiDFilm 94; BioIn 14, 15; ConAu 126; ConTFT 7, 15; CurBio 94; IntAu&W 91, 93; IntMPA 88, 92; LegTOT; MiSFD 9; News 92, 92-1; WhoAm 92, 94, 95, 96, 97; WhoEnt 92; WhoWor 95, 96, 97*

Coetzee, J(ohn) M
South African. Author
Political novels include *From the Heart of the Country,* 1977.
b. Feb 9, 1940 in Cape Town, South Africa
Source: *BioIn 13, 14, 15, 16; CamGLE; ConLC 23, 35, 66; ConNov 91; CurBio 87; CyWA 89; EncWB; FacFETw; MajTwCW; PostFic; RAdv 13-2; WorAu 1975; WrDr 92*

Coeur, Jacques
French. Merchant, Diplomat
Wealthy, influential financial adviser to Charles VII; falsely condemned, imprisoned.
b. 1395 in Bourges, France
d. Nov 25, 1456 in Chios, Ottoman Empire
Source: *BioIn 1, 2, 4, 5, 7, 9, 10, 14; MediFra; NewCol 75; WebBD 83*

Coffey, Paul (Douglas)
Canadian. Hockey Player
Defenseman, Edmonton, 1980-87, Pittsburgh, 1987-92, Detroit, 1993-96; Hartford, 1996; Philadelphia, 1996—; holds NHL records for most goals in season and career points by a defenseman; won Norris Trophy, 1985, 1986, 1995.
b. Jun 1, 1961 in Weston, Ontario, Canada
Source: *BioIn 14, 15; ConNews 85-4; HocEn; HocReg 87; WhoAm 88, 90, 92, 94, 95, 96, 97; WhoMW 96*

Coffield, Kelly
American. Actor
Regular cast member on TV show "In Living Color," 1990—.

Coffin, Charles Albert
American. Business Executive
Developed electric industry in US; formed General Electric Co., 1892, president until 1913.
b. Dec 1844 in Somerset County, Maine
d. Nov 9, 1926 in Portland, Oregon
Source: *BiDAmBL 83; BioIn 1, 10; DcAmB; NatCAB 20; WhAm 1; WorAl*

Coffin, Henry Sloane
American. Clergy
Presbyterian leader in NY Presbytery, 40 yrs; wrote *Religion Yesterday and Today,* 1940.
b. Jan 5, 1877 in New York, New York
d. Nov 25, 1954 in Lakeville, Connecticut
Source: *AmAu&B; ApCAB X; BiDAmM; BioIn 1, 2, 3, 4, 10; CurBio 44, 55; DcAmB S5; DcAmReB 1, 2; LinLib S; LuthC 75; NatCAB 55; ObitOF 79; RelLAm 91; WhAm 3*

Coffin, Howard Earle
American. Engineer
Designed Chalmers, Hudson autos; with Roy Chapin founded Hudson Motor Car Co., 1909.
b. Sep 6, 1873 in West Milton, Ohio
d. Nov 21, 1937 in Sea Island, Georgia
Source: *BiDAmBL 83; BioIn 4; DcAmB S2; NatCAB 16, 30; WebAB 74, 79; WhAm 1*

Coffin, Levi
American. Abolitionist
Organized Underground Railroad in IN, 1826-47, in Cincinnati, 1847-60.
b. Oct 28, 1798 in New Garden, North Carolina
d. Sep 16, 1877 in Cincinnati, Ohio
Source: *ApCAB; BioIn 1, 2, 6, 8, 10; DcNAA; EncSoH; HarEnUS; IndAu 1816; McGEWB; NatCAB 12; OhA&B; TwCBDA; WebAB 74, 79*

Coffin, Robert Peter Tristram
American. Poet, Author, Biographer
Won 1935 Pulitzer for verse *Strange Holiness;* many books concern ME life.
b. Mar 18, 1892 in Brunswick, Maine
d. Oct 29, 1956 in Raleigh, North Carolina
Source: *AmAu&B; AnMV 1926; BioIn 1, 3, 4, 5, 6, 7, 8, 9, 11, 15; ChhPo, S1, S2, S3; CnDAL; ConAmA; DcAmB S5; DcLEL; LngCTC; NatCAB 45; OxCAmL 65; PenC AM; REn; REnAL; Str&VC; TwCA, SUP; WhAm 3; WhLit; WhNAA*

Coffin, William Sloan, Jr.
American. Clergy, Author, Social Reformer
Minister, NYC Presbyterian Riverside Church, 1977-87; leader, SANE/FREEZE, 1988—.
b. Jun 1, 1924 in New York, New York
Source: *BioIn 16; ConAu 103; CurBio 68, 80; EncAI&E; FacFETw; News 90; PolProf J; WhoAm 86; WhoWor 74; WorAlBi*

Coffroth, Jimmy
[James W Coffroth]
"Sunny Jim"
American. Boxing Promoter
Sponsored most of nation's major fights, 1890s-1900s.
b. 1873?
d. Feb 6, 1943 in San Diego, California
Source: *BioIn 10; WhoBox 74*

Coggan, Frederick Donald, Baron
English. Religious Leader
Archbishop of Canterbury, 1974-80; author *Sure Foundation,* 1981.
b. Oct 9, 1909 in London, England
Source: *BioIn 10, 12; BlueB 76; IntAu&W 76, 77, 82; IntWW 74, 75; Who 85; WhoAm 74, 76, 78, 80, 82, 84, 86, 88, 90; WhoRel 92; WhoWor 74, 76, 78, 95, 96, 97*

Coggeshall, L(owell) T(helwell)
American. Scientist
Specialized in prevention and cure of malaria; VP, U of Chicago, 1960-66.
b. May 7, 1901 in Indiana
d. Nov 11, 1987 in Foley, Alabama
Source: *AmMWSc 73P, 76P, 79; BioIn 4, 6; CurBio 63, 88, 88N; IndAu 1917; WhoSSW 73*

Coghill, Nevill Henry Kendall Aylmer
English. Author, Educator, Scholar
Chaucer authority who translated *Canterbury Tales* into modern English, 1951.
b. Apr 19, 1899 in Castletownshend, England
d. Nov 6, 1980 in Oxford, England
Source: *AnObit 1980; BlueB 76; ConAu 13R, 102; ConDr 73, 77D; DcLEL 1940; NewC; REn; WhoThe 77, 81*

Coghlan, Eamonn
"Cockie"
Irish. Track Athlete
Noted indoor miler who established world record, 1981.
b. 1953 in Dublin, Ireland
Source: *BioIn 11, 12, 13; NewYTBS 81*

Coghlan, Rose
Actor
Leading lady of NYC's Wallack Theater, 1877-85.
b. Mar 18, 1851 in Peterborough, England
d. Apr 2, 1932 in Harrison, New York
Source: *DcAmB S1; FamA&A; NatCAB 13; NotAW; NotNAT B; OxCAmT 84; OxCThe 67; PlP&P; WhAm 1; WhoHol B; WhScrn 74, 77; WhThe*

Cohan, George M(ichael)
American. Actor, Dramatist, Producer
"Wrote Over There," 1917; "Give My Regards to Broadway;" life story filmed: *Yankee Doodle Dandy,* 1942; received special Congressional Medal of Honor, 1940.

b. Jul 4, 1878 in Providence, Rhode Island
d. Nov 5, 1942 in New York, New York
Source: *AmAu&B; ASCAP 66; Baker 92; Benet 96; BiDAmM; BioIn 1, 2, 3, 4, 5, 6, 8, 9, 10, 11, 12, 13; CamGWoT; CnMD; CurBio 43; DcAmB S3; DcArts; EncAB-H 1974, 1996; EncMT; EncWT; FamA&A; Film 1; FilmgC; LinLib L, S; McGEWB; McGEWD 72; NatCAB 15; NewGrDO; OxCAmH; OxCAmL 95; OxCThe 67; REn; REnAL; RfGAmL 94; WebAB 74, 79; WhAm 1; WhLit*

Cohan, Josephine
American. Dancer
Talented sister of George M; performed with him in family acts, 1881-1916.
b. 1876 in Providence, Rhode Island
d. Jul 12, 1916 in New York, New York
Source: *BiDD; NotNAT B*

Cohen, Alexander H
American. Producer, Actor
Won two Emmys; producer of Tony Awards, 1967-80; appeared in *The Purple Rose of Cairo,* 1985.
b. Jul 24, 1920 in New York, New York
Source: *BiE&WWA; BioIn 13; BlueB 76; CamGWoT; CelR 90; ConTFT 5; CurBio 65; EncMT; IntWW 74, 91; NotNAT; OxCAmT 84; VarWW 85; WhoAm 80, 82, 90; WhoThe 77, 81; WhoWor 74*

Cohen, Ben(nett)
American. Businessman
Founded, with Jerry Greenfield, Ben & Jerry's Homemade, Inc., an ice cream company, 1978.
b. 1951 in New York, New York
Source: *CurBio 94*

Cohen, Benjamin Victor
American. Lawyer
Counselor to the US Embassy in London, 1941—.
b. Sep 23, 1894 in Muncie, Indiana
d. Aug 15, 1983 in Washington, District of Columbia
Source: *BioIn 1, 7, 13; ConAu 110, P-1; CurBio 41, 83N; FacFETw; IndAu 1917; NewYTBS 83; WhAm 8; WhoAm 74, 76, 78, 80; WhoWorJ 72*

Cohen, Daniel
American. Author
Managing editor, *Science Digest,* 1960-69; writings include *Monsters of Star Trek,* 1980.
b. Mar 12, 1936 in Chicago, Illinois
Source: *Au&Arts 7; AuBYP 2S, 3; BioIn 11, 15, 16, 18, 19; ChlBkCr; ChlLR 3; ConAu 1NR, 20NR, 45; EncSUPP; IntAu&W 77, 82, 91; ScF&FL 92; SixBJA; SmATA 4AS, 8; WrDr 88, 90*

Cohen, Joan Lebold
American. Author
Writes about, photographs current Chinese culture, art; books include *China Today and Her Ancient Treasures,* 1974.
b. Aug 19, 1932 in Highland Park, Illinois
Source: *ConAu 13NR, 25R, 30NR; MacBEP; SmATA 4; WhoAmA 78, 80, 82, 84, 86, 89, 91, 93; WhoAmW 74; WhoE 86, 93*

Cohen, Leonard Norman
Canadian. Singer, Songwriter
Wrote ''Beautiful Losers,'' 1966; ''Bird on a Wire,'' 1969; *I'm Your Man,* 1988.
b. Sep 21, 1934 in Montreal, Quebec, Canada
Source: *Baker 84; BioIn 14, 15; CamGLE; CanWr; CasWL; ConLC 3, 38; ConNov 76, 86; ConPo 75, 85; DcLB 53; IntAu&W 89; OxCCan; OxCCanL; RAdv 13-1; WhoAm 82, 86; WhoCanL 87; WrDr 88*

Cohen, Mickey
[Meyer Cohen]
American. Criminal
Leader of CA gambling rackets, 1940s-50s.
b. Sep 4, 1913 in New York, New York
d. Jul 29, 1976 in Los Angeles, California
Source: *BioIn 11; CopCroC; LegTOT; ObitOF 79*

Cohen, Myron
American. Comedian
Known for dialect, government jokes.
b. Jul 1, 1902 in Grodno, Poland
d. Mar 10, 1986 in Nyack, New York
Source: *LegTOT; NewYTBE 70; WhoCom*

Cohen, Octavus Roy
American. Author
Best known for stories depicting small-town southern blacks.
b. Jun 26, 1891 in Charleston, South Carolina
d. Jan 6, 1959 in Los Angeles, California
Source: *AmAu&B; BenetAL 91; BioIn 3, 4, 5, 6, 14; ConAu 112; CrtSuMy; DcAmB S6; EncMys; LinLib L; NatCAB 46; NotNAT B; OxCAmL 65, 83, 95; REn; REnAL; TwCA, SUP; TwCCr&M 80, 85, 91; WhAm 3; WhNAA*

Cohen, Stanley
American. Biochemist
Discovered the Epidermal Growth Factor, which stimulates the development of nerve cells in the body; awarded Nobel Prize 1986.
b. Nov 17, 1922 in New York, New York
Source: *AmMWSc 73P, 76P, 79, 82, 86, 89, 92, 95; BioIn 15, 20; IntWW 89, 91, 93; LarDcSc; NewYTBS 86; NobelP; NotTwCS; RAdv 14; Who 90, 92, 94; WhoAm 74, 76, 78, 80, 88, 90, 92, 94, 95, 96, 97; WhoMedH; WhoNob 90, 95; WhoScEn 94, 96; WhoSSW 88, 91, 93, 95, 97; WhoWor 89, 91, 93, 95, 96, 97; WorAlBi; WorScD*

Cohen, Wilbur Joseph
American. Educator, Author, Government Official
Helped draft original Social Security Act, mid-1930s; held first Social Security card; secretary of HEW, Johnson administration.
b. Jun 10, 1913 in Milwaukee, Wisconsin
d. May 18, 1987 in Seoul, Korea (South)
Source: *AmEA 74; AmMWSc 73S; BiDrAPH 79; BiDrUSE 71, 89; BioIn 5, 8, 10, 11, 15, 16, 21; BlueB 76; CurBio 68, 87; IntWW 74, 75, 76, 77, 78, 79, 80, 81, 82, 83; IntYB 78, 79, 80, 81, 82; LEduc 74; WhAm 9; WhoAm 74, 76, 78, 80, 82, 84, 86; WhoAmJ 80; WhoAmP 73, 75, 77, 79, 81, 83, 85; WhoSSW 84; WhoWor 74; WhoWorJ 72, 78*

Cohen, William S(ebastian)
American. Government Official, Politician
Rep. senator from ME, 1979-97; wrote *Getting the Most Out of Washington,* 1982; Secretary of Defense, 1997—.
b. Aug 28, 1940 in Bangor, Maine
Source: *AlmAP 80, 92; BiDrUSC 89; BioIn 10, 11, 12, 13, 14; CngDr 87, 89; ConAu 27NR, 108; CurBio 82; IntWW 91; NewYTBS 27; PolProf NF; PolsAm 84; WhoAm 74, 76, 78, 80, 82, 84, 86, 88, 90, 92, 94, 95, 96, 97; WhoAmP 87, 91; WhoE 77, 79, 81, 83, 85, 86, 89, 91, 93, 95, 97; WhoEmL 87; WhoGov 77; WhoWor 80, 82, 84, 87, 89, 91*

Cohn, Al
American. Jazz Musician, Composer
Tenor saxophonist with Big Bands, 1940s; wrote scores for Broadway shows, TV specials.
b. Nov 24, 1925 in New York, New York
d. Feb 14, 1988 in Stroudsburg, Pennsylvania
Source: *AllMusG; AnObit 1988; ASCAP 66; Baker 84; BiDJaz; BioIn 12, 14, 15, 16; CmpEPM; EncJzS; IlEncJ; LegTOT; NewAmDM; NewGrDJ 88; PenEncP; WhoAm 86*

Cohn, Edwin Joseph
American. Biochemist
Worked on the development of blood fractionation, the separation of plasma proteins; helped devise ways to fraction plasma for treatment of wounded soldiers during WW II.
b. Dec 17, 1892 in New York, New York
d. Oct 1, 1953 in Boston, Massachusetts
Source: *BioIn 1, 2, 3, 5; DcAmB S5; DcAmMeB 84; DcScB; InSci; ObitOF 79; WebAB 74, 79; WhAm 3*

Cohn, Ferdinand Julius
Polish. Botanist
Made first systematic attempt to classify bacteria and its fundamental divisions.
b. Jan 24, 1828 in Breslau, Poland
d. Jun 25, 1898 in Breslau, Poland

Source: *AsBiEn; BiESc; BiHiMed; BioIn 9; CamDcSc; DcScB; LarDcSc*

Cohn, Harry
American. Film Executive
Co-founder Columbia Pictures, 1924; dictatorial leadership of business helped establish it as a major motion picture company in the 1930s and 1940s.
b. Jul 23, 1891 in New York, New York
d. Feb 27, 1958 in Phoenix, Arizona
Source: *BiDFilm 94; BioIn 4, 5, 7, 8; DcAmB S6; FacFETw; FilmgC; GangFlm; HalFC 84, 88; IntDcF 2-4; LegTOT; NotNAT A, B; ObitOF 79; OxCFilm; TwYS B; WhAm 3; WorEFlm*

Cohn, Mindy
American. Actor
Played Natalie on TV series "Facts of Life," 1979-88.
b. May 20, 1966 in Los Angeles, California
Source: *BioIn 13; LegTOT; WhoHol 92*

Cohn, Roy (Marcus)
American. Lawyer
Best known as chief counsel to Senator Joseph McCarthy's communist-hunting investigations subcommittee, early 1950s.
b. Feb 20, 1927 in New York, New York
d. Aug 2, 1986 in Bethesda, Maryland
Source: *AnObit 1986; BioIn 3, 6, 7, 8, 10, 11, 12, 14, 15, 16, 18, 20; EncCW; EncMcCE; FacFETw; GayLesB; NewYTBS 86; WhAm 9; WhoAm 74, 76, 78, 80, 82, 84, 86; WhoAmL 78, 79; WhoE 74, 77, 79, 81, 83, 85; WhoWor 76; WhoWorJ 72*

Coit, Margaret Louise
American. Author
Won Pulitzer for first book: *John C Calhoun: American Portrait,* 1951.
b. May 30, 1922 in Norwich, Connecticut
Source: *AmAu&B; AuBYP 2, 3; ConAu 1R, 5NR; CurBio 51; DrAS 74H; ForWC 70; OxCAmL 65; REnAL; SmATA 2; TwCA SUP; WhoAm 84, 90*

Coke, Edward, Sir
English. Judge
Attorney-General to Elizabeth I; prosecuted Raleigh, Essex; wrote *The Petition of Right,* 1628.
b. Feb 1, 1552 in Mileham, England
d. Sep 3, 1634 in Stoke Poges, England
Source: *Alli; BioIn 1, 2, 3, 4, 9, 10, 12, 16, 18; BritAu; CamGEL; CamGLE; DcBiPP; DcEnL; DcNaB; HarEnUS; HisDStE; LinLib L, S; McGEWB; NewC; OxCEng 67, 85, 95; OxCLaw; WhDW*

Coker, Elizabeth Boatwright
American. Author
Wrote novels *India Allen,* 1953; *La Belle,* 1959.
b. Apr 21, 1909
d. Sep 1, 1993 in Hartsville, South Carolina
Source: *BioIn 19; ConAu 45, 142; CurBio 93N; InWom; NewYTBS 93; WhoAm 74, 76, 78, 80, 82, 84, 86, 88, 90; WhoAmW 61, 66, 68, 70, 72, 74, 87, 89, 91; WhoWor 74, 76, 78, 82, 84, 87, 89*

Colasanto, Nicholas
American. Actor
Best known as Coach Ernie Pantusso on TV series "Cheers."
b. Jan 19, 1924 in Providence, Rhode Island
d. Feb 12, 1985 in Los Angeles, California
Source: *ConNews 85-2*

Colavito, Rocky
[Rocco Domenico Colaviro]
American. Baseball Player
Outfielder, 1955-68; led AL in home runs, RBIs, 1965.
b. Aug 10, 1933 in New York, New York
Source: *Ballpl 90; BiDAmSp BB; BioIn 5, 6, 7, 9, 15, 16, 18; WhoProB 73*

Colbert, Claudette
[Lily Claudette Chauchoin]
American. Actor
Won Oscar for *It Happened One Night,* 1934.
b. Sep 13, 1903 in Paris, France
d. Jul 30, 1996 in Bellerive, Barbados
Source: *BiDFilm, 94; BiE&WWA; BioAmW; BioIn 14, 15; BioNews 74; CelR 90; ConTFT 2; CurBio 45, 64; EncAFC; FilmgC; HalFC 88; IntMPA 82, 88, 92; IntWW 89, 91, 93; InWom SUP; LegTOT; MotPP; MovMk; News 97-1; NewYTBS 27, 84; OxCFilm; WhAm 11; Who 82, 85, 88, 90, 92, 94; WhoAm 86, 90, 92, 94, 95, 96; WhoAmW 87; WhoCom; WhoEnt 92; WhoHol 92, A; WhoThe 77; WorAlBi; WorEFlm*

Colbert, Jean-Baptiste
French. Statesman, Government Official
Powerful minister under Louis XIV, 1665-85; created French navy, 1668.
b. Aug 29, 1619 in Reims, France
d. Sep 6, 1683 in Paris, France
Source: *DcBiPP; DcCathB; Dis&D; EncCRAm; HisWorL; IlDcG; OxCArt; OxCFr; OxCLaw; OxCShps; OxDcArt; REn; WebBD 83; WhDW; WorAl*

Colbert, Lester L(um)
American. Auto Executive, Lawyer
Pres., Chrysler Corp., 1950-61.
b. Jun 13, 1905 in Oakwood, Texas
d. Sep 15, 1995 in Naples, Florida
Source: *BioIn 2, 4, 5, 21; BlueB 76; CurBio 51, 95N; EncABHB 5; IntWW 74, 75, 76, 77, 78, 79, 80, 81, 82, 83, 89; WhAm 11; WhoAm 74, 76, 78, 80, 82, 84, 86, 88, 90, 92, 94, 95*

Colbran, Isabella
Spanish. Opera Singer
Dramatic coloratura soprano; married Rossini, starred in his operas.
b. Feb 2, 1785 in Madrid, Spain
d. Oct 7, 1845 in Bologna, Italy
Source: *Baker 84, 92; BioIn 15; InWom; NewEOp 71; OxDcOp*

Colby, Anita
[Anita Katherine Counihan]
"The Face"
American. Actor, Model, Editor
Modeled in the 30s; wrote *Anita Colby's Beauty Book.*
b. Aug 5, 1914 in Washington, District of Columbia
d. Mar 27, 1992 in Oyster Bay, New York
Source: *AmAu&B; AmCath 80; BioIn 8, 10, 12, 17; InWom, SUP; MotPP; NewYTBS 92; WhoAmW 58, 64, 70, 72, 74; WhoHol 92, A*

Colby, Carroll Burleigh
American. Author, Artist
Known for juvenile nature, adventure stories: *Gobbit, the Magic Rabbit,* 1951.
b. Sep 7, 1904 in Claremont, New Hampshire
d. Oct 31, 1977 in New York, New York
Source: *AuBYP 2, 3; BioIn 6, 7, 9; ConAu 1R; MorJA; SmATA 3; WhAm 7; WhoAm 74, 76, 78*

Colby, William E(gan)
American. Government Official
Director, CIA, 1973-76.
b. Jan 4, 1920 in Saint Paul, Minnesota
d. Apr 27, 1996 in Wicomico River, Maryland
Source: *AmCath 80; BioIn 9, 10, 11, 12; BlueB 76; ColdWar 1; ConAu 81, 151; CurBio 75, 96N; EncAI&E; IntWW 74, 75, 76, 77, 78, 79, 80, 81, 82, 83, 89, 91, 93; NewYTBE 73; NewYTBS 77, 92; WhAm 11; WhoAm 74, 76, 78, 80, 82, 84, 86, 88, 90, 92, 94, 95, 96; WhoAmL 79, 83, 92; WhoAmP 75, 77, 79, 81, 83, 85, 87, 89, 91, 93, 95; WhoE 91, 95; WhoGov 75, 77; WhoSSW 73*

Colden, Cadwallader
Irish. Botanist, Author
Held numerous important official positions, 1700s; introduced Linnaeus system to US botany.
b. Feb 7, 1688, Ireland
d. Sep 28, 1776 in Long Island, New York
Source: *Alli; AmAu; AmAu&B; AmBi; AmRev; AmWrBE; ApCAB; BenetAL 91; BiDAmS; BiDrACR; BiHiMed; BiInAmS; BioIn 3, 9, 11, 14, 15; CopCroC; CyAL 1; DcAmAu; DcAmB; DcAmMeB, 84; DcBiPP; DcEnL; DcLB 24, 30; DcNAA; DcNaB; DcScB; Dis&D; Drake; EncAB-H 1974, 1996; EncCRAm; EncNAB; HarEnUS; InSci; McGEWB; OxCAmH; OxCAmL 65, 83, 95; OxCCan; PeoHis; REnAL; REnAW; TwCBDA; WebAB 74,*

79; WebBD 83; WhAm HS; WhAmP; WhAmRev; WhNaAH

Cole, Charles Woolsey
American. Educator, Diplomat
Pres., Amherst College, 1946-60; ambassador to Chile, 1961-64; author of historical works.
b. Feb 8, 1907 in Montclair, New Jersey
d. Feb 6, 1978 in Los Angeles, California
Source: *AmAu&B; BlueB 76; ConAu 69; IntWW 74, 78; Who 74; WhoAm 74*

Cole, Cozy
[William Randolph Cole]
American. Musician
Big band drummer; recorded "Topsy," 1958, only drum solo ever to sell over one million copies.
b. Oct 17, 1909 in East Orange, New Jersey
d. Jan 29, 1981 in Columbus, Ohio
Source: *AnObit 1981; Baker 84; BiDAfM; BiDAmM; BiDJaz; BioIn 16; CmpEPM; DrBlPA, 90; EncJzS; IlEncJ; InB&W 80, 85; LegTOT; NewAmDM; NewYTBS 81; OxCPMus; PenEncP; WhAm 7; WhoAm 74; WhoE 74; WhoJazz 72; WorAl; WorAlBi*

Cole, Dennis
American. Actor
Extensive TV series work includes "Felony Squad," 1966-69; was married to actress Jaclyn Smith.
b. Jul 19, 1943 in Detroit, Michigan
Source: *ConTFT 4; HalFC 88; WhoHol 92, A*

Cole, Edward Nicholas
American. Auto Executive
Pres., GM, 1967-74.
b. Sep 17, 1909 in Berlin, Michigan
d. May 2, 1977 in Kalamazoo, Michigan
Source: *BioIn 4, 5, 6, 8, 9, 10, 11; BioNews 74; BlueB 76; BusPN; CurBio 72; EncABHB 5; IntWW 74; St&PR 75; Ward 77G; Who 74; WhoAm 74; WhoFI 75*

Cole, George
English. Actor
Character parts on stage, film; appeared in TV series A Man of Our Times.
b. Apr 22, 1925 in London, England
Source: *BioIn 13, 19; ConTFT 9; FilmgC; HalFC 84, 88; IntMPA 75, 76, 77, 78, 79, 81, 82, 84, 86, 88, 92, 94, 96; QDrFCA 92; Who 74, 82, 83, 85, 88, 90, 92, 94; WhoHol 92, A; WhoThe 72, 77, 81*

Cole, George Douglas Howard
English. Educator, Author
Oxford professor; wrote books on socialist topics; detective stories with his wife.
b. Sep 25, 1889 in Cambridge, England
d. Jan 14, 1959 in Oxford, England
Source: *BiDMoPL; BioIn 4, 5, 7, 9, 10, 14; ChhPo, S2; DcLEL; DcNaB 1951; EncMys; EvLB; GrBr; LngCTC; McGEWB; NewC; TwCA, SUP; WhAm 3; WhE&EA; WhLit; WhoEc 81, 86; WhoLA*

Cole, Holly
Canadian. Singer
Jazz artist who formed the Holly Cole trio with Aaron Davis and David Piltch, 1985; first album, *Girl Talk*, 1990, and second album, *Blame It On My Youth*, 1991, became a gold records; received Japan's Grand Prix Gold Discs award for best jazz album and best new artist for *Don't Smoke In Bed*, 1993.
b. 1963 in Halifax, Nova Scotia, Canada
Source: *AllMusG*

Cole, Jack
American. Choreographer
Introduced jazz style which became US dance trademark; choreographed dance numbers for Rita Hayworth, Marilyn Monroe.
b. Apr 27, 1914 in New Brunswick, New Jersey
d. Feb 17, 1974 in Los Angeles, California
Source: *BiDD; BiE&WWA; BioIn 4, 10, 13, 14; CamGWoT; CmMov; EncACom; EncMT; FilmgC; HalFC 84, 88; IntDcF 1-4, 2-4; NewYTBS 74; NotNAT B; ObitOF 79; OxCAmT 84; WhAm 6; WhoAm 74; WhoHol B; WhScrn 77, 83; WorEFlm*

Cole, Johnnetta Betsch
American. University Administrator
First black female pres. of Spelman College, 1987—.
b. Oct 19, 1936 in Jacksonville, Florida
Source: *AfrAmBi 1; BioIn 9, 15; BlkWAm; CurBio 94; InB&W 85; NewYTBS 87, 88; NotBlAW 1; WhoAfA 96; WhoAm 90, 92, 94, 95, 96, 97; WhoAmW 89, 91, 93, 95, 97; WhoBlA 80, 85, 88, 90, 92, 94*

Cole, Kenneth Reese
American. Presidential Aide, Business Executive
Special assistant to Richard Nixon, 1969-70; assistant to Gerald Ford, 1974-75.
b. Jan 27, 1938 in New York, New York
Source: *BioIn 9, 10; NewYTBS 74; St&PR 84, 87; WhoAm 74, 76, 78, 80, 82, 84; WhoFI 77*

Cole, Kenneth Stewart
"Father of Biophysics"
American. Physicist
Known for using electrical approach to studying function of living cell membranes.
b. Jul 10, 1900 in Ithaca, New York
d. Apr 18, 1984 in La Jolla, California
Source: *AmMWSc 76P, 79, 82; BioIn 14; BlueB 76; IntWW 80, 81, 82, 83; McGMS 80; WhoAm 80, 82; WhoFrS 84; WhoGov 72, 75*

Cole, Lloyd
English. Songwriter, Singer
Lead singer of Lloyd Cole and the Commotions, 1983-86; went solo, 1990—.
b. Jan 31, 1961 in Buxton, England
Source: *BioIn 14; ConMus 9; EncRk 88; LegTOT; PenEncP*

Cole, Maria
American. Singer
With Duke Ellington Band, 1945-46; widow of Nat King Cole.
b. Aug 1, 1920? in Boston, Massachusetts
Source: *VarWW 85*

Cole, Michael
American. Actor
Played Pete Cochran in TV series "The Mod Squad," 1968-73.
b. Jul 3, 1945 in Madison, Wisconsin
Source: *BioIn 16; Dun&B 90; SmATA 59; WhoHol 92, A*

Cole, Nat King
[Nathaniel Adams Cole]
American. Singer, Bandleader
Known for easy-listening songs including "Mona Lisa," 1950; "Ramblin' Rose," 1962; first black to host TV series, 1950s.
b. Mar 17, 1919 in Montgomery, Alabama
d. Feb 15, 1965 in Santa Monica, California
Source: *AllMusG; ASCAP 66; Baker 78; BiDAmM; BioIn 15, 16, 17, 18, 20, 21; CmpEPM; ConMus 3; CurBio 56, 65; DcAmNB; DrBlPA; FilmgC; HalFC 84, 88; HarEnR 86; IlEncJ; MovMk; NegAl 83; NewYTET; RkOn 74; WhAm 4; WhoHol B; WhoJazz 72; WhoRock 81; WhScrn 74, 77, 83; WorAl*

Cole, Natalie
[Stephanie Natalie Maria Cole]
American. Singer
Won Grammy, 1976, for debut album *Inseparable;* daughter of Nat "King" Cole.
b. Feb 6, 1950 in Los Angeles, California
Source: *AfrAmAl 6; BiDJaz; BioIn 10, 11, 13, 14, 15, 16; BkPepl; CelR 90; ConMus 1; CurBio 91; DcTwCCu 5; DrBlPA, 90; EncPR&S 89; EncRk 88; EncRkSt; HerW 84; InB&W 80, 85; InWom SUP; LegTOT; News 92; PenEncP; RkOn 78; RolSEnR 83; SoulM; WhoAfA 96; WhoAm 86, 90; WhoAmW 81; WhoBlA 77, 85, 92, 94; WhoEnt 92; WhoRock 81; WorAl; WorAlBi*

Cole, Olivia
American. Actor
Best known for role of Mathilda in TV miniseries "Roots," 1977, for which she won an Emmy.
b. Nov 26, 1942 in Memphis, Tennessee

Source: *BioIn 11; BlksAmF; ConTFT 8; DrBlPA; InB&W 85; InWom SUP; WhoAm 82; WhoAmW 81; WhoHol 92*

Cole, Sterling W(illiam)
American. Politician
Rep. congressman from NY, 1935-57; first director of International Atomic Energy Agency, 1957-61.
b. Aug 18, 1904 in Painted Post, New York
d. Mar 15, 1987 in Washington, District of Columbia
Source: *CurBio 54, 87; IntWW 83; St&PR 84; WhoAm 84, 86; WhoUN 75*

Cole, Thomas
American. Artist
One of the founders of the Hudson River School, first American movement in painting.
b. Feb 1, 1801 in Bolton, England
d. Feb 11, 1848 in Catskill, New York
Source: *Alli; AmAu&B; AmBi; AmCulL; ApCAB; ArtsNiC; Benet 87, 96; BenetAL 91; BioIn 1, 4, 5, 6, 7, 8, 9, 10, 11, 12, 13, 14, 15, 16, 17, 19, 20; BriEAA; CyAL 2; DcAmArt; DcAmB; DcArts; DcSeaP; Drake; EncAAH; EncAB-H 1974, 1996; HarEnUS; IlBEAAW; IntDcAA 90; LegTOT; LinLib S; McGDA; McGEWB; NatCAB 7; NewYHSD; OxCAmH; OxCAmL 65, 95; OxCArt; OxDcArt; TwCBDA; WebAB 74, 79; WhAm HS; WorAl; WorAlBi*

Cole, Timothy
[Walter Sylvanus Timotheus Cole]
American. Engraver
Reproduced paintings in wood for *Century; Scribner* mags., 1892-1917; wrote *Wood Engraving: Three Essays,* 1916.
b. Apr 6, 1852 in London, England
d. May 11, 1931 in Poughkeepsie, New York
Source: *AmBi; BioIn 3, 4, 5, 18; DcAmB S1; LinLib L, S; NatCAB 13; WhAm 1; WhAmArt 85; WhNAA*

Coleman, Bessie
"Brave Bessie"
American. Aviator
First black woman to earn a pilot's license; stunt and exhibition pilot.
b. Jan 26, 1893 in Atlanta, Texas
d. Apr 30, 1926 in Jacksonville, Florida
Source: *BioIn 1, 9, 11, 15; BlksScM; EncWHA; HanAmWH; InB&W 80; NotBlAW 1; WomFir*

Coleman, Cy
[Seymour Kaufman]
American. Songwriter
Wrote song "If My Friends Could See Me Now"; score for Tony-award winning *City of Angels,* 1989.
b. Jun 14, 1929 in New York, New York
Source: *AmPS; AmSong; ASCAP 66; Baker 84, 92; BiE&WWA; BioIn 9, 10, 11, 12, 14, 15, 17, 21; BioNews 75; CelR, 90; ConTFT 3, 11; CurBio 90; EncMT; HalFC 84, 88; LegTOT; NewAmDM; NewCBMT; NewGrDA 86; NewGrDO; NewYTBS 86; NotNAT; OxCAmT 84; OxCPMus; PenEncP; WhoAm 74, 76, 78, 80, 82, 84, 86, 88, 90; WhoE 74, 91; WhoEnt 92*

Coleman, Dabney W
American. Actor
Star of TV series "Buffalo Bill," 1983-84; won Golden Globe for "The Slap Maxwell Story," 1988; Emmy for "Sworn to Silence," 1987.
b. Jan 3, 1932 in Austin, Texas
Source: *BioIn 13, 15; CelR 90; ConTFT 3; EncAFC; HalFC 88; IntMPA 92; LesBEnT 92; News 88-3; WhoAm 90; WhoEnt 92; WorAlBi*

Coleman, Gary
American. Actor
Child actor who played Arnold on TV series "Different Strokes," 1978-86.
b. Feb 8, 1968 in Zion, Illinois
Source: *BioIn 12, 13, 14, 15, 16; BlksAmF; ConTFT 3; DrBlPA 90; EncAFC; HalFC 84, 88; InB&W 80, 85; IntMPA 84, 86, 88, 92, 94, 96; LegTOT; WhoAfA 96; WhoBlA 85, 88, 90, 92, 94; WhoHol 92; WhoTelC; WorAl; WorAlBi*

Coleman, James S(amuel)
American. Sociologist, Educator, Author
Champion of integrated public school systems; wrote *Adolescents and the Schools,* 1965.
b. May 12, 1926 in Bedford, Indiana
d. Mar 25, 1995 in Chicago, Illinois
Source: *AmMWSc 73S, 92; BioIn 14, 16, 20, 21; BlueB 76; ConAu 1NR, 13R; CurBio 70, 95N; IndAu 1917; IntWW 83, 91; LEduc 74; PolProf J, NF; RAdv 14; WhAm 11; WhoAm 86, 90; WhoE 74; WhoMW 90; WhoWor 74; WrDr 84, 88*

Coleman, John
American. Meteorologist
Gives national weather report on Good Morning, America.
b. Nov 15, 1935 in Champaign, Illinois

Coleman, Lonnie William
American. Author
Wrote *Beulah Land; Look Away, Beulah Land; The Legacy of Beulah Land.*
b. Aug 2, 1920 in Barstow, Georgia
d. Aug 13, 1982 in Savannah, Georgia
Source: *AmAu&B; AmNov; BiE&WWA; ConAu 77, 107; CurBio 58, 82N; NewYTBS 82; NotNAT*

Coleman, Ornette
American. Jazz Musician
Alto, tenor saxophonist; wrote over 100 jazz compositions; albums include *Song X,* 1986.
b. Mar 19, 1930 in Fort Worth, Texas
Source: *AfrAmAl 6; AllMusG; AmCulL; ASCAP 66; Baker 78, 84, 92; BiDAfM; BiDAmM; BiDJaz; BioIn 5, 6, 7, 9, 10, 11, 12, 13, 14, 15, 16; CelR 90; ConAmC 76, 82; ConMus 5; CurBio 61; DcArts; DcTwCCu 1, 5; DrBlPA, 90; EncJzS; FacFETw; IlEncJ; InB&W 80, 85; LegTOT; NegAl 83, 89; NewAmDM; NewGrDA 86; NewGrDJ 88, 94; NewOxM; OxCPMus; PenEncP; RolSEnR 83; WhoAfA 96; WhoAm 74, 76, 78, 80, 82, 84, 86, 88, 90, 92, 94, 95, 96, 97; WhoBlA 75, 77, 80, 85, 88, 90, 92, 94; WhoEnt 92; WorAl; WorAlBi*

Coleman, Sheldon, Jr.
American. Business Executive
Pres., CEO, Coleman Company, Inc., 1988—, manufacturer of outdoors equipment.
b. 1953
Source: *Dun&B 88; News 90, 90-2*

Coleman, Vince(nt Maurice)
American. Baseball Player
Outfielder, St. Louis, 1985-90, 1995—; NY Mets, 1990-94; NL rookie of year, 1985; holds ML record for stol en bases by rookie; only player to steal 100 bases in first three ML seasons.
b. Sep 22, 1960 in Jacksonville, Florida
Source: *Ballpl 90; BaseReg 86, 87; WhoBlA 92; WorAlBi*

Coleman, William
American. Businessman
Purchased rights for gas lamp, 1903; co. was largest manufacturer of camping equipment, 1960s.
b. 1870
d. 1957
Source: *Entr; WhoColR*

Coleman, William T, Jr.
American. Lawyer, Government Official
Secretary of Transportation, 1975-77.
b. Jul 7, 1920 in Germantown, Pennsylvania
Source: *BiDrUSE 89; BioIn 13, 15; IntWW 83, 89; Law&B 84; NewYTBS 82, 87; WhoAm 84, 90; WhoAmL 92; WhoBlA 75, 92*

Colemon, Johnnie
American. Clergy
Founder and pastor, Christ Unity Temple, Chicago (later Christ Universal Church), 1956—.
b. c. 1921 in Centerville, Alabama
Source: *ConBlB 11*

Coleridge, Hartley
English. Poet, Journalist
Compiled biograhies: *Worthies of Yorkshire,* 1832; eldest son of Samuel Taylor.
b. Sep 19, 1796 in Bristol, England
d. Jan 6, 1849 in Grasmere, England
Source: *Alli; BiD&SB; BioIn 9, 11, 17, 21; CamGEL; CamGLE; CasWL; CelCen; Chambr 3; ChhPo, S2, S3; DcBiPP; DcEnA; DcEnL; DcEuL; DcLB 96; DcLEL; DcNaB; EvLB; LegTOT; NewC; OxCEng 67, 85, 95; PenC ENG*

Coleridge, Mary Elizabeth
English. Author, Poet
Wrote novel *Seven Sleepers of Ephesus,* 1893; verse *Gathered Leaves,* published, 1910.
b. Sep 23, 1861 in London, England
d. Aug 25, 1907 in Harrogate, England
Source: *ConAu 116; DcLB 19; NewC; OxCEng 67*

Coleridge, Samuel Taylor
English. Author, Poet, Critic
Wrote "The Rime of the Ancient Mariner"; "Kubla Khan."
b. Oct 21, 1772 in Ottery Saint Mary, England
d. Jul 25, 1834 in London, England
Source: *Alli; AtlBL; BbD; Benet 87, 96; BiD&SB; BiDLA; BiDPsy; BiDTran; BioIn 1, 2, 3, 4, 5, 6, 7, 8, 9, 10, 11, 12, 13, 14, 15, 16, 17, 18, 19, 20, 21; BlkwCE; BlmGEL; BritAu 19; BritWr 4; CamGEL; CamGLE; CasWL; CelCen; Chambr 3; ChhPo, S1, S2, S3; CnDBLB 3; CnE&AP; CrtT 2, 4; CyWA 58; DcAmC; DcArts; DcBiPP; DcEnA; DcEnL; DcEuL; DcLB 93, 107; DcLEL; DcNaB, C; Dis&D; EncEnl; EncO&P 1, 2, 3; EncPaPR 91; EncWT; EvLB; LegTOT; LinLib L, S; LngCEL; MagSWL; McGEWB; MouLC 3; NewC; NinCLC 9, 54; NotNAT B; OxCEng 67, 85, 95; OxCPhil; OxCThe 67, 83; PenC ENG; PenEncH; PoeCrit 11; RAdv 1, 14, 13-1; RComWL; REn; RfGEnL 91; WebE&AL; WhDW; WomFir; WorAl; WorAlBi; WorLitC; WrPh*

Coleridge-Taylor, Samuel
English. Composer
Wrote *24 Negro Melodies,* 1905; Hiawatha trilogy, 1898-1900.
b. Aug 15, 1875 in London, England
d. Sep 1, 1912 in Thornton, England
Source: *AfrAmAl 6; Baker 78, 84, 92; BiDAfM; BioIn 1, 4, 6, 10, 11, 12, 14, 20; BlkOpe; DcNaB 1912; DrBlPA, 90; InB&W 80, 85; LinLib S; NegAl 76, 83, 89; NewAmDM; NewCol 75; NewGrDO; NewOxM; OxCMus; WhDW*

Coles, Joanna
American. Children's Author
Award-winning science books include *A Snake's Body,* 1981.
b. Aug 11, 1944 in Newark, New Jersey
Source: *ConAu 115*

Coles, Manning
[Cyril Coles and Adelaide Frances Oke Manning]
English. Authors
Invented Tommy Hambleton, intelligence agent; mysteries include *Drink to Yesterday, Toast to Tomorrow,* 1959.
Source: *BioIn 4, 5, 7; ConAu 9R, P-1, X; DcLP 87B; EncMys; LngCTC; PenNWW B; ScF&FL 1; SpyFic; TwCA SUP; TwCCr&M 80, 85, 91; WorAl; WorAlBi*

Coles, Robert
American. Psychiatrist, Author
Prolific author best known for works on the lives of children based on thousands of hours of interviews with them; won Pulitzer, 1973, for volumes 2-3 of *Children of Crisis.*
b. Oct 12, 1929 in Boston, Massachusetts
Source: *AmAu&B; AmMWSc 86, 89, 92, 95; Au&Wr 71; AuBYP 3; BiDrAPA 77; BioIn 8, 9, 10, 11, 13, 16; BlueB 76; CelR, 90; ConAu 3NR, 32NR, 45; CyWA 89; IntAu&W 76, 91, 93; LegTOT; News 95, 95-1; OxCAmL 95; SmATA 23; WhoAm 82, 84, 86, 88, 90, 92, 94, 95, 96, 97; WhoE 93; WhoMedH; WhoUSWr 88; WhoWrEP 89, 92, 95; WorAlBi; WorAu 1970; WrDr 80, 82, 84, 86, 88, 90, 92, 94, 96*

Colette
[Sidonie Gabrielle Colette]
French. Author
Best works include four volume *Claudine,* 1930; *GiGi,* 1943.
b. Jan 28, 1873 in Saint-Sauveur, France
d. Aug 3, 1954 in Paris, France
Source: *AtlBL; Benet 87, 96; BioIn 1, 2, 3, 4, 5, 6, 7, 8, 9, 10, 11, 12, 13, 14, 15, 16, 17, 20, 21; BlmGWL; CasWL; ClDMEL 47; CnMWL; ConAu 104, 131; ContDcW 89; CyWA 58, 89; DcLB 65; DcTwCCu 2; EncEurC; EncWL; EncWT; EuWr 9; EvEuW; FacFETw; FemiCLE; FilmgC; FrenWW; GayLesB; GoodHs; GrFLW; GrWomW; HalFC 84, 88; IntDcWB; ItaFilm; LegTOT; LinLib L, S; LngCTC; MagSWL; MajTwCW; McGEWB; ModFrL; ModRL; ModWoWr; NewGrDO; NotNAT B; Novels; ObitT 1951; OxCEng 67, 85, 95; OxCFilm; OxCFr; PenC EUR; PenNWW B; RAdv 14, 13-2; REn; ShSCr 10; TwCA, SUP; TwCLC 1, 5, 16; TwCWr; WhAm 3; WhDW; WhoTwCL; WorAl; WorAlBi*

Colfax, Schuyler
American. US Vice President
VP under U S Grant, 1869-73; involvement in scandal ended career.
b. Mar 23, 1823 in New York, New York
d. Jan 13, 1885 in Mankato, Minnesota
Source: *AmBi; AmPolLe; ApCAB; BiAUS; BiDrAC; BiDrUSC 89; BiDrUSE 71, 89; BioIn 1, 2, 3, 4, 7, 8, 9, 10, 14; CelCen; CivWDc; CyAG; DcAmB; DcBiPP; Drake; HarEnUS; IndAu 1816; LegTOT; NatCAB 4; PolPar; TwCBDA; VicePre; WebAB 74, 79; WhAm HS; WhAmP; WhCiWar; WorAl; WorAlBi*

Colgate, William
American. Manufacturer
Began soap-making business, 1806; later became Colgate-Palmolive.
b. Jan 25, 1783 in Hollingbourne, England
d. Mar 25, 1857 in New York, New York
Source: *AmBi; ApCAB; BiDAmBL 83; BioIn 4, 16, 18; DcAmB; Entr; NatCAB 13; TwCBDA; WebAB 74, 79; WhAm HS; WorAl; WorAlBi*

Colicos, John
Canadian. Actor
Shakespearean character performer on stage, occasionally films, TV.
b. Dec 10, 1928 in Toronto, Ontario, Canada
Source: *BioIn 6; ConTFT 8; CreCan 1; FilmgC; HalFC 84, 88; NotNAT; OxCCanT; WhoAm 82, 84, 86; WhoHol 92; WhoThe 77*

Coligny, Gaspard de Chatillon
French. Religious Leader
Leader of Huguenots, 1560s; killed in St. Bartholomew's Massacre.
b. Feb 16, 1519 in Chatillon-sur-Loing, France
d. Aug 24, 1572 in Paris, France
Source: *McGEWB; OxCFr; REn*

Collazo, Oscar
Puerto Rican. Attempted Assassin
With Griselio Torresola, tried to assassinate Harry Truman, Nov 1, 1950.
b. 1914
Source: *BioIn 3, 8, 9, 10, 13, 19*

Collett, Alec
English. Hostage
Journalist, one of 7 British citizens taken hostage by Lebanese terrorist goups; after 394 days in captivity, reported slain on Apr 23, 1986.
d. Apr 23, 1986, Lebanon

Collett, Wayne
American. Track Athlete
Sprinter; won silver medal, 1972 Olympics; with Vince Matthews, banned from further competition for not standing at attention on victory stand.
b. Oct 20, 1949 in Los Angeles, California
Source: *BlkOlyM; WhoAm 88; WhoCanF 86; WhoTr&F 73*

Collier, Constance
[Laura Constance Hardie]
English. Actor
Made appearences on London stage, Broadway, films; later became drama coach; autobiography: *Harlequinade,* 1930.
b. Jan 22, 1878 in Windsor, England
d. Apr 25, 1955 in New York, New York
Source: *AmWomPl; BioIn 3, 4, 9, 10; CurBio 54, 55; DcAmB S5; EncAFC; EncWT; Film 1, 2; FilmgC; HalFC 84, 88; MotPP; MovMk; NewC; NotNAT A, B; ObitOF 79; ObitT 1951; OxCThe 67, 83; PlP&P; REn; ThFT; TwYS, A; Vers A; WhoHol B; WhScrn 74, 77, 83; WhThe*

Collier, John
American. Sociologist
Promoted passage of Indian Reorganization Act of 1933, which improved official treatment of Native Americans.
b. May 4, 1884 in Atlanta, Georgia
d. May 8, 1968 in Taos, New Mexico
Source: *AmAu&B; BenetAL 91; BiDSocW; BioIn 3, 6, 8, 10, 11, 13, 14, 15; DcAmB S8; EncAB-H 1974, 1996; NatCAB 54; REnAL; REnAW; WebAB 74, 79; WhAm 5*

Collier, Peter
American. Author
Co-author with David Horowitz, *The Fords: An American Epic,* 1986.
b. Jun 2, 1939 in Hollywood, California
Source: *BioIn 14, 16, 20; ConAu 44NR, 65; IntAu&W 91; LNinSix; NewYTBS 89; WrDr 84, 86, 88, 90, 92*

Collier, William, Sr.
American. Actor, Director, Dramatist
Appeared as comedian on stage, screen for 60 yrs.
b. Nov 12, 1866 in New York, New York
d. Jan 13, 1944 in Beverly Hills, California
Source: *BioIn 3; EncAFC; Film 1, 2; FilmgC; HalFC 84, 88; MovMk; NotNAT B; ObitOF 79; OxCAmT 84; WhAm 2; WhoHol B; WhoStg 1906, 1908; WhScrn 74, 77, 83; WhThe*

Collin, Frank
[Frank Cohn]
American. Political Leader
Son of Jewish refugee who is active in Chicago Nazi Party.
b. Nov 3, 1944? in Chicago, Illinois
Source: *Alli SUP; BioIn 11*

Collinge, Patricia
Irish. Actor
Best known for stage role in *The Little Foxes;* eccentric film roles include *The Nun's Story,* 1958.
b. Sep 20, 1894 in Dublin, Ireland
d. Apr 10, 1974 in New York, New York
Source: *BiE&WWA; WhoHol B; WhScrn 77, 83; WhThe*

Collingwood, Charles Cummings
American. Broadcast Journalist
CBS correspondent who was first American network newsman admitted to N Vietnam, 1968.
b. Jun 4, 1917 in Three Rivers, Michigan
d. Oct 3, 1985 in New York, New York
Source: *BiDAmJo; ConAu 117; CurBio 43, 85; IntWW 83; LesBEnT; WhoAm 74, 84; WhoWor 84*

Collingwood, Robin George
English. Philosopher
Authority on Roman occupation of England; wrote *The Idea of History,* 1945.
b. Feb 22, 1889 in Cartmel Fell, England
d. Jan 9, 1943 in Coniston, England
Source: *BioIn 3, 4, 5, 6, 8, 9, 11, 13, 14, 15, 16; CasWL; CnMWL; DcLEL; DcNaB 1941; LngCTC; LuthC 75; McGEWB; ObitOF 79; OxCEng 67; OxCPhil; PenC ENG; RAdv 14, 13-4; REn; TwCA SUP; WhE&EA*

Collins, Albert
American. Musician, Songwriter
Blues guitarist; single "Frosty," 1962 sold 1 million copies; Grammy award for album *Ice Pickin',* 1978.
b. Oct 1, 1932 in Leona, Texas
d. Nov 24, 1993 in Las Vegas, Nevada
Source: *AnObit 1993; BioIn 19, 20; BluesWW; ConBlB 12; ConMus 4; GuBlues; News 94, 94-2; NewYTBS 93; OnThGG; PenEncP; RolSEnR 83; WhoAfA 96*

Collins, Barbara-Rose
American. Politician
Member of Michigan House of Representatives, 1975-81; Detroit City Council member, 1982-90; Democratic representative from MI, 1991-97.
b. Apr 13, 1939 in Detroit, Michigan
Source: *AfrAmBi 2; AlmAP 92, 96; CngDr 91, 93, 95; ConBlB 7; InB&W 80; NotBlAW 2; WhoAfA 96; WhoAm 92, 94, 95, 96, 97; WhoAmP 75, 77, 79, 81, 83, 85, 87, 89; WhoAmW 81, 83, 91, 93, 95, 97; WhoBlA 92, 94; WhoE 95; WhoGov 77; WhoMW 92, 93, 96; WhoWomW 91; WomPO 78*

Collins, Bootsy
[William Collins]
American. Singer, Musician, Producer
Funk singer; known for trademark "Bootzilla" sunglasses and outrageous clothing; several hit singles and gold albums while in the Rubber Band; producer for stars such as Iggy Pop and Keith Richards.
b. Oct 26, 1951 in Cincinnati, Ohio
Source: *BioIn 11, 16; ConMus 8; NewGrDA 86; RolSEnR 83*

Collins, Cardiss (Hortense Robertson)
American. Politician
First black woman to be elected to US Congress, from IL, 1973; first woman to serve as chairman of Congresssional Black Caucus, 1975.
b. Sep 24, 1931 in Saint Louis, Missouri
Source: *AfrAmAl 6; AfrAmBi 1; AlmAP 78, 80, 82, 84, 88, 92, 96; BiDrUSC 89; BioIn 11; BlkAmsC; CngDr 74, 77, 79, 81, 83, 85, 87, 89, 91, 93, 95; ConBlB 10; InB&W 85; NegAl 89; News 95, 95-3; NotBlAW 1; PolsAm 84; WhoAfA 96; WhoAm 88, 90, 92, 94, 95, 96, 97; WhoAmP 79, 81, 83, 85, 87, 89, 91, 93, 95; WhoAmW 75, 89, 91, 93, 95, 97; WhoBlA 75, 77, 80, 85, 88, 90, 92, 94; WhoGov 75, 77; WhoMW 78, 86, 88, 90, 92, 93, 96; WomCon; WomPO 78*

Collins, Dorothy
[Marjorie Chandler]
Canadian. Singer
Pop singer; star of "Hit Parade," 1950s.
b. Nov 18, 1926 in Windsor, Ontario, Canada
Source: *BiDAmM; BioIn 3, 4, 9, 20; CmpEPM; InWom, SUP; LegTOT; NewYTBE 71; NewYTBS 94; PlP&P A; RadStar; WhoAdv 90; WhoAmW 70; WorAl*

Collins, Eddie
[Edward Trowbridge Collins, Sr]
"Cocky"
American. Baseball Player
Second baseman, 1906-30; had .333 career batting average; Hall of Fame, 1939.
b. May 2, 1887 in Millertown, New York
d. Mar 25, 1951 in Boston, Massachusetts
Source: *Ballpl 90; BiDAmSp BB; BioIn 2, 3, 4, 5, 6, 7, 8, 9, 10, 14, 15, 17; DcAmB S5; LegTOT; WhoProB 73; WhoSpor*

Collins, Eileen
American. Astronaut
First female pilot of the U.S. Space Shuttle, 1995.
b. Nov 19, 1956 in Elmira, New York
Source: *News 95, 95-3*

Collins, Francis S(ellers)
American. Geneticist
Director, National Center for Human Genome Research, 1993—.
b. Apr 14, 1950 in Staunton, Virginia
Source: *AmMWSc 92, 95; CurBio 94*

Collins, Gary
American. TV Personality
Host, "Hour Magazine;" won Emmy, 1984; married to Mary Ann Mobley.
b. Aug 30, 1938 in Boston, Massachusetts
Source: *BioIn 12, 13, 16; ConTFT 6; HalFC 84, 88; IntMPA 92, 94, 96; ItaFilm; LegTOT; VarWW 85; WhoHol 92, A; WhoWrEP 89*

Collins, Jackie
[Jacqueline Jill Collins]
American. Author
Best-selling novels include *Hollywood Wives,* 1983; *Rock Star,* 1988; sister of actress Joan.
b. Oct 4, 1941 in London, England
Source: *ArtclWW 2; BestSel 90-4; BioIn 12, 14, 15, 16; CelR 90; ConAu 22NR, 102; ConPopW; HalFC 84, 88; IntAu&W 91; IntWW 91; InWom SUP; WorAlBi; WrDr 86, 92*

Collins, Janet Faye
American. Dancer, Choreographer
First African-American prima ballerina of Metropolitan Opera, 1951-54; choreographed, *Three Psalms of David.*

b. Mar 2, 1917 in New Orleans, Louisiana
Source: *BiDD; DrBlPA 90; NotBlAW 1; WhoBlA 92*

Collins, Jimmy
[James Joseph Collins]
American. Baseball Player
Third baseman, 1895-1908, known for defensive play; Hall of Fame, 1945.
b. Jan 16, 1873 in Niagara Falls, New York
d. Mar 6, 1943 in Buffalo, New York
Source: *BioIn 2, 3, 7, 14, 15; WhoProB 73*

Collins, Joan Henrietta
English. Actor
Played Alexis Carrington Colby on TV soap opera "Dynasty," 1981-89.
b. May 23, 1933 in London, England
Source: *BioIn 13, 14, 15, 16; CelR 90; ConAu 116; ContDcW 89; ConTFT 8; CurBio 84; DcLP 87B; FilmgC; HalFC 88; IntAu&W 91; IntMPA 92; IntWW 91; InWom SUP; LesBEnT 92; MotPP; MovMk; Who 94; WhoAm 86, 88, 90, 92, 94, 95, 96, 97; WhoAmW 89, 91, 93, 95, 97; WhoEnt 92; WhoHol A; WhoTelC; WhoWor 89, 91, 93, 95, 96, 97; WrDr 92*

Collins, John F(rederick)
American. Politician
Dem. mayor of Boston, 1960-68.
b. Jul 20, 1919
d. Nov 23, 1995 in Boston, Massachusetts
Source: *AmCath 80; BioIn 7, 10, 11; CurBio 96N; PolProf J, K; WhoAm 74, 76, 78, 80; WhoE 74*

Collins, Joseph Lawton, General
"Lightning Joe"
American. Army Officer
Army chief of staff, 1949-53; head of army during Korean War; Ambassador to Viet Nam, 1954-55.
b. May 1, 1896 in New Orleans, Louisiana
d. Sep 12, 1987 in Washington, District of Columbia
Source: *AmCath 80; BiDWWGF; BioIn 2, 3, 5, 7, 11, 15; BlueB 76; CmdGen 1991; CurBio 49, 87; DcAmMiB; GenMudB; HarEnMi; IntWW 74, 75, 76, 77, 78, 79, 80, 81, 82, 83; WebAMB; WhAm 10; Who 74, 82, 83, 85; WhoAm 74, 76*

Collins, Judy
[Judith Marjorie Collins; Mrs. Louis Nelson]
American. Singer
Hits include "Both Sides Now," 1968; "Send in the Clowns," 1975.
b. May 1, 1939 in Seattle, Washington
Source: *Baker 84; BiDAmM; BioIn 7, 8, 10, 11, 12, 14, 15, 17, 18, 19, 21; CelR, 90; ConAu 103; ConMus 4; CurBio 69; DcTwCCu 1; EncFCWM 69, 83; EncRk 88; EncRkSt; FacFETw; GoodHs; InWom SUP; LegTOT; NewAmDM; NewGrDA 86; NewYTBS 76; OxCPMus; PenEncP; RkOn 78; RolSEnR 83; WhoAm 86, 90; WhoAmW 85; WhoEnt 92; WhoHol 92; WhoRock 81; WhoRocM 82; WhoWor 74; WorAlBi*

Collins, Larry
American. Author, Journalist
Middle East correspondent for *Newsweek* mag., 1961-65; novels include *The Fifth Horseman,* 1980.
b. Sep 14, 1929 in Hartford, Connecticut
Source: *AmAu&B; BioIn 12; CelR; ConAu 65, X; IntAu&W 91, 93; IntWW 91, 93; NewYTBS 80; ScF&FL 92; WhoAm 74, 76, 78, 80, 82, 84, 86, 88, 90, 92, 94, 95, 96, 97; WhoWor 74, 76, 78; WrDr 84, 86, 88, 90, 92, 94, 96*

Collins, Lee
American. Jazz Musician
Trumpeter, vocalist; led own ragtime band, Chicago, 1930s-50s.
b. Oct 17, 1901 in New Orleans, Louisiana
d. Jul 7, 1960 in Chicago, Illinois
Source: *AllMusG; BiDAmM; BiDJaz; BioIn 10, 16; CmpEPM; IlEncJ; NewGrDJ 88, 94; NewOrJ; WhoJazz 72*

Collins, Martha Layne Hall
American. Politician
First woman governor of KY, 1979-83; pres., St. Catherine College, 1990—; chaired Dem. National Convention, 1984.
b. Dec 7, 1936 in Bagdad, Kentucky
Source: *AlmAP 88; AmWomM; BioIn 13, 14, 15; CurBio 86; IntWW 91; PolsAm 84; WhoAm 86, 90; WhoAmP 85, 91; WhoAmW 85, 87, 91; WhoSSW 86, 88; WhoWor 89*

Collins, Marva Deloise Nettles
American. Teacher, Social Reformer
Started Chicago's one-room school, Westside Preparatory, 1975.
b. Aug 31, 1936 in Monroeville, Alabama
Source: *BioIn 16; ConAu 111; ConBlB 3; ConHero 1; CurBio 86; InB&W 85; NegAl 89; NotBlAW 1; WhoAm 82, 84, 86, 88, 90; WhoAmW 81, 83, 87, 89, 91, 93; WhoBlA 88, 92; WhoMW 82, 84; WrDr 92*

Collins, Michael
Irish. Revolutionary
Leader in the Sinn Fein movement; commanded Irish Free State Army in Irish Civil War, 1921-22.
b. Oct 16, 1890 in Clonakilty, Ireland
d. Aug 22, 1922 in Beal-na-Blath, Ireland
Source: *BioIn 2, 5, 8, 9, 10, 11, 12, 13, 17, 18; DcCathB; DcIrB 78, 88; DcNaB 1922; DcTwHis; EncRev; FacFETw; HarEnMi; HisDBrE; HisWorL; LinLib S; McGEWB; OxCIri; WebBD 83; WhDW; WhoMilH 76; WorAl; WorAlBi*

Collins, Mike
[Michael Collins]
American. Astronaut
Command module pilot, Apollo 11, first US landing on moon, 1969.
b. Oct 31, 1930 in Rome, Italy
Source: *AmMWSc 73P, 79; AuSpks; BioIn 7, 8, 9, 10, 11, 12, 16, 17, 20; BlueB 76; ConAu 5NR, 53; CurBio 75; EncSF; FacFETw; IntWW 74, 75, 76, 77, 78, 79, 80, 81, 82, 83, 89, 91, 93; LegTOT; LinLib S; SmATA 58; WebAMB; Who 74, 82, 83, 85, 88, 90, 92, 94; WhoAm 74, 76, 78, 80, 82, 84, 86, 88, 90, 92, 94, 95, 96; WhoFI 81; WhoGov 72, 75, 77; WhoSpc; WhoSSW 73, 75, 76; WhoWor 74, 76, 78, 80, 82, 84, 87, 89, 91, 93, 95; WorAl; WorAlBi*

Collins, Phil(ip)
English. Singer, Musician
Drummer, lead singer for Genesis; has successful solo career, including singles "One More Night," 1985; "Groovy Kind of Love," 1988; Grammy award winner, 1986.
b. Jan 30, 1951 in Chiswick, England
Source: *Baker 92; BioIn 13, 14, 15; CelR 90; ConMus 2; CurBio 86; EncRk 88; EncRkSt; HarEnR 86; IntWW 89, 91, 93; LegTOT; OxCPMus; PenEncP; RkOn 85; Who 92, 94; WhoAm 88; WhoEnt 92; WhoHol 92; WhoRocM 82*

Collins, Ray
American. Actor
Appeared in TV series "Perry Mason," 1957-64.
b. Dec 10, 1889 in Sacramento, California
d. Jul 11, 1965 in Santa Monica, California
Source: *BioIn 7; FilmgC; MotPP; MovMk; NotNAT B; RadStar; Vers A; WhoHol B; WhScrn 74, 77; WorAl*

Collins, Stephen
American. Actor
Films include *Star Trek;* starred in TV movie "The Two Mrs. Grenvilles," 1987.
b. Oct 1, 1947 in Des Moines, Iowa
Source: *IntMPA 84, 86, 88, 92, 94, 96; ItaFilm; WhoEnt 92; WhoHol 92*

Collins, Susan M.
American. Politician
Rep. senator, ME, 1997—.
b. Dec 7, 1952
Source: *WhoE 97*

Collins, Ted
American. TV Personality
Known for announcing, producing Kate Smith's radio, TV shows for over 30 yrs.
b. Oct 12, 1899 in New York, New York
d. May 27, 1964 in Lake Placid, New York
Source: *BioIn 3, 6; ODwPR 79*

Collins, Wilkie
[William Collins]
English. Author
Wrote mystery novels *The Woman in White,* 1860; *The Moonstone,* 1868.
b. Jan 8, 1824 in London, England
d. Sep 23, 1889 in London, England
Source: *AtlBL; BbD; Benet 87; BiD&SB; BioIn 1, 2, 3, 4, 5, 7, 8, 9, 10, 11, 14, 15, 16, 17, 18, 19, 21; BlmGEL; BritAu 19; CamGEL; CasWL; Chambr 3; CnDBLB 4; CrtSuMy; CrtT 3; CyWA 58; DcBiA; DcEnA; DcEnL; DcEuL; DcLB 18, 70, 159; DcLEL; EncMys; HalFC 84, 88; HsB&A; LegTOT; LngCEL; MnBBF; NewC; NinCLC 1, 18; NotNAT B; Novels; OxCEng 85; OxCThe 83; PenC ENG; PenEncH; PlP&P; RAdv 1, 14, 13-1; REn; RfGEnL 91; ScF&FL 1, 92; StaCVF; SupFW; TwCCr&M 80A, 85A, 91A; VicBrit; WebE&AL; WhDW; WhoHr&F; WorAl; WorAlBi*

Collins, William
English. Poet
Published 12 memorable *Odes,* 1747.
b. Dec 25, 1721 in Chichester, England
d. Jun 12, 1759 in Chichester, England
Source: *Alli; AtlBL; BbD; Benet 87, 96; BiD&SB; BioIn 1, 3, 5, 7, 8, 9, 10, 12, 17; BlmGEL; BritAu; BritWr 3; CamGEL; CamGLE; CasWL; Chambr 2; ChhPo, S1, S3; CnE&AP; CrtT 2; DcArts; DcEnA; DcEnL; DcEuL; DcLB 109; DcLEL; DcNaB; EvLB; LinLib L; LitC 4; LngCEL; McGEWB; MouLC 2; NewC; OxCEng 67, 85, 95; PenC ENG; RAdv 14, 13-1; REn; RfGEnL 91; WebE&AL; WhDW*

Collinsworth, Cris
[Anthony Cris Collinsworth]
"Cadillac"
American. Football Player
Three-time all-pro wide receiver, Cincinnati, 1981-88; sportscaster, "HBO Sports", 1991—.
b. Jan 27, 1959 in Dayton, Ohio
Source: *BioIn 12; FootReg 87; NewYTBS 82; WhoAm 88*

Collodi, Carlo
[Carlo Lorenzini]
Italian. Author
Story *Pinocchio,* first appeared in newspaper, 1880; English translation, 1892.
b. Nov 24, 1826 in Tuscany, Italy
d. Oct 26, 1890 in Florence, Italy
Source: *AnCL; AuBYP 2, 3; BioIn 1, 2, 3, 5, 7, 8, 13, 19; BkCL; CasWL; ChhPo S2; ChlBkCr; ChlLR 5; DcArts; DcItL 1, 2; EuAu; EvEuW; JBA 34, 51; LegTOT; LinLib L; MajAI; NewCBEL; NewCol 75; NinCLC 54; OxCChiL; SmATA 29; Str&VC; WhoChL*

Collor de Mello, Fernando Affonso
Brazilian. Political Leader
Moderate conservative president of Brazil, 1989-92; first popularly elected president in three decades; resigned after being impeached for corruption.
b. Aug 12, 1949 in Rio de Janeiro, Brazil
Source: *BioIn 16; CurBio 90; IntWW 91; News 92; NewYTBS 90; WhoWor 91*

Collyer, Bud
[Clayton Collyer]
American. TV Personality
Hosted TV game show "To Tell the Truth," 1956.
b. Jun 18, 1908 in New York, New York
d. Sep 8, 1969 in Greenwich, Connecticut
Source: *BioIn 8; LegTOT; LesBEnT; NewYTET; ObitOF 79; RadStar; SaTiSS*

Colman, George
English. Dramatist
Wrote comedies: *The Jealous Wife,* 1761; *The Clandestine Marriage,* 1766; managed Covent Garden, Haymarket theaters.
b. Apr 18, 1732 in Florence, Italy
d. Aug 14, 1794 in London, England
Source: *Alli; BbD; BiD&SB; BioIn 3, 12, 17; BritAu, 19; CamGEL; CamGLE; CamGWoT; CasWL; Chambr 2; DcEnA; DcEnL; DcEuL; DcLB 89; DcLEL; DcNaB; EncWT; EvLB; LinLib L; McGEWD 72, 84; MouLC 2; NewC; NewGrDO; NotNAT A, B; OxCEng 67, 85, 95; OxCThe 67, 83; PenC ENG; PlP&P; REn; RfGEnL 91; WebE&AL*

Colman, George
"The Younger"
English. Dramatist
Wrote comedies, including *John Bull,* 1803.
b. Oct 21, 1762 in London, England
d. Oct 17, 1836 in London, England
Source: *Alli; BbD; BiD&SB; BiDLA, SUP; BioIn 1, 12, 13, 17; BritAu 19; CamGEL; CamGLE; CamGWoT; CasWL; CelCen; Chambr 2; ChhPo, S1; DcBiPP; DcEnA; DcEnL; DcEuL; DcLB 89; DcNaB; EncWT; LinLib L; NewC; NewGrDO; NotNAT A, B; OxCEng 67, 85, 95; OxCThe 67, 83; PenC ENG; REn; RfGEnL 91; WebE&AL*

Colman, Norman Jay
American. Government Official
First secretary of Agriculture, 1889.
b. May 16, 1827 in Otsego County, New York
d. Nov 3, 1911
Source: *AmBi; BiDrUSE 71, 89; BioIn 3, 10; DcAmB; EncAAH; HarEnUS; InSci; TwCBDA; WhAm 1*

Colman, Ronald
American. Actor
Won Oscar for *A Double Life,* 1948; appeared in *A Tale of Two Cities,* 1936.
b. Feb 9, 1891 in Richmond, England
d. May 19, 1958 in Santa Barbara, California
Source: *BiDFilm, 94; BioIn 1, 3, 4, 5, 6, 7, 9, 10, 11, 14, 17; CmMov; CurBio 43, 58; DcArts; EncAFC; EncEurC; Film 1, 2; FilmgC; HalFC 84, 88; IntDcF 1-3, 2-3; LegTOT; MotPP; MovMk; NatCAB 43; NotNAT B; ObitT 1951; OxCFilm; RadStar; SaTiSS; TwYS; WhAm 3; WhoHol B; WhScrn 74, 77, 83; WhThe; WorAl; WorAlBi; WorEFlm*

Colman, Samuel
American. Artist
A founder, first president, American Watercolor Society, 1866.
b. Mar 4, 1832 in Portland, Maine
d. Mar 27, 1920 in New York, New York
Source: *AmBi; ApCAB, X; ArtsAmW 1, 3; BioIn 1, 11, 15; BriEAA; ChhPo; DcAmArt; DcAmB; DcNAA; Drake; EarABI; IlBEAAW; NatCAB 7; NewYHSD; PeoHis; TwCBDA; WhAm 1; WhAmArt 85*

Colombo, Emilio
Italian. Political Leader
Premier of Italy's post-fascist government, 1970-72; minister of Foreign Affairs, 1980-83.
b. Apr 11, 1920 in Potenza, Italy
Source: *CurBio 71; IntWW 74, 75, 76, 77, 78, 79, 80, 81, 82, 83, 89, 91, 93; IntYB 79, 80, 81, 82; NewYTBE 70; Who 82, 83, 85, 88, 90, 92, 94; WhoEIO 82; WhoWor 74, 76, 78, 80, 82, 93*

Colombo, Joseph Anthony
American. Criminal
Headed one of Mafia's biggest crime families; organized Italian-American Civil Rights League, 1970, to fight gangster stereotype.
b. Jun 16, 1923 in New York, New York
d. May 23, 1978 in Newburgh, New York
Source: *BioIn 11; DcAmB S10; EncACr; NewYTBE 70*

Colon, Diego
[Diego Columbus]
Spanish. Statesman
Eldest son of Christopher Columbus; appointed governor of Indies, 1508, and later Viceroy, 1511.
b. 1479?, Portugal
d. Feb 23, 1526 in Montalban, Spain
Source: *BioIn 3, 5, 15; WhAm HS*

Colonius, Lillian
American. Children's Author
Books include *At the Library,* 1967; *Here Comes the Fireboat,* 1967.
b. Mar 19, 1911 in Irvine, California
Source: *BioIn 9; SmATA 3*

Colonna, Jerry
[Gerald Colonna]
American. Comedian, Musician
Accompanied Bob Hope on overseas troop tours; movies with Hope include *Road to Sinapore,* 1940.
b. Sep 17, 1905 in Boston, Massachusetts

d. Nov 21, 1986 in Woodland Hills, California
Source: *ASCAP 66; BioIn 9; ConTFT 4; FilmgC; MovMk; SaTiSS; WhoHol A*

Colonne, Edouard
French. Conductor
Founded Parisian "Concerts Colonne," 1873, premiering works of Berlioz, contemporary composers.
b. Jul 23, 1838 in Bordeaux, France
d. Mar 28, 1910 in Paris, France
Source: *Baker 78, 84, 92; BioIn 2, 8; NewAmDM; NewCol 75; NewGrDM 80; OxCMus; PenDiMP*

Coloradas, Mangas
[Mangas; Mangas Coloradas]
American. Native American Leader
Chief of the Mimbreno Apaches, 1837-1863.
b. 1790? in New Mexico
d. Jan 1863 in Arizona
Source: *NotNaAm*

Colosio Murrieta, Luis Donaldo
Mexican. Politician
Director, Mexican Ministry of Social Development, 1992-93; presidential candidate, assassinated, 1994.
b. Feb 10, 1950 in Magdalena de Kino, Mexico
d. Mar 23, 1994 in Tijuana, Mexico

Colson, Chuck
[Charles Wendell Colson]
American. Presidential Aide
Special counsel to Nixon; became born-again Christian during Watergate trial; wrote *Born Again,* 1976.
b. Oct 16, 1931 in Boston, Massachusetts
Source: *BioIn 9, 10, 11, 12, 13, 14, 15, 16; ConAu 29NR, 102; NewYTBE 73; NewYTBS 74; WhoAm 74, 76, 78, 80, 82, 84, 86, 88, 90, 92, 94, 95, 96, 97; WhoGov 72, 75; WhoRel 92; WhoSSW 73; WhoUSWr 88; WhoWrEP 89, 92, 95; WorAl; WorAlBi; WrDr 92*

Colt, Samuel
American. Inventor
Patented revolving breech pistol, 1835; word "Colt" often synonymous with revolver.
b. Jul 19, 1814 in Hartford, Connecticut
d. Jan 10, 1862 in Hartford, Connecticut
Source: *AmBi; AntBDN F; ApCAB; BiDAmBL 83; BioIn 1, 2, 3, 5, 6, 7, 8, 10, 11, 13, 14, 15, 17, 18; CelCen; CopCroC; DcAmB; DcBiPP; Drake; EncAAH; Entr; HarEnUS; InSci; LegTOT; McGEWB; MorMA; NatCAB 6; OxCAmH; OxCDecA; TwCBDA; WebAB 74, 79; WebAMB; WhAm HS; WhCiWar; WhDW; WorAl; WorAlBi; WorInv*

Colter, Jessie
[Miriam Johnson]
American. Singer
Country-rock hits include "I'm Not Lisa," 1975.
b. May 25, 1947 in Phoenix, Arizona
Source: *BioIn 14; BkPepl; EncFCWM 83; HarEnCM 87; InWom SUP; PenEncP; RkOn 74; WhoAm 84*

Colter, John
American. Explorer
First white man to explore Teton Mt. Range, 1807.
b. 1775 in Staunton, Virginia
d. Nov 1813 in Dundee, Missouri
Source: *BioIn 2, 3, 4, 5, 6, 7, 8, 10, 11, 18, 19, 20; DcAmB; NewCol 75; REnAW; WhAm HS; WhNaAH; WhWE*

Colton, Gardner Quincy
American. Scientist, Inventor
First to successfully use nitrous oxide, or laughing gas, as an anesthetic, 1844.
b. Feb 7, 1814 in Georgia, Vermont
d. Aug 9, 1898 in Rotterdam, Netherlands
Source: *AmBi; ApCAB; DcAmB; DcNAA; HarEnUS; InSci; NatCAB 2; TwCBDA; WhAm HS*

Coltrane, Trane
[John William Coltrane]
American. Jazz Musician
Tenor sax virtuoso; played with Dizzy Gillespie, Miles Davis; helped create "new black music."
b. Sep 26, 1926 in Hamlet, North Carolina
d. Jul 17, 1967 in Huntington, New York
Source: *Baker 84; BiDAmM; IlEncJ; WebAB 74; WhAm 4*

Coluche
[Michel Colucci]
French. Entertainer
Known for vulgar, irreverent humor; most ubiquitous show business star in France.
b. Oct 28, 1944 in Paris, France
d. Jun 19, 1986 in Opio, France
Source: *AnObit 1986; ItaFilm; NewYTBS 86; WhoFr 79*

Colum, Padraic
Irish. Poet
A founder, Irish National Theater; wrote verse *Creatures,* 1927; juvenile book *Children of Odin,* 1920.
b. Dec 8, 1881 in Langford, Ireland
d. Jan 12, 1972 in New York, New York
Source: *AmAu&B; AnCL; ASCAP 66; AuBYP 2, 3; Benet 87, 96; BenetAL 91; BiDIrW; BioIn 1, 2, 3, 4, 5, 7, 8, 9, 10, 12, 13, 14, 17, 19; BkC 3; CamGEL; CamGLE; CamGWoT; CarSB; CasWL; CathA 1930; ChhPo, S1, S2, S3; ChlBkCr; ChlLR 36; CnMD; ConAu 33R, 35NR, 73; ConLC 28; ConPo 70; CrtSuDr; CyWA 89; DcAmB S9; DcArts; DcIrB 78, 88; DcIrL, 96; DcIrW 1, 2; DcLB 19; DcLEL; EncWL; EvLB; FacFETw; FamSYP; IntDcT 2; IriPla; JBA 34, 51; LinLib L, S; LngCTC; MajAI; MajTwCW; McGEWB; McGEWD 72, 84; ModBrL, S1; ModIrL; ModWD; NewC; NotNAT A; ObitT 1971; OxCChiL; OxCEng 85, 95; OxCIri; OxCThe 67, 83; OxCTwCP; PenC ENG; PeoHis; PlP&P; RAdv 1, 14, 13-1; REn; REnWD; RfGEnL 91; SmATA 15; Str&VC; TwCA, SUP; TwCChW 78, 83, 89, 95; TwCWr; WebE&AL; WhAm 5, 7; WhDW; WrChl*

Columba, Saint
Irish. Missionary
Established monastery on island of Iona, 563; wrote three hymns.
b. 521 in Tyrconnell, Ireland
d. Jun 8, 597 in Iona, Scotland
Source: *Benet 87, 96; BiDIrW B; BioIn 1, 2, 3, 4, 5, 6, 7, 8, 9, 10, 11, 12, 14, 17; BlmGEL; CasWL; CyEd; DcBiPP; DcCathB; DcIrW 3; DcNaB; Dis&D; EncEarC; LngCEL; McGEWB; NewC; NewCol 75; OxCEng 67, 85, 95; PenC ENG; REn; WebBD 83; WhDW*

Columban, Saint
Irish. Religious Figure
Missionary to Europe whose practices alienated religious, political powers; founded abbey at Luxeil, 590.
b. 543 in Leinster, Ireland
d. Nov 23, 615 in Bobbia, Italy
Source: *CasWL; CyEd; NewC; NewCol 75; WebBD 83*

Columbo, Russ
[Ruggerio de Rudolpho Columbo]
American. Bandleader, Singer
Baritone; formed band, 1931; died in tragic shooting incident.
b. Jan 4, 1908 in Philadelphia, Pennsylvania
d. Sep 2, 1934 in Hollywood, California
Source: *BiDAmM; BioIn 12, 16; CmpEPM; Film 2; FilmgC; HalFC 84, 88; LegTOT; OxCPMus; PenEncP; RadStar; SaTiSS; WhoHol B; WhScrn 74, 77, 83*

Columbus, Chris
American. Filmmaker, Director
Screenwriter for *Gremlins,* 1984; *Goonies,* 1985; directed *Home Alone,* 1990; *Home Alone 2,* 1992.
b. Sep 10, 1958 in Spangler, Pennsylvania
Source: *BioIn 15; ConTFT 5; IntMPA 92*

Columbus, Christopher
[Cristoforo Colombo]
Italian. Explorer
Sailed from Palos, Spain, Aug 3, 1492; sighted land, San Salvador, Oct 12, 1492.
b. 1451 in Genoa, Italy
d. May 20, 1506, Spain
Source: *AsBiEn; Benet 87, 96; BenetAL 91; BioIn 11, 12, 13; CamDcSc; CasWL; DcEuL; DcScB, S1; EncAB-H 1974, 1996; EncARH; EncCRAm; EncLatA; EvEuW; Expl 93; HisDcSE; HisWorL; LegTOT; McGEWB; NewC; NewYTBS 91; OxCAmH; OxCAmL 65; OxCShps; REn; REnAL; WebAB 74, 79; WhDW; WhNaAH; WhWE; WorAl; WorAlBi*

Colville, Alex
[David Alexander Colville]
Canadian. Artist
Realist painter who captured people, places, animals of Maritime Provinces.
b. Aug 24, 1920 in Toronto, Ontario, Canada
Source: *BioIn 13, 14; CanWW 31, 81, 83, 89; ConArt 77, 83, 89, 96; CreCan 1; CurBio 85; DcArts; DcCAr 81; McGDA; OxCTwCA; OxDcArt; PhDcTCA 77; WhoAm 78, 80, 82, 84, 86, 88, 90, 92, 94, 95, 96, 97; WhoAmA 91*

Colville, Neil McNeil
Canadian. Hockey Player
Center, NY Rangers, 1935-42, 1944-49; Hall of Fame, 1967.
b. Aug 4, 1914 in Edmonton, Alberta, Canada
Source: *HocEn; WhoHcky 73*

Colvin, Sidney, Sir
English. Museum Director
Head of prints, British Museum; wrote on literature, arts: *Early Engraving and Engravers in England,* 1905.
b. Jun 18, 1845 in Norwood, England
d. May 11, 1927 in London, England
Source: *Alli SUP; BiD&SB; BioIn 8, 10, 21; CamGLE; CelCen; Chambr 3; ChhPo S2, S3; DcLB 149; DcLEL; DcNaB 1922; EvLB; LinLib L; LngCTC; NewC; NewCol 75; OxCEng 67, 85, 95; TwCA, SUP; WhLit*

Colwin, Laurie
American. Author
Writings include *Family Happiness,* 1982; *A Big Storm Knocked It Over,* 1993.
b. Jun 14, 1944? in New York, New York
d. Oct 24, 1992 in New York, New York
Source: *AnObit 1992; BioIn 12, 13; ConAu 20NR; ConLC 5, 13, 23, 76, 84; DcLB Y80B; MajTwCW; WorAu 1975; WrDr 92, 94N*

Comaneci, Nadia
[Mrs. Bart Conner]
Romanian. Gymnast
Won three Olympic gold medals, 1976; received seven perfect scores.
b. Nov 12, 1961 in Onesti, Romania
Source: *BioIn 10, 11, 12, 14, 15, 16, 17, 19, 21; BkPepl; CurBio 77; FacFETw; HerW 84; IntDcWB; IntWW 81, 82, 83, 89, 91, 93; InWom SUP; LegTOT; NewYTBS 81; WhoAm 94, 95, 96, 97; WhoWor 91; WorAl; WorAlBi*

Combe, George
Scottish. Author
Founded Phrenological Society, 1820; wrote *The Constitution of Man,* 1828.
b. Oct 21, 1788 in Edinburgh, Scotland
d. Aug 14, 1858 in Farnham, England
Source: *Alli; ApCAB; BiD&SB; BiDTran; BioIn 4, 5; BritAu 19; CelCen; Chambr 3; CyEd; DcBiPP; DcEnL; DcNaB; Drake; EvLB; NatCAB 6; WebBD 83*

Combe, William
"Count Combe"
English. Author
Best known for satirical verses in *Tours of Dr. Syntax,* 1812-21.
b. 1741 in Bristol, England
d. Jun 19, 1823 in London, England
Source: *BiD&SB; BioIn 3, 8; BritAu 19; CamGLE; CasWL; CelCen; Chambr 2; ChhPo, S2, S3; DcLEL; DcNaB; EvLB; NewC; NewCol 75; OxCEng 67, 85, 95; ScF&FL 1; WebBD 83; WebE&AL*

Combs, Earle Bryan
"The Kentucky Colonel"
American. Baseball Player
Outfielder, NY Yankees, 1924-35; had lifetime .350 batting average; Hall of Fame, 1970.
b. May 14, 1899 in Pebworth, Kentucky
Source: *Ballpl 90; BiDAmSp BB; BioIn 14, 15; DcAmB S10; WhoProB 73*

Combs, Sean
"Puffy"
American. Producer, Record Company Executive
President of Bad Boy Entertainment, a division of Arista Records, 1994; produced records by Mary J. Blige, *What's the 411,* 1993, Craig Mack, *Project: Funk Da World,* 1994 and The Notorious B.I.G., *Ready to Die,* 1994.
b. 1971 in New York, New York
Source: *ConMus 16*

Comden, Betty
[Mrs. Steven Kyle]
American. Dramatist
Won Tonys for *Applause,* 1970; *A Doll's Life,* 1982; wrote song "New York, New York," 1945.
b. May 3, 1915 in New York, New York
Source: *AmAu&B; AmPS; AmSong; AmWomD; ASCAP 66; Baker 84, 92; BiDAmM; BiE&WWA; BioIn 5, 6, 8, 9, 10, 12, 15, 16; CamGWoT; CelR 90; CmpEPM; ConAu 2NR, 49; ConDr 82D, 88D; ConTFT 2; CurBio 45; DcLB 44; EncMT; FacFETw; FemiCLE; FilmgC; HalFC 84, 88; IntMPA 86, 92; InWom, SUP; NewCBMT; NewGrDA 86; NotNAT; NotWoAT; OxCAmT 84; OxCFilm; OxCPMus; WhoAm 86, 90; WhoAmW 85, 91; WhoEnt 92; WhoThe 81; WomWMM; WorAlBi; WorEFlm*

Comenius, Johann Amos
"Grandfather of Modern Education"
Czech. Author
Developed new philosophy of education; wrote *Orbis Sensualium Pictus,* 1658, first illustrated textbook, used for 200 yrs.
b. Mar 28, 1592 in Unersky, Moravia
d. Nov 15, 1670 in Amsterdam, Netherlands
Source: *BbD; BiD&SB; BioIn 1, 4, 7, 8, 9, 10, 12, 21; CarSB; CasWL; ChhPo, S1; DcBiPP, A; DcEuL; Dis&D; EuAu; EvEuW; NamesHP; PenC EUR; Str&VC; WhDW*

Comer, Anjanette
American. Actor
Leading roles in films include *Fire Sale,* 1977.
b. Aug 7, 1942 in Dawson, Texas
Source: *BioIn 16; FilmEn; FilmgC; HalFC 84, 88; MotPP; WhoAmW 72; WhoHol 92, A*

Comer, James P(ierpont)
American. Psychiatrist, Writer, Educator
Noted for "Comer Method," a successful plan to turn academically failing low income, minority-dominated schools around; wrote *Maggie's American Dream,* 1988.
b. Sep 25, 1934 in East Chicago, Indiana
Source: *AmMWSc 73S, 76P, 79, 82, 86, 89, 92, 95; BiDrAPA 77, 89; BioIn 14, 16; BlksScM; BlkWr 2; ConAu 43NR, 61; CurBio 91; InB&W 85; St&PR 75, 84, 87, 91, 93, 96, 97; WhoAfA 96; WhoAm 74, 76, 78, 80, 82, 84, 86, 88, 90, 92, 94, 95, 96, 97; WhoBlA 85, 88, 90, 92, 94; WhoE 91; WhoFI 89; WhoMedH; WhoScEn 94, 96*

Comfort, Alexander
English. Author
Biologist, best known for books *The Joy of Sex,* 1972; *A Gormet's Guide to Making Love,* 1973.
b. Feb 10, 1920 in London, England
Source: *AmMWSc 79, 82, 86, 89, 92, 95; Au&Wr 71; BiDrAPA 89; BioIn 4, 10, 11, 13; BlueB 76; ChhPo S3; ConAu 1NR, 1R; ConNov 72, 76, 86; ConPo 70, 75, 80, 91; DcLEL 1940; DcLP 87A; EncWL; EngPo; EvLB; IntAu&W 76, 77, 82, 89, 91; IntWW 74, 75, 76, 77, 78, 79, 80, 81, 82, 83, 89, 91, 93; LngCTC; ModBrL; PenC ENG; TwCA SUP; WhE&EA; Who 74, 82, 83, 85, 88, 90, 92, 94; WhoAm 76, 78, 80, 82, 84, 86, 88, 90, 92, 94, 95, 96, 97; WhoWor 74, 76, 78, 80, 82, 84; WorAl; WorAlBi; WrDr 76, 86, 92*

Comines, Philippe de
French. Historian, Diplomat
Memories written during reigns of Louis XI, Charles VIII were basis for Scott's novel *Quentin Durward.*
b. 1445 in Renescure, Flanders
d. 1511 in Argentan, France
Source: *BbD; BiD&SB; BioIn 7, 10, 12, 16; DcBiPP; Dis&D; McGEWB; NewCol 75; OxCEng 67; REn*

Comiskey, Charlie
[Charles Albert Comiskey]
"Commy"; "Old Roman"
American. Baseball Player, Baseball Executive
Infielder, 1882-94; original owner of Chicago White Sox, 1895; Hall of Fame, 1939.
b. Aug 15, 1859 in Chicago, Illinois

d. Oct 26, 1931 in Eagle River, Wisconsin
Source: *Ballpl 90; BiDAmSp BB; BioIn 3, 4, 7; LegTOT; NatCAB 24; WhoProB 73*

Comissiona, Sergiu
American. Conductor
Music director, Houston Symphony, 1983-88; Baltimore Symphony, 1969-84; Vancouver Symphony, 1990—; named NYC Opera music director, 1986—.
b. Jun 16, 1928 in Bucharest, Romania
Source: *Baker 78, 84, 92; BioIn 9, 10, 11, 15; BioNews 74; CanWW 31; IntWWM 77, 85, 90; MusSN; NewAmDM; NewGrDA 86; NewGrDM 80; NewGrDO; PenDiMP; WhoAm 74, 76, 78, 80, 82, 84, 86, 88, 90, 92, 94, 95, 96, 97; WhoAmM 83; WhoE 81, 83, 85; WhoEnt 92; WhoMus 72; WhoOp 76; WhoSSW 84, 86; WhoWest 92, 94; WhoWor 74, 76, 82, 84, 87, 89, 91, 93, 95, 96, 97*

Commager, Henry Steele
American. Historian, Educator
Histories of the US include *The Growth of the American Republic,* 1930; *The Blue and the Gray,* 1950.
b. Oct 25, 1902 in Pittsburgh, Pennsylvania
Source: *AmAu&B; ApCAB; AuBYP 2, 3; Benet 87; BenetAL 91; BiDAmEd; BioIn 1, 2, 4, 7, 10, 13, 16, 17; BlueB 76; ChhPo S1; CivWDc; ConAu 21R, 26NR; CurBio 46; DcLB 17; DcLEL; DrAS 74H, 78H, 82H; EncWB; IntAu&W 76, 77; IntWW 74, 75, 76, 77, 78, 79, 80, 81, 82, 83, 89, 91, 93; LinLib L, S; MajTwCW; OxCAmH; OxCAmL 65, 83, 95; PenC AM; RAdv 14, 13-3; REn; REnAL; SmATA 23; TwCA SUP; WebAB 74, 79; WhAm 8; WhE&EA; Who 74, 82, 83, 85, 88, 90, 92, 94; WhoAm 76, 78, 80, 82, 86, 88, 90, 97; WhoE 74; WhoWor 74; WorAl; WorAlBi; WrDr 76, 80, 82, 84, 86, 88, 90, 92, 94, 96*

Commager, Steele
[Henry Steele, Jr]
American. Author
Best known for works about the classics: *Odes of Horace: A Critical Study.*
b. Jul 13, 1932 in Bennettsville, South Carolina
d. Apr 2, 1984 in New York, New York
Source: *BioIn 13, 14; ConAu 112; NewYTBS 84; WhoAm 80*

Commodores, The
[William King; Ronald LaPread; Thomas McClary; Walter Clyde Orange; Lionel Richie, Jr; Milan Williams]
American. Music Group
Formed, 1968; number one hits include "Three Times a Lady," 1978; "Sail On," 1979.
Source: *Alli; AntBDN O; ApCAB; BiDAmM; BiDSA; BioIn 14, 15, 16, 18, 19; BkPepl; Chambr 2; DcCanB 9; Drake; EncRk 88; EncRkSt; FolkA 87; HarEnR 86; InB&W 80, 85, 85A; NewAmDM; NewGrDA 86; NewYHSD; PenEncP; RkOn 74, 78; RolSEnR 83; ScFSB; SoulM; TwCSFW 86; WhFla; WhoBlA 85; WhoRock 81*

Commoner, Barry
American. Biologist
Ecology, plant physiology expert; wrote *Science and Survival,* 1966.
b. May 28, 1917 in New York, New York
Source: *AmAu&B; AmMWSc 73P, 76P, 79, 82, 86, 89, 92; AmRef&R; BioIn 7, 8, 9, 10, 11, 12, 16, 17, 20, 21; BlueB 76; CelR; ConAu 33NR, 65; ConIsC 1; CurBio 70; EncWB; EnvEnc; IntWW 74, 75, 76, 77, 78, 79, 80, 81, 82, 83, 89, 91, 93; LNinSix; MajTwCW; NewYTBS 76; NotTwCS; PolPar; WhDW; WhoAm 74, 76, 78, 80, 82, 84, 86, 88, 90, 92, 94, 95, 96, 97; WhoScEn 94, 96; WhoWor 74, 82, 84; WorAl; WorAlBi; WrDr 82, 84, 86, 88, 90, 92, 94, 96*

Commons, John Rogers
American. Economist
First to study American labor movements; wrote *History of Labor in the US,* 1935.
b. Oct 13, 1862 in Hollansburg, Ohio
d. May 11, 1945 in Raleigh, North Carolina
Source: *AmLY; AmRef; AmSocL; BiDAmL; BiDSocW; BioIn 1, 2, 3, 5, 6, 7, 8, 11; DcAmAu; DcAmB S3; DcAmImH; DcNAA; McGEWB; NatCAB 13; OhA&B; OxCAmH; RAdv 14; TwCBDA; WebAB 74, 79; WhAm 2; WhNAA; WhoEc 81; WisWr*

Como, Perry
[Pierino Roland Como]
American. Singer
Popular, easy-going crooner for over 40 years; TV show, 1948-63; hits include "Prisoner of Love," 1956.
b. May 18, 1912 in Canonsburg, Pennsylvania
Source: *AmCath 80; AmPS A, B; Baker 84, 92; BiDAmM; BioIn 12, 14, 16; BkPepl; CelR, 90; CmpEPM; CurBio 47; FilmgC; HalFC 84, 88; IntMPA 77, 82, 84, 86, 88, 92, 94, 96; LegTOT; LesBEnT 92; NewGrDA 86; NewYTET; OxCPMus; PenEncP; RkOn 74; SaTiSS; WhoAm 86, 90; WhoEnt 92; WhoHol 92, A; WhoMus 72; WorAl; WorAlBi*

Compton, Ann (Woodruff)
American. Broadcast Journalist
ABC News White House correspondent, 1979-81, 1984—.
b. Jan 19, 1947 in Chicago, Illinois
Source: *BioIn 10, 11; EncTwCJ; InWom SUP; WhoAm 80, 82, 84, 86, 88, 90, 92, 94, 95, 96, 97; WhoAmW 85, 87, 89, 91, 93, 95, 97*

Compton, Arthur Holly
American. Scientist
Helped develop atomic bomb; won Nobel Prize for X-ray research, 1927; brother of Karl, Wilson.
b. Sep 10, 1892 in Wooster, Ohio
d. Mar 15, 1962 in Berkeley, California
Source: *AmAu&B; AmDec 1920; AsBiEn; BiDAmEd; BiESc; BioIn 1, 3, 4, 5, 6, 7, 13, 14, 15, 17, 20; CamDcSc; ConAu 116; CurBio 40, 58, 62; DcAmB S7; DcScB; EncAB-H 1974, 1996; FacFETw; InSci; LarDcSc; LinLib L, S; McGEWB; NotTwCS; ObitT 1961; OhA&B; OxCAmH; REnAL; WebAB 74, 79; WhAm 4, HSA; WhDW; WhNAA; WhoNob, 90, 95; WorAl; WorScD*

Compton, Fay
[Virginia Lilian Emeline Compton]
English. Actor
Remembered as the supreme Ophelia of her time; wrote *Rosemary,* 1926.
b. Sep 18, 1894 in London, England
d. Dec 12, 1978 in Hove, England
Source: *BiE&WWA; BioIn 11; CnThe; DcNaB 1971; EncWT; Film 1, 2; FilmgC; HalFC 84, 88; IntDcT 3; InWom; ItaFilm; NotNAT, A; ObitOF 79; OxCThe 67, 83; PlP&P; Who 74; WhoHol A; WhoThe 72, 81N; WhScrn 83; WhThe*

Compton, Joyce
[Eleanor Hunt]
American. Actor
Played "dumb blonde" roles in over 50 films, 1920s-30s.
b. Jan 27, 1907 in Lexington, Kentucky
Source: *BioIn 19; EncAFC; Film 2; FilmgC; HalFC 84, 88; IntMPA 86, 92, 94, 96; InWom SUP; MotPP; MovMk; ThFT; WhoHol 92, A*

Compton, Karl Taylor
American. Physicist
Associated with development of atomic bomb, radar, jet rockets; pres., MIT, 1930-49.
b. Sep 14, 1887 in Wooster, Ohio
d. Jun 22, 1954 in New York, New York
Source: *AmAu&B; BiDAmEd; BioIn 1, 2, 3, 4, 5; CurBio 41, 54; DcAmB S5; DcScB; InSci; LinLib S; NatCAB 42; ObitT 1951; OhA&B; OxCAmH; WebBD 83; WhAm 3; WorAl*

Compton, Wilson Martindale
American. University Administrator
Pres. of State College of WA, 1944-51; head of International Information Administration, 1952.
b. Oct 15, 1890 in Wooster, Ohio
d. Mar 7, 1967
Source: *BioIn 1, 2, 3, 5, 7, 8, 10; CurBio 52, 67; NatCAB 54; ObitOF 79; WhAm 4*

Compton-Burnett, Ivy, Dame
English. Author
Wrote witty, chilling social comedies of Edwardian family life: *Mother and Son,* 1955.

b. Jun 5, 1892 in London, England
d. Aug 27, 1969 in London, England
Source: *ArtclWW 2; Benet 87, 96; BioIn 2, 3, 4, 7; CamGEL; CamGLE; CasWL; CnMWL; ConAu 1R, 4NR; ConLC 1, 3, 10, 15; DcArts; DcLEL; EncWL; EvLB; InWom, SUP; LinLib L; LngCEL; LngCTC; ModBrL, S1, S2; ModWoWr; NewC; Novels; OxCEng 67; PenC ENG; PenNWW A; RAdv 1, 14, 13-1; REn; TwCA SUP; TwCWr; WebE&AL; WhAm 5; WhDW; WhoTwCL; WomNov*

Comstock, Ada Louise
American. Educator
First pres., Radcliffe College, 1923-43; first pres., American Assn. of U Women, 1921.
b. Dec 11, 1876 in Moorhead, Minnesota
d. Dec 12, 1973 in New Haven, Connecticut
Source: *AmWomM; BiDAmEd; BioIn 5, 10, 11, 12; EncAB-A 2; NotAW MOD; WhAm 6; WhoAmW 58, 61, 66; WomWWA 14*

Comstock, Anthony
American. Author, Social Reformer
Founder, secretary, Society of Suppression of Vice, 1873-1915.
b. Mar 7, 1844 in New Canaan, Connecticut
d. Sep 21, 1915 in New York, New York
Source: *Alli SUP; AmAu&B; AmBi; AmRef; AmSocL; BenetAL 91; BioIn 2, 9, 10, 13, 15, 17, 19; CnDAL; ConAu 110; CopCroC; DcAmB; DcAmC; DcNAA; GayN; HumSex; LinLib L; LngCTC; McGEWB; NatCAB 15; OxCAmH; OxCAmL 65, 83, 95; PenC AM; REnAL; TwCBDA; TwCLC 13; WebAB 74, 79; WhAm 1*

Comstock, Elizabeth L
English. Abolitionist
Quaker minister who operated stations for underground railroads.
b. Oct 30, 1815 in Maidenhead, England
d. Aug 3, 1891 in Union Springs, New York
Source: *DcAmB; InWom; NotAW; WhAm HS; WhAmP*

Comstock, Henry Tompkins Paige
"Old Pancake"
American. Pioneer
Discovered Comstock Lode, Virginia City, NV, 1859, richest known US silver deposit.
b. 1820 in Trenton, Ontario, Canada
d. Sep 27, 1870 in Bozeman, Montana
Source: *AmBi; BioIn 2; DcAmB; McGEWB; WhAm HS*

Comstock, John Henry
American. Scientist
Entomologist, pioneer in insect, moth classification.
b. Aug 24, 1849 in Janesville, Wisconsin
d. Mar 20, 1931 in Ithaca, New York
Source: *Alli SUP; AmBi; ApCAB; BiDAmEd; BiDAmS; BioIn 1, 3, 9; DcAmAu; DcAmB S1; DcNAA; InSci; NatCAB 4, 22; TwCBDA; WebBD 83; WhAm 1*

Comte, Auguste
French. Philosopher
Founder of positivism, wrote *Ordre et Progres,* 1848.
b. Jan 19, 1798 in Montpellier, France
d. Sep 5, 1857 in Paris, France
Source: *BbD; Benet 87; BiD&SB; BiDPsy; BioIn 1, 2, 3, 4, 5, 6, 7, 8, 11, 14, 19, 20; BlmGEL; CasWL; CelCen; CyEd; DcAmC; DcBiPP; DcEuL; DcSoc; Dis&D; EncUnb; EuAu; EvEuW; LegTOT; LinLib L, S; LngCEL; LuthC 75; McGEWB; NamesHP; NinCLC 54; OxCEng 67, 85, 95; OxCFr; OxCLaw; RAdv 14, 13-3, 13-4; REn; WhDW; WorAl; WorAlBi; WrPh P*

Conacher, Charlie
[Charles William Conacher]
"The Bomber"
Canadian. Hockey Player
Right wing, 1929-41, mostly with Toronto; won Art Ross Trophy, 1934, 1935; Hall of Fame, 1961.
b. Dec 20, 1910 in Toronto, Ontario, Canada
d. Dec 30, 1967 in Toronto, Ontario, Canada
Source: *BioIn 2, 8; HocEn; WhoHcky 73*

Conacher, Lionel Pretoria
Canadian. Athlete, Politician
Won numerous awards in wrestling, boxing, lacrosse, baseball, and hockey; elected Canada's Athlete of the Half Century (1900-50); member, Canadian Parliament, 1949-54.
b. May 24, 1901 in Toronto, Ontario, Canada
d. May 26, 1954 in Ottawa, Ontario, Canada
Source: *BioIn 2, 3, 10; ObitOF 79; PeoHis; WhoHcky 73*

Conant, James Bryant
American. University Administrator, Diplomat
Pres., Harvard U, 1933-53; ambassador to W Germany, 1955-57; wrote on secondary education.
b. Mar 26, 1893 in Dorchester, Massachusetts
d. Feb 11, 1978 in Hanover, New Hampshire
Source: *AmAu&B; AmMWSc 76P; AmSocL; BiDAmEd; BiESc; BioIn 1, 2, 3, 4, 5, 6, 7, 8, 9, 11, 12, 13; ColdWar 1; ConAu 13R, 77; CurBio 41, 51, 78N; DcAmB S10; DcAmDH 80, 89; DcScB S2; EncAB-A 2; EncAB-H 1974, 1996; FacFETw; InSci; IntAu&W 77; IntWW 74, 75, 76, 77; LinLib S; McGEWB; NewYTBS 78; OxCAmH; OxCAmL 65, 83; REnAL; WebAB 74, 79; WhAm 7; Who 74; WhoAm 74, 76, 78; WhoWor 74; WorAl; WorAlBi*

Conaway, Jeff
American. Actor
Starred on Broadway in *Grease;* played Bobby on TV series "Taxi," 1978-81.
b. Oct 5, 1950 in New York, New York
Source: *BioIn 11, 12, 16; ConTFT 2, 5; HalFC 84, 88; IntMPA 81, 82, 84, 86, 88, 92, 94, 96; LegTOT; NewYTBS 78; VarWW 85; WhoHol 92*

Condie, Richard P
American. Conductor
Director, Mormon Tabernacle Choir, 1957-74; brought it to world prominence.
b. Jul 5, 1898 in Springville, Utah
d. Dec 22, 1985 in Salt Lake City, Utah
Source: *BioIn 14; NewYTBS 85; WhoAm 76*

Condit, Carl Wilbur
American. Engineer
Authority on structural engineering; wrote *Rise of the Skyscraper,* 1950.
b. Sep 29, 1914 in Cincinnati, Ohio
Source: *BioIn 16; ConAu 1R, 4NR; DrAS 74H, 78H, 82H; IntAu&W 76, 77, 82; WhoAm 74, 76, 78, 80, 82, 84, 86, 88, 90, 92, 94, 95, 96, 97; WhoEng 88; WhoTech 89; WrDr 76, 80, 86, 92*

Condon, Eddie
American. Bandleader, Jazz Musician
Jazz guitarist noted for "Chicago style" jazz, 1920s; opened NYC nightclub, 1946.
b. Nov 16, 1905 in Goodland, Indiana
d. Aug 3, 1973 in New York, New York
Source: *AllMusG; Baker 92; BioIn 1, 4, 10, 11, 12, 18; CmpEPM; ConAu 45; CurBio 44, 73, 73N; IlEncJ; NewAmDM; NewGrDA 86; NewGrDJ 88, 94; NewYTBE 73; OnThGG; OxCPMus; PenEncP; PeoHis; WhAm 6; WhoAm 74; WhoE 74; WhoJazz 72; WhoMus 72*

Condon, Edward Uhler
American. Physicist
Director, US Bureau of Standards, 1945-51; involved in atomic bomb project, 1943-45; professor, 1954-74.
b. Mar 2, 1902 in Alamogordo, New Mexico
d. Mar 26, 1974 in Boulder, Colorado
Source: *BioIn 1, 2, 3, 7, 8, 10, 11, 18; BioNews 74; DcAmB S9; InSci; LarDcSc; McGMS 80; NewYTBS 74; WebAB 74, 79; WebBD 83; WhAm 6; Who 74; WhoAm 74; WhoWor 74*

Condon, Jackie
[Our Gang]
American. Actor
Child actor who appeared in *Hallroom Boys, Our Gang* comedies, 1922.
b. Mar 25, 1918 in Los Angeles, California
d. Oct 13, 1977 in Inglewood, California
Source: *Film 2; TwYS; WhScrn 83*

Condon, Richard (Thomas)
American. Author
Best-selling novels include *Manchurian Candidate,* 1959; *Prizzi's Honor,* 1982.
b. Mar 18, 1915 in New York, New York
d. Apr 9, 1996 in Dallas, Texas
Source: *AmAu&B; Au&Wr 71; BenetAL 91; BestSel 90-3; BioIn 2, 9, 10, 11, 12, 13, 14, 15, 16; ConAu 1AS, 1R, 2NR, 23NR, 151; ConLC 4, 6, 8, 10, 45; ConNov 72, 76, 82, 86, 91, 96; CurBio 89, 96N; EncSF, 93; IntAu&W 76, 77, 91, 93; IntWW 89, 91, 93; LegTOT; MajTwCW; ModAL, S1; News 96; Novels; PenC AM; RGTwCWr; ScF&FL 1, 2, 92; ScFSB; SpyFic; TwCCr&M 80, 85, 91; WhAm 11; WhoAm 74, 76, 78, 80, 82, 84, 86, 88, 90, 92, 94, 95, 96; WhoEnt 92; WhoSpyF; WhoWor 74, 76, 78; WorAl; WorAlBi; WorAu 1950; WrDr 76, 80, 82, 84, 86, 88, 90, 92, 94, 96*

Condorcet, Marie-Jean-Antoine
French. Philosopher, Mathematician, Revolutionary
Politically prominent during revolution; wrote *Reflexions sur le Commerce des Bles,* 1786.
b. Sep 17, 1743 in Ribemont, France
d. Mar 25, 1794 in Bourg-la-Reine, France
Source: *BbD; BiD&SB; CasWL; DcEuL; EuAu; EvEuW; NewC; OxCEng 67; OxCFr; REn*

Cone, Fairfax Mastick
American. Advertising Executive
Founder, director of Foote, Cone, and Belding, international advertising agency.
b. Feb 21, 1903 in San Francisco, California
d. Jun 20, 1977 in Carmel, California
Source: *BioIn 3, 4, 5, 6, 7, 8, 11; BlueB 76; ConAu 69, 73; CurBio 66; DcAmB S10; IntWW 74, 75, 76; NewYTBS 77; ObitOF 79; St&PR 75; WhAm 7; WhoAdv 72; WhoAm 74, 76, 78*

Cone, James H
American. Theologian, Educator, Author
Regarded as the father of black theology; wrote *A Black Theology of Liberation,*2 1970; *Martin and Malcolm and America,* 1991.
b. Aug 5, 1938 in Fordyce, Arkansas

Cone, Molly Lamken
American. Children's Author
Best known for juvenile fiction *Mishmash* series.
b. Oct 3, 1918 in Tacoma, Washington
Source: *AuBYP 2, 3; BioIn 7, 9, 13; ConAu 1NR, 1R, 16NR, 37NR; DcAmChF 1960; DcLP 87A; ForWC 70; PenNWW A; SmATA 1, 11AS, 28; ThrBJA; WhoAmW 64; WrDr 76, 84, 90*

Cone, Russell Glenn
American. Engineer
Expert on suspense bridges; headed work on Ambassador Bridge (Detroit), Golden Gate Bridge (San Francisco).
b. Mar 22, 1896 in Ottumwa, Iowa
d. Jan 21, 1961 in Vallejo, California
Source: *BioIn 8; DcAmB S7; NatCAB 51; WhAm 4*

Conerly, Charlie
[Charles A. Conerly]
American. Football Player
Quarterback, NY Giants, 1948-61; credited with inventing throwaway pass when trapped.
b. Sep 19, 1921 in Clarksdale, Mississippi
d. Feb 13, 1996 in Memphis, Tennessee
Source: *BioIn 21; WhoFtbl 74; WhoSpor*

Confalonieri, Carlo, Cardinal
Italian. Religious Leader
Dean, College of Cardinals, 1977-86; private secretary of Pope Pius XI, 1920s-30s.
b. Jul 25, 1893 in Seveso, Italy
d. Aug 1, 1986, Vatican City
Source: *AnObit 1986; BioIn 5, 15; IntWW 74, 75, 76, 77, 78, 79, 80, 81, 82, 83; WhoWor 74, 84*

Confrey, Zez
[Edward E. Confrey]
American. Composer
Pianist, bandleader, 1920s; piano works include "Kitten on the Keys."
b. Apr 3, 1895 in Peru, Illinois
d. Nov 22, 1971 in Lakewood, New Jersey
Source: *ASCAP 66; Baker 78, 84, 92; CmpEPM; NewGrDA 86; NewYTBE 71; OxCPMus; PenEncP; WhAm 5*

Confucius
[K'ung-fu-tzu]
Chinese. Philosopher
Developed religious system for management of society; emphasized good family relationships for social stability; philosophy is preserved in the *Lun-yu,* (*The Analects*).
b. Aug 27, 551BC in Tuo, China
d. Nov 21, 479BC in Qufu, China
Source: *BbD; Benet 87, 96; BiD&SB; BioIn 1, 2, 3, 4, 5, 6, 7, 8, 9, 10, 11, 13; CasWL; ClMLC 19; CyEd; DcArts; DcOrL 1; Dis&D; HisWorL; LegTOT; LinLib L; LuthC 75; McGEWB; NewC; OxCEng 85, 95; PenC CL; RAdv 13-4; RComWL; REn; WhDW; WorAl; WorAlBi; WrPh P*

Conger, Clement Ellis
American. Government Official
White House curator since 1970; has added over 500 pieces to building.
b. Oct 15, 1912 in Rockingham, Virginia
Source: *BioIn 9, 11, 13; NewYTBS 77; USBiR 74; WhoAm 74, 76, 78, 80, 82, 84, 86, 88, 90, 92, 94, 95, 96, 97; WhoAmA 78, 91; WhoE 79, 81, 83, 85, 86, 89; WhoGov 72, 75, 77; WhoSSW 73*

Congreve, Richard
English. Essayist, Philosopher
Translated *Catechism of Positive Religion;* wrote *Human Catholicism,* 1877.
b. Sep 14, 1818 in Warwickshire, England
d. Jul 5, 1899 in Hampstead, England
Source: *Alli SUP; BiD&SB; BritAu 19; CelCen; DcBiPP; DcEnL; DcNaB S1; NewC*

Congreve, William
English. Dramatist
Wrote *The Way of the World,* a comedy of manners, 1700.
b. Jan 24, 1670 in Bardsey, England
d. Jan 19, 1729 in London, England
Source: *Alli; AtlBL; BbD; Benet 87, 96; BiD&SB; BiDIrW; BiDLA; BioIn 1, 2, 3, 5, 6, 8, 9, 10, 12, 14, 15, 17, 18; BlkwCE; BlmGEL; BritAu; BritWr 2; CamGEL; CamGLE; CamGWoT; CasWL; Chambr 2; ChhPo S1; CnDBLB 2; CnThe; CrtSuDr; CrtT 2, 4; CyWA 58; DcArts; DcBiPP; DcEnA, A; DcEnL; DcEuL; DcIrB 88; DcIrL, 96; DcIrW 1; DcLB 39, 84; DcLEL; DcNaB; DramC 2; EncEnl; EncWT; EvLB; IntDcT 2; LinLib L, S; LitC 5, 21; LngCEL; MagSWL; McGEWB; McGEWD 72, 84; MouLC 2; NewC; NewGrDO; NotNAT A, B; OxCEng 67, 85, 95; OxCThe 67, 83; PenC ENG; PlP&P; RAdv 14, 13-2; RComWL; REn; REnWD; RfGEnL 91; WebE&AL; WhDW; WorAl; WorAlBi; WorLitC*

Conigliaro, Tony
[Anthony Richard Conigliaro]
American. Baseball Player
Outfielder, 1964-71, mostly with Boston; led AL in home runs, 1965, becoming youngest in MLs to do this; suffered crippling heart attack, 1982.
b. Jan 7, 1945 in Revere, Massachusetts
d. Feb 24, 1990 in Salem, Massachusetts
Source: *AnObit 1990; Ballpl 90; BioIn 7, 8, 9, 13, 16; CurBio 71, 90, 90N; News 90, 90-3; NewYTBE 71; NewYTBS 83, 90; WhoProB 73*

Conkle, Ellsworth Prouty
American. Dramatist, Educator
Works include *Five Plays,* 1947.
b. Jul 10, 1899 in Peru, Nebraska
Source: *AmAu&B; BioIn 19; CnMD; ConAu 65; DrAS 74E, 78E; ModWD; OxCAmL 65, 83; OxCCan*

Conklin, Chester
American. Comedian
Mustachioed silent screen star in *Keystone Cops* series, 1913-22.
b. Jan 11, 1888 in Oskaloosa, Iowa
d. Oct 11, 1971 in Hollywood, California
Source: *BioIn 7, 9; EncAFC; Film 1, 2; FilmgC; HalFC 84, 88; LegTOT; MotPP; MovMk; NewYTBE 72; ObitOF 79; OxCFilm; QDrFCA 92; TwYS; WhoHol B; WhScrn 74, 77, 83*

Conklin, Edwin Grant
American. Biologist
Authority in the field of human evolution, especially cell division and embryology.
b. Nov 24, 1863 in Waldo, Ohio
d. Nov 21, 1952 in Princeton, New Jersey
Source: *BioIn 1, 3, 4, 6, 11, 12, 13; DcAmB S5; DcScB; InSci; NatCAB 12; ObitOF 79; OhA&B; PeoHis; TwCBDA; WhAm 3; WhLit; WhNAA*

Conklin, Gladys Plemon
American. Children's Author
Juvenile science, nature books include *Black Widow Spider—Danger,* 1979.
b. May 30, 1903 in Harpster, Idaho
Source: *AuBYP 2, 3; BiDrLUS 70; ConAu 1R, 4NR; ForWC 70; SmATA 2; WhoAmW 64, 66, 77*

Conklin, Peggy
[Margaret Eleanor Conklin]
American. Actor
Films include *Having Wonderful Time,* 1938.
b. Nov 2, 1912 in Dobbs Ferry, New York
Source: *BiE&WWA; BioIn 15; InWom SUP; NotNAT; OxCAmT 84; ThFT; WhoHol 92, A; WhoThe 72, 77A; WhThe*

Conkling, Roscoe
American. Statesman
Senator from NY, 1867-81; rival of Blaine for Rep. presidential nomination, 1876.
b. Oct 30, 1829 in Albany, New York
d. Apr 18, 1888 in New York, New York
Source: *AmBi; AmPolLe; ApCAB; BiAUS; BiDrAC; BiDrUSC 89; BioIn 3, 9, 15; DcAmB; Drake; EncAB-H 1974, 1996; HarEnUS; LegTOT; LinLib S; McGEWB; NatCAB 3; OxCAmH; OxCSupC; REnAL; TwCBDA; WebAB 74, 79; WhAm HS; WhAmP; WhCiWar; WorAl; WorAlBi*

Conlan, Jocko
[John Bertrand Conlan]
American. Baseball Umpire
ML outfielder for two yrs., NL umpire, 1941-65; wrote autobiography, *Jocko,* 1967; Hall of Fame, 1974.
b. Dec 6, 1899 in Chicago, Illinois
d. Apr 16, 1989 in Scottsdale, Arizona
Source: *AnObit 1989; Ballpl 90; BiDAmSp BB; BioIn 14, 16; LegTOT; NewYTBS 89; WhoProB 73*

Conley, Eugene
American. Opera Singer
Radio tenor beginning 1939; on CBS's "Golden Treasury of Song."
b. Mar 12, 1908 in Lynn, Massachusetts
d. Dec 18, 1981 in Denton, Texas
Source: *Baker 84, 92; BioIn 2, 3, 4, 10, 12, 13; BlueB 76; CurBio 82, 82N; MetOEnc; NewYTBS 81; WhAm 8; WhoAm 74, 76, 78, 80; WhoSSW 82, 84; WhoWor 76, 78, 80*

Conley, Renie
American. Designer
Won Oscar for costumes in *Cleopatra,* 1963; designed Disneyland Park's costumes.
b. Jul 31, 1919 in Republic, Washington
Source: *VarWW 85*

Conn, Billy
[William David Conn]
"The Pittsburgh Kid"
American. Boxer
World light-heavyweight champion, 1939-41; lost bouts to Joe Louis, 1941, 1946; Hall of Fame, 1965.
b. Oct 8, 1917 in East Liberty, Pennsylvania
d. May 29, 1993 in Pittsburgh, Pennsylvania
Source: *AnObit 1993; BiDAmSp BK; BioIn 1, 8, 10, 13, 14; BoxReg; CurBio 41, 93N; LegTOT; WhoBox 74; WhoSpor; WorAl*

Connally, John B.
[John Bowden Connally, Jr.]
American. Lawyer, Politician
Dem. governor of TX, 1963-69; wounded when John Kennedy was assassinated; secretary of Treasury under Richard Nixon, 1971-72.
b. Feb 27, 1917 in Floresville, Texas
d. Jun 15, 1993 in Houston, Texas
Source: *AnObit 1993; BiDrGov 1789; BiDrUSE 71, 89; BioIn 5, 6, 7, 9, 10, 11, 12, 16; BioNews 74; BlueB 76; CurBio 61; EncWB; FacFETw; IntWW 74, 75, 76, 77, 78, 79, 80, 81, 82, 83, 89, 91, 93; NewYTBS 86, 93; PolPar; PolProf K, NF; St&PR 75, 84, 87, 91; WhAm 11; Who 74, 82, 83, 85, 88, 90, 92; WhoAm 74, 76, 78, 80, 82, 84; WhoAmL 79; WhoAmP 73, 75, 77, 79, 81, 83, 85; WhoGov 72; WhoSSW 73, 75, 76; WhoWor 78; WorAl; WorAlBi*

Connally, Tom
[Thomas Terry Connally]
American. Politician
Dem. senator from TX, 1929-53; intermittent chm., Senate Foreign Relations Committee.
b. Aug 19, 1877 in McLennan County, Texas
d. Oct 28, 1963 in Washington, District of Columbia
Source: *AmAu&B; BiDrAC; BiDrUSC 89; BioIn 1, 2, 3, 5, 6, 7, 11; CurBio 41, 49, 64; DcAmB S7; EncMcCE; EncSoH; HisDcKW; PolProf T; WhAm 4; WhAmP*

Connell, Alex
Canadian. Hockey Player
Goalie, 1924-37, mostly with Ottawa; Hall of Fame, 1958.
b. Feb 8, 1902 in Ottawa, Ontario, Canada
d. May 10, 1958 in Ottawa, Ontario, Canada
Source: *HocEn; ObitOF 79; WhoHcky 73*

Connell, Evan Shelby, Jr.
American. Author
Among his fiction writings *The Anatomy Lesson and Other Stories,* 1957; *The Patriot,* 1960.
b. Aug 17, 1924 in Kansas City, Missouri
Source: *AmAu&B; Au&Arts 7; BenetAL 91; BioIn 12, 13, 15; CmCal; ConAu, 1R, 2NR; ConLC 4, 6; ConNov 86, 91; CyWA 89; DcLB Y81A; DcLEL 1940; DrAF 76; DrAPF 91; IntAu&W 76, 77; MajTwCW; ModAL S1; OxCAmL 65; PenC AM; REnAL; WhoAm 74, 76, 78, 80, 82, 84, 86, 88, 90, 92, 94, 95, 96, 97; WhoUSWr 88; WhoWest 94; WhoWor 74; WhoWrEP 89, 92, 95; WrDr 86, 92*

Connelly, Christopher
American. Actor
Played Norman Harrington on TV soap opera "Peyton Place," 1964-69.
b. Sep 8, 1941 in Wichita, Kansas
d. Dec 7, 1988 in Burbank, California
Source: *ConTFT 7; ItaFilm; WhoHol A*

Connelly, Marc(us Cook)
American. Dramatist
Won Pulitzer for *The Green Pastures,* 1930.
b. Dec 13, 1890 in McKeesport, Pennsylvania
d. Dec 21, 1980 in New York, New York
Source: *AmAu&B; AnObit 1980; Benet 87, 96; BenetAL 91; BiDAmM; BiE&WWA; BioIn 1, 4, 5, 8, 10, 12, 13, 14, 15; BlueB 76; CamGLE; CamGWoT; CamHAL; Chambr 3; CnDAL; CnMD; CnThe; ConAmA; ConAmD; ConAmL; ConAu 30NR, 85, 102; ConDr 73, 77, 93; ConLC 7; CrtSuDr; CurBio 69, 81N; CyWA 89; DcAmB S10; DcFM; DcLB 7, Y80A; DcLEL; EncAHmr; EncWT; HalFC 84, 88; IntAu&W 76, 77; IntDcT 2; IntWW 74, 75, 76, 77, 78, 79, 80; LegTOT; LinLib L, S; LngCTC; McGEWD 72, 84; ModAL; ModWD; NewYTBS 80; NotNAT, A; OxCAmL 65, 83, 95; OxCAmT 84; OxCThe 67; PenC AM; PlP&P; REn; REnAL; REnWD; RfGAmL 87, 94; SmATA 25N; TwCA, SUP; WebAB 74, 79; WhAm 7; Who 74; WhoAm 74, 76, 78, 80; WhoHol A; WhoThe 72, 77, 81; WhoWor 74; WhScrn 83; WorAlBi; WrDr 76, 80, 82*

Connelly, One-Eyed
[James Leo Connelly]
American. Eccentric
Best known as gate-crasher at sporting events, political conventions, early 1900s.
b. 1879?
d. Dec 20, 1953 in Zion, Illinois
Source: *BioIn 3, 4, 5*

Conner, Dennis
American. Yachtsman
Skipper of yacht *Stars and Stripes* who lost, regained America's Cup for US, 1983, 1987.

b. Sep 16, 1943 in San Diego, California
Source: *BioIn 15, 16; ConNews 87-2; CurBio 87; NewYTBS 86; WhoAm 94, 95, 96*

Conner, Nadine
American. Opera Singer
Lyric soprano; NY Met. debut, 1942.
b. Feb 20, 1913 in Compton, California
Source: *BioIn 1, 3, 4; CurBio 55; InWom; MetOEnc; NewEOp 71; NewGrDO; WhoAmW 58, 66, 68, 70, 72, 74; WhoHol 92*

Connery, Sean
[Thomas Connery]
Scottish. Actor
Originated film role of James Bond in *Dr. No,* 1962; won Oscar for *The Untouchables,* 1988; starred in *The Rock,* 1996.
b. Aug 25, 1930 in Edinburgh, Scotland
Source: *BiDFilm, 94; BioIn 6, 7, 8, 10, 11, 13, 16; BlueB 76; CelR, 90; CmMov; ConTFT 3, 10; CurBio 66, 93; DcArts; DcTwCCu 1; EncEurC; FacFETw; FilmgC; HalFC 88; IntDcF 1-3, 2-3; IntMPA 75, 76, 77, 78, 79, 81, 82, 84, 86, 88, 92, 94, 96; IntWW 75, 76, 77, 78, 79, 80, 81, 82, 83, 89, 91, 93; ItaFilm; LegTOT; MotPP; MovMk; News 90; OxCFilm; Who 74, 82, 83, 85, 88, 90, 92, 94; WhoAm 80, 82, 84, 86, 88, 90, 92, 94, 95, 96, 97; WhoEnt 92; WhoHol 92, A; WhoWor 74, 93, 95, 96, 97; WorAl; WorAlBi; WorEFlm*

Connick, Harry, Jr.
American. Jazz Musician, Songwriter
Popular jazz pianist, singer; won Grammy Award, 1990, for best jazz vocal performer.
b. Sep 11, 1967 in New Orleans, Louisiana
Source: *AllMusG; BioIn 16; ConMus 4; ConTFT 11; CurBio 90; IntMPA 92, 94, 96; LegTOT; News 91, 91-1; NewYTBS 91; WhoEnt 92*

Conniff, Frank
American. Journalist
Overseas reporter; won Pulitzer for Khruschev interview, 1955.
b. Apr 24, 1914 in Danbury, Connecticut
d. May 25, 1971 in New York, New York
Source: *BiDAmNC; BioIn 9; ConAu 93; WhAm 5*

Conniff, Ray
American. Bandleader
"Ray Conniff" sound launched with album *S'Wonderful,* 1956; combined strong beat with "swing" effect, strong choruses.
b. Nov 6, 1916 in Attleboro, Massachusetts
Source: *Baker 84, 92; BiDAmM; BiDJaz; CmpEPM; EncJzS; IntWWM 90; LegTOT; NewAmDM; NewGrDJ 88, 94; OxCPMus; PenEncP; RkOn 74; WhoAm 74, 76, 78, 80, 82, 84, 86, 88, 90, 92, 94, 95, 96, 97; WhoEnt 92; WhoJazz 72*

Connolly, Cyril Vernon
English. Writer
Editor, *Horizon* mag., 1939-50; wrote *Condemned Playground,* 1945.
b. Sep 10, 1903 in Coventry, England
d. Nov 26, 1974 in London, England
Source: *CasWL; CnMWL; ConAu 53, P-2; ConNov 72; CurBio 47; DcLEL; DcNaB 1971; EncWL; EvLB; GrBr; IntWW 74; LngCTC; ModBrL; NewC; OxCEng 67, 85, 95; PenC ENG; RAdv 1; REn; TwCA SUP; TwCWr; WebE&AL; WhoWor 74*

Connolly, Harold
American. Track Athlete
Hammer thrower; participated in four Olympics; won gold medal, 1956; married Czech discus thrower, Olga Fikotova.
b. Aug 1, 1931 in Somerville, Massachusetts
Source: *BioIn 4, 7, 8, 11; NewYTBS 77; WhoTr&F 73*

Connolly, James B
American. Author
Realistic sea stories included *Out of Gloucester,* 1902.
b. Oct 28, 1868 in Boston, Massachusetts
d. Jan 20, 1957 in Boston, Massachusetts
Source: *AmAu&B; AmLY; BkC 3; CathA 1930; REnAL; TwCA, SUP*

Connolly, Maureen
"Little Mo"
American. Tennis Player
Wimbledon singles champion, 1952-54; won Australian, French, US opens, 1953.
b. Sep 17, 1934 in San Diego, California
d. Jun 21, 1969 in Dallas, Texas
Source: *BioIn 2, 3, 4, 5, 8, 9, 10, 11, 12, 20; BuCMET; CmCal; CurBio 51, 69; EncWomS; GoodHs; GrLiveH; InWom, SUP; LegTOT; NewCol 75; WebAB 74; WomFir; WorAl; WorAlBi*

Connolly, Mike
American. Journalist
Wrote columns for Hollywood trade papers.
b. Jul 10, 1915 in Chicago, Illinois
d. Nov 19, 1966 in Rochester, Minnesota
Source: *WhAm 4*

Connolly, Olga Fikotova
[Mrs. Harold Connolly]
American. Track Athlete
Discus thrower; won gold medal, 1956, as member of Czech Olympic team,; member, four US Olympic teams.
b. Nov 13, 1932 in Praha, Czech Republic
Source: *BioIn 5, 8, 9, 11; InWom SUP; WhoTr&F 73*

Connolly, Sybil
Welsh. Fashion Designer
Known for incorporating rare Irish textiles into her designs.
b. Jan 24, 1921 in Swansea, Wales
Source: *BioIn 4, 6, 16; ConDes 97; EncFash; InWom, SUP; WhoAmW 66, 68, 70, 72, 74; WhoFash 88; WhoWor 74; WorFshn*

Connolly, Tommy
[Thomas Henry Connolly]
American. Baseball Umpire
Umpired first AL game, 1901; first World Series, 1903; with Bill Klem, first umpire elected to Hall of Fame, 1953.
b. Dec 31, 1870 in Manchester, England
d. Apr 28, 1961 in Natick, Massachusetts
Source: *BiDAmSp BB; BioIn 5, 7, 14, 15; DcAmB S7; LegTOT; WhoProB 73*

Connolly, Walter
American. Actor
Versatile performer best remembered for portrayal in *Nothing Sacred,* 1937.
b. Apr 8, 1887 in Cincinnati, Ohio
d. May 28, 1940 in Beverly Hills, California
Source: *BioIn 21; CurBio 40; EncAFC; FilmgC; HalFC 84, 88; MotPP; MovMk; NotNAT B; OlFamFa; OxCFilm; Vers A; WhoHol B; WhScrn 74, 77, 83; WhThe*

Connor, Bull
[Theopilus Eugene Connor]
American. Police Officer
Commissioner of Public Safety during Alabama freedom ride, civil rights demonstrations.
b. Jul 11, 1897 in Selma, Alabama
d. Mar 8, 1973 in Birmingham, Alabama
Source: *BioIn 9, 17*

Connor, George
American. Football Player
Defensive tackle-linebacker, Chicago, 1948-55; Hall of Fame, 1975.
b. Jan 1, 1925 in Chicago, Illinois
Source: *BiDAmSp FB; BioIn 17; LegTOT; WhoFtbl 74; WhoSpor*

Connor, Roger
American. Baseball Player
Infielder, 1880-97; held record for career home runs, 136, broken by Babe Ruth; Hall of Fame, 1976.
b. Jul 1, 1857 in Waterbury, Connecticut
d. Jan 4, 1931 in Waterbury, Connecticut
Source: *Ballpl 90; BiDAmSp BB; BioIn 14, 15, 16, 17; WhoSpor*

Connor, William Neil, Sir
Irish. Journalist
Columnist for London *Daily Mirror,* 1935-67.
b. Apr 26, 1909 in County Derry, Northern Ireland
d. Apr 6, 1967 in London, England
Source: *BioIn 3, 7, 8, 9; DcNaB 1961; LngCTC; ObitOF 79; ObitT 1961; WhAm 4*

Connors, Chuck
[Kevin Joseph Connors]
American. Actor
Starred in TV show "The Rifleman," 1957-62.
b. Apr 10, 1921 in New York, New York
d. Nov 10, 1992 in Los Angeles, California
Source: *AnObit 1992; Ballpl 90; BioIn 15, 18, 19; ConTFT 11; FilmgC; HalFC 84, 88; IntMPA 86, 88, 92; ItaFilm; LegTOT; MotPP; WhoAm 82, 86, 90; WhoEnt 92; WhoHol 92, A; WhoProB 73; WorAl; WorAlBi*

Connors, Dorsey
American. Journalist
TV, radio commentator; columnist, *Chicago Sun Times,* 1965—; wrote *Save Money, Save Yourself,* 1972.
Source: *ConAu 45; ForWC 70; WhoAm 78, 80, 82, 84, 86, 88, 90, 92, 94, 95, 96, 97; WhoAmW 66A, 68, 70, 72, 74, 75, 77, 79, 81, 83, 85, 87, 89, 91, 93, 95, 97; WhoMW 78, 80, 82, 84, 86, 88, 92*

Connors, Jimmy
[James Scott Connors]
American. Tennis Player
Won US Open 1974, 1976, 1978, 1982; won Wimbledon 1974, 1982.
b. Sep 2, 1952 in East Saint Louis, Illinois
Source: *BiDAmSp OS; BioIn 10, 11, 12, 13, 14, 15, 16, 17, 18, 20, 21; BuCMET; CelR 90; CurBio 75; FacFETw; IntWW 81, 82, 83, 89, 91, 93; LegTOT; NewYTBS 77, 85, 87; WhoAm 78, 80, 82, 84, 86, 88, 90, 92, 94, 95, 96, 97; WhoSpor; WhoWor 84, 87, 89, 91, 93, 95, 96; WorAl; WorAlBi*

Connors, Mike
[Krekor Ohanian]
American. Actor
Starred in TV series "Mannix," 1967-74.
b. Aug 15, 1925 in Fresno, California
Source: *BioIn 9; CelR; ConTFT 9; IntMPA 77, 78, 79, 81, 82, 84, 86, 88, 92, 94, 96; ItaFilm; LegTOT; MotPP; WhoAm 76, 78, 80, 82, 84, 86, 88, 90, 92, 94, 95, 96, 97; WhoEnt 92; WhoHol 92, A*

Conover, Harry
American. Businessman
Founder, head of modeling agency, 1939-59; created term "Cover Girl."
b. Aug 29, 1911 in Chicago, Illinois
d. Jul 21, 1965 in New York, New York
Source: *CurBio 49, 65; DcAmB S7; ObitOF 79*

Conquest, Robert
English. Author
Writings include *The Pasternak Affair; Courage of Genius,* 1962; known for works of science fiction, history.
b. Jul 15, 1917 in Malvern, England
Source: *Benet 87; BioIn 8, 10, 14; BlueB 76; CamGLE; ConAu 9NR, 13R, 25NR; ConNov 72; ConPo 70, 75, 80, 85, 91; ConSFA; DcLB 27, 29; DcLP 87A; EncSF; EngPo; IntAu&W 76, 77, 82, 89, 91; IntvTCA 2; IntWW 82; IntWWP 77, 82; LinLib L; LngCTC; OxCEng 85; RAdv 1; ScF&FL 1, 2; ScFSB; TwCWr; Who 74, 82, 83, 85, 88, 90, 92; WhoAm 88, 90; WhoSciF; WorAu 1950; WrDr 76, 80, 82, 84, 86, 88, 90, 92*

Conrad, Charles, Jr.
"Pete"
American. Astronaut
Crew member on Gemini V, 1965; Gemini XI, 1966; Apollo 12, 1969; Skylab, 1973.
b. Jun 2, 1930 in Philadelphia, Pennsylvania
Source: *BioIn 7, 8, 9, 10; BlueB 76; CurBio 65; Dun&B 86, 88, 90; FacFETw; IntWW 74, 75, 76, 77; LinLib S; WhoAm 74, 76, 78, 80, 82, 84, 86, 88, 90; WhoSpc; WhoSSW 73, 75; WhoWor 74, 78; WorAl; WorAlBi; WorDWW*

Conrad, Con
[Conrad K Dober]
American. Songwriter, Publisher
Stage, film composer, 1920s-30s; wrote "Margie," 1920.
b. Jun 18, 1891 in New York, New York
d. Sep 28, 1938 in Van Nuys, California
Source: *AmPS; AmSong; ASCAP 66, 80; BiDAmM; BioIn 4, 6, 15, 16; CmpEPM; Film 2; FilmEn; HalFC 84, 88; NotNAT B; OxCPMus; WhThe*

Conrad, Frank
"Father of American Radio"
American. Engineer, Broadcaster
Transmitted first commercially sponsored broadcast, 1920.
b. May 4, 1874 in Pittsburgh, Pennsylvania
d. Dec 11, 1941 in Miami, Florida
Source: *BioIn 2, 4, 17; DcAmB S3; EncAB-A 18; EncAJ; InSci; NatCAB 35; WhAm 1*

Conrad, Joseph
[Teodor Josef Konrad Koreniowski]
Polish. Author
Wrote *Lord Jim,* 1900; *Heart of Darkness,* 1902; *Victory,* 1915.
b. Dec 3, 1857 in Berdichev, Russia
d. Aug 3, 1924 in Bishopsbourne, England
Source: *AtlBL; BbD; Benet 87, 96; BiD&SB; BioIn 1, 2, 3, 4, 5, 6, 7, 8, 9, 10, 11, 12, 13, 14, 15, 16, 17, 18, 20, 21; BlmGEL; BritWr 6; CamGEL; CamGLE; CasWL; Chambr 3; CnDBLB 5; CnMD; CnMWL; ConAu 104, 131; CyWA 58, 89; DcArts; DcEnA A; DcEuL; DcLB 10, 34, 98, 156; DcLEL; DcNaB 1922; Dis&D; EncMys; EncSF, 93; EncWL, 2, 3; EvLB; FacFETw; FilmgC; GrBr; HalFC 84, 88; JBA 34; LegTOT; LiExTwC; LinLib L, S; LngCEL; LngCTC; MagSWL; MajTwCW; MakMC; McGEWB; ModBrL, S1, S2; ModWD; NewC; Novels; OxCAusL; OxCEng 67, 85, 95; OxCShps; PenC ENG; PenEncH; RAdv 1, 14, 13-1; RComWL; REn; RfGEnL 91; RfGShF; RGTwCWr; ScF&FL 1; ShSCr 9; ShSWr; SmATA 27; SpyFic; TwCA, SUP; TwCLC 1, 6, 13, 25, 43; TwCWr; VicBrit; WebE&AL; WhDW; WhoSpyF; WhoTwCL; WorAl; WorAlBi; WorLitC; WrPh*

Conrad, Kent
American. Politician
Dem. senator from ND, 1987—.
b. Mar 12, 1948
Source: *AlmAP 88, 92, 96; BiDrUSC 89; BioIn 17; CngDr 87, 89, 91, 93, 95; IntWW 89, 91, 93; WhoAm 88, 90, 92, 94, 95, 96, 97; WhoAmP 87, 89, 91, 93, 95; WhoE 95; WhoMW 88, 90, 92, 93, 96; WhoWor 89, 91*

Conrad, Michael
American. Actor
Won Emmy for role of Phil Esterhaus in "Hill Street Blues," 1981, 1982.
b. Oct 16, 1927? in New York, New York
d. Nov 22, 1983 in Los Angeles, California
Source: *BioIn 12; WhoHol A*

Conrad, Paul Francis
American. Cartoonist, Author
LA *Times* syndicated editorial cartoonist, 1973—; won three Pulitzers.
b. Jun 27, 1924 in Cedar Rapids, Iowa
Source: *ConAu 38NR, 113; EncTwCJ; ScFSB; WhoAm 74, 76, 78, 80, 82, 84, 86, 88, 90, 92, 94, 95, 96, 97; WhoAmA 76, 78, 80, 82, 84, 86, 89, 91, 93; WhoWest 74, 87, 89, 92, 94; WorECar*

Conrad, Robert
[Conrad Robert Falk]
American. Actor
Starred in "Hawaiian Eye," 1959-63; "The Wild, Wild West," 1965-69.
b. Mar 1, 1935 in Chicago, Illinois
Source: *BioIn 12, 16; ConTFT 3, 15; FilmgC; GangFlm; HalFC 84, 88; IntMPA 75, 76, 77, 78, 79, 81, 82, 84, 86, 88, 92, 94, 96; LegTOT; MiSFD 9; WhoAm 74, 76, 78, 80, 82, 84, 86, 88, 90, 92, 94, 95, 96, 97; WhoEnt 92; WhoHol 92, A; WorAl; WorAlBi*

Conrad, William
American. Actor
Star of "Cannon," 1971-76; "Nero Wolfe," 1981; "Jake and the Fatman," 1987-92.
b. Sep 27, 1920 in Louisville, Kentucky
d. Feb 11, 1994 in North Hollywood, California
Source: *BioIn 10, 19, 20; BioNews 74; CelR; ConTFT 2, 5, 13; FilmgC; GangFlm; HalFC 84, 88; IntMPA 84, 86, 88, 92, 94; LegTOT; LesBEnT 92; MiSFD 9; MovMk; RadStar; SaTiSS; WhAm 11; WhoAm 76, 78, 80, 82, 84, 86, 88, 90, 92; WhoEnt 92; WhoHol 92, A; WorAl; WorAlBi*

Conreid, Hans
[Frank Foster Conreid]
American. Actor
Comedian in over 100 films; played Uncle Tonoose in "Make Room for Daddy," 1957-64.
b. Apr 1, 1915 in Baltimore, Maryland
d. Jan 5, 1982 in Burbank, California
Source: *AnObit 1982; FilmgC; LegTOT; MotPP; MovMk; NewYTBS 82; RadStar; WhoAm 80; WhoHol A; WhoThe 77; WorAl; WorAlBi*

Conroy, Frank
American. Actor
Played domestic tyrants in *Grand Hotel,* 1932; *The Ox-Bow Incident,* 1943.
b. Oct 14, 1890 in Derby, England
d. Feb 4, 1964 in Paramus, New Jersey
Source: *FilmgC; HalFC 84, 88; MovMk; NotNAT B; PlP&P; Vers A; WhoHbl B; WhScrn 74, 77, 83; WhThe*

Conroy, Frank
American. Writer
Contributed to several mags. including *Harper's.*
b. Jan 15, 1936 in New York, New York
Source: *AmAu&B; BioIn 8, 9, 11, 16, 17, 19, 20; ConAu 77; IntvTCA 2; LegTOT; LiJour; OxCAmL 95; WhoAm 74; WorAu 1980*

Conroy, Jack
[John Wesley Conroy]
American. Author
Books include *Writers in Revolt: The Anvil Anthology,* 1973; *The Disinherited,* 1933.
b. Dec 5, 1899 in Moberly, Missouri
d. Feb 28, 1990 in Moberly, Missouri
Source: *AmAu&B; AmNov; BenetAL 91; BioIn 2, 10, 12, 13, 15, 16, 17, 20; BlueB 76; CamGLE; CamHAL; ConAu 3NR, 5NR, 5R, 131, X; ConNov 72, 76, 82; DcLB Y81B; EncAHmr; EncAL; FacFETw; IntAu&W 76, 77, 82, 86; IntYB 78, 79, 80, 81, 82; Novels; OhA&B; OxCAmL 65, 83, 95; SmATA 19, 65; WhNAA; WhoAm 74, 76, 78, 80, 82, 84, 86; WhoUSWr 88; WhoWrEP 89; WrDr 76, 80, 82, 84*

Conroy, Pat
[Donald Patrick Conroy]
American. Author
Wrote autobiographical novels *The Great Santini,* 1976; *The Water is Wide,* 1972; also wrote *The Prince of Tides,* 1986.
b. Oct 26, 1945 in Atlanta, Georgia
Source: *Au&Arts 8; BiDConC; BioIn 9, 10, 12, 15; ConAu 24NR, 85; ConLC 30, 74; ConPopW; ConTFT 12; CurBio 96; DcLB 6; LegTOT; MajTwCW; WhoAm 82, 84, 86, 88, 90, 92, 94, 95, 96, 97; WhoUSWr 88; WhoWrEP 89, 92, 95; WorAu 1985; WrDr 90, 92*

Considine, Bob
[Robert Bernard Considine]
American. Journalist
Syndicated newspaper columnist; wrote "On the Line column" for nearly 40 yrs.
b. Nov 4, 1906 in Washington, District of Columbia
d. Sep 25, 1975 in New York, New York
Source: *AmAu&B; AuNews 2; BiDAmJo; BiDAmNC; BioIn 1, 5, 7, 10, 11, 16, 21; CathA 1930; CelR; ConAu 61, X; CurBio 47, 75; DcAmB S9; EncTwCJ; NewYTBS 75; REnAL; WhAm 6; WhoAm 74; WhoWor 74, 76; WorAl*

Considine, Tim
American. Actor
Played Mike Douglas on "My Three Sons," 1960-65.
b. Dec 10, 1941 in Louisville, Kentucky
Source: *BioIn 4; WhoHol A*

Constable, John
English. Artist
Romantic landscape painter; influenced Barbizon, impressionist schools.
b. Jun 11, 1776 in East Bergholt, England
d. Mar 30, 1837 in London, England
Source: *AtlBL; Benet 87, 96; BioIn 1, 2, 3, 4, 5, 6, 7, 8, 9, 10, 11, 12, 13, 15, 16; CelCen; ChhPo S1; ClaDrA; DcArts; DcBiPP; DcBrWA; DcNaB; IntDcAA 90; LegTOT; LinLib S; McGDA; McGEWB; NewC; OxCArt; OxCEng 85, 95; OxDcArt; RAdv 14, 13-3; REn; WhDW; WorAl; WorAlBi*

Constant de Rebeque, (Henri) Benjamin
French. Author, Journalist
Best remembered for short novel *Adolphe,* 1816.
b. Oct 25, 1767 in Lausanne, Switzerland
d. Dec 8, 1830 in Paris, France
Source: *AtlBL; CyWA 58; PenC EUR*

Constantine, Eddie
American. Actor
Known for tough-guy roles in French films, 1950s.
b. 1917 in Los Angeles, California
d. Feb 25, 1993
Source: *BioIn 4, 7, 11, 18, 20; EncEurC; FilmgC; GangFlm; HalFC 84, 88; IntDcF 1-3, 2-3; ItaFilm; MotPP; NewYTBS 93; OxCFilm; WhoEnt 92; WorAlBi; WorEFlm*

Constantine, Learie Nicholas Constantine, Baron
Trinidadian. Cricket Player, Government Official
Pioneer in establishing West Indian cricket players in England; knighted, 1962; served on British national Race Relations Board, 1966.
b. Sep 21, 1901 in Diego Martin, Trinidad and Tobago
d. Jul 1, 1971 in London, England
Source: *BioIn 2, 6, 8, 9, 10, 14; DcNaB 1971; GrBr; InB&W 85*

Constantine, Michael
[Constantine Joanides]
American. Actor
Won 1970 Emmy for role of Seymour Kaufman on "Room 222," 1969-74.
b. May 22, 1927 in Reading, Pennsylvania
Source: *BiE&WWA; FilmgC; HalFC 84, 88; IntMPA 96; VarWW 85; WhoAm 74, 76, 78, 80, 82, 84; WhoE 95; WhoEnt 92; WhoHol 92, A; WorAl; WorAlBi*

Constantine I
[Constantine the Great; Flavius Valerius Aurelius Constantinus]
Roman. Ruler
Ruled, 306-377; adopted Christianity, tried to extend rights to Christians; banished Arius, Arianism.
b. Feb 27, 280 in Nassius, Moesia
d. Mar 22, 337 in Nicomedia, Turkey
Source: *LegTOT; NewCol 75; OxCLaw; REn; WebBD 83; WhDW; WorAl*

Constantine V
Byzantine. Ruler
Son of Leo III; during reign, 741-755, summoned council on image worship, 754.
b. 718 in Constantinople, Byzantine Empire
d. Sep 14, 775
Source: *NewCol 75; WebBD 83*

Constantine VI
Byzantine. Ruler
Last of Isaurian emperors; throne seized by mother, Irene, who had him killed.
b. Jan 14, 770? in Constantinople, Turkey
d. Aug 15, 797? in Constantinople, Turkey
Source: *NewCol 75; WebBD 83*

Constantine XII
Greek. Ruler
Succeeded to throne, 1964; left Greece, 1967; deposed, 1973.
b. Jun 2, 1940 in Athens, Greece
Source: *IntWW 81, 91; NewCol 75*

Constantine XI Palaeologus
Byzantine. Ruler
Last emperor of the Eastern Roman Empire, 1449-53.
b. Feb 7, 1405 in Constantinople, Turkey
d. May 29, 1453 in Constantinople, Turkey
Source: *NewCol 75; WebBD 83*

Conte, Lansana
Guinean. Political Leader
President of Guinea, 1984—; assumed leadership in a coup following the death of Sekou Toure.
b. 1934, Guinea

Conte, Richard
[Nicholas Peter]
American. Actor
Often portrayed loner in stage, screen roles, 1940s-70s; film *Call Northside 777* starred Jimmy Stewart, 1948.
b. Mar 24, 1910 in Jersey City, New Jersey
d. Apr 15, 1975 in Los Angeles, California
Source: *CmMov; FilmgC; HolP 40; IntMPA 75; MotPP; MovMk; NewYTBS 75; ObitOF 79; WhAm 6; WhoAm 74; WhoHol C; WhScrn 77; WorAl; WorEFlm*

Conti, Bill
American. Composer
Won Oscar for score of *The Right Stuff,* 1983; TV theme songs include "Dynasty;" "Falcon Crest;" "Cagney and Lacey."
b. Apr 13, 1942 in Providence, Rhode Island
Source: *ConTFT 4, 12; HalFC 88; IntMPA 92, 94, 96; LegTOT; VarWW 85; WhoAm 92, 94, 95, 96, 97; WhoEnt 92*

Conti, Tom
[Thomas Antonio Conti]
Scottish. Actor
Star of BBC TV series "The Glittering Prizes," 1976; won Tony for role in play *Whose Life Is It Anyway?* 1978-79.
b. Nov 22, 1941 in Paisley, Scotland
Source: *BioIn 12; ConTFT 1, 3, 10; CurBio 85; HalFC 84, 88; IntMPA 86, 88, 92, 94, 96; IntWW 91; LegTOT; NewYTBS 79; Who 85, 92; WhoAm 80, 82, 84, 86, 88, 90, 92, 94, 95, 96, 97; WhoEnt 92; WhoHol 92; WhoThe 81; WhoWor 87, 89, 91, 93, 95, 96, 97*

Contino, Dick
American. Musician
Popular nightclub, film accordion player.
b. 1930 in Fresno, California
Source: *BioIn 9; RadStar; WhoHol A*

Converse, Frank
American. Actor
Played Johnny Corso on "NYPD," 1967-69.
b. May 22, 1938 in Saint Louis, Missouri
Source: *BioIn 10; ConTFT 3, 9; HalFC 84, 88; IntMPA 76, 77, 78, 79, 81, 82, 84, 86, 88, 92, 94, 96; ScFEYrs; WhoHol 92, A*

Converse, Frederick J
American. Engineer
Noted innovator of soil mechanics, foundations; projects include Saturn Missile Test Stand for NASA.
b. 1892?
d. Oct 9, 1987
Source: *BioIn 13*

Converse, Frederick Shepherd
American. Composer
Wrote *Pipe of Desire,* first American opera produced by NY Met., 1910.
b. Jan 5, 1871 in Newton, Massachusetts
d. Jun 8, 1940 in Boston, Massachusetts
Source: *AmComp; ApCAB X; ASCAP 66; Baker 78, 84, 92; BiDAmM; BioIn 1, 4, 8, 9, 20; ConAmC 76, 82; CurBio 40; DcAmB S2; NatCAB 14, 30; NewEOp 71; NewGrDA 86; NewGrDO; OxCAmL 65; OxCMus; PenDiMP A; REnAL; WhAm 1*

Converse, Marquis M
American. Manufacturer
Launched Converse Rubber Shoe Co., 1908, making basketball sneakers.
b. Oct 23, 1861 in Lyme, New Hampshire
d. Feb 9, 1931 in Boston, Massachusetts
Source: *Entr; WhAm 1*

Convy, Bert
American. TV Personality
Former baseball player, actor, singer; best known as host of TV game shows: "Tattletales," "Win, Lose, or Draw."
b. Jul 23, 1933 in Saint Louis, Missouri
d. Jul 15, 1991 in Brentwood, California
Source: *BiE&WWA; BioIn 13; IntMPA 88; News 92; NewYTBS 91; NotNAT; WhAm 10; WhoAm 86, 90; WhoHol A; WhoThe 81*

Conway, Jack
American. Actor, Director
Films noted for technical excellence include *A Tale of Two Cities,* 1935.
b. Jul 17, 1887 in Graceville, Minnesota
d. Oct 11, 1952 in Pacific Palisades, California
Source: *BioIn 3; CmMov; DcFM; EncAFC; Film 1; FilmgC; HalFC 84, 88; IlWWHD 1; LegTOT; MiSFD 9N; MovMk; NotNAT B; ObitOF 79; TwYS, A; WhoHol B; WhScrn 74, 77, 83; WorEFlm*

Conway, Jill Kathryn Ker
American. Historian, Writer, Educator
Pres., Smith College, 1975-85; wrote *The Road from Coorain,* 1989.
b. Oct 9, 1934 in Hillston, Australia
Source: *AmWomM; BioIn 16; CanWW 31, 83, 89; ConAu 130; CurBio 91; EncWB; InWom SUP; NewYTBS 89; WhoAm 76, 78, 80, 82, 84, 86, 88, 90, 92, 94, 95, 96, 97; WhoAmW 81, 83, 85, 87, 89, 91, 93, 95; WhoE 77, 89, 91; WhoWor 82*

Conway, Moncure Daniel
American. Clergy, Author
Wrote biographies of Emerson, Carlyle, Hawthorne, Paine.
b. Mar 17, 1832 in Falmouth, Virginia
d. Nov 15, 1907 in Paris, France
Source: *Alli SUP; AmAu; AmAu&B; AmBi; ApCAB; BbD; BiD&SB; BiDSA; BiDTran; BioIn 2, 3, 6, 9, 14, 15; CelCen; Chambr 3; CyAL 2; DcAmAu; DcAmB; DcLB 1; DcLEL; DcNAA; EncUnb; NatCAB 1; OhA&B; OxCAmL 65, 83, 95; PenC AM; REnAL; TwCBDA; WhAm 1; WhLit*

Conway, Shirl
[Shirl Conway Larson]
American. Actor
Nominated for Emmy for "The Nurses," 1963.
b. Jun 13, 1916 in Franklinville, New York
Source: *BiE&WWA; IntMPA 75, 76, 77, 78, 79, 81, 82, 84, 86, 88; InWom; LegTOT; NotNAT; WhoHol 92, A*

Conway, Thomas
[Count de Conway]
American. Army Officer
Revolutionary war general; involved in Conway Cable intrigue.
b. Feb 27, 1735, Ireland
d. 1800
Source: *AmBi; ApCAB; DcAmB; DcAmMiB; Drake; EncCRAm; NatCAB 1; TwCBDA; WebAB 74, 79; WebAMB; WhAm HS; WhAmRev; WorAl; WorAlBi*

Conway, Tim
[Thomas Daniel Conway]
American. Comedian, Actor
Appeared in TV series "McHale's Navy," 1962-66; "The Carol Burnett Show," 1975-78.
b. Dec 15, 1933 in Willoughby, Ohio
Source: *BioIn 12, 16; ConAu 112; ConTFT 3; CurBio 81; EncAFC; HalFC 84, 88; IntMPA 76, 77, 78, 79, 81, 82, 84, 86, 88, 92, 94, 96; LegTOT; LesBEnT 92; NewYTET; WhoAm 78, 80, 82, 84, 86, 88, 90, 92, 94, 95, 96, 97; WhoCom; WhoEnt 92; WhoHol 92, A; WorAl; WorAlBi*

Conway, Tom
[Thomas Charles Sanders]
American. Actor
Brother of actor George Sanders; played title role in "The Falcon," 1942-46.
b. Sep 15, 1904 in Saint Petersburg, Russia
d. Apr 22, 1967 in Culver City, California
Source: *BioIn 10, 17; FilmgC; HalFC 84, 88; HolP 40; MotPP; MovMk; RadStar; WhoHol B; WhScrn 74, 77, 83*

Cony, Edward Roger
American. Journalist
Pres., Dow Jones Publishing Co., 1976-1991; won Pulitzer, 1961 for national reporting.
b. Mar 15, 1923 in Augusta, Maine
Source: *Dun&B 79, 86; EncTwCJ; WhoAm 74, 76, 78, 80, 82, 84, 86, 88; WhoE 74, 75*

Conyers, John, Jr.
American. Politician
Dem. congressman from MI, 1965—; wrote *Anatomy of an Undeclared War,* 1972.

b. May 16, 1929 in Detroit, Michigan
Source: *AfrAmAl 6; AlmAP 78, 80, 82, 84, 88, 92, 96; BiDrAC; BiDrUSC 89; BioIn 7, 8, 9, 10, 11, 12, 17, 19; BlkAmsC; BlueB 76; CivR 74; CngDr 74, 77, 79, 81, 83, 85, 87, 89, 91, 93, 95; ConBlB 4; CurBio 70; DcTwCCu 5; Ebony 1; IntWW 74, 75, 76, 77, 78, 79, 80, 81; NegAl 76, 83, 89; PolProf J, NF; PolsAm 84; WhoAfA 96; WhoAm 74, 76, 78, 80, 82, 84, 86, 88, 90, 92, 94, 95, 96, 97; WhoAmP 73, 75, 77, 79, 81, 83, 85, 87, 89, 91, 93, 95; WhoBlA 75, 77, 80, 85, 88, 90, 92, 94; WhoGov 72, 75, 77; WhoMW 82, 84, 86, 88, 90, 92, 93, 96; WhoWor 78, 80, 82, 96, 97*

Conze, Edward J. D
English. Author
Writings embrace Buddhist philosophies.
b. Mar 18, 1904 in London, England
Source: *Au&Wr 71; BioIn 12; ConAu 13R*

Conzelman, Jimmy
[James Gleason Conzelman]
American. Football Coach
Coach with several pro teams, 1922-42, 1946-48; had greatest success with Chicago Cards; Hall of Fame, 1964.
b. Mar 6, 1898 in Saint Louis, Missouri
d. Jul 31, 1970 in Saint Louis, Missouri
Source: *BioIn 1, 6, 8, 9, 17; ConAu 104; NewYTBE 70; WhoFtbl 74; WhoSpor*

Cooder, Ry(land Peter)
American. Musician
Session guitarist, whose movie scores include *The Long Riders,* 1980; *Crossroad,* 1986.
b. Mar 15, 1947 in Los Angeles, California
Source: *Baker 92; BioIn 10, 11, 12, 13, 14, 15; ConMus 2; ConTFT 8; DcArts; EncFCWM 83; EncPR&S 74, 89; EncRk 88; EncRkSt; HarEnCM 87; HarEnR 86; IlEncRk; LegTOT; NewGrDA 86; OnThGG; PenEncP; RolSEnR 83; WhoAm 80, 82, 84, 86, 88, 90, 92, 94, 95, 96, 97; WhoEnt 92; WhoRock 81*

Coody, Charles
American. Golfer
Turned pro, 1963; won Masters, 1971; has won over $1 million on tour.
b. Jul 13, 1937 in Stamford, Texas
Source: *NewYTBE 71; WhoGolf; WhoIntG*

Coogan, Jackie
[Jack Leslie Coogan]
American. Actor
First child star in movie history, known for role in *The Kid,* 1919; played Uncle Fester on the "Addams Family," 1962-64.
b. Oct 26, 1914 in Los Angeles, California
d. Mar 1, 1984 in Santa Monica, California
Source: *AnObit 1984; BioIn 1, 4, 7, 12, 13, 14, 15; CmCal; ConTFT 1; EncAFC; FacFETw; FilmgC; HalFC 84, 88; IntDcF 1-3; IntMPA 75, 76, 77, 78, 79, 81, 82, 84; LegTOT; MotPP; MovMk; OxCFilm; TwYS; WhoAm 82; WhoCom; WhoHol A; WorAl; WorAlBi*

Cook, Barbara
American. Actor, Singer
Performed on Broadway musical stage, concerts; TV shows include "The Ed Sullivan Show"; "Chevy Show," 1960s.
b. Oct 25, 1927 in Atlanta, Georgia
Source: *BiE&WWA; BioIn 6, 10, 11, 12, 14, 21; CamGWoT; CelR 90; ConTFT 3; CurBio 63; EncMT; InWom; NewAmDM; NewGrDA 86; NewYTBS 80; NotNAT; OxCAmT 84; OxCPMus; PenEncP; WhoAm 82; WhoAmW 66, 68, 70, 72, 74; WhoThe 72, 77, 81*

Cook, Bill
[William Osser Cook]
Canadian. Hockey Player
Right wing, NY Rangers, 1926-37; won Art Ross Trophy, 1927, 1933; Hall of Fame, 1952.
b. Oct 9, 1896 in Brantford, Ontario, Canada
d. May 5, 1986 in Kingston, Ontario, Canada
Source: *BioIn 14, 15; FacFETw; HocEn; NewYTBS 86; WhoHcky 73; WhoSpor*

Cook, Blanche Wiesen
American. Historian
Wrote *Eleanor Roosevelt, Volume One 1884-1933,* 1992.
b. Apr 20, 1941 in New York, New York
Source: *ConAu 4NR, 53; DrAS 74H, 78H, 82H; GayLesB; WhoAm 86, 88, 90, 92, 94, 95, 96, 97; WhoAmW 85, 87, 89, 91; WhoEmL 87*

Cook, Donald
American. Actor
Known for expert characterizations on Broadway, films, 1930s.
b. Sep 26, 1901 in Portland, Oregon
d. Oct 1, 1961 in New Haven, Connecticut
Source: *BioIn 3, 6, 11; CurBio 54, 61; FilmgC; HolP 30; MotPP; MovMk; NotNAT B; ObitOF 79; OxCAmT 84; WhAm 4; WhoHol A, B; WhScrn 74, 77, 83; WhThe*

Cook, Elisha, Jr.
American. Actor
Known for small-time gangster roles; films include *The Maltese Falcon,* 1941; played Francis "Ice Pick" Hofstetler on TV series "Magnum, PI," 1983-88.
b. Dec 26, 1906 in San Francisco, California
d. May 18, 1995 in Los Angeles, California
Source: *BiE&WWA; BioIn 15; CmMov; ConTFT 8, 14; EncAFC; FilmgC; HalFC 84, 88; IntDcF 1-3; IntMPA 86, 92; MovMk; NotNAT; OxCFilm; WhoHol 92, A; WorEFlm*

Cook, Frederick Albert
American. Explorer
Naturalist; claimed to be first to reach N Pole, scale Mt. McKinley.
b. Jun 10, 1865 in Callicoon Depot, New York
d. Aug 5, 1940 in New Rochelle, New York
Source: *BioIn 2, 4, 5, 6, 8, 10, 11, 12, 13, 15, 16, 17, 18; CurBio 40; DcAmAu; DcAmB S2; DcNAA; Expl 93; HarEnUS; InSci; LinLib S; NatCAB 13; NewCol 75; OxCAmH; OxCCan; OxCShps; WhAm 1; WhWE*

Cook, Greg(ory Lynn)
"Blond Bomber"
American. Football Player
Quarterback, Cincinnati, 1969-73; led AFL in passing, 1969.
b. Nov 20, 1946 in Chillicothe, Ohio
Source: *BioIn 8; WhoFtbl 74*

Cook, James, Captain
English. Explorer, Navigator
Discovered New Caledonia on South Sea expedition, 1772-75.
b. Oct 28, 1728 in Morton Village, England
d. Feb 14, 1779 in Kealakekua, Hawaii
Source: *Alli, SUP; ApCAB; AsBiEn; BbD; BbtC; BenetAL 91; BiESc; BiHiMed; BioIn 1, 2, 3, 4, 5, 6, 7, 8, 9, 10, 11, 12, 13, 14, 15, 16, 17, 18, 19, 20, 21; BlkwCE; BritAu; CamDcSc; CamGEL; CamGLE; ChhPo S2; DcBiPP; DcCanB 4; DcLEL; DcNaB; DcScB; Dis&D; Drake; EncCRAm; EncEnl; Expl 93; HisDBrE; HisWorL; LegTOT; LinLib L, S; MacDCB 78; McGEWB; NewC; OxCAmH; OxCAusL; OxCCan; OxCChiL; OxCEng 67, 85, 95; OxCShps; RAdv 14, 13-3; REn; REnAL; WhAm HS; WhDW; WhNaAH; WhWE; WorAl; WorAlBi*

Cook, Joe
American. Entertainer
Large mouth innocent looking clown, famed for juggling act and "Rube Goldberg" inventions.
b. 1890 in Evansville, Indiana
d. May 16, 1959 in Clinton Hollows, New York
Source: *BioIn 5; CmpEPM; EncAFC; EncMT; EncVaud; IndAu 1917; NotNAT B; ObitOF 79; OxCAmT 84; WhoCom; WhoHol B; WhScrn 77, 83; WhThe*

Cook, Lowdrick M
American. Business Executive
Chairman of Atlantic Richfield, 1985-93.
b. 1928
Source: *BioIn 15, 16; Dun&B 90; IntWW 91; WhoAm 84, 86, 90; WhoFI 92; WhoWest 92; WhoWor 87, 91*

Cook, Michael
Canadian. Dramatist
Stage, radio plays include *Deserts of Bohemia,* 1981.
b. Feb 14, 1933 in London, England

Source: *BioIn 11, 15; CamGLE; CamGWoT; CanWW 89; ConAu 93; ConDr 77, 82, 88, 93; ConLC 58; DcLB 53; IntAu&W 91, 93; IntDcT 2; McGEWD 84; OxCCanL; OxCCanT; WhoAm 80, 82, 84; WhoCanL 85, 87, 92; WrDr 80, 82, 84, 86, 88, 90, 92, 94, 96*

Cook, Peter
English. Actor
Won Tony for *Beyond the Fridge,* 1963; films include *The Wrong Box,* 1966.
b. Nov 17, 1937 in Devonshire, England
d. Jan 9, 1995 in London, England
Source: *BiE&WWA; BioIn 8, 10, 12, 20, 21; ConTFT 4, 14; DcArts; FacFETw; FilmgC; HalFC 84, 88; IntMPA 92, 94, 96; ItaFilm; NotNAT; QDrFCA 92; Who 85; WhoHol 92, A; WhoThe 77, 81*

Cook, Robin
American. Author, Physician
Wrote *Coma,* 1977; *Mortal Fear,* 1988; *Contagion,* 1995.
b. May 4, 1940 in New York, New York
Source: *BestSel 90-2; BioIn 11, 12, 13, 16, 17; ConAu 41NR, 108, 111; ConLC 14; ConPopW; EncSF 93; LegTOT; News 96, 96-3; ScF&FL 92; WhoAm 90, 92, 94, 95, 96; WorAlBi; WorAu 1980*

Cook, Thomas
English. Businessman
Founded Thomas Cook and Son tourist agency, 1864; basis for expression "Cook's tour."
b. Nov 22, 1808 in Melbourne, England
d. Jul 19, 1892 in Leicester, England
Source: *BioIn 1, 4, 5, 7, 9, 10, 13, 15; CabMA; DcNaB S1; HisDBrE; LuthC 75; WebBD 83*

Cook, Will Marion
American. Composer, Musician
Created music for black musicals, 1900s; wrote song "Mandy Lou."
b. Jan 27, 1869 in Washington, District of Columbia
d. Jul 19, 1944 in New York, New York
Source: *AfrAmAl 6; ASCAP 66; Baker 92; BiDAfM; BiDAmM; BiDD; BiDJaz; BioIn 1, 2, 5, 9, 13, 14, 18, 21; BlkAWP; BlkCond; CmpEPM; DcAfAmP; DcAmB S3; DcAmNB; DrBlPA, 90; InB&W 80, 85; NewAmDM; NewGrDA 86; NewGrDJ 88, 94; NewGrDO; NotNAT B; OxCAmT 84; OxCPMus; PenEncP; WhoColR*

Cooke, (Alfred) Alistair
American. Broadcaster
Best known for introductions to "Masterpiece Theatre" on PBS.
b. Nov 20, 1908 in Manchester, England
Source: *AmAu&B; AuNews 1; BenetAL 91; BioIn 2, 3, 4, 8, 9, 10, 11, 12, 13, 14, 16, 17, 18; BlueB 76; CelR, 90; ConAu 9NR, 34NR, 57; ConTFT 8; CurBio 74; DcArts; DcLEL 1940; EncMcCE; FacFETw; IntAu&W 76, 77, 89, 91, 93; IntMPA 75, 76, 77, 78, 79, 81, 82, 84, 86, 88, 92, 94, 96; IntWW 74, 75, 76, 77, 78, 79, 80, 81, 82, 83, 89, 91, 93; LegTOT; LesBEnT 92; LngCTC; NewYTBS 88; NewYTET; OxCAmL 65, 83, 95; REnAL; TwCA SUP; Who 74, 82, 83, 85, 88, 90, 92, 94; WhoAm 74, 76, 78, 80, 82, 84, 86, 88, 90, 92, 94, 95, 96, 97; WhoE 95; WhoEnt 92; WhoWor 74, 78; WorAl; WorAlBi; WrDr 76, 80, 82, 84, 86, 88, 90, 92, 94, 96*

Cooke, Christopher M
American. Air Force Officer
Made unauthorized visits to Soviet Embassy working as Titan-missile-launch officer.
b. 1956
Source: *BioIn 12*

Cooke, David Coxe
American. Children's Author
Versatile writer, works include *Sharavathi,* 1966.
b. Jun 7, 1917 in Wilmington, Delaware
Source: *AuBYP 2, 3; BioIn 8, 9; ConAu 1R, 2NR; SmATA 2*

Cooke, Donald
American. Hostage
One of 52 held by terrorists, Nov 1979-Jan 1981.
b. 1955? in Long Island, New York
Source: *NewYTBS 81*

Cooke, Hope
[Maharani of Sikkim Hope Namgyal]
American. Consort
Married Prince Palden Thondup Namgyal, 1963; first native-born American to become queen.
b. Jun 21, 1940 in San Francisco, California
Source: *ArtclWW 2; BioIn 12, 15; ConAu 108; CurBio 67; InWom SUP; NewYTBS 74; WrDr 84, 86, 88*

Cooke, Jack Kent
American. Business Executive, Football Executive
Pioneer in cable television; owner, Washington Redskins, 1960-97; has owned several other pro sports teams.
b. Sep 25, 1912 in Hamilton, Ontario, Canada
d. Apr 6, 1997 in Washington, District of Columbia
Source: *BioIn 8, 9, 11, 14, 15, 16, 17, 18, 19, 20; CanWW 31, 70, 79, 80, 81, 83, 89; CmCal; IntWW 78; IntYB 81, 82; NewYTBS 85; NewYTET; St&PR 75; WhoAm 74, 76, 78, 80, 82, 84, 86, 88, 90, 92, 94, 95, 96, 97; WhoE 83, 85, 86, 91, 93, 95, 97; WhoHcky 73; WhoSSW 80, 82, 84; WhoWest 87, 89, 92*

Cooke, Janet
American. Journalist
Won Pulitzer for contrived story on heroin addiction, 1981; first fakery in Pulitzer history.
b. 1954? in Toledo, Ohio
Source: *BioIn 12, 13, 16; DcAmC; InB&W 85*

Cooke, Jay
American. Banker, Philanthropist
Sold over $1 billion in Union bonds during Civil War.
b. Aug 10, 1821 in Sandusky, Ohio
d. Feb 18, 1905 in Ogortz, Pennsylvania
Source: *AmBi; ApCAB; BiAUS; BiDAmBL 83; BioIn 3, 8, 21; DcAmB; Drake; EncAB-H 1974, 1996; EncABHB 2, 6; HarEnUS; McGEWB; NatCAB 1; OxCAmH; TwCBDA; WebAB 74, 79; WhAm 1, 4; WhCiWar; WorAl; WorAlBi*

Cooke, John Esten
American. Author, Historian
Wrote prewar novels of early VA; served as Jeb Stuart's subordinate officer in Civil War, which was basis for more literature.
b. Nov 3, 1830 in Winchester, Virginia
d. Sep 27, 1886 in Boyce, Virginia
Source: *Alli, SUP; AmAu; AmAu&B; AmBi; ApCAB; BbD; BenetAL 91; BiD&SB; BiDConf; BiDSA; BioIn 1, 3, 5, 7, 8, 11, 12; CamGEL; CasWL; CelCen; Chambr 3; CivWDc; CyAL 2; CyWA 58; DcAmAu; DcAmB; DcBiPP; DcLB 3; DcLEL; DcNAA; Drake; EncSoH; EvLB; FifSWrB; HarEnUS; NatCAB 7; NinCLC 5; Novels; OxCAmH; OxCAmL 65, 83, 95; PenC AM; REnAL; RfGAmL 87, 94; TwCBDA; WhAm HS; WhCiWar*

Cooke, Rose Terry
American. Author, Poet
Notable short stories *Root Bound,* 1885; *Somebody's Neighbors,* 1881.
b. Feb 17, 1827 in Hartford, Connecticut
d. Jul 18, 1892
Source: *Alli SUP; AmAu; AmAu&B; AmBi; AmWom; AmWomWr; ApCAB; ArtclWW 2; BbD; Benet 96; BenetAL 91; BiD&SB; BlmGWL; ChhPo, S2; CnDAL; DcAmAu; DcAmB; DcLB 12, 74; DcLEL; DcNAA; InWom, SUP; LibW; NatCAB 6; NotAW; OxCAmL 65, 83, 95; OxCWoWr 95; PenNWW A; REnAL; TwCBDA; WhAm HS*

Cooke, Sam
American. Singer, Musician
Hits include "You Send Me," 1957; "Another Saturday Night," 1963.
b. Jan 22, 1935 in Chicago, Illinois
d. Dec 11, 1964 in Los Angeles, California
Source: *Baker 84; BiDAfM; BiDAmM; BioIn 12; ConMus 1; DrBlPA, 90; EncPR&S 89; HarEnR 86; InB&W 85; LegTOT; NewAmDM; OxCPMus; PenEncP; RkOn 74; RolSEnR 83; WhoHol B; WhoRock 81; WhoRocM 82; WorAl; WorAlBi*

Cooke, Samuel
American. Businessman
Founder, pres., Penn Fruit Co., 1927-60; pioneer of self-service supermarkets.
b. Dec 29, 1898 in Ukraine, Russia

d. May 22, 1965 in Cheltenham, Pennsylvania
Source: *BioIn 7, 8; DcAmB S7; NatCAB 51; WhAm 4*

Cooke, Terence James
American. Religious Leader
Archbishop of NY, 1968-83.
b. Mar 1, 1921 in New York, New York
d. Oct 6, 1983 in New York, New York
Source: *AmCath 80; AnObit 1983; BioIn 8, 11, 12, 13, 14, 15, 17; BlueB 76; ConAu 108, 110; CurBio 68, 83N; IntWW 74, 75, 76, 77, 78, 79, 80, 81, 82, 83; NewYTBE 73; NewYTBS 79; WhAm 8; WhoAm 80, 82; WhoE 74, 75, 81, 83, 85; WhoRel 75; WhoWor 80, 82; WorAl; WorAlBi*

Cooke, William Fothergil, Sir
English. Engineer
With Charles Wheatstone, invented electric telegraph, 1845.
b. May 4, 1806 in Ealing, England
d. Jun 25, 1879 in Surrey, England
Source: *WebBD 83*

Cook-Lynn, Elizabeth
American. Poet
Published *From the River's Edge,* 1991.
b. Nov 17, 1930 in Fort Thompson, South Dakota
Source: *ConAu 133; ConLC 93; DcNAL; NatNAL; NotNaAm; WhoUSWr 88; WhoWrEP 89, 92, 95; WrDr 94, 96*

Cooley, Denton Arthur
American. Surgeon
Congenital heart disease, transplant specialist who worked with DeBakey, 1950s.
b. Aug 22, 1920 in Houston, Texas
Source: *AmMWSc 76P, 79, 82, 86, 89, 92, 95; BioIn 8, 9, 10, 11, 12, 14, 15, 16; ConAu 126; CurBio 76; IntWW 81, 82, 83, 89, 91, 93; WhoAm 86, 88, 90, 92, 94, 95, 96, 97; WhoScEn 94, 96; WhoSSW 75, 95, 97; WhoWor 74*

Coolidge, Calvin
[John Calvin Coolidge]
"Silent Cal"
American. US President
30th pres; Rep. assumed office on death of Harding, 1923; re-elected, 1924.
b. Jul 4, 1872 in Plymouth, Vermont
d. Jan 5, 1933 in Northampton, Massachusetts
Source: *AmAu&B; AmBi; AmDec 1920; AmPolLe; ApCAB X; Benet 87; BenetAL 91; BiDrAC; BiDrGov 1789; BiDrUSC 89; BiDrUSE 71, 89; BioIn 1, 2, 3, 4, 5, 6, 7, 8, 9, 10, 11, 12, 13, 14, 15, 16, 17, 18, 19, 20; CopCroC; DcAmB; DcAmC; DcAmSR; DcNAA; Dis&D; EncAAH; EncAB-H 1974, 1996; FacFETw; FacPr 89, 93; HealPre; LegTOT; LinLib L, S; McGEWB; NatCAB 24; OxCAmH; OxCAmL 65, 83; PolPar; RComAH; REn; REnAL; VicePre; WebAB 74, 79; WhAm 1; WhAmP; WhDW; WorAl; WorAlBi*

Coolidge, Charles Allerton
American. Architect
Designed Chicago's Art Museum, NY's Rockefeller Institute.
b. Nov 30, 1858 in Boston, Massachusetts
d. Apr 1, 1936 in Long Island, New York
Source: *BiDAmAr; BioIn 3, 4, 5, 15; DcAmB S2; LinLib S; MacEA; NatCAB 13; WebBD 83; WhAm 1*

Coolidge, Dane
American. Author
Expert on Indians, cowboys; many novels on Western life were used as film themes.
b. Mar 24, 1873 in Natick, Massachusetts
d. Aug 8, 1940 in Berkeley, California
Source: *AmAu&B; AmLY; BioIn 2, 11, 14; ChhPo; CmCal; CurBio 40; DcNAA; EncFWF; NatCAB 35; OxCAmL 65, 83; PeoHis; TwCWW 91; WhAm 1; WhLit; WhNAA*

Coolidge, Grace Anne Goodhue
[Mrs. Calvin Coolidge]
American. First Lady
Popular, sociable White House hostess, the opposite of her retiring husband.
b. Jan 3, 1879 in Burlington, Vermont
d. Jul 8, 1957 in Northampton, Massachusetts
Source: *FacPr 89; GoodHs; NotAW MOD; ObitOF 79; WhAm 3; WhNAA*

Coolidge, Rita
American. Singer
Ex-wife of Kris Kristofferson; platinum album *Anytime.Anywhere,* 1977; Grammy award winner.
b. May 1, 1945 in Nashville, Tennessee
Source: *BiDAmM; BioIn 9, 10, 11, 14; BkPepl; EncPR&S 74, 89; EncRk 88; HarEnCM 87; HarEnR 86; IlEncRk; InWom SUP; PenEncP; RkOn 78; WhoAm 86, 88, 90, 92, 94, 95, 96, 97; WhoAmW 95, 97; WhoEnt 92*

Coolidge, William David
American. Inventor
Invented X-ray tube; director of research for GE, 1932-40.
b. Oct 23, 1873 in Hudson, Massachusetts
d. Feb 3, 1975 in Schenectady, New York
Source: *AsBiEn; BioIn 1, 3, 4, 6, 10, 13, 14, 20, 21; DcScB S2; InSci; LarDcSc; LinLib S; NewCol 75; WhAm 6; Who 74; WhoAm 74, 78; WorAl*

Coolio
[Artis Ivey, Jr.]
American. Rapper
Released first major label solo album, *It Takes a Thief,* 1994.
b. Aug 1, 1963 in Los Angeles, California
Source: *News 96*

Coomaraswamy, Ananda Kentish
Ceylonese. Historian
Premier authority on Indian art and culture.
b. Aug 22, 1877 in Colombo, Ceylon
d. Sep 9, 1947 in Needham, Massachusetts
Source: *BioIn 1, 2, 8, 10, 11, 12; ConAu X; DcAmB S4; DcLEL; DcNAA; ObitOF 79; WhAm 2; WhAmArt 85; WhNAA; WhoAmA 91N*

Coombs, Charles Ira
American. Children's Author
Children's information, adventure books include *Young Reader's* series, 1950s; *Be a Winner* series, 1973.
b. Jun 27, 1914 in Los Angeles, California
Source: *AuBYP 2, 3; BioIn 7, 9, 15, 19; ConAu 4NR, 5R, 19NR, 36NR; SmATA 3, 43*

Coon, Carleton Stevens
American. Anthropologist
Wrote on anthropology, human evolution; led expeditions that unearthed Neanderthal bones.
b. Jun 23, 1904 in Wakefield, Massachusetts
d. Jun 3, 1981 in Gloucester, Massachusetts
Source: *AmAu&B; AmMWSc 73S, 76P; Au&Wr 71; BioIn 4, 5, 10, 12, 13; BlueB 76; ConAu 2NR, 5R, 104; CurBio 56, 81; EncAI&E; FifIDA; InSci; IntAu&W 76, 77, 82; IntDcAn; IntWW 74, 75, 76, 77, 78, 79, 80, 81; McGMS 80; NewYTBS 81; WhAm 7; WhoAm 74, 76, 78, 80; WhoWor 74, 76, 78; WorAu 1950*

Cooney, Barbara
American. Children's Author, Illustrator
Caldicott winner for *Chanticleer,* 1958; *Ox-Cart Man,* 1980.
b. Aug 6, 1916 in New York, New York
Source: *AmAu&B; AuBYP 2, 3; BioIn 14, 16; BkP; ChlLR 23; ConAu 3NR, 5R; IlsBYP; IlsCB 1957; MorJA; SmATA 6, 59; Str&VC; WhoAm 86, 90; WhoAmA 84, 86; WhoAmW 87, 91*

Cooney, Gerry
[Gerald Arthur Cooney]
"Great White Hope"
American. Boxer
Heavyweight contender defeated by Larry Holmes, 1982.
b. Aug 24, 1956 in New York, New York
Source: *BioIn 12, 13, 14, 15; LegTOT; NewYTBS 81, 82, 85*

Cooney, Joan Ganz
American. Producer
Pres., Children's TV Workshop, 1970—; shows include "Sesame Street;" "Electric Company;" Medal of Freedom recipient, 1995.
b. Nov 30, 1929 in Phoenix, Arizona
Source: *AmWomM; BioIn 13, 14, 15; BlueB 76; CelR, 90; CurBio 70; ForWC*

70; GoodHs; IntMPA 92, 94, 96; InWom SUP; LesBEnT 92; LibW; NewYTET; St&PR 87, 91, 93, 96, 97; WhoAm 74, 76, 78, 80, 82, 84, 86, 88, 90, 92, 94, 95, 96, 97; WhoAmW 72, 74, 75, 77, 79, 81, 83, 85, 87, 89, 91, 93, 95, 97; WhoE 74; WhoEnt 92; WhoFI 85, 87, 89; WhoWor 76, 78, 80, 82, 84, 87; WorAlBi

Cooney, Rory
American. Composer
Liturgical composer of over 250 songs, some of which are in Catholic churches nationwide; album *Cries of the Spirit: Psalms for Liturgy,* 1991.
b. May 29, 1952 in Delaware, Ohio
Source: *ConMus 6*

Coons, Albert Hewett
American. Scientist, Educator
Developed method of labeling molecules with a fluorochrome.
b. Jun 28, 1912 in Gloversville, New York
d. Sep 30, 1978 in Brookline, Massachusetts
Source: *AmMWSc 73P, 76P; BioIn 5; BlueB 76; CurBio 60; InSci; IntWW 74, 75, 76, 77, 78; McGMS 80; WhAm 7; WhoAm 74, 76, 78; WhoE 74*

Cooper, Alexander
American. Architect, Urban Planner
Partner, Cooper, Robertson & Partners, 1988—; co-designer of Manhattan's Battery Park City.
b. 1936 in Pittsburgh, Pennsylvania
Source: *News 88*

Cooper, Alice
[Vincent Damon Furnier]
American. Singer, Songwriter
One of original "shock-rock" groups, 1970s; hit albums include *Welcome to My Nightmare,* 1975.
b. Feb 4, 1948 in Detroit, Michigan
Source: *Baker 84; BioIn 9, 10, 11, 12, 16; BioNews 74; BkPepl; CelR; ConAu 106; ConMus 8; EncPR&S 89; EncRk 88; EncRkSt; HarEnR 86; LegTOT; NewAmDM; NewGrDA 86; OxCPMus; RkOn 78, 85; VarWW 85; WhoAm 74, 76, 78, 80, 82, 94, 95, 96, 97; WhoEnt 92; WhoHol 92; WorAl; WorAlBi*

Cooper, Annie
[Anna Julia Haywood Cooper]
American. Feminist, Writer, Educator
Her teaching and writings disclosed a modern view of racism and sexism in Western civilization.
b. Aug 10, 1858 in Raleigh, North Carolina
d. Feb 27, 1964 in Washington, District of Columbia
Source: *AmWomWr; BlkWAm; BlmGWL; InB&W 85; NotBlAW 1; OxCWoWr 95*

Cooper, Astley Paston, Sir
English. Surgeon
Surgeon to George IV; wrote many medical books.
b. Aug 23, 1768 in Norwich, England
d. Feb 12, 1841 in London, England
Source: *Alli; BiDLA; BiHiMed; BioIn 1, 2, 3, 5, 9; CelCen; DcBiPP; DcNaB; InSci; LinLib S; OxCMed 86*

Cooper, Cecil Celester
American. Baseball Player
Infielder, Milwaukee 1971-87; led AL in RBIs, 1980, 1983.
b. Dec 20, 1949 in Brenham, Texas
Source: *Ballpl 90; BaseReg 86, 87; BiDAmSp BB; BioIn 12, 13, 16; WhoBlA 80, 92; WhoMW 86*

Cooper, Chuck
[Charles H. Cooper]
American. Basketball Player
First black player in NBA; signed with Boston Celtics, 1950; played six seasons.
b. 1926
d. Feb 5, 1984 in Pittsburgh, Pennsylvania
Source: *AnObit 1984; NewYTBS 84*

Cooper, D. B
American. Criminal
Skyjacker; disappeared after parachuting with ransom money, 1971.
Source: *BioIn 12; DrInf; WhoRocM 82*

Cooper, David (Graham)
South African. Psychiatrist
Developed theory of "anti-psychiatry" which did not treat "madness" as a sickness; wrote *The Language of Madness,* 1978.
b. Feb 11, 1931 in Cape Town, South Africa
d. Jul 29, 1986 in Paris, France
Source: *ConAu 97, 119; FacFETw; IntAu&W 82*

Cooper, Douglas
Canadian. Author
Author of *Amnesia,* 1992.
b. 1960
Source: *ConLC 86*

Cooper, Edward S(awyer)
American. Physician, Educator
First black president of the American Heart Association, 1992-93.
b. Dec 11, 1926 in Columbia, South Carolina
Source: *AfrAmBi 2; BiDrACP 79; BlksScM; WhoAfA 96; WhoBlA 77, 80, 85, 88, 90, 92, 94; WhoE 95; WhoFrS 84; WhoMedH; WhoWor 84, 87, 89*

Cooper, Emil
Russian. Conductor
Directed first Russian performances of Wagner classics; with NY Met., 1944-50.
b. Dec 20, 1877 in Kherson, Russia
d. Nov 19, 1960 in New York, New York
Source: *Baker 78, 84; MetOEnc; NewEOp 71; OxDcOp; PenDiMP*

Cooper, Gary
[Frank James Cooper]
American. Actor
Matinee idol, 1930s-50s; won Oscars for *Sergeant York,* 1941; *High Noon,* 1952; special Oscar, 1960.
b. May 7, 1901 in Helena, Montana
d. May 13, 1961 in Hollywood, California
Source: *AmCulL; BiDFilm, 94; BioIn 1, 2, 3, 4, 5, 6, 7, 8, 9, 10, 11, 12, 14, 16, 17, 19; CmCal; CmMov; CurBio 41, 61; DcAmB S7; DcArts; EncAFC; EncMcCE; FacFETw; Film 2; FilmgC; GangFlm; HalFC 84, 88; IntDcF 1-3, 2-3; LegTOT; MotPP; MovMk; NatCAB 48; NotNAT B; ObitT 1961; OxCFilm; TwYS; WebAB 74, 79; WhAm 4; WhoHol B; WhScrn 74, 77, 83; WorAl; WorAlBi; WorEFlm*

Cooper, Giles (Stannus)
English. Dramatist
Noted radio dramatist; British award for yr's best radio plays was established in his honor, 1978.
b. Aug 9, 1918 in Dublin, Ireland
d. Dec 2, 1966 in Surbiton, England
Source: *BioIn 7, 13; CamGLE; CamGWoT; ConAu 113; ConDr 77F, 82E, 88E; CroCD; DcLB 13; DcLEL 1940; EncWT; LngCTC; NotNAT B; ObitT 1961; ScF&FL 1; WhThe*

Cooper, Gladys, Dame
English. Actor
Career on stage, film, TV spanned more than 60 yrs.
b. Dec 18, 1888 in Lewisham, England
d. Nov 17, 1971 in Henley-on-Thames, England
Source: *BiE&WWA; BioIn 3, 4, 7, 9, 10, 12, 14; CnThe; ConAu 33R; CurBio 56, 72, 72N; EncWT; Film 1, 2; FilmgC; HalFC 84, 88; IntDcF 1-3; InWom, SUP; LegTOT; MGM; MotPP; MovMk; ObitOF 79; ObitT 1971; OxCThe 83; Vers A; WhoHol B; WhoThe 72; WhScrn 74, 77, 83; WhThe; WorAl*

Cooper, Gordon
[Leroy Gordon Cooper, Jr]
American. Astronaut
Made orbit flight in Faith 7, 1963; Gemini V, 1965.
b. Mar 6, 1927 in Shawnee, Oklahoma
Source: *BioIn 6, 7, 9, 10, 13; BlueB 76; CurBio 63; FacFETw; WhoAm 74, 76, 78, 80, 82, 84, 86, 88, 90, 92, 94, 95, 96; WhoFI 87; WhoScEn 94; WhoSpc; WhoSSW 73; WorAl*

Cooper, Henry B
English. Boxer
Held British heavyweight title almost 11 yrs; last fight, 1971.
b. May 3, 1934 in London, England
Source: *BioIn 14, 15; Who 88, 92; WhoBox 74*

Cooper, Jackie
[Our Gang; John Cooper, Jr]
American. Actor
Started acting at age three; starred in *The Champ,* 1931; won Emmys, 1970s for directing.
b. Sep 15, 1922 in Los Angeles, California
Source: *AmMWSc 79, 82, 86, 89, 92, 95; BiDAmM; BiE&WWA; BioIn 15; ConAu 133; ConTFT 2, 8; EncAFC; Film 2; FilmgC; HalFC 84, 88; IntMPA 76, 77, 78, 79, 81, 82, 84, 86, 88, 92, 94, 96; IntWW 81; LesBEnT 92; MGM; MiSFD 9; MovMk; WhoAm 74, 76, 78, 80, 82, 84, 86, 88, 90, 92, 94, 95, 96, 97; WhoEnt 92; WorAl; WorAlBi; WrDr 94, 96*

Cooper, James Fenimore
American. Author
Wrote *The Spy,* 1821; *The Last of the Mohicans,* 1826; first important American novelist.
b. Sep 15, 1789 in Burlington, New Jersey
d. Sep 14, 1851 in Cooperstown, New York
Source: *Alli; AmAu; AmAu&B; AmBi; AmCulL; AmWr; ApCAB; AtlBL; AuBYP 2, 3; BbD; Benet 87, 96; BenetAL 91; BiD&SB; BioIn 1, 2, 3, 4, 5, 6, 7, 8, 9, 10, 11, 12, 13, 14, 15, 16, 17, 19, 20, 21; CamGEL; CamGLE; CamHAL; CarSB; CasWL; CelCen; Chambr 3; ChlBkCr; CnDAL; ColARen; CrtT 3, 4; CyAL 1; CyWA 58; DcAmAu; DcAmB; DcAmC; DcArts; DcBiA; DcBiPP; DcEnA; DcEnL; DcLB 3; DcLEL; DcNAA; Drake; EncAAH; EncAB-H 1974, 1996; EncFWF; EncSF 93; EvLB; FilmgC; HalFC 84, 88; HarEnUS; HsB&A; LegTOT; LinLib L, S; MagSAmL; McGEWB; MemAm; MnBBF; MouLC 3; NatCAB 1; NinCLC 1, 27, 54; Novels; OxCAmH; OxCAmL 65, 83, 95; OxCChiL; OxCEng 67, 85, 95; OxCShps; PenC AM; RAdv 1, 14, 13-1; RComAH; RComWL; REn; REnAL; REnAW; RfGAmL 87, 94; ScFEYrs; SmATA 19; SpyFic; TwCBDA; WebAB 74, 79; WebE&AL; WhAm HS; WhDW; WhNaAH; WhoChL; WhoSpyF; WorAl; WorAlBi; WrChl*

Cooper, John Sherman
American. Diplomat
UN delegate 1949-51, 1968, 1981; former ambassador to India, Nepal, E Germany. Drafted Cooper-Church amendment aimed at barring further U.S. military action in Cambodia during Vietnam War.
b. Aug 23, 1901 in Somerset, Kentucky
d. Feb 21, 1991 in Washington, District of Columbia
Source: *AnObit 1991; BiDrAC; BiDrUSC 89; BioIn 2, 3, 4, 5, 6, 9, 10, 11, 12, 16; BioNews 74; BlueB 76; CurBio 50, 91N; DcAmDH 80, 89; EncCW; EncSoH; IntWW 74, 75, 76, 77, 78, 79, 80, 81, 82, 83; NewYTBS 91; PeoHis; WhAm 10; Who 92; WhoAm 74, 76, 78, 80, 82, 84, 86, 88; WhoAmP 73, 75, 77, 79, 81, 83, 87, 89; WhoGov 72; WhoSSW 73; WorAl; WorAlBi*

Cooper, Joseph D
American. Author
Wrote *The Art of Decision-Making,* 1961, numerous books on photographic techniques.
b. May 25, 1917 in Boston, Massachusetts
d. Mar 25, 1975 in Washington, District of Columbia
Source: *AmMWSc 73S; ConAu 4NR, 5R, 57; CurBio 52; WhAm 6; WhoAm 74; WhoWorJ 72, 78*

Cooper, Kenneth Hardy
"Father of Aerobics"
American. Physician, Author
Credited with coining word aerobics; wrote *Aerobics,* 1968.
b. Mar 4, 1931 in Oklahoma City, Oklahoma
Source: *BioIn 9, 10, 12, 16; ConAu 126, 134; IntAu&W 91*

Cooper, Kent
American. Journalist
General manager, Associated Press, 1925-48.
b. Mar 22, 1880 in Columbus, Indiana
d. Jan 31, 1965 in West Palm Beach, Florida
Source: *AmAu&B; ASCAP 66; BiDAmJo; BioIn 1, 5, 7, 16; ConAu 89; CurBio 44, 65; DcAmB S7; DcLB 29; DrAF 76; EncAJ; EncTwCJ; FacFETw; IndAu 1917; JrnUS; ObitOF 79; WhAm 4*

Cooper, Leon Neil
American. Physicist
Developed the BCS theory of superconductivity, along with John Bardeen and John Robert Schrieffer; won Nobel Prize for Physics, 1972.
b. Feb 28, 1930 in New York, New York
Source: *AmMWSc 92; BiESc; BioIn 9, 10, 15; CamDcSc; Dun&B 88; FacFETw; IntWW 91; LarDcSc; NobelP; St&PR 91; WebAB 79; Who 92; WhoAm 90; WhoE 91; WhoFI 92; WhoNob, 90, 95; WhoTech 89; WhoWor 91; WorAlBi*

Cooper, Lester Irving
American. Writer
Won Emmy, Peabody for "Animals, Animals, Animals," series, 1976.
b. Jan 20, 1919 in New York, New York
d. Jun 6, 1985 in New York, New York
Source: *ConAu 116; WhAm 8; WhoAm 74, 76, 78, 80, 82, 84*

Cooper, Louise Field
American. Author
Novels include *Summer Stranger,* 1947; contributor to the *New Yorker,* 1935-62.
b. Mar 8, 1905 in Hartford, Connecticut
d. Oct 9, 1992 in Woodbridge, Connecticut
Source: *AmAu&B; AmNov; BioIn 2, 4, 18, 19; ConAu 1R, 4NR, 139; CurBio 50, 93N; InWom, SUP; REnAL; ScFSB; TwCA SUP; WhAm 10; WhoAm 74, 76, 78, 80, 82, 84, 86, 88, 90, 92; WhoAmW 58, 66, 68, 70, 72, 74*

Cooper, Melville
American. Actor
Character actor for 50 yrs; films include *The Scarlet Pimpernel,* 1935; *Rebecca,* 1940.
b. Oct 15, 1896 in Birmingham, England
d. Mar 29, 1973 in Woodland Hills, California
Source: *BiE&WWA; BioIn 9; EncAFC; FilmgC; HalFC 84, 88; LegTOT; MovMk; NewYTBE 73; NotNAT B; ObitOF 79; Vers A; WhoHol B; WhScrn 77*

Cooper, Mort(on Cecil)
American. Baseball Player
Pitcher, 1938-49; with brother Walker, helped St. Louis win NL pennant, 1942.
b. Mar 4, 1914 in Atherton, Missouri
d. Nov 17, 1958 in Little Rock, Arkansas
Source: *BiDAmSp Sup; BioIn 3, 5; WhoProB 73*

Cooper, Peter
American. Businessman, Philanthropist
Built first American steam locomotive, *Tom Thumb,* which helped promote rapid growth of railroads in US, 1830.
b. Feb 12, 1791 in New York, New York
d. Apr 4, 1883 in New York, New York
Source: *Alli SUP; AmAu&B; AmBi; AmSocL; ApCAB; BbD; BenetAL 91; BiDAmBL 83; BiD&SB; BiInAmS; BioIn 1, 2, 3, 4, 5, 6, 7, 8, 11, 14, 15, 19; CelCen; DcAmAu; DcAmB; DcAmSR; DcBiPP; DcNAA; Drake; EncAB-H 1974, 1996; EncABHB 3; HarEnUS; InSci; LinLib S; McGEWB; NatCAB 3; OxCAmH; OxCAmL 65, 83, 95; PolPar; REn; REnAL; TwCBDA; WebAB 74, 79; WhAm HS; WhNaAH; WorAl; WorAlBi; WorInv*

Cooper, Samuel
English. Artist
Miniaturist painter; among the subjects for his portraits were Mrs. Pepys, Cromwell, Milton.
b. 1609
d. 1672
Source: *AntBDN J; BioIn 4, 5, 6, 10, 12, 14, 15; DcArts; DcBiPP; DcNaB; McGDA; NewCol 75; OxCArt; OxDcArt; WebBD 83*

Cooper, Thomas
American. Scientist
Political philosopher; wrote *Political Essays,* 1799.
b. Oct 22, 1759 in London, England
d. May 11, 1839 in Columbia, South Carolina
Source: *Alli; AmAu; AmBi; AmWrBE; ApCAB; BenetAL 91; BiDAmEd;*

BiDAmJo; BiDAmS; BiDSA; BiInAmS; BioIn 1, 3, 4, 5, 6, 12, 13, 16, 19; CyAL 2; CyEd; DcAmAu; DcAmB; DcAmMeB; DcNAA; DcNaB; DcScB; Drake; EncAB-H 1974; EncSoH; InSci; McGEWB; NatCAB 11; OxCAmH; OxCAmL 65, 83, 95; PeoHis; REnAL; TwCBDA; WebAB 74, 79; WhAm HS; WhAmP

Cooper, Walker
[William Walker Cooper]
American. Baseball Player
Catcher, 1940-57; with brother Mort, considered one of greatest brother acts in baseball.
b. Jan 8, 1915 in Atherton, Missouri
Source: *Ballpl 90; BaseEn 88; BiDAmSp Sup; BioIn 1, 2, 8; LegTOT; WhoProB 73*

Cooper, Wilhelmina Behmenburg
American. Model, Business Executive
Founded Wilhelmina Models, Inc. in 1967; appeared on record 28 *Vogue* covers, 1960s.
b. May 1, 1940 in Culemborg, Netherlands
d. Mar 1, 1980 in Greenwich, Connecticut
Source: *ConAu 97*

Coors, Adolph
German. Brewer
Opened brewery in Golden, CO, 1880.
b. 1847, Germany
d. Jun 5, 1919 in Virginia Beach, Virginia
Source: *Entr*

Coors, Joseph
American. Brewer
CEO of Adolph Coors Co., 1982-87.
b. Nov 12, 1917 in Golden, Colorado
Source: *BioIn 11, 14; ConAmBL; Dun&B 86, 90; LesBEnT, 92; WhoAm 84, 86, 88, 90, 92, 95; WhoFI 77, 79, 87, 89; WhoWest 87, 92, 94*

Coors, William K
"Bill Coors"
American. Brewer
Pres., CEO, Adolph Coors Co., 1977-85.
b. 1916 in Golden, Colorado
Source: *BioIn 14, 15; ConAmBL; ConNews 85-1; Dun&B 90; St&PR 84, 87, 91; WhoAm 86, 90; WhoFI 83, 85, 89; WhoWest 92*

Coote, Robert
English. Actor
Played Colonel Pickering, Broadway version of *My Fair Lady,* 1956.
b. Feb 4, 1909 in London, England
d. Nov 25, 1982 in New York, New York
Source: *BiE&WWA; BioIn 10, 13; EncAFC; FilmgC; HalFC 84, 88; MotPP; MovMk; NewYTBS 82; NotNAT; Vers A, B; WhoHol A; WhoThe 72, 77, 81*

Coots, J. Fred
American. Songwriter
Wrote "Santa Claus Is Comin' To Town," 1934; "You Go To My Head," 1938.
b. May 2, 1897 in New York, New York
d. Apr 8, 1985 in New York, New York
Source: *AmPS; AmSong; BiDAmM; CmpEPM; EncMT; NewCBMT; NotNAT*

Coover, Robert (Lowell)
American. Author
Wrote *The Origin of the Brunists,* 1966; *A Night at the Movies,* 1987.
b. Feb 4, 1932 in Charles City, Iowa
Source: *AmAu&B; Benet 96; BenetAL 91; BioIn 13, 14, 15; CamGLE; CamHAL; ConAu 3NR, 37NR, 45; ConLC 3, 7, 15, 32, 46, 87; ConNov 72, 76, 82, 86, 91, 96; CurBio 91; CyWA 89; DcArts; DcLB 2, Y81A; DcLEL 1940; DrAF 76; DrAPF 83, 91; EncSF, 93; EncWL 3; IntAu&W 76, 77, 82, 91, 93; IntvTCA 2; MajTwCW; ModAL S1, S2; Novels; OxCAmL 83, 95; PenC AM; PostFic; RAdv 1, 14, 13-1; RfGAmL 94; RfGShF; RGTwCWr; ScF&FL 92; ScFSB; ShSCr 15; WhoAm 74, 76, 78, 80, 82, 84, 97; WhoE 74, 75; WorAu 1970; WrDr 76, 80, 82, 84, 86, 88, 90, 92, 94, 96*

Cope, Edward Drinker
American. Paleontologist
Discovered numerous extinct vertebrate species from the Tertiary Period of geological time.
b. Jul 28, 1840 in Philadelphia, Pennsylvania
d. Apr 12, 1897 in Philadelphia, Pennsylvania
Source: *Alli SUP; AmBi; ApCAB; AsBiEn; BiDAmS; BiESc; BiInAmS; BioIn 2, 4, 7, 8, 9, 10, 13, 18; CelCen; DcAmAu; DcAmB; DcNAA; DcScB, S1; InSci; LarDcSc; LinLib S; NatCAB 7; OxCAmH; PeoHis; TwCBDA; WhAm HS*

Cope, Jack
[Robert Knox Cope]
South African. Author
Writings primarily deal with life in South Africa; shunned in England during WWII due to pacifist views.
b. Jun 3, 1913 in Mooi River, South Africa
Source: *Au&Wr 71; CasWL; ConAu 9R, X; ConNov 72, 76, 82, 86, 91, 96; ConPo 70; DcLEL 1940; EncSoA; IntAu&W 82, 91; IntWWP 77; LiExTwC; ModCmwL; TwCWr; WhoWor 74, 78; WrDr 76, 80, 82, 84, 86, 88, 90, 92, 94, 96*

Cope, Julian
Welsh. Singer, Songwriter
Formed punk band Teardrop Explodes and released debut album, *Kilimanjaro,* 1978; solo albums include *World Shut Your Mouth,* 1984, *Saint Julian,* 1987, *Peggy Suicide,* 1991 and *Twenty Mothers,* 1995.
b. 1957 in Deri, Wales
Source: *ConMus 16; EncRkSt*

Copeau, Jacques
French. Dramatist
Founder of the Theater Vieux Colombier in Paris, 1913.
b. Feb 4, 1878 in Paris, France
d. Oct 20, 1949 in Beaune, France
Source: *CnThe; McGEWD 84; NotNAT B; ObitOF 79; OxCThe 67, 83; PlP&P; WhDW; WhScrn 77; WhThe*

Copeland, Al
Businessman
Founder, owner, Popeyes Famous Fried Chicken and Biscuits, Inc. 1973—.
b. 1944
Source: *BioIn 13, 14; Dun&B 90; News 88-3; WhoAm 90; WhoFI 89; WhoSSW 84*

Copeland, Charles Townsend
English. Educator
English professor, Harvard; taught TS Eliot, Robert Benchley, Heywood Brown.
b. Apr 27, 1860 in Calais, Maine
d. Jul 24, 1952 in Waverly, Massachusetts
Source: *AmAu&B; ApCAB X; BioIn 1, 3, 4, 5, 11; DcAmB S5; GayN; ObitOF 79; OxCAmL 65, 83, 95; REnAL; WhAm 3; WhNAA*

Copeland, Jo
American. Fashion Designer
With Patullo from 1938-72; received Neiman-Marcus Award, 1944.
b. 1899 in New York, New York
d. Mar 20, 1982 in New York, New York
Source: *BioIn 12, 13; NewYTBS 82; WhoAm 80, 82; WorFshn*

Copeland, Lammot du Pont
American. Businessman
Director, E I du Pont de Nemours and Co., 1942-83.
b. May 19, 1905 in Christiana, Delaware
d. Jul 1, 1983 in Mount Cuba, Delaware
Source: *BlueB 76; CurBio 63; IntWW 83; IntYB 82; St&PR 75; WhoAm 82; WhoE 74; WhoFI 74; WhoWor 74*

Copeland, Stewart
American. Songwriter
Wrote hits for rock/pop group, Police: "King of Pain," 1984; film scores include *Bachelor Party,* 1983.
b. Jul 16, 1952 in Maclean, Virginia
Source: *BioIn 12, 13, 15, 16; ConMus 14; ConTFT 5; LegTOT; NewYTBS 89; WhoAm 96, 97; WhoRocM 82*

Copernicus, Nicolaus
[Niklas Kopernik]
Polish. Astronomer
Proposed theory that sun was center of universe, all planets revolved around it, 1543.
b. Feb 19, 1473 in Torun, Poland

d. May 24, 1543 in Frauenburg, Poland
Source: *AstEnc; BbD; Benet 87, 96; BiD&SB; BiDPsy; BiESc; BioIn 1, 2, 3, 4, 5, 6, 7, 8, 9, 10, 11, 12, 13, 14, 15, 16, 17, 18, 19, 20; CamDcSc; CasWL; DcBiPP; DcCathB; DcInv; Dis&D; EncEnl; LuthC 75; McGEWB; NewC; NewCol 75; OxCMed 86; OxCPhil; RAdv 14; REn; WhDW*

Copland, Aaron
American. Composer
America's best-known composer; works include *Billy the Kid,* 1938, *Rodeo,* 1942; won Pulitzer for *Appalachian Spring,* 1944.
b. Nov 14, 1900 in New York, New York
d. Dec 2, 1990 in North Tarrytown, New York
Source: *AmAu&B; AmComp; AmCulL; AnObit 1990; ASCAP 66; Au&Wr 71; Baker 78, 84, 92; Benet 87, 96; BenetAL 91; BiDAmM; BioIn 1, 2, 3, 4, 5, 6, 7, 8, 9, 10, 11, 12, 14, 15, 16, 17, 18, 19, 20, 21; BlueB 76; CelR, 90; CompSN SUP; ConAmC 76, 82; ConAu 5R, 133; ConCom 92; ConMus 2; CpmDNM 81, 82; CurBio 40, 51, 91N; DcArts; DcCM; DcTwCCu 1; EncAAH; EncAB-H 1974, 1996; EncAL; FacFETw; FilmgC; GayLesB; HalFC 84, 88; IntDcB; IntDcF 1-4, 2-4; IntDcOp; IntWW 74, 75, 76, 77, 78, 79, 80, 81, 82, 83, 89, 91N; IntWWM 77, 90; JeAmHC; LegTOT; LinLib S; MakMC; McGEWB; MetOEnc; NewAmDM; NewEOp 71; NewGrDA 86; NewGrDO; NewOxM; News 91, 91-2; NewYTBE 70; NewYTBS 80, 84, 90; OxCAmH; OxCAmL 65; OxCFilm; OxCMus; OxDcOp; PenDiMP A; RAdv 14, 13-3; RComAH; REn; REnAL; WebAB 74, 79; WhAm 10; WhDW; Who 74, 82, 83, 85E, 88, 90, 92N; WhoAm 74, 76, 78, 80, 82, 84, 86, 88, 90; WhoAmM 83; WhoMus 72; WhoWor 74, 76, 78, 80, 82, 84, 87, 89, 91; WhoWorJ 78; WorAl; WorAlBi; WorEFlm*

Copley, John Singleton
American. Artist
Considered greatest American old master; known for perceptive portraits of Paul Revere, Samuel Adams, others.
b. Jul 3, 1733 in Boston, Massachusetts
d. Sep 9, 1815 in London, England
Source: *AmBi; AtlBL; DcAmB; DcBiPP; DcNaB; Drake; EncAR; HarEnUS; NewCol 75; OxCAmH; OxCAmL 65; REn; TwCBDA; WebAB 74; WebBD 83; WhAm HS; WorAl*

Coplon, Judith
American. Spy
Convicted of stealing government papers, passing to Soviet agent, 1950; reversed in Appeals Court.
b. 1921 in New York, New York
Source: *BioIn 1, 2, 4, 19; EncE 75; PolProf T*

Coppard, A(lfred) E(dgar)
English. Author, Poet
First collection of short stories was *Adam and Eve and Pinch Me,* 1921.
b. Jan 4, 1878 in Folkestone, England
d. Jan 13, 1957 in London, England
Source: *BioIn 4, 8, 11, 15; ChhPo, S1, S2; DcLEL; DcNaB 1951; EncWL 2, 3; EvLB; LngCEL; LngCTC; ModBrL; NewC; Novels; OxCEng 67, 95; PenC ENG; REn; RfGShF; RGTwCWr; TwCA, SUP; TwCWr; WhE&EA; WhLit; WhoChL; WhoTwCL; YABC 1*

Coppee, Francois Edouard Joachim
"Poete de Humbles"
French. Poet, Dramatist
Works concerning ordinary people, include verse *Les Humbles,* 1872; play *Le Passant,* 1869.
b. Jan 26, 1842 in Paris, France
d. May 23, 1908 in Paris, France
Source: *BbD; BiD&SB; ClDMEL 47; CnMD; DcCathB; DcEuL; Dis&D; EuAu; LinLib L, S; McGEWD 72; ModWD; NotNAT B; OxCFr; PenC EUR; REn*

Copperfield, David
[David Kotkin]
American. Magician
Combines theater, humor with illusions; performed "illusion of century," 1983, making Statue of Liberty disappear.
b. Sep 16, 1956 in Metuchen, New Jersey
Source: *BioIn 13, 15, 16, 18, 19, 20, 21; CelR 90; ConNews 86-3; ConTFT 7; CurBio 92; WhoAm 90, 92, 94, 95, 96, 97; WhoEnt 92; WhoWor 97*

Coppola, Carmine
American. Composer, Conductor
Father of Francis Ford Coppola; won Oscar for co-writing music for *Godfather II,* 1974.
b. Jun 11, 1910 in New York, New York
d. Apr 26, 1991 in Northridge, California
Source: *AnObit 1991; ASCAP 66; BioIn 2, 10, 12, 17, 18; ConAmC 76A, 82; ConTFT 7, 10; IntMPA 88; LegTOT; News 91; NewYTBS 91; VarWW 85; WhAm 10; WhoAm 82, 84, 86, 88, 90*

Coppola, Francis Ford
American. Director
Films include *The Godfather I, II,* 1972, 1974; *Apocalypse Now,* 1979.
b. Apr 7, 1939 in Detroit, Michigan
Source: *AmDec 1970; BenetAL 91; BiDFilm, 94; BioIn 7, 9, 10, 11, 12, 13, 14, 15, 16, 17, 18, 19, 20, 21; BioNews 75; BkPepl; CelR 90; ConAu 40NR, 77; ConTFT 1, 6, 13; CurBio 74, 91; DcArts; DcLB 44; DcTwCCu 1; FacFETw; FilmgC; GangFlm; HalFC 84, 88; IlWWHD 1; IntDcF 1-2, 2-2; IntMPA 75, 76, 77, 78, 79, 81, 82, 84, 86, 88, 92, 94, 96; IntWW 79, 80, 81, 82, 83, 89, 91, 93; LegTOT; MiSFD 9; MovMk; News 89; NewYTBS 74, 88; OxCFilm; Who 88, 90, 92, 94; WhoAm 76, 78, 80, 82, 84, 86, 88, 90, 92, 94, 95, 96, 97; WhoEnt 92; WhoHol 92; WhoWest 78, 80, 82, 84, 87, 89, 92, 94; WhoWor 95, 96, 97; WorAl; WorAlBi; WorEFlm; WorFDir 2*

Copps, Sheila Maureen
Canadian. Politician
Member, Canadian Parliament, House of Commons, 1984-90; Deputy Direct or, Canadian Liberal Party, 1990—.
b. Nov 27, 1952 in Hamilton, Ontario, Canada
Source: *BioIn 15; CanWW 31, 89; ConNews 86-4; WhoAm 95, 96, 97; WhoAmW 89, 91, 93, 95; WhoFI 96; WhoWor 95, 96*

Copway, George
Canadian. Missionary
Ojibway missionary who was said to be Longfellow's inspiration for the poem *The Song of Hiawatha,* 1855.
b. 1818 in Rice Lake, Ontario, Canada
d. Jan 1869
Source: *Alli; AmAu&B; BiD&SB; BiNAW SupB; BioIn 16, 21; DcAmAu; DcAmB; DcNAA; DcNAL; EncNAB; EncNAR; EncNoAI; MacDCB 78; NatNAL; NotNaAm; OxCAmL 65, 83, 95; REnAL; WhAm HS; WhNaAH*

Coquelin, Benoit Constant
[Coquelin Aine]
French. Actor
His first part, Cyrano de Bergerac, was always associated with his name; with Comedie-Francaise, 1860-92.
b. Jan 23, 1841 in Boulogne-sur-Mer, France
d. Jan 27, 1909 in Pont-aux-Dames, France
Source: *BbD; BiD&SB; BioIn 2, 4; CelCen; LinLib L; NotNAT B; OxCAmT 84; OxCThe 83; WhAm 4, HSA; WhoHol B; WhScrn 83*

Corben, Richard Vance
American. Artist
Horror illustrator who invented fantasy strip "Rowlf."
b. Oct 1, 1940 in Anderson, Missouri
Source: *BioIn 15; ConGrA 1; FanAl; WorECom*

Corbett, James John
"Gentleman Jim"
American. Boxer
Defeated John L Sullivan for heavyweight crown, 1892; portrayed by Errol Flynn in *Gentleman Jim,* 1942; Hall of Famer.
b. Sep 1, 1866 in San Francisco, California
d. Feb 18, 1933 in New York, New York
Source: *AmBi; BiDAmSp BK; BioIn 1, 2, 5, 6, 9, 10, 11, 12, 13, 17; DcAmB S1; Film 1; OxCAmH; WebAB 74, 79; WhAm 4, HSA; WhoBox 74; WhoHol B; WhoStg 1906, 1908; WhScrn 74, 77*

Corbett, John
American. Actor
Plays disc jockey Chris Stevens on TV show "Northern Exposure," 1990—.
Source: *BioIn 17*

Corbett, Scott
[Winfield Scott Corbett]
American. Children's Author
Wrote over 60 books, including *Cutlass Island,* 1962.
b. Jul 27, 1913 in Kansas City, Missouri
Source: *Au&Wr 71; AuBYP 2, 3; BioIn 8, 9, 15, 19; ChILR 1; ConAu 1NR, 1R, 23NR; DcAmChF 1960; FourBJA; IntAu&W 76, 77, 82; MajAI; ScF&FL 1, 2, 92; SmATA 2, 2AS, 42; TwCChW 78, 83, 89; WhoAm 78, 80, 82, 84, 86, 88, 90; WhoUSWr 88; WhoWrEP 89; WrDr 80, 82, 84, 86, 88, 90, 92, 94, 96*

Corbett, Young, III
[Ralph Capabianca Giordano]
Italian. Boxer
World welterweight champion, 1930s.
b. May 27, 1905 in Naples, Italy
d. Jul 20, 1993 in Fresno, California
Source: *BiDAmSp BK; WhoBox 74*

Corbiere, Tristan (Edouard Joachim)
French. Poet
Precursor of the surrealist movement; vol. of poems, *Les Amours Jaunes,* 1873.
b. Jul 18, 1845 in Morlaix, France
d. Mar 1, 1875 in Morlaix, France
Source: *AtlBL; BioIn 1, 5, 7, 8, 9, 11; ClDMEL 47; DcArts; GuFrLit 1; NinCLC 43*

Corbin, Barry
American. Actor
Plays former astronaut Maurice Minnifield on TV show "Northern Exposure," 1990—.
b. Oct 16, in Dawson County, Texas
Source: *BioIn 18; IntMPA 92*

Corbin, Margaret Cochran
"Captain Molly"
American. Historical Figure
Revolutionary War heroine, first woman pensioner of US, 1779.
b. Nov 12, 1751 in Franklin County, Pennsylvania
d. 1800? in Highland Falls, New York
Source: *AmBi; BlkwEAR; DcAmB; EncAmaz 91; EncAR; EncCRAm; EncWHA; InWom, SUP; NotAW; WebAB 74; WebAMB; WhAm HS; WhAmRev*

Corby, Ellen
[Ellen Hansen]
American. Actor
Played Grandma on "The Waltons," 1972-79.
b. Jun 3, 1913 in Racine, Wisconsin
Source: *BioIn 10, 11; ConTFT 9; FilmEn; FilmgC; HalFC 84, 88; InWom SUP; ItaFilm; LegTOT; MovMk; Vers A; WhoAm 76; WhoAmW 72, 74; WhoHol 92, A; WorAl; WorAlBi*

Corby, Mike
[The Babys]
English. Singer, Musician
Keyboardist, guitarist, vocalist with power pop group, 1976-77.
b. Jul 3, 1955 in London, England

Corcoran, Thomas Gardiner
"Tommy the Cork"
American. Lawyer, Politician
Helped draft New Deal legislation, 1930s.
b. Dec 29, 1900 in Pawtucket, Rhode Island
d. Dec 6, 1981 in Washington, District of Columbia
Source: *BioIn 5, 7, 8, 12, 13; CurBio 40, 82, 82N; NewYTBS 81; WhAm 8; WhoAm 74, 76, 78, 80; WhoWor 74*

Corcoran, William Wilson
American. Financier, Philanthropist
Founded Corcoran Art Gallery, Washington, DC, which houses his collection, 1859.
b. Dec 27, 1798 in Baltimore, Maryland
d. Feb 24, 1888 in Washington, District of Columbia
Source: *AmBi; ApCAB; BiAUS; BioIn 8, 9, 12, 15; DcAmB; HarEnUS; NatCAB 3; TwCBDA; WebAB 74, 79; WhAm HS*

Corcos, Lucille
American. Illustrator
Book illustrations include *Treasury of Gilbert and Sullivan,* 1941; *Grimm's Fairy Tales,* 1962; full-page works in *Life; Vogue; Fortune* mags.
b. Sep 21, 1908 in New York, New York
d. Aug 25, 1973
Source: *AmAu&B; AuBYP 2, 3; BioIn 3, 5, 8, 10, 11; ChhPo; ConAu 21R, 134; IlsCB 1946, 1957; SmATA 10; WhAm 6; WhAmArt 85; WhoAm 74; WhoAmA 73, 76N, 78N, 80N, 82N, 84N, 86N, 89N, 91N, 93N; WhoAmW 58, 70, 72, 74*

Cord, Alex
[Alexander Viespi]
American. Actor
TV series include "WEB," 1978; "Airwolf," 1984—.
b. Aug 3, 1931 in Floral Park, New York
Source: *CelR; ConTFT 1, 9; FilmgC; HalFC 84, 88; IntMPA 75, 76, 77, 78, 79, 81, 82, 84, 86, 88, 92; ItaFilm; LegTOT; MotPP; WhoAm 76, 78, 80, 82, 84, 86, 90; WhoEnt 92; WhoHol 92, A*

Cord, E(rret) L(obban)
American. Auto Executive
Designer, 1930s Cord luxury car.
b. 1895 in Warrensburg, Missouri
d. Jan 2, 1974 in Reno, Nevada
Source: *NewYTBS 74*

Corday d'Armount, Charlotte
[Marie Anne Charlotte Corday D'Armount]
French. Revolutionary, Assassin
Murdered Jean Paul Marat in his bath, Jul 13, 1793; guillotined.
b. Jul 27, 1768 in Saint-Saturnin, France
d. Jul 17, 1793 in Paris, France
Source: *InWom; NewCol 75; REn*

Cordero, Angel Tomas
Puerto Rican. Jockey
First jockey to win over $10 million in one year.
b. May 8, 1942 in Santurce, Puerto Rico
Source: *BioIn 6, 10, 12, 13, 14, 15, 16; CelR 90; NewYTBS 82; WhoAm 90; WhoHisp 91, 92, 94; WorAlBi*

Cordero, Helen Quintana
American. Artist
Invented the Storyteller Doll, 1964.
b. 1915
Source: *NotNaAm*

Cordes, Eugene Harold
American. Biochemist
Director, Merck, Sharp and Dohme Research Co., 1979-84; pres. Winthrop Pharms Rach Group Workshop Inc., 1988—; wrote *Biological Chemistry,* 1966.
b. Apr 7, 1936 in York, Nebraska
Source: *AmMWSc 86, 92; WhoAm 74, 76, 78, 80, 82, 84, 86, 88, 90, 92, 94, 95, 96, 97; WhoE 95; WhoMW 96; WhoScEn 94, 96; WhoTech 82, 89; WhoWor 74*

Cordes, Rudolf
German. Hostage
Businessman taken hostage Jan 17, 1987 in Lebanon and released Sep 12, 1988, after 604 days in captivity.

Cordier, Andrew Wellington
American. Diplomat
Exec. asst. to UN Secretary-General, 1946-62.
b. Mar 3, 1901 in Canton, Ohio
d. Jul 11, 1975 in Manhasset, New York
Source: *AmPeW; BiDInt; BioIn 1, 2, 6, 8, 10, 11; BlueB 76; CurBio 50, 75; DcAmB S9; IntWW 74, 75; WhAm 6; Who 74; WhoAm 74; WhoE 74; WhoUN 75; WhoWor 74*

Cordiner, Ralph Jarron
American. Business Executive
Chairman, GE, 1958-63.
b. Mar 20, 1900 in Walla Walla, Washington
d. Dec 4, 1973 in Clearwater, Florida
Source: *BioIn 2, 4, 5, 7, 10, 11, 12; BioNews 74; BusPN; CurBio 51, 74; DcAmB S9; NatCAB 58; NewYTBE 73; WhAm 6; WhoAmP 73*

Cordoba, Francisco Fernandez
Spanish. Soldier, Explorer
Distinguished himself in wars against the Moors; founded Granada, Leon, 1523.
b. 1475
d. 1526
Source: *WebBD 83*

Cordobes, El
[Manuel Benitez Peres]
Spanish. Bullfighter
Highest-paid matador in history, known for courageous, daring feats in ring.
b. May 4, 1936 in Palma del Rio, Spain
Source: *BioIn 6, 7, 8*

Cordtz, Dan
[Howard Dan Cordtz]
American. Broadcast Journalist
With *Wall Street Journal*, 1955-66; economics editor, ABC News, 1974-87.
b. May 1, 1927 in Gary, Indiana
Source: *ConAu 73; WhoAm 80, 82, 84, 86*

Corea, Chick
[Anthony Armando Corea]
American. Jazz Musician
Keyboardist; founded group, Return to Forever, 1971; won five Grammys.
b. Jun 12, 1941 in Chelsea, Massachusetts
Source: *AllMusG; Baker 84; BiDJaz; BioIn 12, 13, 14, 15, 16; ConMus 6; ConNews 86-3; CurBio 88; EncJzS; EncRk 88; FacFETw; IlEncJ; NewAmDM; NewGrDA 86; NewGrDJ 88, 94; PenEncP; RolSEnR 83; WhoAm 74, 76, 80, 82, 84, 86, 88, 90, 92, 94, 95, 96, 97; WhoEnt 92*

Corelli, Arcangelo
Italian. Violinist
Virtuoso; regarded as founder of modern violin technique.
b. Feb 17, 1653 in Fusignano, Italy
d. Jan 8, 1713 in Rome, Italy
Source: *Baker 78, 84, 92; BioIn 1, 2, 3, 4, 7, 8, 11, 12, 14, 20; DcArts; DcBiPP; DcCathB; McGEWB; MusMk; NewAmDM; NewGrDM 80; NewOxM; OxCMus; WhDW*

Corelli, Franco
Italian. Opera Singer
Heroic tenor; NY Met. debut, 1961.
b. Apr 8, 1923 in Ancona, Italy
Source: *Baker 78, 84; BioIn 11, 13; CelR; FacFETw; IntWW 83, 91; IntWWM 90; ItaFilm; MetOEnc; MusSN; NewAmDM; NewEOp 71; NewYTBE 70; PenDiMP; WhoAm 76, 78, 80, 82, 84; WhoAmM 83; WhoHol 92; WhoOp 76; WorAlBi*

Corelli, Marie
[Mary Mackay]
English. Author
Wrote melodramatic novels: *Sorrows of Satan,* 1895; *The Master Christian,* 1900.
b. 1855 in London, England
d. Apr 21, 1924 in Stratford-upon-Avon, England
Source: *ArtclWW 2; BbD; Benet 87, 96; BiD&SB; BioIn 1, 3, 4, 8, 10, 11, 12, 14, 16, 21; BlmGEL; BlmGWL; CamGLE; Chambr 3; ChhPo, S1; ConAu 118; ContDcW 89; DcArts; DcBiA; DcEnA A; DcLB 34, 156; DcLEL; DcNaB 1922; EncBrWW; EncSF, 93; EvLB; FemiCLE; IntDcWB; InWom; LegTOT; LinLib L, S; LngCTC; ModBrL; NewC; OxCEng 67, 85, 95; PenC ENG; REn; RfGEnL 91; ScF&FL 1; ScFEYrs; SJGFanW; StaCVF; SupFW; TwCA, SUP; TwCLC 51; TwCRHW 90, 94; TwCWr; VicBrit; WhoHr&F; WomNov*

Corena, Fernando
Italian. Opera Singer
Leading bass-buffo; NY Met. debut, 1954.
b. Dec 22, 1923 in Geneva, Switzerland
d. Nov 26, 1984, Switzerland
Source: *Baker 84; NewEOp 71; WhoAm 82, 84*

Corey, Irwin
"Professor"
American. Comedian, Actor
Double-talking comedian of stage and screen; films include *Car Wash,* 1976; *The Comeback Trail,* 1982.
b. Jul 29, 1912 in New York, New York
Source: *EncAFC; LegTOT; VarWW 85; WhoCom; WhoHol A*

Corey, Jeff
American. Actor
Played character roles, 1940s; ran acting school, 1940-59; returned to films later in career: *The Last Tycoon,* 1976.
b. Aug 10, 1914 in New York, New York
Source: *BioIn 16; ConTFT 8; FilmgC; HalFC 84, 88; IntMPA 75, 76, 77, 78, 79, 81, 82, 84, 86, 88, 92, 94, 96; Vers B; WhoAm 76, 78, 80, 82, 84, 86, 88, 90, 92, 94, 95, 96, 97; WhoEnt 92; WhoHol 92, A*

Corey, Lewis
[Louis C Fraina]
Italian. Author, Critic
Founded American Communist Party, 1918; changed to democratic principles demonstrated in book, *The Unfinished Task,* 1942.
b. Oct 13, 1894 in Galdo, Italy
d. Sep 16, 1953 in New York, New York
Source: *AmAu&B; BioIn 3, 4; DcAmSR; ObitOF 79; OhA&B; OxCAmL 65, 83; TwCA, SUP*

Corey, Wendell
American. Actor
Former film star; appeared in TV series "The Eleventh Hour," 1962-63; former pres., Academy of Motion Picture Arts and Sciences.
b. Mar 20, 1914 in Dracut, Massachusetts
d. Nov 9, 1968 in Woodland Hills, California
Source: *BiDFilm; BiE&WWA; BioIn 8, 10; FilmgC; GangFlm; HalFC 84, 88; HolP 40; LegTOT; MotPP; MovMk; NotNAT B; ObitOF 79; WhAm 5; WhoHol B; WhScrn 74, 77, 83; WhThe; WorAl; WorEFlm*

Corey, William Ellis
American. Industrialist
Pres., US Steel Corp., the builder of Gary, IN, 1903-11.
b. May 4, 1866 in Braddock, Pennsylvania
d. May 11, 1934
Source: *DcAmB S1; EncABHB 9; NatCAB 14; WhAm 1; WorAl*

Corgan, Billy
[Smashing Pumpkins]
American. Singer, Songwriter
Debut album, *Gish,* 1991.
b. 1968 in Chicago, Illinois

Cori, Carl Ferdinand
American. Biochemist
Discovered steps in glycogen-glucose conversion known as Cori cycle, 1939; Nobelist, 1947.
b. Dec 5, 1896 in Prague, Austria
d. Oct 20, 1984 in Cambridge, Massachusetts
Source: *AmMWSc 73P, 76P, 79, 82; AnObit 1984; AsBiEn; BiESc; BioIn 1, 2, 3, 4, 6; BlueB 76; CamDcSc; CurBio 47; FacFETw; InSci; IntWW 74, 75, 76, 77, 78, 79, 80, 81, 82, 83; LarDcSc; McGMS 80; NotTwCS; OxCMed 86; WebAB 74, 79; WhAm 8; Who 74, 82, 83; WhoAm 74, 76, 78, 80, 82, 84; WhoE 77, 79, 81, 83; WhoFrS 84; WhoNob, 90, 95; WhoWor 74, 76, 78, 82, 84; WorAl*

Cori, Gerty Theresa (Radnitz)
[Mrs. Carl Ferdinand Cori]
American. Biochemist
First woman to win Nobel Prize for medicine, physiology, 1947.
b. Aug 15, 1896 in Prague, Austria
d. Oct 26, 1957 in Saint Louis, Missouri
Source: *AmDec 1940; AmMWSc 76P, 79, 82; AmWomSc; AsBiEn; BiESc; BioIn 1, 2, 3, 4, 5, 6, 7, 12, 14, 15, 19, 20; BlueB 76; CamDcSc; CurBio 58; DcAmB S6; DcAmMeB 84; DcScB; EncWHA; FacFETw; GoodHs; InSci; IntWW 74, 75, 76, 77, 78, 79, 80, 81, 82, 83; InWom, SUP; LarDcSc; LibW; McGMS 80; NatCAB 48; NotAW MOD; NotTwCS; OxCMed 86; WebAB 74, 79; WhAm 3, 8; Who 74, 82, 83; WhoAm 74, 76, 78, 80, 82, 84; WhoAmW 58; WhoE 77, 79, 81, 83; WhoFrS 84; WhoNob, 90, 95; WhoWor 74, 76, 78, 82, 84; WomFir; WorAl; WorScD*

Corigliano, John (Paul)
American. Composer
Composer of "accessible" contemporary music; won acclaim for *The Naked*

Carmen; Concerto for Obe and Orchestra, 1975.
b. Feb 16, 1938 in New York, New York
Source: *AmComp; ASCAP 66; Baker 78, 84, 92; BiDAmM; BioIn 4, 9, 10, 12, 16, 17, 18; CompSN SUP; ConAmC 76, 82; ConCom 92; ConTFT 12; CpmDNM 82; CurBio 89; DcCM; DcTwCCu 1; IntWWM 85, 90; NewAmDM; NewGrDA 86; PenDiMP A; WhoAm 84, 86, 88, 90, 92, 94, 95, 96, 97; WhoAmM 83; WhoEnt 92*

Corinne, Tee A.
American. Artist
Noted for images of female genitalia; published *Wild Lesbian Roses,* 1996.
b. Nov 3, 1943 in Saint Petersburg, Florida
Source: *GayLesB*

Corinth, Lovis
German. Artist
Proponent of Sezession modernistic movement who strongly influenced German expressionism.
b. Jul 21, 1858 in Tapiau, Prussia
d. Jul 12, 1925 in Zandvoort, Netherlands
Source: *BioIn 2, 4, 5, 7, 10, 12, 16, 17; EncTR; IntDcAA 90; McGDA; OxCArt; OxCGer 76, 86; OxCTwCA; OxDcArt; PhDcTCA 77*

Corio, Ann
American. Actor
Best known for stage review *This Was Burlesque.*
b. 1914 in Hartford, Connecticut
Source: *WhoHol 92, A*

Coriolanus, Gaius
Roman. Soldier
Plutarch's story of him is basis for Shakespeare's play *Coriolanus.*
b. 6th cent. BC
Source: *DcBiPP; Dis&D; NewCol 75*

Corle, Edwin
American. Author
Wrote books on the Southwest, *Billy the Kid,* 1953.
b. May 7, 1906 in Wildwood, New Jersey
d. Jun 11, 1956
Source: *AmAu&B; BenetAL 91; BioIn 4, 6, 7, 15; CmCal; DcLB Y85B; EncFWF; NatCAB 46; OxCAmL 65, 83, 95; REnAL; TwCA SUP; TwCWW 91; WhAm 3; WhNAA*

Corley, Pat
American. Actor
Plays Phil, the bar owner, on TV show "Murphy Brown," 1988-95.
b. Jun 1, 1930 in Dallas, Texas
Source: *ConTFT 13; WhoAm 92, 94; WhoEnt 92*

Cormack, Allan MacLeod
American. Scientist, Educator
Shared Nobel Prize in medicine, 1979, for co-inventing CAT-scan (computer-assisted tomography) diagnostic technique.
b. Feb 23, 1924 in Johannesburg, South Africa
Source: *AmMWSc 82, 86, 89, 92, 95; BiESc; BioIn 12, 15, 20; CamDcSc; FacFETw; IntWW 80, 81, 82, 83, 89, 91, 93; LarDcSc; NewYTBS 79; NobelP; Who 82, 83, 85, 88, 90, 92, 94; WhoAm 80, 82, 84, 86, 88, 90, 92, 94, 95, 96, 97; WhoE 81, 83, 85, 86, 89, 91, 93, 95, 97; WhoMedH; WhoNob, 90, 95; WhoScEn 94, 96; WhoWor 80, 82, 84, 87, 89, 91, 93, 95, 96, 97; WorAlBi*

Corman, Gene
American. Producer
Films include *If You Could See What I Hear;* won Emmy for "A Woman Called Golda," 1982.
b. Sep 24, 1927 in Detroit, Michigan
Source: *ConTFT 1, 9; IntMPA 86, 88, 92, 94, 96; VarWW 85*

Corman, Roger William
American. Producer
B horror films include Poe's *The Raven,* 1962; *The Bees,* 1980.
b. Apr 5, 1926 in Detroit, Michigan
Source: *BiDFilm; BioIn 9, 11, 12, 13, 14, 15, 16; CelR 90; ConTFT 7; CurBio 83; DcFM; EncSF; FacFETw; FilmgC; HalFC 84, 88; IntMPA 75, 76, 78, 79, 81, 82, 84, 86, 88, 92, 94; IntWW 82, 83, 89, 91, 93; NewEScF; OxCFilm; PenEncH; WhoAm 74, 76, 78, 80, 82, 84, 86, 88, 90, 92, 94, 95, 96, 97; WhoEnt 92; WhoWor 74, 76, 78, 80, 82, 84; WorEFlm; WorFDir 2*

Corn, Ira George, Jr.
American. Bridge Player
Organized first US pro bridge team, "The Aces," 1968; won three world championships.
b. Aug 22, 1921 in Little Rock, Arkansas
d. Apr 28, 1982 in Dallas, Texas
Source: *BioIn 12, 13; ConAu 35NR, 85, 106; WhAm 8; WhoAm 74, 76, 78, 80, 82; WhoFI 74, 75, 77, 79, 81; WhoSSW 78, 82; WhoWor 78, 80*

Cornea, Aurel
French. Hostage
TV technician held hostage by Lebanese terrorists for 291 days, from Mar 8, 1986-Dec 24.

Corneille
[Cornelis Guillaume van Beverloo]
Dutch. Artist
Abstract colorist, illustrator; co-founded Cobra group, 1947.
b. Jul 3, 1922 in Liege, Belgium
Source: *BioIn 16, 19; ConArt 77, 83, 89, 96; IntWW 91; McGDA; OxCTwCA; OxDcArt; PhDcTCA 77; PrintW 83, 85; WorArt 1950*

Corneille, Pierre
"Father of French Tragedy"
French. Dramatist, Poet
Wrote *Le Cid,* 1637; *Le Menteur,* 1643.
b. Jun 6, 1606 in Rouen, France
d. Oct 1, 1684 in Paris, France
Source: *AtlBL; BbD; Benet 87, 96; BiD&SB; BioIn 1, 2, 3, 5, 7, 9, 10, 14, 15, 20; BlmGEL; CamGWoT; CasWL; CnThe; CyWA 58; DcArts; DcBiPP; DcCathB; DcEuL; Dis&D; EncWT; EuAu; EuWr 3; EvEuW; GuFrLit 2; IntDcT 2; LegTOT; LinLib L, S; LitC 28; LngCEL; MagSWL; McGEWB; McGEWD 72, 84; NewC; NewEOp 71; NewGrDO; NotNAT A, B; OxCEng 67, 85, 95; OxCFr; OxCThe 67, 83; OxDcOp; PenC EUR; PlP&P; RAdv 14, 13-2; RComWL; REn; REnWD; RfGWoL 95; WorAl; WorAlBi*

Cornelius, Don
American. Broadcasting Executive
Creator, producer, and host of syndicated TV show "Soul Train," 1971-93; remains exec. producer.
b. Sep 27, 1936 in Chicago, Illinois
Source: *BioIn 16, 19, 21; ConBlB 4; DrBlPA 90; InB&W 80; WhoAfA 96; WhoBlA 92*

Cornelius, Henry
English. Director
Best known for comedies *Passport to Pimlico,* 1949; *Genevieve,* 1954.
b. Aug 18, 1913, South Africa
d. May 3, 1958 in London, England
Source: *BioIn 4; CmMov; DcFM; FilmgC; HalFC 84, 88; MovMk; OxCFilm*

Cornelius, Peter
German. Composer
Wrote operas *Barbier von Bagdad,* 1858; *Der Cid,* 1865; friend of Liszt, Wagner.
b. Dec 24, 1824 in Mainz, Germany
d. Oct 26, 1874 in Mainz, Germany
Source: *Alli; Baker 78, 84, 92; BioIn 1, 4, 7; Dis&D; EvEuW; IntDcOp; MetOEnc; NewAmDM; NewCol 75; NewEOp 71; NewOxM; OxCMus; OxDcOp; PenDiMP A*

Cornelius, Peter von
German. Artist
Noted for Munich frescoes, reviving German interest in murals.
b. Sep 23, 1783 in Dusseldorf, Germany
d. Mar 6, 1867 in Berlin, Germany
Source: *BioIn 6, 11, 13; CelCen; DcCathB; LinLib S; OxCArt; OxCGer 76, 86; OxDcArt; WhDW*

Cornell, Chris
[Soundgarden]
American. Singer, Songwriter
With group Soundgarden; Grammy for Best Metal Performance "Spoonman," 1994.
b. Jul 20, 1964 in Seattle, Washington

Cornell, Don
[Louis F. Varlaro]
American. Singer
High baritone vocalist; starred with Sammy Kaye's band, 1950s.
b. Apr 21, 1919 in New York, New York
Source: *BiDAmM; CmpEPM; PenEncP*

Cornell, Douglas B
American. Journalist
AP White House correspondent, 1933-69.
b. 1907 in Saint Louis, Missouri
d. Feb 20, 1982 in Detroit, Michigan
Source: *BioIn 12; NewYTBS 82*

Cornell, Ezra
American. Business Executive
Founded Western Union Telegraph Co, 1855; Cornell U, 1865.
b. Jan 11, 1807 in Westchester, New York
d. Dec 9, 1874 in Ithaca, New York
Source: *AmBi; ApCAB; BiDAmBL 83; BioIn 1, 2, 3, 4, 6, 7, 14; CelCen; CyEd; DcAmB; DcBiPP; HarEnUS; InSci; LegTOT; LinLib S; McGEWB; MorMA; NatCAB 4; TwCBDA; WebAB 74, 79; WhAm HS; WorAl; WorAlBi; WorInv*

Cornell, Joseph
American. Artist
An originator of assemblage sculpture, joining unlike objects in unfamiliar positions; work presented in first US exhibition of Surrealists, 1932.
b. Dec 24, 1903 in Nyack, New York
d. Dec 29, 1972 in New York, New York
Source: *BioIn 7, 8, 9, 10, 11, 12, 13, 14, 16, 17, 18, 20; BriEAA; ConArt 77, 83, 89, 96; DcAmArt; DcArts; DcCAA 71, 77, 88, 94; EncWB; FacFETw; McGDA; ModArCr 2; NewYTBE 72; OxCTwCA; OxDcArt; PhDcTCA 77; PrintW 85; WhAm 5; WhoAmA 78N, 80N, 82N, 84N, 86N, 89N, 91N, 93N; WorAlBi; WorArt 1950*

Cornell, Katharine
American. Actor
Played Elizabeth Barrett in *The Barretts of Wimpole Street,* 1931; wed to Guthrie McClintic.
b. Feb 16, 1898 in Berlin, Germany
d. Jun 9, 1974 in Vineyard Haven, Massachusetts
Source: *BiE&WWA; BioAmW; BioIn 1, 2, 3, 4, 5, 6, 8; BioNews 74; CelR; CnThe; ConAu 49; CurBio 41, 52, 74; FamA&A; HerW, 84; IntDcT 3; LinLib S; NewYTBS 74; NotNAT A, B; ObitT 1971; OxCAmL 65; OxCThe 67; PlP&P; WebAB 74; WhAm 6; Who 74; WhoAmW 58, 64, 66, 68, 70, 72, 74; WhoHol A; WhoThe 72; WhoWor 74; WhThe*

Cornell, Lydia
American. Actor
Played Sarah Rush on TV series "Too Close for Comfort," 1980-86.
b. Jul 23, 1957 in El Paso, Texas
Source: *BioIn 12, 13*

Cornfeld, Bernard
American. Financier
Chm. of Investors Overseas Services, 1958-71.
b. Aug 17, 1927 in Istanbul, Turkey
d. Feb 27, 1995 in London, England
Source: *BioIn 7, 8, 9, 10, 11, 12; NewYTBE 70; NewYTBS 95; PolProf NF*

Cornford, Frances Crofts Darwin
American. Poet
Books of poetry include *Spring Morning,* 1915; *Collected Poems,* 1954; granddaughter of Charles Darwin.
b. Mar 30, 1886 in Cambridge, England
d. Aug 19, 1960 in Cambridge, England
Source: *DcLEL; EvLB; InWom SUP; LngCTC; ObitT 1951; REn*

Cornforth, John Warcup, Sir
British. Chemist
Won 1975 Nobel Prize in chemistry.
b. Sep 7, 1917 in Sydney, Australia
Source: *AmMWSc 89, 95; BiESc; BioIn 9, 10, 14, 15, 19, 20, 21; BlueB 76; DeafPAS; FacFETw; IntWW 74, 75, 76, 77, 78, 79, 80, 81, 82, 83, 89, 91, 93; LarDcSc; NobelP; Who 74, 92, 94; WhoAm 88, 90, 92, 94, 95; WhoNob, 90, 95; WhoScEn 94, 96; WhoWor 74, 76, 78, 80, 82, 84, 87, 89, 91, 93, 95, 96, 97*

Corning, Erastus
American. Financier
First pres., NY Central Railroad, 1853-64; NY town named after him.
b. Dec 14, 1794 in Norwich, Connecticut
d. Apr 9, 1872 in Albany, New York
Source: *AmBi; ApCAB; BiAUS; BiDAmBL 83; BiDrAC; BiDrUSC 89; BioIn 3, 5; DcAmB; Drake; EncAB-H 1974, 1996; EncABHB 2; McGEWB; TwCBDA; WhAm HS; WhAmP; WhCiWar*

Corning, Erastus, III
American. Politician
Mayor of Albany, NY, 1942-83; longest tenured mayor in US.
b. Oct 7, 1909 in Albany, New York
d. May 28, 1983 in Boston, Massachusetts
Source: *BioIn 13; NewYTBS 83; PolPar; WhAm 8; WhoAm 74, 76, 78, 80, 82; WhoAmP 73, 75, 77, 79, 81; WhoGov 75, 77*

Cornish, Gene
[The Rascals]
Canadian. Musician
Guitarist with blue-eyed soul group, 1965-71.
b. May 14, 1945 in Ottawa, Ontario, Canada

Cornplanter
American. Native American Leader
Attended several treaty councils that ceded land to the US government, including the Fort Hamar Treaty, 1789, which worsened his position with his tribe.
b. 1732? in Conewaugus, New York
d. Feb 18, 1836
Source: *ApCAB; BioIn 21; Drake; EncAR; HarEnUS; NotNaAm; REnAW; WhAmRev*

Cornwallis, Charles, Marquis
English. Army Officer
Surrendered to George Washington at Yorktown, 1781.
b. Dec 31, 1738 in London, England
d. Oct 5, 1805 in Ghazipur, India
Source: *Alli; AmBi; AmRev; ApCAB; Benet 87; BenetAL 91; BioIn 12; BlkwEAR; CelCen; DcBiPP; DcInB; DcNaB, C; Drake; EncAR; EncCRAm; HarEnMi; HarEnUS; HisDBrE; HisWorL; LinLib S; NatCAB 7; OxCAmH; OxCAmL 65, 83; REn; REnAL; WhAm HS; WhAmRev; WhDW; WhoMilH 76; WorAl*

Cornwell, Patricia (Daniels)
American. Author
Crime novelist; wrote award-winning novel *Postmortem,* 1990; best-sellers *Body of Evidence,* 1991; *Cause of Death,* 1996.
b. Jun 9, 1956 in Miami, Florida
Source: *ConAu 53NR, 134; ConPopW; WhoAmW 97; WrDr 94, 96*

Coroebus
Greek. Olympic Athlete
Won first Olympic race, c. 776 BC.

Corona, Juan
American. Murderer
Convicted of murdering 25 migrant workers, 1970-71.
b. 1934, Mexico
Source: *BioIn 15, 16; CmCal; DrInf; MexAmB; NewYTBE 71*

Coronado, Francisco Vasquez de
"El Dorado"
Spanish. Explorer
Led Mexican expedition searching for wealth of Seven Cities of Cibola, 1540.
b. Feb 25, 1510 in Salamanca, Spain
d. Sep 22, 1554, Mexico
Source: *AmBi; ApCAB; Benet 87, 96; BenetAL 91; DcAmB; DcCathB; DcHiB; EncCRAm; EncLatA; HarEnUS; HisDcSE; McGEWB; OxCAmH; REn; REnAL; REnAW; WebAB 74, 79; WhAm HS; WhDW; WhNaAH; WhWE; WorAl; WorAlBi*

Corot, Jean Baptiste Camille
"Papa"
French. Artist
Barbizon school landscape painter whose works include *Ponte de Mantes,* 1870.
b. Jul 16, 1796 in Paris, France
d. Feb 22, 1875 in Paris, France
Source: *ArtsNiC; AtlBL; Benet 87, 96; BioIn 2, 3, 4, 5, 6, 7, 8, 9, 10, 11, 12, 13; CelCen; DcBiPP; DcCathB; Dis&D; IntDcAA 90; LinLib S; McGEWB;*

NewC; OxCArt; OxCFr; REn; WorAl; WorAlBi

Correggio, Antonio Allegri da
Italian. Artist
Most famous work *The Assumption of the Virgin* in dome of Parma cathedral.
b. Aug 30, 1494 in Correggio, Italy
d. Mar 5, 1534 in Correggio, Italy
Source: *AtlBL; ChhPo, S1; DcArts; DcCathB; REn*

Correia, Natalia
Portuguese. Writer
One of Portugal's best-known writers; poetry anthology "Romantic Sonnets" is an important literary work.
b. Sep 13, 1923 in Sao Miguel, Portugal
d. Mar 16, 1993 in Lisbon, Portugal
Source: *BioIn 18; BlmGWL; EncCoWW; NewYTBS 93*

Correll, Charles J
[Amos 'n Andy]
American. Comedian
Andy of Amos 'n Andy comedy team; on radio, 1928-58.
b. Feb 2, 1890 in Peoria, Illinois
d. Sep 26, 1972 in Chicago, Illinois
Source: *CurBio 72N; NewYTBE 72; ObitOF 79; WebAB 74, 79; WhoHol B; WhScrn 77, 83*

Corri, Adrienne
[Adrienne Riccoboni]
Scottish. Actor
Films include *A Clockwork Orange,* 1971.
b. Nov 13, 1933 in Glasgow, Scotland
Source: *FilmgC; HalFC 84, 88; IntMPA 75, 76, 77, 78, 79, 81, 82, 84, 86, 88, 92, 94, 96; WhoHol A*

Corrigan, Douglas
"Wrong Way"
American. Aviator, Actor
Nicknamed for landing in Ireland after taking off from NY for LA, 1938.
b. Jan 22, 1907 in Galveston, Texas
d. Dec 9, 1995 in Orange, California
Source: *BioIn 2, 7, 8, 16, 21; HalFC 84, 88; InSci; WhoHol 92, A*

Corrigan-Maguire, Mairead
Irish. Social Reformer
With Betty Williams, won Nobel Peace Prize for forming N Ireland Peace Movement, 1976.
b. Jan 27, 1944 in Belfast, Northern Ireland
Source: *BioIn 14, 15, 16; ConHero 1; ContDcW 89; CurBio 78; FacFETw; IntWW 83; InWom SUP; LadLa 86; NewYTBS 77; NobelP; Who 82; WhoNob, 90; WhoWor 97*

Corsaro, Frank
[Francesco Andrea]
American. Actor, Director
Directed many plays, TV shows, operas; with NYC Opera, 1958—; appeared in *Rachel, Rachel,* 1967.
b. Dec 22, 1925 in New York, New York
Source: *BiE&WWA; ConAu 85; ConTFT 7; CurBio 75; IntWW 83, 91; IntWWM 85; MetOEnc; NewGrDA 86; NewYTBE 72; NotNAT; WhoAm 86, 90; WhoAmM 83; WhoEnt 92; WhoThe 81*

Corsi, Jacopo
Italian. Art Patron
Among the orginators of opera; first opera performed at his palace, 1598.
b. 1560 in Celano, Italy
d. 1604 in Florence, Italy
Source: *Baker 78, 84, 92; NewEOp 71*

Corso, Gregory Nunzio
American. Poet
One of the chief spokesmen of the beat movement, 1950s; anti-establishment works appear in "Gasoline," 1958.
b. Mar 26, 1930 in New York, New York
Source: *Benet 87; BenetAL 91; BioIn 15; BlueB 76; ConAu 5NR; ConLC 1, 11; ConPo 80, 85, 91; CroCAP; DcLB 5; DrAP 75; DrAPF 89; MajTwCW; OxCAmL 65, 83; OxCEng 85; PenC AM; RAdv 1; REn; WhoAm 86, 90; WhoAmL 92; WhoWrEP 89; WrDr 86, 92*

Corson, Juliet
American. Author, Teacher
Culinary pioneer, opened NY cooking school, 1876.
b. Jan 14, 1841 in Roxbury, Massachusetts
d. Jun 18, 1897 in New York, New York
Source: *AmWomSc; BiDAmEd; BioIn 20; InWom SUP; LibW; NotAW; WebBD 83*

Cort, Bud
American. Actor
Appeared in *Harold and Maude,* with Ruth Gordon, 1971.
b. Mar 29, 1951 in Rye, New York
Source: *BioIn 16; FilmgC; HalFC 84, 88; IntMPA 86, 92; MovMk; WhoAm 82, 84, 88, 90; WhoEnt 92; WhoHol A*

Cortazar, Julio
French. Author
Argentine writer known for intellectual fiction; lived in exile in Paris following election of Juan Peron.
b. Aug 26, 1914 in Brussels, Belgium
d. Feb 12, 1984 in Paris, France
Source: *AnObit 1984; Benet 87, 96; BenetAL 91; BioIn 6, 7, 8, 9, 10, 13, 14, 15, 16, 17, 18, 20; CasWL; ConAu 12NR, 21R, 32NR; ConFLW 84; ConLC 2, 3, 5, 10, 13, 15, 33, 34, 92; CurBio 74, 84, 84N; CyWA 89; DcArts; DcCLAA; DcHiB; DcLB 113; DcTwCCu 3; EncLatA; EncWL, 2, 3; FacFETw; HispLC; HispWr; IntAu&W 76, 77; IntWW 74, 75, 76, 77, 78, 79, 80, 81, 82, 83; LatAmWr; LegTOT; LiExTwC; LinLib L, S; MajTwCW; ModLAL; NewYTBS 84; Novels; PenC AM; PenEncH; PostFic; RAdv 14, 13-2; RfGShF; RfGWoL 95; ScF&FL 1, 2, 92; ShSCr 7; SpAmA; TwCWr; WhoTwCL; WhoWor 74, 78, 80, 82; WorAlBi; WorAu 1950*

Cortesa, Valentina
Italian. Actor
Appeared in several international films including *Widow's Nest,* 1977.
b. Jan 1, 1925 in Milan, Italy
Source: *FilmgC; HalFC 84, 88; IntMPA 75, 76, 77, 78, 79, 81, 82, 84, 86, 88; MovMk*

Cortez, Hernando
[Hernan Cortes]
Spanish. Conqueror
Conquered Mexico; caused downfall of Aztec empire, 1521.
b. 1485 in Medellin, Spain
d. 1547
Source: *ApCAB; Benet 87, 96; BenetAL 91; BioIn 14, 17, 18, 19, 20; CasWL; DcBiPP; DcEuL; DcSpL; DicTyr; Drake; EncLatA; Expl 93; HarEnMi; HarEnUS; HisDcSE; LinLib S; LitC 31; McGEWB; NewC; OxCAmL 65; OxCSpan; PenC AM; REn; REnAL; WebBD 83; WhAm HS; WhoMilH 76; WorAl; WorAlBi*

Cortez, Ricardo
[Jacob Kranz]
American. Actor
Matinee idol, 1920s; Garbo's first leading man in *The Torrent,* 1926.
b. Sep 19, 1899 in Vienna, Austria
d. May 28, 1977 in New York, New York
Source: *BioIn 8, 11, 14, 17; Film 2; FilmgC; GangFlm; HalFC 84, 88; LegTOT; MotPP; MovMk; NewYTBS 77; ObitOF 79; SilFlmP; WhoHol A; WhoThe 81N; WhScrn 83*

Cortissoz, Royal
American. Journalist, Author
Art, literary editor, *NY Herald Tribune,* 1891-1913.
b. Feb 10, 1869 in New York, New York
d. Oct 17, 1948 in New York, New York
Source: *AmAu&B; BioIn 1, 2, 4; DcAmB S4; DcNAA; EncAJ; LinLib L, S; NatCAB 36; ObitOF 79; TwCA, SUP; WhAm 2; WhLit*

Cortot, Alfred-Denis
French. Pianist, Conductor
One of the foremost pianists of 20th c. France; famous for interpretations of Romantic composers; founded Ecole Normale de Musique, 1918.
b. Sep 26, 1877 in Nyon, Switzerland
d. Jun 15, 1962 in Lausanne, Switzerland
Source: *Baker 84; BioIn 4, 5, 6, 8, 11, 16; FacFETw; MusSN; NewAmDM; ObitOF 79; PenDiMP*

Corum, Martene Windsor
"Bill"
American. Journalist
War correspondent, *NY Journal American,* 1945; sports announcer, "Sports Cavalcade," 1941-58.
b. Jul 20, 1895 in Speed, Missouri
d. Dec 16, 1958 in New York, New York
Source: *BioIn 2; WhAm 3*

Corvo, Baron
[Frederick William Rolfe]
English. Author
Wrote semi-autobiographical *Hadrian the Seventh,* 1904.
b. Jul 22, 1860 in London, England
d. Oct 26, 1913 in Venice, Italy
Source: *AtlBL; BioIn 1, 3, 4, 5, 6, 7, 8, 9, 10, 11, 12; CamGLE; CasWL; CnMWL; DcLB 34, 156; DcLEL; DcNaB MP; EncSF 93; EvLB; LngCTC; ModBrL, S1; NewC; Novels; OxCEng 67, 85, 95; PenC ENG; REn; ScFEYrs; StaCVF; TwCA, SUP; TwCWr; WhDW; WorAl*

Corwin, Edward Samuel
American. Political Scientist
Known for emphasis on historical aspects of constitutional development.
b. Jan 19, 1878 in Plymouth, Michigan
d. Apr 29, 1963 in Princeton, New Jersey
Source: *AmAu&B; BioIn 1, 6, 11, 16; ConAu 113, 122; DcAmB S7; IntEnSS 79; OxCAmH; OxCLaw; OxCSupC; WebAB 74, 79; WhAm 4; WhoFI 87; WhoSSW 86*

Corwin, Norman
American. Screenwriter, Producer, Director
Screenplay, *Lust for Life* was nominated for Oscar, 1956; won many awards in various fields.
b. May 3, 1910 in Boston, Massachusetts
Source: *AmAu&B; ASCAP 66; AuNews 2; BenetAL 91; BiE&WWA; BioIn 1, 2, 3, 4, 11; BlueB 76; CnDAL; ConAu 1NR, 1R, 24NR; ConTFT 1; CurBio 40; IntAu&W 76, 77; IntMPA 75, 76, 77, 78, 79, 81, 82, 84, 86, 88, 92, 94, 96; IntWW 74, 75, 76, 77, 78, 79, 80, 81, 82, 83, 89, 91, 93; LesBEnT 92; LinLib L; NewYTET; NotNAT; OxCAmL 65, 83; REnAL; SaTiSS; ScF&FL 1, 2; TwCA SUP; WhoAm 74, 76, 78, 80, 82, 84, 86, 88, 90, 92, 94, 95, 96, 97; WhoEnt 92; WhoWor 74; WhoWorJ 72, 78; WrDr 76, 80, 82, 84, 86, 88, 90, 92, 94, 96*

Corwin, Thomas
American. Statesman
Whig senator from OH, 1845-50; vehemently opposed Mexican War; minister to Mexico, 1861-64.
b. Jul 29, 1794 in Bourbon County, Kentucky
d. Dec 18, 1865 in Washington, District of Columbia
Source: *Alli SUP; AmBi; ApCAB; BiAUS; BiDrAC; BiDrGov 1789; BiDrUSC 89; BiDrUSE 71, 89; BioIn 1, 2, 3, 7, 10, 16; DcAmB; DcAmDH 80, 89; DcNAA; Drake; HarEnUS; NatCAB 6; NewCol 75; OhA&B; TwCBDA; WhAm HS; WhAmP; WhCiWar*

Cory, John Mackenzie
American. Library Administrator
Director, New York Public Library, 1970-78.
b. Jan 13, 1914
d. Apr 11, 1988
Source: *BiDrLUS 70; BioIn 1, 2, 15, 16; CurBio 49, 88N; NewYTBS 88; WhoLibS 55*

Coryell, Don(ald David)
American. Football Coach
Coach, St. Louis, 1973-77, San Diego, 1978-86; NFL coach of year, 1974.
b. Oct 17, 1924 in Seattle, Washington
Source: *BiDAmSp FB; BioIn 13; FootReg 87; WhoAm 82, 86; WhoWest 82, 84*

Coryell, John Russell
[Nick Carter]
American. Author
With writing team developed fictional detective, Nick Carter; first dime novel in the series, 1886.
b. Dec 15, 1848? in New York, New York
d. Jul 15, 1924 in Mount Vernon, Maine
Source: *AmAu&B; BenetAL 91; DcNAA; EncMys; OxCAmL 65; REn; REnAL*

Coryell, Larry
American. Musician, Composer
Jazz guitarist; work mixes jazz rock/hard rock: *The Firebird & Petrushka,* 1984.
b. Apr 2, 1943 in Galveston, Texas
Source: *AllMusG; BiDJaz; BioIn 12, 15, 16; ConMuA 80A; EncJzS; EncJzS; EncRk 88; HarEnR 86; NewGrDA 86; NewGrDJ 88, 94; OnThGG; PenEncP; RolSEnR 83; WhoAm 78, 80; WhoEnt 92; WhoRock 81; WhoRocM 82*

Cosby, Bill
[William Henry Cosby, Jr.]
American. Actor, Comedian
Star of hit TV series "I Spy," 1965-68; "The Cosby Show," 1984-92.
b. Jul 12, 1937 in Philadelphia, Pennsylvania
Source: *AfrAmAl 6; AfrAmBi 1; AmDec 1980; BestSel 89-4; BiDFilm 94; BioIn 8, 9, 10, 11, 12, 13, 14, 15, 16, 17, 18, 19, 20, 21; BioNews 74; BkPepl; BlksAmF; BlkWr 1, 2; CelR, 90; ConAu 27NR, 42NR, 81, X; ConBlB 7; ConHero 1; ConTFT 3, 9; CurBio 67, 86; DcTwCCu 5; DrBlPA, 90; Ebony 1; EncAFC; EncJzS; FacFETw; FilmgC; HalFC 88; InB&W 80, 85; IntAu&W 91; IntMPA 86, 92; IntWW 93; LegTOT; LesBEnT 92; NegAl 89; SchCGBL; SmATA 66; WhoAfA 96; WhoAm 74, 76, 78, 80, 82, 84, 86, 88, 90, 92, 94, 95, 96, 97; WhoBlA 75, 77, 80, 85, 88, 90, 92, 94; WhoCom; WhoE 93, 95, 97; WhoEnt 92; WhoHol 92, A; WhoUSWr 88; WhoWest 74, 76, 78; WhoWor 74; WhoWrEP 89, 92, 95; WorAl; WorAlBi; WrDr 88, 90, 92, 94, 96*

Cose, Ellis
American. Journalist
Editorial page editor, *New York Daily News,* 1991—; wrote *A Nation of Strangers: Prejudice, Politics, and the Populating of America,* 1992.
b. Feb 20, 1951 in Chicago, Illinois
Source: *ConBlB 5; DcTwCCu 5; WhoAfA 96; WhoAm 96, 97; WhoBlA 77, 80, 85, 88, 90, 92, 94*

Cosell, Howard
[Howard William Cohen]
American. Sportscaster
Known for acerbic style; with ABC, 1956-85; newspaper columnist, *NY Daily News,* 1986-95.
b. Mar 25, 1920 in Winston-Salem, North Carolina
d. Apr 23, 1995 in New York, New York
Source: *Ballpl 90; BiDAmSp OS; BioIn 9, 10, 11, 12, 13, 14, 15, 16, 18; BioNews 74; BkPepl; CelR, 90; ConAu 108; ConTFT 6; CurBio 72, 95N; EncAJ; IntMPA 79, 81, 82, 84, 86, 88, 92, 94; LegTOT; LesBEnT 92; NewYTBS 74; NewYTET; WhoAm 76, 78, 80, 82, 84, 86, 90; WhoE 74; WhoHol 92; WorAl; WorAlBi*

Cosgrave, Liam
Irish. Political Leader
Irish prime minister, 1973-77.
b. Apr 30, 1920 in Dublin, Ireland
Source: *BioIn 9, 10, 11, 16; BlueB 76; CurBio 77; DcTwHis; EncWB; IntWW 74, 75, 76, 77, 78, 79, 80, 81, 82, 83, 89, 91, 93; IntYB 78, 79, 80, 81, 82; NewYTBE 73; Who 74, 82, 83, 85, 88, 90, 92, 94; WhoWor 74, 76, 78, 80*

Cosgrave, William Thomas
Irish. Statesman
President, Irish Free State, 1922-32.
b. Jun 6, 1880 in Dublin, Ireland
d. Nov 16, 1965 in Dublin, Ireland
Source: *BioIn 7; DcIrB 78, 88; DcNaB 1961; DcTwHis; EncRev; HisDBrE; LinLib S; NewCol 75; ObitOF 79; WhAm 4*

Cosimo, Piero di
Italian. Artist, Architect
Painter of religious, mythological works, often in bizarre style *Death of Procris,* c. 1500.
b. 1462
d. 1521
Source: *AtlBL; REn*

Coslow, Sam
American. Songwriter
Songs include "Sing You Sinners," 1930; "Cocktails for Two," 1934.
b. Dec 27, 1905 in New York, New York
d. Apr 2, 1982 in Bronxville, New York

Source: *AmPS; ASCAP 66; CmpEPM; ConAu 29NR, 77, 106; IntMPA 75, 76, 77, 78, 79, 81, 82, 84, 86, 88; NewYTBS 82*

Cossart, Ernest
English. Actor
Usually cast in portly British butler roles: *Charley's Aunt,* 1941.
b. Sep 24, 1876 in Cheltenham, England
d. Jan 21, 1951 in New York, New York
Source: *BioIn 2; EncAFC; Film 1; FilmgC; HalFC 84, 88; NotNAT B; PlP&P; WhoHol B; WhScrn 74, 77, 83; WhThe*

Cossiga, Francesco
Italian. Political Leader
Prime minister of Italy, 1979-80.
b. Jul 26, 1928 in Sassari, Italy
Source: *BioIn 12, 14, 16; CurBio 81; IntWW 77, 78, 79, 80, 81, 82, 83, 89, 91, 93; NewYTBS 79, 88; WhoWor 80, 82, 87, 89, 91, 93*

Cossotto, Fiorenza
Italian. Opera Singer
Mezzo-soprano; NY Met. debut in world premier of *La Gioconda,* 1968.
b. Apr 22, 1935 in Crescentino, Italy
Source: *Baker 78, 84, 92; BioIn 13; IntWWM 90; InWom SUP; MetOEnc; NewAmDM; NewGrDO; NewYTBE 71; OxDcOp; PenDiMP; WhoAm 86, 90, 92, 94, 95, 96, 97; WhoOp 76; WhoWor 89, 91, 93, 95, 96*

Costa, Don
American. Conductor
Arranger of over 200 hit recordings by Frank Sinatra, Perry Como, others.
b. Jun 10, 1925 in Boston, Massachusetts
d. Jan 19, 1983 in New York, New York
Source: *AmPS A; AnObit 1983; Baker 84, 92; BioIn 13; NewYTBS 83; PenEncP; RkOn 74*

Costa, Lucio
Brazilian. Architect
Leader of avant garde movement in Brazil; most famous work is master plan for capital city, Brasilia.
b. 1902 in Toulon, France
Source: *ConArch 80, 87, 94; DcD&D; EncLatA; IntDcAr; IntWW 74, 75, 76, 77, 78, 79, 80, 81, 82, 83, 89, 91, 93; MacEA; McGDA; OxCArt; WhoArch; WhoWor 82, 84*

Costa, Mary
American. Opera Singer
Soprano; NY Met. debut, 1964; starred in film *The Great Waltz,* 1972.
b. Apr 5, 1930 in Knoxville, Tennessee
Source: *Baker 84; BioIn 16; MetOEnc; WhoAm 84; WhoAmM 83; WhoAmW 85, 91; WhoHol A; WhoOp 76; WhoWor 74*

Costa, Victor Charles
American. Fashion Designer
Pres., Victor Costa, Inc., 1973—; best known for bridal creations worn by 35,000 brides, 1965.
b. Dec 17, 1935 in Houston, Texas
Source: *BioIn 15, 16; WhoAm 78, 80, 82, 84, 86, 88, 90, 92, 94, 95, 96, 97; WorFshn*

Costa e Silva, Arthur da
Brazilian. Army Officer, Politician
Led 1964 revolution; pres., 1967-69.
b. Oct 3, 1902 in Taquari, Brazil
d. Dec 17, 1969 in Rio de Janeiro, Brazil
Source: *CurBio 67, 70; DcCPSAm; DcPol; EncLatA; ObitOF 79*

Costa-Gavras
[Kostantinos Gavras]
Greek. Director
Won Oscar for Z, 1969.
b. Feb 13, 1933 in Athens, Greece
Source: *BiDFilm 94; BioIn 9, 10, 12, 14, 16; CelR, 90; ConTFT 6; CurBio 72; FacFETw; FilmgC; HalFC 84, 88; IntMPA 86, 92, 94; IntWW 91; ItaFilm; LegTOT; MovMk; WhoAm 86, 95, 96, 97; WhoFr 79; WhoWor 87, 95, 96, 97; WorAl; WorAlBi*

Costain, Thomas Bertram
American. Author
Wrote best-selling historical novels: *The Black Rose,* 1945; *The Silver Chalice,* 1952.
b. May 8, 1885 in Brantford, Ontario, Canada
d. Oct 8, 1965 in New York, New York
Source: *AmAu&B; AmNov; AuBYP 2, 3; BioIn 2, 3, 4, 7, 8, 12; CanWr; ConAu 5R; CreCan 2; CurBio 53, 65; DcAmB S7; DcLEL, 1940; LinLib L, S; LngCTC; MacDCB 78; OxCAmL 65; OxCCan; REn; REnAL; TwCA SUP; TwCWr; WhAm 4; WorAl*

Costa Mendez, Nicanor
Argentine. Government Official
Foreign minister who led Argentine attack on Falkland Islands, 1982.
b. Oct 30, 1922 in Buenos Aires, Argentina
d. Aug 3, 1992
Source: *BioIn 13, 18; IntWW 74, 82, 83, 89, 91; NewYTBS 82, 92*

Costanza, Midge
[Margaret Costanza]
American. Presidential Aide
Special asst. to Carter, liaison to special interest groups.
b. Nov 28, 1928 in Le Roy, New York
Source: *AmWomM; BioIn 11; CurBio 78; GayLesB; InWom SUP; NewYTBS 78; WhoAm 90; WhoAmP 85; WhoAmW 77; WhoWest 89*

Costas, Bob
[Robert Quinlan Costas]
American. Sportscaster
With NBC Sports since 1980; hosts syndicated radio shows "Sports Flashback;" "Costas Coast to Coast."
b. Mar 22, 1952 in New York, New York
Source: *BioIn 15, 16; CelR 90; ConNews 86-4; ConTFT 12; CurBio 93; LegTOT; LesBEnT 92; WhoAm 88, 90, 92, 94, 95, 96, 97; WhoE 93*

Coste, Dieudonne
French. Aviator
First westward transatlantic flight from Paris to NYC, Sep 1-2, 1930.
b. Nov 4, 1893 in Gascony, France
d. May 18, 1973
Source: *NewYTBE 73*

Costello, Chris
American. Actor, Author
Appeared in movie, *Semi-Tough,* 1978; wrote biography of father Lou Costello, *Lou's on First,* 1982.
b. Aug 15, 1947 in Los Angeles, California
Source: *ConAu 107*

Costello, Dolores
American. Actor
Twenty-year career in films playing sweet, non-exacting roles; married briefly to John Barrymore.
b. Sep 17, 1905 in Pittsburgh, Pennsylvania
d. Mar 1, 1979 in Fallbrook, California
Source: *Film 1, 2; FilmEn; FilmgC; HalFC 84, 88; IntDcF 1-3, 2-3; InWom SUP; LegTOT; MotPP; MovMk; NewYTBS 79; ThFT; TwYS; WhoHol A; WhScrn 83*

Costello, Elvis
[Declan Patrick Aloysius McManus]
English. Singer, Songwriter
Best-known albums: *Armed Forces,* 1979; *Good Year For The Roses,* 1981.
b. Aug 25, 1954 in London, England
Source: *Baker 84, 92; BioIn 11, 13, 15, 16; ConLC 21; ConMus 2; CurBio 83; DcArts; EncPR&S 89; EncRk 88; FacFETw; HarEnCM 87; LegTOT; NewAmDM; News 94; RkOn 85; WhoAm 80, 82, 84, 86, 88, 90, 92, 94, 95, 96, 97; WhoEnt 92; WhoHol 92; WhoNeCM; WhoRocM 82*

Costello, Frank
[Francesco Castiglia]
American. Criminal
Controlled Manhattan's organized crime, 1936-46; witness, Kefauver Senate Investigation, 1950-51.
b. Jan 26, 1891 in Cosenza, Italy
d. Feb 1, 1973 in New York, New York
Source: *BioIn 1, 2, 3, 4, 5, 6, 7, 9, 10, 11, 12, 13, 16; CopCroC; DcAmB S9; DrInf; LegTOT; NewYTBE 73; ObitOF 79; PolProf E*

Costello, John Aloysius
Irish. Political Leader
Prime minister of first coalition government of Eire, 1948-51; head of the Government of Ireland, 1954-76.
b. Jun 20, 1891 in Dublin, Ireland
d. Jan 5, 1976 in Dublin, Ireland
Source: *BioIn 1, 2, 3, 10, 11; BlueB 76; CurBio 48; DcIrB 78, 88; DcNaB 1971; HisDBrE; IntWW 74, 75; LinLib S; PoIre; WhAm 6; Who 74*

Costello, Larry
[Lawrence R Costello]
American. Basketball Player, Basketball Coach
Forward, 1954-68; led NBA in free-throw percentage, 1963, 1965; coach, Milwaukee, 1968-77, Chicago, 1978-79; won NBA championship, 1971.
b. Jul 2, 1931 in Minoa, New York
Source: *BasBi; BiDAmSp BK; BioIn 6; OfNBA 87; WhoBbl 73; WhoSpor*

Costello, Lou
[Abbott and Costello]
American. Actor, Comedian
Starred in over 30 films with Bud Abbott; best known for "Who's On First?" routine.
b. Mar 6, 1906 in Paterson, New Jersey
d. Mar 3, 1959 in Los Angeles, California
Source: *CmMov; CurBio 41, 59; DcAmB S6; EncAFC; FilmgC; HalFC 84, 88; LegTOT; MotPP; MovMk; NotNAT B; ObitT 1951; OxCFilm; WhAm 3; WhoHol B; WhScrn 74, 77, 83; WorAl; WorAlBi; WorEFlm*

Costello, Maurice
"The Dimpled Darling"
American. Actor
One of first matinee stage idols; made film triumph in *A Tale of Two Cities,* 1911.
b. Feb 22, 1877 in Pittsburgh, Pennsylvania
d. Oct 30, 1950 in Hollywood, California
Source: *BioIn 2, 9; Film 1, 2; FilmgC; HalFC 84, 88; IntDcF 1-3, 2-3; MotPP; NotNAT B; SilFlmP; TwYS; WhoHol B; WhScrn 74, 77, 83*

Costello, Robert E
American. Producer
Won Emmys, 1977, 1979 for soap opera "Ryan's Hope."
b. Apr 26, 1921 in Chicago, Illinois
Source: *Law&B 89A; VarWW 85*

Coster, Laurens Janszoon
[Laurens Janszoon Koster]
Dutch. Inventor
Thought by some scholars to have invented moveable type, c. 1430; credit now usually goes to Gutenberg.
b. 1410 in Haarlem, Netherlands
Source: *WebBD 83*

Costigan, James
American. Writer
Won three Emmys for TV shows including "Eleanor and Franklin," 1976.
b. Mar 31, 1928 in Belvedere Gardens, California
Source: *BiE&WWA; ConAu 73; LesBEnT 92; NewYTET; NotNAT; VarWW 85; WhoHol 92*

Costle, Douglas Michael
American. Government Official
First administrator of the EPA, which he helped shape, 1970.
b. Jul 27, 1939 in Long Beach, California
Source: *CurBio 80; IntWW 80, 81, 82, 83; WhoAm 86; WhoAmL 92; WhoE 91, 93; WhoGov 72*

Costner, Kevin (Michael)
American. Actor
Films include *The Untouchables,* 1987; *Bull Durham,* 1988; *JFK,* 1991.
b. Jan 18, 1955 in Lynwood, California
Source: *BiDFilm 94; BioIn 14, 15, 16; CelR 90; ConTFT 5, 9; CurBio 90; DcArts; HalFC 88; HolBB; IntDcF 2-3; IntMPA 92, 94, 96; IntWW 91, 93; LegTOT; MiSFD 9; News 89; NewYTBS 89; WhoAm 90, 92, 94, 95, 96, 97; WhoEnt 92; WorAlBi*

Cotman, John Sell
English. Artist
Norwich school landscape painter, etcher; known for watercolors including *Greta Bridge,* 1805.
b. Aug 16, 1782 in Norwich, England
d. Jul 24, 1865 in London, England
Source: *Alli; AtlBL; BiDLA; BioIn 1, 2, 3, 4, 8, 10, 11, 12; CelCen; ClaDrA; DcArts; DcBiPP; DcBrBI; DcBrWA; DcNaB; IntDcAA 90; McGDA; NewC; OxCArt; OxCShps; OxDcArt; WhDW*

Cotrubas, Ileana
Romanian. Opera Singer
Soprano; NY Met. debut, 1977; noted for lyrico-dramatic roles.
b. Jun 9, 1939 in Galati, Romania
Source: *Baker 84, 92; BioIn 10, 11, 12; ConMus 1; CurBio 81; HalFC 88; IntDcOp; IntWW 78, 91, 93; IntWWM 90; InWom SUP; MetOEnc; NewAmDM; NewGrDO; NewYTBS 77; PenDiMP; WhoAm 86, 90; WhoMus 72; WhoOp 76; WhoSoCE 89; WhoWor 82, 84, 87, 91; WorAlBi*

Cotsworth, Staats
American. Actor
Starred on radio as "Casey, Crime Photographer," 1944-55; films include *Peyton Place,* 1957.
b. Feb 17, 1908 in Oak Park, Illinois
d. Apr 9, 1979 in New York, New York
Source: *BiE&WWA, 78, 79; NewYTBS 79; NotNAT; RadStar; SaTiSS; WhAmArt 85; WhoAmA 73, 76, 78, 80N, 82N, 84N, 86N, 89N, 91N, 93N; WhoHol A; WhoThe 72, 77, 81N; WhScrn 83*

Cott, Ted
American. Radio Executive
Wrote *A Treasury of the Spoken Word,* 1949; won Emmy for outstanding radio operation, 1957.
b. Jan 1, 1917 in Poughkeepsie, New York
d. Jun 13, 1973 in New York, New York
Source: *AmAu&B; BioIn 2, 9, 10; LesBEnT; NewYTBE 73; NewYTET; RadStar; WhAm 6; WhDW; WhoPubR 72*

Cottam, Clarence
American. Biologist
Won Audubon Medal for conservation efforts, 1961; wrote *Insects: A Guide to Familiar American Insects,* 1951.
b. Jan 1, 1899 in Saint George, Utah
d. Mar 30, 1974 in Corpus Christi, Texas
Source: *BioIn 10, 12, 13; BlueB 76; ConAu 97; InSci; NatCAB 58; NatLAC; NewYTBS 74; SmATA 25; WhAm 6; WhoAm 74; WhoWor 74*

Cotten, Joseph
American. Actor
Starred in *Citizen Kane,* 1941; *Journey into Fear,* 1942.
b. May 15, 1905 in Petersburg, Virginia
d. Feb 6, 1994 in Los Angeles, California
Source: *BiDFilm, 94; BiE&WWA; BioIn 1, 3, 4, 6, 10, 11, 14, 15, 19, 20; BioNews 74; CmMov; ConTFT 4, 13; CurBio 43, 94N; DcArts; FilmgC; HalFC 84, 88; IntDcF 1-3, 2-3; IntMPA 75, 76, 77, 78, 79, 81, 82, 84, 86, 88, 92, 94; IntWW 91; ItaFilm; LegTOT; MotPP; MovMk; NewYTBS 94; NotNAT; OxCAmT 84; OxCFilm; PlP&P; RadStar; WhoAm 86, 90; WhoEnt 92; WhoHol 92, A; WhoThe 72, 77, 81; WorAlBi; WorEFlm*

Cotten, Libba
[Elizabeth Cotten]
American. Composer, Musician
Developed the "Cotten picking" guitar-playing style; composer of *Freight Train* and *Washington Blues.*
b. Jan 1892 in Chapel Hill, North Carolina
d. Jun 29, 1987
Source: *BioIn 13; BluesWW; ConMus 16; InB&W 85; InWom SUP; NewAmDM; NewYTBS 83, 87; NotBlAW 1; PenEncP*

Cotten, Michael
[The Tubes]
American. Musician
Keyboardist with The Tubes since late 1960s.
b. Jan 25, 1950 in Kansas City, Missouri

Cotton, Charles
English. Author, Translator
Noted for treatise on fly-fishing, published in fifth edition of Walton's *Compleat Angler,* 1676; translation of Montaigne's *Essays,* 1685.
b. Apr 28, 1630 in Beresford Hall, England

d. Feb 16, 1687 in London, England
Source: *Alli; Benet 87, 96; BiD&SB; BioIn 3, 4, 19; BritAu; CamGEL; CamGLE; CasWL; Chambr 1; ChhPo, S1, S2, S3; CnE&AP; DcBiPP; DcEnL; DcLB 131; DcLEL; DcNaB; EvLB; NewC; OxCEng 67, 85, 95; PenC ENG; REn; RfGEnL 91; WebE&AL*

Cotton, Henry, Sir
[Thomas Henry Cotton]
English. Golfer
Touring pro, 1920s-40s; won British Open, 1934, 1937, 1948.
b. Jan 26, 1907 in Cheshire, England
d. Dec 22, 1987 in London, England
Source: *AnObit 1987; BioIn 1, 9, 13, 15, 19; ConAu 124; IntWW 81, 82, 83; Who 74, 82, 83, 85, 88; WhoGolf*

Cotton, John
[The Patriarch of New England]
American. Religious Leader
Headed Congregationalists in America; preached adherence to authority, resistance to democratic institutions.
b. Dec 4, 1584 in Derby, England
d. Dec 23, 1652 in Boston, Massachusetts
Source: *Alli, SUP; AmAu; AmAu&B; AmBi; AmOrN; AmWrBE; ApCAB; Benet 87, 96; BenetAL 91; BiD&SB; BioIn 3, 6, 7, 8, 13, 14, 17, 19; CamGLE; CamHAL; CnDAL; CyAL 1; DcAmAu; DcAmB; DcAmReB 1, 2; DcLB 24; DcLEL; DcNAA; DcNaB C, S1; EncAB-H 1974, 1996; EncARH; EncCRAm; LuthC 75; McGEWB; OxCAmH; OxCAmL 65, 83, 95; PenC AM; REn; REnAL; TwCBDA; WebAB 74; WhAm HS; WhDW; WorAl; WorAlBi*

Cotton, Norris
American. Politician
Republican senator from NH, 1954-75; wrote column, "Report From Congress," 1949-75.
b. May 11, 1900
d. Feb 24, 1989 in Lebanon, New Hampshire
Source: *BiDrAC; BiDrUSC 89; BioIn 4, 5, 8, 9, 10, 11, 16; BlueB 76; CngDr 74; ConAu 103; CurBio 56, 89N; IntWW 74, 75, 76, 77; NewYTBS 89; PolProf E, K; WhAm 9; WhoAm 74, 76; WhoAmP 73, 75, 77, 79; WhoE 74, 75, 77; WhoGov 72, 75*

Cottrell, Alan Howard, Sir
English. Scientist, Author
Wrote *How Safe Is Nuclear Energy,* 1981.
b. Jul 17, 1919 in Birmingham, England
Source: *BiESc; BlueB 76; CanWW 89; ConAu 10NR; FacFETw; IntAu&W 82; IntWW 83, 91; IntYB 82; McGMS 80; Who 83, 92; WhoEng 88; WhoWor 82, 84; WrDr 84, 92*

Cottrell, Comer J(oseph), Jr.
American. Business Executive
Founder, pres. of Pro-Line, an int'l. ethnic hair care products manufacturer, 1970.
b. Dec 7, 1931 in Mobile, Alabama
Source: *InB&W 85; St&PR 87, 91; WhoBlA 77, 80, 85, 88, 92*

Cottrell, Frederick Gardner
American. Chemist
Invented the electrostatic precipitator.
b. Jan 10, 1877 in Oakland, California
d. Nov 16, 1948 in Berkeley, California
Source: *BioIn 1, 2, 3, 4, 6, 11, 14; DcAmB S4; DcScB; InSci; NatCAB 38; ObitOF 79; WhAm 2*

Coty, Francois Marie Joseph Spoturno
French. Manufacturer, Newspaper Publisher
Founded Coty perfume empire; his conservative, right-wing ideas espoused in his newspapers, including *Le Figaro.*
b. May 3, 1874 in Ajaccio, Corsica, France
d. Jul 25, 1934 in Louveciennes, France
Source: *BiDExR; BiDFrPL*

Coty, Rene (Jules Gustave)
French. Statesman
Last pres. of the fourth French Republic, 1954-59.
b. Mar 20, 1882 in Le Havre, France
d. Nov 22, 1962 in Le Havre, France
Source: *BiDFrPL; BioIn 3, 4, 5, 6, 17; CurBio 54, 63; DcPol; ObitOF 79; ObitT 1961; WhAm 4*

Coubertin, Pierre de, Baron
French. Olympic Official
Revived Olympic games, 1894; pres., IOC, 1894-1925.
b. Jan 1, 1862 in Paris, France
d. Sep 1, 1937 in Geneva, Switzerland
Source: *BioIn 2; WhE&EA; WhLit; WhoLA; WorAl*

Coue, Emile
French. Psychologist
Remembered for his formula for curing by autosuggestion, "Day by day in everyway, I am getting better and better."
b. Feb 26, 1857 in Troyes, France
d. Jul 2, 1926 in Nancy, France
Source: *BiDPsy; BioIn 3, 7; EncO&P 1S1, 2, 3; InSci; NamesHP; NewC; OxCMed 86*

Coues, Elliott
American. Ornithologist
Works include *Key to North American Birds,* 1872.
b. Sep 9, 1842 in Portsmouth, New Hampshire
d. Dec 25, 1899 in Baltimore, Maryland
Source: *Alli SUP; AmAu&B; AmBi; ApCAB; BbD; BbtC; BiDAmS; BiD&SB; BiInAmS; BioIn 3, 9, 12; DcAmAu; DcAmB; DcAmMeB; DcNAA; DcScB; InSci; LinLib S; NatCAB 5; REnAW; TwCBDA; WhAm 1*

Coughlin, Charles Edward, Father
American. Clergy, Radio Performer
Controversial "radio priest" of Depression Era; published *Social Justice,* 1934-42; took violent anti-Roosevelt, anti-Semetic stand.
b. Oct 25, 1891 in Hamilton, Ontario, Canada
d. Oct 27, 1979 in Bloomfield Hills, Michigan
Source: *AmSocL; BiDAmJo; BiDExR; BioIn 1, 4, 5, 7, 9, 10, 11, 12, 13, 14, 15, 16, 19, 21; ConAu 97; CurBio 40, 80, 80N; DcAmB S10; DcAmReB 2; EncAAH; EncAB-H 1974, 1996; EncARH; McGEWB; NewCol 75; OxCAmH; RelLAm 91; SaTiSS; WebAB 74, 79; WorAl*

Coulier, Dave
American. Actor
Host of TV show "American Funniest People;" co-star in TV series "Full House," 1987—.
Source: *BioIn 16*

Coulomb, Charles Augustin de
French. Physicist
Formulated Coulomb's law, 1785, relating to electrical charge and repulsion.
b. Jun 14, 1736 in Angouleme, France
d. Aug 23, 1806 in Paris, France
Source: *AsBiEn; BiESc; BioIn 3, 9, 11, 12; BlkwCE; DcBiPP; DcCathB; DcInv; DcScB; InSci; LarDcSc; McGEWB; NewCol 75; WhDW; WorAl; WorAlBi*

Coulouris, George
English. Actor
Best known for villain roles in films including *For Whom the Bell Tolls,* 1943.
b. Oct 1, 1903 in Manchester, England
d. Apr 25, 1989 in London, England
Source: *AnObit 1989; BiE&WWA; BioIn 16; ConTFT 8; FilmgC; HalFC 84, 88; IntMPA 84, 86, 88; ItaFilm; MovMk; NewYTBS 89; NotNAT; SaTiSS; Vers A; WhoHol A; WhoThe 72, 77, 81*

Coulter, Art(hur Edmund)
"Trapper"
Canadian. Hockey Player
Defenseman, 1931-42, with Chicago, NY Rangers; Hall of Fame, 1974.
b. May 31, 1909 in Winnipeg, Manitoba, Canada
Source: *HocEn; WhoHcky 73*

Coulter, Ernest Kent
American. Social Reformer
Children's court clerk who founded first Big Brother agency, NYC, 1904.
b. Nov 14, 1871 in Columbus, Ohio
d. May 1, 1952 in Santa Barbara, California

Source: *BioIn 2, 4; DcAmB S5; NatCAB 41; ObitOF 79; OhA&B; WhNAA*

Coulter, John Merle
American. Botanist
Founded, edited, *Botanical Gazette,* 1875; wrote *Plant Genetics,* 1918.
b. Nov 20, 1851 in Ningbo, China
d. Dec 23, 1928 in Yonkers, New York
Source: *Alli SUP; AmBi; ApCAB, X; BiDAmEd; BiDAmS; BioIn 2, 6; DcAmAu; DcAmB; DcNAA; DcNaB; IndAu 1816; InSci; LinLib S; NatCAB 11; TwCBDA; WebBD 83; WhAm 1; WhNAA*

Coulter, John William
Canadian. Dramatist
Noted for dramas with Irish themes: *Family Portraits,* 1937.
b. Feb 12, 1888 in Belfast, Northern Ireland
d. Dec 1, 1980 in Toronto, Ontario, Canada
Source: *Au&Wr 71; BioIn 1, 11; CanWW 70, 79; ConAu 3NR, 5R; CreCan 1; IntAu&W 76, 77, 82; OxCCan, SUP*

Country Gentlemen, The
[Eddie Adcock; John Duffey; Bill Emerson; Earl Taylor; Charlie Waller]
American. Music Group
Bluegrass band formed 1957; hit singles *The Rebel Soldier*; *Bringin' Mary Home*; original members are listed above.
Source: *BgBkCoM; BiDAmM; BioIn 17, 20; ConMus 7; EncFCWM 69, 83; HarEnCM 87; InB&W 85; MedHR; NewGrDA 86; NewYTBS 27; PenEncP; WhoAmP 81*

Country Joe and the Fish
[Bruce Barthol; David Cohen; Chicken Hirsch; Joseph McDonald; Barry Melton]
American. Music Group
Appeared at Monterey, Woodstock festivals; albums include *Here We Are Again,* 1969.
Source: *AmMWSc 92, 95; BiDAmM; DrRegL 75; Dun&B 90; EncRk 88; MiSFD 9; MugS; NewAmDM; NewGrDA 86; NewYTBS 82; OnThGG; RkOn 78, 84; RolSEnR 83; WhoAmP 93, 95; WhoRocM 82; WhoTech 95*

Coup, W(illiam) C(ameron)
American. Businessman
With P.T. Barnum founded "The Greatest Show on Earth," 1872.
b. 1837 in Mount Pleasant, Indiana
d. 1895 in Jacksonville, Florida

Couperin
[Armand-Louis Couperin; Charles Couperin; Francois Couperin]
French. Musicians
Family best known as organists at St. Gervais, Paris, 1650-1826.
Source: *Baker 78, 84, 92; BioIn 14, 15; DcCathB; InWom SUP; NewAmDM; NewOxM; OxCMus; PenDiMP A; WhDW*

Couperin, Francois
[LeGrand Couperin]
French. Musician, Composer
Harpsichordist; organist; influenced keyboard technique of Bach; leading French composer of his day.
b. Nov 10, 1668 in Paris, France
d. Sep 12, 1733 in Paris, France
Source: *AtlBL; Baker 78, 84, 92; BioIn 1, 2, 4, 7, 8, 12, 14, 15, 17, 20; DcArts; DcBiPP; DcCathB; EncEnl; LegTOT; LinLib S; McGEWB; MusMk; NewAmDM; NewGrDM 80; NewOxM; OxCFr; OxCMus; PenDiMP A; WhDW*

Couperius, Louis (Marie Anne)
Dutch. Author, Educator
Wrote four-vol. epic *The Books of the Small Souls,* 1914-18.
b. Jun 10, 1863 in The Hague, Netherlands
d. Jul 16, 1923 in De Steeg, Netherlands
Source: *ConAu 115; ConLC 15; CyWA 58; REn*

Coupland, Douglas
Canadian. Author
Wrote novel *Generation X,* 1991.
b. Dec 31, 1961 in Baden-Sollingen, Germany
Source: *ConAu 142; ConCaAu 1; ConLC 85; ConPopW; WrDr 96*

Couples, Fred
[Frederick Stephen Couples]
American. Golfer
Won Masters Tournament, 1992.
b. Oct 3, 1959 in Seattle, Washington
Source: *BioIn 13; CurBio 93; News 94; WhoAm 92, 94, 95, 96, 97; WhoWor 95, 96*

Courant, Richard
American. Mathematician, Educator
Made important contributions in the calculus of variations; promoted New York University's institute of mathematics.
b. Jan 8, 1888 in Lublinitz, Prussia
d. Jan 27, 1972 in New Rochelle, New York
Source: *AmMWSc 73P; BioIn 4, 7, 9, 11, 12, 14, 20; ConAu 33R; CurBio 66, 72N; DcAmB S9; LarDcSc; McGMS 80; NatCAB 58; NewYTBE 72; NotTwCS; ObitOF 79; WhAm 5; Who 92*

Courbet, Gustave
French. Artist
Realist painter whose works include *Burial at Ornans* in the Louvre.
b. Jun 10, 1819 in Ornans, France
d. Dec 31, 1877 in Vevey, Switzerland
Source: *ArtsNiC; AtlBL; Benet 87, 96; BioIn 1, 2, 3, 4, 5, 6, 8, 9, 10, 11, 12, 13, 15, 16, 17, 18; CelCen; ClaDrA; DcArts; DcBiPP; Dis&D; IntDcAA 90; LegTOT; LinLib S; McGDA; OxCArt; OxCFr; OxDcArt; REn; ThHElm; WhDW; WorAl; WorAlBi*

Courboin, Charles
American. Organist
Designed 144 important organs, including Wanamaker's in NYC.
b. Apr 2, 1884 in Antwerp, Belgium
d. Apr 13, 1973 in New York, New York
Source: *Baker 84; BioIn 9*

Couric, Katie
[Katherine Couric; Mrs. Jay Monahan]
American. Broadcast Journalist
Co-anchor NBC News' "Today" show, 1991—.
b. Jan 7, 1957 in Arlington, Virginia
Source: *ConTFT 11; CurBio 93; GrLiveH; IntMPA 96; LegTOT; News 91; WhoAm 92, 94, 95, 96, 97; WhoAmW 93, 95, 97; WhoE 93; WomStre*

Courier, Jim
[James Spencer Courier]
American. Tennis Player
Number one ranked tennis player in the world, February 1992 to April 1993; two-time winner of Australian Open and French Open; finalist at Wimbledon, 1993, and US Open, 1991.
b. Aug 17, 1970 in Sanford, Florida
Source: *BuCMET; IntWW 93; News 93-2; WhoAm 92, 94, 95, 96, 97; WhoSpor; WhoWor 95, 96, 97*

Cournand, Andre Frederic
American. Physiologist
Shared Nobel Prize in medicine with Dickinson Richards, 1956, for development of cardiac catheterization.
b. Sep 24, 1895 in Paris, France
d. Feb 19, 1988 in Great Barrington, Massachusetts
Source: *AmMWSc 73P, 76P, 79, 82, 86; BiESc; BioIn 4, 5, 6, 11; CurBio 57, 88; FacFETw; IntWW 83; LarDcSc; McGMS 80; WebAB 74, 79; Who 74, 82, 83, 85, 88; WhoAm 86; WhoNob; WhoWor 87*

Courneyor, Yvan Serge
"The Roadrunner"
Canadian. Hockey Player
Right wing, Montreal, 1963-79; won Conn Smythe Trophy, 1973; won eight Stanley Cups; Hall of Fame, 1982.
b. Nov 22, 1943 in Drummondville, Quebec, Canada
Source: *BioIn 7, 11*

Cournos, John
Russian. Author
His immigrant life in England is background for books: *The Mask,* 1919; *The Wall,* 1921.
b. Mar 6, 1881 in Kiev, Russia
d. Aug 29, 1966 in New York, New York

Source: *AmAu&B; DcLB 54; DcLEL; LngCTC; OxCAmL 65, 83; REnAL; ScF&FL 1; TwCA, SUP; WhLit; WhoLA*

Cournot, Antoine Augustin
French. Mathematician, Economist
One of first to use mathematics to solve economic problems; study today called econometrics.
b. Aug 28, 1801 in Gray, France
d. Mar 30, 1877 in Paris, France
Source: *BioIn 16; DcScB; GrEconB; McGEWB; NewCol 75; OxCFr; WebBD 83; WhoEc 81, 86*

Courreges, Andre
French. Fashion Designer
Made clothes with an architectural quality; introduced the mini skirt, 1965.
b. Mar 9, 1923 in Pau, France
Source: *AmDec 1960; BioIn 7, 8, 9, 17; ConDes 84, 90, 97; ConFash; CurBio 70; DcArts; DcTwDes; EncFash; FairDF FRA; IntWW 74, 75, 76, 77, 78, 79, 80, 81, 82, 83, 89, 91, 93; LegTOT; WhoAm 74; WhoFash 88; WhoFr 79; WhoWor 74, 78, 80, 82, 84, 87; WorFshn*

Court, Margaret
[Margaret Smith]
Australian. Tennis Player
Wimbledon champ, 1963-65, 1970; US Open champ, 1962, 1965, 1968-70, 1973; Int'l Tennis Hall of Fame, 1979.
b. Jul 16, 1942 in Albury, Australia
Source: *BioIn 6, 9, 10, 11, 12, 14, 17, 20; BioNews 74; CurBio 73; IntWW 81, 82, 83, 89, 91, 93; InWom SUP; LegTOT; NewYTBE 70, 71; WhDW; WhoAm 76, 78, 80, 82; WhoAmW 83; WhoSpor; WhoWor 74; WorAl; WorAlBi*

Courtenay, Tom
[Thomas Daniel Courtenay]
English. Actor
Oscar nominee for *The Dresser,* 1984; *Doctor Zhivago,* 1965; Tony nominee for *Otherwise Engaged,* 1977.
b. Feb 25, 1937 in Hull, England
Source: *BioIn 6, 7, 11, 12, 13, 21; CamGWoT; CelR; ConTFT 1, 5; CurBio 64; FilmgC; HalFC 84, 88; IntMPA 75, 76, 77, 78, 79, 81, 82, 84, 86, 88, 92, 94, 96; IntWW 75, 76, 77, 78, 79, 80, 81, 82, 83, 89, 91, 93; ItaFilm; MotPP; MovMk; NewYTBS 81; OxCFilm; OxCThe 83; Who 74, 82, 83, 85, 88, 90, 92, 94; WhoHol 92, A; WhoThe 72, 77, 81; WhoWor 74; WorAl; WorAlBi; WorEFlm*

Courtneidge, Cicely, Dame
English. Actor
London stage, musical star since 1909; introduced song "The Kings Horses," 1931.
b. Apr 1, 1893 in Sydney, Australia
d. Apr 26, 1980 in London, England
Source: *AnObit 1980; BioIn 3, 9, 10; ConAu 105; DcArts; DcNaB 1971; EncMT; FilmgC; HalFC 84, 88; InWom, SUP; LegTOT; NotNAT A; OxCPMus; OxCThe 83; PenEncP; QDrFCA 92; Who 74; WhoHol A; WhoThe 72, 77, 81; WhScrn 83*

Courtney, Clint(on Dawson)
"Scrap Iron"
American. Baseball Player
Catcher, 1951-61; AL rookie of year, 1952; known for aggressive play.
b. Mar 16, 1927 in Hall Summit, Louisiana
d. Jun 16, 1975 in Rochester, New York
Source: *Ballpl 90; BioIn 3, 10; WhoProB 73*

Courtois, Bernard
French. Chemist
In the course of his work in salt petre production, he discovered manufactured iodine.
b. Feb 8, 1777 in Dijon, France
d. Sep 27, 1838 in Paris, France
Source: *AsBiEn; BiESc; DcInv; DcScB; Dis&D; InSci; LarDcSc; LinLib S*

Courtright, Jim
[Timothy Isaiah Courtright]
"Longhaired Jim"
American. Lawman
Marshal, Ft. Worth, 1876-78; killed by gambler who refused to pay.
b. 1845? in Illinois
d. Feb 8, 1887 in Fort Worth, Texas
Source: *BioIn 4, 5, 10, 11; REnAW*

Cousineau, Tom
American. Football Player
Linebacker, Cleveland, 1982-85, San Francisco, 1986—; highest-paid defensive player at time of signing.
b. May 16, 1957 in Fairview Park, Ohio
Source: *BioIn 12, 13; FootReg 87; NewYTBS 82*

Cousins, Frank
English. Labor Union Official
MP, 1965-66; general secretary, Transport and General Workers Union, 1956-64, 1966-69.
b. Sep 8, 1904 in Bulwell, England
d. Jun 11, 1986 in Chesterfield, England
Source: *AnObit 1986; BioIn 4, 5, 6, 7, 8, 9, 12, 15; BlueB 76; CurBio 86, 86N; DcNaB 1986; FacFETw; IntWW 74, 75, 76, 77, 78, 79, 80, 81, 82, 83; IntYB 78, 79, 80, 81, 82; WhAm 9; Who 74, 82, 83, 85*

Cousins, (Sue) Margaret
American. Children's Author
Books include *Uncle Edgar and the Reluctant Saint,* 1948; *Ben Franklin of Old Philadelphia,* 1952.
b. Jan 26, 1905 in Munday, Texas
d. Jul 30, 1996 in San Antonio, Texas
Source: *AmAu&B; Au&Wr 71; AuBYP 2, 3; BioIn 3, 6, 8, 9, 20, 21; ConAu 1NR, 1R, 152; ContDcW 89; CurBio 96N; DcLB 137; EncTwCJ; ForWC 70; IntAu&W 76, 77, 82, 89, 91; InWom; PenNWW A; SmATA 2; TexWr; WhoAm 74, 76, 78, 80, 82, 84, 86, 88, 90, 92, 94, 95, 96; WhoAmW 58, 61, 64, 66, 68, 70, 72, 74; WhoWor 74; WrDr 76, 80, 82, 84, 86, 88, 90, 92, 94, 96*

Cousins, Norman
American. Editor, Author
Editor *Saturday Review,* 1937-72; author of 25 books on the nature of illness: *Anatomy of an Illness as Perceived by the Patient,* 1979.
b. Jun 24, 1912 in Union Hill, New Jersey
d. Nov 30, 1990 in Westwood, California
Source: *AmAu&B; AmPeW; Benet 87; BioIn 3, 4, 8, 9, 10, 11, 13, 14, 15, 16; CelR 90; ChhPo; ConAu 17R, 33NR; ConHero 1; CurBio 43, 77, 91N; DcLEL 1940; EncAJ; EncTwCJ; EncWB; FacFETw; IntWW 83, 89, 91N; LinLib L, S; MajTwCW; NewYTBE 71; NewYTBS 90; OxCAmL 65, 83, 95; REn; REnAL; TwCA SUP; WebAB 74, 79; Who 85, 90, 92N; WhoAm 86, 90; WhoE 79; WhoUSWr 88; WhoWor 74; WhoWrEP 89; WorAl; WrDr 76, 86, 90*

Cousins, Robin
English. Skater
Won figure skating gold medal, 1980 Olympics.
b. 1957 in Bristol, England
Source: *BioIn 12, 14, 17; NewYTBS 79*

Cousins, Samuel
English. Engraver
Mezzotint engraver who transcribed Thomas Lawrence's works.
b. May 9, 1801 in Exeter, England
d. May 7, 1887 in London, England
Source: *ArtsNiC; CelCen; DcBiPP; DcBrWA; DcNaB; McGDA; NewCol 75*

Cousteau, Jacques (Yves)
French. Oceanographer
Led Calypso expeditions; hosts TV's "Undersea World of Jacques Cousteau," beginning in 1968; won Oscar, 1965, for best documentary; invented the Aqua-lung, 1943.
b. Jun 11, 1910 in Sainte Andre de Cubzac, France
d. Jun 25, 1997 in Paris, France
Source: *AmMWSc 92; AnCL; BiESc; BioIn 3, 4, 5, 6, 7, 8, 9, 10, 11, 12, 13, 14, 15, 16, 18; BioNews 74; CamDcSc; CelR 90; ConAu 15NR, 65; ConHero 2; CurBio 76; DcFM; EncWB; Expl 93; FacFETw; FilmgC; HalFC 88; IntMPA 92; IntWW 83, 91; LarDcSc; LegTOT; LesBEnT 92; MajTwCW; NewYTBS 87; NotTwCS; OxCFilm; OxCShps; REn; WhDW; Who 74, 85, 92; WhoAm 80, 82, 84, 86, 90; WhoOcn 78; WhoUN 75; WhoWor 74, 76, 78, 80, 82, 87, 91; WorAl; WorAlBi; WorEFlm; WorInv*

Cousteau, Jean-Michel
French. Oceanographer
Leader in research, education; works for The Cousteau Society on films, publications; eldest son of Jacques.
b. 1938 in Toulon, France
Source: *News 88-2*

Cousteau, Philippe
French. Oceanographer, Producer
Produced TV series "Undersea World of Jacques Cousteau," 1970-75; Emmy nominee, 1971.
b. Dec 30, 1940 in Toulon, France
d. Jun 28, 1979 in Alverca, Portugal
Source: *BioIn 12; ConAu 89; NewYTBS 79*

Cousy, Bob
[Robert Joseph Cousy]
American. Basketball Player
Guard, Boston, 1950-63; MVP, 1957; 10-time all-star; Hall of Fame, 1970.
b. Aug 9, 1928 in New York, New York
Source: *BasBi; BiDAmSp BK; BioIn 3, 13, 14, 15, 17, 21; CelR; CurBio 58; FacFETw; LegTOT; OfNBA 87; WebAB 74, 79; WhoAm 82, 84, 86, 90; WhoBbl 73; WhoSpor; WorAl; WorAlBi*

Couthon, Georges
French. Politician, Lawyer
Paralyzed, he led army that took Lyons from counter-revolutionaries.
b. Dec 22, 1755 in Orcet, France
d. Jul 28, 1794 in Paris, France
Source: *CmFrR; DcBiPP; Dis&D; OxCFr*

Couve de Murville, (Jacques) Maurice
French. Political Leader
French prime minister, 1968-69; mediator in Lebanese civil war, 1975.
b. Jan 24, 1907 in Reims, France
Source: *BiDFrPL; BioIn 3, 4, 5, 6, 7, 8, 17; DcPol; IntWW 74, 75, 76, 77, 78, 79, 80, 81, 82, 83, 89, 91, 93; IntYB 78, 79, 80, 81, 82; Who 74, 82, 83, 85, 88, 90, 92, 94; WhoFr 79; WhoWor 74, 76, 78*

Couzens, James Joseph, Jr.
American. Businessman, Politician
Ford Motor Co. exec., 1903-15; mayor of Detroit, 1919-22.
b. Aug 26, 1876 in Chatham, Ontario, Canada
d. Oct 22, 1936 in Detroit, Michigan
Source: *AmBi; BiDrAC; DcAmB S2; NatCAB 30; WebAB 74; WhAm 1; WhAmP*

Covarrubias, Miguel
Mexican. Artist, Cartoonist
Contributed to *The New Yorker; Vanity Fair;* author of ethnological books; lithographer; costume, scenery designer.
b. Feb 4, 1904 in Mexico City, Mexico
d. Feb 6, 1957 in Mexico City, Mexico
Source: *BioIn 1, 2, 3, 4, 5, 9, 12, 14, 20; ConArt 83; CurBio 40, 57; EncLatA; IlsCB 1744, 1946; LegTOT; McGDA; ObitOF 79; REnAL; WhAm 3; WhDW; WorECar*

Coveleski, Harry Frank
[Harry Frank Kowalewski]
"The Giant Killer"
American. Baseball Player
Pitcher, 1907-10, 1914-19; known for three wins against NY Giants, knocking them out of pennant race, 1908.
b. Apr 23, 1886 in Shamokin, Pennsylvania
d. Aug 4, 1950 in Shamokin, Pennsylvania
Source: *WhoProB 73*

Coveleski, Stanley Anthony
[Stanislaus Kowalewski]
American. Baseball Player
Pitcher, 1916-28; had 215 career wins; Hall of Fame, 1969.
b. Jul 13, 1889 in Shamokin, Pennsylvania
d. Mar 20, 1984 in South Bend, Indiana
Source: *BiDAmSp BB; WhoProB 73*

Cover, Franklin
American. Actor
Played Tom Willis on TV series "The Jeffersons," 1975-85.
b. Nov 20, 1928 in Cleveland, Ohio
Source: *ConTFT 8; VarWW 85; WhoAm 90; WhoEnt 92; WhoHol 92*

Coverdale, Miles
English. Clergy, Translator
First scholar to translate entire Bible into English, 1535.
b. 1488? in Yorkshire, England
d. Feb 1568? in London, England
Source: *Alli; BbD; Benet 87, 96; BiD&SB; BiDRP&D; BioIn 2, 3, 4, 5, 11, 13; BlmGEL; BritAu; CamGEL; CamGLE; CasWL; Chambr 1; DcEnL; DcEuL; DcLEL; DcNaB, C; EvLB; LinLib L, S; LngCEL; LuthC 75; McGEWB; NewC; OxCEng 67, 85, 95; OxCMus; PenC ENG; REn; WebBD 83; WebE&AL; WhDW*

Coverdell, Paul
American. Politician
Rep. senator from GA, 1993—.
b. Jan 20, 1939
Source: *AlmAP 96; CngDr 93*

Covey, Cyclone
American. Author
Wrote *The Gentle Radical,* 1966.
b. May 21, 1922 in Guthrie, Oklahoma
Source: *ConAu 21R; DrAS 74H, 78H, 82H; WhoAm 74, 76, 78, 80, 82, 84, 86, 88, 90, 92, 94, 95, 96, 97; WhoSSW 73, 91, 93; WhoWor 76*

Covey, Stephen R.
American. Consultant, Author
Founder, Institute for Principle-Centered Leadership; author of *Executive Excellence,* 1984.
b. Oct 24, 1932 in Salt Lake City, Utah
Source: *ConAu 12NR, 33R, 41NR; News 94*

Covici, Pascal
American. Publisher, Editor
Co-owner, Covici-Friede Publishing, 1928-38; promoted John Steinbeck.
b. Nov 4, 1885 in Botosani, Romania
d. Oct 14, 1964 in New York, New York
Source: *DcAmB S7*

Covington, Warren
American. Musician, Bandleader, Singer
Trombonist, 1940s-50s; led Tommy Dorsey's orchestra after Dorsey's death, late 1950s.
b. Aug 7, 1921 in Philadelphia, Pennsylvania
Source: *ASCAP 66; BiDAmM; BiDJaz; CmpEPM; EncJzS; NewGrDJ 88, 94*

Cowan, Jerome
American. Actor
Played Miles Archer in *The Maltese Falcon,* 1941; Dagwood's boss in *Blondie* film series, 1940s.
b. Oct 6, 1897 in New York, New York
d. Jan 24, 1972 in Encino, California
Source: *BiE&WWA; BioIn 9; EncAFC; FilmgC; HalFC 84, 88; MovMk; NewYTBE 72; NotNAT B; ObitOF 79; Vers A; WhoHol B; WhScrn 77, 83*

Cowan, Peter Wilkinshaw
Australian. Author
Short stories include *The Tins & Other Stories,* 1973.
b. Nov 4, 1914 in Perth, Australia
Source: *ConAu 25NR; ConNov 82, 91; IntAu&W 91; IntvTCA 2; WrDr 84, 92*

Coward, Noel Pierce, Sir
English. Dramatist, Composer
Wrote 27 plays, 281 songs; plays include *Private Lives,* 1930; *Blithe Spirit,* 1941.
b. Dec 16, 1899 in London, England
d. Mar 26, 1973 in Kingston, Jamaica
Source: *Au&Wr 71; AuNews 1; BiE&WWA; BioIn 5, 12, 13; BioNews 74; CasWL; Chambr 3; ChhPo S3; CnMD; CnThe; ConDr 73; ConLC 1, 9; CurBio 41, 73; DcFM; DcNaB 1971; EncWL; EvLB; FamA&A; Film 1; FilmgC; LngCTC; MakMC; McGEWD 72; ModBrL, S1; ModWD; MovMk; NewC; NewYTBE 73; NewYTBS 74; OxCEng 67; OxCFilm; TwCA SUP; WebE&AL; WhAm 5; WhoHol B; WhoMus 72; WhScrn 77; WorAl; WorEFlm*

Cowboy Junkies
Canadian. Music Group
Toronto-based country/blues group; known for slow, haunting musical style; hit single "Misguided Angel," 1988.
Source: *BioIn 17; ConMus 4; Dun&B 90; EncRkSt*

Cowdrey, (Michael) Colin
English. Cricket Player, Businessman
Member, England Cricket Team, 1954-75; author *Autobiography of a Cricketer,* 1976.
b. Dec 24, 1932 in Bangalore, India
Source: *BioIn 9, 11; BlueB 76; ConAu 105; IntWW 76, 77, 78, 79, 80, 81, 82, 83, 89, 91, 93; Who 74, 82, 83, 85, 88, 90, 92, 94; WrDr 76, 80, 82, 84, 86, 88, 90, 92, 94, 96*

Cowdry, Edmund Vincent
Canadian. Scientist
Cancer researcher who discovered heartwater.
b. Jul 18, 1888 in MacLeon, Alberta, Canada
d. Jun 25, 1975
Source: *BioIn 1, 10, 13, 14; InSci; NatCAB 61; WhAm 6; WhoAm 74; WhoWor 74*

Cowell, Henry Dixon
American. Composer, Pianist
Introduced innovations: "tone clusters," playing directly on piano strings; invented instrument called Rhythmicon, 1930s.
b. Mar 11, 1897 in Menlo Park, California
d. Dec 10, 1965 in Shady, New York
Source: *Baker 84; DcCM; EncFCWM 69; OxCMus; REnAL; WebAB 74; WhAm 4; WhNAA*

Cowen, Joshua Lionel
American. Inventor, Industrialist
Invented toy electric train, 1900; headed Lionel Corp., 1945-65.
b. Aug 25, 1880 in New York, New York
d. Sep 8, 1965 in New York, New York
Source: *BioIn 1, 2, 3, 6, 7, 12, 18; CurBio 54, 65; DcAmB S7; WhAm 4; WorAl; WorAlBi*

Cowen, Zelman, Sir
Australian. Political Leader
Governor general of Australia, 1977-82; author of books on legal, political subjects.
b. Oct 7, 1919 in Melbourne, Australia
Source: *Au&Wr 71; BioIn 11; BlueB 76; ConAu 1NR, 1R; FarE&A 78, 79, 80, 81; IntAu&W 77, 82, 86, 89, 91; IntWW 78, 79, 80, 81, 82, 83, 89, 91, 93; IntYB 78, 79, 80, 81, 82; Who 74, 82, 83, 85, 88, 90, 92, 94; WhoWor 78, 80, 82, 84, 87, 89, 91, 93, 95, 96, 97; WhoWorJ 72, 78; WrDr 76, 80, 82, 84, 86, 88, 90, 92, 94, 96*

Cowens, Dave
[David William Cowens]
American. Basketball Player
Forward, Boston, 1970-80, Milwaukee, 1982-83; MVP, 1973.
b. Oct 25, 1948 in Newport, Kentucky
Source: *BasBi; BiDAmSp BK; BioIn 10, 11, 12, 13; NewYTBS 76, 78; OfNBA 87; WhoAm 74, 76, 78, 80, 90, 92, 94, 95, 96, 97; WhoBbl 73; WhoE 95; WorAl; WorAlBi*

Cowl, Jane
American. Actor, Dramatist
Co-wrote two plays which became movies, *Lilac Time,* 1928; *Smilin' Through,* 1932.
b. Dec 14, 1884 in Boston, Massachusetts
d. Jun 22, 1950 in Santa Monica, California
Source: *BioIn 2, 3, 5, 10, 16; CamGWoT; EncWT; FacFETw; FamA&A; Film 1; FilmgC; HalFC 84, 88; NotAW; NotNAT B; NotWoAT; OxCAmT 84; OxCThe 83; PlP&P; WhAm 3; WhoHol B; WhScrn 77; WhThe*

Cowles, Fleur Fenton
American. Author, Illustrator
Wrote *The Case of Salvador Dali,* 1960; illustrated *Tiger Flower,* 1968.
b. Feb 13, 1910 in New York, New York
Source: *AmAu&B; Au&Wr 71; AuNews 1; BioNews 74; ConAu 4NR; CurBio 52; EncTwCJ; IntAu&W 91; InWom, SUP; WhoAm 84, 90; WhoAmA 84, 91; WhoWor 80; WrDr 86, 92*

Cowles, Gardner, Jr.
"Mike"
American. Publisher
Founded *Look* mag., 1937; chm., Cowles Communications, Inc.
b. Jan 31, 1903 in Algona, Iowa
d. Jul 8, 1985 in New York, New York
Source: *AmAu&B; AnObit 1985; BiDAmBL 83; BiDAmJo; BioIn 1, 2, 4, 5, 6, 13, 14, 15, 16, 19, 20; ConAu 116; CurBio 43, 85N; DcLB 137; IntWW 74, 75, 76, 77, 78, 79, 80, 81, 82, 83; IntYB 78, 79, 80, 81, 82; LinLib L, S; NewYTBE 71; NewYTBS 83, 85; St&PR 75, 84, 87N; WebAB 74, 79; WhAm 8; WhoAm 74, 76, 78, 80, 82, 84; WhoAmA 73, 76, 78, 80; WhoFI 74; WhoWor 74, 84*

Cowles, Henry Chandler
American. Botanist
Pioneered in plant ecology.
b. Feb 27, 1869 in Kensington, Connecticut
d. Sep 12, 1939 in Chicago, Illinois
Source: *BioIn 4, 6; DcAmB S2; DcNAA; FacFETw; Geog 10; NatCAB 39; WebAB 74, 79; WebBD 83; WhAm 1; WhNAA*

Cowles, John, Sr.
American. Publisher, Business Executive
Owner of several daily newspapers, including *Minneapolis Star.*
b. Dec 14, 1898 in Algona, Iowa
d. Feb 25, 1983 in Minneapolis, Minnesota
Source: *AmAu&B; BiDAmBL 83; BioIn 1, 2, 3, 4, 5, 6, 7, 13; BlueB 76; ConAu 109; CurBio 83, 83N; IntWW 74, 75, 76, 77, 78, 79, 80, 81, 82, 83; IntYB 78, 79, 80, 81, 82; NewYTBS 83; St&PR 75; WhAm 8; WhJnl; WhoAm 74, 76, 78; WhoFI 74; WhoMW 74, 76; WhoWor 74*

Cowles, William Hutchinson, Jr.
American. Publisher
Pres., Spokane Chronicle Co., 1935-68; Cowles Publishing Co., 1946-70.
b. Jul 23, 1902 in Sands Point, New York
d. Aug 12, 1971 in Spokane, Washington
Source: *BioIn 9, 11; NatCAB 57; WhAm 5*

Cowley, Abraham
English. Poet
Originator of English Pindaric ode; best known poem "Davideis," 1656.
b. Jul 24, 1618 in London, England
d. Jul 28, 1667 in Chertsey, England
Source: *Alli; AtlBL; BbD; Benet 87, 96; BiD&SB; BiDRP&D; BioIn 1, 2, 3, 5, 6, 7, 8, 9, 12, 15, 16, 19, 21; BlmGEL; BritAu; BritWr 2; CamGEL; CamGLE; CasWL; Chambr 1; ChhPo, S1, S3; CnE&AP; CroE&S; CrtT 2, 4; CyEd; CyWA 58; DcArts; DcBiPP; DcEnA; DcEnL; DcEuL; DcLB 131, 151; DcLEL; DcNaB; Dis&D; EvLB; LinLib L, S; LngCEL; McGEWB; MouLC 1; NewC; NotNAT B; OxCEng 67, 85, 95; OxCMed 86; OxCThe 67, 83; PenC ENG; REn; RfGEnL 91; WebE&AL*

Cowley, Bill
[William Cowley]
Canadian. Hockey Player
Center, 1934-47, mostly with Boston; won Hart Trophy, 1941, 1943, Art Ross Trophy, 1941; Hall of Fame, 1968.
b. Jun 12, 1912 in Bristol, Quebec, Canada
Source: *HocEn; WhoHcky 73; WhoSpor*

Cowley, Joe
[Joseph Alan Cowley]
American. Baseball Player
Pitcher, Philadelphia, 1984-87; threw no-hitter against California, 1986.
b. Aug 15, 1958 in Lexington, Kentucky
Source: *Ballpl 90; BaseReg 86, 87; BioIn 19*

Cowley, Malcolm
American. Author, Critic
Assistant editor, *New Republic,* 1929-44; wrote autobiographical *Exiles Return,* 1934.
b. Aug 24, 1898 in Belsano, Pennsylvania
d. Mar 27, 1989 in New Milford, Connecticut
Source: *AmAu&B; AmWr S2; AnObit 1989; Au&Wr 71; Benet 87, 96; BenetAL 91; BioIn 1, 2, 4, 6, 7, 10, 11, 12, 13, 14, 15, 16, 17, 19, 20; BlueB 76; CelR; ChhPo, S3; CnDAL; ConAmA; ConAu 3NR, 5R, 55NR, 128, 138; ConLCrt 77, 82; ConPo 70, 75, 80, 85; CurBio 79, 89N; CyWA 89; DcLB 4, 48, Y81A, Y89N; DcLEL; EncWL 2, 3; FacFETw; IntAu&W 76, 77, 82, 86, 89, 91;*

IntvTCA 2; IntWW 74, 75, 76, 77, 78, 79, 80, 81, 82, 83, 89, 91; IntWWP 77, 82; LiExTwC; LinLib L, S; MajTwCW; ModAL, S1, S2; News 89-3; NewYTBS 89; OxCAmL 65, 83, 95; OxCTwCP; PenC AM; RAdv 1, 14, 13-1; REn; REnAL; SixAP; TwCA, SUP; WebAB 74, 79; WebBD 83; WhAm 10; WhNAA; WhoAm 74, 76, 78, 80, 82, 84, 86, 88; WhoE 83, 85, 86, 89; WhoWor 74; WrDr 76, 80, 82, 84, 86, 88

Cowper, Steve Cambreleng
American. Politician
Democratic governor of Alaska, 1987-91, succeeded by Wally Hickel.
b. Aug 21, 1938 in Petersburg, Virginia
Source: *AlmAP 88; IntWW 89, 91, 93; WhoAm 88, 90; WhoAmP 87, 89, 91; WhoWest 87, 92; WhoWor 91*

Cowper, William
English. Poet
Wrote hymn "Oh for a Closer Walk with God," 1779.
b. Nov 15, 1731 in Berkhampstead, England
d. Apr 25, 1800 in Dereham, England
Source: *Alli; AnCL; AtlBL; BbD; Benet 87, 96; BiD&SB; BioIn 1, 2, 3, 4, 5, 6, 7, 8, 9, 11, 12, 13, 14, 15, 16, 17, 18, 19; BlmGEL; BritAu; BritWr 3; CamGEL; CamGLE; CarSB; CasWL; Chambr 2; ChhPo, S1, S2, S3; CnE&AP; CrtT 2, 4; CyEd; CyWA 58; DcArts; DcBiPP; DcEnA; DcEnL; DcEuL; DcLB 104, 109; DcLEL; DcNaB; Dis&D; EncEnl; EvLB; LinLib L, S; LngCEL; LuthC 75; McGEWB; MouLC 2; NewC; NinCLC 8; OxCEng 67, 85, 95; OxCMus; PenC ENG; PoChrch; RAdv 1, 14, 13-1; REn; RfGEnL 91; WebE&AL; WhDW; WorAl; WorAlBi*

Cowsills, The
[Barbara Cowsill; Barry Cowsill; John Cowsill; Paul Cowsill; Richard Cowsill; Robert Cowsill; Susan Cowsill; William Cowsill]
American. Music Group
Family group which inspired TV's "Partridge Family;" hit single theme from *Hair*, 1960s.
Source: *BiDAmM; EncRkSt; RkOn 78, 84; RolSEnR 83; WhoRock 81; WhoRocM 82*

Cox, Alex
English. Screenwriter
Wrote, directed cult films *Repo Man*, 1984; *Sid and Nancy*, 1986.
b. Dec 15, 1954 in Liverpool, England
Source: *BioIn 15; ConTFT 5, 10; HalFC 88; IntMPA 92, 94, 96; LegTOT; MiSFD 9*

Cox, Allyn
American. Artist
Known for completing mural in rotunda of US capitol, 1954, begun 100 yrs. earlier by Constantino Brumidi.
b. Jun 5, 1896 in New York, New York
d. Sep 26, 1982 in Washington, District of Columbia
Source: *BioIn 3, 10, 12, 13; CurBio 54, 83, 83N; NewYTBS 82; WhAm 9; WhAmArt 85; WhoAm 74, 76, 78, 80, 82; WhoAmA 73, 76, 78, 80, 82, 84, 84N, 86N, 89N, 91N, 93N*

Cox, Archibald
American. Lawyer
Watergate prosecutor fired by Solicitor General Robert Bork; replaced by Leon Jaworski.
b. May 17, 1912 in Plainfield, New Jersey
Source: *AuSpks; BioIn 3, 5, 6, 9, 10, 11, 12, 13, 16; BioNews 74; BlueB 76; ConAu 73; CurBio 61; DrAS 78P, 82P; EncWB; FacFETw; IntWW 74, 75, 76, 77, 78, 79, 80, 81, 82, 83, 89, 91, 93; LegTOT; PolProf J, K, NF; Who 82, 83, 85, 88, 90, 92, 94; WhoAm 74, 76, 78, 80, 82, 84, 86, 88, 90, 92, 94, 95, 96, 97; WhoAmL 78, 79, 83, 85, 96; WhoAmP 73, 75, 77, 79, 81, 83, 85, 87, 89, 91, 93, 95; WhoWor 78, 80, 82; WorAl; WorAlBi; WrDr 80, 82, 84, 86, 88, 90, 92, 94, 96*

Cox, Bobby
[Robert Joe]
American. Baseball Manager
Manager, Toronto, 1982-85; AL manager of year, 1985; manager, Atlanta, 1986—.
b. May 21, 1941 in Tulsa, Oklahoma
Source: *Ballpl 90; BaseReg 85; BioIn 19, 21; WhoAm 84, 90, 92, 94, 95, 96, 97; WhoE 85; WhoSSW 91, 95, 97*

Cox, Constance
English. Dramatist
Adapted classics for radio, TV; won Screenwriters Guild Award, 1967, for TV series "The Forsythe Saga."
b. Oct 25, 1915 in Sutton, England
Source: *Au&Wr 71; ConAu 9NR, 21R, 24NR; IntAu&W 82; WhoAmW 77; WhoThe 77, 81; WrDr 76, 80, 82, 84, 86, 88, 90*

Cox, Courteney
American. Actor
Stars in television's "Friends," 1994—.
b. Jun 15, 1964 in Birmingham, Alabama
Source: *ConTFT 7, 15; IntMPA 92, 94, 96; LegTOT; News 96, 96-2; WhoAm 96; WhoHol 92*

Cox, David
English. Artist
Watercolorist of country scenes; published *A Treatise on Landscape Painting*, 1814.
b. Apr 29, 1783 in Deritend, England
d. Jun 7, 1859 in Harborne, England
Source: *ArtsNiC; BioIn 1, 3, 4, 10, 11, 12, 13, 15; CelCen; ClaDrA; DcArts; DcBiPP; DcBrBI; DcBrWA; DcNaB; DcSeaP; DcVicP, 2; McGDA; NewCol 75; OxCArt; OxDcArt; WebBD 83*

Cox, Edward Finch
American. Lawyer
Married Tricia Nixon, Jun 1971.
b. Oct 2, 1946 in Southampton, New York
Source: *BioIn 9, 10; ConAu 29R; WhoAmL 83*

Cox, Gardner
American. Artist
Portrait painter whose subjects include Robert Frost, Dean Acheson, Robert Kennedy.
b. Jan 22, 1906 in Holyoke, Massachusetts
Source: *BioIn 3, 4, 11, 15, 21; NewYTBS 88; WhAm 9; WhAmArt 85; WhoAm 74, 76, 78, 80, 82, 84, 86, 88; WhoAmA 73, 76, 78, 80, 82, 84, 86; WhoWor 80, 82*

Cox, Harvey Gallagher, Jr.
American. Theologian, Social Reformer
Wrote *Secular City*, 1965; believes in socially relevant church.
b. May 19, 1929 in Chester County, Pennsylvania
Source: *AmAu&B; AmSocL; AuNews 1; BioIn 13, 16; ConAu 45, 77; CurBio 68; EncWB; FacFETw; Future; NewYTBS 88; RelLAm 91; TwCSAPR; WhoAm 74, 76, 78, 80, 82, 84, 86, 88, 90; WhoE 74; WhoRel 77, 85, 92; WorAu 1975; WrDr 86, 92*

Cox, Herald Rea
American. Bacteriologist
Developed Orimune, oral liquid polio vaccine, late 1950s, inoculations against Rocky Mountain spotted fever, typhus.
b. Feb 28, 1907 in Rosedale, Indiana
Source: *AmMWSc 76P, 79, 82, 86, 89, 92; BioIn 5, 6; CurBio 61; WhoAm 74*

Cox, Jacob Dolson
American. Government Official
Helped organize Rep. Party in Ohio, 1850s; secretary of interior, 1869-70; attacked patronage.
b. Oct 27, 1828 in Montreal, Quebec, Canada
d. Aug 8, 1900 in Magnolia, Massachusetts
Source: *Alli SUP; AmBi; ApCAB; BiAUS; BiDrAC; BiDrGov 1789; BiDrUSC 89; BiDrUSE 71, 89; BiInAmS; BioIn 3, 7, 10; CivWDc; DcAmAu; DcAmB; DcNAA; Drake; HarEnUS; NatCAB 3, 4, 22; NewCol 75; OhA&B; TwCBDA; WebAB 74, 79; WebAMB; WebBD 83; WhAm 1; WhAmP; WhCiWar*

Cox, James Middleton, Sr.
American. Politician
Dem. governor of OH, 1913-15, 1917-21; US presidential nominee, 1920.
b. Mar 31, 1870 in Jacksonburg, Ohio
d. Jul 15, 1957 in Dayton, Ohio
Source: *ABCMeAm; AmPolLe; ApCAB X; BiDAmJo; BiDInt; BiDrAC; BiDrGov 1789; BiDrUSC 89; BioIn 1, 2, 3, 4, 7, 8, 11; DcAmB S6; DcLB 127; FacFETw;*

JrnUS; LinLib L, S; NatCAB 15, 51; OhA&B; WhAm 3; WhAmP; WhFla

Cox, James Middleton, Jr.
American. Publisher
Pres., *Dayton Daily News,* 1949-56; *Dayton Journal-Herald,* 1948-56; Dayton Newspaper Inc., 1957-58.
b. Jun 27, 1903 in Dayton, Ohio
d. Oct 27, 1974 in Miami, Florida
Source: *BioIn 10; BioNews 74; ConAu 89; DcAmB S9; NewYTBS 74; St&PR 75; WhAm 6; WhoAm 74; WhoMW 74*

Cox, Jean
American. Opera Singer
Outstanding Heldentenor; Bayreuth debut, 1956; acclaimed as Siegfried.
b. Jan 16, 1932 in Gadsden, Alabama
Source: *Baker 84; BioIn 9; IntWWM 90; MetOEnc; NewGrDA 86; PenDiMP; WhoOp 76*

Cox, John Rogers
American. Artist
Landscape painter known for color design *Gray and Gold,* 1942.
b. Mar 24, 1915 in Terre Haute, Indiana
Source: *BioIn 1, 2; DcLP 87A; GrAmP; WhAmArt 85; WhoAm 74, 76, 78; WhoAmA 76, 78, 80, 82, 84*

Cox, Kenyon
American. Artist
Paintings are mainly portraits, figure pieces; also did murals, wrote *Concerning Painting,* 1917.
b. Oct 27, 1856 in Warren, Ohio
d. Mar 17, 1919 in New York, New York
Source: *AmAu&B; AmBi; AmLY; ApCAB; ArtsAmW 1; BioIn 15, 19, 21; BriEAA; ChhPo, S1; DcAmArt; DcAmB; DcNAA; LinLib S; McGDA; NatCAB 5; OhA&B; TwCBDA; WhAm 1; WhAmArt 85*

Cox, Palmer
Canadian. Author, Illustrator
Created "Brownies," series of 14 books for children.
b. Apr 28, 1840 in Granby, Quebec, Canada
d. Jul 24, 1924 in Granby, Quebec, Canada
Source: *Alli SUP; AmAu; AmAu&B; AmBi; ApCAB; ArtsAmW 1; AuBYP 2S, 3; BbD; BenetAL 91; BiD&SB; BioIn 10, 13, 15; CarSB; ChhPo, S1, S2, S3; ChlBkCr; ChlLR 24; CmCal; ConAu 111; DcAmAu; DcAmB; DcLB 42; DcNAA; JBA 34; LinLib L, S; MnBBF; NatCAB 7; OxCAmL 65, 83, 95; OxCChiL; SmATA 24; TwCBDA; TwCChW 83A, 89A, 95A; WhAm 1; WhAmArt 85; WhLit; WorECar*

Cox, Richard Joseph
American. TV Executive
Pres., CBS Cable Division, 1981-83; owner, pres., DCA TV Inc., 1983-90.
b. Aug 21, 1929 in New York, New York
Source: *BioIn 13, 15; ConNews 85-1; WhoAm 78, 80, 82, 84, 86, 88, 90, 92, 94, 95, 96, 97; WhoE 89; WhoEnt 92*

Cox, Wally
[Wallace Maynard Cox]
American. Actor, Comedian
Starred in "Mr. Peepers," 1952-55; regular on "Hollywood Squares."
b. Dec 6, 1924 in Detroit, Michigan
d. Feb 15, 1973 in Los Angeles, California
Source: *BioIn 2, 3, 4, 7, 9, 10, 13; ConAu 41R, 97; CurBio 54, 73, 73N; DcAmB S9; EncAFC; FilmgC; HalFC 84, 88; LegTOT; NewYTBE 73; NewYTET; NotNAT A, B; SmATA 25; WhAm 5; WhoCom; WhoHol B; WhScrn 77, 83; WorAl; WorAlBi*

Coxe, George Harmon
American. Author
Wrote over 60 mystery novels, had several series characters.
b. Apr 23, 1901 in Olean, New York
d. Jan 30, 1984 in Hilton Head Island, South Carolina
Source: *AmAu&B; BioIn 10, 14; ConAu 57; CrtSuMy; EncMys; MnBBF; Novels; REnAL; TwCCr&M 80, 85, 91; WhAm 8; WhoAm 74, 76, 78, 80, 82; WorAu 1950; WrDr 82, 84*

Coxe, Louis Osborne
American. Poet
Wrote blank-verse narrative poem, "The Middle Passage," 1960.
b. 1918 in Manchester, New Hampshire
d. May 25, 1993 in Augusta, Maine
Source: *AmAu&B; BenetAL 91; BiE&WWA; ConAu 13R; ConPo 75, 91; DrAP 75; DrAPF 91; IntAu&W 91; IntWWP 82; McGEWD 84; NotNAT; OxCAmL 65, 83; WhAm 11; WhoAm 86; WorAu 1950; WrDr 86, 92*

Coxey, Jacob Sechler
American. Social Reformer
Leader of 1894 march of unemployed on Washington, DC.
b. Apr 16, 1854 in Selinsgrove, Pennsylvania
d. May 18, 1951 in Massillon, Ohio
Source: *AmRef; AmSocL; BioIn 2, 3, 4, 6, 7, 8, 9, 11, 15, 19, 20; DcAmB S5; DcAmSR; EncAB-H 1974, 1996; GayN; HarEnUS; McGEWB; NatCAB 46; OhA&B; WebAB 74, 79; WhAm 3; WorAl*

Coy, Harold
American. Children's Author
Non-fiction books include *The First Book of Presidents,* 1973.
b. Sep 24, 1902 in La Habre, California
Source: *AuBYP 2, 3; BioIn 7, 9; ConAu 4NR, 5R; IntAu&W 76, 77; SmATA 3; WrDr 76, 80, 82, 84*

Cozzens, James Gould
American. Author
Awarded Pulitzer for *Guard of Honor,* 1948.
b. Aug 19, 1903 in Chicago, Illinois
d. Aug 9, 1978 in Stuart, Florida
Source: *AmAu&B; AmNov; AmWr; Benet 87, 96; BenetAL 91; BioIn 1, 2, 4, 5, 7, 8, 9, 10, 11, 12, 13, 14, 15, 17; BlueB 76; CamGLE; CamHAL; CasWL; CnDAL; ConAmA; ConAu 9NR, 9R, 19NR, 81; ConLC 1, 4, 11, 92; ConNov 72, 76; CurBio 69, 78N; CyWA 58, 89; DcAmB S10; DcAmC; DcLB 9, DS2, Y84A; DcLEL; DcTwCCu 1; DrAF 76; EncWL, 2, 3; FacFETw; IntAu&W 76, 77; IntWW 74, 75, 76, 77, 78; LegTOT; LinLib L, S; LngCTC; MajTwCW; ModAL, S2; NatCAB 61; NewCon; Novels; OxCAmL 65, 83, 95; PenC AM; RAdv 1, 14, 13-1; REn; REnAL; RfGAmL 87, 94; RGTwCWr; ScF&FL 1, 2; TwCA, SUP; TwCWr; WebAB 74, 79; WebE&AL; WhAm 7; Who 74; WhoAm 74, 76, 78; WhoWor 74; WorAl; WorAlBi; WrDr 76*

Crabbe, Buster
[Larry; Clarence Linden]
American. Actor, Swimmer
Starred as Flash Gordon, Buck Rogers in 1930s-40s movie serials.
b. Feb 17, 1908 in Oakland, California
d. Apr 23, 1983 in Scottsdale, Arizona
Source: *AnObit 1983; BioIn 4, 6, 7, 8, 10, 11, 12, 13, 14; ConAu 69; FilmEn; FilmgC; IntDcF 1-3, 2-3; IntMPA 82; MotPP; WhoAm 82; WhoHol A; WorAl; WorAlBi*

Crabbe, George
English. Poet
Wrote realistic narrative poems, "The Village," 1783; "The Borough," 1810.
b. Dec 24, 1754 in Aldeburgh, England
d. Feb 3, 1832 in Trowbridge, England
Source: *Alli; AtlBL; BbD; Benet 87, 96; BiD&SB; BiDLA, SUP; BioIn 1, 2, 3, 4, 5, 7, 8, 9, 10, 11, 12, 16, 17, 20; BlmGEL; BritAu 19; BritWr 3; CamGEL; CasWL; CelCen; Chambr 2; ChhPo, S1, S2, S3; CnE&AP; CrtT 2; CyWA 58; DcArts; DcBiPP; DcEnA; DcEnL; DcEuL; DcLB 93; DcLEL; DcNaB, C; Dis&D; EvLB; LinLib L, S; LngCEL; McGEWB; MouLC 3; NewC; NewGrDO; NinCLC 26; OxCEng 67, 85, 95; OxCMed 86; PenC ENG; PoChrch; RAdv 1, 14, 13-1; REn; RfGEnL 91; WebE&AL; WhDW*

Crabtree, Lotta
American. Actor
Began career entertaining in CA mining camps; appeared in *Old Curiosity Shop,* 1867.
b. Nov 7, 1847 in New York, New York
d. Sep 25, 1924 in Boston, Massachusetts
Source: *AmBi; AmWom; ApCAB; BioAmW; BioIn 1, 2, 5, 6, 8, 11, 15, 16, 17; CmCal; DcAmB; FamA&A; FunnyW; HerW; InWom, SUP; LibW;*

NewCol 75; NewGrDA 86; NotAW; NotNAT A; NotWoAT; OxCAmL 65; TwCBDA; WebAB 74, 79

Craddock, Crash
[Billy Craddock]
"Mr. Country Rock"
American. Singer
Rock and roll performer; member, Dream Lovers since 1974; had hit song "Knock Three Times," 1971.
b. Jun 16, 1940 in Greensboro, North Carolina
Source: *BioIn 14; CounME 74; HarEnCM 87; IlEncCM; PenEncP; WhoAm 86; WhoEnt 92*

Craft, Christine
American. Broadcast Journalist
Sued former employer for age, sex discrimination, 1983; awarded $500,000.
b. 1945? in Canton, Ohio
Source: *BioIn 13, 14; NewYTBS 83*

Craft, Ellen
American. Slave, Abolitionist
Escaped slavery during Civil War; prominent in Boston antislavery movement.
b. 1826 in Clinton, California
d. 1897 in Charleston, South Carolina
Source: *BioIn 18, 21; BlkWAm; DcAmNB; HerW, 84; InB&W 80, 85; InWom SUP; NotAW; NotBlAW 1*

Craft, Robert
American. Conductor
Musical asst., adviser to Igor Stravinsky for 23 yrs.
b. Oct 20, 1923 in Kingston, New York
Source: *AmAu&B; Baker 78, 84; BioIn 5, 7, 8, 9, 10, 11, 13, 14, 16; ConAu 7NR, 9R; CurBio 84; IntAu&W 91, 93; IntWWM 90; NewAmDM; NewGrDA 86; PenDiMP; PeoHis; WhoAm 78, 80, 82, 84, 86; WhoMus 72; WhoWor 74; WorAu 1970; WrDr 76, 80, 82, 84, 86, 88, 90, 92, 94*

Crafts, James Mason
American. Chemist
Research included work on silicon derivatives, catalysis and thermometry.
b. Mar 8, 1839 in Boston, Massachusetts
d. Jun 20, 1917 in Ridgefield, Connecticut
Source: *Alli SUP; AmBi; ApCAB; AsBiEn; BiDAmS; BiESc; BiInAmS; DcAmAu; DcAmB; DcInv; DcNAA; InSci; NatCAB 13; TwCBDA; WhAm 1*

Craig, Cleo F
American. Business Executive
Pres., chm., AT&T, 1951-57.
b. Apr 6, 1895 in Rich Hill, Missouri
d. Apr 21, 1978 in Ridgewood, New Jersey
Source: *CurBio 51, 78; ObitOF 79*

Craig, George N(orth)
American. Politician
Rep. governor, IN, 1953-56.
b. Aug 6, 1909 in Brazil, Indiana
d. Dec 17, 1992 in Indianapolis, Indiana
Source: *BiDrGov 1789; BioIn 2, 3, 4, 18, 19; CurBio 50, 93N; WhoAm 74, 76*

Craig, Gordon
[Edward Henry Gordon Craig]
English. Designer
Published *The Mask,* 1908-29, which featured his designs, theories of stagecraft; wrote *On the Art of the Theatre,* 1911.
b. Jan 16, 1872 in Harpenden, England
d. Jul 30, 1966 in Vence, France
Source: *BioIn 3, 4, 5, 6, 7, 8, 10, 11, 12, 13; CamGWoT; DcNaB 1961; FacFETw; GrBr; GrStDi; LngCTC; OxCEng 85; OxCThe 67, 83; OxCTwCA; OxDcArt; PhDcTCA 77; PlP&P; REn; TwCA, SUP; WhDW*

Craig, Helen
English. Children's Author, Illustrator
Wrote, illustrated prize-winning *Mouse House* series, 1978-83.
b. Aug 30, 1934 in London, England
Source: *AuBYP 3; BioIn 15, 16; ChlBkCr; ConAu 117; SmATA 46, 49*

Craig, Jim
[James Craig]
American. Hockey Player
Goalie, member US Olympic gold medal-winning team, 1980; in NHL, 1980-81.
b. May 31, 1957 in North Easton, Massachusetts
Source: *BioIn 12, 13; HocEn; HocReg 81; NewYTBS 80; WhoSpor*

Craig, Larry Edwin
American. Politician
Rep. senator, ID, 1990—.
b. Jul 20, 1945 in Council, Idaho
Source: *AlmAP 92; BiDrUSC 89; CngDr 89; IntWW 91, 93; PolsAm 84; WhoAm 82, 84, 86, 88, 90, 92, 94, 95, 96, 97; WhoAmP 75, 77, 79, 81, 83, 85, 87, 89, 91, 93, 95; WhoE 95; WhoWest 82, 84, 87, 89, 92, 94, 96*

Craig, Malin
American. Military Leader, Government Official
Commanded every type of military unit; US Army chief of staff, 1935-39.
b. Aug 5, 1875 in Saint Joseph, Missouri
d. Jul 25, 1945 in Washington, District of Columbia
Source: *BiDWWGF; BioIn 3; CmdGen 1991; CurBio 44, 45; DcAmB S3; DcAmMiB; NatCAB 37; WebAMB; WhAm 2*

Craig, May
Irish. Actor
Played in first production of *Playboy of the Western World,* 1907.
b. 1889, Ireland
d. Feb 9, 1972 in Dublin, Ireland
Source: *ConAu 89, 101; DcIrB 78, 88; InWom SUP; NewYTBE 72; NewYTBS 75; ObitOF 79; WhoHol B; WhScrn 77, 83*

Craig, May
[Elizabeth May Craig]
American. Journalist
Served as war correspondent in 1944; popular panelist on "Meet the Press;" noted for persistent questioning at presidential news conferences.
b. Dec 24, 1889 in Coosaw, South Carolina
d. Jul 15, 1975 in Silver Spring, Maryland
Source: *BioIn 1, 2, 10; ConAu 89, 101; CurBio 49, 75, 75N; DcIrB 78, 88; EncAJ; InWom, SUP; NotAW MOD; WhoHol B; WhScrn 77, 83*

Craig, Roger Lee
American. Baseball Manager, Baseball Player
Pitcher, 1955-66; manager, San Diego, 1978-79, San Francisco, 1985-92; known for teaching pitchers split-finger fastball.
b. Feb 17, 1931 in Durham, North Carolina
Source: *BaseReg 87; BioIn 6; WhoAm 88; WhoProB 73; WhoWest 92*

Craig, Roger Timothy
American. Football Player
Fullback, San Francisco, 1983-91; LA, 1991-92; Minnesota, 1992—; set NFL record by becoming the first player ever to run, catch passes for 1,000 yds., 1985.
b. Jul 10, 1960 in Preston, Mississippi
Source: *BioIn 14; FootReg 86, 87; InB&W 85; WhoAm 90; WhoBlA 85, 88, 90, 92; WhoWest 89, 92*

Craig, Wendy
English. Actor
Won BBC TV personality award for "The Nanny," 1970.
b. Jun 20, 1930 in Sacriston, England
Source: *FilmgC; HalFC 88; WhoHol A; WhoThe 81*

Craik, Dinah Maria Mulock
English. Author
Noted for novel *John Halifax, Gentleman,* 1857.
b. Apr 20, 1826 in Stoke-on-Trent, England
d. Oct 12, 1887 in Bromley, England
Source: *Alli SUP; AnCL; ArtclWW 2; BbD; BiD&SB; BioIn 14, 16, 19; BlmGEL; BritAu 19; CarSB; CasWL; ChhPo, S1, S2; DcEnA, A; DcEuL; DcLEL; EncBrWW; EvLB; FamSYP; HsB&A; InWom, SUP; JBA 34; MajAI; NewC; OxCEng 95; REn; ScF&FL 1; Str&VC; VicBrit*

Crain, Jeanne
American. Actor
Oscar nominee for *Pinky,* 1949.
b. May 25, 1925 in Barstow, California
Source: *BiDFilm, 94; BioIn 2, 8, 9, 11; CurBio 51; FilmgC; HalFC 84, 88; IntDcF 1-3; IntMPA 75, 76, 77, 78, 79, 81, 82, 84, 86, 88, 92, 94, 96; InWom, SUP; ItaFilm; LegTOT; MotPP; MovMk; WhoAm 74, 76; WhoAmW 58, 66, 68, 70, 72, 74; WhoHol 92, A; WorAl; WorAlBi; WorEFlm*

Cram, Donald James
American. Chemist
Shared 1987 Nobel Prize in chemistry for developing synthetic molecules that perform like proteins.
b. Apr 22, 1919 in Chester, Vermont
Source: *AmMWSc 76P, 79, 82, 86, 89, 92, 95; BiESc; BioIn 3, 7, 15, 16; FacFETw; IntWW 76, 77, 78, 79, 80, 81, 82, 83, 89, 91, 93; LarDcSc; McGMS 80; NewYTBS 87; Who 90, 92, 94; WhoAm 74, 76, 78, 80, 82, 84, 86, 88, 90, 92, 94, 95, 96, 97; WhoFrS 84; WhoNob 90, 95; WhoScEn 94, 96; WhoUSWr 88; WhoWest 89, 92, 94, 96; WhoWor 89, 91, 93, 95, 96, 97; WhoWrEP 89, 92, 95; WorAlBi*

Cram, Ralph Adams
American. Architect
Gothic revivalist whose works include churches, colleges including Cathedral of John the Divine, NYC, 1912.
b. Dec 16, 1863 in Hampton Falls, New Hampshire
d. Sep 22, 1942 in Boston, Massachusetts
Source: *AmAu&B; AmBi; AmCulL; AmDec 1910; AmLY; BiD&SB; BioIn 13, 15, 19, 21; BriEAA; DcAmAu; DcAmB S3; DcAmC; DcNAA; DcTwDes; EncAAr 1; FacFETw; IntDcAr; MacEA; McGDA; ModArCr 3; NatCAB 15; OxCAmH; OxCAmL 65; PenEncH; REnAL; ScF&FL 1, 92; TwCLC 45; WebAB 74, 79; WebBD 83; WhAm 2, 4A, HSA; WhNAA; WhoArch; WhoHr&F*

Cramer, Floyd
"Mister Keyboards"
American. Singer, Pianist
Member, Grand Ole Opry, 1950s-60s; wrote hit instrumental "Last Date," 1960; established the "Cramer Style."
b. Oct 27, 1933 in Shreveport, Louisiana
Source: *BgBkCoM; BiDAmM; BioIn 14; CounME 74; EncFCWM 69, 83; EncRk 88; HarEnCM 87; IlEncCM; LegTOT; PenEncP; RkOn 74; RolSEnR 83; WhoRock 81*

Cramer, Johann Baptist
German. Pianist, Composer
Wrote sonatas, famed pianoforte studies; founded English firm for publishing, piano-making.
b. Feb 24, 1771 in Mannheim, Germany
d. Apr 16, 1858 in London, England
Source: *Baker 78, 84, 92; BioIn 5, 7, 16; CelCen; DcNaB; NewCol 75; NewOxM; OxCMus; WebBD 83*

Cramm, Gottfried von, Baron
German. Tennis Player, Socialite
One of the outstanding games in tennis history was his five-set loss to Don Budge, 1937.
b. 1909
d. Nov 8, 1976 in Cairo, Egypt
Source: *BioIn 11; EncTR 91; ObitOF 79*

Cramp, Charles Henry
American. Shipping Executive, Architect
Pres., Cramp Shipbuilding Co., 1879-1903.
b. May 9, 1828 in Philadelphia, Pennsylvania
d. Jun 6, 1913 in Philadelphia, Pennsylvania
Source: *AmBi; ApCAB SUP; BiDAmBL 83; DcAmB; HarEnUS; NatCAB 5; OxCShps; TwCBDA; WhAm 1*

Crampton, Bruce Sidney
"Iron Man"
Australian. Golfer
Turned pro, 1957; sixth player to win $1 million on tour (1973).
b. Sep 28, 1935 in Sydney, Australia
Source: *BioIn 13, 15; NewYTBS 75; WhoAm 74, 76, 78, 80, 82, 84, 86, 88; WhoGolf; WhoSSW 84*

Cranach, Lucas
[Lucas Kranach; Lucas Muller]
"The Elder"
German. Artist, Designer
Originated Protestant religious painting; known for altarpieces, portraits of Martin Luther, other reformer friends; court painter to electors of Saxony, 1552-53.
b. Oct 4, 1472 in Kronach, Germany
d. Oct 16, 1553 in Weimar, Germany
Source: *AtlBL; Benet 87, 96; BioIn 4, 5, 6, 7, 8, 9, 10, 14; ClaDrA; DcArts; DcBiPP; Dis&D; IntDcAA 90; LinLib S; LuthC 75; McGDA; McGEWB; OxCArt; OxDcArt; REn; WebBD 83; WhDW; WorAl; WorAlBi*

Crandall, Del(mar Wesley)
American. Baseball Player, Baseball Manager
Catcher, 1949-66; four-time All-Star; manager, 1972-75, 1983-84.
b. Mar 5, 1930 in Ontario, California
Source: *Ballpl 90; BioIn 5, 6, 8, 21; WhoAm 74; WhoProB 73*

Crandall, Prudence
American. Educator, Abolitionist
Tried unsuccessfully, to open school for Negro girls; prosecuted in famed case.
b. Sep 3, 1803 in Hopkinton, Rhode Island
d. Jan 28, 1889 in Elk Falls, Kansas
Source: *AmBi; AmRef; ApCAB; BiDAmEd; BioAmW; BioIn 4, 5, 6, 7, 9, 10, 11, 15, 17, 21; DcAmB; EncWHA; GoodHs; GrLiveH; HerW, 84; InWom, SUP; LibW; McGEWB; NatCAB 2; NewCol 75; NotAW; PeoHis; RComAH; TwCBDA; WebAB 74, 79; WhAm HS; WhAmP*

Crandall, Robert Lloyd
American. Airline Executive
Chm., pres., CEO, American Airlines/AMR Corp., 1985—.
b. Dec 6, 1935 in Westerly, Rhode Island
Source: *BioIn 12, 14, 15, 16; CurBio 92; Dun&B 90; IntWW 81, 82, 83, 89, 91, 93; News 92, 92-1; NewYTBS 84, 90; St&PR 84, 87, 91, 93, 96, 97; WhoAm 78, 82, 84, 86, 88, 90, 92, 94, 95, 96, 97; WhoFI 83, 85, 87, 89, 92, 94, 96; WhoSSW 82, 84, 86, 88, 91, 93, 95, 97; WhoWor 82, 84, 87, 89, 91, 95, 96, 97*

Crane, Bob
American. Actor
Played Colonel Robert Hogan in "Hogan's Heroes," 1965-71.
b. Jul 13, 1928 in Waterbury, Connecticut
d. Jun 29, 1978 in Scottsdale, Arizona
Source: *BioIn 11, 78; WhoAm 74; WhoHol A*

Crane, Cheryl
American.
Daughter of Lana Turner; killed mother's lover, gangster Johnny Stompanato, 1958; wrote autobiography *Detour: A Hollywood Story,* 1988.
b. Jul 26, 1943 in Hollywood, California
Source: *BioIn 15, 16; InWom SUP*

Crane, Daniel B
American. Politician
Rep. congressman from IL, 1979-85; censured by US House, Jul 1983, for sexual relations with page.
b. Jan 10, 1936 in Chicago, Illinois
Source: *AlmAP 80, 82, 84; BiDrUSC 89; BioIn 13; CngDr 79, 81, 83; PolsAm 84; WhoAm 80, 82, 84; WhoAmP 79, 81, 83, 85, 95; WhoMW 80, 82, 84*

Crane, Eva
English. Scientist
Director, International Bee Research Association, 1949-83.
b. Jun 12, 1912 in Wallington, England
Source: *BioIn 19; CurBio 93; WomStre*

Crane, Hart
[Harold Hart Crane]
American. Poet
Major poetry collections: *White Buildings,* 1926; *The Bridge,* 1930.
b. Jul 21, 1899 in Garrettsville, Ohio
d. Apr 27, 1932, At Sea
Source: *AmCulL; Benet 87; BenetAL 91; BioIn 1, 2, 3, 4, 5, 6, 7, 8, 9, 10, 11, 12, 13, 15, 16, 17, 19; CamGEL; CamGLE; CamHAL; ConAu 104, 127; DcAmB S1; DcLB 4, 48; EncAB-H 1974, 1996; EncWL 2, 3; FacFETw; LegTOT; LinLib L; LngCTC; MagSAmL; MajTwCW;*

MakMC; McGEWB; ModAL, S1, S2; OhA&B; OxCAmH; OxCAmL 65, 83; OxCEng 67, 85; PenC AM; PeoHis; PoeCrit 3; RAdv 1, 14, 13-1; REn; REnAL; RfGAmL 87; SixAP; Tw; TwCA, SUP; TwCLC 2, 5; TwCWr; WebAB 74, 79; WebE&AL; WhAm 1; WhDW; WhoTwCL; WorAl; WorAlBi; WorLitC

Crane, Nathalia Clara Ruth
American. Poet, Author
Wrote notable verse collection: *Janitor's Boy* at age 11.
b. Aug 11, 1913 in New York, New York
Source: *AmAu&B; BenetAL 91; ConAmL; DcLEL; InWom SUP; OxCAmL 83; REnAL; ScF&FL 1; WhLit*

Crane, Philip Miller
American. Politician
Conservative congressman who competed with Reagan for presidential nomination, 1980.
b. Nov 3, 1930 in Chicago, Illinois
Source: *AlmAP 82, 92; ASCAP 66; BiDrAC; BiDrUSC 89; BioIn 11, 12, 15; CngDr 83, 89; ConAu 9R; CurBio 80; DcAmC; DrAS 74H; PolsAm 84; WhoAm 74, 76, 78, 80, 82, 84, 86, 88, 90, 92, 94, 95, 96, 97; WhoAmP 73, 75, 77, 79, 81, 83, 85, 87, 89, 91, 93, 95; WhoE 95; WhoGov 72, 75, 77; WhoMW 74, 76, 78, 80, 82, 84, 86, 88, 90, 92, 93, 96; WhoWor 96, 97*

Crane, Roy(ston Campbell)
American. Cartoonist
Wrote "Buz Sawyer" cartoon, 1943-77.
b. Nov 22, 1901 in Abilene, Texas
d. Jul 7, 1977 in Orlando, Florida
Source: *BioIn 13; ConAu 89; EncACom; EncTwCJ; SmATA 22N; WhAm 7; WhAmArt 85; WhoAm 74, 76, 78; WhoAmA 73, 76, 78, 80N, 82N, 84N, 86N, 89N, 91N; WhoWor 74; WorECom*

Crane, Stephen
American. Author
Wrote novels *Maggie: A Girl of the Streets,* 1893; *The Red Badge of Courage,* 1895.
b. Nov 1, 1871 in Newark, New Jersey
d. Jun 5, 1900 in Badenweiler, Germany
Source: *AmAu; AmAu&B; AmBi; AmWr; ApCAB SUP; AtlBL; BbD; Benet 87; BenetAL 91; BiDAmJo; BiD&SB; BioIn 1, 2, 3, 4, 5, 6, 7, 8, 9, 10, 11, 12, 13, 14, 15, 16, 17, 18, 19, 20, 21; CamGEL; CamGLE; CamHAL; CasWL; Chambr 3; ChhPo, S3; CnDAL; CnE&AP; ConAu 109; CrtT 3, 4; CyWA 58; DcAmAu; DcAmB; DcArts; DcLB 12, 54, 78; DcLEL; DcNAA; EncAAH; EncAB-H 1974, 1996; EncAJ; EncFWF; EvLB; GayN; HalFC 84, 88; HarEnUS; JrnUS; LegTOT; LiJour; LinLib L; LngCTC; MagSAmL; McGEWB; ModAL; NatCAB 10; Novels; OxCAmL 65, 83, 95; OxCEng 67, 85, 95; OxCTwCP; PenC AM; PenEncH; PeoHis; RAdv 1, 14, 13-1; RComAH; RComWL; RealN; REn; REnAL; RfGAmL 87, 94; RfGShF; ShSCr 7; ShSWr; TwCBDA; TwCLC 11, 17, 32; WebAB 74, 79; WebE&AL; WhAm 1; WhCiWar; WhDW; WhFla; WorAlBi; WorLitC; YABC 2*

Crane, Walter
English. Illustrator
Noted decorative illustrator, especially of Victorian children's books; prominent in arts, crafts movement, from 1880s.
b. Aug 15, 1845 in Liverpool, England
d. Mar 15, 1915 in London, England
Source: *Alli SUP; AntBDN A, B; ArtsNiC; BioIn 1, 2, 3, 8, 10, 12, 14, 15, 16, 19; CamGLE; CarSB; CelCen; ChhPo, S1, S2, S3; ChlBkCr; ClaDrA; DcArts; DcBrAr 1; DcBrBI; DcBrWA; DcLB 163; DcNaB 1912; DcNiCA; DcTwDes; DcVicP, 2; IlsBYP; JBA 34, 51; LinLib L, S; MacEA; MajAI; McGDA; NewC; OxCArt; OxCChiL; OxCDecA; OxCEng 85, 95; OxDcArt; PenDiDA 89; RAdv 14; SmATA 18; StaCVF; Str&VC; VicBrit; WhLit; WhoChL*

Cranko, John
South African. Dancer, Choreographer
Transformed Stuttgart ballet into major int'l. company, 1961-73.
b. Aug 15, 1927 in Rustenburg, South Africa
d. Jun 26, 1973 in Stuttgart, Germany (West)
Source: *BiDD; BioIn 3, 4, 6, 8, 9, 10, 11, 13, 14; ConAu 45; CurBio 70, 73, 73N; DcArts; EncSoA; FacFETw; IntDcB; NewOxM; NewYTBE 73; ObitOF 79; ObitT 1971; OxCThe 83; WhoWor 74*

Crankshaw, Edward
English. Journalist
Britain's journalistic expert on Soviet policies; wrote *Russia Without Stalin,* 1956.
b. Jan 3, 1909 in Woodford, England
d. Nov 29, 1984, England
Source: *AnObit 1984; BioIn 2, 4, 5, 14; ConAu 23NR, 25R, 114; DcNaB 1981; IntAu&W 76, 77; LngCTC; NewYTBS 84; TwCA SUP; WhE&EA; Who 74, 82, 83, 85; WhoWor 74, 76*

Cranmer, Thomas
English. Religious Leader
Archbishop of Canterbury, 1533; burned at stake for promoting English Reformation, 1556.
b. Jul 2, 1489 in Aslacton, England
d. Mar 21, 1556 in Oxford, England
Source: *Alli; Benet 87, 96; BioIn 1, 2, 3, 4, 5, 6, 7, 8, 9, 10, 11, 12, 19, 20; BlmGEL; BritAu; CamGEL; CamGLE; CasWL; Chambr 1; CroE&S; DcBiPP; DcEnL; DcLB 132; DcLEL; DcNaB; EvLB; LinLib L, S; LngCEL; LuthC 75; McGEWB; NewC; OxCEng 67, 85, 95; OxCMus; PenC ENG; RAdv 14; REn; WebE&AL; WhDW; WorAl; WorAlBi*

Cranston, Alan MacGregor
American. Politician
Dem. senator from CA, 1969-92.
b. Jun 19, 1914 in Palo Alto, California
Source: *AlmAP 92; BiDrAC; BiDrUSC 89; BioIn 13, 16; CngDr 89; CurBio 69; IntWW 74, 91; NewYTBS 90; PolsAm 84; WhoAm 86, 90; WhoAmP 73, 75, 77, 79, 81, 83, 85, 87, 89, 91, 93, 95; WhoGov 72, 75, 77; WhoWest 92; WhoWor 80, 82, 84, 87, 91; WorAl; WorAlBi*

Cranston, Toller
Canadian. Skater
Innovative figure skater; won bronze medal, 1976 Olympics.
b. Apr 20, 1949 in Hamilton, Ontario, Canada
Source: *BioIn 11; CanWW 31, 79, 80, 81, 83, 89; NewYTBS 77*

Crapper, Thomas
English. Engineer
Invented valve and siphon arrangement that made modern flush toilet possible.
b. 1837 in Yorkshire, England
d. Jan 17, 1910
Source: *BioIn 8; WorAl; WorAlBi*

Crapsey, Adelaide
American. Poet
Her poetry was posthumously published in *Verse,* 1914; invented "cinquain verse form."
b. Sep 9, 1878 in New York, New York
d. Oct 8, 1914 in Saranac Lake, New York
Source: *AmAu&B; AmWomWr; ArtclWW 2; BenetAL 91; BioAmW; BioIn 11, 12, 15; ChhPo; CnDAL; ConAmL; DcAmB; DcLB 54; DcNAA; FemiCLE; InWom, SUP; LibW; NotAW; OxCAmL 65, 83, 95; OxCTwCP; REn; REnAL; TwCA; WomWWA 14*

Crashaw, Richard
English. Poet
Best known for writing religious verses.
b. 1613 in London, England
d. Aug 21, 1649 in Loreto, Italy
Source: *Alli; AtlBL; BiD&SB; BiDRP&D; BioIn 1, 2, 3, 5, 6, 7, 9, 10, 11, 12, 17, 19; BritAu; BritWr 2; CasWL; Chambr 1; CnE&AP; CroE&S; CrtT 1; DcArts; DcEnA; DcEnL; DcEuL; DcLEL; DcNaB, C; EvLB; LitC 24; LuthC 75; McGEWB; MouLC 1; NewC; OxCEng 67; PenC ENG; RAdv 1, 14, 13-1; REn; WebE&AL; WhDW*

Crassus, Marcus Licinius Dives
"The Rich"
Roman. Army Officer
With Pompey and Caesar organized First Triumvirate, 60; governor of Syria, 54.
b. 115BC
d. Jun 6, 53BC in Carrhae, Mesopotamia
Source: *REn; WebBD 83*

Crater, Joseph Force
American. Judge
NY Supreme Court jurist; disappeared in 1930; declared legally dead after no trace of him was found; sensational case hinted of political corruption.
b. 1889 in Easton, Pennsylvania
d. 1937?
Source: *BioIn 2, 3, 5, 6, 12, 13, 18; WebAB 74, 79*

Craveirinha, Jose
[Jose G. Vetrinha; Mario Vieira]
"Poet of Mozambique"
Mozambican. Poet, Writer
Played important role in the development of Mozambican Negritude poetry; wrote "I Am Coal."
b. May 28, 1922 in Lourenco Marques, Portuguese East Africa
Source: *AfrA; BioIn 14*

Craven, Frank
American. Actor
Played stage manager in Broadway, film versions of *Our Town.*
b. Aug 24, 1875 in Boston, Massachusetts
d. Sep 1, 1945 in Beverly Hills, California
Source: *AmAu&B; CamGWoT; CurBio 45; DcAmB S3; EncAFC; FilmgC; HalFC 84, 88; MotPP; MovMk; NotNAT B; ObitOF 79; OxCAmT 84; OxCThe 67; Vers A; WhAm 2; WhoHol B; WhScrn 74, 77, 83; WhThe*

Craven, Thomas
American. Critic
Art popularizer, 1930s, promoting American regional art.
b. Jan 6, 1889 in Salina, Kansas
d. Feb 27, 1969
Source: *Alli SUP; AmAu&B; AuBYP 2, 3; BioIn 13; ConAu 97; CurBio 44, 69; REnAL; SmATA 22; TwCA, SUP; WhAm 5*

Crawford, Broderick
[William Broderick Crawford]
American. Actor
Won Oscar, 1949, for *All the King's Men;* known for TV's "Highway Patrol," 1955-59.
b. Dec 9, 1911 in Philadelphia, Pennsylvania
d. Apr 26, 1986 in Rancho Mirage, California
Source: *AnObit 1986; BiDFilm, 94; BiE&WWA; BioIn 2, 4, 6, 7, 10, 11, 14, 15; BioNews 74; CelR; ConNews 86-3; CurBio 50, 86N; EncAFC; FilmgC; GangFlm; IntDcF 1-3, 2-3; IntMPA 75, 76, 77, 78, 79, 81, 82, 84, 86; LegTOT; MotPP; MovMk; NewYTBS 77, 86; WhoAm 74, 76, 78, 80, 82, 84; WhoHol A; WhoWor 74; WorAl; WorAlBi; WorEFlm*

Crawford, Cheryl
American. Producer
Started Actors Studio, 1947, with Robert Lewis, Elia Kazan; produced Broadway hit *Brigadoon.*
b. Sep 24, 1902 in Akron, Ohio
d. Oct 7, 1986 in New York, New York
Source: *AnObit 1986; BiE&WWA; BioIn 1, 2, 3, 5, 11, 12, 15, 16; CamGWoT; ConAu 112, 120; ConNews 87-1; ContDeW 89; ConTFT 4; CurBio 45, 86, 86N; EncMT; EncWT; GrLiveH; InWom, SUP; NewYTBS 80, 86; NotNAT; NotWoAT; OxCAmT 84; OxCThe 83; PlP&P; WhAm 9; WhoAm 74, 76, 78, 80, 82, 84; WhoAmW 58, 61, 64, 66, 68, 70, 72, 74, 75, 77; WhoThe 72, 77, 81; WhoWor 74; WomFir*

Crawford, Christina
American. Actor, Author
Adopted daughter of Joan Crawford; wrote *Mommy Dearest,* 1978; Faye Dunaway starr ed in movie, 1981.
b. Jun 11, 1939 in Hollywood, California
Source: *BioIn 11, 12, 16, 20; ConAu 85; NewYTBS 79; WhoAmW 83, 85, 87; WhoHol 92, A; WhoWor 84; WrDr 80, 82, 84, 86, 88, 90, 92, 94*

Crawford, Cindy
American. Model
Supermodel representing Revlon cosmetics company; host of MTV's "House of Style," 1989-1996.
b. Feb 20, 1966 in De Kalb, Illinois
Source: *BioIn 16, 18; ConTFT 15; CurBio 93; IntWW 93; LegTOT; News 93-3; WhoAm 94, 95, 96, 97; WhoAmW 95; WhoWor 97*

Crawford, Francis Marion
Italian. Author
Wrote romantic novels with historical backgrounds; best known for *In the Palace of the King,* 1900.
b. Aug 2, 1854 in Bagni di Lucca, Italy
d. Apr 9, 1909 in Sorrento, Italy
Source: *Alli SUP; AmAu; AmAu&B; AmBi; ApCAB, X; BbD; BiD&SB; BioIn 1, 5, 7, 12, 15; CamGEL; CamGLE; CamHAL; CelCen; Chambr 3; CnDAL; DcAmAu; DcAmB; DcBiA; DcCathB; DcEnA, A; DcLEL; DcNAA; EvLB; LinLib L, S; LngCTC; NatCAB 2; NotNAT B; OxCAmL 65, 83, 95; OxCEng 67; PenC AM; REn; REnAL; TwCBDA; WebAB 74, 79; WhAm 1*

Crawford, Frederick C(oolidge)
American. Industrialist
Pres., Thompson Products, Inc. (later TRW, Inc.), 1933-53; chm., 1953-58.
b. Mar 19, 1891
d. Dec 9, 1994 in Falmouth, Massachusetts
Source: *BioIn 1, 3, 12; CurBio 95N; InSci; IntYB 78, 79, 80, 81, 82; WhoAm 74; WhoWor 76, 80, 82*

Crawford, James Strickland
American. Jazz Musician
Drummer with Jimmy Lunceford, 1928-43; did free-lance recordings, Broadway shows, 1950s-60s.
b. Jan 4, 1910 in Memphis, Tennessee
Source: *BiDJaz; BioIn 10; CmpEPM; InB&W 80; WhoJazz 72*

Crawford, Joan
[Lucille Fay LeSueur]
"Billie Cassin"
American. Actor
Won Oscar for *Mildred Pierce,* 1945; relationship with daughter subject of novel, film *Mommie Dearest,* 1978, 1981.
b. Mar 28, 1908 in San Antonio, Texas
d. May 10, 1977 in New York, New York
Source: *BiDD; IntWW 74, 75, 76, 77; InWom, SUP; LegTOT; MGM; MovMk; OxCFilm; ThFT; TwYS; WhAm 7; WhoAm 74, 76, 78; WhoAmW 58, 61, 64, 66, 68, 70, 72, 74, 75, 77; WhoWest 74, 76; WhoWor 74; WorAl; WorAlBi*

Crawford, John Edmund
American. Psychologist, Author
Specialist, child psychology; wrote *Better Ways of Growing Up,* 1949, *Milestones for Modern Teens,* 1954.
b. Jan 21, 1904 in Pittsburgh, Pennsylvania
d. Oct 12, 1971
Source: *BioIn 9; ConAu P-2; SmATA 3*

Crawford, Michael
[Michael Patrick Dumble-Smith]
English. Actor, Singer
Won Tony for lead role in musical *Phantom of the Opera,* 1988.
b. Jan 19, 1942 in Salisbury, England
Source: *BioIn 15, 16; CelR 90; ConMus 4; ConTFT 3, 11; CurBio 92; FilmEn; FilmgC; HalFC 84, 88; IntMPA 77, 78, 79, 81, 82, 84, 86, 88, 92, 94, 96; IntWW 82, 83, 89, 91, 93; LegTOT; MotPP; News 94, 94-2; NewYTBS 88; OxCPMus; Who 82, 83, 85, 88, 90, 92, 94; WhoHol 92, A; WhoThe 77, 81*

Crawford, Rusty
[Russell Crawford]
Canadian. Hockey Player
Left wing, 1917-19, with Ottawa, Toronto; Hall of Fame, 1962.
b. Nov 7, 1885 in Cardinal, Ontario, Canada
d. Dec 20, 1971
Source: *HocEn*

Crawford, Sam(uel Earl)
"Wahoo Sam"
American. Baseball Player
Outfielder, 1899-1917; holds ML record for triples, 312; Hall of Fame, 1957.
b. Apr 18, 1880 in Wahoo, Nebraska
d. Jun 15, 1968 in Hollywood, California
Source: *Ballpl 90; BiDAmSp BB; BioIn 3, 7, 8, 14, 15, 17; DcAmB S8; LegTOT; WhoProB 73; WhScrn 83*

Crawford, Thomas
American. Sculptor
Works include equestrian *George Washington,* 1857; *Armed Liberty,* on Capitol dome, 1860.
b. Mar 22, 1813 in New York, New York
d. Oct 10, 1857 in London, England
Source: *AmBi; ApCAB; ArtsNiC; BiAUS; BioIn 6; BriEAA; DcAmArt; DcAmB; DcBiPP; Drake; HarEnUS; IlBEAAW; OxCAmH; OxCAmL 65; OxCArt; TwCBDA; WhAm HS*

Crawford, William Harris
American. Politician
Secretary of treasury, 1816-25; one of four presidential candidates in election decided by Congress, 1824.
b. Feb 24, 1772 in Amherst County, Virginia
d. Sep 15, 1834 in Elberton, Georgia
Source: *AmBi; AmPolLe; ApCAB; BiAUS; BiDrAC; BiDrUSC 89; BiDrUSE 71, 89; BiDSA; BioIn 5, 7, 10, 16; CyAG; DcAmB; DcAmDH 80, 89; Drake; EncAB-H 1974; EncSoH; HarEnUS; McGEWB; NatCAB 5; NewCol 75; OxCAmH; TwCBDA; WebAB 74, 79; WhAm HS; WhAmP*

Crawford, William Hulfish
American. Cartoonist
Political cartoonist Newark, *News,* 1938-77; work appeared in over 700 newspapers.
b. Mar 18, 1913 in Hammond, Indiana
d. Jan 6, 1982 in Washington, District of Columbia
Source: *ConAu 105; WhAm 8; WhoAm 74, 76, 78; WhoAmA 73, 76, 78*

Craxi, Bettino
[Benedetto Craxi]
Italian. Political Leader
First Socialist to become prime minister of Italy, 1983-87.
b. Feb 24, 1934 in Milan, Italy
Source: *BioIn 13, 14, 15; CurBio 84; EncWB; FacFETw; IntAu&W 89; IntWW 78, 79, 80, 81, 82, 83, 89, 91, 93; NewYTBS 83; WhoEIO 82; WhoWor 84, 87, 89, 91, 93; WorAlBi*

Cray, Robert
American. Singer, Songwriter
Guitarist; won Grammys for blues albums *Showdown,* 1987; *Strong Persuader,* 1988.
b. Aug 1, 1953 in Columbus, Georgia
Source: *BioIn 12, 15, 16; ConMus 8; EncRkSt; LegTOT; News 88-2; OnThGG; PenEncP; SoulM; WhoAfA 96; WhoAm 90, 92, 94, 95, 96, 97; WhoBlA 92, 94; WhoEnt 92; WhoRocM 82*

Cray, Seymour R.
American. Computer Executive
Founded computer companies, Cray Research, 1972, Cray Computer, 1989; invented supercomputer, 1960s.
b. Sep 28, 1925 in Chippewa Falls, Wisconsin
d. Oct 5, 1996 in Colorado Springs, Colorado
Source: *BioIn 11, 13, 14, 15; CamDcSc; ConNews 86-3; LarDcSc; LegTOT; NewYTBS 27; PorSil; St&PR 75; WhoAm 84, 88, 90, 92, 94, 95, 96; WhoFrS 84; WhoTech 84, 89, 95; WhoWest 96*

Crazy Horse
[Tim Drummond; Ben Keith; Joe Lala; Ralph Molina; Bruce Palmer; Frank Sampedro; Billy Talbot; Danny Whitten]
American. Music Group
Country-rock group, late 1960s-70s; albums include *Crazy Horse,* 1971.
Source: *ConMuA 80A; DrAPF 97; EncPR&S 89; HarEnR 86; IlEncRk; NewOrJ; OnThGG; OxCAmH; ScF&FL 92; WhoRock 81; WhoRocM 82*

Crazy Horse
American. Native American Chief
One of leaders at Little Big Horn, 1876; led Oglala Sioux in Black Hills.
b. 1842? in Rapid Creek, South Dakota
d. Sep 5, 1877 in Camp Robinson, Nebraska
Source: *AmBi; ApCAB; BioIn 14, 15, 18, 19, 20; DcAmB; EncNAB; HarEnUS; LegTOT; McGEWB; RComAH; REnAW; WebAB 74; WhAm HS; WhNaAH; WhoMilH 76; WorAl*

Creach, Papa
[John Creach]
American. Musician
Rock fiddler; probably was oldest rock-and-roll performer.
b. May 17, 1917 in Beaver Falls, Pennsylvania
Source: *BiDAfM; BiDJaz; BioIn 9, 14; EncJzS; InB&W 80, 85; NewYTBS 94; WhoRock 81*

Cream
[Ginger Baker; Jack Bruce; Eric Clapton]
English. Music Group
First 1960s "supergroup"; hits include "Sunshine of Your Love," 1968.
Source: *AllMusG; BiDJaz A; BioIn 14, 15, 16, 17, 18, 19, 20, 21; ConMuA 80A; ConMus 9; EncPR&S 74, 89; EncRk 88; EncRkSt; HarEnR 86; IlEncRk; NewAmDM; OxCPMus; PenEncP; RkOn 78, 84; RolSEnR 83; WhoAm 74, 76, 78; WhoRock 81; WhoRocM 82; WhoWor 78*

Crean, Robert
American. Dramatist
Dramatist for CBS Playhouse whose plays include *The Defenders,* 1964.
b. 1923
d. May 6, 1974 in New Rochelle, New York
Source: *BioIn 10; LesBEnT; NewYTBS 74; ObitOF 79; WhAm 6*

Creasey, John
English. Author
Crime novelist who wrote under 28 pen names; won Edgar, 1962, for *Gideon's Fire.*
b. Sep 17, 1908 in Southfields, England
d. Jun 9, 1973 in Salisbury, England
Source: *Au&Wr 71; BioIn 4, 5, 6, 7, 8, 9, 10, 14, 17; ConAu 5R, 8NR, 41R; ConLC 11; CorpD; CrtSuMy; CurBio 63, 73, 73N; DcLB 77; EncMys; EncSF, 93; HalFC 84, 88; LegTOT; LngCTC; MajTwCW; MnBBF; NewYTBE 73; Novels; ObitOF 79; ObitT 1971; REn; ScF&FL 1, 2, 92; SpyFic; TwCCr&M 80, 85, 91; TwCSFW 91; TwCWr; WhAm 6; WhE&EA; WhoSpyF; WorAl; WorAlBi; WorAu 1950*

Creavy, Tom
[Thomas Creavy]
American. Golfer
Touring pro, 1920s-30s; won PGA, 1931.
b. Feb 3, 1911 in Tuckahoe, New York
d. Mar 3, 1979 in Delray Beach, Florida
Source: *NewYTBS 79; WhoGolf*

Crebillon, Claude Prosper Jolyot de
French. Author, Dramatist
Works examine the psychology and ethics of sexuality in the aristocratic society of eighteenth-century France.
b. 1707
d. 1777
Source: *BiD&SB; BioIn 6, 7; CasWL; DcBiPP; DcEuL; EuAu; EvEuW; LitC 1, 28; OxCFr; PenC EUR; REn*

Creed, Linda
American. Songwriter
With Thom Bell wrote hits "You Make Me Feel Brand New," 1974, "Could It Be I'm Falling in Love?," 1973.
b. 1949
d. Apr 10, 1986 in Ambler, Pennsylvania
Source: *BioIn 10; InWom SUP*

Creedence Clearwater Revival
[Douglas Ray Clifford; Stuart Cook; John Fogerty; Thomas Fogerty]
American. Music Group
Rock band of late 1960-70s; hits include "Proud Mary," 1969; "Who'll Stop the Rain," 1970.
Source: *BiDAmM; BioIn 14, 15, 19; ConMus 16; EncPR&S 74, 89; EncRk 88; EncRkSt; FacFETw; IlEncRk; NewAmDM; NewGrDA 86; OxCPMus; PenEncP; RkOn 78, 84, 85A; RolSEnR 83; WhoRock 81; WhoRocM 82*

Creel, George Edward
American. Government Official
Chm., Woodrow Wilson's com. on public information, 1917-19, directing govt. propaganda in WW I.
b. Dec 1, 1876 in Lafayette County, Missouri
d. Oct 3, 1953 in San Francisco, California

Source: *ConAu 115; DcAmB S5; DcLB 25; EncAB-H 1974; FacFETw; McGEWB; WebAB 74, 79; WhAm 3*

Creeley, Robert (White)
American. Author, Poet
Edited *Black Mountain Review;* among his collections: *A Form of Women,* 1959.
b. May 21, 1926 in Arlington, Massachusetts
Source: *AmAu&B; Au&Wr 71; Benet 87, 96; BenetAL 91; BioIn 8, 10, 11, 12, 13, 14, 16, 17, 19; BlueB 76; CamGLE; CamHAL; CasWL; ConAu 1R, 10AS, 23NR, 43NR; ConLC 1, 2, 4, 8, 11, 15, 36, 78; ConPo 70, 75, 80, 85, 91, 96; CroCAP; CurBio 88; DcLB 5, 16, 169; DcTwCCu 1; DrAF 76; DrAP 75; DrAPF 89; EncWL 2, 3; FacFETw; IntAu&W 76, 77, 82, 89, 91, 93; IntvTCA 2; IntWW 74, 75, 76, 77, 78, 79, 80, 81, 82, 83, 89, 91, 93; IntWWP 77; LinLib L; MagSAmL; MajTwCW; ModAL, S1, S2; Novels; OxCAmL 83, 95; OxCEng 85, 95; OxCTwCP; PenC AM; RAdv 1, 14, 13-1; REnAL; RfGAmL 87, 94; RGTwCWr; WebE&AL; WhoAm 74, 76, 78, 80, 82, 84, 86, 90, 92, 94, 95, 96, 97; WhoTwCL; WhoUSWr 88; WhoWor 80, 82, 84; WhoWrEP 89, 92, 95; WorAu 1950; WrDr 76, 80, 82, 84, 86, 88, 90, 92, 94, 96*

Cregar, Laird
[Samuel Cregar]
American. Actor
Played Jack the Ripper in *The Lodger,* 1944.
b. Jul 28, 1916 in Philadelphia, Pennsylvania
d. Dec 8, 1944 in Los Angeles, California
Source: *BiDFilm, 94; BioIn 9, 10; CmMov; CurBio 45; FilmgC; HalFC 84, 88; HolP 40; LegTOT; MovMk; NotNAT B; ObitOF 79; WhoHol B; WhScrn 74, 77*

Creighton, Edward
American. Businessman
Pioneer telegraph builder, established coast-to-coast service, 1961.
b. Aug 31, 1820 in Licking County, Ohio
d. Nov 5, 1874 in Omaha, Nebraska
Source: *BioIn 3, 5; DcAmB; DcCathB; NatCAB 22; WhAm HS*

Creighton, Thomas H(awk)
American. Architect, Author
Editor, *Progressive Architecture,* 1946-63.
b. May 19, 1904 in Philadelphia, Pennsylvania
d. Oct 6, 1984 in Honolulu, Hawaii
Source: *AmArch 70; AmAu&B; BioIn 1, 14; ConAu 1R, 5R, 6NR, 114; WhAm 8; WhoAm 74, 76, 78, 80, 82, 84; WhoWest 74, 76, 78*

Cremer, William Randal, Sir
English. Social Reformer
Secretary, Workmen's Peace Assn., 1871-1908; won Nobel Peace Prize, 1903.
b. Mar 18, 1838 in Fareham, England
d. Jul 22, 1908 in London, England
Source: *BioIn 5, 9, 10, 11, 15; DcNaB S2; LinLib S; NewCol 75; WebBD 83; WhoNob*

Cremieux, Isaac-Adolphe
French. Statesman
Co-author of *Code des Cades,* 1835.
b. Apr 30, 1796 in Nimes, France
d. Feb 10, 1880 in Paris, France
Source: *BioIn 11; CelCen; DcBiPP; NewCol 75*

Crenna, Richard
American. Actor
Starred in "Our Miss Brooks," 1952-56; "The Real McCoys," 1957-63; films include *The Flamingo Kid,* 1985.
b. Nov 30, 1927 in Los Angeles, California
Source: *BioIn 13, 15; ConTFT 3; FilmgC; HalFC 84, 88; IntMPA 77, 78, 79, 81, 82, 84, 86, 88, 92, 94, 96; LegTOT; MotPP; MovMk; NewYTBS 86; RadStar; SaTiSS; WhoAm 86, 88, 90, 92, 94, 95, 96, 97; WhoEnt 92; WhoHol A; WorAl; WorAlBi*

Crenshaw, Ben Daniel
American. Golfer
Turned pro, 1973; won Masters, 1984.
b. Jan 11, 1952 in Austin, Texas
Source: *BiDAmSp Sup; BioIn 14, 15, 16; BioNews 75; CelR 90; CurBio 85; NewYTBE 73; NewYTBS 76, 84; WhoAm 84, 86, 90; WhoGolf; WhoIntG*

Crenshaw, Marshall
American. Singer, Musician
Rock singer; guitarist; debut album *Marshall Crenshaw,* 1982 with hit single "Someday, Somewhere."
b. 1954? in Detroit, Michigan
Source: *BioIn 13, 15; ConMus 5; LegTOT; PenEncP; RkOn 85A*

Crescentini, Girolamo
Italian. Opera Singer
One of last, finest Italian male mezzo-sopranos, 1782-1812.
b. Feb 2, 1762 in Urbania, Italy
d. Apr 24, 1846 in Naples, Italy
Source: *Baker 78, 84, 92; BioIn 7, 14; NewEOp 71; NewGrDO; OxDcOp*

Crespin, Regine
French. Opera Singer
Mezzo-soprano, formerly soprano; NY Met., 1962-71; a noted Marschallin.
b. Mar 23, 1927 in Marseilles, France
Source: *Baker 78, 84, 92; BioIn 6, 7, 10, 11, 12, 13; CurBio 79; IntDcOp; IntWW 74, 75, 76, 77, 78, 79, 80, 81, 82, 83, 89, 91, 93; IntWWM 90; InWom SUP; MetOEnc; MusSN; NewAmDM; NewGrDO; OxDcOp; PenDiMP; Who 92; WhoAm 86, 90; WhoAmW 66, 68, 70, 77, 91; WhoEnt 92; WhoFr 79; WhoMus 72; WhoWor 74*

Cresson, Edith Campion
French. Political Leader
First woman prime minister of France, 1991-92.
b. Jan 27, 1934 in Boulogne-Billancourt, France
Source: *BiDFrPL; CurBio 91; IntWW 91; News 92, 92-1; NewYTBS 91; Who 92; WhoWor 84*

Creston, Paul
American. Composer
Wrote over 100 major compositions including six symphonies, choral works, piano pieces.
b. Oct 10, 1906 in New York, New York
d. Aug 24, 1985 in Poway, California
Source: *AmComp; ASCAP 66; Baker 78, 84, 92; BiDAmM; BioIn 1, 3, 6, 8, 11, 14, 20; BlueB 76; CompSN SUP; ConAmC 76, 82; CpmDNM 81; DcCM; IntWWM 77, 85; LegTOT; NewAmDM; NewGrDA 86; OxCMus; PenDiMP A; REnAL; WhAm 8; WhoAm 74, 76, 78, 80, 82, 84; WhoAmM 83; WhoMus 72; WhoWest 74, 76, 78; WhoWor 74, 76*

Cret, Paul P(hilippe)
American. Architect
Designed Washington's Folger Library; Federal Reserve Building, 1937.
b. Oct 23, 1876 in Lyons, France
d. Sep 8, 1945 in Philadelphia, Pennsylvania
Source: *BioIn 1, 10, 12, 13; CurBio 42; DcAmB S3; DcTwDes; EncAAr 2; FacFETw; IntDcAr; MacEA; NatCAB 33; WhAm 2*

Crevecoeur, Michel-Guillaume Jean de
[J Hector St. John]
French. Author
Recorded events, scenes in early American life: *Letters From an American Farmer,* 1782.
b. Jan 31, 1735 in Caen, France
d. Nov 12, 1813 in Sarcelles, France
Source: *AmAu; AmAu&B; BlkwEAR; CasWL; CnDAL; CyWA 58; DcAmB; DcAmImH; DcCathB; DcLEL; DcNAA; EncCRAm; EvLB; HarEnUS; OxCAmL 65, 83, 95; REn; REnAL; WebAB 74; WebE&AL; WhAm HS*

Crews, Harry Eugene
American. Author
Southern gothic novelist who wrote *Florida Frenzy,* 1982.
b. Jun 6, 1935 in Alma, Georgia
Source: *AuNews 1; Benet 87; BenetAL 91; BioIn 13, 15; BioNews 74; ConAu 20NR, 25R; ConLC 23, 49; ConNov 86, 91; DrAF 76; FifSWrA; MajTwCW; NewYTBS 78, 87; PeoHis; PostFic; WhoAm 86, 90; WhoWrEP 89; WorAlBi; WrDr 86, 90*

Crews, Laura Hope
American. Actor
Played Aunt Pittypat in *Gone With the Wind,* 1939.
b. Dec 12, 1879 in San Francisco, California
d. Nov 13, 1942 in New York, New York
Source: *BioIn 16, 21; CmCal; CurBio 43; Film 1; FilmgC; InWom SUP; MotPP; MovMk; NotAW; NotNAT; NotWoAT; OlFamFa; ThFT; Vers A; WhoHol B; WhoStg 1908; WhScrn 74, 77; WhThe*

Crichton, Charles
English. Director
Films include *Hue and Cry,* 1946; *Lavender Hill Mob,* 1951.
b. Aug 6, 1910 in Wallasey, England
Source: *BioIn 15, 17; CmMov; ConTFT 8; DcFM; EncEurC; FilmgC; GangFlm; HalFC 84, 88; IntDcF 1-2, 2-2; IntMPA 75, 76, 77, 78, 79, 81, 82, 84, 86, 88, 92, 94, 96; LegTOT; MiSFD 9; MovMk; OxCFilm; Who 92; WorEFlm; WorFDir 1*

Crichton, James
"The Admirable Crichton"
Scottish. Adventurer, Scholar
Swashbuckling career in France, Italy recounted in historical novel by Ainsworth.
b. Aug 19, 1560 in Eliock, Scotland
d. Jul 3, 1582 in Mantua, Italy
Source: *Alli; BioIn 3, 8, 11; BritAu; CmScLit; DcBiPP; DcNaB, C; LegTOT; NewC; OxCEng 67, 85, 95; WhDW*

Crichton, Michael
[John Michael Crichton; Jeffrey Hudson; John Lange]
American. Author, Director
Won Edgar for *A Case of Need,* 1968; directed *Coma,* 1977; novels include *The Andromeda Strain,*.
b. Oct 23, 1942 in Chicago, Illinois
Source: *AmAu&B; Au&Arts 10; Au&Wr 71; AuNews 2; BioIn 9, 10, 11, 12, 13, 14, 15, 16, 17, 19, 20, 21; CelR, 90; ConAu 13NR, 25R; ConLC 2, 6, 54, 90; ConNov 76, 82; ConTFT 5, 13; CurBio 76, 93; CyWA 89; DcLB Y81B; DcLP 87A; EncSF, 93; FacFETw; FilmgC; HalFC 84, 88; IntAu&W 82, 89, 91, 93; IntMPA 77, 82, 92, 94, 96; LegTOT; LinLib L; MajTwCW; MiSFD 9; NewEScF; News 95, 95-3; Novels; ScF&FL 1, 2, 92; ScFSB; SmATA 9, 49; TwCCr&M 80, 85, 91; TwCSFW 86, 91; Who 90; WhoAm 74, 76, 78, 80, 82, 84, 86, 88, 90, 92, 94, 95, 96, 97; WhoSciF; WhoUSWr 88; WhoWest 80, 82, 84, 89; WhoWor 74; WhoWrEP 89, 92, 95; WorAl; WorAlBi; WorAu 1950, 1970; WorFDir 2; WrDr 76, 80, 82, 86, 88, 90, 92, 94*

Crichton, Robert
American. Author
Wrote *The Great Imposter,* 1958; filmed, 1961; autobiography: *Memoirs of a Bad Soldier,* 1979.
b. Jan 29, 1925 in Albuquerque, New Mexico
d. Mar 23, 1993 in New Rochelle, New York
Source: *AnObit 1993; AuNews 1; BioIn 7, 8, 10; BioNews 74; ConAu 17R, 46NR, 140; IntvTCA 2; WrDr 76, 80, 82, 84, 86, 88, 90*

Crick, Francis Harry Compton
English. Biologist
Co-discovered DNA with James Watson, 1953; shared 1962 Nobel Prize.
b. Jun 8, 1916 in Northampton, England
Source: *AmMWSc 89, 92, 95; AsBiEn; BiESc; BioIn 5, 6, 8, 9, 11, 12, 13, 14, 15, 16; BlueB 76; CamDcSc; CelR 90; ConAu 113, 121; ConHero 1; CurBio 83; FacFETw; IntWW 74, 75, 76, 77, 78, 79, 80, 81, 82, 83, 89, 91, 93; LarDcSc; McGEWB; McGMS 80; NobelP; RAdv 14; ThTwC 87; Who 74, 82, 83, 85, 88, 90, 92, 94; WhoAm 84, 86, 88, 90, 92, 94, 95, 96, 97; WhoFrS 84; WhoMedH; WhoNob, 90, 95; WhoScEn 94, 96; WhoWest 87, 89, 92, 94, 96; WhoWor 74, 78, 80, 82, 84, 87, 89, 91, 93, 95, 96, 97; WorAl; WorAlBi; WorScD; WrDr 86, 92*

Crile, George Washington
American. Surgeon
Developed nerve-block anesthesia.
b. Nov 11, 1864 in Chili, Ohio
d. Jan 7, 1943 in Cleveland, Ohio
Source: *ApCAB X; BioIn 1, 2, 3, 15; CamDcSc; CurBio 43; DcAmB S3; DcAmMeB 84; DcNAA; InSci; LarDcSc; LinLib S; NatCAB 15, 31; OhA&B; OxCMed 86; WebBD 83; WhAm 2; WhNAA*

Crile, George Washington, Jr.
American. Surgeon
Battled unnecessary surgery for thyroid and breast cancer patients; began trend in US toward simple mastectomy or lumpectomy instead of radical mastectomy.
b. Nov 3, 1907 in Cleveland, Ohio
d. Sep 11, 1992 in Cleveland, Ohio
Source: *WhoAm 90*

Crippen, Hawley Harvey
English. Murderer
Capture aided by one of earliest uses of shipboard radio telephone, 1910.
b. Mar 13, 1862 in Coldwater, Michigan
d. Nov 23, 1910 in Pentonville, England
Source: *BioIn 2, 6, 11, 16; DrInf; MurCaTw; OxCMed 86; WhDW*

Crippen, Robert Laurel
American. Astronaut
With Johnson Space Center, 1969—; commander, space shuttle Columbia, 1984; director space shuttle, NASA, 1989-91; director, NASA JFK Space Center, 1992-95; pres., v.p. automation, Lockheed Martin, 1995—.
b. Sep 11, 1937 in Beaumont, Texas
Source: *BioIn 13, 14; BlueB 76; FacFETw; IntWW 74; NewYTBS 84; WhoAm 82, 84, 86, 88, 90, 92, 94, 95, 96, 97; WhoScEn 94, 96; WhoSpc; WhoSSW 73, 75, 76, 95, 97*

Cripps, Stafford, Sir
[Richard Stafford Cripps]
English. Statesman, Lawyer
Chancellor of exchequer, 1947-50; Labor MP, Ambassador to Russia, 1940-42.
b. Apr 24, 1889 in Buckinghamshire, England
d. Apr 21, 1952 in Zurich, Switzerland
Source: *BioIn 1, 2, 3, 4, 10, 12, 13, 14, 15, 21; CurBio 40, 48, 52; DcNaB 1951; DcPol; DcTwHis; FacFETw; GrBr; HisDBrE; HisEWW; InSci; LinLib S; ObitOF 79; ObitT 1951; WhAm 3; WhDW; WhWW-II*

Crisler, Fritz
[Herbert Orin Crisler]
American. Football Coach
Successful college coach, Princeton, 1932-38, U of MI, 1938-48; won nat. championship at MI, 1947.
b. Jan 12, 1899 in Earlville, Illinois
d. Aug 19, 1982 in Ann Arbor, Michigan
Source: *BioIn 1, 4, 5, 6, 10, 13; ConAu 107; CurBio 48, 82, 82N; NewYTBS 82; WhoAm 74; WhoFtbl 74; WhoSpor*

Crisp, Donald
American. Actor
Won Oscar for *How Green Was My Valley,* 1941.
b. Apr 18, 1880 in Aberfeldy, Scotland
d. May 25, 1974 in Van Nuys, California
Source: *BiDFilm, 94; BioIn 10, 21; CmMov; DcAmB S9; EncAFC; Film 1; FilmgC; HalFC 84, 88; IntDcF 1-3, 2-3; LegTOT; MotPP; MovMk; NewYTBS 74; ObitOF 79; OlFamFa; OxCFilm; TwYS, A; Vers A; WhAm 6; WhoHol B; WhScrn 77, 83; WorAl; WorAlBi; WorEFlm*

Crisp, Quentin
[Denis Pratt]
English. Author
Noted for autobiography *The Naked Civil Servant,* 1968.
b. Dec 25, 1908 in Sutton, England
Source: *BioIn 11, 13, 17, 20; ConAu 109, 116; ConTFT 6; GayLesB; GayLL; LegTOT; ScF&FL 92*

Crispin, Edmund
[Robert Bruce Montgomery]
English. Author
Best known for detective novels featuring Gervase Fen. Montgomery.
b. Oct 2, 1921 in Chesham Bois, England
d. Sep 15, 1978 in Plymouth, England
Source: *Au&Wr 71; BioIn 1, 2, 10, 14; ConAu 104; ConLC 22; ConSFA; CrtSuMy; DcLB 87; EncMys; EncSF, 93; LegTOT; Novels; ScF&FL 1, 2;*

TwCCr&M 80, 85, 91; WhoSciF; WorAl; WorAlBi; WorAu 1950

Criss, Peter
[Kiss; Peter Crisscovla]
American. Singer, Musician
Singer, drummer for Kiss, 1972-80; wrote hit song ''Beth'' for wife, 1976.
b. Dec 20, 1947 in New York, New York
Source: *BioIn 12; LegTOT; RkOn 74; RolSEnR 83*

Crist, Judith Klein
American. Critic
Film critic for *TV Guide,* 1966-88; *Saturday Review,* 1980—; Critical Columnist for *Coming Attractions,* 1985-93.
b. May 22, 1922 in New York, New York
Source: *AuNews 1; BioIn 15; BriB; ConAu 17NR, 81; ForWC 70; IntMPA 86, 92; InWom SUP; WhoAm 86, 88, 90; WhoAmW 83, 85, 87, 89, 91; WhoE 74; WhoEnt 92; WhoWorJ 78; WrDr 86, 92*

Cristal, Linda
[Marta Victoria Moya Burges]
Argentine. Actor
Appeared in TV's ''High Chaparral,'' 1967-71.
b. Feb 24, 1936 in Buenos Aires, Argentina
Source: *FilmgC; HalFC 84, 88; MotPP; WhoAmW 72, 74; WhoHol A*

Cristiani, Alfredo
Salvadoran. Political Leader
President, Salvador, 1989-94; member, Nationalist Republican Alliance (Arena).
b. Nov 22, 1947 in San Salvador, El Salvador
Source: *BioIn 16; CurBio 90; DcHiB; IntWW 91; NewYTBS 87, 89; WhoWor 91, 93*

Cristofer, Michael
[Michael Procaccino]
American. Dramatist
Won Pulitzer Prize in drama, 1977, for *The Shadow Box.*
b. Jan 22, 1945 in Trenton, New Jersey
Source: *BiDConC; ConAmD; ConAu 110, 152; ConDr 82, 88, 93; ConLC 28; ConTFT 3; DcLB 7; DcLP 87B; IntAu&W 91; LegTOT; NatPD 77, 81; OxCAmL 83, 95; OxCAmT 84; WhoAm 78, 80, 82, 84, 86, 90, 92, 94, 95; WhoE 79, 81, 85; WhoEnt 92; WhoHol 92; WhoThe 81; WhoWor 95, 96, 97; WorAl; WrDr 86, 92*

Cristofori, Bartolomeo di Francesco
Italian. Inventor
Altered a harpsichord to create the first piano.
b. May 4, 1655 in Padua, Italy
d. Jan 27, 1731 in Florence, Italy
Source: *Baker 84; BioIn 3; NewAmDM*

Crittenden, Christopher
American. Historian
Edited *Historical Societies in the US and Canada: A Handbook,* 1944.
b. Dec 1, 1902 in Wake Forest, North Carolina
d. Oct 13, 1969 in Raleigh, North Carolina
Source: *AmAu&B; BioIn 8, 10; NatCAB 55; WhAm 5*

Crittenden, John Jordan
American. Lawyer, Politician
Held govt. positions, from governor of KY to attorney general, senator, congressman; opposed slavery.
b. Sep 10, 1787 in Versailles, Kentucky
d. Jul 26, 1863 in Frankfort, Kentucky
Source: *AmBi; AmPolLe; ApCAB; BiAUS; BiDrAC; BiDrGov 1789; BiDrUSE 71, 89; BiDSA; BioIn 2, 6, 7, 9, 10, 14; CivWDc; CyAG; DcAmB; Drake; EncAB-H 1974, 1996; HarEnUS; NatCAB 13; OxCSupC; TwCBDA; WebAB 74, 79; WhAm HS; WhAmP; WhCiWar; WorAl*

Crittendon, Thomas Leonidas
American. Army Officer
Served in Union Army, 1861-64; promoted to maj. gen. for distinguished service at Battle of Shiloh, 1862.
b. May 15, 1819 in Russellville, Kentucky
d. Oct 23, 1893 in Annandale, New York
Source: *NewCol 75; TwCBDA; WebAMB; WhAm HS*

Crittenton, Charles Nelson
American. Businessman, Philanthropist
Founded Florence Crittenton Missions for unfortunate women.
b. Feb 20, 1833 in Henderson, New York
d. Nov 16, 1909 in San Francisco, California
Source: *DcAmB; DcAmImH; DcNAA*

Critters
[Don Ciccone; Christopher Darway; Jack Decker; Kenneth Gorka; James Ryan]
American. Music Group
Soft-rock group, 1960s.
Source: *Alli; BiDAmM; BioIn 19; DcCanB 10; DcNAA; Dun&B 90; EncRk 88; PenEncP; RkOn 78; RolSEnR 83; WhoAmP 95; WhoHol 92; WhoRocM 82*

Crivelli, Carlo
Italian. Artist
Produced religious paintings filled with decorative accessories: *Annunciation,* 1486.
b. 1435 in Venice, Italy
d. 1493
Source: *AtlBL; ClaDrA; DcArts; DcCathB; OxCArt*

Croce, Benedetto
Italian. Philosopher
Four-volume *Philosophy of the Spirit,* 1902-17, reacted to 19th c. materialism, attempting to rekindle spiritualism.
b. Feb 25, 1866 in Pescasseroli, Italy
d. Nov 20, 1952 in Naples, Italy
Source: *AtlBL; Benet 87, 96; BiDPsy; BioIn 1, 2, 3, 4, 5, 9, 12, 13, 14; CasWL; ClDMEL 47; ConAu 120; CurBio 44, 53; DcEuL; DcItL 1, 2; EncWL, 2, 3; EuWr 8; EvEuW; FacFETw; LinLib L, S; LngCTC; LuthC 75; McGDA; McGEWB; NewC; ObitT 1951; OxCArt; OxCEng 67, 85, 95; OxCPhil; OxDcArt; PenC EUR; RAdv 14, 13-2, 13-3; REn; ThTwC 87; TwCA, SUP; TwCLC 37; TwCWr; WhAm 3; WhDW; WhE&EA; WhLit; WhoLA; WorAl; WorAlBi*

Croce, Jim
American. Singer, Songwriter
Four gold albums include ''Time in a Bottle,'' 1972; ''Bad Bad Leroy Brown,'' 1973; ''I'll Have to Say I Love You in a Song,'' 1973; killed in plane crash at age 30.
b. Jan 10, 1943 in Philadelphia, Pennsylvania
d. Sep 20, 1973 in Natchitoches, Louisiana
Source: *BioIn 10, 11; BioNews 74; ConMus 3; EncPR&S 74; EncRk 88; EncRkSt; HarEnR 86; NewGrDA 86; OxCPMus; PenEncP; RkOn 74, 78; RolSEnR 83; WhoRocM 82*

Crocker, Charles
American. Railroad Executive
Central Pacific head who used Chinese laborers to link with Union Pacific, 1869.
b. Sep 16, 1822 in Troy, New York
d. Aug 14, 1888 in Monterey, California
Source: *AmBi; ApCAB; BioIn 3, 15; CmCal; DcAmB; GayN; HarEnUS; REnAW; TwCBDA; WebAB 74, 79; WhAm HS; WorAl; WorAlBi*

Crocker, Chester Arthur
American. Educator, Government Official
Assistant Secretary of State for African Affairs, 1981-89.
b. Oct 29, 1941 in New York, New York
Source: *BioIn 12, 13; CurBio 90; IntWW 89, 91, 93; WhoAm 82, 84, 86, 88, 90, 92, 94, 95, 96, 97; WhoAmP 91; WhoE 93, 95, 97*

Crocker, Fay
Uruguayan. Golfer
Turned pro, 1953; won US Women's Open, 1955.
b. Aug 2, 1914 in Montevideo, Uruguay
Source: *BioIn 3; WhoGolf*

Crockett, Davy
[David Crockett]
American. Pioneer
Served as scout under Andrew Jackson during Creek War, 1813-14; died at Alamo.
b. Aug 17, 1786 in Greene City, Tennessee
d. Mar 6, 1836 in San Antonio, Texas
Source: *Alli; AmAu&B; AmBi; ApCAB; Benet 87, 96; BenetAL 91; BiAUS; BiD&SB; BiDrAC; BiDrUSC 89; BiDSA; BioIn 1, 2, 3, 4, 5, 6, 7, 8, 9, 10, 11, 12, 13, 14, 15, 16, 17, 19, 20, 21; CamGEL; CamHAL; CyWA 58; DcAmAu; DcAmB; DcLB 3, 11; DcNAA; Drake; EncAAH; EncAB-H 1974, 1996; EncAHmr; EncSoH; FilmgC; HalFC 84, 88; HarEnUS; HisWorL; LegTOT; LinLib L, S; McGEWB; MemAm; NatCAB 4; NinCLC 8; OxCAmH; OxCAmL 65, 83, 95; OxCFilm; PenC AM; PolPar; RComAH; REn; REnAL; REnAW; TwCBDA; WebAB 74, 79; WebAMB; WhAm HS; WhAmP; WhDW; WhNaAH*

Crockett, George (William), Jr.
American. Lawyer, Politician
First black examiner appointed to a government labor board, 1943; Dem. US Rep. from MI, 1981-91.
b. Aug 10, 1909 in Jacksonville, Florida
Source: *BiDrUSC 89; BioIn 8, 10, 12; BlkAmsC; CngDr 81, 83, 85, 87; ConBlB 10; InB&W 80, 85; WhoAfA 96; WhoAm 82, 84, 86, 88, 90; WhoAmP 81, 83, 85, 87, 89, 91, 93, 95; WhoBlA 85, 88, 90, 92, 94; WhoMW 82, 84, 86, 88, 90*

Crockett, James Underwood
American. Horticulturist
Wrote numerous gardening books; best known for popular *Crockett's Victory Garden*, 1977.
b. Oct 9, 1915 in Haverhill, Massachusetts
d. Jul 11, 1979, Jamaica
Source: *BioIn 11, 12; ConAu 13NR, 33R, 89; WhoE 74*

Crockett, S(amuel) R(utherford)
Scottish. Clergy, Author
Children's books include *Sir Toady Crusoe*, 1905.
b. Sep 24, 1860 in Little Duchrae, Scotland
d. Apr 21, 1914 in Avignon, France
Source: *BbD; BiD&SB; BioIn 3, 8; BritAu 19; CarSB; CasWL; Chambr 3; ChhPo; ConAu 116; DcBiA; DcEnA A; DcLEL; DcNaB 1912; EvLB; LngCEL; LngCTC; NewC; OxCChiL; PenC ENG; REn; ScF&FL 1; StaCVF; TwCA, SUP; TwCChW 78, 83, 89, 95; WhLit; WhoChL*

Croesus
Ruler
Last king of Lydia, defeated by Cyrus the Great, 546 BC; known for great wealth.
b. 560BC
d. 546BC
Source: *HarEnMi; LinLib S; NewC; REn; WhDW*

Croft, Arthur C
American. Publisher
Published *Personnel Journal;* director, American Arbitration Assn., 1950-75.
b. May 26, 1890 in Cleveland, Ohio
d. Sep 6, 1975
Source: *BioIn 2, 3; CurBio 52; WhAm 7*

Croft, Michael
English. Director
Founder, National Youth Theatre, 1956.
b. Mar 8, 1922 in Oswestry, England
d. Nov 15, 1986 in London, England
Source: *AnObit 1986; Au&Wr 71; BlueB 76; ConAu 121; EncWT; EngPo; IntAu&W 76; Who 82; WhoThe 77, 81*

Croft-Cooke, Rupert
English. Author
Detective novels examples of classic British mystery.
b. Jun 20, 1903 in Edenbridge, England
d. Jun 10, 1979 in Bournemouth, England
Source: *Au&Wr 71; BioIn 3, 4, 6, 7, 8, 10, 14; BlueB 76; CathA 1952; ChhPo, S1; ConAu 4NR, 9R, 89; IntAu&W 77; IntWW 74, 75, 76, 77, 78; IntWWP 77; LngCTC; NewC; TwCA, SUP; WhLit; Who 74; WhoWor 74, 76, 78; WrDr 76, 80*

Crofts, Dash
[Seals and Crofts]
American. Singer, Songwriter
Member of soft rock duo with Jim Seals; greatest hits: "Summer Breeze," 1973; "Takin' It Easy," 1978.
b. Aug 14, 1940 in Cisco, Texas
Source: *BkPepl; LegTOT; WhoAm 82; WhoRocM 82*

Crofts, Freeman Willis
Irish. Author
Mystery tales include *French Strikes Oil*, 1952.
b. Jun 1879 in Dublin, Ireland
d. Apr 11, 1957 in Worthing, England
Source: *BioIn 4; ConAu 115; EncMys; LngCTC; WorAl; WorAlBi*

Crohn, Burrill Bernard
American. Physician
Best known for research on ileitis, commonly called Crohn's disease; wrote three books on subject.
b. Jun 13, 1884 in New York, New York
d. Jul 29, 1983 in New Milford, Connecticut
Source: *AnObit 1983; BiDrACP 79; ConAu 110; NewYTBS 83; WhAm 1, 7; WhoWorJ 72*

Croker, Boss
[Richard Croker]
American. Politician
Tammany Hall leader, 1886-1902.
b. Nov 23, 1841 in Clonakilty, Ireland
d. Apr 29, 1922 in New York, New York
Source: *AmBi; ApCAB X; BioIn 7; CopCroC; DcAmB; DcIrB 78, 88; HarEnUS; OxCAmH; WhAm 1*

Croly, Herbert David
American. Journalist
Founder, first editor of liberal journal *The New Republic*, 1914-30.
b. Jan 23, 1869 in New York, New York
d. May 17, 1930 in Santa Barbara, California
Source: *AmAu&B; AmRef; AmSocL; BiDAmJo; BioIn 1, 3, 5, 14, 15, 16, 17, 19, 20; DcAmB S1; DcAmSR; DcNAA; EncAB-H 1974, 1996; EncAJ; JrnUS; McGEWB; OxCAmH; OxCAmL 65, 95; TwCA, SUP; WebAB 74, 79; WebBD 83; WhAm 1; WhAmP*

Croly, Jane Cunningham
"Jennie June"
American. Journalist, Feminist
Edited *Demorest's Monthly Magazine*, 1860-87; founded Sorosis Club, 1868.
b. Dec 19, 1829 in Market Harborough, England
d. Dec 23, 1901 in New York, New York
Source: *Alli SUP; AmAu; AmAu&B; AmRef; AmWomWr; BbD; BiDAmJo; BiDAmNC; BiD&SB; BioIn 15, 16, 21; BlmGWL; BriB; ConAu 118; DcAmAu; DcAmB; DcLB 23; DcNAA; EncAJ; InWom, SUP; JrnUS; LibW; NotAW; OxCAmH; OxCAmL 65, 83, 95; PenNWW A; WhAm 1; WomFir*

Crombie, David Edward
Canadian. Politician
Mayor of Toronto, 1973-78; minister of Multiculturalism, 1986-87; minister of Indian Affairs and Northern Development, 1984-86; Secretary of State, 1986-88; Commissioner of the Royal Commission on the Future of the Toronto Waterfront, 1988—.
b. Apr 24, 1936 in Toronto, Ontario, Canada
Source: *BioIn 11, 13; CanWW 31, 89; IntWW 80, 81, 82, 83, 89, 91; WhoAm 78, 80, 82, 84, 86, 88, 90; WhoE 79, 81, 83, 86, 89*

Crome, John
"Old Crome"
English. Artist
Founded Norwich school of painting; known for romanticized scenes of rural life.
b. Dec 22, 1768 in Norwich, England
d. Apr 22, 1821 in Norwich, England
Source: *Alli; AtlBL; BioIn 1, 2, 4, 5, 8, 10, 11, 12, 13, 15; ClaDrA; DcAmB; DcArts; DcBrWA; DcNaB; IntDcAA 90; LinLib S; McGDA; NewC; OxCArt; OxDcArt; WhDW*

Cromley, Raymond Avolon
American. Journalist
Far-Eastern, Washington correspondent, *Wall Street Journal,* 1938-55; wrote *Veteran's Benefits,* 1966.
b. Aug 23, 1910 in Tulare, California
Source: *WhoAm 74, 76, 78, 80, 82, 84, 86, 88, 90, 92, 94, 95, 96, 97; WhoE 85, 86, 89, 97; WhoWor 74, 76, 78, 80, 82, 84, 87, 89, 91, 93, 95, 96, 97*

Crommelynck, Fernand
Belgian. Dramatist
Wrote plays *Le marchand de regrets,* 1913; *Le cocu magnifique,* 1920 (*The Magnificcent Cuckold*).
b. Nov 19, 1885 in Brussels, Belgium
d. Mar 17, 1970 in Saint-Germain-en-Laye, France
Source: *CasWL; ClDMEL 47; CnMD; ConAu 89; ConLC 75; EncWL; EvEuW; IntDcT 2; McGEWD 72, 84; ModWD; PenC EUR; REn; REnWD; WhThe; WorAu 1950*

Cromwell, Dean Bartlett
"The Maker of Champions"
American. Track Coach
Track and field coach; led US Olympic team, 1948.
b. Sep 20, 1879 in Turner, Oregon
d. Aug 3, 1962 in Los Angeles, California
Source: *BioIn 1, 6, 8; DcAmB S7; WhoTr&F 73*

Cromwell, John
American. Director
Directed *Of Human Bondage,* 1964.
b. Dec 23, 1887 in Toledo, Ohio
d. Sep 26, 1979 in Santa Barbara, California
Source: *BiDFilm; BiE&WWA; CmMov; ConAu 89; DcFM; FilmgC; GangFlm; IntDcF 1-2, 2-2; MovMk; NatPD 77; NotNAT; OxCAmT 84; OxCFilm; WhoHol A; WhoThe 72, 77, 81; WhScrn 83; WorEFlm*

Cromwell, Nolan Neil
American. Football Player
Three-time all-pro safety, LA Rams, 1977-88.
b. Jan 30, 1955 in Smith Center, Kansas
Source: *BioIn 12, 14; FootReg 87; WhoAm 84*

Cromwell, Oliver
"Old Noll"
English. Statesman, Army Officer
Ruled England as Lord Protector, 1653-58, after execution of Charles I; favored religious freedom.
b. Apr 25, 1599 in Huntingdon, England
d. Sep 3, 1658 in London, England
Source: *Alli; Benet 87, 96; BioIn 1, 2, 3, 4, 5, 6, 7, 8, 9, 10, 11, 12, 16, 17, 19, 20; BlmGEL; DcAmSR; DcBiPP; DcNaB; DicTyr; Dis&D; EncCRAm; EncRev; GenMudB; GrLGrT; HalFC 84, 88; HarEnMi; HarEnUS; HisDBrE; HisDStE; HisWorL; LegTOT; LinLib S; LngCEL; LuthC 75; McGEWB; NewC; OxCEng 85, 95; OxCIri; OxCMus; PlP&P; REn; WhDW; WhoMilH 76; WorAl; WorAlBi*

Cromwell, Richard
English. Statesman
Son of Oliver Cromwell, who succeeded father as Lord Protector, 1658-59, until restoration of monarchy, 1660.
b. Oct 4, 1626
d. Jul 13, 1712 in Cheshunt, England
Source: *BioIn 1, 7, 9, 11; DcBiPP; DcNaB; Dis&D; HisDStE; NewCol 75*

Cromwell, Thomas
[Earl of Essex]
English. Statesman
Adviser to Henry VIII who drafted Reformation Acts, 1532; negotiated Henry's marriage to Anne of Cleves, 1539; beheaded for treason, heresy.
b. 1485 in Putney, England
d. Jul 28, 1540 in London, England
Source: *Alli; Benet 87, 96; BioIn 2, 4, 5, 9, 10, 11, 12, 14, 15, 20; BlmGEL; DcEnL; DcNaB, C; LegTOT; LinLib S; LngCEL; LuthC 75; McGEWB; NewC; OxCEng 85, 95; REn; WhDW; WorAl; WorAlBi*

Cronenberg, David
"The King of Venereal Horror"
Canadian. Filmmaker
Works in horror genre include *The Dead Zone,* 1983; *The Fly,* 1986.
b. May 15, 1943 in Toronto, Ontario, Canada
Source: *BiDFilm 94; BioIn 12, 13, 15, 16; CanWW 89; ConAu 138; ConCaAu 1; ConTFT 6, 14; CurBio 92; EncSF 93; HalFC 88; HorFD; IntDcF 2-2; IntMPA 86, 88, 92, 94, 96; IntWW 91, 93; LegTOT; MiSFD 9; NewEScF; News 92, 92-3; PenEncH; WhoAm 95, 96, 97; WhoHol 92; WhoWor 93, 95, 96, 97*

Cronin, A(rchibald) J(oseph)
American. Author
Best known for *The Citadel,* 1937; *Keys of the Kingdom,* 1941.
b. Jul 19, 1896 in Helensburgh, England
d. Jan 6, 1981 in Glion, Switzerland
Source: *Au&Wr 71; Benet 96; BioIn 1, 2, 3, 4, 6, 7, 8, 12, 13, 16; BlueB 76; CasWL; CathA 1930; Chambr 3; ConAu 1R, 5NR, 102; ConNov 76; CurBio 42, 81; DcLEL; DcNaB 1981; EncWL; EvLB; FilmgC; InSci; IntAu&W 76, 77, 82; IntWW 74, 75, 76, 77, 78, 79, 80; LinLib L; LngCTC; ModBrL; NewC; Novels; OxCEng 95; OxCMed 86; PenC ENG; RAdv 1; REn; SmATA 25N; TwCA, SUP; TwCWr; WhAm 7; WhE&EA; WhLit; WhNAA; Who 74; WhoWor 74, 76, 78; WrDr 76, 80, 82*

Cronin, James Watson
American. Physicist, Educator
Shared 1980 Nobel Prize in physics with Val Fitch for researching K-mesons.
b. Sep 25, 1931 in Chicago, Illinois
Source: *AmMWSc 86, 89, 92, 95; BiESc; BioIn 14, 15, 20; CamDcSc; FacFETw; IntWW 81, 82, 83, 89, 91, 93; LarDcSc; NewYTBS 80; NobelP; WhoAm 74, 76, 78, 80, 82, 84, 86, 88, 90, 92, 94, 95, 96, 97; WhoFrS 84; WhoMW 82, 84, 86, 88, 90, 92, 93, 96; WhoNob, 90, 95; WhoScEn 94, 96; WhoWor 82, 84, 87, 89, 91, 93, 95, 96, 97; WorAlBi*

Cronin, Joe
[Joseph Edward Cronin]
American. Baseball Player, Baseball Executive
Infielder, 1926-45; pres., AL, 1959-74; Hall of Fame, 1956.
b. Oct 12, 1906 in San Francisco, California
d. Sep 7, 1984 in Osterville, Massachusetts
Source: *AnObit 1984; Ballpl 90; BiDAmSp BB; BioIn 1, 6, 7, 8, 9, 10, 14, 15, 18; CmCal; CurBio 65, 84, 84N; FacFETw; LegTOT; NewYTBS 84; WhAm 9; WhoAm 82; WhoProB 73*

Cronkite, Walter Leland, Jr.
"Uncle Walter"
American. Broadcast Journalist
Anchored "CBS Evening News," 1962-81; host "Universe" TV series; Television Academy Hall of Fame, 1985.
b. Nov 4, 1916 in Saint Joseph, Missouri
Source: *AuNews 1, 2; BiDAmJo; BioIn 13, 14, 15, 16; BkPepl; BlueB 76; CelR 90; ConAu 69; ConHero 1; ConTFT 6; CurBio 56; DcAmDH 80, 89; EncTwCJ; EncWB; IntMPA 86, 92; IntWW 74, 75, 76, 77, 78, 79, 80, 81, 82, 83, 89, 91, 93; LesBEnT, 92; NewYTBS 81, 89; WebAB 74, 79; WhoAm 86, 90; WhoE 91; WhoWor 74; WorAl; WorAlBi; WrDr 86, 92*

Cronyn, Hume
Canadian. Actor
Won Tony, 1964, for *Hamlet;* best known for *The Gin Game,* 1978, with wife Jessica Tandy.
b. Jul 18, 1911 in London, Ontario, Canada
Source: *BiE&WWA; BioIn 2, 4, 5, 6, 7, 11, 13, 14, 15, 16; CamGWoT; CanWW 31, 70, 79, 80, 81, 83, 89; CelR, 90; ConAu 50NR, 123; ConTFT 1, 7; CurBio 56, 88; FilmgC; GangFlm; HalFC 84, 88; IntDcT 3; IntMPA 75, 76, 77, 78, 79, 81, 82, 84, 86, 88, 92, 94, 96; IntWW 89, 91, 93; LegTOT; MGM; MotPP; MovMk; NewYTBS 74, 82; NotNAT; OxCAmT 84; OxCCanT; OxCThe 83; PlP&P; WhoAm 74, 76, 78, 80, 82, 84, 86, 88, 90, 92, 94, 95, 96, 97; WhoEnt 92; WhoHol 92, A; WhoThe 72, 77, 81; WhoWor 74, 76; WorAl; WorAlBi*

Crook, George
American. Army Officer
Distinguished himself in campaigns against Indians (battle of Powder River, the Rosebud) in 1870s.
b. Sep 23, 1829 in Dayton, Ohio
d. Mar 21, 1890 in Chicago, Illinois

Source: *AmBi; ApCAB; BioIn 12; CivWDc; DcAmB; Drake; GayN; GenMudB; HarEnMi; HarEnUS; OhA&B; TwCBDA; WebAB 74, 79; WebAMB; WhAm HS; WhoMilH 76; WorAl; WorAlBi*

Crookes, William, Sir
English. Physicist
Pioneered in study of vacuum electron tube, forerunner to X-ray, display, cathode-ray tubes; discovered poisonous element thallium, 1861.
b. Jun 17, 1832 in London, England
d. Apr 4, 1919 in London, England
Source: *Alli SUP; AsBiEn; BiDPara; BiESc; BioIn 1, 2, 3, 6, 9, 11, 12, 13, 14, 19; CamDcSc; CelCen; DcInv; DcNaB 1912; DcScB; EncO&P 1, 2, 2S1, 3; EncPaPR 91; InSci; LarDcSc; LinLib S; McGEWB; WebBD 83; WhDW; WhLit; WorAl; WorAlBi; WorInv; WorScD*

Crooks, Richard Alexander
American. Opera Singer
Tenor, NY Met., 1933-43; popular concertizer.
b. Jun 26, 1900 in Trenton, New Jersey
d. 1972
Source: *Baker 84; BiDAmM; NewEOp 71*

Cropsey, Jasper Francis
American. Artist
Hudson River school painter known for autumnal scenes of Catskill Mountains.
b. Feb 18, 1823 in Rossville, New York
d. 1900
Source: *AmBi; ApCAB; BioIn 1, 8, 11, 12, 13, 14, 15, 21; BriEAA; DcAmArt; DcBrBI; Drake; EarABI; McGDA; NatCAB 1; NewYHSD; PeoHis; TwCBDA; WhAm 1*

Crosbie, John (Carnell)
Canadian. Government Official
Minister of international trade, 1988—; responsible for negotiating Canada-US free-trade agreement through Canadian Parliament, 1988.
b. Jan 30, 1931 in Saint John's, Newfoundland, Canada
Source: *BioIn 12, 13, 16; CanWW 31, 70, 79, 80, 81, 83, 89; CurBio 90; IntWW 89, 91, 93; IntYB 78, 79, 80, 81, 82; Who 82, 83, 85, 88, 90, 92, 94; WhoAm 80, 82, 84, 86, 88, 90, 92; WhoE 86, 89, 91, 93; WhoFI 92; WhoWor 89, 91, 93, 95, 96, 97*

Crosby, Alexander L
American. Children's Author
Books include *The Rio Grande,* 1966; *Steamboat Up the Colorado,* 1965.
b. Jun 10, 1906 in Catonsville, Maryland
d. Jan 31, 1980 in Quakertown, Pennsylvania
Source: *AuBYP 2; BioIn 7, 9, 10; ConAu 29R, 93; MorBMP; NewYTBS 80; SmATA 2, 23*

Crosby, Bing
[Harry Lillis Crosby]
American. Actor, Singer
Won Oscar for *Going My Way,* 1944; biggest hit "White Christmas," 1942; crooner known for "road" movies with Bob Hope, Dorothy Lamour.
b. May 2, 1904 in Tacoma, Washington
d. Oct 14, 1977 in Madrid, Spain
Source: *AllMusG, 78; IntWW 74, 75, 76, 77; LegTOT; MotPP; MovMk; NewAmDM; NewGrDA 86; NewGrDJ 88, 94; NewYTBE 70; NewYTBS 77; OxCFilm; RadStar; WebAB 74, 79; WhAm 7; Who 74; WhoAm 74, 76, 78; WhoGolf; WhoHol A; WhoMus 72; WhoProB 73; WhoRock 81; WhoWor 74, 76; WorEFlm*

Crosby, Bob
[George Robert Crosby]
American. Bandleader
Led Dixieland-style big band, 1935-50s; brother of Bing.
b. Aug 23, 1913 in Spokane, Washington
Source: *AllMusG; AnObit 1993; ASCAP 66; Baker 92; BiDAmM; BiDJaz; BioIn 2, 3, 4, 5, 9, 12, 16, 18; CmpEPM; EncJzS; FilmgC; HalFC 84, 88; IlEncJ; IntMPA 75, 76, 77, 78, 79, 81, 82, 84, 86, 88, 92, 94; LegTOT; NewAmDM; NewGrDA 86; NewGrDJ 88, 94; OxCPMus; PenEncP; RadStar; SaTiSS; WhoHol 92, A; WhoJazz 72; WorAl; WorAlBi*

Crosby, Cathy Lee
American. Actor
Co-host of TV show "That's Incredible!," 1980-84.
b. Dec 2, 1949 in Los Angeles, California
Source: *BioIn 13, 14; ForWC 70; IntMPA 86, 92; VarWW 85; WhoHol A*

Crosby, David (Van Cortlandt)
[Crosby, Stills, Nash & Young; The Byrds]
American. Musician, Songwriter
Rhythm guitarist, The Byrds, 1960s; Stills, Nash and Young, 1970s-80s; hit songs include "Deja Vu;" inducted into Rock and Roll Hall of Fame, 1991.
b. Aug 14, 1941 in Los Angeles, California
Source: *BiDAmM; BioIn 9, 13, 14, 15, 16; BkPepl; ConMuA 80A; ConMus 3; EncPR&S 89; EncRk 88; LegTOT; OxCPMus; WhoAm 78, 80, 82, 84; WhoEnt 92; WhoRock 81; WorAlBi*

Crosby, Enoch
American. Spy
Patriot spy during American Revolution, 1776-80; prototype for title character in *The Spy,* by James F. Cooper.
b. 1750 in Cape Cod, Massachusetts
d. 1835
Source: *ApCAB; BioIn 6, 10; Drake; EncAI&E; TwCBDA; WhAmRev*

Crosby, Fanny
[Frances Jane Crosby]
American. Songwriter
Blinded at age 6 weeks; wrote more than 6000 hymns, including "Safe in the Arms of Jesus."
b. Mar 24, 1820 in Putnam County, New York
d. Feb 12, 1915 in Bridgeport, Connecticut
Source: *AmAu&B; AmBi; ApCAB SUP, X; BenetAL 91; BioAmW; BioIn 15, 19; DcAmB; DcAmReB 2; DcNAA; InWom, SUP; LibW; LinLib L, S; LuthC 75; NewGrDA 86; NotAW; RelLAm 91; REnAL; TwCBDA; WebE&AL; WhAm 1; WomWWA 14*

Crosby, Floyd Delafield
American. Filmmaker
Films include *The Raven,* 1935; won Oscar for *Tabu,* 1930-31.
b. Dec 12, 1899 in New York, New York
d. Sep 30, 1985 in Ojai, California
Source: *BioIn 15; VarWW 85*

Crosby, Gary
American. Singer, Actor
Eldest son of the singer Bing Crosby.
d. Aug 24, 1995 in Burbank, California
Source: *MotPP; NewYTBS 95; WhoHol A*

Crosby, Harry
American. Publisher, Poet
Founder, Black Sun Press, 1927, which produced limited editions of T S Eliot, Joyce; obsession with death led to murder, suicide.
b. Jun 4, 1898 in Boston, Massachusetts
d. Dec 10, 1929 in New York, New York
Source: *AmAu&B; BioIn 10, 11, 12, 15, 16; ConAu 107; DcLB 4, 48; DcNAA; LiExTwC*

Crosby, James Morris
American. Business Executive
Founder, chm., Resorts International, Inc., 1968-86; introduced casino gambling to Atlantic City, 1978.
b. May 12, 1927 in Great Neck, New York
d. Apr 10, 1986 in New York, New York
Source: *BioIn 11, 14; NewYTBS 86; WhoAm 82*

Crosby, John
American. Impresario
Inaugurated Santa Fe Opera, 1957; pres., Manhattan School of Music, 1976-86.
b. Jul 12, 1926 in New York, New York
Source: *Baker 78, 84; BioIn 14; CurBio 81; IntWWM 90; NewAmDM; WhoAm 86; WhoWest 74; WhoWor 74*

Crosby, John Campbell
American. Journalist
Radio, TV columnist; collection of his best pieces: *Out of the Blue,* 1952;

wrote espionage/action/adventure novels including *Men in Arms,* 1983.
b. May 18, 1912 in Milwaukee, Wisconsin
d. Sep 7, 1991 in Esmont, Virginia
Source: *AmAu&B; BiDAmNC; BioIn 1, 2, 3, 4, 5, 6, 8; ConAu 1R, 4NR; CurBio 91N; IlsBYP; IntAu&W 77, 89, 91; IntWW 74, 75, 76, 77, 78, 79, 80, 81, 82, 83, 89, 91; REnAL; WhAm 10; WhoAm 74, 76, 78, 80, 82, 84, 86, 88, 90; WhoSSW 80, 82, 84; WhoWor 74; WrDr 76, 94N*

Crosby, Kathryn
[Mrs. Bing Crosby; Kathryn Grandstaff; Kathryn Grant]
American., Actor
Married Bing, 1957, appeared with family in TV Christmas specials.
b. Nov 25, 1933 in Houston, Texas
Source: *BioIn 4, 5, 6, 9, 11, 13; FilmEn; FilmgC; ForYSC; HalFC 80, 84, 88; IntMPA 75, 76, 77, 78, 79, 81, 82, 84, 86, 88, 92, 94, 96; InWom; MotPP; NewYTBE 71; WhoAm 84, 86; WhoEnt 92; WhoHol 92, A; WhoHrs 80*

Crosby, Mary Frances
American. Actor
Played Kristin Shepherd, who shot JR Ewing, on "Dallas," 1979-81; daughter of Bing Crosby.
b. Sep 14, 1959 in Los Angeles, California
Source: *BioIn 11, 12, 14; ConTFT 5; IntMPA 92; VarWW 85*

Crosby, Nathaniel
American. Golfer
Youngest son of Bing; won US Amateur Golf Championship, 1981.
b. Oct 29, 1961 in Los Angeles, California
Source: *BioIn 12, 13; NewYTBS 81*

Crosby, Norm(an Lawrence)
American. Comedian
Night club, TV routines feature mispronounced malapropisms.
b. Sep 15, 1927 in Boston, Massachusetts
Source: *BioIn 13; LegTOT; VarWW 85; WhoAm 86, 88, 90, 92, 94, 95, 96, 97; WhoCom; WhoEnt 92*

Crosby, Percy L
American. Cartoonist
Drew syndicated comic strip Skippy, 1920s-43; became film starring Jackie Cooper, 1931.
b. Dec 8, 1891 in New York, New York
d. Dec 8, 1964 in New York, New York
Source: *WorECom*

Crosby, Sumner McKnight
American. Art Historian, Educator
Books on medieval art, architecture include *The Abbey of St. Denis,* 1953; *The Art Through the Ages,* 1959.
b. Jul 29, 1909 in Minneapolis, Minnesota
d. Nov 16, 1982 in Waterbury, Connecticut
Source: *BioIn 8, 13, 14; ConAu 13R, 108; DrAS 74H, 78H, 82H; NewYTBS 82; WhAm 8; WhoAm 74, 76, 78, 80, 82; WhoAmA 73, 76, 78, 80, 82, 84N, 86N, 89N, 91N, 93N*

Crosby, Stills, Nash & Young
[David Crosby; Graham Nash; Stephen Stills; Neil Young]
American. Music Group
Hits include Woodstock; "Teach Your Children," 1970.
Source: *BiDAmM; BioIn 11, 12, 14, 15, 16, 17, 18, 19, 20, 21; EncFCWM 83; EncPR&S 89; EncRk 88; EncRkSt; FacFETw; IlEncRk; OxCPMus; PenEncP; RkOn 78; RolSEnR 83; Who 92, 94; WhoEnt 92; WhoHol A; WhoRock 81; WhoRocM 82*

Crosley, Powel, Jr.
American. Business Executive, Baseball Executive
Marketed first moderately priced radio, 1921; owner, large radio stations in Cincinnati, Cincinnati Reds, 1933-61; introduced night baseball, 1935.
b. Sep 18, 1886 in Cincinnati, Ohio
d. Mar 28, 1961 in Cincinnati, Ohio
Source: *BiDAmSp BB; BioIn 1, 5, 6, 15; CurBio 47, 61; DcAmB S7; EncABHB 5; WhAm 4; WhoProB 73; WorAl; WorAlBi*

Crosman, Henrietta
American. Actor
Stage actress who made films, 1930s; best known for film *Royal Family of Broadway,* 1930.
b. Sep 2, 1861 in Wheeling, West Virginia
d. Oct 31, 1944 in Pelham Manor, New York
Source: *BioIn 3; CamGWoT; EncAFC; FamA&A; Film 2; HalFC 84, 88; InWom; NotNAT B; ObitOF 79; OxCAmT 84; PlP&P; ThFT; WhoHol B; WhScrn 74, 77, 83; WhThe; WomWWA 14*

Cross, Ben
[Bernard Cross]
English. Actor
Played Olympic runner Harold Abrahams in Oscar-winning *Chariots of Fire,* 1981.
b. Dec 16, 1947? in London, England
Source: *BioIn 12, 13, 14; ConTFT 6; CurBio 84; HalFC 88; IntMPA 92, 94, 96; ItaFilm; NewYTBS 81, 82; WhoHol 92*

Cross, Christopher
[Christopher Geppert]
American. Singer, Songwriter
Known for number one singles "Sailing," 1980; Oscar-winner "Arthur's Theme," 1981.
b. May 3, 1951 in San Antonio, Texas
Source: *BioIn 12, 13; EncPR&S 89; EncRk 88; EncRkSt; HarEnR 86; LegTOT; PenEncP; RkOn 85; RolSEnR 83; WhoAm 84, 86, 88, 90, 92, 94, 95, 96, 97; WhoEnt 92*

Cross, Milton John
American. Radio Performer
Annouced Metropolitan Opera broadcasts, 1931-75.
b. Apr 16, 1897 in New York, New York
d. Jan 3, 1975 in New York, New York
Source: *AmAu&B; BioIn 4, 9, 10; ConAu 53; CurBio 40, 75, 75N; DcAmB S9; NewYTBE 71; ObitOF 79; WhAm 6; WhoAm 74; WhScrn 77; WorAl*

Cross, Wilbur Lucius
American. Educator, Politician
Yale U dean who became governor of CT, 1931-39; wrote autobiography *Connecticut Yankee,* 1943.
b. Apr 10, 1862 in Mansfield, Connecticut
d. Oct 5, 1948 in New Haven, Connecticut
Source: *AmAu&B; BiDAmEd; BiDrGov 1789; BioIn 1, 2, 4, 8; DcAmAu; DcAmB S4; DcLEL; DcNAA; FacFETw; LinLib L, S; ObitOF 79; OxCAmL 65, 83; REnAL; TwCA, SUP; WhAm 2*

Crosse, Rupert
American. Actor
Appeared in film *The Reivers,* 1970; TV series "The Partners," 1971-72.
b. Nov 29, 1928, Nevis
d. Mar 5, 1973, St. Kitts and Nevis
Source: *AfrAmAl 6; DrBlPA; InB&W 80; NegAl 83, 89; WhoHol B; WhScrn 77, 83*

Crossley, Archibald Maddock
American. Pollster
Public opinion analyst; pioneered with Roper, Gallup in polling techniques.
b. Dec 7, 1896 in Fieldsboro, New Jersey
d. May 1, 1985 in Princeton, New Jersey
Source: *BioIn 1, 4, 11; ConAu 116; CurBio 41, 85*

Crossman, Richard Howard Stafford
English. Author
Best known as editor for collection of essays by ex-communists: *The God That Failed.*
b. Dec 15, 1907 in London, England
d. Apr 5, 1974
Source: *Au&Wr 71; ConAu 49, 61; CurBio 47, 74; DcPol; NewYTBS 74; ObitOF 79; ObitT 1971; REn; WhE&EA; Who 74; WhoWor 74; WorAu 1950*

Crothers, Rachel
American. Dramatist
Wrote plays on role of modern woman: *Susan and God,* 1937.
b. Dec 12, 1878 in Bloomington, Illinois
d. Jul 5, 1958 in Danbury, Connecticut
Source: *AmAu&B; AmWomD; ArtclWW 2; BenetAL 91; BioAmW; BioIn 1, 2, 4,*

5; *BlmGWL; CamGLE; CamGWoT; CamHAL; CnDAL; CnMD; CnThe; ConAmA; ConAmD; ConAmL; ConAu 113; ConWomD; DcAmB S6; DcLB 7; DcLEL; EncWL; FacFETw; FemiCLE; FilmgC; HalFC 84, 88; IntDcT 2; InWom, SUP; LibW; LinLib L, S; LngCTC; McGEWD 72, 84; ModWD; NewYTBS 80; NotNAT B; OxCAmL 65, 83, 95; OxCAmT 84; OxCThe 67, 83; OxCWoWr 95; REn; REnAL; REnWD; RfGAmL 87, 94; TwCA, SUP; TwCLC 19; WebAB 74, 79; WhNAA; WhThe; WomWMM*

Crothers, Scatman
[Benjamin Sherman Crothers]
American. Actor, Singer
Known for TV role in "Chico and the Man," 1974-78; film roles in *The Shining*, 1980; *Twilight Zone: The Movie*, 1983.
b. May 23, 1910 in Terre Haute, Indiana
d. Nov 22, 1986 in Los Angeles, California
Source: *AnObit 1986; ConNews 87-1; ConTFT 3; DrBlPA, 90; HalFC 84, 88; LegTOT; NewYTBS 86; WhAm 9; WhoAm 82, 84, 86; WhoHol A*

Crouch, Andrae Edward
American. Singer, Songwriter
The most influential black gospel artist; has won six Grammys.
b. Jul 1, 1942 in Los Angeles, California
Source: *BioIn 11, 13; ConMus 9; DrBlPA 90; InB&W 85; NewGrDA 86; PenEncP; WhoAm 88; WhoBlA 92*

Crouch, Stanley
American. Journalist
Staff writer, *Village Voice*, 1975-80; published essay collections, *Notes of a Hanging Judge*, 1990, and *The American Skin Game*, 1995.
b. Dec 14, 1945 in Los Angeles, California
Source: *BiDJaz; BioIn 13; BlkAWP; ConAu 141; ConBlB 11; CurBio 94; DrAP 75; EncJzS; InB&W 80, 85; LivgBAA; NewGrDJ 88, 94; PenEncP; SelBAAu; WhoAm 96; WrDr 96*

Crouse, Lindsay Ann
American. Actor
Daughter of Russel Crouse; appeared in film *All the President's Men*, 1976.
b. May 12, 1948 in New York, New York
Source: *BioIn 15; ConTFT 4; HalFC 88; IntMPA 86, 92; NewYTBS 81; WhoAm 90; WhoAmW 91; WhoEnt 92*

Crouse, Russel
American. Dramatist
Co-wrote hit Broadway plays *Life with Father*, 1939; *State of the Union*, 1946; wrote book from which *The Sound of Music* was made.
b. Feb 20, 1893 in Findlay, Ohio
d. Apr 3, 1966 in New York, New York
Source: *AmAu&B; AuBYP 2; BenetAL 91; BiE&WWA; BioIn 1, 2, 4, 5, 7, 8, 11; CamGWoT; CnDAL; CnThe; ConAu 77; CurBio 41, 66; EncMT; EncWT; HalFC 84, 88; LinLib L, S; McGEWD 72, 84; ModWD; NewCBMT; NotNAT B; OhA&B; OxCAmL 65, 83, 95; OxCAmT 84; OxCPMus; REn; REnAL; TwCA SUP; WhAm 4; WhE&EA; WhThe; WorAl; WorAlBi*

Crow, John David
American. Football Player
All-America halfback, Texas A & M, 1955-57; won Heisman Trophy, 1957; in NFL, 1958-68.
b. Jul 8, 1935 in Marion, Louisiana
Source: *BiDAmSp FB; BioIn 4, 6, 11, 14; WhoFtbl 74; WhoSpor; WhoSSW 80, 82*

Crow, Sheryl
American. Singer, Songwriter
Grammy, Best Pop Vocal, "All I Wanna Do," 1994.
b. Feb 11, 1964 in Kennett, Missouri
Source: *News 95, 95-2*

Crowder, Enoch Herbert
American. Army Officer
Administered selective civil service, WW I; first Cuban ambassador, 1920s.
b. Apr 11, 1859 in Edinburg, Missouri
d. May 7, 1932 in Washington, District of Columbia
Source: *AmBi; ApCAB X; BioIn 4; DcAmB S1; DcAmDH 80, 89; FacFETw; WebAMB; WhAm 1*

Crow Dog
American. Native American Leader
One of the leaders of the Ghost Dance revival, 1890.
b. 1834? in Horse Stealing Creek, Montana
d. 1911?
Source: *BioIn 21; NotNaAm*

Crow Dog, Mary
[Mary Brave Bird]
American. Political Activist
Life story *Lakota Woman*, 1990, tells of how her involvement with the American Indian Movement gave meaning to her life.
b. 1953
Source: *ConAu 154; ConLC 93; NatNAL; NotNaAm*

Crowe, Cameron
American. Filmmaker, Director
Wrote script for movie *Fast Times at Ridgemont High*, 1982 after attending a high school undercover at age 21; wrote and directed movie *Singles*, 1992.
b. Jul 13, 1957 in Palm Springs, California
Source: *BioIn 16, 18, 21; ConAu 153; ConTFT 13; CurBio 96; IntMPA 94, 96; LegTOT; MiSFD 9; WhoAm 95, 96, 97; WhoWor 95*

Crowe, Colin Tradescant, Sir
British. Diplomat
United Kingdom representative to UN, 1970-73.
b. Sep 7, 1913 in Yokohama, Japan
Source: *BlueB 76; IntWW 74, 75, 76, 77, 78, 79, 80, 81, 82, 83, 89; IntYB 78, 79, 80, 81, 82; Who 74, 82, 83, 85, 88, 90N; WhoGov 72, 75; WhoWor 74, 76, 78*

Crowe, J. D
American. Musician, Singer
Bluerass banjo player for band J.D. Crowe and the New South 1974; known for experimental bluegrass music.
b. Aug 1937 in Lexington, Kentucky

Crowe, William James, Jr.
American. Military Leader
Navy admiral; rose from submarine service to succeed John Vessey as chairman of Joint Chiefs of Staff, 1985-89; succeeded by Colin Powell; Professor of Geopolitics at the Univ. of Oklahoma, 1989—.
b. Jan 2, 1925 in La Grange, Kentucky
Source: *BioIn 14, 15, 16; CurBio 88; IntWW 89, 91, 93; Law&B 89A; NewYTBS 85, 88; WhoAm 78, 82, 84, 86, 88, 90, 94, 95, 96, 97; WhoAmP 91, 95; WhoE 86, 89; WhoSSW 91; WhoWor 89, 95, 96, 97*

Crowell, Luther Childs
American. Inventor
Invented square-bottomed grocer's bag, machine to make it, 1872.
b. Sep 7, 1840 in West Dennis, Massachusetts
d. Sep 16, 1903 in Wellfleet, Massachusetts
Source: *DcAmB; NatCAB 13; WhAm 1*

Crowell, Rodney
American. Singer, Songwriter
Many of his songs recorded by Emmylou Harris; has produced wife Roseanne Cash's albums; top ten single "It's Such a Small World," 1988 sung as duet with Roseanne Cash.
b. Aug 7, 1950 in Houston, Texas
Source: *BgBkCoM; BioIn 14, 16; ConMus 8; HarEnCM 87; HarEnR 86; LegTOT; OnThGG; PenEncP; RkOn 85; RolSEnR 83; WhoEnt 92; WhoNeCM*

Crowfoot
Canadian. Native American Leader
Blackfoot peace crief who signed a treaty with the Canadian government, 1877, formalizing the tribe's relationship with the government.
b. 1830 in Blackfoot Crossing, Alberta, Canada
d. Apr 25, 1890
Source: *NotNaAm; OxCCan*

Crowley, Aleister (Edward Alexander)
"The Great Beast"
English. Author, Magician
Writer of occult lore, Black Magic rites: *Diary of a Drug Fiend,* 1922.
b. Oct 12, 1875 in Leamington, England
d. Dec 1, 1947 in Brighton, England
Source: *AstEnc; Benet 87; BiDAmCu; BioIn 1, 2, 3, 4, 5, 7, 8, 9, 10, 11, 13, 14, 15, 16, 17, 21; ChhPo S1; DcNaB MP; DivFut; EncO&P 1, 1S1, 1S2, 2, 3; EncPaPR 91; EncWW; FacFETw; GayLL; LegTOT; LngCTC; Novels; OxCEng 85, 95; PenEncH; REn; ScF&FL 1, 92; TwCLC 7; WhDW; WhoHr&F; WorAl; WorAlBi*

Crowley, Diane
American. Journalist
Co-winner of nationwide search for Ann Landers' advice column replacement, 1986.
b. 1940?
Source: *BioIn 15; ConAu 135; WhoAm 90*

Crowley, Jim
[Four Horsemen of Notre Dame; James H Crowley]
"Sleepy Jim"
American. Football Player
Running back for Knute Rockne on Notre Dame's championship team, 1924.
b. Sep 10, 1902 in Chicago, Illinois
d. Jan 15, 1986 in Scranton, Pennsylvania
Source: *BioIn 14, 15; NewYTBS 86; WhoFtbl 74; WhoSpor*

Crowley, Leo Thomas
American. Government Official
Held several government posts including first chm. of Federal Deposit Insurance Corp. (FDIC), 1934-42.
b. Aug 15, 1889 in Milton Junction, Wisconsin
d. Apr 15, 1972 in Madison, Wisconsin
Source: *BioIn 1, 9, 13; CurBio 43, 72; DcAmB S9; NewYTBE 72; WhAm 5*

Crowley, Pat
American. Actor
Starred in TV series "Please Don't Eat the Daisies," 1965-67.
b. Sep 17, 1929 in Scranton, Pennsylvania
Source: *ConTFT 8; EncAFC; FilmgC; HalFC 84, 88; MotPP; WhoAm 82, 90; WhoEnt 92; WhoHol A*

Crown, Henry
American. Industrialist, Philanthropist
Chm., General Dynamics, 1970-1986; wealthy philanthropist supported Arie Crown Theater, Chicago; Rebecca Crown Center, Northwestern U; Crown Space Center, Washington, D.C.
b. Jun 13, 1896 in Chicago, Illinois
d. Aug 14, 1990 in Chicago, Illinois
Source: *AnObit 1990; BiDAmBL 83; BioIn 3, 4, 6, 7, 8, 9, 10, 11, 12, 15, 17; BlueB 76; CurBio 72, 90N; Dun&B 86; IntWW 74, 75, 76, 77, 78, 79, 80; IntYB 78, 79, 80, 81, 82; NewYTBS 90; St&PR 75, 84, 87, 91; WhAm 10; WhoAm 74, 76, 78, 80, 82, 84, 86, 88, 90; WhoFI 74, 75, 77; WhoMW 74, 76, 78; WhoWorJ 72, 78*

Crowninshield, Francis Welch
[Arthur Loring Bruce]
American. Editor, Publisher
Edited *Vanity Fair,* 1914-35; one of founders of Museum of Modern Art.
b. Jun 24, 1872 in Paris, France
d. Dec 28, 1947 in New York, New York
Source: *DcAmB S4; DcNAA; REn; REnAL; WhAm 2*

Crowther, Bosley
[Francis Bosley Crowther]
American. Critic
Film critic, *NY Times,* 1940-67; wrote over 200 reviews annually.
b. Jul 13, 1905 in Lutherville, Maryland
d. Mar 7, 1981 in Mount Kisco, New York
Source: *AmAu&B; AnObit 1981; BioIn 4, 5, 8, 12; ConAu 65, 103; CurBio 81, 81N; DcTwCCu 1; EncTwCJ; IntMPA 81; LegTOT; NewYTBS 81; WhAm 7; WhoWor 74; WorAl; WorAlBi*

Crowther, Samuel Adjai
Nigerian. Religious Leader
Explored Niger River, 1841; first African Anglican bishop in Nigeria.
b. 1808 in Ochuga, Yorubaland
d. Dec 31, 1891 in Lagos, Nigeria (Southern)
Source: *BioIn 11; REnAL; WhAm 2; WhNAA*

Crozier, Eric John
English. Producer
Co-founded, English Opera Group, 1947; plays include *Noah Gives Thanks,* 1950; translated several classic operas.
b. Nov 14, 1914 in London, England
Source: *Au&Wr 71; BioIn 12; ChhPo S2; DcLEL 1940; IntAu&W 77, 89; IntWWM 90; LngCTC; Who 74, 82, 83, 85, 88, 90, 92, 94; WhoMus 72*

Crozier, Roger Allan
"The Dodger"
Canadian. Hockey Player
Goalie, 1963-77, mostly with Detroit, Buffalo; won Calder Trophy, 1965, Conn Smythe Trophy, 1966.
b. Mar 16, 1942 in Bracebridge, Ontario, Canada
d. Jan 10, 1996 in Newark, Delaware
Source: *HocEn; WhoHcky 73*

Cruickshank, Andrew John
Scottish. Actor
Star of British theater, film, since 1930s; best known since 1963 for TV series "Dr. Finlay's Casebook."
b. Dec 25, 1907 in Aberdeen, Scotland
d. Apr 29, 1988 in London, England
Source: *FilmgC; PlP&P; Who 74; WhoHol A; WhoThe 81*

Cruikshank, George
English. Artist, Illustrator
Noted for humorous satirical sketches in *Oliver Twist,* 1838; Grimm's *Popular Stories,* 1826.
b. Sep 27, 1792 in London, England
d. Feb 1, 1878 in London, England
Source: *Alli; AntBDN B; ArtsNiC; BioIn 1, 3, 10, 11, 12, 13, 16, 18, 19; BlmGEL; CamGLE; CarSB; CelCen; ChhPo, S1, S2, S3; ClaDrA; DcArts; DcBiPP; DcBrBI; DcBrWA; DcNaB; DcVicP 2; Dis&D; EncEnl; IlsBYP; LinLib L, S; LngCEL; McGDA; NewC; OxCArt; OxCChiL; OxCEng 85, 95; OxDcArt; REn; SmATA 22; StaCVF; Str&VC; VicBrit; WhDW; WorECom*

Cruikshank, Margaret
American. Educator
Faculty member, City College of San Francisco, 1981—, where she teaches gay and lesbian literature.
b. Apr 26, 1940 in Duluth, Minnesota
Source: *GayLesB; GayLL*

Cruise, Tom
[Thomas Cruise Mapother, IV]
American. Actor
Has had roles in six major films, including *Risky Business,* 1983; *Top Gun,* 1986; *Mission Impossible,* 1996; *Jerry Maguire,* 1996.
b. Jul 3, 1962 in Syracuse, New York
Source: *BiDFilm 94; BioIn 13, 14, 15, 16; CelR 90; ConNews 85-4; ConTFT 9; CurBio 87; HalFC 88; IntDcF 2-3; IntMPA 88, 92, 94, 96; IntWW 91, 93; LegTOT; VarWW 85; WhoAm 90, 92, 94, 95, 96, 97; WhoEnt 92; WhoHol 92; WorAlBi*

Crum, Denny
[Denzel Edwin Crum]
American. Basketball Coach
Coach, U of Louisville, 1971—; won NCAA championship, 1980.
b. Mar 2, 1937 in San Fernando, California
Source: *BiDAmSp BK; WhoAm 82, 84, 86, 88, 96, 97; WhoSpor; WhoSSW 88, 95; WorAlBi*

Crumb, George Henry
American. Composer
His works include the 1968 Pulitzer Prize-winning *Echoes of Time and the River.*
b. Oct 24, 1929 in Charleston, West Virginia
Source: *AmComp; AmCulL; Baker 84; BioIn 7, 9, 10, 11, 14, 15, 16; ConAmC 82; ConCom 92; DcArts; EncWB; FacFETw; IntWWM 90; NewAmDM; NewGrDA 86; NewOxM; NewYTBS 75; WhoAm 74, 76, 78, 80, 82, 84, 86, 88, 90, 92, 94, 95, 96, 97; WhoEnt 92*

Crumb, R(obert)
American. Cartoonist
Known for 1970s underground comics with biting satire; started *Zap Comix* series, 1967.
b. Aug 30, 1943 in Philadelphia, Pennsylvania
Source: *BioIn 9, 10, 13, 14, 20; ConAu 106; ConLC 17; CurBio 95; EncACom; MugS; NewYTBE 72; WhoAm 97; WorECom*

Crummell, Alexander
American. Clergy
Episcopal minister who wrote *Africa and America,* 1892.
b. Mar 1819 in New York, New York
d. Sep 1898 in Point Pleasant, New Jersey
Source: *AfrAmAl 6; AfrAmOr; AfrAmPr; Alli SUP; AmAu&B; ApCAB SUP; BioIn 4, 6, 8, 10, 11, 17, 18, 19; BlkWrNE; DcAmAu; DcAmNB; DcAmReB 1, 2; DcNAA; EncAACR; EncARH; InB&W 80, 85; NatCAB 5; OxCAmL 83, 95; RelLAm 91; SelBAAf; SelBAAu; TwCBDA*

Crump, Edward Hull
American. Politician
Boss of Memphis Dem. organization; served four terms as Mayor, two as state representative.
b. 1874 in Holly Springs, Mississippi
d. Oct 16, 1954 in Memphis, Tennessee
Source: *BiDrAC; BiDrUSC 89; BioIn 3, 5, 7, 9, 10, 14; BioNews 74; DcAmB S5; EncSoH; ObitOF 79; St&PR 84; WhAm 3; WhAmP*

Crusaders, The
[Larry Eugene Carlton; Witon Felder; Wayne Henderson; Stix Hooper; Joe Sample]
American. Music Group
Best known for hit single "Uptight (Everything's Alright)," 1966.
Source: *AllMusG; BiDAfM; BiDJaz A; BioIn 17; EncJzS; EncRk 88; EncRkSt; HarEnR 86; InB&W 80, 85, 85A; NewGrDA 86; NewGrDJ 88, 94; PenEncP; RkOn 78, 84; RolSEnR 83; SoulM; WhoAfA 96; WhoBlA 94; WhoRock 81; WhoRocM 82*

Cruyff, Johan
"The Flying Dutchman"
Dutch. Soccer Player
MVP with LA Aztecs, 1979.
b. Apr 25, 1947 in Amsterdam, Netherlands
Source: *BioIn 10, 12; CurBio 81; FacFETw*

Cruz, Arturo
[Arturo Jose Cruz Porras]
Nicaraguan. Politician, Diplomat
Disgust with Sandinistas led to alignment with Contras, early 1980s; aborted candidacy in controversial 1984 pres. election.
b. Dec 18, 1923 in Jinotepe, Nicaragua
Source: *BioIn 14, 15; ConNews 85-1; WhoWor 82*

Cruz, Celia
"Queen of Salsa"
Cuban. Singer
Salsa performer for over forty years; singer with La Sonora Matancera orchestra at Havana's world famous Tropicana nightclub for fifteen years; received Grammy award, 1974; gold records for albums *Celia and Johnny,* 1974, and *Tremendo Trio,* 1983; recipient of NY Music Award for best Latin artist, 1987.
b. Oct 21, 1929 in Havana, Cuba
Source: *ConMus 10; CurBio 83; DcHiB; InWom SUP; NotHsAW 93; WhoAm 96, 97*

Cruz, Stevie
American. Boxer
Won NBA featherweight title, 1986.
b. 1963? in Fort Worth, Texas
Source: *BioIn 15*

Cruzan, Nancy
American. Victim
Subject of U.S. Supreme Court battle over right-to-die option; lived in coma on artificial life support for eight years.
b. 1957
d. Dec 26, 1990 in Mount Vernon, Missouri
Source: *BioIn 16; News 91, 91-3*

Cryer, David
American. Actor
Best known for role in play *The Fantasticks.*
b. Mar 8, 1936 in Evanston, Illinois
Source: *NotNAT; WhoHol 92; WhoThe 77, 81*

Crystal, Billy
[William Crystal]
American. Actor, Comedian
Comedic actor known as versatile mimic; starred in "Soap," 1977-81; movies include *City Slickers,* 1991.
b. Mar 14, 1947 in Long Beach, New York
Source: *BioIn 14, 15, 16; ConNews 85-3; ConTFT 3, 10; CurBio 87; HolBB; IntMPA 84, 86, 88, 92, 94, 96; IntWW 91, 93; LegTOT; QDrFCA 92; WhoAm 86, 88, 90, 92, 94, 95, 96, 97; WhoCom; WhoEnt 92; WhoHol 92; WorAl; WorAlBi*

Crystal, Lester M
American. TV Executive
Won two Emmys; former exec. vp, NBC News.
b. Sep 13, 1934 in Duluth, Minnesota
Source: *LesBEnT 92; VarWW 85; WhoAm 90*

Crystals, The
[Barbara Alston; Lala Brooks; Dee Dee Kenniebrew; Mary Thomas; Pat Wright]
American. Music Group
Brooklyn schoolgirls; 1960s hits include "He's a Rebel," 1962; "Da Doo Ron Ron," 1963.
Source: *BioIn 3, 9, 16, 17, 21; DcLP 87A; DcVicP 2; DcWomA; EncPR&S 89; EncRk 88; EncRkSt; IlEncBM 82; InWom; PenEncP; RkOn 74, 82; RolSEnR 83; SoulM; WhNAA; WhoMus 72; WhoRock 81; WomPO 76, 78*

Csonka, Larry
[Lawrence Richard Csonka]
American. Football Player
Fullback, rushed for 8,081 yds., 1968-80, mostly with Miami; Hall of Fame, 1987.
b. Dec 25, 1946 in Akron, Ohio
Source: *BiDAmSp FB; BioIn 9, 10, 11, 12, 16; BioNews 75; CelR; CurBio 77; LegTOT; NewYTBE 73; NewYTBS 76, 79; WhoAm 82; WhoSpor; WorAl; WorAlBi*

Cuauhtemoc
Aztec. Ruler
Last Aztec ruler who defended empire against Spanish; hanged by Cortes.
b. 1495? in Tenochtitlan, Mexico
d. Feb 26, 1525 in Itzancanal, Mexico
Source: *BioIn 2, 8; DcHiB; EncLatA; McGEWB; NewCol 75; REn*

Cudahy, Michael
American. Meat Packer, Merchant
Partner with Philip D Armour, 1875-90; established Cudahy Packing Co., Omaha, NE.
b. Dec 7, 1841 in Callan, Ireland
d. 1910
Source: *AmBi; BiDAmBL 83; DcAmB; DcCathB; NatCAB 11; NewCol 75; WhAm 1; WorAl; WorAlBi*

Cudlipp, Hugh
Welsh. Journalist
Editor, England's *Daily Mirror,* 1952-63; wrote *Publish and Be Damned,* 1953.
b. Aug 28, 1913 in Cardiff, Wales
Source: *Au&Wr 71; BioIn 3, 5, 6, 8; ConAu 116; IntWW 74, 93; WhE&EA; Who 74; WhoFI 74; WhoWor 74*

Cudworth, Ralph
English. Philosopher, Educator
Wrote *The True Intellectual System of the Universe,* 1678.
b. 1617 in Aller, England
d. Jun 26, 1688 in Cambridge, England
Source: *Alli; BioIn 2, 3, 10; BritAu; CamGEL; CamGLE; CasWL; Chambr 1; DcBiPP; DcEnL; DcEuL; DcNaB; DcScB; EncEnl; EncEth; EvLB; IlEncMy; LuthC 75; McGEWB; NewC; NewCol 75; OxCEng 67, 85; OxCPhil; RAdv 14; REn*

Cuellar, Mike
[Miguel Santana Cuellar]
Cuban. Baseball Player
Pitcher, 1959-77; shared Cy Young Award with Denny McLain, 1969.
b. May 8, 1937 in Santa Clara, Cuba
Source: *Ballpl 90; BioIn 11; WhoHisp 91, 92, 94; WhoProB 73; WhoSpor*

Cueva de Garoza, Juan de la
Spanish. Dramatist, Poet
Introduced historical material, new metric forms into Spanish literature.
b. 1550 in Seville, Spain
d. 1610, Spain
Source: *REn*

Cuffe, Paul
American. Colonizer
Worked to improve conditions of slaves; pioneered efforts to settle free blacks in Sierra Leone, W Africa.
b. Jan 17, 1759 in Cutty Hunk, Massachusetts
d. Sep 9, 1817 in Westport, Massachusetts
Source: *AfrAmAl 6; BiDAmBL 83; BioIn 4, 6, 7, 8, 9, 10, 11, 12, 16; BlkWrNE; DcAmB; DcAmNB; EncAB-H 1974, 1996; InB&W 80; McGEWB; NatCAB 12; RComAH; WhAm HS; WhAmP*

Cugat, Xavier
"Rhumba King"
Spanish. Bandleader
Introduced Americans to tropical rhythms of the rumba, 1930s; with band, the Gigolos, featured in films that made name a household word, 1940s-50s.
b. Jan 1, 1900 in Barcelona, Spain
d. Oct 27, 1990 in Barcelona, Spain
Source: *AnObit 1990; Baker 78, 84, 92; BiDAmM; BioIn 1, 4, 5, 9, 12, 16, 17; CelR; CmpEPM; ConAu 132; CurBio 42, 91N; DcHiB; FacFETw; FilmgC; HalFC 84, 88; ItaFilm; LegTOT; NewAmDM; NewGrDA 86; News 91, 91-2; NewYTBS 90; OxCPMus; PenEncP; RadStar; WhAm 10; WhoAm 74, 76; WhoHol A; WorAl; WorAlBi*

Cui, Cesar Antonovich
Russian. Composer, Soldier
Wrote textbooks on fortification; composed piano works, operas.
b. Jan 18, 1835 in Vilna, Russia
d. Mar 24, 1918 in Petrograd, Union of Soviet Socialist Republics
Source: *Baker 92; BiDSovU; NewAmDM; NewEOp 71; NewGrDO*

Cukor, George (Dewey)
American. Director
Won 1964 Oscar for *My Fair Lady;* last film *Rich and Famous,* 1981.
b. Jul 7, 1899 in New York, New York
d. Jan 24, 1983 in Los Angeles, California
Source: *AnObit 1983; BiDFilm, 94; BiE&WWA; BioIn 5, 7, 8, 9, 10, 11, 12, 13, 14, 15, 17, 20; CelR; CmMov; ConTFT 1; CurBio 83, 83N; DcArts; DcFM; EncAFC; FacFETw; FilmgC; GayLesB; HalFC 84, 88; IlWWHD 1; IntDcF 1-2, 2-2; IntMPA 77, 80; IntWW 74, 75, 76, 77, 78, 79, 80, 81, 82; LegTOT; MakMC; MiSFD 9N; MovMk; NewYTBS 83; NewYTET; OxCFilm; WhAm 8; WhoAm 74, 76, 78, 80, 82; WhoWor 74, 78, 80, 82; WhoWorJ 72, 78; WorAl; WorAlBi; WorEFlm; WorFDir 1*

Culbertson, Ely
American. Bridge Player
Invented contract bridge, became world's top player, 1930s; founded *Bridge World* magazine, 1929.
b. Jul 22, 1891 in Verbilao, Romania
d. Dec 27, 1955 in Brattleboro, Vermont
Source: *AmAu&B; AmPeW; BiDInt; BioIn 2, 4, 6, 12; CurBio 40, 56; DcAmB S5; LegTOT; LinLib L, S; NatCAB 46; ObitT 1951; WebAB 74, 79; WhAm 3; WhE&EA; WorAl; WorAlBi*

Culkin, Macaulay
American. Actor
Starred in *Uncle Buck,* 1989; *Home Alone,* 1990; *Home Alone 2,* 1992; *Richie Rich,* 1995.
b. Aug 26, 1980 in New York, New York
Source: *ConTFT 10; IntMPA 92, 94, 96; LegTOT; News 91, 91-3; NewYTBS 91; WhoAm 94, 95, 96, 97; WhoHol 92*

Cullen, Bill
[William Lawrence Cullen]
American. TV Personality
Had 30-year career hosting over 5,000 game show episodes on TV including "The Price Is Right," "The $25,000 Pyramid," "Name That Tune."
b. Feb 18, 1920 in Pittsburgh, Pennsylvania
d. Jul 7, 1990 in Los Angeles, California
Source: *AnObit 1990; BioIn 3, 4, 5, 17; CurBio 60, 90N; IntMPA 75, 76, 77, 78, 79, 81, 82, 84, 86, 88; LegTOT; LesBEnT, 92; NewYTBS 90; NewYTET; RadStar; SaTiSS; VarWW 85; WhAm 10; WhoAm 74, 76, 78, 80, 82; WorAl; WorAlBi*

Cullen, Countee (Porter)
American. Poet
Wrote *Color,* 1925; *The Black Christ,* 1930.
b. May 30, 1903 in New York, New York
d. Jan 10, 1946 in New York, New York
Source: *AfrAmAl 6; AmAu&B; AnCL; AnMV 1926; Benet 87, 96; BenetAL 91; BioIn 1, 2, 3, 4, 6, 7, 8, 9, 10, 12, 13, 15, 16, 17, 18, 20; BlkAull, 92; BlkAWP; BlkLC; BlkWr 1; BlkWrNE; BroadAu; CamGLE; CamHAL; CasWL; ChhPo, S1; ConAmA; ConAmL; ConAu 108, 124; ConBlB 8; CurBio 46; CyWA 89; DcAmB S4; DcAmNB; DcLB 4, 48, 51; DcLEL; DcNAA; DcTwCCu 5; DrBlPA, 90; EarBlAP; EncAACR; EncWL 2, 3; FacFETw; FourBJA; GayLesB; InB&W 80, 85; LegTOT; LiExTwC; LinLib L; MajTwCW; McGEWB; ModAL, S1; ModBlW; NegAl 76, 83, 89; OxCAmL 65, 83, 95; OxCTwCP; PenC AM; RAdv 1, 14, 13-1; REn; REnAL; RfGAmL 87, 94; RGTwCWr; ScF&FL 1; SchCGBL; SelBAAf; SelBAAu; SmATA 18; Tw; TwCA, SUP; TwCLC 4, 37; WebE&AL; WhAm 2; WhNAA*

Cullen, Paul, Cardinal
Irish. Clergy
Served as Roman Catholic Archbishop of Dublin, 1852-66 when he was appointed prince of the church as cardinal; known for stalwart defense of the church.
b. 1803, Ireland
d. 1878, Ireland
Source: *BioIn 11, 14; CelCen; DcBiPP; DcCathB; DcIrB 78, 88; DcNaB; HisWorL*

Culliford, Peyo
[Pierre Culliford]
Belgian. Author, Cartoonist
Created the Smurfs, 1957; top children's TV show in US, early 1980s.
b. Jun 25, 1928 in Brussels, Belgium
d. Dec 24, 1992 in Brussels, Belgium
Source: *AnObit 1992; BioIn 13, 15, 18, 19; ConAu 124, 140; LegTOT; NewYTBS 92; SmATA 40, 74; WorECom*

Culligan, Emmett J
"Gold Dust"
American. Businessman
Launched water softener firm, 1924.
b. 1893 in Minnesota
d. 1970
Source: *Entr*

Cullinan, Thomas P.
American. Writer
d. Jun 11, 1995 in Cleveland Heights, Ohio
Source: *NewYTBS 95*

Cullum, John
American. Actor
Won Tony awards for *Shenandoah,* 1975; *On the Twentieth Century,* 1978; played "Holling" the pub-owner on TV show "Northern Exposure," 1990-95.
b. Mar 2, 1930 in Knoxville, Tennessee
Source: *BioIn 10, 11; ConTFT 4, 13; DcVicP 2; EncMT; IntMPA 92, 94, 96; LegTOT; NotNAT; VarWW 85; WhoAm 80, 82, 84, 86, 88, 94, 95, 96, 97; WhoHol 92, A; WhoThe 77, 81; WorAl*

Culp, Robert
American. Actor
Starred in "I Spy," 1965-68; "The Greatest American Hero," 1981-83.
b. Aug 13, 1930 in Berkeley, California
Source: *BioIn 16; CelR; ConTFT 3, 14; FilmgC; GangFlm; HalFC 84, 88; IntMPA 77, 78, 79, 81, 82, 84, 86, 88, 92, 94, 96; LegTOT; MiSFD 9; MotPP; WhoAm 76, 78, 80, 82, 84, 86, 88, 90, 92, 94, 95, 96, 97; WhoEnt 92; WhoHol 92, A; WorAl; WorAlBi*

Culpeper, Nicholas
English. Physician
Believed astrology influenced disease, herbs cured it; translated several Latin medical texts into English.
b. 1616 in London, England
d. 1654
Source: *BiESc; BiHiMed; BioIn 1, 3, 9, 18; BritAu; DcBiPP; DcLEL; DcNaB; InSci; OxCEng 85, 95; OxCMed 86; WhDW*

Culture Club
[Boy George; Micheal Craig; Roy Hay; Jon Moss; Helen Terry]
English. Music Group
Most commercially successful of British rock-theater bands, 1980s; first hit "Do You Really Want to Hurt Me?" 1982.
Source: *BioIn 14, 15, 16, 18, 19, 21; EncPR&S 89; EncRk 88; EncRkSt; HarEnR 86; IntAu&W 76X; RkOn 85*

Culvahouse, Art(hur Boggess, Jr.)
"A.B."
American. Lawyer
Protege of Howard Baker, hired 1987 as Pres. Reagan's lawyer.
b. Jul 4, 1948 in Athens, Tennessee
Source: *WhoAmL 92; WhoEmL 91*

Culver, John Chester
American. Politician, Lawyer
Dem. senator from IA, 1975-81.
b. Aug 8, 1932 in Rochester, Minnesota
Source: *BiDrAC; BiDrUSC 89; BioIn 13; CurBio 79; IntWW 83, 91; WhoAm 84; WhoAmP 73, 75, 77, 79, 81, 83, 85, 87, 95; WhoGov 72, 75, 77; WhoMW 74, 76, 78, 80; WhoWor 84*

Cumberland, Richard
English. Theologian
Wrote *De Legibus Naturae,* 1672; often considered father of English utilitarianism.
b. Jul 15, 1631 in London, England
d. Oct 9, 1718 in Peterborough, England
Source: *Alli; DcNaB; NewCol 75*

Cumberland, Richard
English. Dramatist
Wrote over 40 plays, including sentimental comedy *The Brothers,* 1769.
b. Feb 19, 1732 in Cambridge, England
d. May 7, 1811 in London, England
Source: *Alli; BiD&SB; BioIn 3, 9, 12, 16, 17; BlmGEL; BritAu; CamGEL; CamGLE; CamGWoT; CasWL; Chambr 2; CrtSuDr; DcBiPP; DcEnA; DcEnL; DcLB 89; DcLEL; DcNaB; EncWT; EvLB; IntDcT 2; McGEWD 72, 84; NewC; NewCol 75; NotNAT B; OxCEng 67, 85, 95; OxCIri; OxCThe 67, 83; PenC ENG; PlP&P; REn; RfGEnL 91; WebE&AL; WhAmRev*

Cummings, Bob
[Robert Orville Cummings]
American. Actor
Starred in early TV sitcoms, including "Love That Bob," 1954-61; most film roles were light comedies, but also co-starred in Hitchcock's *Dial M for Murder,* 1954.
b. Jun 9, 1908 in Joplin, Missouri
d. Dec 2, 1990 in Los Angeles, California
Source: *BiE&WWA; CurBio 56, 91N; FacFETw; Film 1; FilmgC; HalFC 88; IntMPA 86, 88; LegTOT; LesBEnT 92; MotPP; MovMk; NewYTBS 90; WhoAm 84; WhoHol A; WorAlBi; WorEFlm*

Cummings, Burton
[Guess Who]
Canadian. Singer, Musician
Founding member of Guess Who, 1960s; solo hits include "Stand Tall," 1976.
b. Dec 31, 1947 in Winnipeg, Manitoba, Canada
Source: *RkOn 78, 84; WhoRocM 82*

Cummings, Candy
[William Arthur Cummings]
American. Baseball Player
Pitcher credited with invention of curveball, circa 1867; Hall of Fame, 1939.
b. Oct 17, 1848 in Ware, Massachusetts
d. May 17, 1924 in Toledo, Ohio
Source: *Ballpl 90; BiDAmSp BB; BioIn 3, 7, 14, 15; LegTOT; WhoProB 73; WhoSpor*

Cummings, Constance
[Constance Halverstadt]
American. Actor
Won Tony award for *Wings,* 1979.
b. May 15, 1910 in Seattle, Washington
Source: *BiE&WWA; BioIn 11, 17; CamGWoT; CnThe; ConTFT 4; EncAFC; FilmgC; HalFC 84, 88; HolP 30; IntMPA 75, 76, 77, 78, 79, 81, 82, 84, 86, 88, 92, 94, 96; IntWW 76, 77, 78, 79, 80, 81, 82, 83, 89, 91, 93; InWom, SUP; LegTOT; MotPP; MovMk; NotNAT; OxCThe 83; ThFT; Who 85, 92; WhoAm 86, 90; WhoAmW 91; WhoEnt 92; WhoHol 92, A; WhoThe 72, 77, 81; WorAl*

Cummings, E(dward) E(stlin)
American. Poet, Author
Noted for eccentricity of punctuation, typography; first published work was autobiographical *The Enormous Room,* 1922.
b. Oct 14, 1894 in Cambridge, Massachusetts
d. Sep 3, 1962 in North Conway, New Hampshire
Source: *AmAu&B; AmCulL; AmWr; AnCL; AtlBL; AuBYP 2, 3; Benet 96; BioIn 1, 2, 3, 4, 5, 6, 7, 8, 9, 10, 11, 12, 13, 14, 15, 16, 17, 19; CasWL; CnDAL; CnE&AP; CnMD; CnMWL; ConAmA; ConAmL; ConAu 73; ConLC 15; DcArts; EncAB-H 1974, 1996; EncWL 3; EvLB; LngCTC; MakMC; McGEWB; ModAL S1; ModWD; NotNAT B; OxCAmL 65, 95; OxCEng 67, 95; OxCTwCP; PenC AM; RAdv 1, 14; REn; REnAL; RfGAmL 94; RGTwCWr; SixAP; TwCA, SUP; TwCWr; WebAB 74, 79; WebE&AL; WhAm 4; WhDW; WhoTwCL; WorAl*

Cummings, Nathan
American. Business Executive
Founder, longtime chairman of Consolidated Grocers Corp., a conglomerate of over 50 companies, 1947-68.
b. Oct 14, 1896 in Saint John, New Brunswick, Canada
d. Feb 19, 1985 in Palm Beach, Florida
Source: *BioIn 5, 7, 9, 12, 14, 17, 19; BlueB 76; CelR; ConAmBL; IntWW 74, 75, 76, 77, 78, 79, 80, 81, 82, 83; IntYB 78, 79, 80, 81, 82; NewYTBE 71; NewYTBS 85; St&PR 75, 84; WhAm 8; WhoAm 74, 76, 78, 80, 82, 84; WhoAmJ 80; WhoFI 74; WhoWorJ 72, 78*

Cummings, Quinn
American. Actor
Nominated for Oscar, 1977, for *The Goodbye Girl.*
b. Aug 13, 1967 in Hollywood, California
Source: *BioIn 11, 12; InWom SUP; LegTOT; WhoEnt 92*

Cummings, Terry
[Robert Terrell Cummings]
American. Basketball Player
Forward, San Diego, 1982-84, Milwaukee, 1984-89; San Antonio, 1989—; rookie of year, 1983.
b. Mar 15, 1961 in Chicago, Illinois
Source: *BasBi; BioIn 12, 13, 14, 15, 16; InB&W 85; NewYTBS 85; OfNBA 87; WhoAfA 96; WhoBlA 85, 88, 90, 92, 94; WhoMW 88*

Cummins, George David
American. Religious Leader
Founder, first bishop, Reformed Episcopal Church, 1873.
b. Dec 11, 1822 in Smyrna, Delaware
d. Jun 25, 1876 in Lutherville, Maryland
Source: *Alli SUP; ApCAB; BiDAmCu; BioIn 19; DcAmB; DcAmReB 2; DcNAA; LuthC 75; NatCAB 7; RelLAm 91; TwCBDA; WhAm HS*

Cummins, Peggy
Welsh. Actor
Best known for films *English Without Tears,* 1944; *Late George Apley,* 1946.
b. Dec 18, 1926 in Prestatyn, Wales
Source: *FilmgC; HalFC 84; IntMPA 75, 76, 77, 78, 79, 81, 82, 84, 86, 92; MotPP; WhoHol A; WhoThe 77A; WhThe*

Cunard, Samuel, Sir
Canadian. Shipping Executive
Established first regular steamship service between N America, Europe, 1840; began Cunard Line.

b. Nov 15, 1787 in Halifax, Nova Scotia, Canada
d. Apr 28, 1865 in London, England
Source: *ApCAB; BioIn 3, 8, 11; CelCen; DcBiPP; DcCanB 9; DcNaB; HarEnUS; HisDBrE; LinLib S; MacDCB 78; OxCShps; WorAl; WorAlBi*

Cuneo, Terence Tenison
English. Artist
Portrait and figure painter; best known for works with royal subjects.
b. Nov 1, 1907
Source: *BioIn 14; ClaDrA; DcBrAr 1; DcCAr 81; Who 74, 82, 83, 85, 88, 90, 92, 94; WhoArt 80, 82, 84, 96*

Cunha, Euclides (Rodrigues Pimenta) da
Brazilian. Author
Wrote *Os Sertoes,* 1902, which is considered the finest representation of the Brazilian cry for national unity, identity.
b. Jan 20, 1866 in Santa Rita, Brazil
d. Aug 15, 1909 in Rio de Janeiro, Brazil
Source: *CasWL; McGEWB*

Cunningham, Alan Gordon, Sir
English. Army Officer
Commanded forces that liberated Ethiopia from Italian rule, restored Haile Selassie to throne, 1971.
b. May 1, 1887 in Dublin, Ireland
d. Jan 30, 1983 in Royal Tunbridge Wells, England
Source: *AnObit 1983; BioIn 1, 13; CurBio 46, 83; DcNaB 1981; HarEnMi; HisEAAC; HisEWW; WhAm 8; Who 74, 82, 83*

Cunningham, Andrew Browne, Viscount
Irish. Military Leader
One of great sea commanders of Britain; led Allied naval forces in N Africa, Sicily campaigns, WW II; head of naval staff, 1943-46.
b. Jan 7, 1883 in Dublin, Ireland
d. Jun 12, 1963 in London, England
Source: *BioIn 14, 18; CurBio 41, 63; DcNaB 1961; DcTwHis; GrBr; HarEnMi; HisEWW; OxCShps; WhoMilH 76; WhWW-II*

Cunningham, Bill
[The Box Tops]
American. Musician
Keyboardist, bassist with Memphis-based group, 1966-70.
b. Jan 23, 1950 in Memphis, Tennessee
Source: *BioIn 14*

Cunningham, Billy
[William John Cunninsham]
"Kangaroo Kid"
American. Basketball Player, Basketball Coach
Forward, Philadelphia, 1966-72, 1974-76; coach, Philadelphia, 1978-83; won NBA championship, 1983; Hall of Fame, 1985.
b. Jun 3, 1943 in New York, New York
Source: *BioIn 11, 15; OfNBA 81; WhoAm 82, 84, 86, 88, 90, 92, 94, 95, 96, 97; WhoBbl 73; WhoE 85; WhoSpor*

Cunningham, Glenn Clarence
"Kansas Ironman"
American. Track Athlete
Middle-distance runner; won silver medal, 1,500 meters, 1936 Olympics; set world record in mile, 1938.
b. Aug 4, 1909 in Atlanta, Kansas
d. Mar 10, 1988 in Menifee, Arkansas
Source: *WhoTr&F 73*

Cunningham, Harry Blair
American. Business Executive
Pres., S S Kresge, 1959-67; honorary chm., K-Mart, 1977-1992.
b. Jul 23, 1907 in Home Camp, Pennsylvania
d. Nov 11, 1992 in North Palm Beach, Florida
Source: *BioIn 11, 17, 18, 19; ConAmBL; IntWW 74, 75, 76, 77, 78, 79, 80, 81, 82, 83, 89, 91; St&PR 87; WhoAm 74, 76, 78, 80, 82, 84; WhoFI 74; WhoWor 78*

Cunningham, Imogen
American. Photographer
Experimental, portrait photographer whose career spanned 75 yrs.
b. Apr 12, 1883 in Portland, Oregon
d. Jun 24, 1976 in San Francisco, California
Source: *BioAmW; BioIn 7, 9, 10, 11, 12, 16, 18, 20; BriEAA; CmCal; ConAu 65; ConPhot 82, 88, 95; ContDcW 89; DcAmArt; DcAmB S10; DcArts; FacFETw; GoodHs; GrLiveH; ICPEnP; IntDcWB; InWom SUP; LegTOT; MacBEP; NewYTBS 76; NorAmWA; WhAmArt 85; WhoAmA 78N, 80N, 82N, 84N, 86N, 89N, 91N, 93N; WomArt; WomFir; WorAl; WorAlBi*

Cunningham, Mary Elizabeth
[Mrs. William Agee]
American. Business Executive
Former executive at Bendix, romantically linked to firm's chairman, Wm. Agee; wrote autobiography *Powerplay,* 1984; founded Nurturing Network, 1986.
b. Sep 1, 1951 in Falmouth, Maine
Source: *BioIn 12; CurBio 84; InWom SUP; St&PR 84; WhoAmW 85, 87, 89, 91; WhoFI 85*

Cunningham, Merce
American. Dancer, Choreographer
Martha Graham protege; formed own co., 1952; developed new forms of abstract dance.
b. Apr 16, 1919 in Centralia, Washington
Source: *AmCulL; BiDD; BioIn 11, 12, 13, 14, 16; BlueB 76; CelR 90; CurBio 66; DcArts; DcTwCCu 1; FacFETw; GayLesB; IntDcB; IntWW 74, 75, 76, 77, 78, 79, 80, 81, 82, 83, 89, 91, 93; LegTOT; McGEWB; NewGrDA 86; NewOxM; NewYTBS 82; PeoHis; RAdv 14, 13-3; Who 85, 88, 90, 92, 94; WhoAm 86, 90; WhoE 91; WhoEnt 92; WhoWor 74; WorAl; WorAlBi; WrDr 86, 88, 90*

Cunningham, R. Walter
American. Astronaut, Business Executive
Flew first manned Apollo spacecraft, 1968; founded The Capital Group, 1979-86.
b. Mar 16, 1932 in Creston, Iowa
Source: *BioIn 14; ConAu 103; IntWW 74; WhoAm 84, 86, 90; WhoSpc; WhoWor 74*

Cunningham, Randall
American. Football Player
Quarterback, Philadelphia Eagles, 1985—; Pro Bowl MVP, 1989.
b. Mar 27, 1963 in Santa Barbara, California
Source: *AfrAmBi 1; BioIn 14, 16; CurBio 91; News 90, 90-1; WhoAfA 96; WhoAm 90, 92, 94, 95, 96, 97; WhoBlA 92, 94; WhoE 93, 95; WhoSpor; WorAlBi*

Cunningham, William T(homas)
American. Clergy, Civil Rights Activist
Founder, Focus: Hope, 1967, a Detroit program to train and feed the poor.
b. 1930 in Detroit, Michigan
d. May 26, 1997 in Detroit, Michigan

Cunninghame-Graham, Robert Bontine
English. Author, Traveler
Wrote on S America: *Portrait of a Dictator,* 1933; city Don Roberto, Argentina named for him.
b. May 24, 1852 in London, England
d. Mar 20, 1936 in Buenos Aires, Argentina
Source: *CasWL; DcLEL; DcNaB 1931; EvLB; LngCTC; ModBrL; OxCEng 67; REn; TwCA; WhE&EA; WhLit*

Cuomo, Andrew M.
American. Government Official
Secretary of HUD, 1997—.
b. Dec 6, 1957

Cuomo, Mario Matthew
American. Politician
Dem. governor of NY, 1982-94.
b. Jun 15, 1932 in New York, New York
Source: *AlmAP 88, 92; AmCath 80; AmOrTwC; BioIn 13, 14, 15, 16; CelR 90; ConAu 103; IntWW 91; News 92, 92-2; NewYTBS 86, 88, 91; PolsAm 84; RComAH; Who 92; WhoAm 86, 90, 97; WhoAmP 87, 91; WhoE 81, 91; WhoWor 87, 91, 97; WorAlBi; WrDr 86, 92*

Cuong De
Vietnamese. Prince, Political Activist
Advocated Vietnamese independence from French rule in the early years of the 20th c.
b. 1882
d. Apr 6, 1951 in Tokyo, Japan

Cuppy, Will(iam Jacob)
American. Author, Critic
Satirical "How To's" include *How to Become Extinct,* 1941.
b. Aug 23, 1884 in Auburn, Indiana
d. Sep 19, 1949 in New York, New York
Source: *AmAu&B; BenetAL 91; BioIn 2, 4, 6, 15; ConAu 108; DcAmB S4; DcLB 11; DcNAA; EncAHmr; IndAu 1816; LegTOT; ObitOF 79; REnAL; ScF&FL 1; TwCA, SUP; WhAm 2*

Curb, Mike
[Michael Charles Curb]
American. Politician
Chm., Rep. National Committee, 1982— ; lt. gov. of CA, 1979-83; pres., MGM Records, 1968-74.
b. Dec 24, 1944 in Savannah, Georgia
Source: *BgBkCoM; BioIn 9, 10, 11, 12; EncPR&S 74; EncRk 88; RolSEnR 83; WhoAm 78, 80, 82, 84, 86, 88, 90, 92; WhoAmP 91; WhoWest 80, 82*

Cure, The
English. Music Group
Formed, 1976, in England; music focuses on death and dread; hit albums *Kiss Me, Kiss Me, Kiss Me,* 1987; *Disintegration,* 1989; hit single "Love Song," 1989.
Source: *Alli; AmMWSc 89; BiDBrA; BioIn 1, 3, 11, 15, 16, 17; BioNews 74; ConMus 3; DcArts; DcLP 87A; DcNaB; EncRk 88; EncRkSt; EngPo; InB&W 80; MedHR; NewGrDM 80; NewYHSD; PenEncP; WhoRocM 82; WhsNW 85*

Curel, Francois de
French. Dramatist
Aristocrat who never depended on theater for a living; wrote mainly on inner turmoil, reality, passion.
b. Jun 10, 1854 in Metz, France
d. Apr 25, 1928 in Paris, France
Source: *CasWL; ClDMEL 47; CnMD; Dis&D; EncWT; EvEuW; McGEWD 72, 84; ModFrL; ModWD; NotNAT B; OxCFr; OxCThe 67; PenC EUR; REn; WhoLA; WhThe*

Curie, Eve
[Mrs. Henry R Labouisse]
French. Author, Journalist
Wrote best-selling biography of her mother, *Madame Curie,* 1937.
b. Dec 6, 1904 in Paris, France
Source: *AmAu&B; AnCL; Au&Wr 71; BioIn 3, 6, 9; ConAu P-1; CurBio 40; IntAu&W 76, 77; InWom, SUP; LegTOT; LinLib L, S; SmATA 1; Who 74, 83, 85, 88, 90, 92, 94; WhoAm 74, 76, 78, 80, 82, 84; WhoAmW 61, 64, 66, 68, 70, 72, 74, 75, 79, 81, 83, 85, 87, 89, 91, 93, 95, 97; WhoE 85, 86, 95, 97; WhoFr 79; WhoWor 74, 76, 78, 80, 84, 87, 89, 91, 93, 95*

Curie, Marie
[Mrs. Pierre Curie; Marja Sklodowska]
Polish. Chemist
Discovered new elements polonium, radium, 1898; first to receive two Nobel Prizes, 1903, 1911.
b. Nov 7, 1867 in Warsaw, Poland
d. Jul 4, 1934 in Valence, France
Source: *BioIn 1, 2, 3, 4, 5, 6, 7, 8, 9, 10, 11, 12, 13, 14, 15, 16, 17, 18, 19, 20, 21; CamDcSc; ConAu 118; ConHero 2; ContDcW 89; DcInv; DcScB; Dis&D; FacFETw; GoodHs; HerW, 84; IntDcWB; LadLa 86; LarDcSc; LegTOT; McGEWB; NobelP; NotTwCS; REn; WhDW; WhoNob, 90, 95; WomFir; WorAl; WorAlBi; WorScD*

Curie, Pierre
French. Chemist
Discovered radium, 1898; with wife, investigated radioactivity of radium; received Nobel Prize, 1903.
b. May 15, 1859 in Paris, France
d. Apr 19, 1906 in Paris, France
Source: *AsBiEn; BiESc; BioIn 1, 2, 3, 4, 5, 6, 7, 9, 12, 14, 15, 16, 20; CamDcSc; DcInv; DcScB; Dis&D; FacFETw; InSci; LarDcSc; LegTOT; LinLib S; NobelP; NotTwCS; OxCFr; OxCMed 86; WhDW; WhoNob, 90, 95; WorAl; WorAlBi; WorScD*

Curley, James Michael
American. Political Leader
Boston Dem. boss, 1900-47; four-time mayor; governor of MA, 1935-37.
b. Nov 20, 1874 in Boston, Massachusetts
d. Nov 12, 1958 in Boston, Massachusetts
Source: *BiDrAC; BiDrUSC 89; BioIn 1, 2, 3, 4, 5, 6, 7, 9, 10, 11, 12, 18; DcAmB S6; DcCathB; EncAB-A 5; EncAB-H 1974, 1996; FacFETw; McGEWB; ObitOF 79; OxCAmH; PolPar; WebAB 74, 79; WebBD 83; WhAm 3*

Curly
American. Native American Leader
Crow scout who brought news of the massacre of Gen. George Custer's troops in 1876.
b. 1859?
d. 1935?
Source: *BioIn 21; NotNaAm; WhNaAH*

Curran, Charles Courtney
American. Artist
Won many awards for paintings of OH scenes.
b. Feb 13, 1861 in Hartford, Kentucky
d. Nov 9, 1942 in New York, New York
Source: *ApCAB X; BioIn 10, 19; ChhPo; CurBio 43; NatCAB 13; ObitOF 79; TwCBDA; WhAm 2*

Curran, Charles E(dward)
American. Theologian
Vatican revoked his license to teach moral theology at Catholic U of America, 1986, for publicly dissenting with church views.
b. Mar 30, 1934 in Rochester, New York
Source: *BioIn 14, 15; ConAu 14NR, 21R; CurBio 87; DrAS 74P, 78P, 82P; IntWW 91; News 89-2; RelLAm 91; WhoRel 92; WhoSSW 73, 75, 76, 93; WhoUSWr 88; WhoWrEP 92; WrDr 86, 92*

Curran, Joseph Edwin
"Big Joe"
American. Labor Union Official
Organizer, pres., National Maritime Union, 1937-73.
b. Mar 1, 1906 in New York, New York
d. Aug 14, 1981 in Boca Raton, Florida
Source: *AnObit 1981; BiDAmL; BiDAmLL; BioIn 1, 10, 11, 12; CurBio 81; NewYTBS 81; PolProf E, J, K, NF, T; WhoAm 74; WhoWor 74; WorAl*

Curren, Kevin
South African. Tennis Player
With Steve Denton, won US Clay Court doubles 1980, 81, US Open doubles, 1982.
b. Mar 2, 1958 in Durban, South Africa
Source: *BioIn 14, 15; NewYTBS 86; WhoIntT*

Currie, Barton Wood
American. Editor, Journalist
Edited *The Country Gentleman, Ladies Home Journal,* early 1900s.
b. Mar 8, 1878 in New York, New York
d. May 7, 1962 in Merion, Pennsylvania
Source: *BioIn 6; ConAu 116; WhJnl*

Currie, Finlay
Scottish. Actor
Best known for *Great Expectations,* 1946.
b. Jan 20, 1878 in Edinburgh, Scotland
d. May 9, 1968 in Gerrards Cross, England
Source: *BioIn 8; CmMov; FilmgC; HalFC 84, 88; ItaFilm; MotPP; MovMk; NotNAT B; ObitOF 79; Vers A; WhoHol B; WhScrn 74, 77, 83; WhThe*

Currie, Lauchlin (Bernard)
American. Economist
Wrote *The Supply and Control of Money,* 1934; economic adviser to Pres. Roosevelt, 1939; exiled himself to Colombia after accusations of espionage.
b. Oct 8, 1902
d. Dec 23, 1993 in Bogota, Colombia
Source: *BioIn 1, 2, 4, 12; ConAu 15NR, 73, 143; CurBio 94N*

Currier, Nathaniel
[Currier and Ives]
American. Lithographer
Started lithography business, 1835; partnership with James Ives, 1857.
b. Mar 27, 1813 in Roxbury, Massachusetts
d. Nov 20, 1888 in New York, New York

Source: *AmBi; BenetAL 91; BioIn 1, 2, 3, 4, 9, 10, 11, 13, 16; BriEAA; DcAmB; DcD&D; EncAAH; LegTOT; LinLib L, S; McGDA; McGEWB; NatCAB 21; NewYHSD; OxCAmH; WebAB 74, 79; WhAmArt 85; WhAm HS; WhCiWar; WorAl; WorAlBi*

Curry, Donald
American. Boxer
Undisputed welterweight champion knocking out WBC champ, Milton McCrory, 1985.
b. 1961? in Fort Worth, Texas
Source: *NewYTBS 85, 86*

Curry, John (Anthony)
English. Skater
World champion figure skater, 1976; won gold medal, 1976 Olympics.
b. Sep 9, 1949 in Birmingham, England
d. Apr 15, 1994 in Stratford-upon-Avon, England
Source: *BioIn 11, 12, 14, 17, 19, 20; CurBio 79, 94N; NewYTBE 71; NewYTBS 76, 78, 94; WhAm 11; Who 82, 83, 85, 88, 90, 92, 94; WhoAm 80, 82, 86, 88, 90; WhoE 85*

Curry, John Steuart
American. Artist
Murals, oil paintings deal with rural America.
b. Nov 14, 1897 in Dunavant, Kansas
d. Aug 29, 1946 in Madison, Wisconsin
Source: *ArtsAmW 1, 2; Benet 87; BioIn 1, 4, 5, 7, 10, 11, 13; BriEAA; CurBio 41, 46; DcAmArt; DcAmB S4; DcCAA 71, 77, 88, 94; GrAmP; IlBEAAW; IlsCB 1744; McGDA; ObitOF 79; OxCAmL 65; OxCTwCA; OxDcArt; PhDcTCA 77; REn; REnAL; REnAW; WhAm 2; WhAmArt 85*

Curry, Peggy Simson
American. Author
Wrote *Fire in the Water,* 1951; *So Far From Spring,* 1956.
b. Dec 30, 1912 in Dunure, Scotland
Source: *BioIn 16; ConAu 12NR, 121; CurBio 58; DrAF 76; DrAPF 83, 87; InWom; SmATA 8, 50N; TwCWW 91; WhoAmW 58, 61, 64; WrDr 84, 86*

Curry, Tim
English. Singer, Actor
Played Dr. Frank N. Furter in movie musical *Rocky Horror Picture Show,* 1975; starred in movie *Legend,* 1986; albums include *Fearless,* 1979 with hit single "I Do the Rock."
b. 1947, England
Source: *BioIn 15; ConMus 3; ConTFT 7; HalFC 88; IntMPA 92; RkOn 85; WhoRocM 82*

Curti, Merle Eugene
American. Historian
Political science writings include Pulitzer-winning *Growth of American Thought,* 1943.
b. Sep 15, 1897 in Papillion, Nebraska
d. Mar 9, 1996 in Madison, Wisconsin
Source: *BenetAL 91; BiDAmEd; BioIn 13, 21; ConAu 4NR, 5R, 151; DrAS 74H; IntWW 74, 91; OxCAmH; OxCAmL 65; REnAL; REnAW; TwCA SUP; WhAm 11; WhoAm 74, 76, 78, 80, 82, 84, 86, 88, 90, 92, 94, 95, 96*

Curtice, Harlow Herbert
American. Auto Executive
Pres. of GM, 1953-58.
b. Aug 15, 1893 in Eaton Rapids, Michigan
d. Nov 3, 1962 in Flint, Michigan
Source: *BioIn 1, 3, 4, 5, 6, 9, 11; CurBio 53, 63; EncAB-A 26; EncABHB 5; NatCAB 52; WhAm 4*

Curtin, Andrew Gregg
American. Political Leader
Governor of PA, 1860-68; minister to Russia, 1868-72.
b. Apr 28, 1817 in Bellefonte, Pennsylvania
d. Oct 7, 1894 in Bellefonte, Pennsylvania
Source: *AmBi; ApCAB; BiAUS; BiDrAC; BiDrGov 1789; BiDrUSC 89; CivWDc; DcAmB; Drake; HarEnUS; NatCAB 2, 24; TwCBDA; WhAm HS; WhAmP; WhCiWar*

Curtin, Jane (Therese)
American. Actor, Comedian
Star of NBC TV's "Saturday Night Live," 1975-80; played Allie on "Kate & Allie," 1984-1989; on "3rd Rock from the Sun," 1996—; Emmy award winner, 1984, 1985.
b. Sep 6, 1947 in Cambridge, Massachusetts
Source: *BioIn 14, 15; CelR 90; ConTFT 3; FunnyW; IntMPA 88, 92, 94, 96; LegTOT; VarWW 85; WhoAm 78, 80, 82, 84, 86, 88, 90, 92, 94, 95, 96, 97; WhoAmW 87, 89, 91, 93, 95, 97; WhoCom; WhoEnt 92; WhoHol 92; WorAlBi*

Curtin, John Joseph
Australian. Political Leader
Prime minister of Australia, minister for defense, 1941-45.
b. Jan 8, 1885 in Creswick, Australia
d. Jul 5, 1945 in Canberra, Australia
Source: *CurBio 41, 45; DcNaB 1941; DcPol; DcTwHis; McGEWB; ObitOF 79; WhWW-II*

Curtin, Phyllis Smith
American. Singer
Classical soprano who championed modern American opera; identified with title role, Susannah, 1955.
b. Dec 3, 1927 in Clarksburg, West Virginia
Source: *Baker 84; BlueB 76; CurBio 64; IntWWM 90; MetOEnc; NewAmDM; NewGrDA 86; NewYTBE 72; PenDiMP; WhoAm 84, 88, 90; WhoAmM 83; WhoAmW 77; WhoWor 74*

Curtis, Alan (Harold Neberroth)
American. Actor
Played romantic leads and villains: *Apache Chief,* 1949.
b. Jul 24, 1909 in Chicago, Illinois
d. Feb 1, 1953 in New York, New York
Source: *BioIn 3; EncAFC; FilmgC; HalFC 84, 88; ItaFilm; MotPP; NotNAT B; ObitOF 79; WhoHol B; WhScrn 74, 77, 83*

Curtis, Ann
[The Queen of Amateurs]
American. Swimmer
Holder of seven nat. titles, two world records, 18 American records; first woman and swimmer to receive James E Sullivan Memorial Trophy, 1944.
b. Mar 6, 1926 in San Francisco, California
Source: *BiDAmSp BK; BioIn 1, 6, 11; CurBio 45; EncWomS; InWom, SUP; WomFir*

Curtis, Charles Brent
American. US Vice President
VP under Herbert Hoover, 1929-33.
b. Jan 25, 1860 in Topeka, Kansas
d. Feb 8, 1936 in Washington, District of Columbia
Source: *Alli; AmBi; BiDLA; BiDrAC; BiDrUSE 71; BioIn 16, 21; DcAmB S2; NotNaAm; WebAB 74; WhAm 1; WhAmP*

Curtis, Charles Gordon
American. Inventor
Invented steam turbine, 1896, sold rights to General Electric Co.
b. Apr 20, 1860 in Boston, Massachusetts
d. Mar 10, 1953 in Central Islip, New York
Source: *BioIn 1, 3, 5, 12; InSci; NatCAB 42; ObitOF 79; WhAm 3*

Curtis, Charlotte Murray
American. Newspaper Editor
NY Times columnist best known for society reporting, women's issues; wrote *The Rich and Other Atrocities,* 1976.
b. 1930 in Chicago, Illinois
d. Apr 16, 1987 in Columbus, Ohio
Source: *AuNews 2; ConAu 9R; ForWC 70; InWom SUP; WhoAm 84; WhoAmW 83; WorAl*

Curtis, Cyrus Hermann Kotszchmar
American. Newspaper Publisher
Founded Curtis Publishing Co., 1891; published *Saturday Evening Post; Ladies Home Journal.*
b. Jun 18, 1850 in Portland, Maine
d. Jun 7, 1933 in Wyncote, Pennsylvania
Source: *AmAu&B; AmBi; DcAmB S1; EncAAH; WebAB 74; WhAm 1; WhDW; WorAl*

Curtis, Edward Sheriff
American. Photographer
Interest in Native Americans resulted in 20-volume series *The North American Indian,* 1907-30.
b. Feb 19, 1868 in Madison, Wisconsin
d. Oct 19, 1952 in Los Angeles, California
Source: *AmAu&B; DcAmB S5; EncNAB; ICPEnP; IntDcAn; MacBEP; ObitOF 79; REnAW; WhAm 4; WhNaAH*

Curtis, George William
American. Editor, Author, Lecturer
Wrote series of satires of New York society: *The Potiphar Papers,* 1853; editor of *Harper's Weekly,* 1857.
b. Feb 24, 1824 in Providence, Rhode Island
d. Aug 31, 1892 in Staten Island, New York
Source: *Alli, SUP; AmAu; AmAu&B; AmBi; AmRef; ApCAB; BbD; BenetAL 91; BiDAmJo; BiDAmM; BiD&SB; BiDTran; BioIn 4, 6, 8, 9, 15, 16; CasWL; Chambr 3; ChhPo; CyAL 2; DcAmAu; DcAmB; DcAmC; DcBiA; DcEnL; DcLB 1, 43; DcLEL; DcNAA; Drake; EncAB-H 1974, 1996; EncAJ; EvLB; HarEnUS; JrnUS; LinLib L, S; McGEWB; NatCAB 3; OxCAmH; OxCAmL 65, 83, 95; REn; REnAL; ScF&FL 1; TwCBDA; WebAB 74, 79; WhAm HS; WhAmP*

Curtis, Heber Doust
American. Astronomer, Director
Researched extra-galactic nebulae.
b. Jun 27, 1872 in Muskegon, Michigan
d. Jan 9, 1942 in Ann Arbor, Michigan
Source: *BiESc; BioIn 13; CurBio 42; DcAmB S3; DcScB; FacFETw; InSci; LarDcSc; WhAm 1*

Curtis, Isaac Fisher
American. Football Player
Four-time all-pro wide receiver, Cincinnati, 1973-85.
b. Oct 20, 1950 in Santa Ana, California
Source: *BioIn 11; NewYTBS 82; WhoAm 78, 80; WhoBlA 85, 92; WhoFtbl 74*

Curtis, Jackie
American. Dramatist, Screenwriter
Screenplays include *Women in Revolt,* 1971.
b. Feb 19, 1947 in Stony Creek, Tennessee
Source: *BioIn 14; ConAu 103, X; ConDr 73, 77, 82, 93; NewYTBS 85; WhoE 85; WrDr 76, 80, 82, 84, 86*

Curtis, Jamie Lee
American. Actor
Daughter of Tony Curtis, Janet Leigh; star of film *Halloween,* 1981, TV series "Anything But Love."
b. Nov 22, 1958 in Los Angeles, California
Source: *BiDFilm 94; BioIn 9, 11, 12, 13, 14, 15, 16; CelR 90; ConTFT 6, 13; HalFC 84, 88; HolBB; IntDcF 2-3; IntMPA 84, 86, 88, 92, 94, 96; IntWW 91, 93; InWom SUP; LegTOT; News 95, 95-1; WhoAm 92, 94, 95, 96, 97; WhoAmW 95, 97; WhoEnt 92; WhoHol 92; WorAlBi*

Curtis, Ken
[Curtis Gates]
American. Actor
Made show business debut as singer in swing bands, 1930s; best known as Festus Haggen on "Gunsmoke," 1964-75.
b. Jul 12, 1916 in Lamar, Colorado
d. Apr 28, 1991 in Fresno, California
Source: *BioIn 8, 17; ConTFT 10; HalFC 84, 88; IntMPA 75, 76, 77, 78, 79, 81, 82, 84, 86, 88; LegTOT; NewYTBS 91; WhoHol A*

Curtis, Mike
[James Michael Curtis]
"Animal"
American. Football Player
Four-time all-pro linebacker, 1965-78, mostly with Baltimore; author *Stay Off My Turf,* 1972.
b. Mar 27, 1943 in Rockville, Maryland
Source: *BiDAmSp Sup; BioIn 9, 10; WhoAm 76, 78, 80; WhoFtbl 74*

Curtis, Thomas B(radford)
American. Politician
Rep. congressman from MO, 1951-69.
b. May 14, 1911
d. Jan 10, 1993 in Allegan, Michigan
Source: *BiDrAC; BiDrUSC 89; BioIn 5, 6, 7, 11; BlueB 76; ConAu 61, 140; CurBio 93N; PolProf E, J, K; WhAm 11; WhAmP; WhoAm 74, 76, 78, 80; WhoAmL 79, 83, 85, 87, 90, 92; WhoAmP 73, 75, 77, 79, 81, 83, 85, 87, 89, 91*

Curtis, Tony
[Bernard Schwartz]
American. Actor
Starred in *The Defiant Ones,* 1958; *Some Like it Hot,* 1959.
b. Jun 3, 1925 in New York, New York
Source: *BiDFilm, 94; BioIn 2, 3, 4, 5, 6, 8, 9, 10, 11, 12, 14, 18, 19; CelR, 90; CmMov; ConAu 45NR, 73; ConTFT 3, 9; DcArts; EncAFC; FilmgC; GangFlm; HalFC 84, 88; IntDcF 1-3, 2-3; IntMPA 75, 76, 77, 78, 79, 81, 82, 84, 86, 88, 92, 94, 96; IntWW 79, 80, 81, 82, 83, 89, 91, 93; ItaFilm; LegTOT; MotPP; MovMk; NewYTBE 70; OxCFilm; WhoAm 78, 80, 82, 84, 86, 88, 90, 92, 94, 95, 96, 97; WhoAmJ 80; WhoEnt 92; WhoHol A; WorAl; WorAlBi; WorEFlm*

Curtiss, Glenn Hammond
American. Aircraft Manufacturer, Inventor
Invented seaplane, 1911; established first flying schools.
b. May 21, 1878 in Hammondsport, New York
d. Jul 23, 1930 in Buffalo, New York
Source: *AmBi; ApCAB X; BiDAmBL 83; BioIn 1, 5, 7, 8, 9, 10, 12, 13, 16, 17, 18, 21; DcAmB S1; FacFETw; InSci; LinLib S; McGEWB; NatCAB 15, 22; OxCAmH; WebAB 74, 79; WebAMB; WhAm 1; WhFla; WorAl*

Curtiz, Michael
American. Director
Won Oscar for *Casablanca,* 1942; directed over 100 films for Warner Bros.
b. Dec 24, 1888 in Budapest, Austria-Hungary
d. Apr 11, 1962 in Hollywood, California
Source: *BiDFilm, 94; BioIn 1, 15, 17, 19; CmMov; DcAmB S7; DcArts; DcFM; FilmgC; GangFlm; HalFC 84, 88; IlWWHD 1; IntDcF 1-2, 2-2; ItaFilm; LegTOT; MiSFD 9N; MovMk; ObitOF 79; ObitT 1961; OxCFilm; TwYS; WhAm 4; WhScrn 74, 77, 83; WorEFlm; WorFDir 1*

Curwood, James Oliver
American. Author
Adventure tales of the North woods include *River's Edge,* 1919.
b. Jun 12, 1878 in Owosso, Michigan
d. Aug 13, 1927 in Owosso, Michigan
Source: *AmAu&B; AmBi; ApCAB X; BenetAL 91; BioIn 2, 19; CreCan 1; DcAmB; DcNAA; LinLib L; LngCTC; MichAu 80; MnBBF; OxCAmL 65, 83, 95; OxCCan; REnAL; TwCA, SUP; TwCWW 91; WhAm 1; WhNAA*

Curzon, Clifford Michael, Sir
English. Pianist
Noted for interpretations of Schubert, Brahms; knighted, 1977.
b. May 18, 1907 in London, England
d. Sep 1, 1982 in London, England
Source: *Baker 78; CurBio 82; IntWW 82; IntWWM 77; Who 74; WhoMus 72; WhoWor 78*

Curzon of Kedleston, George Nathaniel Curzon, Marquis
English. Statesman
Viceroy of India, 1898; held various offices in war cabinet; foreign secretary, 1916-24.
b. Jan 11, 1859 in Kedleston Hall, England
d. Mar 20, 1925 in London, England
Source: *ChhPo S1; DcEuL; DcNaB 1922; McGEWB; NewC; WebBD 83; WhDW*

Cusack, Cyril
Irish. Actor
Appeared in TV movies *Catholics; Jesus of Nazareth.*
b. Nov 26, 1910 in Durban, South Africa
Source: *AnObit 1993; BiE&WWA; BioIn 19; BlueB 76; CamGWoT; ConTFT 7; DcArts; EncEurC; Film 1; FilmgC; HalFC 84, 88; IntAu&W 77; IntDcF 1-3, 2-3; IntMPA 75, 76, 77, 78, 79, 81, 82, 84, 86, 88, 92, 94; IntWW 74, 91; ItaFilm; LegTOT; MovMk; NewYTBS 93; NotNAT; OxCIri; OxCThe 83; WhoHol 92, A; WhoThe 72, 77, 81; WhoWor 74, 78, 91; WrDr 80, 82, 84*

Cusack, John
American. Actor
Appeared in films *Eight Men Out,* 1988; *The Grifters,* 1990; *Bullets Over Broadway,* 1994.
b. Jun 28, 1966 in Evanston, Illinois
Source: *ConTFT 8, 15; CurBio 96; IntMPA 92, 94, 96; LegTOT; WhoAm 92, 94, 95, 96, 97; WhoEnt 92*

Cushing, Caleb
American. Diplomat
Special envoy to China, 1843-45, arranged favorable treaties for US.
b. Jan 17, 1800 in Salisbury, Massachusetts
d. Jan 2, 1879 in Newburyport, Massachusetts
Source: *Alli, SUP; AmAu; AmAu&B; AmBi; ApCAB; BiAUS; BiD&SB; BiDrAC; BiDrUSC 89; BiDrUSE 71, 89; BioIn 2, 4, 7, 10, 13; CelCen; CyAG; CyAL 2; DcAmAu; DcAmB; DcBiPP; DcNAA; Drake; HarEnUS; LegTOT; NatCAB 4; OxCAmH; OxCLaw; OxCSupC; TwCBDA; WebAB 74, 79; WhAm HS; WhAmP*

Cushing, Harvey Williams
American. Surgeon
Neurosurgeon who developed techniques that made brain surgery feasible, including sutures to control severe bleeding.
b. Apr 8, 1869 in Cleveland, Ohio
d. Oct 7, 1939 in New Haven, Connecticut
Source: *AmAu&B; AmBi; AmDec 1920; BiESc; BiHiMed; BioIn 14; CamDcSc; DcAmB S2; DcAmMeB 84; DcNAA; DcScB; EncAB-H 1974, 1996; FacFETw; LarDcSc; LinLib L, S; LngCTC; McGEWB; NatCAB 32; OhA&B; OxCAmH; OxCAmL 65; OxCMed 86; REnAL; WebAB 74, 79; WhAm 1; WhDW; WhNAA; WorScD*

Cushing, Peter
English. Actor
Rivals Vincent Price in horror film roles; has played Baron Frankenstein in four movies.
b. May 26, 1913 in Kenley, England
d. Aug 1, 1994 in Canterbury, England
Source: *BioIn 13, 15, 17, 20, 21; CmMov; ConAu 133; ConTFT 4, 13; DcArts; FilmgC; HalFC 84, 88; IntDcF 1-3, 2-3; IntMPA 75, 76, 77, 78, 79, 81, 82, 84, 86, 88, 92, 94; IntWW 82, 83, 89, 91, 93; LegTOT; MotPP; News 95, 95-1; NewYTBS 94; PenEncH; ScF&FL 92; WhoHol 92, A; WhoThe 72, 77, 81; WhoWor 91*

Cushing, Richard James, Cardinal
American. Religious Leader
Archbishop of Boston, 1944-70.
b. Aug 24, 1895 in Boston, Massachusetts
d. Nov 2, 1970 in Boston, Massachusetts
Source: *BioIn 2, 3, 4, 5, 6, 7, 8, 9, 10, 11, 19; ConAu 112; CurBio 70; DcAmB S8; DcAmReB 1, 2; EncARH; NewYTBE 70; ObitOF 79; RelLAm 91; WhAm 5; WorAl*

Cushing, William Barker
American. Military Leader
Union naval hero of the Civil War; known for sinking confederate warship, *Albemarle,* 1864.
b. Nov 4, 1842 in Delafield, Wisconsin
d. Dec 17, 1874 in Washington, District of Columbia
Source: *AmBi; ApCAB; BioIn 4, 5, 7, 9, 10; CivWDc; DcAmB; Drake; HarEnMi; HarEnUS; NatCAB 9; OxCShps; TwCBDA; WebAB 74, 79; WebAMB; WebBD 83; WhAm HS*

Cushman, Austin Thomas
American. Business Executive
Chm., chief exec., Sears, Roebuck, 1962-67; opened 167 stores; sales rose from 6.8 billion, 1966, to 17.2 billion, 1977.
b. 1901 in Albuquerque, New Mexico
d. Jun 12, 1978 in Pasadena, California
Source: *DcAmB S10; NewYTBS 78; ObitOF 79; WhAm 7*

Cushman, Charlotte Saunders
American. Actor
Acclaimed as foremost actress of her day; noted for Shakespearean tragedies; gave farewell performances from 1857-75.
b. Jul 23, 1816 in Boston, Massachusetts
d. Feb 17, 1876 in Boston, Massachusetts
Source: *AmBi; AmWom; ApCAB; DcAmB; Drake; FamA&A; FemPA; NotAW; OxCAmH; OxCAmL 65; OxCThe 67; PlP&P; REnAL; TwCBDA; WebAB 74, 79; WhAm HS; WomFir*

Cushman, Pauline
[Harriet Wood]
"Spy of the Cumberland"
American. Actor, Spy
Spy for the Union; captured, found guilty by Confederates, but rescued by Union advance.
b. Jun 10, 1833 in New Orleans, Louisiana
d. Dec 2, 1893 in San Francisco, California
Source: *AmBi; ApCAB; BioAmW; BioIn 3, 9; CivWDc; DcAmB; EncAI&E; InWom, SUP; NatCAB 23; OxCAmH; TwCBDA; WhAm HS; WhCiWar*

Cushman, Robert Everton, Jr.
American. Army Officer
WW II hero, Vietnam commander, who became deputy director of CIA in 1969; approved burglary of office of Daniel Ellsberg's psychiatrist.
b. Dec 24, 1914 in Saint Paul, Minnesota
d. Jan 2, 1985 in Fort Washington, Maryland
Source: *BioIn 9, 10, 12, 14; BlueB 76; CurBio 85; EncAI&E; HarEnMi; IntWW 82; NewYTBE 73; WebAMB; WhAm 8; WhoAm 74, 76; WhoGov 72, 75; WhoSSW 73; WorDWW*

Custer, Elizabeth Bacon
[Mrs. George Custer]
American. Author
Wrote *Boots and Saddles,* 1885, an account of life in Dakota with husband.
b. Apr 8, 1842 in Monroe, Michigan
d. Apr 4, 1933 in New York, New York
Source: *Alli SUP; AmAu&B; AmBi; AmWomWr; BenetAL 91; BiD&SB; BioIn 17, 18, 19, 20; DcAmAu; DcNAA; HerW; InWom, SUP; OxCAmL 83; PeoHis; REnAL; WhAm 1*

Custer, George Armstrong
American. Army Officer
Youngest general in Union Army, killed at Battle of Little Big Horn by Indians led by Sitting Bull, Crazy Horse.
b. Dec 5, 1839 in New Rumley, Ohio
d. Jun 25, 1876 in Little Big Horn, Montana
Source: *Alli SUP; AmBi; ApCAB; Benet 87, 96; BenetAL 91; BioIn 1, 2, 3, 4, 5, 6, 7, 8, 9, 10, 11, 12, 13, 14, 15, 16, 17, 18, 19, 20, 21; CivWDc; DcAmAu; DcAmB; DcAmMiB; DcNAA; Dis&D; Drake; EncAAH; EncAB-H 1974, 1996; EncNAB; FilmgC; GenMudB; HalFC 84, 88; HarEnMi; HarEnUS; HisWorL; LinLib L, S; McGEWB; NatCAB 4; OhA&B; OxCAmH; OxCAmL 65, 83, 95; OxCChiL; OxCFilm; RComAH; REn; REnAW; TwCBDA; WebAB 74, 79; WebAMB; WhAm HS; WhCiWar; WhDW; WhNaAH; WhoMilH 76; WorAl; WorAlBi*

Custin, Mildred
American. Business Executive
Pres., Bonwit Teller, 1965-69; first woman to head major chain store.
b. Jan 25, 1906 in Manchester, New Hampshire
d. Mar 27, 1997 in Palm Springs, Florida
Source: *BioIn 7, 8; CurBio 67; InWom; St&PR 75, 84; WhoAm 74, 76, 78, 80, 82, 84, 86, 88, 90; WhoAmW 66, 68, 70, 72, 74; WhoFI 75; WorFshn*

Cuthbert, Betty
Australian. Track Athlete
Sprinter; won three gold medals, 1956 Olympics, one gold, 1964 Olympics.
b. Apr 20, 1938 in Sydney, Australia
Source: *BioIn 16; InWom SUP; WhoTr&F 73; WomFir*

Cutler, Dave
Canadian. Football Player
Kicker, Edmonton Eskimos, 1969-74; CFL all-time scoring leader.
b. Oct 17, 1945 in Biggar, Saskatchewan, Canada

Cutler, Manasseh
American. Clergy, Scientist
Ohio River Valley colonizer.
b. May 13, 1742 in Killingly, Connecticut
d. Jul 28, 1823 in Hamilton, Massachusetts

Source: *AmBi; ApCAB; BiAUS; BiDAmS; BiDrAC; BiDrUSC 89; BilnAmS; BioIn 5, 9; DcAmAu; DcAmB; Drake; HarEnUS; InSci; McGEWB; NatCAB 3; NewCol 75; OhA&B; OxCAmH; TwCBDA; WebAB 74, 79; WhAm HS; WhAmRev; WhNaAH*

Cutpurse, Moll
[Mary Frith]
"Queen of Misrule"
English. Criminal
First professional female criminal; dressed as man; pickpocket, highway robber.
b. 1589 in London, England
d. 1662 in London, England

Cuvier, Georges, Baron
"Father of Comparative Anatomy"
French. Zoologist
Devised system of animal classification using four distinct branches, 1790s.
b. Aug 23, 1769 in Montbeliard, France
d. May 13, 1832 in Paris, France
Source: *AsBiEn; BiD&SB; BioIn 2, 4, 7, 8, 11, 12, 14, 15; CelCen; DcInv; EncEnl; McGEWB; NewCol 75; OxCFr; RAdv 14, 13-5; REn; WhDW; WorAlBi*

Cuyler, Kiki
[Hazen Shirley Cuyler]
American. Baseball Player
Outfielder, 1921-38; had lifetime .321 batting average; Hall of Fame, 1968.
b. Aug 30, 1899 in Harrisville, Michigan
d. Feb 11, 1950 in Ann Arbor, Michigan
Source: *Ballpl 90; BiDAmSp BB; BioIn 2, 3; LegTOT; WhoProB 73; WhoSpor*

Cuyp, Aelbert Jacobsz(oon)
Dutch. Artist
Noted for pastoral landscapes: "Piper with Cows."
b. 1620 in Dordrecht, Netherlands
d. Nov 1691 in Dordrecht, Netherlands
Source: *AtlBL; McGDA; NewCol 75; OxCArt*

Cuyp, Jacob Gerritsz(oon)
Dutch. Artist
Acclaimed portrait painter in the 17th century Dutch Baroque tradition.
b. Dec 1594 in Dordrecht, Netherlands
d. 1652 in Dordrecht, Netherlands
Source: *BioIn 3; OxCArt; OxDcArt*

Cuypers, Petrus Josephus Hubertus
Dutch. Architect
Neo-Gothic designer, who built many Catholic churches, Rijksmuseum, 1876.
b. 1827 in Roermond, Netherlands
d. 1921
Source: *BioIn 14; OxCArt; WhoArch*

Cuzzoni, Francesca
Italian. Opera Singer
Soprano popular in London, 1720s; noted Handel soloist.
b. 1700 in Parma, Italy
d. 1770 in Bologna, Italy
Source: *Baker 78, 84, 92; BioIn 7, 14, 15; InWom; NewEOp 71*

Cwiklinska, Mieczyslawa, pseud.
Polish. Actor
Performed comic roles in operettas plays, films.
b. Jan 1, 1880 in Lublin, Poland
d. Jul 28, 1972 in Warsaw, Poland

Cynewulf
English. Poet
Old English religious poet, most praised for "Elene," "Ascension."
b. fl. 8th cent.
Source: *Alli; Benet 87, 96; BiB S; BioIn 3, 12; BritAu; CamGEL; CamGLE; CasWL; Chambr 1; CrtT 1, 4; DcArts; DcCathB; DcEnL; DcNaB; EvLB; LegTOT; LinLib L; LngCEL; LuthC 75; NewC; OxCEng 67, 85, 95; PenC ENG; REn; RfGEnL 91; WebE&AL*

Cyrankiewicz, Josef
Polish. Political Leader
Premier, 1947-52, 1954-70.
b. Apr 23, 1911 in Tarnow, Poland
d. Jan 20, 1989 in Warsaw, Poland
Source: *DcPol; FacFETw; IntWW 82, 89N; IntYB 82; WhoGov 72; WhoSoCE 89*

Cyrano de Bergerac, Savinien de
French. Poet, Soldier
Life romanticized by Edmond Rostand in *Cyrano de Bergerac,* 1897.
b. Mar 6, 1619 in Paris, France
d. Jul 28, 1655 in Paris, France
Source: *BiD&SB; CasWL; Dis&D; EuAu; EvEuW; GuFrLit 2; OxCFr; PenC EUR; REn; WhDW*

Cyril of Alexandria, Saint
Greek. Religious Figure
Patriarch of Alexandria, 412-44, whose writings dealt with problems of the Trinity; feast day, Feb 9.
b. 376 in Alexandria, Egypt
d. Jun 27, 444 in Alexandria, Egypt
Source: *CasWL; DcCathB; McGEWB; WhDW*

Cyrus, Billy Ray
American. Singer
Country singer whose smash single "Achy Breaky Heart," 1992 hit the top of the pop charts.
b. Aug 25, 1961 in Flatwoods, Kentucky
Source: *BgBkCoM; ConMus 11; LegTOT; News 93-1*

Cyrus the Great
[Cyrus the Elder]
Persian. Political Leader
Founded Persian empire, ca. 550 BC; captured Babylon, 538 BC.
b. 600BC, Media
d. 529BC, Asia
Source: *DcBiPP; LinLib S; NewCol 75; REn; WhDW; WorAl; WorAlBi*

Czerny, Karl
Austrian. Composer, Pianist
Beethoven's pupil who wrote widely-used finger exercises.
b. Feb 20, 1791 in Vienna, Austria
d. Jul 15, 1857 in Vienna, Austria
Source: *BioIn 1, 4, 7, 10; CelCen; LegTOT; LinLib S; NewOxM; OxCMus; WhDW*

Czolgosz, Leon F
American. Assassin
Shot William McKinley at Pan-American Exposition, Buffalo, NY, Sep 6, 1901; sent to electric chair.
b. 1873 in Detroit, Michigan
d. Oct 29, 1901 in New York
Source: *Dis&D; HarEnUS; NewCol 75*

D

Dabney, Virginius
American. Editor, Author
Writings include *The Story of Don Miff,* 1886; *Gold That Did Not Glitter,* 1889.
b. Feb 15, 1835 in Gloucester County, Virginia
d. Jun 2, 1894 in New York, New York
Source: *Alli SUP; AmAu; AmAu&B; ApCAB; BiD&SB; BiDSA; DcAmAu; DcAmB; DcNAA; TwCBDA; WhAm HS*

Dabney, Virginius
American. Editor
Won 1948 Pulitzer Prize for editorial writing; editor, Richmond *Times-Dispatch,* 1936-69.
b. Feb 8, 1901
d. Dec 28, 1995 in Richmond, Virginia
Source: *AmAu&B; BioIn 1, 3, 4, 11, 21; BlueB 76; ConAu 1NR, 29NR, 45, 150; CurBio 96N; DrAS 74H, 78H, 82H; EncSoH; EncTwCJ; IntAu&W 82, 91; NewYTBS 95; REnAL; TwCA SUP; WhAm 11; WhoAm 74, 76, 78, 80, 82, 84, 86, 88, 90, 92, 94, 95, 96; WhoWor 74, 76; WrDr 76, 80, 82, 84, 86, 88, 90, 92, 94, 96*

D'Abo, Maryam
English. Actor
Played Kara Milovy in James Bond film *The Living Daylights,* 1987.
b. 1961? in London, England
Source: *BioIn 15; ConTFT 7, 14; LegTOT; WhoHol 92*

Dabrowska, Maria Szumska
Polish. Author
Critically acclaimed saga, *Noce i Dnie,* 1932-34 explored the potential for humans to grow amidst social change.
b. Oct 6, 1889 in Russow, Poland
d. May 19, 1965 in Warsaw, Poland
Source: *CasWL; ConAu 106; ConLC 15; EncCoWW; EncWL 2; InWom SUP; ObitOF 79*

Dabrowski, Jan Henryk
Polish. Military Leader
General; endeared himself to Polish nationalists with his defense of Warsaw in Kosiuszko's uprising; led polish troops in Napoleon's army.
b. Aug 29, 1755 in Pierzchowice, Poland
d. Jun 6, 1818 in Winnogora, Poland
Source: *PolBiDi*

Dache, Lilly
American. Fashion Designer
Designed women's hats; best known for turban, half-hat, snood creations; won Coty, 1943.
b. 1904 in Beigles, France
d. Dec 31, 1989 in Louveciennes, France
Source: *BioIn 16; ConFash; CurBio 41, 90, 90N; FairDF US; InWom, SUP; NewYTBS 90; WhoAm 74; WhoFash, 88; WorFshn*

Dacko, David
African. Political Leader
Ruled as president of tumultuous government of Central African Republic, 1960-65, 1979-81.
b. Mar 24, 1930 in Bouchia, Ubangi-Shari
Source: *AfSS 78, 79, 80, 81, 82; BioIn 6, 7, 12, 21; DcAfHiB 86; FacFETw; IntWW 74, 75, 76, 77, 78, 79, 80, 81, 82, 83, 89, 91, 93; NewYTBS 79; WhoWor 80, 82*

DaCosta, Morton
[Morton Tecosky]
American. Producer, Director
Directed Broadway's biggest hits in the 1950s including *Music Man, Auntie Mame, No Time for Sergeants.*
b. Mar 7, 1914 in Philadelphia, Pennsylvania
d. Jan 29, 1989 in Danbury, Connecticut
Source: *BiE&WWA; BioIn 16; ConTFT 6; FilmgC; HalFC 84, 88; IntMPA 88; NewYTBS 89; NotNAT; OxCAmT 84; VarWW 85; WhoAm 86; WhoE 89; WhoThe 81; WorEFlm*

Daddah, Moktar Ould
Mauritian. Political Leader
First pres., independent Mauritania, 1961-78; promoted national unity.
b. Dec 25, 1924 in Boutilimit, Mauritania
Source: *AfSS 78, 79, 80, 81, 82; BioIn 5, 21; DcAfHiB 86; IntWW 74, 75, 76, 77, 78, 79, 80, 81, 82, 83, 89, 91, 93; IntYB 78; WhoGov 72; WhoWor 74, 76*

Daddario, Emilio Quincy
American. Politician
Dem. representative from CT, 1959-70.
b. Sep 24, 1918 in Newton Centre, Massachusetts
Source: *BiDrAC; BiDrUSC 89; Future; St&PR 75; WhoAm 74, 76, 78, 86, 88, 90, 92, 94, 95, 96, 97; WhoAmP 73, 75, 77, 79, 81, 83, 85, 87, 89, 91, 93, 95; WhoGov 72, 75, 77*

Dadie, Bernard Binlin
Ivoirian. Poet, Dramatist, Author
Works include *Afrique Debout,* 1950; *Un Negre a Paris,* 1959 and *Climbie,* 1953.
b. 1916 in Assini, Cote d'Ivoire
Source: *AfrA, 3; IntDcT 2; IntWWP 77; ModBlW; ModFrL; OxCThe 83; PenC CL; RGAfL*

Dafoe, Allan Roy
Canadian. Physician
Famous for delivering Dionne quintuplets, 1934; served as their guardian for many yrs.
b. May 29, 1883
d. Jun 2, 1943 in North Bay, Ontario, Canada
Source: *BioIn 1, 2; CurBio 43; InSci; MacDCB 78*

Dafoe, Willem
[William Dafoe]
American. Actor
Oscar nominee for supporting actor in *Platoon,* 1987; other films include *To Live and Die in L.A.,* 1985.
b. Jul 22, 1955 in Appleton, Wisconsin

Source: *BioIn 15, 16; ConNews 88-1; ConTFT 7; CurBio 90; HolBB; IntMPA 88, 92, 94, 96; IntWW 91, 93; LegTOT; WhoAm 90, 92, 94, 95, 96, 97; WhoEnt 92; WhoHol 92; WorAlBi*

DaGama, Vasco
Portuguese. Explorer, Navigator
Led expedition around Africa to India, 1497-99, opening first sea route to Asia.
b. 1460 in Sines, Portugal
d. Dec 24, 1524 in Cochin, India
Source: *NewC; NewCol 75; REn; WhAm HS*

Dagmar
[Virginia Ruth Egnor]
American. Actor
Played dumb blonde role of TV variety show "Broadway Open House," 1950; own variety show, "Dagmar's Canteen," 1952.
b. Nov 29, 1926 in Huntington, West Virginia
Source: *JoeFr; LegTOT; LesBEnT*

Dagover, Lil
[Marta Maria Liletta Dagover]
German. Actor
International star of 1920s-30s; heroine of classic *The Cabinet of Dr. Caligari,* 1919.
b. Sep 30, 1897 in Madiven, Dutch East Indies
d. Jan 30, 1980 in Munich, Germany (West)
Source: *AnObit 1980; BioIn 14; ConAu 105; EncEurC; EncTR 91; Film 1, 2; FilmAG WE; FilmEn; FilmgC; HalFC 80, 84, 88; IntDcF 2-3; LegTOT; MovMk; OxCFilm; TwYS; WhoHol A; WhoHrs 80; WorEFlm*

Daguerre, Louis Jacques Mande
French. Inventor
Invented the daguerreotype photograph, 1839.
b. Nov 18, 1787 in Cormeilles en Parisis, France
d. Jul 12, 1851 in Paris, France
Source: *AsBiEn; Benet 87, 96; BioIn 4, 6, 8, 12, 13, 14, 15, 20; CamDcSc; DcBiPP; FilmgC; ICPEnP; McGEWB; NewC; OxCFr; WhCiWar*

Dahl, Arlene
American. Actor
Glamor star of late 1940s-1950s films; has written column, books on beauty; mother of Lorenzo Lamas.
b. Aug 11, 1927 in Minneapolis, Minnesota
Source: *BioIn 1, 4, 9, 11, 14; CelR 90; ConAu 105; ConTFT 2; FilmgC; ForWC 70; HalFC 84, 88; IntAu&W 91; IntMPA 86, 92; InWom, SUP; MGM; MotPP; MovMk; WhoAm 86, 90; WhoAmW 87, 91; WhoE 91; WhoEnt 92; WhoHol A; WhoWest 74; WhoWor 84, 91; WorAl; WorAlBi*

Dahl, Gary
American. Businessman
Invented, marketed the Pet Rock, 1980s.
b. 1937?
Source: *BioIn 12*

Dahl, Roald
American. Author
Wrote macabre children's stories, books for adults, films; *Charlie and the Chocolate Factory,* 1964, adapted for screen as *Willie Wonka and the Chocolate Factory;* wrote screenplay *Chitty Chitty Bang Bang.*
b. Sep 13, 1916 in Llandaff, Wales
d. Nov 23, 1990 in Oxford, England
Source: *AnObit 1990; Au&Arts 15; Au&Wr 71; AuBYP 2, 3; Benet 87, 96; BioIn 3, 5, 6, 8, 9, 10, 11, 12, 13, 15, 16; BioNews 74; CamGLE; ChlBkCr; ChlFicS; ChlLR 1, 7, 41; ConAu 1R, 6NR, 32NR, 37NR, 133; ConLC 1, 6, 18, 79; ConNov 72, 76, 82, 86; ConPopW; ConTFT 6; DcArts; DcLB 139; DcLEL 1940; DcNaB 1986; DrAF 76; DrAPF 80, 91; EncSF, 93; FacFETw; HalFC 80, 84, 88; IntAu&W 76, 77, 82, 89; IntWW 82, 83, 89, 91N; LegTOT; LinLib L; MajAI; MajTwCW; MorBMP; NewC; News 91, 91-2; NewYTBS 90; Novels; OxCChiL; OxCEng 95; PenEncH; PiP; RAdv 1; REn; REnAL; RfGShF; RGTwCWr; ScF&FL 1, 2, 92; ScFSB; SmATA 1, 26, 65, 73; ThrBJA; TwCChW 78, 83, 89; TwCCr&M 80; TwCYAW; VarWW 85; WhAm 10; WhE&EA; Who 82, 83, 85, 88, 90, 92N; WhoAm 74, 76, 78, 80, 82, 84, 86, 88, 90; WhoHr&F; WhoHrs 80; WhoSciF; WhoWor 74, 76, 78; WorAl; WorAlBi; WorAu 1950; WrDr 76, 80, 82, 84, 86, 88, 90*

Dahlberg, Edward
American. Author
Novels include *Bottom Dogs,* 1929; *Because I Was Flesh,* 1964.
b. Jul 22, 1900 in Boston, Massachusetts
d. Feb 27, 1977 in Santa Barbara, California
Source: *AmAu&B; Benet 87, 96; BenetAL 91; BioIn 4, 5, 6, 7, 8, 9, 11, 12, 13, 15, 17; BlueB 76; CamGLE; CamHAL; CelR; ConAu 9R, 31NR, 69; ConLC 1, 7, 14; ConNov 72, 76; DcLB 48; DrAF 76; FacFETw; GrWrEL N; IntAu&W 76, 77; MajTwCW; ModAL, S1; NatCAB 60; Novels; OxCAmL 65, 83, 95; PenC AM; PeoHis; RfGAmL 87, 94; TwCA SUP; TwCWr; WhAm 7; WhoAm 74, 76; WhoWor 74; WrDr 76; WrPh*

Dahlgren, John Adolphus Bernard
American. Naval Officer, Inventor
During naval career developed cannons, guns known as Dahlgrens; nickname for guns was "soda-water bottles."
b. Nov 13, 1809 in Philadelphia, Pennsylvania
d. Jul 12, 1870 in Washington, District of Columbia
Source: *Alli SUP; ApCAB; BioIn 1, 4, 9; DcAmAu; DcAmB; DcAmMiB; DcNAA; Drake; HarEnMi; TwCBDA; WebAB 74, 79; WebAMB; WhAm HS; WhCiWar*

Dahl-Wolfe, Louise
American. Photographer
The doyenne of fashion, portrait photography; with *Harper's Bazaar,* 1936-58.
b. 1895 in San Francisco, California
Source: *BioIn 14, 16; ConAu 130; ConPhot 82, 88; EncFash; ICPEnP; InWom SUP; MacBEP; NewYTBS 84, 89; NorAmWA; WhAmArt 85*

Dahmer, Jeffrey L
American. Murderer
Confessed murderer of 17 young men, some of whom he dismembered and cannibalized, between 1978 and 1991, mostly in Milwaukee, WI.
b. 1959 in Bath Township, Ohio
d. Nov 28, 1994 in Portage, Wisconsin
Source: *NewYTBS 91*

Daiches, David
English. Author
Critical writings include *New Literary Values,* 1936.
b. Sep 2, 1912 in Sunderland, England
Source: *Au&Wr 71; Benet 87, 96; BioIn 4, 14, 16; BlueB 76; ChhPo S1, S3; CmScLit; ConAu 5R, 7NR, 29NR, 54NR; ConLCrt 77, 82; CyWA 89; DcLEL; EvLB; FacFETw; IntAu&W 76, 77, 91, 93; IntWW 74, 75, 76, 77, 78, 79, 80, 81, 82, 83, 89, 91, 93; LinLib L; LngCTC; ModBrL; NewCBEL; OxCEng 85, 95; RAdv 1; REn; TwCA SUP; Who 74, 82, 83, 85, 88, 90, 92, 94; WhoAm 74, 76, 78; WhoWor 74, 76, 78, 84, 87, 89, 91, 93, 95, 96, 97; WhoWorJ 78; WrDr 76, 80, 82, 84, 86, 88, 90, 92, 94, 96*

Dailey, Dan
American. Dancer, Actor
Made Broadway debut in *Babes in Arms,* 1939; films include *The Mortal Storm,* 1940.
b. Dec 14, 1915 in New York, New York
d. Oct 17, 1978 in Hollywood, California
Source: *BiDD; BiDFilm, 81, 94; CmMov; DcAmB S10; FilmgC; ForYSC; MotPP; MovMk; WhoHol A; WhoThe 77; WhScrn 83; WorEFlm*

Dailey, Irene
American. Actor
Won Emmy for role on soap opera "Another World," 1979.
b. Sep 12, 1920 in New York, New York
Source: *BiE&WWA; BioIn 5; ConTFT 3; InWom SUP; NotNAT; VarWW 85; WhoAm 80, 82, 84, 86, 88, 90, 92, 94, 95, 96, 97; WhoEnt 92; WhoHol 92, A; WhoThe 72, 77, 81*

Dailey, Janet
American. Author
America's best-selling romance author; over 60 books include *Calder Born, Calder Bred,* 1987.
b. May 21, 1944 in Storm Lake, Iowa
Source: *ArtclWW 2; BestSel 89-3; BioIn 12, 13, 14, 16; ConAu 17NR, 89; IntAu&W 91; LegTOT; MajTwCW; NewYTBS 81; TwCRGW; TwCRHW 90, 94; TwCWW 82, 91; WhoAm 84, 86, 88, 90, 92, 94, 95, 96, 97; WhoAmW 89, 91, 93, 95, 97; WhoUSWr 88; WhoWrEP 89, 92, 95; WrDr 84, 86, 88, 90, 92, 94, 96*

Daily, Thomas V, Bishop
American. Religious Leader
Roman Catholic bishop of the Archdiocese of Brooklyn, controversial for his anti-abortion stance, condemnation of Dignity USA.
b. Sep 23, 1927 in Belmont, Massachusetts
Source: *News 90; WhoAm 90; WhoE 91; WhoRel 92; WhoSSW 88*

Daimler, Gottlieb (Wilhelm)
German. Auto Manufacturer, Inventor
Founded Daimler Motor Co., 1890, which produced the Mercedes; invented motorcycle, 1885.
b. Mar 17, 1834 in Wurttemberg, Germany
d. Mar 6, 1900 in Stuttgart, Germany
Source: *AsBiEn; BiESc; BioIn 3, 4, 5, 6, 7, 8, 11, 12; InSci; LegTOT; McGEWB; NewCol 75; WebBD 83; WhDW; WorAl; WorAlBi; WorInv*

Daladier, Edouard
French. Political Leader
Radical socialist premier, 1930s; arrested by Vichy, 1940, liberated, 1945.
b. Jun 18, 1884 in Vancluse, France
d. Oct 10, 1970 in Paris, France
Source: *BiDFrPL; BioIn 1, 3, 9, 12, 13, 17, 20; CurBio 40, 70; DcPol; DcTwHis; EncTR, 91; FacFETw; HisEWW; LinLib S; McGEWB; NewYTBE 70; ObitT 1961; REn; WebBD 83; WhDW; WhWW-II; WorAl; WorAlBi*

Dalai Lama, the 14th Incarnate
[Gejong Tenzin Gyatsho]
Tibetan. Ruler, Religious Leader
Exiled religious and political leader of Tibet now living in India; won Nobel Peace Prize, 1989, in recognition of his nonviolent campaign to end China's domination of Tibet.
b. Jul 6, 1935 in Chhija Nangso, Tibet
Source: *Benet 87; BioIn 1, 2, 3, 5, 6, 8, 11, 12, 13, 14, 15, 16, 17, 18, 19, 20; ConHero 2; CurBio 51, 82; FacFETw; FarE&A 79, 81; HeroCon; IntWW 74, 75, 76, 77, 78, 79, 80, 81, 82, 83, 89, 91, 93; LegTOT; McGEWB; News 89-1; NewYTBS 89, 93; NobelP 91; WhDW; WhoNob 90, 95; WhoRel 92; WhoWor 76, 78, 80, 82, 84, 87, 89, 91, 93, 95, 96, 97; WorAlBi*

D'Albert, Eugene
German. Pianist, Composer
20 operas include *Tiefland,* 1903; pupil of Liszt.
b. Apr 10, 1864 in Glasgow, Scotland
d. Mar 3, 1932 in Riga, Union of Soviet Socialist Republics
Source: *Baker 84; BriBkM 80; MusSN; NewEOp 71; OxCMus*

Dale, Alan
American. Musician, Singer
Leading pop singer, 1940s-50s; recorded "Oh, Marie."
b. Jul 9, 1926 in New York, New York
Source: *BioIn 8; CmpEPM*

Dale, Carroll W
American. Football Player
Three-time all-pro end, 1960-73, mostly with Green Bay; a favorite receiver of Bart Starr.
b. Apr 24, 1938 in Wise, Virginia
Source: *WhoFtbl 74*

Dale, Chester
American. Art Collector
His art collection is housed in 10 rooms in Washington's National Gallery.
b. May 3, 1882 in New York, New York
d. Dec 16, 1962 in New York, New York
Source: *CurBio 58, 63; DcAmB S7*

Dale, Clamma Churita
American. Singer
Dramatic soprano of Houston, NYC Opera cos; won awards for *Porgy and Bess,* 1976.
b. Jul 4, 1948 in Chester, Pennsylvania
Source: *Baker 84; BiDAfM; CurBio 79; DrBlPA 90; InB&W 85; IntWWM 90; InWom SUP; MetOEnc; NewYTBS 76; WhoBlA 77, 80, 85, 90, 92*

Dale, Grover
[Grover Robert Aitken]
American. Director, Choreographer
With Michael Bennett, won Tony for *Seesaw,* 1973.
b. Jul 22, 1935 in Harrisburg, Pennsylvania
Source: *BiDD; ConTFT 5; NotNAT; WhoEnt 92; WhoThe 81*

Dale, Henry Hallett
English. Physician
Shared Nobel Prize in medicine, 1936.
b. Jun 9, 1875 in London, England
d. Jul 23, 1968 in Cambridge, England
Source: *Alli SUP; AsBiEn; BiESc; BiHiMed; BioIn 1, 2, 3, 6, 8, 9, 14, 15, 20; CamDcSc; DcNaB, 1961; DcScB, S1; FacFETw; GrBr; InSci; LarDcSc; McGEWB; McGMS 80; NotTwCS; ObitOF 79; ObitT 1961; OxCMed 86; WhAm 5; WhDW; WhoNob, 90, 95*

Dale, Jim
[James Smith]
English. Actor
Starred in Carry On series of films including *Carry On Again, Doctor,* 1969.
b. Aug 15, 1935 in Rothwell, England
Source: *BioIn 12; CelR 90; ConTFT 1, 3; CurBio 81; FilmEn; FilmgC; HalFC 80, 84, 88; IlWWBF; IntMPA 84, 86, 88, 92, 94, 96; ItaFilm; PenEncP; PlP&P A; VarWW 85; Who 74, 82, 83, 85, 88, 90, 92, 94; WhoAm 82, 84, 86, 88, 90, 92, 94, 95, 96, 97; WhoEnt 92; WhoHol 92, A; WhoThe 72, 77, 81*

Dalen, Nils Gustaf
Swedish. Physicist
Won 1912 Nobel Prize for Physics for invention of Solventil.
b. Nov 30, 1869 in Stenstorp, Sweden
d. Dec 9, 1937 in Stockholm, Sweden
Source: *BiESc; BioIn 2, 3, 15, 20; FacFETw; NobelP; WhoNob, 90, 95*

D'Alessio, Kitty
[Catherine Anne D'Alessio]
American. Business Executive
Pres. of US operations, Chanel Inc., 1979-88; vice Chm. of New Ventures and Special Projects for Chanel Inc., 1988—.
b. 1929 in Sea Girt, New Jersey
Source: *BioIn 13, 14, 16; ConNews 87-3; NewYTBS 82, 85; WhoAm 88; WhoAmW 83, 85, 87, 89, 91*

Daley, Arthur (John)
American. Journalist, Author
Sports writer; books include *Knute Rockne,* 1961; column in *NY Times,* 1952-74: "Sports of the Times."
b. Jul 31, 1904 in New York, New York
d. Jan 3, 1974 in New York, New York
Source: *AmAu&B; BiDAmSp OS; BioIn 4, 10; ConAu 45, P-2; CurBio 74N; DcAmB S9; DcLB 171; EncTwCJ; NewYTBS 74; WhAm 6*

Daley, Richard Joseph
American. Politician
Dem. mayor of Chicago, 1955-76; considered last of big-city bosses.
b. May 15, 1902 in Chicago, Illinois
d. Dec 20, 1976 in Chicago, Illinois
Source: *AmPolLe; BioIn 3, 4, 5, 6, 7, 8, 9, 10, 11, 12; CurBio 55; DcAmB S10; EncAB-H 1974, 1996; IntWW 74; WebAB 74, 79; WhAm 7; WhoAm 74, 76, 78; WhoAmP 73, 75; WhoGov 75; WhoMW 74; WhoWor 74*

Daley, Richard Michael
American. Politician
Mayor, Chicago, 1989—; son of Richard Joseph Daley, former mayor.
b. Apr 24, 1942 in Chicago, Illinois
Source: *BioIn 12, 13, 16; CurBio 92; WhoAm 90, 92, 94, 95, 96, 97; WhoAmL 90; WhoAmP 91; WhoE 97; WhoMW 92, 93*

Daley, Robert H
Producer
Films include *Play Misty for Me,* 1971; *Prince of the City,* 1981.
Source: *IntMPA 86; VarWW 85*

Daley, Rosie
American. Cook
Oprah Winfrey's personal chef—she helped the talk show host lose 72 lbs. in eight months.
b. 1961 in South Seaville, New Jersey

Daley, William M.
American. Government Official
US Secretary of Commerce, 1997—.
b. Aug 9, 1948

Dalgleish, Alice
American. Children's Author
Books include *The Bears on Hemlock Mountain,* 1952; *The Columbus Story,* 1955.
b. Oct 7, 1893, Trinidad
d. Jun 11, 1979 in Woodbury, Connecticut
Source: *ALA 80N; AmAu&B; AmPB; AnCL; AuBYP 2; ConAu 73, 89; JBA 34, 51; SmATA 17; Str&VC; WhNAA*

Dalhousie, James Andrew Broun Ramsay, Marquess of
Scottish. Statesman
Youngest governor general of India, 1847-56; worked against suttee, slave trade.
b. Apr 22, 1812 in Midlothian, Scotland
d. Dec 19, 1860 in Midlothian, Scotland
Source: *CelCen; DcBiPP; McGEWB; NewCol 75; WebBD 83*

Dali, Gala
[Mrs. Salvador Dali; Elena Diaranoff]
Model
For over 50 years was inspiration for husband, surrealist painter Salvador Dali.
b. 1893? in Kazan, Russia
d. Jun 10, 1982 in Gerona, Spain
Source: *AnObit 1982; BioIn 12, 13; NewYTBS 82*

Dali, Salvador
Spanish. Artist
Leader of Surrealist Movement; best-known work *Persistence of Memory,* 1931.
b. May 11, 1904 in Figueras, Spain
d. Jan 23, 1989 in Figueras, Spain
Source: *AmAu&B; AnObit 1989; Benet 87, 96; BiDD; BioIn 1, 2, 3, 4, 5, 6, 7, 8, 9, 10, 12, 13, 14, 15, 16, 17, 19, 20; BioNews 74; CelR; ClaDrA; CnOxB; ConArt 77, 83, 89, 96; ConAu 104, 127; CurBio 40, 51, 89N; DancEn 78; DcArts; DcCAr 81; DcHiB; EncFash; EncWT; FacFETw; FilmEn; FilmgC; HalFC 80, 84, 88; IntAu&W 77; IntDcAA 90; IntWW 74, 75, 76, 77, 78, 79, 80, 81, 82, 83, 89N; LegTOT; LinLib L, S; MakMC; McGDA; McGEWB; ModArCr 1; News 89-2; NewYTBS 80, 89; OxCAmH; OxCArt; OxCFilm; OxCSpan; OxCTwCA; OxDcArt; PhDcTCA 77; PrintW 83, 85; REn; WhAm 8, 9; WhDW; Who 74, 82, 83, 85, 88, 90N; WhoAm 74, 76, 78, 80, 82, 86, 88; WhoAmA 76, 78, 80, 82, 84, 86, 89N, 91N, 93N; WhoGrA 62; WhoHrs 80; WhoWor 74, 82, 84, 87, 89; WorAl; WorAlBi; WorArt 1950; WorEFlm*

Dalis, Irene
American. Opera Singer
Leading mezzo-soprano, NY Met., 1957-76; director, Opera San Jose, 1984—.
b. Oct 8, 1925 in San Jose, California
Source: *Baker 84, 92; BioIn 4, 5, 6, 12, 13; IntWWM 90; MetOEnc; NewGrDO; WhoAm 86, 88, 90, 92, 94, 95, 96, 97; WhoAmW 95, 97; WhoEnt 92; WhoWest 87, 89, 92, 94, 96*

Dall, John
[John Jenner Thompson]
American. Actor
Oscar nominee for *The Corn Is Green,* 1946; star of Hitchcock's *Rope,* 1948.
b. 1918 in New York, New York
d. Jan 15, 1971 in Beverly Hills, California
Source: *FilmEn; FilmgC; HalFC 80, 84, 88; MotPP; MovMk; NewYTBE 71; WhoHol B; WhScrn 74, 77, 83*

Dallapiccola, Luigi
Italian. Musician, Composer
First Italian to write atonal music: opera *The Prisoner,* 1948.
b. Feb 3, 1904 in Pisino, Yugoslavia
d. Feb 19, 1975 in Florence, Italy
Source: *Baker 78, 84, 92; BiDAmM; BioIn 2, 3, 4, 5, 7, 8, 10, 12; BriBkM 80; CmOp; CompSN, SUP; CurBio 66; DcArts; DcCM; DcCom&M 79; FacFETw; IntDcOp; IntWW 74; MakMC; McGEWB; MetOEnc; MusMk; MusSN; NewAmDM; NewCol 75; NewEOp 71; NewGrDM 80; NewGrDO; NewOxM; NewYTBS 75; ObitT 1971; OxCMus; OxDcOp; PenDiMP A; WhAm 6; WhDW; Who 74; WhoMus 72; WhoWor 74*

Dalla Rizza, Gilda
Italian. Opera Singer
Soprano; sang over 50 roles at La Scala, 1915-39; admired by Puccini, Toscanini.
b. Oct 12, 1892 in Verona, Italy
d. Jul 5, 1975 in Milan, Italy
Source: *Baker 84, 92; BioIn 8, 10, 12, 14; CmOp; NewEOp 71; NewGrDM 80; NewGrDO; OxDcOp*

Dallas, George Mifflin
American. US Vice President
Second in command under JK Polk, 1844-48.
b. Jul 10, 1792 in Philadelphia, Pennsylvania
d. Dec 31, 1864 in Philadelphia, Pennsylvania
Source: *Alli, SUP; AmBi; AmPolLe; ApCAB; BiAUS; BiDrAC; BiDrUSC 89; BiDrUSE 71, 89; BioIn 1, 4, 7, 8, 9, 10, 11, 14, 16; CelCen; DcAmAu; DcAmB; DcAmDH 80, 89; DcBiPP; DcNAA; Drake; HarEnUS; NatCAB 6; OxCAmH; TwCBDA; VicePre; WebAB 74, 79; WhAm HS; WhAmP*

Dallin, Cyrus Edwin
American. Sculptor
Best known for statues of Paul Revere, Sir Isaac Newton.
b. Nov 22, 1861 in Springville, Vermont
d. Nov 14, 1944 in Boston, Massachusetts
Source: *ApCAB X; BioIn 8, 11, 14; BriEAA; CurBio 45; DcAmArt; DcAmB S3; HarEnUS; IlBEAAW; LinLib S; NatCAB 14; WhAm 2*

Dallis, Nicholas Peter
American. Writer
Creator, "Judge Parker," "Rex Parker, MD," "Apartment 3-G," comic strips.
b. Dec 15, 1911 in New York, New York
d. Jul 6, 1991 in Scottsdale, Arizona
Source: *BiDrAPA 77, 89; BioIn 6, 10; EncTwCJ; WhAm 10; WhoAm 78, 80, 82, 84, 86, 88, 90; WhoWest 76, 78, 80*

Dalmores, Charles
French. Opera Singer
Tenor, with Chicago Opera, 1910-18; noted for his Faust.
b. Jan 1, 1871 in Nancy, France
d. Dec 6, 1939 in Hollywood, California
Source: *Baker 78, 84, 92; BiDAmM; BioIn 14; MetOEnc; NewEOp 71; NewGrDA 86; NewGrDM 80; NewGrDO; NotNAT B; OxDcOp; WhAm 1; WhoStg 1908*

Dalrymple, Ian (Murray)
British. Screenwriter
Won Oscars for *The Citadel; Pygmalion,* 1938.
b. Aug 26, 1903 in Johannesburg, South Africa
Source: *AnObit 1989; BlueB 76; ConAu 115, 128; ConDr 88A; EncEurC; FilmEn; FilmgC; HalFC 80, 84, 88; IlWWBF; IntAu&W 76, 77, 89; IntDcF 1-4, 2-4; IntMPA 75; IntWW 74, 75, 76, 77, 78, 79, 80, 81, 82, 83, 89, 89N; WhE&EA; Who 74, 82, 83, 85, 88, 90N; WhoWor 74, 76, 78*

Dalrymple, Jean
American. Producer, Director
Stage productions include *Hope for the Best,* 1944; *King Lear,* 1957.
b. Sep 2, 1910 in Morristown, New Jersey
Source: *BiE&WWA; BioIn 3, 4, 6, 7, 8, 10, 16; CamGWoT; ConAu 5NR, 5R; CurBio 53; EncMT; IntAu&W 76, 77; InWom; NotNAT, A; NotWoAT; OxCAmT 84; WhoAm 74, 76, 78, 80, 82, 84, 86, 88; WhoAmW 58, 61, 64, 66, 68, 70, 72, 83, 85, 87, 89; WhoE 74, 77, 86, 89; WhoGov 72, 75, 77; WhoThe 72, 77, 81; WrDr 76, 80, 82, 84, 86, 88*

Dalto, Jorge
Argentine. Pianist
Jazz-fusion hits include 1976 Grammy winner "This Masquerade."
b. Jul 7, 1948 in Jorge Perez, Argentina
d. Oct 27, 1987 in New York, New York
Source: *NewYTBS 87*

Dalton, Abby
American. Actor
Played Julia Cumson on TV series "Falcon Crest", 1981-90.
b. Aug 15, 1935 in Las Vegas, Nevada
Source: *BioIn 5; ConTFT 7; VarWW 85; WhoHol 92, A*

Dalton, Charles
American. Actor
Silent films include *Fighting Odds,* 1917; *The Eternal Magdalene,* 1919.
b. Aug 29, 1864
d. Jun 11, 1942 in Stamford, Connecticut
Source: *NotNAT B; WhoHol B; WhoStg 1908; WhScrn 83; WhThe*

Dalton, Emmett
[Dalton Brothers]
American. Outlaw
Realtor, screenwriter after prison term; wrote saga *When the Daltons Rode,* 1931.
b. 1871 in Cass County, Missouri
d. Jul 13, 1937 in Los Angeles, California
Source: *BioIn 15, 17; DrInf; WhScrn 77*

Dalton, Gratton
[Dalton Brothers]
American. Outlaw
Cousin of Younger Brothers; killed by armed citizens after trying to rob two banks at once.
b. 1862 in Cass County, Missouri
d. Oct 5, 1892 in Coffeyville, Kansas
Source: *BioIn 15, 17; DrInf; EncACr*

Dalton, John
English. Scientist
Originated table of atomic weights, 1803; first to thoroughly describe color blindness, 1794.
b. Sep 6, 1766 in Cumberland, England
d. Jul 27, 1844 in Manchester, England
Source: *Alli; AsBiEn; BiDLA; BiDPsy; BiESc; BioIn 1, 2, 3, 4, 5, 6, 7, 9, 12, 14, 15, 20, 21; BritAu 19; CamDcSc; CelCen; DcBiPP; DcNaB; DcScB; Dis&D; InSci; LarDcSc; LinLib S; McGEWB; NamesHP; NewCBEL; OxCMed 86; RAdv 14, 13-5; WhDW; WorAl; WorAlBi; WorScD*

Dalton, John Call
American. Physiologist
First US physician to devote life to experimental physiology; wrote *Doctrines of the Circulation,* 1884.
b. Feb 2, 1825 in Chelmsford, Massachusetts
d. 1889
Source: *Alli SUP; AmBi; ApCAB; BiDAmEd; BiDAmS; BiHiMed; BiInAmS; BioIn 9; DcAmAu; DcAmB; DcAmMeB, 84; DcNAA; DcScB, S1; Drake; NatCAB 10; TwCBDA; WhAm HS*

Dalton, John H.
American. Government Official
Secretary of the Navy, 1997—.
b. Dec 13, 1941

Dalton, John Nichols
American. Politician
Rep. governor of VA, 1978-82; helped build state's Rep. party into one of South's strongest.
b. Jul 11, 1931 in Emporia, Virginia
d. Jul 30, 1986 in Richmond, Virginia
Source: *AlmAP 80; BiDrGov 1789, 1978; BioIn 11; NewYTBS 86; WhAm 9; WhoAm 76, 78, 80, 82, 84, 86; WhoAmL 78, 79; WhoAmP 73, 75, 77, 79, 81, 83, 85; WhoGov 75, 77; WhoSSW 73, 75, 76, 78, 80, 82, 84*

Dalton, Lacy J
American. Singer
Country-western albums include *Hard Times; Lacy J Dalton,* 1980.
b. Oct 13, 1946 in Bloomsburg, Pennsylvania
Source: *BioIn 12, 14, 16; HarEnCM 87; PenEncP; WhoRocM 82*

Dalton, Robert
[Dalton Brothers]
American. Outlaw
Was marshal before becoming bankrobber, trainrobber; killed with brother Gratton trying to rob two banks at once.
b. 1867 in Cass County, Missouri
d. Oct 5, 1892 in Coffeyville, Kansas
Source: *BioIn 10, 15, 17; DcAmB; DrInf; WebAB 74, 79; WhAm HS*

Dalton, Timothy
Welsh. Actor
Played James Bond in film *The Living Daylights,* 1987; *License to Ki ll,* 1990.
b. Mar 21, 1946 in Colwyn Bay, Wales
Source: *BioIn 9, 15, 16; CelR 90; ConTFT 7; CurBio 88; FilmEn; FilmgC; HalFC 88; IntMPA 84, 86, 88, 92; IntWW 89, 91, 93; LegTOT; News 88; VarWW 85; WhoHol A*

Dalton, William
[Dalton Brothers]
American. Criminal
Robbed banks and trains with brothers and Doolin gang; killed by lawmen on front porch.
b. 1873 in Cass County, Missouri
d. 1893
Source: *DrInf; EncACr*

Daltrey, Roger Harry
[The Who]
English. Singer
Appeared in *Tommy,* 1974; hit albums *The Kids Are Alright,; Who Are You?,* 1978.
b. Mar 1, 1944 in London, England
Source: *BioIn 13, 14; BkPepl; ConMus 3; ConTFT 6; EncRk 88; HalFC 88; HarEnR 86; IntMPA 92; OxCPMus; WhoAm 86, 90; WhoEnt 92*

Daly, Arnold
American. Actor
Silent films include *The King's Game,* 1916.
b. Oct 4, 1875 in New York, New York
d. Jan 12, 1927 in New York, New York
Source: *AmBi; CamGWoT; DcAmB; Film 1; NotNAT, A, B; OxCAmT 84; OxCThe 67, 83; PlP&P; REn; WhAm 1; WhoHol B; WhoStg 1906, 1908; WhScrn 74, 77, 83; WhThe*

Daly, Augustin
American. Dramatist
Melodramas include *Under the Gaslight,* 1867; established Broadway theater, Daly's, 1879.
b. Jul 20, 1838 in Plymouth, North Carolina
d. Jun 7, 1899 in Paris, France
Source: *Alli SUP; AmAu; AmAu&B; AmBi; ApCAB; BbD; BenetAL 91; BioIn 1, 3, 4, 6, 8, 11, 12, 13, 14, 16, 19, 20; CamGLE; CamGWoT; CamHAL; CnDAL; CnThe; DcAmB; DcArts; DcNAA; GayN; GrStDi; GrWrEL DR; HsB&A; McGEWD 72, 84; ModWD; NatCAB 1; NotNAT A, B; OxCAmH; OxCAmL 65, 83; OxCAmT 84; OxCPMus; PlP&P; REnAL; REnWD; RfGAmL 87, 94; TwCBDA; WebAB 74, 79; WhAm 1*

Daly, Chuck
[Charles Jerome Daly]
American. Basketball Coach
Coach, Detroit, 1983-1992, where he garnered two NBA championships; coach, NJ, 1992-94; coach, US olympic team, 1992; coach, Orlando, 1997—.
b. Jul 20, 1930 in Saint Mary's, Pennsylvania
Source: *BioIn 16; CurBio 91; LegTOT; OfNBA 87; WhoAm 84, 86, 90, 95, 96, 97; WhoE 95, 97; WhoMW 92; WhoSpor*

Daly, James
American. Actor
Played Dr. Paul Lochner on TV series "Medical Center," 1969-76.
b. Oct 23, 1918 in Wisconsin Rapids, Wisconsin
d. Jul 3, 1978 in Nyack, New York
Source: *BiE&WWA, 78; ItaFilm; LegTOT; NotNAT; WhAm 7; WhoAm 74, 76, 78; WhoHol A; WhoThe 72, 77; WhScrn 83; WorAl*

Daly, John
English. Producer
Films include *Return of the Living Dead,* 1983; *Terminator,* 1984; *Falcon and the Snowman,* 1985.
b. 1937, England
Source: *ConTFT 11; IntMPA 75, 76, 77, 78, 79, 80, 81, 82, 84, 86, 88, 92, 94, 96; VarWW 85*

Daly, John Charles, Jr.
American. TV Personality
Best known for hosting "What's My Line," 1950-67. Voice of America, 1967-.
b. Feb 20, 1914 in Johannesburg, South Africa
d. Feb 24, 1991 in Chevy Chase, Maryland
Source: *BiDAmJo; BioIn 16, 17; ConTFT 13; EncTwCJ; LesBEnT, 92; LinLib L, S; NewYTBS 91; NewYTET; RadStar; WhAm 10; WhoAm 74, 76, 78, 80, 82, 84, 86, 88, 90; WhoE 74; WorAl; WorAlBi*

Daly, Marcus
American. Business Executive, Pioneer
Copper magnate who founded Anaconda Mining Co., 1891, town of Anaconda, MT, 1884.
b. Dec 5, 1841 in Ballyjamesduff, Ireland
d. Nov 12, 1900 in New York, New York
Source: *AmBi; BiDAmBL 83; BioIn 2, 3, 4, 6, 11, 15; DcAmB; GayN; McGEWB; OxCAmH; REnAW; WebAB 74, 79; WhAm 1; WorAl; WorAlBi*

Daly, Mary
American. Theologian
Author of several books and articles on patriarchy and the misogyny of religion; author of *Gyn/Ecology,* 1978.
b. Oct 16, 1928
Source: *AmWomWr SUP; ConAu 25R, 30NR; ConIsC 1; ContDcW 89; DrAS 74P, 78P, 82P; EncARH; EncWB; FemiCLE; FemiWr; GayLesB; GayLL; HanAmWH; IntDcWB; MajTwCW; OxCWoWr 95; RadHan; RAdv 14; WhoAmW 74, 75, 77; WhoRel 75, 77; WomPubS 1925; WrDr 76, 80, 82, 84, 86, 88, 90, 92, 94, 96*

Daly, Maureen Patricia
Irish. Author
Books, *Seventeenth Summer,* 1942; *The Ginger House,* 1964, have been filmed.
b. Mar 15, 1921 in Ulster, Northern Ireland
Source: *AmAu&B; AmNov; ArtclWW 2; Au&Arts 5; AuBYP 2, 3; BioIn 15, 16; BkC 4; CathA 1930; ConAu 11NR; CurBio 46; IntAu&W 91; InWom; MorJA; REnAL; SmATA 1AS, 2; TwCChW 89; WhoAmW 77; WrDr 92*

Daly, Reginald Aldworth
Canadian. Geologist
Authoritative early 20th c. proponent of many widely adopted geologic theories, most notably the theory of magmatic stoping.
b. May 19, 1871 in Napanee, Ontario, Canada
d. Sep 19, 1957 in Cambridge, Massachusetts
Source: *BioIn 4, 5, 6, 20; DcAmB S6; DcScB; InSci; NatCAB 44; NotTwCS; ObitOF 79; OxCCan; WhAm 3; WhE&EA; WhLit; WhNAA*

Daly, Thomas Augustine
American. Journalist, Poet
Columnist, *Philadelphia Evening Bulletin,* 1929-48.
b. May 28, 1871 in Philadelphia, Pennsylvania
d. Oct 4, 1948 in Philadelphia, Pennsylvania
Source: *AmAu&B; AmLY; BiDAmNC; BioIn 1, 4, 5, 6; BkC 1; CathA 1930; ChhPo, S2; CnDAL; ConAmL; DcCathB; DcNAA; OxCAmL 65, 83, 95; REn; REnAL; TwCA, SUP; WhAm 2; WhNAA*

Daly, Timothy
American. Actor
Played in *Diner,* 1982; played Joe in TV series "Wings," 1990-97; brother of Tyne Daly.
b. Mar 1, 1956 in New York, New York
Source: *CelR 90; ConTFT 8, 15; IntMPA 92, 94; LegTOT; WhoAm 94, 95, 96, 97; WhoHol 92*

Daly, Tyne
[Ellen Tyne Daly]
American. Actor
Won two Emmys for role of Mary Beth Lacey in TV series "Cagney and Lacey," 1982-88 .
b. Feb 21, 1944 in Madison, Wisconsin
Source: *BioIn 14, 15, 16; CelR 90; ConTFT 6; CurBio 92; HalFC 84, 88; IntMPA 92; InWom SUP; VarWW 85; WhoAm 86, 90; WhoAmW 87, 91; WhoEnt 92; WhoHol A; WhoTelC; WorAlBi*

Dam, (Carl Peter) Henrik
Danish. Biochemist
Shared Nobel Prize in medicine, 1943, with Edward Doisy for isolating Vitamin K.
b. Feb 21, 1895 in Copenhagen, Denmark
d. Apr 17, 1976 in Copenhagen, Denmark
Source: *AsBiEn; BiESc; BioIn 1, 2, 3, 6, 10, 11, 15, 20; CamDcSc; CurBio 49, 76, 76N; DcScB S2; InSci; IntWW 74, 75, 76; LarDcSc; LinLib S; McGEWB; McGMS 80; NewYTBS 76; NobelP; NotTwCS; WhAm 7; Who 74; WhoNob, 90, 95; WhoWor 74, 76*

Damas, Leon-Gontran
Guyanese. Poet
Poetry concerns racism, French colonialism, and the slave trade; poetry collections include *Pigments,* 1937.
b. Mar 28, 1912 in Cayenne, French Guiana
d. Jan 23, 1978 in Washington, District of Columbia
Source: *BioIn 11, 12; BlkWr 1; CaribW 2; CasWL; ConAu 125; ConLC 84; DcCLAA; EncWL 2, 3; LiExTwC; ModBlW; ModFrL*

D'Amato, Alfonse Marcello
American. Politician
Rep. senator from NY, who upset Javits, 1981—.
b. Aug 1, 1937 in New York, New York
Source: *AlmAP 82, 92; BiDrUSC 89; BioIn 13, 14, 15, 16; CelR 90; CngDr 85, 87, 89; CurBio 83; IntWW 83, 91; NewYTBS 83, 85, 88, 91; PolsAm 84; WhoAm 86, 90; WhoAmP 85, 89; WhoE 81, 91; WhoWor 87, 91; WrDr 86*

D'Amboise, Jacques
[Jacques Joseph d'Amboise Ahearn]
American. Dancer
Director, National Dance Institute; films include *Off Beat,* 1986.
b. Jul 28, 1934 in Dedham, Massachusetts
Source: *BiDD; BioIn 4, 6, 7, 8, 9, 12, 13, 14; CelR, 90; CurBio 64; DancEn 78; FacFETw; IntDcB; LegTOT; NewYTBS 85; WhoAm 86, 90; WhoE 86; WhoEnt 92; WhoHol 92, A*

Damian, Saint
Religious Figure
Martyr; became doctor but accepted no payment; feast day, Sept 27.
d. 303
Source: *BioIn 3, 4, 7; DcCathB*

Damien, Father
[Joseph Damien de Veuster]
Belgian. Missionary
Devoted life to leper colony in Hawaii; died from disease; made famous by Robert Louis Stevenson.
b. Jan 3, 1840 in Tremeloo, Belgium
d. Apr 15, 1889 in Molokai, Hawaii
Source: *AmBi; BioIn 14, 16, 17, 20; McGEWB; NewC; OxCAmL 65, 83, 95; REn; WorAl; WorAlBi*

Damita, Lily
[Liliane-Marie-Madeleine Carre]
French. Actor
Wife of Errol Flynn, 1935-42; films include *Frisco Kid,* 1935.
b. Jul 19, 1901 in Bordeaux, France
Source: *EncAFC; FilmgC; HalFC 88; InWom SUP; MotPP; ThFT*

Damned, The
[Roman Jugg; Rat Scabies; Dave Vanian]
British. Music Group
Hard rock group formed 1976; albums include *Glad It's All Over,* 1984.
Source: *EncRk 88; EncRkSt; HarEnR 86; IlEncRk; OxCPMus; PenEncP; RolSEnR 83; WhoRock 81; WhoRocM 82; WhsNW 85*

Damocles
Courtier
Attended to Dionysius; story told by Cicero.
b. 370?BC in Syracuse, Sicily, Italy
Source: *HispWr; NewC; WebBD 83*

Damon, Cathryn
American. Actor
Best known for role of Mary Campbell in TV spoof, "Soap," 1977-81; won Emmy, 1980.
b. Sep 11, 1931? in Seattle, Washington
d. May 6, 1987 in Los Angeles, California
Source: *AnObit 1987; BioIn 12; HalFC 84; VarWW 85*

Damon, Ralph Shepard
American. Airline Executive
Pres., TWA, 1949-56; developed first skysleeper-Condor, 1933.
b. Jul 6, 1897 in Franklin, New Hampshire
d. Jan 4, 1956 in Mineola, New York
Source: *BioIn 2, 4; CurBio 56; DcAmB S6; InSci; WhAm 3; WorAl*

Damon, Stuart
[Stuart Michael Zonis]
American. Actor
Best known as Dr. Alan Quartermain on TV soap opera General Hospital.
b. Feb 5, 1937 in New York, New York
Source: *BiE&WWA; ConTFT 5; FilmgC; NotNAT; VarWW 85; WhoHol 92; WhoThe 72, 77, 81*

Damon and Pythias
Philosophers
Legendary Greek inseparable friends.
Source: *NewC; WebBD 83*

Damone, Vic
[Vito Farinola]
American. Singer
Starred in own radio show, late 1940s; own TV series, 1956-57, 1967.
b. Jun 12, 1928 in New York, New York
Source: *Baker 84, 92; BiDAmM; BioIn 1, 2, 4, 11, 14, 15; CmpEPM; FilmEn; FilmgC; ForYSC; HalFC 84, 88; IntMPA 84, 86, 88, 92, 94, 96; LegTOT; OxCPMus; PenEncP; RadStar; RkOn 74; WhoAm 74, 78, 80, 82, 84; WhoHol 92, A; WorAl; WorAlBi*

Dampier, William
English. Explorer, Author
Discovered New Britain Islands in Pacific on expedition, 1699-1701.
b. Jun 1652? in East Coker, England
d. Mar 1715 in London, England
Source: *Alli; ApCAB; BioIn 1, 2, 3, 4, 5, 6, 7, 8, 9, 12, 13, 15, 16, 18, 21; BritAu; CamGEL; CamGLE; Chambr 2; DcBiPP; DcLEL; Drake; EvLB; HisDBrE; InSci; McGEWB; NewC; NewCBEL; OxCAusL; OxCEng 67, 85, 95; OxCShps; PenC ENG; REn; WhWE; WorAl; WorAlBi*

Damrosch, Frank Heino
American. Musician
Chorus master, NY Met., 1885-92; conducted children's concerts; son of Leopold.
b. Jun 22, 1859 in Breslau, Prussia
d. Oct 22, 1937 in New York, New York
Source: *BioIn 2, 4; EncAB-A 1; WebBD 83*

Damrosch, Leopold
German. Conductor
Founder, first conductor NYC Oratorio Society, 1873; NY Symphony Society, 1878; father of Walter.
b. Oct 22, 1832 in Posen
d. Feb 15, 1885 in New York, New York
Source: *AmBi; ApCAB; Baker 78, 84, 92; BiDAmM; BioIn 2, 5, 13, 14, 19; BriBkM 80; CmOp; DcAmB; IntDcOp; LinLib S; MetOEnc; NatCAB 2; NewAmDM; NewEOp 71; NewGrDA 86; NewGrDM 80; NewGrDO; OxCAmH; OxCAmL 65; OxDcOp; PenDiMP; TwCBDA; WebAB 74, 79; WhAm HS*

Damrosch, Walter Johannes
German. Conductor, Composer
Directed NY Symphony, 1903-26; formed Damrosch Opera Co., 1895; pioneered in weekly music appreciation broadcasts, 1928.
b. Jan 30, 1862 in Breslau, Prussia
d. Dec 22, 1950 in New York, New York
Source: *ApCAB; ASCAP 66; CurBio 44, 51; DcAmB S4; OxCAmL 65; REn; REnAL; TwCBDA; WebAB 74; WhAm 3; WhScrn 77*

Dana, Bill
American. Comedian, Actor
Films include *The Busybody,* 1967; *The Harrad Summer,* 1974.
b. Oct 5, 1924 in Quincy, Massachusetts
Source: *ASCAP 66, 80; BioIn 17; ConTFT 9; HalFC 84, 88; IntMPA 84, 86, 88, 92, 94, 96; JoeFr; LegTOT; VarWW 85; WhoAm 82, 84; WhoCom; WhoHol 92, A*

Dana, Charles Anderson
American. Journalist
Editor, *NY Tribune,* 1849-62; owner, editor, *NY Sun,* 1868-97.
b. Aug 8, 1819 in Hinsdale, New Hampshire
d. Oct 17, 1897 in West Island, New York
Source: *ABCMeAm; Alli, SUP; AmAu; AmAu&B; AmBi; AmSocL; ApCAB, X; BbD; BiAUS; BiDAmJo; BiDAmM; BiD&SB; BiDTran; BioIn 2, 4, 6, 8, 11, 12, 13, 16, 19, 20; ChhPo; CivWDc; CnDAL; DcAmAu; DcAmB; DcLB 3; DcNAA; Drake; HarEnUS; LinLib L, S; McGEWB; NatCAB 1; OxCAmH; OxCAmL 65, 83, 95; REn; REnAL; TwCBDA; WebAB 74, 79; WhAm HS; WhCiWar*

Dana, James Dwight
American. Geologist
Published several expedition reports; editor, *American Journal of Science,* 1840-95.
b. Feb 12, 1813 in Utica, New York
d. Apr 14, 1895 in New Haven, Connecticut
Source: *Alli, SUP; AmAu; AmBi; ApCAB; BbD; BenetAL 91; BiDAmEd; BiDAmS; BiD&SB; BiESc; BiInAmS; BioIn 2, 5; CelCen; CyAL 1; CyEd; DcAmAu; DcAmB; DcBiPP; DcNAA; DcScB; Drake; HarEnUS; InSci; LarDcSc; LinLib S; NatCAB 6, 30; NewYHSD; OxCAmH; OxCAmL 65, 83; REnAL; TwCBDA; WebAB 74, 79; WebBD 83; WhAm HS; WhWE*

Dana, Margaret Bloxham
American. Writer
Known for consumer attitude research; writings include *Behind the Label,* 1939.
Source: *ForWC 70; IntAu&W 76, 77; WhoAmW 75, 77, 79*

Dana, Richard Henry, Jr.
American. Author
Wrote *Two Years Before the Mast,* 1840.
b. Aug 1, 1815 in Cambridge, Massachusetts
d. Jan 6, 1882 in Rome, Italy
Source: *Alli, SUP; AmAu; AmAu&B; AmBi; AmRef; AmSocL; ApCAB; BbD; Benet 87, 96; BenetAL 91; BiAUS SUP; BibAL; BiD&SB; BioIn 1, 2, 3, 5, 6, 8, 9, 12, 13, 14, 15, 16, 19; CamGEL; CamGLE; CamHAL; CarSB; CasWL; Chambr 3; CivWDc; CmCal; CnDAL; CrtT 3; CyAL 2; CyWA 58; DcAmAu; DcAmB; DcAmSR; DcArts; DcBiPP; DcEnL; DcLB 1; DcLEL; DcNAA; Drake; EncAB-H 1974, 1996; EvLB; GrWrEL N; HarEnUS; LegTOT; LinLib L, S; McGEWB; MorMA; MouLC 4; NatCAB 7; OxCAmH; OxCAmL 65, 83, 95; OxCEng 67, 85, 95; OxCLaw; OxCShps; PenC AM; RAdv 14, 13-3; REn; REnAL; REnAW; RfGAmL 87, 94; SmATA 26; TwCBDA; WebAB 74, 79; WebE&AL; WhAm HS; WhAmP; WhDW; WorAl; WorAlBi*

Dana, Viola
[Violet Flugrath]
American. Actor
Silent screen star of over 50 films: *Revelation,* 1924; made Broadway debut, 1913.
b. Jun 28, 1897 in New York, New York
d. Jul 10, 1987 in Woodland Hills, California

Source: *BiDD; BioIn 10; EncAFC; Film 1, 2; FilmEn; FilmgC; HalFC 80, 84, 88; InWom SUP; SilFlmP; What 5; WhoHol A*

Danby, Thomas Osborne
[Earl of Danby]
English. Statesman
Known for corrupt politics; imprisoned in Tower of London after being impeached, 1678-84.
b. 1632
d. 1712
Source: *NewCol 75; WebBD 83*

Dancer, Stanley
American. Jockey
Harness racing driver whose horses have earned over $14 million since 1940s.
b. Jul 25, 1927 in New Egypt, New York
Source: *BiDAmSp OS; BioIn 9, 10, 13; CelR; CurBio 73; NewYTBS 74*

Dancy, John Albert
American. Broadcast Journalist
With NBC News since 1973; congressional correspondent, 1982-88; Chief diplomatic correspondent 1988; Moscow correspondent, 1994—.
b. Aug 5, 1936 in Jackson, Tennessee
Source: *LesBEnT, 92; PeoHis; WhoAm 80, 82, 84, 86, 88, 90, 92, 94, 95, 96, 97; WhoTelC*

Dandridge, Dorothy
American. Singer, Actor
Starred in Otto Preminger's film *Carmen Jones,* 1954; won Golden Globe for *Porgy and Bess,* 1959.
b. Nov 9, 1922? in Cleveland, Ohio
d. Sep 8, 1965 in West Hollywood, California
Source: *AfrAmAl 6; BioIn 2, 3, 6, 7, 9; BlksAmF; BlksB&W, C; BlkWAm; ConBlB 3; DcAmB S7; DcAmNB; DcTwCCu 5; FilmgC; MotPP; MovMk; NotBlAW 1; WhAm 4; WhoHol B; WhScrn 77, 83*

Dandridge, Ray(mond)
"Hooks"
American. Baseball Player
Third baseman; had 16-yr. career in Negro League, 1930s-40s; Hall of Fame, 1987.
b. 1913 in Richmond, Virginia
Source: *AfrAmSG; Ballpl 90; BiDAmSp BB; BioIn 15, 16, 21; LegTOT; NewYTBS 87; WhoBlA 92; WhoSpor*

Dandridge, Ruby Jean
American. Actor
Began career as maid on radio show "The Judy Canova Show," 1943-53; played Delilah on TV's "Father Knows Best," 1961-62; mother of Dorothy.
b. Mar 3, 1902 in Memphis, Tennessee
d. Oct 17, 1987 in Los Angeles, California
Source: *InB&W 85*

Dandurand, Leo
[Joseph Viateur Dandurand]
American. Hockey Executive
Co-owner, Montreal Canadiens, 1921-37; Hall of Fame, 1963.
b. Jul 9, 1889 in Bourbonnais, Illinois
d. Jun 26, 1964
Source: *BioIn 6; WhoHcky 73*

Dane, Clemence
[Winifred Ashton]
English. Author, Dramatist
Wrote novel, *Regiment of Women,* 1917; play, *Bill of Divorcement,* 1921.
b. 1888 in Blackheath, England
d. Mar 28, 1965 in London, England
Source: *BiE&WWA; CamGLE; CamGWoT; Chambr 3; CnMD; ConAu 93; DcLEL; DcNaB 1961; EncMys; EncSF 93; EngPo; Ent; EvLB; FemiCLE; LngCTC; McGEWD 72, 84; ModBlW; ModBrL; ModWD; ModWoWr; NewC; NotNAT B; OxCEng 85, 95; OxCThe 67, 83; PenNWW A, B; REn; RfGEnL 91; ScF&FL 1, 92; TwCA, SUP; TwCWr; WhoLA; WhThe; WomNov*

Dane, Maxwell
American. Advertising Executive
Founded Doyle Dane Bernbach, Inc., NYC, 1949; pres., United Jewish Appeal, 1982.
b. Jun 7, 1906 in Cincinnati, Ohio
Source: *BlueB 76; St&PR 75, 84, 87, 91, 93, 96; WhoAdv 72, 90; WhoAm 74, 76, 78, 80, 82, 84, 86, 88, 90, 92, 94, 95, 96, 97; WhoAmJ 80; WhoWorJ 72, 78*

Danelli, Dino
[The Rascals]
American. Musician
Drummer with blue-eyed soul group; hit single "How Can I Be Sure," 1967.
b. Jul 23, 1945 in New York, New York

Danelo, Joe
[Joseph Peter Danelo]
American. Football Player
Placekicker, 1975-84, mostly with NY Giants.
b. Sep 2, 1953 in Spokane, Washington
Source: *BioIn 13; FootReg 85; NewYTBS 83*

Danes, Claire
American. Actor
Appeared in *Little Women,* 1994, *Romeo and Juliet,* 1996.
b. Apr 12, 1979 in New York, New York
Source: *ConTFT 15*

Danforth, Dave
[David Charles Danforth]
"Dauntless Dave"
American. Baseball Player
Pitcher, 1911-12, 1916-25; credited with originating "shine ball," 1915.
b. Mar 7, 1890 in Granger, Texas
d. Sep 19, 1970 in Baltimore, Maryland
Source: *Ballpl 90; BioIn 9; NewYTBE 70; WhoProB 73*

Danforth, John Claggett
American. Politician, Clergy
Moderate Rep. senator from MO, 1976-94; heir to Ralston Purina fortune.
b. Sep 5, 1936 in Saint Louis, Missouri
Source: *AlmAP 80; WhoMW 78, 80, 82, 84, 86, 88, 90, 92, 93, 96; WhoRel 85; WhoWor 80, 82, 84, 87, 89, 91, 93, 95*

Danforth, William
[William Daniels]
American. Actor
Appeared in over 5,000 performances of Gilbert & Sullivan operas; played *The Mikado* 1,000 times.
b. May 13, 1869 in Syracuse, New York
d. Apr 16, 1941 in Skaneateles, New York
Source: *CurBio 41; NotNAT B; WhoHol B; WhThe*

Danforth, William H
American. Manufacturer, Business Executive
Founded Ralston Purina, 1893.
b. Sep 10, 1870 in Charleston, Missouri
d. Dec 24, 1952 in Saint Louis, Missouri
Source: *BiDAmBL 83; ObitOF 79; WhAm 3*

D'Angelo, Beverly
American. Actor, Singer
Former rock singer who appeared in films *Paternity,* 1981; *Coal Miner's Daughter,* 1980.
b. Nov 15, 1954? in Columbus, Ohio
Source: *BioIn 15, 16; ConTFT 5; HalFC 84, 88; IntMPA 82, 92, 94, 96; WhoAm 94, 95, 96, 97; WhoAmW 95, 97; WhoEnt 92*

Dangerfield, George Bubb
English. Author
Won 1953 Pulitzer for *The Era of Good Feeling,* which tells of yrs. 1812-1829 in US.
b. Oct 28, 1904 in Berkshire, England
d. Dec 27, 1986 in Santa Barbara, California
Source: *AmAu&B; ConAu 9R; CurBio 53, 87; DrAS 74H; IntAu&W 76, 77; OxCAmL 65; PoIre; WhoAm 74; WhoWor 74; WorAu 1950; WrDr 76, 80, 82, 84, 86*

Dangerfield, Rodney
[Jacob Cohen; Jack Roy]
American. Comedian
Films include *Back to School,* 1986; won Grammy for comedy album *No Respect,* 1980.
b. Nov 22, 1921 in Babylon, New York
Source: *BioIn 12, 14, 15; CelR 90; ConAu 102; ConTFT 3, 14; EncAFC; IntMPA 84, 86, 88, 92, 94, 96; LegTOT; QDrFCA 92; RkOn 85; VarWW 85; WhoAm 90; WhoCom; WhoEnt 92; WhoHol 92, A; WorAl; WorAlBi*

Daniel
Biblical Figure
Visions, life story recorded in Bible; interpreted dreams of King Nebuchadnezzar; escaped from lion's den.
d. 745BC
Source: *BiB S; BioIn 1, 2, 3, 4, 5, 6, 8, 9, 10, 11, 17, 20; DcBiPP; DcBrECP; DcCathB; DcEnL; DcNaB; Dis&D; NewCol 75; WomWrSA*

Daniel, Beth
American. Golfer
Turned pro, 1978; leading money winner on tour, 1980, 1981.
b. Oct 14, 1958? in Charleston, South Carolina
Source: *NewYTBS 78; WhoAm 84, 86, 90; WhoAmW 91; WhoIntG*

Daniel, Clifton, Jr.
American. Journalist
With *NY Times,* 1944-80, associate editor, 1969-77; married to Margaret Truman.
b. Sep 19, 1912 in Zebulon, North Carolina
Source: *BioIn 4, 7, 9, 11, 13, 14, 15; BlueB 76; ConAu 113; IntWW 74, 75, 76, 77, 78, 79, 80, 81, 82, 83; IntYB 78, 79, 80, 81, 82; WhoAm 80; WhoE 74; WhoWor 74; WorAl; WorAlBi*

Daniel, Dan(iel)
American. Journalist
Covered baseball in NYC, 1909-74; founded boxing's *Ring* mag.
b. 1891
d. Jul 1, 1981 in Pompano Beach, Florida
Source: *NewYTBS 81*

Daniel, Price
[Marion Price Daniel]
American. Politician
Dem. governor, TX, 1957-63; US congressman, 1938-45, 1953-57.
b. Oct 10, 1910
d. Aug 25, 1988 in Liberty, Texas
Source: *AmBench 79; BiDrGov 1789; BiDrUSC 89; BioIn 2, 3, 4, 5, 9, 11, 16; CurBio 88N; LinLib S; NewYTBS 88; PolProf E; WhAm 9; WhoAm 78; WhoAmL 78, 79; WhoAmP 75, 77, 79; WhoSSW 76*

Daniel, Samuel
English. Author
Writings include narrative poem *Complaint of Rosamund,* 1592, historical epic *The Civil Wars,* 1595.
b. 1562? in Taunton, England
d. Oct 14, 1619 in Beckington, England
Source: *Alli; AtlBL; BbD; Benet 87, 96; BiD&SB; BiDLA; BiDRP&D; BioIn 1, 3, 5, 7, 8, 10, 12, 14, 16; BlmGEL; BritAu; CamGEL; CamGLE; CamGWoT; CasWL; Chambr 1; ChhPo, S1; CnE&AP; CroE&S; CrtT 1, 4; DcArts; DcBiPP; DcEnA; DcEnL; DcEuL; DcLB 62; DcLEL; DcNaB; EvLB; GrWrEL P; LitC 24; LngCEL; MouLC 1; NewC; NotNAT B; OxCEng 67; OxCThe 67; PenC ENG; PoLE; REn; REnWD; RfGEnL 91; WebE&AL; WhDW*

Danielian, Leon
American. Dancer, Choreographer
Director, American Ballet Theater Schools, 1967-80; professor of dance, Univ. of Texas, 1982-91.
b. Oct 31, 1920 in New York, New York
d. Mar 8, 1997 in Canaan, Connecticut
Source: *BiDD; BioIn 3, 10, 11; CnOxB; DancEn 78; IntDcB; WhoAm 74, 76, 78, 80, 82, 84, 86, 88, 90; WhoEnt 92; WhoWor 74, 76*

Daniell, Henry
English. Actor
Played Prof. Moriarty in Sherlock Holmes film *The Woman in Green,* 1945.
b. Mar 5, 1894 in London, England
d. Oct 31, 1963 in Santa Monica, California
Source: *BioIn 6, 13, 17, 21; CmMov; EncAFC; Film 2; FilmEn; FilmgC; ForYSC; HalFC 80, 84, 88; HolCA; MotPP; MovMk; NotNAT B; OlFamFa; OxCAmT 84; PlP&P; Vers A; WhoHol B; WhoHrs 80; WhScrn 74, 77, 83; WhThe*

Daniell, John Frederic
English. Inventor
Developed Daniell's hygrometer, 1820.
b. Mar 12, 1790
d. Mar 13, 1845
Source: *AsBiEn; BiESc; BioIn 2, 14; CamDcSc; DcNaB; DcScB; WhDW; WorInv*

Daniell, Robert F
American. Business Executive
CEO, United Technologies, 1984-92; chairman, 1992—.
b. 1933 in Milton, Massachusetts
Source: *BioIn 15, 16; Dun&B 90; IntWW 91; St&PR 91; WhoAm 86, 90; WhoE 91; WhoFI 92; WhoWor 91*

Daniels, Bebe
[Virginia Daniels]
American. Actor
Made 200 shorts with Harold Lloyd, 1914-18; wed to Ben Lyon.
b. Jan 14, 1901 in Dallas, Texas
d. Mar 16, 1971 in London, England
Source: *BiDFilm, 81, 94; CmpEPM; EncAFC; Film 1, 2; FilmEn; FilmgC; ForYSC; HalFC 80, 84, 88; IlWWBF, A; IntDcF 1-3, 2-3; InWom, SUP; LegTOT; MotPP; MovMk; NewYTBE 71; NotNAT B; ObitOF 79; ObitT 1971; OxCFilm; OxCPMus; QDrFCA 92; SilFlmP; ThFT; TwYS; What 1; WhoHol A, B; WhScrn 74, 77, 83; WhThe; WomWMM*

Daniels, Billy
American. Singer
Popular vocalist, showman; noted for rendition of "That Old Black Magic."
b. Sep 12, 1915 in Jacksonville, Florida
d. Oct 7, 1988 in Los Angeles, California
Source: *AmPS B; AnObit 1988; CmpEPM; DrBlPA, 90; OxCPMus; PenEncP; WhoHol A*

Daniels, Charlie
[The Charlie Daniels Band]
American. Musician, Songwriter
Nashville session guitarist, who formed Charlie Daniels Band, 1973; wrote Grammy-winning song "Devil Went Down to Georgia," 1979; winner of Grammy award, 1980.
b. Oct 28, 1936 in Wilmington, North Carolina
Source: *Baker 84, 92; BioIn 13, 14; ConAu 138; ConMus 6; EncRk 88; HarEnCM 87; HarEnR 86; IlEncCM; LegTOT; OxCPMus; PenEncP; RkOn 78, 84; WhoAm 80, 82, 84, 86, 88, 90, 92, 94, 95, 96, 97; WhoAmP 91; WhoEnt 92; WhoHol 92; WhoRock 81; WhoRocM 82; WorAlBi*

Daniels, Frank
American. Actor
Began in Vitagraph films, 1915; played in *Kernel Nutt* series.
b. Apr 15, 1856 in Dayton, Ohio
d. Jan 12, 1935 in Palm Beach, Florida
Source: *Film 1; NotNAT B; PlP&P; WhAm 1; WhoHol B; WhoStg 1906, 1908; WhScrn 74, 77; WhThe*

Daniels, Jeff
American. Actor
Films include *Ragtime,* 1982; *Terms of Endearment,* 1984; *Purple Rose of Cairo,* 1985.
b. Feb 19, 1955 in Georgia
Source: *BioIn 14, 16; ConTFT 4, 11; HolBB; IntMPA 88, 92, 94, 96; LegTOT; News 89; VarWW 85; WhoAm 94, 95, 96, 97; WhoEnt 92; WhoHol 92*

Daniels, Jonathan Worth
American. Author, Journalist
FDR's press secretary, 1945, who wrote historical biographies: *Robert E Lee,* 1960; son of Josephus.
b. Apr 26, 1902 in Raleigh, North Carolina
d. Nov 6, 1981 in Hilton Head Island, South Carolina
Source: *AmAu&B; Au&Wr 71; AuBYP 2; BlueB 76; CnDAL; ConAu 49; CurBio 42, 82; IntAu&W 76; IntYB 78, 79, 80, 81, 82; NewYTBS 81; OxCAmL 65; REn; REnAL; ScF&FL 2; TwCA SUP; WhoAm 74, 76, 78, 80; WhoAmP 73, 75, 77, 79; WrDr 80*

Daniels, Josephus
American. Journalist, Government Official
Secretary of Navy, 1913-21; ambassador to Mexico, 1933-41; wrote *Our Navy at War,* 1922.
b. May 18, 1862 in Washington, District of Columbia
d. Jan 15, 1948 in Raleigh, North Carolina

Source: *AmAu&B; ApCAB X; Benet 87; BenetAL 91; BiDAmJo; BiDrUSE 71, 89; BiDSA; BioIn 1, 2, 3, 4, 5, 6, 7, 8, 10, 16; ConAu 122; CurBio 44, 48; DcAmB S4; DcAmDH 80, 89; DcAmMiB; DcAmTB; DcLB 29; DcNAA; DcNCBi 2; EncAB-H 1974, 1996; EncAJ; EncSoH; EncWM; FacFETw; HarEnUS; JrnUS; LinLib L, S; McGEWB; NatCAB 39; OxCAmH; OxCAmL 65, 83, 95; REn; REnAL; TwCBDA; WhAm 2; WhAmP; WhJnl*

Daniels, Mickey
[Our Gang]
Actor
Appeared in first of Our Gang comedies, 1920s.
b. 1914
Source: *EncAFC; Film 2; ForYSC; WhoHol A*

Daniels, William
American. Actor
Won Emmy, 1984, 1986, for role of Dr. Mark Craig on TV series "St. Elsewhere," 1982-88.
b. Mar 31, 1927 in New York, New York
Source: *BiE&WWA; ConTFT 3, 9; EncAFC; FilmEn; ForYSC; HalFC 80, 84, 88; IntMPA 84, 86, 88, 92, 94, 96; NotNAT; PlP&P; WhoAm 86; WhoHol 92, A; WorAlBi*

Daniloff, Nicholas
American. Journalist
Reporter with *US News & World Report;* jailed, accused of spying in Soviet Union, 1986.
b. Dec 30, 1934 in Paris, France
Source: *BioIn 14, 15, 16; ConAu 85; NewYTBS 86*

Danilova, Alexandra
American. Dancer, Choreographer
Best-known ballets include *Le Beau Danube, Swan Lake.*
b. Jan 20, 1904 in Peterhof, Russia
d. Jul 13, 1997 in New York, New York
Source: *BiDD; BiDSovU; BiE&WWA; BioIn 14, 15, 16; ContDcW 89; CurBio 87; FacFETw; GrLiveH; IntDcWB; InWom SUP; Who 85, 92; WhoAm 86, 95; WhoThe 77A; WorAlBi*

Danjon, Andre Louis
French. Astronomer
Invented the Danjon astrolabe and other important instruments used by astronomers.
b. Apr 6, 1890 in Caen, France
d. Apr 21, 1967 in Paris, France
Source: *BioIn 7; McGMS 80*

Dankworth, John Philip William
English. Composer, Conductor
Jazz saxophonist, orchestra leader, 1950s; scored many British films; wed to singer Cleo Laine.
b. Sep 20, 1927 in London, England
Source: *Baker 84; BiDJaz; CmpEPM; HalFC 88; IlEncJ; IntWW 91; IntWWM 90; NewAmDM; NewGrDJ 88; NewGrDM 80; NewOxM; OxCFilm; OxCPMus; PenDiMP; Who 92; WhoMus 72; WhoWor 84*

Dannay, Frederic
[Ellery Queen; Barnaby Ross]
American. Author
Wrote many *Ellery Queen* mysteries with cousin Manfred B Lee; won four Edgars.
b. Oct 20, 1905 in New York, New York
d. Sep 3, 1982 in White Plains, New York
Source: *AmAu&B; AnObit 1982; AuBYP 2, 3; AuSpks; Benet 87; BioIn 2, 3, 4, 8, 10, 11, 12, 13, 14, 17, 20; CelR; ConAu 1NR, 1R, 39NR, 107; ConLC 11; CurBio 82, 82N; DcLB 137; DcLEL; EncMys; EvLB; IntAu&W 77; IntWW 74, 75, 76, 77, 78, 79, 80, 81, 82; LngCTC; MajTwCW; NewYTBS 82; PenC AM; REn; ScF&FL 1; TwCA, SUP; WebAB 74, 79; WhoAm 82; WorAl; WrDr 76, 80, 82*

Danner, Blythe Katharine
[Mrs. Bruce W Paltrow]
American. Actor
Won 1971 Tony for *Butterflies Are Free.*
b. Feb 3, 1943 in Philadelphia, Pennsylvania
Source: *BioIn 10; CelR 90; ConTFT 5; CurBio 81; HalFC 88; IntMPA 82, 92; InWom SUP; NewYTBS 86; VarWW 85; WhoAm 86, 90; WhoAmW 74; WhoEnt 92; WhoHol A; WhoThe 81; WorAl; WorAlBi*

D'Annunzio, Gabriele
Italian. Poet, Author, Soldier
Ardent fascist, courted by Mussolini; numerous writings include *Dead City,* 1902; famed WW I aviator.
b. Mar 12, 1863 in Pescara, Italy
d. Mar 1, 1938 in Vittoriale, Italy
Source: *AtlBL; BiDExR; BioIn 14, 16, 17, 21; CamGWoT; CasWL; ClDMEL 47, 80; CnMD; CnThe; ConAu 104; CyWA 58; DcArts; DcItL 1, 2; DcTwHis; Dis&D; EncRev; EncTR 91; EncWL 2, 3; EncWT; Ent; EuAu; EuWr 8; EvEuW; FacFETw; GrFLW; InSci; IntDcT 2; ItaFilm; LngCTC; MakMC; McGEWB; McGEWD 72, 84; ModRL; ModWD; NewEOp 71; NewGrDM 80; NewGrDO; Novels; OxCEng 67, 85, 95; OxCThe 67, 83; OxDcOp; PenC EUR; PlP&P; RAdv 14, 13-2; RComWL; REn; REnWD; RfGWoL 95; TwCA, SUP; TwCLC 6, 40; TwCWr; WebBD 83; WhDW; WhE&EA; WhoTwCL; WorAl; WorAlBi; WorEFlm*

Danny and the Juniors
[Frank Maffei; Danny Rapp; Joe Terranova; Dave White]
American. Music Group
PA group, formed 1957; recorded classics "At the Hop," 1957; "Rock and Roll Is Here to Stay," 1958.
Source: *EncPR&S 89; EncRk 88; PenEncP; RkOn 74, 82; RolSEnR 83; WhoHol 92; WhoRocM 82*

Danson, Ted
[Edward Bridge Danson, III]
American. Actor
Played Sam Malone on TV comedy "Cheers," 1982-93; starred in film *Three Men and a Baby,* 1987; star of TV's "Ink," 1996-97; winner of two Emmy awards, 1990, 1993.
b. Dec 29, 1947 in San Diego, California
Source: *BioIn 13, 14, 15, 16; CelR 90; ConTFT 1, 4, 11; CurBio 90; HalFC 88; HolBB; IntMPA 86, 88, 92, 94, 96; IntWW 93; LegTOT; VarWW 85; WhoAm 88, 90, 92, 94, 95, 96, 97; WhoEnt 92; WhoHol 92; WorAlBi*

Dante, Nicholas
American. Dramatist
With James Kirkwood, co-wrote *A Chorus Line,* 1976; won Pulitzer, Tony; died of AIDS.
b. Nov 22, 1941 in New York, New York
d. May 21, 1991 in New York, New York
Source: *BiDD; ConTFT 11; NewYTBS 91; VarWW 85; WhoAm 76, 78, 80, 82*

Dante Alighieri
Italian. Poet
Wrote celebrated masterpiece *The Divine Comedy,* 1307-21.
b. May 27, 1265 in Florence, Italy
d. Sep 14, 1321 in Ravenna, Italy
Source: *AtlBL; BbD; BiD&SB; BioIn 1, 2, 3, 4, 5, 6, 7, 8, 9, 10, 11, 12, 13, 14, 17, 18, 19, 20; BlkAWP; CasWL; ChhPo; CyEd; CyWA 58; DcArts; DcBiPP; DcCathB; DcEnL; DcEuL; DcItL 1, 2; EncSF, 93; EuAu; EuWr 1; EvEuW; GrFLW; IlEncMy; LinLib L; LngCEL; LuthC 75; MagSWL; McGEWB; NewC; NewCBEL; NewEOp 71; NewGrDM 80; NewGrDO; OxCEng 67, 85, 95; OxCPhil; OxDcOp; PenC EUR; RAdv 14, 13-2; RComWL; REn; WorAl; WorAlBi; WrPh*

Dantine, Helmut
American. Actor
Known for playing Nazi roles during WW II; films include *Hotel Berlin,* 1945.
b. Oct 7, 1917 in Vienna, Austria
d. May 3, 1982 in Beverly Hills, California
Source: *FilmEn; FilmgC; HalFC 84, 88; IntMPA 82; ItaFilm; LegTOT; MotPP; MovMk; WhoHol A*

Dantley, Adrian (Delano)
"A D"
American. Basketball Player
Forward, Buffalo, 1976-77; Indiana, 1977; LA Lakers, 1977-79; Utah, 1979-86; Detroit, 1986-89; Dallas and Milwaukee, 1989-90; led NBA in scoring, 1981, 1984; 13th player in

NBA history to score 20,000 points in career, 1987.
b. Feb 28, 1956 in Washington, District of Columbia
Source: *BasBi; BiDAmSp BK; BioIn 13, 14; BlkOlyM; LegTOT; NewYTBS 84; OfNBA 87; WhoAfA 96; WhoAm 82, 84, 86, 88, 90; WhoBlA 77, 80, 85, 88, 90, 92, 94; WorAlBi*

Danto, Arthur C(oleman)
American. Writer, Educator
Winner of National Book Award for criticism, 1990; art critic for *Nation,* 1984—.
b. Jan 1, 1924 in Ann Arbor, Michigan
Source: *BioIn 16, 17, 20, 21; CurBio 95; DrAS 74P, 78P, 82P; WhoAm 74, 76, 78, 80, 82, 84, 86, 88, 90, 92, 94, 95, 96, 97; WhoE 74, 97; WhoUSWr 88; WhoWrEP 89, 92, 95; WorAu 1985; WrDr 94, 96*

Danton, Georges Jacques
French. Revolutionary
Leader of French Revolution; major figure in storming of Tuilleries; guillotined by Robespierre.
b. Oct 28, 1759 in Arcis-sur-Aube, France
d. Apr 5, 1794 in Paris, France
Source: *Benet 87, 96; BiDMoER 1; BioIn 1, 4, 5, 8, 9, 11, 12, 13, 15, 16, 20; BlkwCE; CmFrR; DcBiPP; DcEuL; Dis&D; LinLib S; McGEWB; NewC; OxCFr; OxCGer 76; REn; WhDW; WorAl*

Danton, Ray(mond)
American. Actor, Director
Best known for gangster roles *The Rise and Fall of Legs Diamond,* 1960; *Portrait of a Mobster,* 1961.
b. Sep 19, 1931 in New York, New York
d. Feb 11, 1992 in Los Angeles, California
Source: *BioIn 17; ConTFT 11; FilmEn; FilmgC; ForYSC; GangFlm; HalFC 80, 84, 88; HorFD; IntMPA 75, 76, 77, 78, 79, 80, 81, 82, 84, 86, 88, 92; ItaFilm; LegTOT; MiSFD 9N; WhoAm 80; WhoHol 92, A; WhoHrs 80; WorAl; WorEFlm*

Danvers, Dennis
American. Author
Wrote *Wilderness,* 1991, a modern interpretation of traditional werewolf legend.
b. 1947
Source: *ConLC 70; ScF&FL 92*

Danza, Tony
[Anthony Iadanza]
American. Actor
Former middleweight fighter; star of TV series "Taxi," 1982-85; "Who's the Boss ?" 1985-1992.
b. Apr 21, 1951 in New York, New York
Source: *BioIn 12, 15, 16; CelR 90; ConTFT 5; HolBB; IntMPA 88, 92, 94, 96; News 89-1; VarWW 85; WhoAm 92, 94, 95, 96, 97; WhoEnt 92; WhoHol 92; WorAlBi*

Danzig
[Chuck Biscuits; John Christ; Glenn Danzig; Eerie Von]
American. Music Group
Heavy metal band; song themes frequently include the Netherworld and sex; debut album *Danzig,* 1988.
Source: *ConMus 7; WhoRocM 82*

DaPonte, Lorenzo
[Emmanuel Conegliano]
Italian. Poet, Librettist, Educator
Wrote librettos for Mozart's *Marriage of Figaro,* 1786; taught Italian literature, Columbia U, from 1825.
b. Mar 10, 1749 in Ceneda, Italy
d. Aug 17, 1838 in New York, New York
Source: *AmAu&B; ApCAB; BiD&SB; CasWL; CyAL 2; DcAmB; EvEuW; OxCAmH; OxCGer 76; OxCMus; REn; WhAm HS*

Darby, Ken
American. Composer, Conductor
Film conductor who won Oscars for *The King and I,* 1956; *Porgy and Bess,* 1959; *Camelot,* 1967.
b. May 13, 1909 in Hebron, Nebraska
d. Jan 24, 1992 in Los Angeles, California
Source: *CmMov; ConTFT 11; HalFC 84, 88; RadStar; VarWW 85; WhoHol 92*

Darby, Kim
[Deborah Zerby]
American. Actor
Starred with John Wayne in *True Grit,* 1969.
b. Jul 8, 1948 in Hollywood, California
Source: *ConTFT 3; FilmEn; FilmgC; ForYSC; HalFC 88; IntMPA 75, 76, 77, 78, 79, 80, 81, 82, 84, 86, 88, 92, 94, 96; VarWW 85; WhoAm 80, 82; WhoHol 92, A*

D'Arby, Terence Trent
American. Singer, Musician
American expatriate singer; albums include *Introducing the Hardline According to Terence Trent D'Arby,* 1987, which won several British music awards.
b. Mar 15, 1962 in New York, New York
Source: *BioIn 15, 16; ConMus 3; EncPR&S 89; EncRkSt; LegTOT; News 88; PenEncP; SoulM; WhoAfA 96; WhoBlA 92, 94*

Darcel, Denise
American. Singer, Actor
Nightclub performer; Hollywood debut, 1947; played sensuous leads in 1950s films.
b. Sep 8, 1925 in Paris, France
Source: *BioIn 13; FilmEn; FilmgC; ForYSC; HalFC 80, 84, 88; InWom; WhoHol 92, A*

Darcy, Henri Philibert Gaspard
French. Engineer
Pioneered scientific research in ground water hydrology.
b. Jun 10, 1803 in Dijon, France
d. Jan 3, 1858 in Paris, France
Source: *BioIn 12*

D'Arcy, Martin Cyril
English. Clergy, Author
Jesuit professor, philosopher who wrote *Humanism and Christianity,* 1969.
b. Jun 15, 1888 in Bath, England
d. Nov 20, 1976 in London, England
Source: *Au&Wr 71; BioIn 1, 2, 5, 7, 11, 20; BlueB 76; CathA 1930; ConAu 3NR, 5R, 69; CurBio 77; DcNaB 1971; IntAu&W 76; IntWW 74, 75, 76, 77N; LinLib L; NewCBEL; NewYTBS 76; WhAm 7; WhE&EA; Who 74; WhoWor 74, 76*

Darcy, Tom
[Thomas Darcy]
American. Cartoonist
Known for bold lines, facial expressions; won Pulitzer for editorial cartooning, 1970.
b. Jun 7, 1916 in Saint Louis, Missouri
Source: *Dun&B 90; WhoAm 74; WorECar*

Darden, Christopher A.
American. Lawyer
Prosecutor, Los Angeles District Attorney's office, 1981-95; member of the prosecution team in the O. J. Simpson murder trial, 1995.
b. c. Apr 6, 1956 in Richmond, California
Source: *WhoAfA 96*

Darden, Colgate Whitehead
American. Politician, Educator
Dem. governor, 1940s; pres., U of Virginia, 1950s, who fought against school segregation.
b. Feb 11, 1897 in Franklin, Virginia
d. Jun 9, 1981 in Norfolk, Virginia
Source: *BiDrAC; BiDrGov 1789; BiDrUSC 89; BioIn 1, 12; CurBio 48; WhAm 7; WhoAmP 73, 75, 77, 79, 81*

Dare, Virginia
American. Colonial Figure
First child born in America of English parents; disappeared with rest of "lost colony."
b. Aug 18, 1587 in Roanoke Island, North Carolina
d. 1587? in Roanoke Island, North Carolina
Source: *AmBi; ApCAB; Benet 87; BenetAL 91; BioIn 2, 4, 5, 6, 7, 11, 15; ChhPo; DcAmB; DcNCBi 2; Drake; EncCRAm; EncSoH; GoodHs; HarEnUS; HerW; InWom, SUP; LegTOT; LibW; NotAW; OxCAmL 65; REn; WebAB 74,*

79; WhAm HS; WomFir; WorAl; WorAlBi

Dargan, Olive Tilford
American. Poet, Author
Writings include poetic drama, lyric poetry, proletarian novels; best known for *A Stone Came Rolling,* 1935.
b. 1869 in Grayson County, Kentucky
d. Jan 22, 1968 in Asheville, North Carolina
Source: *AmAu&B; AmNov X; AmWomPl; AmWomWr; BiDSA; ChhPo, S2; CnDAL; ConAu 111; DcNCBi 2; InWom SUP; LiHiK; NotNAT B; OxCAmL 65, 83, 95; OxCWoWr 95; PenNWW A; REnAL; SouWr; TwCA, SUP; WhAm 5; WhoAmW 61; WomWWA 14*

Dargomijsky, Alexander
[Alexander Dargomizyhsky]
Russian. Composer
Wrote opera *Esmeralda,* 1847; orchestral work *Baba Yaga,* 1870.
b. Feb 14, 1813 in Tula, Russia
d. Jan 17, 1869 in Saint Petersburg, Russia
Source: *MetOEnc; NewEOp 71; OxCMus*

Darin, Bobby
[Walden Robert Cassotto]
American. Singer, Actor
Best-known song "Mack the Knife," won two Grammys, 1960.
b. May 14, 1936 in New York, New York
d. Dec 20, 1973 in Hollywood, California
Source: *AmPS; Baker 84, 92; BiDAmM; BiDJaz; BioIn 5, 6, 7, 9, 10, 12, 15, 19, 20; ConMus 4; CurBio 63, 74, 74N; DcAmB S9; EncJzS; EncPR&S 89; EncRk 88; EncRkSt; FilmEn; FilmgC; HalFC 80, 84, 88; HarEnR 86; LegTOT; MotPP; MovMk; NewGrDA 86; NewYTBE 73; OxCPMus; PenEncP; PopAmC SUP, SUPN; RkOn 74; RolSEnR 83; WhAm 6; WhoHol B; WhoRock 81; WhScrn 77, 83; WorAl; WorAlBi*

Daringer, Helen Fern
American. Children's Author
Writings include *Yesterday's Daughter,* 1964; *Just Plain Betsy,* 1967.
b. Jun 24, 1892 in Mattoon, Illinois
Source: *BioIn 2, 6, 9; ConAu P-2; CurBio 51; InWom; MorJA; SmATA 1*

Dario, Ruben, pseud.
Nicaraguan. Poet
Spanish Modernist; greatest work, *Cantos de Vida y Esperanza,* 1905.
b. Jan 18, 1867 in Metapa, Nicaragua
d. Feb 6, 1916 in Leon, Nicaragua
Source: *AtlBL; Benet 87, 96; BenetAL 91; BioIn 1, 2, 4, 5, 6, 7, 8, 10, 15, 16, 17, 18; CasWL; ConAu 104, 131; DcArts; DcHiB; DcSpL; DcTwCCu 4; EncLatA; EncWL 2, 3; FacFETw; GrFLW; HispLC; HispWr; LatAmWr; LegTOT; LinLib L; MajTwCW; McGEWB; ModLAL; OxCSpan; PenC AM; RAdv 14, 13-2; REn; RfGWoL 95; TwCA, SUP; TwCLC 4; TwCWr; WhDW; WhoTwCL*

Darion, Joseph
American. Lyricist
Won 1965 Tony for lyrics of *Man of La Mancha.*
b. Jan 30, 1917 in New York, New York
Source: *ASCAP 66, 80; BioIn 10, 12; ConAu 113, X; EncMT; WhoAm 90; WhoEnt 92*

Darius I
[Darius the Great]
Persian. Ruler
King, 521-486 BC; army defeated by Greeks at Battle of Marathon, 490 BC.
b. 558BC
d. 486BC
Source: *McGEWB; REn; WebBD 83*

Dark, Alvin Ralph
"Blackie"
American. Baseball Player, Baseball Manager
Infielder, 1948-60; rookie of year, 1948; won two World Series as manager, 1962, 1974.
b. Jan 7, 1923 in Comanche, Oklahoma
Source: *Ballpl 90; BiDAmSp BB; BioIn 2, 3, 4, 5, 6, 7, 8, 10, 12, 15; CurBio 75; NewYTBS 74; WhoAdv 90; WhoAm 82, 90; WhoProB 73*

Darken, Lawrence Stamper
American. Chemist
Director of fundamental research, US Steel, 1962-71.
b. Sep 18, 1909 in New York, New York
d. Jun 7, 1978 in Boalsburg, Pennsylvania
Source: *AmMWSc 76P, 79; BioIn 8, 11; BlueB 76; IntWW 74, 75, 76, 77, 78, 79; WhAm 7; WhoAm 74, 76, 78*

Darlan, Jean Louis Xavier Francois
French. Government Official
Ex-Vichy commissioner for French and W Africa; assassinated.
b. Aug 7, 1881 in Nerac, France
d. Dec 24, 1942 in Algiers, Algeria
Source: *BioIn 1, 4, 7; CurBio 41, 43; DcTwHis; OxCShps*

Darley, Felix Octavius Carr
American. Illustrator, Author
Illustrated Irving's *Rip Van Winkle,* 1849; *Legend of Sleepy Hollow,* 1850.
b. Jun 23, 1822 in Philadelphia, Pennsylvania
d. Mar 27, 1888 in Claymont, Delaware
Source: *Alli SUP; AmAu&B; AmBi; ApCAB; BenetAL 91; BiD&SB; BioIn 1, 2, 3, 7, 8, 9, 14; BriEAA; CarSB; ChhPo, S1; DcAmArt; DcAmAu; DcAmB; DcNAA; Drake; EarABI, SUP; HarEnUS; IlBEAAW; IlrAm 1880; LinLib L; NatCAB 2; NewYHSD; OxCAmL 65, 83, 95; REnAW; TwCBDA; WhAm HS; WhNaAH*

Darling, Erik
[Weavers]
American. Singer, Musician
Replaced Pete Seeger in the Weavers group, 1958; formed Rooftop Singers, 1962, had gold record with "Walk Right In," 1963.
b. Sep 25, 1933 in Baltimore, Maryland
Source: *BiDAmM; EncFCWM 69; OnThGG; PenEncP; WhoEnt 92*

Darling, Frank Fraser, Sir
Scottish. Scientist, Author
Expert in biology, genetics, agriculture.
b. Jun 23, 1903, Scotland
d. Oct 25, 1979 in Forres, Scotland
Source: *BioIn 15, 19; CmScLit; ConAu 61, 89; DcNaB 1971; IntWW 74; NatLAC; NewCBEL; OxCEng 67, 85, 95; Who 74*

Darling, Jay Norwood
[J N Ding]
American. Cartoonist
On staff, *Des Moines Register;* won two Pulitzers.
b. Oct 21, 1876 in Norwood, Michigan
d. Feb 12, 1962 in Des Moines, Iowa
Source: *AmAu&B; BiDAmJo; BioIn 1, 3, 5, 6, 12, 13, 15, 16; ConAu 93; CurBio 42, 62; DcAmB S7; EncAJ; JrnUS; NatLAC; PeoHis; WhAm 4; WhAmArt 85; WhJnl; WhNAA; WhoAmA 80N, 82N, 84N, 86N, 89N, 91N; WorECar*

Darling, Ron(ald Maurice), Jr.
American. Baseball Player
Pitcher, NY Mets, 1983—; member NL All-Star team, 1985.
b. Aug 19, 1960 in Honolulu, Hawaii
Source: *AsAmAlm; Ballpl 90; BaseReg 86, 87; BioIn 13, 14, 15, 16; CelR 90; LegTOT; NewYTBS 85, 87; WhoAsA 94*

Darlington, Cyril Dean
English. Geneticist
Suggested a theory of evolution that emphasized the role of chromosomes crossing over.
b. Dec 19, 1903 in Chorley, England
d. Mar 26, 1981
Source: *Au&Wr 71; BiESc; BioIn 1, 3; BlueB 76; ConAu 9R, 108; DcNaB 1981; DcScB S2; IntAu&W 77, 82; IntWW 74, 75, 76, 77, 78, 79, 80, 81, 81N; LarDcSc; McGMS 80; WhE&EA; Who 74; WhoWor 74, 76, 78; WrDr 80*

Darman, Richard G(ordon)
American. Government Official
Directer of the Office of Management and Budget, 1989-93; managing director at Carlyle Group, 1993—.
b. May 10, 1943 in Charlotte, North Carolina
Source: *BioIn 12, 13, 16; CurBio 89; IntWW 89, 91, 93; NewYTBS 85, 86, 90; WhoAm 82, 84, 86, 88, 90, 92, 94, 95; WhoAmP 81, 83, 85, 87, 89, 91, 93, 95;*

WhoE 93; WhoFI 77, 79; WhoWor 80, 82

Darnell, Linda (Monetta Eloyse)
American. Actor
Famous for role in *Forever Amber,* 1948.
b. Oct 16, 1923 in Dallas, Texas
d. Apr 10, 1965 in Chicago, Illinois
Source: *BiDFilm, 81; BioIn 1, 7, 15, 17; EvEuW; FilmgC; ForYSC; IntDcF 1-3, 2-3; InWom; MotPP; MovMk; ThFT; WhAm 4; WhoAmW 61; WhScrn 77; WorEFlm*

Darnley, Henry Stuart, Lord
English.
Second husband of Mary Queen of Scots; victim of murder plot.
b. Dec 7, 1545 in Temple Newsom, England
d. Feb 9, 1567 in Edinburgh, Scotland
Source: *Benet 87, 96; DcBiPP; Dis&D; NewC; REn*

Darnton, Robert Choate
American. Author
Wrote award-winning *Literary Underground of the Old Regime,* 1982.
b. May 10, 1939 in New York, New York
Source: *ConAu 113, 116; DrAS 74H, 78H, 82H; IntWW 91, 93; WhoAm 84, 86, 96, 97; WrDr 86, 92*

Darracq, Alexandre
[Pierre Alexandre Darracq]
French. Auto Manufacturer
Helped pioneer mass production of automobiles; built racing cars.
b. Nov 10, 1855 in Bordeaux, France
d. 1931, Monaco

Darragh, Jack
[John Proctor Darragh]
Canadian. Hockey Player
Right wing, Ottawa, 1917-24; Hall of Fame, 1962.
b. Dec 4, 1890 in Ottawa, Ontario, Canada
d. Jun 25, 1924
Source: *HocEn; WhoHcky 73*

Darrell, R(obert) D(onaldson)
American. Critic
First to review mostly recorded music; with *High Fidelity,* 1954-87.
b. Dec 13, 1903 in Newton, Massachusetts
d. May 1, 1988 in Kingston, New York
Source: *AmAu&B; Baker 78, 84, 92; BioIn 4, 15, 16; CurBio 55, 88; IntWWM 77, 80, 85; NewGrDA 86; WhAm 9; WhoAm 74, 76, 78, 80, 82, 84, 86, 88; WhoMus 72; WhoWor 74*

Darren, James
American. Actor, Singer
Starred in *Gidget,* 1959; TV series "The Time Tunnel," 1966-67.
b. Jun 8, 1936 in Philadelphia, Pennsylvania
Source: *BioIn 13; ConTFT 3; EncRk 88; FilmEn; FilmgC; ForYSC; HalFC 80, 84, 88; IntMPA 75, 76, 77, 78, 79, 80, 81, 82, 84, 86, 88, 92, 94, 96; ItaFilm; LegTOT; MiSFD 9; MotPP; MovMk; PenEncP; RkOn 74; WhoHol 92, A; WorAl*

Darrieux, Danielle
French. Actor
Epitome of French femininity; films included *Mayerling,* 1936, *La Ronde,* 1950.
b. May 1, 1917 in Bordeaux, France
Source: *BiDFilm, 81, 94; BioIn 11; DcTwCCu 2; EncEurC; EncWT; FilmAG WE; FilmEn; FilmgC; ForYSC; HalFC 80, 84, 88; IntDcF 1-3, 2-3; IntMPA 75, 76, 77, 78, 79, 80, 81, 82, 84, 86, 88, 92, 94, 96; IntWW 74, 75, 76, 77, 78, 79, 80, 81, 82, 83, 89, 91, 93; InWom, SUP; ItaFilm; LegTOT; MotPP; MovMk; OxCFilm; ThFT; WhoFr 79; WhoHol 92, A; WorEFlm*

Darro, Frankie
[Frank Johnson]
American. Actor
Played tough kids, jockeys in Depression-era films.
b. Dec 22, 1917 in Chicago, Illinois
d. Dec 25, 1976 in Huntington Beach, California
Source: *BioIn 10, 15; EncAFC; Film 2; FilmEn; FilmgC; HalFC 80, 84, 88; MovMk; Vers B; What 4; WhoHol A*

Darrow, Charles Brace
American. Inventor
Invented board game Monopoly.
b. 1889
d. Aug 29, 1967 in Ottsville, Pennsylvania
Source: *BioIn 6, 8; ObitOF 79*

Darrow, Clarence Seward
American. Lawyer
Defense counsel in widely publicized cases: Scopes "monkey" trial, 1925; Leopold-Loeb murder, 1924.
b. Apr 18, 1857 in Kinsman, Ohio
d. Mar 13, 1938 in Chicago, Illinois
Source: *AmAu&B; AmBi; AmOrTwC; AmRef; AmSocL; Benet 96; BioIn 1, 2, 3, 4, 5, 6, 7, 8, 9, 10, 11, 12, 13; DcAmB S2; DcLEL; DcNAA; EncAB-H 1974, 1996; EncUnb; FilmgC; McGEWB; NatCAB 27; OhA&B; OxCAmH; OxCAmL 65, 83, 95; OxCLaw; REn; REnAL; TwCA, SUP; WebAB 74, 79; WebBD 83; WhAm 1; WhNAA; WorAl*

Darrow, Henry
[Henry Thomas Delgado]
American. Actor
Appeared in TV's "High Chaparral," 1967-71, "Harry-O," 1974-75.
b. Sep 15, 1933 in New York, New York
Source: *HispAmA; WhoHisp 92; WhoHol 92, A*

Darrow, Whitney, Jr.
American. Cartoonist
With *New Yorker* mag. since 1934; cartoon books include *You're Sitting on My Eyelashes,* 1943.
b. Aug 22, 1909 in Princeton, New Jersey
Source: *AmAu&B; AuBYP 2S, 3; BioIn 2, 5; ConAu 14NR, 61, 114; CurBio 58; LinLib L; SmATA 13; WhAmArt 85; WhoAm 74, 76, 78, 80, 82; WhoAmA 73, 76, 78, 80, 82, 84, 86, 89, 91, 93; WhoWor 74; WorECar*

Dart, Justin Whitlock
American. Business Executive
Pres., director Rexall Drugs, 1946-75; adviser to Ronald Reagan's kitchen cabinet in CA politics.
b. Aug 7, 1907 in Evanston, Illinois
d. Jan 26, 1984 in Los Angeles, California
Source: *BioIn 1, 7, 8, 10, 12, 13, 14; CurBio 46; Dun&B 79; IntWW 82; IntYB 78, 79, 80, 81, 82; WhoAm 82; WhoWest 82*

Dart, Raymond Arthur
Australian. Anthropologist
Discovered fossil man-ape that was considered link between man, ape in South Africa, 1924.
b. Feb 4, 1893 in Toowong, Australia
d. Nov 22, 1988 in Johannesburg, South Africa
Source: *AfSS 78, 79, 80, 81, 82; AsBiEn; Au&Wr 71; BiESc; BioIn 5, 7; CamDcSc; ConAu 13R, P-1; CurBio 66; EncHuEv; EncSoA; FacFETw; FifIDA; InSci; IntAu&W 76, 77; IntWW 74, 75, 76, 77, 78, 79, 80, 81, 82, 83; LarDcSc; McGMS 80; WhAm 9; WhE&EA; Who 74, 82, 83, 85, 88; WhoLA; WhoWor 74, 76, 78*

Dart, Thurston
English. Musicologist, Musician
Expert in early music; known for contentious interpretations of Bach.
b. Sep 3, 1921 in London, England
d. Mar 6, 1971 in London, England
Source: *Baker 78, 84; BriBkM 80; DcArts; DcNaB 1971; NewAmDM; NewGrDM 80; NewOxM; OxCMus; PenDiMP*

Darvas, Lili
American. Actor
Starred in Max Reinhardt's repertory co., 1926-38.
b. Apr 10, 1906 in Budapest, Austria-Hungary
d. Jul 22, 1974 in New York, New York
Source: *BiE&WWA; ForYSC; NewYTBE 73; NewYTBS 74; NotNAT; ObitOF 79; WhAm 6; WhoAm 74; WhoHol B; WhoThe 72; WhScrn 77; WhThe*

Darvi, Bella
[Bayla Wegier]
American. Actor
Films include *The Racers,* 1955; *Lipstick,* 1963; committed suicide.

b. Oct 23, 1929 in Sosnowiec, Poland
d. Sep 10, 1971 in Monte Carlo, Monaco
Source: *BioIn 9; FilmgC; WhoHol B; WhScrn 74, 77*

Darwell, Jane
[Patti Woodward]
American. Actor
Won 1940 Oscar as Ma Joad in *Grapes of Wrath.*
b. Oct 15, 1879 in Palmyra, Missouri
d. Aug 13, 1967 in Woodland Hills, California
Source: *BiDFilm; CurBio 41, 67; EncAFC; Film 1; FilmEn; FilmgC; HolCA; IntDcF 1-3, 2-3; InWom SUP; LegTOT; MotPP; MovMk; OxCFilm; ThFT; TwYS; Vers A; WhScrn 77; WorAl; WorEFlm*

Darwin, Bernard Richard Meirion
English. Journalist
Wrote weekly golf articles in London *Times* for 43 yrs.
b. Sep 7, 1876 in Downe, England
d. Oct 18, 1961 in Denton, England
Source: *BioIn 2, 4, 6, 10; DcNaB 1961; GrBr; LngCTC; ObitT 1961; WhE&EA; WhLit; WhoGolf; WhoLA*

Darwin, Charles Robert
English. Author, Naturalist
Expounder of theory of evolution through natural selection; best-known work *Origin of the Species,* 1859.
b. Feb 12, 1809 in Shrewsbury, England
d. Apr 19, 1882 in Downe, England
Source: *Alli, SUP; ApCAB SUP; AsBiEn; AtlBL; BbD; Benet 87, 96; BiD&SB; BiESc; BioIn 1, 2, 3, 4, 5, 6, 7, 8, 9, 10, 11, 12, 13, 14, 15, 16; BlmGEL; BritAu 19; CamDcSc; CamGEL; CarSB; CasWL; Chambr 3; CyWA 58; DcBiPP; DcEnA, A; DcEnL; DcEuL; DcLEL; DcNaB; DcScB; Dis&D; EncHuEv; EncUnb; EnvEnc; EvLB; GaEncPs; InSci; LarDcSc; LinLib L; LngCEL; LuthC 75; McGEWB; MouLC 4; NewC; NewCBEL; OxCEng 67, 85, 95; OxCMed 86; OxCShps; PenC ENG; RAdv 14, 13-5; RComWL; REn; VicBrit; WebE&AL; WhDW; WhWE; WorAl*

Darwin, Erasmus
English. Poet, Physician
Wrote long poem *The Botanic Garden,* 1791; *Zoonomia,* 1796; grandfather of Charles.
b. Dec 12, 1731 in Elston Hall, England
d. Apr 18, 1802 in Breadsall Priory, England
Source: *Alli; AsBiEn; BbD; Benet 87, 96; BiD&SB; BiDPsy; BiESc; BioIn 1, 3, 6, 7, 10, 11, 12, 13, 14, 17; BlkwCE; BlmGEL; BritAu; CamGEL; CamGLE; CasWL; Chambr 2; ChhPo, S1; DcBiPP; DcEnA; DcEnL; DcEuL; DcLB 93; DcLEL; DcNaB, C; DcScB; Dis&D; EncEnl; EncSF, 93; EncUnb; EvLB; GrWrEL P; InSci; LarDcSc; LinLib L, S; NamesHP; NewC; NewCBEL; OxCEng 67, 85, 95; OxCMed 86; OxCMus; PenC ENG; REn; RfGEnL 91; WebE&AL*

Darwin, George Howard, Sir
English. Astronomer, Mathematician
Authority on creation of universe, tidal friction; son of Charles.
b. Jul 9, 1845 in Kent, England
d. Dec 7, 1912 in Cambridge, England
Source: *Alli SUP; AsBiEn; BiESc; DcNaB 1912; DcScB; InSci; LinLib L; LuthC 75; NewCol 75; WhLit; WorAl*

Daryush, Elizabeth Bridges
English. Poet
Books of verse include *Collected Poems,* 1976; *Third Book Verses,* 1933.
b. Dec 5, 1887 in London, England
d. Apr 7, 1977 in Stockwell, England
Source: *BioIn 11, 12, 13; ChhPo, S2; ConAu 3NR, 49; ConLC 6; InWom SUP*

Das, Chitta Ranjan
Indian. Politician
Ardent nationalist; founded self-rule party with Nehru, 1922; first mayor of Calcutta, 1924.
b. Nov 5, 1870 in Calcutta, India
d. Jun 16, 1925 in Darjeeling, India
Source: *BioIn 7, 15, 16; HisDBrE; McGEWB; NewCol 75*

Daschle, Thomas Andrew
American. Politician
Dem. senator, SD, 1987—.
b. Dec 9, 1947 in Aberdeen, South Dakota
Source: *AlmAP 92; BiDrUSC 89; CngDr 79, 81, 83, 85, 87, 89; CurBio 95; IntWW 89, 91, 93; PolsAm 84; WhoAm 80, 82, 84, 86, 88, 90, 92, 94, 95, 96, 97; WhoAmP 79, 81, 83, 85, 87, 89, 91, 93, 95; WhoEmL 87; WhoMW 82, 84, 86, 88, 90, 92, 93, 96; WhoWor 89, 91, 96*

Dasgupta, S(urendra) N(ath)
Indian. Author, Philosopher
Philosophy was mixture of Eastern and Western teachings; wrote 5 vol. *History of Indian Philosophy,* 1922-55.
b. Oct 1885 in Kushtia, India
d. Dec 18, 1952 in Lucknow, India
Source: *BioIn 14; ThTwC 87*

Dash, Julie
American. Filmmaker
1st African American woman to write, direct nationally distributed feature-length film; *Daughters of the Dust,* 1992.
b. 1952 in New York, New York
Source: *BlkWAm; ConBlB 4; DcTwCCu 5; DrBlPA 90; NotBlAW 2; ReelWom*

Dash, Samuel
American. Lawyer
Chief counsel US Senate Watergate committee, 1973-74; wrote *The Eavesdroppers,* 1959.
b. Feb 27, 1925 in Camden, New Jersey
Source: *BioIn 9, 10, 12; BioNews 74; ConAu 105; NewYTBE 73; WhoAm 74, 76, 78, 80, 82, 84, 86, 88, 90, 92, 94, 95, 96, 97; WhoAmJ 80; WhoAmL 79, 83, 85; WhoSSW 75, 76*

Dashwood, Elizabeth Monica
[E M Delafield]
English. Author
Comedies of manners include *Provincial Lady in America,* 1934.
b. Jun 9, 1890 in Steying, England
d. Dec 2, 1943 in Cullompton, England
Source: *ConAu 119; NewC; REn; WhE&EA; WhoLA*

da Silva, Benedita
Brazilian. Politician
Member, Brazilian Chamber of Deputies, 1987—.
b. 1942 in Rio de Janeiro, Brazil
Source: *BioIn 19; ConBlB 5*

DaSilva, Howard
[Harold Silverblatt]
American. Actor, Director, Producer
Career spanned 55 yrs; best known for playing Benjamin Franklin in Broadway musical *1776,* 1969.
b. May 4, 1909 in Cleveland, Ohio
d. Feb 16, 1986 in Ossining, New York
Source: *AnObit 1984; BiE&WWA; ConTFT 5; EncMT; FilmEn; FilmgC; ForYSC; HalFC 80, 84; IntMPA 75, 76, 77, 78, 79, 80, 81, 82, 84, 86; MovMk; NewYTBS 74; NotNAT; PlP&P; WhoAm 74, 76, 78, 80, 82, 84; WhoHol A; WhoThe 72, 77, 81; WhoWor 74; WorAl*

Dassault, Marcel
[Marcel Bloch]
French. Aircraft Manufacturer
Built world's most sophisticated warplanes, from biplanes to supersonic Mirage fighters.
b. Jan 22, 1892 in Paris, France
d. Apr 18, 1986 in Paris, France
Source: *AnObit 1986; BioIn 4, 7, 8, 9, 11, 13, 14, 15, 17; ConAu 115, 119; CurBio 86, 86N; FacFETw; IntWW 74, 75, 76, 77, 78, 79, 80, 81, 82, 83; NewYTBS 76, 86; WhoFr 79; WhoWor 74*

Dassin, Jules
American. Director
Married to Melina Mercouri, who starred in his films *Never on Sunday,* 1960, *Topkapi,* 1964.
b. Dec 12, 1911 in Middletown, Connecticut
Source: *BiDFilm, 81, 94; BiE&WWA; BioIn 9, 15; CmMov; ConAu 132; ConDr 77F, 88A; CurBio 71; DcFM; EncEurC; FilmEn; FilmgC; GangFlm; HalFC 80, 84, 88; IIWWHD 1; IntDcF 1-2, 2-2; IntMPA 82, 84, 86, 88, 92, 94, 96; IntWW 74, 75, 76, 77, 78, 79, 80, 81, 82, 83, 89, 91, 93; ItaFilm; LegTOT; MiSFD 9; MovMk; OxCFilm; WhoAm 74, 76, 78, 80, 82, 84; WhoEnt 92; WhoFr 79; WhoHol 92, A; WhoWor 74, 95, 96; WorEFlm; WorFDir 1; WrDr 94*

Dassler, Adolf
"Adi"
German. Manufacturer
Founded Adidas Shoes, 1920; yearly sales now over $700 million.
b. 1901
d. Sep 18, 1978 in Herzogenaurach, Germany (West)
Source: *BioIn 11; ObitOF 79*

Dassler, Horst
Business Executive
Chairman, Adidas Co., 1984-87; one of world's largest sporting goods firms.
b. 1936
d. Apr 10, 1987 in Herzogenaurach, Germany (West)
Source: *AnObit 1987*

Datsolalee
[Louisa Keyser]
American. Artist
Recognized as the greatest basket weaver and designer among the Washo people.
b. 1835
d. 1925
Source: *BioIn 21; EncNAB; InWom SUP; NotNaAm; WhNaAH*

Daubeny, Peter Lauderdale, Sir
English. Director
Plays on London stages include *The Aspern Papers,* 1959; *Chin-Chin,* 1960.
b. Apr 1921 in Wiesbaden, Germany
d. Aug 6, 1975 in London, England
Source: *BioIn 3, 9, 10; CnThe; ConAu 61; DcNaB 1971; EncWT; IntWW 74, 75; OxCThe 67, 83; Who 74; WhoThe 72; WhoWor 74, 76; WhThe*

Daubert, Jake
[Jacob Ellsworth Daubert]
American. Baseball Player
First baseman, Brooklyn, Cincinnati, 1910-24; won NL batting titles, 1913, 1914.
b. May 15, 1885 in Shamokin, Pennsylvania
d. Oct 9, 1924 in Cincinnati, Ohio
Source: *BiDAmSp BB; BioIn 4, 15; WhoProB 73*

Daubigny, Charles Francois
French. Artist
Landscape painter who influenced Impressionists: *Lever de Lune,* 1877.
b. Feb 15, 1817 in Paris, France
d. Feb 19, 1878 in Auvers, France
Source: *ArtsNiC; AtlBL; BioIn 2, 4, 5, 6, 8, 9, 11; ClaDrA; LinLib S; McGEWB; ThHEIm*

D'Aubuisson, Roberto
Salvadoran. Politician
Head of ultra-right Nationalist Republican Alliance Party, pres., Constituent Assembly, 1982-1983; suspected of involvement with death squads.
b. Aug 23, 1944 in Santa Tecla, El Salvador
d. Feb 1992 in San Salvador, El Salvador
Source: *BioIn 13, 14, 16; CurBio 83; EncWB; IntWW 91; NewYTBS 82*

Daudet, Leon
[Alphonse Marie Leon Daudet]
French. Author
Wrote naturalistic novels of contemporary life; stories of Provence include *Tartarin de Tarascon,* 1872.
b. May 13, 1840 in Paris, France
d. Dec 16, 1897 in Saint-Remy-de-Provence, France
Source: *AtlBL; ClDMEL 47; CyWA 58; DcBiA; McGEWB; McGEWD 84; OxCEng 85; OxCFr; PenC EUR; RComWL; REn; WhDW; WorAl*

Daudet, Leon
French. Author, Politician
Wrote 40 books; co-editor, *L'Action Francaise;* supported French Royalist movement; son of Alphonse.
b. Nov 16, 1867
d. Jul 1, 1942
Source: *BiDExR; BiDFrPL; BioIn 1, 16, 17; CasWL; ClDMEL 47, 80; ConAu 121; CurBio 42; DcArts; Dis&D; EncWL; FacFETw; NewC; OxCFr; REn*

Daugherty, Carroll Roop
American. Economist, Educator
Held various government economic positions, 1930s-40s; faculty, Northwestern U, 1946-68; wrote *Labor Problems in American Industry,* 1933.
b. Dec 3, 1900
d. May 11, 1988 in La Jolla, California
Source: *AmAu&B; BioIn 2, 15, 16; BlueB 76; ConAu 125; CurBio 88N; FacFETw; NewYTBS 88; WhAm 9; WhoAm 74, 76, 78, 80, 82, 84, 86, 88; WhoWor 76, 78, 82*

Daugherty, Duffy
[Hugh Daugherty]
American. Football Coach
Head coach, MI State U., 1954-72; won national title, 1965.
b. Sep 8, 1915 in Barnesboro, Pennsylvania
d. Sep 25, 1987 in Santa Barbara, California
Source: *BioIn 15; NewYTBE 73; NewYTBS 87; WhoFtbl 74; WhoSpor*

Daugherty, James Henry
American. Children's Author, Illustrator
Wrote, illustrated history books for children; won Newbery for *Daniel Boone,* 1939.
b. Jun 1, 1889 in Asheville, North Carolina
d. Feb 21, 1974 in Boston, Massachusetts
Source: *ConAu 49; CurBio 40, 74; JBA 34, 51; NewYTBS 74; SmATA 13; WhAm 6; WhoAm 74; WhoAmA 73*

Daugherty, Pat
[Black Oak Arkansas]
American. Musician
Bass guitarist with heavy-metal Dixie boogie group.
b. Nov 11, 1947 in Jonesboro, Arkansas
Source: *WhoRocM 82*

Daugherty, William J
American. Hostage
One of 52 held by terrorists, Nov 1979 - Jan 1981.
b. 1948?
Source: *NewYTBS 81*

D'Aulaire, Edgar Parin
American. Children's Author, Illustrator
With wife, wrote, illustrated children's picture biographies: *Ola,* 1932.
b. Sep 30, 1898 in Munich, Germany
d. May 1, 1986 in Georgetown, Connecticut
Source: *AmAu&B; AnCL; AuBYP 2, 3; BioIn 12, 14, 16, 17, 19; BkCL; ChlBkCr; ChlLR 21; ConAu 29NR, 49, 119; ConICB; CurBio 40; DcLB 22; IlsBYP; IlsCB 1744, 1946, 1957; JBA 51; LinLib L; MajAI; OxCChiL; SmATA 5, 47N, 66; Str&VC; TwCChW 78, 83, 89; WhAm 11; WhoAm 74, 76, 78, 80, 82, 84, 86; WhoAmA 73, 76, 78, 80, 82, 84, 86, 89N, 91N, 93N; WrDr 80, 82, 84, 86*

D'Aulaire, Ingri Mortenson
[Mrs. Edgar Parin D'Aulaire]
American. Children's Author, Illustrator
Won 1940 Caldecott Medal with husband for *Abraham Lincoln,* 1939.
b. Dec 27, 1904 in Kongsberg, Norway
d. Oct 24, 1980 in Wilton, Connecticut
Source: *AmWomWr; AnCL; AuBYP 2; ConAu 49, 102; CurBio 40; DcLB 22; JBA 34, 51; SmATA 5, 24; WhAm 7*

Daumier, Honore Victorin
French. Artist
Noted for over 7,500 lithographs, illustrations satirizing French politics, society.
b. Feb 26, 1808 in Marseilles, France
d. Feb 11, 1879 in Valmondois, France
Source: *AtlBL; McGEWB; OxCFr; REn*

Dauphin, Claude Le Grand Maria Eugene
French. Actor
International film star best known for *April in Paris,* 1952.
b. Aug 19, 1903 in Corbeil, France
d. Nov 17, 1978 in Paris, France
Source: *BiE&WWA; FilmgC; IntMPA 82; MotPP; MovMk; NewYTBS 78; NotNAT; ObitOF 79; WhAm 7; WhoHol A; WhoThe 81; WhoWor 74*

Dauss, George August
"Hooks"
American. Baseball Player
Pitcher, Detroit, 1912-26; won 221 games.
b. Sep 22, 1889 in Indianapolis, Indiana

d. Jul 27, 1963 in Saint Louis, Missouri
Source: *BiDAmSp BB; WhoProB 73*

Dausset, Jean (Baptiste Gabriel Joachim)
French. Scientist
Shared 1980 Nobel Prize in medicine for research contributing to progress in human organ transplants.
b. Oct 19, 1916 in Toulouse, France
Source: *AmMWSc 92; BiESc; BioIn 12, 15, 20; CamDcSc; CurBio 81; FacFETw; IntMed 80; IntWW 82, 91; LarDcSc; McGMS 80; NewYTBS 80; NobelP; NotTwCS; Who 82, 83, 85, 88, 90, 92, 94; WhoAm 88, 90, 92, 94, 95; WhoFr 79; WhoMedH; WhoNob, 90, 95; WhoScEn 94, 96; WhoWor 82, 89, 91, 93, 95, 96, 97; WorAlBi; WorScD*

Dave Clark Five, The
[Dave Clark; Lenny Davidson; Rick Huxley; Denis Payton; Michael Smith]
English. Music Group
British invasion group formed, 1963; hit singles include "Red Balloon," 1968; "Everybody Get Together," 1970.
Source: *Alli; BioIn 14, 15, 16, 17, 18, 20, 21; ConMus 12; DcNAA; EncPR&S 74, 89; EncRk 88; HarEnR 86; IntAu&W 89, 91, 93; LElec; MacDCB 78; OxCCan; PeoHis; RkOn 74, 78; RolSEnR 83; St&PR 93; Who 92, 94; WhoHol 92; WhoRock 81; WhoRocM 82*

Davenant, William, Sir
English. Poet, Dramatist
Siege of Rhodes, 1662, was first English opera.
b. Feb 1606 in Oxford, England
d. Apr 7, 1668 in London, England
Source: *Alli; BbD; Benet 87, 96; BiD&SB; BiDRP&D; BioIn 1, 2, 3, 5, 6, 7, 9, 12, 15; BritAu; CamGEL; CamGLE; CasWL; Chambr 1; ChhPo, S1; CnE&AP; CnThe; CroE&S; CyWA 58; DcEnA; DcEnL; DcEuL; DcLB 58; DcNaB; DcPup; EncWT; Ent; EvLB; GrWrEL DR; LngCEL; McGEWD 72, 84; NewC; NewCBEL; NewGrDM 80; NewGrDO; NotNAT A, B; OxCEng 67, 85; OxCMus; OxCThe 67, 83; PenC ENG; PlP&P; PoLE; REn; REnWD; WebE&AL; WhDW*

Davenport, Charles Benedict
American. Zoologist
Researched eugenics heredity; wrote *Experimental Morphology*, 1897-99.
b. Apr 13, 1866 in Stamford, Connecticut
d. Feb 18, 1944 in Huntington, New York
Source: *AmLY; ApCAB X; BiDAmEd; BiESc; BioIn 1, 2, 14, 17; CurBio 44; DcAmAu; DcAmB S3; DcNAA; DcScB; FacFETw; InSci; LuthC 75; NatCAB 15; NewCol 75; WebBD 83; WhAm 2; WhLit; WhNAA*

Davenport, Eva
English. Actor
Known for stage roles in comedies: *Erminie*.
b. 1858 in London, England
d. Sep 26, 1932 in White Plains, New York
Source: *WhoStg 1908*

Davenport, Fanny Lily Gypsy
American. Actor
Formed own company, 1877; produced, starred in four plays by Sardou.
b. Apr 10, 1850 in London, England
d. Sep 26, 1898 in South Duxbury, Massachusetts
Source: *AmBi; BioIn 13, 16; DcAmB; FamA&A; InWom SUP; LibW; NotAW; NotNAT B; NotWoAT; OxCThe 67; PlP&P; TwCBDA; WhAm HS*

Davenport, Harry George Bryant
American. Actor
Played grandfather roles in films *The Higgins Family* series, 1938-40; *Meet Me in St. Louis*, 1944.
b. Jan 19, 1886 in New York, New York
d. Aug 9, 1949 in Los Angeles, California
Source: *Film 1; FilmgC; MotPP; MovMk; ObitOF 79; OxCThe 67; Vers A; WhoHol B; WhoStg 1906, 1908; WhScrn 74, 77; WhThe*

Davenport, Homer Calvin
American. Cartoonist
Political cartoonist whose most famous cartoon is Uncle Sam's endorsement of T Roosevelt: "He's Good Enough for Me."
b. Mar 8, 1867 in Silverton, Oregon
d. May 2, 1912 in New York, New York
Source: *AmAu&B; AmBi; ArtsAmW 1; BiDAmJo; BioIn 5, 9, 10, 12, 16; DcAmAu; DcAmB; DcNAA; LinLib L, S; NatCAB 11; WhAm 1; WhAmArt 85; WorECar*

Davenport, Marcia
American. Author, Critic
Wrote best-selling *Valley of Decision*, 1942; *East Side, West Side*, 1947.
b. Jun 9, 1903 in New York, New York
d. Jan 16, 1996 in Monterey, California
Source: *AmAu&B; AmNov; AuBYP 2, 3; Baker 78, 84; BenetAL 91; BioIn 1, 2, 3, 4, 5, 8, 14, 17, 18, 21; ConAu 9R, 151; CurBio 44, 96N; DcLEL; IntvTCA 2; InWom, SUP; LinLib L; LngCTC; OxCAmL 65, 83, 95; REn; REnAL; TwCA SUP; TwCRGW; TwCRHW 90; WhoAm 74, 76, 78, 80; WhoAmW 58, 61, 64, 66, 68, 70, 72, 74; WhoWor 74; WrDr 84, 86, 88, 90, 92*

Davenport, Nigel
English. Actor
Character actor who appeared in *Look Back in Anger*, 1959; *Chariots of Fire*, 1981.
b. May 23, 1928 in Shelford, England
Source: *ConTFT 3; FilmEn; FilmgC; HalFC 80, 84, 88; IlWWBF; IntMPA 82, 84, 86, 88, 92, 94, 96; IntWW 89, 91; LegTOT; Who 92; WhoHol 92, A; WhoThe 72, 77, 81*

Davenport, Thomas
American. Inventor
Discovered principle of starting, stopping electric current over wire, 1834.
b. Jul 19, 1802 in Williamstown, Vermont
d. Jul 6, 1851 in Salisbury, Vermont
Source: *AmBi; ApCAB; BilnAmS; BioIn 1, 6; DcAmB; InSci; NatCAB 3; TwCBDA; WebAB 74, 79; WhAm HS; WorInv*

Davenport, Willie D
American. Track Athlete
Hurdler; won gold medal, 1968 Olympics.
b. Jun 8, 1943 in Troy, Alabama
Source: *BiDAmSp OS; BioIn 8, 12; BlkOlyM; InB&W 85; WhoBlA 75, 77, 80, 85, 92; WhoTr&F 73*

David
Hebrew. Ruler, Biblical Figure
Prominent Old Testament figure; second king of Israel, Judah; considered author of many Psalms.
b. 1000BC
d. 960BC
Source: *BiB N; DcOrL 3; JeHun; LegTOT; McGEWB; NewC; NewCol 75; WebBD 83*

David
"Bubble Boy"
American. Patient
Born without any immunity to disease, spent all but last 15 days of life in sterile, plastic bubble.
b. Sep 21, 1971 in Houston, Texas
d. Feb 22, 1984 in Houston, Texas
Source: *BioIn 11, 13*

David, Elizabeth
English. Writer
Influential writer on French, Italian, and English cooking; wrote *Book of Mediterranean Food*, 1950.
d. May 22, 1992 in London, England
Source: *AmEA 74; Au&Wr 71; BlueB 76; ContDcW 89; IntWW 91, 93N; NewYTBS 92; Who 74, 82, 83, 85, 88, 90, 92; WrDr 80, 82, 84, 86, 88, 90, 92, 94N*

David, Felicien Cesar
French. Composer
Known for exotic Oriental melodies; wrote tone poem *Le Desert*, 1844; opera *Lalla-Roukh*, 1862.
b. Apr 13, 1810 in Cadenet, France
d. Aug 29, 1876 in Saint-Germain-en-Laye, France
Source: *Baker 84, 92; CelCen; DcArts; DcBiPP; Dis&D; LinLib S; NewCol 75; NewEOp 71; NewGrDO; OxCMus*

David, Gerard
Dutch. Artist
Paintings include *Madonna with Angels and Saints,* 1509; known for skill in using color.
b. 1460? in Oudewater, Netherlands
d. Aug 13, 1523 in Bruges, Netherlands
Source: *AtlBL; BioIn 15; LegTOT; McGDA*

David, Hal
American. Lyricist
Former partner of Burt Bacharach; won Oscar, 1969, for "Raindrops Keep Fallin' on My Head."
b. May 25, 1921 in New York, New York
Source: *AmPS; AmSong; ASCAP 66, 80; Baker 84, 92; BiDAmM; BioIn 10, 12, 13, 15; CelR, 90; CmpEPM; ConTFT 12; CurBio 80; EncMT; LegTOT; NewGrDA 86; NotNAT; WhoAm 86, 90; WhoE 86, 89; WhoEnt 92*

David, Jacques Louis
French. Artist
Foremost French classicist; named court painter to Napoleon; best known for *Death of Marat,* 1793.
b. Aug 30, 1748 in Paris, France
d. Dec 29, 1825 in Brussels, Belgium
Source: *AtlBL; BioIn 1, 2, 3, 4, 5, 6, 7, 8, 9, 11, 12; CelCen; ClaDrA; CmFrR; DcBiPP; Dis&D; EncEnl; IntDcAA 90; LinLib S; McGEWB; OxCFr; REn*

David, Mack
American. Composer
Film scores include *To Kill a Mockingbird,* 1963; *It's a Mad, Mad, Mad, Mad, World,* 1963.
b. Jul 5, 1912 in New York, New York
Source: *AmPS; ASCAP 66, 80; Baker 84, 92; BiDAmM; BiE&WWA; BioIn 19; CmpEPM; NewGrDA 86; NotNAT; Sw&Ld C; VarWW 85*

David, Saint
Religious Figure
Patron saint of Wales said to have founded 12 monasteries; feast day March 1.
b. 495? in Henfynw, Wales
d. 589? in Mynyw, Wales
Source: *Alli; BioIn 10; DcCathB; LngCEL; NewC; REn*

David d'Angers
[Pierre Jean David]
French. Sculptor
Did national figures—nudes, statues, busts, medallions; executed pediment of Pantheon, Paris.
b. Mar 12, 1788 in Angers, France
d. Jan 4, 1856 in Paris, France
Source: *McGDA; NewCol 75; OxCArt; OxCFr*

David-Neel, Alexandra
French. Explorer, Author
First European woman to enter forbidden Tibetan capital, Lhasa; wrote *My Journey to Lhasa.*
b. Oct 24, 1868
d. Sep 8, 1969 in Digne, France
Source: *BioIn 8, 11, 14, 15, 17, 18, 20, 21; ConAu 25R; EncO&P 1, 2, 3; Expl 93; IntDcWB; WhWE*

Davidovich, Bella
American. Pianist
Deserving Artist of the Soviet Union; soloist, Leningrad Philharmonic for twenty-eight consecutive seasons; taught at Moscow Conservatory, 1962-1978, Juilliard, 1982—.
b. Jul 16, 1928 in Baku, Azerbaijan
Source: *Baker 84, 92; BiDSovU; BioIn 12, 13, 14, 15, 16; CurBio 89; IntWW 89, 91, 93; IntWWM 90; NewGrDA 86; NewYTBS 79, 86; PenDiMP; WhoAm 90, 92, 94, 95, 96, 97; WhoAmW 91, 93; WhoEnt 92*

Davidovich, Lolita
Canadian. Actor
Starred in *Class,* 1983.
b. 1961 in Ontario, Canada
Source: *BioIn 20; ConTFT 10; IntMPA 94, 96; LegTOT; WhoAmW 95*

Davidson, Bruce
American. Photojournalist
Noted for outstanding photo essays.
b. 1933 in Oak Park, Illinois
Source: *BioIn 5, 7, 9, 10, 12, 15; ConPhot 82, 88, 95; ICPEnP; MacBEP; NewYTBS 77*

Davidson, Donald Grady
American. Poet, Critic, Historian
Founded Fugitive School of southern American literature, 1920's.
b. Aug 18, 1893 in Campbellsville, Tennessee
d. Apr 25, 1968 in Nashville, Tennessee
Source: *ConAmA; ConAu 4NR, 5R; ConLC 13; NewYTBE 71; OxCAmL 83; PenC AM; REnAL; TwCA SUP*

Davidson, Garrison H(olt)
American. Army Officer
Commanding general 7th Army in Europe, 1944-66; aide to Patton and Eisenhower during WWII.
b. Apr 24, 1904 in New York
d. Dec 25, 1992 in Oakland, California
Source: *BiDWWGF; BioIn 3, 4, 5, 6, 18, 19; CurBio 57, 93N; NewYTBS 92; WhoAm 74*

Davidson, J. Brownlee
American. Educator, Engineer
Instructor, farm mechanics; designed several pieces of farm equipment including the Iowa dynameter.
b. Feb 15, 1880 in Douglas, Nebraska
d. May 8, 1957 in Denver, Colorado
Source: *BioIn 9; InSci; NatCAB 43; WhAm 3; WhNAA*

Davidson, Jaye
American. Actor, Model
In *The Crying Game,* 1992.
b. 1967 in Riverside, California
Source: *ConBlB 5*

Davidson, Jo
American. Sculptor
Most famous busts include those of Walt Whitman, Will Rogers.
b. Mar 30, 1883 in New York, New York
d. Jan 2, 1952 in Bercheron, France
Source: *BenetAL 91; BioIn 1, 2, 3, 4, 5, 9, 10, 12, 14, 15, 17; BriEAA; CurBio 45, 52; DcAmArt; DcAmB S5; FacFETw; LegTOT; McGDA; ObitT 1951; OxCAmH; OxCAmL 65; REn; REnAL; WebAB 74, 79; WhAm 3; WhAmArt 85; WhoAmA 89N, 91N, 93N*

Davidson, John
"The Poet of Anarchy"
Scottish. Poet, Dramatist
Works noted for rebellious tone: *Fleet Street Eclogues,* 1893, 1895; committed suicide.
b. Apr 11, 1857 in Barrhead, Scotland
d. Mar 23, 1909 in Penzance, England
Source: *AtlBL; BbD; BiD&SB; BioIn 4, 6, 9, 11, 13, 17; BlmGEL; BritAu 19; CamGEL; CamGLE; CasWL; ChhPo, S1, S2, S3; CmScLit; CnE&AP; ConAu 118; DcArts; DcEnA, A; DcEuL; DcLB 19; DcLEL; DcNaB S2; EncSF 93; EvLB; GrWrEL P; LngCTC; ModBrL; NewC; NewCBEL; OxCEng 67, 85, 95; OxCTwCP; PenC ENG; REn; RfGEnL 91; ScF&FL 1; StaCVF; TwCLC 24; WebBD 83; WebE&AL; WhLit*

Davidson, John
American. Singer, Actor
Starred in *The Happiest Millionaire,* 1967; TV series, "That's Incredible," 1980-85.
b. Dec 13, 1941 in Pittsburgh, Pennsylvania
Source: *BioIn 11, 12, 13, 16; BkPepl; ConTFT 7, 15; CurBio 76; HalFC 84, 88; IntMPA 75, 76, 77, 78, 79, 80, 81, 82, 84, 86, 88, 92, 94, 96; LegTOT; MotPP; WhoAm 86, 88, 90; WhoEnt 92; WhoHol 92, A; WorAlBi*

Davidson, Scotty
[Allan M Davidson]
Canadian. Hockey Player
Forward, Toronto Blueshirts, 1912-14; Hall of Fame, 1950; killed in WW I.
b. 1892 in Kingston, Ontario, Canada
Source: *WhoHcky 73*

Davidson, Tommy
American. Actor
Cast regular on TV show "In Living Color," 1990—.
Source: *BioIn 17; WhoAfA 96; WhoBlA 94*

Davie, Alan
Scottish. Artist
Colorful painting style influenced by Picasso, post-war Americans; one-man int'l showings since 1949.
b. Sep 28, 1920 in Grangemouth, Scotland
Source: *BioIn 4, 7, 8; ConArt 77, 83, 89, 96; ConBrA 79; DcBrAr 1; DcCAr 81; IntWW 74, 75, 76, 77, 78, 79, 80, 81, 82, 83, 89, 91, 93; IntWWP 77, 82; McGDA; OxCArt; OxCTwCA; OxDcArt; PhDcTCA 77; TwCPaSc; Who 74, 82, 83, 85, 88, 90, 92, 94; WhoWor 74, 76, 82; WorArt 1950*

Davie, Donald Alfred
English. Author
Writings include *In the Stopping Train,* 1977; professor, Vanderbilt U., Nashville, TN, 1978-88.
b. Jul 17, 1922 in Barnsley, England
d. Sep 18, 1995 in Exeter, England
Source: *Benet 87; BioIn 13, 14, 15; CamGLE; CasWL; ChhPo; ConAu 1R, 3AS; ConLC 5; ConPo 70, 75, 91; CyWA 89; EngPo; FacFETw; IntAu&W 91; IntvTCA 2; IntWW 91; LngCTC; MajTwCW; ModBrL, S1, S2; NewC; OxCEng 85; REn; RfGEnL 91; TwCWr; WhAm 11; Who 90, 92; WhoAm 86, 90; WhoTwCL; WorAu 1950; WrDr 92*

Davies, Arthur Bowen
American. Artist
Painted pastoral scenes, attempted cubism; *Four o'Clock Ladies* was one of his most admired pieces.
b. Sep 26, 1862 in Utica, New York
d. Oct 24, 1928 in Florence, Italy
Source: *AmBi; ArtsAmW 1; BioIn 3, 6, 9, 12, 13; BriEAA; ChhPo; DcAmB; GrAmP; IlBEAAW; McGDA; McGEWB; NatCAB 14, 38; OxCAmH; OxCAmL 65; OxCArt; OxCTwCA; OxDcArt; PhDcTCA 77; WebAB 74, 79; WebBD 83; WhAm 1; WorAl; WorAlBi*

Davies, Bob
[Robert Edris Davies]
"Harrisburg Houdini"
American. Basketball Player
Guard, Rochester, 1945-55; led NBA in assists, 1949; Hall of Fame, 1969.
b. Jan 15, 1920 in Harrisburg, Pennsylvania
Source: *BasBi; BiDAmSp BK; BioIn 3, 16, 17; NewYTBS 90; OfNBA 87; WhoBbl 73; WhoSpor*

Davies, Dave
[David Davies]
English. Singer, Musician
Rhythm guitarist of hard rock-turned pop group; hit single "You Really Got Me," 1964.
b. Feb 3, 1947 in Muswell Hill, England
Source: *BioIn 12, 19; OnThGG; WhoRocM 82*

Davies, Dennis Russell
American. Conductor, Pianist
Music director, St. Paul Chamber Orchestra, 1972-80; co-founder of the Juilliard Ensemble and American Composers Orchestra.
b. Apr 16, 1944 in Toledo, Ohio
Source: *Baker 84, 92; BiDAmM; BioIn 13, 14, 15, 19; BriBkM 80; CurBio 93; IntWWM 90; NewAmDM; NewGrDA 86; NewGrDM 80; NewGrDO; NewYTBS 82; PenDiMP; WhoAm 80, 82, 84, 92, 94, 95, 96, 97; WhoAmM 83; WhoE 97; WhoWor 80, 82, 96, 97*

Davies, Henry Walford, Sir
English. Organist, Composer
Led radio series "Music Lessons in Schools," 1924-34; wrote religious music.
b. Sep 6, 1869 in Oswestry, England
d. Mar 11, 1941 in Wrington, England
Source: *Baker 78, 84; BioIn 4, 5; DcArts; NewOxM; OxCMus; WebBD 83*

Davies, Hunter
Scottish. Author, Editor
Punch columnist since 1979; wrote authorized biography of The Beatles, 1968; *London at Its Best,* 1984.
b. Jan 7, 1936 in Renfrew, Scotland
Source: *BioIn 15, 16; ConAu 12NR, 57; IntAu&W 89, 91; SmATA 45, 55; Who 85, 92; WhoWor 74, 76, 95, 96; WrDr 76, 86, 92, 94, 96*

Davies, Joseph Edward
American. Lawyer, Diplomat
Ambassador to USSR, 1936-38; wrote *Mission to Moscow.*
b. Nov 29, 1876 in Watertown, Wisconsin
d. May 9, 1958 in Washington, District of Columbia
Source: *AmAu&B; BioIn 1, 3, 4, 5, 13, 15, 16, 18; CurBio 42, 58; DcAmB S6; DcAmDH 80, 89; DcPol; EncAB-A 1, 32; NatCAB 61; WhAm 3*

Davies, Leslie Purnell
[Leslie Vardre]
English. Author
Writings include *The Paper Dolls,* 1964; *The Land of Leys,* 1979.
b. Oct 20, 1914 in Cheshire, England
Source: *BioIn 14; DcLP 87A; IntAu&W 76, 77, 93; ScFSB; WhoWor 76; WrDr 76, 80, 82*

Davies, Marion
[Marion Douras]
American. Actor
Mistress of William Randolf Hearst; affair satirized by Orson Welles in *Citizen Kane,* 1941.
b. Jan 3, 1897 in New York, New York
d. Sep 22, 1961 in Hollywood, California
Source: *BiDD; BiDFilm, 81, 94; BioIn 7, 8, 9, 10, 15, 17, 20, 21; EncAFC; Film 1, 2; FilmEn; FilmgC; HalFC 80, 84, 88; IntDcF 1-3, 2-3; InWom SUP; LegTOT; MGM; MotPP; MovMk; NotNAT B; ObitT 1961; OxCFilm; SilFlmP; ThFT; TwYS; WhAm 4; WhoHol B; WhScrn 74, 77, 83; WhThe; WorAl; WorEFlm*

Davies, Peter Maxwell
English. Composer
Founded Orkney Island's annual St. Magnus Festival, 1977; wrote *Eight Songs for a Mad King,* 1969.
b. Sep 8, 1934 in Manchester, England
Source: *Baker 78, 84, 92; BioIn 6, 8, 12, 13, 14, 15, 20, 21; BlueB 76; BriBkM 80; CmOp; CompSN SUP; ConCom 92; CpmDNM 80, 81, 82; CurBio 80; DcArts; DcCom&M 79; FacFETw; IntDcOp; IntWW 74, 75, 76, 77, 78, 79, 80, 81, 82, 83, 89, 91, 93; IntWWM 77, 80, 90; MakMC; MetOEnc; MusMk; NewAmDM; NewGrDM 80; NewGrDO; NewOxM; OxCMus; OxDcOp; PenDiMP, A; PenEncH; Who 82, 83, 85, 88, 90, 92, 94; WhoEnt 92; WhoMus 72; WhoWor 74, 78, 80, 82, 84, 87, 89, 91, 93, 95, 96, 97*

Davies, Ray(mond Douglas)
[The Kinks]
English. Singer, Musician
Lead guitarist for band formed with brother Dave, 1963.
b. Jun 21, 1944 in Muswell Hill, England
Source: *BioIn 14, 15, 19; ConAu 116, 146; ConLC 21; ConMus 5; IlEncRk; LegTOT; WhoAm 80, 82, 84, 86, 88, 90, 92, 94, 95, 96, 97; WhoRocM 82; WorAlBi*

Davies, (William) Robertson
Canadian. Author
One of Canada's most accomplished writers; known for Deptford trilogy.
b. Aug 28, 1913 in Thamesville, Ontario, Canada
d. Dec 2, 1995 in Orangeville, Ontario, Canada
Source: *Au&Wr 71; Benet 96; BenetAL 91; BestSel 89-2; BioIn 6, 9, 10, 11, 12, 15, 16, 17, 20, 21; BlueB 76; CamGLE; CamGWoT; CanWr; CanWW 70, 79, 80, 81, 83, 89; CaP; CasWL; CaW; CnThe; ConAu 17NR, 33R, 42NR, 150; ConCaAu 1; ConDr 73, 77, 82, 88, 93; ConLC 2, 7, 13, 25, 42, 75, 91; ConNov 72, 76, 82, 86, 91, 96; ConPopW; ConTFT 4; CreCan 1; CrtSuDr; CurBio 75, 96N; CyWA 89; DcArts; DcLB 68; DcLEL, 1940; DcLP 87A; DrAS 74E, 78E, 82E; EncWL 3; FacFETw; GrWrEL N; IntAu&W 76, 77, 82, 89, 91, 93; IntLitE; IntvTCA 2; IntWW 77, 78, 79, 80, 81, 82, 83, 89, 91, 93; LegTOT; LngCTC; MagSWL; MajTwCW; McGEWD 72, 84; ModCmwL; NewYTBS 95; Novels; OxCCan; OxCCanL; OxCCan SUP; OxCCanT; OxCEng 95; OxCThe 83; PenC ENG; RAdv 14, 13-1; REnAL; REnWD; RfGEnL 91; RGTwCWr; ScF&FL 92; TwCWr; WhAm 11; WhoAm 74, 76, 78, 80, 82, 84, 86, 88, 90, 92, 94, 95, 96; WhoCanL 85, 87, 92; WhoThe 81; WhoWor 74, 82, 84; WhoWrEP 89, 92; WorAlBi; WorAu*

1950; WorLitC; WrDr 76, 80, 82, 84, 86, 88, 90, 92, 94, 96

Davies, Rodger Paul
American. Diplomat
With US diplomatic service, 1946-74; mainly in Middle East, Southeast Asia.
b. May 7, 1921 in Berkeley, California
d. Aug 19, 1974 in Nicosia, Cyprus
Source: *USBiR 74; WhAm 6; WhoAm 74; WhoGov 72*

Davies, Ronald N(orwood)
American. Judge
Ordered the racial integration of Little Rock High School, 1957.
b. Dec 11, 1904
d. Apr 18, 1996 in Fargo, North Dakota
Source: *AmBench 79; AmCath 80; BiDFedJ; BioIn 4, 5; CurBio 96N; WhAm 11; WhoAm 74, 76, 78, 80, 82, 84, 86, 94, 96; WhoAmL 79, 83, 85, 94; WhoGov 72, 75, 77; WhoMW 74, 76, 93*

Davis, Adelle
American. Nutritionist
Wrote *Let's Cook It Right,* 1947.
b. Feb 25, 1904 in Lizton, Indiana
d. May 31, 1974 in Palos Verdes, California
Source: *AmWomSc; AmWomWr; BioIn 9, 10, 12, 20; BioNews 74; CelR; ConAu 30NR, 37R, 49; CurBio 73, 74N; DcAmB S9; InWom SUP; LegTOT; NewYTBS 74; NotAW MOD; REnAL; WhAm 6; WhoAm 74; WorAl; WorAlBi*

Davis, Al(len)
American. Football Executive
Owner, Oakland/LA Raiders, 1963—.
b. Jul 4, 1929 in Brockton, Massachusetts
Source: *BiDAmSp FB; BioIn 6, 8, 10, 12, 13, 14, 15, 16; CelR 90; CmCal; ConAu 108; ConTFT 1, 4; CurBio 85; NatPD 81; WhoAm 74, 76, 78, 80, 82, 84, 86, 88, 90, 92, 94, 95, 96, 97; WhoEnt 92; WhoFtbl 74; WhoSpor; WhoUSWr 88; WhoWest 74, 76, 80, 82, 87, 89, 92, 94, 96; WhoWrEP 89, 92, 95; WorAlBi*

Davis, Alexander Jackson
American. Architect
Known for gothic, classic styles; designs include state capitol bldgs. in IN, NC, IL.
b. Jul 24, 1803 in New York, New York
d. Jan 14, 1892 in West Orange, New Jersey
Source: *AmBi; AmCulL; ApCAB SUP; BiDAmAr; BioIn 2, 8, 9, 11, 12, 14, 16, 19; BriEAA; DcAmB; DcD&D; DcNAA; DcNCBi 2; EarABI SUP; EncAAr 2; IntDcAr; MacEA; McGDA; McGEWB; NatCAB 22; NewYHSD; OxCAmH; OxCArt; PenDiDA 89; PeoHis; TwCBDA; WhAm HS; WhoArch*

Davis, Andrew Frank
English. Conductor
Musical director, Toronto Symphony Orchestra, 1975-88; music director of Glynde bourne Festival Opera, 1988—
b. Feb 4, 1944 in Ashridge, England
Source: *Baker 84, 92; BioIn 11, 12, 13; BriBkM 80; CanWW 83, 89; CurBio 83; IntWW 83, 91; IntWWM 77, 80, 90; MetOEnc; NewAmDM; NewGrDM 80; NewGrDO; NewYTBS 78; PenDiMP; Who 74, 82, 83, 85, 88, 90, 92, 94; WhoAm 90, 92, 94, 95, 96, 97; WhoE 91, 93; WhoEnt 92*

Davis, Angela (Yvonne)
American. Revolutionary, Author
On FBI's ten most-wanted list, 1970; wrote autobiography, 1974.
b. Jan 26, 1944 in Birmingham, Alabama
Source: *AfrAmAl 6; AfrAmBi 2; AfrAmOr; AmWomWr SUP; BenetAL 91; BiDAmLf; BiDMarx; BioIn 8, 9, 10, 11, 12, 14, 15, 16, 17, 18, 19, 20, 21; BioNews 74; BkPepl; BlkWAm; BlkWr 1, 2; BlkWrNE; CelR; CivR 74; CmCal; ConAu 10NR, 57; ConBlB 5; ConLC 77; ContDcW 89; CurBio 72; DcTwCCu 5; EncAACR; EncAL; EncRev; EncWB; FacFETw; FemiWr; GoodHs; HanAmWH; HerW; HisWorL; InB&W 80; IntDcWB; InWom SUP; LegTOT; LNinSix; MugS; NegAl 76, 89; NewYTBE 70, 71, 72; NotBlAW 1; OxCWoWr 95; RadHan; SchCGBL; SelBAAf; SelBAAu; WhoAfA 96; WhoAm 76; WhoAmW 79; WhoBlA 92, 94; WorAl; WorAlBi; WrDr 92*

Davis, Ann Bradford
American. Actor
Best known for TV series "The Brady Bunch," 1969-74; "The Bob Cummings Show," 1955-59.
b. May 3, 1926 in Schenectady, New York
Source: *ConTFT 3; WhoAm 74, 76, 78, 80, 82, 84; WhoAmW 74, 75; WhoHol A*

Davis, Anthony
American. Composer, Pianist
Composed opera *X: The Life and Times of Malcolm X,* 1986.
b. Feb 20, 1951 in Paterson, New Jersey
Source: *AllMusG; Baker 92; BioIn 12, 13, 16; ConBlB 11; ConMus 17; CurBio 90; InB&W 85; NewGrDA 86; NewGrDJ 88, 94; NewGrDO; WhoAm 90, 96, 97; WhoEnt 92*

Davis, Arthur Vining
American. Business Executive
Founded Aluminum Co. of America; pres., 1908; chm., 1928-62; director, Hotel Waldorf Astoria Corp.
b. May 30, 1867 in Sharon, Massachusetts
d. Nov 17, 1962 in Miami, Florida
Source: *BiDAmBL 83; BioIn 4, 5, 6, 11, 16; DcAmB S7; EncWB; ObitOF 79; WhAm 4, 5; WhFla*

Davis, Barbara
"BD"
American.
Wrote memoir *My Mother's Keeper,* 1985; daughter of Bette Davis.
b. May 1, 1947 in Santa Ana, California

Davis, Benjamin Oliver, Sr.
American. Military Leader
First black general in US Army, 1940.
b. Jul 1, 1877 in Washington, District of Columbia
d. Nov 26, 1970 in North Chicago, Illinois
Source: *AfrAmG; BiDWWGF; BioIn 1, 3, 6, 8, 9, 10; CurBio 42, 71; DcAmB S8; EncAB-H 1974, 1996; InB&W 80, 85; NegAl 76, 83, 89; NewYTBE 70; WebAB 74, 79; WebAMB; WhoColR; WorAl*

Davis, Benjamin Oliver, Jr.
American. Air Force Officer
Member, first group of blacks admitted to air corps, 1941; first black general in air force, 1954.
b. Dec 18, 1912 in Washington, District of Columbia
Source: *AfrAmBi 1; BioIn 3, 4, 5, 6, 7, 8, 9; BlksScM; ConAu 134; ConBlB 2; CurBio 55; DcAmMiB; FacFETw; InB&W 80, 85; InSci; NegAl 89; NewYTBE 70; WebAMB; WhoAm 74, 76, 78, 80; WhoAmP 75, 77, 79, 81, 83, 85, 87, 89, 91, 93, 95; WhoBlA 75, 92; WhoGov 72, 75, 77; WhoSSW 73; WorAl*

Davis, Bette
[Ruth Elizabeth Davis]
American. Actor
Major movie star since 1930s; won Oscars for *Dangerous,* 1935; *Jezebel,* 1938; other films include *The Whales of August,* 1987.
b. Apr 5, 1908 in Lowell, Massachusetts
d. Oct 6, 1989 in Paris, France
Source: *AmCulL; AnObit 1989; BiDFilm, 81, 94; BiE&WWA; BioAmW; BioIn 1, 2, 3, 4, 6, 7, 8, 9, 10, 11, 12, 14, 15, 16, 17, 18, 19, 20, 21; BlueB 76; CelR, 90; CmCal; CmMov; ConAu 21NR, 61, 129, X; ContDcW 89; ConTFT 1, 8; CurBio 41, 53, 89N; DcArts; EncAFC; EncMT; FacFETw; FilmEn; FilmgC; ForYSC; GangFlm; GoodHs; GrLiveH; HalFC 80, 84, 88; HanAmWH; IntDcF 1-3, 2-3; IntDcWB; IntMPA 75, 76, 77, 78, 79, 80, 81, 82, 84, 86, 88; IntWW 74, 75, 76, 77, 78, 79, 80, 81, 82, 83, 89; InWom, SUP; ItaFilm; LegTOT; LibW; LinLib S; MotPP; MovMk; News 90, 90-1; NewYTBE 70; NewYTBS 89; NotNAT, A; OxCFilm; ThFT; WebAB 74, 79; Who 90; WhoAm 86, 88; WhoAmW 58, 61, 64, 66, 68, 70, 72, 74, 75, 89; WhoHol A; WhoHrs 80; WhoThe 77, 81; WhoWor 74, 84; WomFir; WorAl; WorAlBi; WorEFlm*

Davis, Billy, Jr.
[Fifth Dimension]
American. Singer
Vocalist with pop-soul group; had number-one hit "Wedding Bell Blues," 1969.
b. Jun 26, 1940 in Saint Louis, Missouri
Source: *BiDAmM; BioIn 14, 16; InB&W 80, 85; LegTOT; WhoBlA 92*

Davis, Brad
American. Actor
Won Golden Globe Award for best actor in *Midnight Express,* 1978; appeared in *Chariots of Fire,* 1981; television mini-series "Robert Kennedy and His Times."
b. Nov 6, 1949 in Tallahassee, Florida
d. Sep 8, 1991 in Studio City, California
Source: *AnObit 1991; BioIn 11, 17, 18; ConTFT 5, 10; HalFC 84, 88; IntMPA 84, 86, 88; ItaFilm; LegTOT; NewYTBS 91; VarWW 85; WhAm 10; WhoHol 92*

Davis, Burke
American. Children's Author
Writings include *Whisper My Name,* 1949; *Sherman's March,* 1973.
b. Jul 24, 1913 in Durham, North Carolina
Source: *AmAu&B; AuBYP 2, 3; BioIn 3, 4, 5, 7, 9; ConAu 1R, 4NR, 25NR, 50NR; DrAPF 80, 87; IntAu&W 86, 93; SmATA 4; WhoAm 74, 76, 78, 80, 82, 88; WrDr 76, 80, 82, 84, 86, 88, 90, 92, 94, 96*

Davis, Chip
[Louis Chip Davis Davis, Jr]
American. Composer, Musician
Wrote triple-platinum country single "Convoy," 1976; founded classical pop group Mannheim Steamroller; composed platinum album *A Fresh Aire Christmas,*2 1988.
Source: *BioIn 16; ConMus 4; WhoAm 92, 94, 95, 96, 97; WhoEnt 92*

Davis, Clifton
American. Actor, Singer, Composer
Wrote gold-record song "Never Can Say Goodbye", 1970; starred as the Rev. Reuben Gregory on comedy series "Amen," 1986-91.
b. Oct 4, 1945 in Chicago, Illinois
Source: *BioIn 15, 16; ConTFT 6; DrBlPA; LegTOT; VarWW 85; WhoBlA 75, 92; WhoHol 92, A; WorAlBi*

Davis, Clive Jay
American. Music Executive, Lawyer
Pres., Columbia Records, 1966-73; pres., co-owner, Arista Records, 1974—.
b. Apr 4, 1932 in New York, New York
Source: *BioIn 14; BusPN; PenEncP; WhoAm 78, 80, 82, 84, 86, 88, 90; WhoEnt 92*

Davis, Clyde Brion
American. Journalist, Author
Best known for *The Great American Novel,* 1938.
b. May 22, 1894 in Unadilla, Nebraska
d. Jul 19, 1962 in Salisbury, Connecticut
Source: *AmAu&B; AmNov; BenetAL 91; BioIn 2, 3, 4, 6, 12; CnDAL; ConAu 5R; DcLB 9; ObitOF 79; OxCAmL 65, 83, 95; REn; REnAL; TwCA, SUP; WhAm 4; WhE&EA*

Davis, Colin Rex, Sir
English. Conductor
Director, London's Covent Garden Royal Opera since 1971; noted for Mozart, Berlioz interpretations.
b. Sep 25, 1927 in Weybridge, England
Source: *Baker 84, 92; BioIn 13; CurBio 68; IntMPA 92; IntWW 74, 75, 76, 77, 78, 79, 80, 81, 82, 83, 89, 91, 93; IntWWM 77, 90; MetOEnc; NewAmDM; NewGrDO; NewYTBE 72; PenDiMP; Who 92, 94; WhoEnt 92; WhoMus 72; WhoOp 76; WhoWor 74, 76, 78, 80, 82, 84, 87, 89, 91, 93, 95, 96, 97*

Davis, (Thomas) Cullen
American. Oilman
Inherited family's oil business worth over $150 million; acquitted, 1978, of stepdaughter's murder.
b. 1933? in Texas
Source: *BioIn 11, 12, 13, 15*

Davis, David
American. Supreme Court Justice
Associate justice, 1862-77; senator, 1877-83; campaigned for Lincoln's pres. nomination.
b. Mar 9, 1815 in Cecil County, Maryland
d. Jun 26, 1886 in Bloomington, Illinois
Source: *AmPolLe; ApCAB; BiAUS; BiDFedJ; BiDrAC; BiDrUSC 89; BioIn 2, 3, 5, 15; DcAmB; Drake; EncAB-H 1974; HarEnUS; NatCAB 2; OxCSupC; PolPar; SupCtJu; TwCBDA; WebAB 74, 79; WebBD 83; WhAm HS; WhAmP; WhCiWar*

Davis, Dwight Filley
American. Government Official
Secretary of War under Coolidge; governor general, Philippine Islands, 1929-32; donor, 1900, of Davis Cup for world champion tennis.
b. Jul 5, 1879 in Saint Louis, Missouri
d. Nov 28, 1945 in Washington, District of Columbia
Source: *ApCAB X; BiDAmSp OS; BiDrUSE 71, 89; BioIn 4, 10; DcAmB S3; NatCAB 40; ObitOF 79; WhAm 2*

Davis, Edward Michael
American. Government Official
Chief of LA police, 1969-78; member of CA State Senate, 1980—.
b. Nov 15, 1916 in Los Angeles, California
Source: *WhoAmP 81, 83, 85, 87, 89, 91, 93; WhoGov 72, 75, 77; WhoWest 74, 76, 78, 84, 87, 89*

Davis, Elmer Holmes
American. Journalist, Radio Performer
News commentator for CBS, NBC; early opponent of Senator Joseph McCarthy's hearings; books include *Love Among the Ruins,* 1935; *But We Were Born Free,* 1954.
b. Jan 13, 1890 in Aurora, Indiana
d. May 18, 1958 in Washington, District of Columbia
Source: *AmAu&B; CurBio 58; EncAB-H 1974, 1996; IndAu 1816; LesBEnT; OxCAmL 83; PolProf T; REn; REnAL; TwCA SUP; WebAB 79; WhAm 3; WhNAA*

Davis, Eric Keith
"Eric the Red"
American. Baseball Player
Centerfielder, Cincinnati Reds, 1984-91; LA Dodgers, 1992-93, Detroit Tigers, 1993-94.
b. May 29, 1962 in Los Angeles, California
Source: *Ballpl 90; BaseEn 88; BaseReg 86, 87; BioIn 15; ConNews 87-4; WhoAfA 96; WhoAm 90, 92, 94, 95, 96, 97; WhoBlA 88, 92, 94; WhoMW 90; WhoWest 94, 96; WorAlBi*

Davis, Ernie
[Ernest R Davis]
American. Football Player
All-America running back; first black to win Heisman Trophy, 1961; first player chosen in NFL draft, 1962, but died of leukemia before playing a game.
b. Dec 14, 1939 in New Salem, Pennsylvania
d. May 18, 1963 in Cleveland, Ohio
Source: *AfrAmSG; BioIn 13, 14, 16, 21; DcAmB S7; InB&W 80; WhoFtbl 74*

Davis, Frederick C(lyde), X
[Murdo Coombs; Stephen Ransome; Curtis Steele]
American. Author
Wrote several mysteries including *Warning Bell,* 1960.
b. Jun 2, 1902 in Saint Joseph, Missouri
d. 1977
Source: *AmAu&B; ConAu 115; EncSF 93; MnBBF; TwCCr&M 85*

Davis, Gary, Reverend
American. Singer, Musician
Gospel/blues guitarist; recorded *Harlem Street Spirituals,* 1956, *Children of Zion,* 1962, *Pure Religion and Bad Company,* 1962, and *New Blues and Gospel,* 1971.
b. Apr 30, 1896 in Laurens County, South Carolina
d. May 5, 1972 in New York, New York
Source: *BioIn 14, 15, 17; EncFCWM 83; GuBlues; NewAmDM; NewGrDA 86; NewGrDM 80; OnThGG; PenEncP; RolSEnR 83; WhScrn 77, 83*

Davis, Geena
[Virginia Davis]
American. Actor
Won Academy Award for *The Accidental Tourist,* 1989; roles in *Tootsie,* 1982; *The Fly,* 1986.
b. Jan 21, 1957 in Wareham, Massachusetts
Source: *BiDFilm 94; BioIn 16; CelR 90; ConTFT 5, 10; CurBio 91; GrLiveH; IntMPA 88, 92, 94, 96; IntWW 91; LegTOT; News 92, 92-1; WhoAm 90, 94, 95, 96, 97; WhoAmW 91, 95, 97; WhoEnt 92; WorAlBi*

Davis, Gerry
English. Author
Wrote science fiction series *Doctor Who,* 1974-78.
b. Feb 23, 1930 in London, England
Source: *ConAu 117; EncSF 93; IntAu&W 77; ScFSB; TwCSFW 81, 91; WrDr 92*

Davis, Glenn
American. Track Athlete
Hurdler; won gold medals, 1956, 1960 Olympics.
b. Sep 12, 1934 in Wellsburg, West Virginia
Source: *BiDAmSp OS; WhoTr&F 73*

Davis, Glenn W
"Mr. Outside"
American. Football Player
All-America halfback at Army, 1943-46; won Heisman Trophy, 1946; in NFL with LA Rams, 1950-51.
b. Dec 26, 1924 in Claremont, California
Source: *BioIn 14; CurBio 46; WhoFtbl 74*

Davis, Hal Charles
American. Labor Union Official
Pres., American Federation of Musicians International, 1970-78.
b. Feb 27, 1914 in Pittsburgh, Pennsylvania
d. Jan 1, 1978 in New York, New York
Source: *BioIn 11; WhAm 7; WhoAm 74, 76, 78; WhoE 77*

Davis, Harold Lenoir
American. Author
Books include *Honey in the Horn,* 1935, Pulitzer winner.
b. Oct 18, 1896 in Yoncalla, Oregon
d. Oct 31, 1960 in San Antonio, Texas
Source: *AmAu&B; BioIn 2, 3, 4, 5, 12; ChhPo S1; ConAu 89; DcLEL; TwCA, SUP*

Davis, Henry Winter
American. Politician
Rep. congressman, 1850s-60s; denounced Lincoln's reconstruction program in Wade-Davis Manifesto, 1864.
b. Aug 16, 1817 in Annapolis, Maryland
d. Dec 30, 1865 in Baltimore, Maryland
Source: *Alli, SUP; AmBi; ApCAB; BbD; BiAUS; BiD&SB; BiDrAC; BiDrUSC 89; BiDSA; BioIn 10; CivWDc; DcAmAu; DcAmB; DcNAA; Drake; EncSoH; HarEnUS; McGEWB; NatCAB 2; NewCol 75; OxCAmH; TwCBDA; WhAm HS; WhCiWar*

Davis, James Curran
American. Politician
Congressman from GA, 1947-63; advocated racial segregation.
b. May 17, 1895 in Franklin, Georgia
d. Dec 28, 1981 in Atlanta, Georgia
Source: *BiDrAC; BiDrUSC 89; BioIn 4, 12, 13; CurBio 82; NewYTBS 81; WhAm 8; WhAmP; WhoAm 74*

Davis, Janette
American. Singer
Husky-voiced entertainer; with Arthur Godfrey's radio, TV shows, 1940s-50s.
Source: *BioIn 3; CmpEPM; InWom*

Davis, Jefferson
American. Political Leader
Pres. of Confederacy, 1861-65.
b. Jun 3, 1808 in Christian County, Kentucky
d. Dec 6, 1889 in New Orleans, Louisiana
Source: *Alli SUP; AmAu&B; AmBi; AmOrN; AmPolLe; ApCAB; BbD; Benet 87, 96; BenetAL 91; BiAUS; BiD&SB; BiDConf; BiDrAC; BiDrUSE 71, 89; BiDSA; BioIn 1, 2, 3, 4, 5, 6, 7, 8, 9, 10, 11, 12, 13, 14, 16, 17, 18, 19, 20, 21; CelCen; CivWDc; CyAG; DcAmAu; DcAmB; DcAmMiB; DcBiPP; DcNAA; Dis&D; Drake; EncAAH; EncAB-H 1974, 1996; HarEnMi; HarEnUS; HisWorL; LegTOT; LinLib L, S; LiveMA; McGEWB; MemAm; NatCAB 4; OxCAmH; OxCAmL 65, 83, 95; PolPar; RAdv 14, 13-3; RComAH; REn; REnAL; REnAW; TwCBDA; WebAB 74, 79; WebBD 83; WhAm HS; WhAmP; WhCiWar; WorAl; WorAlBi*

Davis, Jim
American. Actor
Played Jock Ewing on TV series "Dallas," 1978-81.
b. Aug 26, 1915 in Edgerton, Missouri
d. Apr 26, 1981 in Northridge, California
Source: *FilmEn; ForYSC; HalFC 84; LegTOT; NewYTBS 81; WhoHol A; WhScrn 83*

Davis, Jim
[James Robert Davis]
American. Cartoonist
Created comic strip character Garfield; syndicated in 500 newspapers.
b. Jul 28, 1945 in Marion, Indiana
Source: *Au&Arts 8; BioIn 13, 14, 16, 21; ConAu 16NR, 41NR, 85; EncTwCJ; LegTOT; SmATA 32; WhoAm 82, 84, 86, 88, 90, 92, 94, 95, 96, 97; WhoAmA 84, 86, 89, 91, 93; WorAlBi*

Davis, Joan
American. Actor, Comedian
Starred in TV series *I Married Joan,* 1952-55.
b. Jun 29, 1907 in Saint Paul, Minnesota
d. May 23, 1961 in Palm Springs, California
Source: *BioIn 2, 3, 7, 9; CurBio 61; EncAFC; FilmEn; FilmgC; Funs; HalFC 84, 88; InWom SUP; LegTOT; MotPP; MovMk; QDrFCA 92; RadStar; SaTiSS; ThFT; WhoCom; WhoHol B; WhScrn 74, 77, 83; WhThe*

Davis, Joe
English. Billiards Player
Developed British game into modern snooker; won first world title in the sport, 1927, held until 1946.
b. Apr 15, 1901 in Whitewell, England
d. Jul 10, 1978 in Hampshire, England
Source: *BioIn 11, 14; ConAu 112*

Davis, John
English. Explorer
Discovered entrance to Baffin Bay, 1587; sighted Falkland Islands, 1592.
b. 1550? in Sandridge, England
d. Dec 29, 1605, At Sea
Source: *Alli; ApCAB; CamGEL; CamGLE; DcCanB 1; DcEnL; DcNaB; Drake; EncCRAm; EvLB; Expl 93; HisDBrE; LinLib L, S; MacDCB 78; McGEWB; NewCBEL; OxCAmH; OxCCan; OxCShps; WhDW; WhWE; WorAl; WorAlBi*

Davis, John Staige
American. Surgeon
Leading plastic surgeon; pres., Southern Surgical Association, 1940.
b. Jan 15, 1872 in Norfolk, Virginia
d. Dec 23, 1946 in Baltimore, Maryland
Source: *BioIn 1, 2; DcAmB S4; DcAmMeB 84; DcNAA; NatCAB 36; NewYTBS 77; WhAm 2; WhoAm 78; WhoSSW 73*

Davis, John Williams
American. Politician, Lawyer
Appeared before US Supreme Court 140 times, more than any other lawyer; ran for US pres., 1924.
b. Apr 13, 1873 in Clarksburg, West Virginia
d. Mar 24, 1955 in New York, New York
Source: *BiDrAC; CurBio 53, 55; DcAmB S5; EncAB-H 1974; WebAB 74; WhAm 3; WhAmP*

Davis, Judy
Australian. Actor
Starred in *My Brilliant Career,* 1981.
b. 1955 in Perth, Australia
Source: *BioIn 12, 14, 15; ConTFT 7; CurBio 93; HalFC 88; IntMPA 92, 96; IntWW 93; WhoAm 96, 97; WhoAmW 97; WhoWor 95, 96*

Davis, Kingsley
American. Sociologist
Professor of sociology, U of S CA in LA, 1977-90; writings include *World Urbanization,* 1972; coined the term "zero population growth."
b. Aug 20, 1908 in Tuxedo, Texas
d. Feb 27, 1997 in Stanford, California
Source: *AmMWSc 73S, 78S; BlueB 76; ConAu 8NR, 13R; IntEnSS 79; IntWW 74, 75, 76, 77, 78, 79, 80; WhoAm 74, 76, 84, 86, 88, 90, 92, 94, 95, 96, 97; WhoEc 81; WhoWest 96; WhoWor 74*

Davis, Loyal
American. Surgeon
Stepfather of Nancy Reagan, known for practice, teaching of brain surgery.
b. Jan 17, 1896 in Galesburg, Illinois
d. Aug 19, 1982 in Scottsdale, Arizona
Source: *AmMWSc 73P, 76P, 79; ConAu 107; NewYTBS 82; WhAm 8; WhoAm 74, 76, 78, 80*

Davis, Mac
American. Singer, Actor, Songwriter
Hit song "I Believe in Music," 1972; starred in *North Dallas Forty,* 1979.
b. Jan 21, 1942 in Lubbock, Texas
Source: *Baker 84, 92; BioIn 11, 12, 14; BkPepl; ConTFT 3; CounME 74, 74A; CurBio 80; EncFCWM 83; EncPR&S 74, 89; EncRk 88; HarEnCM 87; IlEncCM; IntMPA 82, 84, 86, 88, 92, 94, 96; LegTOT; NewYTBS 79; OxCPMus; PenEncP; RkOn 78; WhoAm 78, 80, 82, 84, 86, 88, 90, 92, 94, 95, 96, 97; WhoEnt 92; WhoHol 92; WhoRock 81; WorAl; WorAlBi*

Davis, Mark William
American. Baseball Player
Relief pitcher, 1983—; led ML in saves, 1989; won NL Cy Young Award, 1989.
b. Oct 19, 1960 in Livermore, California
Source: *Ballpl 90; BaseEn 88; BaseReg 88; WorAlBi*

Davis, Martin S
American. Business Executive
Chm., CEO, Paramount Communications (formerly GulfWestern), 1974-94; made unsuccessful bid for Time Inc., 1989.
b. Feb 5, 1927 in New York, New York
Source: *BioIn 14, 15, 16; CurBio 89; Dun&B 90; IntMPA 92; IntWW 91; NewYTBS 91; St&PR 91; WhoAm 90; WhoE 91; WhoEnt 92; WhoFI 92; WhoWor 91*

Davis, Marvin
American. Oilman
Wildcatter, pres., independent Davis Oil Co.
b. Aug 28, 1925 in Newark, New Jersey
Source: *BioIn 11, 12, 13, 16; CelR 90; ConAmBL; NewYTBS 81; WhoAm 94, 95, 96, 97; WhoFI 94, 96; WhoWest 92, 94*

Davis, Meyer
American. Bandleader, Agent
Often played at White House; could provide dance bands in 24-hour notice, 1920s-70s.
b. Jan 10, 1895 in Ellicott City, Maryland
d. Apr 5, 1976 in New York, New York
Source: *BiE&WWA; BioIn 5, 6, 10, 11; BioNews 75; CelR; CmpEPM; CurBio 61, 76N; WhoAm 76*

Davis, Miles Dewey, III
American. Jazz Musician, Composer
Often considered top jazz trumpeter; formed Miles Davis Quintet, 1955; with Charlie Parker, 1940s.
b. May 25, 1926 in Alton, Illinois
d. Sep 28, 1991 in Santa Monica, California
Source: *AfrAmBi 2; AmCulL; Baker 78, 84; BiDAfM; BiDAmM; BiDJaz; BioIn 4, 5, 6, 7, 8, 9, 10, 11, 12, 13, 14, 15, 16; BioNews 74; CelR 90; ConMus 1; CurBio 62, 91N; DrBlPA; EncJzS; EncRk 88; FacFETw; InB&W 80, 85; IntWW 78, 79, 80, 81, 82, 83, 89, 91; MakMC; NegAl 89; NewAmDM; NewOxM; News 92; NewYTBS 85, 91; OxCPMus; PenEncP; RAdv 13-3; WebAB 74, 79; WhAm 10; WhoAm 74, 76, 78, 80, 82, 84, 86, 88, 90; WhoBlA 75, 77, 80, 85, 88, 90, 92, 94N; WhoE 74; WhoMus 72; WhoWor 74; WorAl; WorAlBi*

Davis, Noel
American. Farmer, Inventor
Developed concept of hydrophonics; owner, PhytoFarm, 1983—.
Source: *BioIn 4; News 90, 90-3; WhoBlA 88*

Davis, Ossie
American. Actor, Dramatist
Wrote, directed, starred in *Purlie Victorious,* 1961; plays "Ponder" on TV show "Evening Shade."
b. Dec 18, 1917 in Cogdell, Georgia
Source: *AfrAmAl 6; AmAu&B; Au&Arts 17; BenetAL 91; BiE&WWA; BioIn 5, 6, 8, 9, 10, 12, 13, 14, 16, 17, 18, 19, 20, 21; BlkAmP; BlkAuII, 92; BlkAWP; BlksAmF; BlkWr 1, 2; BroadAu; CamGWoT; CelR, 90; CivR 74; ConAmD; ConAu 26NR, 53NR, 112; ConBlAP 88; ConBlB 5; ConDr 73, 77, 82, 88, 93; ConTFT 2, 9; CurBio 69; DcLB 7, 38; DcTwCCu 5; DrBlPA, 90; EarBlAP; Ent; FilmEn; FilmgC; HalFC 80, 84, 88; InB&W 80, 85; IntMPA 75, 76, 77, 78, 79, 80, 81, 82, 84, 86, 88, 92, 94, 96; LegTOT; LinLib L; LivgBAA; McGEWB; MiSFD 9; MorBAP; MotPP; MovMk; NatPD 81; NegAl 89; NotNAT; OxCAmT 84; PlP&P A; SchCGBL; SelBAAf; SelBAAu; SmATA 81; SouBlCW; SouWr; WhoAfA 96; WhoAm 76, 82, 84, 86, 88, 90, 92, 94, 95, 96, 97; WhoBlA 77, 80, 88, 90, 92, 94; WhoE 93, 95, 97; WhoEnt 92; WhoHol 92, A; WhoThe 72, 77, 81; WhoWor 74; WorAl; WorAlBi; WorAu 1970; WrDr 76, 80, 82, 84, 86, 88, 90, 92, 94, 96*

Davis, Owen
American. Dramatist
Best known for Pulitzer-winning play *Icebound,* 1923.
b. Jan 29, 1874 in Portland, Maine
d. Oct 13, 1956 in New York, New York
Source: *AmAu&B; BenetAL 91; BioIn 1, 2, 4, 5, 6; CamGWoT; CnDAL; CnMD; CrtSuDr; LegTOT; McGEWD 72, 84; ModWD; NatCAB 45; NotNAT A, B; OxCAmL 65, 83, 95; OxCAmT 84; OxCThe 67, 83; REn; REnAL; TwCA, SUP; WhAm 3; WhThe*

Davis, Patti
[Patricia Ann Reagan]
American. Actor, Author
Daughter of Ronald Reagan; wrote controversial *Home Front,* 1986.
b. Oct 22, 1952 in Los Angeles, California
Source: *BioIn 12, 13, 14, 15, 16; ConAu 134; CurBio 86; LegTOT; News 95, 95-1; WhoAmW 97; WrDr 88, 90, 92, 94, 96*

Davis, Peter Frank
American. Producer, Writer
Won 1975 Oscar for controversial Vietnam documentary, *Hearts and Minds;* won Emmy for "The Selling of the Pentagon," 1971.
b. Jan 2, 1937 in Los Angeles, California
Source: *BioIn 16; ConAu 29NR, 54NR; CurBio 83; IntAu&W 86; IntMPA 92; LesBEnT 92; NewYTET; WhoAm 74, 76, 78, 80, 82, 84, 86, 88, 90, 92, 94, 95, 96, 97; WhoE 74, 95; WhoEnt 92; WhoRel 92*

Davis, Phil
American. Cartoonist
Best known for creating cartoon character "Mandrake," 1933.
b. Mar 4, 1906 in Saint Louis, Missouri
d. Dec 16, 1964
Source: *BioIn 1, 7; EncACom; WorECom*

Davis, Rebecca Blaine Harding
American. Author, Journalist
Wrote *Waiting for the Verdict,* 1867; mother of Richard.
b. Jun 24, 1831 in Washington, Pennsylvania
d. Sep 29, 1910 in Mount Kisco, New York
Source: *Alli SUP; AmAu; AmAu&B; AmBi; AmWom; ApCAB; BbD; BiD&SB; DcAmAu; DcAmB; DcBiA; DcLEL; DcNAA; GrWrEL N; InWom SUP; LibW; NatCAB 8; NotAW; OxCAmL 65; REn; REnAL; SouWr; TwCBDA; WhAm 1*

Davis, Rennie
[The Chicago 7]
American. Social Reformer
Coordinated Pentagon march against Vietnam War, 1967; codefendant, Chicago Seven case.
b. May 23, 1941 in Lansing, Michigan

Source: *BiDAmLf; BioIn 10, 11; BioNews 74; HisWorL; MugS; WhoAm 74, 76, 78*

Davis, Richard Harding
American. Author, Journalist
War correspondent in six wars; wrote *The Bar Sinister,* 1903.
b. Apr 18, 1864 in Philadelphia, Pennsylvania
d. Apr 11, 1916 in Mount Kisco, New York
Source: *AmAu&B; AmBi; AmDec 1910; ApCAB X; BbD; Benet 87; BenetAL 91; BibAL; BiDAmJo; BiD&SB; BioIn 3, 4, 5, 6, 8, 9, 10, 12, 13, 14, 16, 18; CamGLE; CamHAL; CarSB; CasWL; Chambr 3; CnDAL; ConAu 114; DcAmAu; DcAmB; DcAmDH 80, 89; DcBiA; DcEnA A; DcLB 12, 23, 78, 79, DS13; DcLEL; DcNAA; EncAJ; EncMys; EvLB; GayN; GrWrEL N; HarEnUS; JBA 34; JrnUS; LiJour; LinLib L, S; LngCTC; McGEWB; MorMA; NatCAB 8; NotNAT B; Novels; OxCAmH; OxCAmL 65, 83, 95; OxCAmT 84; PenC AM; PeoHis; REn; REnAL; RfGAmL 87, 94; ScF&FL 1; TwCA, SUP; TwCBDA; TwCLC 24; WebAB 74, 79; WebE&AL; WhAm 1; WhLit; WhoStg 1906, 1908; WhThe; WorAlBi*

Davis, Sam(uel)
American. Soldier
Confederate with Rutherford Rifles Co; scout with Coleman's scout; hanged by Union for refusing to reveal name of traitor.
b. Oct 6, 1844 in Stewart's Creek, Tennessee
d. Nov 27, 1863 in Giles County, Tennessee
Source: *ApCAB SUP; BioIn 11; EncAI&E; NatCAB 8; WhAm HS*

Davis, Sammi
English. Actor
Films include *Mona Lisa,* 1986; *Hope and Glory,* 1987.
b. Jun 21, 1964? in Kidderminster, England
Source: *BioIn 15, 16; ConTFT 7; IntMPA 92, 96; LegTOT; NewYTBS 89; WhoHol 92*

Davis, Sammy, Jr.
American. Actor, Singer, Dancer
Versatile entertainer; 60-year career spanned vaudeville, stage, movies, recording, nightclubs, TV; last movie role in *Tap,* 1989.
b. Dec 8, 1925 in New York, New York
d. May 16, 1990 in Los Angeles, California
Source: *AfrAmAl 6; AfrAmBi 2; AnObit 1990; Baker 84, 92; BiDAfM; BiDAmM; BiDD; BiE&WWA; BioIn 11, 12, 14, 15, 16; BlksAmF; CelR, 90; CivR 74; ConAu 108, 131; ConMus 4; ConTFT 4, 11; CurBio 56, 78, 90, 90N; DcArts; DcTwCCu 5; DrBlPA, 90; EncAFC; EncMT; Ent; FacFETw; FilmEn; FilmgC; ForYSC; HalFC 80, 84, 88; InB&W 80, 85; IntMPA 75, 76, 77, 78, 79, 80, 81, 82, 84, 86, 88; IntWW 79, 80, 81, 82, 83, 89; IntWWM 90; LegTOT; MotPP; MovMk; NegAl 76, 83, 89; NewAmDM; News 90; NewYTBE 70, 72; NewYTBS 89, 90; NotNAT, A; OxCAmT 84; OxCFilm; OxCPMus; PenEncP; RkOn 74; WebAB 74, 79; WhAm 10; WhoAm 74, 76, 78, 80, 84, 86, 88, 90; WhoBlA 80, 85, 88, 90, 92, 92N; WhoHol A; WhoRock 81; WhoThe 72, 77, 81; WhoWor 74, 76; WorAl; WorAlBi*

Davis, Skeeter
American. Singer
Country-western star; hit song "The End of the World," 1963.
b. Dec 30, 1931 in Dry Ridge, Kentucky
Source: *BgBkCoM; BiDAmM; BioIn 14, 19; ConMus 15; CounME 74, 74A; EncFCWM 69, 83; EncRk 88; HarEnCM 87; IlEncCM; LegTOT; OxCPMus; PenEncP; RkOn 74*

Davis, Spencer
[The Spencer Davis Group]
English. Singer, Musician
Formed rock band featuring Stevie Winwood, 1963-69; known for hit "I'm a Man," 1968.
b. Jul 17, 1942 in Birmingham, England
Source: *EncRk 88; HarEnR 86; LegTOT; PenEncP; RkOn 84; WhoRock 81*

Davis, Stuart
American. Artist
Exhibited at 1913 Armory show; precursor of 1960s pop-art; did abstract works of urban life.
b. Dec 7, 1894 in Philadelphia, Pennsylvania
d. Jun 24, 1964 in New York, New York
Source: *AmCulL; ArtsAmW 3; BioIn 1, 3, 4, 5, 6, 7, 9, 11, 13, 14, 16; BriEAA; ConArt 77, 83; CurBio 64; DcAmArt; DcAmB S7; DcArts; DcCAA 71, 77, 88; EncAB-H 1974, 1996; IlBEAAW; IntDcAA 90; McGDA; McGEWB; OxCAmH; OxCAmL 65; OxCArt; OxCTwCA; OxDcArt; PhDcTCA 77; REn; WebAB 74, 79; WhAm 4; WhAmArt 85; WhDW; WhoAmA 78N, 80N, 82N, 84N, 86N, 89N, 91N, 93N; WorAl; WorAlBi; WorArt 1950*

Davis, Tobe
[Coller Davis]
American. Business Executive, Journalist
Wrote syndicated column *Toby Says.*
b. 1893? in Milwaukee, Wisconsin
d. Dec 25, 1962 in New York, New York
Source: *BioIn 3, 4, 5, 6; CurBio 63; WhoAmW 58*

Davis, Tommy
[Thomas R Davis]
American. Football Player
Kicker, San Francisco, 1959-69; holds NFL record for most consecutive extra points, 234, 1959-65.
b. Oct 13, 1934 in Shreveport, Louisiana
d. Apr 2, 1987 in San Bruno, California
Source: *BioIn 15; WhoFtbl 74*

Davis, Tommy, Jr.
[Thomas Herman Davis]
American. Baseball Player
Outfielder, designated hitter, 1959-76; led NL in batting, RBIs, 1962, in batting, 1963.
b. Mar 21, 1939 in New York, New York
Source: *Ballpl 90; BioIn 15, 20; LegTOT; WhoProB 73; WhoSpor*

Davis, Walter
American. Track Athlete
Member of 1952 Olympic team; set Olympic record in high jump.
b. Jan 5, 1931 in Beaumont, Texas
Source: *BioIn 3, 5; WhoTr&F 73*

Davis, Walter Paul
American. Basketball Player
Forward, Phoenix, 1977-84; Denver, 1988-92; rookie of year, 1978; member of US Olympic Team, 1976.
b. Sep 9, 1954 in Pineville, North Carolina
Source: *BlkOlyM; OfNBA 87; WhoAfA 96; WhoAm 84, 86; WhoBlA 85, 92, 94*

Davis, William Morris
American. Geographer, Geologist
Developed Davisian "cycle of erosion theory," 1880s.
b. Feb 12, 1850 in Philadelphia, Pennsylvania
d. Feb 5, 1934 in Pasadena, California
Source: *Alli SUP; AmBi; AmLY; ApCAB X; BiDAmEd; BiDAmS; BiESc; BioIn 2, 4, 18; CamDcSc; DcAmAu; DcAmB S1; DcNAA; DcScB; FacFETw; Geog 5; InSci; LarDcSc; McGEWB; NatCAB 24; OxCAmH; RAdv 14; TwCBDA; WebAB 74, 79; WebBD 83; WhAm 1; WhDW*

Davis, Willie
[William Henry Davis]
"Comet"
American. Baseball Player
Outfielder, 1960-79, known for speed; had 398 career stolen bases.
b. Apr 15, 1940 in Mineral Springs, Arkansas
Source: *Ballpl 90; BiDAmSp BB; BioIn 10, 15; WhoAm 74, 76; WhoBlA 75, 77; WhoProB 73*

Davison, Bruce
American. Actor
Appeared in films *Willard,* 1971; *Mother, Jugs, and Speed,* 1976; in TV shows, made-for-TV films.
b. Jun 28, 1946 in Philadelphia, Pennsylvania
Source: *ConTFT 4; FilmgC; HalFC 88; IntMPA 81, 92, 94, 96; LegTOT; WhoAm 94, 95, 96, 97; WhoHol 92, A*

Davison, Emily Wilding
English. Feminist
Imprisoned eight times for militant campaigning; force fed during 49 hunger strikes; threw herself under King's horse.
d. Jun 4, 1913
Source: *BioIn 11, 14, 16; IntDcWB*

Davison, Frank Dalby
Australian. Author
Works include *Man-Shy,* 1931.
b. Jun 23, 1893 in Melbourne, Australia
d. May 24, 1970 in Melbourne, Australia
Source: *AuLitCr; BioIn 4, 6, 9, 12; CasWL; ConAu 116; ConLC 15; DcChlFi; DcLEL; OxCAusL; TwCWr*

Davison, Frederic Ellis
American. Army Officer
Major general, 1971-74; received Bronze Star Medal.
b. Sep 28, 1917 in Washington, District of Columbia
Source: *AfrAmBi 1; AfrAmG; BioIn 8, 10, 19; BlksScM; CurBio 74; InB&W 80, 85; NegAl 89; NewYTBE 72; WhoBlA 85, 92; WorDWW*

Davison, Ian Frederic Hay
English. Business Executive
Chief exec., Lloyd's of London, 1983-85.
b. Jun 30, 1931
Source: *BioIn 15; ConNews 86-1; IntWW 83, 89, 91, 93; Who 82, 83, 85, 88, 90, 92, 94*

Davison, Wild Bill
[William Davison]
American. Jazz Musician
Dixieland style cornetist; 50-yr. career as soloist, bandleader.
b. Jan 5, 1906 in Defiance, Ohio
d. Nov 14, 1989 in Santa Barbara, California
Source: *AllMusG; AnObit 1989; Baker 84; BiDAmM; BiDJaz; BioIn 4, 8, 11, 13, 16, 17; CmpEPM; EncJzS; IlEncJ; NewAmDM; NewGrDA 86; NewGrDJ 88, 94; OxCPMus; PenEncP; WhoAm 74; WhoJazz 72*

Davisson, Clinton Joseph
American. Physicist
Shared Nobel Prize in physics, 1937, for discovery of diffraction of electrons by crystals.
b. Oct 22, 1881 in Bloomington, Illinois
d. Feb 1, 1958 in Charlottesville, Virginia
Source: *AsBiEn; BiESc; BioIn 2, 3, 4, 5, 6, 14, 15, 20; CamDcSc; DcAmB S6; DcScB; EncAB-A 38; FacFETw; InSci; LarDcSc; LinLib S; NewCol 75; ObitOF 79; ObitT 1951; WebAB 74, 79; WebBD 83; WhAm 3; WhoNob, 90, 95; WorAl; WorScD*

Davitt, Michael
Irish. Revolutionary
Organized Irish Land League, 1879; United Irish League, 1898.
b. Mar 25, 1846 in Straide, Ireland
d. May 31, 1906 in Dublin, Ireland
Source: *Alli SUP; BiDIrW; BioIn 1, 8, 13, 14; CelCen; DcIrB 78, 88; DcIrW 2; DcNaB S2; HisDBrE; LinLib L, S; NewCol 75; OxCIri; PoIre; WebBD 83; WhLit*

Davout, Louis Nicholas
[Duke d'Auerstadt; Prince d'Eckmuhl]
French. Military Leader
Marshal of France, 1804; fought at Jena, 1806; created duke, 1808, prince, 1809, by Napoleon.
b. May 10, 1770 in Annoux, France
d. Jun 1, 1823 in Paris, France
Source: *BioIn 14; CelCen; DcBiPP; GenMudB; NewCol 75; OxCFr; WebBD 83*

Davy, Humphrey, Sir
English. Scientist
Discovered laughing gas, 1799; invented miner's safety lamp, 1815.
b. Dec 17, 1778 in Cornwall, England
d. May 29, 1829 in Geneva, Switzerland
Source: *Alli; BbD; BiD&SB; BiDLA; BritAu 19; Chambr 2; DcEnL; EvLB; InSci; McGEWB; NewC; OxCEng 85; RAdv 13-5; ScFEYrs; WorAl; WorAlBi*

Dawber, Pam
[Mrs. Mark Harmon]
American. Actor
Played Mindy on TV series "Mork and Mindy," 1978-82; star of "My Sister Sam," 1986-1988.
b. Oct 18, 1951 in Detroit, Michigan
Source: *BioIn 9, 11, 12, 15; CelR 90; ConNews 87-1; ConTFT 4, 7, 15; HalFC 84, 88; HolBB; IntMPA 88, 92, 94, 96; LegTOT; VarWW 85; WhoAm 86, 90, 92, 94, 95, 96, 97; WhoEnt 92; WhoHol 92; WorAlBi*

Dawes, Charles Gates
American. US Vice President, Statesman
Developed Dawes Plan for German war reparations, 1920s, vp under Calvin Coolidge, 1925-29; shared 1925 Nobel Peace Prize.
b. Aug 27, 1865 in Marietta, Ohio
d. Apr 23, 1951 in Evanston, Illinois
Source: *AmAu&B; AmPolLe; ApCAB SUP, X; BiDInt; BiDrAC; BiDrUSC 89; BiDrUSE 71, 89; BioIn 1, 2, 3, 4, 5, 6, 7, 8, 9, 10, 11, 14, 15, 16; DcAmB S5; DcAmDH 80, 89; EncAB-H 1974, 1996; FacFETw; LinLib L, S; NatCAB 14, 42; OhA&B; OxCAmH; VicePre; WebAB 74, 79; WebBD 83; WhAm 3; WhAmP; WhLit; WhoNob, 90, 95; WorAl*

Dawes, Dominique (Margaux)
American. Gymnast
Member of bronze medal winning women's gymnastics team, 1992 Olympics.
b. Nov 20, 1976 in Silver Spring, Maryland
Source: *BioIn 20, 21; ConBlB 11; WhoAfA 96; WhoAmW 97; WhoBlA 94; WhoWor 97*

Dawes, William
American. Revolutionary
Rode with Paul Revere to warn of the British arrival, 1775.
b. Apr 6, 1745 in Boston, Massachusetts
d. Feb 25, 1799 in Boston, Massachusetts
Source: *Alli, SUP; AmBi; ApCAB; DcAmB; WebAMB; WhAm HS; WhAmRev*

Dawkins, Darryl
American. Basketball Player
Forward, Philadelphia, 1975-82, New Jersey, 1982-87; Utah, 1987—; set NBA record for personal fouls in season, 1984.
b. Jan 11, 1957 in Orlando, Florida
Source: *BasBi; BioIn 13, 14, 16; NewYTBS 82, 83, 84; OfNBA 87; WhoAfA 96; WhoBlA 80, 85, 88, 90, 92, 94*

Dawkins, Pete(r M)
American. Football Player
All-America halfback, Army, 1956-58; won Heisman Trophy, 1958; currently investment banker.
b. Mar 8, 1938 in Royal Oak, Michigan
Source: *BiDAmSp FB; BioIn 13, 14, 16; NewYTBS 83, 84, 86, 88; WhoFI 87; WhoFtbl 74*

Dawn, Hazel
"The Pink Lady"
American. Actor, Singer
Starred in Broadway musicals, 1911-20s; silent films, 1914-17.
b. Mar 23, 1898 in Ogden, Utah
d. Aug 28, 1988 in New York, New York
Source: *CmpEPM; EncMT; WhoHol A*

Dawson, Andre (Nolan)
"Hawk"
American. Baseball Player
Outfielder, Montreal 1976-86; Chicago, 1987-92; Boston, 1992-94; Florida, 1994—; NL rookie of year, 1977; led NL in home runs, RBIs, 1987; won NL MVP, 1987, first player ever from last place club.
b. Oct 7, 1954 in Miami, Florida
Source: *AfrAmSG; Ballpl 90; BaseReg 86, 87; BioIn 12, 13; NewYTBS 83; WhoAfA 96; WhoAm 96, 97; WhoBlA 85, 88, 90, 92, 94; WhoWor 96; WorAlBi*

Dawson, Bertrand Edward
[Viscount Dawson of Penn]
English. Physician
Physician to George V; physician-in-ordinary to Edward VIII, George VI, Edward VII.
b. Mar 9, 1864 in Croydon, England
d. Mar 7, 1945 in London, England

Source: *BioIn 14, 15; CurBio 45; DcNaB 1941; GrBr; OxCMed 86*

Dawson, Geoffrey
[George Geoffrey Dawson]
English. Editor
Edited the London *Times,* 1911-41.
b. Oct 25, 1874 in Skipton-in-Craven, England
d. Nov 7, 1944 in London, England
Source: *BioIn 4, 5; ChhPo S2; DcNaB 1941; EncSoA; GrBr; LngCTC; ObitOF 79; WhE&EA*

Dawson, George Mercer
Canadian. Geologist
Dawson City, Yukon's Gold Rush town and capital named for him; first to survey, map Canadian northwest.
b. Aug 1, 1849 in Pictou, Nova Scotia, Canada
d. Mar 2, 1901 in Ottawa, Ontario, Canada
Source: *Alli SUP; ApCAB; BioIn 11; Chambr 3; DcCanB 13; DcNAA; DcNaB S2; MacDCB 78; NewCol 75; OxCCan*

Dawson, John William, Sir
Canadian. Geologist
Pioneer in paleobotany; first president, Royal Society of Canada, 1882; wrote *The Ice Age in Canada,* 1894.
b. Oct 30, 1820 in Pictou, Nova Scotia, Canada
d. Nov 20, 1899 in Montreal, Quebec, Canada
Source: *Alli SUP; ApCAB; BbD; BbtC; BiD&SB; BioIn 2, 9; Chambr 3; DcBiPP; DcCanB 12; DcLEL; DcNAA; DcNaB S1; DcScB; IndAu 1967; InSci; LarDcSc; LinLib S; MacDCB 78; NewCol 75*

Dawson, Len
[Leonard Ray Dawson]
American. Football Player
Quarterback, 1957-75, mostly with Kansas City; 1970 Super Bowl MVP; Hall of Fame, 1987.
b. Jun 20, 1935 in Alliance, Ohio
Source: *BiDAmSp FB; BioIn 9, 10, 17; LegTOT; NewYTBE 70; WhoAm 82, 84; WhoFtbl 74; WorAl; WorAlBi*

Dawson, Richard
English. TV Personality
Starred in TV series "Hogan's Heroes," 1965-71; host of game show "Family Feud," 1976-85.
b. Nov 20, 1932 in Gosport, England
Source: *BioIn 12, 13, 20; ConTFT 8; LegTOT; WhoAm 84, 86, 88; WhoEnt 92; WhoHol 92, A; WorAl; WorAlBi*

Dawson, William L(evi)
American. Politician
Dem. rep. from IL, 1943-70; first black man to chair major House com.
b. Apr 26, 1886 in Albany, Georgia
d. Nov 9, 1970 in Chicago, Illinois
Source: *BiDrAC; BiDrUSC 89; BioIn 1, 4, 5, 7, 9, 10, 11, 17; BlkAmsC; CurBio 45, 70; DcAmB S8; InB&W 80; NewYTBE 70; PolProf E, J, K, T; WhAm 5*

Day, Benjamin Henry
American. Publisher
Founded *NY Sun,* 1833, the first one-cent daily paper.
b. Apr 10, 1810 in West Springfield, Massachusetts
d. Dec 21, 1889 in New York, New York
Source: *AmAu&B; AmBi; BiDAmJo; BioIn 7, 15, 16; DcAmB; DcLB 43; DcNAA; JrnUS; NatCAB 13; NewCol 75; TwCBDA; WebAB 74, 79; WebBD 83; WhAm HS*

Day, Chon
[Chauncey Addison Day]
American. Cartoonist, Author
Known for well-designed gag cartoons; books include *Brother Sebastian at Large,* 1961; cartoon Hall of Famer.
b. Apr 6, 1907 in Chatham, New Jersey
Source: *AmAu&B; WhAmArt 85; WhoAm 80, 82, 84, 86, 88, 90, 92, 94, 95, 96, 97; WhoAmA 73, 76, 78, 80, 82, 84, 86, 89, 91, 93; WhoE 75, 77; WorECar*

Day, Clarence Shepard, Jr.
American. Biographer, Essayist
His autobiography *Life With Father,* 1935, became America's longest-running play, 1940-50.
b. Nov 18, 1874 in New York, New York
d. Dec 28, 1935 in New York, New York
Source: *AmAu&B; ChhPo, S1; ConAmA; CyWA 58; DcAmB S1; DcLEL; DcNAA; EncAHmr; EvLB; LngCTC; OxCAmL 65; PenC AM; REn; REnAL; TwCA, SUP; TwCWr; WebAB 79; WhAm 1; WorAl*

Day, Dennis
[Eugene Denis McNulty]
American. Actor, Singer
Golden-voiced Irish tenor best known as comic target for Jack Benny on radio, TV, film.
b. May 21, 1917 in New York, New York
d. Jun 22, 1988 in Bel Air, California
Source: *AnObit 1988; BiDAmM; BioIn 1, 2, 3, 16; CmpEPM; FilmgC; ForYSC; HalFC 84; MotPP; News 88; NewYTBS 88; OxCPMus; PenEncP; RadStar; SaTiSS; WhoHol A*

Day, Doris
[Doris VonKappelhoff]
American. Actor, Singer
Starred in *The Pajama Game,* 1957; *Pillow Talk,* 1959; star of sit-com, "Doris Day Show," 1968-73.
b. Apr 3, 1924 in Cincinnati, Ohio
Source: *BiDAmM; BiDFilm, 81, 94; BioIn 1, 3, 4, 5, 6, 8, 10, 11, 12, 13, 14, 21; BioNews 74; BkPepl; BlueB 76; CelR, 90; CmMov; ContDcW 89; ConTFT 7; CurBio 54; DcArts; EncAFC; FilmEn; FilmgC; ForYSC; GoodHs; HalFC 80, 84, 88; IntDcF 1-3, 2-3; IntDcWB; IntMPA 75, 76, 77, 78, 79, 80, 81, 82, 84, 86, 88, 92, 94, 96; IntWW 82, 83, 89, 91, 93; InWom, SUP; LegTOT; MotPP; MovMk; NewGrDA 86; OxCFilm; RadStar; RkOn 74; WhoAm 74, 76, 78, 80, 82, 84, 86, 88, 90, 92, 94, 95, 96, 97; WhoAmW 58, 64, 66, 68, 70, 72, 74, 75; WhoCom; WhoEnt 92; WhoHol 92, A; WhoRock 81; WorAl; WorAlBi; WorEFlm*

Day, Dorothy
American. Editor
Founded Catholic Workers movement, 1933.
b. Nov 8, 1897 in New York, New York
d. Nov 29, 1980 in New York, New York
Source: *ABCMeAm; AmCath 80; AmDec 1930; AmRef; AmRef&R; AmSocL; AmWomWr; AnObit 1980; ArtclWW 2; BiDAmJo; BiDAmLf; BiDMoPL; BioAmW; BioIn 1, 2, 3, 6, 8, 9, 10, 11, 12, 13, 14, 15, 16, 17, 18, 19, 20, 21; BioNews 74; CathA 1930; CelR; ConAu 65, 102; ContDcW 89; CurBio 62, 81N; CyWA 89; DcAmB S10; DcAmReB 2; DcLB 29; EncAB-H 1996; EncAJ; EncARH; EncWB; EncWHA; FacFETw; FemiCLE; GoodHs; GrLiveH; HanAmWH; HeroCon; HerW 84; HisWorL; IntDcWB; InWom, SUP; JrnUS; LibW; LinLib L; LNinSix; NewYTBE 72; NewYTBS 80; OxCWoWr 95; RadHan; RAdv 14, 13-4; RComAH; RelLAm 91; SourALJ; TwCSAPR; WebAB 74, 79; WhAm 7; WhoAm 74, 76, 78, 80; WhoAmW 79; WhoE 74; WomComm; WomFir; WomPubS 1925; WorAl; WorAlBi*

Day, Frank
American. Artist, Historian
Maidu painter who had several exhibitions in California; choreographed movements of the traditional Maidu dances.
b. 1902 in Berry Creek, California
d. 1976
Source: *BioIn 21; NotNaAm*

Day, Hap
[Clarence Henry Day]
Canadian. Hockey Player
Left wing, 1924-38, mostly with Toronto; coached Toronto, 1940-50, to four Stanley Cups; Hall of Fame, 1961.
b. Jun 1, 1901 in Owen Sound, Ontario, Canada
d. Feb 1990
Source: *FacFETw; NewYTBS 90; WhoHcky 73*

Day, J(ames) Edward
American. Government Official
Postmaster general under JFK, 1961-63; implemented the Zone Improvement Plan (ZIP) code system, July 1, 1963.
b. Oct 11, 1914 in Jacksonville, Florida
d. Oct 29, 1996 in Hunt Valley, Maryland

Source: *BiDrUSE 71, 89; BioIn 5, 6, 7, 10, 11; BlueB 76; ConAu 17R, 154; CurBio 62; IntWW 74, 75, 76, 77, 78, 79, 80, 81, 82, 83; LinLib S; PolProf K; WhoAm 74, 76, 78, 80, 82, 84, 86, 88, 90, 92, 94, 95, 96, 97; WhoAmL 78, 79, 83, 90, 92, 94; WhoAmP 73, 75, 77, 79, 81, 83, 85, 87, 89, 91, 93, 95; WhoE 91*

Day, James Wentworth
English. Author, Publisher
Writings include *Farming Adventure,* 1943; *In Search of Ghosts,* 1969.
b. Apr 21, 1899 in Exning, England
d. 1983?, England
Source: *ConAu 10NR, 13R, 108; IntAu&W 76, 77; NewCBEL; WhLit; Who 74, 82, 83*

Day, John
English. Dramatist
Wrote allegorical masque *Parliament of Bees,* c. 1607.
b. 1574 in Norfolk, England
d. 1640?
Source: *BiD&SB; BioIn 3, 12, 16; BlmGEL; BritAu; CamGEL; CamGLE; CamGWoT; CasWL; CnThe; CroE&S; DcLB 62; EvLB; GrWrEL DR; NewC; NewCBEL; NewCol 75; NotNAT B; OxCEng 67, 85, 95; OxCThe 67, 83; PenC ENG; REn; REnWD; RfGEnL 91; WebE&AL*

Day, Joseph Paul
American. Real Estate Executive, Insurance Executive
Known for covering largest accident policy ever written, 1898; sold, in auction, over $1 million of real estate holdings, 1937.
b. Sep 22, 1873 in New York, New York
d. Apr 10, 1944 in New York, New York
Source: *BioIn 3; NatCAB 38; ObitOF 79; WhAm 2, 3*

Day, Laraine
[Laraine Johnson]
American. Actor
Played nurse Mary Lamont in *Dr. Kildare* film series, 1940s.
b. Oct 13, 1920 in Roosevelt, Utah
Source: *BioIn 1, 2, 3, 4, 9, 12; CurBio 53; FilmgC; HalFC 84, 88; IntMPA 75, 76, 77, 78, 79, 80, 81, 82, 84, 86, 92, 94, 96; InWom, SUP; MGM; MotPP; MovMk; ThFT; WhoAmW 58A, 68, 70, 72, 74; WhoHol A; WorAl*

Day, Pat
American. Jockey
Professional jockey, 1971—; won 6,000th horse race, Jan. 23, 1994.
b. Oct 13, 1953 in Brush, Colorado
Source: *BioIn 21; News 95, 95-2*

Day, Thomas
English. Author
Wrote children's didactic tale *Sandford and Merton,* 1783-89.
b. Jun 22, 1748 in London, England
d. Sep 28, 1789 in London, England
Source: *Alli; ApCAB; BbD; BiD&SB; BioIn 3, 5, 7, 8, 9, 11, 15; BritAu; CamGLE; CarSB; CasWL; ChhPo; CyEd; CyWA 58; DcBiPP; DcEnA; DcEnL; DcEuL; DcLB 39; DcNaB; Drake; EvLB; LitC 1; NewC; NewCBEL; OxCChiL; OxCEng 67, 85, 95; PenC ENG; WhoChL; YABC 1*

Day, William Rufus
American. Supreme Court Justice
Secretary of State, 1898; high-court judge, 1903-22.
b. Apr 17, 1849 in Ravenna, Ohio
d. Jul 9, 1923 in Mackinac Island, Michigan
Source: *AmBi; AmPolLe; ApCAB SUP, X; BiDFedJ; BiDrUSE 71, 89; BioIn 1, 2, 4, 5, 7, 10, 15, 16; DcAmB; DcAmDH 80, 89; FacFETw; HarEnUS; NatCAB 11, 32; OxCSupC; SupCtJu; TwCBDA; WebAB 74, 79; WebBD 83; WhAm 1*

Dayan, Assaf
Israeli. Actor
Son of Moshe Dayan; appeared in *The Day the Fish Came Out,* 1967.
b. 1945 in Afula, Palestine
Source: *BioIn 8; FilmEn; ItaFilm; WhoHol 92, A*

Dayan, Moshe
Israeli. Soldier, Statesman
Foreign affairs minister; hero of Six-Day War, 1967; negotiated Egypt-Israel peace treaty, 1979.
b. May 20, 1915 in Degania, Palestine
d. Oct 16, 1981 in Tel Aviv, Israel
Source: *AnObit 1981; BioIn 4, 7, 8, 9, 10, 11, 12, 13, 14, 15, 16, 17, 18, 19; CelR; ConAu 21R, 22NR, 105; CurBio 57, 82, 82N; DcMidEa; DcPol; DcTwHis; FacFETw; GenMudB; HarEnMi; HisEAAC; HisWorL; IntAu&W 77; IntWW 74, 75, 76, 77, 78, 79, 80, 81; IntYB 78, 79, 80, 81; LegTOT; LinLib L; McGEWB; MidE 78, 79, 80, 81; NewYTBE 70; NewYTBS 78, 81; PolLCME; WhDW; WhoMilH 76; WhoWor 74, 78, 80; WhoWorJ 72, 78; WorAl; WorAlBi; WorDWW*

Dayan, Yael
Israeli. Politician
Liberal member of the Knesset, 1992—; became first Knesset member to meet with PLO chairman Arafat, 1993.
b. Feb 12, 1939 in Nahalal, Palestine
Source: *AuNews 1; BioIn 8, 10, 14, 15; ConAu 89; WorAu 1950*

Daye, Stephen
English. Printer
First printer in American colonies: *Bay Psalm Book,* 1640.
b. 1594? in London, England
d. Dec 22, 1668 in Cambridge, England
Source: *AmBi; BenetAL 91; NewCol 75; OxCAmH; OxCAmL 65, 83, 95; REn; WebBD 83*

Day-Lewis, Cecil
[Nicholas Blake]
English. Poet, Author
Poet laureate, 1968, wrote numerous detective stories, verse collections.
b. Apr 27, 1904 in Ballintogher, Ireland
d. May 22, 1972 in London, England
Source: *Au&Wr 71; BioIn 3, 4, 5, 6, 8, 9, 10, 12, 13, 14, 17; BlmGEL; CasWL; ChhPo, S1, S3; CnE&AP; CnMWL; ConAu P-1, X; ConLC 1, 6, 10; ConNov 72; ConPo 70, 75; CorpD; CrtSuMy; DcArts; DcIrB 78, 88; DcLB 77; DcLEL; DcNaB 1971; EncMys; EncWL; EngPo; EvLB; GrBr; LinLib L, S; LngCTC; ModBrL, S1; NewC; NewCBEL; Novels; ObitT 1971; OxCEng 67, 85, 95; PenC ENG; PoIre; RAdv 1; REn; ScF&FL 1, 2; TwCA, SUP; TwCChW 78; TwCCr&M 80, 85, 91; TwCWr; WebE&AL; WhAm 5; WhDW; WhoTwCL*

Day-Lewis, Daniel Michael Blake
Irish. Actor
Won best actor Oscar, 1990, for *My Left Foot;* son of England poet laureate, Cecil Day-Lewis.
b. Apr 29, 1957 in London, England
Source: *BioIn 15, 16; ConTFT 6, 9; CurBio 90; FacFETw; HalFC 88; IntMPA 92; IntWW 91; News 89; WhoWor 91*

Dayne, Taylor
American. Singer, Songwriter
Pop vocalist; album *Can't Fight Fate,* 1989 with hit singles "With Every Beat of My Heart" and "Love Will Lead You Back."
b. Mar 7, 1963
Source: *ConMus 4*

Days, Drew S(aunders), III
American. Lawyer
Solicitor general, US Dept. of Justice, 1993—.
b. Aug 29, 1941 in Atlanta, Georgia
Source: *BioIn 11, 12; WhoAfA 96; WhoAm 78, 80, 82; WhoAmL 78, 79; WhoAmP 77, 79, 81, 83, 85, 87, 89, 91, 93, 95; WhoBlA 77, 80, 85, 90, 92, 94; WhoGov 77*

Dazz Band
[Bobby Harris; Keith Harrison; Sennie "Skip" Martin, III; Kenny Pettus; Isaac Wiley, Jr; Michael Wiley]
American. Music Group
Danceable jazz band; won Grammy, 1982, for "Let It Whip."
Source: *RkOn 85*

Deacon, Richard
American. Actor
Known for role of Mel Cooley in "The Dick Van Dyke Show," 1961-66.
b. May 14, 1922 in Philadelphia, Pennsylvania
d. Aug 9, 1984 in Los Angeles, California
Source: *BioIn 14; ConAu 113; EncAFC; FilmgC; MotPP; WhoHol A*

de Acosta, Mercedes
American. Poet, Dramatist
Circle of friends included Greta Garbo, Marlene Dietrich, and Andy Warhol; wrote script for Garbo entitled *Desperate.*
b. 1893
d. 1968
Source: *GayLesB*

Deak, Francis
"Sage of the Nation"
Hungarian. Statesman
Recognized leader of Hungary after defeat of revolution, 1849; fought for political emancipation.
b. Oct 17, 1803 in Sojtor, Hungary
d. Jan 28, 1876 in Budapest, Austria-Hungary
Source: *McGEWB; NewCol 75*

Dean, Arthur H(obson)
American. Lawyer, Government Official
Helped plan creation of Securities Exchange Act, 1938; Trust Indenture Act, 1939.
b. Oct 16, 1898 in Ithaca, New York
d. Nov 30, 1987 in Glen Cove, New York
Source: *BioIn 3, 4, 6, 11, 15, 16; BlueB 76; CurBio 54, 88; IntWW 74, 75, 76, 77, 78, 79, 80, 81, 82, 83; PolProf E, K; St&PR 75; WhAm 9; WhoAm 74, 76, 78, 80, 82; WhoAmL 78, 79; WhoWor 74*

Dean, Basil
English. Actor, Director
Pioneer in stage lighting, who founded Associated Talking Pictures, 1932.
b. Sep 27, 1888 in Croydon, England
d. Apr 22, 1978 in London, England
Source: *BioIn 9; BlueB 76; ConAu 69, 134; DcArts; EncEurC; EncWT; Film 2; FilmEn; FilmgC; HalFC 80, 84, 88; IlWWBF, A; IntDcF 1-4, 2-4; IntWW 74, 75, 76, 77, 78, 78N; ModWD; OxCThe 67; Who 74; WhoThe 81N; WhoWor 74; WhScrn 83; WhThe*

Dean, Christopher
[Torvill and Dean]
English. Skater
With Jayne Torvill, won gold medal in ice dancing, 1984 Olympics.
b. 1959? in Nottingham, England
Source: *BioIn 13, 15; FacFETw*

Dean, Daffy
[Paul Dee Dean]
American. Baseball Player
Pitcher, 1934-43; threw no-hitter, 1934; brother of Dizzy Dean.
b. Aug 14, 1913 in Lucas, Arkansas
d. Mar 17, 1981 in Springdale, Arkansas
Source: *BioIn 7, 12, 17; NewYTBS 81; WebAB 74, 79; WhoProB 73*

Dean, Dizzy
[Jay Hanna Dean]
American. Baseball Player, Sportscaster
Pitcher, 1930-41; won 30 games, 1934 (Denny McLain only pitcher to do it since, 1968); Hall of Fame, 1953.
b. Jan 16, 1911 in Lucas, Arkansas
d. Jul 17, 1974 in Reno, Nevada
Source: *Ballpl 90; BiDAmSp BB; BioIn 2, 3, 4, 5, 6, 7, 8, 9, 10, 13, 14, 15, 17, 18; CurBio 51, 74, 74N; DcAmB S9; FacFETw; LegTOT; NewYTBS 74; WebAB 74, 79; What 2; WhoProB 73; WhoSpor; WorAl; WorAlBi*

Dean, Gordon Evans
American. Banker, Government Official
Member of Lehman Brothers investment bankers, 1953-58; head of US Atomic Energy Commission, 1950-53; Medal of Freedom, 1946.
b. Dec 28, 1905 in Seattle, Washington
d. Aug 15, 1958 in Nantucket, Massachusetts
Source: *BioIn 2, 5, 6, 7; CurBio 58; DcAmB S6; DcAmNB; NatCAB 47, 56; WhAm 3*

Dean, Henry Trendley
American. Dentist
Director, National Institute of Dental Research, 1945-62.
b. Aug 25, 1893 in Winstanley Park, Illinois
d. May 13, 1962 in Chicago, Illinois
Source: *BioIn 4, 6; CurBio 62; WhAm 4*

Dean, Howard
American. Politician
Dem. governor, VT, 1991—.
b. Nov 17, 1948 in New York, New York
Source: *AlmAP 96; BiDrGov 1988; WhoAm 88, 90, 92, 94, 95, 96, 97; WhoAmP 91; WhoE 89, 91, 93, 95, 97; WhoWor 93, 95*

Dean, James Byron
American. Actor
Starred in *East of Eden,* 1955; *Rebel Without a Cause,* 1955; *Giant,* 1956; popular teen idol.
b. Feb 8, 1931 in Marion, Indiana
d. Sep 30, 1955 in Paso Robles, California
Source: *BiDFilm; FilmgC; MotPP; MovMk; OxCFilm; WhAm 4; WhoHol B; WhScrn 74, 77; WorEFlm*

Dean, Jimmy
[Seth Ward]
American. Singer
Country star, best known for song "Big Bad John," 1961.
b. Aug 10, 1928 in Plainview, Texas
Source: *BgBkCoM; BioIn 4, 7, 12, 14, 15; CounME 74, 74A; CurBio 65; Dun&B 86, 88, 90; EncFCWM 83; EncRk 88; HarEnCM 87; IlEncCM; IntMPA 75, 76, 77, 78, 79, 80, 81, 82, 84, 86, 88, 92, 94, 96; LegTOT; PenEncP; RkOn 74; St&PR 84, 87, 91, 93, 96, 97; WhoAm 82, 84, 86, 88, 90, 92, 94, 95, 96, 97; WhoHol 92, A; WhoRock 81; WhoWor 82; WorAl; WorAlBi*

Dean, John Gunther
American. Diplomat
Ambassador to Lebanon, 1978-81; directed pacification in Vietnam, 1970.
b. Feb 24, 1926, Germany
Source: *BioIn 10; BlueB 76; IntWW 74, 75, 76, 77, 78, 79, 80, 81, 82, 83, 89, 91, 93; IntYB 78, 79, 80, 81, 82; MidE 79, 80, 81; USBiR 74; WhoAm 74, 76, 78, 80, 82, 84, 86, 88, 90, 92, 94, 95, 96, 97; WhoAmP 75, 77, 79, 81, 83, 85, 87, 89, 91, 93, 95; WhoWor 80, 82, 87, 89*

Dean, John Wesley
American. Lawyer
Counsel to Richard Nixon, 1971-73; key prosecution witness in Watergate hearings; wrote *Blind Ambition,* 1976.
b. Oct 14, 1938 in Akron, Ohio
Source: *BioIn 9, 10, 11, 12, 13, 14, 15; ConAu 105; WhoAm 74, 76, 78, 80; WhoAmP 73; WhoGov 72; WorAl; WorAlBi*

Dean, Laura
American. Choreographer, Composer
Founded controversial Dean Dancers and Musicians, 1976; composed score for *E nochian,* 1983; known for trademark "spin."
b. Dec 3, 1945 in Staten Island, New York
Source: *BiDD; BioIn 11, 12, 13, 15, 16; CurBio 88; News 89; WhoAm 80, 82, 84, 86, 92; WhoAmW 91, 93; WhoE 83, 86*

Dean, Laura
American. Actor
Had first major role in film *Fame,* 1980.
b. May 27, 1963 in Smithtown, New York
Source: *BioIn 13; ConTFT 3; WhoHol 92*

Dean, Man Mountain
[Frank Simmons Leavitt]
American. Wrestler
Helped make professional wrestling popular with his exciting performances.
b. Jun 30, 1889 in New York, New York
d. May 29, 1953 in Norcross, Georgia
Source: *BioIn 3; DcAmB S5; WebAB 74; WebBD 83*

Dean, Morton
[Nissan Dean]
American. Broadcast Journalist
With CBS News since 1967; part-time anchor of "Newsbreak."
b. Aug 22, 1935 in Fall River, Massachusetts
Source: *ConAu 69; IntMPA 88, 92, 94, 96; WhoAm 86, 88; WhoTelC*

Dean, Patrick (Henry), Sir
English. Diplomat
British ambassador to US, 1965-69; International Adviser to American Express, 1969-94.
b. Mar 16, 1909 in Berlin, Germany
d. Nov 5, 1994 in Kingston, England
Source: *BioIn 5, 6, 7, 20, 21; BlueB 76; CurBio 61, 95N; IntWW 74, 75, 76, 77, 78, 79, 80, 81, 82, 83, 89, 91, 93; IntYB 78, 79, 80, 81, 82; Who 74, 82, 83, 85, 88, 92, 94; WhoWor 74, 76, 78*

Dean, William Frishe
American. Army Officer
Highest ranking officer held captive in Korean War, 1950-53.
b. Aug 1, 1899 in Carlyle, Illinois
d. Aug 24, 1981 in Berkeley, California
Source: *AnObit 1981; BiDWWGF; BioIn 12; CurBio 54, 81; DcAmMiB; MedHR 94; NewYTBS 81; WebAMB*

Deane, Sandy
[Jay and the Americans; Sandy Yaguda]
American. Singer
Part of clean-cut vocal quintet of 1960s.
b. Jan 30, 1943

Deane, Silas
American. Colonial Figure
Secret agent in France for American Revolution, 1776-78.
b. Dec 24, 1737 in Groton, Connecticut
d. Sep 23, 1789 in Deal, England
Source: *AmRev; AmWrBE; ApCAB; BiAUS; BiD&SB; BiDrAC; BiDrUSC 89; BioIn 2, 5, 10, 11, 12, 16; BlkwEAR; CyAG; DcAmAu; DcAmB; DcAmDH 80, 89; Drake; EncAB-H 1974, 1996; EncAI&E; EncAR; EncCRAm; HarEnUS; LegTOT; McGEWB; NatCAB 12; OxCAmH; TwCBDA; WebAB 74, 79; WhAm HS; WhAmP; WhAmRev; WorAl; WorAlBi*

DeAngeli, Marguerite Lofft
American. Children's Author, Illustrator
Won Newbery, 1950, for *A Door in the Wall.*
b. Mar 14, 1889 in Lapeer, Michigan
d. Jun 19, 1987 in Philadelphia, Pennsylvania
Source: *AmAu&B; AmWomWr; Au&ICB; Au&Wr 71; AuBYP 2; AuNews 2; BioIn 14; BkCL; ChhPo, S1; ChlLR 1; ConAu 3NR, 5R; ConICB; CurBio 47; HerW; IlsCB 1744, 1946, 1957; JBA 51; MorBMP; NewbMB 1922; SmATA 1, 27; WhoAm 74; WhoAmA 73*

Dearborn, Henry
American. Government Official
As secretary of War, ordered erection of fort at ''Chikago,'' 1803; Fort Dearborn named for him.
b. Feb 23, 1751 in Hampton, New Hampshire
d. Jun 4, 1829 in Roxbury, Massachusetts
Source: *AmBi; AmRev; ApCAB; BiAUS; BiDrAC; BiDrUSC 89; BiDrUSE 71, 89; BioIn 3, 10; CmdGen 1991; DcAmB; DcAmMeB; DcAmMiB; Drake; EncAR; EncCRAm; HarEnMi; HarEnUS; NatCAB 1; OxCAmH; TwCBDA; WebAB 74, 79; WebAMB; WhAm HS; WhAmP; WhAmRev; WhNaAH; WhoMilH 76*

Dearden, John Francis, Cardinal
American. Religious Leader
Archbishop of Detroit, 1959-80; as pres. of National Conference of Catholic Bishops, was key figure in transformation of US church after Vatican II.
b. Oct 15, 1907 in Valley Falls, Rhode Island
d. Aug 1, 1988 in Southfield, Michigan
Source: *AmCath 80; BioIn 2, 8, 10, 11; BlueB 76; CurBio 69, 88; IntWW 83; RelLAm 91; WhAm 9; WhoAm 74, 76, 78, 80, 82, 84, 86, 88; WhoMW 74, 76, 78, 80; WhoRel 75, 77; WhoWor 74, 84, 87*

Dearie, Blossom
American. Singer, Pianist, Songwriter
Supper-club singer; started Daffodil Records, 1974; first recipient of Mabel Mercer Foundation Award, 1985.
b. Apr 28, 1926 in East Durham, New York
Source: *AllMusG; BiDJaz; BioIn 9, 10, 12, 15, 16; CurBio 89; EncJzS; IntWW 91; InWom SUP; LegTOT; NewGrDA 86; NewGrDJ 88, 94; PenEncP*

Deaver, Michael Keith
American. Presidential Aide
Close adviser to Reagan, deputy chief of staff, 1981-85; involved in controversial lobbying activities.
b. Apr 11, 1938 in Bakersfield, California
Source: *BioIn 10, 13, 14, 15, 16; NewYTBS 81; WhoAm 82, 84, 86, 92, 94, 96; WhoAmP 85*

DeBakey, Michael Ellis
American. Surgeon
Pioneer heart surgeon; implanted first artificial heart in man, 1966; consulted on Russian president Boris Yeltsin's heart surgery, 1996.
b. Sep 7, 1908 in Lake Charles, Louisiana
Source: *AmMWSc 73P, 76P, 79, 82, 86, 89, 92, 95; BioIn 5, 6, 7, 8, 9, 10, 11, 12; BlueB 76; CelR 90; ConAu 73; CurBio 64; IntAu&W 76, 86, 91; IntWW 74, 75, 76, 77, 78, 79, 80, 81, 82, 83, 89, 91, 93; LEduc 74; LegTOT; McGEWB; McGMS 80; NewCol 75; NotTwCS; Who 74, 82, 83, 85, 88, 90, 92, 94; WhoAm 74, 76, 78, 80, 82, 84, 86, 88, 90, 92, 94, 95, 96, 97; WhoFrS 84; WhoMedH; WhoScEn 94, 96; WhoSSW 93, 95, 97; WhoTech 89; WhoWor 74, 76, 78, 80, 82, 84, 87, 89, 91, 93, 95, 96, 97; WorAl; WorAlBi; WrDr 76, 80, 82, 84, 86, 88, 90, 92, 94, 96*

DeBarentzen, Patrick
Danish. Fashion Designer
Opened ready-to-wear house, 1960-71; known for Roman fashions.
Source: *FairDF ITA; WorFshn*

DeBarge
[Bunny DeBarge; Eldra DeBarge; James DeBarge]
American. Music Group
Family singing group from Grand Rapids, MI; had hit single ''Rhythm of the Night,'' 1985.
Source: *BioIn 15; EncRkSt; PenEncP; RkOn 85; SoulM*

DeBarge, Bunny
American. Singer
Vocalist with family group.
b. Mar 10, 1955 in Grand Rapids, Michigan
Source: *LegTOT; RkOn 85*

DeBarge, El(dra)
American. Singer, Musician
Lead singer, keyboardist with family group; also produces group's records.
b. Jun 4, 1961 in Grand Rapids, Michigan
Source: *BioIn 15; LegTOT; RkOn 85; WhoAfA 96*

DeBarge, James
American. Singer, Musician
Vocalist, keyboardist with family group since 1982.
b. Aug 22, 1963 in Grand Rapids, Michigan
Source: *LegTOT*

DeBarge, Mark
American. Singer, Musician
Vocalist, who also plays trumpet and saxophone with family group.
b. Jun 19, 1959 in Grand Rapids, Michigan
Source: *LegTOT; RkOn 85*

DeBarge, Randy
American. Singer, Musician
Vocalist, bass player with family group.
b. Aug 6, 1958 in Grand Rapids, Michigan
Source: *LegTOT; RkOn 85*

DeBartolo, Edward J, Jr.
American. Football Executive
Owner, president, San Francisco 49ers, 1977—; chief administrative officer, DeBartolo Corp., 1979—.
b. Nov 6, 1946 in Youngstown, Ohio
Source: *News 89-3; NewYTBE 73; WhoAm 86, 90; WhoEmL 87; WhoFI 85; WhoMW 92; WhoWest 92*

DeBary, Heinrich Anton
German. Botanist
Founded science of mycology, plant pathology; coined word ''symbiosis,'' 1879.

b. Jan 26, 1831 in Frankfurt am Main, Germany
d. Jan 19, 1888 in Strassburg, Germany
Source: *DcScB; NewCol 75*

DeBeck, Billy
American. Cartoonist
Created comic character Barney Google.
b. Apr 15, 1890 in Chicago, Illinois
d. Nov 11, 1942 in New York, New York
Source: *BioIn 21; EncACom; LegTOT; WorECom*

De Benedetti, Carlo
Italian. Business Executive
As CEO of Olivetti and Co., rescued the corp. from bankruptcy, 1978; currently controls Mondadori-L'Espresso publishing group.
b. Nov 14, 1934 in Turin, Italy
Source: *BioIn 12, 14, 15, 16; CurBio 90; IntWW 79, 80, 81, 82, 83, 89, 91, 93; Who 88, 90, 92, 94; WhoWor 89, 91, 93; WorAlBi*

DeBernardi, Forrest S
"Red"
American. Basketball Player
Known for play on amateur teams, 1920s; Hall of Fame.
b. Mar 3, 1899 in Nevada, Missouri
d. Apr 29, 1970 in Dallas, Texas
Source: *BioIn 9; WhoBbl 73*

Deborah
Biblical Figure
Prophetess, heroine; author of "Song of Deborah" in Bible.
b. fl. 12BC
Source: *DcOrL 3; EncAmaz 91; InWom SUP; WebBD 83; WomWR*

Debost, Michel H
French. Musician
First flutist of Paris Orchestra since 1967; winner of numerous international awards.
b. Jan 20, 1934 in Paris, France
Source: *BriBkM 80; WhoMus 72*

Debray, Regis
[Jules Regis Debray]
French. Government Official
Radical leader in France; appointed as foreign policy adviser by the French pres.
b. Sep 2, 1940 in Paris, France
Source: *BiDNeoM; BioIn 8, 9, 12, 13; CurBio 82; DcCPSAm; EncLatA; IntWW 91, 93; NewYTBE 70; RadHan; WhoAm 74*

Debre, Michel (Jean Pierre)
French. Political Leader
Prime minister of France, 1959-62; Minister of Defense, 1969-73.
b. Jan 15, 1912 in Paris, France
d. Aug 2, 1996 in Montlouis-sur-Loire, France
Source: *BiDFrPL; BioIn 4, 5, 6, 7, 9, 12, 17, 21; CurBio 59, 96N; DcPol; IntAu&W 77, 82; IntWW 74, 75, 76, 77, 78, 79, 80, 81, 82, 83, 89, 91, 93; IntYB 78, 79, 80, 81, 82; NewYTBS 27; PolLCWE; WhDW; Who 85, 92; WhoEIO 82; WhoFr 79; WhoWor 74, 76, 78; WorDWW*

Debrett, John
English. Publisher
Published *Peerage of England, Scotland, Ireland,* 1802; *Baronetage of England,* 1808.
b. 1752
d. 1822
Source: *Alli; Benet 87; BiDLA; NewC; REn; WebBD 83*

Debreu, Gerard
American. Economist
Won Nobel Prize in economics, 1983.
b. Jul 4, 1921 in Calais, France
Source: *AmEA 74; AmMWSc 73S, 78S, 82, 86, 89, 92, 95; BioIn 13, 14, 15; BlueB 76; ConAu 23NR, 37R; GrEconS; IntAu&W 77; IntWW 89, 91, 93; NobelP; Who 85, 88, 92, 94; WhoAm 74, 76, 78, 80, 82, 84, 86, 88, 90, 92, 94, 95, 96, 97; WhoEc 81, 86; WhoFI 85, 87, 89, 92, 94; WhoNob, 90, 95; WhoScEn 96; WhoTech 84, 89; WhoWest 84, 87, 89, 92, 94, 96; WhoWor 87, 89, 91, 93, 95, 96, 97; WorAlBi; WrDr 80, 82, 84, 86, 88, 90, 92, 94, 96*

DeBroca, Philippe Claude Alex
French. Filmmaker
Identified with sophisticated, eccentric comedies: *Le Cavaleur,* 1979.
b. Mar 15, 1933 in Paris, France
Source: *BiDFilm; BioIn 16; ConAu 126; DcFM; FilmgC; HalFC 88; IntMPA 82, 92; MovMk; OxCFilm; WhoWor 74; WorAl; WorAlBi; WorEFlm*

Debs, Eugene Victor
American. Political Leader, Labor Union Official
Founded Social Democratic Party, 1897; ran for pres. five times as socialist.
b. Nov 5, 1855 in Terre Haute, Indiana
d. Oct 20, 1926 in Elmhurst, Illinois
Source: *AmBi; AmLY; AmPeW; AmPolLe; AmRef; AmRef&R; AmSocL; ApCAB X; BiDAmL; BiDAmLL; BiDMoPL; BiDNeoM; BioIn 1, 2, 3, 4, 5, 6, 7, 8, 9, 10, 11, 12, 13; CyAG; DcAmB; DcAmSR; DcNAA; EncAB-H 1974, 1996; EncABHB 2; HarEnUS; HeroCon; IndAu 1816; LinLib S; McGEWB; NatCAB 12; OxCAmH; OxCAmL 65, 83, 95; REn; REnAL; TwCBDA; WebAB 74, 79; WhAm 1; WorAl*

Debus, Kurt Heinrich
American. Government Official
Director of NASA's Cape Canaveral, 1952-74.
b. Nov 29, 1908 in Frankfurt am Main, Germany
d. Oct 10, 1983 in Cocoa, Florida
Source: *AmMWSc 79; AnObit 1983; BioIn 5, 10, 13; BlueB 76; CurBio 73, 83N; FacFETw; IntWW 74, 75, 76, 77, 78, 79, 80, 81, 82, 83; NewYTBS 83; WhAm 8; WhoAm 74, 76; WhoGov 72, 75; WhoSSW 73, 75, 76; WhoWor 74*

Debus, Sigurd Friedrich
German. Terrorist
Red Army extremist who starved to death striking for better prison conditions, 1981.
b. 1943
d. Apr 16, 1981 in Hamburg, Germany (West)
Source: *BioIn 12*

DeBusschere, Dave
[David Albert DeBusschere]
"The Buffalo"
American. Basketball Player
Forward, Detroit, 1962-69, NY Knicks, 1969-73; youngest coach in NBA history, 1964-67; commissioner of ABA, 1975-76; Hall of Fame, 1982.
b. Oct 16, 1940 in Detroit, Michigan
Source: *Ballpl 90; BasBi; BiDAmSp BK; BioIn 7, 10, 12, 13, 14; BioNews 75; CelR; CurBio 73; LegTOT; NewYTBS 82, 85; OfNBA 87; WhoAm 74, 76, 78, 80, 84; WhoBbl 73; WhoE 86; WorAl; WorAlBi*

Debussy, Claude Achille
French. Composer
Creator of musical impressionism; wrote opera *Pelleas et Melisande,* 1902 ; piano piece "Clair de Lune," 1905.
b. Aug 22, 1862 in Saint-Germain-en-Laye, France
d. Mar 25, 1918 in Paris, France
Source: *AtlBL; Baker 84; CompSN; DcCM; MakMC; MusSN; NewGrDM 80; OxCFr; OxCMus; REn; WhDW; WorAl*

DeButts, John Dulany
American. Business Executive
Major influence in telecommunications; joined ATT, 1949; served as director, 1967-81.
b. Apr 10, 1915 in Greensboro, North Carolina
d. Dec 17, 1986 in Winchester, Virginia
Source: *BioIn 11, 14; IntWW 83; LElec; NewYTBS 86; St&PR 87; WhoAm 74, 76, 78, 80, 82, 84, 86; WhoE 74, 75, 77, 79; WhoFI 74, 75, 77, 79; WhoSSW 82, 84*

Debye, Peter Joseph William
American. Chemist
Won Nobel Prize, 1936, for development of theory of dipole movements, diffraction of X-rays.
b. Mar 24, 1884 in Maastricht, Netherlands
d. Nov 2, 1966 in Ithaca, New York
Source: *BiESc; BioIn 2, 3, 4, 6, 7, 8, 9, 11; CurBio 63, 67; DcAmB S8; DcScB; McGEWB; McGMS 80; WhAm 4; WhoNob; WorAl*

DeCamp, L(yon) Sprague
American. Author
Wrote many science-fiction *Conan* books based on character created by Robert E Howard; won Grand Master of Fantasy Award, 1976.
b. Nov 27, 1907 in New York, New York
Source: *AuBYP 2, 3; BenetAL 91; ConAu 1NR, 1R, 20NR; DcLB 8; DcLP 87A; IntAu&W 91; IntvTCA 2; ScFSB; SmATA 9; SupFW; TwCSFW 86, 91; WhoAm 86, 90; WhoUSWr 88; WhoWrEP 89; WorAlBi; WorAu 1950; WrDr 86, 92*

DeCamp, Rosemary
American. Actor
Radio, TV performer; films include *Yankee Doodle Dandy,* 1942.
b. Nov 14, 1910 in Prescott, Arizona
Source: *EncAFC; HalFC 88; IntMPA 92; MotPP; MusMk; RadStar; WhoAm 90; WhoEnt 92; WhoHol A*

Decamps, Alexandre Gabriel
French. Artist
Known for introducing aspect of Orientalism in French art.
b. Mar 3, 1803 in Paris, France
d. Aug 22, 1860 in Fontainebleau, France
Source: *ArtsNiC; BioIn 5, 11; DcBiPP; LinLib S; NewCol 75; WebBD 83*

DeCaprio, Leonardo
American. Actor
Was in *Parenthood,* 1990.
b. 1975

DeCarava, Roy
[Rudolph DeCarava]
American. Photographer
Known for photographs of New York City life.
b. Dec 9, 1919 in New York, New York
Source: *BioIn 21; News 96, 96-3*

DeCarlo, Yvonne
[Peggy Yvonne Middleton]
Canadian. Actor
Played Lily on TV series "The Munsters," 1964-66.
b. Sep 1, 1922 in Vancouver, British Columbia, Canada
Source: *BiDFilm; BioIn 15; CmMov; ConTFT 7; FilmgC; HalFC 84, 88; IntMPA 86, 92; InWom SUP; MotPP; MovMk; PlP&P A; WhoHol A; WorAlBi; WorEFlm*

Decatur, Stephen
American. Naval Officer
Headed navy crew that captured warship *Philadelphia,* 1804; hero of Barbary Wars, 1801-05, War of 1812.
b. Jan 5, 1779 in Sinepuxent, Maryland
d. Mar 22, 1820 in Bladensburg, Maryland
Source: *AmBi; ApCAB; BenetAL 91; BioIn 1, 2, 3, 4, 6, 7, 8, 9, 11, 13, 16; CelCen; DcAmB; DcAmMiB; Drake; EncSoH; GenMudB; HarEnMi; HarEnUS; LinLib S; McGEWB; NatCAB 4; OxCAmH; OxCShps; PeoHis; REn; TwCBDA; WebAB 74, 79; WebAMB; WhAm HS; WhoMilH 76; WorAl; WorAlBi*

Decker, Alonzo G
American. Businessman
Formed business, 1907, with S Duncan Black; produced first electric drill, 1914.
b. Jan 16, 1884 in Baltimore, Maryland
d. Mar 18, 1956 in Towson, Maryland
Source: *BioIn 2; Entr; NatCAB 46; WhAm 3*

Deckers, Jeanine
"The Singing Nun"
Belgian. Religious Figure, Singer
Had hit single "Dominique," 1963; movie *The Singing Nun,* 1966, based on her life.
b. 1933
d. Mar 31, 1985 in Wavre, Belgium
Source: *BioIn 7, 9, 10; ConAu 115*

Decker Slaney, Mary
[Mrs. Richard Slaney]
American. Track Athlete
Once held world record in 5,000 meter run (15:08:26).
b. Aug 4, 1958 in Bunnvale, New Jersey
Source: *BiDAmSp OS; BioIn 13, 14, 15, 16; CelR 90; ContDcW 89; CurBio 83; InWom SUP; NewYTBS 84; WhoAm 84; WhoAmW 85, 87*

DeConcini, Dennis Webster
American. Politician
Dem. senator from AZ, 1977-95.
b. May 8, 1937 in Tucson, Arizona
Source: *AlmAP 80, 92; BiDrUSC 89; BioIn 16; CngDr 87, 89; CurBio 92; IntWW 83, 91; NewYTBS 78; PolsAm 84; WhoAm 86, 90; WhoAmL 79; WhoAmP 85, 91; WhoGov 77; WhoWest 78, 92; WhoWor 87, 91*

DeCordoba, Pedro
American. Actor
Character actor in films, 1915-50, including *Winner Take All,* 1939.
b. Sep 28, 1881 in New York, New York
d. Sep 17, 1950 in Sunland, California
Source: *Film 1; FilmgC; MotPP; MovMk; TwYS; WhoHol B; WhScrn 74, 77; WhThe*

DeCordova, Frederick Timmins
American. Producer
With CBS, NBC, 1953—; won Emmys for "The Tonight Show," 1970s.
b. Oct 27, 1910 in New York, New York
Source: *BioIn 14, 15; ConNews 85-2; ConTFT 7; FilmgC; HalFC 88; IntMPA 92; LesBEnT; WhoAm 86, 90; WhoEnt 92*

Decoster, Charles Theodore Henri
Belgian. Author
Wrote one of the most important works in French-Belgian literature: *La Legen de d'Thyl Ulenspiegel,* 1867.
b. Aug 20, 1827 in Munich, Germany
d. May 7, 1879 in Brussels, Belgium
Source: *BbD; BiD&SB; CasWL; ClDMEL 47; EuAu*

DeCreeft, Jose
American. Sculptor
Works of bronze include Alice in Wonderland 16 foot group, NY, 1957; works exhibited in museums.
b. Nov 27, 1884 in Guadalajara, Spain
d. Sep 10, 1982 in New York, New York
Source: *BioIn 1, 5, 9; BriEAA; CurBio 42; DcAmArt; DcCAA 71, 77; McGDA; WhAm 7; WhAmArt 85; WhoAm 74, 76, 78; WhoAmA 73, 76, 78, 80, 82, 84N*

Decter, Midge
American. Journalist, Writer
Exec. director, Committee for Free World, 1980-90; distinguished fellow, Institute on Religion and Public Life, 1991-95; writings include *Liberal Parents, Radical Children,* 1975.
b. Jul 25, 1927 in Saint Paul, Minnesota
Source: *BioIn 13, 15; CelR 90; ConAu 2NR, 45; CurBio 82; IntAu&W 77; InWom SUP; WhoAm 74, 76, 78, 80, 82, 84, 86, 88, 90, 92, 94, 95, 96, 97; WhoAmW 77, 83; WhoE 74; WhoUSWr 88; WhoWrEP 89, 92, 95; WrDr 76, 80, 82, 84, 86, 88, 90, 92*

DeCuevas, Marquis
American. Ballet Promoter
Colorful ballet impressario; produced extravagant Parisian productions.
b. May 26, 1885 in Santiago, Chile
d. Feb 22, 1961 in Cannes, France
Source: *DcAmB S7*

De Cuir, John
American. Art Director
Won Oscars for *Cleopatra,* 1963; *Hello, Dolly,* 1969; other films include *Ghostbusters,* 1984.
b. Jun 4, 1918 in San Francisco, California
Source: *BioIn 14; FilmEn; FilmgC; HalFC 80, 84, 88; IntMPA 77, 80, 86, 92; VarWW 85*

Dederich, Charles (Edwin)
American. Social Reformer
Founder, Synanon Foundation, Inc., 1958.
b. Mar 22, 1913 in Toledo, Ohio
d. Feb 28, 1997 in Visalia, California
Source: *WhoAm 78*

Dedijer, Vladimir
Yugoslav. Author
Writings include *Letters from America,* 1945; *Sarajevo: 1914,* 1966.
b. Feb 2, 1914 in Belgrade, Yugoslavia

Source: *Au&Wr 71; BioIn 3, 4, 5, 6, 9, 14, 17; ConAu 1R, 4NR, 133; IntAu&W 76, 77, 89; IntWW 74, 75, 76, 77, 78, 79, 80, 81, 82, 83, 89, 91N; NewYTBS 90; WhAm 10; Who 74, 82, 83, 85, 88, 90, 92N; WhoSocC 78; WhoSoCE 89; WhoWor 74, 84, 87, 89, 91*

Dedman, Robert H
American. Businessman, Philanthropist
World's largest owner, operator of private clubs.
b. 1926 in Rison, Arkansas
Source: *BioIn 15; Dun&B 86, 88, 90; NewYTBS 86; WhoAm 90*

DeDuve, Christian Rene Marie Joseph
American. Chemist
Shared 1974 Nobel Prize in medicine for cellular research.
b. Oct 2, 1917 in Thames Ditton, England
Source: *AmMWSc 92; BiESc; BioIn 14, 15; IntWW 91; NobelP; Who 85, 92; WhoAm 90; WhoE 89; WhoNob, 90; WhoWor 84, 91*

Dee, Frances
[Mrs. Joel McCrea]
American. Actor
Co-starred in *The Playboy of Paris,* 1930, with Maurice Chevalier.
b. Nov 26, 1907 in Los Angeles, California
Source: *BioIn 10, 11, 12; EncAFC; FilmEn; FilmgC; ForYSC; HalFC 88; HolP 30; InWom SUP; LegTOT; MotPP; MovMk; ThFT; What 5; WhoHol 92, A; WomWMM*

Dee, John
English. Magician
Practiced magic to entertain; imprisoned for insulting Mary Tudor; released, 1555; wrote on math, astrology.
b. Jul 13, 1527 in London, England
d. Dec 1608 in Mortlake, England
Source: *Alli; Benet 87, 96; BioIn 1, 2, 3, 4, 6, 7, 8, 9, 11, 16, 20; BritAu; CroE&S; DcBiPP; DcLB 136; DcNaB; DcScB; DivFut; EncO&P 1, 2, 3; EncWW; Geog 10; HisDBrE; InSci; LarDcSc; LitC 20; NewC; NewCBEL; NewCol 75; OxCEng 67, 85, 95; OxCLiW 86; OxCMed 86; REn; WhDW*

Dee, Kiki
[Pauline Matthews]
English. Singer
Rock vocalist; formed own band, 1970s; was teamed with Elton John.
b. Mar 6, 1947 in Bradford, England
Source: *BkPepl; EncRk 88; IlEncRk; InWom SUP; LegTOT; PenEncP; RkOn 74, 78; WhoRock 81; WhoRocM 82*

Dee, Ruby
[Mrs. Ossie Davis; Ruby Ann Wallace]
American. Actor
Starred in stage, movie productions of *Raisin in the Sun,* 1959, 1961.
b. Oct 27, 1924 in Cleveland, Ohio
Source: *BiE&WWA; BioIn 5, 6, 9, 10, 12, 13, 16; BlkAWP; BlksAmF; BlksB&W, C; BlkWAm; BlkWr 1; CamGWoT; CelR, 90; ConAu X; ConBlAP 88; ConBlB 8; ConTFT 1, 9; CurBio 70; DcTwCCu 5; DrBlPA 90; Ebony 1; FilmEn; FilmgC; HalFC 84, 88; InB&W 85; IntMPA 82, 84, 86, 88, 92, 94, 96; InWom SUP; MotPP; MovMk; NegAl 89; NewYTBE 70; NotBlAW 1; NotNAT; NotWoAT; WhoAm 86, 90; WhoBlA 75, 88, 92; WhoEnt 92; WhoHol 92, A; WhoThe 81; WomWMM; WorAl; WorAlBi*

Dee, Sandra
[Alexandra Zuck]
American. Actor, Singer
Starred in *Gidget,* 1959; *Tammy Tell Me True,* 1961; was married to Bobby Darin.
b. Apr 23, 1942 in Bayonne, New Jersey
Source: *BioIn 11, 16, 17, 20; EncAFC; FilmEn; FilmgC; ForYSC; HalFC 80, 84, 88; IntMPA 75, 76, 77, 78, 79, 80, 81, 82, 84, 86, 88, 92, 94, 96; InWom, SUP; ItaFilm; LegTOT; MotPP; MovMk; WhoAmW 74; WhoHol 92, A; WorAl; WorAlBi*

Deee-Lite
American. Music Group
Combined dance music with 1970's funk; album *World Clique,* 1990 and single "Groove is in the Heart," earned gold records.
Source: *BioIn 17; ConMus 9; SoulM*

Deeping, (George) Warwick
English. Author
Novels include *Sorrell and Son,* 1925; *Old Pybus,* 1928.
b. May 28, 1877 in Southend, England
d. Apr 20, 1950 in Weybridge, England
Source: *BioIn 2, 4, 7, 14, 21; CamGLE; ConAu 114; DcLB 153; DcLEL; EncSF 93; EvLB; LngCTC; NewC; NewCBEL; Novels; OxCEng 85, 95; OxCMed 86; PenC ENG; REn; ScF&FL 1; TwCA, SUP; TwCRGW; TwCRHW 90, 94; TwCWr; WhE&EA; WhLit; WhoLA*

Deep Purple
[Ritchie Blackmore; Thomas Bolin; David Coverdale; Rod Evans; Roger Glover; Glenn Hughs; Jon Lord; Ian Paige; Nicholas Simper]
American. Music Group
Heavy rock band, formed 1968; hits include "Black Night," 1970.
Source: *BiDAmM; BioIn 15; ConMuA 80A; ConMus 11; EncPR&S 74, 89; EncRk 88; EncRkSt; HarEnR 86; IlEncRk; NewAmDM; OxCPMus; PenEncP; RkOn 78, 84; RolSEnR 83; WhoRock 81; WhoRocM 82*

Deer, Ada E(lizabeth)
American. Government Official
Assistant Secretary for Indian Affairs, Dept. of the Interior, 1993—.
b. Aug 7, 1935 in Keshena, Wisconsin
Source: *CurBio 94; WhoAmP 79, 81, 83, 85, 87, 89, 91, 93, 95*

Deer, Rob(ert George)
American. Baseball Player
Outfielder, 1984—; hit 33 home runs, 1986.
b. Sep 29, 1960 in Orange, California
Source: *Ballpl 90; BaseReg 86, 87; BioIn 15; LegTOT*

DeErdely, Francis
[Ferenc DeErdely]
Hungarian. Artist, Educator
Work permanently exhibited in museums in US, Australia, France, Spain, Belgium.
b. May 3, 1904 in Budapest, Austria-Hungary
d. Nov 28, 1959 in Los Angeles, California
Source: *DcCAA 71; WhAm 4; WhoAmA 82N*

Deere, John
American. Industrialist
Developed, manufactured steel plow, 1837; incorporated Deere and Co., 1868.
b. Feb 7, 1804 in Rutland, Vermont
d. May 17, 1886 in Moline, Illinois
Source: *AmBi; ApCAB X; BiDAmBL 83; BioIn 1, 2, 7, 11, 13, 14, 16, 17, 21; DcAmB; EncAAH; EncAB-A 9; EncAB-H 1974, 1996; Entr; InSci; LegTOT; McGEWB; NatCAB 20; WebAB 74, 79; WhAm HS; WorInv*

Deering, William
American. Manufacturer
Pres., Deering Harvester Co., 1879-1902; merged with International Harvester Co., 1902.
b. Apr 25, 1826 in Paris, Maine
d. Dec 9, 1913 in Coconut Grove, Florida
Source: *AmBi; ApCAB X; BiDAmBL 83; BioIn 15; DcAmB; EncAAH; McGEWB; NatCAB 11; TwCBDA; WhAm 1*

Dees, Morris S(eligman), Jr.
American. Lawyer, Social Reformer
Co-founder, Southern Poverty Law Center, 1971; became target of violence by hate groups for winning millions in civil trials against the Ku Klux Klan and the White Aryan Resistance.
b. Dec 16, 1936 in Mount Meigs, Alabama
Source: *BioIn 7; CurBio 95; News 92, 92-1; WhoAm 76, 78, 80, 82, 84, 90, 92, 95, 96, 97; WhoAmL 78, 79, 92, 94; WhoSSW 93; WhoWor 80, 91*

Defauw, Desire
Belgian. Conductor
Led Chicago Symphony, 1943-47; Gary Orchestra, 1950-58.
b. Sep 5, 1885 in Ghent, Belgium
d. Jul 25, 1960 in Gary, Indiana

Source: *Baker 78, 84, 92; BiDAmM; BioIn 4, 5; CurBio 40, 60; NewAmDM; NewGrDA 86; NewGrDM 80; PenDiMP; WhAm 4*

Defeo, Ronald
American. Murderer
Killing of parents, siblings known as "Amityville Horror"; Long Island, NY house supposedly haunted; subject of films.
b. Sep 26, 1951 in New York, New York
Source: *BioIn 10, 12*

Def Leppard
[Rick Allen; Steve Clark; Phil Collen; Joe Elliott; Rick Savage]
British. Music Group
Heavy metal, new wave group formed 1977; hit singles include "Rock of Ages," 1983; "Pour Some Sugar on Me," 1987.
Source: *BioIn 17, 19; ConMus 3; EncRk 88; EncRkSt; HarEnR 86; IlEncRk; PenEncP; RkOn 85; RolSEnR 83; St&PR 96; WhoAmP 91, 93, 95; WhoHol 92; WhoRocM 82*

Defoe, Daniel
English. Author
Wrote *Robinson Crusoe,* 1719, based on adventures of Alexander Selkirk.
b. Apr 26, 1660 in London, England
d. Apr 26, 1731 in London, England
Source: *Alli; AtlBL; BbD; Benet 87, 96; BiD&SB; BioIn 4, 5, 6, 7, 8, 9, 10, 11, 12, 13; BlkwCE; BlmGEL; BritAu; BritWr 3; CamGEL; CamGLE; CarSB; CasWL; Chambr 2; ChhPo S1; CnDBLB 2; CrtT 2, 4; CyWA 58; DcArts; DcBiA; DcEnA; DcEnL; DcEuL; DcLB 39, 95, 101; DcLEL; DcPup; EncEnl; EncSF, 93; EvLB; FilmgC; GrWrEL N; HalFC 80, 84; HsB&A; LegTOT; LiJour; LinLib L, S; LitC 1; LngCEL; LuthC 75; MagSWL; MajAI; McGEWB; MnBBF; MouLC 2; NewC; NewCBEL; Novels; OxCChiL; OxCEng 67, 85, 95; OxCShps; PenC ENG; RAdv 1, 14; RComWL; REn; RfGEnL 91; ScFEYrs; SmATA 22; WebE&AL; WhDW; WhoChL; WhoHr&F; WorAl; WorAlBi; WorLitC*

Deford, Frank
American. Journalist
Columnist, *Sports Illustrated,* 1962-90; editor of *The National,* a daily sports newspaper, 1990-91.
b. Dec 16, 1938 in Baltimore, Maryland
Source: *Au&Arts 14; BiDAmSp Sup; BioIn 13; ConAu 33R, 45NR; CurBio 96; IntAu&W 89, 91, 93; WhoAm 86, 88, 90, 92; 94, 95, 96, 97; WhoEnt 92; WrDr 76, 80, 82, 84, 86, 88, 90, 92, 94, 96*

DeFore, Don
American. Actor
Appeared in TV shows "Adventures of Ozzie and Harriet," 1952-58, "Hazel," 1961-65.
b. Aug 25, 1917 in Cedar Rapids, Iowa
Source: *BiE&WWA; ConTFT 4; EncAFC; FilmgC; HalFC 88; LegTOT; MotPP; MovMk; NotNAT; VarWW 85; WhoAm 74; WhoHol A*

DeForest, Calvert
American. Actor
Noted for playing Larry "Bud" Melman on NBC's "Late Night With David Letterman."
b. 1923 in New York, New York

DeForest, Lee
"Father of the Radio"
American. Inventor
Patented over 300 inventions, including key component of radio before invention of transistor.
b. Aug 26, 1873 in Council Bluffs, Iowa
d. Jun 30, 1961 in Hollywood, California
Source: *AmDec 1900; ApCAB X; AsBiEn; BiESc; BioIn 1, 2, 3, 4, 5, 6, 7, 8, 9, 11, 12, 13; CmCal; ConAu 112; CurBio 41, 61; DcAmB S7; DcScB; EncAB-H 1974; EncAJ; FacFETw; FilmEn; FilmgC; HalFC 80, 84, 88; InSci; LarDcSc; LegTOT; LinLib S; McGEWB; MemAm; NatCAB 13, 17, 58; NewYTET; NotTwCS; ObitT 1961; OxCAmH; SaTiSS; WebAB 74, 79; WhAm 4; WhDW; WorAl; WorAlBi; WorEFlm; WorInv*

DeFranco, Buddy
American. Jazz Musician, Bandleader
Outstanding modern-style clarinetist with name bands, 1940s-50s; led Glenn Miller band, 1966-74.
b. Feb 17, 1923 in Camden, New Jersey
Source: *AllMusG; Baker 84; BiDJaz; BioIn 15, 16, 19; CmpEPM; EncJzS; IlEncJ; NewAmDM; NewGrDA 86; NewGrDJ 88, 94; PenEncP; WorAl; WorAlBi*

DeFrank, Vincent
American. Conductor
Founder, leader of Memphis Symphony, 1952-84; conductor emeritus, 1984—.
b. Jun 18, 1915 in Long Island, New York
Source: *IntWWM 90; WhoAm 86, 90; WhoSSW 73, 86*

DeFreeze, Donald David
[S(ymbionese) L(iberation) A(rmy)]
"Cinque"
American. Revolutionary
Leader of terrorist group that kidnapped Patricia Hearst, 1974.
b. Nov 16, 1943 in Cleveland, Ohio
d. May 24, 1974 in Los Angeles, California
Source: *BioNews 74; NewYTBS 74*

De Gaetani, Jan
American. Singer
Versatile mezzo-soprano, leading interpreter of new vocal music known for chamber, orchestral performances.
b. Jul 10, 1933 in Massillon, Ohio
d. Sep 15, 1989 in Rochester, New York
Source: *AnObit 1989; Baker 78, 84; BioIn 14, 16; CurBio 77, 89N; InWom SUP; NewAmDM; NewGrDA 86; NewYTBE 73; NewYTBS 81; PenDiMP; WhAm 10; WhoAm 86, 88*

Deganawida
Canadian. Native American Leader
Founded, with Hiawatha, the League of the Iroquois.
b. 1550? in Kingston, Ontario, Canada
d. 1600?
Source: *BioIn 21; NotNaAm*

Degas, (Hilaire Germain) Edgar
French. Artist
Impressionist painter whose favorite subjects were ballet dancers, cafe life.
b. Jul 19, 1834 in Paris, France
d. Sep 27, 1917 in Paris, France
Source: *AtlBL; Benet 87, 96; BiDD; BioIn 1, 2, 3, 4, 5, 6, 7, 8, 9, 10, 11, 12, 13, 14, 15, 16, 17, 19, 20, 21; ClaDrA; CnOxB; DancEn 78; DcArts; DcNiCA; Dis&D; IntDcAA 90; LegTOT; LinLib S; McGDA; McGEWB; ModArCr 3; NewC; OxCFr; OxDcArt; PhDcTCA 77; REn; WhAm 4, HSA; WhDW; WorAl; WorAlBi*

De Gasperi, Alcide
Italian. Statesman, Political Leader
Progressive prime minister, 1945-53, who brought Italy into NATO, tried major reforms.
b. Apr 3, 1881 in Terentino, Italy
d. Aug 19, 1954 in Sella Val Suguna, Italy
Source: *BiDInt; CurBio 46, 54; DcPol; DcTwHis; EncCW; FacFETw; HisEWW; LinLib S; McGEWB; NewCol 75; ObitT 1951; PolLCWE; WebBD 83; WhAm 3; WorAl; WorAlBi*

DeGaulle, Charles Andre Joseph Marie
French. Political Leader
Army general, 1940, who assumed leadership after WW II; first pres., Fifth Republic, 1959-69.
b. Nov 22, 1890 in Lille, France
d. Nov 9, 1970 in Colombey les deux Eglises, France
Source: *BioIn 10; CurBio 40, 49, 60, 70; REn; WhAm 5*

DeGeneres, Ellen
American. Actor, Comedian
Star of ABC's "Ellen," 1994—.
b. Jan 26, 1958 in Metairie, Louisiana
Source: *CurBio 96*

DeGennes, Pierre-Gilles
French. Physicist
Won Nobel Prize, 1991 for discovering rules of molecular behavior.
b. 1932 in Paris, France
Source: *IntWW 91; WhoWor 91*

DeGraff, Robert F(air)
American. Publisher
Co-founded first American paperback co., Pocket Books, 1939.
b. Jun 9, 1895 in Plainfield, New Jersey
d. Nov 1, 1981 in Mill Neck, New York
Source: *BioIn 12, 13; ConAu 105; CurBio 43; DcLB Y81A; ExpInc; WhAm 8*

De Grassi, Alex
American. Musician
Folk guitarist; debut album *Turning: Turning Back,* 1978 lauded as classic.
b. Feb 13, 1952 in Yokosuka, Japan
Source: *BioIn 12; ConMus 6; NewAgMG*

DeHartog, Jan
[F R Eckmar]
Dutch. Author
Translated books include *Captain Jan,* 1976; *The Spiral Road,* 1957.
b. Apr 22, 1914 in Haarlem, Netherlands
Source: *AmAu&B; BioIn 16; CasWL; CnMD; ConAu 1NR, 1R; ConTFT 2; CurBio 70; EncWL; IntWW 74; NotNAT; TwCA SUP; WhoAm 84, 86, 88; WhoWor 87, 91*

DeHaven, Gloria
American. Actor
Co-star in 1940s musicals *Broadway Rythym; Three Little Words; Two Girls and a Sailor.*
b. Jul 23, 1925 in Los Angeles, California
Source: *BiE&WWA; BioIn 16; FilmgC; HalFC 88; InWom SUP; MGM; MotPP; MovMk; WhoAmW 74; WhoHol A*

DeHavilland, Geoffrey, Sir
English. Aircraft Manufacturer
Founded DeHavilland Aircraft Co., produced first commercial jetliner, the Comet.
b. Jul 27, 1882 in Haslemere, England
d. May 21, 1965 in London, England
Source: *BioIn 3, 4, 7, 8, 11, 12, 13, 14; DcNaB 1961; GrBr; ObitOF 79; ObitT 1961; WhAm 4; WhDW*

DeHavilland, Olivia Mary
American. Actor
Played Melanie in *Gone With the Wind,* 1939; won Oscars, 1946, 1949.
b. Jul 1, 1916 in Tokyo, Japan
Source: *BiDFilm; BiE&WWA; BioAmW; BioIn 14; CelR 90; CmMov; ConTFT 6; CurBio 66; FilmgC; HalFC 84, 88; IntMPA 86, 92; IntWW 83, 91; InWom SUP; MotPP; MovMk; ThFT; Who 85, 92; WhoAm 86, 90; WhoEnt 92; WhoHol A; WhoWor 87, 91; WorAlBi; WorEFlm*

Dehmel, Richard
German. Poet
Lyric verse collected in *Woman and the World,* 1896; *Beautiful Wild World,* 1913.
b. Nov 18, 1868, Germany
d. Feb 8, 1920 in Blankenese, Germany
Source: *CasWL; ClDMEL 47; EncWL; EuAu; EvEuW; ModGL; OxCGer 76; PenC EUR; REn*

Dehmelt, Hans Georg
German. Scientist
Won Nobel Prize in physics, 1989, for development of methods to isolate atoms and subatomic particles for study.
b. Sep 9, 1922 in Goerlitz, Germany
Source: *AmMWSc 73P, 76P, 79, 82, 86, 89, 92, 95; IntWW 89, 91, 93; LarDcSc; Who 92, 94; WhoAm 78, 80, 82, 84, 86, 88, 90, 92, 94, 95, 96, 97; WhoFrS 84; WhoNob 90, 95; WhoScEn 94, 96; WhoWest 92, 94, 96; WhoWor 91, 93, 95, 96, 97; WorAlBi*

Dehn, Adolf Arthur
American. Artist
Prolific lithographer, watercolor landscapist.
b. Nov 22, 1895 in Waterville, Minnesota
d. May 19, 1968 in New York, New York
Source: *CurBio 41, 68; DcCAA 71, 77, 88, 94; IlBEAAW; NatCAB 54; WhAm 5; WhAmArt 85*

Dehner, John Forkum
American. Actor
Films include *Thirty Seconds over Tokyo,* 1944; *Airplane II: The Sequel,* 1982.
b. Nov 23, 1915 in New York, New York
d. Feb 4, 1992 in Santa Barbara, California
Source: *ConTFT 7; HalFC 88; VarWW 85*

Dehnert, Henry
"Dutch"
American. Basketball Coach
Known for developing pivot play, 1920s-40s; Hall of Fame.
b. Apr 5, 1898 in New York, New York
d. Apr 20, 1979 in Far Rockaway, New York
Source: *BiDAmSp BK; BioIn 9; NewYTBS 79; WhoBbl 73*

Deighton, Len
[Leonard Cyril Deighton]
English. Author
Best known for spy thrillers: *The Ipcress File,* 1962; movie starred Michael Caine, 1965.
b. Feb 18, 1929 in London, England
Source: *Au&Arts 6; BestSel 89-2; BioIn 6, 7, 9, 10, 12, 14, 17, 18, 19; CamGLE; CnDBLB 8; ConAu 9R, 19NR, 33NR, X; ConLC 4, 7, 22, 46; ConNov 72, 76, 82, 86, 91, 96; ConPopW; CorpD; CrtSuMy; CurBio 84; DcArts; DcLB 87; DcLEL 1940; EncMys; EncSF, 93; FacFETw; HalFC 80, 84, 88; IntAu&W 76, 77, 91, 93; IntMPA 75, 76, 77, 78, 79, 80; IntWW 74, 75, 76, 77, 78, 79, 80, 81, 82, 83, 89, 91, 93; LegTOT; MajTwCW; NewC; NewYTBS 81; Novels; ScF&FL 92; ScFSB; SpyFic; TwCCr&M 80, 85, 91; TwCWr; WhoAm 88, 90, 92, 94, 95, 96, 97; WhoSpyF; WhoWor 74, 78, 80, 82, 84, 87, 89, 91, 93, 95, 96, 97; WorAl; WorAlBi; WorAu 1950; WrDr 76, 80, 82, 84, 86, 88, 90, 92, 94, 96*

Deisenhofer, Johann
German. Scientist
Shared Nobel Prize in chemistry, 1988, for studies on plant protein structures.
b. 1943, Germany
Source: *AmMWSc 92, 95; BioIn 16, 18, 19, 20; LarDcSc; NobelP 91; NotTwCS; Who 90, 92, 94; WhoAm 90, 92, 94, 95, 96, 97; WhoNob 90, 95; WhoScEn 94, 96; WhoSSW 91, 93, 95, 97; WhoWor 91, 93, 95, 96, 97*

Deisenhofer, Johann
German. Biochemist
Co-winner, Nobel Prize for Chemistry, 1988, for identification of proteins fundamental to photosynthesis.
b. Sep 30, 1943 in Zusamaltheim, Germany
Source: *AmMWSc 92, 95; BioIn 16, 18, 19, 20; LarDcSc; NobelP 91; NotTwCS; Who 90, 92, 94; WhoAm 90, 92, 94, 95, 96, 97; WhoNob 90, 95; WhoScEn 94, 96; WhoSSW 91, 93, 95, 97; WhoWor 91, 93, 95, 96, 97*

Deiss, Joseph Jay
American. Author
Writes on archaeology; novels include *The Blue Chips,* 1957.
b. Jan 25, 1915 in Twin Falls, Idaho
Source: *Au&Wr 71; BioIn 8, 11; ConAu 14NR, 33R; IntAu&W 76, 77, 78, 82; SmATA 12; WhoAm 74, 76, 78, 80; WhoWor 74; WrDr 76, 80, 82, 84, 86, 88, 90, 92, 94, 96*

Deitch, Kim
American. Cartoonist
Known for underground comic strips since 1967: "Sunshine Girl;" "Uncle Ed."
b. May 21, 1944
Source: *BioIn 10; MugS*

DeJohnette, Jack
American. Pianist
Jazz pianist and percussionist; receiver of numerous awards; albums *Bitches Brew,* 1970 with Miles Davis; achieved world class status as a drummer on *Live-Evil,* 1970.
b. Aug 9, 1942 in Chicago, Illinois
Source: *AllMusG; BiDJaz; BioIn 11, 12, 14, 15, 16; ConMus 7; DcTwCCu 5; EncJzS; InB&W 85; NewGrDJ 88; PenEncP; WhoAm 90, 97; WhoEnt 92*

DeJong, David Cornel
Dutch. Author
Wrote novel *Old Haven,* 1938; autobiography *With a Dutch Accent,* 1944.
b. Jun 9, 1905 in Blija, Netherlands
d. Sep 5, 1967 in Providence, Rhode Island

Source: *AmAu&B; AmNov; AuBYP 2; ConAu 5R; CurBio 44, 67; OxCAmL 65; REn; REnAL; SmATA 10; TwCA SUP; WhAm 4A*

Dejong, Meindert
American. Children's Author
Won Newbery for *Wheel on the School,* 1954; National Book Award for *Journey from Peppermint Street,* 1969.
b. Mar 4, 1906 in Wierum, Netherlands
d. Jul 16, 1991 in Allegan, Michigan
Source: *AnCL; AnObit 1991; Au&ICB; Au&Wr 71; AuBYP 2, 3; BioIn 2, 3, 4, 6, 7, 8, 9, 10, 14, 15, 17, 18, 19; BkCL; CamGLE; CasWL; ChlBkCr; ChlFicS; ChlLR 1; ConAu 13R, 36NR, 134; CurBio 52, 91N; DcAmChF 1960; DcLB 52; MajAI; MichAu 80; MorBMP; MorJA; NewbMB 1922; NewYTBS 91; OxCChiL; SenS; SmATA 2, 68; TwCChW 78, 83, 89, 95; WhAm 8; WhoAm 74, 76, 78, 80, 82; WrDr 80, 82, 84, 86, 88, 90, 92, 94N*

DeJong, Petrus
Dutch. Political Leader
Prime minister of The Netherlands, 1967-71; member of Senate, 1971-74.
b. Apr 13, 1915 in Apeldoorn, Netherlands
Source: *WhoGov 72; WhoMW 90; WhoRel 92; WhoWor 84*

Dejongh, Peter
American. Engineer
Designed Oak Ridge, TN installation where first atom bomb was built; designed WW II Quonset hut.
b. 1897
d. Jul 5, 1983 in Kearny, New Jersey
Source: *BioIn 13; NewYTBS 83*

Dekker, Albert
American. Actor
Played mad scientists, other villains, 1937-69: *Dr. Cyclops,* 1940; *The Pretenders,* 1947.
b. Dec 20, 1905 in New York, New York
d. May 5, 1968 in Hollywood, California
Source: *BiE&WWA; BioIn 8; FilmgC; ForYSC; HalFC 80, 84, 88; HolCA; MotPP; MovMk; NotNAT B; ObitOF 79; Vers B; WhAm 5; WhoHol B; WhScrn 74, 77; WhThe*

Dekker, Thomas
[Thomas Decker]
English. Dramatist
Wrote comedy *Old Fortunates,* 1599; pamphlet *The Wonderful Yeare 1603,* described London during plague.
b. 1572 in London, England
d. 1632 in London, England
Source: *Alli; AtlBL; BbD; Benet 87, 96; BiD&SB; BioIn 16, 18; BritAu; CasWL; Chambr 1; ChhPo, S1, S2; CnDBLB 1; CnE&AP; CnThe; CroE&S; CrtSuDr; CrtT 1, 4; CyWA 58; DcArts; DcEnA; DcEnL; DcLB 62, 172; DcLEL; EncWT; Ent; EvLB; IntDcT 2; LitC 22; McGEWB; McGEWD 72, 84; MouLC 1; NewC; NewCBEL; OxCEng 67, 85; OxCThe 67, 83; PenC ENG; PlP&P; RAdv 14, 13-2; REn; REnWD; RfGEnL 91; WebE&AL*

De Klerk, F(rederik) W(illem)
South African. Political Leader
Pres., S Africa, 1989-94; released long-held political prisoners including Nelson Mandela; lifted bans on African National Congress, Pan-African Congress.
b. Mar 18, 1936 in Johannesburg, South Africa
Source: *AfSS 82; BioIn 16; CurBio 90; FacFETw; IntWW 79, 80, 81, 82, 83, 89, 91, 93; News 90, 90-1; NewYTBS 90; Who 92, 94; WhoAfr; WhoNob 95; WhoWor 84, 91, 93, 95, 96, 97; WorAlBi*

DeKooning, Elaine Marie Catherine Fried
[Mrs. Willem DeKooning]
American. Artist, Critic
Paintings and portraits combine abstract expressionism and representational style; favorite subjects bullfighters, athletes in action, landscapes.
b. Mar 12, 1920 in New York, New York
d. Feb 1, 1989 in Southampton, New York
Source: *BioIn 13, 16; CurBio 82, 89N; DcCAA 88; InWom SUP; NewYTBS 89; OxDcArt; WhAm 9; WhoAm 86, 88; WhoAmA 73, 86, 89N, 91N; WhoAmW 89; WhoE 89*

deKooning, Willem
American. Artist
Abstract Expressionism leader, 1940s; known for distorted portraits of women.
b. Apr 24, 1904 in Rotterdam, Netherlands
d. Mar 19, 1997 in East Hampton, New York
Source: *AmArt; Benet 87; BioIn 13, 14, 16; CelR 90; ConArt 89; CurBio 84; DcCAA 71, 88; EncAB-H 1974; FacFETw; IntDcAA 90; IntWW 74, 91; OxDcArt; PeoHis; PrintW 85; RComAH; REn; WebAB 74; WhoAm 80, 82, 90; WhoAmA 73, 86, 91N; WhoE 86; WhoWor 74; WorAlBi*

DeKoven, (Henry Louis) Reginald
American. Composer, Critic
Founded, conducted, Washington Philharmonic, 1902-05; wrote operettas *Robin Hood,* 1890, *Student King,* 1906.
b. Apr 3, 1861 in Middletown, Connecticut
d. Jan 16, 1920 in Chicago, Illinois
Source: *AmAu&B; AmBi; ApCAB SUP, X; ASCAP 66; BioIn 1, 3, 5, 6; ChhPo; DcAmB; EncMT; LinLib L, S; NatCAB 26; NewCBMT; OxCAmL 65; REn; REnAL; TwCBDA; WhAm 1*

DeKruif, Paul Henry
American. Bacteriologist, Author
Popular writer on scientific subjects; wrote *Microbe Hunters,* 1926.
b. Mar 2, 1890 in Zeeland, Michigan
d. Feb 28, 1971 in Holland, Michigan
Source: *AmAu&B; BiE&WWA; CurBio 71; InSci; JBA 34; LngCTC; OxCAmL 65; REn; REnAL; SmATA 5; TwCA, SUP; WhAm 5*

Delacorte, George Thomas, Jr.
American. Publisher
Established Dell Publishing Co., Inc., 1921; retired as chm., 1980; financed Central Park's Delacorte Theater.
b. Jun 20, 1894 in New York, New York
d. May 4, 1991 in New York, New York
Source: *BioIn 1, 7, 8, 12, 14; CelR; CurBio 65, 91N; DcLB 91; NewYTBS 79, 85, 91; St&PR 75; WhAm 10; WhoAm 74, 76, 78, 80, 82; WhoAmA 73; WhoWor 74*

Delacroix, (Ferdinand Victor) Eugene
French. Artist
Leading Romantic painter; noted for historical, colorful Moroccan scenes: *Liberty Leading the People,* 1831.
b. Apr 26, 1798 in Charenton, France
d. Aug 13, 1863 in Paris, France
Source: *AtlBL; Benet 87; BioIn 1, 2, 3, 4, 5, 6, 7, 8, 9, 10, 11, 12, 13, 14, 15, 16, 20; ClaDrA; DcArts; DcCathB; EuWr 5; IntDcAA 90; LegTOT; LinLib L, S; McGDA; McGEWB; OxCEng 85, 95; OxCFr; OxDcArt; REn; WhDW; WorAl; WorAlBi*

Delahanty, Ed(ward James)
"Big Ed"
American. Baseball Player
Outfielder, 1888-1903; only man to win batting title in both leagues, 1899, 1902; Hall of Fame, 1945.
b. Oct 31, 1867 in Cleveland, Ohio
d. Jul 2, 1903 in Fort Erie, Ontario, Canada
Source: *Ballpl 90; BiDAmSp BB; BioIn 3, 6, 7, 10, 14, 15, 17, 18, 19; LegTOT; WhoProB 73*

Delahanty, Thomas K
American. Police Officer
Wounded with Ronald Reagan in assassination attempt, 1981.
b. 1935? in Pittsburgh, Pennsylvania
Source: *BioIn 12*

De La Hoya, Oscar
American. Boxer
Won gold medal, 1992 Olympics; WBC super-lightweight champion, 1996—.
b. 1973 in Los Angeles, California
Source: *WhoHisp 94*

DeLaMare, Walter
[Walter Ramal]
English. Author, Poet
Wrote popular children's verse: *Memoirs of a Midget,* 1922.

b. Apr 25, 1873 in Charlton, England
d. Jun 22, 1956 in Twickenham, England
Source: *AnCL; AtlBL; AuBYP 2; BkCL; CarSB; CasWL; Chambr 3; CnE&AP; CyWA 58; OxCEng 85; PenC ENG; REn; TwCA SUP; WhAm 3*

Deland, Margaret Wade
American. Author
Known for short stories *Old Chester Tales,* 1919; novel *Iron Woman,* 1911.
b. Feb 23, 1857 in Allegheny, Pennsylvania
d. Jan 13, 1945
Source: *Alli SUP; AmAu&B; BbD; BiD&SB; Chambr 3; ChhPo, S1, S2; ConAmL; CurBio 45; DcAmAu; DcBiA; DcEnL; DcLEL; DcNAA; GrWrEL N; InWom, SUP; LngCTC; NotAW; OxCAmL 65; REn; REnAL; TwCA, SUP; WhNAA; WomNov*

Delaney, Jack
"Bright Eyes"
Canadian. Boxer
World light-heavyweight champ, 1926.
b. Mar 18, 1900 in Saint Francis, Quebec, Canada
d. Nov 27, 1948 in Katonah, New York
Source: *BiDAmSp BK; BioIn 1, 10; BoxReg; WhoBox 74*

Delaney, Joe Alton
American. Football Player
All-pro running back, Kansas City, 1981-82; drowned trying to rescue three children.
b. Oct 30, 1958 in Henderson, Texas
d. Jun 29, 1983 in Monroe, Louisiana
Source: *NewYTBS 83*

Delaney, Shelagh
English. Dramatist
Wrote *A Taste of Honey,* 1958.
b. Nov 25, 1939 in Salford, England
Source: *Benet 87, 96; BiE&WWA; BioIn 5, 6, 10, 13, 16, 17, 18; BlmGEL; BlmGWL; CamGLE; CamGWoT; CnDBLB 8; CnMD; ConAu 17R, 30NR; ConBrDr; ConDr 73, 77, 82, 88, 93; ConLC 29; ConTFT 6; ConWomD; CroCD; CrtSuDr; CurBio 62; CyWA 89; DcLB 13; DcLEL 1940; EncBrWW; EncWT; Ent; FacFETw; FemiCLE; HalFC 80, 84, 88; IntAu&W 76, 77, 89, 91, 93; IntDcT 2; InWom, SUP; LegTOT; LinLib L; LngCTC; MajTwCW; McGEWD 72, 84; ModWD; NewC; NotNAT; OxCEng 85, 95; PenC ENG; PlP&P; REn; RGTwCWr; TwCWr; Who 74, 82, 83, 85, 88, 90, 92, 94; WhoAmW 68, 70, 72, 74; WhoThe 72, 77, 81; WhoWor 74, 87; WorAu 1950; WrDr 76, 80, 82, 92*

Delaney and Bonnie
[Delaney Bramlett; Bonnie Lynn]
American. Music Group
Southern husband-wife team combining soul, boogie, country; hit album *Down Home,* 1969.
Source: *BioIn 14; HarEnR 86; NewGrDA 86; RkOn 84; WhoRock 81; WhoRocM 82*

Delannoy, Jean
French. Director
Films include *Love and the Frenchwoman,* 1960; *Action Man,* 1967.
b. Jan 12, 1908 in Noisy, France
Source: *BioIn 15; DcFM; DcTwCCu 2; FilmEn; FilmgC; HalFC 80, 84, 88; IntDcF 1-2, 2-2; IntMPA 75, 76, 77, 78, 79, 80, 81, 82, 84, 86, 88, 92, 94; ItaFilm; MiSFD 9; WhoFr 79; WorEFlm; WorFDir 1*

Delano, Isaac O
Nigerian. Author
Books include *The Soul of Nigeria,* 1937; *Iran Orum,* 1953.
b. Nov 4, 1904 in Okenla, Nigeria
Source: *ConAu 25R*

Delano, Jane Arminda
American. Teacher, Nurse
Superintendent, US Army Nurse Corps, 1909-12; chm., American Red Cross Nursing Service; 1918-19.
b. Mar 26, 1858 in Townsend, New York
d. Apr 15, 1919 in Savenay, France
Source: *DcAmMeB 84*

Delany, Annie Elizabeth
"Bessie"
American. Writer, Dentist
Co-author, with her sister, Sarah, of *Having Our Say,* 1993; second black woman to become a dentist in the state of New York.
b. Sep 3, 1891 in Raleigh, North Carolina
d. Sep 25, 1995 in Mount Vernon, New York
Source: *CurBio 95*

Delany, Dana
American. Actor
Played nurse Colleen McMurphy on TV drama "China Beach;" won best actress Emmy, 1988.
b. Mar 11, 1956 in New York, New York
Source: *BioIn 15; ConTFT 10; IntMPA 94, 96; LegTOT; WhoAm 94, 95, 96, 97; WhoAmW 91, 95, 97; WhoEnt 92; WhoHol 92*

Delany, Dana
American. Actor
Played nurse Colleen McMurphy on TV series "China Beach," 1987-91; won best actress Emmy, 1989.
b. Mar 13, 1957 in New York, New York
Source: *BioIn 15; WhoAmW 91; WhoEnt 92*

Delany, Martin Robinson
American. Author, Social Reformer, Soldier
Advocated colonization as solution to slavery; first black commissioned in US Army, 1865.
b. May 6, 1812 in Charletown, Virginia
d. Jan 24, 1885 in Xenia, Ohio
Source: *Alli, SUP; AmAu; AmBi; AmSocL; BiDAmJo; BioIn 6, 8, 9, 11, 14, 15, 16, 17; BlkAmW 1; BlkAWP; DcAmB; DcLB 50; DcNAA; EncAACR; EncAB-H 1974; EncSoH; McGEWB; RfGAmL 94; SchCGBL; WebAB 74, 79; WebBD 83; WhAm HS; WhAmP*

Delany, Samuel R.
[Samuel Ray Delany, Jr.]
American. Author
Helped to make science fiction a respected literary genre; wrote *Babel-17,* 1966.
b. Apr 1, 1942 in New York, New York
Source: *AfrAmAl 6; BenetAL 91; BioIn 12, 13, 14, 15; BlkAWP; BlkLC; BlkWr 1; ConAu 27NR, 81; ConBlB 9; ConGAN; ConLC 8, 14, 38; ConNov 76, 82, 86, 91; ConSFA; CyWA 89; DcLB 8, 33; DrAF 76; DrAPF 80, 91; DrmM 1; EncSF; GayLesB; InB&W 85; IntAu&W 91; IntvTCA 2; LivgBAA; MagSAmL; MajTwCW; NegAl 83, 89; NewEScF; Novels; PeoHis; PostFic; RGSF; RGTwCSF; ScF&FL 1, 2, 92; ScFSB; ScFWr; SchCGBL; SelBAAf; TwCSFW 81, 91; WhoAfA 96; WhoAm 82; WhoBlA 85, 88, 90, 92, 94; WhoSciF; WorAl; WorAlBi; WorAu 1970; WrDr 80, 82, 84, 86, 88, 90, 92*

Delany, Sarah Louise
"Sadie"
American. Writer, Educator
Co-Author, with her sister, Bessie, of *Having Our Say,* 1993.
b. Sep 19, 1889 in Lynch's Station, Virginia
Source: *CurBio 95*

Delaplane, Stanton Hill
American. Journalist
Syndicated travel writer, *San Francisco Chronicle,* 1953-88; won Pulitzer for reporting, 1942.
b. Oct 12, 1907 in Chicago, Illinois
d. Apr 18, 1988 in San Francisco, California
Source: *BiDAmNC; BioIn 15, 16; ConAu 25R, 125; EncTwCJ; WhAm 9; WhoAm 74, 76, 78, 80, 82, 84, 86; WhoWest 74, 76, 78, 87; WhoWor 74*

DeLaRenta, Oscar
American. Fashion Designer
Known for lavish evening clothes; won Coty awards, 1967, 1968.
b. Jul 22, 1932 in Santo Domingo, Dominican Republic
Source: *BioIn 13, 14; BioNews 74; CelR 90; CurBio 70; DcTwDes; EncFash; FacFETw; IntWW 91; WhoAm 86, 90; WhoE 91; WhoFash, 88; WhoHisp 92; WorAlBi; WorFshn*

Delaroche, Hippolyte
[Paul Delaroche]
French. Artist
Large historical paintings include *Joas Saved By Josabeth,* 1822.
b. Jul 17, 1797 in Paris, France
d. Nov 4, 1859 in Paris, France
Source: *ArtsNiC; BioIn 2, 10, 11; CelCen; DcArts; DcBiPP; LegTOT; LinLib S; McGDA; NewCol 75; OxCFr; OxDcArt; WhAmArt 85A*

DeLaRoche, Mazo
Canadian. Author
Best known for novel *Jalna,* 1927, first in a series of an Ontario family chronicle.
b. Jan 15, 1885? in Toronto, Ontario, Canada
d. Jul 12, 1961 in Toronto, Ontario, Canada
Source: *CanNov; CanWr; CasWL; Chambr 3; ConAu 85; ConLC 14; CyWA 58; DcLEL; EvLB; JBA 34; LngCTC; OxCEng 85; PenC ENG; REn; REnAL; TwCA SUP; WhAm 4*

De Larrocha, Alicia
Spanish. Pianist
Foremost interpreter of the Spanish repertoire and "The premier Mozart pianist of her generation."
b. May 23, 1921 in Barcelona, Spain
Source: *BioIn 14, 16; CelR 90; CurBio 68; IntWWM 90; InWom SUP; MusSN; NewAmDM; WhoAm 90; WhoAmM 83; WhoAmW 91; WhoEnt 92; WhoWor 91*

De La Rue, Warren
English. Inventor, Astronomer
Pioneered celestial photography; invented a photoheliograph, which gave first clear pictures of sun, 1858.
b. Jan 18, 1815 in Isle of Guernsey, England
d. Apr 19, 1889 in London, England
Source: *AsBiEn; BiESc; BioIn 14; DcInv; DcNaB; DcScB; InSci; LarDcSc; NewCol 75*

De La Soul
[David (Trugoy the Dove) Jolicoeur; Vincent (Maseo) Mason, Jr; Kelvin (Posdnous) Mercer]
American. Rap Group
Rap trio formed in 1985; debut album *Three Feet High and Rising,* 1989 was smash hit.
Source: *ConMus 7; EncRkSt*

De La Torre(-Bueno), Lillian
American. Writer
Wrote *Elizabeth is Missing,* 1945; self-described "histodetector."
b. Mar 15, 1902
d. Sep 13, 1993 in Colorado Springs, Colorado
Source: *AmAu&B; AuBYP 2, 3; BioIn 1, 2, 3, 4, 7, 14, 19; ConAu X; CrtSuMy; DetWom; EncMys; IntAu&W 89, 91; InWom; REnAL; TwCA SUP; TwCCr&M 80, 85, 91; WrDr 76, 82, 84, 86, 88, 90, 92, 94, 96*

Delaunay, Robert
French. Artist
Known for linking color with movement; works include *Ville de Paris.*
b. Apr 12, 1885 in Paris, France
d. Oct 25, 1941 in Montpellier, France
Source: *AtlBL; BioIn 2, 4, 5, 8, 11, 12, 15, 16; ClaDrA; ConArt 77, 83; DcArts; DcTwCCu 2; EncWB; FacFETw; IntDcAA 90; McGDA; OxCArt; OxCTwCA; OxDcArt; PhDcTCA 77*

Delaunay-Terk, Sonia
French. Artist, Designer
Noted for exuberant use of vibrant color, geometric designs.
b. Nov 14, 1885 in Gradizhsk, Russia
d. Dec 5, 1979 in Paris, France
Source: *BiDWomA; BioIn 4, 5, 8, 10, 11, 12, 13, 15; ConArt 77; CurBio 77, 80; DcArts; DcTwCCu 2; DcWomA; GoodHs; OxCTwCA; OxDcArt; PhDcTCA 77; WhoAmW 70, 74; WhoWor 74, 78*

DeLaurentiis, Dino
Italian. Producer
Best known films *Serpico,* 1974; *King Kong,* 1976; *Blue Velvet,* 1986.
b. Aug 8, 1919 in Torre Annunziata, Italy
Source: *BiDFilm; BioIn 13, 16; CelR 90; CmMov; ConTFT 7; CurBio 65; DcFM; FilmgC; HalFC 88; IntMPA 92; IntWW 83, 91; OxCFilm; WhoAm 86, 90; WhoEnt 92; WhoWest 87; WhoWor 91; WorAl; WorAlBi; WorEFlm*

DeLaurentiis, Federico
Italian. Producer
Son of Dino DeLaurentiis; produced film *King of the Gypsies,* 1978.
b. 1955?
d. 1981 in Kvichak Bay, Alaska
Source: *BioIn 12*

DeLavallade, Carmen
American. Dancer
Appeared on Broadway in *House of Flowers,* 1955; with NYC Center Opera, 1962-65; Yale U dance professor.
b. Mar 6, 1931 in Los Angeles, California
Source: *BiDD; BiE&WWA; BioIn 5, 6, 7, 8, 12, 13, 14; BlkWAm; CurBio 67; DancEn 78; DrBlPA, 90; InB&W 80, 85; InWom; NotNAT; WhoAm 74, 76, 78; WhoAmW 70, 72, 74; WhoBlA 75, 77, 80, 85; WhoHol 92*

Delavigne, Jean Francois Casimir
French. Dramatist, Poet
Historical dramas include *Louis XI,* 1832; wrote song "La Parisienne," 1830.
b. Apr 4, 1793 in Le Havre, France
d. Dec 11, 1843 in Lyons, France
Source: *BbD; BiD&SB; BioIn 7; CasWL; CelCen; DcBiPP; EuAu; EvEuW; McGEWD 84; NewCol 75; NotNAT B; OxCFr; OxCThe 83*

Delaware Prophet
[Neolin]
American. Religious Leader
Spiritual leader who converted the Ottawa Chief Pontiac; authority was from the Master of Life, who was unhappy that the white man dwelled among the Indians.
b. fl. 1760
Source: *EncNAR; EncNoAI; NotNaAm*

Delblanc, Sven
Swedish. Author
Wrote the Swedish novels *The Cassock,* 1963; *Remembrance,* 1970.
b. May 26, 1931 in Swan River, Manitoba, Canada
Source: *DcScanL, 3; WorAu 1975*

Delbruck, Max
American. Scientist
Molecular geneticist who pioneered in bacteriophages research; won Nobel Prize, 1969.
b. Sep 4, 1906 in Berlin, Germany
d. Mar 9, 1981 in Pasadena, California
Source: *AmMWSc 76P, 79; AnObit 1981; BiESc; BioIn 8, 9, 12, 13, 14, 15, 16, 20; CamDcSc; FacFETw; IntWW 74, 75, 76, 77, 78, 79, 80, 81, 81N; LarDcSc; LegTOT; McGMS 80; NewYTBS 81; NobelP; NotTwCS; ThTwC 87; WebAB 74, 79; WhAm 7; Who 74; WhoAm 74, 76, 78, 80; WhoNob, 90, 95; WhoWest 78, 80; WhoWor 80; WorAl; WorAlBi; WorScD*

Delderfield, Ronald Frederick
English. Author, Dramatist
Novels include *Mr. Sermon,* 1963; plays include *And Then There Were None,* 1954.
b. Feb 12, 1912 in London, England
d. Jun 24, 1972 in Sidmouth, England
Source: *Au&Wr 71; BioIn 2, 3, 8, 9, 10, 11, 12, 14; ConAu 37R, 47NR, 73; DcLEL 1940; IntAu&W 76, 77; NewCBEL; NewYTBE 72; SmATA 20; WhE&EA; WhoChL; WhThe*

Deledda, Grazia
[Grazia Madesani]
Italian. Author
Writings depict Sardinian peasantry; won Nobel Prize, 1926.
b. Sep 27, 1875 in Nvoro, Sardinia, Italy
d. Aug 16, 1936 in Rome, Italy
Source: *CasWL; ClDMEL 47; ConAu 123; CyWA 58; EncWL; EvEuW; HerW, 84; InWom, SUP; LegTOT; LinLib L; ModRL; ModWoWr; Novels; PenC EUR; REn; TwCA, SUP; TwCLC 23; TwCWr; WhoNob; WhoTwCL; WorAl*

DeLeeuw, Adele Louise
American. Children's Author
Numerous biographies include *Marie Curie: Woman of Genius,* 1969.
b. Aug 12, 1899 in Hamilton, Ohio
d. Jun 12, 1988 in Plainfield, New Jersey
Source: *AmAu&B; AuBYP 2, 3; BioIn 14, 16; ConAu 1NR, 1R, 125; IntAu&W*

91; JBA 51; OhA&B; SmATA 1, 56N; WhNAA; WhoAmW 77; WrDr 76, 88

Delerue, Georges
French. Composer, Conductor
Won Oscar for score of *A Little Romance,* 1979; Emmy for *Our World,* 1968; wrote scores for *Platoon, Day of the Jackal,* among others.
b. Mar 12, 1925 in Roubaix, France
d. Mar 20, 1992 in Los Angeles, California
Source: *AnObit 1992; ConTFT 7, 11; DcFM; FilmEn; HalFC 88; IntDcF 1-4, 2-4; IntMPA 92; ItaFilm; NewGrDM 80; VarWW 85; WhoFr 79; WorEFlm*

DeLiagre, Alfred
American. Producer, Director
Began stage career, 1930; won Tony for *JB,* 1958.
b. Oct 6, 1904 in Passaic, New Jersey
d. Mar 5, 1987 in New York, New York
Source: *BioIn 15; ConTFT 5; NewYTBS 87; NotNAT; VarWW 85; WhoThe 81*

Delibes, Leo
[Clement Philibert Leo Delibes]
French. Composer
Noted for ballets *La Source,* 1866; *Coppelia,* 1870.
b. Feb 21, 1836 in Saint-Germain-du-Val, France
d. Jan 16, 1891 in Paris, France
Source: *AtlBL; Baker 78, 84; BiDD; BioIn 3, 4, 7, 12, 20; BriBkM 80; CmOp; CmpBCM; CnOxB; DancEn 78; DcCom 77; DcCom&M 79; GrComp; IntDcB; IntDcOp; LegTOT; MetOEnc; MusMk; NewAmDM; NewEOp 71; NewGrDM 80; NewOxM; OxCFr; OxCMus; OxDcOp; PenDiMP A; REn; WhDW*

Delilah
Biblical Figure
Enchantress who discovered Samson's secret source of strength.
Source: *Benet 96; BioIn 2, 4, 5, 6, 7, 11, 17; EncE 75; GoodHs; InWom, SUP; LngCEL*

DeLillo, Don
[Cleo Birdwell]
American. Author
Wrote *White Noise,* 1985; *Libra,* 1988; *Mao II,* 1991; won PEN/Faulkner Award for Fiction, 1992.
b. Nov 20, 1936 in New York, New York
Source: *Benet 96; BenetAL 91; BestSel 89-1; BiDConC; BioIn 13, 16; CamHAL; ConAu 21NR, 81; ConLC 8, 10, 13, 27, 39, 54, 76; ConNov 82, 86, 91, 96; ConPopW; CurBio 89; CyWA 89; DcArts; DcLB 6, 173; DrAPF 80; EncSF 93; IntAu&W 91; LegTOT; MagSAmL; MajTwCW; NewYTBS 91; OxCAmL 95; PostFic; RfGAmL 94; RGTwCWr; ScF&FL 92; WhoAm 86, 88, 90, 92, 94, 95, 96; WorAu 1975; WrDr 82, 84, 86, 88, 90, 92, 94, 96*

Delisle, Guillaume
"Founder of Modern Cartography"
French. Cartographer
Increased accuracy, simplicity of early maps; devised most precise world map of his time, 1700.
b. Feb 28, 1675 in Paris, France
d. Jan 25, 1726 in Paris, France
Source: *DcCathB; DcScB; NewCol 75*

Delisle, Joseph-Nicolas
French. Astronomer
Originated method of observing transits of Venus, Mercury.
b. Apr 4, 1688 in Paris, France
d. Jun 12, 1768 in Paris, France
Source: *DcScB; EncEnl; WebBD 83*

Delius, Frederick
English. Composer
Influenced by European romantics, compositions include opera, choral works.
b. Jan 29, 1862 in Bradford, England
d. Jun 10, 1934 in Grez-sur-Loing, France
Source: *AtlBL; Baker 78, 84, 92; BioIn 1, 2, 3, 4, 5, 6, 7, 8, 9, 10, 11, 12, 13, 14, 15, 16, 20; BriBkM 80; CmOp; CompSN, SUP; DcCM; DcCom 77; DcCom&M 79; DcNaB 1931; DcTwCC; FacFETw; GrBr; IntDcOp; LegTOT; MakMC; MetOEnc; MusMk; NewAmDM; NewEOp 71; NewGrDA 86; NewGrDM 80; NewOxM; OxCEng 85, 95; OxCMus; OxDcOp; PenDiMP A; WhAm 4, HSA; WhDW; WhFla; WorAlBi*

Dell, Floyd
American. Editor, Author, Dramatist
Spokesman for "Jazz Age," 1920s; most successful play comedy *Little Accident,* 1928; editor, *The Liberator,* 1918-24.
b. Jun 28, 1887 in Barry, Illinois
d. Jul 23, 1969 in Bethesda, Maryland
Source: *AmAu&B; AnMV 1926; Benet 87; BenetAL 91; BioIn 4, 6, 8, 9, 12, 20; CamGLE; CamHAL; CnDAL; ConAmA; ConAmL; ConAu 89; DcLB 9; DcLEL; Dis&D; GrWrEL N; LinLib L; LngCTC; ModAL; NotNAT B; OxCAmL 65, 83, 95; PenC AM; PlP&P; REn; REnAL; RfGAmL 87, 94; TwCA, SUP; WebAB 74, 79; WhAm 5; WhNAA; WhThe*

Dell, Gabriel
[Gabriel del Vecchio]
American. Actor
Member of group of actors called the Dead End Kids, from Broadway hit, *Dead End,* 1935; also called Bowery Boys, Eastside Kids in films.
b. Oct 7, 1919, Barbados
d. Jul 3, 1988 in North Hollywood, California
Source: *ConTFT 7; EncAFC; LegTOT; NewYTBE 72; NotNAT; WhoHol A; WhoThe 77; WhThe*

Dell, Michael
American. Computer Executive
Founder of PCs Limited (later Dell Computer Corp.), 1984; CEO of Dell, 1987—.
b. Feb 1965 in Houston, Texas
Source: *ConEn; News 96, 96-2*

DellaCasa, Lisa
[Lisa DellaCase-Debeljevic]
Swiss. Opera Singer
Soprano; with NY Met., 1953-68, noted for Strauss repertory.
b. Feb 1, 1919 in Burgdorf, Switzerland
Source: *Baker 84; BioIn 13, 14; CurBio 56; IntWW 91; IntWWM 90; InWom SUP; MetOEnc; NewAmDM; PenDiMP; WhoMus 72; WhoWor 74*

DellaFemina, Jerry
American. Advertising Executive, Author
Former copywriter, pres; now chm. of DellaFemina, Travisano, & Partners, Inc., 1967—.
b. Jul 22, 1936 in New York, New York
Source: *BioIn 15, 16; ConAmBL; ConAu 111; WhoAdv 72, 90; WhoAm 86, 90; WhoFI 92*

DellaRobbia, Andrea
Italian. Sculptor
Noted for roundels of infants, Florence's Foundling Hospital, 1463-66; nephew of Luca.
b. 1435 in Florence, Italy
d. 1525
Source: *BioIn 9; McGDA; NewCol 75; OxCArt*

DellaRobbia, Giovanni
Italian. Sculptor
Led atelier from 1525; son of Andrea.
b. 1469 in Florence, Italy
d. 1529
Source: *AtlBL; BioIn 10; OxCDecA; WebBD 83*

DellaRobbia, Lucia
Italian. Sculptor
Developed enameling technique of terra-cotta figures, c. 1440; started famed family workshop.
b. Dec 22, 1400 in Florence, Italy
d. Feb 23, 1482 in Florence, Italy
Source: *AtlBL; REn*

Dellenbaugh, Frederick Samuel
American. Artist, Author
Helped draw first map of Grand Canyon region; writings include *A Canyon Voyage,* 1871-73.
b. Sep 13, 1853 in McConnelsville, Ohio
d. Jan 29, 1935
Source: *AmAu&B; AmLY; ArtsAmW 1; DcAmAu; DcAmB S1; DcNAA; IlBEAAW; NatCAB 32; OhA&B; WhAm 1; WhNAA*

Deller, Alfred George
English. Opera Singer
Countertenor; formed ensemble, 1950, specializing in old English music.
b. May 31, 1912 in Margate, England
d. Jul 16, 1979 in Bologna, Italy
Source: *Baker 84; BioIn 5, 7, 8, 9; BlueB 76; BriBkM 80; NewGrDM 80; Who 74*

Dellinger, David T
[The Chicago 7]
American. Author, Editor, Political Activist
Chairman, National Mobilization Committee to End War in Vietnam, 1967-71.
b. Aug 22, 1915 in Wakefield, Massachusetts
Source: *AmPeW; BioIn 10, 11, 13, 14, 16; ConAu 65; CurBio 76; EncAL; EncWB; PolProf J; WhoAm 80, 82; WhoEmL 89; WhoUSWr 88; WhoWrEP 89*

Dello Joio, Norman Joseph
American. Composer
Won 1957 Pulitzer for *Meditations on Ecclesiastes;* noted exponent of neo-classical manner.
b. Jan 24, 1913 in New York, New York
Source: *Baker 84; BiDAmM; BioIn 15, 16; BriBkM 80; ConCom 92; CurBio 57; DancEn 78; DcCM; LEduc 74; MetOEnc; NewAmDM; NewGrDA 86; NewOxM; OxCMus; PenDiMP; WhoAm 86, 90; WhoEnt 92; WhoMus 72*

Dell'Olio, Louis
American. Fashion Designer
Chief designer for Anne Klein, 1984-93; won Cotys, 1982, 1984.
b. Jul 23, 1948 in New York, New York
Source: *BioIn 15, 16; EncFash; IntWW 91, 93; WhoAm 82, 84, 86, 88, 90, 92, 94, 95, 96; WhoE 95; WhoFash, 88*

Dellums, Ronald Vernie
American. Politician
Dem. congressman from CA, 1970—; chairman house armed services committee, 1993—.
b. Nov 24, 1935 in Oakland, California
Source: *AlmAP 92; BiDrUSC 89; BioIn 13, 16; BlkAmsC; CelR 90; CngDr 89; ConBlB 2; CurBio 72; NegAl 89A; PolsAm 84; WhoAfA 96; WhoAm 76, 78, 80, 82, 84, 86, 88, 90; WhoAmP 89, 91; WhoBlA 75, 92, 94; WhoWest 78, 80, 82, 84, 87, 89, 92*

Delmar, Kenny
American. Actor
Played Senator Claghorn on Fred Allen's radio show; films include *Strangers in the City,* 1962.
b. 1911? in Boston, Massachusetts
d. Jul 14, 1984 in Stamford, Connecticut
Source: *BioIn 1, 14; WhoHol A*

Delmar, Vina Croter
American. Author
Novels include *The Laughing Stranger,* 1953; *Grandmere,* 1967.
b. Jan 29, 1905 in New York, New York
Source: *AmAu&B; BenetAL 91; BioIn 14; CnDAL; ConAu 65, 130; OxCAmL 65; REnAL; TwCA, SUP; TwCRHW 90; WrDr 90*

DelMonaco, Mario
Italian. Opera Singer
Tenor, most noted for rendition of Verdi's *Otello,* performed 427 times.
b. Jul 27, 1915 in Florence, Italy
d. Oct 16, 1982 in Mestre, Italy
Source: *Baker 78; CmOp; CurBio 83; IntWW 80, 81; MusMk; MusSN; NewEOp 71; NewGrDM 80; NewYTBS 82; WhoMus 72; WhoOp 76*

Delmonico, Lorenzo
Swiss. Restaurateur
With uncles, established Delmonico's Restaurant, NYC, c. 1834.
b. Mar 13, 1813 in Marengo, Switzerland
d. Sep 3, 1881 in Sharon Springs, New York
Source: *BiDAmBL 83; DcAmB; WebAB 74, 79; WhAm HS*

Delon, Alain
French. Actor
Plays romantic gangster leads; films include *Is Paris Burning?,* 1966.
b. Nov 8, 1935 in Seceaux, France
Source: *BiDFilm, 81, 94; BioIn 6, 7, 9, 11, 14; CelR; ConTFT 14; CurBio 64; DcArts; DcTwCCu 2; EncEurC; FacFETw; FilmAG WE; FilmEn; FilmgC; ForYSC; GangFlm; HalFC 80, 84, 88; IntDcF 1-3, 2-3; IntMPA 75, 76, 77, 78, 79, 80, 81, 82, 84, 86, 88, 92, 94, 96; IntWW 74, 75, 76, 77, 78, 79, 80, 81, 82, 83, 89, 91, 93; ItaFilm; LegTOT; MotPP; MovMk; OxCFilm; WhoFr 79; WhoHol 92, A; WhoWor 74, 76, 78, 82, 84, 89, 91, 93, 95, 96, 97; WorAl; WorAlBi; WorEFlm*

Deloney, Thomas
English. Author
Wrote *The Gentle Craft,* 1598.
b. 1543? in London, England
d. 1600?
Source: *Alli; AtlBL; BiD&SB; BiDRP&D; BioIn 3, 5, 11; BlmGEL; BritAu; CamGEL; CamGLE; CasWL; Chambr 1; ChhPo; CroE&S; CrtT 1; CyWA 58; DcEnL; DcLEL; DcNaB, C; EvLB; GrWrEL N; LngCEL; NewC; NewCBEL; Novels; OxCEng 67, 85; OxCMus; PenC ENG; RAdv 14; REn; RfGEnL 91; WebBD 83; WebE&AL*

DeLong, George Washington
American. Explorer, Naturalist
Died attempting to reach N Pole by way of Bering Strait, 1879-81.
b. Aug 22, 1844 in New York, New York
d. Oct 30, 1881 in Siberia, Russia
Source: *Alli SUP; AmAu&B; AmBi; ApCAB; BbD; BiD&SB; DcAmB; TwCBDA; WhAm HS*

DeLorean, John Zachary
American. Auto Executive, Author
Founded DeLorean Motor Co., 1975.
b. Jan 6, 1925 in Detroit, Michigan
Source: *BioIn 8, 9, 10, 11, 12, 13, 14; BioNews 74; BusPN; ConAu 122; EncABHB 5; FacFETw; PeoHis; WhoAm 74, 76, 78, 80, 82; WhoFI 74, 75, 77, 79, 81; WhoMW 78, 80; WhoWest 92, 94; WhoWor 76, 78, 80, 82*

Deloria, Ella Clara
American. Ethnologist
Wrote *Dakota Grammar,* 1941; *Speaking of Indians,* 1944.
b. Jan 31, 1889 in White Swan, South Dakota
d. 1971 in Vermillion, South Dakota

Deloria, Vine (Victor), Sr.
American. Clergy
Episcopal minister who preached to the Native Americans in South Dakota.
b. Oct 6, 1901 in Saint Elizabeth's Mission,South Dakota
d. Feb 26, 1990
Source: *BioIn 9, 21; EncNAR; EncNoAI; NotNaAm*

Deloria, Vine (Victor), Jr.
American. Lecturer, Political Activist, Author
Professor political science, Univ. of Tucson, 1978-90; Univ. of Colorado, 1990—; known for working to save rights of Native Americans, 1960s—; writings include *Custer Died for Your Sins,* 1969.
b. Mar 26, 1933 in Martin, South Dakota
Source: *AmAu&B; AmSocL; AuSpks; BenetAL 91; BioIn 9, 10, 11, 12, 16; CamGLE; CamHAL; CivR 74; ConAu 5NR, 20NR, 48NR, 53; ConHero 1; ConLC 21; CurBio 74; DcNAL; EncNAB; LNinSix; MajTwCW; MugS; NatNAL; NotNaAm; OxCAmL 95; SmATA 21; WhoAm 74, 76, 78, 82, 84, 86, 88, 90; WhoUSWr 88; WhoWest 78, 89, 92; WhoWrEP 89, 92, 95; WorAu 1975*

Delors, Jacques Lucien Jean
French. Banker, Economist
Pres., European Commission, 1985-95; helped to draft Act of European Unity, which was ratified in 1987.
b. Jul 20, 1925 in Paris, France
Source: *BiDFrPL; BioIn 12, 14, 16; CurBio 89; Future; IntWW 82, 83, 89, 91, 93; News 90-2; NewYTBS 91; Who 82, 83, 85, 88, 90, 92, 94; WhoWor 91*

DeLoutherbourg, Philip James
English. Artist, Designer
Oil painter, dramatic stage designer; introduced act-drops, invented moving peep-show.
b. Oct 31, 1740 in Strassburg, Germany

d. Mar 11, 1812 in Chiswick, England
Source: *DcBrWA; OxCArt*

del Ray, Lester (Ramon Alvarez)
American. Author
Writes science fiction and children's books: *Police Your Planet,* 1975.
b. Jun 2, 1915 in Saratoga, Minnesota
d. May 10, 1993 in New York, New York
Source: *AmAu&B; AuBYP 2, 3; BioIn 13; ConAu 17NR, 65; ConLC 81; DcLB 8; DcLP 87A; IntAu&W 89; MajTwCW; NewEScF; RGTwCSF; SmATA 22; TwCSFW 91; WhoAm 86, 90; WhoUSWr 88; WhoWrEP 89; WorAlBi; WrDr 92*

DelRio, Dolores
[Lolita Dolores Martinez Asunsolo Lopez Negrette]
Mexican. Actor
Best known for *Journey into Fear,* 1942; *The Fugitive,* 1947.
b. Aug 3, 1905 in Durango, Mexico
d. Apr 11, 1983 in Newport Beach, California
Source: *BiDFilm, 81; BioIn 6, 8, 9, 12; CelR; Film 1, 2; FilmEn; FilmgC; ForYSC; HalFC 80; IntMPA 75, 76, 77, 78, 79, 80, 81, 82; InWom; MotPP; MovMk; OxCFilm; TwYS; What 3; WhoHol A; WorAl; WorEFlm*

DelRuth, Roy
American. Director
Directed over 100 features in 40 yr. career.
b. Oct 18, 1895 in Philadelphia, Pennsylvania
d. Apr 27, 1961 in Sherman Oaks, California
Source: *DcAmB S7*

Deluc, Jean Andre
Swiss. Geologist, Meteorologist
Authority on Swiss Alps; tried to reconcile science with biblical book of Genesis.
b. Feb 8, 1727 in Geneva, Switzerland
d. Nov 7, 1817 in Windsor, England
Source: *BiESc; DcNaB; DcScB; NewCol 75*

DeLuca, Giuseppe
Italian. Opera Singer
Baritone, famed bel canto singer; made over 700 appearances in 80 different operas.
b. Dec 29, 1876 in Rome, Italy
d. Aug 27, 1950 in New York, New York
Source: *Baker 84; BiDAmM; CurBio 47, 50; DcAmB S4; MusSN; NewGrDM 80; WhAm 3*

De Lucia, Paco
Spanish. Musician
Guitar player whose eclectic flamenco style incorporates at times jazz, rumba and rock.
b. Dec 1947 in Algeciras, Spain
Source: *BioIn 14; ConMus 1*

DeLue, Donald Harcourt
American. Sculptor
Monuments, memorials include works at Omaha Beach, France; Federal Court Building, Philadelphia.
b. Oct 5, 1897 in Boston, Massachusetts
d. Aug 26, 1988 in Leonardo, New Jersey
Source: *BioIn 4, 10, 16; NewYTBS 88; WhAm 9; WhAmArt 85; WhoAm 74, 76, 78, 84, 86; WhoAmA 86*

DeLugg, Milton
American. Composer, Conductor
Accordionist, bandleader; starred on "Johnny Carson Show," 1950-60.
b. Dec 2, 1918 in Los Angeles, California
Source: *ASCAP 66; CmpEPM; LegTOT*

DeLuise, Dom
American. Comedian, Actor
Appeared in films *Blazing Saddles,* 1974; *The End,* 1978.
b. Aug 1, 1933 in New York, New York
Source: *BioIn 14; ConTFT 9; EncAFC; HalFC 88; IntMPA 92; VarWW 85; WhoAm 86, 90; WhoHol A; WorAlBi*

Delvecchio, Alex Peter
"Fats"
Canadian. Hockey Player
Center, Detroit, 1950-74; won Lady Byng Trophy three times; Hall of Fame, 1977.
b. Dec 4, 1931 in Fort William, Ontario, Canada
Source: *HocEn; WhoHcky 73*

De Maiziere, Lothar
German. Political Leader
First and last freely elected prime minister, German Democratic Republic, Apr 12, 1990-Oct 3, 1990; served only to negotiate reunification of Germany; minister without portfolio, 1990—.
b. Mar 2, 1940 in Nordhausen, Germany
Source: *BioIn 17; CurBio 90; IntWW 91, 93; WhoWor 91*

DeManio, Jack
English. Broadcast Journalist
Host, BBC "Today" show, 1958-71.
b. Jan 26, 1914 in London, England
Source: *BioIn 9; ConAu 61, 127; Who 74, 82, 83, 85, 88, 90N*

DeMar, Clarence
American. Track Athlete
Won Boston Marathon seven times; Olympic team member.
b. 1888
d. Jun 11, 1958 in Reading, Massachusetts
Source: *ObitOF 79*

Demara, Ferdinand Waldo, Jr.
"The Great Imposter"
American. Imposter
Master identity thief; subject of biography, film *The Great Imposter,* 1961.
b. Dec 12, 1921 in Lawrence, Massachusetts
d. Jun 7, 1982 in Anaheim, California
Source: *AnObit 1982; BioIn 4, 5, 6, 12, 13; DrInf; NewYTBS 82*

DeMarco, Tony
American. Actor, Dancer
With partner Sally DeMarco did specialty numbers in 1940s films.
b. 1898 in Buffalo, New York
d. Nov 14, 1965 in Palm Beach, Florida
Source: *BioIn 1, 7; EncAB-A 38; WhoHol B; WhScrn 74, 77, 83*

Demarest, William
American. Actor
Appeared in TV series "My Three Sons," 1967-73.
b. Feb 27, 1892 in Saint Paul, Minnesota
d. Dec 27, 1983 in Palm Springs, California
Source: *AnObit 1983; BioIn 13; ConTFT 2; EncAFC; EncVaud; Film 2; FilmEn; FilmgC; GangFlm; HalFC 80, 84, 88; IntMPA 75, 76, 77, 78, 79, 80, 81, 82, 84; LegTOT; MotPP; MovMk; NewYTBS 83; TwYS; Vers A; WhoHol A; WorAl; WorAlBi*

Demaret, Jimmy
[James Newton Demaret]
American. Golfer
Turned pro, 1938; won over 35 tournaments; first to win Masters three times, 1940, 1947, 1950.
b. May 10, 1910 in Houston, Texas
d. Dec 28, 1983 in Houston, Texas
Source: *AnObit 1983; BiDAmSp OS; BioIn 2, 13, 14, 20; ConAu 111; NewYTBS 83, 84; WhoGolf; WhoSpor*

Demers, Jacques
Canadian. Hockey Coach
NHL coach since 1979; with Detroit, 1986-92; Montreal, 1992—, won Adams Award, 1987, 1988.
b. Aug 25, 1944 in Montreal, Quebec, Canada
Source: *BioIn 15; HocEn; WhoAm 90, 92, 94, 95, 96, 97; WhoE 95, 97; WhoMW 86, 88, 90*

De Mestral, Georges
Swiss. Inventor
Best known for inventing Velcro, 1948, an idea born when he discovered that burrs stuck to his pants consisted of little hooks.
b. 1908? in Nyon, Switzerland
d. Feb 11, 1990 in Commugny, Switzerland
Source: *BioIn 16; NewYTBS 90*

Demetrius I
[Demetrius Poliorcetes]
Macedonian. Ruler
King of Macedonia, 294-285 BC; destroyed Egyptian fleet, 306 BC.
b. 337BC
d. 283BC
Source: *NewCol 75; WebBD 83*

D'Emilio, John
American. Historian
Author of *Intimate Matters: A History of Sexuality in America,* 1988.
b. 1948 in New York, New York
Source: *ConAu 135; GayLesB; GayLL; WrDr 94, 96*

DeMille, Agnes (George)
[Mrs. Walter Foy Prude]
American. Dancer, Author
Choreographed musicals *Oklahoma,* 1943; *Carousel,* 1945; *Brigadoon,* 1947; won Tonys, 1947, 1962; niece of Cecil B.
b. Sep 12, 1905 in New York, New York
d. Oct 7, 1993 in New York, New York
Source: *AmAu&B; BenetAL 91; BioIn 13, 14, 16; BioNews 74; CelR 90; ConAu 30NR, 65; ConTFT 3; CurBio 85; EncMT; FacFETw; HerW, 84; IntWWM 90; InWom, SUP; LibW; NewGrDA 86; NewYTBS 76, 88; NotNAT; NotWoAT; OxCAmT 84; PeoHis; REnAL; WebAB 74, 79; Who 85, 92; WhoAm 86, 90; WhoAmW 85, 91; WhoEnt 92; WhoThe 81; WorAlBi*

DeMille, Cecil B(lount)
American. Director, Producer
With Jesse Lasky, Samuel Goldwyn, formed Jesse Lasky Feature Play Co., 1913; evolved into Paramount Studios; spectacular productions included *The Ten Commandments,* 1956.
b. Aug 12, 1881 in Ashfield, Massachusetts
d. Jan 21, 1959 in Hollywood, California
Source: *AmAu&B; BiDFilm; CmMov; CurBio 42, 59; DcFM; EncAB-H 1974, 1996; FilmgC; MovMk; OxCFilm; REn; REnAL; WhAm 3; WhScrn 77; WorAl; WorEFlm*

Deming, Barbara
American. Author
Published collection of short stories *Wash Us and Comb Us,* 1974.
b. Jul 23, 1917 in New York, New York
d. Aug 2, 1984 in Florida
Source: *AmPeW; AmWomWr SUP; BioIn 11, 12, 14, 15; ConAu 15NR, 85; FemiWr; ForWC 70; GayLesB; RadHan; WhoAmW 58, 61*

Deming, W(illiam) Edwards
American. Consultant
Management specialist, statistician; introduced revolutionary concept of quality control and plant management that enabled Japan to become economic giant; Engineering and Scientific Hall of Fame, 1986.
b. Oct 14, 1900 in Sioux City, Iowa
d. Dec 20, 1993 in Washington, District of Columbia
Source: *AmMWSc 76P, 79, 82, 86, 89; BioIn 12, 13, 16; CurBio 94N; News 92, 92-2; NewYTBS 81; WhoAm 74, 90; WhoFI 92*

Demirel, Suleyman
Turkish. Political Leader
Six-time prime minister; known as moderate man of the people.
b. Oct 6, 1924 in Islamkoy, Turkey
Source: *BioIn 7, 9, 10, 11, 12, 16, 17, 18; CurBio 80; DcPol; EncWB; FacFETw; IntWW 78, 79, 80, 81, 82, 83, 89, 91, 93; IntYB 82; MidE 78, 79, 80, 81, 82; NewYTBS 80; PolLCME; WhoWor 78, 80, 82, 84, 93, 95, 96, 97*

Demjanjuk, John
American. Government Official
Sentenced to death as Treblinka's "Ivan the Terrible," Israeli Supreme Court overturned the conviction, 1993, after sixteen years of controversy.
b. Apr 3, 1921? in Dub Makarenzi, Ukraine
Source: *BioIn 14, 15, 16*

Demme, Jonathan
American. Director
Directed slices of Americana: *Citizens Band,* 1977; *Swing Shift,* 1984.
b. Feb 22, 1944 in Baldwin, New York
Source: *BiDFilm 94; BioIn 14, 15, 16; ConTFT 5, 14; CurBio 85; GangFlm; HalFC 80, 88; IntDcF 1-2, 2-2; IntMPA 80, 81, 82, 84, 86, 88, 92, 94, 96; IntWW 91, 93; LegTOT; MiSFD 9; News 92; WhoAm 90, 92, 94, 95, 96, 97; WhoEnt 92; WorFDir 2*

Demmert, William G., Jr.
American. Educator
Taught at several colleges and universities, including the University of Alaska at Juneau; worked on the development of the Indian Education Act of 1872.
b. Mar 9, 1934 in Klawock, Alaska
Source: *BioIn 21; NotNaAm*

Democritus
"The Laughing Philosopher"
Greek. Philosopher
Developed atomic theory: reality consists of atoms and space between them, anti cipating the modern principles of the conservation of energy and the irreducibility of matter.
b. 460BC in Abdera, Greece
d. 370BC
Source: *Benet 87, 96; BioIn 4, 7, 12; CasWL; DcBiPP; EncEth; Grk&L; LarDcSc; LegTOT; LuthC 75; NewC; OxCClL, 89; OxCEng 85, 95; OxCPhil; PenC CL; REn; WhDW; WorAl; WorAlBi; WorScD; WrPh P*

DeMontebello, Guy-Philippe
American. Museum Director
Director, Metropolitan Museum of Art, 1978—.
b. May 16, 1936 in Paris, France
Source: *BioIn 13, 14, 15, 16; CelR 90; ConAu 45; CurBio 81; NewYTBS 85; Who 83, 92; WhoAm 86, 90; WhoAmA 91; WhoE 91; WhoWor 91*

De Morgan, Augustus
English. Mathematician
A founder, first president, London Mathematical Society, 1865; wrote *Formal Logic,* 1847.
b. Jun 27, 1806 in Madura, India
d. Mar 18, 1871 in London, England
Source: *Alli, SUP; BioIn 13, 15, 18; BritAu 19; CelCen; Chambr 3; ChhPo; CyEd; DcBiPP; DcEnL; DcEuL; DcNaB; DcScB; EncO&P 1, 2, 3; EncPaPR 91; EvLB; InSci; LarDcSc; NewCBEL; NewCol 75; OxCPhil*

De Morgan, William Frend
English. Artist, Author
Potter who made colored lusterware; popular novelist later in life: *Joseph Vance,* 1906; son of Augustus.
b. Nov 16, 1839 in London, England
d. Jan 15, 1917 in London, England
Source: *AntBDN M; BioIn 3, 5, 7, 9, 12; CasWL; Chambr 3; CyWA 58; DcArts; DcBiA; DcD&D; DcEuL; DcLEL; DcNaB 1912; EvLB; GrWrEL N; JBA 34; LinLib L, S; LngCTC; ModBrL; NewC; NewCBEL; NewCol 75; OxCEng 67, 85, 95; PenC ENG; PenDiDA 89; REn; TwCA, SUP; TwCWr*

DeMornay, Rebecca
American. Actor
In films *Risky Business,* 1983; *The Trip to Bountiful,* 1985; daughter of talk show host Wally George.
b. Aug 29, 1962 in Santa Rosa, California
Source: *BioIn 13, 14, 15, 16; ConTFT 3; HalFC 88; IntMPA 92; WhoEnt 92; WorAlBi*

DeMoss, Arthur S
American. Insurance Executive
Pres. of National Liberty Life Insurance Co., 1962-70.
b. Oct 26, 1925 in Albany, New York
Source: *BioIn 9; WhoE 74; WhoFI 74, 75; WhoIns 75, 76, 77, 78, 79, 80, 81, 82, 84*

Demosthenes
Greek. Orator, Statesman
Considered greatest Greek orator; leader of democratic faction, Athens.
b. 384BC in Attica, Greece
d. Oct 322BC in Calavria, Greece
Source: *AncWr; BbD; BiD&SB; BioIn 13, 18, 20; CasWL; ClMLC 13; CyWA 58; DcArts; DcEnL; Grk&L; HarEnMi; HisWorL; LegTOT; LinLib L, S; McGEWB; NewC; OxCClL 89; OxCEng 67; PenC CL; RComWL; REn; RfGWoL 95; WorAl; WorAlBi*

DeMott, Benjamin Haile
American. Author, Educator
Columnist, *Harper's* mag., 1981—; contributing editor, *Atlantic Monthly,* 1977—; novels include *The Body's Cage,* 1959.
b. Jun 2, 1924 in Rockville Centre, New York
Source: *AmAu&B; ConAu 5R; DrAPF 91; DrAS 74E; WhoAm 74, 76, 78, 80, 82, 84, 86; WhoUSWr 88; WhoWrEP 89; WorAu 1950; WrDr 92*

Dempsey, Jack
[William Harrison Dempsey]
"The Manassa Mauler"
American. Boxer
Heavyweight boxing champ, 1919-26, 1931-40; Hall of Fame, 1954.
b. Jun 24, 1895 in Manassa, Colorado
d. May 31, 1983 in New York, New York
Source: *AmDec 1920; AnObit 1983; BiDAmSp BK; BioIn 1, 2, 3, 4, 5, 6, 7, 8, 9, 10, 11, 12, 13, 14, 15, 16, 17, 21; BoxReg; CelR; ConAu 89, 109; CurBio 45, 83N; EncAB-H 1996; FacFETw; Film 2; LegTOT; NewYTBE 70, 73; NewYTBS 83; OxCAmH; WebAB 74, 79; WhoAm 74, 76, 78; WhoBox 74; WhoHol A; WhoSpor; WhoWor 74; WorAl; WorAlBi*

Dempsey, John Noel
American. Politician
Democratic governor of CT, 1961-71.
b. Jan 3, 1915 in Cahir, Ireland
d. Jul 16, 1989 in Killingly, Connecticut
Source: *BiDrGov 1789; BioIn 7, 11, 16; CurBio 61; IntWW 74; WhAmP; WhoAm 74; WhoAmP 73*

Dempsey, Miles Christopher, Sir
English. Army Officer
Led Second Army in D-Day invasion, 1944; commanded forces in South East Asia, Middle East, 1945-47.
b. Dec 15, 1896 in Hoylake, England
d. Jun 6, 1969 in Yattendon, England
Source: *BioIn 1, 8; CurBio 44, 69; DcNaB 1961; HisEWW*

Dempsey, Rick
[John Rikard Dempsey]
American. Baseball Player
Catcher, 1973-90; MVP, 1983 World Series.
b. Sep 13, 1949 in Fayetteville, Tennessee
Source: *Ballpl 90; BaseReg 86, 87; BioIn 13*

Dempsey, Tom
[Thomas Dempsey]
American. Football Player
Birth defect left him with deformed right foot, but became placekicker, 1969-79; with New Orleans, kicked longest field goal in NFL history, 63 yds., 1970.
b. Jan 12, 1947 in Milwaukee, Wisconsin
Source: *BiDAmSp FB; BioIn 9, 10, 12, 13; NewYTBS 83; WhoFtbl 74*

Dempster, Arthur Jeffrey
Canadian. Physicist, Educator
Discovered Uranium-235, 1935, which is the explosive of atomic bomb.
b. Aug 14, 1886 in Toronto, Ontario, Canada
d. Mar 11, 1950 in Stuart, Florida
Source: *AsBiEn; BiESc; BioIn 2, 3; FacFETw; InSci; NatCAB 38; ObitOF 79; WebBD 83; WhAm 2A*

Dempster, Carol
American. Actor
Brief career as star of D W Griffith films in 1920s.
b. 1901 in Duluth, Minnesota
Source: *Film 2; FilmgC; HalFC 80, 84, 88; InWom SUP; MotPP; TwYS; WhoHol A*

Demus, Joreg
Austrian. Pianist
Award-winning Viennese concert performer, made over 200 recordings.
b. Dec 2, 1928 in Saint Poelten, Austria
Source: *Baker 84; BioIn 5; IntWW 78, 91; IntWWM 90; NewAmDM; PenDiMP; WhoMus 72*

Demuth, Charles
American. Artist
Leader of the Precisionist school; known for watercolors, series of flowers, circuses.
b. Nov 8, 1883 in Lancaster, Pennsylvania
d. Oct 23, 1935 in Lancaster, Pennsylvania
Source: *BioIn 14, 15, 16, 20; BriEAA; ConArt 77; DcAmArt; DcAmB S1; DcCAA 71, 77, 88, 94; EncAB-H 1974, 1996; IntDcAA 90; McGDA; McGEWB; OxCAmH; OxCArt; OxCTwCA; OxDcArt; PhDcTCA 77; WebAB 74, 79; WebBD 83; WhAm 4; WhAmArt 85; WhAm HSA; WorAlBi*

Demy, Jacques
French. Director
Best known for film *The Umbrellas of Cherbourg,* 1963; only US film was *Model Shop,* 1971.
b. Jun 5, 1931 in Pont Chateau, France
d. Oct 27, 1990 in Paris, France
Source: *AnObit 1990; BiDFilm, 81, 94; BioIn 12, 16, 17; ConAu 148; ConTFT 9, 10; DcFM; DcTwCCu 2; EncEurC; FacFETw; FilmEn; FilmgC; HalFC 80, 84, 88; IntDcF 1-2, 2-2; IntWW 74, 75, 76, 77, 78, 79, 80, 81, 82, 83, 89, 91N; ItaFilm; MiSFD 9N; MovMk; NewYTBS 90; OxCFilm; WhoFr 79; WhoWor 74, 76, 78; WorEFlm; WorFDir 2*

Dench, Judith Olivia
English. Actor
Stage performances include *Pack of Lies.*
b. Dec 12, 1934 in York, England
Source: *BioIn 13, 14; CamGWoT; CnThe; ContDcW 89; ConTFT 4; FilmgC; HalFC 88; IntMPA 81, 82, 92; IntWW 78, 79, 80, 81, 82, 83, 89, 91, 93; VarWW 85; Who 74, 82, 83, 85, 88, 90, 92, 94; WhoThe 81; WhoWor 82, 84, 87, 89, 91, 93, 95, 96, 97*

Denenberg, Herbert Sidney
American. Journalist, Lawyer
Columnist, *Philadelphia Journal,* 1981-82; writings include *Risk and Insurance,* 1973; won four Emmys.
b. Nov 20, 1929 in Omaha, Nebraska
Source: *AmMWSc 73S, 92; BioIn 9, 10, 11; IntWW 89, 91, 93; WhoAm 74, 76, 78, 80, 82, 84, 86, 88, 90, 92, 94, 95, 96, 97; WhoAmJ 80; WhoE 74, 75, 79, 81, 83, 89, 91, 95; WhoGov 75; WhoIns 75, 79, 80, 81, 82, 84, 86, 88, 90, 92, 93, 94, 97; WhoMedH; WrDr 92*

Deneuve, Catherine
[Catherine Dorleac]
French. Actor
Starred in *Mayerling,* 1968; featured in print, TV ads for Chanel No. 5; image used by French govt. to represent modern "Marianne," 1985.
b. Oct 22, 1943 in Paris, France
Source: *BiDFilm, 81, 94; BioIn 7, 8, 10, 11, 14, 15, 16; BkPepl; CelR, 90; ContDcW 89; ConTFT 2, 4, 14; CurBio 78; DcArts; DcTwCCu 2; EncEurC; FacFETw; FilmAG WE; FilmEn; FilmgC; ForYSC; HalFC 80, 84, 88; IntDcF 1-3, 2-3; IntDcWB; IntMPA 88, 92, 94, 96; IntWW 74, 75, 76, 77, 78, 79, 80, 81, 82, 83, 89, 91, 93; InWom SUP; ItaFilm; LegTOT; MotPP; MovMk; OxCFilm; Who 88, 90, 92, 94; WhoAm 78, 80, 82, 84, 86, 88, 90, 92, 94, 95, 96, 97; WhoAmW 70, 72, 74, 83, 85; WhoEnt 92; WhoFr 79; WhoHol 92, A; WhoHrs 80; WhoWor 78, 80, 82, 84, 87, 89, 91, 93, 95, 96, 97; WomFir; WorAl; WorAlBi; WorEFlm*

Deng Xiaoping
[Teng Hsiaoping]
Chinese. Political Leader
VP of Chinese Communist Party, 1977-87; most powerful member.
b. Aug 22, 1904 in Sichuan, China
d. Feb 19, 1997 in Beijing, China
Source: *BioIn 16, 18, 19, 20, 21; ColdWar 2; CurBio 94; DcTwHis; DicTyr; EncCW; EncRev; FacFETw; HisWorL; IntWW 89, 91, 93; LegTOT; News 95, 95-1; WhoAsAP 91; WhoPRCh 91; WhoWor 84, 87, 91, 93*

Denikin, Anton Ivanovich
Russian. Army Officer
Led White Russian Army against Bolsheviks, 1918-20.
b. 1872
d. Aug 8, 1947 in Ann Arbor, Michigan
Source: *Benet 87, 96; BiDSovU; BioIn 1, 5, 10, 16, 17; BlkwERR; DcTwHis; FacFETw; ObitOF 79; REn; WhoMilH 76; WorAl*

DeNiro, Robert
American. Actor
Won Oscar, 1981, for *Raging Bull;* other films include *The Deer Hunter,* 1979; *The Mission,* 1986; known for role of

Michael Corleone in the *Godfather* series.
b. Aug 17, 1943 in New York, New York
Source: *BioIn 14, 15, 16; BkPepl; CelR 90; ConTFT 4; DcCAA 88; FacFETw; HalFC 88; IntMPA 92; IntWW 91; MovMk; VarWW 85; WhoAm 86, 90; WhoEnt 92; WhoHol A; WorAlBi*

Denis, Maurice
French. Artist, Critic
The spokesman for the Nabis; wrote *History of Religious Art,* 1939.
b. Nov 25, 1870
d. Nov 13, 1943
Source: *BioIn 1, 2, 4, 13, 14, 15, 19; ClaDrA; DcArts; DcTwCCu 2; FacFETw; McGDA; NewCol 75; OxCArt; OxCTwCA; OxDcArt; PhDcTCA 77; ThHElm*

Denison, George Taylor
Canadian. Soldier, Historian
A founder of patriotic "Canada First" movement, 1868; wrote *History of Cavalry,* 1877.
b. Aug 31, 1839 in Toronto, Ontario, Canada
d. Jun 6, 1925 in Toronto, Ontario, Canada
Source: *Alli SUP; ApCAB; BbtC; DcCanB 10; DcNAA; LinLib L; MacDCB 78; OxCCan*

Dennehy, Brian
American. Actor
Films include *Cocoon,* 1985; also known for many TV, stage appearences.
b. Jul 9, 1938 in Bridgeport, Connecticut
Source: *BioIn 14, 16; ConTFT 4, 11; CurBio 91; EncAFC; HalFC 88; IntMPA 92; IntWW 91; VarWW 85; WhoAm 86, 90; WhoEnt 92; WhoHol 92; WorAlBi*

Denneny, Cy(ril)
Canadian. Hockey Player
Left wing, 1917-29, mostly with Ottawa; won Art Ross Trophy, 1924; Hall of Fame, 1959.
b. Dec 23, 1897 in Farran's Point, Ontario, Canada
d. Sep 10, 1970
Source: *HocEn; WhoHcky 73*

Denneny, Michael (Leo)
American. Editor
A founder of *Christopher Street* magazine, 1975; Literary Market Place Editor of the Year, 1994.
b. Mar 2, 1943 in Providence, Rhode Island
Source: *GayLesB*

Denner, Johann Christoph
German. Musician
Invented the clarinet, 1690s.
b. Aug 13, 1655 in Leipzig, Germany
d. Apr 20, 1707 in Nurnberg, Bavaria
Source: *BioIn 2; DcBiPP; MusMk; NewAmDM; NewGrDM 80*

Denning, Alfred Thompson
English. Judge, Author
Investigator of Britain's scandalous Profumo case, 1963.
b. Jan 23, 1899 in Whitchurch, England
Source: *BioIn 13; ConAu 115, 143, X; CurBio 65; IntAu&W 91, 93; IntWW 74, 93; OxCLaw; Who 85; WhoWor 74; WrDr 82, 96*

Denning, Richard
[Louis Albert Denninger]
American. Actor
Films include *Creature from the Black Lagoon,* 1954; *Mary, Queen of Scots,* 1971.
b. Mar 27, 1914 in Poughkeepsie, New York
Source: *BioIn 3, 21; FilmEn; FilmgC; HalFC 80, 84, 88; LegTOT; MotPP; MovMk; VarWW 85; WhAm 8; WhoAm 74, 76, 78, 80, 82; WhoHol 92, A; WhoHrs 80; WorAl*

Dennis, Nigel Forbes
English. Author
Satirist, *Cards of Identity,* 1955 was his best known novel.
b. Jan 16, 1912 in Bletchingley, England
d. Jul 19, 1989 in London, England
Source: *BioIn 13, 16; CamGLE; CamGWoT; ConDr 88, 93; ConNov 86; DcLEL 1940; DcNaB 1986; EncSF 93; FacFETw; IntAu&W 76, 77, 89, 91; IntWWP 77; MajTwCW; ModBrL S2; NewCBEL; NewYTBS 89; OxCEng 85, 95; RGTwCWr; Who 74, 82, 83, 85, 88, 90N; WrDr 88, 90*

Dennis, Patrick
[Virginia Rowens; Edward Everett Tanner, III]
American. Author
Known for *Auntie Mame,* which was adapted to film, Broadway musical *Mame.*
b. May 18, 1921 in Chicago, Illinois
d. Nov 6, 1976 in New York, New York
Source: *AmAu&B; BioIn 4, 5, 6, 7, 10, 11; ConAu 69, 73; CurBio 77, 77N; DcAmB S10; LegTOT; NewYTBS 76; WhAm 7; WhoAm 74, 76; WorAl; WorAu 1950; WrDr 76*

Dennis, Sandy
American. Actor
Won Tony awards for *Splendor in the Grass,* 1963 and *A Thousand Clowns,* 1964; won Oscar, 1966, for *Who's Afraid of Virginia Woolf?*
b. Apr 27, 1937 in Hastings, Nebraska
d. Mar 2, 1992 in Westport, Connecticut
Source: *AnObit 1992; BiE&WWA; BioIn 8, 10, 11, 16, 17, 18, 19; CelR, 90; ConTFT 1, 10; CurBio 69, 92N; FilmEn; FilmgC; ForYSC; HalFC 80, 84, 88; IntMPA 77, 80, 86, 88, 92; IntWW 82, 83, 89, 91; InWom, SUP; LegTOT; MotPP; MovMk; News 92; NewYTBS 92; NotNAT; OxCAmT 84; WhAm 10; WhoAm 74, 76, 78, 80, 82, 84, 86, 88, 90; WhoAmW 68A, 70, 72, 74, 83; WhoEnt 92; WhoHol 92, A; WhoThe 72, 77, 81; WorAl; WorAlBi*

Dennison, George
American. Editor, Author
Wrote *Oilers and Sweepers,* 1979.
b. Sep 10, 1925 in Ashburn, Georgia
d. Oct 8, 1987 in Temple, Maine
Source: *AmAu&B; BioIn 10, 13, 15, 16, 20; ConAu 6AS, 101, 123; MugS*

Dennison, Robert Lee
American. Naval Officer
Naval aide to Truman, 1948-53; retired as admiral, 1963.
b. Apr 13, 1901 in Warren, Pennsylvania
d. Mar 14, 1980 in Bethesda, Maryland
Source: *AnObit 1980; BioIn 5, 12; BlueB 76; CurBio 60, 80, 80N; IntWW 74, 75, 76, 77, 78, 79, 80; IntYB 78, 79, 80; NewYTBS 80; WhAm 7; Who 74; WhoAm 74, 76, 78, 80; WhoFI 74*

Denny, John Allen
American. Baseball Player
Pitcher, 1974-86; led NL in wins, won Cy Young Award, 1983.
b. Nov 8, 1952 in Prescott, Arizona
Source: *Ballpl 90; BaseReg 86, 87; BioIn 13; NegAl 89; WhoAm 86*

Denny, Ludwell
American. Journalist
With Scripps Howard Newspaper Alliance, 1928-59, emeritus, 1960-70.
b. Nov 18, 1894 in Boonville, Indiana
d. Oct 12, 1970
Source: *AmAu&B; ConAu 29R; IndAu 1917; WhAm 5*

Denny, Reginald
American. Victim
Truck driver pulled from truck, beaten on live TV broadcast during 1992 LA riots.
Source: *BioIn 18, 19; ObitOF 79; WhoHol 92*

Denny, Reginald Leigh
[Reginald Leigh Daymore]
English. Actor
Appeared in 200 films including *Leather Pushers* series, 1922-24.
b. Nov 20, 1891 in Richmond, England
d. Jun 16, 1967 in Surrey, England
Source: *BiE&WWA; Film 1; FilmEn; FilmgC; MotPP; MovMk; TwYS; Vers A; WhAm 4; WhoHol B; WhScrn 74, 77; WhThe*

Denny-Brown, Derek Ernest
American. Neurologist, Author
Researched human nervous system; found blood supply to brain influences strokes.
b. Jun 1, 1901 in Christchurch, New Zealand
d. Apr 20, 1981 in Cambridge, Massachusetts
Source: *AmMWSc 76P, 79; BioIn 12, 13; ConAu 103; IntWW 77, 78, 79, 80, 81,*

81N; NewYTBS 81; WhAm 7; WhE&EA; Who 74; WhoAm 74

Denoff, Sam
American. Writer, Producer
Created, produced TV series "That Girl," 1967-71; won Emmys for "The Dick Van Dyke Show," 1964, 1966.
b. Jul 1, 1928 in New York, New York
Source: *ConTFT 4; VarWW 85; WhoEnt 92; WhoWest 89*

Densen-Gerber, Judianne
American. Psychiatrist
Founded Odyssey House, 1966, drug treatment center that doesn't rely on substituting other drugs.
b. Nov 13, 1934 in New York, New York
Source: *AuBYP 2S, 3; BiDrAPA 77, 89; BioIn 9, 12, 13; ConAu 37R; CurBio 83; InWom SUP; WhoAm 74, 76, 78, 80, 82, 84, 88, 90, 92, 94, 95, 96; WhoAmL 83, 85, 87, 90; WhoAmW 70, 72, 74, 75, 77, 79, 81, 83, 95, 97; WhoE 74, 77, 79, 81, 83, 85, 95; WhoMedH; WrDr 76, 80, 82, 84, 86, 88, 90, 92, 94, 96*

Denslow, W(illiam) W(allace)
American. Illustrator
Illustrated original *The Wizard of Oz* children's books, 1900-02.
b. May 5, 1856 in Philadelphia, Pennsylvania
d. Mar 29, 1915
Source: *AmAu&B; ArtsAmW 3; BioIn 9, 11, 12; ChhPo, S1, S2, S3; ChlLR 15; DcNAA; FourBJA; OxCChiL; SmATA 16; WhAm 1; WhAmArt 85*

Densmore, Frances
American. Ethnologist, Musicologist
Leading expert on American Indian cultures; focused on tribal music and songs.
b. May 21, 1867 in Red Wing, Minnesota
d. Jun 5, 1957 in Red Wing, Minnesota
Source: *Baker 78, 84, 92; BenetAL 91; BioIn 1, 4, 11, 15; DcAmB S6; FacFETw; GrLiveH; InWom, SUP; NewGrDA 86; NewGrDM 80; OxCMus; PeoHis; REnAL; REnAW; WhAm 3; WhE&EA; WhNAA; WhoAmL 92; WhoAmW 58*

Densmore, John
[The Doors]
American. Singer, Musician
Drummer, keyboardist with The Doors, mid-60s-1973.
b. Dec 1, 1945 in Los Angeles, California
Source: *LegTOT; WhoRocM 82*

Dent, Alan Holmes
Scottish. Author, Critic, Journalist
Illustrated London News film critic, 1947-68; wrote *Worlds of Shakespeare* book series, 1971-79.
b. Jan 7, 1905 in Ayrshire, Scotland
d. Dec 1978
Source: *Au&Wr 71; ChhPo S2; ConAu 5NR, 9R; DcLEL 1940; IntAu&W 76, 77; LngCTC; Who 74; WhoThe 72, 77; WrDr 76*

Dent, Bucky
[Russell Earl O'Dey]
American. Baseball Player
Shortstop, 1973-84; MVP, 1978 World Series; gm, NY Yankees, 1989-90.
b. Nov 25, 1951 in Savannah, Georgia
Source: *Ballpl 90; BioIn 14, 16, 17; LegTOT; NewYTBS 79; WhoAm 82, 90*

Dent, Edward Joseph
English. Impresario, Musicologist, Educator
Best known British musical scholar of his time; translated Mozart, other operas into English.
b. Jul 16, 1876 in Ribston, England
d. Aug 22, 1957 in London, England
Source: *Baker 78, 84; BioIn 2, 4, 11, 12; DcNaB 1951; NewEOp 71; NewGrDM 80; OxCMus; WhE&EA*

Dent, Phil
"Philby"
Australian. Tennis Player
Won US Open mixed doubles with Billie Jean King, 1976.
b. Feb 14, 1950 in Sydney, Australia
Source: *WhoIntT*

Denton, Jeremiah Andrew, Jr.
American. Politician
Rep. senator from AL, 1981-87; first POW to return from Vietnam.
b. Jul 15, 1924 in Mobile, Alabama
Source: *BiDrUSC 89; BioIn 12, 13; CngDr 85; ConAu 31NR, 69; CurBio 82; IntWW 81, 82, 83; NewYTBS 80; PolsAm 84; WhoAm 76, 78, 80, 82, 84, 86; WhoAmP 85, 91; WhoGov 77; WhoSSW 82, 84, 86; WhoWor 82, 87*

Denton, Steve
"The Bull"
American. Tennis Player
With doubles partner Kevin Curran, won US Clay Court, 1980, 1981, US Open, 1982.
b. Sep 5, 1956 in Kingsville, Texas
Source: *WhoIntT*

Den Uyl, Joop
[Johannes Marten Den Uyl]
Dutch. Politician
Prime minister of The Netherlands, 1973-77, 1977-81, 1982-87.
b. Aug 9, 1919 in Hilversum, Netherlands
d. Dec 24, 1987 in Amsterdam, Netherlands
Source: *BioIn 21*

Denver, Bob
American. Actor
Starred in "The Many Loves of Dobie Gillis," 1959-63; played Gilligan on "Gilligan's Island", 1964-67.
b. Jan 9, 1935 in New Rochelle, New York
Source: *BioIn 16; ConTFT 7; EncAFC; FilmgC; ForYSC; HalFC 80, 84, 88; IntMPA 84, 86, 88, 92, 94, 96; LegTOT; WhoCom; WhoHol 92, A; WorAl; WorAlBi*

Denver, James William
American. Politician
Held various political offices including governor of Territory of KS, 1858.
b. Oct 23, 1817 in Winchester, Virginia
d. Aug 9, 1892 in Washington, District of Columbia
Source: *AmBi; ApCAB; BiAUS; BiDrAC; BiDrATG; BiDrUSC 89; BioIn 7, 17; CivWDc; CmCal; DcAmB; Drake; NatCAB 8; OhA&B; WhAm HS; WhAmP; WhCiWar*

Denver, John
[Henry John Deutschendorf]
American. Singer, Songwriter, Actor
Hits include "Take Me Home Country Road," 1971; "Rocky Mountain High," 1972; appeared in *Oh, God!*, 1977.
b. Dec 31, 1943 in Roswell, New Mexico
Source: *AmSong; ASCAP 80; Baker 84; BgBkCoM; BioIn 10, 11, 12, 14, 15; BioNews 74; BkPepl; CelR 90; ConMuA 80A; ConMus 1; ConTFT 8, 15; CounME 74, 74A; CurBio 75; EncFCWM 83; EncPR&S 89; EncRk 88; EncRkSt; HalFC 80, 84, 88; HarEnCM 87; IlEncCM; IlEncRk; IntMPA 88, 92, 94, 96; IntWW 89, 91, 93; LegTOT; NewAgE 90; NewGrDA 86; OxCPMus; PenEncP; RkOn 78; RolSEnR 83; WhoAm 76, 78, 80, 82, 84, 86, 88, 90, 92, 94, 95, 96, 97; WhoEnt 92; WhoHol 92; WhoRock 81; WorAl; WorAlBi*

Deodato
[Eumir DeAlmeida]
Brazilian. Musician, Composer
Keyboard player best known for background music; albums include *Motion*, 1984.
b. Jun 22, 1942 in Rio de Janeiro, Brazil
Source: *BiDJaz; EncJzS; HarEnR 86; LegTOT; NewGrDJ 88; PenEncP; RkOn 82; WhoAm 84; WhoRocM 82*

DePalma, Brian Russell
American. Director
Inheritor of Alfred Hitchcock's crown "Master of the Macabre"; films include *Dressed to Kill*, 1980; *Body Double*, 1984.
b. Sep 11, 1940 in Newark, New Jersey
Source: *BioIn 11, 13, 14, 15, 16; CelR 90; ConLC 20; ConTFT 6; CurBio 82; FacFETw; FilmgC; HalFC 88; IntMPA 92; IntWW 91; NewYTBE 73; NewYTBS 89; WhoAm 86, 90; WhoEnt 92; WorFDir 2*

De Palma, Ralph
American. Auto Racer
Won 2,557 races out of 2,889 during career, 1908-34.
b. Jan 23, 1884, Italy
d. Mar 31, 1956 in South Pasadena, California
Source: *DcAmB S6; ObitOF 79*

DePaolis, Alessio
Italian. Opera Singer
Lyric tenor; noted for character roles.
b. Apr 5, 1893 in Rome, Italy
d. Mar 9, 1964 in New York, New York
Source: *NewEOp 71; WhAm 4*

Depardieu, Gerard
French. Actor
Won best actor Cesar for *The Last Metro,* 1980; Cannes' Palme d'or for *Under the Sun of Satan,* 1987; Golden Globe for *Green Card,* 1990.
b. Dec 27, 1948 in Chateauroux, France
Source: *BiDFilm 94; BioIn 12, 14, 15; CelR 90; ConTFT 8, 15; CurBio 87; DcArts; DcTwCCu 2; EncEurC; FacFETw; FilmAG WE; FilmEn; HalFC 88; IntDcF 1-3, 2-3; IntMPA 82, 84, 86, 88, 92, 94; IntWW 81, 82, 83, 89, 91, 93; ItaFilm; LegTOT; News 91, 91-2; NewYTBS 81, 87; VarWW 85; WhoAm 94, 95, 96, 97; WhoEnt 92; WhoFr 79; WhoHol 92, A; WhoWor 82, 84, 87, 89, 91, 93, 95, 96, 97*

DeParis, Wilbur
American. Jazz Musician
Trombonist, drummer with Duke Ellington, 1940s; led own bands, NYC, from 1950s.
b. Sep 20, 1900 in Crawfordsville, Indiana
d. Jan 1973 in New York, New York
Source: *AllMusG; BiDJaz; CmpEPM; NewYTBE 73; WhAm 5; WhoJazz 72; WhScrn 77*

De Passe, Suzanne
American. Screenwriter, Producer
Wrote film *Lady Sings the Blues,* 1972; has won several Emmys.
Source: *BioIn 14, 15, 16, 17, 18, 20; ConBlAP 88; InB&W 85; LesBEnT 92; News 90; VarWW 85; WhoAm 86, 90, 92, 94, 95, 96, 97; WhoAmW 85, 91, 93, 95; WhoBlA 92; WhoEnt 92; WhoFI 92, 94, 96; WhoWest 94, 96; WomWMM*

De Patie, David H
American. Producer
Won Oscar for *The Pink Phink,* 1964; Emmy for "The Cat-In-The-Hat," 1982.
b. Dec 24, 1930 in Los Angeles, California
Source: *VarWW 85; WhoAm 88; WhoEnt 92*

DePaul, Gene Vincent
American. Composer
Noted for Oscar-winning score, *Seven Brides for Seven Brothers,* 1954; Songwriter's Hall of Fame, 1985.
b. Jun 17, 1919 in New York, New York
d. Feb 27, 1988 in Los Angeles, California
Source: *CmpEPM*

Depeche Mode
[Vincent Clarke; Andy Fletcher; Dave Gahan; Martin Gore]
English. Music Group
Avant garde pop group formed 1980; hit single "People Are People," 1985.
Source: *ConMus 5; EncRk 88; EncRkSt; MnBBF; PenEncP; WhsNW 85*

Depew, Chauncey Mitchell
American. Politician, Philanthropist
Pres. NY Central Railroad, 1885-99, chm., 1899-1928; Rep. senator, 1899-1911.
b. Apr 23, 1834 in Peekskill, New York
d. Apr 5, 1928 in New York, New York
Source: *AmAu&B; AmBi; ApCAB; BbD; BiDAmBL 83; BiD&SB; BiDrAC; BiDrUSC 89; BioIn 1, 3, 4, 16; DcAmAu; DcAmB; DcNAA; EncABHB 2; HarEnUS; LinLib S; NatCAB 1, 23; REnAL; TwCBDA; WebAB 74, 79; WhAm 1; WhAmP; WhNAA*

DePinies, Jaime
Spanish. Diplomat
Pres. UN General Assembly, 1985-86.
b. Nov 18, 1917 in Madrid, Spain
Source: *BioIn 14, 15; ConNews 86-3; IntWW 91; NewYTBS 85; WhoGov 72; WhoWor 74, 78*

Depp, Johnny
[John Christopher Depp, II]
American. Actor
Played Tom Hanson on TV series "21 Jump Street," 1987-91; starred in 1990 film *Edward Scissorhands.*
b. Jun 9, 1963 in Owensboro, Kentucky
Source: *BioIn 15, 16; ConTFT 10; CurBio 91; IntMPA 92, 94, 96; IntWW 93; LegTOT; News 91, 91-3; WhoAm 92, 94, 95, 96, 97; WhoEnt 92; WhoHol 92; WorAlBi*

DePreist, James Anderson
American. Conductor
Music director and conductor of the Oregon Symphony, 1980—.
b. Nov 21, 1936 in Philadelphia, Pennsylvania
Source: *AfrAmAl 6; Baker 84, 92; BioIn 14, 15; BlkCond; CurBio 90; IntWWM 90; NegAl 89; NewGrDA 86; NewYTBS 87; WhoAfA 96; WhoAm 74, 76, 78, 80, 84, 86, 88, 90, 92, 94, 95, 96, 97; WhoAmM 83; WhoBlA 85, 88, 90, 92, 94; WhoE 79, 83, 85; WhoEnt 92; WhoSSW 75; WhoWest 84, 92, 94, 96; WhoWor 76*

DePriest, Oscar Stanton
American. Politician
Rep. congressman, 1929-35.
b. 1871 in Florence, Alabama
d. May 12, 1951 in Chicago, Illinois
Source: *AfrAmAl 6; AmPolLe; BiDrAC; BlkAmsC; DcAmB S5; DcAmNB; EncAACR; InB&W 80, 85; WhAm 3; WhAmP; WhoColR*

DePugh, Robert Bolivar
[William Robert Bolivar Depugh]
American. Political Activist
Founded Minutemen, 1960, to train Americans to fight guerrilla war against communist takeover.
b. Apr 15, 1923 in Independence, Missouri
Source: *BioIn 11; PolProf J*

DeQuay, Jan E
Dutch. Political Leader
One of founders of Dutch Union, 1940; prime minister of Netherlands, 1959-63.
b. Aug 26, 1901 in S'Hertogenbosch, Netherlands
d. Jul 4, 1985 in Beers, Netherlands
Source: *CurBio 85; IntWW 83; IntYB 82; WhoWor 78*

DeQuincey, Thomas
English. Author
Eloquent prose evident in masterpiece *Confessions of an English Opium Eater,* 1822.
b. Aug 15, 1785 in Greenheys, England
d. Dec 8, 1859 in Edinburgh, Scotland
Source: *Alli; AtlBL; BbD; BiD&SB; BritAu 19; CasWL; Chambr 3; CrtT 2; CyWA 58; DcBiA; DcEnA; MouLC 3; OxCEng 67; PenC ENG; RComWL; REn; WorAl*

Derain, Andre
French. Artist
Known for Fauvist paintings: *The Bathers,* 1907; refused to paint cubism.
b. Jun 10, 1880 in Chatou, France
d. Sep 10, 1954 in Chambourcy, France
Source: *AtlBL; Benet 87, 96; BiDD; BioIn 3, 4, 5, 6, 8, 11, 13, 14, 15, 16, 17, 18, 21; CamGWoT; ClaDrA; CnOxB; DancEn 78; DcArts; DcTwCCu 2; IntDcAA 90; IntDcB; LegTOT; McGDA; McGEWB; OxCArt; OxCTwCA; OxDcArt; PhDcTCA 77; REn; WhDW; WorArt 1950*

Derby, Jane
[Jeanette Barr Derby]
American. Fashion Designer
Opened dress shop, 1930; won Coty award, 1950.
b. May 17, 1895 in Rockymount, Virginia
d. Aug 7, 1965
Source: *BioIn 3, 7; EncFash; InWom SUP; WhAm 4; WhoAmW 58, 66*

DeRegniers, Beatrice Schenk
American. Children's Author
Won Caldecott award for *May I Bring a Friend?* 1964; other books include *Waiting for Mama,* 1984.
b. Aug 16, 1914 in Lafayette, Indiana
Source: *AmAu&B; ArtclWW 2; Au&Wr 71; AuBYP 2, 3; BkP; ConAu 13R, 26NR; DcLP 87A; IndAu 1917; IntAu&W 91; MorJA; OxCChiL; PenNWW A; SmATA 2, 68; WhoAm 86, 90; WrDr 92*

Derek, Bo
[Mary Cathleen Collins; Mrs. John Derek]
American. Actor
Starred with Dudley Moore in *10,* 1979; fourth wife of John Derek.
b. Nov 20, 1956 in Long Beach, California
Source: *BioIn 12, 13, 14, 16; BkPepl; ConTFT 3; HalFC 88; IntMPA 82, 84, 86, 88, 92, 94, 96; InWom SUP; LegTOT*

Derek, John
[Derek Harris]
American. Actor
Starred in *The Ten Commandments,* 1956; former wives Linda Evans, Ursula Andress.
b. Aug 12, 1926 in Hollywood, California
Source: *BioIn 10, 12, 13, 14; CmMov; ConTFT 3; FilmEn; FilmgC; ForYSC; HalFC 80, 84, 88; IntMPA 84, 86, 88, 92, 94, 96; ItaFilm; LegTOT; MiSFD 9; MotPP; MovMk; What 4; WhoHol 92, A; WorAl; WorAlBi; WorEFlm*

Derek and the Dominoes
[Eric Clapton; Jim Gordon; Carl Radle; Bobby Whitlock]
American. Music Group
Encouraged by fame of Cream, formed 1970; albums include *In Concert,* 1973.
Source: *ASCAP 80; BioIn 14, 15, 16, 17, 18, 19, 20, 21; EncPR&S 89; EncRk 88; HarEnR 86; RkOn 78, 82; WhoAm 74, 76, 78; WhoRock 81; WhoRocM 82; WhoWor 78*

Deren, Maya
American. Filmmaker
Producer of avant-garde films; founded Creative Film Foundation, 1955.
b. Apr 29, 1917 in Kiev, Russia
d. Oct 13, 1961 in New York, New York
Source: *BioIn 11, 12, 14, 15, 16, 17, 19, 20; IntDcF 1-2, 2-2; NotAW MOD; RAdv 14; ReelWom; WhoHrs 80; WorFDir 1*

DeReszke, Edouard
Polish. Opera Singer
One of opera's greatest basses, 1870-1903; noted for Mephistopheles in *Faust.*
b. Dec 22, 1853 in Warsaw, Poland
d. May 25, 1917 in Garnek, Poland
Source: *Baker 84; CmOp; NewGrDM 80; WhAm 1*

DeReszke, Jean
[Jan Mieczyslaw]
Polish. Opera Singer
Tenor with NY Met., 1891-1901; often sang with brother Edouard.
b. Jan 14, 1850 in Warsaw, Poland
d. Apr 3, 1925 in Nice, France
Source: *ApCAB SUP; Baker 84; BriBkM 80; NewEOp 71; WhAm 2*

De Ribes, Jacqueline
Fashion Designer
Creates for the American market.
b. 1930 in Paris, France
Source: *BioIn 13, 14, 15, 16; CelR 90; EncFash; NewYTBS 85; WhoFash 88*

Deringer, Henry
American. Inventor
Inventor of the derringer pistol.
b. Oct 26, 1786 in Easton, Pennsylvania
d. 1868
Source: *AntBDN F; CopCroC*

DeRita, Joe
[The Three Stooges]
"Curly Joe"
American. Comedian
Joined The Three Stooges, 1959.
b. Jul 12, 1909 in Philadelphia, Pennsylvania
d. Jul 3, 1993 in Woodland Hills, California
Source: *AnObit 1993; EncAFC; MotPP; WhoHol A*

DeRivera, Jose Ruiz
American. Artist, Sculptor
Began exhibiting work, 1930, in museums, galleries.
b. Sep 18, 1904 in West Baton Rouge, Louisiana
d. Mar 21, 1985 in New York, New York
Source: *BioIn 4, 5; ConArt 83; DcCAA 71; NewYTBS 75; OxCTwCA; WhAm 8; WhoAm 84; WhoAmA 84; WhoE 74*

Derleth, August (William)
American. Author
Wrote *Sac Prairie* saga, 1930s-40s; published science fiction, Arkham House, 1939-71; Derleth Society founded, 1977.
b. Feb 24, 1909 in Sauk City, Wisconsin
d. Jul 4, 1971
Source: *AmAu&B; AmNov; AuBYP 2, 3; Benet 87; BenetAL 91; BiDConC; BioIn 2, 3, 4, 6, 7, 8, 9, 10, 12, 14, 15, 17, 18; BkC 6; ChhPo, S2; CnDAL; ConAu 1R, 4NR, 29R; ConLC 31; ConNov 72; CrtSuMy; DcLB 9; DcLEL; EncMys; EncSF; LegTOT; NewEScF; Novels; OxCAmL 65, 83, 95; REn; REnAL; RGTwCSF; ScF&FL 1, 2, 92; ScFEYrs; ScFSB; SmATA 5; SupFW; TwCA, SUP; TwCCr&M 80, 85, 91; TwCRHW 90; TwCSFW 81, 86, 91; WhAm 5; WhNAA; WhoSciF*

Dern, Bruce MacLeish
American. Actor
Films include *Coming Home,* 1978; *That Championship Season,* 1982.
b. Jun 4, 1936 in Chicago, Illinois
Source: *BkPepl; ConTFT 3; CurBio 78; HalFC 88; IntMPA 92; VarWW 85; WhoAm 74, 76, 78, 80, 82, 84, 86, 88, 90, 92, 94, 95, 96, 97; WhoEnt 92; WhoHol A; WorAl; WorAlBi*

Dern, Laura Elizabeth
American. Actor
Daughter of Bruce Dern; in 1985 film *Mask; Rambling Rose,* 1991.
b. Feb 10, 1967 in Santa Monica, California
Source: *BioIn 14, 15, 16; ConTFT 3; CurBio 92; HalFC 88; IntMPA 92; NewYTBS 86; WhoAm 94; WhoEnt 92*

DeRoburt, Hammer, Sir
Political Leader
Pres. of Nauru, 1968-76, 1987-89.
b. Sep 25, 1923, Nauru
d. Jul 15, 1992 in Melbourne, Australia
Source: *BioIn 10; FarE&A 79, 80, 81; IntWW 80, 81, 82, 83, 89, 91; WhoWor 84, 87, 89, 91*

DeRochemont, Louis
American. Producer
Created newsreels *The March of Time,* 1934; series won Oscar, 1936.
b. Jan 13, 1899 in Chelsea, Massachusetts
d. Dec 23, 1978 in York Harbor, Maine
Source: *CurBio 79N; DcFM; FilmgC; IntMPA 75, 76, 77, 78, 79; ObitOF 79; OxCFilm; WhoAm 74, 76, 78; WhoWor 74; WorEFlm*

De Rochemont, Richard Guertis
American. Filmmaker
Won 1949 Oscar for documentary of Italian Boys Town; with brother Louis, active with March of Time newsreels, 1934-52.
b. Dec 13, 1903 in Chelsea, Massachusetts
d. Aug 4, 1982 in Flemington, New Jersey
Source: *CurBio 45, 82; NewYTBS 82; WhoAm 82*

DeRose, Peter
American. Songwriter, Pianist
Hit songs include "Deep Purple," 1939; in radio series "Sweethearts of the Air," 1923-39.
b. Mar 10, 1900 in New York, New York
d. Apr 23, 1953 in New York, New York
Source: *ASCAP 66; Baker 84; BiDAmM; CmpEPM*

Derr, Kenneth T
American. Business Executive
Chm., CEO, Chevron Corp., 1989—.
b. 1936

Source: *Dun&B 90; IntWW 91; St&PR 91; WhoAm 90; WhoFI 89; WhoWest 92; WhoWor 91*

Derricotte, Juliette Aline
American. Educator
First woman trustee at Talladega, 1918; Fisk U dean of women, 1929-31.
b. Apr 1, 1897 in Athens, Georgia
d. Nov 7, 1931 in Chattanooga, Tennessee
Source: *BioIn 10; DcAmNB; InB&W 80, 85; InWom SUP; NegAl 89; NotBlAW 1*

Derrida, Jacques
French. Philosopher
Invented deconstruction, a poststructuralist form of literary criticism; wrote *Of Grammatology,* 1967; *Writing and Difference,* 1967.
b. Jul 15, 1930 in El-Biar, Algeria
Source: *Benet 96; BenetAL 91; BiDNeoM; BioIn 12; BlmGEL; ClDMEL 80; ConAu 124, 127; ConLC 24, 87; CurBio 93; CyWA 89; DcTwCCu 2; EncWB; EncWL 3; FacFETw; IntWW 89, 91, 93; MakMC; NewYTBS 94; OxCPhil; PostFic; RAdv 14, 13-4; ThTwC 87; WhoWor 93, 95; WorAu 1975*

Derringer, Rick
[Rick Zehringer]
American. Singer, Musician
Singer-guitarist with 1960s McCoys; wrote hit "Hang on, Sloopy," 1965; formed own band, 1976.
b. Aug 4, 1947 in Union City, Illinois
Source: *ConMuA 80A; EncPR&S 89; EncRk 88; HarEnR 86; LegTOT; OnThGG; PenEncP; RkOn 78; WhoRock 81*

Dershowitz, Alan M
American. Lawyer, Writer
Professor, Harvard Law School, 1967—; trial lawyer, 1973—; former clients include Claus von Bulow, Jim Bakker, Leona Helmsley, Patty Hearst; writes synicated column; books include, *Chutzpah,* 1991.
b. Sep 1, 1938 in New York, New York
Source: *BioIn 11, 12, 13, 15; ConAu 11NR, 25R; CurBio 89; DrAS 82P; IntWW 91; News 92, 92-1; WhoAm 90; WhoAmL 92; WrDr 92*

Derthick, L(awrence) G(ridley)
American. Government Official
US commissioner on education, 1956-61.
b. Dec 23, 1905
d. Dec 4, 1992 in Signal Mountain, Tennessee
Source: *BioIn 4; CurBio 93N*

Derwinski, Edward Joseph
American. Government Official
First US Secretary of Veterans Affairs, 1989-93.
b. Sep 15, 1926 in Chicago, Illinois
Source: *BiDrAC; BiDrUSC 89; BiDrUSE 89; BioIn 6, 16; CngDr 89; CurBio 91; IntWW 89, 91, 93; NewYTBS 88; WhoAm 74, 76, 78, 80, 82, 84, 86, 88, 90, 92; WhoAmP 91; WhoE 91, 93; WhoGov 72, 75, 77; WhoMW 74, 76, 78, 80, 82; WhoWor 91, 93*

DeSabata, Victor
Italian. Conductor, Composer
Led La Scala Opera, 1929-53; likened to Toscanini; noted Verdi, Wagner interpreter.
b. Apr 10, 1892 in Trieste, Italy
d. Dec 11, 1967 in Santa Margherita, Italy
Source: *Baker 84; NewEOp 71*

Desai, Morarji (Ranchhodji)
Indian. Political Leader
Held various political posts including prime minister, India, 1977-79.
b. Feb 29, 1896 in Bhadeli, India
d. Apr 10, 1995 in Bombay, India
Source: *BioIn 5, 6, 8, 9, 11, 12, 20, 21; CurBio 58, 78, 95N; DcTwHis; FacFETw; FarE&A 78, 79; IntWW 81, 89, 91, 93; IntYB 82; NewCol 75; NewYTBS 95; Who 82, 85, 90, 92; WhoWor 78; WorAl; WorAlBi*

DeSalvo, Albert
"Boston Strangler"
American. Criminal
Never tried for slayings of 13 women, confessed to psychiatrist; stabbed to death in jail cell.
b. Sep 3, 1931 in Chelsea, Massachusetts
d. Dec 27, 1973 in Walpole, Massachusetts
Source: *BioIn 7, 10, 15*

DeSanctis, Francesco
Italian. Educator, Author, Critic
Founded modern Italian literary criticism.
b. Mar 28, 1817 in Morra Irpino, Italy
d. Dec 19, 1883 in Naples, Italy
Source: *BiD&SB; CasWL; ClDMEL 47; DcEuL; DcItL 1; EuAu; EvEuW; McGEWB; PenC EUR; REn*

DeSantis, Giuseppe
Italian. Director
Advocate of neo-realism in film; made *Bitter Rice,* 1949.
b. Feb 11, 1917 in Fondi, Italy
d. May 16, 1997
Source: *BioIn 15; DcFM; FilmgC; HalFC 88; IntMPA 80, 81, 82, 88; OxCFilm; WorEFlm; WorFDir 1*

DeSapio, Carmine Gerard
[The Miracle Man of Practical Politics]
American. Politician
Dem. held various political posts including NY secretary of state, 1954.
b. Dec 10, 1908 in New York, New York
Source: *BioIn 3, 4, 5, 6, 7, 9, 11; CurBio 55*

Descartes, Rene
French. Mathematician, Philosopher
Known as father of modern philosophy; said "I think, therefore I am"; developed analytical geometry.
b. Mar 31, 1596 in La Haye, France
d. Feb 11, 1650 in Stockholm, Sweden
Source: *BbD; Benet 87, 96; BiD&SB; BiDPsy; BioIn 1, 2, 3, 4, 5, 6, 7, 8, 9, 10, 11, 12, 13, 14, 15, 16, 17, 19, 20, 21; BlkwCE; BlmGEL; CamDcSc; CasWL; CyEd; DcCathB; DcEuL; Dis&D; EncEnl; EncEth; EncUnb; EuAu; EuWr 3; EvEuW; GaEncPs; GuFrLit 2; InSci; LarDcSc; LegTOT; LinLib L; LitC 20, 35; LngCEL; LuthC 75; NamesHP; NewC; NewCBEL; NewGrDM 80; OxCEng 67, 85, 95; OxCFr; OxCMed 86; OxCPhil; PenC EUR; RAdv 14, 13-4, 13-5; REn; WhDW; WorAl; WorAlBi; WorScD; WrPh P*

Deschamps, Eustache
French. Poet
Wrote over 1,000 ballads; first critical treatise on French poetry, 1392.
b. 1346? in Vertus, France
d. 1406?
Source: *BbD; Benet 96; BiD&SB; BlmGEL; CasWL; DcArts; EuAu; EvEuW; LinLib L; MediFra; NewC; OxCEng 67, 85, 95; OxCFr; PenC EUR; REn*

Desert Rose Band
American. Music Group
Los Angeles based country/rock band formed in 1985; country top 40 singles "Ashes of Love," 1987; "Love Reunited," 1987.
Source: *BgBkCoM; BioIn 16, 17; ConMuA 80A; ConMus 4; WhoNeCM, A; WhoRock 81*

DeSeversky, Alexander Procofieff
[Alexander de Seversky]
American. Aeronautical Engineer
A major figure in military aviation, wrote *Victory through Airpower,* 1942.
b. Jun 7, 1894 in Tiflis, Russia
d. Aug 24, 1974 in New York, New York
Source: *CelR; ConAu 53; CurBio 41, 74; InSci; IntWW 74; NewYTBS 74; St&PR 75; WebAB 74; WhAm 6; Who 74; WhoAm 74; WhoFI 74*

Deshaies, Jim
[James Joseph Deshaies]
American. Baseball Player
Pitcher, Houston, 1986-91; San Diego, 1992-93; Minnesota, 1993—; set modern ML record by striking out first eight batters in game April 23, 1986.
b. Jun 23, 1960 in Massena, New York
Source: *Ballpl 90; BaseEn 88; BaseReg 86; BioIn 15; NewYTBS 86*

DeShannon, Jackie
American. Singer, Songwriter
Concert, TV, folk, pop star, 1960s-70s; wrote over 500 songs.

b. Aug 21, 1944 in Hazel, Kentucky
Source: *ASCAP 80; BioIn 12, 14, 19; EncFCWM 83; EncPR&S 74; EncRk 88; LegTOT; PenEncP; RkOn 74; RolSEnR 83; WhoRocM 82*

Deshayes, Catherine
"La Voisin"
French. Criminal
Sorceress who gave poison to aristocracy; killed over 2,000 infants in Black Mass services.
d. Feb 22, 1680 in Paris, France
Source: *BioIn 18; ContDcW 89; IntDcWB*

DeSica, Vittorio
Italian. Actor, Director
Won four Oscars as best director of foreign films.
b. Jul 7, 1901 in Scra, Italy
d. Nov 13, 1974 in Paris, France
Source: *BiDFilm; DcFM; FilmgC; IntMPA 75; IntWW 74; MovMk; NewYTBE 72; OxCFilm; REn; WhAm 6; Who 74; WhoAm 74; WhScrn 77; WorAl; WorEFlm*

Desjardins, Pete
American. Diver
Two-time Olympic gold medal winner in diving, 1928; called best springboard diver in history.
b. 1907
d. May 6, 1985 in Miami, Florida
Source: *WhoSpor*

Desmond, Johnny
[Giovanni Alfredo DeSimone]
"GI Sinatra"
American. Singer, Actor
Popular radio, TV baritone, 1940s-50s; long stint on Breakfast Club Show, 1950s.
b. Nov 14, 1919 in Detroit, Michigan
d. Sep 6, 1985 in Los Angeles, California
Source: *ASCAP 66; CmpEPM; IntMPA 82; WhoHol A*

Desmond, Paul Breitenfeld
American. Jazz Musician
Renowned cool jazz saxist; with Dave Brubeck, 1950s.
b. Nov 25, 1924 in San Francisco, California
d. May 30, 1977 in New York, New York
Source: *CmpEPM; WhoAm 74*

Desmond, William
American. Actor
Silent films include *The Extra Girl,* 1923; talking films include *Phantom of the Opera,* 1943.
b. May 21, 1878 in Dublin, Ireland
d. Nov 3, 1949 in Los Angeles, California
Source: *BioIn 2, 8, 17; Film 1, 2; FilmEn; FilmgC; ForYSC; HalFC 80, 84, 88; LegTOT; MotPP; NotNAT B; ObitOF 79; SilFlmP; TwYS; WhoHol B; WhScrn 74, 77, 83*

Desmoulins, Camille
"Agent of the Lantern"
French. Journalist, Revolutionary
Wrote popular revolutionary pieces; executed by Robespierre.
b. Mar 2, 1760 in Guise, France
d. Apr 5, 1794 in Paris, France
Source: *BioIn 1, 2, 5, 10, 15; CmFrR; DcAmSR; DcBiPP; DcEuL; EvEuW; NewCol 75; OxCFr; REn*

Desormeaux, Kent
"The Kid"
American. Jockey
Holds record for most wins in a single year with 597.
b. 1970 in Maurice, Louisiana
Source: *BioIn 15; News 90, 90-2*

DeSoto, Hernando
Spanish. Explorer
First to see, cross Mississippi River, 1539-42.
b. 1500 in Barcarrota, Spain
d. May 21, 1542 in Ferriday, Louisiana
Source: *AmBi; DcAmB; DcCathB; EncSoH; HarEnUS; LuthC 75; McGEWB; OxCAmH; REn; REnAL; REnAW; WhAm HS; WhFla; WorAl*

DesPres, Josquin
[Josse Depres]
Flemish. Composer
Considered greatest Renaissance composer; wrote over 20 masses, 100 motets; developed antiphonal techniques.
b. 1445? in Conde sur l'Escaut, France
d. Aug 27, 1521 in Conde, France
Source: *AtlBL; Baker 84; NewGrDM 80*

Dessalines, Jean Jacques
[Jacques I]
Haitian. Ruler
Brought to Haiti as slave; with British help, overthrew French, declared himself emperor of the new republic, 1804-06.
b. 1758, Guinea
d. Oct 17, 1806, Haiti
Source: *ApCAB; BioIn 1, 2, 3, 4, 6, 8, 10, 16; Drake; McGEWB; REn; WebBD 83*

Dessau, Paul
German. Composer
Best known for his operas; most successful, *Das Verhor des Lukullus,* 1949 with Bertolt Brecht.
b. Dec 19, 1894 in Hamburg, Germany
d. Jun 28, 1979 in Berlin, German Democratic Republic
Source: *Baker 78, 84, 92; BioIn 1, 2, 12; BriBkM 80; DcArts; DcCM; EncWT; IntWW 74, 75, 76, 77, 78; IntWWM 77; NewAmDM; NewGrDM 80; NewGrDO; NewOxM; OxCGer 76, 86; OxDcOp; WhoMus 72; WhoSocC 78; WhoWor 74*

Desses, Jean
[Jean Dimitre Verginie]
French. Fashion Designer
Opened fashion house, 1938; famous for elegant Greek evening gowns.
b. Aug 6, 1904 in Alexandria, Egypt
d. Aug 2, 1970 in Athens, Greece
Source: *BioIn 4, 9; ConFash; CurBio 56, 70; EncFash; FairDF FRA; NewYTBE 70; WhAm 5; WhoFash, 88; WorFshn*

Destinn, Emmy
[Emma Kittl]
Czech. Opera Singer
Famed dramatic soprano with NY Met., 1908-16; noted for Wagner, Puccini roles.
b. Feb 26, 1878 in Prague, Bohemia
d. Jan 28, 1930 in Budejovice, Czechoslovakia
Source: *Baker 78, 84, 92; BioIn 1, 3, 6, 11, 14, 15; BriBkM 80; CmOp; IntDcOp; MetOEnc; MusSN; NewAmDM; NewEOp 71; NewGrDA 86; NewGrDM 80; NewGrDO; OxDcOp; PenDiMP; WhAm 1; WhScrn 77, 83*

Destouches, Louis-Ferdinand
[Louis-Ferdinand Celine]
French. Author, Physician
Wrote *Journey to End of the Night,* 1934; *Death on Installment Plan,* 1938.
b. May 27, 1894 in Paris, France
d. Jul 4, 1961 in Paris, France
Source: *AtlBL; Benet 87, 96; BiDExR; BioIn 17, 18, 20, 21; CasWL; ClDMEL 47; ConAu 28NR, 85; ConLC 1, 3, 4, 7, 9, 15, 47; CyWA 58, 89; DcLB 72; DcTwCCu 2; EncWL, 3; EuWr 11; EvEuW; FacFETw; GrFLW; GuFrLit 1; LiExTwC; LinLib L; LngCTC; MajTwCW; MakMC; ModFrL; ModRL; Novels; OxCEng 85, 95; OxCFr; PenC EUR; RAdv 14, 13-2; REn; RfGWoL 95; TwCA, SUP; TwCWr; WhoTwCL*

D'Estournelles, Paul Henri Benjamin Balleut de Constant, Baron
French. Diplomat
Awarded 1909 Nobel Peace Prize.
b. Nov 22, 1852 in La Fleche, France
d. May 15, 1924 in Bordeaux, France
Source: *LinLib S; WhoNob, 95*

DeSylva, Buddy
[George Gard DeSylva]
American. Songwriter, Producer
Produced five Shirley Temple films; wrote librettos for numerous George White Scandals, 500 songs including "Sonny Boy," 1928.
b. Jan 27, 1896 in New York, New York
d. Jul 11, 1950 in Oak Park, Illinois
Source: *BioIn 1, 2, 5, 9, 10, 12, 15; CmpEPM; CurBio 43, 50; DcAmB S4; WhAm 3*

Deterding, Henri Wilhelm August, Sir
Dutch. Business Executive
Founded Shell Oil, 1912, largest US foreign controlled co.
b. 1866
d. 1939, Germany
Source: *BioIn 4*

Dett, Robert Nathaniel
American. Composer
Choral pieces evolved from black spirituals: "Chariot Jubilee."
b. Oct 11, 1882 in Drummondsville, Ontario, Canada
d. Oct 2, 1943 in Battle Creek, Michigan
Source: *AmAu&B; ASCAP 66, 80; BiDAmEd; BiDAmM; BioIn 1, 6, 8, 11, 13, 14, 18, 19; BlkAWP; ConAmC 76, 82; CurBio 43, 73; DcAmB S3; DrBlPA, 90; InB&W 80, 85; McGEWB; NewGrDM 80; OxCMus; SelBAAf; SouBlCW; WebBD 83; WhAm 2*

Deukmejian, George
[Courken George Deukmejian, Jr]
American. Politician
Conservative Republican governor of CA, 1983-90; succeeded Jerry Brown; succeeded by Pete Wilson.
b. Jun 6, 1928 in Menands, New York
Source: *AlmAP 84, 88; BiDrGov 1983, 1988; BioIn 13, 14, 15; CelR 90; CurBio 83; IntWW 83, 89, 91, 93; NewYTBS 83; PolsAm 84; Who 85, 88, 90, 92, 94; WhoAm 80, 82, 84, 86, 88, 90, 92, 94, 95, 96, 97; WhoAmL 79; WhoAmP 73, 75, 77, 79, 81, 83, 85, 87, 89, 91, 93, 95; WhoWest 80, 82, 84, 87, 89, 92, 94; WhoWor 84, 87, 89, 91, 93, 95, 96, 97*

Deus, Joao de
Portuguese. Poet
Works include *Flores du Campo,* 1869; developed primer to teach children to read; ideas used in institutions named for him.
b. Mar 8, 1830 in Sao Bartolemeu, Portugal
d. Jan 11, 1896 in Lisbon, Portugal
Source: *BiD&SB; BioIn 1; PenC EUR*

Deutch, John
American. Government Official
Director, Central Intelligence Agency, 1995—.
b. Jul 27, 1938 in Brussels, Belgium
Source: *IntWW 91, 93; News 96*

Deutsch, Adolph
American. Composer
MGM musical director whose scores include Oscar-winning *Oklahoma!,* 1955; *Annie Get Your Gun,* 1950.
b. Oct 20, 1897 in London, England
d. Jan 1, 1980 in Palm Desert, California
Source: *AnObit 1980; ASCAP 66, 80; BioIn 1, 12; CmpEPM; ConAmC 76, 82; FilmEn; GangFlm; HalFC 80, 84, 88; IntDcF 1-4, 2-4*

Deutsch, Babette
[Mrs. Avrahm Yarmolinsky]
American. Author, Poet
Verse concerned with social problems; first book, *Banners,* 1919.
b. Sep 22, 1895 in New York, New York
d. Nov 13, 1982 in New York, New York
Source: *AmAu&B; AmWomWr; AnCL; AnObit 1982; Au&Wr 71; Benet 87, 96; BenetAL 91; BioIn 4, 6, 9, 12, 13, 14, 15; BlueB 76; ChhPo, S1, S2, S3; ConAmL; ConAu 1R, 4NR, 108; ConLC 18; ConPo 70, 75, 80; DcLB 45; DcLEL; DrAP 75; DrAPF 80; DrAS 74E; EvLB; FemiCLE; IntAu&W 76, 77, 82; IntWW 74, 75, 76, 77, 78, 79, 80, 81, 82; IntWWP 77, 82; InWom SUP; LinLib L; LngCTC; MorJA; NewYTBS 82; Novels; OxCAmL 65, 83, 95; OxCTwCP; OxCWoWr 95; PenC AM; RAdv 1; REn; REnAL; SmATA 1, 33N; TwCA, SUP; TwCWr; WhAm 8; WhE&EA; WhNAA; WhoAm 74, 76, 78, 80; WhoAmW 58, 64, 66, 68, 70, 74; WhoWor 74; WhoWorJ 72; WrDr 76, 80, 82*

Deutsch, Harold C(harles)
American. Author
Historical writings include *Hitler and His Generals: The Hidden Crisis,* 1938.
b. Jun 7, 1904 in Milwaukee, Wisconsin
Source: *ConAu 21R; DrAS 74H, 78H, 82H; WhAm 11; WhoMW 93*

Deutsch, Helen
American. Screenwriter, Lyricist
Her screenplays include *National Velvet,* 1944; *Lili,* 1953.
b. Mar 21, 1906 in New York, New York
d. Mar 15, 1992 in New York, New York
Source: *AnObit 1992; ASCAP 66, 80; BioIn 17, 19; ConAu 108, 112, 137; ConTFT 4; IntAu&W 86; IntMPA 80, 84, 92; InWom SUP; SmATA 76; VarWW 85; WomWMM*

Deutsch, Helene R(osenbach)
American. Psychoanalyst
Wrote *The Psychology of Women,* 1944.
b. Oct 9, 1884 in Przemysl, Austria-Hungary
d. Mar 29, 1982 in Cambridge, Massachusetts
Source: *ConAu 106; FacFETw; NewYTBS 82; WorAl*

Deutsch, Karl Wolfgang
American. Political Scientist
Professor emeritus, Harvard U., 1983—; writings include *Advances in Social Sciences,* 1986.
b. Jul 12, 1912 in Prague, Bohemia
d. Nov 2, 1992
Source: *BioIn 16; EncWB; WhAm 11; WhoAm 86, 90; WhoWor 74, 91; WrDr 92*

DeValera, Eamon
Irish. Statesman
Leader of Irish independence movement who was pres., Ireland, 1959-73.
b. Oct 14, 1882 in New York, New York
d. Aug 30, 1975 in Dublin, Ireland
Source: *ChhPo S1; ConAu 89; CurBio 40, 51; DcPol; IntWW 74, 75; REn; WhAm 6; WhDW; Who 74; WhoGov 72, 75; WhoWor 74*

DeValois, Ninette, Dame
[Edris Stannus]
British. Choreographer, Author
Toured with Russian Ballet, Sadler's Wells Ballet; appeared in *The Sleeping Beauty,* 1946.
b. Jun 6, 1898 in Blessington, Ireland
Source: *Au&Wr 71; BiDD; BioIn 13; ConAu 115; ContDcW 89; CurBio 49; IntDcWB; IntWW 83, 91; IntWWM 90; InWom SUP; NewOxM; PlP&P; Who 85, 92; WhoAmW 74; WhThe; WorAlBi*

Devane, William
American. Actor
Star of TV series "Knots Landing," 1983-93.
b. Sep 5, 1939 in Albany, New York
Source: *BioIn 14, 15; CelR 90; ConTFT 3; HalFC 84, 88; IntMPA 92, 94, 96; ItaFilm; LegTOT; WhoAm 86, 90, 92, 94, 95, 96, 97; WhoEnt 92; WhoHol A; WorAl; WorAlBi*

DeVarona, Donna
American. Swimmer, Broadcast Journalist
Youngest member of US Olympic team at 13; won gold medal, 1964.
b. 1947 in San Diego, California
Source: *BiDAmSp BK; BioIn 6, 8, 11, 12, 14, 15; InWom SUP; WhoTelC*

DeVere, Aubrey Thomas
Irish. Poet, Critic
Promoted Celtic literary revival; wrote of Irish lore: *Legends of St. Patrick,* 1872.
b. Jan 10, 1814 in Curragh Chase, Ireland
d. Jan 21, 1902 in Curragh Chase, Ireland
Source: *BritAu 19; CasWL; CelCen; ChhPo S3; DcBiPP; OxCEng 85; REn*

Devereaux, Robert
[Earl of Essex]
English. Courtier
Liked by Queen Elizabeth until his secret marriage caused disfavor; prosecuted for treason, executed; enjoyed literature, writing sonnets.
b. Nov 19, 1566 in Netherwood, England
d. Feb 25, 1601 in London, England
Source: *Alli; NewC; WebBD 83*

Devereux, George
Anthropologist, Author
Studied ethnopsychiatry; writings include *Essays in General Ethnopsychiatry,* 1970.

b. Sep 13, 1908 in Lugos, Austria-Hungary
Source: *BiDPara; ConAu 69; EncO&P 1, 2, 3*

Devers, Gail
[Yolanda Gail Devers]
American. Track Athlete
Won Gold Medal, 100-meter dash, 1992 Summer Olympics.
b. Nov 19, 1966 in Seattle, Washington
Source: *AfrAmSG; ConBlB 7; CurBio 96; EncWomS; WhoSpor*

Devers, Jacob Loucks
American. Army Officer
Influential in revitalizing armed forces, WW II; retired as four-star general, 1949.
b. Sep 8, 1887 in York, Pennsylvania
d. Oct 15, 1979 in Bethesda, Maryland
Source: *BiDWWGF; BioIn 1, 3, 12, 20; CurBio 42, 80; DcAmB S10; DcAmMiB; HarEnMi; NewYTBS 79; WebAMB; WhAm 7; Who 74; WhWW-II*

DeVicenzo, Roberto
Argentine. Golfer
Turned pro, 1938; won British Open, 1967; incorrect scorecard prevented chance to win Masters, 1968.
b. Apr 14, 1923, Argentina
Source: *IntWW 91; WhoGolf*

Devine, Andy
[Jeremiah Schwartz]
American. Actor
Comic sidekick for Roy Rogers; squeaky-voiced character actor of over 300 films.
b. Oct 7, 1905 in Flagstaff, Arizona
d. Feb 18, 1977 in Orange, California
Source: *BioIn 4; LegTOT; MotPP; MovMk; NewYTBS 77; ObitOF 79; OlFamFa; OxCFilm; SaTiSS; TwYS; What 2; WhoHol A; WhScrn 83; WorAl*

Devine, Dan(iel John)
American. Football Coach
Coach, Green Bay, 1971-75; succeeded Ara Parseghian at Notre Dame, 1976-80.
b. Dec 23, 1924 in Augusta, Wisconsin
Source: *BiDAmSp FB; LegTOT; NewYTBS 80; WhoAm 74, 76, 78, 80; WhoFtbl 74; WhoMW 80; WorAl*

Devine, Donald
Canadian. Politician
Progressive-Conservative Party premier of Saskatchewan, 1982—.
b. Jul 5, 1944 in Regina, Saskatchewan, Canada
Source: *Dun&B 90*

Devine, Michael
Irish. Hunger Striker, Revolutionary
IRA member; one of 10 hunger strikers to die in prison, demanding political prisoner rather than criminal status.
b. May 26, 1954? in Londonderry, Northern Ireland
d. Aug 20, 1981 in Belfast, Northern Ireland

DeVinne, Theodore Low
American. Printer
Pioneer in typography, fine printing; founded DeVinne Press, 1908.
b. Dec 25, 1828 in Stamford, Connecticut
d. Feb 16, 1914 in New York, New York
Source: *AmAu&B; AmBi; ApCAB; DcAmAu; DcAmB; DcNAA; OxCAmL 65; REn; REnAL; TwCBDA; WebAB 74, 79; WebBD 83; WhAm 1; WhLit*

DeVita, Vincent Theodore, Jr.
American. Educator, Physician
Noted oncologist, director, National Cancer Institute, 1980-88; with Memorial Sloan-Kettering Cancer Center, 1988-91.
b. Mar 7, 1935 in New York, New York
Source: *AmMWSc 86, 92; BioIn 16; ConNews 87-3; IntMed 80; WhoAm 78, 82, 84, 86, 88, 90, 92, 94, 95, 96, 97; WhoE 83, 95; WhoFrS 84; WhoMedH; WhoScEn 94, 96; WhoSSW 73; WhoWor 82, 96, 97*

DeVito, Danny
[Daniel Michael DeVito]
American. Actor
Played Louie DePalma on TV comedy "Taxi," 1980-83; won Emmy, 1981; in films *Throw Momma from the Train,* 1987, *Twins,* 1988, *War of the Roses,* 1989.
b. Nov 17, 1944 in Neptune, New Jersey
Source: *BiDFilm 94; BioIn 12, 13, 15, 16; CelR 90; ConNews 87-1; ConTFT 6, 13; CurBio 88; EncAFC; HalFC 88; IntMPA 88, 92, 94; IntWW 93; LegTOT; MiSFD 9; NewYTBS 91; QDrFCA 92; WhoAm 86, 90; WhoCom; WhoEnt 92; WhoHol 92; WorAlBi*

DeVito, Tommy
[The Four Seasons]
American. Singer, Musician
One of group's original members, 1962.
b. Jun 19, 1936 in Belleville, New Jersey
Source: *WhoRocM 82*

Devlin, Bernadette Josephine
[Bernadette Devlin McAliskey]
Irish. Political Activist
At age 21, youngest woman elected to British Parliament, 1969-74.
b. Apr 23, 1947 in Cookstown, Northern Ireland
Source: *BioIn 8, 91; WhoWor 74; WorAl; WorAlBi*

Devo
[Bob Casale; Jerry Casale; Bob Mothersbaugh; Mark Mothersbaugh; Alan Myers]
American. Music Group
Weirdly garbed Akron, OH quintet known for synthesizer-oriented rhythm; hit sing le "Whip It," 1980.
Source: *BioIn 18; ConMuA 80A; ConMus 13; ConTFT 14; EncPR&S 89; EncRk 88; EncRkSt; HarEnR 86; NewGrDA 86; PenEncP; RkOn 85; RolSEnR 83; WhoRock 81; WhoRocM 82; WhsNW 85*

De Vorzon, Barry
American. Composer
Wrote "Bless the Beasts and the Children," 1971; Grammy-winning "Nadia's Theme," 1977.
b. Jul 31, 1934 in New York, New York
Source: *HalFC 88; VarWW 85*

DeVos, Richard Marvin
American. Business Executive
Co-founder, pres., Amway Corp, 1959-92.
b. Mar 4, 1926 in Grand Rapids, Michigan
Source: *BioIn 9, 11, 12, 13; ConAmBL; Dun&B 90; St&PR 84, 91; WhoAdv 80; WhoAm 74, 76, 78, 80, 82, 84, 88, 90, 92, 94, 95, 96, 97; WhoFI 74, 77, 81, 83, 85, 87, 89, 92; WhoMW 84, 86, 90; WhoWor 78, 80, 82*

DeVoto, Bernard Augustine
[John August]
American. Author, Journalist, Critic
Won 1948 Pulitzer for *Across the Wide Missouri;* wrote on Americana, Mark Twain.
b. Jan 11, 1897 in Ogden, Utah
d. Nov 13, 1955 in New York, New York
Source: *AmAu&B; AmNov; AuNews 1; CnDAL; ConAmA; DcAmB S5; DcLEL; EncWL; ModAL; OxCAmL 65; PenC AM; REn; REnAL; TwCA SUP; WebAB 79; WhAm 3; WorAl*

DeVries, David Pietersen
Dutch. Colonizer
Founded colonies on Staten Island called New Netherlands, 1630s-40s.
b. 1592 in La Rochelle, France
d. 1655
Source: *ApCAB; DcAmB; HarEnUS; WhAm HS*

DeVries, Hugo
Dutch. Botanist, Educator, Author
His *Mutation Theory,* 1901; *Plant Breeding,* 1907, stressed mutation study.
b. Feb 16, 1848 in Haarlem, Netherlands
d. May 21, 1935 in Amsterdam, Netherlands
Source: *BiESc; EncWB; InSci; LinLib L, S; NewCol 75*

DeVries, Peter
American. Author, Editor
With *New Yorker* mag., 1944-87; books include *The Prick of Noon,* 1984.
b. Feb 27, 1910 in Chicago, Illinois
d. Sep 28, 1993 in Norwalk, Connecticut
Source: *AmAu&B; Au&Wr 71; Benet 87; BenetAL 91; BiE&WWA; BioIn 13; CnDAL; ConAu 17R; ConLC 10, 46, 81; ConNov 76, 91; CyWA 89; DrAPF 91; EncAHmr; IntAu&W 91; IntvTCA 2; IntWW 83, 91; MajTwCW; ModAL S1, S2; OxCAmL 65; PenC AM; Who 92; WhoTwCL; WhoUSWr 88; WhoWrEP 89; WorAu 1950; WrDr 86, 92*

DeVries, William Castle
American. Surgeon
Implanted artificial heart in Barney Clark, 1982; William Schroeder, 1984.
b. Dec 19, 1943 in New York, New York
Source: *AmDec 1980; BioIn 13, 14, 16; CelR 90; CurBio 85; Dun&B 90; IntWW 89, 91, 93; NewYTBS 82; WhoAm 82, 84, 86, 88, 90, 92, 94, 95, 96, 97; WhoFrS 84; WhoSSW 86; WorAlBi*

DeWaart, Edo
Dutch. Conductor
Music director, Minneapolis Orchestra, 1986—; Amsterdam Radio Orchestra, 1988—.
b. Jun 1, 1941 in Amsterdam, Netherlands
Source: *BioIn 16; CurBio 90; IntWW 91; IntWWM 90; MetOEnc; NewGrDA 86; PenDiMP; WhoAm 86, 90; WhoEnt 92; WhoMW 92; WhoWor 74, 91*

Dewaere, Patrick
[Patrick Maurin]
French. Actor
Films include *Beau Pere,* 1981; *Get Out Your Hankerchiefs,* 1978.
b. Jan 26, 1947 in Saint-Brieuc, France
d. Jul 16, 1982 in Paris, France
Source: *AnObit 1982, 1983; BioIn 13; FilmEn; ItaFilm; NewYTBS 82*

Dewar, James, Sir
English. Chemist, Physicist
First to produce liguid hydrogen, 1898; invented Dewar vessel, predecessor of the common thermos bottle.
b. Sep 20, 1842 in Kincardine-on-Forth, Scotland
d. Mar 27, 1923 in London, England
Source: *AsBiEn; BiESc; BioIn 1, 2, 9, 14; CamDcSc; CelCen; DcBiPP; DcInv; DcNaB 1922; DcScB; InSci; LarDcSc; LinLib S; NewCol 75; WhDW; WorAl; WorAlBi; WorInv; WorScD*

Dewar, James A
"Mr. Twinkie"
American. Businessman, Inventor
Invented the Hostess Twinkie snack cake, 1930.
b. 1897?
d. Jun 30, 1985 in Downers Grove, Illinois
Source: *NewYTBS 85*

Dewar, John
Scottish. Manufacturer, Businessman
Opened wine shop, 1846; began making own Scotch; first to package in bottles.
b. 1806 in Perthshire, Scotland
d. 1880
Source: *Entr*

Dewey, Charles Schuveldt
American. Government Official
Agent general of Marshall Plan, 1948, who was a Rep. representative, 1940s.
b. Nov 10, 1882 in Cadiz, Ohio
d. Dec 26, 1980 in Washington, District of Columbia
Source: *BiDrAC; BioIn 1, 2, 12; CurBio 49, 81; WhoAm 74; WhoGov 72, 75*

Dewey, George
American. Naval Officer
Admiral who destroyed eight Spanish warships in Spanish-American War, 1898, to become nat. hero.
b. Dec 26, 1837 in Montpelier, Vermont
d. Jan 16, 1917 in Washington, District of Columbia
Source: *AmBi; ApCAB SUP, X; BioIn 1, 2, 3, 4, 5, 6, 7, 9, 10, 12, 14, 16; CivWDc; DcAmB; DcAmMiB; DcNAA; Dis&D; EncAB-H 1974, 1996; GayN; GenMudB; HarEnMi; HarEnUS; LegTOT; LinLib S; McGEWB; MorMA; NatCAB 9; NewCol 75; OxCAmH; PeoHis; RComAH; REn; TwCBDA; WebAB 74, 79; WebAMB; WebBD 83; WhAm 1; WhCiWar; WhoMilH 76; WorAl; WorAlBi*

Dewey, John
American. Philosopher, Educator
Founded progressive education movement in US; wrote *Democracy and Education,* 1916; leading adherent of pragmatism.
b. Oct 20, 1859 in Burlington, Vermont
d. Jun 1, 1952 in New York, New York
Source: *Alli SUP; AmAu&B; AmDec 1910, 1920; AmPeW; AmRef; AmRef&R; AmSocL; ApCAB X; Benet 87, 96; BenetAL 91; BiDAmEd; BiDMoPL; BiDPsy; BiDTran; BioIn 1, 2, 3, 4, 5, 6, 7, 8, 9, 10, 11, 12, 13, 14, 15, 17, 18, 19, 20, 21; CamGLE; CamHAL; CasWL; ConAmA; ConAu 114; DcAmAu; DcAmB S5; DcAmC; DcAmSR; DcLEL; EncAB-H 1974, 1996; EncAL; EncARH; EncEth; EncUnb; EvLB; FacFETw; GaEncPs; GayN; InSci; LegTOT; LinLib L, S; LngCTC; LuthC 75; MakMC; McGEWB; MemAm; NamesHP; NatCAB 11, 40; ObitT 1951; OxCAmH; OxCAmL 65, 83, 95; OxCEng 67, 85, 95; PenC AM; RAdv 14, 13-3, 13-4; RComAH; REn; REnAL; RfGAmL 87, 94; ThTwC 87; TwCA, SUP; TwCBDA; TwoTYeD; WebAB 74, 79; WebE&AL; WhAm 3; WhDW; WhNAA; WhoTwCL; WorAl; WorAlBi; WrPh P*

Dewey, Melvil
American. Librarian
Devised Dewey Decimal Classification System for cataloging books; founded first library school, 1887.
b. Dec 10, 1851 in Adams Center, New York
d. Dec 26, 1931 in Lake Placid, Florida
Source: *Alli SUP; AmAu&B; AmBi; AmLY; AmRef; ApCAB, X; BenetAL 91; BiDAmEd; BioIn 1, 2, 3, 5, 6, 10, 11, 12, 14, 15, 16, 21; ConAu 118; DcAmAu; DcAmB S1; DcAmLiB; DcArts; DcNAA; HarEnUS; LegTOT; LinLib L, S; McGEWB; MorMA; NatCAB 4, 23; OxCAmH; OxCAmL 65, 83, 95; OxCEng 85, 95; PeoHis; REn; REnAL; TwCBDA; WebAB 74, 79; WhAm 1; WhDW; WhNAA; WorAl; WorAlBi*

Dewey, Thomas Edmund
American. Politician
Lost close presidential race against Harry Truman, 1948; Rep. governor of NY, 1943-55.
b. Mar 24, 1902 in Owosso, Michigan
d. Mar 16, 1971 in Bal Harbour, Florida
Source: *AmPolLe; BiDrGov 1789; BioIn 1, 2, 3, 4, 6, 7, 8, 9, 10, 11, 12, 13; CurBio 40, 71; DcAmB S9; DcPol; EncAB-H 1974, 1996; LinLib S; McGEWB; NewYTBE 71; OxCAmH; PresAR; WebAB 74, 79; WhAm 5; WhDW; WorAl*

Dewhurst, Colleen
Canadian. Actor
Active on stage, screen, TV since mid-1950s; won Tonys for *All the Way Home,* 1962; *Moon for the Misbegotten,* 1974; Emmy for "Murphy Brown," 1989.
b. Jun 3, 1926 in Montreal, Quebec, Canada
d. Aug 22, 1991 in South Salem, New York
Source: *AnObit 1991; BiE&WWA; BioIn 15, 16; BioNews 74; CamGWoT; CelR, 90; CnThe; ConTFT 4; CurBio 74, 91N; Ent; FilmEn; ForYSC; HalFC 80, 84, 88; IntDcT 3; IntMPA 81, 82, 84, 86, 88; InWom SUP; LesBEnT 92; MovMk; News 92, 92-2; NewYTBS 87, 91; NotNAT; NotWoAT; OxCAmT 84; OxCThe 83; PlP&P A; VarWW 85; WhAm 10; WhoAm 86, 88, 90; WhoAmW 91; WhoHol 92, A; WhoThe 77, 81; WorAl; WorAlBi*

DeWilde, Brandon
American. Actor
Nominated for Oscar as child star of movie *Shane,* 1953.
b. Apr 9, 1942 in New York, New York
d. Jul 6, 1972 in Denver, Colorado
Source: *BiE&WWA; FilmgC; MotPP; MovMk; NewYTBE 72; NotNAT B; ObitOF 79; OxCFilm; WhAm 5; WhoHol B; WhScrn 77*

DeWine, Mike
American. Politician
Rep. senator from OH, 1995—.
b. Jan 5, 1947
Source: *AlmAP 96; CngDr 95*

Dewing, Thomas Wilmer
American. Artist
Painted portraits, misty figures, especially of women.
b. May 4, 1851 in Boston, Massachusetts
d. Nov 5, 1938 in New York, New York
Source: *BioIn 3, 4, 13, 15; BriEAA; DcAmArt; DcAmB S2; EncAB-A 11; McGDA; NewCol 75; PhDcTCA 77; TwCBDA; WhAm 1*

DeWint, Peter
English. Artist
Watercolorist, noted for country life scenes.
b. Jan 21, 1784 in Staffordshire, England
d. Jan 30, 1849 in London, England
Source: *DcNaB; McGDA; OxCArt*

DeWitt, Joyce
American. Actor
Played Janet Wood on TV series "Three's Company."
b. Apr 23, 1949 in Wheeling, West Virginia
Source: *BioIn 11, 12; ConTFT 9; IntMPA 82, 86, 88, 92, 94; InWom SUP; LegTOT; WhoAm 80, 82, 84*

DeWitt, William Orville, Sr.
American. Baseball Executive
Held many off-field baseball jobs with several ML teams; as pres. of Detroit, traded managers with Cleveland, 1959, first such deal in ML history.
b. Aug 3, 1902 in Saint Louis, Missouri
d. Mar 3, 1982 in Cincinnati, Ohio
Source: *NewYTBS 82; WhAm 8; WhoAm 74, 76, 78, 80; WhoFI 74, 75; WhoMW 74, 76, 78, 80, 82; WhoProB 73*

DeWohl, Louis
[Ludwig Von Wohl-Musciny]
German. Author
Among his historical novels about saints, about 20 were filmed, dramatized.
b. Jan 24, 1903 in Berlin, Germany
d. Jun 2, 1961 in Lucerne, Switzerland
Source: *BioIn 3, 4, 5, 6; BkC 5; CathA 1952; CurBio 55, 61*

DeWolfe, Billy
[William Andrew Jones]
American. Actor
Character actor in prissy roles; films included *Blue Skies*, 1946, *Call Me Madam*, 1953.
b. Feb 18, 1907 in Wollaston, Massachusetts
d. Mar 5, 1974 in Los Angeles, California
Source: *BiE&WWA; FilmEn; FilmgC; HolP 40; MotPP; MovMk; NewYTBS 74; ObitOF 79; Vers B; WhoHol B; WhoThe 72; WhScrn 77; WorAl*

Dexter, Al
[Clarence Albert Poindexter]
American. Singer, Songwriter
Biggest hit, "Pistol Packin' Mama," 1943, sold over 10 million copies.
b. May 4, 1902 in Jacksonville, Texas
d. Jan 28, 1984 in Lake Lewisville, Texas
Source: *BgBkCoM; BiDAmM; BioIn 14; CmpEPM; ConAu 111; EncFCWM 69, 83; HarEnCM 87*

Dexter, John
English. Director
Stage director, best known for productions of *Equus* and *M. Butterfly*.
b. Aug 2, 1925 in Derby, England
d. Mar 23, 1990 in London, England
Source: *AnObit 1990; BioIn 9, 10, 11, 12, 13, 16, 17, 19, 20; CamGWoT; CmOp; CnThe; ConTFT 10; CurBio 76, 90, 90N; DcNaB 1986; EncWT; Ent; FacFETw; GrStDi; HalFC 88; IntDcOp; IntDcT 3; IntWW 80, 81, 82, 83, 89; IntWWM 90; MetOEnc; NewGrDO; NewYTBS 90; NotNAT; OxCThe 83; OxDcOp; TheaDir; WhAm 10; Who 82, 90; WhoAm 78, 80, 82, 84, 86, 88; WhoOp 76; WhoThe 81; WhoWor 89; WrDr 92*

Dey, Susan Hallock
[Susan Smith]
American. Actor, Model
TV shows include "The Partridge Family," 1970-74; "L.A. Law," 1986-91.
b. Dec 10, 1952 in Pekin, Illinois
Source: *BioIn 15, 16; CelR 90; ConTFT 5; HalFC 88; IntMPA 82, 92; WhoAm 74, 76; WhoEnt 92; WhoHol A; WorAlBi*

De Young, Cliff
American. Actor
Starred in TV movie *Sunshine*, 1973; theatrical films include *The Hunger*, 1983.
b. Feb 12, 1945 in Inglewood, California
Source: *ConTFT 4; HalFC 88; IntMPA 92; VarWW 85*

DeYoung, Dennis
American. Singer
As solo performer had hit single "Desert Moon," 1984.
b. Feb 18, 1947 in Chicago, Illinois
Source: *RkOn 85*

DeYoung, Michel Harry
American. Newspaper Editor
With brother, founded what later became the *San Francisco Chronicle*, 1865, editor-in-chief, 1880-1925.
b. Oct 1, 1849 in Saint Louis, Missouri
d. Feb 15, 1925 in San Francisco, California
Source: *NatCAB 1; WebBD 83; WhAm 1*

Dharmapala, Anagarika
[David Hewivitarne]
Ceylonese. Religious Leader
One of founders of Buddhism in US, Europe.
b. Sep 27, 1864 in Colombo, Ceylon
d. Apr 29, 1933 in Sarnath, India
Source: *BiDAmCu; BioIn 7; EncARH; RelLAm 91*

Dhlomo, R(olfus) R(eginald) R(aymond)
South African. Author
His novel, *An African Tragedy*, 1928, was the first to be written in English by a Zulu.
b. 1901 in Siyamu, South Africa
d. 1971
Source: *AfrA; DcLEL*

Diaghilev, Sergei (Pavlovich)
Russian. Ballet Promoter
Formed Ballet Russe, 1909; productions based on asymmetry, perpetual motion: *The Firebird*, 1910.
b. Mar 19, 1872 in Nizhni-Novgorod, Russia
d. Aug 19, 1929 in Venice, Italy
Source: *Baker 78, 84, 92; BiDSovU; BioIn 1, 2, 3, 4, 5, 6, 7, 8, 9, 10, 11, 12, 13; DcArts; DcPup; DcRusL; EncFash; EncWB; GayLesB; HanRL; LinLib S; NewAmDM; NewEOp 71; OxCTwCA; OxDcArt; RAdv 13-3; REn; WhDW; WhThe; WorAl; WorAlBi*

Dial, Morris Grant
American. Business Executive
Pres. of Union Carbide, 1952-58; emphasized importance of research.
b. Aug 29, 1895 in Chicago, Illinois
d. Oct 4, 1982 in Naples, Florida
Source: *CurBio 56, 83; NewYTBS 82*

Diamand, Peter
Dutch. Director
Director, Edinburgh Festival, 1965-78, Royal Philharmonic Orchestra, 1978-81.
b. Jun 8, 1913 in Berlin, Germany
Source: *BioIn 7; IntWW 74, 75, 76, 77, 78, 79, 80, 81, 82, 83, 89, 91, 93; IntWWM 90; NewGrDM 80; OxDcOp; Who 74, 82, 83, 85E, 88, 90, 92, 94; WhoWor 74, 76, 78*

Diamond, David
American. Composer
Noted for prize-winning symphonies, string quartets; his 50th birthday honored by concerts throughout US.
b. Jul 9, 1915 in Rochester, New York
Source: *AmComp; ASCAP 66; Baker 78, 84; BioIn 14, 16; BlueB 76; CompSN SUP; ConAmC 76, 82; ConCom 92; CurBio 66; DcCM; EncWB; IntWWM 90; LegTOT; LinLib S; NewAmDM; NewGrDA 86; NewYTBS 85; PenDiMP A; REnAL; WhoAm 74; WhoAmM 83; WhoE 74; WhoEnt 92; WhoMus 72; WhoWor 74, 91; WhoWorJ 72*

Diamond, I(sidore) A. L
American. Screenwriter
Films include *Some Like It Hot,* 1959; Oscar-winning *The Apartment,* 1960.
b. Jun 27, 1920 in Unghani, Romania
d. Apr 21, 1988 in Beverly Hills, California
Source: *BioIn 9, 13, 14; CmMov; ConAu 81; ConTFT 1; DcLB 26; EncAFC; FilmEn; FilmgC; HalFC 84; IntDcF 1-4; IntMPA 75, 76, 77, 78, 79, 80, 81, 82, 84, 86, 88; OxCFilm; VarWW 85; WhoAm 86; WorEFlm*

Diamond, Legs
[Jack Diamond; John Thomas Diamond]
American. Criminal
1920s gangster, bootlegger, killer, whose ability to elude police earned him nickname; murdered by other gangsters.
b. 1896 in Philadelphia, Pennsylvania
d. Dec 18, 1931 in Albany, New York
Source: *DrInf; FacFETw; LegTOT*

Diamond, Neil
American. Singer, Songwriter, Actor
Pop singer with over 28 gold, 19 platinum records; number one single "Song Sung Blue," 1972.
b. Jan 24, 1941 in New York, New York
Source: *AmSong; ASCAP 80; Baker 84; BiDAmM; BioIn 9, 10, 11, 12, 14, 15, 16; BioNews 74; BkPepl; CelR, 90; ConAu 108; ConLC 30; ConMus 1; CurBio 81; EncPR&S 89; EncRk 88; EncRkSt; HalFC 84, 88; HarEnR 86; IlEncRk; IntMPA 84, 88, 92, 94, 96; LegTOT; NewGrDA 86; NewYTBE 72; NewYTBS 86; OxCPMus; PenEncP; RkOn 78; RolSEnR 83; WhoAm 74, 76, 78, 80, 82, 84, 86, 90; WhoEnt 92; WhoHol 92; WhoRock 81; WorAl; WorAlBi*

Diamond, Selma
American. Actor
Known for gravel voice, dangling cigarette; appeared in TV series "Night Court."
b. Aug 5, 1920 in London, Ontario, Canada
d. May 13, 1985 in Los Angeles, California
Source: *AnObit 1985; ConAu 116; ConNews 85-2*

Diana, Princess of Wales
[Lady Diana Frances Spencer]
"Lady Di"
English. Princess
Married Prince Charles, 1981; divorced, 1996; mother of Princes William, Henry.
b. Jul 1, 1961 in Sandringham, England
Source: *BioIn 12, 13, 14, 15, 16, 17, 18, 19, 20, 21; ContDcW 89; CurBio 83; EncFash; IntWW 81; InWom SUP; News 93-1; NewYTBS 81; WhoWor 82, 84, 87, 89, 91, 93, 95, 96, 97*

Diane de Poitiers
[Duchess of Valentinois]
Beautiful mistress of France's Henry II from 1536, exercising great influence over him.
b. 1499
d. 1566
Source: *Benet 96; NewCol 75; OxCFr; REn*

Dias, Bartholomew
[Bartholomew Diaz]
Portuguese. Navigator
First to sail around Cape of Good Hope, 1488; opened passage to India.
b. 1450
d. 1500
Source: *EncCRAm; EncSoA; NewCol 75*

Diaz, Justino
Puerto Rican. Opera Singer
Leading bass, Met. Opera Co., 1963—.
b. Jan 29, 1940 in San Juan, Puerto Rico
Source: *Baker 84, 92; BioIn 10; IntWWM 77, 80, 90; MetOEnc; NewAmDM; NewEOp 71; NewGrDA 86; NewGrDM 80; NewGrDO; PenDiMP; WhoAm 74, 76, 78, 80, 82, 84, 86, 88, 90, 92, 94, 95, 96, 97; WhoEnt 92; WhoOp 76; WhoWor 74; WorEFlm*

Diaz, Porfirio
[Jose de la Cruz Porfirio]
Mexican. Political Leader
Overthrew govt., ruled as dictator, 1876-80, 1884-1911.
b. Sep 15, 1830 in Oaxaca, Mexico
d. Jul 2, 1915 in Paris, France
Source: *ApCAB; Benet 87, 96; BiDLAmC; BioIn 1, 6, 7, 8, 9, 10, 11, 12, 14, 16, 18; DcHiB; DicTyr; EncLatA; EncRev; FacFETw; HarEnUS; HisWorL; LegTOT; LinLib S; REn; WhDW; WorAl; WorAlBi*

Diaz de la Pena, Narciso Virgilio
French. Artist
Landscape painter; best known for his scenes from forest of Fontainbleau.
b. 1807 in Bordeaux, France
d. 1876
Source: *NewCol 75; WebBD 83*

Diaz Ordaz, Gustavo
Mexican. Political Leader
Pres. of Mexico, 1964-72; ambassador to Spain, 1977; known for bloody handling of student demonstrations, 1968.
b. Mar 12, 1911 in Puebla, Mexico
d. Jul 15, 1979 in Mexico City, Mexico
Source: *BiDLAmC; BioIn 6, 7, 8, 12, 16; CurBio 65, 79, 79N; DcCPCAm; DcPol; EncLatA; EncWB; IntWW 74, 75, 76, 77, 78; LinLib S; WhoAm 74; WhoSSW 73*

Dibbs, Eddie
[Edward George Dibbs]
"Fast Eddie"
American. Tennis Player
Won German Open, 1973, 1974, 1976; WCT Tournament of Champions, 1981.
b. Feb 23, 1951 in New York, New York
Source: *BioIn 10; WhoAm 78, 80, 82; WhoIntT*

Dibdin, Charles
English. Dramatist, Songwriter
Wrote 30 popular plays, one-man table entertainments; his 1,400 songs include "Tom Bowling."
b. Mar 4, 1745 in Southampton, England
d. Apr 25, 1814 in London, England
Source: *Alli; Baker 78, 84, 92; BbD; BiD&SB; BiDLA, SUP; BioIn 3, 4, 11, 12, 16; BritAu; CamGLE; CamGWoT; CasWL; CelCen; Chambr 2; ChhPo, S1, S2; DcBiPP; DcEnL; DcEuL; DcLEL; DcNaB; DcPup; Ent; EvLB; GrWrEL DR; MusMk; NewAmDM; NewC; NewCBEL; NewGrDM 80; NewGrDO; NewOxM; NotNAT A, B; OxCEng 67, 85, 95; OxCMus; OxCPMus; OxCShps; OxCThe 67, 83; OxDcOp; PenDiMP A; RfGEnL 91; Str&VC; WebBD 83; WhDW*

Dibdin, Thomas Frognall
English. Author, Librarian
Bibliophile who published *Bibliomania,* 1809; *Library Companion,* 1824.
b. 1776 in Calcutta, India
d. Nov 18, 1847 in London, England
Source: *Alli; BiD&SB; BiDLA; BioIn 1, 2, 7, 12; ChhPo S1; DcBiPP; DcEnL; DcEuL; DcLEL; DcNaB; NewC; NewCBEL; OxCEng 67, 85, 95*

Dibdin, Thomas Pitt
English. Dramatist, Songwriter
Thought to have written 2,000 songs, 200 operas, plays; son of Charles.
b. Mar 21, 1771 in London, England
d. Sep 16, 1841 in London, England
Source: *BioIn 9; OxCMus; OxCThe 67; PlP&P*

DiBello, Paul
American. Skier
Handicapped ski champion and coach; won eight gold medals in World Championships for the Disabled.
b. Dec 25, 1950
Source: *BioIn 15; ConNews 86-4*

DiCamerino, Roberta
[Roberta of Venice; Giuliana di Camerino]
Italian. Designer
Fashions are blend of Venetian colors, motifs; known for Venetian cut-velvet handbags.
b. Dec 8, 1920 in Venice, Italy
Source: *WorFshn*

DiCaprio, Leonardo
American. Actor
Appeared in films *Romeo and Juliet,* 1996; *Marvin's Room,* 1996.
b. Nov 11, 1974 in Hollywood, California
Source: *BioIn 20, 21; IntMPA 96; LegTOT; WhoAm 96, 97*

Dichter, Ernest
American. Psychologist
Known for using depth interviewing in marketing research; writings include *Getting Motivated,* 1979.
b. Aug 14, 1907 in Vienna, Austria
d. Nov 21, 1991 in Peekskill, New York
Source: *AmAu&B; AmMWSc 73S, 78S; BioIn 5, 6, 11, 12, 15, 18; BlueB 76; CelR; ConAu 17R, 44NR; CurBio 61, 92N; InSci; IntAu&W 91; IntWW 74, 75, 76, 77, 78, 79, 80, 81, 82, 83, 89, 91; NewYTBS 91; WhAm 10; WhoAdv 72, 90; WhoAm 74, 76, 78, 80, 82, 84, 86, 88, 90; WhoCon 73; WhoWor 74, 76, 78; WrDr 80, 82, 84, 86, 88, 90, 92, 94N, 96*

Dichter, Mischa
American. Musician
Int'l. concert pianist since 1966.
b. Sep 27, 1945 in Shanghai, China
Source: *Baker 84; BioIn 14; IntWW 91; IntWWM 90; NewAmDM; NewGrDA 86; PenDiMP; WhoAm 86, 90*

Dick, Lena Frank
American. Artist
One of the most prominent basket weavers of the Washoe "fancy basketry" period.
b. 1889? in Coleville, California
d. Mar 1965
Source: *BioIn 21; NotNaAm; PeoHis*

Dick, Philip K(indred)
[Richard Phillips]
American. Author
Science fiction writer who won 1962 Hugo award for *Man in the High Castle.*
b. Dec 16, 1928 in Chicago, Illinois
d. Mar 2, 1982 in Santa Ana, California
Source: *AmAu&B; Benet 96; ConAu 2NR, 21R, 49; ConLC 10, 30, 72; ConNov 76, 82; ConPopW; ConSFA; DcLB 8; DrAF 76; EncSF, 93; LinLib L; Novels; ScF&FL 1, 2; WhAm 8; WhoAm 82; WhoSciF; WrDr 76, 80, 82*

Dickason, Olive Patricia
Canadian. Historian
Won the Sir John A. Macdonald prize of the Canadian Historical Association for *Canada's First Nations,* 1992.
b. Mar 6, 1920 in Winnipeg, Manitoba, Canada
Source: *BioIn 21; CanWW 31; ConAu 132; NotNaAm; WrDr 94, 96*

Dickens, Charles (John Huffam)
English. Author, Dramatist
Master storyteller who wrote classics *Pickwick Papers,* 1837; *Christmas Carol,* 1843; *Tale of Two Cities,* 1859.
b. Feb 7, 1812 in Portsmouth, England
d. Jun 9, 1870 in Godshill, England
Source: *Alli, SUP; AtlBL; AuBYP 2, 3; BbD; Benet 87, 96; BiD&SB; BioIn 1, 2, 3, 4, 5, 6, 7, 8, 9, 10, 11, 12, 13, 14, 15, 16, 17, 18, 19, 20; BlmGEL; BritAu 19; BritWr 5; CamGEL; CamGLE; CamGWoT; CarSB; CasWL; CelCen; Chambr 3; ChhPo, S1, S2, S3; CnDBLB 4; CrtSuMy; CrtT 3, 4; CyEd; CyWA 58; DcAmSR; DcArts; DcBiA; DcBiPP; DcEnA, A; DcEnL; DcEuL; DcLB 21, 55, 70, 159, 166; DcLEL; DcNaB, C; DcPup; Dis&D; EncMys; EncO&P 2, 3; EncPaPR 91; EvLB; FamAYP; FilmgC; GrWrEL N; HalFC 80, 84, 88; HsB&A; JBA 34; LegTOT; LiJour; LinLib L, S; LngCEL; MagIlD; MagSWL; MajAI; McGEWB; MnBBF; MouLC 3; NewC; NewCBEL; NewEOp 71; NewGrDO; NinCLC 3, 8, 18, 26, 37, 50; NotNAT B; Novels; OxCAmH; OxCAmL 65, 83, 95; OxCAusL; OxCChiL; OxCEng 67, 85; OxCFilm; OxCThe 67, 83; OxDcOp; PenC AM, ENG; PenEncH; PlP&P; RAdv 1, 14, 13-1; RComWL; REn; RfGEnL 91; RfGShF; ScF&FL 1, 92; ShSCr 17; SmATA 15; StaCVF; Str&VC; SupFW; TwCCr&M 80A, 85A, 91A; TwoTYeD; VicBrit; WebE&AL; WhAm HS; WhDW; WhoChL; WhoHr&F; WhoSpyF; WorAlBi; WorLitC; WrChl*

Dickens, Little Jimmy
American. Singer, Songwriter
Grand Ole Opry guitarist who wrote pop-country novelties: "Hillbilly Fever," 1950.
b. Dec 19, 1925 in Bolt, West Virginia
Source: *BgBkCoM; BiDAmM; BioIn 14, 15; ConMus 7; CounME 74, 74A; EncFCWM 69, 83; HarEnCM 87; IlEncCM; NewAmDM; PenEncP; RkOn 78*

Dickens, Monica Enid
English. Author
Wrote autobiographical series *One Pair of Hands,* 1939; *One Pair of Feet,* 1942; great-granddaughter of Charles.
b. May 10, 1915 in London, England
d. Dec 25, 1992 in Reading, England
Source: *Au&Wr 71; AuBYP 3; BioIn 16; ConAu 2NR, 5R, 46NR, 140; ConNov 72, 76, 91; DcArts; DcLEL; EncBrWW; EvLB; FemiCLE; ForWC 70; IntAu&W 91; IntWW 83, 91; InWom SUP; LngCTC; NewC; NewYTBS 77; OxCEng 95; PenC ENG; REn; SmATA 4, 74; Who 83, 92; WrDr 96*

Dickerson, Eric Demetric
American. Football Player
Running back, LA Rams 1983-87; Indianapolis Colts 1987-91; LA Raiders 1992; Atlanta Falcons 1993-94; has established several NFL records for rushing, including most yds. rushing in season, 1984, breaking O.J. Simpson's record.
b. Sep 2, 1960 in Sealy, Texas
Source: *BiDAmSp FB; BioIn 14, 15, 16; CelR 90; FootReg 87; NegAl 89; NewYTBS 84; WhoAfA 96; WhoAm 86, 88, 90, 92, 94; WhoBlA 85, 92, 94; WhoMW 90; WhoWest 87, 94; WorAlBi*

Dickerson, Ernest
American. Director
Cinematographer, *Malcolm X,* 1992; director, *Surviving the Game,* 1993.
b. c. 1952 in Newark, New Jersey
Source: *ConBlB 6; DcTwCCu 5; IntMPA 92, 94, 96; WhoAm 96, 97*

Dickerson, Nancy Hanschman
American. Broadcast Journalist
Correspondent, NBC News, 1960-70; news analyst on TV's "Inside Washington" since 1971; founder, executive producer, Television Corp. Am., 1980—.
b. Jan 19, 1930 in Milwaukee, Wisconsin
Source: *BioIn 16; ConAu 69; CurBio 62; EncTwCJ; ForWC 70; IntAu&W 89; InWom SUP; LesBEnT, 92; WhoAm 86, 90; WhoAmW 85, 91; WhoSSW 73*

Dickey, Bill
[William Malcolm Dickey]
American. Baseball Player
Catcher, NY Yankees, 1928-46; had .313 career batting average; Hall of Fame, 1954.
b. Jun 6, 1907 in Bastrop, Louisiana
Source: *AnObit 1993; Ballpl 90; BiDAmSp BB; BioIn 1, 2, 3, 6, 7, 8, 9, 10, 14, 15, 19; LegTOT; NewYTBS 93; WhoProB 73; WhoSpor*

Dickey, Herbert Spencer
American. Physician, Explorer
Discovered source of Orinoco River, S America, 1931.
b. Feb 4, 1876 in Highland Falls, New York
d. Oct 28, 1948 in Huigra, Ecuador
Source: *AmAu&B; BioIn 1, 2; NatCAB 36; WhAm 2*

Dickey, James (Lafayette)
American. Poet, Critic
Wrote *Deliverance,* 1970; filmed, 1972, starring Burt Reynolds, Jon Voight.
b. Feb 2, 1923 in Atlanta, Georgia
d. Jan 19, 1997 in Columbia, South Carolina
Source: *AmAu&B; AnCL; AuNews 1, 2; Benet 87, 96; BenetAL 91; BioIn 8, 9, 10, 11, 12, 13, 14, 15, 16; BlueB 76; BroV; CamGEL; CamGLE; CamHAL; CelR, 90; ConAu 2BS, 9NR, 9R, 10NR, 48NR; ConLC 1, 2, 4, 7, 10, 15, 47; ConPo 70, 75, 80, 85, 91, 96; ConPopW; Conv 1; CroCAP; CurBio 68; DcArts; DcLB 5, DS7, Y82A; DcLEL 1940; DcTwCCu 1; DrAF 76; DrAP 75; DrAPF 80, 91; DrAS 74E, 78E, 82E; EncWL, 2, 3; FacFETw; FifSWrA; GrWrEL P; IntAu&W 77, 91, 93; IntvTCA 2; IntWW 74, 75, 76, 77, 78,*

79, 80, 81, 82, 83, 89, 91, 93; IntWWP 77, 82; LegTOT; LinLib L; MagSAmL; MajTwCW; ModAL, S1, S2; Novels; OxCAmL 65, 83, 95; OxCTwCP; PenC AM; RAdv 1, 14, 13-1; RfGAmL 87, 94; RGFAP; RGTwCWr; SouWr; WebAB 74, 79; WebE&AL; WhoAm 74, 76, 78, 80, 82, 84, 86, 88, 90, 92, 94, 95, 96, 97; WhoSSW 73, 75, 76; WhoTwCL; WhoWor 74, 76, 78, 80, 82, 84, 87, 89, 91, 93, 95, 96, 97; WorAl; WorAlBi; WorAu 1950; WrDr 76, 80, 82, 84, 86, 88, 90, 92, 94, 96

Dickinson, Angie
[Angeline Brown]
American. Actor
Starred in TV series "Policewoman," 1974-78; film *Dressed to Kill,* 1980.
b. Sep 30, 1931 in Kulm, North Dakota
Source: *BiDFilm, 81, 94; BioIn 9, 10, 11, 14, 15, 16; BkPepl; CelR 90; ConTFT 6, 13; FilmEn; FilmgC; ForYSC; GangFlm; HalFC 80, 84, 88; IntDcF 1-3, 2-3; IntMPA 84, 86, 88, 92, 94, 96; InWom SUP; ItaFilm; LegTOT; MotPP; MovMk; SweetSg D; WhoAm 74, 82, 88, 90, 92, 94, 95, 96, 97; WhoEnt 92; WhoHol A; WorAl; WorAlBi; WorEFlm*

Dickinson, Edwin W
American. Artist
Painted in Romantic style; never finished *The Fossil Hunters,* 1926-28.
b. Oct 11, 1891 in Seneca Falls, New York
d. Dec 2, 1978 in Cape Cod, Massachusetts
Source: *CurBio 63, 79; DcCAA 71; NewYTBS 78; WhAm 7; WhoAm 78; WhoAmA 73; WhoWor 74; WorArt 1950*

Dickinson, Emily (Elizabeth)
American. Poet
Highly reclusive American literary giant; most works published posthumously.
b. Dec 10, 1830 in Amherst, Massachusetts
d. May 15, 1886 in Amherst, Massachusetts
Source: *AmAu; AmAu&B; AmBi; AmCulL; AmWomWr; AmWr; AnCL; ArtclWW 2; AtlBL; Benet 87, 96; BenetAL 91; BibAL; BiD&SB; BiDTran; BioAmW; BioIn 1, 2, 3, 4, 5, 6, 7, 8, 9, 10, 11, 12, 13, 14, 15, 16, 17, 18, 19, 20, 21; BlmGWL; CamGEL; CamGLE; CamHAL; CasWL; Chambr 3; ChhPo, S1, S2, S3; CnDAL; CnE&AP; ContDcW 89; CrtT 3, 4; CyWA 58; DcAmAu; DcAmB; DcAmC; DcArts; DcLB 1; DcLEL; DcNAA; EncAB-H 1974, 1996; EncWHA; EvLB; FemiCLE; GayLesB; GayN; GoodHs; GrLiveH; GrWomW; GrWrEL P; HanAmWH; HerW, 84; IlEncMy; IntDcWB; InWom, SUP; LegTOT; LibW; LinLib L, S; MagSAmL; ModAL, S1; ModAWWr; MorMA; NatCAB 11, 23; NewGrDA 86; NinCLC 21; OxCAmH; OxCAmL 65, 83, 95; OxCEng 67, 85, 95; OxCWoWr 95; PenBWP; PenC AM; PeoHis; PoeCrit 1; RAdv 1, 14, 13-1; RComAH; RComWL; RealN; REn; REnAL; RfGAmL 87, 94; RGFAP; SmATA 29; Str&VC; TwCBDA; WebAB 74, 79; WebBD 83; WebE&AL; WhAm HS; WhDW; WorAl; WorAlBi; WorLitC; WrPh*

Dickinson, John
American. Statesman
Voted against, refused to sign Declaration of Independence; founded Dickinson College, PA, 1783.
b. Nov 8, 1732 in Talbot County, Maryland
d. Feb 14, 1808 in Wilmington, Delaware
Source: *Alli; AmAu; AmAu&B; AmBi; AmOrN; AmPolLe; AmWrBE; ApCAB; BenetAL 91; BiAUS; BiDAmM; BiD&SB; BiDrAC; BiDrACR; BiDrUSC 89; BioIn 4, 5, 6, 7, 8, 9, 10, 11, 13, 14, 15, 16; BlkwEAR; ChhPo S1; CyAG; CyAL 1; DcAmAu; DcAmB; DcAmC; DcLB 31; DcLEL; DcNAA; Drake; EncAAH; EncAB-H 1974, 1996; EncAR; EncCRAm; EncSoH; HarEnUS; HisDBrE; McGEWB; NatCAB 2; OxCAmH; OxCAmL 65, 83, 95; PenC AM; PeoHis; REnAL; TwCBDA; WebAB 74, 79; WhAm HS; WhAmP; WhAmRev; WorAl; WorAlBi*

Dickman, Joseph Theodore
American. Military Leader
Commanded Third Infantry Division in France, 1917-18; in charge of Third Army in occupied Germany, 1918-19.
b. Oct 6, 1857 in Dayton, Ohio
d. Oct 23, 1927
Source: *AmBi; DcAmB; DcAmMiB; DcNAA; HarEnMi; NatCAB 20; OhA&B; WebAMB; WebBD 83; WhAm 1*

Dickson, Earle Ensign
American. Inventor
Invented adhesive bandage "Band-Aid," 1924.
b. Oct 10, 1892 in Grandview, Tennessee
d. Sep 21, 1961 in New Brunswick, New Jersey
Source: *DcAmB S7; EncAB-A 33; WhAm 4*

Dickson, Gordon Rupert
Canadian. Author
Won Hugo for *Soldier, Ask Not,* 1965; other novels include *Wolfing,* 1969.
b. Nov 1, 1923 in Edmonton, Alberta, Canada
Source: *ConAu 6NR, 9R; ConSFF; DcLB 8; IntAu&W 91; IntvTCA 2; NewEScF; OxCCanL; RGTwCSF; ScFSB; TwCSFW 91; WorAlBi; WrDr 92*

Diddley, Bo
[Ellas Bates McDaniel]
"The Originator"
American. Musician, Songwriter
Best known for "I'm Sorry," 1959; inducted into Rock-'n'-Roll Hall of Fame, 1986.
b. Dec 30, 1928 in Magnolia, Mississippi
Source: *Baker 92; BiDAmM; BiDJaz; BioIn 11, 12, 13, 15, 16, 21; ConMus 3; CurBio 89; DcArts; DcTwCCu 5; DrBlPA, 90; EncPR&S 74, 89; EncRk 88; EncRkSt; HarEnR 86; IlEncRk; LegTOT; MusMk; NewAmDM; NewGrDA 86; OnThGG; OxCPMus; PenEncP; RkOn 74; RolSEnR 83; SoulM; WhoAfA 96; WhoBlA 90, 92, 94; WhoHol 92; WhoRock 81; WhoRocM 82; WorAl; WorAlBi*

Diderot, Denis
[Pantophile Diderot]
French. Editor, Philosopher
Editor, *Encyclopedie,* 1745, first modern encyclopedia; wrote novels, plays, art criticism.
b. Oct 5, 1713 in Langres, France
d. Jul 30, 1784 in Paris, France
Source: *AsBiEn; AtlBL; Baker 78, 84, 92; BbD; Benet 87, 96; BiD&SB; BiDPsy; BioIn 1, 2, 3, 4, 5, 6, 7, 8, 9, 10, 11, 13, 14, 16, 17, 18, 19, 20, 21; BlkwCE; CamGWoT; CasWL; CmFrR; CnThe; CyEd; CyWA 58; DcArts; DcBiPP; DcEuL; DcScB; Dis&D; EncEnl; EncSF; EncUnb; EncWT; Ent; EuAu; EuWr 4; EvEuW; GrFLW; GuFrLit 2; InSci; LegTOT; LinLib L, S; LitC 26; LuthC 75; McGEWB; McGEWD 72, 84; NamesHP; NewC; NewCBEL; NewGrDM 80; NewGrDO; NotNAT B; Novels; OxCArt; OxCEng 67, 85, 95; OxCFr; OxCMus; OxCPhil; OxCThe 67, 83; OxDcArt; OxDcOp; PenC EUR; RAdv 14, 13-2, 13-4; RComWL; REn; REnWD; RfGWoL 95; ScF&FL 1; TwoTYeD; WhDW; WorAl; WorAlBi*

Didion, Joan
American. Author, Screenwriter
Writings include *Democracy,* 1984; co-wrote film *A Star is Born,* 1976.
b. Dec 5, 1934 in Sacramento, California
Source: *AmAu&B; AmWomWr; ArtclWW 2; AuNews 1; Benet 87, 96; BenetAL 91; BioAmW; BioIn 10, 11, 12, 13, 14, 15, 16; BlmGWL; BroV; CelR 90; CmCal; ConAu 5R, 14NR, 52NR; ConLC 1, 3, 8, 14, 32; ConNov 76, 82, 86, 91, 96; ContDcW 89; CurBio 78; CyWA 89; DcArts; DcLB 2, 173, Y81A, Y86A; DcLEL 1940; DcTwCCu 1; DrAF 76; DrAPF 80, 89, 91; EncWL 2, 3; FacFETw; FemiCLE; GrWomW; IntDcWB; IntvTCA 2; IntWW 89, 91, 93; InWom SUP; LegTOT; LiJour; LinLib L; MagSAmL; MajTwCW; ModAL S1, S2; ModAWWr; ModWoWr; NewYTBS 87; Novels; OxCAmL 83, 95; OxCWoWr 95; PostFic; RAdv 14; RfGAmL 94; RGTwCWr; SourALJ; TwCWW 91; WhoAm 78, 80, 82, 84, 86, 88, 90, 92, 94, 95, 96, 97; WhoAmW 72, 79, 81, 83, 85, 87, 89, 91, 93, 95, 97; WhoUSWr 88; WhoWor 93, 95, 96, 97; WhoWrEP 89, 92, 95; WomWMM; WorAl; WorAlBi; WorAu 1970; WrDr 76, 80, 82, 84, 86, 88, 90, 92, 94, 96*

DiDonato, Pietro
American. Author
Wrote autobiographical novel *Christ in Concrete,* 1939; *Naked Author,* 1970.

b. Apr 3, 1911 in West Hoboken, New Jersey
d. Jan 19, 1992 in Stony Brook, New York
Source: *BenetAL 91; CamHAL; ConAu 101; DcAmImH; OxCAmL 65; PeoHis; REnAL; TwCA, SUP*

Diebenkorn, Richard C.
[Richard Clifford Diebenkorn, Jr.]
American. Artist
Exhibits held in museums, galleries; writings include *The Search for Meaning in Modern Art,* 1964.
b. Apr 22, 1922 in Portland, Oregon
d. Mar 30, 1993 in Berkeley, California
Source: *AmArt; AmCulL; BioIn 14, 15; ConArt 77, 83, 89; CurBio 71; DcCAA 71, 88; EncWB; IntWW 83, 89, 91, 93; OxCTwCA; OxDcArt; PrintW 85; WhAm 11; WhoAm 74, 76, 78, 80, 82, 84, 86, 88, 90, 92; WhoAmA 84, 91; WhoWest 74, 76, 78; WhoWor 74*

Diederichs, Nicholaas
South African. Political Leader
Pres. of S Africa, 1975-78.
b. Nov 17, 1904 in Orange Free State, South Africa
d. Aug 21, 1978 in Cape Town, South Africa
Source: *BioIn 11; IntWW 78; WhoWor 78*

Diefenbaker, John George
Canadian. Lawyer, Political Leader
Progressive Conservative prime minister, 1957-63.
b. Sep 18, 1895 in Grey County, Ontario, Canada
d. Aug 16, 1979 in Ottawa, Ontario, Canada
Source: *BioIn 4, 5, 6, 7, 8, 10, 11, 12, 13; BlueB 76; CanWW 70, 79; CurBio 57; DcNaB 1971; DcTwHis; IntWW 74, 75, 76, 77, 78, 79; IntYB 78, 79; McGEWB; OxCCan SUP; WhAm 7; Who 74; WhoAm 74, 76, 78; WhoCan 73, 77, 80; WhoWor 74, 76, 78; WorAl*

Diegel, Leo
American. Golfer
Touring pro, 1920s-30s; won PGA, 1928, 1929; Hall of Fame, 1955.
b. Apr 27, 1899 in Detroit, Michigan
d. May 8, 1951 in North Hollywood, California
Source: *BiDAmSp OS; BioIn 2; ObitOF 79; WhoGolf; WhoSpor*

Diels, Otto Paul Herman
German. Chemist
Shared Nobel Prize, 1950, for discovery of Diels-Alder reaction.
b. Jan 23, 1876 in Hamburg, Germany
d. Mar 7, 1954 in Kiel, Germany (West)
Source: *WhoNob, 90, 95; WorAl*

Diemer, Emma Lou
American. Composer, Organist
Wrote over 100 choral, instrumental works including "Suite for Orchestra," 1981.
b. Nov 24, 1927 in Kansas City, Missouri
Source: *ASCAP 66, 80; Baker 92; BioIn 5, 12, 16; ConAmC 76, 82; ConCom 92; CpmDNM 74, 77, 78, 79, 82; IntWWM 77, 80, 85, 90; InWom SUP; NewGrDA 86; WhoAm 82, 84, 86, 88, 90, 92, 94, 95, 96, 97; WhoAmM 83; WhoAmW 58, 61, 70, 72, 74, 75, 77, 81, 83; WhoEnt 92; WhoWest 80, 92, 94; WomCom*

Dierdorf, Dan(iel Lee)
American. Football Player, Sportscaster
Six-time all-pro center, St. Louis, 1971-83; color commentator for TV's "Monday Night Football."
b. Jun 29, 1949 in Canton, Ohio
Source: *BiDAmSp FB; BioIn 11, 12, 15, 16; NewYTBS 77; WhoAm 90, 92, 94, 95, 96, 97*

Dies, Martin, Jr.
American. Lawyer, Politician
Dem. con., 1931-45, 1953-59; chm. of House committee on un-American activities.
b. Nov 5, 1900 in Colorado, Texas
d. Nov 14, 1972 in Lufkin, Texas
Source: *BiDrAC; BiDrUSC 89; BioIn 7, 9, 10, 17, 21; CurBio 40, 73; DcAmB S9; DcAmC; DcAmSR; EncMcCE; NewYTBE 72; WebAB 74; WebBD 83; WhAm 5; WhAmP*

Diesel, Rudolf Christian Karl
German. Engineer, Inventor
Developed internal combustion engine to run on crude oil, 1893-97.
b. Mar 18, 1858 in Paris, France
d. Sep 29, 1913
Source: *BioIn 12; LarDcSc; NewCol 75; OxCGer 76; WorInv*

Dieterle, William
American. Director
Best known for *The Hunchback of Notre Dame,* 1939, *A Portrait of Jennie,* 1948.
b. Jul 15, 1893 in Ludwigshafen, Germany
d. Dec 9, 1972 in Ottobrunn, Germany (West)
Source: *AmFD; BiDFilm, 81; BioIn 9, 10, 11, 15; CmMov; CurBio 43, 73, 73N; DcFM; EncWT; FilmEn; FilmgC; GangFlm; HalFC 80, 84, 88; IlWWHD 1; IntDcF 1-2, 2-2; ItaFilm; MiSFD 9N; MovMk; NewYTBE 72; ObitOF 79; OxCFilm; WhAm 5; WhoHrs 80; WhScrn 77, 83; WorEFlm; WorFDir 1*

Dietrich, Marlene
[Maria Magdalene von Losch]
American. Actor, Singer
Had glamorous roles in films *The Blue Angel,* 1930; *Destry Rides Again,* 1939; known for sultry looks, long legs.
b. Dec 27, 1901 in Berlin, Germany
d. May 6, 1992 in Paris, France
Source: *AmCulL; AnObit 1992; BiDAmM; BiDFilm, 81, 94; BioIn 14, 15, 17, 18, 19, 20; CelR 90; CmMov; ContDcW 89; ConTFT 10; CurBio 53, 68, 92N; EncTR, 91; Ent; FacFETw; FilmAG WE; FilmEn; FilmgC; GoodHs; GrLiveH; HalFC 80, 84, 88; IntDcF 1-3, 2-3; IntDcWB; IntMPA 88, 92; IntWW 77, 78, 79, 80, 81, 82, 83, 89, 91; InWom SUP; ItaFilm; LegTOT; MotPP; MovMk; NewAmDM; NewGrDM 80; News 92; NewYTBE 72; NewYTBS 76, 92; OxCFilm; OxCPMus; RadStar; ThFT; VarWW 85; WhDW; Who 85, 92; WhoAm 84, 90; WhoAmW 83; WhoEnt 92; WhoHol 92, A; WhoThe 77; WhoWor 91; WomFir; WorAl; WorAlBi; WorEFlm*

Dietrich, Noah
American. Businessman
Chief business adviser to Howard Hughes, 1925-57; wrote *Howard: The Amazing Mr. Hughes,* 1971.
b. Feb 28, 1889 in Batavia, Wisconsin
d. Feb 15, 1982 in Palm Springs, California
Source: *AnObit 1982; BioIn 9; ConAu 45, 106; NewYTBS 82; WhAm 8*

Dietz, Angel DeCora
American. Artist
Championed the use of Native American design in contemporary art; became the first director of the art department at the Carlisle Indian School, PA.
b. May 3, 1871 in Nebraska
d. Feb 6, 1919 in New York, New York
Source: *BioIn 21; EncNAB; NotNaAm*

Dietz, David
American. Broadcast Journalist
Science correspondent, NBC News; won 1937 Pulitzer.
b. Oct 6, 1897 in Cleveland, Ohio
d. Dec 9, 1984 in Cleveland, Ohio
Source: *AmMWSc 73P, 76P, 79, 82; BioIn 14, 15; CurBio 85, 85N; InSci; IntAu&W 76, 77, 82; IntWW 74, 75, 76, 77, 78, 79, 80, 81, 82, 83; IntYB 78, 79, 80, 81, 82*

Dietz, Howard M
American. Songwriter
With Arthur Schwartz, wrote over 500 songs, including "Dancing in the Dark;" "That's Entertainment."
b. Sep 8, 1896 in New York, New York
d. Jul 30, 1983 in New York, New York
Source: *AmAu&B; ASCAP 66; BiDAmM; BiE&WWA; CmpEPM; ConAu 53; ConDr 73; CurBio 65; EncMT; FilmgC; ModWD; NotNAT; REnAL; WhoAm 82; WhoThe 77; WorAl*

Diez, Friedrich Christian
German. Scholar
A founder of Romance philology; wrote grammar of Romantic languages, 1836.
b. Mar 15, 1794 in Giessen, Germany
d. May 29, 1876 in Bonn, Germany

Source: *BiD&SB; BioIn 11; DcBiPP; NewCol 75; WebBD 83*

Diffie, Joe
American. Singer, Songwriter
Country music singer whose first album, *A Thousand Winding Roads*, 1990 produced four number one singles including "Home," "If You Want Me To," "If the Devil Danced in Empty Pockets," and "New Way to Light Up an Old Flame;" recorded *Regular Joe* in 1992 and *Honky Tonk Attitude* in 1993.
b. Dec 28, 1958 in Duncan, Oklahoma
Source: *BgBkCoM; BioIn 20; ConMus 10*

Difford, Chris
English. Singer, Musician
Guitarist, vocalist; collaborated with Glenn Tilbrook on over 600 songs.
b. Apr 11, 1954 in London, England
Source: *LegTOT; OnThGG; WhoRocM 82*

DiFranco, Ani
American. Singer, Songwriter
Released albums *Ani DiFranco*, 1990; *Not A Pretty Girl*, 1995.
b. 1970 in Buffalo, New York
Source: *ConMus 17; News 97-1*

Digby, Kenelm, Sir
English. Diplomat, Author
Believed to have discovered necessity of oxygen to plant life; wrote *Memoirs*, published 1827.
b. Jul 11, 1603 in Gayhurst, England
d. Jun 11, 1665 in London, England
Source: *Alli; BioIn 2, 3, 4, 5, 13, 18; BritAu; CamGEL; CamGLE; Chambr 1; CroE&S; DcBiPP; DcCathB; DcEnA; DcEnL; DcEuL; DcNaB, C; DcScB; Dis&D; EvLB; InSci; NewC; NewCBEL; NewCol 75; OxCEng 67, 85, 95; OxCMed 86; OxCShps; PenC ENG; REn*

Digges, Dudley
Irish. Actor
With Theatre Guild, 1919-30, produced *Pygmalion; Doctor's Dilemma.*
b. Jun 9, 1880 in Dublin, Ireland
d. Oct 24, 1947 in New York, New York
Source: *BioIn 1; DcAmB S4; FamA&A; FilmgC; MovMk; ObitOF 79; OxCThe 67; PlP&P; WhAm 2; WhoHol B; WhScrn 74, 77*

Diggs, Charles Coles, Jr.
American. Politician
Dem. rep. from MI, 1954-80; convicted of defrauding govt. in payroll kickback, 1980.
b. Dec 2, 1922 in Detroit, Michigan
Source: *BiDrAC; BiDrUSC 89; BlkAmsC; CngDr 79; CurBio 57; InB&W 80, 85; NegAl 89A; NewYTBE 71; PolProf J, NF; WhoAm 80; WhoAmP 73, 75, 77, 79, 81, 83, 85, 87, 89, 91, 93, 95; WhoBlA 85; WhoGov 72, 75, 77; WhoMW 74*

Digital Underground
American. Rap Group
Influenced by 1970's funk; earned platinum records for album *Sex Packets*, 1989 and "The Humpty Dance;" original members listed above.
Source: *BioIn 17; ConMus 9*

Dihigo, Martin
Cuban. Baseball Player
Star of Latin American, Negro leagues; failed to join fellow Cubans in MLs because of dark skin; Hall of Fame, 1977.
b. May 24, 1905 in Havana, Cuba
d. May 20, 1971 in Cienfuegos, Cuba
Source: *Ballpl 90; BiDAmSp BB; BioIn 14, 15, 21; InB&W 80; WhoSpor*

Dijkstra, Sjoukje
Dutch. Skater
Three-time world champion figure skater, 1962-64; won gold medal, 1964 Olympics.
b. 1941?
Source: *BioIn 6*

Dill, John Greer, Sir
Irish. Military Leader
Senior British representative on combined Chiefs of Staff committee, WW II.
b. Dec 25, 1881 in Lurgan, Northern Ireland
d. Nov 4, 1944 in Washington, District of Columbia
Source: *BioIn 1, 5, 14, 15; DcNaB 1941; GrBr; HisEWW; WhoMilH 76; WhWW-II*

Dillard, Annie Doak
American. Author
Won Pulitzer for *Pilgrim at Tinker Creek*, 1975.
b. Apr 30, 1945 in Pittsburgh, Pennsylvania
Source: *ArtclWW 2; Au&Arts 6; BenetAL 91; BioIn 13, 16; ConAu 3NR; ConLC 60; CyWA 89; DrAPF 83, 91; FacFETw; FemiCLE; IntAu&W 89; IntWW 91; InWom SUP; MajTwCW; WhoAm 84, 90; WhoAmW 81, 91; WhoUSWr 88; WhoWrEP 89; WorAu 1975; WrDr 92*

Dillard, Harrison
American. Track Athlete
Sprinter, hurdler; won two gold medals each in 1948, 1952 Olympics.
b. Jul 8, 1923 in Cleveland, Ohio
Source: *AfrAmSG; BioIn 10, 11, 12, 16, 21; BlkOlyM; InB&W 80; NewYTBS 79; WhoSpor; WhoTr&F 73*

Diller, Barry Charles
American. Film Executive
CEO, Twentieth Century Fox Film Corp., 1984-85; Fox, Inc., 1985-92. Purchased Silver King Communications, 1995.
b. Feb 2, 1942 in San Francisco, California
Source: *BioIn 9, 11, 12, 14, 15; ConTFT 3; CurBio 86; Dun&B 90; IntMPA 86, 92; IntWW 89, 91; LesBEnT, 92; News 91-1; NewYTBS 84, 86; WhoAm 86, 90; WhoEnt 92; WhoFI 89, 92; WhoWest 92; WorAlBi*

Diller, Phyllis
[Phyllis Driver]
American. Comedian
Known for outrageous appearance, stories about husband, Fang; is also a concert pianist.
b. Jul 17, 1917 in Lima, Ohio
Source: *BioIn 5, 6, 7, 8, 9, 12, 14, 15, 16, 17, 18; CelR, 90; ConAu 22NR, 81; ConTFT 1; CurBio 67; EncAFC; Film 2; FilmEn; FilmgC; ForYSC; FunnyW; Funs; GoodHs; HalFC 80, 84, 88; IntMPA 75, 76, 77, 78, 79, 80, 81, 82, 84, 86, 88, 92, 94, 96; InWom, SUP; JoeFr; LegTOT; MotPP; QDrFCA 92; WhoAm 74, 76, 78, 80, 82, 84, 86, 88, 90, 92, 94, 95, 96, 97; WhoAmW 74, 75, 77, 79, 81, 83; WhoCom; WhoEnt 92; WhoHol 92, A; WhoWor 74; WhoWrEP 89, 92, 95; WorAl; WorAlBi*

Dillinger, John Herbert
American. Criminal, Murderer
"Public Enemy Number One," 1930s; known for daring bank robberies, jail escapes.
b. Jun 28, 1902 in Indianapolis, Indiana
d. Jul 22, 1934 in Chicago, Illinois
Source: *BioNews 74; DcAmB S1; OxCFilm; WebAB 74; WhDW; WorAl*

Dillingham, Charles Bancroft
American. Producer, Manager
Mgr., NYC's Globe Theater, 1910-34; The Hippodrome, 1914-23.
b. May 30, 1868 in Hartford, Connecticut
d. Aug 30, 1934
Source: *BioIn 1; DcAmB S1; EncMT; NotNAT B; OxCThe 67, 83; WebBD 83; WhAm 1; WhThe*

Dillman, Bradford
American. Actor
Appeared in *The Way We Were*, 1973.
b. Apr 13, 1930 in San Francisco, California
Source: *BiE&WWA; BioIn 5, 6; ConTFT 3, 10; CurBio 60; FilmEn; FilmgC; ForYSC; HalFC 80, 84, 88; IntMPA 75, 76, 77, 78, 79, 80, 81, 82, 84, 86, 88, 92, 94, 96; ItaFilm; LegTOT; MotPP; MovMk; NotNAT; WhoAm 80, 82, 84, 86, 88, 90, 92, 94, 95, 96, 97; WhoEnt 92; WhoHol 92, A; WhoWor 95, 96, 97; WorAl; WorAlBi*

Dillon, Diane Claire Sorber
[Mrs. Leo Dillon]
American. Author, Illustrator
Won Caldecott medal with husband, Leo, for illustrating children's tales *Ashanti to Zulu*, 1976.
b. Mar 13, 1933 in Glendale, California
Source: *AuBYP 2S, 3; BiDScF; BioIn 12, 14, 16, 17, 18, 19; BlkAuII, 92;*

ChlBkCr; EncSF, 93; FifBJA; IlrAm 1880; IlsCB 1967; InB&W 80; InWom SUP; MajAI; NewEScF; ScF&FL 92; SmATA 15, 51; WhoAm 78, 80, 82, 84, 90

Dillon, (Clarence) Douglas
American. Banker, Diplomat
Chm. of US & Foreign Securities Corp., 1971-84; ambassador to France, 1953-57.
b. Aug 21, 1909 in Geneva, Switzerland
Source: *BiDAmBL 83; BiDrUSE 71, 89; BioIn 3, 4, 5, 6, 7, 8, 10, 11, 13, 16; CelR; DcAmDH 80, 89; FacFETw; IntYB 78, 79, 80, 81, 82; LinLib S; WhoAm 74, 76, 78, 80, 82, 84, 86, 88, 90, 92, 94, 95, 96, 97; WhoAmP 75, 77, 79, 81, 83, 85; WhoGov 72, 75*

Dillon, George
American. Author, Editor
Editor, *Poetry* Magazine, 1937-50; won 1931 Pulitzer for *Flowering St one.*
b. Nov 12, 1906 in Jacksonville, Florida
d. May 9, 1968 in Charleston, South Carolina
Source: *AmAu&B; BenetAL 91; BioIn 4, 8; ChhPo, S1; ConAmA; ConAu 89; DcLEL; OxCAmL 65, 83, 95; REn; REnAL; TwCA, SUP; WhAm 5; WhFla*

Dillon, Kevin
American. Actor
Films include *Platoon,* 1986; brother of Matt.
b. Aug 19, 1967 in New Rochelle, New York
Source: *ConTFT 8; IntMPA 92*

Dillon, Leo
American. Author, Illustrator
Co-illustrator with wife, Diane, of children's and science fiction books: *Why Mosquitoes Buzz in People's Ears,* 1975.
b. Mar 2, 1933 in New York, New York
Source: *AuBYP 2S, 3; BiDScF; BioIn 12, 14, 16, 17, 18, 19; BlkAull, 92; ChlBkCr; EncSF, 93; FifBJA; IlrAm 1880; IlsCB 1967; InB&W 80; MajAI; NewEScF; ScF&FL 92; SmATA 15, 51*

Dillon, Matt
American. Actor
Played bully in *My Bodyguard,* 1980; starred in *Tex,* 1982.
b. Feb 18, 1964 in New Rochelle, New York
Source: *BioIn 13, 16; CelR 90; ConTFT 5, 15; CurBio 85; HalFC 84, 88; IntDcF 2-3; IntMPA 84, 86, 88, 92, 94, 96; IntWW 91, 93; JohnWSW; LegTOT; News 92, 92-2; NewYTBS 83; WhoAm 88, 90, 92, 94, 95, 96, 97; WhoEnt 92; WhoHol 92; WorAlBi*

Dillon, Melinda
American. Actor
Best known for *Absence of Malice,* 1981.
b. Oct 31, 1939 in Hope, Arkansas
Source: *BiE&WWA; BioIn 6, 11; ConTFT 3, 10; HalFC 84, 88; IntMPA 80, 82, 88, 92, 94, 96; LegTOT; NotNAT; WhoHol 92*

Dillon, Mia
American. Actor
Nominated for Tony for *Crimes of the Heart,* 1982.
b. Jul 9, 1955 in Colorado Springs, Colorado
Source: *ConTFT 4*

Dillon, William A
American. Songwriter
Toured with Harry Lauder, retired 1912.
b. Nov 6, 1877 in Cortland, New York
d. Feb 10, 1966 in Ithaca, New York
Source: *ASCAP 66, 80; BiDAmM; BioIn 4, 7*

Dilthey, Wilhelm Christian Ludwig
German. Philosopher
Developed methods of separating humanities from natural sciences; stressed importance of history in culture.
b. Nov 19, 1833 in Biebrich, Germany
d. Oct 3, 1911 in Seis, Germany
Source: *CasWL; LuthC 75; McGEWB; NewCol 75; OxCGer 76*

DiMaggio, Dom(inic Paul)
"The Little Professor"
American. Baseball Player
Outfielder, Boston, 1940-53; known for fielding and great throwing arm.
b. Feb 12, 1917 in San Francisco, California
Source: *Ballpl 90; BiDAmSp Sup; BioIn 13, 16, 18; St&PR 75, 87; WhoProB 73*

DiMaggio, Joe
[Joseph Paul DiMaggio]
"Joltin' Joe"; "The Yankee Clipper"
American. Baseball Player
Outfielder, NY Yankees, 1936-51; has longest hitting streak in ML history, 56 games, 1941; married Marilyn Monroe, 1954; Hall of Fame, 1955.
b. Nov 24, 1914 in Martinez, California
Source: *AmDec 1940; Ballpl 90; BiDAmSp BB; BioIn 13, 14, 15, 16; CelR, 90; CmCal; CurBio 41, 51; EncAB-H 1996; FacFETw; LegTOT; NewYTBS 81, 84, 87; OxCAmH; WebAB 74, 79; WhoAm 90, 97; WhoHol 92, A; WhoProB 73; WorAl; WorAlBi*

DiMaggio, Vince(nt Paul)
American. Baseball Player
Outfielder, 1937-46; brother of Joe and Dom, but didn't possess their hitting ability; led NL in strikeouts six times.
b. Sep 6, 1912 in Martinez, California
d. Oct 3, 1986 in North Hollywood, California
Source: *Ballpl 90; BioIn 13; NewYTBS 86; WhoProB 73*

DiMeola, Al
American. Musician, Songwriter
Jazz guitarist; albums include *Soaring Through a Dream,* 1985; won Grammy, 1975.
b. Jul 22, 1954 in Jersey City, New Jersey
Source: *AllMusG; BioIn 11, 13, 14, 15; ConMuA 80A; ConNews 86-4; HarEnR 86; PenEncP; WhoEnt 92; WhoRocM 82*

Dimitrios I, Patriarch
Religious Leader
Archbishop of Constantinople; spiritual leader of Eastern Orthodox Christian Church, 1972-91.
b. Sep 8, 1914 in Istanbul, Turkey
d. Oct 2, 1991 in Istanbul, Turkey
Source: *BioIn 15; IntWW 91; NewYTBS 91; WhoWor 91*

Dimitrov, Georgi Mikhailovich
Bulgarian. Political Leader
Prime minister of Bulgaria, 1947-49; won Lenin award, 1945.
b. Jun 18, 1882 in Kovachevtsi, Bulgaria
d. Jul 2, 1949 in Moscow, Union of Soviet Socialist Republics
Source: *ColdWar 2; CurBio 49; DcPol; EncTR; HisEWW; WhAm 3*

Dimitrova, Ghena
Bulgarian. Opera Singer
Soprano; made US debut in *Ernani,* 1981, in Dallas, TX.
b. May 6, 1941 in Beglezh, Bulgaria
Source: *Baker 92; BioIn 14, 16; ConNews 87-1; IntWW 89, 91, 93; IntWWM 90; MetOEnc; NewGrDO; NewYTBS 84; WhoWor 89, 91*

Dimmock, Peter
British. Broadcasting Executive
Headed BBC, 1973; joined ABC Sports, 1977-86; vice-pres., consultant, ABC Video Enterprises, 1984-90; chm. Peter Dimmock Assocs., TV and Media Consultants, 1990—.
b. Dec 6, 1920
Source: *Au&Wr 71; BlueB 76; IntMPA 75, 76, 77, 78, 79, 80, 81, 82, 84, 86, 88, 92, 94; NewYTET; VarWW 85; Who 74, 82, 83, 85, 88, 90, 92; WhoWor 78, 80*

Dine, Jim
American. Artist
Nonconformist works are in museums, one-man shows; wrote *Welcome Home Lovebirds,* 1969.
b. Jun 16, 1935 in Cincinnati, Ohio
Source: *AmArt; BioIn 8, 11, 13, 14, 15, 17, 19, 20; BlueB 76; BriEAA; CelR; ConArt 77, 83, 89, 96; ConDr 73; CurBio 69; DcAmArt; DcArts; DcCAA 71, 77, 88, 94; DcCAr 81; IntWW 91; McGDA; OxCTwCA; OxDcArt; PrintW 83, 85; WhoAm 74, 76, 78, 80, 82, 84, 86, 88, 92, 94, 95, 96; WhoAmA 82, 91; WhoWor 74; WorArt 1950*

Dines, William Henry
English. Meteorologist, Inventor
Invented atmospheric measurement devices including a meteorograph that became British standard.
b. Aug 5, 1855 in London, England
d. Dec 24, 1927 in Benson, England
Source: *CamDcSc; DcNaB 1922; LarDcSc*

Dingell, John David, Jr.
American. Politician
Dem. congressman from MI, 1956—; chm., Energy and Commerce Com. investigating toxic waste.
b. Jul 8, 1926 in Colorado Springs, Colorado
Source: *AlmAP 80, 92; AmCath 80; BiDrAC; BiDrUSC 89; BioIn 8, 12, 13, 14, 15, 16; CngDr 87, 89; IntWW 89, 91; NewYTBS 83, 86, 91; PolsAm 84; WhoAm 74, 76, 78, 80, 82, 84, 86, 88, 90, 92, 94, 95, 96, 97; WhoAmP 87, 91; WhoE 83, 95; WhoGov 72, 75, 77; WhoMW 74, 76, 78, 80, 82, 84, 86, 88, 90, 92, 93, 96*

Dinitz, Simcha
Israeli. Diplomat
Ambassador to US, 1973-78; held various political posts, 1954-78.
b. Jun 23, 1930 in Tel Aviv, Palestine
Source: *IntWW 91; WhoWorJ 72*

Dinkeloo, John Gerard
American. Architect, Engineer
With Roche and Saarinen, designed NYC's CBS Building; Dulles Airport, Washington, DC.
b. Feb 28, 1918 in Holland, Michigan
d. Jun 15, 1981 in Fredericksburg, Virginia
Source: *AmArch 70; BioIn 12, 13; ConArch 87, 94; NewYTBS 81; WhAm 8; WhoAm 74, 76, 78, 80; WhoE 74; WhoFI 75, 77, 79, 81*

Dinkins, David Norman
American. Politician
Succeeded Ed Koch as New York City's 106th and first black mayor, 1990-94.
b. Jul 10, 1927 in Trenton, New Jersey
Source: *BioIn 16; CurBio 90; InB&W 85; IntWW 91; News 90-2; NewYTBS 91; WhoAm 90; WhoAmP 91, 95; WhoBlA 92; WhoE 91*

Dinneen, Bill
[William Henry Dineen]
"Big Bill"
American. Baseball Player, Baseball Umpire
Pitcher, 1899-1909, first to win three games in modern World Series, 1903; AL umpire, beginning 1910.
b. Apr 5, 1876 in Syracuse, New York
d. Jan 13, 1955 in Syracuse, New York
Source: *BaseEn 88; WhoProB 73; WhoSpor*

Dinning, Mark
American. Singer
Known for hit song, "Teen Angel," 1959; banned in Britain because it was so sad.
b. Aug 17, 1935? in Drury, Oklahoma
d. Mar 22, 1986 in Jefferson City, Missouri
Source: *WhoRocM 82*

Dinwiddie, John Ekin
American. Architect, Educator
Designed, built noted "Bay Region" style San Francisco homes, 1930-53.
b. Oct 27, 1902 in Chicago, Illinois
d. Sep 11, 1959 in New Orleans, Louisiana
Source: *BioIn 7; McGDA; NatCAB 48; WhAm 4*

Dinwiddie, Robert
English. Colonial Figure
British administrator in America; VA lt. governor, 1751-58; defended frontier after Braddock's defeat.
b. 1693 in Glasgow, Scotland
d. Jul 27, 1770 in Bristol, England
Source: *AmBi; ApCAB; BiDSA; BioIn 9, 10; DcAmB; EncCRAm; McGEWB; NatCAB 13; WhAm HS; WhNaAH*

Dio, Johnny
[John DioGuardi]
American. Criminal
Labor racketeer; worked with Jimmy Hoffa; sentenced to prison for stock fraud, for 15 yrs.
b. 1915
d. 1979 in Pennsylvania
Source: *BioIn 4; EncACr; FacFETw*

Diocletian
[Gaius Aurelius Valerius Diocletianus]
Roman. Ruler
Ruled, 284-305; persecuted Christians; retired, became interested in gardening.
b. 245
d. 313
Source: *Benet 87; BioIn 5, 7, 9, 10, 11, 14, 17; Dis&D; LinLib S; LuthC 75; McGEWB; NewC; REn; WebBD 83; WhDW; WorAl; WorAlBi*

Diogenes
Greek. Philosopher
Cynic, usually depicted with lantern in search of honest man.
b. 412BC in Sinope, Bohemia
d. 323BC
Source: *AmAu; Benet 87, 96; BioIn 3, 4, 6, 7, 8, 10, 13, 14; Dis&D; LinLib L, S; LuthC 75; NewC; PlP&P; PueRA; REn; WorAl; WorAlBi*

Dion
[Dion and the Belmonts]
American. Singer, Songwriter
Solo hits "Runaround Sue," 1961, "Abraham, Martin, and John," 1968; Rock 'n Roll Hall of Fame, 1989.
b. Jul 18, 1939 in New York, New York
Source: *ASCAP 80; BioIn 12, 14, 16; ConMus 4; EncFCWM 83; EncPR&S 74, 89; EncRk 88; IlEncRk; LegTOT; NewAmDM; NewGrDA 86; OxCClL 89; RkOn 74, 82; WhoRock 81; WorAl; WorAlBi*

Dion, Celine
Canadian. Singer
Sang Grammy Winner "Beauty and the Beast," 1992.
b. Mar 30, 1968 in Charlemagne, Quebec, Canada
Source: *EncRkSt; LegTOT*

Dion and the Belmonts
[Angelo D'Angelo; Dion DiMucci; Carlo Mastangelo; Fred Milano]
American. Music Group
Bronx-born group formed, 1958-60; biggest hits "A Teenager in Love," 1959, "Where or When," 1960.
Source: *BiDAmM; ConMuA 80A; EncPR&S 74; EncRk 88; HarEnR 86; PenEncP; RkOn 74, 82; RolSEnR 83; WhoRocM 82*

Dionne, Emilie
[Dionne Sisters]
Canadian. Quintuplet
One of world's first recorded surviving quintuplets; films *Reunion,* 1936; *Five of a Kind,* 1938, were biographical.
b. May 28, 1934 in Callander, Ontario, Canada
d. Aug 6, 1954 in Saint Agathe, Quebec, Canada
Source: *BioIn 3, 9, 10; InWom, SUP; ObitOF 79; WhoHol 92, B; WhScrn 83*

Dionne, Marcel Elphege
"Beaver"
Canadian. Hockey Player
Center, LA Kings 1971-87; NY Rangers 1987-89; Hall of Fame, 1992; third leading scorer in NHL history behind Howe, Gretzky; third player to score 700 goals.
b. Aug 3, 1951 in Drummondville, Quebec, Canada
Source: *BioIn 13, 14, 15; HocEn; HocReg 87; NewYTBS 85; WhoAm 74, 78, 86, 88, 94; WhoHcky 73*

Dionne, Marie
[Dionne Sisters]
Canadian. Quintuplet
One of world's first recorded surviving quintuplets; films *The Country Doctor,* 1936; *Five of a Kind,* 1938, were biographical.
b. May 28, 1934 in Callander, Ontario, Canada
d. Feb 27, 1970 in Montreal, Quebec, Canada
Source: *BioIn 3, 8, 9, 10; InWom, SUP; ObitOF 79; WhoHol 92, B; WhScrn 74, 77, 83*

Dionne Sisters
[Annette Dionne; Cecile Dionne; Emilie Dionne; Marie Dionne; Yvonne Dionne]
Canadian. Quintuplets
World's first recorded surviving quintuplets; appeared in two films as toddlers.
b. May 28, 1934 in Callander, Ontario, Canada
Source: *BioIn 3, 4, 8, 9, 10, 11, 12, 20; HalFC 84, 88; InWom, SUP; WhoHol 92, B; WhScrn 74, 77, 83; WorAlBi*

Dionysius of Halicarnassus
Greek. Historian
Spent life writing on Roman history in 20 books, also wrote on rhetoric.
b. 30BC
d. 7BC
Source: *CasWL; NewC; PenC CL; WebBD 83*

Dionysius the Elder
Greek. Ruler
Tyrant of Syracuse whose reign was maintained by obedience through fear.
b. 430BC
d. 367BC
Source: *BioIn 1; NewC; WhDW*

Diop, Birago
Senegalese. Poet, Author
Best known for short stories and poetry inspired by the folk tales of West Africa.
b. Dec 11, 1906 in Dakar, Senegal
d. Nov 25, 1989 in Dakar, Senegal
Source: *AnObit 1989; BioIn 14, 16, 17, 21; BlkAull, 92; BlkWr 1; ConAu 125, 130; DcAfHiB 86; EncWL 2, 3; MajTwCW; ModBlW; ModFrL; SchCGBL; SmATA 64; WhoFr 79; WorAu 1975*

Diop, Cheikh Anta
Senegalese. Historian
Promoted the theory that ancient Egyptians were descended from black Africans and Egyptian society influenced the Greek and Roman cultures.
b. Dec 23, 1923 in Diourbel, Senegal
d. Feb 7, 1986 in Dakar, Senegal
Source: *BlkWr 1, 2; ConAu 110, 118, 125; ConBlB 4; InB&W 80; McGEWB; SchCGBL; SelBAAf*

Diop, David
Senegalese. Poet
Works denounced European colonialism and its values; urged political, cultural, economic freedom for Africans.
b. Jul 9, 1927 in Bordeaux, France
d. Aug 1960 in Dakar, Senegal
Source: *AfrA; BioIn 7, 14, 21; DcAfHiB 86; ModBlW; ModFrL*

Dior, Christian
French. Fashion Designer
Introduced long hemlines, full skirts; controversial before accepted, called "new look."
b. Jan 21, 1905 in Granville, France
d. Oct 24, 1957 in Montecatini, Italy
Source: *AmDec 1950; BioIn 1, 3, 4, 5, 15, 16, 17, 21; ConAu 115; ConDes 84; ConFash; CurBio 48, 58; DcArts; DcTwDes; EncFash; Entr; FacFETw; FairDF FRA; LegTOT; NotNAT B; ObitT 1951; WhAm 3; WhoFash 88; WorAl; WorAlBi; WorFshn*

Dioscorides, Pedanius
Greek. Physician, Botanist
Wrote *De Materia Medica,* which was the authority on botany for 1500 yrs.
b. 40?
d. 90?
Source: *BiESc; BioIn 7, 9; CasWL; WebBD 83*

Diouf, Abdou
Senegalese. Political Leader
Prime minister of Senegal, 1970-80; pres., 1981—.
b. Sep 7, 1935 in Louga, Senegal
Source: *AfSS 78, 79, 80, 81, 82; BioIn 13, 15; ConBlB 3; DcAfHiB 86, 86S; IntWW 74, 75, 76, 77, 78, 79, 80, 81, 82, 83, 89, 91, 93; IntYB 79, 80, 81, 82, 82A; NewYTBS 86; WhoAfr; WhoGov 72, 75; WhoWor 74, 76, 78, 80, 82, 84, 87, 89, 91, 93, 95, 96, 97*

DiPrete, Edward Daniel
American. Politician
Rep. governor of RI, 1985-91, defeated by Bruce Sundlun.
b. Jul 8, 1934 in Cranston, Rhode Island
Source: *AlmAP 88; BiDrGov 1983, 1988; IntWW 91; WhoAm 86, 90; WhoAmP 79, 81, 83, 85, 87, 89, 91, 93, 95; WhoE 83, 85, 86, 91; WhoWor 87, 91*

Dirac, Paul Adrien Maurice
English. Mathematician, Physicist
Co-winner of Nobel Prize in physics, 1933; developed quantum-wave theory.
b. Aug 8, 1902 in Bristol, England
d. Oct 20, 1984 in Tallahassee, Florida
Source: *AnObit 1984; AsBiEn; BiESc; BioIn 3, 12, 13, 14, 15, 16, 17, 19, 20, 21; BlueB 76; DcNaB 1981; DcScB S2; FacFETw; InSci; IntWW 74, 75, 76, 77, 78, 79, 80, 81, 82, 83; LarDcSc; McGEWB; McGMS 80; RAdv 14, 13-5; WhAm 8; WhDW; WhE&EA; Who 74, 82, 83; WhoAm 74, 84; WhoNob, 90, 95; WhoWor 74, 82, 84; WorAl; WorScD*

Dire Straits
[John Illsley; Dave Knopfler; Mark Knopfler; Pick Withers]
English. Music Group
Guitar-oriented band, formed 1977; hit single "Walk of Life," 1985.
Source: *BioIn 14, 15, 18, 20; ConMuA 80A; DcArts; EncPR&S 89; EncRk 88; EncRkSt; HarEnR 86; IntWW 93; NewAmDM; PenEncP; RkOn 85; RolSEnR 83; WhoRock 81; WhoRocM 82*

Dirks, Rudolph
American. Cartoonist
One of founding fathers of American comics, created "Katzenjammer Kids," 1897.
b. Feb 26, 1877 in Heinde, Germany
d. Apr 20, 1968 in New York, New York
Source: *BioIn 2, 4, 8, 14, 17; ConAu 106; EncACom; LegTOT; SmATA 31; WorECom*

Dirksen, Everett McKinley
American. Politician
Rep. senator, party leader from IL, 1950s-60s; played major role in passage of civil rights legislation, 1960s; known for oratory.
b. Jan 4, 1896 in Pekin, Illinois
d. Sep 7, 1969 in Washington, District of Columbia
Source: *AmOrTwC; AmPolLe; AuBYP 2S, 3; BiDrAC; BiDrUSC 89; BioIn 2, 3, 4, 5, 6, 7, 8, 9, 10, 11, 12, 16, 17; CurBio 69; DcAmB S8; EncAAH; EncAB-H 1974; EncWB; LinLib S; NatCAB 55; PolPar; PolProf E, J, K, NF, T; WebAB 74, 79; WebBD 83; WhAm 5; WhAmP; WhScrn 77; WorAl; WorAlBi*

DiSabato, Giovanni
American. Biologist
Best known for discovering Interlukin 2, drug used against certain kinds of cancer.
b. Mar 2, 1929 in Venice, Italy
d. Oct 11, 1987 in Nashville, Tennessee
Source: *AmMWSc 82, 86*

DiSalle, Michael Vincent
American. Politician
Dem. OH governor, 1959-63, who headed price stabilization during Korean War.
b. Jan 6, 1908 in New York, New York
d. Sep 15, 1981 in Pescara, Italy
Source: *BiDrGov 1789; BioIn 2, 3, 5, 9, 11, 12; CurBio 51, 81; IntWW 74, 75, 76, 77, 78, 79, 80, 81; NewYTBS 81; PolProf E, K, T; WhAm 8; WhoAm 74, 76, 78, 80*

DiSant'Angelo, Giorgio
American. Fashion Designer
Known for avant-garde accessories and clothing styles ranging from ethnic fantasies to body-clinging elegance; won Cotys, 1968, 1970.
b. May 5, 1936 in Florence, Italy
d. Aug 29, 1989 in New York, New York
Source: *WhoAm 86; WorFshn*

Disney, Doris Miles
American. Author
Novel *Do Not Fold, Spindle, or Mutilate* adapted to film, 1971.

b. Dec 22, 1907 in Glastonbury, Connecticut
d. Mar 8, 1976 in Fredericksburg, Virginia
Source: *AmAu&B*

Disney, Roy E(dward)
American. Broadcasting Executive
VP, Walt Disney Productions, 1970s; pres., Roy E Disney Productions, 1978—; son of Roy Oliver.
b. Jan 10, 1930 in Los Angeles, California
Source: *BioIn 14, 15; ConNews 86-3; Dun&B 90; IntMPA 86, 92; WhoAm 84, 86, 88, 92, 94, 95, 96, 97; WhoEnt 92; WhoFI 89, 94; WhoWest 92, 94; WhoWor 95*

Disney, Roy O(liver)
American. Film Executive
Pres., chm. of board, Walt Disney Productions; co-founder of entertainment empire with brother Walt, 1923.
b. Jun 24, 1893 in Chicago, Illinois
d. Dec 20, 1971 in Burbank, California
Source: *BioIn 7, 9, 11, 15; DcAmB S9; NatCAB 57; NewYTBE 71; ObitOF 79; WhAm 5*

Disney, Walt(er Elias)
[Retlaw Yensid]
American. Cartoonist, Producer
Introduced Mickey Mouse in "Steamboat Willie," 1928; won 29 Oscars; opened Disneyland, 1955, creating family entertainment empire.
b. Dec 5, 1901 in Chicago, Illinois
d. Dec 15, 1966 in Los Angeles, California
Source: *AmCulL; Benet 87; BenetAL 91; BiDAmBL 83; BiDFilm 94; BioIn 1, 2, 3, 4, 5, 6, 7, 8, 9, 10, 11, 12, 13, 14, 15, 16, 17, 18, 19, 20, 21; ChhPo, S1, S2; ChlBkCr; CmCal; ConAu 107; ConHero 1; CurBio 40, 52, 67; DcAmB S8; DcArts; DcFM; DcLB 22; DcTwCCu 1; EncAB-H 1974, 1996; FacFETw; FilmEn; FilmgC; HalFC 80, 84, 88; IntDcF 1-2, 2-4; LegTOT; LinLib L, S; LngCTC; MakMC; McGEWB; MorMA; NatCAB 57; NewYTET; ObitT 1961; OxCAmH; OxCAmL 65, 83, 95; OxCChiL; OxCFilm; RAdv 13-3; RComAH; REn; REnAL; REnAW; SmATA 27, 28; TwYS B; WebAB 74, 79; WhAm 4; WhDW; WhoChL; WhoGrA 62; WhoHol B; WhoHrs 80; WorAl; WorAlBi; WorECar; WorECom; WorEFlm*

Disraeli, Benjamin
[Earl of Benjamin Disraeli Beaconsfield]
"Dizzy"
English. Statesman, Author
Prime minister, 1868, 1874-80; founded modern Conservative Party; popular novels include *Lothair,* 1870.
b. Dec 21, 1804 in London, England
d. Apr 19, 1881 in London, England
Source: *Alli, SUP; AtlBL; BbD; Benet 87, 96; BiD&SB; BioIn 1, 2, 3, 4, 5, 6, 7, 8, 9, 10, 11, 12, 13, 14, 15, 16, 17, 19, 20, 21; BlmGEL; BritAu 19; BritWr 4; CamGEL; CamGLE; CasWL; Chambr 3; CyWA 58; DcAmC; DcBiA; DcEnA, A; DcEnL; DcEuL; DcLB 21, 55; DcLEL; DcNaB; DcPup; Dis&D; EncSF 93; EncUrb; EvLB; FilmgC; GrWrEL N; HalFC 80, 84, 88; HisDBrE; HisWorL; JeHun; LegTOT; LinLib L, S; LngCEL; McGEWB; MouLC 3; NewC; NewCBEL; NinCLC 2, 39; Novels; OxCEng 67, 85, 95; PenC AM, ENG; RAdv 1, 14, 13-1; REn; RfGEnL 91; ScF&FL 1; StaCVF; VicBrit; WebBD 83; WebE&AL; WhDW; WorAl; WorAlBi*

D'Israeli, Isaac
English. Author, Essayist
First, considered best work: *Curiosities of Literature,* 1791-1823; father of Benjamin.
b. May 11, 1766 in London, England
d. Jan 19, 1848
Source: *Alli; BbD; BiD&SB; BioIn 8, 17; BritAu 19; CamGLE; CasWL; CelCen; Chambr 2; ChhPo; DcArts; DcBiPP; DcEnA; DcEnL; DcEuL; DcLB 107; DcLEL; DcNaB, C; EvLB; NewC; NewCBEL; OxCEng 67, 85, 95; OxCMus; PenC AM, ENG; REn*

DiStefano, Giuseppe
Italian. Opera Singer
Tenor; made NY Met. debut, 1948; noted for Verdi, Puccini roles.
b. Jul 24, 1921 in Catania, Sicily, Italy
Source: *Baker 84; FacFETw; IntWW 74; IntWWM 90; MetOEnc; NewAmDM; PenDiMP*

DiSuvero, Mark
American. Sculptor
Abstract expressionist whose massive works of steel, wood beams include LA Tower of Peace, 1966, protesting Vietnam War.
b. Sep 18, 1933 in Shanghai, China
Source: *AmArt; BioIn 13, 14, 15; BriEAA; ConArt 77, 89; CurBio 79; DcAmArt; DcCAA 71, 77, 88; PrintW 85; WhoAm 82, 84, 90; WhoAmA 91*

Dith Pran
American. Photographer
Film *The Killing Fields,* 1984, depicted his ordeal in Cambodia under Khmer Rouge.
b. Sep 27, 1942 in Siem Reap, Cambodia
Source: *BioIn 12, 14, 16; CurBio 96; NewYTBS 80*

Ditka, Mike
[Michael Keller Ditka]
"Hammer"
American. Football Player, Football Coach
Five-time all-pro tight end, 1961-72; coach, Chicago, 1982-92; won 1986 Super Bowl; Hall of Fame, 1988; analyst, NBC Sports, 1992-97; coach, New Orleans, 1997—.
b. Oct 18, 1939 in Carnegie, Pennsylvania
Source: *BiDAmSp FB; BioIn 14, 15, 16, 17, 18, 19, 20; CurBio 87; LegTOT; NewYTBS 84, 86; WhoAm 84, 86, 88, 90, 92, 94, 95, 96; WhoFtbl 74; WhoMW 88, 90, 92; WhoSpor; WorAlBi*

Ditmars, Raymond Lee
American. Naturalist, Author
Herpetologist; worked at NY Zoo as curator of reptiles, mammals.
b. Jun 20, 1876 in Newark, New Jersey
d. May 12, 1942 in New York, New York
Source: *AmAu&B; AuBYP 2, 3; BioIn 2, 5, 7; CurBio 40, 42; DcAmB S3; DcNAA; InSci; JBA 34, 51; LinLib L, S; NatCAB 10; REnAL; TwCA, SUP; WhAm 2; WhNAA*

Ditters, Karl
[Karl Ditters von Dittersdorf]
Austrian. Musician, Composer
44 operas include *Doktor und Apotheker,* 1786; developed German Singspiel.
b. Nov 2, 1739 in Vienna, Austria
d. Dec 24, 1799 in Neuhof, Bohemia
Source: *Baker 78, 84, 92; BioIn 2, 4, 7, 9, 12; BriBkM 80; MetOEnc; MusMk; NewEOp 71; NewGrDM 80; OxCMus; OxDcOp*

Diver, Jenny
[Mary Jones]
English. Criminal
England's greatest pickpocket or "diver"; immortalized in *Beggar's Opera.*
b. 1700?
d. Mar 18, 1740 in London, England

Divine
[Harris Glenn Milstead]
American. Actor
Flamboyant 370-pound female impersonator; starred in several cult films and the commercially successful *Hairspray*, 1988.
b. Oct 19, 1946 in Baltimore, Maryland
d. Mar 7, 1988 in Los Angeles, California
Source: *BioIn 15, 16; ConTFT 7; GayLesB; HalFC 88; LegTOT; News 88-3; NewYTBS 88*

Divine, Arthur Durham
[David Divine; David Rame]
English. Author, Journalist
War, defense correspondent with *Sunday Times,* until 1975; books include *The Opening of the World,* 1973.
b. Jul 27, 1904 in Cape Town, South Africa
Source: *Au&Wr 71; BioIn 2, 16; ConAu 103, 122; DcLEL; DcLP 87A; IntAu&W 77, 82, 89; SmATA 52N; WhE&EA; Who 74, 82, 83, 85, 88N*

Divine, Father Major Jealous
[George Baker]
American. Religious Leader
Founded International Peace Movement, 1919.

b. 1874? in Hutchinson Island, Georgia
d. Sep 10, 1965 in Philadelphia, Pennsylvania
Source: *BioIn 2; CurBio 44; WebAB 74*

Dix, Dorothea Lynde
American. Social Reformer
Instrumental in building state hospitals for the insane.
b. Apr 4, 1802 in Hampden, Maine
d. Jul 17, 1887 in Trenton, New Jersey
Source: *Alli; AmAu; AmAu&B; AmBi; AmJust; AmRef; AmSocL; AmWom; AmWomWr; ApCAB; BiDAmEd; BiD&SB; BiDPsy; BiDSocW; BioAmW; BioIn 1, 2, 3, 4, 5, 6, 7, 8, 9, 10, 11, 12, 15, 16, 17, 19, 21; BlmGWL; CivWDc; CyAG; DcAmAu; DcAmB; DcAmMeB 84; DcLB 1; DcNAA; Dis&D; Drake; EncAB-H 1974, 1996; EncSPD; HerW, 84; InWom, SUP; LibW; McGEWB; NamesHP; NotAW; OxCAmH; OxCAmL 65, 83, 95; TwCBDA; WebAB 74, 79; WhAm HS; WhCiWar; WomFir; WorAl*

Dix, Dorothy
[Elizabeth Meriwether Gilmer]
American. Journalist, Author
Wrote syndicated column on advice to lovelorn, beginning 1896.
b. Nov 18, 1870 in Woodstock, Tennessee
d. Dec 16, 1951 in New Orleans, Louisiana
Source: *AmAu&B; AmWomWr; BenetAL 91; BiDSA; BioAmW; BioIn 15, 16; CurBio 40, 52; DcAmB S5; EncTwCJ; InWom, SUP; LegTOT; LibW; OxCAmL 65; PenNWW B; REn; REnAL; WhAm 3, 5; WhNAA; WomWWA 14*

Dix, John Adams
American. Soldier, Statesman
Major general in Civil War; Rep. governor of NY, 1873-75.
b. Jul 24, 1798 in Boscawen, New Hampshire
d. Apr 21, 1879 in New York, New York
Source: *Alli, SUP; AmBi; ApCAB; BbD; BiAUS; BiD&SB; BiDrAC; BiDrGov 1789; BiDrUSC 89; BiDrUSE 71, 89; BioIn 1, 2, 7, 10, 15, 16; CelCen; CivWDc; CyAL 2; DcAmAu; DcAmB; DcAmDH 80, 89; DcNAA; Drake; HarEnUS; NatCAB 5; TwCBDA; WebAB 74, 79; WebAMB; WebBD 83; WhAm HS; WhAmP; WhCiWar*

Dix, Otto
German. Artist
Realistic work depicted working class life, social criticism; banned by Nazis, WW II.
b. Dec 2, 1891 in Gera, Germany
d. Jun 25, 1969 in Singen, Germany (West)
Source: *Benet 87, 96; BiDMoPL; BioIn 4, 6, 8, 12, 13, 14, 15, 16, 17, 18, 20; ConArt 77, 83; DcArts; EncTR 91; EncWB; FacFETw; IntDcAA 90; LegTOT; McGDA; ModArCr 2; OxCArt; OxCTwCA; OxDcArt; PhDcTCA 77; WhAm 5; WorArt 1950*

Dix, Richard
[Ernest Carlton Brimmer]
American. Actor
Oscar nominee for *Cimarron,* 1931; in DeMille's *The Ten Commandments,* 1923.
b. Jul 18, 1894 in Saint Paul, Minnesota
d. Sep 20, 1949 in Los Angeles, California
Source: *BiDFilm, 81, 94; BioIn 7, 8, 9, 12, 17; CmMov; Film 1, 2; FilmEn; FilmgC; GangFlm; HalFC 80, 84, 88; MotPP; MovMk; NatCAB 37; NotNAT B; SilFlmP; TwYS; WhoHol B; WhoHrs 80; WhScrn 74, 77, 83*

Dixon, Alan John
American. Politician
Dem. senator from IL, 1981-92; replaced Adlai Stevenson III.
b. Jul 7, 1927 in Belleville, Illinois
Source: *AlmAP 88; BiDrUSC 89; CngDr 87, 89; IntWW 81, 82, 83, 89, 91, 93; PolsAm 84; WhoAm 78, 80, 82, 84, 86, 88, 90, 92; WhoAmP 73, 75, 77, 79, 81, 83, 85, 87, 89, 91, 93, 95; WhoGov 72, 75, 77; WhoMW 74, 76, 78, 80, 82, 84, 86, 88, 90, 92; WhoWor 82, 84, 87, 89, 91*

Dixon, Dean
American. Conductor
First black to lead major orchestra, NY Philharmonic, 1944.
b. Jan 10, 1915 in New York, New York
d. Nov 3, 1976 in Zug, Switzerland
Source: *AfrAmAl 6; Baker 78, 84, 92; BiDAmM; BioIn 1, 2, 3, 4, 6, 7, 8, 9, 10, 11, 14, 21; CurBio 43, 77, 77N; DrBlPA, 90; Ebony 1; NegAl 76, 83, 89; NewAmDM; NewGrDA 86; NewGrDM 80; NewYTBS 76; PenDiMP; WhAm 7; WhoAm 74, 76; WhoBlA 75; WhoMus 72*

Dixon, George
English. Navigator
Explored shores of British Columbia, 1780s; wrote *Voyage Round the World,* 1789.
b. 1755?
d. 1800
Source: *ApCAB; Drake; OxCCan; OxCShps; WebBD 83*

Dixon, George
"Little Chocolate"
Canadian. Boxer
Featherweight champ, 1890s; estimates indicate he fought over 800 fights; Hall of Fame, 1956.
b. Jul 29, 1870 in Halifax, Nova Scotia, Canada
d. Jan 6, 1909 in New York, New York
Source: *BioIn 9, 10; BlkWrNE A; BoxReg; DcAmNB; DcCanB 13; InB&W 80, 85; WhoBox 74; WhoSpor*

Dixon, Ivan
American. Actor, Director
Played Cpl. Kinchloe on TV comedy "Hogan's Heroes," 1965-70; has directed many TV shows.
b. Apr 6, 1931 in New York, New York
Source: *BlksAmF; CivR 74; ConTFT 8; DrBlPA, 90; InB&W 80; LegTOT; MiSFD 9; MovMk; WhoAm 80, 82; WhoBlA 80, 92; WhoHol 92, A; WorAl*

Dixon, Jean
[Marie Jacques]
American. Actor
Broadway, film comedienne for 30 yrs; starred in *Gang's All Here,* 1959.
b. Jul 14, 1894 in Waterbury, Connecticut
d. Feb 12, 1981 in New York, New York
Source: *AnObit 1981; BiE&WWA; Film 2; NewYTBS 81; NotNAT; ThFT; WhoHol A; WhThe*

Dixon, Jeane (Pinckert)
American. Astrologer, Author
Proponent of ESP known for horoscopes, annual predictions; began predicting at age eight; predicted the death of US President John F. Kennedy.
b. Jan 5, 1918 in Medford, Wisconsin
d. Jan 25, 1997 in Washington, District of Columbia
Source: *BioAmW; BioIn 7, 8, 9, 10; BkPepl; CelR, 90; ConAu 21NR, 65; CurBio 73; DivFut; EncO&P 1, 2, 3; EncPaPR 91; InWom SUP; LegTOT; WhoAm 80, 82, 90, 94, 95, 96, 97; WhoAmW 74, 95, 97; WhoE 95, 97; WhoSSW 73; WhoWor 91, 97; WhoWrEP 89*

Dixon, Jeremiah
English. Surveyor, Astronomer
With Charles Mason, determined boundary between MD and PA, 1763-78; called Mason-Dixon Line.
d. 1777 in Durham, England
Source: *ApCAB; BioIn 1; HarEnUS; WebAB 74, 79; WhDW*

Dixon, Melvin
American. Author
Authority on African American and West African literature; wrote novel *Vanishing Rooms,* 1991.
b. May 29, 1950 in Stamford, Connecticut
d. Oct 26, 1992 in Stamford, Connecticut
Source: *BioIn 17, 18, 21; ConAu 132; ConGAN; GayLesB; GayLL; SchCGBL; WrDr 92*

Dixon, Mort
American. Lyricist
Wrote "That Old Gang of Mine," 1923; often collaborated with Billy Rose, Harry Warner.
b. Mar 20, 1892 in New York, New York
d. Mar 23, 1956 in Bronxville, New York

Source: *AmPS; ASCAP 66, 80; BiDAmM; BioIn 4; CmpEPM; Sw&Ld C*

Dixon, Paul Rand
American. Government Official
Joined Federal Trade Commission, 1938; commissioner, 1970-83.
b. Sep 29, 1913 in Nashville, Tennessee
Source: *BioIn 5, 8, 9, 11; BlueB 76; CurBio 68; IntWW 74, 75; Law&B 89A; PolProf J, K; WhoAm 74, 76, 78, 80, 82, 86; WhoAmP 73, 75, 77, 79, 81, 83; WhoGov 72, 75, 77; WhoSSW 73, 75*

Dixon, Robert Ellington
American. Military Leader
WW II pilot who signalled sinking of first Japanese carrier: "Scratch one flattop."
b. Apr 22, 1906? in Richland, Georgia
d. Oct 21, 1981 in Virginia Beach, Virginia
Source: *BioIn 12; WhAm 8*

Dixon, Rod
New Zealander. Track Athlete
First foreign male to win NYC Marathon, 1983; won bronze medal, 1,500 meters, 1972 Olympics.
b. 1950?
Source: *BioIn 13; NewYTBS 83*

Dixon, Roland Burrage
American. Anthropologist, Educator
Writings include *Oceanic Mythology,* 1916.
b. Nov 6, 1875 in Worcester, Massachusetts
d. Dec 19, 1934 in Cambridge, Massachusetts
Source: *AmAu&B; AmBi; BioIn 3, 4; DcAmB S1; DcNAA; NatCAB 14, 39; WebBD 83; WhAm 1*

Dixon, Sharon Pratt
American. Politician
Dem. mayor of Washington, DC, 1991—, succeeding Marion Barry; first female African-American mayor of major US city.
b. Jan 30, 1944 in Washington, District of Columbia
Source: *AfrAmAl 6; AfrAmBi 1; ConBlB 1; Dun&B 86, 88, 90; NotBlAW 1; St&PR 87, 91; WhoAmP 77, 79, 81, 83, 85, 87, 89, 91; WhoAmW 91; WhoBlA 80, 85, 88, 90, 92; WhoFI 89; WhoWomW 91*

Dixon, Thomas
American. Author, Clergy
His novel *The Clansman,* 1905, was basis for silent film epic *Birth of a Nation,* 1914.
b. Jan 11, 1865 in Shelby, North Carolina
d. Apr 3, 1946 in Raleigh, North Carolina
Source: *AmAu&B; BiD&SB; BiDSA; CasWL; CnDAL; CurBio 46; DcAmB S4; DcLEL; FilmgC; OxCAmL 65; REnAL; TwCA SUP; WhAm 2*

Dixon, Willie (James)
American. Musician, Songwriter, Producer
Blues musician; work was influential precursor of rock-'n'-roll; won Grammy for *Hidden Charms,* 1989.
b. Jul 1, 1915 in Vicksburg, Mississippi
d. Jan 29, 1992 in Burbank, California
Source: *AmCulL; BiDAfM; BiDAmM; BiDJaz; BioIn 10, 14, 16; BluesWW; ConBlB 4; ConMuA 80A; ConMus 10; CurBio 89, 92N; EncRk 88; GuBlues; InB&W 85; LegTOT; NewYTBS 92; PenEncP; RolSEnR 83; WhAm 10; WhoAm 82, 84, 86, 88, 90; WhoEnt 92; WhoRocM 82*

Djerassi, Carl
American. Chemist, Educator, Writer
Best known for creating birth control pill; chemistry professor, Stanford U, 1959—; National Inventors Hall of Fame, 1978.
b. Oct 29, 1923 in Vienna, Austria
Source: *AmMWSc 73P, 76P, 79, 82, 86, 89, 92, 95; BioIn 4, 5, 10, 11, 12; BlueB 76; ConAu 111, 131; IntAu&W 86, 93; IntWW 74, 75, 76, 77, 78, 79, 80, 81, 82, 83, 89, 91, 93; LarDcSc; McGMS 80; NotTwCS; RAdv 14; St&PR 75; WhoAm 74, 76, 78, 80, 82, 84, 86, 88, 90, 92, 94, 95, 96, 97; WhoFrS 84; WhoScEn 94, 96; WhoWest 87, 89, 92, 94; WhoWor 74, 76, 78, 80, 82, 84, 87; WrDr 92, 94, 96*

Djilas, Milovan
Yugoslav. Author, Politician
VP of Yugoslavia, 1954; won US Freedom Award, 1968; books include *Tito,* 1980.
b. Jun 12, 1911 in Kolasin, Yugoslavia
d. Apr 20, 1995 in Belgrade, Yugoslavia
Source: *Au&Wr 71; BiDNeoM; BioIn 1, 4, 5, 6, 7, 8, 9, 10, 11, 12, 14, 15, 16, 17, 18, 20, 21; ColdWar 2; ConAu 127, 148; CurBio 58, 95N; DcArts; DcPol; DcTwHis; EncCW; EncRev; FacFETw; IntAu&W 77, 89; IntWW 74, 75, 76, 77, 78, 79, 80, 81, 82, 83, 89, 91, 93; LinLib L; McGEWB; NewYTBS 95; RAdv 14, 13-2; WhDW; WhoAm 74, 76, 78; WhoSocC 78; WhoSoCE 89; WhoWor 74; WorAu 1950*

DJ Jazzy Jeff and the Fresh Prince
[Willard Smith; Jeffrey Townes]
American. Rap Group
Rap duo formed 1986; first Grammy in rap category for single *Parents Just Don't Understand,* 1989.
Source: *ConMus 5*

Dlugacz, Judy
American. Record Company Executive
A founder and owner of Olivia Records, 1973; also owns Olivia Cruises and Resorts.
b. 1952
Source: *GayLesB*

Dmytryk, Edward
[The Hollywood Ten]
American. Director
Spent one yr. in jail for communist affiliations, 1947; directed *The Caine Mutiny,* 1954.
b. Sep 4, 1908 in Grand Forks, British Columbia, Canada
Source: *BiDFilm, 81, 94; BioIn 2, 11, 12, 14, 15, 16; CmMov; DcFM; EncMcCE; FilmEn; FilmgC; HalFC 80, 84, 88; IIWWHD 1; IntDcF 1-2, 2-2; IntMPA 75, 76, 77, 78, 79, 80, 81, 82, 84, 86, 88, 92, 94, 96; ItaFilm; LegTOT; MiSFD 9; MovMk; OxCFilm; WorEFlm; WorFDir 1*

Doak, Bill
[William Leopold]
"Spittin' Bill"
American. Baseball Player
Pitcher, 1912-24, 1927-29; one of last in MLs to legally throw spitball.
b. Jan 28, 1891 in Pittsburgh, Pennsylvania
d. Nov 26, 1954 in Bradenton, Florida
Source: *Ballpl 90; BioIn 3; WhoProB 73*

Doar, John Michael
American. Lawyer
Held various political posts, including special counsel for House judiciary comm., 1973-74.
b. Dec 3, 1921 in Minneapolis, Minnesota
Source: *BioIn 7, 8, 10, 11; BioNews 74; NewYTBE 73; NewYTBS 74; PolProf J, K, NF; WhoAm 78*

Dobbs, Mattiwilda
American. Opera Singer
Coloratura soprano; NY Met. debut, 1956; int'l. concert singer.
b. Jul 11, 1925 in Atlanta, Georgia
Source: *AfrAmAl 6; Baker 84, 92; BiDAfM; BioIn 3, 4, 6, 8, 11, 16, 18; BlkOpe; BlkWAm; CmOp; CurBio 55; DcAfAmP; DrBlPA, 90; InB&W 80, 85; IntWW 91; IntWWM 80, 90; InWom; MetOEnc; MusMk; MusSN; NegAl 76, 83, 89; NewAmDM; NewGrDA 86; NewGrDO; NotBlAW 1; PenDiMP; Who 92; WhoAm 86, 88; WhoBlA 85, 92; WhoMus 72; WhoWor 84*

Dobell, Sydney Thompson
[Sydney Yendys]
English. Poet
Wrote *Balder,* 1854; associated with "Spasmodic school."
b. Apr 5, 1824 in Cranbrook, England
d. Aug 22, 1874 in Nailsworth, England
Source: *Alli; BritAu 19; CamGEL; DcEnL; DcNaB; EvLB; NewC; NewCBEL; NinCLC 43; OxCEng 67, 85, 95; REn*

Dobereiner, Johann Wolfgang
German. Chemist
Classed similar triads of elements; discovered catalytic action used in Dobereiner's lamp, 1823.
b. Dec 15, 1780 in Hof, Bavaria

d. Mar 24, 1849 in Jena, Germany
Source: *AsBiEn; BiESc; BioIn 2, 9; CamDcSc; CelCen; DcBiPP; DcScB; InSci; LarDcSc; NewCol 75; WorScD*

Dobie, J(ames) Frank
American. Folklorist, Author, Educator
Numerous books on southwestern history, folklore include *Coronado's Children,* 1931; *Cow People,* 1964.
b. Sep 26, 1888 in Live Oak County, Texas
d. Sep 18, 1964 in Austin, Texas
Source: *AmAu&B; BioIn 1, 2, 3, 4, 5, 7, 8, 9, 10, 11, 14, 15; ConAu 1R; CurBio 45, 64; DcLEL; EncAAH; OxCAmL 65, 95; REn; REnAL; REnAW; TexWr; TwCA SUP; WebAB 74, 79; WhAm 4; WhE&EA; WorAl; WorAlBi*

Dobkin, Alix
American. Singer, Songwriter
Released albums *XXAlix, Love & Politics.*
b. Aug 16, 1940 in New York, New York
Source: *GayLesB*

Dobozy, Imre
Hungarian. Author
Writings include *Spring Wind; New Seed in Cumenia.*
b. Oct 30, 1917, Austria-Hungary
d. Sep 23, 1982
Source: *IntAu&W 76, 77; IntWW 74, 75, 76, 77, 78, 79, 80, 81, 82; WhoSocC 78; WhoSoCE 89*

Dobrovolsky, Georgi Timofeyevich
Russian. Cosmonaut
Flight commander on Soyuz XI spacecraft; crew died during re-entry.
b. Jun 1, 1928 in Odessa, Union of Soviet Socialist Republics
d. Jun 30, 1971
Source: *BioIn 9, 10; NewYTBE 71*

Dobrowen, Issai
Russian. Conductor
Led European orchestras, 1920s-40s; noted for interpreting Musorgsky, Rimsky-Korsakov.
b. Feb 27, 1893 in Nizhni-Novgorod, Russia
d. Dec 9, 1953 in Oslo, Norway
Source: *Baker 84; NewEOp 71*

Dobrynin, Anatoly Fedorovich
[Anatoliy Federovich Dobrynin]
Russian. Diplomat
Soviet ambassador to US, 1962-86.
b. Nov 16, 1919 in Krasnaya Gorka, Union of Soviet Socialist Republics
Source: *BioIn 13, 14; BioNews 74; ConAu 151; CurBio 62; IntWW 74, 75, 76, 77, 78, 79, 91; IntYB 79, 80, 81, 82; Who 90, 92, 94; WhoAm 90; WhoGov 72, 75; WhoUN 75; WhoWor 74, 91*

Dobson, Henry Austin
English. Poet, Essayist
Wrote *Proverbs in Porcelain,* 1877.
b. Jan 18, 1840 in Plymouth, England
d. Sep 2, 1921 in London, England
Source: *Alli SUP; BbD; BritAu 19; CamGEL; CasWL; CelCen; Chambr 3; ChhPo, S1, S2, S3; DcEnA, A; DcLEL; DcNaB 1912; EvLB; NewCBEL; OxCEng 67, 85, 95; PenC ENG; WhLit*

Dobson, Kevin
American. Actor
Played Mac Mackenzie on TV series "Knots Landing," 1982-93.
b. Mar 18, 1944 in Jackson Heights, New York
Source: *BioIn 14; CelR 90; ConTFT 3; IntMPA 92; VarWW 85; WhoAm 86, 88, 90; WhoEnt 92; WhoTelC*

Doby, Larry
[Lawrence Eugene Doby]
American. Baseball Player
Outfielder, 1947-59; first black player in AL, with Cleveland.
b. Dec 13, 1924 in Camden, South Carolina
Source: *Ballpl 90; BiDAmSp BB; BioIn 3, 4, 5, 6, 7, 8, 11, 15, 16; InB&W 80, 85; NewYTBS 87; WhoBlA 75, 77, 80, 85, 90, 92, 94; WhoProB 73; WhoSpor*

Dobyns, Lloyd Allen, Jr.
American. Broadcast Journalist
NBC News correspondent, 1972-86.
b. Mar 12, 1936 in Newport News, Virginia
Source: *ConAu 119; WhoAm 78, 80, 82, 84, 86, 88, 92, 94, 95, 96, 97; WhoSSW 95, 97*

Dockstader, Lew
[George Alfred Clapp]
American. Entertainer
Vaudeville actor, minstrel player; appeared in film *Dan,* 1914.
b. 1856 in Hartford, Connecticut
d. Oct 26, 1924 in New York, New York
Source: *CamGWoT; DcAmB; EncVaud; JoeFr; NatCAB 23; NewGrDA 86; OxCAmT 84; OxCPMus; OxCThe 67, 83; PlP&P; WhScrn 83*

Doctorow, E(dgar) L(aurence)
American. Author, Editor
Combined historical figures, events with fiction in *Ragtime,* 1975.
b. Jan 6, 1931 in New York, New York
Source: *Benet 87; BenetAL 91; BioIn 10, 12, 13, 14, 16; BroV; CamGLE; CamHAL; CelR 90; ConAu 2NR, 33NR, 45, 51NR; ConLC 6, 11, 15, 18, 65; ConNov 91; CyWA 89; DcLB 2; EncSF 93; FacFETw; HalFC 88; IntAu&W 91; IntvTCA 2; IntWW 91; MajTwCW; ModAL S1, S2; NewYTBS 85; Novels; PostFic; RAdv 14, 13-1; RfGAmL 94; TwCRHW 94; TwCWW 91; Who 92; WhoAm 90; WhoUSWr 88; WhoWrEP 89; WorAlBi; WrDr 94, 96*

Dodd, Charles Harold
English. Theologian
Director, New Translation of Bible (NEB), 1950-65; writings include *The Founder of Christianity,* 1970.
b. Apr 7, 1884
d. Sep 22, 1973 in Goring, England
Source: *Au&Wr 71; BioIn 7, 10, 11; ConAu 45; DcEcMov; DcNaB 1971; LuthC 75; NewCBEL; NewYTBE 73; ObitOF 79; RAdv 14; WhAm 6; WhoLA; WhoWor 74*

Dodd, Christopher John
American. Politician
Dem. senator from CT, 1980—; son of former senator Thomas Dodd.
b. May 27, 1944 in Willimantic, Connecticut
Source: *AlmAP 80, 92; BiDrUSC 89; BioIn 10, 13, 16; CelR 90; CngDr 87, 89; CurBio 89; IntAu&W 89; IntWW 91; PolsAm 84; WhoAm 86, 90; WhoAmP 75, 77, 79, 81, 87, 91; WhoE 91; WhoWor 91*

Dodd, Ed(ward) Benton
American. Cartoonist
Cartoon strips include "Back Home Again," 1930-45; "Mark Trail," 1946-1978.
b. Nov 7, 1902 in Lafayette, Georgia
d. May 27, 1991 in Gainesville, Georgia
Source: *BioIn 5, 9, 17; ConAu 31NR, 73, 127, 134; EncACom; EncTwCJ; NewYTBS 91; SmATA 4, 68; WhoAm 74, 86, 90; WhoAmA 76; WorECom*

Dodd, John Bruce, Mrs.
[Sonora Louise Smart]
American. Author, Artist
Founder of Father's Day, first observed, 1910.
b. 1882 in Jenny Lind, Arkansas
d. Mar 22, 1978 in Spokane, Washington
Source: *NewYTBS 78; WhoAmW 58, 61*

Dodd, Thomas Joseph
American. Politician
Dem. senator from CT, 1959-71; censured by Senate for financial irregularities, 1967.
b. May 15, 1907 in Norwich, Connecticut
d. May 24, 1971 in Old Lyme, Connecticut
Source: *BiDrAC; BiDrUSC 89; BioIn 5, 6, 7, 8, 9, 10, 11, 12, 13; CurBio 59, 71; DcAmB S9; NewYTBE 71; WhAm 5; WhAmP*

Dodd, William Edward
American. Historian, Educator
American history professor, U of Chicago, 1908-33; ambassador to Germany, 1933-37.
b. Oct 21, 1869 in Clayton, North Carolina
d. Feb 9, 1940 in Round Hill, Virginia
Source: *AmAu&B; BiDSA; BioIn 1, 3, 4, 8, 16, 18; DcAmB S2; DcAmDH 80, 89; DcNAA; DcNCBi 2; EncAB-A 2; EncSoH; EncTR 91; NatCAB 38;*

OxCAmH; OxCAmL 65; REn; REnAL; WebBD 83; WhAm 1; WhLit

Dodds, Baby
[Warren Dodds]
American. Jazz Musician
New Orleans-style drummer, 1920s-50s; with brother, Johnny's band, 1930s.
b. Dec 24, 1898 in New Orleans, Louisiana
d. Feb 14, 1959 in Chicago, Illinois
Source: *AllMusG; Baker 78, 84, 92; BiDAfM; BioIn 16, 18; CmpEPM; IlEncJ; InB&W 85; NewAmDM; NewGrDA 86; NewGrDJ 88, 94; NewGrDM 80; PenEncP; WhAm 4; WhoJazz 72*

Dodds, Harold Willis
American. Educator, Political Scientist
Pres. of Princeton U, 1933-57.
b. Jun 28, 1889 in Utica, Pennsylvania
d. Oct 25, 1980 in Hightstown, New Jersey
Source: *AmAu&B; AnObit 1981; BiDAmEd; BioIn 1, 4, 11, 12; CurBio 45, 81N; IntWW 74, 75, 76, 77, 78, 79, 80; LinLib L; WhAm 7, 8; WhLit; Who 74; WhoAm 74; WhoGov 72, 75*

Dodds, Johnny
American. Jazz Musician, Bandleader
Clarinetist; led own band, 1930s.
b. Apr 12, 1892 in New Orleans, Louisiana
d. Aug 8, 1940 in Chicago, Illinois
Source: *AllMusG; Baker 78, 84, 92; BiDAmM; BiDJaz; BioIn 6, 16, 17; CmpEPM; DcArts; IlEncJ; InB&W 80; NewAmDM; NewGrDA 86; NewGrDJ 88, 94; NewGrDM 80; NewOrJ; OxCPMus; PenEncP; WhoJazz 72*

Dodge, Bertha Sanford
American. Children's Author
Topics of writing include cultural, ethnic, health: *It Started in Eden,* 1980.
b. Mar 23, 1902 in Cambridge, Massachusetts
Source: *AuBYP 2, 3; BioIn 8, 11; ConAu 2NR, 5R; SmATA 8; WhoAmW 58, 61; WrDr 76, 80, 82, 84, 86, 92, 94, 96*

Dodge, David S
American. Hostage
Former acting pres., American University of Beirut, taken hostage in Lebanon July 20, 1982, released July 21, 1983.
Source: *BioIn 14*

Dodge, Grace Hoadley
American. Educator, Philanthropist
President, YWCA, 1906-14.
b. May 21, 1856 in New York, New York
d. Dec 27, 1914 in New York, New York
Source: *AmBi; AmWom; ApCAB, SUP, X; BiDAmEd; BiDSocW; BioIn 8, 21; DcAmB; InWom SUP; LibW; NatCAB 18; NotAW; WhAm 1; WomFir; WomWWA 14*

Dodge, Grenville Mellen
American. Engineer, Army Officer
Responsible for construction of over 10,000 miles of railroad in US, including most of Union Pacific.
b. Apr 12, 1831 in Danvers, Massachusetts
d. Jan 3, 1916 in Council Bluffs, Iowa
Source: *ApCAB; BiDrAC; BiDrUSC 89; BioIn 1, 5, 7, 12; CivWDc; DcAmB; DcNAA; EncAAH; EncAB-H 1974, 1996; EncABHB 2; EncAI&E; HarEnUS; NatCAB 11, 16; OxCAmH; REnAW; TwCBDA; WebAB 74, 79; WebAMB; WhAm 1; WhCiWar*

Dodge, Henry Chee
American. Native American Leader
First official Navajo interpreter, 1870s-1900s; became first chairman of the Navajo Tribal Council, 1923.
b. 1857?
d. Jan 7, 1947 in Ganado, Arizona
Source: *BioIn 21; EncNoAI; NotNaAm; WhNaAH*

Dodge, Horace Elgin
American. Auto Manufacturer
Built first Dodge car Nov 1914, Detroit, MI.
b. May 17, 1868 in Niles, Michigan
d. Dec 10, 1920 in Palm Beach, Florida
Source: *BioIn 12; EncABHB 4; NatCAB 19; ObitOF 79; WorAl; WorAlBi*

Dodge, John Francis
American. Auto Manufacturer
Pres., Dodge Brothers Co., established 1901, Detroit, MI.
b. Oct 25, 1864 in Niles, Michigan
d. Jan 4, 1920 in New York, New York
Source: *BioIn 12; EncABHB 4; NatCAB 19; WorAl*

Dodge, Mary Elizabeth Mapes
American. Children's Author, Editor
Editor of children's magazine *St. Nicholas,* 1873-1905; wrote *Hans Brinker & the Silver Skates,* 1865.
b. Jan 26, 1831 in New York, New York
d. Aug 21, 1905 in Onteora Park, New York
Source: *Alli SUP; AmAu; AmAu&B; AmBi; BbD; BibAL; BiD&SB; BlmGWL; CarSB; ChhPo, S1, S2; DcAmB; DcBiA; DcNAA; FamAYP; FamSYP; InWom, SUP; JBA 34; LibW; NotAW; OxCAmL 65; REn; REnAL; WebAB 74, 79; WhoChL; WomFir; WorAl*

Dodington, Sven H(enry Marriott)
Canadian. Engineer
Invented tactical air navigation and distant measuring equipment.
b. May 22, 1912 in Vancouver, British Columbia, Canada
d. Jan 13, 1992 in Whippany, New Jersey
Source: *AmMWSc 73P, 79, 82, 86, 92; WhoAm 82, 90; WhoEng 88; WhoTech 82, 84, 89*

Dodsley, Robert
English. Bookseller, Dramatist, Publisher
Founded *Annual Register,* 1758; helped finance Johnson's dictionary.
b. Feb 13, 1703 in Mansfield, England
d. Sep 23, 1764 in Durham, England
Source: *Alli; BbD; BiD&SB; BioIn 3, 8, 12, 14, 16, 17, 21; BlkwCE; BritAu; CamGEL; CamGLE; CamGWoT; CasWL; Chambr 2; DcBiPP; DcEnA; DcEnL; DcEuL; DcLB 95, 154; DcNaB; EvLB; GrWrEL DR; NewC; NewCBEL; NewCol 75; NotNAT B; OxCEng 67, 85, 95; OxCThe 67, 83; REn; RfGEnL 91; WebBD 83*

Dodson, Howard, Jr.
American. Educator, Historian
Chief, The Schomburg Center for Research in Black Culture, 1984—.
b. Jun 1, 1939 in Chester, Pennsylvania
Source: *BioIn 20; ConBlB 7; WhoAfA 96; WhoBlA 77, 80, 85, 88, 90, 92, 94*

Dodson, Owen (Vincent)
American. Dramatist, Poet
Wrote plays *Divine Comedy,* 1938; *New World A-Coming,* 1944.
b. Nov 28, 1914 in New York, New York
d. Jun 21, 1983 in New York, New York
Source: *AmAu&B; AnObit 1983; BiE&WWA; BioIn 1, 12, 13, 14, 16, 17, 19, 20; BlkAmP; BlkAWP; BlkLC; BlkWr 1; BlkWrNE; BroadAu; ConAu 24NR, 65, 110; ConBlAP 88; ConLC 79; DcLB 76; DrAF 76; DrAP 75; DrBlPA, 90; EarBlAP; InB&W 85; LivgBAA; MorBAP; NegAl 76, 83, 89; NewYTBS 83; NotNAT; Novels; PenC AM; SchCGBL; SelBAAf; SelBAAu; SouBlCW; TheaDir; WhAm 8; WhoAm 78, 80; WorAu 1980*

Doe, Samuel Kanyon
Liberian. Political Leader
Pres., 1980-91, whose bloody domestic policies led to his overthrow and violent death in a 1991 coup.
b. May 6, 1951? in Tuzon, Liberia
d. Sep 9, 1990 in Monrovia, Liberia
Source: *BioIn 14, 15, 16; CurBio 81, 90, 90N; DcAfHiB 86; EncWB; InB&W 85; IntWW 82, 91N; IntYB 82; News 91; WhoWor 91*

Doenitz, Karl C
[Karl C Donitz]
German. Naval Officer
Hitler's successor who declared Germany's surrender, 1945; tried, sentenced for war crimes.
b. Sep 16, 1891 in Berlin, Germany
d. Dec 24, 1980 in Hamburg, Germany (West)
Source: *AnObit 1981; ConAu 103; CurBio 42, 81N; EncTR; IntWW 80; WhWW-II*

Doerr, Bobby
[Robert Pershing Doerr]
American. Baseball Player
Second baseman, Boston, 1937-51, known for fielding; MVP in AL, 1944.
b. Apr 7, 1918 in Los Angeles, California
Source: *Ballpl 90; BiDAmSp BB; BioIn 1, 2, 3, 15, 16, 18; LegTOT; WhoProB 73; WhoSpor*

Doesburg, Theo van
[Christian Emil Marie Kupper]
Dutch. Artist
With others founded group, De Stijl; published art review *De Stijl,* 1917.
b. Sep 30, 1883 in Ultrecht, Netherlands
d. Mar 7, 1931 in Davos, Switzerland
Source: *BioIn 1, 4, 10, 12, 13, 15; DcTwDes; EncMA; FacFETw; McGDA; McGEWB; OxCArt; OxCTwCA; OxDcArt; PhDcTCA 77; WebBD 83; WhoArch*

Doggett, Bill
American. Singer, Musician, Songwriter
Popularized use of Hammond organ in R&B; had hit single "Honky Tonk," 1956.
b. Feb 6, 1916 in Philadelphia, Pennsylvania
d. Nov 13, 1996 in New York, New York
Source: *AllMusG; CmpEPM; EncJzS; EncPR&S 74; EncRk 88; HarEnR 86; IlBBlP; NewGrDJ 88, 94; PenEncP; RkOn 74; RolSEnR 83*

Doggett, Thomas
Irish. Actor
Popular comedian; founded sculling prize, Doggett's Coat and Badge, 1716, to commemorate accession of George I; rowed annually on Thames.
b. 1670? in Dublin, Ireland
d. 1721
Source: *CamGWoT; DcIrW 1; NotNAT, A, B; OxCEng 85, 95; OxCThe 67, 83; PlP&P*

Dohanos, Stevan
American. Illustrator, Artist
Member, Society of Illustrators Hall of Fame, NY, 1971.
b. May 18, 1907 in Lorain, Ohio
Source: *BioIn 1, 2, 9, 12, 20; GrAmP; IlrAm 1880, E; NewYTBS 94; WhAmArt 85; WhoAmA 73, 76, 78, 80, 82, 84, 86, 89, 91, 93*

Doheny, Edward Lawrence
American. Oilman
Oil magnate charged with conspiracy, bribery in Teapot Dome Scandal, 1924.
b. Aug 10, 1856 in Fond du Lac, Wisconsin
d. Sep 8, 1935
Source: *DcAmB S1; NatCAB 29; REn; WhAm 1; WorAl*

Doherty, Brian
Canadian. Lawyer, Producer, Dramatist
Founded Shaw Festival at Niagara-on-the-Lake, ON, 1962.
b. Feb 3, 1906 in Toronto, Ontario, Canada
d. 1974
Source: *CanWW 70; ColCR*

Doherty, Kieran
Irish. Hunger Striker, Revolutionary
IRA member; one of 10 hunger strikers to die in prison, demanding political prisoner rather than criminal status.
b. Oct 16, 1956? in Londonderry, Northern Ireland
d. Aug 2, 1981 in Belfast, Northern Ireland
Source: *BioIn 12*

Doherty, Robert Ernest
American. Engineer, Educator
Pres. of Carnegie Institute of Technology, PA, 1909-31; dean of engineering school, Yale U, 1933-36; worked for govt. in WW II.
b. Jan 22, 1885 in Clay City, Illinois
d. Oct 19, 1950 in Scotia, New York
Source: *BioIn 1, 2, 3, 4; CurBio 49, 50; InSci; NatCAB 38; ObitOF 79; WhAm 3*

Doherty, Shannen
American. Actor
Played in "Little House: A New Beginning," 1982-83; played Brenda Walsh on "Beverly Hills, 90210," 1990-94.
b. Apr 12, 1971 in Memphis, Tennessee
Source: *BioIn 15; ConTFT 13; IntMPA 94, 96; LegTOT; News 94, 94-2; WhoAm 95, 96, 97; WhoAmW 95; WhoHol 92*

Dohnanyi, Christoph von
German. Conductor
Led Hamburg State Opera, 1977-84; became music director of Cleveland Orchestra, 1984.
b. Sep 8, 1929 in Berlin, Germany
Source: *Baker 78, 84, 92; BioIn 9, 14, 15, 16; BriBkM 80; CelR 90; CurBio 85; IntWW 91; IntWWM 90; MetOEnc; NewAmDM; NewGrDA 86; NewGrDM 80; NewGrDO; NewYTBS 88; OxDcOp; PenDiMP; WhoAm 88, 96, 97; WhoAmM 83; WhoMW 88, 96; WhoWor 89, 96, 97*

Dohnanyi, Erno von
[Ernst von Dohnanyi]
Hungarian. Composer, Musician, Conductor
Keyboard virtuoso; wrote piano works; grandfather of Christoph.
b. Jul 27, 1877 in Pressburg, Austria-Hungary
d. Feb 9, 1960 in New York, New York
Source: *Baker 78, 84, 92; BioIn 3, 4, 5, 6, 8, 11, 12; BriBkM 80; CompSN; ConAmC 76, 82; DcArts; DcCom 77; DcCom&M 79; FacFETw; MusMk; MusSN; NewGrDM 80; ObitT 1951; OxCMus; WhAm 5*

Dohrn, Bernadine Rae
[The Weathermen]
American. Political Activist
Led militant Weathermen group, 1960s-70s; fled prosecution for breaking antiriot laws; indictments eventually dropped, 1970s.
b. Jan 12, 1942 in Chicago, Illinois
Source: *BiDAmLf; BioIn 13, 14; GoodHs; InWom SUP; MugS; WorAl; WorAlBi*

Doi, Takako
Japanese. Politician
Chm., Japan Socialist Party (JSP), 1986—; first woman to lead a political party in Japan; member of Japan's House of Representatives, 1969—.
b. Nov 30, 1928 in Kobe, Japan
Source: *BioIn 15, 16, 17, 18; ConNews 87-4; ContDcW 89; CurBio 92; IntWW 91; WhoAsAP 91; WhoWomW 91; WhoWor 89, 91, 95, 96, 97; WomFir; WomLaw*

Doisy, Edward Adelbert, Sr.
American. Biochemist
Shared Nobel Prize in medicine, 1943, with Henrick Dam for isolating Vitamin K.
b. Nov 13, 1893 in Hume, Illinois
d. Oct 24, 1986 in Saint Louis, Missouri
Source: *AmMWSc 73S, 76P, 79, 82, 86; AsBiEn; BiESc; BioIn 1, 2, 3, 6, 15, 20; CamDcSc; CurBio 49, 87; InSci; IntWW 74, 75, 76, 77, 78, 79, 80, 81, 82, 83; LarDcSc; McGMS 80; NewYTBS 86; WebAB 74, 79; WhAm 9; Who 74; WhoAm 74, 78, 80, 82, 84, 86; WhoMW 78, 80, 82, 84, 86; WhoNob, 90, 95; WhoWor 74, 82, 84, 87*

Doktor, Paul Karl
American. Musician
Violinist-violist who founded many string ensembles.
b. Mar 28, 1919 in Vienna, Austria
Source: *Baker 84, 92; BioIn 16; IntWWM 77, 80, 90; NewAmDM; NewGrDA 86; NewGrDM 80; NewYTBS 89; PenDiMP; WhAm 10; WhoAm 86, 88; WhoAmM 83; WhoMus 72*

Dolan, Terry
[John Terrance Dolan]
American. Political Activist
"New Right" organizer known for combative approach in political action committees.
b. Dec 20, 1950 in Norwalk, Connecticut
d. Dec 28, 1986 in Washington, District of Columbia
Source: *ConNews 85-2, 87-2*

Dolbier, Maurice (Wyman)
American. Author, Journalist
Editor, *Providence Journal,* from 1967; books include *The Magic Shop,* 1946.
b. May 5, 1912 in Skowhegan, Maine
d. Oct 20, 1993 in Providence, Rhode Island
Source: *AmAu&B; AuBYP 2, 3; BioIn 4, 6, 7, 8, 19, 20; ConAu 65, 143; CurBio*

56, 94N; MorJA; ScF&FL 1; WhoAm 74, 76, 78

Dolby, Ray M(ilton)
American. Inventor
Created Dolby sound, noise reduction system that revolutionized recording industry, c. 1965; National Medal of Technology, 1997.
b. Jan 18, 1933 in Portland, Oregon
Source: *AmMWSc 95; BioIn 13, 15, 16, 18; ConNews 86-1; IlEncRk; LElec; NewYTBS 87; Who 82, 83, 85, 88, 90, 92, 94; WhoAm 78, 80, 82, 84, 86, 88, 90, 92, 94, 95, 96; WhoFI 85; WhoScEn 94, 96*

Dolby, Thomas
[Thomas Morgan Dolby Robertson]
British. Singer, Musician
Keyboardist, who had hit single "She Blinded Me with Science," 1983.
b. Oct 14, 1958 in Cairo, Egypt
Source: *BioIn 13, 14, 16; ConMus 10; EncRk 88; EncRkSt; LegTOT; PenEncP; RkOn 85; WhoRocM 82*

Dolci, Carlo
Italian. Artist
Painted portraits, pious religious subjects.
b. May 25, 1616 in Florence, Italy
d. Jan 17, 1686 in Florence, Italy
Source: *BioIn 10, 19; ClaDrA; DcArts; DcBiPP; DcCathB; McGDA; NewCol 75; OxCArt; OxDcArt; WebBD 83*

Dolci, Danilo
Italian. Architect, Social Reformer
Built Borgo di Dio, a refuge for homeless, in Trappeto, Italy, 1953.
b. Jun 28, 1924 in Sesana, Italy
Source: *Au&Wr 71; BioIn 4, 5, 6, 7, 9, 10, 14; ConAu 116, 127; CurBio 61; IntAu&W 76, 77, 89; IntWW 74, 75, 76, 77, 78, 79, 80, 81, 82, 83, 89, 91, 93; NewYTBE 72; RadHan; TwCWr; Who 74, 82, 83, 85, 88, 90, 92, 94; WhoWor 74, 76, 78; WorAu 1950*

Dole, Charles Minot
"Minnie"
American. Business Executive
Established National Sky Patrol System.
b. Apr 18, 1899 in Tyngsboro, Massachusetts
d. Mar 14, 1976 in Greenwich, Connecticut
Source: *BioIn 13; NatCAB 61; NewYTBS 76*

Dole, Elizabeth Hanford
[Mrs. Robert Dole]
"Liddy"
American. Government Official, Business Executive
First female secretary of transportation, 1983-87; secretary of labor, 1989-90; pres., American Red Cross, 1991—.
b. Jul 29, 1936 in Salisbury, North Carolina
Source: *AmPolLe; AmWomM; BiDrUSE 89; BioIn 13, 14, 15, 16, 17, 18, 19, 20, 21; CelR 90; CngDr 87, 89; CurBio 83; EncWB; IntWW 89, 91, 93; InWom SUP; News 90; NewYTBS 80, 83; WhoAm 78, 80, 82, 84, 86, 88, 90, 92, 94, 95, 96, 97; WhoAmP 85, 87, 89, 91, 93, 95; WhoAmW 83, 85, 87, 89, 91, 93, 95, 97; WhoE 83, 85, 86, 89, 91, 93, 95, 97; WhoFI 92; WhoGov 77; WhoWomW 91; WhoWor 87, 91, 93, 95, 96, 97*

Dole, James
American. Businessman
First to can Hawaiian pineapples before shipment to mainland, early 1900s.
b. Sep 27, 1877 in Boston, Massachusetts
d. May 14, 1958 in Maui, Hawaii
Source: *DcAmB S6; Entr; ObitOF 79; WhAm 3*

Dole, Robert Joseph
American. Politician
Rep. senator from KS, 1969-96; senate majority leader, 1981-87, 1995-96.
b. Jul 22, 1923 in Russell, Kansas
Source: *AlmAP 92; AmPolLe; BiDrAC; BiDrUSC 89; BioIn 8, 9, 10, 11, 12, 13, 14, 15, 16; CelR, 90; CngDr 87, 89; CurBio 72, 87; EncAB-H 1996; EncWB; IntWW 91; NewYTBE 71; NewYTBS 76, 82, 84, 85, 87, 90, 91; PolProf NF; PolsAm 84; PresAR; Who 88, 90, 92, 94; WhoAm 86, 90; WhoAmP 87, 91; WhoGov 72, 75, 77; WhoMW 92; WhoWor 91; WorAlBi*

Dole, Sanford Ballard
Hawaiian. Statesman, Lawyer
First governor of Hawaiian territory, 1900-03.
b. Apr 23, 1844 in Honolulu, Hawaii
d. Jun 9, 1926 in Honolulu, Hawaii
Source: *AmBi; ApCAB SUP, X; BiDrATG; BioIn 4, 16; DcAmB; EncAB-H 1974, 1996; HarEnUS; McGEWB; NatCAB 12; NewCol 75; OxCAmH; TwCBDA; WebAB 74, 79; WebBD 83; WhAm 1; WhAmP*

Dolenz, Mickey
[The Monkees; George Michael Dolenz]
American. Singer
Vocalist, drummer with The Monkees on popular TV series, 1966-68; part of group's late-1980s revival.
b. Mar 8, 1945 in Los Angeles, California
Source: *BioIn 14, 15, 16; ConNews 86-4; LegTOT; WhoAm 92, 94, 95, 96, 97; WhoEnt 92; WhoRocM 82*

Dolin, Anton, Sir
[Sydney Francis Patrick Chippendall Healey-Kay]
English. Dancer, Choreographer
Leading authority on classical ballet who was co-founder, principal dancer, London's Festival Ballet, 1950-61.
b. Jul 27, 1904 in Slinfold, England
d. Nov 25, 1983 in Paris, France
Source: *AnObit 1983; BiDD; BioIn 1, 3, 4, 5, 11, 12, 13, 14, 15; BlueB 76; CanWW 70; CnOxB; CurBio 84N; DancEn 78; DcArts; DcNaB 1981; FacFETw; IntDcB; IntWW 74, 75, 76, 77, 78, 79, 80, 81, 82, 83; NewYTBS 83; WhAm 8; Who 74, 82, 83; WhoAm 74, 76, 78, 80, 82; WhoThe 77A; WhoWor 74; WhThe*

Dollar, Robert
American. Shipping Executive
Founded steamship companies; began first round-the-world passenger service, 1924.
b. Mar 20, 1844 in Falkirk, Scotland
d. May 16, 1932 in San Rafael, California
Source: *BioIn 3, 4; CmCal; DcAmB S1; DcNAA; MacDCB 78; NatCAB 37; WhAm 1*

Dollard, John
American. Psychologist, Author
Race, status authority; wrote classic *Caste and Class in a Southern Town,* 1937.
b. Aug 29, 1900 in Menasha, Wisconsin
d. Oct 8, 1980 in New Haven, Connecticut
Source: *AmAu&B; AmMWSc 73S, 78S; AnObit 1980; BioIn 12; ConAu 102; IntEnSS 79; RAdv 13-3; WhAm 7*

Dollfuss, Engelbert
Austrian. Political Leader
Chancellor, 1932-34; killed by Austrian Nazis.
b. Oct 4, 1892 in Texing, Austria-Hungary
d. Jul 25, 1934 in Vienna, Austria
Source: *BioIn 2, 6, 7, 9; DcCathB; DcPol; DcTwHis; DicTyr; EncTR, 91; FacFETw; LuthC 75; McGEWB; OxCGer 76, 86; REn; WebBD 83; WhDW; WorAl; WorAlBi*

Dolly, Jenny
[Dolly Sisters]
Hungarian. Dancer, Choreographer
Vaudeville twin; starred in Broadway musicals, 1910-20s.
b. Oct 25, 1892 in Budapest, Austria-Hungary
d. Jun 1, 1941 in Hollywood, California
Source: *CmpEPM; CurBio 41; EncVaud; InWom; LegTOT; NotNAT B; WhoHol B; WhScrn 74, 77, 83; WorAl*

Dolly, Rosie
[Dolly Sisters]
Hungarian. Dancer, Choreographer
Vaudeville twin; portrayed by Betty Grable, June Haver in *The Dolly Sisters,* 1945.
b. Oct 25, 1892 in Budapest, Austria-Hungary
d. Feb 1, 1970 in New York, New York
Source: *CmpEPM; EncVaud; LegTOT; ObitT 1961; OxCAmT 84; OxCPMus; WhoHol B; WhScrn 74, 77, 83; WhThe; WorAl*

Dolmetsch, Arnold
[Eugene Arnold Dolmetsch]
English. Antiquarian, Musician
Founded Dolmetsch Foundation, 1928, to cultivate early music, antique instruments.
b. Feb 24, 1858 in Le Mans, France
d. Feb 28, 1940 in Haslemere, England
Source: *Baker 78, 84; BioIn 2, 3, 4, 10, 12, 14; BriBkM 80; DcArts; DcNaB 1931; GrBr; MusMk; NewAmDM; NewGrDA 86; NewGrDM 80; NewOxM; OxCMus; PenDiMP; WebBD 83; WhDW*

Dolomieu, Deodat Guy Gratet de
French. Geologist, Mineralogist
Researched volcanic geology; described "dolomite" mineral named after him, 1791.
b. Jun 24, 1750, France
d. Nov 26, 1801 in Chateauneuf, France
Source: *DcScB; LarDcSc; NewCol 75; WebBD 83*

Domagk, Gerhard
German. Chemist, Physician, Educator
Pathologist; Nobelist in medicine, 1939, for antibacterial effects of sulfonamide.
b. Oct 30, 1895 in Lagow, Germany
d. Apr 24, 1964 in Beirberg, Germany (West)
Source: *BiESc; BioIn 3, 4, 5, 6, 7, 12, 14, 15, 20; CamDcSc; CurBio 58, 64; FacFETw; InSci; McGMS 80; NobelP; NotTwCS; ObitOF 79; ObitT 1961; OxCMed 86; WhDW; WhoNob, 90, 95; WorScD*

Domenichino, Il
[Domenico Zampieri]
Italian. Artist
Major figure in the Baroque eclectic school; chief architect for Vatican, 1621-2 3; Naples, 1630-38.
b. Oct 21, 1581 in Bologna, Italy
d. Apr 6, 1641 in Naples, Italy
Source: *AtlBL; Benet 87; BioIn 1, 4, 6, 13, 19, 20; ClaDrA; DcArts; DcBiPP; DcCathB; IntDcAA 90; LegTOT; LinLib S; McGDA; OxCArt; OxDcArt; REn; WebBD 83; WhDW; WorAl; WorAlBi*

Domenici, Pete V(ichi)
American. Politician
Rep. senator from NM, 1973—; head of Senate Budget Committee, 1981.
b. May 7, 1932 in Albuquerque, New Mexico
Source: *AlmAP 88, 92; BiDrUSC 89; BioIn 12, 13, 14; CngDr 87, 89; CurBio 82; IntWW 91; NewYTBS 81; PolsAm 84; WhoAm 86, 90; WhoAmP 87, 91; WhoGov 77; WhoWest 87, 92; WhoWor 91*

Domenico, Veneziano
[Domenico di Bartolomeo da Venezia]
Italian. Artist
A founder of Florentine school of painting; known for *St. Lucy Altarpiece*, Florence.
b. 1438 in Venice, Italy
d. 1461
Source: *McGDA; McGEWB; NewCol 75; OxCArt*

Domingo, Placido
Spanish. Opera Singer
Versatile operatic tenor who moves easily into the folk and popular milieu for TV performances; recorded, "Perhaps Love," with John Denver, 1981.
b. Jan 21, 1941 in Madrid, Spain
Source: *Baker 78, 84, 92; BiDAmM; BioIn 8, 9, 10, 11, 12, 13, 14, 15, 16; CelR, 90; CmOp; ConMus 1; ConTFT 14; CurBio 72; DcHiB; DcTwCCu 4; EncWB; FacFETw; HalFC 88; IntDcOp; IntWW 77, 78, 79, 80, 81, 82, 83, 89, 91, 93; IntWWM 80, 90; LegTOT; MetOEnc; MusSN; NewAmDM; NewEOp 71; NewGrDA 86; NewGrDM 80; NewGrDO; News 93-2; NewYTBE 72; NewYTBS 74, 77, 83; OxDcOp; PenDiMP; RAdv 14; Who 82, 83, 85, 88, 90, 92, 94; WhoAm 78, 80, 82, 84, 86, 88, 90, 92, 94, 95, 96, 97; WhoAmM 83; WhoEnt 92; WhoHol 92; WhoOp 76; WhoWor 89, 91, 93, 95, 96, 97; WorAl; WorAlBi*

Dominguin, Luis Miguel
[Luis Miguel Gonzalez Lucas]
Spanish. Bullfighter
Considered among the greatest matadors of 20th c.
b. Dec 9, 1926 in Madrid, Spain
d. May 8, 1996 in Soto Grande, Spain
Source: *CurBio 72, 96N*

Dominic, Saint
[Domingo DeGuzman]
Spanish. Religious Figure
Founded Dominican religious order, 1216.
b. 1170
d. 1221
Source: *Benet 87, 96; BioIn 1, 2, 3, 4, 5, 6, 7, 8, 11, 12, 16; DcBiPP; DcCathB; LegTOT; LinLib S; McGEWB; NewCol 75; REn; WebBD 83; WhDW*

Dominick, Peter Hoyt
American. Government Official, Politician
Conservative Rep. senator from CO, 1963-75.
b. Jul 7, 1915 in Stamford, Connecticut
d. Mar 18, 1981 in Hobe Sound, Florida
Source: *BiDrAC; BiDrUSC 89; BioIn 9, 10, 11, 12; BlueB 76; IntWW 74, 75, 76, 77, 78, 79, 80; NewYTBS 81; PolProf J, K; WhAm 7; WhoAm 74, 76, 78; WhoAmP 73, 75, 77, 79; WhoGov 72, 75, 77; WhoWest 74*

Domino, Fats
[Antoine Domino]
American. Singer
Mixed blues with rock; best known for hit song "Blueberry Hill," 1956; Rock and Roll Hall of Fame, 1986; Grammy Lifetime Achievement Award, 1987.
b. Feb 26, 1928 in New Orleans, Louisiana
Source: *AfrAmAl 6; AmPS; AmSong; Baker 84, 92; BiDAfM; BiDAmM; BiDJaz; BioIn 9, 10, 12, 13, 14, 15, 20; BluesWW; ConMus 2; DcTwCCu 5; DrBlPA, 90; EncPR&S 89; EncRk 88; EncRkSt; FacFETw; HarEnR 86; IlEncBM 82; IlEncRk; InB&W 85; LegTOT; MusMk; NewAmDM; NewGrDA 86; OxCPMus; PenEncP; PopAmC SUP; RkOn 74; SoulM; WhoAfA 96; WhoAm 74, 76, 78, 80, 86, 88, 92, 94, 95, 96, 97; WhoBlA 80, 85, 88, 90, 92, 94; WhoEnt 92; WhoRock 81; WorAl; WorAlBi*

Donahue, Elinor
American. Actor
Played Betty Anderson in TV series "Father Knows Best," 1954-62.
b. Apr 19, 1937 in Tacoma, Washington
Source: *BioIn 3, 15, 16; ConTFT 7; IntMPA 92, 94, 96; InWom; WhoAm 78, 80, 82, 84, 88, 90, 92, 94, 95, 96, 97; WhoAmW 95, 97; WhoHol 92, A*

Donahue, Phil
[Philip John Donahue]
American. TV Personality
Host of talk show "Donahue," 1967-96; won Emmys, 1977, 1979; wrote *Donahue: My Own Story*, 1980.
b. Dec 5, 1935 in Cleveland, Ohio
Source: *BioIn 12, 13, 14, 15; BkPepl; CelR 90; ConAu 107; ConTFT 6; CurBio 80; IntMPA 82, 84, 86, 88, 92, 94, 96; IntWW 93; LegTOT; LesBEnT 92; NewYTBS 80; NewYTET; WhoAm 80, 82, 84, 86, 88, 90, 92, 94, 95, 96, 97; WhoE 95; WhoEnt 92*

Donahue, Sam Koontz
American. Musician
Led Big Band, 1940s; directed Dorsey band after Dorsey's death, 1960s.
b. Mar 8, 1918 in Detroit, Michigan
Source: *BgBands 74; BiDAmM; CmpEPM; EncJzS; NewGrDJ 88*

Donahue, Troy
[Merle Johnson, Jr.]
American. Actor
Starred in TV series "Hawaiian Eye," 1962-63; "Surfside Six," 1960-62.
b. Jan 27, 1936 in New York, New York
Source: *ConTFT 8; FilmEn; FilmgC; HalFC 80, 84, 88; IntMPA 82, 92; LegTOT; MotPP; MovMk; VarWW 85; WhoHol A; WorAl; WorAlBi*

Donahue, Woolworth
American. Retailer
Heir to F W Woolworth chain store fortune; cousin of Barbara Hutton.
b. Jan 9, 1913 in New York, New York
d. Apr 5, 1972 in Palm Beach, Florida
Source: *BioIn 9; NewYTBE 72*

Donald, James
Scottish. Actor
Best known for films *Bridge on the River Kwai,* 1957; *The Great Escape,* 1963.
b. May 18, 1917 in Aberdeen, Scotland
d. Aug 3, 1993 in Wiltshire, England
Source: *BioIn 19; FilmEn; FilmgC; ForYSC; HalFC 80, 84, 88; IlWWBF; IntMPA 75, 76, 77, 78, 79, 80, 81, 82, 84, 86; WhoHol 92, A; WhoThe 72, 77A; WhThe*

Donald, Peter
American. Actor
Radio, TV host of "Can You Top This," 1950-51.
b. 1918? in Bristol, England
d. Apr 20, 1979
Source: *BioIn 3, 12; NewYTBS 79; RadStar; SaTiSS*

Donaldson, Sam(uel Andrew)
American. Broadcast Journalist
ABC News White House correspondent, known as one of TV's most aggressive interviewers; co-host, "This Week," 1996—.
b. Mar 11, 1934 in El Paso, Texas
Source: *BioIn 11, 12, 13, 14, 15, 16; CelR 90; ConAu 109, 111; ConTFT 12; CurBio 87; EncTwCJ; IntWW 89, 91, 93; JrnUS; LegTOT; LesBEnT 92; WhoAm 76, 78, 80, 82, 84, 86, 88, 90, 92, 94, 95, 96, 97; WhoE 91, 95, 97; WhoTelC; WorAlBi*

Donaldson, Stephen Reeder
American. Author
Won Fantasy Society Award for leper trilogy *Chronicles of Thomas Covenant,* 1978.
b. May 13, 1947 in Cleveland, Ohio
Source: *BioIn 13; ConAu 89; ConLC 46; DcLP 87A; DrAPF 91; IntAu&W 89, 91, 93; IntvTCA 2; SupFW; WhoAm 82, 84, 86, 88, 90, 92, 94, 95, 96, 97; WhoUSWr 88; WhoWrEP 89, 92, 95; WrDr 92*

Donaldson, Walter
American. Songwriter
Hits songs include "My Buddy," 1922; "My Blue Heaven," 1927.
b. Feb 15, 1893 in New York, New York
d. Jul 15, 1947 in Santa Monica, California
Source: *AmPS; AmSong; ASCAP 66, 80; Baker 84; BiDAmM; BioIn 1, 3, 4, 6, 14, 15, 16; CmpEPM; EncMT; NewAmDM; NewGrDA 86; NewGrDM 80; NotNAT B; OxCPMus; PopAmC; Sw&Ld C; WorAl; WorAlBi*

Donat, Robert
English. Actor
Won Oscar for *Goodbye, Mr. Chips,* 1939.
b. Mar 18, 1905 in Manchester, England
d. Jun 9, 1958 in London, England
Source: *BiDFilm, 81, 94; BioIn 4, 5, 7, 8, 9, 13, 14; DcArts; DcNaB 1951; EncEurC; EncWT; FilmAG WE; FilmEn; FilmgC; ForYSC; HalFC 80, 84, 88; IlWWBF, A; IntDcF 1-3, 2-3; LegTOT; MotPP; MovMk; NotNAT B; ObitT 1951; OxCFilm; OxCThe 67; PlP&P; WhAm 3; WhoHol B; WhScrn 74, 77, 83; WhThe; WorAl; WorAlBi; WorEFlm*

Donatello
[Donatodi Niccolo di Betto Bardi]
Italian. Artist
Considered finest sculptor of his century; masterpeices include *David; John the Evangelist;* mentor of Michelangelo.
b. 1386 in Florence, Italy
d. Dec 13, 1466 in Florence, Italy
Source: *AtlBL; Benet 87, 96; BioIn 1, 2, 4, 5, 6, 7, 9, 10, 11, 12, 13, 14, 15, 21; DcArts; DcCathB; LegTOT; LinLib S; LuthC 75; McGDA; McGEWB; NewCol 75; OxCArt; OxDcArt; REn; WebBD 83; WorAl; WorAlBi*

Donath, Helen
American. Opera Singer
Soprano; a favorite at Salzburg's annual Easter festival.
b. 1940 in Corpus Christi, Texas
Source: *Baker 84, 92; BioIn 9; IntWW 74, 75, 76, 77, 78, 79, 80, 81, 82, 83, 89, 91, 93; IntWWM 77, 80, 90; MetOEnc; NewAmDM; NewGrDA 86; NewGrDM 80; NewGrDO; OxDcOp; PenDiMP; WhoAmM 83; WhoMus 72; WhoOp 76; WhoWor 78*

Donati, Danilo
Italian. Designer
Costume designs include Oscar winners: *Romeo and Juliet,* 1968; *Fellini's Casanova,* 1976.
Source: *ConDes 90; VarWW 85; WhoAmW 70A*

Donegan, Lonnie
Scottish. Singer, Musician
Hits include "Lorelei," 1960; "The Party's Over," 1962.
b. Apr 29, 1931 in Glasgow, Scotland
Source: *EncRk 88; EncRkSt; HarEnR 86; LegTOT; NewGrDJ 88, 94; OnThGG; OxCPMus; PenEncP; RkOn 74, 82; RolSEnR 83; WhoRock 81; WhoRocM 82*

Donen, Stanley
American. Director
Best known for *Arabesque,* 1966.
b. Apr 13, 1924 in Columbia, South Carolina
Source: *BiDD; BiDFilm, 81, 94; BioIn 12, 14, 16; CmMov; DcArts; DcFM; EncAFC; FilmEn; FilmgC; HalFC 80, 84, 88; IlWWHD 1; IntDcF 1-2, 2-2; IntMPA 77, 80, 81, 82, 92, 94, 96; IntWW 74, 75, 76, 77, 78, 79, 80, 81, 82, 83, 89, 91, 93; LegTOT; MiSFD 9; MovMk; OxCFilm; WhoAm 80, 82, 97; WhoEnt 92; WhoWor 74; WorEFlm; WorFDir 2*

Dongen, Kees van
[Cornelius Theodorus Dongen]
French. Artist, Illustrator
Fauvist painter who did landscapes of Holland, Paris; noted for riotous use of color.
b. Jan 26, 1877 in Delfshaven, Netherlands
d. May 28, 1968 in Monte Carlo, Monaco
Source: *BioIn 2, 4, 5, 6, 8, 9, 14, 17; ClaDrA; CurBio 60, 68; DcTwCCu 2; McGDA; OxCArt; OxCTwCA; OxDcArt; PhDcTCA 77*

Donghia, Angelo R
American. Designer
Interior designer noted for bold, contemporary approach to home, commercial furnishings.
b. Mar 7, 1935 in Vandergrift, Pennsylvania
d. Apr 10, 1985 in New York, New York
Source: *ConNews 85-2; NewYTBS 83, 85*

Donizetti, Gaetano
Italian. Composer
A master of musical theater, forerunner of Verdi; wrote *Lucia di Lammermoor,* 1835; *Don Pasquale,* 1843.
b. Nov 29, 1797 in Bergamo, Italy
d. Apr 8, 1848 in Bergamo, Italy
Source: *AtlBL; Baker 78, 84; Benet 87, 96; BioIn 2, 3, 4, 5, 6, 7, 9, 11, 12, 13, 19, 20; BriBkM 80; CmOp; CmpBCM; CnOxB; DcArts; DcCom 77; DcCom&M 79; Dis&D; GrComp; IntDcOp; LegTOT; LinLib S; McGEWB; MetOEnc; MusMk; NewAmDM; NewEOp 71; NewGrDM 80; NewOxM; OxCEng 85, 95; OxCMus; OxDcOp; PenDiMP A; REn; WhDW; WorAl; WorAlBi*

Donleavy, James Patrick
American. Author, Dramatist
Among novels adapted to plays is *The Ginger Man,* 1955.
b. Apr 23, 1926 in New York, New York
Source: *Benet 87; BiDConC; BiDIrW; BioIn 8, 9, 10, 11, 12, 13, 15, 17, 20; CamGLE; CamGWoT; ConAu 9R, 24NR; ConDr 82, 88; ConLC 10, 45; ConNov 86; CurBio 79; CyWA 89; DcLB 6; DcLEL 1940; DrAPF 89; EncAHmr; IntAu&W 77, 82, 86, 89, 91, 93; IntWW 74, 75, 76, 77, 78, 79, 80, 81, 82, 83, 89, 91, 93; MajTwCW; OxCAmL 83; OxCEng 85; Who 74, 82, 83, 85, 88, 90, 92, 94; WhoAm 74, 76, 78, 80, 82, 84, 86, 88, 90, 92, 94, 95, 96, 97; WhoThe 81; WhoWor 74, 76, 78, 80, 82, 84, 87; WorAlBi; WorAu 1950; WrDr 86, 92*

Donlevy, Brian
American. Actor
Best known for tough-guy roles in *Beau Geste,* 1939; *The Great McGinty,* 1940.
b. Feb 9, 1899 in Portadown, Ireland
d. Apr 5, 1972 in Woodland Hills, California

Source: *BiDFilm, 81, 94; BiE&WWA; BioIn 9, 11, 21; EncAFC; FilmEn; FilmgC; HalFC 80, 84, 88; HolP 30; LegTOT; MotPP; MovMk; NewYTBE 72; ObitOF 79; OlFamFa; OxCFilm; WhoHol B; WhoHrs 80; WhScrn 77, 83; WorAl*

Donlon, Mary Honor
American. Judge
First woman from NY to hold a life appointment when named a US Customs Court judge, 1955.
b. 1893? in Utica, New York
d. Mar 5, 1977 in Tucson, Arizona
Source: *BioIn 1, 2, 5, 11; CurBio 49, 77N; NewYTBS 77; WhoAmW 74; WhoGov 72*

Donne, John
English. Poet
Metaphysical poet wrote sonnet "Death Be Not Proud"; poems neglected until 20th c.
b. 1573 in London, England
d. Mar 31, 1631 in London, England
Source: *AtlBL; BioIn 1, 2, 3, 4, 5, 6, 7, 8, 9, 10, 11, 12, 13; BritAu; CasWL; Chambr 1; ChhPo S3; CrtT 1; CyWA 58; DcBiPP; DcEnL; Dis&D; EvLB; HisDStE; LuthC 75; MouLC 1; NewC; NewCol 75; OxCEng 85; PenC ENG; RAdv 1, 14, 13-1; RComWL; REn; WebBD 83*

Donnell, Jeff
[Jean Marie Donnell]
American. Actor
Best known for *Gidget Goes Hawaiian,* 1961; *Gidget Goes to Rome,* 1962.
b. Jul 10, 1921 in South Windham, Maine
d. Apr 11, 1988 in Hollywood, California
Source: *BioIn 15, 16, 18; ConTFT 1; EncAFC; FilmEn; FilmgC; ForYSC; HalFC 80, 84, 88; IntMPA 75, 76, 77, 78, 79, 80, 81, 82, 84, 86, 88; MotPP; SweetSg C; WhoAmW 61; WhoHol A*

Donnellan, Nanci
American. Sportscaster, Radio Performer
Star of ESPN Radio's syndicated show, "Fabulous Sports Babe."
Source: *BioIn 20, 21; News 95, 95-2; NewYTBS 27*

Donnelly, Ignatius
American. Politician, Author
The Great Cryptogram, 1888; *The Cipher in the Plays and on the Tombstone,* 1899, two studies on possibility of Bacon's authorship of Shakespeare's plays.
b. Nov 3, 1831 in Philadelphia, Pennsylvania
d. Jan 1, 1901 in Minneapolis, Minnesota
Source: *Alli, SUP; AmAu; AmAu&B; AmBi; AmPolLe; AmRef; AmSocL; ApCAB; BbD; BenetAL 91; BiAUS; BibAL; BiD&SB; BiDrAC; BiDrUSC 89; BioIn 1, 3, 4, 5, 6, 7, 8, 9, 12, 13, 15, 18, 19; CasWL; ConAu 110; DcAmAu; DcAmB; DcAmSR; DcEnA A; DcLB 12; DcLEL; DcNAA; EncAAH; EncAB-H 1974, 1996; EncO&P 1, 2, 3; EncSF, 93; GayN; GrWrEL N; HarEnUS; McGEWB; NatCAB 1; NewAgE 90; NewEScF; Novels; OxCAmH; OxCAmL 65, 83, 95; PenC AM; Polre; PolPar; REnAL; REnAW; RfGAmL 87, 94; ScF&FL 1; TwCBDA; WebAB 74, 79; WebE&AL; WhAm 1; WhAmP*

Donnelly, Ruth
American. Actor
Films include *Mr. Deeds Goes to Town; The Bells of St. Mary's.*
b. May 17, 1896 in Trenton, New Jersey
d. Nov 17, 1982 in New York, New York
Source: *ASCAP 80; BiE&WWA; BioIn 9, 13; EncAFC; Film 2; FilmEn; FilmgC; ForYSC; HalFC 80, 84, 88; HolCA; InWom SUP; MovMk; NewYTBS 82; NotNAT; ThFT; Vers A; What 3; WhoHol A*

Donner, Frederic Garrett
American. Businessman
Chm., chief exec., GM, 1958-67.
b. 1902 in Three Oaks, Michigan
d. Feb 28, 1987 in Greenwich, Connecticut
Source: *BioIn 5, 6, 8, 15; CurBio 59, 87; EncABHB 5; IntWW 74; NewYTBS 87; St&PR 75; Who 74, 82, 83, 85; WhoGov 75; WhoWor 74*

Donohue, Jack
American. Actor, Dancer, Director
Best known for *Marriage on the Rocks,* 1965; *Assault on a Queen,* 1966.
b. Nov 3, 1912 in New York, New York
d. Mar 27, 1984 in Los Angeles, California
Source: *BiDD; BiE&WWA; ConTFT 2; FilmgC; HalFC 80, 84; IntMPA 80, 81, 82; NotNAT; WhoThe 77; WhThe*

Donoso, Jose
Chilean. Author
Novelist, short story writer; his *El Obsceno Pajaro De La Noche,* 1971, made him famous.
b. Oct 5, 1924 in Santiago, Chile
d. Dec 7, 1996 in Santiago, Chile
Source: *Benet 87, 96; BenetAL 91; BioIn 10, 11, 12, 13, 14, 15, 16; ConAu 32NR, 81; ConFLW 84; ConLC 4, 8, 11, 32; CurBio 78; CyWA 89; DcCLAA; DcHiB; DcLB 113; DcTwCCu 3; EncWB; EncWL, 2, 3; FacFETw; HispLC; HispWr; IntAu&W 76, 77, 82, 89; IntvLAW; IntWW 74, 75, 76, 77, 78, 79, 80, 81, 82, 83, 89, 91, 93; LatAmWr; LiExTwC; MajTwCW; NewYTBS 27; OxCSpan; PenC AM; ScF&FL 92; SpAmA; WhoWor 74, 78, 80, 82, 84, 87, 89, 91, 93; WorAu 1970*

Donovan
[Donovan P Leitch]
Scottish. Singer, Songwriter
Hits include "Sunshine Superman," 1966; "Mellow Yellow," 1966.
b. May 10, 1943 in Glasgow, Scotland
Source: *Baker 92; BioIn 14, 15; ConMus 9; EncFCWM 69; EncPR&S 74; EncRk 88; HarEnR 86; LegTOT; OxCPMus; PenEncP; WorAlBi*

Donovan, Art(hur, Jr.)
American. Football Player
Five-time all-pro tackle, 1950-61, mostly with Baltimore; Hall of Fame.
b. Jun 5, 1925 in New York, New York
Source: *BiDAmSp FB; BioIn 4, 7, 8, 15; LegTOT; WhoAm 86; WhoFtbl 74*

Donovan, Arthur
American. Boxing Referee
Officiated at 14 heavyweight boxing title bouts, more than anyone else in history.
b. Aug 10, 1891 in New York, New York
d. Sep 1, 1980 in New York, New York
Source: *BioIn 12; NewYTBS 80; WhoBox 74*

Donovan, Hedley Williams
American. Journalist
Editor in chief of all Time Inc. publications, 1964-79; wrote *Roosevelt to Reagan: A Reporter's Encounters with Nine Presidents,* 1985.
b. May 24, 1914 in Brainerd, Minnesota
d. Aug 14, 1990 in New York, New York
Source: *BioIn 6, 7, 10, 12, 13, 14, 16; ConAu 110, 115, 132; CurBio 65, 90, 90N; EncTwCJ; IntAu&W 77, 82, 86, 89, 91; IntWW 74, 75, 76, 77, 78, 80, 81, 82, 83, 89, 91N; NewYTBS 90; WhAm 10; Who 74, 90; WhoAm 74, 76, 78, 80, 82, 84, 86, 88, 90; WhoE 74, 75; WhoFI 79, 81; WhoWor 74*

Donovan, King
American. Actor
Films include *The Enforcer,* 1951; on Broadway in *On the Twentieth Century,* 1986.
b. Jan 25, 1918 in New York, New York
d. Jun 30, 1987 in Branford, Connecticut
Source: *BioIn 15; HalFC 84; NewYTBS 87*

Donovan, Raymond James
American. Government Official
Secretary of labor under Ronald Reagan, 1981-85.
b. Aug 31, 1930 in Bayonne, New Jersey
Source: *BiDrUSE 89; BioIn 12, 13, 14, 15, 16; CurBio 82; Dun&B 90; IntWW 91; NatCAB 63N; NewYTBS 80; WhoAm 82, 84, 96; WhoAmP 91; WhoE 81, 83, 85; WhoFI 83, 85; WhoWor 82, 84*

Donovan, Robert John
American. Journalist
Worked for *NY Herald Tribune,* 1937-63; assoc. editor, *LA Times,* 1970-77.
b. Aug 21, 1912 in Buffalo, New York
Source: *AmAu&B; Au&Wr 71; BlueB 76; ConAu 1R, 2NR, 18NR; WhoAm 74, 76,*

78, 80, 82, 84, 86, 88, 90, 92, 94, 95, 96, 97; WhoSSW 95; WhoWor 74, 76

Donovan, William Joseph
"Wild Bill"
American. Public Official
Founded Office of Strategic Services (OSS), 1942, later evolved into CIA; Congressional Medal of Honor, WW II.
b. Jan 1, 1883 in Buffalo, New York
d. Feb 8, 1959 in Washington, District of Columbia
Source: *AmPolLe; BiDWWGF; BioIn 1, 3, 5, 7, 8, 12, 13; CurBio 41, 54, 59; DcAmB S6; DcAmMiB; EncAB-H 1996; EncAI&E; MedHR, 94; NatCAB 47; WebAB 74, 79; WebAMB; WhAm 3; WhWW-II; WorAl*

Doobie Brothers, The
[Jeff Baxter; "Little" John Hartman; Mike Hossack; Tom Johnston; Keith Knudson; Michael McDonald; Tiran Porter; Dave Shogren; Pat Simmons]
American. Music Group
Hit albums include *Minute by Minute,* 1978; *One Step Closer,* 1980.
Source: *BioIn 11; ConMuA 80A; ConMus 3; EncPR&S 74, 89; EncRk 88; EncRkSt; HarEnR 86; IlEncRk; NewAmDM; NewGrDA 86; NewYTBS 75; OnThGG; PenEncP; RkOn 78, 84, 85; RolSEnR 83; WhoRock 81; WhoRocM 82; WhoScEu 91-1*

Doohan, James Montgomery
Canadian. Actor
Played Scotty on "Star Trek," 1966-69; films *Star Trek: The Movie; Star Trek II; Star Trek III.*
b. Mar 3, 1920 in Vancouver, British Columbia, Canada
Source: *BioIn 15, 16; ConTFT 8; IntMPA 92; VarWW 85*

Dooley, Rae
[Rachel Rice Dooley]
Scottish. Actor
Starred with husband Eddie Dowling in Ziegfeld Follies, specialized in bratty kid parts.
b. Oct 30, 1896 in Glasgow, Scotland
d. Jan 28, 1984 in East Hampton, New York
Source: *BiDD; BioIn 9; EncMT; NotNAT; WhoHol A; WhThe*

Dooley, Thomas Anthony, III
American. Missionary, Physician
Established medical facilities in war-torn countries; writings include *Deliver Us from Evil,* 1956.
b. Jan 17, 1927 in Saint Louis, Missouri
d. Jan 18, 1961 in New York, New York
Source: *AmAu&B; BioIn 4, 5, 6, 7, 8, 9, 10, 11, 12; ConAu 93; CurBio 57, 61; DcAmB S7; DcAmMeB 84; DcCathB; InSci; LinLib L; LuthC 75; ObitOF 79; WebAB 74, 79; WebAMB; WebBD 83; WhAm 4A*

Doolittle, Hilda
[H.D; John Helforth]
American. Author, Poet
An early Imagist; wrote verse vol. *Sea Garden,* 1916; prose, *Tribute to Freud,* 1956.
b. Sep 19, 1886 in Bethlehem, Pennsylvania
d. Sep 27, 1961 in Zurich, Switzerland
Source: *AmAu&B; AmWomPl; AmWomWr; AmWr S1; ArtclWW 2; AtlBL; Benet 87, 96; BenetAL 91; BioAmW; BioIn 1, 4, 5, 6, 8, 11, 12, 13, 14, 15, 16, 17, 18, 19, 20; BlmGEL; CamGEL; CamGLE; CamHAL; CasWL; Chambr 3; ChhPo S2, S3; CnDAL; ConAmA; ConAmL; ConAu 35NR, 97; ConLC 3, 8, 14, 31, 34, 73; ContDcW 89; DcArts; DcLB 4, 45; DcLEL; EncWL, 2, 3; EvLB; FacFETw; GayLL; GrWrEL P; HanAmWH; IntDcWB; InWom, SUP; LibW; LiExTwC; LinLib L; LngCTC; MajTwCW; McGEWB; ModAL, S1, S2; ModAWWr; ModWoWr; NewCBEL; NotAW MOD; Novels; OxCAmL 65, 83, 95; OxCEng 85, 95; OxCTwCP; PenBWP; PenC AM; PenNWW A; RAdv 13-1; REn; REnAL; RfGAmL 87, 94; TwCA, SUP; TwCWr; WebAB 74, 79; WebE&AL; WhAm 4; WomFir; WorAl; WorAlBi*

Doolittle, James H(arold)
American. Aviator, Army Officer
Led first aerial raid on Japan, WW II.
b. Dec 14, 1896 in Alameda, California
d. Sep 27, 1993 in Pebble Beach, California
Source: *BiDWWGF; BioIn 1, 2, 3, 4, 5, 6, 7, 8, 9, 10, 11, 12, 15, 16, 17, 18, 19, 20; ConAu 143; CurBio 42, 57, 94N; DcAmMiB; Dun&B 88; EncWB; FacFETw; HarEnMi; HisEWW; IntWW 74, 91; IntYB 78, 79, 80, 81, 82; MedHR 94; OxCAmH; St&PR 75; WebAB 74, 79; WebAMB; WhAm 11; Who 74, 92; WhoAm 74, 76, 78, 80, 82, 84, 86, 88, 90; WhoMilH 76; WhoWest 78; WhWW-II; WorAl; WorAlBi*

Door, Rheta Childe
American. Journalist, Feminist
Covered Russian Revolution, WW I troops in France; wrote *Inside the Russian Revolution,* 1917.
b. Nov 2, 1866 in Omaha, Nebraska
d. Aug 8, 1948 in New Britain, Pennsylvania
Source: *ConAu 116; DcLB 25; WhAm 2*

Doors, The
[John Densmore; Bobby Krieger; Ray Manzarek; Jim Morrison]
American. Music Group
Had number-one song, "Light My Fire," 1967; late 1960s band, controversial for lyrics, lifestyles.
Source: *BiDAmM; BioIn 17; ConAu 40NR, 73, X; ConMuA 80A; ConMus 4; DcArts; EncPR&S 74, 89; EncRk 88; EncRkSt; FacFETw; HarEnR 86; IlEncRk; NewAmDM; NewGrDA 86; NewYTBE 71; ObitOF 79; OxCPMus; PenEncP; RkOn 78, 84; RolSEnR 83; St&PR 93; WhoAmP 93, 95; WhoHol 92; WhoRock 81; WhoRocM 82*

Doppler, Christian Johann
Austrian. Physicist, Mathematician
Directed the Physical Institute, Vienna, 1850-53; known for creating principle called Doppler effect.
b. Nov 30, 1803 in Salzburg, Austria
d. Mar 17, 1853 in Venice, Italy
Source: *AsBiEn; BiESc; CamDcSc; DcInv; DcScB; InSci; LarDcSc; WebBD 83; WhDW; WorAl; WorAlBi; WorScD*

Dorati, Antal
American. Conductor, Composer
Led London's Royal Philharmonic, 1974-81; Detroit Symphony, 1977-81; Stockholm Symphony, 1981-88.
b. Apr 9, 1906 in Budapest, Austria-Hungary
d. Nov 13, 1988 in Gerzensee, Switzerland
Source: *AnObit 1988; Baker 78, 84, 92; BiDAmM; BioIn 1, 2, 4, 6, 9, 11, 12; BlueB 76; BriBkM 80; CnOxB; ConAmC 76, 82; ConAu 127; CpmDNM 82; CurBio 48, 89N; DancEn 78; DcArts; FacFETw; IntWW 74, 75, 76, 77, 78, 79, 80, 81, 82, 83; IntWWM 77, 80, 85; MusMk; MusSN; NewAmDM; NewGrDA 86; NewGrDM 80; NewGrDO; News 89-2; OxDcOp; PenDiMP; WhAm 9; Who 74, 82, 83, 85, 88; WhoAm 74, 76, 78, 80, 82, 84, 86, 88; WhoAmM 83; WhoMus 72; WhoMW 80; WhoOp 76; WhoSSW 73, 75, 76; WhoWor 74, 84, 87, 89; WorAl; WorAlBi*

Dore, Gustave
[Paul Gustave Dore]
French. Artist
Illustrated over 120 books, including many classics, in theatrical style.
b. Jan 6, 1832 in Strasbourg, France
d. Jan 23, 1883 in Paris, France
Source: *AtlBL; Benet 87; BioIn 1, 3, 8, 9, 10, 11, 12, 13, 15, 21; CelCen; ChhPo, S1, S2, S3; ConGrA 1; DcArts; DcBiPP; IlsBYP; IntDcAA 90; LegTOT; OxCArt; OxCChiL; OxCEng 85; OxCFr; OxDcArt; REn; SmATA 19; WhDW; WorECar*

Dorfman, Ariel
Chilean. Author
Wrote novel *Widows,* 1981 (*Viudas*); play *Death and the Maiden,* 1992.
b. May 6, 1942 in Buenos Aires, Argentina
Source: *Benet 96; ConAu 124, 130; ConLC 48, 77; ConWorW 93; DcHiB; DcTwCCu 3; EncWL 3; HispLC; HispWr; LiExTwC; ScF&FL 92; SpAmA; WhoAm 95, 96, 97; WhoWor 91, 95; WorAu 1985; WrDr 94, 96*

Dorfman, Dan
American. Journalist
Financial writer, *Wall Street Journal,* 1967-73; *New York* magazine, 1984-86; *Money* magazine; appears on the

CNBC television network; columnist, *Financial World,* 1997—.
b. Oct 24, 1932 in New York, New York
Source: *BioIn 14, 15, 16; ConAu 116*

Dorgan, Byron Leslie
American. Politician
Dem. senator, ND, 1992—.
b. May 14, 1942 in Dickinson, North Dakota
Source: *AlmAP 92; BiDrUSC 89; BioIn 13; CngDr 89; IntWW 93; PolsAm 84; WhoAm 82, 84, 86, 88, 90, 92, 94, 95, 96, 97; WhoAmP 73, 75, 77, 79, 81, 91; WhoE 95; WhoEmL 87; WhoGov 75, 77; WhoMW 74, 76, 78, 88, 90, 92, 93, 96*

Dorgan, Thomas Aloysius
"Tad"
American. Cartoonist, Journalist
Cartoons, sports columns in *San Francisco Bulletin,* 1892-1902; *NY Journal,* 1902-29; coined term "yes-man," 1913.
b. Apr 29, 1877 in San Francisco, California
d. May 2, 1929 in Great Neck, New York
Source: *AmAu&B; ArtsAmW 1; BioIn 4, 11; CmCal; DcAmB; WebBD 83; WhAm 4; WhAmArt 85; WhAm HSA; WhAmP; WorECom*

Doria, Andrea
"Father of Peace"; "Liberator of Genoa"
Italian. Naval Officer, Statesman
One of greatest Italian military leaders, conquerors of his day; drove French from Genoa, 1528; name given to luxury liner that sank, 1956.
b. Nov 30, 1466 in Oneglia, Italy
d. Nov 25, 1560 in Genoa, Italy
Source: *BioIn 1; GenMudB; HarEnMi; LegTOT; NewCol 75; OxCShps; REn; WebBD 83; WhoMilH 76*

Doriot, Georges Frederic
French. Educator, Business Executive
Founded American Research Development Corp., 1946.
b. Sep 24, 1899 in Paris, France
d. 1987 in Boston, Massachusetts
Source: *BiDWWGF; BioIn 6, 7, 15, 17, 21; BlueB 76; IntWW 74, 75, 76, 77, 78, 79, 80, 81, 82, 83; IntYB 78; NewYTBS 87; St&PR 75; WhoAm 74; WhoFI 74; WorAl*

Dorleac, Francoise
French. Actor
Sister of Catherine Deneuve; starred together in *The Young Girls of Rochefort,* 1967.
b. Mar 21, 1942 in Paris, France
d. Jun 26, 1967 in Nice, France
Source: *BioIn 7, 8, 17; FilmAG WE; FilmEn; FilmgC; ForYSC; ItaFilm; MotPP; ObitOF 79; OxCFilm; WhoHol B; WhScrn 74, 77*

Dorman, Maurice Henry, Sir
English. Political Leader
Held various offices, including governor general of Malta, 1964-71.
b. Aug 7, 1912 in Staffordshire, England
Source: *BlueB 76; IntWW 74, 75, 76, 77, 78, 79, 80, 81, 82, 83, 89, 91, 93; Who 74, 82, 83, 85, 88, 90, 92, 94; WhoGov 72, 75; WhoWor 74, 76, 78*

Dornberger, Walter Robert
German. Engineer
Missile expert who supervised V-2 bombing of London, 1944-45; adviser to US during space race.
b. Sep 6, 1895 in Giessen, Germany
d. Jun 27, 1980 in Hamburg, Germany (West)
Source: *BioIn 6, 7, 12; CurBio 65, 80; InSci; NewYTBS 80*

Dorne, Albert
American. Illustrator
Freelance artist; exhibited in NYC shows, 1934-65; won first NY art directors gold medal award for distinguished career, 1953.
b. Feb 7, 1904 in New York, New York
d. Dec 15, 1965 in New York, New York
Source: *BioIn 1, 2, 4, 5, 6, 7; IlrAm 1880, E; ObitOF 79; WhAm 4; WhAmArt 85*

Dornier, Claude
[Claudius Dornier]
German. Aircraft Manufacturer
Built the DO-X, largest passenger plane at time, 1929.
b. May 14, 1884 in Kempten, Bavaria
d. Dec 5, 1969 in Zug, Switzerland
Source: *BioIn 8, 12; EncTR 91; InSci; ObitOF 79; WebBD 83*

Dorris, Michael (Anthony)
American. Writer
Author of *The Broken Cord,* 1989, an account of a son who suffered fetal alcohol syndrome.
b. Jan 30, 1945 in Louisville, Kentucky
d. Apr 11, 1997 in Concord, New Hampshire
Source: *BestSel 90-1; ChlBkCr; ConAu 19NR, 46NR, 102; CurBio 95; DcNAL; NatNAL; NotNaAm; RfGAmL 94; SmATA 75; TwCWW 91; TwCYAW; WhoAm 76, 78, 80, 82, 84, 86, 88, 90, 92, 94, 95, 96, 97; WhoE 93, 95, 97; WorAu 1985; WrDr 92, 94, 96*

Dors, Diana
[Diana Fluck]
English. Actor
British sex symbol, compared to Marilyn Monroe.
b. Oct 23, 1931 in Swindon, England
d. May 4, 1984 in New Windsor, England
Source: *AnObit 1984; BioIn 11, 12, 13; ConAu 113; ContDcW 89; DcNaB 1981; EncEurC; FacFETw; FilmAG WE; FilmEn; FilmgC; ForYSC; HalFC 80, 84, 88; IlWWBF, A; IntDcF 2-3; IntMPA 75, 76, 77, 78, 79, 80, 81, 82, 84; ItaFilm; LegTOT; MotPP; MovMk; NewYTBS 84; WhoHol A; WhoHrs 80; WorAl*

D'Orsay, Alfred Guillaume, Count
French. Socialite
Famed Paris, London dandy, wit; arbiter of fashion.
b. Sep 4, 1801 in Paris, France
d. Aug 4, 1852 in Paris, France
Source: *DcBiPP; DcNaB; NewCol 75; OxCEng 67*

D'Orsay, Fifi
[Yvonne Lussier]
"The French Bombshell"
Canadian. Actor
Starred in *They Had to See Paris,* 1929; trademark was "Ello beeg boy!"
b. Apr 16, 1904 in Montreal, Quebec, Canada
d. Dec 2, 1983 in Woodland Hills, California
Source: *BioIn 9, 13; EncAFC; FilmEn; FilmgC; HalFC 84, 88; InWom SUP; MotPP; MovMk; NewYTBS 83; ThFT; What 3; WhoHol A*

Dorsett, Tony
[Anthony Drew Dorsett]
"Hawk"; "TD"
American. Football Player
Won Heisman Trophy, 1976; four-time all-pro running back, mostly with Dallas; retired in 1990.
b. Apr 7, 1954 in Aliquippa, Pennsylvania
Source: *AfrAmSG; BiDAmSp FB; BioIn 14, 15, 16; CurBio 80; InB&W 85; LegTOT; NewYTBS 76, 80, 81; WhoAm 82, 84, 86, 88, 92, 95, 96, 97; WhoBlA 85, 92; WhoFtbl 74; WhoSpor; WhoSSW 86; WorAl; WorAlBi*

Dorsey, Bob Rawls
American. Oilman
Gulf Oil Corp., pres., 1965-72, chm., 1972-76.
b. Aug 27, 1912 in Rockland, Texas
Source: *BlueB 76; IntWW 74, 75, 76, 77, 78, 82, 83, 89, 91; NewYTBE 71; St&PR 75; WhoAm 74, 76, 78, 80, 82, 84, 86; WhoE 74; WhoFI 75*

Dorsey, Jimmy
[James Dorsey]
American. Bandleader
Played clarinet, saxophone in his sweet-swing band, 1930s-40s; joined brother Tommy's band, 1953.
b. Feb 29, 1904 in Shenandoah, Pennsylvania
d. Jun 12, 1957 in New York, New York
Source: *AllMusG; ASCAP 66, 80; Baker 78, 84, 92; BgBands 74; BiDAmM; BiDJaz; BioIn 1, 3, 4, 8, 9, 12, 16; CmpEPM; CurBio 42, 57; DcArts; FacFETw; FilmgC; HalFC 80, 84, 88; IlEncJ; LegTOT; NewAmDM; NewGrDA 86; NewGrDJ 88, 94; NewGrDM 80; NotNAT B; ObitT 1951; OxCPMus;*

PenEncP; RadStar; RkOn 74; WhoHol B; WhoJazz 72; WhScrn 74, 77, 83; WorAl; WorAlBi

Dorsey, Thomas Andrew
"Georgia Tom"; "The Professor"
American. Clergy, Composer
Coined term "gospel music," wrote over 400 songs including, "Precious Lord, Take My Hand."
b. Jul 1, 1900 in Villa Rica, Georgia
d. Jan 23, 1993 in Chicago, Illinois
Source: *BioIn 13, 14, 15; BluesWW; DrBlPA, 90; InB&W 80, 85; NewAmDM; NewGrDA 86; OxCPMus; PenEncP; WhoAm 78*

Dorsey, Tommy
[Thomas Francis Dorsey]
"Sentimental Gentleman of Swing"
American. Bandleader
Trombonist who led swing dance bands, 1930s-40s; with brother Jimmy starred in film *The Fabulous Dorseys,* 1947.
b. Nov 19, 1905 in Shenandoah, Pennsylvania
d. Nov 26, 1956 in Greenwich, Connecticut
Source: *AllMusG; ASCAP 80; Baker 78, 84, 92; BgBands 74; BioIn 1, 3, 4, 8, 9, 12, 15, 16, 18, 20; CmpEPM; CurBio 42, 57; DcAmB S6; DcArts; FacFETw; HalFC 80, 84, 88; IlEncJ; LegTOT; MusMk; NewAmDM; NewGrDA 86; NewGrDJ 88, 94; NewGrDM 80; NotNAT B; OxCPMus; PenEncP; RadStar; RkOn 74; WhAm 3; WhoHol B; WhoJazz 72; WhScrn 74, 77, 83; WorAl; WorAlBi*

Dos Passos, John (Roderigo)
American. Author
Wrote fiction based on broad social issues; best known for trilogy *USA,* 1938.
b. Jan 14, 1896 in Chicago, Illinois
d. Sep 28, 1970 in Baltimore, Maryland
Source: *AgeMat; AmAu&B; AmCulL; AmNov; AmWr; AtlBL; Au&Wr 71; Benet 87, 96; BenetAL 91; BiE&WWA; BioIn 1, 2, 3, 4, 5, 6, 7, 8, 9, 10, 11, 12, 13; CamGEL; CamGLE; CamHAL; CasWL; Chambr 3; CnDAL; CnMD; ConAmA; ConAmL; ConAu 3NR, 29R; ConLC 1, 4, 8, 11, 15, 24, 25, 82; CyWA 58; DcAmB S8; DcAmC; DcArts; DcLB 4, 9, DS1; DcLEL; EncAB-H 1974, 1996; EncAL; EncWL, 2, 3; EvLB; FacFETw; GrWrEL N; LegTOT; LiExTwC; LiJour; LinLib L, S; LngCTC; MagSAmL; MajTwCW; McGEWB; ModAL, S1, S2; ModWD; MorMA; Novels; OxCAmL 65, 83, 95; OxCEng 67, 85; PenC AM; PeoHis; RAdv 1, 14, 13-1; REn; REnAL; RfGAmL 87, 94; RGTwCWr; TwCA, SUP; TwCWr; WebAB 74, 79; WebBD 83; WebE&AL; WhAm 5; WhDW; WhNAA; WhoTwCL; WorAl; WorAlBi; WorLitC; WrPh*

Dostoyevsky, Fyodor Mikhailovich
[Fyodor Dostoevski; Fedor Dostoevsky; Fyoder Dostoievsky]
Russian. Author
Wrote novels *Crime and Punishment,* 1886; *The Idiot,* 1887; *Brothers Karamazov,* 1912.
b. Nov 11, 1821 in Moscow, Russia
d. Jan 28, 1881 in Saint Petersburg, Russia
Source: *AtlBL; BbD; Benet 87, 96; BiD&SB; CasWL; ClDMEL 47; CrtSuMy; CyWA 58, 89; DcEuL; DcRusL; EncMys; EncSF; EncWT; EuAu; EvEuW; FilmgC; MagSWL; OxCEng 67; PenC EUR; RAdv 13-2; WorAl*

Dotson, Bob
[Robert Charles Dotson]
American. Broadcast Journalist
Correspondent, NBC News since 1979.
b. Oct 3, 1946 in Saint Louis, Missouri
Source: *ConAu 119, 134; EncTwCJ; IntAu&W 89, 91, 93; Law&B 89A; WhoAm 80, 82, 84, 86, 88, 90, 92, 94, 95, 96, 97; WhoEmL 93; WhoEnt 92; WhoTelC; WrDr 94, 96*

Dott, Gerard
[The Incredible String Band]
Scottish. Singer, Musician
Source: *BiDAmM; ConMuA 80A; EncFCWM 83; EncRk 88; IlEncRk; OxCPMus; PenEncP; RolSEnR 83; WhoRock 81; WhoRocM 82*

Dou, Gerard
[Gerrit Dou]
Dutch. Artist
Studied under Rembrandt; paintings include *The Quack,* 1652.
b. Apr 7, 1613 in Leiden, Netherlands
d. Feb 1675 in Leiden, Netherlands
Source: *AtlBL; BioIn 19; ClaDrA; DcArts; DcBiPP; Dis&D; LinLib S; McGDA; OxCArt; OxDcArt*

Double
[Felix Haug; Kurt Maloo]
Swiss. Music Group
Funky blues band formed 1980s; hit album *Blue,* 1986.

Doubleday, Abner
American. Army Officer, Baseball Pioneer
Folklore calls him inventor of baseball; game's birthplace dedicated as Doubleday Field, 1920, in Cooperstown, NY.
b. Jun 26, 1819 in Ballston Spa, New York
d. Jan 26, 1893 in Mendham, New Jersey
Source: *Alli SUP; AmBi; ApCAB; Ballpl 90; BenetAL 91; BioIn 4, 5, 7, 11, 13, 14; CivWDc; DcAmAu; DcAmB; DcNAA; Drake; HarEnMi; HarEnUS; LegTOT; NatCAB 4; OxCAmH; TwCBDA; WebAB 74, 79; WebAMB; WhAm HS; WhCiWar; WhoProB 73; WorAl; WorAlBi*

Doubleday, Frank Nelson
American. Publisher
Founded Doubleday and Co., 1897.
b. Jan 8, 1862 in New York, New York
d. Jan 30, 1934 in Coconut Grove, Florida
Source: *AmAu&B; ApCAB X; DcAmB S1; LinLib L; NatCAB 13; WebAB 74, 79; WhAm 1; WorAlBi*

Doubleday, Nelson
American. Publisher
Son of Frank Doubleday; founded Nelson Doubleday, Inc., 1910.
b. Jun 16, 1889 in New York, New York
d. Jan 11, 1949 in Oyster Bay, New York
Source: *BiDAmBL 83; BioIn 1, 3; DcAmB S4; EncAB-A 31; NatCAB 37; WhAm 2; WorAl*

Doubleday, Nelson
American. Publisher, Baseball Executive
CEO, Doubleday; majority owner, NY Mets, 1980—.
b. Jul 20, 1933 in Oyster Bay, New York
Source: *BiDAmBL 83; BioIn 13, 15, 16; CelR 90; ConNews 87-1; CurBio 87; Dun&B 88; NewYTBS 86; WhoAm 86, 88; WhoE 91*

Doubrovska, Felia
[Felizata Dluzhnevska; Mrs. Pierre Vladimiroff]
Russian. Dancer
Known for leading roles in Balanchine ballets; taught at School of American Ballet, NYC, 30 yrs.
b. 1896 in Saint Petersburg, Russia
d. Sep 18, 1981 in New York, New York
Source: *AnObit 1981; BiDD; BioIn 11, 18; CnOxB; DancEn 78; FacFETw; IntDcB; NewYTBS 81*

Doucet, Michael
American. Violinist, Singer
Plays Cajun music with rock influences in band, Beausoleil; composed and recorded title track to movie *The Big Easy,* 1987 with Beausoleil.
b. 1951 in Scott, Louisiana
Source: *BioIn 16; ConMus 8*

Doughty, Charles Montagu
English. Poet, Author
Best known for *Travels in Arabia Deserta,* 1888, describing life among the bedouins.
b. Aug 19, 1843 in Suffolk, England
d. Jan 30, 1926 in Kent, England
Source: *Alli SUP; AtlBL; Benet 87, 96; BioIn 1, 4, 5, 6, 7, 9, 11, 12, 13, 14, 15, 16, 18; BritAu 19; CamGEL; CamGLE; CasWL; Chambr 3; ChhPo; CnE&AP; CyWA 58; DcArts; DcLEL; DcNaB 1922; EncWL; EvLB; Expl 93; GrBr; LinLib S; LngCTC; ModBrL; NewC;*

NewCBEL; OxCEng 85, 95; PenC ENG; REn; WhWE

Douglas, Aaron
American. Artist
Major figure in American black art; numerous NYC murals depict black heritage.
b. May 26, 1899 in Topeka, Kansas
d. Feb 2, 1979 in Nashville, Tennessee
Source: *AfrAmAl 6; AfroAA; ArtsAmW 2; BioIn 11; ConBlB 7; DcAmArt; DcAmB S10; DcTwCCu 5; FacFETw; InB&W 80, 85; NegAl 76, 83, 89; NewYTBS 79; WhAmArt 85*

Douglas, Alfred Bruce, Lord
English. Author, Poet
Noted for intimate relationship with Oscar Wilde.
b. Oct 21, 1870 in Worcester, England
d. Mar 20, 1945 in Sussex, England
Source: *BioIn 1, 2, 5, 6, 11, 12, 13, 14; CathA 1930; ChhPo, S2; DcArts; DcCathB; DcLEL; DcNaB 1941; EvLB; LngCTC; NewC; NewCBEL; OxCEng 67, 85, 95; OxCTwCP; PenC ENG; REn; WhoLA*

Douglas, Amanda Minnie
American. Children's Author
Began "Kathie" series with *Kathie's Three Wishes,* 1871.
b. Jul 14, 1837 in New York, New York
d. Jul 18, 1918 in Newark, New Jersey
Source: *Alli SUP; AmAu; AmAu&B; AmWom; AmWomWr; ApCAB; BbD; BiD&SB; CarSB; ChhPo S1, S2; DcAmAu; DcAmB; DcNAA; NatCAB 2; OxCChiL; TwCBDA; WhAm 1; WomNov; WomWWA 14*

Douglas, Buster
[James Douglas]
American. Boxer
Heavyweight fighter; upset Mike Tyson to become heavyweight champion, Feb 1990; lost title to Evander Holyfield, Oct 1990.
b. Apr 7, 1960 in Columbus, Ohio
Source: *News 90; WhoAfA 96; WhoBlA 92, 94*

Douglas, Cathleen Curran Heffernan
[Mrs. William O Douglas]
American. Lawyer
Widow of Supreme Court Justice Douglas; active in women's rights, urban problems; director of National Public Radio, 1977—.
b. Apr 30, 1943
Source: *WhoAm 74, 76, 78, 80, 82, 84; WhoAmL 79; WhoAmW 68, 70, 72, 74, 81, 85*

Douglas, David
Scottish. Botanist
Early explorer of Oregon country; Douglas spruce named for him.
b. 1798 in Scone, Scotland
d. 1834
Source: *ApCAB; BioIn 1, 2, 3, 4, 5, 7, 8, 10, 11, 12, 14; CmCal; DcBiPP; DcNaB; Drake; InSci; LarDcSc; MacDCB 78; OxCCan; WhDW*

Douglas, Donald Willis
American. Aircraft Manufacturer
Founded Douglas Aircraft, 1920; produced DC series for commercial airlines.
b. Apr 6, 1892 in New York, New York
d. Feb 1, 1981 in Palm Springs, California
Source: *CurBio 81; IntWW 78; McGEWB; NewYTBS 81; WebAMB; Who 74; WhoAm 74; WorAl*

Douglas, Donna
[Doris Smith]
American. Actor
Played Elly May Clampett in TV series "The Beverly Hillbillies," 1962-71.
b. Sep 26, 1939 in Baywood, Louisiana
Source: *InWom; MotPP; WhoHol 92, A*

Douglas, Ellen
[Josephine Ayres Haxton]
American. Author
Wrote novels *A Family's Affairs,* 1962; *Apostles of Light,* 1973.
b. Jul 12, 1921 in Natchez, Mississippi
Source: *BioIn 13; ConAu 41NR, 115; ConLC 73; ConNov 91, 96; CyWA 89; LiveMA; PenNWW B; SouWr; WorAu 1980*

Douglas, Emily Taft
[Mrs. Paul Howard Douglas]
American. Author, Politician
Wrote *Margaret Sanger: Pioneer of the Future,* 1970, about early proponent of birth control; liberal Dem. congresswoman from IL, 1945-47.
b. Apr 19, 1899 in Chicago, Illinois
d. Jan 28, 1994 in Briarcliff Manor, New York
Source: *BiDrAC; BiDrUSC 89; BioIn 17, 19, 20; ConAu 107, 143; CurBio 94N; InWom, SUP*

Douglas, Emmitt
American. Civil Rights Leader
LA NAACP head, 1968-81; initiated lawsuit that desegregated local schools, 1956.
b. 1926?
d. Mar 25, 1981 in New Roads, Louisiana
Source: *BioIn 12*

Douglas, Gavin
Scottish. Poet, Translator
Noted for *Aeneid* translation, first classic work translated into English dialect.
b. 1474? in Tantallon Castle, Scotland
d. 1522 in London, England
Source: *Alli; BiD&SB; BioIn 20; BritAu; CamGEL; CasWL; Chambr 1; ChhPo S3; CmScLit; CnE&AP; CrtT 1, 4; DcCathB; DcEnA; DcEuL; DcLEL; DcNaB; EvLB; GrWrEL P; McGEWB; NewC; NewCBEL; OxCEng 67, 85; PenC ENG; REn; RfGEnL 91; WebE&AL*

Douglas, Helen Mary Gahagan
American. Singer, Politician
Dem. rep. from CA, 1944-50; bid for US Senate stopped by opponent Richard Nixon, who insinuated she favored communism; wife of actor Melvyn Douglas.
b. Nov 25, 1900 in Boonton, New Jersey
d. Jun 28, 1980 in New York, New York
Source: *BiDrAC; ConAu 101; CurBio 44, 80; InWom; LibW; NewYTBE 71; NotNAT; WhoAm 74; WhoHol A; WhoThe 77A*

Douglas, James, Sir
"Father of British Columbia"
Canadian. Businessman, Political Leader
First governor of newly-created colony of BC, 1858-64; in office during gold rush.
b. Aug 15, 1803 in Demerara, British Guiana
d. Aug 2, 1877 in Victoria, British Columbia, Canada
Source: *ApCAB; BioIn 1, 7, 9, 11; DcCanB 10; DcNaB MP; HisDBrE; MacDCB 78; NewCol 75; OxCCan; PeoHis*

Douglas, James Henderson, Jr.
American. Government Official, Lawyer
Military adviser to Pres. Dwight D. Eisenhower, 1953-57; Air Force secretary, 1957-59; defense secretary, 1960-61.
b. Mar 11, 1899
d. Feb 24, 1988 in Lake Forest, Illinois
Source: *BioIn 4, 5, 15, 16; CurBio 88N; InSci; St&PR 87; WhAm 9; WhoAm 74, 76, 78*

Douglas, John Leigh
English. Hostage
Teacher, taken hostage Mar 28, 1986 by Lebanese terrorists, found dead 3 weeks later.

Douglas, Keith Castellain
English. Poet, Soldier
WW II casualty whose *Selected Poems,* were edited by Ted Hughes, 1964.
b. Jan 20, 1920 in Tunbridge Wells, England
d. Jun 9, 1944 in Saint Pierre, France
Source: *BioIn 10; DcLEL 1940; DcNaB MP; LngCTC; ModBrL S1; OxCEng 67, 85, 95; PenC ENG; WebE&AL; WhoTwCL; WorAu 1950*

Douglas, Kirk
[Issur Danielovich; Isadore Demsky]
American. Actor
Has appeared in over 70 films including *Lust for Life,* 1956; *Spartac us,* 1960; father of actor Michael; received American Film Institute's Life Achievement Award, 1991.
b. Dec 9, 1916 in Amsterdam, New York

Source: *BestSel 90-4; BiDFilm, 81, 94; BiE&WWA; BioIn 2, 3, 4, 5, 6, 7, 8, 9, 11, 12, 14, 15, 16, 17; BkPepl; CelR, 90; CmMov; ConAu 138; ConTFT 1, 7, 14; CurBio 52; DcArts; DcTwCCu 1; FacFETw; FilmEn; FilmgC; ForYSC; GangFlm; HalFC 80, 84, 88; IntDcF 1-3, 2-3; IntMPA 92, 96; IntWW 74, 75, 76, 77, 78, 79, 80, 81, 82, 83, 89, 91, 93; ItaFilm; LegTOT; MiSFD 9; MotPP; MovMk; NotNAT; OxCFilm; VarWW 85; WhoAm 86, 90, 95, 96, 97; WhoEnt 92; WhoHol 92, A; WhoWor 84; WorAlBi; WorEFlm; WrDr 92*

Douglas, Lloyd Cassel
American. Author, Clergy
Wrote best-sellers *Magnificent Obsession,* 1929; *Green Light,* 1935; *The Robe,* 1942, became first Cinema Scope film, 1953.
b. Aug 27, 1877 in Columbia City, Indiana
d. Feb 13, 1951 in Los Angeles, California
Source: *AmAu&B; AmNov; BioIn 1, 2, 3, 4, 5, 10; ConAu 120; CyWA 58; DcAmB S5; EvLB; FilmgC; IndAu 1917; LngCTC; MichAu 80; OhA&B; OxCAmL 65; PenC AM; RelLAm 91; REn; REnAL; TwCA, SUP; TwCSAPR; TwCWr; WebAB 74, 79; WhAm 3; WhNAA; WorAl*

Douglas, Marjorie
American. Conservationist, Writer
Worked for preservation of FL Everglades; wrote *River of Grass.*
b. Apr 7, 1890 in Minneapolis, Minnesota
Source: *News 93-1*

Douglas, Melvyn
[Melvin Hesselberg]
American. Actor
40-yr. film career highlighted by Oscars for *Hud,* 1963; *Being There,* 1979.
b. Apr 5, 1901 in Macon, Georgia
d. Aug 4, 1981 in New York, New York
Source: *AnObit 1981, 77, 81; WhScrn 83; WorAl; WorAlBi; WorEFlm*

Douglas, Michael Kirk
American. Actor, Producer
Won best producer Oscar for *One Flew Over the Cuckoo's Nest,* 1975, best actor Oscar for *Wall Street,* 1988; son of Kirk.
b. Sep 25, 1944 in New Brunswick, New Jersey
Source: *BkPepl; CelR 90; ConTFT 4; CurBio 87; FilmgC; HalFC 88; IntMPA 92; IntWW 89, 91, 93; VarWW 85; WhoAm 80, 82, 84, 86, 88, 90, 92, 94, 95, 96, 97; WhoEnt 92; WhoHol A; WorAl; WorAlBi*

Douglas, Mike
[Michael Delaney Dowd, Jr.]
American. TV Personality, Singer
Hosted "The Mike Douglas Show," 1960s-70s; has won four Emmys.
b. Aug 11, 1925 in Chicago, Illinois
Source: *BioIn 10, 11, 12, 13; BioNews 75; BkPepl; CelR; ConAu 89; ConTFT 6; CurBio 68; IntMPA 79, 80, 81, 82, 84, 86, 88, 92, 94, 96; LegTOT; LesBEnT 92; NewYTET; RkOn 78, 84; VarWW 85; WhoAm 74, 76, 78, 80, 82; WhoE 74; WhoHol 92, A; WorAl*

Douglas, Norman
Scottish. Author
Best known for Caprian novel *South Wind,* 1917; travel book *Old Calabria,* 1915.
b. Dec 8, 1868 in Aberdeen, Scotland
d. Feb 9, 1952 in Capri, Italy
Source: *AtlBL; Benet 87; BioIn 1, 2, 3, 4, 5, 6, 7, 8, 9, 10, 11, 13, 14, 16; BritWr 6; CamGEL; CasWL; Chambr 3; ChhPo, S1; CnMWL; ConAu 119; CyWA 58; DcArts; DcLB 34; DcLEL; DcNaB 1951; EncSF; FacFETw; GrWrEL N; LegTOT; LinLib L; LngCTC; ModBrL; NewC; NewCBEL; Novels; ObitT 1951; OxCEng 67; PenC ENG; RAdv 1, 13-1; REn; RfGEnL 91; ScF&FL 1; TwCA, SUP; TwCWr; WebE&AL; WhDW; WhoTwCL*

Douglas, Paul
American. Actor
1,024 performances on Broadway in *Born Yesterday.*
b. Nov 4, 1907 in Philadelphia, Pennsylvania
d. Sep 11, 1959 in Hollywood, California
Source: *BiDFilm, 81, 94; BioIn 2, 5, 7, 11; EncAFC; FilmEn; FilmgC; ForYSC; GangFlm; HalFC 80, 84, 88; IntDcF 1-3; ItaFilm; LegTOT; MotPP; MovMk; NotNAT B; ObitOF 79; RadStar; WhoHol B; WhScrn 74, 77, 83; WorAl; WorAlBi; WorEFlm*

Douglas, Paul Howard
American. Economist, Politician
Dem. senator from IL, 1949-67; author of economic books: *The Theory of Wages,* 1934.
b. Mar 26, 1892 in Salem, Massachusetts
d. Sep 24, 1976 in Washington, District of Columbia
Source: *AmAu&B; AmEA 74; AmMWSc 73S; BiDrAC; BiDrUSC 89; BioIn 1, 2, 3, 5, 6, 7, 9, 11, 12; BlueB 76; ConAu 69; CurBio 49, 76; DcAmB S10; IntWW 74, 75, 76; WhAm 7, 9; WhoAm 74, 76; WhoAmP 73; WhoEc 81, 86; WhoWor 74; WorAl*

Douglas, Robert L
American. Basketball Coach, Basketball Executive
Owner, coach Renaissance (NYC) Big Five pro team, 1922-44; first black elected to Hall of Fame.
b. Nov 4, 1884, St. Kitts
d. Jul 16, 1979 in New York, New York
Source: *BiDAmSp BK; InB&W 80; NewYTBS 79; WhoBbl 73*

Douglas, Sholto
[Baron Douglas of Kirtleside; Williom Sholto Douglas]
English. Military Leader
Master of Royal Air Force; chm., British European Airways; wrote *Years of Combat,* 1963.
b. Dec 23, 1893 in Oxford, England
d. Oct 29, 1969 in Northampton, England
Source: *CurBio 43, 69; GrBr; InSci; ObitT 1961; WhAm 5; Who 82, 83; WhWW-II*

Douglas, Stephen Arnold
"Little Giant"
American. Politician
Dem. senator from IL, 1847-61; best known for debates with Lincoln, 1858.
b. Apr 23, 1813 in Brandon, Vermont
d. Jun 3, 1861 in Chicago, Illinois
Source: *AmAu&B; AmBi; AmPolLe; ApCAB; BiAUS; BiDrAC; BiDrUSC 89; BioIn 1, 3, 4, 5, 6, 7, 8, 9, 10, 11, 12, 13, 15, 20; CelCen; CivWDc; CyAG; DcAmB; Dis&D; Drake; EncAAH; EncAB-H 1974, 1996; HarEnUS; LinLib S; McGEWB; NatCAB 2; OxCAmH; OxCAmL 65, 83, 95; REn; REnAL; REnAW; TwCBDA; WebAB 74, 79; WebBD 83; WhAm HS; WhAmP; WhCiWar; WorAl*

Douglas, William Orville
American. Supreme Court Justice
Liberal justice, 1939-75; granted stay of execution to Rosenbergs, 1953.
b. Oct 16, 1898 in Maine, Minnesota
d. Jan 19, 1980 in Washington, District of Columbia
Source: *AmAu&B; AmPolLe; Au&Wr 71; AuBYP 2, 3; BiDFedJ; BioIn 1, 2, 3, 4, 5, 6, 7, 8, 9, 10, 11, 12, 13; CngDr 74, 77, 79; ConAu 9R, 93; CurBio 41, 50, 80; DcAmB S10; DcLEL 1940; DcPol; EncAAH; EncAB-H 1974, 1996; IntAu&W 77; IntWW 74, 75, 76; LinLib S; McGEWB; MinnWr; OxCAmH; OxCAmL 65; OxCLaw; OxCSupC; REn; REnAL; SupCtJu; TwCA SUP; WebAB 74, 79; WhAm 7; Who 74; WhoAm 74, 76, 78, 80; WhoAmL 78, 79; WhoAmP 73, 75, 77, 79; WhoGov 72, 75, 77; WhoPNW; WhoSSW 73, 75; WhoWest 74, 76; WhoWor 74, 78; WorAl; WrDr 76*

Douglas-Home, Alexander Frederick, Sir
Scottish. Politician
Member, House of Lords, 1951; disclaimed peerages for life, 1965; held various political posts, 1960s-70s; prime minister, 1963-64.
b. Jul 2, 1903 in London, England
d. Sep 9, 1995 in Berwickshire, Scotland
Source: *Alli; BioIn 6, 7, 8, 9, 11, 12, 16; ColdWar 1; ConAu 102; DcPol; DcTwHis; EvLB; FacFETw; IntWW 74; NewYTBE 71; PenC ENG; Who 74; WhoWor 74; WrDr 86, 92*

Douglas-Home, Charles
English. Editor, Author
Editor, London *Times,* 1982-85.
b. Sep 1, 1937
d. Oct 29, 1985 in London, England
Source: *AnObit 1985; BioIn 14; ConAu 117; IntAu&W 76; NewYTBS 85; Who 82*

Douglass, Andrew Ellicott
American. Astronomer, Scientist
Noted for research in dating prehistoric ruins by tree rings; coined "term dendochronology."
b. Jul 7, 1867 in Windsor, Utah
d. Oct 20, 1962 in Tucson, Arizona
Source: *AsBiEn; BiESc; BioIn 1, 4, 6, 10, 14; CamDcSc; DcAmB S7; FacFETw; InSci; LarDcSc; NatCAB 16; PeoHis; WebBD 83; WhAm 1, 4*

Douglass, Frederick
[Frederick Augustus W Bailey]
American. Lecturer, Author
Escaped slavery, 1838; took active part in antislavery cause, edited antislavery journal.
b. Feb 14, 1817 in Tuckahoe, Maryland
d. Feb 20, 1895 in Anacosta Heights, Maryland
Source: *ABCMeAm; AfrAmAl 6; AfrAmPr; Alli SUP; AmAu; AmAu&B; AmBi; AmJust; AmRef; AmSocL; ApCAB; BbD; Benet 87, 96; BiDAmJo; BiDAmL; BiD&SB; BiDSA; BioIn 1, 2, 3, 4, 5, 6, 7, 8, 9, 10, 11, 12, 13, 14, 15, 16, 17, 18, 19, 20, 21; BlkAmP; BlkAmW 1; BlkAWP; BlkLC; BlkWrNE; CamGLE; CamHAL; CelCen; Chambr 3; CivWDc; ColARen; CyAG; DcAmAu; DcAmB; DcAmDH 80, 89; DcAmImH; DcAmNB; DcAmSR; DcBiPP, A; DcLB 1, 43, 50, 79; DcNAA; Drake; EncAAH; EncAB-H 1974, 1996; EncAJ; EncSoH; GayN; HarEnUS; InB&W 85; JrnUS; LegTOT; LinLib L, S; McGEWB; MemAm; NatCAB 2; NegAl 76, 89; NinCLC 7, 55; OxCAmH; OxCAmL 65, 83, 95; PeoHis; RadHan; RAdv 13-3; REn; REnAL; SchCGBL; SelBAAf; SelBAAu; SmATA 29; TwCBDA; WebAB 74, 79; WebBD 83; WebE&AL; WhAm HS; WhAmP; WhCiWar; WorAl; WorAlBi; WorLitC*

Douglass, Lathrop
American. Architect, Urban Planner
Designed first shopping center in US, 1950s; developed suburban shopping malls in US, Europe.
b. Sep 5, 1907 in Kansas City, Missouri
d. Jan 21, 1981 in Greenwich, Connecticut
Source: *AmArch 70; AnObit 1981; BioIn 8, 12; NewYTBS 81; WhAm 7; WhoAm 74, 76, 78, 80; WhoFI 74; WhoWor 74, 76*

Doulton, Henry, Sir
English. Artist
Joined father's pottery firm, 1835; introduced stoneware drainpipes, appliances, which made Doulton famous.
b. Jul 25, 1820 in Lambeth, England
d. Nov 18, 1897 in London, England
Source: *AntBDN M; BioIn 9, 14; DcArts; DcNaB S1; WebBD 83*

Dourif, Brad
American. Actor
Received Oscar nomination for *One Flew Over the Cuckoo's Nest,* 1975.
b. Mar 18, 1950 in Huntington, West Virginia
Source: *BioIn 16; ConTFT 7; HalFC 80, 84, 88; IntMPA 88, 92, 94, 96; LegTOT; WhoAm 82; WhoHol 92, A*

Douvillier, Suzanne Theodore Vaillande
"Madame Placide"
American. Dancer
First celebrated American ballerina, 1792; first woman choreographer.
b. Sep 28, 1778 in Dole, France
d. Aug 30, 1826 in New Orleans, Louisiana
Source: *InWom SUP; LibW; NotAW; WomFir*

Dove, Arthur Garfield
American. Artist
Paintings are of large masses of muted colors; worked in collage, nonobjective approach.
b. Aug 2, 1880 in Canandaigua, New York
d. Nov 23, 1946 in Huntington, New York
Source: *AtlBL; BioIn 1, 3, 4, 5, 6, 10, 11, 12, 13, 14, 15, 16, 20; BioNews 75; BriEAA; ChhPo; ConArt 77; DcAmB S4; DcCAA 71; McGDA; McGEWB; OxCTwCA; PhDcTCA 77; WebAB 74, 79; WebBD 83; WhoAmA 76, 78N, 80N, 82N, 84N, 86N, 89N, 91N, 93N*

Dove, Heinrich Wilhelm
German. Physicist
Developed law of gyration, that wind usually shifts in sun's direction.
b. Oct 6, 1803 in Liegnitz, Prussia
d. Apr 4, 1879 in Berlin, Germany
Source: *CelCen; DcBiPP; DcScB; InSci; LarDcSc*

Dove, Rita (Frances)
American. Poet
U.S. Poet Laureate, 1993-95; wrote *Thomas and Beulah,* 1986; won 1987 Pulitzer Prize for Poetry.
b. Aug 28, 1952 in Akron, Ohio
Source: *AfrAmAl 6; AmWomWr SUP; Benet 96; BenetAL 91; BlkWAm; BlkWr 1, 2; ConAu 19AS, 27NR, 42NR, 109; ConBlB 6; ConLC 50, 81; ConPo 91, 96; CurBio 94; DcLB 120; DcTwCCu 5; DrAPF 80; EncWHA; GrWomW; IntAu&W 89, 91, 93; IntWWP 82; ModWoWr; News 94, 94-3; NotBlAW 1; OxCAmL 95; OxCTwCP; OxCWoWr 95; PoeCrit 6; RAdv 14; RfGAmL 94; SchCGBL; WhoAfA 96; WhoAm 88, 90, 92, 94, 95, 96, 97; WhoAmW 89, 91, 93, 95, 97; WhoBlA 88, 90, 92, 94; WhoSSW 95, 97; WhoUSWr 88; WhoWrEP 89, 92, 95; WomFir; WorAu 1980; WrDr 92, 94, 96*

Dove, Ulysses
American. Choreographer, Dancer
Choreographed *Bad Blood,* 1984; *Serious Pleasures,* 1992.
b. Jan 17, 1947 in Jonesville, South Carolina
Source: *BioIn 19; ConBlB 5; DcTwCCu 5; WhoAfA 96; WhoAm 78, 80, 82*

Dovzhenko, Alexander
Ukrainian. Director
Best known for silent films: *Zvenigora, Earth,*
b. Sep 11, 1894 in Sosnytsia, Ukraine
d. Nov 25, 1956 in Moscow, Union of Soviet Socialist Republics
Source: *BiDFilm, 81, 94; BioIn 15, 20; DcFM; FilmEn; FilmgC; HalFC 80, 84, 88; IntDcF 1-2, 2-2; MakMC; MovMk; OxCFilm; WhScrn 74, 77, 83; WomWMM; WorEFlm*

Dow, Charles Henry
American. Financier, Publisher
With Edward D. Jones started *Wall Street Journal,* 1889; laid basis for "Dow Theory," Dow-Jones average.
b. Nov 6, 1851 in Sterling, Connecticut
d. Dec 4, 1902 in New York, New York
Source: *BiDAmJo; BioIn 5, 16, 17, 21; WebAB 74, 79*

Dow, Herbert Henry
American. Chemist, Manufacturer
Founded Dow Chemical Co., 1900.
b. Feb 26, 1866 in Belleville, Ontario, Canada
d. Oct 15, 1930 in Rochester, Minnesota
Source: *BiDAmBL 83; BioIn 6, 9, 15, 16; DcAmB S1; EncAB-A 12, 19; EncAB-H 1974, 1996; GayN; InSci; NatCAB 24; WebAB 74, 79; WhAm 1; WorAl; WorInv*

Dow, Neal
American. Social Reformer, Politician
Drafted strict "Maine Law," 1851; presidential candidate for Prohibitionist Party, 1880.
b. Mar 20, 1804 in Portland, Maine
d. Oct 2, 1897 in Portland, Maine
Source: *AmBi; AmRef; AmSocL; ApCAB; BioIn 4, 6, 7, 11, 15, 19; CivWDc; CyAG; DcAmB; DcAmSR; DcAmTB; DcNAA; EncAB-H 1974, 1996; HarEnUS; McGEWB; NatCAB 5; NewCol 75; OxCAmH; TwCBDA; WebAB 74, 79; WebBD 83; WhAm HS; WhCiWar*

Dow, Tony
American. Actor
Played Wally Cleaver on "Leave It to Beaver," 1957-63.
b. Apr 13, 1945 in Hollywood, California
Source: *BioIn 12, 13; ConTFT 2; WhoHol 92*

Dowd, Maureen (Brigid)
American. Journalist
Op-ed columnist, *The New York Times,* 1995—.
b. Jan 14, 1952 in Washington, District of Columbia
Source: *CurBio 96; News 97-1; WhoAmW 97*

Dowding, Hugh Caswell Tremenheere, Baron
"Stuffy"
British. Air Force Officer
Victorious director, Battle of Britian, 1940; designed improvements to fighter planes.
b. Apr 22, 1882 in Moffat, Scotland
d. Feb 15, 1970 in Kent, England
Source: *ConAu 112; CurBio 40, 70; WhoMilH 76; WhWW-II*

Dowell, Anthony James
English. Dancer
With Royal Ballet since 1961; assoc. director, 1985-86; artistic director, 1986 —.
b. Feb 16, 1943 in London, England
Source: *CurBio 71; FacFETw; IntWW 74, 82, 83, 89, 91, 93; NewYTBS 74; Who 74, 82, 92, 94; WhoAm 80, 82, 84, 86, 88, 90, 92, 94, 95, 96, 97; WhoEnt 92; WhoWor 74, 82, 84, 87, 89, 91, 93, 95, 96, 97; WorAlBi*

Dowie, John Alexander
Scottish. Evangelist
Founded Christian Catholic Apostolic Church; came to US, settled sect near Chicago, 1903-05.
b. May 25, 1847 in Edinburgh, Scotland
d. Mar 9, 1907 in Zion, Illinois
Source: *AmBi; BiDAmCu; BioIn 2, 5, 8; DcAmB; DcNaB S2; LinLib S; LuthC 75; NatCAB 13; PeoHis; RelLAm 91*

Dowland, John
English. Composer, Musician
Greatest lutenist of his age; wrote popular tunes *Songs of Ayres,* 1597-1603.
b. Jan 1563 in Dublin, Ireland
d. Apr 7, 1626 in London, England
Source: *Alli; AtlBL; Baker 84, 92; Benet 96; BiDRP&D; BioIn 3, 4, 7, 9, 11, 12, 13, 20; BritAu; ChhPo S2; CmpBCM; DcArts; DcCom 77; DcCom&M 79; DcLB 172; DcNaB; GrComp; MusMk; NewAmDM; NewC; NewCBEL; NewGrDM 80; NewOxM; OxCEng 67, 85, 95; OxCMus; REn; WhDW*

Dowler, Boyd H
American. Football Player
Two-time all-pro end, 1959-69, 1971, mostly with Green Bay; one of NFL leaders in career receptions.
b. Oct 18, 1937 in Rock Springs, Wyoming
Source: *BiDAmSp FB; WhoFtbl 74*

Dowling, Dan(iel Blair)
American. Cartoonist
Exaggerated, humorous political cartoons appeared in newspapers, 1940-73.
b. Nov 16, 1906 in O'Neill, Nebraska
d. Jul 27, 1993 in Monterey, California
Source: *Alli; BioIn 2, 3, 19; WhoAm 74, 76; WhoAmA 73, 76, 78, 80*

Dowling, Eddie
[Edward Dowling; Joseph Nelson Goucher]
American. Actor, Dramatist, Producer
Won four NY Drama Critics awards; won Pulitzer for *Time of Your Life,* 1940.
b. Dec 11, 1894 in Woonsocket, Rhode Island
d. Feb 18, 1976 in Smithfield, Rhode Island
Source: *ASCAP 66; BiE&WWA; BioIn 1, 8, 10, 11; ConAu 65; CurBio 46, 76, 76N; EncMT; EncVaud; HalFC 80, 84, 88; NewYTBS 76; NotNAT B; OxCAmT 84; PlP&P; WhAm 6; What 2; WhoAm 74; WhoHol C; WhoThe 72, 77A; WhScrn 83; WhThe*

Down, Lesley-Anne
English. Actor
Starred in PBS series "Upstairs, Downstairs"; mini-series "North and South," 1985-86.
b. Mar 17, 1954 in London, England
Source: *BioIn 14, 15; ConTFT 5, 15; FilmEn; HalFC 80, 84, 88; IntMPA 81, 82, 92, 94, 96; LegTOT; WhoEnt 92; WhoHol 92*

Downes, Edward Olin Davenport
American. Musicologist, Broadcaster, Author
Lecturer, NY Met. music series, 1983—; quizmaster, Texaco-Met. Opera Network, 1958—; professor, music history, Julliard School of Music, 1986—.
b. Aug 12, 1911 in Boston, Massachusetts
Source: *Baker 84; DrAS 74H, 78H, 82H; EncAI&E; IntAu&W 86; IntWWM 77, 80, 85, 90; NewAmDM; NewGrDA 86; NewGrDM 80; WhoAm 74, 76, 78, 80, 82, 84, 86, 88, 90, 92, 94, 95, 96, 97; WhoAmM 83; WhoE 74; WhoEnt 92*

Downes, Olin
[Edwin Olin Downes]
American. Critic, Author
Music critic with *NY Times* for 32 yrs; music books include *A Treasury of American Song.*
b. Jan 27, 1886 in Evanston, Illinois
d. Aug 22, 1955 in New York, New York
Source: *AmAu&B; Baker 78, 84; BiDAmM; BioIn 3, 4; CurBio 43, 55; DcAmB S5; EncAJ; NatCAB 41; NewAmDM; NewGrDA 86; NewGrDM 80; OxCAmH; WhAm 3; WhScrn 74, 77, 83*

Downey, Fairfax Davis
American. Author
Wrote more than 50 books on historical, military, or animal themes including *Storming the Gateway,* 1960.
b. Nov 28, 1893 in Salt Lake City, Utah
d. May 31, 1990 in Springfield, New Hampshire
Source: *AmAu&B; ASCAP 66, 80; AuBYP 2, 3; BioIn 1, 2, 8, 9, 16; ChhPo; ConAu 1NR, 1R, 131; CurBio 49, 90, 90N; IntAu&W 76, 82, 91; NewYTBS 90; OxCCan; REnAL; SmATA 3, 66; WhAm 10; WhE&EA; WhNAA; WhoAm 74, 76, 78, 80; WrDr 76, 80, 82, 84, 86, 88, 90*

Downey, Morton
American. Singer
Irish tenor popular, 1930s-40s; made over 1,500 recordings.
b. Nov 14, 1902 in Wallingford, Connecticut
d. Oct 25, 1985 in Palm Beach, Florida
Source: *ASCAP 66; BioIn 1, 2, 8; CurBio 86, 86N; Film 2; ForYSC; What 2; WhoAm 80, 82; WhoHol A*

Downey, Morton, Jr.
American. TV Personality
Hosted talk show bearing his name, 1987-89; known for confrontational, controversial format.
b. 1932
Source: *BioIn 15, 16; LegTOT; News 88*

Downey, Rick
[Blue Oyster Cult]
American. Singer, Musician
Drummer, vocalist with hard rock group since 1981.
b. Aug 29, 1953 in Long Island, New York

Downey, Robert, Jr.
American. Actor
Regular on TV series "Saturday Night Live," 1985-86; starred in film *Chances Are,* 1989.
b. Apr 4, 1965 in New York, New York
Source: *BioIn 16; CelR 90; ConTFT 7, 8, 14; IntMPA 92, 94, 96; LegTOT; WhoAm 94, 95, 96, 97; WhoHol 92; WorAlBi*

Downing, Andrew Jackson
American. Horticulturist, Landscape Architect
Authority on landscape gardening, design.
b. Oct 30, 1815 in Newburgh, New York
d. Jul 28, 1852 in New York
Source: *Alli; AmAu; AmAu&B; AmBi; AmCulL; ApCAB; BiD&SB; BioIn 1, 2, 3, 11, 12, 14, 15, 19; BriEAA; CyAL 2; DcAmAu; DcAmB; DcD&D; DcNAA; Drake; EncAAH; McGDA; McGEWB; NatCAB 11; OxCAmH; OxCArt; TwCBDA; WebAB 74, 79; WhAm HS*

Downs, Hugh (Malcolm)
American. TV Personality
Host of NBC's "Today Show," 1962-72; ABC's newsmagazine "20/20," 1978—.
b. Feb 14, 1921 in Akron, Ohio
Source: *BioIn 4, 5, 6, 7, 8, 9, 10, 12, 13, 15; CelR, 90; ConAu 2NR, 45; ConTFT 5; CurBio 65; EncTwCJ; IntMPA 75, 76, 77, 78, 79, 80, 81, 82, 84, 86, 88, 92, 94, 96; LegTOT; LesBEnT 92; NewYTET; RadStar; WhoAm 74, 76, 78, 80, 82, 84, 86, 88, 90, 92, 94, 95, 96, 97; WhoE 91; WhoEnt 92; WhoHol 92; WorAl; WorAlBi*

Downs, Johnny
American. Actor
Child actor in *Our Gang* series; juvenile lead in 1930s musicals.
b. Oct 10, 1913 in New York, New York
d. Jun 6, 1994 in Coronado, California
Source: *BioIn 10, 20; CmpEPM; EncAFC; Film 2; FilmEn; FilmgC; ForYSC; HalFC 80, 84, 88; What 4; WhoHol 92, A*

Downs, William Randall, Jr.
American. Broadcast Journalist
Most of career was spent covering foreign news; with ABC News, 1964-78.
b. Aug 17, 1914 in Kansas City, Kansas
d. May 3, 1978 in Bethesda, Maryland
Source: *BioIn 11; ConAu 77, 81; WhAm 7; WhoAm 74, 76, 78*

Dowson, Ernest Christopher
English. Author, Poet
Associated with "fin de siecle" period in literature; wrote *Cynara,* 1896.
b. Aug 2, 1867 in Kent, England
d. Feb 23, 1900 in London, England
Source: *AtlBL; BioIn 3, 7, 8, 11, 13, 20; BritAu 19; CamGEL; CasWL; Chambr 3; ChhPo, S1, S2; CnE&AP; ConAu 105; DcLEL; DcNaB MP; EvLB; GrWrEL P; MouLC 4; NewC; NewCBEL; OxCEng 67, 85, 95; PenC ENG; REn; WebE&AL; WorAl*

Doxiadis, Constantinos Apostolos
Greek. Architect
Chief planner for Athens, 1937-38; pres. of own firm, 1951-72; received several honors.
b. May 14, 1913 in Stenimochos, Greece
d. Jun 28, 1975 in Athens, Greece
Source: *BioIn 6, 7, 8, 10, 11; ConArch 87, 94; ConAu 41R, 57; CurBio 64, 75; IntWW 74; WhAm 6; Who 74; WhoWor 74, 76*

Doyle, Arthur Conan, Sir
Scottish. Author, Physician
Introduced Sherlock Holmes in *A Study in Scarlet,* 1887.
b. May 22, 1859 in Edinburgh, Scotland
d. Jul 7, 1930 in Crowborough, England
Source: *Alli SUP; AtlBL; Au&Arts 14; AuBYP 2, 3; BbD; Benet 87, 96; BiD&SB; BiDPara; BiHiMed; BioIn 1, 2, 3, 4, 5, 6, 7, 8, 9, 10, 11, 12, 13, 14, 15, 16, 17, 18, 20, 21; BlmGEL; BritWr S2; CamGEL; CamGLE; CarSB; CasWL; Chambr 3; ChhPo, S1; CmScLit; ConAu 104, 122; CopCroC; CrtSuMy; CyWA 58; DcArts; DcBiA; DcEnA A; DcLB 18, 70, 156; DcLEL; DcNaB 1922; Dis&D; EncMys; EncO&P 2, 3; EncPaPR 91; EncSF, 93; EvLB; FacFETw; FilmgC; GrWrEL N; HalFC 80, 84, 88; JBA 34; LegTOT; LinLib L, S; LngCEL; LngCTC; MagSWL; MajTwCW; McGEWB; MnBBF; ModBrL; NewC; NewCBEL; NewCol 75; NewEScF; NotNAT B; Novels; OxCChiL; OxCEng 67, 85, 95; OxCMed 86; PenC ENG; PenEncH; PlP&P; PoIre; RAdv 1, 14, 13-1; REn; RfGEnL 91; RfGShF; RGSF; ScF&FL 92; ScFEYrs; ScFSB; ScFWr; ShSCr 12; ShSWr; SmATA 24; SpyFic; StaCVF; TwCA, SUP; TwCCr&M 80, 85, 91; TwCLC 7; TwCRHW 90, 94; TwCSFW 81, 86, 91; TwCWr; TwCYAW; VicBrit; WebBD 83; WebE&AL; WhDW; WhLit; WhoChL; WhoHr&F; WhoHrs 80; WhoSpyF; WhoTwCL; WhThe; WorAl; WorAlBi; WorLitC; WrChl*

Doyle, David (Fitzgerald)
American. Actor
Played Bosley in TV series "Charlie's Angels," 1976-81.
b. Dec 1, 1929 in Omaha, Nebraska
d. Feb 26, 1997 in Los Angeles, California
Source: *VarWW 85; WhoAm 78, 80; WhoHol 92, A*

Doyle, Jill
Irish. Actor
Starred in film *Eat the Peach,* 1986.
b. Jan 12, 1965 in Dublin, Ireland
Source: *ConTFT 4*

Doyle, Richard
English. Artist
Regular contributor to *Punch* mag., 1843-50; drew endearing elfish figures in *In Fairyland;* uncle of Arthur Conan.
b. Sep 1824 in London, England
d. Dec 11, 1883 in London, England
Source: *Alli SUP; AntBDN B; BioIn 1, 10, 11, 12, 13; CamGLE; ChhPo, S1, S2, S3; ClaDrA; DcArts; DcBrBI; DcBrWA; DcCathB; DcEuL; DcNaB; DcVicP, 2; McGDA; NewC; OxCArt; OxCChiL; OxCEng 85, 95; OxDcArt; SmATA 21; StaCVF; WhDW; WorECar*

Doyle, Roddy
Irish. Author
Won 1993 Booker Prize for Fiction for *Paddy Clarke Ha Ha Ha.*
b. 1958 in Dublin, Ireland
Source: *Au&Arts 14; ConAu 143; ConLC 81; ConNov 96; DcIrL 96; OxCIri; RGTwCWr; WhoWor 95, 96; WrDr 96*

Dozier, Edward P.
American. Anthropologist
Studied his own people, the Pueblo Indians of the American Southwest; wrote *Mountain Arbiters,* 1966.
b. Apr 23, 1916 in Santa Clara Pueblo, New Mexico
d. May 2, 1971
Source: *BioIn 2, 9, 21; ConAu 29R; EncNAB; EncNoAI; IntDcAn; NotNaAm; REnAW*

Dozier, James Lee
American. Military Leader
Five-star general, kidnapped by Red Brigade terrorists, 1981; freed by Italian police after 42 days.
b. Apr 10, 1931 in Arcadia, Florida
Source: *BioIn 12, 13; NewYTBS 82; WhoAm 88, 90, 92, 94, 95, 96, 97*

Dozier, William
American. Producer
Worked for major studios in the 40s, 50s, 60s; produced TV's "Batman," 1966-68; "Green Hornet," 1966-67 TV series.
b. Feb 13, 1908 in Omaha, Nebraska
d. Apr 24, 1991 in Santa Monica, California
Source: *BioIn 17; ConTFT 10; FilmgC; HalFC 84, 88; LesBEnT 92; NewYTBS 91; NewYTET; WhAm 10; WhoAm 74, 76, 78, 80, 82, 84, 86, 88, 90*

Dr. Dre
[Andre Young]
American. Rapper
Grammy, Best Rap Performance—Solo, "Let Me Ride," 1993; co-host, with Ed Lover, of "Yo! MTV Raps," 1989—.
b. c. 1965 in Compton, California
Source: *ConMus 15; EncRkSt; News 94, 94-3*

Dr. Feelgood
[Buzz Barwell; Lee Brilleaux; Phil Mitchell; Gordon Russell]
English. Music Group
British rhythm and blues revivalists, formed 1970; albums include *Fast Women and Slow Horses,* 1982.
Source: *BiDFedJ; BioIn 2; ConMuA 80A; EncRk 88; EncRkSt; HarEnR 86; IlEncRk; IntWW 77, 78, 79, 80, 81N; NewYTBS 94; PenEncP; RolSEnR 83; Who 74; WhoArt 82N; WhoHol 92; WhoRocM 82*

Dr. Hook
[Rik Elswit; William Francis; Jance Garfat; Dennis Locorriere; Rod Smarr; John Wolters]
American. Music Group
Parody rock group formed 1968; hits include "When You're in Love with a Beautiful Woman," 1979.
Source: *ConMuA 80A; DcLP 87B; EncFCWM 83; EncRk 88; EncRkSt; HarEnR 86; IlEncRk; NewCBEL; NewGrDM 80; PenEncP; RkOn 82;*

RolSEnR 83; Who 90, 92, 94; WhoRock 81; WhoRocM 82

Dr. John
[Malcolm John "Mac" Rebennack]
American. Pianist, Singer
Rock/blues albums include *I Been Hoodood,* 1984; noted for voodoo stage costumes.
b. 1941 in New Orleans, Louisiana
Source: *BioIn 13; ConMus 7; EncRk 88; HarEnR 86; IlEncRk; NewGrDA 86; RolSEnR 83; WhoRocM 82*

Drabble, Margaret
English. Author
Novels include *The Needle's Eye,* 1972; *The Middle Ground,* 1980; sister of A.S. Byatt.
b. Jun 5, 1939 in Sheffield, England
Source: *ArtclWW 2; Au&Wr 71; Benet 87, 96; BioIn 10, 11, 12, 13, 14, 15, 16, 17, 18, 20, 21; BlmGEL; BlmGWL; BlueB 76; CamGEL; CamGLE; CnDBLB 8; ConAu 13R, 18NR, 35NR; ConLC 2, 3, 5, 8, 10, 22, 53; ConNov 72, 76, 82, 86, 91, 96; ConPopW; ContDcW 89; CurBio 81; CyWA 89; DcArts; DcLB 14, 155; DcLEL 1940; EncBrWW; EncWL 2, 3; FacFETw; FemiCLE; FemiWr; GrWomW; IntAu&W 76, 77, 89, 91, 93; IntDcWB; IntvTCA 2; IntWW 74, 75, 76, 77, 78, 79, 80, 81, 82, 83, 89, 91, 93; InWom SUP; LegTOT; LngCTC; MagSWL; MajTwCW; ModBrL S1, S2; ModWoWr; NewYTBS 77; Novels; OxCEng 95; RAdv 1, 14, 13-1; RfGEnL 91; RGTwCWr; SmATA 48; TwCWr; Who 74, 82, 83, 85, 88, 90, 92, 94; WhoAm 74, 76, 78, 82, 84, 86, 88, 90, 92, 94, 95, 96, 97; WhoAmW 70, 72, 74, 75; WhoTwCL; WhoWor 78, 80, 82, 84, 87, 89, 91, 93, 95, 96, 97; WorAl; WorAlBi; WorAu 1970; WrDr 76, 80, 82, 84, 86, 88, 90, 92, 94, 96*

Drabek, Doug(las Dean)
American. Baseball Player
Pitcher, Chicago White Sox, 1983-84; NY Yankees, 1984-86; Pittsburgh Pirates, 1986-92; Houston Astros, 1992—; won NL Cy Young Award, 1990.
b. Jul 25, 1962 in Victoria, Texas
Source: *Ballpl 90; BaseEn 88; BaseReg 88; LegTOT; WhoAm 94, 95, 96, 97; WhoSSW 95*

Drachler, Norman
American. Educator
Superintendent of Detroit Public Schools, 1967-71; consultant to US Office of Education, 1967—.
b. May 20, 1912, Poland
Source: *BioIn 9; LEduc 74; WhoAm 74, 76, 78, 80, 82, 84, 86, 88, 90, 92, 94, 95, 96, 97; WhoWorJ 72, 78*

Drachmann, Holger Henrik Herholdt
Danish. Author
Works include poems, *Muted Melodies,* 1875; play, *Once Upon a Time,* 1885.
b. Oct 9, 1846 in Copenhagen, Denmark
d. Jan 14, 1908 in Hornbaek, Denmark
Source: *BbD; BiD&SB; BioIn 1, 7; CasWL; ClDMEL 47; DcEuL; EuAu; EvEuW; NewCol 75; NotNAT B; OxCThe 67, 83; PenC EUR*

Draco
Greek. Politician
Called founder of Athenian civilization; gave Athens first written code of law, 621 BC.
d. 650BC
Source: *Benet 87; DcBiPP; DicTyr; LegTOT; LinLib L, S; NewC; OxCClL, 89; OxCLaw; REn; WhDW*

Dracula
"Vlad the Impaler"
Hungarian. Prince
Alleged vampire whose life has been subject of many horror films.
b. 1431
d. 1476
Source: *BioIn 9, 10, 13, 15, 16, 17, 18, 20; DicTyr*

Draddy, Vincent de Paul
American. Designer
Chm. of David Crystal, Inc., fashion house known for mass-produced casual clothes including Izod.
Source: *NewYTBS 90; WhoAm 80; WorFshn*

Dragon, Carmen
American. Conductor
Led Hollywood Bowl Symphony; noted for popular music concerts.
b. Jul 28, 1914 in Antioch, California
d. Mar 28, 1984 in Santa Monica, California
Source: *ASCAP 66, 80; Baker 78, 84, 92; BioIn 13, 14; NewGrDA 86; NewYTBS 84; OxCPMus; RadStar; WhoMus 72*

Dragon, Daryl
[The Captain and Tennille]
American. Musician, Songwriter
1970s hits include "Love Will Keep Us Together."
b. Aug 27, 1942 in Studio City, California
Source: *Baker 92; BioIn 13, 21; BkPepl; LegTOT; WorAlBi*

Dragonette, Jessica
Indian. Opera Singer
Light classical soprano; elected Queen of Radio, 1935; starred eight years on Cities Service Concerts, 1930s.
b. Feb 14, 1910? in Calcutta, India
d. Mar 18, 1980 in New York, New York
Source: *AnObit 1980; CmpEPM; WhoAmW 77; WhoMus 72*

Drake, Alfred
[Alfred Capurro]
American. Singer, Actor, Director
Hit Broadway musicals include *Kiss Me Kate,* 1948; won Tony for *Kismet,* 1954.
b. Oct 7, 1914 in New York, New York
d. Jul 25, 1992 in New York, New York
Source: *AnObit 1992; BiE&WWA; BioIn 3, 7, 10, 18, 19; CamGWoT; CelR; CmpEPM; CnThe; CurBio 44, 92N; EncMT; FacFETw; FamA&A; FilmgC; HalFC 80, 84, 88; LegTOT; NotNAT; OxCAmT 84; OxCPMus; PenEncP; VarWW 85; WhoAm 74; WhoHol 92, A; WhoThe 72, 77, 81; WhoWor 74; WorAl*

Drake, Betsy
American. Actor
Married to Cary Grant, 1949-59; films include *Room for One More,* 1952.
b. Sep 11, 1923 in Paris, France
Source: *BioIn 9; FilmEn; FilmgC; ForYSC; HalFC 80, 84, 88; LegTOT; MotPP; WhoHol 92, A*

Drake, Edwin Laurentine
American. Oilman
Established first producing oil well in US, near Titusville, PA, Aug 27, 1859.
b. Mar 29, 1819 in Greenville, New York
d. Nov 8, 1880 in Bethlehem, Pennsylvania
Source: *AmBi; BioIn 4, 6, 7, 8; DcAmB; InSci; LinLib S; NatCAB 26; WebAB 74, 79; WhAm HS; WhDW; WorAl*

Drake, Francis, Sir
English. Naval Officer, Navigator
First Englishman to circumnavigate globe, 1577-80; helped defeat Spanish Armada, 1588.
b. 1540 in Tavistock, England
d. Jan 28, 1596 in Portobelo, Panama
Source: *Alli, SUP; ApCAB; Benet 87, 96; BioIn 1, 2, 3, 4, 5, 6, 7, 8, 9, 10, 11, 12, 13, 15, 16, 17, 18, 19, 20, 21; CmCal; DcCanB 1; DcNaB; Drake; LegTOT; LngCEL; NewC; NewCBEL; OxCAmH; OxCEng 85, 95; OxCMus; REn; REnAL; WhAm HS; WhDW; WhWE; WorAl; WorAlBi*

Drake, Frank Donald
American. Astronomer
Organized search for extra-terrestrial life, called project OZMA, 1960.
b. May 28, 1930 in Chicago, Illinois
Source: *AmMWSc 76P, 79, 82, 86, 89, 92, 95; BiESc; BioIn 6, 7, 8, 17; BlueB 76; ConAu 17R, 29NR; CurBio 63; FacFETw; IntWW 74, 75, 76, 77, 78, 79, 80, 81, 82, 83, 89, 91, 93; WhoAm 74, 76, 78, 80, 82, 84, 86, 88, 90, 92, 94, 95, 96, 97; WhoE 74, 75, 83; WhoFrS 84; WhoScEn 94, 96; WhoTech 89; WhoWest 89, 92, 94; WhoWor 74*

Drake, Joseph Rodman
American. Poet
Wrote *Croaker Papers,* 1819.

b. Aug 17, 1795 in New York, New York
d. Sep 21, 1820 in New York, New York
Source: *Alli; AmAu; AmAu&B; AmBi; ApCAB; BbD; BenetAL 91; BibAL; BiD&SB; BioIn 1, 7, 12; CamGEL; CamHAL; Chambr 3; ChhPo, S2; CnDAL; CyAL 1; DcAmAu; DcAmB; DcLEL; DcNAA; Drake; EvLB; GrWrEL P; LinLib L; NatCAB 5; OxCAmL 65, 83, 95; PenC AM; REn; REnAL; RfGAmL 87, 94; TwCBDA; WhAm HS*

Drake, Nick
English. Singer, Songwriter, Musician
Musician in the English folk movement of the late 1960s; released first album, *Five Leaves Left,* in 1969 and later *Bryter Layter,* 1971 and *Pink Moon,* 1972, all of which received critical acclaim.
b. Jun 18, 1948, Burma
d. Nov 24, 1974 in Tamworth-on-Arden, England
Source: *BioIn 11; ConMuA 80A; ConMus 17; EncRk 88; IlEncRk; OnThGG; PenEncP; RolSEnR 83*

Drake, Stan(ley Albert)
American. Cartoonist
Created comic strip "The Heart of Juliet Jones," 1953; illustrator for *Golf Digest* mag., beginning in 1969; illustrated strip "Blondie."
b. Nov 9, 1921 in New York, New York
d. Mar 10, 1997 in Norwalk, Connecticut
Source: *EncACom; WhoAm 82, 84, 92; WorECom*

Drake, Tom
[Alfred Alderdice]
American. Actor
Appeared in 1940s musicals including *Meet Me in St. Louis,* 1944.
b. Aug 5, 1918 in New York, New York
d. Aug 11, 1982 in Torrance, California
Source: *EncAFC; FilmEn; FilmgC; ForYSC; HalFC 80, 84, 88; MGM; MotPP; MovMk; WhoHol A*

Drapeau, Jean
Canadian. Politician
Mayor of Montreal, 1954-57, 1960-86.
b. Feb 18, 1916 in Montreal, Quebec, Canada
Source: *BioIn 4, 7, 8, 10, 12, 13, 15; BlueB 76; CanWW 31, 70, 79, 80, 81, 83, 89; CurBio 67; IntWW 74, 75, 76, 77, 78, 79, 80, 81, 82, 83, 89, 91, 93; WhoAm 74, 76, 78, 80, 82, 84, 86, 88; WhoCan 73; WhoE 74, 75, 77, 79, 81, 83, 85, 86; WhoWor 74, 76, 78, 80, 82, 84*

Draper, Charles Stark
American. Engineer
Founder, director, Charles Stark Draper Laboratory; invented gyroscope, which stabilized gunsights.
b. Oct 2, 1901 in Windsor, Missouri
d. Jul 25, 1987 in Cambridge, Massachusetts
Source: *AmMWSc 86; BioIn 3, 4, 5, 6, 7, 8, 12, 15, 20; CurBio 65, 87, 87N; FacFETw; InSci; IntWW 74, 75, 76, 77, 78, 79, 80, 81, 82, 83; LElec; McGMS 80; NewYTBS 87; NotTwCS; WhAm 9; WhoAm 74; WhoE 74, 75; WhoWor 74, 76, 78; WorInv*

Draper, Dorothy Tuckerman
American. Interior Decorator
Foremost woman decorator of her time; wrote syndicated column, 1959-67, three bo oks on decorating including, *Decorating Is Fun,* 1939.
b. Nov 22, 1889 in New York, New York
d. Mar 10, 1969 in Cleveland, Ohio
Source: *CurBio 41, 69; InWom; WhAm 5*

Draper, John William
American. Philosopher, Historian
Developed photo-chemistry; made first photograph of moon, 1840.
b. May 5, 1811 in Liverpool, England
d. Jan 4, 1882 in Hastings-on-Hudson, New York
Source: *Alli, SUP; AmAu; AmAu&B; AmBi; ApCAB; AsBiEn; BbD; BiDAmEd; BiDAmS; BiD&SB; BiESc; BiInAmS; BioIn 2, 6, 9, 11, 13; CamDcSc; CelCen; Chambr 3; CyAL 2; CyEd; DcAmAu; DcAmB; DcAmMeB; DcAmReB 2; DcBiPP; DcEnL; DcInv; DcNAA; DcNaB; DcScB; Drake; EvLB; HarEnUS; ICPEnP; InSci; LinLib L, S; McGEWB; NatCAB 3; NewCol 75; OxCAmH; REn; REnAL; TwCBDA; WebAB 74, 79; WhAm HS; WhDW*

Draper, Paul (Nathaniel Saltonstall)
Italian. Dancer
Appeared at Radio City Music Hall, 1940-48; films include *The Time of Your Life,* 1948.
b. Oct 25, 1909 in Florence, Italy
d. Sep 20, 1996 in Woodstock, New York
Source: *BiDD; BiE&WWA; BioIn 17; CnOxB; CurBio 44; DancEn 78; NotNAT; TwCPaSc; Who 92; WhoHol 92, A*

Draper, Ruth
American. Actor
Wrote, performed dramatic monologues, such as *Opening a Bazaar, Three Generations.*
b. Dec 2, 1884 in New York, New York
d. Dec 30, 1956 in New York, New York
Source: *BenetAL 91; BioAmW; BioIn 1, 3, 4, 5, 6, 12, 14, 15, 16; CamGWoT; ContDcW 89; DcAmB S6; EncWT; Ent; FunnyW; InWom, SUP; LibW; NatCAB 45; NotAW MOD; NotNAT A, B; NotWoAT; ObitOF 79; ObitT 1951; OxCAmH; OxCAmT 84; OxCEng 85, 95; OxCThe 67, 83; REnAL; WhAm 3; WhoCom*

Dravecky, Dave
[David Francis Dravecky]
American. Baseball Player
NL pitcher with Padres, 1982-87; Giants, 1987-89; retired due to cancer in pitching arm resulting in amputation; wrote *Comeback,* 1990.
b. Feb 14, 1956 in Youngstown, Ohio
Source: *Ballpl 90; BioIn 16; LegTOT; News 92, 92-1; NewYTBS 89*

Drayton, Michael
English. Author, Poet
Prolific writer of historical, religious verse.
b. 1563 in Warwickshire, England
d. Dec 23, 1631 in London, England
Source: *Alli; AntBDN I; AtlBL; BbD; Benet 87, 96; BiD&SB; BiDRP&D; BioIn 3, 5, 7, 8, 10, 11, 12, 19; BlmGEL; BritAu; CamGEL; CamGLE; CasWL; Chambr 1; ChhPo, S1, S3; CnE&AP; CroE&S; CrtT 1, 4; CyWA 58; DcArts; DcBiPP; DcEnA; DcEnL; DcEuL; DcLB 121; DcLEL; DcNaB; EvLB; GrWrEL P; LinLib L; LitC 8; LngCEL; McGEWB; McGEWD 72, 84; MouLC 1; NewC; NewCBEL; OxCEng 67, 85, 95; OxCLiW 86; PenC ENG; PlP&P; RAdv 14; REn; RfGEnL 91; WebE&AL; WhDW*

Drees, Willem
Dutch. Political Leader
Country's longest-serving prime minister, 1948-58; introduced comprehensive welfare system; ended colonial role in Indonesia, 1949.
b. Jul 5, 1886 in Amsterdam, Netherlands
d. May 14, 1988 in The Hague, Netherlands
Source: *AnObit 1988; BioIn 1, 2, 15, 16, 21; CurBio 49, 88, 88N; EncTR 91; FacFETw; IntWW 74, 75, 76, 77, 78, 79, 80, 81, 82, 83; IntYB 78, 79, 80, 81, 82; NewYTBS 88; PolLCWE; WhAm 7; WhoWor 74, 78*

Dreifus, Claudia
American. Journalist
Writings on women's issues include *Radical Lifestyles,* 1971.
b. Nov 24, 1944
Source: *BioIn 10; ConAu 1NR, 45; ForWC 70; MugS; WhoAmW 75, 77*

Dreiser, Theodore
American. Editor, Author
Wrote *Sister Carrie,* 1900, *An American Tragedy,* 1925; books attacked as immoral.
b. Aug 27, 1871 in Terre Haute, Indiana
d. Dec 28, 1945 in Hollywood, California
Source: *AmAu&B; AmDec 1900; AmLY; AmWr; ApCAB X; AtlBL; Benet 87; BenetAL 91; BiDAmJo; BioIn 1, 2, 3, 4, 5, 6, 7, 8, 9, 10, 11, 12, 13, 14, 15, 16, 17, 19, 20, 21; CamGEL; CamGLE; CamHAL; CasWL; Chambr 3; CnDAL; CnMD; CnMWL; ConAmA; ConAmL; ConAu 106, 132; CyWA 58; DcAmAu;*

DcAmB S3; DcAmImH; DcAmSR; DcBiA; DcLB 9, 12, 102, 137, DS1; DcLEL; DcNAA; EncAB-H 1974, 1996; EncMys; EncUnb; EncWL, 2, 3; EvLB; FacFETw; FilmgC; GayN; GrWrEL N; HalFC 80, 84, 88; IndAu 1816; JrnUS; LegTOT; LiJour; LinLib L, S; LngCTC; MagSAmL; MajTwCW; MemAm; ModAL, S1, S2; ModWD; NatCAB 15, 18, 34; NotNAT B; Novels; OxCAmH; OxCAmL 65, 83; OxCEng 67; PenC AM; RAdv 1, 14, 13-1; RComAH; RComWL; RealN; REn; REnAL; RfGAmL 87; TwCA, SUP; TwCLC 10, 18, 35; TwCWr; WebAB 74, 79; WebE&AL; WhAm 2; WhDW; WhE&EA; WhLit; WhNAA; WhoTwCL; WhThe; WorAlBi; WorLitC; WrPh

Drescher, Fran
American. Actor
Star and co-producer of TV's "The Nanny," 1994—.
b. c. Sep 30, 1957 in New York, New York
Source: *News 95, 95-3; WhoAmW 97; WhoHol 92*

Dressen, Chuck
[Charles Walter Dressen]
American. Baseball Manager
Third baseman, 1925-31; managed for 16 yrs. with several ML clubs; won two pennants with Brooklyn, 1952-53.
b. Sep 20, 1898 in Decatur, Illinois
d. Aug 10, 1966 in Detroit, Michigan
Source: *Ballpl 90; BiDAmSp Sup; BioIn 1, 2, 3, 4, 5, 6, 7, 13, 14; CurBio 51, 66; DcAmB S8; WhAm 4; WhoFtbl 74; WhoProB 73*

Dresser, Davis
[Brett Halliday]
American. Author
Mystery novels include *Framed in Blood,* 1951; *Violence Is Golden,* 1968.
b. Jul 31, 1904 in Chicago, Illinois
d. Feb 4, 1977 in Montecito, California
Source: *AmAu&B; BioIn 6, 10, 11, 14; ConAu 49NR, 69, 77; CorpD; CrtSuMy; CurBio 69, 77; EncMys; LegTOT; TwCCr&M 80, 85, 91; TwCWW 82, 91; WorAu 1950*

Dresser, Louise
[Louise Kerlin]
American. Actor
Starred with Rudolph Valentino in *The Eagle,* 1925; as Al Jolson's mother in *Mammy,* 1930.
b. Oct 5, 1882 in Evansville, Indiana
d. Apr 24, 1965 in Woodland Hills, California
Source: *BioIn 7; FilmgC; InWom; MotPP; MovMk; OxCAmT 84; ThFT; TwYS; WhAm 4, 7; WhoHol B; WhScrn 74, 77; WhThe*

Dressler, Marie
[Leila Marie Koerber]
Canadian. Actor
Won Oscar for *Min and Bill,* 1930, with Wallace Beery.
b. Nov 9, 1869 in Cobourg, Ontario, Canada
d. Jul 28, 1934 in Santa Barbara, California
Source: *BiDFilm, 81, 94; BioIn 2, 3, 6, 7, 9, 10, 11, 15, 16; CamGWoT; CmpEPM; DcAmB S1; EncAFC; EncMT; EncVaud; Film 1, 2; FilmEn; FilmgC; FunnyW; Funs; HalFC 80, 84, 88; IntDcF 1-3, 2-3; InWom; JoeFr; LegTOT; LibW; MGM; MotPP; MovMk; NatCAB 27; NotAW; NotNAT B; NotWoAT; OxCAmT 84; OxCFilm; OxCPMus; OxCThe 67; QDrFCA 92; TwYS; WebAB 74, 79; WhAm 1; WhoCom; WhScrn 74, 77, 83; WhThe; WorAl; WorAlBi; WorEFlm*

Drew, Charles Richard
American. Scientist
Pioneered development of blood banks, 1941; headed blood donor drive, WW II; won 1944 Spingarn Medal.
b. Jun 3, 1904 in Washington, District of Columbia
d. Apr 1, 1950 in Washington, District of Columbia
Source: *AfrAmAl 6; BioIn 1, 2, 3, 4, 5, 6, 7, 8, 9, 10, 11, 13, 16, 17, 18, 19, 20, 21; BlksScM; ConBlB 7; CurBio 44, 50; DcAmB S4; DcAmMeB 84; DcAmNB; EncAACR; EncAB-H 1974, 1996; InB&W 80, 85; InSci; McGEWB; WebAB 74, 79; WhAm 3; WorAl; WorAlBi; WorInv*

Drew, Daniel
American. Financier
Initiated term "robber baron" when he took over Erie Railroad; later went bankrupt, 1876; contributed to Drew U.
b. Jul 29, 1797 in Carmel, New York
d. Sep 18, 1879 in New York, New York
Source: *AmBi; BiDAmBL 83; BioIn 1, 3, 4, 5, 7, 10, 12, 15, 21; DcAmB; DcAmSR; EncABHB 2, 6; EncWM; McGEWB; NatCAB 11; OxCAmH; TwCBDA; WebAB 74, 79; WebBD 83; WhAm HS*

Drew, Elizabeth Brenner
American. Journalist
Washington correspondent for *New Yorker* mag., 1973-92; commentator, "Mo nitor Radio," 1992—.
b. Nov 16, 1935 in Cincinnati, Ohio
Source: *AmWomWr; BioIn 7, 9, 11, 12; ConAu 104; CurBio 79; EncTwCJ; ForWC 70; InWom SUP; WhoAm 86, 90; WhoAmW 75, 77, 87, 91; WhoSSW 75; WorAu 1980*

Drew, John
American. Actor
Appeared in Charles Frohman's Co. with Maude Adams in *The Masked Ball; The Rivals,* 1892-97; uncle of John, Lionel Barrymore.
b. Nov 13, 1853 in Philadelphia, Pennsylvania
d. Jul 9, 1927 in San Francisco, California
Source: *AmAu&B; AmBi; ApCAB X; BioIn 3, 5, 10; CamGWoT; CnThe; DcAmB; DcNAA; EncWT; Ent; FamA&A; Film 1; IntDcT 3; LinLib L, S; NotNAT A, B; OxCAmH; OxCAmT 84; OxCThe 67, 83; PlP&P; TwCBDA; WebAB 74, 79; WhAm 1; WhoStg 1906, 1908; WhThe*

Drew, Louisa Lane
[Mrs. John Drew]
English. Actor
Managed Philadelphia's Arch Street Theatre, 1860-92.
b. Jan 10, 1820 in London, England
d. Aug 31, 1897 in Larchmont, New York
Source: *AmBi; AmWom; ApCAB; BioIn 16; CamGWoT; DcAmB; EncWT; Ent; IntDcT 3; InWom, SUP; LibW; NatCAB 8; NotAW; NotNAT A, B; NotWoAT; OxCAmH; OxCAmT 84; OxCThe 67, 83; PlP&P; TwCBDA; WhAm HS*

Drew, Richard G
American. Engineer
Invented transparent tape, 1930.
b. 1899 in Minnesota
d. Dec 7, 1980 in Santa Barbara, California
Source: *BioIn 1, 12; NewYTBS 80*

Drewry, Guy Carleton
American. Poet
Poet Laureate, Virginia, 1970-91; wrote *A Time for Turning,* 1952.
b. May 21, 1901 in Stevensburg, Virginia
d. Aug 3, 1991
Source: *Au&Wr 71; ConAu 5R, 135; ConLC 70; WhAm 10; WhoAm 74, 76, 78, 80, 82, 84; WhoSSW 73, 75, 76, 78; WhoUSWr 88; WhoWor 74, 76, 78, 80, 82, 84, 87; WhoWrEP 89, 92, 95*

Drewry, John Eldridge
American. Author, Educator
Writings include *Concerning the Fourth Estate,* 1938; *Key to So Much,* 1957.
b. Jun 4, 1902 in Griffin, Georgia
d. Feb 11, 1983
Source: *AmAu&B; BlueB 76; DrAS 74E; IntAu&W 76, 77; WhAm 8; WhJnl; WhNAA; WhoAm 74, 76, 78, 80, 82; WhoWor 76, 78, 80, 82; WrDr 76, 80*

Drexel, Anthony Joseph
American. Banker, Philanthropist
Inherited brokerage firm, Drexel & Co., 1847; son of Francis.
b. Sep 13, 1826 in Philadelphia, Pennsylvania
d. Jun 30, 1893 in Carlsbad, Bohemia
Source: *AmBi; ApCAB; BiDAmBL 83; BioIn 2; DcAmB; EncABHB 6; NatCAB 2; OxCAmH; TwCBDA; WhAm HS*

Drexel, Francis Martin
American. Banker
Founded banking firm, Drexel & Co., 1830s; traveled, painted before becoming broker.
b. Apr 7, 1792 in Dornbirn, Austria
d. Jun 5, 1863 in Philadelphia, Pennsylvania
Source: *ApCAB; DcAmB; NewYHSD; WhAm HS*

Drexel, Mary Katherine
American. Religious Leader
Founder, Catholic Order for Indians and Blacks, 1891.
b. Nov 26, 1858 in Philadelphia, Pennsylvania
d. Mar 3, 1955 in Cornwells Heights, Pennsylvania
Source: *NotAW MOD*

Drexler, Clyde
"The Glide"
American. Basketball Player
Guard for Portland Trailblazers, 1983-94; Houston Rockets, 1994—; member of 1992 US Olympic basketball team.
b. Jun 22, 1962 in New Orleans, Louisiana
Source: *AfrAmSG; BasBi; BioIn 14, 20, 21; ConBlB 4; CurBio 96; LegTOT; News 92; WhoAfA 96; WhoAm 88, 92, 94, 95, 96, 97; WhoBlA 85, 88, 90, 92, 94; WhoSpor; WhoWest 89, 92, 94*

Drexler, Millard S
American. Business Executive
Pres., Gap, Inc., 1983—; currently pres., CEO, Anne Taylor Co.
b. Aug 17, 1944 in New York, New York
Source: *Dun&B 90; News 90-3; WhoAm 90; WhoWest 92*

Drexler, Rosalyn
American. Author
Won 1979 Obie for *The Writer's Opera,* 1974 Emmy for *The Lily Show.*
b. Nov 25, 1926 in New York, New York
Source: *AmAu&B; AmWomD; AmWomWr SUP; BiDWomA; BioIn 6, 9, 10, 15, 16; CamGWoT; ConAmD; ConAu 81; ConDr 73, 77, 82, 88, 93; ConLC 2, 6; ConWomD; DcLP 87A; DrAF 76; DrAPF 91; FemiCLE; IntAu&W 91, 93; InWom SUP; ModAL S1; ModWoWr; NewYTBE 71; NorAmWA; NotNAT; NotWoAT; PenNWW A; WhoAm 76, 78, 80, 82; WorAu 1970; WrDr 76, 80, 82, 84, 86, 88, 90, 92, 94, 96*

Dreyer, Carl Theodore
Danish. Director
Best known for *Day of Wrath; Passion of Joan of Arc; The Word.*
b. Feb 3, 1889 in Copenhagen, Denmark
d. Mar 28, 1968 in Copenhagen, Denmark
Source: *BiDFilm; DcFM; FilmgC; MovMk; ObitOF 79; OxCFilm; WorEFlm*

Dreyer, Johan Ludwig Emil
Danish. Astronomer
Compiled classic *New General Catalogue of Nebulae and Clusters of Stars,* 1888, 1895, 1908.
b. Feb 13, 1852 in Copenhagen, Denmark
d. Sep 14, 1926 in Oxford, England
Source: *NewCol 75; WebBD 83*

Dreyfus, Alfred
French. Army Officer
Wrongly convicted of high treason, 1895, vindicated in 1906; defended by Emile Zola in *J'Accuse,* 1898.
b. Oct 9, 1859 in Mulhouse, France
d. Jul 12, 1935, France
Source: *Benet 87, 96; BiDFrPL; BioIn 1, 4, 5, 6, 7, 8, 9, 10, 12, 14, 16, 17, 20; Dis&D; FilmgC; HalFC 80, 84, 88; HarEnMi; JeHun; LegTOT; LinLib L, S; McGEWB; NewC; OxCEng 85, 95; OxCFilm; REn; WhDW; WhoMilH 76; WorAl; WorAlBi*

Dreyfus, Hubert L(ederer)
American. Author
Philosophy writings include *Sense and Nonsense,* 1964.
b. Oct 15, 1929 in Terre Haute, Indiana
Source: *ConAu 28NR; DrAS 74P, 78P, 82P; IndAu 1917*

Dreyfus, Jack Jonas
American. Financier, Author
Founder, noted investment firm; wrote controversial health book promoting dilantin.
b. 1913 in Alabama
Source: *BioIn 6, 7, 8, 9, 12, 13*

Dreyfus, Pierre
French. Government Official
President of Regie Nationale des Usines Renault, 1955-75.
b. Nov 18, 1907
d. Dec 25, 1994 in Paris, France
Source: *BioIn 4, 5, 6, 13, 17, 20, 21; CurBio 95N; IntWW 74, 75, 76, 77, 78, 79, 80, 81, 82, 83, 89, 91, 93; IntYB 82; Who 74, 82, 83, 85, 88, 90, 92, 94; WhoFr 79; WhoWor 74, 78; WorAl; WorAlBi*

Dreyfuss, Henry
American. Designer
Pioneer in industrial design who believed form followed function; designed ocean liners, farm equipment.
b. Mar 2, 1904 in New York, New York
d. Oct 5, 1972 in Pasadena, California
Source: *BioIn 1, 2, 5, 9, 10, 14; ConAu 37R, 45; ConDes 84, 90, 97; CurBio 48, 59, 72N; DcArts; DcTwDes; EncAB-A 25; FacFETw; McGDA; OxCAmT 84; WhAm 5; WhAmArt 85; WhoAdv 72; WhoWorJ 72, 78; WhThe*

Dreyfuss, Richard (Stephan)
American. Actor
Starred in films *American Graffiti,* 1973, *Jaws,* 1975, *Moon over Parador,* 1988, *Mr. Holland's Opus,* 1995; won oscar for *The Goodbye Girl,* 1977.
b. Oct 29, 1947 in New York, New York
Source: *BiDFilm 94; BioIn 10, 11, 12, 15, 16, 17, 19, 21; BkPepl; CelR 90; ConTFT 1, 5, 12; CurBio 76; EncAFC; HalFC 88; HolBB; IntDcF 1-3, 2-3; IntMPA 86, 88, 92, 94, 96; IntWW 89, 91, 93; LegTOT; News 96, 96-3; NewYTBS 74; VarWW 85; WhoAm 78, 80, 82, 84, 86, 88, 90, 92, 94, 95, 96, 97; WhoEnt 92; WhoHol 92, A; WorAlBi*

Driesch, Hans Adolf Eduard
German. Biologist, Philosopher
Embryology pioneer; noted for philosophy of vitalism.
b. Oct 28, 1867 in Bad Kreuznach, Prussia
d. Apr 17, 1941 in Leipzig, Germany
Source: *BiDPara; BiDPsy; BiESc; BioIn 12; CurBio 41; DcScB; EncO&P 1; EncPaPR 91; FacFETw; InSci; LarDcSc; LuthC 75; McGEWB; NamesHP; NewCol 75*

Drifters, The
[Clyde McPhatter; Billy Pickney; Andrew Thrasher; Gerhart Thrasher]
American. Music Group
Hits included "Save the Last Dance for Me," 1960; "Under the Boardwalk," 1964; Hall of Fame, 1988.
Source: *AmPS A, B; BiDAmM; ConMuA 80A; DcTwCCu 5; EncPR&S 74, 89; EncRk 88; EncRkSt; HarEnR 86; IlEncRk; InB&W 80; NewAmDM; NewGrDA 86; OxCPMus; PenEncP; RkOn 74, 85; RolSEnR 83; SoulM; WhoRock 81; WhoRocM 82*

Drillon, Gordie
[Gordon Drillon]
Canadian. Hockey Player
Left wing, 1936-43, mostly with Toronto; won Art Ross Trophy, Lady Byng Trophy, 1938; Hall of Fame, 1975.
b. Oct 23, 1914 in Moncton, New Brunswick, Canada
Source: *HocEn; WhoHcky 73; WhoSpor*

Drinker, Philip
American. Educator, Engineer
Invented iron lung, 1929.
b. Dec 12, 1894 in Haverford, Pennsylvania
d. Oct 19, 1972 in Fitzwilliam, New Hampshire
Source: *AmMWSc 82; BioIn 6, 7, 8, 9, 11; InSci; NatCAB 57; WhAm 5*

Drinkwater, Charles Graham
Canadian. Hockey Player
Defenseman-forward for amateur Montreal Victorias, 1893, 1895-99; Hall of Fame, 1950.
b. 1873 in Montreal, Quebec, Canada
Source: *WhoHcky 73*

Drinkwater, John
English. Poet, Author, Biographer
Used historical figures for basis of plays: *Robert E. Lee,* 1923.
b. Jun 1, 1882 in Leytonstone, England
d. Mar 25, 1937 in Kilburn, England
Source: *Alli; Benet 87; BiDLA; BioIn 1, 2, 7, 9, 13, 21; CamGLE; CamGWoT; CasWL; Chambr 3; ChhPo, S1, S2, S3; CnMD; CnThe; ConAu 109, 149; CrtSuDr; DcArts; DcLB 10, 19, 149; DcLEL; DcNaB 1931; EncWT; Ent; EvLB; FacFETw; GrWrEL DR; JBA 34; LinLib L, S; LngCTC; McGEWD 72, 84; ModBrL; ModWD; NewC; NewCBEL; NotNAT A, B; OxCEng 67, 85, 95; OxCThe 67, 83; OxCTwCP; PenC ENG; PlP&P; REn; RfGEnL 91; RGTwCWr; Str&VC; TwCA, SUP; TwCLC 57; WebE&AL; WhE&EA; WhLit; WhoLA; WhThe*

Drinkwater, Terry
American. Broadcaster
CBS News correspondent since 1964; covered several presidential campaigns, manned space programs.
b. May 9, 1936 in Denver, Colorado
d. May 31, 1989 in Malibu, California
Source: *BioIn 16; ConAu 69, 128; LesBEnT; NewYTBS 89*

Driscoll, Bobby
American. Actor
Won special Oscar as outstanding juvenile actor, 1949; career faltered in teens; allegedly died from drug overdose.
b. Mar 3, 1937 in Cedar Rapids, Iowa
d. Mar 30, 1968 in New York, New York
Source: *BioIn 9; FilmEn; FilmgC; ForYSC; HalFC 80, 84, 88; HolP 40; LegTOT; WhoHol B; WhScrn 74, 77, 83*

Driscoll, Paddy
[John L Driscoll]
American. Football Player
Running back, 1920-29, mostly with Chicago; known for dropkickng field goals; Hall of Fame, 1965.
b. Jan 11, 1896 in Evanston, Illinois
d. Jun 29, 1968 in Chicago, Illinois
Source: *BioIn 17; LegTOT; WhoFtbl 74; WhoSpor*

Driskell, David C(lyde)
American. Artist, Educator
Professor of art, University of Maryland, 1977—; has been one of the primary people responsible for bringing African American art into the mainstream of American Society.
b. Jun 7, 1931 in Eatonton, Georgia
Source: *AfrAmAl 6; AfroAA; ConAu 102; InB&W 85; WhoAm 74, 76; WhoAmA 73, 76, 78, 80, 82, 84, 86, 89, 91, 93; WhoSSW 73*

Driver, David E.
American. Publishing Executive
Founder and president, The Noble Press, 1988—.
b. Oct 17, 1955 in Chicago, Illinois
Source: *ConBlB 11; WhoAfA 96*

Dropo, Walt(er)
"Moose"
American. Baseball Player
First baseman, 1949-61; led AL in RBIs, 1950; tied ML record for consecutive hits, 12, 1952.
b. Jan 30, 1923 in Moosup, Connecticut
Source: *Ballpl 90; BioIn 1, 2, 3, 4, 5, 18, 19; WhoProB 73*

Dru, Joanne
[Letitia LaCock]
American. Actor
Starred in Westerns *Red River,* 1948; *She Wore a Yellow Ribbon,* 1949; sister of Peter Marshall.
b. Jan 31, 1923 in Logan, West Virginia
d. Sep 10, 1996 in Los Angeles, California
Source: *BiDFilm, 81, 94; BioIn 18; CmMov; FilmEn; FilmgC; ForYSC; GangFlm; HalFC 80, 84, 88; IntMPA 75, 76, 77, 78, 79, 80, 81, 82, 84, 86, 88, 92, 94, 96; InWom, SUP; ItaFilm; LegTOT; MotPP; SweetSg D; WhoHol 92, A; WorAl; WorEFlm*

Drucker, Peter Ferdinand
American. Writer, Educator
Professor of philosophy, politics, 1942-49; chm. in mgt. area, NY U, 1957-62; writings include *The Frontiers of Management,* 1986.
b. Nov 19, 1909 in Vienna, Austria
Source: *AmAu&B; AmMWSc 73P; Au&Wr 71; BioIn 13, 14, 15, 21; ConAu 61; CurBio 64; IntWW 83, 91; NewYTBS 74; PolProf E; Who 85, 92; WhoAm 86, 90, 97; WhoWest 92; WhoWor 87, 91, 97; WorAlBi; WorAu 1970; WrDr 92*

Druckman, Jacob (Raphael)
American. Composer
Electronic composer known for ballet scores; won Pulitzer for orchestral work *Windows,* 1972.
b. Jun 26, 1928 in Philadelphia, Pennsylvania
d. May 24, 1996 in New Haven, Connecticut
Source: *AmComp; ASCAP 80; Baker 78, 84, 92; BioIn 9, 12, 14, 21; BriBkM 80; CompSN SUP; ConAmC 76, 82; ConCom 92; CpmDNM 80, 82; CurBio 81, 96N; DcCM; IntWWM 90; NewAmDM; NewGrDA 86; NewGrDM 80; NewYTBS 27; PenDiMP A; WhAm 11; WhoAm 74, 76, 78, 80, 82, 84, 86, 88, 90, 92, 94, 95, 96; WhoAmM 83; WhoEnt 92*

Drum, Hugh A
American. Military Leader
Lt. general during WW I, II.
b. Sep 19, 1879 in Fort Brady, Michigan
d. Oct 3, 1951
Source: *CurBio 41, 51; DcAmB S5; ObitOF 79; WhAm 3*

Drummond, Roscoe
[James Roscoe Drummond]
American. Journalist
Wrote newspaper column "State of the Nation" for 25 yrs.
b. Jan 13, 1902 in Theresa, New York
d. Sep 30, 1983 in Princeton, New Jersey
Source: *BiDAmJo; BiDAmNC; BioIn 2, 3, 13, 16; ConAu 104, 110; CurBio 83N; EncTwCJ; IntAu&W 77; IntWW 80, 82, 83; NewYTBS 83; WhAm 8; WhoAm 80, 82; WhoSSW 73; WhoWor 74*

Drummond, William Henry
Canadian. Poet, Physician
Wrote poems about French Canadians using their dialects: *The Voyageur,* 1905.
b. Apr 13, 1854 in Mohill, Ireland
d. Apr 6, 1907 in Cobalt, Ontario, Canada
Source: *BenetAL 91; BioIn 1, 7, 17; CamGEL; CamGLE; CanWr; CasWL; ChhPo, S1, S2, S3; CreCan 1; DcAmMeB; DcCanB 13; DcIrL 96; DcLB 92; DcLEL; DcNAA; DcNaB S2; EvLB; LinLib L, S; MacDCB 78; NewC; OxCCan; OxCCanL; OxCEng 67; PoIre; REnAL; TwCA, SUP; TwCLC 25*

Drummond de Andrade, Carlos
Brazilian. Poet, Author
Influential leader of Brazil's modernist movement in literature.
b. Oct 31, 1902 in Itabira, Brazil
d. Aug 17, 1987 in Rio de Janeiro, Brazil
Source: *BioIn 11, 12, 13, 16; CasWL; ConAu 123, 132; ConLC 18; DcArts; EncWL 2; FacFETw; IntWW 83; LatAmWr; WorAu 1970*

Drummond of Hawthornden, William
Scottish. Poet
Collections of Elizabethan verse include *Forth Feasting,* 1617; wrote *History of Scotland,* published in 1655.
b. Dec 13, 1585 in Hawthornden, Scotland
d. Dec 4, 1649 in Hawthornden, Scotland
Source: *Benet 87, 96; BritAu; CamGEL; CamGLE; CasWL; DcLB 121; DcLEL; NewC; NewCol 75; OxCEng 67, 85, 95; REn; WebBD 83; WhDW*

Drury, Allen Stuart
American. Author
Background as Washington journalist was source for his Pulitzer-winning novel, *Advise and Consent,* 1960.
b. Sep 2, 1918 in Houston, Texas
Source: *AmAu&B; Benet 87; BenetAL 91; CelR 90; ConAu 18NR, 57; ConNov 76, 91; FacFETw; HalFC 88; IntAu&W 91; IntWW 91; OxCAmL 65; REnAL; ScFSB; TwCWr; Who 92; WhoAm 80, 82, 90; WhoUSWr 88; WhoWrEP 89; WorAl; WorAu 1950; WrDr 82, 92*

Drury, James
American. Actor
Title star of TV's "The Virginian," 1962-71.
b. Apr 18, 1934 in New York, New York
Source: *BioIn 17; FilmgC; HalFC 80, 84, 88; IntMPA 77, 81, 82, 86, 88, 92, 94, 96; MotPP; WhoHol 92, A*

Druzhinin, Nicolai Mikhailovich
Russian. Historian
Celebrated specialist on 19th-c. Russia, Bolshevik Revolution; authored over 50 works.
b. Jan 13, 1886 in Kursku, Russia
d. Aug 8, 1986
Source: *IntWW 74, 75, 79; WhoSocC 78; WhoWor 74*

Dryden, John
English. Poet, Dramatist
Poet laureate, 1668-89; best-known play *Marriage a la Mode,* 1672.
b. Aug 9, 1631 in Northamptonshire, England
d. May 1, 1700 in London, England
Source: *Alli; AtlBL; BbD; Benet 87, 96; BiD&SB; BioIn 1, 2, 3, 4, 5, 6, 7, 8, 9, 10, 11, 12, 13, 15, 17, 18, 19; BlmGEL; BritAu; BritWr 2; CamGEL; CamGLE; CamGWoT; CasWL; Chambr 1; ChhPo, S1; CnDBLB 2; CnE&AP; CnThe; CrtSuDr; CrtT 2, 4; CyWA 58; DcArts; DcBiPP; DcCathB; DcEnA; DcEnL; DcEuL; DcLB 80, 101, 131; DcLEL; DcNaB, C; DcPup; Dis&D; DramC 3; EncEnl; EncWT; Ent; EvLB; GrWrEL DR, P; HisDStE; IntDcT 2; LegTOT; LinLib L, S; LitC 3, 21; LngCEL; LuthC 75; MagSWL; McGEWB; McGEWD 72, 84; MouLC 1; NewC; NewCBEL; NewEOp 71; NewGrDM 80; NewGrDO; NotNAT A, B; OxCEng 67, 85, 95; OxCMus; OxCThe 67; OxDcOp; PenC ENG; PlP&P; PoChrch; PoLE; RAdv 1, 14, 13-1, 13-2; RComWL; REn; REnWD; RfGEnL 91; RGFBP; WebE&AL; WhDW; WorLitC; WrPh*

Dryden, John Fairfield
American. Businessman, Politician
Founder of Prudential Insurance Company of America; US Senator, NJ, 1902-07.
b. Aug 7, 1939 in Temple Mills, Maine
d. Nov 24, 1911 in Newark, New Jersey
Source: *BiDrAC; BiDrUSC 89; BioIn 7, 16; DcAmB; NatCAB 9; WhAm 1; WhAmP*

Dryden, Ken(neth Wayne)
Canadian. Hockey Player
Goalie, Montreal, 1970-79; won Calder Trophy, 1972, Vezina Trophy five times; Hall of Fame, 1983.
b. Aug 8, 1947 in Islington, Ontario, Canada
Source: *BioIn 9, 10, 11, 12, 14; ConAu 105; HocEn; NewYTBE 71; NewYTBS 84; WhoE 74, 75; WhoHcky 73*

Dryden, Spencer
[Jefferson Airplane]
American. Singer, Musician
Drummer with Jefferson Airplane, 1965-71.
b. Apr 7, 1943 in New York, New York
Source: *LegTOT*

Dryer, Fred
[John Frederick Dryer]
American. Football Player, Actor
Defensive end, NY Giants, 1969-71, LA Rams, 1972-80; plays title role in TV series, "Hunter," 1984—1991.
b. Jul 6, 1946 in Hawthorne, California
Source: *BioIn 14, 16, 17; ConTFT 7; FootReg 81; LegTOT; WhoHol 92; WorAlBi*

Dryfoos, Orvil Eugene
American. Newspaper Publisher
Publisher, *NY Times,* 1961-63; pres., 1957-63.
b. Nov 8, 1912 in New York, New York
d. May 25, 1963 in New York, New York
Source: *BiDAmJo; BioIn 5, 6, 7, 11, 16; CurBio 62, 63; NatCAB 48; ObitOF 79; WhAm 4*

Drysdale, Don(ald Scott)
"Big D"; "Double D"
American. Baseball Player, Sportscaster
Pitcher, Brooklyn, LA Dodgers, 1956-69; set ML record for consecutive scoreless innings pitched (58), 1968, broken by Orel Hershiser, 1988.
b. Jul 23, 1936 in Van Nuys, California
d. Jul 3, 1993 in Montreal, Quebec, Canada
Source: *Ballpl 90; BiDAmSp BB; BioIn 5, 6, 7, 8, 9, 10, 15, 16, 19, 20; CmCal; CurBio 65, 93N; LegTOT; News 94, 94-1; WhAm 11; WhoAm 80, 82, 84, 86, 88, 90, 92; WhoProB 73; WorAl; WorAlBi*

Duane, William
American. Physicist, Educator
Best known for X-ray research.
b. Feb 17, 1872 in Philadelphia, Pennsylvania
d. Mar 7, 1935 in Devon, Pennsylvania
Source: *AmBi; DcAmB S1; DcScB; InSci; WhAm 1; WhNAA*

Duarte (Fuentes), Jose Napoleon
Salvadoran. Political Leader
Christian Democrat president of El Salvador, 1981-82, 1984-89; struggled to bring democracy to country.
b. Nov 23, 1926 in San Salvador, El Salvador
d. Feb 23, 1990 in San Salvador, El Salvador
Source: *BiDLAmC; BioIn 12, 13, 14, 15, 16; ConAu 131; CurBio 81, 90, 90N; DcCPCAm; DcHiB; EncWB; FacFETw; IntWW 83, 89; LegTOT; News 90-3; NewYTBS 84, 88, 90; OxCTwCA; WhoWor 87; WorAlBi*

Du Barry, Marie Jeanne Gomard de Vaubernier, Comtesse
[Madame Du Barry]
French. Mistress
Royal mistress to Louis XV, 1769-74; nursed him until his death; appeared before Revolutionary Tribunal, guillotined.
b. Aug 19, 1746 in Vaucouleurs, France
d. Dec 7, 1793 in Paris, France
Source: *DcBiPP; Dis&D; IntDcWB; NewC; OxCFr*

DuBay, William Bryan
American. Artist, Editor
Editor, *Warren Comics,* 1972-76; created characters Creepy, Errie, Rook.
b. 1948 in San Francisco, California
Source: *FanAl*

Dubcek, Alexander
Czech. Political Leader
First secretary of Communist Party, 1968-69; Soviets crushed his attempts at liberalization, 1968; stripped of power, 1969.
b. Nov 27, 1921 in Uhrovec, Czechoslovakia
d. Nov 7, 1992 in Prague, Czechoslovakia
Source: *AnObit 1992; BiDMarx; BioIn 8, 9, 11, 16; ColdWar 2; CurBio 68, 93N; DcTwHis; EncRev; FacFETw; HisWorL; IntWW 74, 75, 76, 77, 78, 79, 80, 81, 82, 83, 89, 91; McGEWB; NewYTBS 92; RadHan; WhDW; WhoSocC 78; WhoSoCE 89; WhoWor 74, 91, 93*

Dube, Lucky
South African. Singer, Songwriter
Began career as a Zulu "mbaqanga" singer and his group, the Sky Way Band, released the hit song "Zulu Soul" on the *Baxoleleni* album, 1983; his first reggae album, *Rastas Never Die,* 1985, was banned in South Africa; released album, *Slave,* which made him an international star, 1987; albums *Prisoner* went double-platinum in 1990 and *House of Exile* became multi-platinum in 1992; later released album *Trinity* in 1995.
b. 1967 in Ermelo, South Africa
Source: *ConMus 17*

Duberman, Martin
American. Writer
Won Bancroft Prize for *Charles Francis Adams, 1897-1886,* 1961.
b. Aug 6, 1930 in New York, New York
Source: *BlueB 76; ConAu 2NR; ConDr 77, 82, 88; ConLC 8; CroCD; DrAS 74H, 78H, 82H; GayLesB; IntAu&W 77, 82; NatPD 77; WhoAm 74, 76, 78, 96, 97; WhoE 74; WrDr 80, 82, 84, 86, 88, 90, 92, 94, 96*

Dubin, Al
Swiss. Lyricist
Often collaborated with Harry Warren; wrote "42nd Street," "Tiptoe Through the Tulips," 1929.
b. Jun 10, 1891 in Zurich, Switzerland

d. Feb 11, 1945 in New York, New York
Source: *AmPS; AmSong; ASCAP 66, 80; BiDAmM; BioIn 4, 5, 9, 15; CmpEPM; NotNAT B; OxCPMus; Sw&Ld C*

Dubinin, Yuri Vladimirovich
Russian. Diplomat
Soviet ambassador to US, 1986-90; ambassador to France, 1990—.
b. Oct 7, 1930 in Moscow, Union of Soviet Socialist Republics
Source: *BioIn 14, 15, 16; ConNews 87-4; IntWW 89, 91, 93; NewYTBS 86; WhoRus; WhoWor 89*

Dubinsky, David
American. Labor Union Official
Pres., ILGWU, 1932-66; co-founded American Labor Party, 1936.
b. Feb 22, 1892 in Brest-Litovsk, Poland
d. Sep 17, 1982 in New York, New York
Source: *AmDec 1930; AmSocL; AnObit 1982; BiDAmL; BiDAmLL; BioIn 1, 2, 4, 5, 6, 7, 8, 9, 10, 11, 13, 14, 19, 20; ConAu 107; CurBio 83, 83N; DcAmSR; EncAB-H 1974, 1996; FacFETw; IntWW 74, 75, 76, 77, 78, 79, 80, 81, 82; McGEWB; NewYTBS 82; OxCAmH; PolProf E, K, T; WebAB 74, 79; WhAm 8; WhoAm 74, 76; WhoAmP 73, 75, 77, 79; WhoLab 76; WhoWor 74; WorAl; WorAlBi; WorFshn*

DuBois, Guy Pene
American. Artist, Critic
Did genre paintings, illustrations; editor, *Arts and Decoration,* mag., 1913-22.
b. Jan 4, 1884 in New York, New York
d. Jul 18, 1958 in New York, New York
Source: *AmAu&B; Benet 96; CurBio 46, 58; DcCAA 71; WhAm 3*

Du Bois, Raoul Pene
American. Designer
Theatrical set, costume designer for 50 yrs; Broadway hits include *Sugar Babies,* 1979.
b. Nov 29, 1914 in Staten Island, New York
d. Jan 1, 1985 in New York, New York
Source: *BioIn 7; ConDes 90; WhAm 8; WhoAm 84; WhoThe 81*

DuBois, W(illiam) E(dward) B(urghardt)
American. Author, Social Reformer
Prominent in early movements for racial equality; helped create NAACP, 1909; advocated Pan-Africanism.
b. Feb 23, 1868 in Great Barrington, Massachusetts
d. Aug 27, 1963 in Accra, Ghana
Source: *BiDNeoM; ConAmL; ConAu 85; ConBlB 3; ConLC 13; DcAmSR; DcLEL; EncAB-H 1974; EncWL 3; LngCTC; McGEWB; OxCAmL 65, 95; PenC AM; RAdv 14; REn; REnAL; RfGAmL 94; TwCA SUP; WebAB 79; WebE&AL; WhAm 4; WhAmP; WhE&EA; WhNAA*

Du Bois, William Pene
American. Children's Author, Illustrator
Wrote, illustrated 1948 Newbery winner, *The Twenty-One Balloons;* son of Guy Pene.
b. May 9, 1916 in Nutley, New Jersey
d. Feb 5, 1993 in Nice, France
Source: *AmAu&B; AuBYP 2, 3; BioIn 1, 2, 4, 5, 7, 8, 9, 14, 16, 17, 18, 19; ChhPo S1; ChlBkCr; ChlLR 1; ConAu 5R, 17NR; DcAmChF 1960; DcLB 61; EncSF, 93; IlsCB 1744, 1946, 1957; IntAu&W 91; JBA 51; LinLib L; NewbMB 1922; OxCChiL; ScF&FL 1, 2; SmATA 4, 68; Str&VC; TwCChW 78, 83, 89, 95; WhAm 11; WhoAm 82, 84, 86, 88; WhoChL; WrDr 80, 82, 84, 86, 88, 90, 92, 94N*

Dubos, Rene Jules
American. Author, Scientist
Microbiologist whose research resulted in first commerically produced antibiotics won Pulitzer for *So Human an Animal,* 1969.
b. Feb 20, 1901 in Saint-Brice, France
d. Feb 20, 1982 in New York, New York
Source: *AmAu&B; AmMWSc 76P, 79; AsBiEn; BiESc; BioIn 3, 5, 7, 9, 10, 12, 13, 17, 20; BlueB 76; ConAu 48NR; CurBio 82; EncEnv; FacFETw; InSci; IntWW 74, 75, 76, 77, 78, 79, 80, 81; LarDcSc; McGEWB; McGMS 80; NewYTBE 71; NewYTBS 82; OxCMed 86; RAdv 14, 13-5; WebAB 74, 79; WhAm 8; WhoAm 74, 76, 78, 80, 82; WhoE 74; WhoWor 74; WrDr 82*

Dubridge, L(ee) A(lvin)
American. Physicist
Directed a US govt. program at the Massachusetts Institute of Technology devoted to developing radar for the US military during WWII.
b. Sep 21, 1901
d. Jan 23, 1994 in Duarte, California
Source: *AmMWSc 76P, 79, 82, 86, 89, 92; BioIn 1, 3, 5, 7, 8, 9, 13; BlueB 76; CurBio 94N; IndAu 1917; InSci; IntWW 74, 75, 76, 77, 78, 79, 80, 81, 82, 83, 89, 91; WhAm 11; WhoAm 74, 76, 78, 80, 82, 84, 86, 88, 90, 92, 94; WhoScEn 94*

Dubuffet, Jean
French. Artist
Post-WW II artist, known for primitive-style paintings, large-scale representational sculptures.
b. Jul 31, 1901 in Le Havre, France
d. May 12, 1985 in Paris, France
Source: *AnObit 1985; Benet 87, 96; BioIn 1, 2, 4, 5, 6, 7, 8, 9, 10, 11, 12, 13, 14, 15, 17, 20; ConArt 77, 83, 89, 96; ConNews 85-4; CurBio 85, 85N; DcArts; DcCAr 81; DcTwCCu 2; FacFETw; IntDcAA 90; IntWW 74, 75, 76, 77, 78, 79, 80, 81, 82, 83; LegTOT; McGDA; McGEWB; NewYTBE 72; NewYTBS 85; OxCArt; OxCTwCA; OxDcArt; PhDcTCA 77; PrintW 83, 85; WhAm 8, 11; Who 74, 82, 83, 85; WhoArt 80, 82, 84; WhoFr 79; WhoWor 74, 76, 78, 82, 84, 87; WorArt 1950*

Duccio di Buoninsegna
Italian. Artist
Founded Sienese School; noted for Maesta altarpiece, Siena church, 1308-11.
b. 1278 in Siena, Italy
d. 1319 in Siena, Italy
Source: *AtlBL; McGDA; NewCol 75; OxCArt; REn*

Du Chaillu, Paul Belloni
French. Anthropologist, Traveler
Wrote *Stories of the Gorilla Country,* 1868.
b. Jul 31, 1835
d. Apr 20, 1903 in Saint Petersburg, Russia
Source: *Alli SUP; AmAu; AmAu&B; AmBi; ApCAB; BbD; BiD&SB; BiDSA; BiInAmS; CarSB; Chambr 3; DcAmAu; DcAmB; DcEnL; DcNAA; JBA 34; OxCAmL 65, 83, 95; REnAL; TwCBDA*

Duchamp, Marcel
French. Artist
Dadaist painter; *Nude Descending a Staircase,* 1912, among his most controversial works.
b. Jul 28, 1887 in Blainville, France
d. Oct 1, 1968 in Neuilly, France
Source: *AtlBL; Benet 87, 96; BioIn 1, 2, 4, 5, 6, 7, 8, 9, 10, 11, 12, 13, 14, 15, 16, 17, 19, 20, 21; BriEAA; ConArt 77, 83, 89; ConAu 110, 116; CurBio 60, 68; DcArts; DcCAA 71, 77, 88, 94; DcTwCCu 1, 2; FacFETw; FilmEn; GolEC; IntDcAA 90; LegTOT; MakMC; McGDA; McGEWB; ModArCr 3; OxCArt; OxCChes 84; OxCTwCA; OxDcArt; PhDcTCA 77; REn; WhDW; WorAl; WorAlBi; WorArt 1950*

Ducharme, Rejean
Canadian. Author
Works explore the topics of alienation, despair, and the search for identity in the modern world; wrote *The Swallower Swallowed,* 1966 (*L'avalee des avales*).
b. Aug 12, 1941 in Saint-Felix-de-Valois, Quebec, Canada
Source: *ConLC 74; DcLB 60; WhoCanL 85, 87, 92*

Duchin, Eddy
[Edwin Frank Duchin]
"Magic Fingers of Radio"
American. Bandleader, Pianist
Sophisticated musician known for elegant, intricate style; wrote several books on piano technique.
b. Apr 1, 1909 in Cambridge, Massachusetts
d. Feb 9, 1951 in New York, New York
Source: *BiDAmM; BioIn 1, 2, 3, 9, 12; CurBio 47, 51; HalFC 88; LegTOT; RadStar; WhoHol B; WhScrn 74, 77, 83; WorAl; WorAlBi*

Duchin, Peter Oelrichs
American. Bandleader, Pianist
Son of Eddy Duchin; follows father's style in numerous hotel performances.
b. Jul 28, 1937 in New York, New York
Source: *BioIn 15, 16; BioNews 74; BkPepl; CelR 90; WhoAm 74, 76, 78, 80, 82, 84, 86, 88, 90, 92, 94, 95, 96, 97; WhoEnt 92; WhoHol A; WhoWor 96; WorAl; WorAlBi*

Duchovny, David
American. Actor
In TV's "The X-Files," 1993—.
b. Mar 7, 1960 in New York, New York
Source: *IntMPA 96; LegTOT*

Ducis, Jean Francois
French. Dramatist, Poet
Adapted Shakespeare for French stage so drastically that only title remained.
b. Aug 22, 1733 in Versailles, France
d. Mar 31, 1816 in Versailles, France
Source: *BiD&SB; CasWL; CelCen; DcBiPP; DcEuL; EvEuW; NotNAT B; OxCFr; OxCThe 67*

Duclos, Jacques
French. Political Leader
Among founding members of French Communist Party; party secretary, 1931-64.
b. Oct 2, 1896 in Louey, France
d. Apr 25, 1975 in Paris, France
Source: *BiDFrPL; BioIn 1, 2, 3, 10, 17; CurBio 46, 75N; EncCW; IntWW 74; NewYTBS 75; ObitOF 79; ObitT 1971; WhoWor 74, 76*

Ducommun, Elie
Swiss. Educator, Journalist
Directed Berne Peace Bureau; shared 1902 Nobel Peace Prize.
b. Feb 19, 1833 in Geneva, Switzerland
d. Dec 7, 1906 in Bern, Switzerland
Source: *BiDMoPL; BioIn 9, 11, 15; FacFETw; LegTOT; LinLib L; NobelP; WebBD 83; WhoNob, 90, 95*

Dudley, Bill
[William M Dudley]
"Bullet Bill"
American. Football Player
Running back, 1942-53; led NFL in rushing twice; MVP, 1946.
b. Dec 24, 1921 in Bluefield, Virginia
Source: *BiDAmSp FB; BioIn 3, 7, 8, 9, 17; LegTOT; WhoFtbl 74*

Dudley, George S
Canadian. Hockey Executive
Amateur hockey pioneer, best known for arranging for Russian teams to visit Canada; Hall of Fame, 1958.
b. Apr 19, 1894 in Midland, Ontario, Canada
d. May 8, 1960
Source: *WhoHcky 73*

Dudley, Thomas
English. Colonial Figure
Four-time governor, 13-time deputy governor, Massachusetts Bay Colony, 1630s-40s; one of the founders of Harvard U.
b. 1576 in Northampton, England
d. Jul 31, 1653 in Roxbury, Massachusetts
Source: *AmBi; AmWrBE; ApCAB; BiDrACR; DcAmB; Drake; EncCRAm; HarEnUS; McGEWB; NatCAB 7; OxCAmH; TwCBDA; WebAB 74, 79; WebBD 83; WhAm HS*

Duel, Peter
American. Actor
Starred in TV series "Love on a Rooftop," 1966-67; "Alias Smith and Jones," 1971-72.
b. 1940 in Rochester, New York
d. Dec 31, 1971 in Hollywood, California
Source: *BioIn 9; FilmgC; ObitOF 79; WhoHol B; WhScrn 74, 77, 83*

Duerk, Alene B(ertha)
American. Naval Officer
First woman to receive flag rank in US Navy: rear admiral, 1972.
b. Mar 29, 1920 in Defiance, Ohio
Source: *CurBio 73; InWom SUP; NewYTBE 72; WhoAmW 74, 75, 79, 81, 83; WhoGov 72, 75; WorDWW*

Duesenberg, August S
American. Auto Manufacturer
Built luxury and racing cars, 1920s-30s.
b. 1879?
d. Jan 18, 1955 in Indianapolis, Indiana
Source: *BioIn 3; ObitOF 79*

Duesenberg, Frederick S
American. Auto Manufacturer
Built engine for motorcycles adapted for cars, boats, airplanes, 1913.
b. Dec 6, 1876 in Lippe, Germany
d. 1932
Source: *NatCAB 16*

Duff, Howard
American. Actor
Tough-guy actor; starred in TV series "Mr. Adams and Eve," 1957-58; "Felony Squad," 1966-69.
b. Nov 24, 1917 in Bremerton, Washington
d. Jul 9, 1990 in Santa Barbara, California
Source: *BioIn 4; ConTFT 6; FilmEn; FilmgC; ForYSC; GangFlm; HalFC 80, 84, 88; IntMPA 75, 76, 77, 78, 79, 80, 81, 82, 84, 86, 88; ItaFilm; MotPP; MovMk; SaTiSS; WhAm 10; WhoAm 80, 82, 84, 86, 88; WhoHol A; WorAl*

Duff, Mary Ann Dyke
American. Actor
Starred in dramatic roles with Edmund Kean, Junius Brutus Booth, 1812-38.
b. 1794 in London, England
d. Sep 5, 1857 in New York, New York
Source: *AmBi; DcAmB; InWom, SUP; LibW; NatCAB 6; NotAW; WhAm HS*

Duffey, Joseph Daniel
American. Clergy, Sociologist
President, U of MA in Amherst, 1990-91; director, US Information Agency, 1993—; active in liberal Dem. politics, late 1960s-early 1970s.
b. Jul 1, 1932 in Huntington, West Virginia
Source: *BioIn 8, 9, 10, 11, 12, 15; CurBio 71; IntWW 91, 93; NewYTBS 77, 88; WhoAm 74, 78, 80, 82, 84, 86, 88, 90, 92, 94, 95, 96, 97; WhoAmP 79, 91; WhoE 74, 86, 89, 91, 93; WhoWor 82, 84, 87, 89*

Duffy, Ben
[Bernard Cornelius Duffy]
American. Advertising Executive
Helped build Batten, Barton, Durstine & Osborne into second largest ad firm in US, 1946-61.
b. Jan 21, 1902 in New York, New York
d. Sep 1, 1972 in Rye, New York
Source: *Au&Wr 71; BioIn 2, 3, 4, 9, 10, 11; CurBio 52, 72; NatCAB 56; NewYTBE 72; WhAm 5*

Duffy, Clinton Truman
American. Prison Warden
Warden, San Quentin, 1940-52; instituted many penal reforms.
b. Aug 24, 1898 in San Quentin, California
d. Oct 11, 1982 in Walnut Creek, California
Source: *AnObit 1982; BioIn 1, 2, 13; NewYTBS 82*

Duffy, Edmund
American. Cartoonist
Won three Pulitzers, 1931, 1934, 1940, for political cartoons.
b. Mar 1, 1899 in Jersey City, New Jersey
d. Sep 13, 1962 in New York, New York
Source: *AmAu&B; BioIn 1, 5, 6, 15; ConAu 93; DcAmB S7; EncAJ; WebBD 83; WhAm 4; WhAmArt 85; WhoAmA 89N, 91N, 93N; WorECar*

Duffy, Francis Patrick
American. Clergy
Army chaplain during WW I; hero of 1940 film *The Fighting 69th.*
b. May 2, 1871 in Cobourg, Ontario, Canada
d. Jun 26, 1932 in New York, New York
Source: *BioIn 4; DcAmB S1; DcCathB; DcNAA; NatCAB 30; WebAMB; WebBD 83; WhAm 4, HSA*

Duffy, Hugh
American. Baseball Player
Outfielder, 1888-1906; had highest batting average for regular in ML history, .438, 1894; Hall of Fame, 1945.

b. Nov 26, 1866 in River Point, Rhode Island
d. Oct 19, 1954 in Allston, Massachusetts
Source: *Ballpl 90; BiDAmSp BB; BioIn 3, 7, 14, 15; DcAmB S5; LegTOT; WhoProB 73; WhoSpor*

Duffy, James Edson
American. Broadcasting Executive
Pres., ABC TV, 1970-85.
b. Apr 2, 1926 in Decatur, Illinois
Source: *IntMPA 86, 92; LesBEnT, 92; NewYTET; WhoAm 80, 82, 84; WhoE 85; WhoTelC*

Duffy, Julia
American. Actor
Played Stephanie Vander Kellan Harris on TV series "Newhart," 1983-90.
b. Jun 27, 1951 in Saint Paul, Minnesota
Source: *BioIn 14, 15, 16; ConTFT 4; LegTOT; WhoAm 92; WhoEnt 92; WorAlBi*

Duffy, Patrick
American. Actor
Played Bobby Ewing on TV series "Dallas," 1978-91; stars in "Step by Step," 1992—.
b. Mar 17, 1949 in Townsend, Montana
Source: *BioIn 11, 12, 14, 15, 16; CelR 90; ConTFT 3, 11; IntMPA 84, 86, 88, 92, 94, 96; LegTOT; VarWW 85; Who 92; WhoAm 80, 82, 84, 86, 88, 90, 92, 94, 95, 96, 97; WhoEnt 92; WhoHol 92; WorAlBi*

Dufresne, Charles
French. Artist
Prolific painter of exotic, Fauvist-cubist landscapes.
b. Nov 23, 1876 in Millemont, France
d. Aug 8, 1938 in Seyne-sur-Mer, France
Source: *BioIn 4; McGDA; OxCTwCA; PhDcTCA 77*

Dufy, Raoul (Ernest Joseph)
French. Artist
Modernist painter, fabric designer; known for huge panel *History of Electricity,* at 1937 Paris Exhibition.
b. Jun 3, 1877 in Le Havre, France
d. Mar 23, 1953 in Forcalquier, France
Source: *AtlBL; Benet 87, 96; BioIn 1, 2, 3, 4, 5, 6, 8, 9, 10, 12, 13, 14, 15, 16, 17; ClaDrA; CurBio 51, 53; DcArts; DcTwCCu 2; EncFash; FacFETw; IntDcAA 90; LegTOT; McGDA; ModArCr 3; ObitT 1951; OxCArt; OxCTwCA; OxDcArt; PhDcTCA 77; REn; WhAm 3; WhDW; WorAl; WorAlBi; WorArt 1950*

Dugan, Alan
American. Poet
Verse vols. include *Collected Poems 1961-83,* 1983; won Pulitzer, 1963.
b. Feb 12, 1923 in New York, New York
Source: *AmAu&B; BenetAL 91; BioIn 10, 12; ConAu 81; ConLC 2, 6; ConPo 70, 75, 80, 85, 91, 96; CroCAP; CurBio 90; DcLB 5; DcLEL 1940; DrAP 75; DrAPF 80, 87, 91; Focus; IntAu&W 91, 93; IntvTCA 2; IntWWP 77; ModAL, S1; OxCAmL 65, 83, 95; OxCTwCP; PenC AM; RAdv 1, 14, 13-1; REnAL; WhoAm 74; WhoWor 74; WorAu 1950; WrDr 76, 80, 82, 84, 86, 88, 90, 92, 94, 96*

Dugdale, Richard Louis
American. Sociologist
Investigated causes of crime, concluding that heredity, not environment, was prime factor in character development; wrote popular case study, *The Jukes,* 1875.
b. 1841 in Paris, France
d. Jul 23, 1883 in New York, New York
Source: *Alli, SUP; AmBi; ApCAB; BioIn 12; DcAmAu; DcAmB; DcNAA; McGEWB; NewCol 75; WhAm HS*

Dugdale, William, Sir
"Grand Plagiary"
English. Editor, Scholar
Historical books include *The Antiquities of Warwickshire,* 1656; Dugdale Society, founded in 1920, publishes historic documents.
b. Sep 12, 1605 in Shustoke, England
d. Feb 11, 1686 in London, England
Source: *Alli; BiD&SB; BioIn 3; BritAu; CamGEL; CamGLE; CasWL; Chambr 1; CmMedTh; DcBiPP; DcEnA; DcEnL; DcLEL; DcNaB; EvLB; NewC; NewCBEL; OxCEng 67, 85, 95; OxCLaw*

Duggan, Andrew
American. Actor
Character actor on stage, screen, TV; starred in TV series "Twelve O'Clock High," 1965-67.
b. Dec 28, 1923 in Franklin, Indiana
d. May 15, 1988 in Los Angeles, California
Source: *BiE&WWA; BioIn 15, 16; ConTFT 7; FilmgC; ForYSC; HalFC 80, 84, 88; MotPP; WhAm 9; WhoAm 80, 82, 84, 86, 88; WhoHol A; WhoWor 82*

Duggan, Maurice Noel
New Zealander. Author
Writings include *Summer in the Gravel Pit,* 1965; *Collected Stories,* 1981.
b. Nov 25, 1922 in Auckland, New Zealand
d. Jan 1975
Source: *CasWL; ConAu 17NR, 53, 73; ConNov 72, 76; DcLEL 1940; GrWrEL N; OxCChiL; SmATA 30N, 40; TwCChW 83; WebE&AL; WorAu 1975*

Du Guesclin, Bertrand
"The Eagle of Brittany"
French. Military Leader
Considered greatest French warrior of his day; Constable of France, 1370.
b. 1320? in Dinan, France
d. Jul 13, 1380 in Languedoc, France
Source: *BioIn 2, 15, 16; Dis&D; LinLib S; NewCol 75; OxCFr*

Duhamel, Georges
[Denis Thevenin]
French. Author
Writings *Salavin; The Pasquier Chronicles,* give broad picture of French middle-class life from 1880s to WW I.
b. Jun 30, 1884 in Paris, France
d. Apr 13, 1966 in Valmondois, France
Source: *Benet 87, 96; BiDMoPL; BioIn 1, 4, 5, 7, 9, 16, 17; CasWL; ClDMEL 47, 80; ConAu 25R, 35NR, 81; ConLC 8; DcLB 65; DcTwCCu 2; EncWL, 2, 3; EvEuW; GuFrLit 1; LinLib L; LngCTC; MajTwCW; ModFrL; ModRL; ModWD; Novels; ObitT 1961; OxCFr; PenC EUR; REn; ScF&FL 1; TwCA, SUP; TwCWr; WhE&EA; WhoTwCL*

Duhring, Eugen Karl
German. Philosopher, Economist
Positivist; wrote *Capital und Arbeit,* 1865; strongly criticized by Engels in *Anti-Duhring,* 1877.
b. Jan 12, 1833 in Berlin, Germany
d. Sep 21, 1921 in Potsdam, Germany
Source: *EncTR; NewCol 75; WhoEc 81, 86*

Dukakis, Kitty
[Katharine Dickson Dukakis; Mrs. Michael Dukakis]
American.
Married Michael Dukakis, 1963; autobiography *Now You Know,* 1990, details alcohol, drug addiction.
b. Dec 26, 1937? in Cambridge, Massachusetts
Source: *BioIn 15, 16; ConAu 135; NewYTBS 88; WhoAm 90; WhoAmW 91; WhoE 91; WrDr 94*

Dukakis, Michael Stanley
American. Politician
Democratic governor of MA, 1975-79, 1983-91; Democratic presidential candidate, 1988, defeated by George Bush.
b. Nov 3, 1933 in Brookline, Massachusetts
Source: *AlmAP 88; AmPolLe; BiDrGov 1978; BioIn 13, 14, 15, 16; BioNews 75; CelR 90; CurBio 78; FacFETw; IntWW 83, 89, 91, 93; News 88-3; NewYTBS 86, 87, 88; PolsAm 84; Who 90, 92, 94; WhoAm 78, 84, 86, 88, 90, 92, 94, 95; WhoAmP 87, 91, 93, 95; WhoE 83, 85, 86, 89, 91, 93; WhoGov 75, 77; WhoWor 78, 87, 89, 91; WorAlBi*

Dukakis, Olympia
American. Actor
Appeared in *Moonstruck,* 1988; *Mighty Aphrodite,* 1995; won Oscar for *Moonstruck,* 1988; cousin of Michael.
b. Jun 20, 1931 in Lowell, Massachusetts
Source: *BioIn 15, 16; CelR 90; ConTFT 1, 7, 15; CurBio 91; IntMPA 92, 94, 96; LegTOT; News 96; NotNAT; WhoAm 90, 92, 94, 95, 96, 97; WhoAmW 89, 91, 93, 95, 97; WhoEnt 92; WhoHol 92; WorAlBi*

Dukas, Paul Abraham
French. Composer, Critic
Wrote impressionistic opera *Ariane et Barbe-Bleue,* 1907.
b. Oct 1, 1865 in Paris, France
d. May 17, 1935 in Paris, France
Source: *Baker 84; OxCFr; OxCMus*

Duke, Angier Biddle
American. Diplomat, Businessman
US ambassador to El Salvador, 1952-53; to Morocco, 1979-81; heir of American Tobacco Co.
b. Nov 30, 1915 in New York, New York
d. Apr 30, 1995 in Southampton, New York
Source: *BioIn 4, 5, 6, 7, 11, 16, 20, 21; BlueB 76; CelR, 90; CurBio 62, 95N; IntWW 74, 75, 76, 77, 78, 79, 80, 81, 82, 83, 89, 91, 93; PolProf K; WhAm 11; WhoAm 74, 76, 78, 80, 82, 84, 86, 88, 90, 92, 94, 95; WhoAmP 73, 75, 77, 79, 81, 83, 85, 87, 89, 91, 93; WhoWor 80, 82, 87, 89, 91, 93*

Duke, Benjamin Newton
American. Industrialist
Businesses included cotton mills, hotels, power plants.
b. Apr 27, 1855 in Orange County, North Carolina
d. Jan 8, 1929 in New York, New York
Source: *BioIn 10; DcAmB; DcNCBi 2; EncSoH; EncWM; NatCAB 21; WhAm 1; WorAl*

Duke, Bill
American. Director, Actor
Worked in theater, television, film; directed *A Rage in Harlem,* 1991.
b. Feb 26, 1943 in Poughkeepsie, New York
Source: *ConBlB 3; DrBlPA 90; IntMPA 92, 94, 96; WhoAfA 96; WhoHol 92*

Duke, Charles Moss, Jr.
American. Astronaut
Lunar module pilot, Apollo 16, Apr, 1972.
b. Oct 3, 1935 in Charlotte, North Carolina
Source: *FacFETw; IntWW 77; NewYTBE 72; WhoSSW 73, 75; WorDWW*

Duke, David
American.
Former grand Wizard of Ku Klux Klan; presidential candidate for Populist party, 1988; head, National Association for the Advancement of White People; Rep. state representative, LA, 1989-91.
b. 1951 in Tulsa, Oklahoma
Source: *BioIn 10, 11, 16; News 90, 90-2; WhoAmP 91*

Duke, Doris
American. Socialite, Philanthropist
Only child of tobacco magnate James Buchanan Duke; heiress to fortune.
b. Nov 22, 1912 in New York, New York
d. Oct 28, 1993 in Beverly Hills, California
Source: *AnObit 1993; BioIn 10, 16, 17, 18, 19, 20, 21; CelR, 90; InWom, SUP; LegTOT; News 94, 94-2; NewYTBS 93; PenEncP*

Duke, James Buchanan
American. Businessman, Philanthropist
Founded American Tobacco Co., 1890; large benefactor of Trinity College, later renamed Duke University.
b. Dec 23, 1856 in Durham, North Carolina
d. Oct 10, 1925 in New York, New York
Source: *AmBi; BiDAmBL 83; BioIn 1, 3, 5, 7, 8, 9, 10, 14; DcAmB; DcNCBi 2; EncAAH; EncAB-H 1974, 1996; EncSoH; EncWM; FacFETw; LegTOT; McGEWB; MorMA; NatCAB 17; OxCAmH; WebAB 74, 79; WhAm 1; WorAl; WorAlBi*

Duke, Patty
American. Actor
Won Oscar, 1963, Emmy, 1979, for *The Miracle Worker,* playing different roles.
b. Dec 14, 1946 in New York, New York
Source: *BiE&WWA; BioIn 6, 7, 8, 10, 14, 15; BioNews 74; CelR, 90; ConAu 130; ConTFT 3; CurBio 63; FilmEn; FilmgC; ForYSC; HalFC 80, 84, 88; IntMPA 86, 88, 92, 94, 96; InWom, SUP; LegTOT; MotPP; MovMk; NotNAT; WhoAm 74, 76, 78, 80, 86, 88, 90, 92, 94, 95, 96, 97; WhoAmW 66, 68, 70, 72, 74, 79, 89, 91, 93, 95, 97; WhoEnt 92; WhoHol 92, A; WorAl; WorAlBi*

Duke, Red, Dr.
[James Henry Duke]
American. TV Personality
Host of PBS medical show "Body-Watch."
b. 1929
Source: *BioIn 15; ConNews 87-1*

Duke, Robin (Anthony Hare)
English. Government Official, Author
Expert on Japanese culture; wrote *The Pillow Book of Sei Shanagon,* 1979.
b. Mar 21, 1916
d. Nov 27, 1984
Source: *ConAu 115; Who 82*

Duke, Vernon
[Vladimir Dukelsky]
American. Composer
Film scores include *Cabin in the Sky,* 1940; wrote song "April in Paris."
b. Oct 10, 1903 in Pskov, Russia
d. Jan 17, 1969 in Santa Monica, California
Source: *AmPS; AmSong; ASCAP 66, 80; Baker 78, 84, 92; BestMus; BiDAmM; BiDD; BiDSovU; BiE&WWA; BioIn 1, 3, 5, 6, 8, 10, 12, 14, 15, 16, 18; CmpEPM; CnOxB; ConAmC 76, 82; ConAu P-2, X; CurBio 41, 69; DancEn 78; DcAmB S8; DcCM; EncMT; HalFC 80, 84, 88; LegTOT; MusMk; NewAmDM; NewCBMT; NewGrDA 86; NewGrDM 80; NewGrDO; NotNAT A, B; OxCAmT 84; OxCMus; OxCPMus; PenEncP; PopAmC, SUP; WhAm 5; WhThe; WorAl*

Duke, Wayne
American. Athletic Director
Big-Ten Athletic Conference director, 1971-89.
b. Nov 9, 1928 in Burlington, Iowa
Source: *WhoAm 76, 78, 80, 82, 84, 86, 88*

Dukepoo, Frank C.
American. Geneticist
First Hopi to earn a doctorate, 1973; founded the National Native American Honor Society, 1982; conducted research on birth defects in Southwest Native Americans.
b. 1943 in Arizona
Source: *BioIn 9, 21; NotNaAm*

Dukes, David
American. Actor
Appeared in TV mini-series "The Winds of War," 1983; film *Without a Trace,* 1983.
b. Jun 6, 1945? in San Francisco, California
Source: *BioIn 12, 13; CelR 90; ConTFT 7; HalFC 88; IntMPA 92, 94, 96; NewYTBS 79; VarWW 85; WhoAm 82, 90; WhoEmL 91; WhoHol 92; WhoWest 89*

Dulac, Edmund
English. Artist
Created fantastic, intricate scenes for fairy tales: *The Arabian Nights;* designed coronation stamps, 1937, 1953.
b. Oct 22, 1882 in Toulouse, France
d. Mar 25, 1953 in London, England
Source: *AntBDN B; BioIn 1, 2, 3, 8, 10, 11, 12, 14; CarSB; ChhPo, S2; DcBrAr 1; DcBrBI; DcNaB 1951; IlsCB 1744; JBA 51; ObitT 1951; OxCChiL; SmATA 19; TwCPaSc; WhoChL*

Dulbecco, Renato
American. Scientist, Educator
Led team of researchers who shared 1975 Nobel Prize in medicine; researched tumor viruses, cells.
b. Feb 22, 1914 in Catanzaro, Italy
Source: *AmMWSc 73P, 76P, 79, 82, 86, 89, 92, 95; BiESc; BioIn 10, 15, 20; BlueB 76; FacFETw; IntWW 74, 75, 76, 77, 78, 79, 80, 81, 82, 83, 89, 91, 93; LarDcSc; LegTOT; McGMS 80; NobelP; NotTwCS; Who 82, 83, 85, 88, 90, 92, 94; WhoAm 74, 76, 78, 80, 82, 84, 86, 88, 90, 92, 94, 95, 96, 97; WhoMedH; WhoNob, 90, 95; WhoScEn 94, 96; WhoWest 82, 84, 87, 89, 92, 94, 96; WhoWor 74, 76, 78, 80, 82, 84, 87, 89, 91, 93, 95, 96, 97; WorAl; WorAlBi*

Dulfer, Candy
Dutch. Musician
Jazz and pop saxophonist; gold album *Saxuality* with hit single "Lily Was Here"; played for rock stars Prince, Van Morrison, Pink Floyd.
Source: *BioIn 17*

Dullea, Keir
American. Actor
Appeared in *David and Lisa,* 1963; *2001: A Space Odyssey,* 1968.
b. May 30, 1936 in Cleveland, Ohio
Source: *BioAmW; BioIn 7, 8, 9, 13, 14; CelR, 90; ConTFT 4; CurBio 70; FilmEn; FilmgC; HalFC 80, 84, 88; IntMPA 77, 78, 79, 80, 81, 82, 84, 86, 88, 92, 94, 96; ItaFilm; LegTOT; MotPP; MovMk; NewYTBS 86; NotNAT; WhoAm 74, 76, 78, 80, 82, 84, 86, 88, 90, 92; WhoE 89; WhoEnt 92; WhoHol 92, A; WhoHrs 80; WhoThe 77, 81; WorAl*

Dulles, Allen Welsh
American. Lawyer, Diplomat
Director of CIA, 1953-61.
b. Apr 7, 1893 in Watertown, New York
d. Jan 29, 1969 in Washington, District of Columbia
Source: *AmAu&B; AmPolLe; BioIn 1, 2, 3, 4, 5, 6, 8, 9, 11, 12, 18, 20, 21; ColdWar 1; CurBio 49, 69; DcAmB S8; EncAI&E; EncTR; FacFETw; LinLib S; NatCAB 58; ObitOF 79; SpyFic; WhAm 5; WhE&EA; WhWW-II*

Dulles, Eleanor Lansing
American. Diplomat, Educator
Consultant for US state dept., 1970-73.
b. Jun 1, 1895 in Watertown, New York
d. Oct 30, 1996 in Washington, District of Columbia
Source: *AmMWSc 73S; WhoE 89; WhoWor 74*

Dulles, John Foster
American. Lawyer, Government Official
Eisenhower's secretary of state, 1953-59; considered most powerful in US history; advocated development of nuclear weapons.
b. Feb 25, 1888 in Washington, District of Columbia
d. May 24, 1959 in Washington, District of Columbia
Source: *AmAu&B; AmPeW; AmPolLe; BiDInt; BiDrAC; BiDrUSC 89; BiDrUSE 71, 89; BioIn 1, 2, 3, 4, 5, 6, 7, 8, 9, 10, 11, 12, 13, 14, 15, 16, 17, 18, 19, 20; ColdWar 1; ConAu 1NR, 115, 149; CurBio 44, 53, 59; DcAmB S6; DcAmC; DcAmDH 80, 89; DcPol; DcTwHis; EncAB-H 1974, 1996; EncCW; EncMcCE; FacFETw; HisDcKW; HisEAAC; HisEWW; HisWorL; LegTOT; LinLib L, S; McGEWB; NatCAB 43; ObitT 1951; OxCAmH; PolPar; PolProf E, T; RComAH; TwCSAPR; WebAB 74, 79; WhAm 3; WhAmP; WhDW; WorAl; WorAlBi*

Dull Knife
American. Native American Chief
Northern Cheyenne chief best known for Dull Knife Outbreak, 1878.
b. 1828
d. 1879
Source: *BioIn 4, 18; REnAW*

Dulong, Pierre-Louis
French. Chemist, Physicist
Discovered nitrogen chloride, 1813; devised Dulong's Formula to calculate heat value of fuels.
b. Feb 12, 1785 in Rouen, France
d. Jul 18, 1838 in Paris, France
Source: *AsBiEn; BiESc; DcScB; WebBD 83*

Duluth, Daniel (Greysolon)
French. Explorer
Claimed upper Mississippi region, Lake Superior for France, c. 1678.
b. 1636 in Saint-Germain-en-Laye, France
d. Feb 27, 1710 in Montreal, Quebec, Canada
Source: *AmBi; BioIn 4, 5, 7, 9; DcAmB; EncCRAm; NewCol 75; OxCAmH; PeoHis; WebBD 83; WhAm HS; WhNaAH; WhWE*

Dumars, Joe, III
American. Basketball Player
Guard, Detroit, 1985—; MVP, NBA playoffs, 1989; member of Dream Team II, 1994.
b. May 24, 1963 in Shreveport, Louisiana
Source: *BioIn 16, 21; OfNBA 87; WhoAfA 96; WhoAm 92, 94, 95, 96, 97; WhoBlA 92, 94; WhoMW 92, 93; WhoSpor; WorAlBi*

Dumas, Alexandre
French. Dramatist
Play *La Dame aux Camelias,* 1852, basis for Verdi's opera, *La Traviat a.*
b. Jul 27, 1824 in Paris, France
d. Nov 27, 1895 in Paris, France
Source: *AtlBL; BbD; Benet 87, 96; BiD&SB; BioIn 1, 2, 4, 5, 6, 7, 9, 11, 17; CamGWoT; CasWL; CelCen; CnThe; CyWA 58; DcArts; DcBiA; DcBiPP; DcEuL; DramC 1; DrBlPA, 90; EncWT; Ent; EuAu; EvEuW; FilmgC; GuFrLit 1; HalFC 80, 84, 88; HsB&A; InB&W 80, 85; LegTOT; LinLib L, S; McGEWD 72, 84; NewC; NewCBEL; NewEOp 71; NewGrDO; NinCLC 9; NotNAT A, B; OxCEng 67, 85, 95; OxCFr; OxCThe 67, 83; OxDcOp; PenC EUR; RAdv 14, 13-2; RComWL; REn; REnWD; RfGWoL 95; ScF&FL 1; WorAl; WorAlBi*

Dumas, Alexandre Dumas Davy de la Pailleterie
[Dumas Pere]
French. Author, Dramatist
Best known works *The Three Musketeers,* 1844; *The Count of Monte Cristo,* 1845.
b. Jul 24, 1802 in Villers-Cotterets, France
d. Dec 5, 1870 in Puys, France
Source: *AtlBL; BbD; BiD&SB; CarSB; CasWL; CnThe; CyWA 58; DcEuL; EuAu; EvEuW; FilmgC; HsB&A; McGEWD 72; MnBBF; OxCEng 67; PenC EUR; REn*

Dumas, Charles
American. Track Athlete
High jumper; first to jump seven feet, 1956; won gold medal, 1956 Olympics.
b. Dec 2, 1937 in Tulsa, Oklahoma
Source: *BiDAmSp OS; CmCal; WhoTr&F 73*

Dumas, Jean Baptiste Andre
Canadian. Engineer
Electrical engineering professor, 1968—.
b. Jun 4, 1925 in Montreal, Quebec, Canada
Source: *AmMWSc 86, 92; BioIn 14; DcScB; McGEWB*

Dumas, Roland
French. Government Official, Lawyer
French foreign minister, 1984-86 and 1988—; formerly legal counsel to artists, most notably, Pablo Picasso.
b. Aug 23, 1922 in Limoges, France
Source: *BioIn 7, 14; CurBio 90; IntAu&W 89; IntWW 89, 91, 93; Who 88, 90, 92, 94; WhoFr 79; WhoWor 89, 91, 93*

DuMaurier, Daphne
[Lady Browning]
English. Author
Classic gothic novels include *Rebecca,* 1938; *Jamaica Inn,* 1936.
b. May 13, 1907 in London, England
d. Apr 19, 1989 in Par, England
Source: *Au&Wr 71; Benet 87; BiE&WWA; BioIn 13, 14, 15, 16; CamGLE; ConAu 5R, 6NR, 128; ConLC 11, 59; ConNov 86; ContDcW 89; CrtSuMy; CurBio 40, 89N; CyWA 58; DcLEL; EncBrWW; EncMys; EvLB; FacFETw; FemiCLE; FilmgC; HalFC 84, 88; IntAu&W 91; IntWW 83, 89, 89N; InWom, SUP; LngCTC; MajTwCW; NewYTBS 89; NotNAT; OxCEng 85; PenC ENG; PenEncH; RfGEnL 91; SmATA 27, 60; TwCA, SUP; TwCCr&M 91; TwCRHW 90; TwCWr; Who 85, 90N; WhoThe 77A; WhoWor 74; WorAl; WorAlBi; WrDr 86*

DuMaurier, George Louis P. B
English. Author, Artist
Satirized upper classes in *Punch* cartoons, 1864-96; wrote *Trilby,* 1894.
b. Mar 6, 1834 in Paris, France
d. Oct 8, 1896 in London, England
Source: *BbD; BiD&SB; BritAu 19; CasWL; Chambr 3; CyWA 58; DcBiA; DcEuL; DcLEL; EvLB; McGDA; MouLC 4; NewC; NotNAT B; OxCEng 67; PenC ENG; RAdv 1*

DuMaurier, Gerald Hubert, Sir
English. Producer, Actor
Greatest success in *Raffles,* 1906; made hero out of villain; father of Daphne DuMaurier.
b. Mar 26, 1873 in London, England
d. Apr 11, 1934 in London, England
Source: *CnThe; EncWT; Film 2; NewC; NotNAT A, B; OxCThe 67; WhDW; WhoHol B; WhScrn 77; WhThe*

Dumke, Ralph
American. Actor
Supporting actor in *All the King's Men,* 1949; *Invasion of the Body Snatchers,* 1956.
b. Jul 25, 1899 in Indiana
d. Jan 4, 1964 in Sherman Oaks, California
Source: *EncAFC; FilmgC; NotNAT B; RadStar; WhoHol B; WhScrn 74, 77, 83*

Dummar, Melvin
American. Gas Station Attendant
Named heir in will purportedly written by Howard Hughes, later called forgery, 1976.
b. 1944?
Source: *BioIn 10, 11, 15*

DuMont, Allen Balcom
American. Engineer
Pioneer in development of TV; made first feasible cathode ray tube.
b. Jan 29, 1901 in New York, New York
d. Nov 16, 1965 in New York, New York
Source: *BioIn 1, 2, 3, 4, 6, 7; CurBio 66; DcAmB S7; InSci; NewYTET; WhAm 4*

Dumont, Gabriel
Canadian. Native American Leader
Played a major role in the 1885 Northwest Rebellion, led by Louis Riel.
b. 1837? in Winnipeg, Manitoba, Canada
d. 1906 in Batoche
Source: *BioIn 19, 21; DcCanB 13; NotNaAm; WhNaAH*

Dumont, Margaret
[Margaret Baker]
American. Actor
Stately matron in seven Marx Brothers films: *Animal Crackers,* 1930; *A Night at the Opera,* 1935.
b. Oct 20, 1889 in New York, New York
d. Mar 6, 1965 in Los Angeles, California
Source: *BiDFilm, 81, 94; BioIn 7, 11, 21; DcAmB S7; EncAFC; Film 2; FilmEn; FilmgC; HalFC 80, 84, 88; IntDcF 1-3, 2-3; InWom SUP; LegTOT; MotPP; MovMk; ObitOF 79; OlFamFa; OxCFilm; QDrFCA 92; ThFT; Vers A; WhoCom; WhoHol B; WhScrn 74, 77, 83; WorEFlm*

Dumont d'Urville, Jules Sebastian Cesar
French. Navigator
Explored Australia, Oceania Islands, 1826-29; discovered Adelie Coast, Antarctica, 1841.
b. May 23, 1790, France
d. May 8, 1842
Source: *CelCen; DcBiPP; Dis&D; NewCol 75; OxCShps; WhDW*

Dumurcq, Charles
[Alain Gauthier; Charles Gurmukh Sobhraj]
French. Murderer
Subject of Thomas Thompson's book *Serpentine,* 1979.
b. Apr 6, 1944? in Saigon, Vietnam
Source: *BioIn 11, 12*

Dun, Robert Graham
American. Financier
Founded mercantile business, R.G. Dun & Co., 1859; known for quality service.
b. 1826 in Chillicothe, Ohio
d. 1900
Source: *BiDAmBL 83; DcAmB; NatCAB 2; WhAm 1*

Dunant, Jean Henri
Swiss. Philanthropist
Founded Red Cross, 1864; shared first Nobel Peace Prize, 1901.
b. May 8, 1828 in Geneva, Switzerland
d. Oct 30, 1910 in Heiden, Switzerland
Source: *BioIn 1, 2, 3, 4, 5, 6, 7, 8, 9, 11; Dis&D; HisWorL; LinLib L, S; LuthC 75; OxCMed 86; WebBD 83; WhDW; WhoMilH 76; WhoNob, 90, 95; WorAl; WorAlBi*

Dunaway, Faye
[Dorothy Faye Dunaway]
American. Actor
Starred in *Bonnie and Clyde,* 1967; *Chinatown;* on Oscar, 1976, for *Network.*
b. Jan 14, 1941 in Bascom, Florida
Source: *BiDFilm, 81; WorAl; WorAlBi; WorEFlm*

Dunbar, Helen Flanders
American. Psychiatrist, Author
Pioneer in psychosomatic medicine; founded American Psychosomatic Society, 1942.
b. May 14, 1902 in Chicago, Illinois
d. Aug 21, 1959 in South Kent, Connecticut
Source: *AmAu&B; BioIn 5, 12, 19; InWom SUP; NotAW MOD*

Dunbar, Paul Laurence
American. Poet, Author
Published 24 volumes of fiction, poetry; poems used Negro folk material, dialect.
b. Jun 27, 1872 in Dayton, Ohio
d. Feb 9, 1906 in Dayton, Ohio
Source: *AfrAmAl 6; AfrAmW; AmAu; AmAu&B; AmBi; AmDec 1900; AmWr S2; ApCAB SUP; Benet 87, 96; BenetAL 91; BibAL; BiDAfM; BiDAmM; BiD&SB; BioIn 1, 2, 3, 5, 6, 7, 8, 9, 10, 11, 12, 13, 14, 15, 16, 17, 19, 20, 21; BkCL; BlkAmP; BlkAmW 1; BlkAull, 92; BlkAWP; BlkLC; BlkWr 1; CamGEL; CasWL; Chambr 3; ChhPo, S1, S2; CnDAL; ConAu 104, 124; ConBlB 8; CyWA 89; DcAmAu; DcAmB; DcAmNB; DcLB 50, 54, 78; DcNAA; DcTwCCu 5; Dis&D; EarBlAP; EncAACR; FacFETw; GayN; GrWrEL P; InB&W 80, 85; LinLib L, S; MagSAmL; McGEWB; ModBlW; MorBAP; NatCAB 9; NegAl 76, 83, 89; NewGrDA 86; OhA&B; OxCAmL 65, 83, 95; OxCAmT 84; PenC AM; PoeCrit 5; RAdv 1, 13-1; RealN; REn; REnAL; RfGAmL 87, 94; SchCGBL; SelBAAf; SelBAAu; ShSCr 8; SmATA 34; TwCBDA; TwCLC 2, 12; WebAB 74, 79; WebE&AL; WhAm 1; WhFla; WorLitC*

Dunbar, William
Scottish. Poet
Scottish Chaucerian who wrote *Dance of the Seven Deadly Sins,* 1503-08.
b. 1460?
d. 1520?
Source: *Alli; AtlBL; BbD; BiD&SB; BioIn 3, 5, 8, 9, 11, 12, 20, 21; BlmGEL; BritAu; CamGEL; CasWL; Chambr 1; ChhPo, S2; CmScLit; CnE&AP; CrtT 1, 4; DcArts; DcCathB; DcEnA; DcEnL; DcEuL; DcLB 132, 146; DcLEL; DcNaB C; EvLB; GrWrEL P; LinLib L; LitC 20; LngCEL; McGEWB; MouLC 1; NewC; NewCBEL; NewCol 75; OxCEng 67; PenC ENG; REn; RfGEnL 91; WebBD 83; WebE&AL*

Duncan, Augustin
American. Actor, Producer
Brother of Isadora Duncan; co-founder, NY Theatre Guild.
b. Apr 12, 1873 in San Francisco, California
d. Feb 20, 1954 in New York, New York
Source: *BioIn 3, 5; NatCAB 42; NotNAT B; ObitOF 79; OxCAmT 84; WhThe*

Duncan, Charles William, Jr.
American. Government Official, Business Executive
Secretary, US energy dept., 1979-81; pres., Duncan Foods Co., 1958-64.
b. Sep 9, 1926 in Houston, Texas
Source: *BiDrUSE 89; BioIn 12; CngDr 77, 79; CurBio 80; IntWW 77, 78, 79, 80, 81, 82, 83, 89; NewYTBS 79; WhoAm 74, 76, 78, 80, 82, 84, 86, 88, 90, 92, 94, 95, 96, 97; WhoAmP 81; WhoFI 74, 81, 89; WhoGov 77; WhoSSW 95; WhoWor 80, 82, 84*

Duncan, David Douglas
American. Photojournalist
Covered many major events, including Japan's surrender to US aboard *USS Missouri,* 1945.
b. Jan 23, 1916 in Kansas City, Missouri

Source: *AuNews 1; BioIn 2, 4, 5, 7, 8, 9, 10, 11, 16; ConAu 112, 145; ConPhot 82, 88, 95; CurBio 68; EncAJ; EncTwCJ; ICPEnP; LinLib L; MacBEP; WhoAm 74, 76, 78, 80, 82, 84, 86, 88, 92, 94, 95; WhoWor 74, 76; WorAl; WorAlBi*

Duncan, Isadora
American. Dancer
Revolutionized interpretative dancing; wed to Sergei Yesenin; strangled by scarf in freakish car accident.
b. May 27, 1878 in San Francisco, California
d. Sep 14, 1927 in Nice, France
Source: *AmAu&B; AmBi; AmCulL; AmDec 1900; Benet 87; BenetAL 91; BiDD; BioIn 1, 2, 3, 4, 5, 6, 7, 8, 9, 10, 11, 12, 13, 14, 15, 16, 17, 18, 19, 20, 21; CmCal; CmpGMD; CnOxB; ConAu 118; DancEn 78; DcAmB; Dis&D; EncAB-H 1974, 1996; EncFash; EncWHA; GoodHs; HanAmWH; IntDcWB; InWom, SUP; LegTOT; LibW; LinLib S; McGEWB; NatCAB 22; NotAW; NotNAT B; OxCAmH; OxCAmL 65, 83, 95; RAdv 14, 13-3; REn; REnAL; WebAB 74, 79; WhAm 4, HSA; WhDW; WorAl; WorAlBi*

Duncan, Robert Edward
American. Poet
Considered one of greatest American lyric poets of his generation; wrote 14 books of poetry; received first National Poetry Award, 1985.
b. Jan 7, 1919 in Oakland, California
d. Feb 3, 1988 in San Francisco, California
Source: *AmAu&B; Benet 87; BioIn 13; CamGLE; CamHAL; CasWL; ConAu 9R, 124; ConLC 15, 41; ConPo 75, 85; CroCAP; DrAP 75; ModAL S1; PenC AM; RAdv 1, 13-1; REn; REnAL; RfGAmL 87; WhAm 9; WhoAm 86; WorAu 1950; WrDr 86, 88*

Duncan, Sandy
American. Actor
Starred on Broadway as Peter Pan, 1980; starred on TV show "The Hogan Family," 1986-90.
b. Feb 20, 1946 in Henderson, Texas
Source: *BiDD; BioIn 12, 16; CelR 90; ConTFT 2, 7, 14; CurBio 80; EncMT; FilmEn; FilmgC; HalFC 80, 84, 88; IntMPA 75, 76, 77, 78, 79, 80, 81, 82, 84, 86, 88, 92, 94, 96; InWom SUP; LegTOT; LesBEnT 92; WhoAm 80, 82, 84, 86, 88, 90, 92, 94, 95, 96, 97; WhoAmW 95, 97; WhoEnt 92; WhoHol 92, A; WhoThe 77, 81; WorAl; WorAlBi*

Duncan, Sheena
South African. Social Reformer
Member, former pres. of South African women's group, Black Sash; attempts to help blacks with race laws, change whites' views of apartheid through peaceful protest.
b. 1932 in Johannesburg, South Africa
Source: *BioIn 16; ConNews 87-1; DcCPSAf*

Duncan, Todd
[Robert Todd Duncan]
American. Singer
Broadway star; performed in over 1,500 concerts, 1944-65; sang at Lyndon Johnson's inaugural concert.
b. Feb 12, 1903 in Danville, Kentucky
Source: *AfrAmAl 6; BiDAfM; BiDAmM; BiE&WWA; BioIn 1, 2, 3, 9, 10, 14; BlkOpe; CurBio 42; DcAfAmP; DrBlPA, 90; Ebony 1; EncMT; InB&W 80, 85; MetOEnc; NegAl 76, 83, 89; NewAmDM; NewGrDA 86; NotNAT; OxCAmT 84; PlP&P; WhoAfA 96; WhoBlA 75, 77, 80, 85, 90, 92, 94; WhoHol 92, A; WhoThe 77A*

Duncan I
Scottish. Ruler
Succeeded Malcolm II, 1034; overthrown, killed by Macbeth.
d. 1040
Source: *NewC; WebBD 83*

Duncan-Sandys, Edwin, Lord
English. Diplomat, Politician
Negotiated independence for many British territorial colonies, 1960-64; Conservative member of Parliament, 1930s-70s.
b. Jan 24, 1908 in London, England
d. Nov 26, 1987 in London, England
Source: *IntWW 83; Who 85; WhoWor 84*

Duncanson, Robert Scott
American. Artist
Landscape painter commissioned to do series of murals for Taft Museum, Cincinnati, 1840s.
b. 1817 in Cincinnati, Ohio
d. Dec 21, 1872 in Detroit, Michigan
Source: *AfroAA; DcAmArt; InB&W 80; NegAl 83; WhoAmA 82*

Dundee, Angelo Mirena, Jr.
American. Boxing Trainer
Trainer of Muhammad Ali, "Sugar" Ray Leonard.
b. Aug 30, 1921 in Philadelphia, Pennsylvania
Source: *BioIn 13, 14, 15; BioNews 74; InB&W 85; NewYTBS 81*

Dundee, Johnny
[Giuseppe Carrora]
American. Boxer
Popular featherweight champion, 1923-25; Boxing Hall of Fame, 1957.
b. Nov 22, 1893 in Sciacca, Italy
d. Apr 22, 1965 in East Orange, New Jersey
Source: *BiDAmSp BK; BioIn 7; BoxReg; DcAmB S7; WhoBox 74; WhoSpor*

Dunham, Katherine
American. Dancer, Choreographer
First to organize professional black dance troupe; founded own dance school, 1945.
b. Jun 22, 1910 in Chicago, Illinois
Source: *AfrAmAl 6; ArtclWW 2; ASCAP 66; BiDAfM; BiE&WWA; BioAmW; BioIn 1, 2, 3, 4, 5, 6, 8, 9, 10, 11, 12, 13, 14, 15, 16; BlkAWP; BlksAmF; BlkWr 1; ConAu 17NR, 65; ConBlB 4; CurBio 41; DrBlPA, 90; HarlReB; HerW, 84; InB&W 85; IntWW 83, 91; InWom, SUP; ItaFilm; LegTOT; LibW; LivgBAA; NegAl 76, 83, 89; NewYTBS 86, 91; NotBlAW 1; NotNAT, A; NotWoAT; OxCAmT 84; REnAL; SchCGBL; SelBAAf; SelBAAu; WebAB 74, 79; WhoAfA 96; WhoAm 74; WhoBlA 80, 85, 90, 92, 94; WhoE 74; WhoHol A; WhoThe 72, 77, 81; WhoWor 74; WorAl; WorAlBi*

Dunham, Sonny
[Elmer Lewis Dunham]
American. Musician
Trumpeter, bandleader, 1930s-40s; soloist with Glen Gray, 1932-40.
b. Nov 16, 1914 in Brockton, Massachusetts
Source: *BgBands 74; BioIn 9, 12; CmpEPM; NewGrDJ 88, 94; WhoJazz 72*

Dunhill, Alfred Henry
English. Business Executive
Pres., Dunhill Tobacco Group; author *The Gentle Art of Smoking*, 1954.
b. 1896
d. Jul 8, 1971 in Hove, England
Source: *BioIn 9; NewYTBE 71*

Duniway, Abigail Jane Scott
American. Feminist, Suffragist
First registered woman voter in Oregon.
b. Oct 22, 1834 in Groveland, Illinois
d. Oct 11, 1915 in Portland, Oregon
Source: *Alli SUP; AmAu; AmAu&B; AmBi; AmRef; AmWom; DcAmB; DcNAA; EncWHA; HanAmWH; InWom, SUP; LibW; NotAW; REnAW; WhAm 4; WhAmP; WomWWA 14*

Dunlap, William
American. Dramatist, Artist
Wrote 65 plays: *History of American Theater*, 1832; did portrait of George Washington.
b. Feb 11, 1766 in Perth Amboy, New Jersey
d. Sep 28, 1839 in New York, New York
Source: *Alli; AmAu; AmAu&B; AmBi; AmWrBE; ApCAB; BbD; BenetAL 91; BibAL; BiDAmM; BiD&SB; BiDLA; BioIn 7, 8, 9, 10, 12, 13, 14, 16, 19; BriEAA; CamGLE; CamGWoT; CamHAL; CasWL; CnDAL; CnThe; CrtSuDr; CyAL 1, 2; DcAmArt; DcAmAu; DcAmB; DcLB 30, 37, 59; DcNAA; Drake; EncCRAm; EncWT; Ent; EvLB; GrWrEL DR; HarEnUS; IntDcT 2; McGDA; McGEWD 72, 84; NatCAB*

6; NewYHSD; NinCLC 2; NotNAT A, B; OxCAmH; OxCAmL 65, 83, 95; OxCAmT 84; OxCThe 67, 83; OxDcArt; PenC AM; PlP&P; REnAL; REnWD; RfGAmL 87, 94; TwCBDA; WebAB 74, 79; WebE&AL; WhAm HS

Dunlop, Frank
English. Director
Founder, director of Young Vic Theatre, 1969.
b. Feb 15, 1927 in Leeds, England
Source: *BioIn 14; BlueB 76; ConTFT 12; IntWW 93; OxCThe 83; PlP&P A; Who 74, 82, 83, 85, 88, 90, 92, 94; WhoEnt 92; WhoThe 72, 77, 81; WhoWor 78, 80, 82, 84, 87, 89, 91, 93, 95, 96, 97*

Dunlop, John Boyd
Scottish. Inventor
Patented pneumatic tire, 1888.
b. Feb 5, 1840, Scotland
d. 1921
Source: *BioIn 3, 4, 5, 12, 14; DcNaB 1912; Entr; GrBr; InSci; WebBD 83; WhDW; WorAl; WorAlBi; WorInv*

Dunlop, John Thomas
American. Economist
Secretary of Labor under Ford, 1975-76; wrote *Business and Public Policy,* 1980.
b. Jun 5, 1914 in Placerville, California
Source: *AmMWSc 73S, 78S; BiDrUSE 89; BioIn 2, 8, 9, 10, 11, 12; ConAu 5NR, 13R; IntWW 91; NewYTBS 79; St&PR 91; WhoAm 74, 76, 78, 80, 82, 84, 86, 88, 90, 92, 94, 95, 96, 97; WhoAmP 75, 77, 79, 81, 83, 85, 87, 89, 91, 93, 95; WhoE 74, 75, 77, 93; WhoEc 81, 86; WhoGov 75, 77; WhoLab 76; WrDr 92*

Dunn, Alan
American. Cartoonist, Artist
With *New Yorker* mag. for over 40 yrs.
b. Aug 11, 1900 in Belmar, New Jersey
d. May 20, 1974 in New York, New York
Source: *AmAu&B; BioIn 10; ConAu 49, P-2; NewYTBS 74; ScF&FL 1, 2; WhAm 6; WhAmArt 85; WhoAm 74; WhoAmA 73, 76N, 78N, 80N, 82N, 84N, 86N, 89N, 91N; WhoWor 74; WorECar*

Dunn, Holly
American. Singer, Songwriter
Award-winning country music singer; hit single "Daddy's Hands," 1985; regular cast member of the Grand Ole Opry, 1989—.
b. Aug 22, 1957 in San Antonio, Texas
Source: *BgBkCoM; ConMus 7; LegTOT; WhoNeCM*

Dunn, James Howard
American. Actor
Won Oscar for *A Tree Grows in Brooklyn,* 1945.
b. Nov 2, 1905 in New York, New York
d. Sep 3, 1967 in Santa Monica, California
Source: *BiE&WWA; FilmgC; HolP 30; MotPP; MovMk; ObitOF 79; WhoHol B; WhScrn 74, 77; WorAl*

Dunn, Katherine (Karen)
American. Author
Wrote *Geek Love,* 1989.
b. Oct 24, 1945 in Garden City, Kansas
Source: *ConAu 33R; ConLC 71; EncSF 93; ScF&FL 92*

Dunn, Michael
[Gary Neil Miller]
American. Actor
Dwarf actor whose movie credits include *Ship of Fools,* 1965; appeared in TV series "Wild, Wild West," 1965-70.
b. Oct 20, 1934 in Shattuck, Oklahoma
d. Aug 29, 1973 in London, England
Source: *BiE&WWA; BioIn 6, 7, 10; DcAmB S9; FilmEn; FilmgC; ForYSC; ItaFilm; MotPP; MovMk; NewYTBE 73; NotNAT B; WhoHrs 80; WhScrn 77, 83*

Dunn, Mignon
American. Opera Singer
Mezzo-soprano; NY Met. debut, 1958; noted for Wagner, Strauss roles.
Source: *Baker 84; BioIn 6, 10, 13; IntWWM 90; MetOEnc; NewAmDM; NewGrDA 86; NewYTBE 73; WhoAm 74, 76, 78, 80, 82, 84, 86, 88, 90, 92, 94, 95; WhoAmM 83; WhoAmW 66; WhoOp 76*

Dunn, Nora
American. Comedian
Member, "Saturday Night Live" TV series cast, 1985-90; actress in the movie "Passion Fish," 1993.
b. Apr 29, 1952? in Chicago, Illinois
Source: *BioIn 15; ConTFT 11; WhoHol 92*

Dunne, Dominick
American. Author, Journalist
Writes novels based on the lives of the rich and famous; wrote *The Two Mrs. Grenvilles,* 1985 which became a TV miniseries; also a contributing writer to *Vanity Fair* Magazine.
b. Oct 29, 1925 in Hartford, Connecticut
Source: *BestSel 89-1; BiDConC; BioIn 14, 15, 16; CelR 90; ConAu 46NR, 121; ConPopW; ConTFT 9; IntAu&W 91; IntMPA 92, 96; News 97-1; WhoAm 94, 95, 96; WrDr 92, 94, 96*

Dunne, Dominique
American. Actor
Starred in *Poltergeist,* 1982; allegedly strangled by her boyfriend.
b. Nov 20, 1959
d. Nov 4, 1982 in Los Angeles, California

Dunne, Finley Peter
American. Author, Editor
Best known as creator of Mr. Dooley, who commented on political issues for 30 years.
b. Jul 10, 1867 in Chicago, Illinois
d. Apr 24, 1936 in New York, New York
Source: *AmAu&B; AmBi; Benet 87, 96; BenetAL 91; BiDAmJo; BiDAmNC; BiD&SB; BioIn 1, 3, 4, 5, 6, 8, 11, 12, 14, 15, 16, 17; CamGEL; CamHAL; CathA 1930; Chambr 3; ConAmL; ConAu 108; DcAmAu; DcAmB S2; DcAmC; DcAmImH; DcAmSR; DcLB 11, 23; DcLEL; DcNAA; EncAB-H 1974, 1996; EncAHmr; EncAJ; EvLB; GayN; GrWrEL N; JrnUS; LegTOT; LiJour; LinLib L, S; LngCTC; McGEWB; MorMA; NatCAB 14; OxCAmH; OxCAmL 65, 83, 95; OxCEng 67; OxCIri; PenC AM; REn; REnAL; RfGAmL 87, 94; TwCA, SUP; TwCBDA; TwCLC 28; WebAB 74, 79; WhAm 1; WhLit*

Dunne, Griffin
American. Actor, Producer
Produced films *Baby It's You,* 1982; *After Hours,* 1985.
b. Jun 8, 1955 in New York, New York
Source: *BioIn 14; ConTFT 4, 14; HalFC 88; IntMPA 88, 92, 94, 96; LegTOT; VarWW 85; WhoAm 96, 97; WhoHol 92*

Dunne, Irene Marie
American. Actor
Five-time Oscar nominee; best known for lead in *I Remember Mama,* 1948.
b. Dec 20, 1898 in Louisville, Kentucky
d. Sep 4, 1990 in Los Angeles, California
Source: *BiDFilm; BiE&WWA; BioIn 14; CmMov; CmpEPM; CurBio 45, 90N; FacFETw; FilmgC; HalFC 84; IntMPA 86; InWom SUP; MotPP; MovMk; OxCFilm; ThFT; Who 85, 90; WhoAm 74; WhoHol A; WomWMM; WorAl*

Dunne, John Gregory
American. Author
Wrote *True Confessions,* 1977; filmed, 1981.
b. May 25, 1932 in Hartford, Connecticut
Source: *AuNews 1; BenetAL 91; BiDConC; BioIn 9, 10, 12, 13, 14, 15, 16, 18, 20; CmCal; ConAu 14NR, 25R, 50NR; ConLC 28; ConNov 91, 96; CurBio 83; DcLB Y80B; FacFETw; LiJour; NewYTBS 87; OxCAmL 83, 95; TwCCr&M 80; WhoAm 84, 86, 88, 92, 94, 95, 96, 97; WhoUSWr 88; WhoWrEP 89, 92, 95; WorAl; WorAlBi; WorAu 1975; WrDr 82, 84, 86, 88, 90, 92, 94, 96*

Dunne, John William
English. Philosopher, Inventor
Demonstrated immortality of soul, principle of serialism through mathematics; designed first military plane in Britain, 1907.

b. 1875
d. Aug 24, 1949 in London, England
Source: *Benet 87, 96; BioIn 1, 2, 12; DcLEL; DcNaB MP; DivFut; EvLB; InSci; NewCBEL; REn; WhE&EA*

Dunning, John Ray
American. Physicist
Nuclear physicist; key figure in laying the groundwork for the first atomic bomb.
b. Sep 24, 1907 in Shelby, Nebraska
d. Aug 25, 1975 in Key Biscayne, Florida
Source: *AsBiEn; BiESc; BioIn 1, 2, 4, 8, 10, 11; CurBio 48, 75N; DcAmB S9; FacFETw; InSci; IntWW 74, 75; LarDcSc; NewYTBS 75; ObitOF 79; WhAm 6; Who 74; WhoAm 74; WhoE 74; WhoWor 76; WorAl; WorAlBi*

Dunninger, Joseph
American. Astrologer, Magician
Performed telepathic readings on radio, TV.
b. Apr 28, 1896 in New York, New York
d. Mar 9, 1975 in Cliffside Park, New Jersey
Source: *BioIn 1, 2, 3, 4; CurBio 44, 75N; NewYTBS 75; WhAm 6*

Dunnock, Mildred
American. Actor
Oscar nominee for *Death of a Salesman*, 1952, *Baby Doll*, 1956.
b. Jan 25, 1901 in Baltimore, Maryland
d. Jul 5, 1991 in Oak Bluffs, Massachusetts
Source: *AnObit 1991; BiE&WWA; BioIn 15, 16; CamGWoT; ConTFT 8; CurBio 55, 91N; FilmgC; HalFC 84, 88; IntMPA 86, 88; InWom SUP; MotPP; MovMk; NewYTBS 91; NotNAT; NotWoAT; OxCAmT 84; PlP&P; Vers A; WhoAm 86; WhoAmW 74; WhoHol A; WhoThe 81; WorAl*

Dunoyer de Segonzac, Andre
French. Artist
Leader in naturalistic tradition; painting subjects include boxers, dancers.
b. Jul 6, 1884 in Bossy-Saint-Antoine, France
d. Sep 17, 1974 in Paris, France
Source: *BioIn 1, 2, 3, 4, 5, 6, 8, 9, 10, 11; ConAu 53; DcTwCCu 2; IntWW 74; NewYTBS 74; ObitT 1971; OxCArt; OxCTwCA; OxDcArt; PhDcTCA 77; WhAm 6; Who 74; WhoGrA 62; WhoWor 74*

Dunsany, Edward J. M. Plunkett, Baron
[Lord Dunsany]
Irish. Author, Dramatist
Wrote books, plays of fantasy, myth; associated with Abbey Theatre.
b. Jul 24, 1878 in London, England
d. Oct 25, 1957 in Dublin, Ireland
Source: *AtlBL; BioIn 15; CnMD; DcNaB 1951; EncMys; LngCTC; McGEWD 72; ModBrL; ModWD; NewC; Novels; OxCEng 67; PenC ENG; REn; REnWD; TwCA, SUP; TwCWr; WhDW; WhLit*

Duns Scotus, John
"Subtle Doctor"
Scottish. Theologian
Believed in "divine will" rather than "divine intellect"; founded scholastic system called "Scotism."
b. 1266 in Duns, Scotland
d. Nov 8, 1308 in Cologne, Germany
Source: *Alli; BioIn 17, 18; DcLB 115; DcScB; EncEth; LuthC 75; McGEWB; MediFra; NewC; NewCBEL; OxCEng 85, 95; OxCPhil; REn; WrPh P*

Dunton, Davidson
[Arnold Davidson Dunton]
Canadian. Journalist, Businessman
Chm, Canadian Broadcasting Corp., 1945-58; first chm, Ontario Press Council.
b. Jul 4, 1912 in Montreal, Quebec, Canada
d. Feb 7, 1987 in Ottawa, Ontario, Canada
Source: *BioIn 5, 15; CanWW 70, 79, 80, 81, 83; ConAu 121; CurBio 59, 87; IntWW 74, 75, 76, 77, 78, 79, 80, 81, 82, 83; IntYB 78, 79, 80, 81, 82; St&PR 84, 87*

Duong Van Minh
"Big Minh"
Vietnamese. Army Officer
Pres. of Vietnam, 1975.
b. Feb 19, 1916 in My Tho, Vietnam
Source: *BioIn 6, 7, 8, 9, 10; DicTyr; IntWW 74, 75*

Duplessis, Marie
[Alphonsine Plessis]
French. Courtesan, Model
Well-known in Paris, 1840s; first Dame aux Camelias.
b. Jan 15, 1824 in Normandy, France
d. Feb 3, 1847 in Paris, France
Source: *BioIn 2, 3, 4, 7; ContDcW 89; IntDcWB; InWom; OxCFr*

Duplessis, Maurice le Noblet
Canadian. Political Leader
Premier of Quebec, Canada, 1936-39, 1944-59; founded National Union Party.
b. Apr 20, 1890 in Three Rivers, Quebec, Canada
d. Sep 7, 1959 in Schefferville, Quebec, Canada
Source: *CurBio 48, 59; DcCathB; ObitOF 79; ObitT 1951; OxCCan; WhAm 3*

DuPont, Clifford Walter
South African. Political Leader
First pres. of Rhodesia, 1970-75.
b. Dec 6, 1905 in London, England
d. Jun 28, 1978 in Salisbury, Rhodesia
Source: *AfSS 78; BioIn 11; EncSoA; IntWW 74, 75, 76, 77, 78; ObitOF 79; WhoGov 72; WhoWor 74, 76, 78*

DuPont, Eleuthere Irenee
American. Industrialist
Founded gun powder co., textile firm, 1802-04; son of Pierre Samuel DuPont de Nemours.
b. Jun 24, 1771 in Paris, France
d. Oct 31, 1834 in Philadelphia, Pennsylvania
Source: *DcAmB; McGEWB; NewCol 75; OxCAmH; REn; WebBD 83; WhAm HS; WorAl*

DuPont, Henry Francis
American. Business Executive, Philanthropist
Director, EI DuPont de Nemours, 1911-69, GM, 1918-37; founded the Henry Francis Du Pont Winterthur Museum in 1951.
b. May 27, 1880 in Winterthur, Delaware
d. Apr 11, 1969 in Winterthur, Delaware
Source: *BioIn 2, 4, 7, 8, 10, 12, 13; EncSoH; NatCAB 55; WhAm 5*

DuPont, Pierre Samuel
American. Business Executive, Philanthropist
Chairman, EI DuPont de Nemours, 1919-40; pres., General Motors, 1920-23; Longwo od Estate opened to public, 1937.
b. Jan 15, 1870 in Wilmington, Delaware
d. Apr 5, 1954 in Wilmington, Delaware
Source: *BiDAmBL 83; CurBio 40, 54; EncAB-A 26; EncSoH; OxCAmH; WorAl*

DuPont, Pierre Samuel, III
American. Business Executive
Director, Wilmington Trust Co., 1951-66; great-great grandson of founder of chemical firm.
b. Jan 1, 1911 in Wilmington, Delaware
d. Apr 9, 1988 in Rockland, Delaware
Source: *IntWW 74, 75, 76, 77, 78, 79, 80, 81, 82, 83; NatCAB 63N; WhoAm 74, 76, 78, 80; WhoFI 74*

DuPont, Pierre Samuel, IV
American. Politician
Rep. governor of DE, 1977-85; first to declare candidacy for 1988 pres. election, 1986.
b. Jan 22, 1935 in Wilmington, Delaware
Source: *BiDrGov 1978; BiDrUSC 89; BioIn 13, 14, 15; CngDr 74; IntWW 83, 91; MorMA; PolsAm 84; WhoAm 86, 88; WhoAmP 85, 91; WhoE 74, 85; WhoGov 77; WhoWor 84*

DuPont, Samuel Francis
American. Naval Officer
Union Civil War commander; relieved of duty after unsuccessful attack on Charleston, 1863; grandson of Pierre Samuel.
b. Sep 27, 1803 in Bergen Point, New Jersey
d. Jun 23, 1865 in Philadelphia, Pennsylvania
Source: *DcAmB; NatCAB 5; NewCol 75; WebAB 79; WebAMB; WhAm HS*

DuPont de Nemours, Pierre Samuel
French. Economist
Commissioned by Pres. Jefferson to develop educational system for US; influenced French education system.
b. Sep 14, 1739 in Paris, France
d. Aug 7, 1817 in Delaware
Source: *ApCAB; BiD&SB; McGEWB; OxCFr; REn; TwCBDA*

DuPre, Jacqueline
English. Musician
Cellist, Britain's greatest string player; career cut short when stricken with multiple sclerosis, 1972.
b. Jan 26, 1945 in Oxford, England
d. Oct 19, 1987 in London, England
Source: *Baker 78, 84; BioIn 8, 9, 10, 11, 12; BriBkM 80; CurBio 70, 87; IntDcWB; IntWW 74, 75, 76, 77, 78, 79, 80, 81, 82, 83; IntWWM 77, 80; InWom SUP; NewGrDM 80; Who 74, 82, 83, 85, 88; WhoAm 80, 82, 84, 86; WhoMus 72; WhoWor 76, 78*

DuPre, Marcel
French. Composer, Organist
International concertist; made NYC debut, 1921; wrote organ works.
b. May 3, 1886 in Rouen, France
d. May 30, 1971 in Meudon, France
Source: *Baker 78, 84, 92; BioIn 1, 4, 9, 11; BriBkM 80; DcCM; MusMk; MusSN; NewAmDM; NewGrDM 80; NewOxM; NewYTBE 71; OxCMus; PenDiMP; WhAm 5, 7*

Dupree, Minnie
American. Actor
Appeared on stage, screen; films include *Night Club,* 1929.
b. Jan 19, 1873 in San Francisco, California
d. May 23, 1947 in New York, New York
Source: *Film 2; FilmgC; HalFC 80, 84, 88; NotNAT B; ObitOF 79; ThFT; WhoStg 1908; WhScrn 74, 77, 83; WhThe*

DuPrez, Gilbert
French. Opera Singer, Composer
Tenor with Paris Opera, 1837-49; created role of Benvenuto Cellini, 1830s.
b. Dec 6, 1806 in Paris, France
d. Sep 23, 1896 in Passy, France
Source: *Baker 84; CmOp; NewEOp 71; OxDcOp; PenDiMP*

Dupuy, Diane
Canadian. Puppeteer
Founded Famous People Players, puppet troupe largely comprised of mentally handicapped adults.
b. 1948? in Hamilton, Ontario, Canada
Source: *BioIn 15*

Duran, Roberto
"Hands of Stone"
Panamanian. Boxer
One of most feared men in boxing who held world titles in three divisions; record was 77-6, 57 KOs.
b. Jun 16, 1951 in Chorillo, Panama
Source: *BioIn 9, 10, 11, 12, 13, 16; ConAu 131; CurBio 80; DcHiB; HispAmA; HispWr; IntWW 81, 82, 83, 89, 91, 93; LegTOT; WhoBox 74; WhoHisp 91, 92, 94; WhoSpor; WorAl; WorAlBi*

Durand, Asher Brown
American. Artist
Co-founded Hudson River school of landscape painting with Thomas Cole.
b. Aug 21, 1796 in Jefferson, New Jersey
d. Sep 17, 1886 in Jefferson, New Jersey
Source: *AmAu&B; AmBi; ApCAB; BioIn 1, 4, 7, 9, 12, 13, 15, 16; BriEAA; DcAmArt; DcAmB; DcArts; Drake; EarABI; EncASM; HarEnUS; LinLib L, S; McGDA; McGEWB; NatCAB 4; NewYHSD; OxCAmH; OxCAmL 65; TwCBDA; WebAB 74, 79; WhAm HS; WorAl; WorAlBi*

Duran Duran
[Simon LeBon; Nick Rhodes; Andy Taylor; John Taylor; Roger Taylor]
English. Music Group
New Romantic band formed, 1978; hit single "Hungry Like a Wolf," 1982.
Source: *Alli, SUP; BiAUS; BiDBrA; BiDLA; BiDrAC; BiDrUSC 89; BioIn 11, 14, 15, 16, 19, 21; CabMA; CelR 90; Chambr 1, 2; ConMus 4; DcBiPP; DcBrECP; DcLP 87B; DcNaB; DcVicP 2; Drake; Dun&B 88; EncPR&S 89; EncRk 88; EncRkSt; FolkA 87; HarEnR 86; MedHR, 94; NewAmDM; NewCBEL; NewGrDM 80; NotNAT B; OxCPMus; PenDiDA 89; PenEncP; PoIre; RkOn 85; RolSEnR 83; ScF&FL 92; SJGFanW; St&PR 96, 97; WhAm HS; WhoAmP 85, 95; WhoHol 92; WhsNW 85*

Durang, Christopher Ferdinand
American. Dramatist, Actor
Absurdist playwright whose Off-Broadway shows include Obie Award-winning *Sister Mary Ignatius Explains It All for You,* 1979.
b. Jan 2, 1949 in Montclair, New Jersey
Source: *BiDConC; BioIn 11, 12, 13, 15; CamGWoT; ConAu 105; ConDr 82; ConLC 27, 38; ConTFT 3; CurBio 87; CyWA 89; McGEWD 84; NewYTBS 81; WhoThe 81; WorAu 1980; WrDr 92*

Durant, Ariel
[Ida Ariel Ethel Kaufman Durant; Mrs. William James Durant]
American. Author
Collaborated with husband, Will, on *Story of Civilization.*
b. May 10, 1898 in Proskurov, Russia
d. Oct 25, 1981 in Los Angeles, California
Source: *AmWomHi; AmWomWr; AnObit 1981; AuSpks; BioIn 6, 7, 8, 9, 10, 11, 12; CelR; ConAu 4NR, 9R; FacFETw; GrLiveH; LegTOT; NewYTBS 75, 81; RAdv 14, 13-3; WhAm 8; WhoAm 74, 76, 78, 80; WhoAmW 74, 75, 77; WhoWest 74, 76; WhoWor 74, 76*

Durant, Thomas Clark
American. Financier, Railroad Executive
Chief organizer, Union Pacific, who helped build first transcontinental railroad, 1869.
b. Feb 6, 1820 in Lee, Massachusetts
d. Oct 5, 1885 in North Creek, New York
Source: *AmBi; BiDAmBL 83; BioIn 6; DcAmB; McGEWB; REnAW; WebAB 74, 79; WhAm HS; WorAl*

Durant, Will(iam James)
American. Historian, Author
Produced, with wife Ariel, 11-volume, 1926 Pulitzer winner *Story of Civilization.*
b. Nov 5, 1885 in North Adams, Massachusetts
d. Nov 7, 1981 in Los Angeles, California
Source: *AmAu&B; AnObit 1981; AuSpks; Benet 87, 96; BenetAL 91; BioIn 3, 4, 6, 7, 8, 9, 10, 11, 12, 13, 14, 17; BlueB 76; CelR; ConAu 4NR, 9R, 105; CurBio 64, 82, 82N; DcAmSR; DcLEL; EvLB; FacFETw; IntAu&W 76, 77; IntWW 74, 75, 76, 77, 78, 79, 80, 81; LegTOT; LinLib L; LngCTC; MajTwCW; NewYTBS 75, 81; OxCAmH; OxCAmL 65, 83, 95; RAdv 13-3; REn; REnAL; TwCA, SUP; TwoTYeD; WebAB 74, 79; WhAm 7; WhNAA; Who 74, 82; WhoAm 74, 76, 78, 80; WhoWest 74, 76; WhoWor 74, 76, 78, 80; WorAl; WorAlBi*

Durant, William Crapo
American. Auto Manufacturer
Carriage-maker, who co-founded Chevrolet, founded General Motors, 1908.
b. Dec 8, 1861 in Boston, Massachusetts
d. Mar 18, 1947 in New York, New York
Source: *BiDAmBL 83; BioIn 1, 2, 3, 5, 6, 7, 10, 12, 13, 14, 16, 21; DcAmB S4; EncAB-H 1974, 1996; EncABHB 4; McGEWB; NatCAB 15, 36; WebAB 74, 79; WhAm 2; WorAl*

Durante, Francesco
Italian. Composer
Instrumental in development of 18th c. Neapolitan church music.
b. Mar 31, 1684 in Frattamaggiore, Italy
d. Aug 13, 1755 in Naples, Italy
Source: *Baker 78, 84, 92; BioIn 4, 7; BriBkM 80; DcBiPP; GrComp; MusMk; NewEOp 71; NewGrDM 80; NewOxM; OxCMus; OxDcOp*

Durante, Jimmy
[James Francis Durante]
"Ol' Schnozzola"
American. Entertainer
Comedian, singer for over 60 years; nose insured for $100,000 with Lloyd's of London.
b. Feb 10, 1893 in New York, New York
d. Jan 28, 1980 in Santa Monica, California
Source: *AmPS, 78, 79, 80; ItaFilm; JoeFr; LegTOT; MGM; MotPP; MovMk; NewGrDA 86; NewYTBS 80; NewYTET; NotNAT, A; OxCAmT 84; OxCPMus; PenEncP; QDrFCA 92; RadStar; SaTiSS; WebAB 74, 79; WhAm 7; WhoAm 74, 76, 78, 80; WhoCom; WhoHol A; WhoThe 77; WhoWor 74; WhScrn 83; WhThe; WorAl; WorAlBi*

Duranty, Walter
English. Journalist, Author
Correspondent with *NY Times;* won Pulitzer for series on USSR, 1932.
b. May 25, 1884 in Liverpool, England
d. Oct 3, 1957 in Orlando, Florida
Source: *AmAu&B; BenetAL 91; BiDAmJo; BioIn 1, 4, 5, 15, 16, 17, 18; CurBio 43, 58; DcAmB S6; DcLB 29; EncAJ; JrnUS; ObitOF 79; OxCAmL 65, 83; REnAL; TwCA, SUP; WhAm 3*

Duras, Marguerite
[Marguerite Donnadieu]
French. Author
Acclaimed for novels, screenplays; film *Hiroshima Mon Amor,* 1954, won several awards; novel *L'Amant,* 1984, considered her best.
b. Apr 4, 1914 in Gia Dinh, Cochinchina
d. Mar 3, 1996 in Paris, France
Source: *Benet 87, 96; BiDFilm 94; BioIn 6, 7, 10, 11, 12, 13, 14, 15, 16, 17, 18, 19, 20, 21; BlmGWL; CamGWoT; CasWL; ClDMEL 80; CnMD SUP; CnThe; ConAu 25R, 50NR, 151; ConFLW 84; ConLC 3, 6, 11, 20, 34, 40, 68; ContDcW 89; ConTFT 4; ConWorW 93; CroCD; CurBio 85, 96N; CyWA 89; DcArts; DcLB 83; DcTwCCu 2; EncCoWW; EncEurC; EncWL, 2, 3; EncWT; Ent; EvEuW; FacFETw; FemiCLE; FilmEn; FilmgC; FrenWW; GrWomW; GuFrLit 1; HalFC 80, 84, 88; IntAu&W 76, 77, 89, 91; IntDcF 1-2, 2-2; IntDcT 2; IntDcWB; IntWW 74, 75, 76, 77, 78, 79, 80, 81, 82, 83, 89, 91, 93; InWom; ItaFilm; LegTOT; MajTwCW; MakMC; McGEWD 72, 84; MiSFD 9; ModFrL; ModRL; ModWD; ModWoWr; News 96, 96-3; NewYTBS 27, 91; Novels; OxCFilm; OxCThe 83; PenC EUR; RAdv 14, 13-2; ReelWom; REn; REnWD; RfGWoL 95; TwCWr; WhAm 11; WhDW; Who 92; WhoFr 79; WhoThe 72, 77, 81; WhoTwCL; WhoWor 74, 76, 78, 82, 84, 87, 89, 91, 93, 95, 96; WomWMM; WorAl; WorAlBi; WorAu 1950; WorEFlm; WorFDir 2*

Durbin, Deanna
Canadian. Actor
Shared special Oscar with Mickey Rooney, 1938; teenage star, 1930s-40s.
b. Dec 4, 1921 in Winnipeg, Manitoba, Canada
Source: *BiDAmM; BiDFilm, 94; BioIn 7, 9, 11, 15; CmMov; CmpEPM; CurBio 41; FilmEn; FilmgC; HalFC 80, 84, 88; IntDcF 1-3, 2-3; InWom SUP; LegTOT; MotPP; MovMk; OxCFilm; OxCPMus; ThFT; WhoHol 92, A; WorAlBi; WorEFlm*

Durbin, Richard J.
American. Politician
Dem. senator, IL, 1997—.
b. Nov 21, 1944
Source: *AlmAP 84, 88, 92, 96; CngDr 89, 91, 93, 95*

Durcan, Paul
Irish. Poet
Won Whitbread Poetry Prize for *Daddy, Daddy,* 1990.
b. Oct 16, 1944 in Dublin, Ireland
Source: *BiDIrW; ConAu 134; ConLC 43, 70; ConPo 70, 91, 96; DcIrL, 96; EncWL 3; IntAu&W 82, 86, 89, 91, 93; IntWWP 77; OxCIri; OxCTwCP; RGTwCWr; WrDr 92, 94, 96*

Duren, Ryne
[Rinold George Duren]
American. Baseball Player
Relief pitcher, 1954-65; led AL in saves, 20, 1958.
b. Feb 22, 1929 in Cazenovia, Wisconsin
Source: *Ballpl 90; BioIn 5, 7, 11, 13, 14; WhoProB 73*

Durenberger, David Ferdinand
American. Politician
Rep. senator, MN, 1979-95.
b. Aug 19, 1934 in Saint Cloud, Minnesota
Source: *AlmAP 80, 92; BiDrUSC 89; BioIn 11, 13, 14, 15, 16; CngDr 87, 89; CurBio 88; IntWW 89, 91, 93; NewYTBS 87; PolsAm 84; St&PR 75; WhoAm 78, 80, 82, 84, 86, 88, 90, 92, 94, 95; WhoAmP 85, 91; WhoMW 80, 82, 84, 86, 88, 90, 92, 93; WhoWor 80, 82, 84, 87, 89, 91*

Durer, Albrecht
German. Artist
Leading German Renaissance artist; excelled in engraving as well as painting; noted for religious themes.
b. May 21, 1471 in Nuremberg, Germany
d. Apr 6, 1528 in Nuremberg, Germany
Source: *AsBiEn; AtlBL; Benet 87, 96; BioIn 1, 2, 3, 4, 5, 6, 7, 8, 9, 10, 11, 12, 13, 14, 16, 17, 18; ClaDrA; DcArts; DcCathB; DcInv; DcScB; Dis&D; InSci; IntDcAA 90; LegTOT; LinLib L, S; LuthC 75; McGDA; McGEWB; NewC; NewCol 75; OxCArt; OxCEng 85, 95; OxCGer 76, 86; OxDcArt; PenDiDA 89; RAdv 14, 13-3; REn; WhDW; WorAl; WorAlBi*

D'Urfey, Thomas
[Tom D'Urfey]
English. Dramatist, Songwriter
Popular comedies include *The Fond Husband,* 1676; *Madame Fickle,* 1677.
b. 1653 in Exeter, England
d. Feb 26, 1723 in London, England
Source: *Alli; BiD&SB; BioIn 2, 3, 5, 12; BritAu; CamGEL; CamGLE; CamGWoT; CasWL; Chambr 1; ChhPo; DcEnA; DcEnL; DcLB 80; DcNaB, C; EvLB; GrWrEL DR; NewC; NewCBEL; NewGrDM 80; NotNAT B; OxCEng 67, 85, 95; OxCMus; OxCPMus; OxCThe 67, 83; PenC ENG; REn; RfGEnL 91*

Durie, Jo
English. Tennis Player
Britain's number-one woman player, 1983.
b. Jun 27, 1960 in Bristol, England
Source: *BioIn 14; WhoIntT*

Durkee, Eugene R
American. Manufacturer
Introduced first commercially packaged salad dressing, 1857.
b. 1825
d. 1902
Source: *Entr*

Durkheim, Emile
French. Sociologist
A founder of modern sociology; traced origin of religious, moral values to a collective consciousness.
b. Apr 15, 1858 in Epinal, France
d. Nov 15, 1917 in Paris, France
Source: *BiDPsy; BioIn 1, 5, 6, 7, 9, 10, 11, 12, 13, 14, 20; ClDMEL 47, 80; CopCroC; CyWA 89; DcSoc; Dis&D; EncEth; EncUrb; FacFETw; JeHun; LinLib L; LuthC 75; MakMC; McGEWB; NamesHP; NewCol 75; OxCEng 85, 95; OxCFr; OxCLaw; OxCPhil; RAdv 14, 13-3; ThTwC 87; TwCLC 55; WhDW; WorAl; WorAlBi*

Durnan, Bill
[William Ronald Durnan]
Canadian. Hockey Player
Goalie, Montreal, 1943-50; won Vezina Trophy six times; Hall of Fame, 1964.
b. Jan 22, 1916 in Toronto, Ontario, Canada
d. Oct 31, 1972 in Toronto, Ontario, Canada
Source: *BioIn 1, 2, 7, 8, 9, 10; HocEn; NewYTBE 72; WhoHcky 73*

Durning, Charles
American. Actor
Co-starred in *Tootsie,* 1982; plays Harlan on TV show "Evening Shade," 1990—.
b. Feb 28, 1923 in Highland Falls, New York
Source: *ConTFT 5, 14; EncAFC; HalFC 88; IntMPA 86, 92, 96; NotNAT; PlP&P A; WhoAm 80, 82, 84, 86, 88, 90, 92, 94, 95, 96, 97; WhoEnt 92; WhoHol A*

Durocher, Leo Ernest
"Leo the Lip"
American. Baseball Player, Baseball Manager
Infielder, 1928-41; managed for 24 yrs; coined phrase "Nice guys finish last."
b. Jul 27, 1906 in West Springfield, Massachusetts
d. Oct 7, 1991 in Palm Springs, California
Source: *Ballpl 90; BiDAmSp BB; BioIn 1, 2, 3, 4, 5, 6, 7, 8, 9, 10, 12, 14, 15, 16; CurBio 40, 50, 91N; FacFETw; News 92; NewYTBE 71; NewYTBS 81, 87, 91; WebAB 74, 79; WhoAm 82; WhoProB 73; WorAl; WorAlBi*

Durrell, Gerald (Malcolm)
English. Zoologist
Writings on animals include *A Zoo in My Luggage*, 1960; brother of Lawrence.
b. Jan 7, 1925 in Jamshedpur, India
d. Jan 30, 1995 in Saint Helier, England
Source: *Au&Wr 71; AuBYP 2, 3; Benet 87, 96; BioIn 5, 8, 9, 10, 11, 12, 13, 14, 16, 17, 18; BlueB 76; CamGLE; ConAu 4NR, 5R, 25NR, 147; CurBio 85, 87, 95N; DcArts; DcLEL 1940; EnvEnDr; IntAu&W 76, 77, 82, 89, 91, 93; IntWW 74, 75, 76, 77, 78, 79, 80, 81, 82, 83, 89, 91N, 93; LngCTC; MajTwCW; NewC; News 95, 95-3; NotTwCS; REn; ScF&FL 1, 2; SmATA 8, 84; TwCWr; WhAm 11; Who 74, 82, 83, 85, 88, 90, 92, 94; WhoAm 90, 92, 94, 95; WhoWor 74, 76, 78, 84, 87, 89, 91, 93, 95; WorAu 1950; WrDr 76, 80, 82, 84, 86, 88, 90, 92, 94, 96*

Durrell, Lawrence (George)
[Charles Norden]
English. Author
Chief work was four-part novel *Alexandria Quartet*, finished in 1960.
b. Feb 27, 1912 in Darjeeling, India
d. Nov 7, 1990 in Sommieres, France
Source: *AnObit 1990; Au&Wr 71; AuSpks; Benet 87, 96; BioIn 4, 5, 6, 7, 8, 9, 10, 11, 13, 14, 15, 16; BlmGEL; BlueB 76; BritWr S1; CamGEL; CamGLE; CasWL; ChhPo, S3; CnDBLB 7; CnE&AP; CnMD; CnMWL; ConAu 9R, 40NR, 132; ConDr 73, 77, 82, 88, 93; ConLC 1, 4, 6, 8, 13, 27, 41; ConNov 72, 76, 82, 86; ConPo 70, 75, 80, 85, 91; CurBio 63, 91N; CyWA 89; DcArts; DcLB 15, 27, Y90N; DcLEL; DcLP 87A; DcNaB 1986; EncSF, 93; EncWL, 2, 3; EngPo; EvLB; FacFETw; GrWrEL N; IntAu&W 77, 89; IntvTCA 2; IntWW 74, 75, 76, 77, 78, 79, 80, 81, 82, 83, 89, 91; IntWWP 77; LegTOT; LiExTwC; LinLib L, S; LngCEL; LngCTC; MajTwCW; ModBrL, S1, S2; ModWD; NewC; NewCBEL; NewYTBS 90; Novels; OxCEng 67, 85, 95; OxCTwCP; PenC ENG; RAdv 1, 14, 13-1; REn; RfGEnL 91; RGTwCWr; ScF&FL 1, 2, 92; ScFSB; TwCA SUP; TwCSFW 81, 86, 91; TwCWr; WebE&AL; WhAm 10; WhDW; Who 74, 82, 83, 85, 88, 90, 92N; WhoFr 79; WhoTwCL; WhoWor 74, 78, 80, 82, 84, 87, 89, 91; WorAl; WorAlBi; WrDr 76, 80, 82, 84, 86, 88, 90*

Durrenmatt, Friedrich
[Friedrich Duerrenmatt]
Swiss. Author
Writings include *The Visit; The Physicists.*
b. Jan 5, 1921 in Konolfingen, Switzerland
d. Dec 14, 1990 in Neuchatel, Switzerland
Source: *AnObit 1990; Au&Wr 71; Benet 87, 96; BiE&WWA; BiGAW; BioIn 5, 8, 9, 10, 12, 14, 15; CamGWoT; CasWL; ClDMEL 80; CnMD; CnThe; ConAu 17R, 33NR; ConFLW 84; ConLC 1, 4, 8, 11, 15, 43, 45; CroCD; CrtSuMy; CurBio 91N; CyWA 89; DcArts; DcLB 69, 124; EncWL, 2, 3; EncWT; Ent; EuWr 13; EvEuW; FacFETw; GrFLW; IntAu&W 76, 77, 82; IntDcT 2; IntWW 74, 75, 76, 77, 78, 79, 80, 81, 82, 83, 89, 91N; LegTOT; LinLib L; MajMD 1; MajTwCW; McGEWB; McGEWD 72, 84; ModGL; ModWD; NewYTBS 90, 91; NotNAT; OxCAmT 84; OxCEng 85, 95; OxCGer 76, 86; OxCThe 67, 83; PenC EUR; PlP&P; RAdv 14, 13-2; REn; REnWD; RfGWoL 95; TwCCr&M 80B, 85B, 91, 91B; TwCWr; WhAm 10; WhDW; Who 74, 82, 83, 85, 90, 92N; WhoThe 72, 77, 81; WhoTwCL; WhoWor 74, 76, 78, 84, 87, 89, 91; WorAl; WorAlBi; WorAu 1950*

Durrie, George Henry
American. Artist
Genre landscapist, who drew farm, winter scenes reproduced by Currier and Ives.
b. Jun 6, 1820 in Hartford, Connecticut
d. Oct 15, 1863 in New Haven, Connecticut
Source: *BioIn 1, 7, 9; BriEAA; DcAmArt; McGDA; NewYHSD; WhAm HS*

Durslag, Melvin
American. Journalist
Columnist with *LA Examiner & Herald Examiner*, 1953.
b. Apr 29, 1921 in Chicago, Illinois
Source: *Ballpl 90; ConAu 101; WhoAdv 90; WhoAm 74, 76, 78, 80, 82, 84, 86, 88, 90, 92; WhoWest 74, 76*

Dury, Ian
English. Singer, Composer
Blends soul, disco; albums include *Laughter*, 1980.
b. May 12, 1942 in Billericay, England
Source: *BioIn 11, 12; ConMuA 80A; ConTFT 9; EncPR&S 89; EncRk 88; HarEnR 86; LegTOT; OxCPMus; PenEncP; RolSEnR 83; WhoRocM 82; WhsNW 85*

Duryea, Charles Edgar
"Father of the Automobile"
American. Inventor, Manufacturer
Organized Duryea Motor Wagon Co., 1895; sold first car, 1896.
b. Dec 15, 1862 in Canton, Illinois
d. Sep 28, 1938 in Philadelphia, Pennsylvania
Source: *DcAmB S2; OxCAmH; WebAB 74; WhAm 4, HSA*

Duryea, Dan
American. Actor
Character actor, often villain; films include *The Little Foxes*, 1941.
b. Jan 23, 1907 in White Plains, New York
d. Jun 7, 1968 in Los Angeles, California
Source: *BiDFilm, 81, 94; BioIn 1, 8, 9, 10; CmMov; FilmEn; FilmgC; ForYSC; GangFlm; HalFC 80, 84, 88; HolP 40; IntDcF 1-3, 2-3; ItaFilm; LegTOT; MotPP; MovMk; NotNAT B; ObitOF 79; OxCFilm; WhAm 5; WhoHol B; WhScrn 74, 77, 83; WorAl; WorAlBi; WorEFlm*

Duryea, J(ames) Frank
American. Inventor
Designed first successful gasoline-powered car in US; won first auto race, Chicago, 1895.
b. Oct 8, 1869 in Washburn, Illinois
d. Feb 15, 1967 in Saybrook, Connecticut
Source: *BioIn 7, 8; DcAmB S8; OxCAmH*

DuSable, Jean Baptiste
American. Pioneer
Built first house, opened first trading post on site of modern-day Chicago.
b. 1750
d. Aug 28, 1818 in Saint Charles, Missouri
Source: *InB&W 80; WebAB 74; WhAm HS*

Duse, Eleanora
Italian. Actor
Famed tragedienne; made NYC debut, 1893; great rival of Bernhardt.
b. Oct 3, 1858 in Vigevano, Austria
d. Apr 23, 1924 in Pittsburgh, Pennsylvania
Source: *ContDcW 89; Film 2; IntDcWB; InWom SUP; ItaFilm; NotNAT A, B; REn; WhoHol B; WhoStg 1908; WhScrn 74, 77, 83; WorAl; WorAlBi; WorEFlm*

Dussault, Nancy Elizabeth
American. Actor, Singer
Nominated twice for Tonys, 1960s; played wife in TV series "Too Close for Comfort," 1980-83.
b. Jun 30, 1936 in Pensacola, Florida
Source: *BiE&WWA; BioIn 13; ConTFT 4; EncMT; IntMPA 92; InWom SUP; NewYTBS 77; NotNAT; WhoThe 81*

Dutoit, Charles
Swiss. Conductor
Music director, Montreal Symphony Orchestra, 1977-91; artistic director Philadelphia Orchestra 1990-91; music director, Orchestra National de France, 1991—.
b. Oct 7, 1936 in Lausanne, Switzerland

Source: *Baker 78, 84; BioIn 13, 14, 15, 16; CanWW 89; CurBio 87; IntWW 91; IntWWM 90; NewAmDM; NewGrDM 80; NewYTBS 82; PenDiMP; WhoAm 80, 82, 84, 86, 88, 90, 92, 94, 95, 96, 97; WhoE 81, 83, 85, 86, 89, 91, 93, 95, 97; WhoEnt 92; WhoWor 89, 97*

Dutra, Eurico Gaspar
Brazilian. Political Leader
Pres. of Brazil, 1945-50; under his leadership democracy was restored.
b. May 18, 1885 in Cuiaba, Brazil
d. Jun 11, 1974 in Rio de Janeiro, Brazil
Source: *BioIn 1, 10; CurBio 74N; DcCPSAm; DcTwHis; EncLatA; WhAm 6*

Dutra, Olin
American. Golfer
Turned pro, 1924; won PGA, 1932, US Open, 1934; Hall of Fame, 1962.
b. Jan 17, 1901 in Monterey, California
d. May 5, 1983 in Newman, California
Source: *BiDAmSp OS; BioIn 13; LegTOT; WhoGolf*

Dutton, Charles S
American. Actor
Plays title role in TV series "Roc," 1991—.
b. Jan 30, 1951 in Baltimore, Maryland
Source: *BioIn 14; ConTFT 9*

Dutton, E(dward) P(ayson)
American. Publisher
Founded E.P. Dutton publishing house, 1858.
b. Jan 4, 1831 in Keene, New Hampshire
d. Sep 6, 1923 in Ridgefield, Connecticut
Source: *AmAu&B; ChhPo; LinLib L; WhAm 1*

Dutton, Ralph Stawell
English. Historian
Wrote on stately residences: *The English House.*
b. Aug 25, 1898 in Hampshire, England
d. Apr 20, 1985
Source: *ConAu 116; WhE&EA; Who 74, 82, 83, 85*

Dutton, Red
[Mervyn A Dutton]
Canadian. Hockey Player, Hockey Executive
Defenseman, 1926-36; succeeded Frank Calder as president of NHL, 1943-46; Hall of Fame, 1958.
b. Jul 23, 1898 in Russell, Manitoba, Canada
d. Mar 15, 1987 in Calgary, Alberta, Canada
Source: *CanWW 70; HocEn; WhoHcky 73*

Duvalier, Francois
"Papa Doc"
Haitian. Political Leader
Dictator of Haiti, 1957-71; during reign economy declined, terror increased.
b. Apr 14, 1907 in Port-au-Prince, Haiti
d. Apr 21, 1971 in Port-au-Prince, Haiti
Source: *BiDLAmC; BioIn 5, 6, 7, 8, 9, 10, 12, 14, 16, 17; CaribW 2; CurBio 58, 71, 71N; DcCPCAm; DcPol; DcTwHis; DicTyr; EncLatA; EncRev; FacFETw; HisWorL; InB&W 80, 85; InSci; LegTOT; McGEWB; NewYTBE 71; ObitOF 79; ObitT 1971; WhAm 5; WhDW; WorAl; WorAlBi*

Duvalier, Jean-Claude
"Baby Doc"
Haitian. Political Leader
Became "pres. for life" of Haiti, 1970; overthrown in coup, 1986, fled into exile.
b. Jul 3, 1951 in Port-au-Prince, Haiti
Source: *BiDLAmC; BioIn 13, 14, 15, 16; CurBio 72; DcAmImH; DcCPCAm; DicTyr; EncLatA; EncWB; HisWorL; InB&W 80; IntWW 74, 75, 76, 77, 78, 79, 80, 81, 82, 83, 89, 91, 93; IntYB 78, 79, 80, 81, 82; NewYTBE 71; WhoGov 72, 75; WhoWor 74, 84, 91; WorAlBi*

Duvall, Camille
"Golden Goddess of Water Skiing"
American. Skier
Water skier who excels in slalom competitions.
b. 1960
Source: *BioIn 15; ConNews 88-1*

Duvall, Robert Selden
American. Actor
Best known for *Tender Mercies,* 1983; *The Great Santini,* 1980.
b. Jan 5, 1931 in San Diego, California
Source: *BioIn 13, 14, 15; CelR 90; ConAu 116; ConTFT 7; CurBio 77; FilmEn; FilmgC; HalFC 84, 88; IntMPA 86, 92; MovMk; NewYTBE 72; NewYTBS 81; WhoAm 86, 90; WhoEnt 92; WhoHol A; WorAl; WorAlBi*

Duvall, Shelley
American. Actor
Appeared in films *Nashville,* 1975; *Popeye,* 1979.
b. Jul 7, 1949 in Houston, Texas
Source: *BioIn 10, 11, 12, 13, 14, 15, 16; BioNews 74; ConTFT 3; EncAFC; FilmEn; HalFC 80, 84, 88; IntDcF 1-3; IntMPA 82, 84, 86, 88, 92, 94, 96; InWom SUP; LegTOT; LesBEnT 92; NewYTBS 77; WhoAm 80, 82, 84, 86, 88, 90, 92, 94, 95, 96, 97; WhoAmW 89, 91, 93, 95, 97; WhoEnt 92; WhoHol 92, A; WhoWor 95, 96, 97; WorAl; WorAlBi*

Duveen, Joseph, Sir
English. Art Collector
Helped establish major US collections.
b. Oct 14, 1869 in Hull, England
d. May 25, 1939 in London, England
Source: *BioIn 13, 15, 16; DcNaB 1931; GrBr; OxCAmH; OxDcArt; WhAmArt 85; WhE&EA*

Duveneck, Frank
American. Artist, Educator
Noted for brushwork; defined planes of the face on canvas.
b. Oct 9, 1848 in Covington, Kentucky
d. Jan 3, 1919 in Cincinnati, Ohio
Source: *AmBi; ArtsNiC; Benet 87; BiDAmEd; BioIn 4, 7, 8, 9, 15; BriEAA; DcAmArt; DcAmB; LegTOT; LinLib S; McGDA; NatCAB 20; OxCAmL 65; REn; WebAB 74, 79; WhAm 1; WhAmArt 85*

DuVigneaud, Vincent
American. Chemist
Won Nobel Prize, 1955; synthesized penicillin and two pituitary hormones.
b. May 18, 1901 in Chicago, Illinois
d. Dec 11, 1978 in White Plains, New York
Source: *AmMWSc 73P, 76P; AsBiEn; BiESc; BioIn 13, 15; BlueB 76; DcScB; InSci; IntWW 74, 75, 76, 77, 78; McGMS 80; NobelP; WebAB 74, 79; Who 74; WhoAm 74, 76, 78; WhoE 77, 79; WhoNob 90; WhoWor 74; WorAl; WorAlBi*

Duvivier, Julien
French. Director
Best known for films *Pepe le Moko; Maria Chapdelaine.*
b. Oct 8, 1896 in Lille, France
d. Oct 29, 1967 in Paris, France
Source: *BiDFilm, 81, 94; BioIn 8, 15; CurBio 43, 68; DcArts; DcFM; DcTwCCu 2; EncEurC; FilmEn; FilmgC; GangFlm; HalFC 80, 84, 88; IntDcF 1-2, 2-2; ItaFilm; LegTOT; MiSFD 9N; MovMk; ObitOF 79; ObitT 1961; OxCFilm; WorEFlm; WorFDir 1*

Duvoisin, Roger Antoine
American. Children's Author, Illustrator
Numerous works include 1948 Caldecott winner *White Snow, Bright Snow;* wrote *Happy Lion* series.
b. Aug 28, 1904 in Geneva, Switzerland
d. Jun 30, 1980 in Morristown, New Jersey
Source: *AnObit 1980; ConAu 11NR, 101; JBA 51; NewYTBS 80; OxCChiL; SmATA 23N, 30; TwCChW 83*

Duyckinck, Evert Augustus
American. Editor
Co-edited *New York Literary World,* 1847-53; compiled two-volume *Cyclopedia of American Literature,* 1855.
b. Nov 23, 1816 in New York, New York
d. Aug 13, 1878 in New York, New York
Source: *Alli, SUP; AmAu; AmAu&B; AmBi; ApCAB; BbD; BenetAL 91; BiD&SB; BioIn 10, 12, 16, 18; CelCen; CyAL 2; DcAmAu; DcAmB; DcEnL; DcLB 3, 64; DcNAA; Drake; HarEnUS; NatCAB 1; OxCAmL 65, 83, 95; PenC AM; REnAL; TwCBDA; WhAm HS*

Dvorak, Ann
American. Actor
Starred in *Scarface,* 1932.
b. Aug 2, 1912 in New York, New York
d. Dec 10, 1979 in Honolulu, Hawaii
Source: *BioIn 1, 8, 11, 12; EncAFC; Film 2; FilmEn; FilmgC; ForYSC; GangFlm; HalFC 80, 84, 88; HolP 30; InWom SUP; LegTOT; MotPP; MovMk; ThFT; What 2; WhoHol A; WhScrn 83*

Dvorak, Anton
Czech. Composer
Best known for symphony in E minor, *From the New World,* 1892-95.
b. Sep 8, 1841 in Nalahozeves, Bohemia
d. May 1, 1904 in Prague, Bohemia
Source: *AtlBL; BenetAL 91; OxCAmH; OxCAmL 65; REn; REnAL; WhAm HS*

Dwan, Allan
[Joseph Aloysius Dwan]
Canadian. Director
Directed estimated 1,850 films, 1909-61.
b. Apr 3, 1885 in Toronto, Ontario, Canada
d. Dec 21, 1981 in Woodland Hills, California
Source: *AmFD; AnObit 1981; BiDFilm, 81, 94; BioIn 9, 11, 12, 13, 15; DcFM; EncAFC; FacFETw; FilmEn; FilmgC; GangFlm; HalFC 80, 84, 88; IlWWHD 1; IntDcF 1-2, 2-2; IntMPA 75, 76, 77, 78, 79, 80, 81, 82; LegTOT; MiSFD 9N; MovMk; NewYTBS 81; OxCFilm; TwYS A; WhAm 8; WhoAm 76; WhoHrs 80; WorEFlm; WorFDir 1*

Dwiggins, William Addison
American. Type Designer, Illustrator
Known for designing bindings for Knopf publishers, 1936, later did entire books.
b. Jun 19, 1880 in Martinsville, Ohio
d. Dec 25, 1956 in Hingham, Massachusetts
Source: *AmAu&B; BioIn 1, 3, 4, 5, 15, 16; ConDes 84; DcAmB S6; IlsCB 1744, 1946; ObitOF 79; OhA&B; OxCAmL 65; OxCDecA; REnAL; WhAm 3; WhAmArt 85; WhoAmA 80N, 82N, 84N, 86N, 89N, 91N, 93N*

Dwight, Timothy
American. Author
Pres., Yale U., 1795-1817; writings include verse *Conquest of Canaan,* 1785.
b. May 14, 1752 in Northampton, Massachusetts
d. Jan 11, 1817 in New Haven, Connecticut
Source: *Alli; AmAu; AmAu&B; AmBi; AmWrBE; ApCAB; Benet 87, 96; BenetAL 91; BibAL; BiDAmEd; BiDAmM; BiD&SB; BiDLA; BioIn 1, 4, 5, 6, 8, 10, 12, 14, 17, 19; CamGEL; CamGLE; CamHAL; CasWL; CelCen; ChhPo, S1; CnDAL; CyAL 1; CyEd; DcAmAu; DcAmB; DcAmReB 1, 2; DcBiPP; DcEnL; DcLB 37; DcNAA; Drake; EncAB-H 1974, 1996; EncARH; EncCRAm; EvLB; GrWrEL P; HarEnUS; LinLib L, S; LuthC 75; McGEWB; NatCAB 1; NewGrDA 86; NinCLC 13; OxCAmH; OxCAmL 65, 83, 95; PenC AM; PoChrch; REn; REnAL; RfGAmL 87, 94; TwCBDA; WebAB 74, 79; WebE&AL; WhAm HS; WhAmRev*

Dwinell, Lane
American. Politician
Rep. governor of NH, 1955-59; head of Agency for International Development, 1969-71.
b. Nov 14, 1906
d. Mar 27, 1997 in Hanover, New Hampshire
Source: *BiDrGov 1789; BioIn 4, 5; St&PR 75; WhoAm 74, 76, 78, 80; WhoAmP 73, 77, 79, 81, 83, 85, 87, 89, 91, 93, 95*

Dworkin, Andrea
American. Feminist, Writer
Believing that it hurts women, worked to have pornography classified as a form of sex discimination; wrote *Woman Hating,* 1974.
b. Sep 26, 1946 in Camden, New Jersey
Source: *AmWomWr SUP; ConAu 16NR, 21AS, 39NR, 77; ConLC 43; CurBio 94; EncWHA; FemiCLE; FemiWr; GayLL; IntWW 91, 93; JeAmWW; MajTwCW; OxCWoWr 95; RadHan; WomPubS 1925; WrDr 92, 94, 96*

Dwyer, Cynthia
"53rd Hostage"
American. Journalist
Free-lance writer, imprisoned for attempting to free 52 American hostages in Iran; released, Feb 1981.
b. 1931? in Little Rock, Arkansas
Source: *BioIn 12*

Dwyer, Florence Price
American. Politician
Rep. congresswoman from NJ, late 1960s-73.
b. Jul 4, 1902 in Reading, Pennsylvania
d. Feb 29, 1976 in Elizabeth, New Jersey
Source: *BiDrAC; BiDrUSC 89; BioIn 17; NewYTBS 76; WhoAm 74; WhoAmP 73; WhoE 74; WhoGov 75*

Dyce, Alexander
Scottish. Editor
Noted for edition of Shakespeare, 1857, 1864-67; edited Collins's poems, 1827.
b. Jun 30, 1798 in Edinburgh, Scotland
d. May 15, 1869 in London, England
Source: *Alli; BiD&SB; BioIn 9; BritAu 19; CamGLE; CasWL; CelCen; Chambr 3; ChhPo, S1, S2; DcBiPP; DcBrWA; DcEnL; DcEuL; DcNaB; EvLB; NewC; NewCBEL; NewCol 75; OxCEng 85, 95; WebBD 83*

Dyce, William
Scottish. Artist
Historical, portrait painter of House of Parliament frescoes, 1848.
b. Sep 19, 1806 in Aberdeen, Scotland
d. Feb 14, 1864 in Streatham, England
Source: *ArtsNiC; BioIn 1, 4, 6, 8, 10, 11, 12, 13; CelCen; ClaDrA; DcBiPP; DcBrWA; DcNaB; DcVicP, 2; McGDA; NewGrDM 80; OxCArt; OxDcArt; WebBD 83*

Dye, Babe
[Cecil Henry Dye]
Canadian. Hockey Player
Right wing, 1919-31, mostly with Toronto; won Art Ross Trophy, 1923, 1925; Hall of Fame, 1970.
b. May 13, 1898 in Hamilton, Ontario, Canada
d. Jan 2, 1962 in Chicago, Illinois
Source: *BioIn 2; HocEn; WhoHcky 73; WhoSpor*

Dyer, Charles (Raymond)
English. Writer
Novels include *Prelude to Fury,* 1959; screenplays include *Staircase,* 1969.
b. Jul 17, 1928 in Shrewsbury, England
Source: *Au&Wr 71; BiE&WWA; BioIn 10, 13; BlueB 76; ConAu 21R, 44NR; ConBrDr; ConDr 73, 77, 82, 88, 93; ConTFT 6; CroCD; DcLB 13; DcLEL 1940; EncWT; IntAu&W 76, 77, 82, 86, 89, 91; NotNAT; Who 74, 82, 83, 85, 88, 90, 92, 94; WhoHol 92, A; WhoThe 72, 77, 81; WhoWor 76, 78; WrDr 76, 80, 82, 84, 86, 88, 90, 92, 94, 96*

Dyer, Edward, Sir
English. Diplomat, Poet
Most famous poem begins "My mind to me a kingdom is," a description of contentment.
b. 1545? in Somerset, England
d. May 1607 in London, England
Source: *Alli; BiD&SB; BritAu; CasWL; Chambr 1; CnE&AP; CroE&S; DcBiPP; DcEuL; EvLB; NewC; OxCEng 67; REn*

Dyer, Wayne Walter
American. Author
Wrote *Your Erroneous Zones,* 1976; *The Sky's the Limit,* 1980.
b. May 10, 1940 in Detroit, Michigan
Source: *ConAu 25NR, 69; WhoAm 78, 80, 82, 84, 86, 88, 90, 92, 94, 95, 96, 97; WrDr 92*

Dyer-Bennet, Richard
American. Singer
Popular as singer of American, English ballads and folk songs, performing at concert level, 1940s.
b. Oct 6, 1913 in Leicester, England
d. Dec 14, 1991 in Monterey, Massachusetts
Source: *Baker 78, 84, 92; BiDAmM; BioIn 4, 5, 6, 17, 18; CurBio 44, 92N; EncFCWM 69; NewYTBS 91; WhAm 10; WhoAm 74, 76*

Dykes, Jimmy
[James Joseph Dykes]
American. Baseball Player, Baseball Manager
Infielder, 1918-39; managed 21 yrs; with Joe Gordon, involved in first trade of ML managers, 1960.
b. Nov 10, 1896 in Philadelphia, Pennsylvania
d. Jun 15, 1976 in Philadelphia, Pennsylvania
Source: *Ballpl 90; BaseEn 88; BiDAmSp BB; BioIn 1, 2, 5, 6, 10, 15, 18; NewYTBS 76; WhoProB 73; WhScrn 83*

Dykes, John Bacchus
English. Composer, Clergy
Hymns include "Nearer, My God to Thee," "Lead, Kindly Light."
b. Mar 10, 1823 in Kingston-upon-Hull, England
d. Jan 20, 1876 in Ticehurst, England
Source: *Baker 78, 84, 92; BioIn 1, 11; DcNaB; LuthC 75; NewGrDM 80; OxCMus; WebBD 83*

Dykstra, John
American. Auto Executive
Pres. of Ford Motor Co., 1961-63; manufacturing specialist with GM, 1934-47.
b. Apr 16, 1898 in Steins, Netherlands
d. Mar 2, 1972 in Southfield, Michigan
Source: *BioIn 5, 6, 9; CurBio 63, 72N; DcAmB S9; NewYTBE 72; ObitOF 79; WhAm 5*

Dykstra, Lenny
American. Baseball Player
Led Philadelphia Phillies to National League Eastern Division title in 1993; National League All-Star, 1990 and 1993; nominated in 1993 as National League MVP.
b. Feb 10, 1963 in Santa Ana, California
Source: *Ballpl 90; LegTOT; News 93; WhoAm 95, 96, 97; WhoE 95, 97; WhoSpor; WhoWor 95, 96*

Dylan, Bob
[Robert Allen Zimmerman]
American. Singer, Songwriter
Songs include "Blowin' in the Wind," 1962; "The Times They Are a'Changin'," 1964; Rock Hall of Fame, 1988.
b. May 24, 1941 in Duluth, Minnesota
Source: *AmAu&B; AmCulL; AmDec 1960; AmSong; ASCAP 66; Baker 78, 84, 92; BenetAL 91; BgBkCoM; BiDAmM; BioIn 6, 7, 8, 9, 10, 11, 12, 13, 14, 15, 16, 17, 18, 19, 20, 21; BkPepl; BlueB 76; CamGLE; CelR, 90; ConAu 41R; ConLC 3, 4, 6, 12, 77; ConMuA 80A; ConMus 3; ConPo 70, 75, 80, 85, 91, 96; CurBio 91; DcArts; DcLB 16; DcLEL 1940; DcLP 87B; DcTwCCu 1; EncAB-H 1974, 1996; EncFCWM 69, 83; EncPR&S 89; EncRk 88; EncRkSt; FacFETw; HalFC 88; HarEnR 86; IlEncRk; IntAu&W 76, 77, 82, 86, 89, 91; IntWW 74, 75, 76, 77, 78, 79, 80, 81, 82, 83, 89, 91, 93; IntWWP 77, 82; JeHun; LegTOT; LinLib L; LNinSix; MakMC; MiSFD 9; MugS; NewAmDM; NewGrDA 86; NewGrDM 80; NewOxM; NewYTBS 85, 91; OxCEng 85; OxCPMus; OxCTwCP; PenEncP; PolProf J; PopAmC SUP; RComAH; RkOn 78, 84; RolSEnR 83; WebAB 74, 79; WhoAm 74, 76, 78, 80, 82, 84, 86, 88, 90, 92, 94, 95, 96, 97; WhoE 74, 75, 77; WhoEnt 92; WhoHol 92; WhoRock 81; WhoRocM 82; WhoWor 74, 76, 78, 80, 82, 84, 97; WhoWorJ 78; WorAl; WorAlBi; WrDr 76, 80, 82, 84, 86, 88, 90, 92, 94, 96*

Dysart, Richard (Allan)
American. Actor
Plays Leland McKenzie on TV series "L.A. Law," 1986-94; films include *The Terminal Man,* 1974.
b. Mar 30, 1929 in Brighton, Massachusetts
Source: *ConTFT 4; IntMPA 92; LegTOT; NotNAT; VarWW 85; WhoEnt 92; WhoHol 92; WorAlBi*

Dyson, Frank Watson, Sir
English. Astronomer
Astronomer, royal director of Greenwich Observatory, 1910-33; inaugurated radio transmission of Greenwich time, 1920s.
b. Jan 8, 1868 in Measham, England
d. May 25, 1939
Source: *BiESc; BioIn 2, 14, 19; DcNaB 1931; DcScB; FacFETw; InSci; NewCol 75*

Dyson, Freeman John
English. Physicist, Educator
Works in field of mathematical physics, astrophysics; professor, Princeton U., 1953-94.
b. Dec 15, 1923 in Crowthorne, England
Source: *AmMWSc 86, 92; BioIn 13, 14, 16; CamDcSc; ConAu 17NR, 89; CurBio 80; EncWB; FacFETw; IntAu&W 91; IntWW 91; Who 90, 92; WhoAm 86, 90, 97; WhoTech 89; WorAu 1980; WrDr 92*

Dyson, Michael Eric
American. Educator
Director of Institute of African American Research, University of North Carolina, 1994—.
b. Oct 23, 1958 in Detroit, Michigan
Source: *ConAu 154; ConBlB 11; WhoAfA 96; WhoBlA 94*

Dzerzhinsky, Felix Edmundovich
Polish. Politician
Took part in Polish, Russian revolutions; held several high offices in Soviet govt.
b. Sep 11, 1877 in Vilna, Russia
d. Jul 20, 1926 in Moscow, Union of Soviet Socialist Republics
Source: *BlkwERR; CopCroC; DcTwHis; EncE 75; FacFETw; McGEWB; SpyCS*

Dzhanibekov, Vladimir Alexandrovich
Russian. Cosmonaut
Took part in five space missions; best known for helping rehabilitate *Salyut-7* space station, 1985.
b. May 13, 1942 in Iskander, Union of Soviet Socialist Republics
Source: *BioIn 10, 15; ConNews 88-1; FacFETw*

E

Eads, James Buchanan
American. Scientist, Engineer
Built Eads Bridge across the Mississippi at St. Louis, 1867-74.
b. May 23, 1820 in Lawrenceburg, Indiana
d. Mar 8, 1887 in Nassau, Bahamas
Source: *Alli SUP; AmBi; ApCAB; BiInAmS; BioIn 1, 2, 3, 4, 5, 6, 7, 8, 9, 11, 14, 16, 20, 21; DcAmAu; DcAmB; DcAmDH 80, 89; DcAmMiB; DcNAA; EncAB-H 1974, 1996; HarEnUS; IndAu 1917; InSci; LinLib S; MacEA; McGEWB; MorMA; NatCAB 5; OxCAmH; REnAW; TwCBDA; WebAB 74, 79; WhAm HS; WhCiWar*

Eagels, Jeanne
American. Actor
Broadway star as Sadie Thompson in *Rain,* 1922-26; died from heroin overdose.
b. Jun 26, 1894 in Kansas City, Missouri
d. Oct 3, 1929 in New York, New York
Source: *AmBi; BioAmW; BioIn 3, 15, 16; DcAmB; FamA&A; Film 2; FilmEn; FilmgC; HalFC 80, 84, 88; LibW; NotAW; NotNAT A, B; OxCAmT 84; ThFT; TwYS; WhAm 1; WhoHol B; WhScrn 74, 77, 83; WhThe; WorAl*

Eagleburger, Lawrence S.
American. Government Official
Secretary of State, 1992-93.
b. Aug 1, 1930 in Milwaukee, Wisconsin
Source: *BioIn 10, 11, 12, 13, 14; CngDr 89, 91; CurBio 92; IntWW 91; NewYTBS 82; USBiR 74; WhoAm 90; WhoAmP 91; WhoE 89; WhoFI 89; WhoGov 77; WhoWor 84*

Eagles, The
[Don Felder; Glenn Frey; Don Henley; Bernie Leadon; Randy Meiser; Tim Schmidt; Joe Walsh]
American. Music Group
Sold over 40 million albums; *The Long Run,* 1979, was double platinum.
Source: *BgBkCoM; BioIn 14, 15, 16, 17, 18, 21; BkPepl; ConMuA 80A; ConMus 3; DcNaB; EncFCWM 83; EncPR&S 74, 89; EncRk 88; EncRkSt; HarEnCM 87; HarEnR 86; IlEncCM; IlEncRk; NewAmDM; NewGrDA 86; NewGrDM 80; OxCPMus; PenEncP; RkOn 78, 84; RolSEnR 83; St&PR 96; WhoHol 92; WhoNeCM A; WhoRock 81; WhoRocM 82*

Eagleson, Alan
[Robert Alan Eagleson]
"The Eagle"
Canadian. Hockey Player
Exec. director, NHL Players Assn., 1967-89; organized many int'l hockey events.
b. Apr 24, 1933 in Saint Catharines, Ontario, Canada
Source: *BioIn 10, 11, 12, 13, 14, 16, 17; CanWW 83; ConNews 87-4; NewYTBS 80; WhoAm 78, 80, 82; WhoCan 73, 75, 77, 80, 82*

Eagleton, Thomas Francis
American. Politician
George McGovern's running mate, 1972; withdrew due to past history of nervous exhaustion.
b. Sep 4, 1929 in Saint Louis, Missouri
Source: *AmCath 80; BiDrAC; BiDrUSC 89; BioIn 6, 8, 9, 10, 12; BioNews 74; BlueB 76; CngDr 74, 77, 79, 81, 83, 85; ConAu 105; CurBio 73; IntWW 74, 75, 76, 77, 78, 79, 80, 81, 82, 83, 89, 91, 93; NewYTBE 72; PolsAm 84; PresAR; WhoAm 74, 76, 78, 82, 84, 86, 94, 95; WhoAmP 85, 91; WhoGov 72, 75, 77; WhoMW 74, 76, 78, 80, 82, 84, 86, 88; WhoWor 78, 80, 82, 87; WorAl; WorAlBi*

Eaker, Ira Clarence
American. Aviator, Army Officer
Commanded US air forces during WW II; influential in establishing Air Force as separate service branch, 1947.
b. Apr 13, 1896 in Field Creek, Texas
d. Aug 6, 1987 in Camp Springs, Maryland
Source: *AmAu&B; BiDWWGF; BioIn 1, 12, 15; CurBio 42, 87; DcAmMiB; HarEnMi; InSci; WebAMB; Who 74, 82, 83, 85*

Eakins, Thomas
American. Artist
Realist painter known for sporting scenes, surgical operations, portraits.
b. Jul 25, 1844 in Philadelphia, Pennsylvania
d. Jun 25, 1916 in Philadelphia, Pennsylvania
Source: *AmBi; AmCulL; ApCAB; ArtsAmW 1; ArtsNiC; AtlBL; Benet 87, 96; BiDAmEd; BioIn 1, 2, 3, 4, 5, 6, 7, 8, 9, 10, 11, 12, 13, 14, 15, 16, 17, 18, 19, 20, 21; BriEAA; DcAmArt; DcAmB; DcArts; DcSeaP; EncAB-H 1974, 1996; GayN; ICPEnP A; IlBEAAW; IntDcAA 90; LegTOT; MacBEP; McGEWB; MorMA; NatCAB 5; OxCAmH; OxCAmL 65; OxCArt; OxCTwCA; OxDcArt; RComAH; REn; REnAL; WebAB 74, 79; WhAm 1; WhAmArt 85; WhDW; WorAl; WorAlBi*

Eames, Charles
American. Designer, Director, Writer
Designed sets for TV, films; directed, wrote films including *Tops,* 1969.
b. Jun 17, 1907 in Saint Louis, Missouri
d. Aug 21, 1978 in Saint Louis, Missouri
Source: *AmCulL; AmDec 1950; BioIn 1, 2, 5, 7, 8, 9, 10, 11, 12; BriEAA; CmCal; ConArch 80, 87, 94; ConDes 84, 90, 97; CurBio 78N; DcArts; DcD&D; DcTwDes; EncMA; FacFETw; LegTOT; MakMC; McGDA; PenDiDA 89; PeoHis; WebAB 74, 79; WhoAm 74, 76; WhoWor 74; WorAl; WorAlBi; WorEFlm*

Eames, Emma Hayden
American. Opera Singer
Soprano; with NY Met., 1891-1909; extremely popular in both Britain, US.
b. Aug 13, 1865 in Shanghai, China
d. Jun 13, 1952 in New York, New York
Source: *AmWom; NotAW MOD; WomWWA 14*

Eames, Ray
American. Designer
Collaborated with husband, Charles, in designing popular chairs, tables, other furniture: *Eames chair.*
b. 1916 in Sacramento, California

d. Aug 21, 1988 in Los Angeles, California
Source: *AnObit 1988; BioIn 10, 14, 15, 16; ConDes 90, 97; DcArts; DcTwDes; FacFETw; InWom SUP; NewYTBS 88; PeoHis; WhAm 9; WhoAm 88*

Eanes, Antonio dos Santos Ramalho
Portuguese. Political Leader
Pres. of Portugal, 1976-86; first freely elected in 50 yrs.
b. Jan 25, 1935 in Alcains, Portugal
Source: *BioIn 10, 11, 13; CurBio 79; IntWW 89, 91, 93; WhoWor 87*

Earhart, Amelia (Mary)
American. Aviator
First woman to fly solo across Atlantic, 1932; disappeared on round-the-world flight.
b. Jul 24, 1898 in Atchison, Kansas
d. Jul 2, 1937
Source: *AmBi; Benet 87, 96; BioIn 1, 2, 3, 4, 5, 6, 7, 8, 9, 10, 11, 12, 13, 14, 15, 16, 17, 18, 19, 20, 21; ChhPo; ConHero 1; ContDcW 89; DcAmB S2; DcNAA; EncAB-A 2; Expl 93; FacFETw; GoodHs; HerW, 84; InSci; IntDcWB; InWom, SUP; LinLib L, S; NotAW; OxCAmH; REn; WebAB 74, 79; WhAm 1; WomFir; WomWMM; WorAl; WorAlBi*

Earl, Ronnie
American. Musician
Guitarist with blues band, Roomful of Blues 1979-1987; founded band, the Broadcasters, 1987; solo albums *They Call Me Mr. Earl,* 1985; *I Like It When It Rains,* 1986.
Source: *BioIn 18; ConMus 5*

Earle, Alice Morse
American. Author, Historian
Wrote on US colonial past: *Old Time Gardens,* 1901.
b. Apr 27, 1851 in Worcester, Massachusetts
d. Feb 16, 1911 in Hempstead, New York
Source: *AmWomHi; AmWomWr; InWom SUP; LibW; NotAW; OxCAmL 83; OxCWoWr 95*

Earle, Ralph
[Ralph Earl]
American. Artist
Itinerant, primitive painter known for Concord butterflies, stern portraits.
b. May 11, 1751 in Shrewsbury, Massachusetts
d. Nov 24, 1801 in Pendleton, South Carolina
Source: *ApCAB; BioIn 1, 2, 3, 4, 5, 8, 11; BriEAA; DcAmArt; DcAmB; DcBrECP; Drake; EncCRAm; FolkA 87; McGDA; McGEWB; NatCAB 11; NewYHSD; OxCAmH; OxCAmL 65; OxCArt; OxDcArt; TwCBDA; WebAB 74, 79; WhAm HS; WhAmRev*

Earle, Sylvia Alice
American. Scientist
Marine botanist, deep-sea explorer who broke records with "Jim-dive," 1979; co-founder, Deep Ocean Engineering, 1982; first female chief scientist, National Oceanic and Atmospheric Administration, 1990-92.
b. Aug 30, 1935 in Gibbstown, New Jersey
Source: *AmMWSc 73P; BioIn 15, 16; CurBio 92; InWom SUP; NewYTBS 91; WhoAm 82, 86, 88, 90, 92, 94, 95, 96, 97; WhoAmW 83, 89, 91, 93, 95, 97; WhoFrS 84; WhoWest 87, 89, 92, 94*

Early, Gerald
American. Author, Educator
Author of books on black culture; wrote *Tuxedo Junction,* 1990.
b. Apr 21, 1952 in Philadelphia, Pennsylvania
Source: *ConAu 133; CurBio 95; DcTwCCu 5; IntAu&W 93; WhoAfA 96; WhoAm 96, 97; WhoBlA 92, 94; WrDr 94, 96*

Early, Jubal Anderson
American. Military Leader
Confederate general who led Washington, DC, raid, 1864.
b. Nov 3, 1816 in Franklin County, Virginia
d. Mar 2, 1894 in Lynchburg, Virginia
Source: *Alli SUP; AmBi; ApCAB; BbD; BiD&SB; BiDConf; BiDSA; BioIn 1, 2, 4, 5, 16, 17, 18; CivWDc; DcAmAu; DcAmB; DcAmMiB; DcNAA; EncSoH; HarEnUS; LinLib L, S; NatCAB 4, 36; OxCAmH; TwCBDA; WebAB 74, 79; WebAMB; WhAm HS; WhCiWar; WhoMilH 76; WorAl*

Earp, Morgan
American. Lawman
Brother of Wyatt; peace officer, gambler, miner.
b. Apr 24, 1851 in Pella, Iowa
d. Mar 18, 1882 in Tombstone, Arizona
Source: *BioIn 17, 19, 20; CopCroC; REnAW*

Earp, Virgil W
American. Lawman
Brother of Wyatt; gambler, saloonkeeper, peace officer.
b. Jul 18, 1843 in Hartford, Kentucky
d. 1905 in Goldfield, Nevada
Source: *REnAW*

Earp, Wyatt Berry Stapp
American. Lawman
Deputy marshal, Dodge City, KS, 1876-77; survived famous gunfight at OK Corral, 1881.
b. Mar 19, 1848 in Monmouth, Illinois
d. Jan 13, 1929 in Los Angeles, California
Source: *BioIn 3, 4, 5, 6, 7, 8, 10, 11, 12, 13; FilmgC; NewCol 75; OxCFilm; REnAW; WebAB 74, 79; WhAm 4, HS, HSA; WorAl*

Earth, Wind and Fire
[Philip Bailey; Roland Bautista; Jessica Cleaves; Larry Dunn; Johnny Graham; Ralph Johnson; Al McKay; Fred White; Maurice White; Verdine White; Andrew Woolfolk]
American. Music Group
Changed sound of black pop music, 1970s; sold over 19 million albums; won six Grammys for *Touch the World,* 1987.
Source: *Alli; BiDAfM; BioIn 14, 15; ConMuA 80A; ConMus 12; EncPR&S 89; EncRk 88; HarEnR 86; IlEncBM 82; IlEncRk; InB&W 80, 85A; NewAmDM; NewGrDA 86; PenEncP; RkOn 78, 84; RolSEnR 83; SoulM; WhoRock 81; WhoRocM 82*

East, John Porter
American. Politician
Conservative Rep. senator from NC, 1980-86; wrote *Council-Manager Government,* 1965.
b. May 5, 1931 in Springfield, Illinois
d. Jun 29, 1986 in Greenville, North Carolina
Source: *AmMWSc 73S, 78S; BiDrUSC 89; CngDr 81, 83, 85; ConAu 17R, 119; WhAm 9; WhoAm 82, 84; WhoAmP 73, 75, 77, 79, 81, 83, 85; WhoSSW 82, 86; WhoWor 82, 84; WrDr 76, 80, 82, 84*

Eastern Jewel
[Yoshiko Kawashima]
Chinese. Spy
Helped ignite WW II in Far East; beheaded for treason.
b. 1906
d. 1948
Source: *BioIn 19*

Eastlake, Charles Lock, Sir
English. Artist
Served as keeper of National Gallery, 1843-47; known for paintings of Napoleon, Italian banditti, life of Christ.
b. Nov 17, 1793 in Plymouth, England
d. Dec 24, 1865 in Pisa, Italy
Source: *Alli, SUP; ArtsNiC; BiD&SB; BioIn 1, 3, 7, 10, 11; DcBiPP; DcBrWA; DcEnL; DcNaB, C; DcNiCA; DcVicP, 2; LinLib L, S; McGDA; NewC; OxCArt; OxDcArt; REn*

Eastlake, William (Derry)
American. Author
Writings include *The Bamboo Bed,* 1970; *Dancers in the Scalp House,* 1975.
b. Jul 14, 1917 in New York, New York
d. Jun 1, 1997 in Bisbee, Arizona
Source: *AmAu&B; Au&Wr 71; BenetAL 91; BioIn 9, 10, 14; BlueB 76; ConAu 1AS, 5NR, 5R; ConLC 8; ConNov 72, 76, 82, 86, 91, 96; DcLB 6; DcVicP 2; DrAF 76; DrAPF 80, 91; EncFWF; FifWWr; IntAu&W 76, 77, 82; ModAL S1; Novels; OxCAmL 65, 83, 95; PenC AM; PostFic; REnAL; TwCWW 82, 91; WhoAm 74, 76, 78, 80, 82, 84, 86, 88, 90, 92, 94, 95; WhoUSWr 88; WhoWor 74; WhoWrEP 89, 92, 95; WorAu 1950;*

WrDr 76, 80, 82, 84, 86, 88, 90, 92, 94, 96

Eastland, James Oliver
"Big Jim"
American. Politician
Dem. senator from MS, 1941-78; opposed civil rights legislation.
b. Nov 28, 1904 in Doddsville, Mississippi
d. Feb 19, 1986 in Greenwood, Mississippi
Source: *BiDrAC; BiDrUSC 89; BioIn 1, 2, 3, 4, 5, 9, 10, 11, 12; CngDr 74, 77; CurBio 49, 86; EncMcCE; IntWW 83; LiveMA; NewYTBE 72; NewYTBS 86; WhoAm 84; WhoAmP 73, 75, 77, 79; WhoGov 72; WhoSSW 75; WhoWor 74*

Eastman, Carol
[Adrien Joyce]
American. Screenwriter
Won Oscar for screenplay *Five Easy Pieces,* 1970.
Source: *BioIn 9, 15; ConAu 116, X; DcLB 44*

Eastman, Charles Alexander
American. Writer, Physician
Published autobiography *Indian Boyhood,* 1902; practicing physician on several reservations.
b. 1858 in Minnesota
d. 1939
Source: *AmAu&B; AmLY; AmSocL; BiDSocW; BiNAW, B, SupB; BioIn 2, 3, 7, 8, 9, 11, 12, 13, 14, 18, 19, 20, 21; ConAmL; DcAmAu; DcNAL; InSci; JBA 34, 51; NatNAL; NotNaAm; OxCAmL 65, 83, 95; REnAL; TwCLC 55; WhAm 4; WhNaAH; YABC 1*

Eastman, George
American. Inventor, Industrialist
Invented roll film, 1884; the Kodak camera, 1888.
b. Jul 12, 1854 in Waterville, New York
d. Mar 14, 1932 in Rochester, New York
Source: *AmBi; AmSocL; AsBiEn; Baker 78, 84, 92; BiDAmBL 83; BiESc; BioIn 1, 3, 4, 5, 6, 7, 8, 9, 10, 12, 13, 14, 15, 16, 17, 18, 19, 21; DcAmB S1; DcArts; DcFM; DcInv; DcTwDes; EncAB-H 1974, 1996; FacFETw; FilmEn; FilmgC; GayN; HalFC 80, 84, 88; ICPEnP; InSci; LegTOT; LinLib S; MacBEP; McGEWB; MorMA; NatCAB 13, 26; NewGrDA 86; OxCAmH; OxCFilm; OxCMus; RComAH; TwCBDA; WebAB 74, 79; WhAm 1; WhDW; WorAl; WorAlBi; WorEFlm; WorInv*

Eastman, Mary Henderson
American. Author
Wrote Indian tales, anti-Uncle Tom work *Uncle Phillis's Cabin,* 1852.
b. 1818 in Fauquier County, Virginia
d. Feb 24, 1887 in Washington, District of Columbia
Source: *Alli; AmAu&B; AmWomHi; AmWomWr; ApCAB; BiD&SB; BiDSA; BlmGWL; ChhPo; DcAmAu; DcEnL; DcNAA; InWom SUP; LibW; NotAW; OxCAmL 65, 83; REnAL; TwCBDA*

Eastman, Max Forrester
American. Author
Best known for book *Enjoyment of Poetry,* 1913; founder, editor, *The Masses,* 1913-18.
b. Jan 4, 1883 in Canandaigua, New York
d. Mar 25, 1969 in Bridgetown, Barbados
Source: *AmAu&B; AmLY; CasWL; CnDAL; ConAmA; ConAmL; ConAu 9R; CurBio 69; DcAmSR; DcLEL; LngCTC; OxCAmL 65; PenC AM; REn; TwCA SUP; WhE&EA*

Easton, Florence Gertrude
English. Opera Singer
Soprano; with NY Met., 1917-29; sang 150 roles in four languages.
b. Oct 25, 1884 in Middlesborough, England
d. Aug 13, 1955 in New York, New York
Source: *CmOp; InWom; MusSN*

Easton, Sheena
[Sheena Shirley Orr]
Scottish. Singer
Hit pop songs include "Morning Train," 1981; "We've Got Tonight," 1987 (with Kenny Rogers); "U Got the Look," 1987 (with Prince).
b. Apr 27, 1959 in Bellshill, Scotland
Source: *BioIn 13, 14, 15; CelR 90; ConMus 2; EncPR&S 89; EncRk 88; EncRkSt; HarEnR 86; IlEncRk; LegTOT; NewWmR; PenEncP; RkOn 85; RolSEnR 83; VarWW 85; WhoAm 94, 95, 96, 97; WhoAmW 91, 93; WhoEnt 92; WhoHol 92*

Eastwood, Clint
American. Actor, Director
Starred in TV series "Rawhide," 1959-66; movie *Dirty Harry,* 1971; mayor of Carmel, CA, 1986-88.
b. May 31, 1930 in San Francisco, California
Source: *Au&Arts 18; BiDFilm, 81, 94; BioIn 10, 11, 12, 13, 14, 15, 16; BioNews 74; BkPepl; BlueB 76; CelR, 90; ConTFT 1, 6, 13; CurBio 71, 89; DcArts; DcTwCCu 1; FacFETw; FilmEn; FilmgC; ForYSC; GangFlm; HalFC 80, 84, 88; IlWWHD 1; IntDcF 1-3, 2-3; IntMPA 77, 80, 84, 86, 88, 92, 94, 96; IntWW 78, 79, 80, 81, 82, 83, 89, 91, 93; ItaFilm; LegTOT; MiSFD 9; MotPP; MovMk; News 93-3; NewYTBS 85; OxCFilm; WhoAm 86, 88, 90, 92, 94, 95, 96, 97; WhoEnt 92; WhoHol 92, A; WhoHrs 80; WhoWor 91, 93, 95, 96, 97; WorAl; WorAlBi; WorEFlm; WorFDir 2*

Eaton, Cyrus Stephen
American. Financier
Formed Continental Gas & Electric Co., Canada; wrote *The Engineer as Philosopher,* 1961.
b. Dec 27, 1883 in Pugwash, Nova Scotia, Canada
d. May 9, 1979 in Northfield, Ohio
Source: *AmAu&B; BiDAmBL 83; BiDInt; BioIn 1, 3, 4, 5, 6, 7, 8, 10, 11, 12; BioNews 74; BusPN; CanWW 70, 79, 80; CurBio 48, 79; DcAmB S10; FacFETw; IntWW 74, 75, 76, 77, 78; NewYTBE 73; NewYTBS 79; PolProf E, K; WebAB 74, 79; WhAm 7; Who 74; WhoAm 74, 76, 78; WhoFI 74, 75; WhoWor 74, 78; WorAl*

Eaton, John Henry
American. Politician
Youngest ever sworn into Senate; Dem. from TN, 1818-29; secretary of war, 1829-31.
b. Jun 18, 1790 in Halifax County, North Carolina
d. Nov 17, 1856 in Washington, District of Columbia
Source: *Alli; AmBi; ApCAB; BiDrAC; BiDrATG; BiDrUSC 89; BiDrUSE 71, 89; BiDSA; BioIn 10; DcAmAu; DcAmB; DcNAA; DcNCBi 2; EncSoH; NatCAB 5; OxCAmH; PolPar; WhAm HS; WhAmP; WhFla*

Eaton, Mark E
American. Basketball Player
Center, Utah, 1982—; led NBA in blocked shots three years; holds record for blocked shots in season, 1985; defensive player of year, 1989.
b. Jan 24, 1957 in Westminister, California
Source: *NewYTBS 84; OfNBA 87*

Eaton, Mary
American. Actor
In Ziegfeld Follies, 1920-22; starred in *Five O'Clock Girl,* 1927.
b. 1901 in Norfolk, Virginia
d. Oct 10, 1948 in Hollywood, California
Source: *CmpEPM; EncMT; Film 2; HalFC 80, 84, 88; NotNAT B; ObitOF 79; WhoHol B; WhScrn 74, 77, 83; WhThe*

Eaton, Robert James
American. Auto Executive
President of GM Europe, 1988-92; CEO of Chrysler Corp., 1993—.
b. Feb 13, 1940 in Buena Vista, Colorado
Source: *AmMWSc 92, 95; St&PR 84, 87, 91, 93, 96, 97; WhoAm 84, 86, 88, 92, 94, 95, 96, 97; WhoEmL 87; WhoFI 87, 92, 94, 96; WhoMW 92, 93, 96; WhoWor 91, 95, 96, 97*

Eaton, Shirley
English. Actor
Played the girl painted gold in James Bond film *Goldfinger,* 1964.
b. 1936 in London, England
Source: *FilmEn; FilmgC; ForYSC; HalFC 80, 84, 88; MotPP; WhoHol 92, A*

Eaton, Theophilus
English. Colonial Figure, Politician
Founded New Haven, CT, 1638; governor of New Haven colony from 1639.
b. 1590 in Stony Stratford, England
d. Jan 7, 1658 in New Haven, Connecticut
Source: *AmBi; BiDrACR; DcAmB; DcNaB; EncCRAm; NatCAB 6; NewCol 75; OxCAmH; OxCLaw; WhAm HS*

Eaton, Timothy
Canadian. Merchant
Founded Canadian dept. store, Eaton's.
b. 1834
d. Jan 31, 1907
Source: *BioIn 11, 18; DcCanB 13; DcIrB 78, 88; MacDCB 78*

Eaton, Wyatt
American. Artist
Portraitist; a founder of Society of American Artists, 1877.
b. May 6, 1849 in Philipsburg, Quebec, Canada
d. Jun 7, 1896 in Newport, Rhode Island
Source: *AmBi; ApCAB; BriEAA; ChhPo; DcAmB; DcCanB 12; MacDCB 78; NatCAB 8; TwCBDA; WhAm HS*

Eazy-E
[Eric Wright]
American. Rapper
Founder of the rap group N.W.A.
b. c. Sep 7, 1963 in Compton, California
d. Mar 26, 1995 in Los Angeles, California
Source: *BioIn 20, 21; News 95, 95-3; WhoAfA 96*

Eban, Abba
[Aubrey Solomon]
Israeli. Diplomat
UN representative, 1949-59; ambassador to US, 1950-59; wrote *Israel in the World,* 1966.
b. Feb 2, 1915 in Cape Town, South Africa
Source: *BioIn 14, 15, 16, 18; BioNews 75; ConAu 26NR, 57; CurBio 57; EncWB; HisEAAC; IntAu&W 77; IntWW 74, 75, 76, 77, 78, 79, 80, 81, 82, 83, 89, 91, 93; MidE 78, 79, 80, 81, 82; NewYTBS 87; Who 74, 82, 83, 85, 88, 90, 92, 94; WhoWor 74, 76, 78, 82, 84, 87, 89, 91, 93, 95, 96; WhoWorJ 72*

Ebb, Fred
American. Lyricist
With John Kander, wrote song "New York, New York"; won Tonys for *Cabaret,* 1967, *Woman of the Year,* 1980; Songwriter's Hall of Fame, 1983.
b. Apr 8, 1933 in New York, New York
Source: *AmSong; BioIn 15; ConAu 24NR; ConDr 88D; ConTFT 5; LegTOT; NewGrDA 86; OxCAmT 84; OxCPMus; VarWW 85; WhoAm 86; WhoEnt 92; WhoThe 72, 77, 81*

Ebbets, Charles Hercules
American. Baseball Executive
Owner, Brooklyn Dodgers, 1890-1925; built Ebbets Field, Brooklyn, 1913.
b. Oct 29, 1859 in New York, New York
d. Apr 18, 1925 in New York, New York
Source: *BiDAmSp BB; BioIn 15; WhoProB 73*

Eberhard, Johann August
German. Philosopher
Writings include a critical piece on Kantian philosophy in favor of that of Leibnitz, 1772-78.
b. Aug 31, 1739 in Halberstadt, Prussia
d. Jan 6, 1809 in Halle, Germany
Source: *BiD&SB; BioIn 10; DcBiPP; DcEuL; LuthC 75; NewGrDM 80*

Eberhart, Mignon Good
American. Author
Wrote over 50 detective fiction books, including *Murder in Waiting,* 1973; created sleuth nurse, Sarah Keate.
b. Jul 6, 1899 in Lincoln, Nebraska
d. Oct 8, 1996 in Greenwich, Connecticut
Source: *AmAu&B; AmWomWr; AuNews 2; AuSpks; BioIn 14; ConAu 73; CorpD; EncMys; HalFC 84, 88; InWom SUP; LngCTC; REnAL; TwCA, SUP; TwCCr&M 85; TwCRGW; WhNAA; WhoAm 84; WhoWor 74; WorAl; WrDr 86, 88*

Eberhart, Richard (Ghormley)
American. Poet, Dramatist
Won Pulitzer for *Selected Poems 1930-1965,* 1965; also wrote *Ways of Light,* 1980.
b. Apr 5, 1904 in Austin, Minnesota
Source: *AmAu&B; AmWr; Benet 87, 96; BenetAL 91; BiE&WWA; BioIn 3, 4, 5, 6, 7, 8, 9, 10, 11, 12, 14, 15, 17; BlueB 76; CamGLE; CamHAL; CasWL; ChhPo, S3; CnE&AP; ConAu 1R, 2NR; ConLC 1, 3, 11, 19, 56; ConPo 70, 75, 80, 85, 91, 96; DcLB 48; DcLEL; DrAP 75; DrAPF 80, 91; DrAS 74E, 78E, 82E; Focus; GrWrEL P; IntAu&W 77, 82, 89, 91; IntvTCA 2; IntWW 74, 75, 76, 77, 78, 79, 80, 81, 82, 83, 89, 91, 93; IntWWP 77; LegTOT; LinLib L; LngCTC; MajTwCW; ModAL, S1, S2; NewCon; NotNAT; OxCAmL 65, 83, 95; OxCTwCP; PenC AM; RAdv 1, 14, 13-1; REn; REnAL; RfGAmL 87, 94; SixAP; TwCA SUP; TwCWr; WebE&AL; Who 74, 82, 83, 85, 88, 90, 92, 94; WhoAm 74, 76, 78, 80, 82, 84, 86, 88, 90, 92, 94, 95, 96, 97; WhoE 74; WhoTwCL; WhoUSWr 88; WhoWor 74, 76, 78, 80, 82, 84, 87, 91; WhoWrEP 89, 92, 95; WorAl; WorAlBi; WrDr 76, 80, 82, 84, 86, 88, 90, 92, 94, 96*

Eberle, Bob
[The Eberle Brothers; Robert Eberle]
American. Singer, Bandleader
Singer with Dorsey Brothers band; who popularized 1940s hits "Tangerine," 1942; "Green Eyes," 1931.
b. Jul 24, 1916 in Mechanicville, New York
d. Nov 17, 1981 in Glen Burnie, Maryland
Source: *BioIn 3, 10; CmpEPM; NewYTBS 81*

Eberle, Edward Walter
American. Naval Officer
Chief of US naval operations, 1923-28; devised new method of laying mines.
b. Aug 17, 1864 in Denton, Texas
d. Jul 6, 1929 in Washington, District of Columbia
Source: *AmBi; DcAmB; NatCAB 21; WebAMB; WhAm 1*

Eberle, Irmengarde
[Allyn Allen; Phyllis Ann Carter]
American. Author
Among 63 books are *Mustang on the Prairie,* 1968; *Moose Live Here,* 1971.
b. Nov 11, 1898 in San Antonio, Texas
d. Feb 27, 1979
Source: *AmAu&B; AuBYP 2, 3; BioIn 1, 2, 7, 9, 13; BkCL; ConAu 1R, 2NR, 85; CurBio 46; InWom; JBA 51; SmATA 2, 23N; WhoAm 74, 76, 78; WhoAmW 61, 64, 66, 68, 70, 72, 74, 77; WhoWor 74*

Eberle, Mary Abastenia St. Leger
American. Artist
Statuettes include *The White Slave,* 1913.
b. Apr 6, 1878 in Webster City, Iowa
d. Feb 26, 1942 in New York, New York
Source: *DcWomA; NotAW; WomWWA 14*

Eberle, Ray
[The Eberle Brothers]
American. Singer
Star vocalist for Glen Miller, 1940s; brother of Bob.
b. Jan 19, 1919 in Hoosick Falls, New York
Source: *BgBands 74; BioIn 12; CmpEPM; LegTOT; WhScrn 83; WorAl*

Ebers, Georg Moritz
German. Egyptologist, Author
Popularized Egyptology by means of romantic novels: *An Egyptian Princess,* 1864.
b. Mar 1, 1837 in Berlin, Germany
d. Aug 7, 1898 in Tutzing, Germany
Source: *BbD; BiD&SB; BioIn 7; CasWL; DcBiA; EuAu; EvEuW; LinLib L; OxCGer 76, 86; REn*

Ebersol, Dick
[Duncan Dickie Ebersol]
American. TV Executive
President, NBC Sports, 1989—.
b. Jul 28, 1947 in Torrington, Connecticut
Source: *CurBio 96*

Eberstadt, Ferdinand
American. Government Official, Banker
A pioneer in mutual funds investment; held government positions dealing with defense, finance.
b. Jun 19, 1890 in New York, New York
d. Nov 11, 1969
Source: *BioIn 1, 2, 3, 8, 9, 12, 16, 18; CurBio 42, 70; NatCAB 60; WhAm 5*

Ebert, Carl
[Anton Charles Ebert]
American. Producer
Music director of worldwide opera companies.
b. Feb 20, 1887 in Berlin, Germany
d. May 14, 1980 in Santa Monica, California
Source: *AnObit 1980; Baker 84; BioIn 12; BlueB 76; CmOp; EncWT; Film 2; IntDcOp; IntWW 74, 75, 76, 77, 78, 79, 80; IntWWM 77, 80; MetOEnc; NewEOp 71; NewGrDA 86; NewGrDM 80; NewYTBS 80; OxDcOp; Who 74*

Ebert, Friedrich
German. Political Leader
First pres. of German republic, 1919; leading proponent of Weimar constitution.
b. Feb 4, 1871 in Heidelberg, Germany
d. Feb 28, 1925 in Berlin, Germany
Source: *BioIn 8, 9; DcTwHis; Dis&D; EncTR, 91; LinLib S; McGEWB; NewCol 75; OxCGer 76, 86; REn; WebBD 83*

Ebert, Roger (Joseph)
American. Critic
Film critic of TV shows "Sneak Previews," "At the Movies," "Siskel & Ebert," 1975—; won Pulitzer, 1975; film critic, *Chicago Sun-Times,* 1967—.
b. Jun 18, 1942 in Urbana, Illinois
Source: *BioIn 8, 13, 14, 15; ConAu 22NR, 45NR, 69; ConTFT 9; EncTwCJ; LegTOT; WhoAm 74, 76, 78, 80, 82, 84, 86, 88, 90, 92, 94, 95, 96, 97; WhoAmW 83; WhoEnt 92; WhoMW 74, 76, 78, 80, 82, 84, 86, 90, 92, 93, 96; WhoUSWr 88; WhoWrEP 89, 92, 95; WrDr 80, 82, 84, 86, 88, 90, 92, 94, 96*

Ebsen, Buddy
[Christian Rudolf Ebson, Jr.]
American. Actor
Starred in TV series "The Beverly Hillbillies," 1962-71; "Barnaby Jones," 1973-79.
b. Apr 2, 1908 in Belleville, Illinois
Source: *ASCAP 66; BiDD; BioIn 10, 11, 12, 17, 19, 20; CmpEPM; ConTFT 3; CurBio 77; EncAFC; EncMT; EncVaud; FilmEn; FilmgC; HalFC 80, 84, 88; IntMPA 75, 76, 77, 78, 79, 80, 81, 82, 84, 86, 88, 92, 94, 96; LegTOT; LesBEnT 92; MotPP; MovMk; NewYTET; WhoAm 78, 80, 82, 92, 94, 95, 96, 97; WhoHol 92, A; WorAl; WorAlBi*

Eccles, John C(arew), Sir
Australian. Scientist
Shared Nobel Prize in medicine, 1963; wrote *The Understanding of the Brain,* 1973.
b. Jan 27, 1903 in Melbourne, Australia
d. May 2, 1997 in Contra, Switzerland
Source: *AmMWSc 73P; BioIn 15; ConAu 9NR, 65; CurBio 72; IntWW 83; NobelP; Who 85, 88; WhoAm 76, 88; WhoMedH; WhoNob, 95; WhoWor 84, 87, 89, 97; WrDr 88*

Eccles, Marriner Stoddard
American. Economist, Government Official
Member of Federal Reserve Board, 1936-51, chm., 1936-48; directed many financial companies in Utah.
b. Sep 9, 1890 in Logan, Utah
d. Dec 18, 1977 in Salt Lake City, Utah
Source: *AmAu&B; BiDAmBL 83; BioIn 1, 2, 3, 7, 8, 11, 12; CurBio 41, 78; DcAmB S10; EncAB-H 1974, 1996; IntWW 74, 75, 76, 77, 78; IntYB 78; LinLib L, S; NewYTBS 77; PolProf T; St&PR 75; WhAm 7; WhoAm 74, 76, 78; WhoFI 74; WhoWor 74; WorAl*

Ecevit, Bulent
Turkish. Political Leader
Premier of Republic of Turkey, 1974-79.
b. May 28, 1925 in Istanbul, Turkey
Source: *BioIn 10, 11, 12, 16, 17; ConTurW; CurBio 75; EncWB; FacFETw; IntAu&W 89; IntWW 74, 75, 76, 77, 78, 79, 80, 81, 82, 83, 89, 91, 93; IntYB 79, 80, 81, 82; MidE 78, 79, 80, 81, 82; NewCol 75; NewYTBS 77, 80; PolLCME; WhoWor 74, 76, 78, 80, 82, 84, 87, 89, 91, 93, 95*

Echegaray y Eizaguirre, Jose
Spanish. Dramatist
Shared Nobel Prize for Literature, 1904.
b. Apr 19, 1831 in Madrid, Spain
d. Sep 15, 1916 in Madrid, Spain
Source: *BbD; BiD&SB; ClDMEL 47; CnMD; ConAu 104; DcSpL; McGEWD 72; ModRL; ModWD; NotNAT B; OxCThe 67; PenC EUR; REn; TwCWr; WhLit; WhoNob*

Echeverria Alvarez, Louis
Mexican. Political Leader
Pres. of Mexico, 1970-76.
b. Jan 17, 1922 in Mexico City, Mexico
Source: *BioNews 74; CurBio 72; EncWB; IntWW 83; NewYTBE 70; WhoGov 75; WhoSSW 75; WhoWor 74*

Echohawk, John E.
American. Lawyer
Executive director, Native American Rights Fund, 1977—.
b. Aug 11, 1945 in Albuquerque, New Mexico
Source: *BioIn 20, 21; NotNaAm; WhoAmL 79*

Echo-Hawk, Walter R.
American. Lawyer
Attorney with the Native American Rights Fund; cases include the return of Native American remains, 1989-90.
b. Jun 23, 1948 in Oklahoma
Source: *NotNaAm*

Eck, Johann Maier von
German. Theologian
Roman Catholic; strongest of Martin Luther's opponents; first to force him into public opposition to Catholicism.
b. Nov 13, 1486 in Eck, Germany
d. Feb 10, 1543 in Ingolstadt, Bavaria
Source: *DcCathB; McGEWB; NewCol 75; OxCGer 76*

Eckart, William Joseph
American. Designer, Producer
Designed costumes for films *The Pajama Game,* 1957; *The Night They Raided Minsky's,* 1968.
b. Oct 21, 1920 in New Iberia, Louisiana
Source: *BiE&WWA; ConTFT 4; NotNAT; OxCAmT 84; PlP&P; WhoSSW 73; WhoThe 77, 81*

Eckener, Hugo
German. Aeronautical Engineer
Trained German dirigible crews during World War I.
b. Aug 10, 1868 in Flensburg, Prussia
d. Aug 14, 1954 in Friedrichshafen, Germany (West)
Source: *BioIn 3, 4, 8; LinLib S; ObitOF 79; ObitT 1951; WhDW*

Eckersley, Dennis
American. Baseball Player
Relief pitcher Oakland As, 1987—; Cy Young, AL MVP, 1992.
b. Oct 7, 1954 in Oakland, California
Source: *Ballpl 90; BioIn 13, 15, 16, 18, 19*

Eckert, Horst
Polish. Children's Author, Illustrator
Writings, illustrations include *The Magic Auto,* 1971; *The Thieves and the Raven,* 1970.
b. Mar 11, 1931 in Zaborze, Poland
Source: *BioIn 11, 18, 19; ConAu 37R, 38NR; MajAI; SmATA 8, 72*

Eckert, John Presper, Jr.
American. Inventor, Engineer
Co-invented ENIAC, first digital computer to handle coded material, 1946; also co-invented Binac, binary automatic computer.
b. Apr 9, 1919 in Philadelphia, Pennsylvania
d. Jun 3, 1995 in Bryn Mawr, Pennsylvania
Source: *AmMWSc 73P; BioIn 6, 7, 8, 9, 14, 15, 20, 21; HisDcDP; LarDcSc; McGMS 80; WhDW*

Eckert, William Dole
"General Who"; "Spike"; "Unknown Soldier"
American. Baseball Executive
Retired air force officer; served as baseball commissioner, 1965-69; replaced by Bowie Kuhn.
b. Jan 20, 1909 in Freeport, Illinois
d. Apr 16, 1971 in Freeport, Bahamas
Source: *BiDAmSp BB; BioIn 3, 7, 8, 9, 15; NewYTBE 71; WhAm 5; WhoProB 73*

Eckhart, Johannes
"Meister"
German. Philosopher, Mystic
Had conflicts with Church for heresy, 1326; thoughts were influential for Quakers after his death.
b. 1260 in Hochheim, Germany
d. 1327 in Avignon, France
Source: *CasWL; ClMLC 9; EuAu; EvEuW; LinLib L; LuthC 75; NewC; OxCGer 76; PenC EUR; WhDW*

Eckstein, George
American. Writer
Wrote TV shows "The Untouchables," 1959-63; "Gunsmoke," 1955-75; "Dr. Kildare," 1961-66.
b. May 3, 1928 in Los Angeles, California
Source: *ConTFT 2; LesBEnT; VarWW 85*

Eckstein, Gustav
American. Physiologist, Author
Writings include best-seller *Body Has a Head,* 1969.
b. Oct 26, 1890 in Cincinnati, Ohio
d. Sep 23, 1981 in Cincinnati, Ohio
Source: *AmAu&B; AnObit 1981; BioIn 1, 3, 4, 12, 13; ConAu 57, 104; CurBio 42, 81, 81N; InSci; NewYTBS 81; OhA&B; TwCA SUP; WhAm 8; WhE&EA; WhNAA*

Eckstine, Billy
[William Clarence Eckstine]
"The Fabulous Mr. B"
American. Singer
Hits include "Cottage for Sale," 1945; "Prisoner of Love," 1945.
b. Jul 8, 1914 in Pittsburgh, Pennsylvania
d. Mar 8, 1993 in Pittsburgh, Pennsylvania
Source: *AllMusG; AmPS B; AnObit 1993; Baker 78, 84, 92; BgBands 74; BiDAfM; BiDAmM; BiDJaz; BioIn 2, 3, 5, 9, 11, 12, 15, 16; BlksB&W C; CmpEPM; ConMus 1; CurBio 52, 93N; DcTwCCu 5; DrBlPA, 90; EncJzS; EncJzS; FacFETw; IlEncBM 82; IlEncJ; InB&W 80, 85; LegTOT; NewAmDM; NewGrDA 86; NewGrDJ 88, 94; NewGrDM 80; News 93; NewYTBS 93; OxCPMus; PenEncP; WhAm 11; WhoAm 74, 76, 78, 80, 82, 84, 86, 88, 90, 92; WhoBlA 75, 77, 80, 85, 88, 90, 92, 94N; WhoEnt 92; WhoHol 92, A; WhoMus 72*

Eco, Umberto
Italian. Author
Background in semiotics imbues both critical and novelistic work; mystery novel, *The Name of the Rose,* 1981 made into film.
b. Jan 5, 1932 in Alessandria, Italy
Source: *Benet 87, 96; BestSel 90-1; BioIn 13, 14, 15, 16; ConAu 12NR, 33NR, 55NR, 77; ConLC 28, 60; ConPopW; ConWorW 93; CrtSuMy; CurBio 85; CyWA 89; DcArts; DcItL 1; EncSF 93; EncWL 3; FacFETw; IntAu&W 91, 93; IntWW 74, 75, 76, 77, 78, 79, 80, 81, 82, 83, 89, 91, 93; LegTOT; MajTwCW; NewYTBS 89; OxCEng 85, 95; PorSil; RAdv 14; ScF&FL 92; ThTwC 87; WhoAm 74, 94; WhoWor 74, 76, 78, 84, 87, 89, 91, 93, 95, 96; WorAu 1975*

Economaki, Chris(topher Constantine)
American. Publisher, Broadcast Journalist
Award-winning colorcaster for "Wide World of Sports," 1961-83; with CBS Sports, 1984-93; publishes *National Speed Sports News* mag.
b. Oct 15, 1920 in New York, New York
Source: *St&PR 96, 97; WhoAm 84, 86, 90*

Ed, Carl Frank Ludwig
American. Cartoonist
Created character Harold Teen; with *Chicago Tribune,* 1919-59.
b. Jul 16, 1890 in Moline, Illinois
d. Oct 10, 1959 in Evanston, Illinois
Source: *AmAu&B; BioIn 5; WhAm 3; WorECom*

Eda-Pierre, Christiane
French. Opera Singer
Coloratura soprano who was soloist with worldwide symphonic orchestras.
Source: *Baker 84; IntWWM 80, 90; MetOEnc; PenDiMP; WhoOp 76*

Edberg, Stefan
Swedish. Tennis Player
Won Wimbledon singles title, 1988, 1990; first Swedish winner since Bjorn Borg, 1980; won men's singles title at U.S. Open, 1991, 1992; Olympic gold medal winn er, 1984.
b. Jan 19, 1966 in Vastervik, Sweden
Source: *BioIn 15, 16; BuCMET; CurBio 94; IntWW 89, 91, 93; LegTOT; WhoAm 92, 94, 95, 96, 97; WhoSpor; WhoWor 95, 96, 97*

Eddington, Arthur Stanley, Sir
English. Astronomer
Translated theories of relativity into lay terms; worked at Greenwich Observatory, 1906-13.
b. Dec 28, 1882 in Kendal, England
d. Nov 22, 1944 in Cambridge, England
Source: *AsBiEn; BiESc; BioIn 1, 2, 4, 5, 6, 7, 12, 13, 14, 17, 19, 20; Chambr 3; CurBio 41; DcLEL; DcNaB 1941; DcScB; EvLB; FacFETw; GrBr; InSci; LarDcSc; LinLib L, S; LngCTC; LuthC 75; McGEWB; NewC; NewCBEL; NewCol 75; NotTwCS; OxCEng 67; RAdv 14, 13-5; TwCA, SUP; WhE&EA; WhLit; WhoLA; WorScD*

Eddy, Clarence
American. Organist
Noted church, concert organist for over 50 yrs.
b. Jun 23, 1851 in Greenfield, Massachusetts
d. Jan 10, 1937 in Chicago, Illinois
Source: *Alli SUP; Baker 78, 84; BioIn 4; DcAmAu; DcAmB S2; DcNAA; NatCAB 7; NewAmDM; NewGrDA 86; NewGrDM 80; TwCBDA; WhAm 1*

Eddy, Duane
American. Musician
Guitarist whose instrumental hits include "Rebel Rouser," 1958; "Peter Gunn," 1960.
b. Apr 26, 1938 in Corning, New York
Source: *BioIn 11, 13, 20; ConMuA 80A; ConMus 9; EncPR&S 74, 89; EncRk 88; EncRkSt; HarEnR 86; LegTOT; NewGrDA 86; OnThGG; OxCPMus; PenEncP; RkOn 74; RolSEnR 83; WhoHol 92; WhoRock 81; WorAl; WorAlBi*

Eddy, Mary Baker Morse
American. Religious Leader
Founded Christian Science Religious Movement; organized first church, 1879.
b. Jul 16, 1821 in Bow, New Hampshire
d. Dec 3, 1910 in Chestnut Hill, Massachusetts
Source: *Alli SUP; AmAu&B; BiD&SB; CasWL; DcLEL; DcNAA; EncAB-H 1974; HerW; LngCTC; NotAW; OxCAmL 65; OxCEng 67; REn; REnAL; TwCBDA; WebAB 74; WhAm 1*

Eddy, Nelson
American. Singer, Actor
Starred with Jeanette MacDonald 1930's musicals; had voice range of three octaves.
b. Jun 29, 1901 in Providence, Rhode Island
d. Mar 6, 1967 in Miami, Florida
Source: *Baker 78, 84, 92; BiDAmM; BioIn 2, 7, 8, 9, 10, 11, 12, 14, 19, 20; CmMov; CmpEPM; CurBio 43, 67; DcAmB S8; FilmEn; FilmgC; HalFC 80, 84, 88; LegTOT; MetOEnc; MGM; MotPP; MovMk; NatCAB 53; NewAmDM; NewGrDA 86; NotNAT B; ObitT 1961; OxCFilm; OxCPMus; PenDiMP; PenEncP; RadStar; SaTiSS; WhAm 4; WhoHol B; WhScrn 74, 77, 83; WhThe; WorAl; WorAlBi*

Eddy, Sherwood
American. Author
Writings include *Will You Survive After Death,* 1950.
b. Jan 11, 1871 in Leavenworth, Kansas
d. Mar 3, 1963 in Jacksonville, Illinois
Source: *BenetAL 91; OxCAmL 65, 83, 95; REnAL; WhAm 4; WhNAA*

Edel, Leon
[Joseph Leon Edel]
American. Author, Journalist
Writings include *The Middle Years,* 1963; *The Master,* 1972; won Pulitzer, 1963.
b. Sep 9, 1907 in Pittsburgh, Pennsylvania
Source: *AmAu&B; Au&Wr 71; Benet 87, 96; BenetAL 91; BioIn 3, 6, 9, 10, 11, 12, 13, 14, 16, 17, 18; BlueB 76; CanWW 70, 79, 80, 81, 83, 89; ConAu 1NR, 1R, 22NR; ConLC 29; ConLCrt 77, 82; CurBio 63; DcLB 103; DcLEL 1940; DrAS 74E, 78E, 82E; IntAu&W 76, 77, 82, 91; IntWW 74, 75, 76, 77, 78, 79, 80, 81, 82, 83, 89, 91; LegTOT; LinLib L, S; NewYTBE 72; NewYTBS 80; OxCAmL 65, 83; OxCCanL; RAdv 1, 14, 13-1; REn; REnAL; Who 74, 82, 83, 85, 88, 90, 92; WhoAm 74, 76, 78, 80, 82, 84, 86, 88, 90, 92, 94, 95, 96, 97; WhoAmJ 80; WhoUSWr 88; WhoWest 89, 92, 94, 96; WhoWor 74, 76, 78, 80, 82, 84, 87; WhoWrEP 89; WorAu 1950; WrDr 76, 80, 82, 84, 86, 88, 90, 92*

Edelin, Ramona Hoage
American. Educator
Pres., CEO, National Urban Coalition; implemented "Say YES to a Youngster's Future" program.
b. Sep 4, 1945 in Los Angeles, California
Source: *AfrAmAl 6; BioIn 18; NotBlAW 1; WhoAmW 91; WhoBlA 92*

Edelman, Gerald Maurice
American. Chemist
Shared 1972 Nobel Prize in medicine for researching chemical structure of antibodies.
b. Jul 1, 1929 in New York, New York
Source: *AmMWSc 76P, 79, 82, 86, 89, 92, 95; BiESc; BioIn 7, 9, 10, 11, 13, 14, 15; BlueB 76; CamDcSc; ConAu 112; CurBio 95; IntWW 74, 75, 76, 77, 78, 79, 80, 81, 82, 83, 89, 91, 93; LarDcSc; McGMS 80; NobelP; WebAB 74, 79; Who 74, 82, 83, 85, 88, 90, 92, 94; WhoAm 74, 76, 78, 80, 82, 84, 86, 88, 90, 92, 94, 95, 96, 97; WhoE 74, 77, 79, 81, 83, 85, 86, 89, 91; WhoFrS 84; WhoMedH; WhoNob, 90, 95; WhoScEn 94, 96; WhoWest 94, 96; WhoWor 74, 80, 82, 84, 87, 89, 91, 93, 95, 96, 97; WorAl; WorAlBi*

Edelman, Herb
American. Actor
In TV series "The Good Guys," 1968-70; film *The Way We Were,* 1977; had role on TV's "The Golden Girls."
b. Nov 5, 1933 in New York, New York
d. Jul 21, 1996 in Woodland Hills, California
Source: *ConTFT 6; EncAFC; FilmgC; IntMPA 96; WhoEnt 92; WhoHol 92, A*

Edelman, Marian Wright
American. Social Reformer, Author, Lawyer
Founder, pres., Children's Defense Fund, 1973—; wrote *The Measure of Our Success: A Letter to My Children and Yours,* 1992.
b. Jun 6, 1939 in Bennettsville, South Carolina
Source: *AfrAmAl 6; AfrAmBi 1; AfrAmOr; AmSocL; BioIn 14, 15, 16, 18; BlkWAm; BlkWr 1, 2; ConAu 124; ConBlB 5; CurBio 92; Ebony 1; GrLiveH; InWom SUP; NegAl 76, 89; News 90; NewYTBS 86; NotBlAW 1; SchCGBL; WhoAfA 96; WhoAm 74, 76, 78, 80, 82, 84, 86, 88, 90, 92, 94, 95, 96, 97; WhoAmL 90, 92, 94; WhoAmW 70A, 72, 74, 75, 77, 79, 85, 89, 91, 93, 95, 97; WhoBlA 75, 77, 80, 85, 88, 90, 92, 94; WhoE 95; WhoWor 84; WomFir; WomStre*

Edelmann, Otto
Austrian. Opera Singer
Bass-baritone with NY Met., 1954-70.
b. Feb 5, 1917 in Brunn, Austria
Source: *Baker 84; BioIn 13; IntWW 82, 91; IntWWM 90; MetOEnc; NewEOp 71; NewGrDO; OxDcOp; WhoMus 72; WhoWor 74, 89*

Eden, Anthony
[Earl of Avon Robert Anthony Eden]
English. Statesman
Longtime conservative MP, foreign secretary; strong supporter of US; prime minister, 1955-57.
b. Jun 12, 1897 in Durham, England
d. Jan 14, 1977 in Alvediston, England
Source: *BioIn 1, 2, 3, 4, 14, 15, 16, 17, 18, 21; ColdWar 1; ConAu 69, 77; CurBio 40, 51, 77; DcNaB 1971; DcTwHis; EncCW; EncTR 91; FacFETw; GrBr; HisDBrE; HisDcKW; HisEAAC; HisEWW; HisWorL; LegTOT; LinLib L, S; McGEWB; RAdv 13-3; WebBD 83; WhDW; Who 74; WhWW-II; WorAl; WorAlBi*

Eden, Barbara
[Barbara Jean Huffman]
American. Actor
Played title role in TV comedy "I Dream of Jeannie," 1965-70.
b. Aug 23, 1934 in Tucson, Arizona
Source: *BioIn 13, 14, 16; ConTFT 3, 9; FilmEn; FilmgC; ForYSC; HalFC 80, 84, 88; IntMPA 84, 86, 88, 92, 94, 96; InWom SUP; LegTOT; MovMk; WhoAm 74, 84, 86, 88; WhoEnt 92; WhoHol 92, A; WorAl; WorAlBi*

Eden, Dorothy
New Zealander. Author
Wrote romantic fiction: *The Vines of Yarrabee,* 1969; *The Salamanca Drum,* 1979.
b. Apr 3, 1912 in Canterbury, New Zealand
d. Mar 4, 1982 in London, England
Source: *AnObit 1982; BioIn 14; ConAu 81, 106; TwCCr&M 80; TwCRHW 90; WhE&EA; WrDr 76, 80, 82*

Eden, Elizabeth Debbie
[Ernest Aron]
American. Transsexual
Film *Dog Day Afternoon,* 1975, was based on his desire for a sex-change operation, which led to bank robbery.
b. 1946? in Ozone Park, New York
d. Sep 29, 1987 in Rochester, New York

Eden, Nicholas
[Earl of Avon]
English. Government Official
Son of Anthony Eden; under-secretary in Margaret Thatcher's cabinet; last Earl of Avon.
b. Oct 3, 1930 in London, England
d. Aug 17, 1985 in London, England
Source: *BioIn 14; Who 74, 82, 83, 85*

Edenshaw, Charles
Canadian. Artist
Best known for his carvings, made of wood, silver, gold, copper, and agrillite.
b. 1839 in Skidegate, British Columbia, Canada
d. 1920
Source: *BioIn 17, 21; EncNAB; NotNaAm; WhNaAH*

Ederle, Gertrude Caroline
American. Swimmer
First woman to swim English Channel, Calais to Dover, breaking world record, 1926.
b. Oct 23, 1906 in New York, New York
Source: *BiDAmSp BK; ContDcW 89; FacFETw; InWom SUP; LibW; WebAB 74, 79; WhoAmW 61, 64, 66; WhoHol A; WorAlBi*

Edeson, Robert
American. Actor
Noted stage actor who apeared in many DeMille silent films.
b. 1868 in New Orleans, Louisiana
d. Mar 24, 1931 in Hollywood, California
Source: *DcAmB S1; Film 1, 2; FilmEn; ForYSC; MovMk; NotNAT, B; OxCAmT 84; OxCThe 67, 83; SilFlmP; TwYS; WhAm 1; WhoHol B; WhoStg 1906, 1908; WhScrn 74, 77, 83; WhThe*

Edgar
English. Ruler
Younger son of Edmund I; father of Edward the martyr; known for returning monastic houses to Benedictine monks.
b. 943?
d. 975
Source: *BioIn 6, 9; DcBiPP; NewCol 75; WebBD 83*

Edgar, David
English. Dramatist
Prolific stage, TV playwright who stresses political, social themes: *Death Story*, 1972.
b. Feb 26, 1948 in Birmingham, England
Source: *BioIn 13, 14; BlmGEL; CamGLE; CamGWoT; ConAu 12NR, 57; ConBrDr; ConDr 77, 82, 88, 93; ConLC 42; ConTFT 6; DcArts; DcLB 13; IntAu&W 91, 93; IntDcT 2; IntvTCA 2; IntWW 93; MajTwCW; OxCEng 95; RGTwCWr; Who 92; WhoThe 81; WrDr 76, 80, 82, 84, 86, 88, 90, 92, 94, 96*

Edgar, Jim
[James Edgar]
American. Politician
Rep. governor, IL, 1991—, succeeding James Thompson.
b. Jul 22, 1946 in Vinita, Oklahoma
Source: *AlmAP 92, 96; BiDrGov 1988; BioIn 19, 20; IntWW 91, 93; WhoAm 82, 84, 86, 88, 90, 92, 94, 95, 96, 97; WhoAmP 77, 79, 81, 83, 85, 87, 89, 91, 93, 95; WhoMW 88, 90, 92, 93, 96; WhoWor 93, 95, 96, 97*

Edgell, George Harold
American. Author, Museum Director
Headed Boston's Museum of Fine Arts, 1935-54; wrote books on architecture, Sienese painting.
b. Mar 4, 1887 in Saint Louis, Missouri
d. Jun 29, 1954 in Newport, New Hampshire
Source: *BioIn 1, 3, 5, 6; NatCAB 45; WhAm 3; WhAmArt 85; WhE&EA; WhLit*

Edgerton, Harold Eugene
"Doc"
American. Engineer
Invented modern stroboscope, or electronic flash, now standard equipment used in photography, science, oceanographic research.
b. Apr 6, 1903 in Fremont, Nebraska
d. Jan 4, 1990 in Cambridge, Massachusetts
Source: *BioIn 3, 4, 6, 7, 10, 12, 15, 16, 17, 20, 21; BlueB 76; ConAu 5NR, 53, 130; ConPhot 88; CurBio 66, 90, 90N; FacFETw; ICPEnP; InSci; IntWW 74, 75, 76, 77, 78, 79, 80, 81, 82, 83, 89; MacBEP; McGMS 80; NewYTBS 90; WhAm 10; WhAmArt 85; WhoAm 74, 76, 78, 80, 82, 84, 86, 88; WhoFrS 84; WhoTech 89; WrDr 76, 90*

Edgeworth, Maria
English. Children's Author
Novels depict Irish life, moral tales for children.
b. Jan 1, 1767 in Bourton Abbots, England
d. May 22, 1849 in Edgeworthstown, Ireland
Source: *Alli; AtlBL; BbD; Benet 87, 96; BiD&SB; BiDIrW; BiDLA; BioIn 1, 2, 3, 4, 5, 7, 8, 9, 10, 12, 13, 14, 16, 17, 18, 19, 20; BlmGEL; BritAu 19; CamGEL; CamGLE; CarSB; CasWL; CelCen; Chambr 2; ChhPo; ContDcW 89; CrtT 2, 4; CyEd; CyWA 58; DcArts; DcBiA; DcBiPP; DcEnA; DcEnL; DcEuL; DcIrB 78, 88; DcIrL 96; DcIrW 1, 2; DcLEL; DcNaB, C; EncEnl; EvLB; GrWomW; GrWrEL N; IntDcWB; InWom, SUP; LinLib L; McGEWB; MouLC 3; NewC; NewCBEL; NinCLC 1; Novels; OxCChiL; OxCEng 67; OxCIri; PenC ENG; PoIre; RAdv 1, 13-1; REn; SmATA 21; WebE&AL; WhDW; WhoChL*

Edgeworth, Richard Lovell
English. Inventor, Educator
Pioneered in electricity, telegraphy; collaborated with daughter, Maria, on *Practical Education*, 1798.
b. May 31, 1744 in Bath, England
d. Jun 13, 1817 in Edgeworthstown, Ireland
Source: *Alli; BiDIrW; BiDLA; BioIn 2, 7, 9, 13; CelCen; Chambr 2; ChhPo; CyEd; DcBiPP; DcEnA; DcEnL; DcEuL; DcInv; DcIrB 78, 88; DcIrW 2; DcNaB; NewCol 75; OxCIri*

Edison, Thomas Alva
American. Inventor
Changed US lifestyle with over 1,000 inventions including, the phonograph, incandescent lamp.
b. Feb 11, 1847 in Milan, Ohio
d. Oct 18, 1931 in West Orange, New Jersey
Source: *AmBi; AmDec 1900; AmSocL; ApCAB, X; AsBiEn; Benet 87, 96; BiDAmBL 83; BiDAmS; BiDFilm 94; BiESc; BioIn 1, 2, 3, 4, 5, 6, 7, 8, 9, 10, 11, 12, 13; CamDcSc; CelCen; DcAmB S1; DcAmC; DcFM; DcInv; DcScB; DcTwDes; DeafPAS; Dis&D; EncAB-H 1974, 1996; EncAJ; EncPaPR 91; FacFETw; FilmEn; FilmgC; HalFC 80, 84, 88; HarEnUS; InSci; LarDcSc; LinLib L; LngCTC; McGEWB; MemAm; MusMk; NatCAB 3, 25; NewCol 75; NewGrDM 80; NotNAT B; NotTwCS; OxCAmH; OxCFilm; OxCMus; REn; REnAL; TwCBDA; TwoTYeD; WebAB 74, 79; WhAm 1; WhDW; WhFla; WorAl; WorAlBi; WorEFlm; WorInv*

Edley, Christopher Fairfield
American. Lawyer
Pres., CEO, United Negro College Fund, 1973-90.
b. Jan 1, 1928 in Charleston, West Virginia
Source: *BioIn 13; Ebony 1; NegAl 76, 83, 89; WhoAm 82, 84, 86; WhoBlA 92*

Edlund, Richard
American. Special Effects Technician
Won Oscars for visual effects in three *Star Wars* films, 1977, 1980, 1983.
b. Dec 6, 1940 in Fargo, North Dakota
Source: *ConTFT 9; VarWW 85*

Edmiston, Mark Morton
American. Business Executive
Pres., *Newsweek* mag., 1981-86; pres., TVSM Inc., 1987-91; exec. vp *Times Mirror* mag., 1991-92; co-chm., the Jordan Edmiston Group Inc., 1992—.
b. Jul 9, 1943 in Yonkers, New York
Source: *BioIn 16; WhoAm 80, 82, 84, 86, 88, 90, 92, 94, 95, 96, 97; WhoE 85, 86, 89, 91, 93, 95*

Edmonds, Emma E
American. Nurse, Soldier
Wrote popular fictionalized account *Nurse and Spy in the Union Army*, 1865.
b. Dec 1841 in New Brunswick, Canada
d. Sep 5, 1898 in La Porte, Texas
Source: *BioIn 1, 3, 5, 6, 9; InWom SUP; NotAW*

Edmonds, Kenneth
"Babyface"
American. Singer, Songwriter
Grammy, Best R&B Song, "I'll Make Love to You," 1994.
b. c. 1958 in Indianapolis, Indiana
Source: *ConBlB 10; ConMus 12; News 95, 95-3*

Edmonds, Walter Dumaux
American. Author
Known for historical novels of NY; won 1942 Newbery for *Matchlock Gun*.
b. Jul 15, 1903 in Boonville, New York
Source: *AmAu&B; AmNov; AuBYP 2, 3; BenetAL 91; BioIn 1, 2, 4, 5, 6, 7, 9, 10, 12, 13, 14, 15, 19, 21; CnDAL; ConAmA; ConAu 2NR, 5R; CyWA 58; DcAmChF 1960; DcLEL; IntAu&W 82, 91; ModAL; MorBMP; MorJA; NewbMB 1922; OxCAmL 65; PenC AM; REn; REnAL; SmATA 1; TwCA, SUP; TwCChW 89; TwCRHW 90; WhoAm 74, 76, 78, 80, 82, 84, 86, 88, 90, 92, 94, 95, 96, 97; WhoE 89; WrDr 76, 80, 82, 84, 86, 92*

Edmonson, Munro Sterling
American. Anthropologist
Books on cultural topics include one on Mayan mythology: *The Book of Counsel*, 1971.
b. May 18, 1924 in Nogales, Arizona
Source: *AmMWSc 73S, 76P; ConAu 28NR, 33R; FifIDA; IntAu&W 77, 82; WhoAm 74, 76, 78, 80, 82, 84, 86, 88, 90, 92, 94, 95, 96, 97; WhoSSW 93; WrDr 76, 86, 92*

Edmund, Saint
[Edmund the Martyr]
Ruler
Ruled East Anglia, 855-870; refused to renounce faith while being tortured to death.
b. 840? in Nuremberg, Germany
d. 870
Source: *NewC; NewCol 75; WebBD 83*

Edmunds, Dave
Welsh. Musician, Producer
Guitarist who formed Rockpile with Nick Lowe, 1978; hits include "Cruel to be Kind."
b. Apr 15, 1944 in Cardiff, Wales

Source: *BioIn 11, 13; ConMuA 80A, 80B; EncPR&S 89; EncRk 88; EncRkSt; HarEnR 86; IlEncRk; LegTOT; OnThGG; PenEncP; RkOn 78; RolSEnR 83; WhoRock 81*

Edmunds, George Franklin
American. Lawyer, Politician
Senator from VT, 1866-91; drafted much of Civil Rights Act of 1875, helped get it passed, 1877.
b. Feb 1, 1828 in Richmond, Vermont
d. Feb 27, 1919 in Pasadena, California
Source: *AmBi; AmLegL; ApCAB; BiAUS; BiDrAC; BiDrUSC 89; BioIn 7; CyAG; DcAmB; HarEnUS; NatCAB 2; OxCAmH; TwCBDA; WebAB 74, 79; WebBD 83; WhAm 1; WhAmP*

Edson, Gus
American. Cartoonist
Cartoon characters include *Streaky*, 1933-35; *The Gumps*, 1935-66; *Dondi*, 1955-66.
b. Sep 20, 1901 in Stamford, Connecticut
d. Sep 26, 1966 in Stamford, Connecticut
Source: *AmAu; AmAu&B; BioIn 7; EncAB-A 16; ObitOF 79; WhAm 4; WhAmArt 85; WorECom*

Edward
[Edward Antony Richard Louis]
English. Prince
Youngest child of Queen Elizabeth II and Prince Philip; currently seventh in line to British throne.
b. Mar 10, 1964 in London, England
Source: *BioIn 7, 11, 12, 14, 15, 16, 17, 20, 21; LegTOT; Who 82R, 83R, 85R, 88R, 90R, 92R, 94R; WhoWor 95, 96, 97*

Edwardes, George
English. Manager
Noted London theater manager; inventor, developer of modern musical comedy.
b. 1852
d. 1915
Source: *BiDD; BioIn 3, 10; CamGWoT; CnThe; EncMT; EncWT; NotNAT A, B; OxCThe 67, 83; PlP&P; WhDW; WhoStg 1906, 1908; WhThe*

Edward I
English. Ruler
Ruled England, 1272-1307; eldest son of Henry III; buried in Westminster Abbey.
b. Jun 17, 1239 in Westminster, England
d. Jul 7, 1307 in Burgh-on-Sands, England
Source: *BioIn 10; NewCol 75; WebBD 83*

Edward II
[Edward of Carnarvon]
English. Ruler
Ruled England, 1307-27; fourth son of Edward I; captured, imprisoned, forced to resign, murdered, 1327.
b. Apr 25, 1284 in Carnarvon, England
d. Sep 21, 1327 in Berkeley Castle, England
Source: *BioIn 10; DcNaB; NewCol 75; WebBD 83*

Edward III
[Edward of Windsor]
English. Ruler
Ruled England, 1327-77; eldest son of Edward II; claimed French crown in name of mother, Isabella, 1337, assumed title, 1340.
b. Nov 13, 1312 in Windsor, England
d. Jun 21, 1377 in Richmond, England
Source: *BioIn 10; NewCol 75; WebBD 83*

Edward IV
English. Ruler
Ruled England, 1461-70, 1471-83; during reign increased trade, improved public administration.
b. Apr 28, 1442 in Rouen, France
d. Apr 9, 1483 in London, England
Source: *DcBiPP; DcCathB; NewCol 75; WebBD 83; WhDW*

Edwards, Alan
American. Actor
Films include *The White Sister*, 1933; also appeared in silent films.
b. Jun 3, 1900 in New York, New York
d. May 8, 1954 in Los Angeles, California
Source: *Film 2; MotPP; NotNAT B; WhoHol B; WhScrn 74, 77, 83*

Edwards, Anthony
American. Actor
Played Maggie's boyfriend Mike on TV show "Northern Exposure," 1992-93; movie credits include *Top Gun*; *Revenge of the Nerds*. On TV's *ER*.
b. Jul 19, 1962 in Santa Barbara, California
Source: *BioIn 15; ConTFT 6, 14; IntMPA 92, 94, 96; LegTOT; WhoAm 97; WhoHol 92*

Edwards, Blake
[William Blake McEdwards]
American. Producer, Director
Produced *Pink Panther* film series; husband of Julie Andrews.
b. Jul 26, 1922 in Tulsa, Oklahoma
Source: *BiDFilm, 81, 94; BioIn 7, 12, 13, 15, 16, 21; CelR 90; CmMov; ConAu 32NR, 81; ConTFT 1, 6, 15; CurBio 83; DcArts; EncAFC; FilmEn; FilmgC; HalFC 80, 84, 88; IlWWHD 1; IntDcF 1-2, 2-2; IntMPA 75, 76, 77, 78, 79, 80, 81, 82, 84, 86, 88, 92, 94, 96; IntWW 82, 83, 89, 91, 93; LegTOT; LesBEnT, 92; MiSFD 9; MovMk; NewYTBS 95; NewYTET; OxCFilm; WhoAm 74, 76, 78, 80, 82, 84, 86, 88, 92, 94, 95, 96, 97; WhoEnt 92; WhoHol 92; WorAl; WorAlBi; WorEFlm; WorFDir 2*

Edwards, Cliff
"Ukulele Ike"
American. Singer, Actor
Played Ukelele Ike in several films; played sidekick, Harmony, in many Westerns; voice of Jiminy Cricket in *Pinocchio*, 1940.
b. Jun 14, 1895 in Hannibal, Missouri
d. Jul 17, 1971 in Hollywood, California
Source: *BioIn 9, 12, 17; CmpEPM; EncAFC; EncVaud; Film 2; FilmEn; FilmgC; ForYSC; HalFC 80, 84, 88; LegTOT; MotPP; MovMk; NewYTBE 71; OxCPMus; PenEncP; Vers B; What 3; WhoHol B; WhScrn 74, 77, 83*

Edwards, Dennis
[The Temptations]
American. Singer
Original member of Temptations; solo single "Don't Look Any Further," 1984.
b. Feb 3, 1943 in Birmingham, Alabama
Source: *RkOn 85; SoulM; WhoBlA 92; WhoRocM 82*

Edwards, Douglas
American. Broadcast Journalist
CBS News correspondent, 1942-88; anchored network TVs first nightly news show, 1 948; won Peabody, 1955; retired, 1988.
b. Jul 14, 1917 in Ada, Oklahoma
d. Oct 13, 1990 in Sarasota, Florida
Source: *AnObit 1990; BioIn 3, 4, 16, 17, 19; ConAu 110, 118, 132; CurBio 88, 91N; EncAJ; EncTwCJ; FacFETw; IntMPA 75, 76, 77, 78, 79, 80, 81, 82, 84, 86, 88; LesBEnT, 92; NewYTBS 90; NewYTET; RadStar; SaTiSS; WhAm 10; WhoAm 74, 76, 78, 80, 82, 84, 86*

Edwards, Edwin Washington
American. Politician, Lawyer
Controversial Dem. governor of LA, 1972-80, 1984-87, 1991—; acquitted of fraud, 1986; terms marred by scandals.
b. Aug 7, 1927 in Marksville, Louisiana
Source: *AlmAP 88; BiDrAC; BiDrGov 1789, 1978, 1983, 1988; BiDrUSC 89; BioIn 10, 13, 14, 15; IntWW 76, 77, 78, 79, 80, 81, 82, 83, 89, 91, 93; NewYTBS 83, 91; WhoAm 74, 76, 78, 80, 82, 84, 86, 88, 90, 92, 94, 95, 96, 97; WhoAmL 79; WhoAmP 73, 91; WhoGov 72, 75, 77; WhoSSW 73, 75, 76, 78, 80, 84, 86, 88, 95; WhoWor 78, 84, 87*

Edwards, Gus
American. Songwriter
Vaudeville star of int'l fame; portrayed by Bing Crosby in *The Star Maker*, 1939.
b. Aug 18, 1879 in Hohensaliza, Germany
d. Nov 7, 1945 in Los Angeles, California
Source: *AmAu&B; AmPS; AmSong; ASCAP 66, 80; BenetAL 91; BiDAmM; BioIn 2, 4, 6, 9, 15, 16; CmpEPM; CurBio 45; EncVaud; Film 2; NatCAB 34; NewAmDM; NewGrDA 86; NotNAT B; OxCAmT 84; OxCPMus; PopAmC; REnAL; WhScrn 74, 77; WorAl; WorAlBi*

Edwards, Harry, Jr.
American. Sociologist, Consultant
Organized black boycott of 1968 Olympic games; minority affairs consultant for ML baseball, other sports teams.
b. Nov 22, 1942 in East Saint Louis, Missouri
Source: *BioIn 8, 9, 10, 11, 12, 16; CivR 74; ConAu 109, 111; ConBlB 2; EncAACR; InB&W 80, 85; MugS; News 89; SelBAAf; WhoAfA 96; WhoBlA 75, 77, 80, 85, 88, 90, 92, 94; WhoWest 89, 92*

Edwards, India Moffett
American. Journalist, Politician
National Democratic Committee executive, 1940s; persuaded Harry Truman to appoint more women to federal posts; wrote memoirs *Pulling No Punches,* 1977.
b. 1895 in Chicago, Illinois
d. Jan 14, 1990 in Sebastopol, California
Source: *BioIn 2, 3, 11, 16; ConAu 130; CurBio 49, 90, 90N; NewYTBS 90*

Edwards, James Burrows
American. Government Official
Secretary of Energy, 1981-82.
b. Jun 24, 1927 in Hawthorne, Florida
Source: *AmMWSc 92, 95; BiDrGov 1789, 1978; BioIn 12, 13, 14; BlueB 76; CngDr 81; CurBio 82; IntWW 78, 79, 80, 81, 82, 83, 89, 91, 93; NatCAB 63N; NewYTBS 80; WhoAm 76, 78, 80, 82, 84, 86, 88, 90, 92, 94, 95, 96, 97; WhoAmP 73, 75, 77, 79, 81, 83, 85, 87, 89, 91, 93, 95; WhoE 81; WhoGov 75, 77; WhoMedH; WhoSSW 73, 75, 76, 78, 84, 86, 88, 91, 93, 95; WhoWor 82*

Edwards, Joan
American. Singer, Songwriter
Co-starred with Frank Sinatra in radio show "Your Hit Parade," 1941-46.
b. Feb 13, 1919 in New York, New York
d. Aug 27, 1981 in New York, New York
Source: *ASCAP 66; BioIn 3, 12, 19; CmpEPM; CurBio 53, 81, 81N; InWom SUP; NewYTBS 81*

Edwards, Jonathan
American. Author, Theologian
Forceful Calvinist preacher called Puritanism's greatest theologian; wrote *Freedom of the Will,* 1754.
b. Oct 5, 1703 in East Windsor, Connecticut
d. Mar 22, 1758 in Princeton, New Jersey
Source: *Alli; AmAu; AmAu&B; AmBi; AmOrN; AmSocL; AmWr; AmWrBE; ApCAB; AtlBL; BbD; Benet 87, 96; BenetAL 91; BiD&SB; BiDPsy; BioIn 1, 2, 3, 4, 5, 6, 7, 8, 9, 10, 11, 12, 13, 14, 17, 18, 19, 20; BlkwCE; CamGEL; CamGLE; CamHAL; CasWL; CnDAL; CrtT 3, 4; CyAL 1; CyEd; CyWA 58; DcAmAu; DcAmB; DcAmReB 1, 2; DcAmSR; DcBiPP; DcEnL; DcLB 24; DcLEL; DcNAA; Dis&D; Drake; EncAAH; EncAB-H 1974, 1996; EncARH; EncCRAm; EncEnl; EncEth; EncNAR; EvLB; HarEnUS; LegTOT; LinLib L, S; LitC 7; LuthC 75; McGEWB; MouLC 2; NamesHP; NatCAB 5; NewC; OxCAmH; OxCAmL 65, 83, 95; OxCEng 67, 85, 95; OxCPhil; PenC AM; RAdv 14, 13-4; RComAH; RComWL; REn; REnAL; RfGAmL 87, 94; TwCBDA; WebAB 74, 79; WebE&AL; WhAm HS; WhNaAH; WorAl; WorAlBi; WrCNE*

Edwards, Ralph Livingstone
American. Producer, TV Personality
Created, produced, hosted radio (1948-50), TV (1952-61) and syndicated (1971-73) series "This Is Your Life,"; co-exec. producer, "The People's Court,"; created, produced, and hosted "Truth or Consequences."
b. Jun 13, 1913 in Merino, Colorado
Source: *BioIn 18; CelR, 90; ConTFT 3; IntMPA 92; LesBEnT 92; NewYTET; VarWW 85; WhoAm 86; WorAl*

Edwards, Robert Geoffrey
English. Physiologist
Scientist in Dept. of Physiology, Cambridge U., 1963—; editor of scientific text books.
b. Sep 27, 1925
Source: *BioIn 11, 14; IntWW 91, 93; LarDcSc; NewYTBS 78; Who 82, 83, 85, 88, 90, 92, 94*

Edwards, Sherman
American. Composer, Lyricist
Wrote music, lyrics for *1776,* 1969; composed scores for Elvis Presley films, 1960s.
b. Apr 3, 1919 in New York, New York
d. Mar 30, 1981 in New York, New York
Source: *ASCAP 66, 80; BioIn 12; EncMT; WhoAm 74, 76, 78; WhoThe 72, 77*

Edwards, Turk
[Albert Glen Edwards]
American. Football Player
Four-time all-pro tackle, 1932-40, mostly with Washington; Hall of Fame, 1969.
b. Sep 28, 1907 in Mold, Washington
d. Jan 10, 1973 in Seattle, Washington
Source: *BiDAmSp FB; BioIn 6, 9, 17; LegTOT; NewYTBE 73; ObitOF 79; WhoFtbl 74; WhoSpor*

Edwards, Vince(nt)
[Vincent Edward Zoino]
American. Actor
Starred in TV series "Ben Casey," 1961-66.
b. Jul 7, 1928 in New York, New York
d. Mar 11, 1996 in Los Angeles, California
Source: *BioIn 6, 21; ConTFT 7; CurBio 96N; FilmEn; FilmgC; HalFC 80, 84, 88; IntMPA 75, 76, 77, 78, 79, 80, 81, 82, 84, 86, 88, 92, 94, 96; LegTOT; MiSFD 9; MotPP; MovMk; WhoAm 74, 76; WhoHol A; WorAl; WorAlBi*

Edwards, Willard
American. Journalist
Reporter with *Chicago Tribune,* 1925-73.
b. Dec 7, 1902 in Chicago, Illinois
Source: *WhoAm 74, 76, 78, 80; WhoSSW 73, 75*

Edwards, Willard Eldridge
American. Inventor
Originated The Perpetual Calendar, 1919; accepted by US Congress, all other nations.
b. Dec 11, 1903 in Chatham, Massachusetts
d. Aug 15, 1975 in Honolulu, Hawaii
Source: *IntAu&W 76; IntYB 78; WhAm 6, 7; WhoAm 74, 76; WhoWor 74*

Edward the Black Prince
[Edward IV; Edward of Woodstock; Prince of Wales]
English. Prince
Eldest son of Edward III; started hearth tax which led to revolt in 1368.
b. Jun 15, 1330 in Woodstock, England
d. Jun 8, 1376 in London, England
Source: *HarEnMi; HisWorL; LinLib S; McGEWB; NewCol 75; WebBD 83; WhDW*

Edward the Confessor
English. Ruler
Ruled the English, 1042-66; supervised rebuilding of Westminster Abbey; canonized, 1161; feast day, Oct 13.
b. 1002? in Oxford, England
d. Jan 5, 1066
Source: *DcCathB; LngCEL; NewC; NewCol 75; WebBD 83; WhDW*

Edward V
English. Ruler
Crown was seized by uncle, Richard III, 1483; deposed, imprisoned on grounds of illegitimacy.
b. Nov 2, 1470 in Westminster, England
d. Jul 1, 1483? in London, England
Source: *BioIn 10; NewCol 75; WebBD 83*

Edward VI
English. Ruler
Ruled England, Ireland, 1547-53; only child of Henry VIII, Jane Seymour; Henry VIII's only legitimate son.
b. Oct 12, 1537 in Hampton Court, England
d. Jul 6, 1553 in London, England
Source: *BioIn 10; NewCol 75; WebBD 83*

Edward VII
[Edward Albert]
English. Ruler
Son of Queen Victoria who ruled 1901-10; popular monarch known as peacemaker.
b. Nov 9, 1841 in London, England

d. May 6, 1910 in London, England
Source: *NewCol 75; WebBD 83*

Edward VIII
[Edward Albert Christian George Andrew Patrick; Duke of Windsor]
English. Ruler
Reigned, Jan-Dec, 1936; abdicated to marry twice-divorced American Wallis Simpson.
b. Jun 23, 1894 in Richmond, England
d. May 28, 1972 in Paris, France
Source: *Benet 87; BioIn 10, 15; ConAu 33R, X; CurBio 72N; DcNaB 1971; DcPol; NewCol 75; ObitT 1971; REn; WebBD 83; WhAm 5*

Edwy
English. Ruler
Son of Edmund I; succeeded uncle, Eadred, as king, 955.
d. 959
Source: *DcNaB; NewC; NewCol 75; WebBD 83*

Eeckhout, Gerbrand van den
Dutch. Artist
Genre, religious painter; pupil of Rembrandt: *Family of Darius.*
b. Aug 19, 1621 in Amsterdam, Netherlands
d. Sep 29, 1674 in Amsterdam, Netherlands
Source: *BioIn 19; McGDA; NewCol 75; OxCArt*

Eeden, Fredrik Willem van
Dutch. Author
Wrote novel trilogy *The Quest,* 1885-1907; founded Walden farm colony inspired by Thoreau, 1898.
b. May 3, 1860 in Haarlem, Netherlands
d. Jun 16, 1932 in Bussum, Netherlands
Source: *CasWL; NewCol 75*

Efron, Marshall
American. Comedian, Actor, Author
Best known for comedy TV series "The Great American Dream Machine."
b. 1938
Source: *BioIn 9, 10; ConAu 112, 126; NewYTBE 71*

Egan, Eddie
"Popeye"
American. Police Officer
On-duty lifestyle was subject for film *The French Connection,* 1971; played small roles in films, 1970s.
b. 1924
d. Nov 4, 1995 in Fort Lauderdale, Florida
Source: *BioIn 9; HalFC 80, 84, 88*

Egan, John Leopold, Sir
English. Auto Executive
Chairman, Jaguar Cars since 1980; compared to Lee Iacocca for ability to restore co.'s fortunes.
b. Nov 7, 1939 in Rawtenstall, England
Source: *BioIn 16; ConNews 87-2; Who 92; WhoWor 89*

Egan, Raymond B
Canadian. Songwriter
Popular lyricist, 1920s-30s; hits include "Sleepy Time Gal," 1925.
b. Nov 14, 1890 in Windsor, Ontario, Canada
d. Nov 13, 1952 in Westport, Connecticut
Source: *AmPS; ASCAP 66, 80; BiDAmM; CmpEPM*

Egan, Richard
American. Actor
Once considered film successor to Clark Gable, but roles confined to action/ Western movies.
b. Jul 29, 1923 in San Francisco, California
d. Jul 20, 1987 in Santa Monica, California
Source: *FilmgC; IntMPA 75, 76, 77, 78, 79, 80, 81, 82, 84, 86; MotPP; MovMk; NewYTBS 87; WhoHol A*

Egan, Walter Lindsay
American. Singer, Songwriter
Country-rock lyricist, guitarist who had hit album *Hi Fi,* 1979.
b. Jul 12, 1948 in Jamaica, New York
Source: *ASCAP 80; ColdWar 2; ConMuA 80A; RkOn 85*

Egas Moniz, Antonio C. A. F
Portuguese. Physician, Educator
Won Nobel Prize for medicine, 1949.
b. Nov 29, 1874 in Avanca, Portugal
d. Dec 13, 1955 in Lisbon, Portugal
Source: *BiESc; WhoNob*

Egg, Augustus Leopold
English. Artist, Actor
Genre painter; specialized in scenes from Shakespeare, Walter Scott.
b. May 2, 1816 in London, England
d. Mar 26, 1863 in Algiers, Algeria
Source: *ArtsNiC; BioIn 1, 6, 10, 13, 16; CelCen; DcBiPP; DcNaB; DcVicP, 2; VicBrit*

Eggar, Samantha
English. Actor
Won Cannes Film Festival award for *The Collector,* 1965.
b. Mar 5, 1940 in Hampstead, England
Source: *BioIn 16; ConTFT 8; FilmgC; HalFC 84, 88; IlWWBF; IntMPA 75, 76, 77, 78, 79, 80, 81, 82, 86, 92; InWom SUP; MotPP; MovMk; WhoAm 76, 84, 86, 90; WhoAmW 74, 75; WhoEnt 92; WhoHol A; WorAl; WorAlBi*

Eggerth, Marta
Hungarian. Actor, Singer
Starred with husband Jan Kiepura in many filmed operettas in Germany, Austria, 1930s.
b. Apr 17, 1916? in Budapest, Austria-Hungary
Source: *BiE&WWA; ConTFT 1; CurBio 43; NotNAT; PenDiMP; WhoHol A; WhoThe 77A; WhThe*

Eggleston, Edward
American. Author, Clergy
Novels include *The Graysons,* 1888; *The Faith Doctor,* 1891.
b. Dec 10, 1837 in Vevay, Indiana
d. Sep 4, 1902 in Lake George, New York
Source: *Alli SUP; AmAu; AmAu&B; AmBi; ApCAB; BbD; BenetAL 91; BibAL; BiD&SB; BioIn 1, 2, 5, 6, 12, 13, 15; CamGEL; CamGLE; CamHAL; CarSB; CasWL; Chambr 3; ChhPo, S1; CnDAL; ConAu 111; CyAL 2; CyEd; CyWA 58; DcAmAu; DcAmB; DcBiA; DcLB 12; DcNAA; DcRusL; EncAAH; EncWM; EvLB; GrWrEL N; HarEnUS; IndAu 1816; JBA 34; LinLib L, S; McGEWB; NatCAB 6; Novels; OxCAmH; OxCAmL 65, 83, 95; OxCChiL; OxCEng 67, 85, 95; PenC AM; REn; REnAL; RfGAmL 87, 94; SmATA 27; TwCBDA; WebAB 74, 79; WebE&AL; WhAm 1*

Egk, Werner
[Werner Mayer]
German. Composer
Operas include *Peer Gynt,* 1938; *The Magic Violin,* 1935.
b. May 17, 1901 in Auchsensheim, Germany
d. Jul 10, 1983 in Inning, Germany (West)
Source: *AnObit 1983; Baker 78, 84, 92; BioIn 3, 8, 9, 13; BriBkM 80; CmOp; CnOxB; CompSN, SUP; CpmDNM 80; DancEn 78; DcCM; FacFETw; IntDcOp; IntWW 74, 75, 76, 77, 78, 79, 80, 81, 82, 83; IntWWM 80; MetOEnc; NewAmDM; NewEOp 71; NewGrDM 80; NewGrDO; NewOxM; NewYTBS 83; OxCMus; OxDcOp; PenDiMP A; WhoMus 72; WhoWor 74, 80*

Eglevsky, Andre
Russian. Dancer
Best-known roles were in *Swan Lake; Apollo, Leader of the Muses; Les Sylphides.*
b. Dec 21, 1917 in Moscow, Union of Soviet Socialist Republics
d. Dec 4, 1977 in Elmira, New York
Source: *BiDD; BioIn 3, 4, 5, 9, 11, 13; BlueB 76; CnOxB; CurBio 53, 78N; DancEn 78; IntDcB; IntWW 74, 75, 76, 77; LegTOT; WhAm 7; What 3; WhoAm 74, 76, 78; WhoWor 78; WhScrn 83; WorAl; WorAlBi*

Egorov, Youri
Russian. Pianist
Concertist; made NYC debut, 1978; noted for virtuoso technique, romantic style.
b. May 28, 1954 in Kazan, Union of Soviet Socialist Republics
d. Apr 15, 1988 in Amsterdam, Netherlands
Source: *Baker 84, 92; BioIn 11*

Egoyan, Atom
Canadian. Filmmaker
Made *Speaking Parts,* 1989; *Exotica,* 1994.
b. Jul 19, 1960 in Cairo, Egypt
Source: *CanWW 31, 89; ConTFT 15; CurBio 94; IntMPA 96; MiSFD 9; WhoAm 95, 96, 97; WhoWor 95, 96, 97*

Ehmke, Howard Jonathan
"Bob"
American. Baseball Player
Pitcher, 1915-30; known for surprise start and win over Chicago in 1929 World Series.
b. Apr 24, 1894 in Silver Creek, New York
d. Mar 17, 1959 in Philadelphia, Pennsylvania
Source: *BioIn 5, 7, 10; WhoProB 73*

Ehrenberg, Christian Gottfried
German. Scientist
Pioneered in study of microorganisms; wrote *Mikrogeologie,* 1854.
b. Apr 19, 1795 in Delitzsch, Germany
d. Jun 27, 1876 in Berlin, Germany
Source: *BiESc; CelCen; DcBiPP, A; DcScB; InSci; LarDcSc; WebBD 83*

Ehrenburg, Ilya Grigoryevich
[Ilya Ehrenbourg; Ilya Erenburg]
Russian. Author
Prominent Soviet literary figure; 1954 novel *The Thaw* was precursor of expanded intellectual liberalism.
b. Jan 27, 1891 in Kiev, Russia
d. Aug 31, 1967 in Moscow, Union of Soviet Socialist Republics
Source: *BioIn 16; CasWL; ClDMEL 47; ConAu 102; ConLC 18; CurBio 66, 67; DcRusL; EncWL; EvEuW; LngCTC; ModSL 1; PenC EUR; RAdv 13-2; REn; TwCA, SUP; TwCWr; WhDW*

Ehrenreich, Barbara
American. Writer
Author of *Witches, Midwives, and Nurses,,* 1972.
b. Aug 26, 1941 in Butte, Montana
Source: *AmWomWr SUP; BestSel 90-4; ConAu 16NR, 37NR, 73; CurBio 95; FemiWr; IntAu&W 89; MajTwCW; WhoAm 84, 86, 88, 90, 92, 94; WhoAmW 81, 87, 89; WhoEmL 87; WhoWor 96; WorAu 1985*

Ehricke, Krafft Arnold
American. Engineer
Worked for US Army missile program, 1947-52; adviser for Rockwell International; head of Space Global consulting firm.
b. Mar 24, 1917 in Berlin, Germany
d. Dec 11, 1984 in La Jolla, California
Source: *AmMWSc 73P, 79, 82; AnObit 1984; BioIn 4, 5, 6; CurBio 58, 85; WhAm 8; WhoAm 74, 76, 78, 80, 82, 84*

Ehrlich, Bettina Bauer
Austrian. Artist
Self-illustrated books include *Castle in the Sand,* 1951; *Neretta,* 1969.
b. Mar 19, 1903 in Vienna, Austria
Source: *AuBYP 2, 3; BioIn 14; ConAu P-1; DcLP 87A; IlsCB 1946, 1957; MorJA; NewCBEL; OxCChiL; SmATA 1; TwCChW 89; WrDr 92*

Ehrlich, Paul
American. Biologist
Wrote best-selling paperback *The Population Bomb,* 1968.
b. May 29, 1932 in Philadelphia, Pennsylvania
Source: *AmMWSc 82; BioIn 13, 14; ConAu 8NR, 65; CurBio 70; EnvEnc; IntAu&W 91, 93; IntWW 83; LNinSix; NatLAC; WhoAm 84, 88; WhoWest 87; WhoWor 84; WrDr 76, 80, 82, 84, 86, 88, 90, 92, 94, 96*

Ehrlich, Paul Ralph
German. Biologist
Developed immunology, chemotherapy; won Nobel Prize, 1908.
b. Mar 14, 1854 in Strehlen, Prussia
d. Aug 20, 1915 in Homburg, Prussia
Source: *AsBiEn; DcBiPP; DcScB; LinLib S; McGEWB; NewCol 75; WhDW; WhoNob; WorAl*

Ehrlichman, John Daniel
American. Presidential Aide
Served 18 months in prison for involvement in Watergate, 1976-78.
b. Mar 20, 1925 in Tacoma, Washington
Source: *AmPolLe; BioIn 12, 13, 15; BlueB 76; ConAu 45NR, 65; CurBio 79; DrAPF 80, 91; IntAu&W 91; IntWW 75, 76, 77, 78, 79, 80, 81, 82, 83, 89, 91, 93; NewYTBE 73; NewYTBS 74, 75; PolProf NF; SpyFic; WhoAm 74, 76, 78, 80, 82, 84, 86, 88, 90, 92, 94, 95, 96, 97; WhoAmP 73; WhoGov 72; WhoSSW 73, 75; WhoUSWr 88; WhoWor 96; WhoWrEP 89, 92, 95; WorAlBi; WrDr 92*

Ehrling, Sixten
Swedish. Conductor
Head of conducting dept. of Juilliard School, NYC, 1973-88; Manhattan School of Music, 1993—; led Detroit Symphony, 1963-73.
b. Apr 3, 1918 in Malmo, Sweden
Source: *Baker 78, 84; BioIn 10, 11; BioNews 74; BlueB 76; BriBkM 80; HalFC 84; IntWWM 77, 80, 90; MetOEnc; MusSN; NewAmDM; NewGrDA 86; NewGrDM 80; NewGrDO; PenDiMP; WhoAm 74, 76, 78, 80, 82, 84, 86, 88, 90, 92, 94, 95, 96, 97; WhoAmM 83; WhoE 93; WhoEnt 92; WhoMus 72; WhoOp 76; WhoSSW 88; WhoWest 82; WhoWor 74, 76, 91*

Eichelberger, Robert Lawrence
American. Army Officer, Author
Promoted to general, 1954; member, NC State Ports Authority, 1957-61.
b. Mar 9, 1886 in Urbana, Ohio
d. Sep 26, 1961 in Asheville, North Carolina
Source: *AmMWSc 73P; BiDWWGF; BioIn 1, 2, 3, 6, 9; CurBio 43, 61; DcAmB S7; DcAmMiB; HarEnMi; ObitOF 79; WebAMB; WhAm 4; WhoMilH 76; WhWW-II*

Eichenberg, Fritz
American. Illustrator
Designed prize-winning classics, children's books with wood-engravings, lithographs.
b. Oct 24, 1901 in Cologne, Germany
d. Nov 30, 1990 in Peace Dale, Rhode Island
Source: *AnCL; BioIn 1, 3, 4, 5, 6, 8, 10, 11, 12, 13, 14, 16, 17, 19; ChhPo S2; ChlBkCr; ConAu 6NR, 57, 133; ConGrA 3; GrAmP; IlsBYP; IlsCB 1744, 1946, 1957; MajAI; McGDA; MorJA; NewYTBS 90; SmATA 9, 50; Str&VC; WhAm 10; WhAmArt 85; WhoAm 74, 76, 78, 80, 82, 84, 86, 88, 90; WhoAmA 73, 76, 78, 80, 82, 84, 86, 89, 91, 93N; WhoArt 84; WhoGrA 62, 82*

Eichendorff, Joseph Karl Benedict Freiherr von
German. Poet
Best known for poems about his Silesian homeland; wrote novel *Presentiment and the Present,* 1815.
b. Mar 10, 1788 in Ratibor
d. Nov 26, 1857 in Neisse
Source: *AtlBL; BbD; BiD&SB; DcEuL; EuAu; OxCFr; OxCGer 76; PenC EUR; RComWL; REn*

Eichhorn, Lisa
American. Actor
Star of film *The Europeans,* 1979; TV movie "The Wall," 1981.
b. Feb 4, 1952? in Reading, Pennsylvania
Source: *BioIn 12; ConTFT 6; HalFC 84, 88; IntMPA 86, 88, 92, 94, 96; LegTOT; NewYTBS 79; WhoHol 92*

Eichmann, Adolf
[Karl Adolf Eichmann]
Austrian. Government Official
In charge of Hitler's death camps; escaped to Argentina, 1946; captured by Israelis, 1960; hung, 1962.
b. Mar 19, 1906 in Solingen, Germany
d. May 31, 1962 in Ramle, Israel
Source: *BiDExR; BioIn 5, 6, 7, 8, 10, 11, 12, 13, 14, 16, 17, 18, 21; DcAmSR; DcPol; DcTwHis; EncTR, 91; EncWB; FacFETw; HisEWW; HisWorL; LegTOT; NewCol 75; ObitOF 79; REn; SpyCS; WhDW; WhWW-II; WorAl; WorAlBi*

Eiermann, Egon
German. Architect
Leading German architect; most popular work is Kaiser Wilhelm Memorial Church in Berlin.
b. Sep 29, 1904 in Neuendorf, Germany
d. Jul 20, 1970 in Baden-Baden, Germany

Source: *BioIn 6, 9; ConArch 80, 87, 94; EncMA; IntDcAr; MacEA; McGDA; WhoArch*

Eifert, Virginia Snider
American. Children's Author
Award-winning books include *Mississippi Calling,* 1957; *Journeys in Green Places,* 1963.
b. Jan 23, 1911 in Springfield, Illinois
d. Jun 16, 1966
Source: *AmAu&B; Au&Wr 71; AuBYP 2; ConAu 1R; SmATA 2; WhAm 4; WhoAmW 58*

Eiffel, Alexandre Gustave
French. Engineer
Designed Eiffel Tower, 1889, framework for Statue of Liberty, 1885.
b. Dec 15, 1832 in Dijon, France
d. Dec 28, 1923 in Paris, France
Source: *BioIn 12, 14, 15, 18; DcD&D; DcTwDes; EncMA; InSci; MacBEP; McGDA; McGEWB; NewCol 75; OxCArt; WhDW; WhoArch; WorAl*

Eigen, Manfred
German. Chemist
Shared 1967 Nobel Prize in chemistry for developing means to measure fast chemical reactions.
b. May 9, 1927 in Bochum, Germany
Source: *AsBiEn; BiESc; BioIn 8, 14, 15, 19, 20; ConAu 108; FacFETw; IntWW 74, 75, 76, 77, 78, 79, 80, 81, 82, 83, 89, 91, 93; LarDcSc; McGMS 80; NobelP; NotTwCS; Who 74, 82, 83, 85, 88, 90, 92, 94; WhoAm 88, 90, 92, 94, 95; WhoNob, 90, 95; WhoScEn 94, 96; WhoScEu 91-3; WhoThSc 1996; WhoWor 74, 76, 78, 80, 82, 84, 87, 89, 91, 93, 95, 96, 97; WorAl; WorAlBi*

Eigenmann, Rosa Smith
American. Scientist
First prominent woman ichthyologist.
b. Oct 7, 1858 in Monmouth, Illinois
d. Jan 12, 1947 in San Diego, California
Source: *AmWomSc; BiDAmS; BioIn 15, 20; InWom SUP; NotAW; NotWoLS; WomFir; WomSc; WomWWA 14*

Eight, The
[Arthur B Davies; William J Glackens; Robert Henri; Ernest Lawson; George Luks; Maurice Pendergast; Everett Shinn; John Sloan]
American. Artists
Established "Ashcan School" of painting, circa 1907.
Source: *Benet 87, 96; BioIn 18; BriEAA; CurBio 51, 53; DcAmArt; NewCol 75; ObitOF 79; OxCArt; OxCTwCA; PeoHis; RComAH; WhAmArt 85; WhoAmA 78N, 80N, 82N, 84N, 86N*

Eigsti, Karl
American. Designer
Set designer for plays in NYC, including *Eubie,* 1978; *Downriver,* 1985.
b. Sep 19, 1938 in Goshen, Indiana
Source: *BioIn 16; ConTFT 5; WhoThe 77, 81*

Eijkman, Christiaan
Dutch. Physician, Educator
Won Nobel Prize in medicine, 1929, for discovery of antineuritic vitamin.
b. Aug 11, 1858 in Nijkerk, Netherlands
d. Nov 5, 1930 in Utrecht, Netherlands
Source: *AsBiEn; BiESc; BioIn 3, 15, 20; CamDcSc; DcScB; FacFETw; InSci; LarDcSc; NobelP; NotTwCS; OxCMed 86; WhDW; WhoNob, 90, 95; WorScD*

Eikenberry, Jill
[Mrs. Michael Tucker]
American. Actor
Plays Ann Kelsey on TV series "LA Law," 1986-94.
b. Jan 21, 1947 in New Haven, Connecticut
Source: *BioIn 15, 16; ConTFT 5, 14; HalFC 84, 88; IntMPA 84, 86, 88, 92, 94, 96; ItaFilm; LegTOT; VarWW 85; WhoAm 90, 92, 94, 95, 96, 97; WhoAmW 95, 97; WhoEnt 92; WhoHol 92; WorAlBi*

Eilberg, Amy
American. Religious Leader
First woman rabbi in Judaism's Conservative branch, 1985.
b. 1955?
Source: *BioIn 14, 15; ConNews 85-3*

Eilshemius, Louis Michel
"Mahatma of Manhattan's Montparnasse"
American. Artist, Author
Atmospheric landscapes include "Approaching Storm."
b. Feb 4, 1864 in North Arlington, New Jersey
d. Dec 29, 1941 in New York, New York
Source: *AmAu&B; AnMV 1926; ArtsAmW 1; AtlBL; BioIn 1, 4, 5, 6, 11; BriEAA; DcAmArt; DcAmB S3; DcNAA; IlBEAAW; McGDA; NewCol 75; PhDcTCA 77; WhAm 1, 2*

Einaudi, Luigi
Italian. Political Leader
Pres. of Italian Republic, 1948-55; political refugee in Switzerland, 1943-45.
b. Mar 24, 1874 in Cuneo, Italy
d. Oct 30, 1961 in Rome, Italy
Source: *BiDInt; BioIn 1, 3, 6; CurBio 48, 62; NewCol 75; ObitT 1961; WhAm 4; WhoEc 81, 86*

Einem, Gottfried von
Austrian. Composer
Composer of many operas and ballets; first opera, *Dantons Tod,* was produced at the 1947 Salzburg Festival.
b. Jan 24, 1918 in Bern, Switzerland
d. Jul 12, 1996 in Obernduernbach, Austria
Source: *Baker 78, 84, 92; BioIn 2, 3, 7, 8, 11; CmOp; CnOxB; CompSN, SUP; ConCom 92; CurBio 53, 96N; DcCM; IntDcOp; IntWW 74, 75, 76, 77, 78, 79, 80, 81, 82, 83, 89, 91, 93; IntWWM 90; MetOEnc; MusMk; NewAmDM; NewEOp 71; NewGrDM 80; NewGrDO; NewOxM; OxCGer 76, 86; OxCMus; OxDcOp; PenDiMP A*

Einhorn, David
German. Religious Leader
Leader of the Reform movement in Judaism, US; supported liberal views on practice of Judaism.
b. Nov 10, 1809 in Dispeck, Bavaria
d. Nov 2, 1879 in New York, New York
Source: *AmBi; ApCAB; BiGAW; BioIn 2, 4, 5, 7, 12, 13, 14, 16, 19; DcAmB; DcAmReB 1, 2; EncARH; NatCAB 12; NewCol 75; WhAm HS*

Einhorn, Eddie
[Edward Martin Einhorn]
American. Baseball Executive
Pres., Chicago White Sox, 1981—; vice chm. White Soc, 1993—; founder, Sports Vision, 1982—.
b. Jan 3, 1936 in Paterson, New Jersey
Source: *Ballpl 90; BioIn 13; NewYTBS 81; WhoAm 78, 80, 82, 84, 86, 88, 90, 92, 94, 95, 96, 97; WhoMW 88, 90, 92, 93, 96*

Einstein, Albert
American. Physicist
One of greatest scientific intellects who formulated theories of relatively; won Nobel Prize, 1921.
b. Mar 14, 1879 in Ulm, Germany
d. Apr 18, 1955 in Princeton, New Jersey
Source: *AmAu&B; AmPeW; AmSocL; AsBiEn; Benet 87, 96; BenetAL 91; BiDMoPL; BiESc; BioIn 1, 2, 3, 4, 5, 6, 7, 8, 9, 10, 11, 12, 13, 14, 15, 16, 17, 18, 19, 20, 21; CamDcSc; CasWL; ConAu 121, 133; ConHero 2; CurBio 41, 53, 55; DcAmB S5; DcInv; DcLEL; DcScB; DcTwHis; Dis&D; EncAB-H 1974, 1996; EncCW; EncMcCE; EncTR, 91; FacFETw; GolEC; HeroCon; InSci; JeAmHC; JeHun; LarDcSc; LegTOT; LinLib L; LngCTC; LuthC 75; MajTwCW; MakMC; McGEWB; NewYTBE 72; NewYTBS 79; NobelP; NotTwCS; ObitT 1951; OxCAmH; OxCAmL 65; OxCEng 67; OxCPhil; PeoHis; PolProf E, T; RAdv 14, 13-5; RComAH; REn; REnAL; ThTwC 87; TwCLC 65; TwoTYeD; WebAB 74, 79; WhAm 3; WhDW; WhNAA; WhoLA; WhoNob, 90, 95; WorAl; WorAlBi; WorScD*

Einstein, Alfred
German. Musicologist, Critic, Editor
Writings on music include *Mozart, His Character, His Work,* 1945.
b. Dec 30, 1880 in Munich, Germany
d. Feb 13, 1952 in El Cerrito, California
Source: *AmAu&B; Baker 78, 84, 92; BiDAmM; BioIn 2, 3, 4, 12; LngCTC;*

NewGrDA 86; NewGrDM 80; NewGrDO; NewOxM; OxCMus; TwCA SUP; WhAm 3

Einstein, Bob
American. Writer, Producer
Won Emmys for writing "The Smothers Brothers Show," 1969; producing "Van Dyke and Company," 1977.
b. Nov 20, 1940 in Los Angeles, California
Source: *VarWW 85; WhoCom*

Einthoven, Willem
Dutch. Physiologist
Developed the electrocardiogram (EKG), 1895; won Nobel Prize, 1924.
b. May 22, 1860 in Semarang, Dutch East Indies
d. Sep 28, 1927 in Leiden, Netherlands
Source: *AsBiEn; BiESc; BiHiMed; BioIn 3, 5, 6, 9, 12, 15, 20, 21; CamDcSc; DcScB; InSci; LarDcSc; NobelP; NotTwCS; OxCMed 86; WhDW; WhoNob, 90, 95; WorInv*

Eisele, Donn Fulton
American. Astronaut, Businessman
Command module pilot, first Apollo voyage, 1968.
b. Jun 23, 1930 in Columbus, Ohio
d. Dec 2, 1987 in Tokyo, Japan
Source: *USBiR 74; WhAm 9; WhoAm 74, 76, 78, 80, 82, 84, 86; WhoSSW 73, 75; WhoWor 74, 78, 80, 82, 84, 87*

Eiseley, Loren Corey
American. Anthropologist
Professor, U of PA, 1961-77; most interested in evolution; wrote *The Unexpected Universe,* 1969.
b. Sep 3, 1907 in Lincoln, Nebraska
d. Jul 9, 1977 in Philadelphia, Pennsylvania
Source: *AmAu&B; AmMWSc 73S, 76P; Au&Wr 71; ConAu 1R; CurBio 60; DcLEL 1940; InSci; REnAL; WebAB 74; WhoAm 74, 76, 78; WhoE 74; WhoGov 72, 75, 77; WhoWor 74; WorAu 1950*

Eiseman, Florence
American. Designer
Influential children's fashion designer; known for excellent workmanship, top-quality fabrics.
b. Sep 27, 1899 in Minneapolis, Minnesota
d. Jan 8, 1988 in Milwaukee, Wisconsin
Source: *BioIn 7, 13; ColdWar 2; InWom SUP; NewYTBS 84; WhAm 9; WhoAm 74, 76, 82; WhoAmW 70, 72, 74, 81; WhoFash 88; WorFshn*

Eisenhower, David
American.
Grandson of Dwight Eisenhower, husband of Julie Nixon; presidential retreat Camp David named for him.
b. Apr 1, 1947 in West Point, New York
Source: *BioIn 4, 8, 9, 10, 11; NewYTBS 86*

Eisenhower, Dwight D(avid)
"Ike"
American. US President
Allied European military leader, WW II; popular, conservative 34th pres., 1953-61.
b. Oct 14, 1890 in Denison, Texas
d. Mar 28, 1969 in Washington, District of Columbia
Source: *AmAu&B; AmOrTwC; AmPolLe; Benet 96; BiDrAC; BiDrUSE 71, 89; BiDWWGF; BioIn 1, 2, 3, 4, 5, 6, 7, 8, 9, 10, 11, 12, 13; BioNews 74; CmdGen 1991; ColdWar 1; ConAu 65; CurBio 42, 57, 69; DcAmB S8; DcAmMiB; DcPol; DcTwHis; EncAAH; EncAB-H 1974, 1996; EncMcCE; EncSoH; FacPr 89, 93; HarEnMi; HealPre; HisEWW; LinLib L, S; McGEWB; MemAm; NatCAB 56; NewYTBE 71; OxCAmH; OxCAmL 65; RAdv 13-3; REn; REnAL; WebAB 74, 79; WebAMB; WhAm 5; WhAmP; WhDW; WhWW-II; WorAl; WorAlBi*

Eisenhower, John Sheldon Doud
"Young Ike"
American. Diplomat
Son of Dwight and Mamie Eisenhower, father of David; in US Army, 1944-63, in reserves as brigadier general; ambassador to Belgium, 1969-71; author of books about WW II.
b. Aug 3, 1922 in Denver, Colorado
Source: *BioIn 2, 3, 4, 5, 7, 8, 9, 10, 13; BlueB 76; ConAu 14NR, 32NR; CurBio 69; Dun&B 88; IntAu&W 89; IntWW 74, 75, 76, 77, 78, 79, 80, 81, 82, 83, 89, 91, 93; WhoAm 74, 76, 78, 80, 82, 84, 86, 88, 90, 92, 94, 95, 96, 97; WhoAmP 73, 75, 77, 79, 81, 83, 85, 87, 89, 91, 93, 95; WhoE 91, 95; WhoWor 78, 82; WrDr 92*

Eisenhower, Julie Nixon
[Mrs. David Eisenhower]
American., Author
Younger daughter of Richard Nixon; wrote *Special People,* 1977, biography of mother *Pat Nixon: The Untold Story,* 1986.
b. Jul 5, 1948 in Washington, District of Columbia
Source: *BioIn 14, 15, 21; BioNews 74; BkPepl; ConAu 114; GoodHs; InWom SUP; NewYTBE 71; NewYTBS 75, 86; PolProf NF; WorAl*

Eisenhower, Mamie Geneva Doud
[Mrs. Dwight David Eisenhower]
American. First Lady
Her short bangs were fashion fad; served as honorary pres. of Girl Scouts.
b. Nov 14, 1896 in Boone, Iowa
d. Nov 1, 1979 in Washington, District of Columbia
Source: *BioNews 74; CurBio 53, 80; DcAmB S10; FacPr 89; InWom, SUP; WhAm 7; WhoAm 74, 76, 78; WhoAmW 58, 61, 70, 72, 74, 75, 77, 79; WhoGov 72, 75; WhoWor 74*

Eisenhower, Milton Stover
American. University Administrator
Youngest brother of Dwight Eisenhower; adviser to every US pres. from Coolidge to Nixon; served as pres. of three colleges.
b. Sep 15, 1899 in Abilene, Kansas
d. May 2, 1985 in Baltimore, Maryland
Source: *BiDAmEd; BioIn 1, 2, 3, 4, 5, 10, 11, 12, 13, 14, 15, 16; BlueB 76; ConAu 73, 116; CurBio 46, 85; DcAmDH 80, 89; IntWW 74, 75, 76, 77, 78, 79, 80, 81, 82, 83; NewYTBS 85; Who 74, 82, 83, 85; WhoAm 74, 76, 78, 80, 82, 84; WhoAmP 73, 75, 77, 79, 81, 83, 85; WhoE 74; WhoWor 74, 82; WorAl; WorAlBi*

Eisenman, Peter
American. Architect
Member, postmodernistic group, "NY Five"; wrote *House of Cards,* 1981.
b. Aug 11, 1932 in South Orange, New Jersey
Source: *AmDec 1980; BioIn 14, 15, 16, 17, 18; ConArch 80; ConAu 108; DcArts; EncAAr 2; IntDcAr; News 92; WrDr 86*

Eisenstaedt, Alfred
"Eisie"
American. Photojournalist
Photojournalist whose photographs were included on more than 90 *Life* magazine covers.
b. Dec 6, 1898 in Dirschau, Germany
d. Aug 23, 1995 in Martha's Vineyard, Massachusetts
Source: *BiDAmJo; BioIn 1, 3, 4, 6, 7, 8, 10, 11, 12, 14, 15, 16; BioNews 74; ConAu 108, 149; ConPhot 82, 88, 95; CurBio 75, 95N; EncAJ; EncTwCJ; FacFETw; ICPEnP; IntWW 74, 75, 76, 77, 78, 79, 80, 81, 82, 83, 89, 91, 93; LegTOT; MacBEP; ModArCr 3; News 96, 96-1; NewYTBS 88, 95; WhoAm 74, 76, 78, 80, 82, 84, 86, 88, 90, 92, 94, 95; WhoWor 74, 76, 78, 80, 82, 84*

Eisenstein, Sergei Mikhailovich
Russian. Director
Films frequently re-edited to conform to political policy; *October; Battleship Potemkin.*
b. Jan 23, 1898 in Riga, Russia
d. Feb 10, 1948 in Moscow, Union of Soviet Socialist Republics
Source: *BiDFilm; CurBio 46, 48; DcFM; EncWT; FilmgC; McGEWB; MovMk; NewCol 75; NewYTBE 73; ObitOF 79; OxCFilm; REn; WhDW; WomWMM; WorEFlm*

Eisner, Kurt
German. Political Leader
First prime minister, Bavarian Republic, 1918; assassinated.
b. May 14, 1867 in Berlin, Germany
d. Feb 21, 1919 in Munich, Germany
Source: *BiDMoPL; BioIn 16; DcLB 66; EncRev; NewCol 75; OxCGer 76, 86*

Eisner, Michael Dammann
American. Business Executive
Chairman, CEO, Walt Disney Co., 1984—; noted for comeback of company.
b. Mar 7, 1942 in Mount Kisco, New York
Source: *BioIn 11, 14, 15, 16; CurBio 87; Dun&B 90; IntMPA 86, 92; IntWW 91, 93; LesBEnT, 92; News 89-2; St&PR 91; WhoAm 86, 88, 90, 92, 94, 95, 96, 97; WhoEnt 92; WhoFI 83, 89, 92, 94, 96; WhoWest 89, 92, 94, 96; WhoWor 93, 95, 96, 97; WorAlBi*

Eisner, Thomas
German. Biologist
Called "the father of chemical ecology" because of his focus on the chemically related interactions between insects, plants, and other living things.
b. Jun 25, 1929 in Berlin, Germany
Source: *AmMWSc 73P, 76P, 79, 82, 86, 89, 92, 95; BlueB 76; CurBio 93; IntWW 74, 75, 76, 77, 78, 79, 80, 81, 82, 83, 89, 91, 93; NotTwCS; WhoAm 82, 84, 86, 88, 90, 92, 94, 95, 96, 97; WhoE 83, 95; WhoFrS 84; WhoMedH; WhoScEn 94, 96; WhoTech 95*

Eisner, Will(iam E.)
American. Cartoonist
Creator of *The Spirit*, a comic strip that ran 1940-51; published graphic novel *A Contract with God and Other Tenement Stories*, 1978.
b. Mar 6, 1917 in New York, New York
Source: *AmAu&B; AmDec 1940; BioIn 14, 15, 16, 20; ConAu 108; ConGrA 1; CurBio 94; EncACom; SmATA 31; WhoAm 74, 76, 78, 80, 82, 84, 86, 88, 90, 92, 94, 95, 96, 97; WorECom*

Ekberg, Anita
"Ice Maiden"
Swedish. Actor
Films include *La Dolce Vita; Boccaccio '70.*
b. Sep 29, 1931 in Malmo, Sweden
Source: *BioIn 2, 4, 10, 11, 17, 21; ConTFT 7; FilmEn; FilmgC; HalFC 80, 84, 88; IntMPA 77, 78, 79, 80, 81, 82, 84, 86, 88, 92, 94, 96; InWom; ItaFilm; LegTOT; MotPP; MovMk; WhoAm 74; WhoAmW 66, 68, 70, 72, 74; WhoHol 92, A; WorEFlm*

Ekhof, Konrad
German. Actor, Director
A founder of the modern German theater; promoted realism.
b. Aug 12, 1720 in Hamburg, Germany
d. Jun 16, 1778 in Gotha, Germany
Source: *CamGWoT; CnThe; EncWT; Ent; NotNAT B; OxCGer 76, 86; OxCThe 67, 83*

Ekland, Britt
Swedish. Actor
Married Peter Sellers, 1963-68; starred in James Bond film *Man with the Golden Gun*, 1974.
b. Oct 6, 1942 in Stockholm, Sweden
Source: *BioIn 9, 10, 11, 12, 14, 16, 17; ConTFT 7; FilmAG WE; FilmEn; FilmgC; HalFC 80, 84, 88; IntMPA 75, 76, 77, 78, 79, 80, 81, 82, 84, 86, 88, 92, 94, 96; ItaFilm; LegTOT; WhoHol 92, A; WhoHrs 80; WorAl; WorAlBi*

Eklund, Carl Robert
American. Explorer
A founder, first pres. of Antarctican Society, 1959.
b. Jan 27, 1909 in Tomahawk, Wisconsin
d. Nov 4, 1962 in Philadelphia, Pennsylvania
Source: *BioIn 6, 7; DcAmB S7; NatCAB 48*

Eklund, John M(anly)
American. Labor Union Official
Pres., American Federation of Teachers, 1948-52.
b. Sep 14, 1909
d. Jan 11, 1997 in Denver, Colorado
Source: *BiDAmL; BiDAmLL; BioIn 2; BlueB 76; WrDr 76, 80, 82, 84*

Ekwensi, Cyprian Odiatu Duaka
Nigerian. Author
Ibo novelist whose work is characterized by faithful depiction of urban-African life.
b. Sep 26, 1921 in Minna, Nigeria
Source: *AfrA; Benet 87; BioIn 9, 10, 14; BlkWr 1; CamGLE; CasWL; ConAu 18NR, 29R, X; ConLC 4; EncWL 2; IntvTCA 2; IntWW 91; McGEWB; TwCChW 89; WrDr 92*

Elam, Jack
American. Actor
Appeared in over 100 films: *The Way West*, 1967; *Support Your Local Sheriff*, 1969.
b. Nov 13, 1916 in Phoenix, Arizona
Source: *CmMov; ConTFT 2, 6; EncAFC; FilmEn; FilmgC; ForYSC; GangFlm; HalFC 80, 84, 88; HolCA; IntDcF 1-3; IntMPA 82, 84, 86, 88, 92, 94, 96; ItaFilm; MotPP; MovMk; WhoAm 80, 82, 84; WhoFI 79; WhoHol 92, A*

Elazar, David
Israeli. Army Officer
Commanded Israeli troops, October War, 1973; resigned.
b. 1925 in Sarajevo, Yugoslavia
d. Apr 15, 1976 in Tel Aviv, Israel
Source: *BioIn 10; HisEAAC; IntWW 74, 75, 76, 76N; NewYTBS 76; ObitOF 79; WorDWW*

Elder, Lee
American. Golfer
Turned pro, 1959; first black to play in Masters, 1975; 43rd player to win $1 million on tour (1984).
b. Jul 14, 1934 in Dallas, Texas
Source: *AfrAmAl 6; BioIn 10, 11, 12, 14; ConBlB 6; CurBio 76; NegAl 89; NewYTBS 74, 78, 79; WhoAfA 96; WhoBlA 90, 92, 94; WhoGolf; WhoIntG*

Elder, Ruth
"Miss America of Aviation"
American. Aviator, Actor
Made unsuccessful attempts to become first woman to fly across Atlantic, 1927; starred in several vaudeville films.
b. Sep 8, 1905 in Anniston, Alabama
d. Oct 9, 1977 in San Francisco, California
Source: *Film 2; NewYTBS 77; ObitOF 79; WhScrn 83*

Elders, Joycelyn
American. Government Official, Physician
Surgeon general, 1993-94; advocated distribution of contraceptives in school health clinics.
b. Aug 13, 1933 in Schaal, Arkansas
Source: *AmMWSc 92; BioIn 6; BlksScM; ConBlB 6; CurBio 94; LegTOT; News 94, 94-1; NotBlAW 2; WhoAm 90, 96; WhoAmW 91, 95; WhoBlA 92*

Eldjarn, Kristjan
Icelandic. Politician
Pres. of Iceland, 1968-80.
b. Dec 6, 1916 in Tjorn, Iceland
d. Sep 13, 1982 in Cleveland, Ohio
Source: *AnObit 1982; BioIn 13; ConAu 110; FacFETw; IntWW 74, 75, 76, 77, 78, 79, 80, 81, 82; IntYB 78, 79, 80, 81, 82; NewYTBS 82; WhAm 8; WhoGov 72; WhoWor 74, 76, 78*

Eldridge, Florence
[Mrs. Fredric March]
American. Actor
Broadway, film star; appeared with husband in films *Studio Murder Mystery*, 1929; *Les Miserables*, 1935.
b. Sep 5, 1901 in New York, New York
d. Aug 1, 1988 in Santa Barbara, California
Source: *AnObit 1988; BiE&WWA; BioIn 1, 16; CamGWoT; CnThe; CurBio 43, 88N; Film 2; FilmEn; FilmgC; ForYSC; HalFC 80, 84, 88; InWom, SUP; LegTOT; MotPP; MovMk; NewYTBS 88; NotNAT; NotWoAT; OxCAmT 84; ThFT; WhAm 9; WhoAmW 68, 70, 72, 74; WhoHol A; WhoThe 72, 77A; WhThe; WorAl*

Eldridge, Roy
[David Roy Eldridge]
"Little Jazz"
American. Jazz Musician
Trumpeter, drummer; bandleader since 1927; with Goodman, 1950s; became popular as a soloist with Fletcher Henderson band, 1936.
b. Jan 29, 1911 in Pittsburgh, Pennsylvania
d. Feb 26, 1989 in Valley Stream, New York
Source: *AfrAmAl 6; AllMusG; AnObit 1989; ASCAP 80; Baker 84; BiDAfM; BiDAmM; BiDJaz; BioIn 4, 10, 11, 12, 13, 14, 15, 16, 17, 20; CmpEPM; ConMus 9; CurBio 87, 89N, 90; DcTwCCu 5; DrBlPA, 90; EncJzS;*

FacFETw; IlEncJ; InB&W 80, 85; LegTOT; MusMk; NegAl 89; NewAmDM; NewGrDA 86; NewGrDJ 88; NewGrDM 80; News 89-3; NewYTBS 89; OxCPMus; PenEncP; TwCBrS; WhAm 9; WhoAm 74, 76, 78, 80, 82, 84; WhoBlA 85, 88, 90N; WhoJazz 72; WorAl; WorAlBi

Eleanor of Aquitaine
[Eleanor of Guienne]
French. Consort
Marriage to Louis VII annulled; married Henry II, 1154; mother of Richard the Lion-Hearted; story told in Oscar-winning *The Lion in Winter,* 1968.
b. 1122? in Aquitaine, France
d. Apr 1, 1204 in Maine-et-Loire, France
Source: *Benet 87, 96; BioIn 1, 2, 3, 4, 5, 6, 7, 8, 9, 10, 11, 12, 13, 17, 19; BlmGWL; ContDcW 89; DcBiPP; DcEuL; EncAmaz 91; HisWorL; IntDcWB; InWom, SUP; LegTOT; LinLib S; McGEWB; MediFra; NewC; OxCEng 85, 95; REn; WhDW; WomFir; WomWR; WorAl; WorAlBi*

Electric Light Orchestra
[Michael Alberquerque; Bev Bevan; Michael Edwards; Melvyn Gale; Wilf Gibson; Kelly Groucutt; Mik Kaminski; Jeff Lynne; Hugh MacDowell; Richard Tndy; Colin Walker]
English. Music Group
Orchestral rock group formed, 1971; hits include "Roll Over Beethoven," 1973; "Evil Woman," 1976.
Source: *BioIn 12, 17; BkPepl; ConMuA 80A; ConMus 7; EncPR&S 89; EncRk 88; EncRkSt; HarEnR 86; IlEncRk; NewAmDM; PenEncP; RkOn 78, 84; RolSEnR 83; St&PR 96, 97; Who 82, 83, 85, 88, 90, 92, 94; WhoRock 81; WhoRocM 82*

Elegant, Robert Sampson
American. Author, Journalist
Asian news correspondent, 1951-75, who wrote *China's Red Masters,* 1951.
b. Mar 7, 1928 in New York, New York
Source: *AmAu&B; BioIn 11; ConAu 1NR, 1R, 30NR; IntAu&W 77, 91; NewYTBS 80; WhoAm 86, 90, 97; WhoWest 76; WrDr 86, 92*

Elfman, Danny
American. Songwriter, Singer, Composer
Member of the music group Oingo Bingo, 1979-90; has composed over 15 film scores and many TV themes.
b. May 29, 1953 in Amarillo, Texas
Source: *Au&Arts 14; BioIn 15; ConAu 148; ConMus 9; ConTFT 10; IntMPA 92, 94, 96; IntWW 91; WhoAm 94, 95, 96, 97; WhoEnt 92*

Elgar, Edward William, Sir
English. Composer, Conductor, Musician
Best known for oratorios, pomp and circumstance marches, symphonic works in romantic style.
b. Jun 2, 1857 in Broadheath, England
d. Feb 23, 1934 in London, England
Source: *AtlBL; Baker 84, 92; BioIn 1, 2, 3, 4, 5, 6, 7, 8, 9, 10, 12, 13; ConAu 116; DcArts; DcCathB; DcCM; DcNaB 1931; GrBr; LinLib S; McGEWB; NewGrDO; OxCEng 85, 95; OxCMus; REn; WorAl*

Elgart, Les
American. Bandleader
Led popular swing bands, 1950s-60s.
b. Aug 3, 1918 in New Haven, Connecticut
d. Jul 29, 1995 in Dallas, Texas
Source: *BgBands 74; BiDAmM; BioIn 21; CmpEPM; OxCPMus; PenEncP*

Elgin, James Bruce
[Eighth Earl of Elgin]
English. Political Leader
As governor-general of Canada, 1847-54; applied concept of "responsible govt."; viceroy of India, 1862-63.
b. Jul 20, 1811 in London, England
d. Nov 20, 1863 in Dharmsala, India
Source: *ApCAB; BioIn 2, 4, 5, 9, 14; CelCen; Drake; MacDCB 78; McGEWB; NewCol 75; OxCCan*

Elgin, Thomas Bruce
[Seventh Earl of Elgin]
English. Diplomat, Art Collector
As envoy to Constantinople, arranged for Athenian sculpture, *Elgin Marbles,* to be taken to British Museum, 1803-12.
b. Jul 20, 1766
d. Nov 14, 1841 in Paris, France
Source: *Alli; BioIn 1, 8, 10, 14, 18; CelCen; NewCol 75; WebBD 83; WhDW*

Eliade, Mircea
American. Theologian
Wrote on comparative religion: *A History of Religious Ideas,* 1977-85.
b. Mar 9, 1907 in Bucharest, Romania
d. Apr 22, 1986 in Chicago, Illinois
Source: *AmAu&B; AnObit 1986; Au&Wr 71; Benet 87, 96; BiDPara; BioIn 7, 10, 11, 12, 13, 14, 15, 16, 17, 18; CasWL; ConAu 30NR, 65, 119; ConLC 19; CurBio 85, 86, 86N; CyWA 89; DrAS 74P, 78P, 82P; EncO&P 1, 2, 3; EncPaPR 91; EncWB; EncWL, 2, 3; FacFETw; IntEnSS 79; LiExTwC; LinLib L; MajTwCW; MakMC; RAdv 14, 13-2; ScF&FL 1, 92; ThTwC 87; WhAm 9; WhoAm 74, 76, 78, 80, 82, 84; WhoMW 74, 76; WhoRel 77, 85; WhoSocC 78; WhoWor 74, 76; WorAu 1950*

Elias, Rosalind
American. Opera Singer
Mezzo-soprano; made NY Met. debut, 1954; a noted Carmen.
b. Mar 13, 1931 in Lowell, Massachusetts
Source: *Baker 84; BioIn 4, 6, 7, 8, 11, 13; CelR; CmOp; CurBio 67; IntWWM 77, 80, 90; InWom; MetOEnc; MusSN; NewAmDM; NewEOp 71; NewGrDA 86; NewGrDM 80; PenDiMP; WhoAm 76, 78, 80, 82, 84, 86, 88, 90, 92, 94, 95, 96, 97; WhoAmM 83; WhoAmW 66, 68, 70, 72, 74, 83, 95, 97*

Elijah
Biblical Figure
Old Testament prophet whose mission was to destroy worship of foreign gods, restore justice.
b. fl. 875BC
Source: *NewC; NewCol 75*

Elijah Ben Solomon
Polish. Scholar
Called greatest authority on classical Judaism in modern times; wrote over 70 treatises.
b. 1720 in Vilnius, Lithuania
d. 1797 in Vilna, Russia
Source: *BioIn 1, 3, 4, 5, 7, 17; EuAu; McGEWB; NewCol 75*

Elion, Gertrude Bell
American. Biochemist
Shared Nobel Prize, 1988, for research on life-prolonging drug treatments for AIDS, leukemia, gastroduodonal ulcers.
b. Jan 23, 1918 in New York, New York
Source: *AmMWSc 92; BioIn 16; CurBio 95; FacFETw; IntWW 91; InWom SUP; NewYTBS 89; Who 92; WhoAm 90; WhoAmW 91; WhoNob 90; WhoSSW 91; WhoTech 89; WhoWor 91; WorAlBi*

Eliot, Charles William
American. Educator
Pres., Harvard U, 1869-1909; editor, *Harvard Classics,* 1910.
b. Mar 20, 1834 in Boston, Massachusetts
d. Aug 22, 1926 in Maine
Source: *Alli SUP; AmAu; AmAu&B; AmBi; AmDec 1900; AmPeW; AmSocL; ApCAB, X; BiDAmEd; BiD&SB; BiDInt; BioIn 1, 2, 3, 5, 6, 8, 10, 12, 13; CyAG; CyAL 1; DcAmAu; DcAmB; DcAmMeB 84; DcNAA; Dis&D; EncAB-H 1974, 1996; HarEnUS; LinLib L, S; LuthC 75; McGEWB; MemAm; NatCAB 6; NewCol 75; OxCAmH; OxCAmL 65, 83; REn; REnAL; TwCBDA; WebAB 74, 79; WhAm 1; WorAl; WorAlBi*

Eliot, George
[Mary Ann Evans Cross]
English. Author
Popular Victorian novelist stressed moral overtones: *The Mill on the Floss,* 1860.
b. Nov 22, 1819 in Warwickshire, England
d. Dec 22, 1880 in London, England
Source: *Alli SUP; ArtclWW 2; AtlBL; BbD; Benet 87, 96; BiD&SB; BioIn 1, 2, 3, 4, 5, 6, 7, 8, 9, 10, 11, 12, 13, 14, 15, 16, 17, 18, 19, 20, 21; BlmGEL; BlmGWL; BritAu 19; BritWr 5; CamGEL; CamGLE; CasWL; CelCen; Chambr 3; ChhPo, S2, S3; CnDBLB 4; ContDcW 89; CrtT 3, 4; CyWA 58; DcArts; DcBiA; DcEnA, A; DcEnL; DcEuL; DcLB 21, 35, 55; DcLEL; Dis&D; EncBrWW; EncPaPR 91; EvLB;*

FemiCLE; GoodHs; GrWomW; GrWrEL N; HerW, 84; HsB&A; IntDcWB; InWom, SUP; LegTOT; LinLib L, S; LngCEL; MagSWL; McGEWB; MnBBF; MouLC 3; NewC; NewCBEL; NinCLC 4, 13, 23; Novels; OxCEng 67, 85, 95; PenC ENG; PenNWW B; RadHan; RAdv 1, 14, 13-1; RComWL; REn; RfGEnL 91; RfGShF; StaCVF; TwoTYeD; VicBrit; WebE&AL; WhDW; WorAl; WorAlBi; WorLitC; WrPh

Eliot, George Fielding
American. Radio Performer, Author, Lecturer
Military correspondent during WW II; wrote syndicated columns, 1950-67; wrote books on war: *If Russia Strikes,* 1949.
b. Jun 22, 1894 in New York, New York
d. Apr 21, 1971 in Torrington, Connecticut
Source: *AmAu&B; BiDAmNC; BioIn 4, 9, 11; ConAu 29R; CurBio 40, 71, 71N; EncAJ; EncTwCJ; MnBBF; NatCAB 56; REnAL; TwCA, SUP; WhAm 5*

Eliot, John
English. Colonial Figure, Teacher, Missionary
Preached to Native Americans; translated Old, New Testaments into their languages.
b. Aug 5, 1604 in Widford, England
d. May 20, 1690 in Roxbury, Massachusetts
Source: *Alli; AmAu; AmAu&B; AmBi; AmWrBE; ApCAB; BbD; BenetAL 91; BiDAmEd; BiD&SB; BioIn 1, 2, 3, 4, 5, 6, 7, 8, 10, 11, 14, 15, 17, 19; CamGLE; CamHAL; CyAL 1; CyEd; DcAmAu; DcAmB; DcAmReB 1, 2; DcAmSR; DcBiPP; DcLB 24; DcNAA; DcNaB; EncAAH; EncAB-H 1974, 1996; EncARH; EncCRAm; EncNAR; HarEnUS; LinLib L, S; LitC 5; LuthC 75; McGEWB; NatCAB 2; OxCAmH; OxCAmL 65, 83, 95; PenC AM; REn; REnAL; REnAW; TwCBDA; WebAB 74, 79; WhAm HS; WhDW; WhNaAH; WorAl; WorAlBi*

Eliot, Martha May
American. Government Official, Physician
Official of the US Children's Bureau, 1924-56; first woman pres. of American Public Health Association, 1947-48.
b. Apr 7, 1891 in Dorchester, Massachusetts
d. Feb 1978 in Cambridge, Massachusetts
Source: *BiDInt; BiDSocW; BioIn 1, 2, 4, 5, 7, 11, 12, 19; CurBio 48, 78, 78N; InSci; IntWW 74, 75, 76; InWom, SUP; NatCAB 60; WhAm 9; WhoAmW 58, 64, 66, 68, 70; WomFir*

Eliot, T(homas) S(tearns)
English. Poet, Critic
Wrote *Murder in the Cathedral,* 1935, *The Cocktail Party,* 1950; won Nobel Prize, 1948.
b. Sep 26, 1888 in Saint Louis, Missouri
d. Jan 4, 1965 in London, England
Source: *AmCulL; AmWr; AnCL; AtlBL; Benet 96; BioIn 1, 2, 3, 4, 5, 6, 7, 8, 9, 10, 11, 12, 13, 14, 15, 16, 17, 18, 19, 20; BlmGEL; CasWL; Chambr 3; ChhPo S3; CnDAL; CnMD; ConAu 41NR; ConBrDr; ConLC 15; CurBio 62, 65; CyWA 58; DcAmC; DcArts; DcNaB 1961; DcTwHis; EncWL 3; EncWT; EngPo; Ent; GrBr; IntDcT 2; LinLib S; LngCEL; LuthC 75; MakMC; McGEWB; McGEWD 84; ModAL S1; NewCBEL; NotNAT B; OxCAmL 95; OxCEng 85, 95; OxCThe 67; OxCTwCP; PenC ENG; RAdv 14; RComWL; REn; REnAL; RfGAmL 94; RGFAP; RGTwCWr; WebAB 74, 79; WhAm 4; WhDW; WhE&EA; WhLit; WhoNob, 90, 95*

Elisofon, Eliot
American. Photographer, Artist, Filmmaker
Master of color, black and white photography, renowned watercolor artist.
b. Apr 17, 1911 in New York, New York
d. Apr 7, 1973 in New York, New York
Source: *AmAu&B; BioIn 3, 4, 9, 10, 12; ConAu 41R; ConPhot 82, 88; CurBio 72, 73, 73N; EncAJ; EncTwCJ; ICPEnP A; LinLib L; MacBEP; NewYTBE 73; SmATA 21N; WhAm 5; WhoAmA 73, 76N, 78N, 80, 80N, 82N, 84N, 86N, 89N, 91N, 93N*

Elizabeth, the Queen Mother
[Elizabeth Angela Marguerite]
English. Consort
Wife of King George VI; mother of Queen Elizabeth II, Princess Margaret.
b. Aug 4, 1900 in Hertfordshire, England
Source: *BioIn 1, 2, 3, 4, 5, 6, 7, 8, 10, 11, 12, 13, 14, 15, 16, 17, 20; BlueB 76; ContDcW 89; CurBio 81; EncWB; IntWW 74, 75, 76, 77, 78, 79, 80, 82, 83, 89, 91, 93; InWom; NewCol 75; NewYTBS 80; Who 82R, 83R, 85R, 88R, 90R, 92R, 94R; WhoWor 76, 78, 82, 84, 87, 89, 91, 93, 95, 96, 97; WomFir*

Elizabeth I
"Good Queen Bess"; "The Virgin Queen"
English. Ruler
Daughter of Henry VIII, Anne Boleyn; ruled Great Britain, N Ireland, 1558-1603; during reign England became world power.
b. Sep 7, 1533 in Greenwich, England
d. Mar 24, 1603 in Richmond, England
Source: *McGEWB; NewCol 75; WebBD 83*

Elizabeth II
[Elizabeth Alexandra Mary]
English. Ruler
Succeeded father George VI to throne upon his death, 1952; noted horsewoman; allowed TV coverage of royal family.
b. Apr 21, 1926 in London, England
Source: *Benet 87; ContDcW 89; CurBio 44, 55; EncWB; FacFETw; IntWW 91; InWom SUP; NewCol 75; WhoAm 86, 90, 94; WhoWor 91; WomWR; WorAlBi*

Elizabeth of Hungary, Saint
Hungarian. Religious Figure
Daughter of Andrew II, king of Hungary; devoted to religion, charity; canonized, 1235.
b. 1207
d. 1231
Source: *NewCol 75; REn; WebBD 83*

Elizondo, Hector
American. Actor
In TV shows "Popi," 1976; "Casablanca," 1983; film *American Gigolo,* 1980.
b. Dec 22, 1936 in New York, New York
Source: *BioIn 17, 18, 20; ConTFT 2, 7, 14; CurBio 92; HalFC 84, 88; IntMPA 77, 86, 88, 92, 94, 96; LegTOT; WhoAm 84, 86, 88, 90, 92, 94, 95, 96, 97; WhoHisp 91, 92, 94; WhoHol 92, A; WhoThe 77, 81*

Elkin, Benjamin
American. Children's Author
Writings include *King's Wish and Other Stories,* 1960; *Magic Ring,* 1969.
b. Aug 10, 1911 in Baltimore, Maryland
Source: *Alli; Au&Wr 71; AuBYP 2, 3; BioIn 7, 9; ConAu 1R, 4NR; FourBJA; IntAu&W 77; SmATA 3; WhoMW 74; WhoWorJ 72, 78; WrDr 76, 80, 82, 84, 86, 88, 90, 92, 94, 96*

Elkin, Stanley (Lawrence)
American. Author
Novels include *The Magic Kingdom,* 1985; *The Rabbi of Lud,* 1987.
b. May 11, 1930 in New York, New York
d. May 31, 1995 in Saint Louis, Missouri
Source: *AmAu&B; Benet 87, 96; BenetAL 91; BioIn 14, 15, 16, 17, 19, 21; CamGLE; CamHAL; ConAu 8NR, 9R; ConLC 4, 6, 9, 14, 27, 51, 91; ConNov 72, 76, 82, 86, 91, 96; ConPopW; CurBio 87, 95N; CyWA 89; DcLB 2, 28, Y80A; DrAF 76; DrAPF 80, 91; DrAS 74E, 78E, 82E; EncWL; FacFETw; IntAu&W 76, 77, 91, 93; IntWW 89, 91, 93; JeAmFiW; MajTwCW; ModAL S2; NewYTBS 91; Novels; OxCAmL 83, 95; PenC AM; PostFic; RAdv 14, 13-1; RGTwCWr; ScF&FL 92; ShSCr 12; WhAm 11; WhoAm 74, 76, 78, 80, 82, 84, 86, 88, 90, 92, 94, 95; WhoUSWr 88; WhoWrEP 89, 92, 95; WorAlBi; WorAu 1970; WrDr 76, 80, 82, 84, 86, 88, 90, 92, 94, 96*

Elkins, Hillard
"Hilly"
American. Producer
Films include *A Doll's House,* 1972; stage productions include *Streetcar Named Desire,* 1974.
b. Oct 18, 1929 in New York, New York
Source: *CelR; IntMPA 88, 92, 94, 96; NotNAT A; WhoAm 76, 78, 80, 82, 84, 86, 88, 90, 92, 94, 95, 96, 97; WhoEnt 92; WhoThe 72, 77, 81*

Elkins, Stanley Maurice
American. Historian, Educator
American history specialist who wrote *Slavery,* 1959.
b. Apr 29, 1925 in Boston, Massachusetts
Source: *ConAu 102; DrAS 74H, 78H, 82H; EncAAH; WhoAm 74, 76, 78, 80, 82, 84, 86, 88, 90, 92, 94, 95, 96, 97*

Ellender, Allen Joseph
American. Politician
Dem. senator from LA, 1936-71; served as pres. pro tempore of Senate.
b. Sep 24, 1890 in Montegut, Louisiana
d. Jul 27, 1972 in Bethesda, Maryland
Source: *BiDrAC; BiDrUSC 89; CurBio 46, 72; DcAmB S9; NewYTBE 71, 72; WhAm 5; WhAmP; WhoGov 72, 75; WhoSSW 73, 75*

Ellerbee, Linda
American. Broadcast Journalist
Mostly with NBC News, 1978-86; founder, owner, Lucky Duck Prods., 1987—; commentator, CNN, 1989—.
b. Aug 15, 1944 in Bryan, Texas
Source: *Au&Arts 16; BiDAmNC; BioIn 13, 15, 16; ConAu, 110, 115; ConTFT 6; CurBio 86; EncTwCJ; GrLiveH; InWom SUP; LegTOT; LesBEnT 92; News 93-3; WhoAm 80, 82, 84, 86, 88, 90, 92, 94, 95, 96, 97; WhoAmW 91, 93, 95, 97; WhoHol 92; WhoTelC*

Ellery, William
American. Judge, Continental Congressman
Member of Congress, 1776-86; signed Declaration of Independence, 1776; known for ready wit.
b. Dec 22, 1727 in Newport, Rhode Island
d. Feb 15, 1820 in Newport, Rhode Island
Source: *AmBi; ApCAB; BiAUS; BiDrAC; BiDrUSC 89; BioIn 3, 6, 7, 8, 9; CelCen; DcAmB; Drake; EncAR; EncCRAm; HarEnUS; NatCAB 8; TwCBDA; WhAm HS; WhAmP; WhAmRev*

Elliman, Yvonne
[Mrs. William Oakes]
American. Singer
Sang "I Don't Know How to Love Him," in *Jesus Christ Superstar.*
b. Dec 29, 1953 in Honolulu, Hawaii
Source: *EncRk 88; IlEncRk; PenEncP; RkOn 74, 78; WhoAm 80, 82; WhoHol 92; WhoRocM 82*

Ellin, Stanley
American. Author
Mystery writer whose books include *The Eighth Circle,* 1958; *The Key to Nicholas Street,* 1951.
b. Oct 6, 1916 in New York, New York
d. Jul 31, 1986 in New York, New York
Source: *AmAu&B; AnObit 1986; Au&Wr 71; BioIn 5, 10, 11; ConAu 1R, 4NR, 28NR, 119; Conv 3; CrtSuMy; EncMys; MajTwCW; Novels; REnAL; TwCCr&M 80, 85, 91; WorAu 1950; WrDr 76, 80, 82, 84, 86*

Ellingson, Mark
American. Educator
Pres., Rochester NY Institute of Technology, 1936-69.
b. Jun 5, 1904
d. Feb 12, 1993 in Rochester, New York
Source: *BioIn 4, 5, 18, 19; CurBio 93N; WhoAm 74, 76; WhoE 74*

Ellington, Duke
[Edward Kennedy Ellington]
American. Bandleader, Songwriter
Wrote over 5,000 original works, including "Take the A Train," "Moon Indigo"; outstanding jazz personality; won 1959 Spingarn.
b. Apr 29, 1899 in Washington, District of Columbia
d. May 24, 1974 in New York, New York
Source: *AfrAmAl 6; AllMusG; AmComp; AmCulL; AmPS; AmSong; ASCAP 66, 80; Baker 78, 84; BgBands 74; BiDAfM; BiDAmM; BiDD; BiDJaz; BiE&WWA; BioIn 1, 2, 3, 4, 5, 6, 7, 8, 9, 10, 11, 12, 13, 14, 15, 16, 17, 18, 19, 20, 21; BioNews 74; BlkCond; BriBkM 80; CelR; CmpEPM; ConAmC 76, 82; ConAu 49, 97; ConBlB 5; ConHero 2; ConMus 2; CurBio 41, 70, 74, 74N; DcAmB S9; DcArts; DcTwCCu 1, 5; DrBlPA, 90; Ebony 1; EncAB-H 1974, 1996; EncJzS; FacFETw; FilmgC; HalFC 80, 84, 88; IlEncJ; InB&W 80, 85; LegTOT; MakMC; McGEWB; MnPM; MorMA; MusMk; NegAl 76, 83, 89; NewGrDA 86; NewGrDJ 88, 94; NewGrDM 80; NewOxM; NewYTBE 72; NewYTBS 74; NotNAT A, B; ObitT 1971; OxCAmH; OxCMus; OxCPMus; PenDiMP A; PenEncP; PopAmC, SUP, SUPN; RAdv 14, 13-3; RComAH; SelBAAf; SelBAAu; Sw&Ld C; WebAB 74, 79; WhAm 6; Who 74; WhoAm 74; WhoBlA 75; WhoE 74; WhoGov 72; WhoHol B; WhoJazz 72; WhoMus 72; WhoWor 74; WhScrn 77, 83; WorAl; WorAlBi*

Ellington, E. David
American. Computer Executive
Founded NetNoir Inc. with Malcolm CasSelle, 1995.
b. Jul 10, 1960 in New York, New York
Source: *ConBlB 11*

Ellington, Mercer
American. Musician, Bandleader
Son of Duke Ellington; took over orchestra, 1974.
b. Mar 11, 1919 in Washington, District of Columbia
d. Feb 8, 1996 in Copenhagen, Denmark
Source: *AllMusG; ASCAP 66; BiDAfM; BiDJaz; BioIn 12, 16; CmpEPM; ConAu 113; DrBlPA, 90; IlEncJ; InB&W 85; NewAmDM; NewGrDJ 88; PenEncP; WhoAm 82*

Elliot, Cass
[Mamas and the Papas; Ellen Naomi Cohen]
American. Singer
Solo career, 1967-74; hit song "Dream a Little Dream of Me," 1968.
b. Feb 19, 1943 in Arlington, Virginia
d. Jul 29, 1974 in London, England
Source: *BioIn 7, 8, 9; BioNews 74; CelR; NewYTBS 74; WhoHol B; WhoRocM 82*

Elliot, Win
[Irwin Elliot]
American. Radio Performer
Sportscaster on all networks, 1941—; won Football Hall of Fame Citizen award.
b. May 7, 1915 in Chelsea, Massachusetts
Source: *BioIn 1, 2, 3, 9, 21; IntMPA 75, 76; RadStar; SaTiSS; WhoAm 80, 82, 84, 86*

Elliott, Bob
[Bob and Ray; Robert B Elliott]
American. Comedian
Member of comedy team known for satire, ad-libbing; won Peabody Award, 1952, 1957.
b. Mar 26, 1923 in Boston, Massachusetts
Source: *BioIn 3, 4, 5, 9, 10, 13, 16, 17; CelR; ConAu 109, 134; CurBio 57; JoeFr; LegTOT; NewYTBS 89; RadStar; WhoAm 88; WhoHol 92; WrDr 94, 96*

Elliott, Charles Loring
American. Artist
Over 700 portraits include those of James E Freeman, Governor Hunt.
b. Oct 12, 1812 in Scipio, New York
d. Aug 25, 1868 in Albany, New York
Source: *AmBi; ApCAB; ArtsNiC; BioIn 7; BriEAA; DcAmArt; DcAmB; Drake; EarABI; HarEnUS; McGDA; NatCAB 11; NewYHSD; TwCBDA; WhAm HS*

Elliott, Denholm Mitchell
English. Actor
Supporting actor in *Alfie,* 1966; *Raiders of the Lost Ark,* 1981.
b. May 31, 1922 in London, England
d. Oct 6, 1992 in Ibiza, Spain
Source: *BioIn 13, 15; CnThe; ConTFT 4; FilmgC; HalFC 88; IntMPA 86, 92; News 93-2; NewYTBS 86; NotNAT; OxCThe 83; WhAm 10; Who 74, 82, 83, 85, 88, 90, 92; WhoAm 88, 92; WhoEnt 92; WhoHol A; WhoThe 81*

Elliott, Ebenezer
"The Corn Law Rhymer"
English. Poet
Attributed all nat. problems to bread tax, which he condemned in influential *Corn Law Rhymes,* 1831.
b. Mar 17, 1781 in Masborough, England
d. Dec 1, 1849 in Great Haughton, England
Source: *Alli; BbD; BiD&SB; BioIn 2, 9, 12, 16, 17; BritAu 19; CamGLE; CasWL; CelCen; ChhPo, S1, S2, S3; DcBiPP; DcEnA; DcEnL; DcLB 96; DcLEL; DcNaB; EvLB; GrWrEL P; LinLib L; NewC; NewCBEL; OxCEng 67, 85, 95; PenC ENG; PseudAu; REn; RfGEnL 91; VicBrit; WebE&AL*

Elliott, George Paul
American. Author
Writings include *Among the Dangs,* 1961; *Muriel,* 1972.
b. Jun 16, 1918 in Knightstown, Indiana
d. May 3, 1980 in New York, New York
Source: *BioIn 7, 8, 10, 12; ConAu 1R, 2NR; ConLC 2; ConNov 76; ConPo 70, 75; DcLEL 1940; DrAP 75; DrAS 74E, 78E; IndAu 1917; ModAL, S1; OxCAmL 65, 83; WhAm 7; WhoAm 74, 76, 78, 80; WhoWor 74; WrDr 76*

Elliott, Gertrude
[Gertrude Dermott]
American. Actor
Sister of Maxine; starred as Ophelia in *Hamlet,* 1915.
b. 1874 in Rockland, Maine
d. Dec 24, 1950 in Kent, England
Source: *BioIn 2; CamGWoT; Film 1; NotAW; NotNAT B; OxCThe 83; WhAm 3; WhoHol B; WhoStg 1908; WhScrn 74, 77, 83; WhThe; WomWWA 14*

Elliott, Herb
[Herbert James Elliott]
Australian. Track Athlete
Winner of the gold medal, 1960 Olympic Games for the 1,500-metre race; record holder 1,500-metre race, 1958-67; mile race, 1958-62.
b. Feb 25, 1938 in Perth, Australia
Source: *BioIn 4, 5, 7, 9, 10, 12; CurBio 60; WhoTr&F 73*

Elliott, Joe
[Def Leppard]
English. Singer
Lead singer; group named for poster he designed.
b. Aug 1, 1959 in Sheffield, England
Source: *LegTOT*

Elliott, Jumbo
[James Francis Elliott]
American. Athletic Director
Villanova U. track coach, 1935-81; coached 28 Olympic runners.
b. Aug 8, 1915 in Philadelphia, Pennsylvania
d. Mar 22, 1981 in Juno Beach, Florida
Source: *BioIn 6, 11; NewYTBS 79, 81; WhoSpor; WhoTr&F 73*

Elliott, Maxine
[Jessie D McDermott Goodwin]
American. Actor
Star of play written for her *Her Own Way,* 1903; managed own theater, NY, 1908.
b. Feb 5, 1873 in Rockland, Maine
d. Mar 5, 1940 in Juan les Pins, France
Source: *AmBi; ApCAB X; BioAmW; CurBio 40; DcAmB S2; EncWT; FamA&A; Film 1; LibW; NatCAB 14; NotAW; OxCThe 83; WhAm 1; WhoHol B; WhoStg 1906, 1908; WhScrn 74, 77, 83; WomWWA 14*

Elliott, Osborn
American. University Administrator, Editor, Author
Editor *Newsweek,* 1955-76; dean, Columbia U Graduate School of Journ alism, 1979-86.
b. Oct 25, 1924 in New York, New York
Source: *AmAu&B; BioIn 9, 11, 12; BlueB 76; ConAu 1R, 12NR, 69; CurBio 78; EncAJ; EncTwCJ; IntAu&W 77; IntWW 74, 75, 76, 77, 78, 79, 80, 81, 82, 83, 89, 91, 93; NewYTBS 76; St&PR 75; WhoAm 74, 76, 78, 80, 82, 84, 86, 88, 90, 92, 94, 95, 96, 97; WhoE 74, 91, 95; WhoWor 74, 76, 78*

Elliott, Robert Brown
American. Politician
Black Rep. representative from SC, 1871-74; edited *Charleston Leader,* left politics to practice law.
b. Aug 11, 1842 in Boston, Massachusetts
d. Aug 9, 1884 in New Orleans, Louisiana
Source: *AmLegL; ApCAB; BiAUS; BiDrAC; BiDrUSC 89; BioIn 5, 6, 8, 9, 10, 17; BlkAmsC; DcAmNB; EncSoH; InB&W 80, 85; NatCAB 10; TwCBDA; WhAm HS; WhAmP*

Elliott, Sam
American. Actor
In TV's "The Yellow Rose," 1983-84; films include *Butch Cassidy and the Sundance Kid,* 1969.
b. Aug 9, 1944 in Sacramento, California
Source: *ConTFT 3, 11; HalFC 80, 84, 88; IntMPA 84, 86, 88, 92, 94, 96; LegTOT; VarWW 85; WhoAm 88, 90, 92, 94, 95, 96, 97; WhoHol 92, A; WorAlBi*

Ellis, Albert (Isaac)
American. Psychologist
Proposed rational emotive behavior therapy, a cognitive approach to psychological treatment, 1955.
b. Sep 27, 1913 in Pittsburgh, Pennsylvania
Source: *AmAu&B; AmMWSc 73S, 78S, 89, 92, 95; BioIn 15, 16, 20; BlueB 76; ConAu 1R, 2NR, 17NR, 40NR; CurBio 94; GaEncPs; HumSex; IntAu&W 89; RAdv 14, 13-5; WhoAm 74, 76, 78, 80, 82, 84, 86, 88, 90, 92, 94, 95, 96, 97; WhoMedH; WhoWor 74; WrDr 76, 80, 82, 84, 86, 88, 90, 92, 94, 96*

Ellis, Bret Easton
American. Author
Fiction has theme of the abuse of freedom; wrote *Less Than Zero,* 1985; *American Psycho,* 1990.
b. Mar 7, 1964 in Los Angeles, California
Source: *Au&Arts 2; ConAu 51NR, 118, 123; ConLC 39, 71; ConNov 96; ConPopW; CurBio 94; DcArts; IntAu&W 89, 91, 93; LegTOT; WhoAm 92, 94, 95, 96; WrDr 90, 92, 94, 96*

Ellis, Carleton
American. Inventor, Chemist
Held over 750 patents including many in plastics.
b. Sep 20, 1876 in Keene, New Hampshire
d. Jan 13, 1941 in Miami, Florida
Source: *CurBio 41; DcAmB S3; DcNAA; InSci; NatCAB 32; WhAm 1*

Ellis, Dock Phillip, Jr.
American. Baseball Player
Pitcher, 1968-79; threw no-hitter, 1970.
b. Mar 11, 1945 in Los Angeles, California
Source: *Ballpl 90; InB&W 80; WhoAm 74, 76; WhoBlA 75, 77, 80, 85; WhoProB 73*

Ellis, Effie O'Neal
American. Physician
Influential figure in medical policy; stresses family planning; better maternal and child health care.
b. Jun 5, 1913 in Hawkinsville, Georgia
Source: *AmMWSc 79, 82, 86, 89, 92, 95; BioIn 18, 20; BlksScM; BlkWAm; Ebony 1; NotBlAW 1; WhoAfA 96; WhoAmW 85; WhoBlA 75, 77, 80, 85, 88, 90, 92, 94; WhoMW 74, 76*

Ellis, Harry Bearse
American. Journalist, Author
On staff of *Christian Science Monitor,* 1947-85; writings include *The Common Market,* 1965.
b. Dec 9, 1921 in Springfield, Massachusetts
Source: *AmAu&B; AuBYP 2, 3; BioIn 8, 11; BlueB 76; ConAu 1R, 2NR; IntAu&W 77, 82, 89; SmATA 9; WhoAm 74, 76, 78, 80, 82, 84, 86, 88, 90; WhoWor 74, 76; WrDr 76, 80, 82, 84, 86, 88, 90, 92, 94, 96*

Ellis, Havelock
[Henry Havelock Ellis]
English. Psychologist
Seven-vol. *Studies of the Psychology of Sex,* 1897-1928, paved way for modern discussion of sex.
b. Feb 2, 1859 in Croydon, England
d. Jul 8, 1939 in Hintlesham, England
Source: *AtlBL; Benet 87; BiDMoPL; BiDPsy; BioIn 1, 2, 3, 4, 5, 7, 8, 9, 10, 12, 13, 14, 16, 17, 18; BlmGEL; CamGLE; CasWL; ChhPo; ConAu 109; DcLEL; DcNaB 1931; EvLB; FacFETw; GrBr; HumSex; InSci; LegTOT; LinLib L, S; LngCEL; LngCTC; MakMC;*

ModBrL; NamesHP; NewC; NewCBEL; OxCAusL; OxCEng 67, 85, 95; OxCMed 86; RadHan; RAdv 14, 13-5; REn; ScFEYrs; TwCA, SUP; TwCLC 14; VicBrit; WhE&EA; WhLit; WhoLA; WorAl; WorAlBi

Ellis, Herb
American. Musician
Guitarist who joined the Jimmy Dorsey band, 1944-1947; formed the Soft Winds Trio, 1947-1953; played with the Oscar Peterson Trio, 1953-1958; received a Grammy Award for *The Legendary Oscar Peterson Trio Live at the Blue Note,* 1990; recorded *Texas Swings,* 1992.
b. Aug 4, 1921 in Farmersviller, Texas
Source: *AllMusG; BioIn 15, 17; CmpEPM; EncJzS; NewGrDJ 88; OnThGG; PenEncP; RadStar*

Ellis, John Tracy
American. Clergy, Historian
Reform-minded Roman Catholic priest; initiated and encouraged Church's academic self-criticism; books include *American Catholics and the Intellectual Life,* 1956.
b. Jul 30, 1905 in Seneca, Illinois
d. Oct 16, 1992 in Washington, District of Columbia
Source: *AmAu&B; AmCath 80; AnObit 1992; Au&Wr 71; BioIn 3, 4, 10, 16, 17, 18, 19; BkC 5; BlueB 76; CathA 1952; ConAu 1R, 5NR, 46NR, 139; CurBio 90, 93N; DrAS 74H, 78H, 82H; IntWW 89, 91; WhAm 10; WhoAm 74, 76, 78, 80, 82, 84, 86, 88, 90; WhoRel 92*

Ellis, Perry Edwin
American. Fashion Designer
Created the "American Look," easy to wear, youthful garments in natural fibers, colors, 1976.
b. Mar 3, 1940 in Churchland, Virginia
d. May 30, 1986 in New York, New York
Source: *BioIn 12; ConDes 84; ConNews 86-3; CurBio 86; IntWW 91; NewYTBS 82, 86; WhAm 9; WhoAm 80, 82, 84; WhoE 85; WhoFash*

Ellis, Robin
English. Actor
Lead role in BBC TV series "Poldark," shown on PBS.
b. 1944 in London, England
Source: *BioIn 11; NewYTBS 78*

Ellis, Ruth
Welsh. Murderer
Last woman hanged in England; murdered her lover.
b. 1927 in Rhyl, Wales
d. Jul 13, 1955 in London, England
Source: *BioIn 11*

Ellison, Harlan Jay
American. Author
Wrote 42 books including *Shatterday,* 1980; *An Edge in My Voice,* 1985.
b. May 27, 1934 in Cleveland, Ohio
Source: *BenetAL 91; ConAu 5NR, 5R; ConLC 1, 13; DrAPF 91; FacFETw; IntWW 91; MajTwCW; NewEScF; RGTwCSF; TwCSFW 91; WhoAm 86, 90; WhoWrEP 89; WorAlBi; WrDr 86, 92*

Ellison, Ralph (Waldo)
American. Author
Novel *The Invisible Man,* 1952, proclaimed beginning of 1960s civil rights movement.
b. Mar 1, 1914 in Oklahoma City, Oklahoma
d. Apr 16, 1994 in New York, New York
Source: *AfrAmAl 6; AfrAmW; AmAu&B; AmCulL; AmWr S2; Au&Arts 19; Benet 87, 96; BenetAL 91; BioIn 2, 3, 4, 5, 6, 7, 8, 9, 10, 11, 12, 14, 15, 16; BlkAmW 2; BlkAWP; BlkLC; BlkWr 1; BlkWrNE; BlueB 76; CamGEL; CamGLE; CamHAL; CasWL; CnDAL; ConAu 9R, 24NR, 53NR, 145; ConBlB 7; ConLC 1, 3, 11, 54, 86; ConNov 72, 76, 82, 86, 91; CurBio 68, 93, 94N; CyWA 89; DcArts; DcLB 2, 76, Y94N; DcLEL 1940; DcTwCCu 1, 5; DrAF 76; DrAPF 80, 91; Ebony 1; EncAACR; EncAB-H 1974, 1996; EncSoH; EncWL, 2, 3; FacFETw; FifSWrA; GrWrEL N; InB&W 80, 85; IntAu&W 76, 77; IntvTCA 2; IntWW 74, 75, 76, 77, 78, 79, 80, 81, 82, 83, 89, 91, 93; LegTOT; LinLib L, S; LivgBAA; MagSAmL; MajTwCW; McGEWB; ModAL, S1, S2; ModBlW; NegAl 76, 83, 89; NewCon; News 94; Novels; OxCAmL 65, 83, 95; PenC AM; RAdv 1, 14, 13-1; RComAH; REn; REnAL; RfGAmL 87, 94; RfGShF; RGTwCWr; SchCGBL; SelBAAf; SelBAAu; SouWr; TwCWr; TwCYAW; WebAB 74, 79; WebE&AL; WhAm 11; WhoAfA 96; WhoAm 74, 76, 78, 80, 82, 84, 86, 88, 90, 92, 94; WhoBlA 75, 77, 80, 85, 88, 90, 92, 94; WhoE 74; WhoGov 72, 75; WhoTwCL; WhoWor 74, 78; WorAl; WorAlBi; WorAu 1950; WorLitC; WrDr 76, 80, 82, 84, 86, 88, 90, 92, 94, 96*

Ellison, Virginia Howell
[Virginia Tier Howell; Mary A Mapes; Virginia TH Mussey; VH Soski]
American. Children's Author
Writings include *The Pooh Cook Book,* 1969; *Training Pants,* 1946.
b. Feb 4, 1910 in New York, New York
Source: *AuBYP 2S, 3; BiDrLUS 70; BioIn 9; DcLP 87A; IntAu&W 91, 93; PenNWW A; SmATA 4; WrDr 76, 80, 82, 84, 86, 88, 90, 92, 94, 96*

Ellmann, Richard David
American. Critic, Educator
Literary critic; first American to teach English literature at Oxford U; known for his biographies of James Joyce and Oscar Wilde.
b. Mar 15, 1918 in Highland Park, Michigan
d. May 13, 1987 in Oxford, England
Source: *BioIn 1, 5, 7, 10, 14; ConAu 1R, 2NR; DcLEL 1940; DcNaB 1986; DrAS 74E, 78E; IntAu&W 86; NewYTBS 87; OxCEng 85; RAdv 13-1; Who 85, 88N; WhoAm 86; WhoWor 87; WrDr 86*

Ellroy, James
American. Author
Crime novels include *Blood on the Moon,* 1984; *The Black Dahlia,* 1987.
b. 1948?
Source: *BestSel 90-4; BioIn 15; ConAu 138; ConNov 96; DcLB Y91; TwCCr&M 91; WhoAm 96; WrDr 92, 94, 96*

Ellsberg, Daniel
American. Author, Economist, Political Activist
Leaked Pentagon Papers to press, 1971; wrote *Papers on the War,* 1972.
b. Apr 7, 1931 in Chicago, Illinois
Source: *AmPeW; BioIn 9, 10, 12, 13, 14, 15, 16, 18, 20; BioNews 74; ColdWar 1; ConAu 69; CurBio 73; EncCW; EncWB; LinLib S; NewYTBE 71; PeoHis; PolProf NF; WhoAm 74, 76, 78, 80, 82, 84, 86; WhoWor 80, 82, 84; WorAl; WorAlBi*

Ellsberg, Edward
American. Naval Officer, Engineer, Author
Promoted to naval commander by Congress for raising two sunken US submarines; writings include *On the Bottom,* 1929.
b. Nov 21, 1891 in New Haven, Connecticut
d. Jan 24, 1983 in Bryn Mawr, Pennsylvania
Source: *AmAu&B; AmNov; Au&Wr 71; AuBYP 2, 3; BioIn 2, 3, 4, 6, 7, 8, 10, 13, 17; ConAu 5R; CurBio 42, 91N; JBA 34, 51; LinLib L; NewYTBS 83; REnAL; SmATA 7; TwCA, SUP; WebAMB; WhAm 8; WhE&EA; WhoAm 74, 76, 78, 80, 82*

Ellsler, Effie
American. Actor
Played the wronged miller's daughter in melodrama *Hazel Kirk,* 1880s.
b. Sep 17, 1854? in Philadelphia, Pennsylvania
d. Oct 8, 1942 in Los Angeles, California
Source: *InWom SUP; NotAW*

Ellsworth, Lincoln
American. Explorer
First man to cross both Arctic and Antarctic by air.
b. May 12, 1880 in Chicago, Illinois
d. May 26, 1951 in New York, New York
Source: *AmAu&B; BioIn 2, 3, 4, 8, 17, 18, 20; DcAmB S5; EncAB-A 25; Expl 93; FacFETw; InSci; LegTOT; McGEWB; NatCAB 39; NewCol 75; ObitT 1951; OxCAmH; WebAB 74, 79; WebBD 83; WhAm 3; WhDW; WhWE; WorAl; WorAlBi*

Ellsworth, Oliver
American. Supreme Court Justice
Played major role in passage of Judiciary Act, 1789; third chief justice, 1796-99.
b. Apr 29, 1745 in Windsor, Connecticut
d. Nov 26, 1807 in Windsor, Connecticut
Source: *AmBi; AmJust; AmPolLe; ApCAB; BiAUS; BiDFedJ; BiDrAC; BiDrUSC 89; BioIn 1, 2, 5, 8, 9, 11, 15, 16; DcAmB; Drake; EncAB-H 1974, 1996; HarEnUS; LinLib S; NatCAB 1; OxCAmH; OxCLaw; OxCSupC; PolPar; SupCtJu; TwCBDA; WebAB 74, 79; WhAm HS; WhAmP; WhAmRev*

ElMallakh, Kamal
Egyptian. Archaeologist
Discovered 4,700-yr-old funeral boat of the Pharoh Cheops, near Giza, 1954.
b. 1920 in Assuite, Egypt
d. Oct 29, 1987 in Cairo, Egypt
Source: *CurBio 54, 88; IntWW 83; WhoArab 81*

Elman, Mischa
American. Violinist
Among greatest virtuosos of his time; made NY debut, 1908; noted for romantic in terpretations: "Elman Tone."
b. Jan 21, 1891 in Talnoye, Russia
d. Apr 5, 1967 in New York, New York
Source: *ApCAB X; ASCAP 66, 80; Baker 78, 84, 92; BiDAmM; BioIn 1, 2, 3, 4, 5, 7, 8, 9, 11, 14, 15, 17; BriBkM 80; CurBio 45, 67; DcAmB S8; FacFETw; Film 2; LinLib S; MusSN; NewAmDM; NewGrDA 86; NewGrDM 80; ObitT 1961; PenDiMP; WhAm 4; WhScrn 83; WorAlBi*

Elman, Ziggy
[Harry Finkelman]
American. Musician
Trumpet star, 1930s-40s; with Benny Goodman, 1936-40; wrote, recorded hit song "And the Angels Sing," 1939.
b. May 26, 1914 in Philadelphia, Pennsylvania
d. Jun 26, 1968 in Los Angeles, California
Source: *AllMusG; BiDAmM; BiDJaz; BioIn 6, 8; CmpEPM; EncJzS; NewAmDM; NewGrDJ 88, 94; OxCPMus; WhoHol B; WhoJazz 72*

Elmen, Gustav Waldemar
American. Scientist, Engineer
Metallurgist, electrical engineer; developed permalloys used in electrical equipment.
b. Dec 22, 1876 in Stockholm, Sweden
d. Dec 10, 1957 in Englewood, New Jersey
Source: *BioIn 4, 6; NatCAB 43*

Elsasser, Walter M, Dr.
American. Scientist, Educator
Geophysicist; won National Medal of Science, 1987, for research in planetary magnetism, movement of earth's crust.
b. Mar 20, 1904 in Mannheim, Germany
d. Oct 14, 1991 in Baltimore, Maryland
Source: *AmMWSc 73P, 76P, 79, 82, 86, 89, 92; FacFETw; IntWW 74, 75, 76, 77, 78, 79, 80, 81, 82, 83; NewYTBS 91; WhoAm 88, 90*

Elsheimer, Adam
[Adam Tedesco]
German. Artist
Founder of modern landscape painting; works, chiefly done on copper, are usually religious, mythological.
b. Mar 18, 1578 in Frankfurt am Main, Germany
d. Dec 1610 in Rome, Italy
Source: *AtlBL; BioIn 9, 11, 14, 19; ClaDrA; DcArts; IntDcAA 90; McGDA; OxCArt; OxDcArt; WebBD 83; WhDW; WorAl; WorAlBi*

Elson, Edward L(ee) R(oy)
American. Clergy
Chaplain of US Senate, 1969-81; autobiography *Wide Was His Parish,* 1986.
b. Dec 23, 1906
d. Aug 25, 1993 in Washington, District of Columbia
Source: *BioIn 3, 4, 8; ConAu 142; CurBio 93N; IntAu&W 77; WhAm 11; WhoAm 74, 76, 78, 82, 88, 90, 92, 94; WhoGov 72, 75, 77; WhoRel 77, 85, 92*

Elson, Robert Truscott
American. Editor, Journalist
Editor, Time Inc., 1943-69.
b. Jun 21, 1906 in Cleveland, Ohio
d. Mar 11, 1987 in Southampton, New York
Source: *ConAu 77, 121*

Elssler, Fanny
Austrian. Dancer
Introduced folk dancing, especially the tarantella, into theater; made fortune in US tour, 1840s.
b. Jun 23, 1810 in Vienna, Austria
d. Nov 27, 1884 in Vienna, Austria
Source: *BiDD; BioIn 3, 4, 7, 8, 9, 10, 13; CnOxB; ContDcW 89; DancEn 78; IntDcB; IntDcWB; InWom; NewCol 75; NewGrDM 80; NotNAT B; OxCAmT 84; OxCMus; WebBD 83; WomFir; WorAlBi*

Elting, Mary Letha
[Davis Cole; Campbell Tatham]
American. Children's Author
Writings include *Wheels and Noises,* 1950; *The Answer Book,* 1959.
b. Jun 21, 1906 in Creede, Colorado
Source: *AuBYP 2, 3; ConAu 4NR, 9R, 19NR; DcLP 87A; ForWC 70; MorJA; PenNWW A, B; SmATA 2; WhoAmW 79, 81*

Eltinge, Julian
[William Dalton]
American. Actor
Female impersonator in plays *The Crinoline Girl; The Fascinating Widow.*
b. May 14, 1883 in Newtonville, Massachusetts
d. Mar 7, 1941 in New York, New York
Source: *BiDD; CamGWoT; CurBio 41; EncVaud; Film 1, 2; FilmgC; ForYSC; NotNAT B; ObitOF 79; OxCAmT 84; OxCThe 67, 83; TwYS; WhAm 1; WhScrn 74, 77, 83; WhThe*

Elton, Charles Sutherland
English. Zoologist
Director, Bureau of Animal Population, Dept. of Zoological Field Studies, 1932-67.
b. Mar 29, 1900 in Liverpool, England
Source: *BiESc; BioIn 8, 9, 13; FacFETw; IntAu&W 77; IntWW 74, 75, 76, 77, 78, 79, 80, 81, 82, 83, 89, 91, 91N; LarDcSc; Who 74, 82, 83, 85, 88, 90, 92N*

Eluard, Paul
[Eugene Grindel]
French. Author
Early Surrealist, 1919-38; wrote *Poetry and Truth,* 1942.
b. Dec 14, 1895 in Saint-Denis, France
d. Nov 18, 1952 in Charenton, France
Source: *AtlBL; Benet 87, 96; BiDMoPL; BioIn 1, 2, 3, 4, 5, 6, 8, 9, 13; CasWL; ClDMEL 47, 80; CnMWL; ConAu 104; DcArts; DcTwCCu 2; EncWL, 2, 3; EvEuW; FacFETw; GuFrLit 1; LegTOT; LinLib L; ModFrL; ModRL; OxCEng 67, 85, 95; OxCFr; OxCTwCA; PenC EUR; RAdv 14; REn; RfGWoL 95; RGFMEP; TwCA SUP; TwCLC 7, 41; TwCWr; WhDW; WhoTwCL; WorAl; WorAlBi*

Elvira
American. Actor
Creator of character Elvira, Mistress of the Dark; host of "Movie Macabre," 1981—.
b. Sep 17, 1951 in Manhattan, Kansas
Source: *ConNews 88-1; ConTFT 9; WhoEnt 92; WhoHol 92*

Elvira, Pablo
Puerto Rican. Opera Singer
A leading bass-baritone, NY Met. from 1979.
b. Sep 24, 1938 in Santurce, Puerto Rico
Source: *Baker 84; BioIn 13; IntWWM 90; MetOEnc; NewAmDM; NewGrDA 86; NewGrDO; WhoAmM 83; WhoOp 76*

Elway, John Albert
American. Football Player
All-American quarterback, first chosen in NFL draft, 1983; with Denver, known for strong passing.
b. Jun 28, 1960 in Port Angeles, Washington
Source: *BiDAmSp FB; BioIn 13, 14, 15, 16; CurBio 90; FootReg 87; News 90-3; NewYTBS 81, 82, 83; WhoAm 88, 90, 92, 94, 95, 96, 97; WhoWest 87, 89, 92, 94, 96; WorAlBi*

Ely, Joe
American. Musician, Singer
Country-rock singer who had hit album *Notta Gotta Lotta,* 1981.
b. Feb 9, 1947 in Lubbock, Texas
Source: *BgBkCoM; BioIn 12, 14; EncFCWM 83; EncRk 88; HarEnCM 87; NewGrDA 86; PenEncP; RolSEnR 83; WhoAm 94, 95, 96, 97; WhoNeCM*

Ely, Richard Theodore
American. Economist, Social Reformer
Founded Institute for Research in Land Economics, 1920.
b. Apr 13, 1854 in Ripley, New York
d. Oct 4, 1943 in Old Lyme, Connecticut
Source: *Alli SUP; AmLY; AmSocL; ApCAB; BbD; BiDAmEd; BiD&SB; BioIn 1, 2, 3, 4, 5, 6, 7, 8, 12, 13, 14, 15, 16, 19; CurBio 43; DcAmAu; DcAmB S3; DcAmImH; DcAmReB 2; DcNAA; EncAB-H 1974, 1996; GrEconB; HarEnUS; LinLib L; NatCAB 9; OxCAmH; REnAL; TwCBDA; WebAB 74, 79; WhAm 2; WhoEc 81, 86; WisWr*

Ely, Ron
[Ronald Pierce]
American. Actor
Screen's 15th Tarzan who starred in two films, 1970; in TV series, 1968-69.
b. Jun 21, 1938 in Hereford, Texas
Source: *FilmEn; ForYSC; HalFC 84, 88; LegTOT; MotPP; WhoHol 92, A; WhoHrs 80*

Elyot, Thomas, Sir
English. Author
Wrote first Latin-English dictionary, 1538.
b. 1490? in Wiltshire, England
d. Mar 20, 1546 in Carleton, England
Source: *Alli; BiD&SB; BioIn 2, 3, 5, 7, 11, 12, 20; BritAu; CamGEL; CasWL; Chambr 1; CroE&S; CrtT 1; DcEnA; DcEnL; DcEuL; DcLB 136; DcLEL; DcNaB, C; DcPup; EvLB; LitC 11; MouLC 1; NewC; OxCEng 67, 85, 95; OxCLaw; PenC ENG; REn; RfGEnL 91; WebE&AL*

Elytis, Odysseus
[Odysseus Elytis Alepoudhelis]
Greek. Poet, Critic
Awarded Nobel Prize in literature, 1979, for work in poetry.
b. Nov 2, 1911 in Iraklion, Crete
d. Mar 18, 1996 in Athens, Greece
Source: *Benet 87, 96; BioIn 10, 12, 13, 15; ConAu 102, 151; ConFLW 84; ConLC 15, 49; ConWorW 93; CurBio 80, 96N; DcArts; EncWL 2, 3; EuWr 13; FacFETw; IntAu&W 76, 77, 89, 91, 93; IntWW 74, 75, 76, 77, 78, 79, 80, 81, 82, 83, 89, 91, 93; IntWWP 77; LegTOT; LiExTwC; MajTwCW; NewYTBS 27, 79; NobelP; RAdv 14, 13-2; RfGWoL 95; Who 82, 83, 85, 88, 90, 92, 94; WhoNob, 90, 95; WhoWor 82, 84, 87, 89, 91, 93, 95, 96; WorAlBi; WorAu 1950*

Elzevir, Louis
Dutch. Publisher
Founded prestigious publishing firm; noted for typography, small volumes.
b. 1540? in Louvain, Belgium
d. Feb 4, 1617 in Leiden, Netherlands
Source: *DcArts; DcBiPP; EncAJ; NewC*

Emanuel, David
English. Fashion Designer
With wife, Elizabeth, designed Princess Diana's wedding dress, 1981.
b. 1953?, England
Source: *EncFash; NewYTBS 81; Who 92; WhoFash, 88*

Emanuel, Elizabeth
[Mrs. David Emanuel]
English. Fashion Designer
With husband, David, designed Princess Diana's wedding dress, 1981.
b. 1954?
Source: *IntWW 91; NewYTBS 81; Who 92; WhoFash, 88*

Emanuel, James A
American. Author
Writings include *Langston Hughes,* 1967; *Panther Man,* 1970.
b. Jun 21, 1921 in Allande, Nebraska
Source: *BlkAWP; BlkWr 1; ConAu 12NR; ConPo 85, 91; DcLB 41; DrAP 75; DrAPF 91; DrAS 74E, 78E, 82E; InB&W 85; IntAu&W 86; LivgBAA; WhoBlA 92; WrDr 86, 92*

Embry, Wayne Richard
American. Basketball Player, Basketball Executive
Center, 1958-69, mostly with Cincinnati; as general manager, Milwaukee, 1972; first black executive in NBA; now vp, Indiana Pacers.
b. Mar 26, 1937 in Springfield, Ohio
Source: *BioIn 16; InB&W 85; NewYTBE 72; WhoAm 74, 76, 78, 80, 82, 84, 86, 88, 92, 94, 95, 96, 97; WhoBbl 73; WhoBlA 92; WhoMW 88, 90, 92, 93*

Emecheta, Buchi
Nigerian. Author, Sociologist
Wrote *The Joys of Motherhood,* 1979 and *Destination Biafra,* 1981.
b. Jul 21, 1944 in Lagos, Nigeria
Source: *ArtclWW 2; Benet 96; BioIn 12, 13, 16; BlkAuII, 92; BlkLC; BlkWr 1; CamGLE; ConAu 27NR, 81; ConLC 14, 48; ConNov 86, 91; ContDcW 89; EncWL 3; FemiCLE; IntAu&W 82, 89, 91, 93; IntLitE; IntvWPC; LiExTwC; MajTwCW; ModWoWr; RAdv 14, 13-2; ScF&FL 92; SchCGBL; SelBAAf; SmATA 66; TwCChW 89; Who 83, 85, 88, 90, 92, 94; WomFir; WorAu 1975; WrDr 76, 80, 82, 84, 86, 88, 90, 92*

Emerson, Faye Margaret
American. Actor
Hosted late night talk show "Faye Emerson's Wonderful Town," 1950s; once wed to Elliott Roosevelt, "Skitch" Henderson.
b. Jul 8, 1917 in Elizabeth, Louisiana
d. Mar 9, 1983 in Majorca, Spain
Source: *BiE&WWA; CurBio 51, 83N; FilmgC; HolP 40; InWom; MotPP; MovMk; NewYTBS 83; WhAm 8; WhoAmW 68, 70; WhoHol A; WhoThe 77A; WhThe*

Emerson, Gladys Anderson
American. Biochemist, Nutritionist
Leading nutritionist; wrote articles, assoc. editor, *Journalism Nutrition* mag., 1952-56.
b. Jul 1, 1903 in Caldwell, Kansas
Source: *AmMWSc 73P, 76P, 79, 82; AmWomSc; BioIn 3, 5, 11, 12, 14, 20; ContDcW 89; IntDcWB; InWom SUP; LarDcSc; NotTwCS; WhAm 8; WhoAm 74, 76, 78, 80, 82, 84; WhoAmW 58, 61, 64, 66, 68, 70, 72, 74; WhoWor 76, 80, 82; WomFir*

Emerson, Hope
American. Actor
Body measurements (six foot, two inches, 200 lbs) exploited in films *Caged; Adam's Rib.* "Missing."
b. Oct 29, 1898 in Hawarden, Iowa
d. Apr 25, 1960 in Hollywood, California
Source: *FilmgC; ForYSC; MotPP; MovMk; NewYTET; ObitOF 79; Vers A; WhoAmW 70; WhoHol B; WhScrn 74, 77*

Emerson, Keith
[Emerson, Lake, and Palmer; The Nice]
English. Musician
Known for flamboyant performance at keyboards.
b. Nov 1, 1944 in Todmorden, England
Source: *ConMus 5; EncPR&S 89; LegTOT; WhoRocM 82*

Emerson, Peter Henry
English. Photographer
Pioneer in field; wrote classic, *Naturalistic Photography,* 1889.
b. May 13, 1856, Cuba
d. May 12, 1936 in Falmouth, England
Source: *BioIn 8, 10, 11, 13; DcArts; ICPEnP; MacBEP; WhE&EA; WhLit*

Emerson, Ralph Waldo
American. Essayist, Poet, Philosopher
A leading transcendentalist; wrote essay *Self-Reliance,* 1844.
b. May 25, 1803 in Boston, Massachusetts
d. Apr 27, 1882 in Concord, Massachusetts
Source: *Alli, SUP; AmAu; AmAu&B; AmBi; AmCulL; AmOrN; AmPeW; AmRef; AmSocL; AmWr; AnCL; ApCAB; AtlBL; BbD; Benet 87, 96; BenetAL 91; BibAL; BiDAmM; BiD&SB; BiDMoPL; BiDTran; BioIn 1, 2, 3, 4, 5, 6, 7, 8, 9, 10, 11, 12, 13, 14, 15, 16, 17, 19, 20, 21; CamGEL; CamGLE; CamHAL; CasWL; CelCen; Chambr 3; ChhPo, S1, S3; CnDAL; CnE&AP; ColARen; CrtT 3, 4; CyAL 2; CyEd; CyWA 58; DcAmAu; DcAmB; DcAmC; DcAmReB 1, 2; DcAmSR; DcArts; DcBiPP; DcEnA, A;*

DcEnL; DcLB 1, 59, 73; DcLEL; DcNAA; Dis&D; Drake; EncAAH; EncAB-H 1974, 1996; EncARH; EncEnv; EncEth; EncUnb; EvLB; GrWrEL N, P; HarEnUS; LegTOT; LinLib L, S; LuthC 75; MagSAmL; McGEWB; MemAm; MouLC 4; NatCAB 3; NewGrDA 86; NinCLC 1, 38; OxCAmH; OxCAmL 65, 83, 95; OxCEng 67, 85, 95; OxCPhil; PenC AM; RadHan; RAdv 1, 14, 13-1; RComAH; RComWL; REn; REnAL; RfGAmL 87, 94; RGFAP; Str&VC; TwCBDA; TwoTYeD; WebAB 74, 79; WebE&AL; WhAm HS; WhDW; WorAl; WorAlBi; WorLitC; WrPh

Emerson, Roy
Australian. Tennis Player
Member of Australian Davis Cup; never lost a Davis Cup singles match.
b. Nov 3, 1936 in Kingsway, Australia
Source: *BioIn 7, 12; BuCMET; CurBio 65; LegTOT; WhoSpor; WorAl; WorAlBi*

Emerson, Lake, and Palmer
[Keith Emerson; Gregory Lake; Carl Palmer]
English. Music Group
1960s-70s classical rock band known for hit albums: *Trilogy* ; their bigg est song: "Lucky Man," 1971.
Source: *BioIn 9; BkPepl; ConMus 5; EncPR&S 74, 89; EncRk 88; HarEnR 86; NewAmDM; PenEncP; RkOn 84; RolSEnR 83; WhoRocM 82*

Emery, Anne (McGuigan)
American. Author
Writings include *The Sky Is Falling,* 1970; *Step Family,* 1980.
b. Sep 1, 1907 in Fargo, North Dakota
Source: *AuBYP 2, 3; BioIn 2, 3, 6, 7, 9, 14; ConAu 1R, 2NR; ForWC 70; MorJA; SmATA 1, 33; WhoAmW 58, 61, 64, 66, 68, 70, 72*

Eminescu, Mihail
[Mihail Emin]
Romanian. Poet
Influential writer of over 60 poems, one novel; suffered from periods of insanity.
b. Dec 20, 1849 in Botosani, Romania
d. Jun 15, 1889 in Bucharest, Romania
Source: *ClDMEL 47; EuAu; EvEuW*

Emin Pasha
[Eduard Schnitzer]
German. Explorer
Governor of Equatoria, Egyptian Sudan province; abolished slavery, expanded geographical understanding of Central Africa.
b. Mar 8, 1840 in Oppeln, Prussia
d. 1892 in Stanley Falls, Congo
Source: *BioIn 1, 2, 8, 9, 10, 18, 21; DcAfHiB 86; Expl 93; LinLib S; NewCol 75; WebBD 83*

Emmet, Robert
Irish. Revolutionary
Led uprising in Dublin for independence, 1803; gave stirring speech from scaffold before he was hanged.
b. Sep 20, 1178 in Dublin, Ireland
d. Sep 20, 1803 in Dublin, Ireland
Source: *DcIrB 78; DcIrL; McGEWB; NewCol 75; PoIre; REn; WebBD 83*

Emmett, Daniel Decatur
American. Songwriter
Early minstral credited with writing "Dixie," 1859.
b. Oct 29, 1815 in Clinton, Ohio
d. Jun 28, 1904 in Mount Vernon, Ohio
Source: *AmAu; AmAu&B; AmBi; Baker 78, 84, 92; BenetAL 91; BiDAmM; BioIn 1, 3, 4, 6, 9, 14, 15; ChhPo, S1, S2; DcAmB; MusMk; NatCAB 21; NewGrDM 80; OxCAmH; OxCAmL 65, 83, 95; OxCMus; OxCPMus; REnAL; Sw&Ld A; WebAB 74, 79; WhAm 2, HS; WhCiWar; WorAl; WorAlBi*

Emmons, Ebenezer
American. Geologist
Introduced Taconic method of stratigraphy, which was ultimately discredited.
b. May 16, 1799 in Middlefield, Massachusetts
d. Oct 1, 1863 in Brunswick, North Carolina
Source: *Alli SUP; AmBi; ApCAB; BiDAmS; BiInAmS; BioIn 9; CyAL 1; DcAmAu; DcAmB; DcNAA; DcNCBi 2; DcScB; Drake; InSci; NatCAB 8; TwCBDA; WhAm HS*

Empedocles
Greek. Philosopher
First to state principles central to theory of physics; believed blood to be thinking organ.
b. 493BC in Acragas, Italy
d. 433BC
Source: *BbD; BiD&SB; CasWL; Grk&L; IlEncMy; McGEWB; NewC; NewCol 75; PenC CL; WebBD 83*

Empson, William, Sir
English. Poet, Critic
Wrote *Collected Poems of William Empson,* 1949; *Milton's God,* 1961; *Using Biography,* 1985.
b. Sep 27, 1906 in Goole, England
d. Apr 15, 1984 in London, England
Source: *AnObit 1984; Benet 87, 96; BioIn 1, 4, 5, 8, 9, 10, 12, 13, 14, 15, 17, 19; BlmGEL; BlueB 76; BritWr S2; CamGEL; CamGLE; CasWL; ChhPo S3; CnE&AP; CnMWL; ConAu 17R, 31NR, 112; ConLC 3, 8, 19, 33, 34; ConLCrt 77, 82; ConPo 70, 75, 80; CyWA 89; DcArts; DcLB 20; DcLEL; DcNaB 1981; EncWL 2, 3; EngPo; FacFETw; GrWrEL P; IntAu&W 77, 82; IntWW 74, 75, 76, 77, 78, 79, 80, 81, 82, 83; IntWWP 77, 82; LiExTwC; LinLib L; LngCEL; LngCTC; MajTwCW; MakMC; ModBrL, S2; NewC; NewCBEL; OxCEng 67, 85, 95; OxCTwCP; PenC ENG; RAdv 1; REn; RfGEnL 91; RGFMBP; RGTwCWr; TwCA SUP; TwCWr; WebE&AL; WhAm 8; WhDW; Who 74, 82, 83; WhoTwCL; WhoWor 74; WrDr 76, 80, 82, 84*

Endacott, Paul
American. Basketball Player
Played at U of KS, 1921-23; won national championship, named player of yr., 1923; Hall of Fame.
b. Jul 13, 1902 in Lawrence, Kansas
Source: *BiDAmSp BK; BioIn 2; IntWW 74, 75, 76, 77, 78, 79, 80; WhoBbl 73; WhoSpor*

Endara (Galimany), Guillermo
Panamanian. Political Leader
Elected president of Panama, May 1989; sworn into office following overthrow of Manuel Noriega, December 1989.
b. May 12, 1936 in Panama City, Panama
Source: *BioIn 16; CurBio 91; DcCPCAm; IntWW 91; WhoWor 91*

Endecott, John
American. Colonial Figure
Governor of MA, 1640s-50s; persecuted Quakers.
b. 1588? in Devonshire, England
d. Mar 15, 1665 in Boston, Massachusetts
Source: *BioIn 1, 9, 12; DcAmB; DcNaB; Drake; LinLib S; McGEWB; OxCAmH; OxCAmL 65; REn; REnAL; WebAB 74, 79; WhAmP; WhNaAH*

Ender, Kornelia
[Mrs. Roland Matthes]
German. Swimmer
Won four gold medals, 1976 Olympics; called greatest woman swimmer ever.
b. Oct 25, 1958 in Plauen, German Democratic Republic
Source: *BioIn 10, 12, 17, 18; GoodHs; InWom SUP; WomFir*

Enders, John Franklin
American. Physician
Work in virology led to vaccines for polio, measles, German measles, mumps; won Nobel Prize, 1954.
b. Feb 10, 1897 in West Hartford, Connecticut
d. Sep 8, 1985 in Waterford, Connecticut
Source: *AmDec 1950; AmMWSc 76P, 79, 82; AsBiEn; BiESc; BioIn 3, 4, 5, 6, 8, 11; BlueB 76; CamDcSc; CurBio 55, 86; FacFETw; InSci; IntWW 74, 75, 76, 77, 78, 79, 80, 81, 82, 83; LarDcSc; McGEWB; McGMS 80; WebAB 74, 79; WhAm 9; Who 74, 82, 83, 85; WhoAm 74, 76, 78, 80, 84; WhoE 77, 79, 81, 83, 85; WhoNob, 90, 95; WhoWor 74, 82, 84; WorAl*

Endo, Shusaku
Japanese. Author
Oriental-Christian novelist, playwright who wrote *Shiroihito,* 1955; *Chinmoku,* 1966.

b. Mar 27, 1923 in Tokyo, Japan
d. Sep 29, 1996 in Tokyo, Japan
Source: *Benet 87, 96; BioIn 8, 11, 13, 14, 16, 17, 18; ConAu 21NR, 29R, 54NR; ConLC 7, 14, 19, 54; CyWA 89; MajTwCW; RAdv 13-2; WhoWor 91, 93, 95, 96; WorAu 1975*

Enesco, Georges
[Georges Enescu]
Romanian. Violinist, Composer
Wrote opera *Oedipe,* 1936; led NY Philharmonic, 1930s; taught Yehudi Menuhin.
b. Aug 19, 1881 in Liveni, Romania
d. May 4, 1955 in Paris, France
Source: *Baker 78, 84, 92; BioIn 1, 3, 4, 5, 6, 7, 8, 11, 12, 13; BriBkM 80; CompSN, SUP; DcCom&M 79; FacFETw; LegTOT; MusMk; MusSN; NewCol 75; NewGrDM 80; ObitT 1951; OxCMus; PenDiMP; WebBD 83; WhAm 3; WhDW*

Engel, Georgia Bright
American. Actor
Played Georgette on TV series "The Mary Tyler Moore Show," 1972-77.
b. Jul 28, 1948 in Washington, District of Columbia
Source: *ConTFT 2; WhoAm 78, 80, 82, 84*

Engel, Lehman
[Aaron Lehman Engel]
American. Author, Conductor
Conducted over 100 Broadway hits; won two Tonys; wrote autobiography *This Bright Day,* 1973.
b. Sep 12, 1910 in Jackson, Mississippi
d. Aug 29, 1982 in New York, New York
Source: *AmAu&B; AnObit 1982; Baker 78, 84, 92; BiE&WWA; BioIn 1, 2, 4, 5, 10, 13; ConAmC 76, 82; ConAu 31NR, 41R, 107; ConTFT 2; DancEn 78; DcCM; IntWWM 77, 80; LiveMA; NewAmDM; NewGrDA 86; NewGrDM 80; NewYTBS 82; NotNAT, A; OxCAmT 84; OxCPMus; WhAm 8; WhoAm 74, 76, 78, 80, 82; WhoAmJ 80; WhoAmM 83; WhoMus 72; WhoWor 74, 76, 78; WhoWorJ 72, 78*

Engel, Lyle Kenyon
American. Publisher
Founded Book Creations, Inc., 1973; known for fiction vols. *Kent Family Chronicles.*
b. May 12, 1915 in New York, New York
d. Aug 10, 1986 in Miami, Florida
Source: *BioIn 12; ConAu 85, 120; EncSF, 93; WhAm 9; WhoAm 82, 84, 86; WhoE 85, 86*

Engelbreit, Mary
American. Illustrator
Founder of Mary Engelbreit Card Company.
b. c. 1952 in Saint Louis, Missouri
Source: *News 94, 94-3; WhoAmW 97*

Engellau, Gunnar Ludwig
Swedish. Auto Executive
With Volvo, 1956-78, retiring as president; built company into top auto manufacturer.
b. Nov 11, 1907 in Stockholm, Sweden
d. Jan 6, 1988? in Stockholm, Sweden
Source: *IntWW 79, 80, 81, 82, 83; IntYB 82*

Engels, Friedrich
German. Political Leader
One of founders of modern communism with Karl Marx; collaborated on *The Communist Manifesto* with Marx.
b. Nov 28, 1820 in Barmen, Prussia
d. Aug 5, 1895 in London, England
Source: *Benet 87, 96; BiDMarx; BioIn 2, 3, 5, 7, 8, 9, 10, 11, 12, 13, 14, 15, 17, 19, 20, 21; DcAmSR; DcLB 129; DcScB, S1; EncRev; LegTOT; LinLib L, S; LuthC 75; McGEWB; OxCEng 85, 95; OxCGer 76, 86; OxCPhil; RadHan; RAdv 14, 13-3; REn; WhDW; WhoEc 81, 86; WhoMilH 76; WorAl; WorAlBi*

England Dan and John Ford Coley
[John Edward Coley; Danny Seals]
American. Music Group
Formed during early 1970s; had hit song "I'd Really Love to See You Tonight," 1976.
Source: *BioIn 14; EncFCWM 83; PenEncP; RkOn 78; WhoRock 81; WhoRocM 82*

Engle, Clair
American. Politician
Dem. congressman, senator from CA, 1958-64; conservation advocate.
b. Sep 21, 1911 in Bakersfield, California
d. Jul 30, 1964 in Washington, District of Columbia
Source: *BiDrAC; BiDrUSC 89; BioIn 3, 4, 5, 6, 7, 11; CmCal; CurBio 57, 64; DcAmB S7; PolProf E, K; WhAm 4; WhAmP*

Engle, Eloise Katherine
American. Author
Writings include *Dawn Mission,* 1962; *The Winter War,* 1973.
b. Apr 12, 1923 in Seattle, Washington
Source: *BioIn 11; ConAu 1R, 2NR, X; ForWC 70; IntAu&W 86; SmATA 9; WrDr 76, 92*

Engle, Joe Henry
American. Astronaut
Crew member aboard second flight of space shuttle *Columbia,* Nov, 1981.
b. Aug 26, 1932 in Abilene, Kansas
Source: *BioIn 10, 12, 13; NewYTBS 81; WhoSpc; WhoSSW 73; WorDWW*

Engle, Paul (Hamilton)
American. Author, Poet
Award-winning writings include *Embrace: Selected Love Poems,* 1969; *Who's Afraid?,* 1962.
b. Oct 12, 1908 in Cedar Rapids, Iowa
d. Mar 22, 1991 in Chicago, Illinois
Source: *AmAu&B; AnObit 1991; BenetAL 91; BioIn 4, 5, 7, 10, 12, 15, 17, 18; BlueB 76; ChhPo, S1, S2; CnDAL; ConAmA; ConAu 1R, 5NR, 134; ConPo 70, 75, 80, 85, 91; CurBio 42, 91N; DcLB 48; DcLEL; DrAP 75; DrAPF 80, 91; DrAS 74E, 78E, 82E; FacFETw; IntAu&W 91; IntWWP 77, 82; LinLib L; NewCBEL; NewYTBS 91; OxCAmL 65, 83, 95; OxCTwCP; REnAL; SixAP; WhAm 10; WhE&EA; WhoAm 74, 76, 78, 80, 82, 84, 86, 88; WhoUSWr 88; WhoWor 74, 76; WhoWrEP 89; WorAu 1950; WrDr 76, 80, 82, 84, 86, 88, 90*

Englemann, Robert A
American. Hostage
One of 52 held by terrorists, Nov 1979 - Jan 1981.
b. 1947? in Pasadena, California
Source: *NewYTBS 81*

Engler, John Mathias
American. Politician
Governor of Michigan 1991—.
b. Oct 12, 1948 in Mount Pleasant, Michigan
Source: *AlmAP 92; WhoAm 92; WhoAmP 91; WhoGov 77; WhoMW 80, 82, 84, 86, 88, 90, 92*

English, Alex(ander)
American. Basketball Player
Forward, Milwaukee Bucks, 1976-78; Indiana Pacers, 1978-80; Denver Nuggets, 1980-90; Dallas Mavericks, 1990—; led NBA in scoring, 1983; 14th player in NBA history to score 20,000 career pts., 1988.
b. Jan 5, 1954 in Columbia, South Carolina
Source: *BasBi; BiDAmSp BK; BioIn 14, 15; NewYTBS 85; OfNBA 87; WhoAfA 96; WhoAm 84, 86, 88, 90; WhoBlA 88, 90, 92, 94; WhoSpor; WhoWest 87, 89; WorAlBi*

English, Diane
American. Producer
Producer of "Murphy Brown," 1988-92, 1997—.
b. 1948 in Buffalo, New York
Source: *CurBio 93; GrLiveH; LegTOT; NewYTBS 93; WhoAm 94, 95, 96, 97; WhoAmW 95, 97*

English, Doug
[Lowell Douglas English]
American. Football Player
Four-time all-pro defensive lineman, Detroit, 1975-79, 1981-85.
b. Aug 25, 1953 in Dallas, Texas
Source: *ConMus 9; FootReg 85, 86*

English Beat
[''Ranking Roger''; Dave Blockhead; Andy Cox; Wesley Magoogan; Everett Morton; Dave Steele; Dave Wakeling]
English. Music Group
Revivalist group founded 1979-83; hit album *Special Beat Forces,* 1983.
Source: *ConMus 9; EncPR&S 89; RolSEnR 83; WhoRocM 82; WhsNW 85*

Englund, Richard
American. Dancer, Choreographer
Director, company now known as The American Ballet Theatre II, 1972-85; Joffrey II Dancers, 1985-91.
b. 1932 in Seattle, Washington
d. Feb 15, 1991 in New York, New York
Source: *BiDD; News 91, 91-3; NewYTBS 91*

Englund, Robert
American. Actor
Played Freddy Krueger in *Nightmare on Elm Street* films, 1984-89.
b. Jun 6, 1949 in Glendale, California
Source: *BioIn 15, 16; ConTFT 8, 15; CurBio 90; HalFC 88; IntMPA 92, 94, 96*

Engstrom, Elmer William
American. Business Executive
With RCA 41 yrs; played role in development of first color TV tube.
b. Aug 25, 1901 in Minneapolis, Minnesota
d. Oct 30, 1984 in Hightstown, New Jersey
Source: *AmMWSc 79; BioIn 2, 8; BlueB 76; ConNews 85-2; CurBio 51, 85; InSci; IntWW 81; NewYTBS 84; WhAm 8; WhoE 74*

Enke, Karin
German. Skater
Won gold medals in speed skating: 500 meters, 1980 Olympics; 1,500 and 3,000 meters, 1984 Olympics.
b. 1962? in Dresden, German Democratic Republic
Source: *BioIn 12, 13, 15, 16*

Ennis, Del(mer)
American. Baseball Player
Outfielder, 1946-59; had over 100 RBIs in seven seasons; led NL in RBIs, 1950.
b. Jun 8, 1925 in Philadelphia, Pennsylvania
d. Feb 8, 1996 in Huntingdon Valley, Pennsylvania
Source: *Ballpl 90; BiDAmSp BB; BioIn 1, 3, 15, 21; WhoProB 73*

Ennis, Skinnay
American. Singer, Bandleader
Drummer, noted vocalist with Hal Kemp, 1925-38; band often on Bob Hope's radio shows, 1940s.
b. Aug 13, 1908 in Salisbury, North Carolina
d. Jun 5, 1963 in Beverly Hills, California
Source: *BiDJaz; CmpEPM; HalFC 80; WhoJazz 72; WhScrn 77*

Eno, Brian
[Brian Peter George St. John de Baptiste dela Salle Eno]
English. Musician, Producer
Co-founder Roxy Music, 1971; produced albums for David Bowie, Talking Heads, U2.
b. May 15, 1948 in Woodbridge, England
Source: *Baker 92; BioIn 13, 15; ConMuA 80A, 80B; ConMus 8; ConNews 86-2; EncPR&S 89; EncRkSt; HarEnR 86; IlEncRk; LegTOT; NewAgMG; NewAmDM; NewGrDA 86; PenEncP; RolSEnR 83; WhoAm 82, 84, 86, 88, 90, 92, 94, 95, 96, 97; WhoEnt 92; WhoRock 81*

Enoch, Kurt
American. Publisher
Pioneer in paperback publishing with New American Library, Inc., 1947-60.
b. Nov 22, 1895 in Hamburg, Germany
d. Feb 15, 1982, Puerto Rico
Source: *AnObit 1982; BioIn 3, 12; ConAu 106; NewYTBS 82; WhoAmJ 80; WhoE 77, 79, 81; WhoWorJ 78*

Enright, Dennis Joseph
English. Author, Poet
Writings include *Daughters of Earth,* 1972; *The Joke Shop,* 1976.
b. Mar 11, 1920 in Leamington, England
Source: *Au&Wr 71; BioIn 8, 10, 13, 14, 17; ChhPo S2; ConAu 1R; ConLC 4; ConNov 72, 76; ConPo 70, 75, 91; DcLEL 1940; EngPo; IntAu&W 76, 77, 82, 86, 89, 91, 93; IntvTCA 2; IntWW 74, 75, 76, 77, 78, 79, 80, 81, 82, 83, 89, 91, 93; LiExTwC; LngCTC; ModBrL, S1; NewC; PenC ENG; TwCWr; Who 74, 82, 83, 85, 88, 90, 92, 94; WhoTwCL; WhoWor 74, 76, 78, 80; WorAu 1950; WrDr 76, 86, 92*

Enright, Elizabeth
American. Artist, Author, Illustrator
Books for children include Newbery-winner *Thimble Summer,* 1939; adults include *The Moment Before the Rain,* 1959.
b. Sep 17, 1909 in Oak Park, Illinois
d. Jun 8, 1968 in Wainscott, New York
Source: *AmAu&B; AnCL; AuBYP 2, 3; BioIn 1, 2, 4, 5, 7, 8, 11, 14, 19; BkCL; ChlBkCr; ChlLR 4; ConAu 25R, 61; CurBio 47, 68; DcAmChF 1960; DcLB 22; IlsCB 1744, 1946; InWom; JBA 51; LinLib L; MajAI; NewbMB 1922; OxCChiL; SmATA 9; TwCChW 78, 83, 89; WhAm 5; WrChl*

Enrique Tarancon, Vicente, Cardinal
Spanish. Religious Leader
Archbishop of Toledo, Spain, 1969-83.
b. May 14, 1907
d. Nov 28, 1994 in Valencia, Spain
Source: *BioIn 9, 11; CurBio 72, 95N*

Ensor, James Sydney, Baron
Belgian. Artist
Considered most original artist of his time; forerunner of expressionism, surrealism; works include *The Entry of Christ into Brussels,* 1888.
b. Apr 13, 1860 in Ostend, Belgium
d. Nov 19, 1949 in Ostend, Belgium
Source: *AtlBL; WhAm 4; WorAl; WorAlBi*

Entremont, Phillippe
French. Pianist, Conductor
Principal conductor with New Orleans Philharmonic Symphony Orchestra, 1981-85; music director, Denver Symphony, 1986-89; lifetime music director, Vienna Chamber Orchestra, 1975—; nominated for Grammy, 1972.
b. Jun 7, 1934 in Reims, France
Source: *Baker 84; BioIn 14; IntWW 91; IntWWM 90; NewAmDM; NewGrDA 86; PenDiMP; WhoAm 86; WhoEnt 92; WhoMus 72; WhoSSW 86; WhoWest 89; WhoWor 91*

Entwistle, John Alec
[The Who]
English. Musician, Singer
Joined group, 1964; had solo hit ''Too Late the Hero,'' 1981.
b. Sep 10, 1944 in London, England
Source: *BioIn 13; HarEnR 86; WhoAm 82*

Enver Pasha
Turkish. Army Officer, Political Leader
Participated in Young Turk revolution, 1908; by way of coup, became virtual dictator of Turkey, 1913.
b. Nov 23, 1881 in Apana, Turkey
d. Aug 4, 1922 in Bukhara, Turkey
Source: *BioIn 12; EncRev; HarEnMi; HisWorL; McGEWB; NewCol 75; WhoMilH 76*

En Vogue
American. Music Group
Album *Funky Divas,* 1992 had smash single ''My Lovin' (You're Never Gonna Get It).''
Source: *BioIn 21; ConMuA 80B; ConMus 10; EncRkSt; News 94, 94-1; ScF&FL 92; WhoAfA 96; WhoAmP 91, 93, 95; WhoBlA 94*

Enya
Irish. Singer, Composer
Folk-pop singer composed soundtrack for BBC TV series ''The Celts''; albums include *Enya,* 1986; *Watermark,* 1989.
b. 1962 in Gweedore, Ireland
Source: *BioIn 16; ConMus 6; LegTOT; News 92, 92-3*

Enzi, Michael B.
American. Politician
Rep. senator, WY, 1997—.

b. Feb 1, 1944

Epaminondas
Greek. Military Leader
Theban commander; brilliant tactician; defeated Spartans, 371, 362 BC.
b. 410BC
d. 362BC
Source: *McGEWB; NewCol 75; WebBD 83*

Epee, Charles-Michel
French. Educator
Early teacher of deaf mutes; developed one-hand sign alphabet.
b. Nov 25, 1712 in Paris, France
d. Dec 23, 1789 in Paris, France
Source: *LinLib S; NewCol 75; REn*

Ephron, Henry
American. Dramatist, Screenwriter
Films include *Carousel,* 1956; *The Dark Set,* 1957.
b. May 26, 1912 in New York, New York
d. Sep 6, 1992 in Los Angeles, California
Source: *AnObit 1992; BiE&WWA; BioIn 18, 19; ConLC 76; EncAFC; FilmEn; FilmgC; HalFC 80, 84, 88; News 93-2; NotNAT; WomWMM*

Ephron, Nora
American. Author, Screenwriter
Wrote best-seller *Heartburn,* 1983, filmed, 1986; received Oscar nominations for screenplay writing of films *Silkwood,* 1984, *When Harry Met Sally,* 1989.
b. May 19, 1941 in New York, New York
Source: *AuNews 2; BioIn 10, 11, 13, 14, 16; CelR 90; ConAu 12NR, 39NR, 65; ConLC 17, 31; ConTFT 8, 15; CurBio 90; FemiCLE; GrLiveH; IntMPA 94, 96; IntWW 91, 93; LegTOT; MiSFD 9; News 92, 92-3; WhoAm 76, 78, 80, 82, 84, 86, 88, 90, 92, 94, 95, 96, 97; WhoAmW 83, 85, 87, 89, 91, 93, 95, 97; WhoE 93, 95, 97; WhoEmL 87; WhoEnt 92; WhoWor 95, 96, 97; WorAlBi; WorAu 1980; WrDr 96*

Epictetus
Greek. Philosopher
Stoic philosophy based on indifference to external goods.
b. 55?
d. 135?
Source: *BbD; BiD&SB; CasWL; EncEth; LegTOT; NewC; OxCPhil; PenC CL; RComWL; REn*

Epicurus
Greek. Philosopher
Epicureanism described pleasure as highest, only good; the avoidance of pain.
b. 342BC in Samos, Greece
d. 270BC
Source: *BbD; BiD&SB; BioIn 1, 3, 8, 11; BlmGEL; CasWL; DcBiPP; Dis&D; LinLib L, S; LngCEL; McGEWB; NewC; OxCEng 67; PenC CL; RComWL; REn; WhDW*

Epperson, Frank W
American. Inventor
Patented the Popsicle, 1924.
b. 1894
d. Oct 25, 1983 in Fremont, California
Source: *BioIn 13*

Epps, Jack, Jr.
American. Screenwriter
With Jim Cash, wrote screenplays for 1986 films *Top Gun, Legal Eagles.*
b. Nov 3, 1949? in Detroit, Michigan
Source: *BioIn 15; ConAu 133; WrDr 94*

Epstein, Alvin
American. Actor, Director
Had leading roles on stage in *Don Juan; The Tempest;* appeared on several TV shows.
b. May 24, 1925 in New York, New York
Source: *BiE&WWA; ConTFT 9; NotNAT; PlP&P; WhoAm 74, 76, 78, 80, 84, 86, 88, 90, 92, 94, 95, 97; WhoThe 72, 77, 81*

Epstein, Brian
English. Manager
Managed The Beatles, 1961-67; died in swimming pool accident.
b. Sep 19, 1934 in Liverpool, England
d. Aug 27, 1967 in London, England
Source: *BioIn 7, 8, 16; EncRk 88; HarEnR 86; IlEncRk; LegTOT; ObitOF 79; ObitT 1961; PenEncP; WhoRock 81; WhoRocM 82; WorAl; WorAlBi*

Epstein, Edward Jay
American. Author, Educator
Books include *Counterplot,* 1969; contributes to *New Yorker; Esquire* mags.
b. Dec 6, 1935 in New York, New York
Source: *BioIn 8, 11; ConAu 13NR, 17R; WhoWorJ 72, 78*

Epstein, Jacob, Sir
English. Sculptor
Known for peculiar rough-hewn style in bronze busts, Oscar Wilde's tomb in Paris.
b. Nov 10, 1880 in New York, New York
d. Aug 19, 1959 in London, England
Source: *AtlBL; Benet 87, 96; BioIn 1, 2, 3, 4, 5, 6, 7, 8, 9, 14, 15, 16, 17, 19; ConArt 77, 83; ConAu 120; CurBio 45, 59; DcAmB S6; DcArts; DcBrAr 1; DcNaB 1951; DcNiCA; FacFETw; GrBr; IntDcAA 90; LegTOT; LinLib L, S; LngCTC; MakMC; McGDA; McGEWB; NatCAB 44; ObitT 1951; OxCAmL 65; OxCArt; OxCTwCA; OxDcArt; PhDcTCA 77; PolBiDi; REn; REnAL; TwCPaSc; WhAm 2, 3; WhAmArt 85; WhDW; WorArt 1950*

Epstein, Jason
American. Editor, Publishing Executive
Vp./editorial director, Random House, 1958—; inaugurated trade paperback publishing industry with founding of Anchor Books, 1952; co-founder *New York Review of Books,* 1963; Library of America literary series, 1979-89.
b. Aug 25, 1928 in Cambridge, Massachusetts
Source: *BioIn 9, 11, 16; ConAu 57; CurBio 90; News 91, 91-1; NewYTBE 72; PolProf J; WhoAm 74, 76, 78, 80, 82, 84, 86, 88, 90, 92, 94, 95, 96, 97; WhoE 91; WhoFI 87; WorAlBi*

Epstein, Joseph
American. Essayist, Editor, Educator
Editor, *American Scholar,* 1975—; books include *Familiar Territory: Observations on American Life,* 1979; non-fiction, *Divorce in America: Marriage in an Age of Possibility,* 1974.
b. Jan 9, 1937 in Chicago, Illinois
Source: *BioIn 16, 19; ConAu 50NR, 112, 119; CurBio 90; WhoAm 82, 84, 86, 88, 90, 92, 94, 95, 96, 97; WhoE 95; WhoUSWr 88; WhoWor 96; WhoWrEP 89, 92, 95; WorAu 1980; WrDr 90, 92, 94, 96*

Epstein, Julius
American. Writer
Won Oscar for *Casablanca,* 1942.
b. Aug 22, 1909 in New York, New York
Source: *BioIn 14, 15; ConAu 113, 124; DcLB 26; EncAFC; FacFETw; HalFC 88; IntDcF 1-4, 2-4; IntMPA 92; VarWW 85; WhoAm 90*

Epstein, Philip G
American. Screenwriter, Dramatist
Co-wrote film classics *Casablanca,* 1942; *Arsenic and Old Lace,* 1944.
b. Aug 22, 1909 in New York, New York
d. Feb 7, 1952 in Los Angeles, California
Source: *ConAu 117; DcAmB S5; DcLB 26*

Erasmus, Desiderius
[Geert Geerts; Gerhard Gerhards]
Dutch. Author, Philosopher, Scholar
Renaissance humanist who advanced reform in Catholic Church; best known for satire *The Praise of Folly,* 1509.
b. Oct 27, 1469? in Rotterdam, Netherlands
d. Jul 12, 1536 in Basel, Switzerland
Source: *AtlBL; BbD; BiD&SB; CasWL; CroE&S; CyWA 58; DcBiPP; DcEnL; DcEuL; DcSpL; EncUnb; EuAu; LitC 16; LuthC 75; NewCBEL; NewGrDM 80; OxCEng 85; OxCFr; PenC EUR; RComWL; REn; WebBD 83*

Eratosthenes
Greek. Scholar
Head of library at Alexandria, 240BC; measured circumference, tilt of Earth.

b. 275?BC in Cyrene, Greece
d. 195?BC
Source: *BioIn 3, 7, 8, 9; CasWL; CyEd; Geog 2; Grk&L; InSci; PenC CL*

Erdman, Paul E(mil)
Canadian. Author, Economist
Mystery novels include *The Crash of '79,* 1976.
b. May 19, 1932 in Stratford, Ontario, Canada
Source: *AuNews 1; BioIn 12, 14; ConAu 43NR, 61; EncSF 93; ScFSB; TwCCr&M 91; WhoAm 76, 78, 80, 82, 84, 86, 88, 90, 92, 94, 95, 96, 97; WhoWor 89, 91; WorAlBi; WrDr 86, 92*

Erdos, Paul
Hungarian. Mathematician
One of the most prolific mathematicians in history, with more than 1,500 papers to his name; so devoted to mathematics that he had no home or job.
b. 1913, Austria-Hungary
d. Sep 20, 1996 in Warsaw, Poland
Source: *BioIn 15; IntWW 83, 89, 91, 93; NewYTBS 27; WhoWor 87; WhoWorJ 78*

Erdrich, Louise
[Karen Louise Erdrich]
American. Author
Lyrical prize-winning novelist; wrote *The Beet Queen,* 1987.
b. Jul 6, 1954 in Little Falls, Minnesota
Source: *AmWomWr 92, SUP; Au&Arts 10; Benet 96; BenetAL 91; BestSel 89-1; BioIn 14; BlmGWL; ConAu 41NR, 114; ConLC 39, 54; ConNov 91; CurBio 89; CyWA 89; DcLB 152; EncNAB; FemiCLE; GrLiveH; GrWomW; IntAu&W 86, 91; IntWW 91, 93; MagSAmL; MajTwCW; ModWoWr; NatNAL; NotNaAm; OxCAmL 95; OxCWoWr 95; TwCWW 91; WhoAm 86, 88, 90, 92, 94, 95, 96; WhoAmW 91, 93, 95; WhoE 93, 95; WorAu 1980; WrDr 90, 92, 94, 96*

Erhard, Ludwig
German. Economist, Politician
West German chancellor, 1960s, who guided country's post-WW II economic recovery.
b. Feb 4, 1897 in Fuerth, Germany
d. May 7, 1977 in Bonn, Germany
Source: *Au&Wr 71; BioIn 2, 3, 4, 5, 6, 7, 11, 18, 21; ColdWar 1; ConAu 112; CurBio 50, 64, 77, 77N; DcPol; DcTwHis; EncCW; FacFETw; IntAu&W 76, 77; IntWW 74, 75, 76, 77; LinLib S; McGEWB; PolLCWE; WebBD 83; WhDW; Who 74; WhoEc 81, 86; WorAl; WorAlBi*

Erhard, Werner
[John Paul Rosenberg]
American. Educator
Developed est, 1971, an individual, social transformation technique.
b. Sep 5, 1935 in Philadelphia, Pennsylvania
Source: *BioIn 10, 11, 12, 13, 14, 15; BkPepl; CurBio 77; EncO&P 1, 2, 2S1, 3; LegTOT; WhoAm 76, 78, 80, 82, 86, 88, 90, 92; WhoWor 80, 82; WorAlBi*

Eric B. and Rakim
American. Rap Group
Paid in Full, 1987 and *Follow the Leader,* 1988 went gold.
Source: *ConMus 9; DcSeaP; DcVicP 2; NatPD 77, 81; ObitOF 79*

Eric IX
[Eric the Saint; Erik IX Jedvardsson]
Swedish. Ruler
King of Sweden, c. 1150-60, who led Christian crusade to Finland, c. 1157; killed by a Danish prince while attending mass; feast day, May 18.
d. 1161
Source: *BioIn 5; NewCol 75; WebBD 83*

Erickson, Arthur Charles
Canadian. Architect
Principal, Arthur Erickson Architects, 1972—; won American Institute of Architects Gold Medal, 1986; designed Canada's controversial Washington, DC embassy.
b. Jun 14, 1924 in Vancouver, British Columbia, Canada
Source: *BioIn 10, 12, 16; BlueB 76; CanWW 31, 70, 79, 80, 81, 83, 89; ConArch 87, 94; EncWB; IntWW 74, 75, 76, 77, 78, 79, 80, 81, 82, 83, 89, 91, 93; News 89-3; WhoAm 86, 92, 94, 95, 96, 97; WhoArch; WhoCan 73, 75, 77, 80, 82, 84; WhoCanB 86; WhoWest 87, 89, 92, 94, 96; WhoWor 84, 87, 89, 91, 93, 95, 96, 97*

Erickson, Eric
Swedish. Spy
Allied spy, WW II; film based on life *The Counterfeit Traitor,* 1962.
b. 1890 in New York, New York
d. Jan 24, 1983 in Menton, France
Source: *EncE 75; NewYTBS 83*

Erickson, Leif
[William Wycliffe Anderson]
American. Singer, Actor
Best known for role of Big John Cannon on TV series "The High Chaparral."
b. Oct 27, 1911 in Alameda, California
d. Jan 30, 1986 in Pensacola, Florida
Source: *AnObit 1986; BiE&WWA; BioIn 14; FilmEn; FilmgC; ForYSC; HalFC 80, 84, 88; IntMPA 75, 76, 77, 78, 79, 82, 84, 86; LegTOT; MotPP; MovMk; NewYTBS 86; WhoAmP 73; WhoHol A; WorAl*

Ericson, Leif
Icelandic. Navigator, Explorer
Discovered N American coast, circa 1000, which he named Vinland.
b. 975?, Iceland
Source: *BenetAL 91; NewC; NewCol 75; PlP&P; REn; REnAL; WhNaAH; WorAlBi*

Ericsson, John
American. Shipbuilder
Invented ironclad "Monitor" battleship, 1862; began age of modern warships.
b. Jul 31, 1803 in Varmland, Sweden
d. Mar 8, 1889 in New York, New York
Source: *Alli SUP; AmBi; ApCAB; AsBiEn; BiD&SB; BiInAmS; BioIn 1, 3, 4, 5, 6, 10, 12; CelCen; CivWDc; DcAmAu; DcAmB; DcAmMiB; DcBiPP; Drake; HarEnUS; InSci; LinLib S; McGEWB; NatCAB 4; OxCAmH; OxCShps; TwCBDA; WebAB 74, 79; WebAMB; WhAm HS; WhCiWar; WhDW; WorInv*

Eric the Red
[Eirikr Thorvaldsson]
Norwegian. Navigator
Father of Leif Ericson; discovered, colonized Greenland, 982.
b. 950, Norway
d. 1000
Source: *ApCAB; Benet 87, 96; NewCol 75; OxCCan; REn; WhAm HS; WhWE; WorAl; WorAlBi*

Erigena, John Scotus
Irish. Philosopher
Among originators of mysticism during Middle Ages; works include *De Divisione Naturae.*
b. 810?
d. 891?
Source: *Alli; Baker 92; BioIn 15, 17, 18; BritAu; CamGEL; DcBiPP; DcEnL; EvLB; Grk&L; IlEncMy; McGEWB; OxCEng 67*

Erikson, Erik H(omburger)
American. Psychoanalyst
Coined term "identity crisis"; expanded on Freud's thoughts to introduce idea of crises in stages of development.
b. Jun 15, 1902 in Frankfurt am Main, Germany
d. May 12, 1994 in Harwich, Massachusetts
Source: *AmAu&B; AmMWSc 73S, 78S; AmSocL; BioIn 7, 8, 9, 10, 11, 12, 13, 16; ConAu 25R, 33NR, 145; ConLC 86; CurBio 71, 94N; DcLEL 1940; EncAB-H 1974, 1996; FacFETw; IntAu&W 77, 82; IntWW 76, 77, 78, 79, 80, 81, 82, 83, 89, 91, 93; MajTwCW; McGEWB; RAdv 14; WebAB 74, 79; WhAm 11; WhoAm 74, 76, 78, 80, 82, 84, 86, 88, 90, 92, 94; WhoWor 74; WrDr 86, 92, 94, 96*

Erlander, Tage Fritiof
Swedish. Politician
Prime minister, 1946-69; instituted comprehensive school system, social security in Sweden.
b. Jun 13, 1901 in Ransater, Sweden
d. Jun 21, 1985 in Huddinge, Sweden
Source: *ConAu 116; CurBio 47; DcTwHis; IntWW 74, 75, 76, 77, 78, 79, 80, 81, 82, 83; IntYB 78, 79, 80, 81, 82*

Erlanger, Joseph
American. Physiologist
Shared 1944 Nobel Prize for work on nerve impulses.
b. Jan 5, 1874 in San Francisco, California
d. Dec 5, 1965 in Saint Louis, Missouri
Source: *AsBiEn; BiESc; BioIn 3, 5, 6, 7, 8, 14, 15, 20; DcAmB S7; DcAmMeB 84; DcScB; FacFETw; LarDcSc; LegTOT; McGEWB; McGMS 80; NatCAB 51; NobelP; NotTwCS; OxCMed 86; WebAB 74, 79; WebBD 83; WhAm 4; WhDW; WhoNob, 90, 95; WorAl; WorAlBi*

Erman, John
American. Director
Won Emmy for "Who Will Love My Children," 1983.
Source: *IntMPA 88; MiSFD 9; VarWW 85; WhoAm 88*

Ernaux, Annie
French. Author
Wrote novels *Cleaned Out,* 1974; *A Frozen Woman,* 1981.
b. Sep 1, 1940 in Lillebonne, France
Source: *BioIn 21; ConAu 147; ConLC 88*

Ernst, Jimmy
American. Author, Artist
Son of Max Ernst; one of leading abstractionists in US.
b. Jun 24, 1920 in Cologne, Germany
d. Feb 6, 1984 in New York, New York
Source: *AnObit 1984; BioIn 2, 4, 5, 6, 7, 8, 10, 13, 14; ConAu 112; CurBio 84N; DcCAA 71, 77, 88, 94; McGDA; NewYTBS 84; OxCTwCA; PhDcTCA 77; WhAm 9; WhoAm 74, 76, 78, 80, 82, 84, 86, 88; WhoAmA 73, 76, 78, 80, 82, 84, 86N, 89N, 91N, 93N; WhoWor 74; WorArt 1950*

Ernst, Kenneth
American. Cartoonist
Known for clean, tasteful craftmanship; drew "Mary Worth"; "Clyde Beatty."
b. 1918 in Illinois
Source: *BioIn 15; ConGrA 1; WorECom*

Ernst, Max
German. Artist
Co-founded Dadaist group, 1919; helped found Surrealist group, 1931; worked chiefly in sculpture.
b. Apr 2, 1891 in Cologne, Germany
d. Apr 1, 1976 in Paris, France
Source: *ArtsAmW 2; Benet 87, 96; BioIn 1, 4, 5, 6, 7, 8, 9, 10, 11, 12, 13, 14, 15, 16, 17; BioNews 74; CelR; ConArt 77, 83; ConAu 65; CurBio 42, 61, 76N; DcAmB S10; DcArts; FacFETw; IntDcAA 90; IntWW 74, 75, 76; LegTOT; MakMC; McGDA; McGEWB; NewYTBS 76; OxCArt; OxCTwCA; OxDcArt; PhDcTCA 77; REn; WebBD 83; WhAm 7; WhDW; Who 74; WhoAm 74, 76; WhoAmA 78N, 80N, 82N, 84N, 86N, 89N, 91N, 93N; WorAl; WorAlBi; WorArt 1950*

Ernst, Paul Karl Friedrich
German. Author, Critic, Dramatist
Dramas include *Brunhild,* 1909; novels include *Die Selige Insel,* 1909.
b. Mar 7, 1866 in Elbingerode, Germany
d. May 13, 1933 in Saint Georgen, Germany
Source: *CasWL; ClDMEL 47; CnMD; EncWL; EvEuW; McGEWD 72; ModGL; ModWD; OxCGer 76; PenC EUR; WebBD 83; WhoLA*

Ernst, Richard
Swiss. Chemist
Won Nobel Prize, 1991, for developing improvements in nuclear magnetic resonance spectroscopy.
b. Jul 2, 1942 in Elgin, Illinois
Source: *AmMWSc 92; WhoE 91; WhoEmL 87; WhoTech 89*

Erriquez, Elio
Swiss. Hostage
Swiss relief worker held in captivity 312 days by Lebanese terrorist group, Oct 6, 1989-Aug 14, 1990.

Errol, Leon
Australian. Actor
Comedian, dancer; appeared in 60 films, often as hen-pecked husband.
b. Jul 3, 1881 in Sydney, Australia
d. Oct 12, 1951 in Los Angeles, California
Source: *BiDD; BioIn 2; CmpEPM; DcAmB S5; EncAFC; EncMT; EncVaud; Film 2; FilmEn; FilmgC; ForYSC; Funs; HalFC 80, 84, 88; JoeFr; MotPP; MovMk; NotNAT B; OxCAmT 84; PlP&P; QDrFCA 92; Vers B; WhoCom; WhoHol B; WhScrn 74, 77, 83; WhThe*

Erskine, Carl Daniel
"Oisk"
American. Baseball Player
Pitcher, Brooklyn/LA Dodgers, 1948-59; threw two no-hitters, 1952, 1956.
b. Dec 13, 1926 in Anderson, Indiana
Source: *Ballpl 90; BioIn 3, 4, 7, 11; WhoProB 73*

Erskine, John
American. Author, Educator
Wrote humorous versions of famous legends: *Galahad,* 1926.
b. Oct 5, 1879 in New York, New York
d. Jun 2, 1951 in New York, New York
Source: *AmAu&B; AmLY; AmNov; Baker 78, 84, 92; BenetAL 91; BiDAmEd; BiDAmM; BioIn 1, 2, 3, 4, 12, 17; ChhPo, S1; CnDAL; ConAmA; ConAmL; ConAu 112, 154; DcAmB S5; DcLB 9, 102; DcLEL; FacFETw; LinLib L, S; LngCTC; NewGrDA 86; NotNAT B; OxCAmL 65, 83; REnAL; ScF&FL 1; SJGFanW; TwCA, SUP; TwCRHW 90; WebAB 74, 79; WhAm 3; WhLit; WhNAA*

Erte
[Romain de Tirtoff]
Russian. Fashion Designer, Artist
Prolific designer thought to epitomize the elegance of art deco; designed every *Harper's Bazaar* cover, 1915-36.
b. Nov 23, 1892 in Saint Petersburg, Russia
d. Apr 21, 1990 in Paris, France
Source: *AnObit 1990; BiDSovU; BioIn 8, 9, 10, 11, 12, 13, 16, 17; ConDes 84, 90, 97; CurBio 80, 90, 90N; DcArts; EncFash; FacFETw; LegTOT; News 90; NewYTBS 90; PrintW 83, 85; WhoArt 84; WhoFash, 88, 88A; WhoWor 78; WorFshn*

Ertegun, Ahmet (Munir)
American. Businessman, Soccer Executive
Co-founder, Atlantic Records, 1947; pres., NY Cosmos soccer team, 1971-83.
b. Jul 31, 1923 in Istanbul, Turkey
Source: *BioIn 15, 16; CelR, 90; ConMus 10; ConNews 86-3; HarEnR 86; LegTOT; NewGrDJ 88; WhoAm 76, 78, 82, 88, 90, 92, 94, 95, 96, 97; WhoEnt 92; WhoWor 89, 91*

Erteszek, Jan
Polish. Business Executive
Co-founder, with wife, of Olga Co., one of world's leading manufacturers of lingerie.
b. Dec 24, 1913 in Krakow, Poland
d. Jun 27, 1986 in Santa Monica, California
Source: *WhoAm 82, 84*

Ertz, Susan
American. Author
Wrote novel *The Philosopher's Daughter,* 1976.
b. 1894 in Walton-on-Thames, England
d. Apr 11, 1985
Source: *Au&Wr 71; BioIn 4; Chambr 3; ConAu 5R, 116; EncSF 93; InWom; LngCTC; NewC; ScF&FL 1, 92; TwCA, SUP; TwCRGW; TwCRHW 90, 94; TwCWW 82, 91; WhE&EA; Who 85*

Eruzione, Mike
American. Hockey Player
Captain, US Olympic gold medal-winning team, 1980; advisor for film *Miracle on Ice,* 1981, which depicted Olympic triumph.
b. Oct 25, 1954 in Boston, Massachusetts
Source: *BioIn 12, 13; NewYTBS 82*

Ervin, Sam(uel James Jr.)
American. Politician
Folksy Dem. senator from NC, 1954-74; known for role in 1973 Watergate hearings.
b. Sep 27, 1896 in Morganton, North Carolina
d. Apr 23, 1985 in Winston-Salem, North Carolina
Source: *AnObit 1985; BioNews 74; CelR; CngDr 74; ConAu 119; ConNews 85-2; CurBio 55, 73; FacFETw; IntWW*

82; IntYB 82; NewYTBE 70, 73; WhoAm 82; WhoAmP 81; WhoGov 72; WhoSSW 73; WhoWor 80

Erving, Julius Winfield
"Doctor J"
American. Basketball Player
Forward, in ABA, 1971-76; NBA, Philadelphis 76ers 1976-87; three-time MVP; scored over 30,000 career pts.
b. Feb 22, 1950 in Roosevelt, New York
Source: *AfrAmBi 1; BiDAmSp BK; BioIn 9, 10, 11, 12, 13, 14, 15, 16; BkPepl; CelR 90; CurBio 75; FacFETw; InB&W 80, 85; NegAl 89; NewYTBE 72; NewYTBS 75, 76, 85, 87; OfNBA 86; WhoAfA 96; WhoAm 78, 80, 82, 84, 86, 88, 90, 92, 94, 95, 96, 97; WhoBbl 73; WhoBlA 85, 88, 90, 92, 94; WhoE 85, 86, 95; WorAlBi*

Erwin, Pee Wee
[George Erwin]
American. Jazz Musician, Composer
Swing-era trumpeter who played with Benny Goodman, Tommy Dorsey bands, 1930s; led own band, 1940s-50s.
b. May 30, 1913 in Falls City, Nebraska
d. Jun 20, 1981 in Teaneck, New Jersey
Source: *AllMusG; ASCAP 66, 80; BiDAmM; BiDJaz; BioIn 12; CmpEPM; EncJzS; InB&W 85; NewGrDJ 88, 94; WhoJazz 72; WhScrn 83*

Erwin, Stuart
American. Comedian, Actor
Roles in films were usually the hero's friend, Mr. Average: *He Hired the Boss,* 1943.
b. Feb 14, 1902 in Squaw Valley, California
d. Dec 21, 1967 in Beverly Hills, California
Source: *EncAFC; FilmEn; FilmgC; HolCA; MotPP; MovMk; WhoHol B; WhScrn 74, 77, 83*

Esaki, Leo
Japanese. Physicist
Shared Nobel Prize in physics, 1973, for discovery of tunneling in semiconductors; research led to progress in communications, computer networks.
b. Mar 12, 1925 in Osaka, Japan
Source: *AmMWSc 73P, 76P, 79, 82, 86, 89, 92, 95; AsBiEn; BiESc; BioIn 5, 7, 10, 15, 18, 20; CamDcSc; FacFETw; FarE&A 81; IntWW 74, 75, 76, 77, 78, 79, 80, 81, 82, 83, 89, 91, 93; LarDcSc; LElec; McGMS 80; NewYTBE 73; NobelP; NotTwCS; Who 82, 83, 85, 88, 90, 92, 94; WhoAm 76, 78, 80, 82, 84, 86, 88, 90, 92, 94, 95; WhoE 77, 79, 81, 83, 85, 86, 89, 91, 93; WhoFrS 84; WhoNob, 90, 95; WhoScEn 94, 96; WhoWor 78, 80, 82, 84, 87, 89, 91, 93, 95, 96, 97; WorAl; WorAlBi; WorScD*

Esau
Biblical Figure
Son of Isaac who sold his birthright to younger brother, Jacob; followers called Edomites.
Source: *Benet 96; BioIn 4, 5, 10; LngCEL; NewCol 75; WebBD 83*

Escalante, Jaime
Bolivian. Teacher
California teacher who is routinely succesful in getting his disadvantaged students to take and pass advanced math college placement exams; real-life subject of movie *Stand and Deliver,* 1987.
b. Dec 31, 1930 in La Paz, Bolivia
Source: *AmDec 1980; BioIn 13, 16; ConHero 1; DcHiB; HispAmA; LegTOT; NewYTBS 88; WhoHisp 91, 92, 94*

Eschenbach, Christoph
German. Pianist, Conductor
Internationally renowned pianist; has performed with most of world's major orchestras; recorded over a dozen albums; musical director, Houston Symphony Orchestra, 1988—.
b. Feb 20, 1940 in Wroclaw, Poland
Source: *Baker 84, 92; BioIn 8, 11, 16; BriBkM 80; CurBio 89; IntWW 79, 80, 81, 82, 83, 89, 91, 93; IntWWM 85, 90; MusSN; NewAmDM; NewGrDM 80; NewYTBS 74; PenDiMP; Who 88, 90, 92, 94; WhoAm 80, 82, 84, 86, 88, 90, 92, 94, 95, 96, 97; WhoEnt 92; WhoMus 72; WhoSSW 91, 93, 95; WhoWor 74, 78, 80, 82, 84, 87, 89, 93, 95*

Escher, M(aurits) C(ornelis)
Dutch. Artist
Surrealist; paintings mixed reality with symbolism; used math concepts in later works.
b. Jun 17, 1898 in Leeuwarden, Netherlands
d. Mar 27, 1972 in Hilversum, Netherlands
Source: *BioIn 2, 3, 9, 10, 11, 12, 14, 19; DcArts; OxCTwCA; PhDcTCA 77*

Escobar, Sixto
Puerto Rican. Boxer
Won world bantam title, 1930s; last fight, 1940.
b. Mar 23, 1913 in Barceloneta, Puerto Rico
Source: *BioIn 12; HispAmA; WhoBox 74*

Escobar Gaviria, Pablo
Colombian. Criminal
Columbian cocaine trafficker; head, Medellin drug cartel known for terrorizing dynamite and arson attacks.
Source: *BioIn 15*

Escoffier, Georges Auguste
"King of Cooks"
French. Chef
Director of kitchen, Grand Hotel, Monte Carlo; Savoy, Carlton hotels, London; wrote *Ma Cuisine,* 1934.
b. Oct 28, 1846 in Villeneuve-Loubet, France
d. Feb 12, 1935 in Monte Carlo, Monaco
Source: *NewCol 75; WebBD 83; WorAl; WorAlBi*

Escovedo, Alejandro
American. Singer, Songwriter, Musician
Musician who forged the "cow-punk" rock style; formed punk rock group, The Nuns, in 1987; formed country-punk band, Rank and Rile, in 1982; began solo career in 1988, performing with the Alejandro Escovedo Orchestra; recorded *With These Hands,* 1996.
b. 1946 in San Antonio, Texas

Escriva de Balaguer, Josemarie
Spanish. Religious Leader
Founder, Opus Dei religious movement, beatified May 17, 1992 by Pope John Paul II, amidst criticism over the group's unorthodox beliefs.
b. Jan 9, 1902 in Barbastro, Spain
d. Jun 26, 1975 in Rome, Italy
Source: *BioIn 14, 16*

Esenin, Sergei Aleksandrovich
[Sergei Aleksandrovich Yesenin]
Russian. Poet
Cult figure, imagist, who was attacked in literary world for "hooliganism" as a result of alcoholism: *Confessions of a Hooligan,* 1924.
b. Feb 21, 1895 in Konstantinovo, Russia
d. Dec 28, 1925 in Leningrad, Union of Soviet Socialist Republics
Source: *Benet 87, 96; BiDSovU; BioIn 1, 2, 3, 7, 8, 9, 10, 12, 13; CasWL; ClDMEL 47; CnMWL; ConAu 104; EncWL; EvEuW; HanRL; McGEWB; ModSL 1; OxCEng 85, 95; PenC EUR; REn; RfGWoL 95; TwCWr; WhoTwCL; WorAl; WorAu 1950*

Eshkol, Levi
[Levi Shkolnik]
Israeli. Political Leader
A founder of the state of Israel, 1948; premier, 1963-69.
b. Oct 25, 1895 in Oratova, Ukraine
d. Feb 26, 1969 in Jerusalem, Israel
Source: *BioIn 6, 7, 8, 9, 12, 17, 18; ColdWar 2; CurBio 63, 69; DcMidEa; DcPol; DcTwHis; HisEAAC; ObitT 1961; PolLCME; WhAm 5; WhDW*

Esiason, Boomer
[Norman Julius Esiason, Jr.]
American. Football Player
Quarterback, Cincinnati Bengals, 1984-92; NY Jets, 1993—; NFL MVP, 1988.
b. Apr 17, 1961 in West Islip, New York
Source: *BioIn 15, 16; CelR 90; CurBio 95; FootReg 86, 87; News 91, 91-1; WhoAm 90, 92, 94, 95, 96, 97; WhoE 95; WhoMW 90; WhoSpor; WhoWor 96; WorAlBi*

Esmond, Jill
English. Actor
Married to Laurence Olivier, 1930-40; films include *First Lady; Thirteen Women.*
b. Jan 26, 1908 in London, England
d. Jul 28, 1990 in Wimbledon, England
Source: *BioIn 17; FilmEn; FilmgC; ForYSC; HalFC 80, 84, 88; NewYTBS 90; WhoHol A; WhoThe 77A; WhThe*

Esposito, Giancarlo (Giusseppi)
American. Actor
Appeared in *Do the Right Thing,* 1990; *Malcolm X,* 1992.
b. c. 1958 in Copenhagen, Denmark
Source: *BioIn 20; ConBlB 9; DrBlPA 90; IntMPA 94, 96; LegTOT; WhoAfA 96; WhoAm 94, 95, 96, 97; WhoBlA 94*

Esposito, Joseph
"Diamond Joe"
American. Criminal
Labor organizer accused of murder, operating illegal stills during Prohibition.
b. Apr 28, 1872 in Acerra, Italy
d. Mar 21, 1928 in Chicago, Illinois
Source: *DrInf*

Esposito, Phil(ip Anthony)
Canadian. Hockey Player, Hockey Executive
Center, Chicago, 1963-67; Boston, 1967-75; New York, 1975-81; first to score over 70 goals in season (1970-71), second to score over 700 goals in career; Hall of Fame, 1984; general m anager, NY Rangers, 1986-89; coach NY Rangers, 1986-87, 1989; president, general manager, Tampa Bay, 1992—.
b. Feb 20, 1942 in Sault Sainte Marie, Ontario, Canada
Source: *BioIn 8, 9, 10, 11, 12, 14, 15, 20; ConAu 108; CurBio 73; FacFETw; HocEn; LegTOT; NewYTBS 79, 81, 84, 86; WhoAm 78, 80, 82, 88, 94, 95, 96, 97; WhoE 89, 91; WhoHcky 73; WhoSSW 93, 95; WorAl; WorAlBi*

Esposito, Tony
[Anthony James Esposito]
Canadian. Hockey Player, Hockey Executive
Goalie, 1968-84, mostly with Chicago; set modern NHL record for shutouts in seas on, 15 (1969-70); won Vezina Trophy three times; brother of Phil; GM, Pittsburgh, 1988-89; Hall of Fame, 1988.
b. Apr 23, 1944 in Sault Sainte Marie, Ontario, Canada
Source: *BioIn 13; FacFETw; HocEn; WhoAm 80, 82; WhoHcky 73*

Espriu, Salvador
Spanish. Poet, Dramatist, Author
Best known for *Setmana Santa,* 1971.
b. 1913 in Catalonia, Spain
d. Feb 22, 1985 in Barcelona, Spain
Source: *AnObit 1985; BioIn 11, 20; CasWL; ClDMEL 80; ConAu 115, 154; ConLC 9; DcLB 134; EncWL 3; ModSpP S; OxCSpan*

Espy, Mike
[Albert Michael Espy]
American. Government Official
Secretary of Agriculture, 1993-94.
b. Nov 30, 1953 in Yazoo City, Mississippi
Source: *AfrAmBi 2; AlmAP 88, 92; BiDrUSC 89; BioIn 15, 16; BlkAmsC; CngDr 87, 89, 91, 93; ConBlB 6; CurBio 93; IntWW 93; NegAl 89A; WhoAm 88, 90, 92, 94, 95, 96; WhoAmP 89, 91, 93, 95; WhoBlA 92; WhoE 95; WhoFI 94; WhoSSW 88, 91, 93; WhoWor 96*

Esquivel, Juan
Mexican. Bandleader, Musician
Debut album, *To Love Again,* 1956; founded live band The Sights and Sounds of Esquivel!, 1962, disbanded, 1974.
b. Jan 20, 1918 in Tamaulipas, Mexico
Source: *ConMus 17; News 96, 96-2*

Essen, Louis
English. Inventor
Invented the Essen quartz ring clock; built the cesium standard atomic clock, 1958, adopted by Britain as the national standard.
b. Sep 6, 1908 in Nottingham, England
Source: *McGMS 80; Who 74, 82, 83, 85, 88, 90, 92, 94*

Essex, David
[David Cook]
English. Singer, Actor
Drummer whose records include "Rock On," 1973; appeared in films *That'll Be the Day,* 1973; *Stardust,* 1975.
b. Jul 23, 1947 in Plaistow, England
Source: *ConTFT 3, 13; EncPR&S 74; EncRk 88; EncRkSt; HalFC 80, 84, 88; HarEnR 86; IlEncRk; IntMPA 75, 76, 77, 78, 79, 80, 81, 82, 84, 86, 88, 92, 94, 96; IntWW 82, 83, 89, 91, 93; LegTOT; OxCPMus; PenEncP; RkOn 74, 78; RolSEnR 83; WhoHol 92, A; WhoRock 81; WhoRocM 82; WhoThe 81*

Esslin, Martin Julius
British. Author
Writings include *The New Theatre of Europe,* 1970.
b. Jun 8, 1918 in Budapest, Hungary
Source: *BiE&WWA; ConAu 27NR, 85; DrAS 82E; IntAu&W 91; LiExTwC; NotNAT; Who 85, 92; WhoAm 84, 90; WhoThe 81; WrDr 92*

Estaing, Charles Henri Hector, Comte d'
French. Naval Officer
Commanded National Guard at Versailles, 1789; testified in favor of Marie Antoinette during her trial; guillotined as a royalist.
b. Nov 28, 1729 in Auvergne, France
d. Apr 28, 1794 in Paris, France
Source: *AmBi; ApCAB; Drake; NewCol 75; WhAm HS*

Estefan, Gloria
[Gloria Estefan and the Miami Sound Machine]
American. Singer
Leading force, principal singer behind Latin-influenced pop band, Miami Sound Machine; first million-selling album *Primitive Love,* 1986.
b. Sep 1, 1957 in Havana, Cuba
Source: *BioIn 16; CelR 90; ConMus 2, 15; CurBio 95; GrLiveH; LegTOT; News 91; WhoHisp 92*

Estes, Billie Sol
American. Financier, Criminal
Called "world's best salesman" for con-man deals made in TX; served several prison terms.
b. 1925
Source: *BioIn 4, 6, 7, 9, 10, 11, 13; EncACr; PolProf K*

Estes, E(lliott) M(arantette)
"Pete"
American. Auto Executive
Pres. of General Motors, 1974-81.
b. Jan 7, 1916 in Mendon, Michigan
d. Mar 24, 1988 in Chicago, Illinois
Source: *AmMWSc 79; AutoN 79; BioIn 7, 10, 11, 12; BioNews 74; BusPN; CurBio 79, 88; Dun&B 79; IntWW 77, 78, 79, 80, 81, 82, 83; Who 85; WhoAm 84; WhoMW 78*

Estes, Eleanor Ruth Rosenfeld
American. Children's Author
Won Newbery Medal for *Ginger Pye,* 1952.
b. May 9, 1906 in West Haven, Connecticut
d. Jul 15, 1988 in Hamden, Connecticut
Source: *AmAu&B; AmNov; AnCL; AuBYP 2; BkCL; ConAu 1R, 5NR; CurBio 46; IlsCB 1946; InWom; JBA 51; REnAL; SmATA 5, 7; Str&VC; WhoAm 84; WrDr 86*

Estes, Richard
American. Artist
Paintings based on photographs, or, photorealism.
b. May 14, 1932 in Kewanee, Illinois
Source: *AmMWSc 73P, 76P, 79, 82, 86, 89, 92; BioIn 21; ConArt 89, 96; CurBio 95; WhoAm 86, 90, 92, 94, 95, 96, 97; WhoAmA 86, 89, 91, 93*

Estes, Simon Lamont
American. Opera Singer
Renowned bass-baritone; made NY Met. debut, 1982; noted for *The Flying Dutchman.*
b. Feb 2, 1938 in Centerville, Iowa
Source: *AfrAmAl 6; Baker 84, 92; BiDAfM; BioIn 13, 14, 15; CurBio 86; DrBlPA; Ebony 1; InB&W 80, 85; MetOEnc; NegAl 83; NewGrDA 86; NewGrDO; NewYTBS 85; WhoAfA 96; WhoAm 86, 88, 90, 92, 94, 95, 96, 97;*

WhoAmM 83; WhoBlA 75, 77, 80, 85, 88, 90, 92, 94; WhoEnt 92; WhoWor 87

Estevanico
Moroccan. Explorer
Led 1538 Spanish expedition into US Southwest.
b. 1500?
d. 1540
Source: *BioIn 9, 10, 11; Expl 93; InB&W 80, 85; WhNaAH; WhWE*

Estevez (de Galvez), Luis
American. Fashion Designer
Known for dress, sportswear, unusual necklines; set up ready-to-wear store, 1955; won Coty, 1956.
b. Dec 5, 1930 in Havana, Cuba
Source: *BioIn 4; ConFash; EncFash; FairDF US; WhoAm 84, 88; WorFshn*

Estevez, Emilio
American. Actor
Son of actor Martin Sheen; films include *The Breakfast Club; St. Elmo's Fire,* 1985.
b. May 12, 1962 in New York, New York
Source: *BioIn 13, 14, 15; CelR 90; ConNews 85-4; ConTFT 3, 10; DcHiB; HalFC 88; HispAmA; IntMPA 92, 94, 96; IntWW 91, 93; LegTOT; MiSFD 9; WhoAm 92, 94, 95, 96, 97; WhoEnt 92; WhoHisp 91, 92, 94; WhoHol 92*

Esther
Hebrew. Biblical Figure
Married king of Persia without him knowing she was a Jew; persuaded him to stop massacre of Jews; holiday of Purim in her honor.
b. fl. 475BC
Source: *BioIn 9, 11; LegTOT*

Estienne, Henri
French. Printer, Scholar
Patriarch of five generations of famed typographers, scholar-printers.
b. 1531? in Paris, France
d. 1598 in Lyons, France
Source: *CasWL; DcBiPP; DcEuL; EuAu; EvEuW; LinLib L; OxCClL; PenC EUR; REn*

Estleman, Loren D
American. Author
Best-selling mysteries feature tough-guy detective, Amos Walker.
b. Sep 15, 1952 in Ann Arbor, Michigan
Source: *BioIn 14; ConAu 27NR, 85; ConLC 48; IntAu&W 89; TwCCr&M 85; WrDr 86, 90*

Estrada, Erik
[Henry Enrique Estrada]
American. Actor
Played Frank "Ponch" Poncherello on TV series "CHiPS," 1977-83.
b. Mar 16, 1949 in New York, New York
Source: *BioIn 12, 13, 14; ConTFT 3; HalFC 88; IntMPA 84, 86, 88, 92, 94, 96; ItaFilm; LegTOT; VarWW 85; WhoAm 82, 84; WhoHisp 91, 92, 94; WhoHol 92; WorAl*

E-Street Band
[Roy Bittan; Clarence Clemons; Daniel Paul Federici; Nils Lofgren; Patty Scialfa; Garry Wayne Tallent; Max M Weinberg]
American. Music Group
Back-up band for Bruce Springsteen.
Source: *ASCAP 80; BioIn 14, 17; ConMuA 80A; IlEncRk; WhoRock 81; WhoRocM 82*

Estrich, Susan
American. Lawyer, Educator
Professor, Harvard U Law School, 1986-90; first woman pres. *Harvard Law Review,* 1975; Pres. candidate Dukakas' campaign manager, 1987, first woman to direct major campaign.
b. Dec 16, 1952 in Lynn, Massachusetts
Source: *BioIn 16; News 89-1; NewYTBS 88; WhoAmL 92; WhoAmW 91*

Estridge, Philip D
American. Businessman
Pioneered development of IBM Personal Computer, 1980s; is currently best-selling personal computer.
b. 1938?
d. Aug 2, 1985 in Dallas, Texas
Source: *NewYTBS 85*

Etchison, Dennis
[William Dennis Etchison; Jack Martin]
American. Educator, Author
Won World Fantasy Award for *Dark Country,* 1983.
b. Mar 30, 1943 in Stockton, California
Source: *BioIn 15; ConAu 115, 118; PenEncH; ScF&FL 92; WhoHr&F*

Etherege, George, Sir
English. Dramatist
Invented comedy of intrigue; wrote witty comedy *Love in a Tub,* 1664.
b. 1635?
d. 1691 in Paris, France
Source: *Alli; AtlBL; BiD&SB; BioIn 1, 2, 3, 4, 5, 9, 10, 12, 15; BritAu; BritWr 2; CamGLE; CasWL; Chambr 2; CrtSuDr; CrtT 2; CyWA 58; DcArts; DcEnA; DcEnL; DcLEL; DcNaB; EvLB; GrWrEL DR; McGEWD 72, 84; MouLC 1; NewC; NewCol 75; NotNAT A, B; OxCEng 67, 85; OxCThe 83; PenC ENG; PlP&P; RAdv 14, 13-2; REn; REnWD; WebE&AL*

Etheridge, Melissa
American. Singer, Musician, Songwriter
Solo acoustic guitarist; Grammy nomination for single "Bring Me Some Water."
b. May 29, 1961 in Leavenworth, Kansas
Source: *BioIn 16; ConMus 4, 16; CurBio 95; EncRkSt; GayLesB; LegTOT; News 95; WhoEnt 92*

Ethridge, Mark Foster
American. Publisher
Manager, publisher of Louisville papers, 1926-63; campaigned against racism, poverty.
b. Apr 22, 1896 in Meridian, Mississippi
d. Apr 5, 1981 in Moncure, North Carolina
Source: *BioIn 1, 2, 12, 19; ConAu 103; CurBio 46, 81; DcLB 127; EncTwCJ; IntWW 74, 75, 76, 77, 78, 79, 80, 81; PolProf T; WhAm 7; WhoAm 74*

Ethridge, Mark Foster, Jr.
American. Journalist
Editor, *Detroit Free Press,* 1966-73, when paper won Pulitzer for riot coverage, 1968; outspoken critic of Vietnam war, advocated black political power.
b. Jul 29, 1924 in New York, New York
d. Mar 1, 1985 in Chapel Hill, North Carolina
Source: *ConAu 115; IntWW 74; WhoAm 74, 76, 78; WhoMW 74*

Ets, Marie Hall
American. Children's Author
Won Caldecott Medal, 1960, for *Nine Days to Christmas.*
b. Dec 16, 1895 in Milwaukee, Wisconsin
Source: *AnCL; Au&ICB; Au&Wr 71; AuBYP 2, 3; BioIn 14; BkP; ChhPo; ConAu 1R, 4NR; DcAmImH; FamAIYP; IlsBYP; IlsCB 1744, 1946, 1957; InWom, SUP; JBA 51; LinLib L; NewbC 1956; OxCChiL; SmATA 2; Str&VC; TwCChW 89; WhAm 8; WhAmArt 85; WhoAm 82; WhoAmA 73, 76, 78, 80, 82, 84; WhoAmW 72, 74; WrDr 76, 86, 90*

Etscorn, Frank
American. Inventor
Invented nicotine patch, Habitrol, to help smokers break their habit.
Source: *BioIn 18*

Etting, Ruth
American. Singer
Popular Ziegfeld, radio star, 1920s-30s; revived "Shine On Harvest Moon"; Doris Day portrayed her in *Love Me Or Leave Me,* 1955.
b. Nov 23, 1897 in David City, Nebraska
d. Sep 24, 1978 in Colorado Springs, Colorado
Source: *AllMusG; BioIn 10, 11, 12; CmpEPM; EncMT; HalFC 80, 84; SaTiSS; What 5; WhoHol A; WhoThe 77A*

Etty, William
English. Artist
Known for figure compositions, mythological scenes: *Deliverance of Bethulia by Judith.*
b. Mar 10, 1787 in York, England
d. Nov 13, 1849 in York, England
Source: *ArtsNiC; BioIn 1, 3, 5, 10, 11, 13; CelCen; ChhPo; DcArts; DcBiPP; DcBrWA; DcNaB; DcVicP, 2; McGDA; NewCol 75; OxCArt; OxDcArt*

Etzioni, Amitai Werner
American. Sociologist
Director, Center for Policy Reserch, 1968-80, Columbia U; professor, George Washington University, 1980—; writings include *The Active Society,* 1968.
b. Jan 4, 1929 in Cologne, Germany
Source: *AmMWSc 73S, 78S; BioIn 10, 11, 12; ConAu 1R, 5NR, 22NR; CurBio 80; IntAu&W 91; PeoHis; WhoAm 74, 76, 78, 80, 82, 84, 86, 88, 90, 92, 94, 95, 96; WhoE 77, 91; WhoFI 92; WhoWorJ 72; WrDr 86, 92*

Eucken, Rudolf Christoph
German. Philosopher, Author
Idealist whose philosophy centered on ethical activism; won Nobel Prize, 1908.
b. Jan 5, 1846 in Aurich, Germany
d. Sep 15, 1926 in Jena, Germany
Source: *BioIn 15; LinLib L; LuthC 75; OxCGer 76; WhoNob; WorAl*

Euclid
Greek. Mathematician
Best known for treatise on geometry; served as basis for textbooks for many centuries.
b. 323?BC
d. 283?BC
Source: *CasWL; NewC; OxCEng 67; PenC CL; REn*

Eugenides, Jeffrey
American. Author
Wrote *The Virgin Suicides,* 1993.
b. 1960? in Grosse Pointe Park, Michigan
Source: *ConAu 144; ConLC 81; WrDr 96*

Eugenie
[Comtessa de Teba; Eugenia Marie de Montijo de Guzman]
French. Ruler
Wife of Napoleon III and empress, 1853-71; fashion trendsetter of her time.
b. May 5, 1826 in Granada, Spain
d. Jul 11, 1920 in Madrid, Spain
Source: *Benet 87, 96; BioIn 1, 4, 5, 6, 7, 8, 10, 11, 12, 13, 15; ContDcW 89; DcBiPP; DcCathB; Dis&D; EncFash; InWom SUP; LegTOT; OxCFr; REn; WebBD 83*

Eugenie, Princess of York
[Eugenie Victoria Helena]
English. Princess
Second child of Duke and Duchess of York—Prince Andrew and Sarah Ferguson; currently sixth in line to British throne.
b. Mar 23, 1990 in London, England
Source: *BioIn 17*

Eulenspiegel, Till
German. Clown
Peasant known for legendary pranks on tradesmen, townspeople throughout Germany; translation of tales first printed in England, 1560.
b. 1290 in Kheitlingen, Germany
d. 1350 in Lubeck, Germany
Source: *NewC; REn*

Euler, Leonhard
Swiss. Mathematician, Physicist
Known for creativity; developed integral calculus, theories of lunar motion, 1753, 1772; wrote first calculus book.
b. Apr 15, 1707 in Basel, Switzerland
d. Sep 18, 1783 in Saint Petersburg, Russia
Source: *AsBiEn; Baker 84, 92; BiDPsy; BiESc; BioIn 2, 4, 5, 9, 12, 13, 14, 16, 20; CamDcSc; CyEd; DcBiPP; DcInv; DcScB; Dis&D; EncEnl; InSci; LarDcSc; LinLib L, S; LuthC 75; McGEWB; NewCol 75; NewGrDM 80; RAdv 14, 13-5; WebBD 83; WhDW; WorAl; WorAlBi; WorScD*

Euler-Chelpin, Hans Karl August Simon von
Swedish. Chemist
Shared Nobel Prize, 1929, for investigation on fermentation of sugar, structure of coenzyme.
b. Feb 15, 1873 in Augsburg, Germany
d. Nov 6, 1964 in Stockholm, Sweden
Source: *BiESc; BioIn 19, 20; DcScB; LarDcSc; WhoNob, 95; WorAl; WorScD*

Euphorion
Greek. Poet, Scholar
Wrote epics about mythological heroes, satirical verse, elegies.
b. 276BC
Source: *CasWL; Grk&L; NewC; OxCClL 89; OxCThe 67; PenC CL; WebBD 83*

Eupolis
Greek. Poet
Comic poet; rival of Aristophanes; 19 titles survive.
b. 445?BC
d. 441?BC
Source: *CasWL; Grk&L; NewCol 75; OxCThe 83*

Eurich, Alvin C(hristian)
American. Educator
First president, SUNY, 1949-51; founder, chairman, Academy for Educational Development, 1961-87.
b. Jun 14, 1902 in Bay City, Michigan
d. May 27, 1987 in New York, New York
Source: *AmMWSc 73S, 78S; BiDAmEd; BioIn 1, 2, 9, 15; BlueB 76; ConAu 17R, 123; CurBio 49, 87, 87N; Future; LEduc 74; St&PR 75, 84, 87; WhAm 9; WhoAm 74, 76, 78, 80, 82, 84, 86; WhoE 74, 75, 77, 79, 81, 83, 85, 86; WhoFI 74, 75, 77, 79, 81, 83, 85, 87; WhoFrS 84; WhoTech 82, 84, 89; WhoWor 74, 76, 78, 80, 82, 84, 87*

Euripides
Greek. Dramatist
Wrote about 90 tragedies, including *Medea; Electra.*
b. Sep 23, 484?BC in Salamis, Greece
d. Nov 30, 406BC in Pella, Greece
Source: *DramC 4; OxCThe 67; PlP&P; WebBD 83*

Europe, James Reese
[William James Reese Europe]
American. Bandleader, Musician
Most renowned black bandleader in New York during the early 20th century; led the 369th Infantry band during the First World War, 1918-19.
b. Feb 22, 1880 in Mobile, Alabama
d. 1919 in Boston, Massachusetts
Source: *ConBlB 10*

Eurythmics
[Annie Lennox; David Stewart]
British. Music Group
Synthesizer-based duo who had number-one hit "Sweet Dreams," 1983; "Missionary Man," 1986.
Source: *Alli, SUP; ArtsEM; BiDLA SUP; BioIn 14, 15, 16, 18, 19, 20, 21; ConAu X; ConMus 6; DcLP 87B; EncPR&S 89; EncRk 88; EncRkSt; HarEnR 86; PenEncP; RkOn 85; WhoReal 83; WrDr 76, 80, 82, 84, 86, 88, 90, 92, 96*

Eusden, Laurence
English. Poet
Poet laureate, 1718-73.
b. 1688 in Spofforth, England
d. Sep 27, 1730 in Coningsby, England
Source: *Alli; BiD&SB; BioIn 3, 15; BritAu; CamGLE; ChhPo; DcBiPP; DcEnA; DcEnL; DcNaB; EvLB; NewC; NewCBEL; OxCEng 67, 85, 95; PenC ENG; PoIre; PoLE*

Eusebius of Caearea
[Eusebius Pamphili]
Greek. Historian
Bishop of Palestine, 314-339; wrote *Chronicle; Ecclesiastical History.*
b. 264?, Palestine
d. 340?
Source: *NewC; NewCol 75; REn*

Eustachio, Bartolomeo
Italian. Scientist
Discovered Eustachian tube leading from ear drum to throat.
b. 1510 in San Severino, Italy
d. Aug 1574 in Rome, Italy
Source: *AsBiEn; BiHiMed; DcBiPP; DcCathB; EncDeaf; InSci; NewCol 75*

Eustis, Dorothy Leib Harrison Wood
American. Philanthropist
Founded Seeing Eye guide dog training schools, 1929.
b. May 30, 1886 in Philadelphia, Pennsylvania
d. Sep 8, 1946 in New York, New York
Source: *DcAmB S4; InWom SUP; LibW; NotAW*

Euwe, Max
[Machgielis Euwe]
American. Chess Player, Educator
World chess champ, 1935-37; pres., International Chess Federation, 1970-78.
b. May 20, 1901 in Amsterdam, Netherlands
d. Nov 26, 1981 in Amsterdam, Netherlands
Source: *AnObit 1981; BioIn 3, 4, 5, 12, 15, 17; ConAu 105; GolEC; IntAu&W 77, 82; NewYTBS 81; OxCChes 84; Who 74, 82; WhoWor 74, 76*

Evangelista, Linda
Canadian. Model
b. Jun 10, 1965, Canada
Source: *LegTOT*

Evans, Arthur John, Sir
English. Archaeologist
Discovered ancient Minoan civilization of Crete, 1898-1935; wrote *The Palace of Minos,* 1921-35.
b. Jul 8, 1851 in Hemel Hempstead, England
d. Jul 11, 1941 in Youlbury, England
Source: *Alli SUP; BioIn 2, 4, 5, 6, 7, 8, 12, 13, 14, 21; CurBio 41; DcLEL; DcNaB 1941; EvLB; GrBr; InSci; LinLib L; LngCTC; McGDA; McGEWB; NewC; OxCEng 67, 85, 95; WhLit*

Evans, Bergen Baldwin
American. Lexicographer, Author
Master of ceremonies on radio, TV shows; wrote *Word A Day Vocabulary Builder,* 1963.
b. Sep 19, 1904 in Franklin, Ohio
d. Feb 4, 1978 in Highland Park, Illinois
Source: *AmAu&B; Au&Wr 71; CelR; ConAu 4NR, 5R, 77; CurBio 55; DcAmB S10; DrAS 74E; LinLib L; NatCAB 60; NewYTET; OhA&B; WhoAm 74; WhoWor 74*

Evans, Bill
[William John Evans]
American. Pianist, Composer
Jazz virtuoso who formed trio, 1956, won five Grammys.
b. Aug 16, 1929 in Plainfield, New Jersey
d. Sep 1, 1980 in New York, New York
Source: *AllMusG; AmCulL; AnObit 1980; Baker 84, 92; BiDAmM; BiDJaz; BioIn 6, 9, 12, 13, 14, 15, 16, 19, 20; ConMus 17; DcAmB S10; EncJzS; FacFETw; IlEncJ; NewAmDM; NewGrDA 86; NewGrDJ 88, 94; NewGrDM 80; NewYTBS 80; OxCPMus; PenEncP; WhAm 7; WhoAm 80; WhoE 74*

Evans, Billy
[William George Evans]
American. Baseball Umpire
At 22, youngest ML umpire ever; wrote *Umpiring from the Inside,* considered authoritative book on profession; Hall of Fame, 1973.
b. Feb 10, 1884 in Chicago, Illinois
d. Jan 23, 1956 in Miami, Florida
Source: *Ballpl 90; BiDAmSp BB; BioIn 4, 18*

Evans, Bob
[Robert L Evans]
American. Restaurateur
Pres., Bob Evans Farms, Inc., 1944-87; known for fresh country sausage sold in grocery stores, restaurants.
b. Mar 30, 1918 in Sugar Ridge, Ohio
Source: *BusPN; ConAu 32NR; Dun&B 86; WhoAm 82, 84; WhoFI 85; WhoMW 88*

Evans, Bob
[Robert Evans]
American. Actor, Producer
Films include *The Godfather,* 1972; *Chinatown,* 1974; former husband of Ali McGraw, Phyllis George.
b. Jun 29, 1930 in New York, New York
Source: *BiDFilm 81, 94; BioIn 5, 8, 10, 11, 12, 13, 16, 17, 19, 20, 21; BusPN; CelR; ConAu 147; ConTFT 6; DcCAr 81; FilmEn; FilmgC; ForYSC; HalFC 80, 84, 88; IntMPA 75, 76, 77, 78, 79, 80, 81, 82, 84, 86, 88, 92, 94, 96; LegTOT; MotPP; VarWW 85; WhoAm 74, 76, 78, 80, 82, 84, 86, 88; WhoHol 92, A*

Evans, Charles
American. Bibliographer, Librarian
Compiled massive *American Bibliography,* from 1901.
b. Nov 13, 1850 in Boston, Massachusetts
d. Feb 8, 1935
Source: *AmAu&B; BioIn 2, 3, 6, 15, 17; CnDAL; DcAmB S1; DcAmLiB; DcNAA; NatCAB 38; OxCAmH; OxCAmL 65, 83, 95; WhAm 1*

Evans, Chick
[Charles Evans, Jr]
American. Golfer, Author
Amateur player; won US Open, 1916; one of only four amateurs in PGA Hall of Fame.
b. Jul 18, 1890 in Indianapolis, Indiana
d. Nov 6, 1979 in Chicago, Illinois
Source: *BiDAmSp OS; BioIn 1, 6, 10, 12; FacFETw; IndAu 1917; NewYTBS 79; WhAm 8; WhoGolf; WhoSpor*

Evans, Clifford
American. Archaeologist, Author
Curator, Smithsonian Institute, 1951-80; wrote on S American archaeology.
b. Jun 13, 1920 in Dallas, Texas
d. Jan 19, 1981
Source: *AmMWSc 73S, 76P; BioIn 6; FifIDA; PeoHis; WhAm 7; WhoAm 74, 76, 78, 80; WhoGov 72, 75, 77; WhoWor 74, 76*

Evans, Dale
[Mrs. Roy Rogers; Frances Smith]
American. Actor, Evangelist
Starred with husband in TV series "The Roy Rogers Show," 1951-64.
b. Oct 31, 1912 in Uvalde, Texas
Source: *AmAu&B; ASCAP 66, 80; BiDAmM; BioIn 1, 3, 4, 5, 8, 9, 10, 11, 12, 13, 14, 15, 16, 18, 19, 20, 21; BioNews 74; CmCal; CmMov; CmpEPM; ConAu 103, 112; CounME 74, 74A; CurBio 56; DcArts; EncACom; EncFCWM 69, 83; FilmEn; FilmgC; ForYSC; HalFC 80, 84, 88; HarEnCM 87; HolP 40; IlEncCM; InWom SUP; LegTOT; MotPP; MovMk; NewGrDA 86; OxCFilm; RadStar; SaTiSS; SweetSg C; WhoAm 74, 76, 78, 80, 82; WhoAmW 58A, 61, 64, 66, 68, 70; WhoHol 92, A; WhoLibS 66; WorAl; WorAlBi; WorEFlm*

Evans, Daniel Jackson
American. Politician
Rep. governor of WA, 1964-76; senator, 1983-89.
b. Oct 16, 1925 in Seattle, Washington
Source: *AlmAP 88; BiDrGov 1789; BiDrUSC 89; BioIn 7, 8, 10, 11, 12, 13, 15; BlueB 76; CngDr 85, 87; IntWW 74, 75, 76, 77, 78, 79, 80, 81, 82, 83, 89, 91, 93; WhoAm 74, 76, 78, 80, 82, 84, 86, 88, 90, 92, 94, 95, 96, 97; WhoAmP 73, 75, 77, 79, 81, 83, 85, 87, 89, 91, 93, 95; WhoGov 72, 75, 77; WhoWest 74, 76, 78, 87, 89, 92; WhoWor 74, 78, 87, 89*

Evans, Darrell Wayne
American. Baseball Player
Infielder, designated hitter, 1969-89; led AL in home runs, 1985; first player in ML history to hit 30 home runs at age 40, 1987.
b. May 26, 1947 in Pasadena, California
Source: *Ballpl 90; BaseReg 86, 87; BiDAmSp Sup; BioIn 14, 15*

Evans, Edith Mary Booth, Dame
English. Actor
Received Oscar nominations for *Chalk Garden,* 1964; *Tom Jones,* 19 63; *The Whisperers,* 1966.
b. Feb 8, 1888 in London, England
d. Oct 14, 1976 in Kent, England
Source: *BioNews 75; CurBio 56, 77N; Film 1; FilmgC; IntMPA 75; IntWW 74; InWom SUP; MotPP; MovMk; NewC; OxCFilm; OxCThe 67; Who 74; WhoAmW 74; WhoHol A; WorAl; WorEFlm*

Evans, Edward Ratcliffe Garth Russell
[First Baron Mountevans]
English. Naval Officer
Admiral of Royal Navy; wrote *Arctic Solitudes,* 1953, books for boys.
b. Oct 28, 1880 in London, England
d. Aug 20, 1957 in Golaa, Norway
Source: *BioIn 14; CurBio 41, 57; DcNaB 1951; GrBr; ObitOF 79; OxCShps; WhLit*

Evans, Geraint Llewellyn, Sir
Welsh. Opera Singer
Leading British baritone; made NY Met. debut in 1964; noted for Figaro role.
b. Feb 16, 1922 in Pontypridd, Wales

d. Sep 19, 1992 in Aberystwyth, Wales
Source: *Baker 84, 92; BioIn 16; BriBkM 80; CmOp; IntWW 74, 75, 76, 77, 78, 79, 80, 81, 82, 83, 89, 91; IntWWM 77, 80, 85, 90; MetOEnc; MusMk; NewGrDM 80; PenDiMP; Who 74, 82, 83, 85, 88, 90, 92; WhoAm 80, 82, 84, 86, 88, 90, 92; WhoEnt 92; WhoMus 72; WhoOp 76; WhoWor 74, 76, 78, 82, 84, 87, 89, 91*

Evans, Gil
Canadian. Composer
Self-taught musician; collaborated with Miles Davis 1948-50, 1957-59; in later years incorporated rock music with electric sound.
b. May 13, 1912 in Toronto, Ontario, Canada
d. Mar 20, 1988 in Cuernavaca, Mexico
Source: *AllMusG; AnObit 1988; Baker 78, 84; BiDAmM; BiDJaz; BioIn 13, 14, 15, 16; CmpEPM; ConAmC 82; ConMus 17; EncJzS; FacFETw; IlEncJ; LegTOT; NewAmDM; NewGrDA 86; NewGrDJ 88, 94; NewGrDM 80; NewYTBS 88; OxCPMus; PenEncP; WhAm 9; WhoAm 80, 82, 84, 86; WhoE 74; WhoWor 74*

Evans, Harold Matthew
English. Author, Editor
Editor, London *Sunday Times,* 1967-81; editorial director, *US News & World Report,* 1984-86.
b. Jun 28, 1928 in Manchester, England
Source: *BioIn 10, 12, 13, 14; BlueB 76; ConAu 41R; CurBio 85; Dun&B 88; IntAu&W 82, 89, 91, 93; IntWW 75, 76, 77, 78, 79, 80, 81, 82, 83, 89, 91, 93; Who 74, 82, 83, 85, 88, 90, 92, 94; WhoAm 86, 88, 90; WhoFI 92; WhoUSWr 88; WhoWor 74, 76, 78; WhoWrEP 89, 92; WrDr 76, 80, 82, 84, 86, 88, 94*

Evans, Heloise Cruse
American. Journalist
Took over mother's nationally syndicated column "Hints from Heloise," 1977—; books include "Heloise's Beauty Book," 1985.
b. Apr 15, 1951 in Waco, Texas
Source: *WhoAm 82*

Evans, Herbert McLean
American. Physician
Authority on pituitary gland, who discovered Vitamin E, 1922.
b. Sep 23, 1882 in Modesto, California
d. Mar 6, 1971 in Berkeley, California
Source: *BioIn 2, 5, 9, 10, 11, 13; CurBio 59, 71, 71N; DcAmB S9; InSci; NatCAB 57; NewYTBE 71; ObitOF 79*

Evans, Janet
American. Swimmer
Won four gold medals, only American to win three golds in three individual events, 1988 Olympics; won gold medal, 1992 Olympics.
b. Aug 28, 1971 in Fullerton, California
Source: *BiDAmSp Sup; BioIn 15, 16; CurBio 96; EncWomS; LegTOT; News 89-1; NewYTBS 90; WhoAm 97; WhoAmW 93, 95, 97; WhoSpor; WhoWor 95, 96; WorAlBi*

Evans, Jerry
American. Director
Directed several soap operas; won Emmys for "Ryan's Hope," 1979, 1980.
b. Jun 14, 1935 in Santa Monica, California
Source: *VarWW 85*

Evans, John
American. Educator, Government Official
Helped found Northwestern U; suburb of Chicago, Evanston, named for him; governor of CO, 1862-65.
b. Mar 9, 1814 in Waynesville, Ohio
d. Jul 3, 1897 in Denver, Colorado
Source: *AmBi; BiDrATG; BioIn 6, 8, 17; DcAmB; DcAmMeB, 84; DcNaB; EncWM; NatCAB 6; OhA&B; OxCLiW 86; REnAW; TwCBDA; WebAB 74, 79; WhAm HS; WhNaAH*

Evans, Joni
American. Publisher
Chairman, Simon & Schuster, 1974-87; publisher, Random House, 1987—.
b. Apr 10, 1942 in New York, New York
Source: *BioIn 14, 15; InWom SUP; News 91; WhoAm 78, 88, 90, 92; WhoAmW 74, 75, 77; WorAlBi*

Evans, Lee
American. Track Athlete
Sprinter; won gold medals in 400-meters, 1,600 meter relay, 1968 Olympics.
b. Feb 25, 1947 in Mandena, California
Source: *AfrAmSG; BioIn 15; ConAu X; InB&W 80; WhoAfA 96; WhoBlA 77, 80, 85, 88, 90, 92, 94; WhoTr&F 73*

Evans, Linda
[Linda Evenstad]
American. Actor
Played Krystle Carrington on TV soap opera "Dynasty," 1981-89.
b. Nov 18, 1942 in Hartford, Connecticut
Source: *BioIn 13, 14, 15, 16, 17, 21; CelR 90; ConTFT 3; CurBio 86; HalFC 88; IntMPA 86, 88, 92, 94, 96; InWom SUP; LegTOT; LesBEnT 92; VarWW 85; WhoAm 86, 88, 90, 92, 94, 95, 96, 97; WhoAmW 87, 89, 91, 93, 95, 97; WhoEnt 92; WhoHol A; WorAlBi*

Evans, Madge
[Margherita Evans]
American. Actor
Child star, 1915; retired, 1938; films include *Dinner at Eight,* 1933.
b. Jul 1, 1909 in New York, New York
d. Apr 26, 1981 in Oakland, New Jersey
Source: *BiE&WWA; BioIn 12; EncAFC; Film 1, 2; FilmEn; FilmgC; ForYSC; HalFC 80, 84, 88; InWom SUP; MGM; MotPP; MovMk; NewYTBS 81; SilFlmP; ThFT; TwYS; WhoHol A; WhScrn 83; WhThe*

Evans, Mark
Australian. Musician
Bass guitarist with AC-DC, 1974-77.
Source: *Alli SUP; BioIn 12; ChhPo S1; ConAu 65; IntWWM 80, 85, 90; SmATA 19; WhoAmM 83; WhoEnt 92; WhoRocM 82; WhoSSW 88; WhoWest 80; WomWMM*

Evans, Maurice
American. Actor, Manager
Played Samantha's father on TV's "Bewitched," 1964-72; starred in *Hamlet,* 1940s.
b. Jun 3, 1901 in Dorchester, England
d. Mar 12, 1989 in Rottingdean, England
Source: *AnObit 1989; BiE&WWA; BioIn 1, 3, 4, 5, 6, 8, 10, 11, 16; BlueB 76; CamGWoT; CnThe; ConTFT 7; CurBio 61, 89N; EncMT; EncWT; FamA&A; FilmEn; FilmgC; ForYSC; HalFC 80, 84, 88; IlWWBF; IntMPA 75, 76, 77, 78, 79, 80, 81, 82, 84, 86, 88; IntWW 74, 75, 76, 77, 78, 79, 80, 81, 82, 83, 89, 89N; LesBEnT, 92; LinLib L, S; MotPP; MovMk; NewC; NewYTBS 89; NewYTET; NotNAT; OxCAmT 84; OxCThe 67; PlP&P; REn; WhAm 10; Who 85, 90N; WhoAm 74, 76, 78; WhoHol A; WhoThe 72, 77, 81; WhoWor 74, 78, 80, 82; WorAl; WorAlBi*

Evans, Mike
[Michael Jonas Evans]
American. Actor
Played Lionel Jefferson on TV series "The Jeffersons."
b. Nov 3, 1949 in Salisbury, North Carolina
Source: *BioIn 9, 12; ConTFT 3; DrBlPA 90; Who 92; WhoAm 76, 78, 80, 82, 84; WhoHol A*

Evans, Oliver
American. Inventor
Constructed first high-pressure steam engine in America, circa 1800.
b. Sep 13, 1755 in New Castle, Delaware
d. Apr 15, 1819 in New York, New York
Source: *Alli; AmBi; ApCAB; BiDAmBL 83; BiInAmS; BioIn 4, 7, 9, 11, 12, 14, 18, 21; DcAmAu; DcAmB; DcBiPP; DcInv; DcNAA; Drake; EncAAH; EncAB-H 1974, 1996; InSci; LarDcSc; LinLib S; McGEWB; NatCAB 6; OxCAmH; TwCBDA; WebAB 74, 79; WhAm HS; WhDW; WorInv*

Evans, Orrin C
American. Journalist
Reporter, *Philadelphia Bulletin;* first black to cover major stories, 1930s; honored by NAACP, 1971.
d. Aug 7, 1971 in Philadelphia, Pennsylvania
Source: *BioIn 9; NewYTBE 71*

Evans, Ray
American. Composer
Won Oscars for songs "Buttons and Bows," 1948; "Mona Lisa," 1950; "Que Sera Sera," 1956.

b. Feb 4, 1915 in Salamanca, New York
Source: *AmPS; AmSong; BiE&WWA; BioIn 14, 15, 16; CmpEPM; ConTFT 1; FilmEn; FilmgC; HalFC 80, 84, 88; IntMPA 75, 76, 77, 78, 79, 80, 81, 82, 84, 86, 88, 92, 94, 96; LegTOT; NotNAT; Sw&Ld C; VarWW 85*

Evans, Richard Louis
American. Broadcaster
Had radio program on CBS, 1932-71; writings include *An Open Road,* 1968.
b. Mar 23, 1906 in Salt Lake City, Utah
d. Nov 1, 1971 in Salt Lake City, Utah
Source: *AmAu&B; BioIn 9, 10; ConAu 9R; NewYTBE 71; WhAm 5*

Evans, Robley Dunglison
"Fighting Bob"
American. Military Leader
Commander-in-chief, Asiatic Station, 1902-04; Atlantic Fleet, 1907-08; wrote *A Sailor's Log,* 1901.
b. Aug 18, 1846 in Floyd County, Virginia
d. Jan 3, 1912
Source: *AmAu&B; AmBi; ApCAB SUP; BioIn 8; DcAmAu; DcAmB; DcAmMiB; DcNAA; LinLib S; TwCBDA; WebAMB; WhAm 1*

Evans, Ronald Ellwin
American. Astronaut
Command module pilot, Apollo 17, last US manned flight to moon.
b. Nov 10, 1933 in Saint Francis, Kansas
d. Apr 7, 1990 in Scottsdale, Arizona
Source: *BioIn 16; Dun&B 86; IntWW 74; NewYTBS 90; St&PR 87; WhoSSW 73, 75*

Evans, Rowland, Jr.
[Evans and Novak]
American. Journalist
Syndicated columnist, 1963—; wrote *The Reagan Revolution,* 1981, with Robert Novak.
b. Apr 28, 1921 in White Marsh, Pennsylvania
Source: *BiDAmNC; BioIn 7, 14; CelR, 90; ConAu 15NR, 21R; EncAJ; EncTwCJ; FacFETw; JrnUS; LegTOT; WhoAm 74, 76, 78, 80, 82, 84, 86, 88, 90, 92, 94, 95, 96, 97; WhoAmP 87, 89, 91, 93, 95; WhoE 89; WhoSSW 73, 75; WhoWor 74; WrDr 76, 80, 82, 84, 86, 88, 90, 92, 94, 96*

Evans, Walker
American. Photographer, Journalist
Writer, photographer, *Fortune* mag., 1945-65, known for pictures of Dep ression Era.
b. Nov 3, 1903 in Saint Louis, Missouri
d. Apr 10, 1975 in New Haven, Connecticut
Source: *AmAu&B; Benet 87, 96; BioIn 1, 4, 7, 9, 10, 11, 12, 13, 15, 16, 19, 21; BriEAA; ConAu 89; ConPhot 82, 88, 95; CurBio 71, 75N; DcAmArt; DcAmB S9; DcArts; DcTwDes; EncAB-H 1974, 1996; EncAJ; EncWB; FacFETw; ICPEnP; LegTOT; MacBEP; NewYTBS 75; WebAB 74, 79; WhAm 6; WhAmArt 85; WhoAm 74; WhoWor 74*

Evarts, William Maxwell
American. Lawyer, Government Official
Chief counsel in Pres. Andrew Johnson's impeachment case, 1868; secretary of State, 1877-81.
b. Feb 6, 1818 in Boston, Massachusetts
d. Feb 28, 1901 in New York, New York
Source: *AmAu&B; AmBi; AmPolLe; ApCAB; BiAUS; BiDrAC; BiDrUSC 89; BiDrUSE 71, 89; BioIn 1, 3, 4, 10, 12, 16; CivWDc; CyAG; DcAmB; DcAmDH 80, 89; DcNAA; Drake; HarEnUS; McGEWB; NatCAB 3, 27; OxCAmH; TwCBDA; WebAB 74, 79; WhAm 1; WhAmP; WhCiWar*

Eve
Biblical Figure
In Bible as the first woman, created from rib of first man, Adam.
Source: *Benet 96; EncEarC; InWom SUP; NewCol 75; Who 92*

Evelyn, John
English. Author
Wrote vivid account of 1640-1706 cultural life in his *Diary,* published, 1818.
b. Oct 31, 1620 in Wotton, England
d. Feb 27, 1706 in Wotton, England
Source: *Alli; AtlBL; BbD; Benet 87, 96; BiD&SB; BiDBrA, A; BioIn 1, 2, 3, 4, 5, 6, 7, 8, 9, 10, 11, 12, 14, 15, 16; BlmGEL; BritAu; BritWr 2; CamGEL; CamGLE; CasWL; Chambr 1; CroE&S; CyEd; CyWA 58; DcArts; DcBiPP; DcEnA; DcEnL; DcEuL; DcLEL; DcNaB; DcPup; DcScB; Dis&D; EvLB; HisDStE; InSci; LinLib L; LngCEL; McGEWB; NewC; NewCBEL; NewGrDM 80; OxCEng 67, 85, 95; OxCMus; PenC ENG; RAdv 1, 13-1; REn; RfGEnL 91; WebE&AL; WhDW*

Evelyn, Judith
American. Actor
Films include *Rear Window,* 1954; *Giant,* 1956; *Brothers Karamazov,* 1958.
b. 1913 in Seneca, South Dakota
d. May 7, 1967 in New York, New York
Source: *BiE&WWA; BioIn 3, 7; FilmgC; ForYSC; HalFC 80, 84, 88; InWom; MotPP; NotNAT B; ObitOF 79; OxCAmT 84; OxCCanT; WhAm 4; WhoHol B; WhScrn 74, 77, 83; WhThe*

Everest, George, Sir
English. Geographer
Surveyor general of India, 1830-43; Mt. Everest named for him.
b. Jul 4, 1790 in Brecknockshire, Wales
d. Dec 1, 1866 in London, England
Source: *BioIn 8, 14, 17; CelCen; DcBiPP; DcInB; DcNaB, C; NewCol 75; WebBD 83*

Everett, Chad
[Raymon Lee Cramton]
American. Actor
Last performer signed to long-term Hollywood contract when he joined MGM, 1964; played Dr. Joe Gannon on TV series "Medical Center," 1969-76; Golden Globe winner.
b. Jun 11, 1937 in South Bend, Indiana
Source: *BioIn 10, 11, 20; ConTFT 3; FilmgC; HalFC 80, 84, 88; IntMPA 86, 92, 94, 96; LegTOT; MovMk; WhoAm 74, 76, 78, 80, 82; WhoEnt 92; WhoHol A; WorAl; WorAlBi*

Everett, Edward
American. Clergy, Statesman
Co-speaker at dedication of Gettysburg National Cemetery, 1863; pres., Harvard U, 1846-49.
b. Apr 11, 1794 in Dorchester, Massachusetts
d. Jan 15, 1865 in Boston, Massachusetts
Source: *Alli, SUP; AmAu; AmAu&B; AmBi; AmOrN; AmPolLe; ApCAB; BbD; BenetAL 91; BiAUS; BiD&SB; BiDrAC; BiDrGov 1789; BiDrUSC 89; BiDrUSE 71, 89; BiDTran; BioIn 3, 4, 7, 9, 10, 11, 16, 18; CelCen; CivWDc; CyAG; CyAL 1; CyEd; DcAmAu; DcAmB; DcAmDH 80, 89; DcBiPP; DcEnL; DcLB 1, 59; DcNAA; Drake; HarEnUS; LinLib L, S; McGEWB; NatCAB 1, 6; OxCAmH; OxCAmL 65, 83, 95; PenC AM; PeoHis; PresAR; REnAL; TwCBDA; WebAB 74, 79; WhAm HS; WhAmP; WhCiWar*

Evergood, Philip (Howard Francis Dixon)
American. Artist
Produced realistic murals of Depression Era; noted for satiric pictures dealing with social causes.
b. Oct 26, 1901 in New York, New York
d. Mar 11, 1973 in Bridgewater, Connecticut
Source: *BioIn 1, 2, 4, 5, 6, 7, 9, 10, 11, 12, 15, 17; BriEAA; ConArt 83, 89; ConAu 41R; CurBio 44, 60, 73, 73N; DcAmArt; DcCAA 71, 77, 88, 94; EncAL; FacFETw; McGDA; McGEWB; NewYTBE 73; OxCTwCA; OxDcArt; PhDcTCA 77; WhAm 5; WhAmArt 85; WhoAmA 73, 76N, 78N, 80N, 82N, 84N, 86N, 89N, 91N, 93N; WorArt 1950*

Everleigh, Ada
"The Scarlet Sisters"
American. Madam
Known in Chicago for expensive, high-class bordello, 1900s.
b. Feb 15, 1876 in Louisville, Kentucky
d. Jan 3, 1960 in Roanoke, Virginia
Source: *BiDAmBL 83; DcAmB S4; InWom SUP; LibW*

Everleigh, Minna
"The Scarlet Sisters"
American. Madam
Known in Chicago for expensive bordello that was virtually a city landmark.

b. Jul 5, 1878 in Louisville, Kentucky
d. Sep 16, 1948 in New York, New York
Source: *BiDAmBL 83; DcAmB S4; DcAmNB; InWom SUP; LibW; NotAW*

Everly, Don(ald)
[Everly Brothers]
American. Singer, Musician
With brother Phil, had international country hit, "Bye Bye Love," 1957.
b. Feb 1, 1937 in Brownie, Kentucky
Source: *ASCAP 80; Baker 84, 92; BiDAmM; BioIn 12, 13, 14, 15, 16; ConMus 2; CounME 74; EncPR&S 89; IlEncCM; LegTOT; NewAmDM; OxCPMus; WhoRocM 82; WorAl; WorAlBi*

Everly, Phil
[Everly Brothers]
American. Singer, Musician
With brother Don, had two million-selling single, "Cathy's Clown," 1962.
b. Jan 19, 1939 in Chicago, Illinois
Source: *BiDAmM; BioIn 12, 13, 14, 15, 16; ConMus 2; CounME 74; EncPR&S 89; IlEncCM; NewAmDM; OxCPMus; RkOn 74; WhoRocM 82; WorAl; WorAlBi*

Everly Brothers
[Don Everly; Phil Everly]
American. Music Group
Hits include "Wake Up Little Susie," 1957; "Let it Be Me," 1960; disbanded, 1973, reunited, 1983; Rock and Roll Hall of Fame, 1986.
Source: *AmPS A, B; BgBkCoM; BioIn 14, 15, 16, 17, 21; ConMuA 80A; ConMus 2; CounME 74, 74A; DcArts; EncFCWM 69, 83; EncPR&S 74, 89; EncRk 88; EncRkSt; HarEnCM 87; HarEnR 86; IlEncCM; IlEncRk; NewAmDM; NewGrDA 86; OxCPMus; PenEncP; RkOn 74; RolSEnR 83; WhoNeCM C; WhoRock 81; WhoRocM 82; WorAl; WorAlBi*

Evers, James Charles
American. Civil Rights Leader
First black mayor of Fayette, MS, 1969; ran unsuccessfully for governor, 1971; brother of Medgar.
b. Sep 11, 1923 in Decatur, Mississippi
Source: *CurBio 69; InB&W 85; NewYTBE 70; WebAB 74; WhoAmP 91; WhoBlA 92; WorAlBi*

Evers, Jason
American. Actor
In film *Escape from the Planet of the Apes* ; TV shows "Wrangler," 1960; "Channing," 1963-64.
b. Jan 2, 1927 in New York, New York
Source: *HalFC 88; WhoAm 74, 76; WhoHol 92, A*

Evers, Johnny
[John Joseph Evers]
"The Crab"; "The Trojan"
American. Baseball Player
Second baseman, 1902-17; part of Tinker to Evers to Chance double play combination; Hall of Fame, 1946.
b. Jul 21, 1881 in Troy, New York
d. Mar 28, 1947 in Albany, New York
Source: *BiDAmSp BB; BioIn 1, 3, 7, 10; WhoProB 73; WhoSpor*

Evers, Medgar Wiley
American. Civil Rights Leader
Brother of Charles; shot to death in front of home; became martyr for civil rights cause; awarded 1963 Spingarn Medal.
b. Jul 19, 1925 in Decatur, Mississippi
d. Jun 12, 1963 in Jackson, Mississippi
Source: *BioIn 6, 7, 8, 11, 12, 15, 16, 17, 18, 19, 20, 21; ConBlB 3; ConHero 1; DcAmB S7; DcAmNB; InB&W 80, 85; LinLib S; WebAB 74, 79*

Everson, William Oliver
[Brother Antoninus]
American. Poet
Writings include *The Masculine Dead: Poems 1938-40,* 1942; *Waldport Poems,* 1944.
b. Sep 10, 1912 in Sacramento, California
d. Jun 3, 1994 in Santa Cruz, California
Source: *AmAu&B; BenetAL 91; BioIn 8, 10, 12, 13, 16; ConAu 9R, 20NR, X; ConLC 1, 5; ConPo 70, 75, 85, 91; DcLP 87A; DrAP 75; DrAPF 80, 87, 91; IntAu&W 91, 93; IntvTCA 2; IntWWP 77; MajTwCW; OxCAmL 65; PenC AM; PeoHis; RAdv 1; WhAm 11; WhoAm 80, 82, 84, 86, 88, 90, 92, 94; WhoWest 82, 84; WhoWor 89, 91; WorAu 1950; WrDr 76, 86, 92, 94*

Evers-Williams, Myrlie
[Mrs. Medgar Evers]
American. Civil Rights Activist
Chm., NAACP, 1995—.
b. Mar 17, 1933 in Vicksburg, Mississippi
Source: *CurBio 95; News 95; NewYTBS 95; WhoAm 96, 97; WhoAmW 95, 97*

Evert, Chris(tine Marie)
[Mrs. Andy Mill]
American. Tennis Player
Number one female tennis player, 1974-78, 1980-81; won 18 Grand Slam singles titles; first woman to reach $1 million in career tournament earnings.
b. Dec 21, 1954 in Fort Lauderdale, Florida
Source: *BioIn 9, 10, 11, 15, 16; BkPepl; BuCMET; CelR, 90; CurBio 73; EncWomS; FacFETw; GoodHs; GrLiveH; HerW, 84; IntWW 91; InWom SUP; LegTOT; LibW; NewYTBE 72, 73; NewYTBS 74; Who 94; WhoAm 74, 76, 78, 80, 82, 86, 88, 90, 92, 94, 95, 96, 97; WhoAmW 79, 81, 83, 85, 87, 89, 91, 93, 95, 97; WhoWor 78, 80, 87, 89, 91, 93, 95, 96, 97; WorAl; WorAlBi*

Everything But The Girl
[Tracey Thorn; Ben Watt]
English. Music Group
Released albums *Eden,* 1984; *Amplified Heart,* 1994.
Source: *ConMus 15; EncRk 88; EncRkSt; News 96; PenEncP*

Evigan, Greg(ory Ralph)
American. Actor
Starred in TV series "BJ and the Bear," 1979-81, "My Two Dads," 1987-90.
b. Oct 14, 1953 in South Amboy, New Jersey
Source: *BioIn 12, 16; ConTFT 7, 15; IntMPA 94, 96; LegTOT; WhoAm 80, 82, 95, 96, 97*

Evinrude, Ole
American. Inventor, Manufacturer
Built first motor to propel rowboat, 1907; pres., Outboard Marine Corp., 1909-34.
b. Apr 19, 1877 in Christiania, Norway
d. Jul 12, 1934 in Milwaukee, Wisconsin
Source: *BioIn 5, 6, 7, 11, 16, 18, 21; EncAB-A 5; Entr; WorInv*

Evins, David
American. Designer
Well-known shoe designer who won special Coty, 1949; founding member, Council of Fashion Designers of America.
Source: *BioIn 17; NewYTBS 91; WorFshn*

Evren, Kenan
Turkish. Army Officer, Political Leader
Head of Turkish militia who led coup deposing civilian govt., Sep 1980.
b. 1918 in Alasehir, Turkey
Source: *BioIn 12, 13, 14; CurBio 84; FacFETw; IntWW 81, 82, 83, 89, 91, 93; IntYB 81, 82; MidE 80, 81, 82; NewYTBS 80; WhoWor 82, 84, 87, 89, 91*

Evtushenko, Evgeniy Alexandrovich
[Yevgeni Alexandrovich Yevtushenko]
Russian. Poet
Post-Stalin writer who wrote anti-semetic poem *Babi Yar,* 1961.
b. Jul 18, 1933 in Zima, Union of Soviet Socialist Republics
Source: *BiDSovU; BioIn 13; CasWL; ConFLW 84; ConLC 1, 3; DcRusLS; EncWL; EvEuW; HanRL; IntWW 76; IntWWP 77; ModSL 1; PenC EUR; RAdv 13-2; REn; WhoSocC 78; WhoTwCL; WorAu 1950*

Ewald, Johannes
Danish. Poet, Dramatist
Prompted interest in national legends; wrote Danish national anthem, 1779.
b. Nov 18, 1743 in Copenhagen, Denmark
d. Mar 17, 1781 in Copenhagen, Denmark

Source: *BbD; BiD&SB; BioIn 7; CasWL; CnThe; DcEuL; DcScanL; EuAu; EvEuW; LinLib L; NotNAT B; OxCThe 67, 83; PenC EUR; REn; REnWD; WhDW*

Ewbank, Weeb
[Wilbur Charles Ewbank]
American. Football Coach
Spent 22 yrs. in NFL as head coach; best known as coach, NY Jets, 1963-73, for upset Super Bowl win, 1969.
b. May 6, 1907 in Richmond, Indiana
Source: *BiDAmSp FB; BioIn 5, 8, 9, 10, 17; BioNews 75; CelR; CurBio 69; LegTOT; WhoAm 74, 76; WhoE 74; WhoFtbl 74; WhoSpor; WorAl; WorAlBi*

Ewell, Tom
[Yewell Tompkins]
American. Actor
Films include *Adam's Rib,* 1949; *The Seven Year Itch,* 1955.
b. Apr 29, 1909 in Owensboro, Kentucky
d. Sep 12, 1994 in Woodland Hills, California
Source: *BiE&WWA; BioIn 3, 5, 6, 20; BlueB 76; ConTFT 4, 13; CurBio 61, 94N; EncAFC; FilmEn; FilmgC; ForYSC; Funs; HalFC 80, 84, 88; IntMPA 77, 86, 88, 92, 94; LegTOT; MotPP; MovMk; NewYTBE 71; NotNAT; OxCAmT 84; QDrFCA 92; WhoAm 74, 76, 78, 80, 82; WhoHol 92, A; WhoThe 72, 77, 81; WorAl; WorAlBi; WorEFlm*

Ewen, David
American. Author
Numerous books on music, musicians include *Opera,* 1972.
b. Dec 6, 1907 in Lemberg, Austria
Source: *AmAu&B; Au&Wr 71; AuBYP 2, 3; Baker 78, 84, 92; BiE&WWA; BioIn 8, 9, 10, 14, 16; ConAu 1R, 2NR, 118; IntAu&W 77; NewGrDA 86; NewGrDM 80; NewGrDO; OxCAmT 84; REnAL; SmATA 4, 47N; WhAm 9; WhE&EA; WhoAm 74, 76, 78, 80, 82, 84, 86; WhoMus 72; WhoSSW 73, 75; WhoWor 74, 76; WhoWorJ 72, 78; WrDr 76, 80, 82, 84, 86*

Ewen, Frederic
American. Author
Writings include *The Magic Mountain,* 1967; *The Unknown Chekhov,* 1968.
b. Oct 11, 1899 in Lemberg, Austria
Source: *BioIn 16; ConAu 73, 126; IntAu&W 77, 82; NewYTBS 88; WhAm 9; WhoAm 74, 76; WhoWor 74, 76; WrDr 76, 80, 82, 84, 86, 88*

Ewing, Alfred Cyril
English. Author
Writings include *Idealism: A Critical Survey,* 1934.
b. May 11, 1899 in Leicester, England
d. May 1973 in Manchester, England
Source: *Au&Wr 71; ConAu 4NR, 5R; WhAm 6; WhE&EA; WhoWor 74*

Ewing, Buck
[William Ewing]
American. Baseball Player
Greatest catcher of time, 1880-97; Hall of Fame, 1939.
b. Oct 27, 1859 in Hoaglands, Ohio
d. Oct 20, 1906 in Cincinnati, Ohio
Source: *Ballpl 90; BioIn 3, 4, 7, 8, 14, 15, 16, 18, 20; WhoProB 73; WhoSpor*

Ewing, Julianna Horatia (Gatty)
English. Children's Author
Wrote classic tale *Jackanapes,* 1884.
b. Aug 3, 1841 in Ecclesfield, England
d. May 13, 1885 in Bath, England
Source: *BbD; BiD&SB; BritAu 19; CarSB; CasWL; CelCen; DcCanB 11; DcLEL; EvLB; FamSYP; NewC; OxCEng 67; Str&VC; WhoChL*

Ewing, Maria Louise
American. Opera Singer
Soprano opera and concert performer in US, Europe and Japan; repertoire includes frequent performances of Carmen and Salome.
b. Mar 27, 1950 in Detroit, Michigan
Source: *Baker 84; BioIn 11, 12, 13, 14, 16; CurBio 90; InB&W 85; IntWW 91; IntWWM 90; MetOEnc; NewAmDM; NewGrDA 86; PenDiMP; WhoAm 90; WhoAmM 83; WhoEnt 92*

Ewing, Patrick Aloysius
American. Basketball Player
Center, NY Knicks, 1985—; highest paid rookie in NBA history; rookie of year, 1986; part of 1992 Olympic Dream Team.
b. Aug 5, 1962 in Kingston, Jamaica
Source: *BiDAmSp BK; BioIn 13, 14, 15, 16; BlkOlyM; ConNews 85-3; CurBio 91; NewYTBS 80, 82, 84, 85; OfNBA 87; WhoAm 90, 94, 95, 96, 97; WhoBlA 85, 92; WhoE 95; WhoWor 95, 96, 97; WorAlBi*

Ewing, William Maurice
American. Educator, Scientist
Designed SOFAR system which is used to rescue people lost at sea.
b. May 12, 1906 in Lockney, Texas
d. May 4, 1974 in Galveston, Texas
Source: *AsBiEn; Au&Wr 71; BiESc; BioIn 2, 3, 5, 6; CamDcSc; CurBio 53; DcAmB S9; DcScB S2; FacFETw; InSci; McGEWB; McGMS 80; WorAl; WorAlBi; WorScD*

Ewry, Ray C
American. Track Athlete
Winner of eight gold medals in individual events in the 1900, 1904, 1908 Olympics.
b. Oct 14, 1873 in Lafayette, Indiana
d. Sep 29, 1937 in Douglaston, New York
Source: *BioIn 3, 5, 8; WebAB 74, 79; WorAlBi*

Exile
[Buzz Cornelison; Steven Goetzman; Mark Gray; Marlon Hargis; Sonny Lemaire; J P Pennington; Jimmy Stokley; Les Taylor]
American. Music Group
Country group from KY; had number one hit "Kiss You All Over," 1978.
Source: *BgBkCoM; HarEnCM 87; RkOn 85; WhLit; WhoRocM 82; WhsNW 85*

Exley, Frederick (Earl)
American. Writer
Wrote acclaimed trilogy: *A Fan's Notes,* 1968; *Pages from a Cold Island,* 1975; *Last Notes from Home,* 1988.
b. Mar 28, 1929 in Watertown, New York
d. Jun 17, 1992 in Alexandria Bay, New York
Source: *AnObit 1992; BioIn 10, 11, 13, 16; ConAu 81, 138; ConLC 6, 11, 76; CurBio 89, 92N; DcLB 143, Y81B; DrAPF 91; PostFic; RGTwCWr; WorAu 1985*

Exner, Judith Campbell
[Judith Eileen Katherine Immoor]
American.
Alleged mistress of JFK; mobster Sam Giancana; wrote *My Story,* 1977.
b. Jan 11, 1934 in Pacific Palisades, California
Source: *BioIn 10, 11, 12, 16*

Exon, (John) James, (Jr.)
American. Politician
Dem. senator from NE, 1979-97; governor, 1971-79.
b. Aug 9, 1921 in Geddes, South Dakota
Source: *AlmAP 80, 92; BiDrGov 1789, 1978; BiDrUSC 89; BioIn 10; CngDr 79, 81, 83, 87, 89; CurBio 96; IntWW 74, 75, 76, 77, 78, 79, 80, 81, 82, 83, 89, 91; IntYB 78, 79, 80, 81, 82; PolsAm 84; WhoAm 74, 76, 78, 80, 82, 84, 86, 88, 90, 92, 94, 95, 96, 97; WhoAmP 73, 75, 77, 79, 81, 83, 85, 91; WhoE 95; WhoGov 77; WhoMW 76, 88, 90, 92, 93, 96; WhoWor 74, 78, 80, 82, 84, 87, 89, 91*

Expose
American. Music Group
Pop vocal group; album *Exposure,* 1986, broke the Beatles record for the most Top 10 singles from a first album, including single "Come Go With Me."
Source: *ConMus 4*

Eyadema, Etienne Gnassingbe
Togolese. Political Leader
Seized power, 1967; elected head of Togo, 1981—.
b. Dec 26, 1937 in Pya, Togo
Source: *AfSS 82; BioIn 14, 15; DcAfHiB 86; IntWW 83, 91; IntYB 82; WhoAfr; WhoGov 75; WhoWor 80, 82, 84, 87, 89, 91, 93, 95, 96, 97*

Eyen, Tom
American. Dramatist, Director
Won Tony, 1982, for play *Dreamgirls.*
b. Aug 14, 1941 in Cambridge, Ohio
d. May 26, 1991 in Palm Beach, Florida
Source: *AnObit 1991; ConAu 22NR, 25R, 134; ConDr 77, 82, 88, 93; ConLC 70; ConTFT 1, 3, 10; IntAu&W 91, 93; NatPD 77; NewYTBS 91; WhAm 10; WhoAm 74, 76, 78, 80, 82, 84, 86, 88; WhoThe 72, 77, 81; WrDr 82, 84, 86, 88, 90*

Eyre, Edward John
English. Explorer
Explored southern Australia; Lake Eyre and the Eyre Peninsula are named for him.
b. Aug 5, 1815 in Hornsea, England
d. Nov 30, 1901 in Tavistock, England
Source: *ApCAB; BioIn 2, 3, 6, 7, 8, 9, 10, 11, 13, 14, 16, 18, 20; CelCen; DcNaB S2; Expl 93; HisDBrE; McGEWB; NewCBEL; OxCAusL; VicBrit; WhDW; WhWE*

Eysenck, Hans Jurgen
German. Author
Books on psychology, psychotherapy include *Sex, Violence and the Media,* 1978.
b. Mar 14, 1916 in Berlin, Germany
Source: *Au&Wr 71; BioIn 9, 11, 12, 14; BlueB 76; ConAu 4NR, 9R, 25NR; CurBio 72; EncO&P 3; EncPaPR 91; IntAu&W 76, 77, 82, 91; IntMed 80; IntWW 74, 75, 76, 77, 78, 79, 80, 81, 82, 83, 89, 91, 93; MakMC; Who 74, 82, 83, 85, 88, 90, 92, 94; WhoWor 74, 76, 78, 84, 87, 89, 91, 93, 95, 96, 97; WrDr 76, 92*

Eyskens, Gaston, Viscou, Viscount
Belgian. Political Leader
Prime minister of Belgium, 1949, 1958-61, 1968-72.
b. Apr 1, 1905 in Lier, Belgium
d. Jan 3, 1988 in Louvain, Belgium
Source: *AnObit 1988; BioIn 2, 5, 8, 15, 16; CurBio 49, 88, 88N; FacFETw; IntWW 74, 75, 76, 77, 78, 79, 80, 81, 82, 83; IntYB 78, 79, 80, 81, 82; WhoGov 72, 75; WhoWor 74, 76, 78*

Ezekiel
Prophet
Major Hebrew prophet; foretold coming of a messiah, restoration of Jewish ki ngdom, c.586 BC.
Source: *Benet 87, 96; BioIn 1, 2, 3, 4, 7, 10, 17; DcBiPP; DcOrL 3; Dis&D; EncEarC; LegTOT; McGEWB; REn; UFOEn; WhDW*

Ezekiel, Moses Jacob
American. Sculptor
Largely idealized busts include those of Eve, Homer, Christ in the Tomb; also did Arlington National Cemetery's Confederate Monument.
b. Oct 28, 1844 in Richmond, Virginia
d. Mar 27, 1917 in Rome, Italy
Source: *AmBi; ApCAB; ArtsNiC; BioIn 5, 8, 10; DcAmArt; DcAmB; NatCAB 18; TwCBDA; WebBD 83; WhAm 1*

Ezra
Clergy
Shaped ritual of modern Judaism; wrote Book of Ezra, Chronicles I, II in Old Testament.
Source: *Benet 96; BioIn 1, 4, 5, 7, 17; DcOrL 3; EncEarC; McGEWB; NewCol 75; ScF&FL 1; Who 90, 92*

F

Faas, Horst
German. Photographer
Photographer in Vietnam; won Pulitzer for spot news photography, 1972.
b. Apr 28, 1933 in Berlin, Germany
Source: *BioIn 8, 9; WhoAm 74, 76; WhoWor 74*

Fabares, Shelley Michelle Marie
[Mrs. Mike Farrell]
American. Actor, Singer
Played Mary on "The Donna Reed Show," 1958-66; had hit single "Johnny Angel," 1962; appeared with Elvis Presley in *Girl Happy,* 1965, *Clambake,* 1967; plays "Christine" on *Coach,* 1989—.
b. Jan 19, 1944 in Santa Monica, California
Source: *AmPS A; ConTFT 6; FilmgC; HalFC 84, 88; IntMPA 92; RkOn 74, 82; WhoEnt 92; WhoHol A*

Faber, Geoffrey Cust, Sir
English. Publisher, Author
Founded Faber and Faber Publishers, 1927; wrote *Oxford Apostles,* 1933.
b. Aug 23, 1889 in Malvern, England
d. Mar 31, 1961 in Midhurst, England
Source: *BioIn 3, 5, 14, 18; ChhPo, S2; DcNaB 1961; GrBr; NewC; ObitOF 79; ObitT 1961; ScF&FL 1; WhE&EA*

Faber, Red
[Urban Charles Faber]
American. Baseball Player
Pitcher, Chicago White Sox, 1914-33; had four 20-game seasons; Hall of Fame, 1964.
b. Sep 6, 1888 in Cascade, Iowa
d. Sep 25, 1976 in Chicago, Illinois
Source: *Ballpl 90; BioIn 2, 3, 7, 14, 15; LegTOT; WhoProB 73; WhoSpor*

Faberge, Peter Carl
[Karl Gustavovich Faberge]
Russian. Jeweler
Known for lavish Easter eggs designed for czar's court; name lent to cosmetics firm, 1930s.
b. May 18, 1846 in Saint Petersburg, Russia
d. Sep 24, 1920 in Lausanne, Switzerland
Source: *BiDSovU; BioIn 14, 15, 17, 20; DcArts; DcD&D; DcNiCA; Entr; LegTOT; OxCDecA; PenDiDA 89; WorAl; WorAlBi*

Fabi, Teo
Italian. Auto Racer
First rookie in 34 yrs. to win pole position at Indianapolis 500, 1984.
b. 1954? in Milan, Italy
Source: *BioIn 13, 14; NewYTBS 84*

Fabian
[Fabian Forte]
American. Singer, Actor
Teen idol of 1950-60s; 1959 hits include "Turn Me Loose"; "Hound Dog Man."
b. Feb 6, 1943 in Philadelphia, Pennsylvania
Source: *AuBYP 3; BiDAmM; BioIn 13; ConMus 5; EncEarC; EncPR&S 89; EncRk 88; EncRkSt; FilmgC; ForYSC; HalFC 84, 88; HarEnR 86; IntMPA 82, 88, 92, 94, 96; LegTOT; MotPP; PenEncP; RkOn 74; RolSEnR 83; WhoHol A; WhoRocM 82; WorAl; WorAlBi*

Fabian, Robert Honey
English. Detective
With New Scotland Yard, 1923-49; wrote *Fabian of the Yard,* 1950; *London after Dark,* 1954, which were made into TV shorts.
b. Jan 31, 1901 in Ladywell, England
d. Jun 14, 1978 in Epsom, England
Source: *ConAu 77, 81; CurBio 54, 78; NewYTBS 78*

Fabio
[Fabio Lanzoni]
Italian. Model
Posed for the covers of over 350 romance novels in the US; known for mane of long blond hair and bulging muscles.
b. Mar 15, 1961 in Milan, Italy
Source: *LegTOT; News 93; WhoAm 95, 96, 97*

Fabiola, Queen
Belgian.
Wife of King Baudouin of Belgium.
b. Jun 11, 1928
Source: *BioIn 5, 6, 10; InWom SUP; WhoWor 74, 76*

Fabius, Laurent
French. Political Leader
Conservative prime minister, 1984-86, who aimed to modernize France; first Sec., Socialist Party, 1992—.
b. Aug 20, 1946 in Paris, France
Source: *BiDFrPL; BioIn 13, 14, 16; CurBio 85; EncWB; IntWW 82, 83, 89, 91, 93; NewYTBS 84; Who 88, 90, 92, 94; WhoFr 79; WhoWor 84, 87, 95, 96, 97*

Fabray, Nanette
[Ruby Nanette Fabares]
American. Actor
Veteran of stage, screen, TV; won Tony for *Love Life,* 1949, Emmy for best comedienne, 1955, 1956; active in handicapped affairs.
b. Oct 27, 1920 in San Diego, California
Source: *BiDAmM; BiDD; BiE&WWA; BioIn 17; ConTFT 4; CurBio 56; EncAFC; EncMT; Film 2; FilmEn; FilmgC; ForYSC; HalFC 80, 84, 88; IntMPA 75, 76, 77, 78, 79, 80, 81, 82, 84, 86, 88, 92, 94, 96; InWom SUP; LegTOT; MotPP; NotNAT; WhoAm 86, 88; WhoAmW 58, 61, 64, 66, 68, 70, 72, 87, 89; WhoHol 92, A; WhoThe 72, 77; WorAl; WorAlBi*

Fabre, Jean Henri
French. Author, Scientist
Studied insect behavior; wrote *The Marvels of the Insect World,* 1938.
b. Dec 22, 1823 in Saint-Leons, France
d. Oct 11, 1915 in Serigran, France
Source: *AnCL; BiDPsy; BiESc; BioIn 5, 6, 8, 9, 11; CamDcSc; DcScB; Dis&D; InSci; JBA 34, 51; LarDcSc; LinLib L,*

S; LngCTC; NamesHP; OxCFr; RAdv 14, 13-5; REn; SmATA 22

Fabri, Zoltan
Hungarian. Director
Films include *The Fifth Seal,* 1976; *Hungarians,* 1978.
b. Oct 15, 1917 in Budapest, Austria-Hungary
Source: *BioIn 16; DcFM; DrEEuF; FilmEn; FilmgC; HalFC 80, 84, 88; IntDcF 1-2, 2-2; IntWW 74, 75, 76, 77, 78, 79, 80, 81, 82, 83, 89, 91, 93; MiSFD 9; OxCFilm; WhoSocC 78; WhoSoCE 89; WhoWor 74; WorEFlm; WorFDir 2*

Fabricius, Hieronymus ab Aquapendente
Italian. Surgeon
First demonstrated valves in veins, which gave rise to study of blood circulation.
b. 1537 in Aquapendente, Italy
d. 1619
Source: *BiHiMed; BioIn 1, 7, 9; LinLib S; NewCol 75*

Fabritius, Carel
Dutch. Artist
Student of Rembrandt, influenced by Vermeer; paintings include *A View of Delft,* 1652; *The Goldfinch,* 1654.
b. 1622, Netherlands
d. Oct 12, 1654 in Delft, Netherlands
Source: *AtlBL; BioIn 10, 12; DcArts; IntDcAA 90; McGDA; OxCArt; OxDcArt*

Fabrizi, Aldo
Italian. Actor
Best known role in Rossellini's *Open City,* 1945.
b. 1905 in Rome, Italy
Source: *AnObit 1990; BioIn 16, 17; EncEurC; FilmEn; FilmgC; HalFC 80, 84, 88; IntDcF 1-3, 2-3; IntMPA 77, 80, 81, 82, 88; ItaFilm; MovMk; NewYTBS 90; WhoHol A*

Fabry, Charles
French. Physicist
Discovered Earth's ozone layer, which filters out dangerous solar ultraviolet radiation.
b. Jun 11, 1867 in Marseilles, France
d. Dec 11, 1945 in Paris, France
Source: *AsBiEn; BioIn 1, 8, 10, 14; DcScB*

Fabulous Thunderbirds, The
American. Music Group
Blues band whose albums include *Tuff Enuff,* 1986; *Hot Number,* 1987; current members listed above.
Source: *ConMus 1; PenEncP; WhoRocM 82; WhsNW 85*

Face, Roy
[Elroy Leon Face]
American. Baseball Player
Relief pitcher, 1953-69; had 189 career saves; holds ML record for highest winning percentage, .947, 1959.
b. Feb 20, 1928 in Stephentown, New York
Source: *Ballpl 90; BiDAmSp BB; BioIn 15, 17; WhoProB 73*

Faces, The
[Kenney Jones; Ronnie Lane; Ian MacLagan; Rod Stewart; Ron Wood]
British. Music Group
High energy rock band, formed 1968; hit singles include Stay With Me, 1971.
Source: *BiDAmM; BioIn 14, 15, 16, 17, 20; ConMuA 80A; EncPR&S 89; EncRk 88; EncRkSt; HarEnR 86; IlEncRk; OxCPMus; PenEncP; RkOn 78, 84; RolSEnR 83; WhoRock 81; WhoRocM 82*

Factor, Max
American. Cosmetics Executive
Began career as makeup artist; later established own cosmetic co.
b. 1877 in Lodz, Poland
d. Aug 30, 1938 in Beverly Hills, California
Source: *BioIn 9; CmCal; Entr; WhoAm 74, 76; WhoWor 74*

Factor, Max, Jr.
[Francis Factor, Jr.]
American. Cosmetics Executive
Inventor of waterproof mascara, son of the founder of Max Factor cosmetics.
b. Aug 18, 1904 in Saint Louis, Missouri
d. Jun 7, 1996 in Los Angeles, California
Source: *News 96; NewYTBS 27; WhoAm 74, 76; WhoWor 74*

Faderman, Lillian
American. Writer
One of the foremost experts on lesbian history; wrote *Surpassing the Love of Men,* 1981.
b. Jul 18, 1940 in New York, New York
Source: *AmWomHi; BlmGWL; ConAu 16NR, 33R, 37NR; DrAS 74E, 78E, 82E; FemiWr; GayLesB; GayLL*

Fadiman, Clifton Paul
American. Author, Radio Performer
Host of radio's "Information Please," 1938-48; wrote *Party of One,* 1955.
b. May 15, 1904 in New York, New York
Source: *AmAu&B; ConAu 9NR, 61; CurBio 41, 55; IntAu&W 91; IntMPA 86, 88; IntvTCA 2; RAdv 1; REnAL; SmATA 11; TwCA SUP; WhoAm 86, 90; WhoWest 74; WhoWor 74; WorAl; WorAlBi; WrDr 86, 92*

Fagen, Donald
[Steely Dan]
American. Singer, Songwriter
Wrote songs for Steely Dan; solo single "New Frontier," 1983.
b. Jan 10, 1948 in Passaic, New Jersey
Source: *BioIn 11, 12, 13, 16, 18, 19; ConLC 26; ConMus 5; EncPR&S 89; EncRk 88; LegTOT; NewAmDM; PenEncP; RkOn 85; WhoAm 88, 94, 95, 96, 97*

Fagerbakke, Bill
American. Actor
Plays Dawber on TV show "Coach," 1989—.
Source: *WhoHol 92*

Fagunwa, D(aniel) O(lorunfemi)
Nigerian. Author
Well-known novelist in his native land; recognized for his use of the Yoruba language and folk tales in his writings.
b. 1910 in Ondo, Nigeria (Southern)
d. Dec 9, 1963 in Bida, Nigeria
Source: *ConAu 116*

Fahd ibn Abdul Aziz, King
Saudi. Ruler
Formerly Crown Prince, 1973-82; succeeded throne after sudden death of brother, 1982—.
b. 1922 in Riyadh, Saudi Arabia
Source: *BioIn 13, 14, 15; CurBio 79; EncWB; IntWW 75, 76, 77, 78, 79, 80, 83; MidE 78, 79, 80, 81, 82; NewYTBS 75; WhoWor 87, 91*

Fahey, John
American. Musician, Songwriter
Regarded as the father of the contemporary fingerpicking guitar style; released first album, *Blind Joe Death,* 1959 of instrumental guitar songs; also recorded landmark released such as *Fare Forward Voyager,* 1973, *Of Rivers and Religion,* 1972, *John Fahey Visits Washington, D.C.,* 1979 and *The New Possibility,* 1969.
b. Feb 28, 1939 in Takoma Park, Maryland
Source: *BioIn 14; ConMuA 80A; ConMus 17; EncFCWM 83; IlEncRk; NewAmDM; NewGrDA 86; OnThGG; PenEncP; WhoRock 81*

Fahrenheit, Gabriel Daniel
German. Physicist
Invented mercury thermometer, 1714; developed Fahrenheit temperature scale.
b. May 14, 1686 in Danzig, Germany
d. Sep 16, 1736 in The Hague, Netherlands
Source: *AsBiEn; BioIn 6, 7, 9, 12, 13; CamDcSc; DcBiPP; DcInv; Dis&D; InSci; LinLib S; McGEWB; OxCMed 86; REn; WhDW; WorAl*

Fahrenkopf, Frank Joseph, Jr.
American. Politician
Chm., Rep. Nat. Com., 1983-89.
b. Aug 28, 1939 in New York, New York
Source: *BioIn 13; NewYTBS 83; WhoAm 80, 82, 84, 86, 88, 90, 92, 94, 95, 96, 97; WhoAmL 85; WhoE 95; WhoWest 74, 76, 78, 80, 82, 84; WhoWor 84*

Fain, Ferris Roy
"Burrhead"
American. Baseball Player
First baseman, 1947-52; led AL in batting, 1951, 1952.
b. Mar 29, 1922 in San Antonio, Texas
Source: *BioIn 3; WhoProB 73*

Fain, Sammy
American. Singer, Pianist
Prolific songwriter, 1920s-60s; had 10 Oscar nominations; hits include "I'll Be Seeing You," 1938; "That Old Feeling," 1937.
b. Jun 17, 1902 in New York, New York
d. Dec 6, 1989 in Los Angeles, California
Source: *AmPS; AmSong; AnObit 1989; ASCAP 66, 80; Baker 78, 84, 92; BiDAmM; BiE&WWA; BioIn 2, 5, 6, 14, 15, 16, 17; CmpEPM; ConTFT 9; EncMT; FilmEn; IntMPA 77, 80, 86; LegTOT; NewAmDM; NewCBMT; NewGrDM 80; NewYTBS 89; NotNAT; OxCPMus; PenEncP; PopAmC, SUP; Sw&Ld C; WhAm 10; WhoAm 74, 76, 78, 80, 82, 84, 86, 88; WorAl; WorAlBi*

Fairbank, Janet Ayer
American. Author
Books include *The Cortlands of Washington Square,* 1923.
b. 1879 in Chicago, Illinois
d. Dec 28, 1951 in Chicago, Illinois
Source: *AmAu&B; BenetAL 91; ObitOF 79; OxCAmL 65, 83, 95; TwCA SUP; WhAm 3; WhNAA*

Fairbanks, Charles Warren
American. US Vice President
Served as vp under Theodore Roosevelt, 1905-09.
b. May 11, 1852 in Unionville Center, Ohio
d. Jun 4, 1918 in Indianapolis, Indiana
Source: *AmBi; AmPolLe; ApCAB, SUP; BiDrAC; BiDrUSC 89; BiDrUSE 71, 89; BioIn 1, 4, 7, 8, 9, 10, 14; DcAmB; EncWM; HarEnUS; IndAu 1967; NatCAB 11, 14, 39; TwCBDA; VicePre; WebAB 74, 79; WhAm 1; WhAmP*

Fairbanks, Chuck
[Charles Leo Fairbanks]
American. Football Coach
Successful coach at U of OK; in NFL with New England, 1973-79; in USFL with NJ, 1982-83; coach of yr., 1976.
b. Jun 10, 1933 in Detroit, Michigan
Source: *BioIn 12; LegTOT; NewYTBS 74; WhoAm 78, 80, 82, 84, 86, 88; WhoFtbl 74; WhoSSW 73; WorAl*

Fairbanks, Douglas
[Douglas Elton Ulman]
American. Actor
Swashbuckler hero in *The Three Musketeers,* 1921; *Robin Hood,* 1922; married Mary Pickford, 1928-36.
b. May 23, 1883 in Denver, Colorado
d. Dec 12, 1939 in Santa Monica, California
Source: *AmBi; BiDFilm, 81, 94; BioIn 3, 4, 5, 6, 7, 9, 10, 11, 12, 13, 14, 17, 18; CmCal; CmMov; CurBio 40; DcAmB S2; DcArts; EncAFC; FacFETw; Film 1, 2; FilmEn; FilmgC; HalFC 80, 84, 88; IntDcF 1-3, 2-3; LegTOT; LinLib S; MorMA; MotPP; MovMk; NotNAT B; OxCAmH; OxCAmT 84; OxCFilm; SilFlmP; TwYS; WebAB 74, 79; WhAm 1; WhNAA; WhoHol B; WhScrn 74, 77, 83; WhThe; WorAl; WorAlBi; WorEFlm*

Fairbanks, Douglas, Jr.
[Douglas Elton Ulman, Jr.]
American. Actor, Producer
Appeared in over 75 films; married to Joan Crawford, 1928-33.
b. Dec 9, 1909 in New York, New York
Source: *BiDFilm, 81, 94; BioIn 3, 4, 8, 9, 10, 11, 14, 16, 19, 20; BioNews 74; BlueB 76; CelR, 90; CmCal; CmMov; ConTFT 3; CurBio 41, 56; DcArts; Dun&B 90; EncAFC; FacFETw; Film 2; FilmEn; FilmgC; ForYSC; GangFlm; HalFC 80, 84, 88; IntAu&W 89; IntDcF 1-3; IntMPA 75, 76, 77, 78, 79, 80, 81, 82, 84, 86, 88, 92, 94, 96; IntWW 91; LegTOT; MotPP; MovMk; NewYTBS 89; TwYS; WebAB 74, 79; Who 74, 82, 83, 85, 88, 90, 92; WhoAm 86, 90; WhoE 89; WhoEnt 92; WhoThe 77, 81; WhoWor 74, 87, 91; WorAl; WorAlBi; WorEFlm*

Fairbanks, Thaddeus
American. Inventor
Developed platform scale, 1831.
b. Jan 17, 1796 in Brimfield, Massachusetts
d. Apr 12, 1886 in Saint Johnsbury, Vermont
Source: *AmBi; ApCAB; DcAmB; HarEnUS; InSci; NatCAB 10; OxCAmH; TwCBDA; WhAm HS*

Fairchild, David Grandison
American. Botanist
Performed scientific studies on importation of tropical plants.
b. Apr 7, 1869 in East Lansing, Michigan
d. Aug 6, 1954 in Coconut Grove, Florida
Source: *ApCAB X; BioIn 1, 2, 3, 5, 6, 8, 10; DcAmB S5; EncAAH; InSci; LinLib S; WebAB 74, 79; WhAm 3*

Fairchild, John Burr
American. Publisher
Newspapers include *Women's Wear Daily; Daily News Record,* 1960—.
b. Mar 6, 1927 in Newark, New Jersey
Source: *BioIn 8, 9, 10, 12, 14, 16; CelR 90; CurBio 71; DcLP 87A; Dun&B 79, 90; EncFash; EncTwCJ; WhoAm 74, 76, 78, 80, 82, 84, 86, 88, 90, 92, 94, 95, 96, 97; WhoE 74, 75; WhoEnt 92; WhoFash; WhoFI 92; WorFshn*

Fairchild, Morgan
[Patsy Ann McClenny]
American. Actor
Starred in TV series "Flamingo Road," 1981-82; has hosted many TV specials.
b. Feb 3, 1950 in Dallas, Texas
Source: *BioIn 10, 12, 13; ConTFT 5, 14; HalFC 84, 88; IntMPA 84, 86, 88, 92, 94, 96; LegTOT; NewYTBS 82; VarWW 85; WhoEnt 92; WhoHol 92; WorAlBi*

Fairchild, Sherman Mills
American. Inventor
Developed Fairchild aerial camera.
b. Apr 7, 1896 in Oneonta, New York
d. Mar 28, 1971 in New York, New York
Source: *BioIn 2, 3, 5, 8, 9, 10, 12; DcAmB S9; NatCAB 58; NewYTBE 71; WhAm 5*

Faircloth, Lauch
American. Politician
Rep. senator, NC, 1993—.
b. Jan 14, 1928 in Sampson County, North Carolina
Source: *AlmAP 96; BioIn 19; CngDr 93, 95*

Fairfax, Beatrice
[Marie Manning]
American. Journalist
Wrote syndicated column "Advice to the Lovelorn," 1898-1905, 1929-45.
b. Jan 22, 1878 in Washington, District of Columbia
d. Nov 28, 1945 in Allendale, New Jersey
Source: *AmAu&B; CurBio 44, 46; DcAmB S3; DcNAA; EncAJ; InWom; NotAW; REnAL*

Fairfax, Sally
[Sarah Cary Fairfax; Mrs. Will Fairfax]
American.
Wife of George Washington's best friend; object of Washington's lifelong (probably unconsummated) obsession; played by Jaclyn Smith in TV miniseries, 1984.
b. 1730
d. 1811
Source: *BioIn 11, 12*

Fairfax, Thomas
[Baron of Cameron]
English. Army Officer
Commanded New Model Army, 1645, fought against defeated Charles I.
b. Jan 17, 1612 in Leeds Castle, England
d. Nov 12, 1671 in Winchester, Virginia
Source: *Alli; CamGEL; DcBiPP; DcNaB, C; HisDStE; NewC; NewCBEL; PenC ENG; REn; WhDW; WhoMilH 76*

Fairless, Benjamin F
American. Philanthropist, Business Executive
Pres., chm., US Steel, 1938-52; spokesman for American steel industry.

b. May 3, 1890 in Pigeon Run, Ohio
d. Jan 1, 1962 in Ligonier, Pennsylvania
Source: *CurBio 42, 57, 62; DcAmB S7; InSci; PolProf E, T; WhAm 4*

Fairport Convention
[Simon Nichol; Dave Pegg; Bruce Rowland; Dave Swarbrick]
British. Music Group
Music mixes rock, blues, country, cajun; albums include *Farewell Farewell,* 1979.
Source: *ConMuA 80A; EncFCWM 83; EncRk 88; EncRkSt; IlEncRk; OxCPMus; PenEncP; RolSEnR 83; WhoRock 81; WhoRocM 82*

Fairstein, Linda
American. Lawyer
Chief of sex crimes unit, Manhattan Dist. Attorney's office, 1976—; successfully prosecuted celebrated "Preppie Murder" case, 1987.
b. 1948 in Westchester County, New York
Source: *BioIn 16; News 91, 91-1; NewYTBS 90; WhoAmL 92*

Faisal (Ibn Abdul-Aziz al Saud)
Saudi. Ruler
King 1964-75; resisted radical political forces in Arab world; assassinated by nephew.
b. Apr 9, 1906? in Riyadh, Arabia
d. Mar 25, 1975 in Riyadh, Saudi Arabia
Source: *BioIn 16, 17; CurBio 48, 66, 75, 75N; FacFETw; LegTOT; Who 74; WorAl; WorAlBi*

Faisal ibn Musaed
Saudi. Prince
Nephew of Faisal; murdered his uncle.
b. Apr 4, 1944 in Riyadh, Saudi Arabia
d. Jun 18, 1975 in Riyadh, Saudi Arabia
Source: *BioIn 10*

Faisal II
Iraqi. Ruler
King, 1939-58; killed during overthrow of monarchy.
b. May 2, 1935 in Baghdad, Iraq
d. Jul 14, 1958
Source: *CurBio 55, 58; NewCol 75; WebBD 83*

Faison, George
Director, Choreographer
Won Emmy for choreography of *The Wiz,* 1975.
b. 1947
Source: *ConBlAP 88; ConTFT 8; DrBlPA 90; InB&W 80, 85; VarWW 85*

Faith, Adam
[Terence Nelhams]
English. Singer, Actor
Hit songs include "We Are in Love," 1963; in film *Stardust,* 1974.
b. Jun 23, 1940 in London, England
Source: *ConMuA 80A; EncRk 88; EncRkSt; FilmgC; HalFC 84, 88; HarEnR 86; IlEncRk; IlWWBF A; IntWW 89, 91, 93; LegTOT; OxCPMus; PenEncP; RolSEnR 83; WhoHol 92; WhoRock 81*

Faith, Percy
Canadian. Conductor
Nominated for Oscar for film score *Love Me or Leave Me,* 1955; wrote "My Heart Cries for You," 1950; noted for full, mellow sound in albums since 1940s.
b. Apr 7, 1908 in Toronto, Ontario, Canada
d. Feb 9, 1976 in Los Angeles, California
Source: *ASCAP 66, 80; Baker 78, 84, 92; BiDAmM; BioIn 1, 2, 10, 11, 12; CanWW 70; CmpEPM; CreCan 1; DcAmB S10; HalFC 80, 84, 88; LegTOT; NewAmDM; NewGrDA 86; NewYTBS 76; OxCPMus; PenEncP; RadStar; RkOn 74; WhAm 6; WhoAm 74, 76*

Faithfull, Marianne
English. Singer, Actor
Had hit with Jagger/Richard song "As Tears Go By," 1964.
b. Dec 29, 1946 in London, England
Source: *BioIn 12, 77, 81*

Faith No More
[Mike Bordin; Roddy Bottum; Billy Gould; Jim Martin; Mike Patton]
American. Music Group
San Francisco rock band formed 1982; platinum album *The Real Thing,* 1989; current members listed above.
Source: *ConMus 7; DrAPF 80, 83, 85, 87, 89, 91, 93, 97; EncRkSt; ObitOF 79; WhoHol 92*

Faiz, Faiz Ahmad
Pakistani. Poet
Considered Pakistan's poet laureate; wrote *Zindan Namah,* 1950s.
b. Feb 11, 1912? in Sialkot, British India
d. Nov 20, 1984 in Lahore, Pakistan
Source: *CasWL; ConAu 115; DcOrL 2; EncWL 2*

Fakir, Abdul
[Four Tops]
American. Singer
With Motown group formed 1954; achieved success, 1964, with top single "Baby I Need Your Loving."
b. Dec 26, 1938AD in Detroit, Michigan

Falana, Lola
[Loletha Elaine Falana]
"First Lady of Las Vegas"
American. Entertainer
Known for fabulous Las Vegas shows, guest spots on TV specials.
b. Sep 11, 1943 in Camden, New Jersey
Source: *BioIn 8, 10, 12, 13, 16; BkPepl; DrBlPA, 90; InB&W 85; InWom SUP; VarWW 85; WhoAfA 96; WhoAm 82; WhoAmW 72; WhoBlA 85, 88, 90, 92, 94; WhoHol A; WorAlBi*

Falco
[Johann Holzel]
Austrian. Musician
Int'l rock performer known for Mozart character in videos; recorded top-10 hit "Rock Me, Amadeus," 1985.
b. Feb 19, 1957 in Vienna, Austria
Source: *BioIn 16; ConNews 87-2; LegTOT; PenEncP*

Falco, Louis
American. Choreographer, Dancer
Staged dances for movie *Fame,* 1980.
b. Aug 2, 1942? in New York, New York
d. Mar 26, 1993
Source: *BiDD; BioIn 6, 9, 11, 13, 18; CmpGMD; CnOxB; WhAm 11; WhoAm 76, 78, 80, 82, 84, 86, 88, 90, 92; WhoE 83, 85, 86, 91, 93; WhoEnt 92*

Falcone, Giovanni
Italian. Government Official
Public prosecutor whose well-known crusade against the Mafia ended when a bomb blew up a section of highway on which he was traveling.
d. May 23, 1992
Source: *BioIn 18, 19*

Falconetti, Renee Maria
French. Actor
Known for title role in *The Passion of Joan of Arc,* 1927.
b. 1892 in Sermano, France
d. 1946 in Buenos Aires, Argentina
Source: *Film 2; FilmgC; MotPP; OxCFilm; WhoHol B; WhScrn 77; WorEFlm*

Faldo, Nick
[Nicholas Alexander Faldo]
English. Golfer
Turned pro, 1976; 3-time winner of British Open, 1987, 90, 92.
b. Jul 18, 1957 in Hertfordshire, England
Source: *BioIn 16; CurBio 92; IntWW 91, 93; News 93-3; NewYTBS 91; Who 92, 94; WhoAm 96, 97; WhoIntG; WhoSpor; WhoWor 95, 96*

Falk, Lee Harrison
American. Cartoonist, Author
Created comic strips "Mandrake the Magician," 1934; "The Phantom," 1936.
b. 1915 in Saint Louis, Missouri
Source: *BioIn 15; ConAu 97, 133; IntAu&W 82, 86; NatPD 81; WhoAm 78, 80, 82, 86, 90; WorECom*

Falk, Peter
American. Actor
Starred in TV series "Columbo," 1971-78, 1989-90; won Emmy, 1972, 1990.
b. Sep 16, 1927 in New York, New York
Source: *BiE&WWA; BioIn 6, 7, 9, 10, 11, 16, 17; BioNews 75; BkPepl; CelR, 90; ConTFT 1, 6, 13; CurBio 72; EncAFC; FilmEn; FilmgC; ForYSC; HalFC 80, 84, 88; IntDcF 1-3, 2-3;*

IntMPA 75, 76, 77, 78, 79, 80, 81, 82, 84, 86, 88, 92, 94, 96; ItaFilm; LegTOT; LesBEnT 92; MotPP; MovMk; NewYTBE 71; NotNAT; WhoAm 74, 76, 78, 80, 82, 84, 86, 88, 90, 92, 94, 95, 96, 97; WhoCom; WhoEnt 92; WhoHol 92, A; WhoWest 74; WhoWor 74; WorAl; WorAlBi

Falkenburg, Jinx
[Eugenia Lincoln Falkenburg; Jinx McCrary]
American. Model
Highest paid model, 1941; had radio show "Tex and Jinx Show."
b. Jan 21, 1919 in Barcelona, Spain
Source: *BioIn 1, 2, 3, 12, 15; CurBio 53; EncAFC; FilmgC; HalFC 80, 84, 88; InWom; WhoAmW 58, 61, 64; WhoEnt 92; WhoHol 92, A; WorAl*

Falkner, Frank T(ardrew)
English. Physician, Educator
Pediatrician; professor, chm. on child health at U of CA, 198189; prof. pediatrics at U of CA, SF, 1981-89; wrote *Human Growth,* 1978.
b. Oct 27, 1918 in Hale, England
Source: *AmMWSc 76P, 79, 82, 86, 89, 92, 95; IntMed 80; WhoAm 78, 80, 82, 84, 86, 88, 90, 92, 94, 95, 96, 97; WhoMedH; WhoTech 82, 84, 89*

Fall, Albert Bacon
American. Government Official
Secretary of Interior, 1921-23; imprisoned for involvement in Teapot Dome scandal, 1930-32.
b. Nov 26, 1861 in Frankfort, Kentucky
d. Nov 30, 1944 in El Paso, Texas
Source: *AmPolLe; BiDrAC; BiDrUSC 89; BiDrUSE 71, 89; BioIn 3, 6, 7, 9, 10, 13; CurBio 45; DcAmB S3; EncAB-H 1974, 1996; NatCAB 44; OxCAmH; REnAW; WhAm 2; WhAmP; WorAl*

Fall, Bernard B
American. Author
Historian of Vietnamese War: *The Viet-Minh Regime,* 1954.
b. Nov 11, 1926 in Vienna, Austria
d. Feb 21, 1967 in Hue, Vietnam
Source: *AmAu&B; AuSpks; BioIn 7, 8, 10, 11; ConAu 1R, 6NR, 25R, 77; ConLC 11; DcAmB S8; EncAJ; WhAm 4; WorAu 1950*

Falla, Manuel de
Spanish. Composer
Wrote ballet *The Three Cornered Hat,* 1919; impressionistic works rooted in Spanish folk music.
b. Nov 23, 1876 in Cadiz, Spain
d. Nov 14, 1946 in Alta Gracia, Argentina
Source: *AtlBL; Baker 78, 84; Benet 87; BioIn 1, 2, 3, 4, 5, 6, 7, 8, 12, 16, 20; BriBkM 80; CmOp; CnOxB; CompSN, SUP; CurBio 46; DcArts; DcCM; DcCom 77; DcCom&M 79; DcPup; DcTwCC; FacFETw; IntDcOp; LegTOT; LinLib S; McGEWB; MetOEnc; MusMk; NewAmDM; NewEOp 71; NewGrDM 80; NewOxM; OxCMus; OxDcOp; PenDiMP A; REn; WhDW; WorAl; WorAlBi*

Fallaci, Oriana
Italian. Journalist
Interviews with nat leaders collected in *Interviews with History,* 1976 .
b. Jun 29, 1930 in Florence, Italy
Source: *BioIn 9, 10, 11, 12, 14; BlmGWL; ConAu 15NR, 77; ConLC 11; ContDcW 89; CurBio 77; DcItL 2; EncAJ; EncCoWW; FemiWr; IntAu&W 82, 89, 91, 93; IntDcWB; IntWW 78, 79, 80, 81, 82, 83, 89, 91, 93; InWom SUP; MajTwCW; NewYTBE 73; RAdv 14; WhoAm 82, 84, 86, 88, 92, 94, 95, 96; WhoAmW 95; WhoWor 78, 80, 82, 84, 87, 89, 91, 93, 95, 96, 97; WorAu 1975*

Fallada, Hans
[Rudolph Ditzen]
German. Author
Social realist who wrote *Little Man What Now?* 1933.
b. Jul 21, 1893
d. Feb 6, 1947 in Berlin, Germany
Source: *BioIn 1, 4, 9, 14, 16; CasWL; ClDMEL 80; DcLB 56; EncTR 91; EncWL; EvEuW; LngCTC; ModGL; Novels; OxCGer 76, 86; PenC EUR; REn; ScF&FL 1; TwCA, SUP; WhE&EA; WhoTwCL*

Falldin, Thorbjorn Nils Olof
Swedish. Political Leader
First non-Socialist prime minister, 1976-78; 1979-82.
b. Apr 24, 1926 in Hogsjo, Sweden
Source: *CurBio 78; IntWW 83, 91; IntYB 82; NatCAB 44; REnAW*

Fallows, James (Mackenzie)
American. Editor, Journalist
Editor, *U.S. News & World Report,* 1996—.
b. Aug 2, 1949 in Philadelphia, Pennsylvania
Source: *BioIn 12; CurBio 96; WhoAm 80, 82, 84, 86, 88, 90, 92, 94; WhoAmP 77, 79, 81, 83; WhoE 93; WhoGov 77; WhoUSWr 88; WhoWrEP 89, 92, 95; WrDr 92, 94, 96*

Falls, Joe
American. Journalist, Author
Sports writer, editor, *Detroit News,* 1978—; wrote *Man in Motion,* 1973; *The Boston Marathon,* 1977.
b. May 2, 1928 in New York, New York
Source: *Ballpl 90; ConAu 77; WhoAm 86, 90*

Falter, John
American. Illustrator
Illustrated over 150 *Saturday Evening Post* mag. covers.
b. Feb 28, 1910 in Plattsmouth, Nebraska
Source: *BioIn 2, 9, 12, 17; IlrAm 1880; WhoAmA 73, 76, 78, 82, 84, 86, 89N, 91N, 93N*

Faltskog, Agnetha
Swedish. Singer
Known for high vocal range; solo single "Can't Shake Loose," 1983.
b. Apr 5, 1950 in Stockholm, Sweden
Source: *RkOn 85*

Faludi, Susan
American. Writer, Feminist
Best-selling book, *Backlash,* 1991 characterized media distortions of women's issues as retaliation for women asserting themselves.
b. Apr 18, 1959 in New York, New York
Source: *ConAu 138; CurBio 93; FemiWr; LegTOT; News 92; WomStre; WrDr 96*

Falwell, Jerry L
American. Clergy
Prominent fundamentalist spokesman, TV minister; founded Moral Majority, 1979-89.
b. Aug 11, 1933 in Lynchburg, Virginia
Source: *AmOrTwC; BioIn 13, 14, 15, 16; ConAu 102; CurBio 81; DcAmC; EncWB; FacFETw; IntWW 91; LesBEnT 92; RelLAm 91; TwCSAPR; WhoAm 86, 90; WhoRel 85, 92; WhoSSW 88; WorAlBi*

Fame, Georgie
[Clive Powell]
English. Singer, Musician, Composer
Songs include "Sunny," 1966; "Ballad of Bonnie and Clyde," 1967.
b. Jun 26, 1943 in Leigh, England
Source: *BiDJaz; EncJzS; EncJzS; EncRk 88; HarEnR 86; IlEncRk; OxCPMus; PenEncP; RkOn 78, 84; RolSEnR 83; WhoRock 81; WhoRocM 82; WhoWor 74*

Famolare, Joseph P
American. Designer, Businessman
CEO, Famolare, Inc., shoe manufacturer, 1969-89.
b. 1930
Source: *BioIn 12; Dun&B 86, 88; WhoMW 90*

Fanfani, Amintore
"Little Professor"; "Tom Thumb of Itali"
Italian. Political Leader
Five-time prime minister; resigned Apr 1983; wrote over 40 books.
b. Feb 6, 1908 in Tuscany, Italy
Source: *BioIn 3, 4, 5, 6, 7, 9, 10, 13, 16; CurBio 58; EncWB; IntWW 74, 75, 76, 77, 78, 79, 80, 81, 82, 83, 89, 91, 93; IntYB 78, 79, 80, 81, 82; WhoUN 75; WhoWor 74, 78, 80, 82, 89, 91*

Fangio, Juan Manuel
Argentine. Auto Racer
World Grand Prix champion, 1951, 1954, 1957.
b. Jun 24, 1911
d. Jul 17, 1995, Argentina

Source: *BioIn 7, 8, 9, 10, 12, 13, 15, 21; FacFETw; IntWW 81, 82, 83, 89, 91, 93; WhDW; WhoWor 82; WorAl*

Fang Lizhi
Chinese. Educator
Astrophysicist stripped of Communist Party membership for stirring up student unrest, 1987; urges democratization; often compared to Soviet dissident Andrei Sakharov.
b. Feb 12, 1936 in Beijing, China
Source: *BioIn 12, 15; ConAu 135; ConNews 88-1; CurBio 89; IntWW 89, 91, 93; RadHan; WhoPRCh 87, 91*

Fanning, Katherine Woodruff
American. Editor, Journalist
Editor, *Christian Science Monitor,* 1983-88.
b. Oct 18, 1927 in Chicago, Illinois
Source: *BioIn 13, 14, 15, 16; EncTwCJ; NewYTBS 87; WhoAm 74, 76, 78, 80, 82, 84, 86, 88, 90, 92, 94, 95, 96, 97; WhoAmW 74, 75, 87, 89, 91, 93, 95, 97; WhoE 89; WhoWest 82, 84*

Fanon, Frantz (Omar)
American. Psychoanalyst, Philosopher
His *The Wretched of the Earth,* 1961, is considered major contribution to revolutionary thought of Third World countries.
b. Jul 20, 1925, Martinique
d. Dec 6, 1961 in Washington, District of Columbia
Source: *Benet 87, 96; BiDNeoM; BioIn 7, 8, 9, 10, 11, 12, 13, 14, 15; BlkLC; BlkWr 1; CaribW 2; ConAu 89, 116; ConIsC 1; ConLC 74; CyWA 89; DcAfL; DcArts; EncRev; FacFETw; LegTOT; LiExTwC; McGEWB; OxCPhil; RadHan; SchCGBL; SelBAAf; ThTwC 87; WorAu 1950*

Fantin-Latour, (Ignace) Henri
French. Artist
Best known for still lifes, portraits: *Homage a Delacroix,* 1864.
b. Jan 14, 1836 in Grenoble, France
d. Aug 25, 1904 in Bure, France
Source: *ArtsNiC; AtlBL; BioIn 3, 4, 5, 8, 11, 12, 13; NewCol 75; OxCArt; OxDcArt; WebBD 83; WhDW; WorAl; WorAlBi*

Faraday, Michael
English. Scientist
Developed first dynamo; discovered electromagnetic induction and compound bencene.
b. Sep 22, 1791 in Newington, England
d. Aug 25, 1867 in Hampton Court, England
Source: *Alli, SUP; AsBiEn; BbD; BiD&SB; BiDPsy; BiESc; BioIn 1, 2, 3, 4, 5, 6, 7, 8, 9, 10, 11, 12, 13, 14, 15, 16, 17, 18, 20; BritAu 19; CamDcSc; CelCen; Chambr 3; CyEd; DcBiPP; DcEnL; DcInv; DcNaB; DcScB; Dis&D; EncO&P 1, 2, 3; EncPaPR 91; EvLB; InSci; LarDcSc; LinLib S; McGEWB; NewC; NewCol 75; OxCChiL; OxCEng 67, 85, 95; OxCMed 86; OxCMus; RAdv 14, 13-5; REn; VicBrit; WhDW; WorAl; WorAlBi; WorInv; WorScD*

Farago, Ladislas
Hungarian. Author
Books include *The Last Days of Patton,* 1981; *Tenth Fleet,* 1962.
b. Sep 21, 1906 in Csuro, Austria-Hungary
d. Oct 15, 1980 in New York, New York
Source: *AmAu&B; BioIn 6, 9, 10, 12; BioNews 75; CelR; ConAu 10NR, 65, 102; DcAmB S10; EncAI&E; NewYTBS 80; WhAm 7; WhoAm 74, 76, 78, 80; WhoWor 74, 78; WhoWorJ 72, 78*

Farah, James
American. Manufacturer
With brother, William, built small apparel factory into leading maker of men's pants, 1937.
b. 1916?
d. 1964
Source: *Entr*

Farah, William
American. Manufacturer
With brother, James, built small apparel factory into leading maker of men's pants, 1937.
b. 1919
Source: *Dun&B 79, 90; Entr*

Farb, Peter
American. Author, Editor
Book topics include science, natural history, linguistics: *Man's Rise to Civilization,* 1968; *Humankind,* 1978.
b. Jul 25, 1929 in New York, New York
d. Apr 8, 1980 in Boston, Massachusetts
Source: *AmAu&B; AnObit 1980; Au&Wr 71; AuBYP 2S, 3; BioIn 11, 12, 13; ConAu 12NR, 97; NewYTBS 80; SmATA 12, 22N; WhAm 7; WhoAm 74, 76, 78, 80; WhoE 74; WhoWor 74, 78, 80; WorAu 1950, 1970*

Farber, Edward Rolke
American. Inventor
Credited with invention of portable strobe light for still cameras.
b. Jul 22, 1914 in Milwaukee, Wisconsin
d. Jan 22, 1982 in Delafield, Wisconsin
Source: *AnObit 1982; BioIn 12, 13; LElec; NewYTBS 82*

Farber, Simon W
American. Manufacturer
Introduced silver, nickel-plated Farberware, 1910.
b. 1881?
d. 1947
Source: *BioIn 1; Entr*

Farenthold, Frances T(arlton)
American. Political Activist
First woman ever to have name placed in nomination as Dem. VP candidate, 1972.
b. Oct 2, 1926 in Corpus Christi, Texas
Source: *AmCath 80; AmPolW 80; AmWomM; InWom SUP; PolPar; WhoAm 78, 80, 82, 84, 90, 92, 94, 95, 96, 97; WhoAmP 73, 75, 77, 85; WhoAmW 72, 74, 75, 77, 79, 81, 83, 85, 87, 89, 91, 93, 95, 97; WhoE 79; WhoSSW 82, 84, 86, 88, 95, 97; WhoWor 87*

Farentino, James
American. Actor
Starred "The Bold Ones," 1970-72.
b. Feb 24, 1938 in New York, New York
Source: *BioIn 10, 12; ConTFT 2, 7; FilmEn; FilmgC; ForYSC; HalFC 80, 84, 88; IntMPA 75, 76, 77, 78, 79, 80, 81, 82, 84, 86, 88, 92, 94, 96; ItaFilm; LegTOT; MotPP; NewYTBE 73; WhoAm 74, 76, 78, 80, 82, 84, 86, 88, 90, 92, 94, 95, 96, 97; WhoEnt 92; WhoHol 92, A; WhoThe 81*

Fargo, Donna
[Yvonne Vaughan]
American. Singer, Songwriter
Country singer; hits include "Happiest Girl in the USA"; "Funny Face."
b. Nov 10, 1949 in Mount Airy, North Carolina
Source: *BioIn 14; BkPepl; CounME 74, 74A; EncFCWM 83; HarEnCM 87; IlEncCM; PenEncP; RkOn 78; WhoAm 78, 84, 88; WhoEnt 92; WhoWor 84*

Fargo, William George
American. Businessman
With Henry Wells, started express service, Wells, Fargo & Co. during CA gold rush, 1852.
b. May 20, 1818 in Pompey, New York
d. Aug 3, 1881 in Buffalo, New York
Source: *AmBi; ApCAB; BiDAmBL 83; BioIn 4, 6; DcAmB; EncAAH; EncABHB 6; HarEnUS; LinLib S; McGEWB; NatCAB 12; REnAW; TwCBDA; WebAB 74, 79; WhAm HS; WhAmP; WhDW; WorAl*

Farina, Dennis
American. Actor
Star of TV series "Crime Story," 1986-88.
b. Feb 29, 1944 in Chicago, Illinois
Source: *BioIn 15; IntMPA 94, 96; WhoHol 92*

Farina, Giuseppe
Italian. Auto Racer
Won world title, 1950; first to win championship using modern point system.
b. 1906 in Turin, Italy
d. Jun 30, 1966 in Chambery, France
Source: *BioIn 5, 7, 10*

Farina, Richard
American. Author, Singer
Part of folk music scene, 1960s; wrote *Been Down So Long It Looks Like Up To Me,* 1966.
b. 1936 in New York, New York

d. Apr 30, 1966 in Carmel, California
Source: *AmAu&B; BenetAL 91; BiDAmM; BioIn 7; ConAu 25R, 81; ConLC 9; PenEncP; WhScrn 77*

Farinelli
[Carlo Broschi]
"Il Ragazzo"
Italian. Opera Singer
Most famed male soprano of 18th century; women fainted in Venice, London while listening.
b. Jan 24, 1705 in Andria, Italy
d. Jul 15, 1782 in Bologna, Italy
Source: *Baker 78, 84, 92; BioIn 7, 9, 14, 15; BriBkM 80; CmOp; IntDcOp; LegTOT; MetOEnc; MusMk; NewAmDM; NewEOp 71; NewGrDM 80; NewGrDO; OxDcOp; PenDiMP; REn; WhDW*

Farjeon, Eleanor
English. Author
Best known for children's fantasy tales *London Town,* 1916; *Martin Pippin* series, 1930s.
b. Feb 13, 1881 in London, England
d. Jun 5, 1965 in Hampstead, England
Source: *AnCL; ArtclWW 2; AuBYP 2; BioIn 2, 3, 4, 5, 6, 7, 8, 9, 11, 14, 15, 16, 19; BkCL; CamGLE; CasWL; CathA 1952; ChhPo, S1, S2, S3; ChlBkCr; ChlFicS; ChlLR 34; ConAu P-1; DcLB 160; DcLEL; DcNaB 1961; EncBrWW; FacFETw; FemiCLE; GrBr; HerW; InWom, SUP; JBA 34, 51; LinLib L; LngCTC; MajAI; NewC; NewCBEL; ObitT 1961; OxCChiL; OxCEng 85, 95; PenNWW A; ScF&FL 1, 2, 92; SmATA 2; Str&VC; TwCA, SUP; TwCChW 78, 83, 89, 95; TwCWr; WhoChL; WomNov; WrChl*

Farley, Chris
American. Actor
On NBC's "Saturday Night Live," 1990-95.
b. Feb 15, 1964 in Madison, Wisconsin

Farley, James A(loysius)
American. Politician
US postmaster general, 1933-40; managed FDR's campaigns, 1955-67.
b. May 30, 1888 in Grassy Point, New York
d. Jun 9, 1976 in New York, New York
Source: *AmPolLe; BiDrUSE 71, 89; BioIn 1, 2, 3, 4, 5, 9, 10, 11, 12, 13, 16, 17; CathA 1952; ConAu 65; CurBio 44; DcAmB S10; EncAB-A 1; EncAB-H 1974, 1996; Film 1; IntWW 74, 75, 76; LinLib S; OxCAmH; St&PR 75; TwYS; WebAB 74, 79; WhAm 7; WhoAm 76; WhoAmP 73, 75, 77, 79; WhoHol B; WorAl*

Farley, Walter Lorimer
American. Author
Created *Black Stallion* series of children's novels; two have been filmed.
b. Jun 26, 1920 in Syracuse, New York
d. Oct 17, 1989 in Venice, Florida
Source: *AuBYP 3; BioIn 14, 15, 16; ConAu 8NR, 29NR; ConLC 17; CurBio 49, 90N; NewYTBS 89; OxCChiL; SmATA 2, 43; TwCChW 78, 89; WhoAm 74, 76, 86, 88; WhoUSWr 88; WhoWrEP 89; WrDr 86, 90*

Farmer, Arthur Stewart
American. Jazz Musician
Trumpeter, fluegelhornist; led own combo, 1960s.
b. Aug 21, 1928 in Council Bluffs, Arkansas
Source: *BiDAmM; BiDJaz; BioIn 5, 7, 11, 12, 16; CmpEPM; EncJzS; NewAmDM; NewGrDA 86; TwCBrS; WhoAm 74; WhoBlA 75, 77, 80*

Farmer, Don(ald Edwin)
American. Broadcast Journalist
Congressional correspondent, 1975-78; anchor with Cable News Network, 1980-87; anchor, WSB-TV (Atlanta, GA), 1987—.
b. Sep 27, 1938 in Saint Louis, Missouri
Source: *ConAu 65; WhoAm 80, 82, 84*

Farmer, Fannie Merritt
American. Chef
First published *Fannie Farmer Cookbook,* 1896; introduced standard measurements in recipes.
b. Mar 23, 1857 in Boston, Massachusetts
d. Jan 15, 1915 in Boston, Massachusetts
Source: *AmAu&B; AmBi; AmWomSc; AmWomWr; BiDAmEd; BioIn 2, 3, 10, 12, 14, 15, 17, 19, 20, 21; ContDcW 89; DcAmAu; DcAmB; DcNAA; Entr; GayN; GrLiveH; IntDcWB; InWom, SUP; LibW; LinLib S; McGEWB; NatCAB 22; NotAW; OxCAmH; REnAL; WebAB 74, 79; WhAm 1; WomFir; WorAl*

Farmer, Forest Jackson
American. Auto Executive
Pres., Acustar, Inc., 1988—.
b. Jan 15, 1941 in Zanesville, Ohio
Source: *BioIn 16; ConBlB 1; WhoBlA 80, 92*

Farmer, Frances
American. Actor
Stage, film star who spent most of 1940s in mental institution; life was subject of film *Frances,* 1983.
b. Sep 19, 1914 in Seattle, Washington
d. Aug 1, 1970 in Indianapolis, Indiana
Source: *BiDFilm 94; BiDrLUS 70; BioAmW; BioIn 4, 9, 10, 11, 13; BioNews 74; FilmgC; ForYSC; HalFC 80, 84, 88; HolP 30; MotPP; MovMk; NewYTBE 70; NotNAT, A; ObitOF 79; PlP&P; ThFT; WhoAm 78; WhoHol B; WhoWor 74; WhScrn 74, 77, 83; WorAlBi*

Farmer, Gary Dale
Canadian. Actor
Appeared in *The Dark Wind,* 1992.
b. Jun 12, 1953 in Ohswekan, Ontario, Canada
Source: *NotNaAm*

Farmer, James
American. Civil Rights Leader
Founded CORE, 1942, national director, 1961-66; pres., Council on Minority Planning and Strategy, 1973-76.
b. Jan 12, 1920 in Marshall, Texas
Source: *AfrAmAl 6; AfrAmBi 2; AmAu&B; AmDec 1940; BioIn 6, 7, 8, 9, 10, 11, 15, 16; BlueB 76; CivR 74; ConBlB 2; CurBio 64; EncAACR; EncSoH; EncWB; IntAu&W 93; LegTOT; LNinSix; NegAl 76, 83, 89; WhoAfA 96; WhoAm 74, 76, 78, 80, 82, 84, 86, 88, 90, 92, 94, 95, 96, 97; WhoAmP 73, 75, 77, 79, 81; WhoBlA 75, 77, 80, 85, 88, 90, 92, 94; WhoSSW 73, 97; WhoWor 74, 78*

Farmer, Philip Jose
American. Author
Science-fiction books include *Maker of Universes,* 1965.
b. Jan 26, 1918 in Terre Haute, Indiana
Source: *AmAu&B; BioIn 7, 12, 15; ConAu 1R, 4NR, 35NR; ConLC 1, 19; ConSFA; DcLB 8; DcLP 87A; DrAF 76; DrAPF 83, 91; DrmM 1; EncSF, 93; IndAu 1917; IntAu&W 77; IntvTCA 2; LegTOT; LinLib L; MajTwCW; NewEScF; Novels; RAdv 14; RGTwCSF; ScF&FL 1, 2, 92; ScFSB; ScFWr; TwCSFW 81, 86, 91; WhoAm 82, 84, 86, 88; WhoSciF; WhoUSWr 88; WhoWrEP 89, 92, 95; WorAl; WorAlBi; WorAu 1970; WrDr 84, 86, 88, 90, 92, 94, 96*

Farnese, Alessandro
[Duke of Parma]
Spanish. Soldier
Recovered provinces of Netherlands for uncle, Philip II; greatest military expert of time.
b. Aug 27, 1545
d. Dec 3, 1592
Source: *DcBiPP; GenMudB; HisWorL; OxCArt; WhDW; WhoMilH 76*

Farnham, Eliza Wood Burhans
American. Social Reformer, Lecturer
Head, women's dept. of Sing Sing, 1840s; instituted penal reforms.
b. Nov 17, 1815 in Rensselaerville, New York
d. Dec 15, 1864 in New York, New York
Source: *AmRef; BioIn 15, 16, 21; InWom SUP; LibW; NotAW*

Farnham, Sally James
American. Sculptor
Known for military, portraits of pres; did Soldier's and Sailor's monuments, NY, NJ.
b. 1869 in Ogdensburg, New York
d. Apr 28, 1943 in New York, New York
Source: *DcWomA; WhAm 2*

Farnol, Jeffery
English. Author
Popular historical tales include *Amateur Gentleman,* 1913.
b. Feb 10, 1878 in Eastbourne, England
d. Aug 9, 1952 in Eastbourne, England
Source: *BioIn 3, 4, 7, 10, 14; CamGLE; DcNaB 1951; NewC; OxCChiL; OxCEng 85; REn; ScF&FL 1; TwCA, SUP; TwCRGW; TwCRHW 90; TwCWr; WhoLA*

Farnsworth, Philo Taylor
American. Inventor
Received patents for many inventions relating to TV.
b. Aug 19, 1906 in Beaver, Utah
d. Mar 11, 1971 in Salt Lake City, Utah
Source: *BioIn 1, 3, 9, 10, 12; DcAmB S9; InSci; NewCol 75; NewYTBE 71; NewYTET; WebAB 74, 79; WebBD 83; WhAm 5; WorInv*

Farnsworth, Richard
American. Actor
Spent 40 yrs. as stuntman; appeared in films *Comes a Horseman,* 1979; *The Natural,* 1983.
b. Sep 1, 1920 in Los Angeles, California
Source: *BioIn 13; ConTFT 3; HalFC 88; IntMPA 86, 92, 94, 96; VarWW 85; WhoAm 86, 88, 90, 92, 94, 95, 96, 97; WhoEnt 92*

Farnum, Dustin Lancy
American. Actor
Star of Cecil B DeMille's first film *The Squaw Man,* 1914.
b. 1870 in Hampton Beach, Maine
d. Jul 3, 1929 in New York, New York
Source: *DcAmB; Film 1, 2; FilmgC; MotPP; NotNAT B; TwYS; WhAm 1; WhoHol B; WhoStg 1906, 1908; WhScrn 74, 77*

Farnum, William
American. Actor
Debut film *The Spoilers,* 1914; brother of Dustin Farnum.
b. Jul 4, 1876 in Boston, Massachusetts
d. Jun 5, 1953 in Los Angeles, California
Source: *BioIn 3, 8, 9, 17; Film 1, 2; FilmEn; FilmgC; HalFC 80, 84, 88; IntDcF 1-3; MotPP; MovMk; NotNAT B; OxCAmT 84; SilFlmP; TwYS; WhoHol B; WhScrn 74, 77, 83; WhThe*

Farouk I
Egyptian. Ruler
Ruled, 1936-52; incompetent, corrupt; overthrown, forced to abdicate.
b. Feb 11, 1920 in Cairo, Egypt
d. Mar 18, 1965 in Rome, Italy
Source: *CurBio 42, 65; NewCol 75; WebBD 83*

Farquhar, George
English. Dramatist
Comedies include *The Beaux Stratagen,* 1707.
b. 1678 in Londonderry, Northern Ireland
d. Apr 29, 1707 in London, England
Source: *Alli; AtlBL; BbD; Benet 87, 96; BiD&SB; BioIn 1, 3, 5, 7, 8, 9, 12; BlmGEL; BritAu; BritWr 2; CamGEL; CasWL; Chambr 2; CnThe; CrtSuDr; CrtT 2; CyWA 58; DcBiPP; DcEnA; DcEnL; DcIrB 78, 88; DcLEL; DcNaB; EncWT; Ent; EvLB; LinLib L; LitC 21; LngCEL; McGEWD 72; MouLC 2; NewC; NewCBEL; NotNAT B; OxCEng 67, 85; OxCThe 67, 83; PenC ENG; PlP&P; PoIre; RAdv 14, 13-2; REn; REnWD; WebE&AL; WhDW; WorAl; WorAlBi*

Farr, Felicia
[Mrs. Jack Lemmon]
American. Actor
Movies include *Charley Varrick,* 1973; *The Venetian Affair,* 1967.
b. Oct 4, 1932 in Westchester, New York
Source: *FilmEn; FilmgC; ForYSC; HalFC 80, 84, 88; IntMPA 77, 80, 86, 88, 92, 94, 96; MotPP; VarWW 85; WhoHol 92, A*

Farr, Jamie
[Jameel Joseph Farah]
American. Actor
Best known for role as Cpl. Klinger on TV series "M*A*S*H," 1972-83.
b. Jul 1, 1934 in Toledo, Ohio
Source: *BioIn 13; HalFC 84, 88; IntMPA 86, 92, 94, 96; LegTOT; VarWW 85; WhoAm 86, 90; WhoCom; WhoEnt 92; WhoHol 92, A; WhoTelC; WorAlBi*

Farr, Tommy B
Welsh. Boxer
Defeated by Joe Louis in world heavyweight bout, 1937.
b. Mar 12, 1914 in Clydack, Wales
Source: *BioIn 5, 7, 14; FacFETw; NewYTBS 86; WhoBox 74*

Farragut, David Glasgow
"Old Salamander"
American. Military Leader
Civil War hero remembered for saying "Damn the torpedoes, full speed ahead," 1864.
b. Jul 5, 1801 in Knoxville, Tennessee
d. Aug 14, 1870 in Portsmouth, New Hampshire
Source: *AmBi; ApCAB; BioIn 1, 2, 3, 4, 5, 6, 7, 8, 9, 11, 12, 14, 16, 17, 20; CelCen; CivWDc; DcAmB; DcAmMiB; EncAB-H 1974, 1996; EncSoH; GenMudB; HarEnMi; HarEnUS; LinLib S; McGEWB; MorMA; NatCAB 2; OxCAmH; OxCShps; TwCBDA; WebAB 74, 79; WebAMB; WhAm HS; WhCiWar; WhoMilH 76; WorAl; WorAlBi*

Farrakhan, Louis
[Louis Eugene Walcott]
American. Religious Leader
Leader, Nation of Islam, 1977—; promotes black self-help, separatist philosophy; controversial for anti-Semitic, racist rhetoric. Helped organize the Million Man March, 1995.
b. May 11, 1933 in New York, New York
Source: *AfrAmAl 6; AfrAmBi 1; BioIn 13; ConBlB 2; CurBio 92; InB&W 85; LegTOT; News 90; RelLAm 91; WhoAfA 96; WhoAm 95, 96, 97; WhoBlA 85, 88, 90, 92, 94; WhoRel 92; WorAlBi*

Farrand, Beatrix Jones
American. Landscape Architect
Female landscape architect who designed gardens at Dumbarton Oaks, 1920-40.
b. Jun 19, 1872 in New York, New York
d. Feb 27, 1959 in Bar Harbor, Maine
Source: *GrLiveH; InWom SUP; NotAW MOD*

Farrar, Geraldine
American. Opera Singer
Celebrated soprano; sang 500 times in 29 roles, NY Met., 1906-22; often starred with Caruso.
b. Feb 28, 1882 in Melrose, Massachusetts
d. Mar 11, 1967 in Ridgefield, Connecticut
Source: *ApCAB X; ASCAP 66, 80; Baker 78, 84, 92; BiDAmM; BioIn 1, 2, 3, 4, 6, 7, 8, 9, 10, 11, 12, 13, 14, 15, 18, 19, 20; BriBkM 80; CmOp; ContDcW 89; DcAmB S8; EncAB-A 38; FacFETw; Film 1, 2; FilmEn; FilmgC; HalFC 80, 84, 88; IntDcOp; IntDcWB; InWom, SUP; LegTOT; LibW; LinLib S; MetOEnc; MusSN; NatCAB 16; NewAmDM; NewEOp 71; NewGrDA 86; NewGrDM 80; NewGrDO; NewYTBS 82; NotAW MOD; ObitT 1961; OxDcOp; PenDiMP; REn; TwYS; WhAm 4; WhoAmW 58; WhoHol B; WhScrn 74, 77, 83; WomWWA 14; WorAl; WorAlBi*

Farrar, John Chipman
American. Publisher, Author
Founded Farrar, Rinehardt, 1929; Farrar, Strause & Giroux, 1942.
b. Feb 25, 1896 in Burlington, Vermont
d. Nov 6, 1974 in New York, New York
Source: *AmAu&B; BioIn 3, 10; ChhPo, S1, S2, S3; ConAu 53, 65; DcAmB S9; ObitOF 79; REnAL; Str&VC; WhAm 6; WhJnl; WhoAm 74*

Farrar, Margaret (Petherbridge)
American. Editor, Puzzle Maker
Crossword puzzle editor, *NY Times,* 1942-68.
b. Mar 23, 1897 in New York, New York
d. Jun 11, 1984 in New York, New York
Source: *AnObit 1984; BioIn 3, 4, 5, 14; ConAu 113; CurBio 55, 84, 84N; InWom; LibW; NewYTBS 84; WomFir*

Farrell, Charles
American. Actor
Starred with Janet Gaynor in series of romantic films including 1927 silent classics *Sunrise* and *Seventh Heaven;* former mayor of Palm Springs, CA.

b. Aug 9, 1901 in Onset Bay, Massachusetts
d. May 6, 1990 in Palm Springs, California
Source: *AnObit 1990; BioIn 16, 17, 18; CmpEPM; ConTFT 9; EncAFC; Film 2; FilmEn; FilmgC; GangFlm; HalFC 80, 84, 88; IntMPA 75, 76, 77, 78, 79, 80, 81, 82, 84, 86, 88; MovMk; NewYTBS 90; TwYS; VarWW 85; WhoHol A; WhoThe 81*

Farrell, Eileen
American. Opera Singer
Popular soprano; starred in own radio show, 1940s; made NY Met., debut, 1960; noted Wagnerian singer; Grammy winner.
b. Feb 13, 1920 in Willimantic, Connecticut
Source: *Baker 78, 84, 92; BiDAmM; BioIn 18, 21; BlueB 76; BriBkM 80; CelR; CmOp; CurBio 61; IntDcOp; IntWW 74, 75, 76, 77, 78, 79, 80, 81, 82, 83, 89, 91, 93; IntWWM 77, 80, 90; InWom, SUP; LegTOT; LibW; MetOEnc; MusSN; NewAmDM; NewEOp 71; NewGrDA 86; NewGrDM 80; NewGrDO; PenDiMP; RadStar; WebAB 74, 79; WhoAm 74, 76, 78, 80, 82, 84, 86, 94, 95, 96, 97; WhoAmM 83; WhoAmW 58, 61, 64, 66, 68, 70, 72, 74, 75, 83, 85, 87, 95, 97; WhoEnt 92; WhoOp 76; WorAl; WorAlBi*

Farrell, Glenda
American. Actor
Starred as reporter in *Torchy Blane* film series; won Emmy for "Ben Casey," 1963.
b. Jun 30, 1904 in Enid, Oklahoma
d. May 1, 1971 in New York, New York
Source: *BiE&WWA; BioIn 9, 11, 21; EncAFC; Film 2; FilmEn; FilmgC; ForYSC; GangFlm; HalFC 80, 84, 88; HolP 30; InWom SUP; LegTOT; MotPP; MovMk; NewYTBE 71; NotNAT B; OlFamFa; OxCFilm; ThFT; WhAm 5; WhoAmW 72; WhoHol B; WhoThe 72; WhScrn 74, 77, 83; WhThe*

Farrell, James Thomas
American. Author
Best known for *Studs Lonigan* trilogy, 1932-35.
b. Feb 27, 1904 in Chicago, Illinois
d. Aug 22, 1979 in New York, New York
Source: *AmAu&B; AmNov; AmWr; BioIn 1, 2, 3, 4, 5, 6, 7, 8, 9, 10, 11, 12, 13; CasWL; ChhPo S3; CnDAL; ConAmA; ConAu 5R, 89; ConLC 4; ConNov 82A; CurBio 42, 79; DcAmB S10; EncAB-H 1974, 1996; IntAu&W 76, 77; IntWW 74, 75, 76, 77, 78, 79; IntWWP 77; LinLib S; LngCTC; McGEWB; NewYTBS 80; TwCA; WebAB 74, 79; WebE&AL; WhAm 7; WhoAm 74, 76, 78; WhoWor 74; WrDr 76*

Farrell, Johnny
[John J Farrel]
American. Golfer
Touring pro, 1920s; won US Open, 1928, defeating Bobby Jones in playoffs; Hall of Fame, 1961.
b. Apr 1, 1901 in White Plains, New York
d. Jun 14, 1988 in Boynton Beach, Florida
Source: *BioIn 7; WhoGolf*

Farrell, Mike
American. Actor
Played B J Hunnicutt on TV series "M*A*S*H," 1975-83.
b. Feb 6, 1939AD in Saint Paul, Minnesota
Source: *ConTFT 1, 4; IntMPA 92, 94, 96; LegTOT; MiSFD 9; VarWW 85; WhoAm 86, 88, 90, 92, 94, 95, 96, 97; WhoEnt 92; WhoHol 92, A; WhoTelC; WorAlBi*

Farrell, Perry
[Perry Bernstein; Jane's Addiction]
American. Singer
Lead singer, songwriter for Jane's Addiction, 1986-91; gold album, *Ritual de lo Habitual,* 1991.
b. 1960 in New York, New York
Source: *BioIn 18, 19, 20, 21; LegTOT; News 92, 92-2*

Farrell, Suzanne
[Roberta Sue Ficker]
American. Dancer
Principal dancer, NYC Ballet, 1965-69, 1975-89.
b. Aug 16, 1945 in Cincinnati, Ohio
Source: *BiDD; BioIn 7, 8, 9, 10, 11, 12, 13, 14, 15, 16, 17, 18, 21; CelR 90; CnOxB; ConAu 141; ContDcW 89; CurBio 67; DancEn 78; DcTwCCu 1; FacFETw; GrLiveH; IntDcB; IntDcWB; InWom, SUP; LegTOT; LibW; News 96, 96-3; NewYTBS 79; WhoAm 86, 90; WhoAmW 68, 70, 72, 74, 87, 91; WhoE 91; WhoEnt 92; WhoWor 74; WorAl; WorAlBi*

Farrell, Wes
American. Songwriter
Wrote "Hang on Sloopy," 1965; also wrote the music for TV's "The Partridge Family."
d. Feb 29, 1996 in Coconut Grove, Florida
Source: *NewYTBS 27*

Farrere, Claude
[Frederic Charles Pierre Edouard Bargone]
French. Naval Officer, Author
Member of French Academy, 1935; wrote 30 novels, many sea stories.
b. Apr 27, 1876 in Lyons, France
d. Jun 21, 1957 in Paris, France
Source: *BioIn 4; CasWL; EncSF, 93; EncWL; EvEuW; OxCFr; OxCShps; ScF&FL 1; ScFEYrs*

Farrington, Elizabeth Pruett (Mary)
American. Journalist, Politician
Leading advocate of Hawaiian statehood.
b. May 30, 1898 in Tokyo, Japan
d. Jul 21, 1984
Source: *BioIn 14; ConAu 113; CurBio 55, 84, 84N; InWom, SUP; WhAm 8; WhoAm 74, 76, 78, 80; WhoAmP 73, 75, 77, 79, 81; WhoAmW 58, 81, 83; WhoGov 72; WhoWor 78, 80, 82*

Farrow, John Villiers
Australian. Author, Director
Won Oscar for best screenplay *Around the World in 80 Days,* 1956; father of Mia Farrow.
b. Feb 10, 1906 in Sydney, Australia
d. Jan 28, 1963 in Beverly Hills, California
Source: *AmAu&B; BiDFilm; BkC 5; CathA 1930; CmMov; FilmgC; MovMk; WhAm 4; WhNAA; WorEFlm*

Farrow, Mia
[Maria de Lourdes Villiers Farrow]
American. Actor
Played Allison MacKenzie on TV drama "Peyton Place," 1964-66; starred in films *Rosemary's Baby,* 1968, *Hannah and Her Sisters,* 1986; former wife of Frank Sinatra, Andre Previn; memoir, *What Falls Away,* 1996.
b. Feb 9, 1945 in Los Angeles, California
Source: *BiDFilm, 81, 94; BioIn 7, 14, 15, 16; BkPepl; CelR, 90; ContDcW 89; ConTFT 7; CurBio 70; DcArts; EncAFC; FilmEn; FilmgC; ForYSC; HalFC 80, 84, 88; IntMPA 84, 86, 88, 92, 94, 96; IntWW 83, 91; InWom SUP; LegTOT; MotPP; MovMk; NewYTBS 79, 91; OxCFilm; VarWW 85; Who 82, 83, 85, 88, 90, 92; WhoAm 86, 90; WhoAmW 87, 91; WhoEnt 92; WhoHol 92; WhoHrs 80; WorAl; WorAlBi; WorEFlm*

Fascell, Dante Bruno
American. Politician
Dem. congressman from FL, 1954-92.
b. Mar 9, 1917 in Bridgehampton, New York
Source: *AlmAP 92; BiDrAC; BiDrUSC 89; BioIn 5, 13; CngDr 87, 89; CurBio 60; IntWW 91; PolsAm 84; WhoAm 86, 90; WhoAmP 83, 91; WhoGov 72, 75, 77; WhoSSW 86, 91*

Fasch, Johann Friedrich
German. Composer
Wrote operas, church cantatas, 12 Masses, 69 overtures.
b. Apr 15, 1688 in Buttelstedt, Germany
d. Dec 5, 1758 in Zerbst, Germany
Source: *Baker 78, 84, 92; BioIn 9; MusMk; NewAmDM; NewGrDM 80; NewGrDO; NewOxM; OxCMus*

Fassbaender, Brigitte
German. Opera Singer
Had professional debut at the Bavarian State Opera, 1961; retired from

singing, 1994; appeared in productions of *Elektra, Die Walkure.*
b. Jul 3, 1939 in Berlin, Germany
Source: *BioIn 19, 20; CurBio 94; IntDcOp; IntWW 89, 91, 93; IntWWM 77, 80, 85, 90; MetOEnc; NewGrDM 80; NewGrDO; OxDcOp; PenDiMP; WhoAm 90, 92, 94, 95, 96, 97; WhoEnt 92; WhoOp 76*

Fassbinder, Rainer Werner
German. Actor, Author, Director
Films included *The Marriage of Maria Braun,* 1978; *Lili Marleen,* 1980; *Lola,* 1981.
b. May 31, 1946 in Bad Worishofen, Germany
d. Jun 10, 1982? in Munich, Germany (West)
Source: *AnObit 1982; Benet 87, 96; BiDFilm, 81, 94; BioIn 9, 11, 12, 13, 14, 15, 16; ConAu 31NR, 93, 106; ConLC 20; ConTFT 1; CurBio 77, 82, 82N; DcArts; Ent; FilmEn; GayLesB; GayLL; HalFC 80, 84, 88; IntDcF 1-2, 2-2; IntDcT 2; IntWW 78, 79, 80, 81, 82; MiSFD 9N; NewYTBS 77, 82; OxCFilm; WhAm 8; Who 82; WhoAm 82; WhoWor 78*

Fassett, Kaffe
American. Artist
First textile artist to have a solo exhibition at the Victoria and Albert Museum, London, 1988.
b. 1937 in San Francisco, California
Source: *ConFash; CurBio 95; Who 92, 94*

Fast, Howard Melvin
[E V Cunningham]
American. Author
Novels, *Spartacus; Mirage,* were adapted to film, 1960, 1965.
b. Nov 11, 1914 in New York, New York
Source: *AmAu&B; AmNov; AuBYP 2, 3; Benet 87; BenetAL 91; BioIn 13, 14; CamGLE; CamHAL; CnDAL; ConAu 1NR, 1R, 33NR; ConNov 86, 91; CurBio 43, 91; DcLP 87A; EncAL; EncFWF; FacFETw; HalFC 88; IntWW 83, 91; ModAL; NewEScF; NewYTBS 81; OxCAmL 65; PenC AM; ScFSB; TwCCr&M 91; TwCRHW 90; TwCSFW 86, 91; TwCWW 91; WhoAm 86, 90; WhoEnt 92; WhoUSWr 88; WhoWor 87; WhoWrEP 89; WorAlBi; WrDr 86, 92*

Fastolf, John, Sir
[John Falstaff]
English. Soldier
Served during Hundred Years War; present at English defeat by Joan of Arc, 1492; thought by some to be original of Shakespeare's comic character.
b. 1378 in Caister, England
d. Nov 5, 1459 in Caister, England
Source: *BioIn 2, 3, 6, 9; DcNaB; NewC; NewCol 75; OxCEng 85; REn*

Fath, Jacques
French. Fashion Designer
Post WW II coutourier, noted for his "piquant" fashions.
b. Sep 12, 1912 in Vincennes, France
d. Nov 13, 1954 in Paris, France
Source: *BioIn 2, 3, 4, 5, 21; ConFash; CurBio 51, 55; DcTwDes; EncFash; FairDF FRA; ObitOF 79; ObitT 1951; WhAm 3; WhoFash 88; WorFshn*

Fatima
Arab.
Daughter of Mohammed, wife of Ali.
b. 606 in Mecca, Arabia
d. 632 in Medina, Arabia
Source: *DcBiPP; InWom, SUP; NewC; NewCol 75*

Fattah, Chaka
[Arthur Davenport]
American. Politician
Dem. Rep. from PA, 1995—; former assistant director of House of Umoja, Philadelphia.
b. Nov 21, 1956 in Philadelphia, Pennsylvania
Source: *AlmAP 96; BioIn 21; ConBlB 11; WhoAfA 96; WhoAm 96, 97; WhoAmP 87, 89, 91, 93, 95; WhoBlA 92, 94; WhoE 95, 97*

Faubus, Orval E(ugene)
American. Politician, Journalist
Six-term Dem. governor of AR, 1955-67; used National Guard to prevent Little Rock school integration, 1957.
b. Jan 7, 1910 in Combs, Arkansas
d. Dec 14, 1994 in Conway, Arkansas
Source: *BiDrGov 1789; BioIn 4, 5, 6, 7, 8, 9, 11; BlueB 76; CivRSt; CurBio 56, 95N; DcPol; EncSoH; NewCol 75; WhAm 11; WhoAm 74, 76, 78, 80, 82, 86, 90, 92, 94; WhoAmP 73, 75, 77, 79; WhoWor 80, 82*

Fauci, Anthony Stephen
American. Physician
Associate director for AIDS research at the Nat. Institutes of Health, 1988-94; director, Nat. Institute of Allergy and Infectious Diseases, 1984—.
b. Dec 24, 1940 in New York, New York
Source: *AmMWSc 92; BiDrACP 79; BioIn 16; CurBio 88; IntWW 93; NewYTBS 90; WhoAm 86, 88, 90, 92, 94, 95, 96, 97; WhoMedH; WhoScEn 94, 96*

Faulk, John Henry
American. Actor, Radio Performer
Experiences as victim of anti-communist groups, 1950s, dramatized in his book *Fear on Trial;* adapted to TV play, 1976.
b. Aug 21, 1913 in Austin, Texas
d. Apr 9, 1990 in Austin, Texas
Source: *AmAu&B; AnObit 1990; BioIn 3, 6, 7, 8, 10, 11, 16; ConAu 102, 131; EncMcCE; FacFETw; LesBEnT, 92; NewYTBS 90; WhAm 10; WhoAm 74, 76; WhoHol A; WhoSSW 73*

Faulkner, Brian
Irish. Political Leader
Prime minister of N Ireland, 1971-72; tried to resolve Catholic-Protestant conflicts, but without much success.
b. Feb 18, 1921 in Belfast, Northern Ireland
d. Mar 3, 1977 in Belfast, Northern Ireland
Source: *BioIn 9, 10, 11, 12, 16, 17; BlueB 76; CurBio 72, 77, 77N; DcNaB 1971; EncWB; IntWW 75; ObitOF 79; Who 74; WhoAm 74; WhoWor 74, 76*

Faulkner, Eric
[Bay City Rollers]
Scottish. Musician
Guitarist with Beatles-like group founded in 1967; hit albums include *Strangers in the Wild,* 1978.
b. Oct 21, 1955 in Edinburgh, Scotland
Source: *BkPepl; EncRk 88; OxCPMus; PenEncP; RolSEnR 83*

Faulkner, William
American. Author
Wrote *The Sound and the Fury,* 1929; won Nobel Prize, 1949, Pulitzer Prize, 1962.
b. Sep 25, 1897 in New Albany, Mississippi
d. Jul 6, 1962 in Oxford, Mississippi
Source: *AgeMat; AmAu&B; AmDec 1930, 1950; AmNov; AmWr; AtlBL; Au&Arts 7; AuNews 1; Benet 87, 96; BenetAL 91; BioIn 1, 2, 3, 4, 5, 6, 7, 8, 9, 10, 11, 12, 13, 14, 15, 16, 17, 18, 19, 20, 21; BioNews 74; CamGEL; CamGLE; CamHAL; CasWL; Chambr 3; CnDAL; CnMD; CnMWL; ConAmA; ConAu 33NR, 81; ConLC 1, 3, 6, 8, 9, 11, 14, 18, 28, 52, 68; CroCD; CrtSuMy; CurBio 51, 62; CyWA 58, 89; DcFM; DcLB 9, 11, 44, 102, DS2, Y86A; DcLEL; DcTwCCu 1; EncAAH; EncMys; EncWL, 2, 3; FacFETw; FifSWrA; FilmEn; FilmgC; GrWrEL N; HalFC 80, 84, 88; IntDcF 2-4; LegTOT; LinLib L, S; LiveMA; LngCTC; MagSAmL; MajTwCW; MakMC; McGEWB; MemAm; ModAL, S1, S2; ModWD; NatCAB 57; NobelP; NotNAT B; Novels; ObitT 1961; OxCAmH; OxCAmL 65, 83; OxCEng 67; OxCFilm; OxCTwCP; PenC AM; PenEncH; PeoHis; RAdv 1, 14, 13-1; RComAH; RComWL; REn; REnAL; RfGAmL 87, 94; RfGShF; ShSCr 1; ShSWr; SouWr; TwCA, SUP; TwCCr&M 80, 85; TwCWr; WebAB 74; WebE&AL; WhAm 4; WhDW; WhoNob; WhoTwCL; WorAlBi; WorEFlm; WorLitC; WrPh*

Fauntroy, Walter E(dward)
American. Social Reformer, Politician
Dem. con. from DC, 1971-90; chm., Congressional Black Caucus, 1981-83.
b. Feb 6, 1933 in Washington, District of Columbia
Source: *AlmAP 88; BiDrUSC 89; BioIn 12, 13, 14, 15; BlkAmsC; CngDr 74, 77, 79, 81, 83, 85, 87, 89; InB&W 85; NegAl 89A; NewYTBE 71; WhoAm 86, 90; WhoAmP 87, 91; WhoBlA 85, 92; WhoE 91; WhoGov 77*

Faure, Edgar Jean
French. Statesman, Author
Gaullist speaker of National Assembly, 1973-78; held every major govt. job but president.
b. Aug 18, 1908 in Beziers, France
d. Mar 30, 1988 in Paris, France
Source: *BiDFrPL; CurBio 52, 88; IntWW 82, 83; WhAm 11; Who 85; WhoWor 74, 76, 78, 82, 84, 87*

Faure, Elie
French. Art Historian, Critic
Best known for five-volume work *Histoire de l'Art,* 1909-27.
b. Apr 4, 1873 in Saint-Foy, France
d. Oct 31, 1937 in Paris, France
Source: *BioIn 1; CasWL; ClDMEL 47, 80; DcTwCCu 2; Dis&D; OxCFilm; TwCA, SUP; WorEFlm*

Faure, Francois Felix
French. Political Leader
Sixth pres. of French Republic, in office during Dreyfus Affair, 1895-99.
b. Jan 30, 1841 in Paris, France
d. Feb 16, 1899 in Paris, France
Source: *BiDFrPL; BioIn 17; DcCathB; NewCol 75*

Faure, Gabriel Urbain
French. Composer, Musician
Wrote piano works, chamber music; known for grace, delicacy, finesse; wrote *Requiem,* 1888; song "Clair de Lune."
b. May 12, 1845 in Pamiers, France
d. Nov 4, 1924 in Paris, France
Source: *AtlBL; Baker 84; McGEWB; NewCol 75; NewOxM; OxCEng 85; OxCFr; OxCMus; REn*

Fauset, Jessie Redmon
American. Author
First black woman elected to Phi Beta Kappa, 1905; among her works *Comedy: American Style,* 1934.
b. Apr 27, 1882 in Fredericksville, New Jersey
d. Apr 30, 1961 in Philadelphia, Pennsylvania
Source: *AmAu&B; AmWomWr; BioIn 12, 20, 21; BlkAWP; BlkLC; BlkWAm; BlmGWL; ConAu 109; ConLC 19; CyWA 89; DcAmB S7; DcAmNB; DcLB 51; FemiCLE; FemiWr; HanAmWH; HarlReB; InWom SUP; NegAl 83; NotAW MOD; NotBlAW 1; OxCAmL 83, 95; OxCWoWr 95; SchCGBL; TwCA SUP*

Faust, Frederick Schiller
[Max Brand]
American. Author, Poet
Wrote popular westerns; wrote *Dr. Kildare* films.
b. May 29, 1892 in Seattle, Washington
d. May 12, 1944 in Santa Maria Infante, Italy
Source: *AmAu&B; BioIn 14, 15, 16; CurBio 44; DcAmB S3; DcLEL; DcNAA; EncMys; EncSF 93; FifWWr; FilmgC; HalFC 80, 84, 88; LegTOT; LngCTC; MnBBF; NewEScF; OxCAmL 83, 95; RAdv 14; REn; REnAL; REnAW; ScF&FL 1, 92; TwCA, SUP; TwCCr&M 80; TwCWW 82, 91; WebAB 74, 79; WorAl; WorAlBi*

Faust, Gerry
[Gerard Anthony Faust, Jr]
American. Football Coach
Succeeded Dan Devine as football coach at Notre Dame, 1981-85.
b. May 21, 1935 in Dayton, Ohio
Source: *NewYTBS 81*

Faust, Johann
[Johann Faustus]
German. Magician
Was the archtype of character, Dr. Faustus in the writings of Marlowe, Goethe, Mann, also operas by Gounod, Busconi.
b. 1480 in Knittlingen, Germany
d. 1540
Source: *BioIn 1, 6, 12; FilmgC; LinLib L, S; OxCThe 83*

Faust, Lotta
Actor
Appeared on stage in *The Wizard of Oz.*
b. Feb 8, 1880 in New York, New York
d. Jan 25, 1910 in New York, New York
Source: *BiDD; NotNAT B; WhoStg 1908*

Faustino, David
American. Actor
Plays Bud Bundy, the son on TV show "Married.with Children," 1987—.
Source: *BioIn 16, 18*

Favart, Charles Simon
French. Composer
Originated modern light opera; director, Opera Comique, Paris, 1758-69; wrote 150 comedies, operettas.
b. Nov 13, 1710 in Paris, France
d. Mar 12, 1792 in Belleville, France
Source: *Baker 84; BbD; BiD&SB; CasWL; DcBiPP; DcEuL; EvEuW; NewCBEL; NewCol 75; NewEOp 71; OxCFr; OxCMus; OxCThe 83; OxDcOp*

Faversham, William Alfred
English. Actor
Leading man in Charles Frohman's Empire Theatre Co., 1893-1901; in silent films, 1915.
b. Feb 12, 1868 in London, England
d. Apr 7, 1940 in Bay Shore, New York
Source: *AmBi; CurBio 40; DcAmB S2; FamA&A; Film 1, 2; OxCThe 67; PlP&P; TwYS; WhAm 1; WhoHol B; WhScrn 74, 77; WhThe*

Favre, Brett (Lorenzo)
American. Football Player
Quarterback, Atlanta Falcons, 1991-92; Green Bay Packers, 1992—; NFL MVP, 1995, 1996.
b. Oct 10, 1969 in Gulfport, Mississippi
Source: *CurBio 96*

Fawcett, Farrah Leni
American. Actor
Starred in "Charlie's Angels," 1976-77; TV movies "The Burning Bed," 1983; "Poor Little Rich Girl," 1987.
b. Feb 2, 1947 in Corpus Christi, Texas
Source: *BioIn 13, 14, 15, 16; CelR 90; ConTFT 4; HalFC 88; IntMPA 86, 92; InWom SUP; LesBEnT 92; NewYTBS 86; VarWW 85; WhoAm 80, 82, 84, 86, 88, 90, 92, 95, 96, 97; WhoAmW 81, 95, 97; WhoEnt 92; WorAlBi*

Fawcett, George
American. Actor
Silent screen star in D W Griffith films: *Intolerance,* 1916; *Once a Gentleman,* 1930.
b. Aug 25, 1861 in Alexandria, Virginia
d. Jun 6, 1939 in Nantucket, Massachusetts
Source: *Alli SUP; Film 1, 2; MotPP; MovMk; TwYS; WhAm 1; WhoHol B; WhScrn 74, 77; WhThe*

Fawcett, Henry
English. Economist, Statesman
Contributed to passage of 1867 Reform Act; developed postal system.
b. Aug 26, 1833 in Salisbury, England
d. Nov 6, 1884 in Cambridge, England
Source: *Alli SUP; BbD; BiD&SB; BiDBrF 1; BioIn 8, 14, 16; BritAu 19; CelCen; CyEd; DcBiPP; DcEnA; DcEnL; DcInB; DcNaB; Dis&D; EvLB; LinLib S; NewCBEL; NewCol 75; WhoEc 81, 86*

Fawcett, Millicent Garrett, Dame
[Mrs. Henry Fawcett]
English. Feminist
Leader of women's suffrage movement, 1867.
b. Jun 11, 1847 in Aldeburgh, England
d. Aug 5, 1929 in London, England
Source: *Alli SUP; BbD; BiD&SB; BiDBrF 1; BioIn 14, 16, 17; CelCen; ContDcW 89; DcBiPP; DcNaB 1922; EvLB; HisWorL; IntDcWB; InWom SUP; NewC; NewCol 75; VicBrit; WhLit; WomFir*

Fawkes, Guy
English. Soldier
Conspired to blow up English Parliament, King James I, Nov 5, 1605; Guy Fawkes Day celebrated Nov 5.
b. 1570 in York, England
d. Jan 31, 1606 in London, England
Source: *BioIn 2, 4, 5, 6, 7, 8, 11; DcNaB; LegTOT; LinLib S; LuthC 75; NewC; NewCol 75; WhDW; WorAl; WorAlBi*

Fay, Frank
American. Comedian, Actor
Appeared in hit play *Harvey,* 1944; once wed to Barbara Stanwyck.
b. Nov 17, 1897 in San Francisco, California
d. Sep 25, 1961 in Santa Monica, California

Source: *BioIn 1, 2, 6; CmpEPM; EncMT; EncVaud; Film 2; JoeFr; NotNAT A, B; OxCAmT 84; WhoCom; WhoHol B; WhScrn 77; WhThe*

Fay, Michael, Sir
New Zealander. Athlete
b. Apr 10, 1949
Source: *BioIn 16; Who 92*

Faye, Alice
[Ann Leppert]
American. Actor, Singer
Beautiful blonde musical star, 1930s-40s; wife of Phil Harris; in *Alexander's Ragtime Band,* 1938.
b. May 5, 1915 in New York, New York
Source: *BiDAmM; BiDD; BiDFilm; BioIn 2, 9, 10, 12, 13, 14, 15, 16, 18; CelR; CmMov; CmpEPM; DcWomA; EncAFC; FilmgC; ForYSC; HalFC 88; InWom, SUP; LegTOT; MovMk; OxCFilm; OxCPMus; RadStar; ThFT; WhoAm 76; WorAl; WorAlBi; WorEFlm*

Faye, Joey
[Joseph Anthony Palladino]
American. Actor, Comedian
Starred in Minsky's burlesque theatre, 1931-38.
b. Jul 12, 1910 in New York, New York
d. Apr 26, 1997 in Englewood, New Jersey
Source: *BiE&WWA; JoeFr; NotNAT; WhoHol 92, A; WhoThe 72, 77, 81*

Faylen, Frank
[Frank Cusik]
American. Actor
Best known for film *The Lost Weekend,* 1945; was Dobie's father on "The Many Loves of Dobie Gillis," 1959-63.
b. Dec 8, 1907 in Saint Louis, Missouri
d. Aug 2, 1985 in Burbank, California
Source: *FilmEn; FilmgC; ForYSC; HalFC 80, 84, 88; IntMPA 81, 82, 84; MotPP; MovMk; Vers A; WhoHol A*

Fazenda, Louise
American. Actor
In comedies for Mack Sennett's Keystone studio from 1915.
b. Jun 17, 1899 in Lafayette, Indiana
d. Apr 17, 1962 in Beverly Hills, California
Source: *Film 1, 2; FilmEn; FilmgC; MotPP; MovMk; ThFT; TwYS; WhoHol B; WhScrn 74, 77; WorEFlm*

Fearing, Kenneth Flexner
American. Author
Writings include verse *Dead Reckoning,* 1938; mystery novel *Big Clock,* 1946.
b. Jul 28, 1902 in Oak Park, Illinois
d. Jun 26, 1961 in New York, New York
Source: *AmAu&B; AmNov; CnDAL; CnE&AP; ConAmA; ConAu 93; DcLEL; EncMys; ModAL; OxCAmL 65; PenC AM; RAdv 1; REn; TwCA SUP; WebE&AL; WhAm 4; WhoTwCL*

Fears, Tom
[Thomas Jesse Fears]
American. Football Player
End, LA Rams, 1948-56; set NFL record for most receptions in game, 18, 1950; Hall of Fame, 1970.
b. Dec 3, 1923 in Los Angeles, California
Source: *BiDAmSp FB; BioIn 9, 17; CmCal; LegTOT; NewYTBE 70; WhoFtbl 74; WhoSpor*

Feather, Leonard Geoffrey
American. Composer, Critic
Leading jazz spokesman, 1940s-50s; hosted Jazz Club, US series; wrote jazz reference books.
b. Sep 13, 1914 in London, England
Source: *AmAu&B; ASCAP 66; Baker 78, 84; BiDJaz; BioIn 16; CmpEPM; ConAu 61; NewGrDA 86; NewGrDJ 88; OxCPMus; PenEncP; WhoAm 84; WhoUSWr 88; WhoWor 74; WhoWrEP 89; WrDr 92*

Feather, Victor
English. Labor Union Official
Helped to make Trades Union Congress one of Europe's most powerful unions.
b. Apr 10, 1908 in Bradford, England
d. Jul 28, 1976 in London, England
Source: *BioIn 8, 9, 10, 11; CurBio 73, 76N; IntWW 74; NewYTBS 76; Who 74; WhoWor 74, 76*

Febres-Cordero, Leon
Ecuadorean. Political Leader
Social Christian president of Ecuador, 1984-88; succeeded by Rodrigo Cevallos Borja.
b. Mar 9, 1931 in Guayaquil, Ecuador
Source: *BioIn 14, 15; DcCPSAm; IntWW 91; NewYTBS 84; WhoWor 87, 89, 91*

Fechner, Gustav Theodor
German. Philosopher, Physicist
A founder of psychophysics; formulated Fechner's law; wrote *Zendavesta,* 1851.
b. Apr 19, 1801 in Gross-Sarchen, Germany
d. Nov 18, 1887 in Leipzig, Germany
Source: *AsBiEn; Baker 84; BbD; BiD&SB; BiDPsy; BiESc; BioIn 7, 15; CyEd; DcScB; Dis&D; InSci; LarDcSc; LinLib S; LuthC 75; McGEWB; NamesHP; NewCol 75; OxCGer 76, 86*

Federici, Daniel Paul
[E Street Band]
"Phantom"
American. Musician, Singer
Plays keyboards, accordion with Bruce Springsteen's band since 1968.
b. Jan 23, 1950 in Flemington, New Jersey
Source: *WhoRocM 82*

Federko, Bernie
[Bernard Allan Federko]
Canadian. Hockey Player
Center, St. Louis, 1976-89; team's all-time leading goal scorer.
b. May 12, 1956 in Foam Lake, Saskatchewan, Canada
Source: *HocEn; HocReg 87*

Fedin, Konstantin Aleksandrovich
Russian. Author
Wrote of small-town life before and after Revolution: *The Bonfire,* 1962.
b. Feb 24, 1892 in Saratov, Russia
d. Jul 15, 1977 in Moscow, Union of Soviet Socialist Republics
Source: *Benet 87; BiDSovU; BioIn 1, 7, 10, 11; CasWL; ClDMEL 47, 80; ConAu 73, 81; DcRusL; DcRusLS; EncWL 2; EvEuW; HanRL; IntWW 74, 77; ModSL 1; PenC EUR; REn; SovUn; TwCWr; WhDW; WhoSocC 78; WorAl; WorAu 1950*

Fedorenko, Fyodor
Government Official
First accused Nazi war criminal deported by US, 1984; execution date kept secret.
b. 1908?
d. 1987, Union of Soviet Socialist Republics

Fedorenko, Nikolai Trofimovich
Russian. Diplomat
Russian UN ambassador, 1963-68.
b. Nov 9, 1912 in Pyatigorsk, Russia
Source: *BioIn 6, 8; CurBio 67; IntWW 74, 75, 76, 91*

Fedorov, Sergei
Russian. Hockey Player
Center for Detroit Red Wings, 1990—; won Hart Trophy, 1994; Selke Trophy, 1994, 1996.
b. Dec 13, 1969 in Pskov, Union of Soviet Socialist Republics
Source: *BioIn 19, 20*

Feelings, Tom
[Thomas Feelings]
American. Illustrator
Illustrated Caldecott Honor Book, *Mojo Means One,* 1971.
b. May 19, 1933 in New York, New York
Source: *AfroAA; BioIn 8, 9, 11, 12, 16, 18, 19; BkP; BlkAuII, 92; BlkWr 1; ChlBkCr; ChlLR 5; ConAu 25NR, 49; ConBlB 11; IlsBYP; IlsCB 1967; InB&W 80, 85; LivgBAA; MajAI; SchCGBL; SmATA 8, 19AS, 69; ThrBJA; WhoAfA 96; WhoBlA 77, 80, 85, 88, 90, 92, 94; WhoE 77, 79*

Feeney, Chub
[Charles Stoneham Feeney]
American. Baseball Executive
Succeeded Warren Giles as pres. of NL, 1970-86; replaced by A Bartlett Giamatti.
b. Aug 31, 1921 in Orange, New Jersey

d. Jan 10, 1994 in San Francisco, California
Source: *BiDAmSp BB; BioIn 15; WhAm 11; WhoAm 76, 78, 80, 82, 84, 86, 88, 90; WhoE 81, 83; WhoProB 73; WhoWest 87, 89*

Fehr, Donald Martin
American. Baseball Executive
Head of ML Baseball Players Assn., since 1985; avoided strike, 1985; prevented mandatory drug testing.
b. Jul 18, 1948 in Marion, Indiana
Source: *BioIn 14, 16; ConNews 87-2; NewYTBS 85, 89*

Feifel, Herman
American. Psychologist
Pioneer in thanatology, the study of death and dying and the associated coping mechanisms, a field considered taboo when he began his work on it in the 1950s.
b. Nov 4, 1915 in New York, New York
Source: *AmMWSc 73S, 78S, 89, 92, 95; BioIn 20; ConAu 101; CurBio 94; WhoAm 80, 86, 88, 90, 92; WhoFrS 84; WhoThSc 1996; WhoWest 74, 76, 78, 82*

Feiffer, Jules Ralph
"Iconoclast with a Pencil"
American. Cartoonist, Screenwriter
Philosophizing satirist for *Village Voice,* 1956—; wrote screenplay *Carnal Knowledge,* 1971; won Obie, 1969; Pulitzer, 1986.
b. Jan 26, 1929 in New York, New York
Source: *AmAu&B; Au&Arts 3; Au&Wr 71; Benet 87; BioIn 13, 16; CamGWoT; CnThe; ConAu 17R, 30NR; ConDr 88; ConLC 44, 64; CroCD; CurBio 61; DcLB 44; EncACom; EncAHmr; EncTwCJ; FacFETw; FilmgC; HalFC 88; IntAu&W 91; IntWW 83, 91; MajTwCW; McGEWD 72; NotNAT; SmATA 8, 61; WhoAm 86, 90; WhoAmA 91; WhoE 91; WhoEnt 92; WhoUSWr 88; WhoWor 74; WhoWorJ 72; WhoWrEP 89; WorAlBi; WrDr 86, 92*

Feingold, Benjamin Franklin
American. Physician, Author
Developed Feingold diet for hyperactive children removing preservatives, artificially flavored, colored foods; wrote *Why Your Child is Hyperactive,* 1975.
b. Jun 15, 1900 in Pittsburgh, Pennsylvania
d. Mar 23, 1982 in San Francisco, California
Source: *AmMWSc 79; AnObit 1982; BioIn 12; ConAu 106; NewYTBS 82; WhAm 8; WhoAm 76, 78, 80, 82; WhoAmJ 80*

Feingold, Russell D.
American. Politician
Dem. senator, WI, 1993—.
b. Mar 2, 1953 in Janesville, Wisconsin
Source: *AlmAP 96; IntWW 93; WhoAmP 83, 85, 87, 89, 91, 93, 95*

Feininger, Andreas Bernhard Lyonel
American. Photographer
With *Life* mag., 1943-62; known for work in telephoto, close-up photography; noted for poetic views of cities.
b. Dec 27, 1906 in Paris, France
Source: *AmAu&B; BioIn 13, 14, 15, 16; ConAu 20NR, 85; ConPhot 82, 88; CurBio 57; EncTwCJ; ICPEnP; WhAmArt 85; WhoAm 86, 90, 97; WhoAmA 84, 91; WhoWor 76*

Feininger, Lyonel
[Charles Adrian Feininger]
American. Artist, Cartoonist
Pioneer of modern American art whose unique style of dividing forms, space by segmented planes of color was influenced by cubism.
b. Jul 17, 1871 in New York, New York
d. Jan 13, 1956 in New York, New York
Source: *AtlBL; BioIn 1, 2, 3, 4, 5, 6, 7, 10, 11, 12, 13, 14, 17, 18, 20; ConArt 77, 83; ConAu 149; CurBio 55, 56; DcAmArt; DcAmB S6; DcCAA 71, 77, 88, 94; EncTR; IntDcAA 90; McGDA; NatCAB 62; OxCArt; OxCGer 76, 86; OxCTwCA; OxDcArt; PhDcTCA 77; REn; WhAm 3; WorECom*

Feinstein, Dianne
American. Politician
Dem. senator, CA, 1992—; mayor of San Francisco, 1978-88; succeeded assassinated George Moscone.
b. Jun 22, 1933 in San Francisco, California
Source: *AlmAP 96; AmPolW 80; AmWomM; BioIn 10, 11, 12, 13, 14, 15, 16; CngDr 93, 95; CurBio 79, 95; EncWB; GrLiveH; IntWW 89, 91, 93; InWom SUP; LegTOT; News 93-3; NewYTBE 71; NewYTBS 78, 90, 92; PeoHis; PolPar; WhoAm 80, 82, 84, 86, 88, 90, 92, 94, 96, 97; WhoAmP 91; WhoAmW 79, 81, 83, 85, 87, 89, 91, 93, 95, 97; WhoGov 75, 77; WhoWest 80, 82, 84, 87, 89, 92, 94, 96; WomPO 78; WomStre; WorAlBi*

Feinstein, Michael Jay
[Michael Cohen]
American. Musician
Recording, cabaret pianist; known for romantic works by George Gershwin, Cole Porter.
b. Sep 7, 1956 in Columbus, Ohio
Source: *Baker 92; BioIn 15; CurBio 88; NewYTBS 86; WhoAm 90, 92; WhoE 91; WhoEnt 92*

Feis, Herbert
American. Historian
Won Pulitzer, 1961, for history of Potsdam Conference.
b. Jun 7, 1893 in New York, New York
d. Mar 2, 1972 in Winter Park, Florida
Source: *AmAu&B; AmPeW; Au&Wr 71; BiDInt; BioIn 6, 9, 10, 11, 16, 19; ConAu 33R, P-1; CurBio 61, 72, 72N; DcAmB S9; DcAmDH 80, 89; IntAu&W 76; NatCAB 57; NewYTBE 72; OxCAmL 65; WhAm 5; WhoWorJ 72; WorAu 1950*

Fela
Nigerian. Singer, Songwriter, Political Activist
Recording artist whose politically charged songs and activism have made him a controversial figure.
b. 1938 in Abeokuta, Nigeria
Source: *BioIn 11, 13, 14, 15, 17, 18, 21; ConBlB 1; DcArts; EncRk 88; IntWW 89, 91, 93; NewYTBS 77, 86*

Feld, Eliot
American. Dancer, Choreographer
With American Ballet Theater, 1963-70; best-known parts in *Intermezzo,* 1969; *A Footstep of Air,* 1977.
b. Jul 5, 1942 in New York, New York
Source: *BiDD; BioIn 8, 9, 10, 11, 12, 13, 14; CurBio 71; FacFETw; IntDcB; NewGrDA 86; News 96, 96-1; NewYTBE 70; NewYTBS 74; RAdv 14; WhoAm 74, 76, 78, 80, 82, 84, 86, 88, 90, 92, 94, 95, 96, 97; WhoE 74, 79, 81, 83, 85, 86, 89, 91, 93, 95, 97; WhoEnt 92; WhoHol 92; WhoWor 95, 96, 97*

Feld, Fritz
American. Actor
Appeared in 400 major films, 300 TV shows, 500 TV films, since 1920s.
b. Oct 15, 1900 in Berlin, Germany
d. Nov 1994 in Santa Monica, California
Source: *BioIn 15, 19; EncAFC; Film 2; FilmEn; FilmgC; ForYSC; HalFC 80, 84, 88; HolCA; IntMPA 75, 76, 77, 78, 79, 80, 81, 82, 84, 86, 88, 92, 94; MovMk; NewYTBS 93; QDrFCA 92; TwYS; Vers A; WhAm 11; WhoAm 74, 76, 78, 80, 82, 84, 86, 88, 90, 92, 94; WhoAmJ 80; WhoEnt 92; WhoHol 92, A*

Feld, Irvin
American. Businessman, Producer
Pres., producer Ringling Brothers, Barnum & Bailey Circus, 1967-84; founded Clown College, 1968.
b. May 9, 1918 in Hagerstown, Maryland
d. Sep 6, 1984 in Venice, California
Source: *BioIn 11, 12, 14; CelR; CurBio 79, 84N; NewYTBE 70; St&PR 75, 84; WhAm 9; WhoAm 76, 78, 80, 82, 84; WhoWor 78, 80, 82, 84*

Feld, Kenneth Jeffrey
American. Circus Owner
Owner, president, Ringling Brothers and Barnum & Bailey Combined Shows, Inc., 1984—; son of Irvin.
b. 1948 in Washington, District of Columbia
Source: *BioIn 15, 16; Dun&B 88; News 88-2; St&PR 84, 87, 91, 93, 96, 97*

Felder, Don(ald William)
[The Eagles]
American. Musician, Singer, Songwriter
Joined the Eagles as lead guitarist, songwriter, 1973; recorded title song from movie *Heavy Metal,* 1981.

b. Sep 21, 1947 in Gainesville, Florida
Source: *ASCAP 80; OnThGG; RkOn 85; WhoAm 80, 82; WhoRocM 82*

Feldman, Alvin Lindbergh
American. Airline Executive
Pres., Frontier Airlines, Inc., 1971-81.
b. Dec 14, 1927 in New York, New York
d. Aug 9, 1981 in Los Angeles, California
Source: *BioIn 12; WhAm 9; WhoAm 78, 80, 82, 84, 86; WhoFI 81; WhoWest 82*

Feldman, Corey
American. Actor
Lead or primary roles in hit movies *Goonies*, 1985; *Stand by Me*, 1988.
b. Jul 16, 1971 in Reseda, California
Source: *BioIn 15, 16; ConTFT 8, 15; IntMPA 92, 94, 96; LegTOT*

Feldman, Marty
English. Actor
Made American film debut in *Young Frankenstein*, 1974.
b. Jul 8, 1933 in London, England
d. Dec 2, 1982 in Mexico City, Mexico
Source: *AnObit 1982; BioIn 10, 11, 13; ConAu 108; FilmgC; HalFC 80, 84, 88; IntMPA 79, 80, 81, 82; ItaFilm; LegTOT; NewYTBS 82; QDrFCA 92; WhAm 8; WhoAm 78, 80, 82; WhoCom; WhoHol A; WhoHrs 80; WorAl; WorAlBi*

Feldman, Morton
American. Composer
Leading avant-garde composer noted for developing use of hypnotic repetition; operas include *Neither*.
b. Jan 12, 1926 in New York, New York
d. Sep 3, 1987 in Buffalo, New York
Source: *AmComp; AnObit 1987; Baker 78, 84, 92; BiDAmM; BioIn 11; BriBkM 80; CompSN SUP; ConAmC 76, 82; CpmDNM 81; DcArts; DcCM; DcCom&M 79; IntWWM 90; MusMk; NewAmDM; NewGrDA 86; NewGrDM 80; NewGrDO; NewOxM; NewYTBS 87; WhoAm 74; WhoAmM 83; WhoWor 74*

Feldon, Barbara
American. Actor
Best known for role as Agent 99 on TV series "Get Smart," 1965-70.
b. Mar 12, 1939 in Butler, Pennsylvania
Source: *BioIn 13; ConTFT 6; EncAFC; HalFC 80, 84, 88; IntMPA 92; InWom SUP; WhoHol A; WorAlBi*

Feldshuh, Tovah
American. Actor
Played in TV shows "Amazing Howard Hughes"; "Holocaust"; "Beggarman-Thief."
b. Dec 27, 1952 in New York, New York
Source: *BioIn 11, 16; ConTFT 11; HalFC 88; IntMPA 92; LegTOT; WhoAm 86, 88; WhoEnt 92; WhoThe 81*

Feldstein, Martin Stuart
American. Economist
Chm., Council of Economic Advisers, 1982-84; professor of Economics, Harvard University, 1967—.
b. Nov 25, 1939 in New York, New York
Source: *BioIn 11, 12, 13, 14; ConAu 73; GrEconS; IntWW 83, 89, 91, 93; NewYTBS 82; Who 85, 88, 90, 92, 94; WhoAm 74, 76, 78, 80, 82, 84, 86, 88, 90, 92, 94, 95, 96, 97; WhoAmJ 80; WhoE 83, 95, 97; WhoEc 86; WhoFI 81, 83, 85, 87, 89, 92, 94, 96; WhoWor 89, 91; WorAlBi*

Feliciano, Jose
American. Singer, Musician
Blind singer, guitarist; composed theme for TV show "Chico and the Man"; best-known single: "Light My Fire," 1968.
b. Sep 10, 1945 in Lares, Puerto Rico
Source: *ASCAP 80; Baker 84, 92; BiDAmM; BioIn 8, 9, 10, 11, 14, 18, 20; CelR; ConHero 2; ConMus 10; CurBio 69; DcHiB; EncFCWM 83; EncRk 88; EncRkSt; HarEnR 86; LegTOT; OnThGG; PenEncP; RkOn 78, 84; RolSEnR 83; VarWW 85; WhoAm 74, 76, 78, 80, 82, 84, 86, 88, 92, 94, 95, 96, 97; WhoEnt 92; WhoHisp 91, 92, 94; WhoRock 81; WorAl; WorAlBi*

Felker, Clay S
American. Journalist
Founder, editor, publisher, *New York* mag., 1967-77.
b. Oct 2, 1928 in Saint Louis, Missouri
Source: *BioIn 8, 10; CelR; ConAu 73; CurBio 75; EncAJ; EncTwCJ; St&PR 75; WhoAm 74, 76, 78, 80, 82, 84; WhoE 74, 75; WhoFI 74; WhoWor 74*

Fell, John
English. Clergy, Editor
Promoted Oxford University Press, 1670s; designed Fell type.
b. Jun 23, 1625 in Longworth, England
d. Jul 10, 1686 in Oxford, England
Source: *Alli; Benet 87, 96; BioIn 3, 8; BritAu; DcBiPP; DcEnL; DcNaB, C; LuthC 75; NewC; NewCBEL; OxCEng 67, 85, 95; REn*

Fell, Norman
American. Actor
Played Stanley Roper on TV's "Three's Company," 1977-79; "The Ropers," 1979-80.
b. Mar 24, 1925 in Philadelphia, Pennsylvania
Source: *ConTFT 3; EncAFC; HalFC 84, 88; IntMPA 86, 92; WhoAm 74, 78, 80, 82; WhoHol A; WorAl*

Feller, Bob
[Robert William Andrew Feller]
"Rapid Robert"
American. Baseball Player
Pitcher, Cleveland, 1936-41, 1945-56; had 266 career wins, three no-hitters; Hall of Fame, 1962.
b. Nov 3, 1918 in Van Meter, Iowa
Source: *AuBYP 2, 3; Ballpl 90; BiDAmSp BB; BioIn 1, 2, 3, 4, 5, 6, 7, 8, 9, 10, 13, 14, 15, 17; BioNews 74; CurBio 41; LegTOT; NewYTBS 86; WebAB 74, 79; WhoAm 92, 94, 95, 96, 97; WhoEnt 92; WhoHol 92; WhoProB 73; WhoSpor; WhoWor 93; WorAl; WorAlBi*

Fellig, Arthur
"Weegee"
American. Photographer
Black-and-white news photographer known for pictures of NYC violence, 1940s-50s.
b. Jul 12, 1899 in Zloczew, Austria
d. Dec 26, 1968 in New York, New York
Source: *BioIn 8, 10, 11, 13; ConAu 145; ConPhot 82, 88; ICPEnP; LegTOT; MacBEP; WhAmArt 85*

Fellini, Federico
Italian. Screenwriter, Director
Won four Oscars for best foreign film, including *La Dolce Vita*, 1960.
b. Jan 20, 1920 in Rimini, Italy
d. Oct 31, 1993 in Rome, Italy
Source: *AnObit 1993; Benet 87, 96; BiDFilm, 81, 94; BioIn 4, 5, 6, 7, 8, 9, 10, 11, 12, 13, 14, 15, 16; BkPepl; CelR, 90; ConAu 33NR, 65, 143; ConLC 16, 81, 85; ConTFT 1, 7, 12; CurBio 57, 80, 94N; DcArts; DcFM; EncEurC; FacFETw; FilmEn; FilmgC; HalFC 80, 84, 88; IntDcF 1-2, 2-2; IntMPA 75, 76, 77, 78, 79, 80, 81, 82, 84, 86, 88, 92, 94; IntWW 74, 75, 76, 77, 78, 79, 80, 81, 82, 83, 89, 91, 93; ItaFilm; LegTOT; MakMC; McGEWB; MiSFD 9; MovMk; News 94, 94-2; NewYTBS 93; OxCFilm; RAdv 14, 13-3; REn; WhAm 11; WhDW; Who 74, 82, 83, 85, 88, 90, 92, 94; WhoAm 80, 82, 84, 86, 88, 90, 92, 94; WhoHol 92; WhoWor 74, 78, 80, 82, 84, 87, 89, 91, 93; WomWMM; WorAl; WorAlBi; WorEFlm; WorFDir 2*

Fellows, Charles, Sir
English. Archaeologist
Discovered ancient ruins of Lycia, Asia Minor, 1830s-40s; donated collection to British Museum.
b. 1799 in Nottingham, England
d. Nov 8, 1860 in London, England
Source: *Alli; BiD&SB; BritAu 19; DcBiPP; DcNaB; InSci*

Fellows, Edith
American. Actor, Singer
1930s child star in films *Huckleberry Finn; Jane Eyre; Five Little Peppers.*
b. May 20, 1923 in Boston, Massachusetts
Source: *BioIn 9, 10, 14, 15; Film 2; FilmEn; FilmgC; ForYSC; HalFC 80, 84, 88; InWom SUP; ThFT; What 5; WhoEnt 92; WhoHol 92, A*

Fels, Joseph
American. Manufacturer, Philanthropist
Established soap-making business, 1894.

b. Dec 16, 1854 in Halifax, Virginia
d. Feb 22, 1914 in Philadelphia, Pennsylvania
Source: *AmBi; BioIn 5; DcAmB; DcAmSR; NatCAB 20; WhAm 1*

Fels, Samuel Simeon
American. Businessman, Philanthropist
Pres., Fels Naptha Soap Co., 1914-50; founded Crime Prevention Association, 1932.
b. Feb 16, 1860 in Yanceyville, North Carolina
d. Jun 23, 1950 in Philadelphia, Pennsylvania
Source: *BioIn 2, 9; DcAmB S4; DcAmSR; WhAm 3*

Felsenstein, Walter
Austrian. Actor, Director, Producer
Began managing opera companies, 1924; Berlin State Opera, 1940-47; Komische Opera, 1947-75.
b. May 30, 1901 in Vienna, Austria
d. Oct 8, 1975 in Berlin, German Democratic Republic
Source: *Baker 78, 84, 92; BioIn 5, 6, 8, 9, 10; CmOp; ConAu 111; EncWT; IntDcOp; IntWW 74, 75, 76N; MetOEnc; NewEOp 71; NewGrDM 80; NewGrDO; NewYTBS 75; ObitT 1971; OxDcOp; WhoOp 76; WhoSocC 78; WhoWor 74*

Felton, Harold W
American. Author
Writings include *Deborah Sampson: Soldier of the Revolution,* 1976.
b. Apr 1, 1902 in Neola, Iowa
Source: *AuBYP 2, 3; BioIn 6, 8, 9; ConAu 1NR, 1R; MorJA; SmATA 1*

Felton, Rebecca Ann Latimer
American. Politician
Appointed senator from GA, 1922; first woman to sit in Senate.
b. Jun 10, 1835 in Decatur, Illinois
d. Jan 24, 1930 in Atlanta, Georgia
Source: *AmPeW; AmRef; BioIn 15, 17, 19; InWom SUP; LibW; NotAW; WomFir*

Felton, Verna
American. Actor
Played in TV series "December Bride," 1954-61.
b. Jul 20, 1890 in Salinas, California
d. Dec 14, 1966 in North Hollywood, California
Source: *BioIn 4, 7; FilmgC; ForYSC; HalFC 80, 84, 88; InWom; RadStar; SaTiSS; Vers B; WhoHol B; WhScrn 74, 77, 83*

Feltsman, Vladimir
Russian. Pianist
Classical pianist; emigrated to US after years of harassment by Soviet officials; his release became a cause celebre among international organizations.
b. Jan 8, 1952 in Moscow, Union of Soviet Socialist Republics
Source: *Baker 92; BioIn 15, 16; CurBio 88; FacFETw; IntWWM 90; NewYTBS 86, 87; NotTwCP; PenDiMP*

Fender, Freddy
[Baldermar Huerta]
American. Singer, Songwriter
Won Grammy, 1977, for "Before the Next Teardrop Falls."
b. Jun 4, 1937 in San Benito, Texas
Source: *BioIn 10, 12, 14, 21; DcHiB; EncFCWM 83; HarEnCM 87; IlEncCM; LegTOT; NewAmDM; NewGrDA 86; PenEncP; RkOn 74, 78; RolSEnR 83; WhoAm 78, 80, 82, 84, 86, 88, 92, 94, 95, 96, 97; WhoEnt 92; WhoHisp 91, 92, 94; WhoRock 81; WhoSSW 97*

Fender, Leo
[Clarence Leo Fender]
American. Manufacturer
Developed Stratocruiser electric guitar, 1954; pioneer in development of rock music.
b. Aug 10, 1909 in Anaheim, California
d. Mar 21, 1991 in Fullerton, California
Source: *AnObit 1991; BioIn 17, 18; ConMus 10; IlEncRk; NewAmDM; News 92, 92-1; NewYTBS 91; RolSEnR 83; WhAm 10; WhoAm 84, 86, 88, 90*

Fenelon, Fania
[Fanny Goldstein]
French. Author, Singer, Musician
Memoirs, *Playing for Time* 1977, telling horrors of Nazi concentration camps, made into film starring Vanessa Redgrave, 1985.
b. Sep 2, 1918 in Paris, France
d. Dec 20, 1983 in Paris, France
Source: *AnObit 1983; BioIn 11; ConAu 77, 111; NewYTBS 78, 83; WhoWor 80*

Fenelon, Francois de Salignac
French. Author, Theologian
Wrote prose epic *Adventures of Telemachus,* 1699.
b. Aug 6, 1651 in Perigord, France
d. Jan 7, 1715 in Cambrai, France
Source: *AtlBL; BbD; BiD&SB; CasWL; DcEuL; EuAu; LinLib S; McGEWB; NewC; OxCEng 67; OxCFr; PenC EUR; REn*

Fenley, Molissa
American. Choreographer, Dancer
Formed experimental dance company, Molissa Fenley and Dancers, 1977—; works include *Planets,* 1978; *State of Darkness,* 1988.
b. Nov 1954 in Las Vegas, Nevada
Source: *BioIn 12, 13, 14; News 88-3*

Fenn, George Manville
English. Author, Editor
Prolific writer of boys adventure tales.
b. Jan 3, 1831 in Pimlico, England
d. Aug 26, 1909 in Isleworth, England
Source: *Alli SUP; BbD; BiD&SB; BioIn 8; BritAu 19; Chambr 3; ChhPo, S2; DcBiA; DcEnL; DcNaB S2; EvLB; HsB&A; MnBBF; NewC; NewCBEL; NotNAT B; OxCChiL; StaCVF; TwCChW 83A, 89A, 95A; WhLit; WhoChL*

Fenn, Sherilyn
American. Actor
Was in TV's "Twin Peaks;" in TV miniseries, "Liz: The Elizabeth Taylor Story," 1995.
b. Feb 1, 1965 in Detroit, Michigan
Source: *IntMPA 96; LegTOT; WhoAm 94, 95, 96, 97; WhoAmW 95, 97*

Fennell, Frederick
American. Conductor
Founded Eastman Wind Ensemble, 1952, made numerous albums; guest conductor with Boston Pops.
b. Jul 2, 1914 in Cleveland, Ohio
Source: *Baker 78, 84, 92; BioIn 8, 13; IntWWM 85, 90; NewAmDM; NewGrDA 86; PenDiMP; WhoMus 72*

Fennelly, Parker W
American. Radio Performer
Played Titus Moody on "Fred Allen Show," 1940s-50s; commercial spokesman for Pepperidge Farm products.
d. Jan 22, 1988 in Cortland, New York
Source: *BioIn 11; NewYTBS 88; WhoHol A*

Fenneman, George
American. TV Personality
Announcer for Groucho Marx quiz show, "You Bet Your Life," 1950-61.
b. Nov 10, 1919 in Beijing, China
d. May 29, 1997 in Los Angeles, California
Source: *BioIn 3; IntMPA 92, 94, 96; RadStar; WhoEnt 92*

Fenollosa, Ernest Francisco
American. Art Historian
Pioneer Orientalist; later works imitated his style; wrote *The Masters of Ukioye,* 1896.
b. Feb 18, 1853 in Salem, Massachusetts
d. Sep 21, 1908 in London, England
Source: *AmAu; AmBi; BiDSA; BioIn 6; CnDAL; DcAmAu; DcAmB; DcLEL; DcNAA; EncJap; OxCAmH; OxCAmL 65, 83, 95; REn; REnAL; WebAB 74, 79; WebE&AL; WhAm 1*

Fenten, D. X
American. Author, Journalist
Writes syndicated column, "Weekend Gardener," 1974—; author of juvenile books, gardening and computer programs.
b. Jan 3, 1932 in New York, New York
Source: *AuBYP 3; ConAu 5NR; SmATA 4; WrDr 86, 90*

Fenton, Carroll Lane
American. Author, Illustrator
Writer of adult, juvenile natural science books: *Tales Told By Fossils,* 1966.
b. Feb 12, 1900 in Parkersburg, Iowa
d. Nov 16, 1969

Source: *AmAu&B; AuBYP 2, 3; BioIn 6, 7, 8, 10; ConAu 1R, 6NR, 29R; MorJA; NatCAB 55; SmATA 5; WhE&EA*

Fenton, Leslie
English. Actor, Director
Appeared in over 30 films, 1920s-30s, including *Boys Town,* 1938.
b. Mar 12, 1902 in Liverpool, England
Source: *Film 2; FilmEn; FilmgC; GangFlm; HalFC 80, 84, 88; MotPP; MovMk; TwYS; WhScrn 83*

Fenton, Thomas Trail
American. Journalist
Senior European correspondent with CBS News, London, 1979-94; Moscow, 1994—.
b. Apr 8, 1930 in Baltimore, Maryland
Source: *ConAu 102; LesBEnT; WhoAm 74, 76, 78, 80, 82, 84, 86, 88, 90, 92, 94, 95, 96, 97; WhoWor 74, 95, 97*

Fenwick, Millicent Hammond
"Outhouse Millie"
American. Politician
Rep. con. from NJ, 1975-82; defeated in bid for Senate, 1982; inspiration for Doonesbury comic strip character, Lacey Davenport.
b. Feb 25, 1910 in New York, New York
d. Sep 16, 1992 in Bernardsville, New Jersey
Source: *AmPolW 80; AmWomM; BiDrUSC 89; BioIn 13; CngDr 81; ConAu 112, 139; CurBio 77; GoodHs; IntWW 91; News 93-2; NewYTBS 74, 82; WhAm 10; WhoAm 78, 80, 82, 84, 86, 88, 90, 92; WhoAmP 73, 75, 77, 79, 81, 83, 85, 87, 89, 91; WhoAmW 74, 75, 77, 79, 81, 83, 85, 87, 89, 91, 93; WhoE 77, 79, 81, 83, 85, 86, 91, 93; WhoGov 77; WhoWor 87*

Feoktistov, Konstantin Petrovich
Russian. Cosmonaut, Engineer
Has made important engineering contributions to space travel; with team on space craft "Voshkod," 1964.
b. Feb 7, 1926 in Voronezh, Union of Soviet Socialist Republics
Source: *BioIn 15, 17; CurBio 67; IntWW 74, 75, 76, 77; WhoSocC 78; WhoSpc; WhoWor 74*

Ferber, Edna
American. Author
Best-selling novels include 1925 Pulitzer-winning, *So Big; Show Boat,* 1926; *Giant,* 1952.
b. Aug 15, 1887 in Kalamazoo, Michigan
d. Apr 16, 1968 in New York, New York
Source: *AmAu&B; AmNov; AmWomD; AmWomWr; ApCAB X; ArtclWW 2; AuNews 1; Benet 87, 96; BenetAL 91; BiE&WWA; BioAmW; BioIn 1, 2, 3, 4, 5, 6, 8, 9, 10, 11, 12, 14, 16, 17, 20; Chambr 3; CnDAL; CnMD; CnThe; ConAmA; ConAmL; ConAu 5R, 25R; ConLC 18, 93; DcArts; DcLEL; EncWL; EncWT; EvLB; FilmgC; GrWrEL N; HalFC 80, 84, 88; InWom, SUP; LegTOT; LibW; LinLib L, S; LngCTC; MajTwCW; McGEWB; McGEWD 72, 84; ModAL; ModWD; NatCAB 60; NotNAT A, B; Novels; ObitT 1961; OxCAmL 65, 83, 95; OxCAmT 84; OxCThe 67; PenC AM; PlP&P; REn; REnAL; REnAW; SmATA 7; TwCA, SUP; TwCRGW; TwCWr; TwCWW 82; WebAB 74, 79; WhAm 5; WhNAA; WhThe; WisWr; WomNov; WorAlBi*

Ferdinand I
Roman. Ruler
Brother of Charles V; raised in Spain; ruled Holy Roman Empire, 1558-64.
b. Mar 10, 1503 in Alcala de Henares, Spain
d. Jul 25, 1564 in Vienna, Austria
Source: *NewCol 75; WebBD 83*

Ferdinand II
German. Ruler
Catholic Counter-Reformationist; was Holy Roman Emperor, archduke of Austria, King of Bohemia, and King of Hungary.
b. Jul 9, 1578 in Graz, Austria
d. Feb 15, 1637 in Vienna, Austria
Source: *OxCGer 86*

Ferdinand V
[Ferdinand II; Ferdinand III; Ferdinand the Catholic]
Spanish. Ruler
Best known for marrying Isabella of Castile, uniting Spain; established the Inquisition, 1478; aided Columbus.
b. Mar 10, 1452 in Sos, Spain
d. Jan 23, 1516 in Madrigalejo, Spain
Source: *LinLib S; McGEWB; NewCol 75; WebBD 83*

Ferencsik, Janos
Hungarian. Conductor
Director Hungarian State Opera House, 1957-74.
b. Jan 18, 1907 in Budapest, Austria-Hungary
d. Jun 12, 1984 in Budapest, Austria-Hungary
Source: *AnObit 1984; Baker 84, 92; BioIn 14; FacFETw; IntWW 74, 75, 76, 77, 78, 79, 80, 81, 82, 83; IntWWM 77, 80; NewAmDM; NewGrDM 80; NewGrDO; NewYTBS 84; OxDcOp; PenDiMP; WhoOp 76; WhoSocC 78; WhoSoCE 89; WhoWor 82*

Ferguson, Elsie
American. Actor
Silent screen star who played in 16 pictures, 1917-20, including *A Doll's House.*
b. Aug 19, 1885 in New York
d. Nov 15, 1961 in New London, Connecticut
Source: *CurBio 62; Film 1, 2; FilmgC; OxCAmT 84; WhAm 4; WhoHol B; WhThe*

Ferguson, Harry George
English. Industrialist
Contributed to auto, airplane development, invented farm equipment: Ferguson tractor.
b. Nov 4, 1884 in Dromore, Northern Ireland
d. Oct 25, 1960 in Abbotswood, England
Source: *BioIn 3, 4, 5, 6, 9, 10; CurBio 56, 61; DcIrB 78, 88; DcNaB 1951; InSci; ObitOF 79; WhAm 4*

Ferguson, Homer
American. Politician
Senator from MI, 1943-1954.
b. Feb 25, 1888 in Harrison City, Pennsylvania
d. Dec 17, 1982 in Grosse Pointe, Michigan
Source: *BiDrAC; CngDr 79, 81; CurBio 43, 83; IntWW 80, 81; NewYTBS 82; PolProf E, T; WhAm 8; WhoAm 76, 78, 80, 82; WhoAmP 75, 77, 79, 81; WhoGov 75, 77*

Ferguson, Homer Lenoir
American. Shipping Executive
Built battleships for Navy, including USS *Indiana,* 1941.
b. Mar 6, 1873 in Waynesville, North Carolina
d. Mar 14, 1952 in Warwick, Virginia
Source: *BioIn 3, 4; NatCAB 17, 40; WhAm 3; WorAl*

Ferguson, Jay R
American. Actor
Played Taylor on TV show "Evening Shade."
Source: *RkOn 85*

Ferguson, John Bowie
"Fergie"
Canadian. Hockey Player, Hockey Executive
Left wing, Montreal, 1963-71, known for rough style of play; general manager, Winnipeg, 1978-88.
b. Sep 5, 1938 in Vancouver, British Columbia, Canada
Source: *HocEn; WhoAm 74, 76, 84, 86, 88; WhoE 74; WhoFI 75; WhoHcky 73; WhoMW 82, 84, 86, 88, 90*

Ferguson, Maynard
Canadian. Jazz Musician
Headline trumpeter, 1950s; noted for powerful highnote work; led own bands, 1960s-70s; hit album, *Conquistador,* 1978.
b. May 4, 1928 in Verdun, Quebec, Canada
Source: *AllMusG; Baker 84, 92; BgBands 74; BiDAmM; BiDJaz; BioIn 12, 14, 15, 16, 17, 18, 20; CanWW 83, 89; CmpEPM; ConMus 7; CurBio 80; DrBlPA 90; EncJzS; FacFETw; IlEncJ; LegTOT; NewAmDM; NewGrDA 86; NewGrDJ 88, 94; OxCPMus; PenEncP; RkOn 85; TwCBrS; WhoAm 74, 78, 80, 82, 84, 86, 88, 90, 92, 94, 95, 96, 97; WhoBlA 90; WhoEnt 92*

Ferguson, Miriam Amanda
American. Politician
Two term governor of TX, 1924-32.
b. Jun 13, 1875 in Bell County, Texas
d. Jun 25, 1961 in Austin, Texas
Source: *BiDrGov 1789; BioIn 1, 2, 3, 5, 6, 7, 11, 12, 21; DcAmB S7; EncSoH; GoodHs; NotAW MOD; ObitOF 79; WhAm 4; WhAmP; WomFir; WorAl*

Ferguson, Sarah (Margaret)
[Duchess of York]
"Fergie"
English. Writer
Commoner who married Prince Andrew Jul 23, 1986; formally separated, 1992; divorced, 1996; author of children's books; wrote *Sarah Ferguson: Duchess of York: My Story,* 1996.
b. Oct 15, 1959 in London, England
Source: *BioIn 14, 15, 16, 17, 18, 19, 20; ConAu 135; CurBio 87; InWom SUP; LegTOT; News 90, 90-3; SmATA 66; WrDr 94, 96*

Ferguson, Tom R
American. Rodeo Performer
Won the Professional Rodeo Cowboys Assn. all-around cowboy title 6 consecutive times, 1974-79.
b. Dec 20, 1950 in Tahlequah, Oklahoma
Source: *BioIn 10, 11*

Fergusson, Francis
American. Author, Critic
Wrote, lectured on theater; best-known work: *The Idea of a Theater,* 1949.
b. Feb 21, 1904 in Albuquerque, New Mexico
d. Dec 19, 1986 in Princeton, New Jersey
Source: *AmAu&B; BiE&WWA; BioIn 4, 15; BlueB 76; ConAu 3NR, 9R, 121; ConLCrt 77, 82; DrAS 74E, 78E, 82E; IntAu&W 82; NewYTBS 86; NotNAT; REnAL; TwCA SUP; WhAm 9; WhoAm 74, 76, 78, 80, 82, 84, 86; WhoWor 74; WrDr 76, 80, 82, 84, 86*

Fergusson, Harvey
American. Author
Books include *Rio Grande,* 1933; *Home in the West,* 1945.
b. Jan 28, 1890 in Albuquerque, New Mexico
d. Aug 24, 1971 in Berkeley, California
Source: *AmAu&B; AmNov; BenetAL 91; BioIn 2, 4, 8, 9, 10; CmCal; CnDAL; ConAu 33R; EncFWF; FifWWr; OxCAmL 65, 83, 95; REnAL; REnAW; TwCA, SUP; TwCWW 82, 91; WhAm 8; WhLit; WhNAA*

Fergusson, Robert
Scottish. Poet
Known for his poems employing the forms, subjects, and language of his native Scots.
b. 1750 in Edinburgh, Scotland
d. 1774 in Edinburgh, Scotland
Source: *Alli; BbD; BiD&SB; BioIn 3, 13, 17; BlmGEL; BritAu; CamGEL; CamGLE; CasWL; ChhPo, S2, S3; CmScLit; DcEnL; DcLB 109; DcLEL; DcNaB; EvLB; GrWrEL P; LitC 29; NewC; NewCBEL; OxCEng 67, 85, 95; PenC ENG; RfGEnL 91; WebE&AL*

Ferlinghetti, Lawrence Monsanto
American. Author, Poet
Owns San Francisco's first all-paperback book store; identified with "Beat" movement.
b. Mar 24, 1919 in Yonkers, New York
Source: *BenetAL 91; BioIn 14, 15; BlueB 76; CmCal; ConAu 3NR, 5R; ConDr 82; ConLC 10, 27; ConPo 85, 91; CroCAP; CroCD; CurBio 91; DcLB 16; DrAP 75; DrAPF 91; FacFETw; IntAu&W 91; IntvTCA 2; IntWW 83, 91; MajTwCW; ModAL; OxCAmL 83; OxCEng 85; PoeCrit 1; WhoAm 84, 90; WhoWrEP 89; WorAlBi; WrDr 86, 92*

Fermat, Pierre de
French. Mathematician
Discovered analytic geometry, modern theory of numbers, calculus of probabilities.
b. Aug 17, 1601? in Beaumont-de-Lomagne, France
d. Jan 12, 1665 in Castres, France
Source: *AsBiEn; BiESc; BioIn 2, 5, 14, 16, 20; CamDcSc; CyEd; DcBiPP; DcScB; InSci; LarDcSc; McGEWB; RAdv 14, 13-5; WhDW; WorAl; WorAlBi; WorScD*

Fermi, Enrico
American. Physicist
Discovered uranium fission; won Nobel Prize, 1938; developed atomic bomb, 1942-45.
b. Sep 29, 1901 in Rome, Italy
d. Nov 28, 1954 in Chicago, Illinois
Source: *AmDec 1940; AsBiEn; BiESc; BioIn 2, 3, 4, 5, 6, 7, 8, 9, 11, 12, 14, 15, 16, 17, 18, 20; CamDcSc; ConAu 115; CurBio 45, 55; DcAmB S5; DcInv; DcScB; EncAB-H 1974, 1996; EncCW; FacFETw; HisEWW; InSci; LarDcSc; LegTOT; LinLib S; MakMC; McGEWB; McGMS 80; NatCAB 40; NobelP; NotTwCS; ObitT 1951; OxCAmH; PolProf T; RAdv 14, 13-5; ThTwC 87; WebAB 74, 79; WebBD 83; WhAm 3; WhDW; WhoNob, 90, 95; WorAl; WorAlBi; WorScD*

Fernald, John Bailey
American. Director
Known for British stage productions since 1929, including *Dial M for Murder.*
b. Nov 21, 1905 in Mill Valley, California
d. Apr 2, 1985 in London, England
Source: *BlueB 76; ConAu 115, P-2; OxCThe 67; Who 82, 83, 85; WhoThe 77, 81*

Fernandel
[Fernand Contandin]
French. Actor
Popular in *Don Camillo* series of French comedies in which he portrayed an eccentric priest.
b. May 8, 1903 in Marseilles, France
d. Feb 26, 1971 in Paris, France
Source: *BioIn 1, 3, 4, 9, 11; CurBio 71N; DcTwCCu 2; EncEurC; FilmAG WE; FilmEn; FilmgC; ForYSC; HalFC 80, 84, 88; IntDcF 1-3, 2-3; ItaFilm; JoeFr; LegTOT; MotPP; MovMk; NewYTBE 71; ObitT 1971; OxCFilm; QDrFCA 92; WhAm 5; WhoCom; WhoHol B; WhScrn 74, 77, 83; WorEFlm*

Fernandez, Emilio
"El Indio"
Mexican. Director
Award-winner for films with strong, nationalistic tones: *Maria Candelaria,* 1943.
b. Mar 26, 1904 in Hondo, Mexico
d. Aug 6, 1986 in Mexico City, Mexico
Source: *AnObit 1986; BioIn 1; DcFM; FacFETw; FilmEn; FilmgC; HalFC 80, 84, 88; HispAmA; IntDcF 1-2, 2-2; NewYTBS 86; OxCFilm; WhoHol A; WorEFlm*

Fernandez, Joseph
American. Educator
Chancellor, NYC public schools, 1990-93; president, CEO, School Improvement Services, Inc., 1993—.
b. Dec 13, 1935 in East Harlem, New York
Source: *BioIn 16; News 91, 91-3; NewYTBS 90; WhoE 91; WhoHisp 92*

Fernandez, Sid
[Charles Sidney Fernandez]
American. Baseball Player
Pitcher, NY Mets, 1984-93; Baltimore Orioles, 1993-95; Philadelphia Phillies, 1995—; pitched two no-hitters in minor leagues.
b. Oct 12, 1962 in Honolulu, Hawaii
Source: *AsAmAlm; Ballpl 90; BaseReg 86, 87; BioIn 14, 15; LegTOT; NewYTBS 84, 86*

Fernandez-Muro, Jose Antonio
Argentine. Artist
Abstract painter, member of Group of Concrete Artists, 1952; awarded Guggenheim, 1960.
b. Mar 1, 1920 in Madrid, Spain
Source: *IntWW 74, 75, 76, 77, 78, 79, 80, 81, 82, 83, 89, 91, 93; McGDA; OxCTwCA; PhDcTCA 77*

Ferragamo, Salvatore
Italian. Business Executive
Began family-run apparel business in Florence, 1927.
b. Jun 1898 in Bonito, Italy
d. Aug 7, 1960 in Fiumetto, Italy
Source: *BioIn 2, 4, 5, 9, 13, 17; ConFash; DcArts; DcTwDes; EncFash; FairDF ITA; ObitOF 79; WhoFash, 88*

Ferrante, Arthur
[Ferrante and Teicher]
American. Pianist, Composer
Member of two-piano team; popularity peaked in late 1960s, with many records, concerts.
b. Sep 7, 1921 in New York, New York
Source: *ASCAP 66, 80; LegTOT; WhoAm 74*

Ferrare, Christina
[Mrs. Anthony Thomopolos]
American. Model
Former wife of John DeLorean; appeared on mag. covers, some films.
b. 1951
Source: *BioIn 12, 13, 14, 16; LegTOT; WhoHol A*

Ferrari, Enzo
Italian. Auto Executive
Developed the Ferrari, 1940.
b. Feb 18, 1898 in Modena, Italy
d. Aug 14, 1988 in Modena, Italy
Source: *AnObit 1988; BioIn 4, 6, 7, 8, 10, 11, 12, 13, 14, 15, 16, 17, 19; BusPN; ConAu 126; CurBio 67, 88N; Entr; FacFETw; IntWW 74, 75, 76, 77, 78, 79, 80, 81, 82, 83; LegTOT; News 88; NewYTBS 88; Who 74, 82, 83, 85, 88; WhoWor 74, 78; WorAl; WorAlBi*

Ferraris, Galileo
Italian. Explorer, Scientist
Discovered rotary magnetic field, 1885.
b. Oct 31, 1847 in Livorno Vercellese, Sardinia
d. Feb 7, 1897 in Turin, Italy
Source: *DcScB; NewCol 75*

Ferraro, Geraldine Anne
[Mrs. John Zaccaro]
American. Politician
Walter Mondale's running mate, 1984 presidential election; first woman vp candidate.
b. Aug 26, 1935 in Newburgh, New York
Source: *AlmAP 80, 82, 84; AmPolLe; AmPolW 80; AmWomM; BiDrUSC 89; BioAmW; BioIn 13, 14, 15, 16; CngDr 81, 83; ContDcW 89; CurBio 84; EncAB-H 1996; EncWB; FacFETw; HanAmWH; IntWW 89, 91, 93; InWom SUP; NewYTBS 84, 91; PolsAm 84; WhoAm 80, 82, 84, 86, 88, 90, 92, 94, 95, 96, 97; WhoAmP 81, 83, 91; WhoAmW 81, 83, 85, 87, 89, 91, 93, 95, 97; WhoE 81, 83, 85, 93; WhoWor 84; WomFir*

Ferre, Gianfranco
Italian. Fashion Designer
Artistic director, house of Christian Dior, 1989—.
b. Aug 15, 1944 in Legnano, Italy
Source: *BioIn 16; ConDes 90, 97; ConFash; CurBio 91; EncFash; IntWW 91, 93; WhoAm 90, 92, 94, 95, 96, 97; WhoFash 88; WhoWor 91, 95*

Ferre, Maurice Antonio
American. Politician
Mayor of Miami, FL, 1973-85.
b. Jun 23, 1935 in Ponce, Puerto Rico
Source: *AmCath 80; BioIn 13, 16; WhoAm 74, 76, 78, 80, 82, 84; WhoFI 74; WhoGov 75, 77; WhoHisp 91, 92, 94; WhoSSW 75, 76, 78, 84, 86; WhoWor 74, 76*

Ferrell, Conchata Galen
"Chatti"
American. Actor
Won Obie for *The Sea Horse,* 1974.
b. Mar 28, 1943 in Charleston, West Virginia
Source: *ConTFT 8; HalFC 84, 88; IntMPA 92; Who 82; WhoAm 80, 82, 84, 86, 88, 90, 92, 94, 95, 96, 97; WhoAmW 97; WhoEnt 92; WhoHisp 91*

Ferrell, Rachelle
American. Singer, Pianist
Sings both popular and jazz styles; recorded first jazz album, *Somethin' Else,* 1990; her second album, *Rachelle Ferrell,* 1992, was devoted to popular songs which included "Too Late" and "With Open Arms"; released album *First Instrument* in 1995.
b. 1961 in Berwyn, Pennsylvania
Source: *ConMus 17*

Ferrell, Rick
[Richard Benjamin Ferrell]
American. Baseball Player
Catcher, 1929-47; had .281 lifetime batting average; brother of Wes; Hall of Fame, 1984.
b. Aug 12, 1905 in Durham, North Carolina
Source: *Ballpl 90; BiDAmSp BB; BioIn 15, 21; LegTOT; WhoProB 73; WhoSpor*

Ferrell, Wes(ley Cheek)
American. Baseball Player
Pitcher, 1927-41; won 20 games in each of first four full ML seasons; holds ML record for home runs by pitcher, 38.
b. Feb 2, 1908 in Greensboro, North Carolina
d. Dec 9, 1976 in Sarasota, Florida
Source: *Ballpl 90; BiDAmSp BB; BioIn 3, 10, 11, 15, 18; IntWW 76; WhoProB 73*

Ferrer, Jose Vicente
[Jose Vincente Ferrer de Otero y Cintron]
American. Actor
Won 1950 Oscar for *Cyrano de Bergerac*; won 5 Tony Awards; first actor to receive Medal of Arts, 1985.
b. Jan 8, 1912 in Santurce, Puerto Rico
d. Jan 26, 1992 in Coral Gables, Florida
Source: *BiDFilm; BiE&WWA; BioIn 16; CamGWoT; CelR 90; ConTFT 2; CurBio 44; EncMT; FilmgC; HalFC 88; IntMPA 82, 92; IntWW 91; MotPP; MovMk; News 92; NotNAT; OxCFilm; OxCThe 83; WhAm 10; Who 74, 82, 83, 85, 88, 90, 92; WhoAm 74, 76, 78, 80, 82, 84, 86, 88, 90; WhoEnt 92; WhoHisp 92; WhoHol A; WhoThe 77; WorAlBi; WorEFlm*

Ferrer, Mel(chor Gaston)
American. Actor
In film *Lili,* 1953; TV series "Falcon Crest," 1983-84; married to Audrey Hepburn, 1954-68.
b. Aug 25, 1917 in Elberon, New Jersey
Source: *BiDFilm, 81, 94; BiE&WWA; BioIn 2, 4, 14; ConTFT 6; FilmEn; FilmgC; ForYSC; HalFC 80, 84, 88; HispAmA; IntDcF 1-3; IntMPA 75, 76, 77, 78, 79, 80, 81, 82, 84, 86, 88, 92, 94, 96; ItaFilm; LegTOT; MGM; MiSFD 9; MotPP; MovMk; NotNAT; OxCFilm; WhoHol 92, A; WorAl; WorAlBi; WorEFlm*

Ferri, Alessandra Maria
Italian. Dancer
Principal ballerina with American Ballet Theatre (ABT), 1985—; Baryshnikov persuaded her to leave Royal Ballet to join ABT.
b. May 6, 1963 in Milan, Italy
Source: *BioIn 13, 14, 15, 16; ConNews 87-2; NewYTBS 85; WhoAm 86, 88, 90, 92, 94, 95, 96, 97; WhoAmW 95, 97; WhoEnt 92; WhoWor 87, 95*

Ferrier, David, Sir
Scottish. Neurologist
From his experiments with primates originated modern cerebral surgery; wrote *The Functions of the Brain,* 1876.
b. Jan 13, 1843 in Aberdeen, Scotland
d. Mar 19, 1928 in London, England
Source: *Alli SUP; BiESc; BioIn 4, 6, 7; CelCen; DcBiPP; DcNaB 1922; DcScB; InSci; OxCMed 86; WebBD 83; WhLit*

Ferrier, Jim
[James Ferrier]
Australian. Golfer
Turned pro, 1940; won PGA, 1947.
b. Feb 24, 1915 in Sydney, Australia
Source: *BioIn 10, 13, 14, 15; WhoGolf*

Ferrier, Kathleen
English. Opera Singer
Considered remarkable contralto; Benjamin Britten created title roles for her.
b. Apr 22, 1912 in Higher Walter, England
d. Oct 8, 1953 in London, England
Source: *Baker 78, 84; BioIn 1, 2, 3, 4, 5, 8, 9, 11, 14; BriBkM 80; CmOp; ContDcW 89; CurBio 51, 53; FacFETw; IntDcOp; IntDcWB; InWom; MetOEnc; MusMk; MusSN; NewAmDM; NewEOp 71; NewGrDM 80; ObitT 1951; OxCMus; OxDcOp; PenDiMP; WhAm 4, HSA; WhDW; WomFir*

Ferrigno, Lou
American. Actor
Played the Hulk on TV series "The Incredible Hulk," 1977-81; has won many bodybuilding awards, including Mr. Universe, 1973, 1974.
b. Nov 9, 1952 in New York, New York
Source: *BioIn 12, 16; ConTFT 8; ItaFilm; NewYTBS 76; VarWW 85*

Ferril, Thomas Hornsby
American. Poet, Editor
Reporter, dramatic editor, *Rocky Mountain Herald; Denver Times,* 1919-21; won many awards for poetic works.
b. Jun 23, 1896 in Keeseville, New York
Source: *AmAu&B; BenetAL 91; BioIn 4, 10; ChhPo, S1, S2; CnDAL; ConAu 65, 127; ConPo 70, 75, 80; IntWWP 77; OxCAmL 65, 83, 95; REnAL; TwCA SUP; WhAm 10; WhoAm 74, 76, 78, 80, 82, 84, 86, 88; WrDr 76, 80, 82, 84, 86*

Ferris, Barbara Gillian
English. Actor
Began career as dancer at age 15; appears mostly on stage, some films.
b. Oct 3, 1940 in London, England
Source: *ConTFT 5; FilmgC; HalFC 88; NotNAT; WhoHol A; WhoThe 77*

Ferris, George Washington Gale
American. Inventor, Businessman
Invented Ferris Wheel, 1893, for World's Columbian Exposition, Chicago.
b. Feb 14, 1859 in Galesburg, Illinois
d. Nov 22, 1896 in Pittsburgh, Pennsylvania
Source: *ApCAB SUP; BioIn 13, 21; DcAmB; LegTOT; NatCAB 13; WebAB 74, 79; WhAm HS*

Ferry, Bryan
[Roxy Music]
English. Singer, Songwriter
Lead vocalist, principal songwriter for Roxy Music; solo album *Let's Stick Together,* 1976.
b. Sep 26, 1945 in Durham, England
Source: *BioIn 13, 14, 15, 16; ConMuA 80A; ConMus 1; EncRk 88; EncRkSt; HarEnR 86; IlEncRk; LegTOT; OxCMus; OxCPMus; WhoAm 82, 84, 86, 88, 90, 92, 94, 95, 96, 97; WhoRock 81; WhoWor 96, 97*

Fessenden, Reginald Aubrey
Canadian. Inventor
Made first radio broadcast, first two-way telegraphic communication, 1906.
b. Oct 6, 1866 in Milton, Quebec, Canada
d. Jul 22, 1932 in Hamilton, Bermuda
Source: *AmBi; AsBiEn; BiESc; BioIn 5; CamDcSc; DcAmB S1; DcNAA; DcNCBi 2; DcScB; FacFETw; InSci; LarDcSc; NatCAB 15; TwCBDA; WebAB 74, 79; WhAm 1; WorInv*

Fessenden, William Pitt
American. Politician
Whig party member, influential in formation of Rep. party, 1856.
b. Oct 16, 1806 in Boscawen, New Hampshire
d. Sep 8, 1869 in Portland, Maine
Source: *AmBi; ApCAB; BiAUS; BiDrAC; BiDrUSC 89; BiDrUSE 71, 89; BioIn 6, 9, 10, 21; CivWDc; CyAG; DcAmB; DcBiPP; Drake; EncAB-H 1974; HarEnUS; LinLib S; NatCAB 2; OxCAmH; TwCBDA; WebAB 74, 79; WebBD 83; WhAm HS; WhAmP; WhCiWar; WorAl; WorAlBi*

Fetchit, Stepin
[Lincoln Theodore Monroe Andrew Perry]
American. Actor
Known for portrayal of perpetually bemused Uncle Tom-like character; screen debut, 1927.
b. May 30, 1902 in Key West, Florida
d. Nov 19, 1985 in Woodland Hills, California
Source: *AfrAmAl 6; AnObit 1985; BioIn 20; BioNews 74; BlksAmF; ConNews 86-1; DcTwCCu 5; EncAFC; FacFETw; Film 2; FilmEn; FilmgC; HolP 30; MotPP; MovMk; WhoHol A*

Fetis, Francois Joseph
Belgian. Musicologist, Composer
Wrote biographies of musicians, theoretical works; founded *Revue Musicale,* 1827, first musical criticism periodical.
b. Mar 25, 1784 in Mons, Belgium
d. Mar 26, 1871 in Brussels, Belgium
Source: *Baker 84; BiD&SB; DcBiPP; NewCol 75; NewOxM*

Fetti, Domenico
Italian. Artist
Religious artist influenced by Caravaggio, Ruben: *Six Sainted Martyrs,* 1613.
b. 1589 in Rome, Papal States
d. 1623 in Venice, Italy
Source: *BioIn 19; IntDcAA 90; McGDA; OxCArt; OxDcArt*

Fetzer, John Earl
American. Baseball Executive, Businessman
Radio and TV executive; owner, Detroit Tigers, 1956-83.
b. Mar 25, 1901 in Decatur, Indiana
d. Feb 21, 1991 in Honolulu, Hawaii
Source: *Ballpl 90; BioIn 9, 10; IntMPA 86, 92; IntYB 78, 79, 80, 81, 82; LesBEnT 92; NewYTBS 91; St&PR 84, 87, 91; WhAm 10; WhoAm 74, 76, 78, 80, 82, 84, 86, 88, 90; WhoAmW 77; WhoMW 78, 80, 82, 84, 86, 88, 90; WhoProB 73; WhoWor 82*

Feuchtwanger, Lion
German. Author
Historical novels include *Ugly Duchess,* 1923.
b. Jul 7, 1884 in Munich, Germany
d. Dec 21, 1958 in Los Angeles, California
Source: *AmAu&B; Benet 87, 96; BiGAW; BioIn 1, 2, 4, 5, 6, 8, 9, 10, 11, 16; CamGWoT; CasWL; ClDMEL 47, 80; CmCal; CnMD; ConAu 104; CyWA 58; DcAmB S6; DcLB 66; EncGRNM; EncTR, 91; EncWB; EncWL, 2, 3; EncWT; Ent; EvEuW; FacFETw; LiExTwC; LinLib L, S; LngCTC; McGEWD 72, 84; ModGL; ModWD; NotNAT B; Novels; ObitT 1951; OxCEng 67, 85, 95; OxCGer 76, 86; OxCThe 83; PenC EUR; RAdv 14, 13-2; REn; TwCA, SUP; TwCLC 3; WhAm 3; WhE&EA; WorAl; WorAlBi*

Feuer, Cy
American. Director, Producer
Stage productions include *Guys and Dolls; Can-Can; Silk Stockings.*
b. Jan 15, 1911 in New York, New York
Source: *BiE&WWA; BioIn 3, 4, 5; BlueB 76; CelR; EncMT; NotNAT; OxCAmT 84; Who 82; WhoAm 74, 76, 78, 80, 82, 84, 86, 88, 90, 92, 94, 95, 96, 97; WhoE 86, 89, 93, 95, 97; WhoEnt 92; WhoThe 72, 77, 81; WhoWor 74*

Feuerbach, Ludwig Andreas
German. Philosopher
Wrote *The Essence of Christianity,* 1841, an attempt to understand religion from a human point of view.
b. Jul 28, 1804 in Landshut, Bavaria
d. Sep 13, 1872 in Rechenberg, Germany
Source: *BbD; BiD&SB; BioIn 1, 9, 11; CelCen; DcEuL; EncEth; LuthC 75; McGEWB; NewCBEL; NewCol 75; OxCGer 76; OxCPhil; PenC EUR; RAdv 14, 13-4; REn; WhDW; WorAl*

Feuerbach, Paul Johann Anselm
German. Judge
His liberal criminal code, 1813, penal reforms influenced rest of Europe; father of Ludwig, grandfather of Anselm.
b. 1775
d. 1833
Source: *BiD&SB; CelCen; DcBiPP; DcEuL; NewCol 75; OxCLaw*

Feuerbach, Paul Johann Anselm von
German. Artist
Romantic classicist painter famous for "Judgment of Paris," 1870.
b. Nov 14, 1829 in Hainichen, Thuringia
d. May 29, 1880 in Frankfurt am Main, Germany
Source: *NewCol 75; OxCArt; OxCGer 76; PenC EUR; WebBD 83*

Feuermann, Emanuel
American. Musician
Cellist, appeared with many leading US orchestras, 1935—; played chamber music with Rubenstein, Heifetz.
b. Nov 22, 1902 in Kolomea, Ukraine
d. May 25, 1942 in New York, New York

Source: *Baker 78, 84, 92; BiDAmM; BioIn 2, 4, 11, 12; BriBkM 80; CurBio 42; MusSN; NewAmDM; NewGrDA 86; NewGrDM 80; PenDiMP*

Feuillade, Louis
French. Director
Directed over 800 films, 1906-26, wrote almost all of the scripts; best known for his fantasy serials.
b. Feb 19, 1873 in Lunel, France
d. Feb 26, 1925 in Paris, France
Source: *BiDFilm, 81, 94; BioIn 15; DcFM; DcTwCCu 2; EncEurC; FilmEn; FilmgC; HalFC 80, 84, 88; IntDcF 1-2, 2-2; OxCFilm; WorEFlm; WorFDir 1*

Feuillet, Octave
French. Dramatist, Author
Wrote sentimental novel *La Petite Comtesse,* 1857; play *Le Sphinx,* 1874.
b. Jul 11, 1821 in Saint-Lo, France
d. Dec 29, 1890 in Paris, France
Source: *BbD; BiD&SB; BioIn 7; CasWL; DcBiA; DcEuL; Dis&D; EuAu; EvEuW; HsB&A; LinLib L; NinCLC 45; NotNAT B; OxCAmT 84; OxCFr; PenC EUR; REn*

Feulner, Edwin John, Jr.
American. Businessman
Pres., Heritage Foundation, Washington, DC, 1977—.
b. Aug 12, 1941 in Chicago, Illinois
Source: *ConAu 115; DcAmC; WhoAm 82, 84, 86, 88, 90, 92, 94, 95, 96, 97; WhoAmP 73, 75, 77, 79, 81, 83, 85, 87, 89, 91, 93, 95; WhoE 79, 81, 83, 85, 86, 89, 91, 93, 95, 97; WhoFI 79, 81, 83, 85, 87, 89, 92, 94, 96; WhoGov 72, 75, 77; WhoScEn 94; WhoSSW 76, 82, 84, 88; WhoWor 80, 82, 87, 89, 91, 93, 97*

Fey, Thomas Hossler
American. Business Executive
Pres., A & W Beverage Co., 1973-80; pres. Godiva Chocolatier Inc.
b. Sep 17, 1939 in Chicago, Illinois
Source: *WhoAm 82, 84; WhoAmP 91; WhoE 81, 83, 85, 86, 89*

Feydeau, Georges
French. Dramatist
Comedies of manners include *Lady from Maxims,* 1899; *A Flea in Her Ear,* 1907.
b. Dec 8, 1862 in Paris, France
d. Jun 6, 1921 in Rueil-Malmaison, France
Source: *AtlBL; Benet 87, 96; BioIn 17; CamGWoT; CasWL; ClDMEL 80; CnMD; CnThe; ConAu 113; DcArts; EncWL 2, 3; EncWT; Ent; EvEuW; FacFETw; FilmgC; GuFrLit 1; HalFC 80, 84, 88; MajMD 2; McGEWD 72, 84; ModFrL; ModWD; NotNAT A, B; OxCFr; OxCThe 67; PenC EUR; PlP&P; REnWD; TwCLC 22; TwCWr; WhDW; WorAlBi; WorAu 1950*

Feynman, Richard Phillips
American. Physicist
Joint winner of 1965 Nobel Prize in physics for theory of quantum electrodynamics; helped develop atom bomb.
b. May 11, 1918 in New York, New York
d. Feb 15, 1988 in Los Angeles, California
Source: *AmMWSc 73P, 76P, 79, 82, 86; AsBiEn; BiESc; BlueB 76; CamDcSc; ConAu 119, 125, 129; CurBio 55, 86, 88; EncWB; FacFETw; InSci; IntWW 74, 75, 76, 77, 78, 79, 80, 81, 82, 83, 93; LarDcSc; MajTwCW; McGMS 80; RAdv 13-5; WebAB 74, 79; WhAm 9; WhDW; WhoAm 84, 86; WhoNob, 90, 95; WhoUSWr 88; WhoWest 78, 84, 87; WhoWor 74, 84, 87; WhoWrEP 89; WorScD*

Fibak, Wojtek
Polish. Tennis Player
Successful in doubles with Tom Okker; fluent in six languages.
b. Aug 30, 1952 in Poznan, Poland
Source: *BioIn 12; BuCMET; WhoIntT*

Fibiger, Johannes Andreas Grib
Danish. Pathologist
Nobelist, 1926; first to study artificially produced cancer; discovered the *Spiroptera* carcinoma.
b. Apr 23, 1867 in Silkeborg, Denmark
d. Jan 30, 1928 in Copenhagen, Denmark
Source: *BiESc; BioIn 3, 15, 20; InSci; LarDcSc; NewCol 75; OxCMed 86; WebBD 83; WhoNob, 90, 95*

Fichandler, Zelda Diamond
American. Producer, Director
Leader in contemporary regional theater; co-founded Washington's Arena Stage, 1950.
b. Sep 18, 1924 in Boston, Massachusetts
Source: *BioIn 14, 15, 16; CurBio 85, 87; InWom SUP; NewYTBS 85; NotWoAT; TheaDir; WhoSSW 73, 75, 76; WhoThe 81*

Fichte, Johann Gottlieb
German. Philosopher
First Transcendental Idealist; emphasized reason.
b. May 19, 1762 in Rammenau, Germany
d. Jan 27, 1814 in Berlin, Germany
Source: *BbD; Benet 87, 96; BiD&SB; BiDPsy; BioIn 6, 8, 13, 17; BlkwCE; CelCen; CyEd; DcBiPP; DcEuL; DcLB 90; EncEth; EncRev; EvEuW; IlEncMy; LinLib L, S; LuthC 75; McGEWB; NamesHP; NewC; NewCBEL; OxCEng 67, 85, 95; OxCGer 76, 86; OxCLaw; OxCPhil; PenC EUR; RAdv 13-4; REn; WebBD 83; WhDW; WrPh P*

Ficke, Arthur Davidson
American. Poet, Author
Co-founder of satirical "spectrist poetry"; writings include sonnets, romantic vols. of verse, books on Oriental art.
b. Nov 10, 1883 in Davenport, Iowa
d. Nov 30, 1945 in Hudson, New York
Source: *AmAu&B; AmLY; CnDAL; ConAmL; DcLEL; DcNAA; ObitOF 79; OxCAmL 65, 83; REn; REnAL; TwCA, SUP; WhAm 2*

Fickett, Mary
American. Actor
Won 1973 Emmy for role in soap opera "All My Children."
b. May 23, in Bronxville, New York
Source: *Ballpl 90; BiE&WWA; BioIn 13, 15; ForYSC; InWom; NotNAT; VarWW 85; WhoHol A*

Fidler, Jimmie
[James M. Fidler]
American. Journalist, Radio Performer
Gossip columnist; newspaper column appeared in 360 papers, had weekly radio show.
b. Aug 24, 1900 in Saint Louis, Missouri
d. Aug 9, 1988 in California
Source: *BioIn 1, 9, 10, 16; ConAu X; NewYTBS 88; RadStar; WhoHol A*

Fidrych, Mark Steven
"The Bird"
American. Baseball Player
Pitcher, Detroit, 1976-80; known for talking to baseball; AL rookie of year, 1976.
b. Aug 14, 1954 in Worcester, Massachusetts
Source: *CurBio 78; NewYTBS 83; WhoAm 78, 80*

Fiedler, Arthur
American. Conductor
Led Boston Pops Orchestra, 1930-79; credited with elevating it to status of nat. institution through TV series, holiday concerts.
b. Dec 17, 1894 in Boston, Massachusetts
d. Jul 10, 1979 in Brookline, Massachusetts
Source: *AmDec 1970; Baker 78, 84, 92; BiDAmM; BioIn 1, 2, 3, 4, 5, 6, 7, 8, 9, 10, 11, 12, 13, 20; BioNews 74; BriBkM 80; CelR; ConMus 6; CurBio 45, 77, 79N; DcAmB S10; DcArts; IntWWM 77; LegTOT; LinLib S; MusSN; NatCAB 62; NewAmDM; NewGrDA 86; NewGrDM 80; NewYTBE 72; NewYTBS 77, 79; PenDiMP; RadStar; WebAB 74, 79; WhAm 7; WhoAm 74, 76, 78; WhoE 79; WhoWor 74, 78; WorAl; WorAlBi*

Fiedler, Jean(nette Feldman)
American. Children's Author
Writings include *New Brother, New Sister,* 1966.
Source: *BioIn 9; ConAu 11NR, 29R; DrAPF 83, 85, 87, 89, 91, 93, 97; ForWC 70; SmATA 4; WhoAmW 77*

Fiedler, Leslie Aaron
American. Educator, Critic
Best known for *Love and Death in the American Novel,* 1959, rev., 1966.
b. Mar 8, 1917 in Newark, New Jersey
Source: *AmAu&B; Benet 87; BenetAL 91; BioIn 7, 8, 9, 10, 11, 13, 14, 15, 16; BlueB 76; CasWL; ConAu 7NR, 9R; ConLC 24; ConNov 86, 91; CurBio 70; DcLB 67; DcLEL 1940; DrAPF 91; DrAS 74E, 78E, 82E; EncWL 2; IntAu&W 91; IntvTCA 2; IntWW 83, 91; MajTwCW; PenC AM; RAdv 13-1; REnAL; WhoAm 74, 76, 78, 80, 82, 84, 86, 88, 90, 92, 94, 95, 96, 97; WhoAmJ 80; WhoE 74, 86; WhoEnt 92; WhoUSWr 88; WhoWor 74; WhoWorJ 72, 78; WhoWrEP 89, 92, 95; WorAlBi; WorAu 1950; WrDr 86, 92*

Field, Betty
American. Actor
Films include *Of Mice and Men,* 1939; *The Great Gatsby,* 1949; *Peyton Place,* 1957.
b. Feb 8, 1918 in Boston, Massachusetts
d. Sep 13, 1973 in Hyannis, Massachusetts
Source: *BiE&WWA; BioIn 1, 3, 5, 10; CurBio 59, 73, 73N; FilmEn; FilmgC; ForYSC; HalFC 80, 84, 88; HolP 40; InWom, SUP; MotPP; MovMk; NewYTBE 73; NotNAT B; PlP&P; ThFT; WhAm 6; WhoAmW 58, 64, 66, 68, 70, 72, 74; WhoE 74; WhoHol B; WhoThe 72, 77; WhoWor 74; WhScrn 77, 83; WorAl*

Field, Cyrus West
American. Merchant, Financier
Promoter of first Atlantic cable, 1858.
b. Nov 30, 1819 in Stockbridge, Massachusetts
d. Jul 12, 1892 in New York, New York
Source: *AmBi; ApCAB; AsBiEn; BiDAmBL 83; BioIn 3, 5, 7, 8, 9, 10; DcAmB; DcBiPP; Drake; EncAB-H 1974, 1996; HarEnUS; InSci; LinLib S; McGEWB; NatCAB 4; NewCol 75; OxCAmH; TwCBDA; WebAB 74, 79; WhAm HS; WhDW; WorAl*

Field, David Dudley
American. Lawyer, Social Reformer
Noted for legal reform; adopted Code of Civil Procedure, 1848, which was later used throughout US, Britain.
b. Feb 13, 1805 in Haddam, Connecticut
d. Apr 13, 1894 in New York, New York
Source: *Alli SUP; AmBi; AmPeW; AmRef; ApCAB; BiDInt; BiDrAC; BiDrUSC 89; BioIn 3, 15, 17; DcAmAu; DcAmB; DcNAA; Drake; HarEnUS; LinLib S; McGEWB; NatCAB 4; NewCol 75; OxCAmH; OxCLaw; TwCBDA; WebAB 74, 79; WhAm HS*

Field, Eugene
"Poet of Childhood"
American. Poet, Journalist
Popular children's verses include *Little Boy Blue; Wynken, Blynken, and Nod.*
b. Sep 2, 1850 in Saint Louis, Missouri
d. Nov 4, 1895 in Chicago, Illinois
Source: *Alli SUP; AmAu; AmAu&B; AmBi; ApCAB SUP; ASCAP 66, 80; AuBYP 2, 3; BbD; BenetAL 91; BibAL; BiDAmJo; BiDAmM; BiDAmNC; BiD&SB; BiDSA; BioIn 1, 2, 3, 4, 5, 6, 7, 8, 9, 10, 11, 12, 15, 16, 19, 20; CarSB; CasWL; Chambr 3; ChhPo, S1, S2, S3; ChrP; CnDAL; DcAmAu; DcAmB; DcAmBC; DcLB 23, 42, 140, DS13; DcLEL; DcNAA; EncAHmr; EncAJ; EvLB; GayN; GrWrEL P; HarEnUS; JBA 34; JrnUS; LegTOT; LinLib L, S; MajAI; NatCAB 1; NinCLC 3; OxCAmL 65, 83, 95; OxCChiL; OxCEng 67, 85, 95; PenC AM; RAdv 1, 13-1; REn; REnAL; RfGAmL 87, 94; ScF&FL 1; SmATA 16; Str&VC; TwCBDA; WebAB 74, 79; WhAm HS; WorAl; WorAlBi*

Field, John
Irish. Pianist, Composer
Originated keyboard nocturnes, used as models by Chopin; lived mostly in Russia.
b. Jul 26, 1782 in Dublin, Ireland
d. Jan 11, 1837 in Moscow, Russia
Source: *Baker 78, 84, 92; BioIn 1, 4, 7, 8, 9, 10, 12, 13, 16, 17, 20; BriBkM 80; DcCom 77; DcCom&M 79; DcIrB 78, 88; DcNaB; GrComp; MusMk; MusSN; NewAmDM; NewGrDM 80; NewOxM; OxCMus; WhDW*

Field, Kate
[Mary Katherine Keemle]
American. Actor, Author.
Founded weekly "Kate Field's Washington," 1889; wrote *Ten Days in Spain, Hap-Hazard.*
b. Oct 1, 1838 in Saint Louis, Missouri
d. May 19, 1896 in Honolulu, Hawaii
Source: *Alli SUP; AmAu&B; AmWom; AmWomWr; BbD; BiDAmJo; BiD&SB; BiDSA; BioAmW; BioIn 3, 10, 12, 16; DcAmAu; DcAmB; DcNAA; EncAJ; FemiCLE; InWom, SUP; NotAW; NotNAT B; PenNWW A; TwCBDA*

Field, Marshall
American. Merchant
Opened Marshall Field Dept. Store, 1881; donated money to Chicago museums.
b. Aug 18, 1834 in Conway, Massachusetts
d. Jan 16, 1906 in New York, New York
Source: *AmBi; ApCAB SUP; BiDAmBL 83; BioIn 14, 15; DcAmB; EncAB-H 1974; LegTOT; McGEWB; MorMA; OxCAmH; RComAH; TwCBDA; WebAB 74, 79; WhAm 1; WhDW; WorAl; WorAlBi*

Field, Marshall, III
American. Publisher, Philanthropist
Established the *Chicago Sun,* 1941, Field Enterprises, Inc., 1944.
b. Sep 28, 1893 in Chicago, Illinois
d. Nov 8, 1956 in New York, New York
Source: *ABCMeAm; BiDAmBL 83; BioIn 1, 2, 3, 4, 7, 15, 19; CurBio 41, 52, 57; DcAmB S6; DcAmSR; DcLB 127; EncAB-A 28; EncAJ; FacFETw; JrnUS; LegTOT; ObitT 1951; PolProf T; WhAm 3; WorAl; WorAlBi*

Field, Marshall, IV
American. Publisher
Pres., publisher, editor, *Chicago Daily News; Sunday Times.*
b. Jun 15, 1916 in New York, New York
d. Sep 18, 1965 in Chicago, Illinois
Source: *BioIn 1, 2, 4, 5, 6, 7, 14, 15, 19; DcAmB S7; DcLB 127; EncAJ; NatCAB 63; WhAm 4*

Field, Marshall, V
American. Newspaper Publisher
Publisher, *Chicago Sun Times,* 1969-80; chm., Field Enterprises, 1972-84; chm., Field Corp., 1984—; ;pres., World Book-Childcraft International Inc., 1965-80.
b. May 13, 1941 in Charlottesville, Virginia
Source: *BioIn 8, 10, 13, 15; CelR; DcLB 127; WhoAdv 80; WhoAm 74, 76, 78, 80, 82, 84, 86, 88, 90, 92, 94, 95, 96, 97; WhoFI 74, 75, 79, 81, 89, 92, 96; WhoMW 74, 80, 84, 90, 92; WhoWor 74, 76, 78, 80, 82, 84, 87, 89, 91, 93, 95, 96, 97*

Field, Rachel Lyman
American. Children's Author
Writings include 1929 Newbery-winning *Hitty;* adult best-seller *All This and Heaven Too,* 1938.
b. Sep 19, 1894 in New York, New York
d. Mar 15, 1942 in Beverly Hills, California
Source: *ConAmA; ConICB; CurBio 42; DcNAA; FilmgC; JBA 34, 51; LngCTC; NewbMB 1922; NotAW; OxCAmL 65; REnAL; Str&VC; TwCA SUP; TwCWr; WhAm 2*

Field, Ron(ald)
American. Choreographer, Director
Best-known musicals: *Cabaret,* 1966; *Applause,* 1970; won two Tonys, two Emmys.
b. 1934 in New York, New York
d. Feb 6, 1989 in New York, New York
Source: *AnObit 1989; BiDD; BioIn 15, 16; ConTFT 5; EncMT; NewYTBS 89; NotNAT; OxCAmT 84; WhAm 9; WhoAm 86, 88; WhoE 74; WhoThe 77*

Field, Sally Margaret
American. Actor
Won Oscars for *Norma Rae,* 1979; *Places in the Heart,* 1985.
b. Nov 6, 1946 in Pasadena, California
Source: *BioIn 13, 14, 15, 16; BkPepl; CelR 90; ConTFT 3; EncAFC; FilmgC; HalFC 88; IntMPA 86, 92; InWom SUP; LesBEnT 92; WhoAm 74, 86, 90; WhoAmW 74, 91; WhoHol A; WorAlBi*

Field, Stephen Johnson
American. Supreme Court Justice
Served on bench, 1863-97; many of his decisions set standards of constitutional law.
b. Nov 4, 1816 in Haddam, Connecticut
d. Apr 9, 1899 in Washington, District of Columbia
Source: *AmBi; ApCAB; BiAUS; BiDFedJ; BioIn 2, 3, 5, 7, 8, 9, 10, 11; CmCal; DcAmB; DcNAA; Drake; EncAB-H 1974, 1996; HarEnUS; LinLib L, S; McGEWB; NatCAB 1; OxCAmH; OxCAmL 65, 83; OxCSupC; REnAW; SupCtJu; TwCBDA; WebAB 74, 79; WebBD 83; WhAm HS; WhCiWar*

Field, Virginia (Margaret Cynthia St. John)
American. Actor
Known for "other woman" roles; films include *Dream Girl, Imperfect Lady.*
b. Nov 14, 1917 in London, England
d. Jan 2, 1992 in Rancho Mirage, California
Source: *BioIn 10, 17; FilmEn; FilmgC; ForYSC; HalFC 80, 84, 88; IntMPA 77, 80, 86; InWom SUP; MovMk; ThFT; What 5; WhoAmW 77; WhoHol 92, A; WhoThe 77A; WhThe*

Fielder, Cecil Grant
American. Baseball Player
Infielder, Toronto, 1985-88, Detroit, 1990-96, NY Yankees, 1996—; 11th ML player to hit 50 home runs in season (51 in 1990); led AL in home runs, 1990, 1991; led AL in RBIs 1990, 1991, 1992.
b. Sep 21, 1963 in Los Angeles, California
Source: *Ballpl 90; BaseEn 88; News 93-2; WhoAfA 96; WhoAm 94, 95, 96, 97; WhoBlA 92, 94; WhoMW 92, 93, 96*

Fielding, Gabriel
[Alan Gabriel Barnsley]
English. Author
Novels include *The Women of Guinea Lane,* 1986; *Brotherly Love,* 1954.
b. Mar 25, 1916 in Hexham, England
d. Nov 27, 1986 in Bellevue, Washington
Source: *BioIn 6, 8, 10, 15; BlueB 76; ConAu 13R, 121, X; ConNov 72, 76, 82, 86; CurBio 62, 87, 87N; IntAu&W 76, 77; ModBrL, S1; NewC; Novels; RAdv 1; RGTwCWr; WhAm 9; Who 74, 82, 83, 85; WhoAm 74, 76, 78, 80, 82, 84, 86; WorAu 1950; WrDr 76, 80, 82, 84, 86*

Fielding, Henry
English. Author
Perfected English novel in his masterpiece *Tom Jones,* 1749.
b. Apr 22, 1707 in Sharpham Park, England
d. Oct 8, 1754 in Lisbon, Portugal
Source: *Alli; AtlBL; BbD; Benet 87, 96; BiD&SB; BioIn 1, 2, 3, 4, 5, 6, 7, 8, 9, 10, 11, 12, 13, 14, 15, 16, 17, 18, 19, 20; BlkwCE; BlmGEL; BritAu; BritWr 3; CamGEL; CamGLE; CamGWoT; CasWL; Chambr 2; ChhPo, S1; CnDBLB 2; CnThe; CopCroC; CrtSuDr; CrtT 2, 4; CyWA 58; DcArts; DcBiA; DcBiPP; DcEnA; DcEnL; DcEuL; DcLB 39, 84, 101; DcLEL; DcNaB; DcPup; Dis&D; EncEnl; EncWT; Ent; EvLB; GrWrEL DR, N; HalFC 80, 84, 88; IntDcT 2; LegTOT; LinLib L, S; LitC 1; LngCEL; MagSWL; McGEWB; McGEWD 72, 84; MouLC 2; NewC; NewCBEL; NewGrDO; NotNAT B; Novels; OxCEng 67, 85, 95; OxCThe 67, 83; PenC ENG; PlP&P; RAdv 1, 14, 13-1; RComWL; REn; REnWD; RfGEnL 91; ScF&FL 1; WebE&AL; WhDW; WorAl; WorAlBi; WorLitC*

Fielding, Lewis J
American. Psychiatrist
Best known as Daniel Ellsberg's psychiatrist.
b. Oct 2, 1909 in New York, New York
Source: *BiDrAPA 77, 89*

Fielding, Temple Hornaday
American. Author
Best known for producing *Fielding's Travel Guide to Europe,* annually since 1948.
b. Oct 8, 1913 in New York, New York
d. May 18, 1983 in Palma de Majorca, Spain
Source: *AmAu&B; AnObit 1983; BioIn 8, 9, 10, 12, 13; CurBio 69, 83N; NewYTBS 83; WhAm 8; WhoAm 74, 76, 78, 80, 82; WhoWor 74, 76*

Fields, Debbi
[Debra Jane Sivyer Fields]
American. Business Executive
Founded Mrs. Fields Cookies Inc., 1979; gross sales totalled $87 million, 1986.
b. Sep 18, 1956 in Oakland, California
Source: *BioIn 13, 14, 15, 16; ConAmBL; ConEn; ConNews 87-3; LegTOT; WrDr 96*

Fields, Dorothy
American. Songwriter
Won Oscar for lyrics to "The Way You Look Tonight"; contributed lyrics to 400 film songs.
b. Jul 15, 1905 in Allenhurst, New Jersey
d. Mar 28, 1974 in New York, New York
Source: *AmPS; AmSong; AmWomD; AmWomPl; ASCAP 66, 80; BestMus; BiDAmM; BiE&WWA; BioIn 4, 5, 10, 15, 16, 19; CelR; CmpEPM; ConAu 49, 93; ConDr 73; CurBio 58, 74, 74N; DcAmB S9; EncMT; EncWT; FilmEn; InWom, SUP; LegTOT; LibW; NewCBMT; NewYTBS 74; NotNAT B; NotWoAT; OxCAmT 84; Sw&Ld C; WhAm 6; WhoAm 74, 84; WhoHol B; WhoThe 72; WhScrn 77; WhThe; WomFir; WorAl; WorAlBi*

Fields, Freddie
American. Producer
Films include *Looking for Mr. Goodbar,* 1977; *American Gigolo,* 1980.
b. Jul 12, 1923 in Ferndale, New York
Source: *BioIn 8; ConTFT 5; HalFC 84, 88; IntMPA 75, 76, 77, 78, 79, 80, 81, 82, 84, 86, 88, 92, 94, 96; VarWW 85; WhoAm 88, 90, 92, 94, 95, 96, 97; WhoWest 74, 76, 78*

Fields, Gracie
[Grace Stansfield]
English. Comedian
Beloved British night club, music hall entertainer; sang "Biggest aspidastra in the World."
b. Jan 9, 1898 in Rochdale, England
d. Sep 27, 1979 in Capri, Italy
Source: *BiDAmM; BioIn 1, 2, 4, 5, 7, 9, 12, 13, 14; CamGWoT; CmpEPM; ConAu 112; ContDcW 89; CurBio 41, 79, 79N; DcArts; DcNaB 1971; EncEurC; EncVaud; Ent; FacFETw; FilmAG WE; FilmEn; FilmgC; ForYSC; GrBr; HalFC 80, 84, 88; IlWWBF, A; IntDcF 1-3, 2-3; IntDcWB; InWom, SUP; JoeFr; LegTOT; LinLib S; MotPP; MovMk; NewYTBS 79; NotNAT A; OxCFilm; OxCPMus; OxCThe 67; PenEncP; QDrFCA 92; ThFT; Who 74; WhoHol A; WhoThe 77A; WhScrn 83; WhThe; WorAl; WorAlBi*

Fields, James Thomas
American. Publisher, Author
Editor, *Atlantic Monthly,* 1861-71; wrote *Yesterdays with Authors,* 1872.
b. Dec 31, 1817 in Portsmouth, New Hampshire
d. Apr 24, 1881 in Boston, Massachusetts
Source: *Alli, SUP; AmAu; AmAu&B; AmBi; ApCAB; BbD; BibAL; BiD&SB; BioIn 13; ChhPo, S1, S2, S3; CnDAL; CyAL 2; DcAmAu; DcAmB; DcEnL; DcLB 1; DcLEL; DcNAA; Drake; HarEnUS; NatCAB 1; OxCAmL 65; REnAL; TwCBDA; WhAm HS*

Fields, Joseph
American. Screenwriter, Director
Co-wrote book for musicals *Gentlemen Prefer Blondes,* 1949; *Flower Drum Song,* 1958.
b. Feb 21, 1895 in New York, New York
d. Mar 3, 1966 in Beverly Hills, California
Source: *AmAu&B; BiE&WWA; CnMD; ConAu 25R; EncAFC; EncMT; EncWT; FilmEn; McGEWD 72, 84; ModWD; NewGrDA 86; NotNAT B; OxCAmT 84; OxCThe 83; WhThe*

Fields, Kim
American. Actor
Played Tootie on TV series "Facts of Life," 1979-88.
b. May 12, 1969 in Los Angeles, California
Source: *BioIn 12, 13, 14, 15, 16; ConTFT 14; DrBlPA 90; InB&W 80, 85; LegTOT; VarWW 85; WhoAfA 96; WhoBlA 85, 88, 90, 92, 94; WhoHol 92*

Fields, Lew Maurice
[Weber and Fields]
American. Comedian
Member of vaudeville team, Weber and Fields, 1895-1902.
b. Jan 1, 1867 in New York, New York
d. Jul 20, 1941 in Beverly Hills, California
Source: *CurBio 41; EncMT; FamA&A; Film 1; ObitOF 79; OxCThe 67; TwYS; WhAm 1; WhoHol B; WhoStg 1908; WhScrn 74, 77*

Fields, Shep
[Rippling Rhythm Orchestra]
American. Bandleader
Led 1930s-40s orchestra, noted for distinctive bubbling sound.
b. Sep 12, 1910 in New York, New York
d. Feb 23, 1981 in Los Angeles, California
Source: *BiDAmM; BioIn 9, 12, 16; CmpEPM; NewYTBS 81; RadStar; WhoHol A*

Fields, Stanley
American. Actor
Supporting actor in 90 films, 1930-41, including *Island of Lost Souls,* 1933.
b. May 20, 1880 in Allegheny, Pennsylvania
d. Apr 23, 1941 in Los Angeles, California
Source: *CurBio 41; FilmgC; ForYSC; MovMk; WhoHol B; WhScrn 74, 77, 83*

Fields, Totie
[Sophie Feldman]
American. Comedian
Popular nightclub entertainer known for self-deprecating humor.
b. May 7, 1930 in Hartford, Connecticut
d. Aug 2, 1978 in Las Vegas, Nevada
Source: *ConAu 108; GoodHs; LegTOT; NewYTBS 78; WhAm 7; WhoAm 78; WhoCom; WorAl*

Fields, W. C
[Charles Bogle; Otis J Criblecoblis; William Claude Dukenfield; Mahatma Kane Jeeves]
American. Comedian
Vaudeville, stage, radio performer; noted for hard drinking, dislike of children, pets; starred with Mae West in *My Little Chickadee,* 1940.
b. Jan 29, 1880 in Philadelphia, Pennsylvania
d. Dec 25, 1946 in Pasadena, California
Source: *BiDFilm; CmMov; EncMT; FamA&A; Film 1; FilmgC; MotPP; MovMk; OxCFilm; PlP&P; TwYS; WebAB 74; WhAm 2; WhoHol B; WhScrn 77; WorEFlm*

Fiennes, Ralph
English. Actor
Played Amon Goeth in *Schindler's List,* 1993; in *The English Patient,* 1996.
b. Dec 22, 1962 in Suffolk, England
Source: *CurBio 96; IntMPA 96; News 96, 96-2*

Fiennes (Twisleton Wykeham), Ranulph
English. Explorer
Trekked 35,000 miles in a 3-year expedition that circumnavigated the globe via the North and South Poles.
b. Mar 7, 1944 in Windsor, England
Source: *ConAu 3NR, 20NR, 45; News 90, 90-3; WrDr 82, 84, 86, 88, 90, 92*

Fierstein, Harvey (Forbes)
American. Dramatist, Actor
Won best play, actor Tonys for *Torch Song Trilogy,* 1983.
b. Jun 6, 1954 in New York, New York
Source: *BenetAL 91; BioIn 13, 14, 15, 16; CamGWoT; CelR 90; ConAmD; ConAu 123, 129; ConDr 88, 93; ConLC 33; ConPopW; ConTFT 1, 6; CurBio 84; CyWA 89; DcTwCCu 1; GayLesB; GayLL; IntDcT 2; IntMPA 92, 94, 96; IntWW 91; LegTOT; McGEWD 84; NewYTBS 83; OxCAmL 95; WhoAm 90, 92, 94, 95, 96, 97; WhoE 93; WhoEnt 92; WhoHol 92; WrDr 88, 90, 92, 94, 96*

Fifield, Elaine
Australian. Dancer
Performed with Sadler's Wells Ballet, 1947-58; Australian Ballet, 1964-69.
b. Oct 28, 1930 in Sydney, Australia
Source: *BiDD; BioIn 8; CnOxB; WhThe*

Fifth Dimension
[Daniel Beard; William Davis, Jr; Florence LaRue Gordon; Marilyn McCoo; Lamonte McLemore; Ronald Townson]
American. Music Group
Hits include "Up, Up and Away," 1967; "Aquarius," 1969.
Source: *Alli; BiDAfM; BiDAmM; BiDLA; BioIn 14, 15, 16, 17; BioNews 74; CabMA; CelR; DrBlPA 90; EncPR&S 74, 89; EncRk 88; EncRkSt; Film 2; IlEncBM 82; IlEncRk; InB&W 80, 85A; Law&B 89A; NewCBEL; NewYHSD; PenDiDA 89; PenEncP; RkOn 74, 78; RolSEnR 83; St&PR 96, 97; WhoAfA 96; WhoBlA 77, 80, 85, 88, 90, 92, 94; WhoHol 92; WhoRock 81; WhoRocM 82; WorAl*

Figueiredo, Joao Baptista de Oliveira
Brazilian. Political Leader
Pres. of Brazil, 1979-85.
b. Jan 15, 1918 in Rio de Janeiro, Brazil
Source: *BioIn 13, 16; CurBio 80; DcCPSAm; EncWB; IntWW 82, 83, 91; WhoWor 87*

Figueres Ferrer, Jose
Costa Rican. Political Leader
President of Costa Rica, 1953-58, 1970-74, advocating equal treatment for all.
b. Sep 25, 1906 in San Ramon, Costa Rica
d. Jun 8, 1990 in San Jose, Costa Rica
Source: *BiDLAmC; BioIn 16, 17, 20; CurBio 53, 90N; FacFETw; IntWW 74, 75, 76, 77, 78, 79, 80, 81, 82, 83, 89, 91N; McGEWB; NewYTBE 70; NewYTBS 90; WhoGov 72*

Filene, Edward Albert
American. Merchant
Organized, established first credit union in US.
b. Sep 3, 1860 in Salem, Massachusetts
d. Sep 26, 1937 in Paris, France
Source: *AmRef; AmSocL; BiDAmBL 83; BioIn 1, 4, 6, 7, 10, 11, 15, 19; DcAmB S2; DcAmSR; DcNAA; FacFETw; NatCAB 45; WebAB 74, 79; WhAm 1; WhAmP; WorAl*

Filene, Lincoln
American. Merchant
First to apply efficiency techniques, scientific methods to retailing, 1920s; son of Edward.
b. Apr 5, 1865 in Boston, Massachusetts
d. Aug 27, 1957
Source: *BiDAmBL 83; BioIn 4, 6, 10; NatCAB 45; WhAm 3*

Filipovic, Zlata
Yugoslav. Author
Wrote *Zlata's Diary,* 1993—about her family's struggle during siege of Bosnia, 1991-1993.
b. c. Dec 3, 1981 in Sarajevo, Yugoslavia
Source: *News 94*

Fillmore, Abigail Powers
[Mrs. Millard Fillmore]
American. First Lady, Teacher
While in office set up first White House library.
b. Mar 13, 1798 in Stillwater, New York
d. Mar 30, 1853 in Washington, District of Columbia
Source: *AmWom; BioIn 16, 17; FacPr 89; GoodHs; InWom, SUP; NatCAB 6; NotAW*

Fillmore, Caroline Carmichael McIntosh
American.
Second wife of US Pres. Millard Fillmore.
b. Oct 21, 1813 in Morristown, New Jersey
d. Aug 11, 1881 in Buffalo, New York
Source: *BioIn 16; InWom*

Fillmore, Millard
American. US President
Became 13th pres. upon death of Zachary Taylor; Whig, 1850-53; sent Commodore Perry to open up Japan, 1852; supported divisive Compromise of 1850.
b. Jan 7, 1800 in Summerhill, New York
d. Mar 8, 1874 in Buffalo, New York
Source: *AmAu&B; AmBi; AmPolLe; ApCAB; BenetAL 91; BiAUS; BiDrAC; BiDrUSC 89; BiDrUSE 71, 89; BioIn 1, 2, 3, 4, 5, 6, 7, 8, 9, 10, 11, 12, 13, 14, 15, 16, 17, 18, 19, 20, 21; CelCen; CyAG; DcAmB; DcBiPP; Drake; EncAAH; EncAB-H 1974, 1996;*

EncSoH; FacPr 89, 93; HarEnUS; HealPre; LegTOT; LinLib L, S; McGEWB; NatCAB 6; OxCAmH; OxCAmL 65, 83; PolPar; PresAR; RComAH; REnAL; TwCBDA; VicePre; WebAB 74, 79; WhAm HS; WhAmP; WhCiWar; WhDW; WorAl; WorAlBi

Fillmore, Myrtle Page
American. Religious Leader
Co-founded Unity School of Christianity, 1895.
b. Aug 6, 1845 in Pagetown, Ohio
d. Oct 6, 1931 in Unity Farm, Missouri
Source: *BioIn 19; DcAmReB 1, 2; InWom SUP; LibW; NotAW*

Finch, Jon
English. Actor
Films include *Sunday, Bloody Sunday,* 1971; *Frenzy,* 1972.
b. Mar 2, 1941 in Caterham, England
Source: *FilmEn; FilmgC; HalFC 80, 84, 88; IntMPA 80, 81, 82, 84, 86, 88, 92, 96; IntWW 91; WhoHol 92, A; WhoHrs 80*

Finch, Peter
[William Mitchell]
English. Actor
Only actor awarded posthumous Oscar for *Network,* 1976.
b. Sep 28, 1916 in London, England
d. Jan 14, 1977 in Beverly Hills, California
Source: *BiDFilm; ItaFilm; LegTOT; MotPP; MovMk; NewYTBS 77; OxCAusL; OxCFilm; WhAm 7; Who 74; WhoHol A; WhoThe 72, 77A; WhoWor 74, 76; WhScrn 83; WhThe; WorAl; WorAlBi; WorEFlm*

Finch, Rick
[K C and the Sunshine Band; Richard Finch]
American. Musician, Songwriter
Bass player, who also writes songs, produces albums for other singers.
b. Jan 25, 1954 in Indianapolis, Indiana

Finch, Robert Duer Clayton
Canadian. Poet
Poetic style characterized by use of incongruous imagery that reflects variations on literary themes.
b. May 14, 1900 in Freeport, New York
Source: *CanWW 83; CasWL; ConAu 24NR, 57; ConPo 85, 91; DcLB 88; DcLEL; IntAu&W 91; OxCCan; OxCCanL; WrDr 92*

Finch, Robert H(utchison)
American. Government Official
Political adviser to Richard Nixon; secretary of HEW, 1969-70.
b. Oct 9, 1925 in Tempe, Arizona
d. Oct 10, 1995 in Pasadena, California
Source: *BiDrUSE 71, 89; BioIn 12; CurBio 69; IntWW 74, 75, 76, 77, 78, 79, 80, 81, 82, 83; PolProf NF; WhoAm 74, 76, 78, 80; WhoAmP 73, 75, 77, 79, 81, 83, 85, 87, 89, 91, 93, 95; WhoGov 72, 75; WhoSSW 73, 75; WhoWor 74*

Finck, Henry Theophilus
American. Critic
NY Evening Post music critic, 1881-1924; Wagnerian devotee.
b. Sep 22, 1854 in Bethel, Missouri
d. Oct 1, 1926 in Rumford Falls, Maine
Source: *Alli SUP; AmAu&B; AmBi; AmLY; ApCAB; Baker 78, 84; BbD; BiDAmM; BiD&SB; BiDSA; BioIn 3, 7, 9; ChhPo S3; DcAmAu; DcAmB; DcNAA; NatCAB 14; NewGrDM 80; REnAL; TwCBDA; WhAm 1*

Fine, Larry
[The Three Stooges; Laurence Fineburg]
American. Comedian, Actor
Member of original Three Stooges; films include *Snow White and the Three Stooges,* 1961.
b. Oct 5, 1902 in Philadelphia, Pennsylvania
d. Jan 24, 1975 in Woodland Hills, California
Source: *DcAmB S9; EncAFC; LegTOT; MotPP; ObitOF 79; WhScrn 77*

Fine, Sylvia
[Mrs. Danny Kaye]
American. Lyricist, Producer
Wrote comedy scripts for husband; songs include "The Moon Is Blue," "Anatole of Paris."
b. Aug 29, 1913 in New York, New York
d. Oct 28, 1991 in New York, New York
Source: *AnObit 1987, 1991; ASCAP 66; Baker 92; BiDAmM; BiDD; BiDFilm, 81, 94; BiE&WWA; BioIn 1, 2, 3, 4, 5, 6, 7, 8, 9, 10, 11, 12, 13, 19; BlueB 76; CelR; CmMov; CmpEPM; ConAu 121; ConNews 87-2; ConTFT 3; CurBio 87N; DcArts; EncAFC; EncMT; FacFETw; FilmEn; FilmgC; ForYSC; Funs; HalFC 80, 84; IntDcF 1-3, 2-3; IntMPA 75, 76, 77, 78, 79, 80, 81, 82, 84, 86; IntWW 74, 75, 76, 77, 78, 79, 80, 81, 82, 83; JoeFr; LegTOT; MotPP; MovMk; NewAmDM; NewGrDA 86; NewYTBS 87; NewYTET; NotNAT; OxCAmT 84; OxCFilm; OxCPMus; OxCThe 67; PenEncP; QDrFCA 92; RadStar; SmATA 50N; WebAB 74, 79; WhAm 9; WhoAm 74, 76, 78, 80, 82, 84, 86; WhoAmJ 80; WhoAmW 61; WhoCom; WhoHol A; WhoThe 72, 77, 81; WhoUN 75; WhoWor 74, 78, 84, 87; WhoWorJ 72, 78; WorAl; WorAlBi; WorEFlm*

Fineman, Irving
American. Author
Works include *Jacob,* 1941; *Helen Herself,* 1957.
b. Apr 9, 1893 in New York, New York
Source: *AmAu&B; AmNov; Au&Wr 71; BenetAL 91; BioIn 2, 4; ConAu 1R, 5R; IntAu&W 76; OxCAmL 65, 83, 95; REnAL; TwCA, SUP; WhAm 10; WhE&EA; WhNAA; WhoAm 74, 76; WhoWorJ 72; WrDr 76*

Fingers, Rollie
[Roland Glen Fingers]
American. Baseball Player
Relief pitcher, 1968-82, 1984-85; holds ML record for career saves, 324.
b. Aug 25, 1946 in Steubenville, Ohio
Source: *Ballpl 90; BaseReg 86; BiDAmSp BB; BioIn 11, 13, 14, 15; LegTOT; WhoAm 74, 76, 78, 80, 82, 84; WhoProB 73; WhoSpor; WorAl; WorAlBi*

Fingesten, Peter
German. Sculptor
Founder, chairman, art dept. at Pace U, NYC, 1950-86; wrote *East Is East,* 1956.
b. Mar 20, 1916 in Berlin, Germany
d. Sep 9, 1987 in New York, New York
Source: *BioIn 3, 15; ConAu 123; CurBio 54, 87, 87N; DrAS 74P, 78P, 82P; WhAm 9; WhoAm 74, 76, 78; WhoAmA 73, 76, 78, 80, 82, 84, 86; WhoWor 74*

Fini, Leonor
Italian. Artist
Noted theatrical designer, book illustrator; does sensual, surrealistic paintings of women.
b. Aug 30, 1908 in Buenos Aires, Argentina
d. Jan 18, 1996 in Paris, France
Source: *BiDWomA; BioIn 1, 5, 10, 11, 15, 21; CnOxB; ConArt 77; ContDcW 89; DancEn 78; FacFETw; IntDcWB; IntWW 91; InWom SUP; NewYTBS 27; OxCTwCA; PhDcTCA 77; PrintW 85; WomArt, A*

Fink, Mike
"King of the Keelboatmen"
American. Pioneer
Folk hero of Mississippi, Ohio rivers; fame, embellishment of feats similar to Paul Bunyan; Indian fighter, trapper, marksman.
b. 1770? in Fort Pitt, Pennsylvania
d. 1823? in Fort Henry, North Dakota
Source: *BenetAL 91; BioIn 4, 5, 6, 13; CnDAL; NewCol 75; OxCAmH; OxCAmL 65, 83, 95; REnAL; REnAW; WebAB 74, 79*

Finkelstein, Louis, Dr.
American. Clergy, Author
Rabbi, dominant voice of 20th c. conservative Judaism; Chancellor Emeritus, Jewish Theological Seminary of America for 32 years; wrote, edited over 100 books.
b. Jun 14, 1895 in Cincinnati, Ohio
d. Nov 29, 1991 in New York, New York
Source: *AmAu&B; BioIn 1, 2, 3, 5, 16, 17, 18; ConAu 136; CurBio 92N; DrAS 74P, 78P, 82P; EncWB; JeAmHC; LEduc 74; NewYTBS 91; OhA&B; WhAm 10; WhE&EA; WhNAA; WhoAm 74, 76, 78, 80, 82, 84, 86, 88, 90; WhoE 74; WhoWor 74; WhoWorJ 72*

Finlay, Frank
English. Actor
Films include *The Three Musketeers,* 1973.
b. Aug 6, 1926 in Farnworth, England
Source: *BlueB 76; CamGWoT; CnThe; ConTFT 5; FilmEn; FilmgC; HalFC 80, 84, 88; IlWWBF; IntMPA 92, 94, 96; IntWW 89, 91, 93; OxCThe 83; PlP&P; Who 74, 82, 83, 85, 88, 90, 92, 94; WhoAm 92; WhoHol 92, A; WhoThe 77, 81*

Finlay, Virgil
American. Illustrator
Pulp magazine, science fiction artist noted for bubbling and stipple effects.
b. 1914 in Rochester, New York
d. Jan 18, 1971
Source: *BioIn 9, 15; EncSF; FanAl; NewEScF; PenEncH; ScF&FL 1, 92; WhoSciF*

Finletter, Thomas Knight
American. Lawyer, Diplomat
Secretary of Air Force, 1950-53; through his efforts, US air power tripled in 1948.
b. Nov 11, 1893 in Philadelphia, Pennsylvania
d. Apr 24, 1980 in New York, New York
Source: *AmAu&B; AmPeW; BiDInt; BioIn 1, 2, 3, 5, 11, 12; BlueB 76; CurBio 48, 80; DcAmB S10; IntWW 74; NewYTBS 80; PolProf T; WhAm 7; Who 74; WhoAm 74, 76; WhoWor 74*

Finley, Charles O(scar)
American. Businessman, Baseball Executive
Insurance executive; owner, Oakland Athletics, 1960-80; known for bizarre stunts, including colorful team uniforms.
b. Feb 22, 1918 in Ensley, Alabama
d. Feb 19, 1996 in Chicago, Illinois
Source: *Ballpl 90; BiDAmSp BB; BioIn 5, 6, 8, 9, 10, 11; CurBio 74, 96N; NewYTBE 72, 73; WhAm 11; WhoAm 78, 80, 82, 84, 86, 88, 90, 92, 94; WhoHcky 73; WhoProB 73; WorAlBi*

Finley, John Huston
American. Educator, Philanthropist
Pres., NYC College, 1903-13; NY State Commissioner of Education, 1913-21; editor, *NY Times,* 1938-40.
b. Oct 19, 1863 in Grand Ridge, Illinois
d. Mar 7, 1940 in New York, New York
Source: *Alli SUP; AmAu&B; AmBi; ApCAB, X; BbD; BiDAmEd; BiD&SB; BiDSA; BiDSocW; BioIn 1, 4, 8, 9, 10; ChhPo, S1; CurBio 40; DcAmB S2; DcNAA; DrAS 82F; LinLib L, S; NatCAB 13, 30; TwCBDA; WhAm 1, 2; WhJnl*

Finley, Martha
[Martha Farquaharson]
American. Author
Created Elsie Dinsmore series.
b. Apr 26, 1828 in Chillicothe, Ohio
d. Jan 30, 1909
Source: *Alli SUP; AmAu; AmAu&B; BiD&SB; BiDSA; BioIn 2, 4, 8, 12, 15; CarSB; CnDAL; ConAu 118; DcLB 42; FemiCLE; IndAu 1816; LegTOT; LibW; LinLib L; OhA&B; OxCAmL 65; PenNWW A; REnAL; SmATA 43; TwCBDA; TwCChW 83A, 89A, 95A; WhAm 1; WomNov; WorAl; WorAlBi*

Finnbogadottir, Vigdis
Icelandic. Political Leader
Iceland's first female head of state, 1980—.
b. Apr 15, 1930 in Reykjavik, Iceland
Source: *BioIn 12, 13, 14, 15, 18; ConNews 86-2; ContDcW 89; CurBio 87; IntDcWB; IntWW 81, 82, 83, 89, 91, 93; IntYB 82; NewYTBS 82; WhoWomW 91; WhoWor 80, 82, 84, 87, 89, 91, 93, 95, 96, 97; WomFir*

Finney, Albert
English. Actor, Director
Starred in *Tom Jones,* 1963; *Murder on the Orient Express,* 1974.
b. May 9, 1936 in Salford, England
Source: *BiDFilm, 81, 94; BiE&WWA; BioIn 5, 6, 7, 8, 10, 11, 12, 13, 14, 15, 17; BkPepl; BlueB 76; CamGWoT; CelR, 90; CnThe; ConTFT 1, 5; CurBio 63; DcArts; EncEurC; EncWT; Ent; FacFETw; FilmAG WE; FilmEn; FilmgC; ForYSC; HalFC 80, 84, 88; IlWWBF; IntDcF 1-3, 2-3; IntDcT 3; IntMPA 77, 78, 79, 80, 81, 82, 84, 86, 88, 92, 94, 96; IntWW 74, 75, 76, 77, 78, 79, 80, 81, 82, 83, 89, 91, 93; LegTOT; MiSFD 9; MotPP; MovMk; NewYTBS 81; NotNAT; OxCThe 83; PlP&P; Who 85, 92; WhoAm 90, 92, 94, 95, 96, 97; WhoEnt 92; WhoHol 92, A; WhoThe 72, 77, 81; WhoWor 74, 91, 93, 95, 96; WorAl; WorAlBi; WorEFlm*

Finney, Charles Grandison
American. Clergy, Educator
Evangelist; Oberlin College pres., 1851-66.
b. Aug 29, 1792 in Warren, Connecticut
d. Aug 16, 1875 in Oberlin, Ohio
Source: *Alli; AmAu&B; AmBi; AmOrN; AmRef; AmSocL; ApCAB; BiDAmEd; BioIn 2, 3, 4, 5, 6, 7, 8, 10, 11, 12, 14, 15, 16, 17, 18, 19, 21; DcAmAu; DcAmB; DcAmReB 1, 2; DcAmSR; DcNAA; Drake; EncAAH; EncAB-H 1974, 1996; EncARH; LuthC 75; McGEWB; NatCAB 2; OhA&B; OxCAmH; REnAW; TwCBDA; WebAB 74, 79; WhAm HS*

Finney, Jack
[Walter Braden Finney]
American. Author
Wrote science fiction classics *Invasion of the Body Snatchers,* 1954; *Time and Again,* 1970.
b. 1911 in Milwaukee, Wisconsin
d. Nov 14, 1995 in Greenbrae, California
Source: *Au&Wr 71; BioIn 12, 14; ConAu 110, 133, 150; ConSFA; DcLB 8; DcLP 87A; EncSF, 93; IntAu&W 91; LegTOT; NewEScF; RGTwCSF; ScF&FL 1, 92; ScFSB; SJGFanW; TwCCr&M 80, 85, 91; TwCSFW 81, 86, 91; WhoSciF; WorAlBi; WrDr 82, 84, 86, 88, 90, 92, 94, 96*

Finney, Joan Marie McInroy
American. Politician
Dem., first woman governor, KS, 1991-94; defeating incumbent Mike Hayden.
b. Feb 12, 1925 in Topeka, Kansas
Source: *AlmAP 92; IntWW 91, 93; WhoAm 78, 80, 82, 84, 86, 88, 90, 92; WhoAmP 91; WhoAmW 75, 77, 79, 81, 83, 85, 87, 89, 91, 93; WhoMW 78, 80, 82, 84, 86, 88, 90, 92; WhoWor 93*

Finsen, Niels Ryberg
Danish. Physician, Scientist
Used light rays to treat disease, particularly lupus vulgaris; won 1903 Nobel Prize.
b. Dec 15, 1860 in Thorshavn, Denmark
d. Sep 24, 1904 in Copenhagen, Denmark
Source: *AsBiEn; BiESc; BioIn 3, 4, 5, 15; DcScB; FacFETw; InSci; LarDcSc; LinLib S; OxCMed 86; WhDW; WhoNob, 90, 95*

Finsterwald, Dow
American. Golfer
Touring pro, 1950s-60s; won PGA, 1958.
b. Sep 6, 1929 in Athens, Ohio
Source: *BioIn 21; LegTOT; WhoGolf*

Fiorentino, Linda
[Clorinda Fiorentino]
American. Actor
Was in *The Last Seduction* and *Jade.*
b. Mar 9, 1960 in Philadelphia, Pennsylvania
Source: *IntMPA 96*

Fiorito, Ted
American. Bandleader, Songwriter
Had 50-yr. career as pianist, bandleader; wrote song "Toot, Toot, Tootie, Goodbye."
b. Dec 20, 1900 in Newark, New Jersey
d. Jul 22, 1971 in Scottsdale, Arizona
Source: *AmPS; ASCAP 66, 80; BgBands 74; BiDAmM; BioIn 9, 16; CmpEPM; NewGrDA 86; OxCPMus; Sw&Ld C; WhoHol B; WhScrn 74, 77, 83*

Firbank, Louis
[Velvet Underground]
American. Jazz Musician, Songwriter
Lead guitarist, Velvet Underground, 1967-70; albums include *Walk on the Wild Side.*
b. Mar 2, 1942 in New York, New York
Source: *ConAu 117; ConMus 7; EncPR&S 89; EncRk 88; IlEncRk; NewAmDM; OxCPMus; PenEncP; RkOn 84*

Firbank, Ronald
[Arthur Annesley Ronald Firbank]
English. Author
Wrote penetrating novels *Caprice,* 1917; *Prancing Nigger,* 1924.
b. Jan 17, 1886 in London, England
d. May 21, 1926 in Rome, Italy
Source: *AtlBL; Benet 87; BioIn 2, 3, 4, 5, 6, 8, 9, 10, 11, 12, 13, 14; BlmGEL; BritWr S2; CamGEL; CamGLE; CasWL; CnMWL; ConAu 104; DcArts; DcLB 36; DcLEL; EncWL 2, 3; FacFETw; GrWrEL N; LinLib L; LngCEL; LngCTC; MakMC; ModBrL, S1, S2; NewC; Novels; OxCEng 67, 85; PenC ENG; RAdv 1, 14, 13-1; REn; RfGEnL 91; ScF&FL 1; TwCA, SUP; TwCLC 1; TwCWr; WebE&AL; WhDW; WhoTwCL*

Firdausi
[Firdus]
Persian. Poet
Wrote great epic *Shah Namah,* c. 1010, describing Persian kings.
b. 935?
d. 1020?
Source: *AnCL; BiD&SB; BioIn 4; CasWL; McGEWB; NewC; NewCol 75; OxCEng 85; REn; WebBD 83*

Firefall
[Mark Andes; Jock Bartley; Larry Burnett; Michael Clarke; Rick Roberts]
American. Music Group
Pop-country group formed 1974; hit single "You Are the Woman," 1976.
Source: *BioIn 10; ConAu X; PenEncP; PoIre; RkOn 78; RolSEnR 83; SmATA 6, X; Who 74; WhoRock 81; WhoRocM 82; WhoScEu 91-1*

Fireman, Paul
American. Business Executive
Pres., chairman, Reebok, USA, the biggest athletic shoe manufacturer in America; stresses leadership in marketing strategy.
b. Feb 14, 1944 in Cambridge, Massachusetts
Source: *BioIn 16; ConAmBL; ConNews 87-2; CurBio 92; Dun&B 90; St&PR 91; WhoAm 90, 92; WhoE 91; WhoFI 89, 92*

Firestone, Harvey Samuel
American. Manufacturer
Founder, pres., Firestone Tire and Rubber Co, Akron, OH, 1900-38.
b. Dec 20, 1868 in Columbus, Ohio
d. Feb 7, 1938 in Miami Beach, Florida
Source: *AmBi; BiDAmBL 83; BioIn 1, 2, 4, 5, 8, 11, 15, 18; DcAmB S2; DcNAA; LegTOT; McGEWB; NatCAB 32; OhA&B; WebAB 74, 79; WhAm 1; WhFla; WorAl*

Firestone, Harvey Samuel, Jr.
American. Manufacturer
Chairman until 1966, Firestone Tire and Rubber Co; oversaw expansion to worldwide firm.
b. Apr 20, 1898 in Chicago, Illinois
d. Jun 1, 1973 in Akron, Ohio
Source: *BioIn 1, 7, 8, 9, 10; CurBio 44, 73, 73N; DcAmB S9; NewYTBE 73; OhA&B; WhAm 5; WhoFI 74; WhoWor 74*

Firestone, Roy
American. Sportscaster
Noted for cable TV program "Mazda SportsLook," 1984—.
b. Dec 8, 1953 in Miami Beach, Florida
Source: *BioIn 15; News 88-2*

Firkusny, Rudolf
American. Musician
Celebrated 60 yrs. as int'l concert pianist, 1983; favored Czech composers.
b. Feb 11, 1912 in Napajedla, Czech Republic
d. Jul 19, 1994 in Staatsburg, New York
Source: *Baker 78, 84, 92; BioIn 2, 4, 11, 12, 13, 14, 20, 21; BlueB 76; BriBkM 80; CurBio 79, 94N; IntWW 74, 75, 76, 77, 78, 79, 80, 81, 82, 83, 89, 91, 93; IntWWM 77, 80, 85, 90; MusSN; NewAmDM; NewGrDA 86; NewGrDM 80; NewYTBE 73; NewYTBS 94; NotTwCP; PenDiMP; WhAm 11; WhoAm 74, 76, 78, 80, 82, 84, 86, 88, 90, 92, 94; WhoAmM 83; WhoEnt 92; WhoMus 72; WhoWor 74, 76, 78; WorAl; WorAlBi*

Firpo, Luis Angel
"Wild Bull of Pampas"
Argentine. Boxer
Lost to Jack Dempsey in controversial heavyweight title fight, 1923.
b. Oct 11, 1896 in Buenos Aires, Argentina
d. Aug 7, 1960 in Buenos Aires, Argentina
Source: *BioIn 2, 5, 6, 10; WhoBox 74*

Firth, Peter
English. Actor
Made debut as deranged stable boy in stage, film versions of *Equus,* 1975, 1977.
b. Oct 27, 1953 in Bradford, England
Source: *ConTFT 7, 14; FilmEn; HalFC 80, 84, 88; IntMPA 80, 81, 82, 84, 86, 88, 92, 94, 96; IntWW 89, 91, 93; ItaFilm; NewYTBS 74; PlP&P A; WhoHol 92*

Fischer, Anton Otto
German. Illustrator
Cartoonist, marine painter, illustrated Tugboat Annie stories in *Saturday Evening Post,* 1930s-40s.
b. Feb 23, 1882 in Munich, Germany
d. Mar 26, 1962 in Woodstock, New York
Source: *BioIn 1, 5, 6, 11; DcSeaP; IlBEAAW; IlrAm 1880, C; IlsCB 1744, 1946; PeoHis; WhAm 4; WhAmArt 85; WorECar*

Fischer, Bobby
[Robert James Fischer]
American. Chess Player
Defeated Boris Spassky, 1972, in match that received world-wide publicity; world champion, 1972-75; stripped of the title for refusing to defend it; after years of obscurity, returned to defeat Spassky in 1992.
b. Mar 9, 1943 in Chicago, Illinois
Source: *AmDec 1960; BiDAmSp BK; BioIn 14, 15, 16, 17, 18, 19, 20; CelR, 90; ConAu 103; CurBio 63, 94; FacFETw; GolEC; IntWW 74, 75, 76, 77, 78, 79, 80, 81, 82, 83, 89, 91, 93; LegTOT; NewYTBE 73; OxCChes 84; St&PR 87; WebAB 74, 79; WhDW; WhoAm 74, 76, 78, 80, 82; WhoWor 74, 95, 96, 97; WorAl*

Fischer, Carl
American. Publisher
Founded music publishing firm, 1872; published periodical, *Musical Observer,* 1907-23.
b. Dec 7, 1849 in Buttstadt, Thuringia
d. Feb 4, 1923 in New York, New York
Source: *Baker 78, 84, 92; BioIn 9; NewAmDM; NewGrDA 86; NewGrDM 80; OxCSpan*

Fischer, Edmond
American. Biochemist
Co-winner with Edwin Krebs of Nobel Prize in Physiology for discovery of reversible protein phosphorylation, 1992.
b. Apr 6, 1920 in Shanghai, China
Source: *AmMWSc 92; IntWW 91; WhoAm 90; WhoTech 89; WhoWest 87*

Fischer, Emil Herman
German. Chemist
Nobelist, 1902; knwon for expanding science of biochemistry.
b. Oct 9, 1852 in Euskirchen, Prussia
d. Jul 15, 1919 in Berlin, Germany
Source: *DcScB; NewCol 75; WhoNob, 90, 95*

Fischer, Ernst Otto
German. Educator
Won Nobel Prize in chemistry, 1973.
b. Nov 10, 1918 in Munich, Germany
Source: *BiESc; BioIn 10, 14, 15, 19, 20; FacFETw; IntWW 74, 75, 76, 77, 78, 79, 80, 81, 82, 83, 89, 91, 93; IntYB 78, 79, 80, 81, 82; LarDcSc; McGMS 80; NotTwCS; Who 82, 83, 85, 88, 90, 92, 94; WhoAm 76, 78, 80, 82, 84, 86, 88, 90, 92, 94, 95, 96, 97; WhoNob, 90, 95; WhoScEn 94, 96; WhoWor 74, 76, 78, 80, 82, 84, 87, 89, 91, 93, 95, 96, 97; WorAl; WorAlBi*

Fischer, Hans
German. Chemist
Won Nobel Prize, 1902, for work in stereo chemistry.
b. Jul 27, 1881 in Hochstam-Main, Germany
d. Mar 31, 1945 in Munich, Germany

Source: *AsBiEn; BiESc; BioIn 1, 3, 6, 14, 15, 19, 20; CamDcSc; DcScB, S1; FacFETw; InSci; LarDcSc; McGEWB; NobelP; NotTwCS; WhoNob, 90, 95; WorAl; WorAlBi; WorScD*

Fischer, Herman G
American. Manufacturer
With Irving Price, started Fischer-Price Toys, 1930.
b. 1898
d. 1975
Source: *BioIn 6; Entr*

Fischer, John
American. Journalist, Author
Editor-in-chief *Harper's* magazine, 1953-67; wrote best-seller *Why They Behave Like Russians,* 1947.
b. Apr 27, 1910 in Texhoma, Oklahoma
d. Aug 18, 1978 in New Haven, Connecticut
Source: *AmAu&B; BiDrLUS 70; BioIn 1, 3, 11; ConAu 4NR, 9NR, 9R, 81; CurBio 53, 78, 78N; EncTwCJ; IntWW 74, 75, 76, 77, 78; IntYB 78; WhAm 7; Who 74; WhoAm 74, 76, 78; WhoWor 74; WrDr 80*

Fischer, Louis
American. Author
Books include prize-winning *Life of Lenin,* 1964; *Russia Revisited,* 1957.
b. Feb 29, 1896 in Philadelphia, Pennsylvania
d. Jan 15, 1970 in Hackensack, New Jersey
Source: *AmAu&B; Au&Wr 71; Benet 87; BioIn 1, 2, 3, 4, 8, 9, 13; ConAu 25R, P-1; CurBio 40, 70; DcAmB S8; EncAJ; ObitOF 79; REn; REnAL; TwCA SUP; WhE&EA; WhoWorJ 72*

Fischer-Dieskau, Dietrich
German. Singer
Concert, opera baritone noted as a singer of German lieder.
b. May 28, 1925 in Berlin, Germany
Source: *Baker 78, 84; BioIn 4, 5, 6, 7, 8, 10, 11, 12, 14, 16, 17; BriBkM 80; CelR; CmOp; ConAu 97; CurBio 67; DcArts; FacFETw; IntDcOp; IntWW 74, 75, 76, 77, 78, 79, 80, 81, 82, 83, 89, 91, 93; IntWWM 77, 80; MetOEnc; MusMk; MusSN; NewAmDM; NewEOp 71; NewGrDM 80; NewGrDO; NewYTBE 71; NewYTBS 76, 86; OxDcOp; PenDiMP; Who 74, 82, 83, 85, 88, 90, 92, 94; WhoAm 74, 76, 78, 80, 82, 84, 86, 88, 90, 92, 94, 95, 96, 97; WhoEnt 92; WhoMus 72; WhoOp 76; WhoWor 74, 76, 78, 80, 82, 84, 87, 89, 91; WorAl; WorAlBi*

Fischetti, John
American. Editor, Cartoonist
Syndicated political cartoonist; won Pulitzer, 1969; wrote autobiography, *Zinga Za,* 1973.
b. Sep 27, 1916 in New York, New York
d. Nov 8, 1978 in New Haven, Connecticut
Source: *BiDAmJo; BioIn 12, 16; ConAu 102; DcAmB S10; EncTwCJ; NewYTBS 80; WhAm 7, 8; WhoAm 74, 76, 78, 80; WhoAmA 76, 78, 80, 82N, 84N, 86N, 89N, 91N, 93N; WhoWor 74*

Fischl, Eric
American. Artist
Known for paintings that resemble giant movie stills; major exhibition, 1986, NYC's Whitney Museum.
b. Mar 9, 1948 in New York, New York
Source: *AmArt; BioIn 13, 14, 15, 16; ConArt 89, 96; CurBio 86; DcArts; DcCAA 88, 94; IntWW 91, 93; NewYTBS 86; PrintW 83, 85; WhoAm 97; WhoAmA 89, 91, 93; WorArt 1980*

Fish, Albert
[Robert Hayden; Frank Howard; John W Pell; Thomas A Sprague]
"The Moon Maniac"
American. Murderer
Molested 400 children, killed at least six; practiced cannibalism.
b. 1870 in Washington, District of Columbia
d. Jan 16, 1936 in Ossining, New York
Source: *BioIn 17; LegTOT*

Fish, Hamilton
American. Statesman, Author
Secretary of state under U.S. Grant, 1869-77; saved Grant from corruption scandal, negotiated successful treaties; prolific author whose last book, *Tragic Deception,* was written when he was 95.
b. Aug 3, 1808 in New York, New York
d. Sep 6, 1893 in New York, New York
Source: *AmBi; AmPolLe; ApCAB; BiAUS; BiDrAC; BiDrGov 1789; BiDrUSC 89; BiDrUSE 71, 89; BioIn 3, 4, 7, 10, 12, 16; CyAG; DcAmB; DcAmC; DcAmDH 80, 89; DcAmSR; DcBiPP; Drake; EncAB-H 1974, 1996; HarEnUS; LegTOT; LinLib S; McGEWB; NatCAB 4; OxCAmH; TwCBDA; WebAB 74, 79; WebBD 83; WhAm HS; WhAmP; WorAl; WorAlBi*

Fish, Hamilton, III
American. Politician
Rep. con. from NY, 1919-45; known for outspokenness, isolationist views.
b. Dec 7, 1888 in Garrison, New York
d. Jan 18, 1991 in Cold Spring, New York
Source: *AnObit 1991; BiDAmSp FB; BiDrAC; BiDrUSC 89; BioIn 1, 4, 6, 7, 8, 9, 11, 15, 17, 18; CurBio 41, 91N; News 91, 91-3; NewYTBS 91; PolPar; WebBD 83; WhAm 8; WhAmP; WhoFtbl 74; WhoSpor*

Fish, Robert Lloyd
[Robert L Pike]
American. Author
Winner of three Edgars Mystery writers awards: *Isle of Snakes,* 1963.
b. Aug 21, 1912 in Cleveland, Ohio
d. Feb 24, 1981 in Trumbull, Connecticut
Source: *Au&Wr 71; ConAu 13NR, 13R, 103; EncMys; IntAu&W 76, 77; Novels; TwCCr&M 80; WrDr 82*

Fishback, Margaret
American. Poet
Light verse collected in *One to a Customer,* 1937; *Time for a Quick One,* 1940.
b. Mar 10, 1904 in Washington, District of Columbia
d. Sep 25, 1985 in Camden, Maine
Source: *AmAu&B; BioIn 5, 6, 8; ChhPo, S2, S3; CurBio 41, 85, 85N; InWom*

Fishbein, Harry J
American. Bridge Player
Five-time winner of Vanderbilt Cup; world team championship, 1959.
b. 1898
d. Feb 19, 1976 in New York, New York
Source: *BioIn 10; NewYTBS 76*

Fishbein, Morris
American. Physician, Editor, Author
Edited *AMA Journal,* 1924-49; wrote *Popular Medical Encyclopedia,* 1946.
b. Jul 22, 1889 in Saint Louis, Missouri
d. Sep 27, 1976 in Chicago, Illinois
Source: *AmAu&B; AmDec 1930; AmMWSc 73P; BioIn 1, 2, 8, 11; BlueB 76; ConAu 4NR, 5R, 69; CurBio 40, 76N; DcAmMeB 84; EncTwCJ; InSci; IntAu&W 77; IntWW 74, 75, 76; OxCMed 86; St&PR 75; WebAB 74, 79; WhAm 7; WhNAA; WhoAm 74, 76; WhoWor 74; WhoWorJ 72*

Fishbone
[John Bingham; Christopher Dowd; John "Norwood" Fisher; Phillip "Fish" Fisher; Kendall Jones; Walter Kibby; Angelo Moore]
American. Music Group
Funk-rock fusion band formed 1979; hit single "Everyday Sunshine," 1991 from album *The Reality of My Surroundings.*
Source: *ConMus 7; NewCBEL; Who 74, 82, 82S, 83, 85, 88*

Fishburne, Laurence
American. Actor
Appeared in *Apocalypse Now,* 1979, *The Color Purple,* 1985, *Boyz N the Hood,* 1991, *Othello,* 1995.
b. Jul 30, 1961 in Augusta, Georgia
Source: *BioIn 16; ConTFT 7, 14; CurBio 96; DrBlPA; IntMPA 92, 94, 96; News 95, 95-3; WhoAm 94, 95, 96, 97; WhoBlA 92*

Fisher, Amy
"Long Island Lolita"
American. Criminal
Convicted of the attempted murder of Mary Jo Buttafuoco, wife of her alleged lover.
b. Aug 1974 in New York, New York
Source: *LegTOT*

Fisher, Avery
American. Designer
Founder of Fisher Radio Co., foremost makers of audio equipment, 1937—.
b. Mar 4, 1906? in New York, New York
d. Feb 1994 in New Milford, New York
Source: *Baker 84; BioIn 5, 6, 10, 11, 17, 19, 20; CelR 90; NewAmDM; NewYTBE 73; NewYTBS 76, 94*

Fisher, Bud
[Harry Conway Fisher]
American. Cartoonist
Created "Mutt and Jeff" comic strip, 1907.
b. Apr 3, 1885 in Chicago, Illinois
d. Sep 7, 1954 in New York, New York
Source: *AmAu&B; BioIn 3, 6, 15; DcAmB S5; LegTOT; NatCAB 43; WebAB 74; WhAm 3; WhAmArt 85; WorECom*

Fisher, Carrie Frances
American. Actor, Writer
Daughter of Debbie Reynolds, Eddie Fisher; starred in *Star Wars*, trilogy, 1977-84; wrote novel/screenplay *Postcards from the Edge*, 1985.
b. Oct 21, 1956 in Burbank, California
Source: *BioIn 13, 14, 15, 16; BkPepl; CelR 90; ConAu 135; CurBio 91; HalFC 88; IntMPA 92; InWom SUP; News 91, 91-1; NewYTBS 77, 83, 87; WhoAm 86, 90; WhoAmW 85, 87; WhoEnt 92; WhoHol A; WorAlBi; WrDr 92*

Fisher, Clara
American. Actor
Noted comic performer; played male, female roles in career that spanned 72 yrs.
b. Apr 14, 1811 in London, England
d. Nov 12, 1898 in Metuchen, New Jersey
Source: *ApCAB; BioIn 10, 16; DcAmB; FamA&A; InWom, SUP; LibW; NotAW; NotNAT A, B; NotWoAT; OxCAmT 84; OxCThe 67, 83; WhAm HS*

Fisher, Dorothy Frances Canfield
American. Author, Essayist
Numerous novels include *Best Twig*, 1915; *Seasoned Timber*, 1939.
b. Feb 17, 1879 in Lawrence, Kansas
d. Nov 9, 1958 in Arlington, Vermont
Source: *AmAu&B; AmNov; CarSB; Chambr 3; CnDAL; ConAmA; ConAmL; ConAu 114; HerW; REn; REnAL; TwCA SUP; WebAB 79; WhAm 3; WhoAmW 58; WomWWA 14*

Fisher, Eddie
[Edwin Jack Fisher]
American. Singer
"O, My Papa," 1953 million-selling hit; married to Debbie Reynolds, Elizabeth Taylor, Connie Stevens.
b. Aug 10, 1928 in Philadelphia, Pennsylvania
Source: *Baker 84, 92; BiDAmM; BioIn 2, 3, 4, 5, 6, 10, 11, 12, 15, 16; CmpEPM; ConMus 12; CurBio 54; FilmEn; FilmgC; ForYSC; HalFC 80, 84, 88; IntMPA 75, 76, 77, 78, 79, 80, 81, 82, 84, 86, 88, 92, 94, 96; LegTOT; LesBEnT, 92; NewYTET; OxCPMus; PenEncP; RadStar; RkOn 74; WhoAm 74, 76, 78, 80, 82; WhoHol 92, A; WorAl; WorAlBi*

Fisher, Fred
American. Composer
Co-wrote "Peg 'O My Heart," 1913.
b. Sep 30, 1875 in Cologne, Germany
d. Jan 14, 1942 in New York, New York
Source: *AmPS; AmSong; ASCAP 66, 80; BiDAmM; BioIn 1, 6, 11, 15, 16; CmpEPM; NewAmDM; NewGrDA 86; NotNAT B; OxCPMus; PopAmC; Sw&Ld C*

Fisher, Gail
American. Actor
Played Peggy Fair in TV series "Mannix," 1968-74.
b. Aug 18, 1935 in Orange, New Jersey
Source: *BioIn 8, 11, 13; DrBlPA, 90; InB&W 80, 85; NegAl 89; NewYTBE 72; NotBlAW 2; WhoAm 74; WhoBlA 85, 92*

Fisher, Ham(mond Edward)
American. Cartoonist
Created Joe Palooka comic strip.
b. Sep 24, 1900 in Wilkes-Barre, Pennsylvania
d. Dec 27, 1955 in New York, New York
Source: *AmAu&B; DcAmB S5; LegTOT; WhAm 3*

Fisher, Harrison
American. Illustrator
Illustrated books, mag. covers; created "Fisher Girl."
b. Jul 27, 1875 in New York, New York
d. Jan 19, 1934 in New York, New York
Source: *AmAu&B; ArtsAmW 1; DcAmB S1; DcNAA; EncFash; IlrAm 1880, B; WhAm 1; WhAmArt 85*

Fisher, Herbert Albert Laurens
English. Historian
Wrote three-volume *History of Europe*, 1935.
b. Mar 21, 1865 in London, England
d. Apr 18, 1940 in London, England
Source: *BiDInt; BioIn 1, 2, 14, 20; Chambr 3; DcLEL; DcNaB 1931; EvLB; GrBr; LngCTC; NewC; NewCBEL; TwCA, SUP; WhLit*

Fisher, Irving
American. Economist, Author
Devised index numbers for price trend studies; wrote text *Stock MarketCrash*, 1930.
b. Feb 27, 1867 in Saugerties, New York
d. Apr 29, 1947 in New Haven, Connecticut
Source: *AmAu&B; AmLY; ApCAB X; BiDAmEd; BioIn 1, 2, 4, 5, 8, 11, 12, 13, 14, 16, 19, 21; DcAmAu; DcAmB S4; DcAmTB; DcNAA; GrEconB; LinLib S; McGEWB; NatCAB 14; RAdv 14, 13-3; ThTwC 87; TwCBDA; WebAB 74, 79; WhAm 2; WhNAA; WhoEc 81, 86*

Fisher, James Maxwell McConnell
English. Author, Naturalist
Wrote books on birds: *Birds of Britain*, 1942; *Watching Birds*, 1940.
b. Sep 3, 1912 in Clifton, England
d. Sep 25, 1970 in Hendon, England
Source: *Au&Wr 71; BioIn 5, 9, 14; DcNaB 1961; GrBr; WhAm 5*

Fisher, John
English. Clergy, Author
Beheaded for refusing to acknowledge Henry VIII as head of church; canonized, 1935.
b. 1469 in Beverley, England
d. Jun 22, 1535 in London, England
Source: *Alli; BbD; BioIn 1, 2, 4, 5, 7, 8, 9, 11, 16; BritAu; CasWL; DcCathB; DcEnL; DcNaB, C; EvLB; NewCBEL; OxCEng 85, 95*

Fisher, John Arbuthnot
British. Naval Officer
Admiral of the fleet, 1905-10; responsible for preparing Royal Navy for WW I.
b. 1841 in Rambodde, Ceylon
d. 1920
Source: *BioIn 17, 18; DcNaB 1912; DcTwHis; FacFETw; GrBr; HarEnMi; NewCol 75; OxCShps; WhDW; WhoMilH 76*

Fisher, Jules Edward
American. Designer
Won Tonys for light designs in *Pippin*, 1973; *Dancin'*, 1978.
b. Nov 12, 1937 in Norristown, Pennsylvania
Source: *BioIn 15; ConDes 84, 90; ConTFT 4; NotNAT; VarWW 85; WhoAm 84, 86, 88, 90, 92, 94, 95, 96; WhoE 93; WhoEnt 92*

Fisher, M(ary) F(rances) K(ennedy)
[Victoria Bern; Mary Frances Parrish]
American. Author
Best known for her writings on basic human needs, especially food: *The Art of Eating*, 1954.
b. Jul 3, 1908 in Albion, Michigan
d. Jun 22, 1992 in Glen Ellen, California
Source: *AmWomWr SUP; ArtclWW 2; BioIn 2, 6, 9, 11, 13, 15, 16, 17, 18, 19, 20; ConAu 44NR, 77, 138; ConLC 76, 87; ContDcW 89; CurBio 83, 92N; InWom, SUP; OxCAmL 95; PenNWW A, B*

Fisher, Mary
American. AIDS Activist
Founder of Family AIDS Network, Inc.
b. Apr 6, 1948 in Louisville, Kentucky
Source: *BioIn 20, 21; ConAu 148; News 94, 94-3; WhoAmW 97*

Fisher, Terence
English. Director
Joined Hammer films, 1952, directing horror films *Curse of Frankenstein,* 1957; *Island of Terror,* 1966.
b. Feb 23, 1904 in London, England
d. Jun 18, 1980 in Twickenham, England
Source: *AnObit 1980; BiDFilm, 81, 94; BioIn 12, 15, 17; CmMov; DcFM; EncEurC; FilmEn; FilmgC; HalFC 80, 84, 88; HorFD; IlWWBF; IntDcF 1-2, 2-2; IntMPA 75, 76, 77, 78, 79, 80; LegTOT; MiSFD 9N; PenEncH; WhoHrs 80; WorEFlm*

Fisher, Vardis
American. Author
Writings include autobiography *In Tragic Life,* 1932.
b. Mar 31, 1895 in Annis, Idaho
d. Jul 9, 1968 in Jerome, Idaho
Source: *AmAu&B; AmNov; Au&Wr 71; BenetAL 91; BioIn 1, 2, 4, 5, 7, 8, 9, 10, 12, 16; CnDAL; ConAmA; ConAu 5R, 25R; ConLC 7; CyWA 58; DcLB 9; DcLEL; EncFWF; EncSF; FifWWr; GrWrEL N; LinLib L; LngCTC; ModAL; Novels; OxCAmL 65, 83; PenC AM; REn; REnAL; REnAW; RfGAmL 87; ScF&FL 1, 2; TwCA, SUP; TwCWW 82, 91; WhAm 5; WhNAA; Who 74*

Fisher, Welthy (Blakesley Honsinger)
American. Missionary, Educator
Founded India's Literary Village, 1953; wrote memoirs, *To Light a Candle,* 1962.
b. Sep 18, 1879 in Rome, New York
d. Dec 16, 1980 in Southbury, Connecticut
Source: *BioIn 6, 7, 8, 12; ConAu 2NR, 102; CurBio 69, 81, 81N; ForWC 70; IntAu&W 77; InWom SUP; NewYTBS 74, 80*

Fishman, Michael
American. Actor
Played Roseanne's son, D.J., on TV show "Roseanne," 1988-97.

Fisk, Carlton Ernest
"Pudge"
American. Baseball Player
Catcher, Boston Red Sox, 1971-80; Chicago White Sox, 1981—; Al rookie of the year, 1972; holds ML record for home runs by a catcher, 37, 1985.
b. Dec 26, 1947 in Bellows Falls, Vermont
Source: *Ballpl 90; BaseReg 86, 87; BiDAmSp BB; BioIn 10, 11, 12, 14, 15, 16; NewYTBE 73; NewYTBS 85; WhoAm 78, 80, 82, 84, 86, 88, 90, 92, 94, 95, 96, 97; WhoMW 90, 92; WhoProB 73*

Fisk, James Brown
American. Physicist, Business Executive
Head of Bell Laboratories, 1959-73; first research director, Atomic Energy Commission, 1947.
b. Aug 30, 1910 in West Warwick, Rhode Island
d. Aug 10, 1981 in Elizabethtown, New York
Source: *AmMWSc 76P, 79; BioIn 5, 9, 12; BlueB 76; CurBio 59, 81, 81N; InSci; IntWW 74, 75, 76, 77, 78, 79, 80, 81; IntYB 78, 79; LElec; St&PR 75; WhAm 8; Who 74; WhoAm 74, 76, 78; WhoFI 74*

Fisk, Jim
[James Fisk]
American. Financier
Robber baron whose attempt to corner the gold market with Jay Gould resulted in stock market "Black Friday," Sep 24, 1869.
b. Apr 1, 1834 in Bennington, Vermont
d. Jan 7, 1872 in New York, New York
Source: *AmBi; BiDAmBL 83; BioIn 3, 5, 8, 9, 12; DcAmB; DcAmSR; Drake; EncAB-H 1974, 1996; McGEWB; NatCAB 22; OxCAmH; WebAB 74, 79; WhAm HS*

Fiske, Billy
American. Olympic Athlete, Soldier
Won gold medal in 4-man bobsled event at Lake Placid Olympics, 1932; first American to die in WWII.
d. Dec 7, 1941 in Pearl Harbor, Hawaii
Source: *WhoHol 92*

Fiske, John
[Edmund Fisk Green]
"The Largest Author in America"
American. Historian, Philosopher, Author
Known for strong support of Darwinism: *Excursions of an Evolutionist,* 1884; wrote in warm, spirited style.
b. Mar 30, 1842 in Hartford, Connecticut
d. Jul 4, 1901 in Gloucester, Massachusetts
Source: *Alli SUP; AmAu; AmAu&B; AmBi; ApCAB; BbD; BenetAL 91; BibAL; BiD&SB; BiInAmS; BioIn 1, 6, 7, 9, 14, 15, 16, 18; Chambr 3; CyEd; DcAmAu; DcAmB; DcAmDH 80, 89; DcLB 47, 64; DcLEL; DcNAA; EvLB; GayN; HarEnUS; InSci; LinLib L, S; LuthC 75; McGEWB; MorMA; NatCAB 3; OxCAmH; OxCAmL 65, 83, 95; OxCCan; PenC AM; REnAL; TwCBDA; WebAB 74, 79; WebBD 83; WhAm 1*

Fiske, Minnie Maddern
American. Actor
Starred in Henrik Ibsen's *A Doll's House;* helped popularize his plays in US.
b. Dec 19, 1865 in New Orleans, Louisiana
d. Feb 16, 1932 in Hollis, New York
Source: *AmBi; AmWom; ArtclWW 2; BiDSA; BioIn 1, 2, 3, 4, 5, 6, 11, 16; ContDcW 89; DcAmB S1; EncWB; Ent; FamA&A; IntDcT 3; IntDcWB; InWom, SUP; LibW; LinLib S; NatCAB 35; NotAW; NotNAT A, B; NotWoAT; OxCAmH; OxCAmL 65, 83; OxCAmT 84; OxCThe 67, 83; PlP&P; WebAB 74, 79; WhAm 1; WhoHol B; WhoStg 1906, 1908; WhScrn 77; WhThe; WomWWA 14*

Fitch, Aubrey
American. Naval Officer
Commanded US task force planes in Battle of Coral Sea, WW II.
b. Jan 11, 1884 in Saint Ignace, Michigan
d. May 22, 1976 in Newcastle, Maine
Source: *CurBio 45; WhAm 7*

Fitch, Bill
[William Charles Fitch]
American. Basketball Coach
Coach, Cleveland, 1970-79, Boston, 1979-83, Houston, 1983-88; coach of year, 1976, 1980; won NBA championship, 1981.
b. May 19, 1934 in Cedar Rapids, Iowa
Source: *BasBi; BiDAmSp Sup; BioIn 15; NewYTBS 86; OfNBA 87; WhoAm 84, 86, 90; WhoE 91; WhoSSW 84, 88*

Fitch, (William) Clyde
American. Dramatist
Wrote society-oriented dramas: *Nathan Hale,* 1898; *The City,* 1909.
b. May 2, 1865 in Elmira, New York
d. Sep 4, 1909 in Chalons-sur-Marne, France
Source: *AmAu; AmAu&B; AmBi; AmCulL; BbD; BenetAL 91; BibAL; BiDAmM; BiD&SB; BioIn 1, 9, 12, 13, 19, 20; CamGLE; CamGWoT; CamHAL; CarSB; Chambr 3; CnDAL; CnMD; CnThe; ConAu 110; CrtSuDr; DcAmAu; DcAmB; DcLB 7; DcLEL; DcNAA; EncWT; Ent; FacFETw; GayN; GrWrEL DR; IntDcT 2; LinLib L, S; McGEWD 72, 84; ModAL; ModWD; NatCAB 13, 15; NotNAT A, B; OxCAmL 65, 83, 95; OxCAmT 84; OxCThe 67, 83; PenC AM; PlP&P; REnAL; REnWD; RfGAmL 87, 94; TheaDir; TwCBDA; WhAm 1; WhLit; WhoStg 1906, 1908*

Fitch, James Marston
American. Architect, Author
Authority on restoration, historic preservation; wrote *American Building,* 1962.
b. May 8, 1909 in Washington, District of Columbia
Source: *AmAu&B; BioIn 10, 13, 15, 18; ConAu 89; MacEA; WhoAm 74, 76, 84, 86, 88, 90, 92, 94, 95, 96, 97*

Fitch, John
American. Inventor
Built steam boat, 1787; paddlewheeler, 1788.
b. Jan 21, 1743 in Windsor, Connecticut
d. Jul 12, 1798 in Bardstown, Kentucky
Source: *Alli, SUP; AmBi; ApCAB; AsBiEn; BioIn 1, 3, 7, 9, 10, 11, 12, 14, 21; DcAmB; Drake; EncAB-H 1974, 1996; HarEnUS; InSci; LegTOT; LinLib S; McGEWB; NatCAB 6; NewYHSD; OxCAmH; OxCShps; TwCBDA; WebAB 74, 79; WhAm HS; WorAl; WorAlBi; WorInv*

Fitch, Val Logsdon
American. Physicist, Educator
Shared Nobel Prize in physics, 1980, with James Cronin; researched K-mesons.
b. Mar 10, 1923 in Merriman, Nebraska
Source: *AmMWSc 76P, 79, 82, 86, 89, 92, 95; BiESc; BioIn 12, 14, 15, 20; BlueB 76; FacFETw; IntWW 74, 75, 76, 77, 78, 79, 80, 81, 82, 83, 89, 91, 93; LarDcSc; McGMS 80; NobelP; NotTwCS; RAdv 14; WhoAm 74, 76, 78, 80, 82, 84, 86, 88, 90, 92, 94, 95, 96, 97; WhoE 81, 83, 85, 89, 91, 93, 95, 97; WhoFrS 84; WhoNob, 90, 95; WhoScEn 94, 96; WhoWor 82, 84, 87, 89, 91, 93, 95, 96, 97; WorAlBi*

Fittipaldi, Emerson
Brazilian. Auto Racer
Won Formula 1 world championships, 1972, 1974, Indianapolis 500, 1989, 1993.
b. Dec 12, 1946 in Sao Paulo, Brazil
Source: *BioIn 10, 11, 12, 13, 14, 16; CurBio 92; IntWW 77, 78, 79, 80, 81, 82, 83, 89, 91, 93; News 94, 94-2; NewYTBS 84, 89; WhoSpor; WhoWor 82, 95, 96*

Fitts, Dudley
American. Author, Educator
His verse appears in *Two Poems,* 1932; *Poems,* 1929, 1936, 1937.
b. Apr 28, 1903 in Boston, Massachusetts
d. Jul 10, 1968 in Andover, Massachusetts
Source: *AmAu&B; BenetAL 91; BiE&WWA; BioIn 4, 8; ConAu 25R, 93; LinLib L; ModAL; NotNAT B; OxCAmL 65, 83, 95; OxCTwCP; PenC AM; REnAL; TwCA, SUP; WhAm 5*

Fitzgerald, A(rthur) Ernest
American. Financier
Financial management systems deputy, US Air Force, 1973—; uncovered $2 billion excess in Air Force's C-5A transport plane funds.
Source: *BioIn 14, 15; ConNews 86-2*

Fitzgerald, Albert J
American. Labor Union Official
Pres., United Electrical, Radio, and Machine Workers of America, 1941-78; attempted to exclude Communists from CIO.
b. Sep 21, 1906 in Lynn, Massachusetts
d. May 1, 1982 in Boston, Massachusetts
Source: *BiDAmL; BiDAmLL; BioIn 1, 12, 13; CurBio 48, 82, 82N; NewYTBS 82; PolProf T*

Fitzgerald, Barry
[William Joseph Shields]
American. Actor
Won 1944 Oscar for *Going My Way.*
b. Mar 10, 1888 in Dublin, Ireland
d. Jan 4, 1961 in Dublin, Ireland
Source: *BiDFilm, 81, 94; BioIn 1, 5, 6, 7, 10; CurBio 45, 61; DcIrB 78, 88; EncAFC; EncEurC; FacFETw; FilmEn; FilmgC; HalFC 80, 84, 88; HolCA; HolP 40; IntDcF 1-3, 2-3; ItaFilm; LegTOT; MotPP; MovMk; NotNAT B; OxCFilm; OxCThe 83; PlP&P; WhAm 4; WhoHol B; WhScrn 74, 77, 83; WhThe; WorAl; WorAlBi*

Fitzgerald, Ed(ward)
American. Radio Performer
With wife Pegeen broadcast "The Fitzgerald's" radio show for 44 years.
b. 1893 in Troy, New York
d. Mar 22, 1982 in New York, New York
Source: *BioIn 12, 13; CurBio 47; LegTOT; NewYTBS 79, 82*

FitzGerald, Edward
English. Poet, Translator
Best known for translation of Omar Khayyam's *Rubaiyat,* 1859.
b. Mar 31, 1809 in Bredfield, England
d. Jun 14, 1883 in Merton, England
Source: *Alli SUP; AtlBL; BbD; Benet 87, 96; BiD&SB; BioIn 1, 2, 5, 7, 8, 9, 10, 11, 12, 13, 14, 16; BlmGEL; BritAu 19; BritWr 4; CamGEL; CamGLE; CasWL; CelCen; ChhPo, S1, S2, S3; CnE&AP; CrtT 3; CyWA 58; DcArts; DcEnA, A; DcEuL; DcLB 32; DcLEL; DcNaB; DcVicP 2; Dis&D; Drake; EvLB; GrWrEL P; LinLib L, S; LngCEL; MouLC 4; NewC; NewCBEL; NinCLC 9; OxCEng 67, 85, 95; PenC ENG; PoIre; RComWL; REn; RfGEnL 91; VicBrit; WebE&AL; WhDW*

Fitzgerald, Ella
"First Lady of Song"
American. Singer
Jazz singer adept at improvising, scat; won 13 Grammys.
b. Apr 25, 1917 in Newport News, Virginia
d. Jun 15, 1996 in Beverly Hills, California
Source: *ASCAP 66; Baker 84; BiDJaz; BioAmW; BioIn 13, 14, 15, 16; BkPepl; CelR 90; ConMus 1; ContDcW 89; CurBio 56, 90, 96N; DrBlPA 90; EncAB-H 1974; EncWB; HalFC 88; InB&W 85; IntWW 91; IntWWM 90; InWom SUP; NegAl 89; NewAmDM; NewGrDA 86; NewGrDJ 88; News 96; NewYTBS 27, 86; NotBlAW 1; WebAB 79; WhoAm 86, 90; WhoAmW 91; WhoBlA 88, 92; WhoEnt 92; WhoMus 72; WhoWor 84, 91; WorAlBi*

Fitzgerald, F(rancis) Scott (Key)
American. Author
Wrote *This Side of Paradise,* 1920; *The Great Gatsby,* 1925; writings, lifestyle epitomized 1920s "Jazz Age."
b. Sep 24, 1896 in Saint Paul, Minnesota
d. Dec 21, 1940 in Hollywood, California
Source: *Alli SUP; AmAu&B; AmCulL; AmWr; AtlBL; AuNews 1; Benet 96; BioIn 1, 2, 4, 5, 6, 7, 8, 9, 10, 11, 14, 15, 16, 17; BioNews 74; CasWL; Chambr 3; CnDAL; CnMD; CnMWL; CyWA 58; DcAmB S2; DcArts; EncAB-H 1974, 1996; MakMC; McGEWB; ModAL S1; OxCAmL 65, 95; OxCEng 95; PenC AM; REn; RfGShF; RGTwCWr; TwCA SUP; WebAB 74; WhAm 1; WorEFlm*

FitzGerald, Frances
American. Author, Journalist
Won Pulitzer for book about Vietnam, *Fire in the Lake,* 1972.
b. Oct 21, 1940 in New York, New York
Source: *AmWomWr; AuSpks; BenetAL 91; BioIn 7, 8, 9, 11, 12, 13, 14, 15, 17; ConAu 32NR, 41R; CurBio 87; IntWW 89, 91, 93; InWom SUP; LiJour; OxCAmL 83, 95; WhoAm 78, 80, 82, 84, 86, 88; WhoAmW 81, 83; WhoUSWr 88; WhoWrEP 89, 92, 95; WorAu 1980; WrDr 90, 92, 94, 96*

FitzGerald, Garret Michael
Irish. Political Leader
Prime minister of Ireland, 1981-1987; signed historic Anglo-Irish Agreement, 1985.
b. Feb 9, 1926 in Dublin, Ireland
Source: *BioIn 13, 14, 15, 16; CurBio 84; EncWB; IntAu&W 89; IntWW 91; IntYB 79; Who 85, 92; WhoWor 87, 91; WrDr 80, 92*

Fitzgerald, George Francis
Irish. Physicist
Contributions included development of electromagnetic theory of radiation.
b. Aug 3, 1851 in Dublin, Ireland
d. Feb 21, 1901 in Dublin, Ireland
Source: *AsBiEn; BiESc; BioIn 2, 4, 14; CamDcSc; DcIrB 78, 88; DcNaB S2; DcScB; InSci; LarDcSc; NewCol 75*

Fitzgerald, Geraldine
American. Actor
1939 Oscar nominee for *Wuthering Heights.*
b. Nov 24, 1914 in Dublin, Ireland
Source: *BiE&WWA; BioIn 4, 10, 11, 12, 16, 18; CamGWoT; CelR 90; ConTFT 1, 8; CurBio 76; FilmEn; FilmgC; ForYSC; HalFC 84; HolP 30, 40; IlWWBF; IntMPA 75, 76, 77, 78, 79, 80, 81, 82, 84, 86, 88, 92, 94, 96; InWom, SUP; LegTOT; MotPP; MovMk; NewYTBE 71; NotNAT; NotWoAT; ThFT; WhoAm 82, 90; WhoAmW 61; WhoHol 92, A; WhoThe 72, 77, 81; WorAl; WorAlBi*

Fitzgerald, John Dennis
American. Children's Author
Wrote children's *Great Brain* series, 1967-88.
b. 1907 in Vermont
d. May 21, 1988 in Titusville, Florida
Source: *BioIn 12; ChlLR 1; ConAu 93, 126; FifBJA; OxCChiL; SmATA 56N; TwCChW 83; WrDr 86*

Fitzgerald, John Francis
"Honey Fitz"
American. Businessman, Politician
Father of Rose Kennedy; mayor of Boston, 1905-14.

b. Feb 11, 1863 in Boston, Massachusetts
d. Oct 2, 1950 in Boston, Massachusetts
Source: *BiDrAC; BiDrUSC 89; BioIn 2, 6, 8; DcAmB S4; DcCathB; TwCBDA; WhAm 3; WhAmP*

Fitzgerald, Pegeen
American. Radio Performer
With husband Ed, broadcast "The Fitzgeralds" radio talk show.
b. Nov 24, 1910 in Norcatur, Kansas
d. Jan 30, 1989 in New York, New York
Source: *AnObit 1989; BioIn 1, 12, 15, 16; CurBio 47, 89N; ForWC 70; IntMPA 84, 86, 88; InWom; LegTOT; NewYTBS 79, 89; RadStar*

Fitzgerald, Robert Stuart
American. Author, Translator
Poems known for rich imagery, vigorous language; translations of Homer's *Odyssey, Iliad* classics in own right.
b. Oct 12, 1910 in Geneva, New York
d. Jan 16, 1985 in Hamden, Connecticut
Source: *AmAu&B; AmCath 80; AmMWSc 73P; BioIn 3, 4, 7, 11, 12; BlueB 76; CathA 1952; ConAu 1NR, 1R; ConPo 70, 75; DrAP 75; DrAPF 80; DrAS 74E, 78E, 82E; IntAu&W 82; IntWWP 77, 82; ModAL; OxCAmL 65, 83, 95; OxCTwCP; PenC AM; REnAL; TwCA SUP; WhoAm 74, 76, 78, 82; WrDr 76, 80, 84*

Fitzgerald, Zelda
[Mrs. F Scott Fitzgerald; Zelda Sayre]
American., Author
Wrote *Save Me the Waltz,* 1932.
b. Jul 24, 1900 in Montgomery, Alabama
d. Mar 10, 1948 in Asheville, North Carolina
Source: *AmAu&B; AmWomWr; AuNews 1; BioIn 10, 12, 13, 14, 15, 17; BlmGWL; ConAu 117, 126; ContDcW 89; FemiCLE; HanAmWH; IntDcWB; LegTOT; OxCWoWr 95*

Fitzgibbon, Constantine
[Robert Louis Constantine Fitzgibbon]
American. Author
Fiction, non-fiction writer; best work *The Life of Dylan Thomas,* 1965.
b. Jun 8, 1919 in Lenox, Massachusetts
d. Mar 23, 1983 in Dublin, Ireland
Source: *AnObit 1983; BiDIrW; BioIn 13; ConAu 1NR, 2NR, 109; DcLEL 1940; DcNaB 1981; IntWW 74, 83; NewCBEL; ScF&FL 92; TwCSFW 81, 86, 91; Who 74, 82, 83; WhoAm 74, 76, 78, 80, 82; WhoWor 74; WorAu 1950; WrDr 76*

Fitzpatrick, Daniel R
American. Cartoonist
His outspoken political drawings, syndicated from 1912-57, won Pulitzer, 1926, 1955.
b. Mar 5, 1891 in Superior, Wisconsin
d. May 18, 1969 in Saint Louis, Missouri
Source: *ConAu 89; CurBio 41, 69; EncAJ; ObitOF 79; WebBD 83; WorECar*

Fitzpatrick, Thomas
American. Explorer, Naturalist
One of great mountain men; spent life opening up West.
b. 1799 in County Cavan, Ireland
d. Feb 7, 1854 in Washington, District of Columbia
Source: *AmBi; BioIn 4, 5, 10, 12; DcAmB; EncAB-H 1974, 1996; McGEWB; OxCAmH; OxCAmL 65, 83, 95; REnAW; WebAB 74, 79; WhAm HS; WhNaAH; WhWE*

Fitzsimmons, Bob
[Robert Prometheus Fitzsimmons]
English. Boxer
World heavyweight champ, 1897; famed for now outlawed solar-plexus punch.
b. Jun 4, 1862 in Helston, England
d. Oct 22, 1917 in Chicago, Illinois
Source: *AuBYP 2; BioIn 1, 2, 3, 4, 5, 7, 10, 11, 17; DcAmB; DcNAA; Film 1; WebAB 74, 79; WhoBox 74; WhoSpor; WhScrn 83*

Fitzsimmons, Frank Edward
American. Labor Union Official
Teamster pres., 1967-81, following Jimmy Hoffa's disappearance.
b. Apr 7, 1908 in Jeannette, Pennsylvania
d. May 6, 1981 in San Diego, California
Source: *BiDAmL; BiDAmLL; BioIn 9, 10, 11, 12; CurBio 71, 81; IntWW 74, 75, 76, 77, 78, 79, 80, 81, 81N; NewYTBE 71; PolProf J, NF; WhoAm 80; WhoE 79, 81; WhoLab 76*

Fitzsimmons, James E
"Sunny Jim"
American. Horse Trainer
Best known horse trainer of all time; had 2,275 winners totaling over $13 million.
b. Jul 23, 1874 in New York, New York
d. Mar 11, 1966 in Miami, Florida
Source: *BioIn 4, 5, 6, 7, 10*

Fitzwater, Marlin
[Max Marlin Fitzwater]
American. Presidential Aide
Replaced Larry Speakes as presidential press secretary, 1989-93.
b. Nov 24, 1942 in Salinas, Kansas
Source: *BioIn 15, 16; CurBio 88; IntWW 91, 93; LegTOT; WhoAm 86, 88, 90, 92, 94, 95, 96; WhoAmP 87, 89, 91, 93, 95; WhoE 93*

Fix, Paul
American. Actor
Co-star of TV's "The Rifleman," 1958-63.
b. Mar 13, 1902 in Dobbs Ferry, New York
d. Oct 14, 1983 in Santa Monica, California
Source: *Film 2; FilmgC; ForYSC; HalFC 80; HolCA; IntMPA 75, 76, 77, 78, 79, 80, 81, 82, 84, 86; MovMk; TwYS; Vers B; WhoHol A*

Fixico, Donald L.
American. Educator
Published *Termination and Relocation: Federal Indian Policy, 1945-1960,* 1986.
b. Jan 22, 1951 in Shawnee, Oklahoma
Source: *NotNaAm*

Fixx, The
[Charlie Barrett; Cy Curnin; Rupert Greenall; Jamie West-Oram; Adam Woods]
English. Music Group
New wave group who released albums *Shattered Room,* 1982; *Reach the Beach,* 1983.
Source: *PenEncP; RkOn 85*

Fixx, James Fuller
American. Author, Track Athlete
Dean of jogging craze, who collapsed, died while jogging; best selling book *Complete Book of Running.*
b. Apr 23, 1932 in New York, New York
d. Jul 20, 1984 in Hardwick, Vermont
Source: *AnObit 1984; ConAu 13NR, 73; NewYTBS 78, 84; WhAm 8; WhoAm 74, 76, 78, 80, 82, 84*

Fizdale, Robert
American. Musician
Pianist teamed with Arthur Gold since 1944; toured extensively, with works written for them; wrote *Misia,* 1979.
b. Apr 12, 1920 in Chicago, Illinois
d. Dec 6, 1995 in New York, New York
Source: *Baker 78, 84, 92; BioIn 5, 6, 7, 15; NewAmDM; NewGrDA 86; NewGrDM 80; NewYTBS 80, 95; PenDiMP*

Fizeau, Armand Hippolyte Louis
French. Physicist
First to determine velocity of light, 1849.
b. Sep 23, 1819 in Paris, France
d. Sep 18, 1896 in Venteuil, France
Source: *AsBiEn; BiESc; BioIn 8, 14; CamDcSc; DcCathB; DcScB; ICPEnP; LarDcSc; MacBEP; McGEWB; NewCol 75*

Flack, Roberta
American. Singer
Won Grammys for "The First Time Ever I Saw Your Face," 1972; "Killing Me Softly," 1973.
b. Feb 10, 1939 in Black Mountain, North Carolina
Source: *AfrAmAl 6; Baker 84, 92; BiDAfM; BiDJaz; BioIn 13, 16; BkPepl; CelR 90; ConMus 5; CurBio 73; DrBlPA 90; Ebony 1; EncJzS; EncPR&S 89; EncRk 88; HarEnR 86; HerW, 84; IlEncBM 82; IlEncRk; InB&W 85; InWom SUP; LegTOT; NegAl 89; NewGrDA 86; OxCPMus; PenEncP; RolSEnR 83; SoulM; WhoAfA 96; WhoAm 78, 80, 82, 84, 86, 88, 90, 92, 94, 95, 96, 97; WhoAmW 79, 81, 83, 85, 87, 89, 91, 93; WhoBlA 88, 90, 92, 94; WhoEnt 92; WhoHol 92; WhoRock 81; WorAl; WorAlBi*

Flagg, Ernest
American. Architect
Designed US Naval Academy, 1899-1907, Washington's Corcoran Art Gallery.
b. Feb 6, 1857 in New York, New York
d. Apr 10, 1947 in New York, New York
Source: *BiDAmAr; BioIn 1, 17; BriEAA; DcAmB S4; DcNAA; EncAAr 2; IntDcAr; LinLib S; MacEA; McGDA; WhAm 2*

Flagg, Fannie
[Frances Carlton Flagg]
American. Comedian
Films include *Five Easy Pieces,* 1972; *Grease,* 1978.
b. Sep 21, 1944 in Birmingham, Alabama
Source: *BioIn 15; ConTFT 1; ForWC 70; FunnyW; HalFC 88; IntMPA 96; LegTOT; WhoHol A*

Flagg, James Montgomery
American. Artist, Author
His WW I recruiting poster with Uncle Sam, modeled on himself, pointing finger, with caption "I Want You!" brought him fame.
b. Jun 18, 1877 in Pelham Manor, New York
d. May 27, 1960 in New York, New York
Source: *AmAu&B; BenetAL 91; BioIn 1, 5, 10, 12, 15; ChhPo, S2; CurBio 40, 60; DcAmB S6; DcArts; EncAJ; Film 1; IlrAm 1880, B; LegTOT; LinLib L, S; OxCAmL 65, 83, 95; REnAL; WebAB 74, 79; WhAm 4; WhoAmA 89N, 91N, 93N; WhScrn 77, 83; WorECar*

Flagler, Henry Morrison
American. Business Executive
Co-founder, Standard Oil; built railways, hotels in FL, stimulating growth.
b. Jan 2, 1830 in Hopewell, New York
d. May 20, 1913 in West Palm Beach, Florida
Source: *AmBi; ApCAB X; BiDAmBL 83; BioIn 1, 2, 3, 4, 5, 6, 7, 9, 15, 18, 19; DcAmB; EncAB-A 29; EncAB-H 1974, 1996; EncSoH; NatCAB 12, 15; OxCAmH; REnAW; WebAB 74, 79; WhAm 1; WhFla*

Flagstad, Kirsten
Norwegian. Opera Singer
Considered greatest Wagnerian soprano of day; Isolde most celebrated role.
b. Jul 12, 1895 in Hamar, Norway
d. Dec 7, 1962 in Oslo, Norway
Source: *Baker 78, 84; BiDAmM; BioIn 1, 2, 3, 4, 5, 6, 7, 8, 11, 12, 13, 14, 15, 19, 21; BriBkM 80; CmOp; ConAu 112; ContDcW 89; CurBio 47, 63; FacFETw; FilmgC; HalFC 80, 84, 88; IntDcOp; IntDcWB; InWom; LinLib S; MetOEnc; MusMk; MusSN; NewAmDM; NewEOp 71; NewGrDA 86; NewGrDM 80; ObitT 1961; OxDcOp; PenDiMP; REn; WhAm 4; WhDW; WhoHol B; WhScrn 74, 77, 83; WorAl; WorAlBi*

Flaherty, Joe
American. Writer, Actor
Won Emmys for writing "SCTV Network," 1982, 1983.
b. Jun 21, 1940 in Pittsburgh, Pennsylvania
Source: *BiDConC; BioIn 13; VarWW 85*

Flaherty, Ray(mond)
American. Football Player, Football Coach
End, coach, Hall of Fame, 1976.
b. Sep 1, 1904 in Spokane, Washington
Source: *BiDAmSp FB; WhoSpor*

Flaherty, Robert Joseph
American. Director
"Father" of documentary; first was *Nanook of the North,* 1920, about Eskimos.
b. Feb 16, 1884 in Iron Mountain, Michigan
d. Jul 23, 1951 in Dummerston, Vermont
Source: *AmAu&B; AuBYP 2S, 3; Benet 96; BiDFilm; BioIn 1, 2, 3, 5, 7, 9, 10, 11, 12, 14, 15, 16; CurBio 49, 51; DcAmB S5; DcFM; EncAB-H 1974, 1996; EncAJ; FilmEn; FilmgC; ICPEnP A; MacBEP; MovMk; OxCCan; OxCFilm; REn; WebAB 74, 79; WhAm 3; WomWMM; WorEFlm*

Flamininus, Titus Quinctius
"Liberator of Greece"
Roman. Military Leader
Proclaimed independence of Greek city-states, 196, after defeating Macedonian King Philip V at Cynoscephalae.
b. 230?BC
d. 175?BC
Source: *BioIn 9; McGEWB; NewCol 75*

Flammarion, Camille
French. Astronomer
Popularized study of astronomy; wrote *The Atmosphere,* 1872.
b. Feb 25, 1842 in Montigny-le-Roi, France
d. 1925
Source: *BbD; BiD&SB; BiDPara; BioIn 14; ConAu 120; DcBiPP; DcEuL; DcScB; Dis&D; EncO&P 1, 2, 3; EncSF; InSci; LinLib L, S; ScF&FL 1; ScFEYrs; ScFSB; TwCSFW 81A*

Flamsteed, John
English. Astronomer
First Astronomer Royal, 1675; his publication *Historia Coelestis* included first star catalogs, 1712.
b. Aug 19, 1646 in Denby, England
d. Dec 31, 1719 in Greenwich, England
Source: *Alli; AsBiEn; BiESc; BioIn 1, 2, 4, 9, 14, 17; CamDcSc; DcBiPP; DcInv; DcNaB; DcScB; InSci; LarDcSc; LinLib L, S; McGEWB; NewCBEL; OxCShps; WhDW; WorAl; WorAlBi*

Flanagan, Edward Joseph, Father
American. Clergy
Founded Father Flanagan's Home for Boys, 1917; became Boys Town, 1922.
b. Jul 13, 1886 in Roscommon, Ireland
d. May 15, 1948 in Berlin, Germany
Source: *BioIn 1, 2, 3, 5, 6, 8, 9, 11, 15, 20; DcAmB S4; DcCathB; FacFETw; RelLAm 91; WebAB 74, 79; WhAm 2; WhoHol B; WhScrn 74, 77; WorAl*

Flanagan, Hallie Mae Ferguson
American. Historian, Educator
Director of Federal Theatre Project, 1935-39, supervising over 1,000 productions; known for experimental staging, unique drama.
b. Aug 27, 1890 in Redfield, South Dakota
d. Jul 23, 1969 in Washington, District of Columbia
Source: *AmWomM; BioIn 12; NotAW MOD; OxCAmT 84; OxCThe 67, 83; WhThe*

Flanagan, Mike
[Michael Kendall Flanagan]
American. Baseball Player
Pitcher, Baltimore Orioles, 1975-87; Toronto Bluejays, 1987-90; Baltimore Oriol es, 1991-92; won AL Cy Young Award, 1979.
b. Dec 16, 1951 in Manchester, New Hampshire
Source: *Ballpl 90; BaseReg 86, 87; BioIn 12, 13; ConAu 133; WhoAm 80, 82, 84, 86; WhoE 89; WhoSpor*

Flanagan, Tommy (Lee)
American. Pianist
Grammy-nominated jazz pianist; utilizes the single-note, improvised line.
b. Mar 16, 1930 in Detroit, Michigan
Source: *AfrAmAl 6; AllMusG; Baker 92; BiDAfM; BiDAmM; BiDJaz; BioIn 6, 13; CmpEPM; ConMus 16; CurBio 95; DcTwCCu 5; EncJzS; NewGrDA 86; NewGrDJ 88, 94; PenEncP; WhoAm 92, 94, 95, 96, 97*

Flanders, Ed
American. Actor
Actor most noted for his role as Dr. Westphall on television's "St. Elsewhere."
b. Dec 29, 1934 in Minneapolis, Minnesota
d. Feb 22, 1995 in Denny, California
Source: *BioIn 20; ConTFT 6, 14; HalFC 80, 84, 88; News 95, 95-3; NotNAT; WhoHol 92; WorAlBi*

Flanders, Michael
English. Actor, Author
Broadcaster with BBC radio, 1948-75.
b. Mar 1, 1922 in London, England
d. Apr 14, 1975 in Bettws y Coed, Wales
Source: *Au&Wr 71; AuBYP 2, 3; BiE&WWA; BioIn 5, 7, 8, 9, 10; CamGWoT; ChhPo, S1, S2; ConAu 4NR, 5R, 57; CurBio 70, 75, 75N; IntAu&W*

76; IntWW 74, 80; JoeFr; NewYTBS 75; NotNAT B; ObitT 1971; OxCPMus; OxCThe 67; WhAm 6; Who 74; WhoHol C; WhoThe 72; WhoWor 74; WhScrn 77, 83; WhThe

Flanders, Ralph Edward
American. Politician
Rep. senator from VT who introduced censure resolution against Joseph McCarthy, 1954.
b. Sep 28, 1880 in Barnet, Vermont
d. Feb 19, 1970 in Springfield, Vermont
Source: *BiDrAC; BiDrUSC 89; BioIn 1, 2, 3, 4, 5, 8, 9, 11, 12; ConAu P-1; CurBio 48, 70; DcAmB S8; EncAB-A 6; InSci; NewYTBE 70; WhAm 5*

Flandrin, Hippolyte Jean
French. Artist
Follower of Jean Ingres; noted for portraits, religious scenes: *St. Clair Curing the Blind,* 1837.
b. Mar 24, 1809 in Lyons, France
d. Mar 21, 1864 in Rome, Italy
Source: *BioIn 6; ClaDrA; McGDA; NewCol 75*

Flannagan, John Bernard
American. Sculptor
Renowned for animal sculptures: "Triumph of the Egg," 1941.
b. Apr 7, 1895 in Fargo, North Dakota
d. Jan 6, 1942 in New York, New York
Source: *BioIn 5; BriEAA; CurBio 42; DcAmB S3; McGEWB; PhDcTCA 77; WebAB 74, 79; WebBD 83*

Flanner, Janet
American. Journalist, Author
Correspondent, *New Yorker,* Paris, for 50 yrs; wrote *Letter from Paris.*
b. Mar 13, 1892 in Indianapolis, Indiana
d. Jan 7, 1978 in New York, New York
Source: *AmAu&B; AmWomWr; Benet 87, 96; BenetAL 91; BioIn 8, 9, 10, 11, 12, 14, 16, 18; BlmGWL; CelR; ConAu 13NR, 65, 81; CurBio 43, 79N; DcAmB S10; DcLB 4; EncAJ; FacFETw; FemiCLE; GayLL; IndAu 1917; InWom, SUP; LegTOT; LibW; LiExTwC; LiJour; LinLib L; NewYTBS 78; OxCAmL 65, 83, 95; OxCWoWr 95; PenNWW A; REnAL; WhAm 7; WhoAm 74, 76, 78; WhoAmW 61, 64, 66, 68, 68A, 70, 72, 74; WhoWor 74, 76; WorAl; WorAlBi; WorAu 1950; WrDr 76*

Flannery, Susan
American. Actor
Soap opera actress; won Golden Globe for outstanding acting debut in film *The Towering Inferno,* 1974.
b. Jul 31, 1944 in New York, New York
Source: *HalFC 88; WhoHol A*

Flatt, Ernie
American. Choreographer
Won Emmys for "Carol Burnett Show," 1971.
d. Jul 10, 1995 in Taos, New Mexico
Source: *BioIn 7, 9; ConTFT 2; LesBEnT 92; VarWW 85; WhoAm 90; WhoEnt 92*

Flatt, Lester Raymond
[Flatt and Scruggs]
American. Musician, Singer
Teamed with Earl Scruggs 25 yrs; hits include "Rollin' in My Sweet Baby's Arms"; "The Ballad of Jed Clampett," theme from TV's "Beverly Hillbillies."
b. Jun 28, 1914 in Overton County, Tennessee
d. May 11, 1979 in Nashville, Tennessee
Source: *Baker 84; BiDAmM; CmpEPM; CounME 74, 74A; EncFCWM 69, 83; HarEnR 86; IlEncCM; NewYTBS 79*

Flaubert, Gustave
French. Author
Distinctive novelist of Realist school; prosecuted, acquited for *Madame Bovary,* 1857.
b. Dec 12, 1821 in Rouen, France
d. May 8, 1880 in Croisset, France
Source: *AtlBL; BbD; Benet 87, 96; BiD&SB; BioIn 1, 2, 3, 4, 5, 6, 7, 8, 9, 10, 11, 12, 13, 14, 15, 16, 17, 18, 19, 20, 21; BlmGEL; CasWL; CelCen; ClDMEL 47; CyWA 58; DcArts; DcBiA; DcEuL; DcLB 119; Dis&D; EncWT; Ent; EuAu; EuWr 7; EvEuW; GrFLW; GuFrLit 1; LegTOT; LinLib L, S; LngCEL; MagSWL; McGEWB; NewC; NewCBEL; NewEOp 71; NinCLC 2, 10, 19; Novels; OxCEng 67, 85, 95; OxCFr; PenC EUR; RAdv 14, 13-2; RComWL; REn; RfGShF; RfGWoL 95; ScF&FL 1; ShSCr 11; ShSWr; WebBD 83; WhDW; WorAl; WorAlBi; WorLitC*

Flavin, Joseph B(ernard)
American. Business Executive
Chm., CEO, Singer Co., 1975-87.
b. Oct 16, 1928 in Saint Louis, Missouri
d. Oct 7, 1987 in Norwalk, Connecticut
Source: *BioIn 10, 11, 12; Dun&B 79, 86; IntWW 76, 77, 78, 79, 80, 81, 82, 83; LElec; St&PR 75, 84, 87; WhoAm 74, 76, 78, 80, 82, 84, 86; WhoE 83, 85, 86; WhoFI 74, 75, 77, 79, 81, 83, 85, 87; WhoWor 82, 84*

Flavin, Martin Archer
American. Author
Won Pulitzer for *Journey in the Dark,* 1943.
b. Nov 2, 1883 in San Francisco, California
d. Dec 27, 1967 in Carmel, California
Source: *AmAu&B; AmNov; CmCal; CnMD; ConAu 5R, 25R; DcLB 9; DcLEL; McGEWD 84; ModWD; OxCAmL 83; REnAL; TwCA SUP; WhAm 4*

Flaxman, John
English. Artist
Neoclassic Wedgewood pottery designer, 1775-87; known for line drawings of Homer's *Iliad, Odyssey.* 1793.
b. Jul 6, 1755 in York, England
d. Dec 7, 1826 in London, England
Source: *Alli; AntBDN M; AtlBL; BiDLA; BioIn 1, 3, 4, 5, 6, 10, 11, 12, 13, 14, 15, 16; BkIE; BlkwCE; CelCen; ChhPo; DcArts; DcBiPP; DcNaB; DcNiCA; IntDcAA 90; LinLib L, S; McGDA; OxCArt; OxCEng 85, 95; OxDcArt; PenDiDA 89*

Fleck, Bela
American. Musician, Composer
Bluegrass and jazz-oriented banjo player since 1976; formed Bela Fleck and the Fleckstones, circa 1989.
b. Jul 10, 1958 in New York, New York
Source: *AllMusG; BioIn 16; ConMus 8; CurBio 96*

Fleeson, Doris
American. Journalist
First syndicated woman political writer; columns appeared in 100 US papers, 1946-70.
b. May 20, 1901 in Sterling, Kansas
d. Aug 1, 1970 in Washington, District of Columbia
Source: *ABCMeAm; BiDAmJo; BiDAmNC; BioIn 2, 4, 5, 6, 9, 10, 12, 15, 16; BriB; ConAu 93; CurBio 59, 70; DcLB 29; EncAJ; InWom SUP; JrnUS; NewYTBE 70; NotAW MOD; WhAm 5*

Fleetwood, Mick
[Fleetwood Mac]
English. Singer, Musician
Drummer since 1967; recorded 1980 solo album *The Visitor* in Ghana.
b. Jun 24, 1942 in Cornwall, England
Source: *Baker 84, 92; BioIn 11, 13, 14; BkPepl; ConMus 5; EncPR&S 89; LegTOT; OxCPMus; WhoAm 84, 90; WhoEnt 92; WhoRocM 82*

Fleetwood Mac
[Lindsey Buckingham; Mick Fleetwood; Christine McVie; John McVie; Stevie Nicks; Bob Welch; Robert Weston]
English. Music Group
Album *Rumours,* 1977, second biggest selling album of all time.
Source: *BioIn 11, 14, 15, 17, 18, 20; ConAu X; ConMuA 80A; ConMus 5; EncPR&S 74, 89; EncRk 88; EncRkSt; FacFETw; HarEnR 86; IlEncRk; NewAmDM; NewGrDA 86; NewYTBS 80; OxCPMus; PenEncP; RkOn 74, 78; RolSEnR 83; WhoRock 81; WhoRocM 82*

Fleischer, Max
American. Cartoonist
Created cartoon characters Betty Boop, Popeye.
b. Jul 19, 1883 in Vienna, Austria
d. Sep 11, 1972 in Los Angeles, California
Source: *BioIn 9, 11; DcFM; FacFETw; FilmgC; IntDcF 1-2, 2-4; LegTOT; NewYTBE 72; OxCFilm; WorECar; WorEFlm*

Fleischer, Nat(haniel Stanley)
"Mr. Boxing"
American. Author, Publisher
Boxing expert; founded *Ring* magazine, 1922.
b. Nov 3, 1887 in New York, New York
d. Jun 25, 1972 in New York, New York
Source: *DcAmB S9; LegTOT; NewYTBE 72; ObitOF 79; WhoBox 74; WorAl; WorAlBi*

Fleischmann, Charles Louis
American. Manufacturer
Sold first compressed, non-liquid yeast in US, 1868; later produced vinegar, margarine.
b. Nov 3, 1834 in Budapest, Hungary
d. Dec 10, 1897 in Cincinnati, Ohio
Source: *BioIn 9; DcAmB; Entr; NatCAB 22; WhAm HS*

Fleischmann, Peter F(rancis)
American. Publisher
Son of *The New Yorker* co-founder; with *The New Yorker,* 1955-86, president, 1968-75, chairman 1969-86.
b. Jan 27, 1922 in New York, New York
d. Apr 17, 1993 in New York, New York
Source: *Dun&B 79, 86; WhoAm 74, 76, 78, 80, 82, 84; WhoE 77, 79, 81, 83, 85, 86; WhoFI 74; WhoWor 74*

Fleischmann, Raoul H(erbert)
American. Publisher, Manufacturer
Co-founder, publisher, *The New Yorker,* 1925-69.
b. Aug 17, 1885 in Ischl, Austria-Hungary
d. May 11, 1969 in New York, New York
Source: *AmAu&B; BioIn 8; ConAu 115; ObitOF 79; WhAm 5; WhoE 74*

Fleischmann, Sid
[Albert Sidney Fleischmann]
American. Children's Author
Won Newbery for *The Whipping Boy,* 1986.
b. 1920 in New York, New York
Source: *BioIn 8, 11, 13; ConAu 1R; WhoAm 84*

Fleisher, Leon
American. Pianist, Conductor
Brilliant concert pianist, 1952-64; right hand paralyzed, 1965; successful conductor, 1970s; comeback as bimanual pianist, 1982.
b. Jul 23, 1928 in San Francisco, California
Source: *Baker 78, 84, 92; BiDAmM; BioIn 4, 5, 7, 9, 10, 11, 13, 14, 15; BriBkM 80; CurBio 71; IntWWM 77, 80, 90; MusSN; NewAmDM; NewGrDA 86; NewGrDM 80; NewYTBE 70; NotTwCP; PenDiMP; WhoAm 80, 82, 84, 86, 88; WhoAmM 83; WhoE 74, 83; WhoWor 74; WhoWorJ 72, 78*

Fleming, Alexander, Sir
Scottish. Bacteriologist
Discovered penicillin by accident, 1928; shared Nobel Prize, 1945.
b. Aug 6, 1881 in Lochfield, Scotland
d. Mar 11, 1955 in London, England
Source: *AsBiEn; BiESc; BioIn 1, 2, 3, 4, 5, 6, 7, 8, 10, 11, 12, 13, 14, 15, 17, 18, 19, 20; CamDcSc; ConHero 2; CurBio 44, 55; DcInv; DcNaB 1951; DcScB; FacFETw; GrBr; HisEWW; InSci; LarDcSc; LegTOT; LinLib L, S; LngCTC; McGEWB; McGMS 80; NobelP; NotTwCS; ObitOF 79; ObitT 1951; OxCMed 86; RAdv 14; ThTwC 87; WhAm 3; WhDW; WhE&EA; WhoNob, 90, 95; WorAl; WorAlBi; WorScD*

Fleming, Art
[Arthur Fazzin]
American. TV Personality
Host of TV's "Jeopardy," 1964-75.
b. c. 1925 in New York, New York
d. Apr 25, 1995 in Crystal River, Florida
Source: *News 95*

Fleming, Donald M(ethuen)
Canadian. Government Official
A governor of the World Bank, Int'l Monetary Fund, 1957-63; Canadian finance m inister, 1957-62; Conservative MP, 1945-63.
b. May 23, 1905 in Exeter, Ontario, Canada
d. Dec 31, 1986 in Toronto, Ontario, Canada
Source: *BioIn 4, 5, 6, 15; BlueB 76; CanWW 70, 79, 80, 81, 83; ConAu 121, 130; CurBio 59, 87, 87N; IntWW 74, 75, 76, 77, 78, 79, 80, 81, 82, 83; IntYB 78, 79, 80, 81, 82; NewYTBS 87; WhAm 9; Who 74, 82, 83, 85; WhoCan 73, 75, 77, 80; WhoWor 78*

Fleming, Erin
Canadian. Actor
Groucho Marx's companion, 1970-77.
b. Aug 13, 1941? in New Liskeard, Ontario, Canada
Source: *WhoHol A*

Fleming, Ian
British. Actor
Played Dr. Watson in British film series *Sherlock Holmes,* 1930s.
b. Sep 10, 1888 in Melbourne, Australia
d. Jan 1, 1969 in London, England
Source: *FilmgC; HalFC 80, 84, 88; WhoHol B; WhScrn 74, 77, 83; WhThe*

Fleming, Ian Lancaster
English. Author
Created James Bond adventure series; wrote *Dr. No,* 1958; *Goldfinger,* 1959.
b. May 28, 1908 in London, England
d. Aug 12, 1964 in Canterbury, England
Source: *AuBYP 2; ConAu 5R; ConLC 3; CorpD; CurBio 64; DcLEL 1940; DcNaB 1961; EncMys; EncSF, 93; FilmgC; LngCTC; NewC; OxCEng 85, 95; PenC ENG; REn; SmATA 9; SpyFic; TwCYAW; WhAm 4; WhDW; WorAl; WorAu 1950*

Fleming, Joan Margaret
English. Author
Wrote over 30 mysteries, historical romances: *Young Man I Think You're Dying,* 1970.
b. Mar 27, 1908 in Horwich, England
d. Nov 15, 1980, England
Source: *AnObit 1980; ConAu 81, 102; TwCCr&M 80; WrDr 80*

Fleming, John Ambrose, Sir
English. Physicist
Leader in development of electric light in England.
b. Nov 29, 1849 in Lancaster, England
d. Apr 18, 1945 in Sidmouth, England
Source: *AsBiEn; BiESc; BioIn 2, 4, 8, 10, 17, 20, 21; CamDcSc; CurBio 45; DcNaB 1941; DcScB; DeafPAS; EncAJ; InSci; LarDcSc; NewCol 75; NotTwCS; WhDW; WorInv*

Fleming, Peggy Gale
American. Skater
Three-time world champion figure skater, 1966-68; won gold medal, 1968 Olympics.
b. Jul 27, 1948 in San Jose, California
Source: *BiDAmSp BK; BioIn 13; CurBio 68; FacFETw; HerW, 84; InWom, SUP; NewYTBS 81; WhoAm 76, 80, 82, 84, 86, 88, 90, 92, 94, 95, 96, 97; WhoAmW 68, 70, 72, 74, 75; WhoWest 94*

Fleming, Peter
American. Tennis Player
With doubles partner John McEnroe has won Wimbledon, 1979, 1981; US Open, 1979, 1981.
b. Jan 21, 1955 in Summit, New Jersey
Source: *BioIn 12; DcCanB 8; LegTOT; WhoIntT*

Fleming, Renee
American. Opera Singer
Won the first Solti Prize, 1996, after her performance as Donna Anna in Mozart's *Don Giovanni.*
b. Feb 14, 1959 in Indiana, Pennsylvania

Fleming, Rhonda
[Marilyn Lewis]
American. Actor
Played "bad girl" roles, 1945—; films include *Spellboun,d* 1945; *Spiral Staircase,*; *Pony Express,* 1953.
b. Aug 10, 1923 in Los Angeles, California
Source: *BiDFilm, 81; BioIn 1, 21; FilmEn; FilmgC; ForYSC; HalFC 88; IntMPA 80, 81, 82, 84, 86, 92; InWom, SUP; ItaFilm; LegTOT; MotPP; MovMk; MusSN; SweetSg D; WhoAm 82, 90; WhoAmW 61, 89; WhoEnt 92; WhoHol A; WorAl; WorAlBi; WorEFlm*

Fleming, Victor
American. Director
Won Oscar for *Gone With the Wind,* 1939; films include *Wizard of Oz,* 1939; *Treasure Island,* 1934.
b. Feb 23, 1883 in Pasadena, California

d. Jan 6, 1949 in Cottonwood, Arizona
Source: *AmFD; BiDFilm, 81, 94; BioIn 15, 17; DcFM; FilmEn; FilmgC; HalFC 80, 84, 88; IlWWHD 1; IntDcF 1-2, 2-2; LegTOT; MiSFD 9N; MovMk; OxCFilm; TwYS A; WhAm 2; WhoHrs 80; WorEFlm; WorFDir 1*

Fleming, Williamina Paton Stevens
American. Astronomer
With Harvard Observatory, discovered many new stars, 1879-98.
b. May 15, 1857 in Dundee, Scotland
d. May 21, 1911 in Boston, Massachusetts
Source: *AmWomSc; BiDAmS; BiInAmS; BioIn 14, 15, 16, 17, 20, 21; DcAmB; DcScB; FacFETw; GrLiveH; InWom, SUP; LibW; NatCAB 7; NotAW; TwCBDA; WhAm 1; WomSc*

Flemming, Arthur S(herwood)
American. Government Official
Secretary, Health, Education, and Welfare, 1958-61; chairman, US Commission on Civil Rights, 1974-81.
b. Jun 12, 1905 in Kingston, New York
d. Sep 7, 1996 in Alexandria, Virginia
Source: *AmMWSc 73S, 78S; BiDrUSE 71, 89; BioIn 1, 2, 3, 4, 5, 6, 9, 10, 11, 12, 13, 16; BlueB 76; CurBio 60, 96N; EncWM; IntWW 74, 75, 76, 77, 78, 79, 80, 81, 82, 83, 89, 91, 93; LinLib S; NewYTBE 71; PolProf E; WhoAm 80, 82; WhoAmP 73, 75, 77, 79, 81, 83, 85, 87, 89, 91, 93, 95; WhoGov 72, 75, 77*

Flemming, Bill
[William Norman Flemming]
American. Sportscaster
ABC sports commentator, "Wide World of Sports," 1964—.
b. Sep 3, 1926 in Chicago, Illinois
Source: *NewYTET; WhoAm 80, 82, 84, 86; WhoWor 80*

Flesch, Karl
Hungarian. Violinist, Teacher
Founded Curtis String Quartet; wrote classic text on violin playing, 1924-30, translated into 22 languages.
b. Oct 9, 1873 in Moson, Austria-Hungary
d. Nov 15, 1944 in Lausanne, Switzerland
Source: *Baker 84; CurBio 45; NewGrDM 80*

Flesch, Rudolf (Franz)
American. Author
Wrote *Why Johnny Can't Read,* 1955; expert on clear writing, literacy.
b. May 8, 1911 in Vienna, Austria
d. Oct 5, 1986 in Dobbs Ferry, New York
Source: *AmAu&B; AmMWSc 73S, 78S; BioIn 1, 5, 14, 15; ConAu 3NR, 9R, 120; CurBio 86, 86N; NewYTBS 86; WhAm 9; WhoAm 74, 76, 78, 80, 82, 84, 86; WhoE 74; WrDr 76, 80, 82, 84, 86*

Fletcher, Alice Cunningham
American. Ethnologist, Lecturer
Expert on Plains Indians; wrote *The Omaha Tribe,* 1911.
b. Mar 15, 1838 in Havana, Cuba
d. Apr 6, 1923 in Washington, District of Columbia
Source: *AmAu&B; AmBi; AmRef; AmWomSc; Baker 92; BiDAmM; BiDSocW; BioIn 7, 10, 12, 13, 15, 16, 20, 21; CamDcSc; ContDcW 89; DcAmAu; DcAmB; DcNAA; EncNAB; InSci; IntDcAn; IntDcWB; InWom, SUP; LibW; McGEWB; NewGrDA 86; NewGrDM 80; NotAW; OxCMus; WebBD 83; WhAm 1; WhNaAH; WomSc*

Fletcher, Arthur Allen
American. Government Official
First black football player for Baltimore Colts, 1950; as asst. secretary for Wage and Labor Standards, Dept. of Labor, 1969-71, was highest ranking black in Nixon administration.
b. Dec 22, 1924 in Phoenix, Arizona
Source: *BioIn 9, 17; CurBio 71; Ebony 1; EncAACR; InB&W 80; NewYTBE 71; WhoAfA 96; WhoAm 90; WhoAmP 73, 75, 77, 79, 81, 83, 85, 87, 89, 91, 93, 95; WhoBlA 75, 77, 80, 85, 90, 92, 94*

Fletcher, Bramwell
English. Actor
Films include *Raffles,* 1940; *The Mummy,* 1959.
b. Feb 20, 1906 in Bradford, England
Source: *BiE&WWA; BioIn 16; ConAu 125; ConTFT 7; HalFC 88; NewYTBS 88; NotNAT; WhoHol A; WhoThe 77*

Fletcher, Grant
American. Conductor, Composer
Wrote opera *The Carrion Crow,* 1948; works often combine instrumental ensembles.
b. Oct 25, 1913 in Hartsburg, Illinois
Source: *ASCAP 66; Baker 78, 84; ConAmC 76, 82; CpmDNM 72, 78, 79, 80, 81, 82; NewGrDA 86; WhoAmM 83*

Fletcher, John
English. Author, Dramatist
Collaborated with Francis Beaumont in famed partnership; sold 16 plays.
b. Dec 20, 1579 in Rye, England
d. Aug 29, 1625 in London, England
Source: *AtlBL; BbD; BiD&SB; BiDRP&D; BioIn 1, 2, 3, 5, 8, 9, 12, 16, 17, 18; BlmGEL; BritAu; BritWr 2; CamGEL; CamGLE; CamGWoT; CasWL; ChhPo, S1, S3; CnE&AP; CnThe; CroE&S; CrtSuDr; CrtT 1; CyWA 58; DcArts; DcEnA; DcEnL; DcEuL; DcLEL; DcNaB; DramC 6; EncWT; Ent; EvLB; GrWrEL DR; IntDcT 2; LinLib L, S; LitC 33; LngCEL; McGEWB; McGEWD 72, 84; MouLC 1; NewC; NewCBEL; NotNAT A, B; OxCEng 67, 85, 95; OxCMus; OxCThe 67, 83; PenC ENG; PlP&P; RAdv 14, 13-2; REn; REnWD; RfGEnL 91; WebE&AL; WhDW; WorAl; WorAlBi*

Fletcher, John Gould
American. Poet, Critic
Won Pulitzer for *Selected Poems,* 1938.
b. Jan 3, 1886 in Little Rock, Arkansas
d. May 20, 1950 in Little Rock, Arkansas
Source: *AmAu&B; AmLY; AnCL; Benet 87; BenetAL 91; BiDAmM; BioIn 2, 3, 4, 5, 8, 11, 12, 15, 16, 17, 20; CamGLE; CamHAL; CasWL; Chambr 3; ChhPo, S3; CnDAL; ConAmA; ConAmL; ConAu 107; DcAmB S4; DcLB 4, 45; DcLEL; EncWL; EvLB; FacFETw; FifSWrA; GrWrEL P; LegTOT; LinLib L, S; LngCTC; ModAL; NatCAB 42; NewGrDA 86; OxCAmL 65, 83, 95; OxCTwCP; PenC AM; REn; REnAL; RfGAmL 87, 94; SixAP; SouWr; TwCA, SUP; TwCLC 35; WhAm 3; WhE&EA; WhLit; WhNAA*

Fletcher, Louise
American. Actor
Won 1975 Oscar for *One Flew Over the Cuckoo's Nest.*
b. Jul 1934 in Birmingham, Alabama
Source: *BioIn 11, 13; ConTFT 6; FilmEn; HalFC 88; IntMPA 88, 92, 94, 96; InWom SUP; LegTOT; NewYTBS 75, 76; WhoAm 86, 90; WhoAmW 85, 91; WhoEnt 92; WhoHol 92, A; WorAlBi*

Fleury, Andre Hercule de
French. Religious Leader, Statesman
Cardinal; chief advisor to Louis XV, 1726-43.
b. Jun 22, 1653 in Lodeve, France
d. Jan 29, 1743 in Paris, France
Source: *DcCathB; NewCol 75; OxCFr*

Flexner, Abraham
American. Educator, Author
Founded Institute for Advanced Study; wrote biography of *Daniel C Gilman,* 1946.
b. Nov 13, 1866 in Louisville, Kentucky
d. Sep 21, 1959 in Falls Church, Virginia
Source: *AmAu&B; AmDec 1920; AmRef; AmSocL; BiDAmEd; BiDInt; BioIn 3, 4, 5, 6, 8, 9, 14, 15, 19, 20; CurBio 41, 59; DcAmB S6; DcAmMeB 84; EncAB-H 1974, 1996; LinLib L, S; McGEWB; MorMA; NatCAB 52; ObitT 1951; OxCAmH; OxCMed 86; REnAL; TwCA, SUP; WebAB 74, 79; WhAm 3; WhE&EA*

Flick, Elmer Harrison
American. Baseball Player
Outfielder, 1898-1910; had lifetime .315 batting average; Hall of Fame, 1963.
b. Jan 11, 1876 in Bedford, Ohio
d. Jan 9, 1971 in Bedford, Ohio
Source: *BiDAmSp BB; BioIn 6, 7, 9; WhoProB 73*

Flick, Friedrich
German. Industrialist
Owned vast holding co., 1930-72; convicted at Nuremberg trials of using slave labor.
b. Jul 10, 1883 in Ernshorf, Germany

d. Jul 20, 1972 in Lake Constance, Switzerland
Source: *BioIn 4, 6, 8, 9, 14; EncTR, 91; NewYTBE 72; ObitT 1971*

Flinck, Govert
Dutch. Artist
Pupil of Rembrandt, noted for portraits, religious narratives: *Blessing of Jacob.*
b. Jan 25, 1615 in Cleves, Prussia
d. Feb 2, 1660 in Amsterdam, Netherlands
Source: *BioIn 19; ClaDrA; McGDA; NewCol 75; OxCArt; OxDcArt*

Flinders, Matthew
English. Explorer
Known for surveying, charting coasts of Australia, Tasmania.
b. Mar 16, 1774 in Donnington, England
d. Jul 19, 1814 in London, England
Source: *Alli; BioIn 2, 6, 7, 9, 10, 12, 16, 18, 20; CelCen; DcBiPP; DcNaB; Expl 93; HisDBrE; LinLib L, S; McGEWB; NewCBEL; NewCol 75; OxCAusL; OxCShps*

Flint, Austin
American. Physician
Thoracic specialist; popularized binaural stethoscope; wrote classic medical text, 1866.
b. Oct 20, 1812 in Petersham, Massachusetts
d. Mar 13, 1886 in New York, New York
Source: *Alli, SUP; AmBi; ApCAB; BiDAmEd; BiHiMed; BiInAmS; BioIn 1, 2, 9; DcAmAu; DcAmB; DcAmMeB, 84; DcNAA; Drake; InSci; NatCAB 8; OxCMed 86; TwCBDA; WebAB 74, 79; WhAm HS*

Flint, Timothy
American. Clergy, Author
Missionary, described frontier life; his Daniel Boone biography, 1833, helped develop Boone legend.
b. Jul 11, 1780 in North Reading, Massachusetts
d. Aug 16, 1840 in North Reading, Massachusetts
Source: *Alli; AmAu; AmAu&B; AmBi; ApCAB; BbD; BenetAL 91; BibAL; BiD&SB; BiDSA; BioIn 1, 2, 3, 7, 8, 9; CnDAL; CyAL 1; DcAmAu; DcAmB; DcBiPP; DcEnL; DcLB 73; DcLEL; DcNAA; Drake; EncAAH; EncFWF; HarEnUS; NatCAB 6; OhA&B; OxCAmH; OxCAmL 65, 83, 95; REnAL; REnAW; TwCBDA; WebAB 74, 79; WhAm HS*

Flint, William Russell, Sir
Scottish. Artist
Illustrated *Morte d'Arthur;* won silver medal.
b. Apr 4, 1880 in Edinburgh, Scotland
d. Dec 27, 1969 in London, England
Source: *BioIn 2, 9, 14; ClaDrA; DcArts; DcBrAr 1; DcBrBI; DcBrWA; DcNaB 1961; GrBr; ObitOF 79; ObitT 1961; OxDcArt; TwCPaSc; WhE&EA*

Flippen, Jay C
American. Actor
Character actor in films, 1934-71; in TV series "Ensign O'Toole," 1962-64.
b. Mar 6, 1898 in Little Rock, Arkansas
d. Feb 3, 1971 in Hollywood, California
Source: *CmMov; FilmgC; MotPP; MovMk; NewYTBE 71; Vers B; WhoHol B; WhScrn 74, 77*

Flipper, Henry Ossian
American. Soldier, Writer, Engineer
First black graduate of West Point, 1877; first black officer in U.S. Army; wrote *The Colored Cadet at West Point,* 1878.
b. Mar 21, 1856 in Thomasville, Georgia
d. May 3, 1940
Source: *Alli SUP; BioIn 8, 9, 11, 13; BlksScM; ConBlB 3; DcAmMiB; EncAACR; HarEnMi; InB&W 80*

Flock of Seagulls
[Frank Maudsley; Paul Reynolds; Ali Score; Mike Score]
British. Music Group
Hit single, "I Ran," 1982; only British band to win Grammy, 1983.
Source: *HarEnR 86; PenEncP; RkOn 85*

Flood, Curt(is Charles)
American. Baseball Player
Outfielder, 1956-71; fought baseball's reserve clause, 1970; Supreme Court upheld baseball rule.
b. Jan 18, 1938 in Houston, Texas
d. Jan 20, 1997 in Los Angeles, California
Source: *AfrAmSG; AfroAA; Ballpl 90; BiDAmSp BB, FB; BioIn 8, 9, 11, 12, 15, 20, 21; ConAu 115; ConBlB 10; HeroCon; InB&W 80, 85; LegTOT; NewYTBE 70; NewYTBS 81; WhoProB 73*

Flood, Daniel J(ohn)
American. Politician
Dem. congressman from PA, 1944-46, 1948-52, 1954-80.
b. Nov 26, 1904 in Hazelton, Pennsylvania
d. May 28, 1994 in Wilkes-Barre, Pennsylvania
Source: *AmAu&B; BiDrUSC 89; BioIn 11, 12; CngDr 79; CurBio 78, 94N; NewYTBS 78, 80; WhoAm 74, 76; WhoAmP 85; WhoE 74, 75, 77, 79*

Flora, James Royer
American. Author, Illustrator
Self-illustrated children's books include *Grandpa's Ghost Stories,* 1978; *Wanda and the Bumbly Wizard,* 1980.
b. Jan 25, 1914 in Bellefontaine, Ohio
Source: *AuBYP 2, 3; BioIn 14; ConAu 3NR, 5R; ConGrA 3; IlsBYP; IlsCB 1946, 1957; IntAu&W 91; SmATA 1, 6AS, 30; ThrBJA; TwCChW 83, 89; WhoAmA 84, 91; WhoE 89; WrDr 86, 92*

Floren, Myron
American. Musician
Accordion player on "The Lawrence Welk Show."
b. Nov 5, 1919 in Webster, South Dakota
Source: *ASCAP 66, 80; BioIn 12; ConAu 129*

Florence, William Jermyn
[Bernard Conlin]
American. Actor, Songwriter, Dramatist
Wrote, starred in popular comedies, such as *The Irish Boy and the Yankee Girl.*
b. Jul 26, 1831 in Albany, New York
d. Nov 19, 1891 in Philadelphia, Pennsylvania
Source: *AmBi; ApCAB; BioIn 5; CamGWoT; DcAmB; DcNAA; FamA&A; NatCAB 2; NotNAT B; OxCThe 67, 83; PlP&P; PoIre; TwCBDA; WhAm HS*

Flores, Lola
Spanish. Singer
Noted for flamenco singing.
d. May 15, 1995 in Madrid, Spain

Flores, Tom
[Thomas Raymond Flores]
American. Football Coach
Coach, Oakland/LA Raiders, 1979-87; won Super Bowl, 1981, 1984.
b. Mar 21, 1937 in Fresno, California
Source: *BiDAmSp FB; BioIn 13, 16, 19, 20; FootReg 87; HispAmA; MexAmB; NewYTBS 84; WhoAm 86, 90; WhoFtbl 74; WhoHisp 91, 92, 94; WhoSpor; WhoWest 82, 92*

Florey, Howard Walter
English. Scientist, Engineer, Physician
Shared 1945 Nobel Prize for discovering penicillin.
b. Sep 24, 1898 in Adelaide, Australia
d. Feb 21, 1968 in London, England
Source: *AsBiEn; BiESc; BioIn 1, 2, 3, 4, 5, 6, 7, 8, 9, 10; CamDcSc; CurBio 44, 68; DcNaB 1961; DcScB; GrBr; InSci; LarDcSc; McGEWB; NotTwCS; OxCMed 86; WhAm 4A, 5; WhoNob, 90, 95; WorAl; WorScD*

Florio, James Joseph
American. Politician
Dem. governor, NJ, 1990-94; served eight terms as congressman, 1975-94; known for advocacy of consumer and environmental protection laws.
b. Aug 29, 1937 in New York, New York
Source: *AlmAP 88; BiDrUSC 89; BioIn 12, 16; CngDr 83, 89; CurBio 90; News 91-2; NewYTBS 81; PolsAm 84; WhoAm 90; WhoAmP 73, 75, 77, 79, 81, 83, 85, 87, 89, 91, 93, 95; WhoE 91; WhoGov 77*

Florio, John
[Giovanni Florio]
English. Translator, Lexicographer
Compiled Italian-English dictionary, *A World of Words,* 1598; translated Montaigne's essays, 1613.
b. 1553? in London, England
d. 1625 in London, England
Source: *Alli; BiD&SB; BioIn 2, 3, 8, 11; BlmGEL; BritAu; CamGEL; CamGLE; CasWL; Chambr 1; ChhPo S1; CroE&S; CyEd; DcArts; DcEnL; DcEuL; DcLB 172; DcLEL; DcNaB; EvLB; LinLib L; LngCEL; NewC; NewCBEL; OxCEng 67, 85, 95; PenC ENG; REn*

Flory, Paul John
American. Educator, Chemist
Researcher in macronuclear chemistry; won 1974 Nobel Prize.
b. Jun 19, 1910 in Sterling, Illinois
d. Sep 9, 1985 in Big Sur, California
Source: *AmMWSc 76P, 79, 82; BiESc; BioIn 1, 4, 6, 8, 10, 11; ConAu 117; CurBio 75, 85; IntWW 74, 75, 76, 77, 78, 79, 80, 81, 82, 83; LarDcSc; McGMS 80; RAdv 14; WhAm 10; Who 82, 83, 85; WhoAm 74, 76, 78, 80, 82, 84; WhoFrS 84; WhoNob, 90, 95; WhoWest 78, 80, 82, 84; WhoWor 78, 80, 82, 84*

Flotow, Friedrich von, Baron
German. Composer
Wrote romantic operas *Alessandro Stradella,* 1844; *Martha,* 1847.
b. Apr 26, 1812 in Teutendorf, Germany
d. Jan 24, 1883 in Darmstadt, Germany
Source: *AtlBL; Baker 78, 84; BioIn 4, 7, 12; BriBkM 80; CmOp; CmpBCM; DcCom 77; GrComp; MetOEnc; MusMk; OxCMus; OxDcOp; PenDiMP A*

Flowers, Gennifer
[Mrs. Finis Shelnutt]
American. Singer
Cabaret performer whose alleged 12-year affair with AR govenor Bill Clinton threatened to upset his 1992 presidential bid.
b. 1950?

Flowers, Tiger
[Theo Flowers]
"The Georgia Deacon"
American. Boxer
First black to win world middleweight title, 1926.
b. Aug 5, 1895 in Camille, Georgia
d. Nov 16, 1927 in New York, New York
Source: *BioIn 1, 21; BoxReg; WhoBox 74; WhoSpor; WhScrn 83*

Flowers, Wayland Parrott, Jr.
American. Ventriloquist
Known for cabaret shows, TV series with puppet named "Madame."
b. Nov 1939 in Dawson, Georgia
d. Oct 10, 1988 in Hollywood, California
Source: *BioIn 13; ConTFT 5*

Floyd, Carlisle Sessions
American. Composer
His opera *Wuthering Heights* had NY premiere, 1959; also wrote *Of Mice and Men,* 1970.
b. Jun 11, 1926 in Latta, South Carolina
Source: *AmComp; ASCAP 66; Baker 84; BioIn 16; ConAmC 82; CurBio 60; EncWB; IntWWM 90; MetOEnc; NewAmDM; NewGrDA 86; PenDiMP; WhoAm 86, 88; WhoAmM 83; WhoEnt 92*

Floyd, John Buchanan
American. Government Official, Military Leader
US secretary of war, 1857-60; Confederate general, removed from command by Jefferson Davis.
b. Jun 1, 1807 in Blacksburg, Virginia
d. Aug 26, 1863 in Abingdon, Virginia
Source: *AmBi; ApCAB; DcAmB; HarEnUS; NatCAB 5; NewCol 75; TwCBDA; WebAMB*

Floyd, Pretty Boy
[Charles Arthur Floyd]
American. Criminal
"Public enemy No. 1," 1933; killed in gun battle with FBI's Melvin Purvis.
b. Feb 3, 1901 in Akins, Oklahoma
d. Oct 22, 1934 in East Liverpool, Ohio
Source: *BioIn 8, 9; DrInf; EncACr*

Floyd, Raymond Loran
American. Golfer
Turned pro, 1961; won PGA, 1969, 1982, Masters, 1976, US Open, 1986.
b. Sep 14, 1942 in Fort Bragg, North Carolina
Source: *BiDAmSp OS; BioIn 13, 15; NewYTBS 76, 86; WhoAm 84, 86, 90; WhoGolf; WhoIntG*

Floyd, William
American. Statesman, Continental Congressman
Landowner; member first and second Continental Congress; signed Declaration of Independence, 1776.
b. Dec 17, 1734 in Brookhaven, New York
d. Aug 4, 1821 in Westernville, New York
Source: *AmBi; ApCAB; BiAUS; BiDrAC; BiDrUSC 89; BioIn 3, 7, 8, 9; DcAmB; DcNAA; Drake; EncAR; EncCRAm; HarEnUS; NatCAB 4; TwCBDA; WhAm HS; WhAmP; WhAmRev; WhNAA*

Flutie, Doug(las Richard)
American. Football Player
Quarterback; won Heisman Trophy, 1984; played in USFL, 1985, NFL, 1986-89.
b. Oct 23, 1962 in Manchester, Maryland
Source: *BiDAmSp FB; BioIn 13, 14, 15, 16; CurBio 85; FootReg 87; NewYTBS 84*

Flying Burrito Brothers, The
[Chris Ethridge; Chris Hillman; "Sneaky Pete" Kleinow; Gram Parsons]
American. Music Group
Band formed 1969 to introduce country music to rock enthusiasts; hit album *Gilded Place of Sin,* 1969.
Source: *BgBkCoM; BiDAmM; ConMuA 80A; EncFCWM 83; EncPR&S 89; EncRk 88; EncRkSt; HarEnCM 87; HarEnR 86; IlEncCM; IlEncRk; NewGrDA 86; RolSEnR 83; WhoNeCM A; WhoRock 81; WhoRocM 82*

Flynn, Edward Joseph
American. Politician
NY City Democratic "boss," 1922-53.
b. Sep 22, 1891 in New York, New York
d. Aug 18, 1953 in Dublin, Ireland
Source: *BioIn 3; CurBio 40, 53; DcAmB S5; WhAm 3*

Flynn, Elizabeth Gurley
American. Political Leader
Professional revolutionary, 1906-64; first woman nat. chm., US Communist Party, 1961.
b. Aug 7, 1890 in Concord, New Hampshire
d. Sep 5, 1964 in Moscow, Union of Soviet Socialist Republics
Source: *AmRef; AmSocL; AmWomWr; ArtclWW 2; BiDAmL; BiDAmLf; BiDAmLL; BiDMarx; BioIn 1, 4, 6, 7, 8, 9, 10, 12, 15, 16, 19, 20, 21; ConAu 111; ContDcW 89; CurBio 61, 64; DcAmB S7; DcAmImH; EncAL; EncRev; EncWB; EncWHA; FemiCLE; GoodHs; GrLiveH; HanAmWH; IntDcWB; InWom; LibW; NotAW MOD; PeoHis; RadHan; RComAH; WomFir; WorAl; WorAlBi*

Flynn, Errol
American. Actor
Swashbuckling star of 1930s-40s adventure films: *Captain Blood,* 1936; *Robin Hood,* 1938; wrote autobiography, *My Wicked, Wicked Ways.*
b. Jun 20, 1909 in Tasmania, Australia
d. Oct 14, 1959 in Vancouver, British Columbia, Canada
Source: *AmAu&B; BiDFilm, 81, 94; BioIn 1, 5, 6, 7, 8, 9, 10, 11, 12, 13, 14, 16, 17, 18, 20, 21; CmMov; DcArts; EncAFC; FacFETw; FilmEn; FilmgC; ForYSC; HalFC 80, 84, 88; IntDcF 1-3, 2-3; ItaFilm; LegTOT; MotPP; MovMk; NotNAT B; ObitT 1951; OxCAusL; OxCFilm; WhAm 3; WhoHol B; WhScrn 74, 77, 83; WorAl; WorAlBi; WorEFlm*

Flynn, Joe
[Joseph Anthony Flynn]
American. Actor
Played Captain Binghamton in TV series "McHale's Navy," 1962-66.
b. Nov 8, 1925 in Youngstown, Ohio
d. Jul 19, 1974 in Los Angeles, California
Source: *HalFC 80, 84, 88; NewYTBS 74; WhoHol B; WhScrn 77*

Flynn, Raymond (Leo)
American. Politician
Mayor, Boston, 1983-93; US ambassador to the Vatican, 1993—.
b. Jul 22, 1939 in Boston, Massachusetts
Source: *BioIn 13; CurBio 93; LegTOT; NewYTBS 83; WhoAm 86, 88, 90, 92, 94, 95, 96, 97; WhoAmP 91; WhoE 89, 91, 93, 95, 97; WhoWor 95*

Flynn, Sean
American. Photographer, Actor
Son of Errol Flynn; disappeared in Vietnam covering war, 1970.
b. 1941
d. 1970?
Source: *BioIn 6, 8, 9, 10; ForYSC; HalFC 80, 84, 88; ItaFilm; MotPP*

Flynt, Althea Sue
[Mrs. Larry Flynt; Althea Leasure]
American. Publisher
Co-publisher, *Hustler* magazine, 1974-87; editorial director, *Chic* magazine, 1976-87.
b. Nov 6, 1953 in Marietta, Ohio
d. Jun 27, 1987 in Los Angeles, California
Source: *BioIn 11; WhoAm 82, 84, 86, 88; WhoAmW 81, 83*

Flynt, Larry (Claxton)
American. Publisher
Publishes *Hustler* magazine, 1974—; paralyzed in assassination attempt; film based on life, *The People vs. Larry Flynt,* 1996.
b. Nov 1, 1942 in Magoffin County, Kentucky
Source: *AuNews 2; BioIn 10, 13, 14, 15; EncTwCJ; WhoAm 80, 82, 84, 86, 88, 90, 94; WhoWest 82, 84, 87*

Fo, Dario
Italian. Dramatist, Actor
Noted for current-event themes in plays: *We Won't Pay! We Won't Pay!,* 1980.
b. Mar 24, 1926 in Sangiano, Italy
Source: *BioIn 8, 11, 13, 14, 15; CamGWoT; ConAu 116, 128; ConFLW 84; ConLC 32; ConTFT 7; ConWorW 93; CroCD; CurBio 86; CyWA 89; DcArts; DcItL 1, 2; EncWL 2, 3; EncWT; Ent; FacFETw; IntDcT 2; IntWW 91; ItaFilm; MajTwCW; McGEWD 84; NewYTBS 86; OxCEng 85, 95; OxCThe 83; RAdv 14, 13-2; TheaDir; Who 92, 94; WhoWor 95; WorAu 1980*

Foat, Ginny
[Virginia Galluzzo]
American. Feminist
Pres., CA NOW, arrested on 18-yr-old murder charge, 1983; acquitted.
b. Jun 21, 1941 in New York, New York
Source: *BioIn 13, 14*

Foch, Ferdinand
French. Military Leader
Supreme commander of Allied forces, 1918; directed final victorious offensive, WW I.
b. Oct 2, 1851 in Tarbes, France
d. Mar 20, 1929 in Paris, France
Source: *BiDFrPL; BioIn 1, 2, 5, 6, 9, 10, 11, 12, 13, 17, 20; DcCathB; DcTwCCu 2; DcTwHis; FacFETw; HarEnMi; HisWorL; LinLib S; McGEWB; OxCFr; REn; WhDW; WhoMilH 76; WorAl; WorAlBi*

Foch, Nina
[Nina Consuelo Maud Fock]
American. Actor
Oscar nominee for *Executive Suite,* 1954; founder, teacher, Nina Foch Studio, 1973—.
b. Apr 20, 1924 in Leiden, Netherlands
Source: *BiE&WWA; BioIn 1, 10, 18; ConTFT 4; FilmEn; FilmgC; ForYSC; GangFlm; HalFC 80, 84, 88; HolP 40; IntMPA 75, 76, 77, 78, 79, 80, 81, 82, 84, 86, 88, 92, 94, 96; InWom, SUP; LegTOT; MotPP; MovMk; NotNAT; WhoAm 74, 76, 78, 80, 82, 84, 86, 88, 90, 92, 94, 95, 96, 97; WhoAmW 66, 68, 70, 72, 74, 79, 81, 83, 85, 87, 89, 91, 93, 95, 97; WhoEnt 92; WhoHol 92, A; WhoHrs 80; WhoThe 72, 77, 81; WhoWest 80, 82, 84, 87, 89, 92, 94, 96; WhoWor 74, 76, 78; WorAl; WorAlBi*

Focke, Heinrich Karl Johann
"Father of the Helicopter"
German. Inventor
Aviation pioneer, developed helicopter, 1938.
b. 1890
d. Feb 25, 1979 in Bremen, Germany (West)
Source: *BioIn 11; NewYTBS 79; WebBD 83*

Fodor, Eugene
American. Editor, Publisher
Began publishing *Fodor's Travel Guides,* 1949.
b. Oct 5, 1905 in Leva, Austria-Hungary
d. Feb 18, 1991 in Litchfield, Connecticut
Source: *AmAu&B; AnObit 1991; BioIn 17, 18; BioNews 74; ConAu 14NR, 21R, 133; IntAu&W 76; LegTOT; News 91-3; NewYTBS 74, 91; WhAm 10; WhoAm 74, 76, 78, 80, 82, 84, 86, 88, 90; WhoSoCE 89; WhoWor 74*

Fodor, Eugene Nicholas
American. Violinist
Popular concert soloist; shared top honors at Moscow's Tchaikovsky competition, 1974.
b. Mar 5, 1950 in Denver, Colorado
Source: *Baker 78, 84; BioIn 14, 16; CurBio 76; IntWWM 90; NewGrDA 86; WhoAm 76, 78, 80, 82, 84, 86, 88, 92, 94, 95, 96, 97; WhoEnt 92*

Foerster, Friedrich Wilhelm
German. Author, Educator
Books written by him were among first burned by the Nazis, 1930s; wrote *Europe and the German Question,* 1940.
b. Jun 2, 1869 in Berlin, Germany
d. Jan 9, 1966 in Kilchberg, Germany (West)
Source: *BiDMoPL; BioIn 1, 6, 7; CurBio 62, 66; ObitOF 79*

Foerster, Josef Bohuslav
Czech. Composer
Wrote five symphonies, six operas including *Nepremozeni,* 1918.
b. Dec 30, 1859 in Prague, Bohemia
d. May 29, 1951 in Novy Vestec, Czechoslovakia
Source: *Baker 78, 84, 92; BioIn 2; MusMk; NewGrDM 80; NewGrDO; NewOxM; OxCMus; OxDcOp*

Foerster, Norman
American. Author, Educator
Critical writings include *Nature of American Literature,* 1923; *American Criticism,* 1928.
b. Apr 14, 1887 in Pittsburgh, Pennsylvania
Source: *AmAu&B; BenetAL 91; BioIn 3, 4, 9, 12; ChhPo; CnDAL; ConAmA; ConAu 5R; DcLEL; OxCAmL 65, 83; PenC AM; PeoHis; REnAL; TwCA, SUP; WhAm 8; WhLit; WhNAA*

Fogarty, Anne
American. Fashion Designer
Ballerina skirts, tiny waists, petticoats were the "look" she launched in 1950s; won Fashion Critics Award, 1951.
b. Feb 2, 1919 in Pittsburgh, Pennsylvania
d. Jan 15, 1980 in New York, New York
Source: *BioIn 4, 5, 12; ConFash; CurBio 58, 80N; EncFash; InWom, SUP; NewYTBS 80; WhAm 7; WhoAm 74, 76, 78; WhoAmW 58, 61, 64, 66, 68, 70, 72, 74; WhoFash 88; WorFshn*

Fogazzaro, Antonio
Italian. Author, Poet
Popular novels include *The Saint,* 1905; *Leila,* 1910.
b. Mar 25, 1842 in Vicenza, Italy
d. Mar 7, 1911 in Vicenza, Italy
Source: *BbD; Benet 87, 96; BiD&SB; BioIn 1, 5, 9; CasWL; ClDMEL 47, 80; CyWA 58; DcBiA; DcCathB; DcItL 1, 2; EuAu; EvEuW; LinLib L; LngCTC; LuthC 75; McGEWD 72, 84; ModRL; Novels; OxCEng 67, 85, 95; PenC EUR; REn; TwCA, SUP; WhDW*

Fogelberg, Dan(iel Grayling)
American. Composer, Singer
First hit song "Part of the Plan," 1975; recent hit "Leader of the Band," 1982.
b. Aug 13, 1951 in Peoria, Illinois
Source: *ASCAP 80; BioIn 13, 14; ConMus 4; EncFCWM 83; EncRk 88;*

EncRkSt; HarEnCM 87; HarEnR 86; IlEncRk; LegTOT; PenEncP; RkOn 74, 78; RolSEnR 83; WhoAm 76, 80, 82, 84, 86, 88, 90, 92, 94, 95, 96, 97; WhoEnt 92; WhoRock 81; WhoRocM 82

Fogerty, John
American. Singer
Singer, songwriter and guitarist for Creedence Clearwater Revival until group disbanded, 1972; solo hits include "Centerfield," 1973; "The Old Man Down the Road," 1973.
b. May 28, 1945 in Berkeley, California
d. Sep 6, 1990
Source: *BioIn 13, 14, 15; ConMus 2; EncPR&S 89; LegTOT; NewGrDA 86; OnThGG; RkOn 85A; WhoRock 81; WhoRocM 82; WorAlBi*

Foghat
[Roger Earl; David Peverett; Rod Price; Anthony Stevens]
British. Music Group
Formed, 1971; hit single "Slow Ride," 1976.
Source: *BioIn 20; ConMuA 80A; EncPR&S 89; IlEncRk; RkOn 74, 78; RolSEnR 83; WhoRock 81; WhoRocM 82*

Fokine, Michel
American. Dancer
Creator of modern ballet; choreographer of Diaghilev's Ballets Russes in Paris, 1909-14.
b. Apr 26, 1880 in Saint Petersburg, Russia
d. Aug 22, 1942 in Yonkers, New York
Source: *BiDSovU; BioIn 1, 3, 4, 5, 6, 7, 8, 10, 12, 13, 18; BioNews 74; CurBio 42; DancEn 78; DcAmB S3; DcTwCCu 2; LegTOT; LinLib S; NewOxM; NotNAT B; SovUn; WhAm 2; WhDW; WhThe; WorAl; WorAlBi*

Fokker, Anthony Herman Gerard
Dutch. Aircraft Designer
Designed many fighter planes used during WW I; later designed commercial aircraft in US.
b. Apr 6, 1890 in Kediri, Dutch East Indies
d. Dec 23, 1939 in Alpine, New Jersey
Source: *AmBi; BioIn 4, 6, 8, 9, 11, 12; InSci; WhAm 1; WhDW*

Foley, Martha
American. Journalist, Editor
Edited annual *Best American Short Stories,* 1958-76.
b. 1897 in Boston, Massachusetts
d. Sep 5, 1977 in Northampton, Massachusetts
Source: *ArtclWW 2; BenetAL 91; BioIn 11, 20; ConAu 73, 117; CurBio 77N; InWom SUP*

Foley, Red
[Clyde Julian Foley]
American. Singer
Founding father of country music; starred in "Ozark Mountain Jubilee," 1955-61; Hall of Fame, 1967.
b. Jun 17, 1910 in Bluelick, Kentucky
d. Sep 19, 1968 in Fort Wayne, Indiana
Source: *Baker 84; BgBkCoM; BiDAmM; BioIn 4, 8, 14; CmpEPM; CounME 74, 74A; EncFCWM 69, 83; HarEnCM 87; IlEncCM; LegTOT; NewAmDM; NewGrDA 86; OxCPMus; PenEncP; RadStar; SaTiSS; WhoHol B; WhScrn 74, 77, 83; WorAl; WorAlBi*

Foley, Thomas Stephen
American. Politician
Dem. congressman from WA, 1964-95; House majority leader, 1987-89; Speaker of the House, 1989-95.
b. Mar 6, 1929 in Spokane, Washington
Source: *AlmAP 88, 92; AmCath 80; AmPolLe; BiDrAC; BiDrUSC 89; BioIn 10, 13, 15, 16; CngDr 74, 77, 79, 81, 83, 85, 87, 89; CurBio 89; EncAAH; IntWW 89, 91, 93; News 90-1; NewYTBS 82, 86, 89, 90; PolsAm 84; Who 92, 94; WhoAm 74, 76, 78, 80, 82, 84, 86, 88, 90, 92, 94, 95, 96, 97; WhoAmP 73, 75, 77, 79, 81, 83, 85, 87, 89, 91, 93, 95; WhoE 95; WhoGov 72, 75, 77; WhoWest 74, 76, 78, 80, 82, 84, 87, 89, 92, 94, 96; WhoWor 93, 95; WorAlBi*

Folger, Henry Clay
American. Industrialist, Philanthropist
Developed first Shakespeare collection in world—Folger Shakespeare Library, Washington, DC; headed Standard Oil, 1911-28.
b. Jun 18, 1857 in New York, New York
d. Jun 11, 1930 in New York, New York
Source: *AmBi; BenetAL 91; BioIn 1, 6, 13, 15, 20; DcAmB; DcAmBC; DcLB 140; DcNAA; LinLib L, S; NatCAB 23; NewCol 75; NotNAT B; OxCThe 67, 83; REnAL; WhAm 1; WorAl; WorAlBi*

Folger, James A
American. Manufacturer
Started first coffee business at age 15, 1850.
b. 1835
d. 1889
Source: *Entr*

Follett, Ken(neth Martin)
[Myles Symon]
Welsh. Author
Spy thrillers include *Eye of the Needle,* 1978; *The Key to Rebecca,* 1980; non-fiction, *On Wings of Eagles,* 1983.
b. Jun 5, 1949 in Cardiff, Wales
Source: *Au&Arts 6; BestSel 89-4; BioIn 11, 13, 14, 16, 17, 20, 21; ConAu 13NR, 33NR, 54NR, 81; ConLC 18; ConPopW; CrtSuMy; CurBio 90; DcLB 87, Y81B; EncSF 93; IntAu&W 89, 91, 93; IntWW 91, 93; LegTOT; MajTwCW; Novels; ScF&FL 92; SpyFic; TwCCr&M 85, 91; WhoAm 80, 82, 84, 86, 88, 90, 92, 94, 95, 96, 97; WhoSpyF; WhoUSWr 88; WhoWor 80, 82, 84, 87, 91, 93, 95, 96, 97; WhoWrEP 89, 92, 95; WorAlBi; WorAu 1980; WrDr 86, 88, 90, 92, 94, 96*

Folon, Jean-Michel
Belgian. Artist, Illustrator
Designer of magazine covers, bold posters; did book of watercolors *The Eyewitness,* 1980.
b. Mar 1, 1934 in Uccle, Belgium
Source: *BioIn 8, 11, 13, 16; ConDes 84, 90, 97; ConGrA 3; CurBio 81; DcCAr 81; PrintW 83, 85; WorECar*

Folsom, Frank M
American. Businessman, Philanthropist
Pres., RCA, 1949-57; noted for innovative merchandising, advertising concepts for TV.
b. May 14, 1894 in Sprague, Washington
d. Jan 22, 1970 in Scarsdale, New York
Source: *CurBio 70; LesBEnT; NatCAB 55; NewYTBE 70; ObitOF 79; WorAl*

Folsom, James E(lisha)
"Kissin' Jim"
American. Politician
Dem. governor of AL, 1947-51, 1955-59; helped pass law to stifle Ku Klux Klan, 1949.
b. Oct 9, 1908 in Elba, Alabama
d. Nov 21, 1987 in Cullman, Alabama
Source: *BiDrGov 1789; BioIn 1, 2, 4, 6, 11, 15, 16; CurBio 49, 88, 88N; EncSoH; FacFETw; NewYTBE 70; NewYTBS 87; PolProf E*

Folsom, Marion Bayard
American. Government Official
Chief drafter of Social Security Act, 1935; HEW secretary, 1953-61.
b. Nov 23, 1894 in McRue, Georgia
d. Sep 28, 1976 in Rochester, New York
Source: *BiDAmBL 83; BiDrUSE 71; BlueB 76; CurBio 50; IntWW 74; ObitOF 79; WhAm 7; WhoAm 74*

Fonck, Rene
French. Aviator
Credited with shooting down 75 enemy planes during WW I.
b. 1894
d. Jun 18, 1953 in Paris, France
Source: *BioIn 3, 8, 11, 12; InSci; WhoMW 76*

Fonda, Bridget
American. Actor
Co-starred in movies *Singles, Single White Female;* Jane Fonda's niece.
b. Jan 27, 1964 in Los Angeles, California
Source: *ConTFT 8; CurBio 94; IntMPA 92, 94, 96; LegTOT; News 95, 95-1; WhoAm 96, 97; WhoAmW 95, 97*

Fonda, Henry Jaynes
American. Actor
Top film star since 1930s; often cast as upstanding common man; films

include *Grapes of Wrath,* 1940; *On Golden Pond* (Oscar), 1981.
b. May 16, 1905 in Grand Island, Nebraska
d. Aug 12, 1982 in Los Angeles, California
Source: *AmCulL; BiDFilm; BiE&WWA; BkPepl; CmMov; CurBio 82; FilmgC; IntMPA 82; IntWW 78; MotPP; MovMk; NewYTBS 82; OxCFilm; PlP&P; WebAB 74; WhoAm 82; WorEFlm*

Fonda, Jane
[Ted Turner, Mrs.]
American. Actor, Political Activist
Won Oscars for *Klute,* 1971, *Coming Home,* 1978; wrote *Jane Fonda's Workout Book,* 1982; has starred in many fitness videocassettes; daughter of Henry.
b. Dec 21, 1937 in New York, New York
Source: *AmDec 1970; BiDFilm, 81, 94; BiE&WWA; BioAmW; BioIn 5, 6, 7, 8, 9, 10, 11, 12, 13, 14, 15, 16, 17, 18, 20, 21; BkPepl; BlueB 76; CelR, 90; ContDcW 89; ConTFT 1, 7, 14; CurBio 64, 86; DcArts; DcTwCCu 1; EncAFC; EncWB; FacFETw; FilmEn; FilmgC; ForYSC; GoodHs; GrLiveH; HalFC 80, 84, 88; HanAmWH; HeroCon; HerW 84; IntDcF 1-3, 2-3; IntDcWB; IntMPA 77, 78, 79, 80, 81, 82, 84, 86, 88, 92, 94, 96; IntWW 74, 75, 76, 77, 78, 79, 80, 81, 82, 83, 89, 91, 93; InWom, SUP; ItaFilm; LegTOT; LNinSix; MotPP; MovMk; MugS; NewYTBS 74, 80; NotNAT, A; OxCAmT 84; OxCFilm; PolProf NF; WhoAm 74, 76, 78, 80, 82, 84, 86, 88, 90, 92, 94, 95, 96, 97; WhoAmW 79, 81, 83, 85, 87, 89, 91, 93, 95, 97; WhoEnt 92; WhoHol 92, A; WhoHrs 80; WhoThe 72, 77, 81; WhoUSWr 88; WhoWor 78; WhoWrEP 89, 92; WomFir; WomWMM; WorAl; WorAlBi; WorEFlm; WrDr 86, 88, 90, 92, 94, 96*

Fonda, Peter
American. Actor
Wrote, co-produced, and starred in *Easy Rider,* 1969; son of actor Henry, brother of actress Jane.
b. Feb 23, 1940 in New York, New York
Source: *BiDFilm, 81; BioIn 6, 7, 8, 9, 10, 11, 13, 14; BkPepl; CelR 90; ConTFT 2; FilmgC; HalFC 88; IntDcF 1-3; IntMPA 92; MotPP; MovMk; OxCFilm; WhoAm 78, 80, 82, 84, 86, 88, 92; WhoEnt 92; WhoHol A; WorAlBi*

Fong, Hiram Leong
American. Lawyer, Politician
Rep. senator, 1959-77.
b. Oct 1, 1907 in Honolulu, Hawaii
Source: *BiDrAC; WhoWest 74, 92; WhoWor 78*

Fonseca, Harry
American. Artist
Known for his brightly painted "Coyote" series.
b. 1946
Source: *BioIn 21; EncNAB; NotNaAm*

Fonseca, Manuel Deodoro da
Brazilian. Political Leader
First president of Brazil, 1891.
b. Aug 5, 1827 in Alagoas, Brazil
d. Aug 23, 1892 in Rio de Janeiro, Brazil
Source: *BioIn 7, 16; DicTyr; EncLatA; NewCol 75; WebBD 83*

Fontaine, Frank
"Crazy Guggenheim"
American. Comedian, Singer
Best known for appearances on "The Jackie Gleason Show," 1960s.
b. Apr 19, 1920 in Haverhill, Massachusetts
d. Aug 4, 1978 in Spokane, Washington
Source: *BioIn 6, 11; IntMPA 75, 76, 77; LegTOT; WhoHol A; WhScrn 83; WorAl; WorAlBi*

Fontaine, Joan
[Joan de Beauvoir de Havilland]
American. Actor
Won 1941 Oscar for *Suspicion;* sister of Olivia de Havilland.
b. Oct 22, 1917 in Tokyo, Japan
Source: *BiDFilm, 81, 94; BiE&WWA; BioAmW; BioIn 3, 6, 7, 9, 10, 11, 14, 18, 19; CelR, 90; CmMov; ConAu 81; CurBio 44; EncO&P 2; FilmEn; FilmgC; ForWC 70; ForYSC; HalFC 80, 84, 88; IntDcF 1-3, 2-3; IntMPA 75, 76, 77, 78, 79, 80, 81, 82, 84, 86, 88, 92, 94, 96; InWom, SUP; LegTOT; MotPP; MovMk; OxCFilm; ThFT; WhoAm 74, 76, 78, 80, 82, 84; WhoAmW 58, 68, 70, 72, 74, 75, 83; WhoE 74; WhoHol 92, A; WhoHrs 80; WomWMM; WorAl; WorAlBi; WorEFlm*

Fontaine, Marcel
French. Diplomat, Hostage
Diplomat in Lebanon; seized by Islamic Jihad, Mar 22, 1985 and held captive 1,139 days; released May 4, 1988.
d. Jan 20, 1997 in Paris, France

Fontaine, Philip
Canadian. Native American Leader
Grand Chief of the Assembly of Manitoba Chiefs, 1989—.
b. Sep 10, 1944 in Fort Alexander Indian Rese Manitoba, Canada
Source: *BioIn 21; NotNaAm*

Fontana, Domenico
Italian. Architect
Designed portions of the Vatican, helping complete dome of St. Peter's, 1588-90; planned reconstruction of many areas of Rome.
b. 1543 in Melide, Italy
d. 1607 in Naples, Italy
Source: *BioIn 14; DcArts; DcBiPP; DcCathB; DcD&D; LinLib S; MacEA; McGDA; NewCol 75; OxCArt*

Fontana, Tom
American. Writer, Producer
Won Emmy for writing "St. Elsewhere," 1984.
b. Sep 12, 1951 in Buffalo, New York
Source: *ConAu 113, 130; ConTFT 2; IntAu&W 86; St&PR 91; WhoEnt 92; WrDr 96*

Fontane, Theodor
German. Author
Wrote historical novel, *Vor Dem Strum,* 1878; first master of realistic fiction in Germany.
b. Dec 30, 1819 in Neu-Ruppin, Germany
d. Sep 20, 1898 in Berlin, Germany
Source: *Benet 87, 96; BiD&SB; BioIn 1, 3, 5, 7, 11, 12, 13, 16, 18, 19; CasWL; ChhPo S2; ClDMEL 47, 80; CyWA 58; DcArts; DcLB 129; EncWT; EuAu; EuWr 6; EvEuW; GrFLW; LinLib L; McGEWB; NewCBEL; NinCLC 26; Novels; OxCEng 85, 95; OxCGer 76, 86; PenC CL, EUR; RAdv 14, 13-2; REn; RfGWoL 95; WhDW; WorAlBi*

Fontanne, Lynn
[Mrs. Alfred Lunt]
American. Actor
With husband, formed one of great stage duos: *O Mistress Mine,* 1946; *The Visit,* 1960.
b. Dec 6, 1887 in London, England
d. Jul 30, 1983 in Genesee, Wisconsin
Source: *AmCulL; AnObit 1983; BiE&WWA; BioIn 1, 2, 3, 5, 6, 7, 10, 11, 13, 14, 15, 16, 19, 21; BlueB 76; CelR; CnThe; CurBio 41, 83; DcArts; EncWT; Ent; FamA&A; Film 2; FilmEn; FilmgC; HalFC 80, 84, 88; IntWW 74, 75, 76, 77, 78, 79, 80, 81, 82, 83; InWom, SUP; LegTOT; LibW; NewYTBS 83; NotNAT, A; OxCAmT 84; OxCThe 67; PlP&P; ThFT; WebAB 74, 79; WhoAm 82; WhoAmW 77; WhoHol A; WorAl; WorAlBi*

Fonteyn, Margot, Dame
[Mrs. Roberto de Arias; Margaret Hookham]
English. Dancer
Prima ballerina, Britain's Royal Ballet, 1934-75; formed partnership "made in heaven" with Rudolf Nureyev, 1962-79; pres., Royal Academy of Dancing, 1954—.
b. May 18, 1919 in Reigate, England
d. Feb 21, 1991 in Panama City, Panama
Source: *AnObit 1991; BiDD; BioIn 1, 2, 3, 4, 5, 6, 7, 8, 9, 10, 11, 12, 13, 14, 17, 18, 21; BlueB 76; CelR, 90; CnOxB; ConAu 133, X; ContDcW 89; ConTFT 10; CurBio 49, 72, 91N; DancEn 78; DcArts; DcLP 87B; FacFETw; GoodHs; IntDcB; IntDcWB; IntWW 83, 89; InWom, SUP; LegTOT; LinLib S; NewGrDM 80; News 91, 91-3; NewYTBE 72; NewYTBS 74, 91; RAdv 14, 13-3; WhDW; Who 83, 90; WhoAm 82, 90; WhoAmW 75; WhoThe 77A; WhoWor 91; WhThe; WomFir; WorAl; WorAlBi*

Fonyo, Steve
[Stephen Fonyo, Jr]
Canadian. Track Athlete, Victim
After losing leg to cancer, ran 4,924 miles across Canada to raise money for cancer research, 1984-85.
b. Jun 29, 1965 in Montreal, Quebec, Canada
Source: *BioIn 15; ConNews 85-4*

Foot, Michael
English. Politician, Journalist
Leader of Labour party, 1980-83; author *Debts of Honour,* 1980.
b. Jul 23, 1913 in Plymouth, England
Source: *BioIn 1, 2, 4, 9, 10, 11, 12, 13, 14, 15, 16, 21; BlueB 76; ConAu 108; CurBio 50, 81; DcLP 87A; DcPol; EncWB; FacFETw; IntAu&W 91; IntWW 74, 75, 91; IntYB 81, 82; Who 74, 82, 83, 85, 88, 90, 92, 94; WhoWor 74, 76, 78, 82; WrDr 76, 80, 82, 84, 86, 88, 90, 92, 94, 96*

Foote, Andrew Hull
American. Social Reformer
Temperance activist who abolished rum ration in US Navy, 1862; worked to suppress slave trade; wrote *Africa & the American Flag,* 1854.
b. Sep 12, 1806 in New Haven, Connecticut
d. Jun 26, 1863 in New Haven, Connecticut
Source: *Alli; AmBi; ApCAB; BioIn 4, 7; CivWDc; DcAmAu; DcAmB; DcAmMiB; DcAmTB; DcNAA; Drake; HarEnMi; HarEnUS; LinLib S; NatCAB 5; PeoHis; TwCBDA; WebAB 74, 79; WebAMB; WhAm HS; WhCiWar*

Foote, Arthur William
American. Composer, Organist
Wrote overture *In the Mountains,* 1887.
b. Mar 5, 1853 in Salem, Massachusetts
d. Apr 8, 1937 in Boston, Massachusetts
Source: *DcAmB S2; WebBD 83*

Foote, Horton
[Albert Horton Foote, Jr]
American. Author, Screenwriter
Wrote *Trip to Bountiful,* 1953; won Oscars for screenplays of *Tender Mercies,* 1983; *To Kill a Mockingbird,* 1962.
b. Mar 14, 1916 in Wharton, Texas
Source: *AmAu&B; BioIn 10, 14, 15; ConAu 34NR, 51NR, 73; ConDr 73, 82C, 88; ConLC 51, 91; ConTFT 4, 15; CurBio 86; DcLB 26; IntAu&W 91; IntMPA 92, 94, 96; LegTOT; NewYTBS 86; NotNAT; WhoAm 74, 76, 86, 88, 90, 92, 94, 95, 96, 97; WhoEnt 92; WhoThe 81; WhoUSWr 88; WhoWor 95, 96; WhoWrEP 89, 92, 95; WorAu 1950; WrDr 88, 90, 92, 94, 96*

Foote, Samuel
"The English Aristophanes"
English. Dramatist, Actor
One-legged comedian who starred in *Lame Lover,* 1770; mimicked prominent persons; plays include *The Minor,* 1760.
b. Jan 27, 1720 in Truro, England
d. Oct 21, 1777 in Dover, England
Source: *Alli; AnCL; BiD&SB; BioIn 3, 9, 12, 14, 17; BritAu; CamGEL; CamGLE; CasWL; Chambr 2; ChhPo; CrtSuDr; DcEnA; DcEnL; DcNaB; Dis&D; EncWT; EvLB; GrWrEL DR; McGEWD 72, 84; MouLC 2; NewC; NewCBEL; NotNAT A, B; OxCEng 67, 85, 95; OxCThe 67, 83; PenC ENG; PseudAu; REn; WebE&AL*

Foote, Shelby
American. Historian, Writer
Civil War expert; wrote 3-volume *The Civil War: A Narrative,* 1958-74; novels include *Shiloh,* 1952; appeared in highly acclaimed PBS documentary "The Civil War," 1990.
b. Nov 11, 1916 in Greenville, Mississippi
Source: *AmAu&B; BenetAL 91; BioIn 2, 4, 8, 9, 13, 16; ConAu 3NR, 5R, 45NR; ConLC 75; ConNov 72, 76, 82, 86, 91, 96; ConPopW; CurBio 91; DcLB 2, 17; DcLEL 1940; DrAF 76; DrAPF 80; FifSWrA; LegTOT; LiveMA; News 91, 91-2; OxCAmL 83, 95; REnAL; SouWr; TwCA SUP; TwCRHW 90, 94; WhoAm 74, 76, 78, 80, 82, 84, 86, 88, 90, 92, 94, 95, 96, 97; WhoSSW 93, 95, 97; WhoUSWr 88; WhoWrEP 89, 92, 95; WrDr 76, 80, 82, 84, 86, 88, 90, 92, 94, 96*

Forain, Jean-Louis
French. Artist
Etcher, lithographer, caricaturist, known for caustic humor.
b. 1852 in Reims, France
d. 1931 in Paris, France
Source: *DcTwCCu 2; McGDA; OxCFr; OxCTwCA; OxDcArt; PhDcTCA 77; ThHEIm; WorECar*

Foran, Dick John Nicholas
American. Actor
Made series of Warners films as singing cowboy including *My Little Chickadee,* 1940.
b. Jun 18, 1910 in Flemington, New Jersey
d. Aug 10, 1979 in Panorama City, California
Source: *FilmEn; FilmgC; IntMPA 75, 76, 77; NewYTBS 79; WhoHol A*

Forbes, Bertie
[Robert Charles Forbes]
Scottish. Journalist
Founder, editor, *Forbes* mag., 1916; wrote on business, finance.
b. May 14, 1880 in Aberdeen, Scotland
d. May 6, 1954 in New York, New York
Source: *BioIn 7, 8; CurBio 50, 54; NatCAB 47; WebBD 83; WhAm 3*

Forbes, Bryan
English. Screenwriter, Director
Directed *The Stepford Wives,* 1974; *International Velvet,* 1978.
b. Jul 22, 1926 in London, England
Source: *BiDFilm, 81, 94; BioIn 7, 9, 10, 11, 13, 14, 15, 16, 19; BlueB 76; CmMov; ConAu 44NR, 69; ConDr 73, 77A, 82A, 88A; EncEurC; FilmEn; FilmgC; ForYSC; HalFC 80, 84, 88; IlWWBF, A; IntAu&W 76, 77, 82, 89, 91, 93; IntMPA 75, 76, 77, 79, 80, 81, 82, 84, 86, 88, 92, 94, 96; IntWW 74, 75, 76, 77, 78, 79, 80, 81, 82, 83, 89, 91, 93; ItaFilm; MiSFD 9; MovMk; NewYTBE 71; OxCFilm; SmATA 37; Who 74, 82, 83, 85, 88, 90, 92, 94; WhoAm 80, 82, 84, 86, 88, 90, 92, 94, 95; WhoHol 92, A; WhoHrs 80; WhoThe 77; WhoWor 74, 76, 78, 82, 84, 87, 89, 95, 96, 97; WorEFlm; WorFDir 2; WrDr 76, 80, 82, 84, 86, 88, 90, 92, 94, 96*

Forbes, Edward
English. Naturalist
Pioneer in biogeography; wrote *History of British Starfish,* 1841.
b. Feb 12, 1815 in Isle of Man, England
d. Nov 18, 1854 in Wardie, Scotland
Source: *Alli; AsBiEn; BiD&SB; BiESc; BioIn 2, 10; BritAu 19; CamDcSc; CelCen; DcBiPP; DcNaB; DcScB; InSci; LarDcSc*

Forbes, Esther
American. Author
Wrote Pulitzer-winning *Paul Revere and the World He Lived In,* 1942.
b. Jun 28, 1894? in Westboro, Massachusetts
d. Aug 12, 1967 in Worcester, Massachusetts
Source: *AmAu&B; AmNov; AnCL; AuBYP 2, 3; BioIn 1, 2, 3, 4, 5, 6, 7, 8, 9, 11; ChhPo S2; ConAu P-1; CyWA 58; DcLEL; InWom, SUP; MorJA; NewbMB 1922; OxCAmL 65; REn; REnAL; SmATA 2; TwCA, SUP; WhAm 4*

Forbes, Jack D(ouglas)
American. Historian
Has served on many boards relating to Native American studies; wrote *Native Americans of California and Nevada,* 1982.
b. Jan 7, 1934 in Long Beach, California
Source: *AmMWSc 73S; WhoWest 74, 76*

Forbes, John
Scottish. Army Officer
Took over Fort Duquesne, 1758, renaming it Fort Pitt; later became Pittsburgh.
b. 1710 in Dunfermline, Scotland
d. Mar 11, 1759 in Philadelphia, Pennsylvania
Source: *AmBi; ApCAB; BioIn 3, 5, 9, 10; DcAmB; DcCanB 3; DcNaB S1; Drake; EncAAH; EncCRAm; HarEnUS; McGEWB; NatCAB 12; WhAm HS*

Forbes, Kathryn
[Kathryn Anderson McLean]
American. Author
Wrote *Mama's Bank Account,* 1943, which inspired TV series "I Remember Mama," 1949-57.

b. Mar 20, 1909 in San Francisco, California
d. May 15, 1966 in San Francisco, California
Source: *AmAu&B; AmNov; AmWomWr; BenetAL 91; ConAu 29R, P-2, X; CurBio 44, 66; InWom, SUP; REn; REnAL; SmATA 15, X; WorAl; WorAlBi*

Forbes, Malcolm Stevenson
American. Publisher, Editor
Millionaire publisher of *Forbes* magazine, 1957-90; known for extravagant parties.
b. Aug 19, 1919 in New York, New York
d. Feb 24, 1990 in Far Hills, New Jersey
Source: *BioIn 4, 10, 11, 12, 13, 14, 15, 16; CelR 90; ConAu 28NR, 69, 131; CurBio 75, 90, 90N; FacFETw; IntAu&W 89, 91; IntWW 89; News 90, 90-3; NewYTBS 90; St&PR 75, 84, 87, 91N; WhAm 10; WhoAm 74, 76, 78, 80, 82, 84, 86, 88; WhoFI 87, 89; WhoWor 87; WorAlBi*

Forbes, Malcolm Stevenson, Jr.
"Steve Forbes"
American. Publishing Executive
President, Forbes Inc., 1980-90, CEO, 1990—; presidential hopeful, 1996.
b. Jul 18, 1947 in Morristown, New Jersey
Source: *CurBio 96; News 96, 96-2; WhoAm 86, 88, 90, 92, 94, 95, 96, 97; WhoAmP 87, 89, 91, 93, 95; WhoE 83, 85, 86, 89, 91, 93, 95, 97; WhoEmL 87; WhoFI 92, 94, 96*

Forbes, Ralph
[Ralph Taylor]
English. Actor
Starred in silents, early talkies: *Beau Geste,* 1926; *Beau Ideal,* 1931.
b. Sep 30, 1896 in London, England
d. Mar 31, 1951 in New York, New York
Source: *Film 2; FilmEn; FilmgC; ForYSC; MotPP; TwYS; WhoHol B; WhScrn 74, 77, 83; WhThe*

Forbes-Robertson, Johnston, Sir
English. Actor, Manager
Appeared on stage, 1874-1913; said to be greatest Hamlet of his time.
b. Jan 16, 1853 in London, England
d. Nov 6, 1937 in Saint Margaret's Bay, England
Source: *BioIn 1, 2, 3, 4, 7, 9, 10; CamGWoT; ChhPo S2, S3; CnThe; DcNaB 1931; EncWT; Ent; FamA&A; Film 1; IntDcT 3; LinLib L; LngCTC; NewCol 75; NotNAT A, B; OxCAmT 84; OxCThe 67, 83; PlP&P; WhAm 1; WhDW; WhoHol B; WhoStg 1906, 1908; WhScrn 74, 77, 83; WhThe*

Forche, Carolyn (Louise)
American. Poet
Wrote *The Country between Us,* 1982, documenting the horrors against the Salvadoran people during their Civil War in the 1970s; won *Los Angeles Times* Book Award for Poetry for *The Angel of History,* 1994.
b. Apr 28, 1950 in Detroit, Michigan
Source: *AmWomWr SUP; ArtclWW 2; Benet 96; BioIn 12, 13; ConAu 50NR, 109, 117; ConLC 25, 83, 86; ConPo 85, 91, 96; DcLB 5; DrAPF 80; ModWoWr; OxCAmL 95; OxCTwCP; OxCWoWr 95; PoeCrit 10; WhoAm 96; WhoAmW 77, 79; WorAu 1980; WrDr 86, 88, 90, 92, 94, 96*

Ford, Alexander
Polish. Director
Organized Polish army film unit, WW II; director, Film Polski, govt. run film organization.
b. Jan 24, 1908 in Lodz, Poland
Source: *BioIn 15; DcFM; FilmEn; FilmgC; HalFC 80, 84, 88; IntWW 74, 75, 76, 77, 78, 79, 80; WorEFlm; WorFDir 1*

Ford, Anne McDonnell
[Mrs. Deane Johnson]
American.
First wife of Henry Ford II, 1940-64; mother of Charlotte, Ann, Edsel II.
b. Sep 24, 1919 in Rye, New York
d. Mar 29, 1996
Source: *BioIn 5, 13, 15*

Ford, Arthur A
American. Clergy
Psychic medium who lectured on ESP; allegedly broke secret code between Harry Houdini and wife.
b. 1896 in Titusville, Florida
d. Jan 1, 1971 in Miami, Florida
Source: *BioIn 5, 8, 9, 10; EncO&P 1; NewYTBE 71*

Ford, Benson
American. Auto Executive
Grandson of Henry, brother of Henry II; held various executive positions with Ford Motor Co., 1935-78.
b. Jul 20, 1919 in Detroit, Michigan
d. Jul 27, 1978 in Cheboygan, Michigan
Source: *BioIn 1, 2, 3, 4, 11; CurBio 52, 78, 78N; IntWW 74, 75, 76, 77, 78, 79N; NewYTBS 78; St&PR 75; Ward 77; WhAm 7; WhoAm 74, 76, 78; WhoFI 74*

Ford, Betty
[Elizabeth Anne Bloomer Ford; Mrs. Gerald Ford]
American. First Lady
Co-founder, pres., Betty Ford Center for drug rehabilitation, 1982—; wrote *The Times of My Life,* 1979; *Betty: A Glad Awakening,* 1987.
b. Apr 8, 1918 in Chicago, Illinois
Source: *BioIn 13, 14, 15, 16; BioNews 74; BkPepl; CelR 90; ConAu 23NR, 105, X; ConHero 1; FacPr 89; HeroCon; HerW, 84; InWom SUP; LegTOT; NewYTBE 73; NewYTBS 78; WhoAm 86, 90; WhoAmW 77, 91; WhoWest 92; WhoWor 84, 87, 91*

Ford, Bob
[Robert Newton Ford]
"The Dirty Little Coward"
American. Murderer
Fellow gang member who shot Jesse James in back, 1882.
b. 1860
d. Jun 24, 1892 in Creede, Colorado

Ford, Charlotte
American. Socialite, Designer
Daughter of Henry Ford II; etiquette columnist who wrote *Charlotte Ford's Book of Modern Manners.*
b. Apr 3, 1941
Source: *BioIn 8, 10, 11, 13*

Ford, Christina
[Maria Christina Vettore Austin Ford]
Italian.
Second wife of Henry Ford II.
b. 1927
Source: *BioIn 15; NewYTBE 73*

Ford, Constance
American. Actor
Played role of "Ada Hobson" for 25 years on *Another World.*
b. 1924 in New York, New York
d. Feb 26, 1993 in New York, New York
Source: *HalFC 88*

Ford, Corey
[John Riddell]
American. Author
Books include *How to Guess Your Age,* 1950; *The Day Nothing Happened,* 1959.
b. Apr 29, 1902 in New York, New York
d. Jul 27, 1969 in Hanover, New Hampshire
Source: *AmAu&B; BenetAL 91; BioIn 5, 8, 14, 15; ConAu 25R; DcLB 11; EncAHmr; EncAI&E; EncMys; ObitOF 79; REnAL; WhAm 5; WhE&EA; WhNAA*

Ford, Doug
American. Golfer
Turned pro, 1950; won PGA, 1955, Masters, 1957.
b. Aug 6, 1932 in West Haven, Connecticut
Source: *BioIn 5, 10; WhoGolf*

Ford, Edsel Bryant
American. Auto Executive
Son of Henry Ford; pres., Ford Motor Co., 1919-43; the Edsel was named for him.
b. Nov 6, 1893 in Detroit, Michigan
d. May 26, 1943 in Grosse Pointe, Michigan
Source: *BioIn 11, 19; DcAmB S3; EncABHB 5; FacFETw; OxCAmH; WhAm 2; WorAl; WorAlBi*

Ford, Edsel Bryant, II
American. Auto Executive
Son of Henry Ford II; has worked for Ford Motor Co. since 1969; elected board of directors, 1988.
b. 1949
Source: *BioIn 10, 11, 12, 13, 14; BioNews 74; BusPN; NewYTBS 79*

Ford, Eileen
American. Business Executive, Author
With husband founded highly successful model agency, 1946—; author of syndicated column, *Eileen Ford's Model Beauty*.
b. Mar 25, 1922 in New York, New York
Source: *BioIn 13, 15; CelR 90; ConAu 120; CurBio 71; GrLiveH; InWom SUP; LegTOT; WhoAm 86, 90; WhoAmW 85, 91; WhoEnt 92*

Ford, Eleanor Clay
American.
Wife of Edsel B Ford, mother of Henry Ford II.
b. Jun 6, 1896 in Detroit, Michigan
d. Oct 19, 1976 in Detroit, Michigan
Source: *NewYTBS 76; WhoAmA 78N, 80N, 82N, 84N, 86N, 89N, 91N, 93N*

Ford, Ford Madox
[Ford Madox Hueffer]
English. Author, Poet
Founded *English Review*, 1908; wrote *Good Soldier*, 1915, a study of emotional relationships.
b. Dec 17, 1873 in Merton, England
d. Jun 26, 1939 in Deauville, France
Source: *AtlBL; Benet 87, 96; BioIn 1, 2, 4, 5, 6, 7, 8, 9, 11, 12, 13, 14, 15, 16, 17, 18, 19, 21; BlmGEL; BritWr 6; CamGEL; CamGLE; CasWL; Chambr 3; ChhPo, S1; CnDBLB 6; CnMWL; ConAu 104, 132; CyWA 58; DcArts; DcLB 34, 98, 162; DcLEL; DcNaB 1931; EncSF, 93; EncWL 2, 3; EvLB; GrBr; GrWrEL N; LegTOT; LiExTwC; LinLib L; LngCEL; LngCTC; MagSWL; MajTwCW; MakMC; McGEWB; ModBrL, S1, S2; NewC; NewCBEL; Novels; OxCEng 67, 85, 95; OxCTwCP; PenC ENG; RAdv 1, 14, 13-1; REn; REnAL; RfGEnL 91; RGTwCWr; ScF&FL 1; TwCA, SUP; TwCLC 1, 15, 39; TwCRHW 90, 94; TwCWr; WebE&AL; WhAm 2, 3, 4A, HSA; WhDW; WhE&EA; WhoTwCL; WorAl; WorAlBi*

Ford, Gerald R(udolph)
[Gerald King]
American. US President
Rep., 38th pres., 1974-77; succeeded Nixon after his resignation, pardoned him, 1974; withdrew US in fall of S Vietnam, Cambodia, 1975.
b. Jul 14, 1913 in Omaha, Nebraska
Source: *AmOrTwC; AmPolLe; Benet 87; BenetAL 91; BiDrAC; BiDrUSC 89; BiDrUSE 89; BioIn 3, 5, 6, 7, 8, 9, 10, 11, 12, 13, 14, 15, 16; BioNews 74; BkPepl; CelR 90; ColdWar 1; ConAu 110, 114; CurBio 61, 75; DcAmC; DcTwHis; Dun&B 90; EncAAH; EncAB-H 1996; EncWB; FacFETw; FacPr 89, 93; HealPre; HisEAAC; IntWW 74, 75, 76, 77, 78, 79, 80, 81, 82, 83, 89, 91, 93; IntYB 78, 79, 80, 81, 82; NewCol 75; NewYTBE 73; NewYTBS 76; OxCAmL 83; PeoHis; PresAR; RComAH; VicePre; WebAB 79; Who 82, 83, 85, 88, 90, 92, 94; WhoAm 80, 82, 84, 86, 88, 90, 92, 94, 95, 96, 97; WhoAmP 87, 91; WhoGov 72, 75, 77; WhoWest 82, 84, 87, 89, 92, 94, 96; WhoWor 80, 82, 84, 87, 89, 91, 93, 95, 96, 97; WorAlBi*

Ford, Glenn
[Gwyllyn Samuel Newton Ford]
American. Actor
Among his over 100 films are *Gilda*, 1946; *Blackboard Jungle*, 1955; noted for thoughtful leading man roles.
b. May 1, 1916 in Quebec, Canada
Source: *BiDFilm, 81, 94; BioIn 4, 5, 10, 11, 12, 14; BlueB 76; CelR; CmMov; ConTFT 3; CurBio 59; DcArts; EncAFC; FilmEn; FilmgC; ForYSC; HalFC 80, 84, 88; IntDcF 1-3, 2-3; IntMPA 77, 78, 79, 80, 81, 82, 84, 86, 88, 92, 94, 96; ItaFilm; LegTOT; MotPP; MovMk; OxCFilm; WhoAm 74, 76, 78, 80, 82, 84, 86, 88, 90, 92, 94, 95; WhoEnt 92; WhoHol 92, A; WorAl; WorAlBi; WorEFlm*

Ford, Harrison
American. Actor
Best-known roles as Han Solo in *Star Wars* films, Indiana Jones in *Indiana Jones* films; received Oscar nomination for *Witness*, 1985.
b. Jul 13, 1942 in Chicago, Illinois
Source: *BiDFilm 94; BioIn 11, 12, 13, 16; CelR 90; ConTFT 8, 15; CurBio 84; DcArts; DcTwCCu 1; FilmEn; HalFC 84, 88; IntDcF 1-3, 2-3; IntMPA 82, 84, 86, 88, 92, 94, 96; IntWW 89, 91, 93; LegTOT; News 90, 90-2; VarWW 85; WhoAm 78, 80, 82, 84, 86, 88, 90, 92, 94, 95, 96, 97; WhoEnt 92; WhoHol 92; WorAl; WorAlBi*

Ford, Henry
American. Auto Manufacturer
Built first inexpensive auto, Model T, 1909; introduced assembly line, 1913.
b. Jul 30, 1863 in Dearborn, Michigan
d. Apr 7, 1947 in Dearborn, Michigan
Source: *AmAu&B; AmDec 1900, 1920; AmSocL; AsBiEn; BiDAmBL 83; BiDAmSp OS; BioIn 1, 2, 3, 4, 5, 6, 7, 8, 9, 10, 11, 12, 13, 14, 15, 16, 17, 18, 19, 20, 21; ChhPo S3; ConAu 115, 148; CurBio 44, 47; DcAmB S4; DcAmC; DcAmSR; DcInv; DcTwDes; DcTwHis; EncAAH; EncAB-H 1974, 1996; EncABHB 4; Entr; FacFETw; GayN; InSci; LegTOT; LngCEL; MakMC; McGEWB; MemAm; NatCAB 15, 38; NewCol 75; NotTwCS; OxCAmH; PeoHis; RComAH; REn; WebAB 74, 79; WhAm 2; WhDW; WhFla; WorAl; WorAlBi; WorInv*

Ford, Henry, II
"Hank the Deuce"
American. Auto Executive
Grandson of Henry Ford; chm., CEO, Ford Motor Co., 1960-80; credited with revival of co., 1940s.
b. Sep 4, 1917 in Detroit, Michigan
d. Sep 29, 1987 in Detroit, Michigan
Source: *AnObit 1987; AutoN 79; BiDAmBL 83; BioIn 1, 2, 3, 4, 5, 6, 7, 8, 9, 10, 11, 12, 13, 15, 16, 17; BlueB 76; BusPN; CelR; ConAu 111, 123, 148; ConNews 88-1; CurBio 46, 78, 87, 87N; Dun&B 79; EncAB-A 26; EncAB-H 1974, 1996; EncABHB 5; FacFETw; IntWW 74, 75, 76, 77, 78, 79, 80, 81, 82, 83; IntYB 78, 79, 80, 81, 82; LinLib S; McGEWB; NewYTBS 79, 82, 87; OxCAmH; PolProf E, J, K, NF, T; St&PR 75, 84, 87; Ward 77; WhAm 9; Who 74, 82, 83, 85, 88; WhoAm 74, 76, 78, 80, 82, 84, 86; WhoFI 74, 75, 77, 79, 81; WhoMW 74, 76, 78, 80; WhoWor 74, 78, 80, 82, 84, 87; WorAl; WorAlBi*

Ford, Jack
[John Gardner Ford]
American.
Second son of Gerald and Betty Ford.
b. Mar 16, 1952 in Washington, District of Columbia
Source: *BioIn 11, 14, 21*

Ford, Jerry
[Gerard Ford]
American. Business Executive
With wife, Eileen, founded successful modeling agency, 1946.
Source: *ConAu 146; SmATA 78; WhoAmP 79, 81, 83*

Ford, John
English. Dramatist
Melancholy plays include *Broken Heart*, 1633.
b. 1586 in Ilsington, England
d. 1640?
Source: *Alli; AtlBL; BbD; Benet 87, 96; BiD&SB; BiDRP&D; BioIn 3, 4, 5, 7, 12, 16, 17, 18, 20; BlmGEL; BritAu; BritWr 2; CamGEL; CamGLE; CamGWoT; CasWL; ChhPo; CnDBLB 1; CnE&AP; CnThe; CroE&S; CrtSuDr; CrtT 1; CyWA 58; DcArts; DcBiPP; DcEnA; DcEnL; DcLB 58; EncWT; Ent; EvLB; GrWrEL DR; IntDcT 2; LinLib L, S; LngCEL; McGEWB; McGEWD 72, 84; MouLC 1; NewC; NewCBEL; NotNAT A, B; OxCEng 85, 95; OxCThe 67, 83; PenC ENG; PlP&P; RAdv 14, 13-2; REn; REnWD; RfGEnL 91; WebE&AL; WhDW; WorAl; WorAlBi*

Ford, John Sean O'Feeney
American. Director
Best known for western films including *Stagecoach*, 1939; won six Oscars.
b. Feb 1, 1895 in Cape Elizabeth, Maine
d. Aug 31, 1973 in Palm Desert, California
Source: *CmMov; ConAu 45; CurBio 73N; DcFM; EncAB-H 1974; Film 1, 2;*

FilmgC; MovMk; OxCFilm; WebAB 74; WhAm 6; WhoAm 74; WhScrn 77

Ford, Kathleen DuRoss
[Mrs. Henry Ford, II]
American.
Third wife of Henry Ford II.
b. Feb 11, 1940 in Belding, Michigan
Source: *BioIn 10, 11, 12, 15*

Ford, Len
[Leonard Guy Ford, Jr]
American. Football Player
Defensive end, Cleveland, 1950-57; Hall of Fame, 1976.
b. Feb 18, 1926 in Washington, District of Columbia
d. Mar 14, 1972 in Detroit, Michigan
Source: *BiDAmSp FB; BioIn 9; LegTOT; ObitOF 79; WhoSpor*

Ford, Lita
American. Singer, Musician
Heavy metal guitarist and singer; received platinum record for *Lita,* 1986; hit songs include "Close My Eyes Forever" and "Kiss Me Deadly."
b. 1959, England
Source: *BioIn 16; ConMus 9; LegTOT*

Ford, Mary
[Les Paul and Mary Ford; Irene Colleen Summers]
American. Singer, Musician
Popular in early 1950s with husband, Les Paul; known for multiple harmony effect s: "How High the Moon," 1951.
b. Jul 7, 1924AD in Waukesha, Wisconsin
d. Sep 30, 1977 in Los Angeles, California
Source: *BioIn 3, 10, 11, 12; DcAmB S10; InWom SUP; NewGrDA 86; NewYTBS 77; ObitOF 79; RkOn 82; WhScrn 83*

Ford, Michael Gerald
American.
Oldest son of Gerald, Betty Ford.
b. Mar 14, 1950 in Washington, District of Columbia
Source: *BioIn 10, 14*

Ford, Paul
[Paul Ford Weaver]
American. Actor
Stage, film actor who starred in TV series "You'll Never Get Rich," 1955-59; "Baileys of Balboa," 1964-65.
b. Nov 2, 1901 in Baltimore, Maryland
d. Apr 12, 1976 in Mineola, New York
Source: *BiE&WWA; BioIn 10, 13; EncAFC; FilmEn; FilmgC; ForYSC; HalFC 80, 84, 88; ItaFilm; LegTOT; MotPP; MovMk; NatCAB 61; NewYTBS 76; NotNAT, B; OxCAmT 84; WhAm 7; WhoAm 74, 76; WhoE 74; WhoThe 72, 77; WhoWor 74; WhScrn 83; WorAl*

Ford, Paul Leicester
American. Author, Historian
Wrote novel *Janice Meredith,* 1899; 10-volume *Writings of Thomas Jefferson,* 1894.
b. Mar 23, 1865 in New York, New York
d. May 8, 1902 in New York, New York
Source: *Alli SUP; AmAu; AmAu&B; AmBi; ApCAB; BbD; BenetAL 91; BibAL; BiD&SB; BioIn 11; CarSB; Chambr 3; ChhPo S1; CnDAL; DcAmAu; DcAmB; DcAmBC; DcBiA; DcLEL; DcNAA; EvLB; GayN; HarEnUS; JBA 34; LinLib L, S; McGEWB; NatCAB 13; OxCAmL 65, 83, 95; REn; REnAL; TwCBDA; WebAB 74, 79; WhAm 1*

Ford, Phil Jackson
American. Basketball Player
Guard, 1978-85, mostly with Kansas City; rookie of year, 1979.
b. Feb 9, 1956 in Rocky Mount, North Carolina
Source: *BiDAmSp Sup; BioIn 13, 15; BlkOlyM; NewYTBS 86; OfNBA 85*

Ford, Richard
American. Author
Wrote *The Sportswriter,* 1990; *Independence Day,* 1995.
b. Feb 16, 1944 in Jackson, Mississippi
Source: *BenetAL 91; BioIn 13, 15, 16, 17, 19, 21; ConAu 11NR, 47NR, 69; ConLC 46; ConNov 91, 96; CurBio 95; DrAPF 80; IntWW 91, 93; NewYTBS 88; OxCAmL 95; RGTwCWr; WhoAm 97; WorAu 1980; WrDr 80, 82, 84, 86, 88, 90, 92, 94, 96*

Ford, Russ(ell William)
Canadian. Baseball Player
Pitcher, 1909-15; credited with perfecting "emery ball," later outlawed.
b. Apr 25, 1883 in Brandon, Manitoba, Canada
d. Jan 24, 1960 in Rockingham, North Carolina
Source: *Ballpl 90; BioIn 5, 21; WhoProB 73*

Ford, Ruth Elizabeth
American. Actor
On stage in *Dinner at Eight,* 1966; films include *The Keys of the Kingdom,* 1944.
b. Jul 7, 1915 in Hazelhurst, Mississippi
Source: *BiE&WWA; BioIn 16; CelR; ConTFT 7; NotNAT; NotWoAT; WhoAm 84, 86; WhoEnt 92; WhoHol A; WhoThe 77*

Ford, Steven Meigs
American. Actor
Son of Gerald and Betty Ford; starred in TV soap opera "The Young and the Restless," 1981-88.
b. May 19, 1956 in Washington, District of Columbia
Source: *BioIn 10, 14*

Ford, Susan Elizabeth
American.
Only daughter of Gerald and Betty Ford.
b. Jul 6, 1957 in Washington, District of Columbia
Source: *Baker 84; BioIn 10, 11, 14, 15; ConMus 3; EncRk 88; HarEnCM 87; IntMPA 92; LesBEnT; NewGrDA 86; News 92-2; NewYTBS 91; OxCPMus; WhoAm 90; WorAlBi*

Ford, Tennessee Ernie
[Ernest Jennings Ford]
American. Singer
TV star, 1950s-60s; sang gospel, country music; hit song, "Sixteen Tons," 1955; awarded Medal of Freedom, 1984; inducted into Country Music Hall of Fame, 1990.
b. Feb 13, 1919 in Bristol, Tennessee
d. Oct 17, 1991 in Reston, Virginia
Source: *AnObit 1991; ASCAP 66, 80; Baker 84, 92; BgBkCoM; BiDAmM; BioIn 4, 5, 6, 12, 14, 15, 17, 18; CmpEPM; ConMus 3; ConTFT 10; CounME 74, 74A; CurBio 58, 92N; EncFCWM 69, 83; EncRk 88; HarEnCM 87; HarEnR 86; IlEncCM; IntMPA 75, 76, 77, 78, 79, 80, 81, 82, 84, 86, 88, 92; LegTOT; NewGrDA 86; News 92, 92-2; NewYTBS 91; NewYTET; OxCPMus; RkOn 74; WhAm 10; WhoAm 74, 76, 78, 80, 82, 84, 86, 88, 90; WorAl; WorAlBi*

Ford, Wallace
[Samuel Jones Grundy]
English. Actor
Character actor, 1903-65; notable film *The Informer,* 1935.
b. Feb 12, 1898 in Batton, England
d. Jun 11, 1966 in Woodland Hills, California
Source: *BiE&WWA; FilmEn; FilmgC; HolCA; MovMk; NotNAT B; Vers B; WhoHol B; WhScrn 74, 77, 83; WhThe*

Ford, Wendell Hampton
American. Politician
Dem. senator from KY, 1974—.
b. Sep 8, 1924 in Owensboro, Kentucky
Source: *AlmAP 92; BiDrGov 1789; BiDrUSC 89; BioIn 14; BioNews 75; BlueB 76; CngDr 77, 79, 81, 83, 85, 87, 89; IntWW 78, 79, 80, 81, 82, 83, 89, 91, 93; NewYTBS 90; PolsAm 84; WhoAm 74, 76, 78, 80, 82, 84, 86, 88, 90, 92, 94, 95, 96, 97; WhoAmP 91; WhoGov 72, 75, 77; WhoSSW 73, 75, 76, 78, 80, 82, 84, 86, 88, 91, 93, 95, 97; WhoWor 80, 82, 84, 87, 89, 91*

Ford, Whitey
[Edward Charles Ford]
"The Chairman of the Board"
American. Baseball Player
Pitcher, NY Yankees, 1950, 1953-67; holds several World Series records including most wins, 10; Hall of Fame, 1974.
b. Oct 21, 1928 in New York, New York
Source: *Ballpl 90; BiDAmSp BB; BioIn 3, 4, 5, 6, 7, 8, 10, 14, 15, 20; CurBio*

62; NewYTBS 74; WhoAm 76, 78, 80, 82; WhoAmP 91; WhoProB 73; WhoSpor; WorAl; WorAlBi

Ford, William Clay
American. Auto Executive, Football Executive
Brother of Henry Ford II; owner, Detroit Lions football club, 1964—.
b. Mar 14, 1925 in Detroit, Michigan
Source: *BioIn 1, 3, 11, 16; Dun&B 90; IntWW 74, 75, 76, 77, 78, 79, 80, 81, 82, 83, 89, 91, 93; St&PR 84, 87, 91, 93; Ward 77; WhoAm 74, 76, 78, 80, 82, 84, 86, 88, 90, 92, 94, 95, 96, 97; WhoFI 74, 85, 87, 89; WhoMW 74, 78, 80, 82, 84, 86, 88, 90, 92, 93, 96*

Fordice, Kirk
[Daniel Kirkwood Fordice, Jr]
American. Politician
Rep. governor, MS, 1992—.
b. Feb 10, 1934 in Memphis, Tennessee
Source: *AlmAP 96; BiDrGov 1988; BioIn 20; NewYTBS 91; St&PR 87, 91; WhoAm 92, 94, 95, 96, 97; WhoAmP 93, 95; WhoFI 87, 89, 92; WhoSSW 73, 75, 93, 95, 97; WhoWor 91, 93*

Foreigner
[Dennis Elliott; Ed Gagliardi; Lou Gramm; Al Greenwood; Mick Jones; Ian McDonald; Rick Wills]
English. Music Group
Pop-rock hits include "Waiting for a Girl Like You," 1981.
Source: *BioIn 15; ConMuA 80A; EncPR&S 89; EncRk 88; EncRkSt; HarEnR 86; IlEncRk; PenEncP; RkOn 78; RolSEnR 83; WhoHol 92; WhoRock 81; WhoRocM 82*

Foreman, Carl
American. Director
Won best director Oscar for *Bridge Over the River Kwai,* 1957.
b. Jul 23, 1914 in Chicago, Illinois
d. Jun 26, 1984 in Beverly Hills, California
Source: *AnObit 1984; BiDFilm, 81, 94; BioIn 4, 8, 11, 14; BlueB 76; CmMov; ConAu 41R, 113; ConDr 73, 77A; ConTFT 2; DcFM; DcLB 26; EncMcCE; FacFETw; FilmEn; FilmgC; HalFC 80, 84, 88; IntAu&W 76, 77; IntDcF 1-4, 2-4; IntMPA 75, 76, 77, 78, 79, 80, 81, 82, 84; IntWW 74, 75, 76, 77, 78, 79, 80, 81, 82, 83; MiSFD 9N; NewYTBS 84; OxCFilm; VarWW 85; Who 74, 83; WhoAm 74, 76, 78, 82; WhoWor 74, 76, 78; WorEFlm; WrDr 80, 82, 84*

Foreman, Chuck
[Walter Eugene Foreman]
American. Football Player
Five-time all-pro running back, 1973-81, mostly with Minnesota; set NFL record for pass receptions by running back in season, 73, 1975.
b. Oct 26, 1950 in Frederick, Missouri
Source: *BiDAmSp FB; BioIn 11; FootReg 81; NewYTBS 74; WhoAm 78, 80, 82; WhoBlA 77, 80; WhoFtbl 74; WhoSpor*

Foreman, Dave
American. Social Reformer
Co-founder radical Earth First!, environmental group, 1980—; editor *Earth First! Journal,* 1980—.
b. 1947
Source: *EnvEnc; News 90, 90-3*

Foreman, George
American. Boxer
Won gold medal, 1968 Olympics; pro heavyweight champ, 1973-74; made comeback, 1987; heavyweight champion, 1994-95.
b. Jan 10, 1949 in Marshall, Texas
Source: *BiDAmSp BK; BioIn 10, 11, 12, 14, 15, 16; BlkOlyM; CelR; CmCal; ConBlB 1; CurBio 74, 95; FacFETw; InB&W 85; NewYTBE 73; NewYTBS 74, 89, 91; WhoAm 74, 76, 78; WhoBlA 85, 88, 90, 92; WhoBox 74; WorAl; WorAlBi*

Foreman, Richard
American. Dramatist, Director
Established avant-garde theatrical company, Ontological-Hysteric Theater, 1968; won Obie Awards for his plays *Rhoda,* 1976; *Film Is Evil; Radio Is Good,* 1987.
b. Jun 10, 1937 in New York, New York
Source: *BioIn 10, 14, 15, 16, 18, 20; CamGWoT; ConAmD; ConAu 32NR, 65; ConDr 73, 77, 82, 88, 93; ConLC 50; ConTFT 6, 14; CrtSuDr; CurBio 88; GrStDi; IntvTCA 2; McGEWD 84; NatPD 81; NewYTBE 72; NewYTBS 88; PeoHis; TheaDir; WhoAm 94, 95, 96, 97; WhoE 89, 91, 95; WhoEnt 92; WrDr 76, 80, 82, 84, 86, 88, 90, 92, 94, 96*

Forester, Cecil Scott
English. Author
Wrote *Horatio Hornblower* series; *The African Queen,* 1935.
b. Aug 27, 1899 in Cairo, Egypt
d. Apr 2, 1966 in Fullerton, California
Source: *AmAu&B; BioIn 1, 2, 3, 4, 5, 7, 8, 9; ConAu 73; CyWA 58; DcAmB S8; DcLEL; DcNaB 1961; EncMys; EvLB; LngCTC; MnBBF; ModBrL; NatCAB 53; NewC; NewCBEL; OxCShps; RAdv 1; REn; REnAL; SmATA 13; TwCA, SUP; TwCWr; WebE&AL; WhAm 4; WhLit; WhoChL*

Forman, James
American. Civil Rights Leader
Presented Black Manifesto, 1969, a public call for reparations to the black community for years of oppression.
b. Oct 4, 1928 in Chicago, Illinois
Source: *BiDAmLf; BioIn 9, 11, 14, 16, 20; BlkWrNE; CivRSt; ConBlB 7; EncAACR; EncWB; HisWorL; LNinSix; PolProf J, K*

Forman, James Douglas
American. Author
Wrote *A Ballad for Hogskin Hill,* 1979; *That Mad Game; War and the Chance for Peace,* 1980.
b. Nov 12, 1932 in Mineola, New York
Source: *Au&Arts 17; AuBYP 2, 3; ConAu 4NR, 9NR, 9R, 19NR, 42NR; DcAmChF 1960; IntAu&W 76, 77, 82; MajAI; SmATA 8, 70; ThrBJA; WhoAmL 96; WhoE 91*

Forman, Milos
Czech. Director
Won Oscars for *One Flew Over the Cuckoo's Nest,* 1975; *Amadeus,* 1984.
b. Feb 18, 1932 in Caslav, Czechoslovakia
Source: *BiDFilm, 81, 94; BioIn 7, 8, 9, 10, 11, 12, 14, 15, 16; CelR 90; ConAu 109; ConTFT 1, 4; CurBio 71; DcFM; DrEEuF; EncEurC; FacFETw; FilmEn; FilmgC; HalFC 80, 84, 88; IlWWHD 1; IntDcF 1-2, 2-2; IntMPA 77, 78, 79, 82, 84, 86, 88, 92, 94, 96; IntWW 74, 75, 76, 77, 78, 79, 80, 81, 82, 83, 89, 91, 93; LegTOT; MiSFD 9; MovMk; NewYTBE 71; NewYTBS 81; OxCFilm; Who 82, 83, 85, 88, 90, 92, 94; WhoAm 78, 80, 82, 84, 86, 88, 90, 92, 94, 95, 96, 97; WhoEnt 92; WhoHol 92; WhoSocC 78A; WhoSoCE 89; WhoWor 74, 76, 78, 80, 82, 84, 87, 91, 93, 95; WorEFlm; WorFDir 2*

Fornos, Werner H(orst)
[Werner Horst Fahrenhold]
German. Scientist
President, Population Institute, 1982—; leader in the global population stabilization struggle.
b. Nov 5, 1933 in Leipzig, Germany

Forrest, Edwin
American. Actor
First actor to encourage US plays; best known for role in *Othello,* 1826.
b. Mar 9, 1806 in Philadelphia, Pennsylvania
d. Dec 12, 1872 in Philadelphia, Pennsylvania
Source: *AmBi; AmCulL; ApCAB; BenetAL 91; BioIn 2, 3, 4, 5, 7, 8, 9, 10, 11, 13, 14, 19; CamGWoT; CelCen; CnThe; DcAmB; DcBiPP; Drake; EncAB-H 1974, 1996; EncWT; Ent; FamA&A; HarEnUS; IntDcT 3; LinLib L, S; McGEWB; MemAm; NatCAB 5; NotNAT A, B; OxCAmH; OxCAmL 65, 83, 95; OxCAmT 84; OxCThe 67, 83; PlP&P; REnAL; TwCBDA; WebAB 74, 79; WhAm HS*

Forrest, Helen
American. Singer
Big band vocalist, 1930s-40s; made films with Harry James; hosted radio show with Dick Haymes, 1940s.
b. Apr 12, 1918 in Atlantic City, New Jersey
Source: *BioIn 6, 11, 12, 17; CmpEPM; InWom SUP; PenEncP; WhoHol A*

Forrest, Nathan Bedford
American. Military Leader
Confederate war general; first head of original Klu Klux Klan.
b. Jul 13, 1821 in Chapel Hill, Tennessee
d. Oct 29, 1877 in Memphis, Tennessee
Source: *AmBi; ApCAB; BiDConf; BioIn 1, 2, 4, 5, 6, 7, 8, 10, 17, 18, 19; CivWDc; DcAmB; DcAmMiB; EncSoH; GenMudB; HarEnMi; HarEnUS; McGEWB; NatCAB 10; OxCAmH; TwCBDA; WebAB 74, 79; WebAMB; WhAm HS; WhCiWar; WhoMilH 76; WorAl; WorAlBi*

Forrest, Steve
[William Forrest Andrews]
American. Actor
Brother of Dana Andrews; in TV series "SWAT," 1975-76.
b. Sep 29, 1925 in Huntsville, Texas
Source: *ConTFT 7; FilmEn; FilmgC; ForYSC; HalFC 84, 88; IntMPA 84, 86, 92, 94, 96; WhoAm 78, 80, 82, 84, 86; WhoHol A*

Forrestal, James Vincent
American. Government Official
First secretary of Defense, 1947-49.
b. Feb 15, 1892 in Beacon, New York
d. May 22, 1949 in Bethesda, Maryland
Source: *AmAu&B; AmPolLe; BiDrUSE 71, 89; BioIn 1, 2, 5, 6, 7, 8, 10, 12; ColdWar 1; CurBio 42, 48, 49; DcAmB S4; DcAmMiB; DcPol; EncAB-H 1974, 1996; McGEWB; NatCAB 42; WebAB 74, 79; WebAMB; WebBD 83; WhAm 2, 4A; WhWW-II; WorAl*

Forrester, Jay Wright
American. Engineer, Inventor
Electrical engineers; invented the information-storage device used in most digital computers.
b. Jul 14, 1918 in Anselmo, Nebraska
Source: *AmMWSc 73S, 78S, 92; BioIn 4, 10, 15, 20; Future; HisDcDP; IntAu&W 77, 82; LarDcSc; McGMS 80; PorSil; WhoAm 74, 76, 78, 80, 82, 84, 86, 88, 90, 92, 94, 95, 96, 97; WhoE 74, 91; WhoEng 88; WhoFI 83, 85, 92; WhoTech 89*

Forrester, Maureen
Canadian. Opera Singer
Contralto; fine Lieder, oratorio singer; NY Met. debut, 1975.
b. Jul 25, 1931 in Montreal, Quebec, Canada
Source: *Baker 84; BioIn 6, 7, 9, 10, 15; CanWW 89; CreCan 2; CurBio 62; FacFETw; InWom; MetOEnc; MusSN; NewAmDM; NewGrDA 86; PenDiMP; WhoAm 86, 88; WhoMus 72*

Forsch, Bob
[Robert Herbert Forsch]
American. Baseball Player
Pitcher, St. Louis, 1974-88; pitched no-hitters, 1978, 1983.
b. Jan 13, 1950 in Sacramento, California
Source: *Ballpl 90; BaseReg 86, 87; BioIn 21*

Forsch, Ken(neth Roth)
American. Baseball Player
Pitcher, 1970-85; pitched no-hitter, 1979; with brother Bob, only brother combination in MLs to do this.
b. Sep 8, 1946 in Sacramento, California
Source: *Ballpl 90; BaseReg 86*

Forssmann, Werner Theodor Otto
German. Surgeon
Pioneered technique of cardiac catheterization; won Nobel Prize, 1956.
b. Aug 29, 1904 in Berlin, Germany
d. Jun 1, 1979 in Schopfheim, Germany (West)
Source: *BiESc; ConAu 111; CurBio 57, 79; FacFETw; IntWW 76; McGMS 80; NewYTBS 79; Who 74; WhoNob, 90, 95; WhoWor 74, 76; WorAl*

Forster, E(dward) M(organ)
English. Author
Wrote *A Room with a View,* 1908; *A Passage to India,* 1924; both became Oscar-winning films, 1986, 1984.
b. Jan 1, 1879 in London, England
d. Jun 7, 1970 in Coventry, England
Source: *AtlBL; Benet 96; BioIn 1, 2, 3, 4, 5, 6, 7, 8, 9, 10, 11, 12, 13, 14, 15, 16, 17, 18, 19, 20; CasWL; Chambr 3; CnMWL; ConAu 25R, 45NR, P-1; ConLC 1, 2, 3, 4, 9, 10, 13, 15, 22, 45, 77; CyWA 58; DcArts; DcLB 34, 98; DcLEL; DcNaB 1961; EncSF 93; EncWL 3; GayLesB; GayLL; GrBr; HisDBrE; LngCTC; MakMC; McGEWB; NewC; NewCBEL; NewGrDO; OxCEng 67, 95; RAdv 14; RfGShF; RGTwCWr; TwCA SUP; WebE&AL; WhAm 5; WhDW; WhLit; WhoTwCL*

Forster, John
English. Biographer, Critic
Wrote literary biographies, including one of his friend Charles Dickens, 1874.
b. Apr 2, 1812 in Newcastle-upon-Tyne, England
d. Feb 1, 1876 in London, England
Source: *Alli, SUP; BbD; BiD&SB; BioIn 1, 4, 5, 8, 9, 13, 21; BritAu 19; CamGEL; CamGLE; CasWL; CelCen; ChhPo S1; DcBiPP; DcEnA; DcEnL; DcEuL; DcLB 144; DcLEL; DcNaB; EvLB; LinLib L; NewC; NewCBEL; NinCLC 11; NotNAT B; OxCEng 67, 85, 95; OxCThe 67; PenC ENG*

Forster, Robert
American. Actor
Starred in TV series "Banyon," 1972-74.
b. Jul 13, 1942 in Rochester, New York
Source: *ConTFT 2; FilmgC; HalFC 80, 84, 88; IntMPA 82, 92; NewYTBE 72; WhoHol A*

Forster, William Edward
"Buckshot Forster"
English. Statesman
Introduced Elementary Education Act, 1870, the foundation of English compulsory education system.
b. Jul 11, 1818 in Bradpole, England
d. Apr 6, 1886 in London, England
Source: *BioIn 3, 8, 16; CelCen; CyEd; DcBiPP; DcNaB; NewCol 75; VicBrit*

Forsyth, Bill
[William David Forsyth]
Scottish. Filmmaker
Director of gentle comedies; best known for *Gregory's Girl,* 1981; *Local Hero,* 1983.
b. Jul 29, 1947 in Glasgow, Scotland
Source: *BioIn 13, 16; CurBio 89; HalFC 84, 88; IntDcF 2-2; IntMPA 92; IntWW 89, 91, 93; NewYTBS 82; Who 90, 92, 94*

Forsyth, Frederick
English. Author
Won Poe for *The Day of the Jackal,* 1971; other thrillers: *The Odessa File,* 1972.
b. Aug 25, 1938 in Ashford, England
Source: *BestSel 89-4; BioIn 9, 11, 12, 14, 15, 17; CelR 90; ConAu 38NR, 85; ConLC 2, 5, 36; ConNov 82, 86, 91, 96; ConPopW; CrtSuMy; CurBio 86; DcArts; DcLB 87; EncSF 93; HalFC 84, 88; IntAu&W 91, 93; IntWW 91; LegTOT; MajTwCW; Novels; ScF&FL 92; SpyFic; TwCCr&M 80, 85, 91; WhoAm 74, 90, 92, 94, 95, 96; WhoSpyF; WhoWor 84, 87, 89, 91, 93, 95, 96; WorAl; WorAlBi; WorAu 1975; WrDr 76, 82, 84, 86, 88, 90, 92, 94, 96*

Forsyth, Rosemary
American. Actor
Former model; in films *Black Eye,* 1974; *Gray Lady Down,* 1978.
b. Jul 6, 1944 in Montreal, Quebec, Canada
Source: *BioIn 16; FilmEn; FilmgC; HalFC 80, 84, 88; WhoHol 92, A*

Forsythe, Albert E
American. Pilot
Helped open aviation to blacks, 1930s; first black to fly cross-country.
b. 1898 in Nassau, Bahamas
d. May 7, 1986 in Newark, New Jersey
Source: *NewYTBS 86*

Forsythe, Henderson
American. Actor, Director
Won supporting actor Tony for *Best Little Whorehouse in Texas,* 1978; star of TV series "As the World Turns."
b. Sep 11, 1917 in Macon, Missouri
Source: *BiE&WWA; ConTFT 4, 14; NotNAT; VarWW 85; WhoAm 80, 82, 84, 86, 88, 90, 92, 94, 95, 96, 97; WhoEnt 92; WhoHol 92; WhoThe 72, 77, 81*

Forsythe, John
[John Lincoln Freund]
American. Actor
Played Blake Carrington on TV soap opera "Dynasty," 1981-89.
b. Jan 29, 1918 in Penns Grove, New Jersey
Source: *BiE&WWA; BioIn 5, 9, 10, 12, 14, 15, 16; CelR, 90; ConTFT 1, 7, 14; CurBio 73; FilmEn; FilmgC; ForYSC; HalFC 80, 84, 88; IntMPA 75, 76, 77, 78, 79, 80, 81, 82, 84, 86, 88, 92, 94, 96; LegTOT; MotPP; MovMk; NotNAT; WhoAm 74, 76, 78, 80, 82, 84, 86, 88, 90, 92, 94, 95, 96, 97; WhoEnt 92; WhoHol 92, A; WhoThe 72, 77, 81; WhoWest 74, 76; WorAl; WorAlBi*

Fort, Charles Hoy
American. Author
Works descibe psychic phenomena: *Look of the Damned,* 1919.
b. 1874 in Albany, New York
d. May 3, 1932 in New York, New York
Source: *AmAu&B; DcNAA; EncO&P 1; EncSF; OxCAmL 65; REnAL; TwCA; WhoSciF*

Fortas, Abe
American. Supreme Court Justice
Served on bench, 1956-69; resigned under fire after accepting fees from convicted swindler.
b. Jun 19, 1910 in Memphis, Tennessee
d. Apr 5, 1982 in Washington, District of Columbia
Source: *AnObit 1982; BiDFedJ; BioIn 7, 8, 9, 10, 11, 12, 13, 14, 15, 16, 17; BlueB 76; ConAu 106; CurBio 66, 82, 82N; DrAS 74P; FacFETw; IntWW 74, 75, 76, 77, 78, 79, 80, 81, 82, 82N; JeAmHC; LegTOT; LinLib L, S; NewYTBS 82; OxCSupC; PeoHis; PolProf NF; St&PR 75; SupCtJu; WebAB 74, 79; WhAm 8; WhoAm 74, 76, 78, 80, 82; WhoAmL 78, 79; WhoAmP 73, 75, 77, 79, 81, 83, 85; WhoSSW 73; WorAl; WorAlBi*

Forte, Charles, Sir
British. Business Executive
Founded Trusthouse-Forte, PLC, large int'l. hotel, catering firm.
b. Nov 26, 1908 in Monteforte, Italy
Source: *BioIn 10, 11; BlueB 76; DcTwBBL; IntWW 74, 75, 76, 77, 78, 79, 80, 81, 93; NewYTBS 79; Who 74, 82; WhoFI 96; WhoWor 74, 76, 78, 84, 87, 89, 91, 93, 95, 96, 97*

Forten, James
American. Social Reformer
Influential spokesman for the abolition movement.
b. Sep 2, 1766 in Philadelphia, Pennsylvania
d. Mar 4, 1842 in Philadelphia, Pennsylvania
Source: *AfrAmAl 6; AmRef; BiDAmBL 83; BioIn 6, 8, 9, 10, 11, 15, 17, 20; BlksScM; DcAmB; DcAmNB; EncAB-H 1974, 1996; InB&W 80, 85; McGEWB; OxCAmH; WebAB 74, 79; WebBD 83; WhAm HS; WhAmP*

Fortensky, Larry
American.
Seventh husband of actress Elizabeth Taylor.
b. 1952 in Stanton, California

Fortmann, Danny
[Daniel John Fortmann]
American. Football Player
Guard, Chicago, 1936-43; Hall of Fame.
b. Apr 11, 1916 in Pearl River, New York
Source: *BiDAmSp FB; BioIn 6, 8; LegTOT; WhoFtbl 74*

Fortune, Michele
American. Businessman
Pres., CEO, AnnTaylor, women's apparel retailer with 110 stores in 25 states.
b. 1949 in Fresno, California
Source: *CelR 90; Dun&B 90*

Fortune, Timothy Thomas
American. Author, Editor
Ghost writer for Booker T Washington; writings include *The Negro in Politics,* 1885.
b. Oct 3, 1856 in Marianna, Florida
d. Jun 2, 1928 in Philadelphia, Pennsylvania
Source: *Alli SUP; AmAu&B; AmBi; AmRef; BiDAmJo; BioIn 5, 6, 8, 9, 11, 12, 15, 16, 17, 19, 20, 21; BlkAWP; ConAu 112; DcAmNB; DcNAA; EncAACR; EncAB-H 1974, 1996; EncSoH; InB&W 80, 85; NegAl 76; PeoHis; SelBAAf; SelBAAu; SouBlCW; WhoColR*

Fortuny
[Mariano Fortuny y Madrazo]
Spanish. Fashion Designer
Greek-styled, finely-pleated silk dresses were a "status symbol" in 1907.
b. May 11, 1871 in Granada, Spain
d. May 3, 1949 in Venice, Italy
Source: *WhoFash, 88; WorFshn*

Fosbury, Dick
American. Track Athlete
High jumper; developed back-over flop style known as Fosbury Flop; won gold medal, 1968 Olympics.
b. Mar 6, 1947 in Portland, Oregon
Source: *BioIn 17; WhoSpor; WhoTr&F 73; WorAl; WorAlBi*

Foscolo, (Niccolo) Ugo
Italian. Poet, Patriot
Wrote novel *Lost Letters of Jacopo Artis,* 1802.
b. 1778 in Zante, Greece
d. Sep 10, 1827 in London, England
Source: *BbD; Benet 87, 96; BiD&SB; BioIn 2, 3, 5, 7, 9, 12, 13, 14; CasWL; CelCen; DcEuL; DcItL 1, 2; Dis&D; EuAu; EuWr 5; EvEuW; LinLib L; McGEWB; McGEWD 72, 84; NewCBEL; NinCLC 8; OxCEng 85, 95; PenC EUR; RAdv 14, 13-2; REn; WhDW*

Fosdick, Harry Emerson
American. Clergy
Pastor, NYC's Riverside Church, 1926-46; leading spokesman for liberal Protestantism.
b. May 24, 1878 in Buffalo, New York
d. Oct 5, 1969 in Bronxville, New York
Source: *AmAu&B; AmDec 1920, 1930; AmOrTwC; AmPeW; ApCAB X; AuBYP 2, 3; BenetAL 91; BiDAmM; BiDMoPL; BioIn 1, 2, 3, 4, 6, 7, 8, 9, 10, 11, 14, 15, 16, 17, 18, 19; ConAu 25R; CurBio 40, 69; DcAmB S8; DcAmReB 1, 2; EncARH; LinLib L, S; LuthC 75; McGEWB; NatCAB 55; OxCAmH; PrimTiR; RadStar; RelLAm 91; REnAL; TwCA SUP; TwCSAPR; WebAB 74, 79; WhLit; WhNAA; WorAl; WorAlBi*

Fosdick, Raymond Blaine
American. Author, Lawyer
First under-secretary, League of Nations, 1919; pres., Rockefeller Foundation, 1936-48; wrote autobiography, *Chronicle of a Generation,* 1958; brother of Harry Emerson.
b. Jun 9, 1883 in Buffalo, New York
d. Jul 18, 1972 in Newtown, Connecticut
Source: *AmAu&B; AmLY; AmPeW; BiDInt; BioIn 3, 5, 9, 11; CopCroC; CurBio 45, 72; DcAmB S9; LinLib S; NatCAB 57; ObitOF 79; OxCAmH; WhAm 5*

Foss, Joe
[Joseph Jacob Foss]
American. Politician, Football Executive
WW II ace; governor of SD, 1955-63; commissioner of AFL, 1959-66, until league m erged with NFL; National Rifle Assn. pres.
b. Apr 17, 1915 in Sioux Falls, South Dakota
Source: *BiDrGov 1789; BioIn 3, 4, 5, 6, 7, 9, 12, 16; CurBio 55; HarEnMi; InSci; MedHR, 94; News 90, 90-3; WebAMB; WhoAm 90, 92, 94, 95, 96; WhoAmP 73, 75, 77, 79, 81; WhoFtbl 74*

Foss, Lukas
American. Conductor
Led Brooklyn Philharmonic, 1971—; Milwaukee Symphony, 1981—; works include TV opera, *Griffelkin,* 1955.
b. Aug 15, 1922 in Berlin, Germany
Source: *AmComp; ASCAP 66; Baker 78, 84, 92; BiDAmM; BioIn 1, 2, 3, 6, 7, 8, 9, 12, 14, 15; BriBkM 80; CompSN, SUP; ConAmC 76, 82; ConCom 92; CpmDNM 80; CurBio 66; DcArts; DcCM; DcCom&M 79; DcTwCCu 1; IntDcOp; IntWW 75, 76, 77, 78, 79, 80, 81, 82, 83, 89, 91, 93; IntWWM 77, 80, 85, 90; LegTOT; MusMk; NatCAB 63N; NewAmDM; NewEOp 71; NewGrDA 86; NewGrDM 80; NewGrDO; NewOxM; NewYTBS 88; OxCMus; OxDcOp; WhoAm 74, 76, 78, 80, 82, 84, 86, 88, 90, 92, 94, 95, 96, 97; WhoAmM 83; WhoE 74, 83, 85, 86; WhoEnt 92;*

WhoMus 72; WhoMW 82, 84, 86, 88; WhoWor 74, 76, 78, 82, 84, 87, 89, 91, 93, 95, 96, 97

Fosse, Bob
[Robert Louis Fosse]
American. Choreographer, Director
Known for bold, innovative direction; won Oscar for *Cabaret,* 1972; other films include autobiographical *All That Jazz,* 1979.
b. Jun 23, 1927 in Chicago, Illinois
d. Sep 23, 1987 in Washington, District of Columbia
Source: *AmDec 1970; AnObit 1987; BiDFilm, 81, 94; BiE&WWA; BioIn 4, 5, 6, 8, 9, 10, 11, 12, 13; BkPepl; CamGWoT; CelR; CmMov; CnOxB; ConAu 110, 123; ConNews 88-1; ConTFT 1, 5; CurBio 72, 87, 87N; DancEn 78; DcArts; DcTwCCu 1; EncMT; FacFETw; FilmEn; FilmgC; ForYSC; GrStDi; HalFC 80, 84, 88; IlWWHD 1; IntDcF 1-2, 2-2; IntMPA 77, 78, 79, 80, 81, 82, 84, 86; IntWW 83; LegTOT; MiSFD 9N; MovMk; NewYTBS 87; NotNAT; OxCAmT 84; OxCFilm; OxCPMus; RAdv 14; TheaDir; WhAm 9; WhoAm 74, 76, 78, 80, 82, 84, 86; WhoThe 72, 77, 81; WhoWor 74, 76; WorAl; WorAlBi; WorEFlm*

Fossey, Dian
American. Naturalist
At research camp in Rwanda, became leading authority on gorillas, 1966-85; murdered.
b. Jan 16, 1932 in San Francisco, California
d. Dec 27, 1985 in Virunga Mountains, Rwanda
Source: *AnObit 1985; ConAu 34NR, 113, 118; ConHero 1; ConNews 86-1; ContDcW 89; CurBio 85, 86N; EncWHA; FacFETw; GrLiveH; HeroCon; InWom SUP; LegTOT; MajTwCW; NotTwCS; WomFir; WrDr 88*

Foster, Abigail Kelley
American. Abolitionist
Advocate of women's suffrage, temperance, labor reform.
b. Jan 15, 1810 in Pelham, Massachusetts
d. Jan 14, 1887 in Worcester, Massachusetts
Source: *BiDMoPL; DcAmB; HerW, 84; InWom, SUP; LibW; McGEWB; NotAW; WhAm HS; WhAmP*

Foster, David
Canadian. Musician, Songwriter
Keyboardist; recorded many hits with various artists including "Thriller," 1983; won five Grammys.
b. May 1, 1950 in Victoria, British Columbia, Canada
Source: *BioIn 15; ConMus 13; LegTOT; News 88-2; WhoAm 96, 97*

Foster, George Arthur
American. Baseball Player
Outfielder, 1973-86; tied ML record for most consecutive seasons leading NL in RBIs, three, 1976-78.
b. Dec 1, 1949 in Tuscaloosa, Alabama
Source: *BaseReg 86, 87; BiDAmSp BB; BioIn 11, 13, 16; Who 92; WhoAm 80, 82, 86; WhoBlA 75, 77, 92; WorAlBi; WrDr 90*

Foster, Hal
[Harold Ruddle Foster]
American. Cartoonist
Created "Prince Valiant" comic strip.
b. Aug 16, 1892 in Halifax, Nova Scotia, Canada
d. Jul 25, 1982 in Spring Hill, Florida
Source: *AnObit 1982, 1983; BioIn 11; ConAu 107; EncACom; LegTOT; LinLib L; NewYTBS 82; WhoAm 78; WhoAmA 73, 76, 78, 80, 82, 84N, 86N, 89N, 91N, 93N*

Foster, Jodie
[Alicia Christian Foster]
American. Actor, Director
Won Academy Award for best actress, 1988, in *The Accused*; directed *Little Man Tate,* 1991.
b. Nov 19, 1962 in Los Angeles, California
Source: *BiDFilm 94; BioIn 10, 11, 12, 13, 15, 16; BkPepl; CelR 90; ConTFT 2, 7, 14; CurBio 81, 92; DcArts; GrLiveH; HalFC 80, 84, 88; IntDcF 2-3; IntMPA 80, 84, 86, 88, 92, 94, 96; IntWW 91, 93; InWom SUP; ItaFilm; LegTOT; MiSFD 9; News 89-2; NewYTBS 76, 91; WhoAm 82, 84, 86, 88, 90, 92, 94, 95, 96, 97; WhoAmW 83, 85, 91, 93, 95, 97; WhoEnt 92; WhoHol 92, A; WhoHrs 80; WorAl; WorAlBi*

Foster, Joseph C
American. Business Executive
Pres., Foster Grant Co., 1943-69.
b. Oct 30, 1904 in Providence, Rhode Island
d. Nov 10, 1971 in New York, New York
Source: *BioIn 9, 11; NewYTBE 71; WhAm 6*

Foster, Julia
English. Actor
Films include *The Loneliness of the Long Distance Runner,* 1963; *Half a Sixpence,* 1968.
b. 1942 in Lewes, England
Source: *ConTFT 4; HalFC 88; IlWWBF; IntMPA 92; WhoThe 72, 77, 81*

Foster, Norman
[Norman Hoeffer]
American. Director
Leading man, early 1930s; directed numerous hits including *Davy Crockett,* 1955.
b. Dec 13, 1903 in Richmond, Indiana
d. Jul 7, 1976 in Santa Monica, California
Source: *BiDFilm; Film 2; FilmEn; FilmgC; MovMk; NewYTET; WhAm 7; WhoAm 76, 78; WhoHol A; WhoThe 72; WhThe; WorEFlm*

Foster, Paul
American. Dramatist
Plays include *The Madonna in the Orchard,* 1965.
b. Oct 15, 1931 in Penns Grove, New Jersey
Source: *Au&Wr 71; BioIn 10; ConAmD; ConAu 9NR, 21R, 26NR; ConDr 73, 77, 82, 88, 93; IntAu&W 82, 86, 89, 91, 93; NatPD 77; WhoAm 74, 76, 78, 80, 82, 84, 86, 88, 90, 92, 94, 95, 96, 97; WhoE 74; WhoEnt 92; WhoThe 77, 81; WrDr 76, 80, 82, 84, 86, 88, 90, 92, 94, 96*

Foster, Phil
[Fivel Feldman]
American. Comedian
Stand-up comedian best known as Laverne's father on TV series "Laverne and Shirley," 1976-82.
b. Mar 29, 1914 in New York, New York
d. Jul 8, 1985 in Rancho Mirage, California
Source: *BioIn 13; ConNews 85-3; LegTOT; NewYTBS 85; WhoAm 78, 80; WhoHol A; WorAl*

Foster, Pops
[George Murphy Foster]
American. Jazz Musician
Dixieland bassist; 60 yr. career covered pioneer jazz days to 1960s.
b. May 19, 1892 in McCall, Louisiana
d. Oct 30, 1969 in San Francisco, California
Source: *AllMusG; BiDAfM; BiDAmM; BiDJaz; BioIn 9, 10; CmpEPM; EncJzS; InB&W 80, 85; NewAmDM; NewGrDA 86; NewGrDJ 88, 94; WhoJazz 72*

Foster, Preston
American. Actor
Two-fisted hero in films, 1930-68, including *The Last Warning,* 1938.
b. Aug 24, 1900 in Ocean City, New Jersey
d. Jul 14, 1970 in La Jolla, California
Source: *ASCAP 66, 80; FilmgC; HolP 30; MotPP; MovMk; NewYTBE 70; WhoHol B; WhoHrs 80; WhScrn 74, 77, 83*

Foster, Rube
[Andrew Foster]
"The Father of Black Baseball"
American. Baseball Player, Baseball Executive
First baseman in Negro League, early 1900s; dominated black baseball before Jackie Robinson; Hall of Fame, 1981.
b. Sep 17, 1879 in Calvert, Texas
d. Dec 9, 1930 in Kankakee, Illinois
Source: *AfrAmSG; BiDAmSp BB; BioIn 3, 12; DcAmNB; InB&W 80; WhoSpor*

Foster, Stephen Collins
American. Composer
Best known songs "Oh Susanna," 1848; "My Old Kentucky Home," 1853.
b. Jul 4, 1826 in Lawrenceville, Pennsylvania
d. Jan 13, 1864 in New York, New York
Source: *AmAu; AmAu&B; AmBi; AmCulL; ApCAB; AtlBL; Baker 78, 84; BbD; Benet 87, 96; BiDAmM; BiD&SB; BioIn 1, 2, 3, 4, 5, 6, 7, 8, 9, 10, 11, 12, 13, 15, 19, 20; Chambr 3; ChhPo, S1, S2, S3; DcAmAu; DcAmB; DcArts; DcCom 77; DcLEL; DcNAA; Drake; EncAAH; EncAB-H 1996; EncSoH; EvLB; GrWrEL P; HalFC 80; LinLib L, S; McGEWB; MemAm; MusMk; NatCAB 7; NewAmDM; NewGrDM 80; NewOxM; NinCLC 26; OxCAmH; OxCAmL 65, 83, 95; OxCAmT 84; OxCMus; OxCPMus; PoIre; PopAmC; REn; REnAL; RfGAmL 87, 94; Sw&Ld A; TwCBDA; WebAB 74, 79; WhAm HS; WhDW; WhFla; WorAl*

Foster, Susanna
[Suzanne De Lee Flanders Larson]
American. Singer, Actor
Best known for remake of *Phantom of the Opera,* 1943.
b. Dec 6, 1924 in Chicago, Illinois
Source: *BioIn 9, 10, 13, 14, 15; 18; FilmEn; FilmgC; ForYSC; HalFC 80, 84, 88; HolP 40; InWom SUP; LegTOT; MotPP; MovMk; What 3; WhoHol 92, A*

Foster, Tabatha
American. Transplant Patient
Longest survivor of 5-organ transplant operation, Nov. 1, 1987-May 11, 1988.
b. 1985 in Madisonville, Kentucky
d. May 11, 1988 in Pittsburgh, Pennsylvania
Source: *BioIn 15, 16; News 88, 88-3; NewYTBS 88*

Foster, William Zebulon
American. Political Leader, Labor Union Official
Chm., US Communist Party, 1945-56; Communist presidential candidate, 1924, 1928 and 1932.
b. Feb 25, 1881 in Taunton, Massachusetts
d. Sep 1, 1961 in Moscow, Union of Soviet Socialist Republics
Source: *AmAu&B; AmRef; AmSocL; BiDAmL; BiDAmLL; BioIn 1, 3, 4, 6, 12, 13, 15, 16, 19, 20; CurBio 45, 61; DcTwHis; McGEWB; OxCAmH; PolProf T; WebAB 74, 79; WhAm 4; WorAl; WorAlBi*

Foucault, Jean Bernard Leon
French. Physicist
Invented gyroscope, 1852; known for research on speed of light.
b. Sep 18, 1819 in Paris, France
d. Feb 11, 1868 in Paris, France
Source: *AsBiEn; BiESc; BioIn 4, 5, 8, 9, 10, 12, 14, 15; DcBiPP; DcScB; InSci; LarDcSc; LinLib S; MacBEP; McGEWB; NewCol 75; WorAl; WorInv; WorScD*

Foucault, Michel
French. Author, Philosopher
Cultural historian who wrote award-winning *Madness and Civilization,* 1961.
b. Oct 15, 1926 in Poitiers, France
d. Jun 25, 1984 in Paris, France
Source: *AnObit 1984; Benet 87, 96; BiDNeoM; BioIn 8, 12, 13, 14, 15, 16, 17, 18, 19, 20, 21; BlmGEL; ClDMEL 80; ConAu 34NR, 105, 113; ConLC 31, 34, 69; CyWA 89; DcTwCCu 2; EncEth; EncWB; EncWL 3; EuWr 13; FacFETw; GayLesB; GayLL; GuFrLit 1; LegTOT; MajTwCW; MakMC; OxCPhil; PostFic; RadHan; RAdv 14, 13-2, 13-4, 13-5; ThTwC 87; WhoFr 79; WorAu 1970*

Fouche, Joseph
French. Statesman, Revolutionary
Napoleon's minister of police, 1799-1802, 1804-10.
b. May 21, 1759 in Le Pellerin, France
d. Dec 25, 1820 in Trieste, Italy
Source: *Benet 87, 96; BiDMoER 1; CmFrR; CopCroC; LinLib S; McGEWB; NewCol 75; OxCFr; REn; SpyCS*

Fountain, Pete(r Dewey)
American. Jazz Musician
Dixieland clarinetist; starred on Lawrence Welk's show, 1957-60; owned New Orleans club, 1960s-70s.
b. Jul 3, 1930 in New Orleans, Louisiana
Source: *AllMusG; Baker 84, 92; BiDAmM; BiDJaz; BioIn 9; CmpEPM; ConMus 7; EncJzS; NewAmDM; NewGrDJ 88; NewOrJ; WhoAm 74, 76, 78, 80, 82, 84, 86, 88, 90, 92, 94, 95, 96, 97; WhoEnt 92; WhoSSW 73, 75*

Fouquet, Jean
French. Artist
Works include portrait of Charles VII, illuminations for Chevalier's *Book of Hours,* 1450-60.
b. 1420 in Tours, France
d. 1480 in Tours, France
Source: *AtlBL; CmMedTh; IntDcAA 90; LinLib L; McGDA; McGEWB; MediFra; OxCArt; OxCFr; OxDcArt; REn; WhDW*

Fouquet, Nicolas
French. Statesman
Produced illuminations in the *Book of Hours,* 1450-60; introduced Renaissance ideas into French art.
b. 1615 in Paris, France
d. Mar 23, 1680 in Pignerol, France
Source: *Benet 87, 96; BioIn 6, 8, 12, 13; DcBiPP; NewCol 75; OxCFr; REn*

Fouquier-Tinville, Antoine Quentin
French. Lawyer
Revolutionary tribunal prosecutor; Marie Antoinette was one of his victims.
b. Jun 10, 1746 in Herouel, France
d. May 7, 1795 in Paris, France
Source: *BioIn 2; DcBiPP; Dis&D; OxCFr; REn*

Four Chaplains
[George L Fox; Alexander Goode; Clark V Poling; John P Washington]
American. Clergy
Gave life jackets to others, perished when *Dorchester* sunk off coast of Greenland, 1943.
Source: *BioIn 3, 4, 5, 7*

Four Freshmen, The
[Ken Albers; Don Barbour; Ross Barbour; Ray Brown; Bill Comstock; Ken Errair; Bob Flanagan; Hal Kratzch]
American. Music Group
Innovators of tight harmony sound, late 1940s; hit singles "It's a Blue World," 1952;"Graduation Day," 1956.
Source: *BioIn 16, 17, 21; ChhPo; CmpEPM; OxCPMus; PenEncP; RkOn 74; Who 82, 83, 85, 88, 90, 92; WhoRock 81; WhoRocM 82*

Four Horsemen of Notre Dame
[James Crowley; Elmer Layden; Don Miller; Harry Stuhldreher]
American. Football Players
Famed backfield named by *NY Herald Tribune* writer Grantland Rice, 1924.
Source: *BiDAmSp FB; BiDLA; BioIn 1; DrRegL 75; NewYTBE 73; OxCCanL; WhoRocM 82*

Fourier, Francois Marie Charles
French. Philosopher
Utopian socialist, advocate of cooperatives; several French, American settlements sprang from his studies.
b. Apr 7, 1772 in Besancon, France
d. Oct 8, 1837 in Paris, France
Source: *BbD; BiD&SB; BiDTran; BioIn 1, 3, 6, 7, 8, 9, 10, 11, 15; CasWL; DcBiPP; DcEuL; EncUrb; EuAu; LinLib L, S; LuthC 75; McGEWB; NewC; WebBD 83*

Fourier, Jean Baptiste Joseph
French. Mathematician
Discovered theorem of periodic oscillation, related to wave phenomenon, 1822.
b. Mar 21, 1768 in Auxerre, France
d. May 16, 1830 in Paris, France
Source: *AsBiEn; BiD&SB; BioIn 8, 9, 10, 12; CelCen; DcBiPP; DcInv; DcScB; Dis&D; LarDcSc; LinLib S; McGEWB; WhDW; WorAl*

Four Lads, The
[James Arnold; Frank Busseri; Connie Codarini; Bernard Toorish]
Canadian. Music Group
Former choirboys; hit singles "Moments to Remember"; "No Not Much."
Source: *AmPS A, B; CabMA; PenEncP; RkOn 74; WhoRock 81*

Four Musketeers, The
[Jean Borotra; Jacques Brugnon; Henri Cochet; Rene Lacoste]
French. Tennis Players
Quartet who dominated French tennis, 1922-32.
Source: *BioIn 8, 14, 15; NewYTBS 78, 87; ObitOF 79; WhE&EA*

Fournier, Pierre
French. Musician
International concert cellist, 1940s-60s.
b. Jun 24, 1906 in Paris, France
d. Jan 8, 1986 in Geneva, Switzerland
Source: *AnObit 1986; Baker 78, 84; BioIn 4, 5, 7, 11, 14; BriBkM 80; FacFETw; IntWWM 80; MusSN; NewAmDM; NewGrDM 80; PenDiMP; Who 74, 82, 83, 85; WhoFr 79; WhoMus 72; WhoWor 74, 76, 78*

Four Seasons, The
[Tommy DeVito; Bob Gaudio; Nick Massi; Frankie Valli]
American. Music Group
Doo-wop group, begun 1956; number one hits "Sherry"; "Big Girls Don't Cry"; "Rag Doll."
Source: *AmPS A, B; BiDAmM; BioIn 15, 17; ConMuA 80A; EncPR&S 74, 89; EncRk 88; EncRkSt; HarEnR 86; IlEncRk; NewGrDA 86; OxCPMus; PenEncP; RkOn 74, 78; RolSEnR 83; WhoRock 81; WhoRocM 82*

Four Tops
[Renaldo Benson; Abdul Fakir; Lawrence Payton; Levi Stubbs]
American. Music Group
Hits include "Baby I Need Your Loving," 1964; "Reach Out I'll Be There," 1966.
Source: *BiDAmM; BioIn 15; ConMuA 80A; ConMus 11; DcTwCCu 5; EncPR&S 74, 89; EncRk 88; EncRkSt; HarEnR 86; IlEncBM 82; IlEncRk; InB&W 80, 85A; NewAmDM; NewGrDA 86; OxCPMus; PenEncP; RkOn 74, 78, 84; RolSEnR 83; SoulM; WhoAfA 96; WhoBlA 88, 90, 92, 94; WhoRock 81; WhoRocM 82*

Foust, Larry
[Lawrence Michael Foust]
American. Basketball Player
Forward, 1950-62, mostly with Ft. Wayne; led NBA in field goal percentage, 1955.
b. Jun 24, 1928 in Painesville, Ohio
Source: *BasBi; BiDAmSp BK; OfNBA 87; WhoBbl 73*

Fouts, Dan(iel Francis)
American. Football Player
Six-time all-pro quarterback, San Diego, 1973-87; has set several NFL records for passing; Hall of Fame inductee, 1993.
b. Jun 10, 1951 in San Francisco, California
Source: *BiDAmSp FB; BioIn 12, 13, 15; FootReg 87; WhoAm 82, 84, 86, 88, 94, 95, 96, 97; WhoWest 89*

Fowler, Gene
American. Journalist, Author
Wrote outstanding biography of John Barrymore, *Goodnight Sweet Prince,* 1944.
b. Mar 8, 1890 in Denver, Colorado
d. Jul 2, 1960 in Los Angeles, California
Source: *AmAu&B; BenetAL 91; BiDAmJo; BioIn 1, 2, 3, 4, 5, 6, 7, 11, 12, 16; CathA 1952; ConAu 5NR; CurBio 44, 60; DcAmB S6; DcCathB; EncAJ; HalFC 84, 88; NatCAB 48; ObitOF 79; REn; REnAL; TwCA, SUP; WhAm 4; WhE&EA; WhJnl*

Fowler, Henry Watson
English. Lexicographer, Author
Compiled *Dictionary of Modern English Usage,* 1926; *Concise Oxford Dictionary,* 1911.
b. Mar 10, 1858 in Tonbridge, England
d. Dec 27, 1933 in London, England
Source: *Benet 87, 96; BioIn 2, 3, 4, 7, 14, 17; CamGLE; DcLEL; DcNaB 1931; EncAJ; EvLB; GrBr; NewC; NewCBEL; OxCEng 85, 95; REn; TwCA, SUP*

Fowler, Lydia Folger
American. Physician
First woman to receive M D degree, 1850.
b. 1823 in Nantucket, Massachusetts
d. Jan 26, 1879 in London, England
Source: *ApCAB; DcAmAu; DcNAA; IntDcWB*

Fowler, Mark Stapleton
American. Government Official
Chairman, FCC, 1981-87.
b. Oct 6, 1941 in Toronto, Ontario, Canada
Source: *BioIn 13, 14, 15; CurBio 86; LesBEnT, 92; WhoAm 82, 84, 86, 88, 90, 92, 94, 95, 96, 97; WhoFI 83, 85, 87*

Fowler, Orson Squire
American. Author, Lecturer
Noted popularizer of phrenology, 1830s.
b. Oct 11, 1809 in Steuben County, New York
d. Aug 18, 1887 in Sharon Station, Connecticut
Source: *Alli SUP; AmBi; AmRef; ApCAB; BiDAmS; BiInAmS; BioIn 1, 4, 8, 13, 15; DcAmAu; DcAmB; DcNAA; Drake; NatCAB 3; NewCol 75; TwCBDA; WhAm HS*

Fowler, William A(lfred)
American. Physicist
Shared 1983 Nobel Prize for studies on important nuclear reactions in the formation of chemical elements on the universe.
b. Aug 9, 1911 in Pittsburgh, Pennsylvania
d. Mar 14, 1995 in Pasadena, California
Source: *AmMWSc 76P, 79, 82, 86, 89, 92, 95; BiESc; BioIn 10, 13, 14, 15; BlueB 76; CurBio 95N; FacFETw; IntWW 74, 75, 76, 77, 78, 79, 80, 81, 82, 83, 89, 91, 93; LarDcSc; McGMS 80; NobelP; WhAm 11; Who 74, 82, 83, 85, 88, 90, 92, 94; WhoAm 74, 76, 78, 80, 82, 84, 86, 88, 90, 92, 94, 95; WhoAtom 77; WhoFrS 84; WhoGov 72, 75, 77; WhoNob, 90, 95; WhoScEn 94; WhoTech 89; WhoWest 87, 89, 92, 94; WhoWor 84, 87, 89, 91, 93, 95; WorAlBi*

Fowles, John (Robert)
English. Author
Wrote best-sellers *The Collector,* 1963; *French Lieutenant's Woman,* 1969; both filmed, 1965, 1981.
b. Mar 31, 1926 in Leigh-on-Sea, England
Source: *Au&Wr 71; AuBYP 2S, 3; AuSpks; Benet 87, 96; BioIn 7, 8, 10, 11, 12, 13, 14, 15, 16, 17, 18, 20; BlmGEL; BritWr S1; CamGLE; CelR; CnDBLB 8; ConAu 5R, 25NR; ConLC 1, 2, 3, 4, 6, 9, 10, 15, 33, 87; ConNov 72, 76, 82, 86, 91, 96; CurBio 77; CyWA 89; DcArts; DcLB 14, 139; DcLEL 1940; EncSF 93; EncWB; EncWL, 2, 3; FacFETw; HalFC 84, 88; IntAu&W 76, 77, 89, 91; IntvTCA 2; IntWW 74, 75, 76, 77, 78, 79, 80, 81, 82, 83, 89, 91, 93; IntWWP 77; LegTOT; LinLib L; MagSWL; MajTwCW; ModBrL S1, S2; NewC; NewYTBS 77; Novels; OxCEng 85, 95; PostFic; RAdv 1, 14, 13-1; RfGEnL 91; RGTwCWr; ScF&FL 92; SmATA 22; TwCRHW 90, 94; TwCWr; WebE&AL; Who 82, 83, 85, 88, 90, 92, 94; WhoAm 80, 82, 84, 86, 88, 90, 92, 94, 95, 96, 97; WhoWor 74, 76, 78, 80, 82, 84, 87, 89, 91, 93, 95, 96, 97; WorAl; WorAlBi; WorAu 1950; WrDr 76, 80, 82, 84, 86, 88, 90, 92, 94, 96; WrPh*

Fowlie, Wallace
American. Educator, Author
Books include *Climate of Violence,* 1967; *Rimbaud: A Critical Study,* 1967.
b. Nov 8, 1908 in Brookline, Massachusetts
Source: *AmAu&B; AmCath 80; BiE&WWA; BioIn 2, 4, 10, 11, 15, 17; ConAu 5NR, 5R; DrAS 74F, 78F, 82F; ModAL; NotNAT; TwCA SUP; WhoAm 74, 76, 78, 80, 82, 84; WhoSSW 73*

Fox, Carol
American. Impresario, Producer
Founder, manager, Lyric Opera of Chicago, 1952-81; introduced Maria Callas to US audiences.
b. Jun 15, 1926 in Chicago, Illinois
d. Jul 21, 1981 in Chicago, Illinois
Source: *AnObit 1981; Baker 84; BioIn 6, 9, 11, 12; CurBio 78, 81, 81N; InWom SUP; MetOEnc; NewAmDM; NewGrDA 86; NewGrDM 80; NewGrDO; NewYTBS 81; OxDcOp; WhAm 8; WhoAm 74, 76, 78, 80; WhoAmW 64, 66, 68, 70, 72, 79, 81; WhoMW 74, 76, 78, 80; WhoOp 76; WhoWor 74*

Fox, Charles
American. Composer, Conductor
Film scores include *Foul Play,* 1978; *Nine to Five,* 1980; won Emmys for "Love American Style," 1970, 1973.
b. Oct 30, 1940 in New York, New York
Source: *ConAmC 76, 82; ConTFT 12; HalFC 84, 88; VarWW 85; WhoAm 90; WhoEnt 92*

Fox, Charles James
English. Statesman
Liberalist instrumental in abolishing British slave trade.
b. Jan 24, 1749 in London, England
d. Sep 13, 1806 in Chiswick, England
Source: *Alli; AmRev; BbD; Benet 87, 96; BioIn 1, 2, 3, 4, 6, 8, 9, 10, 12, 17, 18, 20; BlmGEL; CasWL; CelCen; ChhPo S1, S2; CmFrR; DcBiPP; DcInB; DcNaB; EncAR; EncCRAm; EvLB; HisDBrE; LinLib L, S; LngCEL; McGEWB; NewC; NewCBEL; OxCEng 85, 95; REn; WhAmRev; WhDW; WorAl*

Fox, Edward
English. Actor
Starred in films *The Day of the Jackal,* 1973; *Gandhi,* 1984.
b. Apr 13, 1937 in London, England
Source: *ConTFT 7; FilmEn; FilmgC; HalFC 80, 84, 88; IlWWBF; IntMPA 78, 79, 80, 81, 82, 84, 86, 88, 92, 94, 96; IntWW 89, 91, 93; MovMk; Who 82, 83, 85, 88, 90, 92, 94; WhoHol 92, A*

Fox, Fontaine Talbot, Jr.
American. Illustrator, Cartoonist
Created syndicated comic strip "Toonerville Folks," 1915-30s.
b. Mar 3, 1884 in Louisville, Kentucky
d. Aug 10, 1964 in Greenwich, Connecticut
Source: *AmAu&B; BioIn 3, 7, 8, 11, 13; ChhPo; ConAu 89; DcAmB S7; NatCAB 51; SmATA 23N; WhAm 4; WorECom*

Fox, George
English. Religious Leader
Founded Society of Friends, the Quakers, 1671; frequently persecuted.
b. Jul 1624 in Leicester, England
d. Jan 13, 1691 in Sussex, England
Source: *Alli; ApCAB; BbD; Benet 87, 96; BiD&SB; BioIn 1, 2, 3, 4, 5, 6, 7, 8, 9, 10, 11, 12, 15, 17, 18, 19, 20; BlmGEL; BritAu; CamGEL; CamGLE; Chambr 1; DcAfL; DcAmReB 1, 2; DcBiPP; DcEuL; DcLEL; DcNaB; Dis&D; DivFut; EncO&P 1, 2, 3; EncPaPR 91; EvLB; HarEnUS; HisDStE; HisWorL; IlEncMy; LegTOT; LinLib L, S; LngCEL; LuthC 75; McGEWB; NatCAB 7; NewC; NewCBEL; OxCAmH; OxCAmL 65; OxCChiL; OxCEng 67, 85, 95; OxCMus; REn; WhDW; WorAl; WorAlBi*

Fox, James
[William Fox]
English. Actor
In films *The Servant,* 1964; *Isadora,* 1968; became an evangelist, 1973-83.
b. May 19, 1939 in London, England
Source: *Alli SUP; BiDFilm 94; BioIn 14; ConTFT 8; DcArts; FilmAG WE; FilmEn; FilmgC; ForYSC; HalFC 80, 84, 88; IlWWBF; IntMPA 75, 76, 77, 78, 79, 80, 81, 82, 84, 86, 88, 92, 94, 96; IntWW 91, 93; ItaFilm; MovMk; VarWW 85; Who 90, 92, 94; WhoHol 92, A*

Fox, John W, Jr.
American. Author
Wrote *Trail of Lonesome Pine,* 1908; *Little Shepherd of Kingdom Come,* 1903.
b. Dec 16, 1863 in Stoney Pointe, Kentucky
d. Jul 8, 1919
Source: *AmAu&B; BbD; BiD&SB; BiDSA; CarSB; CnDAL; ConAmL; DcBiA; DcLEL; DcNAA; EvLB; OxCAmL 65; REn; REnAL; TwCA SUP; TwCWr; WhAm 1*

Fox, Kate
[Catherine Fox]
American. Mystic
With sister, Margaret, pioneered in modern spiritualism, 1850s.
b. 1839 in Bath, New Brunswick, Canada
d. Jul 2, 1892 in New York, New York
Source: *BiDAmCu; BioIn 2, 7, 9; EncO&P 1; InWom, SUP; LibW; NotAW; WebBD 83*

Fox, Margaret
American. Mystic
Toured US, England with act "Rochester Rapping"; exposed as fake, 1888.
b. Oct 7, 1833 in Bath, New Brunswick, Canada
d. Mar 8, 1893 in New York, New York
Source: *Alli, SUP; AmBi; ApCAB; BiDAmCu; BioIn 2, 4, 7, 9, 15, 21; DcAmB; DcNAA; EncO&P 1, 3; InWom, SUP; LibW; LuthC 75; NotAW; OxCAmL 65; WebAB 74, 79; WebBD 83; WhAm HS*

Fox, Matthew (Timothy James)
American. Clergy, Writer
Roman Catholic priest; director, Institute in Culture and Creation Spirituality, 1976—; books include *The Coming of the Cosmic Christ,* 1988.
b. Dec 21, 1940 in Madison, Wisconsin
Source: *BioIn 17, 18; ConAu 109, 126; HeroCon; NewAgE 90; News 92, 92-2; RadHan; RelLAm 91*

Fox, Michael J.
[Michael Andrew Fox]
Canadian. Actor
Played Alex Keaton on TV series "Family Ties," 1982-89; starred in *Back to the Future,* 1985; won Emmys, 1986, 1987; stars in TV series "Spin City," 1996—.
b. Jun 9, 1961 in Vancouver, British Columbia, Canada
Source: *BioIn 14, 15, 16; CanWW 31; CelR 90; ConNews 86-1; ConTFT 5, 12; CurBio 87; HalFC 88; IntDcF 2-3; IntMPA 88, 92, 94, 96; IntWW 91, 93; LegTOT; VarWW 85; WhoAm 88, 90, 92, 94, 95, 96, 97; WhoEnt 92; WhoHol 92; WorAlBi*

Fox, Nellie
[Nelson Jacob Fox]
American. Baseball Player
Infielder, 1947-65; AL MVP, 1959; had lifetime .288 batting average; Hall of Fame, 1997.
b. Dec 25, 1927 in Saint Thomas, Pennsylvania
d. Dec 1, 1975 in Baltimore, Maryland
Source: *Ballpl 90; BioIn 13, 15, 18; CurBio 60, 76, 76N; LegTOT; NewYTBS 75; WhoProB 73; WhoSpor; WorAl; WorAlBi*

Fox, Samantha
English. Singer
Pop singer with gold album *Touch Me,* 1986; top ten hits include, "Naughty Girls," 1987 and "I Wanna Have Some Fun," 1989.
b. 1966, England
Source: *BioIn 16; ConMus 3; LegTOT*

Fox, Terry
[Terrance Stanley Fox]
Canadian. Track Athlete, Victim
After losing leg to cancer began marathon run across Canada to raise money for research; never completed, but raised $24 million.
b. Jul 28, 1958 in Winnipeg, Manitoba, Canada
d. Jun 28, 1981 in New Westminster, British Columbia, Canada
Source: *AnObit 1981; CanWW 81; ConHero 1; FacFETw; HeroCon; NewYTBS 81*

Fox, Uffa
English. Designer, Author
Designed dinghy which transformed sailing into popular sport, 1928; airbourne lifeboat for WW II.
b. Jan 15, 1898 in Cowes, Isle of Wight, England
d. Oct 26, 1972 in Cowes, Isle of Wight, England
Source: *BioIn 4, 7, 9, 12; ConAu 37R; DcNaB 1971; DcTwDes; FacFETw; NewYTBE 72; ObitT 1971; OxCShps*

Fox, Virgil Keel
American. Organist
Established modern organ as concert instrument; noted for dazzling pedal technique, flamboyant showmanship.
b. May 3, 1912 in Princeton, Illinois
d. Oct 25, 1980 in West Palm Beach, Florida
Source: *Baker 84, 92; BlueB 76; BriBkM 80; CurBio 64, 81; DcAmB S10; MusSN; NewYTBS 74; WhoAm 78; WhoMus 72; WhoWor 74*

Fox, William
American. Film Executive
Introduced organ music accompaniment to silent films; introduced *Movietone News,* first successful sound film.
b. Jan 1, 1879 in Tulchva, Hungary
d. May 8, 1952 in New York, New York
Source: *BiDAmBL 83; BioIn 2, 3, 8, 12; CmCal; DcAmB S5; DcFM; FilmEn; FilmgC; HalFC 80, 84, 88; IntDcF 2-4; OxCFilm; WhAm 3; WorEFlm*

Foxman, Abraham H
American. Civil Rights Leader
National director of the Anti-Defamation League of B'nai B'rith, 1987—.
b. May 1, 1940? in Baranovichi, Poland
Source: *BioIn 15; NewYTBS 87*

Foxworth, Robert
American. Actor
Played Chase Gioberti in TV series "Falcon Crest," 1981-87; films include *The Black Marble,* 1980.
b. Nov 1, 1941 in Houston, Texas
Source: *BioIn 13; ConTFT 1, 4; HalFC 84, 88; IntMPA 86, 88, 92, 94, 96; VarWW 85; WhoAm 90; WhoHol 92; WorAlBi*

Foxworthy, Jeff
American. Actor, Comedian
Star of "The Jeff Foxworthy Show," 1995-97.
b. Sep 6, 1958 in Hapeville, Georgia
Source: *News 96, 96-1*

Foxx, Jamie
American. Actor
Regular cast member on TV show "In Living Color," 1990-94; appeared in film *The Truth About Cats & Dogs,* 1996.

Foxx, Jimmie
[Terrance Stanley Fox]
"Double X"; "The Beast"
American. Baseball Player
Infielder, 1925-44; won AL triple crown, 1933; shares ML record for home runs in season by right-handed hitter, 58, 1932; Hall of Fame, 1951.
b. Oct 22, 1907 in Sudlersville, Maryland
d. Jul 21, 1967 in Miami, Florida
Source: *Ballpl 90; BioIn 14, 15, 16, 17, 18; FacFETw; LegTOT; WebAB 74; WhoProB 73; WhoSpor; WorAlBi*

Foxx, Redd
[John Elroy Sanford]
American. Comedian, Actor
Starred as Fred Sanford in TV series "Sanford and Son," 1972-77, 1980.
b. Dec 9, 1922 in Saint Louis, Missouri
d. Oct 11, 1991 in Hollywood, California
Source: *AfrAmAl 6; AfrAmBi 2; AnObit 1991; BioIn 7, 9, 10, 12, 13, 14, 15, 16; BioNews 74; BkPepl; BlksAmF; CelR; ConAu 89, 135; ConBlB 2; ConTFT 2, 10; CurBio 72, 92N; DcTwCCu 5; DrBlPA, 90; Ebony 1; HalFC 80, 84, 88; InB&W 85; IntMPA 84, 86, 88, 92; JoeFr; LegTOT; LesBEnT 92; NegAl 89; News 92, 92-2; NewYTBE 72; NewYTBS 91; WhAm 10; WhoAm 74, 76, 78, 80, 82, 84, 86, 88; WhoBlA 75, 77, 80, 85, 88, 90, 92, 94N; WhoCom; WhoHol 92, A; WorAl; WorAlBi*

Foy, Eddie
[Edward Fitzgerald]
American. Actor
Starred in vaudeville with children as "Eddie and the Seven Little Foys," 1913-27.
b. Mar 9, 1856 in New York, New York
d. Feb 16, 1928 in Kansas City, Missouri
Source: *AmPS B; BiDAmM; BiDD; BioIn 3, 10, 14; CamGWoT; DcAmB; DcNAA; EncMT; Film 1; FilmgC; LegTOT; NotNAT A, B; OxCThe 67, 83; WebAB 74, 79; WhAm 1; WhoHol B; WhScrn 74, 77; WhThe*

Foy, Eddie, Jr.
American. Actor, Dancer
Portrayed famed father in films; starred in Broadway's *Pajama Game,* 1954.
b. Feb 4, 1905 in New Rochelle, New York
d. Jul 15, 1983 in Woodland Hills, California
Source: *BiE&WWA; BioIn 10, 13; CmpEPM; EncAFC; EncMT; Film 2; FilmEn; FilmgC; ForYSC; HalFC 80, 84, 88; LegTOT; NewYTBS 83; NotNAT; OxCAmT 84; OxCPMus; WhoHol A; WhoThe 72, 77*

Foyle, Christina Agnes Lilian
English. Bookseller
Director, W & G Foyle, Ltd., 1963—; daughter of William.
b. Jan 30, 1911 in London, England
Source: *Au&Wr 71; IntWW 77, 78, 79, 80, 81, 82, 83, 89, 91, 93; WhE&EA; Who 85, 92; WhoWor 74*

Foyle, Gilbert Samuel
English. Bookseller
Founded W & G Foyle, Ltd. bookstore in London with brother William.
b. Mar 9, 1886 in London, England
d. Oct 28, 1971
Source: *BioIn 3, 9; CurBio 54, 72, 72N; WhE&EA*

Foyle, William Alfred
English. Bookseller
Founded W & G Foyle, Ltd. bookstore in London with brother Gilbert.
b. Mar 4, 1885 in London, England
d. Jul 4, 1963 in Maldon, England
Source: *BioIn 2, 3, 6, 14; CurBio 54, 63; DcNaB 1961; GrBr; LngCTC; ObitOF 79; ObitT 1961; WhE&EA*

Foyston, Frank C
Canadian. Hockey Player
Center, Detroit, 1926-28; Hall of Fame, 1958.
b. Feb 2, 1891 in Minesing, Ontario, Canada
d. Jan 24, 1966 in Seattle, Washington
Source: *HocEn; WhoHcky 73*

Foyt, A(nthony) J(oseph Jr.)
American. Auto Racer
One of three drivers to win Indianapolis 500 four times.
b. Jan 16, 1935 in Houston, Texas
Source: *BiDAmSp OS; BioIn 13, 14, 15; BusPN; CelR; CurBio 67; FacFETw; NewYTBS 75, 86; WebAB 74; WhoAm 78, 80, 84, 86, 88, 90; WorAlBi*

Fracastoro, Gerolamo
Italian. Physician
His poem, "Syphilis," 1530, gave name to disease.
b. 1478 in Verona, Italy
d. Aug 8, 1553 in Verona, Italy
Source: *BiESc; CasWL; DcBiPP; DcCathB; DcEuL; DcItL 1; REn; WhDW*

Fracci, Carla
Italian. Dancer
Prima ballerina with La Scala Ballet, 1954-67; American Ballet Theater, 1974-77, 1990.
b. Aug 20, 1936 in Milan, Italy
Source: *BiDD; BioIn 5, 6, 8, 9, 10, 11, 12, 13, 14, 20; CnOxB; CurBio 75; DancEn 78; FacFETw; IntDcB; InWom SUP; WhoAmW 74; WhoEnt 92; WhoWor 74, 76, 82, 87, 89, 91, 93, 95; WorAl; WorAlBi*

Fradon, Dana
American. Cartoonist
Contributor to *New Yorker,* 1950—; known for cartoons satirizing local politics.
b. Apr 14, 1922 in Chicago, Illinois
Source: *BioIn 14; WhoAm 74, 80, 82, 84, 86; WhoAmA 76, 78, 80, 82; WorECar*

Fraenkel, Heinrich
Journalist, Author
Publications include *Hitler, The Man and the Myth,* 1978.
b. Sep 28, 1897, Germany
Source: *Au&Wr 71; BioIn 5; DcLP 87A; IntAu&W 76, 77, 82; Who 74, 82, 83, 85; WrDr 76, 80, 82, 84*

Fragonard, Jean-Honore
French. Artist, Engraver
Painted landscapes, elegant outdoor social affairs in Rococo style: *The Swing,* c. 1766.
b. Apr 5, 1732 in Grasse, France
d. Aug 22, 1806 in Grasse, France
Source: *AtlBL; BioIn 14, 15, 16, 19; DcArts; McGDA; OxCFr; OxDcArt; REn; WebBD 83; WorAl; WorAlBi*

Frahm, Sheila
American. Politician
Rep. senator, KS, 1996; filled remainder of Sen. Bob Dole's term.
b. Mar 22, 1945

Source: *WhoAm 95, 96, 97; WhoAmP 89, 91, 93, 95; WhoAmW 91, 93, 95, 97; WhoMW 92, 93, 96*

Frailberg, Selma
American. Psychoanalyst
Wrote *The Magic Years.*
b. 1919 in Detroit, Michigan
d. Dec 19, 1981 in San Francisco, California
Source: *NewYTBS 81; WhoAmW 75; WhoWorJ 72*

Fraker, William A
American. Filmmaker
Cinematographer for *The Exorcist; Looking for Mr. Goodbar; Sharky's Machine.*
b. 1923 in Los Angeles, California
Source: *BioIn 14, 15; ConTFT 9; HalFC 88; IntMPA 92; VarWW 85; WhoAm 90*

Frampton, Peter Kenneth
American. Singer, Songwriter
Solo artist since 1972; album *Frampton Comes Alive!*, 1976, sold over 12 million copies; member of rock band Humble Pie, 1969-71.
b. Apr 22, 1950 in Beckenham, England
Source: *Baker 84; BioIn 15; BkPepl; ConAu 117; ConMus 3; EncPR&S 74, 89; EncRk 88; FacFETw; HarEnR 86; IlEncRk; NewAmDM; OxCPMus; PenEncP; RkOn 74; WhoAm 86, 90; WhoEnt 92; WorAlBi*

Franca, Celia
English. Dancer, Choreographer
Founded National Ballet of Canada, Toronto, 1951.
b. Jun 25, 1921 in London, England
Source: *BiDD, 87, 89, 91, 93, 95, 97; WhoCan 77, 80, 82, 84; WhoEnt 92; WhoWor 74, 87; WorAl; WorAlBi*

Francaix, Jean
French. Composer, Musician
Works include opera: *La Princesse de Cleves,* 1965.
b. May 23, 1912 in Le Mans, France
Source: *Baker 78, 84, 92; BioIn 3, 8; BriBkM 80; CnOxB; CompSN, SUP; ConCom 92; CpmDNM 80; DancEn 78; IntWW 83, 91; IntWWM 77, 80, 90; MusMk; NewAmDM; NewEOp 71; NewGrDM 80; NewGrDO; NewOxM; OxCMus; OxDcOp; PenDiMP, A; WhoFr 79*

France, Anatole
[Jacques Anatole-Francois Thibault]
French. Author
Wrote *Penguin Island,* 1908; won Nobel Prize, 1921.
b. Apr 16, 1844 in Paris, France
d. Oct 12, 1924 in Tours, France
Source: *AtlBL; BbD; Benet 87, 96; BiD&SB; BioIn 1, 2, 3, 4, 5, 6, 8, 9, 10, 14, 15, 17, 19; CasWL; ClDMEL 47, 80; CyWA 58; DcArts; DcBiA; DcEuL; DcLB 123; DcPup; DcTwCCu 2; Dis&D; EncSF, 93; EncUnb; EncWL 2, 3; EvEuW; FacFETw; GuFrLit 1; LegTOT; LinLib L, S; LngCTC; McGEWB; ModFrL; ModRL; NewC; NewEOp 71; NobelP; Novels; OxCEng 67, 85, 95; OxCFr; PenC EUR; PlP&P; RAdv 14, 13-2; RComWL; REn; RfGWoL 95; ScF&FL 1; ScFEYrs; ScFSB; SJGFanW; SupFW; TwCA, SUP; TwCLC 9; TwCWr; WhDW; WhoNob, 90, 95; WhoTwCL; WhThe; WorAl; WorAlBi*

France, Harry Clinton
American. Journalist, Lecturer
Wrote *Managing Money,* 1966.
b. Jul 17, 1890 in Richmondville, New York
d. Jan 18, 1972 in New York, New York
Source: *BioIn 5, 9; WhAm 5*

Francesca da Rimini
Italian. Noblewoman
Killed by husband upon discovery of affair; subject of famous episode in Dante's *Inferno.*
d. 1285
Source: *BioIn 4, 7, 9, 10; InWom, SUP; NewC; REn*

Francescatti, Zino Rene
French. Musician
Brilliant concertist, 1920s-60s; played Beethoven's violin concerto with orchestra at age 10.
b. Aug 9, 1902 in Marseilles, France
d. Sep 17, 1991 in La Ciotat, France
Source: *Baker 84; BioIn 14; BriBkM 80; CurBio 47, 91N; IntWW 91; NewAmDM; NewGrDM 80; NewYTBS 91; PenDiMP; WhAm 10; WhoAm 86, 90; WhoMus 72; WhoWor 74*

Franceschini, Marcantonio
Italian. Artist
Last leader of Bolognese school; painted large frescoes, ceiling decorations.
b. Apr 5, 1648 in Bologna, Italy
d. Dec 14, 1729 in Bologna, Italy
Source: *BioIn 13; DcBiPP; DcCathB; McGDA; NewCol 75*

Franciosa, Anthony
[Anthony Papaleo]
American. Actor
Star of TV series "Name of the Game," 1968-72; "Matt Helm," 1975-76.
b. Oct 25, 1928 in New York, New York
Source: *BiE&WWA; BioIn 4, 5, 6, 10, 14; ConTFT 3; CurBio 61; FilmEn; FilmgC; GangFlm; HalFC 80, 84, 88; IntMPA 77, 78, 79, 80, 81, 82, 84, 86, 88, 92, 94, 96; LegTOT; MotPP; MovMk; NotNAT; WhoAm 74, 76, 78, 80, 82, 84, 86, 88, 90, 92, 94, 95, 96, 97; WhoEnt 92; WhoHol 92, A, B; WhoWor 74; WorAl; WorAlBi*

Francis, Anne
"The Little Queen of Soap Opera"
American. Actor
Played child roles on radio; was TV detective in "Honey West," 1965-66.
b. Sep 16, 1930 in Ossining, New York
Source: *DcLP 87A; FilmEn; FilmgC; ForYSC; GangFlm; HalFC 80, 84, 88; IntMPA 86, 92; LegTOT; MGM; MotPP; MovMk; RadStar; WhoHol 92, A; WorEFlm; WrDr 76*

Francis, Arlene
[Mrs. Martin Gabel; Arlene Francis Kazanjian]
American. Actor
Best known as panelist on TV game show "What's My Line?," 1950-67.
b. Oct 20, 1908 in Boston, Massachusetts
Source: *BiE&WWA; BioIn 3, 4, 5, 6, 10, 11; CelR 90; ConAu 89; ConTFT 5; CurBio 56; FilmgC; ForWC 70; ForYSC; HalFC 80, 84, 88; IntMPA 77, 80, 86, 92, 94, 96; InWom; LegTOT; LesBEnT, 92; NewYTET; NotNAT; SaTiSS; WhoAm 78, 86; WhoHol 92, A; WhoThe 77; WorAl; WorAlBi*

Francis, Connie
[Concetta Maria Franconero]
American. Singer
Popular, award-winning vocalist, 1950s-60s; made eight gold records; starred in, sang title song for *Where the Boys Are,* 1963.
b. Dec 12, 1938 in Newark, New Jersey
Source: *ASCAP 66, 80; BiDAmM; BioIn 6, 12, 14; ConMus 10; CurBio 62; EncAFC; EncPR&S 89; EncRk 88; EncRkSt; FilmEn; FilmgC; ForYSC; HalFC 80, 84, 88; IntMPA 75, 76, 77, 78, 79, 80, 81, 82, 84, 86, 88, 92, 94, 96; InWom, SUP; LegTOT; MotPP; NewGrDA 86; OxCPMus; PenEncP; RkOn 74; RolSEnR 83; WhoHol 92, A; WhoRock 81; WorAl; WorAlBi*

Francis, Dick
Welsh. Author
Ex-champion steeplechase jockey; wrote horse racing mysteries: *Whip Hand,* 1979; *Break-In,* 1986; won Poe for *Forfeit,* 1969.
b. Oct 31, 1920 in Tenby, Wales
Source: *Au&Arts 5; Au&Wr 71; AuSpks; Benet 87, 96; BestSel 89-3; BioIn 12, 13, 14, 15; CelR 90; CnDBLB 8; ConAu 5NR, 5R, 9NR, 42NR; ConLC 2, 22, 42; ConNov 76, 82, 86, 91, 96; CorpD; CrtSuMy; CurBio 81; CyWA 89; DcLB 87; EncMys; FacFETw; IntAu&W 77; IntWW 91; LegTOT; MajTwCW; Novels; TwCCr&M 80, 85, 91; Who 74, 82, 83, 85, 88, 90, 92, 94; WhoAm 84, 86, 88, 90, 92, 94, 95, 96, 97; WorAl; WorAlBi; WorAu 1970; WrDr 76, 80, 82, 84, 86, 88, 90, 92, 94, 96*

Francis, Emile Percy
"The Cat"
Canadian. Hockey Player, Hockey Executive
Goalie, Black Hawks, 1946-48; Rangers, 1948-52, other NHL teams, 1953-60; pres., general manager, St. Louis, 1978—; coach, St. Louis, 1982; pres., general manager, Hartford, 1983—; Hall of Fame, 1982.

b. Sep 13, 1926 in North Battleford, Saskatchewan, Canada
Source: *ConAu 112; CurBio 68; HocEn; WhoAm 86, 88, 90, 92, 94, 95; WhoE 85, 86, 89, 91, 95; WhoHcky 73; WhoMW 82*

Francis, Freddie
English. Filmmaker, Director
Won Oscar for cinematography of *Sons and Lovers,* 1960.
b. 1917 in London, England
Source: *BioIn 11, 17; ConTFT 8, 15; DcFM; EncEurC; FilmEn; FilmgC; HalFC 80, 84, 88; HorFD; IlWWBF; IntDcF 1-4, 2-4; IntMPA 75, 76, 77, 78, 79, 80, 81, 82, 84, 86, 88, 92, 94, 96; MiSFD 9; VarWW 85; WhoAm 90, 92, 94, 95, 96, 97; WhoEnt 92; WhoHrs 80; WhoWor 91*

Francis, Genie
American. Actor
Played Laura on daytime soap opera "General Hospital," 1977-81.
b. May 26, 1962 in Los Angeles, California
Source: *BioIn 12, 13; ConTFT 14; InWom SUP; LegTOT; VarWW 85*

Francis, James Bicheno
"The Father of Modern Hydraulic Engineering"
English. Engineer
Developed hydraulic turbine.
b. May 18, 1815 in Southleigh, England
d. Sep 18, 1892 in Boston, Massachusetts
Source: *Alli, SUP; AmBi; ApCAB; BiInAmS; BioIn 12; DcAmAu; DcAmB; DcNAA; NatCAB 9; TwCBDA; WhAm HS*

Francis, Kay
[Katherine Gibbs]
American. Actor
Glamorous star of 30s films including *The White Angel;* retired, 1946.
b. Jan 13, 1903 in Oklahoma City, Oklahoma
d. Aug 26, 1968 in New York, New York
Source: *BiDFilm, 94; CmMov; EncAFC; Film 2; FilmEn; FilmgC; InWom SUP; MotPP; MovMk; OxCFilm; ThFT; WhAm 5; WhoHol B; WhScrn 74, 77, 83; WorAlBi; WorEFlm*

Francis, Russ(ell Ross)
American. Football Player
Two-time all-pro tight end, New England, 1975-80, San Francisco, 1982-87.
b. Apr 3, 1953 in Seattle, Washington
Source: *BioIn 10, 12; FootReg 87; LegTOT; WhoAm 82; WorAl*

Francis, Sam(uel Lewis)
American. Artist
Abstract expressionist painter, internationally exhibited.
b. Jun 25, 1923 in San Mateo, California
d. Nov 4, 1994 in Santa Monica, California
Source: *AmArt; BioIn 4, 6, 7, 9, 10, 11, 13, 16, 17, 20, 21; BriEAA; CmCal; ConArt 77, 83, 89, 96; CurBio 73, 95N; DcAmArt; DcArts; DcCAA 71, 77, 88, 94; DcCAr 81; IntWW 74, 75, 76, 77, 78, 79, 80, 81, 82, 83, 89, 91, 93; McGDA; OxCTwCA; OxDcArt; PhDcTCA 77; PrintW 83, 85; WhAm 11; WhoAm 74, 76, 82, 84, 86, 88, 90, 92, 94; WhoAmA 73, 76, 78, 80, 82, 84, 86, 89, 91, 93; WhoWor 74; WorAlBi; WorArt 1950*

Francis, Thomas, Jr.
American. Scientist, Educator
Developed first vaccine effective against influenza, 1930s.
b. Jul 15, 1900 in Gas City, Indiana
d. Oct 1, 1969 in Ann Arbor, Michigan
Source: *BiESc; BioIn 1, 5, 8, 11; DcAmMeB 84; FacFETw; InSci; McGMS 80; ObitOF 79; WhAm 5*

Francis, Trevor
English. Soccer Player
Forward; on loan from English team, played two seasons with Detroit, NASL, 1978-79.
b. Apr 19, 1954 in Plymouth, England
Source: *AmEnS; BioIn 12*

Francisco, Peter
American. Soldier
Served in Continental army under Layfayette, 1777; many anecdotes told about physical strength.
b. 1760?
d. 1831 in Richmond, Virginia
Source: *AmRev; ApCAB; BioIn 11, 12, 20; DcNCBi 2; Drake; EncAR; WhAmRev*

Franciscus, James Grover
American. Actor
Played in TV series "Mr. Novak," 1963-65; "Longstreet," 1971-72.
b. Jan 31, 1934 in Clayton, Missouri
d. Jul 9, 1991 in North Hollywood, California
Source: *ConTFT 3; FilmgC; HalFC 84, 88; IntMPA 86, 88; LesBEnT 92; MotPP; News 92, 92-1; NewYTBS 91; WhAm 10; WhoAm 74, 76, 78, 80, 82, 84, 86, 88; WhoHol A*

Francis I
French. Ruler
King, 1515-47; known for patronizing arts, letters; Renaissance in France occurred during reign.
b. Sep 12, 1494 in Cognac, France
d. Mar 31, 1547 in Rambouillet, France
Source: *BioIn 10; NewCol 75; WebBD 83*

Francis of Assisi, Saint
[Giovanni di Bernardone]
Italian. Religious Leader
Called greatest of all Christian saints; founded Franciscans, 1209; often depicted preaching to birds.
b. 1182 in Assisi, Italy
d. Oct 3, 1226 in Porzivncola, Italy
Source: *BioIn 1, 2, 3, 4, 5, 6, 7, 8, 9, 10, 11, 12, 13, 14, 15, 17, 19, 20; CasWL; Dis&D; EncPaPR 91; EuAu; EvEuW; HisWorL; IlEncMy; LinLib L, S; LuthC 75; McGDA; McGEWB; NewC; RComWL; REn; WorAlBi*

Francis Xavier, Saint
Spanish. Missionary
Served in E Indies, Japan, 1540s-50s; patron saint of Roman Catholic missionaries, who believed missionary should adapt to local customs.
b. 1506 in Pamplona, Spain
d. 1557
Source: *McGEWB; NewC*

Franck, Cesar Auguste
French. Organist, Composer
Notable works include piano pieces, oratorios, "Symphony in D-minor," 1888.
b. Dec 10, 1822 in Liege, Belgium
d. Nov 8, 1890 in Paris, France
Source: *AtlBL; Baker 84; Benet 87, 96; BioIn 1, 2, 3, 4, 5, 6, 7, 8, 9, 12, 13; DcArts; LegTOT; LuthC 75; MusMk; NewGrDM 80; OxCFr; OxCMus; REn; WhDW; WorAl*

Franck, James
American. Physicist, Educator
Shared 1925 Nobel Prize; studied effect of an electron upon an atom.
b. Aug 26, 1882 in Hamburg, Germany
d. May 21, 1964 in Gottingen, Germany
Source: *AsBiEn; BiESc; BioIn 3, 4, 5, 6, 7, 9, 14, 15, 20; CamDcSc; CurBio 57, 64; DcAmB S7; DcScB; FacFETw; InSci; LarDcSc; LegTOT; LinLib S; McGMS 80; NobelP; NotTwCS; ObitT 1961; WhAm 4; WhoNob, 90, 95; WorAl; WorAlBi*

Franco
[L'Okanga La Ndju Pene Luambo Makladi]
Zairean. Bandleader, Musician
One of Africa's most popular, influential musicians; created soukous style, a fusion of Afro-Cuban music with jazz, gospel, and African rhythms.
b. Jul 6, 1938? in Suna Bata, Zaire
d. Oct 12, 1989 in Brussels, Belgium
Source: *BioIn 16; FacFETw; NewYTBS 89; PenEncP*

Franco, Francisco
Spanish. Political Leader
Dictator who overthrew republican opposition, headed oppressive regime, 1936-75.
b. Dec 4, 1892 in El Ferrol, Spain
d. Nov 20, 1975 in Madrid, Spain

Source: *BioIn 1, 2, 3, 4, 5, 6, 7, 8, 9, 10, 11, 12, 13, 14, 15, 16, 17, 19, 20, 21; BioNews 75; CurBio 42, 54, 76N; DcHiB; DcPol; DcTwHis; EncCW; EncTR 91; FacFETw; HisEWW; HisWorL; LegTOT; LinLib S; McGEWB; NewYTBS 75; PolLCWE; REn; WhDW; WhoMilH 76; WorAl; WorAlBi*

Franey, Pierre
American. Chef
Former food columnist for the *New York Times;* wrote many cookbooks including *The New York Times Sixty-Minute Gourmet,* 1979.
b. Jan 13, 1921 in Tonnerre, France
d. Oct 15, 1996 in Southampton, England
Source: *ConAu 15NR, 89, 154; NewYTBS 27*

Frank, Anne
German. Diarist
Diary depicted life as Jew during WW II; became best-seller, 1952.
b. Jun 12, 1929 in Frankfurt am Main, Germany
d. Mar 1945 in Bergen-Belsen, Germany
Source: *Au&Arts 12; Benet 87, 96; BioIn 2, 3, 4, 5, 7, 8, 10, 11, 12, 13, 14, 15, 16, 17, 18, 19, 20, 21; BlmGWL; ConAu 113, 133; ConHero 1; DcArts; EncTR, 91; EncWB; FacFETw; HerW, 84; HisEWW; InWom, SUP; JeHun; LegTOT; LinLib L; MajTwCW; RAdv 13-3; REn; SmATA 42; TwCLC 17; TwCWr; WhWW-II; WorAl; WorAlBi; WorLitC*

Frank, Anthony Melchior
American. Banker, Government Official
Postmaster General, 1988-1992.
b. May 21, 1931 in Berlin, Germany
Source: *BioIn 16; CurBio 91; Dun&B 88; News 92; NewYTBS 88; St&PR 87; WhoAm 74, 76, 78, 80, 82, 88, 90, 92, 94, 95, 96, 97; WhoFI 74, 77, 79, 81, 83, 85, 87, 89, 94, 96; WhoWest 84*

Frank, Barney
American. Politician
Dem. congressman from MA, 1981—; gay rights advocate.
b. Mar 31, 1940 in Bayonne, New Jersey
Source: *AlmAP 82, 84, 88, 92, 96; BiDrUSC 89; BioIn 13, 15, 16; CngDr 81, 83, 85, 87, 89, 91, 93, 95; CurBio 95; GayLesB; LegTOT; News 89, 89-2; PolsAm 84; WhoAm 82, 84, 86, 88, 90, 92, 94, 95, 96, 97; WhoAmJ 80; WhoAmP 73, 75, 77, 79, 81, 83, 85, 87, 89, 91, 93, 95; WhoE 79, 81, 83, 85, 86, 89, 91, 93, 95, 97; WhoEmL 87; WhoGov 77*

Frank, Billy, Jr.
American. Political Activist
Worked to settle fishing conflicts in the American northwest; awarded the Albert Schweitzer Award for Humanitarianism, 1992.
b. 1931 in Washington
Source: *BioIn 21; EncNAB; NotNaAm*

Frank, Bruno
German. Author
Best known for his short novels including *The Golden Man,* 1952.
b. Jun 13, 1887 in Stuttgart, Germany
d. Jun 20, 1945 in Beverly Hills, California
Source: *AmAu&B; BiGAW; BioIn 1, 4, 18; ClDMEL 47; CnMD; DcLB 118; EncWL, 2, 3; EncWT; LiExTwC; McGEWD 72, 84; ModGL; ModWD; NotNAT B; ObitOF 79; OxCGer 76, 86; OxCThe 67, 83; REn; TwCA, SUP; WhThe*

Frank, Clinton Edward
American. Football Player
All-America quarterback, Yale, 1935-37; won Heisman Trophy, 1937.
b. Sep 13, 1915 in Saint Louis, Missouri
d. Jul 7, 1992 in Evanston, Illinois
Source: *BiDAmSp FB; BioIn 8, 9, 10, 14; St&PR 84, 87; WhAm 11; WhoAdv 90; WhoAm 74, 76, 78, 80, 82, 84, 86, 88, 90, 92; WhoFI 74, 75; WhoFtbl 74; WhoMW 76, 78*

Frank, Gerold
American. Author
Biographies include *Beloved Infidel,* 1958; *Judy,* 1975.
b. 1907 in Cleveland, Ohio
Source: *Au&Wr 71; BioIn 5, 7, 8, 9; ConAu 109; HalFC 84, 88; IntAu&W 76; LiJour; WhoAm 74, 76, 78, 80, 82, 84, 86, 88, 90, 92, 94, 95; WhoUSWr 88; WhoWor 80, 82, 84, 87, 89; WhoWrEP 89, 92; WorAl*

Frank, Hans
German. Government Official
Hitler's head of programing, 1939 to war's end; hung for war crimes.
b. May 3, 1900 in Karlsruhe, Germany
d. Oct 16, 1946 in Nuremberg, Germany
Source: *BiDExR; BioIn 1, 8, 14, 16, 17, 18, 20; CurBio 41, 46; Dis&D; EncTR, 91; HisEWW; ObitOF 79; WhWW-II*

Frank, Ilya Mikaylovich
Russian. Physicist
Shared Nobel Prize in physics, 1958, for studies on Cherenkov radiation.
b. Oct 23, 1908 in Saint Petersburg, Russia
d. Jun 22, 1990 in Moscow, Union of Soviet Socialist Republics
Source: *BiDSovU; BiESc; IntWW 83, 91N; McGMS 80; NewYTBS 90; NobelP; Who 83, 90; WhoNob, 90, 95; WhoWor 82, 89; WorAl; WorAlBi*

Frank, Jerome David
American. Psychiatrist
Writings include *Sanity and Survival,* 1967.
b. May 30, 1909 in New York, New York
Source: *AmMWSc 73S, 76P; BioIn 15; ConAu 3NR, 5R; WhoAm 74, 76, 78, 80, 82, 84, 86, 88, 90, 92, 94, 95, 96, 97; WhoAtom 77; WhoE 74, 93, 95; WhoMedH; WhoWorJ 72*

Frank, Johann Peter
German. Physician
Physician to Czar Alexander I, 1805-08; founded science of public health.
b. Mar 14, 1745 in Rodalben, Germany
d. Apr 24, 1821 in Vienna, Austria
Source: *BiHiMed; BioIn 5, 6, 9, 11; CopCroC; InSci; WebBD 83*

Frank, Robert
Canadian. Photographer, Filmmaker
Winner of Guggenheim fellowship, 1955 and 1956; won first prize at San Francisco Film Festival, 1959.
b. Nov 9, 1924 in Zurich, Switzerland
Source: *BioIn 15, 16, 20, 21; BriEAA; ConPhot 82, 88, 95; DcAmArt; DcArts; DcCAr 81; DcTwCCu 1; ICPEnP; MacBEP; MiSFD 9; News 95, 95-2; WorEFlm*

Frank, Waldo
American. Author
Included in his works is novel *The Bridegroom Cometh,* 1939.
b. Aug 25, 1889 in Long Branch, New Jersey
d. Jan 9, 1967 in White Plains, New York
Source: *AmAu&B; AmNov; BenetAL 91; BiDAmLf; CamGLE; CamHAL; CnDAL; ConAmA; ConAmL; ConAu 93; CurBio 40, 67; DcLB 9, 63; DcLEL; EncAL; GrWrEL N; JeAmFiW; LinLib L; ModAL; Novels; ObitOF 79; OxCAmL 65, 83; PenC AM; REn; REnAL; RfGAmL 87; ScF&FL 1; TwCA, SUP; WhAm 4; WhE&EA; WhNAA*

Frankau, Gilbert
English. Author
Best known for novel *World Without End,* 1943.
b. Apr 21, 1884 in London, England
d. Nov 4, 1952 in Hove, England
Source: *BioIn 3, 4, 14; ChhPo S1, S2, S3; DcLEL; DcNaB 1951; EncMys; EncSF, 93; EngPo; EvLB; LngCTC; NewC; NewCBEL; ObitOF 79; ObitT 1951; REn; ScF&FL 1; TwCA, SUP; TwCRGW; TwCRHW 90, 94; WhE&EA; WhLit; WhoLA*

Frankau, Pamela
[Mrs. Eliot Naylor]
English. Author
Popular novels include *Winged Horse,* 1953; *The Bridge,* 1957.
b. Jan 8, 1908 in London, England
d. Jun 8, 1967 in Hampstead, England
Source: *AmAu&B; AmWomWr; BioIn 1, 4, 5, 6, 7, 8, 12, 16; CathA 1930; ConAu 25R; DcLEL; EncBrWW; EvLB; FemiCLE; InWom, SUP; LngCTC; NewC; Novels; PenC ENG; PenNWW A; REn; RGTwCWr; ScF&FL 1; TwCA, SUP; TwCWr; WhAm 4; WhLit*

Frankel, Charles
American. Government Official
Philosophy professor; Johnson's assistant secretary of State, 1965-67; resigned to protest Vietnam War.

b. Dec 13, 1917 in New York, New York
d. May 10, 1979 in Bedford Hills, New York
Source: *AmAu&B; Au&Wr 71; BioIn 4, 7, 12, 14; ConAu 4NR, 5R, 89; CurBio 66, 79, 79N; DrAS 74P, 78P; NewYTBS 79; PeoHis; WhAm 7; WhoAm 74, 76, 78; WhoAmP 73, 75, 77; WhoE 74; WhoWorJ 72, 78*

Frankel, Emily
American. Dancer, Choreographer
Performances from 1950-73 include "Electra"; "Four Seasons."
b. 1930 in New York, New York
Source: *BiDD; BioIn 9; CnOxB*

Frankel, Gene
American. Director
Won Obies for *Volpone,* 1958; *Machinal,* 1960.
b. Dec 23, 1923 in New York, New York
Source: *CamGWoT; ConTFT 5; NotNAT; VarWW 85; WhoAm 84, 86, 88, 90, 92, 94, 95, 96, 97; WhoEnt 92; WhoThe 72, 77, 81; WhoWor 97*

Frankel, Max
American. Journalist
Exec. editor *NY Times,* 1986-94; won Pulitzer for international reporting, 1973.
b. Apr 3, 1930 in Gera, Germany
Source: *BioIn 9, 10, 15, 16, 20; ConAu 65; CurBio 87; EncTwCJ; IntAu&W 89, 91, 93; IntWW 89, 91, 93; JrnUS; WhoAm 74, 76, 78, 80, 82, 84, 86, 88, 90, 92, 94, 95, 96, 97; WhoAmJ 80; WhoE 89, 91, 93; WhoSSW 73; WhoUSWr 88; WhoWor 95, 96, 97; WhoWorJ 72, 78; WhoWrEP 89, 92, 95; WorAlBi*

Franken, Al
American. Actor
Cast regular on TV show "Saturday Night Live," 1979-80, 1988—; plays Stuart Smalley, member of several 12-step groups; wrote *Rush Limbaugh is a Big Fat Idiot and Other Observations,* 1995.
b. c. 1952 in Minneapolis, Minnesota
Source: *News 96, 96-3*

Franken, Rose
American. Author, Dramatist
Wrote series of *Claudia* stories, 1939-46, which formed basis for hit play, film, *Claudia,* 1941, 1943.
b. Dec 28, 1898 in Gainesville, Texas
d. Jun 22, 1988 in Tucson, Arizona
Source: *AmAu&B; AmNov; AmWomWr; Au&Wr 71; BiE&WWA; CnMD; CurBio 47; IntAu&W 76, 77; InWom; ModWD; NotNAT; PenNWW A; REn; REnAL; TwCA, SUP; Who 74; WhoAmW 58*

Frankenheimer, John Michael
American. Director
Began career in TV; directed over 125 TV plays; films include *Birdman of Alcatraz,* 1961.
b. Feb 19, 1930 in Malba, New York
Source: *BiDFilm; BioIn 13, 14, 16; BlueB 76; ConTFT 5; CurBio 64; DcFM; FacFETw; FilmgC; HalFC 84, 88; IntDcF 2-2; IntMPA 86, 92; IntWW 91, 93; LesBEnT 92; MovMk; NewYTET; OxCFilm; WhoAm 74, 76, 78, 80, 82, 84, 86, 88, 90, 92, 94, 95, 96, 97; WhoEnt 92; WhoWor 74; WorAlBi; WorEFlm; WorFDir 2*

Frankenstein, Alfred Victor
American. Critic
Music, art critic, *San Francisco Chronicle,* 1934-65; curator, author of books on American art.
b. Oct 5, 1906 in Chicago, Illinois
d. Jun 22, 1981 in San Francisco, California
Source: *AmAu&B; Baker 78, 92; ConAu 1R, 2NR, 102, 104; DrAS 74H, 78H; WhAmArt 85; WhoAm 74, 76, 78, 80; WhoAmA 73, 76, 78, 80, 82N, 84N, 86N, 89N, 91N, 93N; WhoMus 72; WhoWest 74; WhoWor 74*

Frankenthaler, Helen
[Mrs. Robert Motherwell]
American. Artist
Abstract expressionist; had numerous one-woman shows since 1950s.
b. Dec 12, 1928 in New York, New York
Source: *AmArt; AmCulL; BiDWomA; BioAmW; BioIn 4, 5, 6, 7, 8, 9, 10, 11, 12, 13, 14, 16, 19, 20; BlueB 76; BriEAA; CelR, 90; CenC; ConArt 77, 83, 89, 96; ContDcW 89; CurBio 66; DcAmArt; DcArts; DcCAA 71, 77, 88, 94; DcCAr 81; DcTwCCu 1; EncWHA; FacFETw; GoodHs; GrLiveH; IntDcWB; IntWW 74, 75, 76, 77, 78, 79, 80, 81, 82, 83, 89, 91, 93; InWom, SUP; LibW; McGDA; McGEWB; News 90, 90-1; NewYTBS 89; NorAmWA; OxCTwCA; OxDcArt; PhDcTCA 77; PrintW 83, 85; WhoAm 76, 78, 80, 82, 84, 86, 88, 90, 92, 94, 95, 96; WhoAmA 73, 76, 78, 80, 82, 84, 86, 89, 91, 93; WhoAmW 58, 61, 64, 66, 68, 70, 72, 74, 75, 81, 83, 85, 87, 89, 91, 93, 95, 97; WhoArt 80, 82, 84, 96; WhoE 85; WhoWor 74; WomArt; WorAl; WorAlBi; WorArt 1950*

Frankfurter, Alfred Moritz
American. Editor, Critic
Editor, *Art News,* 1936-65.
b. Oct 4, 1906 in Chicago, Illinois
d. May 12, 1965 in Jerusalem, Israel
Source: *BioIn 7; DcAmB S7*

Frankfurter, Felix
American. Supreme Court Justice
Associate justice, 1939-62; prominent advocate of judicial self-restraint.
b. Nov 15, 1882 in Vienna, Austria
d. Feb 22, 1965 in Washington, District of Columbia
Source: *AmAu&B; AmDec 1940; AmPolLe; AmRef; Benet 87; BiDFedJ; BioIn 1, 2, 3, 4, 5, 6, 7, 8, 9, 10, 11, 12, 13, 14, 15, 16, 17, 18, 20; ConAu 124; CopCroC; CurBio 41, 57, 65; DcAmB S7; DcAmSR; DcLEL; EncAB-H 1974, 1996; FacFETw; JeAmHC; LegTOT; LinLib L, S; McGEWB; MorMA; OxCAmH; OxCAmL 65, 83, 95; OxCLaw; OxCSupC; PolProf E, K, T; RComAH; REn; REnAL; SupCtJu; ThTwC 87; WebAB 74, 79; WebBD 83; WhAm 4; WhLit; WhNAA; WorAl; WorAlBi*

Frankie Goes to Hollywood
[Peter Gill; Holly Johnson; Brian Nash; Mark O'Toole; Paul Rutherford]
British. Music Group
Formed 1981; rock/disco hits include "Relax," 1983; "Two Tribes," 1984.
Source: *BioIn 14; EncRk 88; EncRkSt; HarEnR 86; PenEncP; RkOn 85; WhoRocM 82*

Frankl, Viktor E(mil)
Austrian. Psychiatrist, Author
Originator of school of logotherapy who wrote *Man's Search for Meaning,* 1962.
b. Mar 26, 1905 in Vienna, Austria
Source: *ConAu 65; IntMed 80; RAdv 13-5; WhoAm 86, 88; WhoWor 74, 76; WhoWorJ 72*

Franklin, Aretha
"Queen of Soul"
American. Singer
Motown star; hits include "Respect," 1967; "You Make Me Feel Like a Natural Woman," 1967; "Who's Zoomin' Who," 1985; Grammy Award winner, 1967-74 for best female rhythm and blues vocal.
b. Mar 25, 1942 in Memphis, Tennessee
Source: *AfrAmAl 6; AfrAmBi 1; Baker 78, 84, 92; BiDAfM; BiDAmM; BiDJaz; BioIn 6, 8, 9, 10, 11, 12, 14, 15, 16; BkPepl; BlkWAm; CelR, 90; CivR 74; ConBlB 11; ConMus 2, 17; ContDcW 89; CurBio 68, 92; DcArts; DcTwCCu 1, 5; DrBlPA, 90; Ebony 1; EncJzS; EncPR&S 89; EncRk 88; EncRkSt; GrLiveH; HarEnR 86; HerW, 84; IlEncBM 82; IlEncRk; InB&W 80; IntDcWB; IntWW 89, 91, 93; InWom SUP; LegTOT; NegAl 76, 83, 89; NewAmDM; NewGrDA 86; NewYTBS 87; NotBlAW 1; OxCPMus; PenEncP; RolSEnR 83; SoulM; WhoAfA 96; WhoAm 74, 76, 78, 80, 82, 84, 86, 88, 90, 92, 94, 95, 96, 97; WhoAmW 70, 72, 74, 81, 91, 93, 95, 97; WhoBlA 75, 77, 80, 85, 88, 90, 92, 94; WhoHol 92; WhoRock 81; WorAl; WorAlBi*

Franklin, Benjamin
[Richard Saunders]
American. Statesman, Scientist, Author
Published *Poor Richard's Almanack,* 1732-57; invented lightning rod, bifocal glasses; helped draft

Declaration of Independence, Constitution.
b. Jan 17, 1706 in Boston, Massachusetts
d. Apr 17, 1790 in Philadelphia, Pennsylvania
Source: *ABCMeAm; Alli; AmAu; AmAu&B; AmBi; AmOrN; AmPolLe; AmRev; AmWr; AmWrBE; ApCAB; AsBiEn; AtlBL; Baker 78, 84, 92; BbD; Benet 87, 96; BenetAL 91; BiAUS; BiDAmEd; BiDAmJo; BiDAmS; BiDAmSp BK; BiD&SB; BiDPsy; BiDrAC; BiDrACR; BiDrUSC 89; BiESc; BiInAmS; BioIn 1, 2, 3, 4, 5, 6, 7, 8, 9, 10, 11, 12, 13, 14, 15, 16, 17, 18, 19, 20, 21; BlkwCE; BlkwEAR; BriEAA; CamDcSc; CamGEL; CamGLE; CamHAL; CasWL; ChhPo, S1, S2, S3; CmFrR; CnDAL; ColARen; CopCroC; CrtT 3, 4; CyAG; CyAL 1; CyEd; CyWA 58; DcAmAu; DcAmB; DcAmC; DcAmDH 80, 89; DcAmLiB; DcAmMeB; DcAmSR; DcBiPP; DcEnL; DcInv; DcLB 24, 43, 73; DcLEL; DcNAA; DcScB; Dis&D; Drake; EncAAH; EncAB-H 1974, 1996; EncAI&E; EncAJ; EncAR; EncCRAm; EncEnl; EncNAB; EncO&P 1S1, 2, 3; EncSPD; EncUnb; EvLB; GolEC; HarEnUS; HisDBrE; HisWorL; InSci; JrnUS; LarDcSc; LegTOT; LinLib L; LitC 25; MagSAmL; McGEWB; MemAm; MouLC 2; NamesHP; NatCAB 1; NewAmDM; NewC; NewCBEL; NewGrDA 86; NewGrDM 80; NewYHSD; OxCAmH; OxCAmL 65, 83, 95; OxCChes 84; OxCEng 67, 85, 95; OxCMed 86; OxCMus; OxCPhil; PenC AM; PeoHis; RAdv 14, 13-3, 13-5; RComAH; RComWL; REn; REnAL; REnAW; RfGAmL 87, 94; TwCBDA; TwoTYeD; WebAB 74, 79; WebE&AL; WhAm HS; WhAmP; WhAmRev; WhDW; WhNaAH; WhoEc 81, 86; WorAl; WorAlBi; WorInv; WorScD*

Franklin, Bonnie Gail
American. Actor, Dancer
Starred on Broadway in *Applause*, 1970-71; TV series "One Day at a Time," 1 975-84.
b. Jan 6, 1944 in Santa Monica, California
Source: *BioIn 12; ConTFT 7; IntMPA 92; InWom SUP; NewYTBS 80; VarWW 85; WhoAm 78, 80, 82, 84, 86, 88, 90, 92, 94, 95, 96, 97; WhoAmW 79, 81, 83; WhoHol A; WhoRocM 82; WorAl; WorAlBi*

Franklin, Carl
American. Filmmaker
Directed *Full Fathom Five*, 1990; *Devil in a Blue Dress*, 1995.
b. c. 1949 in Richmond, California
Source: *ConBlB 11*

Franklin, Frederic
English. Dancer
With the Monte Carlo Ballet Russe; partner to Alicia Markova, 1937.
b. Jun 13, 1914 in Liverpool, England
Source: *BiDD; BioIn 3, 10, 13, 14; CnOxB; CurBio 43; DancEn 78; IntDcB; WhoAm 74, 76; WhoMW 86*

Franklin, Hardy R.
American. Librarian
President, American Library Association, 1993-94; established a committee to recognize the most effective initiatives established to serve youth in libraries.
b. May 9, 1929 in Rome, Georgia
Source: *BioIn 10, 18; ConBlB 9; WhoAfA 96; WhoAm 78, 80, 82, 88, 92, 95, 96, 97; WhoBlA 75, 77, 80, 85, 94; WhoE 79, 81, 85, 86, 93; WhoLibI 82; WhoLibS 66; WhoWor 96, 97*

Franklin, Irene
American. Actor, Songwriter
Performed on stage in *Sweet Adeline; Merrily We Roll Along.*
b. Jun 13, 1876 in New York, New York
d. Jun 16, 1941 in Englewood, New Jersey
Source: *BioIn 15; CurBio 41; EncVaud; FunnyW; InWom; NotNAT B; OxCAmT 84; WhoCom; WhoHol B; WhScrn 77, 83; WhThe*

Franklin, John, Sir
English. Explorer
Died in search of Northwest Passage, 1845; quest for relics and diaries continues today.
b. Apr 16, 1786 in Spilsby, England
d. Jun 11, 1847, Arctic
Source: *Alli; ApCAB; BioIn 1, 2, 3, 4, 5, 6, 7, 8, 9, 11, 15, 17, 18, 19, 20, 21; BritAu 19; CelCen; DcBiPP; DcCanB 7; DcLB 99; DcNaB; Drake; Expl 93; LinLib S; MacDCB 78; McGEWB; NewC; NewCBEL; OxCAusL; OxCCan; OxCEng 67, 85, 95; OxCShps; WebBD 83; WhDW; WhWE; WorAlBi*

Franklin, John Hope
American. Educator, Historian
History professor, various colleges and universities, 1936-1985; wrote *From Slavery to Freedom: A History of Negro Americans*, 1947.
b. Jan 2, 1915 in Rentiesville, Oklahoma
Source: *AfrAmAl 6; AfrAmBi 2; AmAu&B; AmSocL; BioIn 5, 6, 8, 9, 11, 12, 13, 14, 17, 19, 20, 21; BlkWr 1, 2; BlkWrNE; BlueB 76; ConAu 1NR, 1R, 3NR, 5R, 26NR; ConBlB 5; DcLEL 1940; DrAS 74H, 78H, 82H; Ebony 1; EncAACR; EncAAH; EncAB-H 1996; EncSoH; FacFETw; InB&W 80, 85; IntAu&W 82, 89, 91, 93; IntWW 89, 91, 93; LinLib L; LivgBAA; NegAl 76, 83, 89; RAdv 14, 13-3; SchCGBL; SelBAAf; SelBAAu; WebAB 74, 79; WhoAfA 96; WhoAm 74, 76, 78, 80, 82, 84, 86, 88, 90, 92, 94, 95, 96, 97; WhoBlA 75, 77, 80, 85, 88, 90, 92, 94; WhoSSW 97; WhoUSWr 88; WhoWor 74, 78, 80, 82, 84, 87; WhoWrEP 89, 92, 95; WorAu 1975; WrDr 76, 80*

Franklin, Joseph Paul
[James Clayton Vaughan, Jr.]
American. Murderer
Arrested for killing eight blacks, wounding National Urban League pres. Vernon Jordan, 1980.
b. 1950?
Source: *BioIn 12*

Franklin, Melvin
[The Temptations; David English]
American. Singer
Founding member of The Temptations; hits include "My Girl," 1965.
b. Oct 12, 1942 in Montgomery, Alabama
d. Feb 23, 1995 in Los Angeles, California
Source: *BioIn 20, 21; News 95, 95-3; RolSEnR 83; WhoAfA 96; WhoRocM 82*

Franklin, Miles
[Stella Maria Sarah Franklin]
"Brent of Bin Bin"
Australian. Author
Best known work is autobiographical *My Brilliant Career,* written at 16.
b. Oct 14, 1879 in Talbingo, Australia
d. Sep 19, 1954 in Sydney, Australia
Source: *AuWomWr; Benet 87; BioIn 1, 6, 8, 9, 12, 13, 16, 18, 20; BlmGWL; CamGLE; CasWL; ConAu 104; ContDcW 89; FacFETw; FemiCLE; IntDcWB; LegTOT; LiExTwC; McGEWB; ModCmwL; ModFrL; ModWoWr; OxCAusL; RAdv 13-1; RfGEnL 91; TwCLC 7; TwCWr; WorAu 1975*

Franklin, Pamela
English. Actor
Films include *The Innocents*, 1961; *David Copperfield*, 1969.
b. Feb 4, 1950 in Tokyo, Japan
Source: *BioIn 15, 16; ConTFT 8; FilmEn; FilmgC; ForYSC; HalFC 84, 88; IntMPA 75, 76, 77, 78, 79, 80, 81, 82, 84, 86, 88, 92, 94, 96; WhoHol A; WhoSSW 91*

Franklin, William Buel
American. Military Leader
Union major general, relieved of his command; held responsible for defeat at Fredericksburg, 1862.
b. Feb 27, 1823 in York, Pennsylvania
d. Mar 8, 1903 in Hartford, Connecticut
Source: *AmBi; ApCAB; BioIn 1, 7; CivWDc; DcAmB; HarEnUS; NatCAB 4; TwCBDA; WebAMB; WhAm 1; WhCiWar*

Frankovich, Mike J
American. Producer
With Columbia Pictures, 1955-67; independent, 1967—; films include *Cactus Flower*, 1969; *Butterflies Are Free*, 1972.
b. Sep 29, 1910 in Bisbee, Arizona
d. Jan 1, 1992 in Los Angeles, California
Source: *FilmgC; HalFC 84, 88; IntMPA 86, 92; WhoAm 86, 90; WhoEnt 92; WhoHol A; WhoWest 78; WorEFlm*

Franks, Gary A
American. Politician
First black congressman from CT, 1990—; first black Repub. to serve in the US House of Representatives since 1935.
b. Feb 9, 1953 in Waterbury, Connecticut

Franks, Oliver (Shewell), Sir
English. Government Official
British Ambassador to US, 1948-52; wrote *American Impressions,* 1954.
b. Feb 16, 1905 in Birmingham, England
d. Oct 15, 1992 in Oxford, England
Source: *BioIn 18, 19; BlueB 76; CurBio 48, 93N; DcTwBBL; DcTwHis; HisDcKW; IntWW 74, 81; IntYB 81; NewC; NewYTBS 92; Who 74; WhoWor 74, 76, 78*

Frann, Mary
[Mary Luecke]
American. Actor
Played Joanna Louden in TV series "Newhart," 1982-90.
b. Feb 27, 1943 in Saint Louis, Missouri
Source: *BioIn 13, 14, 15, 16; ConTFT 4; LegTOT; VarWW 85; WhoAm 88; WhoAmW 91; WhoEnt 92*

Franz, Arthur
American. Actor
Films include *Jungle Patrol,* 1948; *Member of the Wedding,* 1952.
b. Feb 29, 1920 in Perth Amboy, New Jersey
Source: *BioIn 17, 78, 79, 80, 81, 82, 84, 86, 88, 92, 94, 96; ItaFilm; LegTOT; VarWW 85; Vers B; WhoHol 92, A; WhoHrs 80*

Franz, Dennis
[Dennis Schlachta]
American. Actor
Appears in TV's "NYPD Blue," 1994—
.
b. Oct 28, 1944 in Maywood, Illinois
Source: *BioIn 20, 21; ConTFT 7, 14; CurBio 95; IntMPA 96; LegTOT; News 95, 95-2; WhoAm 96, 97; WhoHol 92*

Franz, Eduard
American. Actor
Original member of Provincetown Players; appeared in films *Twilight Zone-The Movie,* 1983; *The Ten Commandments,* 1956.
b. Oct 31, 1902 in Milwaukee, Wisconsin
d. Feb 10, 1983 in Los Angeles, California
Source: *FilmEn; ForYSC; HalFC 80, 84, 88; MotPP; VarWW 85; WhoHol A; WhoThe 77*

Franz Ferdinand
Austrian. Political Leader
Archduke, whose assassination, 1914, led to outbreak of WW I.
b. Dec 18, 1863 in Graz, Austria
d. Jun 28, 1914 in Sarajevo, Yugoslavia
Source: *BioIn 14; FacFETw; NewCol 75; OxCGer 76, 86; REn; WebBD 83*

Franz Joseph I
Austrian. Ruler
Emperor of Austria, 1848-1916, king of Hungary, 1867-1916, whose reign was last great age of Austrian political, cultural preeminence.
b. Aug 18, 1830 in Vienna, Austria
d. Nov 21, 1916 in Vienna, Austria
Source: *BioIn 2, 3, 6, 7, 8, 10; DcCathB; NewCol 75; OxCGer 76; REn*

Franz Joseph II
[Prince of Liechtenstein]
Liechtenstein. Ruler
Head of State, 1938-84; oversaw country develop from poor, rural to wealthy tax, banking haven; passed power to son, Crown Prince Hans Adam.
b. Aug 16, 1906, Liechtenstein
d. Nov 13, 1989 in Vaduz, Liechtenstein
Source: *IntWW 91*

Frasconi, Antonio
American. Artist, Author
Woodcut artist, illustrations in children's books: *See and Say,* 1955; designed commemorative stamps, 1963, 1968.
b. Apr 28, 1919 in Montevideo, Uruguay
Source: *AmAu&B; AnCL; AuBYP 2, 3; BioIn 2, 3, 4, 5, 6, 7, 8, 9, 10, 11, 13, 14, 16, 19, 20, 21; BriEAA; ChlBkCr; ChsFB I; ConAu 1NR, 1R, 48NR; CurBio 72; DcCAA 71, 77, 88, 94; IlsCB 1946, 1957; MajAI; McGDA; OxCTwCA; SmATA 6, 11AS, 53; ThrBJA; WhoAm 74, 76, 78, 80, 82, 84; WhoAmA 73, 76, 78, 80, 82, 84, 89, 91, 93; WhoE 74, 93; WhoGrA 62, 82; WhoWor 74*

Fraser, Antonia Pakenham, Lady
English. Author
Wrote *Mary Queen of Scots,* 1969; mysteries featuring Jemima Shore.
b. Aug 27, 1932 in London, England
Source: *ArtclWW 2; Benet 87; BioIn 13, 14, 15, 16; CelR 90; ConAu 44NR, 85; ConLC 32; CrtSuMy; CurBio 74; EncBrWW; EncWB; FemiCLE; IntWW 83, 91; InWom SUP; MajTwCW; NewYTBS 79, 84; OxCEng 85, 95; SmATA 32; ThrtnMM; TwCCr&M 91; Who 85, 92; WhoAm 90; WorAlBi; WrDr 86, 92*

Fraser, Brad
Canadian. Dramatist, Director
Controversial playwright who uses onstage nudity, simulated sex, and profanity; wrote *Unidentified Human Remains,* 1990, winner of the Floyd S. Chalmers Award for best new Canadian play.
b. Jun 28, 1959 in Edmonton, Alberta, Canada
Source: *CanWW 31; CurBio 95; WhoAm 97*

Fraser, Bruce Austin, Sir
[Lord Fraser of North Cape]
"Tubby"
English. Naval Officer
Commander, British Home Fleet, WW II; credited with sinking German battleship *Scharnhorst,* 1943.
b. Feb 5, 1888 in Acton, England
d. Feb 12, 1981 in London, England
Source: *AnObit 1981; BioIn 1; CurBio 43, 81, 81N; DcNaB 1981; Who 74; WhWW-II*

Fraser, Dawn
Australian. Swimmer
Only swimmer to win Olympic medal in same event three successive Olympics—freestyle in 1956, 1960, 1964.
b. Sep 4, 1937 in Balmain, Australia
Source: *BioIn 6, 7, 10, 12, 17; ContDcW 89; GoodHs; IntDcWB; InWom SUP; LegTOT; WomFir; WorAl; WorAlBi*

Fraser, Donald Mackay
American. Politician
Dem. mayor of Minneapolis, 1980-93.
b. Feb 20, 1924 in Minneapolis, Minnesota
Source: *AlmAP 78; WhoMW 74, 76, 78, 80, 82, 84, 86, 88, 90, 92, 93, 96*

Fraser, Douglas Andrew
American. Labor Union Official
Pres., UAW, 1977-83.
b. Dec 18, 1916 in Glasgow, Scotland
Source: *BiDAmL; BioIn 11, 12, 13, 14, 15, 17; BusPN; EncABHB 5; IntWW 78, 79, 80, 81, 82, 83, 89, 91, 93; NatCAB 63N; NewYTBS 77; Ward 77C; WhoAm 78, 80, 82, 84; WhoAmP 79, 81, 83, 85, 87; WhoFI 83*

Fraser, George MacDonald
English. Author
Books include the continuing story of Harry Flashman: *Flashman,* 1969.
b. Apr 2, 1925 in Carlisle, England
Source: *Au&Wr 71; CamGLE; ConAu 2NR, 45, 48NR; ConLC 7; DcLEL 1940; IntAu&W 76, 77, 82, 89, 91, 93; Novels; TwCRHW 90, 94; Who 82, 83, 85, 88, 90, 92, 94; WorAu 1970; WrDr 76, 80, 82, 84, 86, 88, 90, 92, 94, 96*

Fraser, Gretchen Kunigh
American. Skier
Won gold medal in women's slalom, 1948 Olympics.
b. 1919
Source: *BioIn 3, 6, 9, 11; InWom, SUP*

Fraser, Ian
English. Composer, Conductor
Conductor for Liza Minnelli, Sammy Davis, Jr; won five Emmys for musical direction.
b. Aug 23, 1933 in Hove, England
Source: *ASCAP 80; TwCPaSc; VarWW 85; WhoArt 80, 82, 84; WhoEnt 92*

Fraser, James Earle
American. Sculptor
Noted for Old West motifs; best-known sculpture: "The End of the Trail," 1898; des igned buffalo nickel, many medals.
b. Nov 4, 1876 in Winona, Minnesota
d. Oct 11, 1953 in Westport, Connecticut
Source: *BioIn 2, 3, 4, 8, 10, 14, 20; CurBio 51, 54; DcAmB S5; FacFETw; IlBEAAW; LinLib S; NatCAB 16, 40; ObitOF 79; REnAW; WebAB 74, 79; WhAm 3; WhAmArt 85; WhoMW 82*

Fraser, John Malcolm
Australian. Political Leader
Liberal Party prime minister of Australia, 1975-83.
b. Mar 21, 1930 in Melbourne, Australia
Source: *BioIn 10, 11, 12, 13; BlueB 76; DcTwHis; IntWW 74, 75; IntYB 78, 79, 80, 81, 82; NewYTBS 75, 77; Who 82, 83, 85, 88, 90, 92; WhoWor 74, 76, 78, 80, 82, 84, 87; WorAl*

Fratello, Mike
[Michael Robert Fratello]
American. Basketball Coach
Coach, Atlanta, 1983-90; NBA coach of year, 1986.
b. Feb 24, 1947 in Hackensack, New Jersey
Source: *OfNBA 87; WhoAm 84, 86, 88, 90, 92, 94, 95, 96, 97; WhoMW 93; WhoSSW 84, 86, 88*

Fratianne, Linda
American. Skater
World champion figure skater, 1977, 1979; won silver medal, 1980 Olympics.
b. Aug 2, 1960 in Los Angeles, California
Source: *BioIn 11, 12; EncWomS; LegTOT*

Fraunhofer, Joseph von
German. Physicist
Mapped dark lines (Fraunhofer lines) in solar spectrum, 1814; improved micrometers, telescopes.
b. Mar 6, 1787 in Straubing, Bavaria
d. Jun 7, 1826 in Munich, Bavaria
Source: *AsBiEn; BioIn 8, 9, 10, 12, 14; DcCathB; DcInv; DcScB; InSci; LarDcSc; MacBEP; McGEWB; WebBD 83; WhDW; WorInv*

Frawley, William
American. Actor
Played Fred Mertz on TV series "I Love Lucy," 1951-60.
b. Feb 26, 1893 in Burlington, Iowa
d. Mar 3, 1966 in Los Angeles, California
Source: *BioIn 4, 7; Film 1; FilmgC; ForYSC; MotPP; MovMk; Vers B; WhAm 4; WhoHol B; WhScrn 74, 77; WorAl*

Frayn, Michael
English. Author
Books include *The Tin Man,* 1965; *A Very Private Life,* 1968; *Sweet Dreams,* 1973.
b. Sep 8, 1933 in London, England
Source: *Au&Wr 71; Benet 87, 96; BioIn 10, 13, 14, 15, 16; BlmGEL; CamGLE; CamGWoT; ConAu 5R, 30NR; ConBrDr; ConDr 73, 77, 82, 88, 93; ConLC 3, 7, 31, 47; ConNov 72, 76, 82, 86, 91, 96; ConSFA; ConTFT 6; CrtSuDr; CurBio 85; CyWA 89; DcLB 13, 14; DcLEL 1940; EncSF, 93; Ent; IntAu&W 76, 77, 82, 86, 89, 91, 93; IntDcT 2; IntWW 89, 91, 93; LegTOT; MajTwCW; ModBrL, S1, S2; NewC; NewYTBS 85; Novels; OxCEng 85, 95; OxCThe 67, 83; RGTwCWr; ScF&FL 1, 2; ScFSB; SJGFanW; TwCSFW 81, 86, 91; Who 74, 82, 83, 85, 88, 90, 92, 94; WhoThe 77, 81; WhoWor 76; WorAu 1950; WrDr 76, 80, 82, 84, 86, 88, 90, 92, 94, 96*

Frazer, James George, Sir
Scottish. Anthropologist
Best known for lengthy study of magic, religion: *The Golden Bough,* 1915.
b. Jan 1, 1854 in Glasgow, Scotland
d. May 7, 1941 in Cambridge, England
Source: *Alli SUP; AtlBL; Benet 87; BioIn 1, 2, 3, 5, 6, 9, 10, 11, 14, 15, 16, 17, 18; CamGEL; CasWL; Chambr 3; CmScLit; DcEnA A; DcLEL; DcNaB 1941; DcScB; EvLB; GrBr; InSci; IntDcAn; LinLib L, S; LngCTC; LuthC 75; McGEWB; NewC; NewCBEL; OxCEng 67, 85, 95; PenC ENG; RAdv 14, 13-3; REn; TwCA, SUP; VicBrit; WebE&AL; WhLit; WorAl*

Frazetta, Frank
American. Artist, Cartoonist
Drew Buck Rogers, Flash Gordon; known for Tarzan, Conan comic book covers.
b. Feb 9, 1928 in New York, New York
Source: *Au&Arts 14; BiDScF; BioIn 10, 11, 16; ConAu 46NR, 104; EncACom; EncSF, 93; FanAl; IlrAm 1880; NewEScF; PenEncH; ScF&FL 92; SmATA, 58; WhoAm 78, 80, 82, 84, 86, 88, 90, 92, 94, 95, 96, 97; WorECom*

Frazier, Brenda Diana Dudd
[Mrs. Robert F. Chatfield-Taylor]
American. Socialite
Made headlines, 1930s-40s, for glamorous life with friends such as Bette Davis, Duke of Windsor.
b. Jun 9, 1921 in Montreal, Quebec, Canada
d. May 3, 1982 in Boston, Massachusetts
Source: *InWom, SUP; NewYTBS 82*

Frazier, Dallas June
American. Singer, Songwriter
Songs include country hits "Elvira"; "Fourteen Carat Mind," 1982; songwriter interna tional Hall of Fame, 1976.
b. Oct 27, 1939 in Spiro, Oklahoma
Source: *BioIn 14; EncFCWM 83; EncRk 88; PenEncP; WhoAm 78, 80, 82, 84, 86, 88*

Frazier, Edward Franklin
American. Sociologist, Educator
Wrote *The Negro Family in the United States,* 1939.
b. Sep 24, 1897 in Baltimore, Maryland
d. May 17, 1962 in Washington, District of Columbia
Source: *DcAmB S7; WebBD 83*

Frazier, Ian
American. Author
Staff writer, *The New Yorker,* 1975-82; wrote *Great Plains,* 1989.
b. 1951 in Cleveland, Ohio
Source: *ConAu 54NR, 130; ConLC 46; CurBio 96; WrDr 92, 94, 96*

Frazier, Joe
"Smokin' Joe"
American. Boxer
Won gold medal, 1964 Olympics; pro heavyweight champ, 1970-73.
b. Jan 17, 1944 in Beaufort, South Carolina
Source: *AfrAmSG; BiDAmSp BK; BioIn 9, 10, 11, 12, 13; BoxReg; CelR, 90; CurBio 71; FacFETw; InB&W 85; LegTOT; NewYTBE 70; NewYTBS 79, 81; WhoAfA 96; WhoAm 74, 76, 78, 80, 82, 84, 86, 88, 90, 92, 94, 95, 96, 97; WhoBlA 75, 77, 80, 85, 88, 90, 92, 94; WhoBox 74; WhoHol 92*

Frazier, Walt(er Jr.)
"Clyde"
American. Basketball Player
Guard, 1967-80, mostly with NY Knicks; four-time NBA all-star; Hall of Fame, 1986.
b. Mar 29, 1945 in Atlanta, Georgia
Source: *AfrAmSG; BasBi; BioIn 8, 9, 10, 11, 12, 14, 16, 21; CelR; ConAu 103; CurBio 73; InB&W 85; LegTOT; NewYTBE 72, 73; NewYTBS 74, 75, 76, 77, 78; OfNBA 87; WhoAfA 96; WhoAm 74, 76, 78, 80, 82, 92, 94, 95; WhoBbl 73; WhoBlA 75, 77, 80, 85, 88, 90, 92, 94; WhoE 95; WorAl; WorAlBi*

Frears, Stephen Arthur
English. Filmmaker
Films include *My Beautiful Laundrette,* 1986; *Dangerous Liaisons,* 1988.
b. Jun 20, 1941 in Leicester, England
Source: *BioIn 15, 16; ConTFT 6; CurBio 90; IntMPA 92; IntWW 91, 93; Who 88, 90, 92, 94*

Freberg, Stan
American. Composer, Author
Satire on soap operas, "John and Martha," became nat. hit, 1951; developed TV puppet show "Time for Beanie," 1949-54.
b. Aug 7, 1926 in Pasadena, California
Source: *ASCAP 66, 80; BioIn 3, 4, 5, 6, 7, 8, 12, 14, 15, 16; JoeFr; PenEncP; RadStar; RkOn 74, 82; SaTiSS; WhoAdv*

90; WhoAm 74, 76, 88, 90; WhoCom; WhoEnt 92; WhoHol 92, A; WhoWor 89

Frechette, Louis-Honore
Canadian. Poet
Best-known French-Canadian poet of 19th c.: *Les Oiseaux,* 1880.
b. Nov 16, 1839 in Levis, Quebec, Canada
d. May 31, 1908 in Montreal, Quebec, Canada
Source: *ApCAB; BbD; BbtC; BiD&SB; BioIn 17; CamGWoT; CanWr; DcCathB; DcLB 99; DcNaB S2; MacDCB 78; McGEWB; OxCAmL 65; OxCCan; OxCCanT; REn*

Frederic, Harold
American. Author
Produced novel *Damnation of Theron Ware,* 1896.
b. Aug 19, 1856 in Utica, New York
d. Oct 19, 1898 in Henley-on-Thames, England
Source: *Alli SUP; AmAu; AmAu&B; AmBi; AmWr; ApCAB SUP; BbD; BenetAL 91; BibAL; BiD&SB; BioIn 5, 7, 8, 11, 12, 13, 16, 21; CamGLE; CamHAL; CasWL; Chambr 3; CnDAL; CyWA 58; DcAmAu; DcAmB; DcBiA; DcEnA A; DcLB 12, 23, DS13; DcLEL; DcNAA; EncAJ; EvLB; GayN; GrWrEL N; JrnUS; ModAL, S1; NatCAB 5; NinCLC 10; Novels; OxCAmL 65, 83, 95; PenC AM; REn; REnAL; RfGAmL 87, 94; TwCBDA; WebE&AL; WhAm HS*

Frederick, Pauline
[Beatrice Pauline Libby]
American. Actor
Silent screen star beginning 1915 in *Bella Donna; Madame X.*
b. Aug 12, 1885 in Boston, Massachusetts
d. Aug 19, 1938 in Los Angeles, California
Source: *AmBi; ApCAB X; BioAmW; BioIn 7, 9, 11; HalFC 84; InWom; MovMk; NotAW; NotNAT A, B; OxCFilm; WhAm 1; WhScrn 83; WhThe*

Frederick, Pauline
American. Broadcast Journalist
First woman to receive Dupont radio award for news commentating, 1953; career has covered TV, radio, political reporting, analysis, 1940s-70s.
b. Feb 13, 1908 in Gallitzen, Pennsylvania
d. May 9, 1990 in Lake Forest, Illinois
Source: *AnObit 1990; BioIn 2, 3, 4, 5, 6, 7, 10, 16; ConAu 102, 131; CurBio 54, 90; EncTwCJ; FacFETw; HalFC 88; InWom SUP; LesBEnT, 92; NewYTBS 90; RadStar; WhoAm 86; WhoAmW 85, 89; WhoUN 75; WomComm*

Frederick I
[Frederick Barbarossa]
German. Ruler
Thought to be one of greatest German kings, 1152-90; ruled Italy, 1155-90, Holy Roman Empire, 1152-90.
b. 1123?
d. 1190
Source: *BioIn 10; DcNAA; LinLib S; McGEWB; NewC; NewCol 75; OxCGer 76; REn; WebBD 83*

Frederick II
German. Ruler
Son of Henry VI; ruled Holy Roman Empire, 1212-50; noted for interests in science, literature.
b. Dec 26, 1194 in Jesi, Papal States
d. Dec 13, 1250 in Florentino, Italy
Source: *AsBiEn; McGEWB; NewCol 75; WebBD 83*

Frederick II
German. Ruler
King of Prussia, 1740-1786.
b. 1712
d. Aug 17, 1786
Source: *GayLesB*

Frederick III
German. Ruler
Ruled Holy Roman Empire, 1440-93; reign marked by conflict between German princes, Austrian nobles.
b. Oct 18, 1831 in Potsdam, Germany
d. Jun 15, 1888 in Berlin, Germany
Source: *WebBD 83*

Frederick IX
Danish. Ruler
King, 1947-72; known for resisting Germans, allowing female succession to throne, making parliament one house.
b. Mar 11, 1899 in Copenhagen, Denmark
d. Jan 14, 1972 in Copenhagen, Denmark
Source: *NewCol 75; NewYTBE 72; WebBD 83*

Frederick Louis
[Prince of Wales]
English. Prince
Father of King George III of England; had strained relationship with his father, George II.
b. Jan 20, 1707 in Hannover, Germany
d. Mar 20, 1751 in London, England
Source: *BioIn 1, 3, 4, 5, 6, 7, 9, 10, 12, 15, 17; DcBiPP; DcNaB; Dis&D; NewCol 75; WebBD 83*

Fredericks, Carlton
[Harold Carlton Caplan]
American. Nutritionist
Radio host of nutrition, health show, NYC, 1957-87.
b. Oct 23, 1910 in New York, New York
d. Jul 28, 1987 in Yonkers, New York
Source: *AuNews 1; BioIn 6, 8, 10, 15, 16; BioNews 74; ConAu 7NR, 53, 123; NewYTBS 87; WhAm 9; WhoAm 84, 86, 88; WhoE 79, 81, 83, 85; WhoWor 87, 89*

Frederickson, Frank
Canadian. Hockey Player
Forward, 1926-31, with three NHL teams; Hall of Fame, 1958.
b. 1895 in Winnipeg, Manitoba, Canada
Source: *BioIn 10*

Frederickson, H. Gray
American. Producer
Films include *The Good, the Bad and the Ugly;* won Oscar for *The Godfather, Part II,* 1974.
b. Jul 21, 1937 in Oklahoma City, Oklahoma
Source: *IntMPA 92; VarWW 85; WhoAm 86; WhoEnt 92*

Frederick the Great
[Frederick II]
German. Ruler
King of Prussia, 1740-86; son of Frederick William I; noted for social reforms.
b. Jan 24, 1712 in Berlin, Germany
d. Aug 17, 1786 in Berlin, Germany
Source: *Baker 92; BioIn 17, 19, 20; BlkwCE; BriBkM 80; DcBiPP; HarEnMi; HisWorL; LinLib L, S; LitC 14; NewC; NewCol 75; NewGrDM 80; OxCEng 85, 95; OxCFr; OxCMus; PenDiMP; REn; WebBD 83*

Frederick William I
Prussian. Ruler
King, 1713-40; reign marked by internal improvements of kingdom; ordered mandatory schooling, 1717.
b. Aug 15, 1688 in Berlin, Germany
d. May 31, 1740 in Potsdam, Germany
Source: *NewCol 75; WebBD 83*

Frederika Louise
Greek. Consort
Queen of Greece, 1947-64; in self-imposed exile after monarchy overthrow, 1973.
b. Apr 18, 1917 in Blankenburg, Germany
d. Feb 6, 1981 in Madrid, Spain
Source: *BioIn 9, 12; CurBio 55, 81; InWom SUP; NewYTBS 81*

Free
[Kirke; Rabbit Bundrick; Tetsu Kamauchi; Wendell Richardson; Paul Rodgers]
British. Music Group
High-energy band known for understated music; formed, 1968; songs include "All Right Now," 1970; "Free," 1978.
Source: *ConAu 35NR, 128, X; ConMuA 80A; DcNaB; EncRk 88; EncRkSt; HarEnR 86; IlEncRk; MajTwCW; OnThGG; PenEncP; RkOn 78, 84; RolSEnR 83; WhoRock 81; WhoRocM 82*

Free, World B
[Lloyd Free]
American. Basketball Player
Guard, 1975-88, with several NBA teams.

b. Dec 9, 1953 in Atlanta, Georgia
Source: *BioIn 11, 13; OfNBA 87; WhoBlA 85, 92*

Freed, Alan
American. Radio Performer, Songwriter
Unorthodox 1950s dj who introduced term "rock and roll"; career ruined by payola s candal, early 1960s.
b. Dec 15, 1922 in Johnstown, Pennsylvania
d. Jan 20, 1965 in Palm Springs, California
Source: *Baker 84, 92; BioIn 4, 7, 16, 17; DcAmB S1; EncPR&S 89; EncRk 88; HarEnR 86; IlEncRk; LegTOT; NewAmDM; NewGrDA 86; OxCPMus; PenEncP; RolSEnR 83; WhoRock 81; WhoRocM 82; WhScrn 77, 83; WorAl; WorAlBi*

Freed, Arthur
American. Songwriter, Producer
Produced films *Wizard of Oz,* 1939; *Gigi,* 1958; won special Oscar ; wrote "Singin' in the Rain," 1929.
b. Sep 9, 1894 in Charleston, South Carolina
d. Apr 12, 1973 in Los Angeles, California
Source: *AmPS; ASCAP 66, 80; BestMus; BiDAmM; BiDFilm, 81, 94; BioIn 4, 9, 10, 14, 15, 21; CmMov; CmpEPM; ConAu 41R; DcAmB S9; DcFM; FilmEn; FilmgC; HalFC 80, 84, 88; IntDcF 1-4, 2-4; LegTOT; NewYTBE 73; OxCFilm; OxCPMus; Sw&Ld C; WhAm 5; WhoWest 74; WorEFlm*

Freed, Bert
American. Actor
Character actor since 1957; films include *Norma Rae,* 1979.
b. Nov 3, 1919 in New York, New York
Source: *BioIn 20; HalFC 88; WhAm 11; WhoAm 74, 76, 78, 80, 82, 84, 86, 88, 90, 92, 94; WhoEnt 92; WhoHol 92, A*

Freed, James I(ngo)
American. Architect
Designed the United States Holocaust Memorial Museum, Washington, DC, which opened in 1993.
b. Jul 23, 1930 in Essen, Germany
Source: *AmArch 70; BioIn 10, 13, 20; CurBio 94; WhoAm 80, 84, 86, 88, 90, 92, 94, 95, 96, 97*

Freedman, Gerald
American. Director
Won Obie award for *Taming of the Shrew,* 1960.
b. Jun 25, 1927 in Lorain, Ohio
Source: *ASCAP 66, 80; CamGWoT; ConTFT 6; NewYTBE 73; NotNAT; WhoAm 82; WhoOp 76; WhoThe 77, 81*

Freedman, James Oliver
American. University Administrator
President, Dartmouth College, 1987—.
b. Sep 21, 1935 in Manchester, New Hampshire
Source: *BioIn 15; DrAS 74P, 78P, 82P; NewYTBS 87; WhoAm 80, 82, 84, 86, 88, 90, 92, 94, 95, 96, 97; WhoAmL 78, 79; WhoE 91, 93, 95, 97; WhoMW 84, 86, 88; WhoWor 89*

Freedman, Marcia
American. Feminist
Opened the first battered women's shelter in Israel, 1977.
b. 1938
Source: *BioIn 17; GayLesB; WhoWorJ 78*

Freedman, Russell
American. Author
Won Newbery for *Lincoln: A Photobiography,* 1988.
b. Oct 11, 1929 in San Francisco, California
Source: *Au&Arts 4; AuBYP 2, 3; BioIn 8, 16; ChlBkCr; ChlLR 20; ConAu 7NR, 17R, 23NR; ScF&FL 1, 2; SixBJA; SmATA 16, 71*

Freeh, Louis J(oseph)
American. Government Official
Director of the FBI, 1993—.
b. Jan 6, 1950 in Jersey City, New Jersey
Source: *CurBio 96; NewYTBS 93; WhoAmP 93, 95*

Freehan, Bill
[William Ashley Freehan]
American. Baseball Player
Catcher, Detroit, 1961-76; 11-time AL All-Star.
b. Nov 29, 1941 in Detroit, Michigan
Source: *Ballpl 90; BiDAmSp Sup; BioIn 8, 18; WhoAm 74; WhoProB 73*

Freeling, Nicolas
English. Author
Mystery novels feature inspector Van der Valk: *The King of the Rainy Country,* 1966.
b. Mar 3, 1927 in London, England
Source: *AuSpks; Benet 87, 96; BioIn 10, 11, 14; CamGLE; ConAu 1NR, 12AS, 17NR, 49, 50NR; ConLC 38; ConNov 72, 76, 82, 86, 91, 96; CrtSuMy; DcLB 87; DcLP 87A; EncMys; IntAu&W 76, 82, 86, 93; LegTOT; Novels; TwCCr&M 80, 85, 91; TwCWr; Who 74, 82, 83, 85, 88, 90, 92, 94; WorAl; WorAlBi; WorAu 1950; WrDr 76, 80, 82, 84, 86, 88, 90, 92, 94, 96*

Freeman, Al(bert Cornelius), Jr.
American. Actor
Starred in TV shows "Hot 1 Baltimore," 1975; "One Life to Live," 1972-88; appeared in film *Once Upon a Time . When We Were Colored,* 1995.
b. Mar 21, 1934 in San Antonio, Texas
Source: *AfrAmAl 6, 81*

Freeman, Bud
[Lawrence Freeman]
American. Jazz Musician
Great tenor saxist, 1930s-60s; prolific recorder; charter member, "World's Greate st Jazz Band."
b. Apr 13, 1906 in Chicago, Illinois
Source: *AllMusG; AnObit 1991; ASCAP 66, 80; BiDAmM; BiDJaz; BioIn 8, 10, 11, 16; CmpEPM; EncJzS; IlEncJ; NewAmDM; NewGrDA 86; NewGrDJ 88, 94; NewGrDM 80; NewYTBS 91; OxCPMus; PenEncP; WhoAm 74; WhoJazz 72; WhoWor 74*

Freeman, Cliff(ord Lee)
American. Advertising Executive
Executive Creative Director and Chair, Cliff Freeman and Partners, 1987—.
b. Feb 14, 1941 in Vicksburg, Mississippi
Source: *News 96, 96-1; WhoAdv 90; WhoAm 90, 92, 95, 96, 97; WhoE 79*

Freeman, Cynthia
[Beatrice Cynthia Freeman Feinberg]
American. Author
Interior decorator-turned-romance novelist; first novel *A World Full of Strangers,* written at age 50.
b. 1915 in New York, New York
d. Nov 5, 1988 in San Francisco, California
Source: *AnObit 1988; ConAu 29NR, 81, 126; LegTOT; TwCRHW 90, 94*

Freeman, Douglas S
American. Historian, Journalist
Won Pulitzer for *The South to Prosperity,* 1939, and *George Washington,* 1948-54.
b. May 16, 1886 in Lynchburg, Virginia
d. Jun 13, 1953 in Richmond, Virginia
Source: *AmAu&B; ConAu 109; CyWA 58; DcAmB S5; DcLB 17; EncSoH; NatCAB 58; ObitOF 79; ObitT 1951; OxCAmH; OxCAmL 65; REn; REnAL; TwCA SUP; WebAB 74; WhAm 3; WhJnl*

Freeman, Joseph
Author
Marxist critic whose works include *An American Testament,* 1936; *The Long Pursuit,* 1947.
b. Oct 7, 1897 in Ukraine, Russia
d. Aug 9, 1965 in New York, New York
Source: *AmAu&B; AmNov; BenetAL 91; BiDAmLf; BioIn 2, 4, 6, 7, 10; ConAu 89; DcAmB S1, S7; OxCAmL 65, 83, 95; TwCA, SUP; WhAm 4; WhJnl*

Freeman, Mary E. Wilkins
American. Author
Books on rural New England include *Pembroke,* 1894; *Jane Field,* 1893.
b. Oct 31, 1852 in Randolph, Massachusetts
d. Mar 13, 1930 in Metuchen, New Jersey
Source: *AmAu&B; AmBi; AmLY; CarSB; CasWL; CnDAL; ConAmL; ConAu 106; OxCAmL 83; PenC AM; REn; REnAL; TwCLC 9; WebAB 79; WhAm 1*

Freeman, Morgan
American. Actor
Starred in films *Glory, Driving Miss Daisy,* 1989; received Oscar nomination, 1990, for *Driving Miss Daisy*; played Easy Reader on Children's Television Workshop series, "The Electric Company," 1971-75.
b. Jun 1, 1937 in Memphis, Tennessee
Source: *AfrAmAl 6; AfrAmBi 2; BiDFilm 94; BioIn 11, 15, 16; ConBlB 2; ConTFT 6, 15; CurBio 91; DcTwCCu 5; DrBlPA 90; IntMPA 92, 94, 96; IntWW 93; LegTOT; News 90; NewYTBS 87; WhoAfA 96; WhoAm 90, 92, 94, 95, 96, 97; WhoBlA 92, 94; WhoEnt 92; WhoHol 92; WhoThe 81; WorAlBi*

Freeman, Orville Lothrop
American. Government Official
Dem. governor of MN, 1954-61; secretary of agriculture, 1961-69.
b. May 9, 1918 in Minneapolis, Minnesota
Source: *BiDrAPA 89; BiDrGov 1789; BiDrUSE 71, 89; BioIn 4, 5, 6, 7, 8, 10, 11, 12; BlueB 76; CurBio 56; EncAAH; Future; IntWW 74, 75, 83, 89, 91, 93; LinLib S; NewYTBS 80; WhoAm 74, 76, 78, 80, 82, 84, 86, 88, 90, 95, 96, 97; WhoAmP 73, 75, 77, 79, 81, 83, 85, 87, 89, 91, 93, 95; WhoFI 79; WhoWor 78, 80, 82*

Freeman, Paul Lamar
American. Military Leader
Four-star general, US Army; headed NATO, 1962-65; highly decorated for WW II service.
b. 1907
d. Apr 17, 1988 in Monterey, California
Source: *BioIn 4, 15, 16; WhAm 9; WhoAm 74, 76*

Freeman, R(ichard) Austin
English. Author
Detective writer; created scientific detective Dr. John Thorndyke: *The Cat's Eye,* 1927.
b. Apr 11, 1862 in London, England
d. Sep 30, 1943 in Gravesend, England
Source: *Benet 87; BioIn 4, 7, 9, 11, 14; ConAu 152; DcNaB MP; EncMys; EvLB; NewC; REn; TwCA, SUP; TwCCr&M 85; WhE&EA*

Freeman, Seth
American. Writer, Producer
Won Emmy for script of TV show "Lou Grant," 1980.
b. Jan 6, 1945 in Los Angeles, California
Source: *VarWW 85; WhoAm 82*

Freemantle, Brian Harry
English. Author
Mystery writer; created detective Charlie Muffin: *November Man,* 1976.
b. Jun 10, 1936 in Southampton, England
Source: *BioIn 14; ConAu 16NR, 65; DcLP 87A; IntAu&W 91; SpyFic; TwCCr&M 85, 91; WrDr 92*

Freer, Charles Lang
American. Businessman
Donated Freer Gallery, Washington, DC; contains unique work of Whistler.
b. Feb 25, 1856 in Kingston, New York
d. Sep 25, 1919 in New York, New York
Source: *AmBi; BioIn 4, 5, 9, 11, 12, 13; DcAmB; NatCAB 15; PeoHis; WhAm 1; WhAmArt 85; WorAl*

Frehley, Ace
American. Singer, Musician
Guitarist; released solo album, 1978.
b. Apr 27, 1951 in New York, New York
Source: *RkOn 85*

Frei, Eduardo
[Montalva Eduardo Frei]
Chilean. Lawyer, Political Leader
Pres. of Chile, 1964-70.
b. Jan 16, 1911 in Santiago, Chile
d. Jan 22, 1982 in Santiago, Chile
Source: *AnObit 1982; BiDLAmC; BioIn 7, 8, 9, 12, 13, 16, 18; ColdWar 2; ConAu 110; CurBio 65, 82, 82N; DcCPSAm; DcPol; DcTwHis; EncLatA; FacFETw; IntWW 74, 75, 76, 77, 78, 79, 80, 81; IntYB 78, 79, 80, 81, 82, 82A; McGEWB; WhoWor 74*

Freij, Elias
Jordanian. Politician
Mayor of Bethlehem, 1972—.
b. 1920 in Bethlehem, Jordan
Source: *BioIn 14, 15; ConNews 86-4*

Freilicher, Jane
American. Artist
Impressionistic painter recognized for visual irony of her landscapes, often depicting a vase of cut flowers juxtaposed against a cityscape background.
b. Nov 29, 1924 in New York, New York
Source: *BioIn 4, 10, 12, 13, 16; CurBio 89; DcCAA 71, 77, 88, 94; DcCAr 81; InWom SUP; NorAmWA; OxCTwCA; PrintW 85; WhoAm 74, 82, 86, 88, 90, 92, 94, 95, 96, 97; WhoAmA 73, 76, 78, 80, 82, 84, 86, 89, 91, 93; WhoAmW 68A, 70, 72, 74, 75, 81, 83, 85, 87, 95, 97; WhoArt 80; WhoE 74, 83; WorArt 1980*

Frei Ruiz-Tagle, Eduardo
Chilean. Political Leader
Pres., Chile, 1994—.
b. Jun 24, 1942 in Santiago, Chile
Source: *WhoWor 96, 97*

Freleng, Friz
[Isadore Freleng]
American. Director, Producer
Creator of Bugs Bunny, Daffy Duck, Porky Pig, Yosemite Sam, and the Pink Panther.
b. Aug 21, 1906 in Kansas City, Missouri
d. May 26, 1995 in Los Angeles, California
Source: *ASCAP 80; BioIn 20, 21; ConTFT 8, 14; IntDcF 1-4, 2-4; IntMPA 84, 86, 88, 92, 94; News 95; VarWW 85; WhAm 11; WhoAm 78, 80; WhoEnt 92*

Frelich, Phyllis
American. Actor
Deaf actress who won Tony for *Children of a Lesser God,* 1980.
b. Feb 29, 1944 in Devils Lake, North Dakota
Source: *BioIn 12, 21; ConTFT 2; DeafPAS; NewYTBS 80; WhoAm 82, 84, 86, 88, 90, 92, 94; WhoAmW 87, 89; WhoEnt 92; WhoWor 96*

Fremont, John Charles
American. Explorer, Politician
Led three Western expeditions, 1840s; one of first two CA senators; first Rep. candidate for pres., 1856.
b. Jan 21, 1813 in Savannah, Georgia
d. Jul 13, 1890 in New York, New York
Source: *Alli, SUP; AmAu; AmAu&B; AmBi; AmPolLe; ApCAB; BbD; BiAUS; BiD&SB; BiDrAC; BiDrATG; BiDrUSC 89; BiDSA; BioIn 1, 2, 3, 4, 5, 6, 7, 8, 9, 10, 11, 12, 13, 15, 16, 17, 18, 19, 20, 21; CivWDc; CmCal; CyAG; CyAL 2; DcAmAu; DcAmB; DcAmMiB; DcAmSR; DcBiPP; DcNAA; Drake; EncAAH; EncAB-H 1974, 1996; Expl 93; HarEnMi; HarEnUS; HisWorL; InSci; LinLib S; McGEWB; MemAm; NatCAB 4; NewYHSD; OxCAmH; OxCAmL 65, 83, 95; PresAR; REn; REnAL; REnAW; TwCBDA; WebAB 74, 79; WebAMB; WhAm HS; WhAmP; WhCiWar; WhDW; WhNaAH; WhoMilH 76; WhWE; WorAl*

French, Albert
American. Author
Wrote *Billy,* 1993.
b. 1934
d. Jan 4, 1960
Source: *ConLC 86*

French, Daniel Chester
American. Sculptor
Among most famous pieces are "The Minute Man," Concord, MA, 1873; "Lincoln," Lincoln Memorial, Washington, DC, 1922.
b. Apr 20, 1850 in Exeter, New Hampshire
d. Oct 7, 1931 in Stockbridge, Massachusetts
Source: *AmBi; AmCulL; AntBDN C; ApCAB, X; ArtsNiC; BiDTran; BioIn 1, 3, 5, 8, 9, 10, 11, 12, 14, 16, 18, 19; BriEAA; DcAmArt; DcAmB S1; DcArts; GayN; HarEnUS; LinLib S; McGDA; McGEWB; MorMA; NatCAB 1, 8, 31; OxCAmH; OxCAmL 65; OxCArt; OxDcArt; PeoHis; PhDcTCA 77; REnAL; TwCBDA; WebAB 74, 79; WebBD 83; WhAm 1; WhAmArt 85; WorAl; WorAlBi*

French, Jay Jay
[Twisted Sister]
American. Musician
Guitarist with heavy metal group formed 1976.
b. Jul 20, 1954 in New York, New York

French, Marilyn
[Mara Solwoska]
American. Author
Wrote *The Women's Room,* 1977; *The Bleeding Heart,* 1980.
b. Nov 21, 1929 in New York, New York
Source: *AmWomWr SUP; ArtclWW 2; BenetAL 91; BioIn 13, 17, 18; BlmGWL; ConAu 3NR, 31NR, 69; ConLC 10, 18, 60; ConNov 91, 96; ConPopW; CurBio 92; CyWA 89; FemiCLE; FemiWr; IntWW 89, 91, 93; InWom SUP; LegTOT; MajTwCW; OxCAmL 83, 95; OxCWoWr 95; PenNWW A, B; WhoAm 80, 82, 84, 86, 88, 90, 92, 94, 95, 96, 97; WhoAmW 81, 83, 85, 93, 95, 97; WhoUSWr 88; WhoWrEP 89, 92, 95; WorAu 1975; WrDr 82, 84, 86, 88, 90, 92, 94, 96*

French, Robert T
American. Businessman
Started business, 1880, that eventually produced French's mustard, 1904.
b. 1823 in Ithaca, New York
d. 1893
Source: *Entr*

French, Victor
American. Actor
Best known for character roles in TV series "Little House on the Prairie," 1974-77, "Highway to Heaven," 1984-88.
b. Dec 4, 1934 in Los Angeles, California
d. Jun 15, 1989 in Los Angeles, California
Source: *BioIn 14, 16; ConTFT 6; LegTOT; LesBEnT 92; NewYTBS 89; VarWW 85*

Freneau, Philip Morin
American. Poet, Journalist
First professional US journalist; edited *National Gazetter* for Thomas Je fferson, 1791-93; revolutionary poems include "The British Prisonship," 1781.
b. Jan 2, 1752 in New York, New York
d. Dec 18, 1832 in Monmouth County, New Jersey
Source: *Alli; AmAu; AmAu&B; AmBi; ApCAB; AtlBL; Benet 96; BiD&SB; CasWL; Chambr 3; CyWA 58; Drake; EncAB-H 1974, 1996; EncAJ; EncAR; OxCAmH; PenC AM; WhAm HS*

Freni, Mirella
Italian. Opera Singer
Soprano; sang Mimi in La Scala's film version of *La Boheme,* 1963.
b. Feb 27, 1935 in Modena, Italy
Source: *Baker 78, 84, 92; BioIn 7, 11, 12, 15; BriBkM 80; CelR 90; ConMus 14; CurBio 77; IntDcOp; IntWW 78, 79, 80, 81, 82, 83, 89, 91, 93; IntWWM 90; InWom SUP; MetOEnc; MusSN; NewAmDM; NewGrDA 86; NewGrDM 80; NewGrDO; OxDcOp; PenDiMP; WhoAm 80, 82, 84, 86, 88, 90, 92, 94, 95, 96, 97; WhoAmM 83; WhoAmW 83, 85, 87; WhoMus 72; WhoOp 76; WhoWor 78, 82, 84, 87, 89, 91*

Frescobaldi, Girolamo
Italian. Organist, Composer
Organist at St. Peters; noted for keyboard compositions, monothematic writings; greatly influenced Baroque music.
b. 1583 in Ferrara, Italy
d. Mar 2, 1644 in Rome, Italy
Source: *AtlBL; Baker 78, 84, 92; BioIn 3, 4, 7, 12, 13, 14, 16; BriBkM 80; CmpBCM; DcArts; DcCom 77; DcCom&M 79; GrComp; LuthC 75; McGEWB; MusMk; NewAmDM; NewCol 75; NewGrDM 80; NewOxM; OxCMus; WebBD 83; WhDW*

Freshfield, Douglas William
English. Geographer, Mountaineer
Made first ascent of Mt. Elbrus, 1868; numerous mountaineering books include *The Italian Alps,* 1875.
b. Apr 27, 1845 in Hampstead, England
d. Feb 9, 1934 in Forest Rowe, England
Source: *Alli SUP; BioIn 2, 5; DcNaB 1931; NewCBEL; WhE&EA; WhLit*

Fresnel, Augustin-Jean
French. Physicist
Investigated wave theory of light; furthered use of compound lenses in lighthouses.
b. May 10, 1788 in Broglie, France
d. Jul 14, 1827 in Ville-d'Avray, France
Source: *BioIn 3, 10, 12, 14; DcInv; DcScB; McGEWB*

Freuchen, Peter
Danish. Author, Explorer
Explored Arctic, 1906-08; wrote *Eskimo,* 1930; *Arctic Adventure,* 1936.
b. Feb 20, 1886
d. Sep 2, 1957 in Anchorage, Alaska
Source: *AuBYP 2, 3; BioIn 3, 4, 8; ConAu 114; ObitT 1951; PenC EUR; RAdv 14, 13-3; TwCA, SUP; WhAm 3*

Freud, Anna
English. Psychoanalyst
Daughter of Sigmund Freud; authority on childhood mental disorders.
b. Dec 3, 1895 in Vienna, Austria
d. Oct 8, 1982 in London, England
Source: *AnObit 1982; WhoWor 74, 78, 80, 82; WomFir; WomPsyc; WrDr 76, 80, 82*

Freud, Lucian
English. Artist
Prominent modern oil painter of nudes, still life, interiors.
b. Dec 8, 1922 in Berlin, Germany
Source: *BioIn 9, 10, 11, 13, 15, 16; BlueB 76; ConArt 77, 83, 89, 96; ConBrA 79; CurBio 88; DcArts; DcBrAr 1; DcCAr 81; IntWW 74, 75, 76, 77, 78, 79, 80, 81, 82, 83, 89, 91, 93; OxCTwCA; OxDcArt; PhDcTCA 77; TwCPaSc; Who 74, 82, 83, 85, 88, 90, 92, 94; WhoWor 82, 84, 91; WorArt 1950*

Freud, Sigmund
Austrian. Psychoanalyst
Founded psychoanalysis, 1895-1900; first to develop concept of subconscious mind.
b. May 6, 1856 in Freiberg, Moravia
d. Sep 23, 1939 in London, England
Source: *AsBiEn; AtlBL; Benet 87, 96; BiDPara; BiDPsy; BiESc; BiHiMed; BioIn 1, 2, 3, 4, 5, 6, 7, 8, 9, 10, 11, 12, 13, 14, 15, 16, 17, 18, 19, 20, 21; BlmGEL; CasWL; ChhPo S2; ConAu 115, 133; CopCroC; CyWA 58, 89; DcAmSR; DcScB; DcTwHis; Dis&D; EncO&P 1, 2, 3; EncPaPR 91; EncSPD; EncTR 91; EncUnb; EncWL 2, 3; EuWr 8; FacFETw; FilmgC; GaEncPs; GuPsyc; HalFC 80, 84, 88; InSci; JeHun; LegTOT; LiExTwC; LinLib L, S; LngCEL; LngCTC; LuthC 75; MajTwCW; MakMC; McGEWB; NamesHP; NewC; OxCEng 85, 95; OxCGer 76, 86; OxCMed 86; OxCPhil; PenC EUR; RAdv 14, 13-3, 13-5; RComWL; REn; ThTwC 87; TwCA, SUP; TwCLC 52; TwCWr; TwoTYeD; WhAm 4, HSA; WhDW; WhE&EA; WhoLA; WhoTwCL; WorAl; WorAlBi; WrPh P*

Frey, Glenn
[The Eagles]
American. Musician, Songwriter, Singer
Released solo album *No Fun Aloud,* 1982; hits include "You Belong To The City," 1985.
b. Nov 6, 1948 in Detroit, Michigan
Source: *ConMus 3; EncPR&S 89; HarEnR 86; LegTOT; OnThGG; RkOn 85; WhoAm 80, 82, 84, 86, 88, 90, 92, 94, 95, 96, 97; WhoEnt 92; WhoRocM 82*

Frey, Jim
[James Gottfried Frey]
American. Baseball Manager
Minor league outfielder; manager, KC, 1980-81; Chicago Cubs, 1984-86.
b. May 26, 1931 in Cleveland, Ohio
Source: *Ballpl 90; BaseReg 86; BioIn 15; WhoAm 86, 88, 90, 92; WhoMW 82, 90*

Freyse, William
American. Cartoonist
Continued syndicated comic strip by Gene Ahern, "Our Boarding House," 1936-69.
b. 1899 in Detroit, Michigan
d. Mar 3, 1969 in Tucson, Arizona
Source: *BioIn 8; ObitOF 79; WorECom*

Freyssinet, Eugene
[Marie-Eugene-Leon Freyssinet]
French. Engineer
Experimented with and improved pre-stressed concrete, leading to its universal use.
b. Jul 13, 1879 in Objat, France
d. Jun 8, 1962 in Saint Martin-Vesubie, France
Source: *BioIn 2, 4, 6, 10; ConArch 80, 87; DcTwDes; EncMA; FacFETw; MacEA; McGDA; WhoArch*

Frey-Wyssling, Albert F
Swiss. Scientist, Educator
Through studies in submicroscopic morphology prefigured field of molecular biology.
b. Nov 8, 1900 in Kussnacht, Switzerland
d. Aug 30, 1988
Source: *BioIn 4; IntWW 83*

Frick, Ford Christopher
American. Baseball Executive
President of NL, 1934-51; baseball commissioner, 1951-65; founded baseball Hall of Fame, 1938.
b. Dec 19, 1894 in Wawaka, Indiana
d. Apr 8, 1978 in Bronxville, New York
Source: *BiDAmSp BB; BioIn 2, 3, 6, 11; ConAu 89; CurBio 45, 78; DcAmB S10; IndAu 1967; WhAm 7; WhoAm 74, 76, 78; WhoProB 73*

Frick, Gottlob
German. Opera Singer
Bass; noted Wagnerian singer; made NY Met. debut, 1950; retired, 1970.
b. 1906 in Stuttgart, Germany
Source: *Baker 84, 92; BioIn 6; CmOp; IntDcOp; IntWW 74, 75, 76, 77, 78, 79, 80, 81, 82, 83, 89, 91, 93; IntWWM 77, 80, 90; MetOEnc; NewAmDM; NewGrDM 80; NewGrDO; OxDcOp; PenDiMP; WhoWor 74*

Frick, Henry Clay
American. Industrialist, Philanthropist
One of organizers of US Steel; his bequests of art, home to NYC, 1919, were basis for Frick Museum.
b. Dec 19, 1849 in West Overton, Pennsylvania
d. Dec 2, 1919 in New York, New York
Source: *AmBi; ApCAB SUP, X; BiDAmBL 83; BioIn 1, 3, 7, 8, 9, 20, 21; DcAmB; EncAB-H 1974, 1996; EncABHB 3; GayN; LinLib S; McGEWB; NatCAB 10, 23; OxCAmH; OxDcArt; RComAH; WebAB 74, 79; WhAm 1; WhAmArt 85; WorAl; WorAlBi*

Frick, Wilhelm
German. Government Official
Hitler's minister of interior, 1933-43; hanged at Nuremburg trials.
b. Mar 3, 1877 in Alsenz, Germany
d. Oct 16, 1946 in Nuremberg, Germany
Source: *BiDExR; BioIn 1, 14, 16, 18; CurBio 42, 46; Dis&D; EncTR, 91; HisEWW; ObitOF 79; WebBD 83; WhWW-II*

Frickie, Janie
American. Singer, Musician
Had hit single "Down to My Last Broken Heart," 1980; CMA's female vocalist of year, 1982, 1983.
b. Dec 18, 1950 in Whitney, Indiana
Source: *BioIn 11; EncFCWM 83*

Friebus, Florida
American. Actor
Played mother on TV's "The Many Loves of Dobie Gillis," 1959-63; patient on "The Bo b Newhart Show," 1972-78.
b. Oct 10, 1909 in Auburndale, Massachusetts
d. May 27, 1988 in Laguna Niguel, California
Source: *BiE&WWA; ForWC 70; NotNAT*

Fried, Alfred Hermann
Austrian. Author
Founded German Peace Society, 1892; won Nobel Peace Prize, 1911.
b. Nov 11, 1864 in Vienna, Austria
d. May 6, 1921 in Vienna, Austria
Source: *BiDMoPL; BioIn 5, 9, 11, 15; LinLib L; NewCol 75; WebBD 83; WhoNob, 90, 95*

Fried, Gerald
American. Composer
Won Emmy for score of TV mini-series "Roots," 1977.
b. Feb 13, 1928 in New York, New York
Source: *ASCAP 66, 80; BioIn 16; HalFC 88; VarWW 85*

Friedan, Betty (Naomi Goldstein)
American. Feminist, Author
Founded NOW, 1966, pres. until 1970; wrote *The Feminine Mystique*, 1963.
b. Feb 4, 1921 in Peoria, Illinois
Source: *AmAu&B; AmDec 1960; AmOrTwC; AmRef&R; AmSocL; AmWomWr; ArtclWW 2; Benet 96; BenetAL 91; BioIn 6, 9, 10, 11, 12, 13, 14, 15, 18; BkPepl; BlmGWL; BlueB 76; CelR, 90; ConAu 18NR, 65; ConHero 1; ConIsC 2; ConLC 74; ContDcW 89; CurBio 70, 89; DcAmC; EncAB-H 1974; EncWB; EncWHA; FacFETw; FemiCLE; ForWC 70; GoodHs; GrLiveH; HanAmWH; IntDcWB; IntvTCA 2; IntWW 74, 75, 76, 77, 78, 79, 80, 81, 82, 83, 89, 91, 93; InWom SUP; JeHun; LegTOT; LibW; LinLib L; LNinSix; MajTwCW; MakMC; News 94, 94-2; NewYTBE 70, 71; OxCAmL 83, 95; OxCWoWr 95; PeoHis; PolPar; PolProf J, NF; PorAmW; RadHan; RComAH; WebAB 74, 79; WhoAm 74, 76, 78, 80, 82, 84, 86, 88, 90, 92, 94, 95; WhoAmJ 80; WhoAmP 89, 91, 93, 95; WhoAmW 66, 68, 75, 77, 79, 81, 83, 85, 87, 89, 91, 93, 95; WhoEnt 92; WhoUSWr 88; WhoWor 78, 80, 82, 84, 87; WhoWrEP 89, 92, 95; WomChHR; WorAl; WorAlBi; WorAu 1975; WrDr 76, 80, 82, 84, 86, 88, 90, 92, 94, 96*

Friedel, Charles
French. Chemist, Mineralogist
Most valuable work of aromatic hydrocarbons: the Friedel-Crafts reaction, 1877; major contribution to petroleum industry.
b. Mar 12, 1832 in Strasbourg, France
d. Apr 20, 1899 in Mantauban, France
Source: *AsBiEn; BiESc; BioIn 1, 14; CamDcSc; DcInv; InSci; WebBD 83; WhDW*

Friedkin, William
American. Director
Directed *The Exorcist*, 1973; won best director Oscar, 1971, for *The French Connection.*
b. Aug 29, 1939 in Chicago, Illinois
Source: *BiDFilm, 81, 94; BioIn 9, 11, 14, 15, 16; BkPepl; CelR, 90; ConAu 107; ConTFT 5, 15; CurBio 87; FilmEn; FilmgC; GangFlm; HalFC 80, 84, 88; IntDcF 1-2, 2-2; IntMPA 75, 76, 77, 78, 79, 80, 81, 82, 84, 86, 88, 92, 94, 96; IntWW 89, 91, 93; LegTOT; MovMk; WhoAm 74, 76, 78, 80, 82, 84, 86, 88, 92, 94, 95, 96, 97; WhoEnt 92; WhoHrs 80; WhoWest 74, 76, 78, 80, 82; WhoWor 74; WorFDir 2*

Friedlander, Saul
Israeli. Historian
Known for historical works on Germany, Nazism, and the Holocaust; wrote *Prelude to Downfall: Hitler and the United States, 1939-1941*, 1967.
b. Oct 11, 1932 in Prague, Czechoslovakia
Source: *BioIn 12, 17; ConAu 130; ConLC 90; WhoWorJ 72; WorAu 1980*

Friedman, Bruce Jay
American. Author
Wrote films *Doctor Detroit*, 1983; *Splash*, 1984.
b. Apr 26, 1930 in New York, New York
Source: *AmAu&B; Benet 87, 96; BenetAL 91; BioIn 7, 8, 9, 10, 11, 14, 15, 16; CamGWoT; ConAmD; ConAu 9R, 25NR, 52NR; ConDr 73, 77, 82, 88, 93; ConLC 3, 5, 56; ConNov 72, 76, 82, 86, 91, 96; ConTFT 1, 3; CurBio 72; DcLB 2, 28; DcLEL 1940; DrAF 76; DrAPF 80, 87, 91; EncAHmr; IntAu&W 76, 77, 91, 93; JeAmFiW; LinLib L; McGEWD 72, 84; ModAL, S1; NatPD 77, 81; Novels; OxCAmL 83, 95; OxCAmT 84; PenC AM; RAdv 1; VarWW 85; WhoAm 74, 76, 78, 80; WhoThe 81; WorAu 1950; WrDr 76, 80, 82, 84, 86, 88, 90, 92, 94, 96*

Friedman, Herbert
American. Physicist
Pioneered development of rocket, satellite and X-ray astronomy, 1949.
b. Jun 21, 1916 in New York, New York
Source: *AmMWSc 73P, 79, 82, 86, 89, 92, 95; AsBiEn; BiESc; BioIn 6, 7, 8, 13, 16; CamDcSc; ConAu 112; FacFETw; LarDcSc; McGMS 80; WhoAm 74, 76, 78, 80, 82, 86, 88, 90,*

92, 94, 95, 96; WhoE 86; WhoFrS 84; WhoGov 72, 75, 77; WhoScEn 94; WhoSSW 95, 97; WhoWor 89, 91, 93, 95; WrDr 92, 94, 96

Friedman, Jerome
American. Physicist
Shared Nobel Prize in physics, 1990, for breakthrough discoveries about the structure of matter; first to observe traces of quarks, subatomic particles forming the basis of 99% of earth's matter.
b. Mar 28, 1930 in Chicago, Illinois
Source: *AmMWSc 92; NotTwCS; WhoAm 90; WhoNob 90; WhoTech 89*

Friedman, Max
[Heavenly Twins]
American. Basketball Player
Guard with several pro teams, early 1900s, known for defensive play; Hall of Fame.
b. Jul 12, 1889 in New York, New York
d. Jan 1, 1986 in New York, New York
Source: *BiDAmSp BK; WhoBbl 73*

Friedman, Milton
American. Economist, Journalist
Noted conservative monetary expert who won Nobel Prize, 1976; wrote best seller *Free To Choose,* 1980.
b. Jul 31, 1912 in New York, New York
Source: *AmAu&B; AmEA 74; AmMWSc 73S, 78S; AmSocL; Au&Wr 71; BioIn 6, 7, 8, 9, 10, 11, 12, 13, 14, 15, 16, 17, 18, 19, 21; BlueB 76; CelR; ConAu 1NR, 1R, 22NR; ConIsC 1; DcAmC; DcCPSAm; EncAB-H 1974, 1996; EncABHB 7; EncWB; FacFETw; GrEconS; IntAu&W 76, 77, 82, 89, 91, 93; IntWW 74, 75, 76, 77, 78, 79, 80, 81, 82, 83, 89, 91, 93; JeAmHC; LegTOT; LinLib L; MajTwCW; MakMC; NewYTBS 76, 89; NobelP; PolProf J, NF; RAdv 14, 13-3; ThTwC 87; WebAB 74, 79; Who 74, 82, 83, 85, 88, 90, 92, 94; WhoAm 74, 76, 78, 80, 82, 84, 86, 88, 90, 92, 94, 95, 96, 97; WhoAmJ 80; WhoEc 81, 86; WhoFI 79, 81, 83, 89, 92, 94, 96; WhoNob, 90, 95; WhoWest 80, 82, 84, 87, 89, 92, 94, 96; WhoWor 74, 78, 80, 82, 84, 87, 89, 91, 93, 95, 96, 97; WhoWorJ 72, 78; WorAl; WorAlBi; WrDr 76, 80, 82, 84, 86, 88, 90, 92, 94, 96*

Friedman, Stephen
American. Producer
Film work includes *The Last Picture Show,* 1971; *Little Darlings,* 1980.
b. Mar 15, 1937 in New York, New York
d. Oct 4, 1996 in Brentwood, California
Source: *ConTFT 4; HalFC 84, 88; IntMPA 86, 92, 94, 96; St&PR 96, 97; VarWW 85; WhoAm 84, 86; WhoEnt 92; WhoSecI 86*

Friedman, Thomas L(oren)
American. Journalist
Won Pulitzer Prize for international reporting, 1983, 1988; wrote *From Beirut to Jerusalem,* 1989.
b. Jul 20, 1953 in Minneapolis, Minnesota
Source: *ConAu 38NR; CurBio 95; WhoAm 84, 86, 88, 90; WhoE 91, 93; WhoWor 91; WrDr 94, 96*

Friedman, William Frederick
American. Author
Cryptologist who broke "Purple," 1940, the principal Japanese code during WW II; wrote many books on subject.
b. Sep 24, 1891 in Kishinev, Russia
d. Nov 2, 1969 in Washington, District of Columbia
Source: *AmAu&B; BioIn 4, 8, 9, 11, 15; DcAmB S8; EncAI&E; HisDcDP; ObitOF 79; SpyCS; WhAm 5; WhWW-II*

Friedman, Ze'ev
Israeli. Olympic Athlete, Victim
One of 11 members of Israeli Olympic team kidnapped and killed by Arab terrorists during Summer Olympic Games.
b. 1944?
d. Sep 5, 1972 in Munich, Germany (West)
Source: *BioIn 9*

Friedrich, Caspar David
German. Artist
Romantic landscape paintings had mystical tone, limited impact on art: *Man and Woman Gazing at the Moon.*
b. Sep 5, 1774 in Greifswald, Germany
d. May 7, 1840 in Dresden, Germany
Source: *BioIn 6, 9, 10, 11, 12, 13, 14, 15, 17; DcArts; EncEnl; IntDcAA 90; McGDA; McGEWB; NewCol 75; OxCArt; OxCGer 76, 86; OxCShps; OxDcArt; WhDW*

Friedrich, Otto
American. Writer
Author of children's books.
d. Apr 26, 1995 in North Shore, New York
Source: *NewYTBS 95*

Friel, Brian
American. Dramatist
Plays include *The Enemy Within,* 1962; *Philadelphia, Here I Come,* 1965.
b. Jan 9, 1929 in Omagh, Northern Ireland
Source: *Au&Wr 71; Benet 96; BiDIrW; BioIn 10, 13, 14, 16; CamGLE; CamGWoT; CnThe; ConAu 21R, 33NR; ConBrDr; ConDr 73, 77, 82, 88, 93; ConLC 5, 42, 59; ConTFT 10; CrtSuDr; CurBio 74; CyWA 89; DcArts; DcIrL, 96; DcIrW 1; DcLB 13; DcLEL 1940; EncWL 3; FacFETw; IntAu&W 76, 77, 82, 86, 89, 91, 93; IntDcT 2; IntvTCA 2; IntWW 89, 91, 93; IriPla; LegTOT; MajTwCW; McGEWD 72, 84; ModBrL S1, S2; ModIrL; ModWD; NewYTBS 89, 91; NotNAT; OxCIri; OxCThe 83; RAdv 14, 13-2; REnWD; RfGEnL 91; RGTwCWr; Who 74, 82, 83, 85, 88, 90, 92, 94; WhoAm 76, 78, 80, 82, 84, 86, 88, 90, 92, 94, 95, 96, 97; WhoEnt 92; WhoThe 72, 77, 81; WhoWor 74, 76, 95, 96, 97; WorAu 1950; WrDr 76, 80, 82, 84, 86, 88, 90, 92, 94, 96*

Friend, Bob
[Robert Bartmess Friend]
"Warrior"
American. Baseball Player
Pitcher, Pittsburgh, 1951-66; first in MLs to lead league in ERA while playing for last place team, 1955.
b. Nov 24, 1930 in Lafayette, Indiana
Source: *Ballpl 90; BiDAmSp Sup; BioIn 4, 5, 16; WhoProB 73*

Friendly, Alfred
American. Journalist
With *Washington Post,* 1939-71; won Pulitzer for coverage of 1967 Arab-Israeli War.
b. Dec 30, 1911 in Salt Lake City, Utah
d. Nov 7, 1983 in Washington, District of Columbia
Source: *AnObit 1983; BioIn 13, 16; BlueB 76; ConAu 101, 111; IntAu&W 77, 82; IntWW 74, 75, 76, 77, 78, 79, 80, 81, 82, 83; NewYTBS 83; WhoAm 74, 76, 78; WhoWor 78*

Friendly, Ed
[Edwin S Friendly, Jr]
American. Producer
Co-created TV comedy "Laugh-In," 1973; executive producer, TV series "Little House on the Prairie," 1974-82.
b. Apr 8, 1922 in New York, New York
Source: *ConTFT 8; LesBEnT, 92; NewYTET; WhoAm 78, 80, 82, 84, 86, 88; WhoEnt 92; WhoTelC; WhoWor 82, 87, 89, 95, 97*

Friendly, Fred W
[Ferdinand Friendly Wachenheimer]
American. Producer
Known for TV news, public affairs; pres., CBS News, 1964-66.
b. Oct 30, 1915 in New York, New York
Source: *AmAu&B; BiDAmJo; BioIn 15, 16; ConAu 14NR, 21R; ConTFT 6; CurBio 57, 87; EncTwCJ; IntMPA 92; IntWW 83, 91; LesBEnT 92; NewYTET; WhoAm 86, 90; WhoTelC; WorAlBi; WrDr 92*

Fries, Charles W
American. Producer
Films include *The Cat People,* 1982; major supplier of made for TV movies.
b. Sep 30, 1928 in Cincinnati, Ohio
Source: *BioIn 14, 16; ConTFT 2; IntMPA 84, 92; LesBEnT, 92; VarWW 85*

Friese-Greene, William Edward
[William Edward Green]
English. Inventor, Photographer
Built first practical movie camera, 1889; subject of film *The Magic Box,* 1951.
b. Sep 7, 1855 in Bristol, England
d. May 5, 1921 in London, England
Source: *BioIn 1, 2, 3, 4, 10; FilmEn; FilmgC; OxCFilm; WorEFlm*

Friesz, Othon
French. Artist
Designed Gobelin tapestry, *Peace.*
b. Feb 6, 1879 in Le Havre, France
d. Jan 11, 1949 in Paris, France
Source: *BioIn 1, 2, 4, 17; DcTwCCu 2; ObitOF 79; OxCTwCA; OxDcArt; PhDcTCA 77; WhAmArt 85A*

Friganza, Trixie
[Delia O'Callahan]
American. Actor, Singer
Character actress in films including *Gentlemen Prefer Blondes,* 1953.
b. Nov 29, 1870 in Grenola, Kansas
d. Feb 27, 1955 in Flintridge, California
Source: *BiDD; BioIn 3, 4, 15; CmpEPM; EncVaud; Film 2; FunnyW; InWom SUP; OxCAmT 84; TwYS; WhoHol B; WhoStg 1908; WhScrn 74, 77, 83; WhThe*

Frijid Pink
[Thomas Beaudry; Thomas Harris; Richard Stevers; Gary Thompson; Jon Wearing; Craig Webb; Lawrence Zelanka]
American. Music Group
Heavy-metal band, 1970s; biggest hit a remake of "House of the Rising Sun," 1970.
Source: *Alli, SUP; BioIn 4; DcCAr 81; DcNaB; DcNCBi 3; DrAP 75; DrAPF 83, 85, 87, 89, 91, 93, 97; Dun&B 86; FolkA 87; InB&W 80; NewGrDM 80; PenEncH; RkOn 74, 78, 84; WhoAmP 79, 81, 83, 85; WhoRocM 82*

Friml, Rudolf
American. Musician, Composer
Noted for Broadway operettas *Rose Marie,* 1924; *Vagabond King,* 19 25; wrote songs "Indian Love Call," 1924; "The Donkey Serenade," 1937.
b. Dec 7, 1879 in Prague, Bohemia
d. Nov 12, 1972 in Hollywood, California
Source: *AmPS; AmSong; ASCAP 66, 80; Baker 78, 84; BestMus; BiDAmM; BioIn 3, 4, 5, 6, 8, 9, 10, 12, 15, 16; BriBkM 80; CmpEPM; ConAmC 76, 82; EncMT; EncWT; FilmgC; HalFC 80, 84, 88; LegTOT; MusMk; NewAmDM; NewCBMT; NewGrDA 86; NewGrDM 80; NewOxM; NewYTBE 72; NotNAT B; ObitT 1971; OxCAmT 84; OxCPMus; OxDcOp; PenDiMP A; PlP&P; PopAmC, SUP, SUPN; Sw&Ld C; WebAB 74, 79; WhAm 5; WorAl; WorAlBi*

Frings, Joseph Richard
German. Religious Leader
Cardinal who denounced Nazis in sermons during WW II.
b. Feb 6, 1887? in Neuss, Germany
d. Dec 17, 1978 in Cologne, Germany (West)
Source: *BioIn 1, 7, 8, 11; NewYTBS 78; ObitOF 79; WhoWor 76*

Frings, Ketti
[Katherine Hartley]
American. Dramatist, Author
Won Pulitzer for stage adaptation *Look Homeward Angel,* 1968.
b. Feb 28, 1915 in Columbus, Ohio
d. Feb 11, 1981 in Los Angeles, California
Source: *AmAu&B; AmWomD; AmWomWr; AnObit 1981; BenetAL 91; BiE&WWA; ConAu 101, 103; CurBio 60, 81; FilmEn; FilmgC; HalFC 80; McGEWD 72, 84; NatPD 77; NewYTBS 81; NotNAT; NotWoAT; OhA&B; OxCAmL 65; REnAL; ScF&FL 92; WhoAm 80; WhoE 74*

Fripp, Robert
English. Musician
Guitarist for King Crimson, 1969-1984; produced albums for many top musical performers.
b. 1946 in Wimborne Minster, England
Source: *BioIn 12, 14; ConMus 9; EncPR&S 89; EncRk 88; LegTOT; OnThGG; PenEncP*

Frisch, Frankie
[Frank Francis Frisch]
"Dutchman"; "The Fordham Flash"
American. Baseball Player, Baseball Manager
Infielder, 1919-37; had lifetime .316 batting average; Hall of Fame, 1947.
b. Sep 9, 1898 in New York, New York
d. Mar 12, 1973 in Wilmington, Delaware
Source: *Ballpl 90; BiDAmSp BB; DcAmB S9; LegTOT; NewYTBE 73; WhoFtbl 74; WhoProB 73; WhoSpor; WorAl; WorAlBi*

Frisch, Karl von
German. Zoologist, Ethnologist
Won Nobel Prize in medicine, 1973, for research on sense perception and communication in bees.
b. Nov 20, 1886 in Vienna, Austria
d. Jun 12, 1982 in Munich, Germany (West)
Source: *AnObit 1982; AsBiEn; BiESc; BioIn 3, 6, 8, 10, 13, 14, 15, 20; CamDcSc; ConAu 85, 107, 115; CurBio 74, 83N; IntWW 74, 75, 76, 77, 78, 79, 80, 81, 82; LarDcSc; LinLib L; McGEWB; McGMS 80; NewYTBE 73; NobelP; NotTwCS; WhoNob, 95; WhoWor 74; WorAl; WorAlBi*

Frisch, Max
Swiss. Author
Considered dean of German-language literature; plays *The Firebugs, Andorra* became standard theater repertory, translated into 37 languages.
b. May 15, 1911 in Zurich, Switzerland
d. Apr 4, 1991 in Zurich, Switzerland
Source: *AnObit 1991; Benet 87, 96; BiE&WWA; BiGAW; BioIn 6, 7, 8, 9, 10, 11, 12, 13, 14, 15, 17, 18, 19; BioNews 74; CamGWoT; CasWL; ClDMEL 80; CnMD; CnThe; ConAu 32NR, 85, 134; ConFLW 84; ConLC 3, 9, 14, 18, 32, 44; CroCD; CurBio 65, 91N; CyWA 89; DcArts; DcLB 69, 124; EncWL 2, 3; EncWT; Ent; EuWr 13; EvEuW; FacFETw; GrFLW; IntAu&W 76, 77, 91; IntWW 74, 75, 76, 77, 78, 79, 80, 91, 91N; IntWWP 77; LegTOT; LinLib L; MajMD 1; MajTwCW; MakMC; McGEWB; McGEWD 72, 84; ModGL; ModWD; NewYTBS 81, 91; NotNAT; OxCEng 85, 95; OxCGer 76, 86; OxCThe 67; PenC EUR; PostFic; RAdv 14, 13-2; REn; REnWD; TwCWr; WhDW; WhoThe 72, 77, 81; WhoTwCL; WhoWor 74, 91; WorAlBi; WorAu 1950; WrPh*

Frisch, Ragnar Anton Kittil
Norwegian. Economist
Shared 1969 Nobel Prize for developing econometrics, math economics.
b. Mar 2, 1895 in Oslo, Norway
d. Jan 31, 1973 in Oslo, Norway
Source: *ConAu 115; NewYTBE 73; WhAm 5; WhoEc 81, 86; WhoNob*

Frisco, Joe
American. Actor
Vaudevillian; did stuttering comic routine in 1930s films.
b. 1890 in Milan, Illinois
d. Feb 16, 1958 in Woodland Hills, California
Source: *BiDD; BioIn 4, 5; EncAFC; JoeFr; NotNAT B; OxCAmT 84; WhoCom; WhoHol B; WhScrn 74, 77, 83*

Frissell, Toni
American. Photographer
First to photograph formally dressed models outdoors; worked for top fashion magazines from 1931.
b. Mar 10, 1907 in New York, New York
d. Apr 17, 1988 in Saint James, New York
Source: *BioIn 1, 9, 13, 15, 16; ConPhot 82, 88, 95; CurBio 47, 88, 88N; EncFash; ICPEnP A; InWom, SUP*

Frist, Bill
American. Politician
Rep. senator, TN, 1995—.
b. Feb 22, 1952

Fritchie, Barbara
American. Historical Figure
Supposedly waved Union flag at Lee's army as it marched through her town, 1862.
b. 1766 in Frederick, Maryland
d. 1862
Source: *BioIn 4, 5, 7, 8, 10; Dis&D; EncSoH; NatCAB 10; NotAW; WhCiWar*

Frith, William Powell
English. Artist
Known for large, popular pictures of ordinary English life, including *Derby Day,* 1858.
b. Jan 9, 1819 in Aldfield, England
d. Nov 2, 1909 in London, England
Source: *Alli SUP; ArtsNiC; BioIn 4, 5, 6, 10, 12; CelCen; ChhPo; ClaDrA; DcArts; DcBiPP; DcBrBI; DcNaB S2; DcVicP, 2; IntDcAA 90; McGDA; NewCol 75; OxCArt; OxDcArt*

Fritz, Jean Guttery
American. Children's Author
Award-winning novels are usually set in colonial America during Revolutionary War: *Stonewall,* 1979.
b. Nov 16, 1915 in Hankou, China
Source: *AuBYP 2, 3; BioIn 7, 9, 13, 14, 15; ChhPo S2; ChlLR 2, 14; ConAu 1R, 5NR, 16NR, 37NR; DcAmChF 1960; DcLB 52; ForWC 70; IntAu&W 91; MajAI; MorBMP; OxCChiL; SmATA 1, 2AS, 29, 72; ThrBJA; TwCChW 83, 89; WhoAm 84, 92, 94, 95, 96; WhoAmW 83, 89, 91, 93, 95; WrDr 86, 92*

Fritzsche, Hans
German. Government Official
Radio, news propaganda chief under Goebbels; pardoned at Nuremburg trials.
b. Apr 21, 1899 in Dresden, Germany
d. Sep 27, 1953 in Cologne, Germany (West)
Source: *BioIn 1, 2, 3; EncTR; ObitOF 79*

Frizon, Maud
[Maud Frison]
French. Designer
Manufactures colorful, high fashion footwear.
b. 1942? in Paris, France
Source: *BioIn 12, 14, 15, 16; EncFash*

Frizzell, Lefty
[William Orville Frizzell]
American. Singer
Had number-one country hit, ''Saginaw, Michigan,'' 1964; four singles on top-ten lis t at once, 1952.
b. Mar 31, 1928 in Corsicana, Texas
d. Jul 19, 1975 in Nashville, Tennessee
Source: *Baker 84; BgBkCoM; BiDAmM; BioIn 10, 14, 15, 21; ConMus 10; CounME 74, 74A; EncFCWM 69, 83; HarEnCM 87; IlEncCM; LegTOT; NewAmDM; NewGrDA 86; PenEncP; RkOn 78*

Frobe, Gerd
German. Actor
Appeared in nearly 100 movies; best known for role of Goldfinger in James Bond film, 1964.
b. Feb 25, 1912 in Planitz, Germany
d. Sep 5, 1988 in Munich, Germany (West)
Source: *FilmEn; FilmgC; IntMPA 82; MotPP; MovMk; WhoHol A*

Froben, Johann
German. Scholar, Printer
Printed Erasmus's Latin translation of Greek New Testament, 1516; popularized Roman type.
b. 1460 in Hammelburg, Germany
d. Oct 1527 in Basel, Switzerland
Source: *BioIn 5, 7, 9; DcBiPP; DcEuL; OxCGer 76, 86*

Frobisher, Martin
English. Navigator
Made three voyages to New World attempting to discover Northwest Passage, 1576, 1577, 1578.
b. 1535 in Doncaster, England
d. Nov 22, 1594 in Plymouth, England
Source: *Alli; ApCAB; Benet 87, 96; BioIn 3, 4, 7, 8, 9, 11; DcNaB; Drake; EncCRAm; LegTOT; LinLib S; NewC; OxCCan; OxCShps; REn; WhAm HS; WhDW; WhWE; WorAl; WorAlBi*

Froebel, Friedrich Wilhelm August
German. Educator
Founded kindergarten system, 1836.
b. Apr 21, 1782 in Oberweissbach, Germany
d. Jun 21, 1852 in Marienthal, Germany
Source: *BbD; BiD&SB; BioIn 1, 3, 4, 8, 11, 12, 13; LinLib L, S; LngCTC; LuthC 75; McGEWB; NewCBEL; WorAl*

Froese, Bob
Canadian. Hockey Player
Goalie, Philadelphia, 1982-86, NY Rangers, 1986-90; set NHL record for consecutive games without loss at start of career, 13.
b. Jun 30, 1958 in Saint Catharines, Ontario, Canada
Source: *BioIn 13; HocReg 87; NewYTBS 83*

Frohman, Charles
American. Impresario, Producer
Introduced Maude Adams in *Peter Pan,* 1905; helped create ''star'' system; vi ctim of Lusitania disaster.
b. Jun 17, 1860 in Sandusky, Ohio
d. May 7, 1915
Source: *AmBi; BenetAL 91; BiDAmBL 83; BioIn 5, 10; CamGWoT; CnThe; DcAmB; EncMT; EncWT; Ent; LinLib S; NatCAB 11; NotNAT A, B; OxCAmH; OxCAmL 65, 83, 95; OxCAmT 84; OxCPMus; OxCThe 67, 83; PlP&P; REnAL; WebAB 74, 79; WhAm 1; WhoStg 1906, 1908; WhThe*

Frohman, Daniel
American. Manager
With brother Charles was among most noted NYC theater producers, 1880s-90s; pres., Actors Fund of America, 1903-40.
b. Aug 22, 1851 in Sandusky, Ohio
d. Dec 26, 1940 in New York, New York
Source: *AmAu&B; BenetAL 91; BioIn 4, 5; CamGWoT; CurBio 41; DcAmB S2; EncWT; Ent; LinLib L, S; NatCAB 11; NotNAT A, B; OhA&B; OxCAmH; OxCAmL 65, 83, 95; OxCAmT 84; OxCThe 67, 83; PlP&P; REnAL; TwCBDA; WhAm 1; WhThe*

Frohnmayer, John Edward
American. Lawyer, Government Official
Chm., Nat. Endowment for the Arts, 1989-92.
b. Jun 1, 1942 in Medford, Oregon
Source: *BioIn 16; CurBio 90; IntWW 93; NewYTBS 89, 91; WhoAm 90, 92, 94, 95, 96, 97; WhoEnt 92*

Froines, John Radford
[The Chicago 7]
American. Political Activist
Took part in antiwar demonstrations during 1968 Democratic National Convention in Chicago.
b. Jun 13, 1939 in Oakland, California
Source: *BioIn 10, 11; MugS; WhoAm 82; WhoGov 77*

Froissart, Jean
French. Author, Poet
Best-known work: *Chronicles,* originally in four vols., covering 1325-1400.
b. 1333? in Valenciennes, France
d. 1400? in Chimay, France
Source: *AtlBL; BbD; BiD&SB; CasWL; CyWA 58; DcEuL; EuAu; EvEuW; McGEWB; NewC; OxCEng 85; OxCFr; PenC EUR; REn; SmATA 28*

Froman, Jane
American. Actor, Singer
Suffered crippling injuries in 1943 plane crash en route to entertain troops; inspiration for film *With a Song in My Heart,* 1952.
b. Nov 10, 1907 in Saint Louis, Missouri
d. Apr 22, 1980 in Columbia, Missouri
Source: *AmPS A; BioIn 12, 15; CmpEPM; HalFC 84, 88; PenEncP; RadStar; SaTiSS; What 5; WhoHol A*

Fromentin, Eugene
French. Author
Painted exotic scenery; wrote travel books; novel *Dominique,* 1863.
b. Oct 24, 1820 in La Rochelle, France
d. Aug 27, 1876 in La Rochelle, France
Source: *ArtsNiC; BiD&SB; BioIn 1, 5, 7, 13, 15, 19; CasWL; ClaDrA; CyWA 58; DcBiPP; DcCathB; DcEuL; DcLB 123; Dis&D; EuAu; EvEuW; GuFrLit 1; LinLib L, S; McGDA; NinCLC 10; OxCArt; OxCFr; OxDcArt; PenC EUR; WhDW*

Fromholtz, Dianne
Australian. Tennis Player
Won Australian Open doubles, 1977.
b. Aug 10, 1956 in Albury, Australia
Source: *WhoIntT*

Fromm, Erich
American. Psychoanalyst
Dealt with problem of how Western man can come to terms with sense of isolation: *The Art of Loving,* 1956.
b. Mar 23, 1900 in Frankfurt am Main, Germany
d. Mar 18, 1980 in Muralto, Switzerland
Source: *AmAu&B; AmMWSc 73S, 78S; AnObit 1980; Au&Wr 71; Benet 87, 96; BenetAL 91; BiDMoPL; BiDNeoM; BiDPsy; BioIn 4, 5, 7, 8, 9, 10, 11, 12, 13, 14, 16, 17, 21; BlueB 76; ConAu 29NR, 73, 97; CurBio 67, 80, 80N; DcAmB S10; EncAB-H 1974, 1996; EncAL; EncTR; EncWB; FacFETw; GaEncPs; GuPsyc; InSci; IntAu&W 82; IntEnSS 79; IntWW 74, 75, 76, 77, 78, 79; LegTOT; LinLib L; MajTwCW; MakMC; NewYTBS 80; PenC AM; RAdv 14, 13-5; REn; REnAL; ThTwC 87; TwCA SUP; WebAB 74, 79; WhAm 7; WhDW; WhoAm 74, 76, 78, 80; WhoE 74; WhoSSW 73; WhoTwCL; WhoWor 74, 78; WorAl; WorAlBi; WrDr 76, 80*

Fromme, Lynette Alice
"Squeaky"
American. Attempted Assassin, Cultist
Charles Manson follower, convicted of attempting to assassinate Gerald Ford, 1975.
b. Dec 22, 1949 in Santa Monica, California
Source: *BioIn 10, 11, 12, 13; GoodHs; InWom SUP; WorAlBi*

Frondizi, Arturo
Argentine. Lawyer, Politician
Pres. of Argentina, 1958-62.
b. Sep 28, 1908, Argentina
d. Apr 18, 1995 in Buenos Aires, Argentina
Source: *BiDLAmC; BioIn 4, 5, 6, 16, 19, 20, 21; CurBio 58, 95N; DcCPSAm; DcPol; EncLatA; EncWB; IntWW 74, 75, 76, 77, 78, 79, 80, 81, 82, 83, 89, 91, 93; NewYTBS 95; WhoWor 74*

Frontenac, Louis de Buade de
French. Political Leader
Governor-general of New France, late 1600s; promoted French expansion, Indian defeat.
b. May 22, 1622 in Saint-Germain-en-Laye, France
d. Nov 28, 1698 in Quebec, Canada
Source: *ApCAB; DicTyr; Drake; OxCAmL 65; OxCCan; WhAm HS*

Frost, Arthur Burdett
American. Illustrator
Cartoonist with *Life; Colliers* mags; best known for *Uncle Remus* illustrations.
b. Jan 17, 1851 in Philadelphia, Pennsylvania
d. Jun 22, 1928 in Pasadena, California
Source: *AmAu&B; AmBi; ArtsAmW 1; BioIn 2, 3, 4, 5, 12, 19; ChhPo, S1, S2; ChlBkCr; DcAmAu; DcAmB; DcBrBI; DcNAA; IlBEAAW; IlrAm 1880, A; LinLib L, S; NatCAB 11; OxCAmL 65; OxCTwCA; PeoHis; PhDcTCA 77; REnAL; Str&VC; WhAm 1; WorECar*

Frost, David
[David Paradine]
English. TV Personality, Author
Won Emmys, 1970, 1971, for TV interview show; famous for one-on-one interviews with Nixon, Kissinger, others.
b. Apr 7, 1939 in Tenterden, England
Source: *BioIn 8, 9, 10, 11, 12, 15; BlueB 76; CelR, 90; ConAu 31NR, 69; ConTFT 3; CurBio 69; EncAJ; HalFC 80, 84, 88; IntAu&W 91; IntMPA 75, 76, 77, 78, 79, 80, 81, 82; IntWW 74, 91; LegTOT; LesBEnT 92; NewYTBE 71; NewYTET; Who 74, 82, 83, 85, 85E, 88, 90, 92; WhoAm 76, 78, 80, 82, 84, 86, 88, 90; WhoCom; WhoWor 74, 78, 80, 82, 84, 87, 89, 91; WorAlBi; WrDr 80, 82, 84, 86, 88, 90, 92*

Frost, Edwin Brant
American. Astronomer, Lecturer
Director, Yerkes Observatory, 1905-32.
b. Jul 14, 1866 in Brattleboro, Vermont
d. May 14, 1935 in Chicago, Illinois
Source: *AmBi; DcAmB S1; DcNAA; DcScB; InSci; NatCAB 9, 25; TwCBDA; WebBD 83; WhAm 1*

Frost, Robert Lee
American. Poet
Won four Pulitzers; wrote verses on rural New England.
b. Mar 26, 1874 in San Francisco, California
d. Jan 29, 1963 in Boston, Massachusetts
Source: *AmAu&B; AmLY; AmWr; AnCL; AtlBL; CasWL; Chambr 3; CnDAL; ConLC 15; CurBio 42, 63; EncAB-H 1996; ModAL S1; NewYTBE 72; OxCAmL 83; REn; RGTwCWr; TwCA SUP; WhAm 4*

Froude, James Anthony
English. Historian
Wrote *The History of England from the Fall of Wolsey to the Defeat of the Spanish Armada,* 1856-70; Thomas Carlyle's literary executor.
b. Apr 23, 1818 in Dartington, England
d. Oct 20, 1894 in Salcombe, England
Source: *Alli, SUP; AtlBL; BbD; Benet 87; BiD&SB; BioIn 1, 2, 3, 4, 6, 7, 8, 9, 10, 12, 13, 16, 17, 21; BritAu 19; CamGEL; CamGLE; CasWL; CelCen; Chambr 3; DcBiPP; DcEnA, A; DcEnL; DcEuL; DcLB 18, 57, 144; DcLEL; DcNaB S1; EncSoA; EvLB; LinLib L, S; McGEWB; MouLC 4; NewC; NewCBEL; NewCol 75; NinCLC 43; OxCEng 67, 85; OxCShps; PenC ENG; RAdv 13-1; REn; VicBrit; WebE&AL*

Fruehauf, Harvey Charles
American. Manufacturer
Founder, Fruehauf Trailer Co., 1916; built one of first semi-trailers for hauling cargo.
b. Dec 15, 1893 in Grosse Pointe, Michigan
d. Oct 14, 1968 in Detroit, Michigan
Source: *ObitOF 79; WhAm 5*

Frum, Barbara
Canadian. Broadcast Journalist, Author
Host, interviewer, "As It Happens," CBC radio show; "The Journal," TV show; often compared to Barbara Walters.
b. Sep 8, 1937 in Niagara Falls, New York
d. Mar 26, 1992 in Toronto, Ontario, Canada
Source: *AnObit 1992; BioIn 19; CanWW 83, 89; ConAu 101, 137; NewYTBS 92*

Fry, Art
American. Inventor
Scientist for 3M Corp; invented Post-It Notes, 1980.
b. 1932?
Source: *WhoMW 90*

Fry, Charles Burgess
English. Cricket Player, Author
Cricketer who was also 1892 world long jump champion.
b. 1872 in Croydon, England
d. Sep 7, 1956 in London, England
Source: *BioIn 2, 4, 14; DcNaB 1951; GrBr; MnBBF; NewCBEL; ObitOF 79; WhE&EA; WhLit*

Fry, Christopher
English. Dramatist
Wrote plays *The Lady's Not for Burning,* 1949; *Venus Observed,* 1950.
b. Dec 18, 1907 in Bristol, England
Source: *Au&Wr 71; AuBYP 2, 3; Benet 87, 96; BiE&WWA; BioIn 2, 3, 4, 5, 6, 8, 9, 10, 13, 16; BlmGEL; BlueB 76; BritPl; CamGEL; CamGLE; CamGWoT; CasWL; CnMD; CnMWL; CnThe; ConAu 9NR, 17R, 23AS, 30NR; ConBrDr; ConDr 73, 77, 82, 88, 93; ConLC 2, 10, 14; ConPo 70, 75, 80, 85, 91, 96; CroCD; CrtSuDr; CyWA 58; DcArts; DcLB 13; DcLEL; DcLP 87A; EncWL, 2, 3; EncWT; EngPo; Ent; EvLB; FacFETw; GrWrEL DR; IntAu&W 76, 89, 91, 93; IntDcT 2; IntvTCA 2; IntWW 74, 75, 76, 77, 78, 79, 80, 81, 82, 83, 89, 91, 93; IntWWP 77; LegTOT; LinLib L, S; LngCTC; MajTwCW; McGEWD 72, 84; ModBrL, S1; ModWD; NewC; NewCBEL; NotNAT, A; OxCAmT 84; OxCEng 67, 85; OxCThe 67, 83; PenC ENG; PlP&P; RAdv 14, 13-2; REn; RfGEnL 91; RGTwCWr; SmATA 66; TwCA SUP; TwCWr; WebE&AL; Who 74, 82, 83, 85, 88, 90, 92, 94; WhoThe 72, 77, 81; WhoWor 74, 76, 78, 95, 96, 97; WorAl; WorAlBi; WorEFlm; WrDr 76, 80, 82, 84, 86, 88, 90, 92, 94, 96*

Fry, E. Maxwell
[Edwin Maxwell Fry]
English. Architect
Modernist innovator in tropical building.
b. Aug 2, 1899 in Wallasey, England
d. Sep 3, 1987 in Cotherstone, England

Source: *BioIn 7, 10, 11, 14, 16; BlueB 76; ClaDrA; ConArch 80, 87; ConAu 65, 123; DcArts; DcD&D; EncMA; IntWW 74, 75, 76, 77, 78, 79, 80, 81, 82, 83; MacEA; McGDA; OxCArt; Who 74, 82, 83, 85; WhoArch; WhoWor 74, 76, 78*

Fry, Elizabeth Gurney
English. Social Reformer, Philanthropist
Dedicated life to improving condition of the poor, women in prison.
b. May 21, 1780 in Ramsgate, England
d. Oct 12, 1845 in Earlham, England
Source: *Alli; ArtclWW 2; BioIn 6, 7, 8, 9, 10, 11, 16, 17, 21; Dis&D; InWom, SUP; LinLib S; NewCBEL; REn; WomFir*

Fry, Franklin Clark
American. Clergy
Pres., United Lutheran Church, 1944-62; American Lutheran Church, 1962-68.
b. Aug 30, 1900 in Bethlehem, Pennsylvania
d. Jun 6, 1968 in New Rochelle, New York
Source: *BioIn 1, 2, 4, 8, 9, 10; CurBio 46, 68; DcEcMov; LuthC 75; NatCAB 54; ObitOF 79; RelLAm 91; WebAB 74, 79; WhAm 5*

Fry, Roger Eliot
English. Artist, Critic
Introduced modern French painters to English public; coined phrase, Post-Impressionists, 1910.
b. Dec 14, 1866 in London, England
d. Sep 9, 1934 in London, England
Source: *BioIn 1, 2, 3, 4, 7, 9, 10, 12, 13, 14, 15; DcArts; DcNaB 1931; DcTwDes; GrBr; LngCTC; MakMC; ModBrL; NewC; NewCBEL; OxCArt; OxCEng 67, 85, 95; OxCTwCA; REn; TwCA, SUP*

Frye, David
American. Comedian
Stand-up comic, best known for imitation of Richard Nixon.
b. 1934 in New York, New York
Source: *BioIn 9, 10; CurBio 75; JoeFr; WhoCom; WorAl*

Frye, (Herman) Northrop
Canadian. Critic
Literary critic; tracked myths and symbols to biblical sources; wrote *Anatomy of Criticism,* 1957, which became standard work.
b. Jul 14, 1912 in Sherbrooke, Quebec, Canada
d. Jan 22, 1991 in Toronto, Ontario, Canada
Source: *AmAu&B; AnObit 1991; Benet 87, 96; BenetAL 91; BioIn 3, 5, 10, 12, 13; BlueB 76; CamGLE; CanWr; CanWW 70, 79, 80, 81, 83, 89; CasWL; ConAu 5NR, 5R, 8NR, 37NR, 133; ConCaAu 1; ConLC 24, 70; ConLCrt 77, 82; CurBio 83, 91N; CyWA 89; DcArts; DcLB 67, 68; DrAS 74E, 78E, 82E; EncWB; EncWL 2, 3, SUP; FacFETw; IntAu&W 76, 77, 82; IntWW 74, 75, 76, 77, 78, 79, 80, 81, 82, 83, 89, 91N; LegTOT; LinLib L; MajTwCW; NewC; News 91, 91-3; NewYTBS 91; OxCCan; OxCCanL; OxCCan SUP; PenC AM, ENG; RAdv 1, 14, 13-1; ThTwC 87; WhAm 10; WhoAm 74, 76, 78, 80, 82, 84, 86, 88, 90; WhoCan 73; WhoCanL 85, 87, 92; WhoWor 74, 82, 84, 87, 89, 91; WhoWrEP 89; WorAu 1950; WrDr 76, 80, 82, 84, 86, 88, 90*

Fryer, Robert
American. Producer
Won Tonys for *Wonderful Town,* 1953; *Redhead,* 1959; *Sweeney Todd,* 1979.
b. Dec 18, 1920 in Washington, District of Columbia
Source: *BiE&WWA; ConTFT 2; EncMT; HalFC 80, 84, 88; NotNAT; OxCAmT 84; VarWW 85; WhoAm 90; WhoEnt 92; WhoThe 72, 77, 81; WhoWest 89; WhoWor 91*

Fuchida, Mitsuo
Japanese. Naval Officer, Aviator
Imperial Navy commander who led attack on Pearl Harbor, Dec 1941.
b. Dec 3, 1903 in Nagao, Japan
d. May 30, 1976 in Kashiwara, Japan
Source: *BioIn 2, 3, 10; ObitOF 79*

Fuchs, Daniel
American. Author
Won Oscar for *Love Me or Leave Me,* 1955.
b. Jun 25, 1909 in New York, New York
d. Jul 26, 1993 in Los Angeles, California
Source: *AmAu&B; BenetAL 91; BioIn 1, 6, 9, 12, 13, 14, 16, 19; ConAu 5AS, 40NR, 81, 142; ConLC 8, 22, 81; ConNov 72, 76, 82, 86, 91; DcLB 9, 26, 28, Y93N; DrAF 76; DrAPF 80, 91; IntAu&W 76; JeAmFiW; ModAL S1; Novels; OxCAmL 65, 83, 95; PenC AM; PeoHis; REnAL; VarWW 85; WebE&AL; WhoTwCL; WorAu 1970; WrDr 76, 80, 82, 84, 86, 88, 90, 92, 94, 96*

Fuchs, Joseph (Philip)
American. Violinist
International concertist, 1950s-60s; performed new works of modern composers.
b. Apr 26, 1900 in New York, New York
d. Mar 14, 1997 in New York, New York
Source: *Baker 78, 84, 92; BioIn 6, 9, 13, 16; CurBio 62; NewAmDM; NewGrDA 86; NewGrDM 80; NewYTBS 88; WhoAm 74, 76; WhoEnt 92; WhoWor 74*

Fuchs, Klaus
[Emil Klaus Julius Fuchs]
English. Spy, Physicist
Passed American and British A-Bomb research results to USSR.
b. Dec 29, 1911 in Russelsheim, Germany
d. Jan 28, 1988 in Berlin, German Democratic Republic
Source: *AnObit 1988; BioIn 2, 3, 4, 5, 6, 8, 9, 15, 16; ColdWar 1; DcTwHis; EncCW; EncMcCE; FacFETw; InSci; NewYTBS 88; WhoSocC 78; WhoSoCE 89*

Fuchs, Marta
German. Opera Singer
Noted dramatic soprano; often sang at Bayreuth.
b. Jan 1, 1898
d. 1974
Source: *Baker 84, 92; BioIn 10; CmOp; NewEOp 71; NewGrDM 80; NewGrDO; OxDcOp*

Fuchs, Michael J(oseph)
American. TV Executive
Chairman and CEO, HBO, 1984—.
b. Mar 9, 1946 in New York, New York
Source: *CurBio 96; WhoAm 96, 97; WhoE 97*

Fuchs, Vivian Ernest, Sir
English. Geologist, Explorer
With Sir Edmund Hillary, first to cross Antarctica overland, 1957-58.
b. Feb 11, 1908 in Isle of Wight, England
Source: *BioIn 4, 5, 9; ConAu 21NR, 104; CurBio 58; FacFETw; IntWW 74, 75, 76, 77, 78, 79, 80, 81, 82, 83, 89, 91, 93; WhDW; Who 85, 90, 94; WhoWor 87, 91; WrDr 80, 92*

Fudge, Ann (Marie)
American. Business Executive
Pres., Maxwell House Coffee, 1994—.
b. c. 1951 in Washington, District of Columbia
Source: *ConBlB 11; WhoAdv 90; WhoAm 92, 94, 95, 96, 97; WhoAmW 93, 95, 97*

Fuentes, Carlos
Mexican. Author, Dramatist
Writings include *Our Land,* 1974; *A Change of Skin,* 1968.
b. Nov 11, 1928 in Mexico City, Mexico
Source: *Au&Arts 4; AuNews 2; Benet 87, 96; BenetAL 91; BiDAmNC; BioIn 7, 8, 9, 10, 11, 12, 13, 14, 15, 16; CasWL; ConAu 10NR, 32NR, 69; ConFLW 84; ConLC 3, 8, 10, 13, 22, 41, 60; ConWorW 93; CurBio 72; CyWA 89; DcArts; DcCLAA; DcHiB; DcLB 113; DcMexL; DcTwCCu 4; EncLatA; EncWL 2, 3; FacFETw; HispLC; HispWr; IntAu&W 76, 77, 82, 89, 91, 93; IntvLAW; IntWW 74, 75, 76, 77, 78, 79, 80, 81, 82, 83, 89, 91, 93; LatAmWr; LegTOT; LiExTwC; MagSWL; MajTwCW; McGEWB; NewYTBS 88; Novels; OxCSpan; PenC AM; PenEncH; PostFic; RAdv 13-2; RfGShF; RfGWoL 95; ScF&FL 92; SpAmA; TwCWr; Who 88, 90, 92, 94; WhoAm 78, 80, 82, 84, 86, 88, 90, 92, 94, 95, 96, 97; WhoHisp 92, 94; WhoSSW 73; WhoTwCL; WhoWor 78, 80, 82, 84, 87, 89, 91, 93, 95, 96, 97; WorAl; WorAlBi; WorAu 1950; WorLitC*

Fuertes, Louis Agassiz
American. Ornithologist, Artist
Finely detailed paintings illustrate handbooks of birds in eastern, western US.
b. Feb 7, 1874 in Ithaca, New York
d. Aug 22, 1927 in Unadilla, New York
Source: *AmBi; ArtsAmW 2; BioIn 1, 4, 9, 10, 11, 12, 13, 14, 20; DcAmB; DcNAA; LinLib L, S; NatCAB 21; WhAm 1; WhAmArt 85*

Fuess, Claude Moore
American. Educator, Author
Headmaster, Phillips Academy, Andover, MA, 1933-48; known for many biographies: *Daniel Webster,* 1930; *Calvin Coolidge,* 1940.
b. Jan 12, 1885 in Waterville, New York
d. Sep 9, 1963
Source: *AmAu&B; BioIn 1, 3, 4, 6; OxCAmL 65, 83; REnAL; TwCA, SUP; WhAm 4; WhNAA*

Fugard, Athol
[Harold Athol Lannigan Fugard]
South African. Actor, Director, Dramatist
Writes about apartheid in *Sizwe Banzi Is Dead; A Lesson from Aloes.*
b. Jun 11, 1932 in Middleburg, South Africa
Source: *AfSS 79; Au&Arts 17; Benet 87, 96; BioIn 10, 13, 14, 15, 16; CamGEL; CamGLE; CamGWoT; CasWL; CelR 90; CnThe; ConAu 32NR, 85; ConDr 73, 77, 82, 88; ConLC 5, 9, 14, 25, 40, 80; ConTFT 1, 3, 15; CrtSuDr; CurBio 75; CyWA 89; DcArts; DcLEL 1940; DramC 3; EncSoA; EncWB; EncWL 2, 3; EncWT; Ent; FacFETw; GrWrEL DR; IntAu&W 76; IntLitE; IntvTCA 2; IntWW 80, 91, 93; LegTOT; MajTwCW; McGEWD 84; MiSFD 9; ModCmwL; News 92, 92-3; NewYTBE 70; NotNAT; OxCEng 85, 95; OxCThe 83; PlP&P A; RfGEnL 91; TwCWr; Who 82, 83, 85, 88, 90, 92, 94; WhoHol 92; WhoThe 72, 77, 81; WhoTwCL; WhoWor 91; WorAu 1970; WrDr 76, 80, 82, 84, 86, 88, 90, 92, 94, 96*

Fugate, Caril Ann
American. Murderer
Friend of Charles Starkweather allegedly involved in NE murders; spent 18 years in prison.
b. 1943
Source: *BioIn 10; GoodHs; MurCaTw*

Fugger, Jacob
[Jacob II; Jacob the Rich]
German. Merchant
Controlled a chief banking house in 16th-c. Europe; built Fuggerei, low-cost housing near Augsberg.
b. 1459
d. 1525
Source: *NewCol 75; WebBD 83*

Fugs, The
[John Anderson; Lee Crabtree; Pete Kearney; Tuli Kupferberg; Charles Larkey; Vinny Leary; Bob Mason; Ken Pine; Ed Sanders; Peter Stampfield; Ken Weaver]
American. Music Group
Formed theater, music group, 1965; satirized politics, rock, sexual repression.
Source: *Alli, SUP; BiDAmM; BiDBrA; BioIn 3, 4, 5, 6, 14, 15; CabMA; CelCen; ChhPo S1; ConAu X; ConMuA 80A; CurBio 41, 58; DcNaB; DcVicP, 2; DrAPF 83, 85, 87, 89, 91, 93, 97; DrRegL 75; Dun&B 86, 88; EncAR; EncPR&S 74; EncRk 88; EncRkSt; ForYSC; IlEncRk; Law&B 80; LElec; NewCBEL; NewGrDA 86; NewYTBS 74, 92; ObitOF 79; ObitT 1951; PenEncP; RolSEnR 83; WhAm 9; WhE&EA; Who 85N; WhoAm 86; WhoHol A; WhoLibS 55; WhoNeCM; WhoRock 81; WhoRocM 82; WhoScEu 91-1*

Fuhr, Grant Scott
Canadian. Hockey Player
Goalie, Edmonton, 1981-91; Toronto, 1991-93; Buffalo, 1993—; first black player to be on Stanley Cup-winning team; won five Stanley Cups; won Vezina Trophy, 1988.
b. Sep 28, 1962 in Spruce Grove, Alberta, Canada
Source: *BioIn 15, 16; ConBlB 1; HocEn; HocReg 87; WhoAfA 96; WhoBlA 94; WorAlBi*

Fuisz, Robert E
American. Writer, Producer
Won four Emmys for Body Human series including "The Body Human - The Living Code," 1983.
b. Oct 15, 1934 in Pennsylvania
Source: *VarWW 85*

Fujimori, Alberto
Peruvian. Political Leader
Pres., Peru, 1990—, succeeding Alan Garcia Perez; first person of Japanese descent to lead Latin American nation.
b. Jul 28, 1938 in Lima, Peru
Source: *BioIn 16; CurBio 90; DcHiB; IntWW 91; News 92; WhoWor 91, 93*

Fukuda, Takeo
Japanese. Political Leader
Acquitted of 1947 political crimes, 1958; prime minister, 1976-78.
b. Jan 14, 1905, Japan
d. Jul 5, 1995 in Tokyo, Japan
Source: *BioIn 10, 11, 21; CurBio 74, 95N; FarE&A 78, 79, 80, 81; IntWW 74, 75, 76, 77, 78, 79, 80, 81, 82, 83, 89, 91, 93; NewYTBE 71; NewYTBS 76, 77; WhoWor 80, 82; WorAl*

Fukui, Kenichi
Japanese. Chemist
Shared 1981 Nobel Prize in chemistry for theory of chemical reactivity.
b. Oct 4, 1918 in Nara, Japan
Source: *BioIn 12, 15, 19, 20; IntWW 82, 83, 89, 91, 93; LarDcSc; NewYTBS 81; NobelP; NotTwCS; Who 83, 85, 88, 90, 92, 94; WhoAm 88, 90, 92, 94, 95; WhoNob, 90, 95; WhoScEn 94, 96; WhoWor 74, 76, 82, 84, 89, 91, 93, 95, 96, 97; WorAlBi*

Fulani, Lenora
American. Politician, Psychologist
Founder, National Alliance Party.
b. Apr 25, 1950 in Chester, Pennsylvania
Source: *AfrAmOr; ConBlB 11*

Fulbright, J(ames) William
American. Politician
Dem. senator from AR, 1945-74; founder of Fulbright scholarship; Vietnam War critic; books include *The Arrogance of Power,* 1966.
b. Apr 9, 1905 in Sumner, Missouri
d. Feb 9, 1995 in Washington, District of Columbia
Source: *AmOrTwC; AmPolLe; BiDrAC; BiDrUSC 89; BioIn 1, 2, 3, 4, 5, 6, 7, 8, 9, 10, 11, 12, 13, 14, 16; ColdWar 1; ConAu 9R, 147; CurBio 95N; DcAmDH 80, 89; DcPol; DcTwHis; EncAB-H 1974, 1996; EncSoH; FacFETw; IntWW 74, 75, 76, 77; IntYB 78, 79, 80, 81, 82; LinLib L, S; McGEWB; PeoHis; WhAm 11; Who 92, 94; WhoAm 74, 76, 78, 80, 82, 84, 86, 88, 90, 92, 94, 95; WhoAmP 73, 75, 77, 79, 81, 83, 85, 87, 89, 91, 93; WhoGov 72, 75; WhoSSW 73, 75; WhoWor 74, 78, 80, 82, 84, 89; WorAlBi; WrDr 92, 94, 96*

Fulghum, Robert
American. Author
With books *All I Really Need to Know I Learned in Kindergarten,* 1989, and *It Was on Fire When I Lay Down on It,* 1989, became first author ever to capture simultaneously the no. 1 and 2 spots on hardcover best-seller list.
b. Jun 4, 1937 in Waco, Texas
Source: *BestSel 89-2; BioIn 16; CurBio 94; IntAu&W 91; LegTOT; News 96, 96-1; NewYTBS 89; WrDr 92*

Fulks, Joe
[Joseph E Fulks]
"Jumpin' Joe"
American. Basketball Player
Forward, Philadelphia, 1946-54; led NBA in scoring in league's first season, 1947; Hall of Fame, 1977.
b. Oct 26, 1921 in Marshall County, Kentucky
d. Mar 21, 1976 in Eddyville, Kentucky
Source: *BasBi; BioIn 1, 9, 10; OfNBA 87; WhoBbl 73*

Fuller, Alfred Carl
American. Manufacturer
Founded Fuller Brush Co., 1910; introduced the "Fuller Brush Man."
b. Jan 13, 1885 in Kings County, Nova Scotia, Canada
d. Dec 4, 1973 in Hartford, Connecticut
Source: *BiDAmBL 83; BioIn 1, 2, 3, 4, 5, 6, 10, 11, 12; BioNews 74; BusPN;*

ConAu 45; CurBio 50, 74; LegTOT; NatCAB 58; NewYTBE 73; WebAB 74, 79; WhAm 6; WorAl

Fuller, Charles
American. Dramatist
Won Pulitzer for *A Soldier's Play,* 1982; wrote film *A Soldier's Story,* 1984.
b. Mar 5, 1939 in Philadelphia, Pennsylvania
Source: *AfrAmAl 6; BenetAL 91; BioIn 13, 14, 16; BlkAmP; BlkLC; BlkWr 1; CamGWoT; ConAu 108, 112; ConBlB 8; ConDr 88; ConLC 25; ConTFT 7; CrtSuDr; CurBio 89; DramC 1; InB&W 80; LegTOT; MajTwCW; McGEWD 84; NegAl 83, 89; NewYTBS 82; OxCAmL 83, 95; SchCGBL; VarWW 85; WhoAfA 96; WhoAm 82, 84, 86, 88, 90, 92, 94, 95, 96, 97; WhoBlA 80, 85, 88, 90, 92, 94; WhoE 85, 86; WhoEnt 92; WorAlBi; WrDr 88, 90, 92, 94, 96*

Fuller, Edmund
American. Author
Wrote historical novel *A Star Pointed North,* 1946.
b. Mar 3, 1914 in Wilmington, Delaware
Source: *AmAu&B; AuBYP 2, 3; BioIn 8, 10, 12; ChhPo S1; ConAu 77; ConNov 72, 76; DcLEL 1940; DcLP 87A; DrAS 74E; IntAu&W 76, 77; SmATA 21; WorAu 1950; WrDr 76, 80, 82, 84, 86, 88, 90, 92, 94*

Fuller, George
American. Artist
Most important works: *Turkey Pasture in Kentucky,* 1878; *The Romany Girl,* 1879.
b. Jan 17, 1822 in Deerfield, Massachusetts
d. Mar 21, 1884 in Brookline, Massachusetts
Source: *AmBi; ApCAB; ArtsNiC; BioIn 4, 13, 14; BriEAA; DcAmArt; DcAmB; DcAmDH 80; FolkA 87; McGDA; NatCAB 6, 39; NewYHSD; OxCAmL 65; OxCArt; PeoHis; TwCBDA; WhAmArt 85; WhAm HS*

Fuller, Henry Blake
American. Author
Realistic novels of Chicago life include *Cliff-Dwellers,* 1893.
b. Jan 9, 1857 in Chicago, Illinois
d. Jul 29, 1929 in Chicago, Illinois
Source: *AmAu&B; BbD; BibAL; BiD&SB; BioIn 3, 5, 8, 9, 10, 12, 13; CamGEL; CamGLE; CamHAL; CasWL; CnDAL; ConAmL; ConAu 108; DcAmAu; DcAmB; DcLB 12; DcLEL; DcNAA; GayN; GrWrEL N; NatCAB 4, 23; Novels; OxCAmL 65, 83, 95; PenC AM; REn; REnAL; RfGAmL 87, 94; TwCA, SUP; WebE&AL; WhAm 1*

Fuller, Hoyt William
American. Critic, Editor
Editor, *Negro Digest,* 1970; later called *Black World;* started black aesthetic literary movement, 1960s-70s.
b. Sep 10, 1926 in Atlanta, Georgia
d. May 11, 1981 in Atlanta, Georgia
Source: *AnObit 1981; BioIn 12; BlkAWP; ConAmTC; ConAu 53, 103; Ebony 1; LivgBAA; NewYTBS 81; SelBAAu; WhAm 7; WhoAm 76, 78, 80; WhoBlA 77, 80*

Fuller, Ida
American. Social Reformer
Received first US Social Security check, 1940; invested $22 in program, received over $20,000.
b. Sep 6, 1875 in Ludlow, Vermont
d. Jan 27, 1975 in Brattleboro, Vermont
Source: *BioIn 10; NewYTBS 75*

Fuller, Kathryn S(cott)
American. Conservationist
President and CEO, World Wildlife Fund, 1989-.
b. Jul 8, 1946 in New York, New York
Source: *CurBio 94; WhoAm 94, 96, 97; WhoAmW 95, 97; WhoScEn 94*

Fuller, Loie
[Marie Louise Fuller]
American. Dancer, Author
Burlesque, vaudeville performer; appeared in the "Follies Bergere," "Buffalo Bill's Wild West Show"; invented "serpentine dance," theatrical lighting techniques.
b. Jan 15, 1862 in Fullersburg, Illinois
d. Jan 2, 1928 in Paris, France
Source: *AmBi; BioIn 3, 4, 6, 11, 12, 15, 16; CnOxB; ContDcW 89; DancEn 78; DcAmB; DcTwCCu 2; Dis&D; EncVaud; FacFETw; GrLiveH; IntDcWB; InWom, SUP; LegTOT; LibW; NotAW; NotWoAT; WhAm 1; WomFir; WomWMM; WorAl*

Fuller, Margaret
[Sarah Margaret Fuller Ossoli]
American. Critic, Social Reformer
Women's rights leader; first US foreign correspondent, 1848; edited *The Dial,* 1840-42; drowned with family off NY coast.
b. May 23, 1810 in Cambridge, Massachusetts
d. Jul 19, 1850 in Fire Island, New York
Source: *AmAu; AmAu&B; AmBi; AmRef; AmWom; AmWomWr 92; AmWr S2; ArtclWW 2; AtlBL; BbD; Benet 87; BenetAL 91; BiD&SB; BioAmW; BioIn 14, 15, 16, 17, 18, 19, 20, 21; BlmGWL; BriB; CamGEL; CamGLE; CamHAL; ChhPo; CnDAL; CrtT 3, 4; DcAmAu; DcAmB; DcLEL; Dis&D; EncAJ; EncWHA; FemiCLE; GrLiveH; HanAmWH; HerW 84; InWom SUP; JrnUS; LibW; LinLib L; NinCLC 5, 50; NotAW; OxCAmH; OxCAmL 65, 83; OxCEng 67, 85; OxCWoWr 95; PenC AM; PeoHis; PorAmW; RadHan; RAdv 14; RComAH; REn; REnAL; TwCBDA; WebAB 74; WebE&AL; WomFir; WomStre*

Fuller, Millard (Dean)
American. Lawyer, Entrepreneur
President of Habitat for Humanity International, 1976—.
b. Jan 3, 1935 in Lanett, Alabama
Source: *CurBio 95; WhoAm 90, 92, 94, 95, 96, 97; WhoFI 96*

Fuller, Richard Buckminster
"Bucky Fuller"
American. Architect, Author
Developed geodesic dome, circa 1940.
b. Jul 12, 1895 in Milton, Massachusetts
d. Jul 1, 1983 in Los Angeles, California
Source: *AmSocL; AnObit 1983; BioIn 1, 2, 3, 4, 5, 6, 7, 8, 9, 10, 11, 12, 13; BlueB 76; ConArch 80, 87, 94; ConAu 9NR; ConDes 84, 90, 97; CurBio 76, 83N; DcD&D; EncAAr 1, 2; EncAB-H 1974, 1996; EncMA; InSci; IntWW 74, 75, 76, 77, 78, 79, 80, 81, 82, 83; MakMC; McGDA; McGEWB; NewYTBS 74, 83; PenDiDA 89; WebAB 74, 79; WhAm 8; Who 74, 82, 83; WhoAm 74, 76, 78, 80, 82; WhoArch; WhoE 79, 83; WhoWor 74*

Fuller, Robert
American. Actor
In TV Westerns "Laramie," 1959-62; "Wagon Train," 1963-65.
b. Jul 29, 1934 in Troy, New York
Source: *FilmgC; ForYSC; HalFC 80, 84, 88; WhoHol A*

Fuller, Roy Broadbent
English. Poet, Author
Verse collections include *The Ruined Boys,* 1959; *My Child, My Sister,* 1965.
b. Feb 11, 1912 in Failsworth, England
d. Sep 27, 1991 in London, England
Source: *Au&Wr 71; Benet 96; BioIn 14, 18, 21; CasWL; CnE&AP; ConAu 5R, 53NR, 135; ConLC 4, 70; ConNov 76, 91; ConPo 80, 91; FacFETw; IntAu&W 91; IntWW 91; ModBrL; NewC; OxCEng 85, 95; OxCTwCP; PenC ENG; RAdv 1; REn; RfGEnL 91; RGTwCWr; SmATA 87; TwCA SUP; TwCChW 89; TwCCr&M 91; TwCWr; WebE&AL; Who 92; WhoChL; WhoTwCL; WrDr 92, 94N*

Fuller, Samuel
American. Director, Screenwriter
B melodramas include *I Shot Jesse James,* 1949.
b. Aug 12, 1911 in Worcester, Massachusetts
Source: *BiDFilm, 94; BioIn 7, 9, 11, 12, 14, 16; CmMov; ConAu 112, 129; ConTFT 8; CurBio 92; DcFM; FilmEn; FilmgC; HalFC 88; IlWWHD 1; IntAu&W 91; IntDcF 1-2, 2-2; IntMPA 92; MiSFD 9; OxCFilm; ScF&FL 1; TwCCr&M 80; WhoAm 82, 90; WorEFlm; WorFDir 2; WrDr 82, 84, 86, 88, 90*

Fuller-Maitland, John Alexander
English. Critic, Author
Edited *Grove's Dictionary,* 1904-10; best known work, autobiography *A Doorkeeper of Music,* 1929.
b. Apr 7, 1856 in London, England
d. Mar 30, 1936 in Lancashire, England
Source: *Baker 78, 84; BioIn 2; Chambr 3; DcNaB 1931; NewC; OxCMus; WhE&EA; WhoLA*

Fullerton, (Charles) Gordon
American. Astronaut
Aboard the third flight of space shuttle *Columbia,* Apr, 1982.
b. Oct 11, 1936 in Rochester, New York
Source: *BiDrUSC 89; BioIn 13; WhoAm 80, 82, 84, 86, 88, 90; WhoAmP 91; WhoSpc; WhoSSW 73, 75, 76, 78, 84; WhoTech 89; WorDWW*

Fulton, Maude
American. Actor, Dramatist
Starred in own plays *The Brat; Sonny; Humming Bird.*
b. May 14, 1881 in El Dorado, Kansas
d. Nov 4, 1950 in Los Angeles, California
Source: *BioIn 2, 77, 83; WhThe*

Fulton, Richard Harmon
American. Politician
Dem. mayor of Nashville, TN, 1977-87.
b. Jan 27, 1927 in Nashville, Tennessee
Source: *BiDrAC; WhoSSW 75, 76, 78, 84, 86*

Fulton, Robert
American. Engineer
First to develop a practical, profitable steamboat, 1807.
b. Nov 14, 1765 in Lancaster County, Pennsylvania
d. Feb 23, 1815 in New York, New York
Source: *Alli; AmBi; ApCAB; AsBiEn; BiDLA; BiInAmS; BioIn 1, 2, 3, 4, 5, 6, 7, 8, 9, 10, 11, 12, 13, 14, 15, 16, 17; BriEAA; CelCen; DcAmB; DcBiPP; DcBrECP; DcInv; DcNAA; Dis&D; Drake; EncAB-H 1996; HarEnUS; InSci; LegTOT; LinLib S; McGEWB; MemAm; NatCAB 3; NewYHSD; OxCAmH; OxCShps; RComAH; REn; REnAL; TwCBDA; WebAB 74, 79; WebAMB; WhAm HS; WhDW; WorAl; WorAlBi; WorInv*

Funicello, Annette
[Mrs. Glen Holt]
American. Actor, Singer
Disney Mousketeer, 1950s; star of "beach party" films, 1960s.
b. Oct 22, 1942 in Utica, New York
Source: *BiDAmM; BioIn 5, 9, 10, 11, 15, 16; EncAFC; EncRk 88; FilmgC; ForYSC; HalFC 80, 84, 88; IntMPA 96; InWom, SUP; LegTOT; MotPP; WhoHol 92, A; WorAl; WorAlBi*

Funikawa, Gyo
American. Illustrator
Illustrated R L Stevenson's *A Child's Garden of Verses,* 1957.
Source: *BioIn 3, 8, 9; IlsBYP; IlsCB 1967*

Funk, Casimir
American. Biochemist
Best known for naming vitamins, 1912.
b. Feb 23, 1884 in Warsaw, Poland
d. Nov 19, 1967 in Albany, New York
Source: *AsBiEn; BiESc; BiHiMed; BioIn 3, 6, 8, 9, 10, 14; CurBio 45, 68; DcAmB S8; DcInv; DcScB; InSci; JeHun; LarDcSc; WebAB 74, 79; WebBD 83; WhAm 4; WhDW*

Funk, Isaac Kauffman
American. Publisher
Funk and Wagnalls Co. published *Standard Dictionary of the English Language,* 1893.
b. Sep 10, 1839 in Clifton, Ohio
d. Apr 4, 1912 in Montclair, New Jersey
Source: *AmAu&B; AmRef; ApCAB X; BioIn 15; DcAmAu; DcAmB; DcNAA; EncPaPR 91; NatCAB 11; OhA&B; TwCBDA; WebAB 74, 79; WhAm 1*

Funk, Walther
German. Government Official, Banker
Reichsbank pres., 1939-45; responsible for Nazi finances; jailed as war criminal until 1957.
b. Aug 18, 1890 in Trakehnen, Prussia
d. May 31, 1960 in Dusseldorf, Germany (West)
Source: *BioIn 1, 3, 5, 16, 18; CurBio 40, 60; Dis&D; EncTR, 91; ObitOF 79*

Funk, Wilfred John
American. Publisher
Pres., Funk & Wagalls, 1925-40; wrote "Increase Your Word Power" for *Reader's Digest,* 1946-65; son of Isaac.
b. Mar 20, 1883 in New York, New York
d. Jun 1, 1965 in Montclair, New Jersey
Source: *AmAu&B; BioIn 1, 3, 4, 6, 7, 9; ChhPo, S2; ConAu 89; CurBio 55, 65; DcAmB S7; ObitOF 79; WhAm 4*

Funkadelic
[Mickey Atkins; "Tiki" Fulwood; Edward Hazel; William Nelson, Jr; Lucas Tunia Tawl]
American. Music Group
Dance band founded 1969; worked with George Clinton, Parliament; hits include "Knee Deep," 1979.
Source: *Alli; AmEA 74; BiNAW Sup, SupB; BioIn 21; CabMA; DcNaB; EncPR&S 89; IlEncRk; NewAmDM; NewGrDA 86; NewYHSD; OxCLaw; RkOn 78, 84; WhoAtom 77; WhoRock 81; WhoSSW 97*

Funston, Frederick
American. Military Leader
Commanded troops at capture of Vera Cruz, Mexico, 1914.
b. Nov 9, 1865 in New Carlisle, Ohio
d. Feb 19, 1917
Source: *AmBi; ApCAB SUP; BioIn 2, 4, 9, 10, 15, 16; CmCal; DcAmB; DcAmMiB; DcNAA; FacFETw; GenMudB; HarEnMi; HarEnUS; LinLib S; McGEWB; MedHR 94; NatCAB 11; OhA&B; SpyCS; TwCBDA; WebAB 74, 79; WebAMB; WhAm 1*

Funston, George Keith
American. Businessman
Pres. of NY Stock Exchange, 1951-67.
b. Oct 12, 1910 in Waterloo, Iowa
d. May 15, 1992 in Greenwich, Connecticut
Source: *BioIn 2, 3, 4, 7, 11; CurBio 51; IntWW 74, 75, 76, 77, 78, 79, 80, 81, 82, 83, 89; LinLib S; PolProf E, K; St&PR 84; Who 85, 92; WhoAm 74, 76*

Funt, Allen
American. Producer
Creator, host of TV series "Candid Camera."
b. Sep 16, 1914 in New York, New York
Source: *ASCAP 66; BioIn 7, 9, 13, 14; ConAu 146; ConTFT 9; CurBio 66; FilmgC; HalFC 80, 84, 88; IntMPA 82, 84, 86, 88, 92, 94, 96; LegTOT; LesBEnT; MiSFD 9; NewYTET; RadStar; WhoAm 74, 76, 78; WhoHol 92; WorAl; WorAlBi*

Furay, Richie
[Buffalo Springfield; Poco; The Souther-Hillman-Furay Band]
American. Musician
Country-rock singer in various bands; solo single "I Still Have Dreams," 1979.
b. May 9, 1944 in Yellow Springs, Ohio
Source: *BioIn 14; ConMuA 80A; EncFCWM 83; OnThGG; RkOn 85; RkWW 82; RolSEnR 83; WhoRock 81; WhoRocM 82*

Furcolo, (John) Foster
American. Politician
Dem. governor of MA, 1957-61; wrote novel *Let George Do It!,* 1957.
b. Jul 29, 1911
d. Jul 5, 1995 in Cambridge, Massachusetts
Source: *BiDrAC; BiDrUSC 89; BioIn 4, 5, 7, 21; ConAu 149; CurBio 95N; NewYTBS 95; WhoAmP 73*

Furgol, Ed(ward)
American. Golfer
Won US Open, named golfer of year, 1954.
b. Mar 27, 1919 in New York Mills, New York
d. Mar 6, 1997 in Miami, Florida
Source: *BioIn 3, 4, 5; WhoGolf*

Furie, Sidney J
Canadian. Director
Films include *Lady Sings the Blues; Gable and Lombard; Boys in Company C.*
b. Feb 28, 1933 in Toronto, Ontario, Canada
Source: *FilmEn; FilmgC; HalFC 88; IntMPA 92; MovMk; OxCFilm; WorEFlm*

Furillo, Carl Anthony
"Skoonj"; "The Reading Rifle"
American. Baseball Player
Outfielder, Brooklyn/LA Dodgers, 1946-60; won NL batting title, 1953.
b. Mar 8, 1922 in Stony Creek Mills, Pennsylvania
d. Jan 21, 1989 in Stony Creek Mills, Pennsylvania
Source: *Ballpl 90; BiDAmSp Sup; BioIn 3, 16; NewYTBS 89; WhoProB 73*

Furman, Roger
Director
Founder, director, Harlem's Repertory Theater, 1964.
b. 1924?
d. Nov 27, 1983
Source: *BioIn 13; BlkAmW 1; ConAu 111; ConBlAP 88*

Furness, Betty
[Elizabeth Mary Furness]
American. Government Official, Actor, TV Personality
Actress, 1932-37; chm., pres.'s committee on consumer interests, 1967-69; consumer reporter for NBC's "Today" program, 1976-92.
b. Jan 3, 1916 in New York, New York
d. Apr 2, 1994 in New York, New York
Source: *BioIn 3, 5, 7, 8, 9, 10, 12, 13, 19, 20; CelR, 90; CurBio 68, 94N; FilmEn; ForWC 70; ForYSC; IntMPA 82, 84, 86, 88, 92, 94; InWom, SUP; LegTOT; LesBEnT, 92; NewYTBS 94; NewYTET; ThFT; WhAm 11; WhoAm 74, 76, 78, 80, 82, 84, 86, 88, 90, 92, 94; WhoAmW 58, 61, 64, 66, 68, 70, 72, 74, 75, 77, 81, 83, 85, 87, 89; WhoE 74; WhoEnt 92; WhoHol 92, A; WhoSSW 73; WorAl; WorAlBi*

Furniss, Harry
English. Cartoonist, Illustrator
Noted for political lampoons in *Punch,* 1880s-90s; illustrated works of Charles Dickens.
b. Mar 26, 1854 in Wexford, Ireland
d. Jan 14, 1925 in Hastings, England
Source: *AntBDN B; BioIn 8, 12, 13, 14; CelCen; ChhPo, S1, S2; DcBrAr 1; DcBrBI; DcIrB 78, 88; DcNaB 1922; NewCBEL; OxCChiL; WhoChL; WhScrn 77, 83; WorECar*

Furst, Anton
English. Designer
Production designer, won Oscar, 1989, for *Batman.*
d. Nov 24, 1991 in Los Angeles, California
Source: *BioIn 17; ConTFT 8; NewYTBS 91, 92*

Furstenberg, Diane Halfin von
Belgian. Fashion Designer, Author
Began designing, 1971; first effort was jersey wrapdress.
b. Dec 31, 1946 in Brussels, Belgium
Source: *BioIn 13, 16; BioNews 74; BkPepl; CelR 90; InWom SUP; WhoAm 82, 90; WhoAmW 91; WorFshn*

Furstenberg, Egon von
Fashion Designer, Author
Developed ready-to-wear line of fashions; wrote *The Power Look,* 1979.
b. Jun 29, 1946 in Lausanne, Switzerland
Source: *BioIn 12; CelR; WhoAm 82*

Furtseva, Ekaterina Alexeyevna
Russian. Government Official
Minister of culture, 1960-74; promoted cultural exchange with West.
b. Dec 7, 1910 in Vyshni Volochek, Russia
d. Oct 25, 1974 in Moscow, Union of Soviet Socialist Republics
Source: *BioNews 75; CurBio 56, 74N; IntWW 74, 75; NewYTBE 72; NewYTBS 74; WhAm 6; WhoAmW 74; WhoSocC 78; WhoWor 74*

Furtwangler, Wilhelm
[Gustav Heinrich Ernst Martin Wilhelm Furtwangler]
German. Conductor
Led Vienna Symphony, Berlin State Opera, 1930s; absolved of pro-Nazi activities, 1946; noted for interpretations of Wagner, Beethoven.
b. Jan 25, 1886 in Berlin, Germany
d. Nov 30, 1954 in Eberstein, Germany (West)
Source: *Baker 78, 84; BioIn 1, 2, 3, 4, 7, 8, 9, 11, 12, 17, 18, 19, 20; BriBkM 80; CmOp; EncTR, 91; FacFETw; IntDcOp; LinLib S; MetOEnc; MusMk; MusSN; NewAmDM; NewEOp 71; NewGrDM 80; ObitT 1951; OxDcOp; PenDiMP; WhAm 3; WhDW; WorAlBi*

Fury, Billy
[Ronald Wycherly]
English. Singer
Began as rock singer, found success in ballads; hits include "That's Love," 1960; "In Thoughts of You," 1965.
b. Apr 17, 1941 in Liverpool, England
d. Jan 29, 1983 in London, England
Source: *AnObit 1983; BioIn 13; DcNaB 1981; EncRk 88; HalFC 80, 84, 88; HarEnR 86; LegTOT; OxCPMus; PenEncP; RolSEnR 83*

Fuseli, Henry
Swiss. Artist, Author
Romantic painter of eerie imagery including *The Nightmare,* 1781; activ e in Britain.
b. Feb 7, 1741 in Zurich, Switzerland
d. Apr 16, 1825 in London, England
Source: *Alli; AtlBL; BiDLA; BioIn 1, 2, 3, 4, 5, 6, 7, 9, 10, 12, 13, 14, 15; BkIE; CasWL; CelCen; DcArts; DcBrECP; DcBrWA; DcNaB; EncEnl; EuAu; IntDcAA 90; McGDA; McGEWB; NewC; OxCArt; OxCEng 85, 95; OxCGer 76, 86; OxDcArt; PenEncH; WorAl; WorAlBi*

Fussell, Paul
American. Writer
Wrote *The Great War and Modern Memory,* 1975.
b. Mar 22, 1924 in Pasadena, California
Source: *BestSel 90-1; BioIn 12, 13, 16, 17; ChhPo S1; ConAu 8NR, 17R, 21NR, 35NR; ConLC 74; DrAS 74E, 78E, 82E; IntAu&W 91; IntWW 83, 89, 91, 93; MajTwCW; OxCAmL 95; WhoAm 78, 80, 82, 84, 86, 88, 90, 92, 94, 95, 96, 97; WhoWrEP 89, 92, 95; WorAu 1975; WrDr 90, 92, 94, 96*

Fust, Johann
German. Printer
With Gutenberg, issued the first printed book, the Bible, 1450.
b. 1400 in Mainz, Germany
d. Oct 30, 1466 in Paris, France
Source: *DcBiPP; DcCathB; NewC; OxCGer 76, 86*

Futrell, Mary Alice Franklin Hatwood
American. Labor Union Official
Pres., National Education Assn., 1983-89, largest union in US.
b. May 24, 1940 in Altavista, Virginia
Source: *BioIn 13; ConNews 86-1; NewYTBS 83; NotBlAW 1; WhoAm 90; WhoAmW 85, 87, 91*

Futrelle, Jacques
American. Author
Mystery writer whose books include *Blind Man's Bluff,* 1914; died on *Titanic.*
b. Apr 9, 1875 in Pike County, Georgia
d. Apr 15, 1912
Source: *AmAu&B; BiDSA; BioIn 11, 14; ConAu 113; CrtSuMy; CyWA 89; DcNAA; EncMys; EncSF, 93; ScF&FL 1; ScFEYrs; TwCA; TwCCr&M 80, 85, 91; TwCLC 19; WhAm 1*

Futter, Ellen Victoria
American. University Administrator
Youngest exec. of major college who became pres., Barnard College, 1981.
b. Sep 21, 1949 in New York, New York
Source: *BioIn 12, 13, 14, 20, 21; CurBio 85; InWom SUP; NewYTBS 80; WhoAm 84, 86, 88, 90, 92, 94, 95, 96; WhoAmW 85, 87, 89, 91, 93, 95, 97; WhoE 85, 86, 89, 91, 95; WhoWor 96*

Fyffe, Will
Scottish. Actor
Music-hall comedian who specialized in Scottish character sketches.
b. 1885 in Dundee, Scotland

d. Dec 14, 1947 in Saint Andrews, Scotland

Source: *BioIn 1; DcArts; EncWT; Ent; FilmAG WE; FilmgC; IlWWBF; NotNAT B; OxCPMus; OxCThe 67; WhoHol B; WhScrn 74*

G

Gabel, Martin
American. Actor, Director
Won 1961 Tony for *Big Fish, Little Fish;* regular panelist on TV game sho w "What's My Line?"
b. Jun 19, 1912 in Philadelphia, Pennsylvania
d. May 22, 1986 in New York, New York
Source: *BiE&WWA; BioIn 14, 15; ConTFT 4; FilmEn; FilmgC; ForYSC; HalFC 80, 84, 88; LegTOT; MovMk; NewYTBS 86; NotNAT; SaTiSS; VarWW 85; WhoHol A; WhoThe 72, 77, 81; WorAl*

Gabin, Jean
[Jean-Alexis Moncorge]
French. Actor
World-weary hero in films: *Pepe le Moko,* 1937; *Port of Shadows,* 1938.
b. May 17, 1904 in Paris, France
d. Nov 15, 1976 in Neuilly, France
Source: *BiDFilm; IntWW 74, 75, 76; ItaFilm; LegTOT; MotPP; MovMk; OxCFilm; WhAm 7; Who 74; WhoHol A; WhoWor 74; WhScrn 83; WorAl; WorEFlm*

Gable, Clark
[William Clark Gable]
American. Actor
Won Oscar, 1934, for *It Happened One Night;* played Rhett Butler in *Gone With the Wind,* 1939.
b. Feb 1, 1901 in Cadiz, Ohio
d. Nov 16, 1960 in Hollywood, California
Source: *BiDFilm, 81, 94; BioIn 1, 2, 3, 4, 5, 6, 7, 8, 9, 10, 11, 12, 13, 14, 15, 16, 17, 19, 20; CmCal; CmMov; CurBio 45, 61; DcAmB S6; EncAFC; FacFETw; Film 2; FilmEn; FilmgC; ForYSC; GangFlm; HalFC 80, 84, 88; IntDcF 1-3, 2-3; LegTOT; McGEWB; MGM; MotPP; MovMk; NatCAB 60; NotNAT B; ObitT 1951; OxCFilm; WebAB 74, 79; WhAm 4; WhoHol B; WhScrn 74, 77, 83; WhThe; WorAl; WorAlBi; WorEFlm*

Gable, John Clark
American.
Son of Clark Gable.
b. Mar 20, 1961 in Los Angeles, California
Source: *BioIn 6, 9, 13, 16; WhoHol 92*

Gabo, Naum
American. Sculptor
Founded contemporary art movement, Constructivism; wrote *Realist Manifesto,* 1920.
b. Aug 5, 1890 in Briansk, Russia
d. Aug 23, 1977 in Waterbury, Connecticut
Source: *Au&Wr 71; BioIn 1, 3, 6, 7, 8, 9, 11, 12, 13, 14, 15, 16; BriEAA; ConArt 77, 83; ConAu 73, P-2; CurBio 72, 77N; DcAmB S10; DcArts; FacFETw; IntDcAA 90; IntWW 74, 75, 76, 77; LegTOT; MakMC; McGDA; McGEWB; ModArCr 2; NewYTBS 77; ObitOF 79; OxCAmH; OxCArt; OxCTwCA; OxDcArt; PhDcTCA 77; SovUn; WhAm 7; WhDW; WhoAm 74, 76, 78; WhoAmA 76, 78N, 80N, 82N, 84N, 86N, 89N, 91N, 93N; WhoArch; WhoWor 74; WorArt 1950*

Gabor, Dennis
English. Engineer
Invented, developed holography, a three-dimensional photography; won 1971 Nobel Prize in physics.
b. Jun 5, 1900 in Budapest, Austria-Hungary
d. Feb 8, 1979 in London, England
Source: *AmMWSc 73P; Au&Wr 71; BiESc; BioIn 9, 10, 11, 12, 13, 14, 15, 20; BlueB 76; CamDcSc; ConAu 17R, 120; CurBio 72, 79, 79N; DcNaB 1971; DcScB S2; EncWB; FacFETw; ICPEnP; IntAu&W 76; IntWW 74, 75, 76, 77, 78; LarDcSc; MacBEP; McGMS 80; NewYTBE 71; NewYTBS 79; NobelP; NotTwCS; Who 74; WhoE 74; WhoEng 80; WhoNob, 90, 95; WhoWor 74, 76, 78; WorAl; WorAlBi; WorInv; WrDr 80*

Gabor, Eva
Hungarian. Actor
Co-starred with Eddie Albert in TV series "Green Acres," 1965-71.
b. Feb 11, 1921 in Budapest, Hungary
d. Jul 4, 1995 in Los Angeles, California
Source: *BiE&WWA; BioIn 10, 11, 17, 21; BioNews 74; CelR 90; ConTFT 15; CurBio 68, 95N; FilmgC; HalFC 80, 84, 88; InWom SUP; LegTOT; MotPP; MovMk; News 96, 96-1; VarWW 85; WhoAm 82; WhoAmW 74; WhoHol A; WorAl; WorAlBi*

Gabor, Jolie
[Jancsi Tilleman]
Hungarian. Businesswoman
Mother of glamorous Gabor sisters; owned jewelry stores in Palm Springs, CA, and New York City.
b. Sep 29, 1900 in Budapest, Austria-Hungary
d. Apr 1, 1997 in Rancho Mirage, California
Source: *BioNews 74; InWom*

Gabor, Magda
Hungarian. Actor
Eldest sister of famous trio.
b. Jul 10, 1919 in Budapest, Austria-Hungary
d. Jun 6, 1997 in Rancho Mirage, California
Source: *InWom*

Gabor, Mark
American. Author
Author of *The Pin-Up: A Modest History,* 1973.
b. Aug 12, 1939 in New York, New York
Source: *ConAu 81; IntAu&W 76*

Gabor, Zsa Zsa
[Sari Gabor]
Hungarian. Actor
Witty, exotic performer; known for many husbands; films include *Three Ring Circus,* 1954.
b. Feb 6, 1919 in Budapest, Hungary

Source: *BioIn 10, 15, 16; CelR 90; ConTFT 3; CurBio 88; EncAFC; FilmgC; HalFC 80, 84, 88; IntMPA 82, 84, 86, 92; InWom SUP; MotPP; MovMk; WhoAm 82; WhoEnt 92; WhoHol A; WhoHrs 80; WorAl; WorAlBi*

Gabriel
[Gabriel Prosser]
American. Social Reformer
Conceived first major American slave uprising, Aug 30, 1800.
b. 1775 in Richmond, Virginia
d. Sep 1800 in Richmond, Virginia
Source: *AfrAmAl 6; BioIn 4, 9, 10, 11; DcAmNB; InB&W 80, 85; McGEWB; NegAl 76, 83, 89*

Gabriel, Ange-Jacques
French. Architect
Louis XV's chief designer, 1742-75; restoration of Louvre, 1755, among many accomplishments.
b. Oct 23, 1698 in Paris, France
d. Jan 4, 1782 in Paris, France
Source: *AtlBL; IntDcAr; McGDA; McGEWB; WhoArch*

Gabriel, Peter
English. Singer, Songwriter
Genesis main vocalist, songwriter, 1968-75; noted for bizarre theatricals; hit a lbum "Sledgehammer," 1986.
b. May 13, 1950 in London, England
Source: *BioIn 12, 15, 16; CelR 90; ConMuA 80A; ConMus 2, 16; CurBio 90; EncPR&S 89; EncRk 88; EncRkSt; HarEnR 86; IlEncRk; IntWW 89, 91, 93; LegTOT; NewYTBS 86; PenEncP; RkOn 85; RolSEnR 83; WhoAm 90, 92, 94, 95, 96, 97; WhoEnt 92; WhoHol 92; WhoRock 81; WhoRocM 82; WhoWor 93, 95, 96, 97*

Gabriel, Roman, Jr.
"Gabe"
American. Football Player
Four-time all-pro quarterback, LA Rams, 1962-73, Philadelphia, 1973-78; MVP, 1969; wrote autobiography *Player of the Year,* 1970.
b. Aug 5, 1940 in Wilmington, North Carolina
Source: *AsAmAlm; BiDAmSp FB; BioIn 8, 9, 10, 13, 20; ConAu 107; CurBio 75; NewYTBS 83; NotAsAm; WhoAm 74, 76, 78; WhoFtbl 74*

Gabrieli, Giovanni
Italian. Composer, Musician
Developed multiple-choir technique; works mark start of modern orchestration; an organist at St. Mark's, Venice.
b. 1557 in Venice, Italy
d. Aug 12, 1612 in Venice, Italy
Source: *AtlBL; Baker 84; BioIn 4, 7, 8, 10, 11, 12, 14; BriBkM 80; CmpBCM; DcCom 77; DcCom&M 79; EncWT; GrComp; LuthC 75; McGEWB; MusMk; NewCol 75; OxCMus; REn; WebBD 83; WhDW*

Gabrilowitsch, Ossip Salomonovich
American. Conductor, Pianist
Led Detroit Symphony, 1918-36; wed to Mark Twain's daughter, often appeared in concert with her.
b. Jan 26, 1878 in Saint Petersburg, Russia
d. Sep 14, 1936 in Detroit, Michigan
Source: *AmBi; Baker 84; BiDAmM; DcAmB S2; MusSN; NewCol 75; WebBD 83; WhAm 1*

Gacy, John Wayne, Jr.
American. Murderer
Convicted, 1980, of murders of 33 boys in Chicago area, 1972-78.
b. Mar 17, 1942 in Chicago, Illinois
d. May 10, 1994 in Joliet, Illinois
Source: *BioIn 11, 12, 13, 14, 15, 19, 20; EncACr; LegTOT; MurCaTw; News 94; NewYTBS 79*

Gaddis, Thomas (Eugene)
American. Author, Educator
Wrote *The Birdman of Alcatraz,* biography on which 1962 hit film was based.
b. Sep 14, 1908 in Denver, Colorado
d. Oct 10, 1984 in Portland, Oregon
Source: *ConAu 29R, 114; IntAu&W 77; WhoAm 76*

Gaddis, William (Thomas)
American. Author
Best known for first novel *The Recognitions,* 1955; others include *Carpenter's Gothic,* 1985; won National Book Award for Fiction for *A Frolic of His Own,* 1994.
b. Dec 29, 1922 in New York, New York
Source: *AmAu&B; Benet 87, 96; BenetAL 91; BioIn 3, 8, 10, 12, 14, 15, 17, 20; CamGLE; CamHAL; ConAu 17R, 21NR, 48NR; ConLC 1, 3, 6, 8, 10, 19, 43, 86; ConNov 72, 76, 82, 86, 91, 96; CurBio 87; CyWA 89; DcArts; DcLB 2; DcLEL 1940; DrAF 76; DrAPF 80, 87, 91; EncWL 2, 3; FacFETw; GrWrEL N; IntAu&W 76, 77, 91, 93; IntWW 91, 93; LegTOT; MagSAmL; MajTwCW; ModAL S1, S2; NewYTBS 87; Novels; OxCAmL 83, 95; PenC AM; PostFic; RAdv 1, 14, 13-1; RfGAmL 87, 94; RGTwCWr; WhoAm 74, 76, 78, 80, 82, 84, 86, 88, 90, 92, 94, 95, 96, 97; WhoUSWr 88; WhoWrEP 89, 92, 95; WorAlBi; WorAu 1950; WrDr 76, 80, 82, 84, 86, 88, 90, 92, 94, 96*

Gade, Niels Vilhelm
Danish. Composer
Wrote romantic style symphonies, cantatas; founded modern Scandinavian school of composition.
b. Feb 22, 1817 in Copenhagen, Denmark
d. Dec 21, 1890 in Copenhagen, Denmark
Source: *Baker 84; BioIn 4, 7; CelCen; NewCol 75; OxCMus*

Gadsby, Bill
[William Alexander Gadsby]
Canadian. Hockey Player
Defenseman, 1946-66; Hall of Fame, 1970.
b. Aug 8, 1927 in Calgary, Alberta, Canada
Source: *HocEn; WhoHcky 73*

Gadsden, James
American. Statesman
Negotiated treaty to buy strip of land from Mexico, 1853; today called Gadsden Purchase.
b. May 15, 1788 in Charleston, South Carolina
d. Dec 26, 1858 in Charleston, South Carolina
Source: *AmBi; AmPolLe; ApCAB; BiAUS; BioIn 3, 16; DcAmB; DcAmDH 80, 89; Drake; EncSoH; HarEnUS; McGEWB; NatCAB 12; NewCol 75; TwCBDA; WebAB 74, 79; WebBD 83; WhAm HS; WhAmP; WhFla; WhNaAH*

Gadski, Johanna
German. Opera Singer
Soprano; with NY Met., 1898-1904, 1907-17; Wagnerian singer.
b. Jun 15, 1872 in Anklam, Germany
d. Feb 22, 1932 in Berlin, Germany
Source: *Baker 78, 84; BioIn 1, 11, 14; IntDcOp; InWom, SUP; MetOEnc; MusSN; NewEOp 71; NewGrDA 86; NewGrDM 80; NewGrDO; OxDcOp; PenDiMP; WhAm 1*

Gaedel, Eddie
[Edward Carl Gaedel]
American. Baseball Player
Midget who batted against Detroit, Jul 19, 1951, in Bill Veeck promotional gimmick; walked.
b. Jun 8, 1925 in Chicago, Illinois
d. Jun 18, 1961 in Chicago, Illinois
Source: *Ballpl 90; WhoProB 73*

Gag, Wanda
American. Children's Author, Illustrator
Wrote, illustrated modern children's classic *Millions of Cats,* 1928.
b. May 11, 1893 in New Ulm, Minnesota
d. Jun 27, 1946 in New York, New York
Source: *AmAu&B; AnCL; AuBYP 2; BenetAL 91; BioAmW; BioIn 1, 2, 4, 8, 10, 11, 14, 19; ChhPo S2; ChlBkCr; ChlLR 4; ConAu 113; ConICB; CurBio 42; DcAmB S4; DcLB 22; DcNAA; DcWomA; FamAIYP; GrAmP; HerW, 84; IlsCB 1744; JBA 34, 51; LinLib L; McGDA; OxCChiL; RAdv 14; REnAL; TwCA, SUP; TwCChW 78, 83, 89; WhAm 2; WhAmArt 85; WrChl; YABC 1*

Gagarin, Yuri Alexseyevich
Russian. Cosmonaut
First man to travel in space, Apr 12, 1961.
b. Mar 9, 1934 in Gzhatsk, Union of Soviet Socialist Republics
d. Mar 27, 1968 in Moscow, Union of Soviet Socialist Republics

Source: *AsBiEn; CurBio 61, 68; McGEWB; NewCol 75; WhAm 5; WhDW; WorAl*

Gage, Harlow W
American. Business Executive
Manager of GM's overseas division, 1968—.
b. Feb 6, 1911 in Springfield, Massachusetts
Source: *IntWW 91*

Gage, Nicholas
Greek. Journalist, Filmmaker
One of the top investigative reporters in the 1970s; worked at the *NY Times*, 1970-80; wrote *Eleni*, 1985.
b. Jul 23, 1939 in Lia, Greece
Source: *BioIn 13, 14, 16; ConAu 49; CurBio 90; IntAu&W 91; WhoAm 90, 92*

Gage, Thomas
English. Army Officer
Governor of MA, 1774-75; used troops to restrain colonial resistance, which led to bloodshed.
b. 1721 in Firle, England
d. Apr 2, 1787, England
Source: *AmBi; ApCAB; BiDrACR; BioIn 1, 7, 8, 9, 12; DcAmB; DcNaB; EncCRAm; HarEnUS; LinLib S; MacDCB 78; NatCAB 7; OxCAmH; WebBD 83; WhAm HS; WhAmP; WhAmRev; WorAl; WorAlBi*

Gail, Max(well Trowbridge, Jr.)
American. Actor
Played Sergeant Wojciehowicz (Wojo) on TV series "Barney Miller," 1975-81.
b. Apr 5, 1943 in Detroit, Michigan
Source: *ConTFT 2; IntMPA 94, 96; LegTOT; VarWW 85; WhoAm 86, 90; WhoEnt 92*

Gailhard, Pierre
French. Opera Singer, Manager
Bass; managed Paris Opera, 1880s-90s; brought Wagner's works to France.
b. Aug 1, 1848 in Toulouse, France
d. Oct 12, 1918 in Paris, France
Source: *Baker 78, 84, 92; NewEOp 71; NewGrDM 80; NewGrDO; OxDcOp*

Gaines, Boyd
American. Actor
Won 1989 Tony Award for *The Heidi Chronicles*.2
b. May 11, 1953 in Atlanta, Georgia
Source: *ConTFT 8, 15; WhoAm 95, 96, 97; WhoHol 92*

Gaines, Clarence F
American. Businessman
Founded Gaines Dog Food Co., 1928.
b. 1898
d. Jan 2, 1986 in Winter Park, Florida
Source: *NewYTBS 86*

Gaines, Ernest J(ames)
American. Author
Wrote novel, *The Autobiography of Miss Jane Pittman*, 1971; became Emmy-winning TV film, 1974; won 1994 National Book Critics Circle Award for *A Lesson before Dying*, 1993.
b. Jan 15, 1933 in Oscar, Louisiana
Source: *AuBYP 3; AuNews 1; Benet 87; BenetAL 91; BioIn 14; BlkAWP; BlkLC; BlkWr 1, 2; BroV; CamGLE; CamHAL; ConAu 9R, 24NR, 42NR; ConLC 3, 11, 18, 86; ConNov 86, 91, 96; CurBio 94; CyWA 89; DrAPF 87, 91; FifSWrA; InB&W 85; LivgBAA; MajTwCW; ModAL S2; NegAl 89; RfGAmL 94; SelBAAf; SmATA 86; TwCRHW 90, 94; TwCYAW; WhoAm 86, 88, 96; WhoBlA 88, 92; WhoUSWr 88; WhoWrEP 89; WrDr 86, 90*

Gaines, Lee
[Delta Rhythm Boys; Otho Lee Gaines]
American. Composer, Singer
Founded gospel-blues quartet, Delta Rhythm Boys, 1933; popular, 1940s-50s.
b. Apr 21, 1914 in Houston, Mississippi
d. Jul 15, 1987 in Helsinki, Finland
Source: *ASCAP 66, 80; BioIn 15; NewYTBS 87*

Gaines, Steve
[Lynyrd Skynyrd]
American. Musician
Joined band as guitarist, 1976; killed in a private plane crash.
b. 1949?
d. Oct 20, 1977 in McComb, Mississippi
Source: *BioIn 11*

Gaines, William M(axwell)
American. Businessman, Publisher
Founder, publisher *Mad* magazine, 1952.
b. Mar 1, 1922 in New York, New York
d. Jun 3, 1992 in New York, New York
Source: *ConAu 108; ConLC 76; EncACom; EncTwCJ; News 93-1; WhAm 10; WhoAm 76, 78, 80, 82, 84, 86, 88, 90; WhoE 91; WhoEnt 92; WhoFI 89, 92; WhoWor 78, 89, 91, 93*

Gainey, Bob
[Robert Michael Gainey]
Canadian. Hockey Player
Left wing, Montreal, 1973-89; won Selke Trophy four times, Conn Smythe Trophy, 1 979; inducted into Hockey Hall of Fame, 1992.
b. Dec 13, 1953 in Peterborough, Ontario, Canada
Source: *HocEn; HocReg 87; LegTOT; NewYTBS 79; WhoAm 82, 84, 86, 88, 90, 92, 94, 95, 96, 97; WhoE 86; WhoMW 92; WhoSpor; WhoSSW 95; WhoWor 91; WorAl; WorAlBi*

Gainsborough, Thomas
English. Artist
Painted elegant portraits, country children, pastoral subjects; well known for "Blue Boy," 1770.
b. May 14, 1727 in Sudbury, England
d. Aug 2, 1788 in London, England
Source: *AtlBL; Benet 87, 96; BioIn 1, 2, 3, 4, 5, 6, 7, 8, 9, 10, 11, 12, 13, 15, 17; BkIE; BlkwCE; ChhPo; DcArts; DcBiPP; DcBrECP; DcBrWA; DcNaB; EncEnl; IntDcAA 90; LegTOT; LinLib S; McGDA; McGEWB; NewC; OxCArt; OxCEng 85, 95; OxCMus; OxDcArt; RAdv 14, 13-3; REn; WhDW; WorAl; WorAlBi*

Gairy, Eric Matthew, Sir
West Indian. Government Official
Prime minister of Grenada, 1974-79; deposed in coup.
b. Feb 18, 1922 in Saint Andrew's, Grenada
Source: *BiDLAmC; BioIn 12, 13, 16; IntWW 77, 78, 79, 80, 81, 82, 83, 89, 91, 93; IntYB 78, 79, 80, 81, 82; NewYTBS 74; Who 82, 83, 85, 88, 90, 92, 94*

Gaitskell, Hugh (Todd Naylor)
English. Political Leader
Labour Party leader, 1955-63; espoused socialist views.
b. Apr 9, 1906 in London, England
d. Jan 18, 1963 in London, England
Source: *BioIn 1, 2, 3, 4, 5, 6, 7, 8, 9, 10, 12, 13, 14, 15, 18; ColdWar 1; ConAu 112; CurBio 50, 63; DcNaB 1961; DcPol; DcTwHis; EncWB; FacFETw; GrBr; LinLib S; ObitT 1961; WebBD 83; WhAm 4; WhDW; WhoEc 81, 86; WorAl; WorAlBi*

Gajah Mada
Indonesian. Political Leader
Unifier of Indonesian archipelago; prime minister during Majapahit Empire.
d. 1364

Gajdusek, D(aniel) Carleton
American. Scientist
Noted research virologist; expert on strokes, degenerative neurological disorders; won Nobel Prize in medicine, 1976.
b. Sep 9, 1923 in Yonkers, New York
Source: *AmMWSc 76P, 79, 82, 86, 89, 92, 95; BiESc; BioIn 6, 11, 12, 14, 15, 20; CamDcSc; CurBio 81; IntMed 80; IntWW 77, 78, 79, 80, 81, 82, 83, 89, 91, 93; LarDcSc; NewYTBS 76; NobelP; Who 82, 83, 85, 88, 90, 92, 94; WhoAm 78, 80, 82, 84, 86, 88, 90, 92, 94, 95, 96, 97; WhoE 77, 79, 81, 83, 85, 86, 89, 91, 95, 97; WhoFrS 84; WhoGov 72; WhoMedH; WhoNob, 90, 95; WhoScEn 94, 96; WhoWor 78, 80, 82, 84, 87, 89, 91, 93, 95, 96, 97; WrDr 92, 94, 96*

Galamian, Ivan
American. Teacher, Musician
Violinist, on staff of Juilliard School of Music; pupils included Pinchas Zuckerm an, Itzhak Perlman.
b. Jan 23, 1903 in Tabriz, Persia
d. Apr 14, 1981 in New York, New York
Source: *AnObit 1981; Baker 84; BioIn 8, 9, 12, 14; BlueB 76; ConAu 108;*

NewAmDM; NewGrDA 86; NewGrDM 80; NewYTBS 81; PenDiMP; WhAm 7

Galamison, Milton Arthur
American. Clergy, Civil Rights Leader
Pastor, Siloam Presbyterian Church, Brooklyn, 1949-88; active in civil rights movement, especially in desegregation of NYC schools, 1960s.
b. Jan 25, 1923 in Philadelphia, Pennsylvania
d. Mar 9, 1988 in New York, New York
Source: *BioIn 6, 11, 16; InB&W 80; NewYTBS 88; PolProf J; WhoBlA 75, 80, 92N; WhoE 74*

Galanos, James
American. Fashion Designer
Designer of expensive women's fashions; customers include Nancy Reagan.
b. Sep 20, 1924 in Philadelphia, Pennsylvania
Source: *BioIn 5, 6, 7, 9, 12, 14; CelR; ConDes 84, 90, 97; ConFash; CurBio 70; EncFash; IntWW 91, 93; WhoAm 74, 76, 78, 80, 82, 84, 86, 88, 90, 92, 94, 95, 96, 97; WhoFash 88; WorFshn*

Galati, Frank
American. Director
Won two 1990 Tony Awards for *The Grapes of Wrath.*
b. Nov 29, 1943 in Highland Park, Illinois
Source: *WhoAm 90; WhoEnt 92; WhoMW 92*

Galbraith, John Kenneth
American. Economist, Diplomat, Author
Liberal Dem; held numerous advisory posts during Kennedy term; academic career at Harvard, 1949-75; professor at Harvard, 1948-60; books include *The Affluent Society,* 1958; *Money,* 1975.
b. Oct 15, 1908 in Iona Station, Ontario, Canada
Source: *AmAu&B; AmDec 1950; AmEA 74; AmMWSc 73S; AmSocL; Benet 87, 96; BenetAL 91; BioIn 5, 6, 7, 8, 9, 10, 11, 12, 13, 14, 15, 16, 17, 18, 19, 20; CanWW 31, 70, 79, 80, 81, 83, 89; CelR, 90; ConAu 6NR, 21R, 34NR; ConCaAu 1; ConIsC 1; CurBio 75; DcAmDH 80, 89; EncAB-H 1974, 1996; EncCW; EncWB; FacFETw; GrEconS; IntEnSS 79; IntvTCA 2; IntWW 91; LegTOT; LngCTC; MajTwCW; MakMC; OxCAmH; PolProf E, J, K, NF, T; RAdv 14, 13-3; REnAL; ScF&FL 1, 2; ThTwC 87; WebAB 74, 79; Who 74, 82, 83, 85, 88, 90, 92, 94; WhoAm 78, 80, 82, 84, 86, 88, 90, 92, 94, 95, 96, 97; WhoAmP 81, 83, 85, 87, 89, 91, 93, 95; WhoEc 81, 86; WhoFI 83; WhoUSWr 88; WhoWor 89, 93, 95, 96, 97; WhoWrEP 89, 92, 95; WorAl; WorAlBi; WorAu 1950; WrDr 76, 84, 86, 88, 90, 92, 94, 96*

Galbreath, John Wilmer
American. Baseball Executive
Owner, chairman, Pittsburgh Pirates, 1946-85; won three World Series.
b. Aug 9, 1897 in Derby, Ohio
d. Jul 20, 1988 in Columbus, Ohio
Source: *BiDAmSp BB; BioIn 4, 5, 7, 12, 15, 16; St&PR 87; WhAm 9; WhoAm 76, 78, 80, 82; WhoE 74, 81; WhoMW 74, 76, 78, 80; WhoProB 73*

Galbreath, Tony
[Anthony Dale Galbreath]
American. Football Player
Running back, 1976-87; set NFL mark for career pass receptions by running back.
b. Jan 29, 1954 in Fulton, Missouri
Source: *FootReg 87; WhoBlA 80, 85, 90, 92, 94*

Galdikas, Birute M(arija) F(ilomena)
German. Scientist
Studies primates; author of *Reflections of Eden,* 1995.
b. May 10, 1948 in Wiesbaden, Germany
Source: *CurBio 95*

Gale, Eric
American. Musician
Easy-listening blues guitarist; albums include *Blue Horizon,* 1982.
b. Sep 20, 1938 in New York, New York
Source: *AllMusG; BioIn 16; HarEnR 86; NewGrDJ 88, 94; OnThGG; WhoRocM 82*

Gale, Richard Nelson, Sir
English. Army Officer
Led 6th airborne division during Allied invasion of Normandy, 1944.
b. Jul 25, 1896 in London, England
d. Jul 29, 1982 in Kingston-upon-Thames, England
Source: *BioIn 5, 8, 13; ConAu 107; DcNaB 1981; IntWW 82; NewYTBS 82; WhAm 8; Who 74, 82, 83*

Gale, Robert Peter
American. Physician
Known for aiding patients after Chernobyl nuclear crisis, Apr 1986.
b. Oct 11, 1945 in New York, New York
Source: *AmMWSc 76P, 79, 82, 86, 89, 92, 95; BiDrACP 79; BioIn 15, 16; ConNews 86-4; CurBio 87; WhoAm 86, 88, 90, 92, 94, 95, 96, 97; WhoFrS 84; WhoWest 87, 89, 92; WhoWor 89*

Gale, Zona
American. Author, Journalist
Novelist of small-town Midwest life; play *Miss Lulu Bett,* 1920, won Pulitzer.
b. Aug 26, 1874 in Portage, Wisconsin
d. Dec 27, 1938 in Chicago, Illinois
Source: *AmAu&B; AmBi; AmLY; AmPeW; AmWomD; AmWomPl; AmWomWr; AnMV 1926; Benet 87, 96; BenetAL 91; BioAmW; BioIn 4, 5, 6, 12, 15, 16, 20; CamGLE; CamHAL; ChhPo, S2; CnDAL; CnMD; ConAmA; ConAmL; ConAu 105, 153; DcAmB S2; DcLB 9, 78; DcLEL; DcNAA; EvLB; FemiCLE; GrWrEL N; IntDcT 2; InWom, SUP; LegTOT; LibW; LinLib L; LngCTC; McGEWD 72, 84; ModWD; NatCAB 30; NotAW; NotNAT A, B; NotWoAT; Novels; OxCAmL 65, 83, 95; OxCAmT 84; OxCWoWr 95; PenC AM; PenNWW B; REn; REnAL; RfGAmL 87, 94; ScF&FL 1; ScFEYrs; TwCA, SUP; TwCLC 7; TwCWr; WhAm 1; WhNAA; WhThe; WisWr; WomFir; WomNov; WomWWA 14*

Galeano, Eduardo (Hughes)
Uruguayan. Author
Wrote *The Open Veins of Latin America,* 1973; *The Book of Embraces,* 1991.
b. Sep 3, 1940 in Montevideo, Uruguay
Source: *Benet 96; ConAu 13NR, 32NR; ConLC 72; CyWA 89; DcHiB; DcTwCCu 3; HispWr; SpAmA; WhoWor 91; WorAu 1985*

Galella, Ron
American. Photographer
Famous for his pursuit to photograph Jacqueline Onassis.
b. Jan 10, 1931 in New York, New York
Source: *AuNews 1; BioIn 8, 9, 10, 15; BioNews 74; ConAu 14NR, 53; IntAu&W 91; WhoAm 82, 90; WhoE 85; WrDr 76, 80, 82, 84, 86, 88*

Galen
Greek. Physician, Author
Investigated anatomy, physiology; proved that arteries carry blood, not air.
b. 129 in Pergamum, Greece
d. 199
Source: *CamDcSc; CasWL; DcScB; Grk&L; LegTOT; NewC; NewCol 75; OxCClL; OxCEng 85, 95; OxCPhil; OxDcByz; PenC CL, EUR; WebBD 83*

Galento, Tony
[Anthony Galento]
"Two Ton"
American. Boxer
Heavyweight fighter best known for saying, "I'll moider da bum," before each bout.
b. Mar 10, 1909 in Orange, New Jersey
d. Jul 22, 1979 in Livingston, New Jersey
Source: *BioIn 2, 5, 8, 10; NewYTBS 79; WhoBox 74; WhoHol A*

Galiani, Ferdinando
Italian. Economist, Author
Wrote *Della Moneta,* 1750, economic treatise anticipating modern theories of value.
b. Dec 2, 1728 in Chieti, Italy
d. Oct 30, 1787 in Naples, Italy
Source: *BioIn 7, 16, 17, 18; CasWL; DcBiPP; DcCathB; DcEuL; DcItL 1, 2; Dis&D; EncEnl; EuAu; McGEWD 72, 84; OxCFr; OxCLaw; WhoEc 81, 86*

Galileo
[Galileo Galilei]
Italian. Mathematician, Astronomer
Constructed first astronomical telescope, 1609; developed scientific method.
b. Feb 15, 1564 in Pisa, Italy
d. Jan 8, 1642 in Arcetri, Italy
Source: *AsBiEn; Benet 87, 96; BiDPsy; BiESc; BioIn 1, 2, 3, 4, 5, 6, 7, 8, 9, 10, 11, 12, 13, 14, 15, 16, 17, 18, 19, 20, 21; CamDcSc; CasWL; CyEd; DcBiPP; DcCathB; DcEuL; DcItL 1, 2; DcScB; Dis&D; EncEnl; EuAu; EvEuW; InSci; LarDcSc; LegTOT; LuthC 75; McGEWB; NamesHP; NewC; OxCEng 67; OxCMed 86; PenC EUR; RAdv 14, 13-4, 13-5; RComWL; REn; WhDW; WorAl; WorAlBi; WorInv*

Galitzine, Irene, Princess
[Mrs. Silvio Medici]
Italian. Fashion Designer
Known for silk palazzo pajamas, bare back evening dresses, 1960s.
Source: *BioIn 13, 16; EncFash; FairDF ITA; WhoFash 88; WorFshn*

Gall
American. Native American Chief
With Sitting Bull, won Battle of Little Big Horn, 1876; surrendered to U.S. Army, c.1880.
b. 1840? in South Dakota
d. 1894 in Oak Creek, South Dakota
Source: *AmBi; BioIn 1, 21; DcAmB; EncNAB; HarEnMi; NotNaAm; REnAW; WebAB 74, 79; WebAMB; WhAm HS; WhNaAH*

Gall, Franz Joseph
German. Physician
Founder of now-discredited science of phrenology; made important discoveries in cerebral anatomy: idea of localized functions.
b. Mar 9, 1758 in Tiefenbronn, Germany
d. Aug 22, 1828 in Montrouge, France
Source: *AsBiEn; BiDPsy; BiESc; CopCroC; CyEd; DcBiPP; DcInv; DcScB; EncEnl; InSci; LinLib S; NamesHP; NewC; OxCFr; OxCMed 86; REn*

Gallagher, Helen
American. Actor
Won Emmy for her role in TV soap opera "Ryan's Hope," 1976; won Tonys for *No, No, Nanette,* 1970; *Pal Joey,* 1952.
b. Jul 19, 1926 in New York, New York
Source: *BiDD; BiE&WWA; BioIn 3; CelR; ConTFT 5; EncMT; InWom SUP; NewYTBE 71; NotNAT; PlP&P; WhoAm 74, 76, 78, 80, 82; WhoAmW 74, 81, 83; WhoHol 92, A; WhoThe 72, 77, 81*

Gallagher, Richard
"Skeets"
American. Actor
Vaudeville song and dance man; played supporting roles in many 1920s films.
b. Jul 28, 1891 in Terre Haute, Indiana
d. May 22, 1955
Source: *BiDD; BioIn 3, 4, 11; EncAFC; FilmEn*

Gallagher, Rory
Irish. Musician
Blues-rock guitarist who formed trio Taste, 1965-71; Gallagher band, 1971.
b. Mar 2, 1949 in Ballyshannon, Ireland
d. Jun 14, 1995
Source: *ConMuA 80A; EncRk 88; HarEnR 86; IlEncRk; OnThGG; OxCPMus; PenEncP; RolSEnR 83; WhoRock 81*

Gallagher and Lyle
[Benny Gallagher; Graham Lyle]
British. Music Group
Duo formed, 1972-79; Lyle wrote Tina Turner's hit "What's Love Got to do With It?"
Source: *ConMuA 80A; HarEnR 86; IlEncRk; WhoRocM 82*

Galland, Adolf
German. Aviator
Commanded Luftwaffe fighter squadrons, 1943-44; returned to active duty in elite Messerschmitt squadron; shot down and captured, Apr 1945.
b. Mar 19, 1912 in Westerholt, Germany
d. Feb 9, 1996 in Oberwinter, Germany
Source: *BioIn 8, 11, 14, 16, 17, 21; EncTR 91; GenMudB; HarEnMi; NewYTBS 27; WhWW-II*

Gallant, Mavis
Canadian. Author
Short story writer, contributor to *New Yorker,* mag., 1951—.
b. Aug 11, 1922 in Montreal, Quebec, Canada
Source: *ArtclWW 2; Au&Wr 71; Benet 87, 96; BenetAL 91; BioIn 10, 12, 13, 14, 15, 16; BlmGWL; BlueB 76; CamGLE; CanWW 31, 80, 81, 83, 89; ConAu 29NR, 69; ConCaAu 1; ConLC 7, 18, 38; ConNov 72, 76, 82, 86, 91, 96; CurBio 90; DcArts; DcLB 53; DcLEL 1940; DrAF 76; DrAPF 80, 91; EncWL 3; FacFETw; FemiCLE; GrLiveH; IntAu&W 76, 77; IntvTCA 2; InWom SUP; LiExTwC; MajTwCW; ModWoWr; NewC; NewYTBS 85; OxCCan; OxCCanL; OxCCan SUP; RAdv 14, 13-1; RfGEnL 91; RfGShF; RGTwCWr; ShSCr 5; WhoAm 74, 76, 78, 80, 82, 84, 86, 88, 90, 92, 94, 95, 96, 97; WhoAmW 83, 91, 93, 95, 97; WhoCanL 85, 87, 92; WorAu 1950; WrDr 76, 80, 82, 84, 86, 88, 90, 92, 94, 96*

Gallant, Roy Arthur
American. Children's Author
Science writer; books include *Memory: How It Works and How to Improve It,* 1980.
b. Apr 17, 1924 in Portland, Maine
Source: *AuBYP 2, 3; ConAu 4NR, 5R, 29NR; ConLC 17; FifBJA; IntAu&W 91, 93; SmATA 4, 68; WhoE 85, 86; WrDr 76, 80, 82, 84, 86, 88, 90, 92, 94, 96*

Gallatin, Albert
[Abraham Alfonse Albert Gallatin]
American. Financier, Statesman
Secretary of treasury, 1801-14; helped negotiate end of War of 1812.
b. Jan 29, 1761 in Geneva, Switzerland
d. Aug 12, 1849 in Astoria, New York
Source: *Alli; AmAu&B; AmBi; AmPolLe; AmWrBE; ApCAB; BbtC; BenetAL 91; BiAUS; BiD&SB; BiDrAC; BiDrUSC 89; BiDrUSE 71, 89; BioIn 2, 3, 4, 5, 6, 8, 9, 10, 12, 15, 16; CyAG; CyAL 1; DcAmAu; DcAmB; DcAmDH 80, 89; DcLEL; DcNAA; Drake; EncAB-H 1974, 1996; EncABHB 6; HarEnUS; InSci; IntDcAn; LinLib L, S; McGEWB; NatCAB 3; OxCAmH; OxCAmL 65, 83, 95; PeoHis; PolPar; PresAR; REnAL; TwCBDA; WebAB 74, 79; WebBD 83; WhAm HS; WhAmP; WhNaAH; WorAl; WorAlBi*

Gallatin, Albert Eugene
American. Artist, Author
Nonobjective paintings influenced by cubism; author of many books about Whistler.
b. Jul 23, 1881 in Villanova, Pennsylvania
d. Jun 15, 1952 in New York, New York
Source: *AmAu&B; BioIn 1, 2, 3, 5, 11, 20; DcAmBC; McGDA; NatCAB 42; ObitOF 79; WhAm 3; WhAmArt 85; WhLit; WhoAmA 78, 80*

Gallatin, Harry J
American. Basketball Player, Basketball Coach
Forward, NY Knicks, 1948-57, Detroit, 1957-58; led NBA in rebounding, 1954; coach, 1962-66; coach of yr., 1963.
b. Apr 26, 1927 in Roxana, Illinois
Source: *BiDAmSp BK; OfNBA 87*

Gallaudet, Thomas Hopkins
American. Teacher
Established first free school for deaf in US at Hartford, CT, 1817.
b. Dec 10, 1787 in Philadelphia, Pennsylvania
d. Sep 10, 1851 in Hartford, Connecticut
Source: *Alli; AmAu&B; AmBi; AmSocL; ApCAB; BbD; BiDAmEd; BiDAmM; BiD&SB; BiDSocW; BioIn 1, 3, 7, 11, 14, 19; CyEd; DcAmAu; DcAmB; DcAmMeB 84; DcBiPP; DcNAA; Dis&D; Drake; EncDeaf; HarEnUS; LinLib L, S; LuthC 75; McGEWB; NatCAB 9; OxCAmH; TwCBDA; WebAB 74, 79; WhAm HS; WorAl; WorAlBi*

Galle, Emile
French. Artist, Designer
Led modern revival of French art glass, developing new techniques and Art Noveau style.
b. May 8, 1846 in Nancy, France
d. Sep 23, 1904 in Nancy, France
Source: *AntBDN A; BioIn 4, 11, 13, 14, 17; DcArts; DcD&D; DcNiCA; DcTwDes; IlDcG; OxCDecA; PenDiDA 89*

Gallegos, Romulo
Venezuelan. Author, Political Leader, Educator
Pres. of Venezuela, 1948; deposed by military junta.
b. Aug 2, 1884 in Caracas, Venezuela
d. Apr 4, 1969 in Caracas, Venezuela
Source: *Benet 87, 96; BenetAL 91; BiDLAmC; BioIn 1, 4, 5, 7, 8, 9, 10, 16, 17, 18; CasWL; ConAu 131; CyWA 58; DcArts; DcCPSAm; DcHiB; DcSpL; DcTwCCu 3; EncLatA; EncWL 2, 3; FacFETw; HispWr; LatAmWr; MajTwCW; McGEWB; ModLAL; OxCSpan; PenC AM; REn; SpAmA; TwCWr; WhAm 7*

Gallegos, William
American. Hostage
One of 52 held by terrorists, Nov 1979 - Jan 1981.
b. 1959?
Source: *BioIn 12, 15, 16; ConAmBL; Entr; NewYTBS 81; WhoAm 86; WhoWest 92*

Gallen, Hugh J
American. Politician
Dem. governor of NH, 1979-82; defeated in election to third term when refused to rule out tax increase.
b. Jul 30, 1924 in Portland, Oregon
d. Dec 29, 1982 in Boston, Massachusetts
Source: *AlmAP 80, 82; BiDrGov 1978; IntYB 82; NewYTBS 82; WhAm 8; WhoAm 80, 82; WhoAmP 79; WhoE 79, 81; WhoWor 82*

Galliano, John
[Juan Carlos Galliano]
English. Fashion Designer
Head designer, Givenchy, 1995-96; with Christian Dior Couture, 1996—.
b. Nov 28, 1960, Gibraltar
Source: *ConFash; CurBio 96; DcArts*

Gallico, Paul William
American. Author, Journalist
Wrote *The Snow Goose,* 1941; *The Poseidon Adventure,* 1969.
b. Jul 26, 1897 in New York, New York
d. Jul 15, 1976, Monaco
Source: *AmAu&B; AmNov; AuNews 1; BiDAmSp OS; ConAu 5R, 69; ConLC 2; ConNov 76; CurBio 46; DcAmB S10; DcArts; DcLEL; EncSF 93; EvLB; FilmgC; IntAu&W 76, 77; IntWW 74, 75, 76; MajAI; REnAL; SmATA 13; TwCA SUP; TwCWr; WhAm 7; WhoAm 74, 76; WhoWor 74, 76; WorAl; WorAlBi*

Galli-Curci, Amelita
Italian. Opera Singer
Soprano who sang with Metropolitan Opera, 1921-30; best known for role of Gilda in *Rigoletto.*
b. Nov 18, 1882 in Milan, Italy
d. Nov 26, 1963 in La Jolla, California
Source: *Baker 78, 84, 92; BiDAmM; BioIn 6, 7, 11, 12, 13, 14, 15; BriBkM 80; CmOp; DcAmB S7; IntDcOp; InWom SUP; LibW; MetOEnc; MusSN; NewAmDM; NewEOp 71; NewGrDA 86; NewGrDM 80; NewGrDO; ObitT 1961; OxDcOp; PenDiMP; WhAm 4*

Gallieni, Joseph-Simon
French. Army Officer
Led counterattack against Germans at the Marne, 1914; minister of war, 1915-16; made marshal posthumously.
b. Apr 24, 1849 in Saint-Beat, France
d. May 27, 1916 in Versailles, France
Source: *Dis&D; LinLib L; WhoMilH 76*

Galli-Marie, Marie Celestine
French. Opera Singer
Mezzo-soprano; created roles of Mignon, 1866, Carmen, 1875.
b. Nov 1840 in Paris, France
d. Sep 22, 1905 in Vence, France
Source: *Baker 84; NewEOp 71*

Gallitzin, Demetrius Augustine
Russian. Missionary
Founded Catholic colony of Loretto, PA.
b. Dec 22, 1770 in The Hague, Netherlands
d. May 6, 1840 in Loretto, Pennsylvania
Source: *AmBi; ApCAB; BioIn 2, 3, 4, 11; DcAmAu; DcAmB; HarEnUS; NatCAB 23; TwCBDA; WhAm HS*

Gallo, Ernest
American. Vintner
With brother, Julio, marketed wine under own label, beginning 1940.
b. 1910 in Modesto, California
Source: *BusPN; CmCal; ConAmBL; Entr; LegTOT; WhoAm 86*

Gallo, Fortune
Italian. Impresario
Founded NYC's San Carlo Opera, 1909; pioneered in opera sound films.
b. May 9, 1878 in Torremaggiore, Italy
d. Mar 28, 1970 in New York, New York
Source: *Baker 78, 84, 92; BioIn 2, 8, 9; CurBio 49, 70; MetOEnc; NewEOp 71; NewGrDO; NewYTBE 70; NotNAT B; OxCAmT 84; WhAm 5*

Gallo, Frank
American. Artist
Pop artist, sculptor; specializes in life-size figures of epoxy-type materials.
b. Jan 13, 1933 in Toledo, Ohio
Source: *AmArt; BioIn 7, 8, 9; BriEAA; ConArt 77; DcAmArt; DcCAA 71, 77, 88, 94; OxCTwCA; PrintW 83, 85; WhoAm 74, 78, 80, 82, 84, 86, 88; WhoAmA 73, 76, 78, 80, 82, 84, 86, 89, 91, 93*

Gallo, Julio
American. Vintner
Longtime pres. of E&J Gallo Winery; known for mid-priced wine; sells over 150 million gallons a yr.
b. Mar 21, 1910 in Modesto, California
d. May 2, 1993 in Tracy, California
Source: *AnObit 1993; BioIn 9, 10, 11, 15, 16; BusPN; CmCal; ConAmBL; Entr; WhAm 11; WhoAm 86, 88, 92; WhoWest 92*

Gallo, Robert Charles
American. Scientist
Researcher who led team that identified AIDS virus, 1984.
b. Mar 23, 1937 in Waterbury, Connecticut
Source: *AmMWSc 92; BioIn 14, 15; CurBio 86; IntWW 91; News 91-1; WhoAm 78, 80, 82, 84, 88, 90, 92, 94, 95, 96, 97; WhoE 75, 77, 79, 85, 86, 89, 95; WhoFrS 84; WhoScEn 94, 96; WhoTech 89; WhoWor 87, 89, 91, 93, 95, 96, 97*

Galloway, Don
American. Actor
Played Sergeant Ed Brown in TV series "Ironside," 1967-75.
b. Jul 27, 1937 in Brooksville, Kentucky
Source: *ConTFT 2; HalFC 80, 84, 88; VarWW 85; WhoAm 80, 82, 84, 86, 88; WhoHol 92, A*

Gallup, George Horace
American. Pollster
Founded Gallup Poll, 1935; first major success was prediction of re-election of FDR, 1936.
b. Nov 18, 1901 in Jefferson, Iowa
d. Jul 26, 1984 in Tschingel, Switzerland
Source: *AmAu&B; AmMWSc 73S; AmSocL; AnObit 1984; BiDAmJo; BioIn 1, 3, 4, 5, 10, 11, 13, 14, 15, 16, 19; BioNews 74; BlueB 76; ConAu 13R; CurBio 40, 52; EncAB-H 1974, 1996; IntWW 74, 75, 76, 77, 78, 79, 80, 81, 82, 83; IntYB 78, 79, 80, 81, 82; JrnUS; LinLib L, S; LngCTC; REn; REnAL; WebAB 74, 79; WhAm 9; WhoAm 74, 76, 78, 80, 82, 84, 86; WhoWor 74, 76, 78, 80, 82; WorAl*

Galois, Evariste
French. Mathematician
Made important contributions to the theory of equations, numbers, functions, groups of algebraic substitutions; killed in duel.
b. Oct 25, 1811 in Bourg-la-Reine, France
d. May 31, 1832 in Paris, France
Source: *BiESc; BioIn 1, 5, 7, 8, 11, 12, 13, 15; CamDcSc; DcScB; InSci; LarDcSc; NewCol 75; WebBD 83; WhDW*

Galsworthy, John
[John Sinjohn]
English. Author, Dramatist
Known for social satire: *The Forsyte Saga,* 1906-28; won Nobel Prize, 193 2.
b. Aug 14, 1867 in Kingston Hill, England
d. Jan 31, 1933 in Grove Lodge, England
Source: *AtlBL; Benet 87, 96; BioIn 1, 2, 3, 4, 5, 6, 8, 9, 10, 11, 12, 13, 14, 15, 17, 18; BlmGEL; BritPl; BritWr 6;*

CamGEL; CamGLE; CamGWoT; CasWL; Chambr 3; ChhPo, S1, S2, S3; CnDBLB 5; CnMD; CnMWL; CnThe; ConAu 104, 141; CrtSuDr; CyWA 58; DcAmC; DcAmSR; DcArts; DcBiA; DcLB 10, 34, 98, 162; DcLEL; DcNaB 1931; EncPaPR 91; EncSoA; EncWL 2, 3; EncWT; Ent; EvLB; FacFETw; FilmgC; GrBr; GrWrEL DR, N; HalFC 80, 84, 88; IntDcT 2; LegTOT; LinLib L, S; LngCEL; LngCTC; MajMD 1; MakMC; McGEWB; McGEWD 72, 84; ModBrL, S1, S2; ModWD; NewC; NewCBEL; NobelP; NotNAT A, B; Novels; OxCAmT 84; OxCEng 67, 85, 95; OxCThe 67, 83; PenC ENG; PlP&P; RAdv 1, 14, 13-1, 13-2; RComWL; REn; REnWD; RfGEnL 91; RGTwCWr; ShSCr 22; TwCA, SUP; TwCLC 1, 45; TwCWr; WebE&AL; WhDW; WhE&EA; WhoLA; WhoNob, 90, 95; WhoTwCL; WhThe; WorAl; WorAlBi; WorLitC

Galt, John
Scottish. Author
Founded Guelph, ON, 1827; novels of Scottish life include *Annals of the Parish,* 1821.
b. May 2, 1779 in Irvine, Scotland
d. Apr 11, 1839 in Greenock, Scotland
Source: *Alli; ApCAB; BbD; BbtC; BenetAL 91; BiD&SB; BiDLA; BioIn 2, 4, 5, 7, 9, 12, 17, 18; BlmGEL; BritAu 19; CamGEL; CamGLE; CanWr; CasWL; Chambr 3; ChhPo, S2; CmScLit; CyWA 58; DcArts; DcBiA; DcBiPP; DcCanB 7; DcEnA; DcEnL; DcLB 99, 116, 159; DcLEL; DcNaB; EvLB; GrWrEL N; LngCEL; MacDCB 78; NewC; NewCBEL; NinCLC 1; Novels; OxCCan; OxCCanL; OxCEng 67, 85, 95; OxCMus; PenC ENG; RfGEnL 91; RfGShF; ScF&FL 1; WebE&AL*

Galtieri, Leopoldo Fortunato
Argentine. Political Leader
Pres. of Argentina, 1976-82; resigned after unsuccessful war with Great Britain over Falkland Islands.
b. Jul 15, 1926 in Caseros, Argentina
Source: *BiDLAmC; BioIn 12, 13, 16; CurBio 82; DcCPSAm; DicTyr; EncWB; FacFETw; IntWW 82, 83, 89, 91, 93; NewYTBS 82*

Galton, Francis, Sir
English. Scientist, Explorer
Founded modern technique of weather mapping, 1863; early investigator of human intelligence.
b. Feb 16, 1822 in Birmingham, England
d. Jan 17, 1911 in Haslemere, England
Source: *Alli SUP; AsBiEn; BbD; BiD&SB; BiDPsy; BiESc; BiHiMed; BioIn 1, 2, 3, 7, 9, 10, 12, 13; BritAu 19; CamDcSc; CelCen; Chambr 3; ConAu 121; CopCroC; CyEd; DcBiPP; DcEnL; DcLB 166; DcLEL; DcNaB S2; DcScB; Dis&D; EvLB; GaEncPs; InSci; LarDcSc; LinLib L, S; LngCTC; LuthC 75; McGEWB; NamesHP; NewC; NewCBEL; OxCMed 86; OxCMus; RAdv 14; VicBrit; WhDW; WhLit; WorAl; WorAlBi; WorScD*

Galuppi, Baldassare
"Father of Opera Buffa"
Italian. Composer
Thirty comic operas include *Filosofo di Campagna,* 1754.
b. Oct 18, 1706 in Burano, Italy
d. Jan 3, 1784 in Venice, Italy
Source: *Baker 78, 84, 92; BioIn 4, 7; BlkwCE; BriBkM 80; CmOp; GrComp; IntDcOp; MusMk; NewAmDM; NewEOp 71; NewGrDM 80; NewGrDO; NewOxM; OxCMus; OxDcOp; REn*

Galvani, Luigi
Italian. Physicist, Physician
Studied effects of electric impulses on muscle, 1771; many electrical terms derived from his name.
b. Sep 9, 1737 in Bologna, Italy
d. Dec 4, 1798 in Bologna, Italy
Source: *AsBiEn; BiDPsy; BiESc; BioIn 1, 2, 3, 6, 7, 8, 9, 12, 14; CamDcSc; DcCathB; DcInv; DcScB; Dis&D; EncEnl; InSci; LarDcSc; LinLib S; McGEWB; NamesHP; NewC; OxCMed 86; WhDW; WorAl; WorAlBi; WorScD*

Galvez, Bernardo de
Spanish. Colonial Figure
Captain general of LA, the Floridas, 1783; viceroy of New Spain, 1785.
b. Jul 23, 1746? in Macharaviaya, Spain
d. Nov 30, 1786, Mexico
Source: *AmBi; AmRev; ApCAB; BioIn 3, 9, 10, 11, 13, 17, 18, 20, 21; DcAmB; Drake; EncAR; EncCRAm; McGEWB; NatCAB 10; NewCol 75; REnAW; WebBD 83; WhAm HS; WhAmRev*

Galvin, John Rogers
American. Military Leader
NATO supreme allied commander in Europe, 1987-92.
b. May 13, 1929 in Wakefield, Massachusetts
Source: *IntWW 89, 91, 93; News 90; Who 88, 90, 92, 94; WhoAm 82, 84, 88, 90, 92, 94, 95, 96, 97; WhoWor 91, 96, 97*

Galvin, Pud
[James Francis Galvin]
"Gentle Jeems"; "The Little Steam Engine"
American. Baseball Player
Pitcher, 1879-92; won 46 games in each of two consecutive seasons; Hall of Fame, 1965.
b. Dec 25, 1856 in Saint Louis, Missouri
d. Mar 7, 1902 in Pittsburgh, Pennsylvania
Source: *Ballpl 90; BioIn 7, 10, 14, 15; WhoProB 73; WhoSpor*

Galway, James
Irish. Musician
Celebrated flutist; has performed with world-class symphony orchestras; concert artist, 1975-; frequent TV appearences.
b. Dec 8, 1939 in Belfast, Northern Ireland
Source: *Baker 78, 84, 92; BioIn 11, 12, 13, 14, 15; CelR 90; ConAu 105; ConMus 3; CurBio 80; DcArts; IntWW 79, 80, 81, 82, 83, 89, 91, 93; IntWWM 80, 85, 90; LegTOT; NewAmDM; NewGrDM 80; PenDiMP; Who 82, 83, 85, 88, 90, 92, 94; WhoAm 80, 82, 84, 86, 88, 90, 92, 94, 95, 96, 97; WhoAmM 83; WhoEnt 92; WhoWor 82, 84, 87, 89, 91, 93, 95, 96, 97; WorAl; WorAlBi*

Gam, Rita Elenore
American. Actor
Films include *Klute,* 1971; *Night People,* 1954.
b. Apr 2, 1928 in Pittsburgh, Pennsylvania
Source: *BiE&WWA; ConAu 45; FilmgC; ForWC 70; HalFC 88; MotPP; MovMk; NotNAT; PlP&P; WhoAm 82; WhoHol A*

Gamaliel the Elder
Palestinian. Religious Leader, Scholar
Made innovations in Jewish ritual.
d. 50
Source: *NewC*

Gambetta, Leon
French. Lawyer, Statesman
One of formulators of Third Republic; premier, 1881-82.
b. Apr 3, 1838 in Cahors, France
d. Dec 31, 1882 in Ville-d'Avray, France
Source: *BioIn 17; DcBiPP, A; Dis&D; LinLib S; McGEWB; OxCFr; REn; WebBD 83; WorAl; WorAlBi*

Gambino, Carlo
American. Criminal
Leader of NY Mafia family, 1960s-70s.
b. Sep 1, 1902 in Palermo, Sicily, Italy
d. Oct 15, 1976 in Massapequa, New York
Source: *BioIn 9, 11; CopCroC; LegTOT; NewYTBE 71; NewYTBS 76; ObitOF 79*

Gamble, James Norris
American. Manufacturer
Partner in Proctor and Gamble Co; developed Ivory Soap.
b. Aug 9, 1836 in Cincinnati, Ohio
d. Jul 2, 1932 in Westwood, Ohio
Source: *BioIn 4, 10; NatCAB 40; WhAm 1; WorAl*

Gamble, Kenny
American. Songwriter
With Leon Huff won 1989 Grammy for song "If You Don't Know Me By Now."
b. Aug 11, 1943 in Philadelphia, Pennsylvania
Source: *BioIn 9, 12, 16; Ebony 1; InB&W 85; OxCPMus; WhoBlA 88*

Gambling, John Bradley
"The Human Alarm Clock"
American. Radio Performer
Pioneer in morning wake-up programs in NYC, 1925-50.
b. Apr 9, 1897 in Norwich, England
d. Nov 21, 1974 in Palm Beach, Florida
Source: *BioIn 2, 10, 12; CurBio 50, 75; NatCAB 58; NewYTBS 74*

Gamelin, Maurice Gustave
French. Army Officer
Head of Allied forces at outbreak of WW II.
b. Sep 20, 1872 in Paris, France
d. Apr 18, 1958 in Paris, France
Source: *BioIn 1, 4, 5; CurBio 40, 58; DcTwHis; EncTR 91; HarEnMi; WhoMilH 76; WhWW-II*

Gamow, George
American. Physicist
Nuclear physicist noted for his strong support of the big bang theory of the origin of the universe 1948; also contributed to the study of genetics.
b. Mar 4, 1904 in Odessa, Russia
d. Aug 19, 1968 in Boulder, Colorado
Source: *AmAu&B; AsBiEn; BiESc; BioIn 1, 2, 4, 8, 14, 17, 20; CamDcSc; ConAu 93, 102; DcAmB S8; DcScB; EncSF, 93; EncWB; FacFETw; InSci; LarDcSc; LegTOT; McGMS 80; NotTwCS; RAdv 14, 13-5; REnAL; ScF&FL 1; TwCA SUP; WebAB 74, 79; WhAm 5; WhE&EA; WorAl; WorAlBi; WorScD*

Gance, Abel
French. Director, Screenwriter
Pioneer filmmaker who made 1927 silent epic *Napoleon* (revised 1981); used multiple screens, wide angle lenses.
b. Oct 25, 1889 in Paris, France
d. Nov 10, 1981 in Paris, France
Source: *AnObit 1981; Benet 87, 96; BiDFilm, 81, 94; BioIn 10, 11, 12, 13; ConAu 108; ConTFT 2; DcArts; DcFM; DcTwCCu 2; EncEurC; FacFETw; FilmEn; FilmgC; HalFC 80, 84, 88; IntDcF 1-2, 2-2; IntWW 74, 75, 76, 77, 78, 79, 80, 81; ItaFilm; LegTOT; MiSFD 9N; NewYTBS 81; OxCFilm; WhoFr 79; WhoWor 74; WhScrn 83; WorEFlm; WorFDir 1*

Gandhi, Indira Priyadarshini Nehru
Indian. Political Leader
Prime minister, 1966-77, 1978-84; worked for economic planning, social reform; assassinated; daughter of Nehru.
b. Nov 19, 1917 in Allahabad, India
d. Oct 31, 1984 in New Delhi, India
Source: *AnObit 1984; BioNews 74; ColdWar 2; ConNews 85-1; CurBio 59, 66, 84; HerW; InWom, SUP; NewYTBE 72; Who 74; WhoGov 72; WhoWor 74*

Gandhi, Mahatma
[Mohandas Karamchand Gandhi]
Indian. Religious Leader, Lawyer
Known for fasts, civil disobedience which played role in struggle for Indian independence; assassinated.
b. Oct 2, 1869 in Porbandar, India
d. Jan 30, 1948 in New Delhi, India
Source: *AmJust; Benet 87, 96; BiDMoPL; BioIn 1, 2, 3, 4, 5, 6, 7, 8, 9, 10, 11, 12, 13, 14, 15, 16, 17, 18, 19, 20, 21; CasWL; ConAu 121, 132; CurBio 42, 48; DcAfHiB 86; DcLEL; DcNaB 1941; DcTwHis; Dis&D; EncRev; EncSoA; EnvEnc; GrBr; HeroCon; HisDBrE; HisEWW; LegTOT; LinLib L; LuthC 75; MajTwCW; MakMC; McGEWB; OxCEng 67, 85, 95; OxCPhil; PenC CL; PopDcHi; RadHan; REn; TwCLC 59; WhAm 2; WhDW; WhWW-II; WorAl*

Gandhi, Rajiv Ratna
Indian. Political Leader
Son of Indira Gandhi; became India's sixth and youngest prime minister, 1984-89; assassinated while campaigning.
b. Aug 20, 1944 in Bombay, India
d. May 21, 1991 in Sriperumbudur, India
Source: *BioIn 13, 14, 15, 16; CurBio 85, 91N; EncWB; FacFETw; FarE&A 81; IntWW 91; News 91; NewYTBS 84, 91; Who 92N; WhoWor 91; WorAlBi*

Gandhi, Sanjay
Indian.
Son of Indira Gandhi.
b. Dec 14, 1946 in New Delhi, India
d. Jun 23, 1980 in New Delhi, India
Source: *AnObit 1980; BioIn 10, 12, 14; NewYTBS 76*

Gang of Four
[Dave Allen; Hugo Burnham; Andy Gill; Busta Jones; Jon King; Sara Lee]
British. Music Group
Rhythm and blues/disco group, formed 1978; albums include *At the Palace,* 1984; *Mall,* 1991.
Source: *ConMus 8; DcLP 87B; DcTwHis; EncRk 88; HarEnR 86; InB&W 80; OnThGG; PenEncP; RolSEnR 83; ScF&FL 1; WhoHol 92; WhoRocM 82; WhsNW 85*

Gann, Ernest Kellogg
American. Pilot, Author
Barnstorming pilot; awarded Distinguished Flying Award in WWII; wrote many works including *High and the Mighty,* 1952.
b. Oct 13, 1910 in Lincoln, Nebraska
d. Dec 19, 1991 in San Juan Island, Washington
Source: *AmAu&B; AmNov; AuNews 1; BenetAL 91; BioIn 2, 3, 4, 7, 8, 9, 10, 11, 12, 15, 17, 18; BlueB 76; ConAu 1NR, 1R, 136; HalFC 84, 88; NewYTBS 91; TwCRHW 90; TwCWr; WhAm 10; WhoAm 74, 76, 78, 80, 82, 84, 86, 88, 90; WhoEnt 92; WhoPNW; WhoUSWr 88; WhoWest 74; WhoWrEP 89, 92; WorAl; WorAu 1950; WrDr 76, 92*

Gannett, Deborah Sampson
American. Historical Figure
Served in Continental forces, May, 1782-Oct, 1783, disguised as man.
b. Dec 17, 1760 in Plymouth, Massachusetts
d. Apr 29, 1827 in Sharon, Massachusetts
Source: *BioIn 1, 3, 5, 8, 9, 10, 11, 15, 16, 18, 19; BlkWAm; BlkwEAR*

Gannett, Frank Ernest
American. Newspaper Publisher
Founded Gannett Co., 1945; well known for media operations.
b. Sep 15, 1876 in Bristol, New York
d. Dec 3, 1957 in Rochester, New York
Source: *AmAu&B; BiDAmBL 83; BiDAmJo; BioIn 1, 2, 4, 5, 7, 11, 16; CurBio 45, 58; DcAmB S6; DcLB 29; EncAJ; EncTwCJ; NatCAB 48; REnAL; WhAm 3; WhJnl; WhNAA*

Gannett, Lewis Stiles
American. Critic
Wrote book review column for *NY Herald Tribune,* 1931-56; books include *Young China,* 1926.
b. Oct 3, 1891 in Rochester, New York
d. Feb 3, 1966
Source: *AmAu&B; BioIn 1, 4, 7; ChhPo; ConAu 89; CurBio 41, 66; EncAJ; REnAL; TwCA, SUP; WhAm 4, 4A*

Gannett, Ruth
American. Illustrator
Wife of Lewis; won Caldecott, 1946, for *My Mother Is the Most Beautiful Woman in the World.*
b. Aug 12, 1923 in New York, New York
Source: *AuBYP 2, 3; BioIn 14; BkCL; IlsCB 1946; MorJA; SmATA 3, 33; TwCChW 89; WrDr 92*

Gans, Joe
"Old Master"
American. Boxer
World lightweight champ, 1902-08; Hall of Fame, 1954.
b. Nov 25, 1874 in Baltimore, Maryland
d. Aug 10, 1910 in Baltimore, Maryland
Source: *AfrAmSG; BioIn 9, 21; BoxReg; DcAmNB; InB&W 80; WhoBox 74; WhoSpor*

Gantt, Harvey Bernard
American. Architect, Politician
First black mayor, Charlotte, SC, 1983-87; partner, Gantt-Huberman architectural firm, 1971—.
b. Jan 14, 1943 in Charleston, South Carolina
Source: *AfrAmBi 1; BioIn 13, 14, 15, 16; ConBlB 1; WhoAfA 96; WhoAmP 91; WhoBlA 77, 80, 88, 90, 92, 94; WhoSSW 86*

Ganz, Rudolph
Swiss. Conductor, Musician, Composer
Concert pianist, 1900s-20s; led St. Louis Symphony, 1921-27; NY Philharmonic Young People's concerts, 1938-49.
b. Feb 24, 1877 in Zurich, Switzerland
d. Aug 2, 1972 in Chicago, Illinois
Source: *ASCAP 66, 80; Baker 78, 84, 92; BiDAmM; BioIn 1, 4, 7, 9, 11, 20; BriBkM 80; ConAmC 76, 82; DcAmB S9; MusSN; NewAmDM; NewYTBE 72; PenDiMP; WhAm 5*

Gao Gang
Chinese. Government Official
Important leader in the Communist Party and the Chinese government; dismissed from positions for not following Communist policies, 1955.
b. 1902 in Heng Shan, China
d. 1955, China
Source: *EncRev*

Garagiola, Joe
[Joseph Henry Garagiola]
American. Baseball Player, Sportscaster
Catcher, Cardinals, 1946-54; baseball broadcaster on radio and TV, 1955—; regular on "Today" show, 1969-73, 1990-92.
b. Feb 12, 1926 in Saint Louis, Missouri
Source: *Ballpl 90; BiDAmSp OS; BioIn 6, 7, 9, 10, 11, 14, 16, 17; BioNews 74; CelR, 90; ConAu 126, X; CurBio 76; LegTOT; LesBEnT 92; NewYTET; WhoAm 74, 76, 78, 80, 82, 84, 86, 88, 90, 92, 94, 95, 96, 97; WhoE 74, 95; WhoProB 73*

Garamond, Claude
French. Type Designer
Perfected Roman typeface design, which replaced Gothic, 1531.
b. 1499 in Paris, France
d. 1561 in Paris, France
Source: *EncAJ; NewCol 75; WebBD 83; WhDW*

Garand, John Cantius
American. Engineer, Inventor
Developed Garand semi-automatic rifle (M-1) for US Army, 1930.
b. Jan 1, 1888 in Saint Remi, Quebec, Canada
d. Feb 16, 1974 in Springfield, Massachusetts
Source: *CurBio 45, 74; InSci; NewYTBS 74; WebAB 74, 79; WebAMB; WhAm 6*

Garavani, Valentino
Italian. Fashion Designer
Renowned designer, 1960s-70s; clients included Jacqueline Kennedy, Elizabeth Taylor.
b. 1932 in Voghera, Italy
Source: *BioIn 14, 16; WhoAm 96, 97; WhoWor 82, 84, 87, 89, 91, 93, 95, 96, 97; WorFshn*

Garber, Jan
"Idol of the Air Lanes"
American. Bandleader
Led sweet-style dance band, especially popular, 1930s.
b. Nov 5, 1895? in Morristown, Pennsylvania
d. Oct 5, 1977 in Shreveport, Louisiana
Source: *BgBands 74; BioIn 11; CmpEPM; WhScrn 83*

Garbo, Greta
[Greta Lovisa Gustafsson]
Swedish. Actor
Starred in film *Anna Karenina,* 1935; won special Oscar, 1954; famous recluse.
b. Sep 18, 1905 in Stockholm, Sweden
d. Apr 15, 1990 in New York, New York
Source: *AmCulL; AnObit 1990; BiDFilm, 81, 94; BioIn 1, 2, 3, 4, 5, 6, 7, 8, 9, 10, 11, 12, 13, 14, 15, 16, 17, 18, 19, 20, 21; BkPepl; BlueB 76; CelR, 90; CmMov; ContDcW 89; ConTFT 9; CurBio 55, 90, 90N; DcArts; EncAFC; EncEurC; EncFash; FacFETw; Film 2; FilmEn; FilmgC; GayLesB; GoodHs; GrLiveH; HalFC 80, 84, 88; IntDcF 1-3, 2-3; IntDcWB; IntMPA 82, 88; IntWW 89; InWom SUP; LegTOT; LibW; LinLib S; McGEWB; MGM; MotPP; MovMk; News 90, 90-3; NewYTBS 90; OxCAmH; OxCFilm; PeoHis; RComAH; SilFlmP; ThFT; TwYS; WebAB 74, 79; WhAm 10; Who 74, 82, 83, 85, 88, 90; WhoAm 74, 76, 78, 80, 82, 84, 86, 88; WhoAmW 70, 74, 83; WhoWor 78, 80, 82, 84, 87, 89; WorAl; WorAlBi; WorEFlm*

Garcia, Andy
American. Actor
Films include *The Godfather III,* 1991; *Jennifer Eight,* 1992.
b. Apr 12, 1956 in Havana, Cuba
Source: *BiDFilm 94; BioIn 15; ConTFT 8, 15; DcHiB; HispAmA; IntMPA 92, 94, 96; IntWW 93; LegTOT; WhoAm 92, 94, 95, 96, 97; WhoHisp 91, 92, 94; WhoHol 92*

Garcia, Carlos Polestico
Philippine. Political Leader
Pres. of the Philippines, 1957-61.
b. Nov 4, 1896, Philippines
d. Jun 14, 1971 in Quezon City, Philippines
Source: *CurBio 57, 71; NewYTBE 71; ObitOF 79; WhAm 5*

Garcia, Cristina
American. Author, Journalist
Wrote novel *Dreaming in Cuban,* 1992.
b. 1959, Cuba
Source: *ConLC 76*

Garcia, Jerry
[The Grateful Dead; Jerome John Garcia]
American. Musician, Singer
Founder and lead guitarist of acid-rock band, 1965; Top Ten album, *In the Dark,* 1987.
b. Aug 1, 1942 in San Francisco, California
d. Aug 9, 1995 in Forest Knolls, California
Source: *ASCAP 80; Baker 84, 92; BiDAmM; BioIn 9, 11, 14, 15, 16; BkPepl; ConMuA 80A; ConMus 4; CurBio 90, 95N; DcHiB; FacFETw; LegTOT; News 96, 88-3, 96-1; NewYTBS 95; OnThGG; WhAm 11; WhoAm 80, 82, 84, 86, 88, 90, 92, 94, 95; WhoEnt 92; WhoHisp 92, 94; WhoRock 81; WhoRocM 82; WorAl; WorAlBi*

Garcia, Joe
American. Inventor
Invented court game wallyball, combination of volleyball, racquetball, 1979.
b. 1947?, Puerto Rico
Source: *BioIn 15; ConNews 86-4; WhoEmL 87; WhoFI 87; WhoHisp 92; WhoSSW 86*

Garcia, Manuel del Popolo Vincente
Spanish. Opera Singer, Composer
Famed tenor; starred in first US performance of *Don Giovanni,* 1820s.
b. Jan 22, 1775 in Seville, Spain
d. Jun 2, 1832 in Paris, France
Source: *BiDAmM; BriBkM 80; CmOp; NewEOp 71; OxCMus*

Garcia, Manuel Patricio Rodriguez
Spanish. Opera Singer, Teacher
Baritone; wrote respected text on singing technique, 1847; son of Manuel del Popolo.
b. Mar 17, 1805 in Madrid, Spain
d. Jul 1, 1906 in London, England
Source: *Baker 84; NewEOp 71; OxCMus*

Garcia, Mike (Edward Miguel)
"The Big Bear"
American. Baseball Player
Pitcher, 1948-61, mostly with Cleveland; had 142 career wins.
b. Nov 17, 1923 in San Gabriel, California
d. Jan 13, 1986 in Cleveland, Ohio
Source: *Ballpl 90; BioIn 3, 14; WhoProB 73*

Garcia Lorca, Federico
Spanish. Poet, Dramatist
Best-known works include play *Blood Wedding,* 1933; killed during civil war.
b. Jun 5, 1898 in Fuente Vaqueros, Spain
d. Aug 19, 1936 in Granada, Spain
Source: *AtlBL; Benet 87, 96; BioIn 14, 15, 16, 17, 19, 20; CamGWoT; CasWL; ClDMEL 47, 80; CnMD; CnMWL; CnOxB; CnThe; ConAu 104, 131; CyWA 58; DcHiB; DcLB 108; DcSpL; DramC 2; EncWL, 2, 3; EvEuW; FacFETw; GayLesB; GayLL; GrFLW; HispWr; IntDcT 2; LegTOT; LngCTC; MagSWL; MajMD 2; MajTwCW; McGEWB; McGEWD 72, 84; ModRL; ModSpP S; ModWD; NewGrDM 80; NewGrDO;*

OxCEng 85, 95; OxCSpan; OxCThe 67, 83; PenC EUR; PoeCrit 3; RAdv 14; RComWL; REn; REnWD; RfGWoL 95; RGFMEP; TwCA, SUP; TwCLC 7, 49; TwCWr; WhAm 4; WhoTwCL; WorAl; WorAlBi; WorLitC

Garcia-Marquez, Gabriel Jose
Colombian. Author
Won 1982 Nobel Prize in literature for novels, short stories; wrote *One Hundred Years of Solitude,* 1967.
b. Mar 6, 1928 in Aracataca, Colombia
Source: *Au&Arts 3; Benet 87; BenetAL 91; BioIn 13, 14, 15, 16; CasWL; CelR 90; ConAu 28NR; ConFLW 84; ConLC 15, 68; CurBio 73; CyWA 89; DcCLAA; DcLB 113; FacFETw; HispWr; IntWW 91; LatAmWr; LiExTwC; MajTwCW; NobelP; OxCEng 85; PenC AM; PenEncH; PostFic; RAdv 13-2; ShSCr 8; ShSWr; Who 92; WhoNob, 90; WhoWor 89, 91; WorAlBi; WorAu 1950*

Garcia Perez, Alan
Peruvian. Political Leader
President of Peru, 1985-89.
b. May 23, 1949 in Lima, Peru
Source: *BiDLAmC; BioIn 14, 15, 16; CurBio 85; DcCPSAm; IntWW 89, 91, 93; WhoWor 87, 89, 91, 95*

Garcia Robles, Alfonso
Mexican. Diplomat
Shared Nobel Peace Prize, 1982, for work on disarmament; his Treaty of Tlatelolco banned nuclear arms from Latin America, 1967.
b. Mar 20, 1911 in Zamora, Mexico
d. Sep 2, 1991 in Mexico City, Mexico
Source: *BioIn 13, 15, 17; IntWW 74, 75, 76, 77, 78, 79, 80, 81, 82, 83, 89, 91; NewYTBS 82, 91; NobelP; WhAm 11; Who 85, 88, 90, 92N; WhoGov 72; WhoNob, 90, 95; WhoUN 75; WhoWor 74, 76, 78, 84, 87, 89, 91*

Garcia Vargas, Joaquin
Mexican. Actor
Comedy actor noted for slap-stick roles, 1940-80; films include *El Rey de Barrio.*
d. May 13, 1993 in Mexico City, Mexico
Source: *BioIn 18, 19; NewYTBS 93*

Garcia y Sanchez, Damaso Domingo
Dominican. Baseball Player
Infielder, 1978-89; two-time AL All-Star, 1984-85.
b. Feb 7, 1957 in Moca, Dominican Republic
Source: *Ballpl 90; BaseReg 86, 87; BioIn 13; WhoHisp 92*

Gard, Wayne
[Sanford Wayne Gard]
American. Journalist, Historian
Books include *The Great Buffalo Hunt,* 1959; *Rawhide Texas,* 1965.
b. Jun 21, 1899 in Brocton, Illinois
d. Sep 24, 1986 in Dallas, Texas
Source: *AmAu&B; AnMV 1926; BioIn 9, 16; ConAu 1R, 120; EncAAH; REnAW; SmATA 49N; TexWr; WhJnl; WhNAA*

Garden, Mary
Scottish. Opera Singer
Soprano chosen by Debussy for premiere performance of *Pelleas et Melisande,* 1902; awarded French Legion of Honor.
b. Feb 20, 1874 in Aberdeen, Scotland
d. Jan 4, 1967 in Aberdeen, Scotland
Source: *AmCulL; ApCAB X; Baker 78, 84, 92; BioIn 14, 15, 16, 19, 21; CmOp; ContDcW 89; DcAmB S8; FacFETw; Film 1; IntDcOp; IntDcWB; LibW; LinLib S; MetOEnc; MusSN; NewAmDM; NewGrDA 86; NewGrDM 80; NewGrDO; NotAW MOD; OxDcOp; PenDiMP; REn; TwYS; WebAB 74, 79; WhAm 4; WhScrn 74, 77, 83; WomFir*

Gardenia, Vincent
[Vincent Scognamiglio]
American. Actor
Won Tony for *Prisoner of Second Avenue,* 1971; Oscar nominee for *Bang the Drum Slowly,* 1973; *Moonstruck,* 1987; won 1990 Emmy.
b. Jan 7, 1922 in Naples, Italy
d. Dec 11, 1992 in Philadelphia, Pennsylvania
Source: *AnObit 1992; BiE&WWA; BioIn 18, 19; ConTFT 2, 7, 11; EncAFC; FilmgC; HalFC 80, 84, 88; IntMPA 88, 92; ItaFilm; LegTOT; News 93-2; NewYTBS 74; NotNAT; PlP&P A; VarWW 85; WhoAm 86, 90; WhoEnt 92; WhoHol 92, A; WhoThe 77, 81*

Gardiner, Chuck
[Charles Robert Gardiner]
Canadian. Hockey Player
Goalie, Chicago, 1927-34; won Vezina Trophy, 1932, 1934; Hall of Fame, 1945; died from brain tumor.
b. Dec 31, 1904 in Edinburgh, Scotland
d. Jun 13, 1934 in Winnipeg, Manitoba, Canada
Source: *HocEn; WhoHcky 73; WhoSpor*

Gardiner, Herb(ert Martin)
Canadian. Hockey Player
Defenseman, 1926-29, with Chicago, Montreal; won Hart Trophy, 1927; Hall of Fame, 1958.
b. May 8, 1891 in Winnipeg, Manitoba, Canada
d. Jan 11, 1972
Source: *HocEn; WhoHcky 73*

Gardiner, John Eliot
English. Conductor
Best known for his presentations of baroque works; founder, Monteverdi Choir, 1964, and the English Baroque Soloists, 1978.
b. Apr 20, 1943 in Fontmell Magna, England
Source: *Baker 84, 92; BioIn 13, 15, 16; CurBio 91; IntWW 89, 91, 93; IntWWM 80, 90; NewAmDM; NewGrDM 80; NewGrDO; OxDcOp; PenDiMP; Who 82, 83, 85, 88, 90, 92, 94; WhoAm 84*

Gardiner, Muriel
American. Physician
Wrote memoirs of her life in Austrian Underground: *Code Name "Mary",* 1983.
b. Nov 23, 1901 in Chicago, Illinois
d. Feb 6, 1985 in Princeton, New Jersey
Source: *AnObit 1985; BioIn 13, 14, 15, 19; ConAu 77; FacFETw; NewYTBS 85*

Gardiner, Reginald
English. Actor
Familiar character actor; has appeared in 100 films since 1936, including *The Great Dictator,* 1940.
b. Feb 27, 1903 in Wimbledon, England
d. Jul 7, 1980 in Westwood, California
Source: *AnObit 1980; BiE&WWA; BioIn 2, 10, 12; EncAFC; FilmEn; FilmgC; ForYSC; HalFC 80, 84, 88; IlWWBF; MotPP; MovMk; Vers A; What 4; WhoHol A; WhoThe 77; WhScrn 83; WhThe*

Gardner, Alexander
Scottish. Photographer
Known for his photographic coverage of the Civil War and the West; also noted for his photographs of Lincoln.
b. Oct 17, 1821 in Paisley, Scotland
d. Dec 12, 1882 in Washington, District of Columbia
Source: *BiDAmJo; BioIn 16, 17; BriEAA; DcAmArt; DcNAA; ICPEnP; MacBEP; WhCiWar*

Gardner, Ava
[Lucy Johnson]
American. Actor
Screen sex goddess; made over 60 films, 1942-81, including *Mogambo,* 1951, for which she received Oscar nomination; also known for marriages to Mickey Rooney, Artie Shaw, Frank Sinatra.
b. Dec 24, 1922 in Smithfield, North Carolina
d. Jan 25, 1990 in London, England
Source: *AnObit 1990; BiDFilm, 81, 94; BioAmW; BioIn 1, 2, 3, 4, 5, 6, 7, 8, 10, 11, 12, 13, 14, 15, 16, 17, 18; BlueB 76; CelR, 90; ConTFT 3, 9; CurBio 65, 90, 90N; DcArts; DcTwCCu 1; FacFETw; FilmEn; FilmgC; ForYSC; GangFlm; GoodHs; HalFC 80, 84, 88; IntDcF 1-3, 2-3; IntMPA 75, 76, 77, 78, 79, 80, 81, 82, 84, 86, 88; IntWW 74, 75, 76, 77, 78, 79, 80, 81, 82, 83, 89; InWom SUP; ItaFilm; LegTOT; MGM; MotPP; MovMk; News 90, 90-2; NewYTBS 90; OxCFilm; WhAm 10; WhoAm 86, 88; WhoHol A; WorAl; WorAlBi; WorEFlm*

Gardner, Booth
American. Politician
Dem. governor of Washington, 1985—.
b. Aug 21, 1936 in Tacoma, Washington
Source: *AlmAP 88; BiDrGov 1983, 1988; BioIn 16; IntWW 89; WhoAm 86, 88, 90, 92, 96; WhoAmP 85, 87, 89, 91,*

93, 95; WhoWest 87, 89, 92, 96; WhoWor 87, 89, 91, 93

Gardner, Ed(ward Francis)
American. Comedian
Played Archie on radio show "Duffy's Tavern," 1941-51.
b. Jun 29, 1905 in Astoria, New York
d. Aug 17, 1963
Source: *BioIn 1, 2, 6; CurBio 43, 63; JoeFr; WhoHol B; WhScrn 74, 77*

Gardner, Edward George
American. Business Executive
Founded Soft Sheen Products, Inc., 1967.
b. Feb 15, 1925 in Chicago, Illinois
Source: *ConAmBL; Dun&B 90; InB&W 85; WhoBlA 88, 92; WhoFI 85, 87*

Gardner, Erle Stanley
[A A Fair]
American. Author, Lawyer
Wrote Perry Mason detective stories series, basis for movies, radio, TV series.
b. Jul 17, 1889 in Malden, Massachusetts
d. Mar 11, 1970 in Temecula, California
Source: *AmAu&B; Benet 87, 96; BenetAL 91; BioIn 1, 2, 4, 5, 6, 7, 8, 9, 10, 11, 12, 13, 14, 17; CmCal; ConAu 5R, 13NR, 25R; CorpD; CrtSuMy; CurBio 44, 70; DcAmB S8; DcArts; EncMys; EncSF 93; EvLB; FacFETw; FilmgC; GrWrEL N; HalFC 80, 84, 88; LegTOT; LinLib L, S; LngCTC; MajTwCW; MnBBF; NatCAB 62; NewYTBE 70; Novels; ObitT 1961; OxCAmL 65, 83, 95; PenC AM; RAdv 14; REn; REnAL; RfGAmL 87, 94; ScF&FL 92; ScFEYrs; TwCA, SUP; TwCCr&M 80, 85, 91; TwCWr; WebAB 74, 79; WhAm 6; WhE&EA; WhNAA; WorAl; WorAlBi*

Gardner, George
Irish. Boxer
Won middleweight title, 1903.
b. Mar 17, 1877 in Lisdoonvarna, Ireland
d. Jul 8, 1954 in Chicago, Illinois
Source: *BioIn 3; WhoBox 74*

Gardner, Hy
American. Journalist
Syndicated Broadway columnist, *NY Herald Tribune;* host of radio, TV shows, 1930s-40s.
b. Dec 2, 1908 in New York, New York
d. Jun 17, 1989 in Miami, Florida
Source: *AnObit 1989; BiDAmNC; BioIn 16; ConAu 101, 128; NewYTBS 89; WhAm 10; WhoAm 74, 76, 78, 80, 82, 84*

Gardner, Isabella
American. Poet
Verse volumes include *The Looking Glass: New Poems,* 1961.
b. Sep 7, 1915 in Newton, Massachusetts
d. Jul 7, 1981 in New York, New York
Source: *AmWomWr; AnObit 1981; BenetAL 91; BioIn 10, 12, 14; BlueB 76; ConAu 97, 104; IntWWP 77; NewYTBS 81; OxCAmL 83; WhoAm 74; WhoAmW 74; WrDr 82*

Gardner, Isabella Stewart
[Mrs. Jack Gardner]
American. Art Patron, Socialite
In 1899 built Fenway Court to house art treasures, later bequeathed to city of Boston; patron of Bernard Berenson.
b. Apr 14, 1840 in New York, New York
d. Jul 17, 1924 in Boston, Massachusetts
Source: *AmBi; BioIn 15, 16; ContDcW 89; DcAmB; DcArts; EncAB-H 1974, 1996; GayN; GrLiveH; IntDcWB; InWom SUP; LibW; NewGrDA 86; NotAW; WebAB 74, 79; WebBD 83; WhAm 1; WhAmArt 85; WomFir*

Gardner, Jean Louis Charles
French. Architect
Designed Paris Opera House, 1861-75; Monte Carlo casino, 1878.
b. Nov 6, 1825 in Paris, France
d. Aug 3, 1898
Source: *NewCol 75*

Gardner, Jimmy
[James Henry Gardner]
Canadian. Hockey Player
Forward, playing amateur hockey for several Montreal teams, early 1900s; Hall of Fame, 1962.
b. May 21, 1881 in Montreal, Quebec, Canada
d. Nov 7, 1940 in Montreal, Quebec, Canada
Source: *WhoHcky 73*

Gardner, John Champlin, Jr.
American. Author
Wrote *October Light,* 1976; *The King's Indian,* 1974.
b. Jul 21, 1933 in Batavia, New York
d. Sep 14, 1982 in Susquehanna, Pennsylvania
Source: *AnObit 1984; AuBYP 2S; AuNews 1; BioIn 7, 10, 11, 12, 13, 14, 15, 17; ConAu 65, 107; ConLC 10; ConNov 76; CurBio 78, 82; DcLB 2; DcLEL 1940; EncSF; ModAL S1; NewYTBS 82; RAdv 1; SmATA 31N; WhAm 8; WhoAm 74, 76, 78, 80, 82; WrDr 80*

Gardner, John William
American. Government Official
Secretary of HEW, 1965-68; founded, chaired Common Cause, 1970-77.
b. Oct 8, 1912 in Los Angeles, California
Source: *AmAu&B; AmMWSc 73S, 78S; BiDrAPA 89; BiDrUSE 71, 89; BioIn 4, 5, 7, 8, 9, 11, 12, 16; BlueB 76; ConAu 1R, 4NR, 5R; CurBio 56; DcLEL 1940; EncAB-H 1974; EncAI&E; EncWB; IntAu&W 77, 89; IntWW 74, 75, 76, 77, 78, 79, 80, 81, 82, 83, 89, 91, 93; LEduc 74; LinLib L, S; WebAB 74, 79; Who 74, 82, 83, 85, 88, 90, 92, 94; WhoAm 74, 76, 78, 80, 82, 84, 86, 88, 90, 92, 94, 95, 96, 97; WhoAmP 73, 75, 77, 79, 81, 83, 85, 87, 89, 91, 93, 95; WorAl; WorAlBi*

Gardner, Martin
American. Author, Editor
Writings include *The Snark Puzzle Book,* 1973; *Mathematical Magic Show,* 1977.
b. Oct 21, 1914 in Tulsa, Oklahoma
Source: *AmAu&B; AuBYP 2S, 3; BioIn 6, 10, 12, 13, 14, 17, 21; ChhPo, S1, S2, S3; ConAu 46NR, 73; EncSF, 93; RAdv 14; ScF&FL 92; SmATA 16; WhoE 74; WhoSSW 91, 93; WorAu 1980*

Gardner, Mary Sewall
American. Nurse
Wrote classic text *Public Health Nursing,* 1916.
b. Feb 5, 1871 in Newton, Massachusetts
d. Feb 20, 1961 in Providence, Rhode Island
Source: *AmWomWr; BioIn 12, 16; InWom SUP; NotAW MOD*

Gardner, Randy
[Babilonia and Gardner]
American. Skater
With Tai Babilonia, won five national, one world championship in pairs figure skating; injury prevented competition, 1980 Olympics.
b. Dec 2, 1958 in Marina del Rey, California
Source: *BioIn 12, 16; NewYTBS 79; WhoAmP 83, 85, 87, 89, 91; WhoSSW 88*

Gareau, Jacqueline
American. Track Athlete
Real winner of 1980 Boston Marathon, in which Rosie Ruiz was disqualified.
b. Mar 10, 1953
Source: *BioIn 12*

Garfield, Brian Wynne
American. Author
Won Edgar for *Hopscotch,* 1975.
b. Jan 26, 1939 in New York, New York
Source: *BioIn 10, 14, 16; ConAu 6NR; DcLP 87A; EncFWF; Novels; SpyFic; TwCCr&M 91; TwCWW 91; WhoAm 74, 76, 78, 80, 82, 84, 86, 88, 90, 92, 94, 95, 96, 97; WhoEnt 92; WhoUSWr 88; WhoWrEP 89, 92, 95; WrDr 86, 92*

Garfield, James Abram
American. US President
Rep., 20th pres., Mar 4 - Sep 19, 1881; shot in Washington railway station by Charles J Guiteau.
b. Nov 19, 1831 in Cuyahoga County, Ohio
d. Sep 19, 1881 in Elberon, New Jersey
Source: *Alli SUP; AmAu&B; AmBi; AmPolLe; ApCAB; BiAUS; BiD&SB; BiDrAC; BiDrUSC 89; BiDrUSE 71, 89; BioIn 1, 2, 3, 4, 5, 6, 7, 8, 9, 10, 11, 12, 13; CelCen; CivWDc; CyEd; DcAmAu; DcAmB; Dis&D; Drake; EncAAH; EncAB-H 1974; FacPr 89, 93; HarEnUS; HealPre; LinLib S;*

McGEWB; NatCAB 4; OhA&B; OxCAmH; OxCAmL 65, 83; REnAL; TwCBDA; WebAB 74, 79; WhAm HS; WhAmP; WhCiWar; WhDW; WorAl

Garfield, John
[Julius Garfinkle]
American. Actor
Played tough-guy roles in *The Postman Always Rings Twice, Body and Soul;* victim of McCarthy's blacklist.
b. Mar 4, 1913 in New York, New York
d. May 21, 1952 in New York, New York
Source: *BiDFilm, 81, 94; BioIn 1, 2, 3, 6, 7, 9, 10, 11, 13, 14, 15, 17, 18, 19; CmMov; CurBio 48, 52; DcAmB S5; EncMcCE; FilmEn; FilmgC; ForYSC; GangFlm; HalFC 80, 84, 88; IntDcF 1-3, 2-3; LegTOT; MotPP; MovMk; NotNAT A, B; OxCAmT 84; OxCFilm; PlP&P; WhoHol B; WhScrn 74, 77, 83; WhThe; WorAl; WorAlBi; WorEFlm*

Garfield, Leon
English. Author
Completed unfinished Dickens novel, *The Mystery of Edwin Drood,* 1980; won Carnegie Medal for *The God Beneath the Sea,* 1970.
b. Jul 14, 1921 in Brighton, England
d. Jun 2, 1996 in London, England
Source: *Au&Arts 8; Au&Wr 71; AuBYP 2S, 3; BioIn 8, 9, 10, 14, 16; CamGLE; ChlBkCr; ChlFicS; ChlLR 21; ConAu 17R, 38NR, 41NR, 152; ConLC 12; DcLB 161; FourBJA; IntAu&W 89, 91, 93; MajAI; OxCChiL; PiP; ScF&FL 1, 2, 92; SenS; SmATA 1, 32, 76, 90; TwCChW 78, 83, 89; TwCYAW; Who 82, 83, 85, 88, 90, 92, 94; WhoChL; WrDr 76, 80, 82, 84, 86, 88, 90, 92, 94, 96*

Garfield, Lucretia Rudolph
[Mrs. James A Garfield]
American. First Lady
In White House less than seven mos; survived husband by 30 yrs.
b. Apr 19, 1832 in Hiram, Ohio
d. Mar 14, 1918 in Pasadena, California
Source: *AmWom; ApCAB, SUP; BioIn 8, 9, 16, 17, 21; InWom SUP; NatCAB 4; NotAW; TwCBDA; WhAm 1*

Garfinkle, Louis
American. Writer
Wrote award-winning film *The Deer Hunter,* 1982.
b. Feb 11, 1928 in Seattle, Washington
Source: *ConAu 112; IntMPA 75, 76, 77, 78, 79, 80, 81, 82, 84, 86, 88, 92, 94, 96; NatPD 77; VarWW 85; WhoEnt 92; WhoWor 91*

Garfunkel, Art(hur)
[Simon and Garfunkel]
American. Singer, Actor
Best-known songs with Paul Simon include "Mrs. Robinson," 1968; 6-Grammy winner "Bridge Over Troubled Water," 1970.
b. Nov 5, 1941 in Forest Hills, New York
Source: *Baker 84, 92; BioIn 13, 14, 16; BkPepl; CelR, 90; ConMus 4; CurBio 74; EncFCWM 83; EncPR&S 89; EncRk 88; EncRkSt; FilmgC; HalFC 84, 88; HarEnR 86; IlEncRk; IntMPA 92; IntWW 89, 91, 93; LegTOT; NewAmDM; NewGrDA 86; PenEncP; RolSEnR 83; WhoAm 80, 82, 84, 86, 88, 90, 92, 94, 95, 96, 97; WhoEnt 92; WhoRock 81; WorAlBi*

Gargan, William
American. Actor
Played TV's first detective "Martin Kane, Private Eye," 1949.
b. Jul 17, 1905 in New York, New York
d. Feb 16, 1979 in San Diego, California
Source: *BioIn 4, 78, 79; LegTOT; MotPP; MovMk; RadStar; What 5; WhoHol A; WhoThe 77A; WhScrn 83; WhThe; WorAl*

Garibaldi, Giuseppe
Italian. Patriot, Soldier
Major figure in Risorgimento movement for Italian unity, mid-1800s.
b. Jul 4, 1807 in Nice, France
d. Jun 2, 1882 in Caprera, Italy
Source: *ApCAB SUP; Benet 87, 96; BioIn 1, 2, 3, 4, 5, 6, 7, 8, 9, 10, 11, 12, 13, 14, 16, 17, 20; CelCen; DcAmSR; DcBiPP; DcItL 1, 2; DcNiCA; Dis&D; EncPaPR 91; EncRev; HarEnMi; HarEnUS; HisWorL; LegTOT; LinLib S; McGEWB; NewC; OxCFr; REn; WebBD 83; WhAm HS; WhCiWar; WhDW; WhoMilH 76; WorAl; WorAlBi*

Garis, Howard Roger
American. Author
Worked for Stratemeyer syndicate; wrote *Uncle Wiggly* series.
b. Apr 25, 1873 in Binghamton, New York
d. Nov 5, 1962 in Amherst, Massachusetts
Source: *AmAu&B; BioIn 1, 6, 7, 10; CarSB; ConAu 73; DcAmB S7; EncSF; REnAL; SmATA 13; WhAm 4*

Garland, Beverly
[Beverly Lucy Fessenden]
American. Actor
Played in TV shows "My Three Sons," 1969-72; "Scarecrow and Mrs. King," 1983-87.
b. Oct 17, 1926 in Santa Cruz, California
Source: *BioIn 16, 18; FilmEn; FilmgC; ForYSC; GangFlm; HalFC 80, 84, 88; IntMPA 92; LegTOT; MotPP; MovMk; WhoAm 80; WhoHol A; WhoHrs 80*

Garland, Hamlin
[Hannibal Hamlin Garland]
American. Author
Won Pulitzer for autobiographical novel, *A Daughter of the Middle Border,* 1921.
b. Sep 14, 1860 in West Salem, Wisconsin
d. Mar 4, 1940 in Hollywood, California
Source: *AmAu&B; AmBi; AmCulL; AmLY; ApCAB SUP, X; AtlBL; BbD; Benet 87; BenetAL 91; BiD&SB; BiDPara; BioIn 1, 2, 3, 4, 5, 6, 8, 9, 10, 11, 12, 13, 14, 19, 20; CamGEL; CamGLE; CamHAL; CasWL; Chambr 3; ChhPo; CnDAL; ConAmA; ConAmL; ConAu 104; CurBio 40; CyWA 58; DcAmAu; DcAmB S2; DcAmSR; DcBiA; DcLB 12, 71, 78; DcLEL; DcNAA; EncAAH; EncAB-H 1974, 1996; EncFWF; EncO&P 1, 2, 3; EvLB; FacFETw; FifWWr; GayN; GrWrEL N; LegTOT; LinLib L, S; LngCTC; McGEWB; ModAL; NatCAB 8; NotNAT B; Novels; OxCAmL 65, 83; OxCCan; OxCEng 67; PenC AM; RAdv 1, 13-1; REn; REnAL; REnAW; RfGAmL 87; ScF&FL 1; ShSCr 18; Str&VC; TwCA, SUP; TwCBDA; TwCLC 3; TwCWW 82, 91; WebAB 74, 79; WebE&AL; WhAm 1; WhLit; WhNAA; WhNaAH; WisWr; WorAl; WorAlBi*

Garland, Judy
[Frances Ethel Gumm]
American. Actor, Singer
Played Dorothy in *The Wizard of Oz,* 1939; mother of Liza Minnelli, Lorna Luft.
b. Jun 10, 1922 in Grand Rapids, Minnesota
d. Jun 22, 1969 in London, England
Source: *Baker 92; BiDAmM; BiDD; BiDFilm, 81, 94; BioAmW; BioIn 2, 3, 4, 5, 6, 7, 8, 9, 10, 11, 12, 13; CmCal; CmMov; CmpEPM; ConMus 6; ContDcW 89; CurBio 41, 52, 69; DcAmB S8; DcArts; EncAFC; EncWB; FacFETw; FilmEn; FilmgC; GoodHs; GrLiveH; HalFC 80, 84, 88; IntDcF 1-3, 2-3; IntDcWB; InWom, SUP; LegTOT; LibW; MGM; MotPP; MovMk; NewAmDM; NewGrDA 86; NewGrDM 80; NewYTET; NotAW MOD; NotNAT A; ObitT 1961; OxCFilm; OxCPMus; PenEncP; RadStar; SaTiSS; ThFT; WebAB 74, 79; WhAm 5; WhoAmW 58, 64, 66, 68, 70; WhoHol B; WhoHrs 80; WhScrn 74, 77, 83; WorAl; WorAlBi; WorEFlm*

Garment, Leonard
American. Lawyer
Legal counsel to Nixon during Watergate crisis, 1973; urged the firing of Haldeman, Ehrlichman, April 1973.
b. May 11, 1924 in New York, New York
Source: *BioIn 8, 9, 10, 12; NewYTBE 73; PolProf NF; WhoAm 78; WhoAmL 78, 79*

Garn, Jake
[Edwin Jacob Garn]
American. Politician
Rep. senator from UT, 1974—; first politician in space, Apr 12, 1985 on space shuttle *Discovery.*
b. Oct 12, 1932 in Richfield, Utah
Source: *AlmAP 78; WhoSpc; WhoWest 74, 76, 78, 80, 82, 84, 87, 89, 92; WhoWor 80, 82, 84, 87, 89, 91*

Garneau, Marc
Canadian. Naval Officer, Astronaut
Canada's first astronaut; aboard US space shuttle *Challenger*, 1984.
b. Feb 23, 1949 in Quebec, Quebec, Canada
Source: *BioIn 14, 15; CanWW 89; ConNews 85-1; FacFETw; NewYTBS 84; WhoSpc; WhoTech 95*

Garner, Erroll
American. Jazz Musician, Songwriter
Self-taught pianist; popular on TV, 1950s-60s; wrote music to "Misty," 1955.
b. Jun 15, 1921 in Pittsburgh, Pennsylvania
d. Jan 2, 1977 in Los Angeles, California
Source: *AfrAmAl 6; AllMusG; ASCAP 66; Baker 78, 84; BiDAmM; BiDJaz; BioIn 2, 4, 5, 7, 9, 11, 12, 21; CelR; CmpEPM; ConAmC 76, 82; CurBio 59, 77N; EncJzS; LegTOT; MusMk; NegAl 83, 89; NewGrDA 86; NewGrDJ 88; NewGrDM 80; PenEncP; WhoAm 74; WhoBlA 75; WhoE 74; WorAl; WorAlBi*

Garner, James
[James Baumgarner]
American. Actor
Starred in "The Rockford Files," 1974-80; appeared in Polaroid commercials with Mariette Hartley; won Emmy, 1977; inducted into Television Academy Hall of Fame, 1991.
b. Apr 7, 1928 in Norman, Oklahoma
Source: *BiDFilm 94; BioIn 4, 5, 7, 9, 10, 11, 12, 13, 14, 15, 16, 17, 18, 20, 21; BkPepl; CelR, 90; CmMov; ConTFT 3, 9; CurBio 66; EncAFC; FilmEn; FilmgC; ForYSC; HalFC 80, 84, 88; IntDcF 2-3; IntMPA 75, 76, 77, 78, 79, 80, 81, 82, 84, 86, 88, 92, 94, 96; IntWW 82, 83, 89, 91, 93; ItaFilm; LegTOT; LesBEnT 92; MotPP; MovMk; NewYTBE 71; VarWW 85; WhoAm 74, 76, 78, 80, 82, 84, 86, 88, 90, 92, 94, 95, 96, 97; WhoEnt 92; WhoHol 92, A; WorAl; WorAlBi; WorEFlm*

Garner, John Nance
"Cactus Jack"
American. US Vice President
VP under Franklin Roosevelt, 1933-41.
b. Nov 22, 1868 in Blossom Prairie, Texas
d. Nov 7, 1967 in Uvalde, Texas
Source: *AmPolLe; BiDrAC; BiDrUSC 89; BiDrUSE 71, 89; BioIn 1, 2, 3, 4, 5, 6, 7, 8, 9, 10, 11, 12, 14, 20; DcAmB S8; EncAB-H 1974, 1996; EncSoH; FacFETw; LinLib S; PolPar; VicePre; WebAB 74, 79; WhAm 4; WhAmP; WorAl; WorAlBi*

Garner, Peggy Ann
American. Actor
Won special Oscar, 1945, "Outstanding Child Performer" in *A Tree Grows in Broo klyn.*
b. Feb 3, 1931 in Canton, Ohio
d. Oct 17, 1984 in Woodland Hills, California
Source: *BioIn 9, 10, 14, 15; EncAFC; FilmEn; FilmgC; ForWC 70; HalFC 80, 84, 88; HolP 40; IntMPA 75, 76, 77; InWom SUP; LegTOT; MotPP; MovMk; NewYTBS 84; What 3; WhoHol A*

Garnet, Henry Highland
American. Abolitionist, Clergy
Helped enlist first black troops, 1863; first Negro to deliver sermon in House o f Representatives, 1865; minister to Liberia, 1881-82.
b. Dec 23, 1815 in New Market, Maryland
d. Feb 13, 1882 in Monrovia, Liberia
Source: *AfrAmOr; AmBi; AmRef; AmSocL; ApCAB; BioIn 4, 6, 8, 9, 11, 14, 15, 17, 18, 19, 20; BlkWrNE; DcAmB; DcAmNB; DcAmReB 2; InB&W 80, 85; LegTOT; NatCAB 2; NegAl 76, 83, 89; SelBAAf; SelBAAu; TwCBDA; WhAm HS; WhAmP*

Garnett, Constance
English. Translator
Noted for 70-vol. translation of Russian classics into English; mother of David.
b. Dec 19, 1861 in Brighton, England
d. Dec 17, 1946 in Edenbridge, England
Source: *BioIn 16; ContDcW 89; DcLEL; DcNaB 1941; LngCTC; NewC; OxCEng 67; PenC ENG; REn; WhE&EA; WomFir*

Garnett, David
[Leda Burke]
English. Author
Novelist, biographer, fantasy writer who co-founded Nonesuch Press, 1923; wrote award-winning *Lady into Fox*, 1922.
b. Mar 9, 1892 in Brighton, England
d. Feb 17, 1981 in Le Verger Charry, France
Source: *AnObit 1981; Au&Wr 71; Benet 87; BioIn 1, 2, 3, 4, 5, 6, 8, 12, 14; BlueB 76; CamGLE; CasWL; ConAu 5R, 17NR, 103; ConLC 3; ConNov 72, 76; CyWA 58; DcLB 34; DcLEL; DcNaB 1981; EncSF, 93; EncWL; EvLB; GrWrEL N; IntAu&W 76; IntWW 74, 75, 76, 77, 78, 79, 80; LngCTC; ModBrL; NewC; NewCBEL; Novels; OxCEng 85, 95; PenC ENG; REn; RfGEnL 91; RGTwCWr; ScF&FL 1, 2, 92; SJGFanW; SupFW; TwCA, SUP; TwCRHW 90; TwCWr; WhAm 9; WhE&EA; WhLit; Who 74; WhoHr&F; WhoLA; WhoWor 74, 76, 78*

Garnett, Eve C. R
English. Children's Author, Illustrator
Self-illustrated juvenile books include *The Family from One End Street*, 1937.
Source: *Au&Wr 71; AuBYP 2, 3; BioIn 14; ConAu 1R, 2NR, 134; FifBJA; IlsCB 1744, 1946; IntAu&W 82, 91; OxCChiL; SmATA 3; TwCChW 83, 89; WhoArt 82, 84; WhoChL; WrDr 86, 92*

Garnett, Gale
New Zealander. Actor, Singer
Wrote, performed, "We'll Sing in the Sunshine," 1964, which won Grammy.
b. Jul 17, 1942 in Auckland, New Zealand
Source: *RkOn 84; WhoRock 81*

Garnett, Richard
English. Author
Works include *The Twilight of the Gods*, 1888, a collection of original fables; father of David.
b. Feb 27, 1835 in Staffordshire, England
d. Apr 13, 1906 in London, England
Source: *Alli SUP; BbD; BiD&SB; BioIn 1, 15, 16; BritAu 19; CamGLE; CasWL; ChhPo, S1, S3; DcEnA, A; DcEnL; DcLEL; DcNaB S2; EncSF, 93; EvLB; LngCTC; NewC; NewCBEL; OxCEng 67, 85, 95; PenC ENG; REn; ScF&FL 1; SJGFanW; SupFW; WhLit*

Garnier, Jean Louis Charles
French. Architect
Designed Paris Opera House, 1861-75; casino at Monte Carlo, 1878.
b. Nov 6, 1825 in Paris, France
d. Aug 3, 1898 in Paris, France
Source: *McGEWB; NewCol 75; WhoArch*

Garofalo, Janeane
American. Actor, Comedian
Appeared in *Reality Bites*, 1994; *The Truth About Cats and Dogs*, 1996.
b. Sep 28, 1964 in Newton, New Jersey
Source: *News 96*

Garr, Teri Ann
American. Actor
Oscar nominee for role in *Tootsie*, 1982; starred in *Mr. Mom*, 1983.
b. Dec 11, 1949 in Lakewood, Ohio
Source: *BioIn 13, 14, 15, 16; ConTFT 3; EncAFC; HalFC 88; IntMPA 92; InWom SUP; News 88; WhoAm 86, 90; WhoEnt 92; WhoHol A; WorAlBi*

Garraty, John Arthur
American. Historian, Educator, Author
Co-editor of *Encyclopedia of American Biography*, 1974; *Dictionary of American Biography*, (10 vols.), 1974-79.
b. Jul 4, 1920 in New York, New York
Source: *BioIn 10, 13, 21; ConAu 1R, 2NR, 36NR; DcLB 17; DrAS 74H, 78H, 82H; SmATA 23; WhoAm 74, 76, 78, 80, 88, 90, 92; WhoWor 74*

Garrett, Betty
American. Actor
Played in TV shows "All in the Family," 1973-75; "Laverne and Shirley," 1976-82.
b. May 23, 1919 in Saint Joseph, Missouri
Source: *BiDD; BiE&WWA; BioIn 11; CmMov; CmpEPM; ConTFT 4; EncAFC; FilmEn; FilmgC; ForYSC; HalFC 80, 84, 88; IntMPA 84, 86, 88, 92, 94, 96;*

InWom SUP; MGM; MotPP; MovMk; NotNAT; WhoAm 82; WhoHol 92, A; WhoMW 92; WhoThe 72, 77, 81

Garrett, Eileen Jeanette Lyttle
American. Psychic, Publisher
Researcher of telepathy, clairvoyance; established Parapsychology Foundation, 1951-70.
b. Mar 17, 1893 in Beau Park, Ireland
d. Sep 16, 1970 in Nice, France
Source: *AmAu&B; BiDPara; ConAu P-2; NewYTBE 70; WhAm 5*

Garrett, George Palmer, Jr.
American. Author, Educator
Writings include *Death of a Fox,* 1971; *An Evening Performance,* 1985.
b. Jun 11, 1929 in Orlando, Florida
Source: *AmAu&B; BenetAL 91; BioIn 14, 16; ConAu 1NR, 1R, 5AS; ConNov 82, 91; ConPo 80, 91; CyWA 89; DrAP 75; DrAPF 91; IntAu&W 93; OxCAmL 65; RAdv 1; REnAL; WhoAm 74, 76, 78, 80, 82, 84, 86, 88, 90, 92, 94, 95, 96; WhoSSW 95; WhoUSWr 88; WhoWor 74, 78, 80, 82, 84, 89, 91, 96; WhoWrEP 89, 92, 95; WrDr 86, 92*

Garrett, Henry Lawrence, III
American. Government Official
Secretary of the Navy, 1989-92.
b. Jun 24, 1939 in Washington, District of Columbia
Source: *NewYTBS 91, 92; WhoAm 86, 88, 90, 92; WhoAmL 87; WhoWor 91*

Garrett, Joy
American. Actor
Played Jo Johnson on TV soap opera "Days of our Lives," 1986-93.
b. Mar 2, 1946 in Fort Worth, Texas
d. Feb 11, 1993 in Los Angeles, California
Source: *WhoEnt 92*

Garrett, Leif
American. Actor, Singer
Teen idol whose hit single was a remake of "Surfin' USA."
b. Nov 8, 1961 in Hollywood, California
Source: *BioIn 11, 12, 20; ItaFilm; LegTOT; RkOn 78; RolSEnR 83; WhoHol 92; WhoRock 81*

Garrett, Lila
American. Producer, Writer, Director
Won Emmys for "Mother of the Bride," 1974; "The Girl Who Couldn't Lose," 1975.
b. Nov 21, 1925 in New York, New York
Source: *MiSFD 9; VarWW 85*

Garrett, Mike
[Michael Lockett Garrett]
American. Football Player
Running back, KC, San Diego, 1966-70s; won Heisman Trophy, 1965.
b. Apr 12, 1944 in Los Angeles, California
Source: *BiDAmSp FB; BioIn 7, 8, 9, 10, 14; CmCal; WhoAm 74; WhoFtbl 74; WhoSpor*

Garrett, Pat(rick Floyd)
American. Lawman
Best known for killing Billy the Kid, 1881.
b. Jun 5, 1850 in Chambers County, Alabama
d. Feb 29, 1908 in Las Cruces, New Mexico
Source: *BioIn 4, 5, 6, 9, 10, 11, 13; CopCroC; HalFC 80, 84, 88; LegTOT; REnAW*

Garretta, Michel
"Mr. Blood"
French. Physician
Director-General, Nat. Blood Transfusion Center, France; convicted in 1991 for knowingly distributing HIV-contaminated blood products.
b. 1944, France

Garrick, David
English. Actor
Greatest actor of 18th-c. English stage; Garrick Club established for actors in his honor, 1831.
b. Feb 19, 1717 in Hereford, England
d. Jan 20, 1779 in London, England
Source: *Alli; Benet 87, 96; BioIn 1, 2, 3, 4, 5, 6, 7, 8, 9, 10, 11, 12, 13, 14, 15, 17; BlkwCE; BlmGEL; BritAu; CamGEL; CamGLE; CamGWoT; CasWL; Chambr 2; ChhPo S3; CnThe; CrtT 2; DcArts; DcEnA; DcEnL; DcEuL; DcLB 84; DcLEL; DcNaB; EncEnl; EncWT; Ent; EvLB; FilmgC; GrStDi; GrWrEL DR; HalFC 80, 84, 88; IntDcT 3; LegTOT; LinLib L, S; LitC 15; LngCEL; McGEWD 72, 84; MouLC 2; NewC; NewCBEL; NewEOp 71; NewGrDM 80; NewGrDO; NotNAT A, B; OxCEng 67, 85, 95; OxCMus; OxCThe 67, 83; PenC ENG; PlP&P; RAdv 13-3; REn; RfGEnL 91; WhDW*

Garrigou-Lagrange, Reginald Marie
French. Theologian, Philosopher
Preeminent 20th c. Thomistic commentator; wrote *God: His Existence and His Nature,* 1915.
b. Feb 21, 1877 in Auch Gerst, France
d. 1964
Source: *CathA 1930; IlEncMy*

Garrigue, Jean
American. Poet
Poems include "Studies for an Actress," 1973; "Country Without Maps," 1964.
b. Dec 8, 1914 in Evansville, Indiana
d. Dec 27, 1972 in Boston, Massachusetts
Source: *AmAu&B; AmWomWr; Benet 87, 96; BenetAL 91; BioIn 4, 8, 9, 12; ConAu 5R, 20NR, 37R; ConLC 2, 8; ConPo 70, 75, 80A, 85A; DcLEL 1940; FemiCLE; IndAu 1917; IntWWP 77; InWom SUP; LinLib L; ModAL, S1; ModWoWr; OxCAmL 65, 83, 95; PenC AM; RAdv 1; REnAL; TwCA SUP; WhAm 5; WhoAmW 66, 68, 70, 72, 74, 75*

Garriott, Owen
American. Astronaut, Scientist
Science pilot for second Skylab space mission, Jul-Sep, 1973.
b. Nov 22, 1930 in Enid, Oklahoma
Source: *AmMWSc 73P; BioIn 10, 13, 16; IntWW 74; NewYTBE 73; WhoAm 82, 90; WhoGov 75; WhoSpc; WhoSSW 75*

Garrison, David
American. Actor
Tony nominee for *A Day in Hollywood/A Night in the Ukraine,* 1980; other plays include *Torch Song Trilogy,* 1983.
b. Jun 30, 1952 in Long Branch, New Jersey
Source: *BiDD; ConTFT 4*

Garrison, Jim C.
American. Judge, Writer
Investigated J F Kennedy assassination, 1966; concluded he was murdered by New Orleans conspirators, 1967; retired from the LA Court of Appeals, 1991.
b. Nov 20, 1921 in Denison, Iowa
d. Oct 21, 1992 in New Orleans, Louisiana
Source: *ConAu 132; ConLC 76; Dun&B 88; News 93-2; PolProf J; WhoAm 78*

Garrison, Lloyd K(irkham)
American. Lawyer
Leader in social causes; great-grandson of William Lloyd Garrison.
b. Nov 19, 1897 in New York, New York
d. Oct 2, 1991 in New York, New York
Source: *BioIn 1, 17; CurBio 47, 91N; NewYTBS 91; WhAm 10; WhoAm 74, 76, 78; WhoE 74*

Garrison, William Lloyd
American. Abolitionist
Radical founder of antislavery journal *The Liberator,* 1831; after Civil War championed causes of Native Americans, women.
b. Dec 12, 1805 in Newburyport, Massachusetts
d. May 24, 1879 in New York, New York
Source: *ABCMeAm; Alli; AmAu; AmAu&B; AmBi; AmJust; AmOrN; AmPeW; AmRef; AmRef&R; AmSocL; ApCAB; Benet 87, 96; BenetAL 91; BiDAmJo; BiD&SB; BiDMoPL; BiDTran; BioIn 1, 2, 3, 4, 5, 6, 7, 8, 9, 10, 11, 12, 15, 16, 18, 19, 20, 21; CamGEL; CamGLE; CamHAL; Chambr 3; ChhPo, S3; CivWDc; ColARen; CyAG; DcAmAu; DcAmB; DcAmTB; DcEnL; DcLB 1, 43; DcLEL; DcNAA; EncAAH; EncAB-H 1974, 1996; EncAJ; EvLB; HisWorL; JrnUS; LegTOT; LinLib L, S; McGEWB; NatCAB 2; OxCAmH; OxCAmL 65, 83, 95; PeoHis; PolPar;*

RComAH; REn; REnAL; TwCBDA; WebAB 74, 79; WhAm HS; WhAmP; WhCiWar; WhDW; WorAl; WorAlBi

Garrison, Zina
American. Tennis Player
Turned pro 1982; won gold, bronze medals, Summer Olympics, 1988; won French Open, 1990.
b. Nov 16, 1963 in Houston, Texas
Source: *BioIn 12, 13, 16; BlkOlyM; BlkWAm; BuCMET; ConBlB 2; InB&W 85; IntWW 91, 93; NewYTBS 85; WhoAm 92; WhoAmW 93; WhoBlA 88, 90, 92, 94*

Garrod, Dorothy Annie Elizabeth
English. Archaeologist
First woman professor at Cambridge, 1939-52; conducted Palestinian dig which unearthed a 41,000-year-old skeleton, said to represent evolutionary stage between Neanderthal and modern man.
b. May 5, 1892 in London, England
d. Dec 18, 1968 in Cambridge, England
Source: *BioIn 3, 8; EncHuEv*

Garrod, Heathcote William
English. Author, Scholar
Wrote *Wordsworth: Lectures and Essays,* 1923.
b. Jan 21, 1878 in Wells, England
d. Dec 25, 1960 in Oxford, England
Source: *BioIn 5, 14; ChhPo, S1; DcNaB 1951; EngPo; GrBr; NewC; NewCBEL; ObitT 1961*

Garrow, David J
American. Author
Won 1989 Pulitzer for *Bearing the Cross: Martin Luther King, Jr. and the Southern Christian Leadership Conference.*
Source: *ConAu 93; IntAu&W 91; WhoAm 90; WhoSSW 84; WrDr 92*

Garroway, Dave
[David Cunningham Garroway]
American. TV Personality
Original host of the "Today" show, 1952-61.
b. Jul 13, 1913 in Schenectady, New York
d. Jul 21, 1982 in Swarthmore, Pennsylvania
Source: *AnObit 1982; BioIn 2, 3, 4, 5, 6, 8, 10, 13, 14; CelR; ConAu 107; CurBio 52, 82, 82N; IntMPA 77, 80, 81, 82; IntWW 75; LegTOT; NewYTBE 71; NewYTBS 82; NewYTET; RadStar; SaTiSS; WhoAm 80, 82; WorAl; WorAlBi*

Garson, Greer
American. Actor
Won Oscar, 1942, for *Mrs. Miniver.*
b. Sep 29, 1903 in County Down, Northern Ireland
d. Apr 6, 1996 in Dallas, Texas
Source: *BiDFilm; BioIn 21; CmMov; ConTFT 8; CurBio 42; FilmgC; HalFC 88; IntMPA 92; InWom SUP; MotPP; MovMk; News 96; NewYTBS 27; OxCFilm; ThFT; Who 92; WhoAm 82; WhoEnt 92; WhoHol A; WhoThe 77A; WorAlBi; WorEFlm*

Garst, Roswell
American. Agriculturist
Hybrid corn authority; advised Eastern Communists on improved farm methods, 1950s-60s; wrote *No Need for Hunger,* 1964.
b. 1898 in Rockford, Illinois
d. Nov 5, 1977 in Carroll, Iowa
Source: *BioIn 5, 6, 7, 10, 11, 17; CurBio 64, 78, 78N; DcAmB S10; EncAAH; NewYTBS 77; ObitOF 79*

Garth, David
American. Public Relations Executive
Prominent political strategist, 1960—; clients included Ed Koch, John Lindsay.
b. 1930 in Woodmere, New York
Source: *BioIn 11, 12, 14; CurBio 81; PolPar; WhoAm 82, 84, 86, 88, 90*

Garth, Jennie
American. Actor
Plays Kelly Taylor on TV series "Beverly Hills, 90210," 1990—.
Source: *BioIn 18, 19, 20, 21*

Gartner, Michael Gay
American. Broadcasting Executive
Pres. of NBC News, 1988-93.
b. Oct 25, 1938 in Des Moines, Iowa
Source: *BioIn 16; CurBio 90; IntMPA 92; LesBEnT 92; St&PR 84, 87; WhoAm 74, 76, 78, 80, 82, 84, 86, 88, 90, 92, 94, 95, 96, 97; WhoE 91; WhoFI 81, 92; WhoMW 82, 90, 92, 93, 96; WhoSSW 88*

Garver, Kathy
American. Actor
Played Cissy on TV's "Family Affair," 1966-71.
b. Dec 13, 1947 in Long Beach, California
Source: *WhoHol A*

Garvey, Ed(ward Robert)
American. Lawyer, Labor Union Official
Director, NFL Players' Assn., 1971—; chief negotiator, 1982 strike.
b. Apr 18, 1940 in Burlington, Wisconsin
Source: *BioIn 13, 16; WhoAm 78, 80, 82, 84*

Garvey, Marcus Moziah
"Emperor of Kingdom of Africa"
Jamaican. Political Leader
Led Back to Africa movement; founded Universal Negro Improvement Assn., 1914.
b. Aug 17, 1887 in Saint Ann's Bay, Jamaica
d. Jun 10, 1940 in London, England
Source: *AfrAmOr; CurBio 40; DcAmB S2; DcTwHis; EncAB-H 1974, 1996; InB&W 80, 85; LuthC 75; WebAB 74, 79; WhAm 4, HSA; WhAmP*

Garvey, Steve(n Patrick)
American. Baseball Player
First baseman, LA, 1969-82, San Diego, 1983-87; holds many ML, NL fielding records; 10-time NL All-Star.
b. Dec 22, 1948 in Tampa, Florida
Source: *AmCath 80; Ballpl 90; BaseReg 86, 87; BiDAmSp BB; BioIn 10, 11, 12, 13, 14, 15, 16; ConAu 133; LegTOT; NewYTBS 88; WhoAm 78, 80, 82, 84, 86, 88, 92; WhoProB 73; WhoWest 87, 89; WorAlBi; WrDr 94*

Garvin, Clifton Canter, Jr.
American. Business Executive
CEO, Exxon Corp., 1975-85.
b. Dec 22, 1921 in Portsmouth, Virginia
Source: *BioIn 10, 12, 14; CurBio 80; IntWW 83, 91; NatCAB 63N; St&PR 91; Who 82, 83, 85, 88, 90, 92, 94; WhoAm 74, 76, 78, 80, 82, 84, 86, 92; WhoE 77, 79, 81, 83, 85, 86; WhoEng 88; WhoFI 77, 79, 81, 83, 85, 87; WhoTech 89; WhoWor 82, 84, 87; WorAl*

Garwin, Richard Lawrence
American. Physicist
Defense consultant; member of Joint Strategic Target Planning Staff and JASON; outspoken supporter of arms control; played a key role in creating the hydrogen bomb.
b. Apr 19, 1928 in Cleveland, Ohio
Source: *AmMWSc 76P, 79, 82, 86, 89, 92, 95; BioIn 12, 13; WhoAm 80, 82, 84, 90, 92, 94, 96; WhoE 74; WhoFrS 84; WhoScEn 96*

Garwood, Robert Russell
American. Soldier
Marine; only American convicted of treason in Vietnam War, 1981.
b. Dec 22, 1946 in Portsmouth, Virginia
Source: *BioIn 12, 13*

Gary, Elbert Henry
American. Businessman, Philanthropist
Chm., US Steel, 1901-27; Gary, IN named for him.
b. Oct 8, 1846 in Wheaton, Illinois
d. Aug 15, 1927 in New York, New York
Source: *AmBi; ApCAB X; BiDAmBL 83; BioIn 1, 3, 4, 7, 8; DcAmB; EncAB-H 1974, 1996; HarEnUS; LinLib S; McGEWB; NatCAB 14; OxCAmH; WebAB 74, 79; WebBD 83; WhAm 1; WorAl*

Gary, John
[John Gary Strader]
American. Singer
1960s balladeer on TV, radio, records; still active in nightclubs, known for mellow delivery; invented Aqualung diving aid.
b. Nov 29, 1932 in Watertown, New York

Source: *ASCAP 66, 80; BiDAmM; BioIn 7, 8; CurBio 67; WhoAm 74, 76, 90, 92, 94, 95, 96, 97; WhoHol 92, A; WhoSSW 84, 86*

Gary, Raymond
American. Politician
Dem. governor of OK, 1955-59; obtained amendment to state constitution that ended dual financing for black and white schools.
b. Jan 21, 1908
d. Dec 11, 1993 in Madill, Oklahoma
Source: *BioIn 14, 19, 20; CurBio 94N*

Gary, Romain
French. Author, Diplomat
Novels include *A European Education,* 1944; *The Roots of Heaven,* 1956.
b. May 8, 1914 in Vilnius, Russia
d. Dec 2, 1980 in Paris, France
Source: *AnObit 1980, 1981; Au&Wr 71; Benet 87, 96; BioIn 4, 6, 10, 12; CasWL; ClDMEL 80; ConAu 102, 108; ConLC 25; DcLB 83; DcTwCCu 2; EncSF, 93; EncWL; HalFC 84, 88; IntAu&W 76, 77; IntWW 74, 75, 76, 77, 78, 79, 80, 81N; LegTOT; ModFrL; ModRL; NewYTBS 80; Novels; REn; ScF&FL 1, 92; ScFSB; TwCWr; WhAm 7; Who 74, 82N; WhoAm 74, 76; WhoFr 79; WhoWor 74; WorAu 1950; WorEFlm*

Gary Puckett and the Union Gap
[Dwight Cement; Kerry Chater; Gary Puckett; Paul Wheatbread; Mutha Withem]
American. Music Group
Late 1960s rock group known for wearing Civil War uniforms; hits include "Young Girl," 1968, "This Girl Is a Woman Now," 1969.
Source: *BiDAmM; EncPR&S 74; PenEncP; RkOn 84; WhoRocM 82*

Garzarelli, Elaine Marie
American. Business Executive
Financial analyst and exec., Shearson Lehman Brothers, NYC, 1984-94; formed own monet-management firm, Garzarelli Capital Inc., 1995.
b. Oct 13, 1951 in Philadelphia, Pennsylvania
Source: *BioIn 16; CurBio 95; News 92; St&PR 91; WhoAm 90, 92, 94, 95, 96; WhoAmW 87, 89, 91, 93, 95; WhoFI 89, 92, 94, 96*

Gascoyne, David Emery
English. Poet
Writings include *A Short Survey of Surrealism,* 1935; *Collected Poems,* 1982; *Free Spirits I,* 1982.
b. Oct 10, 1916 in Harrow, England
Source: *BioIn 13; CamGLE; CnE&AP; ConAu 10NR, 28NR, 65; ConLC 45; ConPo 80, 91; DcLB 20; EncWL; EngPo; IntWW 82; LngCTC; MajTwCW; ModBrL; OxCEng 85; PenC ENG; RfGEnL 91; TwCWr; WebE&AL; WhoTwCL; WorAu 1950; WrDr 86, 92*

Gaskell, Elizabeth Cleghorn
English. Author
Known for sympathetic portrayal of working class; wrote *Cranford,* 1853.
b. Sep 29, 1810 in London, England
d. Nov 12, 1865 in Alton, England
Source: *Alli SUP; ArtclWW 2; AtlBL; BbD; Benet 87, 96; BiD&SB; BioIn 1, 2, 3, 4, 5, 7, 8, 9, 10, 11, 12, 13, 14, 15, 16, 18, 19, 20, 21; BlmGEL; BritAu 19; CamGEL; CasWL; CelCen; CrtT 3; CyWA 58; DcArts; DcBiA; DcEnA; DcEuL; DcLB 21, 144, 159; DcLEL; DcNaB; EvLB; GrWrEL N; HsB&A; LngCEL; MouLC 3; NewC; NewCBEL; NinCLC 5; OxCEng 67, 85, 95; PenC ENG; RAdv 1; REn; StaCVF; VicBrit; WebE&AL; WomFir; WorAl*

Gass, William Howard
American. Author
Symbolist who develops aesthetic theories in essays: *Habitations of the Word,* 1984.
b. Jul 30, 1924 in Fargo, North Dakota
Source: *AmAu&B; Au&Wr 71; Benet 87; BenetAL 91; BioIn 14, 15; CamGLE; CamHAL; ConAu 17R, 30NR; ConLC 2; ConNov 76, 91; CurBio 86; CyWA 89; DrAPF 91; EncWL; FacFETw; MajTwCW; ModAL S1, S2; PenC AM; PostFic; RAdv 1, 13-1; WhoAm 88; WhoUSWr 88; WhoWrEP 89; WorAu 1950; WrDr 92*

Gasser, Herbert Spencer
American. Physiologist
Shared Nobel Prize in medicine, 1944, with Joseph Erlanger.
b. Jul 5, 1888 in Platteville, Wisconsin
d. May 11, 1963 in New York, New York
Source: *AsBiEn; BiESc; BioIn 1, 3, 6, 7, 11, 13, 14, 15, 20; CamDcSc; CurBio 45, 63; DcAmB S7; DcAmMeB, 84; DcScB; FacFETw; InSci; LarDcSc; LinLib S; McGMS 80; NatCAB 61; NotTwCS; ObitOF 79; OxCMed 86; WebAB 74, 79; WebBD 83; WhAm 4; WhoNob, 90, 95; WorAl*

Gassman, Vittorio
Italian. Actor, Director
Starred in *Bitter Rice,* 1948; *Anna,* 1951; married Shelley Winters, 1952.
b. Sep 1, 1922 in Genoa, Italy
Source: *BiDFilm, 81, 94; BioIn 7, 11, 14, 17, 20; CamGWoT; ConTFT 8; CurBio 64; EncEurC; EncWT; Ent; FilmAG WE; FilmEn; FilmgC; ForYSC; HalFC 80, 84, 88; IntDcF 1-3, 2-3; IntMPA 75, 76, 77, 78, 79, 80, 81, 82, 84, 86, 88, 92, 94, 96; IntWW 74, 75, 76, 77, 78, 79, 80, 81, 82, 83, 89, 91, 93; ItaFilm; LegTOT; MotPP; MovMk; OxCThe 83; TheaDir; WhoAm 82; WhoHol 92, A; WhoWor 74, 84, 87, 89, 91, 93, 95, 96; WorAl; WorEFlm*

Gassner, John Waldhorn
American. Author
Editor, *Best American Plays,* 1947-71; *Reader's Encyclopedia of World Drama,* 1969.
b. Jan 30, 1903 in Sziget, Austria-Hungary
d. Apr 2, 1967 in New Haven, Connecticut
Source: *AmAu&B; ConAu 1R, 3NR, 25R; CurBio 47, 67; EncWT; OxCThe 67, 83; REnAL; WhAm 4; WhNAA*

Gastineau, Mark
[Marcus D Gastineau]
American. Football Player
Five-time all-pro defensive end, NY Jets, 1979-88.
b. Nov 20, 1956 in Ardmore, Oklahoma
Source: *BioIn 13, 14, 15, 16; FootReg 87; LegTOT; NewYTBS 86; WhoAm 86, 88; WhoE 86, 89; WhoSpor*

Gaston, Arthur George
American. Businessman
Began first business, 1923; owned, chaired nine different corporations.
b. Jul 4, 1892 in Demopolis, Alabama
d. Jan 19, 1996 in Birmingham, Alabama
Source: *BioIn 6, 8, 9, 11, 15; InB&W 80; WhoBlA 88, 92*

Gaston, Cito
[Clarence Edwin Gaston]
American. Baseball Manager
ML outfielder, 1969-77; manager, Toronto, 1989—; fourth black manager in ML baseball history.
b. Mar 17, 1944 in San Antonio, Texas
Source: *Ballpl 90; BaseEn 88; BioIn 16; CurBio 93; NewYTBS 89; WhoAfA 96; WhoAm 90, 92, 94, 95, 96, 97; WhoBlA 85, 88, 90, 92, 94; WhoE 91, 95, 97; WhoProB 73; WhoWor 95, 96, 97*

Gates, Daryl F
American. Police Chief
LAPD, 1978-92; criticized for his handling of the 1992 riots.
b. Aug 30, 1926
Source: *BioIn 13; NewYTBS 82; WhoAm 88; WhoWest 84, 92*

Gates, David
American. Singer, Songwriter
Solo guitarist, lead singer of soft-rock group Bread, 1969-73.
b. Dec 11, 1940 in Tulsa, Oklahoma
Source: *ASCAP 80; IlEncRk; LegTOT; RkOn 78; WhoRock 81; WhoRocM 82*

Gates, Henry Louis, Jr.
American. Critic, Author
Renowned critic of black literature; won 1989 American Book Award for *The Signifying Monkey.*
b. Sep 16, 1950 in Keyser, West Virginia
Source: *BioIn 13, 16; BlkWr 1, 2; BlkWrNE; ConAu 25NR, 53NR, 109; ConBlB 3; CurBio 92; DcLB 67; DcTwCCu 1; IntAu&W 86, 91, 93; NegAl 89; NewYTBS 90; RAdv 14;*

SchCGBL; SelBAAf; WhoAfA 96; WhoAm 90, 92, 94, 95, 96, 97; WhoBlA 85, 88, 90, 92, 94; WhoE 86, 89, 91; WhoEmL 87; WhoWor 89, 91; WorAu 1985; WrDr 86, 88, 90, 92, 94, 96

Gates, Horatio
American. Army Officer
Commanded Americans, defeated British at Saratoga, 1777.
b. Jul 26, 1728 in Maldon, England
d. Apr 10, 1806 in New York, New York
Source: *AmBi; AmRev; ApCAB; BioIn 3, 6, 7, 8, 10, 11, 12, 17; DcAmB; DcAmMiB; DcBiPP; DcNaB S1; Drake; EncAR; EncCRAm; EncSoH; HarEnMi; HarEnUS; LegTOT; LinLib S; NatCAB 1; OxCAmL 65; REn; REnAL; TwCBDA; WebAB 74; WebBD 83; WhAm HS; WhAmRev; WorAl; WorAlBi*

Gates, John Warne
"Bet a Million"
American. Financier
Made fortune in manufacturing barbed wire, acquiring interests in steel, iron, coal.
b. May 8, 1855 in Turner Junction, Illinois
d. Aug 9, 1911 in Paris, France
Source: *AmBi; ApCAB X; BiDAmBL 83; BioIn 1, 3, 4, 11, 12, 21; BusPN; DcAmB; EncAB-A 5; EncABHB 3; NatCAB 18; WebAB 74, 79; WhAm 1, 4*

Gates, Larry
American. Actor
Films include *Cat on a Hot Tin Roof,* 1958; *Funny Lady,* 1975; won 1985 Emmy for "Guiding Light" supporting actor.
b. Sep 24, 1915 in Saint Paul, Minnesota
d. Dec 12, 1996 in Sharon, Connecticut
Source: *BiE&WWA; FilmgC; ForYSC; HalFC 80, 84, 88; NotNAT; VarWW 85; WhoAm 84, 86, 88, 90, 92, 94, 95, 96, 97; WhoE 95; WhoEnt 92; WhoHol 92, A; WhoThe 72, 77, 81*

Gates, Pop
[William Gates]
American. Basketball Player
Member, NY Renaissance during game's barnstorming yrs., 1930s-40s; Hall of Fame, 1989.
b. Aug 30, 1917 in Decatur, Alabama
Source: *BiDAmSp Sup; WhoSpor*

Gates, Robert M(ichael)
American. Government Official
Director, CIA, 1991-93.
b. Sep 25, 1943 in Wichita, Kansas
Source: *BioIn 16; CurBio 92; EncAI&E; News 92; NewYTBS 87, 91; WhoAmP 91*

Gates, Thomas Sovereign, Jr.
American. Businessman, Statesman
Secretary of defense under Dwight Eisenhower, 1959-61; authorized Gary Powers U-2 flight.
b. Apr 10, 1906 in Philadelphia, Pennsylvania
d. Mar 25, 1983 in Philadelphia, Pennsylvania
Source: *BiDrUSE 71, 89; BioIn 4, 5, 7, 10, 11, 13; CurBio 57, 83N; IntWW 74, 75, 76, 77, 78, 79, 80, 81, 82, 83; NewYTBS 83; St&PR 75; Who 74; WhoAm 74, 76; WhoAmP 73; WhoE 74*

Gates, William Henry, III
"King of Software"
American. Business Executive, Computer Executive
Cofounded Microsoft Corp., world's largest computer software co., 1975; chairman, CEO, 1982—; at age 31 was the youngest person to become a billionaire; author of *The Road Ahead,* 1995; married to Melinda French.
b. Oct 27, 1955 in Seattle, Washington
Source: *AmDec 1980; BioIn 13, 14, 15; ConAmBL; ConNews 87-4; HisDcDP; IntWW 93; LarDcSc; WhoAm 88, 90, 92, 94, 95, 96, 97; WhoFI 87, 94, 96; WhoScEn 94, 96; WhoWest 87, 89, 92, 94, 96; WhoWor 96, 97*

Gatlin, Larry Wayne
American. Singer, Songwriter
Lead singer in country-pop group Gatlin Brothers; won Grammy for single "Broken Lady," 1976.
b. May 2, 1948 in Seminole, Texas
Source: *Baker 84; BioIn 14; EncFCWM 83; HarEnCM 87; PenEncP; VarWW 85; WhoAm 78, 80, 82, 84, 86, 88, 90, 92, 94, 95, 96, 97; WhoEnt 92*

Gatling, Richard Jordan
American. Inventor
Creator of first practical rapid-firing gun, 1862, forerunner of modern machine gun.
b. Sep 12, 1818 in Maney's Neck, North Carolina
d. Feb 26, 1903 in New York, New York
Source: *AmBi; ApCAB, X; AsBiEn; BioIn 1, 4, 12; CelCen; DcAmB; DcBiPP; DcNCBi 2; Dis&D; EncSoH; HarEnUS; InSci; LinLib S; McGEWB; NatCAB 4; OxCAmH; TwCBDA; WebAB 74, 79; WebAMB; WhAm 1; WhCiWar; WorAl; WorInv*

Gatti-Casazza, Giulio
Italian. Manager
Mgr., Metropolitan Opera, 1908-35; discovered Caruso, Flagstad.
b. Feb 3, 1869 in Udine, Italy
d. Sep 2, 1940 in Ferrara, Italy
Source: *ApCAB X; BiDAmM; BioIn 4, 10, 11, 14; CurBio 40; DcAmB S2; LinLib S; MetOEnc; NewAmDM; NewEOp 71; NewGrDA 86; NewGrDM 80; NewGrDO; OxDcOp; WhAm 1*

Gaud, William Steen, Jr.
American. Government Official
Administrator, controversial US foreign aid program, Agency for International Development (AID), 1966-69.
b. Aug 9, 1905 in New York, New York
d. Dec 5, 1977 in Washington, District of Columbia
Source: *CurBio 69, 78; IntWW 78; NatCAB 60; NewYTBS 77; ObitOF 79; WhAm 7; WhoAm 78; WhoWor 78*

Gaudio, Bob
[The Four Seasons]
American. Musician, Songwriter
Keyboardist with original Four Seasons, 1962-69; wrote group hit songs "Who Loves You," 1975, "December, 1963 (Oh, What a Night)," 1975.
b. Nov 17, 1942 in New York, New York
Source: *BioIn 15; WhoRocM 82*

Gaudi y Cornet, Antonio
Spanish. Architect
Combined constructive elements with sculpture: Sagrada Familia (1883-1926), Casa Mila (1905-10).
b. Jun 25, 1852 in Reus, Spain
d. Jun 10, 1926 in Barcelona, Spain
Source: *BioIn 2, 3, 4, 5, 8, 9, 10, 13; DcBiPP; MacEA; McGEWB; NewCol 75; OxCArt; PhDcTCA 77*

Gauguin, Paul
[Eugene Henri Paul Gauguin]
French. Artist
Post-impressionist painter whose work is noted for massive simplified forms, impassive figures, exotic backgrounds.
b. Jun 7, 1848 in Paris, France
d. May 8, 1903, French Polynesia
Source: *AtlBL; Benet 87; BioIn 1, 2, 3, 4, 5, 6, 7, 8, 9, 10, 11, 12, 13, 14, 15, 16, 17, 18, 19, 20, 21; ClaDrA; DcArts; DcNiCA; DcTwCCu 2; Dis&D; IntDcAA 90; LegTOT; LinLib S; LngCTC; McGDA; McGEWB; NewC; NewCol 75; OxCArt; OxCFr; OxDcArt; PenDiDA 89; PhDcTCA 77; RAdv 14, 13-3; REn; ThHEIm; WebBD 83; WhDW; WorAl; WorAlBi*

Gaulli, Giovanni Battista
[Il Baciccio]
Italian. Artist
Painted altarpieces, portraits: *Assumption of St. Francis Xavier,* in the Gesu, Rome.
b. May 8, 1639 in Genoa, Italy
d. Apr 2, 1709 in Rome, Italy
Source: *BioIn 4, 10, 19; DcCathB; IntDcAA 90; McGDA; McGEWB; OxCArt; OxDcArt*

Gault, Stanley Carleton
American. Business Executive
Chm., CEO, Goodyear Tire and Rubber Co., 1991-96.
b. Jan 6, 1926 in Wooster, Ohio
Source: *BioIn 12; Dun&B 90; St&PR 91; WhoAm 78, 80, 82, 84, 86, 88, 90, 92, 94, 95, 96, 97; WhoFI 85, 87, 89, 92, 94, 96; WhoMW 88, 90, 92, 93, 96; WhoWor 80, 82, 95, 96, 97*

Gault, William Campbell
[Will Duke; Roney Scott]
American. Author
Mystery novels include *Fair Prey,* 1958; works translated into 14 languages.
b. Mar 9, 1910 in Milwaukee, Wisconsin
Source: *AuBYP 2, 3; BioIn 5, 7, 11, 14; ConAu 1NR, 16NR, 37NR, 49; CrtSuMy; EncMys; IntAu&W 91, 93; SmATA 8; TwCCr&M 80, 85, 91; WrDr 82, 84, 86, 88, 90, 92, 94, 96*

Gault, Willie James
American. Football Player, Track Athlete
Wide receiver, Chicago Bears, 1983-88; LA Raiders, 1988.
b. Sep 5, 1960 in Griffin, Georgia
Source: *BioIn 13, 14, 15; FootReg 87; InB&W 85; News 91-2; WhoAfA 96; WhoBlA 85, 88, 90, 92, 94*

Gaunt, William
English. Author, Critic, Artist
London art critic, noted for collective biographies of artists, Victorian social histories.
b. Jul 5, 1900 in Hull, England
d. May 24, 1980 in London, England
Source: *AnObit 1980; Au&Wr 71; BioIn 4, 10, 11; BlueB 76; ConAu 6NR, 9R, 97; DcBrAr 1; IntAu&W 76, 77, 82; LngCTC; TwCA SUP; TwCPaSc; WhE&EA; Who 74; WhoArt 80; WhoWor 76, 78; WrDr 76, 80, 82*

Gauss, Carl Friedrich
[Johann Friedrich Carl Gauss]
German. Mathematician
Proved theorems of algebra, 1799; calculated location of Earth's magnetic poles; unit of magnetic flux named for him.
b. Apr 30, 1777 in Brunswick, Germany
d. Feb 23, 1855 in Gottingen, Germany
Source: *AsBiEn; BiESc; BioIn 15, 16, 20; CyEd; DcBiPP; DcScB; LarDcSc; McGEWB; NamesHP; RAdv 14, 13-5; WhDW; WorAl; WorInv; WorScD*

Gautier, Dick
American. Actor
Played on TV shows "Get Smart," 1966-69; "When Things Were Rotten," 1975.
b. Oct 30, 1937 in Los Angeles, California
Source: *ASCAP 66; FilmgC; HalFC 88; VarWW 85; WhoAm 76, 78, 80, 82, 84, 86, 88, 92, 94, 95, 96, 97; WhoEnt 92; WhoHol A*

Gautier, Felisa Rincon de
American. Politician
Mayor of San Juan, 1946-69.
b. Jan 9, 1897
d. Sep 16, 1994 in San Juan, Puerto Rico
Source: *BioIn 4, 5, 6, 7, 8, 9, 11, 12, 20; CurBio 94N; InWom, SUP*

Gautier, Theophile
[Pierre Jules Theophile Gautier]
French. Poet, Author, Critic
Believed in "art for art's sake"; wrote psychological tale *Mademoiselle de Maupin,* 1835.
b. Aug 31, 1811 in Tarbes, France
d. Oct 23, 1872 in Neuilly-sur-Seine, France
Source: *AtlBL; BbD; Benet 87, 96; BiD&SB; BiDD; BioIn 1, 5, 6, 7, 9, 10, 11, 13, 15, 19; BriBkM 80; CamGWoT; CasWL; CelCen; CnOxB; CyWA 58; DancEn 78; DcArts; DcBiA; DcBiPP; DcEuL; DcLB 119; DcPup; Dis&D; EncWT; EuAu; EuWr 6; EvEuW; GuFrLit 1; IntDcB; LegTOT; LinLib L, S; NewC; NewCBEL; NewEOp 71; NewGrDM 80; NinCLC 1; NotNAT B; Novels; OxCEng 67, 85, 95; OxCFr; OxCThe 83; PenC EUR; PenEncH; RComWL; REn; ScF&FL 1, 92; ShSCr 20; SupFW; ThHElm; WhDW; WhoHr&F; WorAl; WorAlBi*

Gavarni, Paul
[Sulpice Guillaume Chevalier]
French. Caricaturist, Lithographer
Drew witty, satirical scenes of everyday life for *Charivari;* produced over 8,000 drawings.
b. Jan 13, 1804 in Paris, France
d. Nov 23, 1866 in Paris, France
Source: *AtlBL; BioIn 10, 17; DcBrBI; McGDA; NewCol 75; OxCFr*

Gavilan, Kid
"The Hawk"
Cuban. Boxer
Welterweight champ, 1950s; last fight, 1958.
b. Jan 6, 1926 in Camaguey, Cuba
Source: *BioIn 3; BoxReg; LegTOT; WhoBox 74; WhoSpor*

Gavin, James Maurice
American. Army Officer
Paratroop general; commanded 82nd Airborne, took part in D-Day invasion, WW II; served twice as ambassador to France under John F Kennedy.
b. Mar 22, 1907 in New York, New York
d. Feb 23, 1990 in Baltimore, Maryland
Source: *AmAu&B; BiDWWGF; BioIn 3, 4, 5, 6, 7, 8, 11, 12, 16, 17, 20; BlueB 76; ConAu 131, P-1; CurBio 45, 61, 90, 90N; DcAmDH 80, 89; DcAmMiB; FacFETw; IntWW 83, 89; NewYTBS 90; WebAMB; WhoAm 84, 88; WhoFI 74; WhoWor 74; WorAl; WorAlBi*

Gavin, John Anthony Golenor
American. Actor, Business Executive, Diplomat
Reagan's ambassador to Mexico, 1981-86; films include *Imitation of Life,* 1959.
b. Apr 8, 1931 in Los Angeles, California
Source: *BioIn 13; ConTFT 2; CurBio 62; FilmEn; FilmgC; HalFC 84; IntMPA 86; IntWW 83; MotPP; MovMk; VarWW 85; WhAm 9; WhoAdv 90; WhoAm 86, 90; WhoAmP 87; WhoEnt 92; WhoHisp 92; WhoHol A; WhoWor 84*

Gaxton, William
American. Actor
Comedian who co-starred with Mae West in *The Heat's On,* 1943.
b. Dec 2, 1893 in San Francisco, California
d. Feb 2, 1963 in New York, New York
Source: *BioIn 3, 5, 6; CmpEPM; DcAmB S7; EncAFC; EncMT; EncVaud; Film 2; FilmgC; HalFC 80, 84, 88; NotNAT B; OxCAmT 84; OxCPMus; PlP&P; WhoHol B; WhScrn 74, 77, 83; WhThe*

Gay, John
English. Poet, Dramatist
Friend of Swift and Pope; wrote *Beggar's Opera,* 1728.
b. Jun 30, 1685 in Barnstaple, England
d. Dec 4, 1732 in London, England
Source: *Alli; AtlBL; Baker 78, 84, 92; Benet 87, 96; BiD&SB; BioIn 1, 2, 3, 5, 6, 7, 9, 10, 12, 17, 21; BlkwCE; BlmGEL; BritAu; BritWr 3; CamGEL; CamGLE; CamGWoT; CarSB; CasWL; Chambr 2; ChhPo, S1, S2, S3; CnE&AP; CnThe; CrtSuDr; CrtT 2, 4; CyWA 58; DcArts; DcEnA, A; DcEnL; DcEuL; DcLB 84, 95; DcLEL; DcNaB; DcPup; EncEnl; EncWT; Ent; EvLB; GrWrEL DR, P; IntDcOp; IntDcT 2; LegTOT; LinLib L, S; LngCEL; McGEWB; McGEWD 72, 84; MetOEnc; MouLC 2; MusMk; NewAmDM; NewC; NewCBEL; NewEOp 71; NewGrDM 80; NewGrDO; NewOxM; NotNAT A, B; OxCChiL; OxCEng 67, 85, 95; OxCMus; OxCThe 67, 83; OxDcOp; PenC ENG; PlP&P, A; RAdv 14, 13-2; REn; REnWD; RfGEnL 91; RGFBP; WebE&AL; WhDW; WorAl; WorAlBi*

Gay, John
American. Author, Psychoanalyst
Author of *Men Are from Mars, Women Are from Venus,* 1992; *Mars and Venus in the Bedroom,* 1995; specializes in couples therapy.
b. c. 1952 in Houston, Texas

Gay, Peter Jack
American. Author, Educator, Historian
Psychoanalytic historian who won National Book Award for *The Enlightenment,* 1966, 1969.
b. Jun 20, 1923 in Berlin, Germany
Source: *BioIn 14, 15, 16; ConAu 13R, 18NR; CurBio 86; DrAS 82H; IntAu&W 91; IntWW 91; WhoAm 86, 90; WhoUSWr 88; WhoWrEP 89; WorAu 1975; WrDr 86, 92*

Gaye, Marvin Pentz
American. Singer
Had several gold, platinum hits, 1962-83; won two Grammys, 1983; hits include "Ai n't That Peculiar," 1965; "Sexual Healing," 1982.
b. Apr 2, 1939 in Washington, District of Columbia

d. Apr 1, 1984 in Los Angeles, California
Source: *AnObit 1984; BiDAfM; BiDAmM; EncPR&S 74; HarEnR 86; IlEncBM 82; IlEncRk; VarWW 85; WhoAm 82*

Gayle, Addison, Jr.
American. Critic
Critic of black American literature.
b. Jun 2, 1932 in Newport News, Virginia
d. Oct 3, 1991 in New York, New York
Source: *BioIn 11, 16, 17; BlkAull, 92; BlkAWP; BlkWr 1; BroadAu; ConAu 13NR, 25NR, 25R, 135; DcTwCCu 5; InB&W 80, 85; IntAu&W 77; LivgBAA; NegAl 89; NewYTBS 91; SchCGBL; SelBAAf; SelBAAu; WhAm 10; WhoAm 88, 90; WhoBlA 77, 80, 85, 88, 90, 92, 94N*

Gayle, Crystal
[Mrs. Vassilios Gatzimos; Brenda Gail Webb]
American. Singer
Country-pop singer; sister of Loretta Lynn, known for trademark long hair; won G rammy, 1978, for "Don't It Make My Brown Eyes Blue," CMA Outstanding Female Vocalist 1977, 1978.
b. Jan 9, 1951 in Paintsville, Kentucky
Source: *Baker 84, 92; BgBkCoM; BioIn 11, 12, 13, 14, 15, 16; BkPepl; CelR 90; ConMus 1; CurBio 86; EncFCWM 83; EncRk 88; HarEnCM 87; IlEncCM; InWom SUP; LegTOT; NewYTBS 78; OxCPMus; PenEncP; VarWW 85; WhoAm 86, 90; WhoAmW 85; WhoEnt 92; WhoRock 81*

Gayle, Helene Doris
American. Scientist
AIDS researcher and epidemiologist, Centers for Disease Control, Atlanta, GA, 1984—.
b. Aug 16, 1955 in Buffalo, New York
Source: *BioIn 16; BlksScM; ConBlB 3; NotTwCS; WhoAfA 96; WhoBlA 92, 94*

Gay-Lussac, Joseph-Louis
French. Chemist, Physicist
Formulated Gay-Lussac's law of vapor pressure of gases; pioneer in meteorology.
b. Dec 6, 1778 in Saint-Leonard-de-Noblat, France
d. May 9, 1850 in Paris, France
Source: *AsBiEn; BiHiMed; DcScB; McGEWB; NewCol 75; RAdv 14; REn*

Gaynor, Gloria
""Queen of Disco""
American. Singer
Hits include "Never Can Say Goodbye," 1974; "I Will Survive," 1979.
b. Sep 7, 1949 in Newark, New Jersey
Source: *DrBlPA, 90; EncRk 88; IlEncBM 82; InB&W 85; InWom SUP; LegTOT; RkOn 78; RolSEnR 83; SoulM; WhoRock 81*

Gaynor, Janet
[Laura Gainor]
American. Actor
Won first Oscar given, 1928, for *Seventh Heaven.*
b. Oct 6, 1906 in Philadelphia, Pennsylvania
d. Sep 14, 1984 in Palm Springs, California
Source: *AnObit 1984; BiDFilm, 81, 94; BioIn 6, 7, 8, 9, 10, 12, 14, 17, 18, 21; CmMov; EncAFC; Film 2; FilmEn; FilmgC; ForYSC; HalFC 80, 84, 88; IntDcF 1-3, 2-3; InWom, SUP; LegTOT; MotPP; MovMk; NewYTBS 84; OxCFilm; SilFlmP; ThFT; TwYS; VarWW 85; WhAm 8; What 2; WhoHol A; WomFir; WorAl; WorAlBi; WorEFlm*

Gaynor, Mitzi
[Francesca Mitzi Marlene de Charney von Gerber]
American. Singer, Dancer
Starred in film version of *South Pacific,* 1958.
b. Sep 4, 1931 in Chicago, Illinois
Source: *BioIn 2, 4, 5, 11, 13, 15; CmMov; EncAFC; FilmgC; ForYSC; HalFC 88; IntMPA 75, 84, 86, 92, 94, 96; InWom, SUP; LegTOT; MotPP; MovMk; OxCFilm; VarWW 85; WhoAm 82; WhoAmW 58A; WhoHol A; WorAl; WorAlBi; WorEFlm*

Gayoom, Maumoon Abdul
Maldivian. Political Leader
Pres. of Rep. of Maldives, 1978—; Minister of Defense and Nat. Security, 1989—; Minister of Finance, 1989—.
b. Dec 16, 1939
Source: *BioIn 13, 14; FacFETw; FarE&A 78, 79, 81; IntWW 77, 78, 79, 80, 91; WhoWor 80, 82, 84, 87, 89, 91, 93*

Gazda, Ricky
[Southside Johnny and the Asbury Jukes]
American. Musician
Trumpeter with group since 1974.
b. Jun 18, 1952

Gazzaniga, Giuseppe
Italian. Composer
Wrote numerous opera buffa; noted for one-act *Don Giovanni Tenorio,* 1786.
b. Oct 5, 1743 in Verona, Italy
d. Feb 1, 1818 in Crema, Italy
Source: *Baker 78, 84, 92; NewAmDM; NewEOp 71; NewGrDM 80; NewGrDO; OxDcOp*

Gazzara, Ben
[Biago Anthony Gazzara]
American. Actor
Appeared on stage in *Cat on a Hot Tin Roof,* 1955; TV show "Run For Your L ife," 1965-68.
b. Aug 28, 1930 in New York, New York
Source: *BiDFilm, 81, 94; BiE&WWA; BioIn 3, 6, 8, 10, 11, 14, 16, 17; CelR; ConTFT 3; CurBio 67; FilmEn; FilmgC; ForYSC; HalFC 80, 84, 88; IntMPA 76, 77, 78, 79, 80, 81, 82, 84, 86, 88, 92, 94, 96; ItaFilm; LegTOT; MiSFD 9; MotPP; MovMk; NotNAT; OxCAmT 84; OxCFilm; PlP&P A; VarWW 85; WhoAm 74, 76, 78, 80, 82, 84, 86, 88, 90, 92, 94, 95, 96, 97; WhoEnt 92; WhoHol 92, A; WhoThe 72, 77, 81; WorAl; WorAlBi*

Gazzelloni, Severino
Italian. Musician
Internationally noted flutist, largely responsible for renaissance of instrument.
b. Jan 5, 1919 in Roccasecca, Italy
d. Nov 21, 1992 in Roccasecca, Italy
Source: *Baker 84, 92; IntWWM 90; NewAmDM; NewGrDM 80; PenDiMP; WhoMus 72; WhoWor 74*

Gearhart, Sally (Miller)
American. Feminist
Author of *A Feminist Tarot,* 1981.
b. Apr 15, 1931 in Pearisburg, Virginia
Source: *AmWomWr SUP; BioIn 19; ConAu 57; DrAS 74E, 78E, 82E; EncSF 93; FemiCLE; FemiWr; GayLesB; ScF&FL 92*

Geary, Anthony
American. Actor
Best known for role of Luke Spencer on daytime drama "General Hospital."
b. May 29, 1947 in Coalville, Utah
Source: *BioIn 12, 13; ConTFT 2, 6; IntMPA 88, 92, 94, 96; LegTOT; VarWW 85; WhoHol 92; WhoTelC*

Geary, Cynthia
American. Actor
Played Shelly on TV series "Northern Exposure."
Source: *BioIn 20*

Gebbie, Kristine
American. Government Official
White House AIDS coordinator, 1993-94.
b. c. 1944
Source: *News 94, 94-2*

Gebel-Williams, Gunther
German. Animal Trainer
Billed as the greatest wild animal trainer of all time, he performed with Ringling Brothers giving 11,697 performances.
b. Sep 12, 1934 in Schweidnitz, Germany
Source: *BioIn 9, 10, 11, 12, 13, 15, 16; CurBio 71; WhoAm 76, 78, 82, 84, 86, 88, 90, 92, 94; WhoEnt 92*

Ged, William
Scottish. Inventor
Invented stereotyping, patented 1725.
b. 1690 in Edinburgh, Scotland
d. Oct 19, 1749 in Leith, Scotland
Source: *DcBiPP; DcNaB; LinLib L, S; NewCBEL*

Gedda, Nicolai
Swedish. Opera Singer
Lyric tenor; NY Met. debut, 1957.
b. Jul 11, 1925 in Stockholm, Sweden
Source: *Baker 78, 84, 92; BiDAmM; BiDSovU; BioIn 5, 6, 7, 8, 9, 11, 13, 15; BriBkM 80; CmOp; CurBio 65; IntDcOp; IntWW 74, 75, 76, 77, 78, 79, 80, 81, 82, 83, 89, 91, 93; IntWWM 77, 80, 90; MetOEnc; MusMk; MusSN; NewAmDM; NewEOp 71; NewGrDM 80; NewYTBE 72; OxDcOp; PenDiMP; WhoAm 86, 88; WhoAmM 83; WhoMus 72; WhoWor 74, 89; WorAlBi*

Geddes, Barbara Bel
American. Actor
Won Emmy for role as Miss Ellie on TV series "Dallas,"; has appeared in many broadway productions.
b. Oct 31, 1922 in New York, New York
Source: *BiE&WWA; BioIn 1, 2, 3, 11, 13, 16; CelR 90; ConTFT 3; CurBio 48; HalFC 84, 88; IntMPA 92; InWom, SUP; MotPP; NotWoAT; OxCThe 67; WhoAm 74, 76, 84; WhoAmW 58, 61, 64, 66, 68, 70, 72, 74, 91; WhoEnt 92; WhoHol A; WorAlBi*

Geddes, James
American. Engineer
Civil engineer; important figure in the building of the Erie Canal, 1816-22.
b. Jul 22, 1763 in Carlisle, Pennsylvania
d. Aug 19, 1838 in Geddes, New York
Source: *AmBi; ApCAB; BiAUS; BiDrAC; BiDrUSC 89; DcAmB; NatCAB 10; TwCBDA; WhAm HS*

Geddes, Norman Bel
[Norman Melancton Geddes]
American. Designer, Architect
Foremost proponent of "streamline" style in industrial design, 1930s; noted stage designer, 1916-27.
b. Apr 27, 1893 in Adrian, Michigan
d. May 8, 1958 in New York, New York
Source: *BenetAL 91; BioIn 1, 4, 5, 6, 7, 9, 12, 13, 15; CurBio 40, 58; DcAmB S6; LegTOT; LinLib S; MacEA; McGDA; NatCAB 44; NotNAT A, B; OxCThe 67; PlP&P; REn; REnAL; WebAB 74, 79; WhAm 3; WhAmArt 85; WhThe*

Geddes, Patrick, Sir
British. Biologist, Sociologist, Designer
Pioneered in town planning; wrote first report on subject: *City Development,* 1904.
b. Oct 2, 1854 in Ballater, Scotland
d. Apr 16, 1932 in Montpellier, France
Source: *Alli SUP; BbD; BiD&SB; BioIn 2, 3, 4, 8, 9, 10, 11, 12, 13, 17, 18, 21; CmScLit; DcArts; DcNaB 1931; DcSoc; EncUnb; EncUrb; Geog 2; InSci; LinLib L, S; LngCTC; MacEA; McGEWB; NewCol 75; OxCArt; TwCA, SUP; WebBD 83; WhE&EA; WhoLA*

Gedman, Rich(ard Leo, Jr.)
American. Baseball Player
Catcher, Boston, 1981—; rookie of year, 1981.
b. Sep 26, 1959 in Worcester, Massachusetts
Source: *Ballpl 90; BaseEn 88; BaseReg 87, 88*

Geer, Will
American. Actor
Played grandfather on TV series "The Waltons," 1972-78; won 1975 Emmy.
b. Mar 9, 1902 in Frankfort, Indiana
d. Apr 22, 1978 in Los Angeles, California
Source: *BiE&WWA; BioIn 10, 11; FilmEn; FilmgC; ForYSC; HalFC 80, 84, 88; IntMPA 75, 76, 77, 78; LegTOT; MovMk; NewYTBE 72; NewYTBS 78; NotNAT; WhAm 7; WhoAm 78; WhoHol A; WhoThe 72, 77, 81N; WhScrn 83; WorAl; WorAlBi*

Geertz, Clifford James
American. Anthropologist, Author
Wrote books about symbolic and interpretive anthropology: *The Interpretation of Cultures,* 1973.
b. Aug 23, 1926 in San Francisco, California
Source: *AmMWSc 73S; BioIn 14, 16; ConAu 36NR; CyWA 89; IntWW 91; RAdv 13-3; WhoAm 86, 90, 97; WorAu 1980; WrDr 92*

Geeson, Judy
English. Actor
Films include *To Sir With Love.*
b. Sep 10, 1948 in Arundel, England
Source: *ConTFT 8; FilmAG WE; FilmEn; FilmgC; ForYSC; HalFC 80, 84, 88; IlWWBF; IntMPA 75, 76, 77, 78, 79, 80, 81, 82, 84, 86, 88, 92, 94, 96; MovMk; WhoHol 92, A; WhoHrs 80*

Geffen, David
American. Producer
One of most influential people in entertainment industry who produced Tony-winning Broadway musical, *Cats,* 1982.
b. Feb 21, 1943 in New York, New York
Source: *BioIn 9, 10, 12, 13, 14, 15, 16; CelR 90; ConEn; ConMus 8; ConNews 85-3; ConTFT 5; CurBio 92; IntMPA 86, 88, 92, 94, 96; IntWW 93; NewYTBS 82, 85; PenEncP; WhoAm 84, 86, 88, 90, 92, 94, 95, 96, 97; WhoEnt 92; WhoRocM 82*

Gehlen, Reinhard
"Number 30"; "The Doctor"
German. Spy, Author
Head of German Army Intelligence, WW II, who specialized in spying on the Soviets.
b. Apr 3, 1902 in Erfurt, Germany
d. Jun 8, 1979 in Lake Starnberg, Germany (West)
Source: *BioIn 4, 5, 6, 8, 9, 10, 12, 14; ConAu 89; EncE 75; EncTR 91; HisEWW; NewYTBS 79; SpyCS*

Gehrig, Lou
[Henry Louis Gehrig]
"Columbia Lou"; "The Iron Horse"
American. Baseball Player
First baseman, NY Yankees, 1925-39; Hall of Fame, 1939; died of amyotrophic lateral sclerosis (ALS), now commonly called Lou Gehrig's disease. Held the ML record for consecutive games played (2,130) from his retirement in 1939 until Baltimore's Cal Ripken, Jr. broke the record in 1995.
b. Jun 19, 1903 in New York, New York
d. Jun 2, 1941 in New York, New York
Source: *AmDec 1930; Ballpl 90; BiDAmSp BB; BioIn 1, 2, 3, 4, 5, 6, 7, 8, 9, 10, 11, 12, 13, 14, 15, 16, 17, 18, 20, 21; ConHero 2; CurBio 40, 41; DcAmB S3; FacFETw; LegTOT; OxCAmH; WebAB 74, 79; WhAm 4; WhoProB 73; WhoSpor; WhScrn 77, 83; WorAl; WorAlBi*

Gehringer, Charlie
[Charles Leonard Gehringer]
"Mechanical Man"
American. Baseball Player
Second baseman, Detroit, 1924-42; led Al in batting, MVP, 1937; Hall of Fame, 1949.
b. May 11, 1903 in Fowlerville, Michigan
d. Jan 21, 1993 in Bloomfield Hills, Michigan
Source: *AnObit 1993; Ballpl 90; BiDAmSp BB; BioIn 3, 7, 8, 9, 10, 14, 15, 17, 18; LegTOT; NewYTBS 93; WhoProB 73; WhoSpor*

Gehry, Frank Owen
American. Architect
Known for innovative style, use of unorthodox materials like plywood. corrugated cardboard, and chain-link fencing; created ColorCore fish lamps, hockey-inspired line of stick furniture
b. Feb 28, 1929 in Toronto, Ontario, Canada
Source: *AmArch 70; AmCulL; BioIn 14, 15, 16; CanWW 31; ConArch 87; ConNews 87-1; CurBio 87; DcTwDes; EncAB-H 1996; IntWW 89, 91, 93; WhoAm 78, 80, 82, 86, 88, 90, 92, 94, 95, 96, 97; WhoAmA 91; WhoScEn 96; WhoTech 89; WhoWest 84, 87, 89, 92*

Geiberger, Al(len L)
American. Golfer
Turned pro, 1959; won PGA, 1966.
b. Sep 1, 1937 in Red Bluff, California
Source: *BioIn 10, 11, 16, 21; LegTOT; WhoAm 78, 80, 82, 84; WhoGolf; WhoIntG*

Geiger, Abraham
German. Theologian
Leading advocate of Jewish reform movement.

b. 1810 in Frankfurt am Main, Germany
d. Oct 1874
Source: *BioIn 6; DcBiPP; LuthC 75; NewCol 75*

Geiger, Hans
[Johannes Wilhelm Geiger]
German. Physicist
Invented Geiger counter.
b. Sep 30, 1882 in Neustadt an der Haardt, Germany
d. Sep 24, 1945 in Berlin, Germany
Source: *AsBiEn; BioIn 14, 20; InSci; LegTOT; NewCol 75; NotTwCS; WebBD 83; WhDW*

Geiger, Ken
American. Photographer
Won a 1993 Pulitzer in spot news photography for *The Dallas Morning News.*

Geiger, Theodor Julius
German. Sociologist, Educator
First sociology professor, Denmark; known for work on social class structure and mobility.
b. Nov 9, 1891 in Munich, Germany
d. Jun 16, 1952, At Sea

Geikie, Archibald, Sir
Scottish. Geologist
Books include *The Ancient Volcanoes of Great Britain,* 1897.
b. Dec 28, 1835 in Edinburgh, Scotland
d. Nov 10, 1924 in Haslemere, England
Source: *Alli, SUP; BbD; BiD&SB; BiESc; BioIn 2; BritAu 19; CelCen; Chambr 3; DcBiPP; DcEnL; DcNaB 1922; DcScB; Geog 3; InSci; LarDcSc; LinLib S; NewC; NewCol 75; WhLit*

Gein, Ed
American. Murderer
Farmer who was reportedly model for slayer in film *Psycho.*
b. Aug 27, 1906 in Plainfield, Wisconsin
d. Jul 26, 1984 in Madison, Wisconsin
Source: *EncACr; LegTOT; NewYTBS 84*

Geiogamah, Hanay
American. Dramatist, Choreographer
Formed the Native American Theatre Ensemble, early 1970s.
b. 1945
Source: *BioIn 17, 21; ConAu 153; DcNAL; NatNAL; NotNaAm*

Geisel, Ernesto
Brazilian. Political Leader
President of Brazil, 1974-79.
b. Aug 3, 1908 in Bento Goncalves, Brazil
d. Sep 12, 1996 in Rio de Janeiro, Brazil
Source: *BioIn 10, 11; CurBio 75, 96N; DcCPSAm; EncLatA; EncWB; IntWW 83, 91; NewYTBE 73; NewYTBS 77; WhoWor 74*

Gelb, Arthur
American. Journalist, Author
With wife, Barbara, wrote biography *O'Neill,* 1962.
b. Feb 3, 1924 in New York, New York
Source: *BiE&WWA; BioIn 6, 13, 17; ConAu 1R, 21NR; ConTFT 1; DcLB 103; NotNAT; WhoAm 74, 76, 78, 80, 82, 84, 86, 88, 90, 92, 94, 95, 96, 97; WhoE 74, 91; WhoUSWr 88; WhoWrEP 89, 92, 95*

Gelb, Barbara Stone
[Mrs. Arthur Gelb]
American. Author
Best-known works: *So Short a Time,* 1973; *On the Tracks of Murder,* 1975.
b. Feb 6, 1926 in New York, New York
Source: *BioIn 15; ConAu 1R, 21NR; ConTFT 1; DcLB 103; Dun&B 88; NotNAT; St&PR 87; WhoAm 88; WhoFI 85*

Gelb, Lawrence
American. Business Executive
Founded Clairol, Inc., 1931.
b. 1898? in New York, New York
d. Sep 27, 1980 in New York, New York
Source: *NewYTBS 80*

Gelb, Leslie Howard
American. Journalist, Government Official
Diplomatic correspondent for *New York Times;* directed complication of Pentagon Papers; his books analyzed failures of American post-Vietnam foreign.
b. Mar 4, 1937 in New Rochelle, New York
Source: *BiDAmNC; BioIn 14; ColdWar 1; ConAu 19NR, 103; EncTwCJ; WhoAm 78, 80, 82, 84, 86, 88, 90, 92, 94, 95, 96, 97; WhoAmP 79, 81, 83, 85, 87, 89, 91, 93, 95; WhoGov 77*

Gelbart, Larry
American. Producer
Comedy writer for Bob Hope, Sid Caesar; creator of TV's "M*A*S*H."
b. Feb 25, 1928 in Chicago, Illinois
Source: *AmAu&B; ASCAP 66, 80; BioIn 13, 16; BlueB 76; ConAmD; ConAu 73; ConDr 93; ConLC 21, 61; ConTFT 3, 10; IntAu&W 91, 93; IntMPA 86, 92, 96; IntWW 91, 93; LesBEnT, 92; NewYTBS 89; VarWW 85; WhoAm 74, 76, 78, 80, 82, 84, 86, 90, 95, 96, 97; WhoEnt 92; WhoTelC; WhoThe 81; WhoWor 74; WrDr 80, 82, 84, 86, 88, 90, 92*

Gelber, Jack
American. Author, Dramatist
Avant-garde writer of Off-Broadway plays: *The Connection,* 1959; *The Apple,* 1961.
b. Apr 12, 1932 in Chicago, Illinois
Source: *AmAu&B; Benet 87, 96; BenetAL 91; BiE&WWA; BioIn 5, 6, 8, 10, 12, 15; BlueB 76; CamGLE; CamHAL; CasWL; CnThe; ConAmD; ConAu 1R, 2NR; ConDr 73, 77, 82, 88, 93; ConLC 1, 6, 14, 79; ConTFT 5; CroCD; CrtSuDr; DcLB 7; DcLEL 1940; IntAu&W 77; IntDcT 2; IntvTCA 2; McGEWD 72, 84; ModAL; ModWD; NatPD 81; NotNAT; OxCAmL 83, 95; OxCAmT 84; OxCThe 83; PenC AM; PlP&P; REn; REnAL; REnWD; TwCWr; WebE&AL; WhoAm 74, 76, 78, 80, 82, 84, 86, 88, 90, 92, 94, 95, 96, 97; WhoAmJ 80; WhoE 74; WhoEnt 92; WhoThe 72, 77, 81; WhoUSWr 88; WhoWor 74; WhoWrEP 89, 92, 95; WorAu 1950; WrDr 76, 80, 82, 84, 86, 88, 90, 92, 94, 96*

Geldof, Bob
[Boomtown Rats]
"Saint Bob"
Irish. Actor, Musician, Singer
Organizer of Live-Aid, which raised $84 million for African famine, Jul 1985; r unner-up for Nobel Peace Prize, 1986.
b. Oct 5, 1954 in Dublin, Ireland
Source: *BioIn 13, 14, 15, 16; ConHero 1; ConMus 9; ConNews 85-3; CurBio 86; DcArts; EncPR&S 89; EncRk 88; HarEnR 86; IntWW 91, 93; LegTOT; OxCPMus; Who 88, 90, 92, 94; WhoEnt 92; WhoRocM 82; WhoWor 89, 95*

Geldzahler, Henry
American. Art Historian
Cultural affairs commissioner, New York City, 1978-82; promoter of op art.
b. Jul 5, 1935
d. Aug 16, 1994 in Southampton, New York
Source: *BioIn 7, 8, 9, 11, 13; CurBio 78, 94N; NewYTBS 77, 94; WhoAmA 73, 76, 78, 80, 82, 84, 86, 89*

Gelfond, Aleksandr Osipovich
Russian. Mathematician
His study of transcendental numbers led to the establishment of Gelfond's theorem.
b. Oct 24, 1906 in Saint Petersburg, Russia
d. Nov 7, 1968 in Moscow, Russia
Source: *BiDSovU; DcScB*

Geller, Bruce
American. Producer
Produced action TV series "Rawhide"; "Mannix"; "Mission: Impossible," 1960s-70s.
b. Oct 13, 1930 in New York, New York
d. May 21, 1976 in Santa Barbara, California
Source: *ASCAP 66; LesBEnT; NewYTET; WhAm 7; WhoAm 74, 76, 78; WhoWorJ 72, 78*

Geller, Margaret J(oan)
American. Physicist
Worked on three-dimensional maps of galaxies; became permanent staff member of the Smithsonian Astrophysical Observatory, 1983.
b. Dec 8, 1947 in Ithaca, New York
Source: *AmMWSc 76P, 79, 82, 86, 89, 92, 95; NotTwCS; WhoAm 92, 96;*

WhoAmW 87, 89, 91, 93; WhoEmL 87; WhoScEn 94, 96

Geller, Uri
Israeli. Psychic
Psychic powers include ability to bend metal; start, stop watches mentally; phenomenon known as the "Geller Effect."
b. Dec 20, 1946 in Tel Aviv, Palestine
Source: *BiDAmNC; BioIn 10, 11, 13, 14, 15; BioNews 74; ConAu 69; CurBio 78; DivFut; EncO&P 1, 2, 3; EncPaPR 91; IntAu&W 82, 86; LegTOT; ScF&FL 92; UFOEn; WorAl*

Gellhorn, Martha Ellis
American. Author, Journalist
War correspondent, 1938-45; articles collected in *The Faces of War,* 1959; married to Ernest Hemingway, 1940-45.
b. 1908 in Saint Louis, Missouri
Source: *AmAu&B; AmNov; ArtclWW 2; BenetAL 91; BioIn 13, 16; ConAu 77; ConLC 60; ConNov 72, 76, 91; DrAF 76; FemiCLE; IntAu&W 91; IntWW 83, 91; InWom SUP; OxCAmL 83; REnAL; TwCA, SUP; WhoAm 84; WrDr 86, 92*

Gellhorn, Peter
German. Conductor
Led BBC Chorus, 1961-72; conductor for several opera companies.
b. Oct 24, 1912 in Breslau, Germany
Source: *BlueB 76; IntWWM 77, 80, 85, 90; Who 74, 82, 83, 85, 88, 90, 92, 94; WhoMus 72*

Gellhorn, Walter
American. Lawyer
Wrote *When Americans Complain,* 1966.
b. Sep 18, 1906
d. Dec 9, 1995 in New York, New York
Source: *AmAu&B; AuSpks; BioIn 2, 7, 8, 11, 12, 21; ConAu 150; CurBio 96N; DrAS 74P, 78P, 82P; NewYTBS 80; WhAm 11; WhoAm 74, 76, 78, 80, 86, 88, 90, 92, 94, 95, 96; WhoAmL 79, 83; WhoWor 74*

Gellis, Roberta Leah Jacobs
American. Author
Wrote historical *Roselynde Chronicle* series, 1978-81.
b. Sep 27, 1927 in New York, New York
Source: *ArtclWW 2; BioIn 14; ConAu 5R; DcLP 87A; ForWC 70; IntAu&W 91; TwCRHW 90; WhoWrEP 89; WrDr 92*

Gell-Mann, Murray
American. Physicist
Won 1969 Nobel Prize in physics for work on classifying elementary particles, their interactions.
b. Sep 15, 1929 in New York, New York
Source: *AmDec 1960; AmMWSc 73P, 76P, 79, 82, 86, 89, 92, 95; AsBiEn; BiESc; BioIn 4, 5, 6, 7, 8, 9, 10, 14, 15, 18, 19, 20; CamDcSc; CelR; CurBio 66; FacFETw; IntWW 74, 75, 76, 77, 78, 79, 80, 81, 82, 83, 89, 91, 93; LarDcSc; LegTOT; McGEWB; McGMS 80; NobelP; NotTwCS; OxCAmH; RAdv 14; ThTwC 87; WebAB 74, 79; Who 74, 82, 83, 85, 88, 90, 92, 94; WhoAm 74, 76, 78, 80, 82, 84, 86, 88, 90, 92, 94, 95, 96, 97; WhoFrS 84; WhoGov 72, 75, 77; WhoNob, 90, 95; WhoScEn 94, 96; WhoWest 74, 76, 78, 80, 84, 87, 89, 92, 94, 96; WhoWor 74, 78, 80, 82, 84, 87, 89, 91, 93, 95, 96, 97; WorAl; WorAlBi; WorScD; WrDr 86, 88, 90, 92, 94, 96*

Gemayel, Amin
Lebanese. Political Leader
Succeeded assassinated brother as president, 1982-88.
b. 1942 in Bikfaya, Lebanon
Source: *BioIn 13, 14, 16; CurBio 83; DcMidEa; HisEAAC; IntWW 83, 89, 91, 93; NewYTBS 82; WhoWor 84, 87, 89, 91*

Gemayel, Bashir
Lebanese. Political Leader
Pres.-elect who was assassinated in bomb attack before taking office.
b. Nov 10, 1947 in Bikfaya, Lebanon
d. Sep 14, 1982 in Beirut, Lebanon
Source: *AnObit 1982, 1984; BioIn 12, 13; ColdWar 2; DcMidEa; NewYTBS 82*

Gemayel, Pierre, Sheikh
Lebanese. Politician
Founder of Phalange party, 1936; held parliamentary posts, 1958-70; party started civil war, 1975.
b. Nov 1, 1905, Lebanon
d. Aug 30, 1984 in Bikfaya, Lebanon
Source: *AnObit 1984; BioIn 10, 14, 17, 21; DcMidEa; IntWW 74, 75, 76, 77, 78, 79, 80, 81, 82, 83; MidE 78, 79, 80, 81, 82; NewYTBS 82, 84; PolLCME; WhoWor 74*

Geminiani, Francesco
Italian. Violinist, Composer
Virtuoso; wrote first published violin method, 1730.
b. Feb 5, 1687 in Lucca, Italy
d. Sep 17, 1762 in Dublin, Ireland
Source: *Baker 78, 84; BioIn 4, 7, 14; BriBkM 80; CmpBCM; GrComp; MusMk; NewAmDM; NewGrDM 80; NewOxM; OxCMus*

Gemmell, Alan
Scottish. Broadcaster
Radio personality of BBC's "Gardener's Question Time," 1956-86.
b. May 10, 1913 in Glasgow, Scotland
d. Jul 5, 1986 in Isle of Arran, Scotland
Source: *AnObit 1986; Au&Wr 71; IntAu&W 76; Who 83; WhoAm 82; WrDr 84*

Genaro, Frankie
[Frank DiGennara]
American. Boxer
Flyweight champ, early 1930s; last fight, 1934.
b. Aug 26, 1901 in New York
d. 1966
Source: *BiDAmSp BK; BioIn 7; WhoBox 74; WhoSpor; WhScrn 83*

Genauer, Emily
American. Critic, Author
Won Pulitzer for distinguished art criticism, 1974; books include biography, *Marc Chagall,* 1956.
Source: *BioIn 13; ConAu 106; InWom, SUP; WhoAm 74, 76, 78, 80; WhoAmA 73, 76, 78, 80, 82, 84, 86, 89, 91, 93; WhoAmW 58, 64, 66, 68, 70, 72, 77, 81; WhoGov 72, 75; WrDr 80, 82, 84, 86, 88, 90, 92, 94, 96*

Gendron, Maurice
French. Musician
Internationally known concert cellist who recorded with Pablo Casals.
b. Dec 26, 1920 in Nice, France
Source: *AnObit 1990; Baker 84, 92; BioIn 17; IntWWM 77, 80, 90; NewAmDM; NewGrDM 80; NewYTBS 90; PenDiMP; WhoFr 79; WhoMus 72; WhoWor 74*

Geneen, Harold Sydney
American. Businessman
CEO, ITT, 1959-77.
b. Jun 11, 1910 in Bournemouth, England
Source: *BiDAmBL 83; BioIn 5, 8, 9, 10, 11, 12, 14; BlueB 76; CurBio 74; Dun&B 90; IntWW 74, 75, 76, 77, 78, 79, 80, 81, 82, 83, 89, 91, 93; LElec; NewYTBE 72; St&PR 75; WhoAm 74, 76, 78, 80, 82, 84, 86; WhoE 74, 75, 77, 79, 81, 85; WhoFI 79, 81, 83, 85; WhoWor 74, 76, 78, 80, 82, 84, 87*

Genesis
[Tony Banks; Bill Bruford; Phil Collins; Peter Gabriel; Steve Hackett; John Mayhew; Anthony Phillips; Michael Rutherford; John Silver; Daryl Steurmer; Chris Stewart; Chester Thompson]
English. Music Group
Formed 1966 as theatrical cult band; currently pop group with Phil Collins as lead singer.
Source: *AmMWSc 95; AntBDN G; ApCAB; BiDrAPA 77, 89; BioIn 11, 14, 15, 16, 17, 18, 19, 20; ConAu 45; ConMuA 80A; ConMus 4; DrAP 75; DrAPF 80, 83, 85, 87, 89, 91, 93, 97; EncPR&S 89; EncRk 88; EncRkSt; HarEnR 86; IlEncRk; LElec; NewAgMG; NewAmDM; NewYTBS 86, 94; OxCPMus; PenDiDA 89; PenEncP; RkOn 78; Who 85, 88, 90, 92, 94; WhoAm 86, 88, 90, 92, 94; WhoEnt 92; WhoRock 81; WhoRocM 82; WhoScEn 94*

Genet, Arthur Samuel
American. Business Executive
President, Greyhound Corp., 1956, Brink's Inc., 1959-68.
b. Oct 7, 1909 in New York, New York
d. Sep 19, 1968 in Chicago, Illinois
Source: *BioIn 4, 8; ObitOF 79; WhAm 5*

Genet, Edmond Charles Edouard
"Citizen Genet"
American. Statesman
First French minister to US, 1792; recalled for attempts to draw US into France's war with England and Spain.
b. Jan 8, 1763 in Versailles, France
d. Jul 14, 1834 in Schodack, New York
Source: *HarEnUS; LinLib S; NewCol 75; OxCAmH; REn; WebBD 83*

Genet, Jean
French. Dramatist, Author
Wrote of sin, corruption: *Our Lady of the Flowers,* 1942, became cult classic.
b. Dec 19, 1910 in Paris, France
d. Apr 15, 1986 in Paris, France
Source: *AnObit 1986; Benet 87, 96; BiE&WWA; BioIn 10, 11, 12, 13, 14, 15, 16, 17, 18, 19, 20, 21; CamGWoT; CasWL; CelR; ClDMEL 80; CnMD; CnMWL; ConAu 13R, 18NR; ConFLW 84; ConLC 1, 2, 5, 10, 14, 44, 46; ConTFT 3; CroCD; CurBio 43, 74, 86N; CyWA 89; DcArts; DcLB 72, Y86N; DcTwCCu 2; EncWL, 2, 3; EncWT; Ent; EuWr 13; EvEuW; FacFETw; GayLesB; GayLL; GrFLW; GuFrLit 1; IntDcT 2; IntWW 75, 76, 77, 78, 79, 80, 81, 82, 83; LegTOT; LngCTC; MajMD 2; MajTwCW; MakMC; McGEWB; McGEWD 72, 84; ModFrL; ModRL; ModWD; NewYTBS 86; NotNAT, A; Novels; OxCAmT 84; OxCEng 85, 95; OxCThe 67, 83; PenC EUR; PlP&P, A; RAdv 14, 13-2; REn; RfGWoL 95; TwCWr; WhAm 9; WhDW; WhoFr 79; WhoThe 72, 77, 81; WhoTwCL; WhoWor 74; WorAl; WorAlBi; WorAu 1950; WrPh*

Genet, Taras
American. Mountaineer
Became the youngest person at age 12 to reach the summit of Mt. McKinley.
b. 1978

Genevieve, Saint
French. Religious Figure
Patron saint of Paris said to have averted Attila the Hun's attack on city with fasting, prayer.
b. 422? in Nanterre, France
d. 500? in Paris, France
Source: *NewC; NewCol 75; OxCFr; WebBD 83*

Genghis Khan
[Genchiz Khan; Jenghiz Khan; Temujin]
Mongolian. Conqueror
Defeated much of present-day Asia with bold, brilliant moves.
b. 1162, Mongolia
d. Aug 18, 1227 in Kansu, Mongolia
Source: *Benet 87, 96; BioIn 15, 16, 17; DcBiPP; EncE 75; HisWorL; LegTOT; LinLib S; LngCEL; NewC; REn; WebBD 83; WhWE; WorAlBi*

Genn, Leo
English. Actor
Nominated for Oscar for *Quo Vadis,* 1951.
b. Aug 9, 1905 in London, England
d. Jan 26, 1978 in London, England
Source: *BiE&WWA, 78; ItaFilm; MotPP; MovMk; NotNAT; Who 74; WhoHol A; WhoThe 72, 77; WhScrn 83*

Gennaro, Peter
American. Choreographer
Won Tony for *Annie,* 1977; nominee for *Little Me,* 1982.
b. 1924 in Metairie, Louisiana
Source: *BiDD; BiE&WWA; BioIn 3, 5, 6, 7, 8, 10; CelR; CnOxB; ConTFT 4; CurBio 64; DancEn 78; EncMT; LegTOT; NotNAT; OxCAmT 84; WhoAm 86; WhoWor 74; WorAl; WorAlBi*

Genovese, Kitty
American. Victim
Stabbed, as 38 neighbors watched, but did nothing to help.
b. 1935
d. Mar 13, 1964 in New York, New York
Source: *EncACr*

Genovese, Vito
"Don Vitone"
Italian. Criminal
Gangster who rose to power in underworld through narcotics, murder of Albert Anastasia.
b. Nov 27, 1897 in Rosiglino, Italy
d. Feb 14, 1969 in Springfield, Missouri
Source: *BioIn 5, 6, 8, 9, 11; DcAmB S8; DrInf; FacFETw; ObitOF 79; PolProf E*

Genscher, Hans-Dietrich
German. Diplomat
Vice-chancellor, minister of foreign affairs, West Germany, 1974-1992; world's longest-serving foreign minister.
b. Mar 21, 1927 in Reideburg, Germany
Source: *BioIn 13, 16; CurBio 75; EncCW; EncWB; IntWW 91, 93; IntYB 82; NewYTBS 80; PolLCWE; Who 85, 92, 94; WhoEIO 82; WhoWor 84, 91, 93, 95, 96, 97; WorAlBi*

Gentele, Goeran
Swedish. Director
Director, Metropolitan Opera; untimely death in auto accident.
b. Sep 10, 1917 in Stockholm, Sweden
d. Jul 18, 1972 in Sardinia, Italy
Source: *Baker 78, 84, 92; CurBio 72; NewEOp 71; NewYTBE 71, 72; ObitT 1971; WhoMus 72*

Genthe, Arnold
American. Journalist, Photographer
Known for pictures of San Francisco earthquake, presidents; wrote *As I Remember,* 1936.
b. Jan 8, 1869 in Berlin, Germany
d. Aug 8, 1942 in Candlewood Lake, Connecticut
Source: *AmAu&B; BioIn 4, 11, 12; CmCal; ConPhot 82, 88; CurBio 42; DcAmB S3; DcNAA; EncAB-A 12; ICPEnP; MacBEP; WhAm 2; WhAmArt 85*

Gentile, Giovanni
Italian. Philosopher
Reformed Italy's educational system; developed "actual Idealism" philosophy, which gave foundation to Fascism.
b. May 30, 1875 in Castelvetrano, Italy
d. Apr 15, 1944 in Florence, Italy
Source: *BiDExR; BioIn 1, 5, 14; CasWL; ClDMEL 47, 80; ConAu 119; DcItL 1, 2; DcTwHis; EvEuW; FacFETw; LuthC 75; McGEWB; NewCol 75; OxCPhil; RAdv 14, 13-4; ThTwC 87; WebBD 83*

Gentile da Fabriano
Italian. Artist
Gothic-style painter; best-known works: *St. John the Baptist; Adoration of the Magi,* 1422.
b. 1370 in Fabriano, Papal States
d. 1427 in Rome, Italy
Source: *AtlBL; DcArts; McGDA; McGEWB; NewCol 75; OxCArt; OxDcArt; REn; WhDW*

Gentileschi, Artemisia
Italian. Artist
Painted portraits, colorful Biblical scenes including *Judith and Holofernes,* 1618; daughter of Orazio.
b. 1593?, Papal States
d. 1651? in Naples, Italy
Source: *ContDcW 89; DcArts; DcWomA; GoodHs; IntDcAA 90; IntDcWB; InWom SUP; McGDA; NewCol 75; OxCArt; OxDcArt; WomArt*

Gentileschi, Orazio
Italian. Artist
Adopted Caravaggio's chiaroscuro style; court painter to England's Charles I, 1626; known for *The Annunciation,* 1623.
b. Jul 9, 1562 in Pisa, Italy
d. Feb 7, 1639 in London, England
Source: *BioIn 5, 6, 12; McGDA; NewCol 75; OxCArt*

Gentry, Bobbie
[Roberta Streeter]
American. Singer, Songwriter
Wrote, recorded "Ode to Billy Joe," 1967; won three Grammys, adapted to film, 1976 .
b. Jul 27, 1944 in Chicasaw County, Mississippi
Source: *ASCAP 80; Baker 84, 92; BgBkCoM; BioIn 14, 19; CounME 74, 74A; EncFCWM 69, 83; EncRk 88;*

HarEnCM 87; IlEncCM; InWom SUP; LegTOT; NewGrDA 86; OxCPMus; PenEncP; RkOn 78; RolSEnR 83; VarWW 85; WhoAm 78, 80, 86; WhoRock 81

Gentry, Minnie Lee
American. Actor
Stage, TV and film actress; appeared on Broadway 1960s-70s; played Gram Tee on "The Cosby Show."
b. Dec 2, 1915 in Norfolk, Virginia
d. May 11, 1993 in New York, New York
Source: *BlksAmF; DrBlPA 90*

Gentz, Friedrich Von
German. Journalist
Associate of Metternich known for his political writings denouncing the French Revolution and Napoleon.
b. May 2, 1764 in Breslau, Prussia
d. Jun 9, 1832 in Vienna, Austria
Source: *BiD&SB; BiDInt; BioIn 1, 9; CelCen; DcBiPP; DcEuL; OxCGer 76, 86*

Genung, John Franklin
American. Scholar
Works include *A Guidebook to Biblical Literature,* 1919.
b. Jan 27, 1850 in Willseyville, New York
d. Oct 10, 1919 in Amherst, Massachusetts
Source: *Alli SUP; AmAu&B; AmBi; AmLY; BioIn 6; ChhPo S1; DcAmAu; DcAmB; DcNAA; TwCBDA; WebBD 83; WhAm 1*

Geoffrey of Monmouth
English. Author, Religious Figure
His *Historia Regum Britanniae* (History of the Kings of Britain), c. 1135, was probably main source of Arthurian legend.
b. 1100? in Monmouth, Wales
d. 1154
Source: *Alli; BbD; Benet 87, 96; BiB N; BiD&SB; BioIn 1, 3, 7, 8; BritAu; CasWL; Chambr 1; DcArts; DcBiPP; DcCathB; DcEnL; DcLB 146; DcNaB, C; EvLB; LuthC 75; McGEWB; NewC; NewCBEL; NewCol 75; OxCEng 67; OxCFr; PenC ENG; RAdv 13-3; REn; WebE&AL*

Geoffrion, Bernie
[Bernard Geoffrion]
"Boom Boom"
Canadian. Hockey Player
Right wing, 1950-68, mostly with Montreal; first to successfully use slap shot; won Art Ross Trophy, 1955, 1961, Hart Trophy, 1961; Hall of Fame, 1972.
b. Feb 14, 1931 in Montreal, Quebec, Canada
Source: *BioIn 3, 6, 7, 8, 9, 10, 12; HocEn; NewYTBE 70, 72; NewYTBS 79, 80; WhoHcky 73; WhoSpor*

Geoffroy Saint-Hilaire, Etienne
French. Zoologist
Founded teratology with publication of *Philosophie Anotomique,* 1818-22; strongly opposed by Cuvier.
b. Apr 15, 1772 in Etampes, France
d. Jun 19, 1844 in Paris, France
Source: *BioIn 2; BlkwCE; CelCen; DcBiPP; DcScB; Dis&D; InSci; LarDcSc; LinLib S; NewCol 75; OxCFr*

George, Saint
English. Religious Figure
Patron saint of England portrayed in legend as slayer of the dragon.
b. fl. 3rd cent. ?
d. Apr 23, 303 in Diospolis, Palestine
Source: *Benet 96; BlmGEL; LegTOT; NewC; REn*

George, Bill
[William George]
American. Football Player
Eight-time all-pro linebacker, 1952-66, mostly with Chicago; Hall of Fame, 1974.
b. Oct 27, 1930 in Waynesburg, Pennsylvania
d. Sep 30, 1982 in Rockford, Illinois
Source: *BiDAmSp FB; BioIn 6, 17; Dun&B 86, 88, 90; LegTOT; NewYTBS 82; WhoFtbl 74; WhoSpor*

George, Christopher
American. Actor
Played in TV shows "Rat Patrol," 1966-68; "The Immortal," 1970-71.
b. Feb 25, 1929 in Royal Oak, Michigan
d. Nov 29, 1983 in Los Angeles, California
Source: *BioIn 13; FilmEn; FilmgC; HalFC 80, 84, 88; IntMPA 84; ItaFilm; VarWW 85; WhoHol A*

George, Clair
American. Government Official
Deputy Director for Operations, CIA, 1984-87; stood trial on charges of covering up Iran-contra affair.
Source: *BioIn 18*

George, Dan, Chief
[Geswanouth Slaholt]
Canadian. Actor, Native American Chief
Best known for Oscar-winning role as Cheyenne warrior in *Little Big Man,* 1970.
b. Jun 24, 1899 in North Vancouver, British Columbia, Canada
d. Sep 23, 1981 in Vancouver, British Columbia, Canada
Source: *BioIn 21; CelR; ConAu 108; EncNAB; FilmgC; HalFC 88; NewYTBE 71; NotNaAm; WhoAm 76, 78, 80; WhoHol A*

George, Don
American. Songwriter
Best known for "The Yellow Rose of Texas," 1955, adapted from 1860s minstrel song.
b. Aug 27, 1909 in New York, New York
Source: *ASCAP 66, 80*

George, Gladys
American. Actor
Oscar nominee for *Madame X,* 1937; other films include *The Roaring Twenties,* 1939.
b. Sep 13, 1904 in Hatton, Maine
d. Dec 8, 1954 in Los Angeles, California
Source: *BioIn 3; DcAmB S5; EncVaud; Film 1; FilmgC; ForYSC; InWom SUP; MotPP; MovMk; NotNAT B; ThFT; TwYS; Vers A; WhoHol B; WhScrn 74, 77; WhThe*

George, Grace
American. Actor
Married actor, manager William A. Brady; appeared in many of his plays including *The First Mrs. Fraser.*
b. Dec 25, 1879 in New York, New York
d. May 19, 1961 in New York, New York
Source: *BioIn 3, 5, 6; DcAmB S7; FamA&A; HalFC 80, 84, 88; NotNAT B; OxCAmT 84; OxCThe 67, 83; WhoHol B; WhScrn 74, 77, 83; WhThe*

George, Graham Elias
English. Composer
Wrote opera *Evangeline,* ballet, *Peter Pan,* 1948; several anthems.
b. Apr 11, 1912 in Norwich, England
Source: *BiDAmM; CanWW 83, 89; CreCan 2; IntWWM 80, 85; WhoAm 76, 78, 80, 82, 84, 86, 88; WhoE 74, 75; WhoEnt 92; WrDr 76, 80, 82, 84, 86, 88, 90*

George, Henry, Sr.
American. Economist
Known for theory of tax on land, described in *Progress and Poverty,* 1879.
b. Sep 2, 1839 in Philadelphia, Pennsylvania
d. Oct 29, 1897 in New York, New York
Source: *Alli SUP; AmAu; AmAu&B; AmBi; AmRef; AmRef&R; AmSocL; ApCAB, X; BbD; BenetAL 91; BiDAmJo; BiDAmL; BiD&SB; BioIn 1, 2, 3, 4, 5, 7, 8, 9, 10, 11, 12, 13, 14, 15, 16, 17, 19, 20, 21; CamGEL; CamGLE; CamHAL; CasWL; CelCen; CmCal; DcAmAu; DcAmB; DcAmSR; DcLB 23; DcLEL; DcNAA; Dis&D; EncAAH; EncAB-H 1974, 1996; EvLB; GayN; GrEconB; HarEnUS; JrnUS; LinLib L, S; McGEWB; MemAm; NatCAB 4; NewC; OxCAmH; OxCAmL 65, 83, 95; OxCEng 67, 85, 95; PenC AM; PeoHis; PolPar; RAdv 14; RComAH; REn; REnAL; TwCBDA; WebAB 74, 79; WebE&AL; WhAm HS; WhAmP; WhoEc 81, 86; WorAl; WorAlBi*

George, Henry, Jr.
American. Journalist
Books include *The Romance of John Bainbridge,* 1906.
b. Nov 3, 1862 in Sacramento, California
d. Nov 14, 1916 in New York, New York
Source: *AmAu&B; BiDrAC; BiDrUSC 89; BioIn 4; DcAmB; DcNAA; HarEnUS; TwCBDA; WhAm 1; WhAmP*

George, Jean Craighead
American. Artist, Author
Best-known self-illustrated book: *My Side of the Mountain,* 1960; made into movie, 1968.
b. Jul 2, 1919 in Washington, District of Columbia
Source: *AmAu&B; AmWomWr; AnCL; Au&Arts 8; Au&Wr 71; AuBYP 2, 3; BioIn 14, 15, 16, 17, 19; ChlBkCr; ChlLR 1; ConAu 5R, 25NR; ConLC 35; DcAmChF 1960; DcLB 52; FemiCLE; IlsCB 1946; IntAu&W 76, 77, 89, 91, 93; MajAI; MorBMP; MorJA; NewbC 1966; OnHuMoP; OxCChiL; SmATA 2, 68; TwCChW 78, 83, 89; TwCYAW; WhoAm 82, 84, 86, 88, 90, 92, 94, 95, 96, 97; WhoAmW 58, 61, 97; WhoUSWr 88; WhoWrEP 89, 92, 95; WrDr 80, 82, 84, 86, 88, 90, 92, 94, 96*

George, Lynda Day
[Mrs. Christopher George]
American. Actor
Played on TV shows "Mission Impossible," 1971-73; "Silent Force," 1970.
b. Dec 11, 1946 in San Marcos, Texas
Source: *ConTFT 8; VarWW 85; WhoAm 78, 80, 82, 86, 88, 92; WhoAmW 74, 75; WhoEnt 92; WhoHol A*

George, Phyllis
[Mrs. John Y Brown, Jr.]
American. Sportscaster, Beauty Contest Winner
Miss America, 1971; first female network sportscaster, CBS "NFL Today," 1975-85.
b. Jun 25, 1949 in Denton, Texas
Source: *BioIn 9, 10, 11, 12, 13, 14, 16; BkPepl; CelR 90; InWom SUP; LegTOT; LesBEnT 92; VarWW 85; WhoAm 84, 86; WhoAmW 87; WhoEnt 92*

George, Stefan
German. Poet
Most famous work: *The Year of the Soul,* 1897.
b. Jul 12, 1868 in Budesheim, Germany
d. Dec 4, 1933 in Minusio, Switzerland
Source: *AtlBL; Benet 87, 96; CasWL; ClDMEL 47; CnMWL; ConAu 104; CyWA 58; DcArts; EncTR 91; EncWL 2, 3; EuWr 8; EvEuW; FacFETw; IlEncMy; LngCTC; McGEWB; ModGL; OxCGer 76, 86; PenC EUR; RAdv 14, 13-2; REn; TwCA SUP; TwCLC 2; WhDW; WhoTwCL; WorAlBi*

George, Susan
[Mrs. Simon McCorkindale]
English. Actor
Films include *Dirty Mary, Crazy Larry,* 1974; *Mandingo,* 1975.
b. Jul 26, 1950 in London, England
Source: *FilmAG WE; FilmEn; FilmgC; ForYSC; HalFC 80, 84, 88; IlWWBF; IntMPA 77, 80, 84, 86, 88, 92, 94, 96; IntWW 89, 91, 93; InWom SUP; ItaFilm; LegTOT; MovMk; NewYTBE 72; VarWW 85; WhoHol 92, A*

George, Walter Franklin
American. Politician, Government Official
Dem. senator from GA, 1923-57; Eisenhower's NATO ambassador.
b. Jan 29, 1878 in Preston, Georgia
d. Aug 4, 1957 in Vienna, Georgia
Source: *ApCAB X; BiDrAC; BiDrUSC 89; BioIn 1, 2, 3, 4, 11; CurBio 43, 55, 57; DcAmB S6; EncSoH; LinLib S; ObitOF 79; PolProf E, T; WhAm 3; WhAmP*

George, Zelma W(atson)
American. Sociologist, Lecturer
Woman of many careers whose main purpose was to promote communication between different races, cultures, and nations.
b. Dec 8, 1903 in Hearne, Texas
d. Jul 3, 1994 in Cleveland, Ohio
Source: *BiDAfM; BioIn 2, 5, 6, 11, 18, 20; CurBio 61, 94N; Ebony 1; InB&W 80, 85; InWom; NegAl 89A; NotBlAW 1; WhoAfA 96; WhoAm 76, 78, 80; WhoBlA 75, 77, 80, 85, 90, 92, 94*

George Edward Alexander Edmund
[Duke of Kent]
English. Prince
Youngest brother of King George VI.
b. Dec 20, 1902 in London, England
d. Aug 25, 1942 in Dunbreath, Scotland
Source: *DcNaB 1941; ObitOF 79*

George I
[George Louis]
English. Ruler
First king of house of Hanover; succeeded Queen Anne, 1714.
b. May 28, 1660 in Hannover, Prussia
d. Jun 12, 1727 in Osnabruck, Hannover
Source: *DcBiPP; NewCol 75; WebBD 83*

George II
[George Augustus]
English. Ruler
King, 1727-60; son of George I.
b. Nov 10, 1683 in Herrenhausen Palace, Prussia
d. Oct 25, 1760 in London, England
Source: *OxCMus; WebBD 83*

George II
Greek. Ruler
Unpopular king, 1922-23, 1935-47; son of Constantine I; deposed by military junta, 1923.
b. Jul 20, 1890 in Herrenhausen Palace, Hannover
d. Apr 1, 1947
Source: *CurBio 43, 47; NewCol 75; WebBD 83*

George III
[George William Frederick]
English. Ruler
King, 1760-1820; grandson of George II; known for mental attacks, support of policy that led to loss of American colonies.
b. Jun 4, 1738 in London, England
d. Jan 29, 1820 in Windsor, England
Source: *DcBiPP; WebBD 83*

George IV
[George Augustus Frederick]
English. Ruler
Prince regent when George III became mentally deranged, 1811-20; King, 1820-30.
b. Aug 12, 1762 in London, England
d. Jun 25, 1830 in Windsor, England
Source: *NewCol 75; WebBD 83*

George V
[George Frederick Ernest Albert]
English. Ruler
Grandson of Queen Victoria who ruled 1910-36; succeeded by son Edward VIII.
b. Jun 3, 1865 in London, England
d. Jan 20, 1936 in Sandringham, England
Source: *DcBiPP; WebBD 83*

George VI
[Albert Frederick Arthur George; Duke of York]
English. Ruler
Ascended to throne, Dec 11, 1936, upon abdication of brother Edward VIII; father of Queen Elizabeth II.
b. Dec 14, 1895 in Sandringham, England
d. Feb 6, 1952 in Sandringham, England
Source: *CurBio 42, 52; DcBiPP*

Gephardt, Richard Andrew
American. Politician
Moderate Dem. congressman from MO, 1977—; first Dem. to declare 1988 presidential candidacy, 1987.
b. Jan 31, 1941 in Saint Louis, Missouri
Source: *AlmAP 88, 92; BiDrUSC 89; BioIn 12, 14, 15, 16; CngDr 87, 89; ConNews 87-3; CurBio 87; IntWW 89, 91, 93; NewYTBS 87, 90; PolsAm 84; WhoAm 78, 80, 82, 84, 86, 88, 90, 92, 94, 95, 96, 97; WhoAmL 78, 79; WhoAmP 77, 79, 81, 83, 85, 87, 89, 91, 93, 95; WhoGov 75, 77; WhoMW 78, 80, 82, 84, 86, 88, 90, 92, 93, 96; WhoWor 96; WorAlBi*

Gerard, Dave
American. Cartoonist
Drew syndicated comic strip, "Will-Yum," 1953-67.
b. Jun 18, 1909 in Crawfordsville, Indiana

Source: *ConAu 53; WhAmArt 85; WorECar*

Gerard, Eddie
[Edward George Gerard]
Canadian. Hockey Player
Forward, Ottawa, 1917-23; Hall of Fame, 1945.
b. Feb 22, 1890 in Ottawa, Ontario, Canada
d. Aug 7, 1937 in Ottawa, Ontario, Canada
Source: *HocEn; WhoHcky 73; WhoSpor*

Gerard, Francois
French. Artist
Court painter to Napoleon, Louis XVIII; works include *Empress Josephine,* 1802.
b. May 4, 1770 in Rome, Italy
d. Jan 11, 1837 in Paris, France
Source: *AtlBL; DcBiPP; OxCArt; OxDcArt*

Gerard, Gil
American. Actor
Played on TV show "Buck Rogers in the 25th Century," 1979-81.
b. Jan 23, 1943 in Little Rock, Arkansas
Source: *BioIn 16; ConTFT 6; HalFC 84, 88; IntMPA 92, 94, 96; LegTOT; VarWW 85; WhoAm 80, 82*

Gerard, Jean Ignace Isidore
French. Artist, Illustrator
Known for spirited caricatures of social, political life.
b. Sep 13, 1803 in Nancy, France
d. Mar 17, 1847 in Paris, France
Source: *BioIn 15; ConGrA 3; DcBrBI; NewCol 75; OxCFr; SmATA 45; WorECar*

Gerard, John
English. Botanist
Known for *The Herball,* 1597, a history of plants.
b. 1545 in Nantwich, England
d. Feb 1612 in London, England
Source: *BiESc; BioIn 1, 3, 7, 8; BritAu; CamGEL; CamGLE; DcLEL; DcNaB; DcScB; InSci; NewC; NewCol 75; OxCEng 67, 85, 95; OxCMed 86; WhDW*

Gerardo
[Gerardo Mejia, III]
American. Rapper
Had first all-Spanish video on MTV; top 10 single "Rico Suave," 1991.
b. 1965?, Ecuador
Source: *LegTOT; WhoHol 92*

Gerasimov, Innokentii Petrovich
Russian. Geographer, Scientist
Director, Soviet Institute of Geography, 1951-85.
b. Dec 22, 1905 in Kostroma, Russia
d. Mar 30, 1985 in Moscow, Union of Soviet Socialist Republics
Source: *ConAu 115; IntWW 74, 75, 76, 83; WhoSocC 78; WhoWor 74*

Gerasimov, Sergei Appolinarievich
Russian. Director
Joined Communist Party in 1944; films follow party line *By The Lake.*
b. May 21, 1906 in Sverdlovsk, Russia
d. Nov 28, 1985 in Moscow, Union of Soviet Socialist Republics
Source: *BiDFilm; DcFM; FilmgC; IntWW 74, 75, 76, 81; OxCFilm; WhoWor 74; WorEFlm*

Geray, Steven
[Stefan Gyergyay]
Czech. Actor
Character actor in over 100 films from 1941 including *Gentleman Prefer Blondes,* 1953.
b. Nov 10, 1904 in Uzhored, Czechoslovakia
d. Dec 26, 1973
Source: *FilmEn, 78, 79, 80, 81, 82; Vers B; WhoHol A, B; WhScrn 77*

Gerber, Daniel Frank
American. Business Executive, Inventor
Invented strained baby food process, 1928, to feed own baby.
b. May 6, 1898 in Fremont, Michigan
d. Mar 16, 1974 in Fremont, Michigan
Source: *BioIn 2, 6, 9, 10; DcAmB S5, S9; NewYTBS 74; WhAm 6; WhoAm 74; WhoFI 75; WhoWor 74*

Gerber, John
American. Bridge Player
Contract bridge champion; wrote *The Four Club Bid.*
b. 1907? in Portland, Maine
d. Jan 28, 1981 in Houston, Texas
Source: *ConAu 103; NewYTBS 81*

Gere, Richard
American. Actor, Political Activist
Films include *Pretty Woman,* 1990; *An Officer and a Gentleman* 1982; follower of Dalai Lama and AIDS activist.
b. Aug 31, 1949 in Philadelphia, Pennsylvania
Source: *BiDFilm 94; BioIn 13, 14, 15; CelR 90; ConTFT 2, 6, 13; CurBio 80; FilmEn; HalFC 80, 84, 88; HolBB; IntDcF 1-3, 2-3; IntMPA 80, 88, 92, 94, 96; IntWW 89, 91, 93; LegTOT; News 94, 94-3; VarWW 85; Who 92, 94; WhoAm 84, 86, 88, 90, 92, 94, 95, 96, 97; WhoEnt 92; WhoHol 92; WorAlBi*

Gergen, David (Richmond)
American. Government Official
Chief of White House writing/research team, 1971-74; director of White House Office of Communications, 1975-77; adviser to President Bill Clinton, 1993-95.
b. May 9, 1942 in Durham, North Carolina
Source: *BioIn 12; CurBio 94; News 94, 94-1; NewYTBS 93; WhoAm 82, 84, 86, 88, 90, 92, 94, 95, 96, 97; WhoE 81*

Gerhardi, William Alexander
English. Author
Writings include autobiographical novel, *Resurrective,* 1934.
b. Nov 21, 1895 in Saint Petersburg, Russia
d. Jul 5, 1977 in London, England
Source: *Au&Wr 71; BioIn 4, 5; ConAu 25R, 73; ConLC 5; ConNov 72, 76; LngCTC; ModBrL; NewC; OxCEng 67; REn; TwCA, SUP; TwCWr; WhE&EA; WrDr 76*

Gerhardsen, Einar Henry
Norwegian. Political Leader
Prime minister, 1940s-60s; helped determine nation's pro-West stance after WW II.
b. May 10, 1897 in Asker, Norway
d. Sep 19, 1987 in Lilleborg, Norway
Source: *CurBio 49, 87; IntWW 83; WhoWor 74*

Gerhardt, Charles Frederic
French. Chemist
Researched anhydrides of organic acids; developed atomic weight theory.
b. Aug 21, 1816 in Strasbourg, France
d. Aug 19, 1856 in Strasbourg, France
Source: *BiESc; BioIn 2, 14; CamDcSc; DcAmB; DcScB; Dis&D; InSci; LarDcSc; LinLib S; NewCol 75*

Gerhardt, Paul(us)
German. Poet, Theologian
Wrote over 120 Protestant hymns.
b. Mar 12, 1607 in Saxony, Germany
d. May 27, 1676 in Lubbenau, Germany
Source: *BbD; BiD&SB; BioIn 2, 5, 7, 11; CasWL; DcBiPP; DcEnL; DcEuL; DcLB 164; EuAu; EvEuW; LinLib L; LuthC 75; NewGrDM 80; OxCGer 76, 86; PenC EUR; PoChrch*

Gericault, Jean Louis Andre Theodore
French. Artist
Painted bold romantic historical scenes; drew famous *Raft of the Medusa,* 1819.
b. Sep 26, 1791 in Rouen, France
d. Jan 26, 1824 in Paris, France
Source: *AtlBL; ClaDrA; Dis&D; McGDA; McGEWB; NewCol 75; OxCArt; OxCFr; REn*

Germain, George Sackville
English. Soldier, Statesman
British secretary for colonies, 1775-82; often blamed for Britain's defeat in American Revolution.
b. Jan 26, 1716 in London, England
d. Aug 26, 1785 in Withyham, England
Source: *AmRev; DcNaB; EncAR; NewCol 75; WhAmRev*

German, Bruce W
American. Hostage
One of 52 held by terrorists, Nov 1979-Jan 1981.
b. Mar 31, 1936
Source: *NewYTBS 81; USBiR 74*

Germano, Lisa
American. Violinist
Violinist who performed with John Mellencamp's touring band and played on his *Big Daddy* and *Lonesome Jubilee* albums; released first album, *On the Way Down From the Moon Palace,* 1991 and later recorded *Excerpts From a Love Circus,* 1996.
Source: *BioIn 20*

Germer, Lester Halbert
American. Physicist
With Davisson, proved an electron has wave properties, 1927.
b. Oct 10, 1896 in Chicago, Illinois
d. Oct 3, 1971 in Gardiner, New York
Source: *BiESc; BioIn 9; CamDcSc; DcAmB S9; InSci; LarDcSc; NewYTBE 71; WhAm 5*

Germi, Pietro
Italian. Director
Most films set in Italy, depicted poverty-stricken people; directed *Divorce, Italian Style,* 1961.
b. Sep 14, 1904 in Genoa, Italy
d. Dec 5, 1974 in Rome, Italy
Source: *DcFM; FilmgC; IntMPA 75; IntWW 74; MovMk; NewYTBS 74; OxCFilm; WhoHol B; WhScrn 77, 83; WorEFlm*

Gernreich, Rudi
American. Fashion Designer
Introduced topless bathing suits, 1964.
b. Aug 8, 1922 in Vienna, Austria
d. Apr 21, 1985 in Los Angeles, California
Source: *AnObit 1985; BioIn 7, 8, 9, 10, 12, 14, 17; BioNews 74; CelR; CmCal; ConDes 84, 90, 97; ConFash; CurBio 68, 85N; DcTwDes; EncFash; FairDF US; LegTOT; WhAm 8; WhoAm 74, 76, 78, 80, 82, 84; WhoFash 88; WhoWest 74; WhoWor 74; WorAl; WorFshn*

Gernsback, Hugo
American. Inventor, Publisher
Received over 80 patents for radio and electronic devices; published one of first science fiction magazines: *Amazing Stories..*
b. Aug 16, 1884 in Luxembourg, Luxembourg
d. Aug 19, 1967 in New York, New York
Source: *AmAu&B; Benet 87, 96; BenetAL 91; BioIn 6, 7, 8, 12; ConAu 93; DcAmB S8; DcLB 8, 137; EncSF, 93; LegTOT; NewEScF; RGTwCSF; ScF&FL 1; ScFSB; TwCSFW 81, 86, 91; WebAB 74, 79; WhAm 4; WhLit; WhNAA*

Gero, Erno
Hungarian. Government Official
Member, Hungarian Communist Party, 1918-62; as first secretary, called in Soviet troops to quell uprising, 1956.
b. Jul 8, 1898 in Budapest, Austria-Hungary
d. Mar 12, 1980 in Budapest, Hungary
Source: *AnObit 1980; BioIn 1, 2, 12, 18; ColdWar 2; EncCW; EncRev; WhoSocC 78*

Gerold, Karl
German. Journalist
Published, edited leftist daily *Frankfurter Rimdschau.*
b. Aug 29, 1906
d. Feb 28, 1973 in Frankfurt, Germany (West)
Source: *BioIn 9; ConAu 41R; NewYTBE 73*

Gerome, Jean Leon
French. Artist
Historical genre paintings include *The Cock Fight,* 1847.
b. May 11, 1824 in Vesoul, France
d. Jan 10, 1904 in Paris, France
Source: *ArtsNiC; BioIn 1, 5, 8, 9, 11, 13, 15, 16; CelCen; DcBiPP; IntDcAA 90; LinLib S; NewCol 75; OxCArt; OxDcArt; ThHEIm; WhAmArt 85A*

Geronimo
American. Native American Chief
Apache, known for raids before his surrender, 1888; wrote *Geronimo's Story of His Life,* 1906.
b. Jun 1829 in Arizona
d. Feb 17, 1909 in Fort Sill, Oklahoma
Source: *AmBi; ApCAB; Benet 87, 96; BenetAL 91; BioIn 1, 2, 3, 4, 5, 8, 9, 10, 11, 12, 13, 15, 16, 17, 18, 19, 20; DcAmB; DcAmMiB; EncAB-H 1974, 1996; EncNoAI; FilmgC; GayN; GenMudB; HalFC 80, 84, 88; HarEnMi; HisWorL; LegTOT; McGEWB; NatCAB 23; OxCAmH; RComAH; RelLAm 91; REn; REnAL; REnAW; WebAB 74, 79; WebAMB; WhAm 4, HSA; WhDW; WorAl; WorAlBi*

Gerould, Gordon Hall
American. Author, Educator
Books include *Youth in Harley,* 1920; *A Midsummer Mystery,* 1925.
b. Oct 4, 1877 in Goffstown, New Hampshire
d. Jul 27, 1953 in Princeton, New Jersey
Source: *AmAu&B; BenetAL 91; BioIn 3; ChhPo; ObitOF 79; OxCAmL 65, 83, 95; WhAm 3; WhLit*

Gerrard, Roy
English. Children's Author, Illustrator
Books include *Sir Cedric,* 1984.
b. Jan 25, 1935 in Atherton, England
Source: *BioIn 15, 16, 17, 21; ChlBIID; ChlLR 23; ConAu 110; SmATA 45, 47, 90*

Gerry, Elbridge
American. US Vice President
Signed Declaration of Independence; Madison's vp, 1813-14; actions gave rise to term "gerrymander."
b. Jul 17, 1744 in Marblehead, Massachusetts
d. Nov 23, 1814 in Washington, District of Columbia
Source: *Alli; AmBi; AmPolLe; AmWrBE; ApCAB; BiAUS; BiDrAC; BiDrGov 1789; BiDrUSC 89; BiDrUSE 71, 89; BioIn 1, 3, 4, 7, 8, 9, 10, 11, 14, 15, 16, 20; BlkwEAR; DcAmB; Drake; EncAB-H 1974, 1996; EncAR; EncCRAm; HarEnUS; LegTOT; LinLib S; McGEWB; NatCAB 5; OxCAmH; PolPar; REnAL; TwCBDA; VicePre; WebAB 74, 79; WhAm HS; WhAmP; WhAmRev; WorAl; WorAlBi*

Gerry, Elbridge Thomas
American. Lawyer, Social Reformer
Grandson of Elbridge Gerry; co-founded ASPCC, 1875; pres., 1879-1901.
b. Dec 25, 1837 in New York, New York
d. Feb 18, 1927 in New York, New York
Source: *AmBi; ApCAB, X; BiDSocW; BioIn 3; DcAmB; NatCAB 8; TwCBDA; WhAm 1*

Gerry and the Pacemakers
[John Chadwick; Les Maguire; Freddie Marsden; Gerry Marsden]
English. Music Group
Pop group from Liverpool; had hits "Don't Let the Sun Catch You Crying," 1964; "Ferry Cross the Mersey," 1965.
Source: *EncPR&S 89; EncRk 88; HarEnR 86; OxCPMus; PenEncP; RolSEnR 83; Who 74, 82, 83, 85, 88, 90, 92, 94; WhoRocM 82*

Gershon, Karen
[Karen Tripp]
American. Poet
Poetry collections include *Legacies and Encounters,* 1972; *Coming Back from Babylon,* 1979.
b. Aug 29, 1923 in Bielefeld, Germany
d. Mar 24, 1993 in London, England
Source: *AnObit 1993; BioIn 19; ConAu 47NR, 53, 141; ConLC 81; ConPo 80, 85; EngPo; FemiCLE; IntAu&W 82, 91; WhoWorJ 72, 78; WrDr 80, 82, 84, 86, 88, 90, 92, 94, 96*

Gershwin, George
[Jacob Gershvin]
American. Composer
Wrote innovative folk opera *Porgy and Bess,* 1935; semiclassical orchestral works include *Rhapsody in Blue,* 1924; won first Pulitzer for a musical: *Of Thee I Sing,* 1931; often worked with brother.
b. Sep 26, 1898 in New York, New York
d. Jul 11, 1937 in Hollywood, California

Source: *AmBi; AmComp; AmCulL; AmDec 1920; AmPS; AmSong; ASCAP 66, 80; AtlBL; Baker 78, 84, 92; BenetAL 91; BestMus; BiDAmM; BiDD; BioIn 1, 2, 3, 4, 5, 6, 7, 8, 9, 10, 11, 12, 13, 14, 15, 16, 17, 18, 19, 20, 21; BriBkM 80; CamGWoT; CamHAL; CmMov; CmOp; CmpEPM; CnOxB; CompSN, SUP; ConAmC 76, 82; ConMus 11; DcAmB S2; DcArts; DcCM; DcCom 77; DcCom&M 79; DcFM; Dis&D; EncAB-H 1974, 1996; EncMT; EncWT; FacFETw; FilmEn; FilmgC; HalFC 80, 84, 88; IntDcOp; JeAmHC; JeHun; LegTOT; LinLib S; MakMC; McGEWB; McGEWD 72, 84; MemAm; MetOEnc; MnPM; MusMk; NewAmDM; NewCBMT; NewEOp 71; NewGrDA 86; NewGrDM 80; NewGrDO; NewOxM; NewYTBE 73; NotNAT A, B; OxCAmH; OxCAmL 65, 83, 95; OxCAmT 84; OxCFilm; OxCMus; OxCPMus; OxDcOp; PenDiMP A; PenEncP; PlP&P; PopAmC, SUP; RadStar; RAdv 14, 13-3; RComAH; REn; REnAL; Sw&Ld C; WebAB 74, 79; WhAm 1; WhDW; WhThe; WorAl; WorAlBi*

Gershwin, Ira
[Israel Gershvin]
American. Lyricist
Brother of George; wrote lyrics for *Porgy and Bess.*
b. Dec 6, 1896 in New York, New York
d. Aug 17, 1983 in Beverly Hills, California
Source: *AmAu&B; AmCulL; AmPS; AmSong; AnObit 1983; ASCAP 66, 80; Baker 78, 84, 92; BenetAL 91; BestMus; BiDAmM; BiE&WWA; BioIn 2, 4, 5, 7, 9, 10, 11, 12, 13, 15, 18, 19, 20, 21; CamGWoT; CamHAL; CelR; ChhPo S3; CmpEPM; ConAu 108, 110; ConMus 11; CurBio 56, 83, 83N; DcLEL; EncMT; Ent; FacFETw; FilmEn; FilmgC; HalFC 80, 84, 88; IntMPA 75, 76, 77, 78, 79, 80, 81, 82; LegTOT; NewCBMT; NewGrDA 86; NewGrDO; NewYTBS 83; NotNAT, A; OxCAmH; OxCAmL 65, 83, 95; OxCAmT 84; OxCPMus; PlP&P; REnAL; Sw&Ld C; VarWW 85; WhAm 8; WhoAm 74, 76, 78, 80, 82; WhoAmJ 80; WhoMus 72; WhoThe 77A; WhoWor 74, 76; WhoWorJ 72, 78; WhThe; WorAl; WorAlBi*

Gerson, Noel Bertram
American. Author
Wrote historical novels, westerns, biographies, juvenile works under many pseudonyms: *Fifty-Five Days at Peking* and *The Named Maja* both adapted to film.
b. Nov 6, 1914 in Chicago, Illinois
d. Nov 20, 1988 in Boca Raton, Florida
Source: *AmAu&B; Au&Wr 71; AuBYP 2, 3; BioIn 8; ConAu 81, 127; IntAu&W 76; SmATA 22; WhAm 9; WhoAm 74, 76, 78, 80, 82, 84, 86, 88; WhoE 74, 75, 77, 79, 81, 83, 85, 86, 89; WhoUSWr 88; WhoWor 74, 76, 78, 80, 82, 84, 87, 89; WhoWrEP 89; WrDr 76, 84*

Gerstacker, Carl A(llan)
American. Business Executive
Chm., Dow Chemical Co., 1960-76.
b. Aug 6, 1916
d. Apr 23, 1995 in Midland, Michigan
Source: *BioIn 6, 9, 10; CurBio 95N; InSci; IntWW 74, 75, 76, 77, 78, 79, 80, 81, 82, 83; St&PR 75, 84, 87; WhoAm 74, 76, 78, 80, 82, 84, 86; WhoFI 74, 75, 77*

Gersten, Berta
American. Actor
A leading performer in Yiddish theater: *Mirele Efros,* 1939.
b. Aug 20, 1896?
d. Sep 10, 1972
Source: *BioIn 12; InWom SUP; NotAW MOD*

Gerstenberg, Richard Charles
American. Auto Executive
Chief exec., GM, 1972-74.
b. Nov 24, 1909 in Little Falls, New York
Source: *BioIn 9, 10, 11; BioNews 74; BlueB 76; BusPN; EncABHB 5; IntWW 83; NewYTBE 71; NewYTBS 74; Ward 77; Who 74, 82, 83, 85, 88, 90, 92, 94; WhoAm 74, 76, 78, 80; WhoFI 75; WhoMW 74*

Gerstler, Amy
American. Poet
Won National Book Critics Circle Award, 1990 for *Bitter Angel.*
b. Oct 24, 1956 in San Diego, California
Source: *ConAu 146; ConLC 70; WhoUSWr 88*

Gerstner, Louis Vincent, Jr.
American. Business Executive
CEO, RJR Nabisco, 1989-93; pres., American Express, 1985-89; chm. of the board, CEO, IBM, 1993—.
b. Mar 1, 1942 in Mineola, New York
Source: *BioIn 16; CurBio 91; Dun&B 90; IntWW 83, 89, 91, 93; NewYTBS 89, 93; WhoAm 80, 82, 84, 86, 88, 90, 92, 94, 95, 96, 97; WhoE 86, 89, 93, 95, 97; WhoEmL 87; WhoFI 81, 83, 85, 87, 89, 92, 94, 96; WhoWor 82, 84, 87, 89, 95, 96, 97*

Gertrude the Great, Saint
German. Religious Figure
Mystic, known for supernatural visions.
b. Jan 6, 1256 in Eisleben, Germany
d. Nov 17, 1311 in Eisleben, Germany
Source: *BioIn 19; WebBD 83*

Gerulaitis, Vitas
"Lithuanian Lion"
American. Tennis Player
Won Australian Open, 1977; Italian Open, 1977, 1979; Wimbledon doubles, 1975.
b. Jul 26, 1954 in New York, New York
d. Sep 18, 1994 in Southampton, New York
Source: *BioIn 12, 13, 15; BuCMET; CelR 90; CurBio 79, 94N; LegTOT; News 95, 95-1; NewYTBS 94; WhoAm 82, 86; WhoIntT; WhoWor 91*

Gerussi, Bruno
Canadian. Actor, Broadcaster
Played in TV series "The Beachcombers"; radio show Gerussi, 1967-71.
b. 1928 in Medicine Hat, Alberta, Canada
Source: *OxCCanT; WhoThe 72; WhThe*

Gervasi, Frank Henry
American. Journalist
Covered WW II in Europe, N Africa for *Collier's* magazine; information chief for Marshall Plan, 1950-54; author of 10 books; married to Georgia Gibbs.
b. Feb 5, 1908 in Baltimore, Maryland
d. Jan 21, 1990 in New York, New York
Source: *AmAu&B; AuBYP 2S, 3; BioIn 16, 17; ConAu 13R, 130, P-1; CurBio 42, 90, 90N; NewYTBS 90*

Gervin, George
"The Iceman"
American. Basketball Player
Five-time all-star forward, 1972-86, mostly with San Antonio; led NBA in scoring four times, 1978-80, 1982.
b. Apr 27, 1952 in Detroit, Michigan
Source: *AfrAmSG; BasBi; BiDAmSp BK; BioIn 12, 13, 14, 21; InB&W 85; LegTOT; NewYTBS 84; OfNBA 87; WhoAfA 96; WhoAm 82, 84, 86; WhoBlA 77, 80, 85, 88, 90, 92, 94; WhoSpor; WorAl; WorAlBi*

Geschwind, Norman
American. Educator, Physician
Harvard Medical School professor; studied functions of left, right brain.
b. Jan 8, 1926 in New York, New York
d. Jan 4, 1984 in Boston, Massachusetts
Source: *AmMWSc 73P, 76P, 79, 82; BioIn 15; NewYTBS 84; WhAm 8; WhoAm 74, 76, 78, 80, 82, 84; WhoE 74; WhoFrS 84*

Gesell, Arnold
American. Physician
Authority on child development; founder, director, Gesell Institute of Child Development.
b. Jun 21, 1880 in Alma, Wisconsin
d. May 29, 1961 in New Haven, Connecticut
Source: *AmAu&B; AsBiEn; BioIn 3, 4, 5, 6, 7, 9, 14; CurBio 40, 61; GaEncPs; LinLib L, S; NatCAB 49; REnAL; ThTwC 87; WebAB 74; WhAm 4; WhDW; WhE&EA; WhLit*

Gest, Morris
Russian. Producer, Filmmaker
Produced Broadway plays including *The Miracle,* 1924.
b. Jan 7, 1881 in Vilna, Russia
d. May 16, 1942 in New York, New York

Source: *BioIn 3; CurBio 42; DcAmB S3; NatCAB 38; NotNAT B; OxCAmT 84; WhAm 2; WhThe*

Gesualdo, Carlo
Italian. Composer
Noted for his madrigals.
b. 1560 in Naples, Italy
d. Sep 8, 1613 in Naples, Italy
Source: *AtlBL; Baker 78, 84, 92; BioIn 1, 4, 6, 7, 8, 9, 10, 20; BriBkM 80; CmpBCM; GrComp; McGEWB; MusMk; NewAmDM; OxCMus; REn*

Getty, Donald
Canadian. Politician
Progressive-conservative party premier of Alberta, 1985—.
b. Aug 30, 1933 in Westmount, Quebec, Canada
Source: *BioIn 15; CanWW 79, 80, 81, 83, 89; IntWW 89, 91, 93; Who 92; WhoAm 90; WhoWest 92*

Getty, Estelle
American. Actor
Plays Sophia on TV series "The Golden Girls," 1985-92; "The Golden Palace," 1992—; won 1988 Emmy for Best Supporting Actress in a series.
b. Jul 25, 1923 in New York, New York
Source: *BioIn 14, 15, 16; CelR 90; ConTFT 6, 14; CurBio 90; IntMPA 92, 94, 96; LegTOT; WhoAm 90, 92, 94, 95, 96, 97; WhoAmW 91, 95, 97; WhoEnt 92; WhoHol 92; WorAlBi*

Getty, Gordon Peter
American. Businessman, Philanthropist
Fourth son of J Paul Getty, known for endeavors in arts, sciences, rather than business.
b. Dec 20, 1933 in Los Angeles, California
Source: *BioIn 13, 14, 15; CurBio 85; NewYTBS 84; WhoAm 84, 86, 88, 90, 92, 94, 95, 96, 97; WhoWest 96*

Getty, J(ean) Paul
American. Oilman
Became pres. of father's oil co., 1930; major oil deal resulted in control of Arab land where he struck oil, 1953; founded Getty Oil Co, 1956.
b. Dec 15, 1892 in Minneapolis, Minnesota
d. Jun 6, 1976 in Sutton Place, England
Source: *Au&Wr 71; BiDAmBL 83; BioIn 1, 4, 5, 6, 7, 8, 9, 10, 11; BlueB 76; ConAu 65, 69; DcAmB S10; DcArts; EncAB-H 1974, 1996; EncWB; IntWW 74, 75, 76; RComAH; St&PR 75; WebAB 74, 79; WhAm 6, 7; Who 74; WhoAm 74, 76, 78, 80; WhoAmA 73, 76; WhoFI 74, 75; WhoWest 74, 76; WhoWor 74*

Getz, Stan
[Stanley Gayetzby]
American. Jazz Musician
Tenor saxophonist, "cool" jazz exponent popular 1950s-70s; won several awards for bossa-nova recordings.
b. Feb 2, 1927 in Philadelphia, Pennsylvania
d. Jun 6, 1991 in Malibu, California
Source: *AllMusG; AnObit 1991; Baker 84; BioIn 14, 15, 16, 17, 18; CmpEPM; ConMus 12; CurBio 71, 91N; EncJzS; FacFETw; IlEncJ; IntWW 82, 83, 89, 91; IntWWM 90; LegTOT; NewAmDM; NewGrDA 86; NewGrDJ 88; NewGrDM 80; News 91; NewYTBS 91; OxCPMus; PenEncP; VarWW 85; WhAm 10; WhoAm 76, 78, 80, 82, 84, 86, 88, 90; WhoHol 92; WhoWor 74; WorAl; WorAlBi*

Geva, Tamara
Russian. Choreographer, Dancer
Dance roles include *On Your Toes,* 1936; *Errante,* 1934.
b. 1908 in Saint Petersburg, Russia
Source: *BiDD; BiE&WWA; BioIn 9, 13; CnOxB; DancEn 78; EncMT; NotNAT; OxCAmT 84; WhoHol A; WhoThe 77A*

Geyer, Georgie Anne
American. Journalist, Author
Syndicated columnist since 1975; wrote *Buying the Night Flight: The Autobiography of a Woman Foreign Correspondent,* 1983.
b. Apr 2, 1935 in Chicago, Illinois
Source: *BioIn 13, 14, 15, 16; BriB; ConAu 17NR, 29R; CurBio 86; EncTwCJ; ForWC 70; IntAu&W 77, 82, 86, 89, 91, 93; InWom SUP; WhoAm 74, 76, 78, 80, 82, 84, 86, 88, 90, 92, 94, 95, 96, 97; WhoAmW 68, 70, 72, 74, 75, 77, 79, 81, 83, 85, 87, 89, 91, 93, 95; WhoE 95; WhoMW 74, 76; WhoUSWr 88; WhoWor 74, 76; WhoWrEP 89, 92, 95; WrDr 90, 92, 94, 96*

Ghazali, al
"Abu Hamid Muhammad Ibn Muhammad at-Tusi al- Ghazali"
Arab. Philosopher
Renowned theologian; wrote many standard works on theology, philosophy; *Maqasid al-falasifah* translated into Latin.
b. 1058 in Tus, Persia
d. Dec 18, 1111 in Tus, Iran
Source: *CasWL; DcOrL 3; WebBD 83*

Ghelderode, Michel de
[Adolphe-Adhemar-Louis-Michel Martens]
Belgian. Dramatist
Avant-garde plays best known in small Left Bank theaters, Paris: *Hop! Signor,* 1935.
b. Apr 3, 1898 in Ixelles, Belgium
d. Apr 1, 1962 in Brussels, Belgium
Source: *Benet 87, 96; BioIn 2, 3, 5, 6, 7, 10, 20; CamGWoT; CasWL; ClDMEL 80; CnMD; CnThe; ConAu 40NR, 85; ConLC 6, 11; DcPup; DcTwCCu 2; EncWL 2, 3; EncWT; Ent; EuWr 11; IntDcT 2; MajMD 2; McGEWD 72, 84; ModFrL; ModRL; ModWD; NotNAT B; OxCThe 67, 83; PenC EUR; REn; REnWD; TwCWr; WhoTwCL; WorAu 1950*

Gheorghiu-Dej, Gheorghe
Romanian. Political Leader
Head of state, 1961-65; established Romania's independence from Soviet Union.
b. Nov 8, 1901 in Birlad, Romania
d. Mar 19, 1965 in Bucharest, Romania
Source: *BioIn 5, 7, 18, 21; ColdWar 2; CurBio 58, 65; DcPol; DcTwHis; EncCW; EncRev; FacFETw; NewCol 75; ObitT 1961; WhAm 4; WhDW*

Ghezzi, Vic(tor)
American. Golfer
Touring pro, 1930s-40s; won PGA, 1941; Hall of Fame, 1965.
b. Oct 19, 1912 in Rumson, New Jersey
d. May 30, 1976 in Miami Beach, Florida
Source: *BioIn 10; NewYTBS 76; WhoGolf*

Ghiaurov, Nicolai
Bulgarian. Opera Singer
Considered one of finest bass singers since Pinza; noted for Verdi roles.
b. Sep 13, 1929 in Velimgrad, Bulgaria
Source: *Baker 78, 84, 92; BioIn 7, 11, 15; IntDcOp; IntWW 74, 75, 76, 77, 78, 79, 80, 81, 82, 83, 89, 91, 93; IntWWM 90; MetOEnc; MusSN; NewAmDM; NewEOp 71; NewGrDM 80; NewGrDO; OxDcOp; PenDiMP; WhoAm 80, 82, 84, 86, 92, 94, 95, 96, 97; WhoAmM 83; WhoOp 76; WhoSocC 78; WhoSoCE 89; WhoWor 82, 84, 89*

Ghiberti, Lorenzo
"Father of the Renaissance"
Italian. Artist
Sculpted north, east doors of the baptistry of Florence; portals called *Gates of Paradise.*
b. 1378 in Pelago, Italy
d. Dec 1, 1455 in Florence, Italy
Source: *AtlBL; BioIn 1, 5, 6, 7, 15; DcArts; DcBiPP; DcCathB; IntDcAA 90; IntDcAr; LegTOT; LinLib S; LuthC 75; MacEA; McGDA; McGEWB; NewCol 75; OxCArt; OxDcArt; WhDW; WorAl; WorAlBi*

Ghirlandaio, Domenico
[Domenico di Tommaso Bigordi]
Italian. Artist
Among his noted works are wall frescoes in the Sistene Chapel, with Botticelli.
b. 1449 in Florence, Italy
d. Jan 11, 1494 in Florence, Italy
Source: *AtlBL; BioIn 1, 5, 7; DcArts; DcCathB; McGEWB; OxDcArt; WhDW; WorAlBi*

Ghiz, Joseph A
Canadian. Political Leader
Liberal Party premier of Prince Edward Island, 1986-93.
b. Jan 27, 1945 in Charlottetown, Prince Edward Island, Canada
Source: *CanWW 89; IntWW 91; Who 92; WhoAm 90; WhoE 91; WhoEmL 87*

Ghorbal, Ashraf A
Egyptian. Diplomat
Ambassador to US, 1973-84.
b. May 1925 in Alexandria, Egypt
Source: *IntWW 81, 82, 83, 91; WhoWor 78, 80, 82, 84, 87*

Ghormley, Robert Lee
American. Naval Officer
Commanded American, Allied naval forces in Southwest Pacific, WW II; led attack on Solomon Islands, 1942.
b. Oct 15, 1883 in Portland, Oregon
d. Jun 21, 1958 in Washington, District of Columbia
Source: *BiDWWGF; BioIn 1, 4, 5, 17; CurBio 58; HarEnMi; OxCShps; WebAMB; WhAm 3; WhWW-II*

Ghose, Sri Chinmoy Kumar
[Sri Chinmoy]
Indian. Author, Poet
Director, UN Meditation Group; writings stress development of spititual heart over mind: *Yoga and Spiritual Life,* 1970.
b. Aug 27, 1931 in Shakpura, India
Source: *ConAu 2NR, 49; CurBio 76; NewCol 75*

Ghostley, Alice
[Allyce Ghostley]
American. Actor
Played supporting roles on TV: "Bewitched," 1969-72; "Mayberry RFD," 1970-71.
b. Aug 14, 1926 in Eve, Missouri
Source: *BiE&WWA; ConTFT 2; ForYSC; HalFC 80, 84, 88; IntMPA 94, 96; InWom SUP; LegTOT; MotPP; NotNAT; VarWW 85; WhoAm 86; WhoHol 92, A; WhoThe 72, 77, 81; WorAl*

Ghotbzadeh, Sadegh
Iranian. Government Official
Foreign minister who was executed in plot to kill Khomeini and topple government.
b. 1936?
d. Sep 15, 1982 in Tehran, Iran
Source: *AnObit 1982; BioIn 11, 12, 13; IntWW 80; NewYTBS 82*

Giacalone, Anthony
"Tony Jack"
American. Criminal
Mafia leader; allegedly connected with disappearance of Jimmy Hoffa when blood w as found in his car.
b. 1919
Source: *BioIn 10*

Giacometti, Alberto
Swiss. Sculptor
Known for sculptures of wiry, tormented figures: "Man Pointing," 1947.
b. Oct 10, 1901 in Borgonovo, Switzerland
d. Jan 11, 1966 in Chur, Switzerland
Source: *AtlBL; Benet 87, 96; BioIn 1, 2, 3, 4, 5, 6, 7, 8, 9, 10, 11, 12, 13, 14, 15, 16, 17, 20; ConArt 77, 83, 89, 96; CurBio 56, 66; DcArts; FacFETw; IntDcAA 90; LegTOT; MakMC; McGDA; McGEWB; ModArCr 1; ObitT 1961; OxCArt; OxCTwCA; OxDcArt; PhDcTCA 77; REn; WebBD 83; WhAm 4; WhDW; WorAl; WorAlBi; WorArt 1950*

Giacomin, Eddie
[Edward Giacomin]
Canadian. Hockey Player
Goalie 1965-78, mostly with NY Rangers; won Vezina Trophy, 1971; Hall of Fame, 1987.
b. Jun 6, 1939 in Sudbury, Ontario, Canada
Source: *BioIn 8, 9, 11, 15; CurBio 68; HocEn; NewYTBE 72; NewYTBS 87; WhoHcky 73; WhoSpor*

Giaever, Ivar
American. Physicist
Shared 1973 Nobel Prize in physics with Esaki, Josephson, for studying tunneling effects on semiconductors, superconductors.
b. Apr 5, 1929 in Bergen, Norway
Source: *AmMWSc 73P, 79, 82, 86, 89, 92, 95; BiESc; BioIn 12, 15, 20; IntWW 74, 75, 76, 77, 78, 79, 80, 81, 82, 83, 89, 91, 93; LarDcSc; LegTOT; McGMS 80; NobelP; NotTwCS; Who 82, 83, 85, 88, 90, 92, 94; WhoAm 76, 78, 80, 82, 84, 86, 88, 90, 92, 94, 95, 96, 97; WhoE 74, 75, 77, 79, 81, 83, 85, 89, 91, 93, 95, 97; WhoEng 80, 88; WhoFrS 84; WhoNob, 90, 95; WhoScEn 94, 96; WhoWor 78, 80, 82, 84, 87, 89, 91, 93, 95, 96, 97; WorAl; WorAlBi; WorScD*

Giago, Tim
American. Publisher
Founded the *Lakota Times,* later *Indian Country Today,* 1981.
b. Jun 12, 1934 in South Dakota
Source: *EncNAB; NotNaAm*

Giamatti, A(ngelo) Bartlett
American. University Administrator, Baseball Executive
Pres., Yale U, 1978-86, NL of baseball, 1986-89; replaced Peter Ueberroth as baseball commissioner, 1989.
b. Apr 4, 1938 in Boston, Massachusetts
d. Sep 1, 1989 in Martha's Vineyard, Massachusetts
Source: *Ballpl 90; BioIn 11, 12, 13, 15, 16; ConAu 97, 129; CurBio 78, 89, 89N; DrAS 78E, 82E; FacFETw; IntWW 83, 89; News 88, 90-1; NewYTBS 77, 83, 88, 89; Who 85, 90N; WhoAm 78, 80, 82, 84, 86, 88; WhoE 79, 81, 83, 85, 86, 89; WhoWor 84, 87, 89; WorAl; WorAlBi*

Giancana, Sam
[Salvatore Giancana]
"Momo"
American. Criminal
Chicago gang boss who was involved in CIA plot to kill Castro, 1961.
b. Jun 15, 1908 in Chicago, Illinois
d. Jun 19, 1975 in Oak Park, Illinois
Source: *BioIn 11, 17; CopCroC; DcAmB S9; FacFETw; LegTOT*

Giannini, A(madeo) P(eter)
American. Banker
Innovative banking procedures included radical lending policies and establishment of branch banking system.
b. May 6, 1870 in San Jose, California
d. Jun 3, 1949 in San Mateo, California
Source: *BiDAmBL 83; BioIn 1, 2, 3, 4, 6, 7, 8, 9, 10, 12, 15, 16, 18, 20, 21; CmCal; CurBio 47, 49; DcAmB S4; EncABHB 7; EncWB; FacFETw; LinLib S; NatCAB 38; ObitOF 79; PeoHis; REnAW; WebAB 74, 79; WhAm 2; WorAl; WorAlBi*

Giannini, Dusolina
American. Opera Singer
Soprano; with NY Met., 1935-42; prolific recording artist; sister of Vittorio.
b. Dec 19, 1900 in Philadelphia, Pennsylvania
d. Jun 29, 1986
Source: *Baker 84, 92; BioIn 15; IntDcOp; InWom SUP; MetOEnc; NewAmDM; NewGrDA 86; NewGrDM 80; PenDiMP*

Giannini, Giancarlo
Italian. Actor
Known for roles in Lina Wertmuller films including *Love and Anarchy,* 1974.
b. Aug 1, 1942 in Spezia, Italy
Source: *BioIn 12; ConTFT 7; CurBio 79; FilmEn; HalFC 80, 84, 88; IntDcF 1-3, 2-3; IntMPA 77, 78, 79, 80, 81, 82, 84, 86, 88, 92, 94, 96; ItaFilm; LegTOT; VarWW 85; WhoHol 92, A; WhoWor 95, 96, 97; WorAl; WorAlBi*

Giannini, Vittorio
American. Composer
Operas include *The Scarlet Letter,* 1938.
b. Oct 19, 1903 in Philadelphia, Pennsylvania
d. Nov 28, 1966 in New York, New York
Source: *AmComp; ASCAP 66, 80; Baker 78, 84, 92; BiDAmM; BioIn 1, 7, 8, 9, 16; BriBkM 80; CmOp; CompSN, SUP; ConAmC 76, 82; DcCM; NewAmDM; NewEOp 71; NewGrDA 86; NewGrDM 80; NewGrDO; OxCMus; OxDcOp; PenDiMP A; WhAm 4*

Gianninoto, Frank Anthony
American. Designer
Pioneered package design; created Marlboro flip-top box; Howard

Johnson's orange roof; Elsie, the Borden cow.
b. Jan 5, 1903 in Chiaramonte, Italy
d. Apr 8, 1988 in Danbury, Connecticut
Source: *NewYTBS 88; WhoFI 81, 85*

Giap, Vo Nguyen
Vietnamese. Statesman
Founder of Vietnamese Communist Party, 1930s; commanded North Vietnamese forces under Ho Chi-Minh, 1950s.
b. Sep 1, 1912 in Quangblin, Vietnam
Source: *BiDMarx; BioIn 13, 14, 16, 17, 18; ColdWar 2; ConAu X; CurBio 69; DcPol; EncRev; FacFETw; FarE&A 81; GenMudB; HarEnMi; IntWW 83, 91; McGEWB; WhDW; WhoSocC 78; WhoWor 74; WorDWW*

Giardello, Joey
[Carmine Orlando Tilelli]
American. Boxer
Won world middleweight title, 1963-65; inducted into Int'l Boxing Hall of Fame, 1993.
b. Jul 16, 1930 in New York, New York
Source: *BioIn 6, 7, 10, 13; BoxReg; WhoBox 74; WhoSpor*

Giardini, Felice di
Italian. Musician, Composer, Impresario
Violin virtuoso; directed Italian Opera at London's King Theater, 1755-95.
b. Apr 12, 1716 in Turin, Italy
d. Jun 8, 1796 in Moscow, Russia
Source: *Baker 84; WebBD 83*

Giauque, William Francis
American. Chemist, Educator
Won 1949 Nobel Prize for researching matter behavior in zero temperatures.
b. May 12, 1895 in Niagara Falls, Ontario, Canada
d. Mar 29, 1982 in Berkeley, California
Source: *AmMWSc 76P, 79, 82; AsBiEn; BiESc; BioIn 2, 3, 6, 13, 15, 17, 19, 20; BlueB 76; CamDcSc; ConAu 106; CurBio 50, 82; DcScB S2; InSci; IntWW 74, 75, 76, 77, 78, 79, 80, 81, 82; LarDcSc; McGMS 80; NewCol 75; NewYTBS 82; WebAB 74, 79; WhAm 8; WhoAm 74, 76, 78, 80, 82; WhoNob, 90, 95; WhoWest 78, 80; WorAl*

Gibb, Andy
English. Singer, Songwriter, Musician
Albums include *Shadow Dancing,* 1970s.
b. Mar 5, 1958 in Manchester, England
d. Mar 10, 1988 in Oxford, England
Source: *BioIn 11; BkPepl; ConMuA 80A; EncPR&S 89; EncRkSt; LegTOT; News 88-3; RkOn 78, 82; RolSEnR 83; VarWW 85; WhoRock 81; WorAl; WorAlBi*

Gibb, Barry
[The Bee Gees; Douglas Gibb]
English. Singer, Songwriter
Guitarist, songwriter; album *Saturday Night Fever* soundtrack sold 50 million copies, 1976-79.
b. Sep 1, 1946 in Douglas, Isle of Man, England
Source: *BioIn 12; BkPepl; CurBio 81; LegTOT; RkOn 85; VarWW 85; WhoAm 80, 82, 84, 86, 88, 92, 94, 95, 96, 97; WhoEnt 92; WorAlBi*

Gibb, Maurice
[The Bee Gees]
English. Singer, Songwriter
With group of brothers won six Grammys, 1977, 1978, for such hits as *Saturday Night Fever* Soundtrack.
b. Dec 22, 1949 in Manchester, England
Source: *BkPepl; LegTOT; VarWW 85; WhoAm 80, 82, 84, 86, 88, 92, 94, 95, 96, 97; WhoEnt 92; WhoRocM 82; WorAlBi*

Gibb, Robin
[The Bee Gees]
English. Singer, Songwriter
Best known for hit album *Saturday Night Fever,* 1977.
b. Dec 22, 1949 in Manchester, England
Source: *BkPepl; LegTOT; RkOn 85; VarWW 85; WhoAm 80, 82, 84, 86, 88, 92, 94, 95, 96, 97; WhoEnt 92; WhoRocM 82; WorAlBi*

Gibberd, Frederick, Sir
English. Architect, Author
Wrote books on architecture, town planning: *Architecture of England,* 1938.
b. Jan 7, 1908 in Coventry, England
d. Jan 9, 1984 in Harrow, England
Source: *Au&Wr 71; BioIn 13; BlueB 76; ConArch 80, 87, 94; ConAu 111; DcArts; DcBrAr 1; DcD&D; EncMA; IntDcAr; IntWW 74, 75, 76, 77, 78, 79, 80, 81, 82, 83; MacEA; McGDA; Who 74, 82, 83; WhoArt 80, 82; WhoWor 74; WrDr 76, 80, 82, 84*

Gibbon, Edward
English. Historian
Masterpiece was *The History of the Decline and Fall of the Roman Empire,* 1776-1788.
b. May 8, 1737 in Putney, England
d. Jan 16, 1794 in London, England
Source: *Alli; AtlBL; BbD; Benet 87, 96; BiD&SB; BioIn 1, 2, 3, 4, 5, 6, 7, 8, 9, 10, 11, 12, 13, 14, 15, 16, 17, 18; BlkwCE; BlmGEL; BritAu; BritWr 3; CamGEL; CamGLE; CasWL; Chambr 2; CyWA 58; DcArts; DcBiPP; DcEnA; DcEnL; DcEuL; DcLB 104; DcLEL; DcNaB; Dis&D; EncEarC; EncEnl; EvLB; GrWrEL N; HarEnUS; LegTOT; LinLib L, S; LngCEL; LuthC 75; McGEWB; MouLC 2; NewC; NewCBEL; OxCClL; OxCEng 67, 85, 95; OxCMus; PenC ENG; RAdv 13-3; REn; RfGEnL 91; TwoTYeD; WebE&AL; WorAl; WorAlBi*

Gibbon, Lewis Grassic
[James Leslie Mitchell]
Scottish. Author
Best-known work is the trilogy *A Scots Quair,* 1943.
b. Feb 13, 1901 in Auchterless, Scotland
d. Feb 21, 1935 in Welwyn Garden City, England
Source: *Benet 87, 96; BioIn 10, 13, 14; CamGLE; CasWL; Chambr 3; CmScLit; CnMWL; ConAu 104; DcArts; DcLB 15; DcLEL; GrWrEL N; LngCTC; NewCBEL; Novels; OxCEng 85, 95; PenC ENG; REn; RfGEnL 91; RGTwCWr; TwCA, SUP; TwCLC 4; WebE&AL*

Gibbons, Euell
American. Author, Naturalist
Author of books on wild foods, including *Stalking the Good Life,* 1971; widely known as TV commercial spokesman for cereal.
b. Sep 8, 1911 in Clarksville, Texas
d. Dec 29, 1975 in Sunbury, Pennsylvania
Source: *AmAu&B; AuNews 1; AuSpks; BioIn 6, 7, 8, 10, 11, 12; BioNews 74; ConAu 61, P-1, P-2; DcAmB S9; WhoE 74*

Gibbons, Floyd Phillips
American. Journalist
Fast-talking radio commentator, war correspondent; covered WW I, German, Russian revolutions, Spanish civil war.
b. Jul 16, 1887 in Washington, District of Columbia
d. Sep 24, 1939 in Saylorsburg, Pennsylvania
Source: *AmAu&B; AmBi; BioIn 1, 3; CathA 1930; DcAmB S2; DcCathB; DcLB 25; DcNAA; EncAJ; REnAL; TwCA, SUP; WhAm 1*

Gibbons, Grinling
English. Sculptor
Public buildings, palaces, churches were embellished by his woodcarving.
b. Apr 4, 1648 in Rotterdam, Netherlands
d. Aug 3, 1721 in London, England
Source: *AntBDN G; AtlBL; BioIn 3, 4, 6, 7, 9, 15, 16; DcArts; DcBiPP; DcD&D; DcNaB; LinLib S; McGDA; NewC; OxCArt; OxCDecA; OxDcArt; PenDiDA 89; WebBD 83; WhDW*

Gibbons, James, Cardinal
American. Religious Leader
Bishop of Baltimore, 1877, cardinal, 1886; first chancellor, Washington's Catholic U, 1889.
b. Jul 23, 1834 in Baltimore, Maryland
d. Mar 24, 1921 in Baltimore, Maryland
Source: *Alli SUP; AmAu&B; AmBi; AmDec 1910; ApCAB, X; BenetAL 91; BiD&SB; BiDSA; BioIn 1, 3, 4, 6, 8, 11, 14, 15, 19; ChhPo S1; DcAmAu; DcAmB; DcAmReB 1, 2; DcCathB; DcNAA; DcNCBi 2; EncAB-H 1974, 1996; EncARH; EncSoH; HarEnUS; LinLib L, S; LuthC 75; McGEWB; MorMA; NatCAB 1, 29; OxCAmH; RelLAm 91; REnAL; TwCBDA; WebAB 74, 79; WhAm 1*

Gibbons, Kaye
American. Author
Author of novels *Ellen Foster,* 1987; *A Virtuous Woman,* 1989.
b. 1960 in Nash County, North Carolina
Source: *AmWomWr SUP; BioIn 18, 19; ConAu 151; ConLC 50, 88*

Gibbons, Leeza
American. TV Personality
Star of "Entertainment Tonight," 1984—; talk show "Leeza," 1994—.
b. 1957?
Source: *LegTOT*

Gibbons, Orlando
English. Composer, Musician
Organist at Westminster Abbey, 1620s; wrote church music; employed "music anthem" technique.
b. 1583 in Oxford, England
d. Jun 5, 1625 in Canterbury, England
Source: *Alli; Baker 78, 84, 92; BioIn 2, 4, 7, 8; BriBkM 80; CmpBCM; DcArts; DcBiPP; DcCom 77; DcCom&M 79; DcNaB; GrComp; LuthC 75; MusMk; NewAmDM; NewC; NewCBEL; NewCol 75; NewGrDM 80; NewOxM; OxCEng 85, 95; OxCMus; WebBD 83; WhDW*

Gibbons, Stella (Dorothea)
English. Author, Poet
Writings include *The Matchmaker,* 1949; *The Snow Woman,* 1969.
b. Jan 5, 1902 in London, England
d. Dec 19, 1989 in London, England
Source: *AnObit 1989; ArtclWW 2; Au&Wr 71; BioIn 2, 4, 16, 17; BlmGWL; BlueB 76; CamGLE; Chambr 3; ChhPo; ConAu 13R, 130; ConNov 72, 76, 82, 86; DcArts; DcLEL; DcNaB 1986; EncBrWW; EvLB; FemiCLE; IntAu&W 76, 77, 82, 89, 91; IntWW 74, 75, 76, 77, 78, 79, 80, 81, 82, 83, 89; IntWWP 77, 82; InWom SUP; LngCTC; ModBrL; NewC; NewCBEL; NewYTBS 89; Novels; OxCEng 85; PenC ENG; REn; RGTwCWr; TwCA, SUP; TwCWr; WhE&EA; Who 74, 82, 83, 85, 88, 90; WhoWor 74, 76, 78; WrDr 76, 80, 82, 84, 86, 88, 90*

Gibbons, Tom
American. Boxer
Heavyweight champ, defeated by Gene Tunney, 1925; Hall of Famer.
b. Mar 22, 1891 in Saint Paul, Minnesota
d. Nov 19, 1960 in Saint Paul, Minnesota
Source: *WhoBox 74*

Gibbs, Anthony
English. Author
Books include autobiographical *My Own Good Time,* 1969.
b. Mar 9, 1902 in Bolton, England
d. Mar 11, 1975
Source: *BioIn 9; ConAu 29R, P-2; ScF&FL 1, 2, 92; WhE&EA; WhoLA*

Gibbs, Erna Leonhardt
American. Scientist
Best known for developing tool used to interpret brain waves, electroencephalogram (EEG).
b. 1906?
d. Jul 23, 1987 in Chicago, Illinois

Gibbs, Frederic A
American. Neurologist
Epilepsy researcher; first to read EEG waves and predict seizures; founded Gibbs Laboratory, Inc., IL, 1938.
b. Feb 9, 1903 in Baltimore, Maryland
d. Oct 18, 1992 in Northbrook, Illinois
Source: *AmMWSc 73P, 92*

Gibbs, Georgia
"Her Nibs"
American. Singer
1940s-50s pop singer; first hit: "If I Knew You Were Comin' I'd've Baked You a Cake."
b. Aug 26, 1926 in Worcester, Massachusetts
Source: *AmPS A, B; CmpEPM; LegTOT; PenEncP; RkOn 74, 84*

Gibbs, J(osiah) Willard
American. Scientist, Mathematician, Physicist
Yale professor whose complex mathematical theorems formed basic principles of physical chemistry.
b. Feb 11, 1839 in New Haven, Connecticut
d. Apr 28, 1903 in New Haven, Connecticut
Source: *AmBi; ApCAB; AsBiEn; BenetAL 91; BiDAmS; BiESc; BiInAmS; BioIn 1, 2, 3, 4, 5, 6, 8, 10, 11, 13, 14, 17; CamDcSc; DcAmAu; DcAmB; DcNAA; DcScB; EncAB-H 1974, 1996; InSci; LarDcSc; LinLib L, S; McGEWB; MorMA; NatCAB 4; OxCAmH; OxCAmL 65, 83, 95; RAdv 14, 13-5; REnAL; TwCBDA; WebAB 74, 79; WhAm 1; WhDW; WorAl; WorScD*

Gibbs, James
Scottish. Architect
Designed St.-Martins-in-the-Field, 1722-26; Radcliff Library, Oxford U.
b. Dec 23, 1682 in Footdeesmire, Scotland
d. Aug 5, 1754 in London, England
Source: *Alli; AtlBL; BiDBrA; BioIn 2, 3, 4, 5, 6, 13; DcArts; DcD&D; DcNaB; IntDcAr; MacEA; McGDA; McGEWB; OxCArt; WhDW; WhoArch*

Gibbs, Joe Jackson
American. Football Coach
Head coach, Washington, 1981-93; won Super Bowl, 1984, 1988, 1992.
b. Nov 25, 1940 in Mocksville, North Carolina
Source: *BiDAmSp FB; BioIn 13, 16; CurBio 92; FootReg 87; InB&W 85; WhoAm 82, 84, 86, 88, 90, 92, 94, 95, 96, 97; WhoE 83, 85, 86, 89, 91, 95; WorAlBi*

Gibbs, Marla Bradley
American. Actor
Played Florence on TV's "The Jefferson's"; had own series "227," 1985-90.
b. Jun 14, 1931 in Chicago, Illinois
Source: *BioIn 13, 14, 15, 16; BlksAmF; ConTFT 3; DrBlPA 90; InB&W 85; IntMPA 92; InWom SUP; WhoAm 86, 90; WhoBlA 85, 88, 92; WhoEnt 92; WhoTelC; WorAlBi*

Gibbs, Oliver Wolcott
American. Chemist
Developed electrolytic method for determination of copper; Harvard's physico-chemical laboratory named for him.
b. Feb 21, 1822 in New York, New York
d. Dec 9, 1908 in Newport, Rhode Island
Source: *AmBi; ApCAB; DcAmB; DcScB; NatCAB 10; TwCBDA; WebAB 74, 79*

Gibbs, Terri
American. Singer, Musician
Blind country singer; hit single "Somebody's Knockin'," 1981.
b. Jun 15, 1954 in Augusta, Georgia
Source: *BioIn 12, 14; EncFCWM 83; HarEnCM 87, 87A; LegTOT; PenEncP; RkOn 85*

Gibbs, Terry
American. Composer, Conductor, Musician
Big Band vibraphonist; prolific recorder; won Major Bowes contest at age 12.
b. Oct 13, 1924 in New York, New York
Source: *AllMusG; ASCAP 66, 80; Baker 84, 92; BiDAmM; BiDJaz; BioIn 12; CmpEPM; EncJzS; IlEncJ; NewAmDM; NewGrDJ 88, 94; PenEncP*

Gibbs, William Francis
American. Architect
Naval architect; designer of SS United States and WW II Liberty ships.
b. Aug 24, 1886 in Philadelphia, Pennsylvania
d. Sep 6, 1967 in New York, New York
Source: *BiESc; BioIn 1, 2, 4, 6, 8, 9, 20; CurBio 44, 67; DcTwDes; FacFETw; InSci; McGMS 80; NatCAB 53; NotTwCS; ObitT 1961; WebAMB; WhAm 4*

Gibbs, Woolcott
American. Critic
With *New Yorker* mag. as critic, contributor to "Talk of the Town" section, 1940-58.
b. 1902
d. Aug 16, 1958 in Ocean Beach, New York
Source: *EncAJ; OxCAmL 83*

Gibran, Kahlil
American. Poet, Artist
Finest work *The Prophet* translated into 13 languages.
b. Jan 6, 1883 in Bechari, Lebanon

d. Apr 10, 1931 in New York, New York
Source: *AmAu&B; Benet 87; BioIn 1, 2, 3, 4, 5, 7, 9, 10, 13, 14; CasWL; ChhPo S1, S3; ConAu 104, 150; DcNAA; EncO&P 2, 3; EncWB; EncWL 3; FacFETw; LegTOT; LiExTwC; LinLib L; PoeCrit 9; ScF&FL 1; TwCA, SUP; TwCLC 1, 9; WhAmArt 85; WorAl; WorAlBi*

Gibran, Kahlil George
American. Sculptor
Exhibited paintings, 1949-52, life-sized steel sculpture, 1953—.
b. Nov 29, 1922 in Boston, Massachusetts
Source: *ConAu 104; DcAmImH; DcCAA 71, 88; EncO&P 3; FacFETw; LiExTwC; PeoHis; TwCA SUP; WhoAm 86, 90; WhoAmA 73, 76, 78, 80, 82, 84, 86, 89, 91, 93; WhoWor 74; WorAlBi*

Gibson, Althea
American. Tennis Player
First black to win Wimbledon, US championships, 1957, 1958.
b. Aug 25, 1927 in Silver, South Carolina
Source: *AfrAmAl 6; AfrAmBi 1; AfrAmSG; AmDec 1950; BiDAmSp OS; BioIn 4, 5, 6, 7, 8, 9, 10, 11, 12, 13, 14, 15, 16, 17, 18, 20, 21; BlkWAm; BuCMET; ConBlB 8; ContDcW 89; CurBio 57; Ebony 1; EncWomS; GoodHs; GrLiveH; HanAmWH; HerW, 84; InB&W 80, 85; IntDcWB; InWom, SUP; LegTOT; LibW; NegAl 76, 83, 89; NewCol 75; NotBlAW 1; WebAB 74, 79; WhoAfA 96; WhoAm 74, 76, 78, 80, 82, 84, 86, 88, 90, 92, 94, 95, 96, 97; WhoAmW 66, 68, 70, 72, 74, 83, 85, 87, 89, 91, 93, 95, 97; WhoBlA 75, 77, 80, 85, 88, 90, 92, 94; WhoHol 92; WhoSpor; WomFir; WomStre; WorAl; WorAlBi*

Gibson, Bill
[William Gibson]
American. Author
Science-fiction author of cyberpunk; novels include *Neuromancer,* 1981; *Mona Lisa Overdrive,* 1988.
b. Mar 17, 1948 in Conway, South Carolina
Source: *Au&Arts 12; Benet 96; BioIn 15, 17, 18, 19, 21; ConAu 126, 133; ConLC 39, 63; ConTFT 15; DcArts; IntAu&W 91; NewEScF; ScF&FL 92; TwCSFW 86, 91; WhoCanL 87, 92; WrDr 86, 88, 90, 92*

Gibson, Bob
American. Singer, Musician
Folk singer, guitarist; with Bob Camp, 1960s.
b. Nov 16, 1931 in New York, New York
Source: *BioIn 8, 14; EncFCWM 69, 83; InB&W 85; PenEncP; WhoAm 82*

Gibson, Bob
[Robert Gibson]
"Hoot"
American. Baseball Player
Pitcher, St. Louis, 1959-75; set World Series record for strikeouts in game, 17, 1968; won NL Cy Young Award twice, MVP once; Hall of Fame, 1981.
b. Nov 9, 1935 in Omaha, Nebraska
Source: *AfrAmBi 2; AfrAmSG; Ballpl 90; BiDAmSp BB; BioIn 7, 8, 9, 10, 11, 12, 13, 14, 15, 17, 19, 20, 21; Ebony 1; FacFETw; InB&W 80, 85; LegTOT; NegAl 76, 83, 89; WhoAfA 96; WhoAm 74, 76, 82, 84, 86, 88, 90, 92, 94, 95, 96, 97; WhoBlA 75, 77, 80, 85, 88, 90, 92, 94; WhoMW 93; WhoProB 73; WhoSpor; WorAl; WorAlBi*

Gibson, Charles Dana
American. Illustrator
His creation, the "Gibson Girl," set the fashion in women's clothing, hairstyle, 1 890-1914.
b. Sep 14, 1867 in Roxbury, Massachusetts
d. Dec 23, 1944 in New York, New York
Source: *AmAu&B; AmBi; Benet 87; BenetAL 91; BioIn 2, 3, 4, 5, 7, 10; ChhPo; ConGrA 3; CurBio 45; DcAmAu; DcAmB S3; DcArts; DcBrBI; DcLB DS13; DcNAA; EncAJ; EncFash; GayN; IlrAm 1880, A; LinLib L, S; NatCAB 11; OxCAmH; OxCAmL 65, 83, 95; PeoHis; PhDcTCA 77; REn; REnAL; TwCBDA; WebAB 74, 79; WhAm 2; WhAmArt 85; WhScrn 77, 83; WorAl; WorAlBi; WorECar*

Gibson, Charles Dewolf
American. Broadcast Journalist
Replaced David Hartman as co-host, "Good Morning America," 1987—.
b. Mar 9, 1943 in Evanston, Illinois
Source: *WhoAm 84, 86, 88, 90, 92, 94, 95, 96, 97*

Gibson, Debbie
[Deborah Ann Gibson]
American. Singer, Songwriter
Teen singer; had hit album, *Out of the Blue,* 1987.
b. Aug 31, 1971 in Merrick, New York
Source: *BioIn 15, 16; ConMus 1*

Gibson, Don(ald)
American. Singer, Songwriter
Prolific country writer, performer; wrote songs "Sweet Dreams," 1956; "I Can't Stop Loving You," 1958.
b. Apr 3, 1928 in Shelby, North Carolina
Source: *BgBkCoM; BiDAmM; BioIn 14; CounME 74, 74A; EncFCWM 69, 83; EncRk 88; HarEnCM 87; HarEnR 86; IlEncCM; LegTOT; PenEncP; RkOn 74; WhoAm 86*

Gibson, Edward George
American. Astronaut
Pilot of third manned Skylab mission; orbited earth 84 days.
b. Nov 8, 1936 in Buffalo, New York
Source: *AmMWSc 73P, 76P, 79, 82, 86, 89, 92, 95; BioIn 10; St&PR 87; WhoAm 74, 76, 78; WhoSSW 73, 75*

Gibson, Guy
British. Air Force Officer
Led spectacular bombing attacks on German dams, 1943.
b. 1918
d. Sep 1944
Source: *BioIn 5, 8; WhWW-II*

Gibson, Henry
American. Actor, Author
Played on TV show "Laugh-In," 1968-72; wrote *Only Show on Earth.*
b. Sep 21, 1935 in Germantown, Pennsylvania
Source: *ConTFT 3; HalFC 84, 88; IntMPA 82, 84, 86, 88, 92, 94, 96; LegTOT; VarWW 85; WhoAm 74, 76, 78, 80, 82, 84; WhoHol 92, A*

Gibson, Hoot
[Edmund Richard Gibson]
"The Smiling Whirlwind"
American. Actor
Western hero whose films include *Outlaw Trail,* 1944; *Ocean's Eleven,* 1960.
b. Aug 6, 1892 in Tememah, Nebraska
d. Aug 23, 1962 in Woodland Hills, California
Source: *BioIn 7, 8, 12; DcAmB S7; EncAFC; Film 1, 2; FilmEn; FilmgC; HalFC 80, 84, 88; LegTOT; MotPP; MovMk; NotNAT B; OxCFilm; TwYS; WhoHol B; WhScrn 74; WorAl*

Gibson, John
English. Sculptor
Tried, unsuccessfully, to popularize tinted (marble) statues: *Tinted Venus,* 1851-55.
b. Jun 19, 1790 in Gyffin, Wales
d. Jan 27, 1866 in Rome, Italy
Source: *ArtsNiC; BioIn 6, 9, 10; CelCen; DcBiPP; DcNaB; DcNiCA; DcVicP 2; McGDA; NewCol 75; OxCArt; OxDcArt; WhDW*

Gibson, Josh(ua)
American. Baseball Player
One of great hitting stars of Negro baseball, 1930s-40s; Hall of Fame, 1972.
b. Dec 21, 1911 in Buena Vista, Georgia
d. Jan 20, 1947 in Pittsburgh, Pennsylvania
Source: *AfrAmSG; Ballpl 90; BioIn 9, 10, 11, 12, 14, 15, 17, 21; DcAmB S4; DcAmNB; InB&W 80, 85; LegTOT; WhoSpor; WorAl; WorAlBi*

Gibson, Kenneth Allen
American. Politician
First black mayor of Newark, NJ, 1970-86.
b. May 15, 1932 in Enterprise, Alabama
Source: *AfrAmBi 1; BioIn 8, 9, 10, 11, 12, 13; CivR 74; ConBlB 6; CurBio 71; InB&W 80, 85; NewYTBE 70; NewYTBS*

78; WhoAfA 96; WhoAm 74, 76, 78, 80, 82, 84; WhoAmP 73, 75, 77, 79, 81, 83, 85, 87, 89; WhoBlA 75, 77, 80, 85, 88, 90, 92, 94; WhoE 74, 75, 77, 79, 81, 83, 85, 86; WhoGov 72, 75, 77

Gibson, Kirk Harold
"Gibby"
American. Baseball Player
College football All-American, 1978; M.L. outfielder, 1979—, mostly with Detroit; NL MVP, 1988; remembered for dramatic homerun off Dennis Eckersley in 1988 World Series.
b. May 28, 1957 in Pontiac, Michigan
Source: *Ballpl 90; BaseReg 86, 87; BioIn 13, 14, 15, 16; ConNews 85-2; NewYTBS 82, 86; WhoAm 88, 90; WhoWest 89; WorAlBi*

Gibson, Mel
American. Actor, Director
Films include *The Road Warrior,* 1982; and the *Lethal Weapon,* trilogy, 1987-92; *Braveheart,* 1996, winner of best picture and best director Oscars.
b. Jan 3, 1956 in Peekskill, New York
Source: *BiDFilm 94; BioIn 12, 13, 14, 15, 16; CelR 90; ConTFT 6, 13; CurBio 84; DcArts; HalFC 88; HolBB; IntDcF 1-3, 2-3; IntMPA 84, 86, 92, 94, 96; IntWW 89, 91, 93; JohnWSW; LegTOT; News 90, 90-1; VarWW 85; WhoAm 86, 88, 90, 92, 94, 95, 96, 97; WhoEnt 92; WhoHol 92; WhoWor 97; WorAlBi*

Gibson, Michael
American. Conductor
Orchestrated Broadway plays *Barnum,* 1982; *Cabaret,* 1987.
b. Sep 29, 1944 in Wilmington, Delaware
Source: *ConTFT 5; St&PR 87; WhoEnt 92*

Gibson, Walter B(rown)
American. Author
Used 12 pseudonyms; besides *Shadow* series, wrote on magic, games, astrology, etc.
b. Sep 12, 1897 in Philadelphia, Pennsylvania
d. Dec 6, 1985 in Kingston, New York
Source: *BioIn 7, 14; ConAu 108, 110; EncMys; EncSF 93; ScF&FL 1; TwCCr&M 80, 85; WhJnl; WhNAA; WrDr 82, 84, 86*

Gibson, Wilfred Wilson
English. Dramatist, Poet
Verse collections include *Stonefolds,* 1907.
b. Oct 2, 1878 in Hexham, England
d. May 26, 1962 in Virginia Water, England
Source: *CamGLE; ConAu 113; DcLB 19*

Gibson, William
American. Dramatist
Best known plays include Tony-winning *The Miracle Worker,* 1960.
b. Nov 13, 1914 in New York, New York
Source: *BenetAL 91; BiDConC; BiE&WWA; BioIn 3, 4, 5, 10, 12, 13, 14, 15, 17; CamGWoT; CnMD; ConAmD; ConAu 9NR, 9R, 42NR; ConDr 73, 77, 82, 88, 93; ConLC 23; ConTFT 2; CrtSuDr; CurBio 83; DcLB 7; DcLEL 1940; DcLP 87A; Dun&B 86; EncWT; IntAu&W 77, 91; IntvTCA 2; MagSAmL; McGEWD 72, 84; ModAL; ModWD; NatPD 77; NotNAT, A; OxCAmL 83, 95; OxCAmT 84; PenC AM; PlP&P; REnAL; SmATA 66; VarWW 85; WhoAm 74, 76, 78, 80, 82, 84, 86, 88, 90, 92, 94, 95, 96; WhoE 74; WhoThe 72, 77, 81; WhoWor 74; WorAlBi; WorAu 1950; WrDr 76, 80, 82, 84, 86, 88, 90, 92, 94, 96*

Gibson, William F(rank)
American. Civil Rights Leader
Chairman of the NAACP's National Board of Directors, 1985—.
b. 1933 in Greenville, South Carolina
Source: *BioIn 20*

Gidal, Sonia
[Mrs. Tim Gidal]
German. Children's Author
Wrote "My Village" series with husband, 1950s-70.
b. Sep 23, 1922 in Berlin, Germany
Source: *Au&Wr 71; AuBYP 2, 3; BioIn 8, 9; ConAu 5R, 14NR; IntAu&W 76; SmATA 2*

Gidal, Tim
German. Journalist
Photojournalist whose collections are displayed internationally; wrote *Modern Photojournalism: Origin and Evolution,* 1972.
b. May 18, 1909 in Munich, Germany
Source: *BioIn 8, 9, 10, 13, 16, 21; ConAu 5R, 14NR, 20NR, X; ConPhot 82, 88; ICPEnP A; MacBEP; SmATA 2; WhoWor 89, 91*

Giddings, Joshua Reed
American. Politician, Abolitionist
Congressman censured by House for militant antislavery tactics, 1842; resigned, but promptly re-elected.
b. Oct 6, 1795 in Tioga Point, Pennsylvania
d. May 27, 1864 in Montreal, Quebec, Canada
Source: *Alli, SUP; AmAu&B; AmBi; AmOrN; AmPolLe; ApCAB; BiAUS; BiD&SB; BiDrAC; BiDrUSC 89; BioIn 2, 4, 7, 9; CivWDc; DcAmAu; DcAmB; DcAmSR; DcAmTB; DcNAA; Drake; EncAAH; HarEnUS; NatCAB 2; OhA&B; OxCAmH; WebAB 74, 79; WhAm HS; WhAmP; WhCiWar*

Giddings, Paula (Jane)
American. Educator
Book review editor, *Essence,* 1985-90; has been a fellow and visiting scholar at many colleges and universities.
b. Nov 16, 1947 in Yonkers, New York
Source: *ConBlB 11; NotBlAW 1; WhoAfA 96; WhoBlA 92, 94*

Gide, Andre (Paul Guillaume)
French. Author, Critic
Won Nobel Prize for literature, 1947; wrote *The Immoralist,* 1902.
b. Nov 22, 1869 in Paris, France
d. Feb 19, 1951 in Paris, France
Source: *AtlBL; Benet 87, 96; BioIn 1, 2, 3, 4, 5, 6, 7, 8, 9, 10, 11, 12, 13, 14, 15, 16, 17, 18, 20, 21; BlmGEL; CamGWoT; CasWL; ClDMEL 47, 80; CnMD; CnMWL; ConAu 104, 124; CyWA 58; DcArts; DcLB 65; DcTwCCu 2; Dis&D; EncWL, 2, 3; EncWT; Ent; EuWr 8; EvEuW; FacFETw; GayLesB; GayLL; GrFLW; GuFrLit 1; LegTOT; LinLib L, S; LngCTC; MagSWL; MajTwCW; MakMC; McGEWB; ModFrL; ModRL; ModWD; NewC; NobelP; NotNAT B; Novels; ObitT 1951; OxCEng 67, 85, 95; OxCFr; OxCThe 67, 83; PenC EUR; RAdv 1, 14, 13-1, 13-2; RComWL; REn; REnWD; ScF&FL 1; ShSCr 13; TwCA, SUP; TwCLC 5, 12, 36; TwCWr; WhAm 3; WhDW; WhoNob, 90, 95; WhoTwCL; WorAl; WorAlBi; WorLitC; WrPh*

Gidlow, Elsa
Canadian. Poet
Influenced by the classic literature of India; poetry collection, *On a Grey Thread,* 1923.
b. Dec 1898 in Hull, England
d. 1986
Source: *ArtclWW 2; BioIn 15; ConAu 77, 119; DrAPF 80; GayLesB; GayLL; WhoAmW 79, 81*

Gielgud, (Arthur) John, Sir
English. Actor, Director, Producer
Won Oscar for *Arthur,* 1982; distinguished Shakespearean actor with Old Vic, 1920s; won several Tony awards.
b. Apr 14, 1904 in London, England
Source: *BiDFilm, 81, 94; BiE&WWA; BioIn 1, 2, 3, 4, 5, 6, 7, 9, 10, 11, 12, 13, 14, 15, 16, 17, 18, 19, 20; BlmGEL; BlueB 76; CamGWoT; CelR, 90; CnThe; ConAu 111, 147; ConTFT 1, 7, 14; CurBio 47, 84; DcArts; EncEurC; EncWT; Ent; FacFETw; FamA&A; Film 2; FilmAG WE; FilmEn; FilmgC; ForYSC; GayLesB; GrStDi; HalFC 80, 84, 88; IlWWBF, A; IntDcF 1-3, 2-3; IntDcT 3; IntMPA 75, 76, 77, 78, 79, 80, 81, 82, 84, 86, 88, 92, 94, 96; IntWW 74, 75, 76, 77, 78, 79, 80, 81, 82, 83, 89, 91, 93; ItaFilm; LegTOT; MotPP; MovMk; NewC; NewYTBS 84, 91; NotNAT, A; OxCAmT 84; OxCFilm; OxCThe 67, 83; PlP&P; REn; TheaDir; VarWW 85; WhDW; Who 74, 82, 83, 85, 88, 90, 92, 94; WhoAm 80, 82, 84, 86, 88, 90, 92, 94, 95, 96, 97; WhoEnt 92; WhoHol 92, A; WhoThe 72, 77, 81; WhoWor 74, 76, 78, 82, 84, 87, 89, 91, 93, 95, 96, 97; WorAl; WorAlBi; WorEFlm; WrDr 80, 82, 84, 86, 88, 90, 92, 94, 96*

Gielgud, Val Henry
English. Dramatist
Brother of actor John; books include *In Such a Night,* 1974; *A Fearful Thing,* 1975.
b. Apr 28, 1900 in London, England
d. Nov 30, 1981 in Eastbourne, England
Source: *Au&Wr 71; BioIn 2, 7, 12, 14; BlueB 76; ConAu 5NR, 9R; DcLEL; DcNaB 1981; EncMys; IntAu&W 76, 77; IntWW 74, 75, 76, 77, 78, 79, 80, 81; MnBBF; NewCBEL; WhE&EA; WhLit; Who 74, 82, 83N; WhoLA; WhoWor 74, 76, 78; WrDr 76, 84*

Gierek, Edward
Polish. Political Leader
Important in Belgian Underground, WW II; first secretary, Polish United Workers Party, 1970-80.
b. Jan 6, 1913 in Porabka, Poland
Source: *BioIn 9, 10, 11, 12, 18; BioNews 74; ColdWar 2; CurBio 71; DcTwHis; FacFETw; IntWW 74, 75, 76, 77, 78, 79, 80, 81, 82, 83, 89, 91, 93; NewCol 75; NewYTBE 70; NewYTBS 77, 80; PolBiDi; WhoSocC 78; WhoSoCE 89; WhoWor 74, 76, 78, 80; WorAl; WorAlBi*

Gies, Miep
[Hermine Santrouschitz]
Austrian. Secretary
With husband, hid Anne Frank, others, from Nazis; found diary that was published, 1947; story told in made-for-TV movie, 1988.
b. 1909? in Vienna, Austria
Source: *BioIn 15; NewYTBS 87*

Gieseking, Walter Wilhelm
German. Musician
Developed Leimer-Gieseking method of piano study.
b. Nov 5, 1895 in Lyons, France
d. Oct 26, 1956 in London, England
Source: *Baker 92; CurBio 56, 57; NewCol 75; NotTwCP; WhAm 3*

Giesler, Jerry
[Harold Lee Giesler]
American. Lawyer
His first court case, 1910, was defending Clarence Darrow for allegedly bribing a juror.
b. Nov 2, 1886 in Wilton Junction, Iowa
d. Jan 1, 1962 in Beverly Hills, California
Source: *WhAm 4*

Gifford, Frank
[Francis Newton Gifford]
American. Football Player, Sportscaster
Eight-time all-pro running back, NY Giants, 1952-60, 1962-64; MVP, 1956; Hall of Fame, 1977; won Emmy for sportscasting, 1977.
b. Aug 16, 1930 in Santa Monica, California
Source: *BiDAmSp FB; BioIn 4, 5, 6, 7, 8, 9, 11, 13, 15, 16; CelR, 90; ConAu 109; CurBio 64, 95; EncTwCJ; LegTOT; LesBEnT 92; NewYTET; VarWW 85; WhoAm 82, 84, 86, 90; WhoFtbl 74; WhoHol 92, A; WorAl; WorAlBi*

Gifford, Kathie Lee
[Kathie Lee Epstein; Mrs. Frank Gifford]
American. TV Personality, Singer
Co-host, with Regis Philbin, of "The Morning Show," 1985-88; co-host of "Live with Regis and Kathie Lee," a syndicated talk show, 1988—.
b. Aug 16, 1953 in Paris, France
Source: *CelR 90; ConAu 142; CurBio 94; LegTOT; News 92, 92-2; WhoAm 94, 95, 96, 97; WhoAmW 95, 97; WhoE 95; WhoMW 88; WrDr 96*

Gifford, Walter Sherman
American. Philanthropist
Pres., AT&T, 1925-48; ambassador to Britain, 1950-53.
b. Jan 10, 1885 in Salem, Massachusetts
d. May 7, 1966 in New York, New York
Source: *BiDAmBL 83; BioIn 1, 2, 3, 7, 16; CurBio 45, 66; DcAmB S8; DcAmDH 80, 89; LinLib S; ObitT 1961; WhAm 4*

Gift, Roland
[Fine Young Cannibals]
English. Actor, Singer
Lead vocalist for music group Fine Young Cannibals, 1983—.
b. May 28, 1962? in Birmingham, England
Source: *BioIn 16; ConMus 3; LegTOT; News 90-2*

Gigli, Beniamino
Italian. Opera Singer
Much-loved tenor; considered Caruso's successor; with NY Met., 1920-32, 1938-39; acclaimed as Lohengrin.
b. Mar 20, 1890 in Recanati, Italy
d. Nov 30, 1957 in Rome, Italy
Source: *Baker 78, 84, 92; BiDAmM; BioIn 1, 2, 3, 4, 5, 6, 8, 11, 12, 14, 17; BriBkM 80; CmOp; DcArts; FacFETw; FilmgC; HalFC 80, 84, 88; IntDcOp; ItaFilm; MetOEnc; MusMk; MusSN; NewAmDM; NewEOp 71; NewGrDA 86; NewGrDM 80; NewGrDO; ObitT 1951; OxDcOp; PenDiMP; WhoHol B; WhScrn 74, 77, 83*

Gilbert, A(lfred) C(arleton)
American. Business Executive
Invented Erector Set; founder, pres., Gilbert Toy Co.
b. Feb 15, 1884 in Salem, Oregon
d. Jan 24, 1961 in Boston, Massachusetts
Source: *DcAmB S7; PeoHis; WebAB 74; WhAm 4; WhoTr&F 73*

Gilbert, Alfred, Sir
English. Sculptor
Best known work, the Shaftsburg Memorial Fountain, Eros, in London's Piccadilly Circus, 1899.
b. 1854 in London, England
d. 1934 in London, England
Source: *BioIn 2, 3, 8, 13, 14, 15; DcArts; DcBrAr 1; DcNaB 1931; McGDA; OxCArt; OxCTwCA; OxDcArt; PenDiDA 89; PhDcTCA 77; TwCPaSc*

Gilbert, Alfred Carlton, Jr.
American. Manufacturer
Pres., A C Gilbreth Co., 1954-64, makers of recreational equipment.
b. Dec 1, 1919 in New Haven, Connecticut
d. Jun 27, 1964
Source: *DcAmB S7; EncAB-A 32; WhAm 4*

Gilbert, Billy
American. Actor
Trademark was comic sneezing routine used in Disney's *Snow White and the Seven Dwarfs* for the dwarf Sneezy.
b. Sep 12, 1894 in Louisville, Kentucky
d. Sep 23, 1971 in Hollywood, California
Source: *BiE&WWA; BioIn 8, 9; EncAFC; Film 1, 2; FilmEn; FilmgC; ForYSC; JoeFr; MovMk; NotNAT B; TwYS; What 2; WhoCom; WhScrn 74, 77, 83*

Gilbert, Bruce
American. Producer
Films include *Coming Home; China Syndrome; Nine to Five; On Golden Pond.*
b. Mar 28, 1947 in Beverly Hills, California
Source: *BiDrAPA 89; ConTFT 1, 9; IntMPA 81, 92, 94, 96; VarWW 85*

Gilbert, Cass
American. Architect
Designed impressive public buildings: Woolworth Building, NYC, 1913; Supreme Court, Washington, DC, 1935.
b. Nov 24, 1859 in Zanesville, Ohio
d. May 17, 1934 in Brockenhurst, England
Source: *AmBi; AmDec 1910; BioIn 14, 17; BriEAA; DcAmB S1; DcArts; DcD&D; DcTwDes; EncAAr 1, 2; EncAB-A 4; FacFETw; LegTOT; LinLib S; MacEA; MorMA; NatCAB 11, 26; OxCAmH; OxCAmL 65; OxCSupC; TwCBDA; WebAB 74, 79; WebBD 83; WhAm 1; WhAmArt 85; WhoArch; WorAl; WorAlBi*

Gilbert, Grove Karl
American. Geologist
A founder of modern geomorphology; first to describe laccolithic mountain groups; studied Great Lakes, Niagara Falls.
b. May 6, 1843 in Rochester, New York
d. May 1, 1918 in Jackson, Michigan
Source: *Alli SUP; AmBi; ApCAB; BiDAmS; BiInAmS; BioIn 2, 4, 12, 18; DcAmAu; DcAmB; DcNAA; DcScB; Geog 1; InSci; LarDcSc; NatCAB 13; NewCol 75; RAdv 14; TwCBDA; WebAB 74, 79; WhAm 1*

Gilbert, Humphrey, Sir
English. Navigator, Explorer
Founded first British colony in North America at St. John's, Newfoundland, Aug 3, 1583.
b. 1539? in Compton, England
d. Sep 9, 1583, At Sea
Source: *Alli; ApCAB; Benet 87, 96; BenetAL 91; BioIn 3, 8, 9, 10; CamGEL; CamGLE; CasWL; CyEd; DcNaB; Drake; EncCRAm; Expl 93; HarEnUS; HisDBrE; NewC; NewCBEL; NewCol 75; OxCAmH; OxCAmL 65, 83, 95; OxCCan; OxCEng 67; OxCShps; REn; REnAL; WhAm HS; WhDW; WhWE*

Gilbert, John
[John Pringle]
American. Actor
Starred opposite Greta Garbo in several films; talking pictures destroyed career.
b. Jul 10, 1897 in Logan, Utah
d. Jan 9, 1936 in Los Angeles, California
Source: *AmBi; BiDFilm, 81; BioIn 4, 6, 7, 9, 10, 12, 14, 15, 18; CmMov; DcAmB S2; Film 1; FilmgC; IntDcF 2-3; MovMk; NotNAT B; OxCFilm; WhAm 1; WhScrn 74, 77, 83; WorAl; WorAlBi; WorEFlm*

Gilbert, John, Sir
English. Artist, Illustrator
Painted historical scenes; illustrated works of Shakespeare, Scott.
b. Jul 21, 1817 in London, England
d. Oct 5, 1897 in London, England
Source: *AntBDN B, N; ArtsNiC; BioIn 12, 16; CelCen; ChhPo, S1, S2, S3; ClaDrA; DcBiPP; DcBrBI; DcBrWA; DcNaB S1; DcVicP, 2; McGDA; StaCVF; VicBrit*

Gilbert, Martin John
English. Historian
After Randall Churchill's death, became official biographer of Winston Churchill; his 8 volume biography is the longest such work in history.
b. Oct 25, 1936 in London, England
Source: *BioIn 15; CanWW 89; ConAu 9R, 31NR; CurBio 91; DcLEL 1940; IntAu&W 91; IntWW 91; Who 92; WhoWor 91; WorAu 1975; WrDr 92*

Gilbert, Melissa
American. Actor
Played Laura Ingalls Wilder on TV series "Little House on the Prairie," 1974-83.
b. May 8, 1964 in Los Angeles, California
Source: *BioIn 10, 12, 13, 15, 16, 19, 20, 21; CelR 90; ConTFT 2, 5, 14; IntMPA 82, 84, 86, 88, 94, 96; InWom SUP; LegTOT; VarWW 85; WhoAm 92, 94, 95, 96, 97; WhoAmW 95, 97; WhoEnt 92; WhoHol 92; WhoTelC; WorAlBi*

Gilbert, Rod(rigue Gabriel)
Canadian. Hockey Player
Right wing, NY Rangers, 1960-78; scored 406 career goals; won Masterton Trophy, 1976; Hall of Fame, 1982.
b. Jul 1, 1941 in Montreal, Quebec, Canada
Source: *BioIn 8, 10, 11; ConAu 109; CurBio 69; HocEn; NewYTBS 77; WhoAm 82; WhoHcky 73*

Gilbert, Sara
American. Actor
Plays Darlene Conner on TV series "Roseanne," 1988—; films include *Poison Ivy,* 1992.
b. 1975?
Source: *AuBYP 3; BioIn 16; ConTFT 13; LegTOT; WhoAmW 97*

Gilbert, Walter
American. Biologist
Shared Nobel Prize in chemistry with Paul Berg, Frederick Sanger, 1980; helped determine sequence of DNA bases.
b. Mar 21, 1932 in Boston, Massachusetts
Source: *AmMWSc 73P, 76P, 79, 82, 86, 89, 92, 95; BiESc; BioIn 12, 13, 14, 15, 18, 19, 20; CamDcSc; CurBio 92; Dun&B 90; IntWW 81, 82, 83, 89, 91, 93; LarDcSc; News 88-3; NobelP; NotTwCS; St&PR 87; Who 82, 83, 85, 88, 90, 92, 94; WhoAm 74, 76, 78, 80, 82, 84, 86, 88, 90, 92, 94, 95, 96, 97; WhoE 74, 81, 83, 85, 86, 89, 91, 93, 95, 97; WhoFrS 84; WhoNob, 90, 95; WhoScEn 94, 96; WhoWor 82, 84, 87, 89, 91, 93, 95, 96, 97; WorAlBi; WorScD*

Gilbert, William
English. Scientist, Physician
Physician to Queen Elizabeth I; early researcher into electric, magnetic bodies; introduced term "magnetic pole."
b. May 24, 1544 in Colchester, England
d. Dec 10, 1603 in London, England
Source: *Alli; AsBiEn; BiESc; BiHiMed; BioIn 14; BritAu; CamDcSc; CamGLE; DcEnL; DcNaB; DcScB; LarDcSc; McGEWB; NewC; OxCEng 67; WhDW; WorAl; WorAlBi; WorScD*

Gilbert, William S(chwenck), Sir
[Gilbert and Sullivan]
English. Dramatist
Wrote librettos for Gilbert and Sullivan comic operas: *Pirates of Penzance,* 1880; *The Mikado,* 1885.
b. Nov 18, 1836 in London, England
d. May 29, 1911 in Harrow, England
Source: *Alli SUP; AtlBL; AuBYP 2S, 3; Baker 78, 84; BbD; Benet 87, 96; BiD&SB; BioIn 1, 2, 3, 4, 5, 6, 7, 8, 9, 10, 11, 12, 13, 14, 15, 17, 19, 20; BlmGEL; BritAu 19; BritPl; CamGLE; CamGWoT; CasWL; CelCen; Chambr 3; ChhPo, S1, S2, S3; CnE&AP; CnThe; CyWA 58; DcBrBI; DcEnA, A; DcEnL; DcEuL; DcLEL; DcNaB S2; EvLB; FilmgC; LinLib L, S; McGEWB; McGEWD 72; ModWD; MouLC 4; NewAmDM; NewC; NewCBEL; NotNAT A, B; OxCAmT 84; OxCEng 67, 85, 95; OxCThe 67, 83; PenC ENG; PlP&P; RAdv 14, 13-2; REn; REnWD; Str&VC; TwCLC 3; WebE&AL; WhDW; WhLit; WhoStg 1908; WorAl; WorAlBi*

Gilbertson, Mildred Geiger
[Nan Gilbert; Jo Mendel]
American. Children's Author
Books include *The Strange New World Across the Street,* 1979. .
b. Jun 9, 1908 in Galena, Illinois
Source: *ConAu 2NR, 5R; DcLP 87A; ForWC 70; IntAu&W 76, 77, 82; SmATA 2; WhoAmW 83; WrDr 76, 86, 88*

Gilbreth, Frank Bunker
American. Engineer, Lecturer
His family of 12 children was subject of book, film *Cheaper by the Dozen;* efficiency expert.
b. Jul 7, 1868 in Fairfield, Maine
d. Jun 14, 1924 in Montclair, New Jersey
Source: *BiDAmBL 83; BioIn 1, 11, 12, 17, 20; DcNAA; EncAB-A 6, 21; InSci; NatCAB 26; REnAL; WhAm 1*

Gilbreth, Frank Bunker, Jr.
American. Author, Journalist
With sister, Ernestine Carey, wrote of childhood in *Cheaper by the Dozen,* 1948; became film, 1950.
b. Mar 17, 1911 in Plainfield, New Jersey
Source: *AmAu&B; BiDAmNC; BioIn 1, 2, 9; ConAu 9R; ConLC 17; CurBio 49; SmATA 2; St&PR 75, 84; WhoAm 74, 76, 78, 80, 82, 84, 86, 88, 90, 92, 94, 95, 96, 97; WhoSSW 73, 75; WhoWor 74*

Gilbreth, Lillian Moller
American. Engineer
Reared 12 children portrayed in best-selling book, film *Cheaper by the Dozen;* prominent consultant in time-motion studies.
b. May 24, 1878 in Oakland, California
d. Jan 2, 1972 in Phoenix, Arizona
Source: *BiDAmBL 83; BioIn 16, 17, 19, 20, 21; ConAu 33R; CurBio 40, 51, 72; EncAB-A 6; InWom SUP; NewYTBE 72; NotAW; ObitOF 79; REnAL; WebBD 83; WhAm 5, 6; WhoAmW 58, 64, 66, 68, 70, 72; WomPsyc*

Gilder, George
American. Economist, Author
Wrote best-seller, *Wealth and Poverty,* 1981.
b. Nov 29, 1939 in New York, New York
Source: *AuNews 1; BioIn 10, 12, 13, 14, 15; ConAu 9NR, 17R, 26NR; ConIsC 1; CurBio 81; DcAmC; NewYTBS 81; WhoAm 82*

Gilder, Nick
English. Singer
Had number-one single "Hot Child in the City," 1978, from album *City Nights.*
b. Nov 7, 1951 in London, England

Source: *BioIn 11; LegTOT; RkOn 85*

Gildersleeve, Virginia Crocheron
American. Educator
Dean of Barnard College, 1911-47.
b. Oct 3, 1877 in New York, New York
d. Jul 7, 1965 in Centerville, Massachusetts
Source: *AmAu&B; AmPeW; AmWomM; ApCAB X; BiDAmEd; BiDInt; BioIn 1, 3, 5, 6, 7, 12; CurBio 41, 65; DcAmB S7; EncAB-A 2; InWom; NewCol 75; NotAW MOD; WebBD 83; WhAm 4; WhNAA; WhoAmW 58, 61; WomWWA 14*

Gilels, Emil Grigoyevich
Russian. Musician
Pianist known for rich tone, virtuosic power; performed Romantic, classical works, sometimes playing all five Beethoven concertos in succession.
b. Oct 19, 1916 in Odessa, Ukraine
d. Oct 14, 1985 in Moscow, Union of Soviet Socialist Republics
Source: *Baker 84; CurBio 56, 86; IntWW 74; NewGrDM 80; WhoAm 82*

Giles, Warren Crandall
American. Baseball Executive
Replaced Ford Frick as pres. of NL, 1951-69.
b. May 28, 1896 in Tiskilwa, Illinois
d. Feb 7, 1979 in Cincinnati, Ohio
Source: *BiDAmSp BB; BioIn 6, 11; DcAmB S10; NewYTBS 79; WhAm 7; WhoAm 74, 76, 78; WhoProB 73*

Gilford, Jack
[Jacob Gellman]
American. Actor
Versatile comedian; 50-year career began in vaudeville; nominated for Oscar, 1972, for *Save the Tiger;* starred in *Cocoon,* 1985.
b. Jul 25, 1907 in New York, New York
d. Jun 4, 1990 in New York, New York
Source: *AnObit 1990; BiE&WWA; BioIn 11, 15, 16, 17; CamGWoT; ConTFT 2, 11; EncAFC; EncMT; FacFETw; FilmEn; FilmgC; HalFC 80, 84, 88; IntMPA 84, 86, 88; LegTOT; MovMk; News 90; NewYTBS 87, 90; NotNAT; PlP&P; VarWW 85; WhoAm 80, 88; WhoCom; WhoHol A; WorAl; WorAlBi*

Gill, Amory Tingle
"Slats"
American. Basketball Coach
Coach, Oregon State U, 1929-64; career record 599-392; Hall of Fame.
b. May 1, 1901 in Salem, Oregon
d. Apr 5, 1966 in Cornwallis, Oregon
Source: *BioIn 6, 9; WhoBbl 73*

Gill, Brendan
American. Critic, Author
Contributor to *The New Yorker,* 1936—.
b. Oct 4, 1914 in Hartford, Connecticut
Source: *AmAu&B; Benet 87; BiE&WWA; BioIn 2, 4, 10, 13, 14, 16, 17, 21; ConAmTC; ConAu 37NR, 73; ConNov 72, 76, 82, 86, 91, 96; Conv 1; DrAF 76; DrAPF 80, 91; EncTwCJ; IntAu&W 76, 77; IntWW 91, 93; LegTOT; LiJour; MajTwCW; NotNAT, A; Novels; PenC AM; REnAL; TwCA SUP; WhoAm 74, 76, 78, 80, 82, 84, 86, 88, 90, 92, 94, 95, 96, 97; WhoThe 72, 77, 81; WhoUSWr 88; WhoWrEP 89, 92; WrDr 76, 80, 82, 84, 86, 88, 92, 94, 96*

Gill, Eric
English. Author, Sculptor, Engraver
Did wood engravings for prestigious Golden Cockerel Press, from 1924; designed numerous typefaces.
b. Feb 22, 1882 in Brighton, England
d. Nov 18, 1940 in Uxbridge, England
Source: *BioIn 1, 2, 3, 4, 6, 7, 8, 10, 12, 13, 14, 15, 16, 17, 20; BkC 5; CathA 1930; ConAu 120; CurBio 41; DcLB 98; DcLEL; DcNaB 1931; LngCTC; NewCBEL; OxCEng 85; OxCTwCA; OxDcArt; PhDcTCA 77; TwCA SUP; TwCPaSc; WhDW*

Gill, Vince(nt Grant)
American. Singer, Songwriter, Musician
Tenor; country hits include "Turn Me Loose," 1984; "When I Call Your Name," 1990; won 6 Grammys and 9 CMA awards.
b. Apr 12, 1957 in Norman, Oklahoma
Source: *BgBkCoM; BioIn 20, 21; ConMus 7; LegTOT; News 95, 95-2; OnThGG; WhoNeCM; WhoRocM 82*

Gillenson, Lewis W
American. Publisher
Pres., Dodd, Mead, 1982-95; publisher, *Quest Magazine,* 1977-82; pres., Thomas Y. Crowell, Inc., 1971-77.
b. Feb 18, 1918 in New York, New York
d. Sep 4, 1992 in New York, New York
Source: *ConAu 5R; WhoAm 86*

Gilles, D(onald) B(ruce)
American. Dramatist
Wrote *The Girl Who Loved the Beatles.*
b. Aug 30, 1947 in Cleveland, Ohio
Source: *NatPD 77; WorAl*

Gillespie, Dizzy
[John Birks Gillespie]
American. Jazz Musician
Trumpeter responsible for "Be-Bop" sound; wrote *To Be or Not.to Bop,* 197 9; won 2 Emmys 1975, 1980, and a Lifetime Achievement Award, Nat. Assn. of Recording Arts and Sciences, 1989.
b. Oct 21, 1917 in Cheraw, South Carolina
d. Jan 6, 1993 in Englewood, New Jersey
Source: *AfrAmAl 6; AfrAmBi 2; Alli SUP; AllMusG; AmCulL; AmMWSc 73P; AnObit 1993; ASCAP 66, 80; Baker 78, 84, 92; BgBands 74; BiDAfM; BiDAmM; BiDJaz; BioIn 1, 2, 4, 5, 6, 7, 8, 9, 10, 11, 12, 13, 14, 15, 16, 17, 18, 19, 20; BioNews 74; CelR, 90; CmpEPM; ConAu 104; ConBlB 1; ConMus 6; Conv 2; CurBio 57, 93, 93N; DcArts; DcTwCCu 1, 5; DrBlPA, 90; Ebony 1; EncJzS; FacFETw; IlEncJ; InB&W 80, 85; IntWW 78, 79, 80, 81, 82, 83, 89, 91; IntWWM 90; LegTOT; NegAl 83, 89; NewAmDM; NewGrDA 86; NewGrDJ 88, 94; NewGrDM 80; News 93-2; NewYTBE 73; NewYTBS 93; OxCPMus; PenEncP; TwCBrS; VarWW 85; WhAm 10; WhoAm 74, 76, 78, 80, 82, 84, 86, 88, 90, 92; WhoBlA 75, 77, 80, 85, 88, 90, 92, 94N; WhoEnt 92; WorAl; WorAlBi*

Gillett, George Nield, Jr.
American. Business Executive
Chm., Gillett Broadcasting Co., 1978—; owner of several other companies; known for buying TV, radio stations, making them competitive.
b. Oct 22, 1938 in Racine, Wisconsin
Source: *AmCath 80; BioIn 16; ConNews 88-1; Dun&B 88, 90; NewYTBS 88; St&PR 87; WhoAm 76, 78, 80, 82, 84, 86, 88, 90, 94, 95, 96, 97; WhoEnt 92; WhoFI 87, 94; WhoMW 88; WhoSSW 91; WhoWest 92, 96; WhoWor 78, 80, 82*

Gillette, Duane
American. Hostage
One of 52 held by terrorists, Nov 1979 - Jan 1981.
b. 1957?
Source: *NewYTBS 81*

Gillette, King Camp
American. Inventor
Invented safety razor, 1895.
b. Jan 5, 1855 in Fond du Lac, Wisconsin
d. Jul 9, 1932 in Los Angeles, California
Source: *AmBi; BiDAmBL 83; BioIn 1, 7, 11, 15, 16, 17, 18; DcAmB S1; DcNAA; Entr; GayN; InSci; NatCAB 10; WebAB 74, 79; WhAm 1; WhDW; WorAl; WorAlBi*

Gillette, Paul
American. Writer
Author of *Play Misty for Me,* 1971.
b. Oct 1, 1938 in Carbondale, Pennsylvania
d. Jan 6, 1996 in Los Angeles, California
Source: *ConAu 53, 151; NewYTBS 27; WhoUSWr 88; WhoWrEP 89, 92, 95*

Gillette, William Hooker
American. Actor, Dramatist
Starred in play *Sherlock Holmes,* which he adapted from Arthur Conan Doyle's writings.
b. Jul 24, 1853 in Hartford, Connecticut
d. Apr 29, 1937 in Hartford, Connecticut
Source: *AmAu&B; AmBi; ApCAB; BbD; BiD&SB; BioIn 2, 3, 4, 5, 9, 12, 13, 14, 16, 20; Chambr 3; DcAmB S2; DcLEL; FamA&A; FilmgC; IntDcT 3; ModWD; PlP&P; REnAL; RfGAmL 94; TwCBDA; TwYS; WebAB 79; WhAm 1; WhScrn 77*

Gilley, Mickey Leroy
American. Musician
Club named Gilley's was setting for film *Urban Cowboy;* had 1980 pop hit "Stand By Me."
b. Mar 9, 1936 in Natchez, Mississippi
Source: *BioIn 14, 15; ConMus 7; EncFCWM 83; EncRk 88; HarEnCM 87; PenEncP; RkOn 85; WhoAm 78, 80, 82, 84, 86, 88, 90, 92, 94, 95, 96, 97; WhoEnt 92; WhoRock 81; WorAlBi*

Gilliam, Jim
[James William Gilliam]
"Junior"
American. Baseball Player
Infielder, Brooklyn/LA Dodgers, 1953-66, known for consistent play; NL rookie of year, 1953.
b. Oct 17, 1928 in Nashville, Tennessee
d. Oct 8, 1978 in Los Angeles, California
Source: *Ballpl 90; DcAmB S10; WhoBlA 75, 77; WhoProB 73; WhScrn 83*

Gilliam, Terry (Vance)
[Monty Python's Flying Circus; Jerry Gillian]
American. Illustrator, Writer
Created animated sequences for Monty Python comedy TV series, film *Monty Python and the Holy Grail,* 1975.
b. Nov 22, 1940 in Minneapolis, Minnesota
Source: *Au&Arts 19; BiDFilm 94; BioIn 11, 12, 13, 15, 16; ConAu 35NR, 108, 113; ConTFT 5, 12; EncEurC; HalFC 88; IntDcF 2-2; IntMPA 88, 92, 94, 96; IntWW 89, 91, 93; LegTOT; MiSFD 9; ScF&FL 92; VarWW 85; Who 90, 92, 94; WhoAm 80, 82, 84, 86, 88, 90, 92, 94, 95, 96, 97; WhoEnt 92; WhoHol 92; WhoWor 95, 96, 97; WorECar; WorECom*

Gilliatt, Penelope (Ann Douglas Conner)
English. Critic, Writer
Wrote film *Sunday, Bloody Sunday,* 1971; nominated for Oscar; film critic with *New Yorker,* mag. 1968-79.
b. Mar 25, 1932 in London, England
d. May 9, 1993 in London, England
Source: *AnObit 1993; AuNews 2; BioIn 13, 16; ConAu 13R; ConLC 2, 10, 13, 53, 81; ConNov 72, 76, 86, 91; DcLB 14; DcLEL 1940; DrAF 76; DrAPF 80, 91; EncBrWW; EncSF; FacFETw; FemiCLE; FilmgC; HalFC 84, 88; IntAu&W 91; IntWW 83, 91; InWom SUP; Novels; ScF&FL 1, 2; VarWW 85; Who 85, 92; WhoAm 86, 88; WhoE 74; WomWMM; WorAlBi; WorAu 1970; WrDr 76, 92*

Gillies, Clark
"Jethro"
Canadian. Hockey Player
Left wing, 1974-88, mostly with NY Islanders; has won four Stanley Cups.
b. Apr 7, 1954 in Regina, Saskatchewan, Canada
Source: *BioIn 11, 12; HocEn; HocReg 87; NewYTBS 82; WhoAm 80, 82, 84*

Gilligan, Carol
American. Psychologist
Wrote *In a Different Voice,* 1982, which demonstrated that girls place more emphasis on feelings and relationships than boys do.
b. Nov 28, 1936 in New York, New York
Source: *AmDec 1980; BioIn 16; ConAu 142; EncWHA; FemiWr; WhoAm 95; WhoAmW 95; WrDr 96*

Gilligan, John Joyce
American. Politician
Dem. governor of OH, 1971-75.
b. Mar 22, 1921 in Cincinnati, Ohio
Source: *AmCath 80; BiDrAC; BiDrGov 1789; BiDrUSC 89; BioIn 7, 9, 10, 11, 12; IntWW 74, 75, 76, 77, 78, 79, 80, 81; WhoAm 74, 76; WhoAmP 73, 75, 77, 79, 81; WhoGov 72, 75, 77; WhoMW 74, 76*

Gillis, Don
American. Composer
Produced NBC Toscanini-conducted concerts, 1950s; wrote *Symphony No. 5 1/2.*
b. Jun 17, 1912 in Cameron, Missouri
d. Jan 10, 1978 in Columbia, South Carolina
Source: *AmComp; ASCAP 66, 80; Baker 78, 84, 92; BiDAmM; BioIn 1, 2, 3, 11; ConAmC 76, 82; DcCM; DcCom&M 79; NewAmDM; NewGrDA 86; NewGrDM 80; NewGrDO; WhoMus 72*

Gilliss, James Melville
American. Astronomer, Naval Officer
Responsible for the establishment the Naval Observatory, Washington, DC.
b. Sep 6, 1811 in Georgetown, Maryland
d. Feb 9, 1865 in Washington, District of Columbia
Source: *Alli; AmBi; ApCAB; BiDAmS; BilnAmS; BioIn 12, 15; DcAmAu; DcAmB; DcNAA; InSci; NatCAB 9; TwCBDA; WebAB 74, 79; WebAMB; WhAm HS*

Gillman, Sidney
American. Football Coach
Successful coach of several NFL teams: LA Rams, 1955-59, San Diego, 1960-71; Hall of Fame, 1983.
b. Oct 26, 1911 in Minneapolis, Minnesota
Source: *BiDAmSp FB; BioIn 15; CmCal; NewYTBS 81; WhoFtbl 74; WhoSpor*

Gillmore, Frank
American. Labor Union Official
Founder, first pres., Actors Equity Assn., 1929-37.
b. May 14, 1867 in New York, New York
d. Mar 29, 1943 in New York, New York
Source: *BiDAmL; BiDAmLL; CurBio 43; NotNAT B; WhAm 2; WhoStg 1906, 1908; WhScrn 83; WhThe*

Gillott, Jacky
English. Author, Journalist
Early British TV woman newscaster; wrote *Salvage,* 1968.
b. Sep 24, 1939 in Bromley, England
d. Sep 19, 1980 in Somerset, England
Source: *AnObit 1980; BioIn 13; ConAu 102; DcLB 14; IntAu&W 77; InWom SUP; Novels; WrDr 80*

Gillray, James
English. Cartoonist
Political cartoonist whose work covered Napoleonic War, c.1802; credited with introducing English style, format of cartoon to Europe.
b. Aug 13, 1756 in Chelsea, England
d. Jun 1, 1815 in London, England
Source: *Alli; BkIE; DcBrBI; DcBrWA; NewC; NewCol 75; WhDW*

Gilman, Alfred G
American. Scientist
Pioneer in the studies of signal transduction; won Horwitz Prize, 1989.
b. Jul 1, 1941 in New Haven, Connecticut
Source: *AmMWSc 92; WhoAm 90*

Gilman, Daniel Coit
American. Educator
First pres. of Johns Hopkins U, 1875-1901; Carnegie Institution, 1901-04.
b. Jul 6, 1831 in Norwich, Connecticut
d. Oct 13, 1908 in Norwich, Connecticut
Source: *Alli SUP; AmAu&B; AmBi; AmSocL; ApCAB; BenetAL 91; BiDAmEd; BiD&SB; BiDSA; BioIn 1, 2, 3, 5, 6, 8, 14, 19; CmCal; CyEd; DcAmAu; DcAmB; DcAmLiB; DcAmMeB 84; DcNAA; EncAB-H 1974, 1996; EncWB; HarEnUS; LinLib L, S; McGEWB; MorMA; NatCAB 5; OxCAmH; OxCAmL 65, 83, 95; REnAL; TwCBDA; WebAB 74, 79; WebBD 83; WhAm 1*

Gilman, Dorothy
[Dorothy Gilman Butters]
American. Author
Created geriatric sleuth, Mrs. Pollifax, in young people's series.
b. Jun 25, 1923 in New Brunswick, New Jersey
Source: *AmAu&B; Au&Wr 71; AuBYP 2, 3; BioIn 7, 8, 10, 12, 14; ConAu 1R, 2NR, 30NR, X; CrtSuMy; DcLP 87B; FemiCLE; GrWomMW; IntAu&W 91, 93; InWom SUP; LegTOT; ScF&FL 92; SmATA 5; SpyFic; TwCCr&M 80, 85, 91; WhoAm 78, 80, 82, 84, 86, 88, 90, 92; WhoAmW 66, 68, 70; WorAl; WorAlBi; WrDr 82, 84, 86, 88, 90, 92, 94, 96*

Gilman, Lawrence
American. Critic, Author
With *NY Herald Tribune,* 1923-39; wrote *Toscanini and Great Music,* 1938.
b. Jul 5, 1878 in Flushing, New York
d. Sep 8, 1939 in Franconia, New Hampshire
Source: *AmAu&B; ApCAB X; Baker 78, 84, 92; BiDAmM; BioIn 1, 2, 4; DcAmB S2; DcNAA; NatCAB 35; NewGrDA 86; NewGrDM 80; REnAL; TwCA, SUP; WhAm 1*

Gilmore, Artis
American. Basketball Player
Center, 1971-88, with Kentucky in ABA, Chicago, San Antonio and Boston in NBA; ABA MVP, 1972; all-time NBA leader in field goal percentage.
b. Sep 21, 1949 in Chipley, Florida
Source: *BiDAmSp BK; BioIn 13; InB&W 85; LegTOT; NewYTBS 82; WhoAm 78, 80, 82, 84, 86, 88; WhoBbl 73; WhoBlA 88, 92; WhoSpor; WhoSSW 86; WorAl; WorAlBi*

Gilmore, Eddy Lanier King
American. Journalist
Foreign correspondent, Associated Press, 1935-67; won Pulitzer, 1947, for Stalin interview.
b. May 28, 1907 in Selma, Alabama
d. Oct 6, 1967 in London, England
Source: *Au&Wr 71; ConAu 5R; CurBio 47, 67; WhAm 4*

Gilmore, Gary Mark
American. Murderer
First execution, by firing squad, following reinstatement of death penalty.
b. 1941
d. Jan 18, 1977 in Point of Mountain, Utah
Source: *BioIn 11, 12, 13*

Gilmore, Patrick Sarsfield
American. Bandleader
Noted for flamboyant showmanship, wrote "When Johnny Comes Marching Home," 1863.
b. Dec 25, 1829 in County Galway, Ireland
d. Sep 24, 1892 in Saint Louis, Missouri
Source: *AmBi; ApCAB; Baker 78, 84; BioIn 1, 2, 3, 4, 8, 11, 16, 18; ChhPo; DcAmB; DcCathB; DcIrB 78, 88; Drake SUP; NatCAB 3; NewGrDM 80; OxCAmH; PenDiMP; TwCBDA; WebAB 74, 79; WhAm HS*

Gilmore, Virginia
[Sherman Virginia Poole]
American. Actor
Broadway star, 1940s, who starred in 40 films; married to Yul Brynner, 1944-60.
b. Jul 26, 1919 in Del Monte, California
d. Mar 28, 1986 in Santa Barbara, California
Source: *AnObit 1986; BiE&WWA; BioIn 9, 10, 14, 15; FilmEn; FilmgC; ForYSC; HalFC 80, 84, 88; HolP 40; MotPP; MovMk; NotNAT; WhoHol A; WhoThe 77A; WhThe*

Gilmour, Billy
[Hamilton Livingstone Gilmour]
Canadian. Hockey Player
Played on Canadian amateur teams, early 1900s; Hall of Fame, 1962.
b. Mar 21, 1885 in Ottawa, Ontario, Canada
d. Mar 13, 1959 in Mount Royal, Quebec, Canada
Source: *WhoHcky 73*

Gilmour, Dave
[Pink Floyd; David Gilmour]
English. Singer, Musician
Joined group, 1968; his guitar playing is one of band's trademarks.
b. Mar 6, 1944 in Cambridge, England
Source: *BioIn 13; OnThGG; RkOn 85; WhoRocM 82*

Gilmour, Doug
Canadian. Hockey Player
Center, St. Louis Blues, 1983-88, Calgary Flames, 1988-92, Toronto Maple Leafs, 1992—; won Selke Trophy, 1993.
b. Jun 25, 1963 in Kingston, Ontario, Canada
Source: *BioIn 20; News 94, 94-3; WhoAm 95, 96, 97*

Gilot, Francoise
French. Author, Artist
Mistress of Pablo Picasso, 1946-53; had two of his children; wrote *Life with Picasso,* 1964.
b. Nov 26, 1921 in Neuilly-sur-Seine, France
Source: *BioIn 2, 7, 8, 10, 12, 15, 17, 19, 20, 21; ConAu 108; WhoAmW 74, 75; WhoFr 79; WhoWor 74*

Gilpatric, Roswell L(eavitt)
American. Government Official
US Deputy Secretary of Defense, 1961-64.
b. Nov 6, 1904 in New York, New York
d. Mar 15, 1996 in New York, New York
Source: *BioIn 5, 6, 7, 8, 11; ColdWar 1; CurBio 64; PolProf J, K; St&PR 91; WhoAm 90*

Gilpin, Charles Sidney
American. Actor
One of first black actors to win wide stage following; played title role in *The Emperor Jones* which ran for three years.
b. Nov 20, 1878 in Richmond, Virginia
d. May 6, 1930 in Eldridge Park, New Jersey
Source: *AmBi; BiDAfM; BioIn 6, 8, 9, 13; CamGWoT; DcAmB; DcTwCCu 5; FamA&A; InB&W 80, 85; NatCAB 23; OxCThe 67, 83; WebAB 74, 79; WhAm 1; WhoHol B; WhScrn 74, 77*

Gilpin, Laura
American. Photographer, Author
Known for photographic studies of Navaho Indians.
b. Apr 22, 1891 in Colorado Springs, Colorado
d. Nov 30, 1979 in Santa Fe, New Mexico
Source: *BioAmW; BioIn 10, 11, 12, 13; ConAu 111; ConPhot 82, 88, 95; EncWB; GrLiveH; ICPEnP; InWom SUP; MacBEP; NewYTBS 86; NorAmWA; WhAmArt 85; WhoAmA 76, 78, 80N, 82N, 84N, 86N, 89N, 91N, 93N; WhoWest 74*

Gilroy, Frank Daniel
American. Dramatist
TV script writer; won Tony, Pulitzer for *The Subject Was Roses,* 1965.
b. Oct 13, 1925 in New York, New York
Source: *AmAu&B; BenetAL 91; BioIn 6, 7, 10, 12, 15, 18, 19, 21; CamGWoT; ConAu 32NR, 81; ConDr 82, 88; ConTFT 3; CroCD; CurBio 65; DcLB 7; DcLEL 1940; DrAPF 91; HalFC 88; IntAu&W 82; IntMPA 92; McGEWD 84; ModWD; NotNAT; OxCAmL 83; OxCAmT 84; WhoAm 74, 76, 78, 80, 82, 84, 86, 88, 90, 92, 94, 95, 96, 97; WhoE 74; WhoEnt 92; WhoThe 81; WorAlBi; WrDr 86, 92*

Gilruth, Robert Rowe
American. Aeronautical Engineer
Project director, Space Task Group, NASA, 1958-72.
b. Oct 8, 1913 in Nashwauk, Minnesota
Source: *AmMWSc 82, 92; BioIn 2, 5, 6, 9, 12; CurBio 63; FacFETw; IntWW 74, 75, 76, 77, 78, 79, 80, 81, 82, 83, 89, 91, 93; McGMS 80; WhoAm 78, 80, 82, 84, 86, 88, 90, 92, 94, 95, 96, 97; WhoEng 88; WhoFrS 84; WhoGov 72; WhoScEn 94, 96; WhoWor 74, 76, 78*

Gilson, Etienne Henry
French. Philosopher, Historian
Expert on history of philosophy; wrote *Philosophy of St. Thomas Aquinas,* 1919.
b. Jun 13, 1884 in Paris, France
d. Sep 19, 1978 in Cravant, France
Source: *CathA 1930; ConAu 81, 102; IntWW 74; McGEWB; NewCol 75; OxCFr; TwCA, SUP; Who 74; WhoWor 74*

Gilstrap, Suzy
American. Actor
Paraplegic star in TV movie "Skyward," 1980; "Skyward Christmas,"
b. Jan 1966
Source: *BioIn 12, 15*

Gimbel, Adam
American. Retailer
Emigrated to US, 1835; founded dept. store in Philadelphia, 1894.
b. 1815 in Bavaria, Germany
d. 1896
Source: *NewCol 75*

Gimbel, Bernard Feustman
American. Retailer
Grandson of Adam Gimbel; pres., Gimbel Brothers, 1927-53.
b. Apr 10, 1885 in Vincennes, Indiana
d. Sep 29, 1966 in New York, New York
Source: *BiDAmBL 83; BioIn 1, 2, 3, 5, 7, 9; CurBio 50, 66; DcAmB S8; NatCAB 53; WhAm 4; WorAl*

Gimbel, Peter Robin
American. Explorer, Filmmaker
Explored, filmed two TV documentaries on sunken ocean liner *Andrea Doria,* 1976, 1984.
b. Feb 14, 1928 in New York, New York
d. Jul 12, 1987 in New York, New York
Source: *BioIn 11, 12, 13; CurBio 82, 87; NewYTBS 87; WhAm 9; WhoAm 76, 78, 80, 82, 84, 86*

Gimbel, Richard
American. Retailer
Grandson of Adam Gimbel; curator of aeronautical literature at Yale.
b. Jul 26, 1898 in Atlantic City, New Jersey
d. May 27, 1970 in Munich, Germany (West)
Source: *BioIn 8, 9; DcAmBC; NewYTBE 70*

Gimbel, Sophie Haas
"Sophie of Saks Fifth Avenue"
American. Fashion Designer
Created classic clothes for large private clientele, as well as Broadway shows, 1931-65; introduced sweater dress, culotte, balloon skirt; wife of Adam.
b. 1898 in Houston, Texas
d. Nov 28, 1981 in New York, New York
Source: *NewYTBS 81; WhoAmW 74; WorFshn*

Gimpel, Jakob
American. Musician
Brilliant concert pianist, noted for Schumann, Chopin repertoire; won Ben-Gurion award.
b. Apr 16, 1906 in Lemberg, Austria
d. Mar 12, 1989 in Los Angeles, California
Source: *Baker 84, 92; BioIn 16; PenDiMP; WhoAmM 83; WhoMus 72*

Ginastera, Alberto Evaristo
Argentine. Composer
Modern eclectic-style operas include *Beatrix Cenci,* 1971; *Bomarzo,* 1967, was banned from Argentina for its sexual violence content.
b. Apr 11, 1916 in Buenos Aires, Argentina
d. Jun 25, 1983 in Geneva, Switzerland
Source: *Baker 84; BiDAmM; CurBio 71; DcCM; IntWW 74; LatAmCC; McGEWB; MusMk; NewGrDM 80; OxCMus; WhoMus 72; WhoWor 74*

Gingold, Hermione Ferdinanda
English. Actor
Films include *Gigi,* 1958; won Grammy for narration of "Peter and the Wolf."
b. Dec 9, 1897 in London, England
d. May 24, 1987 in New York, New York
Source: *BiE&WWA; ConAu 5R; ConTFT 2, 5; CurBio 58, 87; DcNaB 1986; EncMT; FilmgC; InWom SUP; MotPP; MovMk; NotNAT; PlP&P; VarWW 85; WhAm 9; WhoAm 86; WhoHol A*

Gingold, Josef
American. Violinist
Renowned teacher; has served on many international competition juries.
b. Oct 28, 1909 in Brest-Litovsk, Russia
Source: *Baker 78, 84, 92; BioIn 9, 14, 16, 17, 20, 21; ConMus 6; IntWWM 90; NewAmDM; NewGrDA 86; NewGrDM 80; NewYTBS 95; WhAm 11; WhoAm 84, 86; WhoMus 72; WhoWorJ 72, 78*

Gingrich, Arnold
American. Editor, Author
Published *Esquire,* 1952-76; emphasized magazine's literary qualities.
b. Dec 5, 1903 in Grand Rapids, Michigan
d. Jul 9, 1976 in Ridgewood, New Jersey
Source: *AmAu&B; Au&Wr 71; BenetAL 91; BioIn 5, 6, 9, 10, 11, 13, 20; BlueB 76; CelR; ConAu 65, 69; CurBio 61, 76, 76N; DcLB 137; EncAJ; EncTwCJ; IntAu&W 76, 77; IntWW 74, 75, 76, 77; NatCAB 62; NewYTBS 76; REnAL; St&PR 75; WhAm 7; WhNAA; WhoAm 74, 76; WhoWor 74; WorFshn; WrDr 76*

Gingrich, Newt(on Leroy)
American. Politician
Republican congressman from GA, Speaker of the House, 1995—; known for guer rilla-style tactics.
b. Jun 17, 1943 in Harrisburg, Pennsylvania
Source: *AlmAP 80, 82, 84, 88, 92, 96; BiDrUSC 89; BioIn 14, 16; CelR 90; CngDr 79, 81, 83, 85, 87, 89, 91, 93, 95; ConAu 131; CurBio 89; DrAS 74H, 78H; EncAB-H 1996; IntWW 91, 93; LegTOT; News 91, 91-1; NewYTBS 88, 90; PolsAm 84; WhoAm 80, 82, 84, 86, 88, 90, 92, 94, 95, 96, 97; WhoAmP 79, 81, 83, 85, 87, 89, 91, 93, 95; WhoSSW 80, 86, 88, 91, 95, 97; WhoWor 96, 97; WrDr 94, 96*

Ginott, Haim
American. Author, Psychologist
Book *Between Parent and Child,* 1965, sold over 1.5 million copies, translated into more than 12 languages.
b. Aug 5, 1922 in Tel Aviv, Palestine
d. Nov 4, 1973 in New York, New York
Source: *AmAu&B; ConAu 45; NewYTBE 73; WhAm 6*

Ginsberg, Allen
American. Poet
Associated with "Beat" movement; best-known poem *Howl,* 1956.
b. Jun 3, 1926 in Newark, New Jersey
d. Apr 5, 1997 in New York, New York
Source: *AmAu&B; AmCulL; AmPeW; AmWr S2; AuNews 1; Benet 87, 96; BenetAL 91; BioIn 7, 8, 9, 10, 11, 12, 13, 14, 15, 16, 17, 18, 19, 20, 21; BlueB 76; CamGEL; CamGLE; CamHAL; CasWL; CelR, 90; CmCal; ConAu 1R, 2NR, 41NR; ConLC 1, 2, 3, 4, 6, 13, 36, 69; ConPo 70, 75, 80, 85, 91, 96; CroCAP; CurBio 87; DcLB 5, 16, 169; DcLEL 1940; DcTwCCu 1; DrAP 75; DrAPF 80, 91; EncAB-H 1974, 1996; EncWL, 2, 3; FacFETw; GayLesB; GayLL; GrWrEL P; IntAu&W 77, 82, 89, 91, 93; IntvTCA 2; IntWW 74, 75, 76, 77, 78, 79, 80, 81, 82, 83, 89, 91, 93; IntWWP 77; LegTOT; LinLib L, S; LngCTC; LNinSix; MagSAmL; MajTwCW; MakMC; McGEWB; ModAL, S1, S2; MugS; NewCon; OxCAmL 65, 83, 95; OxCTwCP; PenC AM; PlP&P A; PoeCrit 4; PolProf E, J; RAdv 1, 14, 13-1; RComAH; REn; REnAL; RfGAmL 87, 94; RGFAP; RGTwCWr; ScF&FL 92; TwCWr; WebAB 74, 79; WebE&AL; WhDW; WhoAm 74, 76, 78, 80, 82, 84, 86, 88, 90, 92, 94, 95, 96, 97; WhoE 79, 86, 89, 91, 93, 97; WhoEnt 92; WhoHol 92; WhoTwCL; WhoUSWr 88; WhoWest 82; WhoWor 74, 78, 80, 82, 84, 87, 89, 91, 93, 95, 96, 97; WhoWorJ 72, 78; WhoWrEP 89, 92, 95; WorAlBi; WorAu 1950; WorLitC; WrDr 76, 80, 82, 84, 86, 88, 90, 92, 94, 96*

Ginsberg, Mitchell I(rving)
American. Educator
Expert on social welfare and antipoverty policy.
b. Oct 20, 1915
d. Mar 2, 1996 in New York, New York
Source: *BioIn 9; CurBio 71, 96N; WhAm 11; WhoAm 74, 76, 78, 80, 82, 84, 86; WhoAmJ 80; WhoE 74, 75*

Ginsburg, Charles P
American. Engineer
Contributed to the development of videotape recording, 1956; inducted into the Nat. Inventors Hall of Fame, 1990.
b. Jul 1920
d. Apr 9, 1992 in Eugene, Oregon
Source: *AmMWSc 82, 86, 89, 92; BioIn 9; Dun&B 79, 86; WhoEng 80, 88*

Ginsburg, Douglas Howard
American. Judge
Appointed to Supreme Court by Ronald Reagan, 1987; withdrew name from consideration following news of past marijuana smoking.
b. May 25, 1946 in Chicago, Illinois
Source: *BioIn 15; CngDr 87, 89, 91, 93, 95; NewYTBS 87; OxCSupC; WhoAm 86, 88, 90, 92, 94, 95, 96, 97; WhoAmL 87, 90, 92, 94, 96; WhoAmP 91; WhoE 89, 91, 93, 95, 97*

Ginsburg, Ruth Bader
American. Supreme Court Justice
Became the US Supreme Court's 107th justice, 1993.
b. Mar 15, 1933 in New York, New York
Source: *BioIn 11, 12, 13; CngDr 81, 83, 85, 87, 89, 91, 93; ConAu 53; CurBio 94; DrAS 74P, 78P; InWom SUP; News 93; WhoAm 76, 78, 80, 82, 84, 86, 88, 90, 92, 94, 95, 96, 97; WhoAmJ 80; WhoAmL 78, 79, 83, 85, 87, 90, 92, 94, 96; WhoAmP 91, 93, 95; WhoAmW 70, 72, 74, 75, 77, 81, 83, 85, 87, 89, 95, 97; WhoE 74, 75, 77, 83, 85, 86, 89, 91, 93, 95, 97; WhoWor 95, 96, 97; WomLaw; WomStre*

Ginzburg, Aleksandr Ilich
Russian. Political Activist, Poet
Published underground poetry that led to first arrest, jail sentence, 1960; set up fund for families of political prisoners, 1974.
b. Nov 21, 1936 in Leningrad, Union of Soviet Socialist Republics
Source: *BiDSovU; DcPol; FacFETw; HanRL; IntWW 91; NewYTBS 78, 79*

Ginzburg, Natalia
Italian. Author
Novelist of many family-slanted books, including *The City and the House,* 1987; wrote 8 plays during the years 1965-71.
b. Jul 14, 1916 in Palermo, Sicily, Italy
d. Oct 7, 1991 in Rome, Italy
Source: *AnObit 1991; Benet 87, 96; BioIn 10, 15; BlmGWL; CasWL; ConAu 33NR, 85, 135; ConFLW 84; ConLC 5, 11, 54, 70; ContDcW 89; CurBio 90, 91N; CyWA 89; DcItL 1; EncCoWW; EncWL 2, 3; EncWT; EuWr 13; FacFETw; GrWomW; IntAu&W 77, 89; IntDcWB; IntWW 74, 75, 76, 77, 78, 79, 80, 81, 82, 83, 89, 91; MajTwCW; McGEWD 84; ModWoWr; NewYTBS 91; PenNWW A; RfGWoL 95; WhoWor 74, 91*

Ginzburg, Ralph
American. Publisher, Journalist
Editor, *Moneysworth* mag., 1971—; wrote *Unhurried View of Erotica,* 1956.
b. Oct 28, 1929 in New York, New York
Source: *Au&Wr 71; BioIn 8, 9, 10, 11; ConAu 21R; PolProf J; WhoAdv 80, 90; WhoAm 74, 76, 78, 80, 82, 84, 86, 88, 90, 92, 94, 95, 96, 97; WhoAmJ 80; WhoE 85, 86; WhoUSWr 88; WhoWor 74, 76; WhoWrEP 89, 92, 95*

Gioconda, Lisa Gherardini
[Mona Lisa]
Italian. Noblewoman
Subject of Leonardo da Vinci's famed portrait, which is noted for its enigmatic smile.
b. 1479, Italy
Source: *BioIn 11; InWom SUP*

Giolitti, Giovanni
Italian. Statesman
Five-time premier, 1892-1921; opposed Italy's entry into WW I.
b. Oct 22, 1842 in Mondovi, Sardinia
d. Jul 17, 1928 in Cavour, Italy
Source: *BioIn 8, 10; DcTwHis; FacFETw; McGEWB; NewCol 75; WebBD 83; WhDW*

Giono, Jean
French. Author, Dramatist
Imprisoned for pacifist views, WW II; best-known novels adapted to screen: *Harvest,* 1937; *The Baker's Wife,* 1938.
b. Mar 30, 1895 in Manosque, France
d. Oct 9, 1970 in Manosque, France
Source: *Benet 96; BiDMoPL; BioIn 1, 4, 5, 6, 7, 8, 9, 13, 17; CasWL; ClDMEL 47, 80; CnMD; CnMWL; ConAu 2NR, 29R, 35NR, 45; ConLC 4, 11; CyWA 58, 89; DcArts; DcLB 72; DcTwCCu 2; EncWL, 2, 3; EvEuW; GuFrLit 1; MajTwCW; McGEWD 72, 84; ModFrL; ModRL; ModWD; OxCFilm; OxCFr; PenC EUR; RAdv 14, 13-2; REn; RfGWoL 95; TwCA, SUP; TwCWr; WhDW; WhoTwCL*

Giordano, Luca
"Fa Presto"
Italian. Artist
Student of Ribera; lively, airy compositions combined Neapolitan, Venetian styles; painted ceiling of Escorial, Madrid, 1692.
b. Oct 18, 1632 in Naples, Italy
d. Jan 3, 1705 in Naples, Italy
Source: *BioIn 5, 10, 13, 17, 19; ClaDrA; DcBiPP; DcCathB; IntDcAA 90; McGDA; NewCol 75; OxCArt; WhDW*

Giordano, Umberto
Italian. Composer
Ten operas include *Andrea Chenier,* 1896.
b. Aug 27, 1867 in Foggia, Italy
d. Nov 12, 1948 in Milan, Italy
Source: *Baker 78, 84, 92; BioIn 1, 3, 8, 12, 17; BriBkM 80; CmOp; CmpBCM; CompSN; DcCom 77; DcCom&M 79; IntDcOp; MetOEnc; NewAmDM; NewEOp 71; NewGrDM 80; NewOxM; OxCMus; OxDcOp; PenDiMP A; WebBD 83*

Giorgi, Giovanni
Italian. Physicist
Originator of widely used Giorgi International System of Measurement which utilizes the metre, kilogram, second and joule as units of measurement.
b. Nov 27, 1871 in Lucca, Italy
d. Aug 19, 1950 in Castiglioncello, Italy
Source: *BioIn 2; DcScB; ObitOF 79*

Giorgio, Francesco di
Italian. Architect, Artist, Sculptor
Paintings include *The Rape of Europa, The Chess Players.*
b. 1439 in Siena, Italy
d. 1502 in Siena, Italy
Source: *NewCol 75*

Giorgione
[Giorgio Barbarelli; Giorgio da Castelfranco]
Italian. Artist
Renaissance painter, chief master of Venetian school of his time; influenced contemporaries such as Titian: *The Tempest,* c. 1505.
b. 1477 in Castelfranco, Italy
d. 1510 in Veneto, Italy
Source: *AtlBL; DcBiPP; LegTOT; LinLib S; REn; WebBD 83; WorAl*

Giorno, John
American. Poet
Writings include *Poems,* 1967; *Balling Buddha,* 1970.
b. Dec 4, 1936 in New York, New York
Source: *BioIn 10, 15; ConAu 33R; ConPo 70; DrAP 75; DrAPF 80, 83, 91; IntvTCA 2; IntWWP 77; WhoAmA 86, 89, 91, 93; WhoE 75, 77, 91*

Giotto di Bondone
Italian. Artist, Architect
His paintings among the greatest in Italian, European art; designed campanile, "Giotti's Tower," at cathedral in Florence.
b. 1266? in Vespignano, Italy
d. Jan 8, 1337 in Florence, Italy
Source: *AtlBL; BioIn 1, 2, 3, 4, 5, 6, 7, 8, 10, 11, 12, 13, 18, 20; IlEncMy; MacEA; McGEWB; NewC; OxCArt; OxCEng 85; REn*

Giovanni, Nikki
[Yolande Cornelia Giovanni, Jr.]
"Princess of Black Poetry"
American. Author, Poet
Writings include *My House,* 1972; *The Women and the Men,* 1975.
b. Jun 7, 1943 in Knoxville, Tennessee
Source: *AfrAmAl 6; AmWomWr; ArtclWW 2; AuBYP 2S, 3; AuNews 1; Benet 87; BenetAL 91; BioIn 9, 10, 12, 13, 14, 16; BlkAuII, 92; BlkAWP; BlkLC; BlkWAm; BlkWr 1, 2; BlkWWr; BlmGWL; BroadAu; CamGLE; CamHAL; CelR, 90; ChhPo S2; ChlBkCr; ChlLR 6; CivR 74; ConAu 6AS, 18NR, 29R, 41NR; ConBlB 9; ConLC 2, 4, 19, 64; ConPo 75, 80, 85, 91, 96; CroCAP; CurBio 73; CyWA 89; DcLB 4, 5, 41; DcLEL 1940; DcTwCCu 1, 5; DrAP 75; DrAPF 80, 91; Ebony 1; EncAACR; FacFETw; FemiCLE; FifBJA; GrWomW; InB&W 80, 85; IntvTCA 2; IntWWP 77; InWom SUP; LegTOT; LivgBAA; MagSAmL; MajAl; MajTwCW; ModAWP; ModWoWr; NegAl 76, 83, 89; NotBlAW 1; OxCAmL 83, 95; OxCTwCP; OxCWoWr 95; RAdv 1; RGTwCWr; SchCGBL; SelBAAf; SelBAAu; SmATA 24; SouWr; TwCChW 78, 95; TwCYAW; WhoAfA 96; WhoAm 74, 76, 78, 80, 82, 84, 86, 88, 90, 92, 94, 95, 96; WhoAmW 81, 89, 91, 93, 95; WhoBlA 75, 77, 80, 85, 88, 90, 92, 94; WhoUSWr 88; WhoWrEP 89, 92, 95;*

WorAu 1970; WrDr 76, 80, 82, 84, 86, 88, 90, 92, 96

Giovanni di Paolo
[Giovanni di Grazia]
Italian. Artist
Major painter of Sienese school.
b. 1403 in Siena, Italy
d. 1482 in Siena, Italy
Source: *NewCol 75*

Giovannitti, Arturo
Italian. Poet
Best-known work in *Arrows in the Gale*, 1914.
b. Jan 7, 1884 in Campobasso, Italy
d. Dec 31, 1959 in New York, New York
Source: *AmAu&B; BenetAL 91; BiDAmL; BiDAmLL; ConAmL; DcAmB S6; DcAmSR; EncAL; OxCAmL 65, 83, 95; REn; REnAL; TwCA*

Giovenco, John Vincent
American. Hotel Executive
Pres., CEO, ITT Sheraton, 1993—.
b. Apr 2, 1936 in Chicago, Illinois
Source: *Dun&B 90; St&PR 91; WhoAm 78, 80, 82, 84, 90; WhoFI 89*

Gipp, George
"Gipper"
American. Football Player
All-America running back, Notre Dame, 1917-20; died of pneumonia; Ronald Reagan portrayed him in film *Knute Rockne All American*, 1940.
b. Feb 18, 1895 in Laurium, Michigan
d. Dec 14, 1920 in South Bend, Indiana
Source: *BiDAmSp FB; BioIn 3, 5, 6, 8, 10, 12; WhoFtbl 74; WhoSpor*

Gipson, Lawrence Henry
American. Historian, Educator
Wrote 15-vol. *British Empire Before the American Revolution;* won 1962 Pulitzer for 10th vol., *Thunder Clouds Gather in the West.*
b. Dec 7, 1880 in Greeley, Colorado
d. Sep 26, 1971 in Bethlehem, Pennsylvania
Source: *AmAu&B; Au&Wr 71; BioIn 3, 8, 9, 10, 13; ConAu 3NR, 5R, 33R; CurBio 54, 71, 71N; DcAmB S9; DcLB 17; NewYTBE 70, 71; OxCAmL 65; OxCCan, SUP; WhAm 6; WhE&EA; WhNAA; WorAu 1950*

Gipsy Kings, The
French. Music Group
Flamenco band formed in 1976; has 15 gold & platinum records worldwide; albums include *Gipsy Kings*, 1987; *Mosaique*, 1989.
Source: *ConMus 8; WhoAm 92, 94, 95, 96, 97; WhoEnt 92*

Girard, Stephen
American. Philanthropist
Helped to finance US in War of 1812; founded Girard College, Philadelphia, for poor boys.
b. May 20, 1750 in Bordeaux, France
d. Dec 26, 1831 in Philadelphia, Pennsylvania
Source: *AmBi; ApCAB; BiDAmBL 83; BiDSocW; BioIn 1, 2, 3, 4, 7, 11, 14, 21; CopCroC; CyEd; DcAmB; DcAmImH; Drake; EncAB-H 1974, 1996; EncABHB 6; HarEnUS; LinLib S; LuthC 75; McGEWB; MorMA; NatCAB 7; OxCAmH; TwCBDA; WebAB 74, 79; WebBD 83; WhAm HS*

Girardon, Francois
French. Sculptor
Louis XIV's designer who produced decorative Apollo series for Versailles, 1670s; also designed Richelieu's tomb.
b. 1628 in Troyes, France
d. Sep 1, 1715 in Paris, France
Source: *BioIn 10, 13; DcArts; DcBiPP; DcCathB; IntDcAA 90; LegTOT; McGDA; McGEWB; OxCArt; OxCFilm; OxCFr; OxDcArt; WorAl; WorAlBi*

Girardot, Annie
French. Actor
Won the Cesar (French Oscar) for *No Time For Breakfast*, 1975.
b. Oct 25, 1931 in Paris, France
Source: *FilmAG WE, 80, 84, 86, 88, 92, 94, 96; IntWW 91; ItaFilm; NewYTBE 72; OxCFilm; WhoFr 79; WhoHol 92, A; WorEFlm*

Giraud, Henri Honore
French. Army Officer
Escaped German prison camp, re-establishing French army; military chief, North African campaign, 1943.
b. Jan 18, 1879 in Paris, France
d. Mar 11, 1949 in Dijon, France
Source: *BioIn 1, 2, 3; CurBio 42, 49; EncTR 91; FacFETw; HisEWW*

Giraudoux, Jean
[Hippolyte-Jean Giraudoux]
French. Dramatist, Author, Diplomat
Master of imagery, impressionistic style: *Madwoman of Chaillot*, 1945.
b. Oct 29, 1882 in Bellac, France
d. Jan 31, 1944 in Paris, France
Source: *AtlBL; Au&Wr 71; Benet 87; BioIn 1, 2, 4, 5, 7, 9, 12, 14, 15, 16; CamGWoT; CasWL; ClDMEL 47, 80; CnMD; CnMWL; CnThe; ConAu 104; CurBio 44; CyWA 58; DcLB 65; DcTwCCu 2; EncWL, 2, 3; EncWT; Ent; EuWr 9; EvEuW; FacFETw; GrFLW; GuFrLit 1; HisEWW; LegTOT; LinLib L, S; LngCTC; MajMD 2; McGEWB; McGEWD 72; ModFrL; ModRL; ModWD; NewC; NotNAT A, B; Novels; OxCAmT 84; OxCEng 67, 85, 95; OxCFr; OxCThe 67, 83; PenC EUR; PlP&P; RAdv 14, 13-2; RComWL; REn; REnWD; ScF&FL 1, 92; TwCA, SUP; TwCLC 2, 7; TwCWr; WebBD 83; WhDW; WhoTwCL; WhThe; WorAl; WorAlBi*

Girdler, Tom Mercer
American. Manufacturer
Chairman, Republic Steel, 1930-56.
b. May 19, 1877 in Clark County, Indiana
d. Feb 4, 1965 in Easton, Maryland
Source: *BiDAmBL 83; BioIn 4, 7; CurBio 44, 65; DcAmB S7; IndAu 1917; WhAm 4*

Giroud, Francoise
Swiss. Journalist, Politician
France's first minister of women, 1974-76.
b. Sep 21, 1916 in Geneva, Switzerland
Source: *AuNews 1; BiDFrPL; BioIn 10, 11, 17; ConAu 17NR, 39NR, 81; ContDcW 89; CurBio 75; IntAu&W 82, 86, 89; IntDcWB; IntWW 74, 75, 76, 77, 78, 79, 80, 81, 82, 83, 89, 91, 93; InWom SUP; NewYTBS 74; WhoFr 79; WhoWor 74; WomFir; WomWMM*

Giroux, Robert
American. Editor, Publisher
Chairman, Farrar, Straus, and Giroux, Inc, 1973—.
b. Apr 8, 1914 in New Jersey
Source: *AmCath 80; BioIn 12, 13, 15, 16; ConAu 28NR, 52NR, 107; CurBio 82; WhoAm 74, 76, 78, 80, 82, 84, 86, 88, 90, 92, 94, 95, 96, 97; WhoWor 74*

Girtin, Thomas
English. Artist
Landscape watercolorist; introduced new techniques in shading, tinting: *The White House at Chelsea*, 1800.
b. Feb 18, 1775 in London, England
d. Nov 9, 1802 in London, England
Source: *AtlBL; BioIn 1, 2, 3, 4, 10, 11, 13; DcArts; DcBiPP; DcBrWA; DcNaB; IntDcAA 90; McGDA; OxCArt; OxDcArt*

Giscard d'Estaing, Valery
French. Politician
Pres. of France, 1974-81.
b. Feb 2, 1926 in Koblenz, Germany
Source: *BiDFrPL; BioIn 7, 8, 10, 11, 12, 13, 14, 16, 17, 18, 21; BioNews 74; ColdWar 1; ConAu 111; CurBio 67, 74; DcTwHis; EncCW; EncWB; FacFETw; IntWW 74, 75, 76, 77, 78, 79, 80, 81, 82, 83, 89, 91, 93; IntYB 78, 79, 80, 81, 82; LegTOT; LinLib S; NewYTBS 77, 88; PolLCWE; Who 74, 82, 83, 85, 88, 90, 92, 94; WhoFr 79; WhoWor 76, 78, 80, 82, 84, 87, 89, 91; WorAl; WorAlBi*

Gish, Dorothy
American. Actor
Played in over 75 films, 1912-22, including *Orphans of the Storm.*
b. Mar 11, 1898 in Massillon, Ohio
d. Jun 4, 1968 in Rapallo, Italy
Source: *BiE&WWA; BioAmW; BioIn 1, 2, 3, 5, 6, 8, 10, 11, 12, 14, 15, 16; CurBio 44, 68; DcAmB S8; EncAFC; FamA&A; Film 1, 2; FilmEn; FilmgC;*

ForYSC; HalFC 80, 84, 88; IntDcF 1-3; InWom, SUP; LegTOT; LibW; MotPP; MovMk; NotAW MOD; NotNAT A, B; NotWoAT; ObitT 1961; OxCAmT 84; OxCFilm; SilFlmP; TwYS; WebAB 74, 79; WhoAmW 58A; WhoHol B; WhScrn 74, 77, 83; WhThe; WomWMM; WorAl; WorAlBi; WorEFlm

Gish, Lillian (Diana)
"The First Lady of the Silent Screen"
American. Actor
Starred in D W Griffith classics: *Birth of a Nation,* 1915; revivals in *A Wedding,* 1978; *The Whales of August,* 1987.
b. Oct 14, 1893 in Springfield, Ohio
d. Feb 27, 1993 in New York, New York
Source: *AnObit 1993; BiDFilm, 94; BiE&WWA; BioAmW; BioIn 13, 14, 15, 16, 18, 19, 20, 21; CelR 90; CmMov; ConAu 128; ContDcW 89; ConTFT 4, 11; CurBio 44, 93N; FacFETw; FamA&A; Film 1; GrLiveH; HalFC 88; IntMPA 92; IntWW 91; InWom SUP; LegTOT; MotPP; News 93; NewYTBS 84, 88, 93; NotWoAT; OxCAmT 84; ReelWom; SilFlmP; ThFT; VarWW 85; WebAB 79; Who 92; WhoAm 86, 90; WhoAmW 91; WhoEnt 92; WhoHol A; WhoThe 72, 77, 81; WorAlBi; WorEFlm; WrDr 90*

Gissing, George Robert
English. Author, Critic
Books dealt with poverty, despair: *The Private Papers of Henry Ryecroft,* 1903.
b. Nov 22, 1857 in Wakefield, England
d. Dec 28, 1903 in Saint-Jean-de-Luz, France
Source: *Alli SUP; AtlBL; BbD; BiD&SB; BioIn 1, 3, 5, 6, 7, 8, 9, 10, 11, 12, 13, 14, 15, 16, 17, 20; BlmGEL; BritAu 19; CasWL; Chambr 3; ConAu 105; CyWA 58; DcAmSR; DcArts; DcEnA A; DcEuL; DcLB 18; DcLEL; DcNaB S2; EvLB; GrWrEL N; LngCEL; LngCTC; ModBrL; NewC; NewCBEL; OxCEng 67, 85, 95; PenC ENG; RAdv 1; REn; WebE&AL; WhDW*

Gist, Carole Anne-Marie
American. Beauty Contest Winner
First African-American to become Miss USA; finished first runner-up, Miss Universe pageant, 1990.
b. 1970?
Source: *ConBlB 1*

Gitlow, Benjamin
American. Political Activist
Involved in Socialist, Communist activities.
b. Dec 22, 1891 in Elizabethport, New Jersey
d. Jul 19, 1965
Source: *BiDAmLf; BioIn 7; ConAu 89; DcAmB S7; WhAm 4*

Gittings, Barbara
American. Social Reformer
Helped start the New York Chapter of the Daughters of Bilitis, 1958.
b. Jul 31, 1932 in Vienna, Austria
Source: *BioIn 20; GayLesB; WhoLibI 82*

Giuffre, James Peter
American. Jazz Musician
Clarinetist, saxist; led own trio, 1950s; a major proponent of free-jazz style.
b. Apr 26, 1921 in Dallas, Texas
Source: *Baker 84; BiDAmM; BiDJaz; BioIn 16; ConAmC 82; EncJzS; NewAmDM; NewGrDA 86; NewGrDJ 88; NewGrDM 80; PenEncP; WhoAm 74; WhoE 74; WhoEnt 92*

Giuliani, Rudolph William
American. Politician, Government Official
US attorney, NYC, 1983-89; prosecuted major organized crime, corruption, fraud cases: Ivan Boesky stock-fraud conviction, 1986; Mayor of New York, 1994—.
b. May 28, 1944 in New York, New York
Source: *BioIn 14, 15, 16; CelR 90; CurBio 88; NewYTBS 83, 85, 89; WhoAm 86, 90; WhoAmL 87, 90; WhoAmP 87, 91; WhoE 91*

Giuliani, Veronica, Saint
Italian. Religious Figure
Legendary woman who wiped Jesus' brow as he bore the cross.
Source: *BioIn 1, 2, 5, 6; DcWomA; EncEarC; InWom, SUP; REn*

Giulini, Carlo Maria
Italian. Conductor
Led LA Philharmonic from 1978; Grammy winner, 1971.
b. May 9, 1914 in Barletta, Italy
Source: *Baker 84, 92; BioIn 11, 12, 13; BriBkM 80; CmOp; CurBio 78; DcArts; FacFETw; IntWW 74, 75, 76, 77, 78, 79, 80, 81, 82, 83, 89, 91, 93; IntWWM 77, 80, 90; MetOEnc; MusSN; NewAmDM; NewEOp 71; NewGrDA 86; NewGrDM 80; NewGrDO; NewYTBS 82; OxDcOp; PenDiMP; Who 74, 82, 83, 85, 88, 90, 92, 94; WhoAm 74, 76, 78, 80, 82, 84, 86; WhoAmM 83; WhoMus 72; WhoOp 76; WhoWest 82, 84; WhoWor 78, 80, 82, 84, 87, 91, 93, 95*

Giusti, Dave
[David John Giusti, Jr]
American. Baseball Player
Relief pitcher, 1962-77; led NL in saves, 30, 1971.
b. Nov 27, 1939 in Seneca Falls, New York
Source: *Ballpl 90; BioIn 16; WhoAm 74, 76; WhoProB 73*

Giusti, Giuseppe
Italian. Patriot, Author
Tuscan govt., its grand duke, were targets for much of his satirical poetry: "Il Re traicello," 1841.
b. May 12, 1809 in Monsummano, Italy
d. Mar 31, 1850 in Florence, Italy
Source: *BiD&SB; BioIn 8; CasWL; CelCen; DcCathB; DcEuL; DcItL 1; Dis&D; EvEuW; LinLib L; PenC EUR; REn*

Givenchy, Hubert James Marcel Taffin de
French. Fashion Designer
Opened couture house, 1952; known for elegant day, evening wear.
b. Feb 21, 1927 in Beauvais, France
Source: *BioIn 13, 16; CelR 90; ConDes 90; CurBio 55; DcTwDes; EncFash; Entr; FacFETw; IntWW 91; WhoAm 86, 90, 95, 96; WhoFash, 88; WhoWor 91; WorAlBi; WorFshn*

Givens, Robin
American. Actor
Performed in TV series "Head of the Class"; film *A Rage in Harlem*; married boxer Mike Tyson, 1988, but divorced him following accusations of abuse, 1989.
b. Nov 27, 1964 in New York, New York
Source: *BioIn 15, 16; ConTFT 10; IntMPA 94, 96; LegTOT; WhoBlA 92; WhoEnt 92; WhoHol 92*

Gjellerup, Karl Adolf
Danish. Author
Wrote novel *The Pilgrim Kamanita,* 1906, only work translated into Englis h; shared Nobel Prize, 1917.
b. Jun 2, 1857 in Roholte, Denmark
d. Oct 11, 1919 in Klotzsche, Germany
Source: *BiD&SB; BioIn 1, 7, 15; CasWL; ClDMEL 47; TwCWr; WhoNob; WorAl; WorAlBi*

Glackens, William James
American. Artist
Impressionist; member of realist school The Eight, later known as the Ashcan School: *Hammerstein's Roof Garden,* 1901.
b. Mar 13, 1870 in Philadelphia, Pennsylvania
d. May 22, 1938 in Westport, Connecticut
Source: *AmBi; AtlBL; BioIn 3, 4, 6; BriEAA; DcAmB S2; DcArts; DcCAA 71; IlrAm A; McGDA; McGEWB; NatCAB 38; OxCAmL 65; OxCArt; OxCTwCA; OxDcArt; PhDcTCA 77; WebAB 74, 79; WhAm 1*

Gladstone, James
Canadian. Politician
First Native North American to serve as a senator in the Canadian Parliament, 1958-71.
b. May 21, 1887 in Mountain Hill, Northwest Territories, Canada

d. Sep 4, 1971 in Fernie, British Columbia, Canada
Source: *BioIn 9, 21; MacDCB 78; NotNaAm*

Gladstone, William Ewart
English. Statesman, Author
Four-time British prime minister, 1868-1894; most prominent man in politics of his time.
b. Dec 29, 1809 in Liverpool, England
d. May 19, 1898 in Hawarden, Wales
Source: *Alli, SUP; BbD; Benet 87, 96; BiD&SB; BioIn 1, 2, 3, 4, 5, 6, 7, 8, 9, 10, 11, 12, 13, 14, 15, 16, 17, 19, 20; BlmGEL; CasWL; CelCen; Chambr 3; ChhPo; CyEd; DcBiPP; DcEnA, A; DcEnL; DcLB 57; DcNaB S1; Dis&D; EncO&P 3; EncPaPR 91; EvLB; HisDBrE; HisWorL; LinLib L, S; LngCEL; LuthC 75; McGEWB; NewC; NewCBEL; OxCEng 67, 85, 95; REn; VicBrit; WhDW; WorAl*

Gladys Knight and the Pips
[Langston George; Eleanor Guest; William Guest; Brenda Knight; Gladys Knight; Merald Knight]
American. Music Group
Family group formed in Atlanta, 1952; biggest hit "Midnight Train to Georgia," 1973.
Source: *Alli SUP; BioIn 15, 16, 17, 18; DrRegL 75; EncPR&S 89; HarEnR 86; InB&W 80, 85A; NegAl 89; PenEncP; RolSEnR 83; WhoRocM 82*

Glaisher, James
English. Meteorologist, Balloonist
Established Meteorological Society, 1850; best-known work: *Travels in the Air,* 1867.
b. Apr 7, 1809 in London, England
d. Feb 8, 1903
Source: *Alli SUP; BiD&SB; BioIn 1, 8; DcBiPP; DcNaB S2; DcScB; InSci; LarDcSc; NewCol 75*

Glancy, Diane
American. Writer
Laureate for the Five Civilized Tribes, 1984-86; wrote *One Age in a Dream,* 1986.
b. 1941 in Kansas City, Missouri
Source: *ConAu 24AS, 136; NatNAL; NotNaAm; OxCWoWr 95; WhoUSWr 88; WhoWrEP 89, 92, 95; WrDr 94, 96*

Glanville-Hicks, Peggy
American. Composer, Critic
Wrote opera *The Transposed Heads,* 1954; ballet *A Season in Hell,* 1967.
b. Dec 29, 1912 in Melbourne, Australia
d. Jun 25, 1990 in Sydney, Australia
Source: *AmComp; AnObit 1990; Baker 78, 84, 92; BiDAmM; BioIn 8, 17; CompSN, SUP; ConAmC 76, 82; ContDcW 89; DcCM; IntDcWB; InWom SUP; NewAmDM; NewEOp 71; NewGrDA 86; NewGrDM 80; NewGrDO; NewYTBS 90; OxCMus; WhAm 10; WhoAm 78, 80, 82, 84; WomFir*

Glanzman, Louis S
American. Artist, Illustrator
b. Feb 8, 1922 in Baltimore, Maryland
Source: *BioIn 14; IlrAm 1880, F; IlsBYP; IlsCB 1957; SmATA 36*

Glaser, Donald Arthur
American. Physicist
Nobelist in physics, 1960, for invention of the bubble chamber.
b. Sep 21, 1926 in Cleveland, Ohio
Source: *AmMWSc 76P, 79, 82, 86, 89, 92, 95; AsBiEn; BiESc; BioIn 5, 6, 14, 15, 20; BlueB 76; CamDcSc; CurBio 61; InSci; IntAu&W 77; IntWW 74, 75, 76, 77, 78, 79, 80, 81, 82, 83, 89, 91, 93; LarDcSc; McGMS 80; NatCAB 63N; WebAB 74, 79; WebBD 83; Who 74, 82, 83, 85, 88, 90, 92, 94; WhoAm 74, 90, 92, 94, 95, 96, 97; WhoNob, 90, 95; WhoScEn 94, 96; WhoWest 74, 92, 94, 96; WhoWor 74, 91, 93, 95, 96, 97; WorAl; WorAlBi*

Glaser, Elizabeth
American. Social Reformer
Co-founder, Pediatric AIDS Foundation, 1988.
b. Nov 11, 1947 in New York, New York
d. Dec 3, 1993 in Santa Monica, California
Source: *ConAu 138, 147; News 95, 95-2*

Glaser, Milton
American. Illustrator
Award-winning graphic artist; founder, pres., Push Pin Studios, 1954-74; *New York* mag., 1968-77; designed observation deck, World Trade Center, 1975.
b. Jun 26, 1929 in New York, New York
Source: *AmArt; AmGrD; BioIn 8, 9, 10, 11, 12, 13, 14, 15; ChhPo S2; ConAu 11NR, 17R; ConDes 84, 90, 97; ConGrA 1; CurBio 80; DcTwDes; EncTwCJ; FacFETw; FourBJA; IlrAm 1880, G; IlsBYP; IlsCB 1957; SmATA 11; WhoAdv 90; WhoAm 82, 84, 86, 88, 90, 92, 94, 95, 96, 97; WhoAmA 76, 78, 80, 82, 84, 86, 89, 91, 93; WhoEnt 92; WhoGrA 82*

Glaser, Paul Michael
American. Actor
Played Starsky on TV series "Starsky and Hutch," 1975-79.
b. Mar 25, 1942 in Cambridge, Massachusetts
Source: *BioIn 10, 11; ConTFT 3; HalFC 88; IntMPA 82, 92; VarWW 85; WhoAm 82; WhoEnt 92*

Glasgow, Ellen Anderson Gholson
American. Author
Novels were studies in Southern life; won Pulitzer, 1942; major works: *Barren Ground, The Sheltered Life.*
b. Apr 22, 1873 in Richmond, Virginia
d. Nov 21, 1945 in Richmond, Virginia
Source: *AmAu&B; AmCulL; AmWomWr; AmWr; AtlBL; BiD&SB; BiDSA; BioIn 3, 4, 5, 6, 7, 8, 9, 10, 11, 14, 15, 17, 19, 20, 21; CasWL; Chambr 3; CnDAL; ConAmA; ConAu 104; CurBio 46; DcAmB S3; DcLB 12; EncSoH; EvLB; LibW; McGEWB; NotAW; OxCEng 85, 95; PenC AM; RGTwCWr; TwCA SUP; TwCRHW 94; WebAB 74; WhNAA; WorAl*

Glashow, Sheldon Lee
American. Physicist, Educator
Shared Nobel Prize in physics, 1979, with Abdus Salam and Steven Weinberg.
b. Dec 5, 1932 in New York, New York
Source: *AmMWSc 76P, 79, 82, 86, 89, 92, 95; BiESc; BioIn 12, 14, 15, 16; CamDcSc; IntWW 80, 81, 82, 83, 89, 91, 93; LarDcSc; NobelP; NotTwCS; RAdv 14; St&PR 96, 97; Who 82, 83, 85, 88, 90, 92, 94; WhoAm 74, 76, 78, 80, 82, 84, 86, 88, 90, 92, 94, 95, 96, 97; WhoE 81, 83, 85, 86, 89, 91, 93, 95, 97; WhoFrS 84; WhoNob 90, 95; WhoScEn 94, 96; WhoWor 80, 82, 84, 87, 89, 91, 93, 95, 96, 97; WorAlBi*

Glaspell, Susan Keating
American. Author, Dramatist
Awarded Pulitzer for play *Alison's House,* 1930.
b. Jul 1, 1882 in Davenport, Iowa
d. Jul 27, 1948 in Provincetown, Massachusetts
Source: *AmAu&B; AmNov; Chambr 3; CnDAL; CnMD; ConAmA; ConAmL; ConAu 110; DcAmB S4; DcLB 9; DcLEL; McGEWD 84; OxCAmL 83; OxCThe 83; PlP&P; REn; WhNAA*

Glass, Carter
American. Statesman, Politician
Dem. senator, congressman for 44 yrs; helped draft Federal Reserve Bank Act, 1913.
b. Jan 4, 1858 in Lynchburg, Virginia
d. May 28, 1946 in Washington, District of Columbia
Source: *ApCAB X; BiDrAC; BiDrUSC 89; BiDrUSE 71, 89; BioIn 1, 2, 9, 10, 13; CurBio 41, 46; DcAmB S4; DcNAA; EncAB-H 1974, 1996; EncABHB 7; EncSoH; LegTOT; LinLib S; NatCAB 36; PolPar; WebAB 74, 79; WhAm 2; WhAmP; WhJnl; WorAl; WorAlBi*

Glass, David (Dayne)
American. Business Executive
CEO of Wal-Mart Stores, 1988—.
b. 1935 in Liberty, Missouri
Source: *News 96, 96-1*

Glass, David Victor
English. Sociologist
Pioneered study of demography, Third World understanding; wrote *Social Mobility in Britain,* 1954.
b. Jan 2, 1911 in London, England
Source: *Au&Wr 71; BioIn 1, 13; BlueB 76; ConAu 81, 85; DcNaB 1971; IntWW 74, 75, 76, 77, 78; Who 74*

Glass, Montague (Marsden)
American. Lawyer, Author, Dramatist
Known for humorous books, plays *Potash and Perlmutter,* 1910-26.
b. Jul 23, 1877 in Manchester, England
d. Feb 3, 1934 in Westport, Connecticut
Source: *AmAu&B; AmBi; BenetAL 91; BioIn 15; ChhPo; ConAu 117; DcAmB S1; DcLB 11; DcNAA; EncAHmr; LinLib L, S; NotNAT B; OxCAmT 84; REn; REnAL; TwCA; WhAm 1; WhLit; WhThe*

Glass, Philip
American. Composer
Noted for avant-garde style, use of electric wind instruments; commissioned by N Y Met. to create work, *The Voyage,* for 1992 celebration of Columbus' discovery.
b. Jan 31, 1937 in Baltimore, Maryland
Source: *AmComp; AmCulL; ASCAP 80; Baker 78, 84, 92; BioIn 10, 11, 12, 13, 14, 15, 16; CelR 90; CompSN SUP; ConAmC 76, 82; ConCom 92; ConMus 1; ConTFT 6; CpmDNM 81; CurBio 81; DcArts; EncWB; FacFETw; IntDcOp; IntWW 89, 91, 93; IntWWM 90; LegTOT; MetOEnc; NewAmDM; NewGrDA 86; NewGrDM 80; NewGrDO; News 91; NewYTBS 74, 81, 92; OxDcOp; PenDiMP A; PenEncP; RAdv 14; RolSEnR 83; Who 94; WhoAm 78, 80, 82, 84, 86, 88, 90, 92, 94, 95, 96, 97; WhoAmM 83; WhoE 91, 93, 95, 97; WhoEnt 92; WhoRocM 82; WhoWor 97; WorAlBi*

Glass, Ron
American. Actor
Played Ron Harris on "Barney Miller," 1975-82.
b. Jul 10, 1945 in Evansville, Indiana
Source: *BioIn 11, 12; ConTFT 3; DrBlPA, 90; Dun&B 88; InB&W 80; VarWW 85; WhoAm 86, 88; WhoBlA 92; WhoHol 92*

Glassco, John Stinson
Canadian. Author
Writings include *Memories of Montparnasse,* 1970.
b. Dec 15, 1909 in Montreal, Quebec, Canada
d. Jan 29, 1981 in Montreal, Quebec, Canada
Source: *Au&Wr 71; CanWr; CanWW 70, 79, 80; CasWL; ConAu 15NR, 102; ConNov 72, 76; ConPo 70, 75, 80; OxCCan, SUP; WrDr 76*

Glasscock, Jack
[John Wesley Glasscock]
"Pebbly Jack"
American. Baseball Player
Shortstop, 1879-95; won NL batting title, 1890; had .290 lifetime batting average.
b. Jul 22, 1859 in Wheeling, West Virginia
d. Feb 24, 1947 in Wheeling, West Virginia
Source: *Ballpl 90; BioIn 3*

Glasser, Ira
American. Social Reformer
Exec. director, ACLU, 1978—.
b. Apr 18, 1938 in New York, New York
Source: *BioIn 14, 15; ConAu 137; CurBio 86; News 89-1; WhoAm 90; WhoAmL 83, 92; WrDr 96*

Glasser, Melvin
American. Scientist
Supervised triald of the Salk anti-polio vaccine.
d. Mar 13, 1995 in Washington, District of Columbia

Glasspole, Florizel Augustus
Jamaican. Political Leader
Governor general of Jamaica, 1973-91.
b. Sep 25, 1909 in Kingston, Jamaica
Source: *IntWW 77, 78, 79, 80, 81, 82, 83, 89, 91, 93; IntYB 80, 81, 82; Who 82, 92, 94; WhoWor 78, 80, 82, 84, 87, 89, 91*

Glazer, David
American. Musician
Int'l clarinet soloist; member, NY Woodwind Quintet, 1951-85.
b. May 7, 1913 in Milwaukee, Wisconsin
Source: *Baker 92; IntWWM 80, 85, 90; WhoAm 74, 76, 78, 80, 82, 84, 86, 88; WhoAmM 83; WhoWor 74, 76*

Glazer, Nathan
American. Author
Main sociological works: *The Lonely Crowd,* 1950; *Beyond the Melting Pot,* 1963.
b. Feb 25, 1923 in New York, New York
Source: *AmAu&B; AmMWSc 73S, 78S; BioIn 9, 11, 12, 15, 16; BlueB 76; ConAu 5R; CurBio 70; DcAmC; DcLEL 1940; IntAu&W 82; IntWW 74, 75, 76, 77, 78, 79, 80, 81, 82, 83, 89, 91, 93; LEduc 74; LinLib L; PolProf J, NF; WhoAm 74, 76, 78, 80, 82, 84, 86, 88, 90, 92, 94, 95, 96, 97; WhoAmJ 80; WhoE 77, 86; WhoWorJ 72, 78; WrDr 76, 80, 82, 84, 86, 88, 90, 92, 94, 96*

Glazunov, Alexander Constantinovich
Russian. Composer
Last of Russian National school; master of counterpoint; noted for ballet, *Raymonda.*
b. Aug 10, 1865 in Saint Petersburg, Russia
d. Mar 21, 1936 in Paris, France
Source: *AtlBL; Baker 84; NewGrDM 80; WorAl*

Gleason, Jackie
"The Great One"
American. Actor, Comedian
Best known for role of Ralph Kramden on TV series, "The Honeymooners."
b. Feb 26, 1916 in New York, New York
d. Jun 24, 1987 in Fort Lauderdale, Florida
Source: *AmDec 1950; AnObit 1987; ASCAP 66, 80; BiE&WWA; BioIn 2, 3, 4, 5, 6, 7, 10, 11, 12, 13; CelR; CmpEPM; ConNews 87-4; ConTFT 5; CurBio 55, 87, 87N; DcTwCCu 1; EncAFC; EncMT; FacFETw; FilmEn; FilmgC; ForYSC; GangFlm; HalFC 80, 84, 88; IntMPA 75, 76, 77, 78, 79, 80, 81, 82, 84, 86; JoeFr; LegTOT; LesBEnT; MovMk; NewYTBE 73; NewYTBS 87; NewYTET; OxCAmT 84; OxCPMus; PenEncP; QDrFCA 92; VarWW 85; WebAB 74, 79; WhAm 9; WhoAm 74, 76, 78, 80, 82, 84, 86; WhoCom; WhoHol A; WorAl; WorAlBi*

Gleason, James
American. Actor
Nominated for 1941 Oscar for *Here Comes Mr. Jordan.*
b. May 23, 1886 in New York, New York
d. Apr 12, 1959 in Woodland Hills, California
Source: *BioIn 5, 7, 21; EncAFC; Film 2; FilmEn; FilmgC; ForYSC; HalFC 80, 84, 88; HolCA; LegTOT; MotPP; MovMk; NotNAT B; ObitT 1951; OlFamFa; OxCAmT 84; QDrFCA 92; TwYS; Vers A; WhAm 3; WhoHol B; WhScrn 74, 77, 83; WhThe; WorAl*

Gleason, Joanna
Canadian. Actor
Won Tony for musical *Into the Woods,* 1988.
b. Jun 2, 1950 in Toronto, Ontario, Canada
Source: *BioIn 15, 16; ConTFT 6, 15; NewYTBS 86; WhoAm 94, 95, 96, 97; WhoAmW 91, 93, 95, 97; WhoEnt 92; WhoHol 92*

Gleason, John James
American. Designer
Lighting designer for major NYC productions including *A Streetcar Named Desire,* 1973; *The Magic Flute,* 1987.
b. Apr 10, 1941 in New York, New York
Source: *ConAu 120; ConTFT 5; VarWW 85; WhoAm 84, 86, 88, 90, 92, 94, 95, 96, 97; WhoEnt 92; WhoThe 81*

Gleason, Lucille
American. Actor
Character actress, 1929-45; films include *Klondike Annie, Rhythm of the Range.*
b. Feb 6, 1888 in Pasadena, California
d. May 13, 1947 in Brentwood, California
Source: *FilmgC; WhoHol B; WhScrn 74, 77, 83*

Gleason, Ralph Joseph
American. Journalist, Critic
Founded, edited *Rolling Stone* mag., 1967-75; first jazz critic to take rock music seriously.
b. Mar 1, 1917 in New York, New York

d. Jun 3, 1975 in Berkeley, California
Source: *BioIn 10; CmCal; ConAu 61; DcAmB S9; EncJzS; NewYTBS 75; WhAm 6; WhoAm 74; WhoWest 74*

Gleason, Thomas W(illiam)
American. Labor Union Official
Pres., ILA, 1963-87; vp, AFL-CIO, 1969-87.
b. Nov 8, 1900 in New York, New York
d. Dec 24, 1992 in New York, New York
Source: *BiDAmL; BiDAmLL; BioIn 6, 7, 8, 11, 12; CurBio 65, 93N; PolProf J, K, NF; WhoAm 86; WhoFI 85*

Gleizes, Albert L
French. Artist
Prominent cubist; founding member, Section d'Or group, 1912; works include *Harvest Threshing,* 1912.
b. Dec 8, 1881 in Creteil, France
d. Jun 23, 1953 in Avignon, France
Source: *ConArt 83; ObitT 1951; OxCArt; OxCTwCA; PhDcTCA 77; REn*

Glemp, Jozef, Cardinal
Polish. Religious Leader
Elevated to cardinal Feb 2, 1983, by Pope John Paul II; head of Polish Catholic church, 1981—.
b. Dec 18, 1929 in Inowroclaw, Poland
Source: *BioIn 12, 13, 15; CurBio 82; IntWW 82, 83, 89, 91, 93; NewYTBS 82; WhoRel 92; WhoSoCE 89; WhoWor 82, 84, 87, 89, 91, 95, 96, 97*

Glendower, Owen
Welsh. Revolutionary
Self-proclaimed prince of Wales, 1402; Shakespeare portrayed him in *Henry IV,* Act I.
b. 1359, Wales
d. Sep 20, 1415, Wales
Source: *BioIn 3, 5, 6, 7, 8, 9, 12; DcBiPP; DcNaB; LngCEL; McGEWB; NewC; OxCEng 85, 95*

Glenn, Carroll
American. Violinist
With husband, pianist Eugene List, founded Southern Vermont Music Festival.
b. Oct 28, 1922? in Chester, South Carolina
d. Apr 25, 1983 in New York, New York
Source: *BioIn 1, 9, 13; InWom; NewYTBS 83*

Glenn, John Herschel, Jr.
American. Astronaut, Politician
First American to orbit Earth, Feb 20, 1962; Dem. senator from OH, 1974—.
b. Jul 18, 1921 in Cambridge, Ohio
Source: *AlmAP 92; AnCL; BiDrUSC 89; BioIn 5, 6, 7, 8, 9, 10, 11, 12, 13, 14, 16; BioNews 74; BlueB 76; CelR 90; CngDr 77, 79, 81, 83, 85, 87, 89; ConHero 1; CurBio 62, 76; Dun&B 90; EncWB; IntWW 74, 75, 76, 77, 78, 79, 80, 81, 82, 83, 89, 91, 93; NewYTBE 72; NewYTBS 76; PolProf J, K, NF; PolsAm 84; WebAB 74, 79; WebAMB; WhDW; Who 85, 92; WhoAm 74, 76, 78, 80, 82, 84, 86, 88, 90, 92, 94, 95, 96, 97; WhoAmP 75, 77, 79, 81, 83, 85, 87, 89, 91, 93, 95; WhoGov 75, 77; WhoMW 76, 78, 80, 82, 84, 86, 88, 90, 92, 93, 96; WhoScEn 94, 96; WhoSpc; WhoWor 78, 80, 82, 84, 87, 89, 91; WorAl; WorAlBi*

Glenn, Scott
American. Actor
In films *Urban Cowboy,* 1980; *The Right Stuff,* 1983.
b. Jan 26, 1942? in Pittsburgh, Pennsylvania
Source: *BioIn 13, 16; ConTFT 4, 11; HalFC 84, 88; IntMPA 88, 92, 94, 96; LegTOT; VarWW 85; WhoAm 88, 90, 92, 94, 95, 96, 97; WhoEnt 92*

Glennan, T(homas) Keith
American. Government Official
First head of NASA, 1958-61.
b. Sep 8, 1905
d. Apr 11, 1995 in Mitchellville, Maryland
Source: *AmMWSc 73P, 79, 82, 86, 89, 92, 95; BioIn 1, 2, 5, 8, 13; BlueB 76; CurBio 95N; FacFETw; InSci; IntWW 74, 75, 76, 77, 78, 79, 80, 81, 82, 83, 89, 91, 93; LinLib S; WhoAm 74, 76, 78, 80; WhoEng 80, 88*

Gless, Sharon
American. Actor
Played Chris Cagney on TV series "Cagney and Lacey," 1982-88; won two Emmys.
b. May 31, 1943 in Los Angeles, California
Source: *BioIn 13, 14, 15; ConTFT 6, 13; IntMPA 88, 92, 94, 96; LegTOT; News 89-3; VarWW 85; WhoAm 90; WhoAmW 91; WhoEnt 92; WhoHol 92; WorAlBi*

Glickman, Daniel R.
American. Government Official
Secretary of Agriculture, 1995—.
b. Nov 24, 1944
Source: *CngDr 77; NewYTBS 94; WhoGov 77; WhoMW 78*

Glidden, Joseph Farwell
American. Inventor
Invented the first profitable version of barbed wire; extensively used in Western US to protect livestock and crops from cattle.
b. Jan 18, 1813 in Charlestown, New Hampshire
d. Oct 9, 1906 in De Kalb, Illinois
Source: *AmBi; ApCAB X; DcAmB; EncAAH; NatCAB 23; OxCAmH; WebAB 74, 79; WhAm 4, HS, HSA; WhDW*

Gliere, Reinhold Moritsevich
Russian. Composer
Wrote ballet, *The Bronze Horseman,* 1949; *Symphony No. 3,* 1909-11.
b. Jan 11, 1875 in Kiev, Russia
d. Jun 23, 1956 in Moscow, Union of Soviet Socialist Republics
Source: *Baker 84; BiDD; BioIn 1, 2, 3, 4, 8, 9; DcCM; ObitT 1951*

Glinka, Mikhail Ivanovich
"Father of Russian Music"
Russian. Composer
Wrote first Russian nat. opera, *A Life for the Czar,* 1836; *Russlan and Ludmilla,* 1842, after Pushkin's fairy tale.
b. Jun 1, 1804 in Novospaskoi, Russia
d. Feb 15, 1857 in Berlin, Germany
Source: *AtlBL; Baker 84, 92; Benet 87, 96; BioIn 1, 4, 5, 6, 7, 8, 9, 10, 11, 12, 16, 20; DcArts; IntDcOp; LuthC 75; McGEWB; MusMk; NewAmDM; NewGrDM 80; NewGrDO; PenDiMP A; REn; WhDW; WorAl*

Gloria Estefan and the Miami Sound Machine
[Juan Marcos Avila; Betty Cortez; Emilio Estefan, Jr; Gloria M Estefan; Roger Fisher; Enrique E Garcia; Gustavo Lezcano; Victor Lopez; Wesley B Wright]
Cuban. Music Group
Local club band whose Latin rhythms became popular, 1984; first number one hit "Anything for You" from album *Let it Loose,* 1988.
Source: *Alli; BioIn 17, 21; WhoRocM 82*

Glossop, Peter
English. Opera Singer
Baritone; member of Covent Garden Opera, 1962-66; NY Met. debut, 1967; known for Verdi roles.
b. Jun 6, 1928 in Sheffield, England
Source: *Baker 84, 92; BlueB 76; CmOp; IntDcOp; IntWW 74, 75, 76, 77, 78, 79, 80, 81, 82, 83, 89, 91, 93; IntWWM 77, 80, 90; MetOEnc; NewGrDM 80; NewGrDO; OxDcOp; PenDiMP; Who 74, 82, 83, 85, 88, 90, 92, 94; WhoMus 72; WhoOp 76; WhoWor 74, 76, 78*

Glover, Danny
American. Actor
Starred in *Places in the Heart,* 1984; *The Color Purple,* 1985; trilogy of *Lethal Weapon,* 1987-1992.
b. Jul 22, 1947 in San Francisco, California
Source: *AfrAmAl 6; AfrAmBi 2; BiDFilm 94; BioIn 14, 15, 16; ConBlB 1; ConTFT 5, 12; CurBio 92; DcTwCCu 5; DrBlPA 90; HolBB; InB&W 85; IntMPA 92, 94, 96; LegTOT; NegAl 89; NewYTBS 86; WhoAfA 96; WhoAm 92, 94, 95, 96, 97; WhoBlA 92, 94; WhoEnt 92; WhoHol 92; WorAlBi*

Glover, John
American. Revolutionary
Member MA convention to ratify Constitution, 1788.
b. Nov 5, 1753 in Salem, Massachusetts
d. Jan 30, 1797 in Marblehead, Massachusetts
Source: *AmBi; BioIn 5, 8, 9, 11; DcAmB; WebAB 74; WebBD 83*

Glover, Julian
English. Actor
Films include *Tom Jones,* 1963; *Nicholas and Alexandra,* 1971.
b. Mar 27, 1935 in London, England
Source: *ConTFT 4, 81*

Glover, Savion
American. Dancer, Choreographer
Won Tony Award, Best Choreography, for *Bring In 'Da Noise, Bring In 'Da Funk,* 1996.
b. Nov 19, 1973 in Newark, New Jersey
Source: *CurBio 96; DcTwCCu 5; News 97-1; WhoHol 92*

Glubb, John Bagot, Sir
English. Military Leader, Author
Commanded Arab Legion/Jordanian Army, 1939-56; wrote books on Mideast.
b. Apr 16, 1897 in Preston, England
d. Mar 17, 1986 in Mayfield, England
Source: *AnObit 1984; Au&Wr 71; BioIn 1, 2, 3, 4, 7, 14, 15; BlueB 76; ConAu 5NR, 9R, 118; CurBio 51, 86, 86N; DcMidEa; DcNaB 1986; DcTwHis; FacFETw; HarEnMi; HisEAAC; IntAu&W 76, 77, 82; IntWW 74, 75, 76, 77, 78, 79, 80, 81, 82, 83; IntYB 78, 79, 80, 81, 82; McGEWB; MidE 78, 79, 80, 81, 82; NewYTBS 86; Who 74, 82, 83, 85; WhoWor 74, 76, 78; WrDr 76, 80, 82, 84, 86*

Gluck
[Hannah Gluckstein]
English. Painter
Works featured landscapes, florals, and portraits; had five exhibitions of her work duting her lifetime: 1924, 1926, 1932, 1937, 1973.
b. 1895 in London, England
d. 1978
Source: *BiDWomA; GayLesB*

Gluck, Alma
[Reba Fiersohn]
American. Opera Singer
NY Met. soprano, 1909-12; her recording, "Carry Me Back to Old Virginny," sold two million copies; wife of Efrem Zimbalist.
b. May 11, 1884 in Bucharest, Romania
d. Oct 27, 1938 in New York, New York
Source: *AmBi; Baker 78, 84, 92; BiDAmM; BioIn 1, 2, 4, 6, 11, 12, 14; CmOp; DcAmB S2; IntDcOp; InWom, SUP; LegTOT; LibW; LinLib S; MetOEnc; MusSN; NatCAB 43; NewAmDM; NewEOp 71; NewGrDA 86; NewGrDM 80; NewGrDO; NotAW; PenDiMP; WhAm 1; WomFir*

Gluck, Christoph
[Christoph Willibald von Gluck]
German. Composer
Best-known operas: *Orfeo ed Euridice,* 1762; *Iphigenie en Aulide,* 1774.
b. Jul 2, 1714 in Erasbach, Germany
d. Nov 15, 1787 in Vienna, Austria
Source: *AtlBL; DcArts; DcCathB; LuthC 75; MusMk; NewC; NewGrDM 80; OxCMus; PenDiMP A; REn; WorAl; WorAlBi*

Gluck, Louise
American. Poet
Won 1993 Pulitzer for Poetry for *The Wild Iris.*
b. Apr 22, 1943 in New York, New York
Source: *AmWomWr SUP; ArtclWW 2; Benet 87; BenetAL 91; BioIn 10, 12; BlmGWL; ConAu 33R; ConLC 7, 22, 44, 81; ConPo 70, 75, 80, 91; CroCAP; DcLB 5; DcLEL 1940; DrAP 75; DrAPF 80, 89; FemiCLE; IntAu&W 91, 93; IntWWP 82; LegTOT; OxCTwCP; OxCWoWr 95; PoeCrit 16; RAdv 14, 13-1; WhoAm 90; WhoAmW 91; WhoEmL 87; WhoUSWr 88; WhoWrEP 89; WorAu 1970; WrDr 76, 80, 82, 84, 86, 88, 90, 92, 94, 96*

Glueck, Nelson
American. Theologian, Archaeologist
Discovered King Solomon's copper mines, over 1000 artifacts in Trans-Jordan, the Negev, using Bible as guide, 1930s; pres., Hebrew Union College, 1947-71.
b. Jun 4, 1900 in Cincinnati, Ohio
d. Feb 12, 1971 in Cincinnati, Ohio
Source: *AmAu&B; BioIn 1, 3, 6, 8, 9, 11, 12; ConAu P-2; CurBio 48, 69, 71, 71N; DcAmB S9; InSci; IntDcAn; LinLib L, S; LuthC 75; NatCAB 56; OhA&B; REnAL; WhAm 5*

Glueck, Sheldon
American. Criminologist
Writings include *The Problems of Delinquency,* 1958; professor, Harvard U Law School, 1925-63.
b. Aug 15, 1896 in Warsaw, Poland
d. Mar 10, 1980 in Cambridge, Massachusetts
Source: *AmAu&B; BiDrAPA 77; BioIn 4, 6, 11, 12; BlueB 76; ConAu 5R, 9NR, 97; CurBio 57, 80, 80N; DcAmB S10; DrAS 74P, 78P, 82E, 82P; IntEnSS 79; IntWW 74, 75, 76, 77, 78, 79, 80; NewYTBS 80; OxCAmH; OxCLaw; WebAB 74, 79; WhAm 7; WhNAA; WhoAm 74, 76, 78, 80; WhoWor 74, 76, 78, 80*

Glyn, Elinor Sutherland
English. Author
Adapted her novels to film versions, 1920s; mentor of Clara Bow.
b. Oct 17, 1864 in Isle of Jersey, England
d. Sep 23, 1943 in London, England
Source: *CurBio 43; DcLEL; DcNaB 1941; EvLB; Film 2; FilmgC; InWom, SUP; LngCTC; NewC; OxCEng 85, 95; OxCFilm; REn; TwCA SUP; TwCWr*

Gmeiner, Hermann
Austrian. Social Reformer
Founded SOS-Children's Village movement for orphans, 1949; twice nominated for Nobel Prize.
b. Jun 23, 1919 in Alberschwende, Austria
d. Apr 26, 1986 in Innsbruck, Austria
Source: *BioIn 4, 6, 9, 10, 11, 14, 15; CurBio 63, 86, 86N; NewYTBS 86; WhAm 9; WhoWor 74, 76, 82, 87*

Gneisenau, August Neithardt von
Prussian. Military Leader
Renowned for defense of Kolberg in Napoleonic Wars, early 1800s.
b. Oct 27, 1760 in Schildau, Prussia
d. Aug 23, 1831 in Posen, Prussia
Source: *DcBiPP; NewCol 75; WebBD 83*

Goalby, Bob
[Robert Goalby]
American. Golfer
Turned pro, 1957; won Masters, 1968.
b. Mar 14, 1931 in Belleville, Illinois
Source: *BioIn 7, 8, 10; WhoGolf*

Gobat, Charles Albert
Swiss. Lawyer, Statesman
Shared 1902 Nobel Peace Prize; pres., Bern International Peace Bureau, 1906-14.
b. May 21, 1843 in Tramelan, Switzerland
d. Mar 16, 1914 in Bern, Switzerland
Source: *BioIn 9, 11, 15; WhoNob, 90, 95*

Gobbi, Tito
Italian. Opera Singer
Baritone, best known for portrayal of Scarpia in Puccini's *Tosca,* 1956.
b. Oct 24, 1915 in Bassano, Italy
d. May 5, 1984 in Rome, Italy
Source: *AnObit 1984; BioIn 2, 3, 4, 7, 9, 11, 12, 13, 14, 21; CmOp; ConAu 105, 112, 129; CurBio 57, 84, 84N; IntWW 74, 75, 76, 77, 78, 79; IntWWM 77, 80; MusMk; MusSN; NewEOp 71; NewGrDM 80; WhAm 8; Who 74, 82, 83; WhoAm 78, 80, 82; WhoMus 72; WhoOp 76; WhoWor 74, 76, 78, 82; WorAl; WorAlBi*

Gobel, George Leslie
""Lonesome George""
American. Comedian
Won 1954 Emmy for TV show, "The George Gobel Show."
b. May 20, 1919 in Chicago, Illinois
d. Feb 24, 1991 in Encino, California
Source: *BiDAmM; BioIn 14; ConTFT 7; CurBio 55, 91N; EncAFC; EncFCWM 69; FilmgC; HalFC 88; LesBEnT 92; News 91; NewYTBS 91; VarWW 85; WhAm 10; WhoAm 74; WhoHol A*

Gober, Robert
American. Artist
Creator of many installation pieces.
b. 1954 in Wallingford, Connecticut
Source: *News 96*

Gobineau, Joseph Arthur, Comte de
French. Author, Philosopher
Originator of idea of superiority of Aryan race as scientific theory; wrote essay on *Inequality of Human Races,* 1823-55.
b. Jul 14, 1816 in Ville-d'Avray, France
d. Oct 13, 1882 in Turin, Italy
Source: *BbtC; BiD&SB; BioIn 1, 2, 7, 9, 13; CasWL; ClDMEL 47; EuAu; EvEuW; GuFrLit 1; McGEWB; OxCFr; PenC EUR; REn*

Godard, Benjamin Louis Paul
French. Composer
Wrote operas *La Vivandiere,* 1895; *Jocelyn,* 1881, featuring the famous "Berceuse."
b. Aug 14, 1849 in Paris, France
d. Jan 10, 1895 in Cannes, France
Source: *Baker 84*

Godard, Jean Luc
French. Director
A founder of French New Wave cinema; controversial films include *Breathless,* 1960; *Hail Mary,* 1985.
b. Dec 3, 1930 in Paris, France
Source: *Benet 87; BiDFilm; BioIn 13, 14, 15, 16, 17, 19, 21; ConTFT 7; CurBio 69, 93; DcFM; FacFETw; FilmgC; HalFC 88; IntDcF 2-2; IntMPA 92; IntWW 83, 91; MovMk; NewYTBE 70, 72; OxCFilm; RAdv 13-3; WhoAm 86, 90; WhoEnt 92; WhoWor 84, 91; WomWMM; WorAlBi; WorEFlm; WorFDir 2*

Goddard, Calvin Hooker
American. Criminologist, Historian
Found method of tracing bullets to guns that fired them.
b. Oct 30, 1891 in Baltimore, Maryland
d. Feb 22, 1955 in Washington, District of Columbia
Source: *BioIn 3, 4; CopCroC; DcAmB S5; NatCAB 41; WhAm 3*

Goddard, Paulette
[Marion Levy]
American. Actor
Married Charlie Chaplin, 1936-42, Erich Maria Remarque, 1958-70; appeared in 40 films including *Modern Times,* 1936, with Chaplin.
b. Jun 3, 1905 in Great Neck, New York
d. Apr 23, 1990 in Porto Ronco, Switzerland
Source: *AnObit 1990; BiDFilm; BioAmW; BioIn 14, 16; CmMov; ConTFT 9; CurBio 90N; EncAFC; FacFETw; FilmgC; HalFC 88; IntMPA 88; InWom SUP; NewYTBS 90; OxCFilm; VarWW 85; Who 92; WhoAm 82, 84; WhoHol A; WorAlBi; WorEFlm*

Goddard, Robert Hutchings
"Father of Modern Rocketry"
American. Physicist
Launched first liquid-fueled rocket, 1926.
b. Oct 5, 1882 in Worcester, Massachusetts
d. Aug 10, 1945 in Baltimore, Maryland
Source: *AsBiEn; BiESc; BioIn 1, 2, 3, 4, 5, 6, 7, 8, 9, 10, 11, 12, 13, 14, 16, 17, 18, 20, 21; CamDcSc; ConAu 118; DcAmB S3; DcScB; EncAB-H 1974, 1996; InSci; LarDcSc; McGEWB; MorMA; NatCAB 35; NewCol 75; OxCAmH; PeoHis; WebAB 74, 79; WhAm 2; WhDW; WorAl; WorAlBi*

Godden, Rumer
[Margaret Rumer Haynes Dixon]
English. Author, Poet, Dramatist
Prolific writer of children's stories, adult fiction; six novels adapted for films and TV, including *In This House of Brede,* 1975.
b. Dec 10, 1907 in Sussex, England
Source: *AnCL; Au&Arts 6; Au&Wr 71; AuBYP 2, 3; AuSpks; Benet 87; BioIn 2, 4, 6, 7, 8, 9, 10, 11, 14, 15, 16, 17, 19; BlmGWL; BlueB 76; CamGLE; ChhPo, S1, S2; ChlBkCr; ChlLR 20; ConAu 4NR, 5R, 27NR, 36NR; ConLC 53; ConNov 72, 76, 82, 86, 91; CurBio 76; CyWA 89; DcLB 161; DcLEL; DcLP 87B; EncBrWW; FacFETw; FemiCLE; FilmgC; HalFC 80, 84, 88; IntAu&W 76, 82, 89, 91; IntWW 74, 75, 76, 77, 78, 79, 80, 81, 82, 83, 89, 91, 93; InWom, SUP; LegTOT; LngCTC; ModBrL; MorJA; NewC; Novels; OxCChiL; PenNWW B; PiP; RAdv 1; REn; ScF&FL 1, 2; SmATA 3, 12AS, 36; TwCA, SUP; TwCChW 78, 83, 89, 95; TwCRGW; TwCRHW 90; TwCWr; WhE&EA; Who 85, 88, 90, 92, 94; WhoAm 90, 92, 94, 95, 96, 97; WhoAmW 68, 70, 72, 74, 75; WhoChL; WhoWor 74, 76, 78, 95, 96, 97; WrDr 76, 80, 82, 84, 86, 88, 90, 92, 94, 96*

Godel, Kurt
American. Mathematician
Best known for his theorem, Godel's Proof, 1931.
b. Apr 28, 1906 in Brunn, Austria-Hungary
d. Jan 14, 1978 in Princeton, New Jersey
Source: *AmMWSc 73P, 76P; AsBiEn; BiESc; BioIn 3, 11, 12, 13; BlueB 76; CamDcSc; FacFETw; IntWW 74, 75, 76, 77; LarDcSc; MakMC; McGEWB; McGMS 80; NewCol 75; OxCPhil; RAdv 13-5; ThTwC 87; WhAm 7; Who 74; WhoAm 74, 76; WhoWor 74; WorAl; WorAlBi*

Godey, Louis Antoine
American. Publisher
Established America's leading 19th-c. fashion mag., *Godey's Lady's Book,* 1830.
b. Jun 6, 1804 in New York, New York
d. Nov 29, 1878 in Philadelphia, Pennsylvania
Source: *AmAu; AmAu&B; AmBi; ApCAB; BiDAmJo; DcAmB; JrnUS; NatCAB 22; NewCol 75; REn; WebAB 74, 79; WhAm HS; WorAl; WorAlBi; WorFshn*

Godfrey, Arthur Michael
""Ole Redhead""
American. Actor, Singer
Hosted TV shows, 1948-59, including "The Arthur Godfrey Show."
b. Aug 31, 1903 in New York, New York
d. Mar 16, 1983 in New York, New York
Source: *AnObit 1982; ASCAP 66; BioNews 75; CurBio 48, 83N; NewYTBS 83; WebAB 74, 79; WhoAm 82; WhoHol A*

Godfrey, Isadore
English. Conductor
Led D'Oyly Opera, producer of Gilbert and Sullivan operettas, 1925-68.
b. 1901?
d. Sep 12, 1977 in Sussex, England
Source: *BioIn 11*

Godfrey of Bouillon
French. Ruler, Soldier
Led First Crusade, 1096; captured Jerusalem and became first king, 1099; subject of *Chansons de Geste.*
b. 1058? in Baisyin Brabant, France
d. Jul 18, 1100 in Jerusalem, Palestine
Source: *DcEuL; NewC; NewCol 75*

Godiva, Lady
English. Social Reformer
Made legendary ride naked through Coventry to win tax relief for townspeople.
b. 1010
d. 1067
Source: *InWom; NewC; NewCol 75; REn*

Godkin, E(dwin) L(awrence)
American. Journalist
Founded *The Nation,* 1865, later *NY Evening Post;* fought campaign against Tammany Hall system, NYC.
b. Oct 2, 1831 in Moyne, Ireland
d. May 21, 1902 in Greenway, England
Source: *Alli SUP; AmAu; AmAu&B; AmBi; AmRef; AmSocL; ApCAB; BbD; BiDAmJo; BiD&SB; BioIn 2, 3, 4, 7, 8, 10, 15, 16, 19; DcAmAu; DcAmB; DcIrB 78, 88; DcLEL; DcNAA; DcNaB S2; EncAB-H 1974, 1996; EncAJ; EvLB; HarEnUS; JrnUS; McGEWB; NatCAB 8; OxCAmH; OxCAmL 65, 83, 95; REn; REnAL; TwCBDA; WebAB 74, 79; WhAm 1*

Godolphin, Sidney
English. Statesman
Financed Marlborough's campaigns in war with France, 1702; leader in negotiating Treaty of Union with Scotland, 1707.
b. Jun 15, 1645, England
d. Sep 15, 1712 in Saint Albans, England
Source: *BioIn 18; DcNaB; HisDStE; McGEWB; WebBD 83*

Godowsky, Leopold
American. Musician
Concert pianist who wrote many pieces, arrangements for instrument; developed weight and relaxation theory in piano teaching.
b. Feb 13, 1870 in Vilnius, Lithuania
d. Nov 21, 1938 in New York, New York
Source: *AmBi; ASCAP 66, 80; Baker 78, 84, 92; BiDAmM; BioIn 1, 2, 3, 4, 5, 7, 11, 12, 16, 17, 21; BriBkM 80; ConAmC 76, 82; DcAmB S2; MusMk; MusSN; NatCAB 33; NewAmDM; NewGrDA 86; NewGrDM 80; NotTwCP; OxCMus; PenDiMP; WhAm 1*

Godowsky, Leopold, Jr.
American. Inventor
Co-invented Kodachrome color photography process, 1935.
b. May 27, 1901 in Chicago, Illinois
d. Feb 18, 1983 in New York, New York
Source: *NewYTBS 83*

Godunov, Alexander
[Boris Alexander Godunov]
"Sasha"
American. Dancer, Actor
First Bolshoi Ballet member to defect to US, 1979; films include *Witness,* 1985; *Die Hard,* 1988.
b. Nov 28, 1949 in Sakhalin, Russia
d. May 18, 1995 in West Hollywood, California
Source: *BiDSovU; BioIn 13, 14; CelR 90; CnOxB; ConTFT 4, 14; CurBio 83, 95N; IntMPA 92, 94; IntWW 91; LegTOT; News 95; NewYTBS 79; WhoAm 86, 90; WhoEnt 92; WhoHol 92*

Godunov, Boris Fedorovich
Russian. Ruler
Czar of Russia, 1598-1605; life was subject of play by Pushkin, opera by Mussorgski.
b. 1551 in Moscow, Russia
d. Apr 23, 1605
Source: *McGEWB; NewCol 75; REn; WhDW; WorAl*

Godwin, Edward William
English. Architect, Designer
Best known as designer of wallpaper, furniture, theatrical scenery, and costumes.
b. May 26, 1833 in Bristol, England
d. Oct 6, 1886 in London, England
Source: *Alli SUP; AntBDN G; BioIn 2, 5, 6, 9, 10, 11, 12, 15; DcArts; DcNaB; DcNiCA; MacEA; NotNAT B; OxCArt; OxCDecA; OxCThe 67, 83; OxDcArt; PenDiDA 89; WhoArch*

Godwin, Gail
American. Author
Novelist, short story writer: *Glass People,* 1972; *The Good Husband,* 1994.
b. Jun 18, 1937 in Birmingham, Alabama
Source: *AmWomWr; ArtclWW 2; Benet 87; BenetAL 91; BioIn 12, 13, 14, 15, 17, 19, 20, 21; BlmGWL; ConAu 15NR, 29R; ConLC 5, 8, 22, 31, 69; ConNov 82, 86, 91; CurBio 95; CyWA 89; DcLB 6; DrAF 76; DrAPF 80, 91; FemiCLE; GrWomW; LegTOT; MajTwCW; ModAL S2; ModWoWr; WhoAm 90; WhoAmW 75, 91; WhoUSWr 88; WhoWrEP 89; WorAlBi; WorAu 1975; WrDr 82, 84, 86, 88, 90, 92, 94, 96*

Godwin, Mary Wollstonecraft
English. Author, Feminist
Wrote feminist paper *A Vindication of the Rights of Woman,* 1792; moth er of Mary Shelley.
b. Apr 27, 1759 in London, England
d. Sep 10, 1797 in London, England
Source: *Alli; AtlBL; BbD; BiD&SB; BritAu; CasWL; Chambr 2; CyEd; DcEnA; DcEnL; DcEuL; DcLEL; DcNaB; Dis&D; EvLB; InWom, SUP; NewC; NewCol 75; OxCEng 67; PenC ENG; REn*

Godwin, William
English. Author
Father of Mary Shelley; radical nonconformist, wrote *An Enquiry Concerning Political Justice,* 1793.
b. Mar 3, 1756 in Wisbech, England
d. Apr 7, 1836 in London, England
Source: *Alli; AtlBL; BbD; Benet 87, 96; BiD&SB; BiDLA, SUP; BioIn 1, 2, 3, 5, 6, 7, 8, 9, 10, 11, 12, 13, 14, 15, 16, 17, 18, 19, 20, 21; BlkwCE; BlmGEL; BritAu 19; CamGEL; CamGLE; CasWL; CelCen; Chambr 2; CmFrR; CnDBLB 3; CrtSuMy; CyEd; CyWA 58; DcAmSR; DcArts; DcBiA; DcBiPP; DcEnA; DcEnL; DcEuL; DcLB 39, 104, 142, 158, 163; DcLEL; DcNaB; EncEnl; EncEth; EncMys; EncUnb; EvLB; GrWrEL N; LegTOT; LngCEL; McGEWB; MouLC 3; NewC; NewCBEL; NinCLC 14; Novels; OxCChiL; OxCEng 67, 85, 95; OxCPhil; PenC ENG; RadHan; REn; RfGEnL 91; ScF&FL 1; ScFEYrs; TwCCr&M 80A, 85A, 91A; WebE&AL; WhoEc 81, 86; WorAl; WorAlBi; WrPh P*

Goebbels, Joseph
[Paul Joseph Goebbe]
German. Government Official
Minister of propaganda under Hitler; committed suicide as Berlin fell to Russians.
b. Oct 29, 1897 in Rheydt, Germany
d. May 1, 1945 in Berlin, Germany
Source: *BioIn 1, 2, 3, 5, 6, 7, 8, 9, 10, 11, 12, 13, 14, 15, 16, 17, 19, 20; ConAu 115; CurBio 41; DcPol; EncTR 91; FacFETw; HisEWW; HisWorL; LegTOT; NewCol 75; OxCGer 76; REn; WhDW; WorAl; WorAlBi*

Goerdeler, Karl Friedrich
German. Political Activist
Mayor, Leipzig, 1930-37; planned unsuccesful coup against Hitler, 1944; hanged.
b. Jul 31, 1884 in Schneidemuhl, Germany
d. Feb 2, 1945 in Berlin, Germany
Source: *BioIn 14; ObitOF 79; OxCGer 86*

Goering, Hermann Wilhelm
German. Government Official
Hitler's minister of aviation; founder of Gestapo.
b. Jan 12, 1893 in Rosenheim, Germany
d. Oct 15, 1946 in Nuremberg, Germany
Source: *CurBio 41, 46; DcTwHis; OxCGer 76; REn; WorAl*

Goerlich, John
American. Inventor
Pioneer in automotive parts; invented mufflers; Automotive Hall of Fame, 1990.
d. Oct 7, 1991 in Ottawa Hills, Ohio

Goes, Hugo van der
Flemish. Artist
Best-known work: Portinari altarpiece, Uffizi, Florence, 1476.
b. 1440
d. 1482
Source: *AtlBL; BioIn 2, 10, 13; DcBiPP; Dis&D; OxCArt; REn; WhDW*

Goethals, George Washington
American. Army Officer, Engineer
Chief engineer, Panama Canal, 1913; first governor of Canal Zone, 1914-17.
b. Jun 29, 1858 in New York, New York
d. Jan 21, 1928 in New York, New York
Source: *AmBi; ApCAB X; BioIn 1, 2, 3, 4, 7, 9, 11; DcAmB; DcAmMiB; DcNAA; EncAB-H 1974, 1996; EncLatA; FacFETw; HarEnUS; InSci; LinLib S; McGEWB; NatCAB 14, 24; OxCAmH; WebAB 74, 79; WebAMB; WhAm 1; WorAl; WorAlBi*

Goethe, Johann Wolfgang von
German. Poet, Dramatist, Author
Wrote *Faust,* 1808, 1832; *The Sorrows of Werther,* 1774.
b. Aug 28, 1749 in Frankfurt am Main, Germany
d. Mar 22, 1832 in Weimar, Germany
Source: *AsBiEn; AtlBL; Baker 84, 92; BbD; Benet 87, 96; BiD&SB; BiDPsy; BiDTran; BioIn 1, 2, 3, 4, 5, 6, 7, 8, 9, 10, 11, 12, 13, 14, 17, 18, 19, 20; BlkwCE; BlmGEL; CamGWoT; CasWL; CelCen; ChhPo, S1, S2, S3; CnThe; CyWA 58; DcArts; DcBiA; DcBiPP; DcEnL; DcEuL; DcLB 94; DcPup; DcScB; Dis&D; EncEnl; EncO&P 3; EncPaPR 91; EncUnb; EncWT; Ent; EuAu; EuWr 5; EvEuW; GrFLW; GrStDi; InSci; IntDcT 2; LegTOT; LinLib L; LngCEL; LuthC 75; MagSWL; MajAI; McGEWB; McGEWD 72, 84; MetOEnc; NamesHP; NewC; NewCBEL; NewEOp 71; NewGrDM 80; NewGrDO; NinCLC 4, 22, 34; NotNAT B; Novels; OxCEng 67, 85, 95; OxCFr; OxCGer 76; OxCThe 67; OxDcArt; OxDcOp; PenC EUR; PoeCrit 5; RAdv 14, 13-2; RComWL; REn; REnWD; RfGWoL 95; ScF&FL 1; TwoTYeD; WhDW; WhoHrs 80; WorAl; WorAlBi; WrPh*

Goetz, Delia
American. Author
Books were based on her travels and work in Latin America.
b. Jun 1898?
d. Jun 26, 1996 in Washington, District of Columbia
Source: *AuBYP 2, 3; BioIn 2, 7, 13; ConAu 73, 152; CurBio 96N; InWom; SmATA 22, 91*

Goffstein, Marilyn
American. Children's Author, Illustrator
Goldie the Dollmaker, 1969; *Me and My Captain,* 1974, are among her self-illustrated books.
b. Dec 20, 1940 in Saint Paul, Minnesota
Source: *AuBYP 3; BioIn 14; ConAu 9NR, 21R; DcLB 61; DcLP 87B; PenNWW B; SmATA 8; WhoAmW 77*

Gogarty, Oliver St. John
Irish. Physician, Author
Leader of Sinn Fein movement; wrote memoir *As I Was Going Down Sackville Street,* 1937.
b. Aug 17, 1878 in Dublin, Ireland
d. Sep 22, 1957 in New York, New York
Source: *Benet 87, 96; BiDIrW; BioIn 1, 2, 3, 4, 6, 7, 8, 9, 10, 12, 13, 21; CamGLE; CasWL; CathA 1930; ChhPo, S2, S3; ConAu 109, 150; DcCathB; DcIrB 78, 88; DcIrL, 96; DcIrW 1; DcLB 15, 19; DcLEL; EvLB; GrWrEL P; LiExTwC; LngCTC; ModBrL; ModIrL; NewC; NewCBEL; ObitT 1951; OxCIri; OxCTwCP; PenC ENG; PoIre; REn; RfGEnL 91; RGTwCWr; TwCA, SUP; TwCLC 15; TwCWr; WebE&AL; WhAm 3; WhDW*

Gogol, Nikolai Vasilievich
Russian. Author
First of Russian realists; best known for comedy *The Inspector General,* 1836.
b. Mar 31, 1809 in Sorochintsy, Ukraine
d. Mar 4, 1852 in Moscow, Russia
Source: *AtlBL; BbD; BiD&SB; CamGWoT; CasWL; CnThe; CyWA 58; DcBiA; DcEuL; DcRusL; Dis&D; EuAu; EvEuW; HanRL; McGEWD 84; NewC; OxCThe 67, 83; PenC EUR; PlP&P; RComWL; REnWD; WebBD 83; WhDW*

Go-Go's, The
[Charlotte Caffey; Belinda Carlisle; Gina Schock; Kathy Valentine; Jane Wiedlin]
American. Music Group
Most successful all-female rock group ever, 1978-85; had hit single "We Got the Beat" from album *Beauty and the Beat,* 1982.
Source: *BioIn 15, 16, 17, 18; EncPR&S 89; EncRk 88; EncRkSt; HarEnR 86; NewWmR; PenEncP; RkOn 85; RolSEnR 83; WhoHol 92; WhsNW 85*

Goh Chok Tong
Singaporean. Political Leader
Prime minister, Singapore, 1990—.
b. May 20, 1941, Singapore
Source: *DcMPSA; IntWW 89, 91, 93; Who 92, 94; WhoAsAP 91; WhoWor 89, 91, 93, 95, 96*

Goheen, Robert Francis
American. Educator, University Administrator
Pres., Princeton U, 1957-72; ambassador to India, 1977-80.
b. Aug 15, 1919 in Vengurla, India
Source: *AmAu&B; Au&Wr 71; CurBio 58; DrAS 74F; IntWW 74, 91; LEduc 74; Who 74, 92; WhoAm 82, 90, 97; WhoAmP 87; WhoE 74; WhoWor 74, 84; WorAlBi; WrDr 88*

Goines, Donald
[Al C. Clark]
American. Author
Wrote novels *Whoreson* 1972; *Kenyatta's Last Hit,* 1975.
b. Dec 15, 1937 in Detroit, Michigan
d. Oct 21, 1974 in Highland Park, Michigan
Source: *BioIn 14; BlkLC; BlkWr 1; ConAu 114, 124; ConLC 80; DcLB 33; DcTwCCu 5; InB&W 80; SchCGBL; TwCCr&M 85, 91*

Goizueta, Roberto C(rispulo)
American. Business Executive
With Coca-Cola, 1964—; chm., 1981—.
b. Nov 18, 1931 in Havana, Cuba
Source: *BioIn 12, 14, 15, 16; ConAmBL; CurBio 96; Dun&B 79, 90; IntWW 83, 91; St&PR 91; WhoAm 76, 78, 80, 82, 84, 86, 88, 90, 92, 94, 95, 96, 97; WhoFI 74, 81, 83, 85, 87, 89, 92, 94, 96; WhoHisp 92; WhoSSW 75, 76, 82, 84, 86, 88, 91, 93, 95, 97; WhoWor 82, 84, 87, 89, 91, 93, 95, 96, 97*

Gola, Tom
[Thomas Joseph Gola]
American. Basketball Player
All-position player, 1955-66, mostly with Philadelphia; known for defense; Hall of Fame, 1975.
b. Jan 13, 1933 in Philadelphia, Pennsylvania
Source: *BasBi; BiDAmSp BK; BioIn 3, 4, 5, 6, 10; OfNBA 87; WhoBbl 73; WhoPoA 96*

Golacinski, Alan Bruce
American. Hostage
One of 52 held by terrorists, Nov 1979 - Jan 1981.
b. Jun 4, 1950, Austria
Source: *NewYTBS 81; USBiR 74*

Gold, Andrew
American. Singer
Guitarist, arranger for Linda Ronstadt; wrote hit singles "Lonely Boy," "Thank You for Being a Friend," 1978.
b. Aug 2, 1951 in Burbank, California
Source: *EncRk 88; IlEncRk; LegTOT; OnThGG; PenEncP; RkOn 78; RolSEnR 83; WhoRock 81*

Gold, Arthur
Canadian. Pianist
Part of piano duo with Robert Fizdale for 40 years; known for contemporary music.
b. Feb 6, 1919 in Toronto, Ontario, Canada
d. Jan 3, 1990 in New York, New York
Source: *Baker 84; BioIn 5, 6, 7, 12, 15, 16; ConAu 132; NewAmDM; NewGrDA 86; NewGrDM 80; NewYTBS 90; PenDiMP; Who 92*

Gold, Harry
Spy for the Soviets, 1935-46, who testified in Rosenberg spy trial.
b. 1910 in Bern, Switzerland
d. Aug 28, 1972 in Philadelphia, Pennsylvania
Source: *BioIn 2, 4, 10; NewYTBE 72; NewYTBS 74; SpyCS*

Gold, Herbert
American. Author
Books include *The Man Who Was Not With It,* 1956; *Therefore Be Bold,* 1960.
b. Mar 9, 1924 in Cleveland, Ohio
Source: *AmAu&B; Benet 87, 96; BenetAL 91; BioIn 3, 4, 6, 7, 8, 9, 10, 13, 14, 15, 16, 17, 20; CamGLE; CamHAL; CmCal; ConAu 9R, 17NR, 45NR; ConLC 4, 7, 14, 42; ConNov 72, 76, 82, 86, 91, 96; DcLB 2, Y81A; DcLEL 1940; DrAF 76; DrAPF 80, 91; FacFETw; IntAu&W 76, 77; IntvTCA 2; JeAmFiW; LegTOT; MichAu 80; ModAL; Novels; OxCAmL 65, 83, 95; PenC AM; RAdv 1; REnAL; TwCWr; WhoAm 74, 76, 78, 80, 82, 84, 86, 88, 90; WhoAmJ 80; WhoUSWr 88; WhoWor 74; WhoWorJ 72, 78; WhoWrEP 89, 92, 95; WorAu 1950; WrDr 76, 80, 82, 84, 86, 88, 90, 92, 94, 96*

Gold, Michael
[Irvin Granich]
American. Author, Journalist
Columnist for *The Daily Worker* for 32 yrs; books include *Life of John Brown,* 1924.
b. Apr 12, 1894 in New York, New York
d. May 14, 1967 in Terra Linda, California
Source: *AmAu&B; BenetAL 91; BioIn 4, 6, 7, 12; CamGLE; CamHAL; CnMD; ConAu 45, 97, X; DcLB 28; GrWrEL N; ModWD; Novels; OxCAmL 65, 83; PenC AM; REn; REnAL; TwCA, SUP; WebE&AL*

Gold, Thomas
English. Astronomer
With Bondi and Hoyle devised the steady-state theory of the universe.
b. May 22, 1920 in Vienna, Austria
Source: *AmMWSc 73P, 76P, 79, 82, 86, 89, 92, 95; AsBiEn; BiESc; BioIn 4, 5, 7, 14; BlueB 76; CamDcSc; IntAu&W 77, 82; IntWW 74, 75, 76, 77, 78, 79, 80, 81, 82, 83, 89, 91, 93; LarDcSc; NotTwCS; Who 74, 82, 83, 85, 88, 90,*

92, 94; WhoAm 74, 76, 78, 80, 82, 84, 86, 88, 90, 92, 94, 95, 96, 97; WhoE 74; WhoFrS 84; WorScD

Goldberg, Arthur Joseph
American. Supreme Court Justice
Liberal associate justice, 1962-65; US ambassador to UN, 1965-68, succeeding Adl ai Stevenson.
b. Aug 8, 1908 in Chicago, Illinois
d. Jan 19, 1990 in Washington, District of Columbia
Source: *AmPolLe; BiDAmL; BiDAmLL; BiDFedJ; BiDrUSE 71, 89; BioIn 2, 5, 6, 7, 8, 9, 10, 11, 12, 14, 15, 16; ConAu 65, 130; CurBio 49, 61, 90, 90N; DcPol; EncAB-H 1974; EncAI&E; EncWB; FacFETw; IntAu&W 77; IntWW 74, 75, 76, 77, 78, 79, 80, 81, 82, 83, 89; NewYTBS 90; OxCSupC; PolProf E, J, K; SupCtJu; WebAB 74, 79; WhAm 10; Who 85, 90; WhoAm 74, 76, 78, 80, 82, 84, 86, 88; WhoAmJ 80; WhoAmL 78, 79, 90; WhoAmP 73, 75, 77, 79; WhoSSW 76; WhoWor 78, 80, 82, 84, 87, 89; WhoWorJ 78; WorAl; WorAlBi; WrDr 86, 90*

Goldberg, Bernard
American. Broadcast Journalist
Appears in TV series "48 Hours."
b. Aug 25, 1932 in New York, New York
Source: *IntMPA 78, 79, 80, 81, 82, 84, 86, 88, 92*

Goldberg, Bertrand
American. Architect
His works include Marina City, Chicago, 1959; Stanford U Medical Center, 1967.
b. Jul 17, 1913 in Chicago, Illinois
Source: *AmArch 70; BioIn 10; BioNews 74; ConArch 80, 87, 94; IntWW 82, 83, 89, 91, 93; MacEA; WhoAm 74, 76, 78, 80, 82, 84, 86, 88, 92, 94, 96; WhoTech 84, 89; WhoWor 74, 76*

Goldberg, Gary David
American. Writer, Producer
Creator and writer of TV series, "Family Ties," 1982-89.
b. Jun 25, 1944 in New York, New York
Source: *BioIn 15; ConTFT 10; LesBEnT 92; News 89; WhoAm 80, 82, 84, 86, 88, 90, 92, 94, 95, 96, 97; WhoEnt 92; WhoWest 80*

Goldberg, Leonard
American. Producer
With Aaron Spelling, produced TV series "Charlie's Angels," 1976-81; "Fantasy Island," 1978-84; won Emmy for movie, "Something About Ameliia," 1984.
b. Jan 24, 1934 in New York, New York
Source: *BioIn 9, 12, 15; ConTFT 3, 11; Dun&B 90; IntMPA 84, 86, 88, 92, 94, 96; News 88; NewYTBS 80; VarWW 85; WhoAm 78, 80, 82, 84, 86, 88, 90, 92, 94, 95, 96, 97; WhoEnt 92; WhoFI 89, 92, 94; WhoWor 82*

Goldberg, Rube
[Reuben Lucius Goldberg]
American. Cartoonist
Created comic strips "Mike & Ike," "Lucifer Butts"; known for drawings of absurd mechanical contraptions.
b. Jul 4, 1883 in San Francisco, California
d. Dec 7, 1970 in New York, New York
Source: *AmAu&B; ArtsAmW 2; ASCAP 66; BioIn 1, 2, 5, 6, 7, 8, 9, 10; CmCal; ConAu 5R, X; CurBio 48, 71, 71N; DcAmB S8; EncACom; EncTwCJ; FacFETw; JoeFr; LegTOT; NewYTBE 70; WebAB 74, 79; WhAm 6, 7; WhAmArt 85; WhNAA; WhScrn 77, 83; WorECom*

Goldberg, Whoopi
[Caryn E. Johnson]
American. Actor, Comedian
Star of films *Color Purple*, 1985, *Ghost*, for which she won an Oscar, 1991, *Eddie*, 1996.
b. Nov 13, 1949 in New York, New York
Source: *AfrAmAl 6; BiDFilm 94; BioIn 13, 14, 15, 16; BlksAmF; BlkWAm; CelR 90; ConTFT 3, 6; CurBio 85; DcTwCCu 5; DrBlPA 90; GrLiveH; HalFC 88; HolBB; IntDcF 2-3; IntMPA 88, 92, 94, 96; InWom SUP; LegTOT; NegAl 89; NewYTBS 84; NotBlAW 1; QDrFCA 92; WhoAm 94; WhoAmW 91; WhoBlA 88, 92; WhoCom; WhoEnt 92; WorAlBi*

Goldberger, Joseph
American. Physician
His research during 1913-25 resulted in extinction of B-complex deficiency disease, pellagra.
b. Jul 16, 1874, Austria
d. Jan 17, 1929 in Washington, District of Columbia
Source: *AmBi; AsBiEn; BiESc; BioIn 2, 3, 4, 5, 7, 8, 14; DcAmB; DcAmMeB 84; DcScB; EncSoH; InSci; LarDcSc; NatCAB 21; OxCMed 86; WebAB 74, 79; WhAm 1*

Goldblum, Jeff
American. Actor
Starred in films *The Big Chill*, 1983; *The Fly*, 1986 and sequel *The Fly II*, 1989.
b. Oct 22, 1952 in Pittsburgh, Pennsylvania
Source: *BioIn 13, 14, 15, 16; CelR 90; ConNews 88-1; ConTFT 6; EncAFC; HalFC 84, 88; HolBB; IntMPA 86, 88, 92, 94, 96; IntWW 91, 93; JohnWSW; LegTOT; NewYTBS 78; VarWW 85; WhoAm 88, 90, 92, 94, 95, 96, 97; WhoEnt 92; WhoHol 92; WorAlBi*

Golden, Harry Lewis
American. Author, Editor, Publisher
Popular essay collections include best-selling *Only in America*, 1958; *For 2 Cents Plain*, 1959.
b. May 6, 1903 in Mikulinsty, Austria-Hungary
d. Oct 2, 1981 in Charlotte, North Carolina
Source: *AmAu&B; AnObit 1981; ConAu 1R, 2NR, 104; CurBio 59, 81; JeAmHC; RAdv 1; REnAL; WhoAm 80; WorAu 1950*

Golden, John
American. Dramatist, Producer
Produced plays *Let Us Be Gay*, 1928; *Susan and God*, 1937; *Cla udia*, 1941; wrote song "Poor Butterfly," 1916.
b. Jun 27, 1874 in New York, New York
d. Jun 17, 1955 in New York, New York
Source: *AmAu&B; ASCAP 66, 80; BenetAL 91; BioIn 1, 3, 4, 6; CmpEPM; CurBio 44, 55; DcAmB S5; NatCAB 45; NotNAT A, B; OhA&B; OxCAmT 84; OxCThe 83; PoIre; REnAL; WhAm 3; WhThe*

Golden, Thelma
American. Curator
Curator of "Black Male: Representations of Masculinity in Contemporary American Art," 1994, Whitney Museum of American Art; first black curator at the Whitney.
b. 1965 in New York, New York
Source: *ConBlB 10*

Golden, William
American. Artist
Designed the CBS eye as TV trademark, 1951.
b. Mar 31, 1911 in New York, New York
d. Oct 23, 1959 in Stony Pointe, New York
Source: *BiDLA; BioIn 8, 10; ConDes 84; DcTwDes; WhoGrA 62*

Golden, William Lee
[The Oak Ridge Boys]
American. Singer
Baritone with country-pop group.
b. Jan 12, 1939 in Brewton, Alabama
Source: *WhoAm 80, 82, 84, 86*

Golden Earring
[Rinus Gerritsen; Barry Hay; George Kooymans; Robert Jan Stips; Cesar Zuiderwijk]
Dutch. Music Group
Holland's top rock band since, 1964; hit single "Twilight Zone," 1982.
Source: *RkOn 78, 85; WhoRock 81; WhoRocM 82*

Goldenson, Leonard Harry
American. Film Executive, TV Executive
Chm., chief exec. of ABC since 1972; played pivotal role in history of commercial network TV.
b. Dec 7, 1905 in Scottdale, Pennsylvania
Source: *BiDAmBL 83; BioIn 4, 5, 7, 11, 12, 13, 14, 15; CurBio 57; Dun&B 86; EncTwCJ; IntMPA 92; LesBEnT, 92; St&PR 84; VarWW 85; WhoAm 74, 76, 78, 80, 82, 84, 86; WhoE 74, 83, 85, 86; WhoEnt 92; WhoFI 74, 75, 77, 79, 81, 83, 85; WhoGov 72, 75; WhoTelC; WhoWor 74, 82, 84, 87*

Goldfinger, Nathaniel
American. Labor Union Official
Economist, director of research, AFL-CIO, 1955-76.
b. Aug 20, 1916 in New York, New York
d. Jul 22, 1976 in Silver Spring, Maryland
Source: *AmMWSc 73S; BiDAmL; BioIn 11, 13; NatCAB 61; NewYTBS 76; WhAm 7; WhoAm 74, 76; WhoLab 76*

Goldhaber, Maurice
American. Physicist
Discovered nuclear photoelectric effect, 1934.
b. Apr 18, 1911 in Lemberg, Austria-Hungary
Source: *AmMWSc 73P, 76P, 79, 82, 86, 89, 92, 95; AsBiEn; BiESc; BioIn 13; BlueB 76; IntAu&W 77; IntWW 74, 75, 76, 77, 78, 79, 80, 81, 82, 83, 89, 91, 93; McGMS 80; WhoAm 74, 76, 78, 80, 82, 84, 86, 88, 92, 94, 95, 96, 97; WhoE 95; WhoFrS 84; WhoScEn 94, 96; WorAl; WorAlBi*

Goldie, Grace Wyndham
English. Producer
With BBC, 1944-65; productions include "Press Conference"; "Panorama."
b. 1900?
d. Jun 3, 1986 in London, England
Source: *AnObit 1986; BioIn 6*

Goldin, Daniel S
American. Government Official
NASA administrator, 1992—; combines interest in exploration with fiscal restraint.
b. Jul 23, 1940 in New York, New York
Source: *CurBio 93; Dun&B 90*

Goldin, Horace
American. Magician
Devised magic trick of "sawing a woman in half."
b. Dec 17, 1873 in Vilna, Poland
d. Aug 22, 1939 in London, England
Source: *BioIn 4, 16; CamGWoT; DcAmB S2; MagIlD*

Golding, William (Gerald), Sir
English. Author
Best known for allegorical cult novel *Lord of the Flies,* 1954; won Nobel Prize in literature, 1983.
b. Sep 19, 1911 in Saint Columb Minor, England
d. Jun 19, 1993 in Perranarworthal, England
Source: *AnObit 1993; Au&Arts 5; Benet 87, 96; BioIn 6, 7, 8, 9, 10, 11, 12, 13, 14, 15, 16, 17, 18, 19; BlmGEL; BlueB 76; BritWr S1; CamGEL; CamGLE; CasWL; CelR 90; CnDBLB 7; CnMWL; ConAu 5R, 13NR, 33NR, 54NR, 141; ConLC 1, 2, 3, 8, 10, 17, 27, 58, 81; ConNov 72, 76, 82, 86, 91; CurBio 93N; CyWA 89; DcArts; DcLB 15, 100; DcLEL 1940; EncSF, 93; EncWL, 2, 3; FacFETw; GrWrEL N; IntAu&W 76, 77, 89, 91, 93; IntvTCA 2; IntWW 74, 75, 76, 77, 78, 79, 80, 81, 82, 83, 89, 91, 93; LegTOT; LinLib L; LngCEL; LngCTC; MagSWL; MajTwCW; MakMC; ModBrL, S1, S2; ModWD; NewC; NewEScF; NewYTBS 83, 93; NobelP; Novels; OxCChiL; OxCEng 85, 95; PenC ENG; RAdv 1, 14, 13-1; REn; RfGEnL 91; RGTwCWr; ScF&FL 1, 2, 92; ScFSB; TwCRHW 90, 94; TwCSFW 81, 86, 91; TwCWr; TwCYAW; WebE&AL; WhAm 11; WhDW; WhE&EA; Who 74, 82, 83, 85, 88, 90, 92; WhoAm 80, 82, 84, 86, 88, 90, 92; WhoHr&F; WhoNob, 90, 95; WhoTwCL; WhoWor 74, 78, 80, 82, 84, 87, 89, 91, 93; WorAl; WorAlBi; WorAu 1950; WorLitC; WrDr 76, 80, 82, 84, 86, 88, 90, 92, 94N*

Goldman, Albert
American. Writer
Wrote biographies *Elvis,* 1981; *The Lives of John Lennon,* 1988.
b. Apr 15, 1927 in Dormont, Pennsylvania
d. Mar 28, 1994
Source: *AmAu&B; BestSel 89-2; BioIn 12; ConAu 9NR, 17R, 48NR, 144; ConLC 86; DrAS 74E, 78E, 82E; LiJour; WrDr 92, 94, 96*

Goldman, Bo
American. Screenwriter
Won Oscars for *One Flew Over the Cuckoo's Nest,* 1975; *Melvin and Howard,* 1980.
b. Sep 10, 1932 in New York, New York
Source: *BioIn 19; ConAu 109, 112; ConDr 88A; ConTFT 8; IntAu&W 86; IntDcF 1-4; IntMPA 92, 94, 96; VarWW 85; WhoAm 82, 84, 86, 88, 95, 96, 97; WhoWor 95*

Goldman, Edwin Franko
American. Bandleader, Composer
Composed over 100 marches: "On the Mall," 1924; band held summer outdoor concerts in NYC, 1918-55.
b. Jan 1, 1878 in Louisville, Kentucky
d. Feb 21, 1956 in New York, New York
Source: *ASCAP 66, 80; Baker 78, 84, 92; BiDAmM; BioIn 1, 2, 4, 6, 9; ConAmC 76, 82; CurBio 42, 56; DcAmB S6; NatCAB 41; NewAmDM; NewGrDA 86; NewGrDM 80; NotNAT B; OxCAmH; OxCPMus; PenDiMP; PopAmC; WebAB 74, 79; WhAm 3*

Goldman, Emma
American. Anarchist
Important figure in American radicalism who published *Anarchism and Other Essays,* 1910.
b. Jun 27, 1869 in Kaunas, Lithuania
d. May 14, 1940 in Toronto, Ontario, Canada
Source: *AmBi; AmDec 1900; AmPeW; AmRef; AmSocL; AmWomWr; ArtclWW 2; BenetAL 91; BiDAmL; BiDAmLf; BiDMoPL; BiDNeoM; BioAmW; BioIn 1, 2, 3, 4, 5, 6, 9, 10, 11, 12, 13, 14, 15, 16, 17, 18, 19, 20, 21; ConAu 110, 150; ContDcW 89; CurBio 40; DcAmB S2; DcAmImH; DcAmSR; DcNAA; DcTwHis; EncAB-H 1974, 1996; EncAL; EncRev; EncUnb; EncWHA; FacFETw; FemiCLE; FemiWr; GoodHs; GrLiveH; HanAmWH; HeroCon; HerW, 84; IntDcWB; InWom, SUP; JeAmHC; JeHun; LegTOT; LibW; LiExTwC; LinLib L, S; McGEWB; ModWoWr; NewCol 75; NotAW; OxCAmH; OxCAmL 65, 83, 95; OxCWoWr 95; RadHan; RComAH; REnAL; RfGAmL 94; TwCLC 13; WebAB 74, 79; WhAm 4, HSA; WhAmP; WhLit; WomPubS 1800*

Goldman, Eric Frederick
American. Author, Historian
US history authority; wrote *Rendezvous with Destiny,* 1952; *The Tragedy of Lyndon Johnson,* 1969.
b. Jun 17, 1915 in Washington, District of Columbia
d. Feb 19, 1989 in Princeton, New Jersey
Source: *AmAu&B; BioIn 6, 7, 8, 11, 16; BlueB 76; ConAu 5R, 127; CurBio 64, 89, 89N; DcAmC; DrAS 74H, 78H, 82H; IntAu&W 82; IntWW 83; PolProf J; WhAm 9; WhoAm 74, 76, 78, 80, 84; WhoWor 74, 78; WrDr 76, 80, 86, 90*

Goldman, Francisco
American. Author
Wrote *The Long Night of White Chickens,* 1992.
b. 1955
Source: *ConLC 76*

Goldman, James
American. Dramatist, Author
Films include Oscar winners *Butch Cassidy and the Sundance Kid,* 1969; *All the President's Men,* 1976.
b. Jun 30, 1927 in Chicago, Illinois
Source: *AmAu&B; BiE&WWA; BioIn 10, 12; BlueB 76; ConAmD; ConAu 1NR, 45; ConDr 73, 77, 82, 88, 93; ConTFT 8; FilmgC; HalFC 80, 84, 88; IntAu&W 91, 93; McGEWD 72, 84; NatPD 81; NotNAT; OxCAmT 84; VarWW 85; WhoAm 74, 76, 78, 80, 82, 84, 86, 88, 90, 92, 94, 95, 96, 97; WhoE 74; WhoEnt 92; WhoThe 81; WhoWor 74; WrDr 76, 80, 82, 84, 86, 88, 90, 92, 94, 96*

Goldman, Richard Franko
American. Composer, Bandleader
Wrote "A Sentimental Journey," 1941, numerous works for ensembles.
b. Dec 7, 1910 in New York, New York
d. Jan 19, 1980 in Baltimore, Maryland
Source: *AmAu&B; ASCAP 66; Baker 78, 84, 92; BioIn 1, 12; BlueB 76; ConAmC 76, 82; ConAu 5NR, 9R, 93; DrAS 74H, 78H; IntAu&W 76, 77, 82; IntWWM 77, 80; LEduc 74; NewAmDM; NewGrDA 86; NewYTBS 80; PenDiMP; WhAm 7; WhoAm 74, 76, 78, 80; WhoWor 74; WrDr 76, 80*

Goldman, Ronald Lyle
American. Victim
Friend of Nicole Brown Simpson (Mrs. O.J.) and famous murder victim.
b. Jul 2, 1968 in Illinois
d. Jun 13, 1994 in Los Angeles, California

Goldman, Sylvan N
American. Merchant, Inventor
Depression-era grocery store owner, who invented grocery cart.
b. 1898
d. Nov 25, 1984 in Oklahoma City, Oklahoma
Source: *BioIn 3, 14; St&PR 75*

Goldman, William
American. Author, Screenwriter
Wrote film scripts *Harper,* 1966; *Marathon Man,* 1976; Oscar-winning *Butch Cassidy and the Sundance Kid,* 1969.
b. Aug 12, 1931 in Chicago, Illinois
Source: *AmAu&B; BiDFilm 94; BiE&WWA; BioIn 11, 12, 13, 14, 15, 17, 18, 20, 21; BlueB 76; ConAu 9R, 29NR; ConDr 73, 77A; ConLC 1, 48; ConNov 72, 76, 82, 86, 91, 96; ConTFT 7, 14; CurBio 95; DcLB 44; DcLEL 1940; DrAF 76; DrAPF 80, 89; FilmgC; HalFC 80, 84, 88; IntAu&W 76, 91; IntDcF 1-4, 2-4; IntMPA 78, 79, 80, 81, 82, 84, 86, 88, 92, 94, 96; IntWW 91, 93; JeAmFiW; LegTOT; LinLib L; NewYTBS 78, 79; NotNAT; Novels; PenC AM; ScF&FL 1, 2, 92; SJGFanW; WebE&AL; WhoAm 74, 76, 78, 80, 82, 84, 86, 88, 92, 94, 95, 96, 97; WhoWor 74, 95, 96, 97; WorAlBi; WorAu 1970; WrDr 76, 80, 82, 84, 86, 88, 90, 92, 94, 96*

Goldmann, Nahum
American. Scholar, Government Official
Jewish leader who advocated reconciliation between Israel, Arab nations; pres., World Jewish Congress, 1951-78.
b. Jul 10, 1895 in Wisnewo, Poland
d. Aug 29, 1982 in Bad Reichenhall, Germany (West)
Source: *AnObit 1982; BioIn 15, 16; ConAu 107; CurBio 82, 82N; IntWW 74, 75, 76, 77, 78, 79, 80, 81, 82; MidE 79, 80, 81, 82; NewYTBE 70; NewYTBS 82; Who 74, 82; WhoAmJ 80; WhoRel 75, 77; WhoWor 74, 76, 78; WhoWorJ 72, 78*

Goldmark, Karl
Hungarian. Composer
Noted for opera, *Queen of Sheba,* 1875; overture, *Sakuntala,* 1860.
b. May 18, 1830 in Keszthely, Hungary
d. Jan 2, 1915 in Vienna, Austria
Source: *Baker 78, 84, 92; BioIn 2, 7, 12; BriBkM 80; CmpBCM; DcCom&M 79; GrComp; IntDcOp; MetOEnc; NewAmDM; NewEOp 71; NewGrDM 80; NewGrDO; NewOxM; OxCMus; OxDcOp; PenDiMP A*

Goldmark, Peter Carl
American. Engineer, Inventor
Developed first practical color television system, 1940.
b. Dec 2, 1906 in Budapest, Austria-Hungary
d. Dec 7, 1977 in Westchester County, New York
Source: *AmMWSc 73P, 76P; BioIn 2, 8, 10, 11, 12, 20; BlueB 76; ConAu 73, 77; CurBio 40, 50; DcAmB S10; InSci; IntWW 74, 75, 76, 77; McGMS 80; NatCAB 60; NewYTBE 72; NewYTBS 77; NotTwCS; PenEncP; WhAm 7; WhDW; WhoAm 74, 76, 78; WhoWor 74, 76; WorAl; WorInv*

Goldoni, Carlo
Italian. Dramatist
Established realistic comedy as a dramatic form.
b. Feb 25, 1707 in Venice, Italy
d. Feb 6, 1793 in Paris, France
Source: *AtlBL; Benet 87, 96; BiD&SB; BioIn 5, 7, 8, 10, 11, 13, 14; BlkwCE; CamGWoT; CasWL; CyWA 58; DcArts; DcBiPP; DcCathB; DcEuL; DcItL 1, 2; DcPup; Dis&D; EncEnl; EncWT; Ent; EuAu; EuWr 4; EvEuW; GrFLW; IntDcOp; IntDcT 2; LinLib L, S; LitC 4; McGEWB; McGEWD 72, 84; MetOEnc; NewCBEL; NewEOp 71; NewGrDM 80; NewGrDO; NotNAT A, B; OxCEng 67, 85, 95; OxCThe 67, 83; OxDcOp; PenC EUR; PlP&P; RAdv 14, 13-2; RComWL; REn; REnWD; RfGWoL 95; WhDW; WorAl; WorAlBi*

Goldovsky, Boris
American. Conductor, Director, Pianist
Artistic Director, Goldovsky Opera Institute, 1963—; commentator, NY Met broadcasts, 1946—.
b. Jun 7, 1908 in Moscow, Russia
Source: *Baker 78, 84, 92; BiDAmM; BioIn 1, 2, 7, 8; ConAu 16NR, 81; CurBio 66; IntWWM 77, 80, 90; MetOEnc; NewAmDM; NewEOp 71; NewGrDA 86; NewGrDM 80; OxDcOp; PenDiMP; WhoAm 74, 76, 78, 80, 82, 84, 86, 88, 90, 92, 94, 95, 96, 97; WhoAmJ 80; WhoAmM 83; WhoE 83, 85, 86, 89; WhoEnt 92; WhoMus 72; WhoWor 74*

Goldsboro, Bobby
American. Singer, Songwriter
CMA star of year, 1968; hits include "Honey;" "The Straight Life."
b. Jan 18, 1941 in Marianna, Florida
Source: *BioIn 14; CelR; EncFCWM 83; EncRk 88; LegTOT; PenEncP; RolSEnR 83; VarWW 85; WhoAm 76, 78, 80, 82, 84; WhoRock 81; WorAlBi*

Goldsborough, Louis Malesherbes
American. Naval Officer
Commanded fleet that destroyed Confederate fleet, 1862.
b. Feb 18, 1805 in Washington, District of Columbia
d. Feb 20, 1877 in Washington, District of Columbia
Source: *AmBi; ApCAB; DcAmB; Drake; HarEnMi; HarEnUS; NatCAB 2; NewCol 75; TwCBDA; WebAB 74; WebAMB; WebBD 83; WhAm HS; WhCiWar*

Goldschmidt, Neil Edward
American. Politician
Secretary of transportation under Carter, 1979-81; Dem. governor of Oregon, 1987-91.
b. Jun 16, 1940 in Eugene, Oregon
Source: *AlmAP 88; WhoWest 87, 89, 92; WhoWor 80, 89, 91*

Goldschmidt, Victor Moritz
Norwegian. Mineralogist
Study of thermal metamorphism was precursor to fields of geochemistry and inorganic crystal chemistry.
b. Jan 27, 1888 in Zurich, Switzerland
d. Mar 20, 1947 in Oslo, Norway
Source: *AsBiEn; BiESc; BioIn 1, 2, 6, 14, 17, 19, 20; CamDcSc; DcScB; InSci; LarDcSc*

Goldsmith, Fred Ernest
American. Baseball Player
Pitcher, 1879-84; in some sources, receives credit as co-inventor of curveball, with "Candy" Cummings.
b. May 15, 1852 in New Haven, Connecticut
d. Mar 28, 1939 in Berkley, Michigan
Source: *WhoProB 73*

Goldsmith, James (Michael), Sir
French. Financier
Various business deals have resulted in a net worth of over $2.5 billion.
b. Feb 26, 1933 in Paris, France
d. Jul 18, 1997, Spain
Source: *BioIn 10, 11, 12, 13, 14, 15, 16, 17, 18, 19, 21; BlueB 76; CurBio 88; DcTwBBL; IntWW 76, 77, 78, 79, 80, 81, 82, 83, 89, 91, 93; NewYTBS 84, 86; Who 74, 82, 83, 85, 88, 90, 92, 94; WhoFr 79; WhoWor 78, 80, 82, 84*

Goldsmith, Jerry
American. Composer
Won Oscar, 1976, for *The Omen;* won 1981 Emmy for "Masada."
b. Feb 10, 1929 in Los Angeles, California
Source: *Baker 78, 84, 92; BioIn 15; CmMov; ConAmC 82; ConTFT 3, 14; FilmgC; HalFC 80, 84, 88; IntDcF 1-4, 2-4; IntMPA 92, 94, 96; LegTOT; NewGrDA 86; OxCPMus; PenEncH; WhoAm 86, 88, 90, 92, 94, 95, 96, 97; WhoEnt 92; WorEFlm*

Goldsmith, Judith Ann Becker
American. Feminist
Pres. of NOW, 1982-85.
b. Nov 26, 1938 in Manitowoc, Wisconsin
Source: *BioIn 13, 14; NewYTBS 82, 84; WhoAm 86; WhoAmW 87*

Goldsmith, Oliver
British. Poet, Dramatist, Author
Wrote *The Vicar of Wakefield,* 1766; *She Stoops to Conquer,* 1773.
b. Nov 10, 1728 in Kilkenny West, Ireland
d. Apr 4, 1774 in London, England
Source: *Alli; AtlBL; BbD; BiD&SB; BiDIrW; BioIn 1, 2, 3, 4, 5, 6, 7, 8, 9, 10, 11, 12, 13, 14, 15, 17, 18, 19, 20; BlkwCE; BritAu; BritWr 3; CamGEL; CamGWoT; CarSB; CasWL; Chambr 2; ChhPo, S1, S2, S3; CnE&AP; CrtSuDr; CrtT 2; CyEd; CyWA 58; DcArts; DcBiA; DcBiPP; DcEnA, A; DcEnL; DcEuL; DcIrB 78, 88; DcIrL, 96; DcIrW 1; DcLEL; DcPup; Dis&D; EncEnl; EvLB; GrWrEL DR, N, P; HsB&A; InSci; LinLib L, S; LitC 2; MagSWL; McGEWD 72, 84; MouLC 2; NewC; NewEOp 71; NotNAT A, B; OxCEng 67; OxCIri; OxCMus; PenC ENG; PlP&P; PoIre; RAdv 1, 14, 13-1, 13-2; REn; SmATA 26; WebE&AL; WhDW; WorAl; WorLitC*

Goldstein, Israel
American. Religious Leader
Co-founded National Conference of Christians and Jews, 1928; Brandeis U, 1946.
b. Jun 18, 1896 in Philadelphia, Pennsylvania
d. Apr 11, 1986 in Tel Aviv, Israel
Source: *AmAu&B; BioIn 1, 2, 14, 15, 16; BlueB 76; ConAu 53, 119; CurBio 46, 86, 86N; IntAu&W 77; IntWW 74, 75, 76, 77, 78, 79, 80, 81, 82, 83; MidE 78, 79, 80, 81, 82; WhAm 9; WhoAm 74, 76, 78; WhoAmJ 80; WhoWorJ 72, 78; WrDr 76, 80, 82, 84, 86*

Goldstein, Joseph Leonard
American. Physician, Educator
With Michael S Brown, won Nobel Prize, 1985, for research into role of cholesterol in cardiovascular disease.
b. Apr 18, 1940 in Sumter, South Carolina
Source: *AmMWSc 79, 82, 86, 89, 92, 95; BiDrACP 79; BioIn 14, 15, 20; CamDcSc; CurBio 87; IntWW 89, 91, 93; LarDcSc; NewYTBS 85; NobelP; Who 88, 90, 92, 94; WhoAm 82, 84, 86, 88, 90, 92, 94, 95, 96, 97; WhoFrS 84; WhoMedH; WhoNob, 90, 95; WhoScEn 94, 96; WhoSSW 86, 88, 91, 93, 95, 97; WhoWor 87, 89, 91, 93, 95, 96, 97; WorAlBi*

Goldston, Nathaniel R, III
American. Restaurateur
President, chairman, Gourmet Services Inc., 1975—.
b. Oct 20, 1938 in Omaha, Nebraska
Source: *BioIn 13, 16; WhoBlA 85, 88, 92*

Goldwater, Barry Morris
American. Politician, Author
Rep. senator from AZ, 1953-87; defeated by Lyndon Johnson in landslide 1964 presidential election; father of modern conservatism.
b. Jan 1, 1909 in Phoenix, Arizona
Source: *AmAu&B; AmOrTwC; AmPolLe; BiDrAC; BiDrUSC 89; BioIn 3, 4, 5, 6, 7, 8, 9, 10, 11, 12, 13, 14, 15, 16; CelR 90; CngDr 85; ColdWar 1; CurBio 55, 78; DcAmC; DcPol; Dun&B 88; EncAAH; EncAB-H 1974, 1996; EncWB; FacFETw; IntWW 83, 89, 91, 93; NewYTBS 74, 80; PolProf J, NF; PolsAm 84; PresAR; REnAW; WebAB 74, 79; Who 92; WhoAm 74, 76, 78, 80, 82, 84, 86, 88, 92, 94, 95, 96; WhoAmP 73, 75, 77, 79, 81, 83, 85, 87, 89, 91, 93, 95; WhoGov 72, 75, 77; WhoWest 74, 76, 78, 80, 82, 84, 87, 89, 92, 94; WhoWor 74, 78, 80, 82, 84, 87; WorAl; WorAlBi; WrDr 92*

Goldwater, Barry Morris, Jr.
American. Politician
Son of Barry Goldwater, Rep. congressman from CA, 1969—.
b. Jul 5, 1938 in Los Angeles, California
Source: *AlmAP 82; BiDrAC; BiDrUSC 89; BioIn 13; CngDr 87; WhoAm 78, 80, 82, 84; WhoAmP 87, 91; WhoGov 72, 75, 77; WhoWest 74, 76, 78, 80, 82*

Goldwyn, Samuel
[Samuel Goldfish]
American. Producer
Produced *All Quiet on the Western Front,* 1930; won Oscar for *The Best Years of Our Lives,* 1946; co-founded MGM; noted for malapropisms.
b. Aug 27, 1882 in Warsaw, Poland
d. Jan 31, 1974 in Los Angeles, California
Source: *AmCulL; BenetAL 91; BiDFilm; BioIn 1, 2, 3, 4, 5, 6, 7, 8, 10, 11, 12, 16, 19, 21; BioNews 74; BusPN; CelR; CmCal; CurBio 44, 74N; DcArts; DcFM; FacFETw; FilmEn; FilmgC; GangFlm; HalFC 80, 84, 88; LegTOT; LinLib S; McGEWB; NewYTBS 74; ObitT 1971; OxCFilm; PeoHis; REnAL; WebAB 74, 79; WhAm 6, 7; Who 74; WhoWor 74; WorAlBi; WorEFlm*

Golenpaul, Dan
American. Publisher, Producer
Created radio quiz show, ''Information Please,'' 1930s-40s.
b. 1900
d. Feb 13, 1974 in New York, New York
Source: *BioIn 10; NewYTBS 74; ObitOF 79*

Golgi, Camillo
Italian. Neurologist
Shared 1906 Nobel Prize in medicine; discovered silver nitrate stain for nerve tissue study.
b. Jul 7, 1843 in Corteno, Italy
d. Jan 21, 1926 in Pavia, Italy
Source: *AsBiEn; BiDPsy; BiESc; BiHiMed; BioIn 3, 6, 9, 14, 15, 20; CamDcSc; DcScB; InSci; LarDcSc; NamesHP; NobelP; NotTwCS; OxCMed 86; WebBD 83; WhoNob, 90, 95; WorAl; WorAlBi; WorScD*

Goliath
Biblical Figure
Philistine giant killed by young David with sling and stones.
Source: *BioIn 2, 4, 20; LngCEL; NewCol 75; PenNWW B; WebBD 83*

Gollancz, Victor, Sir
English. Publisher
Founded publishing house, 1928; wrote *A Year of Grace,* 1950.
b. Apr 9, 1893 in London, England
d. Feb 8, 1967 in London, England
Source: *BiDMoPL; BioIn 1, 3, 6, 7, 8, 9, 14, 15, 16, 18; ChhPo S2; ConAu 116; CurBio 63, 67; DcArts; DcLB 112; DcNaB 1961; DcTwBBL; FacFETw; GrBr; LngCTC; ObitOF 79; ObitT 1961; OxCEng 85, 95; WhE&EA*

Golonka, Arlene
American. Actor
Played in Mayberry RFD, 1968-71.
b. Jan 23, 1936 in Chicago, Illinois
Source: *BiE&WWA; NotNAT; WhoHol 92, A*

Golschmann, Vladimir
French. Conductor
Led St. Louis Symphony, 1931-57; Denver Orchestra, 1960s.
b. Dec 26, 1893 in Paris, France
d. Mar 1, 1972 in New York, New York
Source: *Baker 78, 84, 92; BiDAmM; BioIn 1, 2, 3, 4, 9, 11; BriBkM 80; CurBio 51, 72, 72N; MusSN; NewAmDM; NewGrDA 86; NewGrDM 80; NewYTBE 72; PenDiMP; WhAm 5*

Golson, Benny
American. Jazz Musician, Bandleader
Tenor saxist; formed jazztet; first to take band on US State dept. tours.
b. Jan 25, 1929 in Philadelphia, Pennsylvania
Source: *AllMusG; ASCAP 66; BiDAfM; BiDAmM; BiDJaz; BioIn 16, 21; EncJzS; NewAmDM; NewGrDJ 88, 94; PenEncP; WhoAm 74*

Golub, Leon Albert
American. Artist
Figurative painter whose works have strong political overtones.
b. Jan 23, 1922 in Chicago, Illinois
Source: *AmArt; BioIn 13, 14, 16; ConArt 83, 89; CurBio 84; DcAmArt; DcCAA 77, 88; DcCAr 81; McGDA; PrintW 85; WhoAm 84, 90, 97; WhoAmA 84, 91; WhoE 83, 89*

Golub, William Weldon
American. Businessman
Head of Golub Corp., a regional supermarket chain, 1932-82.
b. Oct 7, 1914 in New York, New York
d. Oct 19, 1992 in Schenectady, New York
Source: *WhAm 11; WhoAm 82, 84, 86, 88, 90, 92, 94; WhoAmL 90, 92, 94; WhoE 77, 79, 83*

Gombrowicz, Witold
Polish. Author
Works include *Cosmos*, 1967; winner of International Prize for Literature.
b. Sep 4, 1904 in Moloszyee, Poland
d. Jul 25, 1969 in Nice, France
Source: *Benet 87, 96; BioIn 8, 9, 10, 11, 12, 13; CasWL; ClDMEL 80; CnMD; ConAu 25R, P-2; ConLC 4, 7, 11, 49; CroCD; CyWA 89; DcArts; EncWL 2, 3; EncWT; Ent; EuWr 12; GrFLW; IntDcT 2; LiExTwC; MajMD 2; McGEWD 72, 84; ModSL 2; ModWD; NewCol 75; Novels; OxCThe 83; PenC EUR; PolBiDi; RAdv 14, 13-2; RfGWoL 95; TwCWr; WhAm 5; WhoTwCL; WorAu 1950*

Gomez, Jewelle
American. Writer
Won Lambda Literary awards for fiction and science fiction for *The Gilda Stories*, 1991.
b. Sep 11, 1948 in Boston, Massachusetts
Source: *BlkWr 2; ConAu 142; FemiWr; GayLesB; GayLL; ScF&FL 92; SchCGBL; WrDr 96*

Gomez, Lefty
[Vernon Louis Gomez]
"Goofy"; "The Gay Castilian"
American. Baseball Player
Pitcher, NY Yankees, 1930-42; led AL in wins twice, in strikeouts three times; H all of Fame, 1972.
b. Nov 26, 1909 in Rodeo, California
d. Feb 17, 1989 in Larkspur, California
Source: *AnObit 1989; Ballpl 90; BioIn 1, 2, 3, 5, 8, 9, 14, 15, 16; LegTOT; News 89-3; NewYTBS 89; WhoHisp 91, 91N; WhoProB 73*

Gomez, Marga
American. Entertainer
Works were staged as part of the Whitney Museum's Biennial Performance Series, 1993; works include *Marga Gomez Is Pretty, Witty & Gay.*
Source: *GayLesB*

Gomez, Thomas
American. Actor
Nominated for 1947 Oscar for *Ride a Pink Horse.*
b. Jul 10, 1905 in Long Island, New York
d. Jun 18, 1971 in Santa Monica, California
Source: *BiE&WWA; BioIn 9; CmMov; FilmEn; FilmgC; ForYSC; GangFlm; HalFC 80, 84, 88; HolCA; MovMk; NewYTBE 71; NotNAT B; Vers A; WhoHol B; WhScrn 74, 77, 83*

Gomez-Preston, Cheryl
American. Police Officer
Founded Association for the Sexually Harassed, 1987, after resigning her job because of sexual harassment.
b. Oct 12, 1954 in Detroit, Michigan
Source: *ConBlB 9*

Gompers, Samuel
American. Labor Union Official
Founder, first pres. of AFL, 1886-1924.
b. Jan 27, 1850 in London, England
d. Dec 13, 1924 in San Antonio, Texas
Source: *AmAu&B; AmBi; AmDec 1910; AmJust; AmRef; AmRef&R; AmSocL; ApCAB X; Benet 87, 96; BenetAL 91; BiDAmL; BiDAmLL; BioIn 1, 2, 3, 4, 5, 6, 7, 8, 9, 10, 11, 13, 14, 15, 16, 17, 19, 20, 21; CopCroC; CyAG; DcAmB; DcAmC; DcAmSR; DcNAA; Dis&D; EncAB-H 1974, 1996; FacFETw; GayN; HarEnUS; HisWorL; JeHun; LegTOT; LinLib L, S; McGEWB; MemAm; NatCAB 11; OxCAmH; PolPar; RComAH; REn; REnAL; WebAB 74, 79; WhAm 1; WhAmP; WhLit; WorAl; WorAlBi*

Gomulka, Wladyslaw
Polish. Political Leader
Led Poland's Communist Party, 1956-70.
b. Feb 6, 1905 in Bialobrzegi, Poland
d. Sep 1, 1982 in Warsaw, Poland
Source: *AnObit 1982; BioIn 6, 7, 8, 9, 13; ColdWar 2; CurBio 57, 82, 82N; DcTwHis; EncCW; EncRev; FacFETw; HisWorL; IntWW 74, 75, 76, 77, 78, 79, 80, 81, 82; IntYB 78, 79, 80, 81, 82; LinLib S; McGEWB; NewYTBE 70; NewYTBS 82; PolBiDi; WhAm 8; WhDW; WhoSocC 78; WhoSoCE 89*

Goncharov, Ivan Aleksandrovich
Russian. Author
Russian word for indolence, "oblomovism," derived from his book, *Oblomov*, 1858.
b. Jun 18, 1812 in Simbirsk, Russia
d. Sep 27, 1891 in Saint Petersburg, Russia
Source: *AtlBL; Benet 96; BiD&SB; CasWL; CyWA 58; DcEuL; DcRusL; EuAu; EvEuW; Novels; PenC EUR; REn; WorAl*

Goncourt, Edmond Louis Antoine Huot de
[Edmond Louis DeGoncourt]
French. Author
Collaborated with brother Jules in Brothers Goncourt writing team; endowed annual Goncourt Prize for best prose.
b. May 26, 1822 in Nancy, France
d. Jul 16, 1896 in Champrosay, France
Source: *AtlBL; BbD; BiD&SB; BioIn 1, 2, 4, 5, 6, 7, 9, 10, 11; CasWL; ClDMEL 47; CyWA 58; DcBiA; DcEuL; Ent; EuAu; EvEuW; NewC; NotNAT B; OxCEng 67; OxCFr; OxCThe 67, 83; PenC EUR; REn; WorAl; WorAlBi*

Goncourt, Jules Alfred Huot de
[Jules Alfred DeGoncourt]
French. Author
Collaborated on social histories, novels with brother Edmond; wrote *Madame G ervaisais*, 1869; famed *Goncourt Diary.*
b. Dec 17, 1830 in Paris, France
d. Jun 20, 1870 in Auteuil, France
Source: *BbD; BiD&SB; BioIn 1, 2, 4, 5, 6, 7, 9, 10, 11; BlmGEL; CasWL; ClDMEL 47; CyWA 58; DcEuL; Dis&D; EuAu; EuWr 7; EvEuW; NotNAT B; OxCEng 67; OxCFr; OxCThe 67, 83; PenC EUR; REn; WhDW; WorAl; WorAlBi*

Gondi, Cardinal
French.
A leader of the French Fronde aristocratic rebellion.
b. Sep 1613 in Montmirail, France
d. Aug 24, 1679 in Paris, France

Gong Li
Chinese. Actor
Films include *Farwell My Concubine*, 1993.
b. Dec 31, 1965 in Shenyang, China

Gongora y Argote, Luis de
Spanish. Poet
Castillian balladeer whose later abstruse style was dubbed "Gongorism."
b. Jul 11, 1561 in Cordoba, Spain
d. May 24, 1627 in Cordoba, Spain
Source: *BiD&SB; BioIn 2, 4, 7, 10; CasWL; DcEuL; DcHiB; DcSpL; EuAu; EvEuW; LinLib L; McGEWB; NewCol 75; OxCSpan; PenC EUR; RAdv 14, 13-2; REn; WhDW; WorAlBi*

Gonne, Maud
Irish. Patriot, Philanthropist
Founder of Sinn Fein, loved by Yeats; wrote *A Servant of the Queen*, 1938.
b. 1866 in London, England
d. 1953
Source: *ArtclWW 2; Benet 87, 96; BioIn 1, 3, 7, 10, 11, 12, 16, 17, 18, 19; ContDcW 89; IntDcWB; InWom; LegTOT; NewC; OxCIri; REn; VicBrit; WebBD 83; WomFir; WorAl*

Gonzales, Juan (Alberto)
"Igor"
Puerto Rican. Baseball Player
Plays with the Texas Rangers; led American League in home runs in 1993; led major leagues in home runs in 1992; led American League for three consecutive seasons in RBIs, 1991-1993.
b. Oct 20, 1969 in Arecibo, Puerto Rico

Gonzalez, Henry Barbosa
American. Politician
Dem. congressman, TX, 1961—.
b. May 3, 1916 in San Antonio, Texas
Source: *AlmAP 92; AmCath 80; BiDrAC; BiDrUSC 89; BioIn 5, 6, 7, 8, 9, 10, 11, 16; CngDr 89; CurBio 93; HispAmA; MexAmB; NewYTBS 92; PolProf K; PolsAm 84; WhoAm 90, 92, 94, 95, 96, 97; WhoAmP 73, 75, 77, 79, 81, 83, 85, 87, 89, 91, 93, 95; WhoFI 92; WhoGov 77; WhoHisp 91, 92, 94; WhoSSW 91, 93, 95, 97*

Gonzalez, Jose Ramon
American. University Administrator
Pres., InterAmerican U, 1990—.
b. Jun 11, 1930 in Barranquitas, Puerto Rico
Source: *WhoAm 92, 94, 95, 96, 97; WhoHisp 92; WhoSSW 95, 97; WhoWor 95, 96, 97*

Gonzalez, Pancho
[Richard Alonzo Gonzales]
American. Tennis Player
Eight-time World Pro tennis champ; autobiography *Man with a Racket,* 1959.
b. May 9, 1928 in Los Angeles, California
d. Jul 3, 1995 in Las Vegas, Nevada
Source: *BiDAmSp OS; BioIn 12, 14, 15, 16, 21; BuCMET; ConAu 105; CurBio 49, 95N; MexAmB; WebAB 74, 79; WhoAm 84; WhoHisp 91, 92, 94*

Gonzalez, Xavier
Spanish. Painter, Sculptor
Abstract and figurative sculptor; works include painted murals and the stone relief, *The History of Man,* 1963.
d. Jan 9, 1993 in New York, New York
Source: *ArtsAmW 2; BioIn 1, 2, 3, 5; DcCAA 88; IlsBYP; NewYTBS 93; WhAmArt 85; WhoAmA 91; WhoHisp 92*

Gonzalez Marquez, Felipe
Spanish. Political Leader
First Socialist premier since 1936-39 Civil War; elected 1982—.
b. Mar 5, 1942 in Seville, Spain
Source: *BioIn 11, 13; CurBio 78; IntWW 78, 79, 80, 81, 82, 83, 89, 91, 93; NewYTBS 82; Who 92, 94; WhoWor 78, 84, 87, 89, 91, 95, 96, 97*

Goodall, Jane
[Baroness VanLawick-Goodall]
English. Anthropologist, Author
Expert on chimpanzee behavior after studying them for over 30 yrs. in their natural environment; wrote *In the Shadow of Man,* 1971 and *Through a Window,* 1990.
b. Apr 3, 1934 in London, England
Source: *AmMWSc 95; BioIn 14, 15, 16, 20, 21; ConAu 2NR, 43NR, 45; ConHero 1; ContDcW 89; CurBio 67, 91; EnvEnDr; FacFETw; HerW 84; IntDcWB; IntWW 93; InWom SUP; LarDcSc; LegTOT; MajTwCW; News 91, 91-1; NotTwCS; RAdv 13-5; WhoAm 97; WhoScEn 94, 96; WhoWor 95; WomFir; WomStre; WorAlBi; WrDr 92, 94, 96*

Goodall, John Strickland
English. Artist, Illustrator
Children's books include *Adventures of Paddy Pork,* 1968; *The Story of Main Street,* 1987.
b. Jun 7, 1908 in Heacham, England
d. Jun 3, 1996 in London, England
Source: *BioIn 5, 9, 14; ChlLR 25; ClaDrA; ConAu 33R, 152; DcBrAr 1; IlsCB 1946; SmATA 4, 66; WhoArt 80, 82, 84, 96*

Goode, Richard Stephen
American. Pianist
Concert pianist specializing in chamber music; won Avery Fisher Award, 1980.
b. Jun 1, 1943 in New York, New York
Source: *Baker 92; IntWWM 90; WhoAm 88, 90, 92, 94, 95, 96, 97; WhoAmM 83; WhoEnt 92*

Goode, Wilson
[Willie Wilson Godde]
American. Politician
First black mayor of Philadelphia, 1984-91.
b. Aug 19, 1938 in Seaboard, North Carolina
Source: *BioIn 13, 14, 15; CurBio 85; InB&W 85; NewYTBS 83; WhoAm 86, 90; WhoAmP 91; WhoBlA 88, 92; WhoE 91*

Goodell, Brian Stuart
American. Swimmer
Olympic gold medalist, 1976, for 400, 1500 meter freestyle.
b. Apr 2, 1959 in Stockton, California
Source: *BiDAmSp BK; BioIn 11, 12; NewYTBS 81*

Goodell, Charles Ellsworth
American. Lawyer, Politician
Rep. senator from NY who completed term of Robert Kennedy, 1968-71.
b. Mar 16, 1926 in Jamestown, New York
d. Jan 21, 1987 in Washington, District of Columbia
Source: *BiDrAC; BiDrUSC 89; BioIn 6, 8, 9, 10, 11, 12; ConAu 81; CurBio 68, 87; IntWW 74, 75, 76, 77, 78, 79, 80, 81, 82, 83; WhAm 9; WhoAm 74, 76, 78, 80, 82, 84, 86; WhoAmP 73, 75, 77, 79, 81, 83, 85; WhoE 74*

Gooden, Dwight Eugene
American. Baseball Player
Pitcher, NY Mets, 1984—; NL rookie of year, 1984; youngest ever to win Cy Young Award, 1985.
b. Nov 16, 1964 in Tampa, Florida
Source: *Ballpl 90; BaseReg 86, 87; BioIn 14, 15, 16; CelR 90; ConNews 85-2; CurBio 86; NewYTBS 84, 86, 91; WhoAfA 96; WhoAm 86, 88, 90, 92, 94, 95; WhoBlA 85, 88, 90, 92, 94; WhoE 89, 91, 93, 95; WorAlBi*

Goodeve, Grant
American. Actor
Played David Bradford on TV series "Eight is Enough," 1977-81.
b. Jul 6, 1952 in New Haven, Connecticut
Source: *LegTOT; VarWW 85; WhoHol 92*

Goodfellow, Ebbie
[Ebenezer Ralston Goodfellow]
Canadian. Hockey Player
Center, Detroit, 1929-43; won Hart Trophy, 1940; Hall of Fame, 1963.
b. Apr 9, 1907 in Ottawa, Ontario, Canada
d. Sep 10, 1955
Source: *BioIn 10; HocEn; WhoHcky 73; WhoSpor*

Goodfriend, Lynda
American. Actor
Played Richie's wife on "Happy Days," 1978-83.
b. Oct 31, 1950 in Miami, Florida
Source: *BioIn 12*

Goodhue, Bertram G(rosvenor)
American. Architect
Works include Nebraska state capitol, Rockefeller Chapel, U of Chicago.
b. Apr 28, 1869 in Pomfret, Connecticut
d. Apr 23, 1924 in New York, New York
Source: *AmBi; AmCulL; BiDAmAr; BioIn 11, 13, 19; BriEAA; ChhPo; DcAmAu; DcAmB; DcD&D; DcNAA; DcTwDes; FacFETw; IntDcAr; LinLib S; MacEA; McGDA; NatCAB 19; OxCAmH; OxCAmL 65; WebAB 74, 79; WebBD 83; WhAm 1; WhoArch*

Goodman, Andrew
American. Business Executive
Pres., Bergdorf Goodman, 1951-75.
b. Feb 13, 1907
d. Apr 3, 1993 in Rye, New York
Source: *AnObit 1993; BioIn 9, 10, 18, 19; CurBio 75, 93N; St&PR 75, 84; WhAm 11; WhoAm 74, 76, 78, 80, 82, 84, 86, 88; WhoWorJ 72, 78*

Goodman, Benny
[Benjamin David Goodman]
""King of Swing""
American. Bandleader, Musician
World-renowned clarinetist, bandleader during Big Band era; most popular songs "Stompin' at the Savoy"; "Sing, Sing, Sing."
b. May 30, 1909 in Chicago, Illinois
d. Jun 13, 1986 in New York, New York
Source: *AllMusG; AmCulL; AmDec 1930; AnObit 1986; ASCAP 66, 80; Baker 78, 84, 92; BgBands 74; BiDAmM; BiDJaz; BioIn 1, 2, 3, 4, 5, 6, 7, 8, 9, 10, 11, 12, 13, 14, 15, 16, 17, 18, 19; BioNews 74; BriBkM 80; CelR; CmpEPM; ConAu 119; ConMus 4; ConNews 86-3; CurBio 42, 62, 86, 86N; DcArts; EncAB-H 1974, 1996; EncJzS; EncWB; FacFETw; FilmgC; HalFC 80, 84, 88; IlEncJ; IntWW 74, 75, 76, 77, 78, 79, 80, 81, 82, 83; JeAmHC; JeHun; LegTOT; MnPM; MusMk; NewAmDM; NewGrDA 86; NewGrDJ 88, 94; NewGrDM 80; NewOxM; NewYTBS 86; OxCAmH; OxCPMus; PenDiMP; PenEncP; PeoHis; RadStar; RComAH; VarWW 85; WebAB 74, 79; WhAm 9; WhoAm 74, 76, 78, 80, 82, 84, 86; WhoE 74; WhoHol A; WhoJazz 72; WhoWor 74, 78; WorAl; WorAlBi*

Goodman, Dody
American. Actor
Played Martha Shumway on TV's "Mary Hartman, Mary Hartman," 1976-77; films include *Grease II,* 1982.
b. Oct 28, 1929 in Columbus, Ohio
Source: *BiE&WWA; BioIn 13; ConTFT 4; FilmEn; LegTOT; NewYTBS 76, 83; NotNAT; VarWW 85; WhoAm 86, 88; WhoHol A; WhoThe 77*

Goodman, Ellen Holtz
American. Journalist
Writes syndicated feature, "At Large," 1976—; won Pulitzer for commentary, 1980.
b. Apr 11, 1941 in Newton, Massachusetts
Source: *BiDAmNC; BioIn 14, 15; BriB; ConAu 104; EncTwCJ; InWom SUP; WhoAm 86, 90, 97; WhoAmW 87, 91, 97; WhoE 83; WorAu 1980; WrDr 92*

Goodman, George Jerome Waldo
[Adam Smith]
American. Author
His *The Money Game,* 1968, was published in five languages.
b. Aug 10, 1930 in Saint Louis, Missouri
Source: *AmAu&B; BioIn 8, 12, 13; ConAu 31NR; DcLP 87A; NewYTBS 81; St&PR 87, 91; WhoAm 74, 76, 78, 80, 82, 84, 86, 88, 90, 92, 94, 95, 96, 97; WhoFI 87, 89*

Goodman, John
American. Actor
Played Dan Conner on TV comedy "Roseanne," 1988-97; films include *Sea of Love, Always,* 1989.
b. Jun 20, 1952 in Affton, Missouri
Source: *BioIn 16; ConAu 146; ConTFT 9; Dun&B 90; HolBB; IntMPA 92, 94, 96; News 90, 90-3; NewYTBS 91; WhoAm 94, 95, 96, 97; WhoEnt 92; WhoHol 92; WorAlBi*

Goodman, Johnny
[John G Goodman]
American. Golfer
Fifth amateur player to win US Open, 1933.
b. 1910 in Omaha, Nebraska
d. Aug 8, 1970 in Southgate, California
Source: *BioIn 9; NewYTBE 70; ObitOF 79; WhoGolf*

Goodman, Julian B
American. Broadcasting Executive
Chm. of NBC network, 1974-79.
b. May 1, 1922 in Glasgow, Kentucky
Source: *BioIn 12; CurBio 67; IntMPA 86, 92; IntWW 83, 91; LesBEnT, 92; St&PR 75; VarWW 85; WhoAm 86, 88; WhoE 74; WhoFI 75; WhoWor 74*

Goodman, Linda
American. Writer, Astrologer
Author of *Sun Signs,* 1968.
b. Apr 9, 1925 in Parkersburg, West Virginia
d. Oct 21, 1995 in Colorado Springs, Colorado
Source: *BioIn 21; ConAu 52NR, 89, 150; DivFut*

Goodman, Martin
American. Publisher
Founder, publisher, Marvel Comics in the late 1930s; created the characters Captain America and Spiderman.
b. 1908 in New York, New York
d. Jun 6, 1992 in Palm Beach, Florida

Goodman, Martin Wise
Canadian. Newspaper Executive
Pres. of *Toronto Star* Newspapers, Ltd., 1978-81.
b. Jan 15, 1935 in Calgary, Alberta, Canada
d. Dec 20, 1981 in Toronto, Ontario, Canada
Source: *WhAm 8; WhoAm 78, 80, 82*

Goodman, Mitchell
American. Author
Best known for war novel *The End of It,* 1961.
b. Dec 13, 1923 in New York, New York
d. Feb 1, 1997 in Temple, Maine
Source: *Au&Wr 71; BioIn 8, 10; ConAu 1R, 4NR; DrAF 76; DrAP 75; DrAPF 80, 83, 91; Law&B 89A; LinLib L; MugS*

Goodman, Paul
American. Author, Educator
Books include *Growing Up Absurd,* 1960; plays include *The Young Disciple,* 1955.
b. Sep 9, 1911 in New York, New York
d. Aug 2, 1972 in North Stratford, New Hampshire
Source: *AmAu&B; AmDec 1960; AmNov; Benet 87, 96; BenetAL 91; BiDAmLf; BioIn 2, 4, 7, 8, 9, 10, 11, 12, 13, 14, 17, 19, 20, 21; CamGLE; CamHAL; ConAmD; ConAu 34NR, 37R, P-2; ConDr 73, 93; ConIsC 1; ConLC 1, 2, 4, 7; ConLCrt 77, 82; ConNov 72, 76; ConPo 70; CurBio 72N; DcAmB S9; DcArts; DcLB 130; DcLEL 1940; EncAL; FacFETw; GayLesB; GrWrEL N; IntAu&W 76; LNinSix; MajTwCW; MakMC; ModAL S1; MugS; NewGrDA 86; Novels; OxCAmL 65, 83, 95; OxCTwCP; PenC AM; PolProf J, K; RadHan; RfGAmL 87, 94; RGTwCWr; ThTwC 87; TwCA SUP; WhAm 5; WhoWorJ 72*

Goodman, Robert O, Jr.
American. Naval Officer
Shot down, held by Syrians in Lebanon; released after intercession by Jesse Jackson, 1984.
b. Nov 30, 1956? in San Juan, Puerto Rico
Source: *BioIn 13, 15; WhoBlA 92*

Goodman, Steve(n Benjamin)
American. Songwriter
Best known as author of Arlo Guthrie's 1972 hit "City of New Orleans."
b. Jul 25, 1948 in Chicago, Illinois
d. Sep 20, 1984 in Seattle, Washington
Source: *ASCAP 80; BioIn 13; ConAu 113; ConMuA 80A; EncFCWM 83; EncRk 88; IlEncRk; OnThGG; PenEncP; RolSEnR 83; WhoAm 82; WhoRock 81*

Goodnight, Charles
American. Rancher
Described as "perfect illustration of the cattleman"; opened cattle trails in West ; developed cattalo by breeding buffalo, cattle.
b. Mar 5, 1836 in Macoupin County, Illinois
d. Dec 12, 1929 in Texas
Source: *AmBi; BiDAmBL 83; BioIn 2, 4, 5, 18; DcAmB; EncAAH; McGEWB; REnAW; WebAB 74, 79; WhAm 4, HSA; WhDW*

Goodpaster, Andrew Jackson
American. Army Officer
Commander-in-chief, Supreme Allied Command, Europe, 1969-74, 1977-81.
b. Feb 12, 1915 in Granite City, Illinois
Source: *AmMWSc 73S, 78S; BioIn 3, 8, 9, 11, 12; ConAu 109; CurBio 69; EncWB; IntWW 74, 75, 76, 77, 78, 79, 80, 81, 82, 83, 89, 91, 93; NewYTBS 77; WebAB 74; WebAMB; Who 74, 82, 83, 85, 88, 90, 92, 94; WhoAm 74, 76, 78, 80, 82, 84, 86, 88, 90, 92, 94, 95, 96, 97; WhoE 81; WhoWor 78, 80, 82, 84; WorDWW*

Goodpasture, E(rnest) W(illiam)
American. Pathologist
Developed vaccine for mumps, 1931.
b. Oct 17, 1886 in Montgomery County, Tennessee
d. Sep 20, 1960 in Nashville, Tennessee
Source: *BiESc; BioIn 1, 3, 5, 6, 7; DcAmMeB 84; McGMS 80; ObitOF 79; OxCMed 86; WhAm 4*

Goodrich, Benjamin Franklin
American. Industrialist
Founded B F Goodrich Rubber Co., makers of first solid, pneumatic rubber tires, 1880.
b. Nov 4, 1841 in Ripley, New York
d. Aug 3, 1888 in Manitou Springs, Colorado
Source: *BiDAmBL 83; BioIn 3, 7, 9, 18; DcAmB; Entr; NatCAB 28; WhAm HS; WorAl*

Goodrich, Bert
American. Stunt Performer
First Mr. America, 1939; John Wayne's double in movies.
d. Dec 6, 1991 in Los Angeles, California
Source: *BioIn 8*

Goodrich, Frances
[Mrs. Albert Hackett]
American. Author
With husband, wrote screenplay of *The Diary of Anne Frank,* which won Tony, 1956.
b. 1891 in Belleville, New Jersey
d. Jan 29, 1984 in New York, New York
Source: *AmAu&B; AnObit 1984; BioIn 14, 15; ConAu 111; CurBio 84, 84N; DcLB 26; EncAFC; FilmEn; HalFC 84, 88; IntDcF 1-4, 2-4; InWom SUP; LegTOT; McGEWD 72, 84; NewYTBS 84; ReelWom; VarWW 85; WhoAm 82; WorEFlm*

Goodrich, Gail Charles
"Stumpy"
American. Basketball Player
Guard, 1965-79, mostly with LA; won NBA championship, 1972.
b. Apr 23, 1943 in Los Angeles, California
Source: *BiDAmSp BK; BioIn 9, 10; OfNBA 87; WhoAm 74; WhoBbl 73*

Goodrich, Lloyd
American. Museum Director
Director, NYC Whitney Museum of American Art, 1958-68, emeritus, 1971—; wrote many books on American art.
b. Jul 10, 1897 in Nutley, New Jersey
d. Mar 27, 1987 in New York, New York
Source: *AmAu&B*

Goodrich, Samuel Griswold
[Peter Parley]
American. Publisher
Published *The Tales of Peter Parley About America,* 1827, the first of over 100 books in series.
b. Aug 19, 1793 in Ridgefield, Connecticut
d. May 9, 1860 in New York, New York
Source: *Alli; AmAu; AmAu&B; AmBi; ApCAB; BbD; BbtC; BenetAL 91; BiDAmEd; BiD&SB; BioIn 1, 4, 8, 13, 15, 17; BritAu 19; CarSB; ChhPo, S1, S2, S3; CyAL 2; CyEd; DcAmAu; DcAmB; DcBiPP; DcEnL; DcLB 1, 42, 73; DcNAA; Drake; HarEnUS; LinLib L; NatCAB 5; NewCBEL; OxCAmH; OxCAmL 65, 83, 95; OxCChiL; REn; REnAL; SmATA 23; TwCBDA; WebAB 74, 79; WhAm HS; WhoChL*

Goodson, Mark
American. Producer
With Bill Todman, created "What's My Line"; "The Price Is Right"; and "Family Feud"; won Emmy for Lifetime Achievement; inducted into Television Academy Hall of Fame, 1993.
b. Jan 24, 1915 in Sacramento, California
d. Dec 18, 1992 in New York, New York
Source: *AnObit 1992; BioIn 6, 11, 13, 14, 15; ConTFT 3, 11; CurBio 78, 93N; IntMPA 77, 78, 79, 80, 81, 82, 84, 86, 92; LegTOT; NewYTBS 82; VarWW 85; WhAm 11; WhoAm 74, 76, 78, 80, 82, 84, 86, 88, 90, 92; WhoE 89, 91, 93; WhoEnt 92; WhoTelC; WhoWest 87, 89, 92; WhoWor 74, 76, 78*

Goodwin, Bill
American. Actor
Network radio announcer who appeared on TV and in several films, 1940s-50s.
b. Jul 28, 1910 in San Francisco, California
d. May 9, 1958 in Palm Springs, California
Source: *BioIn 4, 77, 83*

Goodwin, Hannibal Williston
American. Clergy, Inventor
Invented photographic film; received patent, 1898.
b. Apr 30, 1822 in Taughannock, New York
d. Dec 31, 1900
Source: *DcAmB; NatCAB 23; WebBD 83; WhAm HS*

Goodwin, Nat C
American. Actor
Stage and film role of Fagin in *Oliver Twist,* 1912.
b. 1857 in Boston, Massachusetts
d. Jan 31, 1919 in New York
Source: *WhoHol B; WhScrn 74, 77*

Goodwin, Richard N(aradhof)
[Bailey Lavid]
American. Lawyer, Author
Presidential speechwriter, 1960s; developed "Great Society" program.
b. Dec 7, 1931 in Boston, Massachusetts
Source: *BioIn 5, 6, 7, 8, 9, 10, 11, 16; ConAu 111, 146; CurBio 68; IntWW 74, 75, 76; PolProf J, K; WhoAm 80*

Goody, Joan
American. Architect
With Goody, Clancy and Associates since 1961—, now principal; designer of Boston's PaineWebber building.
b. Dec 1, 1935 in New York, New York
Source: *BioIn 15; ConArch 87; InWom SUP; News 90, 90-2; WhoAm 92, 94, 95, 96, 97; WhoE 95, 97*

Goodyear, Charles
American. Inventor
Discovered vulcanization process for rubber, 1839; patented, 1844.
b. Dec 29, 1800 in New Haven, Connecticut
d. Jul 1, 1860 in New York, New York
Source: *AmBi; ApCAB; AsBiEn; BiInAmS; BioIn 2, 3, 4, 5, 6, 7, 8, 9, 11, 14, 16, 18, 21; DcAmB; DcBiPP; Drake; EncAB-H 1974, 1996; Entr; HarEnUS; InSci; LegTOT; LinLib S; McGEWB; MorMA; NatCAB 3; NewCol 75; OxCAmH; TwCBDA; WebAB 74, 79; WhAm HS; WhDW; WorAl; WorAlBi; WorInv*

Goolagong, Evonne
[Mrs. Roger Cawley]
Australian. Tennis Player
Defeated Margaret Court to become fifth youngest Wimbledon singles champ, 1971; won again, 1980.
b. Jul 31, 1951 in Barellan, Australia
Source: *BioIn 7, 9, 10, 11, 12, 13, 14, 16, 21; BioNews 74; BuCMET; CelR; ConAu 89; CurBio 71; GoodHs; HerW, 84; InWom SUP; LegTOT; NewYTBE 71; WhDW; WhoIntT; WhoSpor; WhoWor 74, 76; WorAl; WorAlBi*

Goossens, Eugene, Sir
English. Composer, Conductor
Third generation conductor; autobiography, *Overture and Beginners,* 1951.
b. May 26, 1893 in London, England
d. Jun 13, 1962 in Hillingdon, England
Source: *Baker 78, 84, 92; BioIn 1, 2, 3, 4, 5, 6, 11; BriBkM 80; CurBio 45, 62; DcCM; DcNaB 1961; MetOEnc; MusMk; NewAmDM; NewCol 75; NewEOp 71; NewGrDA 86; NewGrDM 80; NewOxM; ObitOF 79; ObitT 1961; OxCMus; OxDcOp; PenDiMP, A; WhAm 4*

Goossens, Leon Jean
English. Musician
Oboist; wrote oboe compositions, popularizing it as a solo performer; brother of Eugene.
b. Jun 12, 1897 in Liverpool, England
d. Feb 12, 1988 in Tunbridge Wells, England
Source: *Baker 84; DcNaB 1986; IntWW 74, 75, 76, 77, 78, 79, 80, 81, 82, 83; Who 74, 82, 83, 85, 88; WhoMus 72*

Gopallawa, William
Sri Lankan. Diplomat
First pres. of Sri Lanka when name changed from Ceylon, 1972-78.
b. Sep 16, 1897 in Dullewa, Ceylon
d. Jan 30, 1981 in Colombo, Sri Lanka
Source: *AnObit 1981; BioIn 12; FarE&A 78, 79, 80; IntWW 74, 75, 76, 77, 78, 79, 80, 81N; IntYB 78, 79, 80, 81; Who 74, 82N; WhoGov 72; WhoWor 74, 76, 78*

Goranson, Lecy
American. Actor
Plays Becky on TV series "Roseanne," 1988—.
Source: *BioIn 16*

Gorbachev, Mikhail (Sergeyevich)
Russian. Political Leader
Secretary General of USSR Communist Party, 1985-92; initiated glasnost; won Nobel Prize for Peace, 1990; *Time* magazine's Man of the Decade.
b. Mar 2, 1931 in Privolye, Union of Soviet Socialist Republics
Source: *Benet 87, 96; BiDAmNC; BiDSovU; BioIn 13, 14, 15, 16; ColdWar 2; ConAu 132; ConHero 2; ConNews 85-1, 85-2; CurBio 85; DcTwHis; EncCW; EncWB; EnvEnDr; FacFETw; HisWorL; IntWW 81, 82, 83, 89, 91, 93;*

IntYB 82; LegTOT; MajTwCW; NewYTBS 80, 84, 85, 91; NobelP 91; Who 92, 94; WhoNob 90, 95; WhoRus; WhoWor 84, 87, 89, 91, 93, 95, 96, 97; WorAlBi

Gorbachev, Raisa Maksimovna Titorenko
[Mrs. Mikhail Gorbachev]
Russian.
Former Soviet first lady known for her style; married Mikhail in 1956.
b. Jan 5, 1932 in Rubtsovsk, Union of Soviet Socialist Republics
Source: *BiDSovU; BioIn 14, 15, 16; CurBio 88; IntWW 89, 91; WhoWor 91*

Gorbanevskaya, Natalya
Russian. Poet, Translator
Her involvement in 1968 protest, documented in *Red Square at Noon,* 1970.
b. 1936 in Moscow, Union of Soviet Socialist Republics
Source: *BioIn 9; ConAu 111; ConFLW 84; DcRusLS; EncCoWW; HanRL; IntWW 83; RadHan; WorAu 1970*

Gorbatov, Aleksandr Vassil'evich
Russian. Army Officer
Commander of Soviet 3rd army, 1943-45.
b. 1891?
d. Dec 7, 1973 in Moscow, Union of Soviet Socialist Republics
Source: *ConAu 45; NewYTBE 73; ObitOF 79*

Gorcey, Leo
American. Actor
Played Spit, the gang leader, in film series *Dead End Kids; East Side Kids; The Bowery Boys.*
b. Jun 3, 1915 in New York, New York
d. Jun 2, 1969 in Oakland, California
Source: *BioIn 15; EncAFC; FilmEn; FilmgC; ForYSC; GangFlm; HalFC 80, 84, 88; LegTOT; MotPP; MovMk; WhoHol B; WhoHrs 80; WhScrn 74, 77*

Gordeeva, Ekaterina
[Mrs. Sergei Grinkov]
Russian. Skater
Paired with husband Sergei Grinkov, winning gold medals at the 1988 and 1994 Winter Olympics.
b. 1972, Union of Soviet Socialist Republics
Source: *News 96*

Gordimer, Nadine
South African. Author
Anti-apartheid author of *Burger's Daughter,* 1979 and *The Conservationist,* 1974; winner of 1991 Nobel Prize for Literature.
b. Nov 20, 1923 in Springs, South Africa
Source: *AfSS 78, 79, 80, 81, 82; ArtclWW 2; Au&Wr 71; Benet 87, 96; BioIn 3, 5, 7, 9, 10, 11, 12, 13, 14, 15, 16, 17, 18, 20, 21; BlmGEL; BlmGWL; BritWr S2; CamGEL; CamGLE; CasWL; ConAu 3NR, 5R, 28NR; ConLC 3, 5, 7, 10, 18, 33, 51, 70; ConNov 72, 76, 82, 86, 91, 96; ContDcW 89; CurBio 59, 80; CyWA 89; DcArts; DcLB Y91; DcLEL 1940; EncSoA; EncWB; EncWL 2, 3; FacFETw; FemiCLE; GrWomW; GrWrEL N; IntAu&W 76, 77, 82, 89, 91, 93; IntDcWB; IntLitE; IntvTCA 2; IntWW 74, 75, 76, 77, 78, 79, 80, 81, 82, 83, 89, 91, 93; InWom, SUP; LegTOT; MagSWL; MajTwCW; ModCmwL; ModWoWr; NewC; NewYTBS 81, 91; NobelP 91; Novels; OxCEng 85, 95; PenC ENG; RAdv 14, 13-2; RfGEnL 91; RfGShF; RGTwCWr; ShSCr 17; ShSWr; TwCWr; TwCYAW; WhAm 11; Who 74, 82, 83, 85, 88, 90, 92, 94; WhoAm 94, 95, 96, 97; WhoAmW 70, 72, 95, 97; WhoNob 95; WhoTwCL; WhoWor 74, 76, 78, 82, 84, 87, 89, 91, 93, 95, 96, 97; WorAlBi; WorAu 1950; WrDr 76, 80, 82, 84, 86, 88, 90, 92, 94, 96*

Gordon, C. Henry
[Henry Racke]
American. Actor
Suave, cold-hearted villain in films, 1930s.
b. Jun 17, 1883 in New York, New York
d. Dec 3, 1940 in Los Angeles, California
Source: *CurBio 41; FilmEn; FilmgC; MotPP; MovMk; Vers A; WhoHol B; WhScrn 74, 77, 83*

Gordon, Caroline
American. Author, Critic
Southern-theme writer whose novels include *The Malefactors,* 1956.
b. Oct 6, 1895 in Trenton, Kentucky
d. Apr 11, 1981 in Chiapas, Mexico
Source: *AmAu&B; AmNov; AmWomWr; AmWr; AnObit 1981; ArtclWW 2; Benet 87; BenetAL 91; BiDConC; BioAmW; BioIn 2, 3, 4, 5, 7, 8, 9, 12, 13, 15, 16, 17, 20; BlmGWL; CamGLE; CamHAL; CasWL; CathA 1952; ConAu 36NR, 103, P-1; ConLC 6, 13, 29, 83; ConNov 72, 76; CyWA 58, 89; DcLB 4, 9, 102, Y81A; DrAF 76; DrAPF 80; EncWL 2, 3; FemiCLE; FifSWrA; GrWrEL N; IntAu&W 76, 77; InWom, SUP; LiHiK; MajTwCW; ModAL S1; ModWoWr; Novels; OxCAmL 65, 83, 95; OxCWoWr 95; PenC AM; RAdv 1, 14, 13-1; REn; REnAL; RfGAmL 87, 94; RfGShF; ScF&FL 1, 92; ShSCr 15; ShSWr; SouWr; TwCA, SUP; WhAm 7; WhE&EA; WhoAm 74, 76, 78; WhoAmW 70, 72, 74; WrDr 76, 80, 82*

Gordon, Charles George
"Chinese"
English. Army Officer
Soldier who fought in many parts of British Empire; also Taiping Rebellion, China; governor-general, Sudan, 1877-1879.
b. Jan 28, 1833 in Woolwich, England
d. Jan 26, 1885 in Khartoum, Sudan
Source: *Alli SUP; Benet 87, 96; BioIn 3, 4, 5, 6, 7, 8, 9, 10, 12, 13, 14, 15, 16, 21; CelCen; DcAfHiB 86; DcInB; DcNaB; EncSoA; GenMudB; HarEnMi; HisDBrE; HisWorL; LinLib S; McGEWB; NewC; NewCol 75; REn; VicBrit; WhDW; WhoMilH 76; WorAl*

Gordon, David
American. Choreographer
Formed the David Gordon/Pick Up Co., 1978; renowned in the postmodern movement in dance.
b. Jul 14, 1936 in New York, New York
Source: *BioIn 14, 15, 19, 20; CurBio 94; WhoAm 92, 94, 95, 96, 97; WhoE 95*

Gordon, Dexter Keith
American. Jazz Musician
Tenor saxophonist; starred in film *Round Midnight,* 1986 and recorded soundtrack; received Oscar nomination, 1987.
b. Feb 27, 1923 in Los Angeles, California
d. Apr 25, 1990 in Philadelphia, Pennsylvania
Source: *Baker 84, 92; BiDJaz; BioIn 13, 15, 16; ConNews 87-1; FacFETw; InB&W 85; NegAl 89; NewAmDM; NewGrDA 86; NewGrDJ 88; News 90; NewYTBS 90; OxCPMus; PenEncP; WhAm 10; WhoAm 86, 88; WhoBlA 92N*

Gordon, Ed
[Edward Lansing Gordon, III]
American. Broadcast Journalist
Host of Black Entertainment Television's "Lead Story" and "Conversations With Ed Gordon," 1988—.
b. 1960 in Detroit, Michigan
Source: *ConBlB 10*

Gordon, Ellen Rubin
American. Candy Manufacturer
Pres., Tootsie Roll Industries, Inc., 1978—.
b. May 29, 1931 in New York, New York
Source: *BioIn 16; Dun&B 90; St&PR 91; WhoAm 90; WhoAmW 74, 91; WhoMW 92*

Gordon, Gale
[Charles T Aldrich, Jr.]
American. Actor
Played Mr. Wilson on "Dennis the Menace," 1962-64; Mr. Mooney on "The Lucy Show," 1968-74.
b. Feb 2, 1906 in New York, New York
d. Jun 30, 1995 in Escondido, California
Source: *BioIn 4, 18, 21; ConTFT 3, 9, 15; EncAFC; FilmgC; ForYSC; HalFC 88; IntMPA 75, 76, 77, 78, 79, 80, 81, 82, 84, 86, 88, 92, 94; LegTOT; MovMk; News 96, 96-1; RadStar; VarWW 85; WhoHol 92, A; WorAlBi*

Gordon, Jeff
American. Auto Racer
Winner, inaugural Brickyard 400, 1994; Daytona 500, 1997.
b. Aug 4, 1971 in Vallejo, California
Source: *News 96, 96-1; WhoAm 97; WhoSSW 97*

Gordon, Joe
[Joseph Lowell Gordon]
"Flash"
American. Baseball Player, Baseball Manager
Second baseman, 1938-50; AL MVP, 1942; with Jimmy Dykes, involved in first trade of ML managers, 1960.
b. Feb 18, 1915 in Los Angeles, California
d. Jun 7, 1978 in Sacramento, California
Source: *Ballpl 90; BiDAmSp Sup; BioIn 1, 11, 14; NewYTBS 78; WhoProB 73*

Gordon, John Brown
American. Army Officer, Statesman
Confederate leader who participated in surrender agreements.
b. Feb 6, 1832 in Upson County, Georgia
d. Jan 9, 1904 in Miami, Florida
Source: *AmAu&B; AmBi; ApCAB, X; BiAUS; BiDConf; BiDrAC; BiDrUSC 89; BiDSA; BioIn 1, 4, 5, 10; CivWDc; DcAmAu; DcAmB; DcAmMiB; DcNAA; EncSoH; GenMudB; HarEnMi; HarEnUS; McGEWB; NatCAB 1; NewCol 75; TwCBDA; WebAMB; WhAm 1; WhAmP; WhCiWar*

Gordon, John F
American. Auto Executive
Pres., GM, 1958-65.
b. May 15, 1900 in Akron, Ohio
d. Jan 6, 1978 in Royal Oak, Michigan
Source: *IntWW 74; NatCAB 60; NewYTBS 78; ObitOF 79*

Gordon, Kitty
English. Actor
Victor Herbert composed "The Enchantress" for her, 1911.
b. Apr 22, 1878 in Folkestone, England
d. May 26, 1974 in Brentwood, New York
Source: *NewYTBS 74; WhoHol B; WhThe*

Gordon, Mary Catherine
American. Author
Novels of Roman Catholic manners include *Final Payments,* 1978; *Company of Women,* 1981.
b. Dec 8, 1949 in Far Rockaway, New York
Source: *ArtclWW 2; BenetAL 91; BiDConC; BioIn 13, 14, 15, 16; ConAu 102; ConLC 22; ConNov 91; CurBio 81; CyWA 89; DcLB Y81A; DrAPF 91; FemiCLE; HalFC 88; IntAu&W 91; InWom SUP; MajTwCW; WhoAm 84, 88; WhoAmW 91; WorAlBi; WorAu 1975; WrDr 92*

Gordon, Max
American. Producer
Long-running hits include *Born Yesterday,* 1946; *The Solid Gold Cadillac,* 1953.
b. Jun 28, 1892 in New York, New York
d. Nov 2, 1978 in New York, New York
Source: *BiE&WWA; BioIn 6, 9, 11, 12; CurBio 43, 79N; EncMT; NotNAT, A; ObitOF 79; OxCAmT 84; WhAm 7; What 3; WhoAm 74, 76; WhoThe 77A, 81N; WhThe*

Gordon, Michael
American. Director
Blacklisted in the 1950s, he made his comeback with *Pillow Talk,* 1959.
b. Sep 6, 1909 in Baltimore, Maryland
d. Apr 29, 1993 in Los Angeles, California
Source: *BiDFilm, 81, 94; BiE&WWA; ConTFT 1, 12; EncAFC; FilmEn; FilmgC; HalFC 80, 84, 88; IlWWHD 1A; IntMPA 75, 76, 77, 78, 79, 80, 81, 82, 84, 86, 88, 92; LegTOT; MiSFD 9; MovMk; NotNAT; WhAm 11; WhoAm 82, 84, 86, 88, 90, 92; WhoEnt 92; WhoWest 92; WorEFlm*

Gordon, Richard
[Gordon Ostlere]
English. Author
Wrote comic series of novels on medical life: *Bedside Manners,* 1982; *Doctors in the Soup,* 1987.
b. Sep 15, 1921 in London, England
Source: *Au&Wr 71; BioIn 3, 4; ConAu 107; DcArts; DcLEL 1940; DcLP 87A; IntAu&W 76, 77; MnBBF; Novels; TwCWr; Who 74, 92, 94; WrDr 80, 82, 84, 86, 88, 90, 92, 94, 96*

Gordon, Richard Francis, Jr.
American. Astronaut, Football Executive
Piloted Gemini XI, 1966; command module pilot, Apollo XII, second moon-landing flight, 1969.
b. Oct 5, 1929 in Seattle, Washington
Source: *AmMWSc 73P; IntWW 83, 91; LinLib S; WhoAm 78; WhoSpc; WhoSSW 75*

Gordon, Ruth
[Ruth Jones; Mrs. Garson Kanin]
American. Actor
With husband co-wrote *Adam's Rib,* 1952; won Oscar for *Rosemary's Baby,* 1968.
b. Oct 30, 1896 in Wollaston, Massachusetts
d. Aug 28, 1985 in Martha's Vineyard, Massachusetts
Source: *AmAu&B; AmWomD; AmWomWr; AnObit 1985; AuSpks; BiDFilm 81, 94; BiE&WWA; BioIn 1, 3, 7, 8, 9, 11, 12, 14, 15, 16, 18; CamGWoT; CelR; CnThe; ConAu 31NR, 81, 117; ConTFT 1; CurBio 72, 85, 85N; EncAFC; EncWT; Ent; FacFETw; FemiCLE; Film 1; FilmEn; FilmgC; ForYSC; GoodHs; GrLiveH; HalFC 80, 84, 88; IntAu&W 77; IntDcF 1-3, 2-3; IntMPA 75, 76, 77, 78, 79, 80, 81, 82, 84; InWom, SUP; LegTOT; MotPP; MovMk; NatPD 77, 81; NewYTBS 77, 85; NotNAT, A; NotWoAT; OxCAmT 84; OxCFilm; PlP&P; ReelWom; VarWW 85; WhAm 8; WhoAm 74, 76, 78, 80, 82, 84, 86; WhoAmW 58, 64, 66, 68, 70, 72, 74, 83; WhoHol A; WhoHrs 80; WhoThe 72, 77, 81; WhoWor 74; WomWMM; WorAl; WorAlBi; WorEFlm; WrDr 80, 82, 84*

Gordon, Steve
American. Author, Director
Author, director of comedy *Arthur,* 1981.
b. 1940? in Toledo, Ohio
d. Nov 27, 1982 in New York, New York
Source: *BioIn 12; ConAu 108; NewYTBS 82*

Gordon, Thomas
American. Psychologist, Author
Human relations writer whose books include *Leader Effectiveness Training,* 1977.
b. Mar 11, 1918 in Paris, Illinois
Source: *AmMWSc 73S, 78S; BioIn 12; ConAu 29R; WhoAm 78, 80; WrDr 76, 80, 82, 84, 86, 88, 90, 92, 94, 96*

Gordon, Vera
[Vera Nemirou]
American. Actor
Film roles typecast her as Jewish mother; films include *Abie's Irish Rose.*
b. Jun 11, 1886, Russia
d. May 8, 1948 in Beverly Hills, California
Source: *BioIn 1; Film 2; FilmEn; ForYSC; MovMk; NotNAT B; TwYS; WhoHol B; WhScrn 74, 77, 83*

Gordone, Charles Edward
American. Dramatist
Won 1970 Pulitzer for drama *No Place to Be Somebody.*
b. Oct 12, 1925 in Cleveland, Ohio
d. Nov 17, 1995 in College Station, Texas
Source: *AmAu&B; BenetAL 91; BlkWr 1; CamGWoT; ConAmD; ConAu 93; ConBlAP 88; ConDr 82, 88, 93; ConLC 1, 4; DrBlPA 90; InB&W 85; LivgBAA; MajTwCW; McGEWD 72; NotNAT; PlP&P; SelBAAf; WhoAfA 96; WhoAm 86, 90; WhoBlA 92, 94; WhoE 85; WhoEnt 92; WhoThe 81; WrDr 86, 92*

Gordon-Lazareff, Helene
French. Journalist
Editor-in-chief of fashion magazine, *Elle,* 1945-72.
b. Sep 21, 1909 in Rostov-on-Don, Russia
d. Feb 16, 1988 in Lavandou, France
Source: *BioIn 7; ContDcW 89; IntAu&W 89; IntDcWB; IntWW 74, 75, 76, 77, 78, 79, 80, 81, 82, 83; InWom SUP; WhoFr 79; WomFir*

Gordon-Walker of Leyton, Patrick Chrestien Gordon-Walker, Baron
English. Politician
Labour Party leader; cabinet minister during 1950-60s; writings on British politics include *The Commonwealth,* 1962.
b. Apr 7, 1907 in Worthing, England
d. Dec 2, 1980 in London, England

Source: *AnObit 1980; Au&Wr 71; ConAu 29R; CurBio 66; IntAu&W 76; IntWW 78; IntYB 79; WhE&EA; Who 74; WhoWor 74, 76; WrDr 76*

Gordy, Berry, Jr.
American. Music Executive, Film Executive
Founded Motown Records, 1959; signed The Temptations; The Supremes; Hall of Fame, 1988; sold company for $61 million, 1988; director, Gordy Co., 1988—.
b. Nov 28, 1929 in Detroit, Michigan
Source: *AfrAmAl 6; AfrAmBi 1; ASCAP 80; Baker 84, 92; BiDAfM; BiDAmBL 83; BioIn 10, 11, 13, 15, 16; CelR 90; ConAu 148; ConBlB 1; ConMuA 80B; ConMus 6; ConTFT 5; CurBio 75; DrBlPA, 90; EncPR&S 89; HarEnR 86; InB&W 80, 85; IntMPA 80, 86, 92, 94, 96; LegTOT; MiSFD 9; NewGrDA 86; NewYTBS 74; OxCPMus; RolSEnR 83; SoulM; VarWW 85; WhoAfA 96; WhoAm 86, 88, 90, 92, 94, 95, 96, 97; WhoBlA 88, 92, 94; WhoEnt 92; WhoFI 87; WorAl; WorAlBi*

Gordy, Emory, Jr.
American. Musician, Producer, Songwriter
Country music musician; toured and recorded with Neil Diamond, 1971, Elvis Presley, 1973, and John Denver, 1979-1981; joined Emmylou Harris and her Hot Band, 1974-1977; received Grammy Award for *Southern Flavor* for bluegrass album of the year, 1989; also won Country Music Association album of the year award for *When Fallen Angels Fly,* 1994.
b. Dec 24, 1944 in Atlanta, Georgia
Source: *ConMus 17*

Gordy, Robert
American. Artist
Painted flat, whimsical works with repeated patterns and abstracts of human heads.
b. Oct 14, 1933 in Jefferson Island, Louisiana
d. Sep 24, 1986 in New Orleans, Louisiana
Source: *BioIn 8, 11, 15; ConArt 77, 83, 89; DcCAA 88, 94; PrintW 83, 85; WhoAmA 84*

Gore, Albert, Jr.
American. US Vice President
Moderate Dem. senator from TN, 1985-92; VP, 1993—, under Clinton.
b. Mar 31, 1948 in Washington, District of Columbia
Source: *AlmAP 78, 80, 82, 84, 88, 92; BioIn 13, 14, 15, 16, 18; CngDr 77, 79, 81, 83, 85, 87, 89, 91; CurBio 87; EnvEnc; IntWW 89, 91, 93; News 93-2; NewYTBS 83, 91; PolsAm 84; VicePre; Who 94; WhoAm 78, 80, 82, 84, 86, 88, 90, 92, 94, 95, 96, 97; WhoAmP 79, 81, 83, 85, 87, 89, 91, 93, 95; WhoEmL 93; WhoGov 77; WhoSSW 78, 80, 82, 84, 86, 88, 91, 93; WhoWor 89, 91, 96, 97; WorAlBi*

Gore, Albert Arnold
American. Politician
Dem. senator from TN, 1953-70; father of VP Albert Gore.
b. Dec 26, 1907 in Granville, Tennessee
Source: *BiDrAC; BiDrUSC 89; BioIn 2, 3, 4, 5, 6, 7, 9, 11, 12, 13; BlueB 76; CurBio 52; IntWW 74; WhoAm 74, 76, 78, 80, 82; WhoAmP 73, 75, 77, 79; WhoSSW 73, 75; WorAl; WorAlBi*

Gore, Charles
English. Clergy
Bishop of Oxford; wrote *Jesus of Nazareth,* 1929.
b. Jan 22, 1853 in Wimbledon, England
d. Jan 17, 1932 in London, England
Source: *Alli SUP; BiD&SB; BioIn 1, 2, 5, 6, 9, 14; DcNaB 1931; EvLB; GrBr; LngCTC; LuthC 75; NewC; NewCBEL; OxCEng 67, 85, 95; WhE&EA; WhLit; WhoLA*

Gore, Lesley
American. Singer
Early 1960s rock hits include "She's a Fool," 1963; "Young Love," 1966.
b. May 2, 1946 in Tenafly, New Jersey
Source: *BiDAmM; ConMuA 80A; EncRk 88; EncRkSt; InWom SUP; LegTOT; NewGrDA 86; PenEncP; RkOn 74; RolSEnR 83; WhoHol 92, A; WhoRock 81; WhoRocM 82; WorAl; WorAlBi*

Gore, Tipper
[Mary Elizabeth Aitcheson]
American.
Wife of vp Gore; married 1970.
b. Aug 19, 1948 in Washington, District of Columbia
Source: *BioIn 15, 16, 18, 19, 20, 21; ConNews 85-4; WhoAm 94, 95, 96, 97; WhoAmW 93, 95, 97*

Gorecki, Henryk (Mikolaj)
Polish. Composer
Composer in the Polish avante-garde movement; composed *Scontri,* 1960.
b. Dec 6, 1933 in Czernica, Poland
Source: *Baker 78, 84, 92; ConCom 92; CurBio 94; DcArts; IntWW 76, 77, 78, 79, 80, 81, 82, 83, 89, 91, 93; IntWWM 90; NewGrDM 80; OxCMus; WhoSoCE 89; WhoWor 95*

Goren, Charles Henry
American. Bridge Player, Journalist
His method of bridge is most widely used; author of 40 books on bridge, including *Bridge Is My Game,* 1965.
b. Mar 4, 1901 in Philadelphia, Pennsylvania
d. Apr 3, 1991 in Encino, California
Source: *AmAu&B; BioIn 5, 6, 12, 17, 18; ConAu 69, 134; CurBio 59, 91N; News 91; NewYTBS 91; WebAB 74, 79; WhAm 10; WhoAm 80, 82, 84, 86, 88; WhoWor 74; WorAl; WorAlBi; WrDr 90*

Gorey, Edward St. John
American. Author, Illustrator
Won Tony for costumes, set designs for *Dracula,* 1976; known for macabre illustrated children's books.
b. Feb 22, 1925 in Chicago, Illinois
Source: *BenetAL 91; BioIn 13, 15, 16; ConAu 5R, 9NR, 30NR; CurBio 76; DcLB 61; DcLP 87A; IlsBYP; IlsCB 1957; NewYTBE 73; OxCAmL 83; PenEncH; SmATA 27, 29; WhoAm 86, 90; WhoGrA 82; WhoUSWr 88; WhoWrEP 89; WrDr 86, 92*

Gorgas, William Crawford
American. Physician
Army officer best known for anti-mosquito controls which led to eradicating yell ow fever, 1904; US surgeon general, 1914-18.
b. Oct 3, 1854 in Mobile, Alabama
d. Jul 3, 1920 in London, England
Source: *AmBi; ApCAB X; AsBiEn; BiESc; BiHiMed; BiInAmS; BioIn 1, 2, 3, 4, 5, 6, 8, 9, 14, 15, 16; DcAmB; DcAmMeB, 84; DcAmMiB; DcNAA; FacFETw; HarEnUS; InSci; LarDcSc; LinLib S; McGEWB; MorMA; NatCAB 14, 32; NewCol 75; OxCAmH; OxCMed 86; WebAB 74, 79; WebAMB; WhAm 1; WorAl*

Gorges, Ferdinando, Sir
English. Colonial Figure
Received charter for province of Maine, 1639; attempted to colonize New England, promote growth.
b. 1566? in Wraxall, England
d. 1647 in Long Ashton, England
Source: *Alli; AmBi; AmWrBE; ApCAB; BenetAL 91; BioIn 3, 7; DcNaB; Drake; NatCAB 5; NewCol 75; OxCAmL 65, 83, 95; REnAL; WhAm HS*

Gorham, Jabez
American. Merchant
First American silversmith to use machinery; founded Gorham Manufacturing.
b. Feb 18, 1792 in Providence, Rhode Island
d. Mar 24, 1869 in Providence, Rhode Island
Source: *DcAmB; EncASM; NatCAB 23; WhAm HS*

Gorin, Igor
American. Composer, Singer, Actor
Baritone; had radio, operatic roles; made NY Met debut in *La Traviata,* 1964.
b. Oct 26, 1908 in Grodak, Russia
d. Mar 24, 1982 in Tucson, Arizona
Source: *ASCAP 66, 80; Baker 78, 84, 92; ConAmC 76, 82; CurBio 42, 82; WhoAm 74*

Goring, Butch
[Robert Thomas Goring]
Canadian. Hockey Player
Center, 1970-85, mostly with LA, NY Islanders; won Lady Byng, Masterton trophies, 1978, Conn Smythe Trophy, 1981.

b. Oct 22, 1949 in Saint Boniface, Manitoba, Canada
Source: *BioIn 12; HocEn; HocReg 85; WhoAm 82, 84, 86; WhoHcky 73*

Goring, Marius
English. Actor
Films include *Lilli Marlene,* 1944; *The Red Shoes,* 1948; *Exodus,* 1960.
b. May 23, 1912 in Newport, England
Source: *BioIn 19; CnThe; ConTFT 11; EncWT; FilmEn; FilmgC; ForYSC; HalFC 80, 84, 88; IlWWBF; IntMPA 77, 80, 86, 88, 92, 94, 96; IntWW 76, 77, 78, 79, 80, 81, 82, 83, 89, 91, 93; ItaFilm; MotPP; MovMk; PlP&P; VarWW 85; Who 74, 82, 83, 85, 88, 90, 92, 94; WhoHol 92, A; WhoThe 72, 77, 81*

Gorka, John
American. Singer, Songwriter, Musician
Preeminent folk singer of the New Folk Movement; performed with the Razzy Dazzy Spasm Band; as a solo performer released first album, *I Know,* 1987 and later recorded *Land of the Bottom Line,* 1990 and *Temporary Road,* 1993.
b. c. 1958 in New Jersey

Gorkin, Jess
American. Editor, Journalist
Editor *Parade* magazine, 1947-78.
b. Oct 23, 1913 in Rochester, New York
d. Feb 19, 1985 in Longboat Key, Florida
Source: *AmAu&B; BioIn 14; ConAu 115; FacFETw; WhAm 8; WhoAm 74, 76, 78, 80, 82, 84; WhoUSWr 88; WhoWrEP 89, 92*

Gorky, Arshile
[Vosdanig Manoog Adoian]
American. Artist
Abstract expressionist; works include "Dark Green Painting."
b. Oct 25, 1904 in Khorkom Vari, Turkey
d. Jul 21, 1948 in Sherman, Connecticut
Source: *AtlBL; BioIn 1, 2, 3, 4, 6, 7, 8, 10, 11, 12, 13, 14, 15, 17, 19, 20; BriEAA; ConArt 77, 83; DcAmB S4; DcArts; DcCAA 71, 88, 94; IntDcAA 90; LegTOT; McGDA; NewCol 75; REn; WebAB 74, 79; WhAm 4; WhAmArt 85*

Gorky, Maxim
[Aleksey Maksimovich Peshkov]
Russian. Author, Dramatist
Wrote *The Lower Depths,* 1902; *Mother,* 1907; considered father of Soviet literature.
b. Mar 28, 1868 in Nizhni-Novgorod, Russia
d. Jun 14, 1936 in Moscow, Union of Soviet Socialist Republics
Source: *AtlBL; BiD&SB; BioIn 1, 2, 3, 4, 5, 6, 7, 8, 9, 10, 11, 12, 13, 14, 15, 16, 17; CasWL; ClDMEL 47; CnMWL; CnThe; CyWA 58; DcArts; DcRusL; EncWL, 2, 3; EncWT; Ent; EuWr 8; EvEuW; FacFETw; FilmgC; GrFLW; HalFC 80, 84, 88; IntDcT 2; LegTOT; LiExTwC; LinLib L, S; MajMD 2; MakMC; McGEWB; McGEWD 72, 84; ModSL 1; ModWD; NewEOp 71; OxCChiL; OxCEng 67, 85, 95; OxCFilm; OxCThe 67, 83; PenC EUR; PlP&P, A; RAdv 14, 13-2; RComWL; REn; REnWD; TwCA, SUP; TwCLC 8; TwCWr; WhDW; WhLit; WhoTwCL; WorAl; WorAlBi; WorLitC*

Gorman, Carl Nelson
American. Artist
Pioneer of non-Native American art forms such as oil paintings and silk screening.
b. Oct 5, 1907 in Chinle, Arizona
Source: *BioIn 9, 14, 21; EncNAB; NotNaAm; WhoAmA 73, 76, 78, 80, 82*

Gorman, Chester
American. Archaeologist
Unearthed evidence of world's earliest agriculture and Bronze Age society while excavating in Thailand, 1960-70s.
b. Mar 11, 1938 in Oakland, California
d. Jun 7, 1981 in Sacramento, California
Source: *AnObit 1981; BioIn 13; NewYTBS 81*

Gorman, Cliff
American. Actor
Won Tony for *Lenny,* 1971; TV appearences include "Class of '63," 1973.
b. Oct 13, 1936 in New York, New York
Source: *BioIn 8; ConTFT 2, 7; FilmEn; HalFC 80, 84, 88; LegTOT; NotNAT; VarWW 85; WhoAm 74, 76, 78, 80, 82, 84, 86, 88; WhoEnt 92; WhoHol 92; WhoThe 77*

Gorman, Herbert Sherman
American. Author, Journalist
Biographies include *The Mountain and the Plain,* 1936; *The Cry of Dolores,* 1948.
b. Jan 1, 1893 in Springfield, Massachusetts
d. Oct 28, 1954 in Hughsonville, New York
Source: *AmAu&B; AmNov; BioIn 1, 2, 3, 4, 5, 15; ChhPo, S1, S3; CurBio 40, 55; NatCAB 42; OxCAmL 65, 83; REnAL; TwCA, SUP; WhAm 3; WhNAA*

Gorman, Leon Arthur
American. Business Executive
Pres. of L L Bean, 1967—.
b. Dec 20, 1934 in Nashua, New Hampshire
Source: *BioIn 16; ConNews 87-1; Dun&B 90; St&PR 84, 87, 91; WhoAm 82, 90*

Gorman, Leroy
[Bow Wow Wow]
English. Musician
Bassist with group since 1980.
Source: *EncRk 88; PenEncP; RkOn 85; RolSEnR 83; WhoCanL 87; WhsNW 85*

Gorman, Mike
American. Historian, Educator
Taught at Princeton U, 1942-85; wrote *Rendezvous with History,* 1952; special consultant and adviser to Pres. Johnson, 1964-66.
b. Jun 12, 1915 in New York, New York
d. Feb 19, 1989 in Princeton, New Jersey
Source: *BiDrAPA 89; CurBio 89N*

Gorman, R(udolph) C(arl)
American. Artist
Had works exhibited at New York's Metropolitan Museum of Art and the Museum of the American Indian; son of Carl Nelson Gorman.
b. Jul 26, 1931 in Chinle, Arizona

Gorman, Tommy
[Thomas Patrick Gorman]
Canadian. Hockey Coach, Hockey Executive
One of NHL founders; owner, Ottawa Senators, 1917; served as coach, GM of several teams, winning seven Stanley Cups; Hall of Fame, 1963.
b. Jun 9, 1886 in Ottawa, Ontario, Canada
d. May 15, 1961
Source: *WhoHcky 73*

Gorme, Eydie
[Steve and Eydie; Edith Gormenzano; Mrs. Steve Lawrence]
American. Singer
Won 2 Grammys for "We Got Us," 1960; "If He Walked into My Life," 1966; 7 Emmys for "Steve and Eydie Celebrate Irving Berlin," 1979; plus 2 more for "Our Love Is Here to Stay."
b. Aug 16, 1932 in New York, New York
Source: *Baker 84, 92; BioIn 10, 12; BioNews 74; BkPepl; CelR, 90; ConTFT 11; CurBio 65; InWom SUP; PenEncP; VarWW 85; WhoAm 74, 76, 78, 86, 90; WhoAmW 66, 68, 70, 72, 74, 75, 85; WhoEnt 92; WorAl; WorAlBi*

Gorr, Rita
[Marguerite Geirnaert]
Belgian. Opera Singer
Lyric mezzo-soprano concert performer; noted for Wagnerian roles.
b. Feb 18, 1926 in Ghent, Belgium
Source: *Baker 84, 92; BioIn 13; CmOp; IntDcOp; IntWWM 80, 90; InWom SUP; MetOEnc; NewAmDM; NewEOp 71; NewGrDM 80; NewGrDO; OxDcOp; PenDiMP; WhoAmW 74; WhoMus 72*

Gorrie, John
American. Inventor, Physician
Granted patent for mechanical refrigeration, 1851.
b. Oct 3, 1803 in Charleston, South Carolina
d. Jun 16, 1855 in Apalachicola, Florida
Source: *ApCAB SUP; BiHiMed; BioIn 2, 3, 5, 7, 9, 13; DcAmB; DcAmMeB, 84; DcNAA; EncAAH; NatCAB 15; WebAB 74, 79; WhAm HS; WhFla*

Gorshin, Frank John
American. Actor, Comedian
Played the Riddler on "Batman," 1966-68.
b. Apr 5, 1934 in Pittsburgh, Pennsylvania
Source: *BioIn 13; EncAFC; FilmgC; HalFC 84, 88; VarWW 85; WhoAm 74, 76, 84; WhoEnt 92; WhoHol A*

Gorshkov, Sergei
Russian. Naval Officer
As head of Soviet Navy 1956-85, was credited with bringing it into the nuclear era.
b. Feb 26, 1910 in Kamenets-Podolsk, Ukraine
d. May 13, 1988 in Moscow, Union of Soviet Socialist Republics
Source: *AnObit 1988; ColdWar 2; EncCW; IntWW 83; WhoWor 80; WorDWW*

Gortner, Marjoe (Hugh Ross)
American. Evangelist, Actor
Ordained minister, 1948; name is amalgam of Mary and Joseph; won Oscar, 1972, for autobiographical documentary, *Marjoe.*
b. Jan 14, 1945 in Long Beach, California
Source: *BioIn 16; BkPepl; HalFC 84, 88; IntMPA 86, 92; VarWW 85; WhoAm 82; WhoHol A*

Gorton, John Grey, Sir
Australian. Political Leader
Australian prime minister, 1968-71.
b. Sep 9, 1911 in Melbourne, Australia
Source: *BioIn 8, 9, 12; BlueB 76; CurBio 68; DcPol; FarE&A 78, 79; IntWW 74, 75, 76, 77, 78, 79, 80, 81, 82, 83, 89, 91, 93; IntYB 78, 79, 80, 81, 82; NewYTBE 71; WhDW; Who 74, 85, 92, 94; WhoAm 74, 76, 78; WhoGov 72, 75; WhoWor 74, 76*

Gorton, Samuel
American. Religious Leader
His followers, Gortonites, flourished in 1600s, founded Shawomet (later Warwick), RI, 1643.
b. 1592 in Gorton, England
d. 1677 in Warwick, Rhode Island
Source: *Alli; AmBi; AmWrBE; ApCAB; BenetAL 91; BiDrACR; BioIn 13; CyAL 1; DcAmAu; DcAmB; DcNAA; DcNaB; Drake; EncCRAm; HarEnUS; LuthC 75; NewCol 75; OxCAmH; OxCAmL 65, 83, 95; REnAL; WhAm HS*

Gorton, Slade
[Thomas Slade Gorton, III]
American. Politician
Rep. senator from WA, 1981-87, 1989— .
b. Jan 8, 1928 in Chicago, Illinois
Source: *AlmAP 82, 84, 92, 96; BiDrUSC 89; BioIn 13; BlueB 76; CngDr 81, 83, 85, 89, 91, 93, 95; CurBio 93; IntWW 81, 82, 83, 89, 91, 93; PolsAm 84; WhoAm 74, 76, 78, 80, 82, 84, 86, 88, 90, 92, 94, 95, 96, 97; WhoAmL 78, 79, 83, 85; WhoAmP 73, 75, 77, 79, 81, 83, 85, 87, 89, 91, 93, 95; WhoGov 72, 75, 77; WhoWest 74, 76, 78, 80, 82, 84, 87, 89, 92, 94, 96; WhoWor 82, 84, 87, 91*

Goscinny, Rene
French. Cartoonist, Writer
With artist Albert Uderzo, co-created French comic strip *Asterix.*
b. Aug 4, 1926 in Paris, France
d. Nov 5, 1977 in Paris, France
Source: *BioIn 10, 11; ChlLR 37; ConAu 113, 117; SmATA 39, 47; WorECom*

Gosden, Freeman Fisher
[Amos 'n Andy]
American. Comedian
Amos of "Amos 'n Andy" radio show, 1926-58; show denounced by NAACP.
b. May 5, 1899 in Richmond, Virginia
d. Dec 10, 1982 in Los Angeles, California
Source: *AnObit 1982; BioIn 1, 2, 7, 9, 13; ConAu 108; CurBio 47, 83; NewYTBE 72; NewYTBS 82; NewYTET; WebAB 74, 79; WhoHol A; WorAl*

Gosho Heinosuke
Japanese. Director
Films focused on daily lives of Japanese; noted for use of silence and scenes displayed in rapid succesion as cinematic techniques.
b. Feb 1, 1902 in Tokyo, Japan
d. May 1, 1981 in Shizuoka, Japan
Source: *HalFC 84*

Goslin, Goose
[Leon Allen Goslin]
American. Baseball Player
Outfielder, 1921-38; led AL in RBIs, 1924, in batting, 1928; had lifetime .316 batting average; Hall of Fame, 1968.
b. Oct 16, 1900 in Salem, New Jersey
d. May 15, 1971 in Bridgeton, New Jersey
Source: *Ballpl 90; BiDAmSp BB; BioIn 7, 9, 14, 15, 17; DcAmB S9; LegTOT; NewYTBE 71; WhoProB 73; WhoSpor*

Gossage, Goose
[Richard Michael Gossage]
American. Baseball Player
Relief pitcher, 1972—; led AL in saves, 1975, 1978, 1980.
b. Jul 5, 1951 in Colorado Springs, Colorado
Source: *Ballpl 90; BaseReg 87, 88; BiDAmSp BB; BioIn 11, 12, 13, 14, 15; CurBio 84; LegTOT; NewYTBS 77; WhoAm 80, 82, 84, 86, 88; WhoSpor*

Gosse, Edmund William, Sir
English. Author
Promoted Scandinavian literature; wrote autobiography *Father and Son,* 1907.
b. Sep 21, 1849 in London, England
d. May 16, 1928 in London, England
Source: *Alli SUP; BbD; BiD&SB; BioIn 1, 2, 3, 4, 5, 6, 7, 8, 9, 10, 11, 13; CamGEL; CarSB; CasWL; Chambr 3; ChhPo, S1, S2; CnMWL; DcArts; DcEnA, A; DcEnL; DcLEL; DcNaB 1922; EvLB; GrBr; LinLib S; LngCTC; ModBrL; NewC; NewCBEL; NotNAT B; OxCEng 67, 85, 95; PenC ENG; TwCA, SUP; TwCWr; WebE&AL*

Gossec, Francois Joseph
French. Composer
First French symphonist; wrote string quartets, operas, marches, hymns of Revolution.
b. Jan 17, 1734 in Vergnies, Belgium
d. Feb 16, 1829 in Passy, France
Source: *Baker 78; BioIn 4, 7; NewCol 75; NewEOp 71; OxCFr; OxCMus*

Gossett, Bruce
[Daniel Bruce Gossett]
American. Football Player
Two-time all-pro kicker, 1964-74; led NFL in scoring, 1966.
b. Nov 9, 1941 in Cecil, Pennsylvania
Source: *St&PR 87; WhoFtbl 74*

Gossett, Louis, Jr.
American. Actor
Won an Emmy, 1977, for his role in "Roots," and also an Oscar, 1983, for best supporting actor role in *An Officer and a Gentleman,* making him the second black in history to win an Oscar.
b. May 27, 1936 in New York, New York
Source: *AfrAmAl 6; AfrAmBi 2; BiE&WWA; BioIn 13, 14, 15, 16; BlksAmF; CelR 90; ConBlB 7; ConTFT 6, 13; CurBio 90; DcTwCCu 5; DrBlPA 90; HalFC 84, 88; InB&W 80, 85; IntMPA 94, 96; LegTOT; NegAl 89; News 89-3; NotNAT; VarWW 85; WhoAfA 96; WhoAm 78, 80, 82, 84, 86, 88, 90, 92, 94, 95, 96, 97; WhoBlA 80, 85, 88, 90, 92, 94; WhoEnt 92; WhoHol 92; WhoTelC; WorAlBi*

Gottfried, Brian
American. Tennis Player
With doubles partner Raul Ramirez won Wimbledon, 1976; French Open, 1975, 77; Italian Open, 1974-77; WCT World, 1975, 80.
b. Jan 27, 1952 in Baltimore, Maryland
Source: *BioIn 10, 11; BuCMET; LegTOT; WhoAm 82; WhoIntT*

Gottfried, Martin
American. Critic
With *NY Post,* 1974-77; *Saturday Review,* 1977—; *Cue,* 1978—.
b. Oct 9, 1933 in New York, New York
Source: *BiE&WWA; ConAmTC; ConAu 14NR, 21R; DcLEL 1940; NotNAT; WhoAm 78, 80, 82; WhoAmM 83; WhoE 75, 77; WhoThe 81*

Gottfried von Strassburg
German. Poet
Wrote unfinished love epic *Tristan and Isolde,* c. 1210.
b. 1170? in Strassburg, Germany

d. 1215?
Source: *BbD; BiD&SB; CasWL; ClMLC 10; CyWA 58; DcEuL; EuAu; EvEuW; OxCGer 76; PenC EUR; RAdv 14, 13-2; RComWL; REn*

Gotti, John
"Teflon Don"
American. Criminal
Reputed mob leader of the Gambino crime family; convicted on 13 counts listed in federal indictment, 1992.
b. Oct 27, 1940 in New York, New York
Source: *BioIn 14, 15, 16; NewYTBS 87*

Gottlieb, Adolph
American. Artist
Founding member of The Ten, 1935, a group of abstract expressionists; works include *Voyager's Return,* 1946; *Expanding,* 1962.
b. Mar 14, 1903 in New York, New York
d. Mar 4, 1974 in New York, New York
Source: *BioIn 1, 3, 4, 5, 6, 8, 10, 11, 13, 14, 17; BlueB 76; BriEAA; ConArt 77, 83, 89, 96; ConAu 49; CurBio 59, 74, 74N; DcAmArt; DcCAA 71, 77, 88, 94; EncAB-H 1974, 1996; EncWB; McGDA; NewYTBS 74; OxCTwCA; OxDcArt; PhDcTCA 77; PrintW 83, 85; WhAm 6; WhAmArt 85; WhoAm 74; WhoAmA 73, 76N, 78N, 80N, 82N, 84N, 86N, 89N, 91N, 93N; WhoE 74; WhoWor 74; WhoWorJ 72; WorArt 1950*

Gottlieb, Eddie
[Edward Gottlieb]
"The Mogul"
American. Basketball Coach, Basketball Executive
One of NBA's founding fathers; owner, coach, Philadelphia, 1947-55; signed Wilt Chamberlain, 1959; Hall of Fame.
b. Sep 15, 1898 in Kiev, Russia
d. Dec 7, 1979 in Philadelphia, Pennsylvania
Source: *BiDAmSp BK; BioIn 12; NewYTBS 79; WhoBbl 73; WhoSpor*

Gottlieb, Morton Edgar
American. Producer
Won Tony for *Sleuth,* 1970; produced film version, 1972.
b. May 2, 1921 in New York, New York
Source: *BioIn 12; ConTFT 5; Dun&B 88; NewYTBS 82; NotNAT; VarWW 85; WhoAm 78, 80, 82, 84, 86, 88, 90, 92, 94, 95, 96, 97; WhoAmJ 80; WhoE 74, 75, 77, 79, 81, 83, 85, 86, 89; WhoEnt 92; WhoThe 81*

Gottlieb, Robert A(dams)
American. Editor, Business Executive
Pres., Alfred A Knopf Inc., 1973-87; editor, *New Yorker* magazine, 1987-92.
b. Apr 29, 1931 in New York, New York
Source: *BioIn 10, 12, 15, 17, 20; BlueB 76; ConAu 125, 129; CurBio 87; IntWW 89, 91, 93; NewYTBS 87; Who 90, 92, 94; WhoAm 74, 76, 78, 80, 82, 84, 86, 88, 90, 92, 94, 95, 96, 97; WhoE 91, 93; WhoFI 79, 81, 85; WorAlBi*

Gottschalk, Ferdinand
English. Actor
Comedian, character actor in films, 1923-44, including *Grand Hotel,* 1932; *Gold Diggers of 1933,* 1933.
b. 1869 in London, England
d. Oct 10, 1944 in London, England
Source: *Film 2; HalFC 80, 84, 88; MovMk; WhoHol B; WhScrn 74, 77, 83*

Gottschalk, Louis Moreau
American. Musician, Composer
Colorful piano virtuoso; most popular American concert performer of his day; wrote piano music incorporating Latin-American and Creole elements.
b. May 8, 1829 in New Orleans, Louisiana
d. Dec 18, 1869 in Rio de Janeiro, Brazil
Source: *AfrAmAl 6; AmBi; AmComp; AmCulL; ApCAB; Baker 78, 84, 92; BiDAmM; BioIn 1, 3, 4, 5, 7, 8, 9, 10, 11, 12, 13, 14, 16, 17, 19; BriBkM 80; DcAmB; Drake; InB&W 85; LinLib S; McGEWB; MusMk; NegAl 76, 83, 89; NewAmDM; NewGrDA 86; NewGrDM 80; NewGrDO; NewOxM; OxCAmH; OxCAmL 65; OxCMus; OxCPMus; PenDiMP; PeoHis; TwCBDA; WebAB 74, 79; WhAm HS*

Gottschalk, Robert
American. Business Executive
Founder, pres. of Panavision, Inc.
b. Mar 12, 1918 in Chicago, Illinois
d. 1982 in Los Angeles, California
Source: *IntMPA 75, 76, 77, 78, 79, 80, 81, 82*

Gottwald, Klement
Czech. Political Leader
Brought communism to Czechoslovakia, mid-1940s.
b. Nov 23, 1896 in Dedice, Moravia
d. Mar 14, 1953 in Prague, Czechoslovakia
Source: *BioIn 1, 3, 8, 14, 18; ColdWar 2; CurBio 48, 53; DcTwHis; EncRev; EncWB; FacFETw; HisWorL; NewCol 75; ObitT 1951; WebBD 83; WhAm 3; WhDW*

Goucher, John Franklin
American. Clergy, Educator
Pres., Women's College of Baltimore City, now Goucher College.
b. Jun 7, 1845 in Waynesburg, Pennsylvania
d. Jul 19, 1922 in Pikesville, Maryland
Source: *AmAu&B; AmBi; BiDAmEd; DcAmB; EncWM; NatCAB 3, 24; WhAm 1*

Goudge, Elizabeth
English. Author
Best-known novel *Green Dolphin Street,* 1944, was made into a film, 1947.
b. Apr 24, 1900 in Wells, England
d. Apr 1, 1984 in Henley-on-Thames, England
Source: *Au&Wr 71; AuBYP 2, 3; Benet 87, 96; BioIn 1, 2, 3, 4, 8, 9, 10, 13, 14, 15, 16, 19; BlueB 76; ChhPo; ConAu 5NR, 5R, 112; CurBio 40, 84N; EngPo; FemiCLE; InWom, SUP; LegTOT; LngCTC; NewC; NewCBEL; OxCChiL; REn; ScF&FL 1, 2, 92; SmATA 2, 38N; ThrBJA; TwCA, SUP; TwCChW 78, 83, 89; TwCRGW; TwCRHW 90; TwCWr; WhoChL; WrDr 76, 80, 82, 84*

Goudsmit, Samuel Abraham
American. Physicist
With George E. Uhlenbeck developed the theory of electron spin, 1925.
b. Jul 11, 1902 in The Hague, Netherlands
d. Dec 4, 1978 in Reno, Nevada
Source: *AmMWSc 76P; AsBiEn; BiESc; BioIn 3, 10, 11, 12, 20; CamDcSc; ConAu 81; CurBio 79N; DcAmB S10; DcScB S2; FacFETw; InSci; IntAu&W 77; IntWW 74, 75, 76, 77, 78; LarDcSc; NewYTBS 78; ObitOF 79; WhAm 7; WhoAm 74, 76, 78; WhoAtom 77*

Goudy, Frederic William
American. Type Designer
Designer of over 100 different type faces.
b. Mar 8, 1865 in Bloomington, Illinois
d. May 11, 1947 in Marlboro, New York
Source: *AmAu&B; BenetAL 91; BioIn 1, 2, 3, 5, 7, 9; CurBio 41, 47; DcAmB S4; DcNAA; NatCAB 33; NewCol 75; OxCAmL 65; REnAL; WebAB 74, 79; WhAm 2; WhNAA*

Gougelman, Pierre
American. Physician, Inventor
Invented plastic used in manufacture of artificial eyes, 1941.
b. Feb 16, 1877 in Guttenberg, New Jersey
d. Jun 1, 1963 in Thornwood, New York
Source: *BioIn 6, 7; NatCAB 48*

Goulart, Joao
"Jango"
Brazilian. Political Leader
Pres. of Brazil, 1961-64; ousted by a coup after attempting program of radical reforms.
b. Mar 1, 1918 in Sao Borja, Brazil
d. Dec 6, 1976 in Corrientes Province, Argentina
Source: *CurBio 62, 77, 77N; DcPol; EncLatA; IntWW 74; McGEWB; WhAm 7*

Goulart, Ron(ald Joseph)
[Howard Lee; Kenneth Robeson; Frank S Shawn; Con Steffanson]
American. Author
Mystery, science fiction writer; received Edgar Award, 1971, for *After Things Fell Apart.*
b. Jan 13, 1933 in Berkeley, California
Source: *BioIn 8, 10, 14; ConAu 7NR, 25R; ConSFA; CrtSuMy; DcLP 87B; EncSF, 93; IntAu&W 82; NewEScF;*

RGSF; ScF&FL 1, 2, 92; ScFSB; SmATA 6; TwCCr&M 80, 85, 91; TwCSFW 81, 86, 91; WhoAm 82, 84, 86, 88, 90, 92; WhoE 74; WhoUSWr 88; WhoWrEP 89, 92, 95; WrDr 82, 84, 86, 88, 90, 92, 94, 96

Gould, Beatrice Blackmar
American. Editor, Author
With husband, Bruce, edited *Ladies Home Journal* magazine, 1935-62.
b. 1898 in Emmetsburg, Iowa
d. Jan 30, 1989 in Hopewell, New Jersey
Source: *AmAu&B; BioIn 16; BlueB 76; ConAu 127, P-1, P-2; CurBio 47, 89N; IntAu&W 89; IntWW 83, 89; InWom SUP; WhoAmW 74*

Gould, Charles Bruce
American. Editor, Author
Co-edited *Ladies Home Journal* magazine with wife, Beatrice, 1935-62.
b. Jul 28, 1898 in Luana, Iowa
d. Aug 27, 1989 in Hopewell, New Jersey
Source: *AmAu&B; BlueB 76; CurBio 47; IntYB 78, 79, 80, 81, 82*

Gould, Chester
American. Cartoonist
Cartoon comic strip pioneer who created "Dick Tracy," 1931.
b. Nov 20, 1900 in Pawnee, Oklahoma
d. May 11, 1985 in Woodstock, Illinois
Source: *AmDec 1930; AnObit 1985; Au&Arts 7; BioIn 1, 3, 4, 6, 9, 11, 14, 15, 16, 17; ConAu 30NR, 77, 116; ConGrA 1; ConNews 85-2; CurBio 71, 85N; EncACom; EncAJ; EncMys; EncTwCJ; FacFETw; LegTOT; LinLib L; NewYTBS 85; SmATA 43N, 49; WebAB 74, 79; WhAm 8; WhoAm 74, 76, 78, 80, 82, 84; WhoAmA 76, 78, 80, 82; WhoMW 74; WorECom*

Gould, Elliott
[Elliott Goldstein]
American. Actor
Starred in films *Bob and Carol and Ted and Alice,* 1969, *M*A*S*H,* 1970; former husband of Barbra Streisand.
b. Aug 29, 1938 in New York, New York
Source: *BiDFilm 94; BiE&WWA; BioIn 8, 9, 10, 11, 14, 16; BkPepl; BlueB 76; CelR, 90; ConTFT 2, 6, 13; CurBio 71; DcArts; EncAFC; EncMT; FilmEn; FilmgC; ForYSC; HalFC 80, 84, 88; IntDcF 1-3, 2-3; IntMPA 75, 76, 77, 78, 79, 80, 81, 82, 84, 86, 88, 92, 94, 96; IntWW 81, 82, 83, 89, 91, 93; ItaFilm; LegTOT; MovMk; VarWW 85; WhoAm 74, 76, 78, 80, 82, 84, 86, 88, 90, 92, 94, 95, 96, 97; WhoEnt 92; WhoHol 92, A; WhoThe 72, 77, 81; WorAl; WorAlBi*

Gould, George Milbry
American. Physician, Lexicographer
Ophthalmologist, compiled medical dictionaries, devised cemented bifocal lenses, 1889.
b. Nov 8, 1848 in Auburn, Maine
d. Aug 8, 1922 in Atlantic City, New Jersey
Source: *AmAu&B; AmBi; DcAmAu; DcAmB; DcAmMeB; DcNAA; NatCAB 10; OhA&B; WhAm 1*

Gould, Glenn Herbert
Canadian. Pianist, Composer
First N American to play in USSR; noted for idiosyncracies, Brahms interpretations; concentrated on recording after 1964.
b. Sep 25, 1932 in Toronto, Ontario, Canada
d. Oct 4, 1982 in Toronto, Ontario, Canada
Source: *AnObit 1982; Baker 84, 92; CanWW 70, 79, 80, 81; ConMus 9; CreCan 2; CurBio 60, 82; IntWW 82; NewYTBS 75, 82; NotTwCP; WhAm 8; WhoAm 74, 76, 78; WhoMus 72; WhoWor 82; WorAl*

Gould, Gordon
American. Physicist
Coined acronym "laser," 1957.
b. Jul 19, 1920 in New York, New York
Source: *AmMWSc 73P, 76P, 79, 82, 95; BioIn 11, 12, 13, 14, 15, 16; ConNews 87-1; St&PR 91, 93, 96, 97; WhoAm 80, 82, 84, 86, 88, 94, 95, 96; WhoFI 85; WhoFrS 84; WhoScEn 94; WhoSSW 95; WhoTech 82, 84, 89; WorInv*

Gould, Jay
[Jason Gould]
American. Financier
Part owner of many railroads, including the Erie and Union Pacific.
b. May 27, 1836 in Roxbury, New York
d. Dec 2, 1892 in New York, New York
Source: *AmBi; ApCAB, X; BiDAmBL 83; BioIn 1, 3, 4, 6, 8, 11, 12, 15, 16, 21; DcAmB; DcAmSR; DcNAA; EncAB-H 1974, 1996; EncABHB 2; GayN; HarEnUS; LegTOT; LinLib S; McGEWB; NatCAB 7; NewCol 75; OxCAmH; PeoHis; RComAH; REnAW; TwCBDA; WebAB 74, 79; WhAm HS; WhDW; WorAl; WorAlBi*

Gould, Laurence M(cKinley)
American. Explorer, Educator
Second-in-command of R E Byrd's S Pole expedition, 1920s; explored Antarctica, 1950s.
b. Aug 22, 1896 in Lacota, Michigan
d. Jun 20, 1995 in Tucson, Arizona
Source: *AmMWSc 73P, 76P, 79, 82, 86; BioIn 4, 5, 6, 11, 21; CurBio 78, 95N; IntAu&W 77; IntWW 74, 75, 76, 77, 78, 79, 80, 81, 82, 83; WhoAm 74, 76*

Gould, Lois
American. Author
Books include *Such Good Friends,* 1970; *Necessary Objects,* 1972.
b. 1938
Source: *AmAu&B; ArtclWW 2; ConAu 29NR, 77; ConLC 4, 10; DrAPF 83, 87, 91; IntvTCA 2; InWom SUP; MajTwCW; WhoAm 86, 88; WhoUSWr 88; WhoWrEP 89; WorAu 1975; WrDr 86, 92*

Gould, Morton
American. Composer, Conductor
Acclaimed versatile composer; works include ballet *Fall River Legend,* 19 47; led radio's "Chrysler Hour," 1940s.
b. Dec 10, 1913 in Richmond Hill, New York
d. Feb 21, 1996 in Orlando, Florida
Source: *AmComp; ASCAP 66, 80; Baker 78, 84, 92; BiDAmM; BiE&WWA; BioIn 1, 2, 3, 6, 7, 8, 9, 13, 14, 15, 21; BlueB 76; BriBkM 80; CmpEPM; CnOxB; CompSN, SUP; ConAmC 76, 82; ConCom 92; ConMus 16; ConTFT 1, 12; CpmDNM 80, 81, 82; CurBio 45, 68, 96N; DancEn 78; DcCM; DcCom&M 79; DcTwCCu 1; HalFC 84, 88; IntWW 89, 91, 93; IntWWM 77, 80, 90; LegTOT; LinLib S; MusMk; NewAmDM; NewCBMT; NewGrDA 86; NewGrDM 80; NewOxM; NewYTBS 27, 86; NotNAT; OxCMus; OxCPMus; PenEncP; PeoHis; PopAmC, SUP; RadStar; WhAm 11; WhoAm 74, 76, 78, 80, 82, 84, 86, 88, 90, 92, 94, 95, 96; WhoAmJ 80; WhoAmM 83; WhoE 74; WhoEnt 92; WhoHol 92; WhoMus 72; WhoWor 74; WhoWorJ 72, 78*

Gould, Shane
Australian. Swimmer
First woman to win three Olympic gold medals in individual events in world-record times, 1972.
b. Sep 4, 1956 in Brisbane, Australia
Source: *BioIn 9, 10, 11; HerW, 84*

Gould, Stephen Jay
American. Paleontologist, Author
Won American Book Award for *The Panda's Thumb,* 1981; National Book Critics Award for *The Mismeasure of Man,* 1982.
b. Sep 10, 1941 in New York, New York
Source: *AmDec 1980; AmMWSc 73P, 76P, 79, 82, 86, 89, 92, 95; BestSel 90-2; BioIn 11, 12, 13, 14, 15, 16, 17, 18, 20, 21; CamDcSc; ConAu 10NR, 27NR, 77; ConPopW; CurBio 82; EncWB; FacFETw; IntWW 89, 91, 93; LarDcSc; LegTOT; MajTwCW; NewYTBS 83; NotTwCS; RAdv 14, 13-1, 13-5; ThTwC 87; WhoAm 78, 80, 82, 84, 86, 88, 90, 92, 94, 95, 96, 97; WhoE 86, 89, 91, 95; WhoEmL 87; WhoFrS 84; WorAu 1975; WrDr 86, 88, 90, 92, 94, 96*

Goulding, Edmund
American. Director
Films include *Grand Hotel,* 1932; *Nightmare Alley,* 1949.
b. Mar 20, 1891 in London, England
d. Dec 24, 1959 in Hollywood, California
Source: *ASCAP 66, 80; BiDFilm, 81, 94; BioIn 5, 11, 15; CmMov; DcFM; FilmEn; FilmgC; HalFC 80, 84, 88; IlWWHD 1; IntDcF 1-2, 2-2; LegTOT;*

MiSFD 9N; MovMk; NotNAT B; OxCFilm; TwYS, A; WhAm 3; WhScrn 77, 83; WhThe; WorEFlm; WorFDir 1

Goulding, Ray(mond Walter)
[Bob and Ray]
American. Comedian
With Bob Elliott, member of gently offbeat Bob and Ray comedy team, formed late 1940s.
b. Mar 20, 1922 in Lowell, Massachusetts
d. Mar 24, 1990 in Long Island, New York
Source: *AnObit 1990; BioIn 3, 4, 5, 9, 10, 13, 16, 17; CelR; ConAu 36NR, 85, 131; CurBio 57, 90, 90N; JoeFr; LegTOT; NewYTBS 90; RadStar; WhAm 10; WhoAm 74, 76, 78, 80, 82, 84, 86, 88; WorAlBi*

Goulet, Leo D
American. Business Executive
Pres., chief exec., Gerber Products Co., 1983-87.
b. 1926?, Panama
d. Jul 5, 1987 in Fremont, Michigan
Source: *BioIn 15; Dun&B 79, 86, 88; NewYTBS 87; WhoAm 84, 86; WhoFI 87*

Goulet, Michel
Canadian. Hockey Player
Left wing, Quebec, 1979-89, Chicago, 1990-; set NHL record for most pts. by left wing in season, 121 (1983-84).
b. Apr 21, 1960 in Peribonqua, Quebec, Canada
Source: *BioIn 14; HocEn; HocReg 87; WhoAm 88*

Goulet, Robert Gerard
American. Actor, Singer
Broadway debut in *Camelot,* 1960; won Tony, 1968, for *The Happy Time.*
b. Nov 26, 1933 in Lawrence, Massachusetts
Source: *Baker 84, 92; BiE&WWA; BioIn 13; BioNews 74; BlueB 76; CanWW 31, 89; CelR 90; ConTFT 4; CurBio 62; EncMT; FilmgC; HalFC 88; IntMPA 92; NotNAT; PenEncP; VarWW 85; WhoAm 80, 82, 84, 86, 88, 90, 92, 94, 95, 96, 97; WhoEnt 92; WorAlBi*

Gounod, Charles Francois
French. Composer
Wrote operas *Faust,* 1859; *Romeo and Juliet,* 1867; known for lyric rather than dramatic qualities.
b. Jun 17, 1818 in Paris, France
d. Oct 17, 1893 in Saint-Cloud, France
Source: *AtlBL; Baker 78, 84, 92; Benet 87, 96; BioIn 1, 2, 3, 4, 5, 6, 7, 8, 9, 10, 12; CelCen; DcArts; DcCathB; Dis&D; IntDcOp; LegTOT; LinLib S; LuthC 75; McGEWB; NewC; NewCol 75; NewEOp 71; NotNAT B; OxCEng 85, 95; OxCFr; OxCMus; REn; WhDW; WorAl*

Gourdine, Simon (Peter)
American. Lawyer
General counsel, National Basketball Players Association, 1990-95; executive director, 1995-96.
b. Jul 30, 1940 in Jersey City, New Jersey
Source: *BioIn 21; ConBlB 11; WhoAfA 96; WhoAm 76, 78, 80, 82, 84, 86, 88, 90, 92, 94, 95, 96; WhoBlA 85, 88, 90, 92, 94; WhoWor 91, 93, 95, 96, 97*

Gowans, Alan
Canadian. Educator
Writings include *Categorization of Historic Styles in North American Architecture,* 1980.
b. Nov 30, 1923 in Toronto, Ontario, Canada
Source: *AmAu&B; ConAu 1R, 2NR, 18NR, 40NR; DrAS 74H, 78H, 82H; WhoAm 74; WhoAmA 73, 76, 86, 89, 91, 93; WhoE 93; WhoWor 74, 76; WrDr 82, 84, 86, 88, 90, 92, 94, 96*

Gowda, H(aradanahalli) D(odde) Deve
Indian. Political Leader
Prime minister, India, 1996-97.
b. May 18, 1933 in Haradanalli, India
Source: *News 97-1*

Gowdy, Curt(is)
American. Sportscaster
Won four Emmys for hosting TV's "American Sportsman"; covers NFL, baseball games; Hall of Fame, 1984.
b. Jul 31, 1919 in Green River, Wyoming
Source: *Ballpl 90; BiDAmSp OS; BioIn 7, 8, 9, 16; CelR; CurBio 67; IntMPA 75, 76, 77, 78, 79, 80, 81, 82, 84, 86, 88, 92, 94, 96; LegTOT; LesBEnT 92; NewYTET; SaTiSS; VarWW 85; WhoAm 74, 76, 78, 80, 82, 84, 86, 88, 90, 92, 94, 95, 96, 97; WorAl; WorAlBi*

Gowdy, Hank
[Henry Morgan Gowdy]
American. Baseball Player
Catcher, 1910-17, 1919-25, 1929-30; helped Boston win NL pennant, World Series, 1914.
b. Aug 24, 1889 in Columbus, Ohio
d. Aug 1, 1966 in Columbus, Ohio
Source: *Ballpl 90; BioIn 1, 7, 8; WhoProB 73*

Gowers, Ernest Arthur, Sir
English. Linguist
Wrote instructional books on the English language: *Plain Words: A Guide to the Use of English,* 1948.
b. Jun 2, 1880 in London, England
d. Apr 16, 1966 in Midhurst, England
Source: *BioIn 7, 10; ChhPo; ConAu 89; DcLEL 1940; DcNaB 1961; GrBr; LngCTC; NewC; ObitOF 79; ObitT 1961; WorAu 1950*

Gowon, Yakubu
Nigerian. Army Officer
Crushed Biafran secessionist revolt, 1967-70; head of state, 1966-75.
b. Oct 19, 1934 in Pankshin, Nigeria
Source: *AfSS 78, 79, 80, 81, 82; BioIn 8, 9, 10, 18, 21; ColdWar 2; CurBio 70; DcAfHiB 86, 86S; DcPol; DcTwHis; DicTyr; EncRev; FacFETw; InB&W 85; IntWW 74, 75, 76, 77, 78, 79, 80, 81, 82, 83, 89, 91, 93; IntYB 78, 79, 80, 81, 82; NewCol 75; NewYTBS 75; WhDW; Who 88, 90, 92, 94; WhoAfr; WhoGov 72, 75; WhoWor 74, 78, 80, 82; WorDWW*

Goya y Lucientes, Francisco Jose de
Spanish. Artist
Executed portraits, etchings, genre scenes; most noted for depictions of war: *Disasters of War* series, 1810-14.
b. Mar 30, 1746 in Fuendetodos, Spain
d. Apr 16, 1828 in Bordeaux, France
Source: *AtlBL; Benet 87, 96; BioIn 1, 2, 3, 4, 5, 6, 7, 8, 9, 10, 11, 12, 13, 14, 15, 16, 17, 18, 19, 20; BlkwCE; ClaDrA; DcCathB; DeafPAS; Dis&D; EncEnl; NewC; NewCol 75; OxCArt; PenEncH; RAdv 14, 13-3; REn; WhDW; WorAl*

Goyen, Jan Josephszoon van
Dutch. Artist
Created naturalistic landscapes; influenced later Dutch artists.
b. Jan 13, 1596 in Leiden, Netherlands
d. Apr 27, 1656 in The Hague, Netherlands
Source: *NewCol 75; OxCArt*

Goyen, William
American. Author
Wrote novel *The House of Breath,* 1950, which was adapted into play, 1954.
b. Apr 24, 1915 in Trinity, Texas
d. Aug 29, 1983 in Los Angeles, California
Source: *AmAu&B; AnObit 1983; Au&Wr 71; AuNews 2; BenetAL 91; BioIn 10, 11, 13; BlueB 76; ConAu 5R, 6NR, 110; ConLC 5, 8, 14, 40; ConNov 72, 76, 82; DcLB 2, Y83N; DcLEL 1940; DrAF 76; IntAu&W 76; ModAL S2; NewYTBS 83; Novels; OxCAmL 65, 83; PenC AM; REnAL; SouWr; WhoAm 82; WhoE 74; WhoWor 74, 76, 78, 80, 82; WorAu 1950; WrDr 76, 80, 82, 84*

Goytisolo, Fermin
[K C and the Sunshine Band]
Cuban. Musician
Conga player with the Sunshine Band since 1973.
b. Dec 31, 1951 in Havana, Cuba

Gozzoli, Benozzo
[Benozzo di Lese]
Italian. Artist
Frescoes include *The Journey of the Magi,* 1459-60.
b. 1420 in Florence, Italy
d. Oct 4, 1497 in Pistoia, Italy

Source: *AtlBL; BioIn 1, 5, 6, 7, 9; ClaDrA; IntDcAA 90; McGDA; NewCol 75; REn*

Grable, Betty
[Ruth Elizabeth Grable]
American. Actor
WW II pin-up girl; married Jackie Coogan, 1937-40, Harry James, 1943-65.
b. Dec 18, 1916 in Saint Louis, Missouri
d. Jul 2, 1973 in Santa Monica, California
Source: *BiDAmM; BiDFilm, 81, 94; BioAmW; BioIn 1, 4, 5, 9, 10, 12, 15, 19, 21; CelR; CmMov; CmpEPM; ContDcW 89; DcAmB S9; DcArts; EncAFC; FacFETw; Film 2; FilmEn; FilmgC; ForYSC; GoodHs; HalFC 80, 84, 88; IntDcF 1-3, 2-3; InWom, SUP; LegTOT; MotPP; MovMk; NewYTBE 73; NotAW MOD; ObitT 1971; OxCFilm; ThFT; WhAm 5; WhoAmW 58; WhoHol B; WhoThe 72; WhScrn 77, 83; WhThe; WorAl; WorAlBi; WorEFlm*

Gracchus, Gaius Sempronius
Roman. Statesman
Organized reform movement begun by Tiberius; elected tribune of the people, 123 BC.
b. 153BC
d. 121BC in Grove of Furrina, Italy
Source: *Benet 96; BioIn 11; DcBiPP; NewCol 75; WebBD 83*

Gracchus, Tiberius Sempronius
Roman. Government Official
Roman tribune who sought to distribute public land to the peasants and farmers.
b. 169?BC
d. Jun 133 in Rome, Italy
Source: *EncRev*

Grace, J(oseph) Peter, Jr.
American. Business Executive, Philanthropist
Pres., W.R. Grace and Co., 1945-92; has given away millions of dollars to Roman Catholic charities.
b. May 25, 1913 in Manhasset, New York
d. Apr 19, 1995 in New York, New York
Source: *BioIn 3, 5, 6, 7, 8, 11, 12, 13; ConAu 126; CurBio 60, 95N; Dun&B 79, 90; IntWW 91; News 90; NewYTBS 84, 85; St&PR 91; WhoAm 90; WhoE 91; WhoFI 92; WhoWor 84; WorAl; WorAlBi*

Grace, William Russell
"Pirate of Peru"
American. Businessman, Politician
Established W R Grace Co., 1865; underwrote Peruvian nat. debt in exchange for business concessions; first Roman Catholic mayor of NYC, 1880s.
b. May 10, 1832 in Queenstown, Ireland
d. Mar 21, 1904 in New York, New York
Source: *Alli SUP; AmBi; BiDAmBL 83; BioIn 2, 3, 9, 16, 19; DcAmB; DcAmDH 80, 89; DcCathB; McGEWB; NatCAB 36; NewCol 75; TwCBDA; WebAB 74, 79; WhAm 1*

Grade, Lew, Sir
[Lewis Winogradsky]
British. TV Executive
Chm. of Embassy Communications International; films include *The Muppet Movie,* 1977.
b. Dec 25, 1906 in Tokmak, Russia
Source: *BioIn 9, 15, 16, 17, 21; BlueB 76; ConTFT 6; CurBio 79; DcTwBBL; FacFETw; HalFC 80, 84, 88; IntMPA 92, 94, 96; IntWW 74, 75, 76, 93; LegTOT; LesBEnT 92; NewYTET; VarWW 85; Who 74, 85; WhoAm 80, 82, 84, 86, 88, 90, 92, 94, 95, 96, 97; WhoEnt 92; WhoThe 81; WhoWor 74*

Gradishar, Randy Charles
American. Football Player
Six-time all-pro linebacker, Denver, 1974-84.
b. Mar 3, 1952 in Warren, Ohio
Source: *BiDAmSp Sup; BioIn 14; FootReg 81; WhoAm 80, 82; WhoFtbl 74*

Grady, Don
[Don L. Agrati]
American. Actor
Played Robbie Douglas on TV comedy "My Three Sons," 1960-72; was a Mouseketeer on "The Mickey Mouse Club," 1957.
b. Jun 8, 1944 in San Diego, California
Source: *BioIn 18; ConTFT 2; WhoHol 92, A*

Grady, Henry Woodfin
American. Journalist, Orator
Edited *Atlanta Constitution,* 1880-89; known for oration "The New South," 1886.
b. May 24, 1850 in Athens, Georgia
d. Dec 23, 1889 in Atlanta, Georgia
Source: *AmAu; AmBi; BiDAmJo; BiDSA; BioIn 1, 2, 3, 5, 8, 9, 10, 11, 13, 16, 17; DcAmB; DcLB 23; DcLEL; DcNAA; EncAB-H 1974, 1996; EncAJ; EncSoH; EncWM; HarEnUS; JrnUS; McGEWB; NatCAB 1; OxCAmH; OxCAmL 65, 83, 95; REnAL; SouWr; TwCBDA; WebAB 74, 79; WhAm HS*

Graebner, Clark
American. Tennis Player, Businessman
Second-ranking amateur in US, 1968, surpassed only by Arthur Ashe.
b. Nov 4, 1943 in Lakewood, Ohio
Source: *BioIn 8, 9; BuCMET; CurBio 70*

Graf, Herbert
Austrian. Director
Stage director, NY Met., 1936-49.
b. Apr 10, 1903 in Vienna, Austria
d. Apr 1973 in Geneva, Switzerland
Source: *Baker 78, 84, 92; BiDAmM; BioIn 5, 6, 9, 10; CurBio 42, 73, 73N; EncTR; NewYTBE 73; WhAm 5; WhoMus 72*

Graf, Steffi
German. Tennis Player
Number 2 ranked female player; youngest to win French Open, defeating Martina Navratilova, 1987, also 1988, 1993, 1995-96; won Australian Open, 1988-90, 1994; Wimbledon, 1988-89, 1991-93, 1995-96; US Open, 1988-89, 1993-96.
b. Jun 14, 1969 in Mannheim, Germany (West)
Source: *BioIn 15, 16, 18; BuCMET; CelR 90; ConNews 87-4; CurBio 89; FacFETw; IntWW 89, 91, 93; LegTOT; LesBEnT; NewYTBS 87, 88; WhoAm 90, 92, 94, 95, 96, 97; WhoAmW 95, 97; WhoE 95; WhoSpor; WhoWor 93, 95, 96, 97; WorAlBi*

Grafe, Albrecht Friedrich Wilhelm Ernst von
German. Surgeon
Eye surgeon; introduced many new surgical procedures; established the field of modern ophthalmology.
b. May 22, 1828 in Berlin, Germany
d. Jul 20, 1870 in Berlin, Germany

Graff, Henry Franklin
American. Author
Historical writings include *The Presidents: A Reference History,* 1984.
b. Aug 11, 1921 in New York, New York
Source: *AmAu&B; BlueB 76; ChhPo; ConAu 1NR, 1R, 17NR; DrAS 74H, 78H, 82H; IntAu&W 76, 77, 82, 86, 91, 93; WhoAm 74, 76, 78, 80, 82, 84, 86, 88, 90, 92, 94, 95, 96, 97; WhoE 89, 97; WhoWor 78, 80, 82, 84, 87, 89, 91, 93, 95, 96, 97; WrDr 76, 80, 82, 84, 86, 88, 90, 92, 94, 96*

Graffman, Gary
American. Musician
Internationally known concert pianist, 1950s-60s.
b. Oct 14, 1928 in New York, New York
Source: *Baker 78, 84, 92; BioIn 4, 7, 8, 9, 11, 12, 13, 14, 15, 21; BlueB 76; BriBkM 80; CurBio 70; IntWW 74, 75, 76, 77, 78, 79, 80, 81, 82, 83, 89, 91, 93; IntWWM 77, 80, 90; MusSN; NewAmDM; NewGrDA 86; NewGrDM 80; NewYTBE 72, 73; NotTwCP; PenDiMP; WhoAm 74, 78, 80, 82, 84, 88, 90, 92, 94, 95, 96, 97; WhoAmM 83; WhoEnt 92; WhoWor 74, 96, 97*

Grafton, Sue
American. Author
Creator of the character Kinsey Millhone; first book *A Is for Alibi,* 1982.
b. Aug 24, 1940 in Louisville, Kentucky
Source: *Au&Arts 11; BestSel 90-3; BlmGWL; ConAu 31NR, 55NR, 108; ConPopW; CurBio 95; FemiCLE; FemiWr; GrWomMW; IntAu&W 91; RAdv 14; TwCCr&M 91; WhoAm 94, 95,*

96, 97; WhoAmW 93, 95, 97; WorAu 1985; WrDr 92, 94, 96

Graham, Barbara
"Bloody Babs"
American. Murderer
Life and execution portrayed by Susan Hayward in film *I Want to Live,* 1958.
b. 1923
d. Jun 3, 1955 in San Quentin, California
Source: *CmCal; DrInf; EncACr*

Graham, Bill
[Wolfgang Grajonca]
American. Producer
Promoted music groups including the Rolling Stones, Santana; produced Live Aid c oncert, 1986.
b. Jan 8, 1931 in Berlin, Germany
d. Oct 25, 1991 in Vallejo, California
Source: *AnObit 1991; BioIn 8, 9, 10, 11, 14, 15; BkPepl; CmCal; ConMuA 80B; ConMus 10; ConNews 86-4; EncPR&S 74; EncRk 88; HarEnR 86; IlEncRk; LegTOT; MugS; NewGrDA 86; NewGrDJ 88; News 92, 92-2; NewYTBS 91; PenEncP; WhAm 10; WhoAm 78, 80, 82, 84, 86, 88, 90; WhoFI 87; WhoRock 81; WhoWest 87, 89; WorAl; WorAlBi*

Graham, Billy
[William Franklin Graham, Jr]
American. Evangelist
Wrote *The Seven Deadly Sins,* 1955; *Challenge,* 1969; has conducted evangelistic tours throughout the world—Billy Graham Crusades; received Congressional Gold Medal, 1996.
b. Nov 7, 1918 in Charlotte, North Carolina
Source: *AmAu&B; AmDec 1950, 1960, 1970; AmOrTwC; AmSocL; BioIn 2, 3, 4, 5, 6, 7, 8, 9, 10, 11, 12, 13, 14, 15, 16, 17, 18, 19, 20, 21; BioNews 74; BkPepl; BlueB 76; CelR, 90; ChhPo S1; ConAu 9R, 20NR, 42NR, X; ConBlAP 88; ConHero 1; CurBio 51, 73; EncAAH; EncAB-H 1974, 1996; EncARH; EncSoH; FacFETw; IntAu&W 77; IntWW 74, 75, 76, 77, 78, 79, 80, 81, 82, 83, 89, 91, 93; LegTOT; LinLib L, S; McGEWB; News 92, 92-1; OxCAmH; PeoHis; PolProf E, K, NF; PrimTiR; RadStar; RAdv 14, 13-4; RComAH; RelLAm 91; TwCSAPR; WebAB 74, 79; Who 74, 82, 83, 85, 88, 90, 92, 94; WhoAm 74, 76, 78, 80, 82, 84, 86, 88, 90, 92, 94, 95, 96, 97; WhoRel 75, 77, 85, 92; WhoWor 74, 76, 78; WorAl; WrDr 80, 82, 84, 86, 88, 90, 92, 94, 96*

Graham, Bob
[Daniel Robert Graham]
American. Politician
Dem. senator from FL, 1987—; governor, 1979-87.
b. Nov 9, 1936 in Coral Gables, Florida
Source: *AlmAP 80, 92, 96; BiDrUSC 89; BioIn 14, 15, 16, 20; CngDr 87, 89, 91, 93, 95; CurBio 86; IntWW 80, 81, 82, 83, 89, 91, 93; NewYTBS 86; SmATA; TwCChW 89; WhoAm 86, 88; WhoAmP 73, 75, 77, 79, 87; WhoGov 75, 77; WhoSSW 73, 75, 80, 82, 88; WhoWor 91; WrDr 90*

Graham, David
Australian. Golfer
Turned pro, 1962; won PGA, 1979, US Open, 1981.
b. May 23, 1946 in Windsor, Australia
Source: *BioIn 13; Who 92; WhoAm 88; WhoGolf; WhoIntG*

Graham, Donald Edward
American. Newspaper Executive
Son of Katharine Graham; publisher, *Washington Post,* 1979—; pres., Washington Post Co., 1991-93; CEO, 1991—; chairman, 1993—.
b. Apr 22, 1945 in Baltimore, Maryland
Source: *BioIn 11, 12, 14, 15, 16; ConNews 85-4; Dun&B 90; EncTwCJ; IntAu&W 89, 91, 93; IntWW 80, 81, 82, 83, 89, 91, 93; NewYTBS 83; St&PR 84, 87, 91, 93, 96, 97; WhoAm 80, 82, 84, 86, 88, 92, 94, 95, 96, 97; WhoE 89, 93, 95; WhoFI 81; WhoWor 87, 96*

Graham, Ernest Robert
American. Architect
Helped design Merchandise Mart, Field Museum, Chicago; Flatiron Building, NYC.
b. Aug 22, 1866 in Lowell, Michigan
d. Nov 22, 1936
Source: *ApCAB X; BioIn 4; DcAmB S2; EncAB-A 8; WebBD 83; WhAm 1*

Graham, Evarts Ambrose
American. Surgeon
Performed first successful removal of human lung, 1933; gave evidence of correlation between smoking, lung cancer.
b. Mar 19, 1883 in Chicago, Illinois
d. Mar 4, 1957 in Saint Louis, Missouri
Source: *BioIn 2, 3, 4, 5, 11, 13; CurBio 52, 57; DcAmB S6; DcAmMeB 84; InSci; NatCAB 42; OxCMed 86; WhAm 3; WhNAA*

Graham, Fred P(atterson)
American. Journalist
Emmy-winning law correspondent for CBS News, 1972-85.
b. Oct 6, 1931 in Little Rock, Arkansas
Source: *BioIn 16; ConAu 37R; DrAS 74P, 78P, 82P; EncTwCJ; JrnUS; LesBEnT, 92; WhoAm 76, 78, 80, 82, 86, 88, 90, 92, 94, 95, 96, 97; WhoAmL 96; WhoE 95; WhoHol A; WhoTelC; WhoWor 96, 97*

Graham, Gwethalyn
[Gwethalyn Graham Erichsen Brown]
Canadian. Author
Novels include *Earth and High Heaven,* 1944; *Swiss Sonata,* 1948.
b. Jan 18, 1913 in Toronto, Ontario, Canada
d. Nov 24, 1965 in Montreal, Quebec, Canada
Source: *AmAu&B; BenetAL 91; BioIn 1, 7; CanNov; CanWr; ConAu 148; ConCaAu 1; CreCan 1; CurBio 45, 66; DcLB 88; FemiCLE; InWom; LinLib L; MacDCB 78; OxCCan; OxCCanL; REnAL; WhAm 4*

Graham, John
American. Architect
Best known for designing 1962 World's Fair Space Needle, in Seattle.
b. May 8, 1908 in Seattle, Washington
d. Jan 29, 1991 in Seattle, Washington
Source: *BioIn 6, 17; CurBio 91N; NewYTBS 91; WhoAm 74*

Graham, Jorie
American. Poet
Won Pulitzer Prize for *The Dream of the Unified Field: Selected Poems, 1974-1994,* 1996.
b. May 9, 1950 in New York, New York
Source: *AmWomWr SUP*

Graham, Katharine Meyer
American. Newspaper Executive
Pres., Washington Post Co., 1963-73, 1977; chm., 1973-93; CEO, 1973-91; chm., executive committee, 1993—; wrote autobiography, *Personal History,* 1997.
b. Jun 16, 1917 in New York, New York
Source: *AmWomM; AuNews 1; BiDAmBL 83; BioAmW; BioIn 13, 15, 16; BioNews 74; CelR 90; CurBio 71; DcLB 127; Dun&B 90; EncTwCJ; EncWB; EncWHA; ForWC 70; IntWW 74, 83, 89, 91, 93; InWom SUP; LesBEnT 92; LibW; NewYTBS 87; St&PR 75, 87; WhoAm 82, 90; WhoAmW 77, 91; WhoE 91; WhoFI 75, 92; WhoSSW 75; WhoWor 74, 91; WomFir; WorAlBi*

Graham, Larry
[Sly and the Family Stone; Lawrence Graham, Jr]
American. Singer, Musician
Bass guitarist with Sly and the Family Stone until 1972; solo performer since 1980.
b. Aug 14, 1946 in Beaumont, Texas
Source: *BioIn 12; EncPR&S 89; PenEncP; RkOn 85; RolSEnR 83; SoulM; WhoAfA 96; WhoBlA 77, 80, 85, 90, 92, 94*

Graham, Lou
American. Golfer
Turned pro, 1964; won US Open, 1975.
b. Jan 7, 1938 in Nashville, Tennessee
Source: *BioIn 10; WhoGolf*

Graham, Martha
American. Dancer, Choreographer
Doyenne of modern dance; founded Martha Graham Dance Co., 1926; choreographed over 150 works.
b. May 11, 1893 in Pittsburgh, Pennsylvania
d. Apr 1, 1991 in New York, New York

Source: *BioAmW; BioIn 1, 2, 3, 4, 5, 6, 7, 8, 9, 10, 11, 12, 13, 14, 15, 16; BioNews 74; CelR 90; ConAu 129, 134; ContDcW 89; CurBio 44, 61, 91N; DancEn 78; DcArts; EncAB-H 1974; EncWHA; FacFETw; HanAmWH; HerW, 84; IntWW 74, 91, 91N; InWom SUP; LibW; NewGrDA 86; NewOxM; News 91; NewYTBE 70, 73; NewYTBS 86, 89, 91; NotWoAT; RAdv 13-3; RComAH; VarWW 85; WebAB 74; Who 85, 90, 92N; WhoAm 86, 90; WhoAmW 87, 91; WhoE 91; WhoThe 77A; WhoWor 87, 91; WorAl; WorAlBi*

Graham, Nicholas
Canadian. Fashion Designer
Founder, chief designer, Joe Boxer Corp., during the late 1980s; designed an eccentric and fun line of men's boxer shorts and sleepwear.
b. 1960 in Calgary, Alberta, Canada
Source: *News 91*

Graham, Otto Everett, Jr.
''Automatic Otto''
American. Football Player
Quarterback, Cleveland, 1946-55; led NFL in passing six times; Hall of Fame, 1965.
b. Dec 6, 1921 in Waukegan, Illinois
Source: *BiDAmSp FB; BioIn 2, 3, 4, 7, 8, 9, 10; WhoAm 74, 76, 78, 80, 82, 84, 86, 88, 90, 92, 94, 95, 96, 97; WhoFtbl 74; WhoSSW 95, 97; WorAl; WorAlBi*

Graham, Ronny
American. Composer, Actor, Director
Film scores include *To Be Or Not To Be,* 1983; *Finders Keepers,* 1984.
b. Aug 26, 1919 in Philadelphia, Pennsylvania
Source: *ASCAP 66, 80; BiE&WWA; BioIn 17; ConTFT 7; NotNAT; VarWW 85; WhoCom; WhoHol 92, A; WhoThe 72, 77, 81*

Graham, Sheilah
[Lily Shiel]
American. Journalist
Syndicated Hollywood columnist for 33 yrs; known for affair with F Scott Fitzgerald described in autobiographies *Beloved Infidel,* 1958 and *The Rest of the Story,* 1964.
b. Sep 1908 in London, England
d. Nov 17, 1988 in West Palm Beach, Florida
Source: *AmAu&B; AuNews 1; BiDAmJo; BioIn 2, 5, 6, 7, 8, 9, 10, 11; BioNews 74; CelR; ConAu 108; CurBio 69, 89, 89N; EncAJ; InWom SUP; NewYTBS 87; WhoAm 74; WrDr 76, 86*

Graham, Stephen
English. Author
Travel experiences, mainly in Russia, were subject of books: *With Poor Emigrants to America,* 1914.
b. 1884, England
d. Mar 15, 1975 in London, England
Source: *Au&Wr 71; BioIn 4, 7; Chambr 3; ChhPo S3; ConAu 93; DcLEL; EvLB; IntAu&W 76; LngCTC; NewC; NewCBEL; ObitT 1971; REn; TwCA, SUP; WhE&EA; WhLit; Who 74*

Graham, Sylvester
American. Social Reformer
Health evangelist who spoke on diet, wholesome living; invented the graham cracker.
b. Jul 5, 1794 in West Suffield, Connecticut
d. Sep 11, 1851 in Northampton, Massachusetts
Source: *AmBi; AmRef; AmRef&R; AmSocL; ApCAB; BiDTran; BioIn 1, 2, 6, 7, 12, 14, 15, 18, 19, 21; DcAmAu; DcAmB; DcAmMeB 84; DcAmSR; DcNAA; Dis&D; Drake; Entr; McGEWB; NatCAB 5; NewCol 75; TwCBDA; WebAB 74, 79; WhAm HS*

Graham, Thomas
''Father of Colloid Chemistry''
Scottish. Chemist
Formulated Graham's Law of dispersion rate of gases.
b. Dec 20, 1805 in Glasgow, Scotland
d. Sep 16, 1869 in London, England
Source: *Alli; AsBiEn; BiESc; BioIn 4, 6, 8, 14; CamDcSc; CelCen; DcBiPP; DcNaB; DcScB; InSci; LarDcSc; NewCol 75; WebBD 83; WhDW; WorAl; WorAlBi; WorScD*

Graham, Virginia
[Virginia Komiss]
American. TV Personality, Actor
Active in TV, 1950s-60s; honored by many groups for her charitable work; wrote *If I Made It So Can You,* 1979; films include *Slapstick of Another Kind,* 1984.
b. Jul 4, 1912 in Chicago, Illinois
Source: *BioIn 16; CelR; CurBio 56; EngPo; ForWC 70; InWom; VarWW 85; WhoAm 76, 78, 80, 84, 86, 88; WhoAmW 66, 68, 70, 72, 74, 75*

Graham, Wallace H(arry)
American. Physician
Personal physician to Pres. Truman, 1945-53.
b. Oct 9, 1910
d. Jan 4, 1996 in Kansas City, Missouri
Source: *BioIn 1, 21; CurBio 96N; InSci; WhoAm 74, 76*

Graham, William Alexander
American. Politician
A founder of Whig party; senator, governor, secretary of navy.
b. Sep 5, 1804 in Lincoln County, North Carolina
d. Aug 11, 1875 in Saratoga Springs, New York
Source: *AmBi; ApCAB; BiAUS; BiDConf; BiDrAC; BiDrGov 1789; BiDrUSC 89; BiDrUSE 71, 89; BiDSA; BioIn 1, 5, 10; CivWDc; DcAmB; DcNAA; DcNCBi 2; Drake; EncSoH; HarEnUS; NatCAB 4, 6; TwCBDA; WhAm HS; WhAmP; WhCiWar*

Graham, Winston Mawdesley
American. Author
Historical novels include *Poldark's Cornwall,* 1983.
b. Jun 30, 1910 in Manchester, England
Source: *ConAu 2NR, 22NR, 49; ConLC 23; ConNov 72, 86, 91; CrtSuMy; CurBio 55; DcLB 77; IntAu&W 91; Novels; TwCCr&M 85; TwCRHW 90; TwCWr; Who 85, 92; WrDr 86, 92*

Grahame, Gloria
[Gloria Grahame Hallward]
American. Actor
Won 1952 Oscar for *The Bad and the Beautiful.*
b. Nov 28, 1925 in Los Angeles, California
d. Oct 5, 1981 in New York, New York
Source: *BiDFilm, 81, 94; BioIn 1, 11, 12, 16, 17; FilmEn; FilmgC; ForYSC; GangFlm; IntDcF 1-3, 2-3; IntMPA 82; MGM; MotPP; MovMk; NewYTBS 81; WhoHol A; WhoHrs 80; WorEFlm*

Grahame, Kenneth
Scottish. Children's Author
Wrote children's classic *The Wind in the Willows,* 1908.
b. Mar 8, 1859 in Edinburgh, Scotland
d. Jul 6, 1932 in Pangbourne, England
Source: *AnCL; AtlBL; AuBYP 2, 3; Benet 87, 96; BioIn 1, 2, 3, 5, 6, 7, 8, 9, 11, 12, 14, 19, 20, 21; BkCL; CamGLE; CarSB; CasWL; Chambr 3; ChhPo, S1, S3; ChlBkCr; ChlLR 5; CmScLit; CnMWL; ConAu 108, 136; CyWA 58; DcArts; DcLB 34, 141; DcLEL; DcNaB 1931; EvLB; FamSYP; GrBr; GrWrEL N; JBA 34; LegTOT; LinLib L; LngCTC; MajAI; ModBrL; NewC; NewCBEL; OxCChiL; OxCEng 67, 85, 95; PenC ENG; RAdv 14; REn; RfGEnL 91; RGTwCWr; ScF&FL 1A, 92; SJGFanW; StaCVF; Str&VC; TwCA, SUP; TwCChW 78, 83, 89, 95; TwCLC 64; TwCWr; WhDW; WhoChL; WorAl; WorAlBi; WrChl; YABC 1*

Grahame, Margot
English. Actor
Films include *The Informer,* 1934; *The Three Musketeers,* 1935; *Saint Joan,* 1957.
b. Feb 20, 1911 in Canterbury, England
d. Jan 1, 1982
Source: *BioIn 13; FilmEn; FilmgC; ForYSC; HalFC 80, 84, 88; IlWWBF; InWom SUP; ThFT; WhoHol A; WhoThe 77A; WhThe*

Graham Parker and the Rumour
[Bob Andrews; Martin Belmont; Andrew Bodnar; Stephen Goulding; Graham Parker; Brinsley Schwarz]
English. Music Group
Back-up band for Graham Parker, 1975-81; first album *Howlin' Wind,* 1976.
Source: *BioIn 14, 16; ConMuA 80A; EncRk 88; IlEncRk; OnThGG; RkOn 85; St&PR 93; WhoRock 81; WhoRocM 82*

Grahn, Judy
American. Writer
Wrote *Another Mother Tongue—Gay Words, Gay Worlds,* 1984.
b. Jul 28, 1940 in Chicago, Illinois
Source: *AmWomWr SUP; BioIn 13, 19, 20; BlmGWL; ConAu 116; DrAPF 80; FemiCLE; GayLesB; GayLL; OxCWoWr 95; RadHan*

Grainger, Percy Aldridge
American. Pianist, Composer
Experimented with electronic music, novel harmonies; made frequent use of folk tunes: *Children's March.*
b. Jul 8, 1882 in Melbourne, Australia
d. Feb 20, 1961 in White Plains, New York
Source: *AmComp; ASCAP 66; Baker 78, 84; BiDAmM; BioIn 1, 2, 4, 5, 6, 7, 8, 10, 11, 12, 13; ConAmC 76, 82; DcArts; DcCM; LinLib S; NewCol 75; NotNAT B; NotTwCP; OxCAmL 65; OxCMus; WhAm 4; WhDW*

Gram, Hans Christian Joachim
Danish. Physician
Specialized in bacteriological research; developed Gram's stain, 1884.
b. Sep 13, 1853 in Copenhagen, Denmark
d. Nov 14, 1938 in Copenhagen, Denmark
Source: *AsBiEn; BiESc; CamDcSc; DcScB; InSci; LarDcSc; OxCMed 86; WebBD 83*

Gramatky, Hardie
American. Children's Author, Illustrator
Award-winning watercolorist; his self-illustrated *Little Toot,* 1939, has become a perennial children's favorite.
b. Apr 12, 1907 in Dallas, Texas
d. Apr 29, 1979 in Westport, Connecticut
Source: *AmAu&B; AnCL; AuBYP 2, 3; AuNews 1; BioIn 1, 2, 5, 7, 8, 9, 10, 12, 13, 14, 19; BkP; BlueB 76; ChlBkCr; ChlLR 22; ConAu 1R, 3NR, 85; DcLB 22; IlrAm 1880, E; IlsCB 1744, 1946, 1957; JBA 51; LinLib L; MajAI; NewYTBS 79; OxCChiL; SmATA 1, 23N, 30; Str&VC; TwCChW 78, 83, 89, 95; WhAm 7; WhAmArt 85; WhoAm 74, 76; WhoAmA 73, 76, 78, 80N, 82N, 84N, 86N, 89N, 91N, 93N; WhoWor 74; WorECar; WrDr 80*

Gramm, (William) Phil(ip)
American. Economist, Politician
Rep. senator from TX, 1985—; co-author of Gramm-Rudman budget balancing law, 1985.
b. Jul 8, 1942 in Fort Benning, Georgia
Source: *AlmAP 80, 82, 84, 88, 92, 96; BiDrUSC 89; BioIn 12, 13, 14, 15, 19, 20, 21; CngDr 79, 81, 83, 85, 87, 89, 91, 93, 95; CurBio 86; IntWW 89, 91, 93; LegTOT; News 95, 95-2; NewYTBS 95; PolPar; PolsAm 84; WhoAm 80, 82, 84, 86, 88, 90, 92, 94, 95, 96, 97; WhoAmM 83; WhoAmP 79, 81, 83, 85, 87, 89, 91, 93, 95; WhoSSW 80, 82, 84, 86, 88, 91, 93, 95, 97; WhoWor 87, 89, 91*

Gramme, Zenobe Theophile
French. Engineer, Inventor
In 1869 invented the Gramme dynamo electrical generator.
b. Apr 4, 1826 in Jehay-Bodegnee, Belgium
d. Jan 20, 1901 in Bois-Colombes, France
Source: *DcInv; DcScB; InSci; WorInv*

Grammer, Kelsey
American. Actor
Played Frasier Crane on TV series "Cheers," 1984-93. Star of "Frasier," 1993—; Emmy award winner, 1995, 1995.
b. Feb 21, 1955 in Saint Thomas, Virgin Islands of the United States
Source: *BioIn 16; ConTFT 7; CurBio 96; IntMPA 96; LegTOT; WhoEnt 92; WorAlBi*

Grams, Rod
American. Politician
Rep. senator, MN, 1995—.
b. Feb 4, 1948
Source: *AlmAP 96; BioIn 19, 20, 21; CngDr 93, 95; WhoAm 94; WhoAmP 95*

Granados, Enrique
Spanish. Composer, Musician
Noted for series of piano pieces, *Goyescas,* 1916, inspired by Goya's etchings.
b. Jul 27, 1867 in Lerida, Spain
d. Mar 24, 1916
Source: *Baker 78, 84; BioIn 3, 4, 7, 8, 12, 15, 16, 17, 18; BriBkM 80; CmOp; CompSN; DcArts; DcCM; DcCom 77; EncWB; IntDcOp; MetOEnc; MusMk; NewAmDM; NewCol 75; NewEOp 71; NewGrDM 80; NewOxM; OxCMus; OxDcOp; PenDiMP A; WhDW*

Granatelli, Andy
[Anthony Joseph Granatelli]
American. Auto Racer, Businessman
Associated with several firms connected with auto racing, including STP Corp; wrote *They Call Me Mister 500,* 1969.
b. Mar 18, 1923 in Dallas, Texas
Source: *BioIn 8, 9, 10, 17; LegTOT; WhoAm 76*

Grand Funk Railroad
[Donald Brewer; Mark Farner; Craig Frost; Mel Schacher]
American. Music Group
Formed, 1969; most commercially successful heavy metal group, 1970-76; first group to have 10 consecutive platinum albums; sold over 20 million.
Source: *AmMWSc 86; BioIn 16; EncPR&S 74; EncRk 88; EncRkSt; HarEnR 86; NewAmDM; PenEncP; WhoRocM 82*

Grandi, Dino
Italian. Politician
Minister of foreign affairs, 1929-32; ambassador to Great Britain, 1932-39; frequent critic of Mussolini.
b. Jun 4, 1895 in Mordano, Italy
d. May 21, 1988 in Bologna, Italy
Source: *BiDExR; BioIn 15, 16; CurBio 43, 88, 88N; EncRev; FacFETw; HisEWW; IntAu&W 77; IntWW 74, 75, 76, 77, 78, 79, 80, 81, 82, 83; LinLib S; Who 74*

Grandin, Temple
American. Scientist
Supporter of humane treatment of livestock.
b. Aug 29, 1947 in Boston, Massachusetts
Source: *ConAu 154; CurBio 94; WhoAmW 91, 93, 95, 97; WhoEmL 93; WhoMW 92; WhoWest 80, 82, 94*

Grandville
[Jean-Ignace Isidore Gerard]
French. Caricaturist
Did satirical lithographs in which notable people were depicted as animals.
b. Sep 13, 1803 in Nancy, France
d. Mar 17, 1847 in Paris, France
Source: *DcBiPP; Dis&D; McGDA; NewCol 75; OxCChiL; OxCFr; SmATA X*

Grandy, Fred(erick Lawrence)
American. Politician, Actor
Parlayed fame from role on TV series "Love Boat," 1977-86 to win election as Rep. congressman from IA, 1986.
b. Jun 29, 1948 in Sioux City, Iowa
Source: *AlmAP 88, 92; BiDrUSC 89; BioIn 13, 14, 15; CngDr 87, 89, 91, 93; LegTOT; VarWW 85; WhoAm 86, 90, 92, 94, 95, 97; WhoAmP 87, 89, 91, 93, 95; WhoE 95; WhoMW 90, 92, 93*

Grange, Red
[Harold Edward Grange]
"Galloping Ghost"; "Wheaton Ice Man"
American. Football Player
Three-time All-America running back at U of IL, 1923-25; in NFL with Chicago, 1925, 1929-34; Hall of Fame.
b. Jun 13, 1903 in Forksville, Pennsylvania
d. Jan 28, 1991 in Lake Wales, Florida
Source: *AnObit 1991; BiDAmSp FB; BioIn 2, 3, 4, 5, 6, 7, 8, 9, 10, 12, 13, 14, 15, 16, 21; Film 2; LegTOT; News 91, 91-3; NewYTBS 74, 88; OxCAmH; WebAB 74, 79; What 1; WhoFtbl 74; WhoHol A; WhoSpor; WorAl*

Granger, Farley
American. Actor
Played in Hitchcock films *Rope,* 1948; *Strangers on a Train,* 1951.
b. Jul 1, 1925 in San Jose, California
Source: *BiDFilm, 81, 94; BiE&WWA; BioIn 10, 11, 13, 18; ConTFT 3; FilmEn; FilmgC; ForYSC; GangFlm;*

HalFC 80, 84, 88; HolP 40; IntMPA 75, 76, 77, 78, 79, 80, 81, 82, 84, 86, 88, 92, 94, 96; ItaFilm; LegTOT; MotPP; MovMk; NotNAT; VarWW 85; WhoHol 92, A; WorAl; WorAlBi; WorEFlm

Granger, Lester
American. Government Official
Executive director, National Urban League, 1941-61; worked to develop economic opportunities for blacks.
b. Sep 16, 1896 in Newport News, Virginia
d. Jan 9, 1976 in Alexandria, Louisiana
Source: *CurBio 46, 76; WhAm 6; WhoAm 74*

Granger, Stewart
[James Lablache Stewart]
American. Actor, Author
Wrote autobiography *Sparks Fly Upward;* films include *Caesar and Cleopatra,* 1945.
b. May 6, 1913 in London, England
d. Aug 16, 1993 in Santa Monica, California
Source: *AnObit 1993; BiDFilm, 81, 94; BioIn 2, 9, 11, 14, 19; CmMov; ConTFT 8, 12; DcLP 87B; EncEurC; FilmAG WE; FilmEn; FilmgC; ForYSC; HalFC 80, 84, 88; IntDcF 1-3, 2-3; IntMPA 75, 76, 77, 78, 79, 80, 81, 82, 84, 86, 88, 92, 94; IntWW 91, 93; ItaFilm; LegTOT; MGM; MotPP; MovMk; OxCFilm; VarWW 85; Who 74, 82, 83, 85, 88, 90, 92; WhoHol 92, A; WhoThe 77A; WhThe; WorAl; WorAlBi; WorEFlm*

Granick, Harry
[Harry Taylor]
American. Writer, Critic
Won Peabody for "Great Adventures" series, 1944; author of plays, books since 1937 .
b. Jan 23, 1898 in Nova Kraruka, Russia
Source: *ConAu 48NR, 85; ConTFT 4*

Granit, Ragnar Arthur
Swedish. Physiologist
First to show that single nerve fibers in retina could distinguish different wavelengths of light; shared Nobel Prize, 1967.
b. Oct 30, 1900 in Helsinki, Finland
d. Mar 12, 1991
Source: *AsBiEn; BiESc; BioIn 4, 5, 8, 15, 20; IntAu&W 77; IntWW 74, 75, 76, 77, 78, 79, 80, 81, 82, 83, 89, 91; LarDcSc; McGMS 80; NobelP; NotTwCS; WhAm 10; Who 74, 82, 83, 85, 88, 90, 92N; WhoAm 74, 76, 78, 80, 82, 84, 86, 88, 90; WhoNob, 90, 95; WhoWor 74, 76, 78, 80, 82, 84, 87, 89, 91*

Granjon, Robert
French. Type Designer, Engraver
Early printer of music, known for his "caracteres de civilite" based on French Got hic writing.
b. 1545
d. 1588
Source: *NewCol 75; WebBD 83*

Grant, Amy
American. Singer
Christian rock singer whose album *Age to Age,* 1983, sold one million cop ies; *Unguarded* contained hit "Find a Way," 1985; won 5 Grammys, 1982-85, 1988.
b. Nov 25, 1960 in Augusta, Georgia
Source: *BioIn 13, 14, 15; CelR 90; ConMus 7; ConNews 85-4; EncRkSt; LegTOT; WhoAmW 91; WorAlBi*

Grant, Bruce
American. Journalist, Author
Historical children's books include *Longhorn: A Story of the Chisholm Trail,* 1956.
b. Apr 17, 1893 in Wichita Falls, Texas
d. Apr 9, 1977 in Winnetka, Illinois
Source: *AuBYP 2, 3; BioIn 2, 7, 10, 11, 13; ConAu 1R, 6NR, 69; IntYB 82; SmATA 5, 25N*

Grant, Bud
[Harold Peter Grant]
American. Football Coach
Head coach, Minnesota, 1967-83, 1985; compiled 158-96-5 record.
b. May 20, 1927 in Superior, Wisconsin
Source: *BiDAmSp FB; BioIn 12, 14, 15; BioNews 74; FootReg 86; LegTOT; NewYTBS 85; WhoAm 95, 96, 97; WhoFtbl 74; WhoMW 82, 84, 86; WhoSpor*

Grant, Cary
[Archibald Alexander Leach]
"Archie"
American. Actor
One of Hollywood's most enduring leading men; starred in *The Philadelphia Story,* 1940; *North by Northwest,* 1959.
b. Jan 18, 1904 in Bristol, England
d. Nov 29, 1986 in Davenport, Iowa
Source: *AmCulL; AnObit 1986; BiDFilm, 81; BioIn 1, 4, 5, 6, 7, 8, 9, 10, 11, 13, 14, 15, 16, 17, 18, 19, 20; BkPepl; BlueB 76; CelR; CmCal; CmMov; ConNews 87-1; ConTFT 3, 4; CurBio 41, 65, 87, 87N; DcArts; DcNaB 1986; DcTwCCu 1; EncAFC; EncMT; EncVaud; FacFETw; FilmEn; FilmgC; ForYSC; GangFlm; HalFC 80, 84, 88; IntDcF 1-3, 2-3; IntMPA 75, 76, 77, 78, 79, 80, 81, 82, 84, 86; IntWW 74, 75, 76, 77, 78, 79, 80, 81, 82, 83; LegTOT; MotPP; MovMk; NewCol 75; NewYTBS 86; OxCFilm; WebAB 74, 79; WhAm 9; Who 74, 82, 83, 85; WhoAm 74, 76, 78, 80, 82, 84, 86; WhoCom; WhoHol A; WhoHrs 80; WhoWor 74, 78, 80, 82, 84; WorAl; WorAlBi; WorEFlm*

Grant, Duncan (James Corrowr)
English. Artist
Postimpressionist painter; best known for his portraits of Bloomsbury members.
b. Jan 21, 1885 in Rothiemurchus, Scotland
d. May 8, 1978 in Aldermaston, England
Source: *BioIn 4, 7, 11, 14, 15, 16, 17; BlueB 76; ClaDrA; ConArt 77; ConAu 148; DcArts; DcBrAr 1; DcD&D; DcLB DS10; DcNaB 1971; DcTwDes; FacFETw; GayLesB; IntWW 74, 75, 76, 77, 78; McGDA; OxCArt; OxCTwCA; OxDcArt; PhDcTCA 77; TwCPaSc; Who 74; WhoArt 80, 82; WhoWor 74, 76; WorArt 1950*

Grant, Earl
American. Musician
A leading popular organist of 1960s.
b. Jan 20, 1931 in Idabelle, Oklahoma
d. Jun 10, 1970 in Lordsburg, New Mexico
Source: *BiDAfM; DrBlPA, 90; InB&W 80; NewYTBE 70; PenEncP; RkOn 74; WhoHol B; WhScrn 74, 77, 83*

Grant, Eddy
[Edmond Montague Grant]
Guyanese. Singer, Composer
Music has reggae flavor; hits include "Living on the Front Line," 1979; "Electric A venue," 1983.
b. Mar 5, 1948 in Plaisance, British Guiana
Source: *BioIn 13; EncRk 88; EncRkSt; HarEnR 86; LegTOT; OnThGG; PenEncP; RkOn 85*

Grant, Gogi
[Myrtle Audrey Arinsberg; Audrey Grant]
American. Singer
Best known for "The Wayward Wind," one of the most popular records of 1950s.
b. Sep 20, 1924 in Philadelphia, Pennsylvania
Source: *InWom SUP; LegTOT; PenEncP; RkOn 74*

Grant, Gordon
American. Illustrator, Artist
Marine painter whose *Old Ironsides* hangs in Oval Office; best known for illustrations for Tarkington's *Penrod* stories.
b. Jun 7, 1875 in San Francisco, California
d. May 6, 1962 in New York, New York
Source: *AmAu&B; BioIn 1, 3, 5, 6, 13; ConAu 102; CurBio 53, 62; DcSeaP; IlrAm C; IlsCB 1744, 1946; SmATA 25; WhAm 4; WhAmArt 85; WhoAmA 82N; WorECar*

Grant, Harry Johnston
American. Newspaper Publisher
Milwaukee Journal pres., editor, 1935; board chm., 1938-63.
b. Sep 15, 1881 in Chillicothe, Missouri
d. Jul 12, 1963 in Milwaukee, Wisconsin
Source: *BiDAmJo; BioIn 2, 3, 6, 9, 16; DcAmB S7; EncAB-A 39; MnBBF; NatCAB 52; WhAm 4; WhJnl; WhNAA*

Grant, Hugh
English. Actor
Appeared in *Four Weddings and a Funeral,* 1994.
b. Sep 9, 1960 in London, England

Source: *BioIn 19, 20, 21; ConTFT 15; CurBio 95; IntMPA 94, 96; News 95, 95-3; WhoAm 95, 96, 97*

Grant, James
Scottish. Author
His fifty novels include *Romance of War,* 1845; *Harry Ogilvie,* 1856.
b. Aug 1, 1822 in Edinburgh, Scotland
d. May 5, 1887 in Edinburgh, Scotland
Source: *Alli, SUP; BbD; BiD&SB; BritAu 19; CelCen; CmScLit; DcBiA; DcBiPP; DcEnA A; DcEnL; DcLEL; DcNaB; EvLB; NewC; NewCBEL; OxCEng 67, 85, 95; ScF&FL 92; StaCVF*

Grant, Jane
American. Journalist
First woman to cover "city room" desk; with *NY Times,* 1914-30; founded *New Yorker* mag., with husband Harold Ross, 1925.
b. May 29, 1895 in Joplin, Missouri
d. Mar 16, 1972 in Litchfield, Connecticut
Source: *ConAu 33R, P-2; ForWC 70; NewYTBE 72; ObitOF 79*

Grant, Julia Dent
[Mrs. Ulysses S Grant]
American. First Lady
Unpretentious army wife; buried with husband in NY's monumental tomb.
b. Jan 26, 1826 in Saint Louis, Missouri
d. Dec 14, 1902 in Washington, District of Columbia
Source: *AmAu&B; AmWom; ApCAB; BioAmW; BioIn 16, 17; GoodHs; HerW; InWom, SUP; NatCAB 4; NotAW; TwCBDA; WhAm 1*

Grant, Kirby
[Kirby Grant Hoon, Jr.]
American. Actor
Best known as star of TV series "Sky King," 1953-54.
b. Nov 24, 1911 in Butte, Montana
d. Oct 30, 1985 in Titusville, Florida
Source: *BioIn 8, 14; FilmEn; FilmgC; WhoHol A*

Grant, Lee
[Mrs. Joseph Feury; Lyova Haskell Rosenthal]
American. Actor, Director
Won Emmy for "Peyton Place," 1965; Oscar for *Shampoo,* 1975; has directed several TV movies and documentaries.
b. Oct 31, 1931 in New York, New York
Source: *BiE&WWA; BioIn 9, 10, 12; BkPepl; ConTFT 1, 8; CurBio 74; FilmgC; HalFC 84; IntMPA 84, 86, 88, 92, 94, 96; MotPP; MovMk; NewYTBE 70; NotNAT; ReelWom; VarWW 85; WhoAm 74, 76, 78, 82, 84, 86, 88, 90, 92, 94, 95, 96, 97; WhoEnt 92; WhoHol A; WhoWor 95, 96, 97; WorAl; WorAlBi*

Grant, Michael
English. Author, Educator
Ancient history writer whose books include *Jesus: An Historian's Review of the Gospels,* 1977.
b. Nov 21, 1914 in London, England
Source: *Au&Wr 71; Baker 84; BiDJaz; BioIn 9, 10, 12, 13, 16; BlueB 76; ConAu 1R, 4NR, 25NR, 50NR; IntAu&W 86, 89, 91, 93; IntWW 91; IntWWM 90; NewAmDM; NewGrDJ 88; PenDiMP; PenEncP; Who 74, 82, 83, 85, 88, 90, 92, 94; WhoRocM 82; WhoWor 84; WorAu 1975; WrDr 76, 80, 82, 84, 86, 88, 90, 92, 94, 96*

Grant, Mudcat
[James Timothy Grant]
American. Baseball Player
Pitcher, 1958-71; led AL in wins, 1965.
b. Aug 13, 1935 in Lacoochee, Florida
Source: *AmMWSc 92; Ballpl 90; BaseEn 88; BioIn 8; InB&W 80, 85; WhoProB 73*

Grant, Rodney A
American. Actor
Films include *Dances With Wolves,* 1990.
b. 1960 in Winnebago, Nebraska
Source: *News 92, 92-1*

Grant, Ulysses Simpson
[Hiram Ulysses Grant]
American. US President
Union commander-in-chief, Civil War; forced surrender of R E Lee; 18th pres., Rep., 1869-77; term marred by scandals.
b. Apr 27, 1822 in Point Pleasant, Ohio
d. Jul 23, 1885 in Mount McGregor, New York
Source: *Alli SUP; AmAu&B; AmBi; AmPolLe; ApCAB; BbD; BiAUS; BiD&SB; BiDrAC; BiDrUSE 71, 89; BioIn 1, 2, 3, 4, 5, 6, 7, 8, 9, 10, 11, 12, 13; CivWDc; CmdGen 1991; CyAG; DcAmAu; DcAmB; DcAmMiB; DcAmSR; DcBiPP; DcNAA; Dis&D; Drake; EncAAH; EncAB-H 1974, 1996; EncWM; FacPr 89, 93; GenMudB; HarEnMi; HarEnUS; HisWorL; LinLib L, S; McGEWB; NatCAB 4; OhA&B; OxCAmH; OxCAmL 65, 83; REn; REnAL; TwCBDA; WebAB 74, 79; WebAMB; WhAm HS; WhAmP; WhCiWar; WhDW; WhNaAH; WhoMilH 76; WorAl; WorAlBi*

Granville, Bonita
American. Actor
Played Nancy Drew in 1930s film series; produced/directed *Lassie.*
b. Feb 2, 1923 in New York, New York
d. Oct 11, 1988 in Santa Monica, California
Source: *AnObit 1988; BioIn 11, 12, 15, 16; FilmEn; FilmgC; ForYSC; HalFC 80, 84, 88; HolP 30; IntMPA 84, 86, 88; InWom SUP; LegTOT; MotPP; MovMk; ThFT; VarWW 85; WhoHol A*

Granville, Joseph E(nsign)
American. Financier
Stock market advisor; wrote for E F Hutton's *Market Letter,* 1957-63; later published own marketing organ.
b. Aug 20, 1923 in Yonkers, New York
Source: *BioIn 12, 13, 14, 15; ConAu 65; Who 92*

Granville-Barker, Harley
English. Dramatist
Plays include *The Voysey Inheritance,* 1905; *Secret Life,* 1923; wrote series of Prefaces to Shakespearean plays.
b. Nov 25, 1877 in London, England
d. Aug 31, 1946 in Paris, France
Source: *Benet 87, 96; BioIn 14, 15, 17, 20; BlmGEL; BritPl; CamGLE; CamGWoT; CasWL; Chambr 3; CnMD; CnThe; ConAu 104; CrtSuDr; CyWA 58; DcArts; DcLEL; EncWT; Ent; EvLB; FacFETw; GrStDi; LegTOT; LinLib L, S; LngCEL; LngCTC; McGEWD 72, 84; ModBrL; ModWD; NotNAT A, B; OxCEng 85, 95; OxCThe 67, 83; PenC ENG; PlP&P; REnWD; RGTwCWr; TwCA SUP; TwCLC 2; WebE&AL; WhE&EA; WhThe*

Granz, Norman
American. Impresario, Producer
Promoted international jazz concerts; produced jazz records.
b. Aug 6, 1918 in Los Angeles, California
Source: *BiDAmM; BiDJaz; BioIn 1, 3, 4, 9, 11, 12, 13, 16; ConMuA 80B; EncJzS; NewAmDM; NewGrDA 86; NewGrDJ 88, 94; NewGrDM 80; OxCPMus; PenEncP; WhoAm 80, 82, 84; WhoWest 74*

Grapewin, Charley
[Charles Grapewin]
American. Actor
Character actor in over 100 films including *The Grapes of Wrath,* 1940; *Tobacco Road,* 1941.
b. Dec 20, 1869 in Xenia, Ohio
d. Feb 2, 1956 in Corona, California
Source: *BioIn 4; FilmgC; HalFC 80, 84, 88; HolCA; NotNAT B*

Grappelli, Stephane
French. Jazz Musician
Jazz violinist; prominent in Europe for "Le Jazz hot," 1930s with his group, the Quintet of the Hot Club of France.
b. Jan 26, 1908 in Paris, France
Source: *AllMusG; Baker 84, 92; BiDJaz; BioIn 9, 10, 12, 13, 16; CmpEPM; ConMus 10; CurBio 88; DcArts; EncFCWM 83; EncJzS; IlEncJ; IntWW 82, 83, 89, 91, 93; IntWWM 80, 90; NewAmDM; NewGrDJ 88, 94; NewGrDM 80; OxCPMus; PenDiMP; PenEncP; Who 92, 94; WhoAm 92, 94, 95, 96, 97; WhoFr 79; WhoRocM 82; WhoWor 84*

Grass, Gunter (Wilhelm)
German. Author
Best known novel *The Tin Drum,* 1959; film version won best foreign film Oscar, 1980.
b. Oct 16, 1927 in Danzig, Germany
Source: *Benet 87, 96; BioIn 6, 7, 8, 9, 10, 11, 12, 13, 14, 15, 16, 17, 19, 21; CamGWoT; CasWL; CelR, 90; ClDMEL 80; CnMD; CnOxB; ConAu 13R, 20NR; ConFLW 84; ConLC 1, 2, 4, 6, 11, 15, 22, 32, 49, 88; ConWorW 93; CroCD; CurBio 83; CyWA 89; DcArts; DcLB 75, 124; EncWL 2, 3; EncWT; Ent; EuWr 13; EvEuW; FacFETw; GrFLW; IntAu&W 76, 77, 89; IntDcT 2; IntWW 74, 75, 76, 77, 78, 79, 80, 81, 82, 83, 89, 91, 93; IntWWP 77; LegTOT; LiExTwC; LinLib L, S; MagSWL; MakMC; McGEWB; McGEWD 72, 84; ModGL; ModWD; Novels; OxCEng 85, 95; OxCGer 76, 86; PenC EUR; PostFic; PrintW 83, 85; RAdv 14, 13-2; REnWD; RfGWoL 95; ScF&FL 92; TwCWr; WhDW; Who 74, 82, 83, 85, 88, 90, 92, 94; WhoWor 74, 78, 80, 82, 84, 87, 89, 91, 93, 95; WorAl; WorAlBi; WorAu 1950; WorLitC*

Grass, John
[Charging Bear]
American. Native American Chief
Chief of Blackfoot Sioux who defended Indian rights in treaty councils.
b. 1837 in Grand River, South Dakota
d. May 10, 1918 in Fort Yates, South Dakota
Source: *DcAmB; EncNAB; WhAm 4, HSA; WhNaAH*

Grasse, Francois Joseph Paul de, Count
French. Naval Officer
Aided Continental forces in American Revolution.
b. Sep 13, 1722 in Le Bar, France
d. Jan 11, 1788 in Paris, France
Source: *AmBi; HarEnMi; OxCFr; WhAm HS; WorAl*

Grassi, Giovanni Battista
Italian. Zoologist
Proved that Anopheles mosquito carries malaria organism in digestive tract.
b. Mar 27, 1854 in Rovellasca, Italy
d. May 4, 1925 in Rome, Italy
Source: *BiESc; BioIn 6; DcScB; InSci; NewCol 75; WebBD 83*

Grassle, Karen Gene
American. Actor
Played Caroline Ingalls on "Little House on the Prairie," 1973-81.
b. Feb 25, 1944 in Berkeley, California
Source: *BioIn 10; ConTFT 3; VarWW 85; WhoAm 84, 86, 90; WhoEnt 92*

Grassley, Charles Ernest
American. Politician
Rep. senator from IA, 1981—.
b. Sep 17, 1933 in New Hartford, Iowa
Source: *AlmAP 80, 92; BiDrUSC 89; CngDr 77, 79, 81, 83, 85, 87, 89; IntWW 83, 91; WhoAm 86, 90, 92, 94, 95, 96, 97; WhoAmP 85, 89, 91; WhoGov 77; WhoMW 78, 90, 92, 93, 96; WhoWor 84, 87, 91*

Grasso, Ella
[Ella Tambussi]
American. Politician
First woman elected governor in US; Dem., CT, 1975-80.
b. May 10, 1919 in Windsor Locks, Connecticut
d. Feb 5, 1981 in Hartford, Connecticut
Source: *AmCath 80; AmPolW 80, 80A; AnObit 1981; BioIn 8, 10, 11, 12, 15, 16, 17; BioNews 74; CngDr 74; ContDcW 89; CurBio 81N; EncWHA; GoodHs; IntDcWB; IntWW 81N; LibW; NewYTBS 74, 81; WhoAm 74; WhoAmP 73; WhoAmW 77; WhoE 74; WhoGov 75; WomPO 76; WorAl*

Grass Roots, The
[Creed Bratton; Rick Coonce; Warren Entner; Robert Grill; Reed Kailing; Joel Larson; Dennis Provisor]
American. Music Group
Hits include "Temptation Eyes," 1971; "Heaven Knows," 1969.
Source: *EncPR&S 74; EncRkSt; RkOn 74; WhoRocM 82*

Grateful Dead, The
[Jerry Garcia; Mickey Hart; Bill Kreutzmann; Phil Lesh; Robert Hall (Bob) Weir; Vince Welnick]
American. Music Group
Psychedelic band formed, 1965, whose fans are known as "Dead Heads;" current members listed above.
Source: *BioIn 14, 15, 16, 17, 18, 19, 20, 21; BkPepl; ConMus 5; DcArts; DcTwCCu 1; EncPR&S 74, 89; EncRk 88; EncRkSt; FacFETw; HarEnR 86; IlEncRk; NewAmDM; NewGrDA 86; OxCPMus; PenEncP; WhoRocM 82*

Gratian
[Flavius Gratian Augustus]
Roman. Ruler
Ruled empire of Gaul, Spain, Britain; later in reign neglected public affairs for hunting; killed by Maximus' followers.
b. Apr 19, 359 in Sirmium, Roman Empire
d. Aug 25, 383 in Lugdunum, Gaul
Source: *EncEarC; LuthC 75; NewCol 75; OxDcByz; WebBD 83*

Grattan, Clinton Hartley
American. Author
Expert on Australia, Southwest Pacific; wrote *The Lands Down Under,* 1943.
b. Oct 19, 1902 in Wakefield, Massachusetts
d. Jun 25, 1980 in Austin, Texas
Source: *AmAu&B; BioIn 4, 12; ConAu 1R, 101; DrAS 74H, 78H; NewYTBS 80; OxCAmL 65, 83; REnAL; TwCA, SUP; WhAm 7; WhE&EA; WhNAA; WhoAm 74, 76, 78, 80; WhoSSW 73; WrDr 76, 82*

Gratz, Rebecca
American. Philanthropist
Jewish noblewoman who refused to marry the Christian man she loved because of her faith; was model for Rebecca in Scott's *Ivanhoe,* 1819.
b. Mar 4, 1781 in Philadelphia, Pennsylvania
d. Aug 29, 1869
Source: *AmAu&B; AmBi; AmRef; ApCAB SUP; BiDAmEd; BioAmW; BioIn 2, 4, 5, 8, 9, 10, 13, 14, 15, 17, 19, 21; DcAmB; DcAmImH; DcAmReB 2; InWom, SUP; LibW; NatCAB 10; NotAW; REnAL; WhAm HS; WomFir*

Grau, Shirley Ann
American. Author
Awarded Pulitzer for *The Keepers of the House,* 1965.
b. Jul 8, 1929 in New Orleans, Louisiana
Source: *AmAu&B; AmWomWr; ArtclWW 2; Au&Wr 71; AuNews 2; BenetAL 91; BioAmW; BioIn 3, 5, 8, 9, 10, 11, 12, 14, 15, 17, 19; BlmGWL; ConAu 1R, 22NR, 89; ConLC 4, 9; ConNov 72, 76, 82, 86, 91; CurBio 59; CyWA 89; DcLB 2; DcLEL 1940; DrAF 76; DrAPF 91; FemiCLE; FifSWrA; IntAu&W 76, 91; InWom, SUP; LegTOT; LibW; MajTwCW; ModAL; ModWoWr; Novels; OxCAmL 65, 83, 95; PenC AM; REn; REnAL; ShSCr 15; SouWr; WhoAm 74, 76, 78, 80, 82, 84, 86, 88, 90, 92, 94, 95, 96, 97; WhoAmW 58, 61, 64, 66, 68, 70, 72, 74, 75, 77, 83, 85, 87, 89, 91, 93, 95, 97; WhoE 74; WhoEnt 92; WhoSSW 93; WhoWor 74; WhoWrEP 89, 92, 95; WorAl; WorAlBi; WorAu 1950; WrDr 76, 80, 82, 84, 86, 88, 90, 92, 94*

Grauer, Ben(jamin Franklin)
American. Broadcast Journalist
NBC commentator, announcer; covered wide variety of events, 1930-73.
b. Jun 2, 1908 in New York, New York
d. May 31, 1977 in New York, New York
Source: *BioIn 1; NatCAB 60; NewYTBE 73; NewYTBS 77; RadStar; SaTiSS; WhAm 7; WhoAm 74, 76; WhoWor 74, 76; WhoWorJ 72; WhScrn 83*

Grauman, Sid(ney Patrick)
American. Theater Owner
Owner, Chinese Theater restaurant, famous for footprints of stars.
b. Mar 17, 1879 in Indianapolis, Indiana
d. Mar 5, 1950 in Hollywood, California
Source: *BioIn 2; CmCal; HalFC 80, 84, 88; LegTOT; NotNAT B; ObitOF 79; WhoHol B; WhScrn 83*

Gravel, Mike
American. Politician
Dem. senator from Alaska, 1969-75; "Pentagon Papers" affair brought him to wide pu blic attention, 1971.
b. May 13, 1930 in Springfield, Massachusetts
Source: *AlmAP 78, 80; BioIn 8, 9, 10, 12; BlueB 76; CelR; CngDr 74, 77, 79; ConAu 41R; CurBio 72; IntWW 74, 75,*

76, 77, 78, 79, 80, 81, 82, 83, 89, 91, 93; NewYTBE 71; PolProf NF; WhoAm 74, 76, 78, 80, 82; WhoAmP 73, 75, 77, 79, 81, 83, 85, 87, 89, 91, 93, 95; WhoGov 72, 75, 77; WhoWest 74, 76, 78, 80; WhoWor 78, 80, 82; WorAl; WrDr 76, 80, 82, 84

Gravely, Samuel Lee, Jr.
American. Naval Officer
First black admiral in US, 1971; retired 1980.
b. Jun 4, 1922 in Richmond, Virginia
Source: *AfrAmBi 1; AfrAmG; BioIn 7, 9, 11; BlksScM; InB&W 80, 85; NegAl 89; NewYTBE 71; WhoAm 74, 76; WhoBlA 75, 85, 88, 92; WhoGov 75; WhoSSW 73, 75*

Graver, Elizabeth
American. Author
Won 1991 Drue Heinz Literature Prize for *Have You Seen Me?*
b. Jul 2, 1964 in Los Angeles, California
Source: *ConAu 135; ConLC 70; IntAu&W 93; WhoE 97; WrDr 94, 96*

Graves, Alvin Cushman
American. Physicist
Head of nuclear weapons testing at Los Alamos since 1948.
b. Nov 4, 1909 in Washington, District of Columbia
d. Jul 29, 1965 in Del Norte, Colorado
Source: *BioIn 2, 3, 7; CurBio 52, 65; DcAmB S7; InSci*

Graves, Earl Gilbert
American. Publisher
Founder, publisher, business magazine, *Black Enterprises*, 1970—.
b. Jan 9, 1935 in New York, New York
Source: *BioIn 10, 16; ConBlB 1; Ebony 1; EncTwCJ; InB&W 80, 85; NegAl 89; St&PR 91; WhoAdv 80; WhoAm 74, 76, 78, 80, 82, 84, 86, 88, 90, 92, 94, 95, 96, 97; WhoBlA 92; WhoE 95; WhoFI 79, 81, 85, 87, 89, 92, 94, 96*

Graves, John Earl
American. Hostage
One of 52 held by terrorists, Nov 1979-Jan 1981.
b. May 16, 1927 in Detroit, Michigan
Source: *NewYTBS 81; USBiR 74; WhoAm 74, 76, 78; WhoGov 72*

Graves, Michael
American. Architect
Example of his cubist designs is Fargo-Moorhead Cultural Center Bridge, ND, 1977 ; member of postmodernistic group, "NY Five."
b. Jul 9, 1934 in Indianapolis, Indiana
Source: *AmCulL; AmDec 1970; BioIn 12, 13, 14, 15, 16, 17, 19, 21; ConArch 80, 87, 94; ConAu 131; ConDes 84, 90, 97; CurBio 89; DcArts; DcTwCCu 1; DcTwDes; EncAAr 2; EncWB; FacFETw; IntDcAr; PenDiDA 89; PrintW 83, 85; WhoAm 78, 80, 82, 84, 86, 88, 90, 92, 94, 95, 96; WhoAmA 80, 82, 84, 86, 89, 91, 93; WhoE 91, 93, 95*

Graves, Morris Cole
American. Artist
Noted for somber, expressionist bird paintings: *Blind Bird*, 1940.
b. Aug 28, 1910 in Fox Valley, Oregon
Source: *BioIn 3, 4, 5, 6, 13, 14; ConArt 83, 89; CurBio 56; DcAmArt; FacFETw; McGDA; OxCAmH; REn; REnAL; WebAB 74, 79; WhAmArt 85; WhoAm 84, 86, 97; WhoAmA 78, 91*

Graves, Nancy (Stevenson)
American. Artist
Known for sculptures of camels, camouflage paintings, lunar landscapes; work called imaginative, technically exact.
b. Dec 23, 1940 in Pittsfield, Massachusetts
d. Oct 21, 1995 in New York, New York
Source: *AmArt; BiDWomA; BioIn 8, 9, 11, 12, 13, 14, 15, 16, 17, 21; ConAmWS; ConArt 77, 83, 89, 96; CurBio 81, 96N; DcCAA 77, 88, 94; DcCAr 81; InWom SUP; News 89-3; NewYTBS 95; NorAmWA; PrintW 83, 85; WhoAm 84, 86; WhoAmA 73, 76, 78, 80, 82, 84, 86, 89, 91, 93; WhoAmW 85, 91; WorArt 1980*

Graves, Peter
English. Actor
Character actor mainly in British films since 1941.
b. Oct 21, 1911 in London, England
Source: *ConTFT 2, 13; FilmgC; ForYSC; HalFC 80, 84, 88; IlWWBF; IntMPA 75, 76, 77, 78, 79, 80, 81, 82, 84, 86, 88, 92, 94; MotPP; WhoHol 92, A; WhoThe 72, 77, 81*

Graves, Peter
[Peter Aurness]
American. Actor
Played Jim Phelps in "Mission: Impossible," 1967-73; brother of James Arness.
b. Mar 18, 1926 in Minneapolis, Minnesota
Source: *BioIn 9; ConTFT 1; FilmgC; HalFC 84, 88; IntMPA 84, 86, 88, 92, 94, 96; MovMk; VarWW 85; WhoAm 74, 76, 78, 80, 82, 84, 86, 88, 90, 92, 94, 95, 96, 97; WhoEnt 92; WhoHol 92; WorAl; WorAlBi*

Graves, Robert von Ranke
English. Poet, Author
Author of more than 120 novels, books of poetry, criticism, best known for historical novel, *I, Claudius*, 1934.
b. Jul 26, 1895 in London, England
d. Dec 7, 1985 in Deya, Majorca, Spain
Source: *CasWL; CnMWL; ConAu 5NR, 5R; EncWL; EvLB; IntWW 74; LngCTC; ModBrL, S1; NewC; OxCEng 67; PenC ENG; RAdv 1; REn; Who 74; WrDr 76*

Graves, William Sidney
American. Army Officer
Led American expeditionary force in Siberia, 1918-20.
b. Mar 27, 1865 in Mount Calm, Texas
d. Feb 27, 1940 in Shrewsbury, New Jersey
Source: *BioIn 4, 10, 14; DcAmB S2; DcAmMiB; DcNAA; HarEnMi; NewCol 75; WebAMB; WhAm 1; WhNAA*

Gray, Asa
American. Educator, Botanist
Harvard U's famed natural history professor, 1842-73; wrote *Flora of North America*, 1843.
b. Nov 18, 1810 in Sauquoit, New York
d. Jan 30, 1888 in Cambridge, Massachusetts
Source: *Alli, SUP; AmAu; AmAu&B; AmBi; ApCAB; AsBiEn; BbD; BenetAL 91; BiDAmEd; BiDAmS; BiD&SB; BiDTran; BiESc; BiHiMed; BiInAmS; BioIn 3, 4, 5, 6, 8, 9, 11, 14, 16; CelCen; CyAL 2; CyEd; DcAmAu; DcAmB; DcAmMeB; DcBiPP; DcLB 1; DcNAA; DcScB; Drake; EncAAH; EncAB-H 1974, 1996; EncARH; HarEnUS; InSci; LarDcSc; LegTOT; LinLib L, S; McGEWB; MorMA; NatCAB 3; OxCAmH; OxCAmL 65, 83, 95; REn; REnAL; TwCBDA; WebAB 74, 79; WhAm HS; WorAl; WorAlBi*

Gray, Barry
[Bernard Yaraslaw]
American. Radio Performer
Radio interviewer, NYC's WMCA, 1950-89; WOR, 1989-96.
b. Jul 2, 1916 in Red Lion, New Jersey
d. Dec 21, 1996 in New York, New York
Source: *BioIn 10; CelR, 90; ConAu 61; ConTFT 2; WhoAm 90; WhoE 91*

Gray, C(layland) Boyden
American. Lawyer, Government Official
Counsel to Pres. Bush, 1989—93.
b. Feb 6, 1943 in Winston-Salem, North Carolina
Source: *BioIn 16; CurBio 89; WhoAm 82, 84, 86, 90, 92, 94, 95, 96, 97; WhoAmL 83, 85; WhoAmP 91*

Gray, Coleen
[Doris Jenson]
American. Actor
Generally had leads in B-films including *Nightmare Alley*, 1947.
b. Oct 23, 1922 in Staplehurst, Nebraska
Source: *BioIn 1, 4, 18; FilmEn; ForYSC; HalFC 84; IntMPA 75, 76, 77, 78, 79, 81, 84, 86, 88, 92, 94, 96; IntWWM 90; InWom; MotPP; SweetSg D; VarWW 85; WhoAmW 58, 61, 64; WhoEnt 92; WhoHol 92, A; WhoHrs 80*

Gray, Dobie
[Leonard Victor Ainsworth, Jr.]
American. Singer
Husky-voiced country musician; hits include "Drift Away," 1973.
b. Jul 26, 1942 in Brookshire, Texas

Source: *EncRk 88; HarEnR 86; IlEncRk; InB&W 80, 85; LegTOT; PenEncP; RkOn 78, 84; RolSEnR 83; SoulM; WhoRock 81; WhoRocM 82*

Gray, Dolores
American. Actor
Appeared on Broadway in *Annie Get Your Gun,* 1947-50; won Tony for *Carnival in Flanders,* 1954.
b. Jun 7, 1924 in Chicago, Illinois
Source: *BiE&WWA; BioIn 4; CmpEPM; ConTFT 4; EncMT; FilmgC; ForYSC; HalFC 80, 84, 88; MotPP; NotNAT; OxCPMus; PenEncP; VarWW 85; WhoHol 92, A; WhoThe 72, 77, 81*

Gray, Dulcie
[Dulcie Bailey]
British. Actor, Author
Noted for London stage career; writings include mystery/horror books: *Murder in Mind,* 1963.
b. Nov 20, 1919 in Kuala Lumpur
Source: *ConAu 3NR, 5NR, 24NR; ConTFT 5, 13; FemiCLE; FilmEn; FilmgC; HalFC 80, 84, 88; IlWWBF, A; IntAu&W 91; IntMPA 77, 80, 86, 92, 94, 96; ItaFilm; OxCThe 83; TwCCr&M 85, 91; VarWW 85; Who 85, 90, 92; WhoHol 92, A; WhoThe 72, 77, 81; WrDr 86, 90, 92*

Gray, Elisha
American. Inventor
Beat out of telephone patent by Bell, who filed hours earlier, 1876; invented telautograph, 1888.
b. Aug 2, 1835 in Barnesville, Ohio
d. Jan 21, 1901 in Newtonville, Massachusetts
Source: *Alli SUP; AmBi; ApCAB; BiInAmS; BioIn 10, 11, 12; DcAmAu; DcAmB; DcNAA; HarEnUS; InSci; LinLib L, S; NatCAB 4; NewCol 75; OhA&B; TwCBDA; WebAB 74, 79; WhAm 1; WorInv*

Gray, Gilda
[Maryanna Michalski]
American. Actor
Vaudeville performer; films include *Piccadilly,* 1929; created the dance the "shimmy."
b. Oct 24, 1896 in Krakow, Poland
d. Dec 22, 1959 in Hollywood, California
Source: *Film 1; FilmgC; TwYS; WhoHol B; WhScrn 74, 77, 83*

Gray, Glen
[Glen Gray Knoblaugh]
"Spike"
American. Bandleader
Led popular dance band, Casa Loma Orchestra, 1929-50.
b. Jun 7, 1906 in Roanoke, Illinois
d. Aug 23, 1963 in Plymouth, Massachusetts
Source: *BiDAmM; BiDJaz; CmpEPM; DcAmB S7; NewGrDJ 88, 94; WhoHol B; WhScrn 74, 77*

Gray, Gordon
American. Government Official
Secretary of Army, 1949-50; held security posts, 1947-77.
b. May 30, 1909 in Baltimore, Maryland
d. Nov 25, 1982 in Washington, District of Columbia
Source: *BioIn 2, 3, 4, 5, 7, 13; ConAu 109; CurBio 49, 83, 83N; DcNCBi 2; IntWW 74, 75, 76, 77, 78, 79, 80, 81, 82; IntYB 78, 79, 80, 81, 82; NewYTBS 82; PolProf T; WhAm 8; Who 74, 82, 83; WhoAm 74, 76, 78, 80, 82; WhoFI 74, 75; WhoGov 72, 75; WhoSSW 73, 75*

Gray, Hanna (Holborn)
American. Educator
Pres., U of Chicago, 1978-1993; first woman to lead a major American university.
b. Oct 25, 1930 in Heidelberg, Germany
Source: *AmWomM; BioIn 10, 11, 12, 13; CurBio 79; DrAS 74H, 78H, 82H; InWom SUP; LEduc 74; LibW; News 92; NewYTBS 77; Who 82, 83, 85, 88, 90, 92, 94; WhoAm 76, 78, 80, 82, 84, 86, 88, 90, 92, 94, 95, 96, 97; WhoAmW 75, 77, 79, 81, 83, 85, 87, 89, 91, 93, 95, 97; WhoMW 80, 82, 84, 86, 90, 92, 93, 96; WhoWor 80, 82, 84, 87, 89, 91, 93; WorAl; WorAlBi*

Gray, Harold Lincoln
American. Cartoonist
Created comic strip "Little Orphan Annie," 1924, syndicated until 1968.
b. Jan 20, 1894 in Kankakee, Illinois
d. May 9, 1968 in La Jolla, California
Source: *AmAu&B; ConAu 107; DcAmB S8; NatCAB 54; REnAL; WebAB 74, 79; WebBD 83; WhAm 5; WhNAA; WorECom*

Gray, Horace
American. Supreme Court Justice
Served, 1881-1902; appointed by Chester A Arthur.
b. Mar 24, 1828 in Boston, Massachusetts
d. Sep 15, 1902 in Washington, District of Columbia
Source: *AmBi; ApCAB; BiDFedJ; BioIn 2, 3, 5, 15; DcAmB; HarEnUS; NatCAB 1; NewCol 75; OxCSupC; SupCtJu; TwCBDA; WebAB 74, 79; WhAm 1*

Gray, James, Sir
English. Zoologist
Pioneered shift in zoological research from comparative anatomy to investigation of functional changes in living cells and animals.
b. Oct 14, 1891 in London, England
d. Dec 14, 1975 in Cambridge, England
Source: *BioIn 1, 5, 11; BlueB 76; DcNaB 1971; IntWW 74, 75; LarDcSc; ObitT 1971; Who 74; WhoWor 74*

Gray, Linda
American. Actor
Appeared in over 400 TV commercials; played Sue Ellen Ewing on "Dallas," 1978-91.
b. Sep 12, 1940 in Santa Monica, California
Source: *BioIn 12, 13, 14, 15, 16; CelR 90; ConTFT 2; IntMPA 92, 94, 96; InWom SUP; LegTOT; VarWW 85; WhoAm 86, 90, 94, 95, 96, 97; WhoAmW 89, 95; WhoEnt 92; WhoHol 92; WhoTelC*

Gray, Louis Patrick
American. Government Official
Acting director, FBI, 1972-73, who resigned over Watergate; indicted for illegal practices, 1978.
b. Jul 18, 1916 in Saint Louis, Missouri
Source: *BioIn 9, 10, 11, 12; BioNews 74; IntWW 74, 75, 76, 77, 78, 79, 80, 81, 82, 83, 89, 91, 93; NewYTBE 71; WhoAm 74, 76, 78; WhoWor 74, 78*

Gray, Nicholas Stuart
Scottish. Children's Author
Books include *The Seventh Swan,* 1962.
b. Oct 23, 1922, Scotland
d. Mar 17, 1981 in London, England
Source: *AnObit 1981; AuBYP 2S, 3; BioIn 9, 10, 13; ConAu 11NR, 21R, 103; IntAu&W 76, 77; ScF&FL 1, 2, 92; SmATA 4, 27N; TwCChW 78, 83, 89, 95; WhoThe 77; WrDr 76, 80, 82*

Gray, Pete(r)
[Peter J Wyshner]
American. Baseball Player
One-armed outfielder, St. Louis, 1945; in MLs during WW II player shortage; batting average .218 in 77 games.
b. Mar 6, 1917 in Nanticoke, Pennsylvania
Source: *Ballpl 90; BioIn 9, 10, 12, 16; WhoProB 73*

Gray, Simon James Holliday
English. Dramatist
Wrote *Wise Child,* 1968; *Butley,* 1971; *Otherwise Engaged,* 1975.
b. Oct 21, 1936 in Hayling Island, England
Source: *BioIn 10, 11, 12, 13, 14, 15, 16, 17; CamGWoT; ConAu 3AS, 21NR, 21R, 32NR; ConBrDr; ConDr 73, 77, 82, 93; ConLC 36; ConNov 72, 76; CreCan 2; CurBio 83; CyWA 89; DcLEL 1940; EncWT; FacFETw; IntAu&W 91; IntDcT 2; IntWW 81, 82, 83, 89, 91, 93; McGEWD 84; NotNAT; OxCCan, SUP; OxCEng 85, 95; OxCThe 83; RfGEnL 91; VarWW 85; Who 74, 82, 83, 85, 88, 90, 92, 94; WhoThe 77; WhoWor 87, 89, 91, 93, 95, 96; WorAu 1975; WrDr 92, 94, 96*

Gray, Thomas
English. Poet
Poems concerned melancholy, love of nature; "Elegy Written in a Country Churchyard," 1751, best-known piece, epitome of Romantic period.
b. Dec 26, 1716 in London, England
d. Jul 30, 1771 in Cambridge, England
Source: *Alli, SUP; AtlBL; BbD; Benet 87, 96; BiD&SB; BioIn 1, 2, 3, 4, 5, 6, 7, 8, 9, 10, 12, 15, 17, 18; BlkwCE;*

BlmGEL; BritAu; BritWr 3; CamGEL; CamGLE; CasWL; ChhPo, S1, S2, S3; CnDBLB 2; CnE&AP; CrtT 2; CyEd; CyWA 58; DcArts; DcBiPP; DcEnA; DcEnL; DcEuL; DcLB 109; DcLEL; DcNaB; EncEnl; EvLB; GrWrEL P; LegTOT; LinLib L, S; LitC 4; LngCEL; McGEWB; MouLC 2; NewC; NewCBEL; NewGrDM 80; OxCEng 67, 85, 95; OxCLiW 86; PenC ENG; PoeCrit 2; RAdv 1, 14, 13-1; RComWL; REn; RfGEnL 91; RGFBP; WebBD 83; WebE&AL; WhDW; WorAl; WorAlBi; WorLitC

Gray, William H, III
American. Business Executive
Dem. congressman from PA, 1979-91; chm., of House Budget Com., 1985; pres., United Negro College Fund, 1991—.
b. Aug 20, 1941 in Baton Rouge, Louisiana
Source: *AlmAP 88, 92; BioIn 14, 16; CngDr 85, 87, 89; ConBlB 3; CurBio 88; NegAl 89A; NewYTBS 91; WhoAm 86, 90; WhoAmP 87, 91; WhoBlA 88, 92; WhoE 91*

Graydon, James Weir
American. Engineer, Inventor
Invented dynamite gun, aerial torpedo, compound rotary turbines, all bearing his name, late 1800s.
b. Jan 18, 1848 in Indianapolis, Indiana
Source: *CivWDc; NatCAB 13; TwCBDA; WhAm 4*

Grayson, Kathryn
[Zelma Hedrick]
American. Actor
Starred in *Show Boat,* 1951; *Kiss Me Kate,* 1953; *The Vagabond King,* 1956.
b. Feb 9, 1923 in Winston-Salem, North Carolina
Source: *BiDAmM; CmMov; CmpEPM; FilmgC; HalFC 84, 88; IntMPA 75, 76, 77, 78, 79, 80, 81, 82, 84, 86, 88, 92, 94, 96; InWom SUP; MotPP; MovMk; OxCPMus; VarWW 85; WhoAm 84, 86; WhoAmW 85; WhoHol A; WorAl; WorAlBi*

Graziani, Rodolfo
[Marchese DiNeghelli]
Italian. Military Leader
Minister of Defense for Mussolini, WW II; imprisoned by Italian court, 1950.
b. Aug 11, 1882 in Filettino, Italy
d. Jan 11, 1955 in Rome, Italy
Source: *BiDExR; BioIn 1, 2, 3, 4, 21; CurBio 41, 55; EncTR 91; HisEWW; NewCol 75; ObitOF 79; ObitT 1951; WhoMilH 76*

Graziano, Rocky
[Thomas Rocko Barbella]
American. Boxer
Middleweight champ, 1947-48; best remembered for three title fights with Tony Zale; life story filmed as *Somebody Up There Likes Me,* 1956, starring Paul Newman.
b. Jun 7, 1922 in New York, New York
d. May 22, 1990 in New York, New York
Source: *BiDAmSp BK; BioIn 3, 9, 10, 12, 14, 16; BoxReg; CelR, 90; FacFETw; News 90; NewYTBS 90; WhoAm 76; WhoBox 74; WhoHol A; WhoSpor; WorAl; WorAlBi*

Greaza, Walter N
American. Actor
Character actor; played in TV daytime drama "The Edge of Night."
b. Jan 1, 1897 in Saint Paul, Minnesota
d. Jun 1, 1973 in New York, New York
Source: *BiE&WWA; NewYTBE 73; NotNAT B; WhoHol B; WhScrn 77*

Greb, Harry
[Edward Henry Greb]
"The Human Windmill"
American. Boxer
Only fighter to defeat Tunney, 1922; Hall of Fame, 1955.
b. Jun 6, 1894 in Pittsburgh, Pennsylvania
d. Oct 22, 1926 in New York, New York
Source: *BiDAmSp BK; BioIn 1, 4, 6, 7, 15; BoxReg; NewCol 75; WhoBox 74; WhoSpor*

Grebenshikov, Boris
"Aquarium"
Russian. Musician
Founder, guitarist of Russian rock band, Aquarium, 1972—; albums include *Radio Silence,* 1989.
b. Nov 27, 1953 in Leningrad, Union of Soviet Socialist Republics
Source: *BiDSovU; BioIn 15; ConMus 3; IntWW 91; News 90, 90-1; WhoWor 91*

Grebey, Ray
[Clarence Raymond Grebey]
American. Baseball Executive
Employee relations expert; chief negotiator for owners in ML baseball disputes, 1978-83.
b. Mar 10, 1928 in Chicago, Illinois
Source: *BioIn 12; NewYTBS 80; WhoAm 82, 84, 86, 96; WhoFI 89*

Grechko, Andrei Antonovick
Russian. Government Official
Soviet defense minister, commanded Soviet Army, 1967; member of Politburo, 1973-76.
b. Oct 17, 1903 in Golodaevka, Russia
d. Apr 26, 1976 in Moscow, Union of Soviet Socialist Republics
Source: *ColdWar 2; CurBio 68; IntWW 74; NewCol 75; NewYTBE 71; ObitOF 79; WhoWor 74*

Greco, El
[Kyriakos Theotokopoulos]
Spanish. Artist
Works include *Assumption of the Virgin,* 1577; *Burial of the Count of Orgaz,* 1586; noted for elongated figures, mystical mannerism style.
b. 1541 in Candia, Crete
d. Apr 6, 1614 in Toledo, Spain
Source: *AtlBL; BioIn 17, 20; DcArts; McGDA; NewC; NewCol 75; OxCArt; REn*

Greco, Buddy
[Armando Greco]
American. Singer, Songwriter, Pianist
Jazz-styled vocalist, 1950s-70s; on TV, 1950-60.
b. Aug 14, 1926 in Philadelphia, Pennsylvania
Source: *ASCAP 66, 80; BiDAmM; BioIn 10; BioNews 74; CmpEPM; LegTOT; PenEncP; RkOn 74; WhoHol 92*

Greco, Jose
American. Dancer, Choreographer
Debut in *Carmen,* 1937; appeared in *Ship of Fools,* 1965.
b. Dec 23, 1918 in Montorio, Italy
Source: *BiDD; BioIn 2, 3, 6, 10, 11; CelR; ConAu 85; CurBio 52; LegTOT; VarWW 85; WhoAm 74, 76, 78, 80, 82, 84, 86, 88, 90, 92, 94, 95, 96, 97; WhoEnt 92; WhoHol 92, A*

Grede, William John
American. Businessman, Political Activist
Founded Grede Foundries, 1920; served as CEO for 53 yrs; one of the original founders, John Birch Society, 1958.
b. Feb 24, 1897 in Milwaukee, Wisconsin
d. Jun 5, 1989 in Brookfield, Wisconsin
Source: *BioIn 2, 3, 5, 7, 16; CurBio 89N; Dun&B 88; NewYTBS 89; St&PR 87*

Greeley, Andrew Moran
American. Author
Controversial columnist, fiction, nonfiction writer; known for explicit novels with moral overtones: *The Cardinal Sins,* 1981.
b. Feb 5, 1928 in Oak Park, Illinois
Source: *AmMWSc 73S; BiDAmNC; BiDConC; BioIn 9, 10, 11, 12, 13, 16; CelR 90; ConAu 5NR, 5R, 7NR; ConLC 28; CurBio 72; LEduc 74; NewYTBS 82; TwCCr&M 91; WhoAm 84, 86, 97; WhoMW 92, 96; WhoRel 92; WhoUSWr 88; WhoWrEP 89; WorAu 1975; WrDr 90*

Greeley, Dana McLean
American. Religious Leader
First pres., Unitarian Universalist Assn., 1961-69; co-founded World Conference on Religion and Peace.
b. Jul 5, 1908 in Lexington, Massachusetts
d. Jun 13, 1986 in Concord, Massachusetts
Source: *BioIn 6, 7, 8, 15, 19; BlueB 76; ConAu 119; CurBio 64, 86, 86N; DcAmReB 2; WhAm 9; WhoAm 74, 76, 78, 80; WhoWor 74*

Greeley, Horace
American. Publisher
Founded *NY Tribune*, 1841; popularized phrase "Go West, young man."
b. Feb 3, 1811 in Amherst, New Hampshire
d. Nov 29, 1872 in New York, New York
Source: *Alli, SUP; AmAu; AmAu&B; AmBi; AmJust; AmPolLe; AmRef; AmSocL; ApCAB; BbD; Benet 87, 96; BenetAL 91; BiAUS; BiDAmJo; BiD&SB; BiDrAC; BiDrUSC 89; BiDTran; BioIn 1, 2, 3, 4, 5, 6, 7, 8, 9, 10, 11, 12, 13, 14, 15, 16, 18, 19; CamGLE; CamHAL; CasWL; CelCen; Chambr 3; ChhPo; CivWDc; CmCal; CnDAL; CyAG; CyAL 2; DcAmAu; DcAmB; DcAmSR; DcAmTB; DcBiPP; DcCanB 10; DcEnL; DcLB 3, 43; DcNAA; Drake; EncAAH; EncAB-H 1974, 1996; EncAJ; EncO&P 1, 2, 3; EncPaPR 91; EvLB; HarEnUS; JrnUS; LegTOT; LinLib L, S; LuthC 75; McGEWB; MemAm; NatCAB 3; OxCAmH; OxCAmL 65, 83, 95; OxCEng 85, 95; PolPar; PresAR; RComAH; REn; REnAL; REnAW; TwCBDA; WebAB 74, 79; WhAm HS; WhAmP; WhCiWar; WhDW; WorAl; WorAlBi*

Greely, Adolphus Washington
American. Explorer
Told of polar expedition in *Three Years of Arctic Service*, 1886.
b. Mar 27, 1844 in Newburyport, Massachusetts
d. Oct 20, 1935 in Washington, District of Columbia
Source: *Alli SUP; AmAu&B; AmBi; ApCAB, X; BenetAL 91; BiD&SB; BioIn 2, 5, 15; DcAmB S1; DcAmMiB; DcNAA; HarEnMi; HarEnUS; LinLib L, S; McGEWB; MedHR 94; NatCAB 3, 42; NewCol 75; OxCAmH; OxCCan; REnAL; WebAB 74, 79; WebAMB; WhAm 1; WhWE*

Green, Abel
American. Screenwriter, Actor
Wrote film *Mr. Broadway*, 1947; appeared in *Copacabana*, 1947.
b. Jun 3, 1900 in New York, New York
d. May 10, 1973 in New York, New York
Source: *ASCAP 66, 80; BiE&WWA; BioIn 2, 3, 6, 9; CelR; ConAu 41R; EncAJ; EncTwCJ; EncVaud; NewYTBE 73; NotNAT B; OxCAmT 84; WhAm 6; WhoAdv 72; WhoAm 74; WhoThe 72; WhoWorJ 72, 78; WhScrn 77, 83; WhThe*

Green, Adolf
American. Dramatist, Songwriter
Won 5 Tonys for *Hallelujah, Baby*, 1968; *Applause*, 1970; *On the Twentieth Century*, 1978; Songwriter's Hall of Fame, 1980.
b. Dec 2, 1915 in New York, New York
Source: *AmAu&B; ASCAP 66; Baker 84; BioIn 5, 6, 8, 9, 10, 12, 15; CelR 90; CmMov; CmpEPM; ConAu 110; ConDr 82D, 88D; CurBio 45; EncMT; FilmgC; HalFC 88; IntMPA 86, 92; NewCBMT; NotNAT; OxCAmT 84; OxCFilm; OxCPMus; VarWW 85; WhoAm 86; WhoEnt 92; WhoThe 81; WorAlBi; WorEFlm*

Green, Al(bert Leornes)
American. Singer, Songwriter
Hits include "Let's Stay Together," 1972; "I'm Still In Love With You," 1972; released *Your Heart's in Good Hands*, 1995.
b. Apr 13, 1946 in Forrest City, Arkansas
Source: *Baker 84, 92; BiDAfM; BioIn 10, 11, 12; BkPepl; ConBlB 13; ConMus 9; CurBio 96; DrBlPA, 90; EncPR&S 89; EncRk 88; EncRkSt; HarEnR 86; IlEncBM 82; IlEncRk; InB&W 80, 85; LegTOT; NewGrDA 86; NewYTBE 73; PenEncP; RkOn 78; RolSEnR 83; SoulM; WhoAfA 96; WhoAm 82, 84, 86, 88, 90, 92, 94, 95, 96, 97; WhoBlA 88, 90, 92, 94; WhoEnt 92; WhoRock 81; WhoRocM 82*

Green, Anna Katharine
American. Author
Wrote classic detective story *The Leavenworth Case*, 1878.
b. Nov 11, 1846 in New York, New York
d. Apr 11, 1935 in Buffalo, New York
Source: *Alli SUP; AmAu&B; AmBi; AmWom; ApCAB; BbD; BenetAL 91; BiD&SB; BioIn 14; BlmGWL; ConAu 112; CrtSuMy; DcAmAu; DcAmB S1; DcBiA; DcNAA; EncMys; GrWomMW; InWom; LibW; LinLib L; LngCTC; NotAW; OxCAmL 65, 83, 95; PenNWW B; REn; REnAL; TwCA; TwCBDA; TwCCr&M 80, 85, 91; TwCLC 63; WhE&EA; WhNAA; WomWWA 14*

Green, Anne
American. Author
Life in France subject of novels: *A Marriage of Convenience*, 1933; *The Old Lady*, 1947.
b. Nov 11, 1899 in Savannah, Georgia
Source: *AmAu&B; AmNov; BenetAL 91; BioIn 1, 2, 3, 4, 12; CathA 1952; ConAmA; DcLEL; FemiCLE; InWom; LngCTC; OxCAmL 65, 83, 95; REn; REnAL; TwCA, SUP*

Green, Benny
American. Pianist, Composer
Jazz pianist; worked as accompanist for singer Betty Carter, 1982-1987; played with Art Blakey and the Jazz Messengers, 1987-1989 and the Freddie Hubbard quintet, 1989; released debut trio recording, *Lineage*, 1990 with Ray Drummond and Victor Lewis; also released albums *Testifyin'*, 1992 and *The Place to Be*, 1994.
b. Apr 4, 1963 in New York, New York
Source: *AllMusG; ConMus 17*

Green, Brian Austin
American. Actor
Plays David in TV series "Beverly Hills 90210," 1990—.
Source: *BioIn 17, 18, 20, 21*

Green, Constance Windsor McLaughlin
American. Historian, Author
Wrote on nation's capital; won 1963 Pulitzer for *Washington: Village and Capital, 1800-78*.
b. Aug 21, 1897 in Ann Arbor, Michigan
d. Dec 5, 1975 in Annapolis, Maryland
Source: *AmAu&B; ConAu 9R, 61; CurBio 63; ForWC 70; InWom; NotAW MOD; OxCAmL 65; WhAm 6; WhoAm 74; WhoWor 74; WrDr 76*

Green, Dallas
[George Dallas Green, Jr]
American. Baseball Manager, Baseball Executive
Manager, Philadelphia, 1979-82; pres., Chicago Cubs, 1984-87; manager, NY Yankees, 1988-89; NY Mets, 1993—.
b. Aug 4, 1934 in Newport, Delaware
Source: *Ballpl 90; BioIn 12, 13, 14, 15; WhoAm 82, 84, 86, 88, 94, 95, 96, 97; WhoAmA 91; WhoE 91, 95, 97; WhoMW 88; WhoWest 92*

Green, Dennis
American. Football Coach
Head Coach, Minnesota Vikings, 1992—.
b. Feb 17, 1949 in Harrisburg, Pennsylvania
Source: *BioIn 12, 13; ConBlB 5; WhoAfA 96; WhoAm 95, 96, 97; WhoBlA 88, 90, 92, 94; WhoMW 93*

Green, Edith S(tarrett)
American. Politician
Powerful Dem. congressman from OR, 1955-75; worked on education, women's rights, anti-poverty legislation.
b. Jan 17, 1910 in Trent, South Dakota
d. Apr 21, 1987 in Tualatin, Oregon
Source: *AmPolW 80; WomCon*

Green, Gerald
American. Writer
Documentary TV films include Emmy-winner "Holocaust," 1978.
b. Apr 8, 1922 in New York, New York
Source: *AmAu&B; AuSpks; BioIn 3, 4, 6, 8, 9, 10, 11; ConAu 8NR, 13R; DcLB 28; VarWW 85; WhoAm 74, 76, 78, 80, 82, 84, 86, 88, 90, 92, 94, 95, 96; WhoE 89; WhoUSWr 88; WhoWor 74; WhoWrEP 89, 92, 95; WorAu 1950; WrDr 80, 82, 84, 86, 88, 90, 92, 94, 96*

Green, Guy
English. Director
Won 1947 Oscar for *Great Expectations*.
b. 1913 in Frome, England
Source: *BiDFilm, 81, 94; FilmEn; FilmgC; HalFC 80, 84, 88; IlWWBF; IntDcF 1-4, 2-4; IntMPA 75, 76, 77, 78,*

79, 80, 81, 82, 84, 86, 88, 92, 94, 96; ItaFilm; MiSFD 9; VarWW 85; WhoAm 74, 76, 78, 80, 86, 88; WorEFlm

Green, Henry
[Henry Vincent Yorke]
English. Author
Lyrical novelist; works include *Party Going,* 1939; *Loving,* 1945.
b. Oct 29, 1905 in Tewkesbury, England
d. Dec 13, 1973 in London, England
Source: *Benet 87, 96; BioIn 2, 3, 4, 5, 7, 8, 11, 12, 13, 14, 18, 19, 20; BlmGEL; BritWr S2; CamGEL; CamGLE; CasWL; CnMWL; ConAu 49, 85; ConLC 2, 13, 97; ConNov 72, 76; CyWA 58, 89; DcArts; DcLB 15; DcLEL; DcNaB 1971; EncSF 93; EncWL, 2, 3; EvLB; FacFETw; GrWrEL N; IntAu&W 76, 77; LngCEL; LngCTC; MakMC; ModBrL, S1, S2; NewC; NewCBEL; Novels; ObitT 1971; OxCEng 67, 85, 95; PenC ENG; RAdv 1, 14, 13-1; REn; RfGEnL 91; RGTwCWr; ScF&FL 1, 92; TwCA SUP; TwCWr; WebE&AL; Who 74; WhoTwCL*

Green, Hetty
[Henrietta Howland Robinson]
"Witch of Wall Street"
American. Financier
Reputed at that time to be richest woman in US, leaving estate of more than $100 million.
b. Nov 21, 1834 in New Bedford, Massachusetts
d. Jul 3, 1916 in New York, New York
Source: *AmBi; BioAmW; BioIn 15, 16, 17, 21; ContDcW 89; DcAmB; EncABHB 6; GoodHs; IntDcWB; LegTOT; LinLib S; NewCol 75; NotAW; WebAB 74; WhAm 1; WhoAmW 74*

Green, Hubie
[Hubert Green]
American. Golfer
Turned pro, 1970; won US Open, 1977, PGA Tournament, 1985; made 1985 Ryder Cup team.
b. Dec 28, 1946 in Birmingham, Alabama
Source: *BiDAmSp OS; BioIn 10, 11; NewYTBS 76; WhoAm 78, 86, 88, 92, 94, 95, 96; WhoGolf; WhoIntG*

Green, John Richard
English. Historian, Clergy
Wrote *Short History of the English People,* 1874, known for literary quality, emphasis on social trends, not political events.
b. Dec 12, 1837 in Oxford, England
d. Mar 7, 1883 in Menton, France
Source: *Alli SUP; BbD; BiD&SB; BioIn 1, 2, 3, 6, 8, 9, 16, 19; BritAu 19; CamGEL; CamGLE; CasWL; CelCen; DcEnA, A; DcEnL; DcEuL; DcNaB, C; EvLB; LinLib L, S; NewC; NewCBEL; OxCEng 67, 85, 95; PenC ENG; VicBrit*

Green, Johnny
[John W Green]
American. Songwriter
Wrote "Body and Soul," 1930; won Oscars for scores to *Easter Parade,* 1951; *American in Paris,* 1953; *West Side Story,* 1961.
b. Oct 10, 1908 in New York, New York
d. May 15, 1989 in Beverly Hills, California
Source: *AmPS; AmSong; AnObit 1989; ASCAP 66; Baker 84; BiDAmM; BiE&WWA; BioIn 1, 6, 9, 15, 16; CmMov; CmpEPM; ConTFT 3; FilmEn; FilmgC; HalFC 80, 84, 88; IntDcF 1-4, 2-4; IntMPA 84; LegTOT; NewGrDA 86; PenEncP; PopAmC; WhoAm 86, 88; WhoAmM 83; WhoMus 72; WhoWest 74; WhoWor 74, 91*

Green, Julien (Hartridge)
American. Author
Books include *The Closed Garden,* 1928; *Moira,* 1951.
b. Sep 6, 1900 in Paris, France
Source: *Benet 87, 96; BenetAL 91; BioIn 1, 10, 11, 12, 15, 16, 17, 18, 19; CasWL; ClDMEL 47, 80; CnMD; CnMWL; ConAu 21R, 33NR; ConFLW 84; ConLC 3, 11, 77; ConWorW 93; DcLB 4, 72; DcTwCCu 2; EncWL, 2, 3; EvEuW; GuFrLit 1; IntWW 74, 75, 76, 77, 78, 79, 80, 81, 82, 83; MajTwCW; McGEWD 72, 84; ModFrL; Novels; OxCAmL 83, 95; OxCFr; OxCThe 83; PenC EUR; RAdv 14, 13-2; REn; REnAL; REnWD; ScF&FL 1, 2; TwCA; TwCWr; WhoFr 79; WhoTwCL*

Green, Mark J(oseph)
American. Political Activist
Worked with Ralph Nader, 1970-80; active in consumer rights efforts.
b. Mar 15, 1945 in New York, New York
Source: *BioIn 12, 15, 16; ConAu 41R; CurBio 88; NewYTBS 86; WhoAm 80, 82, 84, 86, 88, 90, 92, 94, 95, 96*

Green, Martyn
English. Actor
Lead member of D'Oyly Carte Opera Co., 1922-51.
b. Apr 22, 1899 in London, England
d. Feb 8, 1975 in Hollywood, California
Source: *BiE&WWA; BioIn 1, 2, 3, 5, 10; BriBkM 80; ConAu 57; CurBio 50, 75N; FilmgC; HalFC 80, 84, 88; NewAmDM; NewYTBS 75; NotNAT A, B; ObitT 1971; OxCPMus; WhoHol C; WhoThe 72, 77; WhScrn 77, 83*

Green, Mitzi
American. Actor
Child star who played Annie in *Little Orphan Annie;* Becky Thatcher in *Tom Sawyer, Huckleberry Finn;* retired age 14.
b. Oct 22, 1920 in New York, New York
d. May 24, 1969 in Huntington, California
Source: *BioIn 7, 8, 9, 11; EncAFC; Film 2; FilmEn; FilmgC; ForYSC; HalFC 80, 84, 88; HolP 30; InWom SUP; LegTOT; MotPP; NotNAT B; ThFT; WhoHol B; WhScrn 74, 77, 83; WhThe*

Green, Paul Eliot
American. Dramatist, Screenwriter
Writings portray NC, black themes; wrote 1927 Pulitzer play *In Abraham's Bosom.*
b. Mar 17, 1894 in Lillington, North Carolina
d. May 4, 1981 in Chapel Hill, North Carolina
Source: *AmAu&B; ASCAP 80; Au&Wr 71; AuNews 1; BlueB 76; CnDAL; ConAmA; ConAmL; ConAu 3NR, 5R, 103; ConDr 73; DcLEL; EncWL; EncWT; IntAu&W 76, 77, 82; LngCTC; McGEWB; ModAL; ModWD; NotNAT; OxCAmL 65; OxCThe 67; PenC AM; REn; REnAL; TwCA, SUP; WebAB 74, 79; WebE&AL; WhE&EA; WhLit; WhNAA; Who 74; WhoAm 74, 76, 78, 80; WhoWor 74; WrDr 76*

Green, Paula
American. Advertising Executive
Coined phrase "We try harder" for Avis Rental Car advertising campaign, 1971.
b. Sep 18, 1927 in Hollywood, California
Source: *AdMenW; BioIn 9, 20; WhoAdv 80; WhoAm 74, 76, 78, 80, 82, 84, 90; WhoAmJ 80; WhoAmW 75, 77*

Green, Peter
[Peter Greenbaum]
English. Singer, Musician
Guitarist with Fleetwood Mac in original group, 1967; troubled history resulted in institutionalization; later recordings never matched prior success.
b. Oct 29, 1946 in London, England
Source: *EncRk 88; HarEnR 86; IlEncRk; OnThGG; WhoRocM 82*

Green, Richard R(eginald)
American. Educator
Chancellor, NY Board of Education, 1988-89.
b. May 27, 1936 in Menifee, Arkansas
d. May 10, 1989 in New York, New York
Source: *NewYTBS 88; WhoAm 82; WhoBlA 90N; WhoMW 84*

Green, Rickey Anthony
American. Basketball Player
Guard, 1977—, mostly with Utah; led NBA in steals, 1984.
b. Aug 18, 1954 in Chicago, Illinois
Source: *OfNBA 87; WhoBlA 85, 92*

Green, Wilf(red Thomas)
"Shorty"
Canadian. Hockey Player
Right wing, Hamilton, 1923-25, NY Americans, 1925-27; Hall of Fame, 1962.
b. Jul 17, 1896 in Sudbury, Ontario, Canada
d. Apr 19, 1960

Source: *HocEn; WhoHcky 73*

Green, William
American. Labor Union Official
Succeeded Samuel Gompers as pres. of AFL, 1924-52.
b. Mar 3, 1873 in Coshocton, Ohio
d. Nov 21, 1952 in Coshocton, Ohio
Source: *AmSocL; BiDAmL; BiDAmLL; BioIn 1, 2, 3, 4, 5, 6, 7, 8, 9; CurBio 42, 53; DcAmB S5; EncAB-H 1974; FacFETw; LinLib S; OhA&B; PolProf T; WebAB 74, 79; WhAm 3*

Greenaway, Emerson
American. Librarian
Director, Free Library of Philadelphia, 1951-69; pres., American Library Assn., 1957-58.
b. May 25, 1906 in Springfield, Massachusetts
d. Apr 8, 1990 in New London, New Hampshire
Source: *BiDrLUS 70; BioIn 4, 5, 16, 17; CurBio 90N; WhAm 10; WhoAm 74, 76, 78, 80, 82, 84, 86, 88; WhoE 74; WhoLibI 82; WhoLibS 55, 66*

Greenaway, Kate
[Catherine Greenaway]
English. Illustrator
Watercolorist; known for French empire style figures in children's books including *Mother Goose.*
b. Mar 17, 1846 in London, England
d. Nov 6, 1901 in London, England
Source: *AnCL; ArtclWW 2; AuBYP 2, 3; BiDWomA; BioIn 1, 2, 3, 4, 5, 7, 8, 9, 10, 11, 12, 13, 16, 17, 19, 20; BlmGEL; CamGLE; CarSB; ChhPo, S1, S2, S3; ChlBkCr; ChlLR 6; ClaDrA; ConAu 113, 137; DcArts; DcBrAr 1; DcBrBI; DcBrWA; DcLB 141; DcNaB S2; DcVicP 2; DcWomA; EncBrWW; EncFash; FamAIYP; InWom, SUP; JBA 34, 51; LinLib L; MajAI; McGDA; NewC; NewCBEL; OxCArt; OxCChiL; OxCEng 67, 85, 95; OxDcArt; RAdv 14; StaCVF; VicBrit; WhoChL; WomArt; YABC 2*

Greenaway, Peter
English. Filmmaker
Films include *The Draughtsman's Contract,* 1982, and *The Cook, The Thief, His Wife and Her Lover,* 1989.
b. Apr 5, 1942 in London, England
Source: *BiDFilm 94; BioIn 13; ConAu 127; ConTFT 10; CurBio 91; DcArts; EncEurC; IntDcF 2-2; IntMPA 92, 94, 96; IntWW 89, 91, 93; LegTOT; MiSFD 9; Who 94; WhoWor 95, 96, 97*

Greenbaum, Norman
American. Singer, Songwriter
Hit single, "Spirit in the Sky," sold two million copies, 1970.
b. Nov 20, 1942 in Malden, Massachusetts
Source: *BioIn 8; EncRk 88; PenEncP; RkOn 78; RolSEnR 83*

Greenberg, Clement
American. Critic
Art critic who was an advocate of Jackson Pollock and other Abstract Expressionist artists.
b. Jan 16, 1909 in New York, New York
d. May 7, 1994
Source: *AmAu&B; BioIn 4, 5, 6, 8, 10, 12, 13, 15, 16, 17, 19, 20, 21; ConAu 1R, 2NR, 145; ConLC 86; DcTwCCu 1; EncAB-H 1996; NewYTBS 94; TwCA SUP; WhAmArt 85; WhoAmA 73, 76, 78, 80; WhoWorJ 72, 78; WrDr 76, 80, 82, 84, 86, 88, 90, 92, 94, 96*

Greenberg, Hank
[Henry Benjamin Greenberg]
"Hammerin' Hank"
American. Baseball Player
First baseman, 1930-41, 1945-47; shares ML record for home runs by right-handed hitter, 58, 1938; AL MVP, 1935, 1940; Hall of Fame, 1956.
b. Jan 1, 1911 in New York, New York
d. Sep 4, 1986 in Beverly Hills, California
Source: *Ballpl 90; BiDAmSp BB; BioIn 1, 3, 4, 5, 6, 7, 8, 9, 10, 14, 15, 16, 17; ConNews 86-4; CurBio 47, 86, 86N; FacFETw; LegTOT; NewYTBS 86; What 2; WhoAm 74, 76; WhoProB 73; WhoSpor; WorAl; WorAlBi*

Greenberg, Joanne
[Hannah Green]
American. Author
Wrote autobiographical novel *I Never Promised You a Rose Garden,* 1964; adapted to film, 1977.
b. Sep 24, 1932 in New York, New York
Source: *AmAu&B; AmWomWr; AmWomWr; ArtclWW 2; Au&Arts 12; BioIn 12, 13, 15, 16, 20; ConAu 5NR, 5R, 14NR, 32NR; ConLC 7, 30; ConNov 96; CyWA 89; DrAF 76; DrAPF 80, 91; IntAu&W 89, 91, 93; InWom SUP; PenNWW B; SmATA 23, 25; TwCYAW; WhoAm 74, 76, 78, 80, 82, 84; WhoAmJ 80; WhoAmW 68, 70, 72, 74; WhoUSWr 88; WhoWest 96; WhoWrEP 89, 92, 95; WorAu 1975; WrDr 80, 82, 84, 86, 88, 90, 92, 94, 96*

Greenberg, Stanley B
American. Pollster
Pres. Clinton's poll taker and close adviser.
b. May 10, 1945
Source: *AmMWSc 92*

Greene, Balcomb
American. Artist
Painter, co-founder American Abstract Artists in the 1930s.
b. May 22, 1904 in Niagara Falls, New York
d. Nov 12, 1990 in Montauk Point, New York
Source: *BioIn 3, 4, 5, 6, 7, 17; BlueB 76; BriEAA; ConArt 83, 89; CurBio 91N; DcAmArt; DcCAA 71, 77, 88, 94; McGDA; NewYTBS 90; OxCTwCA; OxDcArt; PhDcTCA 77; WhAm 10; WhAmArt 85; WhoAm 74, 76, 78, 80, 82, 84, 86, 88; WhoAmA 73, 76, 78, 80, 82, 84, 86, 89, 91N, 93N; WhoWor 74, 76*

Greene, Belle da Costa
American. Library Administrator
Director, Pierpont Morgan Library, 1923-48.
b. Dec 13, 1883 in Alexandria, Virginia
d. May 10, 1950 in New York, New York
Source: *BioIn 17, 21; NotAW*

Greene, Bob
[Robert Bernard Greene, Jr.]
American. Journalist
Syndicated columnist, 1976—; wrote *Billion Dollar Baby,* 1974, account of life on road with rock band.
b. Mar 10, 1947 in Columbus, Ohio
Source: *BiDAmNC; BioIn 10, 13, 21; ConAu 27NR, 107; CurBio 95; LegTOT; WhoAm 78, 80, 82, 84, 86, 88, 90, 92, 94, 95, 96, 97; WhoEmL 87; WhoMW 78, 80, 82, 84, 86, 88, 90; WhoUSWr 88; WhoWrEP 89, 92, 95*

Greene, Charles Sumner
American. Architect
With brother, Henry, designed the bungalow style house.
b. Oct 12, 1868 in Brighton, Ohio
d. Jun 11, 1957 in Carmel, California
Source: *AmCulL; BioIn 2, 4, 5, 7, 11, 15, 16, 17, 19; BriEAA; CmCal; ConArch 80, 87; DcAmB S5; DcTwDes; EncAAr 1; EncMA; MacEA; NatCAB 48; PenDiDA 89; PeoHis; WhoArch*

Greene, Gael
American. Author
Books include *Doctor Love,* 1982; *Delicious Sex,* 1986.
b. 1937 in Detroit, Michigan
Source: *BioIn 5; ConAu 10NR, 13R; ConLC 8; Dun&B 90; InWom SUP*

Greene, Graham
Canadian. Actor
Films include *Running Brave,* 1982; *Dances with Wolves,* 1990.
b. 1952 in Ontario, Canada
Source: *NotNaAm*

Greene, Graham (Henry)
English. Author
Wrote 24 novels: *The Power and the Glory,* 1940, *The Heart of the Matter,* 1948.
b. Oct 2, 1904 in Berkhampstead, England
d. Apr 3, 1991 in Vevey, Switzerland
Source: *AnObit 1991; Au&Wr 71; AuBYP 2S, 3; AuNews 2; Benet 87; BiE&WWA; BioIn 1, 2, 3, 4, 5, 6, 7, 8, 9, 10, 11, 12, 13, 14, 15, 16, 17, 18, 19, 20, 21; BlueB 76; BritPl; BritWr S1; CamGEL; CamGLE; CamGWoT; CasWL; CathA 1930; CelR; ChhPo S2; CnDBLB 7; CnMD; CnMWL; CnThe; ConAu 13R, 35NR, 133; ConBrDr;*

ConDr 73, 77, 82, 88, 93; ConLC 1, 3, 6, 9, 14, 18, 27, 37, 70, 72; ConNov 72, 76, 82, 86; CorpD; CroCD; CrtSuDr; CrtSuMy; CurBio 91N; CyWA 58, 89; DcLB 13, 15, 77, 100, 162, Y85A, Y91N; EncEurC; EncMys; EncWL 2, 3; EncWT; Ent; FacFETw; FilmEn; FilmgC; GrWrEL N; HalFC 80, 84, 88; IlWWBF A; IntAu&W 76, 77, 89; IntDcF 2-4; IntWW 74, 75, 76, 77, 78, 79, 80, 81, 82, 83, 89, 91, 91N; ItaFilm; LegTOT; LiExTwC; LinLib L, S; LngCTC; MagSWL; MajTwCW; MakMC; McGEWB; McGEWD 72, 84; ModBrL, S1, S2; ModWD; NewC; NewCBEL; News 91; NewYTBS 85, 91; NotNAT, A; Novels; OxCChiL; OxCEng 67, 85; OxCFilm; OxCThe 67, 83; PenC ENG; PlP&P; RAdv 1, 14, 13-1; REn; RfGEnL 91; ScF&FL 1, 2, 92; ShSWr; SmATA 20; SpyFic; TwCA, SUP; TwCChW 78; TwCCr&M 80, 85, 91; TwCWr; VarWW 85; WebE&AL; WhAm 10; WhDW; WhE&EA; Who 74, 82, 83, 85, 88, 90; WhoAm 80, 82, 84, 86, 88, 90; WhoChL; WhoFr 79; WhoSpyF; WhoThe 72, 77, 81; WhoTwCL; WhoWor 74, 76, 78, 80, 82, 84, 87, 89, 91; WorAl; WorAlBi; WorEFlm; WorLitC; WrDr 76, 80, 82, 84, 86, 88, 90, 92; WrPh

Greene, Henry Mather
American. Architect
One of a team of two brothers whose experimentation with architectural style led to the design of the bungalow.
b. Jan 23, 1870 in Brighton, Ohio
d. Oct 2, 1954 in Pasadena, California
Source: *AmCulL; BioIn 2, 4, 5, 11, 15, 17, 19; BriEAA; CmCal; ConArch 80, 87; DcAmB S5; DcTwDes; EncAAr 1; MacEA; PenDiDA 89; PeoHis; WhoArch*

Greene, Hugh (Carleton), Sir
English. Broadcasting Executive
Director general, BBC, 1960-69; known for liberalization of broadcasting standards.
b. Nov 15, 1910 in Berkhampstead, England
d. Feb 19, 1987 in London, England
Source: *AnObit 1987; BioIn 6, 7, 13, 15; BlueB 76; ConAu 102, 121; CurBio 63, 87, 87N; DcNaB 1986; IntAu&W 77, 82, 86; IntWW 74, 75, 76, 77, 78, 79, 80, 81, 82, 83; IntYB 78, 79, 80, 81, 82; WhAm 9; WhE&EA; Who 74, 82, 83, 85; WhoAm 74, 76, 78; WhoWor 74, 76, 78, 84, 87; WrDr 84, 86*

Greene, Joe
[Charles Edward Greene]
''''Mean Joe''''
American. Football Player
Ten-time all-pro tackle, member ''steel curtain'' defense, Pittsburgh, 1969-81; starred in award-winning Coca Cola commercial, 1970s; won four Super Bowls; Hall of Fame, 1987.
b. Sep 24, 1946 in Temple, Texas
Source: *AfrAmSG; BiDAmSp FB; BioIn 10, 11, 12; ConBlB 10; InB&W 85; LegTOT; WhoAfA 96; WhoAm 78, 80, 82, 84, 86, 88, 90, 92, 94, 95, 96, 97; WhoBlA 77, 80, 85, 88, 90, 92, 94; WhoFtbl 74; WorAl; WorAlBi*

Greene, Lorne
American. Actor
Best known for role of Ben Cartwright on TV western ''Bonanza,'' 1959-73.
b. Feb 12, 1915 in Ottawa, Ontario, Canada
d. Sep 11, 1987 in Santa Monica, California
Source: *AnObit 1987; BiE&WWA; BioIn 7, 8, 12, 15; CanWW 70, 79, 80, 81, 83; CelR; ConNews 88-1; ConTFT 3, 5; CreCan 2; CurBio 67, 87, 87N; FilmEn; FilmgC; ForYSC; HalFC 80, 84, 88; IntMPA 75, 76, 77, 78, 79, 80, 81, 82, 84, 86; LegTOT; MotPP; MovMk; NewYTBS 87; OxCCanT; RkOn 78; VarWW 85; WhAm 9; WhoAm 74, 76, 78, 80, 82, 84, 86; WhoHol A; WhoWor 74; WorAl; WorAlBi*

Greene, Nancy Catherine
Canadian. Skier
Two-time world cup champion skier, 1967, 1968; won gold medal in women's giant Slalom, 1968 Olympics.
b. May 11, 1943 in Ottawa, Ontario, Canada
Source: *BioIn 8, 10; CanWW 31, 70, 79, 80, 81, 83, 89; CurBio 69; InWom SUP; WhoAmW 89*

Greene, Nathanael
American. Army Officer
Won crucial southern campaign over British, 1780-81.
b. Aug 7, 1742 in Potowomut, Rhode Island
d. Jun 19, 1786 in Savannah, Georgia
Source: *AmBi; AmRev; ApCAB; BioIn 3, 4, 5, 6, 7, 8, 9, 10, 12, 13, 15, 16; BlkwEAR; DcAmB; DcAmMiB; EncAB-H 1974, 1996; EncAR; EncCRAm; EncSoH; GenMudB; HarEnMi; HarEnUS; HisWorL; LinLib S; McGEWB; NatCAB 1; OxCAmH; TwCBDA; WebAB 74, 79; WebAMB; WhAm HS; WhAmRev; WhoMilH 76; WorAl; WorAlBi*

Greene, Richard
English. Actor
Played the original Robin Hood in British TV series ''Robin Hood,'' 1950s.
b. Aug 25, 1918 in Plymouth, England
d. Jun 1, 1985 in Norfolk, England
Source: *AnObit 1985; BioIn 4, 11; FilmEn; FilmgC; ForYSC; HolP 30; IlWWBF; MotPP; MovMk; WhoHol A; WorAl*

Greene, Robert
English. Dramatist
His drama *The Honorable History of Friar Bacon and Friar Bungay,* 1594, was a model for Shakespeare's comedies.
b. Jul 11, 1558 in Norwich, England
d. Sep 3, 1592 in London, England
Source: *AtlBL; BioIn 11, 12, 13, 15, 16, 20; BlmGEL; BritAu; CamGLE; CamGWoT; CasWL; CnThe; CrtSuDr; CrtT 4; DcLB 62, 167; EncWT; Ent; GrWrEL N; IntDcT 2; LngCEL; McGEWD 72, 84; NewCBEL; NotNAT B; OxCEng 85, 95; OxCThe 83; PlP&P; RAdv 14, 13-2; REn; REnWD; RfGEnL 91*

Greene, Shecky
[Fred Sheldon Greenfield]
American. Actor, Comedian
Las Vegas comedian since 1953; in film *Tony Rome,* 1967.
b. Apr 8, 1926 in Chicago, Illinois
Source: *BioIn 6, 13; VarWW 85; WhoAm 80, 82, 84, 86, 88, 92, 94, 95, 96, 97; WhoEnt 92; WhoHol A; WhoWor 80, 82*

Greene, Ward
American. Author, Journalist
Novels are marked by action, cool realism: *Route 28,* 1940.
b. Dec 23, 1892 in Asheville, North Carolina
d. Jan 22, 1956
Source: *AmAu&B; AmNov; BenetAL 91; BioIn 2, 3, 4; REnAL; TwCA, SUP; WhAm 3; WhJnl; WhNAA*

Greenfield, Eloise
American. Children's Author
Won Carter G. Woodson Book Award for *Rosa Parks,* 1974; authored several other children's books with black themes.
b. May 17, 1929 in Parmele, North Carolina
Source: *AmWomWr SUP; ArtclWW 2; BioIn 12, 16, 17, 19; BlkAuII, 92; BlkAWP; BlkWAm; BlkWr 1, 2; ChlBkCr; ChlLR 4, 38; ConAu 1NR, 19NR, 43NR, 49; ConBlB 9; DcAmChF 1960; FifBJA; InB&W 80, 85; IntAu&W 77, 82; LivgBAA; MajAI; NotBlAW 2; SchCGBL; SelBAAf; SelBAAu; SmATA 16AS, 19, 61; TwCChW 83, 89, 95; WhoAfA 96; WhoAm 92; WhoBlA 77, 80, 85, 88, 90, 92, 94; WrDr 76, 80, 82, 84, 86, 88, 90, 92, 94, 96*

Greenfield, Howard
American. Songwriter
Co-wrote Grammy-winning ''Love Will Keep Us Together,'' with Neil Sedaka, 1975.
b. Mar 15, 1937? in New York, New York
d. Mar 4, 1986 in Los Angeles, California
Source: *ConAu 118*

Greenfield, Jerry
American. Businessman
Founded, with Ben Cohen, Ben & Jerry's Homemade, Inc., an ice cream company, 1978.
b. 1951 in New York, New York
Source: *CurBio 94; WhoAm 95, 96, 97*

Greenfield, Meg
American. Journalist
Columnist in *Newsweek;* won Pulitzer for editorial writing.
b. Dec 27, 1930 in Seattle, Washington
Source: *BioIn 10, 16; ConAu 123, 128; EncTwCJ; InWom SUP; WhoAm 74, 76, 78, 80, 82, 84, 86, 88, 90, 92, 94, 95, 96, 97; WhoAmW 70A, 72, 74, 75, 79, 81, 83, 91, 93, 95, 97; WhoE 79, 81, 83, 86, 89, 91, 93, 95; WhoSSW 73*

Greenglass, David
American. Spy
Worked at Los Alamos; spied for the Soviets, 1944-46; testified against brother-in-law at Rosenberg trial.
b. 1922 in New York, New York
Source: *BioIn 2, 4, 7; EncMcCE*

Greenhill, Basil
English. Author
Maritime writings include *The British Sea Farce Discovered,* 1979.
b. Feb 26, 1920 in Weston-super-Mare, England
Source: *Au&Wr 71; ConAu 2NR, 5R, 17NR; IntAu&W 89, 91; OxCCan SUP; Who 83, 90; WrDr 84, 92*

Greenough, Horatio
American. Sculptor
Neo-classical works include *Washington,* currently in Smithsonian Institution.
b. Sep 6, 1805 in Boston, Massachusetts
d. Dec 18, 1852 in Somerville, Massachusetts
Source: *Alli; AmAu; AmAu&B; AmBi; ApCAB, X; ArtsNiC; BenetAL 91; BiAUS; BiDTran; BioIn 3, 4, 5, 6, 7, 8, 9, 10, 11, 12, 14; BriEAA; CyAL 2; DcAmArt; DcAmB; DcBiPP; DcLB 1; DcNAA; DcTwDes; Drake; HarEnUS; LinLib S; McGDA; NatCAB 6; NewYHSD; OxCAmH; OxCAmL 65, 83, 95; OxCArt; OxDcArt; PeoHis; REnAL; TwCBDA; WebAB 74, 79; WhAm HS*

Greenspan, Alan
American. Government Official
Economist; named chm., Federal Reserve Board, 1987, replacing Paul Volcker.
b. Mar 6, 1926 in New York, New York
Source: *AmEA 74; AmMWSc 73S; BioIn 8, 10, 11, 12, 13, 16; BioNews 74; CurBio 74, 89; EncABHB 7; IntWW 75, 76, 77, 78, 79, 80, 81, 82, 83, 89, 91, 93; LegTOT; News 92, 92-2; NewYTBS 79, 87, 89; PolProf NF; St&PR 75; Who 90, 92, 94; WhoAm 76, 78, 80, 82, 84, 86, 88, 90, 92, 94, 95, 96, 97; WhoAmP 77, 79, 81, 83, 85, 87, 89, 91, 93, 95; WhoE 83, 85, 86, 89, 91, 93, 95, 97; WhoFI 83, 85, 87, 89, 92, 94, 96; WhoGov 75, 77; WhoWor 78, 80, 82, 84, 87, 89, 91, 93, 95, 96, 97; WorAlBi*

Greenspan, Bud
American. Producer, Director
Known for sports documentaries for TV, albums.
b. Sep 18, 1927 in New York, New York
Source: *BioIn 10, 13, 14; ConAu 103; LesBEnT, 92; WhoAm 90; WhoEnt 92*

Greenstreet, Sydney Hughes
English. Actor
Best known roles in *The Maltese Falcon,* 1941; *Casablanca,* 1942.
b. Dec 27, 1879 in Sandwich, England
d. Jan 19, 1954 in Los Angeles, California
Source: *BiDFilm; CmMov; CurBio 43, 54; DcAmB S5; HolP 40; MotPP; OxCFilm; Vers A; WhoHol B; WhScrn 74, 77; WorEFlm*

Greenwood, Charlotte
American. Actor
Comedienne best known for her high kicking dance routines.
b. Jun 25, 1893 in Philadelphia, Pennsylvania
d. Jan 18, 1978 in Los Angeles, California
Source: *BiDD; BiE&WWA; BioIn 3, 15; CmpEPM; EncAFC; EncMT; EncVaud; Film 1, 2; FilmEn; FilmgC; ForYSC; FunnyW; IntMPA 75, 76, 77, 78; InWom, SUP; MotPP; MovMk; NotNAT; OxCAmT 84; RadStar; ThFT; Vers A; WhoHol A; WhoThe 77A; WhScrn 83; WhThe*

Greenwood, Chester
American. Inventor
Created the earmuff, 1873.
b. Dec 4, 1858 in Farmington, Maine
d. Jul 5, 1937 in Farmington, Maine
Source: *BioIn 10; EncAB-A 10; NatCAB 27; WorAl*

Greenwood, Joan
English. Actor
Films include *The Man in the White Suit,* 1951.
b. Mar 4, 1921 in London, England
d. Mar 2, 1987 in London, England
Source: *AnObit 1987; BiDFilm, 81, 94; BiE&WWA; BioIn 3, 11, 15; CnThe; ConTFT 4; CurBio 54, 87, 87N; EncEurC; FilmAG WE; FilmEn; FilmgC; HalFC 80, 84, 88; IlWWBF; IntDcF 1-3, 2-3; IntMPA 77, 80, 84, 86; InWom, SUP; MotPP; MovMk; NewYTBS 87; NotNAT; OxCFilm; VarWW 85; Who 74, 82, 83, 85; WhoHol A; WhoThe 72, 77, 81; WorEFlm*

Greenwood, Lee
American. Singer, Songwriter
Country performer who recorded single "I O U," 1983.
b. Oct 27, 1942 in Los Angeles, California
Source: *BgBkCoM; BioIn 13; ConMus 12; LegTOT; RkOn 85; WhoAm 88; WhoEnt 92*

Greer, Germaine
English. Author, Educator
Wrote one of the first successful feminist books, *The Female Eunuch,* 1970 although *Sex and Destiny,* 1984 was called anti-feminist by the critics.
b. Jan 29, 1939 in Melbourne, Australia
Source: *ArtclWW 2; AuNews 1; AuSpks; AuWomWr; BioIn 9, 10, 11, 12, 13, 14, 16, 17, 21; BlmGWL; BlueB 76; CelR; ConAu 33NR, 81; ContDcW 89; CurBio 71, 88; DcLEL 1940; DcLP 87A; EncWB; FacFETw; FemiCLE; FemiWr; HanAmWH; IntAu&W 76, 77, 86, 89, 91, 93; IntDcWB; IntWW 74, 75, 76, 77, 78, 79, 80, 81, 82, 83, 89, 91, 93; InWom SUP; LegTOT; LiJour; MajTwCW; MakMC; NewYTBE 71; OxCAusL; RadHan; Who 82, 83, 85, 88, 90, 92, 94; WhoAm 78, 80, 82, 84, 86, 88, 90, 92, 94, 95, 96, 97; WhoAmW 74, 75, 77, 81, 83; WhoUSWr 88; WhoWor 74, 76, 78; WorAu 1985; WrDr 76, 80, 82, 84, 86, 88, 90, 92, 94, 96*

Greer, Hal
[Harold Everett Greer]
American. Basketball Player
Guard, 1958-73, mostly with Philadelphia; Hall of Fame, 1981.
b. Jun 26, 1936 in Huntington, West Virginia
Source: *AfrAmSG; BasBi; BiDAmSp BK; BioIn 10, 21; InB&W 80; OfNBA 87; WhoAfA 96; WhoAm 74, 76; WhoBbl 73; WhoBlA 75, 77, 80, 92, 94; WhoSpor*

Greer, Howard
American. Fashion Designer
Leading Hollywood designer, 1940s-50s.
b. 1896
d. Apr 20, 1974
Source: *NewYTBS 74; ObitOF 79*

Greer, Jane
American. Actor
Brief career in films *You're in the Navy Now; Desperate Search.*
b. Sep 9, 1924 in Washington, District of Columbia
Source: *BioIn 1, 78, 79, 80, 81, 82, 84, 86, 88, 92, 94, 96; InWom SUP; LegTOT; MotPP; MovMk; ODwPR 91; VarWW 85; WhoHol 92, A*

Greer, Sonny
[William Alexander Greer]
American. Musician
Drummer, Duke Ellington Orchestra for over 30 years.
b. Dec 13, 1903 in Long Branch, New Jersey
d. Mar 23, 1982 in New York, New York
Source: *BiDAfM; BiDAmM; BioIn 12, 13; CmpEPM; EncJzS; IlEncJ; InB&W 80; NewAmDM; NewYTBS 82; WhoJazz 72*

Greg, Walter Wilson, Sir
English. Bibliographer
Pres., Bibliographical Society, 1930-32; edited many Elizabethan plays.
b. 1875
d. 1959

Source: *BioIn 5; DcLEL; DcNaB 1951; NewCBEL; ObitT 1951; OxCEng 67, 85, 95; PenC ENG; REn*

Gregg, Forrest
[Alvis Forrest Gregg]
American. Football Player, Football Coach
Seven-time all-pro offensive tackle, 1956, 1958-71, mostly with Green Bay; coached Cleveland, Cincinnati, Green Bay in NFL; Hall of Fame, 1977.
b. Oct 18, 1933 in Birthright, Texas
Source: *BiDAmSp FB; FootReg 86; LegTOT; WhoAm 84, 86, 88, 92, 94, 95; WhoFtbl 74; WhoMW 82, 84, 86, 88; WhoSpor*

Gregg, John Robert
American. Inventor
Invented the widely used Gregg shorthand system.
b. Jun 17, 1867 in Rockcorry, Ireland
d. Feb 23, 1948 in New York, New York
Source: *AmAu&B; AmLY; BiDAmEd; BioIn 1, 2, 5, 6; DcAmB S4; DcIrB 78, 88; DcNAA; EncAB-A 10; InSci; WhAm 2; WhNAA*

Gregg, Judd
American. Politician
Governor, NH 1989-93; rep. senator, NH, 1993—.
b. Feb 14, 1947 in Nashua, New Hampshire
Source: *AlmAP 82, 84, 88, 92, 96; BiDrGov 1988; BiDrUSC 89; BioIn 19, 20; CngDr 81, 83, 85, 87, 93, 95; IntWW 89, 91, 93; PolsAm 84; WhoAm 82, 86, 88, 90, 92, 94, 95, 96, 97; WhoAmP 91; WhoE 81, 83, 85, 86, 89, 91, 93, 95, 97; WhoWor 91, 93, 95, 96, 97*

Gregg, William
"Father of Southern Textile Industry"
American. Industrialist
Early cotton manufacturer; wrote *Essays on Domestic Industry,* 1845.
b. Feb 2, 1800 in Monongalia County, West Virginia
d. Sep 13, 1867
Source: *AmBi; BiDAmBL 83; BiDConf; BioIn 2, 3, 7, 11; DcAmB; EncAB-H 1974; EncSoH; McGEWB; TwCBDA; WebAB 74, 79; WhAm HS; WhCiWar*

Greg Kihn Band, The
[Greg Douglass; Greg Kihn; Larry Lynch; Gary Phillips; Steve Wright]
American. Music Group
Rock band formed 1975; eighth album *Kihnspiracy* contained hit single "Jeo pardy," 1983.
Source: *BioIn 13; Dun&B 90; RkOn 85; RolSEnR 83; WhoRocM 82*

Gregor, Arthur
American. Poet
Writings include *Embodiment and Other Poems,* 1982.
b. Nov 18, 1923 in Vienna, Austria
Source: *BioIn 13, 14, 17; ConAu 10AS, 11NR, 25NR, 25R; ConLC 9; ConPo 70, 75, 80, 85, 91, 96; DrAP 75; DrAPF 80; IntAu&W 76, 77; IntWWP 77; LiExTwC; LinLib L; OxCTwCP; SmATA 36; WhoAm 74, 76, 78, 80, 82, 84, 86, 88, 90; WhoAmJ 80; WhoE 83; WhoUSWr 88; WhoWrEP 89, 92, 95; WorAu 1980; WrDr 76, 80, 82, 84, 86, 88, 90, 92, 94, 96*

Gregorian, Vartan
American. University Administrator
Pres., Brown U, 1989—; pres., NY Public Library, 1981-88; former college professor.
b. Apr 8, 1934 in Tabriz, Iran
Source: *BioIn 12, 13, 14, 16; ConAu 29R; CurBio 85; DrAS 82H; IntWW 89, 91, 93; News 90, 90-3; NewYTBS 88; WhoAm 78, 80, 82, 84, 86, 88, 90, 92, 94, 95, 96, 97; WhoE 75, 77, 79, 81, 83, 85, 86, 89, 91, 93, 95, 97; WhoLibI 82; WhoWor 82, 91, 93, 95, 96, 97*

Gregory, Bettina Louise
American. Journalist
Correspondent, ABC News, 1974—; White House correspondent, 1979—.
b. Jun 4, 1946 in New York, New York
Source: *BioIn 12; ConAu 69; EncTwCJ; InWom SUP; WhoAm 80, 82, 84, 86, 88, 90, 92, 94, 95, 96, 97; WhoAmW 85, 87, 89, 93, 95, 97; WhoEmL 87*

Gregory, Cynthia Kathleen
American. Dancer
Principal dancer with American Ballet Theatre, 1967-91.
b. Jul 8, 1946 in Los Angeles, California
Source: *BiDD; BioIn 7, 13, 16; CelR 90; CurBio 77; FacFETw; InWom SUP; News 90, 90-2; NewYTBE 73; WhoAm 74, 76, 78, 80, 82, 84, 86, 88, 92, 94, 95; WhoAmW 72, 74, 75, 79, 81, 83, 85, 89, 91, 93; WorAl; WorAlBi*

Gregory, Dick
[Richard Claxton Gregory]
American. Comedian, Author, Political Activist
Noted for social consciousness expressed through fasting, lifestyle; first black comedian to perform for white audiences; owner, Dick Gregory Health Enterprises.
b. Oct 12, 1932 in Saint Louis, Missouri
Source: *AmAu&B; BioIn 5, 6, 7, 8, 9, 10, 11, 12, 16; BioNews 74; BlkWr 1; BlkWrNE; BlueB 76; CelR; CivR 74; CivRSt; ConAu 7NR, 45; ConBlB 1; ConHero 1; CurBio 62; DcTwCCu 5; DrBlPA, 90; Ebony 1; EncAACR; EncWB; HeroCon; InB&W 80, 85; JoeFr; LegTOT; LivgBAA; LNinSix; NegAl 76, 83, 89; NewAgE 90; News 90, 90-3; NotNAT A; PolProf J; SchCGBL; SelBAAf; SelBAAu; WhoAfA 96; WhoAm 74, 76, 78, 80, 82, 84, 86, 88, 92, 94, 95, 96, 97; WhoAmP 73, 75, 77, 79, 81, 83, 85, 87, 89, 91, 93, 95; WhoBlA 75, 77, 80, 85, 88, 90, 92, 94; WhoCom; WhoEnt 92; WhoHol 92, A; WorAl; WorAlBi; WrDr 76, 80, 82, 84, 86, 88, 90, 92, 94, 96*

Gregory, Frederick D(rew)
American. Astronaut
First black to pilot a space shuttle, 1985.
b. Jan 7, 1941 in Washington, District of Columbia
Source: *AfrAmAl 6; BlksScM; WhoAfA 96; WhoBlA 80, 85, 88, 90, 92, 94*

Gregory, Horace Victor
American. Poet
Among prominent American poets; known for combining classic, contemporary lyrics; won 1965 Bollinger prize for *Collected Poems.*
b. Apr 10, 1898 in Milwaukee, Wisconsin
d. Mar 11, 1982 in Shelburne Falls, Massachusetts
Source: *AmAu&B; AnObit 1982; BlueB 76; CnDAL; ConAmA; ConAu 3NR, 5NR, 106; ConPo 75; DcLEL; DrAP 75; IntAu&W 77; IntWW 74, 75, 76, 77, 78, 79, 80, 81, 82; NewYTBS 82; OxCAmL 65; PenC AM; REn; REnAL; TwCA SUP; WhoAm 74, 76, 78, 80, 82; WhoE 74; WhoWor 74; WrDr 80*

Gregory, Isabella Augusta Persse, Lady
Irish. Dramatist
A founder, Irish National Theater; directed Abbey Theater, 1904; her plays depict Irish peasants.
b. Mar 5, 1852 in Roxborough, Ireland
d. May 22, 1932? in Coole, Ireland
Source: *AtlBL; BioIn 14, 15, 16, 18; Chambr 3; DcLEL; EvLB; IriPla; LngCTC; ModBrL, S1; ModWD; PenC ENG; PlP&P; REn; TwCA SUP; TwCWr; WebE&AL; WhoLA*

Gregory, James
American. Actor
Starred on Broadway in *Death of a Salesman;* in films *PT-109; The In-Laws.*
b. Dec 23, 1911 in New York, New York
Source: *BiE&WWA; BioIn 12; ConTFT 3; DcScB; FilmEn; FilmgC; ForYSC; HalFC 80, 84, 88; MotPP; MovMk; NotNAT; VarWW 85; WhoAm 74, 76, 78, 80, 82, 84, 86, 88, 90, 92, 94, 95, 96, 97; WhoHol 92, A; WhoWest 94, 96*

Gregory the Great, Saint
[Pope Gregory I]
Italian. Religious Leader
Doctor of the Church who extended its temporal power; supposedly responsible for Gregorian chant.
b. Feb 3, 540 in Rome, Italy
d. Mar 12, 604 in Rome, Italy
Source: *BioIn 17, 18, 19, 20; CasWL; CyEd; DcCathB; HisWorL; LuthC 75;*

NewCol 75; NewGrDM 80; OxDcByz; PenC EUR; RAdv 14, 13-4; REn; WebBD 83

Gregory XIII, Pope
[Ugo Boncompagni]
Italian. Religious Leader
Catholic reformer who created Gregorian calendar, 1582, replacing Julian calendar.
b. Jun 7, 1502 in Bologna, Italy
d. Apr 10, 1585 in Rome, Italy
Source: *McGEWB; NewCol 75; WebBD 83*

Gregory XV, Pope
[Alessandro Ludovisi]
Italian. Religious Leader
Reformed papal elections; founded Congregation for Propagation of Faith, 1622, to coordinate missionary activities.
b. Jan 9, 1554 in Bologna, Papal States
d. Jul 8, 1623 in Rome, Papal States
Source: *DcCathB; WebBD 83*

Gregson, John
English. Actor
Played in British TV police series "Gideon's Way."
b. Mar 15, 1919 in Liverpool, England
d. Jan 8, 1975 in Porlock Weir, England
Source: *BioIn 10, 13; CmMov; FilmAG WE; FilmEn; FilmgC; ForYSC; HalFC 80, 84, 88; IlWWBF; IntMPA 75; ObitT 1971; WhoHol C; WhScrn 77, 83*

Grene, Marjorie
American. Author
Works include *Philosophy in and out of Europe and Other Essays,* 1976.
b. Dec 13, 1910 in Milwaukee, Wisconsin
Source: *Au&Wr 71; ConAu 8NR, 13R, 25NR; DrAS 74P, 82P; WhoAmW 74*

Grenfell, Joyce Irene
English. Actor
Presented her own monologues in one-woman shows, 1939; character actress in film *Yellow Rolls Royce.*
b. Feb 10, 1910 in London, England
d. Nov 30, 1979 in London, England
Source: *BiE&WWA; ConAu 81, 89; CurBio 58, 80; DcNaB 1971; EncMT; FilmgC; GrBr; IntWW 74, 75, 76, 77, 78, 79; IntWWP 77; InWom, SUP; MotPP; MovMk; NewYTBS 79; NotNAT; OxCThe 67, 83; Who 74; WhoAmW 74; WhoHol A; WhoThe 77*

Grenfell, Wilfred Thomason, Sir
English. Author, Physician, Missionary
Built hospitals, schools in Labrador, Newfoundland; supported mission with writings: *Adrift on an Ice-Pan,* 1909.
b. Feb 28, 1865 in Parkgate, England
d. Oct 9, 1940 in Charlotte, Vermont
Source: *AmLY; BenetAL 91; BioIn 1, 2, 3, 4, 5, 6, 7, 8, 10, 12, 17; CurBio 40; DcLB 92; DcLEL; DcNAA; DcNaB 1931; EvLB; InSci; LinLib L, S; LngCTC; LuthC 75; MacDCB 78; NewC; OxCCan; OxCCanL; OxCMed 86; REn; REnAL; TwCA, SUP; WhAm 1; WhE&EA; WhLit; WhNAA*

Grentz, Theresa Shank
American. Basketball Coach
Head coach, women's basketball team, Rutgers U, 1976—; head coach, US Olympic team, 1992; named Nat. Coach of the Yr., 1987.
Source: *BioIn 15*

Grenville, Richard, Sir
English. Naval Officer
Led colonizing expedition to Roanoke Island, NC, 1585; subject of Tennyson's poem "The Revenge"; cousin of Sir Walter Raleigh.
b. Jun 15, 1542 in Cornwall, England
d. Sep 1591
Source: *Alli; AmBi; ApCAB; BioIn 1, 3, 6, 11; DcNaB; HarEnUS; HisDBrE; NewC; OxCShps; REn; WhoMilH 76*

Gres, Alix
French. Fashion Designer
Known for Grecian-styled, draped jersey gowns.
b. Nov 30, 1903 in Paris, France
d. Nov 24, 1993, France
Source: *BioIn 13, 14, 16, 20, 21; CurBio 80; DcTwDes; EncFash; FairDF FRA; InWom SUP; NewYTBS 94; WhoFash 88; WorFshn*

Grese, Irma
German. Government Official
Camp guard in charge of 18,000 female prisioners at Auschwitz; known for brutality; sentenced to death.
b. 1923
d. Dec 13, 1945 in Hamelin, Germany
Source: *BioIn 1, 7; EncTR; InWom, SUP*

Gresham, Thomas, Sir
English. Financier
Founded Royal Exchange, London, 1560s; Gresham's law: "bad money drives out good."
b. 1518? in London, England
d. Nov 21, 1579 in London, England
Source: *DcNaB; NewC; NewCol 75; WhDW*

Gretchaninov, Aleksandr Tikhonovich
[Aleksandr Tikhonovich Grechaninov]
American. Composer
Music rooted in Russian national tradition; wrote popular song "Over the Steppes."
b. Oct 25, 1864 in Moscow, Russia
d. Jan 3, 1956 in New York, New York
Source: *Baker 84; BiDSovU; LuthC 75; NewCol 75; NewEOp 71; ObitOF 79; OxCMus*

Gretry, Andre Ernest Modeste
"The Moliere of Music"
French. Composer
Founded French opera-comique; 50 operas included *Lucile,* 1769.
b. Feb 10, 1741 in Liege, Belgium
d. Sep 24, 1813 in Montmorency, France
Source: *Baker 78, 84; BioIn 1, 4, 7, 9, 11, 12, 15; BlkwCE; BriBkM 80; CmOp; DcBiPP; DcCom 77; Dis&D; GrComp; MusMk; NewAmDM; NewCol 75; NewEOp 71; NewGrDM 80; NewOxM; OxCFr; OxCMus*

Grettenberger, John O
American. Business Executive
General Manager, Cadillac, 1984—.
b. 1937 in Okemos, Michigan

Gretzky, Wayne
"The Great Gretzky"
Canadian. Hockey Player
Center, Edmonton, 1978-88, Los Angeles, 1988-96, St. Louis, 1996, New York Rangers, 1996—; has set numerous NHL scoring records, including most goals in one season, 92 (1981-82), and most career points, passing Gordie Howe, 1989; won Hart Trophy, 1980-87, 1990, 1991, 1994; Art Ross Trophy, 1981-87, 1990, 1991, 1994; Conn Smythe Trophy, 1985, 1988; Lady Byng Trophy, 1980, 1991, 1992, 1994.
b. Jan 26, 1961 in Brantford, Ontario, Canada
Source: *AmDec 1980; BioIn 11, 12, 13, 14, 15, 16, 18; CanWW 31, 83, 89; CelR 90; CurBio 82; FacFETw; HocEn; HocReg 87; LegTOT; News 89-2; NewYTBS 81, 82, 84, 85; WhoAm 84, 86, 88, 90, 92, 94, 95; WhoWest 87, 89, 92, 94; WhoWor 95; WorAlBi*

Greuze, Jean-Baptiste
French. Artist
Painted portraits, murals, sentimental genre scenes.
b. Aug 21, 1725 in Tournus, France
d. Mar 21, 1805 in Paris, France
Source: *EncEnl; McGDA; McGEWB; NewCol 75; OxCArt*

Grevy, Francois Paul Jules
French. Political Leader
President of Third Republic, 1879-87; resigned over ministerial complications.
b. Aug 15, 1807 in Mont-sous-Vaudrey, France
d. Sep 19, 1891 in Mont-sous-Vaudrey, France
Source: *LinLib S; NewCol 75*

Grew, Joseph Clark
American. Statesman
Ambassador to Japan, 1931-41; warned US of possible Japanese attack on Pearl Harbor.
b. May 27, 1880 in Boston, Massachusetts
d. May 25, 1965 in Manchester, Massachusetts

Source: *AmAu&B; BioIn 1, 3, 7, 9, 10; CurBio 41, 65; DcAmB S7; DcAmDH 80, 89; EncAB-H 1974, 1996; NatCAB 55; ObitOF 79; WebAB 74, 79; WhAm 4; WhNAA; WhWW-II*

Grew, Nehemiah
English. Scientist
Botanist; from microscopic studies, first to observe sex in plants; wrote *Anatomy of Plants,* 1682.
b. 1641 in Mancetter Parish, England
d. Mar 25, 1712 in London, England
Source: *Alli; AsBiEn; BioIn 2, 9, 12; DcBiPP; DcInv; DcNaB; DcScB; Dis&D; InSci; LarDcSc; NewCBEL; NewCol 75*

Grey, Charles
English. Statesman
Prime minister, 1830-34; passed Reform Bill, 1832.
b. Mar 13, 1764 in Fallodon, England
d. Jul 17, 1845 in Howick, England
Source: *BioIn 12; CelCen; DcBiPP; DcNaB, C; McGEWB; NewCol 75; WhDW; WorAl; WorAlBi*

Grey, Jane, Lady
[Lady Jane Dudley]
English. Ruler
Ruled for nine days; imprisoned, beheaded by Mary I's troops.
b. Oct 1537 in Bradgate, England
d. Feb 12, 1554 in London, England
Source: *Alli; Benet 87, 96; BioIn 1, 2, 3, 4, 5, 6, 7, 8, 9, 10, 11, 12, 14, 15, 20; ContDcW 89; DcBiPP; DcLB 132; DcNaB; Dis&D; FemiCLE; GoodHs; HerW, 84; IntDcWB; InWom, SUP; LegTOT; LinLib S; NewCol 75; REn; WhDW; WomWR; WorAl; WorAlBi*

Grey, Jennifer
American. Actor
Films include *Ferris Bueller's Day Off,* 1986; *Dirty Dancing,* 1987; daughter of Joel.
b. Mar 26, 1960 in New York, New York
Source: *BioIn 15, 16; CelR 90; ConTFT 15; IntMPA 92, 94, 96; LegTOT; NewYTBS 87; WhoAm 95, 96, 97; WhoAmW 95, 97; WhoHol 92*

Grey, Joel
[Joel Katz]
American. Singer, Actor, Dancer
Won Tony for *Cabaret,* 1967; Oscar for film, 1972.
b. Apr 11, 1932 in Cleveland, Ohio
Source: *BiDD; BioIn 7, 8, 9, 10, 11, 15, 16; CelR, 90; ConTFT 4; CurBio 73; EncMT; FilmEn; HalFC 80, 84, 88; IntMPA 77, 78, 79, 80, 81, 82, 84, 86, 88, 92, 94, 96; LegTOT; NewAmDM; NewYTBS 87; NotNAT; OxCAmT 84; OxCPMus; St&PR 75, 84; VarWW 85; WhoAm 74, 76, 78, 80, 82, 84, 86, 88, 90, 92, 94, 95, 96, 97; WhoEnt 92; WhoHol 92, A; WhoThe 72, 77, 81; WhoWor 74; WorAl; WorAlBi*

Grey, Virginia
American. Actor
Began career as Little Eva in *Uncle Tom's Cabin,* 1927.
b. Mar 22, 1917 in Los Angeles, California
Source: *BioIn 10, 18; EncAFC; Film 2; FilmEn; FilmgC; ForYSC; GangFlm; HalFC 80, 84, 88; IntMPA 82, 92, 94, 96; InWom SUP; MGM; MovMk; SweetSg C; ThFT; VarWW 85; What 5; WhoHol 92, A*

Grey, Zane
American. Author
Sixty best-selling Westerns include *Riders of the Purple Sage,* 1912; books sold over 13 million copies during lifetime.
b. Jan 31, 1872 in Zanesville, Ohio
d. Oct 23, 1939 in Altadena, California
Source: *AmBi; BioIn 1, 2, 3, 4, 5, 6, 7, 8, 9, 10, 11, 12, 13, 14, 16, 17; CamGLE; CamHAL; CmCal; ConAu 104, 132; DcAmB S2; DcLB 9; DcLEL; EncAAH; EncFWF; EvLB; FifWWr; FilmgC; GrWrEL N; LngCTC; MajTwCW; Novels; OxCAmL 65, 83, 95; OxCAusL; PenC AM; RAdv 14; REn; REnAL; RfGAmL 87, 94; TwCA, SUP; TwCLC 6; TwCWr; TwCWW 82, 91; WebAB 74; WebBD 83; WebE&AL; WhAm 1; WhNAA; WorAl*

Grey of Fallodon, Edward, Viscount
English. Statesman
Foreign secretary, 1905-16; shaped Britain's WW I policy.
b. Apr 25, 1862 in London, England
d. Sep 7, 1933
Source: *InSci; NewC; NewCol 75; TwCA, SUP*

Grey Owl
[(Archibald) George Stansfeld Belaney]
English. Naturalist, Author
Wrote best-seller on Indian lore: *Pilgrims on the Wild,* 1935.
b. Sep 1888 in Hastings, England
d. Apr 13, 1938 in Prince Albert, Saskatchewan, Canada
Source: *BenetAL 91; BioIn 13, 16, 17, 20; CanWr; ChlLR 32; CreCan 1; DcLB 92; DcLEL; DcNAA; OxCCan; OxCChiL; TwCChW 78, 83, 89, 95; WhoChL*

Gribble, Harry Wagstaff Graham
English. Dramatist, Director
Wrote Broadway hit *Elizabeth and Essex,* 1930; directed *Johnny Belinda,* 1940.
b. Mar 27, 1896 in Sevenoaks, England
d. Jan 28, 1981 in New York, New York
Source: *BiE&WWA; ConAu 102; CurBio 45, 81; NewYTBS 81; NotNAT; WhThe*

Grieg, Edvard Hagerup
Norwegian. Composer, Musician
Considered founder, Norwegian National School of Composition; 100 works include *Peer Gynt* suites.
b. Jun 15, 1843 in Bergen, Norway
d. Sep 4, 1907 in Bergen, Norway
Source: *AtlBL; Baker 78, 84, 92; BioIn 1, 2, 3, 4, 5, 6, 7, 8, 9, 10, 12; BriBkM 80; CmpBCM; CnOxB; DcArts; DcCom 77; DcCom&M 79; GrComp; LinLib S; McGEWB; MusMk; NewCol 75; NewGrDM 80; NewGrDO; NotNAT B; OxCMus; REn; WhDW; WorAl*

Grieg, Nordahl Brun
[Johan Nordahl Brun Grieg]
Norwegian. Writer, Political Activist
Voiced opposition in poetry and on radio to German occupation of Norway in WW II; death in Allied bombing raid made him national hero.
b. Nov 1, 1902 in Bergen, Norway
d. Dec 2, 1943 in Berlin, Germany
Source: *BioIn 1; CamGWoT; CasWL; ChhPo, S1; ClDMEL 47, 80; CnMD; CnThe; ConAu 107; DcScanL; EncWL, 2; EvEuW; McGEWD 72; ModWD; NotNAT B; OxCThe 67, 83; PenC EUR; REn; REnWD; TwCLC 10; TwCWr; WhoTwCL*

Grier, Barbara
American. Editor, Publisher
Co-founder and publisher of Naiad Press, 1973; editor of the first national lesbian magazine, *Ladder,* 1957-72.
b. Nov 4, 1933 in Cincinnati, Ohio
Source: *GayLesB*

Grier, David Allen
American. Actor
Films include *A Soldiers Story,* 1984; TV series "In Living Color," 1990-94.
b. Jun 30, 1955 in Detroit, Michigan
Source: *DrBlPA 90; WhoBlA 92*

Grier, Pam(ela Suzette)
American. Actor
Films include *On The Edge,* 1985; *Something Wicked This Way Comes,* 1983; TV show "Roots II."
b. May 26, 1949 in Winston-Salem, North Carolina
Source: *BioIn 10, 11, 16; BioNews 74; BlksAmF; ConBlB 9; DcTwCCu 5; DrBlPA 90; HalFC 80, 84, 88; InB&W 80, 85; IntMPA 94, 96; InWom SUP; NotBlAW 2; VarWW 85; WhoAm 82; WhoEnt 92; WhoHol 92*

Grier, Robert Cooper
American. Supreme Court Justice
Served, 1846-70; appointed by Polk.
b. Mar 5, 1794 in Cumberland County, Pennsylvania
d. Sep 25, 1870 in Philadelphia, Pennsylvania
Source: *AmBi; ApCAB; BiAUS; BiDFedJ; BioIn 2, 5; DcAmB; Drake; NatCAB 2; OxCSupC; SupCtJu; TwCBDA; WebAB 74, 79; WebBD 83; WhAm HS; WhCiWar*

Grier, Rosey
[Roosevelt Grier]
American. Football Player, Actor
Tackle, 1955-56, 1958-66; member LA Rams' "Fearsome Foursome" defensive line; has appeared in several films, TV shows; wrote *The Rosey Grier Needlepoint Book for Men,* 1973.
b. Jul 14, 1932 in Cuthbert, Georgia
Source: *BiDAmSp FB; BioIn 8, 9, 10, 11, 13, 15; ConAu 113, X; ConBlB 13; CurBio 73, 75; DrBlPA, 90; HalFC 84, 88; InB&W 80, 85; LegTOT; NewYTBE 70, 73; WhoAfA 96; WhoBlA 75, 77, 80, 90, 92, 94; WhoFtbl 74; WhoHol 92, A*

Griese, Arnold
American. Author
Juvenile books include *Do You Read Me,* 1976; *The Wind is Not a River,* 1979.
b. Apr 13, 1921 in Lakota, Iowa
Source: *BioIn 11; ConAu 1NR, 49; LEduc 74; SmATA 9*

Griese, Bob
[Robert Allen Griese]
American. Football Player
Six-time all-pro quarterback, Miami, 1967-80; led NFL in passing, 1977; Hall of Fame, 1990.
b. Feb 3, 1945 in Evansville, Indiana
Source: *BiDAmSp FB; BioIn 7, 9, 10, 11, 13, 17; CelR; WhoAm 78, 80, 82, 84, 86; WhoFtbl 74; WhoSpor; WorAl; WorAlBi*

Griffes, Charles Tomlinson
American. Composer
Impressionist works, often adapted from Oriental, Russian schools include *The White Peacock,* 1915.
b. Sep 17, 1884 in Elmira, New York
d. Apr 8, 1920 in New York, New York
Source: *AmComp; ASCAP 66, 80; Baker 78, 84; BiDAmM; BioIn 1, 2, 3, 4, 6, 7, 8, 9, 13, 14, 19; BriBkM 80; CompSN; ConAmC 76, 82; DcAmB; DcCom&M 79; EncWB; FacFETw; MusMk; NatCAB 33; NewCol 75; NewGrDM 80; OxCAmH; OxCAmL 65; OxCMus; WebBD 83; WhAm 4, HSA*

Griffey, Ken
[George Kenneth Griffey]
American. Baseball Player
Infielder-outfielder, 1974-92, mostly with Cincinnati; f ather of Ken, Jr; first father-son combination to play in MLs at same time, on the same team (1990).
b. Apr 10, 1950 in Donora, Pennsylvania
Source: *Ballpl 90; BaseEn 88; BiDAmSp Sup; BioIn 12; LegTOT; NewYTBS 82, 89; WhoAfA 96; WhoBlA 85, 88, 90, 92, 94*

Griffey, Ken, Jr.
[George Kenneth Griffey, Jr.]
American. Baseball Player
Outfielder, Seattle, 1989—; son of Ken; first father-son combination to play in MLs at the same time, on the same team (1990).
b. Nov 21, 1969 in Donora, Pennsylvania
Source: *AfrAmSG; BioIn 15; ConBlB 12; CurBio 96; News 94, 94-1; NewYTBS 89; WhoAfA 96; WhoAm 92, 94, 95, 96, 97; WhoBlA 90, 92, 94; WhoSpor; WhoWest 94, 96*

Griffin, Archie Mason
American. Football Player
Running back; only player to win Heisman Trophy twice, 1974, 1975; in NFL with Cincinnati, 1976-83.
b. Aug 21, 1954 in Columbus, Ohio
Source: *BiDAmSp FB; BioIn 10, 11, 12, 14, 16; InB&W 85; NewYTBS 75, 82; WhoBlA 85, 90, 92; WhoFtbl 74; WorAl*

Griffin, Bob
[Robert Paul Griffin]
American. Politician, Lawyer
Senator from MI, 1966-79.
b. Nov 6, 1923 in Detroit, Michigan
Source: *BiDrAC; BiDrUSC 89; BioIn 5, 7, 8, 9, 10, 11, 12; BlueB 76; CngDr 74, 77; CurBio 60; DrAS 82E; IntWW 83, 91; NewYTBE 72; PolProf E, J, NF; WhoAm 84, 86, 90, 92, 94, 95, 96, 97; WhoAmL 90, 92, 94, 96; WhoAmP 73, 75, 77, 79, 81, 83, 85, 87, 89, 91, 93, 95; WhoGov 77; WhoMW 74, 90, 92, 93, 96; WhoWor 74; WorAlBi*

Griffin, Dale
[Mott the Hoople]
"Buffin"
English. Musician
Drummer with hard-rock group, 1969-74.
b. Oct 24, 1948 in Ross-on-Wye, England
Source: *WhoRocM 82*

Griffin, John Howard
American. Author, Photographer
Chemically blackened skin to better understand racial problems in US; wrote *Black Like Me,* 1961.
b. Jun 16, 1920 in Dallas, Texas
d. Sep 9, 1980 in Fort Worth, Texas
Source: *AmAu&B; AmCath 80; AnObit 1980; Au&Wr 71; AuNews 1; BioIn 3, 4, 5, 6, 9, 10, 11, 12, 13, 16; BlueB 76; ConAu 1R, 2NR, 101; ConLC 68; CurBio 60, 80N; DcAmB S10; EncAACR; FacFETw; IntAu&W 76; LiJour; LinLib L, S; NewYTBS 80; Novels; SouWr; WhAm 7; WhoAm 74, 76, 78, 80; WhoRel 75, 77; WhoWor 74; WorAu 1950; WrDr 76, 80, 82*

Griffin, Marvin
[Samuel Marvin Griffin]
American. Politician
Governor of GA, 1955-59; George Wallace's vp running mate, 1968.
b. Sep 4, 1907 in Bainbridge, Georgia
d. Jun 13, 1982 in Tallahassee, Florida
Source: *BiDrGov 1789; BioIn 4, 5, 6, 11, 12, 13; ConAu 108; CurBio 82N; PolProf E; WhoAmP 73, 75, 77, 79*

Griffin, Merv(yn Edward)
American. TV Personality
Hosted "The Merv Griffin Show," 1965-80s; produces TV game shows "Wheel of Fortune," "Jeopardy."
b. Jul 6, 1925 in San Mateo, California
Source: *BioIn 6, 8, 12, 15, 16, 17; BkPepl; CelR, 90; CmpEPM; ConAmBL; ConAu 130; ConTFT 3; CurBio 67; ForYSC; IntMPA 75, 76, 77, 78, 79, 80, 81, 82, 84, 86, 88, 92, 94, 96; LegTOT; LesBEnT 92; NewYTBS 88; NewYTET; VarWW 85; WhoAm 86, 90; WhoEnt 92; WhoFI 89, 92; WhoHol 92, A; WorAl; WorAlBi; WrDr 94, 96*

Griffin, Walter Burley
American. Architect
As a city planned, he designed Canberra, Australia.
b. Nov 24, 1876 in Maywood, Illinois
d. Feb 13, 1937 in Lucknow, India
Source: *BioIn 2, 6, 7, 10, 12, 21; ConArch 80; EncAB-H 1974; EncUrb; IntDcAr; MacEA; OxCArt; WhoArch*

Griffis, Stanton
American. Diplomat
Ambassador to Poland, 1947; Egypt, 1948; Argentina, 1949; Spain, 1951.
b. May 2, 1887 in Boston, Massachusetts
d. Aug 29, 1974 in New York, New York
Source: *BioIn 1, 3, 10, 16; CurBio 44, 74, 74N; DcAmDH 89; NewYTBS 74; ObitOF 79; St&PR 75; WhAm 6; WhoAm 74*

Griffith, Andy
[Andrew Griffith]
American. Actor
Made stage and film debut in *No Time for Sergeants,* 1955; played Andy Taylor on TV comedy "The Andy Griffith Show," 1960-68; "Matlock," 1986-95.
b. Jun 1, 1926 in Mount Airy, North Carolina
Source: *BiE&WWA; BioIn 4, 5, 6, 10, 11, 14, 15, 16, 17, 21; BioNews 74; CelR, 90; ConTFT 3, 10; CurBio 60; EncAFC; FilmEn; FilmgC; ForYSC; HalFC 80, 84, 88; IntMPA 75, 76, 77, 78, 79, 80, 81, 82, 84, 86, 88, 92, 94, 96; LegTOT; MotPP; VarWW 85; WhoAm 74, 76, 78, 80, 82, 84, 86, 88, 90, 92, 94, 95, 96, 97; WhoCom; WhoEnt 92; WhoHol 92, A; WorAl; WorAlBi*

Griffith, Arthur
Irish. Political Leader
Founded Sinn Fein movement, 1902; president, Irish Free State, 1922.
b. Mar 31, 1872 in Dublin, Ireland
d. Aug 12, 1922 in Dublin, Ireland
Source: *BiDIrW; BioIn 3, 5, 11, 13, 17; DcIrL, 96; DcIrW 2; DcNaB 1922; DcTwHis; EncRev; FacFETw; HisDBrE; NewCol 75; WebBD 83*

Griffith, Clark Calvin
"Old Fox"
American. Baseball Player, Baseball Manager, Baseball Executive
Pitcher, 1891-1914; manager, 1901-20; owner, Washington, Minnesota franchises, 1920-55; Hall of Fame, 1946.
b. Nov 20, 1869 in Stringtown, Missouri
d. Oct 27, 1955 in Washington, District of Columbia
Source: *BiDAmSp BB; BioIn 2, 3, 4, 7; CurBio 50, 56; DcAmB S5; WhAm 3; WhoProB 73*

Griffith, Corinne
American. Actor
Films include *Papa's Delicate Condition,* 1963; known as "Orchid Lady" for her beauty.
b. Nov 24, 1896 in Texarkana, Texas
d. Jul 13, 1979 in Santa Monica, California
Source: *ASCAP 66; BioIn 8, 9, 10, 12; EncAFC; Film 1; FilmEn; FilmgC; InWom SUP; MotPP; MovMk; ThFT; TwYS; What 2; WhoHol A*

Griffith, D(avid Lewelyn) W(ark)
American. Director, Actor
Introduced techniques that changed movies into art form; films include *Birth of a Nation,* 1915.
b. Jan 22, 1875 in Floydsfork, Kentucky
d. Jul 23, 1948 in Hollywood, California
Source: *Benet 96; BiDFilm; CmMov; ConAu 150; DcAmB S4; DcFM; EncAB-H 1974, 1996; Film 1; FilmgC; MorMA; MovMk; OxCAmL 65, 95; OxCFilm; REn; REnAL; TwYS; WebAB 74; WhAm 2; WhScrn 77; WorEFlm*

Griffith, Darrell Steven
"Dr. Dunkenstein"
American. Basketball Player
Guard, Utah, 1980-91; rookie of year, 1981.
b. Jun 16, 1958 in Louisville, Kentucky
Source: *BioIn 10, 12, 13; NewYTBS 80, 84; OfNBA 87; WhoAfA 96; WhoBlA 92, 94*

Griffith, Emile Alphonse
American. Boxer
Won world middleweight crown, 1966.
b. Feb 3, 1938, Virgin Islands of the United States
Source: *BiDAmSp BK; BioIn 6, 7, 10, 11; NewYTBS 77; WhoBox 74; WorAlBi*

Griffith, Ernest S(tacey)
American. Political Scientist
Director of the Congressional Reference Service, Library of Congress, 1940-58; wrote *The Impasse of Democracy,* 1939.
b. Nov 28, 1896
d. Jan 17, 1997 in Portland, Oregon
Source: *Au&Wr 71; BioIn 1; ChhPo S1; IntAu&W 76, 77, 82; IntWW 74, 75, 76, 77, 78, 79, 80, 81, 82, 83; WhE&EA; WhoAm 74, 76, 78, 80; WhoSSW 73; WhoWor 74; WrDr 76, 80, 82, 84, 86, 88, 90*

Griffith, Hugh Emrys
Welsh. Actor
Won Oscar for *Ben Hur,* 1959.
b. May 30, 1912 in Anglesey, Wales
d. May 14, 1980 in London, England
Source: *AnObit 1980; BiE&WWA; FilmgC; HalFC 84; IntMPA 77; IntWW 78, 79, 80; MotPP; MovMk; NewYTBS 80; NotNAT; WhAm 7; Who 74; WhoHol A; WhoThe 81N; WhScrn 83*

Griffith, Mark Winston
American. Banker
To help revitalize the community, co-founded, with Errol T. Louis, the Central Brooklyn Federal Credit Union, 1993.
b. Feb 6, 1963 in New York, New York
Source: *BioIn 20*

Griffith, Melanie
American. Actor
Oscar nominee for *Working Girl,* 1988; also starred in *Shining Through,* 1992; daughter of Tippi Hedren.
b. Aug 9, 1957 in New York, New York
Source: *BiDFilm 94; BioIn 10, 15, 16; CelR 90; ConTFT 6, 13; CurBio 90; HolBB; IntMPA 88, 92, 94, 96; Law&B 89A; LegTOT; News 89-3; VarWW 85; WhoAm 90, 92, 94, 95, 96, 97; WhoAmW 95, 97; WhoEnt 92; WhoHol 92, A; WorAlBi*

Griffith, Nanci
American. Singer, Songwriter
Storytelling folksinger influenced by Southern literary tradition, music; albums include *Lone Star State of Mind,* 1987.
b. Jul 6, 1953 in Austin, Texas
Source: *BgBkCoM; BioIn 15, 16; ConMus 3; EncRkSt; PenEncP; WhoNeCM*

Griffiths, John Willis
American. Architect
Naval designs influenced clipper ships for China trade, 1845; constructed gunboat propelled by twin screws.
b. Oct 6, 1809 in New York, New York
d. Mar 30, 1882 in New York, New York
Source: *Alli, SUP; AmBi; ApCAB; DcAmAu; DcAmB; DcNAA; Drake; NatCAB 8; TwCBDA; WebAB 74, 79; WebAMB; WhAm HS*

Grignard, Francois Auguste Victor
French. Chemist
Nobel Prize winner, 1912; noted for discovering Grignard reagent, furthering organic chemistry.
b. May 6, 1871 in Cherbourg, France
d. Dec 13, 1935 in Lyons, France
Source: *AsBiEn; BiESc; BioIn 14, 15, 19, 20; DcScB; NotTwCS; WhoNob, 90, 95; WorAl*

Grigorovich, Yuri Nikolaevich
Russian. Dancer, Choreographer
Head choreographer/artistic director, Bolshoi Ballet, 1964-95.
b. Jan 2, 1927 in Leningrad, Union of Soviet Socialist Republics
Source: *BiDD; BioIn 10; ConAu 126; CurBio 75; IntWW 74, 75, 83, 89, 91; WhoEnt 92; WhoWor 74, 82, 84, 89*

Grigson, Geoffrey Edward Harvey
English. Author, Poet
Poetry volumes include *Several Observations,* 1939; prose *Essays from the Air,* 1951.
b. Mar 2, 1905 in Pelynt, England
d. Nov 25, 1985 in Broad Town, England
Source: *Au&Wr 71; AuBYP 2; ConAu 118; ConLC 7, 39; ConPo 85; DcLB 27; DcLEL; DcNaB 1981; EvLB; LngCTC; OxCEng 85, 95; PenC ENG; TwCA SUP; Who 85; WrDr 86*

Grillo, John
English. Dramatist, Actor
Bizarre plays include *Hello Goodbye Sebastian,* 1965.
b. Nov 29, 1942 in Watford, England
Source: *BioIn 10; ConAu 117; ConBrDr; ConDr 73, 77, 82, 88, 93; ConTFT 12; WrDr 76, 80, 82*

Grillparzer, Franz
Austrian. Dramatist
Best-known works include *The Golden Fleece,* 1821; *The Waves of Sea and Love,* 1831.
b. Jan 15, 1791 in Vienna, Austria
d. Jan 21, 1872 in Vienna, Austria
Source: *AtlBL; BbD; Benet 87, 96; BiD&SB; BioIn 1, 2, 5, 7, 9, 10, 12, 13, 20; CamGWoT; CasWL; CelCen; CnThe; CyWA 58; DcArts; DcBiPP; DcCathB; DcEuL; DcLB 133; Dis&D; EncWT; Ent; EuAu; EuWr 5; EvEuW; GrFLW; IntDcT 2; LinLib L, S; McGEWB; McGEWD 72, 84; NewCBEL; NewGrDM 80; NewGrDO; NinCLC 1; NotNAT B; OxCGer 76, 86; OxCThe 67, 83; OxDcOp; PenC EUR; RAdv 14, 13-2; RComWL; REn; REnWD; RfGWoL 95; WhDW; WorAl; WorAlBi*

Grimaldi, Joseph
English. Clown
Popular attraction in Covent Garden, 1806-23; created archetypal clown "Joey."
b. Dec 18, 1778 in London, England
d. May 31, 1837 in London, England
Source: *BiDD; CamGWoT; CnThe; DcNaB; EncWT; Ent; IntDcT 3; NewC; NewCol 75; OxCThe 67, 83; PlP&P; WhDW*

Grimes, Burleigh Arland
"Ol' Stubblebeard"
American. Baseball Player
Pitcher, 1916-34; one of last to legally use spitball; Hall of Fame, 1964.

b. Aug 18, 1893 in Clear Lake, Wisconsin
d. Dec 10, 1985 in Clear Lake, Wisconsin
Source: *BiDAmSp BB; WhoProB 73*

Grimes, J. William
American. TV Executive
Pres., CEO, cable sports network, ESPN, 1982-88; pres., Univision Holdings, 1988-91; pres., Multimedia Inc., 1995—.
b. Mar 7, 1941 in Wheeling, West Virginia
Source: *BioIn 16; Dun&B 79; WhoAm 86; WhoTelC*

Grimes, Martha
American. Author, Educator
Uses British pubs for the titles and settings of her mystery novels: *The Anodyne Necklace,* 1983, *The Deer Leap,* 1985.
Source: *BestSel 90-1; BioIn 15, 17, 21; ConAu 113, 117; ConPopW; CrtSuMy; DetWom; FacFETw; LegTOT; MajTwCW; TwCCr&M 91; WhoAm 94, 95, 96; WhoAmW 89, 91, 93, 95, 97; WorAlBi; WorAu 1985; WrDr 92, 94, 96*

Grimes, Tammy Lee
American. Actor
Won Tonys for *Unsinkable Molly Brown,* 1961; *Private Lives,* 1970; married Christopher Plummer, 1956-60.
b. Jan 30, 1934 in Lynn, Massachusetts
Source: *BiE&WWA; BioIn 5, 6, 7, 12, 13; CelR 90; ConTFT 9; CurBio 62; EncMT; HalFC 84, 88; IntMPA 86, 92; InWom, SUP; MotPP; NotNAT; OxCAmT 84; VarWW 85; WhoAm 86, 88; WhoEnt 92; WhoHol A; WhoThe 81; WhoWor 74*

Grimke, Angelina Emily
American. Abolitionist, Author
Wrote anti-slavery pamphlets; sister of Sarah.
b. Feb 20, 1805 in Charleston, South Carolina
d. Oct 26, 1879 in Hyde Park, Massachusetts
Source: *AmAu&B; AmBi; AmRef; AmWomWr; ApCAB; BenetAL 91; BioIn 3, 4, 5, 6, 7, 8, 10, 11, 12, 13, 15, 16, 17, 18, 19, 20, 21; BlmGWL; ContDcW 89; DcAmB; DcAmReB 1, 2; DcNAA; EncAB-H 1974, 1996; EncARH; EncWHA; FemiCLE; GoodHs; HanAmWH; HerW 84; IntDcWB; InWom; LibW; McGEWB; NatCAB 2; NotAW; PenNWW A; TwCBDA; WebAB 74, 79; WhAm HS; WhAmP; WhCiWar; WomFir; WorAl; WorAlBi*

Grimke, Angelina Emily Weld
American. Poet, Dramatist
Wrote 3-act play *Rachel,* produced in 1916 and published in 1921; most of her poetry remains unpublished.
b. Feb 27, 1880 in Boston, Massachusetts
d. Jun 10, 1958 in New York, New York
Source: *GayLesB; InB&W 85; NotBlAW 1*

Grimke, Archibald H(enry)
American. Lawyer
Editor of the *Hub,* 1883-85, a Republican-sponsored newspaper dedicated to the welfare of black people in the Boston area; US consul to Santo Domingo, 1894-98; won Spingarn Medal, 1919.
b. Aug 17, 1849 in Charleston, South Carolina
d. 1930 in Washington, District of Columbia
Source: *AmAu&B; AmBi; AmLY; AmSocL; BioIn 4, 8, 19, 20; DcAmAu; DcAmB; DcNAA; InB&W 80, 85; McGEWB; NatCAB 26; WhAm 1; WhoColR*

Grimke, Charlotte Lottie Forten
American. Author, Educator
Wrote *Journal of Charlotte L Foster,* published 1953, depicting blacks in 19th c. America.
b. Aug 17, 1837? in Philadelphia, Pennsylvania
d. Jul 23, 1914 in Washington, District of Columbia
Source: *BlkAmW 1; ConAu 117; NotAW*

Grimke, Sarah Moore
American. Abolitionist, Lecturer
With sister Angelina, lectured for American Anti-Slavery Society and women's rights from 1835.
b. Nov 26, 1792 in Charleston, South Carolina
d. Dec 23, 1873 in Hyde Park, Massachusetts
Source: *AmBi; AmRef; AmSocL; AmWom; AmWomWr; ApCAB; ArtclWW 2; BenetAL 91; BiDMoPL; BiDSA; BioIn 3, 4, 5, 6, 7, 8, 10, 11, 12, 13, 15, 16, 17, 18, 19, 20, 21; BlmGWL; ContDcW 89; DcAmAu; DcAmB; DcAmReB 1, 2; DcAmSR; DcNAA; EncAB-H 1974; FemiCLE; GoodHs; HanAmWH; IntDcWB; InWom, SUP; LibW; McGEWB; NatCAB 2; NotAW; OxCAmL 83, 95; OxCWoWr 95; WebAB 74, 79; WhAm HS; WhAmP; WhCiWar; WomFir; WorAl; WorAlBi*

Grimm, Charlie
[Charles John Grimm]
"Jolly Cholly"
American. Baseball Player, Baseball Manager
First baseman, 1916-36; managed Chicago Cubs to three pennants.
b. Aug 28, 1899 in Saint Louis, Missouri
d. Nov 15, 1983 in Scottsdale, Arizona
Source: *NewYTBS 83; WhoProB 73*

Grimm, Jakob Ludwig Karl
[Brothers Grimm]
German. Folklorist
Best known for collection of German folk tales, *Grimm's Fairy Tales,* 1812-15; collaborated with brother; noted philologist.
b. Jan 4, 1785 in Hanau, Germany
d. Sep 20, 1863 in Berlin, Germany
Source: *AnCL; AtlBL; AuBYP 2, 3; BbD; BiD&SB; BioIn 1, 3, 6, 7, 8, 9, 12, 13; CarSB; CasWL; ChhPo, S3; DcArts; DcEuL; EuAu; EvEuW; FamSYP; LinLib L, S; NewC; NinCLC 3; OxCEng 67; OxCGer 76; PenC EUR; REn; Str&VC; WhoChL*

Grimm, Wilhelm Karl
[Brothers Grimm]
German. Folklorist
Co-author, *Grimm's Fairy Tales,* 1812-15, English translation, 1823; noted philologist.
b. Feb 24, 1786 in Hanau, Germany
d. Dec 16, 1859 in Berlin, Germany
Source: *AnCL; AtlBL; AuBYP 2; BiD&SB; CarSB; CasWL; ChhPo S3; DcEuL; EuAu; EvEuW; FamSYP; PenC EUR; REn; Str&VC*

Grimond, Jo(seph)
Scottish. Politician
Innovative leader, British Liberal Party, 1956-67.
b. Jul 29, 1913 in Saint Andrews, Scotland
d. Oct 24, 1993 in Orkney Islands, Scotland
Source: *BioIn 5, 6, 7, 10, 11, 12, 19, 20, 21; BlueB 76; ConAu 108, 143; CurBio 94N; DcPol; DcTwHis; IntAu&W 77, 82; IntWW 74, 75, 76, 77, 78, 79, 80, 81, 82, 83, 93; IntYB 78, 79, 80, 81, 82; Who 74, 82, 83; WhoWor 74, 76, 78; WrDr 76, 80, 82, 84, 86, 88, 90, 92, 94, 96*

Grimsby, Roger
American. Broadcast Journalist
Six-time Emmy Award winning TV "Eyewitness News" anchor.
d. Jun 23, 1995 in New York
Source: *BioIn 21; NewYTBS 95*

Grinkov, Sergei
Russian. Skater
Winner of two Olympic gold medals with his wife.
b. Feb 4, 1967 in Moscow, Union of Soviet Socialist Republics
d. Nov 20, 1995 in Lake Placid, New York
Source: *News 96, 96-2; NewYTBS 95*

Gris, Juan
[Jose Victoriano Gonzales]
Spanish. Artist
Major contributor to synthetic Cubism; works are of geometric form; spent most of life in France.
b. Mar 23, 1887 in Madrid, Spain
d. May 11, 1927 in Boulogne-sur-Seine, France
Source: *AtlBL; Benet 87, 96; BioIn 1, 2, 4, 5, 8, 9, 10, 11, 12, 13, 14, 16, 17; ConArt 77, 83; DcArts; DcTwCCu 2; IntDcAA 90; LegTOT; MakMC; McGDA; McGEWB; NewCol 75; OxCArt; OxCTwCA; OxDcArt; PhDcTCA 77; WhDW*

Grisham, John
American. Author
Author of *A Time to Kill,* 1989; *The Firm,* 1991; *The Pelican Brief,* 1992; *The Client,* 1993; *The Chamber,* 1994.
b. 1955 in Arkansas
Source: *Au&Arts 14; ConAu 47NR, 138; ConLC 84; ConNov 96; ConPopW; CurBio 93; News 94; WhoAm 94, 95, 96, 97; WhoAmP 89; WrDr 94, 96*

Grisi, Giulia
Italian. Opera Singer
Celebrated prima donna soprano; made annual London appearances, 1830s-50s.
b. Jul 28, 1811 in Milan, Italy
d. Nov 29, 1869 in Berlin, Prussia
Source: *Baker 78, 84, 92; BioIn 3, 7, 14, 15, 19; BriBkM 80; CmOp; ContDcW 89; IntDcOp; IntDcWB; MetOEnc; NewAmDM; NewCol 75; NewEOp 71; NewGrDM 80; NewGrDO; OxCFr; OxDcOp; PenDiMP*

Grisman, David
American. Musician
Mandolin player of American folk, bluegrass, and jazz music traditions; contributed mandolin tracks fo Grateful Dead landmark album *American Beauty,* 1970; joined Jerry Garcia, John Kahn, Vassar Clements, and Peter Rowan to form the bluegrass band, Old and in the Way, and released album *Old and In the Way,* 1974; also albums *Home Is Where the Heart Is,* 1988, *Dawg 90',* 1990, and *Dawganova,* 1995.
b. Mar 23, 1945 in Passaic, New Jersey
Source: *BioIn 14, 15; ConMus 17; EncFCWM 83; NewGrDA 86; PenEncP*

Grissom, Virgil Ivan
"Gus"
American. Astronaut
Third man in space, 1961; killed during simulation of Apollo I launching.
b. Apr 3, 1926 in Mitchell, Indiana
d. Jan 27, 1967 in Cape Canaveral, Florida
Source: *BioIn 5, 6, 7, 8, 9, 10, 12, 13; CurBio 65, 67; DcAmB S8; IndAu 1967; WhAm 4; WorAl*

Grist, Reri
American. Opera Singer
Coloratura soprano; made NY Met. debut, 1966.
b. 1934 in New York, New York
Source: *Baker 84, 92; BioIn 6, 7, 8, 9, 11, 16; DrBlPA 90; InB&W 80, 85; IntDcOp; IntWW 82, 83; IntWWM 90; MetOEnc; MusSN; NegAl 89; NewGrDA 86; NewYTBE 70; PenDiMP; WhoAm 74; WhoAmM 83; WhoBlA 75, 92; WhoMus 72; WhoWor 74*

Griswold, Alfred Whitney
American. Educator, Historian
Pres. of Yale U, 1950-63.
b. Oct 27, 1906 in Morristown, New Jersey
d. Apr 19, 1963 in New Haven, Connecticut
Source: *AmAu&B; BiDAmEd; BioIn 2, 3, 5, 6, 8, 9; CurBio 50, 63; DcAmB S7; LinLib L, S; NatCAB 53; WhAm 4*

Griswold, Erwin N(athaniel)
American. Educator, Lawyer
Dean, Harvard U Law School, 1946-67; US Solicitor General, 1967-73.
b. Jul 14, 1904
d. Nov 29, 1994 in Boston, Massachusetts
Source: *BioIn 4, 6; BlueB 76; ConAu 147, P-1; CurBio 95N; DrAS 74P, 78P; IntWW 74, 75, 76, 77, 78, 79, 80, 81, 82, 83, 89, 91, 93; OxCLaw; PolProf J; WhAm 11; WhoAm 74, 76, 78, 80, 82, 84, 86, 88, 90, 92, 94; WhoAmL 78, 79, 83, 85, 87, 90, 92, 94; WhoAmP 73, 75, 77, 79, 81, 83, 85, 87, 89, 91, 93, 95; WhoAmW 58, 61, 64, 66, 68, 72; WhoE 86, 89; WhoGov 72; WhoWor 74, 89, 91*

Grivas, Georgios Theodoros
Cypriot. Military Leader
Led right-wing guerilla group, EOKA, to unite Cyprus with Greece, 1955-59.
b. May 23, 1898 in Trikomo, Cyprus
d. Jan 27, 1974 in Limassol, Cyprus
Source: *CurBio 64, 74; EncRev; NewCol 75*

Grizodubova, Valentina (Stepanovna)
Russian. Aviator
Set world distance record for women, flying almost 4000 miles nonstop, 1938.
b. 1910?
d. Apr 28, 1993, Russia
Source: *AnObit 1993; BioIn 1; CurBio 93N*

Grizzard, George
American. Actor
Broadway appearances include *The Happiest Millionaire,* 1958; *The Cou ntry Girl,* 1972; *The Royal Family,* 1975.
b. Apr 1, 1928 in Roanoke Rapids, North Carolina
Source: *BiE&WWA; BioIn 7, 10, 11, 15; CnThe; ConTFT 6; CurBio 76; FilmgC; ForYSC; HalFC 84, 88; IntMPA 80, 81, 82, 84, 86, 88, 92, 94, 96; LegTOT; NewYTBE 72; NotNAT; PlP&P; VarWW 85; WhoAm 74, 76, 78, 80, 82, 92, 94, 95, 96, 97; WhoHol 92, A; WhoThe 72, 77, 81; WhoWor 74; WorAl*

Grizzard, Lewis M., Jr.
American. Writer
Wrote *Elvis Is Dead, and I Don't Feel So Good Myself,* 1984; *Chili Dawgs Always Bark at Night,* 1989.
b. Oct 20, 1946 in Columbus, Georgia
d. Mar 20, 1994 in Atlanta, Georgia
Source: *ConLC 86*

Groat, Dick
[Richard Morrow Groat]
American. Baseball Player
Shortstop, 1952, 1955-67; won NL batting title, NL MVP, 1960.
b. Nov 4, 1930 in Swissvale, Pennsylvania
Source: *Ballpl 90; BasBi; BiDAmSp BK; BioIn 4, 5, 6, 12; CurBio 61; WhoBbl 73; WhoProB 73; WhoSpor*

Grock
Swiss. Clown
In Europe, widely known for his comedy act using a piano and violin.
b. Jan 10, 1880 in Reconvilier, Switzerland
d. Jul 14, 1959 in Imperia, Italy
Source: *BioIn 1, 2, 3, 4, 5, 9, 11; CamGWoT; EncVaud; EncWT; Ent; FilmgC; HalFC 80, 84, 88; NotNAT A; ObitOF 79; ObitT 1951; OxCThe 67, 83; WhDW; WhoCom; WhScrn 77, 83*

Grodin, Charles
[Charles Grodinsky]
American. Actor, Director, Writer
Films include *Heartbreak Kid,* 1972; *The Woman in Red,* 1984; *Movers and Shakers,* 1985.
b. Apr 21, 1935 in Pittsburgh, Pennsylvania
Source: *BioIn 9, 11, 12, 16; CelR, 90; ConTFT 3, 9; CurBio 95; EncAFC; FilmEn; HalFC 80, 84, 88; IntMPA 80, 84, 86, 88, 92, 94, 96; LegTOT; NotNAT; VarWW 85; WhoAm 74, 76, 80, 82, 84, 86, 88, 90, 92, 94, 95, 96, 97; WhoEnt 92; WhoHol 92, A; WhoThe 77, 81; WorAl; WorAlBi*

Groening, Matt
American. Cartoonist
Created TV's first animated prime-time series, "The Simpsons," 1990; writes a weekly comic strip, "Life in Hell," 1979—; wrote *The Big Book of Hell,* 1990.
b. Feb 15, 1954 in Portland, Oregon
Source: *Au&Arts 8; BiDAmNC; BioIn 14, 15, 16, 18; ConAu 138; ConTFT 10; CurBio 90; EncACom; LegTOT; News 90; SmATA 81; WhoAm 90; WhoEnt 92; WrDr 92, 94, 96*

Grofe, Ferde
American. Composer
Wrote *Grand Canyon Suite,* 1931.
b. Mar 27, 1892 in New York, New York
d. Apr 3, 1972 in Santa Monica, California
Source: *AmComp; ASCAP 66, 80; Baker 78, 84, 92; BioIn 1, 6, 8, 9, 10; CmpEPM; CurBio 40, 72N; DcAmB S9; DcCom&M 79; FacFETw; LegTOT; MnPM; MusMk; NewAmDM; NewGrDA 86; NewGrDJ 88; NewYTBE 72; OxCMus; OxCPMus; PopAmC, SUP; RadStar; WebAB 74, 79; WhAm 5*

Grogan, Steve(n James)
American. Football Player
Quarterback, New England, 1975-90; led NFL in passing average, 1980, 1981.
b. Jul 24, 1953 in San Antonio, Texas
Source: *BioIn 11, 14; FootReg 87; NewYTBS 76; WhoAm 78, 80, 82, 84, 90, 92*

Groh, David Lawrence
American. Actor
Played Joe Girard on TV comedy "Rhoda," 1974-77; starred in Broadway production of *Chapter Two,* 1978.
b. May 21, 1939 in New York, New York
Source: *BioIn 10; ConTFT 3; VarWW 85; WhoAm 82, 84, 86*

Grolier, Jean
[Jean Grolier de Servieres]
French. Government Official
Known for collection of 3,000 bound books; NY bibliophile club, the Grolier Club, named for him, 1884.
b. 1479 in Lyons, France
d. Oct 22, 1565 in Paris, France
Source: *DcBiPP; NewCol 75; OxCDecA; PenDiDA 89*

Gromyko, Andrei Andreevich
Russian. Diplomat
Pres., USSR, 1985-88; Soviet foreign affairs minister, 1957-85.
b. Jul 18, 1909 in Starye Gromyky, Russia
d. Jul 2, 1989 in Moscow, Union of Soviet Socialist Republics
Source: *AnObit 1989; BiDSovU; BioIn 1, 2, 3, 4, 5, 6, 7, 8, 9, 10, 11, 12, 13, 14, 15, 16, 18; ColdWar 2; CurBio 43, 58, 89, 89N; EncWB; FacFETw; IntWW 74, 75, 89; IntYB 78, 79, 80, 81, 82; News 90, 90-2; NewYTBS 84, 85, 89; WhDW; Who 74, 82, 83, 85, 88, 90N; WhoSocC 78; WhoWor 87, 89*

Gronchi, Giovanni
Italian. Politician
Pres. of Italy, 1955-62.
b. Sep 10, 1887 in Pontedera, Italy
d. Oct 17, 1978 in Rome, Italy
Source: *BioIn 3, 4, 6, 11, 12; CurBio 55, 79N; FacFETw; IntWW 74, 75, 76, 77, 78; ObitOF 79; WhAm 8; Who 74; WhoAtom 77*

Gronouski, John A(ustin)
American. Diplomat, Economist, Government Official
State commissioner on taxation, WI, 1960-63; postmaster general, 1963-65; ambassador to Poland, 1965-69.
b. Oct 26, 1919
d. Jan 7, 1996 in Green Bay, Wisconsin
Source: *AmCath 80; AmEA 74; AmMWSc 73S, 78S; BiDrUSE 71, 89; BioIn 6, 7, 8, 10, 11; BlueB 76; CurBio 96N; IntWW 74, 75, 76, 77, 78, 79, 80, 81, 82, 83, 89, 91; LEduc 74; LinLib S; PolProf J; WhAm 11; WhoAm 74, 76, 78, 80; WhoAmP 73, 75, 77, 79; WhoPoA 96; WhoSSW 86*

Grooms, Red
[Charles Roger Grooms]
American. Artist
Produces animated, experimental films; mixed-media constructions.
b. Jun 2, 1937 in Nashville, Tennessee
Source: *AmArt; BioIn 7, 9, 10, 12, 13, 14, 15; BriEAA; ConArt 77, 83, 89, 96; CurBio 72; DcAmArt; DcCAA 71, 77, 88, 94; DcCAr 81; EncWB; FacFETw; OxCTwCA; PrintW 83, 85; WhoAm 74, 76, 78, 80, 82, 84, 86, 88, 90, 92, 94, 95, 96; WhoAmA 73, 76, 78, 80, 82, 84, 86, 89, 91, 93; WorArt 1950*

Groote, Gerhard
[Geerte Groete]
Dutch. Mystic, Social Reformer
Founded religious order, Brothers of the Common Life.
b. 1340 in Deventer, Netherlands
d. Aug 20, 1384 in Deventer, Netherlands
Source: *BioIn 14; DcCathB; LuthC 75; NewCol 75*

Gropius, Walter Adolf
German. Architect
Co-designed Pan Am Building, NYC with Pietro Belluschi.
b. May 18, 1883 in Berlin, Germany
d. Jul 5, 1969 in Boston, Massachusetts
Source: *AmAu&B; AtlBL; ConArch 87, 94; CurBio 41, 52, 69; DcArts; EncAAr 1, 2; NewCol 75; OxCAmH; REn; WebAB 74, 79; WebBD 83; WhAm 5; WhE&EA*

Gropper, William
American. Artist
Liberal cartoonist for *NY Herald Tribune,* 1919-35; executed murals for public buildings, illustrated his own children's books.
b. Dec 3, 1897 in New York, New York
d. Jan 6, 1977 in Manhasset, New York
Source: *AmAu&B; Au&Wr 71; BioIn 1, 2, 5, 6, 8, 11, 12, 14, 17; BriEAA; ConAu 89, 102; CurBio 40, 77N; DcAmArt; DcAmB S10; DcCAA 71, 77, 88, 94; EncAL; FacFETw; GrAmP; IlBEAAW; IlsCB 1946; IntWW 74, 75, 76; McGDA; NewYTBS 77; OxCTwCA; OxDcArt; PhDcTCA 77; REnAL; WebAB 74, 79; WhAm 7; WhAmArt 85; Who 74; WhoAm 74, 76; WhoAmA 73, 76, 78N, 80N, 82N, 84N, 86N, 89N, 91N, 93N; WhoWor 74; WhoWorJ 72, 78; WorArt 1950; WorECar*

Groppi, James E
American. Political Activist, Clergy
Former priest who gained national attention by leading 200 consecutive marches in support of open housing in Milwaukee, 1960s.
b. Nov 16, 1930 in Milwaukee, Wisconsin
d. Nov 4, 1985 in Milwaukee, Wisconsin
Source: *BioIn 14, 15, 16; NewCol 75; NewYTBE 70; NewYTBS 85; WhoMW 74, 76, 78*

Gros, Antoine Jean
French. Artist
Romantic painter of Napoleon's war campaigns: *Napoleon at Eylau,* 1808.
b. Mar 16, 1771 in Paris, France
d. Jun 26, 1835 in Paris, France
Source: *AtlBL; BioIn 4, 5, 7, 8, 9, 11, 12, 15; ClaDrA; DcBiPP; McGDA; NewCol 75; OxCArt; OxCFr; OxDcArt*

Grosbard, Ulu
American. Director
Films include *True Confessions,* 1981; *Falling in Love,* 1984; plays: *The Subject Was Roses,* 1964.
b. Jan 9, 1929 in Antwerp, Belgium
Source: *BiE&WWA; BioIn 12, 13, 16; CamGWoT; ConAu 25NR, 25R; ConTFT 2; FilmEn; HalFC 84, 88; IntMPA 92, 94, 96; LegTOT; MiSFD 9; NotNAT; TheaDir; VarWW 85; WhoAm 74, 76, 86, 88, 90, 92, 94, 95, 96, 97; WhoEnt 92; WhoThe 72, 77, 81; WhoWor 74*

Gross, Chaim
American. Sculptor
Among his compositions in modern art museums: *Handlebar Riders,* 1935; *Family of Three,* 1948.
b. Mar 17, 1904 in Kolomea, Austria
d. May 4, 1991 in New York, New York
Source: *AmArt; AmAu&B; BioIn 2, 4, 5, 6, 7, 10, 12, 13, 14, 17; BriEAA; CurBio 41, 66, 91N; DcAmArt; DcCAA 71, 77, 88, 94; McGDA; NewYTBS 74, 91; PhDcTCA 77; PrintW 83, 85; WhAm 10; WhAmArt 85; WhoAm 74, 76, 82, 84, 88; WhoAmA 73, 76, 78, 80, 82, 84, 86, 89, 91, 93N; WhoAmJ 80; WhoWor 74; WhoWorJ 72, 78; WorArt 1950*

Gross, Courtlandt Sherrington
American. Airline Executive
Co-founded Lockheed Aircraft Corp.
b. Nov 21, 1904 in Boston, Massachusetts
d. Jul 16, 1982 in Villanova, Pennsylvania
Source: *AnObit 1982; BioIn 1, 7, 13; NewYTBS 82; St&PR 75; WhAm 8; WhoAm 74, 76, 78, 80; WhoE 74; WhoFI 74*

Gross, H(arold) R(oyce)
American. Politician
Conservative Rep. congressman from IA, 1949-75.
b. Jun 30, 1899 in Arispe, Iowa
d. Sep 22, 1987 in Washington, District of Columbia
Source: *BiDrAC; BiDrUSC 89; BioIn 6, 7, 9, 10, 11, 15; CngDr 74; CurBio 64, 87, 87N; NewYTBS 87; PolProf E, J, K; WhAm 9; WhoAm 74, 76; WhoAmP 73, 75, 77, 79; WhoGov 72, 75, 77; WhoMW 74*

Gross, Michael
American. Actor
Played Steven Keaton on TV series "Family Ties," 1982-89.
b. Jun 21, 1947 in Chicago, Illinois
Source: *BiDrAPA 89; BioIn 11, 16; ConAu 93; ConTFT 6, 13; IntMPA 92, 94, 96; LegTOT; NewYTBS 84; VarWW 85; WhoAdv 90; WhoAm 92, 94; WhoEnt 92; WhoHol 92; WhoRel 92; WorAlBi*

Gross, Milt
American. Cartoonist
Created popular comic strips, early 1900s: "Banana Oil"; "Dear Dollink."
b. Mar 4, 1895 in New York, New York
d. Nov 29, 1953
Source: *AmAu&B; BenetAL 91; BiDAmNC; BioIn 3; ChhPo S3; DcAmB S5; DcLB 11; EncACom; REnAL; WhAm 3; WhAmArt 85*

Gross, Robert Ellsworth
American. Aircraft Manufacturer
Bought Lockheed Aircraft Corp., 1932; developed Polaris missile.
b. May 11, 1897 in Boston, Massachusetts
d. Sep 3, 1961 in Santa Monica, California
Source: *BiDAmBL 83; BioIn 1, 3, 4, 6; InSci; ObitOF 79; WhAm 4; WorAl*

Gross, Samuel Daniel
American. Surgeon, Author
Notable books include the *Elements of Pathological Anatomy,* 1839; *A System of Surgery,* 1859.
b. Jul 8, 1805 in Easton, Pennsylvania
d. May 6, 1884 in Philadelphia, Pennsylvania
Source: *BioIn 1, 9; DcAmB; NatCAB 8; OxCMed 86; WebAB 79; WhAm HS*

Grossinger, Jennie
American. Hotel Executive
Owned Grossinger's, noted Catskill mountain resort.
b. Jun 16, 1892 in Vienna, Austria
d. Nov 20, 1972 in Sullivan County, New York
Source: *AmWomM; BiDAmBL 83; BioAmW; BioIn 4, 8, 9, 10, 12; CurBio 56, 73, 73N; DcAmB S9; EncWB; InWom, SUP; NewYTBE 72; NotAW MOD; WhAm 5; WhoAmW 61, 64, 66, 68, 70, 72, 74; WorAl; WorAlBi*

Grossman, Lawrence K(ugelmass)
American. Broadcasting Executive
Pres. of PBS, 1976-83; pres. of NBC News, 1984-1988.
b. Jun 21, 1931 in New York, New York
Source: *BioIn 11, 12, 13, 14, 15, 16; EncTwCJ; LesBEnT, 92; NewYTET; WhoAdv 90; WhoAm 74, 76, 78, 80, 82, 84, 86, 88, 90; WhoFI 83, 85; WhoTelC*

Grosvenor, Gerald Cavendish
[Duke of Westminster]
English. Businessman
Controls international property empire, making him Britain's richest man.
b. Dec 22, 1951 in London, England
Source: *BioIn 7, 14, 15, 16; NewYTBS 84; Who 82, 83, 85, 88, 92, 94; WhoWor 91*

Grosvenor, Gilbert Hovey
American. Geographer, Editor
Driving force behind growth of *National Geographic* mag., 1899-1966.
b. Oct 28, 1875 in Constantinople, Turkey
d. Feb 4, 1966 in Baddeck, Nova Scotia, Canada
Source: *AmAu&B; ApCAB X; BioIn 1, 2, 3, 5, 6, 7, 8; CurBio 46, 66; DcAmB S8; InSci; JrnUS; LinLib L, S; REnAL; WebAB 74, 79; WebBD 83; WhAm 4; WhDW; WhNAA*

Grosvenor, Melville Bell
American. Publisher
Pres., National Geographic Society, 1957-67; edited mag., 1957-77.
b. Nov 26, 1901 in Washington, District of Columbia
d. Apr 22, 1982 in Miami, Florida
Source: *AmAu&B; WhoSSW 73, 75, 76; WhoWor 74, 76*

Grosz, George Ehrenfried
American. Artist
Violent drawings were social critiques; series included *Ecce Homo,* 1922; *The Stickman,* 1947.
b. Jul 26, 1893 in Berlin, Germany
d. Jul 6, 1959 in Berlin, Germany (West)
Source: *AmAu&B; AtlBL; CurBio 42, 59; OxCGer 76; REn; WhAm 3; WhoGrA 62*

Grosz, Karoly
Hungarian. Political Leader
Prime Minister of Hungary, 1987-1990; succeeded Janos Kadar as Communist Party chief, 1988-89.
b. Aug 1, 1930 in Miskolc, Hungary
d. Jan 7, 1996 in Goedoelloe, Hungary
Source: *BioIn 16; ColdWar 2; CurBio 88, 96N; IntWW 89, 91; NewYTBS 88; WhAm 11; WhoSoCE 89; WhoWor 89, 91*

Grote, George
English. Historian, Philosopher
Wrote classic *History of Greece,* 1845-56.
b. Nov 17, 1794 in Clay Hill, England
d. Jun 18, 1871 in London, England
Source: *Alli, SUP; BbD; BiD&SB; BioIn 3, 4, 6; BritAu 19; CamGEL; CamGLE; CelCen; Chambr 3; CyEd; DcBiPP; DcEnA; DcEnL; DcEuL; DcLEL; DcNaB, C; EvLB; LinLib L, S; NewC; NewCBEL; NewCol 75; OxCClL; OxCEng 67, 85, 95; PenC ENG; REn*

Groth, John August
American. Artist, Journalist
Illustrated, wrote introductions for books: *Grapes of Wrath,* 1947; *War and Peace,* 1961; *Exodus,* 1962.
b. Feb 26, 1908 in Chicago, Illinois
d. Jun 27, 1988 in New York, New York
Source: *ConAu 101; CurBio 43; IlBEAAW; IlrAm E; SmATA 21; WhAmArt 85; WhoAm 86; WhoAmA 73, 76, 78, 80, 82, 84, 86*

Grotius, Hugo
[Hugo de Groot]
Dutch. Scholar
Beliefs in conscience of humanity influenced American thinking; wrote *De Jur e Belli ac Pacis,* 1625.
b. Apr 10, 1583 in Delft, Netherlands
d. Aug 28, 1645 in Rostock, Germany
Source: *BbD; Benet 87, 96; BiD&SB; BioIn 1, 2, 7, 8, 12, 18, 20; CasWL; CyEd; DcBiPP; DcEuL; EncEth; EuAu; EvEuW; HisWorL; LinLib L, S; LuthC 75; McGEWB; NewC; NewCBEL; NewCol 75; OxCEng 67, 85, 95; OxCPhil; REn; WhDW; WorAl; WorAlBi*

Grotowski, Jerzy
Polish. Director
Internationally known in the experimental theatre movement; advocate of audience participation.
b. Aug 11, 1933 in Rzeszow, Poland
Source: *BioIn 8, 9, 10, 12, 14, 20; BlmGEL; CamGWoT; ConAu 105; CurBio 70; DcArts; EncWB; EncWT; Ent; FacFETw; GrStDi; IntDcT 3; IntWW 74, 75, 76, 77, 78, 79, 80, 81, 82, 83, 89, 91, 93; MakMC; McGEWD 84; NotNAT A; OxCThe 83; RadHan; TheaDir; WhoAm 92, 94, 95, 96, 97; WhoSocC 78; WhoSoCE 89; WhoWor 74, 76, 78, 84, 87, 91, 93, 95, 96, 97*

Group of Seven
[Frank Carmichael; Lauren Harris; A(lexander) Y(oung) Jackson; Frank Johnston; Arthur Lismer; J(ames) E(dward) H(ervey) MacDonald; F(rederick) H(orseman) Varley]
Canadian. Artists
Canadian art movement inspired by northern Ontario landscapes; offically formed, exhibited, 1920.
Source: *ColCR; OxCTwCA; OxDcArt; TwCCr&M 91*

Grove, Andrew S.
[Andras Grof]
American. Business Executive
President and CEO of Intel Corp, 1987—.
b. 1936 in Budapest, Hungary
Source: *AmMWSc 73P, 79, 82, 86, 89, 92, 95; BioIn 11, 12; ConAu 130; Dun&B 86, 88, 90; LElec; News 95, 95-3; St&PR 93, 96, 97; WhoAm 84, 86, 88, 90, 92, 94, 95, 96, 97; WhoFI 87, 89, 94, 96; WhoFrS 84; WhoScEn 96; WhoWest 84, 87, 89, 92, 94, 96; WrDr 94, 96*

Grove, Frederick Philip
Canadian. Author
Wrote novels of Canadian pioneer life: *Our Daily Bread,* 1928.
b. Feb 14, 1872, Sweden
d. Aug 18, 1948 in Simcoe, Ontario, Canada
Source: *BioIn 1, 2, 3, 4, 8, 9, 10; CanNov; CanWr; CasWL; DcLEL; EncSF; LinLib L; LngCTC; McGEWB; ModCmwL; OxCCan; PenC ENG; REnAL; WebE&AL; WhNAA*

Grove, George, Sir
English. Author, Engineer
Compiled *Grove's Dictionary of Music and Musicians,* four vols., 1879-89; built lighthouses in West Indies.
b. Aug 13, 1820 in London, England
d. May 28, 1900 in London, England
Source: *Alli SUP; Baker 78, 84, 92; Benet 87, 96; BiD&SB; BioIn 1, 12, 21; BriBkM 80; Chambr 3; DcBiPP; DcEnL; DcNaB, S1; LinLib L, S; NewC; NewCBEL; NewCol 75; NewGrDM 80; NewOxM; OxCEng 67, 85; OxCMus; REn; WebBD 83; WhDW*

Grove, Lefty
[Robert Moses Grove]
"Mose"
American. Baseball Player
Pitcher, 1925-41; had 300 career wins, 2,266 strikeouts; Hall of Fame, 1947.
b. Mar 6, 1900 in Lonaconing, Maryland
d. May 22, 1975 in Norwalk, Ohio
Source: *Ballpl 90; BiDAmSp BB; BioIn 2, 3, 4, 6, 7, 8, 9, 10, 13, 14, 15, 16, 17, 18, 20; DcAmB S9; FacFETw; LegTOT; NewCol 75; NewYTBS 75; WhoProB 73; WhoSpor; WorAl; WorAlBi*

Grove, William Robert, Sir
Welsh. Physicist
Invented two voltaic cells: Grove Cell, Grove Gas Cell; early supporter of energy conservation.
b. Jul 11, 1811 in Swansea, Wales
d. Aug 1, 1896 in London, England
Source: *AsBiEn; BiESc; BioIn 7; CamDcSc; CelCen; DcBiPP; DcEnL; DcInv; DcNaB C, S1; DcScB; InSci; LarDcSc*

Groves, Charles Barnard, Sir
English. Composer
Leads major British operas, orchestras; with Royal Philharmonic since 1967.
b. Mar 10, 1915 in London, England
Source: *Baker 84; BlueB 76; IntWW 83; IntWWM 85; WhAm 10; Who 85, 92; WhoMus 72; WhoWor 87, 89*

Groves, Leslie Richard
American. Army Officer
Director of Manhattan Project, which developed atomic bomb, 1942-47.
b. Aug 17, 1896 in Albany, New York
d. Jul 13, 1970 in Washington, District of Columbia
Source: *BiDWWGF; BioIn 1, 3, 9, 11; CurBio 45, 70; DcAmB S8; DcAmMiB; HisDcDP; NatCAB 56; NewYTBE 70; NotTwCS; WebAMB; WhAm 5; WorAl; WorAlBi*

Groves, Wallace
"The Father of Freeport"
American. Financier
Developed scrub land into Freeport, the second largest city, and major resort in Bahamas.
b. Mar 20, 1901 in Norfolk, Virginia
d. Jan 30, 1988 in Coral Gables, Florida
Source: *BioIn 7, 15; BlueB 76; IntWW 74, 75, 76, 77, 78, 79, 80, 81, 82, 83, 89; IntYB 78, 79, 80, 81, 82; WhAm 10; WhoAm 74, 76, 78, 80, 82, 84, 86, 88; WhoWor 74*

Groza, Alex John
[Fabulous Five]
American. Basketball Player
Center, top scorer, U of KY, 1947-49; member US Olympic team, won gold medal, 1948.
b. Oct 7, 1926 in Martins Ferry, Ohio
d. Jan 21, 1995 in San Diego, California
Source: *BiDAmSp Sup; BioIn 2, 10, 16; WhoBbl 73*

Groza, Lou(is)
"The Toe"
American. Football Player
Offensive tackle-kicker, Cleveland, 1946-67; led NFL in field goals five times; Hall of Fame, 1974.
b. Jan 25, 1924 in Martins Ferry, Ohio
Source: *BiDAmSp FB; BioIn 1, 7, 10, 12, 16, 17; LegTOT; WhoFtbl 74; WorAl*

Gruber, Frank
American. Author, Screenwriter
Most of film scripts were Westerns; wrote mystery novels, some of which were adapted to film: *Twenty plus Two,* 1961.
b. Feb 2, 1904 in Elmer, Minnesota
d. Dec 9, 1969
Source: *AmAu&B; BioIn 1, 5, 8, 9, 14; ConAu 25R, P-1; CurBio 41, 70; EncFWF; EncMys; FilmEn; FilmgC; HalFC 80, 84, 88; TwCCr&M 80, 85, 91; TwCWW 82, 91*

Gruber, Franz-Xaver
Austrian. Organist
Choral director; wrote music for Christmas hymn, "Silent Night," 1818.
b. 1787, Germany
d. Jun 7, 1863
Source: *NewCol 75; WebBD 83*

Gruber, Kelly
American. Baseball Player
Third baseman, Toronto Blue Jays, 1984-91; CA Angels, 1992—.
b. Feb 26, 1962 in Houston, Texas
Source: *Ballpl 90; BioIn 19; LegTOT*

Grubert, Carl Alfred
American. Military Leader
Youngest four-star general in history, 1951; commander of NATO, 1953-56; pres. of American Red Cross, 1957-64.
b. Sep 10, 1911 in Chicago, Illinois
d. May 30, 1983 in Washington, District of Columbia
Source: *CurBio 83N; NewYTBS 83; WhoAm 74; WhoAmA 73, 76, 78, 80N, 82N, 84N, 86N, 89N, 91N, 93N*

Grucci, Felix
American. Business Executive
Head of Fireworks by Grucci, Long Island, NY, 1980—; first to synchronize fireworks with music, 1960.
b. May 28, 1905 in New York, New York
Source: *AnObit 1993; BioIn 12, 16, 18; ConNews 87-1; NewYTBS 80*

Gruelle, Johnny
[John Barton Gruelle]
American. Cartoonist, Author
Created series *Raggedy Ann,* 1918, *Raggedy Andy,* 1920.
b. Dec 24, 1880 in Arcola, Illinois
d. Jan 9, 1938 in Miami Beach, Florida
Source: *AmAu&B; ASCAP 66, 80; BenetAL 91; BioIn 2, 10, 14, 19, 20; ChhPo, S1, S2; ChlLR 34; DcLB 22; DcNAA; EncACom; FanAl; IndAu 1816; OhA&B; REnAL; TwCChW 83, 89, 95; WorECar*

Gruen, Victor
American. Architect
Specialized in planning, building shopping centers in US.
b. Jul 18, 1903 in Vienna, Austria
d. Feb 14, 1980 in Vienna, Austria
Source: *AmArch 70; AnObit 1980; BioIn 4, 5, 6, 8, 12, 21; ConArch 80; ConAu 10NR; CurBio 59, 80, 80N; EncMA; FacFETw; IntAu&W 77, 82; IntWW 74, 75, 76, 77, 78, 79; MacEA; McGDA; NewCol 75; NewYTBS 80; WhAm 7; WhoWor 78; WrDr 80*

Gruenberg, Louis
American. Composer
Wrote opera *The Emperor Jones,* 1933.
b. Aug 3, 1884, Russia
d. Jun 9, 1964 in Beverly Hills, California
Source: *AmComp; ASCAP 66, 80; Baker 78, 84, 92; BioIn 2, 3, 6, 8; CompSN, SUP; ConAmC 82; DcCM; HalFC 84, 88; IntDcOp; LegTOT; MetOEnc; NatCAB 50; NewAmDM; NewCol 75; NewEOp 71; NewGrDA 86; NewGrDM 80; NewGrDO; NotNAT B; ObitOF 79; OxCAmL 65; OxCMus; PenDiMP A; WhAm 4*

Gruenberg, Sidonie Matsner
American. Author
Wrote *The Wonderful Story of How You Were Born,* 1952.
b. Jun 10, 1881 in Vienna, Austria

d. Mar 11, 1974 in New York, New York
Source: *AmAu&B; AuBYP 2; BiDAmEd; BioIn 10; ChhPo; ConAu 49, P-1; CurBio 74N; InWom, SUP; NotAW MOD; SmATA 2; WhAm 6; WhNAA; WhoAmW 58, 64, 66, 68, 70, 72, 74*

Gruenther, Alfred Maximillian
American. Military Leader
Youngest four-star general in US history; Supreme Military Commander, NATO, 1953-56.
b. Mar 3, 1899 in Platte Center, Nebraska
d. May 30, 1983 in Washington, District of Columbia
Source: *AmCath 80; BiDWWGF; ConAu 109; CurBio 50, 83N; IntWW 74; NewCol 75; NewYTBS 83; Who 83*

Grumman, Leroy Randle
American. Industrialist, Designer
Founder, pres., Grumman Aircraft, 1930-46; designed Hellcat, Avenger aircraft.
b. Jan 4, 1895 in Huntington, New York
d. Oct 4, 1982 in Manhasset, New York
Source: *AnObit 1982; BioIn 8, 11, 13; CurBio 45, 83; EncAB-A 29; InSci; IntWW 74, 75, 76, 77, 78, 79, 80, 81, 82, 83N; NewYTBS 82; WebAB 74; WebAMB; WhAm 8; WhoAm 74; WhoWor 74; WorAl*

Grundy, Hugh
[The Zombies]
English. Singer, Musician
Drummer with "beat group" band, 1963-67; hits include "She's Not There," 1964.
b. Mar 6, 1945 in Winchester, England
Source: *WhoRocM 82*

Grunewald, Matthias
[Mathis Gothardt]
German. Artist
Considered finest painter of German Gothic school; masterpiece, *Isenheim Altarpiece,* 1515, is now in Colmar.
b. 1480? in Wurzburg, Germany
d. Aug 1528 in Halle, Germany
Source: *AtlBL; NewCol 75; OxCGer 76; REn; WebBD 83*

Grunwald, Henry Anatole
American. Journalist, Businessman
Editor-in-chief, Time, Inc., 1979-87; US ambassador to Austria, 1987-90.
b. Dec 3, 1922 in Vienna, Austria
Source: *AmAu&B; BioIn 8, 9, 11; ConAu 107; Dun&B 86, 88; EncTwCJ; IntWW 89, 91, 93; NewYTBS 87; St&PR 84, 87; WhoAm 74, 76, 78, 80, 82, 84, 86, 88, 90; WhoAmP 91; WhoE 83, 85, 86, 89; WhoWor 87, 89, 91*

Grusin, Dave
American. Filmmaker
Won Grammy for *Harlequin,* 1985 and Oscar for *The Milagro Beanfield War,* 1989.
b. Jun 26, 1934 in Littleton, Colorado
Source: *AllMusG; BiDAmM; BiDJaz; BioIn 14, 15, 16; ConMus 7; ConNews 87-2; ConTFT 10; EncJzS; HalFC 80, 88; IntMPA 92; LegTOT; NewGrDJ 88, 94; VarWW 85; WhoAm 90, 92, 94, 95, 96, 97; WhoEnt 92; WhoRocM 82*

Grzimek, Bernhard
German. Zoologist
Directed Zoological Garden in Frankfurt; edited *Grzimek's Animal Life Encyclopedia.*
b. Apr 24, 1909 in Neisse, Silesia
d. Mar 13, 1987 in Frankfurt, Germany
Source: *BioIn 9, 10, 15; ConAu 121, 133; CurBio 73, 87, 87N; NewYTBS 87*

Guadagni, Gaetano
Italian. Opera Singer
Famed male contralto, soprano, 1740s-70s.
b. 1725 in Lodi, Italy
d. Nov 1792 in Padua, Italy
Source: *Baker 78, 84, 92; BioIn 7, 14; CmOp; IntDcOp; NewAmDM; NewEOp 71; NewGrDM 80; OxDcOp; PenDiMP*

Guaraldi, Vince(nt Anthony)
American. Pianist, Composer
Wrote, performed jazz-oriented scores for "Charlie Brown" TV specials; authored "Cast Your Fate to the Wind," one of first jazz compositions on a national Top 40 list.
b. Jul 17, 1928 in San Francisco, California
d. Feb 6, 1976 in Menlo Park, California
Source: *AllMusG; BiDAmM; BiDJaz; ConMus 3; EncJzS; NewGrDJ 88, 94*

Guardi, Francesco
Italian. Artist
Noted for imaginary landscapes, views of Venice.
b. Oct 5, 1712 in Venice, Italy
d. Jan 1, 1793 in Venice, Italy
Source: *AtlBL; Benet 87; BioIn 2, 3, 4, 5, 9; ClaDrA; DcArts; EncEnl; IntDcAA 90; McGDA; McGEWB; NewCol 75; OxCArt; OxDcArt; REn; WhDW*

Guardini, Romano
Italian. Religious Leader, Philosopher
Leading Catholic theologian who founded German Catholic Youth Movement after WW II.
b. Feb 17, 1885 in Verona, Italy
d. Oct 1, 1968 in Munich, Germany (West)
Source: *BioIn 1, 2, 3, 5, 8, 20; CathA 1930*

Guardino, Harry
American. Actor
Played on Broadway in *Woman of the Year;* films include *Dirty Harry,* 1971; *Any Which Way You Can,* 1980.
b. Dec 23, 1925 in New York, New York
d. Jul 17, 1995 in Palm Springs, California
Source: *BiE&WWA; BioIn 21; ConTFT 9, 15; FilmEn; FilmgC; ForYSC; HalFC 80, 84, 88; IntMPA 75, 76, 77, 78, 79, 80, 81, 82, 84, 86, 88, 92, 94, 96; ItaFilm; LegTOT; MovMk; VarWW 85; WhAm 11; WhoAm 78, 80, 82, 84, 86, 88, 90, 92, 94, 95; WhoEnt 92; WhoHol 92, A*

Guare, John
American. Dramatist
Won 1971 Tony for best musical: *Two Gentlemen of Verona;* wrote *The House of Blue Leaves,* 1986.
b. Feb 5, 1938 in New York, New York
Source: *ASCAP 80; Benet 96; BenetAL 91; BiDConC; BioIn 10, 12, 13, 16; CamGWoT; CelR, 90; ConAu 21NR, 73; ConDr 73, 77, 82, 88; ConLC 8, 14, 29, 67; ConTFT 1, 8; CrtSuDr; CurBio 82; CyWA 89; DcArts; DcLB 7; DcTwCCu 1; Ent; FacFETw; IntAu&W 82, 91, 93; MajTwCW; McGEWD 84; ModAL S2; NatPD 77, 81; NotNAT; OxCAmL 95; OxCAmT 84; OxCThe 83; PlP&P A; RAdv 14; VarWW 85; WhoAm 74, 76, 78, 80, 82, 84, 86, 88, 90, 92, 94, 95, 96, 97; WhoE 74, 93, 95; WhoEnt 92; WhoThe 77, 81; WorAlBi; WorAu 1970; WrDr 76, 80, 82, 84, 86, 88, 90, 92, 94, 96*

Guarneri, Giuseppe Antonio
[Giuseppe Del Gesu]
Italian. Violin Maker
Most noted in family of violin makers; signed his labels with cross and IHS.
b. Jun 8, 1687 in Cremona, Italy
d. 1745
Source: *NewCol 75; WebBD 83*

Guarnieri, Johnny
[John Albert Guarnieri]
American. Jazz Musician
Jazz pianist who performed with Benny Goodman and Artie Shaw bands during the Swing Era.
b. Mar 23, 1917 in New York, New York
d. Jan 7, 1985 in Livingston, New Jersey
Source: *AllMusG; AnObit 1985; ASCAP 66, 80; BioIn 14; CmpEPM; EncJzS; FacFETw; IlEncJ; NewGrDJ 94; NewYTBS 85; OxCPMus; PenEncP; WhoJazz 72*

Guarrera, Frank
American. Opera Singer
Baritone; made NY Met. debut, 1948; noted for Italian roles.
b. Dec 3, 1923 in Philadelphia, Pennsylvania
Source: *Baker 84, 92; BioIn 1, 4, 13; IntWWM 90; MetOEnc; NewEOp 71; WhoAm 84, 86; WhoAmM 83*

Guattari, Felix
French. Philosopher
Influenced post-1968 French intellectuals; wrote a series of books with Gilles Deleuze, including *L'Anti-Oedipe,* 1972.
b. Apr 30, 1930 in Colombes, France

d. Aug 29, 1992 in Paris, France
Source: *BiDNeoM; NewYTBS 92*

Guber, Peter
[Howard Peter Guber]
American. Producer
Produced *Missing,* 1982; *Flashdance,* 1983.
b. Mar 1, 1942 in Boston, Massachusetts
Source: *BioIn 12, 16; ConTFT 2, 4; IntMPA 86, 92, 94, 96; NewYTBS 89; VarWW 85; WhoAm 92, 94, 95, 96, 97; WhoEnt 92*

Gucci, Aldo
Italian. Business Executive
Headed family leather goods empire, making high-quality luggage, chic accessories, beginning 1950s in US.
b. May 26, 1909 in Florence, Italy
d. Jan 19, 1990 in Rome, Italy
Source: *BioIn 8, 13, 14, 16; CelR, 90; EncFash; FairDF ITA; LegTOT; NewYTBS 90; WhAm 10; WhoAm 76, 78, 80, 82, 84, 86; WorFshn*

Gucci, Guccio
Italian. Merchant, Manufacturer
Made Gucci loafer, other leather goods, beginning 1906.
b. 1881
d. 1953
Source: *DcTwDes; Entr; FacFETw; WorFshn*

Gucci, Maurizio
Italian. Business Executive
Nephew of Aldo Gucci; named pres. of Gucci Shops, 1984.
b. 1948? in Florence, Italy
d. Mar 27, 1995 in Milan, Italy
Source: *BioIn 14, 15, 16; ConNews 85-4; EncFash; NewYTBS 85; PenDiDA 89*

Gucci, Rodolfo
Italian. Fashion Designer
With brothers, made Gucci name synonymous with quality, elegance in fashion.
b. 1902?
d. May 15, 1983 in Milan, Italy
Source: *WorFshn*

Guccione, Bob
[Robert Charles Joseph Edward Sabatini Guccione]
American. Publisher
Founder, publisher, adult magazine *Penthouse,* 1965; and science magazine *Omni,* 1978.
b. Dec 17, 1930 in New York, New York
Source: *BioIn 8, 9, 10, 11, 12, 13, 14, 15, 17, 20, 21; CelR, 90; ConNews 86-1; CurBio 94; EncTwCJ; IntWW 93; LegTOT; WhoAm 84, 86, 92, 95, 96, 97*

Guccione, Bob, Jr.
[Robert Guccione, Jr]
American. Publisher, Editor
Founder, publisher of rock and roll magazine, *Spin,* 1985; son of Bob.
b. 1956 in New York, New York
Source: *AmDec 1980; BioIn 14; News 91; NewYTBS 85*

Guderian, Heinz Wilhelm
German. Military Leader
Army general who developed concept of blitzkrieg warfare during WW II.
b. Jun 17, 1888 in Kulm, Prussia
d. May 15, 1954 in Schwangau bei Fussen, Germany (West)
Source: *BioIn 3, 10, 11; EncTR; ObitT 1951; WhoMilH 76; WhWW-II; WorAl*

Guedalla, Philip
English. Author, Historian
Historical works include *The Hundred Days,* 1934; *The Hundred Years,* 1936.
b. Mar 12, 1889 in Maida Vale, England
d. Dec 16, 1944 in London, England
Source: *BioIn 1, 4, 5, 12, 13; ChhPo; CurBio 45; DcLEL; DcNaB 1941; EvLB; LinLib L, S; LngCTC; ModBrL; NewC; NewCBEL; OxCEng 67, 85, 95; REn; TwCA, SUP; TwCWr; WhAm 2; WhE&EA; WhLit; WhNAA*

Gueden, Hilde
Austrian. Opera Singer
Soprano; former Vienna State Opera star; with NY Met., 1951-60; noted for Mozart, Strauss roles.
b. Sep 15, 1917 in Vienna, Austria
d. Sep 17, 1988 in Vienna, Austria
Source: *Baker 78, 84, 92; BioIn 5, 11; CurBio 55, 88; IntDcOp; IntWW 83; IntWWM 80; InWom SUP; MetOEnc; MusSN; NewAmDM; NewEOp 71; NewGrDM 80; NewGrDO; PenDiMP; WhoMus 72; WhoWor 74*

Guenther, Charles John
American. Author
Award-winning works include *Modern Italian Poets,* 1961; librarian, 1943-75.
b. Apr 29, 1920 in Saint Louis, Missouri
Source: *BiDrLUS 70; BioIn 9, 10; ConAu 29NR; DrAP 75; DrAPF 91; IntAu&W 82, 89; IntWWP 82; WhoAm 86, 88, 97; WhoUSWr 88; WhoWor 84, 87, 89; WhoWrEP 89; WrDr 86, 92*

Guerard, Albert Joseph
American. Author, Educator
Books include *The Bystander,* 1958; *Christine Annette,* 1985.
b. Nov 2, 1914 in Houston, Texas
Source: *AmAu&B; BioIn 2, 4, 12, 15; BlueB 76; ConAu 1R, 2AS, 2NR; ConNov 86, 91; CurBio 46; DrAPF 91; DrAS 82E; OxCAmL 83; TwCA SUP; WhoAm 86, 90, 97; WhoUSWr 88; WhoWest 74; WrDr 86, 92*

Guercino, Il
[Giovanni Francesco Barbieri]
"The Squinting One"
Italian. Artist
Religious, Baroque artist, painted illusionistic ceiling at Casino Ludovisi, Rome, 1621.
b. Feb 8, 1591 in Cento, Papal States
d. Dec 22, 1666 in Bologna, Papal States
Source: *AtlBL; BioIn 3, 8, 9, 12, 13, 17, 19; DcArts; Dis&D; IntDcAA 90; McGDA; McGEWB; NewCol 75; OxCArt; WebBD 83*

Guerin, Camille
French. Scientist
With Albert Calmette developed a tuberculosis vaccine known as Bacillus Calmette-Guerin (BCG), 1921.
b. Dec 22, 1872 in Poitiers, France
d. Jun 9, 1961 in Paris, France
Source: *BioIn 5, 6; OxCMed 86*

Guerin, Jules
American. Artist
Painted murals in Lincoln Memorial, Washington, DC; LA state capitol.
b. Nov 18, 1866 in Saint Louis, Missouri
d. Jun 13, 1946 in Neptune, New Jersey
Source: *ApCAB X; ArtsAmW 3; BioIn 1; ChhPo; IlrAm 1880; NewCol 75; ObitOF 79; WhAm 2; WhAmArt 85*

Guerin, Richard V
American. Basketball Player, Basketball Coach
Guard, 1956-70, mostly with NY Knicks; coach, 1964-72, with St. Louis, Atlanta; NBA coach of yr., 1968.
b. May 29, 1932 in New York, New York
Source: *BiDAmSp BK; BioIn 6; OfNBA 87*

Guerrero, Francisco
Spanish. Composer
Wrote contrapuntal sacred music, many secular songs.
b. May 1527? in Seville, Spain
d. Nov 8, 1599 in Seville, Spain
Source: *Baker 84; BriBkM 80; NewOxM; OxCMus*

Guerrero, Pedro
Dominican. Baseball Player
Infielder-outfielder, LA, 1978-88; St. Louis, 1988—; three-time All-Star; World Series MVP, 1981.
b. Jun 2, 1956 in San Pedro de Macoris, Dominican Republic
Source: *Ballpl 90; BaseReg 86, 87; BioIn 13, 16, 21; LegTOT; NewYTBS 85; WhoAm 86, 88, 90, 92; WhoAmP 87; WhoBlA 92, 94; WhoHisp 91, 92, 94; WhoMW 92; WorAlBi*

Guerrero, Roberto
Colombian. Auto Racer
Winner of 1984 Indy 500; 1984 CART Rooke of the Yr.
b. Nov 16, 1958 in Antioquia, Colombia

Source: *BioIn 14, 16; WhoHisp 91, 92, 94*

Guess Who
[Chad Allan; Bob Ashley; Randy Bachman; Burton Cummings; Bruce Decker; David Inglish; Jim Kale; Greg Leskiw; Vance Masters; Don McDougall; Gary Peterson; Domenic Troiano; Bill Wallace; Ralph Watts; Kurt Winter]
Canadian. Music Group
Top Canadian band, 1960s-70s; hit singles "These Eyes," 1969; "No Time," 1970.
Source: *ConAu X; DrRegL 75; EncPR&S 74, 89; EncRk 88; EncRkSt; HarEnR 86; MiSFD 9; NewAmDM; PenEncP; RolSEnR 83; SmATA X; WhoAmP 85; WhoRock 81; WhoRocM 82*

Guest, C. Z
American. Author
Wrote *C.Z. Guest's Garden Planner and Date Book,* 1987.
b. Feb 19, 1920 in Boston, Massachusetts
Source: *BioIn 14, 16; CelR 90; NewYTBS 76*

Guest, Edgar A(lbert)
American. Poet, Journalist
Popular homespun verse collections include *Heap o' Livin'!,* 1916; hosted Detroit radio show, 1931-42.
b. Aug 20, 1881 in Birmingham, England
d. Aug 5, 1959 in Detroit, Michigan
Source: *AmAu&B; BiDAmNC; BioIn 1, 2, 3, 5, 6; ChhPo, S1, S2, S3; CnE&AP; ConAu 112; CurBio 41, 59; DcAmB S6; LinLib S; MichAu 80; NatCAB 44; OxCAmL 65, 83, 95; PenC AM; REn; REnAL; WebAB 74, 79; WebBD 83; WhAm 3; WhNAA*

Guest, Judith Ann
American. Author
Wrote *Ordinary People,* 1976; made into Oscar-winning movie, 1980.
b. Mar 29, 1936 in Detroit, Michigan
Source: *ArtclWW 2; Au&Arts 7; ConAu 13NR, 15NR, 77; ConLC 8, 30; DrAPF 91; MajTwCW; WhoAm 78, 80, 82, 84, 86, 88, 90, 92, 94, 95, 96; WhoAmW 95; WhoUSWr 88; WhoWrEP 89, 92, 95; WrDr 86, 92*

Guevara, Che
[Ernesto Guevara de la Serna]
Argentine. Revolutionary
Marxist intellectual with Castro in Cuban takeover, 1950s; tried to spread revolution to Latin America, Africa.
b. Jun 14, 1928 in Rosario, Argentina
d. Oct 8, 1967, Bolivia
Source: *BioIn 14, 15, 16, 17, 18; ColdWar 2; ConLC 87; CurBio 63, 67; DcHiB; HispLC; LegTOT; MakMC; RadHan; ThTwC 87; WebBD 83; WorAl; WorAlBi*

Gueye, Lamine
Senegalese. Politician
Played an important role in Senegalese politics and government, 1940s-60s.
b. 1891 in Medine, French Sudan
d. Jun 10, 1968 in Dakar, Senegal
Source: *BioIn 21; DcAfHiB 86; McGEWB*

Guffey, Burnett
American. Filmmaker
Won Oscars for *From Here to Eternity,* 1953; *Bonnie and Clyde,* 1967.
b. May 26, 1905 in Del Rio, Tennessee
d. May 30, 1983 in Goleta Valley, California
Source: *BioIn 13, 14; CmMov; DcFM; FilmEn; FilmgC; GangFlm; HalFC 80, 84, 88; IntDcF 1-4, 2-4; IntMPA 75, 76, 77, 78, 79, 80, 81, 82; VarWW 85; WorEFlm*

Guggenheim, Daniel
American. Financier, Philanthropist
Helped to form the American Smelting and Refining Co; endowed fund for Promotion of Aerona utics, 1926; son of Meyer.
b. Jul 9, 1856 in Philadelphia, Pennsylvania
d. Sep 28, 1930 in Port Washington, New York
Source: *AmBi; AmSocL; BiDAmBL 83; BioIn 3, 5, 16, 19; DcAmB; EncAB-H 1974, 1996; EncABHB 8; InSci; NatCAB 12, 22; NewCol 75; OxCAmH; WebAB 74, 79; WhAm 1; WorAl; WorAlBi*

Guggenheim, Harry Frank
American. Publisher
Ambassador to Cuba, 1929-33; co-founder of Long Island newspaper *Newsday,* 1939; son of Daniel.
b. Aug 23, 1890 in West End, New Jersey
d. Jan 22, 1971 in Sands Point, New York
Source: *BiDAmBL 83; BioIn 4, 5, 7, 9, 10, 11, 13, 16; ConAu 89; CurBio 56, 71; DcAmB S9; DcAmDH 80, 89; EncAJ; InSci; NatCAB 57; NewCol 75; NewYTBE 71; ObitOF 79; WhoAmA 78N, 80N, 82N, 84N, 86N, 89N, 91N, 93N*

Guggenheim, Meyer
American. Industrialist, Philanthropist
Founder of Guggenheim fortune who acquired near-monopoly in copper industry.
b. Feb 1, 1828 in Langnau, Switzerland
d. Mar 15, 1905 in Palm Beach, Florida
Source: *AmBi; AmSocL; BiDAmBL 83; BioIn 5, 8, 11, 14, 16, 19; DcAmB; McGEWB; NatCAB 12; OxCAmH; WebAB 74, 79; WebBD 83; WorAl; WorAlBi*

Guggenheim, Peggy
[Marguerite Guggenheim]
American. Art Collector, Socialite
Collected 20th c. art; patron to Jackson Pollock, Robert Motherwell.
b. Aug 26, 1898 in New York, New York
d. Dec 23, 1979 in Venice, Italy
Source: *Au&Wr 71; BioAmW; BioIn 1, 4, 5, 6, 7, 8, 10, 12, 13, 14, 15, 16; BlueB 76; BriEAA; CelR; ConAu 105; ContDcW 89; CurBio 62, 80N; DcAmB S10; FacFETw; IntDcWB; IntWW 74, 75, 76, 77, 78, 79; InWom, SUP; LegTOT; NewYTBS 74, 79; PeoHis; RComAH; WhAm 7; WhoAm 74, 76, 78; WhoAmA 73, 76, 78, 80N, 82N, 84N, 86N, 89N, 91N, 93N; WhoAmW 70, 72, 74; WhoArt 80; WhoWor 74; WomFir; WorAl; WorAlBi*

Guggenheim, Solomon Robert
American. Philanthropist
Founded Guggenheim Museum of Modern Art, NYC, 1937; brother of Daniel.
b. Feb 2, 1861 in Philadelphia, Pennsylvania
d. Nov 3, 1949 in Sands Point, New York
Source: *BioIn 2, 4, 16; DcAmB S4; NatCAB 12, 39; NewCol 75; ObitOF 79; WhAm 2*

Guggenheimer, Minnie
American. Philanthropist
Known for patronage of musical endeavors; founded annual summer concert series at City College of NY.
b. Oct 22, 1882 in New York, New York
d. May 23, 1966 in New York, New York
Source: *BioAmW; BioIn 2, 3, 4, 7; CurBio 62, 66; WhAm 4; WhoAmW 66, 68*

Gui, Vittorio
Italian. Conductor, Composer
Founder, Florence Maggio Musicale, 1933; noted interpreter of Gluck, Rossini.
b. Sep 14, 1885 in Rome, Italy
d. Oct 16, 1975 in Florence, Italy
Source: *Baker 78, 84, 92; BioIn 4, 10, 11; CmOp; IntWW 74, 75; IntWWM 77, 80; MetOEnc; MusSN; NewAmDM; NewEOp 71; NewGrDM 80; NewGrDO; NewYTBS 75; ObitT 1971; OxCMus; OxDcOp; PenDiMP; Who 74; WhoMus 72*

Guicciardini, Francesco
Italian. Historian, Statesman
Wrote *Story of Italy,* chief historical piece of 16th c; Florentine, friend of Medicis.
b. Mar 6, 1483 in Florence, Italy
d. May 22, 1540 in Santa Margherita a Montici, Italy
Source: *Benet 96; BiD&SB; CasWL; DcCathB; DcEuL; DcItL 1, 2; EuAu; EvEuW; LinLib L; McGEWB; NewC; NewCBEL; OxCEng 67, 85, 95; PenC EUR; REn; WebBD 83; WhDW*

Guido d'Arezzo
[Guy of Arezzo; Fra Guittone; Guido Aretinus]
Italian. Musician, Religious Figure
Benedictine music theorist; devised four-line staff, system of solmization.
b. 990?, Italy
d. 1050, Italy
Source: *Baker 84; BioIn 13; McGEWB; NewCol 75*

Guido of Sienna
[Guido da Siena]
Italian. Artist
Considered innovator of Italian art; broke away from Byzantine style; authenticity, date of painting *Madonna Hodetria* disputed.
b. fl. 13th cent. AD
Source: *McGDA; NewCol 75; OxCArt; OxDcArt*

Guidry, Ron(ald Ames)
"Gator"; "Louisiana Lightning"
American. Baseball Player
Pitcher, NY Yankees, 1975-89; won Cy Young Award, 1978.
b. Aug 28, 1950 in Lafayette, Louisiana
Source: *Ballpl 90; BaseReg 86, 87; BiDAmSp BB; BioIn 11, 12, 13, 14, 15, 16; CurBio 79; LegTOT; NewYTBS 89; WhoAm 80, 82, 84, 86, 88; WhoE 89; WorAl; WorAlBi*

Guilbert, Yvette
French. Singer
Favorite Paris, London cabaret performer whose long black gloves were trademark.
b. Jan 20, 1867 in Paris, France
d. Feb 4, 1944 in Aix-en-Provence, France
Source: *Baker 78; BioIn 4, 6, 7, 8; EncWT; Ent; Film 2; InWom SUP; NotNAT B; OxCThe 67; WhAm 4; WhThe*

Guillaume, Charles Edouard
French. Scientist
Won 1920 Nobel Prize in physics for discovering anomalies in nickel steel alloys.
b. Feb 15, 1861 in Fleurier, Switzerland
d. Jun 13, 1938 in Sevres, France
Source: *AsBiEn; BiESc; BioIn 3, 6, 15, 20; DcScB; InSci; LarDcSc; LinLib S; WhE&EA; WhoLA; WhoNob, 90, 95; WorAl*

Guillaume, Robert
[Robert Peter Williams]
American. Actor
Best known for role of Benson on TV's "Soap," 1977-81 and spin-off "Benson," 1979-86; won 2 Emmys 1979, 1986.
b. Nov 30, 1927 in Saint Louis, Missouri
Source: *AfrAmBi 2; BioIn 12, 13, 14, 15; BlkOpe; BlksAmF; ConBlAP 88; ConBlB 3; ConTFT 3, 9; DrBlPA, 90; HalFC 84, 88; InB&W 85; IntMPA 86, 92; NewYTBS 77; VarWW 85; WhoAm 86; WhoBlA 88, 92; WhoCom; WhoEnt 92; WorAlBi*

Guillem, Sylvie
French. Dancer
Etoile, Paris Opera Ballet Co., 1985-89; principal dancer, The Royal Ballet, 1989—; ballets include *Cinderella, Swan Lake.*
b. Feb 23, 1965? in Le Blanc-Mesnil, France
Source: *BioIn 15, 16; ConTFT 10; IntDcB; IntWW 89, 91, 93; News 88-2; WhoEnt 92*

Guillemin, Roger Charles Louis
American. Physiologist
Shared 1977 Nobel Prize in medicine for identifying, synthesizing three brain hormones.
b. Jan 11, 1924 in Dijon, France
Source: *AmMWSc 82, 86, 92; BioIn 11, 12, 13; IntWW 83, 91; NewYTBS 77; NobelP; Who 85, 92; WhoAm 86, 90; WhoNob, 90; WhoWest 92; WhoWor 84, 87, 89; WorAlBi*

Guillen, Jorge
Spanish. Poet
Member, "Generation of 1927" group of Spanish poets; verses include *Cantico, Clamor.*
b. Jan 18, 1893 in Valladolid, Spain
d. Feb 6, 1984 in Malaga, Spain
Source: *AnObit 1984; Benet 87, 96; BioIn 1, 4, 8, 10, 11, 12, 13, 14, 17; CasWL; ClDMEL 47, 80; CnMWL; ConAu 89, 112; ConFLW 84; ConLC 11; DcHiB; DcLB 108; DcSpL; EncWL 2, 3; EvEuW; FacFETw; HispWr; LiExTwC; LinLib L; MakMC; ModRL; ModSpP S; OxCSpan; PenC EUR; RAdv 14, 13-2; REn; RfGWoL 95; RGFMEP; TwCWr; WhAm 8; WhoTwCL; WorAlBi; WorAu 1950*

Guillen, Ozzie
[Barrios Guillen; Jose Oswaldo]
Venezuelan. Baseball Player
Infielder, Chicago White Sox, 1985—; AL rookie of the year, 1985.
b. Jan 20, 1964 in Ocumare del Tuy, Venezuela
Source: *Ballpl 90; BaseReg 86, 87; BioIn 13, 14; LegTOT; WhoAm 94, 95; WhoHisp 91, 92, 94*

Guillen (y Batista), Nicolas (Cristobal)
Cuban. Poet
Published collections *Motivos de son,* 1930; *West Indies, Ltd.,* 1934.
b. Jul 10, 1902 in Camaguey, Cuba
d. 1989
Source: *AnObit 1989; Benet 87, 96; BenetAL 91; BioIn 14, 15, 16, 18; BlkLC; BlkWr 1, 2; CaribW 4; CasWL; ConAu 116, 125, 129; ConLC 48, 79; DcCLAA; DcSpL; DcTwCCu 4; DcTwCuL; EncLatA; EncWB; EncWL 2, 3; HispLC; HispWr; IntAu&W 77; IntWW 74, 75, 76, 77, 78, 79, 80, 81, 82, 83, 89; IntWWP 77; LatAmWr; LiExTwC; ModLAL; NewYTBS 89; PenC AM; RAdv 14, 13-2; SchCGBL; SelBAAf; SpAmA; WhoSocC 78; WhoWor 74; WorAu 1950*

Guillotin, Joseph Ignace
French. Physician
Proposed all capital punishment be by decapitation; name used for machine, the guillotine.
b. May 28, 1738 in Saintes, France
d. Mar 26, 1814 in Paris, France
Source: *BioIn 7; CmFrR; DcBiPP; Dis&D; NewC; OxCMed 86; WhDW; WorAl*

Guimard, Hector Germain
French. Architect
Designer of Art Nouveau buildings.
b. Mar 10, 1867 in Lyons, France
d. May 20, 1942 in New York, New York
Source: *BioIn 8, 9, 11; DcTwDes; MacEA; OxDcArt; PenDiDA 89; WhoArch*

Guinan, Matthew
American. Labor Union Official
Pres., AFL-CIO's Transport Workers Union, 1966-79.
b. Oct 14, 1910, Ireland
d. Mar 22, 1995 in Lauder Hill, Florida
Source: *BiDAmL; BioIn 10, 20, 21; CurBio 74, 95N; WhoLab 76*

Guinan, Texas
[Mary Louise Cecilia Guinan]
""First Lady of the Speakeasies""
American. Actor
Nightclub owner known for saying "Hello, Sucker!"; Betty Hutton portrayed her in movie *Incendiary Blonde,* 1945.
b. 1889? in Waco, Texas
d. Nov 5, 1933 in Vancouver, British Columbia, Canada
Source: *Film 1; NotAW; TwYS; WhoHol A; WhScrn 74, 77*

Guiney, Louise Imogene
American. Poet, Essayist
Poem collections include *A Roadside Harp,* 1893; *England and Yesterday,* 1898.
b. 1861 in Boston, Massachusetts
d. Nov 2, 1920 in Chipping Camden, England
Source: *AmBi; DcAmB; DcCathB; OxCAmL 83; WhAm 1*

Guinier, Lani
[Carol Lani Guinier]
American. Lawyer, Educator
Professor, Univ. of Pennsylvania Law School, 1988—; withdrew nomination to assistant attorney general, Civil Rights Division, Dept. of Justice, 1993.
b. Apr 19, 1950 in New York, New York
Source: *ConBlB 7; NewYTBS 93; NotBlAW 2; WhoBlA 80, 85*

Guinness, Alec, Sir
English. Actor
Versatile stage, screen performer; played eight roles in *Kind Hearts and Coronets,* 1949; won Oscar for *The Bridge on the River Kwai,* 1958; played Ben Kenobi, *Star Wars,* 1977.
b. Apr 2, 1914 in London, England
Source: *BiDFilm, 81; BiE&WWA; BioIn 1, 2, 3, 4, 5, 6, 7, 8, 9, 10, 11, 12, 13, 14, 15, 16; BlueB 76; CamGWoT; CelR, 90; CmMov; CnThe; ConTFT 1, 8, 15; CurBio 50, 81; DcArts; EncEurC; EncWT; Ent; FacFETw; FamA&A; FilmAG WE; FilmEn; FilmgC; ForYSC; GangFlm; HalFC 80, 84, 88; IlWWBF, A; IntDcF 1-3, 2-3; IntDcT 3; IntMPA 75, 76, 77, 78, 79, 80, 81, 82, 84, 86, 88, 92, 94, 96; IntWW 74, 75, 76, 77, 78, 79, 80, 81, 82, 83, 89, 91, 93; ItaFilm; LegTOT; LinLib S; MotPP; MovMk; NewC; NewYTBE 72; NotNAT, A; OxCAmT 84; OxCFilm; OxCThe 67, 83; PlP&P; QDrFCA 92; REn; VarWW 85; Who 74, 82, 83, 85, 88, 90, 92, 94; WhoAm 78, 80, 82, 84, 86, 88, 90, 92, 94, 95, 96, 97; WhoCom; WhoEnt 92; WhoHol 92, A; WhoHrs 80; WhoThe 72, 77, 81; WhoWor 74, 76, 78, 80, 82, 84, 87, 89, 91, 93, 95, 96, 97; WorAl; WorAlBi; WorEFlm*

Guion, Connie Myers
American. Physician
Internist; first female professor of clinical medicine, Cornell Medical College, 1946-52.
b. Aug 9, 1882 in Lincolnton, North Carolina
d. Apr 29, 1971
Source: *BioIn 2, 6, 7, 9, 11; CurBio 62; DcNCBi 2; InWom, SUP; WhAm 7; WhoAmW 58*

Guion, David Wendel Fentress
American. Songwriter
Wrote Western melodies including "Home On the Range," 1908.
b. Dec 15, 1892 in Ballinger, Texas
d. Oct 17, 1981 in Dallas, Texas
Source: *ASCAP 66; BioIn 1, 6, 7, 12; OxCAmL 65*

Guisewite, Cathy Lee
American. Cartoonist
Created syndicated "Cathy" comic strip, 1976; wrote *The Cathy Chronicles,* 1978; TV special "Cathy" won an Emmy, 1987.
b. Sep 5, 1950 in Dayton, Ohio
Source: *BioIn 11, 13; ConAu 111, 113; CurBio 89; EncACom; EncTwCJ; IntAu&W 86; SmATA 57; WhoAm 80, 82, 84, 86, 88, 92, 94, 95; WhoAmW 81, 89, 91, 93, 95, 97*

Guiteau, Charles Julius
American. Murderer
Shot, killed James Garfield, Washington, DC, Jul 2, 1881; hanged.
b. Sep 8, 1844 in Freeport, Illinois
d. Jun 30, 1882 in Washington, District of Columbia
Source: *Alli SUP; WhAm HS*

Guiterman, Arthur
American. Poet
Known for humorous verse; American ballad *Brave Laughter,* 1943.
b. Nov 20, 1871 in Vienna, Austria
d. Jan 11, 1943 in Pittsburgh, Pennsylvania
Source: *AmAu&B; AmLY; ApCAB X; BenetAL 91; BiDAmM; BioIn 4, 5, 8; ChhPo, S1, S2; CnDAL; ConAu 120; DcLB 11; DcNAA; EncAJ; EvLB; LinLib L; OxCAmL 65, 83, 95; REn; REnAL; Str&VC; TwCA, SUP; WhAm 2; WhLit; WhNAA*

Guitry, Sacha
French. Filmmaker, Dramatist, Actor
More than 90 of his plays were produced; writer, director, and actor in many French films.
b. Feb 21, 1885 in Saint Petersburg, Russia
d. Jul 24, 1957 in Paris, France
Source: *Benet 87; BiDFilm, 81, 94; BioIn 1, 2, 4, 8, 12, 15, 20; CamGWoT; CasWL; ClDMEL 47, 80; CnMD; CnThe; DcFM; DcTwCCu 2; Dis&D; EncEurC; EncWT; Ent; EvEuW; FilmAG WE; FilmEn; FilmgC; HalFC 80, 84, 88; IntDcF 1-2, 2-2; ItaFilm; LegTOT; McGEWD 72, 84; ModFrL; ModWD; MovMk; NotNAT A, B; ObitT 1951; OxCFilm; OxCFr; OxCThe 67, 83; PenC EUR; PlP&P; REn; TwCA, SUP; WhDW; WhE&EA; WhoHol B; WhScrn 74, 77, 83; WhThe; WorEFlm; WorFDir 1*

Guizot, Francois Pierre Guillaume
French. Historian, Statesman
Prime Minister, 1840-48; his policies helped foment Revolution of 1848 which swept him from power.
b. Oct 4, 1787 in Nimes, France
d. Oct 12, 1874 in Val-Richer, France
Source: *BbD; BioIn 6, 10, 11; CelCen; CyEd; DcBiPP; DcEuL; Dis&D; EvEuW; LinLib L, S; LuthC 75; McGEWB; NewC; NewCol 75; OxCEng 67; OxCFr; REn; WhDW*

Gulager, Clu
American. Actor
Films include *The Last Picture Show,* 1971.
b. Nov 16, 1928 in Holdenville, Oklahoma
Source: *ConTFT 7; FilmgC; HalFC 88; IntMPA 84, 92, 94, 96; VarWW 85; WhoHol 92, A*

Gulbenkian, Calouste S
British. Art Collector, Oilman
Founder, Iraq Petroleum Co.,; major stockholder in merger of Royal Dutch and Shell oil.
b. 1869, Turkey
d. Oct 20, 1955 in Lisbon, Portugal
Source: *BioNews 74; BusPN; ObitOF 79; ObitT 1951; WhDW*

Gulbenkian, Nubar Sarkis
Iranian. Financier
Colorful, eccentric son of Calouste; director of Iraq Petroleum Co., 1955-72.
b. Jun 2, 1896 in Kadi Keui, Ottoman Empire
d. Jan 10, 1972 in Cannes, France
Source: *BioIn 5, 7, 9; NewYTBE 72; ObitOF 79; ObitT 1971*

Gulda, Friedrich
Austrian. Pianist
Brilliant classic concertist, 1940s-50s; wrote, performed jazz pieces, 1960s-70s.
b. May 16, 1930 in Vienna, Austria
Source: *Baker 78, 84, 92; BioIn 3, 4, 8, 9, 14; IntWWM 77, 80, 90; NewAmDM; NewGrDJ 88, 94; NewGrDM 80; NewYTBS 85; PenDiMP; WhoMus 72*

Guldahl, Ralph
American. Golfer
Touring pro, 1930s-40s; won US Open, 1937, 1938; Masters, 1939; Hall of Fame, 1963.
b. Nov 22, 1912 in Dallas, Texas
d. Jun 11, 1987 in Sherman Oaks, California
Source: *AnObit 1987; BioIn 6, 10, 13, 15; WhoGolf*

Gulick, Luther (Halsey)
American. Educator
Founded Camp Fire Girls with wife Charlotte, 1910; helped develop basketball.
b. Dec 4, 1865 in Honolulu, Hawaii
d. Aug 13, 1918 in South Casco, Maine
Source: *AmAu&B; AmBi; AmRef; ApCAB X; BiDAmEd; BiInAmS; BioIn 5, 9, 10, 12, 15; DcAmB; DcAmMeB; DcNAA; LinLib S; NatCAB 26; WebAB 74, 79; WhAm 1; WhoBbl 73*

Gulick, Luther (Halsey)
American. Political Scientist
Assisted the Roosevelt Administration in improving civil service.
b. Jan 17, 1892
d. Jan 10, 1993 in Vermont
Source: *AmMWSc 73S, 78S; BioIn 12, 17, 18, 19, 20; CurBio 93N; WhNAA; WhoAm 74, 76, 78, 80, 90, 92; WhoWor 74*

Gullstrand, Allvar
Swedish. Scientist
Won 1911 Nobel Prize in medicine for research on the dioptrics of the eye; developed new theory of optical images, researched astigmatism.
b. Jun 5, 1862 in Landskrona, Sweden
d. Jul 28, 1930 in Stockholm, Sweden
Source: *BiESc; BioIn 3, 15, 20; DcScB; InSci; LinLib S; NewCol 75; NobelP; NotTwCS; OxCMed 86; WhoNob, 90, 95; WorScD*

Gumbel, Bryant (Charles)
American. Broadcast Journalist
Hosted "NBC Sports," 1975-82; won Emmys 1976, 1977; host, "Today" show, 1982-97.
b. Sep 29, 1948 in New Orleans, Louisiana
Source: *AfrAmAl 6; AfrAmBi 1; BioIn 12, 13, 14, 15, 16, 17, 18, 20, 21; CelR 90; CurBio 86; DcTwCCu 5; DrBlPA 90; InB&W 85; IntMPA 86, 92, 94, 96; IntWW 93; LegTOT; LesBEnT 92; News 90, 90-2; NewYTBS 90; VarWW 85; WhoAfA 96; WhoAm 82, 84, 86, 88, 90, 92, 94, 95, 96, 97; WhoBlA 77, 80, 85, 88, 90, 92, 94; WhoE 91, 93, 95; WhoEnt 92; WorAlBi*

Gumbel, Greg(ory)
American. Sportscaster
Sportscaster, ESPN, 1981-89; CBS, 1990-94; NBC, 1995—; brother of Bryant.
b. May 3, 1946 in New Orleans, Louisiana
Source: *BioIn 13, 20; ConBlB 8; CurBio 96; News 96; WhoAfA 96; WhoBlA 94*

Gumbleton, Thomas J
American. Religious Leader
Bishop, Detroit, 1968—; visited hostages in Iran; critic of US foreign policy, urges disarmament.
b. Jan 26, 1930 in Detroit, Michigan
Source: *BioIn 10; WhoAm 86, 90; WhoMW 92; WhoRel 92*

Gumilev, Nikolai
Russian. Poet
Writings include *Pearls,* 1910; *Pillar of Fire,* 1921; executed by Bolsheviks.
b. Apr 3, 1886 in Kronstadt, Russia
d. Aug 25, 1921 in Leningrad, Union of Soviet Socialist Republics
Source: *FacFETw; NewCol 75; WorAlBi*

Gummere, William Stryker
American. Football Pioneer
With William Leggett, set up rules organized first American football game, 1869.
b. Jun 24, 1850 in Trenton, New Jersey
d. Jan 26, 1933 in Newark, New York
Source: *BioIn 11; DcAmB S1; NatCAB 13; WhAm 1; WhoFtbl 74*

Gund, Agnes
American. Museum Director, Philanthropist
Museum of Modern Art pres., 1991—; generous donor of art treasures; founder, NY's Studio in a School project, 1977.
b. 1938 in Cleveland, Ohio
Source: *BioIn 19; News 93-2; WhoAmA 93*

Gungl, Joseph
Hungarian. Composer, Bandleader
Bandmaster; composed over 300 popular dances, marches.
b. Dec 1, 1810 in Zsambek, Hungary
d. Jan 31, 1889 in Weimar, Germany
Source: *Baker 78, 84, 92; MusMk; NewGrDM 80; OxCMus*

Gunn, Hartford Nelson, Jr.
American. TV Executive
Founder, pres., PBS, 1971-80.
b. Dec 24, 1926 in Port Washington, New York
d. Jan 2, 1986 in Boston, Massachusetts
Source: *BioIn 10; ConNews 86-2; NewYTBS 86; NewYTET; WhAm 9; WhoAm 76, 78, 80, 82; WhoE 79; WhoFI 74, 75, 77, 79; WhoWor 76, 78, 80, 82*

Gunn, Moses
American. Actor, Director
Broadway plays include *First Breeze of Summer,* 1975; *I Have a Dream,* 1977; joined Negro Ensemble Co., 1967-68.
b. Oct 2, 1929 in Saint Louis, Missouri
d. Dec 17, 1993 in Guilford, Connecticut
Source: *AnObit 1993; BioIn 8, 14, 15, 19, 20; CamGWoT; ConBlB 10; ConTFT 4, 12; DrBlPA, 90; FilmEn; HalFC 80, 84, 88; InB&W 80; IntMPA 77, 80, 84, 86, 88, 92, 94; LegTOT; VarWW 85; WhAm 11; WhoAfA 96; WhoAm 74, 76, 78, 80, 82, 84, 86, 88, 90, 92, 94; WhoBlA 75, 77, 80; WhoHol 92, A; WhoThe 72, 77, 81*

Gunn, Thom(son William)
English. Poet
Works include *The Passages of Joy,* 1982; won The Lenore Marshall/*Nation* Poetry Prize, 1993.
b. Aug 29, 1929 in Gravesend, England
Source: *AmAu&B; Au&Wr 71; Benet 87, 96; BioIn 4, 10, 12, 13, 16; BlmGEL; BlueB 76; CamGEL; CamGLE; CasWL; ChhPo, S1, S2; CnDBLB 8; ConAu 9NR, 17R, 33NR; ConLC 3, 6, 18, 32, 81; ConPo 70, 75, 80, 85, 91, 96; CurBio 88; DcLB 27; DrAP 75; DrAPF 91; DrAS 74E, 78E, 82E; EngPo; Focus; GayLL; GrWrEL P; IntAu&W 77, 82, 86, 89, 91, 93; IntWW 74, 75, 76, 77, 78, 79, 80, 81, 82, 83, 89, 93; IntWWP 77, 82; LegTOT; LinLib L; LngCTC; MajTwCW; MakMC; ModBrL, S1, S2; OxCEng 85, 95; OxCTwCP; PenC ENG; RAdv 1, 13-1; REn; RfGEnL 91; RGFMBP; RGTwCWr; St&PR 91; TwCWr; WebE&AL; Who 74, 82, 83, 85, 88, 90, 92, 94; WhoAm 74, 76, 78, 80, 82, 84, 86, 88, 92, 94, 95, 96, 97; WhoTwCL; WhoUSWr 88; WhoWor 74; WhoWrEP 89, 92, 95; WorAu 1950; WrDr 76, 80, 82, 84, 86, 88, 90, 92, 94, 96*

Gunning, Lucille C
American. Physician
As director of physical medicine and rehabilitation at the Children's Medical Center, Dayton, OH, developed a program for treating children with disabilities with other children in the hospital.
b. Feb 21, 1922 in New York, New York
Source: *NotBlAW 1*

Gunnison, Foster
American. Architect
Pioneer in prefabricated housing, c. 1930s.
b. Jun 9, 1896 in New York, New York
d. Oct 19, 1961 in Saint Petersburg, Florida
Source: *BioIn 7; DcAmB S7; NatCAB 49; WhAm 4*

Guns n' Roses
[Slash; Steven Adler; Duff McKagan; Axl Rose; Izzy Stradlin]
American. Music Group
Formed 1985; heavy metal album *Appetite for Destruction,* 1987, went platinum.
Source: *BioIn 16, 17, 18, 19, 20, 21; ConMus 2; EncRkSt; WhoAm 94; WhoEnt 92*

Gunther, Hans F. K
German. Anthropologist, Author
Laid groundwork for Nazi doctrine: *A Short Ethnology of the German People,* 1929; proponent of Nordic supremacy.
b. Feb 16, 1891 in Freiburg, Germany
d. Sep 25, 1968 in Freiburg, Germany (West)
Source: *EncTR*

Gunther, John
American. Author
Wrote *Inside Europe,* 1936; *Death Be Not Proud,* 1949.
b. Aug 30, 1901 in Chicago, Illinois
d. May 29, 1970 in New York, New York
Source: *AmAu&B; AmNov; AuBYP 2, 3; Benet 87; BenetAL 91; BioIn 1, 2, 3, 4, 5, 6, 7, 8, 9, 16, 17; ConAu 9R, 25R; CurBio 61, 70; DcAmB S8; EncAJ; EvLB; FacFETw; JrnUS; LegTOT; LinLib L, S; LngCTC; ObitT 1961; OxCAmL 65, 83, 95; PenC AM; RAdv 14, 13-3; REn; REnAL; ScF&FL 1, 2; SmATA 2; TwCA, SUP; WebAB 74, 79; WhAm 6; WorAl; WorAlBi*

Gunzberg, Nicolas de, Baron
"Nicky"
American. Fashion Editor
Elegant senior fashion editor, *Vogue* mag., from 1940s.
b. 1904 in Paris
d. Feb 20, 1981 in New York, New York
Source: *NewYTBS 81; WorFshn*

Guo Moruo
Chinese. Scholar, Writer
Important 20th c. figure in Chinese intellectual and literary life.
b. Nov 1892 in Shawan, China
d. Jun 12, 1978 in Beijing, China
Source: *BioIn 16, 18; McGEWD 84*

Guptill, Arthur Leighton
American. Publisher, Author
Founder, pres., Watson-Guptill Publications, specialists in art books, 1937; art director, *Gourmet* mag., 1941-53.
b. Mar 19, 1891 in Gorham, Maine
d. Feb 29, 1956 in Stamford, Connecticut
Source: *BioIn 3, 4; CurBio 55, 56; ObitOF 79; WhAm 3; WhNAA*

Gurdjieff, George Ivanovitch
Armenian. Mystic
Founder, Institute for the Harmonious Development of Man, 1919.
b. 1872?
d. Oct 29, 1949 in Neuilly, France
Source: *BioIn 10; ObitOF 79; OxCEng 85*

Gurganus, Allan
American. Author
Won Los Angeles Times Book Award for *White People,* 1991; also wrote *The Oldest Living Confederate Widow Tells All,* 1989.
b. Jun 11, 1947 in Rocky Mount, North Carolina
Source: *Benet 96; BestSel 90-1; ConAu 135; ConGAN; ConLC 70; ConPopW; GayLL; IntAu&W 91; WorAu 1985; WrDr 94, 96*

Gurie, Sigrid
[Sigrid Gurie Haukelid]
American. Actor
Protege of Sam Goldwyn; publicized as "The Siren of the Fjords," brief film career .
b. May 18, 1911 in New York, New York
d. Aug 14, 1969 in Mexico City, Mexico
Source: *BioIn 8, 21; FilmEn; FilmgC; HalFC 80, 84, 88; InWom SUP; ThFT; WhoHol B; WhScrn 74, 77, 83*

Gurney, A(lbert) R(amsdell), Jr.
[Pete Gurney]
American. Dramatist
Plays describe WASP society: *Scenes from American Life,* 1971.
b. Nov 1, 1930 in Buffalo, New York
Source: *AmMWSc 92; Benet 96; BioIn 13, 14, 15, 16, 17; CamGWoT; ConAmD; ConAu 32NR, 77; ConDr 77, 82, 88, 93; ConLC 30, 32, 50, 54; ConTFT 4; CurBio 86; CyWA 89; DrAPF 80, 87; DrAS 74E, 78E, 82E; IntAu&W 91, 93; NatPD 77, 81; NewYTBS 83, 89; ScF&FL 1; WhoAm 74, 76, 78, 80, 82, 84, 86, 88, 90, 92, 94, 95, 96, 97; WhoE 93, 95, 97; WhoEnt 92; WhoThe 81; WhoUSWr 88; WhoWrEP 89, 92, 95; WorAu 1980; WrDr 80, 82, 84, 86, 88, 90, 92, 94, 96*

Gurney, Dan
American. Auto Racer, Businessman
Driver, 1955-70; owner, All American Racers, Inc; manager, Eagle Racing Team, 1964, which had Indy 500 winners, 1968-75.
b. Apr 13, 1931
Source: *BiDAmSp OS; BioIn 6, 7, 8, 10, 12, 13; BioNews 74; WhoAm 86, 90; WhoEnt 92; WhoWest 92*

Gurney, Edward John
American. Politician, Lawyer
Rep. senator from FL, 1969-75.
b. Jan 12, 1914 in Portland, Maine
d. May 14, 1996 in Winter Park, Florida
Source: *BiDrAC; BiDrUSC 89; BioIn 8, 9, 10, 11, 12; BioNews 74; BlueB 76; CngDr 74; IntWW 74, 75; WhoAm 74, 76, 78, 80, 82, 84, 86, 88, 90; WhoAmP 73, 75, 77, 79, 81, 83, 85, 87, 89, 91, 93, 95; WhoGov 72, 75; WhoSSW 73, 75*

Gustaf Adolf VI
Swedish. Ruler
Reigned 1950-73; founded Swedish Institute in Rome; succeeded by grandson, Carl Gustaf XVI.
b. Nov 11, 1882 in Stockholm, Sweden
d. Sep 15, 1973 in Helsingborg, Sweden
Source: *BioIn 10; ConAu 45; NewCol 75*

Gustafson, Karin
American. Actor
Film debut in *Taps,* 1981.
b. Jun 23, 1959 in Miami, Florida
Source: *ConTFT 3*

Gustavus Adophus
[Gustav II Adolph]
Swedish. Ruler
Son of Charles IX; ruled, 1611-32; victorious in battle with Russia, 1613-17.
b. Dec 9, 1594 in Stockholm, Sweden
d. Nov 6, 1632 in Lutzen, Saxony
Source: *NewC; NewCol 75; OxCGer 76; WebBD 83*

Guston, Philip
American. Artist
Muralist for WPA projects, 1936-40, developed into abstract expressionist; works include *Altar,* 1953.
b. Jun 27, 1913 in Montreal, Quebec, Canada
d. Jun 7, 1980 in Woodstock, New York
Source: *AnObit 1980; BioIn 9, 10, 11, 12, 13, 14, 15, 16, 20; BriEAA; ConArt 77, 83, 89, 96; CurBio 71, 80N; DcAmArt; DcArts; DcCAA 71, 77, 88, 94; DcCAr 81; DcTwCCu 1; EncWB; NewCol 75; NewYTBS 80; OxCTwCA; OxDcArt; PhDcTCA 77; WhAm 7; WhoAm 74, 76, 78, 80; WhoAmA 73, 76, 78, 80, 82N, 84N, 86N, 89N, 91N, 93N; WhoWor 74; WorArt 1950*

Gutenberg, Johann Gensfleischzur Laden Zum
German. Printer
Believed to be first European to print using moveable type, ca. 1454; famed for 42-line Bible.
b. Feb 23, 1400? in Mainz, Germany
d. Feb 3, 1468? in Mainz, Germany
Source: *NewC; NewCol 75; OxCGer 76; REn*

Guterson, David
American. Author
Wrote *The Country Ahead of Us, the Country Behind,* 1989; *Snow Falling on Cedars,* 1994.
b. May 4, 1956 in Seattle, Washington
Source: *ConAu 132; ConLC 91; CurBio 96; WhoAm 96, 97; WrDr 94, 96*

Gutfreund, Yosef
Israeli. Olympic Athlete, Victim
One of 11 members of Israeli Olympic team kidnapped and killed by Arab terrorists during Summer Olympic games.
b. 1931?, Romania
d. Sep 5, 1972 in Munich, Germany (West)

Guth, Alan Harvey
American. Physicist
Known for revolutionary theories of cosmology, expanded on Big Bang theory.
b. Feb 27, 1947 in New Brunswick, New Jersey
Source: *AmMWSc 82, 86, 89, 92, 95; BioIn 15, 16; CurBio 87; IntWW 89, 91, 93; WhoAm 82, 84, 86, 88, 90, 92, 94, 95, 96; WhoE 95; WhoFrS 84; WhoScEn 94, 96; WhoTech 89*

Guthrie, A(lfred) B(ertram), Jr.
American. Journalist, Author
Novels include Pulitzer-winner *The Way West,* 1950.
b. Jan 13, 1901 in Bedford, Indiana
d. Apr 26, 1991 in Choteau, Montana
Source: *AmAu&B; AmNov; Benet 96; BenetAL 91; BiDrAPA 89; BioIn 1, 2, 4, 5, 7, 8, 10, 14, 15, 16, 17, 18; CnDAL; ConAu 57, 134; ConLC 23, 70; ConNov 72, 76, 82, 86; CurBio 91N; CyWA 58; DcLB 6; DcLEL 1940; DrAF 76; DrAPF 89, 91; HalFC 84, 88; IndAu 1917; ModAL; NewYTBS 91; Novels; OxCAmL 65, 83, 95; REnAL; REnAW; SmATA 62, 67; TwCA SUP; TwCWW 91; WhAm 10; WhoAm 74, 76, 78, 80, 82, 84, 86, 88, 90; WhoPNW; WhoWest 74, 76; WhoWor 74; WrDr 76, 84, 90*

Guthrie, Arlo Davy
American. Singer
Son of Woody Guthrie; best known for hit "Alice's Restaurant," 1969.
b. Jul 10, 1947 in New York, New York
Source: *AmAu&B; BenetAL 91; BioIn 7, 11, 12, 13, 14, 15; BkPepl; CelR 90; ConAu 113; ConMus 6; CurBio 82; EncFCWM 69, 83; EncRk 88; FacFETw; HalFC 88; HarEnR 86; NewAmDM; NewGrDA 86; OxCPMus; PenEncP; WhoAm 82; WorAlBi*

Guthrie, Edwin Ray
American. Psychologist
His studies dealt with the psychology of learning and the role association plays.
b. Jan 9, 1886 in Lincoln, Nebraska
d. Apr 23, 1959 in Seattle, Washington
Source: *BiDPsy; BioIn 5; DcAmB S6; McGEWB; NamesHP*

Guthrie, Janet
American. Auto Racer
First woman to qualify and drive in Indianapolis 500, 1977.
b. Mar 7, 1938 in Iowa City, Iowa
Source: *BiDAmSp OS; BioIn 10, 11, 12, 17; CurBio 78; EncWomS; HerW 84; InWom SUP; LegTOT; LibW; NewYTBS 76; WhoAm 78, 80, 82, 84, 86, 88, 90, 92, 94, 95, 96, 97; WhoAmW 83, 85, 87, 89, 95, 97; WhoWor 80, 82, 84, 87, 89; WomFir; WorAl; WorAlBi*

Guthrie, Samuel
American. Physician
Discovered chloroform, 1831.
b. 1782 in Brimfield, Massachusetts
d. Oct 19, 1848 in Sackets Harbor, New York
Source: *AmBi; ApCAB; AsBiEn; BiDAmS; BiESc; BiInAmS; BioIn 1; DcAmB; DcAmMeB, 84; DcNAA; Drake; InSci; LarDcSc; LinLib S; NatCAB 11; NewCol 75; TwCBDA; WhAm HS*

Guthrie, Tyrone, Sir
[William Tyrone Guthrie]
English. Director
Director, London's Old Vic, 1933-45; Stratford's Shakespeare Festival, 1953-57.
b. Jul 2, 1900 in Tunbridge Wells, England
d. May 15, 1971 in Newbliss, Ireland
Source: *BiE&WWA; BioIn 3, 4, 5, 6, 8, 9, 10, 11, 12, 17, 20; CamGWoT; CmOp; CnThe; ConAu 29R, 123; CreCan 1; CurBio 54, 71, 71N; DcAmB S9; DcArts; DcIrB 78, 88; DcNaB 1971; EncWB; EncWT; Ent; FacFETw; GrStDi; IntDcOp; LinLib S; MetOEnc; NewC; NewCBEL; NewGrDO; NewYTBE 71; NotNAT A, B; ObitOF 79; ObitT 1971; OxCAmL 83; OxCAmT 84; OxCCanT; OxCThe 67, 83; OxDcOp; PlP&P; TheaDir; WhAm 5; WhE&EA; WhoHol B; WhoThe 72; WhScrn 83; WhThe; WorAl; WorAlBi*

Guthrie, Woody
[Woodrow Wilson Guthrie]
American. Songwriter
Folksinger, balladeer; wrote over 1000 songs, 1930s-40s, including "This Land is Your Land," 1956; Hall of Fame, 1988; father of Arlo.
b. Jul 14, 1912 in Okemah, Oklahoma
d. Oct 3, 1967 in New York, New York
Source: *AmAu&B; AmCulL; AmDec 1930; AmSocL; AmSong; Baker 78, 84, 92; BenetAL 91; BgBkCoM; BiDAmM; BioIn 6, 7, 8, 9, 10, 11, 12, 13, 14, 15, 16, 17, 18, 19, 20, 21; BluesWW; CmpEPM; ConAu 93, 113; ConLC 35; ConMuA 80A; ConMus 2; CounME 74, 74A; CurBio 63, 67; DcAmB S8; DcArts; EncAB-H 1974, 1996; EncAL; EncFCWM 69, 83; EncRk 88; EncWB; FacFETw; HarEnCM 87; HarEnR 86; IlEncCM; IlEncRk; LegTOT; MusMk; NewAmDM; NewGrDA 86; NewGrDM 80; ObitOF 79; OnThGG; OxCAmL 95; OxCPMus; PenEncP; PeoHis; RComAH; REnAW; RolSEnR 83; WebAB 74, 79; WhAm 4; WhoRock 81; WhoRocM 82; WorAl; WorAlBi*

Gutierrez, Cesar Dario
"Coca"
Venezuelan. Baseball Player
Infielder, 1967, 1969-71; holds ML record for consecutive hits in one game, seven 1971.
b. Jan 26, 1943 in Coro, Venezuela
Source: *Ballpl 90; BaseEn 88; BioIn 10; WhoProB 73*

Gutman, Roy
American. Journalist
Newsday reporter; won a 1993 Pulitzer for international reporting.
b. Mar 5, 1944 in New York, New York
Source: *ConAu 131*

Gutsu, Tatiana
Russian. Gymnast
Won gold medal in all-around competition and silver for uneven bars at the 1992 Summer Olympics.

Guttenberg, Steve
American. Actor
Starred in films *Cocoon,* 1985, *Three Men and a Baby,* 1987.
b. Aug 24, 1958 in New York, New York
Source: *BioIn 12, 13, 14, 15; ConTFT 2, 6; EncAFC; HalFC 88; HolBB; IntMPA 86, 88, 92, 94, 96; LegTOT; QDrFCA 92; VarWW 85; WhoAm 88, 90, 92, 94, 95, 96, 97; WhoEnt 92; WhoHol 92; WorAlBi*

Gutzkow, Karl Ferdinand
German. Writer, Critic
A leader, Young Germany literary group; wrote nine-vol. social novel *Die Ritter vom Geiste,* 1850-52.
b. Mar 17, 1811 in Berlin, Prussia
d. Dec 16, 1878 in Sachsenhausen, Prussia
Source: *BbD; BiD&SB; BioIn 6, 7, 8; CasWL; CelCen; DcEuL; EncWT; EuAu; EvEuW; McGEWD 72, 84; NewCol 75; NotNAT B; OxCGer 76, 86; OxCThe 67, 83; PenC EUR; REn*

Guy, Buddy
American. Musician
Influential blues guitarist, stage performer.
b. Jul 30, 1936 in Lettsworth, Louisiana
Source: *BiDAmM; BiDJaz; BioIn 8; ConMuA 80A; ConMus 4; EncRk 88; NewGrDA 86; OnThGG; PenEncP; WhoAm 92, 94, 95, 96, 97; WhoRocM 82*

Guy, Jasmine
American. Actor
Played Whitley Gilbert, "A Different World," 1987-93; movies include *School Daze,* 1988.
b. Mar 10, 1964 in Boston, Massachusetts
Source: *BioIn 15, 16; ConBlB 2; ConTFT 9; DcTwCCu 5; DrBlPA 90; LegTOT; WhoAfA 96; WhoBlA 92, 94; WhoEnt 92; WhoHol 92*

Guy, Ray
[William Ray Guy]
American. Football Player
Punter, Oakland, LA Raiders, 1973-87; led NFL in punting three times; played in seven Pro Bowls.
b. Dec 22, 1949 in Swainsboro, Georgia
Source: *BiDAmSp FB; BioIn 9, 11, 16; FootReg 86; LegTOT; WhoAm 78; WhoFtbl 74; WorAl*

Guy, Rosa Cuthbert
American. Author
Young adult books include *The Disappearance,* 1979; *I Heard a Bird Sing,* 1986.
b. Sep 1, 1928 in San Fernando, Trinidad and Tobago
Source: *ArtclWW 2; Au&Arts 4; BioIn 12, 15, 16; BlkAWP; BlkWr 1; ConAu 14NR, 17NR, 17R; ConBlAP 88; ConLC 26; DcLB 33; DrAPF 89; FemiCLE; FifBJA; OxCChiL; SmATA 14; TwCChW 83; WhoBlA 92; WrDr 84, 88*

Guy-Blache, Alice
French. Director
World's first woman director; first film *La Fee aux Choux,* 1896; made US films, 1910-20.
b. Jul 1, 1873 in Paris, France
d. 1968 in Mahwah, New Jersey
Source: *BioIn 15; DcFM; FilmEn; FilmgC; HalFC 80, 84, 88; MovMk; OxCFilm; WorFDir 1*

Guyer, David Leigh
American. Social Reformer
President of Save the Children Federation, 1977-87.
b. Sep 24, 1925 in Pasadena, California
d. May 14, 1988 in Honolulu, Hawaii
Source: *BioIn 16; BlueB 76; ConNews 88-1; WhoAm 74, 76, 78, 80*

Guyer, Tennyson
American. Politician
Representative from OH since 1973; noted for patriotic speeches.
b. Nov 29, 1913 in Findlay, Ohio
d. Apr 12, 1981 in Alexandria, Virginia
Source: *AlmAP 78, 80; BiDrUSC 89; BioIn 12; CngDr 74, 77, 79; WhAm 8; WhoAm 74, 76, 78, 80; WhoAmP 73, 75, 77, 79; WhoGov 75, 77; WhoMW 76, 78, 80*

Guynemer, Georges Marie
French. Pilot
WWI combat ace; with 53 air victories, he gained recognition as the first of Frances's elite combat pilots.
b. Dec 24, 1894 in Paris, France
d. Sep 11, 1917 in Poelcapelle, Belgium
Source: *BioIn 7, 9, 12*

Guyon, Joe
[Joseph Guyon]
American. Football Player
All-America tackle-running back; in pros, 1919-25, 1927; Hall of Fame.
b. Nov 26, 1892 in Mohnomen, Minnesota
d. Nov 27, 1971
Source: *Ballpl 90; BioIn 8, 9, 17; LegTOT; WhoFtbl 74*

Guyot, Arnold Henry
American. Scientist
Meteorological observations led to founding of US Weather Bureau; wrote *Creation,* 1884.
b. Sep 28, 1807 in Boudevilliers, Switzerland
d. Feb 8, 1884 in Princeton, New Jersey
Source: *Alli SUP; AmBi; AsBiEn; BbD; BiDAmEd; BiDAmS; BiD&SB; BiESc; BiInAmS; BioIn 1, 5, 11, 18; CyAL 1; CyEd; DcAmAu; DcAmB; DcBiPP; DcNAA; DcScB; Drake; Geog 5; HarEnUS; InSci; LinLib L; TwCBDA; WhAm HS*

Guyton, Tyree
American. Artist
Creator of the "Heidelberg Project," a project in Detroit which transformed part of a neighborhood into a work of art using discarded objects to embellish abandoned houses, sidewalks, and empty lots.
b. Aug 24, 1955 in Detroit, Michigan
Source: *ConBlB 9; WhoAfA 96; WhoBlA 90, 92, 94*

Guzman, Antonio
[Silvestre Antonio Guzman Fernandez]
Dominican. Political Leader
Pres., 1978-82; freed political prisoners, abolished state censorship.
b. Feb 12, 1911 in La Vega, Dominican Republic
d. Jul 4, 1982 in Santo Domingo, Dominican Republic
Source: *AnObit 1982; BioIn 11, 12, 13; DcCPCAm; IntWW 80; WhoWor 78, 80*

Guzman, Nuno Beltran de
Spanish. Conqueror
First pres. of New Spain, 1528; founded Mexican cities Guadalajara, Culiacan.
d. 1544
Source: *ApCAB; BioIn 6; NewCol 75; WhWE*

Gwaltney, John Langston
American. Anthropologist
Professor of Anthropology, Syracuse U, 1971—; books on subject include *A Self-Portrait of Black America,* 1980.
b. Sep 25, 1928 in Orange, New Jersey
Source: *BioIn 12; BlksScM; ConAu 33R, 77; InB&W 85; IntAu&W 89; SelBAAf; SelBAAu; WhoAm 82, 84, 86, 88, 90, 92; WhoBlA 85, 92; WrDr 76, 80, 82, 84, 86, 88, 90, 92, 94, 96*

Gwathmey, Charles
American. Architect
Co-author, *Five Architects,* 1972, as member of "White School" postmodernis t group of architects.
b. Jun 19, 1938 in Charlotte, North Carolina
Source: *AmArch 70; BioIn 10, 15, 16, 21; ConArch 80, 87, 94; CurBio 88; DcTwDes; IntDcAr; IntWW 91, 93; WhoAm 78, 80, 82, 84, 86, 92, 94, 95, 96, 97*

Gwathmey, Robert
American. Artist
Combined modernist style with social themes of the underprivileged.
b. Jan 24, 1903 in Richmond, Virginia
d. Sep 21, 1988 in Southampton, New York
Source: *AnObit 1988; BioIn 1, 6, 11, 14, 16, 17; BriEAA; CurBio 43, 88N; DcAmArt; DcCAA 71, 77, 88, 94; McGDA; OxCTwCA; OxDcArt; PhDcTCA 77; WhAm 9; WhAmArt 85; WhoAm 74, 76, 78, 80, 84, 86; WhoAmA 73, 76, 78, 80, 82, 84, 86, 89N, 91N, 93N; WorArt 1950*

Gwenn, Edmund
Welsh. Actor
Won Oscar for role of Santa Claus in *Miracle on 34th Street,* 1947.
b. Sep 26, 1875 in Glamorgan, Wales
d. Sep 6, 1959 in Woodland Hills, California
Source: *BiDFilm; BioIn 5; CurBio 43, 59; EncAFC; Film 1, 2; FilmAG WE; FilmEn; FilmgC; ForYSC; HalFC 80, 84, 88; HolCA; IlWWBF; IntDcF 1-3; ItaFilm; LegTOT; MotPP; MovMk; NotNAT B; OxCFilm; Vers A; WhoHol B; WhoHrs 80; WhScrn 74, 77, 83; WhThe; WorAl; WorAlBi*

Gwilym, Mike
Welsh. Actor
Played on PBS shows "How Green Was My Valley"; "The Racing Game."
b. Mar 5, 1949 in Neath, Wales
Source: *BioIn 11; ConTFT 6; WhoHol 92; WhoThe 77, 81*

Gwinnett, Button
American. Patriot, Continental Congressman
Signed Declaration of Independence, 1776; his signature is extremely rare; died following duel.
b. 1735 in Gloucester, England
d. May 16, 1777 in Saint Catherine's Island, Georgia
Source: *AmBi; AmRev; ApCAB; BiAUS; BiDrAC; BiDrACR; BiDrUSC 89; BioIn 3, 4, 5, 7, 8, 9, 10, 12; DcAmB; Drake; EncAR; EncCRAm; EncRev; HarEnUS; LegTOT; TwCBDA; WebAB 74, 79; WhAm HS; WhAmP; WhAmRev; WorAl; WorAlBi*

Gwyn, Nell
[Eleanor Gwyn]
English. Actor
Noted for comedy performances; mistress of Charles II, 1668-85; bore him two sons.
b. Feb 2, 1650 in London, England
d. Nov 13, 1687 in London, England
Source: *Benet 87, 96; BioIn 2, 3, 4, 5, 8, 9, 10, 11, 15, 16; ContDcW 89; DcNaB; IntDcWB; LegTOT; NewC; NotNAT A, B; OxCEng 85, 95; REn; WorAl; WorAlBi*

Gwynn, Tony
[Anthony Keith Gwynn]
American. Baseball Player
Outfielder, San Diego, 1982—; won NL batting title, 1984, 1987, 1988, 1989, 1994, 1995, 1996.
b. May 9, 1960 in Los Angeles, California
Source: *AfrAmSG; Ballpl 90; BaseReg 86, 87; BioIn 16; CurBio 96; LegTOT; News 95, 95-1; NewYTBS 91; WhoAfA 96; WhoAm 86, 88, 90, 92, 94, 95, 96, 97; WhoBlA 88, 90, 92, 94; WhoSpor; WhoWest 87, 89, 92, 94, 96; WorAlBi*

Gwynne, Fred
[Frederick Hubbard Gwynne]
American. Actor
Played Herman Munster in TV comedy "The Munsters," 1964-68; starred in films *O n the Waterfront,* 1954, *Cotton Club,* 1984.
b. Jul 10, 1926 in New York, New York
Source: *AnObit 1993; BioIn 13, 14, 15; ConAu 113; ConTFT 2, 8, 12; GangFlm; HalFC 84, 88; IlsBYP; IntMPA 84, 86, 88, 92, 94; ItaFilm; LegTOT; NotNAT; SmATA 27, 41; VarWW 85; WhAm 11; WhoAm 80, 82, 84, 86, 88, 90, 92; WhoCom; WhoEnt 92; WhoHol 92, A; WhoThe 77, 81*

Gyllenhammar, Pehr Gustaf
Swedish. Business Executive, Auto Executive
Chairman, Volvo A B; founder European Roundtable, executives' lobby group.
b. Apr 28, 1935 in Gothenburg, Sweden
Source: *BioIn 9, 10, 11, 12, 14, 16; ConAu 13NR, 73; IntWW 74, 75, 76, 77, 78, 79, 80, 81, 82, 83, 89, 91, 93; NewYTBE 73; Who 85, 88, 90, 92, 94; WhoAm 92, 94, 95, 96, 97; WhoE 93; WhoFI 94, 96; WhoWor 78, 80, 82, 84, 87, 89, 91, 93, 95, 96, 97*

H

Haack, Morton R
American. Designer
Designed costumes for films: *Planet of the Apes,* 1968; *Please Don't Eat the Daisies,* 1960.
b. Jun 26, 1924 in Los Angeles, California
Source: *VarWW 85*

Haacke, Hans Christoph
German. Artist, Sculptor
Controversial graphic artist known for visual attacks on society; had first one-man show in US, 1986.
b. Aug 12, 1936 in Cologne, Germany
Source: *AmArt; BioIn 9, 10; ConArt 83; CurBio 87; IntWW 91; OxCTwCA; WhoAm 82, 84; WhoAmA 76, 78, 80, 82, 84, 86, 89, 91, 93; WhoE 75, 77, 91*

Haakon VII
Norwegian. Ruler
First king of independent Norway after separation from Sweden, 1905-57.
b. Aug 3, 1872 in Charlottenlund, Denmark
d. Sep 21, 1957 in Oslo, Norway
Source: *CurBio 57; HisEWW; LinLib S; ObitOF 79; ObitT 1951; WhAm 3; WhWW-II*

Haas, Ernst
Austrian. Photojournalist
Noted for his originality in the use of color in still photography; famous photo story: "The Miracle of Greece," late 1940s.
b. Mar 2, 1921 in Vienna, Austria
d. Sep 12, 1986 in New York, New York
Source: *AmArt; AnObit 1986; BioIn 3, 4, 6, 8, 10, 15; ConAu 120; ConPhot 82, 88, 95; ICPEnP; MacBEP; NewYTBS 86; WhoAmA 80, 82, 84, 86*

Haas, Robert D(ouglas)
American. Business Executive
Began with Levi Strauss & Co., 1973; Chm. of the board, 1989—.
b. Apr 3, 1942 in San Francisco, California
Source: *ConAmBL; ConNews 86-4; IntWW 93; St&PR 84, 87; WhoAm 86, 88, 90, 92, 94, 95, 96, 97; WhoFI 89, 92, 94, 96; WhoWest 87, 89, 92, 94, 96; WhoWor 95, 96*

Haas, Walter A(braham), Sr.
American. Business Executive
Pres., Levi Strauss Co., 1928-56, director, 1956-59; turned family jean co. into American institution.
b. 1899 in San Francisco, California
d. Dec 7, 1979 in San Francisco, California
Source: *NewYTBS 79; St&PR 75; WhAm 7; WhoAm 74, 76, 78; WhoFI 74, 75, 77; WhoWorJ 72*

Haas, Walter A(braham), Jr.
American. Business Executive
Pres., Levi Strauss Co., 1956-72. Owner, Oakland Athletics, 1980-94.
b. Jan 24, 1916 in San Francisco, California
d. Sep 20, 1995 in San Francisco, California
Source: *BioIn 5; ConAmBL; Dun&B 86; St&PR 87, 91; WhoAm 84, 86, 90; WhoFI 81, 83, 89, 92; WhoWest 82, 89, 92*

Haavelmo, Trygve Magnus
Norwegian. Economist
Forerunner in the field of economic prediction based on statistical probability theory; won the Nobel Memorial Prize in Economic Science, 1989.
b. Dec 13, 1911 in Skedsmo, Norway
Source: *BioIn 16; IntWW 91; NewYTBS 89; WhoFI 92; WhoNob 90; WhoWor 91; WorAlBi*

Habash, Georges
Palestinian. Political Leader
Founded Popular Front for Liberation of Palestine (PFLP), radical Marxist faction of PLO, 1967.
b. 1925? in Lydda, Palestine
Source: *BioIn 13, 15, 16; ColdWar 2; ConNews 86-1; CurBio 88; EncWB; IntWW 83, 91; NewYTBE 70*

Habberton, John
American. Author
Noted for popular novel *Helen's Babies,* 1876.
b. Feb 24, 1842 in New York, New York
d. Feb 24, 1921
Source: *Alli SUP; AmAu; AmAu&B; AmBi; ApCAB; BbD; BenetAL 91; BiD&SB; BioIn 8, 15; CarSB; CelCen; Chambr 3; DcAmAu; DcAmB; DcBiA; DcEnL; DcNAA; EncAHmr; EvLB; HarEnUS; NatCAB 4; OxCAmL 65, 83, 95; REnAL; TwCBDA; WhAm 1; WhLit; WhoChL*

Haber, Fritz
German. Chemist
Won 1918 Nobel Prize for developing Haber process, which produced ammonia; directed Germany's chemical warfare, WW I.
b. Dec 9, 1868 in Breslau, Prussia
d. Jan 29, 1934 in Basel, Switzerland
Source: *AsBiEn; BiESc; BioIn 1, 3, 5, 6, 7, 8, 12, 13, 19; CamDcSc; DcScB; InSci; LarDcSc; LinLib S; McGEWB; NobelP; NotTwCS; WhDW; WhoNob, 90, 95; WorInv*

Haber, Joyce
[Joyce Haber Cramer]
American. Journalist
Columnist with *LA Times,* 1966-75; contributing editor *LA* mag., 1977-79.
b. Dec 28, 1932 in New York, New York
Source: *AnObit 1993; ConAu 65, 142; IntMPA 75, 76, 77, 78, 79, 80, 81, 82, 84, 86, 88, 92, 94, 96; LegTOT; WhAm 11; WhoAm 78, 80, 82, 84, 86, 88, 90, 92, 94; WhoWor 82, 84, 87, 89, 91, 93; WrDr 82*

Haberl, Franz Xaver
German. Musicologist
Published *Kirchenmusikalisches Jahrbuch,* 1885-1907; founded famed school of church music, 1874; edited 33-vol. edition of Giovanni Palestrina's works, 1879-94.
b. Apr 12, 1840 in Oberellenbach, Bavaria
d. Sep 5, 1910 in Regensburg, Germany
Source: *Baker 78, 84, 92; DcCathB; NewGrDM 80; OxCMus*

Haberlandt, Gottlieb
Austrian. Botanist
His study of physiological plant anatomy led him to become the first to work with plant tissue culture, 1921.
b. Nov 28, 1854 in Ungarisch-Altenburg, Hungary
d. Jan 30, 1945 in Berlin, Germany
Source: *DcScB*

Habib, Philip Charles
American. Diplomat
Ambassador to Korea, 1971-74; special Middle East envoy, 1981-83.
b. Feb 25, 1920 in New York, New York
Source: *AnObit 1992; BioIn 11, 12, 13, 14, 16, 19; BlueB 76; CurBio 81, 92N; DcAmDH 89; FarE&A 78, 79, 80, 81; HisEAAC; IntWW 78, 79, 80, 81, 82, 83, 89, 91; MidE 81, 82; NewYTBS 81; PolProf J; USBiR 74; WhAm 10; WhoAm 74, 76, 78, 80, 82, 84, 86, 88, 90; WhoAmP 75, 77, 79, 81, 83, 85, 87, 89, 91; WhoGov 72, 75, 77; WhoWor 74, 76, 87, 89, 91*

Habre, Hissene
Chadian. Political Leader
Pres. of Chad, 1982-90; ousted in coup.
b. 1942 in Faya Largeau, Chad
Source: *AfSS 81, 82; BioIn 13, 14, 15, 20, 21; ConBlB 6; CurBio 87; DcAfHiB 86, 86S; IntWW 83; WhoWor 87, 89*

Habyarimana, Juvenal
Rwandan. Political Leader
Pres. of Rwanda, 1973-94.
b. Aug 3, 1937 in Gasiza, Ruanda-Urundi
d. Apr 6, 1994 in Kigali, Rwanda
Source: *AfSS 79, 80, 81, 82; BioIn 19, 20, 21; ConBlB 8; DcAfHiB 86; IntWW 74, 75, 80, 81, 82, 83, 89, 91, 93; WhAm 11; WhoAfr; WhoWor 82, 84, 87, 89, 91, 93*

Hack, Shelley
American. Model, Actor
Revlon's "Charlie Girl" in TV commercials; starred in TV series "Charlie's Angels," 1979.
b. Jul 6, 1952 in Greenwich, Connecticut
Source: *BioIn 12, 15; ConTFT 7; IntMPA 86, 92, 94, 96; VarWW 85; WhoAm 82*

Hacker, Marilyn
American. Poet
Published poetry collections *Assumptions,* 1985; *Going Back to the River,* 1990.
b. Nov 27, 1942 in New York, New York
Source: *AmWomWr; ArtclWW 2; BioIn 12, 19; BlmGWL; ConAu 77; ConLC 5, 9, 23, 72, 91; ConPo 80, 85, 91, 96; DcLB 120; DrAP 75; DrAPF 80; FemiCLE; FemiWr; GayLesB; IntAu&W 91, 93; IntWWP 77, 82; OxCTwCP; OxCWoWr 95; ScF&FL 1; WhoAm 78, 80, 82; WhoAmJ 80; WorAu 1975; WrDr 82, 84, 86, 88, 90, 92, 94, 96*

Hackett, Albert
American. Author
With wife won Pulitzer for play adaptation of *The Diary of Anne Frank,* 1955.
b. Feb 16, 1900 in New York, New York
d. Mar 16, 1995 in New York, New York
Source: *AmAu&B; AuBYP 2, 3; BenetAL 91; BiE&WWA; BioIn 4, 8, 11, 14, 15, 20, 21; CmMov; ConDr 88A; CurBio 56, 95N; DcLB 26; EncAFC; Film 1, 2; FilmEn; FilmgC; HalFC 80, 84, 88; LegTOT; ModWD; NewYTBS 95; NotNAT; OxCAmL 65, 83; OxCAmT 84; REnAL; TwYS; VarWW 85; WhoAm 74, 76, 78; WhoHol 92; WorEFlm*

Hackett, Bobby
[Robert Leo Hackett]
American. Jazz Musician
Guitarist, cornetist; led own band, 1940s-50s.
b. Jan 31, 1915 in Providence, Rhode Island
d. Jun 7, 1976 in Chatham, Massachusetts
Source: *AllMusG; Baker 84, 92; BgBands 74; BiDAmM; BiDJaz; BioIn 1, 9, 10, 11, 12, 16, 20; CmpEPM; DcAmB S10; EncJzS; IlEncJ; LegTOT; NewAmDM; NewGrDA 86; NewGrDJ 88, 94; NewYTBS 76; OxCPMus; PenEncP; TwCBrS; WhAm 7; WhoAm 74, 76; WhoJazz 72; WorAl; WorAlBi*

Hackett, Buddy
[Leonard Hacker]
American. Comedian
Starred in *God's Little Acre,* 1958; *The Love Bug,* 1969; known for popular stand-up acts on TV, in nightclubs.
b. Aug 31, 1924 in New York, New York
Source: *ASCAP 66, 80; BiE&WWA; BioIn 4, 7, 10; CelR; ConAu 108; ConTFT 8; CurBio 65; Dun&B 90; EncAFC; FilmEn; FilmgC; ForYSC; HalFC 80, 84, 88; IntMPA 77, 80, 84, 86, 88, 92, 94, 96; JoeFr; LegTOT; MotPP; MovMk; QDrFCA 92; VarWW 85; WhoAm 74, 76, 78, 80, 82, 84, 86, 88, 90, 92, 94, 95, 96, 97; WhoCom; WhoEnt 92; WhoHol 92, A; WorAl; WorAlBi*

Hackett, Francis
American. Author, Editor
Wrote *Story of the Irish Nation,* 1922; *Francis the First,* 1935.
b. Jan 21, 1883 in Kilkenny, Ireland
d. Apr 24, 1962 in Virum, Denmark
Source: *AmAu&B; BenetAL 91; BiDIrW; BioIn 4, 6, 9; ConAu 89, 108; DcAmB S7; DcIrL, 96; DcIrW 1, 2; EncAJ; LinLib L, S; LngCTC; OxCAmL 65, 83; REnAL; TwCA, SUP; WhAm 4; WhE&EA; WhLit*

Hackett, Joan
American. Actor
Starred in *The Group,* 1966; nominated for Oscar, 1982, for *Only When I Laugh.*
b. Mar 1, 1934 in New York, New York
d. Oct 8, 1983 in Encino, California
Source: *AnObit 1983; BiE&WWA; BioIn 6, 12, 13, 14; FilmgC; ForWC 70; HalFC 80, 84, 88; IntMPA 84; LegTOT; MovMk; NewYTBE 72; NewYTBS 83; NotNAT; VarWW 85; WhoAm 82; WhoAmW 83; WhoHol A; WorAl*

Hackett, Raymond
American. Actor
Leading man in silents, early talkies, 1918-31.
b. Jul 15, 1902 in New York, New York
d. Jun 9, 1958 in Hollywood, California
Source: *Film 1; FilmEn; FilmgC; ForYSC; HalFC 80, 84, 88; MotPP; NotNAT B; SilFlmP; WhoHol B; WhScrn 74, 77, 83; WhThe*

Hackett, Steve
English. Musician
Guitarist with Genesis, 1970-77.
b. Feb 12, 1950 in London, England
Source: *BioIn 15; OnThGG*

Hackford, Taylor
American. Director, Producer
Films include *An Officer and A Gentleman,* 1983; *Against All Odds,* 1984.
b. Dec 31, 1944 in Santa Barbara, California
Source: *BioIn 13; ConTFT 3, 13; HalFC 88; IntMPA 86, 92, 94, 96; LegTOT; MiSFD 9; VarWW 85; WhoAm 84, 86, 88, 95, 96, 97; WhoEnt 92*

Hackman, Gene
[Eugene Alden Hackman]
American. Actor
Won Oscars for *The French Connection,* 1972; *Unforgiven,* 1992.
b. Jan 30, 1931 in San Bernardino, California
Source: *BioIn 9, 10, 11, 16, 17, 19; BioNews 74; BkPepl; CelR, 90; CmMov; ConTFT 5; CurBio 72; DcArts; FilmEn; FilmgC; ForYSC; HalFC 88; IntDcF 1-3, 2-3; IntMPA 84, 86, 92; IntWW 79, 80, 81, 82, 83, 89, 91, 93; MovMk; News 89-3; NewYTBE 71; NewYTBS 89; OxCFilm; VarWW 85; WhoAm 86, 90; WhoEnt 92; WhoHol 92, A; WorAl; WorAlBi*

Hackney, (Francis) Sheldon
American. Educator
Chairman of the National Endowment for the Humanities, 1993—.
b. Dec 5, 1933 in Birmingham, Alabama
Source: *BioIn 18, 19, 21; ConAu 41R; DrAS 74H, 78H, 82H; News 95, 95-1; NewYTBS 93; WhoAm 74, 76, 78, 82, 86, 88, 90, 92, 94, 95, 96, 97; WhoAmP 93, 95; WhoE 81, 83, 85, 86, 89; WhoWor 87, 89, 91, 93*

Hadamard, Jacques Salomon
French. Mathematician
Independently of Poussin, established the validity of the prime number theorem, 1896.
b. Dec 8, 1865 in Versailles, France
d. Oct 7, 1963 in Paris, France
Source: *BioIn 6, 7, 17, 20; DcScB; LarDcSc; WhAm 5*

Haddad, Saad
Lebanese. Army Officer
Renegade army major; formed own militia, made seperate peace with Israel to keep Syria from annexing Lebanon.
b. 1937? in Marjayoun, Lebanon
d. Jan 14, 1984 in Marjayoun, Lebanon
Source: *BioIn 12, 13; NewYTBS 84*

Hadden, Briton
American. Publisher
Co-founded *Time* mag. with Henry Luce, 1923.
b. Feb 18, 1898 in New York, New York
d. Feb 27, 1929 in New York, New York
Source: *AmDec 1920; BioIn 1, 2, 8, 10, 17; DcLB 91; EncAJ; EncTwCJ; NatCAB 28; REnAL*

Haden, Charlie
American. Jazz Musician
Acoustic bassist played with the Ornette Coleman Quartet in the late 1950s; albums include *Dream Keeper,* 1991.
b. 1937 in Shenandoah, Iowa
Source: *AllMusG; BiDJaz; BioIn 15, 16; ConMus 12; EncJzS; NewGrDA 86; NewGrDJ 88, 94; PenEncP; WhoAm 88*

Haden, Francis Seymour, Sir
English. Artist, Surgeon
Noted etcher; helped familiarize public with Rembrandt's etchings; Whistler's brother-in-law.
b. Sep 16, 1818 in London, England
d. Jun 1, 1910 in Alresford, England
Source: *Alli SUP; ArtsNiC; BioIn 9, 11; CelCen; DcBrWA; DcNaB S2; Dis&D; InSci; McGDA; NewCol 75; WhLit*

Haden, Pat(rick Capper)
American. Football Player
Quarterback, LA Rams, 1976-81; recipient of Rhodes Scholarship.
b. Jan 23, 1953 in Westbury, New York
Source: *BioIn 11, 12, 13; FootReg 81; NewYTBS 78, 81, 82; WhoAm 80, 82, 84*

Hadley, Arthur Twining
American. University Administrator
President, Yale U, 1899-1921; wrote *Railroad Transportation,* 1885, first thorough treatment of topic.
b. Apr 25, 1856 in New Haven, Connecticut
d. Mar 6, 1930 in Kobe, Japan
Source: *Alli SUP; AmAu&B; AmBi; AmLY; ApCAB, X; BbD; BiDAmEd; BiD&SB; BioIn 1, 8, 12; DcAmAu; DcAmB; DcNAA; HarEnUS; LinLib L, S; NatCAB 9, 32; NewCol 75; OxCAmH; REnAL; TwCBDA; WebAB 74, 79; WhAm 1; WhoEc 81, 86*

Hadley, Henry Kimball
American. Composer
Romantic operas include *Cleopatra's Night,* 1920; foundation organized for music advancement, 1938.
b. Dec 20, 1871 in Somerville, Massachusetts
d. Sep 6, 1937 in New York, New York
Source: *AmBi; AmComp; ASCAP 66; Baker 84; BiDAmM; DcAmB S2; NewGrDM 80; OxCMus; WhAm 1*

Hadley, Jerry
American. Opera Singer
Tenor who has performed at major opera houses throughout the US and Europe since 1979.
b. Jun 16, 1952 in Princeton, Illinois
Source: *BioIn 15, 20; CurBio 91; IntWWM 90; MetOEnc; NewGrDO; NewYTBS 86; OxDcOp; WhoAm 88, 90, 92, 94, 95, 96, 97*

Hadley, Reed
[Reed Herring]
American. Actor
Starred in TV series "Racket Squad," 1951-53; "Public Defender," 1954.
b. Jan 8, 1911 in Petrolia, Texas
d. Dec 11, 1974 in Los Angeles, California
Source: *BioIn 3, 10; FilmEn; FilmgC; ForYSC; HalFC 80, 84, 88; Vers B; WhoHol B; WhScrn 77, 83*

Hadrian
[Adrian; Publius Aelius Hadrianus]
Roman. Ruler
Emperor, 117-38; during reign erected many buildings, including temple of Venus and Roma.
b. Jan 24, 76 in Italica, Spain
d. Jul 10, 138 in Baiae, Italy
Source: *Benet 87, 96; BioIn 1, 3, 4, 5, 6, 7, 8, 9, 11, 12, 15, 17, 18, 20; CasWL; DcBiPP; DicTyr; Dis&D; EncEarC; GayLesB; Grk&L; HarEnMi; HisWorL; LegTOT; LinLib S; MacEA; McGEWB; NewC; OxCClL, 89; PenC CL; REn; WebBD 83; WhDW; WorAl; WorAlBi*

Haeckel, Ernst Heinrich Philipp August
German. Zoologist
Advocate of Darwinism who theorized that growing organisms mirror species development; coined term "ecology."
b. Feb 15, 1834 in Potsdam, Prussia
d. Aug 8, 1919 in Jena, Germany
Source: *BioIn 9, 14; Dis&D; EncWB; InSci; LarDcSc; LuthC 75; OxCMed 86; WorAl*

Haenigsen, Harry William
American. Cartoonist
Created comic strips "Our Bell," 1939-66; "Penny," 1943-70.
b. Jul 14, 1902 in New York, New York
Source: *AmAu&B; EncACom; WhAmArt 85; WhoAm 74; WorECar*

Hafey, Chick
[Charles James Hafey]
American. Baseball Player
Outfielder, 1924-35, 1937; won NL batting title, 1931; had .317 lifetime average; Hall of Fame, 1971.
b. Feb 12, 1903 in Berkeley, California
d. Jul 2, 1973 in Calistoga, California
Source: *Ballpl 90; BiDAmSp BB; LegTOT; WhoProB 73; WhoSpor*

Ḥafiz, Shams-al-Din Muhammad
Persian. Poet
Considered greatest Persian lyric poet; principal work: "Divan."
b. 1320 in Shiraz, Persia
d. 1389
Source: *CasWL; IlEncMy; OxCEng 67; PenC CL; RComWL*

Hafstad, Lawrence R(andolph)
American. Physicist
With two colleagues at the Carnegie Institute of Technology, split atomic nuclei, 1939.
b. Jun 18, 1904
d. Oct 12, 1993 in Oldwick, New Jersey
Source: *AmMWSc 73P, 76P, 79, 82, 86, 89, 92; BioIn 3, 4; CurBio 94N; InSci; IntYB 78, 79, 80; LElec; McGMS 80; WhoAm 74, 76, 78, 80; WhoEng 80*

Hagan, Cliff(ord Oldham)
"Lil Abner"
American. Basketball Player
Forward-center, St. Louis, 1956-66, Dallas, 1967-70; won NBA championship, 1958; Hall of Fame, 1977.
b. Dec 9, 1931 in Owensboro, Kentucky
Source: *BasBi; BiDAmSp BK; OfNBA 87; WhoAm 80, 82, 84; WhoBbl 73*

Hagar, Sammy
[Van Halen]
American. Singer, Musician
Lead singer, second guitarist with Van Halen, 1986-96; released 10 albums during nine yr. solo career.
b. Oct 13, 1949 in Monterey, California
Source: *BioIn 16; EncPR&S 89; HarEnR 86; PenEncP; RkOn 85; RolSEnR 83; WhoEnt 92*

Hagedorn, Hermann
American. Author, Poet
Noted for works on Theodore Roosevelt.

b. Jul 18, 1882 in New York, New York
d. Jul 27, 1964 in Santa Barbara, California
Source: *AmAu&B; AmLY; BenetAL 91; BioIn 4, 5, 7; ChhPo, S1, S2; ConAmL; ConAu 116; OxCAmL 65, 83, 95; REnAL; TwCA, SUP; WhAm 4; WhE&EA; WhLit*

Hagegard, Hakan
Swedish. Opera Singer
Lyric baritone; starred in Ingmar Bergman's film version of *The Magic Flute,* 1975.
b. Nov 25, 1945 in Karlstad, Sweden
Source: *Baker 84, 92; BioIn 11, 13, 14; CurBio 85; IntWWM 90; MetOEnc; NewAmDM; PenDiMP; WhoAm 82, 84, 92; WhoOp 76; WhoWor 80, 82, 84, 87, 89, 91, 93, 95*

Hagel, Chuck
American. Politician
Rep. senator, NE, 1997—.
b. Oct 4, 1946

Hagelstein, Peter
American. Inventor, Physicist
Developed laser device that was basis for Strategic Defense Initiative, or "Star Wars," 1979.
b. 1955?
Source: *BioIn 15, 16; ConNews 86-3*

Hagen, Jean
[Jean Shirley Verhagen]
American. Actor
Starred in TV series "Make Room for Daddy," 1953-57; films *Singin' in the Rain* , 1952; *Adam's Rib,* 1949.
b. Aug 3, 1923 in Chicago, Illinois
d. Aug 29, 1977 in Woodland Hills, California
Source: *EncAFC; FilmEn; FilmgC; GangFlm; IntMPA 77; MotPP; MovMk; VarWW 85; WhoHol A; WhoThe 81N; WhScrn 83*

Hagen, Johann Georg
Austrian. Astronomer, Clergy
Jesuit priest; while director of the Vatican Observatory discovered what is now known as Hagen's clouds.
b. Mar 6, 1847 in Bregenz, Austria
d. Sep 5, 1930 in Rome, Italy
Source: *AmBi; BioIn 9; DcCathB; WhE&EA; WhoLA*

Hagen, John Peter
American. Physicist
Directed Project Vanguard, America's first major space probe, 1958; expert in microwave electronics, radar, rocketry.
b. Jul 31, 1908 in Amherst, Nova Scotia, Canada
d. Aug 26, 1990 in Las Vegas, Nevada
Source: *AmMWSc 73P, 76P, 79; BioIn 4, 6; CurBio 57, 90, 90N; NewYTBS 90; Who 90, 92N*

Hagen, Uta Thyra
American. Actor
Won Tonys for *The Country Girl,* 1951; *Who's Afraid of Virginia Woolf?* 1963.
b. Jun 12, 1919 in Gottingen, Germany
Source: *BiE&WWA; BioIn 13, 15, 16; CamGWoT; ConTFT 2; CurBio 63; IntWW 74, 75, 76, 77, 78, 79, 80, 81, 82, 83, 89, 91, 93; InWom, SUP; NotNAT; OxCAmT 84; OxCThe 83; PeoHis; PlP&P; VarWW 85; WhoAm 86, 90, 92, 94, 95, 96, 97; WhoAmW 89, 91, 93, 95, 97; WhoEnt 92; WhoHol A; WhoThe 81; WhoWor 84; WorAl; WrDr 90, 92*

Hagen, Walter Charles
"The Haig"
American. Golfer
First important American golfer, 1920s; won five PGA titles, four British Opens, two US Opens; charter member, Hall of Fame, 1940.
b. Dec 21, 1892 in Rochester, New York
d. Oct 5, 1969 in Traverse City, Michigan
Source: *DcAmB S8; NewCol 75; NewYTBS 77; ObitOF 79; WebAB 74, 79; WhoGolf*

Hagenbeck, Carl
German. Animal Dealer, Animal Trainer
Introduced training methods that replaced the cruel, harsh treatment of the past.
b. Jun 10, 1844 in Hamburg, Germany
d. Apr 14, 1913 in Hamburg, Germany
Source: *BioIn 14; Ent*

Hagerty, James Campbell
American. Government Official, Journalist
Pres. Eisenhower's White House press secretary, 1952-60.
b. May 9, 1909 in Plattsburg, New York
d. Apr 11, 1981 in Bronxville, New York
Source: *BiDAmJo; BioIn 3, 4, 5, 6, 8, 11, 12, 13; BlueB 76; ConAu 103; CurBio 81; IntWW 78; LesBEnT; PolProf E; Who 82N; WhoFI 74; WhoPubR 72; WhoWor 74*

Hagg, Gunder
Swedish. Track Athlete
Long distance runner; set 15 world marks, 1940s.
b. Dec 31, 1918 in Sorbygden, Sweden
Source: *BioIn 9; IntWW 89; WhoTr&F 73*

Haggar, Joseph M(arion)
[Maroun Hajjar]
Syrian. Manufacturer
Opened Haggar Apparel Co., 1926; today is largest manufacturer of men's clothing.
b. 1892 in Jazzini, Syria
d. Dec 15, 1987 in Dallas, Texas
Source: *BioIn 1, 11, 12; Entr; St&PR 84*

Haggard, Henry Rider, Sir
English. Author
Wrote *King Solomon's Mines,* 1885; *She,* 1887.
b. Jun 22, 1856 in Bradenham, England
d. May 14, 1925 in London, England
Source: *Alli SUP; BbD; BiD&SB; BioIn 1, 2, 3, 5, 7, 8, 11, 12, 13, 14, 15, 16, 20; CamGLE; Chambr 3; ConAu 108; CyWA 58; DcAfHiB 86; DcBiA; DcEnA A; DcEuL; DcLEL; DcNaB 1922; EncPaPR 91; EncSF; EncSoA; EvLB; HisDBrE; LinLib L, S; LngCTC; MnBBF; ModBrL; NewC; NewCBEL; Novels; OxCChiL; OxCEng 67; PenC ENG; REn; TwCA, SUP; VicBrit; WebE&AL; WhLit; WhoChL*

Haggard, Merle Ronald
American. Singer, Songwriter
Gravelly-voiced country singer; hits include "Okie from Muskogee," 1969; won Gramm y, 1984.
b. Apr 6, 1937 in Bakersfield, California
Source: *AmSong; Baker 78, 84, 92; BiDAmM; BioIn 13, 14, 15, 16; CelR 90; ConAu 112; ConMus 2; CurBio 77; EncFCWM 83; EncRk 88; HarEnCM 87; HarEnR 86; NewAmDM; NewGrDA 86; OxCPMus; PenEncP; RkOn 84; VarWW 85; WhoAm 74, 76, 78, 80, 82, 84, 86, 88, 94, 95, 96, 97; WhoEnt 92; WhoNeCM C; WhoThe 77; WhoWor 78; WorAl; WorAlBi*

Haggart, Bob
[Robert Sherwood]
American. Composer, Musician
Bassist with Bob Crosby, 1935-42; co-led World's Greatest Jazz Band, 1970s.
b. Mar 13, 1914 in New York, New York
Source: *AllMusG; ASCAP 66; BiDJaz; BioIn 18; CmpEPM; EncJzS; NewGrDJ 88, 94; WhoJazz 72*

Haggerty, Dan
American. Actor
Starred in TV series "Life and Times of Grizzly Adams," 1977-78.
b. Nov 19, 1941 in Hollywood, California
Source: *ConTFT 3; Dun&B 90; HalFC 84, 88; LegTOT; VarWW 85; WhoAm 78, 80, 82, 84*

Hagler, Marvelous Marvin
[Marvin Nathaniel Hagler]
American. Boxer
WBA, WBC middleweight champ, 1980-87; inducted into Int'l Boxing Hall of Fame, 1993.
b. May 23, 1952 in Newark, New Jersey
Source: *ConNews 85-2; IntWW 89, 91; NegAl 89; NewYTBS 81, 87; WhoAm 86, 90; WhoBlA 88, 90, 92; WhoE 91*

Hagman, Larry
American. Actor
Played Tony Nelson on TV comedy "I Dream of Jeannie," 1965-70, J R

Ewing on TV series "Dallas," 1978-91; son of Mary Martin.
b. Sep 21, 1931 in Fort Worth, Texas
Source: *BioIn 12, 13, 14, 15, 16; CelR 90; ConTFT 3, 14; CurBio 80; EncAFC; FilmgC; HalFC 88; IntMPA 82, 84, 86, 88, 92, 94, 96; LegTOT; MiSFD 9; VarWW 85; WhoAm 84, 86, 90, 92, 94, 95, 96, 97; WhoEnt 92; WhoHol A; WorAl; WorAlBi*

Hague, Albert
American. Composer
Won Tony, 1959, for *Redhead.*
b. Oct 13, 1920 in Berlin, Germany
Source: *AmPS; ASCAP 66, 80; BiDAmM; BiE&WWA; BioIn 6, 13, 14; ConTFT 4; EncMT; NewCBMT; NotNAT; OxCPMus; PopAmC; WhoAm 94; WhoEnt 92; WhoHol 92; WhoThe 72, 77, 81*

Hague, Frank
American. Politician
Dem. mayor, political boss of Jersey City, 1917-47.
b. Jan 17, 1876 in Jersey City, New Jersey
d. Jan 1, 1956 in Jersey City, New Jersey
Source: *BioIn 1, 3, 4, 6, 7, 8, 9, 15; CopCroC; DcAmB S6; McGEWB; ObitOF 79; PolPar; PolProf T; WhAm 3*

Hague, Raoul (Heukelekian)
American. Sculptor
Known for his abstract wood sculptures of tree trunks.
b. Mar 28, 1905 in Constantinople, Ottoman Empire
d. Feb 17, 1993 in Woodstock, New York
Source: *BioIn 7; BriEAA; McGDA; PhDcTCA 77; WhAm 11; WhoAm 74, 76, 78, 80, 82, 84, 86, 88, 90, 92; WhoAmA 91, 93; WorArt 1950*

Hahn, Archie
American. Track Athlete
Sprinter; won three gold medals, 1904 Olympics, one gold, 1906 Olympics; wrote classic *How to Sprint.*
b. 1880 in Milwaukee, Wisconsin
d. Jan 21, 1955 in Charlottesville, Virginia
Source: *BioIn 3; ObitOF 79; WhoSpor; WhoTr&F 73*

Hahn, Carl Horst
German. Auto Executive
Chairman, Volkswagen, 1982-92.
b. Jul 1, 1926 in Chemnitz, Germany
Source: *BioIn 13, 14, 15; ConNews 86-4; Dun&B 90; IntWW 74, 75, 76, 77, 78, 79, 80, 81, 82, 83, 89, 91, 93; St&PR 84; Who 85, 88, 90, 92, 94; WhoAm 86, 90, 92; WhoFI 87, 89, 92; WhoMW 88, 90; WhoWor 84, 87, 89, 91, 93*

Hahn, Emily
American. Author
Numerous books on China include *Soong Sisters,* 1941; longtime contributor to *The New Yorker.*
b. Jan 14, 1905 in Saint Louis, Missouri
d. Feb 18, 1997 in New York, New York
Source: *AmAu&B; AmWomWr; AuBYP 2, 3; BioIn 1, 2, 3, 4, 7, 8, 9, 11, 12, 13, 15, 20, 21; ConAu 1NR, 1R, 11AS, 27NR; CurBio 42; FemiCLE; IntAu&W 91; InWom, SUP; LngCTC; REnAL; SmATA 3; TwCA SUP; WhNAA; WhoAm 74, 76, 78, 80, 82, 84, 86, 88, 90, 94, 97; WhoAmW 58, 64, 66, 68, 70, 72, 74, 75, 77, 83, 85, 93; WhoE 74; WhoWor 74, 76; WrDr 80, 82, 84, 86, 88, 90, 92, 94, 96*

Hahn, Jessica
American. Secretary
Part of PTL scandal involving Jim Bakker, 1987; posed in *Playboy* magazine later.
b. Jul 7, 1959 in Massapequa, New York
Source: *BioIn 15, 16; LegTOT; News 89*

Hahn, Otto
German. Chemist
Won Nobel Prize in chemistry, 1944, for discovery of nuclear fission.
b. Mar 8, 1879 in Frankfurt am Main, Germany
d. Jul 28, 1968 in Gottingen, Germany (West)
Source: *AsBiEn; BiESc; BioIn 1, 2, 3, 4, 6, 7, 8, 9, 12, 14, 15, 19, 20; CamDcSc; ConAu 112; CurBio 51, 68; DcScB; EncTR 91; FacFETw; InSci; LarDcSc; LegTOT; McGEWB; McGMS 80; NobelP; NotTwCS; ObitOF 79; ObitT 1961; REn; WhAm 5; WhDW; WhoNob, 90, 95; WorAl; WorAlBi; WorScD*

Hahnemann, Samuel
[Christian Friedrich Samuel Hahnemann]
German. Physician
Founded Homeopathy, 1796.
b. Apr 10, 1755 in Meissen, Saxony
d. Jul 2, 1843 in Paris, France
Source: *BioIn 3, 6, 10; CelCen; DcBiPP; DcScB; LinLib S; OxCMed 86; WhDW*

Haid, Charles
American. Actor
Played Andy Renko on TV series "Hill Street Blues," 1981-87.
b. Jun 2, 1944? in San Francisco, California
Source: *BioIn 13; ConTFT 7; IntMPA 92; VarWW 85; WhoAm 90; WhoEnt 92; WhoTelC*

Haider, Michael Lawrence
American. Business Executive
CEO, chm., Standard Oil Co., 1965-69.
b. Oct 1, 1904 in Mandan, North Dakota
d. Aug 14, 1986 in Atherton, California
Source: *AmMWSc 79; BioIn 7, 8, 11; St&PR 75; WhAm 9; Who 74, 82, 83, 85, 88; WhoEng 80*

Haig, Alexander Meigs, Jr.
American. Army Officer, Government Official
Commander in chief, US European Command, 1974-78; Reagan's secretary of State, 1981-82; Rep. presidential candidate, 1987-88.
b. Dec 2, 1924 in Philadelphia, Pennsylvania
Source: *AmPolLe; BiDrUSE 89; BioIn 9, 10, 11, 12, 13, 14, 15, 16, 17, 18; BioNews 74; BlueB 76; CngDr 81; ColdWar 1; CurBio 73, 87; DcAmDH 89; DcCPSAm; FacFETw; HarEnMi; IntWW 74, 75, 76, 77, 78, 79, 80, 81, 82, 83, 89, 91, 93; IntYB 78, 79, 80, 81, 82; NewAmDM; NewGrDJ 88; NewYTBE 73; NewYTBS 80, 87; PenEncP; WebAMB; Who 82, 83, 85, 88, 90, 92, 94; WhoAm 74, 76, 78, 80, 82, 84, 86, 88, 90, 92, 94, 95, 96, 97; WhoAmP 85; WhoE 81, 83; WhoFI 89; WhoGov 77; WhoSSW 73, 75; WhoWor 82, 84, 87, 89, 91, 93, 95, 96, 97; WorAl; WorAlBi*

Haig, Douglas
British. Military Leader
Commanded British forces in France, 1915-18.
b. Jun 19, 1861 in Edinburgh, Scotland
d. Jan 29, 1928 in London, England
Source: *BioIn 12, 16, 17; DcNaB 1922; DcTwHis; FacFETw; GenMudB; GrBr; HarEnMi; HisWorL; McGEWB; WhDW; WhoMilH 76; WorAl; WorAlBi*

Haigh, Kenneth
English. Actor
Appeared in *Cleopatra,* 1963.
b. Mar 25, 1931 in Mexboro, England
Source: *BiE&WWA; CnThe; ConTFT 2; FilmgC; HalFC 88; NotNAT; PlP&P; WhoHol 92, A; WhoThe 77, 81*

Haile Selassie, I
[Tafari Makonnen]
"Lion of Judah"
Ethiopian. Ruler
Autocratic ruler of Ethiopia, 1930-74.
b. Jul 23, 1892 in Harar, Ethiopia
d. Aug 27, 1975 in Addis Ababa, Ethiopia
Source: *BioIn 10, 11, 12, 13, 20, 21; ColdWar 2; CurBio 41, 54, 75, 75N; DcAfHiB 86; DcTwHis; DicTyr; FacFETw; HisEWW; HisWorL; InB&W 80, 85; IntWW 74; LinLib S; McGEWB; NewYTBS 75; REn; WhDW; Who 74; WhoGov 72; WhoWor 74; WhWW-II; WorAl; WorAlBi*

Hailey, Arthur
Canadian. Author
Wrote *Hotel,* 1965; *Airport,* 1968; *Wheels,* 1971.
b. Apr 5, 1920 in Luton, England
Source: *AmAu&B; Au&Wr 71; AuNews 2; Benet 87; BenetAL 91; BestSel 90-3; BioIn 7, 9, 10, 11, 13, 14; BlueB 76; CanWr; CanWW 31, 70, 83; ConAu 1R, 2NR, 36NR; ConCaAu 1; ConLC 5; ConNov 72, 76, 82, 86, 91, 96; ConPopW; ConTFT 6; CreCan 2;*

CurBio 72; DcLB 88, Y82B; DcLEL 1940; EncSF; HalFC 84, 88; IntAu&W 76, 89, 91; IntWW 74, 75, 76, 77, 78, 79, 80, 81, 82, 83, 89, 91, 93; LegTOT; LinLib L; MajTwCW; NewYTBS 79; Novels; OxCCan; OxCCanL; VarWW 85; Who 82, 83, 85, 88, 90, 92, 94; WhoAm 76, 78, 80, 82, 84, 86, 88, 90, 92, 94, 95, 96, 97; WhoCanL 85, 87; WhoE 74; WhoEnt 92; WhoWor 74, 76, 78, 80, 82, 84, 87, 89, 91, 93, 95, 96, 97; WhoWrEP 89, 92; WorAl; WorAlBi; WorAu 1970; WrDr 76, 80, 82, 84, 86, 88, 90, 92, 94, 96

Hailwood, Mike
[Stanley Michael Bailey Hailwood]
English. Motorcycle Racer, Auto Racer
Considered one of greatest motorcycle racers of all time; died in auto accident.
b. Apr 4, 1940 in Oxford, England
d. Mar 23, 1981 in Eastbourne, England
Source: *AnObit 1981; BioIn 11, 12; ConAu 108; EncMot*

Haines, Jesse Joseph
"Pop"
American. Baseball Player
Pitcher, 1920-37; known for throwing knuckleball; had 210 career wins; Hall of Fame, 1970.
b. Jul 22, 1893 in Clayton, Ohio
d. Aug 5, 1978 in Dayton, Ohio
Source: *BiDAmSp BB; BioIn 8, 11; WhoProB 73*

Haines, Randa
American. Director
Drama films include *The Doctor,* 1991; *Children of a Lesser God,* 1986.
b. Feb 20, 1945 in Los Angeles, California
Source: *ConTFT 10; IntMPA 96; LegTOT; WhoAmW 97*

Haines, Robert Terrel
American. Actor
Starred in vaudeville, radio, film, and on stage in career spanning four decades.
b. Feb 3, 1870 in Muncie, Indiana
d. May 6, 1943 in New York, New York
Source: *Film 1, 2; NotNAT B; TwYS; WhAm 5; WhoStg 1906, 1908; WhScrn 74, 77; WhThe*

Haines, William
American. Actor
Appeared in silent films and early talkies; retired to become interior decorator.
b. Jan 1, 1900 in Staunton, Virginia
d. Nov 26, 1973 in Santa Monica, California
Source: *BioIn 2, 10, 17; EncAFC; Film 2; FilmEn; FilmgC; ForYSC; Funs; HalFC 80, 84, 88; MotPP; MovMk; SilFlmP; TwYS; What 4; WhoHol B; WhScrn 77, 83*

Hainsworth, George
Canadian. Hockey Player
Goalie, 1926-37, mostly with Montreal; holds NHL record for most shutouts in season, 22, 1929; won Vezina Trophy three times; Hall of Fame, 1961.
b. Jun 26, 1895 in Toronto, Ontario, Canada
d. Oct 9, 1950 in Gravenhurst, Ontario, Canada
Source: *HocEn; ObitOF 79; WhoHcky 73; WhoSpor*

Hair, Jay D(ee)
American. Environmentalist
President and CEO, National Wildlife Federation, 1981—.
b. Nov 30, 1945 in Miami, Florida
Source: *AmMWSc 95; CurBio 93; NatLAC; WhoAm 82, 84, 86, 88, 90, 94, 96, 97; WhoScEn 94, 96; WhoWor 96*

Haire, Bill Martin
American. Fashion Designer
Designer of Eastern airline uniforms, 1980—; founder, Bill Haire, Ltd., 1981—.
b. Sep 30, 1936 in New York, New York
Source: *WhoAm 80, 82, 84, 86, 88, 90, 92; WhoFash 88; WhoWor 80, 82; WorFshn*

Haise, Fred W(allace, Jr.)
American. Astronaut
Crew member, Apollo 13, 1970; Apollo 16, 1972.
b. Nov 14, 1933 in Biloxi, Mississippi
Source: *AmMWSc 73P; BioIn 8, 10; IntWW 74, 75, 76, 77; NewYTBE 70; WhoAm 84, 86, 88; WhoGov 75; WhoSpc; WhoSSW 75*

Haitink, Bernard
Dutch. Conductor
Director, Amsterdam's Concertgebouw, since 1964; led London's Philharmonic, 1976-79; knighted, 1978.
b. Mar 4, 1929 in Amsterdam, Netherlands
Source: *Baker 78, 84; BioIn 5, 7, 8, 9, 11, 12, 13; BriBkM 80; CurBio 77; DcArts; IntWW 74, 75, 76, 77, 78, 79, 80, 81, 82, 83, 89, 91, 93; IntWWM 77, 80, 90; MetOEnc; MusMk; MusSN; NewAmDM; NewGrDM 80; OxDcOp; PenDiMP; Who 74, 82, 83, 85, 88, 90, 92, 94; WhoEnt 92; WhoFash; WhoMus 72; WhoWor 74, 91; WorAlBi*

Hakluyt, Richard
English. Geographer
Compiled accounts of English voyages of discovery: *Principal Navigations,* 1589.
b. 1552
d. Nov 23, 1616 in London, England
Source: *Alli; AnCL; AtlBL; BenetAL 91; BiD&SB; BiDSA; BioIn 1, 3, 4, 5, 6, 8, 9, 11, 20; BritAu; CamGEL; CamGLE; CasWL; Chambr 1; CroE&S; CyEd; CyWA 58; DcEnA; DcEnL; DcEuL; DcLEL; DcNaB; DcScB; EncCRAm; EvLB; HisDBrE; InSci; LitC 31; McGEWB; NewC; OxCAmH; OxCAmL 65, 83, 95; OxCCan; OxCEng 67, 85, 95; OxCShps; PenC ENG; RAdv 14, 13-3; REn; REnAL; RfGEnL 91; WebE&AL; WhAm HS; WhWE*

Halaby, Najeeb E(lias)
American. Financier
Pres., Halaby International Corp., 1973—; chm., Dulles Access Rapid Transit Inc., 1985—.
b. Nov 19, 1915 in Dallas, Texas
Source: *BioIn 5, 6, 8, 9, 11, 12; BlueB 76; ConAu 108; CurBio 61; IntWW 83; Ward 77; Who 82, 83, 85, 88, 90, 92, 94; WhoAm 84, 86, 90; WhoE 74; WhoFI 74; WhoWor 74*

Halas, George Stanley
"Papa Bear"
American. Football Coach, Football Executive
Football pioneer; one of founders of NFL; founder, pres., Chicago Bears, 1920-64; coached, 1920-67; charter member, Hall of Fame, 1963.
b. Feb 2, 1895 in Chicago, Illinois
d. Oct 31, 1983 in Chicago, Illinois
Source: *AnObit 1983; BiDAmSp FB; BioIn 4, 5, 6, 7, 8, 9, 12, 13, 14, 17, 21; ConAu 111; EncAB-H 1974, 1996; NewYTBS 83; WebAB 74, 79; WhAm 8; WhoAm 74, 76, 78, 80, 82; WhoFtbl 74; WhoMW 80, 82; WhoWor 80, 82*

Halasz, Laszlo
American. Conductor, Pianist
Music director, Nat. Grand Opera, 1985—; Toscanini Award, 1972.
b. Jun 6, 1905 in Debrecen, Austria-Hungary
Source: *Baker 78, 84, 92; BioIn 1, 2; CmOp; CurBio 49; IntWWM 90; MetOEnc; NewEOp 71; NewGrDO; WhoAm 76, 78, 80, 82, 86, 88; WhoOp 76*

Halberstam, David
American. Journalist
Won Pulitzer, 1964; critical writings of Vietnam War include *The Best and the Brightest,* 1972.
b. Apr 10, 1934 in New York, New York
Source: *AmAu&B; Benet 96; BenetAL 91; BestSel 89-4; BioIn 9, 10, 11, 12, 13, 15, 18, 19, 20, 21; BlueB 76; CelR, 90; ColdWar 1; ConAu 10NR, 45NR, 69; CurBio 73; DcLEL 1940; EncAJ; EncTwCJ; IntAu&W 91; LegTOT; LiJour; OxCAmL 95; PolProf K; WhoAm 74, 76, 78, 80, 82, 84, 86, 88, 90, 92, 94, 95, 96, 97; WhoE 95; WhoUSWr 88; WhoWor 74; WhoWrEP 89, 92, 95; WorAlBi; WorAu 1970; WrDr 76, 80, 82, 84, 86, 88, 90, 92, 94, 96*

Halberstam, Michael Joseph
American. Physician, Author
Editor, *Modern Medicine,* 1976-80; wrote *Pills in Your Life,* 1972.

b. Aug 9, 1932 in New York, New York
d. Dec 5, 1980 in Washington, District of Columbia
Source: *AmMWSc 79; BioIn 12; ConAu 65, 102; WhAm 7; WhoAm 76, 78, 80*

Haldane, J(ohn) B(urdon) S(anderson)
English. Scientist
Best known for work in genetics; helped develop heart-lung machine.
b. Nov 5, 1892 in Oxford, England
d. Dec 1, 1964 in Bhubaneswar, India
Source: *AsBiEn; BiESc; BioIn 4, 7, 8, 9, 12, 13, 14, 16, 18, 20; DcLEL; DcNaB 1961; DcScB; EncSF 93; EvLB; FacFETw; GrBr; LarDcSc; LngCTC; McGEWB; McGMS 80; NewC; NewCBEL; NotTwCS; OxCEng 67, 95; RAdv 14, 13-5; TwCA, SUP; TwCChW 95; UFOEn; WebBD 83; WhE&EA; WhLit; WorAl; WorScD*

Haldane, John Scott
Scottish. Physiologist
Developed method of stage decompression by which divers can be safely brought to surface.
b. May 3, 1860 in Edinburgh, Scotland
d. Mar 14, 1936 in Oxford, England
Source: *BiESc; BiHiMed; BioIn 2, 5, 9, 14; DcNaB 1931; DcScB; GrBr; InSci; LarDcSc; NewCBEL; OxCMed 86; WhE&EA; WhLit; WhoLA*

Haldeman, H(arry) R(obbins)
American. Government Official
Convicted for involvement in Watergate, 1975; jailed, 1977-78; chief of staff to Pres. Nixon.
b. Oct 27, 1926 in Los Angeles, California
d. Nov 12, 1993 in Santa Barbara, California
Source: *AmPolLe; BioIn 8, 9, 10, 11, 12, 13; ConAu 143; IntWW 91; NewYTBE 72, 73; NewYTBS 74; St&PR 87; WhoAm 86, 90; WhoAmP 73; WhoGov 75; WhoSSW 75; WhoWor 74; WorAlBi*

Haldeman-Julius, Emanuel
American. Publisher
Founded popular 10-cent reprint series *Little Blue Books,* 1919.
b. Jul 30, 1889 in Philadelphia, Pennsylvania
d. Jul 31, 1951 in Girard, Kansas
Source: *AmRef; BioIn 2, 5, 11, 14, 15, 16; DcAmB S5; EncUnb; PeoHis; RelLAm 91; WebAB 74, 79; WhAm 3*

Hale, Alan
[Rufus Alan McKahan]
American. Actor
Character actor best known as Errol Flynn's sidekick in films such as *The Adventures of Robin Hood,* 1938.
b. Feb 10, 1892 in Washington, District of Columbia
d. Jan 22, 1950 in Hollywood, California
Source: *BioIn 2, 7, 17, 21; CmMov; EncAFC; Film 1, 2; FilmEn; FilmgC; ForYSC; HalFC 80, 84, 88; HolCA; IntMPA 82; LegTOT; MotPP; MovMk; NotNAT B; OlFamFa; TwYS; Vers A; WhoHol A, B; WhScrn 74, 77, 83*

Hale, Alan, Jr.
American. Actor
Played the Skipper on TV series "Gilligan's Island," 1964-67; son of Alan.
b. Mar 8, 1918 in Los Angeles, California
d. Jan 2, 1990 in Los Angeles, California
Source: *AnObit 1990; BioIn 16, 17; ConTFT 9; EncAFC; FilmgC; ForYSC; HalFC 80, 84, 88; IntMPA 77, 80, 84, 86, 88; LegTOT; NewYTBS 90; VarWW 85; WhoHol A*

Hale, Barbara
American. Actor
Played Della Street on TV series "Perry Mason," 1957-66; mother of actor William K att.
b. Apr 18, 1922 in De Kalb, Illinois
Source: *BioIn 1, 10; ConTFT 7; FilmgC; ForYSC; HalFC 80, 84, 88; IntMPA 75, 76, 77, 78, 79, 80, 81, 82, 84, 86, 88, 92, 94, 96; LegTOT; MotPP; MovMk; VarWW 85; WhoAmW 74; WhoEnt 92; WhoHol 92, A*

Hale, Clara (McBride)
"Mother Hale"
American. Social Reformer
Founded Hale House, 1969, in Harlem to care for babies born to drug-addicted mothers.
b. Apr 1, 1905 in Philadelphia, Pennsylvania
d. Dec 18, 1992 in New York, New York
Source: *AfrAmBi 2; AnObit 1992; BioIn 9, 11, 13; CurBio 85, 93N; InB&W 80; InWom SUP; News 93-3; NotBlAW 1*

Hale, Edward Everett
American. Clergy, Author
Active in founding Unitarian Church of America; wrote short story *Man Without a Country,* made into opera, produced by Met. Opera Co., 1937.
b. Apr 3, 1822 in Boston, Massachusetts
d. Jun 10, 1909 in Roxbury, Massachusetts
Source: *Alli, SUP; AmAu; AmAu&B; AmBi; AmRef; ApCAB; BbD; BenetAL 91; BiDAmM; BiD&SB; BiDSocW; BiDTran; BioIn 1, 2, 3, 4, 5, 7, 9, 12, 15; CarSB; Chambr 3; ChhPo, S1, S2, S3; CnDAL; ConAu 119; CyAL 2; CyWA 58; DcAmAu; DcAmB; DcAmTB; DcBiPP; DcEnL; DcLB 1, 42, 74; DcLEL; DcNAA; Drake; EncSF, 93; EvLB; HarEnUS; JBA 34; LinLib L, S; LuthC 75; McGEWB; NatCAB 1; NewEScF; OxCAmH; OxCAmL 65, 83, 95; OxCChiL; PenC AM; RelLAm 91; REn; REnAL; ScF&FL 1; ScFEYrs; SmATA 16; TwCBDA; WebAB 74, 79; WhAm 1*

Hale, George Ellery
American. Astronomer, Educator
Organizer, director, Yerkes, Mount Wilson observatories; found magnetic fields in sunspots; invented spectroheliograph.
b. Jun 29, 1868 in Chicago, Illinois
d. Feb 21, 1938 in Pasadena, California
Source: *AmBi; AmDec 1900; AsBiEn; BiESc; BioIn 2, 3, 4, 5, 7, 8, 9, 13, 14, 18, 19, 20, 21; CamDcSc; CmCal; DcAmB S2; DcNAA; DcScB; EncAB-H 1974, 1996; EncWB; InSci; LarDcSc; LinLib S; NatCAB 11, 38; NewCol 75; NotTwCS; OxCAmH; RAdv 14; TwCBDA; WebAB 74, 79; WhAm 1; WhDW; WhNAA; WorAl*

Hale, Janet Campbell
American. Author
Nominated for the Pulitzer Prize for *The Jailing of Cecelia Capture,* 1985.
b. Jan 11, 1946
Source: *NotNaAm*

Hale, Lorraine
American. Social Reformer
Co-founded, with mother Clara Hale, Hale House, 1969.
b. c. 1926 in Philadelphia, Pennsylvania
Source: *BioIn 20; ConBlB 8*

Hale, Lucretia Peabody
American. Author
Wrote children's tale *The Peterkin Papers,* 1880.
b. Sep 2, 1820 in Boston, Massachusetts
d. Jun 12, 1900 in Belmont, Massachusetts
Source: *Alli SUP; AmAu; AmAu&B; AmBi; AmWomWr; ApCAB; BenetAL 91; BiD&SB; BioIn 1, 3, 4, 5, 8, 12, 13, 15, 19; BlmGWL; CarSB; ChhPo S2; ConAu 122, 136; DcAmAu; DcAmB; DcLB 42; DcNAA; FamSYP; FemiCLE; InWom, SUP; JBA 34; LibW; MajAI; NatCAB 5; NotAW; OxCAmH; OxCAmL 65, 83, 95; REnAL; SmATA 26; TwCBDA; TwCChW 78A; WebAB 74, 79; WhAm 1; WhoChL; WomFir*

Hale, Nancy
American. Author, Journalist
Wrote fiction, biography, and memoirs, and short stories documenting changing American Upper-class manners: *The Prodigal Women,* 1942; was *New York Times'* first woman reporter, 1935.
b. May 6, 1908 in Boston, Massachusetts
d. Sep 24, 1988 in Charlottesville, Virginia
Source: *AmAu&B; AmWomWr; Au&Wr 71; BenetAL 91; BioIn 1, 2, 4, 7, 8, 12, 14, 16; BlmGWL; ConAu 5NR, 5R, 126; ConNov 72, 76, 82, 86; CyWA 89; DcLB 86, Y80B, Y88N; DrAF 76; DrAPF 80; FemiCLE; IntAu&W 76, 77, 82; InWom; LinLib L; NewYTBS 88; OxCAmL 65, 83, 95; REn; REnAL; SmATA 31, 31N, 57; TwCA SUP; WhAm 9; WhoAm 74, 76, 78, 80, 82, 84, 86, 88; WhoAmW 58, 61, 64, 66, 68, 70, 72, 74; WhoSSW 73;*

WhoUSWr 88; WhoWor 74, 76; WrDr 76, 80, 82, 84, 86, 88

Hale, Nathan
American. Revolutionary, Spy
By Washington's request volunteered to gather information on British; hanged by British as a spy.
b. Jun 6, 1755 in Coventry, Connecticut
d. Sep 22, 1776 in New York, New York
Source: *AmBi; AmRev; ApCAB; Benet 87, 96; BenetAL 91; BioIn 1, 2, 3, 4, 5, 6, 7, 8, 9, 10, 11, 12; BlkwEAR; DcAmB; DcAmSR; Drake; EncAI&E; EncAR; EncCRAm; EncRev; HarEnUS; LegTOT; LinLib S; NatCAB 1; OxCAmH; OxCAmL 65, 83, 95; REn; REnAL; TwCBDA; WebAB 74, 79; WebAMB; WhAm HS; WhAmRev; WorAl; WorAlBi*

Hale, Sarah Josepha Buell
[Cornelia]
American. Journalist, Author
Edited *Godey's Lady's Book,* 1837-77; wrote verse "Mary Had a Little Lamb," 1830.
b. Oct 24, 1788 in Newport, New Hampshire
d. Apr 30, 1879 in Philadelphia, Pennsylvania
Source: *EncAB-H 1996; NotAW; OxCAmL 83; PenNWW B; WomComm*

Hales, Stephen
"Father of Plant Physiology"
English. Physiologist
Made early studies of sap circulation in plants; one of first to measure blood pressure, heart capacity.
b. Sep 17, 1677 in Bekesbourne, England
d. Jan 4, 1761 in Teddington, England
Source: *Alli; AsBiEn; BiESc; BiHiMed; BioIn 1, 2, 4, 6, 9, 10, 12, 14; BlkwCE; CamDcSc; DcBiPP; DcEnL; DcInv; DcNaB; DcScB; Dis&D; EncEnl; InSci; LarDcSc; McGEWB; NewCBEL; NewCol 75; OxCMed 86; WhDW; WorScD*

Ha-Levi, Judah
Spanish. Religious Leader, Poet
b. c. 1075 in Tudela, Spain
d. Jul 1141, Egypt
Source: *CasWL; OxCSpan*

Halevy, Jacques Francois Fromental Elie
[Jacques Francois F Elie Levy]
French. Composer
Wrote "grand" opera *La Juive,* 1835; comic opera *L'Eclair,* 1835.
b. May 27, 1799 in Paris, France
d. Mar 17, 1862 in Nice, France
Source: *Baker 84; BioIn 3, 4, 6, 7; DcBiPP; NewEOp 71; OxCMus; WebBD 83*

Halevy, Ludovic
French. Librettist, Author
With Henri Meilhac, wrote libretti for Bizet's *Carmen,* Offenbach's light operas; best known novel: *L'Abbe Constantin.*
b. Jan 1, 1834 in Paris, France
d. May 8, 1908 in Paris, France
Source: *BbD; BiD&SB; BioIn 5, 6, 7; CasWL; CelCen; CmOp; CyWA 58; DcArts; DcBiA; DcBiPP; DcEuL; EuAu; EvEuW; LinLib L, S; McGEWD 72, 84; ModWD; NewGrDO; NotNAT B; OxCAmT 84; OxCFr; OxCPMus; OxCThe 83; PlP&P; REn; WebBD 83; WhLit*

Haley, Alex (Murray Palmer)
American. Author, Journalist
Pulitzer-winning novel *Roots,* 1976, had largest hard cover printing in US publishing history; became most-watched dramatic show in TV history; 1976 Spingarn winner.
b. Aug 11, 1921 in Ithaca, New York
d. Feb 10, 1992 in Seattle, Washington
Source: *AfrAmAl 6; AnObit 1992; AuSpks; Benet 87; BenetAL 91; BioIn 11, 13, 14, 15, 16; BkPepl; BlkLC; BlksCm; BlkWr 1; ConAu 77; ConBlB 4; ConHero 2; ConLC 8, 12, 76; ConPopW; CurBio 77; CyWA 89; DcLB 38; DcTwCCu 5; Ebony 1; FacFETw; InB&W 85; LegTOT; LivgBAA; MajTwCW; MorBAP; NegAl 83, 89; News 92; OxCAmL 83; PeoHis; SchCGBL; SelBAAf; SelBAAu; SouWr; WhoAm 86, 88; WhoBlA 88, 92; WhoUSWr 88; WhoWest 74; WhoWrEP 89; WorAlBi; WorAu 1975; WrDr 80, 82, 84, 86, 88, 90, 92*

Haley, Bill
[Bill Haley and the Comets; William John Clifton Haley, Jr]
"Father of Rock 'n' Roll"
American. Singer, Musician
Hits "Rock Around the Clock," 1955; "Shake, Rattle, and Roll," 1954; paved way for E lvis Presley, The Beatles.
b. Jul 6, 1925 in Highland Park, Michigan
d. Feb 9, 1981 in Harlingen, Texas
Source: *AnObit 1981; ASCAP 66, 80; Baker 84, 92; BiDAmM; BioIn 21; ConMus 6; EncPR&S 89; EncRk 88; HarEnCM 87; HarEnR 86; IlEncCM; LegTOT; NewAmDM; NewGrDA 86; NewGrDM 80; NewYTBS 81; OxCPMus; PenEncP; RolSEnR 83; WhoRock 81; WhScrn 83; WorAlBi*

Haley, Jack
American. Actor
Best known for role of the Tin Man in film *Wizard of Oz,* 1939.
b. Aug 10, 1898 in Boston, Massachusetts
d. Jun 6, 1979 in Los Angeles, California
Source: *BiE&WWA; EncMT; EncVaud; FilmgC; MovMk; WhoAm 74; WhoHol A; WhoThe 77A; WhScrn 83*

Haley, Jack, Jr.
[John J Haley]
American. Director, Producer
Has produced many TV specials and awards shows; directed film *That's Entertainment,* 1974; son of Jack Haley; former husband of Liza Minnelli.
b. Oct 25, 1933 in Los Angeles, California
Source: *BioIn 10; ConAu 135; ConTFT 2; HalFC 88; IntMPA 92, 94, 96; LegTOT; LesBEnT, 92; MiSFD 9; VarWW 85; WhoAm 74, 76, 78, 80, 82, 84, 86, 88, 92, 94, 95, 96, 97; WhoEnt 92; WhoTelC; WhoWest 74, 76; WrDr 94, 96*

Haley, William John, Sir
English. Newspaper Executive, Broadcasting Executive
Director-general, BBC, 1944-52; editor-in-chief, London *Times,* 1952-66.
b. May 24, 1901 in Isle of Jersey, England
d. Sep 6, 1987 in Isle of Jersey, England
Source: *BioIn 1, 2, 3, 8, 9; CurBio 48, 87, 87N; DcNaB 1986; IntAu&W 77, 89; IntWW 74, 75, 76, 77, 78, 79, 80, 81, 82, 83; WhE&EA; Who 85; WhoAm 74, 76; WhoWor 74, 76, 78*

Halfin, Eliezer
Israeli. Olympic Athlete, Victim
One of 11 members of Israeli Olympic team kidnapped and killed by Arab terrorists during Summer Olympic games.
b. 1948?, Union of Soviet Socialist Republics
d. Sep 5, 1972 in Munich, Germany (West)
Source: *BioIn 9*

Haliburton, Thomas Chandler
[Sam Slick]
Canadian. Judge, Author
Created humorous character Sam Slick who appears in *The Clockmaker,* 1836-40.
b. Dec 17, 1796 in Windsor, Nova Scotia, Canada
d. Aug 27, 1865 in Isleworth, England
Source: *Alli, SUP; BbD; BbtC; Benet 87, 96; BenetAL 91; BiD&SB; BioIn 9, 11, 13, 15, 17; BritAu 19; CamGEL; CamGLE; CanWr; CasWL; Chambr 3; DcBiPP; DcCanB 9; DcEnA; DcEnL; DcLB 11, 99; DcLEL; DcNAA; DcNaB; EncAHmr; EvLB; GrWrEL N; LinLib L, S; MacDCB 78; McGEWB; NatCAB 5; NewC; NinCLC 15; OxCAmL 65; OxCCan; OxCEng 67, 85, 95; PenC ENG; RAdv 14, 13-1; REn; REnAL; RfGEnL 91; RfGShF; StaCVF; WebE&AL*

Halifax, Edward Frederick Lindley Wood
English. Statesman
Viceroy to India, 1925-31; ambassador to US, 1941-46.
b. Apr 16, 1881 in Exeter, England

d. Dec 23, 1959 in York, England
Source: *BioIn 19; CurBio 40, 60; DcNaB 1951; DcTwHis; FacFETw; McGEWB; WhAm 3; WhDW*

Hall, Adrian
American. Director
Award-winning stage work includes *Buried Child,* 1979; won special Tony, 1981.
b. Dec 3, 1927 in Van, Texas
Source: *BioIn 14, 16; ConAu 22NR, 106; ConTFT 5; GrStDi; NotNAT; WhoThe 81; WhoWrEP 89, 92, 95*

Hall, Anthony Thomas Charles
American. Actor
Films include *The Breakfast Club,* 1985; *Out of Bounds,* 1986.
b. Apr 14, 1968 in Boston, Massachusetts
Source: *BioIn 14, 15; ConNews 86-3; ConTFT 7; HalFC 88; IntMPA 88, 92*

Hall, Arsenio
American. Comedian, Actor
Talk show host, "The Arsenio Hall Show," 1988-94; films include *Coming to America,* 1988; *Harlem Nights,* 1989.
b. Feb 12, 1955 in Cleveland, Ohio
Source: *AfrAmBi 1; BioIn 15, 16; CelR 90; ConTFT 7; CurBio 89; DrBlPA 90; InB&W 85; IntMPA 92; NegAl 89; News 90, 90-2; NewYTBS 89; WhoAm 92, 94, 95, 96, 97; WhoBlA 92; WorAlBi*

Hall, Asaph
American. Astronomer
Discovered the two satellites of Mars, 1877.
b. Oct 15, 1829 in Goshen, Connecticut
d. Nov 22, 1907 in Annapolis, Maryland
Source: *AmBi; ApCAB; AsBiEn; BiDAmS; BiESc; BiInAmS; BioIn 8, 11, 14; CamDcSc; DcAmB; DcNAA; DcScB; HarEnUS; InSci; LarDcSc; McGEWB; NatCAB 11, 22; TwCBDA; WebAB 74, 79; WhAm 1*

Hall, Bridget
American. Model
Began modeling at age nine; by age 16, had already graced the covers of 22 magazines.
b. Dec 14, 1977 in Dallas, Texas

Hall, Camilla Christine
[S(ymbionese) L(iberation) A(rmy)]
"Gabi"
American. Revolutionary
Member of terrorist group that kidnapped Patricia Hearst, 1974.
b. Mar 24, 1946
Source: *BioIn 10; GoodHs; InWom SUP; PeoHis*

Hall, Charles Francis
American. Explorer
Led Arctic expeditions, 1860-71; wrote *Arctic Researches Among the Esquimaux,* 1864; died in Arctic.
b. 1821 in Rochester, New Hampshire
d. Nov 8, 1871
Source: *Alli SUP; AmAu&B; AmBi; ApCAB; BioIn 1, 5, 8, 9, 11, 12, 15, 18; CelCen; DcAmAu; DcAmB; DcCanB 10; DcNAA; Expl 93; HarEnUS; InSci; NatCAB 3; NewCol 75; OhA&B; OxCCan; OxCShps; TwCBDA; WhAm HS; WhDW; WhWE*

Hall, Charles Martin
American. Scientist
Developed electrolytic process used in aluminum refining, co-founded ALCOA, 1890.
b. Dec 6, 1863 in Thompson, Ohio
d. Dec 27, 1914 in Daytona Beach, Florida
Source: *AmBi; AsBiEn; BiESc; BiInAmS; BioIn 2, 3, 4, 6, 7, 8, 11, 12, 14, 15, 21; DcAmB; DcScB; InSci; LarDcSc; LinLib S; NatCAB 13; WebAB 74, 79; WhAm 1; WhDW; WorAl; WorInv*

Hall, Daryl
[Hall and Oates]
American. Singer, Musician
Recorded 3 gold albums with John Oates; hits include "Sara Smile," "She's Gone," and "Kiss on My List.".
b. Oct 11, 1949 in Pottstown, Pennsylvania
Source: *BioIn 13, 14, 15; CelR 90; OxCPMus; RkWW 82; SoulM; WhoAm 82, 84, 86, 88, 90, 92, 94, 95, 96, 97; WhoEnt 92; WhoRocM 82; WorAlBi*

Hall, Deidre
American. Actor
Plays Marlena Evans on TV soap *Days of Our Lives,* 1975-87; 1991—.
b. Oct 31, 1948 in Milwaukee, Wisconsin
Source: *BioIn 11, 16; InWom SUP; LegTOT; WhoAm 96, 97*

Hall, Donald Andrew
American. Poet
Wrote first verse collection, *Exiles and Marriages,* 1955; edited many poetry anthologies.
b. Sep 20, 1928 in New Haven, Connecticut
Source: *AmAu&B; AuBYP 2, 3; Ballpl 90; BioIn 13, 14, 15, 16; CnE&AP; ConAu 2NR, 5R; ConLC 37, 59; ConPo 85; CurBio 84; DcLEL 1940; FifBJA; PenC AM; RAdv 1, 13-1; REn; REnAL; SmATA 23; Who 92; WhoAm 86, 88; WhoUSWr 88; WorAu 1950; WrDr 86, 92*

Hall, Donald Joyce
American. Business Executive
With Hallmark Cards since 1953; chm. of the board, 1983—; son of Joyce Clyde Hall.
b. Jul 9, 1928 in Kansas City, Missouri
Source: *Benet 87; BioIn 10, 13, 14, 15; ConAu 7AS; ConLC 37; ConPo 85; CurBio 84; Dun&B 90; FifBJA; RAdv 13-1; WhoAm 74, 76, 78, 80, 82, 84, 86, 88, 92, 94, 95, 96, 97; WhoFI 83, 85, 87, 89, 92, 94, 96; WhoMW 84, 88, 90, 92; WhoUSWr 88; WhoWor 84; WrDr 88*

Hall, Edd
American. TV Personality
Announcer, "The Tonight Show," 1992—.
b. 1959?

Hall, Edwin Herbert
American. Physicist, Educator
Discovered Hall Effect, 1879.
b. Nov 7, 1855 in Great Falls, Maine
d. Nov 20, 1938 in Cambridge, Massachusetts
Source: *BiDAmS; BioIn 4, 10; DcAmB S2; DcNAA; DcScB; InSci; NatCAB 39; WebBD 83; WhAm 1; WorScD*

Hall, Fawn
American. Secretary
Worked for Oliver North; involved in Iran-Contra controversy, 1987.
b. 1959? in Annandale, Virginia
Source: *BioIn 15; LegTOT; NewYTBS 87*

Hall, G(ranville) Stanley
American. Psychologist
Pioneer in American child, educational psychology; established one of earliest psychological laboratories; first president, American Psychological Association, 1892.
b. Feb 1, 1844 in Ashfield, Massachusetts
d. Apr 24, 1924 in Worcester, Massachusetts
Source: *Alli SUP; AmBi; AmPeW; AmSocL; BiDAmEd; BiD&SB; BiDPsy; BioIn 1, 4, 7, 8, 9, 12, 15, 16, 18, 19; DcAmAu; DcAmB; DcAmMeB 84; DcNAA; Dis&D; EncPaPR 91; LinLib L, S; McGEWB; NamesHP; NatCAB 39; NewCol 75; OhA&B; OxCAmH; OxCAmL 65, 95; RAdv 14; REnAL; TwCA, SUP; WebAB 74, 79; WhAm 1; WorAl; WorAlBi*

Hall, Glenn Henry
"Mr. Goalie"
Canadian. Hockey Player
Goalie, 1952-71, mostly with Chicago; won Vezina Trophy three times, Conn Smythe Trophy, 1968; Hall of Fame, 1975.
b. Oct 3, 1931 in Humboldt, Saskatchewan, Canada
Source: *BioIn 6, 8, 9, 10, 11; HocEn; WhoHcky 73*

Hall, Gus
[Arvo Kusta Halberg]
American. Political Activist
Leading American communist; two-time presidential candidate.

b. Oct 8, 1910 in Iron, Minnesota
Source: *BiDAmLf; BioIn 9, 10, 11, 13, 14; BioNews 74; ConAu 108, 137; CurBio 73; EncAL; FacFETw; NewYTBS 84; PolPar; PolProf J, K; WhoAm 78, 80, 82, 84, 86, 88, 90, 92, 94, 95, 96; WhoAmP 73, 75, 77, 79, 81; WrDr 96*

Hall, Huntz
[Henry Hall]
American. Actor
Played Dippy in *The Dead End Kids;* Satch in *The Bowery Boys* film series, 1930s-40s.
b. Aug 15, 1920 in New York, New York
Source: *BioIn 15, 16; EncAFC; FilmEn; FilmgC; ForYSC; GangFlm; HalFC 80, 84, 88; IntMPA 77, 80, 84, 86, 88, 92; JoeFr; LegTOT; MovMk; VarWW 85; WhoHol 92, A; WhoHrs 80*

Hall, James
American. Geologist
Authority on invertebrate paleontology, stratigraphic geology; wrote classic *Geology of New York,* 1843.
b. Sep 12, 1811 in Hingham, Massachusetts
d. Aug 7, 1898 in Bethlehem, New Hampshire
Source: *Alli; AmBi; ApCAB; BiDAmS; BiESc; BiInAmS; BioIn 2, 11; DcAmAu; DcAmB; DcBiPP; DcNAA; DcScB; Drake; HarEnUS; InSci; LarDcSc; NatCAB 3; OxCAmH; TwCBDA; WebAB 74, 79; WhAm HS; WhDW*

Hall, James, Sir
Scottish. Chemist, Geologist
Founded experimental geology.
b. Jan 17, 1761 in Dunglass, Scotland
d. Jun 23, 1832 in Edinburgh, Scotland
Source: *Alli; AsBiEn; BiDLA; BiESc; BioIn 5; DcBiPP; DcEnL; DcNaB; DcScB; InSci; LarDcSc; WhDW; WorScD*

Hall, James Norman
American. Author
Co-wrote novels of S Pacific with Charles Nordhoff: *Mutiny on the Bounty,* 1932.
b. Apr 22, 1887 in Colfax, Iowa
d. Jul 6, 1951 in Papeete, Tahiti, French Polynesia
Source: *AmAu&B; AmNov; AuBYP 2, 3; Benet 87; BenetAL 91; BioIn 1, 2, 3, 4, 5, 7, 8, 9, 12; ConAu 123; CyWA 58; DcAmB S5; DcLEL; JBA 34; LegTOT; LinLib L, S; MnBBF; OxCAmL 65, 83, 95; OxCAusL; PenC AM; PeoHis; REn; REnAL; SmATA 21; TwCA, SUP; TwCLC 23; WhAm 3; WhLit; WhNAA*

Hall, Jerry (Faye)
"Tall Hall"
American. Model
Top fashion model in the 1970-80s; married to Mick Jagger.
b. Jul 2, 1956 in Mesquite, Texas
Source: *AmMWSc 92; BioIn 12, 13, 14, 16; CelR 90; IntWW 91, 93; LegTOT*

Hall, Joe
[Joseph Henry Hall]
"Bad Joe"
Canadian. Hockey Player
Forward, Montreal, 1917-19; Hall of Fame, 1961; died from influenza during Stanley Cup playoffs.
b. Apr 5, 1882 in Staffordshire, England
d. Apr 5, 1919 in Seattle, Washington
Source: *HocEn; WhoHcky 73*

Hall, Joe Beasman
American. Basketball Coach
Coach, U of KY, 1971-85.
b. Nov 30, 1928 in Cynthiana, Kentucky
Source: *Dun&B 90; WhoAm 80, 82, 84, 90; WhoFI 89; WhoSSW 80*

Hall, Joseph M
[The Hostages]
American. Hostage
One of 52 held by terrorists, Nov 1979 - Jan 1981.
b. 1950? in Oklahoma
Source: *NewYTBS 81*

Hall, Joyce Clyde
American. Business Executive
Founded Hallmark Cards, Inc., 1910.
b. Dec 29, 1891 in David City, Nebraska
d. Oct 29, 1982 in Leawood, Kansas
Source: *BiDAmBL 83; BioIn 2, 3, 4, 5, 6, 7, 8, 9, 11, 13, 15, 18; CurBio 83; FacFETw; InWom SUP; NewYTBS 82; WebAB 74, 79; WhAm 8; WhoAm 74, 76, 78, 80, 82; WhoAmA 73; WhoFI 83; WorAl*

Hall, Juanita
American. Singer, Actor
Best known for Broadway role of Bloody Mary in *South Pacific,* 1949
b. Nov 6, 1901 in Newport, New Jersey
d. Feb 28, 1968 in Keyport, New Jersey
Source: *BiE&WWA; BioIn 8, 18; BlkWAm; CmpEPM; DcAmNB; EncMT; FilmgC; HalFC 80, 84, 88; LegTOT; MotPP; NotBlAW 1; NotNAT B; WhAm 4; WhoHol B; WhScrn 74, 77*

Hall, Lloyd Augustus
American. Chemist
Patented over 25 methods of preserving, sterilizing foods.
b. Jun 20, 1894 in Elgin, Illinois
d. Jan 2, 1971 in Altadena, California
Source: *BioIn 4, 5, 9, 11, 20; BlksScM; DiAASTC; InB&W 80, 85; NegAl 76, 83, 89; NotTwCS; WhAm 5*

Hall, Lyman
American. Statesman, Continental Congressman
Early GA patroit; signed Declaration of Independence, 1776; GA governor, 1783.
b. Apr 12, 1724 in Wallingford, Connecticut
d. Oct 19, 1790 in Burke County, Georgia
Source: *AmBi; AmRev; ApCAB; BiAUS; BiDrAC; BiDrACR; BiDrUSC 89; BioIn 3, 5, 7, 8, 9; DcAmB; Dis&D; Drake; EncAR; EncCRAm; EncSoH; NatCAB 2; TwCBDA; WhAm HS; WhAmP; WhAmRev*

Hall, Manly Palmer
Canadian. Author
Founded Philosophical Research Society, 1934; author of many books on philosophy, religion.
b. Mar 18, 1901 in Peterborough, Ontario, Canada
d. Aug 29, 1990 in Los Angeles, California
Source: *AstEnc; Au&Wr 71; ConAu 93, 132; EncAB-A 8; EncO&P 1, 2, 3; IntAu&W 76, 77; NewAgE 90; RelLAm 91; WhE&EA; WhNAA; WhoAm 76, 78, 80; WhoWest 74, 76, 78, 80; WrDr 76*

Hall, Monty
[Monty Halparin]
Canadian. TV Personality
Host of "Let's Make a Deal," 1963-77.
b. Aug 25, 1924 in Winnipeg, Manitoba, Canada
Source: *BioIn 13, 16; BioNews 74; CanWW 70, 79, 80, 81, 83, 89; ConAu 108; ConTFT 4; LesBEnT 92; VarWW 85; WhoAm 86, 90; WhoEnt 92; WorAlBi*

Hall, Peter Reginald Frederick, Sir
English. Director
Nat. Theatre Co. director, 1973-88.
b. Nov 22, 1930 in Bury Saint Edmunds, England
Source: *Baker 92; BiE&WWA; CnThe; ConAu 133; CroCD; DcArts; EncWT; FacFETw; FilmgC; HalFC 88; IntDcT 3; IntWW 74, 75, 76, 77, 78, 79, 80, 81, 82, 83, 89, 91, 93; IntWWM 90; NewGrDO; NotNAT A; OxCFilm; OxCThe 67, 83; PlP&P; VarWW 85; Who 74, 82, 83, 85, 90, 92, 94; WhoAm 92, 94, 95, 96, 97; WhoEnt 92; WhoOp 76; WhoThe 81; WhoWor 74, 76, 78, 80, 82, 84, 87, 89, 91, 93, 95; WorEFlm; WrDr 94, 96*

Hall, Radclyffe
[Marguerite Radclyffe-Hall]
English. Author, Poet
Wrote *The Well of Loneliness,* 1928, censored for lesbian theme.
b. Aug 12, 1880 in Bournemouth, England
d. Oct 7, 1943 in London, England
Source: *CurBio 43; DcNaB MP; FemiCLE; GayLesB; LngCTC; ModBrL; NewC; RadHan; REn; RfGEnL 91; TwCA SUP; TwCWr; WhoLA*

Hall, Rich
American. Comedian
TV show: "The Rich Hall Show," 1987.
Source: *BioIn 13; WhoHol 92*

Hall, Tom T
"The Storyteller"
American. Singer, Songwriter
Wrote song "Harper Valley PTA"; sold over 4.5 million copies.
b. May 25, 1936 in Olive Hill, Kentucky
Source: *Baker 84; BioIn 14, 15, 16; ConAu 102; ConMus 4; EncRk 88; HarEnCM 87; NewAmDM; NewGrDA 86; PenEncP; RkOn 74, 84; VarWW 85; WhoAm 86, 90; WhoEnt 92*

Hall and Oats
[Daryl Hall; John Oates]
American. Music Group
Pop-rock hits include "Rich Girl," 1977; "Maneater," 1982.
Source: *BiDBrA; BioIn 14, 15; CelR 90; Dun&B 88; EncRk 88; HarEnR 86; IlEncRk; NewGrDA 86; OxCPMus; RkOn 84; WhoRock 81; WhoRocM 82*

Halle, Charles, Sir
English. Pianist, Conductor
Founded, led Halle Concerts, 1858-95, in Manchester, England; became famed Halle Orchestra.
b. Apr 11, 1819 in Hagen, Germany
d. Oct 25, 1895 in Manchester, England
Source: *Baker 78, 84, 92; BioIn 1, 3, 7, 8, 9, 10, 12, 16; BriBkM 80; CelCen; DcNaB S1; MusMk; NewAmDM; NewGrDM 80; OxCMus; OxDcOp; PenDiMP*

Halleck, Charles Abraham
"Mr. Republican"
American. Lawyer, Politician
Congressman from IN, 1935-67, who served as both majority, minority leader.
b. Aug 22, 1900 in Demotte, Indiana
d. Mar 3, 1986 in Lafayette, Indiana
Source: *BiDrAC; BiDrUSC 89; BioIn 1, 3, 5, 6, 7, 11; CurBio 86; IntWW 74, 75, 76, 77; WhAmP; WhoAm 82*

Halleck, Fritz-Greene
American. Poet
Member, NYC's Knickerbocker group; with Joseph Rodman Drake wrote *Croaker Papers.*
b. Jul 8, 1790 in Guilford, Connecticut
d. Nov 19, 1867 in Guilford, Connecticut
Source: *Alli, SUP; AmAu; AmAu&B; AtlBL; BbD; BiD&SB; CasWL; CnDAL; CyAL 1; DcEnL; DcLEL; EvLB; OxCAmL 65; REn; REnAL*

Halleck, Henry Wager
American. Military Leader
General in chief of the Union army, 1862-64; replaced by Grant.
b. Jan 16, 1815 in Westernville, New York
d. Jan 9, 1872 in Louisville, Kentucky
Source: *Alli, SUP; AmBi; ApCAB; BioIn 1, 3, 6, 7, 11, 12, 15; CelCen; CivWDc; CmdGen 1991; DcAmAu; DcAmB; DcAmMiB; DcNAA; EncAB-H 1974, 1996; HarEnMi; HarEnUS; NatCAB 4; OxCAmH; OxCLaw; PeoHis; TwCBDA; WebAB 74, 79; WebAMB; WhAm HS; WhCiWar; WhoMilH 76; WorAl; WorAlBi*

Haller, Albrecht von
Swiss. Scientist
One of first to study experimental physiology; conducted landmark experiments in irritability of muscle tissue; wrote 8-vol. Elementa Physiologiae Corporis Humani, 1757-66.
b. Oct 16, 1708 in Bern, Switzerland
d. Dec 12, 1777 in Bern, Switzerland
Source: *AsBiEn; BiD&SB; BiDPsy; BiESc; BioIn 2, 5, 7, 9, 10, 11, 12, 14; BlkwCE; CamDcSc; CasWL; DcBiPP; DcEuL; DcLB 168; DcScB; EncEnl; EuAu; EvEuW; InSci; LinLib L, S; LuthC 75; McGEWB; NamesHP; NewCBEL; NewCol 75; OxCGer 76, 86; PenC EUR; WhDW; WorAl; WorAlBi*

Halley, Edmund
English. Astronomer
Predicted comets seen 1531, 1607, 1682 were same; known as Halley's Comet.
b. Nov 8, 1656 in Haggerston, England
d. Jan 14, 1742 in Greenwich, England
Source: *Alli; AsBiEn; BiESc; BioIn 12, 13; DcBiPP; DcEnL; DcInv; InSci; LegTOT; LinLib S; McGEWB; NewC; NewCBEL; OxCShps; REn; WorAl; WorAlBi*

Halliburton, Richard
American. Author, Explorer
Wrote *The Royal Road to Romance,* 1925; *The Flying Carpet,* 1932.
b. Jan 9, 1900 in Brownsville, Tennessee
d. Mar 23, 1939, At Sea
Source: *AmAu&B; AmBi; BenetAL 91; BioIn 2, 5, 6, 7, 21; CnDAL; ConAu 114, 135; DcNAA; EvLB; LinLib L, S; NatCAB 35; OxCAmL 65, 83; REnAL; SmATA 81; TwCA, SUP; WhAm 1, 1C; WhE&EA; WhNAA*

Halliday, Johnny
[Jean-Phillippe Smet]
French. Singer
European rock star, 1960s; hit "Let's Twist Again," 1961.
b. Jun 15, 1943 in Paris, France
Source: *PenEncP; RolSEnR 83*

Halliday, Richard
American. Producer
Producer, stage production of *Sound of Music,* stage, film productions of *Peter Pan;* married Mary Martin, 1940.
b. Apr 3, 1905 in Denver, Colorado
d. Mar 3, 1973 in Brasilia, Brazil
Source: *BiE&WWA; BioIn 9; ConAu 41R; NewYTBE 73; NotNAT B; WhAm 5; WhoE 74*

Hallstein, Walter
German. Diplomat, Statesman
Founder of European Economic Community (Common Market), pres., 1958-67.
b. Nov 17, 1901 in Mainz, Germany
d. Mar 29, 1982 in Stuttgart, Germany
Source: *AnObit 1982; BioIn 2, 3, 5, 6, 7, 12, 13, 18; ColdWar 1; ConAu 106; CurBio 82, 82N; FacFETw; IntWW 74, 75, 76, 77, 78, 79, 80, 81, 82, 82N; IntYB 78, 79, 80, 81, 82; NewYTBS 82; WhAm 8; Who 74, 82; WhoWor 74, 76, 78*

Hallstrom, Ivar
Swedish. Composer
Many operas, operettas include *The Vikings,* 1877.
b. Jun 5, 1826 in Stockholm, Sweden
d. Apr 11, 1901 in Stockholm, Sweden
Source: *Baker 78, 84; NewEOp 71; NewGrDM 80; OxCMus; OxDcOp*

Halop, Billy
American. Actor
Original Leader of Dead End Kids on stage, several films of 1930s-40s.
b. Feb 11, 1920 in New York, New York
d. Nov 9, 1976 in California
Source: *BioIn 15; SaTiSS; WhoHol A; WhScrn 83*

Halop, Florence
American. Actor
Played bailiff on TV series "Night Court," 1985-86.
b. Jan 23, 1923 in New York, New York
d. Jul 15, 1986 in Los Angeles, California
Source: *BioIn 15; NewYTBS 86; RadStar; WhoHol A*

Halper, Albert
American. Author
Studies of industrial life in large urban cities are subject of books: *Union Square,* 1933.
b. Aug 3, 1904 in Chicago, Illinois
Source: *AmAu&B; AmNov; Au&Wr 71; BenetAL 91; BioIn 1, 2, 4, 9, 12, 13; CamGLE; CamHAL; CnDAL; ConAmA; ConAu 3NR, 5R, 111; DcLB 9; DcLEL; JeAmFiW; OxCAmL 65, 83, 95; REn; REnAL; TwCA, SUP; WhAm 8; WhNAA; WhoAm 74, 76, 78, 80, 82; WhoAmJ 80*

Halpert, Edith Gregor
American. Art Collector
American folk art expert; assembled artifacts shown at Colonial Williamsburg, 1940.
b. Apr 25, 1900? in Odessa, Russia
d. Oct 6, 1970 in New York, New York
Source: *BioIn 9, 12, 17; DcAmB S8; InWom, SUP; NotAW MOD; WhAm 5; WhoAmW 58, 61, 64, 66, 68, 70, 72*

Hals, Frans
Dutch. Artist
Famed portraitist known for characterization: *Laughing Cavalier.*
b. 1581? in Antwerp, Spanish Netherlands
d. Sep 1, 1666 in Haarlem, Netherlands
Source: *AtlBL; BioIn 1, 2, 3, 4, 5, 6, 7, 8, 9, 10, 11; DcArts; LegTOT;*

McGEWB; OxCArt; OxDcArt; REn; WebBD 83; WorAl; WorAlBi

Halsey, Margaret (Frances)
American. Author
Wrote bestseller *With Malice Toward Some,* 1938.
b. Feb 13, 1910 in Yonkers, New York
d. Feb 4, 1997 in White Plains, New York
Source: *AmAu&B; ArtclWW 2; BioIn 3, 8, 11; ConAu 81; InWom SUP; REnAL*

Halsey, William Frederick, Jr.
"Bull"
American. Naval Officer
Commanded US 3rd Fleet, 1944-45.
b. Oct 30, 1882 in Elizabeth, New Jersey
d. Aug 16, 1959 in Fishers Island, New York
Source: *BiDWWGF; BioIn 1, 5, 6, 7, 8, 9, 10, 11, 15, 16; CurBio 42, 59; DcAmB S6; DcAmMiB; DcTwHis; HarEnMi; HisEWW; LinLib S; McGEWB; OxCAmH; OxCShps; WebAB 74, 79; WebAMB; WhAm 3; WhoMilH 76; WorAl*

Halsman, Philippe
American. Photographer
Noted for honest realism in portraits; has over 100 *Life* covers to credit.
b. May 2, 1906 in Riga, Russia
d. Jun 25, 1979 in New York, New York
Source: *AmAu&B; Au&Wr 71; AuBYP 2, 3; BioIn 2, 4, 5, 7, 12, 13; ConAu 10NR, 21R, 89; ConPhot 82, 88; CurBio 79, 79N; DcAmB S10; EncTwCJ; ICPEnP; MacBEP; NewYTBS 79; WhAm 7; WhAmArt 85; WhoAm 76, 78; WhoAmA 80N, 82N, 84N, 86N, 89N, 91N, 93N; WhoWor 74, 76*

Halstead, William S
American. Inventor
His over 80 patents include the technology for adding stereo sound in films; developed multiplexor.
b. 1903? in Mount Kisco, New York
d. Jul 7, 1987 in Los Angeles, California
Source: *NewYTBS 87*

Halsted, William Stewart
American. Surgeon
Established first surgical residency program, introduced sterile techniques to operating room procedures, 1890, at John Hopkins Hospital.
b. Sep 23, 1852 in New York, New York
d. Sep 7, 1922 in Baltimore, Maryland
Source: *AmBi; AsBiEn; BiDAmEd; BiESc; BiHiMed; BioIn 1, 2, 3, 4, 6, 7, 9, 11, 16; DcAmB; DcAmMeB, 84; DcNAA; DcScB; EncAB-H 1974, 1996; InSci; NatCAB 20; OxCAmH; OxCMed 86; WebAB 74, 79; WhAm 1; WorAl; WorScD*

Halston
[Roy Halston Frowick]
American. Fashion Designer
Launched modern-era of fashion retailing by mass marketing his name; created the spare shape, including pillbox hat made famous by Jackie Kennedy, and simple sportswear, considered America's contribution to fashion.
b. Apr 23, 1932 in Des Moines, Iowa
d. Mar 26, 1990 in San Francisco, California
Source: *AmDec 1970; AnObit 1990; BioIn 13, 14, 15, 16; BkPepl; CelR, 90; ConDes 84, 90, 97; ConFash; CurBio 72, 90, 90N; DcTwDes; EncFash; Entr; FacFETw; LegTOT; News 90, 90-3; NewYTBE 73; NewYTBS 87, 90; WhAm 10; WhoAm 76, 78, 80, 82, 84, 86, 88; WhoE 85; WhoFash 88; WorAl; WorAlBi; WorFshn*

Ham, Jack Raphael
American. Football Player
Seven-time all-pro linebacker, key performer Pittsburgh's "steel curtain" defense, 1971-82; won four Super Bowls; Hall of Fame, 1988.
b. Dec 23, 1948 in Johnstown, Pennsylvania
Source: *BiDAmSp FB; BioIn 9, 14; NewYTBE 70; WhoFtbl 74*

Hambleton, Hugh George
Canadian. Spy, Economist
Convicted of spying for Soviets while working for NATO, 1956-61.
b. May 4, 1922 in Ottawa, Ontario, Canada
Source: *BioIn 13; CanWW 70, 79, 80, 81*

Hamblin, Ken
American. Radio Performer
Host of "The Ken Hamblin Show," 1994—, a syndicated conservative call-in program.
b. 1940 in New York, New York
Source: *BiDAmNC; ConBlB 10*

Hambro, Leonid
American. Pianist
Official pianist, NY Philharmonic Orchestra, 1948-60s; toured with Victor Borge.
b. Jun 26, 1920 in Chicago, Illinois
Source: *NewGrDJ 88; WhoAm 74, 76, 86; WhoAmM 83*

Hamburger, Philip
American. Writer
Staff writer, *The New Yorker,* 1939—; published collection of writings, *Our Man Stanley,* 1963.
b. Jul 2, 1914 in Wheeling, West Virginia
Source: *AmAu&B; Au&Wr 71; BlueB 76; ConAu 5R; IntAu&W 76, 77, 82, 86, 89, 91; LinLib L; WhoAm 74, 76, 78, 80, 82, 84, 86, 88, 90; WhoWor 82, 84, 87, 89; WrDr 76, 80, 82, 84, 86, 88, 90, 92, 94, 96*

Hamel, Veronica
American. Model, Actor
Played Joyce Davenport on TV series "Hill Street Blues," 1981-87.
b. Nov 20, 1945 in Philadelphia, Pennsylvania
Source: *BioIn 12, 14; ConTFT 7; IntMPA 92; InWom SUP; VarWW 85; WhoAm 90; WhoAmW 91; WhoEnt 92*

Hamen y Leon, Juan van der
Spanish. Artist
Known for still lifes; portraits include *The Cook,* 1930.
b. 1596 in Madrid, Spain
d. 1631 in Madrid, Spain
Source: *BioIn 17, 19; McGDA*

Hamer, Dean H.
American. Geneticist
Published study that showed a link between male homosexuality and a gene in the X chromosome called Xq28, 1993.
b. May 29, 1951 in Montclair, New Jersey
Source: *AmMWSc 79, 82, 86, 89, 92, 95; WhoTech 82, 84, 89, 95*

Hamer, Fannie Lou Townsend
American. Civil Rights Leader
Founder of MS Freedom Dem. Party, 1972.
b. Oct 6, 1917 in Montgomery County, Mississippi
d. Mar 14, 1977 in Mound Bayou, Mississippi
Source: *AfrAmBi 2; AmRef; AmSocL; BioIn 11, 15, 17, 18, 19, 20, 21; InB&W 80, 85; InWom SUP; NewYTBS 77; NotBlAW 1; ObitOF 79; PolProf J*

Hamer, Robert
English. Director
Best known for *Kind Hearts and Coronets,* 1949.
b. Mar 31, 1911 in Kidderminster, England
d. Dec 4, 1963 in London, England
Source: *BiDFilm, 81, 94; BioIn 12, 15, 21; CmMov; DcFM; EncEurC; FilmEn; FilmgC; HalFC 80, 84, 88; IlWWBF; IntDcF 1-2, 2-2; MiSFD 9N; MovMk; NotNAT B; ObitT 1961; OxCFilm; WorEFlm; WorFDir 1*

Hamer, Rusty
[Russell Craig Hamer]
American. Actor
Played Rusty in TV series "Make Room for Daddy," 1953-64, "Make Room for Granddaddy," 1970-71; suicide victim.
b. Feb 15, 1947 in Tenafly, New Jersey
d. Jan 18, 1990 in De Ridder, Louisiana
Source: *BioIn 16; LegTOT; WhoHol A*

Hamill, Dorothy Stuart
American. Skater
World champion figure skater, 1976; won gold medal, 1976 Olympics; co-

owner, pres., The Ice Capades, 1993-95.
b. Jul 26, 1956 in Chicago, Illinois
Source: *BiDAmSp BK; BkPepl; CurBio 76; InWom SUP; NewYTBS 76, 77; WhoAm 86, 88; WhoAmW 85*

Hamill, Mark
"Motor-Mouth"
American. Actor
Played Luke Skywalker in *Star Wars*, trilogy, 1977-83.
b. Sep 25, 1952 in Oakland, California
Source: *BkPepl; CelR 90; ConTFT 5; FilmEn; HalFC 80, 84, 88; IntMPA 86, 88, 92, 94; VarWW 85; WhoAm 86, 90; WhoEnt 92; WhoHol 92; WorAlBi*

Hamill, Pete
[William Hamill]
American. Journalist
Wrote *The Gift*, 1973; *Flesh and Blood*, 1977.
b. Jun 24, 1935 in New York, New York
Source: *BiDAmNC; BiDConC; BioIn 8, 13, 16; CelR, 90; ConAu 18NR, 25R; ConLC 10; IntMPA 77, 80, 86, 92, 94; LiJour; VarWW 85; WhoAm 76, 78, 80, 82, 84, 86, 88, 92, 94, 95, 96, 97; WhoHol 92; WhoUSWr 88; WhoWrEP 89, 92, 95; WomWMM*

Hamilton, Alexander
American. Politician, Author
First US treasury secretary, 1789-95; strong federalist, planned US fiscal system.
b. Jan 11, 1755, West Indies
d. Jul 12, 1804 in New York, New York
Source: *Alli; AmAu; AmAu&B; AmBi; AmPolLe; ApCAB; BbD; BenetAL 91; BiAUS; BiD&SB; BiDrAC; BiDrUSE 71; CopCroC; CyAL 1; CyWA 58; DcAmB; DcAmC; DcEnL; DcLB 37; Drake; EncAB-H 1974, 1996; EncABHB 6; EncAJ; EncCRAm; EncEnl; HisWorL; JrnUS; LegTOT; McGEWB; MemAm; NinCLC 49; OxCAmH; OxCAmL 83, 95; RComAH; REn; REnAL; TwCBDA; WebAB 74, 79; WhAmP; WorAl; WorAlBi*

Hamilton, Alice
American. Physician, Social Reformer
Pioneer in industrial toxicology.
b. Feb 27, 1869 in New York, New York
d. Sep 22, 1970 in Hadlyme, Connecticut
Source: *AmPeW; AmRef; AmSocL; AmWomSc; AmWomWr; BiDMoPL; BiDSocW; BioAmW; BioIn 1, 2, 4, 5, 6, 7, 8, 9, 11, 12; ContDcW 89; DcAmB S8; DcAmImH; DcAmMeB 84; EncAB-H 1974, 1996; GoodHs; GrLiveH; HanAmWH; HerW, 84; HisWorL; InSci; IntDcWB; InWom, SUP; McGEWB; NotAW MOD; NotTwCS; NotWoLS; RComAH; WhAm 5; WhNAA; WhoAmW 58; WomFir; WomStre*

Hamilton, Andrew
American. Lawyer
Helped establish freedom of the press in 1735 libel trial.
b. 1676, Scotland
d. Aug 4, 1741 in Philadelphia, Pennsylvania
Source: *AmBi; ApCAB; BioIn 2, 6, 7, 9, 12, 15; DcAmB; Drake; EncCRAm; HarEnUS; MacEA; NatCAB 13; TwCBDA; WhAm HS*

Hamilton, Billy
[William Robert Hamilton]
"Sliding Billy"
American. Baseball Player
Outfielder, 1888-1901; won NL batting title, 1891, 1893; led NL in stolen bases seven times; Hall of Fame, 1961.
b. Feb 16, 1866 in Newark, New Jersey
d. Dec 16, 1940 in Worcester, Massachusetts
Source: *Ballpl 90; BiDAmSp BB; BioIn 7, 14, 15; WhoProB 73; WhoSpor*

Hamilton, Bob
[Robert Hamilton]
American. Golfer
Touring pro, 1940s; won PGA, 1944.
b. Jan 10, 1916 in Evansville, Illinois
Source: *BioIn 5; St&PR 91; WhoGolf*

Hamilton, Carrie
American. Actor
Daughter of Carol Burnett; in film *Tokyo Pop*, 1987, with mother in TV mo vie "Hostage," 1988.
b. Dec 5, 1963 in New York, New York
Source: *BioIn 15, 16; ConTFT 6; LegTOT*

Hamilton, Charles
American. Handwriting Expert
Operated Charles Hamilton Galleries, 1953-80, an auction house specializing in autographs; wrote *American Autographs*, 1983.
b. Dec 24, 1913
d. Dec 11, 1996 in New York, New York
Source: *AuBYP 2S, 3; BioIn 8, 10, 11, 12, 17; BlueB 76; ConAu 3NR, 5R, 20NR, 49NR; CurBio 76; IntAu&W 91, 93; SmATA 65; WrDr 80, 82, 84, 86, 88, 90, 92, 94, 96*

Hamilton, Charles Harold St. John
English. Author
Wrote boys adventure series, weekly papers; used over 20 pseudonyms in 5,000 stories.
b. Aug 8, 1875 in Ealing, England
d. Dec 24, 1961 in Kent, England
Source: *BioIn 3, 6, 7, 8, 10, 14; ConAu 73; MnBBF; OxCEng 67; SmATA 13; WhoChL*

Hamilton, Denis, Sir
English. Business Executive
Chairman of Reuters from 1979; chairman, Times Newspapers, 1971-80.
b. Dec 6, 1918 in South Shields, England
d. Apr 7, 1988 in London, England
Source: *AnObit 1988; BioIn 15, 16; BlueB 76; ConAu 109, 125; IntAu&W 77, 82; IntWW 76, 77, 78, 79, 80, 81, 82, 83; IntYB 78, 79, 80, 81, 82; WhAm 11; WhoWor 74, 78, 80, 82, 89*

Hamilton, Edith
American. Author
Mythology expert; wrote *The Greek Way*, 1930; *The Roman Way*, 1932.
b. Aug 12, 1867 in Dresden, Germany
d. May 31, 1963 in Washington, District of Columbia
Source: *AmAu&B; AmWomM; AmWomPl; AmWomWr; AnCL; BenetAL 91; BioAmW; BioIn 3, 4, 5, 6, 7, 8, 9, 11, 12; ConAu 77; CurBio 63; DcAmB S7; DcArts; EncAB-H 1974, 1996; HerW, 84; InWom, SUP; LibW; LinLib L, S; NatCAB 52; NotAW MOD; RAdv 14; RComAH; REn; REnAL; SmATA 20; TwCA, SUP; WebAB 74, 79; WhAm 4; WhNAA; WhoAmW 58, 64*

Hamilton, Emma, Lady
[Amy Lyon]
English. Mistress
Mistress of Horatio Nelson; known for her beauty.
b. Apr 26, 1761 in Great Neston, England
d. Jan 15, 1815 in Calais, France
Source: *Alli; Benet 87, 96; BiDLA; BioIn 2, 3, 4, 5, 6, 7, 8, 9, 10, 11, 13, 15, 16, 18; ContDcW 89; DcNaB; IntDcWB; NewC; REn*

Hamilton, Floyd (Garland)
American. Criminal
Public enemy number one, 1930s; pardoned for work with ex-convicts.
b. 1908?
d. Jun 26, 1984 in Grand Prairie, Texas
Source: *BioIn 9; ConAu 113*

Hamilton, George, IV
"Gorgeous George"
American. Actor
Star, producer of *Love at First Bite*, 1979; *Zorro, the Gay Blade*, 1981.
b. Aug 12, 1939 in Memphis, Tennessee
Source: *BioIn 5, 7, 12, 14; CelR, 90; ConAu X; ConTFT 3; FilmEn; FilmgC; ForYSC; HalFC 80, 84, 88; IntMPA 77, 78, 79, 80, 81, 82, 84, 86, 88, 92, 94, 96; ItaFilm; LegTOT; MnBBF; MotPP; MovMk; VarWW 85; WhoAm 76, 78, 80, 82; WhoHol 92, A; WorAl; WorAlBi*

Hamilton, Grace Towns
American. Politician
First African-American woman elected to the Georgia legislature, 1966-84; promoter of racial integration.
b. Feb 10, 1907 in Atlanta, Georgia
d. Jun 17, 1992 in Atlanta, Georgia

Source: *AfrAmBi 2; BlkWAm; InB&W 85; InWom SUP; NotBlAW 1; WhoAm 76, 78, 80, 82, 84, 86, 88; WhoAmW 66, 68, 70, 74, 75, 77, 79, 81, 83; WhoBlA 85, 90, 92, 94N; WhoGov 77; WomPO 78*

Hamilton, Guy
British. Director
Best known for James Bond films *Goldfinger*, 1964; *Diamonds Are Forever*, 1971.
b. 1922 in Paris, France
Source: *BiDFilm, 81, 94; BioIn 19; CmMov; ConTFT 8; FilmEn; FilmgC; HalFC 80, 84, 88; IlWWBF; IntMPA 75, 76, 77, 78, 79, 80, 81, 82, 84, 86, 88, 92, 94, 96; ItaFilm; MiSFD 9; VarWW 85; WhoAm 82; WhoEnt 92; WhoHrs 80; WorEFlm*

Hamilton, Ian Standish Monteith, Sir
English. Army Officer, Author
British commander at Gallipoli, WW I.
b. Jan 16, 1853 in Corfu, Ionian Islands
d. Oct 12, 1947 in London, England
Source: *Alli SUP; BioIn 1, 5, 7, 11; ChhPo, S1; DcInB; DcNaB 1941; EncSoA; HarEnMi; ObitOF 79; WhoMilH 76*

Hamilton, Joe
[Joseph Henry Michael Hamilton, Jr]
American. Producer
Emmy-winning producer; ex-husband of Carol Burnett; TV programs include "The Carol Burnett Show," 1967-78.
b. Jan 6, 1929 in Los Angeles, California
d. Jun 11, 1991 in Brentwood, California
Source: *BioIn 11; ConTFT 8, 10; LesBEnT 92; NewYTBS 91; WhAm 11; WhoAm 74, 76, 78, 80, 82, 84, 86, 88, 92; WhoEnt 92*

Hamilton, Lee Herbert
American. Politician
Dem. congressman from IN, 1964—; foreign affairs expert; co-chaired Iran Contra hearings, 1987.
b. Apr 20, 1931 in Daytona Beach, Florida
Source: *AlmAP 92; BiDrAC; BiDrUSC 89; BioIn 16; CngDr 74, 77, 79, 81, 83, 85, 87, 89; CurBio 88; NewYTBS 86; WhoAm 74, 76, 78, 80, 82, 84, 86, 88, 90, 92, 94, 95, 96, 97; WhoAmP 73, 75, 77, 79, 81, 83, 85, 87, 89, 91, 93, 95; WhoGov 72, 75, 77; WhoMW 80, 82, 86, 88, 90, 92, 93, 96*

Hamilton, Linda
American. Actor
Starred in the *Terminator* films, 1984, 1991; played Catherine Chandler on TV series, "Beauty and the Beast," 1987-89.
b. Sep 26, 1957 in Salisbury, Maryland
Source: *BioIn 16; CelR 90; ConTFT 7, 8; IntMPA 92; LegTOT*

Hamilton, Margaret Brainard
American. Actor
Best known for role of Miss Gulch/ Wicked Witch of the West in film *The Wizard of Oz*, 1939.
b. Sep 12, 1902 in Cleveland, Ohio
d. May 16, 1985 in Salisbury, Connecticut
Source: *BiE&WWA; ConNews 85-3; ConTFT 2; FilmgC; ForWC 70; IntMPA 82; MovMk; NotNAT; ThFT; VarWW 85; Vers A; WhoHol A*

Hamilton, Murray
American. Actor
Had supporting roles in films *The Graduate; The Hustler; Jaws; Jaws 2.*
b. Mar 24, 1923 in Washington, District of Columbia
d. Sep 1, 1986 in Washington, District of Columbia
Source: *BioIn 15; EncAFC; FilmgC; HalFC 80, 84, 88; NewYTBS 86; NotNAT*

Hamilton, Nancy
American. Actor, Songwriter
Wrote lyrics for Oscar-winning documentary on Helen Keller, 1956.
b. Jul 27, 1908 in Sewickley, Pennsylvania
d. Feb 18, 1985 in New York, New York
Source: *AmWomD; ASCAP 66, 80; BiE&WWA; BioIn 14, 19; CmpEPM; ConAu 115; EncMT; InWom; NotNAT; OxCPMus; WhoAmW 61*

Hamilton, Neil
American. Actor
Films include *Madame X*, 1966; *Which Way to the Front?*, 1970.
b. Sep 9, 1899 in Lynn, Massachusetts
d. Sep 24, 1984 in Escondido, California
Source: *BiE&WWA; BioIn 13, 14; ConTFT 2; Film 2; FilmEn; FilmgC; ForYSC; HalFC 80, 84, 88; MovMk; NotNAT; SilFlmP; TwYS; VarWW 85; What 5; WhoHol A; WhThe*

Hamilton, Patrick
[Anthony Walter Patrick Hamilton]
English. Dramatist, Actor, Author
Plays include *Angel Street*, 1938.
b. Mar 17, 1904 in Hassocks, England
d. Sep 23, 1962 in Sheringham, England
Source: *BioIn 4, 6, 9, 13, 14; CnMD; ConAu 113; ConLC 51; DcLB 10; DcLEL; EncMys; EncWT; Ent; HalFC 80, 84, 88; LngCTC; ModWD; NewCBEL; NotNAT B; OxCEng 85; REn; ScF&FL 1; TwCA SUP; TwCCr&M 80, 85, 91; TwCWr; WhoTwCL; WhThe*

Hamilton, Roy
American. Singer
Baritone of 1950s; hits include "Ebb Tide," 1954; "Unchained Melody," 1955.
b. Apr 16, 1929 in Leesburg, Georgia
d. Jul 20, 1969 in New Rochelle, New York
Source: *BiDAmM; BioIn 8, 16; DrBlPA, 90; EncRk 88; IlEncBM 82; PenEncP; RkOn 74; RolSEnR 83; WhoRock 81*

Hamilton, Scott
American. Skater
Four-time world champion figure skater, 1981-84; won gold medal, 1984 Olympics.
b. Aug 28, 1958 in Toledo, Ohio
Source: *BiDAmSp BK; BioIn 12, 13; CurBio 85; FacFETw; LegTOT; NewYTBS 83; WhoMW 90; WhoSpor; WorAlBi*

Hamilton, Virginia
American. Author
Won Edgar for *The House of Dies Drear*, 1969.
b. Mar 13, 1936 in Yellow Springs, Ohio
Source: *AmWomWr; ArtclWW 2; Au&Arts 2; Au&ICB; AuBYP 2; AuNews 1; BioIn 14, 15, 16, 17, 18, 19, 20, 21; BlkAWP; BlkWr 1, 2; BlmGWL; CamGLE; ChhPo S2; ChlBkCr; ChlLR 1, 11, 40; ConAu 20NR, 25R, 37NR; ConBlB 10; ConLC 26; DcLB 32, 33, 52; DcTwCCu 5; InB&W 80; MajAI; MajTwCW; MorBMP; NewbC 1966; NotBlAW 1; OnHuMoP; OxCChiL; ScF&FL 92; SchCGBL; SmATA 4, 56; TwCChW 78, 83, 89; WhoAfA 96; WhoAm 76, 78, 80, 82, 84, 86, 88, 90, 92, 94, 95, 96, 97; WhoAmW 74, 81, 83, 85, 87, 89, 91, 93, 95, 97; WhoBlA 85, 88, 90, 92, 94; WhoMW 92; WhoUSWr 88; WhoWrEP 89, 92, 95; WrDr 80, 82, 84, 86, 88, 90, 92*

Hamilton, William
American. Cartoonist, Author
New Yorker cartoonist, 1965—; wrote syndicated "Now Society" column since 1973.
b. Jun 2, 1939 in Palo Alto, California
Source: *BioIn 10, 11, 12, 15, 18; ConAu 15NR, 69; ConGrA 1; IntAu&W 91; WhoAm 78, 80, 82, 84, 86, 88, 90; WorECar*

Hamilton, William, Sir
Scottish. Philosopher
Influenced by Kant; wrote "Philosophy of the Unconditioned," 1829.
b. Mar 8, 1788 in Glasgow, Scotland
d. May 6, 1856 in Edinburgh, Scotland
Source: *Alli; BiD&SB; BiDPsy; BioIn 6, 16; BritAu 19; CamGEL; CamGLE; CasWL; CelCen; CmScLit; CyEd; DcBiPP; DcEnL; DcNaB; DcScB; EvLB; LinLib L, S; LuthC 75; NamesHP; NewC; NewCBEL; OxCEng 67, 85, 95; OxCPhil; VicBrit*

Hamilton, William Rowan, Sir
Irish. Mathematician, Astronomer
Devised law of varying action; developed theories of geometrical optics, 1827, of quaternions, 1843.
b. Aug 4, 1805 in Dublin, Ireland
d. Sep 2, 1865 in Dublin, Ireland
Source: *Alli; AsBiEn; BiDIrW; BiESc; BioIn 3, 4, 6, 7, 8, 11, 12, 14, 15, 16,*

17, 21; CamDcSc; CelCen; DcBiPP; DclrB 78, 88; DclrL 96; DclrW 1, 2; DcNaB; DcScB; InSci; LarDcSc; LinLib S; McGEWB; NewC; NewCol 75; OxCEng 67, 85, 95; OxClri; Polre; RAdv 13-5; WorAl; WorScD

Hamlin, Hannibal
American. US Vice President
VP under Lincoln, 1861-65.
b. Aug 27, 1809 in Paris Hill, Maine
d. Jul 4, 1891 in Bangor, Maine
Source: *AmBi; AmPolLe; ApCAB; BiAUS; BiDrAC; BiDrGov 1789; BiDrUSC 89; BiDrUSE 71, 89; BioIn 1, 3, 4, 7, 8, 9, 10, 14, 17, 21; CivWDc; CyAG; DcAmB; Drake; HarEnUS; LegTOT; LinLib S; NatCAB 2; PolPar; TwCBDA; VicePre; WebAB 74, 79; WhAm HS; WhAmP; WhCiWar; WorAl; WorAlBi*

Hamlin, Harry Robinson
American. Actor
Starred in TV series "L.A. Law," 1986-91; films include *Making Love,* 19 82.
b. Oct 30, 1951 in Pasadena, California
Source: *BioIn 13, 15, 16; ConTFT 6; HalFC 84; IntMPA 82, 92; NewYTBS 79; VarWW 85; WhoAm 84, 86, 88, 90, 92, 94, 95, 96, 97; WhoEmL 93; WhoEnt 92; WorAlBi*

Hamlin, Talbot Faulkner
American. Author
Won Pulitzer for biography *Benjamin Henry Latrobe,* 1956.
b. Jun 16, 1889 in New York, New York
d. Oct 7, 1956 in Beaufort, South Carolina
Source: *AmAu&B; BioIn 3, 4, 6; CurBio 54, 56, 57; DcAmB S6; MacEA; NatCAB 46; ObitOF 79; OxCAmL 65; WhAm 3; WhAmArt 85*

Hamlisch, Marvin Frederick
American. Composer, Musician
Won Oscars for scoring *The Way We Were, The Sting,* 1974; has won 4 Grammys, 9 Tonys; a Pulitzer for *A Chorus Line,* 1975.
b. Jun 2, 1944 in New York, New York
Source: *AmSong; ASCAP 66; Baker 84; BioIn 14, 15; BioNews 74; BkPepl; CelR 90; ConMus 1; ConTFT 4; HalFC 88; IntMPA 92; IntWW 91; IntWWM 90; NewAmDM; OxCAmT 84; OxCPMus; VarWW 85; WhoAm 86, 90; WhoEnt 92*

Hammarskjold, Dag (Hjalmar Agne Carl)
Swedish. Statesman
Secretary general, UN, 1953-61; won Nobel Peace Prize, 1961; died in plane crash.
b. Jul 29, 1905 in Jonkoping, Sweden
d. Sep 18, 1961 in Ndola, Rhodesia
Source: *BiDInt; BioIn 3, 4, 5, 6, 7, 8, 9, 10, 11, 12, 13, 14, 15, 16, 17, 18, 19, 20; ColdWar 1; ConAu 77; ConHero 1; CurBio 53, 61; DcPol; DcTwHis; EncCW; EncSoA; FacFETw; GayLesB; HisDcKW; HisEAAC; HisWorL; IlEncMy; LegTOT; LinLib L, S; McGEWB; NobelP; ObitT 1961; OxCLaw; RAdv 13-3; REn; WhAm 4; WhoNob, 90, 95; WhoUN 75; WorAl; WorAlBi*

Hammarskjold, Hjalmar
[Knut Hjalmar Leonard Hammarskjold]
Swedish. Political Leader
Prime minister, 1914-17; chm., Nobel Prize Foundation, 1929-47; father of Dag.
b. Feb 4, 1862 in Tuna, Sweden
d. Oct 12, 1953 in Stockholm, Sweden
Source: *BioIn 3; ObitOF 79; WebBD 83*

Hammer
[Stanley Kirk Burrell]
American. Rapper, Dancer
Rap singer; album *Please Hammer Don't Hurt 'Em* has sold more than 6 mill ion copies to become rap's all-time best seller; *Too Legit to Quit,* 1991; won 5 American Music Awards, 3 Grammys and a People's Choice Award, 1991.
b. Mar 29, 1963 in Oakland, California
Source: *BioIn 18; CurBio 91; LegTOT; News 91, 91-2; WhoBlA 92*

Hammer, Armand
American. Financier, Manufacturer
One of world's most powerful men; chairman, Occidental Petroleum, 1957-90; known for philanthropic interests, int'l investments.
b. May 21, 1898 in New York, New York
d. Dec 10, 1990 in Los Angeles, California
Source: *AmDec 1930; AnObit 1990; BiDAmBL 83; BioIn 7, 8, 9, 10, 11, 12, 13, 14, 15, 16, 17, 18, 19, 20; BioNews 74; BlueB 76; BusPN; CelR 90; ConAu 134; CurBio 73, 91N; Dun&B 79, 86, 88, 90; EncCW; EncWB; FacFETw; IntWW 74, 75, 76, 77, 78, 79, 80, 81, 82, 83, 89, 91N; JeAmHC; LegTOT; News 91, 91-3; NewYTBE 72, 73; NewYTBS 81, 87, 90; PolProf NF; St&PR 75, 91; WhAm 10; Who 85, 88, 90, 92N; WhoAm 74, 76, 78, 80, 82, 84, 86, 88, 90; WhoAmA 78, 80, 82, 84, 86, 89, 91N, 93N; WhoFI 74, 75, 77, 79, 81, 83, 85, 87, 89; WhoWest 74, 76, 78, 80, 82, 84, 87, 89; WhoWor 78, 80, 82, 84, 87, 89, 91; WorAl; WorAlBi*

Hammer, Barbara J.
American. Filmmaker
Has been called "the mother of lesbian film," made *Out of South Africa,* 1995.
b. May 15, 1939 in Hollywood, California
Source: *GayLesB*

Hammer, Jan
[Mahavishnu Orchestra]
Czech. Musician, Composer
Pianist with Mahavishnu Orchestra, 1971-73; best known for soundtrack performances, production for TV series "Miami Vice," 1984-89.
b. Apr 17, 1948 in Prague, Czechoslovakia
Source: *AllMusG; ASCAP 80; BiDJaz; BioIn 11, 14, 15, 16; ConMuA 80A; ConNews 87-3; ConTFT 10; EncJzS; LegTOT; NewAgMG; NewGrDJ 88, 94; PenEncP; WhoEnt 92; WhoRock 81*

Hammer, Richard
American. Author
Won Edgars for fact crime books: *CBS Murders,* 1987; *The Vatican Connection,* 1983.
b. Mar 22, 1928 in Hartford, Connecticut
Source: *BioIn 10; ConAu 11NR, 25R; SmATA 6; WhoEnt 92; WhoMW 86, 90*

Hammerstein, Oscar
German. Manager, Impresario
Built operatic theaters in NY, Philadelphia, London, 1898-1910; father of Oscar II.
b. May 8, 1846 in Berlin, Germany
d. Aug 1, 1919 in New York, New York
Source: *Baker 78, 84, 92; DcAmB; EncMT; MetOEnc; NewAmDM; NewEOp 71; NewGrDA 86; NewGrDO; OxCAmL 65; OxCMus; OxDcOp; WhAm 1; WhoStg 1906, 1908*

Hammerstein, Oscar, II
[Rodgers and Hammerstein]
American. Lyricist
Wrote lyrics for *Oklahoma!,* 1943; *Carousel,* 1945; *South Pacific,* 1949; with Richard Rogers, one of Broadway's most respected, successful teams.
b. Jul 12, 1895 in New York, New York
d. Aug 22, 1960 in Doylestown, Pennsylvania
Source: *AmAu&B; AmPS; AmSong; ASCAP 66, 80; Baker 78, 84; Benet 87; BenetAL 91; BestMus; BiDAmM; BioIn 1, 2, 3, 4, 5, 6, 7, 9, 10, 11, 12, 14, 15, 16, 17, 18; BriBkM 80; CamGWoT; CamHAL; ChhPo S1, S3; CmpEPM; CnDAL; ConAu 101; CurBio 44, 60; DcAmB S6; DcArts; EncMT; EncWT; Ent; FacFETw; FilmEn; FilmgC; HalFC 80, 84, 88; LegTOT; LinLib L, S; McGEWD 72, 84; ModWD; MorMA; NatCAB 45; NewAmDM; NewCBMT; NewGrDA 86; NewGrDM 80; NewOxM; NotNAT A, B; ObitT 1951; OxCAmH; OxCAmL 65, 83, 95; OxCAmT 84; OxCPMus; OxCThe 67; OxDcOp; PlP&P; REn; REnAL; Sw&Ld C; WebAB 74, 79; WhAm 4; WhScrn 77, 83; WhThe; WorAl; WorAlBi*

Hammett, Dashiell
[Samuel Dashiell Hammett]
American. Author
Created fictional detective Sam Spade in *The Maltese Falcon,* 1930.
b. May 27, 1894 in Saint Mary's County, Maryland
d. Jan 10, 1961 in New York, New York
Source: *AgeMat; AmAu&B; AmCulL; AuNews 1; Benet 87; BenetAL 91; BioIn*

2, 4, 6, 7, 8, 10, 11, 12, 13, 14, 15, 17, 19, 20, 21; BlmGEL; CamGEL; CamGLE; CamHAL; CasWL; CmCal; CmMov; CnDAL; CnMWL; ConAu 81; ConLC 3, 5, 10, 19, 47; CorpD; CrtSuMy; CyWA 58, 89; DcAmB S7; DcFM; DcLB DS6; DcLEL; EncAB-H 1974, 1996; EncMcCE; EncMys; EncWB; EncWL 3; EvLB; FacFETw; FilmEn; FilmgC; GangFlm; GrWrEL N; HalFC 80, 84, 88; LegTOT; LinLib L; LngCTC; MagSAmL; MajTwCW; MnBBF; ModAL, S1, S2; Novels; ObitT 1961; OxCAmL 65, 83; OxCEng 67, 85; OxCFilm; PenC AM; PolProf T; RAdv 14; REn; REnAL; RfGAmL 87; ScF&FL 1; ScFEYrs; ShSCr 17; ShSWr; TwCA, SUP; TwCCr&M 80, 85, 91; TwCWr; WebAB 74, 79; WebE&AL; WhAm 4; WhE&EA; WhoTwCL; WorAl; WorAlBi; WorEFlm

Hammon, Jupiter
American. Poet
First black poet published in US, 1761.
b. 1720
d. 1800
Source: *AfrAmAl 6; AmAu; AmAu&B; BenetAL 91; BioIn 4, 7, 8, 9, 13, 14, 15; BlkAWP; CamGEL; CamGLE; CamHAL; DcAmB; DcNAA; InB&W 80; LegTOT; NegAl 76, 83, 89; OxCAmL 65, 83, 95; REnAL; SelBAAf; SelBAAu; WhAm HS*

Hammon, William McDowell
American. Physician
Renowned for experiments with gamma globulin in the 1950s that aided in the discovery of Salk vaccine.
b. Jul 20, 1904 in Columbus, Ohio
d. Sep 19, 1989 in Seminole, Florida
Source: *AmMWSc 76P, 79; BiDrAPH 79; BioIn 3, 4, 16; BlueB 76; CurBio 89N; InSci; NewYTBS 89; WhAm 10; WhoAm 74, 76; WhoTech 84*

Hammond, Bray
American. Author, Banker
Won Pulitzer for *Banks and Politics in America: From the Revolution to the Civil War,* 1958.
b. Nov 20, 1886 in Springfield, Missouri
d. Jul 20, 1968 in Thetford, Vermont
Source: *AmAu&B; BioIn 8, 10; DcAmB S8; NatCAB 55; ObitOF 79; OxCAmL 65; WhAm 5*

Hammond, E(dward) Cuyler
American. Scientist
First medical researcher to link cigarette smoking and lung cancer, 1952.
b. Jun 14, 1912 in Baltimore, Maryland
d. Nov 3, 1986 in New York, New York
Source: *AmMWSc 73P; BioIn 4, 11, 15, 16; ConNews 87-1; CurBio 57, 87; InSci; IntYB 78; WhAm 9; WhoAm 74, 76*

Hammond, James Henry
''''Mudsill Hammond''''
American. Politician
SC senator, 1857-60; advocated states' rights; made famous ''Cotton is King'' speech, 1858.
b. Nov 17, 1807 in Newbury District, South Carolina
d. Nov 13, 1864 in Beech Island, South Carolina
Source: *Alli, SUP; AmBi; AmPolLe; ApCAB; BiDrAC; BiDrGov 1789; BiDrUSC 89; BiDSA; BioIn 7, 13, 14, 16, 20; CyAL 2; DcAmAu; DcAmB; DcNAA; EncAAH; EncAB-H 1974, 1996; EncSoH; HarEnUS; McGEWB; NatCAB 12; NewCol 75; TwCBDA; WhAm HS; WhAmP; WhoColR*

Hammond, John Hays, Jr.
American. Inventor
Made extensive contributions to radio remote control.
b. Apr 13, 1888 in San Francisco, California
d. Feb 12, 1965 in New York, New York
Source: *Baker 78, 84, 92; BioIn 1, 5, 6, 7; NatCAB 15; WhAm 4*

Hammond, John Henry, Jr.
American. Music Executive
VP, Columbia Records; discovered Billie Holiday, Aretha Franklin, Bob Dylan; contributed to development of jazz.
b. Dec 15, 1910 in New York, New York
d. Jul 10, 1987 in New York, New York
Source: *AmCulL; CurBio 79, 87; EncJzS; HarEnR 86; News 88-2; NewYTBS 87; WhoAm 78*

Hammond, Laurens
American. Inventor
Manufactured keyboard instruments including Hammond organ, chord organ, 1940s-50s.
b. Jan 11, 1895 in Evanston, Illinois
d. Jul 1, 1973 in Cornwall, Connecticut
Source: *Baker 78, 84, 92; ConAu 104; DcAmB S9; NewAmDM; NewYTBE 73; ObitOF 79; WhAm 6; WhoAm 74; WhoMus 72*

Hammurabi
Babylonian. Ruler
Started to build tower of Babel; established written code of law.
b. 1792BC
d. 1750BC
Source: *CopCroC; HisWorL; LegTOT; NewCol 75; WebBD 83; WorAl; WorAlBi*

Hamner, Earl Henry, Jr.
American. Author
Creator of TV series ''The Waltons,'' ''Falcon Crest.''
b. Jul 10, 1923 in Schuyler, Virginia
Source: *AuNews 2; BioIn 11, 14; ConAu 73; ConLC 12; ConTFT 6; IntMPA 92; LesBEnT 92; VarWW 85; WhoAm 76, 78, 80, 82, 84, 86, 88, 92, 94, 95, 96, 97*

Hampden, John
English. Statesman
Symbolized resistance to royal tyranny by refusal to honor Charles I's taxation for ship money, 1636.
b. 1594 in London, England
d. Jun 24, 1643 in Thame, England
Source: *Alli; Benet 87, 96; BioIn 1, 3, 9, 11, 12; DcBiPP; DcNaB; HisDStE; LinLib S; McGEWB; NewC; OxCEng 85, 95; REn; WhDW*

Hampden, Walter
[Walter Hampden Dougherty]
American. Actor
Starred in *Hamlet, Cyrano de Bergerac;* fourth pres., Players' Club, 1927-54.
b. Jun 30, 1879 in New York, New York
d. Jun 11, 1955 in Los Angeles, California
Source: *BioIn 2, 3, 4, 6, 10; CamGWoT; CurBio 53, 55; DcAmB S5; EncWT; FamA&A; Film 1; FilmEn; FilmgC; ForYSC; HalFC 80, 84, 88; HolCA; LinLib S; MotPP; MovMk; NatCAB 44; NotNAT B; OxCAmT 84; OxCThe 67, 83; REn; REnAL; Vers B; WebAB 74, 79; WhAm 3; WhoHol B; WhoStg 1908; WhScrn 74, 77, 83; WhThe*

Hampshire, Susan
English. Actor
Won Emmys, 1970, 71, 73; appeared in series ''The Forsythe Saga,'' ''The First Churchi lls.''
b. May 12, 1942 in London, England
Source: *BioIn 13; ConAu 112, 129; ConTFT 2, 14; CurBio 74; FilmgC; HalFC 84; IlWWBF; IntAu&W 93; IntMPA 82, 92; IntWW 83, 89, 91, 93; InWom SUP; LegTOT; NewYTBE 70; VarWW 85; Who 82, 83, 85, 88, 90, 92, 94; WhoAm 74, 76, 78, 80, 82, 84, 86, 88, 90, 92, 94, 95; WhoAmW 83, 85, 87; WhoEnt 92; WhoHol A; WhoThe 77, 81; WhoWor 78, 91; WorAl*

Hampson, Frank
English. Cartoonist, Author
Created science fiction cartoon character Dan Dare, 1950.
b. Dec 21, 1918? in Manchester, England
d. Jul 8, 1985 in Surrey, England
Source: *AnObit 1985; BiDScF; BioIn 14, 15; ConAu 117; DcNaB 1981; EncSF; SmATA 46N; WorECom*

Hampson, Thomas
American. Opera Singer
Baritone; noted roles at the Metropolitan Opera include Figaro and Don Giovanni.
b. Jun 28, 1955 in Elkhart, Indiana
Source: *Baker 92; BioIn 16; ConMus 12; CurBio 91; IntWWM 90; LegTOT; NewGrDO; NewYTBS 91; WhoAmM 83*

Hampton, Christopher James
British. Dramatist
Wrote 1971 Tony Award winner *The Philanthropist.*
b. Jan 26, 1946 in Fayal, Azores

Source: *Au&Wr 71; BioIn 11, 13, 14; CamGWoT; CnThe; ConAu 25R; ConLC 5, 6; ConTFT 7; DcLEL 1940; IntAu&W 76, 91; IntWW 83, 91; OxCEng 85; VarWW 85; Who 85, 92; WhoThe 77; WhoWor 91; WrDr 80, 92*

Hampton, Henry
American. Filmmaker
President and founder, Blackside, Inc. (a film and TV production co.), 1968—.
b. Jan 8, 1940 in Saint Louis, Missouri
Source: *ConBlB 6*

Hampton, Hope
American. Socialite, Actor
Silent film star, NYC socialite; noted for lavish dress.
b. 1901 in Houston, Texas
d. Jan 2, 1982 in New York, New York
Source: *Film 2; FilmgC; InWom; MotPP; NewYTBS 82; TwYS; WhoHol A*

Hampton, James
American. Actor
In films *Condorman,* 1981; *The China Syndrome,* 1979.
b. Jul 9, 1936 in Oklahoma City, Oklahoma
Source: *ConTFT 7; IntMPA 92, 94, 96; VarWW 85; WhoHol 92, A*

Hampton, Lionel Leo
"Hamp"; "King of Vibes"
American. Bandleader, Jazz Musician
Top vibraphonist pioneer who formed big band, 1940; theme song: "Flying Home."
b. Apr 12, 1913 in Louisville, Kentucky
Source: *BiDJaz; BioIn 15; CelR 90; CurBio 71; DrBlPA 90; InB&W 80; NewGrDA 86; PenEncP; VarWW 85; WhoAm 78, 80, 82, 84, 86, 88, 92, 94, 95, 96, 97; WhoBlA 80, 85, 88; WhoE 74; WhoEnt 92; WhoHol A; WorAlBi*

Hampton, Wade
American. Army Officer
Confederate leader whose troops of artillery, infantry, cavalry were known as "Ha mpton's Legion."
b. Mar 28, 1818 in Charleston, South Carolina
d. Apr 11, 1902 in Columbia, South Carolina
Source: *AmBi; AmPolLe; ApCAB; BiDConf; BiDrAC; BiDrGov 1789; BiDrUSC 89; BioIn 2, 3, 4, 5, 9, 11, 14, 16, 17; CivWDc; DcAmB; Drake; EncAB-H 1974, 1996; EncSoH; GenMudB; HarEnMi; HarEnUS; LegTOT; LinLib S; McGEWB; NatCAB 12; OxCAmH; PolPar; TwCBDA; WebAB 74, 79; WebAMB; WhAm 1; WhAmP; WhCiWar; WhoMilH 76; WorAl; WorAlBi*

Hamsun, Knut
[Knut Pedersen]
Norwegian. Author
Won 1920 Nobel Prize for *The Growth of the Soil,* 1917; wrote Neo-Romantic novels of farmers, laborers.
b. Aug 4, 1859 in Lom, Norway
d. Feb 19, 1952 in Noerholmen, Norway
Source: *AtlBL; Benet 87; BiDExR; BioIn 1, 2, 3, 4, 5, 8, 12, 15; CasWL; ClDMEL 47; CnMD; ConAu 104, 119; CyWA 58, 89; DcArts; DcBiA; DcScanL; Dis&D; EncTR 91; EncWL 2, 3; EncWT; EuWr 8; EvEuW; FacFETw; GrFLW; LegTOT; LinLib L, S; LngCTC; MagSWL; MajTwCW; McGEWB; NobelP; NotNAT B; Novels; ObitT 1951; OxCEng 85, 95; OxCThe 83; PenC EUR; RAdv 14, 13-2; REn; REnWD; RfGWoL 95; TwCA SUP; TwCLC 2, 14, 49; WebBD 83; WhAm 3, 4; WhDW; WhE&EA; WhoLA; WhoNob, 90, 95; WhoTwCL; WorAl; WorAlBi*

Hanauer, Chip
[Lee Edward Hanauer]
American. Boat Racer
Hydroplane racer; won record ninth American Powerboat Assn. Gold Cup, 1993.
b. Jul 1, 1954 in Seattle, Washington
Source: *BioIn 14, 15; ConNews 86-2*

Hancock, Herbie
[Herbert Jeffrey Hancock]
American. Jazz Musician, Composer
Pianist who won Grammy, 1984, for electronic jazz composition "Rockit," also for "Call Sheet Blues," 1988; won an Oscar for *Round Midnight,* 1986.
b. Apr 12, 1940 in Chicago, Illinois
Source: *AfrAmAl 6; AllMusG; Baker 84, 92; BiDAfM; BiDAmM; BiDJaz; BioIn 10, 11, 12, 13, 14, 15, 16, 17, 18, 20; BioNews 74; BlkCS; ConMuA 80A; ConMus 8; ConNews 85-1; ConTFT 8; CurBio 88; DcTwCCu 5; DrBlPA, 90; EncJzS; EncPR&S 89; EncRk 88; FacFETw; HarEnR 86; IlEncJ; IlEncRk; InB&W 80, 85; LegTOT; NegAl 83, 89; NewAmDM; NewGrDA 86; NewGrDJ 88, 94; OxCPMus; PenEncP; RkOn 85; RolSEnR 83; WhoAfA 96; WhoAm 74, 76, 78, 80, 82, 84, 86, 88, 90, 92, 94, 95, 96, 97; WhoBlA 75, 77, 80, 85, 88, 90, 92, 94; WhoE 74; WhoEnt 92; WhoHol 92; WhoRock 81; WhoRocM 82; WhoWest 96; WorAlBi*

Hancock, John
American. Statesman, Continental Congressman
First to sign Declaration of Independence, 1776, in very bold handwriting; elected MA governor nine times, 1780-93.
b. Jan 12, 1737 in Braintree, Massachusetts
d. Oct 8, 1793 in Quincy, Massachusetts
Source: *Alli; AmBi; AmPolLe; ApCAB; Benet 87, 96; BiAUS; BiDAmBL 83; BiDrAC; BiDrACR; BiDrGov 1789; BiDrUSC 89; BiDrUSE 71, 89; BioIn 1, 3, 4, 6, 7, 8, 9, 10, 11, 12, 16; BlkwEAR; CyAG; DcAmB; DcAmSR; DcBiPP; Drake; EncAB-H 1974, 1996; EncAR; EncCRAm; EncRev; HarEnUS; HisWorL; LegTOT; LinLib L, S; McGEWB; NatCAB 1; OxCAmH; PeoHis; RComAH; REn; REnAL; TwCBDA; WebAB 74, 79; WebAMB; WhAm HS; WhAmP; WhAmRev; WorAl; WorAlBi*

Hancock, John D
American. Director
Films include *Bang the Drum Slowly,* 1973; *Baby Blue Marine,* 1976.
b. Feb 12, 1939 in Kansas City, Missouri
Source: *FilmEn; IntMPA 81; MovMk; VarWW 85; WhoAm 86, 90; WhoEnt 92*

Hancock, Winfield Scott
American. Army Officer
Battle of Gettysburg, Indian Wars hero; Dem. presidential candidate, 1880, lost to Garfield.
b. Feb 14, 1824 in Montgomery County, Pennsylvania
d. Feb 9, 1886 in Governor's Island, New York
Source: *AmBi; AmPolLe; ApCAB; BioIn 5, 7, 8, 13, 16, 21; CelCen; CivWDc; DcAmB; DcAmMiB; DcBiPP; Drake; GenMudB; HarEnMi; HarEnUS; LinLib S; NatCAB 4; NewCol 75; OxCAmH; PresAR; TwCBDA; WebAB 74, 79; WebAMB; WhAm HS; WhCiWar; WhNaAH; WorAl; WorAlBi*

Hand, Learned
[Billings Learned Hand]
American. Judge
Considered one of greatest jurists in US history; wrote opinion in Alcoa antitrust case, 1945.
b. Jan 27, 1872 in Albany, New York
d. Aug 18, 1961 in New York, New York
Source: *AmAu&B; AmJust; BiDFedJ; BioIn 1, 2, 3, 4, 5, 6, 9, 10, 11, 15, 18, 19, 20; CurBio 50, 61; DcAmB S7; EncAB-H 1974; FacFETw; LegTOT; LinLib L, S; McGEWB; ObitT 1961; OxCAmH; OxCLaw; OxCSupC; PolProf T; WebAB 74, 79; WhAm 4*

Handel, George Frideric
[Georg Friedrich Handel]
English. Composer
Master of baroque music who composed 46 operas; best-known work: *The Messiah* , 1741.
b. Feb 23, 1685 in Halle, Saxony
d. Apr 14, 1759 in London, England
Source: *AtlBL; Baker 78, 84, 92; Benet 87, 96; BioIn 1, 2, 3, 4, 5, 6, 7, 8, 9, 10, 11, 12, 13, 14, 15, 16, 17, 18, 20, 21; BriBkM 80; CmOp; CmpBCM; CnOxB; DcArts; DcCom 77; GrComp; IntDcOp; LegTOT; McGEWB; MetOEnc; MusMk; NewAmDM; NewC; NewEOp 71; NewGrDM 80; NewGrDO; NewOxM; OxCEng 85, 95; OxCMus; OxDcOp; PenDiMP A; RAdv 14, 13-3; REn*

Handelman, Stanley Myron
American. Comedian
TV appearances include "The Merv Griffin Show," "A Cry for Love."
Source: *VarWW 85; WhoHol 92*

Handford, Martin
English. Illustrator, Children's Author
Bestselling children's author of *Where's Waldo?* books.
b. Sep 27, 1956 in London, England
Source: *Benet 87; BioIn 9, 10, 11, 12, 14; CamGWoT; CasWL; ChlLR 22; ConAu 33NR, 77; ConLC 5, 8, 10, 15, 38; CroCD; CurBio 73; CyWA 89; DcLB 85; DrAPF 91; EncWL 2; FacFETw; LiExTwC; MajMD 1; MajTwCW; McGEWD 84; OxCGer 86; PostFic; SmATA 64; WorAu 1970*

Handke, Peter
Austrian. Author
Austria's foremost living author; won first Grillparzer Prize, 1991.
b. Dec 6, 1942 in Griffin, Austria
Source: *Benet 87, 96; BioIn 9, 10, 11, 12, 13, 14, 17, 19; CamGWoT; CasWL; ClDMEL 80; ConAu 33NR, 77; ConFLW 84; ConLC 5, 8, 10, 15, 38; ConWorW 93; CroCD; CurBio 73; CyWA 89; DcArts; DcLB 85, 124; DrAF 76; DrAPF 80; EncWL 2, 3; EncWT; Ent; FacFETw; IntDcT 2; LiExTwC; MagSWL; MajMD 1; MajTwCW; MakMC; McGEWD 72, 84; ModGL; Novels; OxCGer 76, 86; OxCThe 83; PlP&P A; PostFic; RAdv 14, 13-2; WhoWor 95; WorAu 1970*

Handler, Elliot
American. Manufacturer
With wife, introduced Barbie doll, 1958, named for daughter, Barbara; Ken named for son.
b. 1916 in Denver, Colorado
Source: *BioIn 17; ConAmBL; WhoAm 74; WhoFI 74, 75*

Handler, Ruth
[Mrs. Elliot Handler]
American. Manufacturer
With husband, introduced Barbie doll, 1958, named for daughter, Barbara.
b. Nov 4, 1916 in Denver, Colorado
Source: *BioIn 9, 12, 15, 17, 19, 20, 21; ConAmBL; InWom SUP; WhoAm 74; WhoAmW 75; WhoFI 74, 75*

Handlin, Oscar
American. Educator, Historian
Studies of Americans and immigration include 1952 Pulitzer-winner, *The Uprooted.*
b. Sep 29, 1915 in New York, New York
Source: *AmAu&B; Au&Wr 71; BenetAL 91; BioIn 2, 3, 4, 8, 12, 13, 14; BlueB 76; ConAu 1R, 5NR, 23NR; DcLB 17; DcLEL 1940; DrAS 74H, 78H, 82H; EncAAH; IntAu&W 76, 77; IntWW 89, 91, 93; JeAmHC; LegTOT; LinLib L; McGEWB; OxCAmL 65; RAdv 14, 13-3; REnAL; ThTwC 87; TwCA SUP; WebAB 74, 79; Who 74, 82, 83, 85, 88, 90, 92, 94; WhoAm 74, 76, 78, 80, 82, 84, 86, 88, 90, 92, 94, 95, 96, 97; WhoAmJ 80; WhoE 74; WhoLibI 82; WhoWor 74, 82, 84, 87; WhoWorJ 72, 78; WorAl; WorAlBi; WrDr 76, 80, 82, 84, 86*

Hands, Terry
[Terence David Hands]
English. Director
London stage productions include *Cyrano de Bergerac,* 1985.
b. Jan 9, 1941 in Aldershot, England
Source: *BioIn 13, 14; CamGWoT; ConTFT 5, 13; EncWT; Ent; IntDcT 3; IntWW 79, 80, 81, 82, 83, 89, 91, 93; NewYTBS 85; OxCThe 83; Who 82, 83, 85, 88, 90, 92, 94; WhoAm 94, 95, 96, 97; WhoThe 72, 77, 81; WhoWor 82, 84, 87, 89, 91, 93, 95, 96, 97*

Handsome Lake
American. Religious Leader
Had visions; preached the message of "Gaiwiio" (the Good Word).
b. 1735? in Conewaugus, New York
d. Aug 10, 1815
Source: *AmBi; BioIn 4; DcAmReB 1, 2; EncARH; EncNoAI; NotNaAm; WhNaAH*

Handy, Thomas Troy
American. Army Officer
Deputy chief-of-staff to generals Marshall, Eisenhower; commander of all US troops in Europe, 1944-54.
b. Mar 11, 1892 in Spring City, Tennessee
d. Apr 14, 1982 in San Antonio, Texas
Source: *BiDWWGF; BioIn 1, 2, 3, 12, 13; CurBio 51, 82; NewYTBS 82; WebAMB; WhAm 8; Who 74, 82, 83*

Handy, W(illiam) C(hristopher)
"Father of the Blues"
American. Songwriter, Bandleader
First to compile, publish "blues" music; led own band, 1903-21; wrote "St. Louis Blues," 1914; "Memphis Blues," 1912.
b. Nov 16, 1873 in Florence, Alabama
d. Mar 29, 1958 in New York, New York
Source: *AfrAmAl 6; AmAu&B; AmPS; ASCAP 66, 80; Baker 92; BiDAmM; BiDJaz; BioIn 1, 3, 4, 5, 6, 8, 9, 12, 13, 14, 15, 20; ConAmC 76, 82; CurBio 41, 58; DcAmB S6; EncAB-H 1974, 1996; InB&W 80, 85; LinLib S; McGEWB; MemAm; NatCAB 60; NewGrDJ 94; NewGrDM 80; NotNAT B; ObitT 1951; OxCAmL 65, 95; OxCMus; REnAL; SelBAAf; SouBlCW; WebAB 74, 79; WhAm 3; WhoJazz 72*

Hanes, John Wesley
American. Manufacturer
Launched Hanes Hosiery Mills, producing men's, women's stockings.
b. 1850
d. 1903
Source: *DcNCBi 3; Entr*

Hanes, Pleasant H
American. Manufacturer
Launched P H Hanes Knitting Co., 1902, making underwear.
b. Oct 16, 1845 in Fulton Davie County, North Carolina
d. Jun 9, 1925 in Winston-Salem, North Carolina
Source: *Entr; NatCAB 22*

Haney, Carol
American. Choreographer, Dancer
In Broadway musical *Pajama Game,* 1954; choreographed *Funny Girl,* 1964.
b. Dec 24, 1924 in Bedford, Massachusetts
d. May 10, 1964 in Saddle River, New Jersey
Source: *BiDD; BioIn 3, 4, 6; EncMT; FilmgC; InWom, SUP; NotNAT B; WhAm 4; WhoAmW 64; WhoHol B; WhScrn 74, 77; WorAl; WorAlBi*

Haney, Chris
Canadian. Photojournalist, Inventor
With Scott Abbott, John Haney, invented board game Trivial Pursuit, 1979.
b. 1949?
Source: *BioIn 13, 14, 15; ConNews 85-1*

Haney, John
Canadian. Inventor
With Chris Haney, Scott Abbott, invented board game Trivial Pursuit, 1979.
Source: *BiDrAPA 89; ConNews 85-1; WhoE 91*

Hanfmann, George Maxim Anossov
American. Archaeologist, Educator
Field director, Harvard-Cornell expedition, 1958-76, that uncovered ancient capital of Lydia.
b. Nov 20, 1911 in Saint Petersburg, Russia
d. Mar 13, 1986 in Cambridge, Massachusetts
Source: *BioIn 8, 14, 15; CurBio 67, 86; DrAS 74H, 78H, 82H; WhAm 9; WhoAm 74, 76, 78, 80, 82, 84; WhoAmA 84*

Hanfstaengl, Ernst Franz Sedgwick
"Putzi"
German. Author
Foreign press chief, 1932-37; friend of Hitler, who entertained Fuhrer at piano.
b. Feb 11, 1887 in Munich, Germany
d. Nov 6, 1975 in Munich, Germany (West)
Source: *BioIn 10; EncTR; NewYTBS 75; ObitOF 79*

Hani, Chris
South African. Political Activist
Participant in talks between the African National Congress and the South African government, 1990-93; became

general secretary of South Africa's communist party, 1991.
b. Jun 28, 1942 in Cofimvaba, South Africa
d. Apr 10, 1993, South Africa
Source: *ConBlB 6; EncRev; IntWW 91, 93; News 93*

Hanika, Sylvia
German. Tennis Player
Tour player since 1978; voted most improved, 1979.
b. Nov 30, 1959 in Munich, Germany (West)
Source: *WhoIntT*

Hanks, Nancy
[Mrs. Thomas Lincoln]
American.
Mother of Abraham Lincoln; died when son was nine.
b. Feb 5, 1784 in Campbell County, Virginia
d. Oct 5, 1818 in Spencer County, Indiana
Source: *DcNCBi 3; HerW; WhAm 8*

Hanks, Nancy
American. Government Official
Chm., National Endowment for the Arts, 1969-77.
b. Dec 31, 1927 in Miami Beach, Florida
d. Jan 7, 1983 in New York, New York
Source: *AnObit 1983*

Hanks, Tom
American. Actor
TV show "Bosom Buddies," 1980-82; string of comedies include *Splash,* 1984; *The Money Pit,* 1986; *Big,* 1988 and *The Burbs,* 1989 among others. Academy Award (Best Actor) for *Forrest Gump,* 1995.
b. Jul 9, 1956 in Concord, California
Source: *BiDFilm 94; BioIn 13, 14, 15, 16; CelR 90; ConTFT 5, 12; CurBio 89; EncAFC; HalFC 88; HolBB; IntDcF 2-3; IntMPA 88, 92, 94, 96; IntWW 91; LegTOT; News 89-2; QDrFCA 92; VarWW 85; WhoAm 90, 92, 94, 95, 96, 97; WhoCom; WhoEnt 92; WhoHol 92; WorAlBi*

Hanley, William
American. Dramatist
Films include *The Gypsy Moths;* plays include *No Answer.*
b. Oct 22, 1931 in Lorain, Ohio
Source: *BenetAL 91; BiDrAPA 89; BiE&WWA; BioIn 10; CnMD SUP; ConAmD; ConAu 41R; ConDr 73, 77, 82, 88, 93; ConTFT 2; CroCD; DcLEL 1940; DrAF 76; DrAPF 80, 89, 91; ModWD; MorBAP; NotNAT; WhoAm 74, 76, 78; WhoE 74, 75, 77; WhoThe 72, 77, 81; WrDr 76, 80, 82, 84, 86, 88, 90, 92, 94, 96*

Hanna, Mark
[Marcus Alonzo Hanna]
American. Businessman, Politician
Major power in Rep. Party, 1885-1904; retired from business to run campaign for William McKinley; became his closest adviser.
b. Sep 24, 1837 in New Lisbon, Ohio
d. Feb 15, 1904 in Washington, District of Columbia
Source: *AmBi; AmPolLe; ApCAB SUP, X; BiDAmBL 83; BiDrAC; BiDrUSC 89; BioIn 3, 6, 10, 11, 17; CyAG; DcAmB; EncAB-H 1974, 1996; GayN; HarEnUS; LinLib S; McGEWB; NatCAB 11, 22; OhA&B; OxCAmH; OxCAmL 65; RComAH; REnAL; REnAW; TwCBDA; WebAB 74, 79; WhAm 1; WhAmP; WorAl*

Hanna, William Denby
[Hanna and Barbera]
American. Cartoonist
With Joseph Barbera, created cartoons "Tom and Jerry," "Yogi Bear," and "The Flintstones."
b. Jul 14, 1910 in Melrose, New Mexico
Source: *BioIn 12, 13, 16; CelR 90; ConTFT 8; CurBio 83; FilmgC; IntMPA 82; OxCFilm; VarWW 85; WhoAm 74, 76, 78, 82, 84, 86, 88, 90, 92, 94, 95, 96, 97; WhoEnt 92; WhoTelC; WorECar; WorEFlm*

Hannagan, Steve
[Stephen Jerome Hannagan]
American. Public Relations Executive
Promoted Indy 500, ski resorts, Miami Beach, FL; created advertising that made these places popular.
b. Apr 4, 1899 in Lafayette, Indiana
d. Feb 5, 1953 in Nairobi, British East Africa
Source: *BioIn 1, 3, 9; CurBio 44, 53; DcAmB S5; EncAJ; WhAm 3*

Hannah, Barry
American. Author
Writes novels set in the American South; novels include *Geronimo Rex,* 1972; *Boomerang,* 1989.
b. Apr 23, 1942 in Meridian, Mississippi
Source: *BenetAL 91; ConAu 43NR, 108, 110; ConLC 23, 38, 90; ConNov 86, 91, 96; DcLB 6; DrAPF 80; IntAu&W 91, 93; MajTwCW; PostFic; WhoAm 94, 95, 96, 97; WhoSSW 91; WorAu 1980; WrDr 88, 90, 92, 94, 96*

Hannah, Daryl
American. Actor
Films include *Splash,* 1984; *Legal Eagles,* 1986; and *Steel Magnolias,* 1989.
b. Dec 3, 1960 in Chicago, Illinois
Source: *BioIn 13, 14, 15, 16; CelR 90; ConNews 87-4; ConTFT 4; CurBio 90; HalFC 88; IntMPA 88, 92, 94, 96; IntWW 91, 93; LegTOT; VarWW 85; WhoAm 90, 94, 95, 96, 97; WhoAmW 95, 97; WhoEnt 92; WhoHol 92; WorAlBi*

Hannah, John Alfred
American. University Administrator
Pres., MSU, 1941-69; transformed it from an agricultural college to a major university.
b. Oct 9, 1902 in Grand Rapids, Michigan
d. Feb 23, 1991 in Kalamazoo, Michigan
Source: *AmMWSc 73P, 76P; BioIn 2, 3, 4, 6, 7, 8, 11, 12; CurBio 91N; InSci; IntWW 74, 75, 76, 77, 78, 79, 80, 81, 82, 83; LinLib S; NewYTBS 91; WhoAm 74, 76, 80, 82, 84; WhoGov 72; WhoMW 82, 84; WhoSSW 73; WhoUN 75; WhoWor 74*

Hannah, John Allen
"Hog"
American. Football Player
Six-time all-pro guard, New England, 1973-82.
b. Apr 4, 1951 in Canton, Georgia
Source: *BiDAmSp FB; BioIn 12; FootReg 81; WhoE 86*

Hannah, Marc (Regis)
American. Computer Scientist
One of the founders of Silicon Graphics Incorporated, 1982; designs computers that are used to create special effects for movies.
b. Oct 13, 1956 in Chicago, Illinois
Source: *BioIn 19, 20; ConBlB 10; WhoAfA 96; WhoBlA 85, 88, 90, 92, 94*

Hannibal
Military Leader
Carthaginian general, who with 35,000 soldiers, elephants, crossed Alps into Italy, 221 BC; known for tactical genius.
b. 247BC, Africa
d. 183BC in Libyssa, Bithynia
Source: *Benet 87, 96; BioIn 1, 2, 3, 4, 5, 6, 7, 8, 10, 12, 13, 15, 17, 19, 20; DcBiPP; Dis&D; GenMudB; HisWorL; InB&W 85; LegTOT; LinLib S; NewCol 75; OxCClL, 89; REn; WhDW; WorAl; WorAlBi*

Hannum, Alex(ander Murray)
American. Basketball Coach
Coached NBA championship teams, St. Louis, 1965, Philadelphia, 1967.
b. Jul 19, 1923 in Los Angeles, California
Source: *BasBi; BiDAmSp BK; BioIn 7; WhoBbl 73*

Hansberry, Lorraine
American. Author, Dramatist
Wrote *A Raisin in the Sun,* 1959; first play by black woman produced on Broadway.
b. May 19, 1930 in Chicago, Illinois
d. Jan 12, 1965 in New York, New York
Source: *AfrAmAl 6; AfrAmW; AmAu&B; AmWomD; AmWomWr; ArtclWW 2; AuNews 2; Benet 87; BenetAL 91; BiE&WWA; BioAmW; BioIn 5, 6, 7, 8, 9, 10, 12, 13, 14, 15, 16, 17, 18, 19, 20, 21; BlkAmP; BlkAWP; BlkLC; BlkWr 1; BlmGWL; CamGLE; CamGWoT;*

CamHAL; CasWL; CnMD SUP; ConAu 3BS, 25R, 109; ConBlAP 88; ConBlB 6; ConDr 77F, 82E, 88E; ConLC 17, 62; ContDcW 89; CroCD; CrtSuDr; CurBio 65; CyWA 89; DcLB 7, 38; DcLEL 1940; DcTwCCu 1, 5; DramC 2; DrBlPA, 90; EncAL; EncWL 2, 3; EncWT; Ent; FacFETw; FemiCLE; GayLesB; GoodHs; GrLiveH; GrWomW; GrWrEL DR; HalFC 84, 88; HanAmWH; HerW 84; IntDcWB; InWom; LegTOT; LibW; LinLib L; MagSAmL; MajTwCW; McGEWD 72, 84; ModAL S1; ModBlW; ModWD; ModWoWr; MorBAP; NatCAB 60; NegAl 76, 83, 89; NewCon; NotAW MOD; NotBlAW 1; NotNAT B; NotWoAT; OxCAmL 83, 95; OxCWoWr 95; PeoHis; PlP&P, A; RAdv 14, 13-2; REnAL; RfGAmL 87; SchCGBL; SelBAAf; SelBAAu; WhAm 4; WhoAmW 64; WomFir; WorAl; WorAlBi; WorAu 1950

Hansberry, William Leo
American. Educator
Professor of history, Howard Univ., 1929-59; pioneer in the study of ancient African history.
b. Feb 25, 1894 in Gloster, Mississippi
d. Nov 3, 1965 in Chicago, Illinois
Source: *BioIn 5, 7; ConBlB 11; DcAmNB; InB&W 80, 85; SelBAAf; SelBAAu*

Hansell, Haywood Shepherd, Jr.
American. Military Leader
US Air Force officer, directed strategic bombing of Germany and Japan in World War II; adviser to Joint Chiefs of Staff during Korean War.
b. Sep 28, 1903 in Fort Monroe, Virginia
d. Nov 14, 1988 in Hilton Head Island, South Carolina
Source: *BiDWWGF; BioIn 16; CurBio 45, 89N; NewYTBS 88*

Hansen, Alvin Harvey
American. Economist
Leading American exponent of Keynesian economics; wrote many books, served on government boards.
b. Aug 23, 1887 in Viborg, South Dakota
d. Jun 6, 1975 in Alexandria, Virginia
Source: *AmAu&B; BioIn 1, 9, 10, 11, 14, 15; ConAu 57, P-1; CurBio 45; DcAmB S9; EncAB-H 1974, 1996; IntWW 74, 75; McGEWB; NatCAB 63; WebAB 74, 79; WebBD 83; WhAm 6; WhE&EA; Who 74; WhoAm 74; WhoEc 81, 86*

Hansen, Clifford Peter
American. Politician
Rep. senator from WY, 1967-79.
b. Oct 16, 1912 in Zenith, Wyoming
Source: *BiDrAC; WhoWest 74, 76, 78, 89, 92, 94*

Hansen, Fred Morgan
American. Track Athlete
Pole vaulter; won gold medal, 1964 Olympics.
b. Dec 29, 1940 in Cuero, Texas
Source: *BioIn 7; CurBio 65; WhoTr&F 73*

Hansen, Georges
French. Hostage
French TV crew member taken hostage by Lebanese terrorists and held for 104 days, Mar. 8, 1986-June 20, 1986.
b. 1941, France

Hansen, James E(dward)
American. Scientist
Director, NASA's Goddard Institute for Space Studies, 1981—; reported that Earth's average global temperature has been, and still is, on the rise.
b. Mar 29, 1941 in Charter Oak, Iowa
Source: *CurBio 96*

Hansen, Joseph
[Rose Brock; James Colton; James Coulton]
American. Author, Poet
Created detective character Dave Brandstetter; wrote novel *Skinflick,* 1980.
b. Jul 19, 1923 in Aberdeen, South Dakota
Source: *BioIn 13, 14; ConAu 16NR, 17AS, 29R, 44NR; ConGAN; ConLC 38; CrtSuMy; DcLP 87A; DrAPF 80, 91; GayLL; IntAu&W 77, 82, 89, 91, 93; IntvTCA 2; Novels; TwCCr&M 80, 85, 91; WrDr 82, 84, 86, 88, 90, 92, 94, 96*

Hansen, Peter Andreas
German. Astronomer
Developed theories of motion for comets, moon; lunar theory published in *Fundamenta,* 1838.
b. Dec 8, 1795 in Tondern, Denmark
d. Mar 28, 1874 in Gotha, Germany
Source: *DcBiPP; DcScB; InSci*

Hansen, William Webster
American. Physicist
Contributed greatly to the early development of microwave technology.
b. May 27, 1909 in Fresno, California
d. May 23, 1949 in Palo Alto, California
Source: *BioIn 1, 2, 3, 16; DcAmB, S4; DcScB; InSci; ObitOF 79; WhAm 3*

Hanslick, Eduard
Czech. Critic
Early supporter of Brahms; known for being temperamental, yet brilliant.
b. Sep 11, 1825 in Prague, Bohemia
d. Aug 6, 1904 in Baden, Austria
Source: *Baker 78, 84, 92; BbD; BiD&SB; BioIn 9, 10, 12, 14; NewAmDM; NewEOp 71; NewGrDM 80; NewGrDO; NewOxM; OxCMus; OxDcOp; WhDW*

Hansom, Joseph Aloysius
English. Inventor
Patented safety cab, 1834, two-wheeled, one-horse enclosed cab.
b. Oct 26, 1803 in York, England
d. Jun 29, 1882 in London, England
Source: *BiDBrA; DcArts; DcNaB; InSci; MacEA; NewC; WhoArch*

Hanson, Duane (Elwood)
American. Sculptor
Specializes in plastic human effigies set in realistic situations.
b. Jan 17, 1925 in Alexandria, Minnesota
d. Jan 6, 1996 in Boca Raton, Florida
Source: *AmArt; BioIn 9, 11, 12, 13, 14, 15, 21; ConArt 77, 83, 89, 96; CurBio 83, 96N; DcAmArt; DcCAA 77, 88, 94; FacFETw; IntWW 89, 91, 93; NewYTBS 27; OxDcArt; WhAm 11; WhoAm 76, 78, 80, 82, 84, 86, 88, 90, 94, 95, 96; WhoAmA 73, 76, 78, 80, 82, 84, 86, 89, 91, 93; WhoSSW 84; WorArt 1950*

Hanson, Howard
American. Composer, Conductor, Educator
Directed Rochester, NY's School of Music, 1924-64; varied works include opera, *Merry Mount,* 1934; Pulitzer-winner *Fourth Symphony,* 1944.
b. Oct 28, 1896 in Wahoo, Nebraska
d. Feb 26, 1981 in New York, New York
Source: *AmComp; AnObit 1981; ASCAP 66, 80; Baker 78, 84; BiDAmEd; BiDAmM; BioIn 1, 2, 3, 4, 6, 7, 8, 9, 11, 12, 13, 16, 19; BlueB 76; BriBkM 80; CompSN, SUP; ConAmC 76, 82; ConAu 103; CurBio 41, 66, 81, 81N; DcCM; DcCom&M 79; DrAS 74H, 78H; IntWW 74, 75, 76, 77, 78, 79, 80, 81, 81N; IntWWM 77, 80; LegTOT; LinLib S; McGEWB; MetOEnc; NewAmDM; NewEOp 71; NewGrDA 86; NewGrDM 80; NewOxM; NewYTBS 81; OxCAmH; OxCAmL 65; PenDiMP A; WebAB 74; WhAm 7, 8; WhoAm 74, 76, 78, 80; WhoE 74; WhoMus 72; WhoWor 74, 76, 78; WorAlBi*

Hanson, John
American. Colonial Figure
First pres. of Continental Congress, 1781-82.
b. Apr 13, 1721 in Charles County, Maryland
d. Nov 22, 1783 in Oxon Hill, Maryland
Source: *AmBi; BioIn 1, 3, 4, 7, 12; DcAmB; DcAmSR; EncAR; NewCol 75; WebAB 74, 79; WhAm HS; WhAmRev; WorAlBi*

Han Suyin
[Elizabeth Comber]
Chinese. Author
Wrote "A Many Splendored Thing," 1952; "The Enchantress," 1985.
b. Sep 12, 1917 in Beijing, China
Source: *Au&Wr 71; BioIn 3, 4, 5, 7, 8, 10, 11, 12, 14; ConAu 17R; DcLP 87B; FemiCLE; IntAu&W 89; IntWW 74, 89, 91, 93; InWom SUP; NewYTBS 85; RGTwCWr; TwCWr; Who 74, 90, 92, 94; WorAu 1950; WrDr 76, 90, 92, 94, 96*

Han Yongun
[Manhae]
Korean. Clergy, Poet, Political Activist
Struggled for Korean independence from Japanese rule; sought to popularize and renew Buddhist faith in Korea.
b. 1879, Korea
d. 1944, Korea

Hapgood, Norman
American. Editor, Author
Edited *Collier's*, 1903-12; *Harper's Weekly*, 1913-16; wrote biographies of American statesmen.
b. Mar 28, 1868 in Chicago, Illinois
d. Apr 29, 1937
Source: *AmAu&B; AmBi; AmRef; ApCAB X; BenetAL 91; BiDAmJo; BiD&SB; BioIn 4, 11, 15, 16, 17; DcAmAu; DcAmB S2; DcAmSR; DcLB 91; DcNAA; EncAB-A 9; EncAJ; GayN; LinLib L, S; McGEWB; NatCAB 27; NotNAT B; OxCAmL 65, 83, 95; OxCAmT 84; REnAL; TwCA; TwCBDA; WhAm 1; WhE&EA; WhLit*

Harald
Norwegian. Ruler
Son of King Olav V; succeeded father to throne upon his death, 1991.
b. Feb 21, 1937 in Oslo, Norway
Source: *AuBYP 3; BioIn 10; IntWW 91, 93; WhoWor 95, 96, 97*

Hara Takashi
Japanese. Political Leader
First commoner, professional politician to be prime minister, 1918-21; assassinated.
b. Mar 15, 1856 in Morioka, Japan
d. Nov 4, 1921 in Tokyo, Japan
Source: *BioIn 8; DcTwHis; McGEWB; NewCol 75; WebBD 83*

Harbach, Otto Abels
American. Lyricist
Often collaborated with Oscar Hammerstein; hits include "Smoke Gets in Your Eyes ," 1933.
b. Aug 18, 1873 in Salt Lake City, Utah
d. Jan 24, 1963 in New York, New York
Source: *AmAu&B; ASCAP 66; BiDAmM; BioIn 2, 3, 4, 5, 6, 9, 10, 12; CmpEPM; CurBio 50, 63; EncMT; NatCAB 52; NewCBMT; REnAL; WhAm 4*

Harbert, Chick
[Melvin R Harbert]
American. Golfer
Touring pro, 1940s-50s; won PGA, 1954; Hall of Fame, 1968.
b. Feb 20, 1915 in Dayton, Ohio
d. Sep 2, 1992 in Ocala, Florida
Source: *BioIn 18; WhoGolf; WhoSpor*

Harbison, John Harris
American. Composer, Educator
Noted long-time MIT music professor; won a 1987 Pulitzer Prize for "The Flight into Egypt."
b. Dec 20, 1938 in Orange, New Jersey
Source: *Baker 78, 84; BioIn 13, 15; ConCom 92; CurBio 93; DcCM; IntWWM 90; NewAmDM; NewGrDA 86; WhoAm 84, 90; WhoEnt 92; WhoMW 92*

Harburg, E(dgar) Y(ipsel)
""Yip""
American. Lyricist
Wrote lyrics for "Somewhere Over the Rainbow," from *Wizard of Oz*, 1939; al so wrote lyrics for song "Only a Paper Moon," play *Finian's Rainbow*.
b. Apr 8, 1896 in New York, New York
d. Mar 5, 1981 in Los Angeles, California
Source: *AmPS; ASCAP 66, 80; BiDAmM; BiE&WWA; BioIn 12, 19; CmpEPM; ConAu 85, 103; ConDr 73, 77D; CurBio 80, 81; EncMT; NewYTBS 81; NotNAT; WhAm 7; WhoAm 80; WorAl*

Hardaway, Anfernee (Deon)
"Penny"
American. Basketball Player
WIth Orlando Magic, 1993-96; Miami Heat, 1996—.
b. Jul 18, 1971 in Memphis, Tennessee
Source: *ConBlB 13; News 96, 96-2*

Hardee, William Joseph
American. Army Officer
Confederate general, surrendered to Sherman in NC, Apr, 1865; wrote *Rifle and Light Infantry Tactics*, 1855, used as army textbook.
b. Oct 12, 1815 in Savannah, Georgia
d. Nov 6, 1873 in Wytheville, Virginia
Source: *Alli SUP; BiDConf; BiDSA; BioIn 1, 5, 7, 11, 17; CivWDc; DcAmAu; DcAmB; DcAmMiB; DcNAA; EncSoH; GenMudB; HarEnMi; HarEnUS; NatCAB 4; WebAMB; WhAm HS; WhCiWar*

Harden, Arthur, Sir
English. Chemist
Shared Nobel Prize in chemistry, 1929, for studies of alcoholic fermentation and enzymes.
b. Oct 12, 1865 in Manchester, England
d. Jun 17, 1940 in Bourne, England
Source: *AsBiEn; BiESc; BioIn 1, 2, 3, 6, 14, 15, 19, 20; CamDcSc; DcNaB 1931; DcScB; InSci; LarDcSc; NobelP; NotTwCS; WhE&EA; WhoNob, 90, 95; WorAl; WorAlBi; WorScD*

Hardie, James Keir
Scottish. Labor Union Official
Coal miner who founded Scottish Labor Party, 1888.
b. Aug 15, 1856 in Legbrannock, Scotland
d. Sep 26, 1915 in Glasgow, Scotland
Source: *BiDMoPL; BioIn 4, 6, 8, 9, 10, 11, 13; DcNaB 1912; LinLib L, S; McGEWB; NewCol 75; VicBrit*

Hardin, Helen
American. Artist
Known for her works in acrylics and casein.
b. 1946 in Albuquerque, New Mexico
d. Jun 9, 1984 in Albuquerque, New Mexico
Source: *BioIn 9; NotNaAm*

Hardin, John Wesley
American. Murderer
A Texas gunslinger, he killed over 20 men, 1868-77.
b. May 26, 1853 in Bonham County, Texas
d. Aug 19, 1895 in El Paso, Texas
Source: *BioIn 4, 5, 6, 11, 13, 15, 17, 18, 21; DrInf; EncAAH; PeoHis; REnAW; WhAm HS*

Hardin, Louis Thomas
"Moondog"
American. Musician
Blinded at 13, he invented new string instrument, new drum.
b. May 26, 1916 in Marysville, Kansas
Source: *ASCAP 80; BioIn 3, 11, 16, 19; ConAmC 82; PenEncP*

Hardin, Tim
American. Songwriter, Singer
Wrote song "If I Were a Carpenter," recorded by Bobby Darin, Bob Seger, others.
b. Dec 23, 1941 in Eugene, Oregon
d. Dec 29, 1980 in Hollywood, California
Source: *AnObit 1980; BiDJaz; BioIn 12; ConAu 102; EncRk 88; EncRkSt; HarEnR 86; IlEncRk; PenEncP; RolSEnR 83; WhoRock 81*

Harding, Ann
[Dorothy Walton Gatley]
American. Actor
1930s film star; received Oscar nomination for *Holiday*, 1930.
b. Aug 17, 1904 in San Antonio, Texas
d. Sep 1, 1981 in Sherman Oaks, California
Source: *BiE&WWA; BioIn 10; Film 2; FilmgC; IntMPA 75, 76, 77, 78, 79, 80, 81, 82; MotPP; MovMk; NotNAT; OxCFilm; ThFT; WhoHol A; WhoThe 77A*

Harding, Chester
American. Artist
Portraitist; popular in London, Boston; sitters included John Marshall, 1828.
b. Sep 1, 1792 in Conway, Massachusetts
d. Apr 1, 1866 in Boston, Massachusetts
Source: *Alli SUP; AmBi; ApCAB; ArtsNiC; BioIn 1, 2, 3, 4, 9, 14; BriEAA; DcAmArt; DcAmB; DcBiPP; Drake; FolkA 87; IlBEAAW; McGDA; NatCAB 4; NewCol 75; NewYHSD; OxCAmL 65; TwCBDA; WebAB 74, 79; WhAm HS*

Harding, Chester
American. Army Officer, Engineer
Division engineer at Panama Canal, 1907-17; governor of Panama Canal, 1917-21.
b. Dec 31, 1866 in Enterprise, Mississippi
d. Nov 11, 1936 in Vineyard Haven, Massachusetts
Source: *WhAm 1; WhAmArt 85*

Harding, Florence Kling De Wolfe
[Mrs. Warren G Harding]
American. First Lady
Ambitious divorcee who pushed Warren into presidency; burned his executive papers.
b. Aug 15, 1860 in Marion, Ohio
d. Nov 21, 1924 in Marion, Ohio
Source: *BioIn 16, 17, 19; GoodHs; NatCAB 20; NotAW*

Harding, John Wesley
English. Singer, Songwriter
Noted lyricist; albums include *Here Comes the Groom,* 1990.
b. Oct 22, 1965 in Hastings, England
Source: *BioIn 19; ConMus 6*

Harding, Warren G(amaliel)
American. US President
Rep., 29th pres., 1921-23; administration was plagued with corruption, scandal.
b. Nov 2, 1865 in Corsica, Ohio
d. Aug 2, 1923 in San Francisco, California
Source: *AmAu&B; AmBi; AmDec 1920; AmPolLe; ApCAB X; Benet 96; BiDAmJo; BiDrAC; BiDrUSC 89; BiDrUSE 71, 89; BioIn 1, 2, 3, 4, 5, 6, 7, 8, 9, 10, 11, 12, 13; DcAmB; DcAmSR; DcNAA; Dis&D; EncAAH; EncAB-H 1974, 1996; FacPr 89, 93; HealPre; LinLib L, S; McGEWB; NatCAB 19; OhA&B; OxCAmH; OxCAmL 65, 83; REn; REnAL; St&PR 75; WebAB 74, 79; WhAm 1; WhAmP; WhDW; WorAl*

Hardison, Kadeem
American. Actor
Plays Dwayne Wayne on TV series "A Different World," 1988—; films include *White Men Can't Jump.*
b. 1966
Source: *BioIn 16; IntMPA 96*

Hardwick, Billy
American. Bowler
Pro bowler, 1960s-70s; bowler of year, 1963, 1969; PBA Hall of Fame.
b. 1932
Source: *BiDrAPA 89; NewYTBS 74*

Hardwick, Elizabeth
American. Author
First woman recipient of Nathan Drama Criticism Award, 1967.
b. Jul 27, 1916 in Lexington, Kentucky
Source: *AmAu&B; AmWomWr; AmWr S3; ArtclWW 2; Benet 96; BenetAL 91; BioIn 10, 12, 13, 15, 16; BlmGWL; BlueB 76; ConAu 3NR, 5R, 32NR; ConLC 13; ConNov 82, 86, 91; CurBio 81; DcLB 6; FacFETw; FemiCLE; IntAu&W 76, 77; IntWW 89, 91, 93; InWom SUP; LiHiK; MajTwCW; ModAWWr; NotWoAT; Novels; OxCAmL 83, 95; OxCWoWr 95; RGTwCWr; SouWr; WhoAm 74, 76, 78, 80, 82, 84, 86, 88, 90, 94, 95, 96, 97; WhoAmW 66, 68, 70, 72, 74, 85, 87, 89, 93, 95, 97; WhoE 95, 97; WhoUSWr 88; WhoWrEP 89, 92, 95; WorAu 1950; WrDr 76, 80, 82, 84, 86, 88, 90, 92*

Hardwicke, Cedric Webster, Sir
English. Actor
Character actor in authoritative, villain roles: *The Hunchback of Notre Dame,* 1939; *Suspicion,* 1941.
b. Feb 19, 1893 in Lye, England
d. Aug 6, 1964 in New York, New York
Source: *BiDFilm; BiE&WWA; CurBio 49, 64; DcAmB S7; DcNaB 1961; Film 1; FilmgC; GrBr; LngCTC; MotPP; MovMk; NewC; OxCFilm; OxCThe 67, 83; PlP&P; WhAm 4; WhE&EA; WhScrn 77*

Hardy, Godfrey Harold
English. Mathematician
Formulated Hardy-Weinberg law of genetics, 1908.
b. Feb 7, 1877 in Cranleigh, England
d. Dec 1, 1947 in Cambridge, England
Source: *BiESc; BioIn 1, 2, 5, 6, 7, 11, 12, 14, 20; CamDcSc; DcNaB 1941; DcScB; GrBr; LarDcSc; NewCBEL; NotTwCS*

Hardy, Oliver
[Laurel and Hardy; Oliver Norvell Hardy, Jr.]
American. Comedian
First film with Laurel: *Putting Pants on Philip,* 1926.
b. Jan 18, 1892 in Harlem, Georgia
d. Aug 7, 1957 in North Hollywood, California
Source: *BiDFilm; BioIn 2, 4, 5, 7, 8, 9, 10, 11, 12, 14, 15, 16, 17, 18, 20; CmMov; DcAmB S6; DcArts; EncAFC; Film 1, 2; FilmEn; FilmgC; ForYSC; Funs; HalFC 80, 84, 88; JoeFr; LegTOT; MGM; MotPP; MovMk; NotNAT B; OxCFilm; RAdv 13-3; TwYS; WebAB 74, 79; WhoHol B; WhoHrs 80; WhScrn 74, 77, 83; WorAl; WorAlBi; WorEFlm*

Hardy, Porter, Jr.
American. Politician
US rep. from VA, 1947-69.
b. Jun 1, 1903
d. Apr 19, 1995 in Virginia Beach, Virginia
Source: *BiDrAC; BiDrUSC 89; BioIn 4, 20, 21; CurBio 95N; WhAmP; WhoAm 76; WhoAmP 75, 77, 79, 81, 83*

Hardy, Thomas
English. Author, Poet
Wrote *Far From the Madding Crowd,* 1874; *Tess of the D'Ubervilles,* 1891.
b. Jun 2, 1840 in Higher Bockhampton, England
d. Jan 11, 1928 in Dorchester, England
Source: *Alli SUP; AnCL; AtlBL; BbD; Benet 87, 96; BiD&SB; BioIn 1, 2, 3, 4, 5, 6, 7, 8, 9, 10, 11, 12, 13, 14, 15, 16, 17, 18, 19, 20, 21; BlmGEL; BritAu 19; BritWr 6; CamGEL; CamGLE; CasWL; CelCen; Chambr 3; ChhPo, S1, S2, S3; CnDBLB 5; CnE&AP; CnMWL; ConAu 104, 123; CrtSuDr; CrtT 3, 4; CyWA 58; DcArts; DcBiA; DcEnA, A; DcEnL; DcEuL; DcLB 18, 19, 135; DcLEL; DcNaB 1922; Dis&D; EncWL, 2, 3; EvLB; FilmgC; GrBr; GrWrEL N, P; HalFC 80, 84, 88; LegTOT; LinLib L, S; LngCEL; LngCTC; MagSWL; MajTwCW; McGEWB; ModBrL, S1, S2; ModWD; NewC; NewCBEL; NewEOp 71; Novels; OxCEng 67, 85, 95; OxCMus; OxCTwCP; OxDcOp; PenC ENG; PenEncH; PoeCrit 8; RAdv 1, 14, 13-1; RComWL; REn; RfGEnL 91; RfGShF; RGFMBP; RGTwCWr; ScF&FL 92; ShSCr 2; SmATA 25; TwCLC 4, 10, 18, 32, 48, 53; TwCWr; VicBrit; WebE&AL; WhDW; WhE&EA; WhLit; WhoChL; WhoLA; WhoTwCL; WorAl; WorAlBi; WorLitC*

Hare, David
American. Photographer, Sculptor, Artist
Prominent figure of the first generation NY School artists; noted for Indian photographs, abstract sculpture and paintings of mythological subjects.
b. Mar 10, 1917 in New York, New York
d. Dec 21, 1992 in Jackson Hole, Wyoming
Source: *BioIn 1, 4, 5, 13, 18; BriEAA; ConArt 77, 83, 89, 96; DcAmArt; DcCAA 71, 77, 88, 94; McGDA; NewYTBS 92; OxCTwCA; OxDcArt; PhDcTCA 77; WhAm 11; WhoAm 82, 84, 86, 88, 90, 92; WhoAmA 73, 76, 78, 80, 82, 84, 86, 89, 91, 93; WorArt 1950*

Hare, David
English. Dramatist
Award-winning playwright: *Knuckle,* 1974; *Plenty,* 1978.
b. Jun 5, 1947 in Saint Leonards, England
Source: *BiDFilm 94; BioIn 10, 11, 12, 13, 16; BlmGEL; CamGLE; CamGWoT; CnThe; ConAu 39NR, 97; ConBrDr; ConDr 73, 77, 82, 88, 93; ConLC 29, 58; ConTFT 4, 11; CrtSuDr; CurBio 83; CyWA 89; DcArts; DcLB 13; DcLEL 1940; EncWT; Ent; FacFETw; IntAu&W 76, 82, 89, 91, 93; IntDcT 2; IntMPA 92, 94, 96; IntWW 89, 91, 93; MajTwCW; McGEWD 84; MiSFD 9; NewYTBS 82, 85; OxCEng 95; OxCThe 83; RAdv 14, 13-2; RGTwCWr; Who 82, 83, 85, 88, 90, 92, 94; WhoAm 82, 84, 86, 88, 90, 92, 94, 95, 96, 97; WhoEnt 92; WhoThe 77, 81; WhoWor 84, 87, 89, 91, 93, 95, 96, 97; WorAu 1980; WrDr 76, 80, 82, 84, 86, 88, 90, 92, 94, 96*

Hare, Ernie
[The Happiness Boys; Thomas Ernest Hare]
American. Singer
Teamed with Billy Jones in radio act, 1921-39; among early stars, they performed first commercial jingles for many products.
b. 1883
d. 1939
Source: *BioIn 5; RadStar; WhScrn 83*

Hare, James Henry
English. Journalist
Covered major wars, 1898-1918; pioneered in aerial photography.
b. Oct 3, 1856 in London, England
d. Jun 24, 1946 in Teaneck, New Jersey
Source: *BioIn 1, 8, 11; DcAmB S4; ObitOF 79; WhAm 2*

Hare, John, Sir
English. Actor, Manager
Noted character actor; managed Garrick Theatre, 1889-95, built for him by W S Gilbert.
b. May 16, 1844 in Giggleswick, England
d. Dec 28, 1921 in London, England
Source: *BioIn 16; CamGWoT; CelCen; DcNaB 1912; EncWT; NewCol 75; NotNAT B; OxCThe 67, 83; PlP&P; VicBrit; WhoStg 1908; WhScrn 77, 83; WhThe*

Hare, Raymond A(rthur)
American. Diplomat
Began foreign service, 1927; involved in Middle Eastern, Near Eastern, and South Asian affairs.
b. Apr 3, 1901
d. Feb 9, 1994 in Washington, District of Columbia
Source: *BioIn 4, 5, 16, 19, 20; BlueB 76; CurBio 94N; DcAmDH 89; IntWW 74, 75, 76, 77, 78, 79, 80, 81, 82, 83, 89, 91, 93; IntYB 78, 79, 80, 81, 82; MidE 78, 79, 80, 81, 82; WhoAm 74, 76, 78, 80; WhoWor 74, 76, 78*

Hare, William
[Burke and Hare]
Irish. Murderer
With William Burke murdered 15 people, sold bodies to school of anatomy.
b. 1792? in Londonderry, Northern Ireland
d. 1870
Source: *BioIn 1, 4, 10*

Harewood, Dorian
American. Actor
Appeared in TV mini-series "Roots—The Next Generations," 1979-81; film, *Again st All Odds,* 1984.
b. Aug 6, 1951 in Dayton, Ohio
Source: *BioIn 11, 14, 15; ConTFT 7; DrBlPA 90; HalFC 84, 88; InB&W 80, 85; IntMPA 92; NewYTBS 76; VarWW 85; WhoBlA 85, 90, 92; WhoHol 92*

Harewood, George Henry Hubert Lascelles, Earl
English. Director, Critic
Directed English National Opera, 1970s, Edinburgh Festival, 1960s; edited *Kobbe's Opera Book.*
b. Feb 7, 1923 in Leeds, England
Source: *Au&Wr 71; Baker 84; BioIn 7, 8, 13, 14; ConAu 125; CurBio 65; IntAu&W 86; IntWW 81, 93*

Harger, Rolla
American. Scientist
Invented the Drunkometer, first instrument to test driver's toxication level.
b. Jan 14, 1890 in Decatur County, Kansas
d. Aug 8, 1983 in Indianapolis, Indiana
Source: *AnObit 1983; IndAu 1917; NewYTBS 83*

Hargis, Billy James
American. Evangelist
Founded, led Christian Crusade, 1966—; ultraconservative revivalist; had TV series "Pray for America," 1979-83.
b. Aug 3, 1925 in Texarkana, Texas
Source: *AmDec 1970; AmOrTwC; BioIn 6, 8, 9, 10, 17; CelR; CurBio 72; PrimTiR; RelLAm 91; TwCSAPR; WhoAm 76, 78, 80, 82, 84, 86, 88, 90, 92, 94, 95, 96, 97; WhoRel 85, 92; WhoSSW 73; WhoWor 78, 80, 82, 84, 87, 89, 91, 93*

Hargrave, Lawrence
Australian. Aeronautical Engineer
Invented box kite; contributed greatly to field of aeronautics with studies of wing surfaces.
b. Jan 29, 1850 in Greenwich, England
d. Jul 6, 1915 in Sydney, Australia
Source: *BioIn 2, 6, 9, 11, 12, 16, 21; InSci*

Hargreaves, James
English. Engineer, Inventor
Invented spinning jenny, 1764.
b. 1720?
d. Apr 22, 1778 in Nottinghamshire, England
Source: *BioIn 3, 12, 14; DcInv; DcNaB; NewCol 75; OxCDecA; WhDW*

Hargrove, Roy
American. Jazz Musician
Jazz trumpeter; albums include *The Vibe,* 1992.
b. 1970 in Texas

Haring, Georg Wilhelm Heinrich
[Willibald Alexis]
German. Author
Journalist; historical novels include *Walladmor,* 1824; *Schloss Avalon,* 1827.
b. Jun 29, 1798 in Breslau, Germany
d. Dec 16, 1871 in Arnstadt, Germany
Source: *BbD; BiD&SB; CasWL; DcEnL; DcEuL; DcLB 133; EuAu; EvEuW; LinLib L; OxCGer 76, 86; REn; WebBD 83*

Haring, Keith
American. Artist
Graffiti artist known for drawings in NYC subways; died of AIDS.
b. May 4, 1958 in Kutztown, Pennsylvania
d. Feb 16, 1990 in New York, New York
Source: *AmDec 1980; AnObit 1990; BioIn 13, 15, 16, 17, 20; CelR 90; CurBio 86, 90, 90N; DcCAA 88, 94; DcTwCCu 1; GayLesB; LegTOT; News 90, 90-3; NewYTBS 90; PrintW 83, 85; WhoAmA 86, 89, 91N, 93N; WorArt 1980*

Harjo, Chitto
[Wilson Jones]
American. Native American Leader
Member of the Crazy Snake Movement, 1900-1909, which demanded that the Creek National Council and the President of the United States enforce the Treaty of 1832, which guaranteed the Five Nations a specified amount of land in Oklahoma.
b. 1846 in Arbeka, Oklahoma
d. Apr 11, 1911
Source: *BioIn 21; EncNoAI; NotNaAm*

Harjo, Joy
American. Poet
Published collections of poetry *The Last Song,* 1975; *In Mad Love and War,* 1990.
b. May 9, 1951 in Tulsa, Oklahoma
Source: *AmWomWr SUP; BenetAL 91; BioIn 19, 21; BlmGWL; ConAu 35NR, 114; ConLC 83; ConPo 96; DcLB 120; DcNAL; DrAPF 80; EncNAB; FemiCLE; Focus; IntAu&W 86, 89; IntWWP 82; InWom SUP; ModWoWr; NatNAL; NotNaAm; OxCAmL 95; RfGAmL 94; WhoUSWr 88; WhoWrEP 89, 92, 95*

Harjo, Susan Shown
American. Native American Leader
President of the Morningstar Institute, an Indian advocacy group, 1990s.
b. 1945

Harkes, John
American. Soccer Player
Member of US National Team, 1990—; plays with Washington United, 1996—
b. Mar 8, 1967 in Kearny, New Jersey
Source: *News 96*

Harkin, Thomas R(ichard)
American. Politician
Dem. congressman from IA, 1974-85, senator, 1985—; entered 1992 presidential primaries, withdrew in March.
b. Nov 19, 1939 in Cumming, Iowa
Source: *AlmAP 88; BiDrUSC 89; BioIn 14, 15; CngDr 87; CurBio 92; IntWW 91; NewYTBS 91; PolsAm 84; WhoAm*

86, 90, 92, 94, 95, 96, 97; WhoAmP 87; WhoGov 77; WhoMW 76, 78, 80, 82, 84, 86, 90, 92, 93, 96; WhoWor 91

Harkins, William Draper
American. Chemist
First to demonstrate process of nuclear fusion.
b. Dec 28, 1873 in Titusville, Pennsylvania
d. Mar 7, 1951 in Chicago, Illinois
Source: *AsBiEn; BiESc; BioIn 2, 5, 11, 14, 15; DcAmB S5; DcScB; NatCAB 42; WhAm 3; WorAl; WorAlBi*

Harkness, Anna M. Richardson
American. Philanthropist
Widow of oil magnate; left large endowments to Yale U.
b. Oct 25, 1837 in Dalton, Ohio
d. Mar 27, 1926 in New York, New York
Source: *InWom SUP; LibW; NotAW*

Harkness, Edward Stephen
American. Businessman, Philanthropist
Heir to Standard Oil fortune; donated over $100 million to medical educational institutions.
b. Jan 22, 1874 in Cleveland, Ohio
d. Jan 29, 1940
Source: *AmBi; BioIn 2, 4; CurBio 40; DcAmB S2; LinLib S; WhAm 1*

Harkness, Rebekah West
American. Philanthropist, Composer
Founded Harkness Ballet, 1964-74; Rebekah Harkness Foundation, to support dance companies, 1959.
b. Apr 17, 1915 in Saint Louis, Missouri
d. Jun 17, 1982 in New York, New York
Source: *ASCAP 66*

Harlan, John Marshall, I
American. Supreme Court Justice
Associate justice, 1877-1911; Hayes appointee; noted for forceful, often bitter dissents.
b. Jun 1, 1833 in Boyle County, Kentucky
d. Oct 14, 1911 in Washington, District of Columbia
Source: *AmBi; AmPolLe; AmRef; ApCAB; BiDSA; BioIn 2, 3, 5, 7, 9, 13, 15, 18, 20, 21; DcAmB; DcAmSR; DcNAA; EncAACR; EncAB-H 1974, 1996; EncSoH; FacFETw; HarEnUS; LinLib L, S; McGEWB; NatCAB 1; OxCAmH; OxCLaw; OxCSupC; PeoHis; RComAH; SupCtJu; TwCBDA; WebAB 74, 79; WhAm 1; WorAl*

Harlan, John Marshall, II
American. Supreme Court Justice
Conservative who served 1955-71; advocated judicial restraint.
b. May 20, 1899 in Chicago, Illinois
d. Dec 29, 1971 in Washington, District of Columbia
Source: *AmDec 1960; BiDFedJ; BioIn 3, 4, 5, 6, 7, 8, 9, 10, 11, 12, 13, 15, 17, 18; ConAu 33R; CurBio 55, 72N; DcAmB S9; EncWB; FacFETw; LegTOT; LinLib L, S; NatCAB 57; ObitT 1971; OxCSupC; PeoHis; PolProf E, J, K, NF; SupCtJu; WebAB 74, 79; WhAm 5; WhoSSW 73*

Harlan, Louis R
American. Author
Won Pulitzer, 1984, for biography *Booker T Washington: The Wizard of Tuskegee.*
b. Jul 13, 1922 in West Point, Mississippi
Source: *BioIn 14; ConAu 21R, 25NR; ConLC 34; DrAS 74H, 78H, 82H; NewYTBS 84; WhoAm 90; WhoE 89*

Harlan, Veit
German. Director
Under Goebbels turned out Nazi propaganda films, including *Jew Suess,* 1940.
b. Sep 22, 1899 in Berlin, Germany
d. Apr 13, 1964 in Capri, Italy
Source: *BiDFilm, 81, 94; BioIn 6, 14; DcFM; EncEurC; EncTR 91; FilmEn; FilmgC; HalFC 80, 84, 88; OxCFilm; WhScrn 77, 83*

Harlech, William David Ormsby-Gore, Baron
English. Diplomat
Confidant of John F Kennedy who was British ambassador to Washington, 1961-65.
b. May 20, 1918 in London, England
d. Jan 26, 1985 in Shrewsbury, England
Source: *BioIn 7, 8, 11; IntWW 81; NewYTBS 85; Who 85; WhoWor 74*

Harley, Bill
[William Harley]
American. Entertainer
Children's performer; albums include *Monsters in the Bathroom,* 1984; *Grownups Are Strange,* 1990.
Source: *Alli; BioIn 2; ConMus 7*

Harlow, Bryce Nathaniel
American. Presidential Aide, Business Executive
Powerful adviser to Ford, Nixon, Eisenhower; lobbyist, governmental relations ex pert.
b. Aug 11, 1916 in Oklahoma City, Oklahoma
d. Feb 17, 1987 in Washington, District of Columbia
Source: *BioIn 11, 12; IntWW 74, 75, 76, 77, 78, 79, 80, 81, 82, 83; WhAm 9; WhoAm 74, 76; WhoWor 78*

Harlow, Jean
[Harlean Carpenter]
"Blonde Bombshell"
American. Actor
Platinum blonde star of *Hell's Angels,* 1930; *Dinner at Eight,* 1933; sex queen of 1930s.
b. Mar 3, 1911 in Kansas City, Missouri
d. Jun 7, 1937 in Los Angeles, California
Source: *BiDFilm, 81, 94; BioAmW; BioIn 4, 6, 7, 9, 10, 11, 12, 14, 15, 17, 19, 20; CmCal; ContDcW 89; DcAmB S2; DcArts; EncAFC; FacFETw; Film 2; FilmEn; FilmgC; ForYSC; GangFlm; GoodHs; HalFC 80, 84, 88; IntDcF 1-3, 2-3; IntDcWB; InWom, SUP; LegTOT; LibW; MGM; MotPP; MovMk; NatCAB 27; NotAW; NotNAT B; OxCFilm; ThFT; TwYS; WebAB 74, 79; WhAm 4, HSA; WhoHol B; WhScrn 74, 77, 83; WorAl; WorAlBi; WorEFlm*

Harman, Fred
American. Cartoonist
Created syndicated "Red Ryder" comic strips for 25 yrs.
b. Feb 9, 1902 in Saint Joseph, Missouri
d. Jan 2, 1982 in Phoenix, Arizona
Source: *BioIn 1, 11, 12, 14, 17; ConAu 106; IlBEAAW; NewYTBS 82; SmATA 30N; WhAmArt 85; WorECom*

Harman, Hugh
American. Cartoonist
With Rudolf C. Ising created *Looney Tunes* and *Merry Melodies* cartoon series.
b. 1903 in Pagosa Springs, Colorado
d. Nov 26, 1982 in Chatsworth, California
Source: *AnObit 1982; BioIn 13, 14; ConAu 108; DcFM; HalFC 84, 88; SmATA 33N; WorECar*

Harman, Jeanne Perkins
American. Writer, Journalist
Syndicated feature writer for over 80 newspapers; writes travel books and articles.
b. Jul 27, 1919 in Baxter Springs, Kansas
Source: *BioIn 10; ConAu 11NR, 39NR, 69; ForWC 70; WhoSSW 91*

Harmon, Claude
American. Golfer
Won Masters, 1948; only player not on PGA tour to accomplish this.
b. Jul 14, 1916 in Savannah, Georgia
d. Jul 23, 1989 in Houston, Texas
Source: *BioIn 1, 16; NewYTBS 89; WhoGolf*

Harmon, Ernest N(ason)
American. Army Officer
Commanded First Armored Division, North African, Italian campaigns, WW II; one of army's most decorated officers.
b. Feb 26, 1894 in Lowell, Massachusetts
d. Nov 13, 1979 in White River Junction, Vermont
Source: *BiDWWGF; BioIn 1, 4, 6, 9, 12; CurBio 46, 80N; FacFETw; HarEnMi; NewYTBS 79; WebAMB; WhAm 7; WhoAm 74*

Harmon, Mark
American. Actor
Son of Tom Harmon and Elyse Knox; starred in "St. Elsewhere," 1984-86; "Reasonable Doubts," 1991-93; films include the role of Ted Bundy in TV movie "The Deliberate Stranger," 1986; *Summer School,* 1987.
b. Sep 2, 1951 in Burbank, California
Source: *BioIn 9, 11, 14, 15, 16; CelR 90; ConNews 87-1; ConTFT 7, 15; HalFC 84, 88; HolBB; IntMPA 82, 88, 92, 94, 96; LegTOT; LesBEnT 92; VarWW 85; WhoAm 90, 92, 94, 95, 96, 97; WhoEnt 92; WhoHol 92; WorAlBi*

Harmon, Tom
[Thomas Dudley Harmon]
"Old 98"
American. Football Player
Two-time All-America halfback, U of MI, 1938-40; won Heisman Trophy, 1940; in NFL with LA Rams, 1946-47; father of Mark Harmon.
b. Sep 28, 1919 in Rensselaer, Indiana
d. Mar 15, 1990 in Los Angeles, California
Source: *BioIn 10, 14, 16, 17; FacFETw; IndAu 1917; IntMPA 75, 76, 77, 78, 79, 80, 81, 82, 84, 86, 88; LegTOT; News 90, 90-3; NewYTBS 90; VarWW 85; WhoFtbl 74; WhoHol A*

Harmsworth, Harold Sidney
[First Viscount Rothermere]
English. Businessman
With brother Alfred, owned many newspapers, revolutionized British journalism.
b. Apr 26, 1868 in London, England
d. Nov 26, 1940, Bermuda
Source: *BioIn 14; CurBio 41; DcNaB 1931; DcTwBBL; GrBr; LngCTC; NewC; WorAl*

Harnett, William Michael
American. Artist
Master of Trompe L'oeil (Fool the Eye); still life works include *After the H unt,* 1885.
b. Aug 10, 1848 in Clonakilty, Ireland
d. Oct 29, 1892 in New York, New York
Source: *BioIn 1, 2, 3, 4, 5, 9, 11, 12, 15, 17, 18, 19, 20; BriEAA; DcAmArt; LinLib S; McGDA; McGEWB; OxCAmH; OxCArt; OxDcArt; WebAB 74, 79*

Harney, Benjamin Robertson
American. Composer
Known for early ragtime compositions.
b. Mar 6, 1871
d. Mar 1, 1938 in Philadelphia, Pennsylvania
Source: *BiDAmM; BioIn 4, 6; DcAmB S2*

Harnick, Sheldon Mayer
American. Lyricist
Won Tony awards for *Fiorello,* 1960; *Fiddler on the Roof,* 1964.
b. Apr 30, 1924 in Chicago, Illinois
Source: *BiE&WWA; BioIn 15; CamGWoT; CelR 90; EncMT; IntWW 74, 75, 76, 77, 78, 79, 80, 81, 82, 83, 89, 91, 93; NewCBMT; NewGrDA 86; NotNAT; OxCAmT 84; OxCPMus; PlP&P; VarWW 85; WhoAm 74, 76, 78, 80, 82, 84, 86, 88, 90, 92, 94, 95, 96, 97; WhoE 95; WhoEnt 92; WhoWor 74*

Harnoncourt, Nikolaus
Austrian. Conductor
Created the Concentus Musicus of Vienna, 1953; recorded all of Bach's cantatas in 45 volumes.
b. Dec 6, 1929 in Berlin, Germany
Source: *Baker 84, 92; BioIn 12, 17; BriBkM 80; CurBio 91; IntWW 79, 80, 81, 82, 83, 89, 91, 93; IntWWM 77, 80, 85, 90; NewAmDM; NewGrDM 80; NewGrDO; PenDiMP; WhoWor 74, 76, 82, 84, 87, 89, 91, 93, 95; WorAlBi*

Harnwell, Gaylord Probasco
American. Physicist, Educator
Pres., U of Pennsylvania, 1953-70.
b. Sep 29, 1903 in Evanston, Illinois
d. Apr 18, 1982 in Haverford, Pennsylvania
Source: *AmMWSc 73P, 76P, 79, 82; BioIn 3, 4, 5, 12, 13; ConAu 106; CurBio 82; NewYTBS 82; WhoAm 80*

Harold II
[Harold Godwineson]
English. Ruler
King who reigned after brother-in-law, Edward the Confessor's death, 1066; conquered Wales, killed in battle.
b. 1022?
d. Oct 15, 1066 in Hastings, England
Source: *McGEWB; WebBD 83*

Harp, Holly
American. Fashion Designer
Designer noted for hand-painted dresses.
d. Apr 24, 1995
Source: *InWom SUP; NewYTBS 95*

Harper, Ben
American. Singer, Songwriter, Musician
Blues influenced guitarist and social lyricist; toured with blues artist Taj Mahal, 1992-1993; released debut album, *Welcome to the Cruel World,* in 1994 and later released *Fight for Your Mind,* in 1995.
b. Oct 28, 1969 in California
Source: *ConMus 17*

Harper, Chandler
American. Golfer
Turned pro, 1934; won PGA, 1950; Hall of Fame, 1969.
b. Mar 10, 1914 in Portsmouth, Virginia
Source: *BioIn 15, 20; WhoGolf; WhoSpor*

Harper, Elijah
Canadian. Native American Leader
Member of the Manitoba legislature, 1981—; put aboriginal demands at the top of Canada's constitutional agenda.
b. 1949 in Manitoba, Canada
Source: *BioIn 20, 21; EncNAB; NotNaAm*

Harper, Fletcher
[Harper Brothers]
American. Publisher
Member, famed publishing firm, from 1825; added *Harper's Weekly,* 1857; *Harper's Bazaar,* 1867; promoted schoolbook trade.
b. Jan 31, 1806 in Newton, New York
d. May 29, 1877 in New York, New York
Source: *AmAu&B; BiDAmBL 83; DcAmB; DcLB 79; EncAJ; JrnUS; NatCAB 1; TwCBDA; WebAB 74, 79; WhAm HS; WhCiWar*

Harper, Frances Ellen Watkins
American. Poet
Among earliest US black writers; wrote anti-slavery verse, 1850s-60s; co-organizer, National Assn. of Colored Women.
b. Sep 24, 1825 in Baltimore, Maryland
d. Feb 22, 1911 in Philadelphia, Pennsylvania
Source: *AfrAmOr; AfrAmW; Alli SUP; AmPeW; AmWomWr, 92; ArtclWW 2; Benet 96; BenetAL 91; BioIn 15, 17, 18, 19, 20, 21; BlkAmW 1; BlkAWP; BlkLC; BlkWAm; BlkWr 1; BlkWrNE; ChhPo S1; ConAu 111, 125; DcAmB; DcAmNB; DcAmReB 1, 2; DcAmTB; DcLB 50; DcNAA; EncWHA; FemiCLE; HanAmWH; InB&W 80, 85; InWom SUP; LegTOT; LibW; ModAWWr; NotAW; OxCAmL 95; OxCWoWr 95; RfGAmL 94; SchCGBL; SelBAAf; SelBAAu; TwCLC 14; WomFir*

Harper, Heather Mary
[Mrs. Buck]
British. Opera Singer
Soprano who had Covent Garden debut, 1962; toured US annually since 1967.
b. May 8, 1930 in Belfast, Northern Ireland
Source: *Baker 84, 92; IntWW 83, 91; IntWWM 90; InWom SUP; MetOEnc; NewAmDM; NewGrDM 80; NewGrDO; PenDiMP; Who 92, 94; WhoAm 78, 80, 82, 84, 86, 88, 90, 92, 94, 95, 96, 97; WhoAmM 83; WhoOp 76; WhoWor 84, 89, 91, 93, 95*

Harper, James
[Harper Brothers]
American. Publisher
Co-founded with brother John, J & J Harper, 1817; became reform mayor of NYC, 1844.
b. Apr 13, 1795 in Newton, New York
d. Mar 27, 1869 in New York, New York
Source: *AmAu&B; AmBi; ApCAB; BiDAmBL 83; DcAmB; DcNaB; Drake; EncAB-H 1974, 1996; LegTOT; NatCAB 1; TwCBDA; WebAB 74, 79; WhAm HS; WhDW; WorAl*

Harper, John
[Harper Brothers]
American. Publisher
With brother James, co-founded J & J Harper, 1817; adopted firm name Harper Brothers, 1833.
b. Jan 22, 1797 in Newton, New York
d. Apr 22, 1875 in New York, New York
Source: *DcAmB; Drake; NatCAB 1; TwCBDA; WebAB 74, 79*

Harper, Joseph Wesley
[Harper Brothers]
American. Publisher
Admitted to brothers' firm, 1823; chief editor, critic.
b. Dec 25, 1801 in Newton, New York
d. Feb 14, 1870 in New York, New York
Source: *DcAmB; Drake; NatCAB 1; TwCBDA; WebAB 74, 79*

Harper, Ken
American. Producer
Best-known Broadway musical, *The Wiz*, opened, 1975; won seven Tonys.
b. 1940?
d. Jan 20, 1988 in New York, New York

Harper, Marion, Jr.
American. Advertising Executive
Pres. and chm., McCann-Erickson, later Interpublic Group, 1948-68.
b. May 14, 1916 in Oklahoma City, Oklahoma
d. Oct 25, 1989 in Oklahoma City, Oklahoma
Source: *AdMenW; BioIn 1, 3, 5, 6, 8, 12, 13, 16, 17, 20; CurBio 90N; NewYTBS 89; WhAm 10; WhoAm 74*

Harper, Tess
[Tessie Jean Washam]
American. Actor
In movies *Silkwood, Tender Mercies.* 1983.
b. Aug 15, 1950 in Mammoth Spring, Arkansas
Source: *BioIn 13; ConTFT 7; IntMPA 92; LegTOT; WhoHol 92*

Harper, Valerie
American. Actor
Won four Emmys for role of Rhoda in "The Mary Tyler Moore Show," 1970-74; "Rhoda," 1974-78; star of TV show "Valerie," 1986-87; starred in numerous made for TV movies.
b. Aug 22, 1940 in Suffern, New York
Source: *BioIn 12, 14, 15; BioNews 75; BkPepl; CelR 90; ConTFT 5; CurBio 75; EncAFC; FilmEn; HalFC 80, 84, 88; HerW; IntMPA 80, 82, 84, 86, 88, 92, 94, 96; InWom SUP; LegTOT; LesBEnT; NewYTBE 71; NewYTBS 74; VarWW 85; WhoAm 76, 78, 80, 82, 84, 86, 88, 90, 92, 94, 95, 96, 97; WhoAmW 95; WhoCom; WhoEnt 92; WhoHol 92, A; WorAl; WorAlBi*

Harper, William Rainey
American. Educator
First pres., U of Chicago, 1891-1906; noted Hebraic scholar.
b. Jul 26, 1856 in New Concord, Ohio
d. Jan 10, 1906 in Chicago, Illinois
Source: *AmAu&B; AmBi; ApCAB; BiDAmEd; BioIn 3, 4, 7, 8, 12, 14, 15, 16, 19; CyEd; DcAmAu; DcAmB; DcAmReB 2; DcNAA; EncAB-H 1974, 1996; HarEnUS; LinLib L, S; LuthC 75; McGEWB; MorMA; NatCAB 11; OhA&B; OxCAmH; REnAL; TwCBDA; WebAB 74, 79; WhAm 1; WorAl; WorAlBi*

Harpignies, Henri
French. Artist
Landscape painter of Barbizon School; in first Impressionist exhibition, 1874.
b. Jun 28, 1819 in Valenciennes, France
d. Aug 28, 1916 in Saint-Prive, France
Source: *ArtsNiC; Dis&D; McGDA; OxCArt; OxCFr; OxDcArt*

Harrah, Bill
[William Fisk Harrah]
American. Gambler, Businessman
Founded Harrah's Casino, 1937; Harrah's Tahoe Casino, 1955.
b. Sep 2, 1911 in Pasadena, California
d. Jun 30, 1978 in Rochester, Minnesota
Source: *BioIn 7, 10, 11, 12; DcAmB S10; WhAm 7; WhoAm 78*

Harrar, J(acob) George
American. Botanist
Pres. of Rockefeller Foundation, 1961-72.
b. Dec 2, 1906 in Painesville, Ohio
d. Apr 18, 1982 in Scarsdale, New York
Source: *AmMWSc 73P, 76P, 79, 82; AnObit 1982; BioIn 6, 7, 9, 12, 13; BlueB 76; ConAu 110; CurBio 64, 82, 82N; IntWW 74, 75, 76, 77, 78, 79, 80, 81, 82, 83; LEduc 74; McGMS 80; NewYTBS 82; St&PR 75; WhAm 8; WhoAm 74, 76, 78, 80, 82*

Harrell, Andre (O'Neal)
American. Music Executive
Founder and president of Uptown Records, 1987-92; president, Uptown Entertainment, 1992—.
b. c. 1962
Source: *ConBlB 9; ConMus 16*

Harrell, Lynn Morris
American. Musician
Cello soloist with major US, European symphonies since early 70's; TV appearances include "Live from Lincoln Center."
b. Jan 30, 1944 in New York, New York
Source: *Baker 84; BioIn 11, 13; ConMus 3; CurBio 83; IntWW 91; IntWWM 90; NewAmDM; NewGrDA 86; NewYTBS 77; PenDiMP; Who 94; WhoAm 78, 80, 82, 84, 86, 88, 90, 92, 94, 95, 96, 97; WhoAmM 83; WhoEnt 92; WhoWest 92, 94, 96*

Harrelson, Ken(neth Smith)
"Hawk"
American. Baseball Player
Infielder-outfielder, 1963-71; led AL in RBIs, 1968; known for flamboyance.
b. Sep 4, 1941 in Woodruff, South Carolina
Source: *Ballpl 90; BioIn 8, 9, 12, 14; CurBio 70; WhoAm 86, 90; WhoProB 73*

Harrelson, Woody
[Woodrow Tracy Harrelson]
American. Actor
Played Woody Boyd on TV comedy "Cheers," 1985-93; won Emmy 1989; films include *White Men Can't Jump,* 1992, *Indecent Proposal,* 1993; *The People vs. Larry Flynt,* 1996.
b. Jul 23, 1961 in Midland, Texas
Source: *BioIn 16; IntMPA 92, 94, 96; LegTOT; WhoAm 94, 95, 96, 97; WhoEnt 92; WhoHol 92; WorAlBi*

Harridge, Will(iam)
American. Baseball Executive
Pres. of AL, 1931-58, succeeded by Joe Cronin; Hall of Fame, 1972.
b. Oct 16, 1881 in Chicago, Illinois
d. Apr 9, 1971 in Evanston, Illinois

Harrigan, Edward
"Ned"
American. Actor, Dramatist
Known for comedy sketches on NY immigrant life, late 19th c; *The Mulligan Guard Picnic,* 1878.
b. Oct 26, 1845 in New York, New York
d. Jun 6, 1911 in New York, New York
Source: *AmAu; AmAu&B; AmPS; BenetAL 91; BiDAmM; BiD&SB; BioIn 3, 4, 11, 12; ChhPo S2; CnThe; DcAmAu; DcAmB; DcAmImH; DcNAA; EncMT; EncVaud; EncWT; Ent; FamA&A; McGEWD 72, 84; ModWD; NatCAB 11; NotNAT B; OxCAmL 65, 83, 95; OxCAmT 84; OxCThe 67; PlP&P; PoIre; REnAL; REnWD; Sw&Ld B; WhAm 1*

Harriman, E(dward) Roland (Noel)
American. Financier
Chm., Union Pacific Railroad, 1946-49; brother of W Averell.
b. Dec 24, 1895 in New York, New York
d. Feb 16, 1978 in Arden, New York
Source: *CurBio 51, 78, 78N; DcAmB S10; IntWW 74, 75, 76, 77, 78; IntYB 78; NewYTBS 78; St&PR 75; WhAm 5, 7; WhNAA; WhoAm 74; WhoFI 74; WhoGov 72*

Harriman, Edward Henry
American. Businessman, Philanthropist
Railroad financier; headed Union Pacific, 1880-90s; organized first Boys Club, 1876; father of W Averell.
b. Feb 25, 1848 in Hampstead, New York
d. Sep 9, 1909 in Orange County, New York

Source: *AmBi; ApCAB X; BiDAmBL 83; BioIn 1, 2, 3, 7, 8, 11, 12, 13, 14, 15, 21; CmCal; DcAmB; EncAB-H 1974, 1996; EncABHB 2; GayN; HarEnUS; InSci; LinLib S; McGEWB; MorMA; NatCAB 14; OxCAmH; REnAW; WebAB 74, 79; WebBD 83; WhAm 1; WorAl*

Harriman, Pamela
American. Government Official
US Ambassador to France, 1993-97.
b. Mar 20, 1920 in Farnborough, England
d. Feb 5, 1997 in Paris, France
Source: *News 94*

Harriman, W(illiam) Averell
American. Government Official, Statesman
Dem. who served four presidents in diplomatic roles.
b. Nov 15, 1891 in New York, New York
d. Jul 26, 1986 in Yorktown Heights, New York
Source: *AmDec 1950; BiDrGov 1789; BiDrUSE 71, 89; BioIn 1, 2, 3, 4, 5, 6, 7, 8, 9, 10, 11, 12, 13; ColdWar 1; ConAu 111, 119; ConNews 86-4; CurBio 41, 46, 86; DcAmDH 80, 89; DcPol; DcTwHis; EncAB-H 1974, 1996; IntWW 74, 75, 76, 78, 79, 80, 82, 83; IntYB 78, 79, 80; LinLib S; McGEWB; NewYTBS 81, 86; OxCAmH; PolProf E, J, K, T; St&PR 75, 84, 87; WebAB 74; WhAm 9; WhDW; Who 74, 82, 83, 85; WhoAm 74, 76, 78, 80, 82, 84, 86; WhoAmP 73, 75, 77, 79, 81, 83, 85; WhoWor 74, 78; WhWW-II; WorAl*

Harrington, Michael
[Edward Michael Harrington]
American. Politician, Author
Wrote *The Other America,* 1962, bringing poverty into arena of public dis cussion; co-chaired the Dem. Socialists of America, 1981-89.
b. Feb 24, 1928 in Saint Louis, Missouri
d. Jul 31, 1989 in Larchmont, New York
Source: *AmAu&B; AmPeW; AmSocL; AnObit 1989; Benet 87; BenetAL 91; BiDAmL; BiDAmLf; BiDNeoM; BioIn 8, 11, 16, 18, 19, 20; CelR, 90; ConAu 17R, 19NR, 129; ConIsC 1; CurBio 69, 88, 89, 89N; EncAB-H 1974, 1996; EncAL; EncWB; FacFETw; LegTOT; LinLib L; LNinSix; NewYTBE 72; NewYTBS 89; OxCCan; PolProf J, K; RadHan; RComAH; WhAm 10; WhoAm 74, 76, 78, 80, 82, 84, 86, 88; WhoUSWr 88; WhoWrEP 89; WorAl; WorAlBi; WorAu 1975; WrDr 80, 82, 84, 86, 88*

Harrington, Oliver W(endell)
American. Cartoonist
Freelance political cartoonist, 1932—; created Bootsie, 1935, a black man contending with racism in American society.
b. Feb 14, 1912 in Valhalla, New York

Harrington, Pat
[Daniel Patrick Harrington, Jr.]
American. Actor
Played Schneider on TV series "One Day at a Time," 1975-84.
b. Aug 13, 1929 in New York, New York
Source: *BioIn 14; ConTFT 3; IntMPA 84, 86, 88, 92, 94, 96; LegTOT; VarWW 85; WhoAm 86, 90; WhoCom; WhoHol 92*

Harris, Alice
American. Civil Rights Activist
Founded Parents of Watts, 1979, a non-profit Los Angeles-based community service organization.
b. Jan 14, 1934 in Gadsden, Alabama
Source: *BioIn 20; ConBlB 7*

Harris, Arthur Travers, Sir
"Bomber Harris"
English. Military Leader
Head of Britain's Bomber Command, WW II; believed key to victory was massive night bombing raids on German cities.
b. Apr 13, 1892 in Cheltenham, England
d. Apr 5, 1984 in Goring, England
Source: *BioIn 1, 11, 13, 14; CurBio 42, 84, 84N; DcNaB 1981; EncTR 91; FacFETw; HarEnMi; InSci; IntWW 74, 75, 76, 77, 78, 79, 80, 81, 82, 83; NewYTBS 84; Who 74, 82, 83, 85N*

Harris, Augustus, Sir
English. Impresario
Celebrated manager, London's Covent Garden, 1888-96; introduced day's most famous singers.
b. 1852 in Paris, France
d. Jun 22, 1896 in Folkestone, England
Source: *Baker 78, 84; CnThe; MetOEnc; NewEOp 71; NewGrDM 80; NotNAT B; OxCThe 67; OxDcOp*

Harris, Barbara
American. Actor
Films include *Plaza Suite,* 1971; *Nashville,* 1975; won Tony for *The Apple Tree,* 1966.
b. Jul 25, 1935 in Evanston, Illinois
Source: *BiDAmM; BiE&WWA; BioIn 7, 8; CelR; ConTFT 4; HalFC 84; IntMPA 84, 86, 88, 92, 94, 96; InWom, SUP; LegTOT; MotPP; NewYTBE 72; NotBlAW 1; VarWW 85; WhoAm 74, 76, 78, 80, 82, 84, 86, 88, 90, 92, 94, 95; WhoAmW 68, 70, 72, 74, 83; WhoE 74; WhoEnt 92; WhoHol A; WhoWor 74; WorAl; WorAlBi*

Harris, Barbara Clementine
American. Religious Leader
First female bishop in the history of the Episcopal church and the worldwide Anglican Communion, 1989.
b. Jun 12, 1930 in Philadelphia, Pennsylvania
Source: *AfrAmBi 1; AmDec 1980; NewYTBS 88; NotBlAW 1; RelLAm 91; WhoAm 92, 94, 95, 96, 97; WhoAmW 91, 93; WhoBlA 92; WhoE 95, 97; WhoRel 92*

Harris, Bertha
American. Author
Wrote novels *Catching Stardove,* 1969; *Lover,* 1976.
b. Dec 17, 1937 in Fayetteville, North Carolina
Source: *AmWomWr; ConAu 29R; DrAPF 80; FemiCLE; GayLesB*

Harris, Bucky
[Stanley Raymond Harris]
American. Baseball Player, Baseball Manager
Infielder, 1919-29, 1931; managed for 29 yrs; Hall of Fame, 1975.
b. Nov 8, 1896 in Port Jervis, New York
d. Nov 8, 1977 in Bethesda, Maryland
Source: *Ballpl 90; BiDAmSp BB; BioIn 1, 2, 5, 6, 11, 14, 15; CurBio 48, 78, 78N; DcAmB S10; LegTOT; NewYTBS 77; WhoProB 73; WhoSpor*

Harris, Derek
English. Journalist
Editor and columnist for the London *Times.*
b. Feb 3, 1929 in Littleover, England
d. Apr 6, 1995, England

Harris, E. Lynn
American. Author
Wrote *Invisible Life,* 1991, portraying the problems faced by black homosexuals and bisexuals; also wrote *Just As I Am,* 1994.
b. 1955 in Flint, Michigan
Source: *CurBio 96*

Harris, Ed
American. Actor
Was in *Apollo 13,* 1995.
b. Nov 28, 1950 in Tenafly, New Jersey
Source: *ConTFT 6, 14; IntMPA 86, 88, 92, 94; LegTOT; WhoHol 92; WorAlBi*

Harris, Emily Schwartz
[S(ymbionese) L(iberation) A(rmy); Mrs. William Harris]
American. Revolutionary
With husband, kidnapped Patricia Hearst, 1974.
b. Feb 11, 1947 in Baltimore, Maryland
Source: *BioIn 10; InWom SUP; NewYTBS 75; WorAlBi*

Harris, Emmylou
American. Singer, Songwriter
Won 7 Grammys awards; CMA female vocalist of year, best album, *Roses in the Snow,* 1980.
b. Apr 2, 1947 in Birmingham, Alabama
Source: *Baker 84, 92; BioIn 10, 11, 13, 14, 15, 16; BkPepl; ConMuA 80A; ConMus 4; CurBio 94; EncFCWM 83; EncRk 88; EncRkSt; HarEnCM 87; HarEnR 86; IlEncRk; InWom SUP; LegTOT; NewAmDM; NewGrDA 86; News 91, 91-3; OxCPMus; PenEncP;*

RkOn 85; RolSEnR 83; VarWW 85; WhoAm 82, 84, 86, 88, 90, 92, 94, 95, 96, 97; WhoAmW 89, 91, 93, 95, 97; WhoEnt 92; WhoHol 92; WhoNeCM A; WhoRock 81; WorAlBi

Harris, Franco
American. Football Player
Nine-time all-pro running back, Pittsburgh, 1972-84; rushed for over 1,000 yds. in each of eight seasons, tying NFL record; Hall of Fame, 1990.
b. Mar 7, 1950 in Fort Dix, New Jersey
Source: *AfrAmSG; BiDAmSp FB; BioIn 9, 10, 11, 12, 13, 14, 17, 20, 21; CelR; CurBio 76; InB&W 80; LegTOT; NewYTBE 73; NewYTBS 83, 84; WhoAfA 96; WhoAm 78, 80, 82, 84; WhoBlA 77, 80, 85, 90, 92, 94; WhoFtbl 74; WhoSpor; WorAl; WorAlBi*

Harris, Frank
[James Thomas Harris]
American. Author, Journalist
Works include *The Man Shakespeare,* 1909; controversial Wilde biography, 1916; erotic three-vol. *My Life and Loves.*
b. Feb 14, 1856 in County Galway, Ireland
d. Aug 26, 1931 in Nice, France
Source: *AmBi; Benet 87, 96; BenetAL 91; CamGLE; CnDAL; CnMD; ConAmL; ConAu 109, 150; DcArts; DcIrB 78, 88; DcIrL 96; DcLB 156; DcLEL; DcNaB 1931; EncSF 93; EvLB; FacFETw; LegTOT; LinLib L, S; LngCTC; McGEWB; ModBrL; NewC; NotNAT B; OxCAmL 65, 83, 95; OxCEng 67, 85, 95; OxCIri; PenC ENG; RAdv 1, 13-1; RfGEnL 91; ScF&FL 1; StaCVF; TwCA, SUP; TwCLC 24; TwCWr; WhAm 1; WhLit; WhoTwCL; WorAl; WorAlBi*

Harris, Fred Roy
American. Politician
Dem. senator from OK, 1964-73.
b. Nov 13, 1930 in Walters, Oklahoma
Source: *BiDrAC; BiDrUSC 89; BioIn 7, 8, 9, 10, 11, 12; CurBio 68; IntWW 74; WhoAm 86, 90; WhoAmP 73, 91; WhoGov 75; WhoSSW 73; WrDr 92*

Harris, Harwell Hamilton
American. Architect, Educator
A leading exponent of "California style" architecture, 1940s-50s.
b. Jul 2, 1903 in Redlands, California
d. Nov 18, 1990 in Raleigh, North Carolina
Source: *AmArch 70; BioIn 6, 17; ConArch 80, 87, 94; CurBio 62, 91N; IntWW 82, 83, 89, 91N; MacEA; McGDA; NewYTBS 90; WhAm 11; WhoAm 74, 76, 78, 80, 82, 84, 86, 88, 90; WhoSSW 73, 75, 76; WhoWor 74*

Harris, James Andrew
American. Chemist
Co-discovered chemical elements: 104, 105—Unnilpentium, Unnilquadium.
b. Mar 26, 1932 in Waco, Texas
Source: *BlksScM; InB&W 85; WhoAfA 96; WhoBlA 80, 85, 88, 90, 92, 94*

Harris, Jean Witt Struven
American. Murderer
Convicted of murder of former lover, Dr. Herman Tarnower, 1980; wrote autobiography *Stranger in Two Worlds,* 1986.
b. 1924
Source: *BioIn 12, 13, 16; InWom SUP*

Harris, Jed
[Jacob Horowitz]
American. Producer, Director
Had four Broadway hits in 1928: *Broadway; Coquette; The Front Page; The Royal Family;* considered theater genius.
b. Feb 25, 1900 in Vienna, Austria
d. Nov 14, 1979 in New York, New York
Source: *BiE&WWA; BioIn 1, 2, 6, 12, 13; CamGWoT; ConAu 89; DcAmB S10; GrStDi; NewYTBS 79; NotNAT, A; OxCAmT 84; TheaDir; WhAm 7; WhoAm 74; WhoThe 77A; WhThe*

Harris, Joe Frank
American. Politician
Democratic governor of GA, 1983-91, succeeded by Zell Miller.
b. Feb 16, 1936 in Cartersville, Georgia
Source: *AlmAP 84, 88; BiDrGov 1983, 1988; BioIn 20; PolsAm 84; WhoAm 84, 86, 88, 90, 92, 94, 95, 96, 97; WhoAmP 85, 87, 89, 91, 93, 95; WhoSSW 84, 86, 88, 91, 93; WhoWor 84, 87, 89, 91, 93, 95, 96, 97*

Harris, Joel Chandler
American. Author
Editor, *Atlanta Constitution,* 1890-1900; created Uncle Remus character.
b. Dec 9, 1848 in Eatonton, Georgia
d. Jul 3, 1908 in Atlanta, Georgia
Source: *Alli SUP; AmAu; AmAu&B; AmBi; AmCulL; AnCL; ApCAB, X; AtlBL; AuBYP 2, 3; BbD; Benet 87, 96; BenetAL 91; BibAL; BiDAmJo; BiDAmNC; BiD&SB; BiDSA; BioIn 1, 2, 3, 4, 5, 6, 7, 8, 10, 11, 12, 13, 14, 15, 16, 17, 19, 20; CamGEL; CamGLE; CamHAL; CarSB; CasWL; Chambr 3; ChhPo, S1, S2, S3; ChlBkCr; CnDAL; ConAu 104, 137; CyWA 58; DcAmAu; DcAmB; DcAmC; DcAmSR; DcArts; DcBiA; DcCathB; DcEnA A; DcLB 11, 23, 42, 78, 91; DcLEL; DcNAA; EncAAH; EncAB-H 1974, 1996; EncAHmr; EncAJ; EncSoH; EvLB; FamAYP; FifSWrB; GayN; GrWrEL N; HalFC 84, 88; HarEnUS; JBA 34; JrnUS; LegTOT; LinLib L, S; MajAI; McGEWB; MemAm; NatCAB 1; Novels; OxCAmL 65, 83, 95; OxCChiL; OxCEng 67, 85, 95; PenC AM; RAdv 1, 14, 13-1; REn; REnAL; RfGAmL 87, 94; RfGShF; ShSCr 19; SouWr; Str&VC; TwCBDA; TwCChW 78A, 83A, 89A, 95A; TwCLC 2; WebAB 74, 79; WebE&AL; WhAm 1; WhDW; WhLit; WhoChL; WorAl; WorAlBi; WrChl; YABC 1*

Harris, Jonathan
American. Actor
Starred in TV series "Lost in Space," 1965-68.
b. Nov 6, 1919? in New York, New York
Source: *FilmgC; HalFC 80, 84; WhoEnt 92; WhoHol A; WhoWest 89*

Harris, Joseph Pratt
American. Political Activist, Educator
Invented automatic voting machine, Harris Votamatic, 1962.
b. Feb 18, 1896 in Candor, North Carolina
d. Feb 13, 1985 in Berkeley, California
Source: *BioIn 14; ConAu 1R, 115; WhoAm 74, 76*

Harris, Julie
American. Actor
Starred in "Knots Landing," 1981-88; won 2 Emmys, 5 Tonys; films include *Member of the Wedding,* 1952; *East of Eden,* 1955.
b. Dec 2, 1925 in Grosse Pointe Park, Michigan
Source: *AuBYP 2S, 3; BiDFilm, 81; BiE&WWA; BioIn 2, 3, 4, 5, 6, 7, 9, 10, 11, 13; BioNews 74; CamGWoT; CelR, 90; CnThe; ConAu 103; ConTFT 2, 8; CurBio 56, 77; EncWT; Ent; FacFETw; FilmEn; FilmgC; ForYSC; GoodHs; GrLiveH; HalFC 80, 84, 88; IntMPA 75, 76, 77, 78, 79, 80, 81, 82, 84, 86, 88, 92, 94, 96; IntWW 79, 80, 81, 82, 83, 89, 91, 93; InWom, SUP; LegTOT; MotPP; MovMk; NotNAT; NotWoAT; OxCAmT 84; OxCFilm; PlP&P A; WhoAm 74, 76, 78, 80, 82, 84, 86, 88, 90, 92; WhoAmW 58, 64, 66, 68, 70, 72, 74, 75, 81, 83; WhoEnt 92; WhoHol 92, A; WhoHrs 80; WhoThe 72, 77, 81; WhoWor 74; WorAl; WorAlBi*

Harris, LaDonna (Crawford)
American. Social Reformer
Feminist, Comanche Indian; ran for VP on Citizens Party ticket, 1980.
b. Feb 15, 1931 in Temple, Oklahoma
Source: *BioIn 8, 9, 10, 11, 12, 19, 21; CivR 74; EncNAB; InWom SUP; NewYTBE 70; NewYTBS 80; NotNaAm; REnAW; WhoAmW 68, 70, 72, 74, 75, 77; WhoSSW 73*

Harris, Lauren
[Group of Seven]
Canadian. Artist
Painted simplified Canadian landscapes.
b. Oct 23, 1885 in Brantford, Ontario, Canada
d. Jan 29, 1970 in Vancouver, British Columbia, Canada
Source: *CreCan 2; IlBEAAW; MacDCB 78; McGDA*

Harris, Leonard
American. Writer, Actor
Writer for "CBS This Morning," 1987—; appeared in films *Taxi Driver,* 1976; *Hero at Large,* 1978.

b. Sep 27, 1929 in New York, New York
Source: *BiDrAPA 89; ConAu 9NR, 65; Dun&B 90; ScF&FL 92; St&PR 91; WhoMW 88; WrDr 80, 82, 84, 86, 88, 90, 92, 94, 96*

Harris, Leslie
American. Director, Screenwriter
Made first feature film, *Just Another Girl on the IRT,* 1992.
b. 1961 in Cleveland, Ohio
Source: *ConBlB 6*

Harris, Louis
American. Pollster
Founded public opinion, marketing research firm, Louis Harris and Associates, Inc., 1956.
b. Jan 6, 1921 in New Haven, Connecticut
Source: *AmMWSc 73S, 78S; BioIn 7, 11, 21; BlueB 76; CelR; ConAu 13R; Dun&B 88, 90; EncAJ; EncTwCJ; PolProf K; WebAB 74, 79; WhoAm 74, 76, 78, 80, 82, 84, 86, 88, 90, 92, 94, 95, 96, 97; WhoWor 74*

Harris, MacDonald
American. Author
Wrote novels *Herma,* 1981; *Hemingway's Suitcase,* 1991.
b. Sep 7, 1921 in South Pasadena, California
d. Jul 24, 1993 in Newport Beach, California
Source: *BioIn 12, 19, 21; ConLC 9, 81; EncSF 93; ScF&FL 92; SJGFanW; WhoUSWr 88; WorAu 1985; WrDr 80, 82, 84, 86, 88, 90, 92, 94, 96*

Harris, Marcelite Jordan
American. Air Force Officer
Brigadier general; first African-American woman Air Force general.
b. Jan 16, 1943 in Houston, Texas
Source: *NotBlAW 1; WhoAm 92, 94, 95, 96, 97; WhoAmW 93, 95, 97; WomStre*

Harris, Mark
American. Author, Educator
Works include *The Southpaw,* 1953; edited *Heart of Boswell,* 1981.
b. Nov 19, 1922 in Mount Vernon, New York
Source: *AmAu&B; Au&Wr 71; Ballpl 90; BenetAL 91; BioIn 5, 7, 8, 10, 12, 13, 14, 15; ConAu 2NR, 3AS, 5R, 55NR; ConLC 19; ConNov 72, 76, 82, 86, 91, 96; CyWA 89; DcLB 2, Y80A; DcLEL 1940; DcLP 87A; DrAF 76; DrAPF 80, 87; DrAS 74E, 78E, 82E; IntAu&W 76, 77, 82; IntvTCA 2; JeAmFiW; OxCAmL 65, 83, 95; RAdv 1; WhoAm 74, 76, 78, 80, 82, 84, 86, 88, 90, 92, 94, 95, 96, 97; WhoAmJ 80; WhoUSWr 88; WhoWor 74; WhoWrEP 89, 92, 95; WorAu 1970; WrDr 76, 80, 82, 84, 86, 88, 90, 92, 94, 96*

Harris, Neil Patrick
American. Actor
Played title role in TV series "Doogie Howser, MD," 1989-93.
b. Jun 15, 1973 in Albuquerque, New Mexico
Source: *BioIn 16; ConTFT 11; IntMPA 94, 96; LegTOT; Who 88; WhoHol 92*

Harris, Patricia Roberts
American. Government Official
Ambassador to Luxembourg, 1965-67; secretary of HUD, 1977-79; HEW, 1979-80.
b. May 31, 1924 in Mattoon, Illinois
d. Mar 23, 1985 in Washington, District of Columbia
Source: *AfrAmAl 6; AfrAmBi 1; AmPolLe; AmPolW 80; AmWomM; AnObit 1985; BiDrUSE 89; BlkWAm; BlueB 76; CivR 74; ConBlB 2; ConNews 85-2; ContDcW 89; CurBio 65, 85N; Ebony 1; EncAACR; EncWB; FacFETw; GoodHs; InB&W 80, 85; IntDcWB; IntWW 74, 75, 76, 77, 78, 79, 80, 81, 82, 83; IntYB 79, 80, 81, 82; InWom, SUP; LibW; NewYTBS 76, 79; NotBlAW 1; WhAm 8; WhoAm 74, 76, 78, 80, 82, 84; WhoAmL 78, 79; WhoAmP 73, 75, 77, 79, 81, 83; WhoAmW 58, 70, 72, 74, 75, 77, 79, 81, 83, 85; WhoBlA 75; WhoE 77, 79, 81, 83, 85; WhoSSW 76; WhoWor 78, 80; WomFir; WomStre; WorAl; WorAlBi*

Harris, Phil
American. Comedian, Bandleader
Showman who led band from 1930s; with Jack Benny's radio show, 1936-46; husband of Alice Faye; popularized song "That's What I Like About the South."
b. Jun 24, 1904 in Linton, Indiana
d. Aug 11, 1995 in Rancho Mirage, California
Source: *BiDAmM; CmpEPM; FilmgC; HalFC 84, 88; IntMPA 86, 88; MotPP; OxCPMus; PenEncP; RadStar; VarWW 85; WhoCom; WhoHol 92, A; WorAlBi*

Harris, Richard, Sir
Irish. Actor
Won Golden Globe for *Camelot,* 1968; appeared in *A Man Called Horse,* 1970.
b. Oct 1, 1930 in Limerick, Ireland
Source: *BiDFilm, 94; BioIn 13; BkPepl; CelR, 90; CurBio 64; EngPo; FilmgC; ForYSC; HalFC 88; IntMPA 75, 76, 77, 78, 79, 80, 81, 82, 84, 86, 88, 92, 94, 96; LegTOT; MotPP; MovMk; NewYTBE 72; OxCFilm; PenEncP; RkOn 84; VarWW 85; WhoAm 86, 90; WhoHol 92, A; WhoThe 77A; WorEFlm*

Harris, Robert
English. Actor
Veteran Shakespearean actor; made Broadway debut in Noel Coward's "Easy Virtue."
d. May 18, 1995 in London, England
Source: *Alli SUP; BioIn 11, 12, 16; CabMA; DrAPF 83, 85; Dun&B 88; IntAu&W 86X; IntMPA 82, 84, 86, 88, 92; Law&B 80, 84, 89A, 92; NewYTBS 95; WhoAmP 77; WhoHol 92*

Harris, Robert Alton
American. Murderer
Killed two teen-age boys, 1978; execution, April 21, 1992, first in California in 25 yrs.
b. 1953?
d. Apr 22, 1992 in San Quentin, California
Source: *BioIn 15*

Harris, Robin
American. Actor, Comedian
Appeared in films *Do the Right Thing,* 1989; *Mo'Better Blues,* 1990.
b. Aug 30, 1953 in Chicago, Illinois
d. Mar 18, 1990 in Chicago, Illinois
Source: *BioIn 16, 17, 20; ConBlB 7*

Harris, Rosemary Ann
English. Actor
Won Tony for *Lion in Winter,* 1966.
b. Sep 19, 1930 in Ashby, England
Source: *AuBYP 3; BiE&WWA; BioIn 16; CurBio 67; FilmgC; HalFC 84; IntMPA 92; MotPP; NotNAT; NotWoAT; OxCThe 83; VarWW 85; WhoAm 78, 80, 86, 88, 90, 92, 96, 97; WhoAmW 95, 97; WhoHol A; WhoWor 74, 76*

Harris, Roy
[Leroy Ellsworth Harris]
American. Composer
Numerous works include *Symphony No. 3,* 1939; overture, *When Johnny C omes Marching Home,* 1935.
b. Feb 12, 1898 in Lincoln County, Oklahoma
d. Oct 1, 1979 in Santa Monica, California
Source: *AmComp; Baker 78, 84; BiDAmM; BioIn 1, 2, 3, 4, 5, 6, 7, 8, 9, 11, 12, 17, 20; BlueB 76; BriBkM 80; CmCal; CompSN, SUP; ConAmC 82; CurBio 40, 79, 79N; DcAmB S10; DcArts; DcCM; DcCom&M 79; IntWW 74, 78, 79; LegTOT; LinLib S; MusMk; NewAmDM; NewCol 75; NewGrDA 86; NewGrDM 80; NewOxM; OxCAmH; OxCAmL 65; PenDiMP A; REn; REnAL; WebAB 74; WhDW; WhoWor 74*

Harris, Sam Henry
American. Producer
Credited with 28 Broadway plays, 1920s-30s, including three Pulitzer winners.
b. Feb 3, 1872 in New York, New York
d. Jul 3, 1941 in New York, New York
Source: *BioIn 5; CurBio 41; DcAmB S3, S5; EncMT; ObitOF 79; WhAm 1; WhoStg 1906, 1908*

Harris, Sydney J(ustin)
American. Journalist, Author
Wrote syndicated column *Strictly Personal,* 1944-86; among several books since 1953: *Pieces of Eight,* 1982.
b. Sep 14, 1917 in London, England

d. Dec 7, 1986 in Chicago, Illinois
Source: *AmAu&B; BiDAmNC; BioIn 15; ConAu 11NR, 61, 120; WhAm 9; WhoAm 74, 76, 78, 80, 82, 84, 86; WhoMW 74, 84, 86*

Harris, Thomas Anthony
American. Author
Wrote 1969's *I'm OK—You're OK.*
b. 1910
d. May 4, 1995 in Sacramento, California
Source: *BiDrAPA 77; WhoAm 74, 76, 78*

Harris, Willard Palmer
"Bill Harris"
American. Jazz Musician
Trombonist; with Woody Herman, 1940s; with Red Norvo, 1960s.
b. Oct 28, 1916 in Philadelphia, Pennsylvania
d. 1973
Source: *AllMusG; BiDAmM; BiDJaz; CmpEPM; EncJzS; IlEncJ; NewAmDM; NewGrDA 86; NewGrDJ 88, 94; WhoJazz 72*

Harris, William
[S(ymbionese) L(iberation) A(rmy)]
American. Revolutionary
With wife Emily, kidnapped Patricia Hearst, 1974.
b. Jan 22, 1945 in Fort Sill, Oklahoma
Source: *BioIn 10, 11, 13; Dun&B 88, 90; NewYTBS 75; WorAl; WorAlBi*

Harris, William Bliss
[Amos Pettingill]
American. Editor, Author
Automotive writer, *Fortune,* 1937-60; wrote periodical *White Flower Farm Garden Book.*
b. 1901? in Denver, Colorado
d. Jun 22, 1981 in Falmouth, Massachusetts
Source: *BioIn 12; ConAu 104; NewYTBS 81*

Harrison, Anna Tuthill Symmes
[Mrs. William Henry Harrison]
American. First Lady
Wife of William Henry, grandmother of Benjamin Harrison.
b. Jul 25, 1775 in Morristown, New Jersey
d. Feb 25, 1864 in North Bend, Ohio
Source: *AmWom; ApCAB; FacPr 89; GoodHs; NatCAB 3; NotAW; TwCBDA*

Harrison, Benjamin
American. Continental Congressman
Governor of VA, signer of Declaration of Independence; ancestor of two US presidents.
b. Apr 5, 1726? in Charles City, Virginia
d. Apr 24, 1791 in Charles City, Virginia
Source: *AmBi; ApCAB; BiDrAC; BiDrACR; BiDrUSC 89; BiDSA; BioIn 3, 7, 8; DcAmB; Drake; EncAR; EncSoH; NatCAB 10; TwCBDA; WhAm HS; WhAmP; WhAmRev*

Harrison, Benjamin
American. US President
Rep., 23rd pres., 1889-93; grandson of William Henry; election decided by electoral college; popular vote favored Grover Cleveland.
b. Aug 20, 1833 in North Bend, Ohio
d. Mar 13, 1901 in Indianapolis, Indiana
Source: *Alli SUP; AmAu&B; AmBi; AmPolLe; ApCAB, SUP; BenetAL 91; BiD&SB; BiDrAC; BiDrUSC 89; BiDrUSE 71, 89; BioIn 1, 2, 3, 4, 5, 6, 7, 8, 9, 10, 11, 12, 13, 14, 15, 16, 17, 18, 19, 20; CivWDc; CyAG; DcAmAu; DcAmB; DcNAA; EncAAH; EncAB-H 1974, 1996; EncSoH; FacPr 89, 93; GayN; HarEnUS; HealPre; IndAu 1816; LegTOT; LinLib L, S; McGEWB; NatCAB 1; OhA&B; OxCAmH; OxCAmL 65, 83; PolPar; PresAR; RComAH; REnAL; TwCBDA; WebAB 74, 79; WhAm 1; WhAmP; WhCiWar; WhDW; WorAl; WorAlBi*

Harrison, Caroline Lavinia Scott
[Mrs. Benjamin Harrison]
American. First Lady
First wife of Benjamin Harrison; died in White House two weeks before husband was defeated for second term.
b. Oct 1, 1832 in Oxford, Ohio
d. Oct 25, 1892 in Washington, District of Columbia
Source: *AmWom; ApCAB SUP; FacPr 89; GoodHs; InWom; NatCAB 1, 4; NotAW; TwCBDA*

Harrison, G(eorge) Donald
American. Designer
Designed or altered many of the best 20th c. church organs, including those at St. John the Divine in NY and Mormon Tabernacle.
b. Apr 21, 1889 in Huddersfield, England
d. Jun 14, 1956 in New York, New York
Source: *BioIn 4; NewGrDA 86; NewGrDM 80; ObitOF 79*

Harrison, George
[The Beatles]
English. Singer, Songwriter
Most mysterious of group who launched solo career with gold album *All Things Must Pass,* 1970; known for benefits for Bangladesh, interest in Eastern mysticism; had revival with album *Cloud Nine,* 1987.
b. Feb 25, 1943 in Liverpool, England
Source: *Baker 78, 84, 92; BioIn 6, 7, 8, 9, 10, 11, 12, 13, 16; BkPepl; BlueB 76; CelR, 90; ConMuA 80A; ConMus 2; ConTFT 8; CurBio 66, 89; EncPR&S 89; EncRk 88; EncRkSt; FilmEn; ForYSC; HarEnR 86; IlEncRk; IntMPA 88, 92, 94, 96; IntWW 74, 75, 76, 77, 78, 79, 80, 81, 82, 83, 89, 91, 93; IntWWM 77; LegTOT; MotPP; NewGrDM 80; OnThGG; OxCPMus; PenDiMP; PenEncP; RkOn 78, 84; RolSEnR 83; VarWW 85; WhoAm 80, 82, 84, 86, 88, 90, 92, 94, 95, 96, 97; WhoEnt 92; WhoHol 92, A; WhoRock 81; WhoRocM 82; WhoWor 74, 78, 80, 82, 84, 87, 89, 91, 93, 95, 97; WorAl; WorAlBi*

Harrison, Gregory
American. Actor
Played Gonzo Gates in "Trapper John, MD," 1979-86.
b. May 31, 1950 in Avalon, California
Source: *BioIn 12, 13; ConTFT 3; Dun&B 88; HolBB; IntMPA 84, 86, 88, 92, 96; LegTOT; VarWW 85; WhoAm 80, 82, 84, 86, 88, 90; WhoEnt 92; WhoHol 92*

Harrison, Jenilee
American. Actor
Played Jamie Ewing Barnes on TV series "Dallas," 1984-91.
b. Jun 12, 1959? in Northridge, California
Source: *BioIn 14*

Harrison, Joan (Mary)
English. Screenwriter
Wrote screenplays for *Rebecca,* 1940; *Saboteur,* 1942.
b. Jun 20, 1909
d. Aug 14, 1994 in London, England
Source: *ConAu 104, 146; ConLC 86; IntDcF 1-4, 2-4; WhoAm 74, 76; WhoAmW 64, 66, 68, 70, 72, 74, 75*

Harrison, Kathryn
American. Author
Wrote *Thicker Than Water,* 1991.
b. Mar 20, 1961 in Los Angeles, California
Source: *ConAu 144; ConLC 70; WrDr 96*

Harrison, Mary Scott Lord Dimmick
[Mrs. Benjamin Harrison]
American.
Second wife of Benjamin Harrison, married 1896.
b. Apr 30, 1858 in Honesdale, Pennsylvania
d. Jan 5, 1948 in New York, New York
Source: *BiCAW; BioIn 16; FacPr 89; InWom, SUP; NotAW; ObitOF 79; WhAm 2; WhDW; WomWWA 14; WorAl*

Harrison, Noel
English. Singer, Actor
Had 1960s hit single: "Suzanne"; starred in "The Girl from UNCLE"; son of actor Rex.
b. Jan 29, 1936 in London, England
Source: *BioIn 7; ItaFilm; WhoHol A; WhoRocM 82*

Harrison, Peter
American. Architect
Called first real architect in America; introduced Neo-Palladian style in US.
b. Jun 14, 1716 in York, England
d. Apr 30, 1775 in New Haven, Connecticut
Source: *AmCulL; BiDAmAr; BioIn 1, 5, 9, 14, 15, 19; BriEAA; DcAmB; EncAAr*

1, 2; EncCRAm; IntDcAr; MacEA; McGDA; McGEWB; NatCAB 23; OxCAmH; OxCArt; WebAB 74, 79; WebBD 83; WhAm HS; WhoArch

Harrison, Rex, Sir
[Reginald Carey Harrison]
English. Actor
Won 1957 Tony, 1964 Oscar for role of Henry Higgins in *My Fair Lady;* considered a master of light comedy.
b. Mar 5, 1908 in Huyton, England
d. Jun 2, 1990 in New York, New York
Source: *AnObit 1990; BiDFilm, 81, 94; BiE&WWA; BioIn 1, 2, 4, 5, 6, 7, 8, 9, 10, 11, 12, 14, 15, 16; BlueB 76; CamGWoT; CelR, 90; CnThe; ConAu 131; ConTFT 4, 9; CurBio 47, 86, 90, 90N; DcArts; DcNaB 1986; EncAFC; EncEurC; EncMT; EncWT; Ent; FacFETw; FamA&A; Film 2; FilmAG WE; FilmEn; FilmgC; ForYSC; HalFC 80, 84, 88; IlWWBF, A; IntDcF 1-3, 2-3; IntMPA 75, 76, 77, 78, 79, 80, 81, 82, 84, 86, 88; IntWW 75, 76, 77, 78, 79, 80, 81, 82, 83, 89; LegTOT; MotPP; MovMk; NewC; News 90; NewYTBS 81, 90; NotNAT, A; OxCAmT 84; OxCFilm; OxCPMus; PlP&P; VarWW 85; Who 85, 90; WhoAm 84, 88; WhoHol A; WhoThe 72, 77, 81; WorAl; WorAlBi; WorEFlm; WrDr 80, 82, 84, 86, 88, 90*

Harrison, Ross Granville
American. Zoologist
Known for research in animal-tissue cultures, embryology.
b. Jan 13, 1879 in Germantown, Pennsylvania
d. Sep 30, 1959 in New Haven, Connecticut
Source: *BioIn 2, 3, 6, 11; DcAmB S6; DcScB; NatCAB 15; ObitOF 79; OxCMed 86; WebAB 79; WhAm 3*

Harrison, Wallace Kirkman
American. Architect
Designed Rockefeller Center, 1930; UN Building, 1947.
b. Sep 28, 1895 in Worcester, Massachusetts
d. Dec 2, 1981 in New York, New York
Source: *BioIn 1, 3, 5, 7, 12, 13, 16, 17; BlueB 76; ConArch 87, 94; CurBio 47, 82; EncAAr 1, 2; EncMA; IntWW 74, 75, 76, 77, 78, 79, 80, 81; McGDA; WhAm 8; WhoAm 74, 76, 78, 80; WhoArch; WhoWor 74, 78, 80; WorAl*

Harrison, William Henry
American. US President
Ninth pres., Mar 4-Apr 4, 1841; first pres. to die in office.
b. Feb 9, 1773 in Charles City County, Virginia
d. Apr 4, 1841 in Washington, District of Columbia
Source: *Alli; AmAu&B; AmBi; AmPolLe; ApCAB; BenetAL 91; BiAUS; BiDrAC; BiDrATG; BiDrUSC 89; BiDrUSE 71, 89; BioIn 1, 2, 3, 4, 5, 6, 7, 8, 9, 10, 11, 12, 13, 14, 15, 16, 17, 18, 19, 20; CelCen; CyAG; DcAmB; DcAmMiB; DcAmSR; DcBiPP; Drake; EncAAH; EncAB-H 1974, 1996; EncSoH; FacPr 89, 93; HarEnMi; HarEnUS; HealPre; LinLib L, S; McGEWB; NatCAB 3; OhA&B; OxCAmH; OxCAmL 65, 83; PolPar; PresAR; RComAH; REn; REnAL; REnAW; TwCBDA; WebAB 74, 79; WebAMB; WhAm HS; WhAmP; WhDW; WhNaAH; WorAl; WorAlBi*

Harrison, William Kelly, Jr.
American. Military Leader
General; influential negotiator in truce talks that ended Korean War, 1951-52.
b. Sep 7, 1895 in Washington, District of Columbia
d. May 25, 1987 in Bryn Mawr Terrace, Pennsylvania
Source: *BiDWWGF; BioIn 2, 3, 11, 12; CurBio 52, 87; PolProf E*

Harroun, Ray
American. Auto Racer, Engineer
Winner of the first Indy 500, 1911.
b. Jan 12, 1879
d. Jan 19, 1968 in Anderson, Indiana
Source: *BioIn 8; ObitOF 79; WhoSpor*

Harry, Debbie
[Deborah Ann Harry]
American. Singer
First punk star to appear in commercial; hit songs with Blondie, 1975-83, include "Call Me," 1980; solo album, *Rockbird,* 1987.
b. Jul 11, 1945 in Miami, Florida
Source: *BioIn 12, 13; BkPepl; ConAu 129; ConMus 4; ConTFT 8; CurBio 81; IntWW 93; NewGrDA 86; News 90, 90-1; NewWmR; NewYTBS 79; RkOn 85; VarWW 85; WhoAm 82, 84, 86, 88, 90, 92, 94, 95, 96, 97; WhoAmW 95; WhoEnt 92; WhoHol 92; WhoRocM 82; WorAlBi*

Harryhausen, Ray
American. Special Effects Technician
Trick film specialist: *Clash of the Titans,* 1981.
b. Jun 29, 1920 in Los Angeles, California
Source: *BioIn 11, 12; CmMov; ConTFT 8; EncSF, 93; FilmgC; HalFC 80, 84, 88; IntDcF 1-4, 2-4; IntMPA 77, 80, 92, 94, 96; IntWW 91, 93; NewEScF; ScF&FL 92; WhoEnt 92; WhoHrs 80*

Harsch, Joseph Close
American. Journalist
Books include *Does Our Foreign Policy Make Sense?,* 1948.
b. May 25, 1905 in Toledo, Ohio
Source: *AmAu&B; Au&Wr 71; BiDAmNC; BioIn 3; ConAu 102; CurBio 44; IntAu&W 76, 77, 89, 91; IntWW 74, 75, 76, 77, 78, 79, 80, 81, 82, 83, 89, 91, 93; Who 74, 82, 83, 85, 88, 90, 92, 94; WhoAm 86, 88*

Harsh, George
Canadian. Criminal, Aviator
While a WW II prisoner of war he planned escape of 126 Allied soldiers, the basis for film *The Great Escape,* 1963.
b. 1908?
d. Jan 25, 1980 in Toronto, Ontario, Canada
Source: *BioIn 9, 12; ConAu 93; FacFETw; NewYTBS 80*

Harshaw, Margaret
American. Opera Singer
Soprano with NY Met., 1942-64; noted for Wagnerian roles.
b. May 12, 1912 in Narbeth, Pennsylvania
Source: *Baker 78, 84; BioIn 2, 4, 13; CmOp; IntWWM 90; InWom; NewAmDM; NewEOp 71; NewGrDM 80; OxDcOp; PenDiMP; WhoMus 72*

Hart, Charles
English. Lyricist, Composer
Wrote lyrics for Tony-winner *The Phantom of the Opera,* 1986.
b. Jun 3, 1961 in London, England
Source: *ConTFT 4; WhoEnt 92*

Hart, Frances Noyes
American. Author
Mysteries include *The Bellamy Trial,* 1927.
b. Aug 10, 1890 in Silver Spring, Maryland
d. Oct 25, 1943 in New Canaan, Connecticut
Source: *AmAu&B; AmWomWr; BenetAL 91; BioIn 14; ConAu 112; EncMys; LngCTC; OxCAmL 65, 83, 95; REnAL; TwCA SUP; TwCCr&M 80, 85, 91; WhAm 2; WhE&EA; WhNAA*

Hart, Gary Warren
[Gary Warren Hartpence]
American. Politician
Dem. senator from CO, 1975-87; vied for presidential nomination, 1984, 1988; scandal-ridden 1988 campaign rocked party.
b. Nov 28, 1936 in Ottawa, Kansas
Source: *BiDrUSC 89; BioIn 13, 14, 15, 16; CngDr 85; ConAu 114, 124; CurBio 76; EncWB; FacFETw; IntWW 91; NewYTBS 87; PolProf NF; SpyFic; WhoAm 86, 88; WhoAmP 85, 91; WhoGov 77; WhoWest 87; WhoWor 84, 87*

Hart, George Overbury
"Pop"
American. Artist
Watercolorist; his best-known landscape: *Santo Domingo;* lithograph: *Springtime New Orleans.*
b. May 10, 1868 in Cairo, Illinois
d. Sep 9, 1933
Source: *BioIn 15; BriEAA; DcAmB S1; EncAB-A 11; GrAmP; McGDA; WhAm 1; WhAmArt 85*

Hart, Jim
[James Warren Hart]
American. Football Player
Four-time all-pro quarterback, 1966-84, mostly with St. Louis.
b. Apr 29, 1944 in Evanston, Illinois
Source: *BiDAmSp FB; BioIn 8, 11; WhoAm 78, 80, 82, 84, 86, 88, 90, 92, 94, 95, 96, 97; WhoEnt 92; WhoFtbl 74; WhoMW 82, 84; WhoSpor*

Hart, John
American. Continental Congressman
Farmer; signed Declaration of Independence, 1776; died before independence was won.
b. 1711? in Stonington, Connecticut
d. May 11, 1779 in Hopewell, New Jersey
Source: *AmBi; ApCAB; BiAUS; BiDrAC; BioIn 1, 7, 8, 9, 11; DcAmB; Drake; EncAR; EncCRAm; TwCBDA; WhAm HS; WhAmP; WhAmRev*

Hart, John Richard
American. Broadcast Journalist
Correspondent, NBC News, 1975-88.
b. Feb 1, 1932 in Denver, Colorado
Source: *BioIn 18; Dun&B 90; WhoAm 82, 84, 88, 92; WhoTelC; WrDr 92*

Hart, Johnny
[John Lewis Hart]
American. Cartoonist
Draws "BC," 1958—; "The Wizard of Id," 1964—.
b. Feb 18, 1931 in Endicott, New York
Source: *AmAu&B; AuNews 1; BioIn 4, 10, 13; BioNews 74; BlueB 76; ConAu 4NR, 49; EncACom; EncTwCJ; IntAu&W 77; LegTOT; WhoAm 74, 76, 78, 80, 82, 84, 86, 88, 90, 92, 94, 95, 96, 97; WhoAmA 76, 78, 80, 82, 84, 86, 89, 91, 93; WhoWest 94; WorECom*

Hart, Josephine
Irish. Author
Wrote the Gothic novel *Damage,* 1991.
b. 1942? in Mullingar, Ireland
Source: *ConAu 138; ConLC 70; ConPopW; WrDr 96*

Hart, Leon J
American. Football Player
All-America end, Notre Dame, 1946-49; won Heisman Trophy, 1949; in NFL with Detroit, 1950-57.
b. Nov 2, 1928 in Turtle Creek, Pennsylvania
Source: *BiDAmSp FB; BioIn 2, 14; WhoFtbl 74*

Hart, LeRoy
American. Inventor
Designed Moon Shoes, plastic catapulting footwear, 1990.
Source: *BioIn 18; WhoFI 92*

Hart, Lorenz
[Rogers and Hart]
American. Lyricist
Collaborated with Richard Rodgers for 25 yrs; wrote lyrics for musicals; songs include "Blue Moon"; "Where or When."
b. May 2, 1895 in New York, New York
d. Nov 22, 1943 in New York, New York
Source: *AmPS; ASCAP 66, 80; Baker 78, 84; Benet 87; BenetAL 91; BestMus; BioIn 3, 5, 9, 10, 11, 12, 13, 15, 16, 20, 21; CamGWoT; CmpEPM; CrtSuDr; CurBio 40; CyWA 89; DcAmB S3; EncMT; Ent; FacFETw; HalFC 84, 88; LegTOT; McGEWD 72, 84; MnPM; NewAmDM; NewCBMT; NewGrDA 86; NewGrDM 80; NotNAT B; ObitOF 79; OxCAmT 84; OxCFilm; OxCPMus; OxCThe 83; PlP&P; REnAL; Sw&Ld C; WhAm 4; WhThe; WorAlBi*

Hart, Mary
American. TV Personality
Co-host of syndicated TV series "Entertainment Tonight," 1982—.
b. Nov 8, 1951 in Madison, South Dakota
Source: *BioIn 15, 16; CelR 90; ConNews 88-1; ConTFT 11; WhoAm 95, 96, 97; WhoAmW 95; WorAlBi*

Hart, Mickey
[The Grateful Dead; Michael Hart]
American. Singer, Musician
Drummer with group since 1967; released solo album, *Rolling Thunder,* 1972.
b. Sep 11, 1943 in New York, New York
Source: *BioIn 15; CurBio 94; News 91, 91-2; WhoRocM 82*

Hart, Moss
[Robert Arnold Conrad]
American. Director, Dramatist, Author
Won Tony for directing *My Fair Lady,* 1959.
b. Oct 24, 1904 in New York, New York
d. Dec 20, 1961 in Palm Springs, California
Source: *AmAu&B; AmCulL; Benet 87, 96; BenetAL 91; BestMus; BiDAmM; BioIn 1, 2, 4, 5, 6, 7, 12, 15, 17, 19, 21; CamGWoT; CamHAL; CasWL; CnDAL; CnMD; CnThe; ConAu 89, 109; ConLC 66; CrtSuDr; CurBio 40, 60, 62; CyWA 89; DcAmB S7; DcArts; DcLB 7; EncAHmr; EncMT; EncWT; Ent; FacFETw; FilmEn; FilmgC; GrWrEL DR; HalFC 80, 84, 88; LegTOT; LngCTC; McGEWD 72, 84; ModWD; NatCAB 46; NewCBMT; NewGrDA 86; NotNAT A, B; ObitT 1961; OxCAmL 65, 83, 95; OxCAmT 84; OxCPMus; OxCThe 67, 83; PenC AM; PlP&P; REn; REnAL; REnWD; RfGAmL 87, 94; TwCA, SUP; WebAB 74, 79; WebE&AL; WhAm 4; WhThe; WorAl; WorAlBi; WorEFlm*

Hart, Pearl
American. Outlaw
Last bandit to rob stagecoach in US, 1899.
b. 1878
d. 1925
Source: *BioIn 3, 11; EncACr*

Hart, Philip Aloysius
"Conscience of the Senate"
American. Politician
Popular liberal Dem. senator from MI, 1958-76.
b. Dec 10, 1912 in Bryn Mawr, Pennsylvania
d. Dec 26, 1976 in Washington, District of Columbia
Source: *BiDrAC; BiDrUSC 89; BioIn 5, 6, 8, 9, 10, 11, 12; CngDr 74; CurBio 59, 77; DcAmB S10; NatCAB 60; NewYTBS 75, 76; WhoAm 74; WhoAmP 73; WhoGov 75; WhoMW 74; WhoWor 74*

Hart, William Surrey
American. Actor, Author
Stone-faced Western star, 1914-27; wrote Western novels, autobiography, *My Life: East and West,* 1929.
b. Dec 6, 1870 in Newburgh, New York
d. Jun 23, 1946 in Newhall, California
Source: *AmAu&B; BiDFilm; BioIn 12, 13; CmMov; CurBio 46; Film 1; FilmgC; MnBBF; MotPP; MovMk; OxCFilm; TwYS; WebAB 74, 79; WhAm 2; WhScrn 77; WorEFlm*

Hartack, Billy
[William John Hartack, Jr]
American. Jockey
Rode KY Derby winner five times; leading money maker, 1957.
b. Dec 9, 1932 in Ebensburg, Pennsylvania
Source: *BiDAmSp OS; BioIn 4, 5, 6, 10, 11; FacFETw; LegTOT; WorAlBi*

Hart-Davis, Rupert
[Charles Rupert Hart-Davis]
English. Publisher, Editor, Author
Founded Rupert Hart-Davis, publishers, 1942.
b. Aug 28, 1907, England
Source: *BioIn 10, 12, 14; ChhPo S1; ConAu 115, 134; DcLB 112; IntAu&W 77, 89, 91; Who 74, 82, 83, 85, 88, 90, 92; WorAu 1950; WrDr 86, 88, 90, 92*

Harte, (Francis) Bret
American. Author, Journalist
Wrote popular stories *The Outcasts of Poker Flat; Tennessee's Partner; Miggles.*
b. Aug 25, 1836 in Albany, New York
d. May 5, 1902 in London, England
Source: *Alli SUP; AmAu; AmAu&B; AmBi; AmWr S2; AtlBL; AuBYP 2, 3; BbD; Benet 87; BenetAL 91; BibAL; BiD&SB; BioIn 1, 3, 4, 5, 6, 7, 8, 9, 10, 11, 12, 13, 14, 15, 16; CamGEL; CamGLE; CamGWoT; CamHAL; CasWL; Chambr 3; ChhPo, S1, S2, S3; CmCal; CnDAL; ConAu 104; CrtT 3;*

CyAL 2; CyWA 58; DcAmAu; DcAmB; DcArts; DcBiA; DcEnA, A; DcEnL; DcLB 12, 64, 74, 79; DcLEL; DcNAA; EncAAH; EncAHmr; EncFWF; EvLB; FifWWr; GrWrEL N; HalFC 84, 88; LegTOT; LinLib L, S; MagSAmL; MouLC 4; NotNAT B; Novels; OxCAmH; OxCAmL 65, 83; OxCEng 67, 85, 95; PenC AM; PeoHis; RAdv 1, 13-1; RealN; REn; REnAL; REnAW; RfGAmL 87; ShSCr 8; SmATA 26; TwCLC 1, 25; WebAB 74, 79; WebE&AL; WhDW; WorAl; WorAlBi; WorLitC

Hartford, George Huntington
American. Merchant, Businessman
Co-founded Great Atlantic and Pacific Tea Company (A&P), 1869.
b. Sep 5, 1833 in Augusta, Maine
d. Aug 29, 1917 in Spring Lake, New Jersey
Source: *BiDAmBL 83; DcAmB S5; WhAm 4, HSA*

Hartford, George Ludlum
American. Merchant, Businessman
Son of George H Hartford; became chm. of A&P; tasted coffee samples daily.
b. Nov 7, 1864 in New York, New York
d. Sep 23, 1957 in Montclair, New Jersey
Source: *BiDAmBL 83; BioIn 2, 4, 7; DcAmB S5; WhAm 3*

Hartford, Huntington
American. Financier, Art Patron
Heir to A&P fortune; developed Paradise Island, Nassau; founded Gallery of Modern Art, NYC, 1964.
b. Apr 18, 1911 in New York, New York
Source: *AmAu&B; BiE&WWA; BioIn 5, 6, 7, 8, 10, 15, 17; BlueB 76; CelR; ConAu 17R; CurBio 59; IntWW 74, 75, 76, 77, 78, 79, 80, 81, 82, 83, 89, 91, 93; WhoAm 74, 76, 78, 80, 82, 84, 86, 88, 90, 92, 94, 95, 96; WhoAmA 73, 76, 78, 80, 82, 84, 86; WhoE 74; WhoGov 72, 75; WrDr 80, 82, 84*

Hartford, John Augustine
American. Merchant, Businessman
Son of George H Hartford; became pres. of A&P.
b. Feb 10, 1872 in Orange, New Jersey
d. Sep 20, 1951 in New York, New York
Source: *BiDAmBL 83; BioIn 2, 3; DcAmB S5; WhAm 3*

Hartford, John Cowan
American. Singer, Songwriter
Wrote "Gentle on My Mind," 1967; recorded by Glen Campbell, 200 others.
b. Dec 30, 1937 in New York, New York
Source: *BiDAmM; BioIn 14; ConMus 1; EncFCWM 83; EncRk 88; HarEnCM 87; RolSEnR 83; WhoAm 80, 82, 84, 86, 88, 90, 92, 94, 95, 96, 97; WhoEnt 92; WhoRock 81*

Hartke, Stephen Paul
American. Composer
Early atonal symphonic compositions gave way to tonal pieces; wrote *Pacific Rim,* 1988.
b. Jul 6, 1952 in Orange, New Jersey
Source: *ConAmC 76, 82; ConMus 5; CpmDNM 80; IntWWM 90; WhoAm 95, 96, 97*

Hartke, Vance
American. Politician
Dem. senator from IN, 1959-77; wrote *The American Crisis in Vietnam,* 1968.
b. May 31, 1919 in Stendal, Indiana
Source: *BioIn 5, 6, 7, 9, 10, 11, 12; BlueB 76; CngDr 74; ConAu 25R; CurBio 60; IndAu 1917; IntWW 74, 75, 76, 77, 78, 79, 80, 81, 82, 83; WhoAm 74, 76; WhoAmP 73, 75, 77, 79, 81, 83, 85, 87, 89, 91, 93, 95; WhoGov 72, 75, 77; WhoWor 74; WorAl; WorAlBi*

Hartley, David
English. Philosopher
Founder of associational psychology; wrote *Observations on Man,* 1749.
b. Aug 8, 1705 in Armley, England
d. Aug 28, 1757 in Bath, England
Source: *Alli; BiDPsy; BioIn 1, 2, 3; BlkwCE; BlmGEL; BritAu; CamGEL; CamGLE; CasWL; CyEd; DcBiPP; DcEnA; DcEnL; DcNaB; DcScB; Dis&D; EncEnl; EvLB; LngCEL; McGEWB; NamesHP; NewCBEL; NewCol 75; OxCEng 67, 85, 95; OxCPhil; PenC ENG; REn; WebE&AL; WrPh P*

Hartley, Fred Lloyd
American. Business Executive
Joined Union Oil Co. as maintenance worker, 1939, built it into mulitbillion-dollar Unocal Oil.
b. Jan 16, 1917 in Vancouver, British Columbia, Canada
d. Oct 19, 1990 in Los Angeles, California
Source: *AmMWSc 82, 92; BioIn 7, 13, 14; CanWW 70, 79, 80, 81, 83, 89; Dun&B 90; IntWW 89; NewYTBS 83, 90; St&PR 91; WhAm 10; WhoAm 74, 76, 78, 80, 82, 84, 86, 88, 90; WhoEng 88; WhoFI 87, 89; WhoWest 84, 87, 89; WhoWor 82, 84, 87, 89*

Hartley, Hal
American. Filmmaker
Films influenced by Jean-Luc Godard; made *Simple Men,* 1992.
b. Nov 3, 1959 in Lindenhurst, New York
Source: *CurBio 95; IntMPA 96; LegTOT*

Hartley, L(eslie) P(oles)
English. Author
Best-known novel: *The Go-Between,* 1953.
b. Dec 30, 1895 in Peterborough, England
d. Dec 13, 1972 in London, England
Source: *Au&Wr 71; Benet 96; BioIn 4, 6, 7, 9, 10, 11, 13, 15, 17, 20; CamGEL; CasWL; ConAu 45; ConLC 2; ConNov 72, 76; DcArts; DcLEL; DcNaB 1971; EncSF 93; EncWL, 3; EvLB; IntAu&W 76, 77; LngCEL; LngCTC; ModBrL, S1; NewC; NewCBEL; OxCEng 85, 95; PenC ENG; RAdv 1, 14; REn; RfGShF; RGTwCWr; TwCA SUP; TwCWr; WebE&AL; WhAm 5; WhE&EA; WhoTwCL*

Hartley, Mariette
[Mrs. Patrick Boyriven]
American. Actor
Best known for Polaroid commercials with James Garner; won Emmy for "The Incredib le Hulk," 1979.
b. Jun 21, 1940 in New York, New York
Source: *BioIn 12, 13, 14, 15; CelR 90; ConTFT 1, 4; HalFC 80, 84, 88; IntMPA 86, 88, 92, 94, 96; LegTOT; VarWW 85; WhoAm 86, 88, 90, 92, 94; WhoAmW 91, 93, 95; WhoEnt 92; WhoHol A*

Hartley, Marsden
American. Artist
Painted still-lifes, harsh landscapes of Maine, US Southwest; used flat, somber forms.
b. Jan 4, 1877 in Lewiston, Maine
d. Sep 2, 1943 in Ellsworth, Maine
Source: *ArtsAmW 1, 3; AtlBL; BenetAL 91; BioIn 1, 2, 3, 4, 5, 6, 8, 9, 10, 12, 14, 15, 16, 17, 18, 20; BriEAA; ConArt 77; ConAu 123; CurBio 43; DcAmArt; DcAmB S3; DcCAA 71, 77, 88, 94; DcLB 54; IlBEAAW; LegTOT; McGDA; McGEWB; OxCAmL 65; OxCTwCA; OxDcArt; PeoHis; REnAL; WhAmArt 85*

Hartline, Haldan Keffer
American. Scientist
Shared Nobel Prize in medicine, 1967, for work with vision.
b. Dec 22, 1903 in Bloomsburg, Pennsylvania
d. Mar 17, 1983 in Fallston, Maryland
Source: *AmMWSc 73P, 76P, 79, 82; AsBiEn; BiESc; BioIn 8, 12, 13; BlueB 76; IntWW 74, 75, 76, 77, 78, 79, 80, 81, 82, 83; LarDcSc; McGMS 80; NewYTBS 83; NotTwCS; WebAB 74, 79; WhAm 8, 9; Who 74, 82, 83; WhoAm 74, 76, 78, 82; WhoE 74, 77, 79, 81, 83; WhoFrS 84; WhoNob; WhoWor 74, 76, 78, 80, 82; WorAl; WorAlBi*

Hartman, Dan
American. Singer, Musician, Songwriter
Pop singer who had hit single "I Can Dream About You," 1984.
Source: *BioIn 19; PenEncP; RkOn 85; RolSEnR 83; WhoEnt 92; WhoRocM 82*

Hartman, David Downs
American. TV Personality
Hosted ABC's "Good Morning America," 1975-87.
b. May 19, 1935 in Pawtucket, Rhode Island
Source: *BioIn 12, 13, 14, 15, 16; BkPepl; CurBio 81; HalFC 88; IntMPA 92; LesBEnT; NewYTBS 85; NewYTET; VarWW 85; WhoAm 74, 76, 78, 80, 82,*

84, 86, 88, 90, 92; WhoEnt 92; WhoHol A; WorAl; WorAlBi

Hartman, Elizabeth
"Biff"
American. Actor
Oscar nominee for first film: *A Patch of Blue,* 1965; committed suicide.
b. Dec 23, 1941 in Boardman, Ohio
d. Jun 11, 1987 in Pittsburgh, Pennsylvania
Source: *BioIn 8; FilmEn; FilmgC; ForYSC; HalFC 80, 84, 88; IntMPA 86; VarWW 85*

Hartman, Grace
American. Comedian
Wife of Paul, formed comedy dance team.
b. 1907 in San Francisco, California
d. Aug 8, 1955 in Van Nuys, California
Source: *BiDD; BioIn 1, 2, 4; CurBio 42, 55; EncVaud; InWom; NotNAT B; WhoHol B; WhScrn 74, 77, 83*

Hartman, Lisa
American. Actor, Singer
Played Ciji Dunne on TV series "Knots Landing," 1982, Cathy Geary on "Knots Landing," 1984-86; albums include *Til My Heart Stops,* 1988.
b. Jun 1, 1956 in Houston, Texas
Source: *BioIn 14; CelR 90; ConTFT 3, 9; IntMPA 94, 96; LegTOT; WhoAm 94, 95, 96; WhoHol 92*

Hartman, Paul
American. Actor
Comic dance team with wife Grace on Broadway; won Tony, 1948, for *Angel in the Wings.*
b. Mar 1, 1904 in San Francisco, California
d. Oct 2, 1973 in Los Angeles, California
Source: *BiE&WWA; MovMk; NewYTBE 73; NotNAT B; WhAm 6; WhoAm 74; WhoHol B; WhoWorJ 72; WhScrn 77, 83*

Hartman, Phil
Canadian. Actor
Was in cast of TV's "Saturday Night Live," 1986-94; stars in NBC's "NewsRadio," 1995—.
b. Sep 24, 1948 in Brantford, Ontario, Canada
Source: *ConTFT 7, 14; IntMPA 96; LegTOT; News 96, 96-2; WhoHol 92*

Hartmann, Franz
German. Mystic, Physician, Author
Wrote *Occult Science in Medicine,* 1893.
b. Nov 22, 1838, Bavaria
d. Aug 7, 1912 in Kempten, Bavaria
Source: *ConAu 115; DivFut; EncO&P 1, 1S2, 2, 3; ScF&FL 1*

Hartmann, Rudolph
German. Producer, Manager
Led noted German orchestras, 1920s-60s; revised many Strauss works.
b. Oct 11, 1900 in Ingolstadt, Germany
Source: *Baker 84; MetOEnc; NewEOp 71; NewGrDM 80*

Hartmann, Sadakichi
[Carl Sadakichi Hartmann]
American. Author
"Bohemian" identified with NYC's Greenwich Village, Hollywood; wrote privately pu blished plays: *Buddha,* 1897; *Moses,* 1934.
b. Nov 8, 1869 in Nagasaki, Japan
d. Nov 21, 1944 in Saint Petersburg, Florida
Source: *AmAu&B; ArtsAmW 2; OxCAmL 65, 83; REnAL; WhAm 5; WhAmArt 85; WhScrn 77*

Hartmann von Aue
[Hartmann von Ouwe]
German. Poet
Credited with introducing Arthurian legend into medieval Germany.
b. c. 1170
d. c. 1210
Source: *BiD&SB; CasWL; ClMLC 15; CyWA 58; DcCathB; DcEuL; EuAu; EvEuW; LinLib L; OxCGer 76; PenC EUR; REn*

Hartnell, Norman Bishop, Sir
English. Fashion Designer
Queen Elizabeth's official dressmaker; has clothed the royal family since 1938.
b. Jun 12, 1901 in Hassocks, England
d. Jun 8, 1979 in Windsor, England
Source: *CurBio 53, 79; DcNaB 1971; IntWW 77, 78, 79; NewYTBS 79; Who 74; WhoWor 78*

Hartnett, Gabby
[Charles Leo Hartnett]
"Old Tomato Face"
American. Baseball Player
Catcher, 1922-41; NL MVP, 1935; hit home run that won pennant for Cubs, 1938; Hall of Fame, 1955.
b. Dec 20, 1900 in Woonsocket, Rhode Island
d. Dec 20, 1972 in Park Ridge, Illinois
Source: *Ballpl 90; BiDAmSp BB; BioIn 1, 7, 8, 9, 10, 13, 14, 15, 16, 17; DcAmB S9; LegTOT; NewYTBE 72; WhoProB 73; WhoSpor*

Hartt, Frederick
American. Art Historian
Noted Renaissance scholar and art historian.
b. May 22, 1914 in Boston, Massachusetts
d. Oct 31, 1991 in Washington, District of Columbia
Source: *BioIn 17; DrAS 74H, 78H, 82H; FacFETw; NewYTBS 91; WhAm 10; WhoAm 74, 76, 78, 80, 82, 84, 86, 88, 90; WhoAmA 73, 76, 78, 80, 82, 84, 86, 89, 91, 93N; WhoE 89, 91; WhoWor 74*

Hartung, Hans
[Heinrich Ernst Hartung]
French. Artist
Early abstract expressionist; black splashes reminiscent of Japanese calligraphy.
b. Sep 21, 1904 in Leipzig, Germany
d. Dec 7, 1989 in Antibes, France
Source: *AnObit 1989; BioIn 3, 4, 5, 6, 8, 10, 11, 13, 15, 16, 17; ClaDrA; ConArt 83, 89; ConAu 130; CurBio 58, 90, 90N; DcCAr 81; FacFETw; IntWW 74, 75, 76, 77, 78, 79, 80, 81, 82, 83, 89; McGDA; NewYTBS 89; OxCTwCA; OxDcArt; PhDcTCA 77; PrintW 85; WhoArt 80, 82, 84; WhoFr 79; WorArt 1950*

Hartz, James Leroy
American. Broadcast Journalist
Co-hosted "Today Show," 1974; "Over Easy," 1979.
b. Feb 3, 1940 in Tulsa, Oklahoma
Source: *AuNews 2; BioIn 10, 11; BioNews 74; IntMPA 82, 92; LesBEnT 92; VarWW 85*

Harun-Al-Rashid
[Caliph of Bagdad]
Arab. Political Leader
Fifth caliph of Abbasid dynasty, 786-809; reign marked by grandeur and noble style.
b. 764? in Rayy, Persia
d. Mar 24, 809? in Tus, Persia
Source: *McGEWB; NewCol 75; OxCEng 85; WhDW*

Harunobu, Suzuki
Japanese. Artist
Master of woodblock printing; perfected brocade painting; admired by Degas in 19th c.
b. 1718 in Edo, Japan
d. 1770 in Edo, Japan
Source: *BioIn 4, 10; McGDA; McGEWB; NewCol 75; OxCArt; WhDW*

Harvard, Beverly
American. Police Chief
First black woman to head a police force; police chief of Atlanta, 1994—.
b. 1950 in Macon, Georgia
Source: *ConBlB 11; News 95, 95-2*

Harvard, John
English. Clergy
Left library, estate money toward founding of new college; named in his honor, 1639.
b. Nov 26, 1607 in London, England
d. Sep 14, 1638 in Boston, Massachusetts
Source: *AmBi; ApCAB; Benet 87, 96; BioIn 1, 18; CyAL 1; CyEd; DcAmB; DcNaB; Drake; HarEnUS; LinLib L, S; LuthC 75; NatCAB 6; OxCEng 85, 95; REn; TwCBDA; WebAB 74, 79; WhAm HS; WhDW; WorAl; WorAlBi*

Harvey, Anthony (Kesteven)
English. Director
Best known for *Lion in Winter,* 1968; *They Might Be Giants,* 1972.
b. Jun 3, 1931 in London, England
Source: *BioIn 13, 16; BlueB 76; ConTFT 1, 9; FilmEn; FilmgC; HalFC 80, 84, 88; IntMPA 75, 76, 77, 78, 79, 80, 81, 82, 84, 86, 88, 92, 94, 96; IntWW 74, 75, 76, 77, 78, 79, 80, 81, 82, 83, 89, 91, 93; MiSFD 9; VarWW 85; WhoAm 80, 82, 84, 86, 88, 90; WhoHol 92; WhoWor 76, 78, 82, 84, 87, 91, 93, 95, 96, 97*

Harvey, Doug(las Norman)
Canadian. Hockey Player
Defenseman, 1947-69, mostly with Montreal; won Norris Trophy seven times; Hall of Fame, 1973.
b. Dec 19, 1924 in Montreal, Quebec, Canada
d. Dec 26, 1989 in Montreal, Quebec, Canada
Source: *BioIn 6, 8, 9, 10, 16, 17; HocEn; WhoHcky 73; WhoTech 89*

Harvey, Frank Laird
English. Screenwriter
Wrote screenplay for *Poltergeist,* 1946.
b. Aug 11, 1912 in Manchester, England
Source: *Au&Wr 71; ConAu 5R; FilmgC; HalFC 88; IntAu&W 77; WhoThe 72, 77*

Harvey, Fred(erick Henry)
American. Restaurateur
His "Harvey Houses" in Santa Fe depots were famous throughout Southwest.
b. Jun 27, 1835 in London, England
d. Feb 9, 1901 in Leavenworth, Kansas
Source: *BioIn 7, 12; WebAB 74, 79*

Harvey, George Brinton M
American. Publisher
Pres., Harper Bros. publishing house, 1900-15; edited *North American Review* for 27 yrs.
b. Feb 16, 1864 in Peacham, Vermont
d. Aug 20, 1928
Source: *AmAu&B; AmBi; DcAmB; NatCAB 13; WhAm 1*

Harvey, Hayward Augustus
American. Inventor
Invented carburizing process for strengthening steel plate, widely used in warship construction.
b. Jan 17, 1824 in Jamestown, New York
d. Aug 28, 1893 in Orange, New Jersey
Source: *ApCAB SUP; DcAmB; InSci; NatCAB 13; WhAm HS*

Harvey, Laurence
[Larushke Mischa Skikne]
English. Actor
Oscar nominee for *Room at the Top,* 1958.
b. Oct 1, 1928 in Janiskis, Lithuania
d. Nov 25, 1973 in London, England
Source: *BiDFilm, 81, 94; BiE&WWA; BioIn 4, 5, 6, 8, 10, 11, 13, 14; BioNews 74; CurBio 61, 74, 74N; DcArts; FilmAG WE; FilmEn; FilmgC; ForYSC; HalFC 80, 84, 88; IlWWBF, A; IntDcF 1-3, 2-3; ItaFilm; LegTOT; MotPP; MovMk; NewC; NewYTBE 73; NotNAT A, B; ObitT 1971; OxCFilm; WhAm 6; Who 74; WhoHol B; WhoThe 72; WhoWor 74; WhScrn 77, 83; WhThe; WorAl; WorAlBi; WorEFlm*

Harvey, Paul
[Paul Harvey Aurandt]
"Voice of US Heartland"
American. Broadcast Journalist
Opinionated, colorful ABC News commentator, 1944—; wrote *Paul Harvey's For What It's Worth,* 1991.
b. Sep 4, 1918 in Tulsa, Oklahoma
Source: *AmAu&B; BiDAmNC; BioIn 6, 8, 10, 11, 13, 14, 15, 21; CelR; ConAu 102; CurBio 86; DcAmC; EncTwCJ; JrnUS; LegTOT; LesBEnT 92; News 95, 95-3; NewYTET; RadStar; SaTiSS; WhoAm 74, 76, 78, 80, 82, 84, 86, 88, 90, 92, 94, 95, 96, 97; WhoWor 78, 80, 82*

Harvey, Polly Jean
English. Singer, Songwriter, Musician
Named best songwriter and best new female singer by *Rolling Stone,* 1993.
b. c. 1970 in Yeovil, England
Source: *ConMus 11; News 95*

Harvey, William
English. Physician
Physician to James I, 1618; Charles I, 1631; published treatise on theory of blood circulation, 1628.
b. Apr 1, 1578 in Folkestone, England
d. Jun 3, 1657 in London, England
Source: *Alli; AsBiEn; Benet 87, 96; BiDPsy; BiESc; BiHiMed; BioIn 1, 2, 3, 4, 5, 6, 7, 8, 9, 10, 11, 12, 13, 14, 15, 16, 18, 19, 20; BritAu; CamDcSc; CamGEL; CamGLE; DcBiPP; DcEnL; DcInv; DcNaB, C; DcScB; InSci; LarDcSc; LinLib S; McGEWB; NamesHP; NewC; OxCEng 67, 85, 95; OxCMed 86; RAdv 14; REn; WebBD 83; WhDW; WorAl; WorAlBi; WorScD*

Harvey, William Hope
"Coin Harvey"
American. Economist
Advocated bimetallism; wrote *Coin's Financial School,* 1894.
b. Aug 16, 1851 in Buffalo, Virginia
d. Feb 11, 1936
Source: *AmRef; BiDSA; BioIn 1, 4, 9, 12, 15; DcAmAu; DcAmB S2; DcNAA; EncAAH; EncSoH; NatCAB 18; OhA&B; OxCAmL 65, 83, 95; REnAL; WebAB 74, 79; WhAm 1; WhNAA*

Harwell, Ernie
American. Broadcaster, Author
Was announcer for NY Giants, Brooklyn Dodgers, Baltimore Orioles, and Detroit Tigers; wrote *Tuned to Baseball,* 1985; Hall of Fame, 1981.
b. Jan 25, 1918 in Atlanta, Georgia
Source: *Ballpl 90; BioNews 74; ConAu 128, X; NewYTBS 91*

Harwood, Vanessa Clare
Canadian. Dancer
Star, National Ballet of Canada, 1970-86.
b. Jun 14, 1947 in Cheltenham, England
Source: *BiDD; CanWW 31, 83, 89; IntWWM 85; WhoAm 78, 80, 82, 84, 86, 88, 90, 92, 94, 95, 96, 97; WhoE 81, 83, 85, 86; WhoEmL 87; WhoEnt 92*

Hasani, Ali Nasir Muhammad
Political Leader
Pres., People's Democratic Republic of Yemen, 1980-86.
b. 1938
Source: *BioIn 11; WhoWor 84*

Hasegawa, Kazuo
Japanese. Actor
Warrior hero in many Japanese films since 1927.
b. Feb 29, 1908, Japan
Source: *FilmEn; IntDcF 1-3, 2-3; JapFilm; OxCFilm*

Hasek, Jaroslav
Czech. Author
Four-vol. series *The Good Soldier Schweik,* 1920-23, is considered a satirical masterpiece.
b. Apr 30, 1883 in Prague, Bohemia
d. Jan 3, 1923 in Lipuice, Czechoslovakia
Source: *Benet 87, 96; BioIn 1, 10, 11, 12, 13, 17; CasWL; ClDMEL 47, 80; ConAu 104, 129; DcArts; EncWL 2, 3; EncWT; EuWr 9; EvEuW; FacFETw; GrFLW; LngCTC; MajTwCW; MakMC; ModSL 2; Novels; PenC EUR; RAdv 14, 13-2; REn; RfGShF; RfGWoL 95; TwCA, SUP; TwCLC 4; TwCWr; WebBD 83; WhDW; WhoTwCL; WorAlBi*

Hasford, Jerry Gustav
American. Author
Novels include *The Short-Timers,* 1979; *The Phantom Blooper,* 1990.
b. Nov 28, 1947 in Haleyville, Alabama
d. Jan 29, 1993, Greece
Source: *ConLC 81*

Hashimoto, Ryutaro
Japanese. Political Leader
Prime minister of Japan, 1996—.
b. Jul 29, 1937 in Soja, Japan
Source: *IntWW 89, 91, 93; WhoAsAP 91; WhoWor 91, 97*

Haskell, Arnold Lionel
English. Journalist
Dance critic for several newspapers; wrote popular ballet texts: *Ballet Russe,* 1968.
b. Jul 19, 1903 in London, England
d. Nov 14, 1980 in Bath, England
Source: *AnObit 1980; Au&Wr 71; BioIn 2, 3, 10, 12; CnOxB; ConAu 5R, 108; DancEn 78; IntAu&W 77; IntWW 74, 75, 76, 77, 78, 79, 80, 81; NewCBEL;*

NewYTBS 80; SmATA 6; WhE&EA; Who 74; WhoWor 74

Hasluck, Paul Meernaa, Sir
Australian. Political Leader, Author
Liberal MP, 1949-69; governor general, 1969-74; wrote *The Poet in Australia,* 1975.
b. Apr 1, 1905 in Fremantle, Australia
Source: *BioIn 13, 14, 15; ConAu 109; CurBio 46; IntWW 83, 91; NewYTBS 86; Who 85, 92; WhoGov 75; WhoWor 74, 89; WrDr 86, 92*

Hass, H(enry) B(ohn)
American. Chemist
Helped discover gas chromatography; helped develop atomic bomb, 1942-46.
b. Jan 25, 1902 in Huntington, Ohio
d. Feb 13, 1987 in Manhasset, New York
Source: *AmMWSc 73P, 76P, 79, 82, 86; BioIn 4, 5, 8, 15; BlueB 76; CurBio 56, 87, 87N; InSci; McGMS 80; WhAm 9; WhoAm 76*

Hassam, Childe
[Frederick Childs Hassam]
American. Artist
Major American Impressionist; known for NYC, New England scenes.
b. Oct 17, 1859 in Boston, Massachusetts
d. Aug 27, 1935 in East Hampton, New York
Source: *AmBi; ApCAB X; ArtsAmW 3; BioIn 4, 5, 7, 8, 12; BriEAA; ClaDrA; DcAmArt; DcArts; FacFETw; GayN; LegTOT; LinLib S; NatCAB 10; OxCAmH; OxCAmL 65; OxDcArt; PhDcTCA 77; WebAB 74, 79; WhAm 1; WhAmArt 85; WorAl; WorAlBi*

Hassan II
[Mawley Hasan Muhammad Ibn Yusuf; King of Morocco]
Moroccan. Ruler
King since 1961; son of King Mohammed V.
b. Jul 9, 1929 in Rabat, Morocco
Source: *BioIn 10; CurBio 64; IntWW 83, 91; NewYTBS 86; PolLCME; WhoWor 84, 87, 91; WorAlBi*

Hasse, Johann Adolph
"Il Caro Sassone"
German. Composer
Wrote over 100 operas including *Sesostrate,* 1726; wed to prima donna Faustina Bordoni.
b. Mar 25, 1699 in Bergedorf, Germany
d. Dec 16, 1783 in Venice, Italy
Source: *Baker 78, 84; BioIn 3, 4, 7, 9, 10; BriBkM 80; DcBiPP; GrComp; IntDcOp; MusMk; NewEOp 71; NewGrDM 80; OxCMus*

Hassel, Odd
Norwegian. Chemist
Shared 1969 Nobel Prize in chemistry with Derek Barton.
b. May 17, 1897 in Kristiania, Norway
d. May 11, 1981 in Oslo, Norway
Source: *AnObit 1981; BioIn 2, 8, 9, 15, 19, 20; ConAu 108; IntWW 74, 75, 76, 77, 78, 79, 80, 81, 81N; LarDcSc; McGMS 80; NobelP; NotTwCS; Who 74; WhoNob, 90, 95; WhoWor 74, 76, 78, 80*

Hasselhoff, David
American. Actor
Appeared in soap opera "The Young and the Restless"; star of "Knight Rider;" "Baywatch."
b. Jul 17, 1952 in Baltimore, Maryland
Source: *BioIn 13, 14; ConTFT 7, 14; IntMPA 88, 92, 94, 96; LegTOT; VarWW 85; WhoAm 96, 97; WhoHol 92; WhoTelC*

Hassenfeld, Stephen David
American. Business Executive
Chairman, CEO, Hasbro Industries, 1974-89, toy manufacturers who have produced GI Joe, Mr. Potatohead.
b. Jan 19, 1942 in Providence, Rhode Island
d. Jun 25, 1989 in New York, New York
Source: *BioIn 14, 16; ConAmBL; ConNews 87-4; Dun&B 90; NewYTBS 89; St&PR 84, 87; WhAm 10; WhoAm 82, 84, 86, 88; WhoE 89; WhoFI 87, 89*

Hasso, Signe Eleonora Cecilia
Swedish. Actor
Sweden's leading lady; first Hollywood starring role: *Assignment in Brittany,* 1943.
b. Aug 15, 1915 in Stockholm, Sweden
Source: *BiE&WWA; FilmgC; ForWC 70; HalFC 84; HolP 40; IntAu&W 82; MotPP; MovMk; NotNAT; WhoAm 74, 76, 78, 80, 82, 84, 86, 88, 90, 92, 94, 95, 96, 97; WhoE 74; WhoEnt 92; WhoHol A; WhoThe 77*

Hastie, William Henry
American. Judge, Politician
First black Federal Appeals judge, 1949; governor, Virgin Islands, 1946-49; Spingarn winner, 1943.
b. Nov 17, 1904 in Knoxville, Tennessee
d. Apr 14, 1976 in East Norriton, Pennsylvania
Source: *BiDFedJ; BioIn 1, 2, 6, 7, 8, 9, 10, 11, 13; CurBio 44, 76; EncAACR; EncAB-H 1974, 1996; EncSoH; InB&W 80, 85; IntWW 74; LinLib S; OxCAmH; WebAB 74, 79; WhAm 7; WhoE 74; WhoGov 72*

Hastings, Alcee L
American. Politician
Dem. congressman, FL, 1993—.
b. Sep 5, 1936 in Altamonte Springs, Florida
Source: *BioIn 15; InB&W 85; NewYTBS 87; WhoAm 88; WhoAmL 90; WhoBlA 92; WhoSSW 88*

Hastings, Thomas
American. Architect
Building designs include NY Public Library.
b. Mar 11, 1860 in New York
d. Oct 22, 1929
Source: *AmBi; ApCAB X; BiDAmAr; BioIn 1, 14, 16; DcAmB; LinLib S; McGDA; NatCAB 11, 33; WhAm 1; WhAmArt 85; WhoArch*

Hastings, Warren
English. Statesman
Governor of Bengal, governor-general of India, 1750; impeached for corruption, 1 788, acquitted.
b. Dec 17, 1732 in Churchill, England
d. Aug 22, 1818 in Daylesford, England
Source: *Alli; Benet 87, 96; BiDLA; BioIn 1, 2, 3, 4, 6, 7, 8, 9, 10, 11, 12; DcBiPP; DcInB; DcNaB; HisDBrE; HisWorL; LinLib S; McGEWB; NewC; NewCBEL; OxCEng 85, 95; REn; WhDW; WorAl; WorAlBi*

Hatathli, Ned
American. Educator
Helped found the Navajo Community College, 1969.
b. Oct 11, 1923 in Coalmine Mesa, Arizona
d. Oct 16, 1972 in Many Farms, Arizona
Source: *BioIn 21; EncNAB; EncNoAI; NotNaAm; WhAm 6*

Hatch, Carl A
American. Lawyer, Politician
Dem. senator from NM, 1933-49; US district judge, 1949-63.
b. Nov 27, 1889 in Kirwin, Kansas
d. Sep 15, 1963 in Albuquerque, New Mexico
Source: *BiDrAC; CurBio 44, 63; WhAm 4*

Hatch, Orrin G(rant)
American. Politician
Rep. senator from UT, 1977—.
b. Mar 22, 1934 in Pittsburgh, Pennsylvania
Source: *AlmAP 80, 92; BiDrUSC 89; BioIn 11, 12, 13, 14; CelR 90; CngDr 77, 79, 81, 83, 85, 87, 89; CurBio 82; IntWW 77, 78, 79, 80, 81, 82, 83, 89, 91, 93; PolsAm 84; WhoAm 78, 80, 82, 84, 86, 88, 90, 92, 94, 95, 96, 97; WhoAmP 77, 79, 81, 83, 85, 87, 89, 91, 93, 95; WhoGov 77; WhoWest 78, 80, 82, 84, 87, 89, 92, 94, 96; WhoWor 80, 82, 87, 89, 91*

Hatch, Richard Lawrence
American. Actor
Replaced Michael Douglas on TV series "The Streets of San Francisco," 1976-77.
b. May 21, 1946 in Santa Monica, California
Source: *VarWW 85; WhoAm 88; WhoEmL 91; WhoWest 89*

Hatcher, Richard Gordon
American. Politician
First black mayor of Gary, IN, 1967-88.
b. Jul 10, 1933 in Michigan City, Indiana
Source: *AfrAmBi 1; BioIn 8, 9, 10, 11, 13; CivR 74; CurBio 72; Ebony 1;*

EncAACR; InB&W 80, 85; WhoAfA 96; WhoAm 86, 88; WhoAmL 78, 79; WhoAmP 85, 91; WhoBlA 75, 77, 80, 85, 88, 90, 92, 94; WhoGov 75; WhoMW 74, 88; WorAlBi

Hatcher, Teri
American. Actor
Plays Lois Lane on ABC's "Lois and Clark: The New Adventures of Superman," 1993-97.
b. Dec 8, 1964 in Sunnyvale, California

Hatfield, Bobby
[Righteous Brothers]
American. Singer
With Bill Medley had hit single "Unchained Melody," 1965.
b. Aug 10, 1940 in Beaver Dam, Wisconsin
Source: *IntMPA 75, 76, 77, 78, 79, 80, 81, 82, 84, 86, 88, 92; WhoRocM 82*

Hatfield, Hurd
American. Actor
Starred in film *The Picture of Dorian Gray,* 1945.
b. Dec 7, 1918 in New York, New York
Source: *BiDFilm, 81; BiE&WWA; BioIn 14; FilmEn; FilmgC; ForYSC; HalFC 80, 84, 88; IntMPA 84, 86, 88, 92, 94, 96; ItaFilm; LegTOT; MotPP; MovMk; NotNAT; VarWW 85; WhoHol 92, A; WhoHrs 80*

Hatfield, Mark Odom
American. Politician
Rep. senator from OR, 1967-97; wrote *Between a Rock and a Hard Place,* 1977.
b. Jul 12, 1922 in Dallas, Oregon
Source: *AlmAP 92; BiDrAC; BiDrUSC 89; BioIn 5, 6, 7, 8, 9, 10, 11, 12, 13, 14; CelR 90; CngDr 87, 89; CurBio 84; IntWW 83, 89, 91; IntYB 81, 82; NewYTBS 91; PolsAm 84; WhoAm 86, 90; WhoAmP 73, 75, 77, 79, 81, 83, 85, 87, 89, 91, 93, 95; WhoGov 75, 77; WhoRel 75; WhoWest 74, 76, 78, 80, 82, 84, 89, 92; WhoWor 87, 91*

Hatfield, Richard
Canadian. Politician
Progressive-Conservative Party premier of New Brunswick, 1970-87.
b. Apr 9, 1931 in Woodstock, New Brunswick, Canada
Source: *BioIn 13, 14, 15; CanWW 83, 89; IntWW 89; Who 90, 92N; WhoAm 90; WhoE 89*

Hathaway, Anne
[Mrs. William Shakespeare]
English.
Married Shakespeare, 1582; home is open for tours in Stratford-upon-Avon.
b. 1557 in Temple Grafton, England
d. Aug 6, 1623 in Stratford-upon-Avon, England
Source: *InWom; NewC; OxCEng 85; REn*

Hathaway, Donny
American. Singer, Songwriter
Best known for duets with Roberta Flack: "Where Is the Love," 1972; "The Closer I G et to You," 1978.
b. Oct 1, 1945 in Chicago, Illinois
d. Jan 13, 1979 in New York, New York
Source: *Baker 84, 92; BiDAfM; BioIn 11, 16; DcAmB S10; EncPR&S 89; EncRk 88; EncRkSt; HarEnR 86; IlEncBM 82; InB&W 85; LegTOT; PenEncP; RkOn 74, 78; RolSEnR 83; SoulM; WhoBlA 77; WhoRock 81*

Hathaway, Henry
[Henri Leopold de Fiennes]
American. Director
Best known for directing *True Grit,* 1969.
b. Mar 13, 1898 in Sacramento, California
d. Feb 11, 1985 in Los Angeles, California
Source: *AmFD; BiDFilm, 81, 94; BioIn 10, 14, 15; CmMov; DcFM; FacFETw; FilmEn; FilmgC; GangFlm; HalFC 80, 84, 88; IlWWHD 1; IntDcF 1-2, 2-2; IntMPA 75, 76, 77, 78, 79, 80, 81, 82, 84; LegTOT; MiSFD 9N; MovMk; NewYTBS 85; OxCFilm; VarWW 85; WorEFlm; WorFDir 1*

Hathaway, Sibyl Collings
[Dame of Sark]
English. Ruler, Author
Feudal master of Channel Island; Seigneur of Sark, 1927-74; wrote *Maid of Sark,* 1939.
b. Jan 13, 1884 in Guernsey
d. Jul 14, 1974 in London, England
Source: *ConAu 1R, 103; Who 74*

Hathaway, Stanley Knapp
American. Politician
Rep. governor of WY, 1967-74.
b. Jul 19, 1924 in Osceola, Nebraska
Source: *BiDrGov 1789; BiDrUSE 89; IntWW 83; NewYTBS 75; WhoAm 74; WhoAmL 83, 85, 87; WhoAmP 85, 91; WhoFI 89, 92, 94; WhoGov 75; WhoWest 74, 76, 96; WhoWor 97*

Hathaway, Starke R
American. Psychologist, Author
Co-developer of Minnesota Multiphasic Personality Inventory, 1930s; widely used during WW II.
b. Aug 22, 1903 in Central Lake, Michigan
d. Jul 4, 1984 in Minneapolis, Minnesota
Source: *AmMWSc 73S; AnObit 1984; ConAu 5R, 113; NewYTBS 84; WhAm 8; WhoAm 74*

Hathaway, William Dodd
American. Politician
Dem. congressman from ME, 1965-78, senator, 1973-79.
b. Feb 21, 1924 in Cambridge, Massachusetts
Source: *BiDrAC; BiDrUSC 89; BioIn 9, 10, 11; BlueB 76; CngDr 74, 77; DrAPF 91; IntWW 74, 75, 76, 77, 78, 79, 80, 81, 82, 83; WhoAm 74, 76, 78, 92, 94, 95, 96, 97; WhoAmP 73, 75, 77, 79, 81, 91; WhoE 74, 75, 77, 79; WhoFI 94, 96; WhoGov 72, 75, 77*

Hatlo, Jimmy
American. Cartoonist
Created comic character Little Iodine.
b. Sep 1, 1898 in Providence, Rhode Island
d. Nov 30, 1963 in Carmel, California
Source: *BioIn 2, 3, 6, 13; ConAu 93; DcAmB S7; EncACom; EncAJ; EncTwCJ; LegTOT; SmATA 23N; WhAm 4*

Hatoyama Ichiro
Japanese. Political Leader
Helped found Liberal-Democratic Party, 1955; as prime minister, bettered relations with other Asian nations and the USSR.
b. Jan 1, 1883 in Tokyo, Japan
d. Mar 7, 1959 in Tokyo, Japan
Source: *BioIn 2, 3, 4, 5; CurBio 55, 59; IntWW 91; ObitOF 79; WhAm 3*

Hatta, Mohammad
"Father of the Indonesian Cooperative Movement"
Indonesian. Politician
Helped to establish Indonesian independence; served as prime minister, 1948-50; vp, 1950-56.
b. Aug 12, 1902 in Bukittinggi, Dutch East Indies
d. Mar 14, 1980 in Jakarta, Indonesia
Source: *AnObit 1980; BioIn 1, 2, 13, 16, 17; ConAu 97; CurBio 49, 91N; DcMPSA; EncRev; EncWB; IntWW 74, 75, 76, 77, 78, 79*

Hatton, Christopher, Sir
English. Statesman
Lord chancellor, 1587; favorite of Elizabeth I; one of several responsible for Mary Queen of Scots' sentence.
b. 1540 in Holdenby, England
d. Nov 20, 1591 in London, England
Source: *Alli; BiDRP&D; BioIn 1, 3, 11, 13; DcBiPP; DcNaB, C; NewC; NewCBEL; OxCEng 67, 85, 95; OxCLaw*

Hauer, Rutger
Dutch. Actor
Films include *Blade Runner,* 1982; *A Breed Apart,* 1984.
b. Jan 23, 1944 in Breukelen, Netherlands
Source: *ConTFT 7, 14; HalFC 84, 88; IntMPA 82, 84, 86, 88, 92, 94, 96; IntWW 91, 93; LegTOT; NewYTBS 81; VarWW 85; WhoHol 92*

Hauff, Wilhelm
German. Author
Best-known historical novel: *Lichtenstein,* 1826.
b. Nov 29, 1802 in Stuttgart, Wurttemberg
d. Nov 18, 1827 in Stuttgart, Wurttemberg

Source: *AuBYP 2; BiD&SB; BioIn 7, 8, 10, 17; CasWL; DcBiA; DcBiPP; DcLB 90; EuAu; EvEuW; OxCChiL; OxCGer 76, 86; PenC EUR; REn; ScF&FL 1; SupFW; WhoChL; WhoHr&F*

Haug, Hans
Swiss. Composer
Wrote choral music; opera *Tartuffe,* 1937.
b. Jul 27, 1900 in Basel, Switzerland
d. Sep 15, 1967 in Lausanne, Switzerland
Source: *Baker 78, 84, 92; BioIn 8; NewEOp 71; NewGrDM 80; NewGrDO*

Hauge, Gabriel
American. Economist
Eisenhower adviser, speechwriter, 1952-58.
b. Mar 7, 1914 in Hawley, Minnesota
d. Jul 24, 1981 in New York, New York
Source: *AnObit 1981; BioIn 3, 4, 9, 11, 12; CurBio 53, 81, 81N; EncAB-A 24; IntWW 74, 75, 76, 77, 78, 79, 80, 81; PolProf E; St&PR 75; Ward 77; WhAm 9; WhoAm 74, 76, 78, 80; WhoE 74, 77, 79, 81; WhoFI 74, 75, 79, 81; WhoWor 74, 76, 78, 80*

Haughey, Charles James
Irish. Political Leader
Prime minister during prison hunger strikes, 1979-81.
b. Sep 16, 1925 in Castlebar, Ireland
Source: *BioIn 12, 13, 14, 15, 16; BlueB 76; CurBio 81; DcTwHis; IntWW 74, 75, 76, 77, 78, 79, 80, 81, 82, 83, 89, 91, 93; NewYTBS 79, 82, 87; Who 82, 83, 85, 88, 90, 92, 94; WhoEIO 82; WhoWor 76, 78, 80, 82, 84, 87, 89, 91*

Haughton, Billy
[William R Haughton]
American. Horse Trainer, Jockey
Won 4,910 races, $40.2 million for harness racing, training; Hall of Fame, 1968.
b. Nov 23, 1923 in Gloversville, New York
d. Jul 15, 1986 in Valhalla, New York
Source: *BioIn 6, 8, 10, 15; NewYTBS 86; WorAl*

Haughton, Daniel Jeremiah
American. Business Executive
Joined Lockheed Aircraft Corp., 1939; chairman, 1967-76.
b. Sep 7, 1911 in Dora, Alabama
d. Jul 5, 1987 in Marietta, Georgia
Source: *BioIn 7, 8, 9, 10, 11, 15; BlueB 76; CurBio 74, 87; IntWW 74, 75, 76, 77, 78, 79, 80, 81, 82, 83; NewYTBE 71, 72; NewYTBS 76, 87; WhAm 9; Who 74, 82, 83, 85, 88, 90; WhoAm 74, 76; WhoFI 74, 75; WhoGov 72, 75; WhoWest 74, 76*

Hauk, Minnie
American. Opera Singer
Celebrated soprano; starred in first American performance of Carmen.
b. Nov 16, 1851 in New York, New York
d. Feb 6, 1929 in Triebschen, Switzerland
Source: *AmBi; AmWom; Baker 78, 84, 92; BiDAmM; CmOp; DcAmB; InWom, SUP; LibW; MetOEnc; NewAmDM; NewEOp 71; NewGrDA 86; NewGrDM 80; NewGrDO; NotAW; OxDcOp; PenDiMP; WhAm 4, HS*

Haupt, Herman
American. Engineer
Pioneered transportation of pipe-line oil; invented compressed air drill; chief of construction of military railroads during Civil War.
b. Mar 26, 1817 in Philadelphia, Pennsylvania
d. Dec 14, 1905 in Jersey City, New Jersey
Source: *Alli, SUP; AmBi; ApCAB; BiInAmS; BioIn 7, 8, 10, 12, 14; CivWDc; DcAmAu; DcAmB; DcAmMiB; DcNAA; EncABHB 2; NatCAB 10; TwCBDA; WhAm 1; WhCiWar*

Hauptman, Herbert Aaron
American. Physicist
With Jerome Karl, won Nobel Prize, 1985, for studies of molecular structure of crystals.
b. Feb 14, 1917 in New York, New York
Source: *AmMWSc 73P, 76P, 79, 82, 86, 89, 92, 95; BioIn 14, 15, 19, 20; LarDcSc; NewYTBS 85; NobelP; Who 88, 90, 92, 94; WhoAm 86, 88, 90, 92, 94, 95, 96, 97; WhoE 74, 86, 89, 91, 93, 95, 97; WhoNob, 90, 95; WhoScEn 94, 96; WhoTech 82, 89; WhoWor 87, 89, 91, 93, 95, 96, 97; WorAlBi*

Hauptman, William
American. Dramatist
Won Tony for *Big River,* 1985.
b. Nov 26, 1942 in Wichita Falls, Texas
Source: *ConAu 128; ConDr 88; ConTFT 4; IntAu&W 91; WhoAm 94, 95, 96, 97; WhoEnt 92; WrDr 92*

Hauptmann, Bruno Richard
German. Criminal, Murderer
Kidnapped son of Charles Lindbergh, Mar 1, 1932; convicted, executed for murder.
b. Nov 26, 1899 in Kamenz, Germany
d. Apr 3, 1936 in Trenton, New Jersey
Source: *AmBi; BioIn 1, 2, 6, 8, 10, 11, 12, 13; CopCroC; MurCaTw; NewCol 75; WorAl*

Hauptmann, Gerhart Johann Robert
German. Author, Poet
Leading Naturalist playwright: *The Weavers,* 1892; won Nobel Prize, 1912.
b. Nov 15, 1862 in Bad Salzbrunn, Prussia
d. Jun 6, 1946 in Agnetendorf, Germany
Source: *AtlBL; BiD&SB; CasWL; CIDMEL 47; CnMD; CnThe; CurBio 46; CyWA 58; EncWL; EvEuW; LngCTC; ModWD; PenC EUR; REn; TwCA SUP; WhAm 2; WhoNob*

Haury, Emil W
American. Anthropologist
Excavations led to the identification of prehistoric Mogollon Indian culture in the American Southwest.
b. May 2, 1904 in Newton, Kansas
d. Dec 5, 1992 in Tucson, Arizona
Source: *BioIn 8, 14, 16; ConAu 65; IntWW 91; WhoAm 90*

Hauser, Gayelord
American. Nutritionist
Pioneer in health foods who advocated yogurt, wheat germ; wrote *Look Younger, Live Younger,* 1950.
b. May 17, 1895 in Tubingen, Germany
d. Dec 2, 1984 in North Hollywood, California
Source: *AmDec 1950; AnObit 1984; BioIn 1, 2, 3, 4; CelR; CurBio 85N; NewYTBS 74; WhAm 9; WhoAm 76, 78, 80, 82*

Hauser, Philip M(orris)
American. Educator
With U.S. Bureau of the Census from 1932 to the late 1940s.
b. Sep 27, 1909
d. Dec 13, 1994 in Chicago, Illinois
Source: *AmMWSc 73S; BioIn 4, 6, 8; BlueB 76; CurBio 95N; IntWW 74, 75, 76, 77, 78, 79, 80, 81, 82, 83, 89, 91, 93; WhAm 11; WhoAm 74, 76, 78, 80, 82, 84, 86, 88, 90; WhoWor 82; WrDr 82, 84, 86, 88, 90, 92, 94*

Haushofer, Karl Ernst
German. Geographer, Military Leader
Geographer who used geopolitical theories to justify Germany's expansion; influenced, advised Hitler on foreign affairs.
b. Aug 27, 1869 in Munich, Bavaria
d. Mar 13, 1946 in Pahl, Germany (West)
Source: *BiDExR; CurBio 46; EncTR; McGEWB; NewCol 75; REn*

Hauy, Rene Just
French. Mineralogist
Helped found science of crystallography by discovering geometric law of crystallization.
b. Feb 28, 1743 in Saint-Just-en-Chaussee, France
d. Jun 1, 1822 in Paris, France
Source: *AsBiEn; BiESc; CamDcSc; DcBiPP; DcCathB; DcScB; InSci; LarDcSc; NewCol 75; WhDW*

Havel, Vaclav
Czech. Political Leader, Dramatist
Pres., Czechoslovakia, 1989-92; won Obie, 1970.
b. Oct 5, 1936 in Prague, Czechoslovakia
Source: *Au&Wr 71; Benet 87, 96; BioIn 14, 15, 16; CamGWoT; CasWL; CIDMEL 80; CnThe; ColdWar 2; ConAu*

36NR, 104; ConFLW 84; ConHero 2; ConLC 25, 58, 65; ConTFT 9; ConWorW 93; CroCD; CurBio 85, 95; CyWA 89; DcArts; DcTwHis; DramC 6; EncRev; EncWL, 2, 3; EncWT; Ent; FacFETw; HeroCon; IntAu&W 76, 77, 91, 93; IntDcT 2; IntWW 74, 75, 76, 77, 78, 79, 80, 81, 82, 83, 89, 91, 93; MagSWL; MajTwCW; McGEWD 84; ModSL 2; ModWD; News 90, 90-3; NewYTBS 79, 86, 87; OxCThe 83; RadHan; RAdv 14, 13-2; REnWD; Who 92, 94; WhoEnt 92; WhoSocC 78; WhoSoCE 89; WhoWor 91, 93, 95, 96, 97; WorAlBi; WorAu 1970

Havell, Robert, Jr.
English. Engraver
Did aquatints for Audubon's *Birds of America,* 1827-38.
b. Nov 25, 1793 in Reading, England
d. Nov 11, 1878 in Tarrytown, New York
Source: *AntBDN B; BioIn 1, 2; DcAmB; GrBIl; NatCAB 22; NewYHSD; WhAm HS*

Havens, Richie
American. Singer, Musician
Black folksinger who had hit single "Here Comes the Sun," 1971.
b. Jan 21, 1941 in New York, New York
Source: *BioIn 8, 9, 14; ConMus 11; DrBlPA, 90; EncFCWM 83; EncRk 88; EncRkSt; HarEnR 86; IlEncBM 82; InB&W 80; LegTOT; OnThGG; PenEncP; RkOn 74, 78; RolSEnR 83; WhoHol 92; WhoRocM 82*

Haver, June
[Mrs. Fred MacMurray; June Stovenour]
American. Actor
Personified *The Girl Next Door,* title of movie she starred in, 1953.
b. Jun 10, 1926 in Rock Island, Illinois
Source: *BiDAmM; BioIn 9; CmMov; CmpEPM; FilmEn; FilmgC; ForYSC; HalFC 80, 84, 88; InWom SUP; LegTOT; MotPP; MovMk; VarWW 85; What 3; WhoHol 92, A*

Havighurst, Walter Edwin
American. Author
Works of Great Lakes region include *Long Ships Passing,* 1942.
b. Nov 28, 1901 in Appleton, Wisconsin
Source: *AmAu&B; AmNov; Au&Wr 71; AuBYP 2, 3; BenetAL 91; BioIn 14; CnDAL; ConAu 1NR, 1R, 29NR; DrAS 82E; MorJA; OhA&B; OxCAmL 65, 83; REnAL; SmATA 1; TwCA SUP; WhoAm 74; WrDr 76, 86, 88*

Haviland, Virginia
American. Librarian
Organized, headed children's book division of Library of Congress, 1963-81.
b. May 21, 1911 in Rochester, New York
d. Jan 6, 1988 in Washington, District of Columbia
Source: *AuBYP 2S, 3; BiDrLUS 70; BioIn 10, 15, 16; ChhPo S1, S2; ConAu 12NR, 17R, 124; FourBJA; OxCChiL; SmATA 6, 54N; WhAm 9; WhoAm 74, 76, 78, 80, 82; WhoAmW 61, 64, 66, 68, 70, 72, 74, 75, 77; WhoLibI 82; WhoLibS 66; WhoSSW 73*

Havlicek, John
"Hondo"
American. Basketball Player
Four-time all-star forward-guard, Boston, 1962-78; won eight NBA championships; Hall of Fame, 1983; named one of the top 50 players in NBA history by the NBA, 1996.
b. Apr 8, 1940 in Martins Ferry, Ohio
Source: *BasBi; BiDAmSp BK; BioIn 6, 8, 9, 10, 11, 12, 16; LegTOT; NewYTBS 78; OfNBA 87; WhoAm 74, 76, 90, 92, 94, 95; WhoBbl 73; WhoE 95; WhoSpor; WorAl; WorAlBi*

Havoc, June
[Ellen Evangeline Hovick]
"Baby June"
American. Actor
Sister of Gypsy Rose Lee; author of two autobiographies, numerous plays.
b. Nov 8, 1916 in Seattle, Washington
Source: *BiE&WWA; BioIn 3, 5, 10, 12, 16; CmpEPM; ConAu 107; FilmEn; FilmgC; ForYSC; HalFC 80, 84, 88; HolP 40; IntMPA 77, 80, 84, 86, 88, 92, 94, 96; InWom, SUP; LegTOT; MotPP; MovMk; NewYTBS 80; NotNAT, A; NotWoAT; VarWW 85; WhoAm 84, 86, 88, 90, 92, 94, 95, 96, 97; WhoAmW 68; WhoEnt 92; WhoHol 92, A; WhoThe 72, 77, 81; WorAl*

Hawerchuk, Dale
Canadian. Hockey Player
Center, Winnipeg, 1981-89, Buffalo, 1990—; youngest NHL player to score 100 pts. in season (1981-82); won Calder Trophy, 1982.
b. Apr 4, 1963 in Toronto, Ontario, Canada
Source: *BioIn 12; HocEn; HocReg 87; NewYTBS 81; WhoAm 96, 97; WhoMW 86; WhoSpor; WorAlBi*

Hawes, Elizabeth
American. Fashion Designer, Feminist, Author
Wrote best-seller *Fashion Is Spinach,* 1938.
b. Dec 16, 1903 in Ridgewood, New Jersey
d. Sep 6, 1971 in New York, New York
Source: *AmDec 1930; BioAmW; BioIn 2, 9, 12, 15, 16, 17; ConFash; CurBio 91N; EncAL; EncFash; InWom, SUP; NotAW MOD; WhAm 5; WhoAmW 58, 61, 64, 66, 68; WorFshn*

Hawes, Harriet Ann Boyd
American. Archaeologist
Led excavations at Gournia, Crete; discovered early Bronze Age Minoan site, 1901.
b. Oct 11, 1871 in Boston, Massachusetts
d. Mar 31, 1945 in Washington, District of Columbia
Source: *AmWomSc; DcAmB S3; InWom SUP; LibW; NotAW; WhAm 3A; WomWWA 14*

Hawke, Bob
[Robert James Lee Hawke]
Australian. Political Leader
Labor Party leader, succeeded Malcolm Fraser as prime minister, 1983-91.
b. Dec 9, 1929 in Bordertown, Australia
Source: *BioIn 12, 13, 14, 15; BlueB 76; ConAu 152; CurBio 83; DcTwHis; FarE&A 78, 79, 80, 81; IntWW 74, 75, 76, 77, 78, 79, 80, 81, 82, 83, 89, 91, 93; IntYB 78, 79, 80, 81, 82; NewYTBS 83; Who 82, 83, 85, 88, 90, 92, 94; WhoAsAP 91; WhoUN 75; WhoWor 78, 80, 82, 87, 89, 91, 93*

Hawke, Ethan
American. Actor, Director
Co-founder of the New York theatre company, Malaparte. Was in *Dead Poets Society.*
b. Nov 6, 1970 in Austin, Texas
Source: *BioIn 20, 21; ConTFT 12; IntMPA 92, 94, 96; LegTOT; WhoAm 95, 96, 97*

Hawkes, John Clendennin Burne, Jr.
American. Author
Avant-garde novels include *The Cannibal,* 1949; *Passion Artist,* 1949.
b. Aug 17, 1925 in Stamford, Connecticut
Source: *AmAu&B; Benet 87; BenetAL 91; BioIn 13, 14; CamGLE; CamHAL; ConAu 1R, 2NR; ConDr 82; ConLC 15, 27, 49; ConNov 86, 91; CroCD; DcLEL 1940; DcLP 87B; DrAF 76; DrAPF 91; EncWL; IntAu&W 91; IntvTCA 2; IntWW 83, 91; MajTwCW; ModAL, S1, S2; RAdv 13-1; RfGAmL 87; WhoAm 90; WhoTwCL; WhoUSWr 88; WhoWor 74; WhoWrEP 89; WorAlBi; WrDr 86, 92*

Hawking, Stephen William
English. Educator, Physicist, Author
Mathematics professor; has developed significant physics theories; wrote best-seller *A Brief History of Time,* 1988; suffers from Lou Gehrig's disease.
b. Jan 8, 1942 in Oxford, England
Source: *BiESc; BioIn 11, 12, 13, 14, 15, 16; BlueB 76; ConAu 129, X; ConLC 65; CurBio 84, 90; FacFETw; IntAu&W 91, 93; IntWW 89, 91, 93; LarDcSc; McGMS 80; News 90, 90-1; RAdv 14; Who 82, 83, 85, 88, 90, 92, 94; WhoWor 82, 84, 91; WorAlBi; WorScD; WrDr 80, 82, 84, 86, 88, 92*

Hawkins, Bean
[Coleman Hawkins]
American. Jazz Musician
Tenor saxist, noted for 1939 recording of "Body and Soul"; led own band, 1940s.

b. Nov 21, 1904 in Saint Joseph, Missouri
d. May 19, 1969 in New York, New York
Source: *AfrAmAl 6; AllMusG; Baker 78, 84; BiDAfM; BiDAmM; BiDJaz; BioIn 4, 5, 6, 8, 10, 11; CmpEPM; ConBlB 9; ConMus 11; DcTwCCu 5; DrBlPA, 90; EncJzS; FacFETw; IlEncJ; InB&W 80, 85; LegTOT; MusMk; NegAl 76, 83, 89; NewAmDM; NewGrDA 86; NewGrDJ 88; NewGrDM 80; ObitT 1961; PenEncP; WhAm 5; WhoJazz 72; WhScrn 77, 83; WorAl; WorAlBi*

Hawkins, Coleman
"Bean"; "Father of the Tenor Saxophone"; "Hawk"
American. Musician
Jazz saxophonist; helped launch bebop.
b. Nov 21, 1904 in Saint Joseph, Missouri
d. May 19, 1969 in New York, New York
Source: *AfrAmAl 6; AllMusG; Baker 78, 84; BiDAfM; BiDAmM; BiDJaz; BioIn 4, 5, 6, 8, 10, 11; CmpEPM; ConBlB 9; ConMus 11; DcTwCCu 5; DrBlPA, 90; EncJzS; FacFETw; IlEncJ; InB&W 80, 85; LegTOT; MusMk; NegAl 76, 83, 89; NewAmDM; NewGrDA 86; NewGrDJ 88; NewGrDM 80; ObitT 1961; PenEncP; WhAm 5; WhoJazz 72; WhScrn 83; WorAl; WorAlBi*

Hawkins, Connie
"The Hawk"
American. Basketball Player
As NY high school player banned from NBA, 1962-69, for allegedly introducing players to a man convicted of fixing games; Phoenix Suns, 1969-76; Hall of Fame, 1992.
b. Jul 17, 1942 in New York, New York
Source: *BasBi; BioIn 8, 9, 10, 12, 21; WhoAfA 96; WhoAm 74, 76; WhoBbl 73; WhoBlA 75, 77, 80, 85, 90, 92, 94; WhoSpor*

Hawkins, Erick
[Frederick Hawkins]
American. Dancer, Choreographer
With Martha Graham Dance Company, 1939-51.
b. Apr 23, 1909
d. Nov 23, 1994 in New York, New York
Source: *BiDD; BioIn 12, 13; CmpGMD; CnOxB; CurBio 95N; DancEn 78; NewYTBS 94*

Hawkins, Erskine (Ramsey)
""20th-Century Gabriel""
American. Songwriter, Bandleader
Big band leader noted for high-note trumpet playing; theme was "Tuxedo Junction."
b. Jul 26, 1914 in Birmingham, Alabama
d. Nov 11, 1993 in Willingboro, New Jersey
Source: *AllMusG; AnObit 1993; ASCAP 66, 80; BgBands 74; BiDAmM; BiDJaz; BioIn 16, 18, 19, 20; BlkCond; CmpEPM; CurBio 94N; DrBlPA, 90; EncJzS; InB&W 80, 85; NewAmDM; NewGrDJ 88, 94; NewYTBS 88; OxCPMus; PenEncP; WhoBlA 92; WhoJazz 72*

Hawkins, Gus
[Augustus Freeman Hawkins]
American. Politician
Dem. congressman from CA, 1962-90; co-author, Humphrey-Hawkins Full Employment and Balanced Growth Act.
b. Aug 31, 1907 in Shreveport, Louisiana
Source: *AlmAP 84, 88; BiDrAC; BiDrUSC 89; BioIn 6, 9, 10, 11, 12, 13, 14; BlkAmsC; CngDr 87, 89; CurBio 83; InB&W 80, 85; NegAl 89A; NewYTBS 90; PolProf J, NF; PolsAm 84; WhoAm 74, 76, 78, 80, 82, 84, 86, 88, 90, 96; WhoAmP 85, 91; WhoBlA 85, 88, 92; WhoGov 72, 75, 77; WhoWest 74, 76, 78, 80, 82, 84, 87, 89, 92*

Hawkins, Jack
English. Actor
Lost voice, 1966, due to cancer, but continued to act, with speaking parts dubbed by others.
b. Sep 14, 1910 in London, England
d. Jul 18, 1973 in London, England
Source: *BiDFilm, 81, 94; BioIn 4, 5, 7, 10, 13; CmMov; CurBio 59, 73, 73N; DcArts; EncEurC; FilmAG WE; FilmEn; FilmgC; ForYSC; HalFC 80, 84, 88; IlWWBF, A; IntDcF 1-3, 2-3; ItaFilm; LegTOT; MotPP; MovMk; NewYTBE 73; NotNAT B; ObitT 1971; OxCFilm; PlP&P; WhAm 5; WhoHol B; WhoHrs 80; WhScrn 77, 83; WhThe; WorAl; WorAlBi; WorEFlm*

Hawkins, John, Sir
[Sir John Hawkyns]
English. Naval Officer
Naval expeditions with relative, Sir Francis Drake, brought about break between England and Spain, defeated Spanish Armada, 1587.
b. 1532 in Plymouth, England
d. Nov 12, 1595, West Indies
Source: *Alli; Benet 87, 96; BioIn 1, 2, 3, 4, 5, 7, 8, 9, 11, 18; CamGEL; CamGLE; DcNaB; HisDBrE; LinLib S; McGEWB; NewC; NewCBEL; OxCAmH; OxCEng 67, 85, 95; OxCShps; REn; WhDW; WhWE; WorAl; WorAlBi*

Hawkins, Osie Penman, Jr.
American. Opera Singer
Wagnerian baritone with NY Met. from 1941.
b. Aug 16, 1913 in Phoenix City, Alabama
Source: *BioIn 13; IntWWM 90; MetOEnc; WhoAm 74, 76, 78, 80, 82, 84, 86, 88, 90, 92, 94, 95, 96, 97; WhoEnt 92; WhoSSW 82, 84, 86; WhoWor 78, 82*

Hawkins, Paula Fickes
[Mrs. Walter E Hawkins]
American. Politician
Rep. senator from FL, 1980-87; first woman elected to Senate based on own career.
b. Jan 24, 1927 in Salt Lake City, Utah
Source: *BiDrUSC 89; BioIn 13, 14, 15; CngDr 85, 87; CurBio 85; IntWW 83; InWom SUP; NewYTBS 80; PolsAm 84; WhoAm 84, 88; WhoAmP 91; WhoAmW 85, 87, 89; WhoSSW 86, 88; WhoWor 84, 87*

Hawkins, Ronnie
American. Singer
Rock 'n' roll hits include "Forty Days," "Mary Lou," 1959.
b. Jan 10, 1935 in Huntsville, Arkansas
Source: *BioIn 12, 14, 16, 21; ConMuA 80A; EncFCWM 83; EncRk 88; EncRkSt; HarEnCM 87; HarEnR 86; IlEncRk; NewGrDA 86; PenEncP; RkOn 82; RolSEnR 83; WhoRock 81*

Hawkins, Screamin' Jay
[Jalacy J Hawkins]
American. Singer, Pianist
Known for wild stage antics; wrote song "I Put a Spell on You."
b. Jul 18, 1929 in Cleveland, Ohio
Source: *BioIn 13; ConMus 8; EncRk 88; HarEnR 86; InB&W 85; LegTOT; PenEncP; RkOn 74, 82; RolSEnR 83; SoulM; WhoHol 92; WhoRock 81; WhoRocM 82*

Hawkins, Tramaine
[Tramaine Aunzola Davis]
American. Singer
Gospel singer; recorded "O Happy Day," 1969 with the Edwin Hawkins Singers and "Christian People," 1970 with the Andrae Crouch and the Disciples; received Grammy Awards for single "The Lord's Prayer," 1980 and album *Tramaine Hawkins Live,* 1990; released *To A Higher Place* in 1994.
b. Oct 11, 1951 in San Francisco, California
Source: *BlkWAm; ConMus 17*

Hawkins, Walter Lincoln
American. Chemist
His work at AT&T's Bell Laboratories earned him 18 US patents; invented an additive that gave long life to plastic coatings on cable wire.
b. Mar 21, 1911 in Washington, District of Columbia
d. Aug 20, 1992 in San Marcos, California
Source: *AfrAmBi 2; AmMWSc 73P, 76P, 79, 82, 86, 89, 92; BioIn 9, 14, 18, 20; BlksScM; DiAASTC; WhAm 10; WhoAfA 96; WhoAm 74, 76, 78, 80, 82, 84, 88, 90, 92; WhoBlA 77, 80, 85, 88, 90, 92, 94; WhoFrS 84*

Hawks, Howard Winchester
American. Director, Producer
Best known for films *Bringing Up Baby,* 1938; *The Big Sleep,* 1946.
b. May 30, 1896 in Goshen, Indiana
d. Dec 26, 1977 in Palm Springs, California
Source: *AmCulL; BiDFilm; CmMov; CurBio 72, 80N; DcAmB S10; DcFM; FacFETw; FilmgC; HalFC 84; IntMPA 77; MakMC; MovMk; OxCFilm; TwYS; WebAB 74, 79; WhAm 7; WhoAm 74, 76, 78; WhoWor 74; WorEFlm*

Hawkwind
[Dave Brock; Alan Davey; Clive Deamer; Huw Lloyd Langton]
British. Music Group
Noted for live performances, rock band formed 1969; success tainted by bad publi city, drug use; hit single, "Silver Machine," 1972.
Source: *ConMuA 80A; EncRk 88; EncRkSt; HarEnR 86; IlEncRk; OnThGG; RolSEnR 83; WhoRock 81; WhoRocM 82*

Hawley, Cameron
American. Author
Wrote best-selling novel *Executive Suite,* 1952; later film called *Cash McCall,* 1955.
b. Sep 19, 1905 in Howard, South Dakota
d. Mar 9, 1969 in Marathon, Florida
Source: *AmAu&B; BioIn 3, 4, 5, 8, 10; ConAu 1R, 25R; CurBio 57; NatCAB 54; ObitOF 79; WhAm 5*

Hawn, Goldie (Jean)
American. Actor
Won Oscar for *Cactus Flower,* 1969; other films include *Protocol,* 1984, *The First Wives Club,* 1996.
b. Nov 21, 1945 in Washington, District of Columbia
Source: *BiDFilm 81, 94; BioIn 8, 9, 11, 12, 13, 14, 15, 16; BioNews 74; BkPepl; CelR, 90; ConTFT 1, 5, 12; CurBio 71; EncAFC; FilmEn; FilmgC; FunnyW; HalFC 80, 84, 88; IntDcF 1-3, 2-3; IntMPA 75, 76, 77, 78, 79, 80, 81, 82, 84, 86, 88, 92, 94, 96; IntWW 89, 91, 93; InWom SUP; ItaFilm; JoeFr; LegTOT; MotPP; MovMk; NewYTBE 73; NewYTBS 80; QDrFCA 92; VarWW 85; WhoAm 74, 76, 78, 80, 82, 84, 86, 88, 90, 92, 94, 95, 96, 97; WhoAmW 74, 83, 85, 87, 89, 91, 93, 95, 97; WhoCom; WhoEnt 92; WhoHol 92, A; WorAl; WorAlBi*

Haworth, Leland John
American. Physicist
Director, Brookhaven Nuclear Energy Laboratory, 1948-61.
b. Jul 11, 1904 in Flint, Michigan
d. Mar 5, 1979 in Port Jefferson, New York
Source: *AmMWSc 73P, 76P, 79; BioIn 2, 3, 6, 11, 12; BlueB 76; CurBio 50, 79; DcAmB S10; InSci; IntAu&W 77; IntWW 74, 75, 76, 77, 78, 79; NewYTBS 79; WhAm 7; WhoAm 74, 76, 78; WhoE 74*

Haworth, Ted
[Edward S Haworth]
American. Director
Won Oscar for movie *Sayonara,* 1958.
b. 1917 in Cleveland, Ohio
d. Feb 18, 1993 in Provo, Utah
Source: *HalFC 84, 88*

Haworth, Walter Norman, Sir
English. Chemist
Won Nobel Prize, 1937, for work on constitution of carbohydrates, vitamin C.
b. Mar 19, 1883 in Chorley, England
d. Mar 19, 1950 in Birmingham, England
Source: *AsBiEn; BioIn 14, 15, 19, 20; DcScB; InSci; WhE&EA; WhoNob, 90, 95; WorAl*

Hawthorne, Julian
American. Author
Wrote novel *Garth,* 1877, biographical *Hawthorne and His Circle,* 1903; son of Nathaniel.
b. Jun 22, 1846 in Boston, Massachusetts
d. Jul 14, 1934 in San Francisco, California
Source: *Alli SUP; AmAu&B; AmBi; ApCAB; BbD; BenetAL 91; BiD&SB; BioIn 4, 7, 9, 15, 17, 21; CarSB; CelCen; Chambr 3; ChhPo, S2; DcAmAu; DcAmB S1; DcBiA; DcCathB; DcEnA, A; DcEnL; DcNAA; EncMys; LinLib L; NatCAB 2, 25; OxCAmL 65, 83, 95; PenEncH; REnAL; ScF&FL 1; ScFEYrs, A; TwCA; TwCBDA; TwCLC 25; WhAm 1; WhLit; WhNAA; WhoHr&F*

Hawthorne, Nathaniel
American. Author
Wrote *The Scarlet Letter,* 1850; *The House of Seven Gables,* 1851.
b. Jul 4, 1804 in Salem, Massachusetts
d. May 19, 1864 in Plymouth, New Hampshire
Source: *Alli, SUP; AmAu; AmAu&B; AmBi; AmCulL; AmWr; ApCAB; AtlBL; Au&Arts 18; AuBYP 2S, 3; BbD; Benet 87, 96; BenetAL 91; BiAUS; BibAL; BiD&SB; BiDTran; BioIn 1, 2, 3, 4, 5, 6, 7, 8, 9, 10, 11, 12, 13, 14, 15, 16, 17, 18, 19, 20, 21; CamGEL; CamGLE; CamHAL; CarSB; CasWL; CelCen; Chambr 3; ChhPo S1, S2, S3; ChlBkCr; CnDAL; ColARen; CrtT 3, 4; CyAL 2; CyWA 58; DcAmAu; DcAmB; DcAmC; DcAmSR; DcArts; DcBiA; DcBiPP; DcEnA, A; DcEnL; DcLB 1, 74; DcLEL; DcNAA; DcPup; Dis&D; Drake; EncAAH; EncAB-H 1974, 1996; EncSF, 93; EncWW; EvLB; FamAYP; FilmgC; GrWrEL N; HalFC 80, 84, 88; HarEnUS; LegTOT; LinLib L, S; LuthC 75; MagSAmL; McGEWB; MemAm; MouLC 3; NatCAB 3; NewEOp 71; NewEScF; NewGrDA 86; NinCLC 2, 10, 17, 23, 39; Novels; OxCAmH; OxCAmL 65, 83, 95; OxCChiL; OxCEng 67, 85, 95; PenC AM; PenEncH; PeoHis; RAdv 1, 14, 13-1; RComAH; RComWL; REn; REnAL; RfGAmL 87, 94; RfGShF; ScF&FL 1; ScFEYrs; ScFSB; ShSCr 3; ShSWr; Str&VC; SupFW; TwCBDA; WebAB 74, 79; WebE&AL; WhAm HS; WhDW; WhoChL; WhoHr&F; WorAl; WorAlBi; WorLitC; WrChl; WrPh; YABC 2*

Hawtrey, Ralph George, Sir
English. Economist
Stated multiplier concept in economics; influenced Keynes.
b. Nov 22, 1879 in Slough, England
d. Mar 21, 1975 in London, England
Source: *BioIn 1; DcNaB 1971; GrEconS; IntWW 74; WhAm 6; WhE&EA; WhoEc 81, 86*

Hay, George Dewey
"Solomon Ol' Judge"
American. Radio Executive, Radio Performer
Founder of "Grand Ole Opry," longest running program on American radio.
b. Nov 9, 1895 in Attica, Indiana
d. May 9, 1968 in Virginia Beach, Virginia
Source: *BioIn 14; ConMus 3; EncFCWM 69, 83; HarEnCM 87; IlEncCM; NewGrDA 86*

Hay, George W
Canadian. Hockey Player
Left wing, 1926-34, mostly with Detroit; Hall of Fame, 1958.
b. Jan 10, 1898 in Listowel, Ontario, Canada
d. Jul 13, 1975
Source: *HocEn; WhoHcky 73*

Hay, Harry
American. Social Reformer
Organized the Mattachine Foundation, 1950.
b. Apr 7, 1912 in Worthing, England
Source: *BioIn 20; GayLesB*

Hay, John
American. Businessman
Co-founder, Celestial Seasonings, herbal tea co., 1971; sold to Kraft for $36 million, 1984.
b. 1945?
Source: *WhoAmL 87; WhoEmL 87; WhoWor 89*

Hay, John Milton
American. Statesman
Secretary of State, 1898-1905; devised Open Door policy toward China, 1899.
b. Oct 8, 1838 in Salem, Indiana
d. Jul 1, 1905 in Newbury, New Hampshire
Source: *AmAu; AmAu&B; BiDrUSE 71; CasWL; DcAmB; DcBiA; DcNAA; EncAB-H 1974, 1996; EvLB; IndAu 1816; OhA&B; OxCAmL 65; PenC AM; REn; REnAL; WhAm 1; WhAmP*

Hay, Oliver Perry
American. Paleontologist
Authority on Pleistocene vertebrata of North America; wrote *Fossil Turtles,* 1908.
b. May 22, 1846 in Saluda, Indiana
d. Nov 2, 1930 in Washington, District of Columbia
Source: *AmBi; BiDAmS; DcAmB; DcNAA; IndAu 1917; NatCAB 22; WhAm 1; WhNAA*

Haya de la Torre, Victor Raul
Peruvian. Political Leader
Founder, APRA party, 1920s; party was outlawed 1931-34, 1935-45.
b. Feb 22, 1895 in Trujillo, Peru
d. Aug 2, 1979 in Lima, Peru
Source: *BiDLAmC; BioIn 12, 16; ConAu 89; CurBio 42, 79, 79N; DcCPSAm; DcSpL; DcTwHis; IntWW 74, 75, 76, 77, 78; McGEWB; NewCol 75; NewYTBS 79; OxCSpan; WhoWor 74*

Hayakawa, S(amuel) I(chiye)
"Sleeping' Sam"
American. Educator, Politician
Wrote *Language in Thought and Action;* conservative Rep. senator from CA, 1977-83.
b. Jul 18, 1906 in Vancouver, British Columbia, Canada
d. Feb 27, 1992 in San Francisco, California
Source: *AmAu&B; AmMWSc 73S, 78S; AnObit 1992; BenetAL 91; BiDAmEd; BiDrUSC 89; BioIn 3, 4, 5, 8, 9, 10, 11, 13; BlueB 76; CngDr 77, 79, 81; ConAu 13R, 20NR, 137; CurBio 59, 92N; DrAS 74F, 78F, 82F; IntAu&W 77; IntWW 74, 75, 76, 77, 78, 79, 80, 81, 82, 83, 89, 91; IntYB 78, 79, 80, 81, 82; LEduc 74; News 92, 92-3; NotAsAm; REn; REnAL; TwCA SUP; WebAB 74, 79; WhAm 10; WhoAm 74, 76, 78, 80, 82, 84, 86, 88, 90; WhoAmP 77, 79, 81, 83, 85, 87, 89, 91; WhoGov 77; WhoWest 74; WhoWor 78, 80, 82; WorAl; WorAlBi; WrDr 76*

Hayakawa, Sessue (Kintaro)
Japanese. Actor
Oscar nominee for *Bridge on the River Kwai,* 1957.
b. Jun 10, 1886 in Chiba, Japan
d. Nov 23, 1974 in Tokyo, Japan
Source: *BioNews 74; CurBio 62, 74; Film 1; FilmgC; MotPP; MovMk; NewYTBE 73; OxCFilm; SilFlmP; TwYS; WhAm 6; WhoHol B; WhScrn 77*

Hayden, Carl Trumball
American. Politician
Dem. senator from AZ, 1927-69; credited with longest senatorial tenure.
b. Oct 2, 1877 in Tempe, Arizona
d. Jan 25, 1972 in Mesa, Arizona
Source: *BiDrAC; CurBio 51, 72; NewYTBE 72; WhAm 5, 6; WhAmP*

Hayden, Melissa
[Mildred Herman]
Canadian. Dancer
Dancer, NYC Ballet Co., 1950-73; wrote *M H: Off Stage and On,* 1961.
b. Apr 25, 1928 in Toronto, Ontario, Canada
Source: *BiDD; BioIn 3, 4, 6, 7, 9, 10, 11, 13; CanWW 70, 83; CurBio 55; InWom, SUP; LegTOT; NewYTBE 73; WhoAm 74; WhoAmW 58, 61, 64, 66, 70, 72, 74, 75; WhoHol A; WhoWor 74; WorAlBi*

Hayden, Mike
[John Michael Hayden]
American. Politician
Republican governor of KS, 1987-91, defeated by Joan Finney.
b. Mar 16, 1944 in Colby, Kansas
Source: *AlmAP 88; BiDrGov 1983, 1988; BioIn 17, 20; IntWW 89, 91, 93; WhoAm 84, 86, 88, 90; WhoAmP 85, 87, 89, 91, 93, 95; WhoGov 75, 77; WhoMW 88, 90; WhoWor 91*

Hayden, Robert Earl
American. Poet
Works include verse volume *Angle of Ascent: New and Selected Poems,* 1975.
b. Aug 4, 1913 in Detroit, Michigan
d. Feb 25, 1980 in Ann Arbor, Michigan
Source: *AmAu&B; BlkAWP; ChhPo S1, S2; ConAu 69, 97; ConLC 5, 9, 14; ConPo 70, 75; CroCAP; DcLEL 1940; DrAP 75; LivgBAA; NewYTBS 80; SelBAAu; SmATA 19, 26N; WhAm 7; WhoAm 76, 80; WrDr 76, 80*

Hayden, Russell
[Pate Lucid]
"Lucky"
American. Actor
Played Lucky Jenkins in *Hopalong Cassidy* western films.
b. Jun 12, 1912 in Chico, California
d. Jun 9, 1981 in Palm Springs, California
Source: *BioIn 8, 10, 12; FilmEn; FilmgC; ForYSC; HalFC 80, 84, 88; IntMPA 75, 76, 77, 78, 79, 80, 81; NewYTBS 81; What 5; WhoHol A; WhScrn 83*

Hayden, Sterling Relyea Walter
[John Hamilton; Stirling Hayden]
American. Actor, Author
Rugged character actor; best known for roles in *The Asphalt Jungle,* 1950; *Dr. Strangelove,* 1964; wrote of wanderlust, love of sea in popular novel *Voyage,* 1976.
b. Mar 26, 1916 in Montclair, New Jersey
d. May 23, 1986 in Sausalito, California
Source: *BiDFilm; ConAu 111, 119; CurBio 78; FilmgC; HalFC 84; HolP 40; IntMPA 86; MotPP; MovMk; OxCFilm; WhoAm 84; WhoHol A; WorEFlm*

Hayden, Tom
[The Chicago 7; Thomas Emmett Hayden]
American. Political Activist, Politician
Co-founded SDS (Students for Democratic Society), 1961; liberal Dem. CA assembly man, 1982-92; member, CA state senate, 1992—.
b. Dec 11, 1939 in Royal Oak, Michigan
Source: *AmAu&B; AmDec 1960; AmSocL; BioIn 13, 16; ConAu 107; EncWB; LegTOT; LNinSix; PolProf NF; WhoAm 82, 84, 86, 88, 90, 95, 96, 97; WhoAmP 83, 85, 87, 89, 91, 93, 95; WhoUSWr 88; WhoWest 89, 92, 94; WhoWrEP 89, 92, 95; WorAlBi; WrDr 90, 92, 94, 96*

Haydn, Hiram Collins
American. Editor, Author
Novels include *Hands of Esau,* 1962; edited literary series.
b. Nov 3, 1907 in Cleveland, Ohio
d. Dec 2, 1973 in Vineyard Haven, Massachusetts
Source: *AmAu&B; AmNov; Au&Wr 71; CnDAL; ConAu 45, P-1; ConNov 72; DcLEL 1940; NewYTBE 73; OhA&B; OxCAmL 65; REnAL; TwCA SUP; WhAm 6; WhoWor 74*

Haydn, Joseph
[Franz Joseph Haydn]
Austrian. Composer
Composed *Surprise Symphony,* 1791; influenced work of Beethoven, Mozart.
b. Mar 31, 1732 in Rohrau, Austria
d. May 31, 1809 in Vienna, Austria
Source: *AtlBL; Baker 78, 84; Benet 87, 96; BioIn 1, 2, 3, 4, 5, 6, 7, 8, 9, 10, 11, 12, 13, 14, 16, 17, 18, 20, 21; BlkwCE; BriBkM 80; CelCen; CmOp; CmpBCM; CnOxB; DcArts; DcBiPP; DcCathB; DcCom 77; DcCom&M 79; DcPup; Dis&D; EncEnl; GrComp; IntDcOp; LegTOT; LinLib S; LuthC 75; McGEWB; MetOEnc; MusMk; NewAmDM; NewC; NewCol 75; NewEOp 71; NewGrDM 80; NewOxM; OxCEng 85; OxCGer 76; OxCMus; OxDcOp; PenDiMP A; RAdv 14, 13-3; REn; WhDW; WorAl; WorAlBi*

Haydn, Richard
English. Actor, Director
Starred in *Please Don't Eat the Daisies,* 1960; *The Sound of Music,* 1965.
b. 1905 in London, England
d. Apr 25, 1985 in Pacific Palisades, California
Source: *AnObit 1985; BioIn 15; ConAu 115; EncAFC; FilmEn; FilmgC; ForYSC; HalFC 80, 84, 88; IntMPA 82; MovMk; VarWW 85; Vers B; WhoAm 74; WhoHol A; WorEFlm*

Haydon, Benjamin Robert
English. Artist, Author
Painted portraits, Biblical, historical scenes; admired by many prominent Romant ics; wrote witty autobiography, 1853.
b. Jan 26, 1786 in Plymouth, England
d. Jun 22, 1846 in London, England

Source: *Alli; BioIn 1, 2, 3, 5, 6, 11, 13, 14, 16, 17, 18; BritAu 19; CamGEL; CamGLE; CasWL; CelCen; ChhPo, S1; ClaDrA; DcArts; DcBiPP; DcBrWA; DcLB 110; DcLEL; DcNaB; DcPup; DcVicP, 2; McGDA; NewC; NewCBEL; NewCol 75; OxCArt; OxCEng 67, 85, 95; OxDcArt; REn*

Haydon, Julie
[Donella Donaldson]
American. Actor
Broadway roles include *The Glass Menagerie,* 1940s; widow of George Jean Nathan.
b. Jun 10, 1910 in Oak Park, Illinois
d. Dec 24, 1994 in La Crosse, Wisconsin
Source: *BiE&WWA; BioIn 1, 12, 16, 20; ConTFT 1, 15; FilmEn; ForYSC; InWom SUP; NewYTBS 80; NotNAT; NotWoAT; OxCAmT 84; PlP&P; ThFT; WhoHol 92, A; WhoThe 77A; WhThe*

Hayek, Friedrich August von
German. Economist, Author
Shared Nobel Prize in economics, 1974.
b. May 8, 1899 in Vienna, Austria
d. Mar 23, 1992 in Freiburg, Germany
Source: *AnObit 1992; BioIn 4, 6, 10, 11, 12, 13, 16; BlueB 76; ConAu 93; CurBio 45; DcTwHis; IntEnSS 79; IntWW 74, 75, 76, 77, 78, 83, 91; LngCTC; MajTwCW; NewCBEL; OxCPhil; RAdv 14; ThTwC 87; TwCA SUP; WhAm 10; WhE&EA; Who 74, 82, 85, 92; WhoAm 74; WhoEc 86; WhoNob, 90, 95; WhoWor 74, 76, 82, 91; WorAl; WorAlBi; WrDr 76, 80, 82, 84, 86, 88, 90*

Hayes, Alfred
American. Banker
Pres., Federal Reserve Bank, NY, 1956-75.
b. Jul 4, 1910 in Ithaca, New York
d. Oct 22, 1989 in New Canaan, Connecticut
Source: *BioIn 4, 7, 16, 17; BlueB 76; CurBio 90N; IntWW 74, 75, 76, 77, 78, 79, 80, 81, 82, 83; IntYB 78, 79, 80, 81, 82; St&PR 75; WhAm 10; WhoAm 74, 76, 78, 80, 82, 84*

Hayes, Alfred
American. Author
Novels include *Shadow of Heaven,* 1947; *The Big Time,* 1944.
b. Apr 17, 1911 in London, England
d. Aug 14, 1985 in Sherman Oaks, California
Source: *AmAu&B; AmNov; AnObit 1985; BenetAL 91; BioIn 4; ConAu 106, 117; ModAL; OxCAmL 65, 83, 95; REn; REnAL; TwCA SUP; WhoAm 74*

Hayes, Bob
[Robert Lee Hayes]
"World's Fastest Human"
American. Track Athlete, Football Player
Sprinter; won gold medal, 1964 Olympics; receiver in NFL, 1965-75, mostly with Dallas.
b. Dec 20, 1942 in Jacksonville, Florida
Source: *AfrAmSG; BiDAmSp OS; BioIn 7, 8, 9, 10, 17, 19, 21; BlkOlyM; CurBio 66; LegTOT; NegAl 76, 83, 89; WhoSpor; WhoTr&F 73*

Hayes, Carlton Joseph Huntley
American. Historian, Educator
Specialist in history of modern naturalism: *Naturalism: A Religion,* 1960.
b. May 16, 1882 in Afton, New York
d. Sep 3, 1964 in Afton, New York
Source: *AmAu&B; AmLY; BiDAmEd; BioIn 1, 2, 4, 7, 11, 12, 16; CathA 1930; ConAu 1R; DcAmB S7; LngCTC; REnAL; TwCA SUP; WhAm 4; WhNAA*

Hayes, Elvin Ernest
"Big E"
American. Basketball Player
Three-time all-star center, 1968-84, mostly with Washington; led NBA in scoring, 1969, in rebounding, 1970, 1974.
b. Nov 17, 1945 in Rayville, Louisiana
Source: *BiDAmSp BK; BioIn 14; ConAu 111; InB&W 85; NewYTBS 85; OfNBA 87; WhoAm 82, 84; WhoBbl 73; WhoBlA 85, 90, 92; WorAlBi*

Hayes, Gabby
[George Francis Hayes]
American. Actor
Comic sidekick in over 200 westerns.
b. May 7, 1885 in Wellsville, New York
d. Feb 9, 1969 in Burbank, California
Source: *BiE&WWA; CmMov; DcAmB S8; FilmgC; LegTOT; MotPP; MovMk; OxCFilm; PlP&P; Vers B; WhoHol B; WhScrn 74, 77; WorAl; WorAlBi*

Hayes, Helen
[Helen Hayes Brown; Mrs. Charles MacArthur]
"First Lady of the American Theater"
American. Actor
Won Oscars for *The Sin of Madelon Claudet,* 1931; *Airport,* 1970; adoptive mother of James MacArthur.
b. Oct 10, 1900 in Washington, District of Columbia
d. Mar 17, 1993 in Nyack, New York
Source: *AmCulL; AnObit 1993; BiDFilm 94; BiE&WWA; BioAmW; BioIn 1, 2, 3, 4, 5, 6, 7, 8, 9, 10, 11, 12, 14, 15, 16, 17, 18, 19, 20; BlueB 76; CamGWoT; CelR, 90; CnThe; ConAu 138, 140; ContDcW 89; ConTFT 11; CurBio 42, 93N; EncAB-H 1996; EncWB; EncWT; Ent; FacFETw; FamA&A; Film 1, 2; FilmEn; FilmgC; ForYSC; GoodHs; GrLiveH; HalFC 80, 84, 88; IntDcT 3; IntDcWB; IntMPA 92, 94; IntWW 74, 75, 76, 77, 78, 79, 80, 81, 82, 83, 89, 91; InWom, SUP; LegTOT; LibW; LinLib L, S; MGM; MovMk; News 93; NewYTBS 83, 93; NotNAT, A; NotWoAT; OxCAmH; OxCAmL 65; OxCAmT 84; OxCFilm; OxCThe 67, 83; PlP&P; RadStar; REn; SaTiSS; ThFT; VarWW 85; WebAB 74, 79; WhAm 11; Who 74, 82, 83, 85, 88, 90, 92; WhoAm 74, 76, 78, 80, 84, 86, 88, 90, 92; WhoAmW 58, 61, 64, 66, 68, 70, 72, 74, 75, 77, 83, 85, 87, 89, 91, 93; WhoE 74; WhoEnt 92; WhoHol 92, A; WhoThe 72, 77, 81; WhoWor 74, 78; WorAl; WorAlBi; WorEFlm*

Hayes, Ira Hamilton
American. Soldier
One of the Marines who helped raise the US flag on Mount Suribachi during the battle of Iwo Jima.
b. Jan 12, 1923 in Sacaton, Arizona
d. Jan 24, 1955 in Arizona
Source: *EncNAB; NotNaAm*

Hayes, Isaac
"Black Moses"
American. Musician, Songwriter
Won Grammy, Oscar for score of *Shaft,* 1971; rhythm, blues vocalist.
b. Aug 20, 1942 in Covington, Tennessee
Source: *AfrAmAl 6; Baker 84; BiDAfM; BiDAmM; BiDJaz; BioIn 8, 9, 10, 12, 15; BioNews 74; CelR; ConAmC 76, 82; ConMus 10; CurBio 72; DrBlPA, 90; Ebony 1; EncJzS; EncPR&S 89; EncRkSt; HarEnR 86; IlEncBM 82; InB&W 80, 85; IntMPA 96; LegTOT; NewAmDM; NewGrDA 86; NewYTBE 72; OxCPMus; PenEncP; RkOn 78; SoulM; VarWW 85; WhoAfA 96; WhoAm 74, 76, 78, 80, 82, 84, 86, 88, 90, 92, 94, 95, 96, 97; WhoBlA 75, 77, 80, 85, 88, 90, 92, 94; WhoEnt 92; WhoHol 92, A; WorAl; WorAlBi*

Hayes, Isaac Israel
American. Explorer
Led Arctic expeditions to prove existence of navigable open seas around North Pole, 1860s; wrote several books of experiences: *The Land of Desolation,* 1871.
b. Mar 5, 1832 in Chester County, Pennsylvania
d. Dec 17, 1881 in New York, New York
Source: *Alli SUP; AmAu&B; AmBi; ApCAB; BbD; BiD&SB; BiInAmS; BioIn 1; DcAmAu; DcAmB; DcAmMeB; DcBiPP; DcCanB 11; DcNAA; Drake; HarEnUS; NatCAB 3; OxCCan; OxCShps; REnAL; TwCBDA; WhAm HS; WhWE*

Hayes, James C.
American. Politician
Mayor of Fairbanks, AK, 1992—; first black to be elected a mayor in that state.
b. May 25, 1946 in Sacramento, California
Source: *ConBlB 10*

Hayes, John Michael
American. Screenwriter
Won awards for scripts for *Rear Window,* 1954; *To Catch a Thief,* 1955.
b. May 11, 1919 in Worcester, Massachusetts

Source: *BioIn 14; ConAu 108; DcLB 26; FilmEn; FilmgC; HalFC 80, 84, 88; IntDcF 1-4, 2-4; IntMPA 75, 76, 77, 78, 79, 80, 81, 82, 84, 86, 88, 92, 94, 96; VarWW 85; WhoMW 90; WorEFlm*

Hayes, Lester
American. Football Player
Five-time all-pro cornerback, Oakland/ LA Raiders, 1977-86; led NFL in interceptions, 1980.
b. Jan 22, 1955 in Houston, Texas
Source: *BioIn 12; FootReg 87; NewYTBS 81; WhoAfA 96; WhoAm 86, 88; WhoBlA 88, 90, 92, 94*

Hayes, Lucy Webb
[Mrs. Rutherford B Hayes]
"Lemonade Lucy"
American. First Lady
First president's wife to graduate from college; refused to serve alcohol at White House.
b. Aug 28, 1831 in Chillicothe, Ohio
d. Jun 25, 1889 in Fremont, Ohio
Source: *AmWom; ApCAB; BioAmW; BioIn 14, 16, 17; GoodHs; InWom; NatCAB 3; NotAW; TwCBDA; WhAm HS*

Hayes, Patrick Joseph, Cardinal
American. Religious Leader
Archbishop of NY, 1919-38.
b. Nov 20, 1867 in New York, New York
d. Sep 4, 1938 in Monticello, New York
Source: *AmBi; ApCAB X; BioIn 1, 4, 6, 8; DcAmB S2; DcCathB; LinLib S; McGEWB; NatCAB 16; RelLAm 91; WhAm 1*

Hayes, Peter Lind
American. Entertainer
With wife, Mary Healy, popular TV, radio personality, 1950s; hosted TV series "Wh en Television Was Live," 1975.
b. Jun 25, 1915 in San Francisco, California
Source: *AmAu&B; ASCAP 66, 80; BiE&WWA; BioIn 1, 2, 3, 4, 5; ConTFT 1; CurBio 59; ForYSC; IntMPA 77, 80, 84, 86, 88, 92, 94, 96; NotNAT; VarWW 85; WhoAm 74, 76, 78, 80, 82, 84, 86, 88, 90, 92, 94, 95, 96, 97; WhoHol 92, A*

Hayes, Robert Michael
American. Lawyer, Social Reformer
Counsel, Nat. Coalition for the Homeless, 1982-89 whose lawsuits gained rights for the homeless.
b. Nov 12, 1952 in New York, New York
Source: *CurBio 89; St&PR 96, 97*

Hayes, Roland
American. Opera Singer
Tenor who sang arias, folk songs, 1920s-40s; pioneered black singers on concert stage.
b. Jun 3, 1887 in Curryville, Georgia
d. Dec 31, 1976 in Boston, Massachusetts
Source: *AfrAmAl 6; Baker 78, 84, 92; BiDAfM; BiDAmM; BioIn 1, 3, 4, 5, 6, 8, 9, 10, 11, 18, 19; BriBkM 80; ConBlB 4; ConMus 13; CurBio 77, 77N; DcAfAmP; DcTwCCu 5; DrBlPA, 90; EncAACR; LinLib S; MusSN; NegAl 76, 83, 89; NewAmDM; NewGrDA 86; NewGrDM 80; PenDiMP; WebAB 74, 79; WhAm 7; WhoAm 74; WhoBlA 75*

Hayes, Rutherford B(irchard)
American. US President
Rep., 19th pres., 1877-81; won by one vote in newly created electoral college; ended Reconstruction period in South.
b. Oct 4, 1822 in Delaware, Ohio
d. Jan 17, 1893 in Fremont, Ohio
Source: *AmAu&B; AmBi; AmPolLe; ApCAB; BiAUS; BiDrAC; BiDrGov 1789; BiDrUSC 89; BiDrUSE 71, 89; BioIn 1, 2, 3, 4, 5, 6, 7, 8, 9, 10, 11, 12, 13; CelCen; CivWDc; CyAG; DcAmB; DcBiPP A; Drake; EncAAH; EncAB-H 1974, 1996; EncSoH; FacPr 89, 93; HarEnUS; HealPre; LinLib L, S; McGEWB; NatCAB 3; OhA&B; OxCAmH; OxCAmL 65, 83; REnAL; TwCBDA; WebAB 74, 79; WhAm HS; WhAmP; WhCiWar; WhDW; WorAl*

Hayes, Woody
[Wayne Woodrow Hayes]
American. Football Coach
Head coach, Ohio State, 1951-79; compiled 238-72-10 record; won two national championships.
b. Feb 14, 1913 in Clifton, Ohio
d. Mar 12, 1987 in Upper Arlington, Ohio
Source: *AnObit 1987; BiDAmSp FB; BioIn 4, 6, 8, 9, 10, 11, 12, 19; BioNews 75; CelR; ConAu 121; ConNews 87-2; CurBio 75, 87, 87N; LegTOT; NewYTBS 74; WhoAm 76, 78; WhoSpor; WorAl*

Hayford, John Fillmore
American. Engineer
Civil engineer, geodesist; proposed theory of isostasy.
b. May 19, 1868 in Rouses Point, New York
d. Mar 10, 1925 in Evanston, Illinois
Source: *DcAmB; DcNAA; DcScB; InSci; NatCAB 14; WhAm 1*

Hayman, Richard
American. Conductor
Led pop concerts with Detroit Symphony, 1970-90; St. Louis Symphony, 1976-90.
b. Mar 27, 1920 in Cambridge, Massachusetts
Source: *ASCAP 66, 80; Baker 84; CmpEPM; IntWWM 90; NewGrDA 86; RkOn 74; WhoAm 90; WhoEnt 92*

Haymes, Dick
[Richard Haymes]
American. Singer
Star film vocalist noted for mellow voice, 1940s; rivaled by Crosby, Sinatra; hosted radio show with Helen Forrest, sang "Little White Lies."
b. Sep 13, 1917 in Buenos Aires, Argentina
d. Mar 28, 1980 in Los Angeles, California
Source: *CmpEPM; FilmgC; HolP 40; IntMPA 77; MotPP; NewYTBS 80; WhoHol A*

Hayne, Robert Young
American. Politician
A leader of states' rights; debated Daniel Webster in Senate debates that delineated differences between North and South, 1830.
b. Nov 10, 1791 in Colleton District, South Carolina
d. Sep 24, 1839 in Asheville, North Carolina
Source: *AmBi; AmPolLe; ApCAB; BiAUS; BiDrAC; BiDrGov 1789; BiDrUSC 89; BioIn 9, 13; DcAmB; Drake; EncAAH; EncAB-H 1974; EncSoH; HarEnUS; LinLib S; McGEWB; NatCAB 3, 12; NewCol 75; OxCAmH; TwCBDA; WebAB 74, 79; WhAm HS; WhAmP*

Haynes, Elwood
American. Inventor
Built one of America's first successful horseless carriages, 1893; patented stainless steel, 1919.
b. Oct 14, 1857 in Portland, Indiana
d. Apr 13, 1925 in Kokomo, Indiana
Source: *AmBi; ApCAB X; EncABHB 4; FacFETw; IndAu 1967; LegTOT; NatCAB 13, 25; OxCAmH; WhAm 1*

Haynes, George Edmund
American. Sociologist
Wrote *The Clinical Approach to Race Relations*, 1946; charter member, NAACP.
b. May 11, 1880 in Pine Bluff, Arkansas
d. Jan 8, 1960 in New York, New York
Source: *AmAu&B; BiDSocW; BioIn 1, 5, 6, 17, 20; ConBlB 8; DcAmB S6; DcAmNB; EncAACR; InB&W 85; NatCAB 44; WhAm 3; WhNAA; WhoColR; WorAl*

Haynes, Lloyd
[Samuel Lloyd Haynes]
American. Actor
Best known portrayal of history teacher Pete Dixon on TV series "Room 222," 1969-7 4.
b. Oct 19, 1935 in South Bend, Indiana
d. Dec 31, 1986 in Coronado, California
Source: *InB&W 80; WhoHol A*

Haynes, Marques Oreole
American. Basketball Player
Guard, Harlem Globetrotters, 1947-53; known as world's greatest dribbler.
b. Mar 10, 1926 in Sand Spring, Oklahoma
Source: *BiDAmSp BK; BioIn 10; InB&W 85; NewYTBE 73; WhoBbl 73*

Haynie, Hugh
American. Cartoonist
Liberal political cartoonist, *Louisville Courier-Journal;* syndicated with Los Angeles Times, 1958—.
b. Feb 6, 1927 in Reedville, Virginia
Source: *BlueB 76; ConAu 121; ConGrA 3; EncTwCJ; WhoAm 74, 76, 78, 80, 82, 84, 86, 97; WhoAmA 76, 78, 80, 82, 84, 86, 89, 91, 93; WhoSSW 73, 75; WhoWor 84, 87, 89; WorECar*

Haynie, Sandra
American. Golfer
Turned pro, 1961; won US Women's Open, 1974.
b. Jun 4, 1943 in Fort Worth, Texas
Source: *BiDAmSp Sup; BioIn 10, 13; ConAu 121; LegTOT; NewYTBS 82; WhoGolf*

Haynsworth, Clement Furman, Jr.
American. Judge
Served on US Court of Appeals, 1957-64; chief justice, 1964-81.
b. Oct 30, 1912 in Greenville, South Carolina
Source: *BiDFedJ; BioIn 8, 9, 10, 12, 15, 16; NatCAB 12; NewYTBS 89; OxCSupC; PolProf NF; WhAm 10; WhoAm 74, 76, 78, 80, 82, 84, 86, 88; WhoAmL 78, 79, 85, 90; WhoAmP 73, 75, 77; WhoGov 72, 75, 77; WhoSSW 73, 78, 80, 82, 84, 88*

Hays, Brooks
American. Politician, Author
Congressman from AR; tried to mediate Little Rock's integration crisis, 1950s.
b. Aug 9, 1898 in Russellville, Arkansas
d. Oct 11, 1981 in Chevy Chase, Maryland
Source: *AnObit 1981; CurBio 58, 82, 82N; IntAu&W 77; IntWW 74, 75, 76, 77, 78, 79, 80, 81; PolProf E; WhAm 8; WhoAm 74, 76, 78, 80, 82; WhoWor 76, 78; WrDr 76, 80, 82, 84*

Hays, Lee
[The Weavers]
American. Singer, Songwriter
Folk singer with The Weavers, 1948-63; co-wrote "If Had a Hammer," with Pete Seeger.
b. 1914 in Little Rock, Arkansas
d. Aug 26, 1981 in North Tarrytown, New York
Source: *AnObit 1981; Baker 84, 92; BiDAmM; BioIn 12, 14, 16; EncFCWM 69, 83; NewYTBS 81*

Hays, Robert
American. Actor
Starred in *Airplane!,* 1980; *Airplane II,* 1982.
b. Jul 24, 1947 in Bethesda, Maryland
Source: *BioIn 16; ConTFT 6; DrAPF 89, 91; EncAFC; FolkA 87; HalFC 84; IntMPA 84, 86, 88, 92, 94, 96; LegTOT; VarWW 85; WhoAm 88, 92; WhoEnt 92; WorAlBi*

Hays, Wayne Levere
American. Politician
Congressman who retired from office after involvement with Elizabeth Ray, 1976.
b. Jun 13, 1911 in Bannock, Ohio
Source: *BiDrAC; BiDrUSC 89; BioIn 3, 7, 10, 11, 12, 16, 17; BioNews 74; CngDr 74; CurBio 74, 89N; NewYTBS 89; PolProf E, K, NF; WhAm 9; WhoAm 74, 76; WhoAmP 85, 87; WhoFI 83; WhoGov 75; WhoMW 76*

Hays, Will Harrison
American. Lawyer
Pres., MPPDA; screen censor, known for "Purity Seal" which was needed for film dis tribution, 1921-45.
b. Nov 5, 1879 in Sullivan, Indiana
d. Mar 7, 1954 in Sullivan, Indiana
Source: *BioIn 2, 3, 4, 10, 12, 13; CurBio 43, 54; DcAmB S5; DcFM; FilmgC; IndAu 1917; NatCAB 61; OxCFilm; WhAm 3; WorEFlm*

Hayter, Stanley William
English. Artist
Pioneer of graphic art; influenced Picasso, Miro; founded print shop, 1927.
b. Dec 27, 1901 in London, England
d. May 4, 1988 in Paris, France
Source: *BioIn 2, 5, 6, 10, 11, 13, 14, 15, 16; ConArt 77, 83, 89, 96; ConAu 125; CurBio 45, 88, 88N; DcBrAr 1; DcNaB 1986; FacFETw; IntWW 74, 75, 76, 77, 78, 79, 80, 81, 82, 83; McGDA; NewYTBS 88; OxCTwCA; PhDcTCA 77; TwCPaSc; Who 74, 82, 83, 85, 88; WhoAmA 73; WhoArt 80, 82, 84; WhoWor 74, 76, 78; WorArt 1950*

Hayton, Lennie
[Leonard George Hayton]
American. Composer, Conductor
Noted pianist-arranger, 1920s-60s; MGM music director, 1940-53; once wed to singer Lena Horne.
b. Feb 13, 1908 in New York, New York
d. Apr 24, 1971 in Palm Springs, California
Source: *ASCAP 66, 80; Baker 78, 84, 92; BiDAmM; BiDJaz; BioIn 9; CmMov; CmpEPM; ConAmC 76, 82; EncJzS; EncJzS; HalFC 84, 88; NewGrDJ 88, 94; NewYTBE 71; PenEncP; RadStar; WhoJazz 72*

Hayward, Brooke
American. Author, Actor
Daughter of Leland, Margaret Sullavan; wrote *Haywire,* 1977.
b. Jul 5, 1937 in Los Angeles, California
Source: *BioIn 5, 11, 12, 15; BkPepl; ConAu 81; InWom SUP; NewYTBS 77; WhoHol 92*

Hayward, John Davy
English. Editor
Editorial adviser to Cresset Press; editorial director of *Book Collector.*
b. Feb 2, 1905 in London, England
d. Sep 17, 1965 in Chelsea, England
Source: *DcLEL; DcNaB 1961; GrBr; LngCTC; WhLit*

Hayward, Leland
American. Producer
Top Hollywood agent, 1940s; produced Broadway hits *South Pacific,* 1949; *Sound of Music,* 1959.
b. Sep 13, 1902 in Nebraska City, Nebraska
d. Mar 18, 1971 in Yorktown Heights, New York
Source: *BiE&WWA; BioIn 1, 2, 4, 9, 11, 13; CamGWoT; CurBio 49, 71, 71N; DcAmB S9; EncMT; FilmEn; FilmgC; HalFC 80, 84, 88; InSci; LegTOT; LesBEnT; NatCAB 62; NewYTBE 71; NewYTET; NotNAT B; ObitOF 79; OxCAmT 84; WhoThe 72; WhThe; WorAl; WorAlBi*

Hayward, Louis
[Seafield Grant]
American. Actor
Played swashbucklers in 1940s adventure films; last film was *Terror in the Wax Museum,* 1973.
b. Mar 19, 1909 in Johannesburg, South Africa
d. Feb 21, 1985 in Palm Springs, California
Source: *AnObit 1985, 80, 84; ItaFilm; MotPP; MovMk; NewYTBS 85; VarWW 85; What 5; WhoHol A; WhoHrs 80; WorEFlm*

Hayward, Susan
[Edythe Marrener]
American. Actor
Won Oscar for *I Want to Live,* 1958.
b. Jun 30, 1917 in New York, New York
d. Mar 14, 1975 in Beverly Hills, California
Source: *BiDFilm; CmMov; CurBio 53; FilmgC; IntMPA 75; InWom; MotPP; MovMk; NotAW MOD; OxCFilm; ThFT; WhAm 6; WhoAm 74; WhScrn 77; WorAlBi; WorEFlm*

Haywood, Eliza
English. Author
Popular scandalous novels include *Memoirs of a Certain Island,* 1725.
b. 1693?
d. Feb 25, 1756 in London, England
Source: *ArtclWW 2; BiDEWW; BioIn 9, 11, 12; BlkwCE; BlmGEL; BritAu; CamGLE; CasWL; ContDcW 89; DcBrAmW; DcLB 39; DcLEL; DcNaB; EncEnl; EncSF; IntDcWB; InWom; LitC 1; NewCol 75; OxCEng 85, 95; RfGEnL 91; ScF&FL 1; WomFir*

Haywood, Spencer
American. Basketball Player
Two-time all-star forward-center, 1969-83, with six NBA teams; member US Olympic team, 1968.
b. Apr 22, 1949 in Silver City, Mississippi
Source: *BasBi; BiDAmSp BK; BioIn 8, 9, 10, 16; BlkOlyM; InB&W 80, 85;*

NewYTBS 75, 76; OfNBA 87; WhoAfA 96; WhoBbl 73; WhoBlA 77, 80, 85, 90, 92, 94

Haywood, William Dudley
"Big Bill Haywood"
American. Labor Union Official
Helped organize IWW in the early 1900s.
b. Feb 4, 1869 in Salt Lake City, Utah
d. May 18, 1928 in Moscow, Union of Soviet Socialist Republics
Source: *AmBi; AmRef; AmSocL; BenetAL 91; BiDAmL; BiDAmLf; BiDAmLL; BiDMarx; BioIn 1, 2, 4, 6, 7, 8, 9, 11, 12, 13, 15, 16, 19; DcAmB; DcNAA; EncAB-H 1974, 1996; EncAL; EncRev; McGEWB; PeoHis; RComAH; REnAW; WebAB 74, 79; WhAm 4, HSA*

Hayworth, Rita
[Margarita Carmen Cansino]
"The Love Goddess"
American. Actor
Made 60 films in 37 yrs; known for WW II pinup photo in *Life* mag., 1941.
b. Oct 17, 1918 in New York, New York
d. May 14, 1987 in New York, New York
Source: *AnObit 1987; BiDD; BiDFilm, 81, 94; BioAmW; BioIn 1, 2, 4, 5, 6, 9, 10, 11, 13, 15, 16, 17, 18, 21; BlueB 76; CmMov; ConNews 87-3; ContDcW 89; CurBio 60, 87, 87N; DcArts; DcHiB; FacFETw; FilmEn; FilmgC; ForYSC; GangFlm; GrLiveH; HalFC 80, 84, 88; HispAmA; IntDcF 1-3, 2-3; IntDcWB; IntMPA 86; InWom SUP; ItaFilm; LegTOT; MotPP; MovMk; NewYTBS 87; NotHsAW 93; OxCFilm; ThFT; VarWW 85; WhAm 9; WhoAm 74, 76, 78, 80, 82; WhoAmW 66, 68, 70, 72, 74; WomWMM; WorAl; WorAlBi; WorEFlm*

Hazam, Lou(is J)
American. Producer
Pioneer in producing TV documentaries, 1950s.
b. Jan 3, 1911 in Norwich, Connecticut
d. Sep 6, 1983 in Silver Spring, Maryland
Source: *AnObit 1983; BioIn 13; ConAu 110; LesBEnT; NewYTBS 83; NewYTET*

Hazan, Marcella Maddalena
Italian. Author
Wrote *The Classic Italian Cookbook,* 1973.
b. Apr 15, 1924? in Cesenatico, Italy
Source: *BioIn 11, 15; ConAu 116; IntAu&W 89; WhoAm 80, 82, 84, 86, 88, 90, 92, 94, 95, 96, 97; WhoAmW 95, 97*

Hazeltine, (Louis) Alan
American. Inventor, Physicist
Aided commercial development of radio by inventing neutrodyne circuit.
b. Aug 7, 1886 in Morristown, New Jersey
d. May 24, 1964 in Maplewood, New Jersey
Source: *BioIn 1, 6, 7, 12; InSci; WhAm 4, 7*

Hazelton, Nika
American. Author
Author of 30 cookbooks, among them *International Cookbook,* 1967 which became a standard for serious cooks.
b. 1908? in Rome, Italy
d. Apr 14, 1992 in New York, New York
Source: *BioIn 13, 16*

Hazelwood, Joe
[Joseph J Hazelwood]
American. Criminal
Captain, Exxon Valdez, convicted of negligence after the tanker struck a reef in Prince William Sound, AK, dumping 11 million gallons of oil.
Source: *BioIn 16*

Hazelwood, Lee
American. Singer, Songwriter
Best known for duets with Nancy Sinatra: "Jackson," 1967; "Some Velvet Morning," 1968.
b. Jul 9, 1929 in Mannford, Oklahoma
Source: *BiDAmM; OxCPMus; RolSEnR 83*

Hazen, William Babcock
American. Military Leader
Army's chief signal officer, 1880; organized Adolphus Greely's polar expedition, 1881; court-martialed for criticizing superiors, 1885.
b. Sep 27, 1830 in West Hartford, Vermont
d. Jan 16, 1887 in Washington, District of Columbia
Source: *Alli SUP; AmBi; ApCAB; BiInAmS; BioIn 7, 10; CivWDc; DcAmAu; DcAmB; DcNAA; Drake; HarEnUS; NatCAB 3; NewCol 75; OhA&B; TwCBDA; WebAMB; WhAm HS; WhCiWar; WhNaAH*

Hazlitt, William
English. Author
Wrote *Characters of Shakespeare's Plays,* 1817; *Lectures on the English Poets,* 1818.
b. Apr 10, 1778 in Maidstone, England
d. Sep 18, 1830 in London, England
Source: *Alli; AtlBL; Benet 87, 96; BiD&SB; BiDLA; BioIn 1, 2, 3, 4, 5, 6, 7, 8, 9, 10, 11, 12, 13, 14, 17; BlkwCE; BlmGEL; BritAu 19; BritWr 4; CamGEL; CamGLE; CamGWoT; CasWL; CelCen; Chambr 3; ChhPo S3; CrtT 2, 4; CyWA 58; DcArts; DcBiPP; DcEnA, A; DcEnL; DcEuL; DcLB 110, 158; DcLEL; DcNaB; DcPup; EncWT; EvLB; GrWrEL N; LegTOT; LiJour; LinLib L, S; LngCEL; McGEWB; MouLC 3; NewC; NewCBEL; NinCLC 29; NotNAT A, B; OxCEng 67, 85, 95; OxCThe 67, 83; OxDcArt; PenC ENG; RAdv 1, 14, 13-1; RComWL; REn; RfGEnL 91; WebE&AL; WhDW*

Hazzard, Shirley
Australian. Author
Novelist and short-story writer; best-seller *The Transit of Venus,* 1980, won the Nat. Book Critics Circle Award in 1981.
b. Jan 30, 1931 in Sydney, Australia
Source: *AmAu&B; ArtclWW 2; Au&Wr 71; AuLitCr; AuWomWr; BenetAL 91; BioIn 12, 13, 14, 16, 17; BlmGWL; CamGLE; ConAu 4NR, 9R; ConLC 18; ConNov 72, 76, 82, 86, 91, 96; CurBio 91; DcLB Y82B; DcLEL 1940; DrAF 76; DrAPF 80; FemiCLE; IntAu&W 76, 82, 89, 91, 93; IntLitE; IntWW 89, 91, 93; InWom SUP; MajTwCW; ModWoWr; NewYTBS 76, 80, 82; Novels; OxCAmL 83, 95; OxCAusL; RAdv 14; RGTwCWr; WhoAm 74, 76, 78, 80, 82, 84, 86, 88, 90, 92, 94, 95, 96, 97; WhoAmW 70, 72, 74, 75, 83, 85, 87, 89, 91, 93, 95, 97; WhoUSWr 88; WhoWrEP 89, 92, 95; WorAu 1970; WrDr 76, 80, 82, 84, 86, 88, 90, 92, 94, 96*

Head, Bessie Emery
South African. Author
Exiled from S Africa; wrote *Maru,* 1971; *A Question of Power,* 197 3.
b. Jul 6, 1937 in Pietermaritzburg, South Africa
d. Apr 17, 1986 in Serowe, Botswana
Source: *AfSS 82; ConNov 82; DcLEL 1940; WrDr 84*

Head, Edith
American. Fashion Designer
Leading Hollywood designer with 1,000 screen credits; dressed many stars; nomina ted for 34 Oscars, won eight.
b. Oct 28, 1907 in San Bernardino, California
d. Oct 24, 1981 in Hollywood, California
Source: *BioIn 1, 2, 4, 5, 10; CelR; CmCal; ContDcW 89; CurBio 45, 82; FacFETw; FilmEn; FilmgC; HalFC 80, 84, 88; IntDcWB; IntMPA 77, 80, 81; LegTOT; ReelWom; WhoAm 80; WhoAmW 74; WomFir; WorAlBi*

Head, Edmund Walker, Sir
"Grandfather of Confederation"
English. Colonial Figure
Governor-in-chief of Canada, 1854-61.
b. 1805 in Raleigh, England
d. Jan 28, 1868 in London, England
Source: *Alli, SUP; ApCAB; BioIn 4; BritAu 19; DcBiPP; DcCanB 9; DcEnL; DcNaB; Drake; MacDCB 78; OxCCan; REnAL*

Head, Howard
American. Inventor
Invented the Head metal ski, aluminum sandwich ski and the Prince tennis racket.
b. Jul 31, 1914 in Philadelphia, Pennsylvania
d. Mar 3, 1991 in Baltimore, Maryland
Source: *BioIn 6, 11, 12, 14, 19; Entr; NewYTBS 91; WhAm 10; WhoAm 82, 84, 86, 88, 90*

Healey, Ed(ward)
American. Football Player
Tackle, Chicago, 1922-27; Hall of Fame, 1964.

b. Dec 18, 1894 in Springfield, Massachusetts
Source: *BiDAmSp FB; BioIn 8, 9, 17; LegTOT; WhoFtbl 74*

Healey, Jack
American. Social Reformer
Exec. director, Amnesty International 1981—
b. 1938
Source: *News 90, 90-1*

Healey, Jeff
[Jeff Healy Band]
Canadian. Singer, Songwriter
Rock/jazz/blues guitarist who inspired, recorded soundtrack for movie *Road House,* 1989; hits include "Confidence Man," 1989.
b. 1966 in Toronto, Ontario, Canada
Source: *BioIn 16; ConMus 4*

Healy, Bernadine
American. Government Official, Physician
First woman to head Nat. Institutes of Health, 1991-93.
b. Aug 2, 1944 in New York, New York
Source: *AmMWSc 92; CurBio 92; News 93-1; NewYTBS 91; NotTwCS; WhoAm 90; WhoAmW 91; WhoE 86; WhoMW 90*

Healy, George Peter Alexander
American. Artist
Portraitist whose subjects include Webster, Longfellow; works include *Webster's Reply to Hayne.*
b. Jul 15, 1813 in Boston, Massachusetts
d. Jun 24, 1894 in Chicago, Illinois
Source: *AmBi; ApCAB; BioIn 2, 3, 4, 8, 9, 11; BriEAA; DcAmArt; DcAmB; DcBiPP; DcNAA; Drake; McGDA; NatCAB 11, 15; NewYHSD; TwCBDA; WhAmArt 85; WhAm HS*

Healy, Katherine
American. Dancer, Actor
Won gold medal, Varna International Ballet Competition; in film *Six Weeks,* 1982.
b. 1969? in New York, New York
Source: *BioIn 11, 12, 13; WhoHol 92*

Healy, Mary
[Mrs. Peter Lind Hayes]
American. Entertainer
Teamed with husband, Peter Lind Hayes, for radio, TV shows, 1950s; wrote *Only Twenty-Five Minutes from Broadway,* 1961.
b. Apr 14, 1918 in New Orleans, Louisiana
Source: *BiE&WWA; BioIn 3, 4, 5; ForYSC; InWom; NotNAT; WhoAm 74, 76, 78, 80, 82, 84, 86, 88, 90, 92, 94, 95, 96, 97; WhoAmW 58, 61, 64, 66, 68, 72, 74, 95, 97; WhoEnt 92; WhoHol 92, A*

Healy, T(imothy) M(ichael)
Irish. Political Leader
Led anti-Parnell nationalists; first governor general, Irish Free State, 1922-28.
b. May 17, 1855 in Bantry, Ireland
d. Mar 26, 1931 in Dublin, Ireland
Source: *Alli SUP; BioIn 2; CelCen; DcCathB; DcIrB 78, 88; DcNaB 1931; NewCol 75*

Healy, Ted
American. Actor
Films include *Reckless,* 1935; *Hollywood Hotel,* 1937.
b. Oct 1, 1896 in Houston, Texas
d. Dec 21, 1937 in Los Angeles, California
Source: *EncAFC; EncVaud; FilmgC; ForYSC; WhoHol B; WhScrn 74, 77, 83*

Healy, Timothy S(tafford)
American. Library Administrator, University Administrator
Jesuit priest; succeeded Vartan Gregorian as pres., NY Public Library, 1989-92; pres., Georgetown U, 1976-89.
b. Apr 25, 1923 in New York, New York
d. Dec 30, 1992 in Newark, New Jersey
Source: *BioIn 16, 17, 18, 19; ConAu 41R, 46NR, 140; CurBio 93; News 90-2; NewYTBS 76; WhAm 11; WhoAm 78, 80, 82, 84, 86, 88, 90; WhoE 75, 77, 79, 81, 83, 85, 86, 89, 91; WhoEnt 92; WhoWor 80, 82, 84, 87, 89, 91, 93*

Heaney, Seamus (Justin)
Irish. Poet
Volumes of poetry include *Eleven Poems,* 1965; *Bog Poems,* 1975; won Nobel Prize for literature, 1995.
b. Apr 13, 1939 in Mossbawn, Northern Ireland
Source: *Benet 87, 96; BiDIrW; BioIn 10, 12, 13, 14, 15, 16; BlmGEL; BritWr S2; CamGLE; ChhPo S2; CnDBLB 8; ConAu 25NR, 48NR, 85; ConLC 5, 7, 14, 25, 37, 74, 91; ConPo 70, 75, 80, 85, 91, 96; CurBio 82; DcArts; DcIrL 96; DcLB 40; DcLEL 1940; EncWL 2, 3; FacFETw; GrWrEL P; IntAu&W 89, 91, 93; IntvTCA 2; IntWW 89, 91, 93; IntWWP 77; LegTOT; MajTwCW; ModBrL S1, S2; ModIrL; News 96, 96-2; OxCEng 85, 95; OxCIri; OxCTwCP; RAdv 14, 13-1; RfGEnL 91; RGTwCWr; Who 82, 83, 85, 88, 90, 92, 94; WhoAm 90, 92, 94, 95, 96, 97; WhoE 97; WhoNob 95; WhoWor 80, 82, 84, 87, 89, 91, 93, 95, 96, 97; WorAu 1970; WrDr 76, 80, 82, 84, 86, 88, 90, 92, 94, 96*

Heard, Gerald
[Henry Fitzgerald Heard]
English. Author
Writer on science, mystical religion; spiritual influence on Huxley, Isherwood: *Human Venture,* 1955.
b. Oct 6, 1889 in London, England
d. Aug 14, 1971 in Santa Monica, California
Source: *AmAu&B; Au&Wr 71; BiDMoPL; BiDPara; BioIn 1, 4, 9, 14, 15, 17; ConAu 21R, 29R, P-2, X; EncMys; EncO&P 1, 2, 3; EncPaPR 91; EncSF, 93; LngCTC; NewC; NewCBEL; OxCEng 85; REn; RGTwCSF; TwCA, SUP; TwCSFW 81; WhAm 5; WhE&EA*

Heard, John
American. Actor
Films include *Cat People,* 1982; *CHUD,* 1984; won Obie for *Othello and Split,* 1980.
b. Mar 7, 1945 in Washington, District of Columbia
Source: *BioIn 11; ConTFT 5; HalFC 88; IntMPA 82, 92; VarWW 85; WhoEnt 92*

Hearn, Lafcadio
[Patricio Lafcadio Tessima Carlos Hearn; Koizumi Yakumo]
Japanese. Author, Journalist
Introduced Japanese culture to the West through his works.
b. Jun 27, 1850 in Levkas, Ionian Islands
d. Sep 26, 1904 in Okubo, Japan
Source: *Alli SUP; AmAu; AmAu&B; AmBi; AnCL; AtlBL; BbD; Benet 87; BenetAL 91; BibAL; BiDAmNC; BiD&SB; BiDSA; BioIn 1, 2, 3, 4, 5, 6, 8, 9, 10, 11, 12, 13, 14, 15, 16, 17, 18, 20, 21; CamGEL; CamGLE; CamHAL; CasWL; Chambr 3; ChhPo, S3; CnDAL; ConAu 105; CrtT 3; CyWA 58; DcAmAu; DcAmB; DcBiA; DcEuL; DcIrL 96; DcLB 12, 78; DcLEL; DcNAA; Dis&D; EncAB-H 1974, 1996; EncJap; EvLB; GayN; GrWrEL N; LegTOT; LiJour; LinLib L, S; McGEWB; ModAL; MorMA; NatCAB 1; NewC; Novels; OhA&B; OxCAmH; OxCAmL 65, 83, 95; OxCEng 67, 85, 95; PenC AM, ENG; PenEncH; PeoHis; PoIre; RAdv 1; REn; REnAL; RfGAmL 87; ScF&FL 1, 92; SouWr; TwCLC 9; WebAB 74, 79; WhAm 1; WhoHr&F*

Hearne, Samuel
English. Explorer
First man to reach Arctic Ocean over land, 1771-72.
b. 1745 in London, England
d. Nov 1792, England
Source: *Alli; ApCAB; BbtC; BenetAL 91; BioIn 1, 2, 3, 5, 6, 8, 9, 12, 14, 17, 18; DcBiPP; DcCanB 4; DcLB 99; DcLEL; DcNaB; Drake; EncCRAm; Expl 93; IntDcAn; MacDCB 78; McGEWB; NewCBEL; OxCCan; OxCShps; WhDW; WhNaAH; WhWE*

Hearns, Thomas
"Detroit Hit Man"; "Motor City Cobra"; "Tommy Hearns"
American. Boxer
First boxer to win championship titles in six different weight classes.
b. Oct 18, 1958 in Grand Junction, Tennessee
Source: *AfrAmBi 1; AfrAmSG; BiDAmSp Sup; BioIn 12, 13, 14, 16; CurBio 83; InB&W 85; IntWW 89, 91, 93; NegAl 89; NewYTBS 81; WhoAfA 96; WhoAm*

84, 86, 88, 92, 94, 95, 96, 97; WhoBlA 85, 88, 90, 92, 94; WhoSpor

Hearst, David W(hitmire)
American. Publisher
Son of W R Hearst; published *LA Herald-Express,* 1950.
b. Dec 2, 1916 in New York, New York
d. May 13, 1986 in Los Angeles, California
Source: *Dun&B 79; IntWW 83; NewYTBS 86; WhoAm 78*

Hearst, Millicent Veronica Willson
[Mrs. William Randolph, Sr.]
American. Philanthropist
Married Hearst, 1903-51; best known for establishing Free Milk Fund for Babies, 1926.
b. Jul 16, 1882 in New York, New York
d. Dec 6, 1974 in New York, New York
Source: *BioNews 75; NewYTBS 74; ObitOF 79*

Hearst, Patty
[Patricia Campbell Hearst]
"Tanya"
American. Victim, Author
Kidnapped by SLA, Feb 5, 1974; wrote *Every Secret Thing,* 1982; granddaughter of William Randolph Hearst.
b. Feb 20, 1954 in San Francisco, California
Source: *BioAmW; BioIn 10, 11, 12, 13, 16; BioNews 74; BkPepl; CelR 90; ConAu 136; CurBio 82; FacFETw; InWom SUP; LegTOT; NewYTBS 74, 77; PolProf NF; WorAl; WorAlBi; WrDr 94*

Hearst, Randolph Apperson
American. Newspaper Executive
Pres., Hearst Foundation, 1972—; president, San Francisco Examiner, 1972—; father of Patty Hearst Shaw.
b. Dec 2, 1915 in New York, New York
Source: *BioIn 2, 10, 17; BioNews 74; IntWW 74, 79, 80, 81, 82, 83, 89, 91, 93; NewYTBS 74; St&PR 91; WhoAm 74, 76, 78, 80, 82, 84, 86, 88, 90, 92, 94, 95, 96, 97; WhoFI 81, 89, 92; WhoWest 76, 78, 80, 82, 84, 87, 89*

Hearst, William Randolph
American. Newspaper Publisher
Founder of newspaper chain with yellow journalism reputation; movie *Citizen Kane,* 1941, based on his life.
b. Apr 29, 1863 in San Francisco, California
d. Aug 14, 1951 in Beverly Hills, California
Source: *ABCMeAm; AmAu&B; AmDec 1900; AmSocL; Benet 87, 96; BenetAL 91; BiDAmBL 83; BiDAmJo; BiDAmNC; BiDrAC; BiDrUSC 89; BioIn 1, 2, 3, 4, 5, 6, 7, 8, 9, 10, 11, 12, 13, 14, 15, 16, 17, 18, 19, 20, 21; CmCal; ConAu 118; DcAmBC; DcAmB S5; DcAmSR; DcFM; DcLB 25; EncAB-H 1974, 1996; EncACom; EncAJ; FacFETw; FilmEn; FilmgC; GayN; HalFC 80, 84, 88; HarEnUS; JrnUS; LegTOT; LinLib L, S; LngCTC; McGEWB; MemAm; NatCAB 14, 39; ObitT 1951; OxCAmH; OxCAmL 65, 83, 95; OxCFilm; PolPar; RComAH; REn; REnAL; REnAW; WebAB 74, 79; WhAm 3; WhAmP; WhDW; WhE&EA; WhJnl; WhLit; WorAl; WorAlBi; WorEFlm*

Hearst, William Randolph, Jr.
American. Editor, Publisher
Editor-in-chief, Hearst Newspapers, 1956-93; won Pulitzer for int'l correspondence, 1956.
b. Jan 27, 1908 in New York, New York
d. May 14, 1993 in New York, New York
Source: *AmAu&B; BioIn 2, 3, 4, 5, 18, 19; BlueB 76; CelR, 90; ConAu 139; CurBio 55, 93N; DcLB 127; EncPR&S 89; IntAu&W 89; IntWW 74, 75, 76, 77, 78, 79, 80, 81, 82, 83, 89, 91, 93; IntYB 78, 79, 80, 81, 82; NewYTBS 93; St&PR 75, 84, 87, 91, 93; WhAm 11; Who 74, 82, 83, 85, 88, 90, 92; WhoAm 74, 76, 78, 80, 82, 84, 86, 88, 90, 92; WhoE 77, 79, 81, 83; WhoWor 78, 80, 82, 84, 87, 89, 91, 93; WorAlBi; WrDr 96*

Hearst, William Randolph, III
American. Newspaper Executive
Publisher, *San Francisco Examiner,* 1984—; son of William Randolph, Jr., cousin of Patty Hearst.
b. Jun 18, 1949 in Washington, District of Columbia
Source: *BioIn 10, 14, 15; CurBio 55; IntWW 83; WhoAm 86, 88, 90, 92, 94, 95, 97; WhoWest 87, 89, 92, 94; WhoWor 82*

Heart
[Mark Andes; Denny Carmassi; Mike Derosier; Roger Fisher; Steve Fossen; Howard Leese; Ann Wilson; Nancy Wilson]
American. Music Group
Heavy metal band led by sisters, Ann, Nancy Wilson since 1972; album *Dreamboat Annie* sold 2.5 million copies, 1976.
Source: *Alli; BioIn 15, 18, 20, 21; BioNews 74; ConMuA 80A; ConMus 1; DcLP 87B; EncPR&S 89; EncRkSt; HarEnR 86; IlEncRk; NewWmR; PenEncP; RkOn 74, 78; RolSEnR 83; WhoAmW 66; WhoRock 81; WhoRocM 82; WomPO 78*

Heath, Catherine
English. Author
Wrote novels *Stone Walls,* 1973; *Joseph and The Goths,* 1975.
b. Nov 17, 1924 in London, England
d. Nov 27, 1991
Source: *BioIn 13; ConAu 30NR, 93, 136; ConLC 70; DcLB 14; IntAu&W 76, 77, 82; WrDr 76, 80, 82, 84, 86, 88, 90, 92, 94N*

Heath, Edward Richard George
English. Political Leader
Prime minister, 1970-74; named Knight Companion of the Most Noble Order of the Garter by Queen Elizabeth, 1992.
b. Jul 9, 1916 in Broadstairs, England
Source: *ColdWar 1; CurBio 62; IntWW 83, 89, 91; NewYTBE 70, 71; Who 90, 92; WhoWor 84, 87, 91*

Heath, Lawrence S
American. Candy Manufacturer
Merchant who began making Heath Bar, 1931.
b. 1869
d. 1956
Source: *Entr*

Heath, Ted
English. Bandleader, Musician
Trombonist who led own band from 1945; in films, 1960s.
b. Mar 30, 1902 in London, England
d. Nov 18, 1969 in Virginia Water, England
Source: *BiDJaz; BioIn 2, 4, 8; CmpEPM; WhoHol B; WhScrn 74, 77, 83*

Heath, William
American. Army Officer
Last surviving Revolutionary War major general; commanded Eastern Department, Hudson Valley, 1777-79.
b. Mar 2, 1737 in Roxbury, Massachusetts
d. Jan 24, 1814 in Roxbury, Massachusetts
Source: *Alli; AmBi; AmRev; ApCAB; BioIn 8; DcAmB; DcNAA; Drake; EncAR; HarEnUS; NatCAB 1; TwCBDA; WebAMB; WhAm HS; WhAmRev*

Heatherton, Joey
American. Actor, Singer, Dancer
Films include *Happy Hooker Goes to Washington,* 1977; *Bluebeard,* 1972.
b. Sep 14, 1944 in Rockville Centre, New York
Source: *BiDAmM; BioIn 15, 16; FilmEn; FilmgC; ForYSC; HalFC 80, 84, 88; IntMPA 84, 86, 88, 92, 94, 96; LegTOT; MotPP; VarWW 85; WhoAm 74; WhoHol 92, A; WorAl*

Heatherton, Ray(mond Joseph)
American. Actor, Singer
Broadway, radio vocalist, 1930s; led dance combo, 1940s; hosted children's TV sh ow, "Merry Mailman"; father of Joey.
b. Jun 1, 1910 in Jersey City, New Jersey
Source: *BiE&WWA; CmpEPM; NotNAT*

Heaton, Leonard
American. Military Leader, Physician
Surgeon General under four presidents, 1959-69.
b. 1902 in Parkersburg, West Virginia

d. Sep 11, 1983 in Washington, District of Columbia
Source: *NewYTBS 83*

Heatter, Gabriel
American. Radio Performer, Journalist
Opening words for his news broadcasts, "Ah-there's good news tonight," became nat. catch phrase.
b. Sep 17, 1890 in New York, New York
d. Mar 30, 1972 in Miami Beach, Florida
Source: *BiDAmJo; BioIn 1, 5, 6, 7, 9, 11, 16; ConAu 89; CurBio 41, 72, 72N; DcAmB S9; EncAJ; JrnUS; NewYTBE 72; RadStar; SaTiSS; WebAB 74, 79; WhAm 8; What 1; WhScrn 77, 83*

Heatwave
["Bilbo" Berger; Keith Bramble; Calvin Duke; Keith Harrison; Billy Jones; Johnnie Wilder; Keith Wilder]
Music Group
Soul/pop band formed 1975; hits include platinum single "Boogie Nights," 1977.
Source: *BioIn 5; CurBio 41; EncRkSt; HarEnR 86; OnThGG; RkOn 78, 84; SoulM; WhoHol 92; WhoRocM 82*

Heavy D
[Dwight Myers]
Jamaican. Rapper
Rap singer who formed Heavy D and the Boyz group in mid-1980s; received platinum records for *Living Large*, 1987, *Big Tyme*, 1989, and *Peaceful Journey*, 1991; received gold record for *Blue Funk* in 1993.
b. 1967, Jamaica
Source: *ConMus 10*

Hebbel, Friedrich
[Christian Friedrich Hebbel]
German. Dramatist
Psychological tragedies include trilogy *Die Niebelungen*, 1862.
b. Mar 18, 1813 in Wesselburen, Germany
d. Dec 13, 1863 in Vienna, Austria
Source: *Benet 87; BiD&SB; BioIn 1, 5, 7, 8, 19; CamGWoT; CasWL; CnThe; CyWA 58; DcBiPP; DcEuL; DcLB 129; Dis&D; EncWT; Ent; EuAu; EuWr 6; EvEuW; GrFLW; McGEWB; McGEWD 72, 84; NewCBEL; NewCol 75; NewEOp 71; NinCLC 43; NotNAT, A, B; OxCGer 76, 86; OxCThe 67, 83; PenC EUR; RAdv 14, 13-2; RComWL; REn; REnWD*

Heber, Reginald
English. Religious Leader
Anglican bishop of Calcutta, 1822-26; wrote beloved hymns including "Holy, Holy, Holy."
b. Apr 21, 1783 in Malpas, England
d. Apr 3, 1826 in Trichinopoly, India
Source: *Alli; BbD; BiD&SB; BiDLA; BioIn 9, 14; BritAu 19; CamGEL; CamGLE; CasWL; CelCen; Chambr 3; ChhPo, S1, S2, S3; DcBiPP; DcEnA; DcEnL; DcInB; DcNaB; EvLB; LinLib L, S; LuthC 75; MnBBF; NewC; NewCBEL; NewCol 75; OxCEng 67, 85; PenC ENG; PoChrch; WebE&AL*

Hebert, Bobby Joseph
American. Football Player
Quarterback, MI Panthers, USFL, 1983-85; USFL player of year, 1983; with NFL New Orleans, 1985-92, Atlanta, 1993—.
b. Aug 19, 1960 in Baton Rouge, Louisiana
Source: *BioIn 14; FootReg 87*

Hebert, F(elix) Edward
American. Politician, Editor
Dem. con. from LA, 1941-76; wrote award-winning expose of Huey Long, 1939.
b. Oct 12, 1901 in New Orleans, Louisiana
d. Dec 29, 1979 in New Orleans, Louisiana
Source: *AmCath 80; BiDrAC; BiDrUSC 89; BioIn 2, 5, 9, 10, 11, 12; CngDr 74; ConAu 106, 110; CurBio 51, 80, 80N; DcAmB S10; EncTwCJ; NewYTBS 79; PolProf E, J, K, NF, T; WhAm 7; WhoAm 74, 76, 78; WhoAmP 73, 75, 77, 79; WhoGov 72, 75, 77; WhoSSW 73, 75, 76*

Hebert, Jay
American. Golfer
Touring pro, 1950s-60s; won PGA, 1960; brother of Lionel.
b. Feb 14, 1923 in Lafayette, Louisiana
d. May 25, 1997 in Houston, Texas
Source: *WhoGolf*

Hebert, Lionel
American. Golfer
Turned pro, 1957; won PGA, 1957; brother of Jay.
b. Jan 20, 1928 in Lafayette, Louisiana
Source: *WhoGolf*

Hebner, Richie
[Richard Joseph Hebner]
American. Baseball Player
Infielder, 1968-85; established NL playoff record for most series played, eight.
b. Nov 26, 1947 in Brighton, Massachusetts
Source: *Ballpl 90; BaseReg 86; BioIn 9, 15; WhoAm 74; WhoProB 73*

Heche, Ann
American. Actor
Starred in *Volcano*, 1997.
b. May 25, 1969

Hechinger, Fred Michael
American. Author
Books on education include *Growing Up in America*, 1975.
b. Jul 7, 1920 in Nuremberg, Germany
d. Nov 6, 1995 in New York, New York
Source: *AmAu&B; BioIn 10; BlueB 76; ConAu 77; EncTwCJ; NewYTBS 76; WhAm 11; WhoAm 74, 76, 78, 80, 82, 84, 86, 88, 90, 92, 94, 95, 96; WhoE 74, 93; WhoWorJ 72; WrDr 76, 86, 92*

Hecht, Anthony Evan
American. Poet
Won Pulitzer, 1968, for *The Hard Hours*, which featured empathetic perspective on human suffering.
b. Jan 16, 1923 in New York, New York
Source: *BenetAL 91; BioIn 14, 15; ConPo 91; CurBio 86; DrAPF 89, 91; IntAu&W 91; IntWW 91; LinLib L; WhoAm 84, 90; WhoTwCL; WhoUSWr 88; WhoWrEP 89; WrDr 90, 92*

Hecht, Ben
American. Author, Dramatist
Wrote novels of city life; co-wrote many Hollywood, Broadway hits, including *Front Page*, 1928.
b. Feb 28, 1893 in New York, New York
d. Apr 18, 1964 in New York, New York
Source: *AmAu&B; Benet 87, 96; BenetAL 91; BiDFilm, 94; BioIn 3, 4, 6, 7, 8, 10, 11; CmMov; CnDAL; CnMD; CnThe; ConAmA; ConAmL; ConAu 85; ConLC 8; CurBio 42, 64; DcArts; DcFM; DcLEL; EncAFC; EncMys; FacFETw; FilmEn; IntDcF 1-4, 2-4; JeAmFiW; LegTOT; LngCTC; MiSFD 9N; OxCAmL 65; PenC AM; REn; REnAL; RGTwCWr; ScF&FL 1; SJGFanW; TwCA, SUP; WhAm 4; WorAl*

Hecht, Chic
American. Politician
Republican senator from NV, 1983-89.
b. Nov 30, 1928 in Cape Girardeau, Missouri
Source: *CngDr 83, 85, 87; LegTOT; PolsAm 84; WhoAm 84, 86, 88, 90, 92, 94, 95, 96, 97; WhoAmP 73, 75, 77, 79, 83, 85, 87, 89, 91, 93, 95; WhoWest 84, 87, 89, 92, 94, 96; WhoWor 87, 89, 93, 95, 96, 97*

Hecht, George Joseph
American. Publisher
Founded *Parents' Magazine; Humpty Dumpty*.
b. Nov 1, 1895 in New York, New York
d. Apr 23, 1980 in New York, New York
Source: *BioIn 1, 2, 12, 13; ConAu 97; CurBio 47, 80; EncAB-A 28; EncTwCJ; NewYTBS 75, 80; SmATA 22; St&PR 75; WhAm 7; WhNAA; WhoAm 74, 76, 78, 80; WhoWorJ 72*

Hecht, Harold
American. Producer
Won best picture Oscar, 1955, for *Marty*.
b. Jun 1, 1907 in New York, New York
d. May 25, 1985 in Beverly Hills, California
Source: *AnObit 1985; BioIn 14; FacFETw; FilmEn; FilmgC; HalFC 80, 84; IntMPA 75, 76, 77, 78, 79, 80, 81, 82, 84; NewYTBS 85; VarWW 85; WhAm 8; WhoAm 74, 76, 78; WorEFlm*

Heck, Barbara Ruckle
"Mother of Methodism"
Irish. Religious Leader
Helped establish first Methodist chapel in America, 1768.
b. 1734 in County Limerick, Ireland
d. Aug 17, 1804 in Augusta, Ontario, Canada
Source: *ApCAB; BioIn 19; DcAmB; DcAmReB 2; EncCRAm; EncWM; InWom; LibW; MacDCB 78; NatCAB 13; NotAW; OxCCan; WhAm HS*

Heckart, Eileen
[Anna Eileen Heckart]
American. Actor
Won 1972 Oscar for *Butterflies Are Free.*
b. Mar 29, 1919 in Columbus, Ohio
Source: *BiE&WWA; BioIn 4, 5, 6, 10, 14, 16; CelR; ConTFT 4; CurBio 58; EncAFC; FilmEn; FilmgC; ForYSC; HalFC 80, 84, 88; IntMPA 77, 80, 84, 86, 88, 92, 94, 96; InWom, SUP; LegTOT; MotPP; MovMk; NewYTBE 73; NotNAT; OxCAmT 84; PlP&P; VarWW 85; WhoAm 74, 76, 78, 80, 82, 84, 86, 88, 90, 92, 95, 96, 97; WhoAmW 64, 66, 68, 70, 72, 74, 75, 83, 85, 87, 89, 91, 93, 95, 97; WhoE 74; WhoEnt 92; WhoHol 92, A; WhoThe 72, 77, 81; WhoWor 82; WorAl; WorAlBi*

Heckel, Erich
German. Artist
Expressionist; a founder of Die Bruecke school of painting, 1905; art denounced by Nazis.
b. Jul 31, 1883 in Dobeln, Germany
d. Jan 27, 1970 in Radolfzell, Germany (West)
Source: *BioIn 4, 6, 8, 14, 17, 20; ConArt 77, 83; DcArts; EncTR 91; FacFETw; McGDA; NewYTBE 70; OxCArt; OxCGer 76, 86; OxCTwCA; OxDcArt; PhDcTCA 77*

Heckerling, Amy
American. Director
Comedy films include *Fast Times at Ridgemont High,* 1982; *Look Who's Talking,* 1989.
b. May 7, 1954 in New York, New York
Source: *BioIn 14, 16; ConAu 139; ConNews 87-2; ConTFT 6, 10; HalFC 88; IntMPA 88, 92, 94, 96; LegTOT; MiSFD 9; WhoAmW 91, 93, 95; WhoEnt 92*

Heckert, Richard Edwin
American. Business Executive
Chairman, CEO, DuPont Co., 1986-89.
b. Jan 13, 1924 in Oxford, Ohio
Source: *AmMWSc 73P; BioIn 10, 15, 16; ConNews 87-3; Dun&B 86, 88; IntWW 89, 91, 93; St&PR 84, 87, 91, 93, 96, 97; WhoAm 82, 84, 86, 88, 92, 94; WhoE 89, 91; WhoFI 83, 85, 87, 89; WhoWor 84, 89*

Heckler, Margaret Mary
American. Government Official, Diplomat
Secretary of Health and Human Services under Reagan, 1983-85; ambassador to Ireland, 1985-89.
b. Jun 21, 1931 in Flushing, New York
Source: *AmWomM; BiDrAC; BiDrUSC 89; BiDrUSE 89; BioIn 13, 14, 15; CngDr 83, 85; CurBio 83; EncWB; InWom SUP; NewYTBS 85; WhoAm 74, 76, 78, 80, 82, 84, 86, 88; WhoAmP 85, 89; WhoAmW 87, 89, 91, 93; WhoE 74, 85; WhoGov 77; WhoWor 89, 91*

Heckscher, August
American. Author, Journalist
Wrote *The Politics of Woodrow Wilson,* 1956; *When La Guardia Was Mayor,* 1978.
b. Sep 16, 1913 in Huntington, New York
d. Apr 5, 1997 in New York, New York
Source: *AmAu&B; Au&Wr 71; AuSpks; BiE&WWA; BioIn 5, 6, 7, 10, 11, 13; BlueB 76; ConAu 1R, 35NR; CurBio 41, 58; EncAI&E; IntAu&W 76, 89; IntWW 74, 75, 76, 77, 78, 79, 80, 81, 82, 83, 89, 91, 93; WhoAm 74, 76, 92, 94, 95, 96, 97; WhoE 74, 91; WhoGov 72, 75, 77; WhoScEn 94*

Hedges, Michael
American. Singer, Songwriter
Innovator in acoustic guitar technique; recorded first three albums live; *Aerial Boundaries,* 1984, earned Grammy nomination.
b. Dec 31, 1953 in Enid, Oklahoma
Source: *ConMus 3; NewAgMG*

Hedison, David
[Albert David Hedison, Jr; David Heditsian]
American. Actor
In films *Greatest Story Ever Told,* 1965; *Live and Let Die,* 1973.
b. May 20, 1928 in Providence, Rhode Island
Source: *ConTFT 8; FilmgC; HalFC 88; MotPP; VarWW 85; WhoAm 88; WhoHol A; WhoHrs 80*

Hedren, Tippi
[Natalie Kay Hedren]
American. Actor
Cool blonde star of Hitchcock films: *The Birds,* 1963; *Marnie,* 1964; mother of Melanie Griffith.
b. Jan 19, 1935 in New Ulm, Minnesota
Source: *BiDFilm, 81, 94; BioIn 6, 11, 14; ConTFT 7; FilmEn; FilmgC; ForYSC; HalFC 80, 84, 88; IntDcF 1-3; IntMPA 94, 96; LegTOT; MotPP; VarWW 85; WhoAm 74, 76; WhoHol A*

Hedtoft (-Hansen), Hans Christian
Danish. Political Leader
Prime minister, 1947-50, 1953-55; brought Denmark into NATO, 1949.
b. Apr 21, 1903 in Aarhus, Denmark
d. Jan 29, 1955 in Stockholm, Sweden
Source: *BioIn 1, 2, 3, 4; CurBio 49, 55; ObitOF 79; WhAm 3*

Heem, Jan Davidsz(oon) de
Dutch. Artist
Known for realistic still lifes, portraits: *Still Life with Books,* 1628.
b. 1606 in Utrecht, Netherlands
d. Apr 6, 1684? in Antwerp, Belgium
Source: *BioIn 19; ClaDrA; McGDA; OxCArt; OxDcArt*

Heenan, John Carmel
"The Benicia Boy"
American. Boxer
Heavyweight bare knuckles champ, 1858; fought famed 42-round bout with Tom Sayers, 1860.
b. May 2, 1833 in West Troy, New York
d. Oct 28, 1873 in Green River Station, Wyoming
Source: *BiDAmSp BK; BioIn 2; DcAmB; WebBD 83; WhAm HS*

Heffelfinger, Pudge
[William Walter Heffelfinger]
"Heff"
American. Football Player
Three-time All-America guard, Yale, 1888-91; thought to be first paid player, 1892.
b. Dec 20, 1867 in Minneapolis, Minnesota
d. Apr 2, 1954 in Blessing, Texas
Source: *BiDAmSp FB; BioIn 3, 5, 6, 10; DcAmB S5; WebAB 74, 79; WhoFtbl 74; WhoSpor*

Heflin, Howell Thomas
American. Politician
Dem. senator, AL, 1979-96.
b. Jun 19, 1921 in Poulan, Georgia
Source: *AlmAP 92; BiDrUSC 89; BioIn 11; CngDr 79, 81, 83, 85, 87, 89; NewYTBS 90; PolsAm 84; WhoAm 74, 76, 78, 80, 82, 84, 86, 88, 90, 92, 94, 95, 96, 97; WhoAmL 78, 79; WhoAmP 73, 75, 79, 81, 83, 85, 87, 89, 91, 93, 95; WhoGov 75, 77; WhoSSW 75, 76, 80, 82, 84, 86, 88, 91, 93, 95, 97; WhoWor 80, 82, 84, 87, 89, 91*

Heflin, Van Emmett Evan
American. Actor
Won Oscar for *Johnny Eager,* 1942; also in film *Shane,* 1953.
b. Dec 13, 1910 in Walters, Oklahoma
d. Jul 23, 1971 in Hollywood, California
Source: *BiDFilm; BiE&WWA; CmMov; CurBio 43, 71; FilmgC; MotPP; MovMk; OxCFilm; PlP&P; WhAm 5; WhoHol B; WhScrn 77; WorEFlm*

Hefner, Christie
[Christine Ann Hefner]
American. Business Executive, Publishing Executive
Daughter of Hugh Hefner; CEO, Playboy Enterprises, 1988—.
b. Nov 8, 1952 in Chicago, Illinois
Source: *AmWomM; BioIn 12, 13, 14, 15, 16; CelR 90; ConAmBL; ConNews 85-1;*

CurBio 86; Dun&B 90; EncTwCJ; LegTOT; NewYTBS 79, 91; St&PR 87, 91, 93, 96, 97; WhoAdv 90; WhoAm 90; WhoAmW 85, 91; WhoEnt 92; WhoFI 89, 92; WhoMW 90

Hefner, Hugh Marston
American. Publisher
Founded adult mags. *Playboy,* 1953; *VIP,* 1963-75; *Oui,* 1972-81.
b. Apr 9, 1926 in Chicago, Illinois
Source: *AuNews 1; BioIn 13, 14, 15, 16; BioNews 74; BkPepl; CelR 90; ConAmBL; ConAu 110; CurBio 68; Dun&B 90; EncAB-H 1996; EncTwCJ; IntWW 83, 91; NewYTBS 79; St&PR 87, 91; WebAB 74; WhoAm 86, 90, 97; WhoEnt 92; WhoFI 75; WhoMW 74; WhoWor 74; WorAlBi*

Hefti, Neal Paul
American. Composer, Publisher
Trumpeter, Big Band arranger, 1940s-50s; film scores include *Barefoot in the Park,* 1967.
b. Oct 29, 1922 in Hastings, Nebraska
Source: *ASCAP 66; Baker 84; BiDAmM; BiDJaz; BioIn 13; CmpEPM; NewAmDM; NewGrDA 86; NewGrDJ 88; OxCPMus; PenEncP; VarWW 85; WhoAm 74, 76, 78, 80, 82, 84*

Hegan, Jim
[James Edward Hegan]
American. Baseball Player, Baseball Coach
Catcher, Cleveland, 1941-57; known for defense, handling one of best pitching staffs assembled—Feller, Lemon, Garcia, Wynn.
b. Aug 3, 1920 in Lynn, Massachusetts
d. Jun 17, 1984 in Swampscott, Massachusetts
Source: *Ballpl 90; BiDAmSp Sup; BioIn 2, 4, 5, 8, 14; WhoProB 73*

Hegel, Georg Wilhelm Friedrich
German. Philosopher
His absolute idealism influenced Sartre, Marx, others.
b. Aug 27, 1770 in Stuttgart, Wurttemberg
d. Nov 14, 1831 in Berlin, Germany
Source: *BbD; BiD&SB; BiDPsy; BiDTran; BioIn 2, 6, 7, 8, 9, 10, 12, 13, 14, 17, 20, 21; CasWL; CelCen; CyEd; DcBiPP; DcEuL; DcLB 90; Dis&D; EncEth; EncUnb; EuAu; EvEuW; IlEncMy; LinLib L, S; LngCEL; LuthC 75; McGEWB; NamesHP; NewC; NewCBEL; NinCLC 46; OxCEng 67, 85, 95; OxCGer 76, 86; OxCLaw; OxCPhil; PenC EUR; RAdv 14, 13-4; REn; WebBD 83; WhDW*

Heger, Robert
Alsatian. Conductor, Composer
Led many German symphonies, from 1913; wrote four operas, symphonies.
b. Aug 19, 1886 in Strassburg, Germany
d. Jan 14, 1978 in Munich, Germany (West)
Source: *Baker 78, 84, 92; CmOp; MetOEnc; NewEOp 71; NewGrDM 80; NewGrDO; OxDcOp; PenDiMP; Who 74; WhoMus 72*

Heggen, Thomas Orls, Jr.
American. Author, Dramatist
His wartime experiences were used for plot of popular novel: *Mister Roberts;* adapted to stage, film, 1950s.
b. Dec 23, 1919 in Fort Dodge, Iowa
d. May 19, 1949 in New York, New York
Source: *AmAu&B; CyWA 58; McGEWD 84; NatCAB 38; ObitOF 79; OxCAmL 83; PenC AM; REnAL; TwCA SUP; WhAm 2*

Heggie, O. P
Australian. Actor
Films include *Anne of Green Gables,* 1934; *Bride of Frankenstein,* 1935.
b. Nov 17, 1879 in Angaston, Australia
d. Feb 7, 1936 in Los Angeles, California
Source: *FilmgC; MovMk; TwYS; WhoHol B; WhScrn 74, 77*

Hegyes, Robert
American. Actor
Played Epstein on TV series "Welcome Back, Kotter," 1975-79.
b. May 7, 1951 in New Jersey
Source: *BioIn 11; WhoHol 92*

Heidegger, Martin
German. Author, Philosopher
Focused on human condition without effects of religion; principal work *Being and Time,* 1927.
b. Sep 26, 1889 in Messkirch, Germany
d. May 26, 1976 in Messkirch, Germany (West)
Source: *Benet 87, 96; BiDExR; BioIn 2, 4, 5, 6, 8, 9, 10, 11, 12, 13, 14, 15, 16, 17, 19, 20, 21; CasWL; ClDMEL 80; ConAu 34NR, 65, 81; ConLC 24; CurBio 72, 76N; EncEth; EncTR; FacFETw; IntEnSS 79; IntWW 74, 75, 76; LegTOT; LinLib L; LngCTC; LuthC 75; MajTwCW; MakMC; McGEWB; OxCGer 76, 86; OxCPhil; RAdv 14, 13-4; REn; ThTwC 87; TwCA SUP; TwCWr; WhAm 6; WhDW; Who 74; WorAl; WorAlBi; WrPh P*

Heiden, Eric Arthur
American. Skater
Speed skater; first to win five individual Olympic gold medals, 1980; first spe ed skater to receive the Sullivan Award, 1981.
b. Jun 14, 1958 in Madison, Wisconsin
Source: *BiDAmSp OS; BioIn 13, 14, 15; CurBio 80; FacFETw; NewYTBS 80, 81, 84, 86; WorAlBi*

Heiden, Konrad
German. Historian, Author
Expert on Hitler, said to have coined term "Nazi" as derisive nickname.
b. Aug 7, 1901 in Munich, Germany
d. Jul 18, 1966 in New York, New York
Source: *BioIn 7, 10; ConAu 116; CurBio 44, 75, 75N; EncGRNM; WhAm 6*

Heidenstam, Carl Gustaf Verner von
Swedish. Author, Poet
First volume of poetry *Pilgrimage and Wanderyears,* 1888, challenged contemporary Swedish literature; won Nobel Prize, 1916.
b. Jul 6, 1859 in Olshammar, Sweden
d. May 20, 1940 in Ovralid, Sweden
Source: *BiD&SB; CasWL; ConAu 104; DcScanL; EvEuW; McGEWB; REn; WhoNob*

Heidt, Horace Murray
American. Bandleader
Led band, 1930s-50s; starred in radio talent shows "Pot of Gold," 1938-41; "Youth O pportunity Program," 1948-53.
b. May 21, 1901 in Alameda, California
d. Dec 1, 1986 in Los Angeles, California
Source: *AmPS A, B; BioIn 1, 2, 8, 9, 12, 13; CmpEPM; VarWW 85; WhoHol A*

Heifetz, Jascha
American. Violinist
Child prodigy who had debut at age five; considered best classical violinist of c; playing noted for silken tone, careful regard for composer's markings.
b. Feb 2, 1901 in Vilnius, Lithuania
d. Dec 10, 1987 in Los Angeles, California
Source: *AmCulL; AnObit 1987; ASCAP 66, 80; Baker 78, 84; BiDAmM; BiDSovU; BioIn 1, 2, 3, 5, 6, 8, 9, 10, 11, 12, 14, 15, 16, 19; BriBkM 80; CelR; CurBio 44, 88, 88N; DcArts; DcTwCCu 1; FacFETw; IntWW 74, 75, 76, 77, 78, 79, 80, 81, 82, 83; IntWWM 77, 80; LegTOT; LinLib S; MusMk; MusSN; NewAmDM; NewGrDA 86; NewGrDM 80; News 88-2; NewYTBS 87; PenDiMP; REn; VarWW 85; WebAB 74, 79; WhAm 9; Who 74, 82, 83, 85, 88; WhoAm 74, 76, 78, 80, 82, 84, 86; WhoAmM 83; WhoHol A; WhoMus 72; WhoWor 74, 78; WorAl; WorAlBi*

Height, Dorothy Irene
American. Social Reformer
Pres., Nat. Council of Negro Women, 1957—.
b. Mar 24, 1912 in Richmond, Virginia
Source: *AfrAmBi 1; BioIn 9, 10, 12, 13; BlkWAm; ConBlB 2; InWom SUP; NegAl 89; NewYTBS 79; WhoAmW 85; WhoBlA 92*

Heilbrun, Carolyn Gold
American. Author
Writes mysteries, as well as books on feminist issues, including best-seller *Writing a Women's Life,* 1988.
b. Jan 13, 1926 in East Orange, New Jersey
Source: *BioIn 16; ConAu 28NR; CurBio 93; FemiCLE; IntWW 91, 93; NewYTBS*

92; OxCWoWr 95; TwCCr&M 91; WhoAm 84, 86, 88, 90, 92, 94, 95, 96, 97; WhoAmW 85, 87, 89, 91, 93, 95, 97; WhoUSWr 88; WhoWrEP 89, 92, 95; WrDr 92

Heilmann, Harry Edwin
"Slug"
American. Baseball Player
Outfielder, 1914-30, 1932; won AL batting title four times; had lifetime .342 average; Hall of Fame, 1952.
b. Aug 3, 1894 in San Francisco, California
d. Jul 9, 1951 in Southfield, Michigan
Source: *BiDAmSp BB; BioIn 2, 3, 7; DcAmB S5; WhoProB 73*

Heim, Jacques
French. Fashion Designer
First couturier to introduce ready-to-wear as an extension of French couture.
b. May 8, 1899 in Paris, France
d. Jan 8, 1967 in Paris, France
Source: *BioIn 1, 7; ConFash; EncFash; FairDF FRA; ObitOF 79; ObitT 1961; WhAm 4; WorFshn*

Heimlich, Henry Jay
American. Physician, Author
Developed anti-choking maneuver named for him: "Heimlich Maneuver."
b. Feb 3, 1920 in Wilmington, Delaware
Source: *AmMWSc 95; BioIn 11, 13; ConAu 102; CurBio 86; NotTwCS; WhoAm 78, 80, 82, 84, 86, 88, 90, 92, 94, 95, 96, 97; WhoMW 74, 76, 78, 80, 82, 84; WhoScEn 94, 96; WhoWorJ 78*

Hein, Mel(vin John)
American. Football Player
Eight-time all-pro center, NY Giants, 1931-45; NFL MVP, 1938; Hall of Fame, 1963.
b. Aug 22, 1909 in Redding, California
d. Jan 31, 1992 in San Clemente, California
Source: *AnObit 1992; BiDAmSp FB; BioIn 3, 6, 8, 10, 17, 19; LegTOT; NewYTBS 74; WhoFtbl 74*

Heindorf, Ray
American. Composer, Conductor
Head of Warner Bros. music dept; won Oscars for orchestrations of *Yankee Doodle Dandy,* 1942; *Music Man,* 1962.
b. Aug 25, 1908 in Haverstraw, New York
d. Feb 3, 1980 in Los Angeles, California
Source: *ASCAP 80; CmMov; CmpEPM; FilmEn; FilmgC; HalFC 84, 88; IntMPA 77*

Heine, Heinrich
[Christian Johann Heinrich Heine]
German. Poet, Critic
Wrote satirical poetry including *The Harz Journey,* 1826.
b. Dec 13, 1797 in Dusseldorf, Prussia
d. Feb 17, 1856 in Paris, France
Source: *AtlBL; BbD; Benet 87, 96; BiD&SB; BioIn 1, 2, 3, 4, 5, 6, 7, 8, 9, 10, 11, 12, 13, 14, 16, 17, 20, 21; CasWL; ChhPo, S1, S2, S3; CnOxB; CyWA 58; DcAmSR; DcArts; DcEuL; DcLB 90; Dis&D; EuAu; EuWr 5; EvEuW; GrFLW; JeHun; LegTOT; LinLib L, S; LuthC 75; MagSWL; McGEWB; NewC; NewCBEL; NewEOp 71; NewGrDM 80; NewGrDO; NinCLC 4, 54; OxCEng 67, 85, 95; OxCFr; OxCGer 76, 86; OxCMus; OxDcOp; PenC EUR; RAdv 14, 13-2; RComWL; REn; RfGWoL 95; WhDW; WorAl; WorAlBi*

Heinemann, Edward H
American. Aircraft Designer
Designed numerous innovative aircraft including the Dauntless dive bomber; received Nat. Medal of Science, 1983.
b. Mar 14, 1908 in Saginaw, Michigan
d. Nov 26, 1991 in San Diego, California
Source: *AmMWSc 92; BioIn 2, 3, 11, 12; WhoAm 90; WhoEng 88; WhoTech 89*

Heinemann, Gustav Walter
German. Political Leader
First Social Democrat to be elected pres. of Germany, 1969-74; opposed Hitler.
b. Jul 23, 1899 in Schwelm, Germany
d. Jul 7, 1976 in Essen, Germany (West)
Source: *CurBio 69, 76N; IntWW 74, 75, 76; NewYTBS 76; WhAm 7; WhoGov 75; WhoWor 74*

Heinemann, William
English. Publisher
Founded publishing company, 1890; firm known for its contemporary fiction, translations of European and classical works.
b. May 18, 1863 in Surbiton, England
d. Oct 5, 1920 in London, England
Source: *BiD&SB; BioIn 14, 18; DcLB 112; DcNaB 1912; GayN; GrBr; LngCTC; NewC; NewCBEL; StaCVF*

Heinkel, Ernst Heinrich
German. Aeronautical Engineer
Designed, constructed first rocket-powered aircraft.
b. Jan 24, 1888 in Grunbach, Germany
d. Jan 30, 1958 in Stuttgart, Germany
Source: *BioIn 4, 5; EncTR 91; ObitOF 79*

Heinlein, Robert Anson
American. Author
Won four Hugos; classics include *The Moon is a Harsh Mistress,* 1966.
b. Jul 7, 1907 in Butler, Missouri
d. May 8, 1988 in Carmel, California
Source: *AmCulL; AuBYP 3; BioIn 3, 4, 6, 7, 10, 11, 12, 13; ConAu 1NR, 1R; ConLC 3, 8, 14; ConNov 86; CurBio 55, 88; IntAu&W 76; MorJA; NewYTBS 80; PenC AM; REnAL; RfGAmL 94; SmATA 9; TwCA SUP; WebAB 74, 79; WhAm 9; WhoAm 74, 76, 78, 80, 82, 84, 86; WhoUSWr 88; WhoWor 76, 78, 80, 82, 84, 87; WorAl; WrDr 86*

Heinsohn, Tommy
[Thomas William Heinsohn]
American. Basketball Player
Six-time all-star forward, Boston, 1957-65; rookie of year, 1958; won eight NBA championships; Hall of Fame, 1986.
b. Aug 26, 1934 in Jersey City, New Jersey
Source: *BiDAmSp BK; BioIn 5, 6, 8, 10, 11, 16; ConAu 118, X; NewYTBE 73; WhoAm 74, 76, 78; WhoBbl 73*

Heinz, Henry John
American. Manufacturer
Founded H J Heinz Co., 1876; originated "57 varieties" slogan, 1896.
b. Oct 11, 1844 in Pittsburgh, Pennsylvania
d. May 14, 1919 in Pittsburgh, Pennsylvania
Source: *BiDAmBL 83; BioIn 9, 10, 11, 15, 18, 20; DcAmB; EncAB-A 1; EncWM; GayN; NatCAB 5, 26; WebAB 74, 79; WhAm 1; WhDW; WorAl; WorAlBi*

Heinz, Henry John, II
American. Business Executive, Philanthropist
Pres., chairman, of grandfather's ketchup, pickle co., active in political, cultural causes.
b. Jul 10, 1908 in Sewickley, Pennsylvania
d. Feb 23, 1987 in Hobe Sound, Florida
Source: *BioIn 1, 2, 3, 5, 10, 15, 16; ConNews 87-2; CurBio 47, 87; IntWW 74, 75, 76, 77, 78, 79, 80, 81, 82, 83; IntYB 78, 79, 80, 81, 82; WhAm 10; Who 74, 82, 83, 85; WhoAm 74, 76, 78, 80, 82, 84, 86; WhoE 79, 81, 83, 85, 86; WhoFI 74, 75, 77, 79, 81, 83, 85; WhoWor 74, 76, 78, 80, 82, 87; WorAl; WorAlBi*

Heinz, John
[Henry John Heinz, III]
American. Politician
Liberal Rep. senator from PA, 1976-91.
b. Oct 23, 1938 in Pittsburgh, Pennsylvania
d. Apr 4, 1991 in Merion, Pennsylvania
Source: *AlmAP 80; AnObit 1991; BiDrUSC 89; BioIn 9, 11, 12, 14, 15, 16; CelR 90; CngDr 74, 77, 79, 81, 83, 85, 87, 89; CurBio 81, 91N; IntWW 77, 78, 79, 80, 81, 82, 83, 89, 91, 91N; News 91; NewYTBS 91; PolsAm 84; WhAm 10; WhoAm 74, 76, 78, 80, 82, 84, 86, 88, 90; WhoAmP 73, 75, 79, 81, 83, 85, 87, 89; WhoE 74, 75, 77, 79, 81, 83, 85, 86, 89, 91; WhoGov 75, 77; WhoWor 80, 82, 84, 87, 89, 91; WorAlBi*

Heisenberg, Werner Karl
German. Physicist
Won 1932 Nobel Prize for discoveries that led to knowledge of the allotropic forms of hydrogen.
b. Dec 5, 1901 in Wurzburg, Germany
d. Feb 1, 1976 in Munich, Germany (West)

Source: *AsBiEn; BiESc; CamDcSc; ConAu 65; CurBio 57; DcScB S2; FacFETw; InSci; IntWW 74; LarDcSc; McGEWB; NotTwCS; WhAm 6; Who 74; WhoNob, 90, 95; WhoWor 74, 76; WorAl; WorAlBi; WorScD*

Heiser, Victor George
American. Physician, Author
Wrote best-selling *An American Doctor's Odyssey,* 1936; first pres., International Leprosy Assn.
b. Feb 5, 1873 in Pennsylvania
d. Feb 27, 1972 in New York, New York
Source: *AmAu&B; BioIn 1, 2, 3, 9; ConAu 33R; CurBio 42, 72; InSci; NewYTBE 72; WhAm 5; WhNAA*

Heiskell, Andrew
American. Publisher
Chm., CEO, Time Inc., 1960-80.
b. Sep 13, 1915 in Naples, Italy
Source: *AmAu&B; BioIn 7, 12, 13; BlueB 76; CurBio 66; Dun&B 79; EncTwCJ; IntWW 74, 75, 76, 77, 78, 79, 80, 81, 82, 83, 89, 91, 93; NewYTBS 80; St&PR 75; Who 74, 82, 83, 85, 88, 90, 92, 94; WhoAm 74, 76, 78, 80, 82, 84, 86; WhoE 74; WhoEnt 92; WhoFI 74, 75, 77, 79, 81; WhoWor 74*

Heisman, John William
American. Football Coach
Collegiate coach for 36 yrs; one of football's greatest innovators, credited with center snap, modern signals; Heisman Trophy named for him.
b. Oct 23, 1869 in Cleveland, Ohio
d. Oct 3, 1936 in New York, New York
Source: *BiDAmSp FB; BioIn 4, 6, 7; NewYTBS 84; WhoFtbl 74*

Heiss, Carol Elizabeth
American. Skater
Captured gold medal in figure skating at 1960 Winter Olympics.
b. Jan 20, 1940 in New York, New York
Source: *BiDAmSp BK; BioIn 4, 5, 6, 7, 8, 9, 10, 11, 12, 13; CurBio 59; HalFC 88; HerW 84; InWom SUP*

Hejduk, John
American. Architect
Dean, Cooper Union School of Architecture, 1975; member of "NY Five," leaders in p ostmodernistic architecture.
b. Jul 19, 1929 in New York, New York
Source: *BioIn 13, 14, 15, 16, 17; ConArch 80, 87; IntDcAr; MacEA; WhoAm 86, 90; WhoE 85A, 86, 89*

Helburn, Theresa
American. Producer
With Theatre Guild, 1918-53; produced *Oklahoma,* 1943.
b. Jan 12, 1887 in New York, New York
d. Aug 18, 1959 in Weston, Connecticut
Source: *AmAu&B; AmWomD; AmWomPl; BenetAL 91; BioIn 3, 5, 12, 13, 16; CamGWoT; ChhPo; CurBio 44, 59; DcAmB S6; EncMT; InWom, SUP; NatCAB 61; NotAW MOD; NotNAT A, B; NotWoAT; ObitOF 79; OxCAmH; OxCAmT 84; PlP&P; REnAL; WhAm 3; WhThe*

Helck, Peter
[Clarence Peter Helck]
American. Artist, Illustrator
Automobiles serve as painting subjects; entered illustrators Hall of Fame, 1968.
b. Jun 17, 1893 in New York, New York
Source: *BioIn 6, 7, 11, 12, 16; ConAu 1NR, 1R; IlrAm D; WhoAm 74, 76, 78, 80, 82, 84; WhoAmA 73, 76, 78, 80, 82, 84, 86, 89N, 91N, 93N*

Held, Al
American. Artist
Paintings developed from abstract expressionism to massive black and white geometrics: *Albany Mural,* 1971.
b. Oct 12, 1928 in New York, New York
Source: *AmArt; BioIn 7, 8, 10, 12, 13, 14, 15, 16, 19, 21; BriEAA; ConArt 77, 83, 89, 96; CurBio 86; DcAmArt; DcCAA 71, 77, 88, 94; DcCAr 81; IntWW 89, 91, 93; OxCTwCA; OxDcArt; PhDcTCA 77; PrintW 85; WhoAm 74, 82, 86, 88, 90, 92, 94, 95, 96, 97; WhoAmA 73, 76, 78, 80, 82, 84, 86, 89, 91, 93; WorArt 1950*

Held, Anna
American. Actor
Broadway star; first wife of Flo Ziegfeld; starred in *Anna Held,* 1902; known for expressive eyes, milk baths.
b. Mar 8, 1873 in Paris, France
d. Aug 12, 1918 in New York, New York
Source: *BiDD; CmpEPM; EncMT; EncVaud; FamA&A; Film 1; HalFC 80, 84, 88; InWom; LegTOT; NewGrDA 86; NotAW; NotNAT B; OxCAmT 84; OxCPMus; WhAm 1; WhoHol B; WhoStg 1906, 1908; WhScrn 77, 83; WhThe; WomWWA 14*

Held, John, Jr.
American. Cartoonist, Illustrator
His line drawings captured spirit of "flaming youth" and "flappers" during 1920s.
b. Jan 10, 1889 in Salt Lake City, Utah
d. Mar 2, 1958 in Belmar, New Jersey
Source: *AmAu&B; AmDec 1920; ArtsAmW 3; BenetAL 91; BioIn 4, 5, 6, 7, 8, 9; ChhPo S1; DcAmB S6; EncAB-A 30; EncACom; EncAJ; IlrAm 1880, C; OxCAmH; OxCAmL 65, 83, 95; REnAL; ScF&FL 1; WebAB 74, 79; WhAm 3; WhAmArt 85; WhoAmA 80N, 82N, 84N, 86N, 89N, 91N, 93N; WorECom*

Helen of Troy
Greek. Legendary Figure
Daughter of Zeus and Leda; was abducted by Paris and taken to Troy; husband's at tempts to reclaim her led to Trojan War.
Source: *InWom, SUP; NewCol 75*

Helfgott, David
Australian. Pianist
Life was portrayed in 1996 film *Shine.*
b. May 19, 1947 in Melbourne, Australia

Heliogabalus
[Varius Avitus Bassianus]
Roman. Ruler
King, 218-222; imposed Baal worship on Rome; adopted Alexander as heir; killed w hen he tried to depose Alexander.
b. 204 in Emesa, Syria
d. 222
Source: *BioIn 5, 9, 10, 11, 14; Dis&D; NewC; REn; WebBD 83*

Helion, Jean
French. Artist
Pioneer in abstract school of painting, 1929-39; later works tended toward reality.
b. Apr 21, 1904 in Couterne, France
d. Oct 27, 1987 in Paris, France
Source: *AnObit 1987; BioIn 1, 5, 7, 11, 13, 14, 15, 16, 18, 20; ConArt 77, 83, 89, 96; ConAu 124; CurBio 43, 88, 88N; DcCAr 81; IntWW 74, 75, 76, 77, 78, 79, 80, 81, 82, 83; McGDA; NewYTBS 87; OxCTwCA; PhDcTCA 77; WhoFr 79; WhoWor 74, 76, 78; WorArt 1950*

Helland-Hansen, Bjorn
Norwegian. Oceanographer
Changed oceanography from descriptive to scientific discipline based on physics, chemistry.
b. Oct 16, 1877 in Christiania, Norway
d. Sep 7, 1957 in Bergen, Norway
Source: *BioIn 4; DcScB S2*

Heller, Joseph
American. Author, Dramatist
Wrote contemporary American masterpiece, *Catch-22,* 1961.
b. May 1, 1923 in New York, New York
Source: *AmAu&B; AuNews 1; Benet 87, 96; BenetAL 91; BiDrAPA 89; BioIn 8, 9, 10, 11, 12, 13, 14, 15, 16; BioNews 74; BlueB 76; CamGEL; CamGLE; CamHAL; CasWL; CelR 90; ConAu 1BS, 5R, 8NR, 42NR; ConDr 73, 77, 82, 93; ConLC 1, 3, 5, 8, 11, 36, 63; ConNov 72, 76, 82, 86, 91, 96; ConPopW; CurBio 73; CyWA 89; DcArts; DcLB 2, 28, Y80A; DcLEL 1940; DcTwCCu 1; DrAF 76; DrAPF 80, 89; EncAHmr; EncWL 2, 3; FacFETw; GrWrEL N; HalFC 84, 88; IntAu&W 76, 89, 91, 93; IntvTCA 2; IntWW 83, 89, 91, 93; LegTOT; LinLib L; MagSAmL; MajTwCW; ModAL, S1, S2; NewYTBS 79, 86; NotNAT; Novels; OxCAmL 65, 83, 95; OxCEng 85, 95; PenC AM; RAdv 1, 13-1; RfGAmL 87, 94; RGTwCWr; ScF&FL 92; TwCWr; TwCYAW; WebE&AL; WhoAm 74, 76, 78, 80, 82, 84, 86, 92, 94, 95, 96, 97; WhoTwCL; WhoUSWr 88; WhoWrEP 89, 92, 95; WorAl; WorAlBi; WorAu 1950; WorLitC; WrDr 76, 80, 82, 84, 86, 88, 90, 92, 94, 96*

Heller, Walter Wolfgang
American. Economist, Government Official
Consultant, CBO, 1975-87; mem. Trilateral Commission, 1978-87; author of numerous books on economics.
b. Aug 27, 1915 in Buffalo, New York
d. Jun 15, 1987 in Seattle, Washington
Source: *BioIn 5, 6, 8, 10, 11, 12; BlueB 76; ConNews 87-4; CurBio 87; IntAu&W 77, 82, 86; IntWW 74, 75, 76, 77, 78, 79, 80, 81, 82, 83; PolProf J, K; WhAm 9; WhoAm 74, 76, 78, 80, 82, 84, 86; WhoAmP 73, 75, 77, 79, 81, 83, 85; WhoWor 74; WrDr 82*

Hellerman, Fred
[The Weavers]
American. Singer, Musician, Songwriter
Folksinger; original member, The Weavers, 1948-64; co-wrote song "Kisses Sweeter Than Wine," 1951.
b. May 13, 1927 in New York, New York
Source: *ASCAP 66, 80; BiDAmM; EncFCWM 69; OnThGG; WhoAm 74, 76, 78, 80, 82, 84, 90, 92; WhoE 74; WhoEnt 92*

Hellinger, Mark
American. Journalist
News columnist, NYC, 1930s-40s; headed own film co. from 1937; Broadway theater named for him.
b. Mar 21, 1903 in New York, New York
d. Dec 21, 1947 in Hollywood, California
Source: *AmAu&B; BenetAL 91; BiDAmJo; BiDFilm, 81, 94; BioIn 1, 3, 16; CmMov; CurBio 47, 48; DcFM; DcNAA; EncAJ; FilmEn; FilmgC; GangFlm; HalFC 80, 84, 88; NotNAT A, B; OxCFilm; REnAL; WhAm 2; WhScrn 77, 83; WorEFlm*

Hellman, Lillian
American. Dramatist, Author
Wrote *The Little Foxes,* 1939; movie *Julia,* based on *Pentimento,* 1973.
b. Jun 20, 1905 in New Orleans, Louisiana
d. Jun 30, 1984 in Vineyard Haven, Massachusetts
Source: *AmAu&B; AmCulL; AmWomWr; ArtclWW 2; AuNews 1, 2; Benet 87, 96; BenetAL 91; BiE&WWA; BioAmW; BioIn 1, 2, 4, 5, 7, 8, 9, 10, 11, 12; BioNews 74; CamGEL; CasWL; CelR; CnDAL; CnMD; CnThe; ConAu 112; ConDr 73, 82; ConLC 2, 4, 18, 52; CroCD; CrtSuDr; CurBio 60, 84N; CyWA 58, 89; DcFM; DramC 1; EncAB-H 1974, 1996; EncMcCE; EncSoH; EncWL 2, 3; EncWT; Ent; FacFETw; FemiCLE; FifSWrA; FilmEn; FilmgC; GangFlm; GoodHs; GrLiveH; GrWomW; HalFC 80, 84, 88; HanAmWH; InWom, SUP; LegTOT; LibW; LinLib L; MagSAmL; MajMD 1; McGEWB; McGEWD 72, 84; ModAL, S1, S2; ModAWWr; ModWD; ModWoWr; NewYTBE 73; OxCAmL 65, 83, 95; OxCAmT 84; OxCFilm; OxCThe 67, 83; OxCWoWr 95; PenC AM; PlP&P; PolProf T; RAdv 14, 13-2; ReelWom; REn; REnAL; REnWD; RfGAmL 87; SouWr; TwCA, SUP; VarWW 85; WebAB 74, 79; WebE&AL; WhE&EA; WhoAm 82; WhoAmW 58, 61, 64, 66; WhoThe 72, 77, 81; WhoTwCL; WhoWorJ 72, 78; WorAl; WorAlBi; WorEFlm*

Hellmann, Richard
American. Manufacturer
Began selling Hellmann's Mayonnaise, 1912; merged with General Foods, 1927.
b. 1876 in Vetschau, Germany
d. Feb 2, 1971 in Greenwich, Connecticut
Source: *BioIn 9; Entr; NewYTBE 71*

Helm, Levon
[The Band]
American. Musician, Singer, Actor
Played Loretta Lynn's father in *Coal Miner's Daughter,* 1980.
b. May 26, 1943 in Marvell, Arkansas
Source: *BioIn 19, 20; ConTFT 7; RkWW 82; WhoRocM 82*

Helmholtz, Hermann Ludwig Ferdinand von
German. Physicist, Physiologist
First to outline principle of energy conservation; invented ophthalmoscope, 1850.
b. Aug 31, 1821 in Potsdam, Germany
d. Sep 8, 1894 in Charlottenburg, Germany
Source: *AsBiEn; BbD; BiDPsy; BiESc; BioIn 1, 4, 7, 9, 11, 14, 15, 20; DcScB; Dis&D; EncDeaf; ICPEnP; InSci; LinLib S; LuthC 75; MacBEP; McGEWB; NamesHP; RAdv 14, 13-5; REn; WorAl*

Helmond, Katherine
American. Actor
Starred as Jessica Tate on TV's "Soap," 1977-80; "Who's the Boss," 1984-92.
b. Jul 5, 1934 in Galveston, Texas
Source: *BioIn 11, 14, 21; ConTFT 3, 15; HalFC 88; IntMPA 92, 94, 96; Who 90; WhoAm 82, 84, 86, 88, 90, 92, 94, 95, 96, 97; WhoAmW 95, 97; WhoEnt 92; WorAlBi*

Helmont, Jan Baptista van
Belgian. Chemist
First to use word "gas" to designate aeriform fluids; isolated carbon dioxide.
b. Jan 12, 1580 in Brussels, Belgium
d. Dec 30, 1644 in Vilvoorde, Belgium
Source: *BioIn 1, 6, 9, 12, 13; DcScB; McGEWB; NewCol 75*

Helmore, Tom
English. Actor
Films include *Designing Woman,* 1957; *Vertigo,* 1958.
b. Jan 4, 1912 in London, England
Source: *BiE&WWA; DcVicP 2; NotNAT; WhoHol A*

Helms, Jesse Alexander, Jr.
American. Politician, Journalist
Rep. senator from NC, 1973—.
b. Oct 18, 1921 in Monroe, North Carolina
Source: *AlmAP 88, 92; AmOrTwC; AmPolLe; BiDrUSC 89; BioIn 13, 14, 15, 16; CngDr 87, 89; ConAu 124; CurBio 79; DcAmC; IntWW 91; PolProf NF; PolsAm 84; WhoAm 74, 76, 86, 90; WhoAmP 87, 91; WhoGov 77; WhoSSW 91; WhoWor 84, 91; WorAlBi*

Helms, Richard McGarrah
American. Government Official
CIA Deputy Director, 1965-73; ambassador to Iran, 1973-76.
b. Mar 30, 1913 in Saint Davids, Pennsylvania
Source: *BioIn 6, 7, 8, 9, 10, 11, 12, 13; ColdWar 1; CurBio 67; DcAmDH 89; EncAI&E; IntWW 91; NewYTBE 71, 73; NewYTBS 77; PolProf J, K, NF; USBiR 74; WhoAm 74, 76, 78, 82, 84, 86, 88, 90, 92, 94, 95, 96, 97; WhoAmP 77, 79; WhoGov 75; WhoSSW 73; WhoWor 74, 76, 78*

Helmsley, Harry B(rakmann)
American. Businessman
Real estate tycoon; Manhattan's largest landlord; bought Empire State Building for $65 million, 1961; indicted for tax evasion, 1988.
b. Mar 4, 1909 in New York, New York
d. Jan 4, 1997 in Scottsdale, Arizona
Source: *BioIn 8, 9, 11, 12, 13, 14, 15, 16; CurBio 85; Dun&B 90; NewYTBE 73; NewYTBS 80; St&PR 87, 91; WhoAm 86, 90; WhoE 91; WhoFI 87*

Helmsley, Leona Mindy Rosenthal
[Mrs. Harry Helmsley]
American. Hotel Executive
Presided over husband's 26 luxury hotels, 1980-89; known for tough rules, passion for details; convicted on tax evasion charges, 1992.
b. Jul 4, 1920 in Marbletown, New York
Source: *BioIn 13, 14, 15, 16; ConNews 88-1; Dun&B 90; NewYTBS 80, 88; WhoAm 86, 88; WhoAmW 87, 91; WhoFI 85, 87*

Heloise
[Heloise and Abelard]
French. Religious Figure
Best known for love affair with Pierre Abelard; immortalized in their letters.
b. 1098?
d. May 15, 1164 in Paraclete Abbey, France
Source: *EncCoWW; IntDcWB; InWom SUP; LegTOT; NotWoLS; OxCFr; REn; WorAl*

Heloise
[Heloise Bowles Reese]
American. Journalist, Author
Wrote syndicated column *Hints from Heloise,* 1961-77.
b. May 4, 1919 in Fort Worth, Texas

d. Dec 28, 1977 in San Antonio, Texas
Source: *ConAu 9R, 73; DcAmB S10; InWom; LegTOT; PenNWW A, B*

Heloise
[Ponce Kiah Marchelle Heloise Cruse Evans]
American. Writer
Writes column "Hints from Heloise," 1977—, a columns of household tips.
b. Apr 15, 1951 in Waco, Texas
Source: *CurBio 96; WhoAm 84, 86, 88, 90, 92, 94, 95, 96, 97; WhoAmW 81, 85, 87, 89, 91, 93, 95, 97; WhoEmL 87; WhoSSW 95, 97*

Helper, Hinton Rowan
American. Writer
One of few Southerners to oppose slavery, he penned economic arguments against it in *The Impending Crisis of the South,* 1857.
b. Dec 27, 1829 in Davie County, North Carolina
d. Mar 9, 1909 in Washington, District of Columbia
Source: *Alli, SUP; AmAu; AmAu&B; AmBi; AmRef; AmSocL; ApCAB; Benet 87; BenetAL 91; BiD&SB; BiDSA; BioIn 1, 3, 7, 8, 9, 14, 15, 19; CnDAL; DcAmAu; DcAmB; DcNAA; DcNCBi 3; Drake SUP; EncAAH; EncAB-H 1974, 1996; EncSoH; HarEnUS; McGEWB; MorMA; OxCAmH; OxCAmL 65, 83, 95; REn; REnAL; TwCBDA; WebAB 74, 79; WhAm 1; WhCiWar*

Helpmann, Robert Murray, Sir
Australian. Dancer, Actor
Flamboyant star of British ballet, 1934-50; known for theatricality; films include *The Mango Tree,* 1981.
b. Apr 9, 1909 in Mount Gambier, Australia
d. Sep 28, 1986 in Sydney, Australia
Source: *BiDD; BiE&WWA; BlueB 76; CurBio 50, 86; DcNaB 1986; FilmgC; IntWW 74, 75, 76, 77, 78, 79, 80, 81, 82, 83; MovMk; NewYTBS 86; NotNAT; OxCThe 67, 83; PlP&P; VarWW 85; Who 74, 82, 83, 85; WhoHol A; WhoThe 81; WhoWor 74, 76, 78*

Helprin, Mark
American. Author
Best-selling novelist; works include *A Soldier of the Great War,* 1991; *Ellis Island and Other Stories,* 1981.
b. Jun 28, 1947 in New York, New York
Source: *BenetAL 91; BioIn 12, 13; ConAu 47NR, 81; ConLC 7, 10, 22, 32; ConPopW; CurBio 71, 91; CyWA 89; DcLB Y85B; EncSF 93; IntAu&W 89, 91, 93; MajTwCW; NewYTBS 84, 91; OxCAmL 95; ScF&FL 92; SJGFanW; TwCSFW 86; WhoAm 82, 84, 86, 88, 90, 92, 94, 95, 96, 97; WhoWest 94; WorAu 1975; WrDr 86, 88, 90, 92, 94, 96*

Hemans, Felicia Dorothea Browne
English. Poet
Wrote verses "The Boy Stood on the Burning Deck"; "England's Dead."
b. Sep 25, 1793 in Liverpool, England
d. May 16, 1835 in Dublin, Ireland
Source: *Alli; BbD; BiD&SB; BioIn 15, 16, 17, 18; BritAu 19; CarSB; CasWL; ChhPo S2, S3; DcEnA; DcEnL; DcEuL; DcLEL; EncBrWW; EvLB; GrWrEL P; InWom, SUP; NewC; NewCBEL; OxCEng 67, 95; PoChrch; REn; WebE&AL*

Hemings, Sally
"Black Sally"
American. Slave
Believed by some to have been mistress of Thomas Jefferson; subject of book by Barbara Chase-Riboud, 1979.
b. 1773
d. 1835
Source: *BioIn 4, 6, 9, 11, 12, 17, 18, 19, 20, 21; BlkWAm; DcAmNB; InB&W 80, 85; InWom SUP; NotBlAW 1*

Hemingway, Ernest (Miller)
American. Journalist, Author
Wrote *A Farewell to Arms,* 1929; *For Whom the Bell Tolls,* 1940; won Nobel Prize, 1954.
b. Jul 21, 1899 in Oak Park, Illinois
d. Jul 2, 1961 in Ketchum, Idaho
Source: *AmAu&B; AmCulL; AmDec 1920, 1950; AmNov; AmWr; ArizL; Au&Arts 19; AuNews 2; Benet 87, 96; BenetAL 91; BiDAmJo; BioIn 6, 7, 8, 9, 10, 11, 13, 14, 15, 16, 17, 18, 19, 20, 21; CasWL; Chambr 3; ChhPo S1, S2, S3; CnDAL; CnMD; CnMWL; ConAmA; ConAmL; ConAu 34NR, 77; ConLC 1, 3, 6, 8, 10, 13, 19, 30, 34, 39, 41, 44, 50, 61, 80; CyWA 58, 89; DcAmB S7; DcArts; DcLB 4, 9, 102, DS1, Y81A, Y87A, Y92; DcLEL; DcTwCCu 1; EncAB-H 1974, 1996; EncTwCJ; EncWL, 2, 3; EvLB; FilmgC; GrWrEL N; HalFC 80, 84, 88; LegTOT; LiExTwC; LiJour; LinLib L, S; LngCTC; MagSAmL; MajTwCW; MakMC; MemAm; MichAu 80; ModAL, S1, S2; ModWD; NatCAB 57; NewYTBS 85; NobelP; NotNAT B; ObitT 1961; OxCAmL 65, 83, 95; OxCEng 67, 85, 95; PenC AM; RAdv 1, 14, 13-1; RComAH; RComWL; REn; REnAL; RfGAmL 87, 94; RfGShF; RGTwCWr; ShSCr 1; ShSWr; Tw; TwCA, SUP; TwCWr; WebAB 74, 79; WebBD 83; WebE&AL; WhAm 4; WhDW; WhFla; WhoNob, 90, 95; WhoTwCL; WorAl; WorAlBi; WorEFlm; WorLitC*

Hemingway, Leicester
American. Author
Younger brother of Ernest Hemingway; wrote biography *My Brother, Ernest Hemingway.*
b. Apr 1, 1915 in Oak Park, Illinois
d. Sep 13, 1982 in Miami, Florida
Source: *BioIn 3, 13; ConAu 107*

Hemingway, Margaux
American. Model, Actor
Granddaughter of Ernest Hemingway; starred in *Lipstick,* 1976; killed herself by taking an overdose of phenobarbital.
b. Feb 19, 1955 in Portland, Oregon
d. Jun 1996 in Santa Monica, California
Source: *BioIn 10, 11, 12, 16; BkPepl; ConTFT 13; CurBio 78, 96N; HalFC 84, 88; IntMPA 88, 92; InWom SUP; ItaFilm; LegTOT; News 97-1; NewYTBS 27; VarWW 85; WhoAm 80; WhoHol 92, A*

Hemingway, Mariel
American. Actor
Granddaughter of Ernest Hemingway; starred in *Lipstick,* 1976; *Manhattan,* 1979; TV series "Civil Wars," 1991-93.
b. Nov 21, 1961 in Mill Valley, California
Source: *BioIn 11, 13, 14, 15, 16; ConTFT 2, 3, 12; HalFC 84, 88; IntMPA 86, 88, 92, 94, 96; LegTOT; VarWW 85; WhoAm 94, 95, 96, 97; WhoAmW 95, 97; WhoEnt 92; WhoHol 92*

Hemingway, Mary Welsh
[Mrs. Ernest Hemingway]
American. Author, Journalist
Fourth wife of Ernest Hemingway; foreign correspondent during WW II; wrote autobiography *How It Was,* 1976.
b. Apr 5, 1908 in Walker, Minnesota
d. Nov 27, 1986 in New York, New York
Source: *BioAmW; ConAu 73, 121; Conv 1; CurBio 68, 87; ForWC 70; InWom, SUP; WhoAmW 74; WhoE 75, 77, 79; WrDr 80, 82, 84*

Hemion, Dwight
American. Director, Producer
Won Emmy for TV special "Frank Sinatra: A Man and His Music," 1965.
b. Mar 14, 1926 in New Haven, Connecticut
Source: *ConTFT 8; LesBEnT 92; NewYTET; VarWW 85; WhoAm 82, 90; WhoEnt 92; WhoWest 89, 92*

Hemmings, David Leslie Edward
[Leslie Edward]
English. Actor
Starred in films *Blow-Up,* 1966, *Camelot,* 1967.
b. Nov 18, 1941 in Guildford, England
Source: *BioIn 14; ConTFT 7; FilmgC; HalFC 88; IntMPA 82, 92; IntWW 82, 83, 89, 91, 93; MotPP; MovMk; VarWW 85; Who 74, 82, 83, 85, 88, 90, 92, 94; WhoAm 84; WhoEnt 92; WhoHol A; WhoWor 84, 87, 91, 93, 95, 96, 97; WorAlBi; WorEFlm*

Hempel, Frieda
German. Opera Singer
Brilliant soprano; with NY Met., 1912-19; noted for Jenny Lind recitals, 1920s.
b. Jun 26, 1885 in Leipzig, Germany
d. Oct 7, 1955 in Berlin, Germany (West)

Source: *ApCAB X; Baker 78, 84, 92; BioIn 1, 3, 4, 11, 14; CmOp; IntDcOp; InWom, SUP; MetOEnc; MusSN; NewAmDM; NewEOp 71; NewGrDA 86; NewGrDM 80; NewGrDO; OxDcOp; PenDiMP; WhAm 3*

Hemphill, Essex
American. AIDS Activist, Poet
Edited *Brother to Brother,* a compilation of writings by black gay men.
b. 1957 in Chicago, Illinois
d. Nov 5, 1995
Source: *ConBlB 10; GayLesB; RAdv 14; SchCGBL*

Hemphill, Paul
American. Author
Writer of the Southern experience: *The Nashville Sound,* 1970, deals with rise and popularity of country music.
b. Feb 18, 1936 in Birmingham, Alabama
Source: *AuBYP 2S, 3; AuNews 2; BioIn 10, 11, 15, 19; ConAu 12NR, 29NR, 49, 55NR; DcLB Y87B; WrDr 92*

Hemsley, Sherman
American. Actor
Played George Jefferson on "The Jeffersons," 1975-85; star of "Amen," 1986-91.
b. Feb 1, 1938 in Philadelphia, Pennsylvania
Source: *BioIn 10, 12, 15; BlksAmF; ConTFT 3; DrBlPA, 90; InB&W 80, 85; IntMPA 92, 94, 96; LegTOT; VarWW 85; WhoAfA 96; WhoAm 86, 88, 90, 92, 94; WhoBlA 85, 88, 90, 92, 94; WhoCom; WhoEnt 92; WhoHol 92; WhoTelC*

Hench, Philip Showalter
American. Scientist, Physician, Engineer
Shared Nobel Prize in medicine, 1950 with Edward Kendall for work on hormones of the adrenal cortex.
b. Feb 28, 1896 in Pittsburgh, Pennsylvania
d. Mar 30, 1965 in Ocho Rios, Jamaica
Source: *AsBiEn; BiESc; BioIn 2, 3, 4, 7, 15, 20; CurBio 50, 65; DcAmB, S7; DcAmMeB 84; FacFETw; InSci; LarDcSc; McGMS 80; NotTwCS; ObitOF 79; ObitT 1961, 1971; OxCMed 86; WebAB 74, 79; WebBD 83; WhAm 4; WhoNob, 90, 95; WorAl; WorScD*

Henderson, Arthur
"Founding Father of the Labor Party"
British. Diplomat
Won Nobel Peace Prize, 1934, for part he played as president, League of Nations World Disarmament Conference.
b. Sep 13, 1863 in Glasgow, Scotland
d. Oct 20, 1935 in London, England
Source: *BiDInt; BioIn 2, 3, 9, 11, 14, 15, 16, 18; DcNaB, 1931; EncWM; FacFETw; GrBr; LinLib S; McGEWB; NobelP; WhDW; WhoNob, 90, 95*

Henderson, Arthur
English. Statesman
Labor leader; led International Disarmament Conference of League of Nations, 1932; won Nobel Peace Prize, 1934.
b. Aug 27, 1893
d. Aug 28, 1968 in London, England
Source: *IntYB 78; WhE&EA; WhoLA*

Henderson, Bruce
American. Consultant
Pioneer in business strategy consulting.
b. Apr 30, 1915 in Nashville, Tennessee
d. Jul 20, 1992 in Nashville, Tennessee
Source: *St&PR 75, 84; WhoAm 90; WhoFI 89; WhoWor 91*

Henderson, Fletcher
[James Fletcher Henderson]
"Smack"
American. Bandleader, Composer
Pianist; first jazzman to use written arrangements; organized his first band, 19 23.
b. Dec 18, 1897 in Cuthbert, Georgia
d. Dec 29, 1952 in New York, New York
Source: *AfrAmAl 6; AllMusG; ASCAP 66, 80; Baker 84; BiDAmM; BiDJaz; ConMus 16; DcAmB S5; DcTwCCu 5; FacFETw; NegAl 89; NewAmDM; NewGrDA 86; NewGrDJ 88; OxCPMus; PenEncP; WhoJazz 72*

Henderson, Florence
American. Actor, Singer
Starred in TV series "The Brady Bunch," 1969-75.
b. Feb 14, 1934 in Dale, Indiana
Source: *BiE&WWA; BioIn 3, 4, 8, 9, 17; CelR 90; ConTFT 2; CurBio 71; EncMT; HalFC 80, 84, 88; IntMPA 96; InWom, SUP; LegTOT; NotNAT; VarWW 85; WhoAm 80, 82, 84, 86, 88, 90, 92, 94, 95, 96, 97; WhoAmW 68, 70, 72, 74; WhoEnt 92; WhoHol 92, A; WhoThe 72, 77, 81; WorAl; WorAlBi*

Henderson, Gordon
American. Fashion Designer
Launched clothing line, "But Gordon," 1990; won Perry Ellis Award for best new fashion design talent, 1990.
b. 1957 in San Joaquin Valley, California
Source: *ConBlB 5; ConFash*

Henderson, Jimmy
[Black Oak Arkansas]
American. Musician
Guitarist with heavy-metal, Dixie boogie group.
b. May 20, 1954 in Jackson, Mississippi
Source: *WhoAdv 90; WhoE 89; WhoEmL 89, 91; WhoRocM 82*

Henderson, Joe
American. Jazz Musician
Saxophonist influenced by Strayhorn; albums include *Lush Life,* 1992.
b. Apr 24, 1937 in Lima, Ohio
Source: *AfrAmAl 6; AllMusG; ConMus 14; CurBio 96; EncJzS; IlEncJ; NewGrDA 86; NewGrDJ 88, 94; WhoAm 94, 95, 96, 97*

Henderson, Lawrence Joseph
American. Author, Biochemist
Wrote *Order of Nature,* 1917; *Blood,* 1928.
b. Jun 3, 1878 in Lynn, Massachusetts
d. Feb 10, 1942 in Cambridge, Massachusetts
Source: *BiDAmEd; BiHiMed; BioIn 3, 5, 8, 9; CurBio 42; DcAmB S3; DcAmMeB 84; DcNAA; DcScB; InSci; OxCMed 86; WebBD 83; WhAm 1*

Henderson, Leon
"The Price Czar"
American. Government Official
Powerful FDR aide; directed rationing, price ceilings, first half of WW II.
b. May 26, 1895 in Millville, New Jersey
d. Oct 19, 1986 in Oceanside, California
Source: *AmPolLe; AnObit 1986; BioIn 1, 5, 15; CurBio 40, 87, 87N; LinLib S; WhAm 9*

Henderson, Leon N(esbit)
American. Educator
Professor of education, 1945-60, head of department, 1956-60, U of FL.
b. Feb 22, 1906 in Baker, Florida
d. Feb 7, 1960 in Gainesville, Florida
Source: *WhAm 4*

Henderson, Ray
American. Songwriter
Noted pianst-composer; often teamed with B DeSylva, Lew Brown; scored Jolson films; portrayed in film *Best Things in Life Are Free,* 1956.
b. Dec 1, 1896 in Buffalo, New York
d. Dec 31, 1971 in Greenwich, Connecticut
Source: *AmPS; AmSong; ASCAP 66, 80; Baker 78, 84; BiDAmM; BiE&WWA; BioIn 1, 4, 5, 6, 9, 10, 12, 14, 15, 16; CmpEPM; ConAmC 76, 82; DcAmB S8; EncMT; HalFC 80, 84, 88; NewAmDM; NewCBMT; NewGrDA 86; NewGrDM 80; NewYTBE 71; NotNAT B; OxCAmT 84; OxCPMus; PopAmC, SUP; Sw&Ld C; WhThe*

Henderson, Rickey (Henley)
American. Baseball Player
Outfielder, Oakland Athletics, 1979-84, 1989-93, 1994—, NY Yankees, 1985-89, Toronto Blue Jays, 1993-94; broke Lou Brock's ML record for stolen bases, 1991; MVP, AL, 1990; MVP, American Championship Series, 1989; Winner AL Gold Glove, 1981
b. Dec 25, 1958 in Chicago, Illinois
Source: *AfrAmBi 1; AfrAmSG; Ballpl 90; BaseReg 86, 87; BiDAmSp BB; BioIn 12, 13, 14, 15, 16; CelR 90; CurBio 90; InB&W 85; NegAl 89; NewYTBS 84, 86; WhoAfA 96; WhoAm 86, 88, 90, 92, 94, 95, 96, 97; WhoBlA 85, 88, 90, 92, 94; WhoE 86, 89; WhoWest 92, 94, 96; WorAlBi*

Henderson, Robert W
American. Librarian, Historian
Sports historian; wrote *Ball, Bat, and Bishop,* 1947; disputed myth that Abner Doubleday invented baseball.
b. Dec 25, 1888 in South Shields, England
d. Aug 19, 1985 in Hartford, Connecticut
Source: *AmAu&B; WhoLibS 55*

Henderson, Skitch
[Lyle Henderson; Lyle Russell Cedric Henderson]
American. Bandleader, Pianist
Played piano on Sinatra, Crosby radio shows; led band on Steve Allen's original "Tonight Show," 1950s.
b. Jan 27, 1918 in Halstad, Minnesota
Source: *ASCAP 66, 80; Baker 84, 92; BgBands 74; BioIn 4, 5, 6, 7, 10, 21; CelR, 90; CmpEPM; CurBio 66; IntMPA 77, 80, 86, 88, 92, 94, 96; IntWWM 77; LegTOT; NewAmDM; NewGrDA 86; NewYTBE 72; NewYTBS 27; PenEncP; RadStar; VarWW 85; WhoAm 86, 88, 90, 92, 94, 95, 96, 97; WhoE 97; WhoEnt 92*

Henderson, Vivian Wilson
American. Educator, Economist
Pres., Atlanta's Clark College, 1965-76.
b. Feb 10, 1923 in Bristol, Tennessee
d. Jan 25, 1976 in Atlanta, Georgia
Source: *BioIn 8, 10, 11; ConAu 61, 65; Ebony 1; NewYTBS 76; ObitOF 79; WhAm 6; WhoAm 74, 76; WhoBlA 75; WhoRel 75*

Hendrick, Burton Jesse
American. Biographer, Journalist
Won Pulitzers for *Victory at Sea,* 1920; *Life of Walter Page,* 1922; *Training of an American,* 1928.
b. Dec 28, 1870 in New Haven, Connecticut
d. Mar 23, 1949 in New York, New York
Source: *AmAu&B; BioIn 1, 2, 3, 4, 7; ChhPo S2; DcAmB S4; DcLEL; NatCAB 38, 47; ObitOF 79; OxCAmL 65; REnAL; TwCA, SUP; WhAm 2; WhNAA*

Hendricks, Barbara
American. Opera Singer
Famous for her impressive lyric sopranos; debuted at NY Metropolitan Opera in *Der Rosenkavalier,* 1986.
b. Nov 20, 1948 in Stephens, Arkansas
Source: *AfrAmAl 6; Baker 84, 92; BioIn 16; BlkWAm; BriBkM 80; ConBlB 3; ConMus 10; CurBio 89; InB&W 85; IntWW 89, 91, 93; IntWWM 90; MetOEnc; NegAl 89; NewGrDA 86; NewGrDO; NewYTBS 86; OxDcOp; PenDiMP; WhoAfA 96; WhoAm 78, 80, 82, 84, 86, 88, 90, 92, 94, 95, 96, 97; WhoAmM 83; WhoAmW 91, 93; WhoBlA 85, 88, 90, 92, 94; WhoOp 76; WhoWor 91*

Hendricks, Ted
[Theodore Paul Hendricks]
"Mad Stork"
American. Football Player
Seven-time all-pro linebacker, 1969-83, mostly with Oakland/LA; set NFL record for safeties in career (4); Hall of Fame, 1990.
b. Nov 1, 1947 in Guatemala City, Guatemala
Source: *BiDAmSp FB; BioIn 12, 13, 14; NewYTBS 82; WhoAm 78; WhoFtbl 74; WhoSpor*

Hendricks, Thomas Andrews
American. US Vice President
VP under Grover Cleveland, 1885.
b. Sep 7, 1819 in Zanesville, Ohio
d. Nov 25, 1885 in Indianapolis, Indiana
Source: *AmPolLe; ApCAB; BiDrAC; BiDrUSC 89; BiDrUSE 71, 89; BioIn 1, 4, 7, 8, 9, 10, 14; DcAmB; HarEnUS; NatCAB 2; TwCBDA; VicePre; WebAB 74, 79; WhAm HS; WhAmP; WhCiWar*

Hendrix, Jimi
[James Marshall Hendrix]
American. Musician, Singer
Innovative electric guitarist; hits include "Purple Haze," 1967; died of drug overdose.
b. Nov 27, 1942 in Seattle, Washington
d. Sep 18, 1970 in London, England
Source: *AfrAmAl 6; AmCulL; AmDec 1960; Baker 78, 84, 92; BiDAfM; BiDAmM; BioIn 8, 9, 10, 11, 12, 13; BluesWW; ConBlB 10; ConMus 2; DcAmB S8; DcArts; DcTwCCu 1, 5; DrBlPA, 90; EncPR&S 89; EncRk 88; EncRkSt; FacFETw; HarEnR 86; IlEncBM 82; IlEncRk; InB&W 80, 85; LegTOT; NegAl 89; NewAmDM; NewGrDA 86; NewYTBE 70; OnThGG; OxCPMus; PenEncP; RolSEnR 83; SoulM; WhAm 5; WhoHol B; WhoRock 81; WhoRocM 82; WhScrn 77; WorAl; WorAlBi*

Hendry, Ian
English. Actor
Best known for *Theatre of Blood,* 1973.
b. Jan 13, 1931 in Ipswich, England
Source: *FilmgC; HalFC 80, 84, 88; IlWWBF; IntMPA 75, 76, 77, 78, 79, 80, 81, 82, 84; ItaFilm; WhoHol A*

Henie, Sonja
American. Skater
Won gold medals in figure skating, 1928, 1932, 1936 Olympics; starred in film *Wintertime,* 1943.
b. Apr 8, 1912 in Kristiania, Norway
d. Oct 12, 1969 in Los Angeles, California
Source: *BiDD; BiDFilm 94; BioIn 2, 3, 5, 6, 7, 8, 9, 10, 11, 12, 19, 21; CmMov; CmpEPM; CurBio 40, 52, 70; DcAmB S8; FacFETw; Film 2; FilmEn; FilmgC; IntDcF 1-3, 2-3; InWom SUP; MotPP; MovMk; NotAW MOD; OxCFilm; WhAm 5; WhoSpor; WhScrn 74, 77, 83; WorAl; WorAlBi*

Henize, Karl G(ordon)
American. Astronomer, Astronaut
Specialist for numerous Apollo, Skylab, Space Shuttle Missions; with NASA from 1967; recipient of Flight Achievement Award, American Astroautical Society, 1985; recipient of NASA Medal for Exceptional Scientific Achievement, 1974.
b. Oct 17, 1926 in Cincinnati, Ohio
d. 1994 in Mount Everest
Source: *AmMWSc 76P, 79, 82, 86, 89, 92, 95; BioIn 10, 15; BlueB 76; IntWW 74, 75, 76, 77; WhAm 11; WhoAm 74, 76, 78, 80, 82, 84, 86, 88, 90; WhoGov 75, 77; WhoScEn 94; WhoSpc; WhoSSW 73, 75, 76; WhoWor 74, 76, 78, 80, 82, 84*

Henke, Tom
American. Baseball Player
Toronto Blue Jays' right-handed relief pitcher who was the highest paid for that position in 1992 for over $3.6 million.
Source: *Ballpl 90*

Henkle, Henrietta
[Henrietta Buckmaster]
American. Author, Journalist
Novels on black life include *Let My People Go,* 1941; *Deep River,* 1949.
b. 1909 in Cleveland, Ohio
d. Apr 26, 1993 in Chestnut Hill, Massachusetts
Source: *AmAu&B; AmWomWr; BioIn 1, 2, 10, 13; ConAu 69; CurBio 46, 83N; DcLP 87A; FemiCLE; InWom, SUP; OhA&B; ScF&FL 92*

Henle, Guy
American. Editor
Exec. editor *Consumer Reports,* 1972-83.
b. Dec 22, 1920 in New York, New York
d. May 11, 1992 in Scarsdale, New York
Source: *BioIn 17, 18; WhAm 10; WhoAm 74, 76, 78, 80, 82, 84, 86, 88, 90; WhoE 74*

Henley, Beth
[Elizabeth Becker Henley]
American. Dramatist
Won Pulitzer, 1981, for *Crimes of the Heart,* filmed 1986.
b. May 8, 1952 in Jackson, Mississippi
Source: *AmWomD; AmWomWr SUP; ArtclWW 2; Benet 87; BenetAL 91; BioIn 12, 13, 15, 16; CamGWoT; CelR 90; ConAmD; ConAu 3BS, 32NR, 107; ConDr 88, 93; ConLC 23; ConTFT 1, 12; ConWomD; CrtSuDr; CurBio 83; CyWA 89; DcLB Y86B; DcTwCCu 1; DramC 6; FemiCLE; FemiWr; GrLiveH; GrWomW; IntAu&W 89, 91, 93; IntDcT 2; IntWW 89, 91, 93; InWom SUP; LegTOT; MajTwCW; ModWoWr; NatPD 81; NewYTBS 81; OxCAmL 83, 95; OxCWoWr 95; RAdv 14, 13-2; VarWW 85; WhoAm 84, 88, 90, 92, 94, 95, 96, 97; WhoAmW 85, 87, 89, 91, 93, 95; WhoEnt 92; WhoHol 92; WhoWor 95,*

96, 97; WorAu 1980; WrDr 88, 90, 92, 94, 96

Henley, Don
[The Eagles]
American. Singer, Musician, Songwriter
As solo performer, won 1990 Grammy for "The End of the Innocence."
b. Jul 22, 1947 in Linden, Texas
Source: *BioIn 14, 15, 16; ConMus 3; EncPR&S 89; EncRkSt; LegTOT; RkOn 85; WhoEnt 92*

Henley, William Ernest
English. Author, Poet
Editor, man-of-letters; best known for poem "Invictus."
b. Aug 23, 1849 in Gloucester, England
d. Jul 11, 1903 in Woking, England
Source: *Alli SUP; AtlBL; Benet 87, 96; BiD&SB; BioIn 1, 2, 9, 10, 11, 13, 15, 16, 21; BritAu 19; CamGEL; CasWL; Chambr 3; ChhPo, S1, S2, S3; CnE&AP; ConAu 105; DcEnA, A; DcEuL; DcLB 19; DcLEL; DcNaB S2; Dis&D; EvLB; GrWrEL P; LinLib S; LngCTC; MouLC 4; NewC; NewCBEL; NotNAT B; OxCEng 67; PenC ENG; REn; TwCLC 8; VicBrit; WebE&AL; WhDW*

Hennard, George, Jr.
American. Murderer
Crashed truck into Luby's Cafeteria (Killeen, TX); opened fire on lunch crowd, killing 23; worst mass-murder in U.S. history, 1991.
b. Oct 15, 1956 in Sayre, Pennsylvania
d. Oct 16, 1991 in Killeen, Texas

Hennebique, Francois
French. Engineer
Patented complete building system based on use of reinforced concrete, 1892.
b. 1842 in Neuville-Saint-Vaast, France
d. 1921 in Paris, France
Source: *BioIn 10, 13; IntDcAr; MacEA; WhoArch*

Hennepin, Louis
French. Explorer
Explored Great Lakes with La Salle, 1678-79; wrote *Description de la Louisia ne,* 1683.
b. Apr 7, 1640? in Ath, Belgium
d. 1701?
Source: *AmBi; ApCAB; BenetAL 91; BiDSA; BioIn 4, 8, 13; DcAmB; DcBiPP; DcCathB; Drake; EncCRAm; EncNAR; HarEnUS; LinLib L, S; LuthC 75; NewCBEL; OxCAmH; OxCAmL 65, 83, 95; REn; REnAL; WebAB 74, 79; WhAm HS; WhNaAH; WhWE*

Henner, Jean Jacques
French. Artist
Drew historical subjects, female portraits, sensuous nudes in Italian settings: "Sleeping Bather," 1863.
b. Mar 5, 1829 in Bernwiller, France
d. Jul 23, 1905 in Paris, France
Source: *ClaDrA; McGDA; WhAmArt 85A*

Henner, Marilu
American. Actor
Played Elaine Nardo on TV comedy "Taxi," 1978-83; "Evening Shade," 1990-94.
b. Apr 6, 1953 in Chicago, Illinois
Source: *BioIn 11, 14, 16; ConTFT 2, 7; IntMPA 92; InWom SUP; VarWW 85; WhoEnt 92; WhoTelC*

Henning, Anne
American. Skater
Won speed skating gold medal, 1972 Olympics.
b. 1956 in Northbrook, Illinois
Source: *BioIn 10; InWom SUP; NewYTBS 76*

Henning, Doug(las James)
Canadian. Magician
Created, starred in musical *The Magic Show;* host of TV specials.
b. May 3, 1947 in Fort Gary, Manitoba, Canada
Source: *BioIn 10, 11, 13, 14; CanWW 31, 81, 83, 89; CurBio 76; LegTOT; NewYTBS 74, 83; VarWW 85; WhoAm 78, 80, 82, 84, 86, 88, 90, 92, 94, 95, 96, 97; WhoEnt 92*

Henning, Linda Kaye
American. Actor
Played Betty Jo Bradley on TV series "Petticoat Junction," 1963-70.
b. Sep 16, 1944 in Toluca Lake, California
Source: *BioIn 18; ConTFT 3; IntMPA 77, 88, 92, 94, 96; WhoHol A*

Henreid, Paul
[Paul G Julius VonHernreid]
Italian. Actor, Director
Discovered by Otto Preminger, 1933; starred in *Casablanca,* 1943.
b. Jan 10, 1908 in Trieste, Italy
d. Mar 29, 1992 in Santa Monica, California
Source: *AnObit 1992; BiDFilm, 81, 94; BioIn 13, 14, 17, 18, 19; CmMov; ConTFT 12; CurBio 43, 92N; FilmEn; FilmgC; ForYSC; HalFC 88; IntDcF 1-3, 2-3; IntMPA 77, 78, 79, 80, 81, 82, 92; ItaFilm; LegTOT; MotPP; MovMk; NewYTBS 92; OxCFilm; VarWW 85; WhoAm 82, 90; WhoEnt 92; WhoHol A; WorAl; WorAlBi; WorEFlm*

Henri, Robert
American. Artist
A major influence on group of now-famous artists known as the Ashcan School.
b. Jun 25, 1865 in Cincinnati, Ohio
d. Jul 12, 1929 in New York, New York
Source: *AmBi; AmCulL; AmDec 1900; ArtsAmW 1, 2; AtlBL; BiDAmEd; BioIn 1, 3, 4, 5, 6, 7, 8, 9, 13, 14, 17, 19, 20; BriEAA; ConArt 77; DcAmArt; DcAmB; DcArts; DcNAA; EncAB-H 1974, 1996; FacFETw; GayN; IlBEAAW; LegTOT; LinLib S; McGDA; NatCAB 15; OhA&B; OxCAmH; OxCAmL 65; OxCArt; OxCTwCA; OxDcArt; PhDcTCA 77; REnAL; WebAB 74, 79; WhAm 1; WhAmArt 85; WhNAA; WorAl; WorAlBi*

Henrich, Tommy
[Thomas David Henrich]
"Old Reliable"
American. Baseball Player
Infielder-outfielder, NY Yankees, 1937-50; one of baseball's first free agents, 1937.
b. Feb 20, 1913 in Massillon, Ohio
Source: *Ballpl 90; BioIn 14, 16, 18; LegTOT; NewYTBE 71; WhoProB 73*

Henriksen, Lance
American. Actor
His films include *Aliens,* 1986, 1992; and *Jennifer 8,* 1992.
b. 1940 in New York, New York

Henrit, Robert
English. Musician
Drummer with Argent, 1969-76.
b. May 2, 1946 in Boxbourne, England
Source: *WhoRocM 82*

Henry, Buck
[Buck Zuckerman]
American. Screenwriter, Actor
Wrote, appeared in film: *The Graduate,* 1967; wrote *Protocol,* 1984.
b. Dec 9, 1930 in New York, New York
Source: *BioIn 9, 12, 14; ConAu 77; ConDr 73, 77A, 88A; ConTFT 9; DcLB 26; EncAFC; FilmEn; FilmgC; HalFC 80, 84, 88; IntDcF 1-4, 2-4; IntMPA 77, 80, 92, 94, 96; ItaFilm; LegTOT; MiSFD 9; NewYTBE 70; VarWW 85; WhoAm 86, 90, 92, 94, 95, 96, 97; WhoCom; WhoEnt 92; WhoHol 92, A*

Henry, Charlotte
American. Actor
Had title role in *Alice in Wonderland,* 1933.
b. Mar 3, 1913 in Charlotte, New York
d. Apr 1980 in San Diego, California
Source: *FilmEn; FilmgC; ForYSC; HalFC 84, 88; WhoHol A*

Henry, Clarence
""Frogman""
American. Singer
Rhythm and blues singer best known for froglike voice, hit single "Ain't Got No H ome," 1956.
b. Mar 19, 1937 in Algiers, Louisiana
Source: *EncRk 88; PenEncP; RolSEnR 83; WhoRock 81*

Henry, David D(odds)
American. University Administrator
Pres., U of IL, 1955-71.
b. Oct 21, 1905
d. Sep 4, 1995 in Naples, Florida
Source: *BiDAmEd; BioIn 5, 7, 21; BlueB 76; ConAu 106, 149; CurBio 95N; IntWW 74, 75, 76, 77, 78, 79, 80, 81, 82, 83; LEduc 74; WhoAm 74, 76, 80*

Henry, Edward Lamson
American. Artist
Illustrated American history, railroad scenes in detailed, naturalistic manner.
b. Jan 12, 1841 in Charleston, South Carolina
d. May 9, 1919 in New York, New York
Source: *AmBi; ApCAB, X; BioIn 9, 10, 12, 15; BriEAA; DcAmArt; DcAmB; HarEnUS; McGDA; NatCAB 5; NewYHSD; TwCBDA; WhAm 1*

Henry, Edward Richard, Sir
English. Government Official
London police commissioner who adopted system of taking fingerprints to identify criminals.
b. Jul 26, 1850
d. 1931
Source: *BioIn 2, 5, 6, 9, 13; CopCroC; DcInB; DcNaB 1931*

Henry, George William
American. Psychiatrist
Director, Brooklea Farm Sanitarium; wrote *Sex Variants,* 1941.
b. Jun 13, 1889 in Oswego, New York
d. May 23, 1964 in Greenwich, Connecticut
Source: *AmAu&B; BioIn 6; EncAB-A 10; WhAm 4*

Henry, Joe
American. Singer, Songwriter
Released first album, *Talk of Heaven,* 1986 and later recorded *Shuffletown,* 1990, *Kindness of the World,* 1992 and *Trampoline,* 1996; collaborated with sister-in-law, recording artist Madonna, on song "Guilt by Association" for *Sweet Relief II: Gravity of the Situation, The Songs of Vic Chestnutt,* 1996.

Henry, Joseph
American. Inventor, Physicist
Invented electromagnetic telegraph, basis for commercial telegraphic system.
b. Dec 17, 1797 in Albany, New York
d. May 13, 1878 in Washington, District of Columbia
Source: *Alli, SUP; AmBi; AmSocL; ApCAB; AsBiEn; BiAUS; BiDAmS; BiESc; BiInAmS; BioIn 1, 2, 3, 4, 5, 6, 7, 8, 9, 10, 11, 12, 13, 14, 15, 16, 19, 21; CamDcSc; CelCen; DcAmAu; DcAmB; DcBiPP; DcNAA; DcScB; Drake; EncAB-H 1974, 1996; HarEnUS; InSci; LarDcSc; LinLib S; McGEWB; NatCAB 3; NewCol 75; OxCAmH; OxCAmL 65, 83, 95; RAdv 13-5; REnAL; WebAB 74, 79; WhAm HS; WhDW; WorAl; WorAlBi; WorInv; WorScD*

Henry, Lenny
English. Actor, Comedian
Founded Crucial Films, 1993; appeared in numerous TV specials in England.
b. Aug 28, 1958 in Dudley, England
Source: *ConBlB 9; WhoHol 92*

Henry, Marguerite
American. Children's Author
Won 1949 Newbery for *King of the Wind.*
b. Apr 13, 1902 in Milwaukee, Wisconsin
Source: *AmAu&B; AmWomWr; Au&ICB; Au&Wr 71; AuBYP 2, 3; BioIn 1, 2, 3, 4, 7, 8, 11, 12, 14, 18, 19; BkCL; ChlBkCr; ChlLR 4; ConAu 9NR, 17R; CurBio 47; DcLB 22; IntAu&W 86; InWom, SUP; JBA 51; LinLib L; MajAI; NewbMB 1922; OxCChiL; SmATA 7AS, 11, 69; TwCChW 83, 89, 95; WhoAm 84, 86, 90; WhoUSWr 88; WhoWrEP 89; WrDr 76, 86, 92*

Henry, Martha
[Martha Buhs]
American. Actor, Director
Leader of London, ON's Grand Theater, from 1988; Canadian Stratford Festival star, 1962—.
b. Feb 17, 1938 in Detroit, Michigan
Source: *BioIn 13; CanWW 31, 89; NotNAT, A; OxCCanT*

Henry, O
[William Sydney Porter]
American. Author, Journalist
Wrote short stories with surprise endings; noted for tale *Gift of the Magi.*
b. Sep 11, 1862 in Greensboro, North Carolina
d. Jun 5, 1910 in New York, New York
Source: *AmAu&B; AmBi; AtlBL; AuBYP 2S, 3; BibAL; BiDSA; BioIn 1, 2, 3, 4, 5, 6, 7, 8, 9, 10, 11, 12, 13, 14, 17; CasWL; Chambr 3; CnDAL; ConAu 104, 131; CyWA 58; DcAmB; DcLB 12, 78, 79; DcLEL; DcNAA; Dis&D; EncFWF; EncMys; EncSoH; EvLB; FifSWrA; GrWrEL N; LinLib L, S; LngCTC; MajTwCW; McGEWB; NatCAB 15; OhA&B; OxCAmL 65, 83, 95; OxCEng 67; PenC AM; RAdv 13-1; RealN; REn; REnAL; SouWr; TwCA, SUP; TwCLC 1; WebAB 74, 79; WebE&AL; WhAm 1; YABC 2*

Henry, Patrick
American. Revolutionary, Patriot
Led radical faction in VA, 1775; famous for saying, "Give me liberty or give me death."
b. May 29, 1736 in Studley, Virginia
d. Jun 6, 1799 in Charlotte County, Virginia
Source: *Alli; AmAu; AmAu&B; AmBi; AmOrN; AmPolLe; AmRev; ApCAB; BbD; Benet 87, 96; BenetAL 91; BiAUS; BiD&SB; BiDrAC; BiDrACR; BiDrUSC 89; BiDSA; BioIn 1, 2, 3, 4, 5, 6, 7, 8, 9, 10, 11, 12, 13, 14, 15, 16, 17, 18, 20, 21; BlkwEAR; CyAG; DcAmAu; DcAmB; DcAmC; DcAmSR; DcBiPP; Drake; EncAAH; EncAB-H 1974, 1996; EncAR; EncNAB; EncRev; EncSoH; HarEnUS; HisDBrE; HisWorL; LegTOT; LinLib L, S; LitC 25; McGEWB; MorMA; NatCAB 1; OxCAmH; OxCAmL 65, 83, 95; PolPar; RComAH; REn; REnAL; REnAW; TwCBDA; WebAB 74, 79; WhAm HS; WhAmP; WhAmRev; WhDW; WorAl; WorAlBi*

Henry, Pete
[Wilbur F Henry]
"Fats"
American. Football Player
Tackle, 1920s, with Canton Bulldogs, Pottsville Maroons; Hall of Fame, 1963.
b. Oct 31, 1897 in Mansfield, Ohio
d. Feb 7, 1952 in Washington, District of Columbia
Source: *BioIn 6, 8, 17; WhoFtbl 74*

Henry, William M
American. Journalist
Award-winning *Los Angeles Times* columnist, 1911-70.
b. Aug 21, 1890 in San Francisco, California
d. Apr 13, 1970 in Chatsworth, California
Source: *ConAu 89; WhAm 5, 8*

Henry I
[Henry Beauclerc]
English. Ruler
King of England, 1100-35, ascending to throne following death of brother, William II; long suspected of arranging brother's death; youngest son of William the Conqueror.
b. 1069 in Selby, England
d. Dec 1, 1135 in Lyons-la-Foret, France
Source: *LinLib S; McGEWB; NewC; WebBD 83*

Henry II
English. Ruler
First Plantagenet king of England, 1154-89; began development of common law.
b. Mar 5, 1133 in Le Mans, France
d. Jul 6, 1189 in Chinon, France
Source: *WebBD 83; WhDW*

Henry III
English. Ruler
Plantagenet king, 1216-72; captured during Baron's War, 1264; rescued by son Edward I, 1265, who later succeeded him.
b. Oct 1, 1207 in Winchester, England
d. Nov 16, 1272 in Westminster, England
Source: *BioIn 10; OxCMus; WebBD 83*

Henry IV
[Henry of Lancaster; Henry Bolingbroke]
English. Ruler
King of England, 1399-1413.
b. Apr 3, 1367 in Spilsby, England
d. Mar 20, 1413 in London, England
Source: *BioIn 10; BlmGEL; LngCEL; NewC; WebBD 83*

Henry of Wales
[Henry Charles Albert David]
"Harry"
English. Prince
Second son of Prince Charles and Princess Diana; third in line to British throne behind father and brother, William of Wales.
b. Sep 15, 1984 in London, England

Henry the Navigator
Portuguese. Prince
Never went on voyage but established school of navigation, improved compass, helped voyagers in coastal African trips.
b. Mar 4, 1394 in Porto, Portugal
d. Nov 13, 1460 in Sagres, Portugal
Source: *AsBiEn; Benet 87, 96; BioIn 1, 2, 3, 4, 5, 6, 7, 8, 9, 10, 11, 12, 17, 18, 19, 20; DcBiPP; DcCathB; EncCRAm; Expl 93; HisWorL; LinLib S; McGEWB; REn; WebBD 83; WhDW; WhWE; WorAl; WorAlBi*

Henry V
English. Ruler
Lancastrian king of England, 1413-22; acquired Norway, France, 1417-20.
b. Aug 9, 1387 in Monmouth, Wales
d. Aug 31, 1422 in Bois de Vincennes, France
Source: *WebBD 83; WhDW*

Henry VI
English. Ruler
King of England, son of Henry V; ruled during War of Roses.
b. Dec 6, 1421 in Windsor, England
d. May 21, 1471 in London, England
Source: *WebBD 83; WhDW*

Henry VII
[Henry Tudor]
English. Ruler
King of England, 1485-1509; first Tudor monarch; marriage of daughter to James IV of Scotland brought two countries together.
b. Jan 28, 1457 in Pembroke, Wales
d. Apr 21, 1509 in Richmond, England
Source: *NewC; WhDW*

Henry VIII
English. Ruler
Most renowned of English kings, 1509-47; break with Roman church led to English Reformation; father of Elizabeth I.
b. Jun 28, 1491 in Greenwich, England
d. Jan 28, 1547 in Westminster, England
Source: *CasWL; NewCol 75; REn; WebBD 83; WhDW*

Henry William Frederick Albert
[Duke of Gloucester]
English. Prince
Uncle of Queen Elizabeth II, last surviving son of King George V; best known as soldier, horseman.
b. Mar 31, 1900 in Sandringham, England
d. Jun 9, 1974 in Northamptonshire, England
Source: *DcNaB 1971; IntWW 74; NewYTBS 74*

Hensley, Pamela Gail
American. Actor
Played CJ on TV series "Matt Houston."
b. Oct 3, 1950 in Los Angeles, California
Source: *BioIn 13; IntMPA 88; VarWW 85; WhoAm 76, 78, 80, 82*

Hensley, William L.
American. Native American Leader
Co-founder of the Alaska Federation of Natives, 1966.
b. Jun 17, 1941 in Kotzebue, Alaska
Source: *BioIn 12, 21; Dun&B 86, 88; NotNaAm; WhoAm 96; WhoWest 89*

Henslowe, Philip
English. Theater Owner
Built London's Rose Theatre, 1587; his company was main rival of Shakespeare's; wrote *Diary,* 1592-1603, a major source of information on Elizabethan theater.
b. 1550? in Lindfield, England
d. Jan 6, 1616 in London, England
Source: *BioIn 14, 19; CamGWoT; DcNaB; Ent; NewCol 75; OxCEng 85; OxCThe 83*

Henson, Brian
American. Puppeteer
Created Teenage Mutant Ninja Turtles, TV series *Dinosaurs,* 1991—; pres, Jim Henson Productions, 1991—, after father's death; Emmy Award winner.
b. 1964 in New York, New York
Source: *News 92, 92-1; WhoEnt 92*

Henson, Jim
[James Maury Henson]
American. Puppeteer
Emmy and Grammy winning creator of Muppets who first appeared on "Sesame Street," 1969; "The Muppet Show," 1976-81; directed several movies, including *The Muppet Movie,* 1979.
b. Sep 24, 1936 in Greenville, Mississippi
d. May 16, 1990 in New York, New York
Source: *AmDec 1970; AnObit 1990; ASCAP 80; BioIn 11, 12, 13, 14, 15, 16; CelR 90; ConAu 106, 124, 131; ConHero 2; ConTFT 1, 11; CurBio 77, 90, 90N; EncAB-H 1996; HalFC 84, 88; IntMPA 80, 81, 82, 84, 86, 88; LegTOT; LesBEnT 92; MiSFD 9N; News 90, 89-1; NewYTBS 79, 90; SmATA 43, 65; VarWW 85; WhAm 10; WhoAm 78, 80, 82, 84, 86, 88; WhoTelC; WorAl; WorAlBi*

Henson, Josiah
American. Slave, Clergy
Prototype of Uncle Tom in *Uncle Tom's Cabin.*
b. Jun 15, 1789 in Charles County, Maryland
d. May 15, 1883 in Dresden, Ontario, Canada
Source: *AfrAmAl 6; AfrAmPr; AmAu; AmAu&B; AmBi; ApCAB; BenetAL 91; BioIn 1, 2, 5, 6, 8, 9, 10, 17; BlkWrNE; CivWDc; DcAmB; DcAmNB; DcBiPP A; DcCanB 11; DcNAA; EncSoH; InB&W 80; MacDCB 78; McGEWB; NatCAB 22; OxCAmL 65, 83, 95; OxCCan; REnAL; WhAm HS; WhCiWar*

Henson, Lisa
American. Publisher
Daughter of Jim Henson; first woman pres. of *The Harvard Lampoon.*
b. 1960?
Source: *BioIn 13; IntMPA 92, 96; NewYTBS 82; WhoAmW 97*

Henson, Maria
American. Journalist
Won Pulitzer Prize for editorial writing, 1992.

Henson, Matthew Alexander
American. Explorer
Accompanied Robert Peary expedition to N Pole, 1909.
b. Aug 8, 1866 in Charles County, Maryland
d. Mar 9, 1955 in New York, New York
Source: *AfrAmAl 6; BioIn 1, 2, 3, 4, 6, 7, 8, 9, 10, 11, 12, 13, 15, 16, 17, 18, 20, 21; DcAmB S5; DcAmNB; InB&W 85; WhWE*

Hentoff, Nat(han Irving)
American. Critic, Journalist
Writer on jazz-turned civil libertarian; writings focused on improving education.
b. Jun 10, 1925 in Boston, Massachusetts
Source: *AmAu&B; Au&Arts 4; AuBYP 2; BenetAL 91; BiDAmNC; BioIn 7, 8, 9, 13, 14, 15, 16; ChhPo S2; ChlBkCr; ChlLR 1; ConAu 1R, 5NR, 6AS, 25NR; ConLC 26; CurBio 86; DcAmChF 1960; EncTwCJ; IntAu&W 77; LinLib L; MajAI; NewGrDA 86; NewGrDJ 88, 94; REnAL; SmATA 27, 42, 69; ThrBJA; TwCChW 78, 83, 89; TwCYAW; WhoAm 74, 76, 78, 80, 82, 84, 86, 88, 90, 92, 94, 95, 96, 97; WhoE 74, 89; WhoUSWr 88; WhoWor 74; WhoWrEP 89, 92, 95; WrDr 76, 86, 92*

Henty, George Alfred
English. Children's Author
Wrote 80 boys adventure tales including *With Clive in India,* 1884.
b. Dec 8, 1832 in Trumpington, England
d. Nov 16, 1902 in Weymouth, England
Source: *Alli SUP; BbD; BiD&SB; BioIn 2, 4, 8, 10, 11, 12, 13, 14, 16, 17, 20; BritAu 19; CarSB; CasWL; Chambr 3; DcBiPP; DcBrBI; DcLEL; DcNaB S2; EvLB; HisDBrE; JBA 34; LngCTC;*

MnBBF; NewC; NewCBEL; OxCEng 67; OxCShps; PenC ENG; TwCChW 78A; VicBrit; WhoChL

Henze, Hans Werner
German. Composer
Works include operas *Boulevard Solitude,* 1952; *The Bassarids,* 19 66; *La Cubana,* 1973.
b. Jul 1, 1926 in Gutersloh, Germany
Source: *Baker 78, 84, 92; BiDD; BioIn 6, 7, 8, 9, 11, 12, 13, 15, 17, 20; BriBkM 80; CmOp; CnOxB; CompSN, SUP; ConCom 92; CurBio 66; DancEn 78; DcArts; DcCM; DcCom 77; DcCom&M 79; FacFETw; IntDcB; IntDcOp; IntWW 74, 75, 76, 77, 78, 79, 80, 81, 82, 83, 89, 91, 93; IntWWM 77, 80, 90; MakMC; McGEWB; MetOEnc; MusMk; NewAmDM; NewEOp 71; NewGrDM 80; NewGrDO; NewOxM; NewYTBE 72; OxCEng 85, 95; OxCGer 76, 86; OxCMus; OxDcOp; PenDiMP A; WhDW; Who 74, 82, 83, 85, 88, 90, 92, 94; WhoAm 74; WhoMus 72; WhoWor 74, 82, 84, 87, 89, 91, 93, 95, 96, 97*

Hepbron, George
American. Basketball Referee
First official in NY area; wrote first handbook of game, *How to Play Basketball,* 1904; Hall of Fame.
b. Aug 27, 1863 in Still Pond, Maryland
d. Apr 30, 1946 in Newark, New Jersey
Source: *BasBi; WhoBbl 73*

Hepburn, Audrey (Edda)
[Edda Van Heemstra Hepburn-Ruston]
American. Actor
Won Oscar for *Roman Holiday,* 1953; starred in *My Fair Lady,* 1964 ; special ambassador, UN Int'l Children's Emergency Fund, 1988-92.
b. May 4, 1929 in Brussels, Belgium
d. Jan 20, 1993 in Tolochenaz, Switzerland
Source: *AnObit 1993; BiDFilm, 81, 94; BiE&WWA; BioIn 2, 3, 4, 5, 6, 7, 8, 9, 10, 11, 12, 14, 16, 17, 18, 19, 20, 21; BkPepl; BlueB 76; CelR, 90; ContDcW 89; ConTFT 7, 11; CurBio 54, 93N; DcArts; DcTwCCu 1; EncAFC; EncFash; FilmEn; FilmgC; ForYSC; GoodHs; HalFC 80, 84, 88; IntDcF 1-3, 2-3; IntDcWB; IntMPA 75, 76, 77, 78, 79, 80, 81, 82, 84, 86, 88, 92, 94; IntWW 74, 75, 76, 77, 78, 79, 80, 81, 82, 83, 89, 91; InWom, SUP; ItaFilm; LegTOT; MotPP; MovMk; News 93-2; NewYTBS 80, 93; NotNAT; OxCFilm; VarWW 85; WhAm 11; Who 74, 82, 83, 85, 88, 90, 92; WhoAm 74, 76, 78, 80, 82, 84, 86, 88, 90, 92; WhoAmW 64, 66, 68, 70, 72, 74, 83; WhoEnt 92; WhoHol 92, A; WorAl; WorAlBi; WorEFlm*

Hepburn, Katharine (Houghton)
American. Actor
Received Oscars for *Guess Who's Coming to Dinner,* 1967, *The Lion in Winter,* 1968, *On Golden Pond,* 1981; other films include *The Philadelphia Story,* 1940, several with Spencer Tracy, and *The African Queen,* 1951; received Cannes Int'l Film Festival Best Actress Award for *Long Day's Journey Into Night,* 1962.
b. May 12, 1907 in Hartford, Connecticut
Source: *AmCulL; BiDFilm 94; BiE&WWA; BioAmW; BioIn 13, 14, 15, 16, 17, 18, 19, 20, 21; BioNews 74; BkPepl; CamGWoT; CelR 90; CmMov; ConHero 1; ContDcW 89; ConTFT 5; CurBio 69; EncAFC; EncFash; EncMcCE; EncMT; EncWB; FacFETw; FamA&A; FilmEn; FilmgC; GrLiveH; HalFC 80, 84, 88; HanAmWH; IntDcF 1-3, 2-3; IntDcWB; IntMPA 92, 94, 96; IntWW 91; InWom SUP; MGM; News 91, 91-2; NewYTBS 85, 91; NotWoAT; OxCAmT 84; ThFT; VarWW 85; WebAB 79; Who 85, 92; WhoAm 86, 92, 94, 95, 96, 97; WhoAmW 87, 93, 95, 97; WhoEnt 92; WhoHol 92, A; WhoWor 87, 93, 95, 96, 97; WorAlBi*

Hepplewhite, George
English. Cabinetmaker, Furniture Designer
Influenced by Chippendale; designs reflect neoclassic style of Robert Adam.
d. 1786 in London, England
Source: *AntBDN G; BioIn 3, 7; DcArts; DcD&D; DcNaB MP; LegTOT; LinLib S; McGDA; McGEWB; OxCDecA; PenDiDA 89; WebBD 83; WorAl; WorAlBi*

Heppner, Ben
Canadian. Opera Singer
Heroic tenor in both German and Italian operas; recorded *Herodiade,* 1996.
b. Jan 14, 1956 in Murrayville, British Columbia, Canada
Source: *NewGrDO*

Hepworth, Barbara, Dame
[Jocelyn Barbara Hepworth]
English. Sculptor
Designed large geometric shapes from wood, stone; introduced the "hole," painted hollows to abstract sculpture.
b. Jan 10, 1903 in Wakefield, England
d. May 20, 1975 in Saint Ives, England
Source: *Benet 87; BiDWomA; BioIn 1, 2, 3, 4, 5, 6, 7, 8, 9, 10, 11, 12, 14, 16, 17, 20, 21; ConArt 77, 83, 89; ContDcW 89; CurBio 57, 75, 75N; DcArts; DcBrAr 1, 2; DcNaB 1971; FacFETw; GoodHs; GrBr; IntDcAA 90; IntDcWB; IntWW 74, 75; InWom, SUP; LegTOT; MakMC; McGDA; McGEWB; ModArCr 2; NewYTBS 75; ObitOF 79; ObitT 1971; OxCArt; OxCTwCA; OxDcArt; PhDcTCA 77; PrintW 83, 85; TwCPaSc; WhAm 6; WhDW; Who 74; WhoAmW 64, 66, 68, 70, 72, 74; WhoWor 74; WomArt; WorAl; WorAlBi; WorArt 1950*

Heraclitus of Ephesus
"The Weeping Philosopher"
Greek. Philosopher
Known for idea of flux: "Nothing is; everything is becoming."
b. 540?BC in Ephesus, Asia Minor
d. 480?BC
Source: *AsBiEn; DcScB; McGEWB; NewCol 75; WebBD 83*

Herber, Arnie
[Arnold Herber]
"Flash"
American. Football Player
Quarterback, 1930-40, 1944-45, mostly with Green Bay; known for passes to Don Hutson; Hall of Fame, 1966.
b. Apr 2, 1910 in Green Bay, Wisconsin
d. Oct 14, 1969 in Green Bay, Wisconsin
Source: *BiDAmSp FB; BioIn 8, 17; LegTOT; WhoFtbl 74; WhoSpor*

Herbert, A(lan) P(atrick), Sir
English. Author, Statesman
MP, 1935-50; wrote *Secret Battle,* 1919.
b. Sep 24, 1890 in Elstead, England
d. Nov 11, 1971 in London, England
Source: *Au&Wr 71; BioIn 1, 2, 3, 4, 5, 9, 10, 11, 13, 14; CamGLE; ChhPo, S1, S2, S3; ConAu 33R, 97; ConNov 72; DcLB 10; DcLEL; DcNaB 1971; EncSF 93; EngPo; Ent; EvLB; GrBr; LinLib L; LngCTC; ModBrL; NewC; NewCBEL; OxCEng 85, 95; PenC ENG; REn; RGTwCWr; ScF&FL 1; TwCA, SUP; TwCWr; WhE&EA; WhoThe 72; WhThe*

Herbert, Anthony B
American. Army Officer
Much-decorated lieutenant colonel; in book *Soldier,* 1973, described US A rmy atrocities in Vietnam; sued "60 Minutes" for libel.
b. 1930
Source: *BioIn 9, 12, 13; ConAu 77; NewYTBE 71*

Herbert, Frank (Patrick)
American. Author
Author of *Dune* series; won Nebula, 1965; Hugo, 1966; adapted to film, 1984.
b. Oct 8, 1920 in Tacoma, Washington
d. Feb 11, 1986 in Madison, Wisconsin
Source: *AmAu&B; AnObit 1986; Benet 87, 96; BenetAL 91; BioIn 10, 11, 12, 13; ConAu 5NR, 43NR, 53, 118; ConLC 12, 23, 35, 44, 85; ConPopW; CyWA 89; DcArts; DcLB 8; DrmM 1; EncSF, 93; IntAu&W 77; LegTOT; MagSAmL; MajTwCW; NewEScF; Novels; RAdv 14; RGSF; RGTwCSF; ScF&FL 1, 2, 92; ScFSB; ScFWr; SmATA 9, 37, 47N; TwCSFW 81, 86, 91; TwCYAW; WhAm 9; WhoAm 74, 76, 78, 80, 82, 84; WhoSciF; WorAl; WorAlBi; WorAu 1970; WrDr 76, 80, 82, 84, 86*

Herbert, George
English. Author
Wrote verse volume *The Temple,* 1633; prose work *A Priest to the Temp le.*
b. Apr 3, 1593 in Montgomery Castle, Wales
d. Mar 1, 1633 in Bremerton, England
Source: *Alli; AtlBL; BbD; Benet 87, 96; BiD&SB; BiDRP&D; BioIn 1, 2, 3, 5, 6, 7, 8, 9, 10, 11, 12, 14, 16, 18, 19;*

BlmGEL; BritAu; BritWr 2; CamGEL; CamGLE; CasWL; ChhPo, S1, S2, S3; CnDBLB 1; CnE&AP; CroE&S; CrtT 1, 4; CyWA 58; DcArts; DcBiPP; DcEnA; DcEnL; DcEuL; DcLB 126; DcLEL; DcNaB; EvLB; GrWrEL P; IlEncMy; LinLib L; LitC 24; LngCEL; LuthC 75; McGEWB; MouLC 1; NewC; NewCBEL; NewGrDM 80; OxCEng 67, 85, 95; OxCLiW 86; PenC ENG; PoeCrit 4; RAdv 1, 14, 13-1; REn; RfGEnL 91; RGFBP; WebE&AL; WhDW

Herbert, George Edward Stanhope Molyneux
[Earl of Canarvon]
English. Egyptologist, Archaeologist
Discovered, with Howard Carter, tomb of Tutankhamen, 1922.
b. Jun 26, 1866 in Newbury, England
d. Apr 6, 1923 in Cairo, Egypt
Source: *DcNaB 1922; WebBD 83*

Herbert, Hugh
American. Actor
Comedian whose signature was fluttery hands and expression "Woo-Woo!"
b. Aug 10, 1887 in Binghamton, New York
d. Mar 13, 1951 in Hollywood, California
Source: *BioIn 21; EncAFC; Film 2; FilmEn; FilmgC; ForYSC; HalFC 80, 84, 88; HolCA; MotPP; MovMk; NotNAT B; OlFamFa; QDrFCA 92; Vers A; WhoHol B; WhoHrs 80; WhScrn 74, 77, 83*

Herbert, John
[John Herbert Brundage]
Canadian. Dramatist, Director
Known for drama of prison life: *Fortune and Men's Eyes,* 1967.
b. Oct 13, 1926 in Toronto, Ontario, Canada
Source: *BioIn 10, 11, 15; CanWW 83, 89; CaP; ColCR; ConAu 101; ConDr 73, 77, 82, 88, 93; DcLB 53; Dun&B 88; IntAu&W 82; McGEWD 84; OxCCanL; OxCCan SUP; OxCCanT; St&PR 87; WhoAm 88; WhoCanL 85, 87, 92; WrDr 76, 80, 82, 84, 86, 88, 90, 92, 94, 96*

Herbert, Victor
American. Conductor, Composer
Wrote over 40 operettas including *Babes in Toyland,* 1903.
b. Feb 1, 1859 in Dublin, Ireland
d. May 27, 1924 in New York, New York
Source: *AmBi; AmPS; AmSong; ApCAB X; ASCAP 66, 80; Baker 78, 84; BenetAL 91; BestMus; BiDAmM; BiDD; BioIn 1, 2, 3, 4, 5, 6, 7, 8, 9, 10, 11, 12; BriBkM 80; CamGWoT; CmOp; CmpEPM; DcAmB; DcArts; EncMT; FacFETw; GayN; HalFC 80, 84, 88; LegTOT; LinLib S; McGEWD 72, 84; MetOEnc; MorMA; MusMk; NatCAB 12, 22; NewAmDM; NewCBMT; NewEOp 71; NewGrDA 86; NewGrDM 80; NewOxM; NotNAT B; OxCAmH; OxCAmL 65, 83, 95; OxCAmT 84; OxCMus; OxCPMus; OxDcOp; PenDiMP A; PenEncP; PlP&P; PopAmC; REn; REnAL; Sw&Ld B; TwCBDA; WebAB 74, 79; WhAm 1; WhoStg 1906, 1908; WhThe; WorAl; WorAlBi*

Herblock
[Herbert Lawrence Block]
American. Cartoonist
Political cartoonist, Washington *Post,* 1946—; won Pulitzers, 1942, 1954, 1979; coined term McCarthyism, 1950.
b. Oct 13, 1909 in Chicago, Illinois
Source: *AmAu&B; AmSocL; BioIn 1, 2, 3, 4, 5, 6, 9, 10, 11, 14, 16, 17, 19; CelR, 90; ConAu X; CurBio 54; EncAB-H 1974; EncTwCJ; IntWW 83, 89, 91, 93; LegTOT; NewYTBS 84; WebAB 74, 79; WhoAm 74, 76, 78, 80, 82, 84, 86, 88, 90, 92, 94, 95, 96, 97; WhoAmA 76, 78, 80, 82; WhoE 89, 91, 93; WhoSSW 73, 75, 82; WhoWor 74, 84; WorAl; WorAlBi; WorECar*

Herbst, Josephine Frey
American. Author
Noted for trilogy of the Trexler family, 1933-39.
b. Mar 5, 1897 in Sioux City, Iowa
d. Jan 28, 1969 in New York, New York
Source: *AmAu&B; AmNov; ArtclWW 2; BioAmW; ConAmA; ConAu 5R; InWom, SUP; OxCAmL 65; REn; REnAL; TwCA, SUP; WebE&AL; WhAm 5; WhE&EA; WhNAA; WhoAmW 58, 70*

Herder, Johann Gottfried von
German. Poet, Critic
Prominent in Sturm und Drang movement, he wrote some of first studies of comparative religion, mythology.
b. Aug 25, 1744 in Mohrungen, Prussia
d. Dec 18, 1803 in Weimar, Germany
Source: *AtlBL; BbD; BiD&SB; BioIn 1, 2, 3, 5, 7, 10; BlkwCE; CasWL; ChhPo S1; DcArts; DcBiPP; DcEuL; Dis&D; EuAu; EuWr 4; EvEuW; InSci; LinLib L, S; LuthC 75; McGEWB; NewC; NewCBEL; NinCLC 8; OxCEng 67; OxCGer 76; PenC EUR; RAdv 14, 13-2; RComWL; REn; WebBD 83; WorAl*

Herdt, Gilbert
American. Anthropologist
Studies the changing gay/lesbian culture; the emerging identities of gays/ lesbians, and the impact of AIDS.
b. Feb 29, 1949 in Oakley, Kansas
Source: *GayLesB*

Herelle, Felix d'
Canadian. Scientist
Microbiologist, credited with discovering the bacteriophage.
b. Apr 25, 1873 in Montreal, Quebec, Canada
d. Feb 22, 1949 in Paris, France
Source: *BioIn 2, 20; DcScB*

Hereward the Wake
Anglo-Saxon. Revolutionary
Famous outlaw; led rebels against William the Conqueror, 1070; subject of legends.
Source: *EncE 75; LngCEL; NewCol 75; OxCEng 67, 85; WebBD 83*

Herford, Oliver
American. Author, Illustrator
Self-illustrated books include *Little Book of Bores,* 1906.
b. Dec 1, 1863 in Sheffield, England
d. Jul 5, 1935 in New York, New York
Source: *AmAu&B; AuBYP 2S, 3; BenetAL 91; BiD&SB; BioIn 2, 5, 8; CarSB; ChhPo, S1, S2, S3; DcAmAu; DcAmB S1; DcNAA; EvLB; LngCTC; NewC; OxCAmL 65, 83, 95; REnAL; TwCA, SUP; WhAmArt 85; WorECar*

Hergesheimer, Joseph
American. Author
Novels of manners include *Three Black Pennys,* 1917; *Java Head,* 1919.
b. Feb 15, 1880 in Philadelphia, Pennsylvania
d. Apr 25, 1954 in Sea Isle City, New Jersey
Source: *AmAu&B; Benet 87; BenetAL 91; BioIn 1, 3, 4, 5, 6, 7, 11, 12, 17; CasWL; Chambr 3; CnDAL; ConAmA; ConAmL; ConAu 109; CyWA 58; DcAmB S5; DcBiA; DcLB 9, 102; DcLEL; EvLB; GrWrEL N; LinLib L, S; LngCTC; NatCAB 47; Novels; ObitT 1951; OxCAmL 65, 83, 95; OxCEng 67; PenC AM; REn; REnAL; RfGAmL 87, 94; TwCA, SUP; TwCLC 11; TwCWr; WhAm 3; WhE&EA; WhFla; WhLit; WhNAA*

Herkimer, Nicholas
American. Military Leader
Revolutionary war hero; killed in Battle of Oriskany; NY town named for him.
b. Nov 10, 1728 in Herkimer, New York
d. Aug 16, 1777 in Little Falls, New York
Source: *AmBi; ApCAB; BioIn 11; DcAmB; Drake; EncAR; HarEnMi; OxCAmH; TwCBDA; WebAMB; WhAm HS; WhAmRev; WhNaAH; WhoMilH 76; WorAl; WorAlBi*

Herlie, Eileen
[Eileen Herlihy]
Scottish. Actor
Played Queen Gertrude in *Hamlet,* opposite Laurence Olivier, 1948, Richard Burton, 1964.
b. Mar 8, 1920 in Glasgow, Scotland
Source: *BiE&WWA; Ent; FilmEn; FilmgC; HalFC 88; InWom SUP; MovMk; NotNAT; OxCThe 83; VarWW 85; Who 74, 82, 83, 85, 88, 90, 92, 94; WhoHol A; WhoThe 72, 77, 81*

Herlihy, James Leo
American. Author
Works include *Midnight Cowboy,* 1965.
b. Feb 27, 1927 in Detroit, Michigan

d. Oct 21, 1993 in Los Angeles, California
Source: *AmAu&B; Au&Wr 71; BenetAL 91; BiE&WWA; BioIn 6, 7, 10, 15, 19, 20; BlueB 76; CelR; ConAmD; ConAu 1R, 2NR, 143; ConDr 73, 77, 82, 88, 93; ConLC 6; ConNov 72, 76, 82, 86, 91; ConTFT 1, 12; CurBio 61, 94N; DcLEL 1940; DrAF 76; DrAPF 80, 87, 89; HalFC 84, 88; IntAu&W 76, 77; LegTOT; LinLib L; NotNAT; Novels; OxCAmL 83, 95; RGTwCWr; WhAm 11; WhoAm 74, 76, 78, 80, 82, 84, 86, 88, 90, 92, 94; WhoE 74, 75; WhoEnt 92; WhoHol 92; WhoWor 74, 76, 78, 80; WorAl; WorAu 1950; WrDr 76, 80, 82, 84, 86, 88, 90, 92, 94, 96*

Herman, Alexis M.
American. Government Official
US Secretary of Labor, 1997—.
b. Jul 16, 1947
Source: *AfrAmBi 2; AmCath 80; BioIn 11, 12; IntDcWB; InWom SUP; NewYTBS 94; NotBlAW 2; WhoAfA 96; WhoAm 80; WhoAmP 77, 79, 81, 83, 85, 87, 89, 91, 93, 95; WhoAmW 79, 81; WhoBlA 77, 80, 85, 88, 90, 92, 94; WhoGov 77*

Herman, Babe
[Floyd Caves Herman]
American. Baseball Player
Outfielder-infielder, 1926-37, 1945; known for milestone plays: hit first ML home run in night game, 1935; tripled into double play, 1926.
b. Jun 26, 1903 in Buffalo, New York
d. Nov 27, 1987 in Glendale, California
Source: *Ballpl 90; BiDAmSp BB; BioIn 1, 2, 3, 5, 6, 8, 9, 12, 14, 15, 18; LegTOT; NewYTBS 79; WhoProB 73*

Herman, Billy
[William Jennings Bryan Herman]
American. Baseball Player
Second baseman, 1931-47; 10-time All-Star known for fielding; had .304 lifetime batting average; Hall of Fame, 1975.
b. Jul 7, 1909 in New Albany, Indiana
d. Sep 5, 1992 in West Palm Beach, Florida
Source: *Ballpl 90; BiDAmSp BB; BioIn 10, 14, 15, 18, 19; LegTOT; NewYTBS 92; WhoProB 73; WhoSpor*

Herman, George Edward
American. Broadcast Journalist
Moderator on TV show "Face the Nation," 1969-84; Washington, DC correspondent, 1954-87.
b. Jan 14, 1920 in New York, New York
Source: *VarWW 85; WhoAm 74, 76, 78, 80, 82, 84, 86, 88, 90, 92, 94, 95, 96, 97; WhoAmJ 80; WhoE 91; WhoWor 74, 76*

Herman, Jerry
American. Songwriter
Won Tony, two Grammys for *Hello Dolly!* 1964; Tony for best score, *La Cage Aux Follies*, 1984; Theatre Hall of Fame, 1985.
b. Jul 10, 1933 in New York, New York
Source: *AmSong; ASCAP 66, 80; Baker 78, 84, 92; BestMus; BiDAmM; BiE&WWA; BioIn 7, 9, 10, 12, 14, 15; CelR, 90; ConAmC 76, 82; ConTFT 1, 3; CurBio 65; DcTwCCu 1; EncMT; HalFC 88; NewAmDM; NewCBMT; NewGrDA 86; NewGrDM 80; NotNAT; OxCPMus; PlP&P; PopAmC SUP; VarWW 85; WhoAm 86, 88, 90; WhoE 85; WhoEnt 92; WhoThe 77, 81; WorAlBi*

Herman, Pee-Wee
[Paul Rubens]
American. Comedian
His child-like character became basis for hit film *Pee-wee's Big Adventure,* 1985; children's TV show "Pee-wee's Playhouse," 1986-91 won six Emmys.
b. Jul 27, 1952 in Peekskill, New York
Source: *BioIn 14, 15, 16; CelR 90; ConNews 87-2; ConTFT 9; CurBio 88; IntMPA 92, 94; WhoCom; WhoHol 92*

Herman, Woody
[Woodrow Charles Herman]
American. Bandleader, Musician
Directed high-quality swing orchestras for over 50 yrs; recording of "Woodchoppe r's Ball" sold over one million copies; won three Grammys.
b. May 16, 1913 in Milwaukee, Wisconsin
d. Oct 29, 1987 in Los Angeles, California
Source: *AllMusG; AnObit 1987; ASCAP 66; Baker 78, 84, 92; BgBands 74; BiDAmM; BiDJaz; BioIn 1, 2, 4, 8, 9, 10, 11, 12, 13; BioNews 74; CmpEPM; ConMus 12; CurBio 73, 88, 88N; DcArts; EncJzS; FacFETw; IlEncJ; IntWWM 77; LegTOT; MusMk; NewAmDM; NewGrDA 86; NewGrDJ 88, 94; NewGrDM 80; NewYTBS 87; OxCPMus; PenEncP; VarWW 85; WhAm 9; WhoAm 74, 76, 78, 80, 82, 84, 86; WhoHol A; WhoJazz 72; WhoMus 72; WhoWest 74, 76; WorAl; WorAlBi*

Hermann, Jane Pomerance
American. Director
Director, American Ballet Theatre, 1989-92.
b. Oct 1, 1935 in New York, New York
Source: *WhoAm 90, 92; WhoE 93; WhoEnt 92*

Hermannsson, Steingrimur
Icelandic. Political Leader
Prime minister of Iceland, 1983-91.
b. Jun 22, 1928, Iceland
Source: *IntWW 83, 89, 91, 93; IntYB 79, 80, 81, 82; WhoFI 96; WhoOcn 78; WhoWor 80, 82, 84, 87, 89, 91, 93, 95, 96, 97*

Herman's Hermits
[Karl Greene; Keith Hopwood; Derek Leckenby; Peter Noone; Barry Whitwam]
English. Music Group
Part of "British Invasion," 1960s; had ten hits, 1964-66: "Mrs. Brown You've Got a Lovely Daughter," 1965; disbanded after 1971.
Source: *BioIn 16; ConMuA 80A; ConMus 5; EncPR&S 74, 89; EncRk 88; EncRkSt; HarEnR 86; IlEncRk; NewAmDM; OxCPMus; PenEncP; RkOn 78; RolSEnR 83; WhoHol 92, A; WhoRocM 82*

Hermening, Kevin Jay
[The Hostages]
American. Hostage
One of 52 held by terrorists, Nov 1979 - Jan 1981.
b. 1960? in Milwaukee, Wisconsin
Source: *BioIn 12; NewYTBS 81; WhoAmP 91*

Hermes, Thierry
French. Designer
Saddle, harness maker; founded co., 1830s, which supplied riding equipment to nobility; now specializes in luggage, handbags, jewelry.
Source: *WorFshn*

Hern, Riley
[William Milton Hern]
Canadian. Hockey Player
Goalie with several amateur teams, early 1900s; Hall of Fame, 1962.
b. Dec 5, 1880 in Saint Marys, Ontario, Canada
d. Jun 24, 1929 in Montreal, Quebec, Canada
Source: *WhoHcky 73*

Hernandez, Aileen Clark
American. Feminist
Succeeded Betty Friedan as president of NOW, 1971.
b. May 23, 1926 in New York, New York
Source: *BioIn 9; CurBio 71; InWom SUP; NegAl 89; WhoBlA 92*

Hernandez, Keith
[Guillermo Villaneuva Hernandez]
American. Baseball Player
First baseman, 1974-90; won NL batting title, 1979; holds several records for defensive play.
b. Oct 20, 1953 in San Francisco, California
Source: *Ballpl 90; BaseReg 86, 87; BiDAmSp BB; BioIn 12, 13, 14, 15, 16, 19, 20; CurBio 88; HispAmA; NewYTBS 83, 86; WhoAm 80, 82, 84, 86, 88, 90; WhoE 89; WhoHisp 91, 92, 94; WhoSpor; WorAlBi*

Hernandez, Willie (Guillermo Villaneuva)
American. Baseball Player
Relief pitcher, 1977-89; won AL Cy Young Award, MVP, 1984.
b. Nov 14, 1955 in Aguada, Puerto Rico
Source: *BaseReg 86, 87; BiDrAPA 89; ConNews 85-1; WhoAm 86, 88; WhoHisp 92*

Hernandez-Colon, Rafael
Puerto Rican. Politician
Governor of Puerto Rico, 1973-77.
b. Oct 24, 1936 in Ponce, Puerto Rico
Source: *BiDLAmC; BioIn 9, 10, 16; CurBio 73; DcCPCAm; EncLatA; EncWB; IntWW 74, 75, 76, 77, 78, 79, 80, 81, 82, 83, 89, 91, 93; WhoAm 74, 76, 78, 86, 88, 92; WhoAmP 73, 75, 77, 79, 81, 83, 85, 87, 89, 91, 93, 95; WhoGov 75, 77; WhoHisp 91, 92, 94; WhoSSW 73, 75, 76, 86, 88, 91, 93; WhoWor 87, 89, 91, 93*

Herne, Chrystal Katharine
American. Actor
Starred in Pulitzer-winning play *Craig's Wife,* 1925-27.
b. Jun 17, 1882 in Dorchester, Massachusetts
d. Sep 19, 1950 in Boston, Massachusetts
Source: *DcAmB S4; InWom SUP; LibW; NotAW; NotWoAT*

Herod Antipas
Palestinian. Ruler
Son of Herod the Great who executed John the Baptist, sent Jesus to Pontius Pilate.
b. 4BC
d. 39AD
Source: *REn*

Herodotus
"Father of History"
Greek. Historian
Wrote *History,* which tells of rise of Persia, development of Greek city-states, Greco-Asian world, published in 15th c. AD.
b. c. 485BC in Halicarnassus, Asia Minor
d. c. 425BC in Thurii, Italy
Source: *AtlBL; BbD; BiD&SB; CasWL; ClMLC 17; CyWA 58; DcEnL; DcEuL; NewC; OxCEng 67; PenC CL; RComWL; REn; WhDW*

Herod the Great
Ruler, Biblical Figure
King of Judea who ordered the killing of all males under age two for fear of losing throne to Jesus.
b. 73BC
d. 4BC in Jericho, Judea
Source: *Benet 87, 96; BioIn 17, 18; DcBiPP; Dis&D; HisWorL; LegTOT; McGEWB; NewC; OxCClL, 89; REn; WhDW; WorAlBi*

Herold, Ferdinand
[Louis Joseph Ferdinand Herold]
French. Composer
Wrote operas *La Clochette,* 1817; *Marie,* 1826; *Zampa,* 1831.
b. Jan 28, 1791 in Paris, France
d. Jan 19, 1833 in Paris, France
Source: *Baker 84; BioIn 4, 7; BriBkM 80; CmOp; CnOxB; DcBiPP; GrComp; IntDcOp; MetOEnc; MusMk; NewAmDM; NewEOp 71; NewGrDM 80; NewOxM; OxCMus; OxDcOp*

Heroult, Paul Louis Toussaint
French. Chemist
Devised electric-arc furnace, used in steelmaking.
b. Apr 10, 1863 in Thury-Harcourt, France
d. May 9, 1914 in Antibes, France
Source: *AsBiEn; BiESc; BioIn 2, 3, 15; DcScB; InSci; LarDcSc*

Herrera, Carolina
[Maria Carolina Josefina Pacanins y Nino]
Venezuelan. Fashion Designer
Designer of ready-to-wear elegant clothing; established own firm in 1981.
b. Jan 8, 1939 in Caracas, Venezuela
Source: *BioIn 14, 15, 16; CelR 90; ConFash; CurBio 96; DcHiB; EncFash; News 97-1; NotHsAW 93; WhoAm 94, 95, 96, 97; WhoAmW 95, 97; WhoFash 88; WhoHisp 92, 94*

Herrera, Paloma
Argentine. Dancer
Principal dancer, American Ballet Theatre, 1995—.
b. Dec 21, 1975 in Buenos Aires, Argentina
Source: *News 96, 96-2; WhoAm 95, 96, 97; WhoAmW 95, 97*

Herrera Campins, Luis
Venezuelan. Political Leader
Co-founder of the Social Christian Party, 1946; pres. of Venezuela, 1979-83.
b. May 4, 1925 in Acariqua, Venezuela
Source: *BiDLAmC; BioIn 11, 12, 16; CurBio 80; DcCPSAm; IntWW 79, 80, 81, 82, 83, 89, 91, 93; IntYB 80, 81, 82; NewYTBS 78; WhoWor 80, 82, 84*

Herrick, Elinore Morehouse
American. Government Official
Labor expert; director, NY regional National Labor Relations Board, 1935-42.
b. Jun 15, 1895 in New York, New York
d. Oct 11, 1964
Source: *BiDAmL; CurBio 47, 65; InWom, SUP; NotAW MOD; WhAm 4*

Herrick, James Bryan
American. Physician
Discoverer of sickle-cell anemia.
b. Aug 11, 1861 in Oak Park, Illinois
d. Mar 7, 1954 in Chicago, Illinois
Source: *BiHiMed; BioIn 1, 2, 3, 5, 9; DcAmMeB 84; NatCAB 42; OxCMed 86; WhAm 3*

Herrick, Robert
English. Author, Poet
A major Cavalier poet; love lyrics, pastorals include "To Daffadils"; verse collection *Hesperides,* 1648.
b. 1591 in London, England
d. Oct 1674 in Dean Prior, England
Source: *Alli; AnCL; AtlBL; BbD; Benet 87, 96; BiD&SB; BiDRP&D; BioIn 1, 2, 3, 4, 5, 6, 7, 10, 12, 14, 15, 19; BlmGEL; BritAu; BritWr 2; CamGEL; CamGLE; CasWL; Chambr 1; ChhPo, S1, S2; CnE&AP; CroE&S; CrtT 1, 4; CyWA 58; DcArts; DcBiPP; DcEnA; DcEnL; DcEuL; DcLB 126; DcLEL; DcNaB; Dis&D; EvLB; GrWrEL P; LinLib L, S; LitC 13; LngCEL; LngCTC; McGEWB; MouLC 1; NewC; NewCBEL; OxCEng 67, 85, 95; OxCMus; PenC ENG; PoeCrit 9; RAdv 1, 14, 13-1; REn; RfGEnL 91; RGFBP; WebE&AL; WhDW; WorAl; WorAlBi*

Herriman, George
American. Cartoonist
Created cartoon character Krazy Kat.
b. Aug 22, 1880 in New Orleans, Louisiana
d. Apr 25, 1944 in Hollywood, California
Source: *AmDec 1910; BenetAL 91; BioIn 14, 15, 17; ChhPo; DcAmB S3; EncACom; LegTOT; NewYTBS 86; REnAL; WebAB 74; WorECom*

Herriot, Edouard
French. Statesman, Political Leader
Radical socialist who held several political posts, including premier.
b. Jul 5, 1872 in Troyes, France
d. Mar 26, 1957 in Lyons, France
Source: *Baker 78, 84; BiDFrPL; BiDInt; BioIn 1, 2, 3, 4, 5, 6, 10, 12, 17; CurBio 46, 57; Dis&D; FacFETw; HisEWW; LinLib L, S; ObitT 1951; REn; WebBD 83; WhAm 3; WhE&EA*

Herriot, James
[James Alfred Wight]
Scottish. Veterinarian, Author
Wrote *All Creatures Great and Small,* 1972; *All Things Bright and Beautiful,* 1974.
b. Oct 3, 1916 in Glasgow, Scotland
d. Feb 23, 1995 in Thirsk, England
Source: *Au&Arts 1; AuBYP 3; Benet 87; BioIn 10, 11, 12, 15, 16; ChlBkCr; ConAu 40NR, 77, 148; ConLC 12; ConPopW; CyWA 89; DcArts; DcLP 87B; IntAu&W 91; IntWW 82, 83, 89, 91, 93; LegTOT; NewYTBS 95; SmATA 44, 55, 86, X; TwCYAW; Who 82, 83, 85, 88, 90, 92, 94; WhoAm 94, 95; WhoWor 84, 87, 89, 91, 93, 95; WorAl; WorAlBi; WorAu 1975; WrDr 86, 92, 94, 96*

Herrmann, Bernard
American. Composer
Wrote over 60 radio, movie scores; known for themes of Hitchcock films: *Psycho,* 1960.
b. Jun 29, 1911 in New York, New York
d. Dec 24, 1975 in Los Angeles, California
Source: *AmComp; Baker 78, 84, 92; BiDAmM; BiDFilm 94; BioIn 1, 2, 3, 9, 10, 11, 15, 17; CmMov; CmpEPM; ConAmC 76, 82; ConMus 14; DcAmB S9; DcArts; DcFM; FacFETw; FanAl; FilmEn; HalFC 80, 84, 88; IntDcF 1-4, 2-4; IntMPA 75, 76; IntWWM 77; ItaFilm; LegTOT; MusMk; NewAmDM; NewGrDA 86; NewGrDM 80; NewGrDO; NewOxM; NewYTBS 75; OxCFilm; OxCMus; OxCPMus; PenEncH; RadStar; WhAm 6; WhoAm 74, 76; WhoHrs 80; WorEFlm*

Herrmann, Edward
American. Actor
Won Tony, 1976, for *Mrs. Warren's Profession;* played FDR on TV's "Eleanor and Franklin."
b. Jul 21, 1943 in Washington, District of Columbia
Source: *BioIn 13, 15; ConTFT 6; HalFC 84, 88; IntMPA 88, 92, 94, 96; ItaFilm; LegTOT; NewYTBS 83; VarWW 85; WhoAm 84, 90; WhoEnt 92; WhoHol 92*

Herschbach, Dudley Robert
American. Chemist, Educator
Shared Nobel Prize in Chemistry, 1986; conceived "crossed molecular beam technique" for studying chemical reactions.
b. Jun 18, 1932 in San Jose, California
Source: *AmMWSc 73P, 76P, 79, 82, 86, 89, 92, 95; BioIn 7, 13, 15; BlueB 76; IntWW 74, 75, 76, 77, 78, 79, 80, 81, 82, 83, 89, 91, 93; LarDcSc; NobelP; Who 88, 90, 92, 94; WhoAm 74, 76, 78, 80, 82, 84, 88, 90, 92, 94, 95, 96, 97; WhoE 74, 89, 91, 93, 95, 97; WhoFrS 84; WhoNob 90, 95; WhoScEn 94, 96; WhoTech 89; WhoWor 74, 76, 78, 89, 91, 93, 95, 96, 97*

Herschel, John Frederick William, Sir
English. Astronomer
Studied double stars, Milky Way; first to apply "positive" and "negative" terms to p hotographic images; son of William.
b. Mar 7, 1792 in Slough, England
d. May 11, 1871 in Collingwood, England
Source: *Alli, SUP; AsBiEn; BiD&SB; BiESc; BioIn 4, 7, 8, 9, 10, 13, 14, 16, 18, 19, 21; BritAu 19; CamDcSc; CamGLE; CelCen; Chambr 3; DcArts; DcBiPP; DcEnL; DcInv; DcNaB; DcScB; EncSoA; EvLB; ICPEnP; InSci; LarDcSc; LinLib S; McGEWB; NewC; NewCBEL; NewCol 75; VicBrit; WorInv*

Herschel, William Frederick, Sir
English. Astronomer
Discovered Uranus, 1781; theorized on the history of stars; first to hypothesize sun was in motion.
b. Nov 15, 1738 in Hannover, Hannover
d. Aug 25, 1822 in Slough, England
Source: *Alli; McGEWB; NewC; REn; WorAl*

Hersey, John (Richard)
American. Author, Journalist
Pulitzer Prize-winning author of *A Bell for Adano,* 1944; *Hiroshima,* 1946.
b. Jun 17, 1914 in Tianjin, China
d. Mar 24, 1993 in Key West, Florida
Source: *AmAu&B; AmCulL; AmNov; AnObit 1993; Benet 87, 96; BenetAL 91; BioIn 1, 2, 4, 5, 7, 8, 9, 10, 12, 13, 14, 15, 16, 17, 18, 19; BlueB 76; CasWL; CelR, 90; ChhPo S3; CnDAL; ConAu 17R, 33NR, 140; ConLC 1, 2, 7, 9, 40, 81, 97; ConNov 72, 76, 82, 86, 91; ConPopW; CurBio 44, 93N; CyWA 58, 89; DcLB 6; DcLEL 1940; DrAF 76; DrAPF 89, 91; DrAS 74E, 78E, 82E; EncAJ; EncSF, 93; EncTwCJ; FacFETw; HalFC 84, 88; IntAu&W 76, 77, 89, 91, 93; IntWW 74, 75, 76, 77, 78, 79, 80, 81, 82, 83, 89, 91; JrnUS; LegTOT; LiJour; LinLib L, S; LngCTC; MajTwCW; ModAL; NewEScF; NewYTBS 93; Novels; OxCAmL 65, 83, 95; PenC AM; RAdv 1; REn; REnAL; ScF&FL 1, 2; ScFSB; SmATA 25, 76; SourALJ; TwCA SUP; TwCSFW 81, 86; WebAB 74, 79; WhAm 11; Who 74, 82, 83, 85, 88, 90, 92; WhoAm 74, 76, 78, 80, 82, 84, 86, 88, 90, 92; WhoE 74; WhoUSWr 88; WhoWor 74, 76, 78, 80, 82, 84; WhoWrEP 89, 92; WorAl; WorAlBi; WrDr 76, 80, 82, 84, 86, 88, 90, 92, 94N*

Hersh, Seymour
American. Journalist
Won 1970 Pulitzer, int'l reporting, for articles on My Lai massacre.
b. Apr 8, 1937 in Chicago, Illinois
Source: *AmAu&B; AuNews 1; BioIn 13, 14, 15; ConAu 15NR, 73; CurBio 84; EncTwCJ; JrnUS; WhoAm 86, 90*

Hershey, Alfred D(ay)
American. Scientist
Shared 1969 Nobel Prize in medicine for researching viruses.
b. Dec 4, 1908 in Owosso, Michigan
d. May 22, 1997 in Syosset, New York
Source: *AmMWSc 73P, 76P, 79, 86, 89, 92, 95; BiESc; BioIn 8, 9, 12, 15, 20; BlueB 76; CamDcSc; CurBio 70; IntWW 74, 75, 76, 77, 78, 79, 80, 81, 82, 83, 89, 91, 93; LarDcSc; McGMS 80; NotTwCS; WebAB 74, 79; Who 74, 82, 83, 85, 88, 90, 92, 94; WhoAm 78, 80, 82, 84, 86, 88, 90, 92, 94, 95, 96, 97; WhoE 77, 79, 81, 83, 85, 86, 89, 91, 93, 95, 97; WhoMedH; WhoNob, 90, 95; WhoScEn 94, 96; WhoWor 80, 82, 84, 87, 89, 91, 93, 95, 96, 97; WorAl; WorAlBi; WorScD*

Hershey, Barbara
[Barbara Herzstein; Barbara Seagull]
American. Actor
In TV series "The Monroes," 1966-67; films *Shy People,* 1987 and *A World Apart,* 1988 won her 2 Cannes awards for best actress.
b. Feb 5, 1948 in Hollywood, California
Source: *BioIn 8, 9, 12, 13, 15, 16; ConTFT 3, 10; CurBio 89; FilmEn; FilmgC; GangFlm; HalFC 80, 84, 88; IntMPA 77, 84, 86, 88, 92, 94, 96; IntWW 91; LegTOT; News 89-1; NewYTBS 87; VarWW 85; WhoAm 86, 88, 90, 92, 94, 95, 96, 97; WhoAmW 93, 95, 97; WhoEnt 92; WhoHol 92, A; WhoWor 95, 96, 97; WorAlBi*

Hershey, Lenore
American. Editor
Editor-in-chief, *Ladies Home Journal,* 1973-81.
b. Mar 20, 1920 in New York, New York
d. Feb 28, 1997 in New York, New York
Source: *BioIn 13, 14; InWom SUP; WhoAm 74, 76, 80, 82; WhoAmW 85*

Hershey, Lewis Blaine
American. Army Officer
As director of Selective Service, 1941-70, supervised drafting of over 14,000,000 men for service in WW II, Korea, Vietnam.
b. Sep 12, 1893 in Steuben City, Indiana
d. May 20, 1977 in Angola, Indiana
Source: *BiDWWGF; BioIn 1, 2, 3, 7, 8, 9, 11, 14; CurBio 41, 51, 77; DcAmB S10; IntWW 74, 75, 76, 77; NewYTBS 77; ObitOF 79; WebAMB; WhAm 7; WhoAm 74, 76; WhoAmP 73, 75, 77; WhoGov 72, 75; WhoSSW 73; WorAl*

Hershey, Milton Snavely
American. Candy Manufacturer
Founded Hershey Chocolate Co., 1903.
b. Sep 13, 1857 in Dauphin City, Pennsylvania
d. Oct 13, 1945 in Hershey, Pennsylvania
Source: *BioIn 1, 3, 4, 6, 9, 16, 17, 18, 20; CurBio 45; DcAmB S3; NatCAB 33; WebAB 74, 79; WhAm 2; WorAl*

Hershfield, Harry
American. Cartoonist
Created comic strip Abie the Agent.
b. Oct 13, 1885 in Cedar Rapids, Iowa
d. Dec 15, 1974 in New York, New York
Source: *BioIn 10; ConAu 53; EncACom; Film 2; NewYTBS 74; RadStar; WhScrn 77, 83; WorECom*

Hershiser, Orel Leonard, IV
American. Baseball Player
Pitcher, LA, 1983—; set ML record for consecutive scoreless innings pitched, 1988, formerly held by Don Drysdale; MVP, 1988 World Series; won NL Cy Young Award, 1988.
b. Sep 16, 1958 in Buffalo, New York

Source: *Ballpl 90; BaseEn 88; BaseReg 88; BioIn 15, 16; CurBio 90; News 89-2; WhoAm 90, 92, 94, 95, 96, 97; WhoMW 96; WhoWest 89, 92, 94; WorAlBi*

Hersholt, Jean
Danish. Actor
Special Oscar, Jean Hersholt Humanitarian Award, given in his honor since 1956; star of radio show "Dr. Christian," 1937-54.
b. Jul 12, 1886 in Copenhagen, Denmark
d. Jun 2, 1956 in Beverly Hills, California
Source: *BioIn 4, 5, 7, 17, 21; ChhPo; CurBio 56; EncAFC; Film 1, 2; FilmEn; FilmgC; HalFC 80, 84, 88; HolCA; IntDcF 1-3; MGM; MotPP; MovMk; NatCAB 42; NotNAT B; OlFamFa; RadStar; SaTiSS; SilFlmP; TwYS; WhAm 3; WhoHol B; WhScrn 74, 77, 83; WorEFlm*

Herskovits, Melville Jean
American. Anthropologist, Educator
Professor at Northwestern U, 1927-63; founded first program for African studies at university level in US.
b. Sep 10, 1895 in Bellefontaine, Ohio
d. Feb 25, 1963 in Evanston, Illinois
Source: *AmAu&B; BioIn 1, 4, 6, 7, 9, 10; CurBio 48, 63; EncAACR; EncAB-H 1974, 1996; InSci; McGEWB; NamesHP; OhA&B; OxCAmH; RAdv 14, 13-3; REnAL; TwCA SUP; WebAB 74, 79; WhAm 4*

Herter, Christian Archibald
American. Diplomat, Editor
Rep. governor of MA, 1952-56; Eisenhower's secretary of State, 1959-60; headed trade talks with European Common Market for Kennedy, Johnson.
b. Mar 28, 1895 in Paris, France
d. Dec 30, 1966 in Washington, District of Columbia
Source: *AmPolLe; BiDrAC; BiDrUSC 89; BiDrUSE 71, 89; BioIn 1, 3, 4, 5, 6, 7, 8, 9, 10, 11, 16, 18; ColdWar 1; CurBio 47, 58, 67; DcAmB, S8; DcAmDH 80, 89; LinLib S; NewCol 75; WhAm 1, 4, 8, HS; WhAmP; WorAl*

Hertz, Alfred
"Father of the Hollywood Bowl"
American. Conductor
Conducted first American performance of Parsifal, NY Met., 1903; founded Hollywood Bowl concerts, 1922.
b. Jul 15, 1872 in Frankfurt am Main, Germany
d. Apr 17, 1942 in San Francisco, California
Source: *ApCAB X; Baker 78, 84, 92; BiDAmM; BioIn 2, 4, 11; CmCal; CurBio 42; DcAmB S3; MetOEnc; MusSN; NatCAB 31; NewAmDM; NewEOp 71; NewGrDA 86; NewGrDM 80; NewGrDO; OxDcOp; PenDiMP; WhAm 2*

Hertz, Gustav Ludwig
German. Scientist
Shared 1925 Nobel Prize in physics for discovering laws governing the collision of an electron and an atom.
b. Jul 22, 1887 in Hamburg, Germany
d. Oct 30, 1975 in Berlin, German Democratic Republic
Source: *BiESc; DcScB; LarDcSc; WhoNob, 90, 95; WhoWor 74; WorAl; WorAlBi*

Hertz, Heinrich Rudolph
German. Physicist
In confirming Maxwell's electromagnetic theory, produced, studied electromagneti c waves, also called radio waves, 1885-89.
b. Feb 22, 1857 in Hamburg, Germany
d. Jan 1, 1894 in Bonn, Germany
Source: *AsBiEn; BioIn 2, 3, 4, 5, 6, 8, 9, 11, 12; CamDcSc; DcScB; Dis&D; LinLib S; McGEWB; NewCol 75; OxCMus; REn; WhDW*

Hertz, John Daniel
American. Business Executive
Founded Yellow Cab Co., 1915; Hertz Drive-Ur-Self Corp., 1924.
b. Apr 10, 1879 in Ruttka, Austria
d. Oct 8, 1961 in Los Angeles, California
Source: *BioIn 4, 6; DcAmB S7; EncABHB 5; ObitOF 79; WhAm 4*

Hertzberg, Arthur
American. Author, Religious Leader
VP, World Jewish Congress, 1975-91; Pres., American Jewish Policy Foundation, 1978—; wrote *Being Jewish in America,* 1979.
b. Jun 9, 1921 in Lubaczow, Poland
Source: *BioIn 10, 16, 17; BlueB 76; ConAu 17R; CurBio 75; NewYTBE 72; WhoAm 74, 76, 78, 80, 82, 84, 86, 88, 90, 92, 94, 95, 96, 97; WhoAmJ 80; WhoE 75, 77, 79, 81, 83, 85, 86, 89; WhoRel 85, 92; WrDr 92, 94, 96*

Hertzsprung, Ejnar
Danish. Astronomer
Associated color with true brightness in stars, providing a way to measure their distance from Earth.
b. Oct 8, 1873 in Frederiksberg, Denmark
d. Oct 21, 1967 in Roskilde, Denmark
Source: *AsBiEn; BiESc; BioIn 1, 6, 8, 11, 14, 20; CamDcSc; DcScB; InSci; LarDcSc; NotTwCS; WhDW; WorAl; WorAlBi; WorScD*

Hervey, Jason
American. Actor
Played Wayne on TV series "The Wonder Years," 1988-93.
b. Apr 6, 1972
Source: *BioIn 16; ConTFT 8; LegTOT*

Hervieu, Paul-Ernest
French. Dramatist, Author
Wrote novel *Amitie,* 1900; plays: *The Passing of the Torch,* 1901; works dealt with problems of natural law, social injustice.
b. Sep 9, 1857 in Neuilly-sur-Seine, France
d. Sep 25, 1915 in Paris, France
Source: *EuAu; McGEWD 84; ModWD; OxCFr; OxCThe 67*

Herzberg, Gerhard
Canadian. Chemist
Won Nobel Prize in chemistry, 1971, for studies of molecules.
b. Dec 25, 1904 in Hamburg, Germany
Source: *AmMWSc 73P, 76P, 79, 82, 86, 89, 92, 95; BiESc; BioIn 2, 4, 8, 9, 10, 11, 14, 15, 19, 20; BlueB 76; CamDcSc; CanWW 31, 70, 79, 80, 81, 83, 89; CurBio 73; EncWB; IntAu&W 77, 82, 86; IntWW 74, 75, 76, 77, 78, 79, 80, 81, 82, 83, 89, 91, 93; IntYB 78, 79, 80, 81, 82; LarDcSc; McGMS 80; NobelP; NotTwCS; Who 74, 82, 83, 85, 88, 90, 92, 94; WhoAm 78, 80, 82, 84, 86, 88, 90, 92, 94, 95, 96, 97; WhoCan 73, 75, 77, 80, 82; WhoE 91, 97; WhoFrS 84; WhoNob, 90, 95; WhoScEn 94, 96; WhoWest 94, 96; WhoWor 76, 78, 80, 82, 84, 87, 89, 91, 93, 95, 96, 97; WrDr 76, 80, 82, 84, 86, 88, 90, 92, 94, 96*

Herzen, Aleksandr Ivanovich
Russian. Author, Revolutionary
Published *The Bell,* 1857-67, leading journal of Russian reformers; wrote popular novel *Who is to Blame,* 1847.
b. Apr 6, 1812 in Moscow, Russia
d. Jan 21, 1870 in Paris, France
Source: *Benet 87, 96; CasWL; EuAu; HanRL; McGEWB; NewCBEL; NewCol 75; NinCLC 10; OxCEng 67; REn; WebBD 83*

Herzl, Theodor
"Father of Modern Zionism"
Hungarian. Journalist
Founder of Zionism, 1897, who supported creation of Jewish settlement in Palestine.
b. May 2, 1860 in Budapest, Hungary
d. Jul 3, 1904 in Edlach, Austria
Source: *BioIn 1, 2, 3, 4, 5, 6, 7, 9, 10, 11, 12, 13, 15, 16, 17, 19, 20; EncTR 91; EuAu; FacFETw; HisEAAC; JeHun; LuthC 75; McGEWB; NewCol 75; OxCGer 76, 86; TwCLC 36; WhDW; WorAl; WorAlBi*

Herzog, Arthur, Jr.
American. Songwriter
Wrote blues song "God Bless the Child," made famous by Billie Holiday.
b. 1901? in New York, New York
d. Sep 1, 1983 in Detroit, Michigan

Herzog, Chaim
Israeli. Political Leader
Pres., 1983-93; ambassador to UN, 1973-78.

b. Sep 17, 1918 in Belfast, Northern Ireland
d. Apr 17, 1997 in Tel Aviv, Israel
Source: *BioIn 13, 15, 16; ConAu 42NR, 103; CurBio 88; DcMidEa; FacFETw; IntWW 77, 78, 79, 80, 81, 82, 83, 89, 91, 93; IntYB 78, 79, 80, 81, 82; MidE 78, 79, 80, 81, 82; NewYTBS 75, 76, 83; Who 88, 90, 92, 94; WhoAm 76, 78; WhoWor 78, 80, 82, 84, 87, 89, 91, 93, 95, 96, 97; WhoWorJ 72, 78*

Herzog, Werner
[Werner H Stipetic]
German. Director
Films include *Aguirre, the Wrath of God,* 1972, *Fitzcarraldo,* 198 2.
b. Sep 5, 1942 in Sachrang, Germany
Source: *BiDFilm, 81, 94; BioIn 11, 12, 13, 14, 15, 16; CelR 90; ConAu 89; ConLC 16; ConTFT 7, 14; CurBio 78; DcArts; EncEurC; FacFETw; FilmEn; HalFC 80, 84, 88; IntDcF 1-2, 2-2; IntMPA 84, 86, 88, 92, 94, 96; IntWW 78, 79, 80, 81, 82, 83, 89, 91, 93; LegTOT; MiSFD 9; OxCFilm; VarWW 85; WhoWor 80, 82, 84, 87, 89, 93, 95, 96, 97; WorFDir 2*

Herzog, Whitey
[Dorrel Norman Elvert Herzog]
American. Baseball Manager
Outfielder, 1956-63; manager, St. Louis, 1980-90; won World Series, 1982; NL manager of year, 1985.
b. Nov 9, 1931 in New Athens, Illinois
Source: *Ballpl 90; BaseReg 87; BioIn 12, 13, 16; LegTOT; WhoAm 74, 78, 80, 82, 84, 86, 88, 90, 92, 94, 95, 96, 97; WhoMW 82, 88, 90; WhoProB 73; WhoWest 92, 94, 96; WorAlBi*

Hesburgh, Theodore Martin
American. Clergy, University Administrator
Served as pres. of Notre Dame longer than anyone, 1952-87.
b. May 25, 1917 in Syracuse, New York
Source: *AmCath 80; BioIn 3, 4, 5, 6, 8, 9, 10, 11, 12, 13, 14, 15, 16; BlueB 76; ConAu 13R; CurBio 55, 82; DrAS 74P, 78P, 82P; EncWB; FacFETw; IndAu 1917; IntWW 83, 91; LEduc 74; NewYTBE 71; PolProf J, K, NF; RelLAm 91; WhoAm 74, 76, 78, 80, 82, 84, 86, 88, 90, 92, 95, 96, 97; WhoGov 72; WhoMW 74, 78, 80, 82, 84, 86, 88, 90; WhoRel 77, 85, 92; WhoWor 74, 78, 84, 87; WorAl; WorAlBi*

Heschel, Abraham Joshua
Polish. Religious Leader
First Jewish scholar on staff of Union Theological Seminary.
b. 1907 in Warsaw, Poland
d. Dec 23, 1972 in New York, New York
Source: *AmAu&B; BioIn 7, 8, 9, 10, 11, 13, 14, 16, 17, 19, 20; ConAu 4NR, 5R, 37R, 81; CurBio 73, 73N; DcAmB S9; DcAmReB 1, 2; EncARH; IntAu&W 77; McGEWB; NewYTBE 73; RAdv 14, 13-4; RelLAm 91; ThTwC 87; WhAm 5; WhoE 74, 75, 85A*

Heseltine, Michael Ray Dibdin
Welsh. Government Official
Defense minister in Margaret Thatcher's Conservative gov't., 1983-86; member, Parliament, 1986-92; secretary, Dept. of Trade and Industry, 1992—.
b. Mar 21, 1933 in Swansea, Wales
Source: *BioIn 9, 12, 13, 16; BlueB 76; CurBio 85; FacFETw; IntWW 74, 75, 76, 77, 78, 80, 81, 82, 83, 89, 91, 93; Who 74, 92, 94; WhoWor 84, 87, 93, 95, 97*

Heseltine, Philip Arnold
[Peter Warlock]
English. Composer, Author
Musical writings include *The English Ayre,* 1926; composed song cycle *The Curlew.*
b. Oct 30, 1894 in London, England
d. Dec 17, 1930 in London, England
Source: *Baker 78, 84; BioIn 15, 16, 20; BriBkM 80; DcArts; DcCom&M 79; MagIlD; MusMk; NewGrDM 80; NewOxM; OxCEng 85, 95; OxCMus*

Hesiod
"Father of Greek Didactic Poetry"
Greek. Poet
Wrote *Works and Days, Theogony, The Shield of Heracles.*
b. fl. c. 700, Greece
Source: *AtlBL; BbD; Benet 87; BiD&SB; CasWL; ClMLC 5; CyWA 58; GrFLW; NewC; OxCClL 89; OxCEng 67, 85; PenC CL; RAdv 14, 13-2; RComWL; REn; RfGWoL 95; WorAlBi*

Hess, Leon
American. Oilman, Football Executive
Chm. and CEO, Amerada Hess Corp., 1971—; owner NY Jets, 1963—.
b. Mar 13, 1914 in Asbury Park, New Jersey
Source: *BioIn 8, 11, 12, 15; ConAmBL; Dun&B 79, 86, 88, 90; NewYTBS 75; St&PR 93, 96, 97; WhoAm 76, 78, 80, 82, 84, 86, 88, 90, 92, 94, 95, 96, 97; WhoE 81, 83, 85, 86, 89, 91, 95, 97; WhoFI 74, 75, 77, 79, 81, 83, 85, 87, 89, 92, 94, 96; WhoWor 82, 84, 87, 89*

Hess, Myra, Dame
English. Pianist
Among great performers of her day; made London debut, 1907; created Dame, 1941.
b. Feb 25, 1890 in London, England
d. Dec 26, 1965 in London, England
Source: *Baker 78, 84, 92; BioIn 1, 2, 3, 4, 5, 7, 8, 11, 14, 21; BriBkM 80; ContDcW 89; CurBio 43, 66; DcNaB 1961; FacFETw; GrBr; IntDcWB; InWom, SUP; LegTOT; MusMk; MusSN; NewAmDM; NewGrDM 80; NotTwCP; ObitT 1961; PenDiMP; WhAm 4; WomFir; WorAl; WorAlBi*

Hess, Richard
American. Artist, Illustrator
Invented paint-by-number art kits in the 1950s; specialized in graphic political commentary.
b. May 27, 1934 in Royal Oak, Michigan
d. Aug 5, 1991 in Torrington, Connecticut
Source: *AmGrD; BioIn 10, 15, 17; ConGrA 2; IlrAm 1880; NewYTBS 91*

Hess, Rudolf
[Walter Richard Rudolf Hess]
German. Government Official
Hitler's deputy; coined phrase "Heil Hitler!".
b. Apr 26, 1894 in Alexandria, Egypt
d. Aug 17, 1987 in Berlin, Germany (West)
Source: *AnObit 1987; BiDExR; BioIn 1, 3, 4, 5, 6, 7, 8, 9, 10, 11, 12, 14, 15, 16, 17, 18, 19, 21; ConAu 123; ConNews 88-1; CurBio 41, 87, 87N; DcPol; DcTwHis; Dis&D; EncTR, 91; EncWB; FacFETw; HisEWW; IntWW 82, 83; LegTOT; NewYTBS 74, 87; OxCGer 76, 86; REn; WhDW*

Hess, Sol
American. Cartoonist
Founded cartoon strip "The Nebbs," 1923.
b. Oct 14, 1872 in Northville, Illinois
d. Dec 31, 1941 in Chicago, Illinois
Source: *WorECom*

Hess, Victor Francis
American. Physicist, Educator
Won Nobel Prize in physics, 1936, for discovery of cosmic radiation.
b. Jun 24, 1883 in Waldstein, Austria
d. Dec 17, 1964 in Mount Vernon, New York
Source: *AsBiEn; BiESc; BioIn 3, 6, 7, 14, 15, 20; CamDcSc; CurBio 63, 65; EncAB-A 37; InSci; LarDcSc; McGEWB; ObitOF 79; WhAm 4; WhE&EA; WhoNob*

Hess, Walter Rudolf
Swiss. Physician, Educator
Won Nobel Prize in medicine, 1949, for discovery of interbrain function.
b. Mar 17, 1881 in Frauenfeld, Switzerland
d. Aug 12, 1973 in Locarno, Switzerland
Source: *BiDPsy; BiESc; BioIn 2, 3, 6, 10, 15, 20; CamDcSc; InSci; LarDcSc; McGEWB; McGMS 80; NotTwCS; WhAm 6; WhoNob; WhoWor 74*

Hesse, Eva
German. Artist, Sculptor
Major conceptualist sculptor; created disquieting hanging modular forms.
b. Jan 11, 1936 in Hamburg, Germany
d. May 29, 1970 in New York, New York
Source: *BiDWomA; BioIn 8, 9, 10, 11, 12, 13, 14, 16, 17, 18, 19, 20; ConArt 77, 83, 89, 96; ContDcW 89; DcAmArt; DcCAA 77, 88, 94; DcTwCCu 1; EncWB; EncWHA; IntDcWB; InWom*

SUP; NewYTBE 70; NorAmWA; NotAW MOD; WhoAmA 78N, 80N, 82N, 84N, 86N, 89N, 91N, 93N; WorArt 1980

Hesse, Hermann
Swiss. Author
Known for imagination, accuracy of psychological, cultural observations; won Nobel Prize, 1946.
b. Jul 2, 1877 in Calw, Germany
d. Aug 9, 1962 in Montagnola, Switzerland
Source: *AtlBL; Benet 87, 96; BioIn 1, 2, 3, 4, 5, 6, 7, 8, 9, 10, 11, 12, 13, 14, 15, 16, 17, 20; CasWL; ClDMEL 47, 80; ConAu P-2; ConLC 1, 2, 3, 6, 17, 25, 69; CurBio 62; CyWA 58, 89; DcArts; DcLB 66; EncO&P 1, 2, 3; EncSF, 93; EncWL, 2, 3; EuWr 9; EvEuW; FacFETw; GrFLW; LegTOT; LinLib L, S; MagSWL; MajTwCW; MakMC; McGEWB; ModGL; NobelP; Novels; ObitT 1961; OxCEng 85, 95; OxCGer 76, 86; PenC EUR; RAdv 14, 13-2; RComWL; REn; RfGWoL 95; ScF&FL 1, 92; ScFSB; SmATA 50; TwCA, SUP; TwCWr; WhAm 4; WhDW; WhoNob; WhoTwCL; WorAl; WorAlBi; WorLitC; WrPh*

Hesselius, John
American. Artist
Portraitist influenced by Feke and Wollaston: "Charles Calvert and His Slave," 176 1.
b. 1728 in Philadelphia, Pennsylvania
d. Apr 9, 1778 in Bellefield, Maryland
Source: *BioIn 4, 11, 12; BriEAA; DcAmArt; DcAmB; EncCRAm; FolkA 87; McGDA; NatCAB 23; NewYHSD; WhAm HS*

Hesseman, Howard
American. Actor
Played Dr. Johnny Fever on TV comedy "WKRP in Cincinnati," 1978-82; star of TV comedy "Head of the Class," 1986-91.
b. Feb 27, 1940 in Lebanon, Oregon
Source: *BioIn 12, 13, 15; ConTFT 3; IntMPA 88, 92, 94, 96; LegTOT; VarWW 85; WhoAm 80, 82, 84, 86, 88, 90, 92, 94, 95, 96, 97; WhoEnt 92; WhoHol 92; WhoWor 80, 82; WorAlBi*

Heston, Charlton
American. Actor
Starred in *Ten Commandments,* 1957; won Oscar for *Ben Hur,* 1959; president of Screen Actors Guild, 1966-71.
b. Oct 4, 1922 in Evanston, Illinois
Source: *BiDFilm; BiE&WWA; BioIn 3, 4, 5, 6, 7, 8, 10, 11, 12, 13, 16; BkPepl; CelR 90; CmMov; ConAu 108; ConTFT 1, 3, 15; CurBio 57, 86; FacFETw; FilmgC; HalFC 88; IntMPA 92; IntWW 91; MotPP; MovMk; VarWW 85; Who 85, 92; WhoAm 86, 90; WhoEnt 92A; WhoHol 92; WhoThe 72, 77, 81; WhoWor 91; WorAlBi*

Heth, Charlotte
American. Musicologist
Collected and published materials relating to Native American Music; published *Music of the Sacred Fire,* 1978.
b. Oct 29, 1937
Source: *NotNaAm*

Hevelius, Johannes
[Johannes Hevel]
German. Astronomer
Recorded pioneer study of lunar topography in *Selenographia,* 1647.
b. Jan 28, 1611 in Danzig, Poland
d. Jan 28, 1687 in Danzig, Poland
Source: *AsBiEn; BiESc; BioIn 9, 14; DcScB; InSci; LarDcSc; NewCol 75; WorAl; WorAlBi*

Hevesy, George Charles von
Hungarian. Chemist
Won Nobel Prize, 1943, for discovery of hafnium and work on use of isotopes as tracer elements.
b. Aug 1, 1885 in Budapest, Austria-Hungary
d. Jul 5, 1966 in Freiburg im Breisgau, Germany (West)
Source: *CurBio 59, 66; DcScB; LarDcSc; McGMS 80; WhoNob, 90, 95*

Hewes, Henry
American. Critic
Drama critic with *Saturday Review,* 1952-73; won Pulitzers, 1968, 1981.
b. Apr 9, 1917 in Boston, Massachusetts
Source: *AmAu&B; BiE&WWA; ConAmTC; ConAu 13R; NotNAT; OxCAmT 84; OxCThe 67; WhoAm 74, 76, 78, 80, 82, 84, 86, 88, 90, 92, 94, 95, 96, 97; WhoEnt 92; WhoThe 72, 77, 81; WhoWor 74, 76, 84*

Hewes, Joseph
American. Merchant, Continental Congressman
Signed Declaration of Independence, 1776; was virtually first head of US Navy.
b. Jan 23, 1730 in Kingston, New Jersey
d. Nov 10, 1779 in Philadelphia, Pennsylvania
Source: *AmBi; ApCAB; BiAUS; BiDrAC; BiDrUSC 89; BioIn 1, 3, 7, 8, 9; DcAmB; DcNCBi 3; Drake; EncAR; HarEnUS; NatCAB 10; TwCBDA; WhAm HS; WhAmP; WhAmRev*

Hewish, Antony
English. Scientist
Discovered pulsars; shared 1974 Nobel Prize in physics.
b. May 11, 1924 in Fowey, England
Source: *AmMWSc 89, 92, 95; BiESc; BioIn 10, 13, 14, 15, 20; BlueB 76; CamDcSc; IntAu&W 77, 82; IntWW 74, 75, 76, 77, 78, 79, 80, 81, 82, 83, 89, 91, 93; LarDcSc; McGMS 80; NobelP; NotTwCS; Who 74, 82, 83, 85, 88, 90, 92, 94; WhoNob, 90, 95; WhoWor 78, 80, 82, 84, 87, 89, 91, 93, 95, 96; WorAl; WorAlBi; WorScD*

Hewitt, Abram Stevens
American. Industrialist
Co-founded Cooper, Hewitt iron-manufacturing co., 1845; made first US-made steel, 1870; NYC mayor, 1887-88.
b. Jul 31, 1822 in Haverstraw, New York
d. Jan 18, 1903 in Ringwood, New Jersey
Source: *AmBi; ApCAB; BiAUS; BiDAmBL 83; BiDrAC; BiDrUSC 89; BioIn 8, 11, 12, 17; DcAmB; EncAB-H 1974, 1996; EncABHB 3; HarEnUS; McGEWB; NatCAB 3; OxCAmH; TwCBDA; WebAB 74, 79; WhAm 1, 4; WhAmP; WorAl*

Hewitt, Alan
American. Actor
Film work included *That Touch of Mink,* 1962; *Sweet Charity,* 1969; recorded over 200 books for the blind.
b. Jan 21, 1915 in New York, New York
d. Nov 7, 1986 in New York, New York
Source: *BiE&WWA; ConTFT 1, 2, 4; NotNAT; WhoHol A*

Hewitt, Bill
[William E Hewitt]
American. Football Player
Four-time all-pro defensive end, 1932-39, 1943; Hall of Fame, 1971; killed in auto crash.
b. Oct 8, 1909 in Bay City, Michigan
d. Jan 14, 1947 in Sellersville, Pennsylvania
Source: *BioIn 6, 17; LegTOT; WhoFtbl 74; WhoSpor*

Hewitt, Don S.
American. Broadcasting Executive
Creator, producer of CBS TV news program "60 Minutes," 1968—; named to NATAS Hall of Fame, 1990; recipient of Peabody Award, 1989.
b. Dec 14, 1922 in New York, New York
Source: *BioIn 13, 14, 15, 16; ConAu 119, 146; CurBio 88; EncAJ; EncTwCJ; LesBEnT, 92; WhoAm 74, 76, 78, 80, 82, 84, 86, 88, 90, 92, 94, 95, 96; WhoE 74, 93; WhoEnt 92*

Hewitt, Foster
[William Foster Hewitt]
Canadian. Broadcaster
First to broadcast a hockey game, from Toronto, 1923; longtime voice of CBCs "Hoc key Night in Canada," known for unique style; Hall of Fame, 1965.
b. Nov 21, 1903 in Toronto, Ontario, Canada
d. Apr 21, 1985 in Toronto, Ontario, Canada
Source: *BioIn 8, 14, 15; ConAu 115; WhoHcky 73*

Hewitt, Henry Kent
American. Naval Officer
Led naval operations, invasion of N Africa, WW II; invasion of S France, 1944; appointed Admiral, 1949.

b. Feb 11, 1887 in Hackensack, New Jersey
d. Sep 15, 1972 in Middlebury, Vermont
Source: *BiDWWGF; BioIn 1, 9, 11; CurBio 43, 72; DcAmB S9; DcAmMiB; HarEnMi; NatCAB 57; ObitOF 79; OxCShps; WebAMB; WhAm 5*

Hewitt, J(ohn) N(apoleon) B(rinton)
American. Anthropologist
He was the twentieth century's foremost authority on the Iroquois.
b. 1859 in New York
d. 1937
Source: *BiNAW, B, SupB; EncNAB; WhAm 4; WhNaAH*

Hewitt, Martin
American. Actor
Had screen debut in *Endless Love,* with Brooke Shields, 1981.
b. Feb 19, 1958 in San Jose, California
Source: *BioIn 12; DcLP 87B*

Hewitt, Peter Cooper
American. Inventor
Electrical engineer; devised mercury-vapor lamp 1901, an important development in elctrical lighting.
b. May 5, 1861 in New York, New York
d. Aug 25, 1921 in Paris, France
Source: *AmBi; ApCAB X; DcAmB; InSci; LinLib S; NatCAB 14; WhAm 1*

Hewitt, William Archibald
Canadian. Journalist
Sports editor, *Toronto Star* for 31 yrs; credited with introducing goal nets in Hockey; Hall of Fame, 1945.
b. May 15, 1875 in Cobourg, Ontario, Canada
d. Sep 8, 1951
Source: *WhoHcky 73*

Hewlett, William
American. Businessman, Engineer
With David Packard, launched Hewlett-Packard, high-tech electronic, information systems, 1939.
b. May 20, 1913 in Ann Arbor, Michigan
Source: *AmMWSc 92; BiDrAPA 89; BioIn 15, 16; ConAmBL; Entr; LegTOT; NotTwCS; WhoAm 78, 80, 82, 84, 86, 88, 90; WhoFI 77, 79, 81, 83, 87, 89; WhoWest 87, 89, 92; WhoWor 87*

Hextall, Bryan Aldwyn
Canadian. Hockey Player
Right wing, NY Rangers, 1936-48; won Art Ross Trophy, 1942; Hall of Fame, 1969; sons Bryan, Dennis played in NHL.
b. Jul 31, 1913 in Greenfell, Saskatchewan, Canada
d. Jul 24, 1984 in Portage La Prairie, Manitoba, Canada
Source: *HocEn; NewYTBS 84, 85; WhoHcky 73*

Hextall, Ron(ald Jeffrey)
Canadian. Hockey Player
Goalie, Philadelphia, 1986-92, NY Islanders, 1993—; won Conn Smythe, Vezina trophies, 1986, 1987; first goalie ever to score a goal, 1987-88.
b. May 3, 1964 in Winnipeg, Manitoba, Canada
Source: *BioIn 16; HocReg 86, 87; News 88-2; WhoAm 92, 94, 95, 96, 97; WorAlBi*

Hexum, Jon-Erik
American. Actor
In TV series "Cover-Up," 1984; accidentally killed himself playing Russian Roulett e.
b. Nov 5, 1957 in Englewood, New Jersey
d. Oct 18, 1984 in Los Angeles, California
Source: *ConTFT 2; LegTOT*

Heydrich, Reinhard Tristan Eugen
"The Hangman of Europe"
German. Government Official
Aide to Himmler in Gestapo; early director of death camps; assassinated.
b. Mar 9, 1904 in Halle, Germany
d. Jun 4, 1942 in Lidice, Czechoslovakia
Source: *BiDExR; CurBio 42; NewCol 75; SpyCS; WebBD 83*

Heyer, Georgette
English. Author
Wrote historical, mystery novels set in Regency London: *A Blunt Instrument,* 1938, *The Spanish Bride,* 1940.
b. Aug 6, 1902 in Wimbledon, England
d. Jul 4, 1974 in London, England
Source: *Au&Wr 71; Benet 87; BioIn 4, 10, 14, 16, 17; BlmGWL; ConAu 49, 93; ConPopW; CorpD; CrtSuMy; DcLB 77; DcLEL; DcNaB 1971; DetWom; EncBrWW; EncMys; FemiCLE; GrWomMW; InWom SUP; LngCTC; MajTwCW; NewC; NewYTBS 74; Novels; ObitOF 79; ObitT 1971; OxCChiL; OxCEng 85, 95; PenNWW A; REn; TwCA, SUP; TwCCr&M 80, 85, 91; TwCRGW; TwCRHW 90, 94; TwCWr; WhAm 6; WhE&EA; WhLit; Who 74; WhoAm 74; WhoAmW 66, 72; WhoWor 74; WorAl*

Heyerdahl, Thor
Norwegian. Anthropologist, Explorer
Wrote *Kon-Tiki,* 1950; *Aku-Aku: The Secret of Easter Island,* 1958.
b. Oct 6, 1914 in Larvik, Norway
Source: *Au&Wr 71; BioIn 1, 2, 3, 4, 5, 6, 8, 9, 10, 11, 12, 15, 16; CelR; ConAu 5NR, 5R, 22NR; ConHero 2; ConLC 26; CurBio 47, 72; DcTwHis; EnvEnDr; FacFETw; InSci; IntAu&W 76, 77, 82, 89, 91, 93; IntDcAn; IntWW 74, 75, 76, 77, 78, 79, 80, 81, 82, 83, 89, 91, 93; LegTOT; LinLib L, S; LngCTC; MajTwCW; OxCShps; RAdv 14, 13-3; SmATA 2, 52; TwCA SUP; TwCWr; WhDW; Who 74, 82, 83, 85, 88, 90, 92, 94; WhoAm 80, 82, 84, 86, 88; WhoScEn 94; WhoWor 74, 76, 78, 82, 84, 87, 91, 93, 95; WorAl; WorAlBi; WrDr 76, 80, 82, 84, 86, 88, 90, 92, 94, 96*

Heym, Stefan
German. Author
Novels include *Five Days in June,* 1974.
b. Apr 10, 1913 in Chemnitz, Germany
Source: *AmAu&B; AmNov; Au&Wr 71; BenetAL 91; BiGAW; BioIn 2, 4, 18; ConAu 4NR, 9R; ConFLW 84; ConLC 41; ConWorW 93; CurBio 43; DcLB 69; EncWL 3; IntAu&W 76, 77, 82, 86; IntWW 91, 93; LiExTwC; ModGL; OxCGer 76, 86; PenC EUR; RAdv 14; REnAL; ScF&FL 92; TwCA SUP; WhE&EA; WhoSocC 78; WhoSoCE 89; WrDr 80*

Heymans, Corneille Jean Francois
Belgian. Physician, Educator
Won Nobel Prize in medicine, 1938, for studies of respiratory function.
b. Mar 28, 1892 in Ghent, Belgium
d. Jul 18, 1968 in Knokke, Belgium
Source: *BiESc; LarDcSc; WhDW; WhoNob, 90, 95*

Heyns, Roger W(illiam)
American. Psychologist
Chancellor, U. of CA at Berkeley, 1965-71; wrote *The Psychology of Personal Adjustment,* 1958.
b. Jan 27, 1918
d. Sep 11, 1995 in Volos, Greece
Source: *AmMWSc 73S; BioIn 7, 8, 9, 11; CurBio 95N; LEduc 74; PolProf J; WhAm 11; WhoAm 74, 76, 78, 80, 82, 84, 86, 88, 90, 92, 94, 95, 96; WhoGov 72, 75, 77; WhoSSW 73; WhoWest 96*

Heyrovsky, Jaroslav
Czech. Scientist
Won Nobel Prize in chemistry, 1959, for discovery of polarography.
b. Dec 20, 1890 in Prague, Bohemia
d. Mar 27, 1967 in Prague, Czechoslovakia
Source: *AsBiEn; BiESc; BioIn 5, 6, 7, 8, 14, 15, 19, 20; CamDcSc; CurBio 61, 67; DcScB; InSci; LarDcSc; McGMS 80; NobelP; NotTwCS; WhAm 4; WhoNob, 90, 95*

Heyse, Paul Johann Ludwig von
German. Author
Master of novella; won Nobel Prize for literature, 1910.
b. Mar 15, 1830 in Berlin, Germany
d. Apr 2, 1914 in Munich, Germany
Source: *BioIn 1, 5, 7, 15, 19; CasWL; ClDMEL 47, 80; EuAu; EvEuW; NotNAT B; OxCGer 76; PenC EUR; REn; WhoNob, 90, 95; WorAl*

Heyward, (Edwin) DuBose
American. Author
Major writer of Harlem Renaissance; wrote *Porgy,* 1925; adapted as opera *Porgy and Bess,* 1935.

b. Aug 31, 1885 in Charleston, South Carolina
d. Jun 16, 1940 in Tryon, North Carolina
Source: *AmAu&B; ASCAP 66, 80; Benet 87, 96; BenetAL 91; BioIn 3, 4, 5, 8, 10, 12, 15; BriBkM 80; CamGLE; CamHAL; ChhPo; CnDAL; CnMD; ConAmA; ConAmL; ConAu 108; CrtSuDr; CurBio 40; CyWA 58; DcAmB S2; DcLB 7, 9, 45; DcLEL; DcNAA; EncSoH; EvLB; GrWrEL N; LegTOT; LinLib L, S; LngCTC; McGEWD 72, 84; ModAL; ModWD; NatCAB 60; NotNAT A, B; Novels; OxCAmL 65, 83, 95; OxCAmT 84; PenC AM; PlP&P; REn; REnAL; RfGAmL 87, 94; RGTwCWr; ScF&FL 1; SmATA 21; SouWr; TwCA, SUP; TwCLC 59; TwCWr; WebAB 74, 79; WhAm 1; WhE&EA; WhThe*

Heyward, Thomas, Jr.
American. Lawyer, Continental Congressman
Soldier, planter, patroit; signed Declaration of Independence from SC, 1776.
b. Jul 28, 1746 in Saint Helena's, South Carolina
d. Mar 6, 1809 in Saint Luke's, South Carolina
Source: *AmBi; ApCAB; BiAUS; BiDrAC; BiDrUSC 89; BioIn 7, 8, 9, 11; DcAmB; EncAR; EncCRAm; EncSoH; HarEnUS; NatCAB 1; TwCBDA; WhAm HS; WhAmP; WhAmRev*

Heywood, Eddie, Jr.
American. Musician, Composer
Jazz pianist; recorded "Begin the Beguine," 1944; wrote "Canadian Sunset," 1956.
b. Dec 4, 1915 in Atlanta, Georgia
d. Jan 1, 1989 in Miami Beach, Florida
Source: *AllMusG; AnObit 1989; Baker 92; BiDAmM; BiDJaz; BioIn 10, 16; CmpEPM; DrBlPA 90; EncJzS; FacFETw; IlEncJ; InB&W 85; LegTOT; NewAmDM; NewGrDJ 88, 94; NewYTBS 89; OxCPMus; PenEncP; WhoJazz 72*

Heywood, Thomas
English. Dramatist
Said to have written 220 plays including *The Captives,* 1634.
b. c. 1574 in Lincolnshire, England
d. Aug 16, 1641 in London, England
Source: *Alli; AtlBL; BbD; BiD&SB; BioIn 16; BlmGEL; BritAu; CasWL; Chambr 1; ChhPo; CnThe; CroE&S; CrtT 1; CyWA 58; DcEnA; DcEnL; DcEuL; DcLEL; Ent; EvLB; McGEWD 72; MouLC 1; NewC; NewCBEL; OxCEng 67, 85, 95; OxCThe 67; PenC ENG; REn; REnWD; WebE&AL*

Heyworth, James
American. TV Executive
Pres., CEO, HBO, 1980-83; pres., CEO, Viewer's Choice, 1989—.
b. Sep 22, 1942 in Chicago, Illinois
Source: *Dun&B 86; St&PR 87; WhoAm 84, 86, 90; WhoEnt 92; WhoFI 83, 92; WhoTelC*

Hiassen, Carl
American. Author
Novels include *Double Whammy,* 1987; *Strip Tease,* 1993; works blend humor with serious messages.
b. Mar 12, 1953 in Fort Lauderdale, Florida

Hiatt, John
American. Singer, Songwriter
Composer of over 600 songs, including "Thing Called Love," popularized on Bonnie Raitt's *Nick of Time,* 1989.
b. 1952 in Indianapolis, Indiana
Source: *BgBkCoM; BioIn 12, 15; ConMus 8; EncRkSt; OnThGG; PenEncP; RolSEnR 83; WhoAm 94, 95, 96, 97; WhoFash*

Hiawatha
American. Legendary Figure
Subject of Henry Wadsworth Longfellow's *Song of Hiawatha,* 1855.
b. 1450?
Source: *EngPo; NewCol 75; OxCAmL 65; WebAB 74; WhNaAH*

Hibberd, Andrew Stuart
English. Broadcaster
BBC announcer, 1924-51.
b. Oct 5, 1893 in Canford Magna, England
d. Nov 1983
Source: *ConAu 111; Who 74, 82, 83*

Hibbert, Eleanor Alice Burford
[Philippa Carr; Elbur Ford; Victoria Holt; Jean Plaidy Kellow; Kathleen Kellow; Jean Plaidy; Ellalice Tate]
English. Author
Prolific writer of Gothic romances since 1950s; best known as Victoria Holt; died on cruise in the Mediterranean.
b. 1906 in London, England
d. Jan 18, 1993, At Sea
Source: *AmAu&B; ArtclWW 2; Au&Wr 71; BestSel 90-4; BioIn 14, 18, 19; BlmGWL; ConAu 9NR, 17R, 28NR, 140, X; ConLC 7, 81; ConPopW; CorpD; DcLP 87A; EncMys; FacFETw; FemiCLE; IntAu&W 91; InWom SUP; Novels; PenNWW B; SmATA 2, 74; TwCCr&M 85, 91; TwCRGW; TwCRHW 90, 94; TwCWr; Who 92; WhoAm 86; WhoAmW 74, 75, 77; WhoWor 91; WorAl; WorAlBi; WorAu 1950; WrDr 76, 84, 86, 88, 90, 92, 94N*

Hibbler, Al
American. Singer
Popular baritone with Duke Ellington's orchestra, 1943-51.
b. Aug 16, 1915 in Little Rock, Arkansas
Source: *BiDAmM; BiDJaz; BioIn 4, 10; CmpEPM; DrBlPA, 90; NegAl 89; NewGrDJ 88; PenEncP; RkOn 74*

Hibbs, Ben
American. Journalist
Editor, *Saturday Evening Post,* 1942-62.
b. Jul 23, 1901 in Fontana, Kansas
d. Mar 29, 1975 in Penn Valley, Pennsylvania
Source: *AmAu&B; BioIn 1, 5, 6, 10, 12, 16, 20; ConAu 65, 104; CurBio 46, 75, 75N; DcLB 137; EncTwCJ; IntWW 74; NatCAB 58; WhAm 6; WhE&EA; WhJnl; WhoAm 74*

Hickel, Wally
[Walter Joseph Hickel]
American. Politician
Independent governor, AK, 1966-69; 1990-94, succeeding Steve Cowper.
b. Aug 18, 1919 in Claflin, Kansas
Source: *AlmAP 92; AmCath 80; BiDrGov 1789; BioIn 8, 9, 10, 11, 12, 16, 17, 18, 20; ConAu 41R; CurBio 69; Dun&B 90; IntWW 74, 75, 76, 77, 78, 79, 80, 81, 82, 83, 89, 91, 93; PolProf NF; WhoAm 74, 76, 78, 80, 82, 84, 86, 88, 90, 92, 94, 95, 96, 97; WhoAmP 73, 75, 77, 79, 81, 83, 85, 87, 89, 91, 93, 95; WhoFI 96; WhoWest 89, 92, 94, 96; WhoWor 74, 76, 78, 93, 95, 96, 97*

Hickenlooper, Bourke B
American. Politician
Rep. senator from IA, 1945-69; governor of IA, 1943-45; co-sponsored Atomic Energy Act, 1954.
b. Jul 21, 1896 in Blockton, Iowa
d. Sep 4, 1971 in Shelter Island, New York
Source: *BiDrAC; CurBio 47, 71, 71N; NewYTBE 71; PolProf E, J, K, T; WhAm 5; WhAmP*

Hickerson, John Dewey
American. Government Official
Helped write treaty that later established NATO; Asst. Secretary of State, 1949-53; served as ambassador to Finland, 1955-59; to the Philippines 1959-62.
b. Jan 26, 1898 in Crawford, Texas
d. Jan 18, 1989 in Bethesda, Maryland
Source: *BioIn 2, 5, 16; CurBio 89N*

Hickey, James Aloysius, Cardinal
American. Religious Leader
Archbishop of Washington, DC, 1980—; made cardinal, 1988.
b. Oct 11, 1920 in Midland, Michigan
Source: *AmCath 80; BioIn 13; IntWW 89, 91, 93; RelLAm 91; WhoAm 74, 76, 78, 80, 82, 84, 86, 88, 90, 95, 96, 97; WhoE 83, 85, 86, 91, 93, 95; WhoMW 80; WhoRel 77, 85, 92; WhoWor 91, 95, 96, 97*

Hickey, Margaret A.
American. Editor
Public affairs editor, *Ladies Home Journal;* founder, director, School for Secretaries, 1933-69.
b. Mar 14, 1902 in Kansas City, Missouri
d. Dec 7, 1994 in Tucson, Arizona
Source: *BioIn 20, 21; CurBio 44, 95N; InWom; WhAm 11; WhoAdv 90; WhoAm 74, 76, 78, 80, 82, 84, 86, 88, 90, 92; WhoGov 77; WhoWor 74*

Hickey, William
English. Lawyer, Traveler
Noted for *Memoirs,* 1749-1809, published 1913-25, describing voyages, colorful life.
b. 1749 in Westminster, England
d. 1830
Source: *BiDIrW; BioIn 6, 8, 10, 14; DcArts; DcIrW 2; DcLEL; DcNaB MP; OxCEng 67, 85, 95; PenC ENG*

Hickman, Darryl
American. Actor
Juvenile actor in 1940s films; became producer, 1960s; executive producer, TV so ap "Love of Life."
b. Jul 28, 1931 in Los Angeles, California
Source: *BiE&WWA; BioIn 15, 16; ConTFT 5; FilmEn; FilmgC; ForYSC; HalFC 80, 84, 88; IntMPA 82, 92; MovMk; VarWW 85; WhoHol A*

Hickman, Dwayne B
American. Actor
Starred in "The Many Loves of Dobie Gillis," 1959-63.
b. May 18, 1934 in Los Angeles, California
Source: *BioIn 15, 16; FilmgC; HalFC 88; MotPP; MovMk; VarWW 85; WhoHol A*

Hickman, Fred(erick Douglass)
American. Sportscaster
Cohost of "Sports Tonight," CNN, 1980-84, 1986—.
b. Oct 17, 1951 in Springfield, Illinois
Source: *ConBlB 11; WhoAfA 96; WhoBlA 94*

Hickman, Herman Michael, Jr.
American. Football Player, Football Coach
All-America guard, U of TN, 1931; in pros, 1932-34; coach, Yale, 1949-52; first football player to have successful TV show, 1950s.
b. Oct 1, 1911 in Johnson City, Tennessee
d. Apr 25, 1958 in Washington, District of Columbia
Source: *BiDAmSp Sup; CurBio 51, 58; WhAm 3; WhoFtbl 74; WhScrn 83*

Hickock, Richard Eugene
American. Murderer
Subject of Truman Capote's *In Cold Blood,* who murdered family with partner Perry Smith, 1959.
b. Jun 6, 1931 in Kansas City, Missouri
d. Apr 14, 1965 in Lansing, Kansas
Source: *BioIn 7; MurCaTw*

Hickok, Lorena A
American. Author, Journalist
Reporter who frequently covered the Roosevelts; wrote young people's books on Eleanor and Franklin.
b. 1892 in East Troy, Wisconsin
d. May 3, 1968 in Rhinebeck, New York
Source: *AuBYP 2; BioIn 7, 8, 10; ConAu 73; SmATA 20*

Hickok, Wild Bill
[James Butler Hickok]
American. Entertainer, Pioneer
Toured with Buffalo Bill as legendary gunfighter, 1872-74; killed while playing poker.
b. May 27, 1837 in Troy Grove, Illinois
d. Aug 2, 1876 in Deadwood, South Dakota
Source: *AmBi; Benet 87; BenetAL 91; BioIn 1, 2, 3, 4, 5, 6, 7, 8, 9, 10, 11, 12, 13, 14, 15, 17; CopCroC; DcAmB; FilmgC; HalFC 80, 84, 88; LegTOT; McGEWB; OxCAmH; OxCAmL 65, 83, 95; PeoHis; REn; REnAL; REnAW; WebAB 74, 79; WhAm HS; WhCiWar; WhDW; WhNaAH; WorAl; WorAlBi*

Hicks, David Nightingale
English. Designer, Interior Decorator
Designer of fabric, sheets, furniture, carpet, etc; author, *David Hicks on Decoration,* 1966.
b. Mar 25, 1929 in Essex, England
Source: *BioIn 16; ConDes 90; DcTwDes; IntAu&W 77; IntWW 91; WhAm 9; Who 82, 92; WhoWor 78, 84*

Hicks, Edward
American. Artist
Quaker folk painter remembered for beloved *The Peaceable Kingdom.*
b. Apr 4, 1780 in Attleboro, Pennsylvania
d. Aug 23, 1849 in Newtown, Pennsylvania
Source: *AmCulL; AmFkP; BioIn 1, 2, 3, 4, 5, 6, 7, 9, 10, 12, 13, 15, 19; BriEAA; DcAmArt; FolkA 87; IlBEAAW; LegTOT; McGDA; McGEWB; NewCol 75; NewYHSD; OxCAmH; OxDcArt; PeoHis; REn; WebAB 74, 79; WebBD 83; WhAm HS; WorAl; WorAlBi*

Hicks, Elias
American. Religious Leader
Led liberal faction of Quakers; followers called Hicksites.
b. Mar 19, 1748 in Hempstead Township, New York
d. Feb 27, 1830 in Jericho, New York
Source: *Alli; AmAu&B; AmBi; AmRef; AmWrBE; ApCAB; BbD; BenetAL 91; BiDAmCu; BiD&SB; BioIn 3, 9, 15, 19; CelCen; DcAmAu; DcAmB; DcAmReB 1, 2; DcAmSR; DcNAA; Drake; HarEnUS; LinLib S; LuthC 75; NatCAB 11; OxCAmL 65, 83, 95; REnAL; TwCBDA; WebAB 74, 79; WhAm HS*

Hicks, Granville
American. Author
Spokesman for American proletarian literary movement; wrote *John Reed: The Making of a Revolutionary,* 1936.
b. Sep 9, 1901 in Exeter, New Hampshire
d. Jun 18, 1982 in Franklin Park, New Jersey
Source: *AmAu&B; AmNov; AnObit 1982; Benet 87, 96; BenetAL 91; BiDAmLf; BioIn 1, 2, 4, 6, 7, 12, 13, 14; CnDAL; ConAmA; ConAu 9R, 13NR, 107; ConLCrt 77, 82; ConNov 72, 76, 82; CurBio 82, 82N; DcLEL; EncAL; EncMcCE; EncSF 93; IntAu&W 76, 77; IntWW 74, 75, 76, 77, 78, 79, 80, 81, 82; LegTOT; NewYTBS 82; OxCAmL 65, 83, 95; PenC AM; RAdv 1; REn; REnAL; ScF&FL 1, 92; TwCA, SUP; WhAm 8; WhLit; WhoAm 74, 76, 78; WhoWor 74, 76, 78; WrDr 76, 80, 82*

Hicks, John Richard, Sir
English. Economist
Shared 1972 Nobel Prize for contributions to economic equilibrium theory.
b. Apr 8, 1904 in Leamington Spa, England
d. May 20, 1989 in Blockley, England
Source: *BioIn 14, 15, 16; DcNaB 1986; IntAu&W 77, 82; IntEnSS 79; IntWW 74, 75, 76, 77, 78, 79, 80, 81, 82, 83, 89; NewYTBS 89; RAdv 14; WhAm 10; Who 82, 85, 92; WhoNob, 90, 95; WhoWor 74, 76, 78, 80, 82, 84, 87, 89; WrDr 94N*

Hicks, Louise Day
American. Politician
Advocate of neighborhood school concept; opposed MA school desegregation plans, 1960s; first woman to run for Boston mayor.
b. Oct 16, 1923 in Boston, Massachusetts
Source: *BiDrUSC 89; BioIn 17; CurBio 74; InWom SUP; WhoAm 74, 76; WhoAmP 73, 75, 77, 79; WhoAmW 74; WhoE 74; WhoGov 72, 75; WomPO 78*

Hicks, Tony
[The Hollies; Anthony Hicks]
English. Musician
Guitarist with Hollies since 1962.
b. Dec 16, 1943 in Nelson, England
Source: *OnThGG; WhoRocM 82*

Hicks, Ursula Kathleen Webb
English. Economist, Editor
Co-founder, editor for 27 yrs. *Review of Economics.*
b. Feb 17, 1896 in Dublin, Ireland
d. Jul 16, 1985 in Blockley, England
Source: *ConAu 117; Who 85*

Hidalgo, Elvira de
Spanish. Opera Singer, Teacher
Last of Spanish soprani d' agilita; only teacher of Maria Callas.
b. Dec 27, 1882 in Barcelona, Spain
d. Jan 21, 1980 in Milan, Italy
Source: *CmOp; MetOEnc; PenDiMP*

Hidalgo y Costilla, Miguel
Mexican. Clergy, Revolutionary
Led lower classes in fight for independence from Spain, 1810.
b. May 8, 1753 in Corralejo, Mexico
d. Jul 30, 1811 in Chihuahua, Mexico

Source: *ApCAB; Benet 87, 96; BiDLAmC; BioIn 3, 5, 7, 8, 9, 10, 13, 16, 17, 18, 19, 20; Drake; EncLatA; EncRev; LegTOT; McGEWB; NewCol 75; REn; WhDW*

Higbe, Kirby
[Walter Kirby Higbe]
American. Baseball Player
Pitcher, 1937-49; helped Brooklyn win pennant, 1941, but asked to be traded, 1947, for refusal to play on same team with Jackie Robinson.
b. Apr 8, 1915 in Columbia, South Carolina
d. May 6, 1985 in Columbia, South Carolina
Source: *Ballpl 90; BioIn 3, 11, 14; ConAu 116; WhoProB 73*

Higginbotham, Jack
[Jay C Higginbotham]
American. Musician
Trombonist, vocalist; recorded with Fletcher Henderson, Louis Armstrong, from 1930s; led own band, 1960s.
b. May 11, 1906 in Atlanta, Georgia
d. May 26, 1973 in New York, New York
Source: *Baker 84; BiDAfM; BiDAmM; BiDJaz; BioIn 9; EncJzS; InB&W 80, 85; WhAm 6; WhoJazz 72; WorAl*

Higgins, Andrew J
American. Shipping Executive
Higgins Industries built landing craft during WW II, ships during Korean War.
b. Aug 28, 1886 in Columbus, Nebraska
d. Aug 1, 1952 in New Orleans, Louisiana
Source: *CurBio 52; DcAmB S5; WhAm 3*

Higgins, Bertie
[Elbert Higgins]
American. Singer, Songwriter
Recorded hit single, "Key Largo," 1982.
b. 1946? in Tarpon Springs, Florida
Source: *LegTOT; RkOn 85*

Higgins, Colin
French. Writer
Films include *Harold and Maude,* 1971; *Nine to Five,* 1980; TV movies include *Out on a Limb,* 1987.
b. Jul 28, 1941 in Noumea, New Caledonia
Source: *BioIn 14, 16; ConAu 30NR, 33R, 126; ConTFT 1, 5; DcLB 26; HalFC 84, 88; IntMPA 86, 88; MiSFD 9N; VarWW 85; WhAm 9; WhoAm 82, 84, 86, 88; WrDr 76, 80*

Higgins, George V
American. Author, Lawyer
Wrote *Kennedy for the Defense,* 1980.
b. Nov 13, 1939 in Brockton, Massachusetts
Source: *BenetAL 91; BioIn 13, 14, 16; ConAu 5AS, 17NR, 77; ConLC 18; ConNov 86, 91; DrAPF 89, 91; IntAu&W 91; IntWW 91; MajTwCW; TwCCr&M 85; WhoAm 86, 90; WhoWrEP 89; WorAlBi; WorAu 1975; WrDr 86, 92*

Higgins, Marguerite
American. Journalist
Korean, Vietnam War correspondent who won 1951 Pulitzer for int'l reporting.
b. Sep 3, 1920, Hong Kong
d. Jan 3, 1966 in Washington, District of Columbia
Source: *AmAu&B; AmDec 1950; AmWomWr; BiDAmJo; BiDAmNC; BioIn 2, 3, 4, 5, 7, 8, 9, 12, 13, 15, 16, 21; BriB; ConAu 5R, 25R; CurBio 51, 66; DcAmB S8; DcAmDH 80, 89; EncAJ; EncTwCJ; GoodHs; GrLiveH; HisDcKW; InWom, SUP; JrnUS; LegTOT; NotAW MOD; WhAm 4; WomComm; WomFir; WomStre; WorAlBi*

Higgins, William R
American. Hostage
Lt. Col., USMC, taken hostage by Lebanese terrorist groups; was executed after 530 days in captivity.
b. 1946?
d. Jul 1989, Lebanon
Source: *BioIn 15*

Higginson, Thomas Wentworth Storrow
American. Clergy, Author
Unitarian minister, slavery opponent; led first colored regiment in Civil War, 1862-64; friend of Emily Dickinson.
b. Dec 22, 1823 in Cambridge, Massachusetts
d. May 9, 1911 in Cambridge, Massachusetts
Source: *AmAu; AmAu&B; AmBi; AmRef; AmSocL; ApCAB; BbD; BiD&SB; CasWL; Chambr 3; CnDAL; CyAL 2; DcAmB; DcLEL; Drake; McGEWB; NatCAB 1; OxCAmL 65; REn; REnAL; TwCBDA; WebAB 74, 79; WhAm 1*

Highet, Gilbert Arthur
American. Author, Educator
Noted for popularizing intellectual topics; wrote *Anatomy of Satire,* 1962.
b. Jun 22, 1906 in Glasgow, Scotland
d. Jan 20, 1978 in New York, New York
Source: *AmAu&B; Au&Wr 71; ChhPo S2; ConAu 1R; CurBio 64; DcLEL 1940; DrAS 74F; IntWW 74; LngCTC; NewC; NewCBEL; NewYTBE 72; RAdv 1; REnAL; TwCA SUP; Who 74; WhoAm 74; WhoWor 74; WrDr 76*

Highsmith, Patricia
[Patricia Plangman]
American. Author
Award-winning crime novels include *The Talented Mr. Ripley,* 1955, and *Found in the Street,* 1986.
b. Jan 1, 1921 in Fort Worth, Texas
d. Feb 5, 1995 in Locarno, Switzerland
Source: *AmWomWr; ArtclWW 2; Au&Wr 71; Benet 96; BenetAL 91; BioIn 10, 12, 14, 15, 16, 17, 18, 19, 20, 21; BlueB 76; CamGLE; ConAu 1NR, 1R, 20NR; ConLC 2, 4, 14, 42; ConNov 72, 76, 82, 86, 91; ConPopW; CrtSuMy; CurBio 90, 95N; DcArts; DcLP 87A; DetWom; EncMys; FacFETw; FemiCLE; GrWomMW; HalFC 80, 84, 88; IntAu&W 76, 77, 82, 89, 91; IntWW 82, 83, 89, 91, 93; InWom SUP; LegTOT; MajTwCW; News 95, 95-3; NewYTBS 88; Novels; OxCAmL 95; OxCEng 85, 95; PenNWW A; RAdv 14; RGTwCWr; ScF&FL 92; TwCCr&M 80, 85, 91; WhAm 11; Who 74, 82, 83, 85, 88, 90, 92, 94; WhoHr&F; WhoTwCL; WhoWor 76, 89; WorAl; WorAlBi; WorAu 1950; WrDr 76, 80, 82, 84, 86, 88, 90, 92*

Hightower, Florence Josephine Cole
American. Children's Author
Wrote adventure mysteries for children: *Secret of the Crazy Quilt,* 1972.
b. Jun 9, 1916 in Boston, Massachusetts
d. Mar 6, 1981 in Boston, Massachusetts
Source: *AuBYP 2; ConAu 103; SmATA 4; WhoAmW 72, 74, 75*

Hightower, John Marmann
American. Journalist
AP Washington bureau reporter, 1936-71; known for detailed reporting; won Pulitzer, 1952.
b. Sep 17, 1909 in Coal Creek, Tennessee
d. Feb 9, 1987 in Santa Fe, New Mexico
Source: *BioIn 3; CurBio 52, 87; WhoAm 84, 86*

Hightower, Rosella
American. Dancer
Leading ballerina, Grand Ballet de Monte Carlo, 1947-61; noted for enormous repertoire.
b. Jan 30, 1920 in Ardmore, Oklahoma
Source: *BiDD; BioIn 1, 3, 4, 9, 11, 12, 13, 14, 21; CnOxB; DancEn 78; InWom; LegTOT; NotNaAm; WhoWor 84*

Highway, Thomson
Canadian. Dramatist
Plays include *The Rez Sisters,* 1986.
b. 1951 in Manitoba, Canada
Source: *NotNaAm*

Highway 101
[Paulette Carlson; Jack Daniels; Scott (Cactus) Moser]
American. Music Group
Country band formed, 1986; hits include "The Bed You Made for Me; Whiskey, If You Were a Woman," 1987.
Source: *BgBkCoM; ConMus 4; WhoNeCM*

Higinbotham, William A(lfred)
American. Physicist
Electronics group leader in atomic bomb development.
b. Oct 25, 1910
d. Nov 10, 1994 in Gainesville, Georgia
Source: *AmMWSc 73P, 76P, 79, 82, 86, 89, 92, 95; BioIn 1; CurBio 95N; InSci;*

LElec; WhAm 11; WhoAm 74, 76, 78, 80, 82, 84, 86, 88, 90, 92, 94; WhoE 89; WhoEng 80, 88; WhoTech 82, 84, 89

Higuera, Teddy
[Teodoro Higuera Valenzuela]
Mexican. Baseball Player
Pitcher, Milwaukee, 1985—; first Mexican to win 20 games in AL, 1986.
b. Nov 9, 1958 in Las Mochis, Mexico
Source: *Ballpl 90; BaseReg 86, 87; BioIn 15; WhoHisp 92*

Hilberseimer, Ludwig Karl
American. Architect
Pioneered in regional planning; founded city planning department of Bauhaus Scho ol, 1928; wrote *Nature of Cities,* 1955.
b. Sep 14, 1885 in Karlsruhe, Germany
d. May 6, 1967 in Chicago, Illinois
Source: *BioIn 7; ConArch 87, 94; MacEA; WebBD 83; WhAm 4*

Hilbert, David
German. Mathematician
Known for work in geometry, integral equations; posed 23 famous questions of significance for 20th c. mathematicians, some of which remain unsolved.
b. Jan 23, 1862 in Konigsberg, Prussia
d. Feb 14, 1943 in Gottingen, Germany
Source: *AsBiEn; BiESc; BioIn 9, 13, 14, 20; CamDcSc; DcScB; FacFETw; InSci; LarDcSc; NotTwCS; OxCPhil; RAdv 14, 13-5; ThTwC 87; WorScD*

Hildebrand, Adolf von
German. Artist
Noted for public monuments, realistic portrait busts.
b. Oct 6, 1847 in Marburg, Germany
d. Jan 18, 1921 in Munich, Germany
Source: *BioIn 9; McGDA; NewCol 75; OxDcArt*

Hildegarde, Loretta Sell
"The First Lady of Supper Clubs"
American. Singer
Nightclub, radio pianist, vocalist; popular, 1940s; wore evening gowns, long gloves.
b. Feb 1, 1906 in Adell, Wisconsin
Source: *CelR 90; CmpEPM; CurBio 44; InWom SUP; OxCPMus*

Hildegard of Bingen, Saint
"Sybil of the Rhine"
German. Religious Figure
Benedictine nun; noted for prophecies recorded in *Scivias.*
b. 1098 in Bockelheim, Franconia (West)
d. Sep 17, 1179 in Rupertsberg, Franconia (West)
Source: *BioIn 4, 5, 11; CasWL; ContDcW 89; DcScB; InSci; IntDcWB; LuthC 75; McGDA; MediWW; NewAmDM; NewGrDM 80; NotWoLS; OxDcOp; WomFir; WomSc*

Hildesheimer, Wolfgang
German. Dramatist, Writer
Wrote *Mozart,* 1977, examining the composer from a psychoanalytic perspective.
b. Dec 9, 1916 in Hamburg, Germany
d. Aug 21, 1991 in Poschiavo, Switzerland
Source: *AnObit 1991; Benet 96; BioIn 17, 18, 19, 21; CamGWoT; CasWL; ClDMEL 80; CnMD; ConAu 101, 135; ConLC 49, 70; CroCD; CyWA 89; DcLB 69, 124; EncWL 2, 3; EncWT; Ent; IntAu&W 76, 77, 82, 89; IntWW 74, 75, 76, 77, 78, 79, 80, 81, 82, 83, 89, 91; McGEWD 72; ModGL; ModWD; NewYTBS 91; OxCGer 76, 86; PenC EUR; ScF&FL 92; WhAm 10; WhoWor 74, 76, 78; WorAu 1985*

Hildreth, Horace A(ugusta)
American. Politician
US Ambassador to Pakistan, 1953-57; governor of ME, 1945-49; pres. of ME Senate, 1943-45.
b. Dec 2, 1902 in Gardiner, Maine
d. Jun 2, 1988 in Portland, Oregon
Source: *BiDrGov 1789; BioIn 16; CurBio 88N; NewYTBS 88; WhAm 9*

Hilfiger, Tommy
[Thomas Jacob Hilfiger]
American. Fashion Designer
Founded Tommy Hilfiger USA, 1985; company became the second-largest menswear manufacturer in the US, 1994.
b. 1951 in Elmira, New York
Source: *CurBio 96*

Hill, Abram
American. Theater Owner
Founder, American Negro Theater, NYC, 1940, which was the starting place for Harry Belafonte, Sidney Poitier, Ruby Dee.
b. Jan 20, 1911 in Atlanta, Georgia
d. Oct 6, 1986 in New York, New York
Source: *BioIn 10; BlkAmP; CurBio 45, 86N; DrBlPA, 90; EarBlAP; MorBAP; SouBlCW*

Hill, Ambrose Powell
American. Military Leader
Confederate lt. general; led first attack, Battle of Gettysburg; killed in action.
b. Nov 9, 1825 in Culpeper, Virginia
d. Apr 2, 1865 in Petersburg, Virginia
Source: *AmBi; ApCAB; BiDConf; BioIn 1, 4, 5, 6, 15; CivWDc; DcAmB; DcAmMiB; Drake; EncSoH; GenMudB; HarEnMi; HarEnUS; LinLib S; NatCAB 4; OxCAmH; TwCBDA; WebAB 74, 79; WebAMB; WhAm HS; WhCiWar*

Hill, Anita Faye
American. Educator, Lawyer
Tenured law professor, U. of Oklahoma, 1988—; accused Supreme Court Justice Clarence Thomas of sexual harassment at his televised confirmation hearing.
b. Jul 30, 1956 in Morris, Oklahoma
Source: *ConAu 153; CurBio 95; EncWHA; NewYTBS 91; WhoAfA 96; WhoAmW 95; WhoBlA 94; WhoSSW 95*

Hill, Archibald Vivian
English. Physiologist
Nobelist, 1922; discovered the production of heat in muscles.
b. Sep 26, 1886? in Bristol, England
d. Jun 3, 1977 in Cambridge, England
Source: *AsBiEn; BiESc; BioIn 1, 2, 3, 6, 11, 14, 15, 20; BlueB 76; DcLEL; DcNaB 1971; GrBr; InSci; IntAu&W 76, 77; IntWW 74, 75, 76, 77; LarDcSc; McGEWB; WhE&EA; Who 74; WhoLA; WhoNob, 90, 95; WorScD*

Hill, Arthur
Canadian. Actor
Won 1962 Tony for *Who's Afraid of Virginia Woolf?,* starred in TV show "Ow en Marshall, Counselor at Law," 1971-74.
b. Aug 1, 1922 in Melfort, Saskatchewan, Canada
Source: *BiE&WWA; BioIn 6, 10, 11; CamGWoT; ConTFT 10; CurBio 77; FilmEn; FilmgC; ForYSC; HalFC 80, 84, 88; IntMPA 75, 76, 77, 78, 79, 80, 81, 82, 84, 86, 88, 92, 94, 96; LegTOT; MotPP; NewYTBE 71; NotNAT; OxCAmT 84; PlP&P; VarWW 85; Who 92; WhoAm 82, 88, 92, 94, 95; WhoEnt 92; WhoHol 92, A; WhoThe 72, 77, 81; WorAl; WorAlBi*

Hill, Benny
[Alfred Hawthorn Hill; Benjamin Hill]
English. Comedian
Off-color, slapstick star of internationally syndicated TV series, "The Benny Hill Show."
b. Jan 21, 1924 in Southampton, England
d. Apr 20, 1992 in Teddington, England
Source: *BioIn 13; ConTFT 5; CurBio 83; HalFC 88; IntMPA 82; News 92; VarWW 85; WhoHol A; WhoTelC; WhoWor 87*

Hill, Billy
American. Songwriter
Numerous hits include "The Last Round-Up," 1933; "Empty Saddles," 1936.
b. Jul 14, 1899 in Boston, Massachusetts
d. Dec 24, 1940 in Boston, Massachusetts
Source: *AmPS; CmpEPM; NotNAT B; OxCPMus; PopAmC*

Hill, Calvin
American. Football Player
Four-time all-pro running back, 1969-74, 1976-81, mostly with Dallas; rookie of year, 1969.
b. Jan 2, 1947 in Baltimore, Maryland
Source: *BiDAmSp FB; BioIn 8, 9, 10, 12, 13; NewYTBS 75, 81; WhoAfA 96; WhoAm 74, 76, 78; WhoBlA 75, 77, 80, 85, 88, 90, 92, 94; WhoFtbl 74*

Hill, Chippie
[Bertha Hill]
American. Jazz Musician
Vocalist with Ma Rainey's troupe; made numerous recordings with Louis Armstrong.
b. Mar 15, 1905? in Charleston, South Carolina
d. May 7, 1950 in New York, New York
Source: *Baker 84, 92; BiDAfM; BiDAmM; BiDJaz; BioIn 16, 19; BluesWW; CmpEPM; GuBlues; InB&W 80, 85; InWom SUP; NewGrDJ 88, 94; OxCPMus; PenEncP; WhoJazz 72*

Hill, Dan
Canadian. Singer
Soft rock singer; had hit single "Sometimes When We Touch," 1977.
b. Jun 3, 1954 in Toronto, Ontario, Canada
Source: *BioIn 11; Dun&B 88; LegTOT; RkOn 74, 78; WhoIns 92*

Hill, Faith
American. Singer
Country singer in the "Young Country" Movement; released debut album, *Take Me As I Am,* 1994; later recorded *It Matters To Me,* 1995; received *Billboard* top female country artist award, 1994, and *TNN/Music City News* Star of Tomorrow Award, 1995.
b. Sep 21, 1967 in Jackson, Mississippi

Hill, Geoffrey
English. Poet
Award-winning verse vols. include *Mercian Hymns,* 1971.
b. Jun 18, 1932 in Bromsgrove, England
Source: *BioIn 12, 13, 14, 15; BlmGEL; CamGEL; CamGLE; CnDBLB 8; CnE&AP; ConAu 21NR, 81; ConLC 5, 8, 18, 45; ConPo 70, 75, 80, 85, 91, 96; DcLB 40; DcLEL 1940; EncWL 2, 3; EngPo; FacFETw; GrWrEL P; IntAu&W 77, 82; IntvTCA 2; IntWW 89, 91; IntWWP 77; MajTwCW; ModBrL S1, S2; NewCBEL; OxCEng 85, 95; OxCTwCP; RfGEnL 91; RGFMBP; Who 82, 83, 85, 88, 90, 92; WorAu 1950, 1970; WrDr 76, 80, 82, 84, 86, 88, 90, 92, 94, 96*

Hill, George Birkbeck Norman
English. Author, Educator
Authority on life, works of Samuel Johnson; edited James Boswell's classic *Life of Johnson,* 1887.
b. Jun 7, 1835 in Tottenham, England
d. Feb 27, 1903 in London, England
Source: *BritAu 19; DcLEL; DcNaB S2; NewCBEL*

Hill, George Roy
American. Director
Directed *Butch Cassidy and the Sundance Kid,* 1969; *The Sting,* 1973; won Oscar for *The Sting.*
b. Dec 20, 1922 in Minneapolis, Minnesota
Source: *BiDFilm, 81, 94; BiE&WWA; BioIn 10, 11, 13, 14, 16; CelR 90; ConLC 26; ConTFT 1, 6; CurBio 77; FilmEn; FilmgC; GangFlm; HalFC 80, 84, 88; IlWWHD 1; IntDcF 1-2, 2-2; IntMPA 86, 92; IntWW 83, 89, 91; MiSFD 9; MovMk; NewYTBS 75; NotNAT; OxCFilm; VarWW 85; WhoAm 78, 80, 82, 84, 86, 90; WhoEnt 92; WhoThe 72, 77, 81; WorAlBi; WorEFlm; WorFDir 2*

Hill, George Washington
American. Business Executive
Pres., American Tobacco Co., 1925-46; introduced Lucky Strike cigarettes, 1917; sponsored radio's "Your Hit Parade," from 1935.
b. Oct 22, 1884 in Philadelphia, Pennsylvania
d. Sep 13, 1946 in Matapedia, Quebec, Canada
Source: *BiDAmBL 83; BioIn 1, 7; CurBio 46; DcAmB S4; ObitOF 79; WebAB 74, 79; WhAm 2*

Hill, George William
American. Astronomer
Expert in celestial mechanics; most important theory concerned effects of planets on moon's motion.
b. Mar 3, 1838 in New York, New York
d. Apr 16, 1914 in West Nyack, New York
Source: *ApCAB; BiDAmS; BiInAmS; BioIn 17; DcAmB; DcNAA; DcScB; InSci; NatCAB 13; TwCBDA; WhAm 1*

Hill, Grace Livingstone
American. Author
Popular novels sold over three million copies: *April Gold,* 1936.
b. Apr 16, 1865 in Wellsville, New York
d. Feb 23, 1947 in Swarthmore, Pennsylvania
Source: *NotAW; REnAL*

Hill, Graham
[Norman Graham Hill]
English. Auto Racer
Won world Grand Prix championship, 1962, 1968; author, *Life at the Limit,* 1969.
b. Feb 15, 1929 in London, England
d. Nov 30, 1975 in London, England
Source: *BioIn 6, 7, 8, 9, 10, 11, 12; BioNews 74; BlueB 76; ConAu 108; CurBio 73, 76N; DcNaB 1971; LegTOT; NewYTBS 75; ObitT 1971; WhAm 7; WhDW; Who 74; WhoWor 76; WhScrn 83; WorAl; WorAlBi*

Hill, Grant
American. Basketball Player
Forward for Detroit Pistons, 1994—.
b. Oct 5, 1972 in Dallas, Texas
Source: *ConBlB 13; News 95, 95-3; WhoAm 97*

Hill, Herbert
American. Civil Rights Leader
Labor director, NAACP, 1961-72; wrote *Anger and Beyond,* 1966.
b. Jan 24, 1924 in New York, New York
Source: *BioIn 9, 11; CivR 74; CivRSt; ConAu 65; CurBio 70; EncWB; PolProf J, K*

Hill, Howard
American. Archer, Actor
First white man to kill elephant with bow and arrow; stand-in archer in several Errol Flynn movies.
b. 1899
d. Feb 4, 1975 in Birmingham, Alabama
Source: *BioIn 10; NewYTBS 75; WhoHol C; WhScrn 77, 83*

Hill, James Jerome
"The Empire Builder"
American. Railroad Executive
Founded Great Northern Railway, 1890; his stock market battles caused panic of 1901.
b. Sep 16, 1838 in Guelph, Ontario, Canada
d. May 29, 1916 in Saint Paul, Minnesota
Source: *AmBi; ApCAB X; BbtC; BiDAmBL 83; BioIn 1, 2, 3, 4, 5, 8, 9, 10, 11, 12, 13, 15, 16, 17, 19, 21; CyAG; DcAmB; DcNAA; EncAB-H 1974, 1996; LinLib S; MacDCB 78; McGEWB; MemAm; NatCAB 13, 33; OxCAmH; REnAW; WebAB 74, 79; WebBD 83; WhAm 1; WorAl*

Hill, Jesse, Jr.
American. Insurance Executive
President, CEO, Atlantic Life, 1973—.
b. 1927 in Saint Louis, Missouri
Source: *Ballpl 90; BiNAW Sup, SupB; Dun&B 86, 88, 90; InB&W 80; WhoBlA 88, 92*

Hill, Jimmy
[James William Thomas Hill]
English. Sportscaster
Soccer analyst on BBC since 1973.
b. 1928
Source: *BioIn 11; Who 92*

Hill, Joe
[Joel Emmanuel Haaglung; Joseph Hillstrom]
American. Labor Union Official, Songwriter
Member, IWW; best known for song "The Preacher and the Slave," which contained phrase "pie in the sky."
b. Oct 7, 1879 in Gavle, Sweden
d. Nov 19, 1915 in Salt Lake City, Utah
Source: *AmDec 1910; AmRef; AmSocL; BenetAL 91; BiDAmL; BiDAmLL; BioIn 7, 8, 9, 11, 14, 15, 16, 17, 19; EncAL; NewGrDA 86; OxCAmL 95; REnAW; WebAB 74; WhAm 4, HSA*

Hill, Lester
American. Politician
Dem. senator from AL, 1938-68.
b. Dec 29, 1894 in Montgomery, Alabama
d. Dec 20, 1984 in Montgomery, Alabama
Source: *CurBio 85*

Hill, Lynn
American. Athlete
One of the world's top five rock climbers; first woman to complete a grade 5.14 climb.
b. 1961 in Los Angeles, California
Source: *BioIn 16, 19; News 91, 91-2; NewYTBS 89*

Hill, Morton A(nthony)
American. Social Reformer, Clergy
Founder, pres., Morality in Media, Inc., 1962-85; co-authored Hill-Link Report on obscenity, 1970.
b. Jul 13, 1917 in New York, New York
d. Nov 4, 1985 in New York, New York
Source: *AmCath 80; BioIn 14, 15; NewYTBS 85; WhoRel 75, 77*

Hill, Norbert S., Jr.
American. Educator
Chair, Oneida tribe education committee, 1970-74; executive director, American Indian Science and Engineering Society, 1983—.
b. Nov 26, 1946 in Warren, Michigan
Source: *NotNaAm; WhoAm 96; WhoWest 96*

Hill, Patty Smith
American. Educator
Emphasized creativity and natural instincts in kindergarten education, diverging from Friedrich Froebel's more structured approach.
b. Mar 27, 1868 in Anchorage, Kentucky
d. May 25, 1946 in New York, New York
Source: *AmRef; BiDAmEd; BioIn 1, 3, 10, 13, 15; ChhPo, S1; DcAmB S4; DcNAA; InWom, SUP; LibW; NotAW; WhAm 2; WomFir*

Hill, Phil(ip Toll)
American. Auto Racer
First American to gain world driving championship, 1961.
b. Apr 20, 1927 in Miami, Florida
Source: *BioIn 5, 6, 7, 8, 10, 12; WhoSpor*

Hill, Rowland, Sir
English. Educator, Government Official
Postal reformist; originated penny postage, 1839.
b. Dec 3, 1795 in Kidderminster, England
d. Aug 27, 1879 in Hampstead, England
Source: *Alli; BioIn 2, 3, 4, 5, 7, 8, 9, 12, 14, 16; CelCen; DcBiPP; DcNaB; LinLib S; NewC; OxCEng 67; VicBrit*

Hill, Thomas
English. Artist
Noted for western, Yosemite Valley scenes: "Muir Glacier."
b. Sep 11, 1829 in Birmingham, England
d. 1908 in Raymond, California
Source: *ApCAB; ArtsAmW 1; ArtsNiC; BioIn 1, 9, 14, 17; CmCal; DcAmArt; DcAmB; Drake; EarABI; IlBEAAW; NatCAB 3; NewYHSD; REnAW; WhAm 1; WhAmArt 85*

Hill, Virginia
"The Flamingo"
American. Actor, Criminal
Appeared in 1930s musicals; mistress of gangsters Joe Adonis, Bugsy Siegel; key witness, 1951 Kefauver Crime Investigation.
b. Aug 26, 1916 in Lipscomb, Alabama
d. Mar 24, 1966 in Salzburg, Austria
Source: *BioIn 2, 3, 7, 19; LegTOT; WhoHol B; WhScrn 77*

Hillary, Edmund Percival, Sir
New Zealander. Explorer, Mountaineer
With Tenzing Norkay was first to reach summit of Mt. Everest, 1953.
b. Jul 20, 1919 in Auckland, New Zealand
Source: *AsBiEn; Au&Wr 71; BioIn 13, 16; ConHero 1; CurBio 54; EncWB; FacFETw; FarE&A 78, 79, 80, 81; IntAu&W 91; IntWW 74, 75, 76, 77, 78, 79, 80, 81, 82, 83, 89; LngCTC; RAdv 13-3; WhDW; Who 74, 92; WhoWor 74, 89, 97; WorAl; WorAlBi; WrDr 76, 92*

Hillcourt, William
"Green Bar Bill"
American. Writer
Principal author of the *Official Boy Scout Handbook;* wrote an advice column for *Boys' Life* mag., 1929-88.
b. Aug 6, 1900 in Aarhus, Denmark
d. Nov 9, 1992 in Manlius, New York
Source: *AmAu&B; AnObit 1992; AuBYP 2, 3; BioIn 7, 13, 18, 19; ConAu 46NR, 93, 139; SmATA 27; WhoAm 74, 76, 78, 80, 82, 84, 86, 88, 90*

Hillegrass, C(lifton) K(eith)
"Cliff"
American. Publisher
Founder, Cliff Notes, Inc., 1958; pres., 1958-83; chm., 1983—; co. known for its study guides.
b. Apr 18, 1918 in Rising City, Nebraska
Source: *BioIn 13, 15; BioNews 74; News 89; WhoAm 90*

Hillel
Scholar
Jewish scholar whose sayings resemble Jesus Christ's: "Do not unto others that which is hateful unto thee."
d. 9
Source: *BioIn 1, 2, 4, 5, 6, 7, 9, 17, 19; NewCol 75; WebBD 83; WhDW*

Hillenkoetter, Roscoe H(enry)
American. Business Executive
First director of CIA, 1947-50.
b. May 8, 1897 in Saint Louis, Missouri
d. Jun 18, 1982 in New York, New York
Source: *AnObit 1982; BioIn 1, 2, 4, 12, 13; CurBio 82, 82N; EncAI&E; FacFETw; NewYTBS 82; PolProf T; WebAMB; WhAm 8; WhoAm 74, 76, 78, 80, 82*

Hiller, Arthur
American. Director
Best known for *Love Story,* 1970.
b. Nov 22, 1923 in Edmonton, Alberta, Canada
Source: *BiDFilm, 81, 94; CanWW 70, 89; ConTFT 1, 8; EncAFC; FilmEn; FilmgC; HalFC 80, 84, 88; IlWWHD 1; IntDcF 1-2; IntMPA 75, 76, 77, 78, 79, 80, 81, 82, 84, 86, 88, 92, 94, 96; ItaFilm; LegTOT; MiSFD 9; MovMk; VarWW 85; WhoAm 74, 76, 78, 80, 82, 84, 86, 88, 90, 92, 94, 95, 96, 97; WhoEnt 92; WorAlBi*

Hiller, Johann Adam
Prussian. Composer
Credited with originating the singspiel; his singspiels include "Die Jagd," 1770.
b. Dec 25, 1728 in Wendisch-Ossig, Prussia
d. Jun 16, 1804 in Leipzig, Germany
Source: *Baker 78, 84, 92; BioIn 7; BlkwCE; BriBkM 80; DcBiPP; GrComp; LuthC 75; NewAmDM; NewEOp 71; NewGrDM 80; NewGrDO; NewOxM; OxCGer 76, 86; OxCMus; OxDcOp*

Hiller, John Frederick
American. Baseball Player
Pitcher, Detroit, 1967-70, 1972-80; suffered heart attack, 1971; led AL in saves, 38, 1973.
b. Apr 8, 1943 in Scarborough, Ontario, Canada
Source: *Ballpl 90; BioIn 9, 10, 11; WhoProB 73*

Hiller, Wendy, Dame
English. Actor
Won 1958 Oscar for *Separate Tables.*
b. Aug 15, 1912 in Bramhall, England
Source: *BiE&WWA; BioIn 1, 9, 19; CnThe; ConTFT 6; CurBio 41; DcArts; EncEurC; Ent; FilmAG WE; FilmEn; FilmgC; ForYSC; HalFC 80, 84, 88; IlWWBF; IntDcF 1-3; IntDcT 3; IntMPA 77, 78, 79, 80, 81, 82, 84, 86, 88, 92, 94, 96; IntWW 76, 77, 78, 79, 80, 81, 82, 83, 91; InWom, SUP; LegTOT; MotPP; MovMk; NotNAT; OxCFilm; OxCThe 83; ThFT; VarWW 85; Who 74, 82, 83, 85, 88, 90, 92, 94; WhoAm 82, 90; WhoAmW 66, 68, 70, 72, 74, 77; WhoEnt 92; WhoHol 92, A; WhoThe 72, 77, 81; WorAl; WorAlBi*

Hillerman, John Benedict
American. Actor
Played Jonathan Higgins on "Magnum PI," 1980-88; won Emmy, 1987.
b. Dec 20, 1932 in Denison, Texas
Source: *BioIn 13; ConTFT 3, 8; HalFC 88; IntMPA 92; VarWW 85; WhoAm 82, 86, 88; WhoEnt 92; WhoHol A; WorAlBi*

Hillerman, Tony
American. Author
Detective novelist concerned with Native American culture: *Dance Hall of the Dead,* 1974.

b. May 27, 1925 in Sacred Heart, Oklahoma
Source: *Au&Arts 6; BenetAL 91; BestSel 89-1; BioIn 8, 10, 12, 14, 16; ConAu 21NR, 29R, 42NR; ConLC 62; ConPopW; CrtSuMy; CurBio 92; EncFWF; IntAu&W 91; NewYTBS 89; RAdv 14; RfGAmL 94; SmATA 6; TwCCr&M 80, 85, 91; TwCWW 91; TwCYAW; WhoAm 92, 94, 95, 96, 97; WhoUSWr 88; WhoWest 92, 94; WhoWrEP 89, 92, 95; WorAlBi; WrDr 82, 84, 86, 88, 90, 92, 94, 96*

Hillery, Patrick John
Irish. Political Leader
Pres. of the Republic of Ireland, 1976-90.
b. May 2, 1923 in Milltown Malvay, Ireland
Source: *BioIn 9, 11; BlueB 76; IntWW 74, 75, 76, 77, 78, 79, 80, 81, 82, 83, 89, 91, 93; IntYB 78, 79, 80, 81, 82; NewYTBE 70; NewYTBS 76; Who 82, 83, 85, 88, 92, 94; WhoWor 74, 76, 78, 80, 82, 84, 87, 89, 91, 93, 95, 96, 97*

Hilliard, David
American. Civil Rights Activist
With Black Panther Party, 1967-74; wrote autobiography, *This Side of Glory,* 1993.
b. May 15, 1942 in Rockville, Alabama
Source: *BlkWr 2; ConAu 142; ConBlB 7; SchCGBL; WrDr 96*

Hilliard, Nicholas
English. Artist
Best known for miniature portraits of Queen Elizabeth I set in jeweled lockets.
b. 1537 in Exeter, England
d. Jan 7, 1619 in London, England
Source: *AntBDN J; BioIn 1, 2, 3, 4, 5, 6, 10, 11, 12; DcBiPP; DcNaB; NewCol 75; OxCArt*

Hilliard, Robert Cochran
American. Actor
Best known for play *Girl of the Golden West,* 1905.
b. May 28, 1857 in New York, New York
d. Jun 6, 1927 in New York, New York
Source: *NatCAB 22; NotNAT A, B; WhAm 1; WhoStg 1906, 1908; WhThe*

Hillier, James
Canadian. Physicist
Research director, RCA Corp., 1976-78; member, Inventors Hall of Fame, 1980.
b. Aug 22, 1915 in Brantford, Ontario, Canada
Source: *AmMWSc 73P, 76P, 79, 82, 86, 89, 92, 95; AsBiEn; BiESc; BioIn 3, 5, 10, 12; BlueB 76; CanWW 31, 70, 79, 80, 81, 83, 89; LarDcSc; LegTOT; LElec; McGMS 80; St&PR 75; WhoAm 74, 76, 78, 80, 92, 94, 95, 96, 97; WhoE 79, 81, 83, 93; WhoEng 80, 88; WhoFI 74, 75; WhoScEn 94; WhoWor 80, 95, 96; WorAl; WorAlBi*

Hillings, Patrick J(ohn)
American. Politician
Rep. congressman from CA, 1951-58; FL director of Pres. Reagan's campaign, 1980.
b. Feb 19, 1923
d. Jul 20, 1994 in Rancho Mirage, California
Source: *BioIn 4; CurBio 94N; WhoAmP 73, 75, 77, 79*

Hillis, Margaret
American. Conductor, Musician
Choral director, Chicago Symphony Chorus, 1957-94; founded American Choral Foundation, 1954; music director, conductor, Elgin Symphony Orchestra. 1971-85.
b. Oct 1, 1921 in Kokomo, Indiana
Source: *Baker 78, 84, 92; BioIn 4, 6, 10, 11, 12, 13; BriBkM 80; GrLiveH; IntWWM 90; InWom SUP; NewAmDM; NewGrDA 86; NewGrDM 80; PenDiMP; WhoAm 74, 76, 78, 80, 82, 84, 86, 88, 90, 92, 94, 95, 96, 97; WhoAmM 83; WhoAmW 58, 64, 66, 68, 70, 72, 74, 75, 79, 81, 83, 85, 87, 89, 91, 93, 95, 97; WhoEnt 92; WhoMW 74, 84; WhoWor 76, 78, 95; WomCom*

Hillis, W(illiam) Daniel, (Jr.)
American. Computer Scientist
Founder of Thinking Machines Corporation, 1983.
b. Sep 25, 1958 in Baltimore, Maryland
Source: *CurBio 95*

Hillman, Chris
[The Byrds; The Flying Burrito Brothers; The Souther-Hillman-Furay Band]
American. Musician
Blue-grass mandolinist; solo works include ''Slippin' Away.''
b. Dec 4, 1942 in Los Angeles, California
Source: *BioIn 14; ConMuA 80A; EncFCWM 83; EncRk 88; HarEnCM 87; OnThGG; PenEncP; WhoNeCM A; WhoRock 81; WhoRocM 82*

Hillman, Sidney (Simcha)
American. Labor Union Official
Pres., Amalgamated Clothing Workers of America, 1914-46; vp, CIO, 1935-40.
b. Mar 23, 1887 in Zagare, Lithuania
d. Jul 10, 1946 in Point Lookout, New York
Source: *AmDec 1940; AmSocL; BiDAmL; BiDAmLL; BioIn 1, 2, 3, 5, 6, 7, 8, 9, 14, 15, 17, 19, 20; CurBio 40, 46; DcAmB S4; DcAmImH; DcAmSR; EncAB-H 1974, 1996; FacFETw; LinLib S; McGEWB; OxCAmH; PolPar; WebAB 74, 79; WhAm 2; WorAl; WorAlBi*

Hillquit, Morris
[Morris Hillkowitz]
American. Political Leader
Led founding of Social Dem. Party, 1897; socialist candidate for mayor of NYC, 1917, 1932.
b. Aug 1, 1869 in Riga, Latvia
d. Oct 7, 1933 in New York, New York
Source: *AmBi; AmLY; AmPeW; AmRef; BiDAmL; BiDAmLf; BiDAmLL; BiDMoPL; BioIn 1, 2, 6, 7, 11, 12, 15; DcAmB S1; DcAmSR; DcNAA; EncAL; EncRev; LinLib L, S; McGEWB; NatCAB 44; OxCAmH; PolPar; REnAL; WebAB 74, 79; WhAm 1; WhAmP*

Hills, Argentina (Schifano)
American. Publisher
Publisher, editor, San Juan, PR's *El Mundo,* 1960-87; wed to Lee Hills, 1963.
b. Oct 4, 1921 in Pola, Italy
Source: *ConAu 136; WhoAmW 77, 79, 81, 83, 85, 87; WhoSSW 75; WhoWor 84, 87*

Hills, Austin H
American. Merchant
With brother, Reuben, first to introduce vacuum-packed coffee in cans, 1900.
b. 1851
d. 1933
Source: *Entr*

Hills, Carla Anderson
American. Government Official
US trade representative, 1989-93; chm., Urban Institute, 1983-88; member, Trilateral Commission, 1977-82; secretary, HUD, 1975 -77.
b. Jan 3, 1934 in Los Angeles, California
Source: *AfrAmBi 1; AmPolW 80; AmWomM; BiDrUSE 89; BioIn 16, 17, 18, 19; CurBio 75, 93; GoodHs; IntDcWB; IntWW 75, 76, 77, 78, 79, 80, 81, 82, 83, 89, 91, 93; InWom SUP; LibW; News 90, 90-3; NewYTBS 75, 88; St&PR 91; WhoAm 76, 78, 80, 82, 84, 86, 88, 90, 92, 94, 95, 96, 97; WhoAmL 79, 83, 85, 87, 90, 94, 96; WhoAmP 75, 77, 79, 81, 83, 85, 87, 89, 91, 93, 95; WhoAmW 74, 75, 77, 79, 83, 87, 89, 91, 93, 95, 97; WhoE 93, 95, 97; WhoFI 92; WhoSSW 76; WhoWomW 91; WomFir; WorAlBi*

Hills, Lee
American. Editor
Exec. editor, *Detroit Free Press,* 1951-69; editorial chm., Knight-Ridder Newspapers, 1979-81; won Pulitzer, 1956.
b. May 28, 1906 in Granville, North Dakota
Source: *BioIn 2, 11, 19; ConAu 101; DcLB 127; Dun&B 79; EncTwCJ; St&PR 75, 84, 87, 91, 93, 96; WhoAm 74, 76, 78, 80, 82, 84, 86, 94, 95, 96, 97; WhoFI 77, 79, 81; WhoMW 74, 76; WhoSSW 73, 75, 80, 82, 95, 97; WhoWor 74, 82*

Hills, Reuben W
American. Merchant
With brother, Austin, first to introduce vacuum-packed coffee in cans, 1900.
b. 1856
d. 1934
Source: *Entr*

Hills, Roderick M
American. Lawyer, Government Official
Counsel to Gerald Ford, 1975; husband of Carla Hills.
b. Mar 9, 1931 in Seattle, Washington
Source: *IntWW 91; WhoAm 82, 90; WhoE 89*

Hillyer, Robert
American. Poet, Author, Educator
Poetry volumes include *The Seventh Hill,* 1928; won 1933 Pulitzer for *Collected Verses.*
b. Jun 3, 1895 in East Orange, New Jersey
d. Dec 24, 1961 in Wilmington, Delaware
Source: *AmAu&B; BenetAL 91; CamGLE; CamHAL; CnDAL; CnE&AP; ConAmA; ConAu 89; CurBio 40, 62; DcLB 54; DcLEL; OxCAmL 65, 83; OxCTwCP; PenC AM; REn; REnAL; TwCA SUP; WhAm 4; WhNAA*

Hilton, Conrad Nicholson
American. Hotel Executive
Formed Hilton Hotel Corp., 1946; wrote autobiography, *Be My Guest,* 1957.
b. Dec 25, 1887 in San Antonio, New Mexico
d. Jan 3, 1979 in Santa Monica, California
Source: *BiDAmBL 83; BioIn 1, 2, 3, 4, 5, 6, 7, 8, 9, 11, 12; DcAmB S10; EncAB-A 33; IntWW 74, 75, 76, 77, 78; IntYB 78, 79; St&PR 75; WebAB 74, 79; Who 74; WhoAm 74; WhoFI 75; WhoWor 74; WorAl*

Hilton, Daisy
[The Hilton Sisters]
English. Entertainer
Siamese twin in films *Freaks,* 1932; *Chained for Life,* 1950.
b. Feb 5, 1908? in Brighton, England
d. Jan 4, 1969 in Charlotte, North Carolina
Source: *BioIn 8; EncVaud; WhScrn 77, 83*

Hilton, James
English. Author
Best-known novels are *Lost Horizon,* 1933; *Goodbye, Mr. Chips,* 1934.
b. Sep 9, 1900 in Leigh-on-Sea, England
d. Dec 20, 1954 in Long Beach, California
Source: *Benet 87, 96; BenetAL 91; BioIn 1, 2, 3, 4, 5, 14; CamGLE; ChhPo S1; ConAu 108; CurBio 42, 55; CyWA 58; DcArts; DcLB 34, 77; DcLEL; DcNaB 1951; EncMys; EncSF, 93; EvLB; FacFETw; FilmEn; FilmgC; HalFC 80, 84, 88; LegTOT; LngCTC; MnBBF; ModBrL; NewC; NewCBEL; NewEScF; Novels; ObitT 1951; OxCEng 85, 95; PenC ENG; REn; REnAL; RGTwCWr; ScF&FL 1; ScFSB; SJGFanW; SmATA 34; TwCA, SUP; TwCLC 21; TwCSFW 81; TwCWr; WhAm 3; WhE&EA; WhLit; WorAl; WorAlBi*

Hilton, Violet
[The Hilton Sisters]
English. Entertainer
One of Siamese twin in vaudeville act; made film *Chained for Life,* 1950.
b. Feb 5, 1908? in Brighton, England
d. Jan 4, 1969 in Charlotte, North Carolina
Source: *BioIn 8; EncVaud; WhScrn 77, 83*

Hilton, William Barron
American. Hotel Executive
Pres., CEO, Hilton Hotels Corp.
b. 1927 in Dallas, Texas
Source: *BioIn 10, 11, 12, 13; BusPN; St&PR 84, 87, 91, 93, 96, 97; Who 92; WhoWest 78*

Himes, Chester Bomar
American. Author
Wrote detective novel *Cotton Comes to Harlem,* which became 1970 film.
b. Jul 29, 1909 in Jefferson City, Missouri
d. Nov 12, 1984 in Moraira, Spain
Source: *AmAu&B; AmNov; BioIn 1, 2, 5, 9, 10, 11, 12, 13; BlkAWP; ConLC 2, 4, 18; ConNov 72, 76; DcLEL 1940; DrAF 76; EncWL; InB&W 80, 85; LivgBAA; ModAL, S1; OhA&B; PenC AM; RAdv 1; SelBAAu; WebE&AL; WhoAm 74, 76, 78, 80, 82, 84; WhoBlA 75, 77, 80; WorAu 1950; WrDr 76*

Himmler, Heinrich
German. Government Official
Head of SS, 1929, which merged with Gestapo, 1934; minister of interior, 1943-45; captured by British; committed suicide.
b. Oct 7, 1900 in Munich, Germany
d. May 23, 1945 in Luneburg, Germany
Source: *BiDExR; BioIn 1, 3, 4, 5, 7, 8, 9, 12, 13, 14, 16, 17, 19, 20; CurBio 45; DcPol; DcTwHis; EncRev; EncTR, 91; FacFETw; HisEWW; HisWorL; LegTOT; LinLib S; McGEWB; NewCol 75; OxCGer 76, 86; REn; SpyCS; WebBD 83; WhDW; WhWW-II; WorAl; WorAlBi*

Hinckley, John Warnock, Jr.
American. Attempted Assassin
Acquitted, 1982, by reason of insanity for shooting Ronald Reagan, Mar 30, 1981.
b. May 29, 1955 in Ardmore, Oklahoma
Source: *BioIn 12, 13, 14, 15; NewYTBS 81; WorAlBi*

Hinde, Thomas, Sir
[Sir Thomas Wiles Chitty]
English. Author
Novels include *Daymare,* 1980.
b. Mar 26, 1926 in Felixstowe, England
Source: *Au&Wr 71, 3; IntAu&W 76, 91; IntvTCA 2; IntWW 91; ModBrL S1, S2; NewC; Novels; RGTwCWr; TwCWr; Who 74, 92; WorAu 1950; WrDr 76, 82, 84, 86, 88, 90, 92, 94, 96*

Hindemith, Paul
German. Musician, Composer
Music banned by Nazis; best known for opera *Mathis the Painter,* 1938.
b. Nov 16, 1895 in Hanau, Germany
d. Dec 28, 1963 in Frankfurt, Germany (West)
Source: *AmComp; AmCulL; AtlBL; Baker 78, 84, 92; Benet 87, 96; BiDAmM; BiDD; BioIn 1, 2, 3, 4, 5, 6, 7, 8, 9, 10, 11, 12, 13, 14, 16, 19, 20, 21; BriBkM 80; CmOp; CnOxB; CompSN, SUP; ConAmC 76, 82; ConAu 112; CurBio 64; DancEn 78; DcArts; DcCM; DcCom 77; DcCom&M 79; DcTwCC, A; EncTR, 91; FacFETw; IntDcB; IntDcOp; LegTOT; LinLib S; LuthC 75; MakMC; McGEWB; MetOEnc; MusMk; NewAmDM; NewEOp 71; NewGrDA 86; NewGrDM 80; NewGrDO; NewOxM; NotNAT B; ObitT 1961; OxCAmH; OxCGer 76, 86; OxCMus; OxDcOp; PenDiMP A; RAdv 14, 13-3; REn; WhAm 4; WhDW; WorAl; WorAlBi*

Hindenburg, Paul Ludwig Hans Anton von Beneckendorff und
German. Army Officer, Political Leader
Pres., 1925-34, who appointed Adolph Hitler chancellor, 1933.
b. Oct 2, 1847 in Posen, Prussia
d. Aug 2, 1934 in Neudeck, Germany
Source: *McGEWB; NewCol 75; WebBD 83*

Hinderas, Natalie Leota Henderson
American. Pianist
One of first black musicians to establish a solid career in classical music.
b. Jun 15, 1927 in Oberlin, Ohio
d. Jul 22, 1987 in Philadelphia, Pennsylvania
Source: *BioIn 10, 11; BlkWAm; InB&W 85; NewYTBE 72; NewYTBS 87; WhoBlA 85*

Hine, Lewis Wickes
American. Photographer, Sociologist
Focused on social problems, especially those of child laborers and immigrants; documented construction of Empire State Building, *Men at Work,* 1932.
b. Sep 26, 1874 in Oshkosh, Wisconsin
d. Nov 3, 1940 in Hastings-on-Hudson, New York
Source: *AmSocL; BiDAmJo; BiDSocW; BioIn 4, 8, 10, 11, 13, 14, 15, 16, 18, 19, 20; BriEAA; DcAmArt; DcAmB S2; DcAmImH; DcTwDes; FacFETw; ICPEnP; MacBEP; WebAB 74, 79; WhAmArt 85*

Hines, Duncan
American. Author, Publisher
His books, *Adventures in Good Eating,* 1936-59, influenced the culinary and sanitary practices of American restaurants.
b. Mar 26, 1880 in Bowling Green, Kentucky

d. Mar 15, 1959 in Bowling Green, Kentucky
Source: *AmAu&B; BioIn 1, 3, 4, 5, 6, 14; CurBio 59; DcAmB S6; Entr; LegTOT; NatCAB 43; WebAB 74, 79; WhAm 3; WorAl; WorAlBi*

Hines, Fatha
[Earl Kenneth Hines]
American. Jazz Musician
Member, Down Beat Magazine Hall of Fame; leading influence in swing, jazz piano styles.
b. Dec 28, 1905 in Duquesne, Pennsylvania
d. Apr 22, 1983 in Oakland, California
Source: *ASCAP 66; BiDAfM; CurBio 83N; EncAB-H 1974, 1996; EncJzS; InB&W 80; IntWW 75, 76, 77, 78, 79, 80, 81, 82, 83; NewYTBS 83; WhoAm 80, 82; WhoBlA 77, 80; WhoJazz 72*

Hines, Gregory Oliver
American. Dancer, Actor
Tap dancer, known for jazz numbers in musical *Eubie,* 1978; films include *White Nights,* 1985; *A Rage in Harlem,* 1991; won 1992 Tony for *Jelly's Last Jam.*
b. Feb 14, 1946 in New York, New York
Source: *AfrAmBi 1; BioIn 14, 15; BlksAmF; CelR 90; ConTFT 3; CurBio 85; DrBlPA 90; HalFC 88; InB&W 85; IntMPA 92; NegAl 89; News 92; NewYTBS 78; VarWW 85; WhoAfA 96; WhoAm 82, 84, 86, 88, 90, 92, 94, 95, 96, 97; WhoBlA 92, 94; WhoEnt 92*

Hines, Jerome
American. Opera Singer
A leading basso, NY Met., from 1947; noted for *Boris Godunov.*
b. Nov 9, 1921 in Hollywood, California
Source: *ASCAP 80; Baker 78, 84; BiDAmM; BioIn 3, 4, 5, 6, 8, 10, 11, 12, 13, 17; BioNews 75; CmOp; ConAu 130; CurBio 63; DcTwCCu 1; IntWWM 80, 90; LegTOT; MetOEnc; MusSN; NewAmDM; NewEOp 71; NewGrDA 86; NewGrDM 80; OxDcOp; PenDiMP; WhoAm 74, 78, 80, 82, 84, 86, 88; WhoAmM 83; WhoEnt 92; WhoMus 72; WhoOp 76; WorAl; WorAlBi; WrDr 94, 96*

Hines, Jim
American. Track Athlete
Sprinter; won gold medal in 100-meters, 400-meter relay, 1968 Olympics.
b. Sep 10, 1946 in Dumas, Arkansas
Source: *BioIn 7; WhoSpor; WhoTr&F 73*

Hines, John E(lbridge)
American. Religious Leader
Presiding bishop, Protestant Episcopal Church of US, 1964-74.
b. Oct 3, 1910 in Seneca, South Carolina
d. Jul 19, 1997 in Austin, Texas
Source: *BioIn 8, 10; BlueB 76; CurBio 68; IntWW 74, 75, 76, 77, 78; RelLAm 91; WhoAm 74, 76; WhoE 75; WhoRel 75; WhoWor 74*

Hingle, Pat
[Martin Patterson Hingle]
American. Actor
Films include *Splendor in the Grass,* 1961; *Norma Rae,* 1979.
b. Jul 19, 1924 in Denver, Colorado
Source: *BiE&WWA; BioIn 5, 7; BlueB 76; CamGWoT; ConTFT 2, 8; CurBio 65; FilmgC; ForYSC; HalFC 88; IntMPA 82, 92, 94, 96; MotPP; MovMk; NotNAT; OxCAmT 84; VarWW 85; WhoAm 74, 76, 78, 80, 82, 84, 86, 88, 90, 92, 94, 95, 96, 97; WhoE 74; WhoEnt 92; WhoHol A; WhoThe 77; WorAl; WorAlBi*

Hingson, Robert A(ndrew)
American. Physician
Invented anesthetic technique for childbirth called continuous caudal anesthesia, 1941-43.
b. Apr 13, 1913
d. Oct 9, 1996 in Lake City, Florida
Source: *AmMWSc 73P, 76P, 79, 82, 86; BioIn 8; WhoAm 74, 76, 78, 80, 82, 88, 90, 92, 94, 95, 96, 97; WhoE 93, 97; WhoMedH; WhoRel 75, 77, 85; WhoScEn 96; WhoWor 89, 91, 93, 95*

Hinkle, Paul
"Tony"
American. Basketball Coach
Coach, Butler U, 1927-42, 1946-70, with career 561-393 record; Hall of Fame.
b. Dec 19, 1899 in Logansport, Indiana
d. 1992
Source: *BiDAmSp BK; BioIn 9; WhoBbl 73*

Hinkle, W. Clarke
American. Football Player
Four-time all-pro fullback, Green Bay, 1932-41; led NFL in scoring, 1938; Hall of Fame, 1964.
b. Apr 10, 1912 in Toronto, Ontario, Canada
d. Nov 9, 1988 in Bern, Switzerland
Source: *BioIn 8, 9; WhoFtbl 74*

Hinrichs, Gustav
German. Conductor
Organized opera co., Philadelphia, 1885; led American premieres of *Cavalleria Rusticana,* 1891; *Pagliacci,* 1893.
b. Dec 10, 1850 in Mecklenburg, Germany
d. Mar 26, 1942 in Mountain Lakes, New Jersey
Source: *Baker 78, 84, 92; BiDAmM; BioIn 3; CurBio 42; NatCAB 38; NewEOp 71; NewGrDA 86; NewGrDO*

Hinshelwood, Cyril Norman, Sir
English. Chemist
Shared Nobel Prize, 1956, for basic studies in kinetics.
b. Jun 19, 1897 in London, England
d. Oct 9, 1967 in London, England
Source: *AsBiEn; BiESc; BioIn 1, 4, 6, 8, 10, 14, 15, 19, 20; CamDcSc; CurBio 57, 67; DcNaB 1961; DcScB; GrBr; InSci; LarDcSc; McGEWB; WhAm 4, 5; WhE&EA; WhoNob, 90, 95; WorAl*

Hinton, Christopher, Sir
[Lord Hinton of Bankside]
English. Engineer
Leading figure in development of Britain's atomic energy industry.
b. May 12, 1901 in Tisbury, England
d. Jun 22, 1983 in London, England
Source: *AnObit 1983; AsBiEn; BioIn 3, 4, 6, 7; CurBio 57; DcNaB 1981; DcTwBBL; InSci; IntWW 82, 83; IntYB 78, 79, 82; McGMS 80; Who 82, 83; WhoEng 80; WhoWor 74, 76, 78; WorAl; WorAlBi*

Hinton, S(usan) E(loise)
American. Author
Writes books for teenagers: *The Outsiders,* 1967; *That Was Then, This Is Now,* 1971.
b. 1948 in Tulsa, Oklahoma
Source: *Au&Arts 2; AuBYP 3; BenetAL 91; BioIn 12, 13, 16; ChlLR 23; ConAu 32NR, 81; ConLC 30; DcLP 87B; MajTwCW; OxCChiL; PenNWW B; SmATA 19, 58; TwCChW 83, 89; WhoAm 86, 88, 92, 94, 95, 96, 97; WhoAmW 91, 93, 95, 97; WorAlBi; WrDr 86, 92, 94, 96*

Hinton, Walter
American. Aviator
Best known for Friendship Flight, 1922, from NYC to Rio de Janeiro; mapped parts of Amazon jungle from air, 1924.
b. Nov 10, 1889 in Van Wert, Ohio
d. Sep 28, 1981 in Pompano Beach, Florida
Source: *AnObit 1981; BioIn 11; InSci; NewYTBS 81; OhA&B; WhAm 8*

Hinton, William Augustus
American. Physician
First black Harvard professor, 1949; wrote *Syphilis and Its Treatment,* 1936.
b. Dec 15, 1883 in Chicago, Illinois
d. Aug 8, 1959 in Canton, Massachusetts
Source: *BioIn 1, 2, 5, 11, 20; BlksScM; ConBlB 8; DcAmMeB 84; DcAmNB; DiAASTC; InB&W 80, 85; NotTwCS; ObitOF 79; SelBAAf; SelBAAu*

Hipparchus
Greek. Astronomer
Catalogued over 1,000 stars; originated method of using latitude, longitude to indicate geographical position.
b. 160?BC in Nicaea, Asia Minor
d. 127?BC
Source: *BioIn 3, 7, 8; CasWL; CyEd; InSci; PenC CL*

Hippocrates
"The Father of Medicine"
Greek. Physician
Credited with having devised physicians' code of ethics known as "Hippocratic oat h"; still administered to new doctors.
b. 460BC in Island of Cos, Greece
d. 377BC in Larissa, Greece

Source: *AsBiEn; Benet 87, 96; BiDPsy; BiHiMed; BioIn 1, 2, 3, 4, 5, 6, 7, 9, 10, 12; CamDcSc; CasWL; CyEd; DcBiPP; InSci; LarDcSc; LegTOT; LinLib L, S; McGEWB; NamesHP; NewC; NewCBEL; OxCClL, 89; OxCEng 67, 85, 95; OxCMed 86; PenC CL; REn; WhDW; WorAl; WorAlBi*

Hippolytus, Saint
"The Presbyter"
Religious Leader
First antipope, leader of first schism in Catholic church; eventually was reconciled.
b. 170?
d. 235?, Sardinia
Source: *EncEarC; LuthC 75; NewCol 75; WebBD 83*

Hires, Charles E
American. Manufacturer
Invented, manufactured root beer, 1876.
b. Aug 19, 1851 in Roadstown, New Jersey
d. Jul 31, 1937 in Haverford, Pennsylvania
Source: *DcAmB S2; Entr; WebAB 74; WhAm 4, HSA*

Hirohito
Japanese. Ruler
Emperor of Japan, 1926-89; surrendered to US to end WW II, 1945.
b. Apr 29, 1901 in Tokyo, Japan
d. Jan 7, 1989 in Tokyo, Japan
Source: *AnObit 1989; BioIn 1, 2, 3, 4, 5, 6, 7, 8, 9, 10, 11, 12, 13, 14, 15, 16, 18, 19, 20, 21; CurBio 42, 76, 89, 89N; DcPol; DcTwHis; EncJap; FacFETw; FarE&A 78, 79, 80, 81; HisEWW; HisWorL; IntWW 74, 75, 76, 77, 78, 79, 80, 81, 82, 83, 89N; LegTOT; LinLib S; McGEWB; News 89-2; NewYTBS 75, 89; REn; WhAm 9; WhDW; Who 90N; WhoGov 72; WhoWor 76, 78, 80, 82, 84, 87, 89; WhWW-II; WorAl; WorAlBi*

Hiroshige, Ando
Japanese. Artist
Member, Ukiyo-e school; master of colored woodcut; noted for landscapes which influenced European impressionists.
b. 1797 in Edo, Japan
d. Oct 12, 1858 in Edo, Japan
Source: *DcArts; LinLib S; McGDA; McGEWB; NewCol 75; OxCArt; WebBD 83; WhDW*

Hirsch, Crazylegs
[Elroy Leon Hirsch]
American. Football Player
End, 1946-57, mostly with LA; led NFL in scoring, 1951; Hall of Fame.
b. Jun 17, 1923 in Wausau, Wisconsin
Source: *BiDAmSp FB; BioIn 3, 7, 8, 9; LegTOT; WhoAm 76, 80, 82, 84; WhoFtbl 74; WhoHol A; WhoSpor*

Hirsch, E(ric) D(onald), Jr.
American. Writer
Wrote *Innocence and Experience: An Introduction to Blake,* 1964.
b. Mar 22, 1928 in Memphis, Tennessee
Source: *BioIn 17; ConAu 25R, 27NR, 51NR; ConLC 79; WhoAm 74, 76, 78, 80, 82, 84, 86, 88, 90, 92, 94, 95, 96, 97; WhoAmJ 80; WhoSSW 84, 86, 95; WorAu 1985; WrDr 94, 96*

Hirsch, John Stephen
Canadian. Director
Cofounded Manitoba Theater center; best known for his work at Ontario's Stratford Festival and served as director, 1965-85.
b. May 1, 1930 in Siofok, Hungary
d. Aug 1, 1989 in Toronto, Ontario, Canada
Source: *CamGWoT; CanWW 89; ConTFT 6; CreCan 2; CurBio 89N; OxCCanT; OxCThe 83; WhoAm 76, 78, 80, 82, 84, 86, 88; WhoMW 88*

Hirsch, Joseph
American. Artist
Drew caricatures, scenes of social injustice.
b. Apr 25, 1910 in Philadelphia, Pennsylvania
d. Sep 21, 1981 in New York, New York
Source: *AnObit 1981; BioIn 1, 4, 6, 9, 12; ChhPo S1; DcAmArt; DcCAA 71; GrAmP; McGDA; PrintW 83, 85; WhAm 8; WhAmArt 85; WhoAm 74, 76, 78, 80, 84; WhoAmA 73, 76, 78, 80, 82N, 84N, 86N, 89N, 91N, 93N*

Hirsch, Judd
American. Actor
TV series include "Taxi," 1978-83; "Dear John," 1988-92; won 1986 Tony for *I'm Not Rappaport;* won Emmy for best actor in "Taxi," 1981 and 1983; won Golden Globe Award for "Dear John," 1988.
b. Mar 15, 1935 in New York, New York
Source: *BioIn 12, 13, 14, 16, 17; CamGWoT; CelR 90; ConTFT 1, 4, 11; CurBio 84; HalFC 88; IntMPA 86, 88, 92, 94, 96; IntWW 89, 91, 93; LegTOT; LesBEnT 92; VarWW 85; WhoAm 78, 80, 82, 84, 86, 88, 90, 92, 94, 95, 96, 97; WhoAmJ 80; WhoE 93, 95, 97; WhoEnt 92; WhoHol 92; WhoTelC; WhoThe 81; WorAl; WorAlBi*

Hirschfeld, Al(bert)
American. Cartoonist, Artist, Author
Well-known theatrical caricaturist with *NY Times,* 1925—; recipient of Stage Directors and Choregraphers Award, 1992.
b. Jun 21, 1903 in Saint Louis, Missouri
Source: *AmArt; AmAu&B; BiE&WWA; BioIn 9, 11, 12, 13, 14, 15, 17, 18, 19, 20, 21; CelR; ConArt 77; ConAu 1R, 2NR; ConTFT 1; CurBio 71; EncAJ; LesBEnT; News 92, 92-3; NewYTBS 83; NotNAT; OxCAmT 84; PeoHis; WhoAm 74, 76, 78, 80, 82, 84, 86, 88, 90, 92, 94, 95, 96, 97; WhoAmA 73, 76, 78, 80, 82, 84, 86, 89, 91, 93; WhoAmJ 80; WhoE 86, 89, 91, 93; WhoEnt 92; WhoWorJ 72, 78; WorArt 1950; WorECar*

Hirschfeld, Magnus
German. Physician
Founded the German homosexual movement.
b. May 14, 1868 in Kolberg, Prussia
d. May 14, 1935 in Nice, France
Source: *ConAu 148; EncTR 91; GayLesB; GayLL; HumSex*

Hirschfelder, Joseph Oakland
American. Chemist
Authority on nuclear energy; contributed to the development of the atomic bomb at Los Alamos.
b. May 27, 1911 in Baltimore, Maryland
d. Mar 30, 1990 in Madison, Wisconsin
Source: *AmMWSc 73P, 76P, 79, 82, 86, 89, 92; BiInAmS; BioIn 2, 7, 11, 16, 17; BlueB 76; ConAu 131; CurBio 90N; InSci; IntWW 74, 75, 76, 77, 78, 79, 80, 81, 82, 83, 89, 91N; McGMS 80; NewYTBS 90; WhAm 10; WhoAm 74, 76, 78, 86, 88; WhoFrS 84*

Hirschorn, Joel
"Diamond Joel"
American. Lawyer
Defense attorney who specializes in defending major drug smugglers.
b. Mar 13, 1943 in New York, New York
Source: *BioIn 14, 15; ConNews 86-1; WhoAmL 87; WhoEmL 87; WhoEng 88; WhoTech 89; WhoWor 84*

Hirshfield, Morris
American. Artist
Self-taught "primitive" painter; started painting at age 65; drew nudes, landscape s, animals.
b. Apr 10, 1872, Russia-Poland
d. 1946
Source: *AmFkP; BioIn 1, 2, 12, 13, 14, 20; BriEAA; CurBio 43; FacFETw; FolkA 87; McGDA; MusmAFA; OxCTwCA; PhDcTCA 77*

Hirshhorn, Joseph Herman
American. Art Collector, Financier
Uranium tycoon; donated $50 million art collection for Washington's Hirshhorn Museum, 1966.
b. Aug 11, 1899 in Mitau, Russia
d. Aug 31, 1981 in Washington, District of Columbia
Source: *BioIn 3, 4, 5, 6, 7, 8, 9, 10, 12; CanWW 70; CurBio 66, 81N; NewYTBS 81; WhoAmA 78; WhoE 74; WorAl*

Hirt, Al(ois Maxwell)
"Round Mound of Sound"
American. Jazz Musician
Trumpeter whose hits include "Bourbon Street," 1961; "Cotton Candy," 1964; Grammy for "Java."

b. Nov 7, 1922 in New Orleans, Louisiana
Source: *AllMusG; Baker 84, 92; BiDAmM; BiDJaz; BioIn 5, 6, 7, 8, 10, 20; CmpEPM; ConMus 5; CurBio 67; IntMPA 75, 76, 77, 78, 79, 80, 81, 82, 84, 86, 88, 92, 94, 96; LegTOT; NewAmDM; NewGrDA 86; NewGrDJ 88, 94; NewOrJ; PenEncP; RkOn 78; TwCBrS; VarWW 85; WhoAm 74, 76, 78, 80; WhoHol 92; WhoSSW 73, 75, 76; WorAl; WorAlBi*

His, Wilhelm
German. Scientist
Anatomist, embryologist; founded science of histogenesis; helped to establish neuron theory.
b. Jul 9, 1831 in Basel, Switzerland
d. May 1, 1904 in Leipzig, Germany
Source: *BiESc; BiHiMed; BioIn 1, 4, 9; CamDcSc; DcScB; InSci; LarDcSc; OxCMed 86*

Hiss, Alger
American. Government Official, Lawyer
Alleged Soviet spy convicted of perjury, 1950; after three years in prison, sought to have verdict, allegations re-examined.
b. Nov 11, 1904 in Baltimore, Maryland
d. Nov 15, 1996 in New York, New York
Source: *AmDec 1940, 1950; Au&Wr 71; BioIn 1, 2, 3, 4, 5, 6, 7, 8, 9, 10, 11, 12, 13, 14, 15, 16; ColdWar 1; ConAu 33R, 154; CopCroC; CurBio 47; DcPol; DcTwHis; EncAB-H 1974, 1996; EncAL; EncCW; EncMcCE; EncWB; FacFETw; LegTOT; NewYTBS 27, 88; OxCAmH; PeoHis; PolPar; PolProf T; SpyCS; WebAB 74, 79; What 1; WhDW; Who 74, 82, 83, 85, 88, 90, 92, 94; WorAl; WorAlBi*

Hitch, Charles J(ohnston)
American. University Administrator
Pres., U of CA, 1968-75.
b. Jan 9, 1910 in Boonville, Missouri
d. Sep 11, 1995 in San Leandro, California
Source: *AmEA 74; AmMWSc 73S, 78S; BioIn 5, 7, 8, 9, 11; BlueB 76; CurBio 70, 95N; EncAI&E; Future; IntWW 74, 75, 76, 77, 78, 79, 80, 81, 82, 83, 89, 91, 93; LEduc 74; PolProf K; WhAm 11; WhoAm 74, 76, 78, 80, 82, 84, 86, 88, 90, 92, 94, 95; WhoSSW 76; WhoWest 74; WhoWor 74, 76, 78, 80, 82, 84, 87, 89*

Hitchcock, Alfred Joseph, Sir
"Master of Suspense"
English. Director
Famous thrillers include *North by Northwest,* 1959; *Psycho,* 1960; won 1940 Oscar for *Rebecca.*
b. Aug 13, 1899 in London, England
d. Apr 29, 1980 in Bel Air, California
Source: *AmCulL; Au&Wr 71; BiDFilm; BioIn 1, 2, 3, 4, 5, 6, 7, 8, 9, 10, 11; BioNews 74; CmMov; ConAu 97; ConLC 16; CurBio 41, 60, 80N; DcAmB S10; DcFM; DcNaB 1971; FilmgC; GrBr; IntAu&W 77; IntWW 74, 75, 76, 77, 78, 79, 80; MakMC; McGEWB; OxCAmH; OxCFilm; RAdv 14; WebAB 74, 79; WhAm 7; Who 74; WhoAm 74, 76, 78, 80; WhoWest 74, 76; WhoWor 74, 78; WorAl; WorEFlm*

Hitchcock, Edward
American. Geologist, University Administrator
A founder, first president, American Assn. of Geologists, 1840; president, Amherst College, 1844-54.
b. May 24, 1793 in Deerfield, Massachusetts
d. Feb 27, 1864 in Amherst, Massachusetts
Source: *Alli, SUP; AmBi; ApCAB; BbD; BiDAmEd; BiDAmS; BiD&SB; BiInAmS; BioIn 9, 17, 19; CyAL 1; CyEd; DcAmAu; DcAmB; DcAmReB 1, 2; DcBiPP; DcEnL; DcNAA; DcScB; Drake; InSci; LarDcSc; LinLib S; NatCAB 5; OxCAmH; PeoHis; REnAL; TwCBDA; WhAm HS*

Hitchcock, Henry Russell
American. Educator, Historian
Writings on architecture considered foremost in field: *Frank Lloyd Wright,* 1928; *Modern Architecture,* 1929.
b. Jun 3, 1903 in Boston, Massachusetts
d. Feb 19, 1987 in New York
Source: *BioIn 3, 6, 9, 12, 15, 16, 17; DcD&D; IntAu&W 77; IntWW 78, 83; Who 85; WhoAm 74, 76, 78, 80, 82, 84, 86; WhoAmA 73, 76, 78, 80, 82, 84, 86, 89N, 91N, 93N; WhoWor 74; WrDr 86*

Hitchcock, Lambert
American. Cabinetmaker, Furniture Designer
Hitchcock chair, 1826, an early example of mass production, is collector's item today.
b. Jun 28, 1795 in Cheshire, Connecticut
d. 1852
Source: *AntBDN G; BioIn 3, 9, 15; CabMA; DcD&D; DcNiCA; LinLib S; NewCol 75; OxCDecA; PenDiDA 89*

Hitchcock, Raymond
American. Actor
Vaudeville, film comedian who did three films for Mack Sennett, 1915.
b. Oct 22, 1865 in Auburn, New York
d. Dec 24, 1929 in Beverly Hills, California
Source: *BioIn 3; CmpEPM; DcAmB; EncMT; EncVaud; Film 1, 2; MotPP; NotNAT B; OxCAmT 84; OxCPMus; TwYS; WhScrn 77, 83; WhThe*

Hitchcock, Robyn
English. Singer, Songwriter
Founded punk-rock band the "Soft Boys," 1976-81; reformed as the "Egyptians," 1984—; albums include *Globe of Frogs,* 1988.
b. 1953 in London, England
Source: *BioIn 15; ConMus 9*

Hitchcock, Tommy
[Thomas Hitchcock, Jr]
American. Polo Player
Dominated the game of polo for nearly 20 yrs., 1922-39; considered greatest American player of all time.
b. Feb 11, 1900 in Aiken, South Carolina
d. Apr 19, 1944 in Salisbury, England
Source: *BiDAmSp OS; BioIn 3, 5, 6, 10, 12; CurBio 44; DcAmB S3; NatCAB 38; OxCAmH; WebAB 74, 79; WebAMB; WhoSpor*

Hitchings, George Herbert
American. Biochemist
Shared 1988 Nobel Prize in medicine for research on life-prolonging drug treatments for AIDS, leukemia and other diseases.
b. Apr 18, 1905 in Hoquiam, Washington
Source: *AmMWSc 73P, 76P, 79, 82, 86, 89, 92, 95; BiESc; BioIn 11; CamDcSc; IntWW 83, 89, 91, 93; LarDcSc; NewYTBS 89; Who 90, 92, 94; WhoAm 74, 76, 78, 80, 86, 88, 90, 92, 94, 95, 96; WhoFI 96; WhoFrS 84; WhoMedH; WhoNob 90, 95; WhoScEn 94, 96; WhoSSW 86, 88, 91, 93, 95; WhoTech 89; WhoWor 91, 93, 95, 96, 97*

Hite, Robert Ernest, Jr.
[Canned Heat]
"The Bear"
American. Singer
Blue-grass vocalist; hit song "On the Road Again."
b. Jan 26, 1943 in Torrance, California
d. Apr 5, 1981 in Los Angeles, California
Source: *WhoAm 74; WhoRocM 82; WhoWor 74*

Hite, Shere
[Shirley Diana Gregory]
American. Author
Writings center on cultural research in human sexuality; controversial works kno wn as "Hite Reports."
b. Nov 2, 1942 in Saint Joseph, Missouri
Source: *BioIn 15; ConAu 31NR, 81; ConPopW; CurBio 88; IntWW 91; InWom SUP; LegTOT; MajTwCW; WhoAm 86, 90; WhoAmW 85, 91; WhoUSWr 88; WhoWrEP 89; WorAlBi*

Hitler, Adolf
[Adolf Schickelgruber]
"Der Fuhrer"
German. Political Leader
Founded National Socialism; invasion of Poland, 1939, started WW II; engineered Holocaust, in which over six million Jews and their supporters were murdered.
b. Apr 20, 1889 in Braunau, Austria
d. Apr 30, 1945 in Berlin, Germany
Source: *Benet 87, 96; BiDExR; BioIn 1, 2, 3, 4, 5, 6, 7, 8, 9, 10, 11, 12, 13, 14, 15, 16, 17, 18, 19, 20, 21; ConAu 117, 147; CurBio 57; DcAmC; DcPol; DcTwHis; DicTyr; Dis&D; EncRev; EncTR, 91; FacFETw; FilmgC; HalFC*

80, 84, 88; HarEnMi; HisEWW; HisWorL; LegTOT; LinLib L, S; LuthC 75; McGEWB; NewYTBE 72, 73; OxCEng 67, 85, 95; OxCGer 76, 86; REn; TwCLC 53; WhAm 4; WhDW; WhoMilH 76; WhWW-II; WorAl; WorAlBi

Hitotsubashi
[Tokugawa Keiki Yoshinobu]
Japanese. Ruler
Last shogun of Japan, 1866-67; aided in peaceful transition of power to emperor; became prince, 1902.
b. 1837
d. 1902
Source: *WebBD 83*

Hittorf, Johann Wilhelm
German. Physicist
Pioneered in electrochemical research; the Hittorf tube named for him.
b. Mar 27, 1824 in Bonn, Germany
d. Nov 28, 1914 in Munster, Prussia
Source: *AsBiEn; BiESc; DcScB; InSci; LarDcSc; LinLib S*

Ho, David D.
[Da-I Ho]
American. Scientist
Treated some of the first people infected with HIV, 1981; CEO, Aaron Diamond AIDS Research Center, 1990—.
b. Nov 3, 1952, Taiwan
Source: *AsAmAlm; BioIn 20; NotAsAm; WhoAsA 94*

Ho, Don
American. Singer
Best known entertainer in Hawaii; popularized song "Tiny Bubbles," 1967.
b. Aug 13, 1930 in Kakaako, Hawaii
Source: *BioIn 8, 12; LegTOT; VarWW 85; WhoAm 74, 90; WhoWest 92; WhoWor 74*

Ho, Ying-Chin
Chinese. Government Official
Chief of staff, Nationalist army, 1929; minister of war, 1930-44; fled to Taiwan, 1949.
b. 1899 in Xingyi, China
d. Oct 21, 1987 in Taipei, Taiwan
Source: *CurBio 42, 88, 88N*

Hoad, Lew(is A.)
Australian. Tennis Player
Won Wimbledon singles titles, 1956, 1957, and doubles, 1953, 1955, 1956.
b. Nov 23, 1934
d. Jul 3, 1994, Spain
Source: *BioIn 20; BuCMET; CurBio 94N; NewYTBS 94*

Hoagland, Dennis Robert
American. Botanist
Developed Hoagland's solution for water culture of plants, studied ion absorption in plants.
b. Apr 2, 1884 in Golden, Colorado
d. Sep 5, 1949 in Oakland, California
Source: *BioIn 1, 2, 4, 6, 7; DcAmB S4; DcNAA; DcScB; InSci; NatCAB 47*

Hoagland, Edward Morley
American. Author
Novels include *Cat Man,* 1956; *The Moose on the Wall,* 1974.
b. Dec 21, 1932 in New York, New York
Source: *Benet 87; BenetAL 91; BioIn 13, 16; ConAu 1R, 2NR, 31NR; ConLC 28; ConNov 86, 91; CurBio 82; CyWA 89; DcLB 6; DrAPF 89; IntAu&W 86; SmATA 51; TwCWW 91; WhoAm 90; WhoUSWr 88; WhoWrEP 89; WrDr 86, 92*

Hoare, Samuel John Gurney, Sir
English. Diplomat
Ambassador to Spain, 1940-44; Conservative MP, 1910-44.
b. Feb 24, 1880 in London, England
d. May 7, 1959 in London, England
Source: *BioIn 14; CurBio 40, 59; DcNaB 1951; DcTwHis; GrBr; HisEWW*

Hoban, James
American. Architect
Designed White House, 1792, rebuilt following British destruction, 1814.
b. 1762 in Callan, Ireland
d. Dec 8, 1831 in Washington, District of Columbia
Source: *AmBi; BiAUS; BriEAA; DcAmB; DcIrB 78, 88; LegTOT; MacEA; McGDA; OxCAmH; OxCAmL 65; WebAB 74, 79; WebBD 83; WhAm HS; WorAl; WorAlBi*

Hoban, Russell
American. Artist, Author
Writes children's books: *The Atomic Submarine; Bedtime for Frances,* 1960; adult fiction includes *Riddley Walker,* 1986.
b. Feb 4, 1925 in Lansdale, Pennsylvania
Source: *AuBYP 2, 3; BenetAL 91; BioIn 6, 8, 9, 10, 12, 14, 15; CamGLE; ChlBkCr; ChlLR 3; ConAu 5R, 23NR; ConNov 86, 91; DcAmChF 1960; DcLB 52; IlrAm G; IntAu&W 91; IntWW 91; LegTOT; LiExTwC; MajTwCW; NewEScF; Novels; OxCAmL 95; OxCChiL; PostFic; ScF&FL 1, 2, 92; ScFSB; SmATA 1, 40; ThrBJA; TwCChW 78, 83, 89; TwCSFW 86, 91; Who 85, 92; WhoAm 86; WorAu 1975; WrDr 80, 82, 84, 86, 88, 90, 92, 94, 96*

Hobart, Alice Tisdale Nourse
American. Author
Best-known works include *Oil for the Lamps of China,* 1933; *Venture into Darkness,* 1955.
b. Jan 28, 1882 in Lockport, New York
d. Mar 14, 1967 in Oakland, California
Source: *AmAu&B; AmNov; ConAu 5R; InWom; ObitOF 79; REnAL; TwCA SUP; WhAm 4; WhNAA*

Hobart, Garret Augustus
American. US Vice President
Served as VP under William McKinley, 1897-99.
b. Jun 3, 1844 in Long Branch, New Jersey
d. Nov 21, 1899 in Paterson, New Jersey
Source: *AmBi; AmLegL; AmPolLe; ApCAB SUP; BiDrAC; BiDrUSC 89; BiDrUSE 71, 89; BioIn 1, 4, 7, 8, 9, 10, 14; DcAmB; HarEnUS; NatCAB 11; TwCBDA; VicePre; WebAB 74, 79; WhAm 1; WhAmP*

Hobart, Rose
American. Actor
Featured in "other woman" roles; best known for *Farmer's Daughter,* 1940.
b. May 1, 1906 in New York, New York
Source: *BiE&WWA; BioIn 14, 20; EncAFC; FilmEn; FilmgC; ForWC 70; ForYSC; HalFC 80, 84, 88; InWom SUP; MovMk; NotNAT; ThFT; WhoEnt 92; WhoHol 92, A; WhoThe 77A; WhThe*

Hobbema, Meindert
Dutch. Artist
Last of 17th-c. Dutch landscapists; most famous work: *The Avenue, Middelharnis,* 1689.
b. c. 1638, Netherlands
d. Dec 7, 1709 in Amsterdam, Netherlands
Source: *AtlBL; Benet 87; BioIn 5, 19; DcArts; IntDcAA 90; LinLib S; McGDA; OxCArt; OxDcArt; REn; WhDW; WorAl; WorAlBi*

Hobbes, Thomas
English. Author, Philosopher
Father of modern analytical philosophy; best-known work *Leviathan,* 1651.
b. Apr 5, 1588 in Westport, England
d. Dec 4, 1679 in Hardwick Hall, England
Source: *Alli; AtlBL; Benet 87, 96; BiD&SB; BiDPsy; BioIn 1, 2, 3, 4, 5, 6, 8, 9, 10, 11, 12, 13, 14, 15, 20, 21; BlkwCE; BlmGEL; BritAu; CamGEL; CamGLE; CasWL; Chambr 1; CroE&S; CrtT 2, 4; CyEd; CyWA 58; DcAmC; DcBiPP; DcEnA; DcEnL; DcEuL; DcLB 151; DcLEL; DcNaB; DcScB; DcSoc; Dis&D; EncEnl; EncEth; EncUnb; EvLB; GrWrEL N; HisDStE; LegTOT; LinLib L, S; LngCEL; LuthC 75; McGEWB; MouLC 1; NamesHP; NewC; NewCBEL; OxCEng 67, 85, 95; OxCLaw; OxCPhil; PenC ENG; RAdv 14, 13-3, 13-4; RComWL; REn; RfGEnL 91; TwoTYeD; WebE&AL; WhDW; WorAl; WorAlBi; WrPh P*

Hobbs, Leonard Sinclair
"Luke"
American. Aircraft Designer
Developed J-57, gas turbine engine which powered first American jets, 1952.
b. Dec 20, 1896 in Carbon, Wyoming
d. Nov 1, 1977 in Hartford, Connecticut
Source: *BioIn 3, 11; CurBio 78; InSci; NewYTBS 77; ObitOF 79; WorAl*

Hobby, Oveta Culp
American. Government Official, Publisher
Co-editor, publisher, *Houston Post*, 1931-53; director of WACS, 1942-45; first secretary, dept. of HEW, 1953-55.
b. Jan 19, 1905 in Killeen, Texas
d. Aug 16, 1995 in Houston, Texas
Source: *AmDec 1940; AmPolLe; AmPolW 80; AmWomM; BiDrUSE 71, 89; BioIn 13, 18, 19, 21; BlueB 76; ConAu 81; CurBio 42, 53, 95N; DcAmMiB; DcLB 127; EncTwCJ; ForWC 70; GoodHs; GrLiveH; IntWW 74, 75, 76, 77, 78, 79, 80, 81, 82, 83, 89, 91, 93; InWom, SUP; LegTOT; LibW; LinLib L, S; PolProf E; St&PR 75, 87, 91, 93, 96; TexWr; WebAMB; WhAm 11; WhoAm 74, 76, 78, 80, 84, 86, 88, 90, 92; WhoAmP 73, 75, 77; WhoAmW 58, 61, 64, 66, 68, 70, 72, 74, 75, 77, 81, 83, 85; WhoSSW 73, 75, 76, 78; WhoWor 74, 76, 78; WomFir; WorAl; WorAlBi*

Hobson, Geary
American. Educator
Coordinated Returning the Gift, An International Native Writers Festival, 1992.
b. Jun 12, 1941 in Arkansas
Source: *BioIn 21; ConAu 122; NotNaAm*

Hobson, Harold
English. Critic
Influential drama critic, *Christian Science Monitor*, 1932-72; *The Sunday Times*, 1947-76.
b. Aug 4, 1904 in Rotherham, England
d. Mar 13, 1992
Source: *BiE&WWA; BioIn 12; BlueB 76; ConAu 81, 137; CroCD; DcLEL 1940; EncWT; IntAu&W 77, 82, 89, 91; LngCTC; NotNAT; OxCEng 85; OxCThe 83; ScF&FL 1; Who 74, 82, 83, 85, 88, 90, 92; WhoThe 72, 77, 81; WhoWor 87; WrDr 80, 82, 84, 86, 88, 90, 92, 94, 96*

Hobson, John Atkinson
English. Economist
Pioneer of oversaving theory of business cycle: *Confessions of an Economic Heretic*, 1938.
b. Jul 6, 1858 in Derby, England
d. Apr 1, 1940 in London, England
Source: *BiDInt; BioIn 2, 3, 5, 8, 11, 14, 16, 17; CurBio 40; DcNaB 1931; GrEconB; HisDBrE; NewC; NewCBEL; WhLit; WhoEc 81, 86*

Hobson, Laura Zametkin
American. Author
Wrote *Gentleman's Agreement*, 1947, which explored anti-Semitism in US.
b. Jun 19, 1900 in New York, New York
d. Feb 28, 1986 in New York, New York
Source: *AmAu&B; AmNov; ConAu 17R; ConLC 7; ConNov 86; CurBio 47, 86; REn; REnAL; TwCA SUP; WhoAm 82; WhoAmW 85; WrDr 86*

Hobson, Richmond Pearson
American. Military Leader
Commander of Merrimac during famous naval maneuver, 1898.
b. Aug 17, 1870 in Greensboro, Alabama
d. Mar 16, 1937 in New York, New York
Source: *AmAu&B; AmBi; ApCAB SUP; BiDInt; BiDrAC; BiDSA; BioIn 4, 5, 6, 12; DcAmAu; DcAmB S2; DcAmTB; DcNAA; EncSoH; HarEnUS; MedHR, 94; NatCAB 9; TwCBDA; WebAMB; WhAm 1*

Hobson, Valerie Babette
British. Actor
Leading lady in British films, 1936-54; retired, married to John Profumo since 1954.
b. Apr 14, 1917 in Larne, Northern Ireland
Source: *FilmEn; FilmgC; HalFC 88; InWom SUP; MovMk; OxCFilm; ThFT; Who 74, 92; WhoHol A*

Hochhuth, Rolf
German. Author, Dramatist
Due to subject matter (guilt, moral responsibility), his play *The Deputy* brought him int'l fame, 1963.
b. Apr 1, 1931, Germany
Source: *Benet 87, 96; BioIn 6, 8, 9, 10, 11, 12, 19; CamGWoT; CasWL; ClDMEL 80; CnMD; CnThe; ConAu 5R, 33NR; ConFLW 84; ConLC 4, 11, 18; ConWorW 93; CroCD; CurBio 76; CyWA 89; DcArts; DcLB 124; EncWL, 2, 3; EncWT; Ent; IntAu&W 76, 77, 89, 91, 93; IntDcT 2; IntWW 83, 89, 91, 93; MajMD 1; MajTwCW; MakMC; McGEWD 72, 84; ModGL; ModWD; NotNAT; OxCGer 76, 86; OxCThe 83; PenC EUR; RAdv 14, 13-2; REnWD; TwCWr; WhoThe 72, 77, 81; WhoWor 74; WorAu 1950*

Ho Chi Minh
[Nguyen Tat Thanh Thank]
"Uncle Ho"
Vietnamese. Political Leader, Revolutionary
Founder, first pres., N Vietnam, 1945-69; legendary figure instrumental in spread of Communism throughout Southeast Asia.
b. May 19, 1890 in Hoang Tru, Vietnam
d. Sep 3, 1969 in Hanoi, Vietnam
Source: *BiDMarx; BioIn 8, 9, 10, 11, 12, 13, 14, 15, 18, 19, 20; ColdWar 2; ConAu 112; CurBio 49, 66, 69; DcMPSA; DcOrL 2; DcPol; DcTwHis; DicTyr; EncCW; EncRev; FacFETw; GrLGrT; HarEnMi; HisWorL; LegTOT; LinLib L, S; MakMC; ObitT 1961; RAdv 14; WhDW; WorAl; WorAlBi*

Hochoy, Solomon, Sir
West Indian. Politician
Governor-general, Trinidad and Tobago, 1962-72.
b. Apr 20, 1905, Jamaica
Source: *BlueB 76; IntWW 74, 75, 76, 77, 78, 79, 80, 81, 82, 83; IntYB 78, 79, 80, 81, 82; Who 74, 82, 83; WhoGov 72, 75; WhoWor 74, 76, 78*

Hockenberry, John (Charles)
American. Broadcast Journalist
Correspondent with National Public Radio, 1981—.
b. Jun 1956 in Dayton, Ohio
Source: *CurBio 96*

Hocking, Silas
English. Religious Leader
Wrote reminiscences, *My Book of Memory*, 1923.
b. Mar 24, 1850 in Saint Stephen, England
d. Mar 4, 1937 in Perranporth, England
Source: *Chambr 3; DcNaB 1931; EvLB; LngCTC; NewC; OxCChiL; WhE&EA; WhLit*

Hocking, William Ernest
American. Educator
Harvard U professor of philosophy, 1914-43; books include *Man and the State*, 1926; *Human Nature and Its Remaking*, 1918.
b. Aug 1, 1873 in Cleveland, Ohio
d. Jun 12, 1966 in Madison, New Hampshire
Source: *AmAu&B; BiDAmEd; BioIn 3, 4, 6, 7, 10; ConAu P-1; CurBio 62, 66; DcAmB S8; EncWB; LuthC 75; NatCAB 54; OhA&B; OxCAmH; OxCAmL 65, 83, 95; OxCPhil; RAdv 14, 13-4; REnAL; TwCA SUP; WebAB 74, 79; WhAm 4; WhLit; WhNAA*

Hockney, David
English. Artist
Graphic, pop artist whose early success came with a set of satirical etchings: *The Rake's Progress*, 1963; master of the double portrait.
b. Jul 9, 1937 in Bradford, England
Source: *AmArt; AmCulL; Au&Arts 17; Benet 87, 96; BioIn 7, 9, 10, 11, 12, 13, 14, 15, 16; BlueB 76; CelR 90; ConArt 77, 83, 89, 96; ConAu 116, 150; ConBrA 79; ConPhot 88, 95; ConTFT 10; CurBio 72; DcArts; DcCAr 81; FacFETw; GayLesB; ICPEnP A; IntDcAA 90; IntDcOp; IntWW 74, 75, 76, 77, 78, 79, 80, 81, 82, 83, 89, 91, 93; IntWWM 90; LegTOT; MakMC; MetOEnc; NewGrDO; News 88-3; OxCTwCA; OxDcArt; OxDcOp; PhDcTCA 77; PrintW 83, 85; TwCPaSc; WhDW; Who 74, 82, 83, 85, 88, 90, 92, 94; WhoAm 80, 82, 84, 86, 88, 90, 92, 94, 95, 96, 97; WhoAmA 93; WhoEnt 92; WhoWest 89, 92, 94, 96; WhoWor 74, 82, 84, 87, 89, 91, 93, 95, 96, 97; WorAlBi; WorArt 1950; WrDr 80, 82, 84, 86, 88, 90, 92*

Hodel, Donald P(aul)
American. Government Official
Interior secretary under Reagan, 1985-89; energy secretary, 1982-85.
b. May 23, 1935 in Portland, Oregon
Source: *BiDrUSE 89; BioIn 12, 13, 14, 15, 16; CngDr 83, 85, 87; CurBio 87;*

IntWW 83, 89, 91, 93; NewYTBS 82, 85; WhoAm 74, 82, 84, 86, 88; WhoAmP 73, 75, 77, 79, 81, 83, 85, 87, 89, 91, 93, 95; WhoE 83, 85, 86, 89; WhoFI 87; WhoWor 87, 89

Hodge, Frederick Webb
English. Anthropologist
Indian authority who led expeditions to Southwest, 1884-86; co-founded American Anthropological Assn.
b. Jan 5, 1864 in Plymouth, England
d. Sep 28, 1956 in Santa Fe, New Mexico
Source: *AmAu&B; AmLY; ApCAB SUP; BenetAL 91; BioIn 4, 5, 6; DcAmAu; HarEnUS; IntDcAn; NatCAB 10, 43; OxCAmH; OxCAmL 65, 83, 95; OxCCan; REnAL; REnAW; TwCBDA; WhAm 3; WhE&EA; WhLit; WhNaAH*

Hodge, John Reed
"The Patton of the Pacific"
American. Army Officer
Led American Division in Pacific during WW II.
b. Jun 12, 1893 in Golconda, Illinois
d. Nov 12, 1963 in Washington, District of Columbia
Source: *BiDWWGF; BioIn 1, 3, 6, 7, 8; CurBio 45, 64; DcAmB S7; HarEnMi; NatCAB 51; WebAMB; WhAm 4*

Hodges, Courtney
American. Military Leader
Commander, US First Army, WW II.
b. Jan 5, 1887 in Perry, Georgia
d. Jan 16, 1966 in San Antonio, Texas
Source: *CurBio 41, 66; WhAm 4*

Hodges, Craig Anthony
American. Basketball Player
Guard, San Diego, 1982-84, Milwaukee, 1984-88; Chicago, 1988-92.
b. Jun 29, 1960 in Park Forest, Illinois
Source: *OfNBA 87; WhoAfA 96; WhoBlA 85, 88, 90, 92, 94*

Hodges, Eddie
[Samuel Edward Hodges]
American. Actor
Films include *Adventures of Huckleberry Finn,* 1960; *Advise and Consent,* 1961.
b. Mar 5, 1947 in Hattiesburg, Mississippi
Source: *BiE&WWA; BioIn 4, 5; EncRk 88; ForYSC; MotPP; RkOn 74; WhoHol 92, A*

Hodges, Gil(bert Raymond)
American. Baseball Player, Baseball Manager
Infielder, 1943, 1947-63; managed NY Mets to pennant, World Series victory, 1969.
b. Apr 4, 1924 in Princeton, Indiana
d. Apr 2, 1972 in West Palm Beach, Florida
Source: *Ballpl 90; BioIn 13, 15, 17, 18; ConAu 109; CurBio 62, 72, 72N; FacFETw; LegTOT; NewYTBE 72; WhAm 5; WhoProB 73; WhoSpor; WhScrn 83; WorAl; WorAlBi*

Hodges, Johnny
[John Cornelius Hodges]
"Rabbit"
American. Jazz Musician
Alto saxist with Duke Ellington, 1928-51, 1955-70.
b. Jul 25, 1906 in Cambridge, Massachusetts
d. May 11, 1970 in New York, New York
Source: *ASCAP 66; Baker 78, 84, 92; BiDAfM; BiDAmM; BiDJaz; BioIn 8, 13, 15, 16; CmpEPM; EncJzS; IlEncJ; InB&W 80, 85; LegTOT; MusMk; NewAmDM; NewGrDM 80; NewYTBE 70; WhAm 5; WhoJazz 72; WorAl; WorAlBi*

Hodges, Luther Hartwell
American. Government Official
Dem. governor of NC, 1954-60; secretary of commerce, 1961-65.
b. Mar 9, 1898 in Pittsylvania County, Virginia
d. Oct 6, 1974 in Eden, North Carolina
Source: *BiDrGov 1789; BiDrUSE 71, 89; BioIn 3, 4, 5, 6, 7, 8, 10, 11; ConAu 53; CurBio 56, 74; DcAmB S9; DcNCBi 3; EncSoH; IntWW 74; PolProf E, K; WhAm 6; WhoAm 74; WhoAmP 73; WhoFI 74, 75*

Hodgkin, Alan Lloyd, Sir
English. Physiologist
Shared 1963 Nobel Prize for research in electrical, chemical events in nerve cell damage.
b. Feb 5, 1914 in Banbury, England
Source: *AsBiEn; BiESc; BioIn 2, 5, 6, 14, 15, 18, 20; BlueB 76; CamDcSc; ConAu 140; IntWW 74, 75, 76, 77, 78, 79, 80, 81, 82, 83, 89, 91, 93; LarDcSc; McGEWB; NotTwCS; Who 85, 92, 94; WhoAm 76, 78, 80, 88, 90, 92, 94, 95; WhoMedH; WhoNob, 90, 95; WhoScEn 94, 96; WhoWor 74, 76, 78, 80, 82, 84, 87, 89, 91, 93, 95, 96, 97; WorAl; WorAlBi; WorScD*

Hodgkin, Dorothy Mary Crowfoot
English. Educator
Won 1964 Nobel Prize in chemistry for work on vitamin B-12.
b. May 12, 1910 in Cairo, Egypt
Source: *BiESc; BioIn 14, 15, 16; InSci; IntWW 91; InWom, SUP; LadLa 86; NobelP; Who 82, 83, 85, 88, 90, 92, 94; WhoAm 90; WhoNob, 90; WhoWor 91*

Hodgkin, Howard
English. Artist
Known for his miniature abstract pictures and Indian paintings during the 1970s-1980s; *In the Black Kitchen,* 1990, took 6 yrs. to complete.
b. Aug 6, 1932 in London, England
Source: *BioIn 12, 13, 14, 15, 17, 20; ConArt 77, 83, 89, 96; ConBrA 79; CurBio 91; DcCAr 81; FacFETw; IntWW 89, 91, 93; NewYTBS 90; OxCTwCA; OxDcArt; PrintW 83, 85; TwCPaSc; Who 82, 83, 85, 88, 90, 92, 94; WorArt 1980*

Hodgson, James Day
American. Government Official
Secretary of labor, 1970-73; ambassador to Japan, 1974-77.
b. Dec 3, 1915 in Dawson, Minnesota
Source: *BiDrUSE 89; WhoSSW 73; WhoWor 78*

Hodiak, John
American. Actor
Best known for film *Lifeboat,* 1944.
b. Apr 16, 1914 in Pittsburgh, Pennsylvania
d. Oct 19, 1955 in Tarzana, California
Source: *BioIn 4, 10; CmMov; FilmEn; FilmgC; ForYSC; GangFlm; HalFC 80, 84, 88; HolP 40; LegTOT; MGM; MotPP; MovMk; NotNAT B; RadStar; SaTiSS; WhoHol B; WhScrn 74, 77, 83; WorAl; WorAlBi*

Hodler, Ferdinand
Swiss. Artist
Post-Impressionist; used parallelism compositions; awarded Gold Medal, 1900 Paris World's Fair.
b. Mar 14, 1853 in Bern, Switzerland
d. May 19, 1918 in Geneva, Switzerland
Source: *BioIn 4, 5, 9, 13, 14, 15; ClaDrA; DcArts; IntDcAA 90; McGDA; McGEWB; OxCArt; OxCTwCA; OxDcArt; PhDcTCA 77*

Hoe, Richard March
American. Inventor
Developed Hoe rotary press, which improved speed of printing, 1846-47.
b. Sep 12, 1812 in New York, New York
d. Jun 7, 1886 in Florence, Italy
Source: *AmBi; ApCAB; BioIn 3; DcAmB; HarEnUS; InSci; LinLib S; McGEWB; NatCAB 7; OxCAmH; OxCAmL 65, 83, 95; TwCBDA; WebAB 74, 79; WhAm HS*

Hoess, Rudolf Franz
German. Soldier
Commanded Auschwitz concentration camp, 1940-45; hanged for war crimes, 1947.
b. Nov 25, 1900 in Baden-Baden, Germany
d. Apr 15, 1947 in Auschwitz, Poland
Source: *BiDExR; BioIn 14, 16; EncTR*

Hoest, Bill
[William Hoest]
American. Cartoonist
Created syndicated cartoons "The Lockhorns," 1968; "Agatha Crumm," 1977.
b. Feb 7, 1926 in Newark, New Jersey
d. Nov 7, 1988 in New York, New York
Source: *BioIn 8, 16, 17; ConAu 69; EncACom*

Hofer, Andreas
Austrian. Patriot
Prominent in organization of Tyrol militia, late 1700s; led insurrection against Bavaria, 1809; betrayed to French, court-martialed, shot.
b. Nov 22, 1767 in Saint Leonhard, Austria
d. Feb 20, 1810 in Mantua, Italy
Source: *BioIn 4, 5, 9; CelCen; DcBiPP; DcCathB; LinLib S; NewC; OxCGer 76, 86*

Hofer, Karl
German. Artist
Expressionist, known for emaciated mannequin figures.
b. Oct 11, 1878 in Karlsruhe, Germany
d. Apr 3, 1955 in Berlin, Germany (West)
Source: *BioIn 3, 4, 17; McGDA; ObitOF 79; OxCArt; PhDcTCA 77*

Hoff, Jacobus Henricus van't
Dutch. Chemist
First recipient of Nobel Prize in Chemistry, 1901.
b. Aug 30, 1852 in Rotterdam, Netherlands
d. Mar 1, 1911 in Berlin, Germany
Source: *BioIn 2, 3, 6, 8, 9, 19; WhDW*

Hoff, Sydney
American. Illustrator, Author
Cartoonist for syndicated comic strip, "Laugh It Off," 1957-71; children's book il lustrator: *Danny and the Dinosaur,* 1958.
b. Sep 4, 1912 in New York, New York
Source: *AmAu&B; AuBYP 2, 3; BioIn 7, 8, 9, 11, 15; ConAu 4NR, 5R; EncACom; IlsCB 1957; IntAu&W 91; SmATA 4AS, 9; ThrBJA; TwCChW 83; WhoAm 86, 90, 92, 94, 95, 96, 97; WhoSSW 84; WrDr 86, 92*

Hoffa, Jimmy
[James Riddle Hoffa]
American. Labor Union Official
Pres., Teamsters, 1957-71; believed killed following abduction from MI restaurant; declared dead, Dec 8, 1982.
b. Feb 14, 1913 in Brazil, Indiana
d. Jul 30, 1975? in Bloomfield Hills, Michigan
Source: *AmSocL; BiDAmL; BiDAmLL; BioIn 3, 4, 5, 6, 7, 8, 9, 10, 11, 12, 13; CurBio 72, 83; DcAmB S9; EncAB-H 1996; IndAu 1967; IntWW 74, 75, 76; LegTOT; NewYTBE 71, 72; WebAB 74, 79; WhDW; WhoAm 74, 76; WhoWor 74; WorAl*

Hoffenstein, Samuel Goodman
American. Poet
Best-known work: *Poems in Praise of Practically Nothing,* 1928.
b. Oct 8, 1890, Lithuania
d. Oct 6, 1947 in Hollywood, California
Source: *AmAu&B; BioIn 4, 8; ConAu 111; DcLB 11; REnAL; TwCA SUP; WhAm 2*

Hoffer, Eric
American. Author, Philosopher
Wrote *The True Believer,* 1951; awarded Presidential Medal of Freedom, 1983.
b. Jul 25, 1902 in New York, New York
d. May 21, 1983 in San Francisco, California
Source: *AnObit 1983; Benet 87, 96; BioIn 2, 4, 6, 7, 8, 10, 11, 13, 14; CelR; CmCal; ConAu 13R, 18NR, 109; ConIsC 2; CurBio 65, 83N; DcAmC; LegTOT; LinLib L; NewYTBS 83; PolProf J; RAdv 1; WebAB 74, 79; WhAm 8; WhoAm 74, 76, 78, 80, 82; WorAl; WorAlBi; WorAu 1950; WrDr 76, 80, 82, 84*

Hoffman, Abbie
[The Chicago 7; Abbott Hoffman; Spiro Igloo]
American. Author, Political Activist
Flamboyant revolutionary, antiwar activist; co-founded Yippies; tried as one of Chicago 7 for conspiring to disrupt Democratic National Convention, 1968; wrote *Revolution for the Hell of It,* 1968; suicide victim.
b. Nov 30, 1936 in Worcester, Massachusetts
d. Apr 12, 1989 in New Hope, Pennsylvania
Source: *AmAu&B; AmDec 1970; AmSocL; AnObit 1989; BiDAmLf; BioIn 10, 11, 12, 15, 16; CelR; ConAu 8NR, 21R, 35NR, 128; CurBio 81, 89, 89N; DcAmC; EncAL; EncWB; FacFETw; HisWorL; IntvTCA 2; LegTOT; MajTwCW; MugS; News 89-3; NewYTBE 70; NewYTBS 89; PolProf J; RadHan; RComAH; WhoAm 76, 78; WhoE 74, 75*

Hoffman, Al
American. Composer, Author
Wrote popular stage scores, 1930s-50; hit songs include "Mairz Doats," 1944.
b. Sep 25, 1902 in Minsk, Russia
d. Jul 21, 1960 in New York, New York
Source: *ASCAP 66, 80; BiDAmM; BioIn 5, 14; CmpEPM; OxCPMus; Sw&Ld C*

Hoffman, Charles Fenno
American. Poet
Contributed to *Knickerbocker* mag., 1800s; best-known novel: *Greyslaer: A Romance of the Mohawk,* 1840.
b. Feb 7, 1806 in New York, New York
d. Jun 7, 1884 in Harrisburg, Pennsylvania
Source: *Alli; AmAu; AmAu&B; AmBi; ApCAB; BenetAL 91; BibAL; BiDAmM; BiD&SB; BioIn 1, 3, 10, 12; CamGEL; CamGLE; CamHAL; CasWL; ChhPo; CnDAL; CyAL 2; DcAmAu; DcAmB; DcBiA; DcEnL; DcLB 3; DcLEL; DcNAA; Drake; EvLB; GrWrEL P; HarEnUS; NatCAB 8; Novels; OxCAmL 65, 83, 95; PenC AM; REnAL; RfGAmL 87, 94; TwCBDA; WhAm HS*

Hoffman, Dustin (Lee)
American. Actor
Starred in *The Graduate,* 1967; won Oscars for *Kramer vs. Kramer,* 1979 and *Rainman,* 1988; won Emmy for TV movie *Death of a Salesman,* 1986.
b. Aug 8, 1937 in Los Angeles, California
Source: *AmMWSc 92; BiDFilm 81, 94; BioIn 8, 9, 10, 11, 12, 13, 14, 15, 16, 17, 18, 19, 20, 21; BkPepl; BlueB 76; CamGWoT; CelR, 90; ConTFT 1, 7, 14; CurBio 69, 96; DcArts; DcTwCCu 1; Ent; FacFETw; FilmEn; FilmgC; ForYSC; GangFlm; HalFC 80, 84, 88; IntDcF 1-3, 2-3; IntMPA 75, 76, 77, 78, 79, 80, 81, 82, 84, 86, 88, 92, 94, 96; IntWW 77, 78, 79, 80, 81, 82, 83, 89, 91, 93; ItaFilm; LegTOT; MotPP; MovMk; OxCFilm; VarWW 85; Who 82, 83, 85, 88, 90, 92, 94; WhoAm 74, 76, 78, 80, 82, 84, 86, 88, 90, 92, 94, 95, 96, 97; WhoAmJ 80; WhoE 91, 97; WhoEnt 92; WhoHol 92, A; WhoThe 72, 77, 81; WhoWor 91, 93, 96; WorAl; WorAlBi*

Hoffman, Irwin
American. Conductor
Has led Florida Gulf Coast Symphony since 1968.
b. Nov 26, 1924 in New York, New York
Source: *Baker 84; BioIn 14; CreCan 1; IntWWM 77, 80, 85, 90; WhoAm 74, 76, 78, 80, 82, 84, 86, 88, 90, 92, 94, 95, 96, 97; WhoAmM 83; WhoEnt 92; WhoMus 72; WhoSSW 73, 75, 76; WhoWor 74, 91, 95, 96, 97*

Hoffman, Julius Jennings
American. Judge
Presided over controversial "Chicago Seven" trial, 1969-70.
b. Jul 7, 1895 in Chicago, Illinois
d. Jul 1, 1983 in Chicago, Illinois
Source: *BioIn 8, 9, 11, 12, 13; ConAu 110; NewYTBS 83; PolProf NF; WhAm 8; WhoAm 82; WhoAmJ 80; WhoGov 77*

Hoffman, Malvina
American. Sculptor
Her greatest achievement: group of 101 life-size bronze statues, *Races of Mankind,* for the Field Museum, Chicago, 1930-35.
b. Jun 15, 1887 in New York, New York
d. Jul 10, 1966 in New York, New York
Source: *AmAu&B; BioIn 1, 2, 4, 5, 7, 8, 10, 14, 16, 20; ContDcW 89; CurBio 40, 66; DcAmArt; FacFETw; InWom; LegTOT; LibW; McGDA; OxCAmH; REnAL; WhAm 4; WhoAmA 89N, 91N, 93N; WomFir*

Hoffman, Paul Gray
American. Auto Executive, Statesman
First administrator of Marshall Plan, WW II; directed UN Development Program, 1959-72.
b. Apr 26, 1891 in Chicago, Illinois
d. Oct 8, 1974 in New York, New York
Source: *AmPeW; BiDAmBL 83; BiDInt; BioIn 1, 2, 3, 4, 5, 7, 8, 9, 10, 11, 13; CurBio 46, 74; DcAmB S9; DcAmDH 89; EncABHB 5; IntWW 74; LinLib S; NewYTBE 71; NewYTBS 74; WhAm 6; Who 74; WhoAm 74; WhoWor 74*

Hoffman, Rob
American. Publisher
Co-founder of *National Lampoon* following graduation from Harvard, 1969.
b. 1948?
Source: *WhoIns 92*

Hoffman, Robert C
"Mr. Physical Fitness"
American. Weightlifter, Businessman
Champion weightlifter; Olympic weightlifting coach, 1933.
b. 1899 in Tifton, Georgia
d. Jul 18, 1985 in York, Pennsylvania
Source: *ConAu 116*

Hoffmann, E(rnst) T(heodor) A(madeus)
German. Author
Master of weird, macabre; Offenbach's opera *Tales of Hoffmann* based on his work.
b. Jan 24, 1776 in Konigsberg, Prussia
d. Jun 25, 1822 in Berlin, Germany
Source: *Baker 78, 84, 92; BbD; Benet 96; BioIn 1, 3, 4, 5, 7, 8, 9, 10, 11, 13, 14, 15, 17; CamGWoT; CnOxB; DcArts; EncSF 93; EvEuW; IntDcOp; McGEWB; NewCBEL; NewEOp 71; NewGrDO; NinCLC 2; OxCEng 85, 95; OxCGer 86; PenC EUR; RAdv 14; RfGWoL 95; WorECar*

Hoffmann, Heinrich
German. Children's Author
Wrote children's classic *Struwwelpeter,* 1847, collection of graphic stories stressing morality.
b. Jun 1, 1809 in Frankfurt am Main, Germany
d. Sep 20, 1894 in Frankfurt am Main, Germany
Source: *BiD&SB; BioIn 8; EvEuW; NewCBEL; OxCEng 85, 95; OxCMed 86; WhoChL; WorECar; WrChl*

Hoffmann, Jan
German. Skater
World champion figure skater, 1980.
b. 1960?, German Democratic Republic

Hoffmann, Roald
American. Chemist
Shared 1981 Nobel Prize in chemistry for research on chemical reactions.
b. Jul 18, 1937 in Zloczow, Poland
Source: *AmMWSc 73P, 76P, 79, 82, 86, 89, 92, 95; BiESc; BioIn 8, 10, 12, 15, 16, 17, 19, 20; BlueB 76; ConAu 142; DrAPF 91; IntWW 74, 75, 76, 77, 78, 79, 80, 81, 82, 83, 89, 91, 93; LarDcSc; McGMS 80; NobelP; NotTwCS; RAdv 14; Who 83, 85, 88, 90, 92, 94; WhoAm 74, 76, 78, 80, 82, 84, 86, 88, 90, 92, 94, 95, 96, 97; WhoAmJ 80; WhoE 74, 83, 85, 86, 89, 91, 93, 95, 97; WhoFrS 84; WhoNob; WhoScEn 94, 96; WhoWor 82, 84, 89, 91, 93, 95, 96, 97; WhoWorJ 78; WorAlBi; WrDr 96*

Hoffner, Joseph, Cardinal
German. Religious Leader
Archbishop of Cologne, 1969-87; opposed liberalization of Roman Catholic Church.
b. Dec 24, 1906 in Trier, Germany
d. Oct 16, 1987 in Cologne, Germany (West)
Source: *BioIn 11, 15; IntWW 74, 75, 76, 77, 78, 79, 80, 81, 82, 83; NewYTBS 87; WhAm 11; WhoWor 74, 76, 78, 80, 82, 84, 87*

Hoffs, Susanna
[The Bangles]
American. Singer
Lead vocalist with all-female rock group, 1981-91; hits include "Walk Like an Egyptian," 1986; began solo career, 1991.
b. Jan 17, 1959 in Los Angeles, California
Source: *BioIn 15, 16; News 88-2*

Hofheinz, Roy Mark
American. Business Executive
Conceived idea of domed, air-conditioned stadium so Houston could attract NL baseball franchise, 1960.
b. Apr 10, 1912 in Beaumont, Texas
d. Nov 21, 1982 in Houston, Texas
Source: *BioIn 4, 6, 7, 8, 11, 12, 13, 21; CelR; NewYTBS 82; WhoAm 74, 76; WhoProB 73; WhoSSW 73, 75*

Hofmann, August Wilhelm von
German. Chemist
Noted for work in organic chemistry; a founder of German Chemical Society, 1867.
b. Apr 8, 1818 in Giessen, Germany
d. May 2, 1892 in Berlin, Germany
Source: *AsBiEn; BioIn 2, 5, 6, 8; CamDcSc; DcScB; InSci; LarDcSc; LinLib S; McGEWB; NewCol 75; WorInv*

Hofmann, Hans
German. Artist
His paintings inspired Abstract Expressionism movement.
b. Mar 21, 1880 in Weissenberg, Germany
d. Feb 17, 1966 in New York, New York
Source: *BioIn 1, 2, 3, 4, 5, 6, 7, 8, 9, 10, 11, 12, 13, 14, 17; BriEAA; CmCal; ConArt 77, 83; CurBio 58, 66; DcAmArt; DcAmB S8; DcArts; DcCAA 71, 77, 88, 94; IntDcAA 90; McGDA; McGEWB; OxCAmH; OxCTwCA; OxDcArt; PhDcTCA 77; REn; WebAB 74, 79; WhAm 4; WhAmArt 85; WhDW; WhoAmA 78N, 80N, 82N, 84N, 86N, 89N, 91N, 93N; WorAlBi; WorArt 1950*

Hofmann, Josef Casimir
American. Musician
Child prodigy, int'l concert pianist; famous for Chopin, Liszt interpretations.
b. Jan 20, 1876 in Podgorze, Poland
d. Feb 16, 1957 in Los Angeles, California
Source: *Baker 84; BioIn 9, 11; DcAmB S6; LinLib S; NatCAB 53; NewGrDM 80; NotTwCP; ObitT 1951; OxCAmH; OxCMus; WhAm 3*

Hofmannsthal, Hugo von
Austrian. Poet, Dramatist
Noted as librettist of Richard Strauss's operas.
b. Feb 1, 1874 in Vienna, Austria
d. Jul 15, 1929 in Rodaun, Austria
Source: *AtlBL; Benet 87, 96; BioIn 14, 15, 18, 21; BriBkM 80; CamGWoT; CasWL; ClDMEL 47, 80; CmOp; CnMD; CnMWL; CnThe; ConAu 106, 153; DcLB 81, 118; DcPup; DramC 4; EncWL, 2, 3; EncWT; Ent; EuWr 9; EvEuW; FacFETw; GrFLW; IntDcOp; IntDcT 2; LinLib L; MajMD 1; McGEWB; McGEWD 72, 84; MetOEnc; ModGL; ModWD; NewAmDM; NewC; NewCBEL; NewEOp 71; NewGrDM 80; NewGrDO; NotNAT B; OxCEng 85, 95; OxCGer 76, 86; OxCMus; OxCThe 67, 83; OxDcOp; PenC EUR; RAdv 14, 13-2; REn; REnWD; RGFMEP; TwCA SUP; TwCLC 11; TwCWr; WhDW*

Hofsiss, Jack Bernard
American. Director
Won Tony for *Elephant Man,* 1979.
b. Sep 28, 1950 in New York, New York
Source: *BioIn 15; VarWW 85; WhoAm 80, 82, 84*

Hofstadter, Richard
American. Historian
Analyst of American society; won Pulitzers for *The Age of Reform, Anti-Intellectualism in American Life.*
b. Aug 6, 1916 in Buffalo, New York
d. Oct 24, 1970 in New York, New York
Source: *AmAu&B; AmSocL; Benet 87, 96; BioIn 4, 8, 9, 10, 11, 13, 14, 15, 18, 19; ConAu 1R, 4NR, 29R; CurBio 56, 70; DcAmB S8; DcLB 17; EncAAH; EncAB-H 1974, 1996; EncWB; IntEnSS 79; LegTOT; OxCAmL 65, 83, 95; PenC AM; PolProf E; RAdv 14, 13-3; RComAH; REn; REnAL; ThTwC 87; WebAB 74, 79; WhAm 5; WorAl; WorAlBi; WorAu 1950*

Hofstadter, Robert
American. Physicist, Educator
Shared Nobel Prize in physics, 1961, with R L Moessbauer.
b. Feb 5, 1915 in New York, New York
d. Nov 17, 1990 in Palo Alto, California
Source: *AmMWSc 73P, 76P, 79, 82, 86, 89, 92; AnObit 1990; AsBiEn; BiESc; BioIn 6, 12, 14, 15, 17, 18, 20, 21; BlueB 76; CamDcSc; CurBio 91N; FacFETw; IntWW 74, 75, 76, 77, 78, 79, 80, 81, 82, 83, 89, 91N; LarDcSc; LegTOT; McGMS 80; NewYTBS 90; NobelP; NotTwCS; WebAB 74, 79; WhAm 10; Who 74, 82, 83, 85, 88, 90, 92N; WhoAm 74, 76, 78, 80, 82, 84, 86, 88, 90; WhoNob, 90, 95; WhoTech 82,*

84, 89, 95N; WhoWest 78, 80, 82, 84, 87, 89; WhoWor 74, 76, 78, 80, 82, 84, 87, 89, 91; WhoWorJ 78; WorAl; WorAlBi; WorScD

Hogan, Ben
[William Benjamin Hogan]
American. Golfer
One of the giants of modern golf; turned pro, 1931; won four US Opens, two Maste rs, one British Open, two PGAs; wrote *Power Golf,* 1948.
b. Aug 13, 1912 in Dublin, Texas
d. Jul 25, 1997 in Fort Worth, Texas
Source: *AmDec 1950; BiDAmSp OS; BioIn 1, 2, 3, 4, 5, 6, 7, 8, 9, 10, 11, 12, 13, 15, 16, 17, 18, 19; CelR; CurBio 48; FacFETw; IntWW 83, 91; LegTOT; NewYTBS 90; WebAB 74, 79; WhDW; WhoAm 76, 78, 80, 82, 84, 86, 88, 90, 92, 94, 95, 96; WhoGolf; WhoSpor; WorAl; WorAlBi*

Hogan, Hulk
[Terry Gene Bollea]
"Hulkamania"
American. Wrestler
Former World Wrestling Federation heavyweight champion.
b. Aug 11, 1953 in Augusta, Georgia
Source: *BioIn 14, 15, 16, 18; ConNews 87-3; ConTFT 13; IntMPA 96; LegTOT*

Hogan, Linda
American. Poet
Published poetry collections *Daughters, I Love You,* 1981; *Savings,* 1988.
b. Jul 16, 1947 in Denver, Colorado
Source: *AmWomWr SUP; BenetAL 91; BlmGWL; ConAu 45NR, 120; ConLC 73; GrWomW; NatNAL; NotNaAm; OxCAmL 95; OxCWoWr 95; TwCWW 91; WrDr 92, 94, 96*

Hogan, Paul
Australian. Actor
Wrote, directed, starred in *Crocodile Dundee,* 1986; *Crocodile Dundee II,* 1988; married co-star Linda Kozlowski, 1990.
b. Oct 8, 1939 in Lightning Ridge, Australia
Source: *BioIn 14, 15, 16; ConTFT 7, 14; CurBio 87; IntMPA 92, 94, 96; IntWW 91; WhoEnt 92; WhoHol 92; WhoWor 91, 95, 96; WorAlBi*

Hogarth, Burne
American. Cartoonist
Created, drew "Tarzan," 1937-50; pres., Pendragon Press, 1975-79.
b. Nov 25, 1911 in Chicago, Illinois
d. Jan 28, 1996 in Paris, France
Source: *BioIn 15, 17, 21; ConAu 93, 151; ConGrA 1; EncACom; IntAu&W 82; LegTOT; SmATA 63, 89; WhAm 11; WhoAm 90, 92, 94, 95, 96; WhoAmA 80, 82, 84, 86, 89, 91, 93; WhoE 81; WhoWest 87, 89, 92, 94, 96; WhoWor 87, 89, 91, 93; WorECom*

Hogarth, William
English. Artist, Engraver
Engraved series of morality scenes: *Rake's Progress,* 1735; *Marriage a la Mode,* 1745.
b. Nov 10, 1697 in London, England
d. Oct 26, 1764 in London, England
Source: *Alli; AntBDN Q; AtlBL; Benet 87, 96; BiHiMed; BioIn 1, 2, 3, 4, 5, 6, 7, 8, 9, 10, 11, 12, 13, 14, 15, 17, 18, 19; BkIE; BlkwCE; BlmGEL; CamGLE; ChhPo, S3; ClaDrA; ConGrA 2; DcArts; DcBiPP; DcBrECP; DcNaB; DcPup; Dis&D; EncEnl; IntDcAA 90; LegTOT; LinLib L, S; LngCEL; McGDA; McGEWB; NewC; NewCBEL; OxCArt; OxCEng 85, 95; OxCMus; OxDcArt; REn; WhDW; WorAl; WorAlBi; WorECom*

Hoge, James Fulton, Jr.
American. Editor
Editor, *Foreign Affairs,* 1992—; publisher, president, *New York Daily News,* 1985-91.
b. Dec 25, 1935 in New York, New York
Source: *BioIn 8, 10, 11; St&PR 91; WhoAm 74, 76, 78, 80, 82, 84, 86, 88, 90, 92, 94, 95, 96, 97; WhoE 86, 89, 91, 93, 95; WhoFI 89, 92; WhoMW 74, 76, 82*

Hogg, Ima
American. Philanthropist
Hogg Mental Health Foundation, Houston Symphony were two of civic projects she founded, supported.
b. Jul 10, 1882 in Mineola, Texas
d. Aug 19, 1975 in London, England
Source: *BioIn 10, 12, 13; InWom SUP; NewGrDA 86; NewYTBS 75; NotAW MOD*

Hogg, James
"The Ettrick Shepherd"
Scottish. Author
Wrote *The Queen's Wake,* 1813; *The Mountain Bard,* 1807.
b. 1770 in Ettrick, Scotland
d. Nov 21, 1835 in Yarrow, Scotland
Source: *Alli; AtlBL; BbD; Benet 87, 96; BiD&SB; BiDLA, SUP; BioIn 1, 2, 7, 8, 9, 12, 15, 17, 18; BlmGEL; BritAu 19; CamGEL; CamGLE; CasWL; CelCen; ChhPo, S1, S2; CmScLit; DcArts; DcEnA; DcEnL; DcEuL; DcLB 93, 116, 159; DcLEL; DcNaB, C; EvLB; GrWrEL N; LinLib L; LngCEL; MouLC 3; NewC; NewCBEL; NewCol 75; NinCLC 4; Novels; OxCEng 67, 85, 95; PenC ENG; RAdv 14; REn; RfGEnL 91; ScF&FL 1; SupFW; WebE&AL; WhoHr&F*

Hogrogian, Nonny
American. Illustrator
Children's book illustrator; won Caldecott for *Always Room for One More,* 1966.
b. May 7, 1932 in New York, New York
Source: *AuBYP 2, 3; BioIn 7, 8, 9, 10, 12, 14, 15; BkP; ChhPo S2; ChlBkCr; ChlLR 2; ConAu 2NR, 45, 49NR; IlsBYP; IlsCB 1957; MajAI; NewbC 1966; OxCChiL; SmATA, 1AS, 7, 74; ThrBJA; WhoAm 74, 76, 78; WhoAmA 76, 78; WhoAmW 68, 72; WhoE 74*

Hogwood, Christopher
English. Conductor, Musician
Founded Academy of Ancient Music, 1974.
b. Sep 10, 1941 in Nottingham, England
Source: *Baker 84; BioIn 13, 14, 15; ConAu 120, 127; CurBio 85; IntWW 91; IntWWM 90; NewAmDM; PenDiMP; Who 92; WhoAm 90; WhoEnt 92; WhoMus 72; WhoMW 92; WorAlBi*

Hohman, Donald
[The Hostages]
American. Hostage
One of 52 held by terrorists, Nov 1979 - Jan 1981.
b. 1943? in Yuma City, California
Source: *NewYTBS 81*

Hoiby, Lee
American. Composer, Pianist
Virtuoso concert pianist/romantic composer best known for opera *Summer and Smoke,* 1971, based on play by Tennessee Williams.
b. Feb 17, 1926 in Madison, Wisconsin
Source: *AmComp; ASCAP 66, 80; Baker 78, 84, 92; BiDAmM; BioIn 9, 12, 15; ConAmC 76, 82; CpmDNM 79; CurBio 87; DcCM; IntWWM 85, 90; MetOEnc; NewAmDM; NewGrDA 86; NewGrDM 80; NewGrDO; WhoAm 82, 84, 86, 88, 90, 92, 94, 95, 96, 97; WhoAmM 83; WhoEnt 92*

Hokinson, Helen
American. Cartoonist
Satirized middle-aged clubwomen in *The New Yorker,* 1925-49.
b. 1899 in Mendota, Illinois
d. Nov 1, 1949 in Washington, District of Columbia
Source: *DcAmB S4; NotAW; WebAB 74, 79*

Hokusai, Katsushika
Japanese. Engraver
Wood block prints, such as *Crabs,* had great effect on Western art.
b. Oct 1760 in Edo, Japan
d. May 10, 1849 in Edo, Japan
Source: *DcArts; McGEWB; OxCArt; REn; WhDW; WorECom*

Holabird, William
American. Architect
Established skeleton method of construction for tall buildings with Tacoma Building, 1888.
b. Sep 11, 1854 in Amenia Union, New York
d. Jul 19, 1923 in Evanston, Illinois
Source: *BiDAmAr; DcAmB; DcD&D; EncAAr 1; EncMA; IntDcAr; MacEA; McGDA; NatCAB 24; WebAB 74, 79; WhAm 1; WhoArch*

Holbein, Hans, the Elder
German. Artist
Late Gothic painter; religious works include altarpieces for Augsburg cathedral, 1493, several other churches.
b. 1465? in Augsburg, Germany
d. 1524 in Isenheim, France
Source: *McGDA; NewCol 75; OxDcArt; WebBD 83*

Holbein, Hans, the Younger
German. Artist
Called one of world's greatest portraitists; subjects included Erasmus, Henry VIII, Sir Thomas More; son of Hans the Elder.
b. 1497 in Augsburg, Germany
d. 1543 in London, England
Source: *AtlBL; Benet 87, 96; BioIn 1, 2, 3, 4, 5, 6, 7, 8, 9, 11, 12, 13; ClaDrA; DcArts; DcNaB; Dis&D; IntDcAA 90; LegTOT; LinLib S; LuthC 75; McGDA; McGEWB; NewC; OxCArt; OxCEng 85, 95; OxCGer 76, 86; OxDcArt; PenDiDA 89; REn; WebBD 83; WorAl; WorAlBi*

Holbrook, Hal
[Harold Rowe Holbrook, Jr]
American. Actor
Won Tony, NY Drama Critics citation for *Mark Twain Tonight,* 1966; won Emmy awards for "The Pueblo," 1973, "Sandburg's Lincoln," 1974-75, "The Senator," 1970-71; TV series "Evening Shade," 1990-94.
b. Feb 17, 1925 in Cleveland, Ohio
Source: *BiE&WWA; BioIn 5, 6, 7, 10, 14; BioNews 74; CamGWoT; CelR, 90; ConTFT 1, 7, 15; CurBio 61; FilmEn; FilmgC; HalFC 80, 84, 88; IntMPA 75, 76, 77, 78, 79, 80, 81, 82, 84, 86, 88, 92, 94, 96; LegTOT; LesBEnT 92; MotPP; NewYTBE 73; NotNAT; OxCAmT 84; VarWW 85; WhoAm 74, 76, 78, 80, 82, 84, 86, 88, 90, 92, 94, 95, 96, 97; WhoEnt 92; WhoHol 92, A; WhoThe 72, 77, 81; WorAl; WorAlBi*

Holbrook, Josiah
American. Educator
Founded lyceum movement for adult education, 1826; published weekly *Family Lyceum,* 1832.
b. 1788 in Derby, Connecticut
d. Jun 17, 1854 in Lynchburg, Virginia
Source: *AmAu; AmRef; BenetAL 91; BiDAmEd; BioIn 11, 14, 15; ChhPo S2; CyEd; DcAmB; DcNAA; McGEWB; NewCol 75; OhA&B; OxCAmH; OxCAmL 65, 83, 95; REnAL; WebAB 74, 79; WhAm HS*

Holbrook, Stewart Hall
American. Author, Journalist
Made history entertaining, yet accurate in books such as *The Age of Moguls,* 1953; *Wyatt Earp: US Marshall,* 1956.
b. Aug 22, 1893 in Newport, Vermont
d. Sep 3, 1964 in Portland, Oregon
Source: *AmAu&B; AuBYP 2, 3; BioIn 2, 4, 5, 7, 8, 9; ConAu P-1; DcAmB S7; NatLAC; OxCAmL 65, 83; REnAL; REnAW; SmATA 2; ThrBJA; TwCA SUP; WhAm 4; WhNAA; WhoPNW*

Holbrooke, Josef
English. Composer
Wrote Celtic-type trilogy, *The Cauldron of Anwyn,* 1912-29.
b. Jul 5, 1878 in Croydon, England
d. Aug 5, 1958 in London, England
Source: *Baker 78, 84; NewEOp 71; NewGrDM 80; ObitT 1951; WhLit*

Holbrooke, Richard
American. Diplomat
US ambassador to Germany, 1993-94.
b. c. 1941 in Scarsdale, New York
Source: *BioIn 10, 11; ConAu 135; IntYB 78, 79, 80, 81, 82; News 96, 96-2; WhoAmP 77, 79, 81, 83, 85, 87, 89, 91, 93, 95; WrDr 94, 96*

Holden, Fay
[Fay Hammerton]
English. Actor
Portrayed Mickey Rooney's mother in Andy Hardy film series.
b. Sep 26, 1895 in Birmingham, England
d. Jun 23, 1973 in Los Angeles, California
Source: *BioIn 9, 10; EncAFC; FilmEn; FilmgC; ForYSC; InWom SUP; MGM; MotPP; MovMk; NewYTBE 73; ThFT; Vers A; WhoHol B; WhScrn 77, 83*

Holden, William
[William Franklin Beedle, Jr.]
American. Actor
Starred in over 50 films; won Oscar for *Stalag 17,* 1953.
b. Apr 17, 1918 in O'Fallon, Illinois
d. Nov 16, 1981 in Santa Monica, California
Source: *AnObit 1981; BiDFilm, 81, 94; BioIn 2, 3, 4, 5, 6, 7, 8, 10, 11, 12, 13, 14, 16, 17, 18; BkPepl; BlueB 76; CelR; CmMov; CurBio 82, 82N; DcArts; DcTwCCu 1; FilmEn; FilmgC; ForYSC; GangFlm; HalFC 80, 84, 88; IntDcF 1-3, 2-3; IntMPA 75, 76, 77, 78, 79, 80, 81, 82; IntWW 79, 80, 81; ItaFilm; LegTOT; MotPP; MovMk; NewYTBS 81; OxCFilm; WhoAm 80; WhoHol A; WhScrn 83; WorAl; WorAlBi; WorEFlm*

Holder, Eric H., Jr.
American. Lawyer
First black to serve as US attorney for DC, 1993—.
b. c. 1951 in New York, New York
Source: *ConBlB 9; WhoAm 95, 96, 97; WhoAmL 94, 96*

Holder, Geoffrey
Actor
Won Tony Awards as director, costume designer of *The Wiz,* 1975.
b. Aug 1, 1930 in Port of Spain, Trinidad and Tobago
Source: *AfrAmAl 6; AfroAA; BiDD; BiE&WWA; BioIn 3, 13, 14, 15; BlkAWP; BlkOpe; CaribW 1; CnOxB; ConTFT 10; CurBio 57; DancEn 78; DcTwCCu 5; DrBlPA, 90; InB&W 85; NegAl 89; NotNAT; PlP&P A; ScF&FL 1; VarWW 85; WhoAfA 96; WhoAm 74, 78, 80, 82, 84, 86, 88, 92, 94, 95; WhoBlA 75, 77, 80, 85, 88, 90, 92, 94; WhoEnt 92; WhoHol 92, A; WhoThe 77, 81*

Holdereid, Kristine
American. Student
First woman to finish at head of class at US Naval Academy, 1984.
b. 1963?
Source: *BioIn 15*

Holderlin, Friedrich
German. Poet
Central figure of the German Classical-Romantic period.
b. Mar 20, 1770 in Lauffen, Germany
d. Jun 7, 1843 in Tubingen, Germany
Source: *AtlBL; Benet 87, 96; BiD&SB; BioIn 14, 17, 20; DcArts; DcEuL; DcLB 90; Dis&D; EncWT; EuAu; EuWr 5; GrFLW; LinLib L; McGEWD 72, 84; NewCBEL; NinCLC 16; OxCEng 85, 95; OxCGer 76, 86; PenC EUR; PoeCrit 4; RAdv 14, 13-2; RComWL; REn; WorAlBi; WrPh*

Holdren, Judd Clifton
American. Actor
Starred in 1950s film series *Captain Video; Zombies of the Stratosphere; Last Planet.*
b. Oct 16, 1915 in Iowa
d. Mar 11, 1974 in Los Angeles, California
Source: *WhoHol B; WhScrn 77*

Holiday, Billie
[Eleanora Fagan]
"Lady Day"
American. Singer
Renowned jazz vocalist; autobiography, *Lady Sings the Blues,* 1956, inspired film, 1972.
b. Apr 7, 1915 in Baltimore, Maryland
d. Jul 17, 1959 in New York, New York
Source: *AfrAmAl 6; AllMusG; AmCulL; AmDec 1940; Baker 78, 84; BiDAfM; BiDAmM; BiDJaz; BioAmW; BioIn 1, 4, 5, 6, 9, 10, 11, 12, 13, 14, 15, 16, 17, 18, 19, 20, 21; BlkWAm; CmpEPM; ConBlB 1; ConMus 6; ContDcW 89; DcAmB S6; DcAmNB; DcArts; DcTwCCu 5; DrBlPA, 90; EncWB; FacFETw; GoodHs; GrLiveH; HalFC 80, 84, 88; HanAmWH; HerW 84; IlEncJ; InB&W 80, 85; InWom, SUP; LegTOT; LibW; MusMk; NegAl 76, 83, 89; NewAmDM; NewGrDA 86; NewGrDJ 88, 94; NewGrDM 80; NewYTBE 72; NotAW MOD; NotBlAW 1; ObitT 1951; OxCPMus; PenEncP; RAdv 14; WebAB 74, 79; WhoHol B; WhoJazz 72; WomFir; WorAl; WorAlBi*

Holifield, Chet
[Chester Earl Holifield]
American. Politician
Chairman, Joint Committee on Atomic Energy, 1961-71; dem. rep. from CA, 1943-73.
b. Dec 3, 1903 in Mayfield, Kentucky
d. Feb 5, 1995 in Redlands, California
Source: *BiDrAC; BiDrUSC 89; BioIn 4, 5, 7, 10, 11, 12, 20, 21; CngDr 74; CurBio 55, 95N; PolProf E, J, K, NF; WhoAm 74, 76; WhoAmP 73, 75, 77; WhoGov 72, 75; WhoWest 74, 76*

Holinshed, Raphael
English. Editor
Best-known work *The Chronicles of England, Scotlande, and Irelande,* 1578.
d. 1580?
Source: *AtlBL; BbD; Benet 87, 96; BiD&SB; BioIn 3, 11; BlmGEL; BritAu; CamGEL; CamGLE; CasWL; CroE&S; DcBiPP; DcEnA; DcEnL; DcLB 167; DcNaB; LinLib L, S; LngCEL; NewC; NotNAT B; OxCEng 67, 85, 95; REn; RfGEnL 91*

Holladay, Wilhelmina Cole
"Billie"
American. Museum Director
Founded National Museum of Women in the Arts, Washington, DC, 1987.
b. Oct 10, 1922 in Elmira, New York
Source: *BioIn 15; CurBio 87; WhoAm 92; WhoAmA 86, 91; WhoAmW 83, 85, 87, 89, 91, 93, 95; WhoE 91; WhoWor 84, 87, 89, 91; WomFir*

Holland, Charles
American. Opera Singer
Expatriate; first black man to perform in Paris Opera House; Carnegie Hall debut, 1982.
b. Dec 27, 1909 in Norfolk, Virginia
d. Nov 7, 1987 in Amsterdam, Netherlands
Source: *AnObit 1987; Baker 92; BioIn 13; InB&W 85; NewAmDM; NewGrDA 86; NewGrDO*

Holland, Clifford Milburn
American. Engineer
Expert on underwater tunnel construction; chief engineer, NYC Holland Tunnel, 1919-24.
b. Mar 13, 1883 in Somerset, Massachusetts
d. Oct 27, 1924 in Battle Creek, Michigan
Source: *AmBi; ApCAB X; BioIn 3, 4, 8; DcAmB; InSci; NatCAB 19; WhAm 1*

Holland, Endesha Ida Mae
American. Dramatist
Won Lorraine Hansberry Award, 1981, for best play *The Second Doctor Lady.*
b. Aug 29, 1944 in Greenwood, Mississippi
Source: *ConBlAP 88; ConBlB 3; ConTFT 11; InB&W 85; WhoE 97; WhoEnt 92; WhoWor 96*

Holland, Jerome Heartwell
American. Diplomat, Business Executive
Ambassador to Sweden, 1970-72; chairman, American Red Cross, 1979-85.
b. Jan 9, 1916 in Auburn, New York
d. Jan 13, 1985 in New York, New York
Source: *BiDAmSp Sup; BioIn 6, 8, 9; ConAu 114; InB&W 80, 85; NewYTBS 85; SelBAAf; SelBAAu; WhAm 8; WhoAm 74, 76, 82, 84; WhoGov 72, 75*

Holland, John Philip
American. Inventor
Developed first submarine used by US Navy, 1900.
b. Feb 24, 1841 in Liscannor, Ireland
d. Aug 12, 1914 in Newark, New Jersey
Source: *ApCAB X; BioIn 3, 5, 6, 7, 14, 17, 20; DcAmImH; DcIrB 78, 88; LinLib S; WebAB 74*

Holland, Leland James
[The Hostages]
American. Hostage
One of 52 held by terrorists, Nov 1979 - Jan 1981.
b. 1928? in Shullsburg, Wisconsin
d. Oct 2, 1990 in Washington, District of Columbia
Source: *BioIn 12; NewYTBS 81, 90*

Holland, Robert, Jr.
American. Business Executive
Pres. and CEO, Ben & Jerry's Homemade Ice Cream, Inc., 1995-96.
b. Apr 1940 in Michigan
Source: *ConAu 33R; ConBlB 11; WhoAfA 96; WhoAm 96, 97; WhoFI 96*

Holland, Tom
American. Writer
Horror film screenplays include *Psycho II,* 1983; *Fright Night,* 1985.
b. Jul 11, 1943 in Poughkeepsie, New York
Source: *ConTFT 4; IntAu&W 91*

Holland, William Jacob
American. Naturalist, Clergy, Educator
Lepidoptera expert; wrote *Moth Book,* 1903.
b. Aug 16, 1848, Jamaica
d. Dec 13, 1932 in Pittsburgh, Pennsylvania
Source: *AmAu&B; AmBi; AmLY; BiDAmS; BioIn 9; DcAmAu; DcAmB S1; DcNAA; InSci; NatCAB 13; TwCBDA; WhAm 1*

Holland-Dozier-Holland
American. Composers
Motown songwriting and production team; wrote 37 Top 10 pop/r&b hits from 1963-67, including "Baby, I Need Your Loving," "Reach Out I'll Be There."
Source: *ConMus 5; EncRk 88; LegTOT; NewGrDA 86; OxCPMus; PenEncP; RolSEnR 83; SoulM; WhoBlA 77, 80; WhoRock 81; WhoRocM 82*

Hollander, John
American. Poet
Poetry collections include *The Night Mirror,* 1971, and *Harp Lake,* 1988.
b. Oct 28, 1929 in New York, New York
Source: *AmAu&B; AuBYP 2, 3; Benet 96; BenetAL 91; BioIn 8, 10, 12, 13, 15, 16; CamGLE; CamHAL; ChhPo, S1; ConAu 1NR, 1R, 52NR; ConLC 2, 5, 8, 14; ConPo 70, 75, 80, 85, 91, 96; CurBio 91; DcLB 5; DcLEL 1940; DrAP 75; DrAPF 80, 89, 91; DrAS 74E, 78E, 82E; IntAu&W 77, 82, 86, 89, 91; IntWW 78, 79, 80, 81, 82, 83, 89, 91, 93; IntWWP 77, 82; LinLib L; ModAL S2; OxCAmL 65, 83, 95; OxCTwCP; PenC AM; REnAL; RGTwCWr; SmATA 13; WhoAm 74, 76, 78, 80, 82, 84, 86, 88, 90, 92, 94, 95, 96, 97; WhoE 74; WhoTwCL; WhoUSWr 88; WhoWrEP 89, 92, 95; WorAu 1950; WrDr 76, 80, 82, 84, 86, 88, 90, 92, 94, 96*

Hollander, Xaviera
Dutch. Author
Former call girl who wrote of her experiences in *The Happy Hooker,* 1972.
b. 1943?
Source: *BioIn 12; InWom SUP; LegTOT*

Hollerith, Herman
American. Inventor
His invention of a tabulating machine was an important step in the development of the electronic computer.
b. Feb 29, 1860 in Buffalo, New York
d. Nov 17, 1929 in Washington, District of Columbia
Source: *BioIn 6, 8, 9, 12, 13, 14, 15; CamDcSc; DcAmB S1; HisDcDP; LarDcSc; RAdv 14; WebAB 74, 79; WhAm 4, HSA; WorInv*

Holley, Robert W(illiam)
American. Scientist, Educator
Shared 1968 Nobel Prize in medicine.
b. Jan 28, 1922 in Urbana, Illinois
d. Feb 11, 1993 in Los Gatos, California
Source: *AmMWSc 73P, 76P, 79, 82, 86, 89, 92; AsBiEn; BiESc; BioIn 7, 8, 14, 15, 18, 19, 20; CurBio 67, 93N; IntWW 91; LarDcSc; McGMS 80; NobelP; NotTwCS; WebAB 74, 79; WhAm 11; Who 92; WhoAm 74, 76, 78, 80, 82, 84, 86, 88, 90, 92; WhoE 74; WhoFrS 84; WhoNob, 90, 95; WhoTech 89; WhoWest 76, 78, 80, 82, 84, 87, 89, 92; WhoWor 74, 76, 78, 80, 82, 84, 87, 89, 91, 93; WorAl; WorAlBi; WorScD*

Holliday, Doc
[John Henry Holliday]
American. Dentist, Gambler, Criminal
Frontier gambler who was friend of Wyatt Earp and with him at OK Corral gunfight, 1882.
b. 1851 in Griffin, Georgia
d. Nov 8, 1887 in Glenwood Springs, Colorado
Source: *BioIn 11; LegTOT; OxCFilm; REnAW*

Holliday, Jennifer Yvette
American. Singer, Actor
Star of Broadway's *Dream Girls,* who had hit single from show: "And I'm Te lling You I'm Not Going," 1982.
b. Oct 19, 1960 in Riverside, Texas
Source: *BioIn 13; ConTFT 6; CurBio 83; DrBlPA 90; InB&W 80, 85; InWom SUP; NewYTBS 81; NotBlAW 1; PenEncP; RkOn 85; VarWW 85; WhoAm 88, 90, 92, 94, 95, 96, 97; WhoAmW 87, 89, 91, 93; WhoBlA 92; WhoEnt 92*

Holliday, Judy
[Judith Tuvim]
American. Actor
Won Oscar, 1950, for *Born Yesterday.*
b. Jun 21, 1922 in New York, New York
d. Jun 7, 1965 in New York, New York
Source: *BiDFilm, 94; BiE&WWA; BioAmW; BioIn 2, 3, 4, 5, 7, 11, 16, 17; CmMov; CurBio 51, 65; EncAFC; EncMcCE; EncMT; Ent; FilmEn; FilmgC; Funs; GoodHs; HalFC 80, 84, 88; InWom, SUP; LegTOT; MotPP; MovMk; NotNAT B; OxCAmT 84; OxCFilm; OxCPMus; QDrFCA 92; WhAm 4; WhoCom; WhScrn 77; WorAlBi; WorEFlm*

Holliday, Polly Dean
American. Actor
Starred in TV series "Alice," 1976-80; in own series Flo, 1981.
b. Jul 2, 1937 in Jasper, Alabama
Source: *BioIn 12, 13; ConTFT 7; InWom SUP; VarWW 85; WhoAm 80, 82, 84, 86, 88, 90, 92, 94, 95, 96, 97; WhoAmW 95, 97*

Hollies, The
[Bernie Calvert; Allan Clarke; Bobby Elliott; Eric Haydock; Tony Hicks; Graham Nash; Mikael Rikfors; Terry Sylvester]
English. Music Group
Most consistently successful band after The Beatles; hit single "He Ain't Heavy, He's My Brother," 1970.
Source: *BioIn 11, 12, 16, 17, 18; ConMuA 80A; EncPR&S 89; EncRk 88; EncRkSt; HarEnR 86; IlEncRk; OxCPMus; PenEncP; RkOn 78; RolSEnR 83; WhoRock 81; WhoRocM 82*

Holliger, Heinz
Swiss. Musician
International prize-winning oboist.
b. May 21, 1939 in Langenthal, Switzerland
Source: *Baker 78, 84, 92; BioIn 13, 14, 15; BriBkM 80; ConCom 92; CurBio 87; DcArts; DcCM; IntWW 74, 75, 76, 77, 78, 79, 80, 81, 82, 83, 89, 91, 93; IntWWM 90; NewAmDM; NewGrDM 80; NewOxM; PenDiMP; Who 82, 83, 85, 88, 90, 92, 94; WhoWor 82*

Holliman, Earl
[Anthony Numkena]
American. Actor
Starred, with Angie Dickinson, in TV series "Police Woman," 1974-78.
b. Sep 11, 1928 in Delhi, Louisiana
Source: *BioIn 5; ConTFT 3; FilmEn; FilmgC; HalFC 80, 84, 88; IntMPA 77, 84, 86, 88, 92, 94, 96; ItaFilm; LegTOT; MotPP; VarWW 85; WhoAm 78, 80, 82, 84, 86; WhoEnt 92; WhoHol 92, A*

Holling, Holling C(lancy)
American. Author, Naturalist
Wrote geo-historical fiction books for children: *Paddle to the Sea,* 1941.
b. Aug 2, 1900 in Holling Corners, Michigan
d. Sep 7, 1973 in California
Source: *AmAu&B; Au&ICB; AuBYP 2, 3; BioIn 1, 2, 3, 5, 7, 8, 12, 13; ConAu 106; IlsCB 1946, 1957; JBA 51; MajAI; SmATA 15; Str&VC; TwCChW 95*

Hollings, Ernest Frederick
"Fritz"
American. Politician
Dem. senator from SC, 1966—; govenor of SC, 1959-63.
b. Jan 1, 1922 in Charleston, South Carolina
Source: *AlmAP 78; WhoSSW 75, 76, 78, 80, 82, 84, 86, 88, 91, 93, 95; WhoWor 80, 82, 84, 87, 89, 91*

Holloman, Bobo
[Alva Lee Holloman]
American. Baseball Player
Pitcher, St. Louis Browns, 1953; one of three pitchers to throw a no-hitter in first ML appearance.
b. Mar 27, 1924 in Thomaston, Georgia
Source: *Ballpl 90; BioIn 3, 10; WhoProB 73*

Holloway, Emory
American. Author, Educator
Awarded Pulitzer Prize for biography of Walt Whitman, 1927.
b. Mar 16, 1885 in Marshall, Missouri
d. Jul 30, 1977 in Bethlehem, Pennsylvania
Source: *AmAu&B; BioIn 4, 11, 17; ConAu 49, 73; DcLB 103; DrAS 74E; OxCAmL 65, 83; REnAL; TwCA, SUP; WhAm 7; WhE&EA; WhLit; WhNAA*

Holloway, Stanley
English. Actor
Played Eliza Doolittle's father in *My Fair Lady,* 1964.
b. Oct 1, 1890 in London, England
d. Jan 30, 1982 in Littlehampton, England
Source: *AmPS B; AnObit 1982; BiDD; BiE&WWA; BioIn 4, 6, 8, 12, 13; BlueB 76; ConAu 106; CurBio 82, 82N; EncMT; EncWT; Ent; FacFETw; Film 2; FilmAG WE; FilmEn; FilmgC; ForYSC; HalFC 80, 84, 88; IlWWBF, A; IntDcF 1-3; IntMPA 77, 80, 82; LegTOT; MovMk; NewC; NewYTBS 82; NotNAT, A; OxCPMus; QDrFCA 92; WhAm 8; Who 74, 82; WhoHol A; WhoThe 72, 77, 81; WorAl*

Holloway, Sterling Price
American. Actor
Voice of many Disney animals, including Winnie the Pooh; supporting actor in over 100 films.
b. Jan 4, 1905 in Cedartown, Georgia
d. Nov 22, 1992 in Los Angeles, California
Source: *AnObit 1992; BiE&WWA; ConTFT 5; EncAFC; FilmgC; HalFC 88; IntMPA 92; MotPP; MovMk; NotNAT; PlP&P; VarWW 85; Vers B; WhoAm 86, 88; WhoEnt 92; WhoHol A*

Holloway, Wanda
American. Criminal
Texas mother convicted for putting a contract on a mother of a teen-age cheerleader, when her own daughter didn't make the squad.
b. 1954?

Hollowood, Albert Bernard
English. Editor, Economist
Editor, *Punch* magazine, 1957-68; wrote *Funny Money,* 1975.
b. Jun 3, 1910 in Burslem, England
d. Mar 28, 1981 in Guildford, England
Source: *Au&Wr 71; ConAu 9R, 103; IntWW 78; WhAm 7; WhE&EA; Who 74; WhoAm 74, 76; WrDr 80*

Holly, Buddy
[Buddy Holly and the Crickets; Charles Hardin Holley Holly]
American. Singer, Songwriter
Pioneered early, upbeat rock-and-roll: "Peggy Sue," 1957.
b. Sep 7, 1936 in Lubbock, Texas
d. Feb 3, 1959 in Clear Lake, Iowa
Source: *AmCulL; Baker 84, 92; BgBkCoM; BioIn 9, 10, 11, 12, 13, 15, 17, 19, 21; ConMuA 80A; ConMus 1; DcArts; EncPR&S 89; EncRk 88; FacFETw; HarEnCM 87; HarEnR 86; IlEncCM; IlEncRk; LegTOT; OnThGG; OxCPMus; PenEncP; RkOn 74; RolSEnR 83; TwCLC 65; WhAm 4; WhoRock 81; WorAl; WorAlBi*

Holly, James Theodore
American. Clergy
First Protestant Episcopal bishop of Haiti, 1874-1911.
b. Oct 3, 1829 in Washington, District of Columbia
d. 1911 in Port-au-Prince, Haiti
Source: *BioIn 5, 9; DcAmB; DcAmNB; InB&W 80; NatCAB 5; WhAm 1*

Holly, Lauren
[Mrs. Jim Carrey]
American. Actor
Appears on TV's "Picket Fences."
Source: *BioIn 17, 19, 20, 21; WhoHol 92*

Hollyer, Samuel
English. Engraver
Engravings include presidents Washington to Grant, Dickens, Tennyson, Longfellow.
b. Feb 24, 1826 in Landon, England

d. 1919
Source: *DcAmB; NewYHSD; WhAm 4; WhAmArt 85*

Hollywood Ten
[Alvah Bessie; Herbert Biberman; Lester Cole; Edward Dmytryk; Ring Lardner, Jr; John Howard Lawson; Albert Maltz; Samuel Ornitz; Adrian Scott; Dalton Trumbo]
American. Filmmakers
Blacklisted group who refused to testify before House Un-American Activities Committee about alleged membership in Communist Party; sentenced to jail, 1948.
Source: *BioIn 10, 14, 15, 16, 21; ConAu 131; ConDr 88A; Conv 1; CurBio 40, 41; DcLP 87A; DrAPF 83, 85, 87, 89, 91, 93, 97; FilmEn; FilmgC; HalFC 80, 88; IntvTCA 2; MajTwCW; NewYTBE 70; NewYTBS 76, 85; ObitOF 79; OxCFilm; PeoHis; PlP&P; SourALJ; WhoAmJ 80; WhoHol 92; WhoThe 81N*

Holm, Celeste
American. Actor
Won 1947 Oscar for *Gentleman's Agreement;* plus numerous TV appearances.
b. Apr 29, 1919 in New York, New York
Source: *BiDAmM; BiE&WWA; BioIn 2, 3, 7, 10, 11, 16, 18; CamGWoT; CelR 90; CmpEPM; ConTFT 1, 11; CurBio 44; EncAFC; EncMT; FilmEn; FilmgC; ForYSC; HalFC 80, 84, 88; HolP 40; IntMPA 77, 80, 84, 86, 88, 92, 94, 96; InWom SUP; LegTOT; MotPP; MovMk; NotNAT; NotWoAT; OxCAmT 84; OxCFilm; VarWW 85; WhoAm 74, 76, 84, 86, 88, 90, 92, 94, 95, 96, 97; WhoAmW 58, 61, 64, 66, 68, 95, 97; WhoEnt 92; WhoHol 92, A; WhoThe 72, 77; WorAl; WorAlBi*

Holm, Eleanor
American. Swimmer, Actor
Played Jane in *Tarzan's Revenge,* 1938; married to Billy Rose 14 years.
b. Dec 6, 1913
Source: *BiDAmSp BK; EncWomS; InWom SUP; WhoHol 92, A*

Holm, Hanya
[Johanna Kuntze]
American. Choreographer
Kiss Me, Kate, 1948 was only one of the many Broadway musicals she choreographed.
b. 1898 in Worms am Rhein, Germany
d. Nov 3, 1992 in New York, New York
Source: *BiDD; BioIn 1, 3, 4, 8, 11, 16; CnOxB; ContDcW 89; CurBio 54; FacFETw; HerW 84; IntDcWB; InWom SUP; LegTOT; NotNAT, A; NotWoAT; OxCAmT 84; WhoAm 90; WhoAmW 91; WhoThe 81*

Holm, Ian
[Ian Holm Cuthbert]
English. Actor
Received Oscar nomination for *Chariots of Fire,* 1981.
b. Sep 12, 1931 in Goodmayes, England
Source: *BiDFilm 94; ConTFT 2, 9; FilmEn; FilmgC; HalFC 88; IlWWBF; IntMPA 84, 86, 88, 92, 94, 96; IntWW 89, 91, 93; LegTOT; OxCThe 83; VarWW 85; Who 82, 83, 85, 88, 90, 92, 94; WhoAm 90, 92, 94, 95, 96, 97; WhoEnt 92; WhoHol 92, A; WhoThe 72, 77, 81; WhoWor 74, 95, 96, 97*

Holm, John Cecil
American. Dramatist, Actor
Co-wrote Broadway comedy *Three Men on a Horse.*
b. Nov 4, 1904 in Philadelphia, Pennsylvania
d. Oct 24, 1981 in Rhode Island
Source: *ASCAP 80; BenetAL 91; BiE&WWA; BioIn 1, 12; ConAu 116; ModWD; NotNAT; REnAL; ScF&FL 1, 92; WhoThe 72, 77, 81*

Holman, Bill
American. Cartoonist
Created, drew comic strip "Smokey Stover," 1935-75.
b. 1903 in Crawfordsville, Indiana
d. Feb 27, 1987 in New York, New York
Source: *ConGrA 3; EncACom; WorECom*

Holman, Eugene
American. Oilman
Pres., chm., Standard Oil Corp., 1944-60.
b. May 2, 1895 in San Angelo, Texas
d. Aug 12, 1962 in New York, New York
Source: *BiDAmBL 83; BioIn 1, 2, 5, 6; CurBio 48, 62; InSci; WhAm 4*

Holman, Libby
American. Singer, Actor
In Broadway musicals, 1920s-30s; torch singer known for sultry rendition of "Body and Soul."
b. May 23, 1906 in Cincinnati, Ohio
d. Jun 18, 1971 in Stamford, Connecticut
Source: *BiDAmM; BiE&WWA; BioAmW; BioIn 9, 12, 14, 15; CmpEPM; EncMT; NewYTBE 71; NotNAT B; OxCAmT 84; OxCPMus; PlP&P; What 1; WhoHol B; WhScrn 77, 83; WhThe*

Holman, Nat(han)
"Mister Basketball"
American. Basketball Player, Basketball Coach
Guard, Boston, 1921-28; one of first to have scoring average in double figures; coach, City College of NY, 37 yrs; Hall of Fame.
b. Oct 18, 1896 in New York, New York
d. Feb 12, 1995 in New York, New York
Source: *BasBi; BiDAmSp BK; BioIn 1, 2, 3, 4, 6, 8, 9, 10, 14, 20, 21; LegTOT; WhoAmJ 80; WhoBbl 73; WhoSpor; WhoWorJ 72, 78; WorAl*

Holme, Constance
English. Author
Wrote of common folk of English country life: *The Lonely Plough,* 1914; *The Trumpet in the Dust,* 1921.
b. Oct 7, 1880 in Milnthorpe, England
d. Jun 17, 1955 in Arnside, England
Source: *BioIn 14, 16; ConAu 118; DcLB 34; DcLEL; EvLB; FemiCLE; LngCTC; NewCBEL; OxCEng 67; TwCA SUP*

Holmes, Anna Marie
Canadian. Dancer
Performances with husband, David, include *Romeo and Juliet, Taras Bulba.*
b. Apr 17, 1943 in Mission City, British Columbia, Canada
Source: *BiDD; CreCan 1; IntWWM 85; WhoAmW 89; WhoEnt 92; WhoSSW 86*

Holmes, Arthur
English. Geologist, Educator
Laid foundations of isotope geology.
b. Jan 14, 1890 in Hebburn, England
d. Sep 20, 1965 in London, England
Source: *BiESc; BioIn 4, 7, 8, 20; CamDcSc; ConAu 116; DcNaB 1961; DcScB; InSci; LarDcSc; McGEWB; McGMS 80; NotTwCS; ObitT 1961; WhAm 4; WhE&EA; WhLit*

Holmes, Burton
American. Producer
Presented travelogues, 1890-1958; known for tag line: "Sun sinks slowly in the We st."
b. Jan 8, 1870 in Chicago, Illinois
d. Jul 22, 1958 in Hollywood, California
Source: *BioIn 1, 3, 5, 6, 10, 11; CurBio 58; NatCAB 44; WhAm 3; WhE&EA; WhNAA; WhoHol B; WhScrn 74, 77, 83*

Holmes, David
Canadian. Dancer
Known for performances with London Festival Ballet, Les Grandes Ballets Canadiens.
Source: *AmMWSc 92; ApCAB; BiAUS; BioIn 8, 16; CanWW 89; CreCan 2; Drake; ODwPR 91; Who 92; WhoAm 90; WhoAmA 91; WhoE 91*

Holmes, Hap
[Harold Holmes]
Canadian. Hockey Player
Goalie, Toronto, 1917-19, Detroit, 1926-28; Hall of Fame, 1972.
b. Apr 15, 1889 in Aurora, Ontario, Canada
d. Jun 27, 1941 in Florida
Source: *HocEn; WhoHcky 73*

Holmes, John Clellon
American. Author
Coined term "beat" describing literary, social rebels after WW II; *Nothing Mor e to Declare,* 1967, regarded as

definitive chronicle of Beat Generation.
b. Mar 12, 1926 in Holyoke, Massachusetts
d. Mar 30, 1988 in Middletown, Connecticut
Source: *AmAu&B; AnObit 1988; Au&Wr 71; BioIn 13, 15, 16, 20; CamGLE; ConAu 4NR, 9R, 125; ConLC 56; ConNov 72, 76, 82, 86; DcLB 16; DcLEL 1940; DrAF 76; DrAPF 80; IntAu&W 76, 77, 82, 89; NewYTBS 88; Novels; OxCAmL 65, 83, 95; PenC AM; RGTwCWr; WhAm 9; WhoAm 74, 76, 78, 80, 82, 84, 86; WhoE 74; WhoUSWr 88; WrDr 76, 80, 82, 84, 86, 88*

Holmes, John Haynes
American. Clergy, Social Reformer
Modernist Unitarian who combined religious, political beliefs; wrote *I Speak for Myself,* 1959.
b. Nov 9, 1879 in Philadelphia, Pennsylvania
d. Apr 3, 1964 in New York, New York
Source: *AmAu&B; AmDec 1930; AmLY; AmPeW; BenetAL 91; BiDAmLf; BiDAmM; BiDMoPL; BiDSocW; BioIn 1, 4, 5, 6, 7, 9, 12, 19; ChhPo S1; ConAu 89; CurBio 41, 64; DcAmB S7; DcAmReB 1, 2; DcAmSR; LinLib L, S; McGEWB; NatCAB 15; RelLAm 91; REnAL; TwCA SUP; WhAm 4; WhNAA*

Holmes, Larry
American. Boxer
Heavyweight champ, 1978-85; career record 48-2; lost title to Michael Spinks.
b. Nov 3, 1949 in Cuthbert, Georgia
Source: *AfrAmBi 1; AfrAmSG; BiDAmSp BK; BioIn 11, 12, 13, 16; CelR 90; CurBio 81; InB&W 85; IntWW 81, 82, 83, 89, 91, 93; LegTOT; NewYTBS 87; WhoAfA 96; WhoAm 80, 82, 84, 86, 88, 90, 92, 94, 95; WhoBlA 85, 88, 90, 92, 94; WhoSpor; WorAl; WorAlBi*

Holmes, Mary Jane Hawes
American. Author
Sentimental novels include *Lena Rivers,* 1856; *Marian Grey,* 1863.
b. Apr 5, 1825 in Brookfield, Massachusetts
d. Oct 6, 1907 in Brockport, New York
Source: *NotAW*

Holmes, Oliver Wendell, Sr.
American. Poet, Author, Essayist
First dean, Harvard Medical School, 1847-53; wrote *Elsie Venner,* 1861.
b. Aug 29, 1809 in Cambridge, Massachusetts
d. Oct 7, 1894 in Boston, Massachusetts
Source: *Alli, SUP; AmAu; AmAu&B; AmBi; AmCulL; AmWr S1; ApCAB; AsBiEn; AtlBL; BbD; Benet 87, 96; BenetAL 91; BibAL; BiDAmM; BiD&SB; BiDTran; BiESc; BiHiMed; BioIn 1, 2, 3, 4, 5, 6, 7, 8, 9, 10, 11, 12, 14, 16, 19; CamGEL; CamGLE; CamHAL; CasWL; CelCen; Chambr 3; ChhPo, S1, S2, S3; CnDAL; ColARen; CrtT 3, 4; CyAL 2; CyWA 58; DcAmAu; DcAmB; DcAmC; DcAmMeB, 84; DcAmSR; DcArts; DcBiA; DcBiPP; DcEnA; DcEnL; DcLB 1; DcLEL; DcNAA; Dis&D; Drake; EncAB-H 1974, 1996; EncPaPR 91; EvLB; GrWrEL N, P; HarEnUS; InSci; LegTOT; LinLib L, S; McGEWB; MorMA; MouLC 4; NatCAB 2; NewGrDA 86; NinCLC 14; Novels; OxCAmH; OxCAmL 65, 83, 95; OxCEng 67, 85, 95; OxCMed 86; PenC AM; PoChrch; RAdv 1, 14, 13-1; REn; REnAL; RfGAmL 87, 94; ScF&FL 1; ScFEYrs; SmATA 34; Str&VC; TwCBDA; WebAB 74, 79; WebE&AL; WhAm HS; WhDW; WorAl; WorAlBi; WorScD*

Holmes, Oliver Wendell, Jr.
"The Great Dissenter"
American. Supreme Court Justice
Liberal Supreme Court justice, 1902-32, known for frequent disagreement with conservative majority.
b. Mar 8, 1841 in Boston, Massachusetts
d. Mar 6, 1935 in Washington, District of Columbia
Source: *Alli SUP; AmAu&B; AmBi; AmDec 1910; AmJust; AmPolLe; ApCAB, X; AtlBL; Benet 87, 96; BenetAL 91; BiDFedJ; BioIn 1, 2, 3, 4, 5, 6, 7, 8, 9, 10, 11, 12, 13, 14, 15, 16, 17, 18, 19, 20, 21; CamGEL; CamHAL; CivWDc; ConAu 114; CopCroC; DcAmAu; DcAmB S1; DcAmC; DcNAA; EncAB-H 1974, 1996; FacFETw; GayN; HarEnUS; LegTOT; LinLib L, S; McGEWB; MemAm; NatCAB 12, 27; OxCAmH; OxCAmL 65, 83, 95; OxCLaw; OxCSupC; PeoHis; RAdv 13-3; RComAH; REn; REnAL; SupCtJu; ThTwC 87; TwCBDA; WebAB 74, 79; WhAm 1; WhAmP; WhCiWar; WhDW; WorAl; WorAlBi*

Holmes, Rupert
American. Singer, Songwriter
Wrote, recorded number one single "Escape (The Pina Colada Song)," 1979.
b. Feb 24, 1947 in Cheshire, England
Source: *ASCAP 80; BioIn 12, 15; ConDr 88D; ConTFT 13; LegTOT; NewYTBS 75; PenEncP; RkOn 85; WhoAm 82*

Holmes, Taylor
American. Actor
Had title role in *Ruggles of Red Gap,* 1918.
b. May 16, 1872 in Newark, New Jersey
d. Sep 30, 1959 in Hollywood, California
Source: *EncAFC; Film 1, 2; FilmgC; ForYSC; HalFC 80, 84, 88; MotPP; MovMk; TwYS; Vers A; WhScrn 74, 77, 83*

Holmes, Tommy
[Thomas Francis Holmes]
"Kelly"
American. Baseball Player
Outfielder, 1942-52; had 37-game hitting streak, 1945, longest in NL until broken by Pete Rose, 1978.
b. Mar 29, 1917 in New York, New York
Source: *Ballpl 90; BiDAmSp BB; BioIn 15, 20; WhoProB 73*

Holroyd, Michael De Courcy Fraser
English. Biographer
Works include *Lytton Strachey,* 1967-68; *Augustus John,* 1976 and *Bernard Shaw,* 1988-91.
b. Aug 27, 1935 in London, England
Source: *BioIn 8, 11, 16; ConAu 4NR, 18NR, 35NR, 53; CurBio 89; DcLEL 1940; IntAu&W 91; IntWW 91; MajTwCW; OxCEng 85, 95; Who 92, 94; WhoAm 90; WorAu 1970; WrDr 92*

Holst, Gustav Theodore
English. Musician, Composer
Remembered for symphonic suite, *The Planets,* 1914-17.
b. Sep 21, 1874 in Cheltenham, England
d. May 25, 1934 in London, England
Source: *Baker 78, 84; BioIn 1; BriBkM 80; DcCM; DcNaB 1931; GrBr; MusMk; NewGrDM 80; OxCMus; WhDW; WorAl*

Holt, A(ndrew) D(avid, Jr.)
American. University Administrator
Pres., U of TN, 1959-70; increased enrollment, funding.
b. Dec 4, 1904 in Milan, Tennessee
d. Aug 7, 1987 in Knoxville, Tennessee
Source: *BioIn 2; CurBio 49, 87, 87N*

Holt, Fritz
[George William Holt, III]
American. Producer
Best known for co-producing Broadway hit *La Cage Aux Folles,* 1983; revival of *Gypsy,* 1974.
b. 1941? in San Francisco, California
d. Jul 14, 1987 in Montclair, New Jersey

Holt, Harold Edward
Australian. Political Leader
Prime minister, 1966-67; supported Lyndon Johnson's escalation of Vietnam War.
b. Aug 5, 1908 in Sydney, Australia
d. Dec 17, 1967 in Port Philip Bay, Australia
Source: *BioIn 7, 8, 9; CurBio 66, 68; ObitT 1961; WhAm 4*

Holt, Henry
American. Publisher
Founded Henry Holt & Co. publishers, 1873; books include *The Cosmic Relations and Immortality,* 1919.
b. Jan 3, 1840 in Baltimore, Maryland
d. Feb 13, 1926 in New York, New York
Source: *Alli SUP; AmAu&B; AmBi; BiDPara; BioIn 4, 6; DcAmAu; DcAmB; DcNAA; EncO&P 1, 2, 3; MnBBF; NatCAB 9, 31; TwCBDA; WhAm 1*

Holt, Ivan Lee
American. Clergy
Pres. of World Methodist Conference, movement for Protestant unity.
b. Jan 9, 1886 in De Witt, Arkansas
d. Jan 12, 1967 in Atlanta, Georgia
Source: *BioIn 1, 7; EncWM; RelLAm 91; WhAm 4*

Holt, Jack
[Charles John Holt]
American. Actor
Father of Tim Holt; hero in many silent Westerns.
b. May 31, 1888 in Winchester, Virginia
d. Jan 18, 1951 in Los Angeles, California
Source: *BioIn 2; Film 1, 2; FilmEn; FilmgC; ForYSC; GangFlm; HalFC 80, 84, 88; MotPP; MovMk; NotNAT B; SilFlmP; TwYS; WhoHol B; WhScrn 74, 77, 83*

Holt, John Caldwell
American. Educator, Author
Wrote *How Children Fail,* 1964; sparked debate about quality of education in US.
b. Apr 14, 1923 in New York, New York
d. Sep 14, 1985 in Boston, Massachusetts
Source: *BioIn 8, 11, 14, 16, 17, 20; ConAu 69; CurBio 85; WhoAm 82*

Holt, Tim
[Charles John Holt, Jr.]
American. Actor
Best known for *Treasure of the Sierra Madre,* 1948.
b. Feb 5, 1918 in Beverly Hills, California
d. Feb 15, 1973 in Shawnee, Oklahoma
Source: *BioIn 8, 9, 10, 12, 15, 20; FilmEn; FilmgC; ForYSC; HolP 40; MotPP; MovMk; NewYTBE 73; What 2; WhoHol B; WhScrn 77*

Holtz, Lou
American. Actor
Comedian in revues, on radio in "Rudy Vallee Show"; "Bing Crosby Show."
b. Apr 11, 1898 in San Francisco, California
Source: *BiE&WWA; ConNews 86-4; EncMT; JoeFr; NotNAT; OxCAmT 84; WhoThe 77A; WhThe*

Holtz, Lou(is Leo)
American. Football Coach
Succeeded Gerry Faust as head football coach at Notre Dame, 1986-96.
b. Jan 6, 1937 in Follansbee, West Virginia
Source: *BiDAmSp Sup; BioIn 11, 12, 16; ConNews 86-4; CurBio 89; NewYTBS 76, 85; WhoAm 82, 84, 86, 88, 90, 92, 94, 95, 96, 97; WhoMW 93, 96; WorAlBi*

Holtzman, Elizabeth
American. Politician
Dem. congresswoman from NY, 1974-80.
b. Aug 11, 1941 in New York, New York
Source: *AlmAP 78; WomPO 78; WomStre; WorAl; WorAlBi*

Holum, Dianne
American. Skater
Won speed skating gold medal, 1972 Olympics.
b. 1952 in Northbrook, Illinois
Source: *BiDAmSp OS; BioIn 12; ConAu 123; InWom SUP; NewYTBE 72*

Holyfield, Evander
"The Real Deal"
American. Boxer
Became heavyweight boxing champion, 1990, defeated Buster Douglas; lost crown in 1992 to Riddick Bowe; regained championship, 1993-94; won bronze 1984, Olympics.
b. Oct 19, 1962 in Atmore, Georgia
Source: *AfrAmBi 1; BioIn 15, 16; BlkOlyM; ConBlB 6; CurBio 93; News 91, 91-3; NewYTBS 91; WhoBlA 92; WhoSpor*

Holyoake, Keith Jacka, Sir
New Zealander. Political Leader
Prime minister, 1960-72; governor general, 1977-80.
b. Feb 11, 1904 in Pahiatua, New Zealand
d. Dec 8, 1983 in Wellington, New Zealand
Source: *AnObit 1983; BioIn 5, 6, 13, 14; CurBio 84N; DcTwHis; EncWB; FacFETw; IntWW 74, 75, 76, 77, 78, 79, 80, 81, 82, 83; NewYTBS 83; Who 74, 82, 83; WhoGov 72; WhoWor 74, 78, 80, 82*

Holzer, Harold
American. Author, Editor
Award-winning books on Abraham Lincoln include *The Lincoln Image,* 1984.
b. Feb 5, 1949 in New York, New York
Source: *ConAu 39NR, 116; ODwPR 91; WhoE 93, 95, 97*

Holzer, Jenny
American. Artist
Her textual works consist of statements from bland to inflammatory, such as "Money creates taste," which have appeared on T-shirts to huge LED signboards during 1980s.
b. Jul 29, 1950 in Gallipolis, Ohio
Source: *BioIn 13, 15, 16; ConArt 89, 96; CurBio 90; IntWW 89, 91, 93; NewYTBS 89; NorAmWA; WhoAm 95, 96, 97; WhoAmA 84, 86, 89, 91, 93; WhoE 89, 95, 97; WorArt 1980*

Holzman, Red
[William Holzman]
American. Basketball Coach
Coach, 1953-82, mostly with NY; won NBA championships, 1970, 1973; coach of yr., 1970; Hall of Fame, 1985.
b. Aug 10, 1920 in New York, New York
Source: *BasBi; BiDAmSp BK; BioIn 15, 16; ConAu 101; LegTOT; NewYTBE 73; OfNBA 87; WhoAm 74, 76, 78, 80; WhoBbl 73; WhoE 81; WhoSpor; WorAl*

Home, Daniel Douglas
English. Psychic
Noted spiritualist medium; seances attended by prominent people.
b. Mar 20, 1833, Scotland
d. Jun 21, 1886 in Auteuil, France
Source: *Alli SUP; AmBi; ApCAB; BiDPara; DcNaB; Drake; NewC; OxCEng 67; REn*

Home, William Douglas
English. Dramatist
Plays include *Now Barabbas,* 1947; *The Chiltern Hundreds,* 1947; *The Reluctant Debutante,* 1956.
b. Jun 3, 1912 in Edinburgh, Scotland
d. Sep 23, 1992 in Alresford, England
Source: *AnObit 1992; Au&Wr 71; BiE&WWA; BioIn 3, 4, 9, 10, 11, 12, 13, 16, 18, 19; CamGLE; CamGWoT; CnMD; CnThe; ConAu 102, 139; ConDr 73, 77, 82, 88, 93; ConLC 76; CroCD; DcLB 13; DcLEL 1940; EncWT; Ent; GrWrEL DR; IntAu&W 76, 77, 89, 91, 93; ModWD; NotNAT; OxCThe 83; PlP&P; Who 74, 82, 83, 85, 88, 92; WhoThe 72, 77, 81; WorAu 1970; WrDr 76, 80, 82, 84, 86, 88, 90, 92, 94N*

Homer
Greek. Author
Credited with writing *The Iliad; The Odyssey.*
b. 750BC
Source: *AtlBL; BbD; Benet 87; BiD&SB; CasWL; ClMLC 16; CyWA 58; DcBiA; DcEnL; DcEuL; EncSF; GrFLW; NewC; OxCClL 89; OxCEng 67; PenC CL; PlP&P; RAdv 13-2; RComWL; WorAlBi*

Homer, Louise
[Louise Dilworth Beatty]
American. Opera Singer
Leading contralto with NY Met., 1900-19; starred with Enrico Caruso in *Samson and Dalila.*
b. Apr 28, 1871 in Sewickley, Pennsylvania
d. May 6, 1947 in Winter Park, Florida
Source: *Baker 78, 84; BiDAmM; BioAmW; BioIn 14, 21; BriBkM 80; CmOp; DcAmB S4; IntDcOp; MetOEnc; MusSN; NewEOp 71; NewGrDA 86; NewGrDM 80; NotAW; OxDcOp; PenDiMP; WhAm 2; WomWWA 14*

Homer, Sidney
American. Composer
Published over 100 songs: "Song of the Shirt," "Sweet and Low"; husband of Louise.
b. Dec 9, 1864 in Boston, Massachusetts
d. Jul 10, 1953 in Winter Park, Florida
Source: *ASCAP 66, 80; Baker 78, 84, 92; BenetAL 91; BiDAmM; BioIn 1, 3, 21; EncAB-A 24; NewGrDA 86; NewGrDM 80; OxCAmL 65, 83; OxCMus; REnAL; WhAm 3*

Homer, Winslow
American. Artist
Excelled in watercolors of seascapes, including *Breaking Storm, Maine Coast.*
b. Feb 24, 1836 in Boston, Massachusetts
d. Sep 29, 1910 in Prouts Neck, Maine
Source: *AmBi; AmCulL; ApCAB; ArtsNiC; AtlBL; Benet 87, 96; BioIn 1, 2, 3, 4, 5, 6, 7, 8, 9, 10, 11, 12, 13, 14, 15, 16, 17, 18, 19, 21; BriEAA; ChhPo, S1, S2, S3; CivWDc; DcAmArt; DcAmB; DcArts; DcSeaP; EarABI, SUP; EncAB-H 1974, 1996; GayN; IntDcAA 90; LegTOT; LinLib S; McGDA; McGEWB; MorMA; NatCAB 11; NewYHSD; OxCAmH; OxCAmL 65; OxCArt; OxCChiL; OxDcArt; PeoHis; RComAH; REn; REnAL; TwCBDA; WebAB 74, 79; WhAm 1; WhAmArt 85; WhCiWar; WhDW; WhFla; WorAl; WorAlBi*

Homer and Jethro
[Kenneth C Burns; Homer Haynes]
American. Musicians
Country music comedy duo; known for parodies of popular songs after WW II; "Baby Its Cold Outside," 1948, "Hound Dog in Winter," 1953.
Source: *BgBkCoM; BiDAmM; CounME 74, 74A; EncFCWM 69, 83; HarEnCM 87; IlEncCM; PenEncP; WhoCom*

Homolka, Oscar
Austrian. Actor
Oscar nominee for *I Remember Mama,* 1948.
b. Aug 12, 1903 in Vienna, Austria
d. Jan 27, 1978 in Sussex, England
Source: *BiDFilm; BiE&WWA; ForYSC; MovMk; NotNAT; OxCFilm*

Honda, Ishiro
Japanese. Director
Directed Godzilla monster movie series in the 1950s.
b. 1912, Japan
d. Feb 28, 1993 in Tokyo, Japan
Source: *AnObit 1993*

Honda, Soichiro
Japanese. Auto Executive
Began producing motorcycles, 1948; founded Honda Motor Co., 1973, first Japanese auto company to build factories in U.S; inducted into Automotive Hall of Fame, 1989.
b. Nov 17, 1906 in Iwata Gun, Japan
d. Aug 5, 1991 in Tokyo, Japan
Source: *AnObit 1991; BioIn 7, 8, 10, 11, 13, 15, 16, 17, 18, 19; ConNews 86-1; Entr; FarE&A 78, 79, 80, 81; IntWW 74, 75, 76, 77, 78, 79, 80, 81, 82, 83, 89, 91; LegTOT; News 92, 92-1; NewYTBS 77, 91; WhAm 10; WhoFI 74; WhoWor 74, 78, 80, 82; WorAlBi*

Hone, William
English. Author
Wrote political satires; popular compilation of facts: *Every Day Book,* 1826-27.
b. Jun 3, 1780 in Bath, England
d. Nov 6, 1842 in Tottenham, England
Source: *Alli; BiD&SB; BioIn 4, 6, 9, 17; BritAu 19; CasWL; CelCen; Chambr 2; DcAmB; DcEnL; DcLB 110, 158; DcLEL; DcNaB; DcPup; EvLB; NewC; NewCBEL; NewCol 75; OxCEng 67, 85, 95*

Honecker, Erich
German. Politician
First, general secretary, central committee, Socialist Unity Party; most powerful man in East Germany, 1971-89.
b. Aug 25, 1912 in Wiebelskirchen, Germany
d. May 29, 1994 in Santiago, Chile
Source: *BioIn 9, 10, 12, 13, 16; CurBio 72, 94N; DcTwHis; EncCW; EncGRNM; EncWB; FacFETw; IntWW 74, 75, 76, 77, 78, 79, 80, 81, 82, 83, 89, 91, 93; IntYB 82; News 94; NewYTBE 73; NewYTBS 94; PolLCWE; WhAm 11; WhoSocC 78; WhoSoCE 89; WhoWor 74, 76, 78, 80, 82, 84, 87, 89, 91*

Honegger, Arthur
[Les Six]
French. Composer
Member of avant-garde "Group of Six"; wrote *Le Roi David,* 1921; *Pacifi c 231,* 1923, describing a locomotive; composed several film scores.
b. Mar 10, 1892 in Le Havre, France
d. Nov 27, 1955 in Paris, France
Source: *AtlBL; Baker 78, 84; Benet 87; BiDD; BioIn 1, 2, 3, 4, 6, 7, 8, 9, 12, 20; BriBkM 80; CmOp; CnOxB; CompSN, SUP; CurBio 41, 56; DancEn 78; DcArts; DcCM; DcCom 77; DcCom&M 79; DcFM; DcTwCC; DcTwCCu 2; FacFETw; FilmEn; FilmgC; HalFC 80, 84, 88; IntDcB; IntDcF 1-4, 2-4; IntDcOp; ItaFilm; LegTOT; LuthC 75; McGEWB; MetOEnc; MusMk; NewAmDM; NewEOp 71; NewGrDM 80; NewGrDO; NewOxM; NotNAT B; ObitT 1951; OxCFilm; OxCMus; OxDcOp; PenDiMP A; REn; WhAm 4; WhDW; WorEFlm*

Honeycombs, The
[Denis Dalziel; Ann "Honey" Lantree; John Lantree; Martin Murray; Alan Ward]
English. Music Group
"British Invasion" group, formed 1963; first to have female drummer.
Source: *EncRkSt; PenEncP; RkOn 78; RolSEnR 83*

Honeydrippers, The
[Jeff Beck; Jimmy Page; Robert Plant; Nile Rodgers]
English. Music Group
Formed to record album of old rock songs: hit single "Sea of Love," 1984.
Source: *BioIn 14, 15, 16, 17, 18, 19; ConMuA 80A, 80B; EncPR&S 89; NewGrDA 86; NewYTBS 85; RkOn 85; WhoAfA 96; WhoBlA 94; WhoRocM 82*

Honeyman-Scott, James
[The Pretenders]
"Jimmy Honeyman-Scott"
English. Musician
Guitarist, keyboardist with British pop group, 1980-82.
b. Oct 27, 1957 in Hereford, England
d. Jun 16, 1982 in London, England

Honeywell, Mark Charles
American. Inventor, Manufacturer
Founded Honeywell Heating Specialty Co., 1906; improved water heating systems controls.
b. Dec 29, 1874 in Wabash, Indiana
d. Sep 13, 1964 in Indianapolis, Indiana
Source: *BioIn 7, 9; NatCAB 52; WhAm 4*

Honwana, Luis Bernardo
Mozambican. Writer
Noted African short story writer; stories reflect village life in his native country; works include *Nos Matamos a Cao Tinhosa,* 1964
b. Nov 1942 in Lourenco Marques, Mozambique
Source: *AfrA; BioIn 14; LiExTwC*

Hooch, Pieter de
Dutch. Artist
Genre painter: *Courtyard of a Dutch House,* 1658.
b. Dec 20, 1629? in Rotterdam, Netherlands
d. 1683? in Amsterdam, Netherlands
Source: *AtlBL; BioIn 7, 12, 19; ClaDrA; DcArts; IntDcAA 90; McGDA; McGEWB; NewCol 75; OxCArt; OxDcArt; WhDW*

Hood, Darla Jean
[Our Gang]
American. Actor
Curly-headed sweetheart of *Our Gang* comedies, 1935-42.
b. Nov 4, 1931 in Leedey, Oklahoma
d. Jun 13, 1979 in Canoga Park, California
Source: *BioIn 10; NewYTBS 79; WhoHol A*

Hood, John Bell
American. Military Leader
Confederate general; led Confederate Army in unsuccessful defense of Atlanta, 1864.

b. Jun 1, 1831 in Owingsville, Kentucky
d. Aug 30, 1879 in New Orleans, Louisiana
Source: *Alli SUP; AmBi; ApCAB; BenetAL 91; BiDConf; BiDSA; BioIn 1, 2, 5, 7, 8, 9, 11, 13, 17, 19; CivWDc; DcAmAu; DcAmB; DcAmMiB; DcNAA; EncSoH; HarEnMi; HarEnUS; LinLib S; NatCAB 4; OxCAmH; TwCBDA; WebAB 74, 79; WebAMB; WhAm HS; WhCiWar; WhoMilH 76; WorAl; WorAlBi*

Hood, Raymond Matthewson
American. Architect
Collaborated on Rockefeller Center, NYC, 1930s, Tribune Tower, Chicago, 1922.
b. Mar 29, 1881 in Pawtucket, Rhode Island
d. Aug 14, 1934 in Stamford, Connecticut
Source: *AmBi; DcAmB S1; WebBD 83; WhAm 1*

Hood, Thomas
English. Author
Edited *Comic Annuals,* 1830-42; wrote serious poem "Song of the Shirt," 184 3.
b. May 23, 1799 in London, England
d. May 3, 1845 in London, England
Source: *Alli; AnCL; AtlBL; BbD; Benet 87, 96; BiD&SB; BioIn 1, 2, 3, 4, 6, 8, 9, 10, 12, 13, 15, 16, 17; BlmGEL; BritAS; BritAu 19; BritWr 4; CamGEL; CamGLE; CarSB; CasWL; CelCen; Chambr 3; ChhPo, S1, S2, S3; CnE&AP; CrtT 2, 4; DcArts; DcBrBI; DcBrWA; DcEnA; DcEnL; DcEuL; DcLB 96; DcLEL; DcNaB; EvLB; GrWrEL P; LinLib L, S; LngCEL; MouLC 3; NewC; NewCBEL; NinCLC 16; OxCEng 67, 85, 95; PenC ENG; PenEncH; REn; RfGEnL 91; ScF&FL 1; Str&VC; VicBrit; WebE&AL; WhDW*

Hooft, Pieter Corneliszoon
Dutch. Historian
Noted for history of Netherlands revolt against Spain, *Nederlandsche Historien,* 1628-47.
b. Mar 16, 1581 in Amsterdam, Netherlands
d. May 21, 1647 in The Hague, Netherlands
Source: *BiD&SB; BioIn 7; CasWL; DcEuL; EvEuW; NewCol 75; OxCThe 83; PenC EUR; RfGWoL 95*

Hook, Sidney
American. Philosopher, Educator
Social philosopher; with NYU, 1927-69; strong exponent of liberal democracy; one of the early analyzers of Marxism.
b. Dec 20, 1902 in New York, New York
d. Jul 12, 1989 in Stanford, California
Source: *AmAu&B; AmDec 1940; AnObit 1989; BiDAmEd; BiDAmLf; BioIn 2, 3, 4, 8, 9, 11, 12, 13, 14, 15, 16, 17, 18, 21; BlueB 76; CelR; ColdWar 1; ConAu 7NR, 9R, 129; CurBio 88, 89N; DcAmC; DrAS 74P, 78P, 82P; EncAB-H 1996; EncAL; EncUnb; EncWB; FacFETw; IntAu&W 82, 86, 91; IntEnSS 79; IntWW 74, 75, 76, 77, 78, 79, 80, 81, 82, 83, 89; LEduc 74; MakMC; NewYTBS 87, 89; OxCPhil; PeoHis; PolProf E; RAdv 14, 13-4; REnAL; ThTwC 87; TwCA SUP; WhAm 10; WhE&EA; Who 74, 82, 83, 85, 88, 90, 92; WhoAm 74, 76, 78, 80, 82, 84, 86, 88; WhoAmJ 80; WhoWorJ 72, 78; WrDr 80, 82, 84, 86, 88*

Hook, Theodore Edward
English. Author, Humorist
Edited *John Bull,* 1820; popular racy novels include *Maxwell,* 1830.
b. Sep 22, 1788 in London, England
d. Aug 24, 1841 in London, England
Source: *Alli; BbD; BiD&SB; BiDLA; BioIn 9, 10, 12; BritAu 19; CamGEL; CamGLE; CasWL; CelCen; Chambr 3; ChhPo, S1; DcBiPP; DcEnA; DcEnL; DcEuL; DcLEL; DcNaB; EvLB; GrWrEL N; NewC; NewCBEL; OxCEng 67, 85, 95*

Hooke, Robert
English. Scientist, Philosopher
Discovered Hooke's Law of Elasticity, 1678; invented spiral spring in watches; c onstructed early telescope; coined term "cell."
b. Jul 18, 1635 in Isle of Wight, England
d. Mar 3, 1703 in London, England
Source: *Alli; AsBiEn; BiDBrA; BiESc; BiHiMed; BioIn 2, 3, 4, 5, 6, 7, 9, 11, 12, 13, 14, 15, 18; CamDcSc; DcBiPP; DcD&D; DcEnL; DcInv; DcNaB; DcScB; Dis&D; InSci; LarDcSc; MacEA; McGDA; McGEWB; NewCBEL; NewCol 75; NewGrDM 80; OxCArt; OxCMed 86; WhDW; WorAl; WorAlBi; WorInv; WorScD*

Hooker, Brian
American. Dramatist, Librettist
Wrote librettos for Broadway shows, 1920s-30s, including *Vagabond King,* 1925.
b. Nov 2, 1880 in New York, New York
d. Dec 28, 1946 in New London, Connecticut
Source: *ASCAP 66, 80; BenetAL 91; BiDAmM; BioIn 1; ChhPo, S1; CmpEPM; DcNAA; EncMT; NewEOp 71; NotNAT B; OxCAmL 65, 83; OxCAmT 84; REn; REnAL; WhAm 2*

Hooker, John Lee
"Doctor Feelgood"; "Godfather of Blues"; "King of the Boogie"; "The Hook"
American. Singer
One of the earliest recorded blues greats; had rhythm and blues million-seller, 1949, "Boogie Chillin'."
b. Aug 22, 1917 in Clarksdale, Mississippi
Source: *BiDAfM; BiDAmM; BioIn 12, 16; BluesWW; ConMus 1; DcArts; DcTwCCu 5; DrBlPA 90; EncFCWM 69, 83; EncPR&S 89; EncRk 88; GuBlues; HarEnR 86; IlEncBM 82; IlEncJ; InB&W 85; LegTOT; NewAmDM; NewGrDA 86; NewGrDM 80; OnThGG; OxCPMus; PenEncP; RolSEnR 83; WhoAfA 96; WhoAm 74, 76, 78, 80, 82, 84, 86, 88, 90, 92, 94, 95, 96, 97; WhoBlA 75, 77, 80, 85, 88, 90, 92, 94; WhoEnt 92; WhoRock 81; WhoRocM 82*

Hooker, Joseph
"Fighting Joe"
American. Military Leader
Union general in Civil War; commanded Army of the Potomac, 1862-63.
b. Nov 13, 1814 in Hadley, Massachusetts
d. Oct 31, 1879 in Garden City, New York
Source: *AmBi; ApCAB; BioIn 1, 3, 6, 7, 20; CivWDc; DcAmB; DcAmMiB; HarEnMi; HarEnUS; LinLib S; NatCAB 4; OxCAmH; TwCBDA; WebAB 74, 79; WebAMB; WhAm HS; WhCiWar; WhoMilH 76; WorAl; WorAlBi*

Hooker, Richard
English. Theologian
Staunch Anglican; opposed Calvinism, defended Church of England, 1590s.
b. Mar 1554 in Heavitree, England
d. Nov 2, 1600 in Bishopsbourne, England
Source: *Alli; BbD; Benet 87, 96; BiD&SB; BioIn 1, 2, 3, 4, 6, 7, 9, 10, 11, 12; BritAu; CamGLE; CasWL; Chambr 1; CroE&S; CrtT 1, 4; DcEnA; DcEnL; DcEuL; DcLB 132; DcLEL; DcNaB; EvLB; LuthC 75; McGEWB; NewC; NewCBEL; OxCEng 67, 85, 95; PenC ENG; REn; RfGEnL 91; WebE&AL*

Hooker, Thomas
English. Clergy
Emigrated to MA, 1633; founded Hartford, CT, 1636.
b. Jul 7, 1586 in Marfield, England
d. Jul 19, 1647 in Hartford, Connecticut
Source: *Alli; AmAu; AmAu&B; AmBi; AmWrBE; ApCAB; BenetAL 91; BiD&SB; BioIn 3, 4, 9, 11, 14, 17, 19; CamGLE; CamHAL; CnDAL; CyAL 1; DcAmAu; DcAmB; DcAmReB 1, 2; DcAmSR; DcBiPP; DcLB 24; DcLEL; DcNaB; Drake; EncAB-H 1974, 1996; EncARH; EncCRAm; HarEnUS; LinLib L, S; LuthC 75; McGEWB; NatCAB 6; NewC; OxCAmH; OxCAmL 65, 83, 95; PenC AM; REnAL; WebAB 74, 79; WhAm HS; WhDW; WorAl; WorAlBi; WrCNE*

Hooker, William Jackson, Sir
English. Botanist
First director, Royal Botanic Gardens at Kew, 1841-65; fern expert; wrote *British Flora,* 1830.
b. Jul 6, 1785 in Norwich, England
d. Aug 12, 1865 in Kew, England
Source: *Alli, SUP; BbD; BbtC; BiD&SB; BiDLA; BiESc; BioIn 2, 4, 8, 14; BritAu 19; CelCen; DcBiPP; DcBrWA; DcNaB; DcScB; InSci; LarDcSc; NewC; NewCBEL; NewCol 75; WhDW*

Hooks, Bell
[Gloria Jean Watkins]
American. Writer
Writer on racism in the United States; wrote *Yearning: Race, Gender, and Cultural Politics,* 1990.
b. Sep 25, 1952 in Hopkinsville, Kentucky
Source: *AmWomWr SUP; ConBlB 5; ConLC 94; CurBio 95; DcTwCCu 5; NotBlAW 2; RadHan; WhoAm 97*

Hooks, Benjamin Lawson
American. Civil Rights Leader, Clergy
Executive Director, NAACP, 1977-93, succeeding Roy Wilkins; won Spingarn, 1986.
b. Jan 31, 1925 in Memphis, Tennessee
Source: *AfrAmBi 1; AfrAmOr; AmSocL; BioIn 9, 10, 11, 12, 13, 14, 16; BioNews 74; CelR 90; CivR 74; CurBio 78; Ebony 1; EncAACR; EncWB; InB&W 80, 85; LesBEnT 92; NegAl 76, 89; NewYTBE 72; NewYTBS 76, 79, 92; NewYTET; WhoAfA 96; WhoAm 86, 90, 92, 94, 95, 96, 97; WhoAmL 83; WhoAmP 91; WhoBlA 80, 85, 88, 90, 92, 94; WorAlBi*

Hooks, Jan
American. Actor
TV shows include *Saturday Night Live,* 1986-91; *Designing Women,* 1991—.
b. 1958

Hooks, Kevin
American. Actor
Best known for role of Morris Thorpe on TV series "The White Shadow," 1978-81.
b. Sep 19, 1958 in Philadelphia, Pennsylvania
Source: *BioIn 10, 12, 15; ConTFT 9; DrBlPA, 90; IntMPA 92, 94, 96; MiSFD 9; WhoEnt 92; WhoHol 92*

Hooks, Robert
American. Actor
Founder, Negro Ensemble Co; appeared in TV series "NYPD," 1967-69.
b. Apr 18, 1937 in Washington, District of Columbia
Source: *BioIn 8, 9, 12; ConTFT 5; CurBio 70; DrBlPA, 90; Ebony 1; FilmEn; FilmgC; HalFC 80, 84, 88; InB&W 85; IntMPA 92, 94, 96; NotNAT; PlP&P A; VarWW 85; WhoAm 74, 76, 80, 82; WhoBlA 75, 77, 80; WhoHol 92, A; WhoThe 77, 81*

Hooper, Harry Bartholomew
American. Baseball Player
Outfielder, 1909-25, known for defensive play; Hall of Fame, 1971.
b. Aug 24, 1887 in Bell Station, California
d. Dec 18, 1974 in Santa Cruz, California
Source: *BiDAmSp BB; BioIn 7, 10; DcAmB S9; WhoProB 73*

Hooper, Tom
[Charles Thomas Hooper]
Canadian. Hockey Player
Played amateur hockey, early 1900s; Hall of Fame, 1962.
b. Nov 24, 1883 in Rat Portage, Ontario, Canada
d. Mar 23, 1960
Source: *WhoHcky 73*

Hooper, William
American. Lawyer, Continental Congressman
Signed Declaration of Independence as North Carolina delegate; absent during vote, but signed later.
b. Jun 17, 1742 in Boston, Massachusetts
d. Oct 14, 1790 in Hillsboro, North Carolina
Source: *AmBi; ApCAB; BiAUS; BiDrAC; BiDrUSC 89; BioIn 7, 8, 9, 12; DcAmB; DcNCBi 3; Drake; EncAR; EncCRAm; HarEnUS; NatCAB 5; PeoHis; TwCBDA; WhAm HS; WhAmP; WhAmRev*

Hoopes, Darlington
American. Politician
Quaker Socialist party leader who ran for vp of US on Socialist ticket, 1932; chaired party, 1946-57, 1968; party's candidate for pres., 1952, 1956.
b. Sep 11, 1896 in Vale, Maryland
d. Sep 25, 1989 in Sinking Spring, Pennsylvania
Source: *BiDAmLf; BioIn 3, 16; CurBio 89N; NewYTBS 89; WhoAm 74, 76; WhoAmP 73, 75, 77, 79; WhoE 74*

Hooton, Earnest Albert
American. Anthropologist
Included among his non-scientific writngs: *Why Men Behave Like Apes & Vice Versa,* 1940.
b. Nov 20, 1887 in Clemansville, Wisconsin
d. May 3, 1954 in Cambridge, Massachusetts
Source: *AmAu&B; BioIn 3, 4, 12, 13; CopCroC; CurBio 40, 54; DcAmB S5; EncHuEv; InSci; LinLib L, S; NatCAB 40; REnAL; TwCA, SUP; WebAB 74, 79; WhAm 3; WhE&EA*

Hoover, Herbert C(lark)
American. US President
31st pres., Rep., 1929-33; administration dominated by early yrs. of Great Depression.
b. Aug 10, 1874 in West Branch, Iowa
d. Oct 20, 1964 in New York, New York
Source: *AmAu&B; AmLY; AmOrTwC; AmPeW; AmPolLe; ApCAB X; Benet 96; BiDAmBL 83; BiDInt; BiDrAC; BiDrUSE 71, 89; BioIn 1, 2, 3, 4, 5, 6, 7, 8, 9, 10, 11, 12, 13; ConAu 89, 108; CurBio 43; DcAmB S7; DcPol; Dis&D; EncAAH; EncAB-H 1974, 1996; EncTR 91; FacPr 89, 93; InSci; LinLib L, S; McGEWB; MorMA; NatCAB 56; OxCAmH; OxCAmL 65, 83; REn; REnAL; WebAB 74, 79; WhAm 4; WhAmP; WhDW; WhLit; WhNAA; WorAl*

Hoover, J(ohn) Edgar
American. Government Official
Director of FBI, 1924-72; established fingerprint file, crime lab.
b. Jan 1, 1895 in Washington, District of Columbia
d. May 2, 1972 in Washington, District of Columbia
Source: *AmAu&B; AmPolLe; BioIn 1, 2, 3, 4, 5, 6, 7, 8, 9, 10, 11, 12, 13, 14, 15, 16, 18, 19, 20; ConAu 2NR; CurBio 72N; DcAmB S9; DcPol; DcTwHis; EncAB-A 5; EncAB-H 1974, 1996; McGEWB; OxCAmH; PolProf E, J, K, NF, T; SpyCS; WebAB 74, 79; WhAm 5; WhDW; WhoGov 72; WhScrn 77*

Hoover, Lou Henry
[Mrs. Herbert Hoover]
American. First Lady
Dignified, brilliant White House hostess; she and husband translated *De Re Metallica.*
b. Mar 29, 1875 in Waterloo, Iowa
d. Jan 7, 1944 in New York, New York
Source: *CmCal; CurBio 44; GoodHs; HerW; InWom; NotAW; ObitOF 79; WhAm 2; WomFir*

Hoover, William K
"Boss"
American. Businessman
Purchased rights to suction sweeper, 1908; marketed by offering 10-day free, in-home trial.
b. 1849
d. 1932
Source: *Entr*

Hope, Bob
[Leslie Townes Hope]
American. Comedian, Actor
Made annual trips to entertain American troops, 1940-91; won 4 special Oscars ; theme song: "Thanks for the Memory."
b. May 29, 1903 in Eltham, England
Source: *AmAu&B; BestSel 90-4; BiDFilm, 94; BiE&WWA; BioIn 1, 2, 3, 4, 5, 6, 7, 8, 9, 10, 11, 12, 13, 14, 15, 16, 17, 21; BkPepl; CelR, 90; CmpEPM; ConAu 43NR, 101; ConHero 1; ConTFT 3; CurBio 41, 53; DcArts; EncAFC; EncMT; EncVaud; EncWB; FacFETw; FilmEn; FilmgC; ForYSC; Funs; HalFC 80, 84, 88; IntAu&W 91; IntDcF 1-3, 2-3; IntMPA 75, 76, 77, 78, 79, 80, 81, 82, 84, 86, 88, 92, 94, 96; IntWW 79, 80, 81, 82, 83, 89, 91, 93; JoeFr; LegTOT; LesBEnT 92; MovMk; NewYTBS 89; ODwPR 91; OhA&B; OxCAmT 84; OxCFilm; OxCPMus; QDrFCA 92; RadStar; SaTiSS; WebAB 74, 79; Who 82, 83, 85, 88, 90, 92, 94; WhoAm 78, 80, 82, 84, 86, 88, 90, 92, 94, 95, 96, 97; WhoCom; WhoEnt 92; WhoGolf; WhoHol 92, A; WhoHrs 80; WhoProB 73; WhoWor 89, 91, 93, 95, 96, 97; WhThe; WorAl; WorAlBi; WorEFlm; WrDr 90, 92, 94, 96*

Hope, John
American. Civil Rights Activist, Educator
President, Atlanta Baptist College (later Morehouse College), 1906-31; president, Atlanta University, 1929-36.
b. Jun 2, 1868 in Augusta, Georgia
d. Feb 20, 1936 in Atlanta, Georgia
Source: *AmBi; AmDec 1900; BiDAmEd; BioIn 1, 4, 5, 6, 8, 9, 20; ConBlB 8; DcAmB S2; DcAmNB; EncAACR; EncSoH; InB&W 80, 85; McGEWB; NatCAB 28; WebAB 74, 79; WhAm 1*

Hope-Hawkins, Anthony, Sir
English. Author
Books include *The Prisoner of Zenda,* 1894; *The Dolly Dialogues,* 1894.
b. Feb 7, 1863 in London, England
d. Jul 8, 1933 in Tadworth, England
Source: *BiD&SB; Chambr 3; CyWA 58; DcBiA; DcEnA A; DcLEL; EvLB; FilmgC; LngCTC; ModBrL; NewC; OxCChiL; OxCEng 85; PenC ENG; REn; TwCA SUP; WhoChL*

Hopkin, Mary
Welsh. Singer
Discovered by the Beatles; best-known song: "Those Were the Days," 1968.
b. May 3, 1950 in Ystradgynlais, Wales
Source: *BioIn 8; EncRk 88; EncRkSt; PenEncP; RkOn 78; RolSEnR 83; WhoAm 74; WhoRock 81; WhoRocM 82*

Hopkins, Anthony (Philip), Sir
Welsh. Actor
Won Emmy, 1976, for "The Lindbergh Kidnapping Case"; films include *Magic,* 1978; *The Elephant Man,* 1980; *The Silence of the Lambs,* 1991; *Shadowlands,* 1993; *Nixon,* 1995.
b. Dec 31, 1937 in Port Talbot, Wales
Source: *BiDFilm 94; BioIn 10, 12, 15; CelR 90; CnThe; ConTFT 1, 8; CurBio 80; DcArts; EncEurC; FilmEn; HalFC 88; IntDcF 1-3, 2-3; IntMPA 86, 88, 92, 94, 96; IntWW 89, 91, 93; ItaFilm; LegTOT; News 92; NewYTBS 87; PlP&P; VarWW 85; Who 74, 82, 83, 85, 88, 90, 92, 94; WhoAm 78, 80, 82, 84, 86, 88, 90, 92, 94, 95, 96, 97; WhoEnt 92; WhoHol 92, A; WhoThe 72, 77, 81; WhoWor 89, 91, 93, 95, 96, 97; WorAl; WorAlBi; WrDr 92*

Hopkins, Arthur
American. Director, Producer
Best known for plays *Poor Little Rich Girl; Glory Road.*
b. Oct 4, 1878 in Cleveland, Ohio
d. Mar 22, 1950 in New York, New York
Source: *AmAu&B; CamGWoT; GrStDi; NotNAT A, B; OhA&B; OxCAmT 84; REn; REnAL; WhThe*

Hopkins, Bo
American. Actor
Known for "tough guy" roles: *The Wild Bunch,* 1969; *American Graffiti,* 1973.
b. Feb 2, 1942 in Greenwood, South Carolina
Source: *ConTFT 3; FilmEn; HalFC 84, 88; IntMPA 92, 94, 96; ItaFilm; LegTOT; VarWW 85; WhoEnt 92; WhoHol 92, A*

Hopkins, Claude
American. Musician
Pianist who led popular swing band, 1930s-50s.
b. Aug 3, 1903 in Washington, District of Columbia
d. Feb 19, 1984 in New York, New York
Source: *AllMusG; ASCAP 66; Baker 84; BgBands 74; BiDAfM; BiDAmM; BiDJaz; BioIn 10, 13, 16; CmpEPM; DrBlPA 90; EncJzS; IlEncJ; InB&W 85; NewGrDA 86; NewGrDJ 88; OxCPMus; PenEncP; WhoJazz 72*

Hopkins, Esek
American. Naval Officer
First commander, Continental navy, 1775-78.
b. Apr 26, 1718 in Scituate, Rhode Island
d. Feb 26, 1802 in Providence, Rhode Island
Source: *AmBi; AmRev; ApCAB; BioIn 6, 7; BlkwEAR; DcAmB; DcAmMiB; Drake; EncAR; HarEnMi; HarEnUS; LinLib S; McGEWB; NatCAB 2; OxCAmH; OxCShps; TwCBDA; WebAB 74, 79; WebAMB; WhAm HS; WhAmRev; WorAl; WorAlBi*

Hopkins, Frederick Gowland, Sir
English. Biochemist, Physician
Won Nobel Prize in medicine, 1929, for discovery of growth-stimulating vitamins.
b. Jun 30, 1861 in Eastbourne, England
d. May 16, 1947 in Cambridge, England
Source: *AsBiEn; BiESc; BiHiMed; BioIn 1, 2, 3, 4, 5, 6, 9, 14, 15, 20; CamDcSc; DcNaB 1941; DcScB; GrBr; InSci; LarDcSc; McGEWB; NewCol 75; NobelP; NotTwCS; OxCMed 86; WhoNob, 90, 95; WorAl; WorScD*

Hopkins, Gerard Manley
English. Poet
Jesuit college professor; poems, edited by Robert Bridges, are contained in one vol., published in 1918.
b. Jun 28, 1844 in Stratford-upon-Avon, England
d. Jun 8, 1889 in Dublin, Ireland
Source: *AnCL; AtlBL; Benet 87, 96; BioIn 1, 2, 3, 4, 5, 6, 7, 8, 9, 10, 11, 12, 13, 14, 16, 17, 18, 21; BlmGEL; BritAu 19; BritWr 5; CamGEL; CamGLE; CasWL; Chambr 3; ChhPo, S1, S2; CnDBLB 5; CnE&AP; CnMWL; CrtT 3, 4; CyWA 58; DcArts; DcCathB; DcLB 35, 57; DcLEL; DcNaB MP; EvLB; GrWrEL P; IlEncMy; LegTOT; LinLib L, S; LngCEL; LngCTC; MagSWL; McGEWB; ModBrL, S1, S2; NewC; NewCBEL; NinCLC 17; OxCEng 67, 85, 95; OxCLiW 86; PenC ENG; PoeCrit 15; RAdv 1, 14, 13-1; RComWL; REn; RfGEnL 91; RGFBP; VicBrit; WebE&AL; WhDW; WhoTwCL; WorAl; WorAlBi; WorLitC; WrPh*

Hopkins, Harry Lloyd
American. Presidential Aide
Commerce secretary, relief administrator, close adviser to FDR.
b. Aug 17, 1890 in Sioux City, Iowa
d. Jan 29, 1946 in New York, New York
Source: *AmPolLe; AmRef; BiDrUSE 71, 89; BiDSocW; BioIn 1, 2, 3, 4, 5, 6, 8, 10, 11, 15, 16, 17, 18; ColdWar 1; CurBio 41, 46; DcAmB S4; DcPol; DcTwHis; EncAAH; EncAB-H 1974, 1996; HisEWW; LinLib S; McGEWB; NatCAB 42; OxCAmH; WebAB 74, 79; WebBD 83; WhAm 2; WhAmP; WhWW-II*

Hopkins, John Henry
American. Religious Leader, Author
First Episcopal bishop of VT, 1832; wrote *The American Citizen,* 1857.
b. Jan 30, 1792 in Dublin, Ireland
d. Jan 9, 1868 in Rock Pointe, Vermont
Source: *Alli, SUP; AmAu; AmAu&B; ApCAB; BbD; BiD&SB; BioIn 1, 2, 7, 9; CyAL 2; DcAmAu; DcAmB; DcBiPP; DcNAA; Drake; MacEA; NatCAB 11; NewYHSD; PoIre; TwCBDA; WhAm HS*

Hopkins, Johns
American. Financier, Philanthropist
Bequeathed $7 million for founding of Johns Hopkins U, Johns Hopkins Hospital.
b. May 19, 1795 in Anne Arundel, Maryland
d. Dec 24, 1873 in Baltimore, Maryland
Source: *AmBi; ApCAB; BiDAmBL 83; BioIn 1, 4, 10, 14; DcAmB; HarEnUS; LegTOT; MorMA; TwCBDA; WhAm HS*

Hopkins, Lightnin'
[Sam Hopkins]
American. Singer, Musician
Blues singer, guitarist, whose nickname was derived from partner "Thunder Smith"; recorded 100 singles.
b. Mar 15, 1912 in Centerville, Texas
d. Jan 30, 1982 in Houston, Texas
Source: *AnObit 1982; Baker 84, 92; BiDAfM; BiDAmM; BiDJaz; BioIn 12, 13, 14; BluesWW; ConAu 106; ConMus 13; DcTwCCu 5; EncFCWM 69, 83; EncRk 88; FacFETw; GuBlues; IlEncJ; InB&W 80, 85; LegTOT; NewAmDM; NewGrDA 86; NewGrDM 80; NewYTBS 82; OnThGG; OxCPMus; PenEncP; RolSEnR 83; WhAm 8; WhoAm 82; WhoRock 81; WhoRocM 82; WorAl; WorAlBi*

Hopkins, Mark
American. Educator
Professor of philosophy, 1830-87; pres., Williams College, 1836-72.
b. Feb 4, 1802 in Stockbridge, Massachusetts
d. Jun 17, 1887 in Williamstown, Massachusetts
Source: *Alli, SUP; AmAu; AmAu&B; AmBi; ApCAB; BbD; BenetAL 91;*

BiDAmEd; BiD&SB; BioIn 1, 3, 4, 6, 11, 17, 19; CyAL 1; CyEd; DcAmAu; DcAmB; DcAmReB 1, 2; DcAmTB; DcNAA; Drake; HarEnUS; LinLib L, S; LuthC 75; McGEWB; NatCAB 6; OxCAmH; OxCAmL 65, 83, 95; REnAL; TwCBDA; WebAB 74, 79; WhAm HS; WorAl; WorAlBi

Hopkins, Miriam
American. Actor
Sophisticated blonde in films: *Design for Living,* 1933; *Becky Sharp,* 1935.
b. Oct 18, 1902 in Bainbridge, Georgia
d. Oct 9, 1972 in New York, New York
Source: *BiDFilm, 81, 94; BiE&WWA; BioIn 9, 11, 14; DcAmB S9; EncAFC; FilmEn; FilmgC; ForYSC; HalFC 80, 84, 88; InWom, SUP; LegTOT; MotPP; MovMk; NewYTBE 72; NotNAT B; OxCFilm; ThFT; WhAm 5; WhoHol B; WhScrn 77, 83; WhThe; WorAl; WorAlBi; WorEFlm*

Hopkins, Stephen
American. Merchant, Judge
Signed Declaration of Independence, 1776.
b. Mar 7, 1707 in Providence, Rhode Island
d. Jul 13, 1785 in Providence, Rhode Island
Source: *Alli; AmBi; AmWrBE; ApCAB, X; BenetAL 91; BiAUS; BiDrAC; BiDrACR; BiDrUSC 89; BioIn 3, 7, 8, 9; BlkwEAR; CyAG; DcAmAu; DcAmB; DcBiPP; DcNAA; Drake; EncAR; HarEnUS; NatCAB 10; OxCAmH; OxCAmL 65, 83, 95; PeoHis; REnAL; TwCBDA; WhAm HS; WhAmP; WhAmRev; WorAl; WorAlBi*

Hopkins, Telma Louise
[Tony Orlando and Dawn]
American. Actor, Singer
Part of singing group Dawn; co-starred in TV series "Gimme a Break," "Family Matters," 1989—.
b. Oct 28, 1948 in Louisville, Kentucky
Source: *BioIn 14; ConTFT 6; DrBlPA 90; InB&W 80, 85; WorAlBi*

Hopkinson, Francis
American. Continental Congressman, Lawyer, Poet, Composer
Signed Declaration of Independence for NJ, 1776; wrote satires against British; helped design American flag, 1777; considered among first American composers.
b. Sep 21, 1737 in Philadelphia, Pennsylvania
d. May 9, 1791 in Philadelphia, Pennsylvania
Source: *Alli; AmAu; AmAu&B; AmBi; AmComp; AmWrBE; ApCAB; Baker 78, 84, 92; BbD; BenetAL 91; BiDAmM; BiD&SB; BiDFedJ; BiDrAC; BiDrUSC 89; BioIn 1, 3, 4, 7, 8, 9, 10, 11, 12, 14; CamGLE; CamHAL; CasWL; ChhPo, S1; CnDAL; CyAL 1; DcAmAu; DcAmB; DcAmSR; DcLB 31; DcLEL; DcNAA; EncAR; EncCRAm; EvLB; GrWrEL P; HarEnUS; LinLib L, S; LitC 25; McGEWB; NatCAB 5; NewAmDM; NewGrDA 86; NewGrDM 80; NewYHSD; OxCAmH; OxCAmL 65, 83, 95; OxCMus; PenC AM; REn; REnAL; RfGAmL 87, 94; TwCBDA; WebAB 74, 79; WhAm HS; WhAmP; WhAmRev; WorAl; WorAlBi*

Hoppe, Arthur Watterson
American. Journalist
Columnist with *San Francisco Chronicle,* 1960—; wrote *The Martial Arts,* 1985.
b. Apr 23, 1925 in Honolulu, Hawaii
Source: *BioIn 21; ConAu 3NR, 5R; IntAu&W 91; WhoAm 86, 90, 97; WhoWest 74; WrDr 86, 92*

Hoppe, Willie
[William F Hoppe]
American. Billiards Player
Acknowledged as greatest billiards player in history of game, 1903-52.
b. Oct 11, 1887 in New York, New York
d. Feb 1, 1959 in Miami, Florida
Source: *BioIn 1, 2, 3, 4, 5, 10; CurBio 47, 59; OxCAmH; WebAB 74; WhoSpor; WorAl; WorAlBi*

Hopper, De Wolfe
[William De Wolfe Hopper]
American. Actor
Noted for recitations of "Casey at the Bat."
b. Mar 30, 1858 in New York, New York
d. Sep 23, 1935 in Kansas City, Missouri
Source: *AmAu&B; Film 1; WebAB 74; WhoStg 1908*

Hopper, Dennis
American. Actor, Director
Cult figure who directed, starred in *Easy Rider,* 1969; also starred in *Blue Velvet,* 1986.
b. May 17, 1936 in Dodge City, Kansas
Source: *BiDFilm 94; BioIn 7, 8, 9, 11, 13, 14, 15, 16; CelR; ConAu 114; ConTFT 4, 13; CurBio 87; DcArts; FilmEn; FilmgC; ForYSC; HalFC 88; IntDcF 1-3, 2-3; IntMPA 75, 76, 77, 78, 79, 80, 81, 82, 84, 86, 88, 92, 94, 96; IntWW 89, 91, 93; LegTOT; MiSFD 9; MotPP; MovMk; NewYTBE 70; NewYTBS 83, 94; VarWW 85; WhoAm 74, 76, 78, 80, 82, 84, 86, 88, 90, 92, 94, 95, 96, 97; WhoEnt 92; WhoHol 92, A; WorAl; WorAlBi*

Hopper, Edward
"Painter of Loneliness"
American. Artist
Known for starkly realistic scenes of city streets, theater interiors, lunch cou nters, etc.: "Early Sunday Morning," 1930.
b. Jul 22, 1882 in Nyack, New York
d. May 15, 1967 in New York, New York
Source: *AmCulL; ArtsAmW 1; AtlBL; Benet 87, 96; BioIn 1, 2, 3, 4, 5, 6, 7, 8, 9, 10, 11, 12, 13, 14, 16, 17, 18, 19, 20, 21; BriEAA; ConArt 77, 83; CurBio 50, 67; DcAmArt; DcAmB S8; DcArts; DcCAA 71, 77, 88, 94; EncAB-H 1974, 1996; FacFETw; GrAmP; IlBEAAW; IntDcAA 90; LegTOT; McGDA; McGEWB; ModArCr 2; ObitT 1961; OxCAmH; OxCArt; OxCTwCA; OxDcArt; PeoHis; PhDcTCA 77; REn; WebAB 74, 79; WhAm 4; WhAmArt 85; WhoAmA 78N, 80N, 82N, 84N, 86N, 89N, 91N, 93N; WorAl; WorAlBi; WorArt 1950*

Hopper, Grace Brewster Murray
"Amazing Grace"; "Grand Old Lady of Software"
American. Military Leader, Mathematician, Educator
Rear admiral who was oldest active military officer, 1943-86; co-invented comput er language COBOL; first female as an individual to win Nat. Medal of Technology, 1991; coined computer term "bug.".
b. Dec 9, 1906 in New York, New York
d. Jan 1, 1992 in Arlington, Virginia
Source: *AmMWSc 82, 92; BioIn 13, 16; HisDcDP; InWom SUP; LElec; NewYTBE 71; PorSil; WhoAm 74, 76, 78, 80, 82, 90; WhoAmW 70, 72, 74, 83, 89, 91; WhoEng 88; WhoFrS 84; WomFir; WomMath*

Hopper, Hedda
[Elda Furry]
American. Journalist, Actor
Began 28-year career as Hollywood gossip columnist, 1938; famous for her hats.
b. Jun 2, 1890 in Hollidaysburg, Pennsylvania
d. Feb 1, 1966 in Hollywood, California
Source: *AmAu&B; BiDAmNC; BioIn 1, 3, 4, 6, 7, 9, 12, 14; CmCal; ConAu 89, 113; ContDcW 89; CurBio 42, 66; DcArts; EncAFC; EncAJ; EncTwCJ; Film 1; FilmEn; FilmgC; HalFC 80, 84, 88; IntDcWB; InWom; LegTOT; LibW; MovMk; NotNAT B; OxCFilm; RadStar; ReelWom; ThFT; TwYS; WebAB 74, 79; WhAm 4; WhoAmW 58, 64; WhScrn 74, 77, 83; WorAl; WorAlBi; WorEFlm*

Hopper, William
American. Actor
Starred as Paul Drake on TV's "Perry Mason," 1957-65; son of Hedda Hopper.
b. Jan 26, 1915 in New York, New York
d. Mar 6, 1970 in Palm Springs, California
Source: *BioIn 8; EncAFC; FilmgC; HalFC 80, 84, 88; WhoHol B; WhoHrs 80; WhScrn 74, 77, 83*

Hoppner, John
English. Artist
Portrait painter to Prince of Wales, 1789; said to be illegitimate son of George III.
b. Apr 4, 1758 in London, England
d. Jan 23, 1810 in London, England
Source: *AtlBL; BioIn 1, 4, 15; DcArts; DcBiPP; DcBrECP; DcBrWA; DcNaB;*

IntDcAA 90; McGDA; NewCol 75; OxCArt; OxDcArt

Hopwood, Avery
American. Dramatist
Wrote farces, mystery plays: *Getting Gertie's Garter,* 1921; *Why Men Leave Home,* 1922; Hopwood Literary Prize, U of MI, established in his honor, 1931.
b. May 28, 1882 in Cleveland, Ohio
d. Jul 1, 1928 in Juan les Pins, France
Source: *AmAu&B; BenetAL 91; CamGWoT; CnDAL; DcAmB; DcNAA; EncMys; McGEWD 72, 84; ModWD; NotNAT B; OhA&B; OxCAmL 65, 83, 95; OxCAmT 84; PeoHis; REnAL; WhThe*

Horace
[Quintus Horatius Flaccus]
Roman. Poet, Satirist
His *Ars Poetica* was used as style handbook by 16th-, 17th-c. neoclassicists.
b. Dec 8, 65BC in Venosa, Italy
d. Nov 27, 8BC in Rome, Italy
Source: *AncWr; AtlBL; BbD; Benet 87, 96; BiD&SB; BioIn 1, 2, 3, 4, 5, 7, 8, 9, 10, 12, 13; BlmGEL; CamGWoT; CasWL; ChhPo; CyWA 58; DcArts; DcEnL; DcEuL; DcPup; Dis&D; GrFLW; Grk&L; LegTOT; LinLib L, S; LngCEL; MagSWL; McGEWB; NewC; NewCBEL; NewGrDM 80; OxCClL, 89; OxCEng 67, 85, 95; PenC CL; RAdv 14, 13-2; RComWL; REn; RfGWoL 95; WebBD 83; WhDW; WorAl; WorAlBi*

Horan, James David
American. Historian, Author
Historian who specialized in, wrote several books on Old West.
b. Jul 27, 1914 in New York, New York
d. Oct 13, 1981 in New York, New York
Source: *AmAu&B; ConAu 9NR, 105; IntWW 81; WhoAm 80*

Horchow, S(amuel) Roger
American. Businessman, Author
Publisher of catalogue offering elegant, expensive goods: *The Horchow Collection.*
b. Jul 3, 1928 in Cincinnati, Ohio
Source: *BioIn 16; ConAu 106; St&PR 84, 91; WhoAm 86, 90, 92, 94, 95, 96, 97; WhoSSW 80, 91, 93, 95*

Horder, Thomas Jeeves
[First Baron Horder]
English. Physician
Foremost clinician of his time whose patients included George V, George VI, Elizabeth II.
b. Jan 7, 1871 in Shaftesbury, England
d. Aug 13, 1955 in Petersfield, England
Source: *CurBio 55; DcNaB 1951; GrBr; InSci; ObitT 1951; OxCMed 86; WhE&EA*

Hordern, Michael
English. Actor
Character actor in films from 1940, in many PBS Shakespeare plays.
b. Oct 3, 1911 in Berkhampstead, England
d. May 2, 1995 in Oxford, England
Source: *BioIn 13, 81*

Hore-Belisha, Leslie, Baron
English. Political Leader, Lawyer
He introduced traffic control poles, or "Belisha Beacons," while minister of transportation, 1934-37.
b. Sep 7, 1893 in Kilburn, England
d. Feb 16, 1957 in Reims, France
Source: *CurBio 41, 57; DcNaB 1951; EncTR 91; GrBr*

Horgan, Paul
American. Author
Won Pulitzers for *Great River,* 1954; *Lamy of Santa Fe,* 1975.
b. Aug 1, 1903 in Buffalo, New York
d. Mar 8, 1995 in Middletown, Connecticut
Source: *AmAu&B; AmCath 80; AmNov; Au&Wr 71; AuBYP 2, 3; Benet 87, 96; BenetAL 91; BiDConC; BioIn 1, 2, 3, 4, 5, 6, 7, 8, 9, 10, 13, 14, 15, 17, 19, 20, 21; BlueB 76; CathA 1930; ChhPo; CnDAL; ConAu 9NR, 35NR; ConLC 9, 53; ConNov 72, 76, 82, 86, 91; CurBio 71, 95N; CyWA 89; DcLB 2, 102, Y85B; DcLEL; DrAF 76; DrAPF 80, 91; DrAS 74H, 78H, 82H; EncFWF; FifWWr; IlsCB 1744; IntAu&W 82, 91; IntvTCA 2; IntWW 89, 91, 93; LegTOT; MajTwCW; Novels; OxCAmL 65, 83, 95; RAdv 13-3; REnAL; REnAW; ScF&FL 1, 2; SmATA 13, 84; TwCA SUP; TwCWW 82, 91; WhE&EA; WhNAA; WhoAm 74, 76, 78, 80, 82, 84, 86, 88, 90, 92, 94, 95; WhoE 74; WhoGov 72; WhoWor 74, 78, 80, 82, 84, 87, 89; WrDr 76, 80, 82, 84, 86, 88, 90, 92, 94, 96*

Horikoshi, Jiro
Japanese. Aeronautical Engineer
Designed the Zero fighter plane used during WW II.
b. 1904?
d. Jan 11, 1982 in Tokyo, Japan
Source: *AnObit 1982; ConAu 110; NewYTBS 82*

Horlick, Alexander James
American. Manufacturer
Son of William, pres. of Horlick's Malted Milk Corp., 1939-47.
b. Oct 3, 1873 in Racine, Wisconsin
d. Jun 6, 1950 in Racine, Wisconsin
Source: *BioIn 2, 4, 5; NatCAB 39; WhAm 3*

Horlick, William
American. Industrialist
Founder of malted milk and company bearing his name.
b. Feb 23, 1846 in Gloucester, England
d. Sep 25, 1936 in Racine, Wisconsin
Source: *BioIn 4, 5; DcAmB S2; NatCAB 27; WhAm 1; WorAl; WorAlBi*

Hormel, George Albert
American. Meat Packer
Founder, pres. George A Hormel & Co., 1892-1928; produced first canned hams in US.
b. Dec 4, 1860 in Buffalo, New York
d. Jun 5, 1946 in Los Angeles, California
Source: *BioIn 1; DcAmB S4; WhAm 2; WorAl*

Horn, Alfred Aloysius
[Alfred Aloysius Smith]
"Trader"
English. Adventurer, Author
African West Coast merchant; wrote best-seller *Trader Horn,* 1927.
b. 1854? in Lancashire, England
d. Jun 26, 1927 in Whitstable, England
Source: *DcAfHiB 86; EncSoA; IlBEAAW; LngCTC; TwCA, SUP; WhAmArt 85*

Horn, Paul Joseph
American. Musician
Flutist, Grammy Award winner, 1966; made recordings in Taj Mahal, Giza pyramids, 1976.
b. Mar 17, 1930 in New York, New York
Source: *ASCAP 66; BiDAmM; BlueB 76; ConAmC 76; EncJzS; NewAgE 90; NewAgMG; NewGrDJ 88; PenEncP; WhoAm 74, 76, 78, 80, 82, 84, 86, 88, 90, 92, 94, 95, 96, 97; WhoEnt 92; WhoWest 74, 76, 78*

Horn, Shirley
American. Singer, Pianist
Jazz albums include *You Won't Forget Me,* 1991; *Here's to Life,* 1992; has recorded with Miles Davis, Branford and Wynton Marsalis, Johnny Mandel, and Toots Thielemans.
b. May 1, 1934 in Washington, District of Columbia
Source: *AllMusG; BiDAmM; BlkWAm; ConMus 7; InWom SUP; NewGrDJ 88, 94; NotBlAW 2; PenEncP; WhoEnt 92*

Horn, Tom
American. Lawman, Murderer
Hired by WY Cattleman's Assn. to eliminate small ranchers, rustlers; hanged for murder.
b. 1860 in Memphis, Missouri
d. Nov 20, 1903 in Cheyenne, Wyoming
Source: *BioIn 1, 6, 7, 10, 11, 14, 15, 16, 17, 19; DcAmB; EncACr; REnAW; WhNaAH*

Horne, Lena Calhoun
American. Singer, Actor
Nightclub entertainer known for song "Stormy Weather"; starred on Broadway in "Lena Horne: The Lady and Her Music," 1980-82; won Spingarn, 1982.
b. Jun 30, 1917 in New York, New York
Source: *AfrAmBi 2; Baker 92; BiE&WWA; BioAmW; BioIn 16; BkPepl; BlksAmF; CelR 90; CurBio 85; DrBlPA 90; EncMT; FacFETw; FilmgC; HalFC 88; IntMPA 92; InWom SUP; MotPP; MovMk; NegAl 89; NewAmDM;*

NewYTBE 72; NotBlAW 1; NotNAT; OxCPMus; PenEncP; VarWW 85; WhoAm 86, 90; WhoBlA 88, 92; WhoEnt 92; WorAlBi

Horne, Marilyn Berneice
American. Opera Singer
Mezzo-soprano who dubbed Dorothy Dandridge's voice in *Carmen Jones,* film, 1954.
b. Jan 16, 1934 in Bradford, Pennsylvania
Source: *Baker 84; BioIn 13, 15; CelR 90; ConAu 133; ConMus 9; CurBio 67; IntWW 83, 91; IntWWM 90; InWom SUP; MetOEnc; NewAmDM; NewGrDA 86; NewYTBE 70, 71; NewYTBS 91; PenDiMP; VarWW 85; WhoAm 86, 90; WhoAmM 83; WhoAmW 85; WhoEnt 92; WhoWor 91; WorAlBi*

Horner, Bob
[James Robert Horner]
American. Baseball Player
Infielder, Atlanta, 1978-86, St. Louis, 1988-89; 11th ML player to hit four home runs in one game, 1986.
b. Aug 6, 1957 in Junction City, Kansas
Source: *Ballpl 90; BaseReg 86, 87; BioIn 12, 15, 16*

Horner, Harry
Czech. Director
Films include Oscar winners: *The Heiress,* 1949; *The Hustler,* 1961.
b. Jul 24, 1910 in Holitsch, Czech Republic
d. Dec 5, 1994
Source: *BioIn 20; ConDes 84, 90, 97; FilmEn; FilmgC; HalFC 80, 84, 88; IntDcF 1-4, 2-4; IntMPA 75, 76, 77, 78, 79, 80, 81, 82, 84, 86, 88, 92, 94; WhoAm 74, 76, 78, 80, 82, 84, 86, 88, 90, 92, 94; WhoEnt 92; WhoWor 74, 76; WorEFlm*

Horner, Jack
[John R Horner]
American. Paleontologist
Discovered nesting sites of dinosaurs, 1978.
b. 1946 in Shelby, Montana
Source: *BioIn 13, 14, 15, 16; ConNews 85-2; CurBio 92; WhoWest 92*

Horner, James
American. Composer
Produced scores for films *Star Trek II,* 1982; *Glory,* 1989; *Apollo 13,* 1995.
b. 1953 in Los Angeles, California

Horner, Matina Souretis
American. Educator
Pres., Radcliffe College, 1972-89.
b. Jul 28, 1939 in Boston, Massachusetts
Source: *AmMWSc 78S; AmWomM; BioIn 13; BlueB 76; CurBio 73; EncWB; GoodHs; InWom SUP; LEduc 74; WhoAm 74, 76, 78, 80, 82, 84, 86, 88, 90, 92, 94, 95, 96, 97; WhoAmW 74, 75, 79, 81, 83, 85, 87, 89, 91, 93, 95, 97; WhoE 75, 77, 79, 81, 83, 85, 86, 89; WhoIns 92; WhoWor 87, 89, 91, 93, 95, 96, 97*

Horner, Red
[George Reginald Horner]
Canadian. Hockey Player
Defenseman, Toronto, 1928-40; led league in penalties eight yrs; Hall of Fame, 1965.
b. May 28, 1909 in Lynden, Ontario, Canada
Source: *BioIn 2; HocEn; WhoHcky 73; WhoSpor*

Horney, Karen Danielson
American. Psychoanalyst
Founded American Institute of Psychoanalysis, 1941.
b. Sep 16, 1885 in Hamburg, Germany
d. Dec 4, 1952 in New York, New York
Source: *AmAu&B; AmWomWr; CurBio 41, 53; DcAmB S5; InWom; NewYTBE 73; TwCA SUP; WhAm 3*

Hornsby, Bruce
[Bruce Hornsby and the Range]
American. Singer, Songwriter, Musician
Had number one single "Way It Is" from debut album of same name, 1986; won Grammy for best new artist, 1987; second album, *Scenes from the Southside,* 1988.
b. Nov 23, 1954 in Williamsburg, Virginia
Source: *BioIn 15, 16; ConMus 3; EncRkSt; LegTOT; News 89-3; WhoEnt 92*

Hornsby, Rogers
"Rajah"
American. Baseball Player, Baseball Manager
Infielder, 1915-37; had highest lifetime batting average for right-handed hitter, .358; Hall of Fame, 1942.
b. Apr 27, 1896 in Winters, Texas
d. Jan 5, 1963 in Chicago, Illinois
Source: *Ballpl 90; BiDAmSp BB; BioIn 1, 2, 3, 4, 5, 6, 7, 8, 9, 10, 13, 14, 15, 16, 17, 19, 20, 21; CurBio 52, 63; DcAmB S7; FacFETw; LegTOT; NewYTBE 73; WebAB 74, 79; WhAm 4, HSA; WhoProB 73; WhoSpor; WorAl; WorAlBi*

Hornung, Ernest William
English. Author
Best known for stories featuring A J Raffles and sidekick, Bunny, similar to Doyle's Holmes/Watson tales.
b. Jun 7, 1866 in Middlesborough, England
d. Mar 22, 1921 in Saint-Jean-de-Luz, France
Source: *BbD; BiD&SB; BioIn 1, 2, 14; Chambr 3; ConAu 108; CorpD; DcLEL; DcNaB MP; EncMys; EvLB; LngCTC; MnBBF; NewC; REn; TwCA, SUP; TwCWr; WhLit*

Hornung, Paul Vernon
"The Golden Boy"
American. Football Player
Two-time All-America running back, won Heisman Trophy, 1956; with Green Bay, 1957-66; led NFL in scoring three times; suspended, 1963, with Alex Karras for gambling; Hall of Fame, 1986.
b. Dec 23, 1935 in Louisville, Kentucky
Source: *BiDAmSp FB; BioIn 6, 7, 8, 9, 14, 16; CurBio 63; FacFETw; WhoFtbl 74; WorAlBi*

Horovitz, Adam
American. Rapper
Known as King Ad-Rock of a white rap group, 1983—; first album *Licensed to Ill,* 1987 went platinum; son of Israel.
b. 1968
Source: *BioIn 16; News 88, 88-3*

Horovitz, Israel Arthur
American. Dramatist
Plays include *The Bottom; The Widow's Blind Date,* 1983.
b. Mar 31, 1939 in Wakefield, Massachusetts
Source: *Benet 87; BenetAL 91; BioIn 13, 14; CelR 90; ConDr 73, 88; ConLC 56; ConTFT 3; CroCD; DrAP 75; DrAPF 87, 89; IntAu&W 86; ModAL S1; NatPD 77; NewYTBS 86; NotNAT; VarWW 85; WhoAm 86, 90, 97; WhoE 97; WhoEnt 92; WhoThe 81; WrDr 86, 92*

Horowitz, David Joel
American. Author
Co-author, with Peter Collier, *The Fords: An American Epic,* 1986.
b. Jan 10, 1939 in New York, New York
Source: *BioIn 16; NewYTBS 89; WhoAm 76, 78, 80, 82, 84, 86, 88, 92, 94, 95, 96; WhoUSWr 88; WhoWrEP 89, 92, 95*

Horowitz, Paul
American. Physicist
Best known for world-wide network used to study, search for extraterrestrial radio signals.
b. Dec 28, 1942 in New York, New York
Source: *AmMWSc 92; BioIn 17; News 88, 88-2; WhoAm 78, 80, 82, 84, 86, 96*

Horowitz, Vladimir
American. Pianist
Dominated 20th-c. concert pianism with delicate pedaling, daring finger work; left Soviet Union, 1925, returning to Moscow to perform, 1986; won numerous Grammys.
b. Oct 1, 1904 in Kiev, Russia
d. Nov 5, 1989 in New York, New York
Source: *AnObit 1989; Baker 78, 84; BiDAmM; BiDSovU; BioIn 1, 2, 3, 4, 5, 6, 7, 8, 9, 10, 11, 12, 13, 14, 15, 16, 17, 18, 21; BlueB 76; BriBkM 80; CelR, 90; ConMus 1; CurBio 43, 66, 90, 90N; DcArts; EncWB; FacFETw; IntWW 74, 75, 76, 77, 78, 79, 80, 81, 82, 83, 89; IntWWM 77, 80; LegTOT; LinLib S; MusMk; MusSN; NewAmDM; NewGrDA*

86; NewGrDM 80; News 90; NewYTBS 74, 75, 78, 80, 83, 86, 89; PenDiMP; RAdv 14, 13-3; VarWW 85; WhAm 11; Who 74, 82, 83, 85, 88, 90; WhoAm 74, 76, 78, 80, 82, 84, 86, 88; WhoAmM 83; WhoMus 72; WhoWor 74, 76, 78, 80, 82, 84, 87, 89; WhoWorJ 78; WorAl; WorAlBi

Horrigan, Edward, Jr.
American. Business Executive
Vice chm., RJR Nabisco, Inc., 1985—; noted for tackling the anti-cigarette lobbies.
b. Sep 23, 1929 in New York, New York
Source: *Dun&B 90; News 89-1; WhoAm 90; WhoFI 89; WhoSSW 91; WhoWor 89*

Horrocks, Brian Gwynne, Sir
British. Army Officer
Helped to defeat Rommel's forces in Africa, 1942; his forces annihilated at Arnhem, 1944.
b. Sep 7, 1895 in Rainkhet, India
d. Jan 6, 1985 in Fishbourne, England
Source: *BioIn 5, 10, 11; CurBio 85; DcNaB 1981; HisEWW; IntAu&W 82; IntWW 74, 75, 76, 77, 78, 79, 80, 81, 82, 83; Who 74, 82, 83, 85; WhoWor 74, 76, 78; WhWW-II; WrDr 76, 80*

Horrocks, Jeremiah
[Jeremiah Horrox]
English. Astronomer
Made first observation of transit of Venus, 1639.
b. 1617? in Toxteth Park, England
d. Jan 3, 1641 in Toxteth Park, England
Source: *BiESc; BioIn 8; DcNaB; InSci; NewCol 75*

Horsbrugh, Florence
Scottish. Statesman
Conservative minister of education, 1951-54; responsible for evacuating over one million women, children from London, WW II.
b. 1889 in Edinburgh, Scotland
d. Dec 6, 1969 in Edinburgh, Scotland
Source: *CurBio 52, 70; DcNaB 1961; InWom, SUP*

Horse Capture, George, Sr.
American. Curator
Curator, Plains Indian Museum of the Buffalo Bill Historical Center, Cody, WY, 1980-90.
b. Oct 20, 1936 in Fort Belknap Reservation, Montana
Source: *NotNaAm*

Horsley, Lee
American. Actor
Starred in TV series "Matt Houston," 1982-84.
b. May 15, 1955 in Muleshoe, Texas
Source: *BioIn 13; ConTFT 3; IntMPA 92, 94, 96; LegTOT; VarWW 85; WhoHol 92; WhoTelC; WorAlBi*

Horst, Horst P(aul)
American. Photographer
Longtime fashion photographer for *Vogue.*
b. Aug 14, 1906 in Weissenfels-an-der-Saale, Germany
Source: *BioIn 13; ConPhot 82, 88, 95; CurBio 92; ICPEnP; MacBEP*

Horst, Louis
American. Dancer
Musical director, Martha Graham Dance Company, 1926-48.
b. Jan 12, 1884 in Kansas City, Missouri
d. Jan 23, 1964 in New York, New York
Source: *Baker 92; BiDD; BioIn 3, 6, 10, 14, 18; CnOxB; DancEn 78; DcAmB S7; DcCM; NewGrDA 86; WebBD 83; WhAm 4*

Horthy de Nagybanya, Nicholas
[Miklos von Nagybanya]
Hungarian. Naval Officer, Political Leader
Dictator of Hungary, 1920-44; aided Hitler in WW II.
b. Jun 18, 1868 in Kenderes, Austria-Hungary
d. Mar 9, 1957 in Estoril, Portugal
Source: *CurBio 57; LinLib S; McGEWB*

Horton, Edward Everett
American. Actor
Known for tag line in comic roles: "Oh dear, oh dear" ; often Fred Astaire's sideki ck.
b. Mar 18, 1887 in New York, New York
d. Sep 29, 1970 in Encino, California
Source: *BiE&WWA; BioIn 1, 9; CurBio 70; FilmgC; IntDcF 1-3; MotPP; MovMk; NewYTBE 70; OxCFilm; TwYS; Vers A; WhAm 5; WhScrn 77; WorEFlm*

Horton, Johnny
""Singing Fisherman""
American. Singer
Country singer who crossed over to pop charts; hit single "Battle of New Orleans", 1959.
b. Apr 30, 1927 in Tyler, Texas
d. Nov 5, 1960 in Austin, Texas
Source: *BiDAmM; EncFCWM 69; EncRk 88; LegTOT; ObitOF 79; RkOn 74; RolSEnR 83; WhoRock 81*

Horton, Peter William
American. Actor, Director
Played Gary on TV series "Thirtysomething," 1987-91.
b. Aug 20, in Bellevue, Washington
Source: *BioIn 16; ConTFT 8; WhoEnt 92*

Horton, Robert
American. Actor
Starred in TV series "Wagon Train," 1957-62, "A Man Called Shenandoah," 1965-66.
b. Jul 29, 1924 in Los Angeles, California
Source: *BioIn 6; FilmgC; ForYSC; HalFC 80, 84, 88; IntMPA 75, 76, 77, 78, 79, 80, 81, 82, 84, 86, 88, 92, 94, 96; LegTOT; MotPP; VarWW 85; WhoE 74, 75; WhoHol 92, A; WhoThe 77A; WhoWest 74*

Horton, Tim
[Miles Gilbert Horton]
Canadian. Hockey Player
Defenseman, 1949-74, mostly with Toronto; killed in car accident; Hall of Fame, 1977.
b. Jan 12, 1930 in Cochrane, Ontario, Canada
d. Feb 21, 1974 in Saint Catharines, Ontario, Canada
Source: *BioIn 10; HocEn; NewYTBS 74; ObitOF 79; WhoHcky 73*

Horton, Willie
American. Murderer
Convicted murderer who committed another murder while out on furlough in MA; used in Pres. Bush's media campaign leading to Dukakis' downfall.
Source: *BioIn 14, 15, 19; NewYTBS 79, 85*

Horton, Willie
[William Wattison Horton]
American. Baseball Player
Outfielder-designated hitter, 1963-80, mostly with Detroit; had 325 career home runs.
b. Oct 18, 1942 in Arno, Virginia
Source: *Ballpl 90; BiDAmSp BB; BioIn 8, 9, 14, 15; NewYTBS 85; WhoBlA 92; WhoProB 73*

Horvath, Leslie
American. Football Player
All-America quarterback, Ohio State U, 1940-42, 1944; won Heisman Trophy, 1944; in NFL with LA Rams, 1947-48.
b. 1923? in South Bend, Indiana
d. Nov 16, 1995 in Glendale, California
Source: *WhoFtbl 74*

Hosea
Prophet
Call for Israel to repent sins recorded in Old Testament book of Hosea.
Source: *Benet 87, 96; BioIn 2, 3, 4, 5, 6, 7, 10; DcBiPP; DcOrL 3; Dis&D; EncRev; LegTOT; McGEWB*

Hosking, Eric J
English. Ornithologist, Photographer
One of his many self-illustrated bird books: *British Birds,* 1961-76.
b. Oct 2, 1909 in London, England
Source: *BioIn 16; ConAu 17NR; ConPhot 82, 88; ICPEnP A; IntAu&W 86; Who 85, 90, 92N*

Hoskins, Allen Clayton
[Our Gang]
''Farina''
American. Actor
Played pigtailed Farina in over 100 *Our Gang* episodes.
b. Aug 9, 1920 in Chelsea, Massachusetts
d. Jul 26, 1980 in Oakland, California
Source: *BioIn 12; DrBlPA, 90; WhoHol A*

Hoskins, Bob
English. Actor
Cockney actor; won Cannes best actor honors for *Mona Lisa,* 1986; starred in *Who Framed Roger Rabbit,* 1988.
b. Oct 26, 1942 in Bury Saint Edmunds, England
Source: *BiDFilm 94; BioIn 13, 15, 16, 17; ConTFT 1, 2, 3, 10; CurBio 90; DcArts; DcLP 87A; EncEurC; GangFlm; HalFC 84, 88; IntDcF 2-3; IntMPA 86, 88, 92, 94, 96; IntWW 89, 91, 93; ItaFilm; LegTOT; MiSFD 9; News 89-1; NewYTBS 86; VarWW 85; WhoAm 90, 92, 94, 95, 96, 97; WhoEnt 92; WhoHol 92, A; WhoThe 77, 81; WhoWor 95, 96, 97; WorAlBi*

Hosmer, Craig
[Chester Craig Hosmer]
American. Lawyer, Politician
Rep. representative from CA, 1953-75; lobbied for nuclear energy; died on cruise ship.
b. May 16, 1915 in Borea, California
d. Oct 11, 1982, At Sea
Source: *BiDrAC; BiDrUSC 89; BioIn 4, 5, 11, 13; BlueB 76; CngDr 74; CurBio 83, 83N; NewYTBS 82; WhAm 8; WhoAm 74, 76, 78, 80, 82; WhoAmP 73, 75, 77, 79, 81; WhoGov 72, 75; WhoSSW 76; WhoWest 74*

Hosmer, Harriet Goodhue
American. Sculptor
Her most popular statue: *Puck,* of which she made 30 copies.
b. Oct 9, 1830 in Watertown, Massachusetts
d. Feb 21, 1908 in Watertown, Massachusetts
Source: *AmBi; AmWom; ApCAB; BiDWomA; BioIn 1, 3, 5, 6, 7, 10, 11; BriEAA; DcAmB; DcWomA; Dis&D; Drake; EncWHA; HanAmWH; HarEnUS; IntDcWB; InWom, SUP; LibW; McGDA; NatCAB 1, 8; NewYHSD; NotAW; OxCAmH; TwCBDA; WhAm 1*

Hosokawa, Morihiro
Japanese. Politician
Prime Minister of Japan, 1993-94.
b. Jan 14, 1938 in Kyushu, Japan
Source: *BioIn 19, 20; CurBio 94; News 94, 94-1; NewYTBS 93; WhoWor 89, 91, 95*

Hotchkiss, Benjamin Berkeley
American. Inventor
Invented Hotchkiss machine gun, 1872; magazine rifle, 1875.
b. Oct 1, 1826 in Watertown, Connecticut
d. Feb 14, 1885 in Paris, France
Source: *AmBi; ApCAB; DcAmB; InSci; NatCAB 6; TwCBDA; WhAm HS; WorInv*

Hotchner, Aaron Edward
American. Author, Editor
Long association with Ernest Hemingway resulted in memoir *Papa Hemingway,* 1966.
b. Jun 28, 1920 in Saint Louis, Missouri
Source: *AmAu&B; ConAu 27NR, 69; IntAu&W 91; IntvTCA 2; WhoAm 74, 76, 78, 80, 82, 84, 86, 88, 90, 92, 94, 95, 96, 97; WhoE 74; WhoWor 74, 76; WrDr 86, 92*

Hot Chocolate
[Errol Brown; Tony Connor; Larry Ferguson; Harvey Hinsley; Patrick Olive]
British. Music Group
Hit soul singles since early 1970s include ''Brother Louie,'' 1973; ''I Gave You My He art,'' 1984.
Source: *BiDJaz A; BioIn 15, 17; ConMuA 80A; DcLP 87A; DrAPF 89, 91, 93, 97; EncRk 88; EncRkSt; HarEnR 86; IlEncRk; IntAu&W 86X; PenEncP; RkOn 78, 84; RolSEnR 83; WhoRock 81*

Hottelet, Richard C(urt)
American. Journalist
UN correspondent, CBS News, 1960-85.
b. Sep 22, 1917 in New York, New York
Source: *EncTwCJ; LesBEnT, 92; WhoAm 74, 76, 78, 80, 82, 84, 86; WhoWor 74, 76*

Hotter, Hans
German. Opera Singer
Bass-baritone known for Wagnerian roles.
b. Jan 19, 1909 in Offenbach am Main, Germany
Source: *Baker 78, 84, 92; BioIn 11, 13, 14; BriBkM 80; CmOp; IntDcOp; IntWW 74, 75, 76, 77, 78, 79, 80, 81, 82, 83, 89, 91, 93; IntWWM 77, 80, 90; MetOEnc; MusMk; NewAmDM; NewEOp 71; NewGrDM 80; NewGrDO; OxDcOp; PenDiMP; Who 85, 92, 94; WhoMus 72; WhoWor 74*

Hot Tuna
[Jack Casady; Papa John Creach; Jorma Kaukonen; Sammy Piazza; Will Scarlett; Bob Steeler]
American. Music Group
Satellite group of Jefferson Airplane, 1972-78.
Source: *BioIn 9; ConMuA 80A; DcLP 87B; EncPR&S 89; IlEncRk; RolSEnR 83; WhoRock 81; WhoRocM 82*

Houbregs, Bob
American. Basketball Player
Center, 1954-58; Hall of Fame, 1987.
b. Mar 12, 1932 in Seattle, Washington
Source: *BasBi; BiDAmSp BK; WhoBbl 73; WhoSpor*

Houdin, Jean Eugene Robert
'''Father of Modern Conjuring''''
French. Magician
First magician to use electricity; debunked ''fakes''; Harry Houdini named himself a fter him.
b. Dec 6, 1805 in Blois, France
d. Jun 13, 1871 in Blois, France
Source: *DcBiPP; Dis&D; NewCol 75; WebBD 83*

Houdini, Harry
[Ehrich Weiss; Erik Weisz]
American. Magician
America's most celebrated magician; known for escapes from bonds, many of which have not been duplicated; worked to improve quality, ethics of industry.
b. Mar 24, 1874 in Budapest, Hungary
d. Oct 31, 1926 in Detroit, Michigan
Source: *AmBi; Benet 87; BioIn 1, 2, 3, 4, 5, 6, 7, 8, 9, 10, 11, 12, 13, 14, 15, 16, 17, 19, 20, 21; CamGWoT; DcAmB; DcAmBC; DcArts; DcNAA; DcPup; EncO&P 1, 2, 3; EncPaPR 91; EncVaud; FacFETw; Film 1, 2; FilmEn; FilmgC; JeHun; LegTOT; LinLib S; MagIlD; NatCAB 22; NewCol 75; OxCAmH; OxCAmT 84; OxCFilm; TwYS; WebAB 74, 79; WebBD 83; WhAm 1; WhDW; WhoHol B; WhoHrs 80; WhScrn 74, 77, 83; WorAl; WorAlBi*

Houdon, Jean Antoine
French. Sculptor
Neoclassicist; did busts of Voltaire, Thomas Jefferson, George Washington, Napoleon I.
b. Mar 20, 1741 in Versailles, France
d. Jul 15, 1828 in Paris, France
Source: *ApCAB; AtlBL; Benet 87, 96; BioIn 1, 2, 6, 7, 10, 11, 12, 13; DcBiPP; DcCathB; Dis&D; Drake; EncEnl; IntDcAA 90; LinLib S; McGDA; McGEWB; NatCAB 8; NewYHSD; OxCAmH; OxCArt; OxCFr; REn; WorAl; WorAlBi*

Houdry, Eugene Jules
''Mr. Catalysis''
American. Inventor
Developed catalytic cracking process, 1927.
b. Apr 18, 1892 in Domont, France
d. Jul 18, 1962 in Upper Darby, Pennsylvania
Source: *BioIn 1, 3, 5, 6; DcAmB S7*

Hough, Henry Beetle
American. Journalist
Edited Martha's Vineyard *Vineyard Gazette,* from 1920s.
b. Nov 8, 1896 in New Bedford, Massachusetts
d. Jun 6, 1985 in Edgartown, Massachusetts
Source: *AmAu&B; AmNov; AnObit 1985; BenetAL 91; BioIn 2, 4, 5, 9, 11, 12, 14; ConAu 1R, 2NR, 116; NewYTBS 85;*

REnAL; TwCA SUP; WhoAm 74, 76, 78, 80, 82

Hough, John
English. Director
Directed movie *Eyewitness,* 1981; TV series "The Avengers," "The Saint," 1960 s.
b. Nov 21, 1941 in London, England
Source: *ConTFT 2; FilmEn; HalFC 80, 84, 88; HorFD; IntMPA 80, 92, 94, 96; MiSFD 9; VarWW 85*

Houghton, Amory
American. Business Executive, Government Official
Pres., Corning Glass Works, 1930-71; ambassador to France, 1958-61.
b. Jul 27, 1899 in Corning, New York
d. Feb 21, 1981 in Charleston, South Carolina
Source: *AnObit 1981; BiDAmBL 83; BioIn 1, 4, 6, 7, 11, 12, 16, 19; CurBio 81, 81N; DcAmDH 80, 89; IntWW 74, 75, 76, 77, 78, 79, 80; IntYB 78, 79, 80, 81; St&PR 75; WhAm 8; WhoAm 74, 76, 78, 80, 82; WhoFI 74, 75, 77, 79, 81*

Houghton, Henry Oscar
American. Publisher
Founded Houghton-Mifflin publishing house, 1880.
b. Apr 30, 1823 in Sutton, Vermont
d. Aug 25, 1895 in North Andover, Massachusetts
Source: *AmAu&B; AmBi; ApCAB; DcAmB; NatCAB 1; TwCBDA; WhAm HS*

Houghton, Katharine
American. Actor
Niece of Katharine Hepburn; starred with her in *Guess Who's Coming to Dinner ?* 1967.
b. Mar 10, 1945 in Hartford, Connecticut
Source: *BioIn 8; ConAu 130; FilmgC; HalFC 80, 84, 88; WhoAm 74, 76, 78, 80, 82, 84, 86, 88, 90, 92, 94, 95, 96, 97; WhoAmW 95, 97; WhoE 93, 95, 97; WhoEnt 92; WhoHol 92, A; WrDr 94, 96*

Houk, Ralph George
"Major"
American. Baseball Manager
Played 91 games in eight-yr. career, 1947-54; best known for 20 yrs. as manager, mostly with Yankees; won three World Series.
b. Aug 9, 1919 in Lawrence, Kansas
Source: *Ballpl 90; BiDAmSp BB; BioIn 5, 6, 7, 12, 13, 15; CurBio 62; NewYTBS 81; WhoAm 74, 76, 78, 80, 82, 84; WhoE 74, 83, 85; WhoProB 73*

Hounsfield, Godfrey Newbold, Sir
English. Scientist
Shared Nobel Prize in medicine, 1979, for co-inventing CAT-scan (computer-assisted tomography), which revolutionized diagnosis.
b. Aug 28, 1919 in Newark, England
Source: *AmMWSc 89; BiESc; BioIn 12, 15, 20; CamDcSc; CurBio 80; FacFETw; IntWW 80, 81, 82, 83, 89, 91, 93; LarDcSc; News 89-2; NobelP; Who 74, 82, 88, 92, 94; WhoMedH; WhoNob, 90, 95; WhoScEn 94, 96; WhoWor 80, 82, 84, 87, 89, 91, 93, 95, 96, 97; WorAlBi*

Houphouet-Boigny, Felix
Ivoirian. Politician
President of Republic of the Ivory Coast, 1960-93.
b. Oct 18, 1905? in Yamoussouko, Cote d'Ivoire
d. Dec 7, 1993 in Yamoussouko, Cote d'Ivoire
Source: *AfSS 78, 79, 80, 81, 82; AnObit 1993; BiDFrPL; BioIn 4, 5, 6, 7, 8, 9, 13, 15; ConBlB 4; CurBio 58, 91, 94N; DcAfHiB 86; DcPol; DcTwHis; FacFETw; InB&W 80, 85; IntWW 74, 75, 76, 77, 78, 79, 80, 81, 82, 83, 89, 91, 93; IntYB 78, 79, 80, 82; McGEWB; NewYTBS 93; WhAm 11; WhoAfr; WhoFr 79; WhoGov 72; WhoWor 74, 76, 78, 80, 82, 84, 87, 89, 91, 93*

House, Edward Mandell
"Colonel House"
American. Diplomat
Adviser to Woodrow Wilson; chief liaison with Allied leaders during WW I.
b. Jul 26, 1858 in Houston, Texas
d. Mar 28, 1938 in New York, New York
Source: *AmAu&B; AmBi; AmPolLe; ApCAB X; BenetAL 91; BiDInt; BioIn 1, 3, 4, 5, 6, 7, 9, 11, 12, 15, 16, 17; DcAmB S2; DcAmDH 80, 89; DcNAA; EncAB-H 1974, 1996; EncSF 93; EncSoH; FacFETw; LinLib L, S; McGEWB; OxCAmH; OxCAmL 65, 83, 95; ScF&FL 1; ScFEYrs; TexWr; WebAB 74, 79; WhAm 1; WhAmP; WorAl*

House, Son
[Eddie James House]
American. Musician
Legendary Delta blues singer who gave lessons to Robert Johnson and Muddy Waters.
b. c. Mar 21, 1902 in Clarksdale, Mississippi
d. Oct 19, 1988 in Detroit, Michigan
Source: *BiDAmM; BioIn 8, 20; BluesWW; ConBlB 8; ConMus 11; DcTwCCu 5; EncFCWM 69, 83; GuBlues; InB&W 85; NewAmDM; NewGrDA 86; OnThGG; PenEncP; RolSEnR 83*

Household, Geoffrey Edward West
English. Author
Wrote adventure stories: classic thriller *Rogue Male,* 1939.
b. Nov 30, 1900 in Bristol, England
d. Oct 4, 1988 in Banbury, England
Source: *ConAu 77; ConNov 86; DcLEL 1940; EncMys; IntAu&W 76, 77, 89, 91; LngCTC; NewC; OxCEng 85; SmATA 14; TwCA SUP; TwCCr&M 85; Who 74, 82, 83, 85, 88; WhoSpyF; WhoWor 74, 76*

Houseman, John
[Jacques Haussmann]
American. Actor, Director, Producer
Won Oscar, 1973, for *The Paper Chase;* recreated role in TV series.
b. Sep 22, 1902 in Bucharest, Romania
d. Oct 31, 1988 in Malibu, California
Source: *AnObit 1988; BiDFilm, 81, 94; BiE&WWA; BioIn 5, 6, 9, 10, 11, 12, 13; CamGWoT; CelR; CnThe; ConAu 110, 127; ConTFT 2, 7; CurBio 59, 84, 89N; DcArts; FacFETw; FilmEn; FilmgC; GangFlm; HalFC 80, 84, 88; IntAu&W 77, 89, 91; IntDcF 1-4, 2-4; IntDcT 3; IntMPA 75, 76, 77, 78, 79, 80, 81, 82, 84, 86, 88; IntWW 76, 77, 78, 79, 80, 81, 82, 83; ItaFilm; LegTOT; News 89-1; NewYTBE 72; NewYTBS 88; NotNAT, A; OxCAmT 84; PlP&P; TheaDir; VarWW 85; WhAm 9; WhoAm 74, 76, 78, 80, 82, 84, 86, 88; WhoHol A; WhoOp 76; WhoThe 72, 77, 81; WhoWor 74, 78, 80, 82, 84, 87; WorAl; WorAlBi; WorEFlm; WrDr 88*

Houser, Allan
American. Sculptor
Created the memorial bronze "Coming of Age" for the Denver Art Museum, 1977.
b. Jun 30, 1914 in Apache, Oklahoma
d. Aug 22, 1994 in Santa Fe, New Mexico
Source: *BioIn 5, 8, 9, 10, 17, 18, 20, 21; NotNaAm*

Houser, Clarence
American. Track Athlete
Discus thrower, shot putter; won gold medals in both, 1924 Olympics, gold medal in discus, 1928 Olympics.
b. Sep 25, 1901 in Wennigin, Missouri
Source: *BioIn 20; WhoTr&F 73*

Housman, A(lfred) E(dward)
English. Poet, Scholar
Best known for *A Shropshire Lad,* 1896.
b. Mar 26, 1859 in Fockbury, England
d. Apr 30, 1936 in Cambridge, England
Source: *AnCL; AtlBL; Benet 96; BioIn 1, 2, 3, 4, 5, 8, 9, 10, 11, 12, 13, 14, 15, 16, 17, 18; CasWL; Chambr 3; ChhPo, S1, S2, S3; CnE&AP; CnMWL; CyWA 58; DcArts; DcLEL; DcNaB 1931; EncPaPR 91; EncWL, 3; EvLB; FacFETw; GayLL; GrBr; LinLib S; McGEWB; ModBrL S1; NewC; NewCBEL; OxCEng 67, 85, 95; OxCTwCP; PenC ENG; RAdv 14; REn; RGTwCWr; TwCA, SUP; VicBrit; WebBD 83; WhDW; WhoLA*

Housman, Laurence
English. Author, Dramatist
Brother of A E; wrote over 100 novels, fairy tales, self-illustrated books of verse; *Victoria Regina,* 1935, was one of his most successful plays.

b. Jul 18, 1865 in Bromsgrove, England
d. Feb 20, 1959 in Glastonbury, England
Source: *AntBDN B; AuBYP 2S; Benet 87, 96; BiDBrF 2; BioIn 1, 3, 4, 5, 12, 13, 17, 19; BritPl; CamGEL; CamGLE; CamGWoT; Chambr 3; ChhPo, S1, S2, S3; CnMD; ConAu 106; DcBrAr 1; DcBrBI; DcEnA A; DcLB 10; DcLEL; DcNaB 1951; EncSF, 93; EvLB; GrWrEL DR; IlsCB 1744; JBA 34; LegTOT; LngCTC; McGEWD 72, 84; ModBrL; ModWD; NewC; NewCBEL; NotNAT A, B; ObitT 1951; OxCChiL; OxCEng 67, 85, 95; OxCThe 67, 83; PenC ENG; REn; RfGEnL 91; RGTwCWr; ScF&FL 1; SJGFanW; SmATA 25; StaCVF; TwCA, SUP; TwCLC 7; WhAm 3; WhE&EA; WhLit; WhoHr&F; WhoLA; WhThe*

Houssay, Bernardo Alberto
Argentine. Physiologist, Educator
Shared Nobel Prize, 1947, for discovery of role of pituitary hormones in sugar metabolism.
b. Apr 10, 1887 in Buenos Aires, Argentina
d. Sep 21, 1971 in Buenos Aires, Argentina
Source: *AsBiEn; BiESc; BioIn 1, 2, 3, 4, 6, 9, 10, 15, 20; CurBio 48, 71, 71N; DcScB S1; InSci; LarDcSc; McGEWB; McGMS 80; NewYTBE 71; OxCMed 86; WhAm 5; WhoNob, 90, 95; WorAl*

Houston, Charles Hamilton
American. Lawyer, Civil Rights Leader
Member of NAACP's legal committee, 1940s; awarded Spingarn Medal, 1950.
b. Sep 3, 1895 in Washington, District of Columbia
d. Apr 22, 1950 in Washington, District of Columbia
Source: *AfrAmAl 6; BioIn 1, 2, 3, 6, 8, 11, 12, 17, 19, 21; ConBlB 4; CurBio 50; DcAmB S4; InB&W 80; NatCAB 38; OxCSupC; PeoHis; WhAm 3*

Houston, Cissy
[Sweet Inspirations; Emily Drinkard Houston]
American. Singer
Gospel-soul singer; first to record "Midnight Train to Georgia"; mother of Whitney Houston.
b. 1932 in Newark, New Jersey
Source: *BioIn 15, 16; ConMus 6; DrBlPA 90; LegTOT; PenEncP; RolSEnR 83; SoulM*

Houston, James Archibold
Canadian. Children's Author, Illustrator
Self-illustrated Eskimo books include *The White Archer,* 1967; *Akavak,* 1968.
b. Jun 12, 1921 in Toronto, Ontario, Canada
Source: *BioIn 14, 15, 16; CanWW 89; ChlLR 3; ConAu 65; CurBio 87; FourBJA; IntAu&W 91; OxCChiL; SmATA 13; TwCChW 89; WhoAm 90; WhoAmA 91; WhoCanL 87; WhoEnt 92; WrDr 92*

Houston, Ken(neth Ray)
American. Football Player
Nine-time all-pro defensive back, 1967-80, mostly with Washington; holds NFL record for career TDs on interceptions; Hall of Fame, 1986.
b. Nov 12, 1944 in Lufkin, Texas
Source: *BiDAmSp FB; BioIn 11; FootReg 81; LegTOT; WhoAfA 96; WhoAm 80, 82; WhoBlA 77, 80, 85, 88, 90, 92, 94; WhoFtbl 74*

Houston, Sam(uel)
American. Army Officer, Statesman
First pres., Republic of Texas, 1836-38, 1841-44; hero of Battle of San Jacinto, 1836.
b. Mar 2, 1793 in Lexington, Virginia
d. Jul 26, 1863 in Huntsville, Texas
Source: *AmAu&B; AmBi; AmPolLe; ApCAB; BenetAL 91; BiAUS; BiDrAC; BiDrGov 1789; BiDrUSC 89; BiDSA; BioIn 1, 2, 3, 4, 5, 6, 7, 8, 9, 10, 11, 12, 13, 14, 15, 16, 17, 18, 19, 20, 21; CyAG; DcAmB; Drake; EncAAH; EncAB-H 1974, 1996; EncSoB; EncSoH; GenMudB; HalFC 80, 84, 88; HarEnMi; HarEnUS; HisWorL; LinLib S; McGEWB; MorMA; NatCAB 9; OxCAmH; PeoHis; PolPar; RComAH; REn; REnAL; REnAW; TwCBDA; WebAB 74, 79; WebAMB; WebBD 83; WhAm HS; WhAmP; WhCiWar; WhDW; WhNaAH; WorAl; WorAlBi*

Houston, Whitney
American. Singer
Won Grammy, 1986, for top female pop vocalist; hits include "How Will I Know," 1987; won Emmy for performance on The Grammy Awards, 1986; film debut *The Bodyguard,* 1992.
b. Aug 9, 1963 in East Orange, New Jersey
Source: *AfrAmAl 6; AfrAmBi 1; Baker 92; BioIn 14, 15, 16; CelR 90; ConBlB 7; ConMus 8; ConNews 86-3; ConTFT 12; CurBio 86; DcArts; DcTwCCu 5; DrBlPA 90; EncPR&S 89; EncRkSt; HarEnR 86; IntWW 93; LegTOT; NewYTBS 85; NotBlAW 2; OxCPMus; PenEncP; SoulM; WhoAfA 96; WhoAm 90, 92, 94, 95, 96, 97; WhoAmW 89, 91, 93, 95, 97; WhoBlA 90, 92, 94; WhoEnt 92; WorAlBi*

Hovey, Richard
American. Poet
Proclaimed joy of open road in *Songs from Vagabondia* series, 1894, 1901.
b. May 4, 1864 in Normal, Illinois
d. Feb 24, 1900 in New York, New York
Source: *AmAu; AmAu&B; AmBi; ApCAB SUP; BbD; BenetAL 91; BibAL; BiDAmM; BiD&SB; BioIn 4, 8, 10, 12, 15; CamGEL; CamGLE; CamHAL; Chambr 3; ChhPo, S1, S2, S3; CnDAL; DcAmAu; DcAmB; DcLB 54; DcLEL; DcNAA; GayN; GrWrEL P; NatCAB 6; OxCAmL 65, 83, 95; PenC AM; REn; REnAL; RfGAmL 87, 94; TwCBDA; WhAm 1*

Hoveyda, Amir Abbas
Iranian. Political Leader
Prime minister of Iran, 1965-77, who was Shah's adviser; executed by Islamic court.
b. Feb 18, 1919 in Tehran, Persia
d. Apr 7, 1979 in Tehran, Iran
Source: *BioIn 9, 12; CurBio 71, 79, 79N; IntWW 74, 75, 76, 77, 78; WhoWor 76, 78*

Hovhaness, Alan
American. Composer
Numerous works include "And God Created Great Whales," 1970, with recorded humpback whale voices.
b. Mar 8, 1911 in Somerville, Massachusetts
Source: *AmComp; Baker 78, 84; BiDAmM; BioIn 1, 2, 4, 5, 6, 7, 8, 9, 12, 16, 19; BlueB 76; BriBkM 80; CnOxB; CompSN, SUP; ConAmC 82; ConCom 92; CpmDNM 72, 73, 74, 76, 79, 80; CurBio 65; DancEn 78; DcCM; DcTwCCu 1; FacFETw; IntWWM 77, 80, 90; MusMk; NewAmDM; NewGrDA 86; NewGrDM 80; NewGrDO; NewOxM; OxCMus; OxDcOp; PenDiMP A; WhoAm 74, 76, 78, 80, 82, 84, 86, 88, 90, 92, 94, 95; WhoEnt 92; WhoWor 74, 76*

Hoving, Jane Pickens
American. Singer
Leader of the 1930s singing trio Pickens Sisters; sang in the Ziegfeld Follies, 1936; Broadway play *Boys and Girls Together,* 1940.
b. 1909? in Macon, Georgia
d. Feb 21, 1992 in Newport, Rhode Island
Source: *WhoAm 86; WhoAmW 85*

Hoving, Thomas Pearsall Field
American. Art Historian
Director of NY's Metropolitan Museum of Art, 1967-77; wrote *King of the Confessors,* 1981; *Tutankhamum: The Untold Story,* 1977.
b. Jan 15, 1931 in New York, New York
Source: *BioIn 7, 8, 9, 10, 11, 12, 13, 15; ConAu 101; CurBio 67; IntWW 74, 75, 76, 77, 83, 91; Who 85, 92; WhoAm 86, 90; WhoAmA 84, 91; WhoE 74, 85; WhoWrEP 89*

Hoving, Walter
American. Business Executive
Head of Tiffany & Co., 1955-80; rebuilt store into highly successful and profitable jewelry enterprise.
b. Dec 2, 1897 in Stockholm, Sweden
d. Nov 27, 1989 in Newport, Rhode Island
Source: *AnObit 1989; BioIn 1, 2, 5, 12, 16, 17; CelR; CurBio 46, 90, 90N; NewYTBS 89; St&PR 75; WhAm 10; WhoAm 74, 76, 78, 80, 82, 84; WhoWor 74, 76; WorAl*

Howar, Barbara
American. Journalist, Author
Her book, *Laughing All the Way,* 1973, tells inside story of Washington l ife during Kennedy, Johnson administrations; TV show "Entertainment Tonight," 1982-87.
b. Sep 27, 1934 in Raleigh, North Carolina
Source: *AuNews 1, 2; BioIn 16; CelR 90; ConAu 89; CurBio 89; WhoAm 86; WrDr 76*

Howard, Anthony
English. Editor
Books include *The Road to Number 10,* 1965; edited *The Crossman Diaries,* 1964-70.
b. Feb 12, 1934 in London, England
Source: *ConAu 109; IntAu&W 91; IntWW 83, 91; Who 85, 92; WhoAm 76; WhoWor 76*

Howard, Bronson Crocker
American. Dramatist
First professional American playwright; 21 plays include *Shenandoah,* 1888.
b. Oct 7, 1842 in Detroit, Michigan
d. Aug 4, 1908 in Avon, New Jersey
Source: *AmAu&B; CnThe; EncWT; McGEWD 72; ModWD; OxCAmL 65; OxCThe 67; REnAL; REnWD; WhAm 1*

Howard, Catherine
English. Consort
Fifth wife of Henry VIII, 1540; beheaded for adultery.
b. 1520
d. 1542
Source: *DcBiPP; InWom; OxCGer 76; WebBD 83*

Howard, Clint
American. Actor
Starred in TV's "Gentle Ben," 1967-69; brother of Ron Howard.
b. Apr 20, 1959 in Burbank, California
Source: *ConTFT 7, 15; IntMPA 96; WhoHol 92, A*

Howard, Cordelia
American. Actor
Original Little Eva in *Uncle Tom's Cabin,* on stage, 1853.
b. Feb 1, 1848 in Providence, Rhode Island
d. Aug 10, 1941 in Belmont, Massachusetts
Source: *BioIn 16; CurBio 41; InWom SUP; NotAW; NotNAT B; NotWoAT; OxCAmT 84*

Howard, Curly
[The Three Stooges; Jerry Howard]
American. Comedian
Member of popular 1940s comedy team.
b. Oct 22, 1903 in New York, New York
d. Jan 19, 1952 in San Gabriel, California
Source: *EncAFC; HalFC 84; MotPP; ObitOF 79; WhoHol B*

Howard, Desmond
"Magic"
American. Football Player
Wide receiver with Washington, Jacksonville, and Green Bay, 1992—; Heisman Trophy winner, 1991; Super Bowl MVP, 1996.
b. May 15, 1970 in Cleveland, Ohio
Source: *BioIn 21*

Howard, Ebenezer, Sir
English. Urban Planner
Founded English garden-city movement, 1800s.
b. Jan 29, 1850 in London, England
d. May 1, 1928 in Welwyn Garden City, England
Source: *BioIn 8, 9, 10, 14, 15, 16, 18; DcArts; DcD&D; DcNaB, 1922; EncMA; EncUrb; GrBr; MacEA; NewCol 75; RadHan*

Howard, Eddy
American. Bandleader, Songwriter, Actor
Vocalist, 1930s; led band, 1940s-50s; wrote "Careless."
b. Sep 12, 1909 in Woodland, California
d. May 23, 1963 in Palm Desert, California
Source: *ASCAP 66; BgBands 74; CmpEPM; WhAm 4; WhoHol B; WhScrn 74, 77, 83*

Howard, Elston Gene
"Ellie"
American. Baseball Player
Catcher, 1955-68, mostly with Yankees; first black to win MVP, 1963; first black coach in AL, 1969.
b. Feb 23, 1929 in Saint Louis, Missouri
d. Dec 14, 1980 in New York, New York
Source: *BiDAmSp Sup; BioNews 74; CurBio 81; DcAmB S10; InB&W 80, 85; WhAm 7; WhoAm 74, 76, 78, 80; WhoBlA 75, 77; WhoProB 73*

Howard, Eugene
[Eugene Levkowitz]
American. Comedian, Actor
Known for vaudeville act with brother: . "Eugene and Willie Howard."
b. 1881 in Neustadt, Germany
d. Aug 1, 1965 in New York, New York
Source: *BiE&WWA; EncVaud; Film 2; NotNAT B; OxCPMus; WhoHol B; WhScrn 74, 77, 83*

Howard, Frank Oliver
"Hondo"; "The Capital Punisher"
American. Baseball Player
Outfielder, 1958-73, known for tremendous home run power; led AL in home runs, 1968, 1970, RBIs, 1970.
b. Aug 8, 1936 in Columbus, Ohio
Source: *Ballpl 90; BiDAmSp BB; BioIn 5, 6, 8, 9; CurBio 72; WhoProB 73*

Howard, Guy Wesley
American. Clergy
Itinerant preacher; wrote autobiographical *Walkin' Preacher of the Ozarks,* 1945.
b. Nov 7, 1891 in Chariton, Iowa
d. May 12, 1966 in Raytown, Missouri
Source: *BioIn 7*

Howard, James John
American. Politician
Dem. congressman from NJ, 1965-88; chairman, House Public Works, Transportation Committee, 1981-88.
b. Jul 24, 1927 in Irvington, New Jersey
d. Mar 25, 1988 in Washington, District of Columbia
Source: *BiDrAC; BiDrUSC 89; CngDr 83, 85; WhoAm 86; WhoAmP 85; WhoGov 72, 75, 77*

Howard, Jane Temple
American. Journalist, Author
Books include *Families,* 1978; *Margaret Mead: A Life,* 1984.
b. May 4, 1935 in Springfield, Illinois
d. Jun 27, 1996 in New York, New York
Source: *BioNews 74; ConAu 13NR, 29R, 152; WhAm 11; WhoAm 76, 78, 80, 84, 86, 88; WhoAmW 85; WhoUSWr 88; WhoWrEP 89, 92, 95; WrDr 76, 80, 82, 84, 86, 94, 96*

Howard, John (Winston)
Australian. Political Leader
Prime minister, Australia, 1996—.
b. Jul 26, 1939 in Earlwood, Australia
Source: *BioIn 16; FarE&A 78, 79, 80, 81; IntWW 89, 91, 93; Who 82, 83, 85, 88, 90, 92, 94; WhoAsAP 91; WhoWor 91, 97*

Howard, Joseph Edgar
American. Entertainer, Songwriter
Wrote songs "Hello, My Baby"; "I Wonder Who's Kissing Her Now."
b. Feb 12, 1878 in New York, New York
d. May 19, 1961 in Chicago, Illinois
Source: *AmPS; ASCAP 66, 80; BiDAmM; CmpEPM; NotNAT B*

Howard, Ken(neth Joseph, Jr.)
American. Actor, Singer
Won Theatre World Award for play *1776;* starred in TV series "White Shadow," 1978-81.
b. Mar 28, 1944 in El Centro, California
Source: *BioIn 13, 15; ConTFT 4; FilmEn; HalFC 80, 84, 88; IntMPA 84, 86, 88, 92, 94, 96; LegTOT; NotNAT; VarWW 85; WhoAm 86, 90; WhoEnt 92; WhoHol 92, A; WhoThe 72, 77, 81; WorAl; WorAlBi*

Howard, Leslie
[Leslie Stainer]
English. Actor
Played Ashley Wilkes in *Gone with the Wind,* 1939.
b. Apr 3, 1893 in London, England
d. Jun 2, 1943, At Sea
Source: *BiDFilm, 81, 94; BioIn 2, 3, 4, 5, 6, 7, 8, 9, 10, 12, 14, 18; CmMov; DcAmB S3; DcArts; DcNaB 1941; EncEurC; EncWT; FacFETw; FamA&A; Film 1, 2; FilmEn; FilmgC; ForYSC;*

GrBr; IlWWBF, A; IntDcF 1-3, 2-3; MiSFD 9N; MovMk; NotNAT A, B; OxCAmT 84; OxCFilm; REn; WhAm 2; WhoHol B; WhScrn 74, 77, 83; WhThe; WorAl; WorAlBi; WorEFlm

Howard, Moe
[The Three Stooges]
American. Comedian
Last survivor of 1940s comedy team.
b. Jun 19, 1897 in New York, New York
d. May 4, 1975 in Hollywood, California
Source: *DcAmB S9; EncAFC; ForYSC; HalFC 84; LegTOT; MotPP; ObitOF 79; WhoHol C; WhScrn 77, 83*

Howard, Oliver Otis
American. Army Officer
Union Civil War general; founded Howard Univ., 1867, in Washington, DC.
b. Nov 8, 1830 in Leeds, Maine
d. Oct 26, 1909 in Burlington, Vermont
Source: *Alli SUP; AmAu&B; AmBi; ApCAB; BenetAL 91; BiD&SB; BiDSocW; BioIn 1, 3, 7, 8, 9, 21; CivWDc; ConAu 109; DcAmAu; DcAmB; DcAmMiB; DcAmTB; DcNAA; Drake; EncAACR; EncAB-H 1974, 1996; HarEnMi; HarEnUS; LinLib L, S; McGEWB; MedHR 94; NatCAB 4; OxCAmH; REnAW; TwCBDA; WebAB 74, 79; WebAMB; WhAm 1; WhCiWar; WhNaAH; WorAl; WorAlBi*

Howard, Robert Ervin
[Patrick Ervin]
American. Author
Fantasy writer known for popular *Conan the Barbarian* series.
b. Jan 22, 1906 in Peaster, Texas
d. Jun 12, 1936 in Cross Plains, Texas
Source: *BioIn 11, 13, 14, 15, 16, 17; ChhPo; ConAu 105; EncSF; FanAl; ScF&FL 1; ScFEYrs; WhNAA; WhoHr&F; WhoSciF*

Howard, Ron(ald William)
American. Actor, Director
Played Opie on "The Andy Griffith Show," 1960-68, Richie Cunningham on "Happy Days," 1974-80; directed *Splash,* 1984; *Cocoon,* 1985; *Apollo 13,* 1995.
b. Mar 1, 1954 in Duncan, Oklahoma
Source: *Au&Arts 8; BiDFilm 94; BioIn 11, 12, 13, 14, 15, 16; BkPepl; CelR 90; ConTFT 1, 4, 11; CurBio 79, 95; Dun&B 88; FilmEn; HalFC 88; IntMPA 75, 76, 77, 78, 79, 80, 81, 82, 84, 86, 88, 92, 94, 96; IntWW 91, 93; LegTOT; LesBEnT 92; MiSFD 9; NewYTBS 85, 89; VarWW 85; WhoAm 86, 88, 90, 92, 94, 95, 96, 97; WhoEnt 92; WhoHol 92, A; WhoWor 95, 96, 97; WorAl; WorAlBi*

Howard, Roy Wilson
American. Journalist
Pres., United Press, 1912-21; pres., chm., Scripps-Howard Newspapers, 1925-53.
b. Jan 1, 1883 in Gano, Ohio
d. Nov 20, 1964 in New York, New York
Source: *AmAu&B; BiDAmJo; BioIn 2, 4, 5, 6, 7, 16; ConAu 89; CurBio 40, 65; DcAmB S7; EncTwCJ; LinLib L, S; WebAB 74, 79; WhAm 4; WhNAA; WorAl*

Howard, Shemp
[The Three Stooges; Samuel Howard]
American. Comedian
Member of 1940s comedy team.
b. Mar 17, 1900 in New York, New York
d. Nov 22, 1955 in Hollywood, California
Source: *FilmgC; HalFC 84; MotPP; WhScrn 83*

Howard, Sidney Coe
American. Dramatist, Journalist
Won Oscar for screenplay of *Gone With the Wind,* 1939; won Pulitzer for *They Knew What They Wanted,* 1924.
b. Jun 26, 1891 in Oakland, California
d. Aug 23, 1939 in Tyringham, Massachusetts
Source: *AmAu&B; AmBi; CasWL; CnDAL; CnMD; CnThe; ConAmA; ConAmL; DcAmB S2; DcLEL; HalFC 84; McGEWD 84; OxCAmL 83; OxCThe 83; TwCA SUP; WebAB 79; WhAm 1*

Howard, Susan
[Jeri Lynn Mooney]
American. Actor
Played Donna Culver Krebs on TV series "Dallas," 1978-87.
b. Jan 28, 1943 in Marshall, Texas
Source: *BioIn 10, 14, 15; VarWW 85; WhoAm 86, 88; WhoAmW 87, 89; WhoEnt 92; WhoHol 92*

Howard, Tom
British. Actor
Starred in two-reel comedies, 1930-36.
b. Jun 16, 1885 in County Tyrone, Ireland
d. Feb 27, 1955 in Long Branch, New Jersey
Source: *BioIn 1, 3, 4; RadStar; WhoHol B; WhScrn 74, 77*

Howard, Trevor Wallace
English. Actor
Starred in over 70 films spanning five decades; known for portrayal of military officers, including Captain Bligh in *Mutiny on the Bounty,* 1962.
b. Sep 29, 1916 in Cliftonville-Margate, England
d. Jan 7, 1988 in London, England
Source: *CmMov; ConTFT 4; CurBio 64, 88; FilmgC; IntMPA 86; IntWW 74, 75, 76, 77, 78, 79, 80, 81, 82, 83; MovMk; News 88-2; NewYTBS 88; OxCFilm; VarWW 85; WhAm 9; Who 74, 82, 83, 85, 88; WhoThe 81; WhoWor 82, 84, 87, 89; WorEFlm*

Howard, Willie
American. Comedian
Starred on Broadway with brother Eugene from 1912; on radio, 1930s.
b. Apr 13, 1886 in Neustadt, Germany
d. Jan 14, 1949 in New York, New York
Source: *CamGWoT; CmpEPM; DcAmB S4; EncAFC; EncMT; EncVaud; JoeFr; NotNAT B; OxCAmT 84; OxCPMus; WhAm 3; WhoCom; WhScrn 77*

Howatch, Susan
American. Author
Books include *Penmarric,* 1971, adapted to BBC TV serial; *Sins of th e Fathers,* 1981; *Wheel of Fortune,* 1985; *Glittering Images,* 1988.
b. Jul 14, 1940 in Leatherhead, England
Source: *AuNews 1; BioIn 9, 10, 14, 15; ConAu 24NR, 45, 55NR; ConPopW; IntAu&W 76, 77, 91, 93; IntWW 91, 93; InWom SUP; Novels; ScF&FL 1, 2, 92; TwCRGW; TwCRHW 90, 94; WrDr 76, 80, 82, 84, 86, 88, 90, 92, 94, 96*

Howe, Clarence Decatur
Canadian. Politician, Economist
Liberal Cabinet member, 1935-57.
b. Jan 15, 1886 in Waltham, Massachusetts
d. Dec 31, 1960 in Montreal, Quebec, Canada
Source: *BioIn 1, 2, 3, 4, 5, 6, 8, 12, 13; CurBio 45, 61; DcNaB 1951; InSci; ObitOF 79; WhAm 4*

Howe, Edgar Watson
"Sage of Potato Hill"
American. Editor, Author
Wrote *Story of a Country Town,* 1883, early example of realism.
b. May 3, 1853 in Treaty, Indiana
d. Oct 3, 1937 in Atchison, Kansas
Source: *ABCMeAm; Alli SUP; AmAu&B; AmBi; BiDAmJo; BiD&SB; BioIn 2, 3, 4, 5, 6, 8, 9, 10, 12, 13; CasWL; CnDAL; CyWA 58; DcAmAu; DcAmB S2; DcNAA; EncAAH; EncAJ; EncTwCJ; IndAu 1816; McGEWB; OxCAmL 65; REn; REnAL; TwCA, SUP; WebAB 74, 79; WebE&AL; WhAm 1*

Howe, Elias
American. Inventor
Patented first sewing machine, 1846.
b. Jul 9, 1819 in Spencer, Massachusetts
d. Oct 3, 1867 in New York, New York
Source: *AmBi; ApCAB; AsBiEn; BioIn 1, 3, 4, 6, 8, 10, 11, 12, 13, 21; DcAmB; DcBiPP; Drake; EncAB-H 1974, 1996; HarEnUS; InSci; LegTOT; LinLib S; McGEWB; MemAm; NatCAB 4; OxCAmH; TwCBDA; WebAB 74, 79; WhAm HS; WorAl; WorAlBi; WorInv*

Howe, Geoffrey Richard Edward, Sir
Welsh. Government Official
Chancellor of Exchequer, conservative Thatcher govt., 1979-83.
b. Dec 20, 1926 in Port Talbot, Wales
Source: *BioIn 13, 16; CurBio 80; EncWB; FacFETw; IntWW 83; IntYB 79; NewYTBS 79; Who 85, 92; WhoWor 84, 87, 91; WorAlBi*

Howe, Gordie
[Gordon Howe]
American. Hockey Player
Right wing, 1946-80, mostly with Detroit; holds several NHL records including most career goals, 801; won Hart Trophy, Art Ross Trophy six times; Hall of Fame, 1972.
b. Mar 31, 1928 in Saskatoon, Saskatchewan, Canada
Source: *BioIn 3, 5, 6, 8, 9, 10, 11, 12, 14, 15, 16; BioNews 74; CanWW 31, 70, 79, 80, 81, 83, 89; CurBio 62; FacFETw; HocEn; LegTOT; NewYTBE 73; NewYTBS 74, 77, 78, 79, 80; WhoAm 74, 76, 78, 80, 82, 84, 86, 88, 90, 92, 94, 95, 96, 97; WhoE 89, 91, 93; WhoHcky 73; WhoSpor; WorAl; WorAlBi*

Howe, Harold, II
American. Educator
US commissioner of education, 1965-68; advocated desegregation of schools.
b. Aug 17, 1918 in Hartford, Connecticut
Source: *BioIn 7, 8, 9, 11; BlueB 76; CivRSt; CurBio 67; IntWW 74, 75, 76, 77, 78, 79, 80, 81, 82, 83, 89, 91, 93; NewYTBE 70; PolProf J; WhoAm 76, 80, 82, 84, 86, 96, 97*

Howe, Irving
American. Author, Editor, Critic
Publications include *Sherwood Anderson: A Critical Study,* 1951; *Thomas Hardy,* 1967.
b. Jun 11, 1920 in New York, New York
d. May 5, 1993 in New York, New York
Source: *AmAu&B; AmSocL; AnObit 1993; Benet 87, 96; BenetAL 91; BiDAmLf; BioIn 3, 4, 10, 11, 12, 13, 14, 15, 16; BlueB 76; ConAu 9R, 21NR, 50NR, 141; ConLC 81, 85; ConLCrt 77, 82; CurBio 78, 93N; CyWA 89; DcLB 67; DcLEL 1940; DrAS 74E, 78E, 82E; EncAL; EncWL 2, 3; FacFETw; JeAmHC; LNinSix; MajTwCW; ModAL; NewYTBS 93; OxCAmL 83, 95; PolProf J, NF; RAdv 1, 14, 13-1; REnAL; ScF&FL 92; TwCA SUP; WhAm 11; WhoAm 74, 76, 78, 80, 82, 84, 86, 88, 90, 92; WhoAmJ 80; WhoRel 92; WhoUSWr 88; WhoWor 74; WhoWorJ 72, 78; WhoWrEP 89, 92; WorAl; WorAlBi; WrDr 80, 82, 84, 86, 88, 90, 92, 94N*

Howe, James Wong
American. Filmmaker
Cameraman who helped establish distinctive look of Warner Brothers pictures, 1940.
b. Aug 28, 1899 in Guangdong Province, China
d. Jul 12, 1976 in Hollywood, California
Source: *AsAmAlm; BioIn 3, 5, 8, 9, 10, 11, 12, 20; CurBio 43, 76N; DcAmB S10; DcArts; DcFM; FilmEn; FilmgC; GangFlm; HalFC 80, 84, 88; IntDcF 1-4, 2-4; IntMPA 75, 76; NatCAB 59; NewYTBS 76; NotAsAm; OxCFilm; WhAm 7; WhoAm 74, 76; WhoWor 74, 76; WorEFlm*

Howe, Joseph
Canadian. Author, Politician
Premier of Nova Scotia, 1863-66; against Nova Scotia entry into Canadian union.
b. Dec 13, 1804 in Halifax, Nova Scotia, Canada
d. Jun 1, 1873 in Nova Scotia, Canada
Source: *Alli; ApCAB; BbtC; BenetAL 91; BioIn 1, 5, 8, 10, 12, 13, 17; BritAu 19; CanWr; Chambr 3; DcBiPP; DcCanB 10; DcLB 99; DcLEL; DcNaB; Drake; HisDBrE; LinLib L; MacDCB 78; McGEWB; OxCCan; OxCCanL; REnAL*

Howe, Julia Ward
[Mrs. Samuel Gridley Howe]
American. Author, Social Reformer
Wrote poem, ''Battle Hymn of the Republic,'' 1862; became theme for Union Army.
b. May 27, 1819 in New York, New York
d. Oct 17, 1910 in Newport, Rhode Island
Source: *Alli, SUP; AmAu; AmAu&B; AmBi; AmPeW; AmRef; AmSocL; AmWom; AmWomWr; ApCAB, X; ArtclWW 2; BbD; Benet 87, 96; BenetAL 91; BibAL; BiCAW; BiDAmM; BiD&SB; BiDMoPL; BiDTran; BioAmW; BioIn 15, 16, 17, 19, 20, 21; BlmGWL; CamGEL; CamGLE; CamHAL; Chambr 3; ChhPo, S1, S2, S3; CivWDc; CnDAL; ConAu 117; CyAL 2; DcAmAu; DcAmB; DcAmSR; DcEnL; DcLB 1; DcLEL; DcNAA; Drake; EncAB-H 1974, 1996; EncARH; EncWHA; EvLB; FemiWr; FemPA; GoodHs; GrLiveH; HanAmWH; HarEnUS; HerW; InWom, SUP; LibW; LinLib L, S; McGEWB; NatCAB 1; NewGrDA 86; NotAW; NotNAT B; OxCAmH; OxCAmL 65, 83, 95; OxCEng 67; OxCWoWr 95; PenC AM; PenNWW A; REn; REnAL; TwCBDA; TwCLC 21; WebAB 74, 79; WebE&AL; WhAm 1; WhAmP; WhCiWar; WomFir; WorAl; WorAlBi*

Howe, Louis McHenry
American. Journalist, Secretary
FDR's secretary, 1913-30; a political mentor who greatly influenced both Eleanor and Franklin's success.
b. Jan 14, 1871 in Indianapolis, Indiana
d. Apr 18, 1936 in Fall River, Massachusetts
Source: *BioIn 2, 3, 4, 6, 8, 11; DcAmB S2; NatCAB 27; WhAm 1; WhAmP*

Howe, Mark De Wolfe
American. Editor, Author
Wrote nonfiction texts, biographies of New England life; won 1924 Pulitzer for *Barrett Wendell.*
b. May 22, 1906 in Boston, Massachusetts
d. Feb 28, 1967 in Cambridge, Massachusetts
Source: *AmAu&B; ConAu 89; WhAm 4; WhNAA*

Howe, Mark Steven
American. Hockey Player
Defenseman, in WHA, 1973-77, in NHL, Hartford Whalers, 1977-82, Philadelphia Flyers, 1982—; son of Gordie.
b. May 28, 1955 in Detroit, Michigan
Source: *BiDAmSp BK; BioIn 10, 11, 13; HocReg 87; WhoAm 88, 90*

Howe, Oscar
American. Artist
Among the first Native Americans to combine traditional and modern forms in his art; won the Grand Purchase Prize in the 1947 Indian Art Annual.
b. May 13, 1915 in Joe Creek, South Dakota
d. Oct 7, 1983
Source: *BioIn 6, 8, 9, 13, 21; EncNoAI; IlBEAAW; NotNaAm; WhAm 9; WhoAm 80, 82; WhoAmA 73, 76, 78, 80, 82, 84, 86, 89, 91, 91N, 93, 93N*

Howe, Quincy
American. Editor, Broadcaster
Pioneered in news commentary, analysis; wrote *A World History of Our Times,* 1947-53.
b. Aug 17, 1900 in Boston, Massachusetts
d. Feb 17, 1977 in New York, New York
Source: *AmAu&B; IntWW 74, 75, 76; NewYTBS 77; RadStar; REnAL; WhAm 7; WhoAm 74, 76*

Howe, Richard
English. Naval Officer
Led British navy in America, 1776-78.
b. Mar 19, 1725 in London, England
d. Aug 5, 1799 in London, England
Source: *Alli; ApCAB; Drake; HarEnUS*

Howe, Samuel Gridley
American. Educator, Social Reformer
First to educate a blind deaf-mute child, Laura Dewey Bridgman, 1837; pioneer in education of mentally retarded children.
b. Nov 10, 1802 in Boston, Massachusetts
d. Jan 9, 1876 in Boston, Massachusetts
Source: *Alli; AmAu; AmAu&B; AmBi; ApCAB; DcAmB; DcNAA; Drake; EncAB-H 1974; OxCAmL 65; REn; REnAL; TwCBDA; WebAB 74; WhAm HS*

Howe, Steve
American. Baseball Player
Relief pitcher, 1980—, currently with NY Yankees; banned for life for drug and alcohol abuse, June 1992, but reinstated by arbitrator, Nov 1992; charged with carrying an unlicensed gun, 1996.
b. Mar 10, 1958 in Pontiac, Michigan
Source: *Ballpl 90; BioIn 16; NewYTBS 85*

Howe, Susan
American. Poet
Published collection of poems, *Defenestration of Prague,* 1983; also wrote *My Emily Dickinson,* 1985.
b. Jun 10, 1937 in Boston, Massachusetts
Source: *BioIn 19, 20, 21; ConLC 72; ConPo 96; DcLB 120; FemiWr; GrWomW; OxCWoWr 95; WrDr 96*

Howe, Syd(ney Harris)
Canadian. Hockey Player
Center, 1929-46, mostly with Detroit; first player to score six goals in one game (1944); Hall of Fame, 1965.
b. Sep 28, 1911 in Ottawa, Ontario, Canada
Source: *HocEn; WhoHcky 73*

Howe, Tina
American. Dramatist
Wrote several plays, including the Obie winning *Coastal Disturbances,* 1986.
b. Nov 21, 1937 in New York, New York
Source: *AmWomD; AmWomWr SUP; BioIn 13, 15, 16; ConAmD; ConAu 109; ConDr 88, 93; ConLC 48; ConTFT 7, 15; ConWomD; CrtSuDr; CurBio 90; DcTwCCu 1; FemiCLE; GrLiveH; IntAu&W 91, 93; NotWoAT; OxCWoWr 95; WhoAm 95, 96, 97; WhoAmW 85, 95, 97; WhoE 95, 97; WhoEnt 92; WorAu 1985; WrDr 88, 90, 92, 94, 96*

Howe, William, Viscount
English. Military Leader
Commanded British troops early in American Revolution; captured NYC, 1776; occu pied Philadelphia, 1777.
b. Aug 10, 1729 in London, England
d. Jul 12, 1814 in Plymouth, England
Source: *Alli; AmBi; AmRev; ApCAB; BenetAL 91; BlkwEAR; DcNaB; Drake; EncAR; EncCRAm; HarEnMi; HarEnUS; LinLib S; NatCAB 7; OxCAmH; OxCAmL 65, 83, 95; REnAL; WhAm HS; WhAmRev; WhoMilH 76; WorAl; WorAlBi*

Howell, Albert S
American. Businessman
With Donald Bell, formed Bell and Howell Co., 1907, to make, service equipment for film industry.
b. Apr 17, 1879 in West Branch, Michigan
d. Jan 3, 1951 in Chicago, Illinois
Source: *DcAmB S5; EncAB-A 8; Entr*

Howell, Bailey E
American. Basketball Player
Forward, 1959-71, with four NBA teams; won NBA championships with Boston, 1968-69.
b. Jan 20, 1937 in Middletown, Tennessee
Source: *BiDAmSp BK; OfNBA 87*

Howell, Clark
American. Journalist, Editor
Member of Democratic National Committee, 1892-1924; won Pulitzer, 1929, for campaign against municipal graft.
b. Sep 21, 1863 in Barnwell County, South Carolina
d. Nov 14, 1936 in Atlanta, Georgia
Source: *AmBi; AmLegL; BiDAmJo; BiDSA; BioIn 4, 13, 14, 16; DcAmB S2; DcLB 25; DcNAA; EncSoH; JrnUS; LinLib L; NatCAB 1; WhAm 1; WhAmP; WhJnl*

Howell, Harry
[Henry Vernon Howell]
Canadian. Hockey Player
Defenseman, 1953-76, mostly with NY Rangers; won Norris Trophy, 1967; Hall of Fame, 1979.
b. Dec 28, 1932 in Hamilton, Ontario, Canada
Source: *BioIn 8; HocEn; WhoHcky 73; WhoSpor*

Howell, William H(enry)
American. Physiologist
Discovered anticoagulant, heparin.
b. Feb 20, 1860 in Baltimore, Maryland
d. Feb 6, 1945 in Baltimore, Maryland
Source: *Alli SUP; BioIn 2, 11; CurBio 45; DcAmB S3; DcAmMeB 84; DcNAA; DcScB; InSci; OxCMed 86; WhAm 2; WhNAA*

Howells, Anne Elizabeth
English. Opera Singer
Lyric coloratura mezzo-soprano known for numerous recordings.
b. Jan 12, 1941 in Southport, England
Source: *Baker 84, 92; BioAmW; CmOp; IntWW 78, 79, 80, 81, 82, 83, 89, 91, 93; IntWWM 77, 80, 90; NewGrDM 80; PenDiMP; Who 74, 92; WhoMus 72; WhoOp 76*

Howells, William Dean
American. Author, Editor
Pre-eminent man of letters; edited *Atlantic Monthly,* 1871-81; *Harper's,* 1880s; wrote *Rise of Silas Lapham,* 1885.
b. Mar 1, 1837 in Martins Ferry, Ohio
d. May 10, 1920 in New York, New York
Source: *Alli SUP; AmAu; AmAu&B; AmBi; AmCulL; AmRef; AmSocL; AmWr; ApCAB, X; AtlBL; BbD; Benet 87, 96; BenetAL 91; BibAL; BiDAmJo; BiD&SB; BioIn 1, 2, 3, 4, 5, 6, 7, 8, 9, 10, 11, 12, 13, 14, 15, 16, 17, 18, 19, 20; CamGEL; CamGLE; CamGWoT; CamHAL; CarSB; CasWL; Chambr 3; ChhPo, S1, S2; CnDAL; ConAu 104, 134; CrtT 3, 4; CyAL 2; CyWA 58; DcAmAu; DcAmB; DcAmSR; DcArts; DcBiA; DcEnA, A; DcEnL; DcLB 12, 64, 74, 79; DcLEL; DcNAA; Drake; EncAB-H 1974, 1996; EncAL; EncSF, 93; EncWL; EvLB; GayN; GrWrEL N; HarEnUS; JrnUS; LegTOT; LinLib L, S; MagSAmL; McGEWB; McGEWD 72, 84; ModAL, S1; ModWD; MorMA; NatCAB 1; NotNAT B; Novels; OhA&B; OxCAmH; OxCAmL 65, 83, 95; OxCAmT 84; OxCChiL; OxCEng 67, 85, 95; PenC AM; PlP&P; RAdv 1, 14, 13-1; RComAH; RComWL; RealN; REn; REnAL; RfGAmL 87, 94; ScFEYrs; ScFSB; TwCBDA; TwCLC 7, 17, 41; TwCSFW 81, 86, 91; WebAB 74, 79; WebE&AL; WhAm 1; WhAmArt 85; WhLit; WorAl; WorAlBi*

Howes, Frank Stewart
English. Critic, Educator
London *Times* music critic since 1925.
b. Apr 2, 1891 in Oxford, England
d. Sep 28, 1974 in Combe, England
Source: *ConAu 115; IntWW 74; WhAm 6; Who 74; WhoMus 72; WhoWor 74*

Howes, Sally Ann
English. Actor, Singer
Child star of 1940 British films, later in *Chitty Chitty Bang Bang,* 1968.
b. Jul 20, 1934 in London, England
Source: *BiE&WWA; ConTFT 5; EncMT; FilmgC; ForYSC; HalFC 88; MotPP; MovMk; NotNAT; OxCPMus; VarWW 85; Who 85, 92; WhoHol A; WhoThe 77*

Howitt, Mary
English. Translator, Children's Author
Known for translations of Scandinavian fairy tales.
b. Mar 12, 1799 in Coleford, England
d. Jan 30, 1888 in Rome, Italy
Source: *Alli, SUP; BbD; BiD&SB; BioIn 3, 10; BritAu 19; CarSB; CasWL; ChhPo, S1, S2, S3; DcEnA; DcEnL; DcEuL; DcLB 110; DcNaB; EvLB; FemiCLE; HsB&A; NewC; NewCBEL; OxCChiL; StaCVF*

Howitt, William
English. Author
Wrote *Book of the Seasons,* 1831.
b. Dec 18, 1792 in Heanor, England
d. Mar 3, 1879 in Rome, Italy
Source: *Alli, SUP; BbD; BiD&SB; BioIn 3, 16, 17; BritAu 19; CarSB; CasWL; CelCen; ChhPo, S1, S2, S3; DcEnA; DcEnL; DcEuL; DcLB 110; DcNaB; EncO&P 1, 2, 3; EvLB; NewC; NewCBEL; OxCAusL; OxCChiL; StaCVF; VicBrit*

Howland, Alfred Cornelius
American. Artist
Drew landscapes; New England genre scenes: *Old Farm,* 1887.
b. Feb 12, 1838 in Walpole, New Hampshire
d. 1909 in Pasadena, California
Source: *ApCAB; ArtsAmW 2; BioIn 11; DcAmB; EarABI; NatCAB 7; NewYHSD; TwCBDA; WhAm 1; WhAmArt 85*

Howland, Beth
American. Actor
Played Vera on TV series "Alice," 1976-85.

b. May 28, 1941 in Boston, Massachusetts
Source: *ConTFT 3; VarWW 85; WhoAm 86; WhoTelC*

Howland, Michael
[The Hostages]
American. Hostage
One of 52 held by terrorists, Nov 1979-Jan 1981.
b. 1947?
Source: *BioIn 12; NewYTBS 81*

Howlin' Wolf
[Chester Arthur Burnett]
American. Singer, Songwriter
Had rhythm and blues hits, 1954-64: "Little Red Rooster"; "Back Door Man."
b. Jun 10, 1910 in West Point, Mississippi
d. Jan 10, 1976 in Chicago, Illinois
Source: *AfrAmAl 6; AmCulL; BiDAfM; BiDAmM; BioIn 7, 8, 9, 10, 12, 15, 17, 19, 20; BluesWW; ConBlB 9; ConMus 6; DcAmB S10; DcArts; EncPR&S 74, 89; EncRk 88; EncRkSt; HarEnR 86; IlEncBM 82; InB&W 80, 85; LegTOT; NewAmDM; NewGrDA 86; NewYTBS 76; OnThGG; OxCPMus; RolSEnR 83; WhAm 7; WhoRock 81; WhoRocM 82; WhScrn 83*

Howser, Dick
[Richard Dalton Howser]
American. Baseball Player, Baseball Manager
Infielder, 1961-68; had 507-425 career record as manager of NY Yankees, KC Royals; led KC to world championship, 1985.
b. May 14, 1937 in Miami, Florida
d. Jun 17, 1987 in Kansas City, Missouri
Source: *AnObit 1987; Ballpl 90; BioIn 12; ConNews 87-4; WhoAm 82*

Hoxha, Enver
Albanian. Political Leader
Founded Albanian Communist Party, 1941; prime minister, 1944-54; kept country internationally isolated.
b. Oct 16, 1908 in Gjirokaster, Albania
d. Apr 11, 1985 in Tirana, Albania
Source: *AnObit 1985; BioIn 1, 6, 9, 10, 13, 14, 15, 17, 18; ColdWar 2; CurBio 50, 85N; DcPol; DcTwHis; DicTyr; EncCW; EncRev; EncWB; FacFETw; IntWW 74, 75, 76, 77, 78, 79, 80, 81, 82, 83; IntYB 78, 79, 80, 81, 82; NewYTBS 85; WhDW; WhoSocC 78; WhoSoCE 89; WhoWor 74, 78, 80, 82, 84; WhWW-II*

Hoyle, Edmond
English. Lawyer
Game expert who codified card game rules; "according to Hoyle" has come to mean by "highest authority."
b. 1672
d. Aug 29, 1769 in London, England
Source: *Alli; BiD&SB; BioIn 3; BritAu; DcNaB; NewC; NewCBEL; OxCEng 67; WhDW*

Hoyle, Fred, Sir
English. Author, Astronomer
Wrote *Nature of the Universe,* 1951, including Steady State Theory, that the universe is steadily expanding.
b. Jun 24, 1915 in Bingley, England
Source: *AsBiEn; Au&Wr 71; Benet 87, 96; BiESc; BioIn 4, 5, 6, 10, 12, 13, 14, 15; BlueB 76; CamDcSc; ConAu 3NR, 5R, 29NR, 55NR; ConNov 72; ConSFA; DcLEL 1940; EncSF, 93; FacFETw; InSci; IntAu&W 76, 77, 91, 93; IntWW 74, 75, 76, 77, 78, 79, 80, 81, 82, 83, 89, 91, 93; LarDcSc; LegTOT; LinLib L; MajTwCW; McGMS 80; NewEScF; NotTwCS; Novels; RGSF; RGTwCSF; ScF&FL 1, 2, 92; ScFSB; ScFWr; ThTwC 87; TwCSFW 81, 86, 91; TwCWr; Who 74, 82, 83, 85, 88, 90, 92, 94; WhoScEn 96; WhoSciF; WhoWor 74, 76, 78, 82, 87, 96; WorAu 1950; WorScD; WrDr 76, 80, 82, 84, 86, 88, 90, 92, 94, 96*

Hoyt, LaMarr
[Dewey Lamarr Hoyt]
American. Baseball Player
Pitcher; won AL Cy Young Award, 1983; banned from baseball, 1987, for drug involvement.
b. Jan 1, 1955 in Columbia, South Carolina
Source: *Ballpl 90; BaseReg 86, 87; BioIn 13; WhoAm 86*

Hoyt, Lawrence W
American. Publisher
Founded Walden Book Co., 1962.
b. 1901 in Brighton, Massachusetts
d. Dec 17, 1982 in Bridgeport, Connecticut
Source: *BioIn 13; NewYTBS 82*

Hoyt, Palmer
[Edwin Palmer Hoyt]
American. Newspaper Publisher
Publisher, editor, *Denver Post,* 1946-71; *Portland Oregonian,* 1938-46.
b. Mar 10, 1897 in Roseville, Illinois
d. Jun 25, 1979 in Denver, Colorado
Source: *BiDAmJo; BioIn 1, 2, 3, 9, 12; ConAu 89; CurBio 43, 79, 79N; DcLB 127; EncAJ; EncTwCJ; NewYTBS 79; St&PR 75*

Hoyt, Waite Charles
"Schoolboy"
American. Baseball Player
Pitcher, 1918-38; one of first athletes to become broadcaster; Hall of Fame, 1969.
b. Sep 9, 1899 in New York, New York
d. Aug 25, 1984 in Cincinnati, Ohio
Source: *BiDAmSp BB; BioIn 2, 3; WhoProB 73*

Hrabosky, Al(an Thomas)
"The Mad Hunganian"
American. Baseball Player
Relief pitcher, 1970-82; led NL in saves, 22, 1975.
b. Jul 21, 1949 in Oakland, California
Source: *Ballpl 90; BaseEn 88; BioIn 10, 12; LegTOT; WorAl*

Hrawi, Elias
Lebanese. Political Leader
Pres., Lebanon, 1989—.
b. Sep 4, 1925 in Zahle, Lebanon

Hrbek, Kent Alan
American. Baseball Player
First baseman, Minnesota, 1981—.
b. May 21, 1960 in Bloomington, Minnesota
Source: *Ballpl 90; BaseEn 88; BaseReg 87, 88; BioIn 13*

Hrdlicka, Ales
American. Anthropologist
Pioneer in studies of Neanderthal man and the theory that American Indians migrated from Asia through the Bering Strait.
b. Mar 29, 1869 in Humpolec, Bohemia
d. Sep 5, 1943 in Washington, District of Columbia
Source: *AmAu&B; AmLY; ApCAB X; BioIn 2, 3, 13, 20; DcAmB S3; DcNAA; DcScB; EncHuEv; EncWB; InSci; IntDcAn; LinLib L, S; NatCAB 35; NotTwCS; ObitOF 79; PeoHis; REnAL; WebAB 74, 79; WhAm 2; WhNAA*

Hrushevsky, Mykhailo
Ukrainian. Historian, Statesman
Pres., Republic of Ukraine from 1918; wrote 10-vol. *History of Ukraine,* 1899-1937.
b. 1866
d. 1934
Source: *BlkwERR; CasWL; NewCol 75*

Hruska, Roman Lee
American. Politician
Rep. senator from NE, 1954-76.
b. Aug 16, 1904 in David City, Nebraska
Source: *BiDrAC; BiDrUSC 89; BioIn 4, 5, 6, 9, 10, 11, 12; BlueB 76; CngDr 74; CurBio 56; IntWW 74, 75; PolProf E, J, K, NF; WhoAm 74, 76, 78, 80, 82, 84, 86, 88, 90, 92, 94, 95, 96; WhoAmP 73, 75, 77, 79, 81, 83, 85, 87, 89, 91, 93, 95; WhoGov 72, 75, 77; WhoMW 74, 76; WhoWor 74, 76*

Hsia Kuei
Chinese. Artist
Renowned landscape artist in album leaf form; co-founded the Ma-Hsia school of painting.
b. 12th cent. in Hangzhou, China

Hsiung Shih-Li
Chinese. Philosopher
Great Chinese philosopher who formed an ontological system that combined Buddhist, Confucian and Western ideas.
b. 1885 in Huang-Kang, China
d. 1968 in Beijing, China

Hua Guofeng
Chinese. Politician, Statesman
Premier, chm., Chinese Communist Party, 1976-77; responsible for the arrest of the "Gang of Four."
b. 1919 in Shanxi Province, China
Source: *BioIn 13; ColdWar 2; CurBio 77; IntWW 83, 91; NewYTBS 78; WhoPRCh 87; WhoWor 91; WorAlBi*

Huang Hua
[Wang Rumei]
Chinese. Diplomat, Government Official
Minister of Foreign Affairs, People's Republic of China, 1976-82; Ambassador to the United Nations, 1871-76.
b. 1913 in Jiangsu, China
Source: *BioIn 18; ColdWar 2; IntWW 89, 91, 93; WhoPRCh 91*

Huarte, John G
American. Football Player
All-America quarterback, won Heisman Trophy, 1964; had minor NFL career, 1966-72.
b. Apr 6, 1944 in Anaheim, California
Source: *BiDAmSp FB; BioIn 7, 13, 14; NewYTBS 83; WhoFtbl 74*

Hubay, Jeno
Hungarian. Violinist, Composer
Operas include *Anna Karenina,* 1915.
b. Sep 14, 1858 in Budapest, Hungary
d. Mar 12, 1937 in Vienna, Austria
Source: *Baker 78, 84, 92; BioIn 2, 14; BriBkM 80; NewEOp 71; NewGrDM 80; NewGrDO; NewOxM; OxCMus; PenDiMP*

Hubbard, Cal
[Robert Calvin Hubbard]
American. Football Player, Baseball Umpire
Played pro football, 1927-36; AL umpire, 1936-52; only man elected to both football (1963), baseball (1976) Halls of Fame.
b. Oct 11, 1900 in Keytesville, Missouri
d. Oct 17, 1977 in Saint Petersburg, Florida
Source: *Ballpl 90; BioIn 6, 8, 11, 14, 17, 20; LegTOT; NewYTBS 77; WhoFtbl 74; WhoProB 73; WhoSpor; WorAl; WorAlBi*

Hubbard, Elbert Green
[Fra Elbertus]
American. Author, Publisher
Established Roycroft Press and inspirational mags; wrote *A Message to Garcia,* 1899; died on Lusitania.
b. Jun 19, 1856 in Bloomington, Illinois
d. May 7, 1915, At Sea
Source: *AmAu&B; AmBi; BbD; BiD&SB; ChhPo S3; CnDAL; DcAmB; DcLEL; DcNAA; EncAHmr; EvLB; OxCAmL 65; REn; REnAL; TwCA, SUP; WebAB 79*

Hubbard, Freddie
[Frederick Dewayne Hubbard]
American. Jazz Musician, Bandleader
Trumpeter and bandleader known for his jazz-rock fusion; won Grammy for *First Light,* 1972.
b. Apr 7, 1938 in Indianapolis, Indiana
Source: *AllMusG; Baker 84, 92; BiDAfM; BiDAmM; BiDJaz; BioIn 11, 12, 16, 17, 20, 21; DcTwCCu 5; DrBlPA, 90; EncJzS; IlEncJ; InB&W 80, 85; NewAmDM; NewGrDA 86; NewGrDJ 88, 94; News 88; PenEncP; TwCBrS; WhoAfA 96; WhoAm 74, 76, 78, 80, 82, 84, 86, 88, 90, 92, 94, 95, 96, 97; WhoBlA 75, 77, 80, 92, 94; WhoEnt 92*

Hubbard, Kin
[Frank McKinney Hubbard]
American. Journalist
Created cartoon character "Abe Martin," home-cured philosopher, 1906-29.
b. Sep 1, 1868 in Bellefontaine, Ohio
d. Dec 26, 1930 in Indianapolis, Indiana
Source: *AmAu&B; AmBi; BenetAL 91; BiDAmNC; BioIn 2, 6; ConAu 113; DcAmB; DcLB 11; DcNAA; IndAu 1816; LegTOT; OhA&B; OxCAmL 65, 83, 95; REnAL; TwCA, SUP; WebAB 74, 79; WhAm 1; WhAmArt 85; WhNAA*

Hubbard, L(afayette) Ron(ald)
American. Religious Leader
Founded Church of Scientology, 1954, based on his book *Dianetics: The Modern Science of Mental Health.*
b. Mar 13, 1911 in Tilden, Nebraska
d. Jan 24, 1986 in San Luis Obispo, California
Source: *Au&Wr 71; BioIn 6, 8, 9, 10, 12, 13; ConAu 52NR, 77; ConPopW; DcAmReB 2; EncO&P 1, 2; EncSF, 93; IntAu&W 76, 77, 86; ScF&FL 1; ScFSB; SJGFanW; WhoAm 76, 78, 80, 82, 84; WhoE 81, 83, 85; WhoHr&F; WhoRel 77, 85; WhoSciF; WhoSSW 73, 75, 76, 78; WhoWor 76, 78, 80, 82, 84; WorAl; WrDr 76, 80, 82, 84, 86*

Hubbard, Orville Liscum
American. Politician
Mayor of Dearborn, MI, 1941-77; holder national record for full-time mayor, until passed by Erastus Corning, III.
b. Apr 2, 1903 in Union City, Michigan
d. Dec 16, 1982 in Detroit, Michigan
Source: *BioIn 2, 5, 7, 8, 13; NewYTBS 82; WhAm 8; WhoAm 74, 76, 78; WhoAmP 73, 75, 77, 79, 81; WhoGov 77; WhoMW 78*

Hubbell, Carl Owen
"King Carl"; "The Meal Ticket"
American. Baseball Player
Pitcher, NY Giants, 1928-43; holds ML record for consecutive wins, 24, 1936-37; Hall of Fame, 1947.
b. Jun 22, 1903 in Carthage, Missouri
d. Nov 19, 1988 in Scottsdale, Arizona
Source: *BiDAmSp BB; BioIn 2, 3, 4, 5, 6, 7, 8, 9, 10; OxCAmH; WhoProB 73*

Hubble, Edwin Powell
American. Astronomer
Proved existence of star systems beyond Milky Way, 1925.
b. Nov 20, 1889 in Marshfield, Missouri
d. Sep 28, 1953 in San Marino, California
Source: *AsBiEn; BiESc; BioIn 1, 3, 5, 8, 12, 14, 15, 16, 17, 19, 20, 21; CamDcSc; DcAmB S5; DcScB; FacFETw; InSci; LarDcSc; LinLib L, S; McGEWB; NatCAB 42; ObitT 1951; OxCAmH; RAdv 14, 13-5; REnAL; ThTwC 87; WebAB 74, 79; WhAm 3; WhDW; WhE&EA; WorAl*

Hubel, David Hunter
American. Scientist, Educator
Shared Nobel Prize in medicine, 1981, for vision research.
b. Feb 27, 1926 in Windsor, Ontario, Canada
Source: *AmMWSc 73P, 76P, 79, 82, 86, 89, 92, 95; BiESc; BioIn 12, 13, 15; BlueB 76; CamDcSc; IntWW 74, 75, 76, 77, 78, 79, 80, 81, 82, 83, 89, 91, 93; LarDcSc; NewYTBS 81; Who 83, 85, 88, 90, 92, 94; WhoAm 74, 76, 78, 80, 82, 84, 86, 88, 90, 92, 94, 95, 96, 97; WhoE 74, 83, 85, 86, 89, 91, 93, 95, 97; WhoFrS 84; WhoMedH; WhoNob, 90, 95; WhoScEn 94, 96; WhoTech 89; WhoWor 84, 87, 89, 91, 93, 95, 96, 97*

Huber, Robert
German. Biochemist
Shared the 1988 Nobel Prize for Chemistry for identifying a protein complex structure in bacterial photosynthesis.
b. Feb 20, 1937 in Munich, Germany
Source: *AmMWSc 92, 95; BioIn 16, 18, 19, 20; IntWW 89, 91, 93; LarDcSc; NobelP 91; NotTwCS; Who 90, 92, 94; WhoNob 90, 95; WhoScEn 94, 96; WhoScEu 91-3; WhoWor 80, 91, 93, 95, 96, 97; WorAlBi*

Huberman, Bronislaw
Austrian. Violinist
Int'l concertist; founded Palestine Symphony Orchestra, 1936, composed largely of Jewish musicians; exiled by Nazi oppression.
b. Dec 19, 1882 in Czestochowa, Poland
d. Jun 16, 1947 in Nant Corsier, Switzerland
Source: *Baker 78, 84, 92; BioIn 1, 2, 4, 11, 14; CurBio 41, 47; MusSN; NewAmDM; NewGrDM 80*

Hubert, Conrad
American. Inventor, Businessman
Invented small electric lamp, forerunner of flashlight; established Eveready Flashlight Co., 1898.
b. Apr 15, 1856 in Minsk, Russia
d. Feb 14, 1928 in Cannes, France
Source: *DcAmB; NatCAB 24, 44; WhAm 4*

Hubert, Saint
Religious Figure
Patron saint of hunters and trappers.
b. 655?
d. 727
Source: *McGDA; OxCFr*

Hubley, Season
American. Actor
Starred as Priscilla Presley in TV movie *Elvis,* 1978; theatrical films include *Hardcore,* 1978.
b. May 14, 1951 in New York, New York
Source: *BioIn 11; ConTFT 4; HalFC 88; IntMPA 94, 96; LegTOT; VarWW 85; WhoEnt 92; WhoHol 92, A*

Huch, Ricarda (Octavia)
German. Poet, Author
Novels include *The Deruger Trail,* 1929.
b. Jul 18, 1864 in Brunswick, Germany
d. Nov 17, 1947 in Frankfurt am Main, Germany
Source: *Benet 87, 96; BioIn 1, 2, 3, 4, 14, 16; BlmGWL; CasWL; ClDMEL 47, 80; ConAu 111; ContDcW 89; DcLB 66; EncCoWW; EncTR, 91; EncWL, 2, 3; EvEuW; IntDcWB; InWom, SUP; LinLib L; McGEWB; ModGL; ModWoWr; OxCGer 76, 86; PenBWP; PenC EUR; REn; TwCA, SUP; TwCLC 13; WhE&EA; WhoLA*

Hucknall, Mick
[Simply Red]
"Red"
English. Singer
Known for flaming red hair; had number one hit "Holding Back the Years," 1986.
b. Jun 8, 1960 in Manchester, England
Source: *BioIn 15; LegTOT*

Huddleston, Trevor
[Ernest Urban Trevor Huddleston]
English. Religious Leader
Bishop of Mauritius, Archbishop of Indian Ocean, since 1978.
b. Jun 15, 1913 in Bedford, England
Source: *AfSS 81, 82; BioIn 3, 4, 6, 7, 8, 9, 10, 21; BlueB 76; CurBio 63; EncSoA; IntWW 74, 75, 76, 77, 78, 79, 80, 81, 82, 83, 89, 91; Who 85, 88, 90, 92; WhoAm 74; WhoWor 74, 95, 96; WrDr 76, 80, 82, 84, 86, 88, 90, 92, 94, 96*

Huddleston, Walter Darlington
American. Politician
Dem. senator from KY, 1972-79.
b. Apr 15, 1926 in Cumberland County, Kentucky
Source: *BiDrUSC 89; BioIn 10, 11; CngDr 83; IntWW 83, 91; NewYTBS 78; PolsAm 84; WhoAm 74, 76, 78, 80, 82, 84, 88; WhoAmP 85, 91, 93, 95; WhoGov 75, 77; WhoSSW 73, 75, 76, 78, 80, 82; WhoWor 80, 82*

Hudlin, Reginald
American. Filmmaker
Collaborated with brother Warrington on *House Party,* 1990; *Boomerang,* 1992.
b. c. 1962 in East Saint Louis, Missouri

Hudlin, Warrington
American. Filmmaker
Collaborated with brother Reginald on *House Party,* 1990; *Boomerang,* 1992.
b. c. 1953 in East Saint Louis, Missouri
Source: *ConTFT 11; WhoAm 96, 97*

Hudson, Henry
English. Navigator
Made several attempts to find Northwest Passage; first white man to go up Hudson River, 1609, which was named for him.
b. Sep 12, 1575?, England
d. Jun 23, 1611? in Hudson Bay, Canada
Source: *Alli; AmBi; ApCAB; BioIn 1, 2, 3, 4, 5, 6, 7, 8, 10, 11, 12, 15, 17, 18, 19; DcAmB; Drake; EncAB-H 1974; LegTOT; McGEWB; NatCAB 9; OxCCan; REn; REnAL; TwCBDA; WebAB 74; WhAm HS*

Hudson, Joseph Lowthian
English. Businessman
Founded J L Hudson Co., Detroit's best-known dept. store, 1881; pres., 1891-1912.
b. Oct 17, 1846 in Newcastle-upon-Tyne, England
d. Jul 15, 1912 in Worthing, England
Source: *BiDAmBL 83; BioIn 3, 7; NatCAB 47; WhAm 1*

Hudson, Lou(is C)
American. Basketball Player
Five-time all-star forward-guard, 1966-79, mostly with Atlanta; known for jump shot.
b. Jul 11, 1944 in Greensboro, North Carolina
Source: *BasBi; BiDAmSp BK; InB&W 80; OfNBA 87; WhoAfA 96; WhoBbl 73; WhoBlA 77, 80, 85, 90, 92, 94*

Hudson, Rochelle
American. Actor
Played Natalie Wood's mother in *Rebel Without a Cause,* 1955.
b. Mar 6, 1915 in Oklahoma City, Oklahoma
d. Jan 17, 1972 in Palm Desert, California
Source: *BioIn 9; FilmgC; MotPP; MovMk; NewYTBE 72; ThFT; What 3; WhoHol B; WhScrn 77*

Hudson, Rock
[Roy Fitzgerald; Roy Harold Scherer]
American. Actor
Known for light romantic comedy: *Pillow Talk,* 1959; nominated for Oscar for *Giant,* 1956.
b. Nov 17, 1925 in Winnetka, Illinois
d. Oct 2, 1985 in Beverly Hills, California
Source: *AnObit 1985; BiDFilm, 94; BioIn 3, 4, 5, 6, 9, 10, 11, 13, 14, 15, 16, 17, 18, 20; BkPepl; CelR; CmMov; ConNews 85-4; ConTFT 2; CurBio 61, 85N; DcArts; DcTwCCu 1; EncAFC; FacFETw; FilmEn; FilmgC; ForYSC; GayLesB; HalFC 80, 84, 88; IntDcF 1-3, 2-3; IntMPA 75, 76, 77, 78, 79, 80, 81, 82; ItaFilm; LegTOT; MotPP; MovMk; NewYTBS 85; OxCFilm; VarWW 85; WhAm 9; WhoAm 74, 76, 78, 80, 82, 84; WhoHol A; WhoWest 74; WhoWor 74; WorAl; WorAlBi; WorEFlm*

Hudson, Walter
American.
Labelled the heaviest man alive by Guinness, he weighed 1,025 pounds at his death.
d. Dec 24, 1991 in Hempstead, New York
Source: *ASCAP 80; BioIn 15, 17, 18, 19*

Hudson, William Henry
English. Author, Naturalist
Wrote *Green Mansions,* 1904; *The Book of a Naturalist,* 1919.
b. Aug 4, 1841 in Quilmes, Argentina
d. Aug 18, 1922 in London, England
Source: *Alli SUP; AnCL; AtlBL; Benet 87, 96; BioIn 1, 2, 3, 5, 6, 8, 9, 12, 13, 14, 15, 17; CarSB; CasWL; Chambr 3; ChhPo S1, S2, S3; CyWA 58; DcBiA; DcEuL; DcLEL; DcNaB 1922; Dis&D; EncSF; EvLB; GrBr; InSci; LinLib S; LngCTC; ModBrL; NewC; NewCBEL; OxCEng 67; OxCSpan; PenC ENG; RAdv 1, 14, 13-1; REn; ScFSB; TwCA, SUP; TwCWr; WebE&AL; WhDW*

Hudson Brothers, The
[Bill Hudson; Brett Hudson; Mark Hudson]
American. Music Group
Hit singles include "Rendevous," 1975; starred in own weekly TV show, "The Razzle Dazzle Comedy Hour," 1975.
Source: *AfroAA; BioIn 16; RkOn 84; WhoAmP 87, 89, 91; WhoRocM 82*

Huebner, Clarence R
American. Army Officer
Commander, First Division, campaigns in Sicily, France, Germany, WW II.
b. Nov 24, 1888 in Bushton, Kansas
d. Sep 23, 1972 in Washington, District of Columbia
Source: *CurBio 49, 72N; FacFETw; NewYTBE 72; WhAm 5*

Hues Corporation, The
[Tommy Brown; H Ann Kelly; St. Clair Lee; Karl Russell; Fleming Williams]
American. Music Group
Disco-soul group formed 1969; had hit single "Rock the Boat," 1974.
Source: *BluesWW; InB&W 80; RkOn 78; RolSEnR 83; WhoRock 81*

Huey Lewis and the News
[Mario Cipollina; Johnny Colla; Bill Gibson; Chris Hayes; Sean Hopper; Huey Lewis]
American. Music Group
Pop/rock group formed 1982; hits include "Heart and Soul," 1983; "If This Is It," 1984.
Source: *BioIn 14, 15, 16; EncPR&S 89; EncRk 88; PenEncP; RkOn 85; WhoRocM 82*

Huff, Leon
American. Songwriter
With Kenny Gamble won 1989 Grammy for "If You Don't Know Me By Now."
b. Apr 8, 1942 in Camden, New Jersey
Source: *BiDAfM; BioIn 9, 12; NewGrDA 86; WhoBlA 92*

Huff, Sam
[Robert Lee Huff]
American. Football Player
Five-time all-pro linebacker, NY Giants, 1956-63, Washington, 1964-68.
b. Oct 4, 1934 in Edna Gas, West Virginia
Source: *BiDAmSp FB; BioIn 5, 6, 7, 8, 10, 11, 15, 16, 17; LegTOT; WhoFtbl 74; WhoSpor*

Huffington, Arianna
[Arianna Stassinopoulos]
Greek. Writer
Wrote *Fourth Instinct: The Call of the Soul,* 1994.
b. Jul 15, 1950 in Athens, Greece
Source: *BioIn 12, 13; ConAu 114; News 96, 96-2; WrDr 76, 80, 82, 84, 86, 88, 90, 92, 94, 96*

Hufstedler, Shirley (Ann) M(ount)
American. Judge, Government Official
First secretary of Education, Carter administration, 1979-81.
b. Aug 24, 1925 in Denver, Colorado
Source: *AmAu&B; AmWomM; BiDrUSE 89; BioIn 13; CurBio 80; GoodHs; InWom SUP; NewYTBS 79; WhoAm 84, 86, 90; WhoAmL 79, 92; WhoAmW 85, 87, 91; WhoGov 77; WhoWest 78; WhoWor 84, 87*

Hugel, Max
American. Businessman, Government Official
Resigned as CIA director, 1981, for alleged earlier stock market practices.
b. 1925 in New York, New York
Source: *BioIn 2, 4, 12, 13; St&PR 75; WhoAdv 90; WhoFI 85*

Huggins, Charles B(renton)
American. Surgeon
Won 1966 Nobel Prize in medicine for cancer research.
b. Sep 22, 1901 in Halifax, Nova Scotia, Canada
d. Jan 12, 1997 in Chicago, Illinois
Source: *AmMWSc 73P, 76P, 79, 82, 86, 89, 92, 95; BiESc; BioIn 15; BlueB 76; CanWW 83, 89; ConAu 115; CurBio 65; IntWW 83, 91; LarDcSc; McGMS 80; NobelP; WebAB 74, 79; Who 85, 92; WhoAm 86, 88, 90, 92, 94, 95, 96, 97; WhoMedH; WhoMW 74, 76, 78, 80, 82, 84, 86, 88, 90, 92, 93, 96; WhoNob, 90, 95; WhoScEn 94, 96; WhoWor 74, 87, 89, 91, 93, 95, 96, 97; WorAl; WorAlBi*

Huggins, Miller James
"Hug"; "The Mighty Mite"
American. Baseball Player, Baseball Manager
Second baseman, 1904-16; managed Yankees, 1918-29; Hall of Fame, 1964.
b. Mar 27, 1879 in Cincinnati, Ohio
d. Sep 25, 1929 in New York, New York
Source: *BiDAmSp BB; DcAmB; WhAm 4, HS, HSA; WhoProB 73*

Huggins, William, Sir
English. Astronomer
Pioneered in spectroscopic photography; made first observations of a nova by a spectroscope, 1866.
b. Feb 7, 1824 in London, England
d. May 12, 1910 in London, England
Source: *Alli SUP; AsBiEn; BiESc; BioIn 14, 17; CamDcSc; DcBiPP; DcNaB S2; DcScB; InSci; LarDcSc; LinLib S; McGEWB; NewCol 75; WhDW; WhLit; WorAl; WorAlBi; WorScD*

Hughan, Jessie Wallace
American. Political Activist
Active pacifist, socialist party member; founder, War Resister's League, 1923-55.
b. Dec 25, 1876 in New York, New York
d. Apr 10, 1955 in New York, New York
Source: *NotAW MOD; WhAm 5; WhNAA; WomWWA 14*

Hugh Capet
French. Ruler
Succeeded Louis V, 987, over Charles of Lower Lorraine.
b. 938
d. 996
Source: *DcCathB; NewCol 75; WebBD 83*

Hughes, Albert
American. Director
Directed *Menace II Society,* 1993; brother of director Allen Hughes.
b. Apr 1, 1972 in Detroit, Michigan
Source: *ConBlB 7*

Hughes, Allen
American. Director
Directed *Menace II Society,* 1993; brother of director Albert Hughes.
b. Apr 1, 1972 in Detroit, Michigan
Source: *ConBlB 7*

Hughes, Arthur
English. Artist, Illustrator
Pre-Raphaelite whose paintings are characterized by detail, bright palette: *Home from the Sea,* 1856; *The Long Engagement,* 1859.
b. Jan 27, 1832 in London, England
d. Dec 22, 1915 in Kew Green, England
Source: *ArtsNiC; BioIn 1, 5, 6, 8, 14, 16; ChhPo, S1; ClaDrA; DcBrAr 1; DcBrBI; DcBrWA; DcNaB 1912; DcVicP, 2; McGDA; OxCArt; StaCVF; VicBrit; WhoChL*

Hughes, Barnard
American. Actor
TV series include "Doc," 1975-76, "Mr. Merlin," 1981-82, "The Cavanaughs," 1986-87, "Blossom," 1991-93; won 1978 Emmy; won Tony for best actor in *Da,* 1978.
b. Jul 16, 1915 in Bedford Hills, New York
Source: *BioIn 12; CamGWoT; ConTFT 1, 7; CurBio 81; HalFC 80, 84, 88; IntMPA 84, 86, 88, 92, 94, 96; NewYTBS 78; NotNAT; VarWW 85; WhoAm 80, 82, 84, 86, 88, 90, 92, 94, 95, 96, 97; WhoE 85; WhoEnt 92; WhoHol 92, A; WhoThe 77, 81*

Hughes, Charles Evans
American. Supreme Court Justice
US chief justice, 1930-41; resisted attempts to pack the court with pro-FDR justices.
b. Apr 11, 1862 in Glens Falls, New York
d. Aug 27, 1948 in Osterville, Massachusetts
Source: *AmAu&B; AmDec 1900, 1930; AmJust; AmPolLe; ApCAB X; BenetAL 91; BiDFedJ; BiDInt; BiDrGov 1789; BiDrUSE 71, 89; BioIn 1, 2, 3, 4, 5, 6, 7, 8, 9, 10, 11, 12, 15, 16, 18; CurBio 41, 48; CyAG; DcAmB S4; DcAmDH 80; DcAmSR; DcNAA; DcTwHis; EncAB-H 1974, 1996; FacFETw; HarEnUS; LinLib L, S; McGEWB; NatCAB 14, 39; NewCol 75; ObitOF 79; OxCAmH; OxCLaw; OxCSupC; PolPar; RComAH; REn; REnAL; SupCtJu; WebAB 74, 79; WhAm 2; WhAmP; WorAl; WorAlBi*

Hughes, Emmet John
American. Author, Journalist
Columnist, *Newsweek,* 1963-68; speechwriter for Dwight Eisenhower and Nelson Rockefeller.
b. Dec 26, 1920 in Newark, New Jersey
d. Sep 20, 1982 in Princeton, New Jersey
Source: *AmAu&B; AnObit 1982; BioIn 1, 3, 5, 6, 7, 8, 11, 13; ConAu 69, 107; CurBio 82, 82N; EncTwCJ; PolPar; PolProf E; WhAm 8; Who 74, 82, 83; WhoAm 74, 76, 78; WhoWor 74, 76*

Hughes, Francis
Irish. Hunger Striker, Revolutionary
IRA member; one of 10 hunger strikers to die in prison, demanding political prisoner rather than criminal status.

b. Feb 28, 1956 in Bellaghy, Northern Ireland
d. May 12, 1981 in Belfast, Northern Ireland
Source: *BioIn 12*

Hughes, George
American. Illustrator
Cover artist for the *Saturday Evening Post*, 1948-62, whose style depicted post-WW II life in suburban America.
b. 1907 in New York, New York
d. Nov 1989
Source: *BioIn 2, 18; IlrAm 1880, E*

Hughes, Harold E(verett)
American. Politician
Dem. governor of Iowa, 1963-69; US senator, 1969-74; made Iowa's liquor laws more liberal.
b. Feb 10, 1922
d. Oct 24, 1996 in Glendale, Arizona
Source: *BiDrAC; BiDrUSC 89; BioIn 6, 7, 8, 9, 10, 11, 12; CngDr 74; DcAmTB; IntWW 74, 75, 76, 77, 78, 79, 80, 81, 82, 83; St&PR 96, 97; WhoAm 74, 76; WhoAmP 73, 75, 77, 79, 81, 83, 85, 87, 89, 91, 93, 95; WhoGov 72, 75; WhoWor 74*

Hughes, Holly
American. Entertainer
Performances include *Dress Suits to Hire*, 1987.
b. Mar 10, 1955 in Saginaw, Michigan
Source: *GayLesB*

Hughes, Howard Robard
American. Aviator, Industrialist
Amassed huge fortune through film production, real estate, aircraft manufacture, 1930s; known in later years for reclusive, eccentric lifestyle.
b. Dec 24, 1905 in Houston, Texas
d. Apr 5, 1976 in Houston, Texas
Source: *BiDAmBL 83; BiDFilm; BioIn 1, 3, 4, 5, 6, 7, 8, 9, 10, 11, 12, 13; CurBio 41, 76; DcAmB S10; DcFM; EncAB-H 1974, 1996; EncWB; FacFETw; FilmgC; InSci; IntMPA 75; IntWW 74, 75, 76; OxCFilm; REnAW; WebAB 74, 79; WebBD 83; WhAm 6; WhoAm 74, 76, 78; WhoFI 74, 75; WhoWor 74; WorAl; WorEFlm*

Hughes, Irene Finger
American. Journalist
Psychic researcher; author of column, "ESPecially.Irene."
Source: *ConAu 103; EncO&P 3; InWom SUP; WhoAmW 70, 72, 74*

Hughes, John
American. Filmmaker
Noted for teen films *Sixteen Candles*, 1984 and *The Breakfast Club*, 1985; comedies include box-office hits *Home Alone*, 1990, 1992.
b. 1950 in Detroit, Michigan
Source: *Au&Arts 7; BiDFilm 94; ConAu 124, 129; ConTFT 12; CurBio 91; Dun&B 88, 90; IntMPA 96; LegTOT; MiSFD 9; NewYTBS 86*

Hughes, Langston
[James Langston Hughes]
American. Poet, Author, Journalist
Expressed Negro view of America in *Shakespeare in Harlem*, 1942; 1959 Spingarn winner.
b. Feb 1, 1902 in Joplin, Missouri
d. May 22, 1967 in New York, New York
Source: *AfrAmAl 6; AfrAmW; AgeMat; AmAu&B; AmCulL; AmDec 1920; AmWr S1; AnCL; ASCAP 66, 80; Au&Arts 12; AuBYP 2, 3; Benet 87; BenetAL 91; BiDAfM; BiDAmM; BiDAmNC; BiE&WWA; BioIn 1, 2, 3, 4, 5, 6, 7, 8, 9, 10, 11, 12, 13, 14, 15, 16, 17, 18, 19, 20, 21; BkCL; BlkAmP; BlkAmW 1; BlkAuII, 92; BlkAWP; BlkLC; BlkWr 1; BroadAu; CamGLE; CamHAL; CasWL; ChhPo, S1, S2, S3; ChlBkCr; ChlLR 17; CnDAL; CnMD; ConAmA; ConAu 1NR, 1R, 25R, 34NR; ConBlAP 88; ConBlB 4; ConHero 2; ConLC 1, 5, 10, 15, 35; ConPo 75; CroCD; CurBio 40, 67; CyWA 89; DcAmB S8; DcAmNB; DcArts; DcLB 4, 7, 48, 51, 86; DcLEL; DcTwCCu 5; DramC 3; DrBlPA, 90; EarBlAP; EncAACR; EncAB-H 1974, 1996; EncAL; EncJzS; EncWL, 2, 3; EncWT; Ent; FacFETw; FourBJA; GayLesB; GrWrEL P; LegTOT; LiExTwC; LinLib L, S; LngCTC; MagSAmL; MajTwCW; McGEWB; McGEWD 72, 84; ModAL, S1, S2; ModBlW; ModWD; MorBAP; NegAl 76, 83, 89; NewGrDA 86; NotNAT A, B; Novels; OxCAmL 65, 83; OxCTwCP; PenC AM; PeoHis; PoeCrit 1; RAdv 1, 14, 13-1; RComAH; REn; REnAL; RfGAmL 87; RGFAP; SchCGBL; SelBAAf; SelBAAu; ShSCr 6; ShSWr; SixAP; SmATA 4, 33; SouWr; Str&VC; TwCA, SUP; TwoTYeD; WebAB 74, 79; WebE&AL; WhAm 4; WhDW; WhE&EA; WhoTwCL; WorAl; WorAlBi; WorLitC; WrChl*

Hughes, Richard Arthur Warren
Welsh. Author, Dramatist
Wrote *High Wind in Jamaica*, 1929.
b. Apr 19, 1900 in Weybridge, England
d. Apr 28, 1976 in Merionethshire, Wales
Source: *Au&Wr 71; BioIn 4, 5, 6, 7, 8, 14, 15, 17, 21; CasWL; ChhPo, S2; ConAu 5R; ConLC 1; ConNov 72, 76; CyWA 58; DcArts; DcLEL; DcNaB 1971; EncWL; EvLB; GrWrEL N; IntAu&W 76; LngCTC; ModBrL, S1; NewC; NewCBEL; OxCEng 67, 85, 95; PenC ENG; RAdv 1; REn; RGTwCWr; SmATA 8; TwCA, SUP; TwCChW 95; TwCWr; WhAm 7; WhoChL; WhoLA; WhoTwCL; WrDr 76*

Hughes, Richard J(oseph)
American. Judge, Politician
Dem. governor of NJ, 1962-70; chief justice, NJ Supreme Court, 1974-70; wrote desicion allowing parents of comatose Karen Ann Quinlan to remove her from a respirator.
b. Aug 10, 1909
d. Dec 7, 1992 in Boca Raton, Florida
Source: *AmBench 79; BiDrGov 1789; BioIn 6, 7, 11; BlueB 76; CurBio 93N; PolProf J, K; WhoAm 74, 78; WhoAmL 78, 79; WhoAmP 73, 75, 77, 79; WhoE 74, 79, 81*

Hughes, Robert Studley Forrest
Australian. Critic, Author
Art critic, *Time* mag., 1970—; wrote *Art of Australia*, 1966, *The Fatal Shore*, 1987.
b. Jul 28, 1938 in Sydney, Australia
Source: *CurBio 87; Who 85, 92; WhoAm 84, 90, 97; WhoAmA 84*

Hughes, Rupert
American. Author
Wrote novel *Man Without a Home*, 1935; biography *George Washington*, 1930.
b. Jan 31, 1872 in Lancaster, Missouri
d. Sep 9, 1956 in Los Angeles, California
Source: *AmAu&B; AnMV 1926; ApCAB X; ASCAP 66, 80; Baker 78, 84, 92; BenetAL 91; BioIn 1, 4; ChhPo, S1, S2; CmCal; ConAmL; DcAmAu; DcAmB S6; NewGrDA 86; NotNAT B; OhA&B; OxCAmL 65, 83, 95; OxCAmT 84; REnAL; ScF&FL 1; TwCA, SUP; TwYS, A; WhAm 3; WhE&EA; WhLit; WhNAA; WhoStg 1908; WhScrn 77, 83; WhThe*

Hughes, Sarah Tilghman
American. Judge
Administered oath of office to L B Johnson after assassination of J F Kennedy, 1963.
b. Aug 2, 1896 in Baltimore, Maryland
d. Apr 23, 1985 in Dallas, Texas
Source: *AmBench 79; BiDFedJ; GoodHs; InWom, SUP; WhAm 8; WhoAm 74, 76, 78, 80, 82, 84; WhoAmL 79; WhoAmP 73; WhoAmW 58, 64, 66, 68, 70, 72, 74, 79, 81, 83; WhoGov 72, 75, 77; WhoSSW 73, 76*

Hughes, Ted
[Edward J Hughes]
English. Poet
Poet laureate of England, 1984—; writer of award-winning children's verse.
b. Aug 17, 1930 in Mytholmroyd, England
Source: *AuBYP 2S, 3; Benet 87, 96; BioIn 7, 9, 10, 11, 12, 13, 14, 15, 16, 17, 19, 21; BlmGEL; BlueB 76; BritWr S1; CamGEL; CamGLE; CasWL; ChhPo, S1, S2, S3; ChlBkCr; ChlFicS; ChlLR 3; CnE&AP; ConAu 1NR, 1R, 33NR; ConLC 2, 4, 9, 14, 37; ConPo 70, 75, 80, 85, 91, 96; CurBio 79; DcArts; DcLB 40, 161; DcLEL 1940; EncSF, 93; EncWB; EncWL, 2, 3; EngPo; FacFETw; GrWrEL P; IntAu&W 76, 77, 89, 91, 93; IntWW 74, 75, 76, 77, 78, 79, 80, 81, 82, 83, 89, 91, 93; IntWWP 77; LegTOT; LinLib L; LngCEL; LngCTC; MagSWL; MajAl; MajTwCW;*

MakMC; ModBrL, S1, S2; NewC; OxCChiL; OxCEng 85, 95; OxCTwCP; PenC ENG; PoeCrit 7; RAdv 1, 14, 13-1; RfGEnL 91; RGFMBP; RGTwCWr; ScF&FL 92; SmATA 27, 49; TwCChW 78, 83, 89; TwCWr; TwCYAW; WebE&AL; WhDW; Who 74, 82, 83, 85, 88, 90, 92, 94; WhoAm 82, 84, 86, 88, 90, 92, 94, 95, 96, 97; WhoTwCL; WhoWor 74, 76, 78, 82, 84, 87, 89, 91, 93, 95, 96, 97; WorAl; WorAlBi; WorAu 1950; WrDr 76, 80, 82, 84, 86, 88, 90, 92, 94, 96

Hughes, Thomas
English. Social Reformer, Author
Wrote classic *Tom Brown's School Days,* 1857.
b. Oct 20, 1822 in Uffington, England
d. Mar 22, 1896 in Brighton, England
Source: *Alli SUP; BbD; BiD&SB; BioIn 3, 4, 5, 6, 8, 9, 12, 13, 14, 16; BritAu 19; CamGEL; CamGLE; CarSB; CasWL; ChhPo S3; CyWA 58; DcArts; DcBiA; DcEnA; DcEnL; DcEuL; DcLB 18, 163; DcLEL; DcNaB S1; EvLB; GrWrEL N; JBA 34; LegTOT; LinLib L, S; LuthC 75; MnBBF; MouLC 4; NewC; NewCBEL; Novels; OxCChiL; OxCEng 67, 85, 95; PenC ENG; REn; RfGEnL 91; SmATA 31; StaCVF; TwCChW 83A, 89A, 95A; VicBrit; WhoChL; WorAl; WorAlBi*

Hugo, Adele
French.
Daughter of Victor Hugo whose life was filmed as *Story of Adele H.,* 1975.
b. Jul 30, 1830 in Paris, France
d. Apr 21, 1915 in Paris, France
Source: *BioIn 11*

Hugo, Victor Marie
French. Dramatist, Author
Best known for *Les Miserables,* 1862.
b. Feb 26, 1802 in Besancon, France
d. May 22, 1885 in Paris, France
Source: *AtlBL; BioIn 2, 3, 4, 5, 6, 7, 8, 9, 10, 11, 13; CasWL; DcBiPP; DcEnL; DcEuL; EncMys; EuAu; EvEuW; HsB&A; McGEWD 72; MnBBF; NewC; OxCEng 67; OxCFr; OxCThe 67; PenC EUR; RComWL; REn*

Huie, William Bradford
American. Author, Journalist
Known for books dealing with violence in civil rights movement in South: *The Klansman,* 1967; also wrote *The Execution of Private Slovik,* 1954, later filmed.
b. Nov 13, 1910 in Hartselle, Alabama
d. Nov 23, 1986 in Guntersville, Alabama
Source: *AmAu&B; AnObit 1986; Au&Wr 71; AuNews 1; AuSpks; BioIn 4, 6, 8, 10, 11, 15; ConAu 7NR, 9R, 121; ConNov 72, 76, 82, 86; FacFETw; IntAu&W 76, 77, 82, 86; NewYTBS 86; REnAL; TwCA SUP; WhAm 9; WhoAm 74, 76, 78, 80, 82, 84, 86; WhoSSW 73; WhoWor 74; WrDr 76, 80, 82, 84, 86*

Huizenga, H(arry) Wayne
American. Business Executive
Chm., CEO, Blockbuster Video, 1987—; part owner, Miami Dolphins, Joe Robbie Stadium, Miami, 1989—; owner, Florida Marlins, 1992—.
b. Dec 29, 1939 in Evergreen Park, Illinois
Source: *BioIn 16; CurBio 95; Dun&B 88; News 92; WhoAm 94, 95, 96, 97; WhoFI 92; WhoSSW 93, 95*

Hulagu Khan
Mongolian. Ruler
Grandson of Genghis Khan, brother of Kublai Khan; fought for control of Baghdad and Syria.
b. 1217
d. 1265
Source: *NewCol 75; WebBD 83*

Hulbert, Jack
English. Entertainer
Appeared in film *The Camels Are Coming.*
b. Apr 24, 1892 in Ely, England
d. Mar 25, 1978 in London, England
Source: *BiDD; BioIn 11; ConAu 115; EncMT; FilmgC; HalFC 80, 84, 88; IlWWBF, A; OxCPMus; QDrFCA 92; Who 74; WhoHol A; WhoThe 72, 77; WhScrn 83*

Hulce, Thomas
American. Actor
Made debut in *Those Lips, Those Eyes,* 1980; nominated for Oscar, 1984, for title role in *Amadeus.*
b. Dec 6, 1953 in White Water, Wisconsin
Source: *BioIn 14; ConTFT 3, 9; HalFC 88; IntMPA 92; IntWW 91; VarWW 85; WhoAm 90; WhoEnt 92; WorAlBi*

Hull, Bobby
[Robert Marvin Hull]
"The Golden Jet"
Canadian. Hockey Player
Left wing, 1957-80, mostly with Chicago; known for speed, vicious slap shot; won Hart Trophy twice, Art Ross Trophy three times; Hall of Fame, 1983.
b. Jan 3, 1939 in Point Anne, Ontario, Canada
Source: *BioIn 7, 8, 9, 10, 11, 12, 16, 20, 21; CanWW 31, 81, 83, 89; CelR; CurBio 66; FacFETw; LegTOT; NewYTBE 73; NewYTBS 78, 80; WhoAm 74, 76, 78, 80, 82, 84, 86, 88, 90, 92, 94, 95, 96, 97; WhoHcky 73; WhoMW 74; WhoSpor; WorAl; WorAlBi*

Hull, Brett (A.)
"The Golden Brett"
Canadian. Hockey Player
NHL right wing, 1986-88, with St. Louis, 1988—; son of Bobby; only player besides Gretzky to score 50 goals in 50 games more than once; 6th NHL player to score 70 goals in one season (1989-90); MVP, 1992; won Hart Trophy, 1991.
b. Aug 9, 1964 in Belleville, Ontario, Canada
Source: *BioIn 14, 15; CurBio 92; HocReg 87; News 91; NewYTBS 86; WhoAm 92, 94, 95, 96, 97; WhoMW 92; WhoSpor*

Hull, Cordell
American. Statesman
Helped establish UN, "good neighbor policies," 1945; won Nobel Peace Prize, 1945.
b. Oct 2, 1871 in Overton County, Tennessee
d. Jul 23, 1955 in Bethesda, Maryland
Source: *AmDec 1930; AmPeW; AmPolLe; BiDInt; BiDrAC; BiDrUSC 89; BiDrUSE 71, 89; BioIn 1, 2, 4, 5, 6, 7, 9, 10, 11, 15, 16, 17, 21; CurBio 40, 55; DcAmB S5; DcAmDH 80, 89; DcPol; DcTwHis; EncAAH; EncAB-H 1974, 1996; EncSoH; EncTR 91; FacFETw; HisEWW; HisWorL; LegTOT; LinLib S; McGEWB; NobelP; ObitOF 79; ObitT 1951; OxCAmH; PolPar; WebAB 74, 79; WebBD 83; WhAm 3; WhAmP; WhoNob, 90, 95; WhWW-II; WorAl; WorAlBi*

Hull, Henry
American. Actor
Created role of Jeeter Lester in *Tobacco Road,* Broadway, 1934; title in film *The Werewolf of London,* 1935.
b. Oct 3, 1890 in Louisville, Kentucky
d. Mar 8, 1977 in Cornwall, England
Source: *BiE&WWA; MotPP; MovMk; NewYTBS 77; NotNAT; OxCAmT 84; PlP&P; TwYS; Vers A; WhoHol A; WhoHrs 80; WhoThe 77A; WhScrn 83; WhThe*

Hull, Isaac
American. Military Leader
Led sinking of British ship *Guerriere,* 1812.
b. Mar 9, 1773 in Huntington, Connecticut
d. Dec 13, 1843 in Philadelphia, Pennsylvania
Source: *AmBi; ApCAB; BioIn 1, 2, 7, 13, 15; DcAmB; DcAmMiB; HarEnMi; LegTOT; LinLib S; NatCAB 13; OxCAmH; OxCShps; REn; TwCBDA; WebAB 74, 79; WebAMB; WhAm HS; WorAl; WorAlBi*

Hull, John Edwin
American. Military Leader
Commanded UN forces in the Far East, 1953-55.
b. May 26, 1895 in Greenfield, Ohio
d. Jun 10, 1975
Source: *BioIn 3, 4, 10, 12; CurBio 54; IntWW 74, 75, 76, 77, 78, 79, 80, 81; WhAm 6*

Hull, Josephine
[Josephine Sherwood]
American. Actor
Won 1950 Oscar for *Harvey;* one of Cary Grant's murderous aunts in *Arsenic and Old Lace,* 1942.

b. Jan 3, 1884 in Newton, Massachusetts
d. Mar 12, 1957 in New York, New York
Source: *BioAmW; CurBio 53, 57; EncAFC; FilmEn; FilmgC; HalFC 80, 84, 88; LegTOT; MotPP; MovMk; PlP&P; ThFT; Vers B; WhAm 3; WhoHol B; WhScrn 74, 77; WomWWA 14*

Hull, Warren
American. Actor, Singer
Host of radio, TV quiz show, "Strike It Rich."
b. Jan 17, 1903 in Gasport, New York
d. Sep 21, 1974 in Waterbury, Connecticut
Source: *BioIn 3, 10; FilmEn; FilmgC; ForYSC; HalFC 80, 84, 88; LegTOT; NewYTBS 74; NewYTET; RadStar; SaTiSS; WhoHol B; WhScrn 77, 83*

Hulman, Tony, Jr.
[Anton Hulman]
American. Auto Racing Executive, Business Executive
Pres., Indianapolis Speedway who began each race saying "Gentlemen, start your engines."
b. Feb 11, 1901 in Terre Haute, Indiana
d. Oct 27, 1977 in Indianapolis, Indiana
Source: *BiDAmSp OS; BioIn 1, 21; NewYTBS 77; St&PR 75; WhScrn 83*

Hulme, Kathryn Cavarly
American. Author
Wrote *The Wild Place,* 1953; best-selling biography *Nun's Story,* 1957.
b. Jan 6, 1900 in San Francisco, California
d. Aug 25, 1981 in Lihue, Hawaii
Source: *AmAu&B; WhoAm 74; WhoAmW 77; WhoWor 74*

Hulme, Thomas Ernest
English. Philosopher
Led anti-Romantic movement called Imagism in early 1900s.
b. Sep 16, 1883 in Endon, England
d. Sep 28, 1917, France
Source: *Benet 87; BioIn 1, 5, 9, 10, 12, 13, 14, 15; BlmGEL; CasWL; Chambr 3; ChhPo S1; DcEuL; LngCTC; ModBrL; NewCBEL; OxCEng 67; PenC ENG; REn; TwCA, SUP; WebE&AL; WhoTwCL*

Human League, The
[Ian Burden; Joe Callis; Joanne Catherall; Phil Oakey; Susanne Sulley; Philip Wright]
English. Music Group
Electro-pop band formed 1977; best successes in US: "Don't You Want Me," 1982; "Human," 1987.
Source: *BioIn 4; ConMus 17; EncRk 88; EncRkSt; HarEnR 86; IlEncRk; OxCPMus; PenEncP; RkOn 85; RolSEnR 83; WhoRocM 82; WhsNW 85*

Humbard, Rex
American. Evangelist
TV, radio evangelist since 1930; reaches 20 million people on 360 stations.
b. Aug 13, 1919 in Little Rock, Arkansas
Source: *BioIn 9, 10, 11, 12, 14, 15; ConAu 111; CurBio 72; NewYTBE 73; PrimTiR; RelLAm 91; WhoAm 82, 84, 86*

Humble Pie
[David Clem Clemson; Peter Frampton; Steve Marriott; Gregory Ridley; Jerry Shirley]
English. Music Group
Hard-rock band, 1968-75; had hit album *Smokin',* 1972.
Source: *BioIn 15, 21; ConMuA 80A; EncPR&S 89; EncRk 88; EncRkSt; HarEnR 86; IlEncRk; NewYTBS 76; PenEncP; RkOn 78; RolSEnR 83; WhoRock 81; WhoRocM 82*

Humboldt, Alexander, Freiherr von
German. Explorer, Scientist
Traveled through Latin America, 1799-1804; discovered Peruvian current bearing name.
b. Sep 14, 1769 in Berlin, Germany
d. May 6, 1859 in Berlin, Germany
Source: *BiD&SB; BioIn 1, 2, 3, 4, 5, 6, 7, 8, 9, 10, 11, 17, 18, 19, 20; CasWL; DcEuL; EuAu; NewC; OxCEng 67; OxCGer 76, 86; OxCSpan; PenC EUR; REn*

Humboldt, Wilhelm Freiherr von
German. Statesman, Author
Noted philologist who wrote on Basque, Java languages; brother of Alexander.
b. Jun 22, 1767 in Potsdam, Prussia
d. Apr 8, 1835 in Tegel, Prussia
Source: *BiD&SB; CasWL; DcEuL; EuAu; OxCGer 76; PenC EUR; REn*

Hume, Brit
[Alexander Britton Hume]
American. Broadcast Journalist
ABC nat. correspondent, 1976-87; White House correspondent, 1976—.
b. Jun 22, 1943 in Washington, District of Columbia
Source: *BioIn 16; ConAu 119, 126; EncTwCJ; IntAu&W 91; LesBEnT 92; WhoAm 80, 82, 84, 86, 88, 90, 94, 95, 96, 97; WhoE 95, 97; WhoWor 96, 97*

Hume, David
Scottish. Philosopher
Philosophical skeptic who influenced metaphysical thought; wrote classic *History of England,* 1754-62.
b. Apr 26, 1711 in Edinburgh, Scotland
d. Aug 25, 1776 in Edinburgh, Scotland
Source: *Alli; AtlBL; BbD; Benet 87, 96; BiD&SB; BiDPsy; BiESc; BioIn 1, 2, 3, 4, 5, 6, 7, 8, 9, 10, 11, 12, 13, 14, 16, 17, 21; BlkwCE; BlkwEAR; BlmGEL; BritAu; CamGEL; CamGLE; CasWL; Chambr 2; CmScLit; CyEd; CyWA 58; DcAmC; DcBiPP; DcEnA; DcEnL; DcEuL; DcLB 104; DcLEL; DcNaB; DcScB; EncEnl; EncEth; EncUnb; EvLB; GrEconB; LegTOT; LinLib L, S; LitC 7; LngCEL; LuthC 75; McGEWB; MouLC 2; NamesHP; NewC; NewCBEL; OxCEng 67, 85, 95; OxCLaw; OxCPhil; PenC ENG; RAdv 14, 13-4; REn; TwoTYeD; WebE&AL; WhDW; WhoEc 81, 86; WorAl; WorAlBi; WrPh P*

Hume, John
Irish. Politician
Member, Northern Ireland Assembly, 1973-75, 1982-86; British Parliament, 1983—.
b. Jan 18, 1937 in Londonderry, Northern Ireland
Source: *BioIn 9, 12, 14, 16; ConNews 87-1; IntWW 82, 83, 89, 91, 93; Who 82, 83, 85, 88, 90, 92, 94; WhoEIO 82; WhoWor 87, 91, 97*

Humes, Helen
American. Singer
Jazz singer who sang with Count Basie, 1938-42; had hit song "Be Baba Leba," 1945.
b. Jun 23, 1913 in Louisville, Kentucky
d. Sep 13, 1981 in Santa Monica, California
Source: *AllMusG; AnObit 1981; ASCAP 80; Baker 84, 92; BiDAfM; BiDAmM; BiDJaz; BioIn 4, 10, 12, 16, 17; BluesWW; CmpEPM; DrBlPA 90; EncJzS; InB&W 85; InWom SUP; NewGrDA 86; NewGrDJ 88, 94; NewYTBS 81; NotBlAW 2; OxCPMus; PenEncP; WhoJazz 72; WhScrn 83*

Humes, James Calhoun
American. Lawyer
Speechwriter for presidents Nixon, Ford; wrote *Churchill: Speaker of the Century,* 1980.
b. Oct 31, 1934 in Williamsport, Pennsylvania
Source: *ConAu 1NR, 45; WhoAm 74, 76, 78, 80, 82, 84, 86, 88, 90, 92, 94, 95, 96, 97; WhoAmL 96; WhoE 97; WhoGov 72, 75; WhoSSW 73, 75; WhoWor 76, 78, 93*

Hummel, Berta
[Sister Maria Innocentia]
German. Artist
Hummel figurines inspired by her drawings; international industry by 1935.
b. May 21, 1909 in Massing, Bavaria
d. Nov 6, 1946 in Siessen, Germany
Source: *BioIn 12, 15, 17; ChhPo S2; Entr; SmATA 43*

Hummel, Johann Nepomuk
German. Composer, Pianist
Helped develop art of piano playing; wrote opera *Mathilde von guise,* 1810.
b. Nov 14, 1778 in Pressburg, Germany
d. Oct 17, 1837 in Weimar, Germany
Source: *Baker 78, 84, 92; BioIn 1, 2, 7, 9, 10, 11; BriBkM 80; CelCen; DcBiPP; MusMk; NewAmDM; NewGrDM 80; NewGrDO; NewOxM; OxCMus; OxDcOp; PenDiMP A*

Hummel, Lisl
Austrian.
Known for use of silhouettes in fairy tales, children's books.
Source: *BioIn 1; ChhPo; ConICB; IlsCB 1744, 1946; InWom*

Hump
[Etokeah]
American. Native American Leader
Served with Red Cloud during the wars of 1866-68; known as a nontreaty chief because of his refusal to sign the Treaty of Fort Laramie in 1866.
b. 1848 in South Dakota
d. 1908
Source: *BioIn 21; EncNAB; NotNaAm*

Humperdinck, Engelbert
German. Composer
Wrote opera *Hansel and Gretel,* 1893.
b. Sep 1, 1854 in Siegburg, Germany
d. Sep 27, 1921 in Neustrelitz, Germany
Source: *AtlBL; Baker 78, 84, 92; BioIn 3, 4, 7, 8, 10, 12, 16; BriBkM 80; CmOp; CmpBCM; DcArts; DcCom 77; DcCom&M 79; DcPup; Dis&D; GrComp; IntDcOp; LegTOT; LinLib S; MetOEnc; MusMk; NewAmDM; NewEOp 71; NewGrDM 80; NewGrDO; NewOxM; OxCGer 76; OxCMus; OxDcOp; PenDiMP A; REn; WorAl; WorAlBi*

Humperdinck, Engelbert
[Arnold George Dorsey]
English. Singer
Nightclub, TV singer, most popular 1960s-70s; picked stage name from music dictionary; albums include *Release Me,* 1966.
b. May 3, 1936 in Madras, India
Source: *Baker 78, 84, 92; BiDAmM; BioIn 8, 9, 11, 13; BkPepl; CelR, 90; EncPR&S 89; LegTOT; NewGrDA 86; OxCPMus; PenEncP; RkOn 78; VarWW 85; WhoAm 78, 80, 82, 84, 86, 88, 90, 92, 94, 95, 96, 97; WhoEnt 92; WhoHol 92; WhoRock 81; WhoWor 74, 84; WorAl; WorAlBi*

Humphrey, Doris
American. Dancer, Choreographer
Artistic director for Jose Limon, 1946; founded Julliard Dance Theater, 1955.
b. Oct 17, 1895 in Oak Park, Illinois
d. Dec 29, 1958 in New York, New York
Source: *BiDD; BioAmW; BioIn 1, 3, 4, 5, 7, 8, 9, 10, 11, 12, 15, 17, 18, 20, 21; CmpGMD; CnOxB; ContDcW 89; CurBio 42, 59; DancEn 78; DcAmB S6; DcArts; IntDcWB; InWom, SUP; LibW; NotAW MOD; RAdv 14; WhAm 3; WhoAmW 58; WorAl; WorAlBi*

Humphrey, Elliott S
American. Animal Trainer
Trained first guide dogs for blind.
b. 1889 in Saratoga Springs, New York
d. Jun 6, 1981 in Phoenix, Arizona
Source: *NewYTBS 81*

Humphrey, George Magoffin
American. Statesman
Secretary of Treasury, 1953-57.
b. Mar 8, 1890 in Cheboygan, Michigan
d. Jan 20, 1970 in Cleveland, Ohio
Source: *BiDAmBL 83; BiDrUSE 71, 89; BioIn 1, 3, 4, 5, 6, 8, 9, 10, 11; CurBio 53, 70; DcAmB S8; EncABHB 9; NatCAB 55; NewYTBE 70; PolProf E; WhAm 5; WorAl*

Humphrey, Gordon John
American. Politician
Conservative Republican senator from NH, 1979-91.
b. Oct 9, 1940 in Bristol, Connecticut
Source: *AlmAP 80, 88; BiDrUSC 89; CngDr 85, 87, 89; IntWW 89, 91, 93; NewYTBS 78; PolsAm 84; WhoAm 80, 82, 84, 86, 88, 90; WhoAmP 85, 91; WhoE 79, 81, 83, 85, 86, 89, 91; WhoEmL 87; WhoWor 80, 82, 87, 89, 91*

Humphrey, Hubert Horatio, Jr.
"The Happy Warrior"
American. US Vice President
Thirty-two yr. public service career included 23 yrs. as Dem. senator from MN, 5 yrs. as vp under Johnson.
b. May 27, 1911 in Wallace, South Dakota
d. Jan 13, 1978 in Waverly, Minnesota
Source: *AmOrTwC; AmPolLe; BiDrAC; BiDrUSC 89; BiDrUSE 71, 89; BioIn 1, 2, 3, 4, 5, 6, 7, 8, 9, 10, 11, 12, 14, 17, 18; BlueB 76; ColdWar 1; ConAu 69, 73; CurBio 49, 66, 78; DcAmB S10; EncAACR; EncAAH; EncAB-H 1974, 1996; EncWB; FacFETw; IntWW 74, 75, 76, 77; NewYTBS 78; VicePre; WebAB 74, 79; WebBD 83; WhAm 7; WhDW; Who 74; WhoAm 74, 76, 78; WhoAmP 73, 75, 77; WhoGov 72, 75, 77; WhoMW 74, 76; WhoWor 74; WorAl*

Humphrey, Muriel Fay Buck
[Mrs. Hubert Humphrey]
American., Politician
Completed husband's final senate term, 1978-79.
b. Feb 20, 1912 in Huron, South Dakota
Source: *BiDrUSC 89; BioIn 13; WhoAm 74, 76, 78, 80, 82, 86; WhoAmW 66, 68, 70, 72, 74, 79, 81; WhoMW 74, 76, 78*

Humphreys, Christmas
[Travers Christmas Humphreys]
English. Author
Most writings reflect belief in Buddhism: *The Development of Buddhism in England,* 1937.
b. Feb 15, 1901 in London, England
d. Apr 13, 1983 in London, England
Source: *AnObit 1983; Au&Wr 71; BioIn 12, 13; ChhPo S1, S2; ConAu 77, 109; DcNaB 1981; EncO&P 3; EngPo; IntAu&W 76, 82; IntWW 74, 75, 76, 77, 78, 79, 80, 81, 82, 83, 83N; IntWWP 77, 82; WhE&EA; Who 74, 82, 83; WhoWor 74, 76, 78*

Humphreys, Joshua
American. Architect
First US Naval constructor, 1794-1801; designed speedy frigates like the *Constitution.*
b. Jun 17, 1751 in Delaware County, Delaware
d. Jan 12, 1838 in Haverford, Pennsylvania
Source: *AmBi; ApCAB; BioIn 3; DcAmB; DcAmMiB; EncCRAm; NatCAB 5; TwCBDA; WebAB 74, 79; WebAMB; WhAm HS*

Humphries, Barry
[John Barry Humphries]
Australian. Actor
Best known as "Dame Edna Everage," a character he portrays in the form of a rhinestone eyeglass-wearing Australian housewife.
b. Feb 17, 1934 in Melbourne, Australia
Source: *CamGWoT; ConAu 129; DcLP 87A; Ent; HalFC 88; IntAu&W 89, 91; IntWW 89, 91; News 93-1; OxCAusL; Who 83, 85, 88, 90, 92; WhoHol 92; WhoThe 81*

Humphries, Rolfe
[George Rolfe Humphries]
American. Poet
Award-winning verse volumes include *Wind of Time,* 1951.
b. Nov 20, 1894 in Philadelphia, Pennsylvania
d. Apr 22, 1969 in Redwood City, California
Source: *AmAu&B; BenetAL 91; BioIn 4, 8, 12, 17; ChhPo S1; CnDAL; ConAu 3NR, 5R, 25R; DcAmB S8; LinLib L; OxCAmL 65, 83; OxCLiW 86; OxCTwCP; RAdv 1; REnAL; ScF&FL 1, 2; TwCA, SUP; WhAm 5*

Humphry, Ann Wickett
American. Social Reformer
Co-founder, Hemlock Society, a right-to-die group, 1978; committed suicide, 1991.
b. 1942?
d. Oct 8, 1991 in Willamette Valley, Oregon
Source: *NewYTBS 91*

Humphry, Derek John
English. Social Reformer, Author
Founder, Hemlock Society, a right-to-die group, 1980; wrote *Final Exit,* a suicide manual, 1991.
b. Apr 29, 1930 in Bath, England
Source: *ConAu 41R; CurBio 95; IntAu&W 86, 89, 91, 93; News 92; WhoUSWr 88; WhoWest 87, 89, 92, 94; WhoWor 87, 89, 93; WhoWrEP 89, 92, 95*

Hu Na
Chinese. Tennis Player
Defected to US; China suspended cultural exchanges in retaliation, 1983.
b. Apr 1963
Source: *BioIn 13*

Hundertwasser, Friedensreich
[Friedrich Stowasser]
Austrian. Artist
Abstract painter who developed grammar of vision theory: *Regenstag* series.
b. Dec 15, 1928 in Vienna, Austria
Source: *BioIn 15; ConArt 77, 83, 89, 96; EncWB; IntWW 74, 75, 76, 77, 78, 79, 80, 81, 82, 83, 89, 91, 93; WhoArt 84; WhoWor 74, 78, 84, 87, 89, 91, 93, 95, 96*

Huneker, James Gibbons
American. Critic, Author
Music, drama critic from 1900; wrote musical biographies *Ivory, Apes, and Peacocks,* 1915; *Painted Veils,* 1920.
b. Jan 31, 1860 in Philadelphia, Pennsylvania
d. Feb 9, 1921 in New York, New York
Source: *AmAu&B; AmBi; ApCAB X; Benet 87; BenetAL 91; BiDAmM; BioIn 1, 2, 4, 5, 6, 7, 10, 12, 13, 15, 16; CnDAL; ConAmL; DcAmAu; DcAmB; DcLEL; DcNAA; EncAJ; EncWT; GrWrEL N; LinLib L, S; LngCTC; NatCAB 14; Novels; OxCAmL 65; OxCMus; OxCThe 67, 83; PenC AM; PeoHis; RAdv 1; REn; REnAL; TwCA, SUP; WebAB 74, 79; WhAm 1*

Hung-Wu
[Chu Yuan-Chang]
Chinese. Ruler
Emperor of China, 1368-98; founded Ming dynasty.
b. Oct 21, 1328 in Hao-Chou, China
d. Jun 24, 1398, China
Source: *McGEWB*

Hunnicutt, Arthur
American. Actor
Received Oscar nomination for *The Big Sky,* 1952.
b. Feb 17, 1911 in Gravelly, Arkansas
d. Sep 27, 1979 in Woodland Hills, California
Source: *BioIn 12, 78, 79, 80; MovMk; Vers A; WhoHol A; WhScrn 83*

Hunnicutt, Gayle
American. Actor
Starred in TV movies "The Golden Bowl"; "A Man Called Intrepid."
b. Feb 6, 1943 in Fort Worth, Texas
Source: *BioIn 21; FilmEn; FilmgC; HalFC 88; IntMPA 86; ItaFilm; VarWW 85; WhoAmW 70A, 72, 74; WhoHol 92, A*

Hunsaker, Jerome Clarke
American. Aeronautical Engineer
Founded nation's first course in aeronautical engineering at MIT, 1914; built first effective wind tunnel in US, 1914.
b. Aug 26, 1886 in Creston, Louisiana
d. Sep 10, 1984 in Boston, Massachusetts
Source: *AmMWSc 73P; AnObit 1984; BiESc; BioIn 2, 3, 8, 12; BlueB 76; CurBio 42; InSci; IntWW 74; McGMS 80; NewYTBS 84; WebAB 74, 79; WebAMB; WhAm 7, 8; WhoAm 74, 76*

Hun Sen
Cambodian. Politician
Both foreign minister, 1978—, and prime minister, 1985-93, of Cambodia.
b. Apr 1951 in Kroch Chhmar, Cambodia
Source: *BioIn 16; CurBio 90; DcMPSA; IntWW 91; WhoAsAP 91; WhoWor 91*

Hunt, E(verette) Howard
American. Presidential Aide, Author
Consultant to Nixon, 1971-72; jailed for involvement in Watergate, 1973-74, 1975-77.
b. Oct 9, 1918 in Hamburg, New York
Source: *AmAu&B; BioIn 9, 10, 11, 12, 13, 14; ConAu 2NR, 45, 47NR; ConLC 3; IntAu&W 93; SpyFic; WhoAm 74, 76, 78, 86; WrDr 86, 88, 94, 96*

Hunt, Frazier
"Spike"
American. Journalist
War correspondent for *Chicago Tribune,* WW I; wrote *The Long Trail from Texas,* 1940.
b. Dec 1, 1885 in Rock Island, Illinois
d. Dec 24, 1967 in Newtown, Pennsylvania
Source: *AmAu&B; BioIn 8; ConAu 93; WhAm 4*

Hunt, George Wylie Paul
American. Politician, Statesman
First governor of AZ, 1911; re-elected three times.
b. Nov 1, 1859 in Huntsville, Maryland
d. Dec 24, 1934
Source: *BiDrGov 1789; BioIn 1, 6, 8, 10, 17; DcAmB S1; NatCAB 29; REnAW; WhAm 1; WhAmP*

Hunt, Guy
[H. Guy Hunt]
American. Politician
Rep. governor of Alabama, 1987-93; removed from office after being convicted of using $200,000 from his inaugural fund for personal debts.
b. Jun 17, 1933 in Holly Pond, Alabama
Source: *AlmAP 88; BiDrGov 1983, 1988; WhoAm 90; WhoAmP 87, 91; WhoSSW 91; WhoWor 91*

Hunt, H(aroldson) L(afayette)
American. Oilman
Billionaire who at height of wealth had a weekly income of over $1 million.
b. Feb 17, 1889 in Vandalia, Illinois
d. Nov 29, 1974 in Dallas, Texas
Source: *AmDec 1930; BiDAmBL 83; BiDAmNC; BioIn 8, 9, 10, 11, 12, 13; BusPN; CelR; CurBio 70, 75; DcAmB S9; EncAB-H 1974, 1996; MemAm; NatCAB 63; NewYTBS 74; REnAW; WebAB 74, 79; WhAm 6; WhoAm 74*

Hunt, Helen
American. Actor
Star of numerous films, made-for-TV movies, and TV series "Mad About You," 1992—; starred in 1996's *Twister;* won Emmy for best actress in a comedy series, 1996.
b. Jun 15, 1963 in Los Angeles, California
Source: *BenetAL 91; ConTFT 8; CurBio 96; IntMPA 92, 94, 96; InWom SUP; LegTOT; News 94; WhoAm 94, 95, 96, 97; WhoAmW 95, 97; WhoHol 92*

Hunt, Holman
[William Holman Hunt]
English. Artist
A founder of pre-Raphaelite Brotherhood, 1848; painted *Light of the World,* 1854.
b. Apr 2, 1827 in London, England
d. Sep 7, 1910 in London, England
Source: *ArtsNiC; AtlBL; Benet 87; BioIn 3, 4, 6, 8, 9, 10, 11, 12, 13, 14, 15, 16, 17; CelCen; ClaDrA; DcArts; DcBiPP; DcBrAr 1; DcBrBI; DcBrWA; DcNaB S2; DcVicP, 2; IntDcAA 90; LegTOT; LinLib L, S; LuthC 75; McGDA; McGEWB; NewCBEL; NewCol 75; OxCArt; OxCEng 85; OxDcArt; REn; VicBrit; WhDW; WorAl; WorAlBi*

Hunt, Jack Reed
American. Engineer, Pilot
Piloted longest non-stop, non-refueled trans-Atlantic blimp flight, 1958.
b. May 17, 1918 in Red Oak, Iowa
d. Jan 7, 1984 in Ormond Beach, Florida
Source: *BioIn 13; LEduc 74; NewYTBS 84; WhoFla*

Hunt, James
English. Auto Racer
Known for winning World Grand Prix Championship, 1976, despite rain, fog.
b. Aug 29, 1947 in Epsom, England
d. Jun 15, 1993 in London, England
Source: *BioIn 11, 12, 15, 19*

Hunt, James Baxter, Jr.
American. Politician
Dem. governor, NC, 1977-85; 1993—.
b. May 16, 1937 in Greensboro, North Carolina
Source: *BiDrGov 1789, 1978, 1983, 1988; BioIn 13, 14; CurBio 93; IntWW 93; PolsAm 84; WhoAm 76, 78, 80, 82, 84, 88, 90, 92, 94, 95, 96, 97; WhoAmL 79; WhoAmP 73, 75, 77, 79, 81, 83, 85, 87, 89, 91, 93, 95; WhoGov 75, 77; WhoSSW 76, 78, 80, 82, 95, 97; WhoWor 82*

Hunt, John, Baron
[Henry Cecil John Hunt]
English. Mountaineer
Led Hillary's Mt. Everest expedition, 1953; described event in *The Ascent of Everest,* 1953.
b. Jun 22, 1910 in Marlborough, England
Source: *BioIn 3, 4, 12; ConAu 109*

Hunt, Lamar
American. Football Executive
Owner, KC Chiefs, 1959—; founder, first pres., AFL, 1959; pres., AFC, 1970—; Hall of Fame, 1973.
b. Aug 2, 1932 in Dallas, Texas
Source: *BiDAmSp FB; BioIn 13, 15, 16, 21; BuCMET; CelR, 90; Dun&B 86, 88, 90; WhoAm 80, 82, 84, 86, 88, 90, 92, 94, 95, 96, 97; WhoFtbl 74; WhoMW 90, 92, 93, 96*

Hunt, Leigh
[James Henry Leigh Hunt]
English. Author, Poet
Associated with Byron, Shelley, Keats; wrote verse "Abou Ben Adhem," 1834; edited literary periodicals.
b. Oct 19, 1784 in Southgate, England
d. Aug 28, 1859 in Putney, England
Source: *Alli; AtlBL; BbD; Benet 87; BiD&SB; BiDLA; BioIn 1, 2, 3, 4, 5, 6, 7, 8, 9, 10, 11, 12, 14, 17, 21; BlmGEL; BritAu 19; CamGEL; CamGLE; CamGWoT; CasWL; CelCen; Chambr 3; ChhPo, S1, S2, S3; CnE&AP; CrtT 2, 4; DcBiPP; DcEnA; DcEnL; DcEuL; DcLB 96, 110, 144; DcLEL; DcNaB; Dis&D; EvLB; GrWrEL N; LinLib L, S; LngCEL; MouLC 3; NatCAB 24; NewC; NewCBEL; NinCLC 1; NotNAT B; OxCEng 67, 85; OxCMus; OxCThe 67, 83; PenC ENG; RAdv 1, 14; REn; RfGEnL 91; ScF&FL 1; WebE&AL; WhAm 3; WhDW*

Hunt, Linda
American. Actor
Won Oscar, 1983, for role of man in *The Year of Living Dangerously.*
b. Apr 2, 1945 in Morristown, New Jersey
Source: *BioIn 13, 16; ConTFT 3, 9; CurBio 88; HalFC 88; IntMPA 86, 88, 92, 94, 96; LegTOT; NewYTBS 83; VarWW 85; WhoAm 88, 90, 92, 94, 95, 96, 97; WhoAmA 91; WhoAmW 87, 89, 91, 93, 95, 97; WhoEnt 92; WhoHol 92; WorAlBi*

Hunt, Lois
American. Actor, Singer
Soprano, NY Met., 1949-53; on Broadway in *Sound of Music,* 1961-62.
b. Nov 26, 1925 in York, Pennsylvania
Source: *BioIn 1, 2; WhoAm 74, 76; WhoAmW 68, 70, 72*

Hunt, Marsha
American. Author
Star of the London production of *Hair;* wrote *Joy,* 1991.
b. 1946
Source: *BioIn 20; BlkWr 2; ConAu 143; ConLC 70; InB&W 80*

Hunt, Martita
English. Actor
Played Miss Havisham in 1947 film *Great Expectations.*
b. Jan 30, 1900, Argentina
d. Jun 13, 1969 in London, England
Source: *BiE&WWA; BioIn 8, 9; FilmAG WE; FilmEn; FilmgC; ForYSC; HalFC 80, 84, 88; IlWWBF; ItaFilm; LegTOT; MotPP; MovMk; NotNAT B; ObitT 1961; Vers A; WhoHol B; WhScrn 74, 77, 83; WhThe*

Hunt, Nelson Bunker
"Bunky"
American. Business Executive
Played prominent role in silver crash of Mar 27, 1980; fortune estimated at $1.4 billion.
b. Feb 22, 1926 in Eldorado, Texas
Source: *BioIn 10, 11, 12, 13, 14, 15, 16, 17, 19; CurBio 80; Dun&B 79, 86; NewYTBS 76; WhoAm 82, 84, 86, 88; WhoFI 87; WhoSSW 84*

Hunt, Pee Wee
[Walter Hunt]
American. Jazz Musician
Trombonist; vocalist with Glen Gray, 1929-43; led Dixieland combos, 1950s-60s.
b. May 10, 1907 in Mount Healthy, Ohio
Source: *AmPS A; BiDJaz; CmpEPM; NewGrDJ 88, 94; OxCPMus; PenEncP; WhoJazz 72*

Hunt, Richard (Howard)
American. Sculptor
Sculptor of abstract works of welded steel and bronze based on natural forms.
b. Sep 12, 1935 in Chicago, Illinois
Source: *AfrAmAl 6; AmArt; BioIn 6, 8, 10, 13, 17, 20, 21; ConArt 83, 89, 96; ConBlB 6; DcAmArt; DcCAA 71, 77, 88, 94; DcCAr 81; DcTwCCu 5; Ebony 1; InB&W 80, 85; NegAl 76, 83, 89; PrintW 83, 85; WhoAfA 96; WhoAm 74, 76, 78, 80, 82, 84, 92, 94, 95, 96; WhoAmA 73, 76, 78, 80, 82, 84, 86, 89, 91, 93; WhoBlA 75, 77, 80, 85, 88, 90, 92, 94; WhoGov 72, 75; WhoMW 80, 82, 92*

Hunt, Richard Morris
American. Architect
Works include base of Statue of Liberty; NYCs Tribune Building.
b. Oct 31, 1828 in Brattleboro, Vermont
d. Jul 31, 1896 in Newport, Rhode Island
Source: *Alli SUP; AmBi; ApCAB; BioIn 1, 3, 4, 8, 9, 10, 12; BriEAA; DcAmB; Drake; LinLib S; McGDA; McGEWB; NatCAB 6; OxCAmH; OxCAmL 65; TwCBDA; WebAB 74; WhAm HS; WhoArch*

Hunt, Walter
American. Inventor
Invented the safety pin, fountain pen, and other practical items.
b. Jul 29, 1796 in Martinsburg, New York
d. Jun 8, 1859 in New York, New York
Source: *BioIn 4; InSci; NatCAB 19; WebAB 74, 79; WorInv*

Hunt, William Morris
American. Artist
Portraitist; introduced Millet, French Barbizon school to US; brother of Richard Morris.
b. Mar 31, 1824 in Brattleboro, Vermont
d. Sep 8, 1879 in Isles of Shoals, Vermont
Source: *AmBi; AmCulL; ApCAB; ArtsNiC; BiDAmEd; BioIn 2, 7, 8, 9, 12, 17, 19; BriEAA; DcAmArt; DcAmB; DcNAA; Drake; LinLib S; McGDA; NewYHSD; OxCAmH; OxCAmL 65; TwCBDA; WebAB 74, 79; WhAmArt 85; WhAm HS*

Hunter, Alberta
American. Singer, Songwriter
Blues singer; performed with jazz greats, wrote own songs; remarkable comeback at age 82.
b. Apr 1, 1895 in Memphis, Tennessee
d. Oct 17, 1984 in New York, New York
Source: *AllMusG; AnObit 1984; ASCAP 66; Baker 84, 92; BiDAfM; BiDJaz; BioAmW; BioIn 11, 12, 13, 14, 15, 16, 18, 19, 20; BlkWAm; BluesWW; ConMus 7; CurBio 79, 85N; DcTwCCu 5; DrBlPA 90; GayLesB; InB&W 80, 85; InWom SUP; LegTOT; NewGrDA 86; NewGrDJ 88, 94; NewYTBS 84; NotBlAW 1; OxCPMus; PenEncP; RolSEnR 83; WhoJazz 72*

Hunter, Catfish
[James Augustus Hunter]
American. Baseball Player
Pitcher, 1965-79; threw perfect game, 1968; Hall of Fame, 1987.
b. Apr 18, 1946 in Hertford, North Carolina
Source: *Ballpl 90; BiDAmSp BB; BioIn 10, 11, 12, 14, 15, 16, 17; CmCal; LegTOT; NewYTBS 75; WhoAm 74, 76, 78, 80, 82; WhoProB 73; WhoSpor; WorAlBi*

Hunter, Clementine
"Black Grandma Moses"
American. Artist
One of the South's most important folk artists; known for primitive visions of rural life.
b. Jan 19, 1887 in Natchitoches, Louisiana
d. Jan 1, 1988 in Natchitoches, Louisiana
Source: *AfroAA; NotBlAW 1*

Hunter, Dard
American. Printer, Author
Authority on papermaking, printing; wrote *My Life with Paper,* 1958.
b. Nov 29, 1883 in Steubenville, Ohio
d. Feb 20, 1966
Source: *AmAu&B; BenetAL 91; BioIn 1, 3, 4, 5, 6, 7, 8; ConAu 25R, P-1; CurBio 60, 66; OhA&B; OxCAmL 65, 83, 95; REnAL; WhAm 4; WhE&EA; WhNAA*

Hunter, Evan
[Ed McBain]
American. Author, Screenwriter
Books include *The Blackboard Jungle,* 1954; *Kiss,*; films include *The Birds,* 1962.
b. Oct 15, 1926 in New York, New York
Source: *AmAu&B; ASCAP 66, 80; Au&Wr 71; AuBYP 2, 3; Benet 87, 96; BenetAL 91; BioIn 4, 5, 8, 10, 12, 13, 14, 15, 17, 18, 21; BlueB 76; CamGLE; CamHAL; ConAu 5NR, 5R, 38NR; ConLC 11, 31; ConNov 72, 76, 82, 86, 91, 96; ConPopW; CurBio 56; DcLB Y82B; DcLEL 1940; DcLP 87B; DrAF 76; DrAPF 80, 87; EncMys; EncSF, 93; FacFETw; FilmgC; HalFC 80, 84, 88; IntAu&W 76, 77, 89; IntWW 74, 75, 76, 77, 78, 79, 80, 81, 82, 83, 89, 91, 93; LegTOT; MajTwCW; PenC AM; REn; REnAL; ScF&FL 1, 2, 92; ScFSB; SmATA 25; TwCCr&M 91; TwCSFW 81, 86, 91; VarWW 85; Who 82, 83, 85, 88, 90, 92, 94; WhoAm 74, 76, 78, 80, 82, 84, 86, 88, 90, 92, 94, 95, 96; WhoE 74; WhoTwCL; WhoUSWr 88; WhoWor 74; WhoWrEP 89, 92, 95; WorAl; WorAlBi; WorAu 1950; WorEFlm; WrDr 76, 80, 82, 84, 86, 88, 90, 92, 94, 96*

Hunter, Glenn
American. Actor
Played title role on stage, in film *Merton of the Movies,* 1922-24.
b. 1897 in Highland, New York
d. Dec 30, 1945 in New York, New York
Source: *CurBio 46; FilmgC; HalFC 80, 84, 88; MotPP; TwYS; WhoHol B; WhScrn 74, 77, 83*

Hunter, Holly
American. Actor
Oscar nominee for *Broadcast News,* 1988; won Emmy for TV miniseries "Roe vs. Wade," 1989; Golden Globe Award, Best Actress, *The Piano,* 1993.
b. Mar 20, 1958 in Conyers, Georgia
Source: *BiDFilm 94; BioIn 14, 15, 16; ConTFT 6, 13; CurBio 94; IntMPA 88, 92, 94, 96; LegTOT; News 89; NewYTBS 84; WhoAm 90, 92, 94, 95, 96, 97; WhoAmW 91, 93, 95, 97; WhoEnt 92; WhoHol 92; WhoWor 95, 96, 97; WorAlBi*

Hunter, Howard
American. Religious Leader
President of the Mormon church, 1994—

b. 1907 in Boise, Idaho
Source: *News 94*

Hunter, Ian
South African. Actor
Played nice guys in Hollywood films: *Adventures of Robin Hood,* 1938.
b. Jun 13, 1900 in Cape Town, South Africa
d. Sep 24, 1975, England
Source: *BioIn 11; ConMuA 80A; Film 2; FilmEn; FilmgC; ForYSC; HalFC 80, 84, 88; HolP 30; IlWWBF; IntMPA 75; MotPP; MovMk; WhoHol A; WhScrn 77, 83; WhThe*

Hunter, Ian
[Mott the Hoople]
English. Singer, Musician
Leader of Mott the Hoople; had solo hit "Just Another Night," 1979.
b. Jun 3, 1946 in Shrewsbury, England
Source: *BioIn 11, 12; ConMuA 80A; IlEncRk; LegTOT; RkOn 85; RolSEnR 83; WhoRock 81; WhoRocM 82*

Hunter, Ivory Joe
American. Singer, Songwriter
Rhythm and blues singer-pianist, 1950s; had gold record "Since I Met You Baby," 1956.
b. Oct 11, 1911 in Kirbyville, Texas
d. Nov 8, 1974 in Memphis, Tennessee
Source: *BiDAmM; BioIn 10, 15; DcAmB S9; EncFCWM 69; GuBlues; RkOn 74; WhoRock 81*

Hunter, Jeffrey
[Henry Herman McKinnies]
American. Actor
Played Jesus Christ in 1961 film *King of Kings;* generally in action pictures, 1951-69.
b. Nov 23, 1926 in New Orleans, Louisiana
d. May 27, 1969 in Van Nuys, California
Source: *BiDFilm; BioIn 18; FilmEn; FilmgC; MovMk; WhoHol B; WhScrn 74, 77, 83; WorEFlm*

Hunter, John
English. Surgeon
Surgeon to George III, 1776; investigated circulation, venereal diseases.
b. Feb 13, 1728 in Long Calderwood, Scotland
d. Oct 16, 1793 in London, England
Source: *Alli; BiESc; BiHiMed; BioIn 1, 2, 3, 4, 5, 6, 7, 8, 9, 12, 13, 16, 20; BlkwCE; DcBiPP; DcNaB; DcScB; EncEnl; InSci; LarDcSc; LinLib S; NewC; NewCBEL; OxCEng 67; OxCMed 86; WhDW; WorInv*

Hunter, Kim
[Janet Cole]
American. Actor
Won 1951 Oscar for *Streetcar Named Desire,* for role of Stella.
b. Nov 12, 1922 in Detroit, Michigan
Source: *BiE&WWA; BioIn 2, 3, 6, 12, 14, 15, 16, 17; CamGWoT; ConAu 61; ConTFT 3; CurBio 52, 61; FilmEn; FilmgC; ForYSC; HalFC 80, 84, 88; IntMPA 75, 76, 77, 78, 79, 80, 81, 82, 84, 86, 88, 92, 94, 96; InWom, SUP; ItaFilm; LegTOT; MotPP; MovMk; NotNAT; NotWoAT; VarWW 85; WhoAm 74, 76, 78, 80, 82, 84, 86, 88, 90, 92, 94, 95, 96, 97; WhoAmW 58, 61, 64, 66, 68, 70, 72, 74, 83, 85, 87, 89, 91, 93, 95, 97; WhoEnt 92; WhoHol 92, A; WhoThe 72, 77, 81; WhoWor 74, 76; WorAl; WorAlBi*

Hunter, Madeline Cheek
American. Educator
Professor of Education, U of CA, LA, 1982—; known for mechanical approach to education using behavioral psychology.
b. 1916
Source: *BioIn 14; News 91*

Hunter, Ross
[Martin Fuss]
"Last of the Dream Merchants"
American. Producer
Films include *Flower Drum Song,* 1961; *Airport,* 1970; famous for great scale of stories, sumptuous sets.
b. May 6, 1920 in Cleveland, Ohio
d. Mar 10, 1996 in Los Angeles, California
Source: *CmMov; CurBio 67, 96N; FilmgC; HalFC 84; IntMPA 86; MotPP; VarWW 85; WhoAm 84; WhoHol A; WhoWor 74; WorEFlm*

Hunter, Tab
[Arthur Gelien]
American. Actor
Teen idol, 1950s; in films *Damn Yankees,* 1958; *Ride the Wild Surf,* 1964.
b. Jul 11, 1931 in New York, New York
Source: *BioIn 5, 11, 14; FilmEn; FilmgC; ForYSC; HalFC 80, 84, 88; IntMPA 75, 76, 77, 78, 79, 80, 81, 82, 84, 86, 88, 92, 94, 96; ItaFilm; LegTOT; MotPP; MovMk; PenEncP; RkOn 74; VarWW 85; WhoHol 92, A; WhoRock 81; WorAl; WorAlBi*

Hunter, Thomas
Irish. Educator
Founded NY's Hunter College, 1870.
b. Oct 19, 1831 in Ardglass, Ireland
d. Oct 14, 1915 in New York, New York
Source: *BiDAmEd; DcAmB; DcNAA; NatCAB 22; WhAm 4, HSA; WorAl; WorAlBi*

Hunter, William
English. Surgeon, Scientist
First professor of anatomy, Royal Academy, 1768; developed study of obstetrics; brother of John.
b. May 23, 1718 in Long Calderwood, Scotland
d. Mar 30, 1783 in London, England
Source: *Alli; BiESc; BiHiMed; BioIn 1, 2, 3, 4, 6, 7, 9, 11; DcBiPP; DcEnL; DcNaB; DcScB; EncEnl; InSci; McGEWB; NewC; NewCBEL; OxCMed 86*

Hunter-Gault, Charlayne
American. Broadcast Journalist
Won 1983 Emmy for reporting in Grenada after the US invasion.
b. Feb 27, 1942 in Due West, South Carolina
Source: *BioIn 12, 15; BlkWAm; BlkWr 2; ConAu 141; ConBlB 6; CurBio 87; DcTwCCu 5; GrLiveH; InB&W 80, 85; JrnUS; NegAl 89; NotBlAW 1; SchCGBL; WhoAm 76, 95, 96, 97;*

WhoAmW 95, 97; WhoBlA 80, 92; WhoUSWr 88; WhoWrEP 89, 92, 95; WomStre

Hunthausen, Raymond Gerhardt
American. Religious Leader
Archbishop of Seattle, 1975-91.
b. Aug 21, 1921 in Anaconda, Montana
Source: *AmCath 80; BioIn 13, 14, 15; CurBio 87; WhoAm 74, 76, 78, 80, 84, 86, 88, 90; WhoRel 75, 77, 85, 92; WhoWest 76, 78, 80, 84, 87, 89, 92*

Huntington, Collis Potter
American. Railroad Executive
Built Central Pacific Railroad of CA, which joined with Union Pacific in UT, 1869.
b. Oct 22, 1821 in Harwinton, Connecticut
d. Aug 13, 1900 in Raquette Lake, New York
Source: *ApCAB; BiDAmBL 83; BioIn 3, 8, 12, 15; DcAmB; EncAB-A 30; EncAB-H 1974, 1996; HarEnUS; McGEWB; NatCAB 15; NewCol 75; OxCAmH; REnAW; TwCBDA; WebAB 74, 79; WhAm 1*

Huntington, Daniel
American. Artist
Works include *Mercy's Dream, The Sibyl;* portraits of presidents Lincoln, Van Buren.
b. Oct 14, 1816 in New York, New York
d. Apr 18, 1906 in New York, New York
Source: *AmBi; ApCAB; ArtsNiC; BioIn 7, 11, 12; BriEAA; DcAmArt; DcAmB; DcBiPP; Drake; EarABI; HarEnUS; McGDA; NatCAB 5; NewYHSD; TwCBDA; WhAm 1; WhAmArt 85*

Huntington, Ellsworth
American. Geographer, Explorer
Explored Euphrates River, 1901, Iran, Asia Minor; books include *Earth and Sun,* 1923.
b. Sep 16, 1876 in Galesburg, Illinois
d. Oct 17, 1947 in New Haven, Connecticut
Source: *AmAu&B; AmLY; BiDAmEd; BioIn 1, 3, 4, 10, 18; DcAmB S4; DcNAA; GayN; NatCAB 37; NewCol 75; REnAL; WebAB 74, 79; WhAm 2; WhNAA*

Huntington, Henry Edwards
American. Railroad Executive, Philanthropist
Founded CA's $30 million Huntington Library and Art Collection.
b. Feb 27, 1850 in Oneonta, New York
d. May 23, 1927 in Philadelphia, Pennsylvania
Source: *AmBi; AmDec 1900; BiDAmBL 83; BioIn 1, 2, 6, 13, 15, 17, 20, 21; DcAmB; LinLib S; NatCAB 15; WebAB 74, 79; WhAm 1; WorAl*

Huntington, Henry S, Jr.
American. Social Reformer
Pioneer in organized nudism; founded early nudist camp, 1933; wrote *Defense of Nudism,* 1958.
b. 1882 in Gorham, Maine
d. Feb 16, 1981 in Philadelphia, Pennsylvania
Source: *NewYTBS 81*

Huntington, Samuel
American. Judge, Continental Congressman
Pres., Continental Congress, 1779-81; signed Declaration of Independence, 1776; governor of CT, 1786-98.
b. Jul 3, 1731 in Windham, Connecticut
d. Jan 5, 1796 in Norwich, Connecticut
Source: *AmBi; ApCAB; BiAUS; BiDrAC; BiDrACR; BiDrGov 1789; BiDrUSC 89; BiDrUSE 71, 89; BioIn 7, 8, 9, 11; DcAmB; Drake; EncAR; EncCRAm; HarEnUS; NatCAB 10; TwCBDA; WhAm HS; WhAmP; WhAmRev*

Huntley, Chet
[Chester Robert Huntley]
American. Broadcast Journalist
Teamed with David Brinkley for nightly newscasts, 1956-70; author *The Generous Years,* 1968.
b. Dec 10, 1911 in Cardwell, Montana
d. Mar 20, 1974 in Bozeman, Montana
Source: *AuNews 1; AuSpks; BiDAmJo; BioIn 3, 4, 5, 6, 7, 8, 9, 10, 11, 14, 16, 19; CelR; ConAu 49, 97; CurBio 56, 74, 74N; DcAmB S9; EncAJ; EncTwCJ; FacFETw; JrnUS; LegTOT; NewYTBE 70; NewYTBS 74; WhAm 6; WhoAm 74; WhoHol B; WhoWor 74; WhScrn 77*

Hunyadi, Janos
[John Huniades]
Hungarian. Military Leader
Commanded Hungarian army, 1452-56; conquered Turks, 1456.
b. 1385?
d. 1465
Source: *LinLib S; McGEWB; NewC; NewCol 75; WhDW*

Hupp, Louis Gorham
American. Manufacturer
With brother Robert, founded Hupp Motor Car Co., 1908-41, producing Hupmobiles.
b. Nov 13, 1872 in Kalamazoo, Michigan
d. Dec 10, 1961 in Detroit, Michigan
Source: *DcAmB S7*

Huppert, Isabelle
French. Actor
Won 1978 best actress award, Cannes Festival, for *Violette Noziere.*
b. Mar 16, 1955 in Paris, France
Source: *BiDFilm 94; BioIn 11, 12, 16; ConTFT 7; CurBio 81; DcArts; EncEurC; FilmEn; HalFC 84, 88; IntDcF 1-3, 2-3; IntMPA 88, 92, 94, 96; InWom SUP; ItaFilm; LegTOT; VarWW 85; WhoHol 92*

Hurd, Clement
American. Illustrator
Best known for children's classic *Goodnight Moon,* continuously in print since 1947.
b. Jan 12, 1908 in New York, New York
d. Feb 5, 1988 in San Francisco, California
Source: *AuBYP 2, 3; BioIn 1, 5, 6, 7, 8, 9, 12, 15, 16, 17, 19; ChhPo S1; ChlBkCr; ConAu 9NR, 24NR, 29R, 124; IlsCB 1744, 1946, 1957, 1967; MorJA; SmATA 2, 54N, 64*

Hurd, Douglas
English. Government Official
Secretary of State for Foreign and Commonwealth Affairs of Great Britain and N Ireland, 1989-95.
b. Mar 8, 1930 in Marlborough, England
Source: *BioIn 14, 16, 17, 19; ConAu 10NR, 25R; CurBio 90; IntAu&W 91; ScF&FL 1, 2; Who 83, 85, 88, 90, 92; WhoSpyF*

Hurd, Peter
American. Artist, Illustrator
Best known for works of open, sun-drenched mountains, valleys of southwest US.
b. Feb 22, 1904 in Roswell, New Mexico
d. Jul 9, 1984 in Roswell, New Mexico
Source: *AmArt; AnObit 1984; BioIn 1, 2, 4, 6, 7, 9, 10, 14, 17; ConICB; CurBio 57, 84N; DcAmArt; GrAmP; IlBEAAW; IlsCB 1744; McGDA; WhAm 9; WhAmArt 85; WhoAm 74, 76, 78, 80, 82, 84, 86; WhoAmA 73, 76, 78, 80N, 82, 84, 86N, 89N, 91N, 93N; WhoWor 74, 76*

Hurkos, Peter
[Peter Van der Hurk]
Dutch. Psychic, Actor
Films include *The Boston Strangler,* 1968; *Boxoffice,* 1982.
b. May 21, 1911 in Dordrecht, Netherlands
d. Jun 1, 1988 in Los Angeles, California
Source: *AnObit 1988; BioIn 6, 9, 10, 11, 15, 16, 17; BioNews 74; ConAu 125; EncO&P 1, 2, 3; EncPaPR 91; VarWW 85; WhoWest 82, 84*

Hurley, Elizabeth
English. Actor, Model
Replaced Paulina Porizkova as the face of Estee Lauder; co-starred in *Austin Powers,* 1997.
b. Jun 10, 1965 in Hampshire, England

Hurley, Jack B
"The Old Professor"
American. Boxing Promoter
Handled fighters for over 50 yrs., but never had a champion; known for wit, honesty.
b. Dec 9, 1897 in Moorhead, Minnesota
d. Nov 16, 1972 in Seattle, Washington
Source: *BioIn 5, 7, 9; NewYTBE 72*

Hurley, Patrick Jay
American. Lawyer, Diplomat
Secretary of War, 1929-33; ambassador to China, 1944-45.
b. Jan 8, 1883 in Oklahoma
d. Jul 30, 1963 in Santa Fe, New Mexico
Source: *BiDrUSE 71, 89; BiDWWGF; BioIn 1, 3, 4, 6, 9, 10, 11; CurBio 44, 63; DcAmB S7; DcAmDH 80, 89; EncAB-A 39; NatCAB 53; PolProf T; WhAm 4; WhWW-II*

Hurok, Sol(omon Isaievich)
American. Impresario, Author
Brought world-famous artists to US, including Segovia, Rubinstein, Pavlova, Nureyev.
b. Apr 9, 1888 in Pogar, Russia
d. Mar 5, 1974 in New York, New York
Source: *Baker 78, 84; BiDAmM; BiDD; BiDSovU; BiE&WWA; BioIn 13, 19, 20, 21; BioNews 74; CelR; ConAu 49; FacFETw; LegTOT; LinLib L, S; NatCAB 61; NewGrDA 86; NewGrDM 80; NewYTBE 73; NewYTBS 74; NotNAT B; OxCAmT 84; WebAB 74; WhAm 6; Who 74; WhoAm 74; WhoThe 72; WhoWor 74; WhoWorJ 72; WhThe; WorAl; WorAlBi*

Hurrell, George
American. Photographer
Noted for classic black and white shots of legendary Hollywood Stars, 1920s-50s.
b. 1904 in Cincinnati, Ohio
d. May 17, 1992 in Van Nuys, California
Source: *BioIn 12, 13, 14; ICPEnP A; LegTOT; MacBEP*

Hurson, Martin
Irish. Hunger Striker, Revolutionary
IRA member; one of 10 hunger strikers to die in prison, demanding political prisoner rather than criminal status.
b. Sep 13, 1954 in Cappagh, Northern Ireland
d. Jul 13, 1981 in Belfast, Northern Ireland
Source: *BioIn 12*

Hurst, Fannie
American. Author
Wrote popular novels including *Imitation of Life,* 1933; adapted to film, 1934.
b. Oct 19, 1889 in Hamilton, Ohio
d. Feb 23, 1968 in New York, New York
Source: *AmAu&B; AmLY; AmNov; AmWomD; AmWomPl; AmWomWr; ArtclWW 2; Benet 96; BenetAL 91; BioIn 1, 2, 4, 5, 6, 7, 8, 9, 11, 12, 14, 20; BlmGWL; ChhPo; ConAmA; ConAmL; ConAu 25R, P-1; DcAmB S8; DcAmImH; DcBiA; DcLB 86; Dis&D; EvLB; FacFETw; FilmgC; HalFC 80, 84, 88; InWom, SUP; JeAmFiW; JeAmWW; LegTOT; LibW; LngCTC; NotAW MOD; NotNAT B; ObitT 1961; OhA&B; OxCAmL 65, 83, 95; REn; REnAL; ScF&FL 1, 2; TwCA, SUP; TwCRGW; TwCWr; WhNAA; WhThe; WorAl; WorAlBi*

Hurst, George
English. Conductor
Teacher, conductor, Peabody Conservatory, Baltimore, 1947-55; conducted BBC Northern Symphony, 1958-68.
b. May 20, 1926 in Edinburgh, Scotland
Source: *Baker 84, 92; IntWWM 77, 80, 90; NewAmDM; NewGrDM 80; PenDiMP; Who 74, 82, 83, 85, 88, 90, 92, 94; WhoMus 72*

Hurston, Zora Neale
American. Dramatist, Author
Her writings chronicle rural black life: *Mules and Men,* 1935; *Tell My Horse,* 1938.
b. Jan 7, 1903 in Eatonville, Florida
d. Jan 28, 1960 in Fort Pierce, Florida
Source: *AfrAmAl 6; AmAu&B; AmNov; AmWomWr; ArtclWW 2; BlkAmP; BlkAWP; CamGLE; CamHAL; ConAu 85; ConBlB 3; ConLC 7; CurBio 42, 60; CyWA 89; DcAmB S6; DcAmNB; DrBlPA, 90; EncWB; GrWrEL N; InB&W 85; IntDcWB; InWom; LegTOT; LibW; MajTwCW; ModBlW; MorBAP; NegAl 76, 83, 89; NotAW MOD; NotBlAW 1; OxCAmL 65, 83; REnAL; RGTwCWr; SelBAAf; SelBAAu; SouBlCW; SouWr; TwCA, SUP; WhE&EA; WhFla*

Hurt, John
English. Actor
Starred in *The Elephant Man,* 1980; *Champions,* 1984.
b. Jan 22, 1940 in Chesterfield, England
Source: *BiDFilm 94, 81; WorAlBi*

Hurt, Mary Beth Supinger
American. Actor
In films *The World According to Garp,* 1982; *A Change of Seasons,* 1980; Tony nominee for *Crimes of the Heart,* 1981.
b. Sep 26, 1948? in Marshalltown, Iowa
Source: *BioIn 14; ConTFT 4; HalFC 84, 88; IntMPA 86, 92; NewYTBS 76, 86; VarWW 85; WhoAm 90; WhoEnt 92; WhoThe 81; WorAlBi*

Hurt, Mississippi John
American. Singer, Musician
Hits include "Candy Man Blues," 1928; dropped out of business for 35 yrs., made comeback in 1963.
b. Mar 8, 1892 in Teoc, Mississippi
d. Nov 2, 1966 in Grenada, Mississippi
Source: *BiDAmM; BioIn 14; DrBlPA, 90; EncFCWM 69, 83; WhoRocM 82*

Hurt, William
American. Actor
Won Oscar for *Kiss of the Spider Woman,* 1985; other films include *Br oadcast News,* 1987; *The Accidental Tourist,* 1988.
b. Mar 20, 1950 in Washington, District of Columbia
Source: *BiDFilm 94; BioIn 14, 15, 16, 17, 19; CelR 90; ConNews 86-1; ConTFT 1, 5, 12; CurBio 86; DcArts; HalFC 84, 88; HolBB; IntDcF 1-3, 2-3; IntMPA 86, 88, 92, 94, 96; IntWW 89, 91, 93; LegTOT; VarWW 85; WhoAm 82, 84, 86, 88, 90, 92, 94, 95, 96, 97; WhoEnt 92; WhoHol 92; WhoWor 95, 96, 97; WorAlBi*

Hus, Jan
[John Huss]
Czech. Religious Leader
Burned at stake for urging reform; his loyalists started political party, fought civil war, as Hussites.
b. 1369 in Husinec, Bohemia
d. Jul 6, 1415 in Constance, Germany
Source: *BioIn 1, 2, 3, 5, 6, 7, 8, 9, 10, 12, 13, 17, 18, 20; CasWL; DcEuL; EuAu; EvEuW; HisWorL; NewC; PenC EUR; REn; WebBD 83*

Husain, Zakir
Indian. Political Leader
First Muslim to be elected pres. of India, 1967-69.
b. Feb 8, 1897 in Hyderabad, India
d. May 3, 1969 in New Delhi, India
Source: *BioIn 8, 9, 18; ObitT 1961*

Husak, Gustav
Czech. Political Leader
Pres., Czechoslovak Socialist Republic, 1975-89.
b. Jan 10, 1913 in Dubravka, Slovakia
d. Nov 18, 1991 in Bratislava, Czechoslovakia
Source: *AnObit 1991; BioIn 9, 11, 13, 14, 15; ColdWar 2; CurBio 71, 92N; DicTyr; EncCW; EncRev; EncWB; FacFETw; IntWW 74, 75, 76, 77, 78, 79, 80, 81, 82, 83, 89, 91; IntYB 82; NewYTBE 71; NewYTBS 91; WhAm 10; WhoSocC 78; WhoSoCE 89; WhoWor 74, 76, 78, 80, 82, 84, 87, 89, 91; WorAl; WorAlBi*

Husch, Gerhard
German. Opera Singer
Baritone; noted lieder singer.
b. Feb 2, 1901 in Hannover, Germany
d. Nov 21, 1984 in Munich, Germany
Source: *AnObit 1984; Baker 84; BioIn 14; MetOEnc; NewCol 75; NewEOp 71; NewGrDM 80; OxDcOp; PenDiMP; WhoMus 72*

Hu Shih
Chinese. Scholar
Contributor in establishing the vernacular as China's nat. language, 1922.
b. Dec 17, 1891 in Shanghai, China
d. Feb 24, 1962, Taiwan
Source: *Benet 96; EncWL 3; RAdv 14; WhAm 4*

Husing, Ted
American. Sportscaster
One of America's leading sports announcers, on radio since 1924.
b. Nov 27, 1901 in New York, New York
d. Aug 10, 1962 in Pasadena, California

Source: *Ballpl 90; BiDAmJo; BioIn 16; CurBio 42, 62; RadStar; SaTiSS; WhoHol B; WhScrn 77, 83*

Husky, Ferlin
American. Singer
Country, pop recording star on radio, TV.
b. Dec 3, 1927 in Flat River, Missouri
Source: *BgBkCoM; BiDAmM; BioIn 14, 15; CounME 74, 74A; EncFCWM 69, 83; HarEnCM 87; IlEncCM; PenEncP; RkOn 74; VarWW 85; WhoAm 74, 80, 82, 84; WhoHol 92; WhoRock 81*

Hussein, I, King
[Hussein (Ibn Talal); King of Jordan]
Jordanian. Ruler
Descendant of Mohammed, who succeeded father to throne, 1952—.
b. Nov 14, 1935 in Amman, Jordan
Source: *BioIn 2, 3, 4, 5, 6, 7, 8, 9, 10, 11, 12, 13, 14, 15, 16, 17, 18, 19, 20; CurBio 55, 86; DcPol; DcTwHis; EncWB; HisEAAC; IntWW 75, 76, 77, 78, 79, 80, 81, 82, 83, 89, 91, 93; MidE 78, 79, 80, 81, 82; NewYTBS 79, 90; PolLCME; WhDW; Who 92; WhoWor 80, 84, 87, 91*

Hussein, Ibrahim
Kenyan. Track Athlete
Three-time winner of the Boston Marathon, 1988, 1991-92; 1992 time was second-fastest marathon ever; was first African winner in 1988.
Source: *BioIn 15*

Hussein, Saddam (Al-Tikriti)
Iraqi. Political Leader
Pres., Iraq, 1979—, whose invasion of Kuwait, 1990, led to defeat in the Persian Gulf War, 1991; prime minister of Iraq, 1994—.
b. Apr 28, 1937 in Tikrit, Iraq
Source: *BioIn 13, 14, 16; ColdWar 2; CurBio 81; DcMidEa; DcTwHis; FacFETw; HisEAAC; IntWW 77, 78, 79, 80, 81, 82, 83, 89, 91; LegTOT; News 91, 91-1; NewYTBS 80, 82, 90; PolLCME; WhoArab 81; WhoWor 78, 80, 82, 84, 87, 89, 91, 93, 95, 96, 97*

Husseini, Haj Amin
Palestinian. Political Leader
Anti-Zionist leader of Arab world, 1940s-50s; Nazi collaborator, WW II.
b. 1893 in Jerusalem, Palestine
d. Jul 4, 1974 in Beirut, Lebanon
Source: *BioIn 10, 12, 16; IntWW 74; NewYTBE 71; NewYTBS 74; WhoWor 74*

Husserl, Edmund
German. Philosopher
Originated philosophic study called phenomenology.
b. Apr 8, 1859 in Prossnitz, Moravia
d. Apr 27, 1938 in Freiburg, Germany
Source: *Benet 87, 96; BiDPsy; BioIn 2, 9, 10, 12, 13, 14; ConAu 116, 133; FacFETw; LuthC 75; MakMC; McGEWB; NamesHP; OxCPhil; RAdv 14, 13-4; REn; ThTwC 87; WhDW; WorAu 1950; WrPh P*

Hussey, Christopher Edward Clive
English. Architect
On editorial staff of *Country Life,* 1920-70; wrote *English Gardens and Landscapes,* 1967.
b. Oct 21, 1899 in London, England
d. Mar 20, 1970 in London, England
Source: *AmArch 70; BioIn 14; DcNaB 1961; GrBr; WhE&EA; WhLit*

Hussey, Olivia
English. Actor
Starred as Juliet in screen version of *Romeo and Juliet,* 1969.
b. Apr 17, 1951 in Buenos Aires, Argentina
Source: *ConTFT 7, 15; FilmEn; FilmgC; HalFC 80, 84, 88; IntMPA 92, 94, 96; ItaFilm; LegTOT; MotPP; VarWW 85; WhoHol 92, A*

Hussey, Ruth Carol
[Ruth Carol O'Rourke]
American. Actor
Oscar nominee for *The Philadelphia Story,* 1940.
b. Oct 30, 1915 in Providence, Rhode Island
Source: *BiE&WWA; EncAFC; FilmgC; HalFC 84, 88; InWom SUP; MotPP; MovMk; NotNAT; ThFT; VarWW 85; WhoAm 84; WhoEnt 92; WhoHol A; WhoThe 77A*

Husted, Marjorie Child
American. Cook
Consultant to General Mills, 1948; helped create Betty Crocker character; edited Betty Crocker Cookbook, 1951.
b. 1892 in Minneapolis, Minnesota
d. Dec 23, 1986 in Minneapolis, Minnesota
Source: *BioIn 1, 2; CurBio 49, 87, 87N; InWom SUP; LibW; NewYTBS 86*

Huston, Anjelica
American. Actor
Won best supporting actress Oscar for *Prizzi's Honor,* 1986; and an Oscar nomination for *Enemies, A Love Story,* 1990; daughter of John.
b. Jul 8, 1951 in Los Angeles, California
Source: *BiDFilm 94; BioIn 8, 14, 15, 16; ConTFT 4, 11; CurBio 90; FacFETw; HalFC 84, 88; IntDcF 2-3; IntMPA 88, 92, 94, 96; IntWW 91, 93; LegTOT; News 89; NewYTBS 89; VarWW 85; WhoAm 90, 92, 94, 95, 96, 97; WhoAmW 91, 93, 95, 97; WhoEnt 92; WhoHol 92; WorAlBi*

Huston, John
Irish. Actor, Director
Won Oscar for *Treasure of the Sierra Madre,* 1948; also directed *The African Queen,* 1952; *Prizzi's Honor,* 1985.
b. Aug 5, 1906 in Nevada, Missouri
d. Aug 28, 1987 in Middletown, Rhode Island
Source: *AmFD; AnObit 1987; Benet 87, 96; BenetAL 91; BiDFilm, 81, 94; BioIn 1, 2, 3, 4, 5, 6, 7, 8, 9, 10, 11, 12, 13, 14, 15, 16, 17, 18, 20; BlueB 76; CelR; CmMov; ConAu 34NR, 73, 123; ConDr 73, 77A; ConLC 20; ConNews 88-1; ConTFT 5; CurBio 81, 87, 87N; DcArts; DcFM; DcLB 26; DcTwCCu 1; FacFETw; FilmEn; FilmgC; GangFlm; HalFC 80, 84, 88; IlWWHD 1; IntAu&W 77, 89, 91; IntDcF 1-2, 2-2; IntMPA 77, 78, 79, 80, 81, 82, 84, 86; IntWW 74, 75, 76, 77, 78, 79, 80, 81, 82, 83; ItaFilm; LegTOT; MiSFD 9N; MovMk; NewYTBS 87; OxCFilm; RAdv 14; REnAL; VarWW 85; WebAB 74, 79; WhAm 9; Who 74, 82, 83, 85; WhoAm 74, 76, 78, 80, 82, 84, 86; WhoHol A; WhoWor 74; WorAl; WorAlBi; WorEFlm; WorFDir 1*

Huston, Walter
[Walter Houghston]
American. Actor
Won 1948 Oscar for *The Treasure of the Sierra Madre,* which his son John directed.
b. Apr 6, 1884 in Toronto, Ontario, Canada
d. Apr 7, 1950 in Beverly Hills, California
Source: *BiDFilm, 81, 94; BioIn 1, 2, 3, 4, 7, 9, 13, 21; CamGWoT; CurBio 49, 50; DcAmB S4; DcArts; EncMT; EncVaud; EncWT; Ent; FamA&A; Film 2; FilmEn; FilmgC; ForYSC; GangFlm; HalFC 80, 84, 88; IntDcF 1-3, 2-3; LegTOT; MotPP; MovMk; NatCAB 61, 62; NotNAT B; OlFamFa; OxCAmT 84; OxCCanT; OxCFilm; PlP&P; WebAB 74, 79; WhAm 4; WhoHol B; WhScrn 74, 77, 83; WhThe; WorAl; WorAlBi; WorEFlm*

Hustvedt, Siri
American. Author
Wrote *The Blindfold,* 1992.
b. Feb 19, 1955 in Northfield, Minnesota
Source: *ConAu 137; ConLC 76; WrDr 96*

Hutchence, Michael
Australian. Singer
Lead singer; had top 10 singles "New Sensation," "Devil Inside" from album *Kick,* 1988.
b. Jan 22, 1960 in Sydney, Australia
Source: *BioIn 16; LegTOT; WhoHol 92*

Hutcheson, Francis
Scottish. Philosopher
Wrote *Inquiry into Original of Our Ideas of Beauty and Virtue,* 1725; coi ned phrase "moral sense."
b. Aug 8, 1694 in County Down, Ireland
d. 1746 in Glasgow, Scotland
Source: *Alli; BiD&SB; BioIn 3, 7, 13, 14, 21; BlkwCE; BritAu; CasWL; Chambr 2; DcBiPP; DcEnA; DcEnL; DcEuL; DcIrB 78, 88; DcLB 31A; DcNaB; EncEnl; EncEth; EvLB;*

HarEnUS; NewC; NewCol 75; OxCArt; OxCEng 67, 85, 95; OxCIri; OxCPhil; OxDcArt; PenC ENG; RAdv 14; WhoEc 81, 86

Hutchins, Bobby
[Our Gang]
"Wheezer"
American. Actor
Joined "Our Gang" series, 1929.
Source: *EncAFC; Film 2; HalFC 88; WhoHol 92*

Hutchins, Robert Maynard
American. Lawyer, Educator
At age 30 was made pres., U of Chicago; made controversial, important innovations in the curriculum, 1929-51.
b. Jan 17, 1899 in New York, New York
d. May 14, 1977 in Santa Barbara, California
Source: *AmAu&B; AmSocL; BenetAL 91; BiDAmEd; BiDInt; BioIn 1, 2, 3, 4, 5, 6, 7, 8, 10, 11, 12, 14, 16, 17, 18, 19; BlueB 76; ConAu 69; CurBio 40, 54, 77N; DcAmB S10; EncAB-H 1974, 1996; FacFETw; IntWW 74, 75, 76, 77; McGEWB; OxCAmH; OxCAmL 65, 83, 95; RComAH; REnAL; ThTwC 87; WebAB 74, 79; WhAm 7, 8; WhNAA; Who 74; WhoAm 74, 76, 80, 82, 84; WhoWor 74*

Hutchins, Thomas
American. Geographer
Named by Congress "geographer of the United States," 1781; plotted Seven Ranges in the West.
b. 1730 in Monmouth County, New Jersey
d. Apr 28, 1789 in Pittsburgh, Pennsylvania
Source: *Alli; AmBi; AmRev; ApCAB; BiDAmS; BiInAmS; BioIn 12; DcAmAu; DcAmB; DcBiPP; DcNAA; Drake; EncCRAm; HarEnUS; InSci; NatCAB 9; NewCBEL; NewCol 75; TwCBDA; WebAB 74, 79; WebAMB; WhAm HS; WhAmRev*

Hutchins, Will
[Marshall Lowell Hutchason]
American. Actor
Starred in TV series "Sugarfoot," 1957-61; "Blondie," 1968.
b. May 5, 1932 in Atwater, California
Source: *FilmgC; ForYSC; HalFC 80, 84, 88; VarWW 85; WhoHol 92, A*

Hutchinson, Anne
[Anne Marbury]
English. Religious Leader
Belief in covenant of grace opposed Puritan covenant of works; banished from MA Bay, 1637.
b. 1591 in Alford, England
d. Aug 1643 in Long Island, New York
Source: *AmBi; ApCAB; ArtclWW 2; BenetAL 91; BiCAW; BioAmW; BioIn 3, 4, 5, 6, 7, 8, 9, 10, 11, 12; CamHAL; ContDcW 89; DcAmB; DcAmReB 1; DcAmSR; Drake; EncAB-H 1974; EncARH; EncWHA; GrLiveH; HerW, 84; HisWorL; IntDcWB; LibW; McGEWB; NotAW; OxCAmH; OxCAmL 65, 83, 95; OxCWoWr 95; PorAmW; RComAH; REn; REnAL; TwCBDA; WebAB 74, 79; WhAm HS; WhAmP; WomFir; WorAl; WorAlBi*

Hutchinson, Thomas
English. Colonial Figure
Royal governor of MA, 1770-74; noted loyalist; upheld British authority; exiled in England, from 1774.
b. Sep 9, 1711 in Boston, Massachusetts
d. Jun 3, 1780 in Brompton, England
Source: *Alli; AmAu; AmAu&B; AmBi; AmPolLe; AmWrBE; ApCAB; BenetAL 91; BiDrACR; BioIn 1, 2, 3, 4, 5, 9, 10, 12, 13, 14, 17, 18; BlkwEAR; CyAG; CyAL 1; DcAmAu; DcAmB; DcAmC; DcBiPP; DcLB 30, 31; DcNAA; DcNaB; Drake; EncAB-H 1974, 1996; EncAR; EncCRAm; HarEnUS; LinLib L, S; McGEWB; NatCAB 7; NewCBEL; OxCAmH; OxCAmL 65, 83, 95; PenC AM; RComAH; REnAL; TwCBDA; WebAB 74, 79; WhAm HS; WhAmRev; WorAl; WorAlBi*

Hutchinson, Tim
American. Politician
Rep. senator, AR, 1997—.
b. Aug 11, 1949
Source: *AlmAP 96; BioIn 19; CngDr 93, 95; WhoAm 94, 95, 96, 97; WhoSSW 95*

Hutchison, Kay Bailey
American. Politician
Rep. senator from TX, 1993—.
b. Jul 22, 1943
Source: *AlmAP 96; NewYTBS 93; WhoAm 82, 92, 94, 96, 97; WhoAmL 79, 83; WhoAmP 81, 91, 93, 95; WhoAmW 91, 93, 95, 97; WhoSSW 93, 95, 97*

Hutson, Don(ald M)
"Alabama Antelope"
American. Football Player
Wide receiver, Green Bay, 1935-45; led NFL in receiving, eight times, in scoring, five times; Hall of Fame, 1963.
b. Jan 31, 1913 in Pine Bluff, Arkansas
d. Jun 26, 1997 in Rancho Mirage, California
Source: *BioIn 15, 16, 17, 20; LegTOT; NewYTBE 71; WhoFtbl 74; WorAl; WorAlBi*

Hutt, William Ian Dewitt
Canadian. Director, Producer
Member, Stratford, ON Shakespeare Festival Co., as actor, director, since 1953.
b. May 2, 1920 in Toronto, Ontario, Canada
Source: *BioIn 16; BlueB 76; CanWW 83, 89; CreCan 1; OxCCanT; OxCThe 83; WhoAm 78, 80, 82, 84, 86, 88; WhoEnt 92; WhoThe 81*

Hutton, Barbara Woolworth
"Poor Little Rich Girl"
American. Socialite
Granddaughter of FW Woolworth, heir to family fortune; married seven times; life story subject of TV mini series, 1987.
b. Nov 14, 1912 in New York, New York
d. May 11, 1979 in Los Angeles, California
Source: *DcAmB S10; GoodHs; NewYTBS 79; WhAm 7*

Hutton, Betty
[Betty Thornburg]
American. Actor, Singer
Blonde bombshell of 1940s films; noted for *Annie Get Your Gun,* 1950.
b. Feb 26, 1921 in Battle Creek, Michigan
Source: *BiDAmM; BiDD; BiE&WWA; BioIn 1, 2, 3, 9, 10, 15; CmMov; CmpEPM; CurBio 50; EncAFC; FilmEn; FilmgC; ForYSC; HalFC 80, 84, 88; IntDcF 1-3, 2-3; IntMPA 75, 76, 77, 78, 79, 80, 81, 82, 84, 86, 88, 92, 94, 96; InWom, SUP; LegTOT; MotPP; MovMk; OxCFilm; OxCPMus; PenEncP; VarWW 85; WhoHol 92, A; WorAl; WorAlBi*

Hutton, Bouse
[John Bower Hutton]
Canadian. Hockey Player
Goalie on Ottawa amateur teams, 1898-1904; Hall of Fame, 1962.
b. Oct 24, 1877
d. Oct 27, 1962
Source: *WhoHcky 73*

Hutton, Edward F
American. Banker, Business Executive
Founded E F Hutton investment firm.
b. 1877 in New York, New York
d. Jul 11, 1962 in Westbury, New York
Source: *BioIn 2, 5, 6; WhAm 4*

Hutton, Ina Ray
"Blond Bombshell of Swing"
American. Bandleader, Singer
Founded one of first all-female orchestras, 1935-40.
b. Mar 3, 1916 in Chicago, Illinois
d. Feb 19, 1984 in Ventura, California
Source: *AnObit 1984; BiDJaz; BioIn 9, 10, 12, 13; InWom SUP; LegTOT; NewGrDJ 88, 94; WhoJazz 72*

Hutton, James
Scottish. Geologist
Founder of modern geology; findings appear in *Theory of the Earth,* 1795.
b. Jun 3, 1726 in Edinburgh, Scotland
d. Mar 26, 1797 in Edinburgh, Scotland
Source: *Alli; AsBiEn; BiDLA, SUP; BiESc; BioIn 1, 2, 5, 7, 11, 12, 13, 15; BlkwCE; CamDcSc; DcBiPP; DcEnL; DcNaB; DcScB; EncEnl; InSci; LarDcSc; McGEWB; NewCBEL; RAdv 14; WhDW; WorAl; WorAlBi; WorScD*

Hutton, Jim
American. Actor
Starred in films *Where the Boys Are,* 1960; *The Trouble with Angels,* 1966; father of Timothy Hutton.
b. Mar 31, 1934 in Binghamton, New York
d. Jun 2, 1979 in Los Angeles, California
Source: *FilmgC; HalFC 80, 84, 88; IntMPA 77; LegTOT; MotPP; MovMk; WhoHol A; WhScrn 83*

Hutton, Lauren
[Mary Laurence Hutton]
American. Actor, Model
Film career since 1968; films include *The Gambler,* 1974; *American Gigolo,* 1979.
b. Nov 17, 1943 in Charleston, South Carolina
Source: *BioIn 13, 15, 16; BioNews 75; BkPepl; CelR 90; ConTFT 3; CurBio 94; FilmEn; HalFC 80, 84, 88; IntMPA 86, 92, 94, 96; InWom SUP; ItaFilm; LegTOT; VarWW 85; WhoEnt 92; WhoHol 92, A; WorAlBi*

Hutton, Robert
[Robert Bruce Winne]
American. Actor
Had boy-next-door roles in 1940s films: *And Baby Makes Three,* 1949.
b. Jun 11, 1920 in Kingston, New York
Source: *BioIn 10, 17, 20; ConTFT 9, 13; FilmEn; FilmgC; ForYSC; HalFC 80, 84, 88; HolP 40; IntMPA 75, 76, 77, 78, 79, 80, 81, 82, 84, 86, 88, 92, 94; MotPP; VarWW 85; WhoHol 92, A; WhoHrs 80*

Hutton, Timothy James
American. Actor
Won Oscar for *Ordinary People,* 1980; star of *The Falcon and the Snowman,* 1985; married Debra Winger.
b. Aug 16, 1960 in Malibu, California
Source: *BioIn 13; ConNews 86-3; ConTFT 6; HalFC 84, 88; IntMPA 86, 92; IntWW 91; VarWW 85; WhoAm 86, 90; WhoEnt 92; WorAlBi*

Huxley, Aldous (Leonard)
English. Author, Critic
Best known for *Brave New World,* 1932; *Brave New World Revisited,* 1958.
b. Jul 26, 1894 in Godalming, England
d. Nov 22, 1963 in Los Angeles, California
Source: *AmAu&B; AtlBL; Au&Arts 11; Benet 87, 96; BiDMoPL; BiDPara; BioIn 1, 2, 3, 4, 5, 6, 7, 8, 9, 10, 11, 12, 13, 14, 15, 16, 17, 18, 20; BlmGEL; BritWr 7; CamGEL; CamGLE; CasWL; Chambr 3; ChhPo, S1, S2; CmCal; CnDBLB 6; CnMD; CnMWL; ConAu 44NR, 85; ConLC 1, 3, 4, 5, 8, 11, 18, 35, 79; CyWA 58, 89; DcAmB S7; DcAmC; DcArts; DcLB 36, 100, 162; DcLEL; DcNaB 1961; Dis&D; EncO&P 1, 2, 3; EncPaPR 91; EncSF, 93; EncWL, 2, 3; EvLB; FacFETw; FilmEn; GrBr; GrWrEL N; HalFC 80, 84, 88; IlEncMy; LegTOT; LinLib L, S; LngCEL; LngCTC; MagSWL; MajTwCW; MakMC; McGEWB; ModBrL, S1, S2; ModWD; NewC; NewCBEL; NewEScF; NewGrDO; NotNAT B; Novels; ObitT 1961; OxCEng 67, 85, 95; OxCTwCP; PenC ENG; RAdv 1, 14, 13-1; REn; RfGEnL 91; RGTwCSF; RGTwCWr; ScF&FL 1, 92; ScFSB; ScFWr; SmATA 63; TwCA, SUP; TwCSFW 81, 86, 91; TwCWr; TwCYAW; WebE&AL; WhAm 4; WhDW; WhE&EA; WhLit; WhoSciF; WhoTwCL; WorAl; WorAlBi; WorLitC; WrPh*

Huxley, Andrew Fielding, Sir
English. Scientist, Educator
Shared Nobel Prize in medicine, 1963.
b. Nov 22, 1917 in London, England
Source: *AsBiEn; BiESc; BioIn 6, 14, 15, 20; FacFETw; IntMed 80; IntWW 74, 75, 76, 77, 78, 79, 80, 81, 82, 83, 89, 91, 93; LarDcSc; NobelP; NotTwCS; Who 74, 82, 83, 85, 88, 90, 92, 94; WhoAm 74, 76, 82, 88, 92, 94; WhoMedH; WhoNob, 90, 95; WhoScEn 94, 96; WhoWor 74, 91, 93, 95, 96, 97; WorAl; WorAlBi*

Huxley, Elspeth Josceline Grant
English. Author
Books include *Man from Nowhere,* 1965; *Scott of the Antarctic,* 1978.
b. Jul 23, 1907 in London, England
d. Jan 10, 1997 in Tetbury, England
Source: *BioIn 14, 15, 16; ConAu 28NR, 77; DcLB 77; DcLEL; EncMys; IntAu&W 91; IntWW 83, 91; LngCTC; SmATA 62; TwCCr&M 85, 91; TwCWr; Who 85, 92; WhoAmW 74; WhoWor 74; WorAu 1950; WrDr 86, 92*

Huxley, Julian Sorell, Sir
English. Biologist, Author
First director-general of UNESCO, 1946-48; explained complexities of science to layman; advocated evolutionary humanism.
b. Jun 22, 1887 in London, England
d. Feb 14, 1975 in London, England
Source: *Benet 87; BiDInt; BiESc; BioIn 1, 3, 4, 5, 6, 9, 10, 11; Chambr 3; ConAu 9R, 57; CurBio 42, 63; DcNaB 1971; FacFETw; GrBr; InSci; IntWW 74; LarDcSc; LegTOT; OxCEng 67, 85, 95; OxCFilm; PenC ENG; RAdv 13-5; REn; TwCA, SUP; TwCWr; WhAm 6; WhDW; Who 74; WhoLA; WhoUN 75; WhoWor 74*

Huxley, Laura Archera
Italian. Author
Wife of Aldous; writings include *This Timeless Moment: A Personal View of Aldous Huxley,* 1968.
Source: *AmAu&B; NewYTBE 71; WhoAmW 66, 68, 89*

Huxley, Thomas Henry
English. Biologist
Foremost defender of Darwin's theories; wrote *Man's Place in Nature,* 1863.
b. May 4, 1825 in Ealing, England
d. Jun 29, 1895 in Eastbourne, England
Source: *Alli, SUP; AsBiEn; AtlBL; BbD; Benet 87, 96; BiD&SB; BiDPsy; BiESc; BioIn 1, 2, 3, 4, 5, 6, 7, 8, 9, 10, 11, 12, 13, 14, 16, 17, 20; BlmGEL; BritAu 19; CamDcSc; CamGEL; CamGLE; CasWL; CelCen; Chambr 3; ChhPo S2; CrtT 3; CyEd; CyWA 58; DcArts; DcBiPP; DcEnA, A; DcEnL; DcEuL; DcLEL; DcNaB C, S1; DcScB; Dis&D; EncHuEv; EncUnb; EvLB; InSci; LinLib L, S; LngCEL; LuthC 75; McGEWB; MouLC 4; NamesHP; NewC; NewCBEL; OxCEng 67; OxCMed 86; PenC ENG; RAdv 14, 13-5; REn; TwoTYeD; VicBrit; WebE&AL; WorAl*

Huxtable, Ada Louise
[Ada Louise Landman]
American. Critic, Editor
Architecture critic for *NY Times,* 1963-82; won Pulitzer Prize for distinguished criticism, 1970; wrote *Pier Luigi Nervi,* 1960.
b. 1921 in New York, New York
Source: *AmWomWr; BenetAL 91; BioIn 7, 8, 9, 10, 11, 12, 13, 15, 16; BlueB 76; BriB; ConAu 120, 127, 132; ConDr 88; ConLC 55; ConTFT 5; CurBio 73, 89; IntAu&W 91; IntWW 83, 91; InWom SUP; NewYTBS 88; WhoAm 86, 90; WhoAmA 84, 91; WhoE 74; WhoEnt 92; WorAu 1975; WrDr 86, 88, 90, 92, 94, 96*

Hu Yaobang
Chinese. Politician
General secretary, Chinese Communist Party, 1980-87; championed change; death triggered political crisis.
b. Nov 20, 1915 in Liuyang City, China
d. Apr 15, 1989 in Beijing, China
Source: *AnObit 1989; BioIn 13, 14, 15, 16, 18; ColdWar 2; CurBio 89N; DcTwHis; FacFETw; IntWW 89, 89N, 91; News 89; NewYTBS 89; WhAm 11; WhoPRCh 87; WhoWor 84*

Huygens, Christian
Dutch. Physicist, Astronomer
Discovered rings of Saturn, 1655; developed wave theory of light, 1678.
b. Apr 14, 1629 in The Hague, Netherlands
d. Jun 8, 1695 in The Hague, Netherlands
Source: *AsBiEn; BiDPsy; DcEuL; DcScB; Dis&D; InSci; LinLib L, S; McGEWB; NamesHP; NewCol 75; WebBD 83*

Huysmans, Joris Karl
[Charles Marie Georges]
French. Author
Wrote realist novels *Marthe,* 1876; *Rebours,* 1884.
b. Feb 5, 1848 in Paris, France
d. May 12, 1907 in Paris, France
Source: *AtlBL; BbD; Benet 87, 96; BiD&SB; BioIn 1, 2, 3, 4, 5, 7, 10, 11; CasWL; ClDMEL 47, 80; CyWA 58; DcCathB; Dis&D; EncWL; EuWr 7; EvEuW; LinLib S; McGEWB; ModFrL; ModRL; NewCBEL; OxCFr; REn;*

ScF&FL 1; WhDW; WhLit; WhoTwCL; WorAlBi

Hvorostovsky, Dmitri
Russian. Opera Singer
Baritone; won BBC Cardiff singer of the World Competition, 1989.
Source: *BioIn 17, 19, 21*

Hwang, David Henry
American. Dramatist
His drama, *M. Butterfly,* won best play Tony, 1988; won Obie for *The Dance and the Railroad,* 1981 and *F.O.B.,* 1980; his *The Voyage,* was commissioned for 1992 celebration of Columbus discovery.
b. Aug 11, 1957 in Los Angeles, California
Source: *AsAmAlm; BenetAL 91; BioIn 12, 13; ConAmD; ConAu 127, 132; ConDr 88, 93; ConLC 55; ConTFT 5, 12; CrtSuDr; CurBio 89; DramC 4; IntAu&W 91, 93; LegTOT; NatPD 81; NewYTBS 81; NotAsAm; OxCAmL 95; RAdv 14, 13-2; RfGAmL 94; WhoAm 90, 92, 94, 95, 96, 97; WhoAsA 94; WhoEnt 92; WorAu 1985; WrDr 88, 90, 92, 94, 96*

Hyams, Joe
[Joseph Hyams]
American. Author
Wrote *Bogart and Bacall: A Love Story,* 1966; *Zen in the Martial Arts,* 1979.
b. Jun 6, 1923 in Cambridge, Massachusetts
Source: *AmAu&B; BioIn 4, 10; ConAu 7NR, 17R, 22NR, 45NR; WhoAm 74, 76, 78, 80, 82, 84, 86, 88, 92, 94, 95, 96; WhoEnt 92; WhoUSWr 88; WhoWor 78; WhoWrEP 89, 92, 95; WrDr 76, 80, 82, 84, 86, 88, 90, 92, 94, 96*

Hyatt, Alpheus
American. Scientist
Founded new school of invertebrate paleontology; helped establish Marine Biological Laboratory, Woods Hole, MA.
b. Apr 5, 1838 in Washington, District of Columbia
d. Jan 15, 1902 in Cambridge, Massachusetts
Source: *Alli SUP; AmBi; ApCAB; BiDAmEd; BiDAmS; BiD&SB; BiInAmS; BioIn 1, 2, 3; DcAmAu; DcAmB; DcNAA; DcScB; InSci; NatCAB 3, 23; NewCol 75; TwCBDA; WebAB 74, 79; WhAm 1*

Hyatt, Joel
[Joel Zylberberg]
American. Lawyer, Businessman
Co-founder, Hyatt Legal Services, 1977.
b. May 6, 1950 in Cleveland, Ohio
Source: *BioIn 11, 14, 15, 18; ConNews 85-3; WhoAm 86, 90; WhoAmL 87; WhoEmL 89; WhoMW 88*

Hyde, Henry John
American. Politician
Rep. congressman, IL, 1975—; known for his Hyde amendments—riders tacked on bills to restrict public funding of abortions.
b. Apr 18, 1924 in Chicago, Illinois
Source: *BiDrUSC 89; BioIn 12; NewYTBS 80; WhoAm 78, 80, 82, 84, 86, 88, 90, 92, 94, 95, 96, 97; WhoAmP 73, 75, 77, 79, 81, 83, 85, 87, 89, 91, 93, 95; WhoE 95; WhoMW 80, 82, 84, 86, 88, 90, 92, 93, 96*

Hyde-White, Wilfrid
English. Actor
Played Colonel Pickering in film version of *My Fair Lady,* 1964.
b. May 12, 1903 in Gloucester, England
d. May 6, 1991 in Los Angeles, California
Source: *AnObit 1991; BiE&WWA; BioIn 13, 17, 18; ConTFT 11; FilmAG WE; FilmEn; FilmgC; ForYSC; HalFC 80, 84, 88; IntMPA 77; IntWW 83, 91, 91N; LegTOT; MovMk; NewYTBS 91; NotNAT; OxCFilm; WhAm 10; Who 74, 82, 83, 85, 88, 90, 92N; WhoAm 82, 84, 86, 88, 90; WhoHol A; WhoThe 72, 77, 81; WorAlBi*

Hyer, Martha
American. Actor
Received 1959 Oscar nomination for *Some Came Running.*
b. Aug 10, 1924 in Fort Worth, Texas
Source: *BioIn 16; FilmEn; FilmgC; ForYSC; HalFC 84, 88; IntMPA 86, 88, 92, 94, 96; ItaFilm; MotPP; SweetSg C; WhoAm 84; WhoAmW 77; WhoHol 92, A*

Hyland, Brian
American. Singer
Pop singer who had novelty hit, "Itsy Bitsy Teenie Weenie Yellow Polkadot Bikini," 1960.
b. Nov 12, 1943 in Woodhaven, New York
Source: *EncRk 88; EncRkSt; PenEncP; RkOn 74; RolSEnR 83; WhoRock 81*

Hyland, Diana
[Joan Diana Genter]
American. Actor
Played Joan Bradford on TV series "Eight Is Enough"; died after first season.
b. Jan 25, 1936 in Cleveland Heights, Ohio
d. Mar 27, 1977 in Los Angeles, California
Source: *BiE&WWA; BioIn 11; ForYSC; HalFC 80, 84, 88; LegTOT; WhoAm 74; WhoHol A; WhScrn 83*

Hyland, Harry
[Harold Hyland]
Canadian. Hockey Player
Right wing, Ottawa, Montreal Wanderers, 1917-18; Hall of Fame, 1962.
b. Jan 2, 1889 in Montreal, Quebec, Canada
d. Aug 8, 1969 in Montreal, Quebec, Canada
Source: *HocEn; WhoHcky 73*

Hyman, Earle
American. Actor
Active on stage since early 1940s; films include *The Bamboo Prison,* 1955; played Rusell Huxtable on "The Cosby Show."
b. Oct 11, 1926 in Rocky Mount, North Carolina
Source: *AfrAmAl 6; BiE&WWA; BioIn 14, 16; CamGWoT; ConTFT 3, 11; DrBlPA, 90; InB&W 80; NegAl 76, 83, 89; NotNAT; WhoAfA 96; WhoAm 84, 86, 88, 90, 92, 94, 95; WhoBlA 77, 80, 85, 88, 90, 92, 94; WhoEnt 92; WhoHol 92, A; WhoThe 72, 77, 81; WorAlBi*

Hyman, Libbie Henrietta
American. Zoologist
Specialist in invertebrate and vertebrate zoology; reference books include her 6-volume *The Invertebrates.*
b. Dec 6, 1888 in Des Moines, Iowa
d. Aug 3, 1969 in New York, New York
Source: *AmWomSc; BiESc; BioIn 4, 5, 8, 9, 12, 16; DcScB S2; InSci; InWom, SUP; LarDcSc; LibW; NotAW MOD; NotTwCS; NotWoLS; WhAm 5; WhNAA; WhoAmW 58, 66, 68*

Hynde, Chrissie
[The Pretenders; Christine Ellen Hynde]
American. Singer, Songwriter
Founded British rock group The Pretenders, 1978; comback hit "I'll Stand By You."
b. Sep 7, 1951? in Akron, Ohio
Source: *BioIn 12, 13, 15, 16; CurBio 93; EncPR&S 89; LegTOT; NewGrDA 86; News 91, 91-1*

Hyndman, Henry Mayers
English. Political Leader
Founder of British socialism; organized Democratic Federation, 1881, which became Socialist Party, 1911.
b. Mar 7, 1842 in London, England
d. Nov 22, 1921 in Hampstead, England
Source: *Alli SUP; BbD; BiD&SB; BiDMarx; BioIn 5, 6, 11, 16; CelCen; DcNaB 1912; LinLib L, S; NewCBEL; WhoEc 81, 86*

Hynek, J(oseph) Allen
American. Astronomer
Consultant to US Air Force on UFO's; author *The UFO Experience,* 1951.
b. May 1, 1910 in Chicago, Illinois
d. Apr 27, 1986 in Scottsdale, Arizona
Source: *AmMWSc 73P, 76P, 79, 82, 86; BioIn 7, 14, 15; ConAu 81, 119; CurBio 68, 86, 86N; EncO&P 1S1, 2, 3; FacFETw; NewYTBS 86; UFOEn; WhoAm 74; WhoWor 74*

Hypatia
Alexandrian. Philosopher, Mathematician
Famous for her beauty, eloquence, learning; ordered murdered by St. Cyril of Alexander.
d. 415
Source: *BioIn 4, 8, 10; DcBiPP; EncEarC; NewCol 75; OxCClL, 89*

Hyperides
Greek. Statesman, Orator
His oldest surviving papyrus manuscript: *Against Athenogenes.*
b. 389BC in Athens, Greece
d. 323BC
Source: *CasWL; Grk&L; OxCClL*

Hyslop, James Hervey
American. Philosopher
Writings include *Logic and Argument,* 1879; *Life After Death,* 1918.
b. Aug 18, 1854 in Xenia, Ohio
d. Jun 17, 1920 in New York, New York
Source: *AmAu&B; AmBi; AmLY; BiDPara; BiInAmS; DcAmAu; DcAmB; DcNAA; EncO&P 1, 2, 3; EncPaPR 91; HarEnUS; LiveLet; NatCAB 10, 14, 26; OhA&B; TwCBDA; WhAm 1*

I

Iacocca, Lee
[Lido Anthony Iacocca]
American. Auto Executive
Chm., CEO, Chrysler Corp., 1979-92; 1985 autobiography is best non-fiction seller in publishing history.
b. Oct 15, 1924 in Allentown, Pennsylvania
Source: *AmMWSc 89, 92; BestSel 89-1; BiDAmBL 83; BiDAmNC; BioIn 6, 8, 9, 10, 11, 13, 14, 15, 16; BioNews 74; BusPN; CelR 90; ConAu 125, X; ConHero 1; CurBio 71, 88; Dun&B 90; EncABHB 5; EncWB; FacFETw; IntAu&W 91; IntWW 83, 91; LegTOT; News 93-1; NewYTBE 71; NewYTBS 78, 79, 80, 86; St&PR 84, 87, 91; Ward 77; WhoAm 74, 76, 78, 80, 82, 84, 86, 88, 90, 92, 94, 95, 96, 97; WhoFI 74, 77, 79, 81, 83, 85, 87, 89, 94; WhoMW 74, 76, 78, 82, 84, 86, 88, 90, 93; WhoWor 74, 78, 82, 87, 89, 91; WorAlBi; WrDr 90, 92, 96*

Iakovos, Demetrios A. Coucouzis, Archbishop
Greek. Religious Leader
Greek Orthodox archbishop of North, South America, Holy Synod of Ecumenical Patriarchate, 1959—.
b. Jul 29, 1911 in Imvros, Turkey
Source: *BioIn 9; CurBio 60; IntWW 91; RelLAm 91; WhoAm 86, 90; WhoE 86; WhoMW 92; WhoRel 92; WhoWor 87*

Ian, Janis
[Janis Eddy Fink]
American. Singer, Songwriter
Won Grammy, 1975, for "At Seventeen."
b. May 7, 1950 in New York, New York
Source: *BioIn 7, 8, 10, 11, 14, 15; BkPepl; ConAu 105; ConLC 21; ConMus 5; EncFCWM 83; EncPR&S 74, 89; EncRk 88; HarEnR 86; InWom SUP; LegTOT; NewAmDM; NewGrDA 86; RkOn 74; VarWW 85; WhoAm 84; WhoRocM 82; WorAl; WorAlBi*

Ian and Sylvia
[Sylvia Fricker; Ian Tyson]
Canadian. Music Group
Husband-wife folksinging duo, formed 1959; sang country music, 1960s.
Source: *BgBkCoM; BioIn 8; CounME 74, 74A; EncFCWM 69, 83; PenEncP; RolSEnR 83; WhoAm 74, 76; WhoAmW 68, 70, 72, 74; WhoRocM 82*

Iba, Hank
[Henry Payne Iba]
"Iron Duke"
American. Basketball Coach
Successful college coach, mostly at OK State, 1935-70; had 767-338 career record ; coached gold medal-winning Olympic teams, 1964, 1968; Hall of Fame, 1968.
b. Aug 6, 1904 in Easton, Missouri
d. Jan 15, 1993 in Stillwater, Oklahoma
Source: *BasBi; BiDAmSp BK; BioIn 8, 9, 10, 16, 18; WhoBbl 73; WhoSpor*

Ibarruri, Dolores Gomez
"La Pasionaria"
Spanish. Revolutionary
A founder of the Communist Party of Spain, 1920; popular, controversial political figure during Spanish Civil War.
b. Dec 9, 1895 in Gallarta, Spain
d. Nov 12, 1989 in Madrid, Spain
Source: *BiDMarx; BioIn 13, 15, 16; ContDcW 89; CurBio 67, 90, 90N; EncCoWW; FacFETw; IntAu&W 89; InWom, SUP; NewYTBS 89; WomWrS; WorAlBi*

Ibert, Jacques (Francois Antoine)
French. Composer
Director, Paris Opera, French Academy in Rome; wrote music for films, 1937-55.
b. Aug 15, 1890 in Paris, France
d. Feb 5, 1962 in Paris, France
Source: *Baker 78, 84, 92; BiDD; BioIn 2, 3, 4, 6, 8, 14, 17; BriBkM 80; CmOp; CnOxB; CompSN; DancEn 78; DcCM; DcCom&M 79; DcFM; FacFETw; FilmEn; HalFC 80, 84, 88; IntDcF 1-4, 2-4; LegTOT; MetOEnc; MusMk; NewAmDM; NewCol 75; NewEOp 71; NewGrDM 80; NewGrDO; NewOxM; NotNAT B; OxCFilm; OxCMus; OxDcOp; PenDiMP A; WhAm 4; WhDW; WhoMus 72; WorEFlm*

Iberville, Pierre Le Moyne, Sieur d'
"Le Cid Canadien"
Canadian. Explorer, Soldier
Explored Mississippi, discovered Lake Pontchartrain; founded French territory of LA, 1699.
b. Jul 20, 1661 in Montreal, Quebec, Canada
d. Feb 7, 1728 in Ottawa, Ontario, Canada
Source: *AmBi; ApCAB; BiDSA; DcAmB; DcCathB; EncCRAm; EncSoH; HarEnUS; LinLib S; MacDCB 78; OxCAmH; OxCCan; REn; REnAL; WebAB 79; WhNaAH; WhWE; WorAlBi*

Ibn Batutah
[Muhammad ibn 'abd Allah]
Arab. Traveler
Traveled extensively for 30 yrs. beginning ca. 1325; considered most reliable source for geography of his time.
b. 1304? in Tangiers, Morocco
d. 1378? in Fez, Morocco
Source: *BiD&SB; NewC; NewCol 75*

Ibn Khaldun
Tunisian. Historian
Arab historian of great renown; crowning achievement was the philosophy of history, *Mugaddimah,* 1379.
b. May 27, 1332 in Tunis, Tunisia
d. Mar 17, 1406 in Cairo, Egypt
Source: *Benet 96; BioIn 2, 4, 7, 8, 9, 12, 17, 20; DcAfHiB 86; LinLib L; OxCPhil; RAdv 13-4; WhDW*

Ibn Saud
[Abdul Aziz ibn Saud]
Saudi. Ruler
Founder of Saudi Arabia, 1932, who was king, 1932-53.
b. 1880 in Riyadh, Arabia

d. Nov 9, 1953, Saudi Arabia
Source: *BioIn 19; CurBio 43, 54; DcPol; NewCol 75; WebBD 83*

Ibsen, Henrik Johan
Norwegian. Dramatist, Author
Depicted 19th c. women in *A Doll's House,* 1879; *Hedda Gabler,* 1890.
b. Mar 20, 1828 in Skien, Norway
d. May 23, 1906 in Christiania, Norway
Source: *AtlBL; BbD; Benet 96; BiD&SB; CasWL; ClDMEL 47; CnMD; CnThe; CyWA 58; DcEuL; EncWL; EuAu; McGEWD 72; NewC; OxCEng 67; PenC EUR; RComWL; REn*

Ibuse, Masuji
Japanese. Author
Author of novel *Black Rain,* 1966, about the atomic bombing of Hiroshima.
b. Feb 15, 1898 in Hiroshima, Japan
d. Jul 10, 1993 in Tokyo, Japan
Source: *AnObit 1993; Benet 87; BioIn 16, 17, 19; CasWL; ConLC 22, 81; DcOrL 1; EncWL 2; NewYTBS 93; Novels; PenC CL; RAdv 13-2; WhoTwCL; WorAu 1980*

Icaza (Coronel), Jorge
Ecuadorean. Author
Novels depicted oppression of Ecuadorean Indians as in *Huasipungo,* 1934.
b. Jul 10, 1906 in Quito, Ecuador
d. May 26, 1978 in Quito, Ecuador
Source: *Benet 87, 96; BenetAL 91; BioIn 5, 16, 18; CasWL; ConAu 85, 89; CyWA 58; DcCLAA; DcHiB; DcSpL; EncLatA; EncWL 2, 3; HispWr; IntAu&W 76, 77; IntWW 74, 75, 76, 77, 78; LatAmWr; LinLib L; ModLAL; OxCSpan; PenC AM; SpAmA*

Iceberg Slim
[Robert Beck]
American. Author
Wrote *Pimp: The Story of My Life,* 1967.
b. Aug 4, 1918 in Chicago, Illinois
d. Apr 28, 1992 in Los Angeles, California
Source: *ConBlB 11; InB&W 80, 85*

Ice Cube
[O'Shea Jackson]
American. Rapper
Hit albums include *Death Certificate,* 1991.
b. Jun 15, 1969 in Los Angeles, California
Source: *ConBlB 8; ConMus 10; ConTFT 13; CurBio 95; DcTwCCu 5; IntMPA 96; WhoAfA 96; WhoBlA 94*

Iceman
Russian. Victim
Mummified body of a Bronze Age hunter found in an Italian glacier near Austria, 1991.
b. 1921

Ice-T
[Tracy Marrow]
American. Rapper
Known for his controversial song "Cop Killer," from the album *Body Count;* films include *New Jack City,* 1991.
b. Feb 16, 1958 in Newark, New Jersey
Source: *ConBlB 6; ConMus 7; CurBio 94; DcTwCCu 5; News 92*

Ichikawa, Fusae
Japanese. Feminist, Politician
Founded Woman's Suffrage League of Japan; elected to Parliament, 1953-71; 1974-81.
b. May 15, 1893 in Onishi, Japan
d. Feb 11, 1981 in Tokyo, Japan
Source: *AnObit 1981; BioIn 12, 14, 21; NewYTBS 81*

Ickes, Harold LeClair
"Honest Harold"
American. Government Official
FDR's secretary of interior; ardent reformer, conservationist also headed Public Works Administration, 1930s.
b. Mar 15, 1874 in Blair County, Pennsylvania
d. Feb 3, 1952 in Washington, District of Columbia
Source: *AmAu&B; BiDrUSE 71; CurBio 41, 52; DcAmB S5; EncAAH; EncAB-H 1974; McGEWB; NatCAB 40; NewCol 75; OxCAmH; REnAL; WebAB 74, 79; WhAm 3*

Idei, Nobuyuki
Japanese. Business Executive
Pres., Sony Corp., 1995—.
b. Nov 22, 1937, Japan

Idle, Eric
[Monty Python's Flying Circus]
English. Actor, Author
Co-winner, 1983 Cannes Film Festival for *Monty Python's Meaning of Life.*
b. Mar 29, 1943 in Durham, England
Source: *BioIn 13, 16; ConAu 35NR, 116; ConLC 21; ConTFT 5; IntMPA 92, 94, 96; LegTOT; MiSFD 9; QDrFCA 92; VarWW 85; WhoAm 94, 95, 96, 97; WhoCom; WhoEnt 92; WhoHol 92; WhoWor 95, 96, 97*

Idol, Billy
[Willem Wolfe Broad]
English. Singer
Punk rock teen idol; hit singles in early 1980's include "Eyes Without a Face," "Rebel Yell."
b. Nov 30, 1955 in London, England
Source: *BioIn 13, 14, 15; CelR 90; ConMus 3; CurBio 94; EncPR&S 89; EncRk 88; EncRkSt; HarEnR 86; LegTOT; PenEncP; RkOn 85; WhoEnt 92; WhoRocM 82; WorAlBi*

Idris I
[Sayyid Muhammad Idris as-Sanusi]
Liberian. Ruler
First, only king of Libya, 1951-69; deposed by Khadafy.
b. Mar 13, 1890 in Jaghbub, Libya
d. May 25, 1983 in Cairo, Egypt
Source: *CurBio 56, 83; IntWW 74, 82, 83; MidE 81, 82; NewYTBS 83*

Iger, Robert A
American. TV Executive
Pres., ABC Television Network Group, 1992-94.
b. 1951 in New York
Source: *BioIn 16; IntMPA 92; LesBEnT 92; WhoEnt 92*

Iglesias, Julio
[Julio Iglesias de la Cueva]
Spanish. Singer, Songwriter
Master of love song; has sold over 100 million albums.
b. Sep 23, 1943 in Madrid, Spain
Source: *BioIn 13, 14, 15, 16; CelR 90; ConMus 2; CurBio 84; DcHiB; LegTOT; PenEncP; RkOn 84, 85; WhoAm 86, 88, 90, 92, 94, 95, 96, 97; WhoEnt 92; WhoHisp 91, 92, 94; WhoWor 84, 87, 91, 93, 95; WorAlBi*

Ignatius of Loyola, Saint
[Inigo do Onez y Loyola]
Spanish. Religious Leader
Founded Society of Jesus or Jesuits, 1540; concerned with education, missionary work; canonized 1622.
b. Dec 24, 1491 in Loyola, Spain
d. Jul 31, 1556 in Rome, Italy
Source: *BioIn 16, 17, 19, 20; CasWL; DcSpL; EuAu; LegTOT; LinLib L; McGEWB; NewC; RAdv 14, 13-4; REn; WorAl; WorAlBi*

Igoe, Hype
[Herbert A Igoe]
American. Journalist, Cartoonist
Sports writer known for boxing column "Pardon My Glove."
b. Jun 13, 1885
d. Feb 11, 1945 in New York, New York
Source: *CurBio 45; EncAJ; WhJnl*

Ike, Reverend
[Frederick Joseph Eikerenkoetter, II]
American. Evangelist, Educator
Founder, pres., United Christian Evangelist Assn., 1962—; Reverend Ike Foundation, 1973—.
b. Jun 1, 1935 in Ridgeland, South Carolina
Source: *BioIn 10, 11, 13; BkPepl; EncO&P 1, 3; WhoAm 76, 78, 80, 82, 84, 86; WhoBlA 90, 92; WhoE 85, 86, 89; WhoRel 92*

Ike and Tina Turner
American. Music Group
Husband-wife rock and roll singing duo; first hit: "A Fool in Love," 1960.
Source: *BiDAmM; EncPR&S 74; IlEncRk*

Ikhnaton, Pharaoh
Egyptian. Ruler
Ruled ancient Egypt c. 1379-1358 BC; changed religious beliefs from polytheism to monotheism.
b. fl. 14th cent. BC
d. 1354BC
Source: *BioIn 1, 3, 4, 5, 6, 7, 8, 9, 10, 11, 12, 14, 16; Dis&D; IlEncMy; LuthC 75; McGEWB; NewC; NewCol 75; WebBD 83; WhDW; WorAl; WorAlBi*

Ikle, Fred Charles
American. Government Official
Known for his opposition to the theory of Mutual Assured Destruction and his support for strategic defenses.
b. Aug 24, 1924 in Samaden, Switzerland
Source: *AmMWSc 73S; BioIn 9, 13; BlueB 76; ColdWar 1; ConAu 45; IntAu&W 77; IntWW 75, 76, 77, 78, 79, 80, 81, 82, 83, 89, 91, 93; USBiR 74; WhoAm 74, 76, 78, 80, 82, 84, 86, 88, 90, 92, 94, 95, 96, 97; WhoAmP 77, 79, 81, 83, 85, 87, 89, 91, 93, 95; WhoGov 75, 77; WrDr 92*

Ilg, Frances Lillian
American. Author, Physician, Educator
Co-founded, Gesell Institute of Child Development, 1950-70; wrote books on child care, development.
b. Oct 11, 1902 in Oak Park, Illinois
d. Jul 26, 1981 in Manitowish Waters, Wisconsin
Source: *AmAu&B; BioIn 4, 12; ConAu 107; CurBio 56, 81; InWom, SUP; NewYTBS 81; WhoAmW 66*

Iliescu, Ion
Romanian. Political Leader
Became pres. of Romania, 1990—, after the execution of Nicolae Ceausescu in the first free elections since 1937.
b. Mar 3, 1930 in Oltenita, Romania
Source: *BioIn 16; CurBio 90; IntWW 74, 75, 76, 77, 78, 79, 80, 81, 82, 83, 89, 91, 93; IntYB 78, 79, 80, 81, 82; WhoSocC 78; WhoSoCE 89; WhoWor 91, 93, 95, 96, 97*

Ilitch, Mike
[Michael Ilitch]
American. Businessman, Sports Executive
Founder, owner, Little Caesars' Pizza, 1959—; owner, Detroit Red Wings, 1982—; Detroit Tigers, 1992—.
b. Jul 20, 1929 in Detroit, Michigan
Source: *Dun&B 88, 90; News 93; WhoAm 86, 90; WhoMW 86, 90*

Ilizarov, Gavril A
Russian. Surgeon
Orthopedic surgeon; developed what is known as the Ilizarov procedure to correct deformed bones.
b. 1921 in Caucasus, Union of Soviet Socialist Republics
d. Jul 24, 1992 in Kurgan, Union of Soviet Socialist Republics

Illia, Arturo Umberto
Argentine. Political Leader
Won first Argentinian presidential election based on proportional representation, 1963; ousted in coup, 1966.
b. Aug 4, 1900 in Cordoba, Argentina
d. Jan 18, 1983 in Cordoba, Argentina
Source: *AnObit 1983; BiDLAmC; BioIn 6, 7, 13, 16; CurBio 65, 83; DcCPSAm; EncLatA; IntWW 81, 82, 83*

Illich, Ivan
American. Educator
Former Roman Catholic priest who founded Intercultural Center of Documentation (CIDOC) in Mexico, 1961.
b. Sep 4, 1926 in Vienna, Austria
Source: *AuNews 2; BioIn 6, 8, 9, 10, 11, 12, 13, 14, 17, 21; ConAu 10NR, 35NR, 53; CurBio 69; DcTwHis; FacFETw; Future; IntAu&W 89; IntWW 75, 76, 77, 78, 79, 80, 81, 82, 83, 89, 91, 93; MajTwCW; MakMC; RadHan; RAdv 14; ThTwC 87; WhoAm 74, 76, 78, 80, 82, 84, 86, 88, 90, 92, 94, 95, 96, 97; WhoSSW 73, 75, 76; WhoWor 74, 76, 78; WrDr 80, 82, 84, 86, 88, 90, 92, 94, 96*

Illingworth, Leslie Gilbert
Welsh. Cartoonist
Cartoonist for *Daily Mail,* 1939-68.
b. Sep 2, 1902 in Barry, Wales
d. Dec 20, 1979 in Hastings, England
Source: *BioIn 12; DcBrAr 2; Who 74; WorECar*

Ilyushin, Sergei Vladimirovich
Russian. Aircraft Designer
Designed IL-2, or dive bomber, Soviet fighter plane of WW II.
b. Mar 31, 1894 in Diyalora, Russia
d. Feb 9, 1977 in Moscow, Union of Soviet Socialist Republics
Source: *FacFETw; IntWW 74, 75, 76, 77; NewYTBS 77; Who 74; WhoWor 74; WhWW-II*

Iman
[Iman Mohamed Abdulmajid; Mrs. David Bowie]
American. Model, Author
Cover model for major int'l mags; wrote *African Fairy Tales.*
b. Jul 25, 1955 in Mogadishu, Italian Somaliland
Source: *BioIn 10, 11, 12, 13, 14, 15, 16; ConBlB 4; CurBio 95; InB&W 80, 85; LegTOT; WhoAm 96, 97; WhoAmW 95; WhoWor 97*

Imlach, Punch
[George Imlach]
Canadian. Hockey Coach, Hockey Executive
Coach, general manager, Toronto, 1958-69; won four Stanley Cups; Hall of Fame, 1984.
b. Mar 15, 1918 in Toronto, Ontario, Canada
d. Dec 1, 1987 in Toronto, Ontario, Canada
Source: *BioIn 7, 8, 9, 15; HocEn; WhAm 9; WhoAm 76, 78; WhoE 74; WhoHcky 73; WhoSpor*

Immelmann, Max
German. Aviator
Developed maneuver known as "Immelmann turn"; one of the founders of German technique of air combat.
b. 1890
d. Jul 18, 1916
Source: *BioIn 12; EncSoA; HarEnMi; WebBD 83*

Impellitteri, Vincent R(ichard)
American. Politician
Dem. mayor of NYC, 1950-53; first mayor of NYC elected without political party support.
b. Feb 4, 1900 in Isnello, Sicily, Italy
d. Jan 29, 1987 in Bridgeport, Connecticut
Source: *BioIn 1, 2, 3, 4, 7; CurBio 51, 87; PolProf T*

Impressions, The
[Fred Cash; Sam Gooden; Ralph Johnson; Reggie Torrian]
American. Music Group
Soul vocal group formed 1958; pre-Temptations hits include "Gypsy Woman," 1961; "It's Alright," 1963.
Source: *Alli; BiDAfM; BiDAmM; BioIn 15; ConMuA 80A; EncPR&S 89; EncRk 88; EncRkSt; HarEnR 86; IlEncRk; InB&W 80, 85A; NewAmDM; NewGrDA 86; OxCPMus; RkOn 74, 82; RolSEnR 83; SoulM; WhoRock 81; WhoRocM 82*

Imus, Don
[John Donald Imus, Jr.]
American. Radio Performer
Host of nationally syndicated "Imus in the Morning," radio program; with WNBC-AM, New York, 1971-77, 1979-87; WFAN-AM, 1987—.
b. Jul 23, 1940 in Riverside, California
Source: *BioIn 9, 12; CurBio 96; News 97-1*

Inatome, Rick
American. Business Executive
Founder, Computer Mart, 1976 (name changed to Inacom, 1991); pres., CEO, Inacomp Computer Centers, 1982—.
b. Jul 27, 1953 in Detroit, Michigan
Source: *BioIn 13, 15; ConNews 85-4; Dun&B 90; WhoAm 88, 90, 92, 94, 95, 97; WhoAsA 94; WhoFI 81, 83, 89, 92, 94; WhoMW 82, 84, 86; WhoWor 82*

Ince, Thomas H(arper)
American. Director, Producer
Wrote, directed, produced films including *Civilization,* 1916.
b. Nov 6, 1882 in Newport, Rhode Island
d. Nov 19, 1924 in Beverly Hills, California

Source: *BiDFilm, 81, 94; BioIn 11, 12, 13; CmMov; DcFM; FacFETw; Film 1; FilmEn; FilmgC; HalFC 80; MovMk; OxCFilm; TwYS A; WhAm 1; WhoHol B; WhScrn 74, 77; WorEFlm*

Incredible String Band, The
[Gerard Dott; Mike Heron; Malcolm LeMaistre; "Licorice" (Christina) McKechnie; Rose Simpson; Robin Williamson]
Scottish. Music Group
Albums include *Changing Horses; I Looked Up.*
Source: *BiDAmM; BioIn 19; ConMuA 80A; DrAPF 85, 87, 89, 91, 93, 97; EncFCWM 83; EncPR&S 74; EncRk 88; IlEncRk; OxCPMus; PenEncP; RolSEnR 83; WhoHol 92; WhoRock 81; WhoRocM 82*

Indiana, Robert
[Robert Clarke]
American. Artist
Creates art out of words; called designer of trivia.
b. Sep 13, 1928 in New Castle, Indiana
Source: *AmArt; BioIn 6, 7, 9, 10, 14, 16, 17; BlueB 76; BriEAA; CelR; ConArt 77, 83, 89, 96; CurBio 73; DcAmArt; DcCAA 71, 77, 88, 94; DcCAr 81; IntWW 74, 75, 76, 77, 78, 79, 80, 81, 82, 83, 89, 91, 93; OxCTwCA; OxDcArt; PhDcTCA 77; PrintW 83, 85; WhoAm 74, 76, 78, 80, 82, 84, 86, 88, 90, 92, 94, 95, 96; WhoAmA 73, 76, 78, 82, 84, 86, 89, 91, 93; WhoUSWr 88; WhoWor 74; WorArt 1950*

Indigo Girls
American. Music Group
Folk/pop duo; hits include "Closer to Fine," and accompanying video, 1989.
Source: *ConMus 3; EncRkSt; News 94*

Indurain, Miguel
[Miguel Angel Indurain-Larraya]
Spanish. Cyclist
Champion, Tour de France, 1991, 1992, 1993.
b. Jul 16, 1964 in Villava, Spain
Source: *DcHiB; News 94, 94-1; WhoWor 95, 96*

Indy, Paul (Marie Theodore Vincent d')
French. Composer, Author
Wrote opera *Le Chant de la Cloche,* 1883; revived interest in Gregorian chant; made Wagner known in France.
b. Mar 27, 1851 in Paris, France
d. Dec 2, 1931 in Paris, France
Source: *AtlBL; Baker 84; LinLib L, S; NewEOp 71; OxCFr; OxCMus; WebBD 83*

Inescort, Frieda
[Frieda Wightman]
Scottish. Actor
Character actress in films *Mary of Scotland,* 1936; *Pride and Prejudice,* 1940.
b. Jun 29, 1901 in Edinburgh, Scotland
d. 1976
Source: *BioIn 10; EncAFC; FilmEn; FilmgC; ForYSC; HalFC 80, 88; InWom SUP; MotPP; MovMk; ThFT; What 4; WhoHol C; WhoHrs 80; WhScrn 83; WhThe*

Iness, Sim
American. Track Athlete
Discus thrower; won gold medal, 1952 Olympics.
b. Jul 9, 1930 in Keota, Oklahoma
Source: *WhoTr&F 73*

Infeld, Leopold
Polish. Physicist, Author
Worked with Albert Einstein on relativity and quantum theory.
b. Aug 20, 1898 in Krakow, Poland
d. Jan 16, 1968 in Warsaw, Poland
Source: *AmAu&B; BioIn 6, 8, 12; CurBio 63, 68; DcScB; InSci; WhAm 4; WhE&EA*

Ing, Dean
American. Author
Science-fiction author; books include *Blood of Eagles,* 1987; *Nemesis Mission,* 1991.
b. Jun 17, 1931 in Austin, Texas
Source: *ConAu 23NR, 106; EncSF 93; IntAu&W 91, 93; NewEScF; ScF&FL 92; ScFSB; TwCSFW 86, 91; WrDr 88, 90, 92, 94, 96*

Inge, William Motter
American. Dramatist
Wrote *Come Back, Little Sheba,* 1950; *Bus Stop,* 1955.
b. May 3, 1913 in Independence, Kansas
d. Jun 10, 1973 in Hollywood Hills, California
Source: *ConLC 8; CurBio 53, 73; McGEWD 72; ModAL; ModWD; OxCAmL 65; OxCThe 67; PenC AM; PlP&P; REn; REnAL; REnWD; TwCA SUP; WebE&AL; WhAm 5; WorEFlm*

Inge, William Ralph
"The Gloomy Dean"
English. Religious Leader, Author
Divinity professor, Oxford 1907-1911; dean, St. Paul's Cathedral, London, 1911-1934.
b. Jun 6, 1860 in Craike, England
d. Feb 26, 1954 in Wallingford, England
Source: *Alli SUP; BioIn 2, 3, 4, 5, 6, 8, 14; Chambr 3; ConAu 116; DcLEL; DcNaB 1951; EncWB; EvLB; GrBr; IlEncMy; LinLib L, S; LngCTC; LuthC 75; NewC; NewCBEL; OxCEng 67, 85, 95; ThTwC 87; TwCA, SUP; WhE&EA; WhLit; WhoLA; WorAl*

Ingelow, Jean
English. Poet, Author
Wrote novel *John Jerome,* 1886, three series of *Poems,* 1871-85.
b. Mar 17, 1820 in Boston, England
d. Jul 20, 1897 in London, England
Source: *Alli SUP; BbD; BiD&SB; BioIn 2, 3, 8, 9, 14, 16; BlmGWL; BritAu 19; CamGEL; CamGLE; CarSB; CasWL; Chambr 3; ChhPo, S1, S2; DcBiA; DcEnA; DcEnL; DcEuL; DcLB 35, 163; DcLEL; DcNaB C, S1; EncBrWW; EvLB; FemiCLE; InWom, SUP; JBA 34; LinLib L, S; NewC; NewCBEL; NinCLC 39; OxCChiL; OxCEng 67, 85, 95; PenC ENG; PenNWW A; SJGFanW; SmATA 33; StaCVF; TwCChW 78A, 83A, 89A, 95A; VicBrit; WhoChL; WomNov*

Ingels, Marty
[Martin Ingerman]
American. Comedian, Actor
Films include *Guide for a Married Man.*
b. Mar 9, 1936 in Brooklyn, Michigan
Source: *BioIn 11; ConTFT 5; EncAFC; FilmEn; FilmgC; ForYSC; HalFC 80, 84, 88; IntMPA 75, 76, 77, 78, 79, 80, 81, 82, 84, 86, 88, 92, 94, 96; LegTOT; WhoAm 74, 76, 78, 80, 82, 84, 86, 88, 90, 92, 94, 95, 96, 97; WhoEnt 92; WhoHol 92, A; WhoWest 84, 87*

Ingersoll, Ralph McAllister
American. Journalist, Publisher
VP, general manager, Time, Inc., 1935-38; publisher, 1937-39.
b. Dec 8, 1900 in New Haven, Connecticut
d. Mar 8, 1985 in Miami Beach, Florida
Source: *AmSocL; Au&Wr 71; BioIn 1, 4, 5, 6, 12; BlueB 76; ChhPo; ConAu P-1; CurBio 40; DcLB 127; FacFETw; IntAu&W 77; IntWW 74, 75, 76, 77, 78, 79, 80, 81, 82, 83; IntYB 78, 79, 80, 81, 82; REnAL; TwCA SUP; WhAm 8, 9; WhE&EA; WhNAA; Who 74, 82, 83, 85; WhoAm 74, 76, 78, 80, 82, 84; WhoE 74*

Ingersoll, Ralph McAllister, II
American. Publisher
CEO, chairman of family-owned publishing firm, R J Company, 1973— .
b. Jun 14, 1946 in New York, New York
Source: *BioIn 15; News 88, 88-2; WhoAm 90; WhoE 79, 81, 83; WhoFI 85, 87*

Ingersoll, Robert Green
American. Lawyer, Orator
Noted trial lawyer; IL attorney general 1867-69; published influential, religious lectures.
b. Aug 11, 1833 in Dresden, New York
d. Jul 21, 1899 in New York, New York
Source: *Alli SUP; AmAu; AmAu&B; AmBi; AmOrN; AmRef; ApCAB, X; BbD; BiD&SB; BioIn 1, 2, 3, 4, 5, 6, 7, 9, 10, 11, 12, 14, 15, 16, 17, 19; DcAmAu; DcAmB; DcAmReB 1, 2; DcNAA; EncAB-H 1974, 1996; EncARH; EncUnb; HarEnUS; LinLib L, S; LuthC 75; McGEWB; NatCAB 9; OxCAmH; OxCAmL 65, 83, 95; RelLAm 91; REn; REnAL; TwCBDA; TwoTYeD; WebAB 74, 79; WhAm 1; WhAmP*

Ingersoll, Simon
American. Inventor
Patented rotating shaft for steam engine, 1858; 16 improvements of drill machinery, four for life line thrower, 1873-83.
b. Mar 3, 1818 in Stanwich, Connecticut
d. Jul 24, 1894
Source: *AmBi; BioIn 9; DcAmB; WhAm HS*

Ingersoll, Stuart H
American. Military Leader
Navy admiral who commanded Sixth, Seventh fleets.
b. 1898?
d. Jan 29, 1983 in Newport, Rhode Island
Source: *BioIn 13; NewYTBS 83, 84*

Ingold, Christopher Kelk, Sir
English. Chemist, Writer, Educator
Chm. of chemistry, U College of London, 1930-61; published over 400 theoretical papers.
b. Oct 28, 1893 in London, England
d. Dec 8, 1970 in London, England
Source: *BiESc; BioIn 1, 7, 9, 12; DcNaB 1961; InSci; LarDcSc; WhE&EA*

Ingraham, Hubert
Bahamian. Political Leader
Succeeded Lynden O. Pindling as Prime Minister, Bahamas, 1992—.
b. Aug 4, 1947 in Pine Ridge, Bahamas

Ingram, James
American. Singer, Songwriter
With Patti Austin, had hit single "Baby Come to Me," 1982.
b. Feb 16, 1956? in Akron, Ohio
Source: *BioIn 15; Dun&B 88; InB&W 85; LegTOT; RkOn 85; WhoAm 90*

Ingram, Rex
American. Actor
Best known as slave Jim in film *Adventures of Huckleberry Finn,* 1939.
b. Oct 20, 1895 in Cairo, Illinois
d. Sep 19, 1969 in Los Angeles, California
Source: *AfrAmAl 6; BiE&WWA; BioIn 2, 19; BlksAmF; ConBlB 5; DrBlPA, 90; FilmEn; FilmgC; ForYSC; HalFC 80, 84, 88; HolCA; MovMk; NegAl 76, 83, 89; NotNAT B; OxCFilm; Vers A; WhoHol B; WhoHrs 80; WhScrn 74, 77, 83; WhThe; WorAl*

Ingrassia, Paul
American. Journalist
Reporter with the *Wall Street Journal;* won a 1993 Pulitzer Prize for beat reporting.
b. Aug 18, 1950 in Laurel, Mississippi
Source: *WhoAm 90; WhoFI 83*

Ingres, Jean Auguste Dominique
French. Artist
Famed Draughtsman; did portraits, sensual nudes in neoclassic linear style: *Madame Riviere,* 1806.
b. Aug 29, 1780 in Montauban, France
d. Jan 13, 1867 in Paris, France
Source: *AtlBL; Benet 87, 96; BioIn 1, 2, 3, 4, 5, 6, 7, 8, 9, 10, 11, 12, 13, 15, 16; ClaDrA; DcCathB; Dis&D; IntDcAA 90; LinLib S; McGEWB; NewC; NewCol 75; OxCArt; OxCFr; REn*

Ingstad, Helge Marcus
Norwegian. Author
Wrote on travels in Canada: *Land of Feast and Famine,* 1933; researched Apache Indians, Eskimo groups, 1936-68.
b. Dec 30, 1899 in Meraker, Norway
Source: *ConAu 65; IntAu&W 76, 77, 82, 89; IntWW 74, 75, 76, 77, 78, 79, 80, 81, 82, 83, 89, 91, 93; OxCCan; WhoWor 74, 76, 78*

Inhofe, James M.
American. Politician
Rep. senator, OK, 1994—.
b. Nov 17, 1934
Source: *AlmAP 88, 92, 96; CngDr 87, 89, 91, 93, 95; WhoAm 88, 90, 92, 94, 95, 96, 97; WhoIns 75, 76, 77, 78, 79, 80, 82, 84, 86; WhoSSW 88, 91, 93, 95, 97*

Ink Spots, The
[Billy Bowen; Charlie Fuqua; Orville Jones; Bill Kenny; Herb Kenny; Ivory Watson]
American. Music Group
Biggest hit "If I Didn't Care," 1939.
Source: *AmPS A, B; BiDAfM; BiDJaz A; BioIn 18; CmpEPM; DcTwCCu 5; DrBlPA, 90; EncRk 88; InB&W 80, 85, 85A; NewAmDM; NewGrDA 86; NewYTBS 78; ObitOF 79; OxCPMus; PenEncP; RolSEnR 83; WhoHol 92; WhoRock 81*

Inman, Bobby Ray
American. Business Executive
Deputy director, CIA, 1981-82; pres., CEO, Microelectronics and Computer Technologies Corp., 1983-86; Secretary of Defense nominee that withdrew his nam e from consideration, 1994.
b. Apr 4, 1931 in Rhonesboro, Texas
Source: *BioIn 11, 12, 13, 14, 15, 16; ConNews 85-1; EncAI&E; NewYTBS 93; St&PR 91; WhoAm 78, 80, 82, 84, 86, 88, 90, 92, 94, 95, 96, 97; WhoAmP 81, 83, 85, 87, 89, 91, 93; WhoFrS 84; WhoGov 75; WhoSSW 78*

Inman, Henry
American. Artist
Historical, portrait painter; founded National Academy of Design; director, PA Academy of Fine Arts.
b. Oct 28, 1801 in Utica, New York
d. Jan 17, 1846 in New York, New York
Source: *AmBi; AntBDN J; ApCAB; BenetAL 91; BioIn 1, 4, 5, 7, 9, 11; BriEAA; DcAmArt; DcAmB; Drake; FolkA 87; HarEnUS; IlBEAAW; LinLib S; McGDA; NatCAB 5, 9; NewCol 75; NewYHSD; TwCBDA; WebAB 74, 79; WebBD 83; WhAm HS*

Innaurato, Albert
American. Dramatist
Won Obie for *Gemini,* 1977.
b. Jun 2, 1948 in Philadelphia, Pennsylvania
Source: *BiDConC; BioIn 11, 12, 15, 16; CamGWoT; ConAu 115, 122; ConDr 82, 88; ConLC 21, 60; ConTFT 4; CrtSuDr; CurBio 88; CyWA 89; IntAu&W 91; McGEWD 84; NatPD 77, 81; OxCAmT 84; WhoAm 86, 88, 90; WhoThe 81; WorAu 1980; WrDr 84, 86, 88, 90, 92, 94, 96*

Innes, Hammond
[Ralph Hammond-Innes]
English. Author
Writings include *Fire in the Snow,* 1947; *The Last Voyage,* 1978.
b. Jul 15, 1913 in Horsham, England
Source: *AmAu&B; ConNov 72, 76, 82, 86, 91; CurBio 54; DcLP 87B; IntvTCA 2; IntWW 83, 91; LinLib L; LngCTC; NewCBEL; Novels; REn; TwCCr&M 80, 85, 91; TwCWr; Who 85, 92; WhoWor 74; WorAu 1950; WrDr 76, 86, 92, 94*

Inness, George
American. Artist
Landscape artist; influenced by Hudson River and Barbizon schools.
b. May 1, 1825 in Newburgh, New York
d. Aug 3, 1894, Scotland
Source: *AmBi; AmCulL; ApCAB; ArtsAmW 1; ArtsNiC; AtlBL; BioIn 1, 3, 4, 6, 7, 8, 9, 11, 14, 15, 19; BriEAA; DcAmArt; DcAmB; DcArts; Drake; HarEnUS; IlBEAAW; LegTOT; LinLib S; McGDA; McGEWB; NatCAB 2; NewCol 75; NewYHSD; OxCAmH; OxCAmL 65; OxCArt; OxDcArt; REn; TwCBDA; WebAB 74, 79; WhAmArt 85; WhAm HS; WhFla; WorAl; WorAlBi*

Innis, Roy Emile Alfredo
American. Civil Rights Leader
Nat. director, CORE, 1968-82; nat. chm., 1982—.
b. Jun 6, 1934 in Saint Croix, Virgin Islands of the United States
Source: *AmSocL; BioIn 14; CurBio 69; InB&W 85; IntWW 74, 75, 76, 77, 78, 79, 80, 81, 82, 83, 89, 91, 93; NegAl 89; WhoAfA 96; WhoAm 74, 76, 78, 80, 82, 84, 86, 88, 90, 92, 94, 95, 96, 97; WhoBlA 85, 88, 90, 92, 94; WhoUN 75*

Innocent XI, Pope
[Benedetto Odescalchi]
Italian. Religious Leader
During 1676-89 pontificate, stressed moral reform, clashed frequently with Louis XIV; considered finest pontiff of 17th c.
b. May 19, 1611 in Como, Italy

d. Aug 12, 1689 in Rome, Italy
Source: *DcCathB; NewCol 75; WebBD 83*

Inonu, Ismet
Turkish. Statesman
First prime minister Republic of Turkey, 1923-1937; pres., 1938-1950.
b. Sep 24, 1884 in Iznik, Ottoman Empire
d. Dec 25, 1973 in Ankara, Turkey
Source: *BioIn 1, 6, 7, 10, 11, 17; CurBio 41, 64, 74, 74N; DcTwHis; EncWB; FacFETw; HisEWW; LinLib S; NewCol 75; NewYTBE 73; ObitT 1971; PolLCME; WhAm 6, 7; Who 74; WhWW-II*

Inouye, Daniel Ken
American. Politician
Dem. senator from HI, 1963—; co-chaired Iran-Contra hearings, 1987.
b. Sep 7, 1924 in Honolulu, Hawaii
Source: *AlmAP 92; AsAmAlm; BiDrAC; BiDrUSC 89; BioIn 5, 6, 8, 9, 10, 11, 12, 13, 15, 16; BlueB 76; CngDr 74, 77, 79, 81, 83, 85, 87, 89; CurBio 60, 87; IntWW 74, 75, 76, 77, 78, 79, 80, 81, 82, 83, 89, 91, 93; NewYTBS 86; PolsAm 84; WhoAm 74, 76, 78, 80, 82, 84, 86, 88, 90, 92, 94, 95, 96, 97; WhoAmL 78, 79; WhoAmP 73, 75, 77, 79, 81, 83, 85, 87, 89, 91, 93, 95; WhoGov 72, 75, 77; WhoWest 74, 76, 78, 80, 82, 84, 87, 89, 92, 94, 96; WhoWor 74, 76, 78, 80, 82, 84, 87, 89, 91; WorAl; WorAlBi*

Insull, Samuel
English. Business Executive
Public utilities exec. who headed many Edison electrical companies including Commonwealth Edison Co., 1907-30; chm., 1930-32.
b. Nov 11, 1859 in London, England
d. Jul 16, 1938 in Paris, France
Source: *AmBi; AmDec 1930; ApCAB X; BiDAmBL 83; BioIn 2, 3, 4, 5, 6, 9, 14, 15, 18, 19, 21; DcAmB S2; DcAmSR; EncAB-H 1974, 1996; EncABHB 1; LinLib S; McGEWB; NatCAB 14; NewCol 75; OxCAmH; WebAB 74, 79; WhAm 1*

INXS
[Garry Gary Beers; Andrew Farriss; Jon Farriss; Tim Farriss; Michael Hutchence; Kirk Pengilly]
Australian. Music Group
Rock group formed in 1979; albums include *The Swing,* 1984; *Kick,* 1987.
Source: *BioIn 16, 17; CelR 90; ConMus 2; EncRkSt; PenEncP; RkOn 85*

Ionesco, Eugene
French. Author, Dramatist
Theater of the absurd: *The Bald Prima Donna,* 1950; *The Rhinoceros,* 1959.
b. Nov 26, 1909 in Slatina, Romania
d. Mar 28, 1994 in Paris, France
Source: *Benet 87; BioIn 13, 14, 15; CamGWoT; CelR 90; ConAu 144; ConFLW 84; ConLC 1, 4, 6, 9, 11, 15, 41, 86; ConTFT 4; CurBio 94N; CyWA 89; EuWr 13; FacFETw; GrFLW; GuFrLit 1; IntAu&W 89; IntDcT 2; IntWW 83, 91; LiExTwC; MajMD 2; MajTwCW; McGEWD 72; OxCAmT 84; OxCEng 85; PenC EUR; PlP&P; RAdv 13-2; RComWL; REn; REnWD; RfGWoL 95; SmATA 7; TwCWr; Who 85, 92; WhoAm 86, 90; WhoEnt 92; WhoThe 81; WhoTwCL; WhoWor 84, 91; WorAlBi; WorAu 1950*

Ippolitov-Ivanov, Mikhail Mikhailovich
Russian. Composer
Awarded "People's Artist of the Republic," 1923; conductor, Moscow Opera, 1925.
b. Nov 9, 1859 in Gatchina, Russia
d. Jan 26, 1935 in Moscow, Union of Soviet Socialist Republics
Source: *BiDSovU; BioIn 4, 9; NewCol 75*

Iqbal, Mahomed, Sir
[Sir Muhammad Iqbal]
Indian. Poet, Philosopher
Pres., Muslim League, 1930; advocated Pakistani independence.
b. Nov 9, 1877 in Sialkot, India
d. Apr 21, 1938 in Lahore, India
Source: *BioIn 14, 18, 19; EncWL 2, 3; McGEWB; NewCol 75; WebBD 83; WorAu 1970*

Iredell, James
American. Jurist
Associate justice, US Supreme Court, 1790-99; supported ratification of Constitution.
b. Oct 5, 1751 in Lewes, England
d. Oct 2, 1799 in Edenton, North Carolina
Source: *AmBi; AmWrBE; ApCAB; BiDFedJ; BioIn 2, 3, 5, 15; BlkwEAR; DcAmB; DcNCBi 3; Drake; EncSoH; NatCAB 1; NewCol 75; OxCSupC; PeoHis; SupCtJu; TwCBDA; WebAB 74, 79; WebBD 83; WhAm HS; WhAmRev*

Ireland, Jill
[Mrs. Charles Bronson]
American. Actor
Starred with Charles Bronson in several films: *Breakheart Pass,* 1976; autobiography *Life Wish,* 1987, deals with her fight with cancer; died of cancer.
b. Apr 24, 1936 in London, England
d. May 18, 1990 in Malibu, California
Source: *AnObit 1990; BioIn 10, 11, 14, 15, 16; ConAu 131, 135; ConTFT 9; FilmEn; FilmgC; HalFC 80, 84, 88; IlWWBF; IntMPA 77, 78, 79, 80, 81, 82, 84, 86, 88; ItaFilm; LegTOT; News 90; NewYTBS 90; VarWW 85; WhoAm 76, 84; WhoHol A; WorAlBi*

Ireland, John
Canadian. Actor
Oscar nominee for *All the King's Men,* 1949.
b. Jan 30, 1915 in Victoria, British Columbia, Canada
d. Mar 21, 1992 in Santa Barbara, California
Source: *BiE&WWA; CmMov; ConTFT 8; FilmgC; HalFC 84, 88; IntDcF 1-3; IntMPA 75, 76, 77, 78, 79, 80, 81, 82, 84, 86, 88, 92; MovMk; NotNAT; OxCFilm; WorAl; WorAlBi*

Ireland, John Nicholson
English. Composer
Wrote piano pieces, orchestral works, 100 songs to words of noted authors.
b. Aug 13, 1879 in Inglewood, England
d. Jun 12, 1962 in Washington, England
Source: *Baker 84; BriBkM 80; DcCM; MusMk; NewCol 75; NewGrDM 80; OxCMus; VarWW 85; WhAm 4*

Ireland, Kathy
American. Model
Known for modeling swimsuits in *SI* magazine.
Source: *BioIn 17; LegTOT; WhoHol 92*

Ireland, Patricia
American. Political Activist
Pres., NOW, 1991—.
b. Oct 19, 1945 in Oak Park, Illinois
Source: *CurBio 92; News 92; NewYTBS 91; WhoAm 94, 95, 96, 97; WhoAmW 93, 95, 97*

Ireland, William Henry
English. Imposter
Wrote two "pseudo-Shakespearean" plays, *Vortigern and Rowena; Henry II.*
b. 1777
d. 1835
Source: *Alli; BiDLA; BioIn 4, 7, 8, 9; BlkwCE; CamGLE; CasWL; Chambr 2; ChhPo; DcEnL; DcLEL; DrInf; EvLB; LinLib L; NewC; OxCEng 85, 95; REn*

Irene
[Irene Gibbons]
American. Fashion Designer
Leading film designer, 1950s, who also had ready-to-wear line; replaced Adrian as designer for MGM.
b. Dec 8, 1907 in Baker, Montana
d. Nov 15, 1962 in Hollywood, California
Source: *BioIn 1, 6; CurBio 46, 63; EncFash; FilmgC; HalFC 84; InWom; NotNAT B; WhScrn 83; WorFshn*

Irene
Dutch. Princess
Daughter of Queen Julianna and Prince Bernhard; sister of Christina.
b. Aug 5, 1939 in Soestdijk, Netherlands
Source: *BioIn 2, 6; WhoWor 76*

Irish, Ned
[Edward Simmons Irish]
American. Basketball Executive
Founder, pres., NY Knicks, 1946-74; promoted college basketball at Madison Square Garden; Hall of Fame.

b. May 6, 1905 in Lake George, New York
d. Jan 21, 1982 in Venice, Florida
Source: *BasBi; BiDAmSp BK; BioIn 1, 5, 9, 12, 21; NewYTBS 82; WhAm 8; WhoAm 74, 76; WhoBbl 73*

Irish Hunger Strikers
[Michael Devine; Kieran Doherty; Francis Hughes; Martin Hurson; Kevin Lynch; Raymond McCreesh; Joe McDonnell; Thomas McIlwee; Patrick O'Hara; Bobby Sands]
Irish. Revolutionaries
IRA members who starved themelves to death in Belfast's Maze Prison, 1981, demanding they be known as political prisoners rather than criminals.
Source: *Alli SUP; AmEA 74; BioIn 17; WhoRocM 82*

Irish Rovers, The
[Jimmy Ferguson; Wilcil McDowell; George Millar; Joe Millar; Will Millar]
Canadian. Music Group
Hits include "The Unicorn," 1968; "Wasn't That a Party," 1981; N Ireland-born musicians have had TV series, concert successes.
Source: *Alli; BioIn 20; ColCR; CurBio 49; RkOn 78A, 85*

Iron Butterfly
[Erik Braun; Ronald Bushy; Lee Dorman; Doug Ingle; Michael Pinera; Lawrence Reinhardt]
American. Music Group
Heavy metal group; albums include *Sun and Steel,* 1975; *Iron Butterfly,* 1970.
Source: *BiDAmM; ConMuA 80A; EncPR&S 74, 89; EncRk 88; EncRkSt; HarEnR 86; IlEncRk; PenEncP; RkOn 74, 78; RolSEnR 83; WhoRock 81; WhoRocM 82*

Iron Maiden
[Clive Burr; Paul Di'Anno; Steve Harris; Dave Murray; Adrian Smith; Dennis Stratton]
British. Music Group
Heavy metal band named after medieval torture device; formed in 1977; albums include *Piece of Mind,* 1983.
Source: *ConMus 10; EncPR&S 89; EncRk 88; EncRkSt; HarEnR 86; PenEncP; RolSEnR 83; WhoRel 92; WhoRocM 82*

Irons, Jeremy John
English. Actor
Best known role in *French Lieutenant's Woman,* 1981; won best actor Oscar, 1991, for *Reversal of Fortune.*
b. Sep 19, 1948 in Cowes, Isle of Wight, England
Source: *BioIn 13, 14, 15, 16; CamGWoT; CelR 90; ConTFT 7; CurBio 84; HalFC 84, 88; IntMPA 84; IntWW 82, 83, 91; News 91; NewYTBS 84; Who 92; WhoAm 84, 86, 88, 90, 92, 94, 95, 96, 97; WhoEnt 92; WhoWor 89, 91, 95, 96, 97; WorAlBi*

Ironside, Christopher
English. Artist, Designer
Works include coats of arms, tapestries, coinages.
b. Jul 11, 1913, England
d. Jul 13, 1992
Source: *Who 74, 82, 83, 85, 88, 90, 92*

Ironside, Henry Allan
"Archbishop of Fundamentalism"
Canadian. Clergy
Popular broadcaster; pastor of Chicago's Moody Memorial Church, 1930s-40s.
b. Oct 14, 1876 in Toronto, Ontario, Canada
d. Jan 15, 1951 in Rotorua, New Zealand
Source: *BioIn 1, 2, 11, 12, 17, 19; ConAu 115; CurBio 45, 51; DcAmB S5; WhAm 3; WhE&EA; WhNAA*

Ironside, William Edmund
Scottish. Army Officer
Chief of Imperial General Staff, 1939-40; commander-in-chief of Home Forces, 1940.
b. May 6, 1880 in Ironside, Scotland
d. Sep 22, 1959 in London, England
Source: *CurBio 40, 59; DcNaB 1951*

Irsay, Robert
American. Football Executive
Owner, Baltimore Colts, 1972-97; moved team to Indianapolis, 1984.
b. Mar 5, 1923 in Chicago, Illinois
d. Jan 14, 1997 in Indianapolis, Indiana
Source: *Ballpl 90; BioIn 14, 15, 16; WhoAm 84, 86, 88, 90, 92, 94, 95, 96, 97; WhoMW 88, 90, 92, 93*

Irvin, Dick
[James Dickenson Irvin]
Canadian. Hockey Player
Forward, Chicago, 1926-29; coach, Toronto, 1931-32, Montreal, 1940-55; won four Stanley Cups; Hall of Fame, 1958.
b. Jul 19, 1892 in Limestone Ridge, Ontario, Canada
d. May 16, 1957 in Montreal, Quebec, Canada
Source: *BioIn 2, 4; HocEn; WhoHcky 73; WhoSpor*

Irvin, Michael (Jerome)
American. Football Player
With the Dallas Cowboys, 1988—.
b. Mar 5, 1966 in Fort Lauderdale, Florida
Source: *BioIn 19, 20, 21; News 96, 96-3; WhoAfA 96; WhoAm 94, 95, 96, 97; WhoSSW 95; WhoWor 95, 96*

Irvin, Monte
[Monford Merrill Irvin]
American. Baseball Player
Star outfielder in Negro Leagues before playing in ML, 1949-56; led NL in RBIs, 1951; Hall of Fame, 1973.
b. Feb 25, 1919 in Columbia, Alabama
Source: *Ballpl 90; BiDAmSp BB; BioIn 2, 3, 7, 11, 14, 15, 16, 19, 20; InB&W 80; LegTOT; NewYTBE 73; WhoAfA 96; WhoBlA 75, 77, 80, 85, 88, 90, 92, 94; WhoProB 73; WhoSpor*

Irvin, Rea
American. Artist
Created first *New Yorker* cover, introducing best known character, Eustace Tilley.
b. Aug 26, 1881 in San Francisco, California
d. May 28, 1972 in Frederiksted, Saint Croix, Virgin Islands of the United States
Source: *ArtsAmW 2; BioIn 9; ChhPo S1; ConAu 93; DcWomA; NewYTBE 72; WhAm 5; WhAmArt 85; WhoAmA 73, 76N, 78N, 80, 80N, 82N, 84N, 86N, 89N, 91N, 93N; WorECar*

Irvin, Robert W
American. Journalist
Automotive writer for 30 yrs; editor, *Automotive News;* publisher, *Auto Week.*
b. Mar 3, 1933 in Highland Park, Michigan
d. Dec 1, 1980 in Chicago, Illinois
Source: *BioIn 9, 12; ConAu 103; Ward 77, 77F*

Irving, Amy
American. Actor
Films include *Yentl,* 1983; *Micki & Maude,* 1984.
b. Sep 10, 1953 in Palo Alto, California
Source: *BioIn 11, 12, 13, 14, 15, 16; CelR 90; ConTFT 1, 4, 11; HalFC 84, 88; IntMPA 84, 86, 88, 92, 94, 96; IntWW 91, 93; LegTOT; NewYTBS 88; VarWW 85; WhoAm 88, 90, 92, 94, 95, 96, 97; WhoAmW 83, 85, 87, 89, 91, 95, 97; WhoEnt 92; WhoHol 92; WorAlBi*

Irving, Clifford Michael
American. Author
Served 17 months in prison for writing false autobiography of Howard Hughes.
b. Nov 5, 1930 in New York, New York
Source: *Au&Wr 71; AuNews 1; BioIn 9, 10, 11, 13; BioNews 74; ConAu 1R, 2NR; DcLP 87A; FacFETw; IntAu&W 91; NewYTBE 72; Who 92; WrDr 76, 86, 92*

Irving, Edward
Scottish. Mystic, Religious Leader
Influential in founding of Catholic Apostolic Church; deposed from Scottish church.
b. Aug 4, 1792 in Annan, Scotland
d. Dec 7, 1834 in Glasgow, Scotland
Source: *Alli; BbD; BiDAmCu; BioIn 1, 2, 3, 5; BritAu 19; CamGLE; CelCen; Chambr 3; CmScLit; DcBiPP; DcEnL; DcNaB; EncO&P 1, 2, 3; EvLB; LuthC 75; NewC; NewCBEL; NewCol 75; WhDW*

Irving, George Steven
[George Irving Shelasky]
American. Actor
Won Tony for *Irene,* 1973; began Broadway career with *Oklahoma,* 1943.
b. Nov 1, 1922 in Springfield, Massachusetts
Source: *ConTFT 4; NotNAT; WhoAm 84, 86, 88, 90, 92, 94, 95, 96, 97; WhoEnt 92; WhoThe 81*

Irving, Henry, Sir
[John Henry Brodribb]
English. Actor
Noted for Shakespearean roles; first actor to be knighted, 1895.
b. Feb 6, 1838 in Glastonbury, England
d. Oct 13, 1905 in Bradford, England
Source: *BioIn 1, 2, 3, 4, 5, 7, 8, 9, 10, 11, 12, 14, 15, 16, 20, 21; BlmGEL; CamGWoT; CelCen; CnThe; DcArts; DcNaB S2; EncWT; Ent; FamA&A; GrStDi; HarEnUS; IntDcT 3; LinLib L, S; LngCEL; NewC; NewCol 75; NotNAT A, B; OxCAmT 84; OxCEng 85, 95; OxCThe 67, 83; PlP&P; REn; TheaDir; VicBrit; WhAm 1; WhDW; WorAl; WorAlBi*

Irving, Isabel
American. Actor
Active on stage from 1887 to 1936.
b. Feb 28, 1871 in Bridgeport, Connecticut
d. Sep 1, 1944 in Nantucket, Massachusetts
Source: *InWom; NotNAT B; WhAm 2; WhoStg 1906, 1908; WhThe; WomWWA 14*

Irving, John
American. Author
Novels *The World According to Garp,* 1978 and *The Hotel New Hampshire,* 1981 were adapted to film.
b. Mar 2, 1942 in Exeter, New Hampshire
Source: *Au&Arts 8; Benet 87; BenetAL 91; BestSel 89-3; BioIn 8, 11, 12, 13, 14, 16, 17, 20, 21; CelR 90; ConAu 25R, 28NR; ConLC 13, 23, 38; ConNov 82, 86, 91; CurBio 79; CyWA 89; DcArts; DcLB 6, Y82A; DcTwCCu 1; DrAPF 80, 89; EncWL 3; FacFETw; HalFC 84, 88; LegTOT; MagSAmL; MajTwCW; ModAL S2; Novels; OxCAmL 83; PostFic; RAdv 14, 13-1; WhoAm 82; WorAl; WorAlBi; WorAu 1975; WrDr 80, 82, 84, 86, 88, 90, 92*

Irving, Jules
American. Actor, Producer, Director
Artistic director, Repertory Theatre of Lincoln Center, 1964-72; co-founder, San Francisco Actors Workshop, 1952-64.
b. Apr 13, 1925 in New York, New York
d. Jul 28, 1979 in Reno, Nevada
Source: *BiE&WWA, 77, 81; WhScrn 83*

Irving, Laurence Sidney
English. Actor
Had roles in his own plays, *Peter the Great, Unwritten Law;* son of Henry Irving.
b. Dec 21, 1871 in London, England
d. May 29, 1914
Source: *EncWT; OxCThe 67; WhLit; WhThe*

Irving, Robert Augustine
American. Conductor
Led NYC Ballet, 1958-89; England's Royal Ballet, 1949-58; received *Dance Magazine* Award for Lifetime Achievement, 1984.
b. Aug 28, 1913 in Winchester, England
d. Sep 13, 1991 in Winchester, England
Source: *Baker 84; BioIn 16; IntAu&W 91; IntWW 83, 91; IntWWM 90; NewYTBS 91; PenDiMP; WhAm 10; Who 90, 92N; WhoAm 86, 88; WhoAmM 83; WhoE 86; WhoMus 72*

Irving, Washington
[Diedrich Knickerbocker]
American. Author
Wrote *Rip Van Winkle, Legend of Sleepy Hollow,* 1820.
b. Apr 3, 1783 in New York, New York
d. Nov 28, 1859 in Tarrytown, New York
Source: *Alli; AmAu; AmAu&B; AmBi; AmCulL; AmWr; ApCAB; AtlBL; BbD; Benet 87, 96; BenetAL 91; BiAUS; BibAL; BiD&SB; BioIn 1, 2, 3, 4, 5, 6, 7, 8, 9, 10, 11, 12, 13, 14, 15, 16, 18, 19, 20, 21; CamGEL; CamGLE; CamHAL; CarSB; CasWL; CelCen; Chambr 3; ChhPo, S2, S3; ChlBkCr; CnDAL; ColARen; CrtT 3, 4; CyAL 1; CyWA 58; DcAmAu; DcAmB; DcAmC; DcAmDH 80, 89; DcArts; DcBiA; DcBiPP; DcEnA; DcEnL; DcLB 3, 11, 30, 59, 73, 74; DcLEL; DcNAA; DcPup; DcSpL; Dis&D; Drake; EncAAH; EncAB-H 1974, 1996; EncAHmr; EncFWF; EvLB; FamAYP; GrWrEL N; HalFC 84, 88; HarEnUS; LegTOT; LinLib L, S; MagSAmL; McGEWB; MemAm; MouLC 3; NatCAB 3; NewEOp 71; NewGrDA 86; NewYHSD; NinCLC 2, 19; NotNAT B; Novels; OxCAmH; OxCAmL 65, 83, 95; OxCAmT 84; OxCCan; OxCChiL; OxCEng 67, 85, 95; OxCSpan; OxCThe 67, 83; PenC AM; PenEncH; PlP&P; RAdv 1, 14, 13-1; REn; REnAL; REnAW; RfGAmL 87, 94; RfGShF; ScF&FL 1, 92; ShSCr 2; ShSWr; SupFW; TwCBDA; WebAB 74, 79; WebE&AL; WhAm HS; WhDW; WhoChL; WhoHr&F; WisWr; WorAl; WorAlBi; WorLitC; WrChl; YABC 2*

Irwin, Bill
[William Mills Irwin]
American. Actor, Choreographer
Performing artist; best-known act, *The Regard of Flight,* 1982, was highest grossing show at American Palace Theatre, NYC.
b. Apr 11, 1950 in Santa Monica, California
Source: *BioIn 13, 14, 15, 16; CamGWoT; ConTFT 7; CurBio 87; IntMPA 92, 94, 96; LegTOT; News 88-3; NewYTBS 82, 84; WhoHol 92*

Irwin, Hale S
American. Golfer
Turned pro, 1968; won US Open, 1974, 1979, 1990; oldest player to win US Open.
b. Jun 3, 1945 in Joplin, Missouri
Source: *BiDAmSp OS; BioIn 13, 14; NewYTBS 74, 75, 85; WhoAm 74, 86, 90; WhoGolf; WhoIntG*

Irwin, James Benson
American. Astronaut, Author
Eighth American to walk on moon (Apollo 15), 1971; with NASA, 1966-72; wrote *To Rule the Night.*
b. Mar 17, 1930 in Pittsburgh, Pennsylvania
d. Aug 8, 1991 in Glenwood Springs, Colorado
Source: *BioIn 9, 10, 16, 17, 18; BlueB 76; FacFETw; News 92, 92-1; NewYTBE 71; NewYTBS 74, 91; WhAm 10; WhoAm 74, 76, 78, 80, 82, 84, 86, 88, 90; WhoTech 89; WhoWest 76, 78, 80, 82, 84; WhoWor 74, 76, 78, 80, 82, 84, 87, 89, 91; WorDWW*

Irwin, Margaret
English. Author
Writings include *None So Pretty,* 1930; *The Bride,* 1939.
b. 1889 in London, England
d. 1967
Source: *BioIn 3, 8, 14, 15, 17; ConAu 93; CurBio 46, 91N; DcLEL; LngCTC; NewCBEL; PenEncH; ScF&FL 92; TwCA SUP; TwCRGW; TwCRHW 90; TwCWr; WhoHr&F; WhoLA*

Irwin, May
[May Campbell]
Canadian. Actor
Made screen history in Thomas Edison's *The Kiss,* 1896; denounced as immoral; noted farce comedienne with Tony Pasteur, 1877-83.
b. Jun 27, 1862 in Whitby, Ontario, Canada
d. Oct 22, 1938 in New York, New York
Source: *AmBi; BiDAmM; BioIn 3, 4, 6, 15, 16; DcAmB S2; EncVaud; FamA&A; Film 1; FilmEn; FunnyW; InWom, SUP; LibW; MotPP; NewAmDM; NewGrDA 86; NotAW; NotNAT B; NotWoAT; OxCAmT 84; OxCCanT; OxCPMus; OxCThe 83; TwYS; WhAm 1; WhoHol B; WhoStg 1906, 1908; WhScrn 74, 77, 83; WhThe; WomWWA 14*

Irwin, Robert
American. Artist
Avant-garde painter; works involve dot paintings, light and perception.
b. Sep 12, 1928 in Long Beach, California
Source: *AmArt; BioIn 9, 10, 11, 12, 13, 18, 19; ConArt 77, 83, 89, 96; CurBio 93; DcAmArt; DcCAA 71, 77, 88, 94;*

DcCAr 81; OxCTwCA; WhoAmA 73, 76, 78, 80, 82, 84, 86, 89, 91, 93

Irwin, Wallace (Admah)
American. Journalist, Author
Writings include *Pilgrims into Folly,* 1917; *Mated,* 1926; *Young Wife,* 1936; brother of Will.
b. Mar 15, 1875 in Oneida, New York
d. Feb 14, 1959 in Southern Pines, North Carolina
Source: *AmAu&B; Benet 87; BenetAL 91; BioIn 4, 5; ChhPo S1, S2; CmCal; CnDAL; ConAmL; DcAmAu; LinLib L, S; OxCAmL 65, 83, 95; REn; REnAL; Str&VC; TwCA, SUP; WhAm 3; WhScrn 77, 83*

Irwin, Will(iam Henry)
American. Journalist
Books on his experiences as a WW I reporter include *Christ or Mars?,* 1923; brother of Wallace.
b. Sep 14, 1873 in Oneida, New York
d. Feb 24, 1948 in New York, New York
Source: *AmAu&B; AmPeW; ApCAB X; BenetAL 91; BiDAmJo; BiDInt; BioIn 1, 2, 4, 12, 14, 16; ChhPo S1; CmCal; ConAu 117; DcAmB S4; DcLB 25; DcNAA; Dis&D; EncAJ; EncMys; JrnUS; LinLib L, S; NatCAB 35; OxCAmL 65, 83, 95; REnAL; ScF&FL 1; TwCA, SUP; WhAm 2; WhE&EA; WhLit; WhNAA; WhScrn 77*

Isaac
Biblical Figure
Only son of Abraham and Sarah; married Rebecca; father of Esau, Jacob; offered as a sacrifice by Abraham to God.
Source: *Benet 96; BioIn 1, 2, 4, 5, 7, 8, 10, 11, 17; DcCanB 4; DcCathB; EncEarC; LngCEL; McGDA; NewCol 75*

Isaacs, Alick
Scottish. Bacteriologist
Co-discovered chemotherapeutic agent, Interferon.
b. Jul 17, 1921 in Glasgow, Scotland
d. Jan 26, 1967 in London, England
Source: *BiESc; BioIn 8, 14, 20; CamDcSc; DcNaB 1961; GrBr; LarDcSc; NotTwCS; ObitOF 79; ObitT 1961*

Isaacs, Susan
American. Author
Wrote *Compromising Positions,* 1978; *Shining Through,* 1988.
b. Dec 7, 1943 in New York, New York
Source: *ArtclWW 2; BestSel 89-1; BioIn 14, 15, 17, 19, 20, 21; ConAu 20NR, 41NR, 89; ConLC 32; ConPopW; CurBio 93; IntAu&W 91, 93; MajTwCW; WhoAm 94, 95, 96, 97; WhoE 91, 93, 95, 97; WhoEnt 92; WorAu 1985; WrDr 84, 86, 88, 90, 92, 94, 96*

Isaak, Chris
American. Singer, Songwriter, Actor
Pop musician influenced by jazz and rockabilly; formed band, Silvertone, 1981; first Top 10 hit "Wicked Game," 1991, was featured in *Wild at Heart* soundtrack.
b. Jun 26, 1956 in Stockton, California
Source: *BioIn 14, 15; ConMus 6; ConTFT 15; CurBio 93; EncRkSt; LegTOT; WhoAm 94, 95, 96, 97*

Isabella I
[Isabela La Catolica]
Spanish. Ruler
Queen of Castile, 1474; financed Columbus' voyage, 1492.
b. Apr 22, 1451 in Madrigal de las Altas Torr, Spain
d. Nov 26, 1504 in Medina del Campo, Spain
Source: *LinLib S; NewCol 75; WebBD 83*

Isabella II
[Maria Isabella Louisa]
Spanish. Ruler
Queen of Spain, 1833-1868; had strifeful reign; abdicated in favor of son, Alfonso XII, 1870.
b. Oct 10, 1830 in Madrid, Spain
d. Apr 19, 1904 in Paris, France
Source: *McGEWB; NewCol 75; WebBD 83*

Isaiah
Hebrew. Prophet
His prophesies are collected in book of Old Testament; the first, longest book of the Major Prophets.
b. fl. 8th cent. BC
Source: *BioIn 1, 2, 3, 4, 5, 6, 7, 8, 10, 17, 20; DcBiPP; DcOrL 3; EncEarC; LegTOT; McGEWB; NewC; NewCol 75; WhDW; WorAl; WorAlBi*

Isbell, Marion William
American. Hotel Executive
Founded Ramada Inc. motel chain, 1929.
b. Aug 12, 1905 in Whitehaven, Tennessee
d. Oct 20, 1988 in Scottsdale, Arizona
Source: *BioIn 14, 15, 16; ExpInc; NatCAB 63N; NewYTBS 88; WhAm 9; WhoAm 74, 76, 78, 80, 82; WhoFI 79, 81, 83, 85; WhoWest 78, 80, 82*

Ishak, Yusof bin
Singaporean. Political Leader
First elected pres. of Singapore, 1963-70.
b. Aug 12, 1910
d. Nov 23, 1970, Singapore
Source: *ConAu 104; NewYTBE 70; ObitOF 79*

Isham, Samuel
American. Artist, Author
Wrote *The History of American Painting,* 1905.
b. May 12, 1855 in New York, New York
d. Jun 12, 1914
Source: *AmAu&B; BioIn 2; DcAmB; DcNAA; LinLib L; NatCAB 35; WhAm 1; WhAmArt 85*

Isherwood, Christopher (William)
[Christopher William Bradshaw-Isherwood]
American. Author, Dramatist
Play *Cabaret,* 1966 was based on his stories *Goodbye to Berlin,* 1935.
b. Aug 26, 1904 in Cheshire, England
d. Jan 4, 1986 in Santa Monica, California
Source: *AmAu&B; AnObit 1986; Au&Wr 71; Benet 87; BenetAL 91; BioIn 1, 2, 3, 4, 7, 8, 9, 10, 11, 12, 13, 14, 15, 17, 18, 20; BlmGEL; BlueB 76; BritWr 7; CamGEL; CamGLE; CamGWoT; CasWL; CelR; CmCal; CnMD; CnMWL; ConAu 13R, 35NR, 117; ConDr 73, 77, 82; ConGAN; ConLC 1, 9, 11, 14, 44; ConNov 72, 76, 82; CurBio 72, 86N; CyWA 89; DcLB 15, Y86N; DcLEL; DrAF 76; DrAPF 80; EncWB; EncWL 2, 3; EncWT; EvLB; FacFETw; GayLesB; GrWrEL N; HalFC 80, 84, 88; IntAu&W 77; IntWW 74, 75, 76, 77, 78, 79, 80, 81, 82, 83; IntWWP 77; LegTOT; LiExTwC; LinLib L; LngCTC; MagSWL; MajTwCW; McGEWD 72, 84; ModBrL, S1, S2; ModWD; NewC; NewCBEL; NewYTBE 73; NewYTBS 86; Novels; OxCAmL 65, 83, 95; OxCEng 67; PenC ENG; PlP&P; RAdv 1, 14, 13-1; REn; REnAL; RfGEnL 91; ShSWr; TwCA, SUP; TwCWr; VarWW 85; WebE&AL; WhAm 9; WhDW; WhE&EA; Who 74, 82, 83, 85; WhoAm 74, 76, 78, 80, 82, 84; WhoTwCL; WhoWor 74, 76, 78; WhThe; WorAl; WorAlBi; WrDr 76, 80, 82, 84, 86; WrPh*

Ishi
American.
Identified as the "last wild Indian" in North America; last known survivor of the Yahi tribe of Northern California.
b. 1862?
d. Mar 25, 1916
Source: *EncNAB; NotNaAm; WhNaAH*

Ishiguro, Kazuo
British. Author
Writings deal with how people come to terms with past mistakes, failures; won Booker Prize, 1989, for *The Remains of the Day.*
b. Nov 8, 1954 in Nagasaki, Japan
Source: *BestSel 90-2; BioIn 16, 17, 21; ConAu 49NR, 120; ConLC 27, 56, 59; ConNov 91, 96; CurBio 90; DcArts; IntAu&W 91, 93; IntWW 91, 93; LiExTwC; MagSWL; MajTwCW; NewYTBS 90; OxCEng 95; RGTwCWr; Who 88, 90, 92, 94; WhoE 89; WhoWor 89, 91, 93, 95, 96; WorAu 1985; WrDr 84, 88, 90, 92, 94, 96*

Ising, Rudolf C
American. Cartoonist
With Hugh Harman created *Looney Tunes* and *Merry Melodies* cartoon series; won an Oscar, 1940.

b. 1912?
d. Jul 18, 1992 in Newport Beach, California

Isley Brothers, The
[Ernie Isley; Marvin Isley; O'Kelly Isley; Ronald Isley; Rudolph Isley]
American. Music Group
Rhythm and Blues group formed, 1957; hits include "It's Your Thing," 1969; "Harvest For the World," 1976; Rock and Roll Hall of Fame, 1992.
Source: *ASCAP 80; BiDAmM; BioIn 11, 16; ConMus 8; DcTwCCu 5; EncPR&S 74, 89; EncRk 88; EncRkSt; HarEnR 86; IlEncBM 82; IlEncRk; InB&W 80, 85A; NewGrDA 86; OxCPMus; PenEncP; RkOn 82; SoulM; WhoRocM 82*

Ismail, Raghib
"Rocket"
American. Football Player
Wide receiver, Toronto, Canadian Football League, 1991-92, LA Raiders, NFL, 1993—; *Sporting News* College Player of the Year, 1990.
b. Nov 18, 1969 in Newark, New Jersey
Source: *BioIn 16; WhoAm 94, 95, 96, 97; WhoWest 94*

Ismay, Hastings Lionel, Baron
English. Military Leader
A leading military advisor to Churchill, WW II; secretary-general, NATO, 1952-57.
b. Jun 21, 1887 in Naini Tal, India
d. Dec 17, 1965 in Wormington Orange, England
Source: *CurBio 66; DcNaB 1961; EncCW; GrBr; HisDBrE; HisEWW; WhWW-II*

Ismay, Joseph Bruce
English. Business Executive
Chairman of the White Star Line at the time of the sinking of the R.M.S. Titanic, 1912.
b. Dec 12, 1862 in Crosby, England
d. Oct 17, 1937 in London, England
Source: *BioIn 2; DcNaB 1931*

Isocrates
Greek. Orator, Teacher
Founded Athenian school of oratory; developed literary form of rhetorical essays.
b. 436BC in Athens, Greece
d. 338BC in Athens, Greece
Source: *AncWr; BbD; BiD&SB; BioIn 12; BlmGEL; CasWL; CyEd; DcArts; DcBiPP; Grk&L; LegTOT; LinLib L, S; LngCEL; McGEWB; NewC; NewCol 75; OxCClL, 89; PenC CL; REn; WhDW*

Isozaki, Arata
Japanese. Architect
Prominent in Japan since late 1960s; American buildings include Los Angeles Muse um of Contemporary Art and of the Team Disney office-block, which features mouse-ear shape and functions as a giant sundial; uses basic geometrical forms.
b. Jul 23, 1931 in Oita, Japan
Source: *BioIn 11, 12, 13, 14, 15, 16; ConArch 80, 87, 94; CurBio 88; DcArts; DcTwDes; IntDcAr; IntWW 83, 89, 91, 93; News 90, 90-2; WhoAm 94, 95, 96; WhoWor 84, 87, 89, 91, 93, 95, 96, 97*

Israels, Josef
Dutch. Artist
Known for peasant genre watercolors, portraits and etchings.
b. Jan 27, 1824 in Groningen, Netherlands
d. Aug 12, 1911 in The Hague, Netherlands
Source: *ArtsNiC; LinLib S; McGDA; NewCol 75; WebBD 83*

Issel, Dan(iel Paul)
American. Basketball Player
Forward-center, ABA Kentucky, 1970-75, NBA Denver, 1975-85; led ABA in scoring, 1971.
b. Oct 25, 1948 in Batavia, Illinois
Source: *BasBi; BiDAmSp BK; BioIn 10, 13, 14; NewYTBS 85; OfNBA 87; WhoAm 82, 84, 94, 95; WhoBbl 73; WhoWest 94; WorAl; WorAlBi*

Issigonis, Alec Arnold Constantine, Sir
British. Engineer
Designed the Morris Minor, bringing economical motoring to millions of Britons.
b. 1906 in Smyrna, Turkey
d. Oct 2, 1988 in Birmingham, England
Source: *BlueB 76; IntWW 75, 76, 77, 78, 79, 80, 81, 82, 83; Who 85; WhoWor 76, 78, 82*

Istomin, Eugene George
American. Musician
Int'l concert soloist; with Pablo Casals, annual Casals Festivals, from 1950.
b. Nov 26, 1925 in New York, New York
Source: *Baker 84, 92; BioIn 14, 15; IntWW 74, 75, 76, 77, 78, 79, 80, 81, 82, 83, 89, 91, 93; IntWWM 90; NewAmDM; NewGrDA 86; NewYTBE 71; NewYTBS 87; PenDiMP; WhoAm 86, 88; WhoMus 72; WhoWor 74*

Itami, Juzo
Japanese. Filmmaker
Best known for "Noodle Westerns"; his comedies include *The Funeral,* 1984; *A Taxing Woman,* 1987, won 9 Japanese Academy Awards.
b. 1933 in Kyoto, Japan
Source: *BioIn 16; CurBio 90; EncJap; IntDcF 2-2; IntMPA 92, 94, 96; IntWW 91, 93; JapFilm; MiSFD 9; NewYTBS 89*

Ito, Hirobumi
Japanese. Statesman
Four-time premier who was important in Japan's modernization, supporter of Western ideas.
b. Sep 2, 1841 in Choshu Province, Japan
d. Oct 26, 1909 in Harbin, China
Source: *BioIn 15, 20; HisWorL; LegTOT; McGEWB; NewCol 75; WorAl; WorAlBi*

Ito, Lance
American. Judge
Superior Court Judge, Los Angeles County, Calif., 1989—; presided over O.J. Simpson murder trial, 1994-95.
b. c. 1950 in Los Angeles, California
Source: *News 95, 95-3*

Ittner, William Butts
American. Architect
Designed numerous early 20th century schools, Masonic buildings.
b. Sep 4, 1864 in Saint Louis, Missouri
d. Jan 26, 1936 in Saint Louis, Missouri
Source: *WhAm 1*

Iturbi, Amparo
Spanish. Pianist
Often performed with brother, Jose.
b. Mar 12, 1899 in Valencia, Spain
d. Apr 21, 1969 in Beverly Hills, California
Source: *Baker 84; BioIn 8, 18; DcHiB; NotHsAW 93; WhoHol B; WhScrn 77, 83*

Iturbi, Jose
Spanish. Composer, Conductor
Pianist; appeared in films, 1940s; helped to popularize classical music.
b. Nov 28, 1895 in Valencia, Spain
d. Jun 28, 1980 in Los Angeles, California
Source: *AnObit 1980; Baker 78, 84, 92; BiDAmM; BioIn 1, 2, 4, 5, 10, 11, 12; BriBkM 80; CelR; CurBio 43, 80N; DcAmB S10; FacFETw; FilmEn; FilmgC; ForYSC; HalFC 80, 84, 88; IntWW 74, 75, 76, 77, 78, 79, 80; IntWWM 77, 80; LegTOT; MGM; MovMk; MusSN; NewAmDM; NewGrDA 86; NewGrDM 80; NewYTBS 80; PenDiMP; RadStar; WhAm 7; What 5; Who 74; WhoAm 74, 76, 78, 80; WhoHol A; WhoMus 72; WhoWor 74, 76, 78; WorAl; WorAlBi*

Iturbide, Augustin de
[Augustin I]
Mexican. Army Officer, Ruler
Won Mexican independence from Spain, 1821; Emperor, 1822-23.
b. Sep 27, 1783 in Valladolid, Mexico
d. Jul 19, 1824 in Padillla, Mexico
Source: *ApCAB; BioIn 1, 2, 3, 8, 9, 10; CmCal; DcBiPP; EncLatA; HarEnUS; NewCol 75*

Ivan, Tommy
[Thomas N Ivan]
Canadian. Hockey Coach, Hockey Executive
Coach, Detroit, 1947-54; won three Stanley Cups; GM, Chicago, 1954-77; won Stanley Cup, 1961; Hall of Fame, 1974.

b. Jan 31, 1911 in Toronto, Ontario, Canada
Source: *WhoAm 90; WhoHcky 73*

Ivan III
[Ivan Vasilyevich]
"Ivan the Great"
Russian. Ruler
Czar of Russia, 1462-1505; compiled first Russian code of law.
b. Jan 22, 1440 in Moscow, Russia
d. Oct 27, 1505 in Moscow, Russia
Source: *HisWorL; NewCol 75; WebBD 83*

Ivan IV
[Ivan Grozny]
"Ivan the Terrible"
Russian. Ruler
Grandson of Ivan III; czar of Russia at age three; assumed title 1547.
b. Aug 25, 1530 in Kolomenskoye, Russia
d. Mar 17, 1584 in Moscow, Russia
Source: *CasWL; DcRusL; HisWorL; NewCol 75; OxDcOp; REn; WhoMilH 76*

Ivanov, Konstantin Konstantinovich
Russian. Conductor
Led USSR State Symphony, 1946-75; has had numerous world tours.
b. May 21, 1907 in Efremov, Russia
Source: *Baker 84; BiDSovU; IntWW 74, 75, 76, 77, 78, 79, 80; PenDiMP; SovUn; WhoSocC 78; WhoWor 74*

Ivask, Ivar Vidrik
American. Poet
Editor of *World Literature Today,* 1967-91; poetry includes *Gespiegelte Erde,* 1967; *Snow Lessons,* 1986.
b. Dec 17, 1927 in Latvia, Estonia
d. Sep 23, 1992, Ireland
Source: *ConAu 24NR, 37R, 139; ConLC 14, 76; DrAS 74F, 78F, 82F*

Iveagh, Arthur Francis Benjamin Guinness, Lord
English. Business Executive
Chm., 1962-86; pres., 1986-92, Guinness P.L.C. brewing co.
b. May 20, 1937
d. Jun 18, 1992 in London, England
Source: *BioIn 18; IntWW 81, 91; Who 92; WhoWor 82, 84*

Ivens, Joris
[Georg Henri Anton Ivens]
Dutch. Director
Known for documentaries; *The Spanish Earth,* 1937, was considered his masterpiece.
b. Nov 18, 1898 in Nijmegen, Netherlands
d. Jun 28, 1989 in Paris, France
Source: *AnObit 1989; BiDFilm, 81, 94; BioIn 9, 12, 15, 16, 17; ConAu 129; DcFM; EncEurC; FacFETw; FilmEn; FilmgC; HalFC 80, 84, 88; IntDcF 1-2, 2-2; ItaFilm; MovMk; NewYTBS 89; OxCFilm; WhoWor 74, 76; WorEFlm; WorFDir 1*

Ives, Burl (Icle Ivanhoe)
American. Actor, Singer
Foremost folksinger since 1940s; won 1959 Oscar for *The Big Country;* noted for role of Big Daddy in *Cat on a Hot Tin Roof,* 1958.
b. Jun 14, 1909 in Hunt, Illinois
d. Apr 14, 1995 in Anacortes, Washington
Source: *AmAu&B; ASCAP 66, 80; Baker 78, 84, 92; BiDAmM; BiE&WWA; BioIn 1, 2, 3, 4, 5, 7, 8, 12, 14, 20, 21; ChhPo S2; CmMov; CmpEPM; ConAu 103, 148; ConMus 12; ConTFT 3; CounME 74, 74A; CurBio 46, 60, 95N; DcTwCCu 1; EncFCWM 69, 83; FacFETw; FilmEn; FilmgC; ForYSC; HalFC 80, 84, 88; IntAu&W 77; IntMPA 75, 76, 77, 78, 79, 80, 81, 82, 84, 86, 88, 92, 94, 96; IntWW 74, 75, 76, 77, 78, 79, 80, 81, 82, 83, 89, 91, 93; LegTOT; LinLib L; MotPP; MovMk; NewAmDM; NewGrDA 86; News 95; NotNAT; OxCPMus; PenEncP; PlP&P; RadStar; REnAL; RkOn 74; VarWW 85; WhoAm 74, 76, 78, 80, 82, 84, 86, 88, 92, 94, 95; WhoEnt 92; WhoHol 92, A; WhoMus 72; WhoRock 81; WhoThe 72, 77, 81; WhoWor 74; WorAl; WorAlBi; WorEFlm*

Ives, Charles Edward
American. Composer
Unconventional style of composition included polytonal harmonies, unusual rhythms; won 1947 Pulitzer for *Symphony Number Three.*
b. Oct 20, 1874 in Danbury, Connecticut
d. May 11, 1954 in New York, New York
Source: *AmComp; AmCulL; AtlBL; Baker 78, 84, 92; Benet 96; BenetAL 91; BiDAmM; BioIn 1, 2, 3, 4, 5, 6, 7, 8, 9, 10, 11, 12, 13, 14, 15, 16, 17, 18, 19, 20; BioNews 74; ConAmC 76, 82; ConAu 113, 149; CurBio 47, 54; DcAmB S3, S5; DcArts; DcCM; DcCom&M 79; EncAB-H 1974, 1996; MakMC; McGEWB; NatCAB 42; NewCol 75; NewGrDM 80; OxCAmL 65; RAdv 14, 13-3; REn; REnAL; WebAB 74, 79; WhAm 3; WorAl*

Ives, Frederic Eugene
American. Inventor
Pioneer in modern photography; developed halftone process of photoengraving.
b. Feb 17, 1856 in Litchfield, Connecticut
d. May 27, 1937 in Philadelphia, Pennsylvania
Source: *AmBi; ApCAB X; BiDAmJo; BioIn 4; DcAmB S2; DcNAA; ICPEnP; InSci; NatCAB 13, 15; NewCol 75; WebAB 74, 79; WhAm 1; WorInv*

Ives, Herbert Eugene
American. Inventor, Physicist
Helped to develop television.
b. Jul 31, 1882 in Philadelphia, Pennsylvania
d. Nov 13, 1953 in Upper Montclair, New Jersey
Source: *BioIn 2, 3, 4; DcScB; EncAB-A 25; InSci; LinLib S; NatCAB 15, 41; NewCol 75; WhAm 3*

Ives, James Merritt
[Currier and Ives]
American. Artist
Partner, from 1857, with Nathaniel Currier, Currier and Ives Lithograph Publishers.
b. Mar 5, 1824 in New York, New York
d. Jan 3, 1895 in Rye, New York
Source: *AmAu&B; BenetAL 91; BioIn 2, 3, 4, 9, 10, 11, 13; DcAmB; EncAAH; McGDA; NewCol 75; NewYHSD; REn; REnAL; WebAB 74, 79; WhAm HS; WhCiWar; WorAl; WorAlBi*

Ivey, Judith
American. Actor
Won Tony Awards for *Steaming,* 1982; *Hurlyburly,* 1984; played B.J. on TV's "Designing Women," 1992-93.
b. Sep 4, 1951 in El Paso, Texas
Source: *BioIn 13, 14; CelR 90; ConTFT 1, 8; CurBio 93; IntMPA 86, 88, 92, 94, 96; LegTOT; NewYTBS 86; WhoAm 86, 88, 90, 92, 94, 95, 96, 97; WhoAmW 89, 91, 93, 95, 97; WhoEnt 92; WhoHol 92*

Ivogun, Maria
[Ilse VonGunther]
Hungarian. Opera Singer
Leading coloratura soprano of German opera, 1913-33.
b. Nov 11, 1891 in Budapest, Austria-Hungary
d. Oct 3, 1987 in Beatenberg, Switzerland
Source: *AnObit 1987; Baker 78, 84, 92; BioIn 12, 15; CmOp; IntDcOp; InWom; MetOEnc; NewEOp 71; NewGrDM 80; NewGrDO; NewYTBS 87; OxDcOp; PenDiMP*

Ivory, James
American. Director, Producer
With Ismail Merchant and Ruth Prawer Jhabvala has for 30 yrs. produced stylish, quality, independent films: *Shakespeare Wallah, The Bostonians, Howard's End.*
b. Jun 7, 1928 in Berkeley, California
Source: *BiDFilm 94; BioIn 12, 14, 15, 16; ConAu 109; ConTFT 1, 6, 13; CurBio 81; DcArts; FilmEn; FilmgC; GayLesB; HalFC 80, 84, 88; IntDcF 1-2, 2-2; IntMPA 84, 86, 88, 92, 94, 96; IntWW 91; LegTOT; MiSFD 9; OxCFilm; VarWW 85; Who 92; WhoAm 90; WhoEnt 92; WorFDir 2*

Iwama, Kazuo
Japanese. Business Executive
Pres., 1976-82; board chm., 1978-82, Sony Corp.
b. Feb 7, 1919 in Anjo City, Japan
d. Aug 24, 1982 in Tokyo, Japan

Source: *AnObit 1982; BioIn 13; FarE&A 78, 79, 80, 81; IntWW 77, 78, 79, 80, 81, 82; LElec; NewYTBS 82; WhoWor 78, 82*

Iwatani, Toro
Japanese. Inventor
Developed video game "Pac-Man."
b. 1955?

Iwerks, Ub(be)
American. Cartoonist
Developed character of Mickey Mouse for Walt Disney, 1927; won Oscars, 1959, 1965.
b. Mar 24, 1901 in Kansas City, Missouri
d. Jul 7, 1971 in Burbank, California
Source: *BioIn 9; DcFM; FilmEn; FilmgC; IntDcF 1-4, 2-4; OxCFilm; WorECar; WorEFlm*

Izac, Edouard V(ictor Michel)
American. Government Official
WW I navy hero; Democratic congressman from CA, 1937-47.
b. Dec 18, 1891 in Cresco, Iowa
d. Jan 18, 1990 in Fairfax, Virginia
Source: *BiDrAC; BiDrUSC 89; BioIn 7, 16; CurBio 45, 90, 90N; MedHR; NewYTBS 90; WhoAmP 75, 77, 79*

Izetbegovic, Alija
Bosnian. Politician
President of Bosnia and Herzegovina, 1990-96; chairman of a three-member presidency, 1996—.
b. Aug 8, 1925 in Bos Samac, Yugoslavia
Source: *BioIn 19; CurBio 93; IntWW 93; News 96; WhoWor 95, 96, 97*

J

Jaabari, Mohammed Ali, Sheik
Palestinian. Politician
Mayor of Hebron, Israel for 36 yrs.
b. 1900, Jordan
d. May 29, 1980 in Hebron, Israel
Source: *BioIn 12; NewYTBS 80*

Jabir al-Ahmad al-Jabir Al Sabah, Sheikh
Kuwaiti. Political Leader
Emir of Kuwait, 1978—.
b. Jun 29, 1926 in Kuwait City, Kuwait
Source: *BioIn 16; CurBio 88; IntWW 91; NewYTBS 90*

Jablonski, Henryk
Polish. Historian, Political Leader
Pres., Polish Council of State, 1972-85; writings include *School, Teacher, Education,* 1972.
b. Dec 27, 1909 in Waliszewo, Poland
Source: *BioIn 10; IntWW 74, 75, 76, 77, 78, 79, 80, 81, 82, 83, 89, 91, 93; IntYB 78, 79, 80, 81, 82; WhoSocC 78; WhoSoCE 89; WhoWor 74, 76, 78, 80, 82, 84, 87*

Jabotinsky, Vladimir Evgenevich
Russian. Religious Leader
Founder, pres., World Union of Zionist-Revisionists, 1922; New Zionist Organization, 1935.
b. Oct 18, 1880 in Odessa, Russia
d. Aug 3, 1940 in Hunter, New York
Source: *CurBio 40; McGEWB*

Jack, Homer A(lexander)
American. Clergy
Co-founder of National Committee for a Sane Nuclear Policy, 1957.
b. May 19, 1916
d. Aug 5, 1993 in Swarthmore, Pennsylvania
Source: *AmPeW; Au&Wr 71; BioIn 5, 6, 13; ConAu 14NR, 41R, 142; CurBio 93N; IntAu&W 82; WhoAm 76, 78, 80, 82, 84, 86, 88, 90; WhoE 77; WhoRel 75, 77, 85, 92; WhoUN 75; WhoWor 74*

Jackee
[Jackee Harry]
American. Actor
Played Sandra Clark on TV comedy "227," 1985-89; won Emmy, 1987; TV show "Royal Family," 1991—.
b. Aug 14, 1957 in Winston-Salem, North Carolina
Source: *BioIn 15, 16; ConTFT 5; DrBlPA 90; LegTOT; WhoBlA 92; WorAlBi*

Jacklin, Tony
[Anthony Jacklin]
"Jacko"
English. Golfer
Turned pro, 1962; won British Open, 1969, US Open, 1970.
b. Jul 7, 1944 in Scunthorpe, England
Source: *BioIn 8, 9, 10, 13, 16, 21; BlueB 76; ConAu 85; IntAu&W 82; IntWW 81, 82, 83, 89, 91, 93; NewYTBE 70; Who 74, 82, 83, 85, 88, 90, 92, 94; WhoGolf; WhoIntG; WhoWor 84, 87, 89, 91, 93, 95, 96, 97*

Jackson, A(lexander) Y(oung)
[Group of Seven]
Canadian. Artist
Co-founder, Group of Seven, 1920; drew rural Quebec arctic scenes.
b. Oct 3, 1882 in Montreal, Quebec, Canada
d. Apr 6, 1974 in Kleinburg, Ontario, Canada
Source: *BioIn 1, 2, 3, 5, 10, 12; CanWW 70; CreCan 2; DcArts; DcBrAr 2; FacFETw; IlBEAAW; MacDCB 78; McGDA; OxCTwCA; OxDcArt; Who 74; WhoAmA 73, 76N, 78N, 80N, 82N, 84N, 86N, 89N, 91N, 93N*

Jackson, Alan Eugene
American. Singer, Songwriter
Country albums include *Here in the Real World,* 1990; *Don't Rock the Jukebox,* 1991; 2 CMA awards, 1990.
b. Oct 17, 1958 in Newnan, Georgia
Source: *ConMus 7*

Jackson, Andrew
"Old Hickory"; "Tribune of the People"
American. US President
First Dem. pres., 1829-37; military hero of War of 1812; introduced spoils system, boosted expansionism.
b. Mar 15, 1767 in Waxhaw, South Carolina
d. Jun 8, 1845 in Nashville, Tennessee
Source: *Alli; AmAu&B; AmBi; AmOrN; AmPolLe; ApCAB; Benet 87, 96; BenetAL 91; BiAUS; BiDrAC; BiDrUSC 89; BiDrUSE 71, 89; BiDSA; BioIn 1, 2, 3, 4, 5, 6, 7, 8, 9, 10, 11, 12, 13, 14, 15, 16, 17, 18, 19, 20, 21; CelCen; CyAG; DcAmB; DcAmMiB; DcBiPP; DcNCBi 3; Dis&D; Drake; EncAAH; EncAB-H 1974, 1996; EncSoH; FacPr 89, 93; GenMudB; HarEnMi; HarEnUS; HealPre; HisWorL; LegTOT; LinLib L, S; McGEWB; MemAm; NatCAB 5; OxCAmH; OxCAmL 65, 83, 95; OxCSupC; PolPar; PresAR; RComAH; REn; REnAL; REnAW; TwCBDA; WebAB 74, 79; WebAMB; WhAm HS; WhAmP; WhAmRev; WhDW; WhFla; WhNaAH; WhoMilH 76; WorAl; WorAlBi*

Jackson, Anne
[Mrs. Eli Wallach]
American. Actor
Appeared on stage with husband Eli Wallach in *The Typists,* 1963; *The Tiger,; The Waltz of the Toreadors,* 1973.
b. Sep 3, 1926 in Allegheny, Pennsylvania
Source: *AmMWSc 92; BiE&WWA; BioIn 6, 8, 12, 14, 20; ConTFT 1, 7; CurBio 80; EncAFC; FilmEn; FilmgC; ForYSC; HalFC 88; HerW 84; IntMPA 86, 88, 92, 94, 96; InWom, SUP; LegTOT; MotPP; MovMk; NotNAT; OxCAmT 84; VarWW 85; WhoAm 80, 86, 90, 95, 96, 97; WhoAmW 91, 95, 97; WhoEnt 92; WhoHol 92, A; WhoThe 72, 77, 81; WorAlBi*

Jackson, Aunt Molly
[Mary Magdalene Garland]
American. Singer
Songs include "The Death of Harry Simms," 1931; prominent figure in coal mine union organization, 1930s.
b. 1880 in Clay City, Kentucky
d. Sep 1, 1960
Source: *BgBkCoM; BioIn 19; EncFCWM 69; InWom SUP; NewGrDA 86*

Jackson, Bo
[Vincent Edward Jackson]
American. Football Player, Baseball Player
Played professional football with LA Raiders, 1987-91; played professional baseball, with KC, 1986-91; White Sox, 1991-93; California Angels, 1994-95; All-star MVP, 1989; Heisman Trophy recipient, 1985.
b. Nov 30, 1962 in Bessemer, Alabama
Source: *AfrAmBi 1; AfrAmSG; Ballpl 90; BaseEn 88; BaseReg 87, 88; BioIn 13, 14, 15, 16, 18; ConAu 141; ConNews 86-3; CurBio 91; LegTOT; NewYTBS 84, 86; WhoAfA 96; WhoAm 92, 94, 95, 96, 97; WhoBlA 92; WhoMW 93, 96; WhoSpor; WhoWest 94, 96; WorAlBi*

Jackson, Busher
[Ralph Harvey Jackson]
Canadian. Hockey Player
Left wing, 1929-44, mostly with Toronto; won Art Ross Trophy, 1932; Hall of Fame, 1971.
b. Jan 19, 1911 in Toronto, Ontario, Canada
d. Jun 25, 1966 in Toronto, Ontario, Canada
Source: *HocEn; WhoHcky 73; WhoSpor*

Jackson, Charles Reginald
American. Author
Wrote novel, *The Lost Weekend,* 1944, which was filmed, 1945; won Oscar.
b. Apr 6, 1903 in Summit, New Jersey
d. Sep 21, 1968 in New York, New York
Source: *AmAu&B; AmNov; ConAu 101; CyWA 58; LngCTC; OxCAmL 65; REn; REnAL; TwCA, SUP; WhAm 5*

Jackson, Charles Thomas
American. Scientist, Physician
Suggested idea of telegraph to Samuel Morse; discovered surgical anesthesia.
b. Jun 21, 1805 in Plymouth, Massachusetts
d. Aug 28, 1880 in Somerville, Massachusetts
Source: *Alli; AmBi; ApCAB; AsBiEn; BbtC; BiDAmS; BiESc; BiInAmS; BioIn 1, 3, 7, 21; DcAmAu; DcAmB; DcAmMeB, 84; DcBiPP; DcNAA; DcScB; Drake; EarABI; FolkA 87; HarEnUS; InSci; LinLib S; NatCAB 3; NewYHSD; TwCBDA; WebAB 74, 79; WhAm HS*

Jackson, Chevalier
American. Scientist
Best known for developing methods for seeing into stomach, larynx, esophagus; successful at removing foreign bodies from lungs, throat.
b. Nov 4, 1865 in Greentree, Pennsylvania
d. Aug 16, 1958 in Philadelphia, Pennsylvania
Source: *BioIn 1, 5, 8; CurBio 40; DcAmB S6; DcAmMeB 84; InSci; OxCMed 86; WhAm 3; WhAmArt 85; WhNAA*

Jackson, Freddie
American. Singer, Songwriter
Pop/soul romantic balladeer; albums *Rock Me Tonight, Just Like the First Time* went platinum.
b. Oct 2, 1958 in New York, New York
Source: *BioIn 14, 16; ConMus 3; DrBlPA 90; WhoAfA 96; WhoBlA 92, 94*

Jackson, George
American. Criminal
Robber who wrote *Soledad Brother,* 1970.
b. Sep 23, 1941 in Chicago, Illinois
d. Aug 21, 1971 in San Quentin, California
Source: *BioIn 9, 10, 11; BlkWr 1; ConAu 111, 120; MugS; SchCGBL; SelBAAf; SelBAAu*

Jackson, Glenda
English. Actor
Won Oscars for *Women in Love,* 1970; *A Touch of Class,* 1973.
b. May 9, 1936 in Birkenhead, England
Source: *BiDFilm 94; BioIn 9, 14, 15, 16; BkPepl; CamGWoT; CelR, 90; ContDcW 89; ConTFT 4; CurBio 71; DcArts; EncAFC; EncEurC; Ent; FacFETw; FilmEn; FilmgC; HalFC 88; IlWWBF; IntDcF 1-3, 2-3; IntDcT 3; IntMPA 84, 86, 88, 92, 94, 96; IntWW 74, 75, 76, 77, 78, 79, 80, 81, 82, 83, 89, 91, 93; InWom SUP; ItaFilm; LegTOT; MovMk; NewYTBE 71; NewYTBS 83; OxCFilm; OxCThe 83; VarWW 85; Who 74, 82, 83, 85, 88, 90, 92, 94; WhoAm 76, 78, 80, 82, 84, 86, 88, 90, 92, 94, 95; WhoAmW 81, 83, 95, 97; WhoEnt 92; WhoHol 92, A; WhoThe 72, 77, 81; WhoWor 74, 82, 84, 87, 89, 91, 93, 95, 96, 97; WomFir; WorAl; WorAlBi*

Jackson, Gordon Cameron
Scottish. Actor
Won Emmy for role of Hudson the butler in PBS series "Upstairs, Downstairs," 1970s.
b. Dec 19, 1923 in Glasgow, Scotland
d. Jan 14, 1990 in London, England
Source: *ConTFT 5; FilmgC; IntMPA 82; IntWW 89; VarWW 85; Who 85, 88, 90; WhoAm 88; WhoThe 77*

Jackson, Helen Maria Hunt Fiske
[Saxe Holm]
American. Author
Wrote *Ramona,* 1884; worked toward betterment of Native Americans.
b. Oct 18, 1831 in Amherst, Massachusetts
d. Aug 12, 1885 in San Francisco, California
Source: *Alli SUP; AmAu; AmAu&B; AmBi; AmWom; ApCAB; BbD; BiD&SB; CarSB; CasWL; McGEWB; NotAW; OxCAmL 83; REn; TwCBDA; WebAB 79; WhAm HS*

Jackson, Henry Martin
"Scoop"
American. Politician
Dem. senator from WA, 1953-83; prominent member, Armed Services Committee.
b. May 31, 1912 in Everett, Washington
d. Sep 1, 1983 in Everett, Washington
Source: *AlmAP 82; WhoPNW; WhoWest 74, 76, 78, 80, 82, 84; WhoWor 74, 78, 80, 82; WorAl*

Jackson, Hurricane
[Thomas Jackson]
American. Boxer
Heavyweight contender, defeated by Floyd Patterson, 1957; barred, due to alleged brain damage, 1958.
b. Aug 9, 1931 in Sparta, Georgia
d. Feb 14, 1982 in New York, New York
Source: *BioIn 3, 4, 12; NewYTBS 82; WhoBox 74*

Jackson, Isaiah Allen
American. Conductor
First black music director of the Royal Ballet, 1987-90, and the Dayton Philharmonic Orchestra, 1987—; music dir., Youngstown (Ohio) Symphony, 1996.
b. Jan 22, 1945 in Richmond, Virginia
Source: *Baker 92; BioIn 16; BlkCond; ConBlB 3; DrBlPA; InB&W 85; IntWWM 90; NewAmDM; PenDiMP; WhoAfA 96; WhoAm 84; WhoAmW 83; WhoBlA 80, 85, 88, 90, 92, 94; WhoEnt 92; WhoMW 92*

Jackson, Jackie
[The Jackson Five; The Jacksons; Sigmund Esco Jackson]
American. Singer
Oldest in group of singing brothers; first hit, "I Want You Back," 1970, sold over two million copies; solo album *Jackie Jackson,* 1973.
b. May 4, 1951 in Gary, Indiana
Source: *EncPR&S 89; InB&W 80; LegTOT; OxCPMus; RkOn 84*

Jackson, Janet Damita
American. Singer, Actor
Won Grammy, Best Music Video—Long Form, *Rhythm Nation 1814,* 1989; Grammy, Best R&B Song, "That's the Way Love Goes," 1993.
b. Jun 16, 1966 in Gary, Indiana

Source: *BioIn 13, 14, 15, 16; CelR 90; ConMus 3; CurBio 91; InB&W 80, 85; News 90; PenEncP; RkOn 85; WhoAm 92, 94, 95, 96, 97; WhoAmW 95; WhoBlA 92; WhoEnt 92; WorAlBi*

Jackson, Jermaine La Jaune
[The Jackson Five; The Jacksons]
American. Singer, Musician
Has had consistent solo career: "Let's Get Serious," 1980.
b. Dec 11, 1954 in Gary, Indiana
Source: *BioIn 15; EncPR&S 89; EncRk 88; InB&W 85; OxCPMus; PenEncP; RkOn 84; WorAlBi*

Jackson, Jesse Louis
American. Civil Rights Leader, Religious Leader
Founded Operation PUSH, 1971; chm., National Rainbow Coalition; Dem. presidential candidate, 1984, 1988.
b. Oct 8, 1941 in Greenville, South Carolina
Source: *AfrAmBi 1; AfrAmOr; AmOrTwC; AmSocL; BiDAmNC; BioIn 8, 9, 10, 11, 12, 14, 15, 16; BkPepl; CelR 90; ConBlB 1; ConHero 1; CurBio 86; EncAB-H 1996; EncWB; FacFETw; IntWW 89, 91, 93; NegAl 89; NewYTBS 89; PolProf J; RComAH; RelLAm 91; WebAB 74, 79; WhoAfA 96; WhoAm 74, 76, 78, 80, 82, 84, 86, 88, 90, 92, 94, 95, 96, 97; WhoAmP 87, 89, 91, 93; WhoBlA 80, 85, 88, 90, 92, 94; WhoMW 74, 80, 82, 84, 86, 88, 90; WhoRel 75, 77, 92; WhoWor 84, 87; WorAlBi*

Jackson, Joe
[Joseph Jefferson Jackson]
"Shoeless Joe"
American. Baseball Player
Outfielder, 1908-20; had .356 lifetime batting average; banned from game for part in "Black Sox" scandal, 1919 World Series.
b. Jul 16, 1888 in Brandon Mills, South Carolina
d. Dec 5, 1951 in Greenville, South Carolina
Source: *BioIn 2, 3, 5, 10; LegTOT; WhoProB 73*

Jackson, Joe
English. Singer
Had hit single "Steppin' Out," 1982; cut eclectic live album *Big World,* 1986; *Laughter and Lust,* 1991.
b. Aug 11, 1954 in Burton-on-Trent, England
Source: *BioIn 13; ConMus 4; CurBio 96; EncPR&S 89; EncRk 88; EncRkSt; HarEnR 86; PenEncP; RkOn 85; WhoEnt 92*

Jackson, John Adams
American. Sculptor
Best known for busts including Musidora, 1873; Hylas, 1875.
b. Nov 5, 1825 in Bath, Maine
d. Aug 30, 1879 in Pracchia, Italy
Source: *AmBi; ApCAB; ArtsNiC; BriEAA; DcAmB; NatCAB 8; NewYHSD; TwCBDA; WhAm HS*

Jackson, John Hughlings
English. Neurologist
Studied speech defects in brain disease; identified Jacksonian epilepsy, 1863.
b. Apr 4, 1835 in Green Hammerton, England
d. Oct 7, 1911 in London, England
Source: *BiDPsy; BioIn 3, 4, 5, 6, 8, 9, 13, 21; DcNaB S2; DcScB; InSci; LarDcSc; NamesHP; OxCMed 86; WebBD 83*

Jackson, Kate
American. Actor
TV series include "The Rookies," 1972-76; "Charlie's Angels," 1976-79; "Scarecrow and Mrs. King," 1983-87.
b. Oct 29, 1949 in Birmingham, Alabama
Source: *BioIn 13, 14, 15; BkPepl; CelR 90; ConTFT 3; HalFC 88; IntMPA 84, 86, 88, 92, 94, 96; InWom SUP; VarWW 85; WhoAm 86, 88; WhoAmW 89, 91; WhoEnt 92; WhoHol A; WhoTelC; WorAl; WorAlBi*

Jackson, La Toya
American. Singer
One of Jackson family; wrote autobiography *La Toya,* 1992, about growing up in the Jackson family and alleged abuse.
b. May 16, 1966 in Gary, Indiana
Source: *BioIn 14, 16; RkOn 85A*

Jackson, Laura Riding
American. Poet
Wrote *Lives of Wives,* 1939.
b. Jan 16, 1901 in New York
d. Sep 2, 1991 in Sebastian, Florida
Source: *AmAu&B; AmWomWr; ConLC 70; ConPo 70, 75; DcLB 48; IntWWP 77; RAdv 13-1; RGFAP; TwCA SUP; WhoAm 86; WrDr 76*

Jackson, Madeline Manning
American. Track Athlete
Middle-distance runner; won gold medal in 800 meters, 1968 Olympics.
b. Jan 11, 1948 in Columbus, Ohio
Source: *BiDAmSp OS; BioIn 8, 11, 12; HerW 84; InB&W 80; WhoTr&F 73*

Jackson, Mahalia
American. Singer
Best known for gospel songs "I Believe," "He's Got the Whole World in His Hands."
b. Oct 25, 1911 in New Orleans, Louisiana
d. Jan 27, 1972 in Evergreen Park, Illinois
Source: *AmCulL; Baker 78, 84, 92; BiDAmM; BiDJaz; BioAmW; BioIn 3, 4, 5, 6, 7, 8, 9, 10, 11, 12, 13, 15, 17, 18, 19, 20; BlkWAm; CmpEPM; ConBlB 5; ConMus 8; ContDcW 89; CurBio 57, 72, 72N; DcAmB S9; DcArts; DrBlPA, 90; EncJzS; EncRk 88; FacFETw; GoodHs; GrLiveH; HerW, 84; InB&W 80, 85; IntDcWB; InWom, SUP; LegTOT; LibW; LinLib S; NegAl 76, 83, 89; NewAmDM; NewGrDA 86; NewGrDM 80; NewYTBE 72; NotAW MOD; NotBlAW 1; ObitT 1971; OxCPMus; PenEncP; PrimTiR; RelLAm 91; RolSEnR 83; WebAB 74, 79; WhAm 5; WhoAmW 58, 64, 66, 68, 70, 72; WhoHol B; WhScrn 77, 83; WorAl; WorAlBi*

Jackson, Mark
American. Basketball Player
Guard, NY Knicks, 1987-92, LA Clippers, 1993—; average 10.6 assists per game highest ever by NBA rookie; rookie of year, 1988.
b. Apr 1, 1965 in New York, New York
Source: *BasBi; BioIn 15, 16; OfNBA 87; WhoBlA 92; WhoWrEP 89*

Jackson, Marlon David
[The Jackson Five; The Jacksons]
American. Singer
Biggest selling hit was "I'll Be There," 1970.
b. Mar 12, 1957 in Gary, Indiana
Source: *BioIn 14, 15, 16; EncPR&S 89; InB&W 80; OxCPMus; RkOn 84*

Jackson, Maynard Holbrook, Jr.
American. Politician
First black mayor of Atlanta, GA, 1974-82; 1990-94.
b. Mar 23, 1938 in Dallas, Texas
Source: *BioIn 8; WhoSSW 73, 75, 76, 78, 80, 82; WorAlBi*

Jackson, Michael Joseph
[The Jackson Five; The Jacksons]
"King of Pop"
American. Singer, Songwriter, Actor
Lead singer with group of brothers during the 60s-70s; solo career made him cult figure: best-selling album of all time *Thriller,* 1982; other albums include *Bad,* 1987; *Dangerous,* 1992; winner of numersous Grammys.
b. Aug 29, 1958 in Gary, Indiana
Source: *AfrAmBi 1; Baker 84, 92; BioIn 12, 13, 14, 15, 16; BkPepl; CelR 90; ConMus 1; CurBio 83; DrBlPA 90; EncPR&S 89; EncRk 88; FacFETw; HarEnR 86; IlEncBM 82; InB&W 80, 85; IntMPA 92; IntWW 89, 91, 93; NegAl 89; NewAmDM; NewYTBS 87; OxCPMus; PenEncP; RkOn 85; VarWW 85; Who 92; WhoAm 84, 86, 88, 90, 92, 94, 95, 96, 97; WhoBlA 88, 92; WhoEnt 92A; WhoWor 93, 95, 96, 97; WorAlBi*

Jackson, Milt(on)
"Bags"
American. Jazz Musician
Pioneer bop vibist; helped develop progressive jazz.
b. Jan 1, 1923 in Detroit, Michigan
Source: *AllMusG; Baker 84, 92; BiDAfM; BiDAmM; BiDJaz; BioIn 5, 7, 9, 11, 13, 14, 15, 16, 18; CmpEPM; ConMus 15; DcTwCCu 5; DrBlPA, 90; EncJzS; IlEncJ; InB&W 80; LegTOT;*

NewAmDM; NewGrDA 86; NewGrDJ 88, 94; NewGrDM 80; NewYTBS 88; OxCPMus; PenEncP; WhoAfA 96; WhoAm 74, 76, 78, 80, 82, 84, 86, 88, 92, 94, 95, 96, 97; WhoBlA 75, 77, 80, 85, 88, 90, 92, 94; WhoEnt 92; WorAl; WorAlBi

Jackson, Peter B
West Indian. Boxer, Actor
Popular British heavyweight champ, 1892; in film *Uncle Tom's Cabin;* Hall of Fame.
b. Jul 3, 1861 in Saint Croix, Australia
d. Jul 13, 1901 in Roma, Australia
Source: *WhoBox 74*

Jackson, Phil(ip D.)
American. Basketball Coach
Coach, Chicago Bulls, 1989—; won NBA championships, 1991, 1992, 1993, 1996.
b. Sep 17, 1945 in Deer Lodge, Montana
Source: *BioIn 10; CurBio 92; LegTOT; News 96, 96-3; WhoBbl 73; WhoSpor*

Jackson, Rachel Donelson Robards
[Mrs. Andrew Jackson]
American. First Lady
Caused scandal when she married Jackson before divorcing first husband.
b. Jun 15, 1767 in Pittsylvania County, Virginia
d. Dec 22, 1828 in Nashville, Tennessee
Source: *Alli; AmAu&B; AmBi; AmOrN; AmPolLe; ApCAB; Benet 87, 96; BenetAL 91; BiAUS; BiDrAC; BiDrUSC 89; BiDrUSE 71, 89; BiDSA; BioIn 1, 2, 3, 4, 5, 6, 7, 8, 9, 10, 11, 12, 13, 14, 15, 16, 17, 18, 19, 20, 21; CelCen; CyAG; DcAmB; DcAmMiB; DcBiPP; DcNCBi 3; Dis&D; Drake; EncAAH; EncAB-H 1974, 1996; EncSoH; FacPr 89, 93; GenMudB; GoodHs; HarEnMi; HarEnUS; HealPre; HerW; HisWorL; InWom, SUP; LegTOT; LinLib L, S; McGEWB; MemAm; NatCAB 5; NotAW; OxCAmH; OxCAmL 65, 83, 95; OxCSupC; PolPar; PresAR; RComAH; REn; REnAL; REnAW; TwCBDA; WebAB 74, 79; WebAMB; WhAm HS; WhAmP; WhAmRev; WhDW; WhFla; WhNaAH; WhoMilH 76; WorAl; WorAlBi*

Jackson, Randy
[The Jacksons; Steven Randall Jackson]
American. Singer
Joined singing brothers as drummer, 1974.
b. Oct 29, 1961 in Gary, Indiana
Source: *BioIn 11; EncPR&S 89; InB&W 80; RkOn 84*

Jackson, Reggie
[Reginald Martinez Jackson]
"Mr. October"
American. Baseball Player
Outfielder-designated hitter, 1967-87; holds numerous ML, AL hitting records; led AL in home runs four times; AL MVP, 1973; Baseball Hall of Fame, 1993.
b. May 18, 1946 in Wyncote, Pennsylvania
Source: *AfrAmAl 6; AfrAmBi 2; AfrAmSG; Ballpl 90; BaseReg 86, 87; BiDAmSp BB; BioIn 8, 10, 11, 12, 13; BkPepl; CelR 90; CmCal; ConAu 112; CurBio 74; InB&W 80; LegTOT; NewYTBE 73; NewYTBS 76, 77, 82, 84, 85; WhoAm 78, 80, 82, 84, 86, 88, 92, 94, 95, 96, 97; WhoBlA 80, 85, 88, 90; WhoE 95; WhoProB 73; WhoSpor; WhoWest 87, 89; WorAl; WorAlBi*

Jackson, Robert Houghwout
American. Supreme Court Justice
Chief US prosecutor, major Nazi war criminal trials, 1945.
b. Feb 13, 1892 in Spring Creek, Pennsylvania
d. Oct 9, 1954 in Washington, District of Columbia
Source: *BiDFedJ; BiDrUSE 71, 89; BioIn 1, 2, 3, 4, 5, 6, 9, 10, 11, 13, 15; CopCroC; DcAmB S5; DcTwHis; EncAB-A 4; EncAB-H 1974, 1996; LinLib S; McGEWB; OxCAmH; OxCSupC; SupCtJu; WebAB 74, 79; WhAm 3; WorAl*

Jackson, Samuel L(eroy)
American. Actor
Appeared in *Jungle Fever,* 1991; *Pulp Fiction,* 1994; *A Time to Kill,* 1996.
b. c. 1949 in Washington, District of Columbia
Source: *CurBio 96*

Jackson, Shirley Ann
American. Physicist
First African-American female to earn Ph.D. at MIT; work deals with theoretical physics.
b. Aug 5, 1946 in Washington, District of Columbia
Source: *AfrAmAl 6; AmMWSc 76P, 79, 82, 86, 89, 92, 95; BioIn 10, 11, 18, 19, 20, 21; BlksScM; ConBlB 12; DiAASTC; NotBlAW 1; NotTwCS; WhoAfA 96; WhoAm 96, 97; WhoAmW 87, 97; WhoBlA 92, 94; WhoE 81, 85, 86; WhoEmL 87*

Jackson, Shirley (Hardie)
American. Author
Wrote stories dealing with supernatural in everyday setting: *The Lottery,* 1949.
b. Dec 14, 1919 in San Francisco, California
d. Aug 8, 1965 in North Bennington, Vermont
Source: *AmAu&B; AmNov; AmWomWr; ArtclWW 2; Au&Arts 9; Benet 87, 96; BenetAL 91; BioAmW; BioIn 2, 3, 4, 6, 7, 8, 9, 10, 14, 15, 16, 20; BlmGWL; CamGLE; CamHAL; ConAu 1R, 4NR, 25R, 52NR; ConLC 11, 60, 87; ConNov 76, 82A; CyWA 89; DcAmB S7; DcLB 6; DcLEL 1940; EncSF, 93; FacFETw; FemiCLE; GrWomW; GrWrEL N; InWom, SUP; LegTOT; LngCTC; ModAL; ModWoWr; NewCon; Novels; OxCAmL 65; OxCWoWr 95; PenC AM; PenEncH; RAdv 1, 14, 13-1; REn; REnAL; RfGAmL 87; RGTwCWr; ScF&FL 1, 2, 92; ScFSB; ShSCr 9; SmATA 2; SupFW; TwCA SUP; TwCCr&M 80; TwCRGW; TwCRHW 90; WhAm 4; WhoAmW 58, 64, 66; WhoHr&F; WorAl; WorAlBi; WorLitC*

Jackson, Stonewall
[Thomas Jonathan Jackson]
American. Military Leader
Outstanding Confederate general; defeated Union at second Battle of Bull Run, 1862; killed by fire from his own troops.
b. Jan 21, 1824 in Clarksburg, West Virginia
d. May 10, 1863 in Guinea Station, Virginia
Source: *AmBi; ApCAB; Benet 87; BenetAL 91; BiDConf; BioIn 1, 2, 3, 4, 5, 6, 7, 8, 9, 10, 11, 12, 13, 15, 16, 17, 18, 19, 21; CelCen; CivWDc; DcAmB; DcAmMiB; Dis&D; Drake; EncAB-H 1974, 1996; EncSoH; GenMudB; HarEnMi; HarEnUS; LinLib S; McGEWB; NatCAB 4; OxCAmH; REn; REnAL; REnAW; SpyCS; TwCBDA; WebAB 74, 79; WebAMB; WhAm HS; WhCiWar; WhDW; WhoMilH 76; WorAl*

Jackson, Tito
[The Jackson Five; The Jacksons; Toriano Adaryll Jackson]
American. Singer, Musician
Had 13 top 20 singles: "ABC" was number one, 1970.
b. Oct 15, 1953 in Gary, Indiana
Source: *InB&W 80; LegTOT; OxCPMus; RkOn 84*

Jackson, Travis Calvin
"Stonewall"
American. Baseball Player
Shortstop, NY Giants, 1922-36; had .291 career batting average; Hall of Fame, 1982.
b. Nov 2, 1903 in Waldo, Arkansas
d. Jul 27, 1987 in Waldo, Arkansas
Source: *BiDAmSp BB; BioIn 8; NewYTBS 87; WhoProB 73*

Jackson, William Henry
American. Artist, Photographer
Best known for photographic record of development of West.
b. Apr 4, 1843 in Keeseville, New York
d. Jun 30, 1942 in New York, New York
Source: *AmAu&B; ArtsAmW 1; BioIn 1, 5, 6, 7, 9, 10, 13, 15, 16; BriEAA; DcAmArt; DcAmB S3; DcNAA; ICPEnP; IlBEAAW; MacBEP; REnAW; WhAm 2; WhAmArt 85; WhNaAH*

Jackson Five, The
[Jackie Jackson; Jermaine Jackson; Marlon Jackson; Michael Jackson; Tito Jackson]
American. Music Group
Motown group from Gary, IN; hits include "ABC," "I'll Be There," 1970.

Source: *BiDAfM; BiDAmM; BioIn 9, 10, 11, 12, 14, 15, 16; CelR; EncPR&S 74; EncRk 88; IlEncBM 82; NewYTBS 84, 87; OxCPMus; RkOn 74, 78, 84; RolSEnR 83; SoulM; WhoRocM 82; WorAl*

Jacksons, The
[Jackie Jackson; Marlon Jackson; Michael Jackson; Randy Jackson]
American. Music Group
Family singing group formed 1976 after leaving Motown label as The Jackson Five; hit albums include *Triumph,* 1981; *Victory,* 1984; disbanded following 1984 *Victory* tour.
Source: *BioIn 14, 15, 16; ConMuA 80A; ConMus 7; DrRegL 75; EncPR&S 89; HarEnR 86; IlEncRk; NewYTBS 84, 87; OxCPMus; PenEncP; RkOn 84; RolSEnR 83; VarWW 85; WhoRock 81; WhoRocM 82*

Jack the Ripper
English. Murderer
Nickname from ferocity of crimes; five London women killed, 1888; never caught.
Source: *BioIn 9, 16, 21; DrInf; EncO&P 3; EncPaPR 91; HalFC 84, 88; OxCEng 85; OxCLaw; VicBrit; WorAl; WorAlBi*

Jacob
Biblical Figure
Younger twin of Esau, sons of Isaac, Rebecca; vision of angels on ladder basis of phrase "Jacob's Ladder."
b. 1838?BC
d. 1689BC
Source: *DcBiPP; NewCol 75; REn*

Jacob, Francois
French. Geneticist
Co-winner, 1965 Nobel Prize, for work on viruses, cellular genetics.
b. Jun 17, 1920 in Nancy, France
Source: *AmMWSc 95; AsBiEn; BiESc; BioIn 7, 8, 13, 14, 15, 16, 17, 20; ConAu 102; CurBio 66; IntMed 80; IntWW 74, 75, 76, 77, 78, 79, 80, 81, 82, 83, 89, 91, 93; McGMS 80; NewYTBS 88; NobelP; NotTwCS; ThTwC 87; Who 74, 82, 83, 85, 88, 90, 92, 94; WhoAm 74, 88, 90, 92, 94, 95; WhoFr 79; WhoMedH; WhoNob, 90, 95; WhoScEn 94, 96; WhoScEu 91-2; WhoWor 74, 76, 78, 80, 82, 84, 87, 89, 91, 93, 95, 96, 97; WorAl; WorAlBi; WorScD*

Jacob, John Edward
"Jake"
American. Social Reformer
Pres., National Urban League, 1982—.
b. Dec 16, 1934 in Trout, Louisiana
Source: *AfrAmBi 1; CurBio 86; NegAl 83; WhoAfA 96; WhoAm 82, 84, 86, 88, 90, 92, 94, 95, 96; WhoBlA 85, 88, 90, 92, 94; WhoE 91, 93, 95; WhoSSW 73; WhoWest 74*

Jacob, Max
French. Poet, Artist
Poems were written in surrealistic style before its actual beginning: *Le Cornet a Des,* 1917.
b. Jul 11, 1876 in Quimper, France
d. Mar 5, 1944 in Drancy, France
Source: *Benet 87; BioIn 1, 2, 5, 6, 7, 9, 10; CasWL; ClDMEL 47, 80; CnMWL; ConAu 104; DcTwCCu 2; EncWL 2, 3; EvEuW; GuFrLit 1; LegTOT; ModFrL; ModRL; OxCFr; PenC EUR; REn; RfGWoL 95; TwCLC 6; WhoTwCL; WorAu 1950*

Jacobi, Abraham
American. Physician
Founder of pediatrics in US; established first children's clinic, 1860.
b. May 6, 1830 in Westphalia, Germany
d. Jul 10, 1914 in Bolton Landing, New York
Source: *Alli SUP; AmBi; ApCAB, X; BiDSocW; BiHiMed; BiInAmS; BioIn 1, 2, 4, 5, 8, 9, 10, 12; DcAmAu; DcAmB; DcAmMeB, 84; DcNAA; InSci; LinLib S; McGEWB; NatCAB 9; NewCol 75; OxCMed 86; TwCBDA; WebAB 74, 79; WhAm 1*

Jacobi, Carl Gustav Jacob
German. Mathematician
Known for studies of elliptic functions, differential equations, dynamics.
b. Dec 10, 1804 in Potsdam, Germany
d. Feb 18, 1851 in Berlin, Germany
Source: *DcScB; LarDcSc; NewCol 75*

Jacobi, Derek George
English. Actor
Won 1977 Emmy for "The Tenth Man;" won 1985 Tony for *Much Ado About Nothing.*
b. Oct 22, 1938 in London, England
Source: *ConTFT 4; CurBio 81; IntMPA 86; NewYTBS 84; OxCThe 83; VarWW 85; WhoAm 97; WhoThe 77; WhoWor 84, 97*

Jacobi, Friedrich Heinrich
German. Philosopher
Developed philosophy of feeling and faith, Gefuehlsphilosophie, opposing rationalism of Spinoza, Kant.
b. Jan 25, 1743 in Dusseldorf, Germany
d. Mar 10, 1819 in Munich, Germany
Source: *BbD; Benet 87, 96; BiD&SB; BioIn 17; BlkwCE; CasWL; CelCen; DcBiPP; DcLB 94; EncEnl; EvEuW; LinLib L; LuthC 75; McGEWB; NewCol 75; OxCGer 76, 86; OxCPhil; REn*

Jacobi, Lou
Canadian. Actor
Starred in film *Irma La Douce,* 1963.
b. Dec 28, 1913 in Toronto, Ontario, Canada
Source: *BiE&WWA; ConTFT 7; EncAFC; FilmEn; HalFC 80, 84, 88; LegTOT; NotNAT; VarWW 85; WhoAm 74, 76, 78, 80, 82, 84, 88; WhoEnt 92; WhoHol 92, A; WhoThe 72, 77, 81*

Jacobi, Mary Corinna Putnam
American. Physician
First woman member of NY Academy of Medicine; wrote *The Value of Life.*
b. Aug 31, 1842 in London, England
d. Jun 10, 1906 in New York, New York
Source: *Alli SUP; AmBi; AmWom; ApCAB; BiDAmEd; BiD&SB; BiInAmS; DcAmB; InWom SUP; LibW; McGEWB; NatCAB 8; NotAW; TwCBDA; WhAm 1*

Jacobs, Al(bert T)
American. Lyricist, Composer
Wrote over 300 songs including "This Is My Country," "There'll Never Be Another You."
b. Jan 22, 1903 in San Francisco, California
d. Feb 13, 1985 in Laurel, Maryland
Source: *ASCAP 66, 80; CmpEPM; ConAu 115*

Jacobs, Helen (Hull)
American. Tennis Player, Author
First to win both US singles and doubles titles four successive yrs, 1932-35.
b. Aug 6, 1908 in Globe, Arizona
d. Jun 2, 1997 in Easthampton, New York
Source: *AmAu&B; Au&Wr 71; AuBYP 2, 3; BiDAmSp OS; BioIn 1, 7, 8, 9, 11, 12; BuCMET; CmCal; ConAu 9R; EncWomS; GoodHs; IntAu&W 76, 77, 82; InWom, SUP; LegTOT; PenNWW A; SmATA 12; What 1; WhoAm 74, 76, 78, 80, 82, 84, 86, 88, 90, 92, 94, 95, 96, 97; WhoAmW 58, 68, 70, 72, 74; WhoSpor; WorAl; WorAlBi; WrDr 76, 80, 82, 84, 86, 88, 90, 92, 94, 96*

Jacobs, Joe
American. Physician
Appointed director of Office of Alternative Medicine, National Institutes of Health, 1992.
b. c. 1945 in New York, New York
Source: *News 94, 94-1*

Jacobs, Joe B
"Yussel the Muscle"
American. Boxing Promoter
Managed numerous champs including Max Schmeling, Tony Galento.
b. May 7, 1897 in New York, New York
d. Apr 24, 1940 in New York, New York
Source: *BioIn 12; CurBio 40; WhoBox 74*

Jacobs, Joseph
American. Author, Folklorist
Compiled *Celtic Fairy Tales,* 1891.
b. Aug 29, 1854 in Sydney, Australia
d. Jan 30, 1916 in Yonkers, New York
Source: *Alli SUP; AmAu&B; AmBi; AnCL; BiD&SB; BioIn 1, 2, 3, 8, 13, 16, 19, 20; BritAu 19; CarSB; Chambr 3; ChlBkCr; ConAu 111, 136; DcAmAu; DcAmB; DcLB 141; DcNAA; JBA 34; MajAI; NatCAB 24; NewCBEL; OxCChiL; RAdv 14; REnAL; SmATA 25; Str&VC; WebBD 83; WhAm 1; WhLit; WhoChL; WrChl*

Jacobs, Lou
American. Clown
Master clown, Ringling Brothers and Barnum and Bailey Circus, 1925-85; his face was circus' emblem.
b. 1903 in Bremerhaven, Germany
d. Sep 13, 1992 in Sarasota, Florida
Source: *BioIn 18, 20; NewYTBS 92*

Jacobs, Michael S
American. Boxing Promoter
Sponsored Joe Louis; founded 20th Century Sporting Club.
b. Mar 10, 1880 in New York, New York
d. Jan 25, 1953 in New York, New York
Source: *WhoBox 74*

Jacobs, Raymond
American. Businessman
With wife founded the Earth Shoe Co., 1970.
b. 1924?
d. Mar 17, 1993 in Torrington, Connecticut
Source: *WhoMW 92*

Jacobs, Sally
English. Designer
Stage, costume designs include *A Midsummer Night's Dream,* 1970; *Endgame,* 1980.
b. Nov 5, 1932 in London, England
Source: *ConDes 84, 90, 97; ConTFT 5; WhoThe 72, 77, 81*

Jacobs, W(illiam) W(ymark)
English. Author
Wrote sea stories, humor; noted for tale *Monkey's Paw,* 1902.
b. Sep 8, 1863 in London, England
d. Sep 1, 1943 in London, England
Source: *BbD; Benet 87, 96; BiD&SB; BioIn 4, 5, 8, 15, 20; CasWL; Chambr 3; DcArts; DcBiA; DcEnA A; DcLEL; DcNaB 1941; EncMys; EvLB; LngCTC; MnBBF; ModBrL; NewC; NewCBEL; NotNAT B; OxCEng 67, 95; OxCShps; PenC ENG; REn; RfGShF; TwCA, SUP; TwCWr; WhE&EA; WhLit; WhoLA; WhThe*

Jacobs, Walter L
American. Business Executive
Founded Hertz Rent-a-Car, 1954; first car rental agency.
b. Jun 15, 1896 in Chicago, Illinois
d. Feb 7, 1985 in Miami, Florida
Source: *BioIn 14; FacFETw; NewYTBS 85; WhoAm 74, 76*

Jacobsen, Arne
Danish. Architect
Known for simple, neat designs of homes, buildings, furniture: St. Catherine's College, Oxford, 1960.
b. Feb 11, 1902 in Copenhagen, Denmark
d. Mar 24, 1971 in Copenhagen, Denmark
Source: *BioIn 6, 9, 11, 12, 14; ConArch 80, 87, 94; ConDes 84, 90, 97; DcD&D; DcTwDes; EncMA; IntDcAr; MacEA; McGDA; ObitT 1971; PenDiDA 89; WhoArch*

Jacobsen, David P
American. Hostage
Director, American U of Beirut medical center, taken hostage for 523 days, released Nov. 2, 1986.

Jacobsen, Hugh Newell
American. Architect
Modernist architect; known for his work on the addition to the US Capitol Building, 1992.
b. Mar 11, 1929 in Grand Rapids, Michigan
Source: *AmArch 70; BioIn 13; ConArch 80, 87, 94; WhoAm 74, 76, 82, 84, 86, 88, 92, 94, 95, 96, 97; WhoSSW 73*

Jacobsen, Jens Peter
Danish. Author
First to translate, introduce Darwin's works to Denmark.
b. Apr 7, 1847 in Thisted, Denmark
d. May 30, 1885 in Thisted, Denmark
Source: *Benet 87, 96; BiD&SB; BioIn 1, 5, 7, 8; CasWL; ClDMEL 47, 80; CyWA 58; DcEuL; DcScanL; Dis&D; EuAu; EvEuW; LinLib L; McGEWB; NinCLC 34; Novels; PenC EUR; RAdv 14, 13-2; REn; WhDW*

Jacobson, Leon Orris
American. Scientist, Educator
Longtime professor of medicine, U of Chicago.
b. Dec 16, 1911 in Sims, North Dakota
d. Sep 18, 1992 in Chicago, Illinois
Source: *AmMWSc 73P, 76P, 82, 86, 89, 92; BiDrACP 79; BioIn 6; CurBio 62, 93N; IntWW 74, 75, 76, 77, 78, 79, 80, 81, 82, 83, 89, 91; LEduc 74; McGMS 80; WhAm 10; WhoAm 74, 76, 78, 80, 82, 84, 86, 88, 90, 92; WhoFrS 84; WhoWor 84, 87, 89*

Jacobson, Michael Faraday
American. Social Reformer
Co-founder, director, Center for Science in the Public Interest, 1971—; books include *The Fast Food Guide,* 1986; *The Booze Merchants,* 1983.
b. Jul 29, 1943 in Chicago, Illinois
Source: *AmMWSc 86; ConAu 13NR; WhoAm 86, 88, 90, 92, 94, 95, 96, 97; WhoWor 87*

Jacobsson, Ulla
Swedish. Actor
Films include *Smiles of a Summer Night,* 1957.
b. May 23, 1929? in Gothenburg, Sweden
d. Aug 22, 1982 in Vienna, Austria
Source: *BioIn 13; FilmEn; FilmgC; HalFC 80, 84, 88; WhoHol A; WorEFlm*

Jacoby, Oswald
American. Bridge Player, Journalist, Author
Called best card player in world, 1950; syndicated bridge columnist, 1949-84.
b. Dec 8, 1902 in New York, New York
d. Jun 27, 1984 in Dallas, Texas
Source: *AmAu&B; AnObit 1984; BioIn 2, 3, 11, 12, 14; ConAu 107, 113; WhAm 8*

Jacquard, Joseph Marie
French. Inventor
Developed Jacquard loom, 1801, first loom to weave designs in cloth.
b. Jul 7, 1752 in Lyons, France
d. Aug 7, 1834 in Oullins, France
Source: *AntBDN P; BioIn 14, 15, 21; CamDcSc; DcBiPP; InSci; LinLib S; NewCol 75; REn; WhDW*

Jacquet, Illinois (Robert Russell)
American. Jazz Musician
Tenor saxist; led own combos, 1940s-70s; recorded "Flying Home."
b. Oct 31, 1922 in Broussard, Louisiana
d. Feb 28, 1990 in Oakland, California
Source: *AllMusG; Baker 84; BiDAmM; CmpEPM; ConMus 17; DrBlPA, 90; IlEncJ; NewAmDM; NewGrDJ 88; OxCPMus; PenEncP*

Jacuzzi, Candido
American. Inventor, Businessman
Developed Jacuzzi whirlpool, 1950s, first as therapeutic aid, then as trendy item.
b. 1903 in Casarsa de Delicia, Italy
d. Oct 7, 1986 in Sun City, Arizona
Source: *AnObit 1986; BioIn 16; ConNews 87-1; Entr*

Jadlowker, Hermann
Russian. Opera Singer
Tenor with NY Met., 1910-13; made over 200 records.
b. Jul 5, 1879 in Riga, Russia
d. May 13, 1953 in Tel Aviv, Israel
Source: *Baker 84; BioIn 2; NewEOp 71*

Jaeckel, Richard (Hanley)
American. Actor
Oscar nominee for *Sometimes a Great Notion,* 1971; character actor usually in role of the heavy.
b. Oct 26, 1926 in Long Beach, California
d. Jun 14, 1997 in Woodland Hills, California
Source: *ConTFT 5; FilmEn; FilmgC; ForYSC; HalFC 80, 84, 88; IntMPA 75, 76, 77, 78, 79, 80, 81, 82, 84, 86, 88, 92, 94, 96; MotPP; MovMk; VarWW 85; Vers A; WhoEnt 92; WhoHol A; WorAlBi*

Jaeger, Andrea
"Rocky"
American. Tennis Player
Youngest player ever to turn pro, 1980.
b. Jun 4, 1965 in Chicago, Illinois
Source: *HerW 84; NewYTBS 83; WhoIntT*

Jaeger, Gustav, Dr.
English. Designer
Sportswear line founded, 1884.
b. 1808 in Leipzig, Germany
d. 1871
Source: *ArtsNiC; WorFshn*

Jaeger, Werner Wilhelm
American. Philosopher, Author
Prominent 20th-c. classical humanist; *Paideia,* 1934, standard of classical studies.
b. Jul 30, 1888 in Lobberich, Prussia
d. Oct 19, 1961 in Boston, Massachusetts
Source: *BioIn 5, 6, 7, 13; DcAmB, S7; NatCAB 47; WhAm 4; WhE&EA*

Jaegers, Albert
American. Sculptor
Known for busts of marble, bronze; commissioned to do statue of Baron von Steuben by US government.
b. Mar 28, 1868 in Elberfeld, Germany
d. Jul 22, 1925 in Suffern, New York
Source: *NatCAB 16; WhAm 1; WhAmArt 85*

Jaffe, Harold W
American. Physician
Researcher/writer on epidemiology of sexually transmitted diseases, including AIDS.
b. Apr 26, 1946 in Newton, Massachusetts

Jaffe, Herb
American. Producer
Horror films include *Motel Hell,* 1980; *The Gate,* 1986.
b. 1921 in New York, New York
d. Dec 7, 1991 in Beverly Hills, California
Source: *ConTFT 5, 10; IntMPA 92; NewYTBS 91*

Jaffe, Rona
American. Author
Wrote *The Last Chance,* 1976; *Class Reunion,* 1979.
b. Jun 12, 1932 in New York, New York
Source: *AmAu&B; ArtclWW 2; AuNews 1; BestSel 90-3; BioIn 5, 9, 10, 12; BioNews 75; ConAu 24NR, 73; InWom, SUP; LegTOT; MajTwCW; NewYTBS 79; Novels; WhoAm 80, 82, 84, 86, 90, 92, 94, 95, 96, 97; WhoAmW 81, 83, 85, 87, 89, 91, 93, 95, 97; WhoUSWr 88; WhoWorJ 72; WhoWrEP 89, 92, 95; WorAlBi; WrDr 76, 86*

Jaffe, Sam
American. Actor
Played Dr. Zorba on TV's "Ben Casey," 1961-66.
b. Mar 8, 1893 in New York, New York
d. Mar 24, 1984 in Beverly Hills, California
Source: *BiE&WWA; ConTFT 1; ForYSC; GangFlm; HalFC 84, 88; HolCA; IntMPA 82; ItaFilm; MotPP; NotNAT; WhoAm 82; WhoHol A; WhoThe 72, 77, 81*

Jaffe, Sam(uel Anderson)
American. Broadcast Journalist
ABC News correspondent, 1961-69; covered Vietnam War.
b. 1924 in San Francisco, California
d. Feb 8, 1985 in Bethesda, Maryland
Source: *ConAu 115; VarWW 85*

Jaffee, Allan
American. Cartoonist, Author
Illustrator for *Mad* magazine; created their "Fold-In."
b. Mar 13, 1921 in Savannah, Georgia
Source: *ConAu 116; EncACom; SmATA 37; WorECom*

Jaffee, Irving
American. Skater
Won two speed skating gold medals, 1932 Olympics.
b. 1907?
d. Mar 20, 1981 in San Diego, California
Source: *BioIn 12; NewYTBS 81*

Jagan, Cheddi (Berret)
Guyanese. Politician
First premier of British Guiana (now Guyana), 1961-64; general secretary, People's Progressive Party, 1970-97; president of Guyana, 1992-97.
b. Mar 22, 1918, British Guiana
d. Mar 6, 1997 in Washington, District of Columbia
Source: *BiDLAmC; BiDMarx; BioIn 3, 4, 6, 7, 8, 16, 17; CurBio 63; DcCPSAm; DcPol; IntAu&W 82; IntWW 74, 75, 76, 77, 78, 79, 80, 81, 82, 83, 89, 91, 93; IntYB 79, 80, 81, 82; Who 74, 82, 83, 85, 88, 90, 92, 94; WhoWor 74, 76, 78, 84, 95, 96, 97*

Jagan, Janet
[Mrs. Cheddi Jagan]
Guyanese. Politician, Newspaper Editor
General secretary, People's Progressive Party (PPP), 1950-70; int'l. secretary, PPP, 1970-84; exec. secretary, PPP, 1970-91; editor, *Mirror Newspaper,* 1973—.
b. Oct 20, 1920 in Chicago, Illinois
Source: *BiDLAmC; BioIn 16, 17; IntWW 74, 75, 76, 77, 78, 79, 80, 81, 82, 83, 89, 91, 93; WhoWor 74, 76, 84, 91*

Jagel, Frederick
American. Opera Singer, Teacher
Tenor; sang title role in first US performance of *Peter Grimes,* 1948.
b. Jun 10, 1897 in New York, New York
d. Jul 5, 1982 in San Francisco, California
Source: *Baker 78, 84, 92; BiDAmM; BioIn 1, 13; IntWWM 77, 80; MetOEnc; NewAmDM; NewEOp 71; NewGrDA 86; NewGrDO; NewYTBS 82*

Jagendorf, Moritz Adolf
American. Folklorist, Author
Wrote *Till Ulenspiegel's Merry Pranks,* 1938.
b. Aug 24, 1888 in Czernowitz, Austria
d. Jan 8, 1981 in Ithaca, New York
Source: *AnCL; AuBYP 2; BioIn 3, 6, 8, 9, 12, 13; ConAu 5R, 102; IntAu&W 77; MorJA; NewYTBS 81; SmATA 2, 24N; WhNAA; WrDr 76, 80*

Jaggar, Thomas Augustus
American. Geologist
Specialist in volcano experiments; wrote *Volcanology,* 1931.
b. Jan 24, 1871 in Philadelphia, Pennsylvania
d. Jan 17, 1953
Source: *BioIn 3; DcAmAu; DcAmB S5; DcScB; OhA&B; WhAm 3; WhNAA*

Jagger, Bianca Teresa
[Bianca Perez Mora Macias]
English. Socialite, Actor
Married to Mick Jagger, 1971-79; youngest member, best-dressed Hall of Fame; since divorce, has become political and environmental activist in Nicaragua.
b. May 2, 1950 in Managua, Nicaragua
Source: *BioNews 75; BkPepl; CurBio 87*

Jagger, Dean
American. Actor
Oscar winner for *Twelve O'Clock High,* 1950.
b. Nov 7, 1903 in Columbus Grove, Ohio
d. Feb 5, 1991 in Santa Monica, California
Source: *AnObit 1991; BioIn 17, 18; ConTFT 11; Film 2; FilmEn; FilmgC; ForYSC; GangFlm; HalFC 80, 84, 88; HolCA; IntMPA 75, 76, 77, 78, 79, 80, 81, 82, 84, 86, 88; LegTOT; MotPP; MovMk; NewYTBS 91; VarWW 85; WhoAm 82; WhoHol A; WhoHrs 80; WhoThe 77A; WorAlBi*

Jagger, Mick
[The Rolling Stones; Michael Philip Jagger]
English. Singer, Musician, Songwriter
Formed Rolling Stones, 1962; hits include "Satisfaction," "Honky Tonk Woman"; first solo album in 1985; films include *Freejack;* Rock and Roll Hall of Fame, 1989.
b. Jul 26, 1943 in Dartford, England
Source: *BioIn 13; BioNews 75; BkPepl; BlueB 76; CelR 90; ConMus 7; CurBio 72; EncPR&S 89; FacFETw; FilmgC; IntMPA 84, 86, 88, 92, 94, 96; IntWW 77, 78, 79, 80, 81, 82, 83, 89, 91, 93; LegTOT; NewAmDM; VarWW 85; WhoAm 78, 80, 82, 84, 86, 88, 90, 92, 94, 95, 96, 97; WhoEnt 92; WhoHol 92, A; WhoRocM 82; WhoWor 84, 87, 89, 91, 93, 95, 96, 97; WorAl; WorAlBi*

Jagr, Jaromir
Czech. Hockey Player
With Pittsburgh Penguins, 1990—; won Art Ross Trophy, 1995.
b. Feb 15, 1972 in Kladno, Czechoslovakia
Source: *BioIn 21; News 95*

Jahan, Marine
French. Dancer
Did dance scenes in *Flashdance,* 1983, for Jennifer Beals, but didn't get credit in film.
b. Sep 17, 1958 in Le Plessis-Aux-Bois, France
Source: *WhoAmW 91; WhoEmL 93; WhoEnt 92*

Jahangir
[Conqueror of the World]
Indian. Ruler
Son of Akbar; ruled India, 1605-27; pleasant ruler who enjoyed the arts.
b. Aug 30, 1569 in Sikri, India
d. Nov 7, 1627 in Bhimbar, India
Source: *BioIn 9, 10, 11, 18; HisWorL; NewC; NewCol 75; WebBD 83; WhDW*

Jahn, Friedrich Ludwig
German. Gymnastics Pioneer
Considered father of gymnastics; opened first athletic field, Berlin, 1811.
b. Aug 11, 1778 in Lanz, Germany
d. Oct 15, 1852 in Freyburg, Germany
Source: *CyEd; DcBiPP; EncTR 91; LinLib S; NewCol 75; OxCGer 76, 86*

Jahn, Helmut
"The Baron of High Tech"
American. Architect
Designed Southwest Center, Houston; winner of national architecture awards.
b. Apr 1, 1940 in Allersberg, Germany
Source: *BioIn 12, 13; ConArch 80, 87, 94; ConNews 87-3; CurBio 89; IntDcAr; WhoAm 78, 80, 82, 84, 86, 88, 90, 92, 94, 95, 96, 97; WhoMW 82, 84, 86, 88, 92, 93, 96; WhoTech 82, 84, 89, 95*

Jahoda, Gloria (Adelaide Love)
American. Author
Writings include *Annie,* 1960; *The Trail of Tears,* 1976.
b. Oct 6, 1926 in Chicago, Illinois
d. Jan 13, 1980 in Tallahassee, Florida
Source: *AuNews 1; ConAu 1R, 4NR, 104; ForWC 70; IntAu&W 76; WhoAmW 77; WrDr 76, 80*

Jakes, John (William)
American. Author
Wrote *Kent Family Chronicles,* 1974-80 including *The Bastard;* also trilogy containing *Heaven and Hell,* 1987.
b. Mar 31, 1932 in Chicago, Illinois
Source: *AuBYP 2S, 3; BenetAL 91; BestSel 89-4; BioIn 11, 14, 16, 17; ConAu 10NR, 43NR, 57; ConLC 29; ConPopW; ConSFA; CurBio 88; DcLB Y83B; EncSF, 93; IndAu 1967; IntAu&W 82, 89; LegTOT; MajTwCW; NewEScF; OxCCan SUP; RAdv 14; RGSF; ScF&FL 1, 2, 92; ScFSB; SJGFanW; SmATA 62; TwCRHW 90, 94; TwCSFW 81, 86, 91; TwCWW 82, 91; WhoAm 78, 80, 82, 84, 86, 88, 90, 92, 94, 95, 96, 97; WhoUSWr 88; WhoWrEP 89, 92, 95; WrDr 82, 84, 86, 88, 90, 92, 94, 96*

Jakes, Milos
Czech. Politician
General secretary, Czechoslovak Communist Party, 1987-89.
b. Aug 12, 1922 in Ceske Chalupy, Czechoslovakia
Source: *BioIn 15, 16; ColdWar 2; IntWW 80, 81, 82, 83, 89; NewYTBS 87; WhoSocC 78; WhoSoCE 89; WhoWor 89, 91*

Jakobovits, Immanuel
German. Religious Leader
Chief Rabbi of Great Britain and the Commonwealth, 1967-91.
b. Feb 8, 1921 in Konigsberg, Germany
Source: *BioIn 7; BlueB 76; ConAu 108; CurBio 88; IntWW 74, 75, 76, 77, 78, 79, 80, 81, 82, 83, 93; Who 74, 82, 83, 85, 88; WhoRel 92; WhoWor 74, 78; WhoWorJ 72, 78*

Jakobson, Roman
American. Linguist
Leading authority on Slavic languages.
b. Oct 11, 1896 in Moscow, Russia
d. Jul 18, 1982 in Boston, Massachusetts
Source: *AmAu&B; AnObit 1982; Benet 96; BioIn 14, 20; BlmGEL; BlueB 76; ConAu 31NR, 77, 107; DrAS 74F, 78F, 82F; FifIDA; IntEnSS 79; IntWW 74, 75, 76, 77, 78, 79, 80, 81, 82, 83N; NewYTBE 71; NewYTBS 82; OxCEng 85, 95; ThTwC 87; WhAm 8; Who 74, 82; WhoAm 74, 76, 78, 80, 82; WhoE 77; WorAu 1970*

Jamal, Ahmad
American. Jazz Musician
Pianist known for concerts, recordings; only artist to have album on nat. top-10 list for 108 straight weeks: *But Not for Me.*
b. Jul 7, 1930 in Pittsburgh, Pennsylvania
Source: *AllMusG; BiDAfM; BiDAmM; BiDJaz; BioIn 5, 6, 10, 12, 13, 16, 19, 20; BioNews 74; DcTwCCu 5; DrBlPA, 90; EncJzS; InB&W 85; NewAmDM; NewGrDA 86; NewGrDJ 88, 94; PenEncP; VarWW 85; WhoAfA 96; WhoBlA 75, 77, 80, 85, 88, 90, 92, 94*

James, Art
[Denver Dixon; Art Mix]
American. Actor, Producer, Director
Western star, 1920s-30s; films include *Mormon Conquest,* 1938.
b. Oct 15, 1890 in Dearborn, Michigan
d. Nov 9, 1972 in Hollywood, California
Source: *WhoHol B; WhScrn 77, 83*

James, Bob
American. Jazz Musician
Uses funk influence in music; hit albums include *Foxie,* 1983.
b. Dec 25, 1939 in Marshall, Montana
Source: *AllMusG; ConMuA 80A, 80B; ConTFT 12; EncJzS; HarEnR 86; NewGrDJ 88, 94; WhoEnt 92*

James, Daniel, Jr.
"Chappie"
American. Government Official
First black four-star general in US, 1975.
b. Feb 11, 1920 in Pensacola, Florida
d. Feb 25, 1978 in Colorado Springs, Colorado
Source: *AfrAmAl 6; AfrAmBi 1; AfrAmG; BioIn 4, 8, 9, 10, 11, 13, 17, 18, 19; BlksScM; CurBio 76, 78, 78N; DcAmB S10; Ebony 1; EncWB; InB&W 80, 85; NegAl 76, 83, 89; USBiR 74; WebAMB; WhAm 7; WhoAm 76, 78; WhoBlA 75; WhoGov 72, 75, 77; WhoWest 78; WorAlBi; WorDWW*

James, Dennis
American. TV Personality
Game shows include "Chance of a Lifetime," 1952-56; daytime "Name That Tune," 1980s.
b. Aug 24, 1917 in Jersey City, New Jersey
d. Jun 3, 1997 in Palm Springs, California
Source: *IntMPA 75, 76, 77, 78, 79, 80, 81, 82, 84, 86, 88, 92, 94, 96; NewYTET; VarWW 85; WhoHol 92*

James, Edwin
American. Explorer
Writings of travels include *An Account of an Expedition from Pittsburgh to The Rocky Mountains,* 1822-23.
b. Aug 27, 1797 in Weybridge, Vermont
d. Oct 28, 1861
Source: *Alli; AmAu&B; ApCAB; BenetAL 91; BiDAmS; BiInAmS; BioIn 2, 6, 7; DcAmAu; DcAmB; DcAmMeB; DcNAA; HarEnUS; InSci; REnAL; REnAW; TwCBDA; WhAm HS*

James, Elmore
American. Musician
Blues performer; hits include "Dust My Broom," 1951; Rock and Roll Hall of Fame, 1992.
b. Jan 27, 1918 in Richland, Mississippi
d. May 24, 1963 in Chicago, Illinois
Source: *BioIn 18; BluesWW; ConMus 8; DcArts; EncRk 88; GuBlues; OnThGG; OxCPMus; PenEncP; RolSEnR 83; WhoRocM 82*

James, Etta
[Jamesetta Hawkins]
American. Singer
Influential performer who bridged r & b and rock; charted ten Top 10 hits, 1960-63; Rock and Roll Hall of Fame, 1993.
b. 1938 in Los Angeles, California
Source: *AfrAmBi 2; BiDAfM; BioIn 11, 20, 21; BlkWAm; ConBlB 13; ConMus 6; DcTwCCu 5; EncPR&S 89; EncRk 88; GuBlues; InB&W 80, 85; LegTOT; NewAmDM; NewGrDA 86; News 95, 95-2; PenEncP; RkOn 74; RolSEnR 83; SoulM; WhoAfA 96; WhoAmW 97; WhoBlA 92, 94; WhoRock 81*

James, Frank
[Alexander Franklin James]
American. Outlaw
Only brother of Jesse James; after brother's death he surrendered to governor's office.
b. Jan 10, 1843 in Clay County, Missouri
d. Feb 18, 1915 in Clay County, Missouri
Source: *BioIn 2, 7, 8, 9, 10, 11, 12, 13; CopCroC; HalFC 84; OxCAmH; REnAW; WhCiWar*

James, G(eorge) P(ayne) R(ainsford)
English. Author
Historical novels include *Life of the Black Prince,* 1836.
b. Aug 9, 1799 in London, England
d. May 9, 1860 in Venice, Italy
Source: *Alli; BbD; BiD&SB; BritAu 19; CamGEL; CamGLE; CasWL; Chambr 3; ChhPo S1; DcBiA; DcEnA; DcEnL; DcEuL; DcLEL; DcNaB; Dis&D; EvLB; HsB&A; MnBBF; NewC; NewCBEL; OxCEng 67, 85, 95; StaCVF; WebE&AL; WhoHr&F*

James, Harry
American. Bandleader
Brilliant trumpeter; led popular dance band for 40 yrs; wed to Betty Grable, 1943-65.
b. Mar 15, 1916 in Albany, Georgia
d. Jul 5, 1983 in Las Vegas, Nevada
Source: *AllMusG; AnObit 1983; ASCAP 66, 80; Baker 84; BgBands 74; BioIn 2, 6, 9, 10, 12, 13, 16, 20; CmpEPM; ConMus 11; CurBio 83N; FacFETw; FilmEn; FilmgC; ForYSC; HalFC 80, 84, 88; HolP 40; IlEncJ; IntMPA 75, 76, 77, 78, 79, 80, 81, 82; LegTOT; MovMk; NewAmDM; NewGrDA 86; NewGrDJ 88; NewYTBS 83; OxCPMus; PenEncP; RadStar; VarWW 85; WhoHol A; WorAl; WorAlBi*

James, Henry, Sr.
American. Philosopher, Writer, Lecturer
Writings on social, religious issues include *Christianity the Logic of Creation,* 1857.
b. Jun 3, 1811 in Albany, New York
d. Dec 18, 1882 in Cambridge, Massachusetts
Source: *Alli SUP; AmAu; AmAu&B; AmBi; ApCAB; BbD; BenetAL 91; BiD&SB; BiDTran; BioIn 1, 2, 3, 4, 5, 8, 10, 12, 13, 14, 16, 17, 20, 21; CamGEL; CamHAL; CyAL 2; DcAmAu; DcAmB; DcNAA; Drake; LuthC 75; NatCAB 13; NinCLC 53; OxCAmH; OxCAmL 65, 83, 95; PenC AM; REnAL; TwCBDA; WebAB 74, 79; WhAm HS; WorAl; WorAlBi*

James, Henry, (Jr.)
American. Author
Master of psychological novel; wrote *The Aspern Papers,* 1888; *The Turn of the Screw,* 1898.
b. Apr 15, 1843 in New York, New York
d. Feb 28, 1916 in London, England
Source: *Alli SUP; AmAu; AmAu&B; AmBi; AmCulL; AmWr; ApCAB; AtlBL; BbD; Benet 87, 96; BenetAL 91; BibAL; BiD&SB; BiDTran; BioIn 1, 2, 3, 4, 5, 6, 7, 8, 9, 10, 11, 12, 13, 14, 15, 16, 17, 18, 19, 20, 21; BlmGEL; BritWr 6; CamGEL; CamGLE; CamHAL; CasWL; CelCen; CnDAL; CnMD; CnMWL; CnThe; ConAu 104, 132; CrtSuDr; CrtT 3, 4; CyWA 58, 89; DcAmAu; DcAmB; DcAmC; DcArts; DcBiA; DcEnA, A; DcEnL; DcEuL; DcLB 12, 71, 74, DS13; DcLEL; DcNAA; DcNaB 1912; DcPup; Dis&D; EncAB-H 1974, 1996; EncWL 2, 3; EncWT; EvLB; FacFETw; GayLesB; GayN; GrBr; GrWrEL N; HalFC 80, 84, 88; HarEnUS; JrnUS; LegTOT; LiExTwC; LinLib L, S; LngCEL; LngCTC; LuthC 75; MagSAmL; MajTwCW; McGEWB; McGEWD 72, 84; MemAm; MetOEnc; ModAL, S1; ModBrL, S1, S2; ModWD; NatCAB 1; NewC; NewCBEL; NewEOp 71; NewGrDA 86; NewGrDO; NotNAT B; Novels; OxCAmH; OxCAmL 65, 83, 95; OxCAmT 84; OxCEng 67, 85, 95; OxCThe 67, 83; OxDcOp; PenC AM, ENG; PenEncH; PeoHis; RAdv 1, 14, 13-1; RComAH; RComWL; RealN; REn; REnAL; REnWD; RfGAmL 87, 94; RfGEnL 91; RfGShF; RGTwCWr; ScF&FL 1, 92; ShSCr 8; ShSWr; SupFW; ThHElm; TwCBDA; TwCLC 2, 11, 24, 40, 47, 64; TwCWr; WebAB 74, 79; WebE&AL; WhAm 1, 4A, HSA; WhDW; WhLit; WhoHr&F; WhoTwCL; WorAl; WorAlBi; WorLitC; WrPh*

James, Jesse Woodson
American. Outlaw
Leader of outlaw gang known for spectacular bank, train robberies; killed by Robert Ford for reward.
b. Sep 5, 1847 in Centerville, Missouri
d. Apr 3, 1882 in Saint Joseph, Missouri
Source: *AmBi; FilmgC; OxCAmL 65; OxCFilm; REn; REnAL*

James, John
American. Actor
Played Jeff Colby on TV dramas "Dynasty," 1981-85, 1987-89, "The Colbys," 1985-87.
b. Apr 18, 1956 in Minneapolis, Minnesota
Source: *BioIn 13; ConTFT 8; LegTOT*

James, Marquis
American. Author
Biographer who won 1929 Pulitzer for *The Raven: A Biography of Sam Houston.*
b. Sep 29, 1891 in Springfield, Missouri
d. Nov 19, 1955
Source: *AmAu&B; BenetAL 91; BioIn 1, 2, 4, 6; ConAu 144; DcAmB S5; JrnUS; LinLib L, S; NatCAB 44; OxCAmL 65, 83, 95; REnAL; TwCA, SUP; WhAm 3; WhE&EA; WhNAA*

James, Montague Rhodes
English. Scholar, Author
Provost of Eton, 1918-36; wrote on art, literature of Middle Ages.
b. Aug 1, 1862 in Goodnestone, England
d. Jun 12, 1936 in Eton, England
Source: *BioIn 2, 4, 12, 13, 14, 15; DcLEL; DcNaB 1931; EvLB; GrBr; LngCTC; NewC; NewCBEL; OxCEng 67; PenC ENG; TwCA, SUP; TwCWr; WhDW; WhE&EA; WhLit; WhoLA*

James, P(hyllis) D(orothy)
English. Author
Writings include *Cover Her Face,* 1962; *The Black Tower,* 1975.
b. Aug 3, 1920 in Oxford, England
Source: *ConLC 18; ConNov 96; ConPopW; CurBio 80; DcArts; EncBrWW; EncMys; IntAu&W 93; IntWW 89; NewYTBS 86; OxCEng 95; RGTwCWr; Who 82, 83, 85, 88, 90; WhoAm 90, 92, 94, 95, 96, 97; WhoWor 93, 95, 96, 97; WrDr 94, 96*

James, Philip
American. Composer, Conductor
Works include prize-winning orchestra suite *Station WGZBX,* 1932.
b. May 17, 1890 in Jersey City, New Jersey
d. Nov 1, 1975 in Southampton, New York
Source: *ASCAP 66, 80; Baker 78, 84, 92; BioIn 1, 10, 12; ConAmC 76, 82; NatCAB 59; NewAmDM; NewGrDA 86; NewGrDM 80; OxCMus; RadStar; WhAm 6, 7; WhoAm 74, 76*

James, Rick
[James Johnson]
American. Singer, Songwriter
Funk star; double platinum album *Street Songs,* 1981, included single "Superfreak."
b. Feb 1, 1952 in Buffalo, New York
Source: *BioIn 12, 13; EncPR&S 89; EncRk 88; HarEnR 86; IlEncBM 82; IlEncRk; InB&W 80, 85; LegTOT; NewGrDA 86; RkOn 85; SoulM*

James, Skip
[Nehemiah James]
American. Musician, Singer
Blues pioneer, rediscovered, 1960s; hit song "I'm So Glad."
b. Jun 9, 1902 in Bentonia, Mississippi
d. Oct 3, 1969 in Philadelphia, Pennsylvania
Source: *BiDAfM; BiDAmM; BiDJaz; BioIn 7, 8, 12, 17, 20; BluesWW; EncFCWM 69; EncJzS; GuBlues; InB&W 80, 85; OnThGG; PenEncP; WhoRock 81; WhoRocM 82*

James, Sonny
[Jimmy Loden]
"The Southern Gentleman"
American. Singer
Country vocalist; recorded best-selling "Young Love," 1957.
b. Mar 1, 1929 in Hackleburg, Alaska

Source: *BgBkCoM; BiDAmM; BioIn 14; CounME 74, 74A; EncFCWM 69, 83; HarEnCM 87; IlEncCM; LegTOT; PenEncP; RkOn 74; VarWW 85; WhoHol 92; WhoRock 81*

James, Will(iam Roderick)
American. Author, Illustrator
Self-illustrated books include *All in the Day's Riding,* 1933; *Book of Cowboy Stories,* 1951.
b. Jun 6, 1892 in Great Falls, Montana
d. Sep 3, 1942 in Hollywood, California
Source: *AmAu&B; ArtsAmW 1; AuBYP 2, 3; BenetAL 91; BioIn 1, 2, 3, 4, 7, 8, 12, 13, 14, 15, 16, 19, 20; ChlBkCr; ConAu 137; CurBio 42; DcAmB S3; DcNAA; EncAAH; IlBEAAW; JBA 34, 51; LinLib L; MajAI; NatCAB 35; NewbMB 1922; OxCAmL 65, 83, 95; REnAL; REnAW; SmATA 19; TwCA, SUP; TwCChW 78, 83, 89, 95; TwCWW 82, 91; WhAm 2; WhAmArt 85; WhLit; WhNAA*

James, William
American. Psychologist, Philosopher
One of founders of pragmatism who wrote *The Meaning of Truth,* 1909.
b. Jan 11, 1842 in New York, New York
d. Aug 26, 1910 in Chocorua, New Hampshire
Source: *AmAu; AmAu&B; AmBi; AmDec 1900; AmPeW; AmSocL; AmWr; ApCAB; AsBiEn; AtlBL; Benet 87, 96; BiDAmEd; BiDAmS; BiD&SB; BiDPara; BiDPsy; BiDTran; BiInAmS; BioIn 1, 2, 3, 4, 5, 6, 7, 8, 9, 10, 11, 12, 13, 14, 15, 16, 17, 18, 19, 20, 21; CamGEL; CamGLE; CamHAL; CasWL; ConAu 109; CyEd; CyWA 58; DcAmAu; DcAmB; DcAmC; DcAmMeB; DcAmReB 1, 2; DcAmSR; DcEuL; DcLEL; DcNAA; DcScB; EncAB-H 1974, 1996; EncARH; EncEth; EncO&P 1, 2, 3; EncPaPR 91; EvLB; GaEncPs; GayN; GuPsyc; HarEnUS; IlEncMy; InSci; LegTOT; LinLib L, S; LngCTC; LuthC 75; McGEWB; MemAm; ModAL, S1; NamesHP; NatCAB 18; NewC; OxCAmH; OxCAmL 65, 83, 95; OxCEng 67, 85, 95; OxCMed 86; OxCPhil; PenC AM; RAdv 14, 13-3, 13-4, 13-5; RComAH; RComWL; REn; REnAL; RfGAmL 87, 94; ThTwC 87; TwCBDA; TwCLC 15, 32; TwoTYeD; WebAB 74, 79; WebE&AL; WhAm 1; WhDW; WhLit; WhoTwCL; WorAl; WorAlBi; WrPh P*

James Gang
[Tom Bolin; James Fox; Phil Giallombardo; "Bubba" Keith; Roy Kenner; Dale Peters; Richard Shack; Dom Troiano; Joseph Fidler Walsh; Bob Webb]
American. Music Group
Vocal, instrumental rock group; albums include *Yer Album,* 1969.
Source: *Alli SUP; BioIn 7; ConAu X; DcLP 87A; EncPR&S 74; EncRk 88; IlEncRk; Law&B 89A, 92; PenEncP; RkOn 78; RolSEnR 83; WhoRock 81; WhoRocM 82*

James I
Scottish. Ruler
King of Scotland, 1406-37.
b. Jul 25, 1394 in Dunfermline, Scotland
d. Feb 20, 1437 in Perth, Scotland
Source: *CasWL; NewCol 75; WebBD 83*

James I
[James VI]
English. Ruler
As James I, King of England, 1603-25; as James VI, King of Scotland, 1567-1625; son of Mary Queen of Scots.
b. Jun 19, 1566 in Edinburgh, Scotland
d. Mar 27, 1625 in Theobalds, England
Source: *WebBD 83*

James II
Scottish. Ruler
King of Scotland, 1437-60.
b. Oct 16, 1430 in Edinburgh, Scotland
d. Aug 3, 1460 in Roxburgh Castle, Scotland
Source: *DcCathB; DcNaB; WebBD 83*

James II
English. Ruler
King of England, Scotland, Ireland, 1685-88.
b. Oct 14, 1633? in London, England
d. Sep 16, 1701 in Saint-Germain-en-Laye, France
Source: *McGEWB; WebBD 83*

James III
Scottish. Ruler
King of Scotland, 1460-88.
b. May 10, 1451 in Stirling, Scotland
d. Jun 11, 1488 in Sauchieburn, Scotland
Source: *DcCathB; DcNaB; OxCMus; WebBD 83*

James IV
Scottish. Ruler
King of Scotland, 1488-1513; marriage to Margaret Tudor led to union of crowns of England, Scotland.
b. Mar 17, 1473 in Stirling Castle, Scotland
d. Sep 9, 1513 in Branxton, England
Source: *DcNaB; Dis&D; OxCMus; WebBD 83*

Jameson, House
American. Actor
Played father in radio, TV series "The Aldrich Family," 1949-53.
b. Dec 17, 1902 in Austin, Texas
d. Apr 23, 1971 in Danbury, Connecticut
Source: *BiE&WWA; BioIn 9; NotNAT B; PlP&P; RadStar; WhScrn 74, 77*

Jameson, Leander Starr, Sir
"Doctor Jameson"
British. Political Leader
S African statesman; led unsuccessful Jameson raid, 1895, to overthrow Boer govt; prime minister, Cape Colony, 1904-08; helped found Unionist Party, 1910.
b. Feb 3, 1853 in Edinburgh, Scotland
d. Nov 26, 1917 in London, England
Source: *BioIn 2, 12, 16, 17, 21; DcAfHiB 86; DcNaB 1912; EncSoA; HisDBrE; LinLib S; McGEWB; NewC; NewCol 75; OxCMed 86; VicBrit; WhDW*

Jameson, Margaret Storm
English. Author
Best-known novels include *Cousin Honore; Europe to Let,* 1940; *Cloudless May,* 1943.
b. 1891 in Whitby, England
d. Sep 30, 1986 in Cambridge, England
Source: *ConAu 81; DcLEL; EvLB; IntAu&W 76, 77, 82; LngCTC; ModBrL; NewC; PenC ENG; REn; Who 85; WomFir*

James the Greater, Saint
[Saint James the Elder]
Hebrew. Biblical Figure
One of three apostles to witness Jesus' transfiguration, agony in Garden of Gethsemane; feast day: Jul 25.
d. c. 44AD in Jerusalem, Palestine
Source: *Benet 87, 96; BioIn 3, 4, 5, 6, 8, 9, 11; DcCathB; LuthC 75; McGDA; REn*

James the Less, Saint
Biblical Figure
One of twelve apostles; feast day: May 3.
Source: *McGDA; REn*

James V
Scottish. Ruler
King of Scotland, 1513-42.
b. Apr 10, 1512 in Linlithgow, Scotland
d. Dec 14, 1542 in Solway Moss, England
Source: *DcCathB; DcNaB; OxCMus; WebBD 83*

Jamieson, Bob
[Robert John Jamieson]
American. Broadcast Journalist
NBC News correspondent; won 1981 Emmy for coverage of Iranian hostage crisis.
b. Feb 1, 1943 in Streator, Illinois
Source: *ConAu 110, 116; WhoAm 80, 82, 84, 86, 95, 96, 97*

Jamison, Judith
American. Dancer, Choreographer
Performer with the Alvin Ailey Dance Theater, 1965-80; appointed artistic director, 1990—; starred in *Sophisticated Ladies.*
b. May 10, 1943 in Philadelphia, Pennsylvania
Source: *AfrAmBi 2; BioNews 74; ConBlB 7; ContDcW 89; CurBio 73; DcTwCCu 5; DrBlPA, 90; Ebony 1; InB&W 80; IntDcWB; NewYTBE 72; WhoAfA 96; WhoAm 86, 95, 96, 97; WhoAmW 95, 97; WhoBlA 75, 92, 94; WhoE 95, 97; WomFir*

Jamison, Philip Duane, Jr.
American. Artist
Realistic watercolorist, known for flowers, interiors, ME landscapes.
b. Jul 3, 1925 in Philadelphia, Pennsylvania
Source: *WhoAm 74, 76, 78, 86; WhoAmA 84; WhoE 74*

Jammes, Francis
French. Author, Poet
Wrote about rural life, animals, nature; later turned to religious themes.
b. Dec 2, 1868 in Tournay, France
d. Nov 1, 1938 in Hasparren, France
Source: *Benet 87, 96; BioIn 1, 2, 3, 5; CasWL; CathA 1930; ChhPo; ClDMEL 47, 80; DcTwCCu 2; EncWL, 2, 3; EvEuW; GuFrLit 1; LinLib L; ModFrL; ModRL; NewC; OxCEng 67; OxCFr; PenC EUR; REn; TwCA, SUP; WhoTwCL*

Jampolis, Neil Peter
American. Designer
Won Tony for lighting design of *Sherlock Holmes,* 1975; did set, costume designs for *The Life and Adventures of Nicholas Nickleby,* 1981.
b. Mar 14, 1943 in New York, New York
Source: *ConTFT 5; NotNAT; VarWW 85; WhoAm 74, 76, 78, 80, 82, 84, 86, 88, 92, 94, 95, 96; WhoEnt 92; WhoOp 76; WhoThe 81*

Janacek, Leos
Czech. Composer
A leading exponent of musical nationalism; wrote *Her Foster Daughter,* 1904.
b. Jul 3, 1854 in Hukvaldy, Moravia
d. Aug 12, 1928 in Prague, Czech Republic
Source: *Baker 78, 84, 92; BioIn 1, 2, 3, 4, 5, 6, 7, 8, 9, 10, 11, 12, 13, 14, 16, 17, 18, 20; BriBkM 80; CmOp; CnOxB; CompSN, SUP; DcArts; DcCM; DcCom 77; DcCom&M 79; DcTwCC, A; FacFETw; IntDcOp; LegTOT; MakMC; McGEWB; MetOEnc; MusMk; NewAmDM; NewEOp 71; NewGrDM 80; NewGrDO; NewOxM; OxCMus; OxDcOp; PenDiMP A; RAdv 14; WebBD 83; WhDW; WorAl; WorAlBi*

Jan and Dean
[Jan Berry; Dean Torrance]
American. Music Group
Surf music duo, 1958-66; hit debut single "Jennie Lee," sold 10 million albums.
Source: *AmPS A; BiDAmM; ConMuA 80A; DrRegL 75; EncPR&S 74, 89; EncRk 88; HarEnR 86; IlEncRk; LegTOT; NewGrDA 86; PenEncP; RkOn 74; RolSEnR 83; WhoRock 81; WhoRocM 82; WorAl; WorAlBi*

Janaszak, Steve
American. Hockey Player
Member US Olympic gold medal-winning team, 1980.
b. Jan 7, 1957 in Saint Paul, Minnesota
Source: *HocReg 81*

Jancso, Miklos
Hungarian. Director
Films include *Round-Up,* 1965; *Red Psalm,* 1972.
b. Sep 27, 1922 in Vac, Hungary
Source: *BiDFilm; DcFM; FilmgC; IntWW 83; OxCFilm; WorEFlm*

Janes's Addiction
American. Music Group
Hard rock/metal band formed in 1986; album *Ritual de lo Habitual,* 1990 went gold; disbanded, early 1990s.
Source: *ConAu 49; ConMus 6*

Janeway, Eliot
American. Economist, Author, Lecturer
Writings on economic topics include *You and Your Money,* 1972; husband of Elizabeth.
b. Jan 1, 1913 in New York, New York
d. Feb 8, 1993 in New York, New York
Source: *AmAu&B; AnObit 1993; BioIn 8, 9, 11, 13; BlueB 76; ConAu 112, 130, 140; CurBio 70, 93N; IntAu&W 89; IntWW 74, 75, 76, 77, 78, 79, 80, 81, 82, 83, 89, 91, 93; LegTOT; LinLib L; NewYTBS 93; WhAm 11; WhoAm 74, 76, 78, 80, 82, 84, 86, 88, 92; WhoE 85, 86, 89, 91, 93; WhoWor 74, 76, 78, 80, 82; WorAl; WorAlBi; WrDr 76, 80, 82, 84, 86, 88, 90, 92, 94, 96*

Janeway, Elizabeth Hall
[Mrs. Eliot Janeway]
American. Author
Writings include *Powers of the Weak,* 1980; *Cross Sections: From a Decade of Change,* 1982.
b. Oct 7, 1913 in New York, New York
Source: *AmAu&B; AmNov; AnObit 1993; ArtclWW 2; Au&Wr 71; AuBYP 2; AuNews 1; BioIn 8, 9, 11, 13; BlueB 76; ConAu 2NR, 45, 112, 130, 140; CurBio 44, 93N; DcAmChF 1960; IntAu&W 89; IntWW 74, 75, 76, 77, 78, 79, 80, 81, 82, 83, 89, 91, 93; InWom, SUP; LegTOT; LinLib L; NewYTBS 79, 93; REnAL; SmATA 19; TwCA SUP; WhAm 11; WhoAm 74, 76, 78, 80, 82, 84, 86, 88, 90, 92, 94, 95, 96, 97; WhoAmW 85, 89, 91, 93, 95, 97; WhoE 85, 86, 89, 91, 93; WhoUSWr 88; WhoWor 74, 76, 78, 80, 82; WhoWrEP 89, 92, 95; WorAl; WorAlBi; WrDr 76, 80, 82, 84, 86, 88, 90, 92, 94, 96*

Janifer, Laurence M(ark)
[Larry M Harris]
American. Author
Writings include *The Protector,* 1960; used over 400 pseuds. for stories in mags.
b. Mar 17, 1933 in New York, New York
Source: *ConAu 5NR, 9R; ConSFA; EncSF, 93; IntAu&W 91; NewEScF; RGSF; ScF&FL 1, 2, 92; ScFSB; TwCSFW 81, 86, 91; WhoSciF; WrDr 84, 86, 88, 90, 92, 94, 96*

Janigo, Antonio
Italian. Musician, Conductor
International cello soloist; founded ensemble, Solisti di Zagreb, 1950.
b. Jan 21, 1918 in Milan, Italy
d. May 1, 1989
Source: *Baker 78; NewGrDM 80*

Janis, Byron
American. Pianist
First American sent in cultural exchange to USSR, 1960, 1962; discovered unknown Chopin waltzes.
b. Mar 24, 1928 in McKeesport, Pennsylvania
Source: *Baker 78, 84, 92; BioIn 2, 3, 7, 8, 9, 10, 11, 12, 14, 21; BriBkM 80; CelR, 90; CurBio 66; IntWWM 77, 80; MusSN; NewAmDM; NewGrDA 86; NewGrDM 80; NotTwCP; PenDiMP; WhoAm 74, 76, 78, 80, 82, 84, 86, 88, 92, 94; WhoAmM 83; WhoE 74; WhoEnt 92; WhoMus 72*

Janis, Conrad
American. Actor, Musician
Starred as Mindy's father in TV show "Mork and Mindy," 1978-81.
b. Feb 11, 1928 in New York, New York
Source: *BiDAmM; BiE&WWA; BioIn 3, 12; CmpEPM; ConTFT 4; FilmgC; MotPP; NotNAT; VarWW 85; WhoAm 86; WhoAmA 73, 76, 78, 80, 82, 84, 86, 89, 91, 93; WhoE 75, 77; WhoHol 92, A; WhoThe 72, 77, 81*

Janis, Elsie
[Elsie Bierbower]
American. Actor
First American to entertain troops in WW I.
b. Mar 16, 1889 in Columbus, Ohio
d. Feb 26, 1956 in Beverly Hills, California
Source: *AmWomD; AmWomPl; ASCAP 66, 80; BioIn 3, 4, 5, 14, 16, 19; CmpEPM; DcAmB S6; EncAFC; EncMT; EncVaud; FamA&A; Film 1, 2; FilmgC; HalFC 80, 84, 88; InWom; NotNAT A, B; NotWoAT; ObitT 1951; OhA&B; OxCAmT 84; OxCPMus; TwYS; WhAm 3; WhoHol B; WhoStg 1906, 1908; WhScrn 74, 77, 83; WhThe; WomWWA 14*

Janis, Sidney
American. Art Collector
Art dealer who donated his multi-million-dollar private collection to Museum of Modern Art, 1967.
b. Jul 8, 1896 in Buffalo, New York
d. Nov 23, 1989 in New York, New York
Source: *AmAu&B; AnObit 1989; Au&Wr 71; BioIn 5, 9, 15, 16, 17; ConAu 130; CurBio 90N; IntAu&W 76; NewYTBS 86,*

89; WhAm 10; WhoAm 74, 76, 78, 80, 82, 84; WhoAmA 73, 76, 78, 80, 82, 84, 86, 89, 91N, 93N; WhoWor 74

Janklow, Morton Lloyd
American. Agent, Lawyer
Lawyer turned literary agent; partner, Janklow and Nesbit Associates, 1989—; noted for getting clients lucrative deals.
b. May 30, 1930 in New York, New York
Source: *BioIn 11, 16; News 89; NewYTBS 89; WhoAm 74, 76, 78, 80, 82, 84, 86, 88, 90, 92, 94, 95, 97; WhoWor 76, 78, 80, 82, 84, 87, 89, 91, 93, 95*

Janney, Leon
American. Actor
Radio series include "The Parker Family"; "Chick Carter."
b. Apr 1, 1917 in Ogden, Utah
d. Oct 28, 1980 in Guadalajara, Mexico
Source: *BiE&WWA; BioIn 1, 12; Film 2; ForYSC; HalFC 84, 88; NewYTBS 80; NotNAT; RadStar; SaTiSS; WhoHol A; WhScrn 83*

Janney, Russell Dixon
American. Author, Producer
Co-wrote, produced hit Broadway musical *The Vagabond King,* 1925.
b. Apr 14, 1885 in Wilmington, Ohio
d. Jul 14, 1963 in New York, New York
Source: *DcAmB S7*

Jannings, Emil
American. Actor
Won Oscar for *The Last Command; The Way of All Flesh,* 1928.
b. Jul 26, 1886 in Rorschach, Switzerland
d. Jan 3, 1950 in Lake Wolfgang, Austria
Source: *BiDFilm, 83; WorAl; WorAlBi; WorEFlm*

Janov, Arthur
American. Psychologist
Developed method known as "primal therapy," which involves the screams of patients.
b. Aug 21, 1924 in Los Angeles, California
Source: *BioIn 12; ConAu 116; CurBio 80*

Janowicz, Vic(tor Felix)
American. Football Player
All-America halfback, Ohio State U, 1949-51; won Heisman Trophy, 1950; in NFL with Washington, 1954-55; first Heisman winner to play ML baseball, 1953-54.
b. Feb 26, 1930 in Elyria, Ohio
d. Feb 27, 1996 in Columbus, Ohio
Source: *Ballpl 90; BaseEn 88; BiDAmSp FB; BioIn 2, 5, 14, 21; WhoFtbl 74; WhoPoA 96*

Janowitz, Morris
American. Sociologist, Political Scientist
Noted for his work in sociological theory and post-WW II civil-military concerns.
b. Oct 22, 1919 in Paterson, New Jersey
d. Nov 7, 1988 in Chicago, Illinois
Source: *AmMWSc 73S, 78S; BioIn 16; ConAu 13R, 127; NewYTBS 88; RAdv 14; WhAm 9; WhoAm 74, 76, 78, 86, 88; WhoMW 84; WhoWor 74*

Janowitz, Tama
American. Writer
Best-selling author of *Slaves of New York,* 1986; starred in the first "literary video" on MTV, *A Cannibal in Manhattan,* 1987.
b. Apr 12, 1957 in San Francisco, California
Source: *BioIn 12, 15, 16; CelR 90; ConAu 52NR, 106; ConLC 43; ConNov 91, 96; ConPopW; CurBio 89; DrAPF 91; LegTOT; OxCWoWr 95; WhoUSWr 88; WhoWrEP 89, 92, 95; WorAu 1985; WrDr 90, 92, 94, 96*

Jansen, Cornelis Otto
Flemish. Theologian
Founded Roman Catholic reform movement or Jansenism.
b. Oct 28, 1585 in Acquoi, Netherlands
d. May 6, 1638, Spanish Netherlands
Source: *McGEWB; NewCol 75*

Jansen, Dan
American. Skater
Won gold medal, made world record in 1000 meter event, 1994 Olympics.
b. Jun 17, 1965 in Milwaukee, Wisconsin
Source: *CurBio 94*

Janson, Horst Woldemar
American. Educator, Author
Wrote *History of Art,* 1962.
b. Oct 4, 1913 in Saint Petersburg, Russia
d. Sep 30, 1982
Source: *AnObit 1982; AuBYP 2, 3; BioIn 8, 10, 11, 13, 14; ConAu 1R; DrAS 74H, 78H, 82H; NewYTBS 82; SmATA 9; WhAm 8; WhoAm 74, 76, 78, 80; WhoAmA 73, 76, 78, 80, 82, 84N, 86N, 89N, 91N, 93N; WhoArt 80, 82, 84; WhoWor 74, 76; WrDr 76, 80*

Janssen, David
[David Harold Meyer]
American. Actor
Starred in TV series "The Fugitive," 1963-67; "Harry-O," 1974-76.
b. Mar 27, 1931 in Naponee, Nebraska
d. Feb 13, 1980 in Malibu Beach, California
Source: *ASCAP 80, 78, 79, 80; MotPP; MovMk; WhAm 7; WhoAm 74, 78, 80; WhoHol A; WhoWor 74; WhScrn 83*

Janssen, Herbert
American. Opera Singer
Baritone, N.Y. Met., 1939-51; Wagnerian soloist.
b. Sep 22, 1895 in Cologne, Germany
d. Jun 3, 1965 in New York, New York
Source: *Baker 78, 84; BioIn 1, 7, 10; CmOp; NewEOp 71; PenDiMP*

Janssen, Pierre Jules Cesar
French. Astronomer
Established Mont Blanc observatory, 1893; pioneered in celestial photography.
b. Feb 22, 1824 in Paris, France
d. Dec 23, 1907 in Meudon, France
Source: *AsBiEn; BiESc; BioIn 14; DcScB; InSci; MacBEP; NewCol 75; WhDW*

Janssen, Werner
American. Conductor, Composer
Organized Hollywood's Janssen Symphony, 1940-52; wrote "New Year's Eve in New York," 1952.
b. Jun 1, 1899 in New York, New York
d. Sep 21, 1990 in New York, New York
Source: *ASCAP 66, 80; Baker 78, 84, 92; BioIn 4, 17; ConAmC 76, 82; DcCM; FacFETw; HalFC 84, 88; NewAmDM; NewGrDA 86; NewGrDM 80; PenDiMP; WhoAm 74*

Jantzen, Carl
American. Manufacturer
Invented rib-stitch method of making bathing suits; co-founded int'l line of swim wear, 1925.
b. 1883, Denmark
d. 1939
Source: *Entr*

January, Don(ald)
American. Golfer
Turned pro, 1956; won PGA, 1967.
b. Nov 20, 1929 in Plainview, Texas
Source: *BioIn 12, 21; NewYTBS 80; WhoAm 78, 80, 82; WhoGolf*

Janzen, Daniel Hunt
American. Biologist, Educator
Since mid 1960s has experimented with growing a tropical forest in Costa Rica; professor of biology, U of PA, 1976—.
b. Jan 18, 1939 in Milwaukee, Wisconsin
Source: *AmMWSc 73P, 76P, 79, 82, 86, 89, 92, 95; BioIn 16; IntWW 89, 91, 93; WhoAm 82, 86, 88, 90, 92, 94, 95, 96; WhoTech 89*

Japrisot, Sebastien
[Jean Baptiste Rossi]
French. Author
Writer of mystery novels including *Trap for Cinderella,* 1962.
b. 1931
Source: *BioIn 16; ConLC 90; TwCCr&M 80B, 85B, 91B*

Jardine, Al(lan)
[The Beach Boys]
American. Singer, Musician
Vocalist, guitarist; hits with group include *Ten Years of Harmony,* 1981.
b. Sep 3, 1942 in Lima, Ohio
Source: *BioIn 11; BkPepl; RolSEnR 83; WhoRocM 82*

Jarman, Claude, Jr.
American. Actor
Won special Oscar for debut in *The Yearling,* 1946.
b. Sep 27, 1934 in Nashville, Tennessee
Source: *BioIn 10, 78, 79, 80, 81, 82, 84, 86, 88, 92, 94, 96; MGM; MotPP; MovMk; VarWW 85; What 4; WhoHol 92, A*

Jarman, Derek
English. Filmmaker
Films include *The Angelic Conversation,* 1985; *Edward II,* 1991.
b. 1942 in Northwood, England
d. 1994
Source: *BiDFilm 94; BioIn 16, 17, 18, 19, 20; ConAu 144; ConTFT 9, 13; DcArts; EncEurC; GayLesB; HalFC 88; IntDcF 2-2; IntWW 89, 91, 93; MiSFD 9; TwCPaSc; Who 88, 90, 92, 94*

Jarman, John
American. Politician
Dem. congressman from OK, 1951-77.
b. Jul 17, 1915 in Sallisaw, Oklahoma
d. Jan 15, 1982 in Oklahoma City, Oklahoma
Source: *BiDrAC; WhoSSW 73, 75, 76*

Jarmusch, Jim
American. Filmmaker
Director whose fresh approach to storytelling won the Camera d'Or at Cannes for *Stranger than Paradise,* 1984; other films include *Mystery Train,* 1989.
b. 1953 in Akron, Ohio
Source: *BiDFilm 94; BioIn 14, 15, 16; ConAu 132; ConTFT 3, 9; CurBio 90; IntDcF 2-2; IntMPA 88, 92, 94, 96; IntWW 91, 93; LegTOT; MiSFD 9; WhoEnt 92; WrDr 94*

Jaroszewicz, Piotr
Polish. Politician
Chm., Council of Ministers, 1970-80; pres., Chief Council of Union of Fighters for Freedom and Democracy, 1972-80.
b. Oct 8, 1909 in Nieswicz, Poland
d. Sep 2, 1992 in Warsaw, Poland
Source: *AnObit 1992; BioIn 12, 18, 19; IntWW 74, 75, 76, 77, 78, 79, 80, 81, 82, 83; NewYTBE 70; WhoSocC 78; WhoSoCE 89; WhoWor 74, 76, 78*

Jarre, Jean-Michel
French. Composer, Musician
Writes synthesizer music influenced by new instruments, foreign cultures, outer space; albums include *Oxygene,* 1977.
b. Aug 24, 1948, France
Source: *ConMus 2; EncRkSt; IntWW 91; LegTOT; NewAgMG*

Jarre, Maurice
French. Composer
Won Oscars for scores *Lawrence of Arabia,* 1962; *Doctor Zhivago,* 1966.
b. Sep 13, 1924 in Lyons, France
Source: *Baker 78, 84, 92; BioIn 18; CmMov; ConTFT 5, 12; DcFM; FilmEn; FilmgC; HalFC 80, 84, 88; IntDcF 1-4, 2-4; IntMPA 75, 76, 77, 78, 79, 80, 81, 82, 84, 86, 88, 92, 94, 96; ItaFilm; LegTOT; MusMk; NewAmDM; NewGrDM 80; OxCFilm; OxCPMus; VarWW 85; WorEFlm*

Jarreau, Al(wyn Lopez)
"Acrobat of Scat"
American. Singer, Songwriter
Jazz vocalist known for ability to mimic musical instruments; had million-selling album *Breakin' Away,* 1981.
b. Mar 12, 1940 in Milwaukee, Wisconsin
Source: *AfrAmBi 2; Baker 92; BioIn 11, 12; ConAu 116, 117; ConMus 1; CurBio 92; DrBlPA 90; EncRkSt; IlEncBM 82; InB&W 80, 85; LegTOT; NewGrDA 86; NewGrDJ 88, 94; PenEncP; RkOn 85; SoulM; VarWW 85; WhoAfA 96; WhoAm 80, 82, 84, 86, 88, 90, 92, 94, 95, 96, 97; WhoBlA 77, 80, 85, 88, 90, 92, 94; WhoEnt 92; WorAlBi*

Jarrell, Randall
American. Author, Poet
Noted for critical writing: *The Woman at the Washington Zoo,* 1960.
b. May 6, 1914 in Nashville, Tennessee
d. Oct 14, 1965 in Chapel Hill, North Carolina
Source: *AmAu&B; AmCulL; AmWr; AnCL; AuBYP 2, 3; Benet 87, 96; BenetAL 91; BioIn 3, 4, 5, 7, 8, 9, 10, 11, 12, 13, 14, 15, 16, 17, 19; CamGLE; CamHAL; CasWL; ChhPo, S1, S3; ChlBkCr; ChlLR 6; CnDAL; CnE&AP; ConAu 2BS, 5R, 6NR, 25R, 34NR; ConLC 1, 2, 6, 9, 13, 49; ConLCrt 77, 82; ConPo 75, 80A, 85A; CroCAP; DcAmB S7; DcAmChF 1960; DcLB 48, 52; DcLEL 1940; DcNCBi 3; DcTwCCu 1; EncWB; EncWL, 2, 3; FacFETw; FifSWrA; GrWrEL P; LegTOT; LinLib L; MajAI; MajTwCW; ModAL, S1, S2; NewCon; Novels; OxCAmL 65, 83, 95; OxCChiL; OxCEng 85, 95; OxCTwCP; PenC AM; RAdv 1, 14, 13-1; REn; REnAL; RfGAmL 87, 94; RGFAP; RGTwCWr; ScF&FL 1, 2; SixAP; SmATA 7; SouWr; ThrBJA; TwCA SUP; TwCChW 78, 83, 89, 95; TwCWr; WebAB 74, 79; WebE&AL; WhAm 4; WhoAmA 89N, 91N, 93N; WhoTwCL; WorAl; WorAlBi*

Jarrett, Keith
American. Musician
Noted jazz pianist, 1960s-70s; specialized in Bartok performances, 1980s.
b. May 8, 1945 in Allentown, Pennsylvania
Source: *AllMusG; Baker 84, 92; BiDAmM; BiDJaz; BioIn 11, 12, 13; ConAmC 76, 82; ConMus 1; CurBio 85; DcArts; EncJzS; IntWW 78, 79, 80, 81, 82, 83, 89, 91, 93; IntWWM 90; LegTOT; NewAmDM; NewGrDA 86; NewGrDJ 88, 94; News 92; NewYTBS 79; PenEncP; WhoAm 74, 80, 82, 84, 86, 88, 92, 94, 95, 96, 97; WhoAmM 83; WhoEnt 92; WhoRock 81*

Jarriel, Tom
[Thomas Edwin Jarriel]
American. Broadcast Journalist
Correspondent, ABC News since 1965; contributor to "20/20."
b. Dec 29, 1934 in La Grange, Georgia
Source: *ConAu 109, 120; ConTFT 13; NewYTET; VarWW 85; WhoAm 76, 78, 84, 86, 88, 92, 94, 95, 96, 97; WhoE 95; WhoTelC*

Jarring, Gunnar Valfrid
Swedish. Diplomat
Ambassador to US, 1958-64; to USSR, 1964-73; to Mongolia, 1965-73; special representative to UN, 1967-91.
b. Oct 12, 1907 in Brunnby, Sweden
Source: *BioIn 4, 5, 8, 9; CurBio 57; IntYB 78, 79, 80, 81, 82; NewYTBE 70; Who 85; WhoUN 75; WhoWor 82, 84*

Jarry, Alfred
French. Poet, Dramatist
Wrote first theatrical work of the absurd: *Ubu Roi,* 1896.
b. Oct 8, 1873 in Laval, France
d. Nov 1, 1907 in Paris, France
Source: *Benet 87; BioIn 1, 2, 4, 5, 7, 9, 14; CamGWoT; CasWL; ClDMEL 47, 80; CnMD; CnThe; ConAu 104, 153; CyWA 89; DcArts; DcPup; DcTwCCu 2; EncSF, 93; EncWL, 2, 3; EncWT; Ent; EuAu; EuWr 9; EvEuW; FacFETw; GrFLW; GuFrLit 1; LngCTC; MajMD 2; McGEWD 72, 84; ModFrL; ModRL; ModWD; NotNAT B; OxCFr; OxCThe 67, 83; PenC EUR; RComWL; REn; REnWD; ScF&FL 92; ShSCr 20; TwCLC 2, 14; WhDW; WhoTwCL; WorAlBi*

Jaruzelski, Wojciech Witold
Polish. Political Leader
Career soldier; head of Poland, 1981-90.
b. Jul 6, 1923 in Kurow, Poland
Source: *BioIn 12, 13; CurBio 82; NewYTBS 81, 84; WhoSocC 78; WhoWor 87; WorDWW*

Jarvi, Neemi
Estonian. Conductor
Music director, Detroit Symphony Orchestra, 1990—.
b. Jun 7, 1937 in Tallinn, Estonia
Source: *CurBio 93*

Jarvik, Robert Koffler
American. Physician, Inventor
Designed Jarvik-7, artificial heart, 1972; first used in Barney Clark, 1982.
b. May 11, 1946 in Midland, Michigan
Source: *BioIn 12, 13; ConNews 85-1; CurBio 85; IntWW 89, 91, 93; LegTOT; NewYTBS 82; WhoAm 84, 86; WhoWest 87; WhoWor 87*

Jarvis, Anna
American. Social Reformer
Founded Mother's Day to commemorate anniversary of mother's death.
b. May 1, 1864 in Grafton, West Virginia
d. Nov 24, 1948 in West Chester, Pennsylvania
Source: *WomWWA 14*

Jarvis, Doug(las)
Canadian. Hockey Player
Center, 1975—; broke Garry Unger's NHL record for consecutive games played, 1986; streak ended at 964, 1987.
b. Mar 24, 1955 in Brantford, Ontario, Canada
Source: *BioIn 15; HocEn; HocReg 86, 87*

Jarvis, Gregory
American. Astronaut
Crew member who died in explosion of space shuttle, *Challenger.*
b. Aug 24, 1944 in Detroit, Michigan
d. Jan 28, 1986 in Cape Canaveral, Florida
Source: *ConHero 1; NewYTBS 86; WhoSpc*

Jarvis, Howard Arnold
American. Social Reformer
Force behind CA's Proposition 13, which reduced property taxes 57%, 1978.
b. Sep 22, 1902 in Magna, Utah
d. Aug 11, 1986 in Los Angeles, California
Source: *BioIn 11, 12; CurBio 79; NewYTBS 78; WhAm 9*

Jarvis, John Wesley
American. Artist
Noted for full-length portraits of military heroes; nephew of John Wesley.
b. 1781 in South Shields, England
d. Jan 14, 1839 in New York, New York
Source: *AmBi; BioIn 1, 2, 9; DcAmB; EarABI; EncWM; WhAm HS*

Jason, Rick
American. Actor
Starred in TV series "Combat," 1962-67.
b. May 21, 1926 in New York, New York
Source: *FilmgC; ForYSC; IntMPA 75, 76, 77, 78, 79, 80, 81, 82, 84, 86, 88, 92, 94, 96; MotPP; VarWW 85; WhoHol A*

Jasper, John J
American. Clergy
Minister, Sixth Mount Zion Church, Richmond, VA; wrote sermon "De Sun Do Move," 1850.
b. Jul 4, 1812 in Fluvanna County, Virginia
d. Mar 28, 1901
Source: *BioIn 3, 6, 8; REnAL*

Jaspers, Karl
German. Author, Philosopher, Physician, Educator
Promoted existentialism; influenced modern theology, psychiatry.
b. Feb 23, 1883 in Oldenburg, Germany
d. Feb 26, 1969 in Basel, Switzerland
Source: *Benet 87, 96; BioIn 3, 4, 8, 9, 10, 12, 14, 18, 19, 21; CasWL; ConAu 25R, 122; EncTR, 91; FacFETw; IntEnSS 79; LegTOT; LuthC 75; McGEWB; OxCGer 76, 86; OxCPhil; RAdv 14, 13-4; REn; ThTwC 87; TwCA SUP; TwCWr; WhAm 9; WhDW; WorAlBi; WrPh P*

Jastrow, Robert
American. Author, Astronomer
Writings include *Until the Sun Dies,* 1977; *The Enchanted Loom,* 1981.
b. Sep 7, 1925 in New York, New York
Source: *AmMWSc 73P; WhoScEn 94, 96; WhoWor 74; WorAu 1975; WrDr 76, 80, 82, 84, 86, 88, 90, 92, 94, 96*

Jaures, Jean Leon
French. Political Leader
Co-founded French Socialist Party, 1905; assassinated by patriotic fanatic.
b. Sep 3, 1859 in Castres, France
d. Jul 31, 1914 in Paris, France
Source: *Benet 87, 96; BiDFrPL; BiDMoPL; BioIn 1, 2, 4, 6, 10; DcAmSR; McGEWB; NewCol 75; OxCFr; REn; WhDW; WhoMilH 76*

Jausovec, Mima
Yugoslav. Tennis Player
Winner French Open, 1977; Italian Open, 1976.
b. Jul 20, 1956 in Maribor, Yugoslavia
Source: *WhoIntT*

Javits, Jacob Koppel
American. Politician
Liberal Rep. senator from NY, 1956-80, who championed civil rights, ERA.
b. May 18, 1904 in New York, New York
d. Apr 7, 1986 in West Palm Beach, Florida
Source: *AmAu&B; BiDrAC; BiDrUSC 89; BioIn 1, 2, 4, 5, 7, 8, 9, 10, 11, 12, 13; CngDr 79; ColdWar 1; ConAu 1NR, 1R; CurBio 48, 58; IntWW 74, 75, 76, 77, 78, 79, 80, 81, 82, 83; JeAmHC; NewYTBS 74, 80; PolProf J, K, NF; WhAm 9; WhoAm 74, 76, 78, 80, 82, 84; WhoAmJ 80; WhoAmL 79; WhoAmP 73, 75, 77, 79, 81, 83, 85; WhoE 74, 75, 77, 79, 81; WhoGov 72, 75, 77; WhoWor 74, 78, 80, 82, 84; WorAl*

Jawara, Alhaji Dawda Kairaba, Sir
Gambian. Political Leader
Leader, People's Progressive Party, Gambia, 1960—; first prime minister, 1966-70; president, 1970-1994; vice president, Senegambia Confederati on, 1982—.
b. May 16, 1924 in Barajally, Gambia
Source: *McGEWB; Who 85; WhoWor 84*

Jaworski, Leon
American. Government Official, Lawyer
Special Watergate prosecutor, 1973-74; prosecutor at Nuremberg trials.
b. Sep 19, 1905 in Waco, Texas
d. Dec 9, 1982 in Wimberley, Texas
Source: *AmDec 1970; WhoSSW 73; WorAl; WorAlBi*

Jaworski, Ron(ald Vincent)
"The Polish Rifle"
American. Football Player
Quarterback, 1974—, mostly with Philadelphia.
b. Mar 23, 1951 in Lackawanna, New York
Source: *BioIn 12; FootReg 87; WhoAm 82, 84*

Jay, John
American. Supreme Court Justice
First chief justice of Supreme Court, 1789-95; wrote five *Federalist* papers.
b. Dec 12, 1745 in New York, New York
d. May 17, 1829 in Bedford, New York
Source: *Alli; AmAu&B; AmBi; AmJust; AmPolLe; AmRev; AmWrBE; ApCAB; Benet 87, 96; BenetAL 91; BiAUS; BiDFedJ; BiDrAC; BiDrGov 1789; BiDrUSC 89; BiDrUSE 71, 89; BioIn 1, 2, 3, 4, 5, 6, 7, 8, 9, 10, 11, 12, 14, 15, 16; CopCroC; CyAG; CyAL 1; CyWA 58; DcAmAu; DcAmB; DcAmC; DcAmDH 80; DcAmSR; DcBiPP; DcLB 31; DcNAA; Drake; EncAAH; EncAB-H 1974, 1996; EncAR; EncCRAm; EncEnl; HarEnUS; HisWorL; LegTOT; LinLib L, S; McGEWB; MorMA; NatCAB 1; OxCAmH; OxCAmL 65, 83, 95; OxCLaw; OxCSupC; RComAH; REn; REnAL; SupCtJu; TwCBDA; WebAB 74, 79; WhAm HS; WhAmP; WhAmRev; WorAl; WorAlBi*

Jay, Karla
American. Educator, Writer
Series editor of New York University's *The Cutting Edge: Lesbian Life and Literature.*
b. Feb 22, 1947 in New York, New York
Source: *ConAu 85; GayLesB; GayLL; WhoE 95*

Jay, Peter
English. Editor, Broadcaster
Chm., Nat. Council for Voluntary Organizations, 1981-86; editor, *Banking World,* 1983-86; broadcaster, BBC, 1990—.
b. Feb 7, 1937 in London, England

Source: *BioIn 11; BlueB 76; ConAu 109; CurBio 78; EncSF 93; IntAu&W 86, 89, 91, 93; IntWW 76, 77, 78, 79, 80, 81, 82, 83, 89, 91, 93; IntYB 78, 79, 80, 81, 82; NewYTBS 78; ScF&FL 92; Who 74, 82, 83, 85, 88, 90, 92, 94; WhoFI 89; WhoWor 76, 78, 91; WrDr 86, 88, 90, 92, 94*

Jay, Ricky
American. Magician
Began performing at age seven; star of many stage, film, and television performances; performed in show *Ricky Jay & His 52 Assistants.*
b. c. 1949 in New York, New York
Source: *ConTFT 14; CurBio 94; News 95, 95-1*

Jay and the Americans
[David "Jay" Black; Sandy Deane; Howie Kane; Marty Sander; John "Jay" Traynor; Kenny Vance]
American. Music Group
Clean-cut, Brooklyn-based group; hits included "Cara Mia," 1965; "This Magic Moment," 1969.
Source: *BiDAmM; ConMuA 80A; EncPR&S 89; EncRk 88; NewAmDM; PenEncP; RkOn 74; RolSEnR 83; WhoHol 92; WhoRock 81; WhoRocM 82*

Jayewardene, J(unius) R(ichard)
Sri Lankan. Political Leader
Exec. pres., Sri Lanka, 1978-88; committed to Western-style democracy, free enterprise system.
b. Sep 17, 1906 in Colombo, Ceylon
d. Nov 1, 1996 in Colombo, Sri Lanka
Source: *BioIn 13; CurBio 84; EncWB; FacFETw; IntWW 93; IntYB 78, 79, 80, 81, 82; Who 82, 83, 85, 88, 90, 92, 94; WhoWor 78, 80, 82, 84, 87, 89, 91*

Jayston, Michael
[Michael James]
English. Actor
Best known for film *Nicholas and Alexandra,* 1971.
b. Oct 29, 1936 in Nottingham, England
Source: *ConTFT 5; FilmgC; HalFC 80, 84, 88; VarWW 85; WhoHol A; WhoThe 72, 77, 81*

Jeakins, Dorothy
American. Designer
Won Oscars for costumes in *Samson and Delilah,* 1950; *The Night of the Iguana,* 1964.
b. Jan 11, 1914 in San Diego, California
d. Nov 21, 1995 in Santa Barbara, California
Source: *BiE&WWA; BioIn 21; ConTFT 1, 10, 15; IntDcF 1-4, 2-4; NewYTBS 95; NotNAT*

Jean, Prince
[Jean Benoit Guillaume Marie Robert Louis Antoin d'Aviano]
Luxembourg. Ruler
Grand Duke of Luxembourg, 1964—; son of Charlotte, Felix; married Princess Josephine Charlotte.
b. Jan 5, 1921 in Colmar, France
Source: *BioIn 3, 17; IntWW 74, 75; NewCol 75; WhoWor 74, 76, 78, 80, 82, 84, 87, 89, 91, 93, 95, 96, 97*

Jeanmaire, Renee Marcelle
"Zizi"
French. Actor, Dancer, Singer
Wife of Roland Petit and leading dancer of Ballets Roland Petit, Casino de Paris.
b. Apr 29, 1924 in Paris, France
Source: *CurBio 52; FilmEn; IntWW 74, 75, 76, 77, 78, 79, 80, 81, 82, 83, 89, 91; WhoWor 82*

Jeans, James Hopwood, Sir
English. Mathematician, Astronomer
Considerable work done on kinetic theory of gases, multiple star systems, radiation.
b. Sep 11, 1877 in Lancashire, England
d. Sep 17, 1946 in Dorking, England
Source: *AsBiEn; BiESc; BioIn 1, 2, 3, 4, 5; Chambr 3; CurBio 41, 46; DcLEL; DcNaB 1941; DcScB; EvLB; GrBr; InSci; LarDcSc; LinLib L, S; LngCTC; LuthC 75; McGEWB; NewC; NewCBEL; OxCEng 67; TwCA, SUP; WebBD 83; WhLit; WorAl*

JEB
[Joan E(lisabeth) Biren]
American. Photographer
Photographs published in *Eye to Eye: Portraits of Lesbians,* 1979.
b. Jul 13, 1944 in Washington, District of Columbia
Source: *GayLesB*

Jeffers, (John) Robinson
American. Poet, Dramatist
Verse expressed contempt for human society; wrote *Medea,* 1946; *Give Your Heart to the Hawks,* 1933.
b. Jan 10, 1887 in Pittsburgh, Pennsylvania
d. Jan 20, 1962 in Carmel, California
Source: *AmAu&B; AmWr S2; AtlBL; Benet 87, 96; BenetAL 91; BioIn 1, 2, 3, 4, 5, 6, 7, 8, 9, 10, 11, 12, 14, 15, 16, 17; CamGEL; CamGLE; CamHAL; CasWL; ChhPo S1, S2, S3; CmCal; CnDAL; CnE&AP; CnMD; CnMWL; ConAmA; ConAmL; ConAu 35NR, 85; ConLC 2, 3, 11, 15, 54; CyWA 58; DcAmB S7; DcArts; DcLB 45; DcLEL; Dis&D; EncWL 2, 3; EncWT; EvLB; FacFETw; FifWWr; GrWrEL P; LegTOT; LinLib L, S; LngCTC; MagSAmL; MajTwCW; McGEWB; McGEWD 72, 84; ModAL, S1, S2; ModWD; NotNAT A, B; OxCAmL 65, 83, 95; OxCAmT 84; OxCEng 67, 85, 95; OxCTwCP; PenC AM; PeoHis; RAdv 1, 14, 13-1; REn; REnAL; RfGAmL 87, 94; RGFAP; RGTwCWr; SixAP; Tw; TwCA, SUP; TwCWr; WebAB 74, 79; WebE&AL; WhAm 4; WhDW; WhLit; WhNAA; WhoTwCL; WorAl; WorAlBi; WorLitC; WrPh*

Jefferson, Blind Lemon
American. Singer
Country-blues singer, 1920s; album issued 1968: *Blind Lemon Jefferson: 1926-29.*
b. Jul 11, 1897 in Couchman, Texas
d. Dec 29, 1929 in Chicago, Illinois
Source: *Baker 84, 92; BiDAmM; DcTwCCu 5; DrBlPA, 90; IlEncJ; LegTOT; NewAmDM; NewGrDA 86; NewGrDM 80; OnThGG; PenEncP; RolSEnR 83; WorAl; WorAlBi*

Jefferson, John Larry
American. Football Player
Four-time all-pro wide receiver, 1978-85; led NFL in receiving, 1980, in TDs, 1978, 1980.
b. Feb 3, 1956 in Dallas, Texas
Source: *BiDAmSp FB; FootReg 86; WhoAm 82, 84, 86; WhoBlA 80*

Jefferson, Joseph
American. Actor
Identified with title role in play *Rip Van Winkle;* had 72-yr. stage career.
b. Feb 20, 1829 in Philadelphia, Pennsylvania
d. Apr 23, 1905 in Palm Beach, Florida
Source: *AmAu&B; AmBi; ApCAB; BbD; BenetAL 91; BiD&SB; BioIn 1, 2, 3, 4, 5, 7, 8, 11, 13; CamGWoT; CelCen; DcAmAu; DcAmB; DcNAA; Drake; EncWT; Ent; FamA&A; Film 1; HarEnUS; IntDcT 3; McGEWB; MemAm; NatCAB 1; NewYHSD; NotNAT A, B; OxCAmH; OxCAmL 65, 83, 95; OxCAmT 84; OxCThe 67, 83; PlP&P; REnAL; REnWD; TwCBDA; WebAB 74, 79; WhAm 1; WhAmArt 85; WhoHol B; WhScrn 77, 83*

Jefferson, Martha
[Mrs. Thomas Mann Randolph]
American.
Eldest daughter of Thomas Jefferson; headed father's household after mother's death.
b. Sep 27, 1772 in Albemarle County, Virginia
d. Oct 10, 1836 in Washington, District of Columbia
Source: *BioIn 11; HerW; NatCAB 3, 5; NotAW*

Jefferson, Martha Wayles Skelton
[Mrs. Thomas Jefferson]
American.
Married Thomas Jefferson, Jan 1, 1772; died before he became pres., 1801.
b. Oct 19, 1748 in Charles City, Virginia
d. Sep 6, 1782 in Albemarle County, Virginia
Source: *AmWom; ApCAB; BioIn 8, 9, 16, 17; EncSoH; FacPr 89; NatCAB 3; NotAW; TwCBDA; WhAm HS, HSA*

Jefferson, Mary
[Mrs. John Wayles Eppes]
"Marie"; "Polly"
American.
Daughter of Thomas Jefferson in constant competition with older sister, Martha; died in childbirth during father's second term as pres.
b. Aug 1, 1778 in Albemarle County, Virginia
d. Apr 17, 1804 in Albemarle County, Virginia
Source: *BioIn 1, 3, 6, 7*

Jefferson, Thomas
"Red Fox"
American. US President
Third pres., 1801-09; wrote Declaration of Independence, 1776; negotiated LA Purchase, 1803; organized Lewis, Clark expedition, 1803.
b. Apr 13, 1743 in Albemarle County, Virginia
d. Jul 4, 1826 in Albemarle County, Virginia
Source: *Alli; AmAu&B; AmBi; AmCulL; AmOrN; AmPolLe; AmRef; AmWrBE; ApCAB; AsBiEn; AtlBL; BbD; Benet 87, 96; BenetAL 91; BiAUS; BiDAmEd; BiDAmS; BiD&SB; BiDrAC; BiDrACR; BiDrUSC 89; BiDrUSE 71, 89; BiDSA; BiInAmS; BioIn 1, 2, 3, 4, 5, 6, 7, 8, 9, 10, 11, 12, 13, 14, 15, 16, 17, 18, 19, 20, 21; BlkwCE; BlkwEAR; BriEAA; CamGEL; CamGLE; CamHAL; CasWL; CelCen; Chambr 3; ChhPo S3; CmFrR; ColARen; CyAG; CyAL 1; CyEd; CyWA 58; DcAmAu; DcAmB; DcAmBC; DcAmC; DcAmDH 80, 89; DcAmLiB; DcAmReB 1, 2; DcBiPP; DcD&D; DcLB 31; DcLEL; DcNAA; DcScB; Dis&D; Drake; EncAAH; EncAAr 1, 2; EncAB-H 1974, 1996; EncAR; EncARH; EncCRAm; EncEnl; EncEth; EncRev; EncUnb; EncUrb; EvLB; FacPr 89, 93; FifSWrB; FolkA 87; HarEnUS; HealPre; HisWorL; InSci; IntDcAr; LegTOT; LinLib L; LuthC 75; MacEA; McGDA; McGEWB; MemAm; NatCAB 3; NewCBEL; NinCLC 11; OxCAmH; OxCAmL 65, 83, 95; OxCArt; OxCLaw; OxCPhil; OxCSupC; PenC AM; PolPar; PresAR; RAdv 14, 13-3; RComAH; RComWL; REn; REnAL; REnAW; RfGAmL 87, 94; SouWr; TwCBDA; TwoTYeD; VicePre; WebAB 74, 79; WebE&AL; WhAm HS; WhAmP; WhAmRev; WhDW; WhNaAH; WhoArch; WorAl; WorAlBi; WorInv*

Jefferson, Thomas
American. Actor
Son of Joseph Jefferson, 5th generation of theatrical family; entered films with D W Griffith, 1909.
b. 1859
d. Apr 2, 1923 in Hollywood, California
Source: *Film 1, 2; FilmEn; NotNAT B; TwYS; WhoHol B; WhScrn 74, 77, 83*

Jefferson Starship
[Marty Balin; John Barbata; Craig Chaquico; Papa John Creach; Aynsley Dunbar; David Freiberg; Paul Kantner; Jorma Kaukonen; Pete Sears; Grace Slick; Mickey Thomas]
American. Music Group
Founded, 1965, as Jefferson Airplane; several members formed Starship, 1974; best-selling hit "White Rabbit," 1967.
Source: *BioIn 9; ConMuA 80A; ConMus 5; EncPR&S 74, 89; EncRk 88; FacFETw; HarEnR 86; IlEncRk; PenEncP; RkOn 78, 84; RolSEnR 83; WhoAm 74; WhoRock 81; WhoRocM 82*

Jeffords, James Merrill
American. Politician
Rep. senator, VT, 1989—.
b. May 11, 1934 in Rutland, Vermont
Source: *AlmAP 92; BiDrUSC 89; IntWW 89, 91, 93; PolsAm 84; WhoAm 74, 76, 78, 80, 82, 84, 86, 88, 90, 92, 94, 95, 96, 97; WhoAmP 73, 75, 77, 79, 81, 83, 85, 87, 89, 91, 93, 95; WhoE 74, 77, 79, 81, 83, 85, 86, 89, 91, 93, 95, 97; WhoGov 72, 75, 77; WhoWor 91*

Jeffrey, Francis Jeffrey, Lord
Scottish. Author
Known for founding the *Edinburgh Review;* editor until 1829.
b. Oct 23, 1773 in Edinburgh, Scotland
d. Jan 26, 1850 in Edinburgh, Scotland
Source: *Alli; BbD; BiD&SB; BioIn 1, 4, 6, 10, 11; BritAu 19; CasWL; Chambr 3; CrtT 2; DcEnA; DcEnL; DcEuL; DcLEL; OxCLaw*

Jeffreys, Anne
[Mrs. Robert Sterling]
American. Actor
Played Marion Kerby in TV series "Topper," 1953-56, with husband.
b. Jan 26, 1923 in Goldsboro, North Carolina
Source: *BiE&WWA; BioIn 18; EncAFC; FilmEn; FilmgC; ForYSC; HalFC 80, 84, 88; IntMPA 82, 92, 94, 96; InWom, SUP; LegTOT; MotPP; MovMk; NotNAT; SweetSg C; VarWW 85; WhoHol 92, A; WhoThe 72, 77, 81; WorAl; WorAlBi*

Jeffreys, Garland
American. Singer, Songwriter
Soul singer who blends rock, jazz, reggae; album *Escape Artist,* 1981.
b. 1944 in New York, New York
Source: *BioIn 12, 19; IlEncBM 82; NewGrDA 86; PenEncP; RolSEnR 83*

Jeffries, James Jackson
"The Boilermaker"
American. Boxer, Actor
Won heavyweight championship of world, 1899-1904; retired undefeated, 1905.
b. Apr 15, 1875 in Carroll County, Ohio
d. Mar 3, 1953 in Burbank, California
Source: *BiDAmSp BK; BioIn 1, 2, 3, 5, 6, 9, 10, 11; DcAmB S5; Film 1; WhoPubR 76; WhScrn 77*

Jeffries, Leonard
American. Educator
City College, New York, professor of black studies, 1972—.
b. Jan 19, 1937 in Newark, New Jersey
Source: *ConBlB 8*

Jeffries, Lionel Charles
English. Actor
Character actor, 1950—; directed films including *The Railway Children,* 1971; *Water Babies,* 1979.
b. Jun 10, 1926 in London, England
Source: *FilmgC; MovMk; VarWW 85; Who 74, 82, 83, 85, 88, 90, 92, 94; WhoHol A; WhoWor 74*

Jeffries, Richard
English. Author
Wrote classic autobiography *Story of My Heart,* 1883.
b. Nov 6, 1848 in North Wiltshire, England
d. Aug 14, 1887 in Worthing, England
Source: *DcEuL; REn; WhoChL*

Jellicoe, Ann
[Patricia Ann Jellicoe]
English. Dramatist
Plays include *The Sport of My Mad Mother,* 1964.
b. Jul 15, 1927 in Middlesborough, England
Source: *ArtclWW 2; Benet 87; BioIn 9, 10, 12, 13; BlmGEL; BlmGWL; BlueB 76; CamGLE; CnThe; ConAu 85; ConDr 73, 77, 82, 88; ConLC 27; ConTFT 2; CroCD; DcLB 13; DcLEL 1940; EncBrWW; EncWT; FemiCLE; IntAu&W 76, 89, 91; LegTOT; McGEWD 72, 84; ModWD; NewC; NotNAT; OxCEng 85; REnWD; TwCChW 78, 83, 89; TwCWr; Who 74, 82, 83, 85, 88, 90, 92; WhoThe 72, 77, 81; WorAu 1950; WrDr 76, 80, 82, 84, 86, 88, 90, 92, 94, 96*

Jellicoe, John Rushworth
English. Naval Officer
Commanded Atlantic Fleet, 1910-16; governor general of New Zealand, 1920-24.
b. Dec 5, 1859 in Southampton, England
d. Nov 20, 1935 in Kensington, England
Source: *BioIn 12; DcNaB 1931; DcTwHis; FacFETw; GrBr; HarEnMi; LinLib S; McGEWB; OxCShps; WhE&EA; WhoLA*

Jellinek, Elvin Morton
American. Physiologist
Promoted scientific study of alcoholism.
b. Aug 15, 1890 in New York, New York
d. Oct 22, 1963 in Palo Alto, California
Source: *BioIn 1, 6, 7; CurBio 47, 64; DcAmTB; InSci; WhAm 4*

Jemison, Alice Mae
American. Political Activist
Oposed the Bureau of Indian Affairs, the Indian Reorganization Act, and the Selective Service Act.
b. Oct 9, 1901 in Cattaraugus Indian ReservaNew York
d. Mar 1964
Source: *BioIn 12, 21; NotNaAm*

Jemison, Mae C(arol)
American. Astronaut, Physician
First black woman astronaut selected by NASA, 1987; mission specialist, Discovery flight, 1991.
b. Oct 17, 1956 in Decatur, Alabama
Source: *BioIn 15, 16; BlksScM; ConBlB 1; CurBio 93; NegAl 89; News 93-1; NewYTBS 92; NotBlAW 1; WhoAmW 93; WhoBlA 92*

Jen, Gish
[Lillian Jen]
American. Author
Wrote *Typical American,* 1991, which focusses on cultural assimilation.
b. 1955
Source: *AsAmAlm; ConLC 70; NotAsAm; WhoAsA 94; WrDr 94, 96*

Jenco, Lawrence M
American. Hostage, Religious Figure
Roman Catholic priest taken hostage by Lebanese terrorist groups on Jan 8, 1985; released after 564 days on Jul 26, 1986.
b. Nov 27, 1934 in Joliet, Illinois
d. Jul 19, 1996 in Chicago, Illinois
Source: *BioIn 15*

Jenifer, Franklyn Green
American. University Administrator
Pres., Howard U, Washington, DC, 1990-94; succeeding James E. Cheek; pres., U of Texas, Dallas, 1994—.
b. Mar 26, 1939 in Washington, District of Columbia
Source: *BioIn 15; ConBlB 2; WhoAfA 96; WhoAm 90; WhoBlA 92, 94*

Jenkins, Allen
[Al McConegal]
American. Actor
Played character roles in 175 films from 1931.
b. Apr 9, 1900 in New York, New York
d. Jul 20, 1974 in Santa Monica, California
Source: *BioIn 4, 78, 79, 80, 81, 82; MovMk; OlFamFa; Vers A; What 4*

Jenkins, Carol Elizabeth Heiss
American. Skater
Five-time world champion figure skater, 1956-60; won gold medal, 1960 Olympics.
b. Jan 20, 1940 in New York, New York
Source: *BiDAmSp BK; CurBio 59; FilmgC; GoodHs; HerW*

Jenkins, Dave
[David W Jenkins]
American. Skater
Three-time world champion figure skater, 1957-59; won gold medal, 1960 Olympics.

Jenkins, Ferguson Arthur
"Fergie"
Canadian. Baseball Player
Pitcher, 1965-83; won at least 20 games for six straight seasons; won NL Cy Young Award, 1971; Hall of Fame, 1991.
b. Dec 13, 1943 in Chatham, Ontario, Canada
Source: *BiDAmSp Sup; BioIn 8, 9, 10, 11; NewYTBE 71; WhoAm 78, 80, 82, 84, 92, 94, 95, 96, 97; WhoBlA 85; WhoE 95; WhoProB 73*

Jenkins, Gordon
American. Composer, Conductor
Best known for 1945 composition *Manhattan Tower Suite,* in praise of NY.
b. May 12, 1910 in Webster Groves, Missouri
d. May 1, 1984 in Malibu, California
Source: *AnObit 1984; ASCAP 66, 80; Baker 84, 92; BiDAmM; BioIn 13, 14; CmpEPM; ConAu 112; OxCPMus; PenEncP; RadStar*

Jenkins, Hayes Alan
American. Skater
Four-time world champion figure skater, 1953-56; won gold medal, 1956 Olympics.
b. Mar 23, 1933 in Akron, Ohio
Source: *BiDAmSp BK; BioIn 4, 7, 17; CurBio 56; LegTOT; WhoAmL 90, 96; WhoSpor*

Jenkins, Newell
American. Conductor
Founded NY's Clarion Music Society, 1957.
b. Feb 8, 1915 in New Haven, Connecticut
d. Dec 24, 1996 in Hillsdale, New York
Source: *Baker 84; IntWWM 77, 80, 90; NewAmDM; NewGrDA 86; NewGrDM 80; WhoAm 90, 96; WhoAmM 83; WhoE 74, 75, 83, 85, 86, 89; WhoEnt 92*

Jenkins, Paul
American. Artist
Noted for "pouring" pigments on floor canvasses; wrote *Painters Country,* 1958.
b. Jul 12, 1923 in Kansas City, Missouri
Source: *AmArt; BioIn 5, 6, 7, 14; ConArt 77, 83, 89, 96; DcAmArt; DcCAA 71, 77, 88, 94; OxCTwCA; PrintW 83, 85; WhoAm 74, 76, 78, 82, 84, 86, 88, 90, 92, 94, 95, 96, 97; WhoAmA 73, 76, 78, 80, 82, 84, 86, 89, 91, 93; WhoE 81, 83; WhoWor 74, 76; WorArt 1950*

Jenkins, Ray Howard
American. Lawyer
Noted for insistent manner of questioning as Senate counsel in McCarthy hearings, 1954.
b. Mar 18, 1897 in Unaka, North Carolina
d. Dec 26, 1980 in Knoxville, Tennessee
Source: *BioIn 3, 7, 8, 9, 12; CurBio 54, 81; EncMcCE; WhAm 7; WhoAm 74*

Jenkins, Roy Harris
Welsh. Political Leader
Co-founder, Social Dem. Party in Britain, 1981; member, British House of Commons, 1948-87.
b. Nov 11, 1920 in Abersychan, Wales
Source: *Au&Wr 71; ColdWar 1; ConAu 13NR; CurBio 66, 82; DcLEL 1940; IntWW 83; IntYB 81; NewYTBE 70; OxCLaw; Who 85; WhoWor 84, 97; WorAu 1950; WrDr 86*

Jenner, Bruce
American. Track Athlete, Sportscaster
Won gold medal in decathlon, 1976 Olympics.
b. Oct 28, 1949 in Mount Kisco, New York
Source: *BioIn 11, 12, 13, 15; BkPepl; ConAu 110; CurBio 77; LegTOT; NewYTBS 76, 77, 78; VarWW 85; WhoAm 78, 80, 82, 84, 86, 88, 90, 92, 94, 95, 96, 97; WhoHol 92; WhoSpor; WhoWest 96; WorAl; WorAlBi*

Jenner, Edward
English. Physician
Discovered vaccine used against smallpox, 1796; paved way for science of immunology.
b. May 17, 1749 in Berkeley, England
d. Jan 26, 1823 in Berkeley, England
Source: *Alli; AsBiEn; BiDLA; BiESc; BiHiMed; BioIn 1, 2, 3, 4, 5, 6, 7, 8, 9, 10, 11, 12, 13, 14, 15, 18, 20; BlkwCE; CamDcSc; CelCen; DcBiPP; DcNaB, C; DcScB; EncEnl; InSci; LarDcSc; LinLib S; McGEWB; NewC; NewCBEL; NewCol 75; OxCMed 86; REn; WhDW; WorAl; WorAlBi; WorScD*

Jenner, William, Sir
English. Scientist, Engineer, Physician
Discovered separate identities of typhus, typhoid fevers, 1847; physician to Queen Victoria, 1861.
b. 1815 in Chatham, England
d. Dec 7, 1898
Source: *Alli SUP; BiHiMed; BioIn 2, 4, 9; CelCen; DcBiPP; DcNaB C, S1; InSci; OxCMed 86; WebBD 83*

Jenner, William Ezra
American. Politician
Ultraconservative Republican senator from IN, 1944-45, 1947-59.
b. Jul 21, 1908 in Marengo, Indiana
d. Mar 9, 1985 in Bedford, Indiana
Source: *BiDrAC; BiDrUSC 89; BioIn 2, 3, 4, 5, 11; CurBio 85; NewYTBS 85; WhAm 8*

Jenney, William LeBaron
"Father of the Skyscraper"
American. Architect, Engineer
Innovative construction methods resulted in design for skyscrapers.
b. Sep 25, 1832 in Fairhaven, Massachusetts
d. Jun 15, 1907 in Los Angeles, California
Source: *AmBi; ApCAB SUP; BiDAmAr; BioIn 3, 10, 11; DcAmB; DcNAA; EncAAr 1; EncMA; HarEnUS; MacEA; NatCAB 10; OxCAmH; TwCBDA; WebAB 74, 79; WhAm 1; WhDW; WhoArch; WorAl*

Jennings, Bill
[William Jennings]
Canadian. Hockey Executive
Pres., NY Rangers; spearheaded expansion of NHL, 1967; Jennings Trophy for goalies named in his honor; Hall of Fame, 1975.
Source: *Alli; BiDLA; BioIn 14; NewYHSD*

Jennings, Elizabeth Joan
English. Author
Writings include *Let's Have Some Poetry,* 1960; *Selected Poems,* 1979.
b. Jul 18, 1926 in Boston, England
Source: *Au&Wr 71; ConAu 61; ConLC 14; ConPo 85; LngCTC; ModBrL S1; NewC; PenC ENG; RAdv 1; TwCWr; WebE&AL; Who 85; WhoTwCL; WrDr 86*

Jennings, Gary
[Gayne Jennings]
American. Author
Books of juvenile non-fiction, self illustrated, include *March of the Gods,* 1976.
b. Sep 20, 1928 in Buena Vista, Virginia
Source: *AuBYP 2, 3; BioIn 8, 11, 12; ConAu 5R, 9NR, 29NR; SmATA 9; TwCRHW 90, 94*

Jennings, Hugh(ey Ambrose)
"Ee-Yah"
American. Baseball Player, Baseball Manager
Infielder, 1891-1903; managed Detroit, 1907-20, during Ty Cobb's prime; Hall of Fame, 1945.
b. Apr 2, 1870 in Pittston, Pennsylvania
d. Feb 1, 1928 in Scranton, Pennsylvania

Jennings, Paul Joseph
American. Labor Union Official
Co-founded International Union of Electrical Workers, 1949; on Nixon's "political opponents" list, 1970s.
b. Mar 19, 1918 in New York, New York
d. Sep 7, 1987 in West Hempstead, New York
Source: *BiDAmL; BiDAmLL; BioIn 8, 11, 12; CurBio 69, 87; PolProf J, NF; WhoLab 76*

Jennings, Peter (Charles)
Canadian. Broadcast Journalist
Anchor, "ABC World News Tonight," 1983—; recipient of 7 Emmy awards.
b. Jul 29, 1938 in Toronto, Ontario, Canada
Source: *BioIn 13, 14, 15, 16, 17, 18, 19, 21; CanWW 31; CelR 90; ConAu 114, 134; ConTFT 6; CurBio 83; EncTwCJ; IntMPA 88, 92, 94, 96; JrnUS; LegTOT; LesBEnT; VarWW 85; WhoAm 74, 76, 78, 80, 82, 84, 86, 88, 90, 92, 94, 95, 96, 97; WhoE 74, 91; WhoTelC*

Jennings, Talbot
American. Dramatist, Screenwriter
Co-authored screenplays *The Good Earth,* 1937; *Mutiny on the Bounty,* 1935.
b. 1895? in Shoshone, Ohio
d. May 30, 1985 in East Glacier Park, Montana
Source: *CmMov; ConAu 116; FilmEn; IntMPA 84; VarWW 85*

Jennings, Waylon
American. Singer
Country music singer; prominent in the outlaw movement; won 1969 Grammy for "MacArthur Park;" 1976 album *Wanted The Outlaw,* was first country LP to go platinum; wrote TV series "The Dukes of Hazzard," theme song, 1979.
b. Jun 15, 1937 in Littlefield, Texas
Source: *Baker 84; BgBkCoM; BiDAmM; BioIn 12, 13, 20; BkPepl; CelR 90; ConLC 21; ConMuA 80A; ConMus 4; CounME 74, 74A; CurBio 82; EncFCWM 69, 83; EncRk 88; HarEnCM 87; HarEnR 86; IlEncCM; IlEncRk; LegTOT; NewGrDA 86; OxCPMus; PenEncP; RkOn 78; RolSEnR 83; VarWW 85; WhoAm 78, 80, 82, 84, 86, 88, 94, 95, 96, 97; WhoHol A; WhoRock 81; WhoSSW 97; WorAlBi*

Jenrette, John Wilson, Jr.
American. Politician
Former congressman convicted in ABSCAM scandal, 1980; served two-year sentence, 1984-86.
b. May 19, 1936 in Conway, South Carolina
Source: *AlmAP 80; WhoSSW 76, 78, 80*

Jens, Salome
American. Actor
Films include *Angel Baby,* 1961; *Harry's War,* 1981.
b. May 8, 1935 in Milwaukee, Wisconsin
Source: *BiE&WWA; ConTFT 5; FilmEn; FilmgC; ForYSC; HalFC 80, 84, 88; IntMPA 84, 86, 88, 92, 94, 96; LegTOT; MotPP; NotNAT; VarWW 85; WhoEnt 92; WhoHol 92, A; WhoThe 72, 77, 81*

Jensen, Adolph
German. Composer
Published about 160 songs; similar to Schumann's works.
b. Jan 12, 1837 in Konigsberg, Germany
d. Jan 23, 1879 in Baden-Baden, Germany
Source: *Baker 84; NewGrDM 80; NewOxM; OxCMus*

Jensen, Alfred Julio
Guatemalan. Artist
Did bright, checkerboard works inspired by architecture, mathematical themes.
b. Dec 11, 1903 in Guatemala City, Guatemala
d. Apr 4, 1981 in Livingston, New Jersey
Source: *BioIn 7, 10, 12; DcCAA 77; FacFETw; WhAm 7; WhoAm 80; WhoAmA 78*

Jensen, Arthur Robert
American. Psychologist, Author
Writings include *Genetics and Education,* 1973; *Educational Differences,* 1973.
b. Aug 24, 1923 in San Diego, California
Source: *AmMWSc 73S, 78S; BioIn 8, 9, 10; BlueB 76; ConAu 1R, 2NR; CurBio 73; IntAu&W 89; IntWW 75, 76, 77, 78, 79, 80, 81, 82, 83, 89, 91, 93; LEduc 74; WhoAm 74, 76, 78, 80, 82, 84, 96, 97; WhoFrS 84; WhoWest 74, 76, 84, 87, 89, 94, 96; WhoWor 82; WrDr 76, 80, 82, 84, 86, 88, 90, 92, 94, 96*

Jensen, Jackie
[Jack Eugene Jensen]
"Golden Boy"
American. Baseball Player
Outfielder, 1950-61; led AL in RBIs three times; AL MVP, 1958.
b. Mar 9, 1927 in San Francisco, California
d. Jul 14, 1982 in Charlottesville, Virginia
Source: *Ballpl 90; BiDAmSp Sup; BioIn 2, 3, 5, 8, 10, 13; CmCal; CurBio 59, 82, 82N; NewYTBS 82; WhoSpor*

Jensen, Johannes Hans Daniel
German. Physicist, Educator
Shared Nobel Prize in physics, 1963, for developing shell model of atomic nucleus.
b. Jun 25, 1907 in Hamburg, Germany
d. Feb 11, 1973 in Heidelberg, Germany (West)
Source: *BiESc; BioIn 14, 15; WhoNob, 90, 95*

Jensen, Johannes Vilhelm
Danish. Author
Won Nobel Prize in literature, 1944, for multi-volume *Himmerlandshistorier.*
b. Jan 30, 1873 in Farso, Denmark
d. Nov 25, 1950 in Copenhagen, Denmark
Source: *Benet 87, 96; BioIn 1, 2, 3, 4, 5, 9; CasWL; ClDMEL 47, 80; CyWA 58; DcScanL; EncWL 2, 3; EvEuW; Novels; PenC EUR; REn; TwCA, SUP; TwCWr; WhAm 3; WhoNob, 90, 95; WorAl*

Jensen, Mike
[Michael C Jensen]
American. Broadcast Journalist
NBC News correspondent who specializes in business, economics.
b. Nov 1, 1934 in Chicago, Illinois
Source: *ConAu 49, 127; WhoAm 86; WhoEc 81; WhoTelC*

Jensen, Oliver Ormerod
American. Author, Editor
Co-founder, editor, *American Heritage* magazine, 1954-76, senior editor, 1976-80, 1983-86; wrote *Railroads in America,* 1975.
b. Apr 16, 1914 in Ithaca, New York
Source: *CurBio 45; DrAS 82H; IntAu&W 89; St&PR 75; WhoAm 74, 76, 78, 80, 82, 84, 86, 88, 90, 92, 94, 95, 96, 97; WhoE 74; WhoWor 74, 76*

Jensen, Virginia Allen
American. Author
Books for children include *Lars Peter's Birthday,* 1959; *Sara and the Door,* 1975.
b. Sep 21, 1927 in Des Moines, Iowa
Source: *ConAu 1NR, 45; SmATA 8*

Jepsen, Roger William
American. Politician
Conservative Rep. senator from IA, 1979-85.
b. Dec 23, 1928 in Cedar Falls, Iowa
Source: *AlmAP 80; BiDrUSC 89; CngDr 79, 81, 83; IntWW 83; WhoAm 80, 82, 84, 86, 88, 92; WhoAmP 73, 75, 77, 79, 81, 83, 85, 87, 89, 91, 93, 95; WhoFI 92; WhoMW 80, 82, 84, 86; WhoWor 80, 82, 84*

Jepson, Helen
American. Opera Singer
Soprano with NY Met., 1935-43.
b. Nov 25, 1906 in Akron, Ohio
Source: *Baker 84; BiDAmM; BioIn 4, 6, 10, 13; InWom, SUP; NewEOp 71; RadStar; WhoHol A*

Jeremiah
Hebrew. Prophet
One of major Old Testament prophets who foretold destruction of temple in Jerusalem.
b. 650BC in Anathoth, Judea
d. 570BC, Egypt
Source: *DcOrL 3; LegTOT; NewC; WhDW; WorAl; WorAlBi*

Jergens, Adele
American. Actor
Played brassy blonde in 50 B-films, including *The Day the World Ended,* 1956.
b. Nov 26, 1917 in New York, New York
Source: *BioIn 10, 18; EncAFC; FilmEn; FilmgC; IntMPA 82, 94, 96; InWom SUP; LegTOT; MotPP; SweetSg D; VarWW 85; What 5; WhoHol 92, A*

Jergens, Andrew
American. Manufacturer
Headed firm which made toilet soap, 1882.
b. 1852
d. Jan 1929
Source: *Entr*

Jerger, Alfred
Austrian. Opera Singer
Bass-baritone; recorded *Der Rosenkavalier* at age 80.
b. Jun 9, 1889 in Brunn, Austria
d. Nov 18, 1976 in Vienna, Austria
Source: *Baker 84, 92; BioIn 11; CmOp; MetOEnc; NewEOp 71; NewGrDM 80; NewGrDO; OxDcOp; PenDiMP*

Jeritza, Maria
[Mitzi Jedlicka]
American. Opera Singer
Soprano with NY Met., 1921-32; noted for her Tosca, Carmen.
b. Oct 6, 1887 in Brunn, Austria
d. Jul 10, 1982 in Orange, New Jersey
Source: *AnObit 1982; Baker 78, 84, 92; BioIn 1, 2, 3, 5, 8, 9, 11, 12, 13, 14, 15; CmOp; ConAu 107; FacFETw; IntDcOp; IntWWM 77, 80; InWom SUP; LegTOT; MetOEnc; MusSN; NewAmDM; NewEOp 71; NewGrDA 86; NewGrDM 80; NewGrDO; NewYTBS 82; OxDcOp; PenDiMP; WhAm 8; What 2*

Jerne, Niels Kaj
Danish. Scientist
Shared 1984 Nobel Prize in medicine; a leading immunologist, he was awarded for his three theories crucial to the field.
b. Dec 23, 1911 in London, England
Source: *AmMWSc 89, 92, 95; IntWW 83, 89, 91, 93; WhAm 11; Who 82, 83, 85, 88, 90, 92, 94; WhoAm 88, 90; WhoNob, 90, 95; WhoScEn 94; WhoWor 87, 89, 91, 93*

Jerome, Jerome Klapka
English. Author
Known for humorous novel, *Three Men in a Boat,* 1889; morality play, *Passing of the Third Floor Back,* 1908.
b. May 2, 1859 in Walsall, England
d. Jun 14, 1927 in Northampton, England
Source: *Alli SUP; BbD; BiD&SB; BioIn 2, 5, 10, 13; CasWL; Chambr 3; CyWA 58; DcBiA; DcEnA A; DcLEL; DcNaB 1922; EncWT; EvLB; GrBr; HalFC 80; LinLib S; LngCTC; McGEWD 72; MnBBF; ModBrL; ModWD; NewC; NewCBEL; NotNAT A, B; OxCEng 67; OxCThe 67, 83; PenC ENG; REn; TwCA; TwCWr; WhDW; WhLit; WhoStg 1908; WhThe*

Jerome, Saint
Roman. Religious Figure
Translated Bible into Latin; feast day: Sep 30.
b. 345 in Strido, Dalmatia
d. 420 in Bethlehem, Judea
Source: *CasWL; NewC; OxCEng 67; PenC CL; RComWL; REn*

Jerry Murad's Harmonicats
[Al Fiore; Don Les; Jerry Murad]
American. Music Group
Harmonica group best known for 1947 hit "Peg o' My Heart."
Source: *CmpEPM; RkOn 74*

Jerusalem, Siegfried
German. Opera Singer
World-class tenor specializing in Wagnerian roles.
b. Apr 17, 1940 in Oberhausen, Germany
Source: *Baker 84, 92; CurBio 92; IntDcOp; IntWW 89, 91, 93; IntWWM 85, 90; MetOEnc; NewGrDO; OxDcOp; PenDiMP*

Jessel, George Albert
American. Actor
Called "Toastmaster General" for many appearances as MC.
b. Apr 3, 1898 in New York, New York
d. May 24, 1981 in Los Angeles, California
Source: *AmPS B; ASCAP 66; BiE&WWA; BioNews 74; CmMov; CmpEPM; ConAu 89, 103; CurBio 43, 81; EncMT; NotNAT; TwYS; WebAB 74, 79; WhAm 7; WhoAm 80; WhoHol A*

Jessup, Philip Caryl
American. Diplomat
Member, US delegation to UN; helped negotiate end of Soviet blockade in Berlin, 1949.
b. Jan 5, 1897 in New York, New York
d. Jan 31, 1986 in Newtown, Pennsylvania
Source: *AmAu&B; BioIn 1, 2, 3, 5, 7; ConAu 77; CurBio 86; DcAmDH 80, 89; IntWW 74; REnAL; WebAB 74, 79; Who 74; WhoAm 76; WhoWor 74*

Jessup, Richard
American. Author
Wrote *The Cincinnati Kid,* 1964; movie starred Steve McQueen, 1965.
b. Jan 1, 1925 in Savannah, Georgia
d. Oct 22, 1982 in Nokomis, Florida
Source: *AmAu&B; BioIn 13, 14; ConAu 108; NewYTBS 82; TwCCr&M 85, 91; TwCWW 82, 91; WrDr 84*

Jesus Christ
[Anointed One; King of the Jews; Messiah; Son of God; Son of Man]
Roman. Religious Leader
Central figure of Christianity, one of world's largest, most influential religions; Christians believe him to be the "Son of God."
b. 4?BC in Bethlehem, Judea
d. 29?AD in Jerusalem, Judea
Source: *DcBiPP; McGEWB; NewCol 75; REn; WebBD 83; WhDW; WorAl*

Jeter, Michael
American. Actor
Won a 1990 Tony for *Grand Hotel;* plays Herman Styles on TV series "Evening Shade," 1990-94; Emmy award winner, 1992.
b. Sep 20, 1952 in Lawrenceberg, Tennessee
Source: *ConTFT 11; IntMPA 92, 94, 96; WhoAm 94, 95, 96, 97; WhoEnt 92; WhoHol 92*

Jethro Tull
[Mick Abrahams; Ian Anderson; Barriemore Barlow; Martin Barre; Clive Bunker; Glenn Cornick; John Evan; Jeffrey Hammond-Hammond]
English. Music Group
Successful rock/heavy metal band; popular 1970's singles include "Living in the Past," 1972; Grammy for *The Crest of a Knave,* 1988.
Source: *BioIn 11; ConMuA 80A; ConMus 8; EncPR&S 74, 89; EncRk 88; EncRkSt; HarEnR 86; IlEncRk; NewAmDM; OxCPMus; PenEncP; RkOn 78, 84; RolSEnR 83; WhoRock 81; WhoRocM 82*

Jett, Joan
[Joan Jett and the Blackhearts; The Runaways; Joan Larkin]
American. Singer, Musician
Had pop-heavy metal single "I Love Rock 'n Roll," 1982.
b. Sep 22, 1960 in Philadelphia, Pennsylvania
Source: *ConMus 3; ConTFT 4; CurBio 93; EncPR&S 89; EncRk 88; LegTOT; NewWmR; OnThGG; RkOn 85; RolSEnR 83; WhoHol 92; WhoRocM 82; WorAlBi*

Jewett, Frank Baldwin
American. Engineer, Business Executive
First pres., Bell Telephone Laboratories, Inc; did pioneer research on long-distance and transcontinental phone lines.
b. Sep 5, 1879 in Pasadena, California
d. Nov 18, 1949 in Summit, New Jersey
Source: *BioIn 1, 2, 3, 15; DcAmB S4; DcScB; InSci; NotTwCS; St&PR 87; WhAm 2; WhoAm 86; WhoTech 89*

Jewett, Henry
American. Actor
Built Repertory Theatre of Boston, 1924; first in US.
b. Jun 4, 1862 in Warrnambool, Australia
d. Jun 24, 1930 in West Newton, Massachusetts
Source: *NatCAB 22; WhoStg 1906, 1908*

Jewett, Sarah Orne
American. Author
Stories depict New England countryside charm; works include *A Country Doctor,* 1884; *The Life of Nancy,* 1895.
b. Sep 3, 1849 in South Berwick, Maine
d. Jun 24, 1909 in South Berwick, Maine
Source: *Alli SUP; AmAu; AmAu&B; AmBi; AmWom; AmWomWr, 92; AmWr; ApCAB; ArtclWW 2; AtlBL; AuBYP 2, 3; BbD; Benet 87, 96; BenetAL 91; BibAL; BiD&SB; BioAmW; BioIn 1, 2, 3, 4, 5, 6, 7, 8, 9, 11, 12, 13, 16, 17, 18, 19, 20, 21; BlmGWL; CamGEL; CamGLE; CamHAL; CarSB; CasWL; Chambr 3; ChhPo, S1, S2; CnDAL; ConAu 108, 127; ContDcW 89; CrtT 3, 4; CyWA 58; DcAmAu; DcAmB; DcBiA; DcLB 12, 74; DcLEL; DcNAA; Dis&D; EncAAH; EncWHA; EvLB; FemiCLE; FemiWr; GayLesB; GayN; GrLiveH; GrWomW; GrWrEL N; HanAmWH; HarEnUS; IntDcWB; InWom, SUP; JBA 34; LegTOT; LibW; LinLib L, S; MagSAmL; McGEWB; ModAL; ModAWWr; ModWoWr; NatCAB 1; NotAW; Novels; OxCAmL 65, 83, 95; OxCEng 67, 85, 95; OxCWoWr 95; PenC AM; PenNWW A; RAdv 1, 14, 13-1; REn; REnAL; RfGAmL 87; ShSCr 6; ShSWr; SmATA 15; TwCBDA; TwCLC 1, 22; WebAB 74, 79; WebE&AL; WhAm 1; WomFir; WomNov; WorAl; WorAlBi*

Jewison, Norman
American. Director
Best known for *Fiddler on the Roof,* 1971; won 3 Emmys.
b. Jul 21, 1926 in Toronto, Ontario, Canada
Source: *BiDFilm, 81, 94; CanWW 70, 79, 80; CelR 90; ConAu 113; ConTFT 1, 6; CurBio 79; EncAFC; FilmEn; FilmgC; HalFC 80, 84, 88; IlWWHD 1; IntDcF 1-2, 2-2; IntMPA 77, 82, 96; LegTOT; MiSFD 9; MovMk; NewYTET; OxCFilm; VarWW 85; WhoAm 82; WorAlBi; WorEFlm; WorFDir 2*

Jewtraw, Charlie
[Charles Jewtraw]
American. Skater
Won speed skating gold medal—the first event at the first Winter Olympics, 1924.
b. 1900?
d. Jan 26, 1996 in Hobe Sound, Florida
Source: *BioIn 13, 21; WhoSpor*

Jezebel
Phoenician. Princess
Wife of King Ahab; name is used symbolically for a wicked woman.
b. fl. 9th cent. BC
Source: *Benet 96; BioIn 2, 3, 4, 5, 6, 7, 11, 17, 19; ContDcW 89; DcBiPP; EncAmaz 91; GoodHs; InWom; LngCEL; NewCol 75; WebBD 83*

J Geils Band, The
[Stephen Jo Bladd; Magic Dick; Jerome Geils; Seth Justman; Danny Klein; Peter Wolf]
American. Music Group
Combined blues, doo-woop, rhythm and blues, pop; had hit album *Freeze-Frame,* single "Centerfold," 1981.
Source: *BioIn 7; HarEnR 86; NewAmDM; NewGrDA 86; RolSEnR 83; WhoRocM 82; WhoWor 89*

Jhabvala, Ruth Prawer
British. Author
For over 25 yrs., part of the Merchant Ivory film-making team; won Oscar for *A Room with a View,* screenplay adaptation 1986; books include *Poet and Dancer,* 1993.
b. May 7, 1927 in Cologne, Germany
Source: *ArtclWW 2; Au&Wr 71; Benet 87, 96; BlmGWL; CamGLE; ConAu 1R, 2NR, 29NR, 51NR; ConLC 4, 8, 29, 94; ConNov 72, 76, 82, 86, 91, 96; ContDcW 89; ConTFT 1, 6, 13; CurBio 77; CyWA 89; DcArts; DcLB 139; DcLEL 1940; DrAPF 80; EncBrWW; EncEurC; EncWL 2, 3; FacFETw; GrLiveH; GrWomW; GrWrEL N; IntAu&W 76, 82, 91, 93; IntDcF 1-4, 2-4; IntLitE; IntMPA 88, 92, 94, 96; IntWW 77, 78, 79, 80, 81, 82, 83, 89, 91, 93; InWom SUP; LegTOT; LiExTwC; MajTwCW; ModCmwL; ModWoWr; NewC; NewYTBE 73; NewYTBS 83; Novels; OxCEng 85, 95; RAdv 13-2; RfGEnL 91; RGTwCWr; TwCRHW 94; TwCWr; Who 82, 83, 85, 88, 90, 92, 94; WhoAm 90, 92, 94, 95, 96, 97; WhoAmW 95, 97; WhoUSWr 88; WhoWor 87, 89, 91, 93, 95, 96, 97; WhoWrEP 89, 92, 95; WorAu 1950; WrDr 76, 92, 94, 96*

Jiang Zemin
Chinese. Political Leader
Pres., China, 1993—.
b. Aug 17, 1926 in Yangzhou City, China
Source: *CurBio 95; IntWW 89, 91, 93; News 96, 96-1; WhoAsAP 91; WhoPRCh 91; WhoWor 91, 93, 95, 96, 97*

Jillian, Ann
[Mrs. Andrew Murcia; Ann Jura Nauseda]
American. Actor
Starred on Broadway in *Sugar Babies,* 1979-80; starred in own life story, 1987, which focused on her double mastectomy, 1985.
b. Jan 29, 1951 in Cambridge, Massachusetts
Source: *BioIn 12; ConHero 1; ConNews 86-4; ConTFT 1, 4; HolBB; IntMPA 86, 88, 92, 94, 96; VarWW 85; WhoHol 92*

Jimenez, Juan Ramon
Spanish. Poet
Best known for prose poem "Platero y Yo," 1917; won 1956 Nobel Prize.
b. Dec 24, 1881 in Monguer, Spain
d. May 29, 1958 in San Juan, Puerto Rico
Source: *AnCL; AtlBL; Benet 87, 96; BioIn 1, 2, 3, 4, 5, 6, 8, 9, 10, 11; CasWL; ClDMEL 47, 80; CnMWL; ConAu 104, 131; CyWA 58; DcArts; DcHiB; DcLB 134; DcSpL; EncWL, 2, 3; EuWr 9; EvEuW; FacFETw; GrFLW; HispLC; HispWr; LiExTwC; LinLib L, S; MajTwCW; McGEWB; ModRL; ModSpP S; OxCSpan; PenC EUR; PoeCrit 7; RAdv 14, 13-2; REn; RGFMEP; TwCLC 4; TwCWr; WhAm 3; WhDW; WhoNob,*

90, 95; WhoTwCL; WorAl; WorAlBi; WorAu 1950

Jinnah, Mohammed Ali
Indian. Political Leader
Principal founder, first governor-general of Pakistan, 1947.
b. Dec 25, 1876 in Karachi, Pakistan
d. Sep 11, 1948 in Karachi, Pakistan
Source: *DcPol; WhAm 2; WhDW*

Joachim, Joseph
Hungarian. Violinist, Composer
Violin virtuoso; founded famed Joachim Quartet, 1869; wrote "Hungarian Concerto," 1857.
b. Jun 28, 1831 in Kisstee, Hungary
d. Aug 15, 1907 in Berlin, Germany
Source: *Baker 78, 84, 92; BioIn 1, 2, 4, 8, 9, 14; BriBkM 80; CelCen; DcArts; DcBiPP; LinLib S; MusMk; NewAmDM; NewCol 75; NewGrDM 80; NewOxM; OxCMus; PenDiMP; WebBD 83; WhDW*

Joanis, John W
American. Insurance Executive
Founder, chairman, Sentry Insurance Co.
b. Jun 13, 1918 in Hopewell, Virginia
d. Nov 19, 1985 in Marshfield, Wisconsin
Source: *BioIn 14; Dun&B 86; St&PR 84; WhoAm 82, 84; WhoIns 75, 76, 77, 78, 79, 80, 81, 82, 84, 86*

Joan Jett and the Blackhearts
[Ricky Byrd; Lee Crystal; Joan Jett; Gary Ryan]
American. Music Group
Had hit single "I Love Rock 'n Roll," 1982.
Source: *BioIn 14, 19, 20, 21; ConTFT 4; EncRk 88; EncRkSt; HarEnR 86; RkOn 85; WhoRocM 82; WhsNW 85*

Joan of Arc, Saint
[Jeanne d'Arc]
"Maid of Orleans"
French. Historical Figure
Led troops to victory over English, 1429; tried for heresy, burned at stake.
b. Jan 6, 1412 in Domremy, France
d. May 30, 1431 in Rouen, France
Source: *Benet 87, 96; BioIn 1, 2, 3, 4, 5, 6, 7, 8, 9, 10, 11, 12, 13, 16, 17, 19, 20; BlmGEL; ContDcW 89; DcCathB; Dis&D; EncAmaz 91; EncPaPR 91; EncWW; FilmgC; GenMudB; HarEnMi; HerW, 84; HisWorL; IntDcWB; InWom, SUP; LegTOT; LngCEL; LuthC 75; McGDA; McGEWB; NewC; NewCol 75; OxCEng 85, 95; OxCFr; OxDcOp; REn; WebBD 83; WhDW; WomFir; WomStre; WorAl; WorAlBi*

Job
Biblical Figure
Story told in Old Testament Book of Job; revered for his patience.
Source: *BioIn 1, 2, 4, 5, 6, 10, 15, 17; Dis&D; FolkA 87; LngCEL; NewCol 75; OxCSpan; OxDcByz; WhoRel 77; WorECar*

Jobert, Michel
French. Diplomat
Minister of Foreign Affairs, 1973-74; of Foreign Trade, 1981-83.
b. Sep 11, 1921 in Meknes, French Morocco
Source: *BiDFrPL; BioIn 9, 10, 17; CurBio 75; IntWW 75, 76, 77, 78, 79, 80, 81, 82, 83, 89, 91, 93; IntYB 82; NewYTBS 74; Who 74, 82, 83, 85, 88, 90, 92; WhoFr 79; WhoWor 78, 80, 82, 84, 95*

Jobim, Antonio Carlos
Brazilian. Composer
One of the creators of the bossa nova; his album *Jazz Samba,* 1962, spurred the craze in the US; inducted into the Songwriters Hall of Fame, 1991.
b. Jan 25, 1927 in Rio de Janeiro, Brazil
d. Dec 8, 1994 in New York, New York
Source: *AllMusG; BiDAmM; BioIn 20, 21; CurBio 91, 95N; EncJzS; NewGrDJ 88, 94; OxCPMus*

Jobin, Raoul
Canadian. Opera Singer
Tenor; made NY Met. debut, 1940; mostly French repertory.
b. Apr 8, 1906 in Quebec, Quebec, Canada
d. Jan 13, 1974 in Quebec, Quebec, Canada
Source: *BioIn 10; CanWW 70; CmOp; CreCan 1; MacDCB 78; MetOEnc; NewAmDM; NewEOp 71; NewGrDM 80; NewGrDO; OxCMus; OxDcOp; PenDiMP; WhAm 6*

Jobs, Steven Paul
American. Business Executive
Co-founder, Apple Computer Inc., 1976, formed second computer co., Next. Developed WebObjects, allowing users to form sites on the World Wide Web.
b. 1955
Source: *BioIn 13; ConAmBL; CurBio 83; HisDcDP; IntWW 89, 91, 93; LElec; WhoAm 84, 86, 88, 92, 94, 95, 96, 97; WhoFI 87, 89, 92; WhoFrS 84; WhoScEn 94; WhoWest 84, 87, 89, 92, 94*

Jochum, Eugen
German. Conductor
Founded Bavarian Radio Symphony, 1949; conducted it until 1960.
b. Nov 2, 1902 in Babenhausen, Germany
d. Mar 26, 1987 in Munich, Germany (West)
Source: *AnObit 1987; Baker 78, 84, 92; BioIn 4, 11; BriBkM 80; FacFETw; IntWW 74, 75, 76, 77, 78, 79, 80, 81, 82, 83; IntWWM 77, 80; MetOEnc; NewAmDM; NewEOp 71; NewGrDM 80; NewGrDO; NewYTBS 78, 87; OxDcOp; PenDiMP; WhoMus 72; WhoOp 76; WhoWor 74*

Joel, Billy
[William Martin Joel]
American. Singer, Songwriter
Had five 1 songs from album *An Innocent Man,* 1983; albums include platinum *52nd Street,* 1978.
b. May 9, 1949 in Hicksville, New York
Source: *AmSong; ASCAP 80; Baker 84, 92; BioIn 10, 11, 12, 13, 14, 15, 17, 18, 19, 20, 21; BioNews 74; BkPepl; CelR 90; ConAu 108; ConLC 26; ConMuA 80A; ConMus 2, 12; CurBio 79; EncPR&S 89; EncRk 88; EncRkSt; HarEnR 86; IlEncRk; LegTOT; NewGrDA 86; News 94, 94-3; OxCPMus; PenEncP; RkOn 78; RolSEnR 83; WhoAm 80, 82, 84, 86, 88, 90, 92, 94, 95, 96, 97; WhoEnt 92; WhoRock 81; WhoRocM 82; WhoWor 80, 82, 87; WorAl; WorAlBi*

Joffre, Joseph Jacques Cesaire
French. Military Leader
Commander of French army credited with directing orderly French retreat before German advance, 1914.
b. Jan 12, 1852 in Rivesaltes, France
d. Jan 13, 1931 in Paris, France
Source: *BiDFrPL; BioIn 1, 2, 6, 10, 11, 17; DcTwHis; HarEnMi; LinLib S; McGEWB; OxCFr; WhoMilH 76; WorAl*

Joffrey, Robert
[Abdullah Jaffa Bey Khan]
American. Choreographer
Founder, artistic director, Joffrey Ballet Co., 1956, renowned for wide-ranging repertory.
b. Dec 24, 1930 in Seattle, Washington
d. Mar 25, 1988 in New York, New York
Source: *AnObit 1988; BiDD; BioIn 3, 5, 6, 7, 8, 9, 10, 11, 12; BioNews 74; CnOxB; CurBio 67, 88, 88N; DancEn 78; FacFETw; IntDcB; LegTOT; NewGrDA 86; News 88-3; NewYTBE 72; NewYTBS 88; RAdv 14; WhAm 9; WhoAm 76, 78, 80, 82, 84, 86; WhoE 79, 81, 83, 85, 86; WhoWor 74, 78, 80, 82, 84, 87; WorAl; WorAlBi*

Jofre, Eder
Brazilian. Boxer
World bantamweight champ, 1961-65.
b. Mar 26, 1936 in Sao Paulo, Brazil
Source: *BioIn 6; BoxReg; WhoBox 74*

Johannesen, Grant
American. Pianist
International concertist, 1950s-60s; esteemed for French, American works.
b. Jul 30, 1921 in Salt Lake City, Utah
Source: *Baker 78, 84, 92; BioIn 3, 5, 6, 7, 10, 12, 14, 15, 21; BioNews 75; ConAmC 76, 82; CurBio 61; IntWWM 77, 80, 90; NewGrDA 86; NewGrDM 80; NotTwCP; PenDiMP; WhoAm 74, 76; WhoAmM 83; WhoE 85; WhoMus 72*

Johansen, David
American. Singer, Songwriter
Lead singer for New York Dolls, 1971-75; solo performer from 1975; film

credits include *Married to the Mob,* and *Scrooged.*
b. Jan 9, 1950 in Staten Island, New York
Source: *BioIn 12, 13, 14, 15, 16; ConMus 7; ConTFT 14; LegTOT; RolSEnR 83; WhoAm 94, 95, 96, 97*

Johansen, Gunnar
American. Pianist, Composer
First performing musician to hold post of artist-in-residence at an American U, 1939-76; composed orhestral, chamber and choral works.
b. Jan 21, 1906 in Copenhagen, Denmark
d. May 25, 1991 in Blue Mounds, Wisconsin
Source: *Baker 78, 84, 92; BioIn 8, 11, 14, 15, 17; ConAmC 82; IntWWM 80; NewGrDA 86; NewYTBS 91; WhoMW 74, 76*

Johanson, Donald Carl
American. Anthropologist
Unearthed most complete skeleton known to anthropologists, 1974.
b. Jun 28, 1943 in Chicago, Illinois
Source: *AmMWSc 95; BioIn 12, 13; ConAu 107; CurBio 84; IntAu&W 86; IntWW 89, 91, 93; LarDcSc; NewYTBS 79; WhoAm 82, 84, 86, 88, 90, 92, 94, 95, 96, 97; WhoEmL 87, 89; WhoMW 76, 78; WhoScEn 94, 96; WhoWest 87, 89, 92, 94, 96*

Johansson, Ingemar
[Jens Ingemar Johansson]
Swedish. Boxer
Heavyweight boxing champion, 1959-60; fought Floyd Patterson.
b. Sep 22, 1932 in Gothenburg, Sweden
Source: *BioIn 5, 6, 9, 10, 11, 12, 13; CurBio 59; What 4; WhoBox 74; WhoHol A*

John, King of England
"John Lackland"
English. Ruler
Son of Henry II; forced by English barons to sign Magna Carta, 1215.
b. Dec 24, 1167 in Oxford, England
d. Oct 29, 1216 in Newark, England
Source: *Benet 87, 96; BioIn 1, 2, 4, 5, 6, 7, 8, 9, 10, 11, 12, 13, 14, 17, 21; DcCathB; DcNaB, C; DicTyr; Dis&D; LegTOT; LinLib S; LuthC 75; McGEWB; MediFra; NewC; NewCol 75; REn; WhDW; WorAl; WorAlBi*

John, Augustus Edwin
English. Artist
Noted for portraits of celebrities including Shaw, Yeats; remembered as nonconformist.
b. Jan 4, 1878 in Tenby, Wales
d. Oct 31, 1961 in Fordingbridge, England
Source: *AtlBL; CurBio 41, 62; OxCEng 67; WhAm 4*

John, Elton
[Reginald Kenneth Dwight]
English. Singer, Songwriter
Has recorded over 25 albums; hits include "Rocket Man," 1972; "Philadelphia Freedom," 1975; "Wrap Her Up," 1985; Grammy award, 1981; rock and Roll Hall of Famd, 1994.
b. Mar 25, 1947 in Pinner, England
Source: *Baker 78, 84, 92; BioIn 9, 10, 11, 12; BioNews 74; BkPepl; CelR, 90; ConMuA 80A; ConMus 3; CurBio 75; DcArts; EncPR&S 89; EncRk 88; EncRkSt; FacFETw; GayLesB; HalFC 80, 84, 88; HarEnR 86; IlEncRk; LegTOT; NewAmDM; News 95; NewYTBE 71; NewYTBS 74; OxCPMus; PenEncP; RkOn 78; RolSEnR 83; VarWW 85; WhoAm 76, 78, 80, 82, 84, 86, 88, 90, 92, 94, 95, 96, 97; WhoEnt 92; WhoHol 92, A; WhoRock 81; WhoRocM 82; WhoWor 91, 95, 96, 97; WorAl; WorAlBi*

John, Gwendolyn Mary
Welsh. Artist
Painted interiors, austere female portraits; Whistler's pupil.
b. 1876 in Haverfordwest, Wales
d. 1939 in Dieppe, France
Source: *McGDA; WomArt*

John, John P(ico)
"Mr. John"
American. Designer
Designs include custom-made dresses, hats, furs for women, perfumes, beginning in 1948.
b. Mar 14, 1906 in Florence, Italy
d. Jun 25, 1993 in New York, New York
Source: *BioIn 4; CurBio 56, 93N; EncFash; WhoAm 74*

John, Tommy
[Thomas Edward John, Jr]
American. Baseball Player
Pitcher, 1965-89, last team NY Yankees; left elbow surgically reconstructed, 1974; won 20 or more games in three seasons since.
b. May 22, 1943 in Terre Haute, Indiana
Source: *Ballpl 90; BaseReg 86, 87; BiDAmSp BB; BioIn 11, 13; CurBio 81; IndAu 1967; LegTOT; NewYTBS 77, 78, 83; WhoAm 76, 78, 80, 82, 84, 86; WhoProB 73; WorAl; WorAlBi*

John of Gaunt
[Duke of Lancaster; Earl of Derby; Earl of Richmond]
English. Prince
Fourth son of Edward III; house of Tudor descended from him.
b. Mar 1340 in Ghent, Belgium
d. Feb 3, 1399 in London, England
Source: *Benet 87, 96; BioIn 1, 3, 6, 7, 9, 18; DcNaB; LngCEL; McGEWB; NewC; NewCol 75; OxCEng 85, 95; REn; WebBD 83*

John of Salisbury
English. Author
Most learned scholarly writer of his time; wrote *Policraticus,* 1159.
b. 1120 in Salisbury, England
d. Oct 25, 1180 in Chartres, France
Source: *Alli; BiB N; BritAu; CasWL; DcEnL; DcEuL; EvLB; NewC; OxCEng 67, 95; PenC ENG; RAdv 13-4*

John of the Cross, Saint
[Juan de Yepes y Alvarez; San Juan de la Cruz]
"Ecstatic Doctor"
Spanish. Poet
Poems are a mix of religion, poetic imagery; canonized, 1726.
b. Jun 24, 1542 in Avila, Spain
d. Dec 14, 1591 in Penuela, Spain
Source: *AtlBL; Benet 87, 96; BioIn 1, 2, 3, 4, 5, 6, 7, 9, 10, 11; CasWL; DcBiPP; DcCathB; DcEuL; DcSpL; EuAu; EvEuW; GrFLW; LinLib L; LitC 18; LuthC 75; McGEWB; NewC; OxCEng 85, 95; PenC EUR; RAdv 14, 13-2; RComWL; REn; RfGWoL 95; WorAl; WorAlBi*

John Paul I, Pope
[Albino Luciani]
Italian. Religious Leader
Pope for 34 days, 1978, before dying of heart attack.
b. Oct 17, 1912 in Belluno, Italy
d. Sep 28, 1978, Vatican City
Source: *BioIn 14, 16; ConAu 81; CurBio 78; IntWW 74, 75, 76, 77, 78, 79; WhoWor 74, 78*

John Paul II, Pope
[Karol Jozef Wojtyla]
Polish. Religious Leader
First non-Italian pope since Renaissance, 1978—; most traveled, known for conservatism in doctrine, expanding college of cardinals.
b. May 18, 1920 in Wadowice, Poland
Source: *BioIn 11; BkPepl; ColdWar 2; ConAu 106; CurBio 79; NewYTBS 82, 85; WhoAm 86, 92, 94, 95, 96, 97; WhoRel 92; WhoSoCE 89; WhoWor 91, 93, 95, 96, 97*

Johns, Glynis
English. Actor
Noted for role of mother in film *Mary Poppins,* 1964; won Tony for *A Little Night Music,* 1973.
b. Oct 5, 1923 in Pretoria, South Africa
Source: *BiE&WWA; BioIn 10, 11; BlueB 76; ConTFT 5, 12; CurBio 73; FilmAG WE; FilmEn; FilmgC; ForYSC; HalFC 80, 84, 88; IlWWBF; IntMPA 75, 76, 77, 78, 79, 80, 81, 82, 84, 86, 88, 92, 94, 96; InWom SUP; LegTOT; MotPP; MovMk; NewYTBE 73; NotNAT; OxCFilm; VarWW 85; Who 74; WhoAm 76; WhoAmW 74, 75; WhoHol 92, A; WhoHrs 80; WhoThe 72, 77, 81; WorAl; WorAlBi*

Johns, Jasper, (Jr.)
American. Artist
Pop artist known for using flags, letters, numbers in work.
b. May 15, 1930 in Augusta, Georgia
Source: *AmArt; AmCulL; Benet 87; BiDD; BioIn 5, 6, 7, 8, 9, 10, 11, 12, 13; BlueB 76; BriEAA; CelR, 90; CnOxB; ConArt 77, 83, 89, 96; CurBio 67, 87; DcAmArt; DcArts; DcCAA 71, 77, 88, 94; DcCAr 81; DcTwCCu 1; EncAB-H 1974, 1996; FacFETw; GayLesB; IntDcAA 90; IntWW 74, 75, 76, 77, 78, 79, 80, 81, 82, 83, 89, 91, 93; LegTOT; MakMC; McGDA; McGEWB; NewCol 75; OxCArt; OxCTwCA; OxDcArt; PhDcTCA 77; PrintW 83, 85; RComAH; WhoAm 74, 76, 78, 80, 82, 84, 86, 88, 92, 94, 95, 96, 97; WhoAmA 73, 76, 78, 80, 82, 84, 86, 89, 91, 93; WhoWor 74, 78, 80, 82, 84, 87, 89, 91, 93, 95; WorAl; WorAlBi; WorArt 1950*

Johnson, Alex(ander)
American. Baseball Player
Outfielder, 1964-76; won AL batting title, 1970.
b. Dec 7, 1942 in Helena, Arkansas
Source: *Ballpl 90; BioIn 9; InB&W 80; WhoAm 74, 76; WhoProB 73*

Johnson, Amy
English. Aviator
Solo flights include round-trip flight from London to Tokyo, 1931; flew across Atlantic from England to US, 1933.
b. 1903 in Kingston-upon-Hull, England
d. Jan 5, 1941
Source: *BioIn 3, 4, 5, 6, 7, 8, 9, 11, 14, 15, 16, 18, 20; ContDcW 89; CurBio 41; DcNaB 1941; Expl 93; FacFETw; GrBr; HerW, 84; IntDcWB; WhDW*

Johnson, Andrew
American. US President
Dem., 17th pres., 1865-69; succeeded Lincoln on his assassination; survived impeachment by Congress, 1868.
b. Dec 29, 1808 in Raleigh, North Carolina
d. Jul 31, 1875 in Carter Station, Tennessee
Source: *AmAu&B; AmBi; AmPolLe; ApCAB; Benet 87, 96; BenetAL 91; BiAUS; BiDrAC; BiDrGov 1789; BiDrUSC 89; BiDrUSE 71, 89; BioIn 1, 2, 3, 4, 5, 6, 7, 8, 9, 10, 11, 12, 13, 14, 15, 16, 17, 18, 19, 20, 21; CelCen; CivWDc; CyAG; DcAmB; DcAmSR; DcBiPP; DcNAA; DcNCBi 3; Drake; EncAAH; EncAB-H 1974, 1996; EncSoH; FacPr 89, 93; HarEnUS; HealPre; LegTOT; LinLib L, S; McGEWB; NatCAB 2; NewCol 75; OxCAmH; OxCAmL 65, 83; PolPar; RComAH; REn; REnAL; TwCBDA; WebAB 74, 79; WhAm HS; WhAmP; WhCiWar; WhDW; WorAl; WorAlBi*

Johnson, Arno Hollock
American. Economist, Advertising Executive, Author
J Walter Thompson economist, 1926-67; wrote *Marketing Opportunities.*
b. Jan 12, 1901 in Jacksonville, Florida
d. Jul 20, 1985 in Delray Beach, Florida
Source: *ConAu 116; IntYB 81; WhoAm 78*

Johnson, Arte
American. Actor, Comedian
Best known for character acting in TV's "Laugh-In," 1968-71; popularized expression "Velly interesting"; won Emmy, 1969.
b. Jan 20, 1934 in Benton Harbor, Michigan
Source: *ConTFT 3; HalFC 84, 88; IntMPA 86, 88, 92, 94, 96; LegTOT; VarWW 85; WhoAm 78, 80, 82, 84; WhoHol A*

Johnson, Ban
[Byron Bancroft Johnson]
American. Baseball Executive
First president of AL, 1901-27; helped game become national pastime; Hall of Fame, 1937.
b. Jan 8, 1864 in Norwalk, Ohio
d. Mar 18, 1931 in Saint Louis, Missouri
Source: *Ballpl 90; BioIn 3, 7, 14, 15, 21; DcAmB; WhAm 1; WhoProB 73*

Johnson, Ben
American. Actor
Won Oscar for *The Last Picture Show,* 1971.
b. Jun 13, 1920 in Pawhuska, Oklahoma
d. Apr 8, 1996 in Mesa, Arizona
Source: *BioIn 8, 12, 21; CmMov; FilmEn; FilmgC; ForYSC; HalFC 84; IntMPA 86; MovMk; NewYTBS 27; VarWW 85; WhoHol A*

Johnson, Ben
[Benjamin Sinclair Johnson, Jr.]
"Big Ben"
Canadian. Track Athlete
Sprinter stripped of 1988 Olympic gold medal after testing positive for steroid use; banned for life, 1993, after testing positive again.
b. Dec 30, 1961 in Falmouth, Jamaica
Source: *ConBlB 1; CurBio 88; FacFETw; IntWW 89, 91, 93*

Johnson, Betsey Lee
American. Fashion Designer
Designer of children's, maternity, women's clothes; owner, NYC's Betsey Johnson store, 1979—.
b. Aug 10, 1942 in Hartford, Connecticut
Source: *CurBio 94; WhoAm 80, 82, 84, 86, 88, 90, 92, 94, 95, 96, 97; WhoAmW 91, 93, 95, 97; WorFshn*

Johnson, Beverly
American. Model
First black woman on cover of *Vogue,* 1975; won outstanding US model award, 1975.
b. Oct 13, 1952 in Buffalo, New York
Source: *BioIn 10, 11; ConBlB 2; CurBio 94; DcTwCCu 5; InB&W 80, 85; NegAl 76; NotBlAW 1; WhoAfA 96; WhoAmW 95; WhoBlA 85, 94; WhoHol 92*

Johnson, Bill
[William D Johnson]
American. Skier
First American to win gold medal, men's downhill, 1984 Olympics.
b. 1961? in Los Angeles, California
Source: *NewYTBS 84, 85*

Johnson, Billy
[William Arthur Johnson]
"White Shoes"
American. Football Player
Three-time all-pro wide receiver, 1974; set NFL record for punt return yds. in career.
b. Jan 21, 1952 in Boothwyn, Pennsylvania
Source: *FootReg 87; WhoAfA 96; WhoBlA 77, 80, 85, 88, 90, 92, 94; WhoFI 81, 83*

Johnson, Bob
American. Hockey Coach
Coached Pittsburgh to first Stanley Cup, 1991; Hockey Hall of Fame, 1992.
b. Mar 4, 1941 in Minneapolis, Minnesota
d. Nov 26, 1991
Source: *NewYTBS 91*

Johnson, Bunk
[William Geary Johnson]
American. Jazz Musician
Early Dixieland trumpeter; rediscovered, 1937, by jazz aficionados.
b. Dec 27, 1879 in New Orleans, Louisiana
d. Jul 7, 1949 in New Iberia, Louisiana
Source: *Baker 78, 84; BiDAfM; BiDAmM; BiDJaz; BioIn 16; CmpEPM; IlEncJ; InB&W 80, 85; LegTOT; NewGrDM 80; WhAm 4; WhoJazz 72; WorAl; WorAlBi*

Johnson, Celia, Dame
English. Actor
Starred in films *Brief Encounter,* 1945, *In Which We Serve,* 1942.
b. Dec 18, 1908 in Richmond, England
d. Apr 25, 1982 in Nettlebed, England
Source: *AnObit 1982, 81*

Johnson, Charles Richard
American. Author
Fiction writer; *Middle Passage,* 1990 won Nat. Book Award.
b. Apr 23, 1948 in Evanston, Illinois
Source: *ConAu 116; ConLC 7; DcLB 33*

Johnson, Chic
[Olsen and Johnson; Harold Ogden Johnson]
American. Actor, Comedian
Vaudeville star with Ole Olsen, 1914; *Hellzapoppin* became great Broadway, film success, 1941.
b. Mar 5, 1891 in Chicago, Illinois
d. Feb 1962 in Las Vegas, Nevada
Source: *BioIn 2, 6, 16; DcAmB S7; FilmEn; FilmgC; HalFC 80, 84, 88; JoeFr; LegTOT; MovMk; NotNAT B; WhoHol B; WhScrn 74, 77, 83; WhThe*

Johnson, Ching
[Ivan Wilfred Johnson]
Canadian. Hockey Player
Defenseman, 1926-38, mostly with NY Rangers; Hall of Fame, 1958.
b. Dec 7, 1898 in Winnipeg, Manitoba, Canada
d. Jun 16, 1979 in Silver Spring, Maryland
Source: *BioIn 12; HocEn; NewYTBS 79; WhoHcky 73*

Johnson, Clarence Leonard
"Kelly"
American. Aeronautical Engineer
Created America's first production jet fighter and a generation of spy planes, including the U2 and SR71 Blackbird.
b. Feb 27, 1910 in Ishpeming, Michigan
d. Dec 21, 1990 in Burbank, California
Source: *AmMWSc 73P, 82; BioIn 8, 10, 11, 12, 17, 20; CurBio 68; WebAMB; WhAm 10; WhoAm 74, 76; WhoFI 74*

Johnson, Cletus Merlin
American. Artist
Known for shadowbox constructions of imaginary facades.
b. Nov 19, 1941 in Elizabeth, New Jersey
Source: *WhoAm 82; WhoAmA 76, 78, 80, 82*

Johnson, Cornelius
American. Track Athlete
High jumper; won gold medal, 1936 Berlin Olympics.
b. Aug 21, 1913 in Los Angeles, California
d. Feb 15, 1946 in San Francisco, California
Source: *BioIn 1, 6; BlkOlyM; WhoSpor; WhoTr&F 73*

Johnson, Crockett
[David Johnson Leisk]
American. Cartoonist, Author
Created comic strip "Barnaby," 1941-62; author, illustrator of several children's books.
b. Oct 20, 1906 in New York, New York
d. Jul 11, 1975 in Norwalk, Connecticut
Source: *Au&Wr 71; AuBYP 2; BioIn 1, 5, 8, 9, 10, 13, 14; BkP; ChlBkCr; ConAu 57; CurBio 84, 84N; EncACom; IlsCB 1946, 1957; LinLib L; NewYTBS 75; OxCChiL; SmATA 1; ThrBJA; TwCChW 78, 83, 89, 95; WhAm 6; WhoAmA 73, 76, 78N, 80N*

Johnson, Davey
[David Allen Johnson]
American. Baseball Player, Baseball Manager
Second baseman, 1965-78; set ML record for home runs by second baseman in one season, 43, 1973; manager, NY Mets, 1984-90; Cincinnati Reds, 1993-95; Baltimore Orioles, 1996—.
b. Jan 30, 1943 in Orlando, Florida
Source: *Ballpl 90; BaseReg 86, 87; BiDAmSp Sup; BioIn 10; WhoAm 86, 88, 94, 95, 96, 97; WhoE 89, 91, 97; WhoMW 93, 96; WhoProB 73; WhoSpor; WorAlBi*

Johnson, Dennis Wayne
American. Basketball Player
Guard, 1976-90, mostly with Boston; won three NBA championships; NBA All-Defensive Team, 1979-86.
b. Sep 18, 1954 in San Pedro, California
Source: *BiDAmSp BK; NewYTBS 84; OfNBA 87; WhoAm 84, 86; WhoBlA 88*

Johnson, Dink
[Oliver Johnson]
American. Jazz Musician
Drummer, pianist, clarinetist with Kid Ory, 1920s.
b. Oct 28, 1892 in New Orleans, Louisiana
d. Nov 29, 1954 in Portland, Oregon
Source: *BiDJaz; BluesWW; InB&W 80, 85; NewGrDJ 88, 94; NewOrJ; OxCPMus; WhoJazz 72*

Johnson, Don
[Donald Wayne]
American. Actor
Played Sonny Crockett on TV series "Miami Vice," 1984-89; portrays Nash Bridges on series of same name, 1997.
b. Dec 15, 1949 in Flat Creek, Missouri
Source: *CelR 90; ConNews 86-1; CurBio 86; HolBB; IntMPA 94, 96; LegTOT; WhoHol 92; WorAlBi*

Johnson, Earvin, Jr.
"Magic"
American. Basketball Player
Guard, LA Lakers, 1979-92, 1996; NBA MVP, 1987, 1989, 1990; won 1992 Olympic gold medal with US "Dream Team;" retired twice 1991, 1992 after testing HIV positive; announced third comeback, 1996, but did not finish season before retiring again.
b. Aug 14, 1959 in Lansing, Michigan
Source: *AfrAmAl 6; AfrAmBi 1; BiDAmSp BK; BioIn 12, 13, 14, 15, 16, 17, 18, 19, 20, 21; ConAu 141; ConBlB 3; CurBio 82; InB&W 80, 85; IntWW 93; News 88; NewYTBS 86; OfNBA 87; WhoAfA 96; WhoAm 82, 84, 86, 88, 90, 92, 94, 95, 96, 97; WhoBlA 85, 88, 90, 92, 94; WhoWest 87, 89, 92, 94, 96*

Johnson, Eastman
American. Artist
Painted genre pictures of black life in the South, portraits of presidents, authors.
b. Jul 29, 1824 in Lovell, Maine
d. Apr 5, 1906 in New York, New York
Source: *AmBi; ApCAB; ArtsNiC; BioIn 1, 4, 7, 9, 10, 13, 14, 16; BriEAA; DcAmArt; DcAmB; DcArts; DcBiPP; Drake; HarEnUS; LegTOT; LinLib S; McGDA; NatCAB 9; NewYHSD; OxCAmL 65; REnAW; TwCBDA; WebAB 74, 79; WhAm 1; WhAmArt 85; WhNaAH*

Johnson, Eddie Bernice
American. Politician
First black woman elected to Congress from North Texas, 1993—.
b. Dec 3, 1935 in Waco, Texas
Source: *AlmAP 96; BioIn 19, 20; CngDr 93, 95; ConBlB 8; WhoAfA 96; WhoAm 94, 95, 96, 97; WhoAmP 87, 89, 91, 93, 95; WhoAmW 89, 91, 93, 95, 97; WhoBlA 94; WhoSSW 91, 95, 97; WhoWomW 91*

Johnson, Eleanor M
American. Publisher
Founded *The Weekly Reader,* 1928, which was read by two-thirds of today's US adults as children.
b. Dec 10, 1892? in Washington County, Maryland
d. Oct 8, 1987 in Gaithersburg, Maryland
Source: *LEduc 74; NewYTBS 87*

Johnson, Eliza McCardle
[Mrs. Andrew Johnson]
American. First Lady
Taught Andrew to read, write; semi-invalid unable to assume White House duties.
b. Oct 4, 1810 in Leesburg, Tennessee
d. Jan 15, 1876 in Greeneville, Tennessee
Source: *AmWom; ApCAB; BioIn 16, 17; FacPr 89; GoodHs; InWom, SUP; NatCAB 2; NotAW; TwCBDA*

Johnson, Emily Pauline
Canadian. Author, Entertainer
First Native Canadian to have her likeness and name commenorated on a postage stamp; published poetry collection, *Songs of the Great Dominion,* 1889.
b. Mar 10, 1861 in Chiefswood, Ontario, Canada
d. Mar 7, 1913 in Vancouver, British Columbia, Canada
Source: *BioIn 1, 7, 10, 11, 17, 21; EncNAB; InWom, SUP; NotNaAm*

Johnson, Eyvind Olof Verner
Swedish. Author
Won 1974 Nobel Prize in literature for his novels, short stories.
b. Jul 29, 1900 in Overlvlea, Sweden
d. Aug 25, 1976 in Stockholm, Sweden
Source: *ConAu 73; DcScanL; WhoNob, 90, 95*

Johnson, F(rederick) Ross
Canadian. Business Executive
CEO of the RJR Nabisco Co. until 1989 when the largest leveraged buyout in corporate history occurred.
b. Dec 13, 1931 in Winnipeg, Manitoba, Canada
Source: *BioIn 15, 16; CanWW 89; CurBio 89; Dun&B 88; IntWW 81, 82, 83, 89, 91, 93; NewYTBS 88; St&PR 91; WhoAm 74, 76, 78, 84; WhoFI 79, 81, 89, 92; WhoSSW 88, 91, 93, 97; WhoWor 78, 84, 91*

Johnson, George E(llis)
American. Business Executive
Founder, pres., Johnson Products Co., 1954—; first black-owned co. to be listed on major US stock exchange, 1971.
b. Jun 16, 1927 in Richton, Mississippi
Source: *InB&W 80, 85; WhoAfA 96; WhoBlA 88, 90, 92, 94; WhoFI 81, 83, 85; WhoGov 75*

Johnson, Gerald White
[Charles North]
American. Journalist, Author
Editorial writer, *Baltimore Sun,* 1939-43; mystery novels include *Number Thirty Six,* 1933.
b. Aug 6, 1890 in Riverton, North Carolina
d. Mar 23, 1980 in Baltimore, Maryland
Source: *AmAu; AmAu&B; AnCL; AuBYP 2, 3; BioIn 2, 3, 4, 7, 9, 12, 13, 14; CnDAL; ConAu 85, 97; DcNCBi 3; EncSoH; EncTwCJ; JrnUS; OxCAmL 65; REnAL; SmATA 19, 28N; SouWr; ThrBJA; TwCA SUP; WhAm 7; WhNAA; WhoAm 74, 76, 78, 80; WhoWor 74*

Johnson, Gus, Jr.
American. Basketball Player
Forward, 1963-73, mostly with Baltimore.
b. Dec 13, 1938 in Akron, Ohio
d. Apr 28, 1987 in Akron, Ohio
Source: *BasBi; BiDAmSp BK; BioIn 7, 10, 12; NewYTBS 87; OfNBA 87; WhoBbl 73; WhoBlA 92N*

Johnson, Hall
American. Composer
Organized Hall Johnson Choir heard in movie *Lost Horizon;* founded Negro Choir, 1925.
b. Mar 12, 1888 in Athens, Georgia
d. Apr 30, 1970 in New York, New York
Source: *ASCAP 66, 80; BiDAmM; BioIn 8, 9, 11, 14, 18; BlkAmP; BlkAWP; BlksBF; ConAmC 76; CurBio 45, 70; DcAfAmP; DrBlPA, 90; EarBlAP; MorBAP; NewAmDM; NewGrDA 86; NewGrDM 80; NotNAT B; WhAm 8; WhoHol B; WhScrn 77, 83*

Johnson, Harold
American. Boxer
World lightweight champ, 1954-63; last fight, 1971; inducted into Int'l Boxing Hall of Fame, 1993.
b. Aug 9, 1928 in Manayunk, Pennsylvania
Source: *BioIn 9; BoxReg; InB&W 80; WhoAmP 73; WhoBox 74; WhoSpor*

Johnson, Henry
American. Soldier
Black who was first American given Croix de Guerre by France in WW I; received no honors from his own country, died in poverty.
b. 1897 in Winston-Salem, North Carolina
d. Jul 2, 1929 in Washington, District of Columbia
Source: *AfrAmAl 6; BioIn 4, 8; DcAmNB; InB&W 80, 85; NegAl 76, 83, 89*

Johnson, Herbert Fisk
American. Businessman, Philanthropist
Served as exec. for SC Johnson & Son, Inc., later known as Johnson's Wax.
b. Nov 15, 1899 in Racine, Wisconsin
d. Dec 13, 1978 in Racine, Wisconsin
Source: *BioIn 11; IntYB 78; NewYTBS 78; WhAm 7*

Johnson, Hewlett
"Red Dean of Canterbury"
English. Religious Leader
Dean of Canterbury, 1924-63; won Stalin Peace Prize, 1951.
b. Jan 25, 1874 in Manchester, England
d. Oct 22, 1966 in Canterbury, England
Source: *BioIn 1, 2, 3, 4, 6, 7, 8, 14; CurBio 43, 66; DcLEL 1940; DcNaB 1961; GrBr; LngCTC; ObitT 1961; WhAm 4; WhE&EA; WhLit*

Johnson, Hiram Warren
American. Politician
A founder of Progressive Party, ran as Theodore Roosevelt's VP candidate, 1912; firmly isolationist senator from CA, 1917-45.
b. Sep 2, 1866 in Sacramento, California
d. Aug 6, 1945 in Bethesda, Maryland
Source: *AmPolLe; ApCAB X; BiDrAC; BiDrUSC 89; BioIn 1, 2, 4, 5, 7, 8, 9; CurBio 41, 45; DcAmB S3; EncAB-H 1974, 1996; LinLib S; McGEWB; NatCAB 15, 40; NewCol 75; OxCAmH; REnAW; WebAB 74, 79; WebBD 83; WhAm 2; WhAmP; WorAl*

Johnson, Howard Brennan
American. Restaurateur
Pres., director, chm. Howard Johnson Co., 1964-81.
b. Aug 23, 1932 in Boston, Massachusetts
Source: *BioIn 7, 11; CurBio 66; WhoAm 82; WhoFI 74; WhoWor 74*

Johnson, Howard Deering
American. Restaurateur
Began ice cream business, 1924; first Howard Johnson's restaurant opened, 1929 in MA.
b. 1896? in Boston, Massachusetts
d. Jun 20, 1972 in New York, New York
Source: *DcAmB S9; FacFETw; NewYTBE 72; WebAB 74, 79; WhAm 5*

Johnson, Hugh Samuel
American. Government Official
Devised plan for selective draft, 1917; headed office, 1917-18.
b. Aug 5, 1882 in Fort Scott, Kansas
d. Apr 15, 1942 in Washington, District of Columbia
Source: *AmAu&B; BioIn 1, 2, 5; CurBio 40, 42; DcAmB S3; DcAmMiB; DcNAA; EncAB-H 1974; NatCAB 42; WebAB 74, 79; WebAMB; WhAm 2*

Johnson, J. J
[James Louis Johnson]
American. Jazz Musician
Noted bop era trombonist; with Count Basie, 1940s.
b. Jan 22, 1924 in Indianapolis, Indiana
Source: *Baker 84; BiDAfM; BiDAmM; BiDJaz; BioIn 4, 5, 8, 11, 15, 16, 17, 20; CmpEPM; ConAmC 76, 82; EncJzS; IlEncJ; InB&W 80, 85; NewGrDM 80; OxCPMus; TwCBrS; WhoAm 74, 76; WhoBlA 75, 77, 80, 85; WhoFI 75, 77; WhoJazz 72*

Johnson, Jack
[John Arthur Johnson]
American. Boxer
First black man to win heavyweight crown, 1908-15; Hall of Fame, 1954.
b. Mar 31, 1878 in Galveston, Texas
d. Jun 10, 1946 in Raleigh, North Carolina
Source: *AfrAmAl 6; AfrAmSG; AmDec 1900; BioIn 1, 2, 3, 6, 7, 8, 9, 10, 11, 12, 13, 15, 16, 17, 20, 21; BlksB&W C; BoxReg; ConAu 115; ConBlB 8; CurBio 46; DcAmB S4; DcAmNB; DcTwCCu 5; FacFETw; InB&W 80, 85; LegTOT; NegAl 76, 83, 89; PeoHis; WebAB 74; WhAm 2; WhoBox 74; WhoSpor; WhScrn 77, 83; WorAl; WorAlBi*

Johnson, James Price
American. Songwriter, Pianist
Wrote lyrics, music for hit "Charleston," 1923; song gave its name to popular 1920s dance.
b. Feb 1, 1891 in New Brunswick, New Jersey
d. Nov 17, 1955 in New York, New York
Source: *ASCAP 66; Baker 84; BiDAmM; BioIn 1, 6, 7, 12; CmpEPM; IlEncJ; InB&W 80, 85; NewGrDM 80; WhoJazz 72*

Johnson, James Ralph
American. Author
Wrote *Little Red,* 1966; *Animals and Their Food,* 1972.
b. May 20, 1922 in Fort Payne, Alabama
Source: *AuBYP 2, 3; BioIn 8, 9; ConAu 1R, 2NR; IntAu&W 76, 77, 82, 86, 89, 91, 93; SmATA 1; WhoAmA 76, 78, 80, 82, 84, 86, 89, 91, 93; WhoWest 78, 92, 94, 96; WrDr 76, 80, 82, 84, 86, 88, 90, 92, 94, 96*

Johnson, James Weldon
American. Author
Wrote *The Book of American Negro Poetry,* 1921; *Negro Americans, What Now?* 1934.
b. Jun 17, 1871 in Jacksonville, Florida
d. Jun 26, 1938 in Wiscasset, Maine
Source: *AfrAmAl 6; AfrAmW; AmAu&B; AmBi; AnCL; AnMV 1926; ASCAP 66, 80; Baker 78, 84, 92; Benet 87, 96; BenetAL 91; BiDAfM; BiDAmM; BioIn 1, 2, 4, 6, 7, 8, 9, 10, 12, 13, 14, 15, 16, 17, 18, 19, 20, 21; BlkAmW 1; BlkAuII, 92; BlkAWP; BlkLC; BlkWr 1; BlkWrNE; CamGLE; CamHAL; CasWL; ChhPo, S1, S2, S3; ChlLR 32; ConAmA; ConAmL; ConAu 104, 125; ConBlB 5; CyWA 89; DcAfAmP; DcAmB S2; DcAmNB; DcArts; DcLB 51; DcLEL; DcNAA; DcTwCCu 5; DrBlPA, 90; EncAACR; EncAB-H 1974, 1996; EncSoH; EncWL 2, 3; FacFETw; FifSWrA; FourBJA; GrWrEL P; HisWorL; InB&W 80, 85; LegTOT; LinLib L; MajTwCW; McGEWB; ModAL S1; ModBlW; NegAl 76, 83, 89; NewAmDM; NewGrDA 86; OxCAmH; OxCAmL 65, 83, 95; OxCAmT 84; OxCPMus; OxCTwCP; PenC AM; RAdv 1, 14, 13-1; RComAH; REn; REnAL; RfGAmL 87, 94; SchCGBL; SelBAAf; SelBAAu; SixAP; SouBlCW; SouWr; Tw; TwCA, SUP; TwCLC 3, 19; WebAB 74, 79; WebE&AL; WhAm 1; WhAmP; WhFla; WhLit; WhNAA; WhoColR A*

Johnson, Jimmy
[James William Johnson]
American. Football Coach
Head coach, U of Miami, 1983-88; Dallas Cowboys, 1989-94; Miami Dolphins, 1996—; first coach to win a national college title and a Super Bowl.
b. Jul 16, 1943 in Port Arthur, Texas
Source: *BiDAmSp Sup; CurBio 94; News 93-3; WhoAm 90, 92, 94, 95, 96, 97; WhoMW 92; WhoSpor; WhoSSW 93, 97; WhoWor 95*

Johnson, John Harold
American. Publisher
Publishing, Johnson Publishing Co., 1942—; produces *Ebony, Jet, Tan* and *Hue*; awarded Spingarn Medal, 1966.
b. Jan 19, 1918 in Arkansas City, Arkansas
Source: *AfrAmBi 1; BiDAmBL 83; BioIn 2, 3, 5, 6, 8, 9, 10, 11; ConBlB 3; EncAB-H 1974, 1996; EncTwCJ; EncWB; FacFETw; InB&W 80, 85; IntWW 83; JrnUS; LegTOT; SelBAAf; SelBAAu; WebAB 74, 79; WhoAm 86; WhoBlA 88; WhoFI 75; WhoIns 86; WhoMW 74, 76, 78, 80, 82, 84, 86*

Johnson, John Henry
"Big John"
American. Football Player
Three-time all-pro running back, 1954-66; Hall of Fame, 1987.
b. Nov 24, 1929 in Waterproof, Louisiana
Source: *BiDAmSp FB; BioIn 6, 17; WhoFtbl 74; WhoSpor*

Johnson, Josephine Winslow
[Mrs. Grant G Cannon]
American. Author
First novel, *Now in November,* won Pulitzer for fiction, 1935.
b. Jan 20, 1910 in Kirkwood, Missouri
d. Feb 27, 1990 in Batavia, Ohio
Source: *AmAu&B; AmNov; AnMV 1926; CnDAL; ConAmA; ConNov 86; DcLEL; NewYTBS 90; OxCAmL 83; REnAL; TwCA SUP; WhAm 10; WhNAA; WhoAm 86; WrDr 86*

Johnson, Joshua
American. Artist
Former slave; self-taught portrait painter.
b. 1796
d. 1824
Source: *AfroAA*

Johnson, Judy
[William Julius Johnson]
American. Baseball Player
Standout third baseman in Negro Leagues, 1930s; sixth black player elected to Hall of Fame, 1975.
b. Oct 26, 1899 in Snow Hill, Maryland
d. Jun 14, 1989 in Wilmington, Delaware
Source: *Ballpl 90; BiDAmSp BB; BioIn 16; NewYTBS 89; WhoSpor*

Johnson, Kevin
American. Basketball Player
Point guard, Phoenix Suns, 1988—.
b. Mar 4, 1966 in Sacramento, California
Source: *BioIn 16, 17, 21; News 91, 91-1; WorAlBi*

Johnson, Lady Bird
[Claudia Alta Taylor Johnson; Mrs. Lyndon Johnson]
American. First Lady
Promoted national conservation programs; wrote *White House Diary,* 1971.
b. Dec 22, 1912 in Karnack, Texas
Source: *BioIn 14; WhoSSW 73, 84, 86, 91, 93, 95, 97; WhoWor 74, 76*

Johnson, Larry
[Larry Demetric Johnson]
American. Basketball Player
Forward from NV-Las Vegas named NBA rookie of the year, 1992, averaging 19.2 points, 11 rebounds and 3.6 assists that season.
b. Mar 14, 1969 in Tyler, Texas
Source: *News 93-3; WhoAfA 96; WhoAm 94, 95, 96, 97; WhoBlA 94; WhoSSW 95*

Johnson, Lionel Pigot
English. Journalist, Editor
Wrote *Art of Thomas Hardy,* 1894.
b. Mar 15, 1867 in Broadstairs, England
d. Oct 4, 1902 in London, England
Source: *AtlBL; BioIn 13, 15, 16; BritAu 19; CamGEL; CasWL; Chambr 3; ChhPo, S2, S3; CnE&AP; ConAu 117; DcEnA A; DcEuL; DcLB 19; DcLEL; DcNaB S2; EvLB; GrWrEL P; LngCTC; NewC; NewCBEL; OxCEng 67, 85, 95; PenC ENG; PoIre; REn; WebE&AL*

Johnson, Lonnie
[Alonzo Johnson]
American. Musician, Singer
Jazz and blues guitarist; appeared as a guest musician with Louis Armstrong's Hot Five, 1927, and with Duke Ellington and the Chocolate Dandies, 1928; recorded his biggest hit "Tomorrow Night" in 1948; travelled with the American Folk Blues Festival, 1963; performed last show with Buddy Guy at Toronto's Massey Hall, 1970.
b. Feb 8, 1899 in New Orleans, Louisiana
d. Jun 6, 1970
Source: *ConMus 17; NewAmDM; PenEncP*

Johnson, Luci Baines
American.
Younger daughter of Lyndon Johnson.
b. Jul 2, 1947 in Washington, District of Columbia
Source: *BioIn 6, 7, 8, 9, 10, 21; BioNews 74; NewYTBE 71*

Johnson, Lynda Bird
[Mrs. Charles Robb]
American.
Elder daughter of Lyndon Johnson.
b. Mar 19, 1944 in Washington, District of Columbia
Source: *BioIn 6; BioNews 74*

Johnson, Lyndon B(aines)
American. US President
Dem., 36th pres., 1963-69; domestic improvements overshadowed by US involvement in S. Vietnam.
b. Aug 27, 1908 in Stonewall, Texas
d. Jan 22, 1973 in Johnson City, Texas
Source: *AmAu&B; AmDec 1960; AmPolLe; Benet 96; BenetAL 91; BiDrAC; BiDrUSC 89; BiDrUSE 71, 89; BioIn 2, 3, 4, 5, 6, 7, 8, 9, 10, 11, 12, 13; ConAu 23NR, 41R, 53; CopCroC; CurBio 51, 64, 73; DcAmB S9; EncAAH; EncAB-H 1974, 1996; EncCW; EncMcCE; EncSoH; FacFETw; FacPr 89, 93; HealPre; HisEAAC; HisWorL; LegTOT; LinLib L; McGEWB; NatCAB 58; NewYTBE 71, 73; ObitOF 79; ObitT 1971; OxCAmH; OxCAmL 65, 83; RAdv 13-3; REn; VicePre; WebAB 74, 79; WhAm 5; WhAmP; WhDW; WhoGov 72; WhoSSW 73; WorAl; WorAlBi*

Johnson, Lynn-Holly
American. Skater, Actor
Former Ice Capades star; starred in movie *Ice Castles,* 1979.
b. 1959 in Chicago, Illinois
Source: *BioIn 12; WhoHol 92*

Johnson, Mark
American. Hockey Player
Center, 1980-90, mostly with New Jersey; member US Olympic gold medal-winning team, 1980.
b. Sep 22, 1957 in Madison, Wisconsin
Source: *HocEn; HocReg 87*

Johnson, Marques Kevin
American. Basketball Player
Forward, Milwaukee, 1977-84, LA Clippers, 1984-88; college player of yr., 1977.
b. Feb 8, 1956 in Natchitoches, Louisiana
Source: *BiDAmSp Sup; OfNBA 87; WhoAfA 96; WhoAm 80, 82, 84, 86, 88, 90, 92; WhoBlA 88, 92, 94; WhoEmL 89; WhoWest 87, 89; WhoWor 82*

Johnson, Martin Elmer
American. Author, Filmmaker, Explorer
Made African, S Seas expeditions, filming vanishing wildlife.
b. Oct 9, 1884 in Rockford, Illinois
d. Jan 13, 1937 in Los Angeles, California
Source: *AmAu&B; AmBi; BioIn 6, 7, 9, 10, 14, 15, 16, 18, 19, 20; DcFM; DcNAA; Film 1; LinLib L, S; NatCAB 24, 28; REnAL; TwYS; WhAm 1; WhScrn 77*

Johnson, Michael
American. Track Athlete
Won gold medals in the 200- and 400-meter races, 1996 Olympics.
b. Sep 13, 1967 in Dallas, Texas
Source: *AfrAmSG; ConBlB 13; CurBio 96; WhoWor 97*

Johnson, Moose
[Ernest Johnson]
Canadian. Hockey Player
Left-wing defenseman with several amateur Canadian teams, early 1900s; played with longest stick ever; Hall of Fame, 1952.
b. 1886 in Montreal, Quebec, Canada
d. Mar 25, 1963 in White Rock, British Columbia, Canada
Source: *WhoHcky 73*

Johnson, Mordecai Wyatt
American. University Administrator
First black pres., Howard U, the largest black U in country, 1926-60.
b. Jan 12, 1890 in Paris, Texas
d. Sep 10, 1976 in Washington, District of Columbia
Source: *BiDAmEd; BioIn 1, 3, 4, 6, 8; CurBio 41; DcAmB S10; EncAACR; InB&W 80, 85; ObitOF 79; WhAm 7*

Johnson, Nicholas
American. Government Official, Lawyer, Writer
FCC commissioner, 1966-73; wrote *Test Pattern for Living,* 1972.
b. Sep 23, 1934 in Iowa City, Iowa
Source: *AmAu&B; BioIn 8, 9, 10; BlueB 76; CelR; ConAu 29R; CurBio 68; EncAJ; LesBEnT; NewYTBE 71; NewYTET; WhoAm 74, 76, 78, 80, 82, 84, 86, 88, 92, 94, 95, 96, 97; WhoGov 72; WhoSSW 73; WhoUSWr 88; WhoWor 74, 76; WhoWrEP 89, 92, 95; WrDr 76, 80, 82, 84, 86, 88, 90, 92, 94, 96*

Johnson, Nunnally
American. Director, Screenwriter, Producer
Best-known films *The Grapes of Wrath,* 1940; *The Three Faces of Eve,* 1957.
b. Dec 5, 1897 in Columbus, Georgia
d. Mar 25, 1977 in Los Angeles, California
Source: *AmAu&B; BenetAL 91; BiDFilm, 81, 94; BioIn 1, 6, 8, 9, 11, 12, 14, 17; ChhPo; CmMov; ConAu 69, 81; CurBio 41, 77, 77N; DcFM; DcLB 26; EncAFC; FilmEn; FilmgC; HalFC 80, 84, 88; IntDcF 1-4, 2-4; IntMPA 75, 76, 77; ItaFilm; LegTOT; MiSFD 9N; OxCFilm; REnAL; WhAm 7; WhoAm 74, 76; WhoWor 74; WorEFlm*

Johnson, Osa Helen Leighty
[Mrs. Martin Johnson]
American. Explorer
Accompanied husband on expeditions; co-author *Safari,* 1928.
b. Mar 14, 1894 in Chanute, Kansas
d. Jan 7, 1953 in New York, New York
Source: *AmAu&B; AuBYP 2; BioIn 14, 15, 16, 18, 19, 20; CurBio 40, 53; DcAmB S5; InWom, SUP; LibW; NatCAB 39; REnAL; WhAm 3; WhScrn 77; WomWMM*

Johnson, Pamela Hansford
[Mrs. C P Snow; Baroness Pamela Hansford Johnson Snow]
English. Author, Critic
Versatile writer of psychological novels, literary studies: *Catherine Carter,* 1952.
b. May 29, 1912 in London, England
d. Jun 18, 1981 in London, England
Source: *AnObit 1981; ArtclWW 2; Au&Wr 71; Benet 87, 96; BioIn 1, 4, 5, 8, 10, 12, 13, 16, 17; BlmGEL; BlmGWL; BlueB 76; CamGLE; ConAu 1R, 2NR, 28NR, 104; ConLC 1, 7, 27; ConNov 72, 76, 82; CurBio 48, 81, 81N; DcArts; DcLB 15; DcLEL; DcNaB 1981; EncBrWW; EncWL; EvLB; FacFETw; FemiCLE; GrWrEL N; IntAu&W 76, 77, 82; IntWW 74, 75, 76, 77, 78, 79, 80, 81; InWom, SUP; LngCEL; LngCTC; MajTwCW; ModBrL, S1; ModWoWr; NewC; NewCBEL; NewYTBS 81; OxCEng 85, 95; REn; RfGEnL 91; RGTwCWr; TwCA SUP; TwCWr; WebE&AL; WhAm 8; Who 74; WhoAmW 66, 68, 70, 72, 74, 75, 77; WhoWor 74, 76, 78; WrDr 76, 80, 82*

Johnson, Paul (Bede)
English. Journalist
Once with the *New Statesman,* a liberal British journal, he became a conservative and has written columns for the *Sunday Telegraph* and *Spectator.*
b. Nov 2, 1928 in Barton, England
Source: *Au&Wr 71; BestSel 89-4; BioIn 7, 12, 15, 16, 20, 21; BlueB 76; ConAu 17R, 34NR; CurBio 94; IntAu&W 77, 89, 91, 93; IntWW 77, 78, 79, 80, 81, 82, 83, 89, 91, 93; OxCEng 85, 95; Who 74, 82, 83, 85, 88, 90, 92, 94; WhoWor 74, 76; WorAu 1985; WrDr 76, 80, 82, 84, 86, 88, 90, 92, 94, 96*

Johnson, Pete
American. Football Player
Running back, 1977-84, mostly with Cincinnati; suspended by NFL for drug involvement, 1983; acquitted in court, 1988.
b. Mar 2, 1954 in Peach County, Georgia
Source: *BioIn 13; FootReg 85*

Johnson, Philip Cortelyou
American. Architect, Author
Designed Lincoln Center, 1964 and Manhattan's AT&T headquarters, 1978 among others.
b. Jul 8, 1906 in Cleveland, Ohio
Source: *AmCulL; Benet 96; BioIn 3, 4, 5, 6, 7, 9, 10, 11, 12, 13, 14, 15, 16, 17, 18, 19, 20, 21; BriEAA; ConArch 87, 94; ConAu 106; CurBio 57; DcArts; EncAAr 1, 2; EncAB-H 1996; IntWW 74, 75, 76, 77, 78, 79, 80, 81, 82, 83, 89, 91, 93; McGDA; McGEWB; WebAB 74, 79; Who 74, 82, 83, 85, 88, 90, 92, 94; WhoAm 74, 76, 78, 80, 82, 84, 86, 88, 92, 94, 95, 96; WhoAmA 73, 76, 78, 80, 82, 84; WhoArch; WhoE 85; WhoWor 78, 84, 87, 89, 91, 93, 95; WorAl*

Johnson, Pierre Marc
Canadian. Politician
Conservative who succeeded Rene Levesque as leader of Parti Quebecois; opposition leader, 1985-87.
b. Jul 5, 1946 in Montreal, Quebec, Canada
Source: *BioIn 14, 15; CanWW 31, 81, 83, 89; ConNews 85-4; IntWW 89, 91, 93; NewYTBS 85; WhoAm 86, 88, 90; WhoE 86, 89; WhoEmL 87; WhoWor 89*

Johnson, Rafer Lewis
American. Track Athlete
Won silver medal in decathlon, 1956 Olympics; gold medal, 1960 Olympics; lights Summer Olympic flame, 1984.
b. Aug 18, 1935 in Hillsboro, Texas
Source: *BiDAmSp OS; BioIn 4, 5, 6, 7, 8, 9, 16, 18, 21; CurBio 61; FilmgC; WhoAm 76, 78, 80, 82, 84; WhoBlA 80, 85, 90, 92; WhoHol A; WhoTr&F 73*

Johnson, Randy
[Randall David Johnson]
American. Baseball Player
Pitcher, Seattle Mariners, 1989—; won Cy Young Award, 1995.
b. Sep 10, 1963 in Walnut Creek, California

Source: *Ballpl 90; News 96, 96-2; WhoAm 94, 95, 96, 97; WhoSpor; WhoWest 94, 96*

Johnson, Raynor Carey
English. Physicist, Author
Books on parapsychology include *Nurslings of Immortality,* 1957.
b. Apr 5, 1901 in Leeds, England
d. 1987
Source: *Au&Wr 71; BiDPara; ConAu 115; EncO&P 1*

Johnson, Reverdy
[The Trimmer]
American. Lawyer, Diplomat
Landmark cases include "Brown vs. Maryland," 1827; "Dred Scott vs. Sanford," 1857.
b. May 21, 1796 in Annapolis, Maryland
d. Feb 10, 1876 in Annapolis, Maryland
Source: *AmBi; ApCAB; BiAUS, SUP; BiDMoPL; BiDrAC; BiDrUSC 89; BiDrUSE 71, 89; BiDSA; BioIn 6, 8, 10, 16; CelCen; CivWDc; DcAmB; DcAmDH 80, 89; DcBiPP; Drake; EncSoH; HarEnUS; NatCAB 4; TwCBDA; WebAB 74, 79; WhAm HS; WhAmP*

Johnson, Richard
English. Actor
Films include *Take All of Me,* 1978; *The Comeback,* 1982.
b. Jul 30, 1927 in Upminster, England
Source: *BiE&WWA; ConTFT 5, 15; FilmAG WE; FilmEn; FilmgC; HalFC 80, 84, 88; IlWWBF; IntMPA 75, 76, 77, 78, 79, 80, 81, 82, 84, 86, 88, 92, 94, 96; ItaFilm; MovMk; VarWW 85; WhoHol 92, A; WhoThe 72, 77, 81*

Johnson, Richard Mentor
American. US Vice President
VP under Martin Van Buren, 1837-41.
b. Oct 17, 1781 in Beargrass, Kentucky
d. Nov 19, 1850 in Frankfort, Kentucky
Source: *AmPolLe; ApCAB; BiDrAC; BiDrUSE 71, 89; BiDSA; DcAmMiB; Drake; EncSoB; HarEnUS; LinLib S; NatCAB 6; TwCBDA; WebAB 79; WhAm HS; WhAmP*

Johnson, Robert
American. Singer
Delta blues singer during 1930s; songs include, "I Believe I'll Dust My Broom," and "Sweet Home Chicago," 1936-37.
b. May 8, 1911 in Hazelhurst, Mississippi
Source: *BlksB&W; ConBlB 2; ConMus 6; DcTwCCu 5; InB&W 80; OnThGG; OxCPMus; PenEncP; RolSEnR 83*

Johnson, Robert
[K C and the Sunshine Band]
American. Musician
Drummer with the Sunshine Band since 1973.
b. Mar 21, 1953 in Miami, Florida
Source: *WhoRocM 82*

Johnson, Robert Louis
American. Broadcasting Executive
CEO, cable TV's Black Entertainment Television Network, 1979—; chm., pres., CEO, BET Holdings, Inc., 1993—.
b. Apr 8, 1946 in Hickory, Mississippi
Source: *ConBlB 3; CurBio 94; Dun&B 90; WhoAm 88, 90, 92, 94, 95, 96, 97; WhoBlA 90; WhoEnt 92; WhoFI 85, 92, 94, 96; WhoWor 96, 97*

Johnson, Robert Willard
American. Educator
Professor, Purdue U, 1964—; affiliated with the Credit Research Center, 1974-90; writings include *Capital Budgeting,* 1977.
b. Dec 23, 1921 in Denver, Colorado
Source: *AmMWSc 73S, 78S; ConAu 17R; WhoAm 74, 76, 78, 80, 82, 84, 86, 88, 90, 92, 94, 95, 96, 97; WhoCon 73; WhoEc 81; WrDr 76, 80, 86*

Johnson, Samuel
[Dr. Johnson]
"Great Cham of Literature"
English. Lexicographer, Critic
Wrote first great critique of Shakespeare, 1765; *Dictionary of the English Language,* 1755.
b. Sep 18, 1709 in Litchfield, England
d. Dec 13, 1784 in London, England
Source: *Alli; AtlBL; BbD; Benet 87, 96; BiD&SB; BioIn 1, 2, 3, 4, 5, 6, 7, 8, 9, 10, 11, 12, 13, 14, 15, 16, 17, 18, 19, 20, 21; BlkwCE; BlmGEL; BritAu; BritWr 3; CamGEL; CamGLE; CamGWoT; CasWL; ChhPo, S1, S2, S3; CnDBLB 2; CnE&AP; CrtT 2, 4; CyEd; CyWA 58; DcAmC; DcArts; DcBiA; DcBiPP; DcEnA, A; DcEnL; DcEuL; DcLB 39, 95, 104, 142; DcLEL; DcNaB; DcPup; Dis&D; EncEnl; EncPaPR 91; EncSF, 93; Ent; EvLB; GrWrEL N, P; LinLib L, S; LitC 15; LngCEL; LuthC 75; MagSWL; McGEWB; MouLC 2; NewC; NewCBEL; NotNAT B; OxCAmL 65, 83, 95; OxCEng 67, 85, 95; OxCMus; OxCPhil; OxCThe 67, 83; PenC ENG; PlP&P; RAdv 14, 13-1; RComWL; REn; RfGEnL 91; RGFBP; WebBD 83; WebE&AL; WhDW; WorAl; WorAlBi; WorLitC*

Johnson, Samuel C
American. Manufacturer
Established firm which became major wax manufacturer, 1886.
b. 1833
d. 1919
Source: *Entr*

Johnson, Sonia
American. Feminist
ERA support led to excommunication by Mormon Church, 1979; wrote *From Housewife to Heretic,* 1981.
b. Feb 27, 1936? in Malad, Idaho
Source: *BioIn 12, 14, 15, 17; ConAu 118; CurBio 85; InWom SUP; NewYTBS 79*

Johnson, Steve
[Clarence Stephen Johnson]
American. Basketball Player
Forward, 1981—, with several NBA teams; led NBA in field goal percentage, 1986.
b. Nov 3, 1957 in Akron, Ohio
Source: *OfNBA 87; WhoAfA 96; WhoBlA 92, 94*

Johnson, Tim
American. Politician
Dem. senator, SD, 1997—.
b. Dec 28, 1946
Source: *AlmAP 88, 92, 96; CngDr 87, 89, 91, 93, 95*

Johnson, Tom
[Thomas Christian Johnson]
Canadian. Hockey Player
Defenseman, 1947-48, 1950-65, mostly with Montreal; won Norris Trophy, 1959; Hall of Fame, 1970.
b. Feb 18, 1928 in Baldur, Manitoba, Canada
Source: *BioIn 10; HocEn; WhoE 74; WhoHcky 73*

Johnson, U(ral) Alexis
American. Diplomat
In foreign service beginning in 1935; served as ambassador to Czechoslovakia, 1953-58, Thailand, 1958-61, Japan, 1966-69.
b. Oct 17, 1908 in Falun, Kansas
d. Mar 24, 1997 in Raleigh, North Carolina
Source: *BioIn 4, 5, 7, 8, 11, 12, 14, 16; ConAu 143; CurBio 55; DcAmDH 80, 89; EncCW; IntWW 82; IntYB 82; PolProf NF; USBiR 74; WhoAm 78; WhoAmP 81; WhoGov 72, 77; WhoWor 74; WrDr 96*

Johnson, Van
"The Voiceless Sinatra"
American. Actor
Bobby-soxers idol in MGM films throughout 1940s; later free-lanced, did TV, dinner-theater shows.
b. Aug 25, 1916 in Newport, Rhode Island
Source: *BiDFilm, 81; BiE&WWA; BioIn 1, 6, 11, 15, 16; CelR, 90; CmMov; CmpEPM; ConTFT 4; CurBio 45; EncAFC; FilmEn; FilmgC; ForYSC; HalFC 80, 84, 88; IntDcF 1-3, 2-3; IntMPA 75, 76, 77, 78, 79, 80, 81, 82, 84, 86, 88, 92, 94, 96; ItaFilm; LegTOT; MGM; MotPP; MovMk; OxCFilm; VarWW 85; WhoAm 78, 80, 82, 84, 86, 92; WhoHol 92, A; WhoThe 77, 81; WorAl; WorAlBi; WorEFlm*

Johnson, Virginia (Alma Fairfax)
American. Dancer, Choreographer
With Dance Theatre of Harlem, 1969—, as soloist and prima ballerina.
b. Jan 25, 1950 in Washington, District of Columbia
Source: *BioIn 14, 15, 16, 17; BlkWAm; ConBlB 9; CurBio 85; DcTwCCu 5; InB&W 80, 85; IntDcB; IntWWM 85;*

InWom SUP; NotBlAW 2; WhoAfA 96; WhoAm 78, 84, 86, 92, 94, 95, 96, 97; WhoAmW 95; WhoBlA 88, 90, 92, 94; WhoEnt 92

Johnson, Virginia E
[Masters and Johnson]
American. Psychologist
Researcher in human sexuality; wrote, with then husband William H Masters, *Human Sexual Response,* 1966.
b. Feb 11, 1925 in Springfield, Missouri
Source: *AmAu&B; AuNews 1; CurBio 76; EncAB-H 1974; NewYTBE 70; WhoAm 74; WhoAmW 77; WrDr 86*

Johnson, Wallace Edward
American. Hotel Executive
Co-founder, Holiday Inns hotel chain, 1953-79.
b. 1902?
d. Apr 27, 1988 in Memphis, Tennessee
Source: *BioIn 2, 6*

Johnson, Walter
[Thomas Walter Johnson]
American. Historian, Educator
Wrote on American history: *William Allen White's America,* 1947.
b. Jun 27, 1915 in Nahant, Massachusetts
d. Jun 14, 1985 in Ludington, Michigan
Source: *BioIn 4, 14; BlueB 76; ConAu 89, 116; CurBio 57, 85, 85N; DrAS 74H, 78H, 82H; IntAu&W 77, 82; IntWW 74, 75, 76, 77, 78, 79, 80, 81, 82, 83; WhoAm 74, 76, 78, 80, 82, 84; WhoUSWr 88; WhoWest 74, 76; WhoWor 74; WrDr 80, 82, 84, 86*

Johnson, Walter Perry
"Barney"; "The Big Train"
American. Baseball Player, Baseball Manager
Pitcher, 1907-27; holds ML record for shutouts, 110; second in career wins, 416; Hall of Fame, 1936.
b. Nov 6, 1887 in Humboldt, Kansas
d. Dec 10, 1946 in Washington, District of Columbia
Source: *BiDAmSp BB; BioIn 1, 2, 3, 4, 5, 6, 7, 8, 9, 10; DcAmB S4; OxCAmH; WebAB 74, 79; WhAm 4, HSA; WhoProB 73; WorAl*

Johnson, William
American. Supreme Court Justice
Appointed by Jefferson, served 1804-34.
b. Dec 27, 1771 in Charleston, South Carolina
d. Aug 4, 1834 in New York, New York
Source: *ApCAB; BiAUS; BiDFedJ; BiDSA; BioIn 2, 3, 5, 15, 17; DcAmB; DcNAA; Drake; EncSoH; HarEnUS; LinLib L; NatCAB 2; OxCSupC; SupCtJu; TwCBDA; WebAB 74, 79; WhAm HS*

Johnson, William, Sir
Irish. Government Official
Superintendant of Indian affairs north of Ohio River, 1756.
b. 1715 in Smithtown, Ireland
d. Jul 11, 1774 in Johnstown, New York
Source: *Alli; AmBi; AmRev; ApCAB; BenetAL 91; BioIn 1, 2, 4, 5, 7, 8, 9, 10, 11, 12, 16, 18, 20; BlkwEAR; DcAmB; DcAmMiB; DcCanB 4; DcIrB 78, 88; DcNaB; Drake; EncAB-H 1974, 1996; EncAR; EncCRAm; EncNAB; HarEnMi; HarEnUS; HisDBrE; MacDCB 78; McGEWB; NatCAB 5; OxCAmH; OxCAmL 65, 83, 95; OxCCan; REnAL; REnAW; WebAB 74, 79; WebAMB; WhAm HS; WhAmRev; WhDW; WhNaAH*

Johnson, William Henry
American. Painter
Landscape and portrait painter; themes focused on the South and African heritage.
b. Mar 18, 1901 in Florence, South Carolina
d. Apr 13, 1970 in Long Island, New York
Source: *AfroAA; ConBlB 3; InB&W 80, 85*

Johnston, Albert Sidney
American. Military Leader
Served in Mexican War for the Union 1845; served in Civil War for Confederate Army, 1861.
b. Feb 2, 1803 in Washington, Kentucky
d. Apr 6, 1862 in Shiloh, Tennessee
Source: *AmBi; ApCAB; BiDConf; BioIn 1, 4, 5, 6, 7, 17; CivWDc; DcAmB; DcAmMiB; Drake; EncSoH; GenMudB; HarEnMi; HarEnUS; LinLib S; NatCAB 29; REnAW; TwCBDA; WebAB 74, 79; WebAMB; WhAm HS; WhCiWar; WhoMilH 76*

Johnston, Annie Fellows
American. Children's Author
Wrote *Little Colonel* series, 1896-1910.
b. May 15, 1863 in Evansville, Indiana
d. Oct 5, 1931 in Pewee Valley, Kentucky
Source: *AmAu&B; AmWomPl; AmWomWr; ArizL; BenetAL 91; BiDSA; BioIn 15; CarSB; ChhPo; ConAu 116; DcAmAu; DcAmB; DcLB 42; DcNAA; IndAu 1816; InWom SUP; JBA 34; LibW; LiHiK; NatCAB 13; NotAW; OxCAmL 65, 83, 95; OxCChiL; REnAL; SmATA 37; TwCA, SUP; WhAm 1; WomWWA 14*

Johnston, Basil H.
Canadian. Author
Wrote *Indian School Days,* 1988; received the Order of Ontario, 1989.
b. Jul 13, 1929 in Parry Island Indian Reserv Ontario, Canada
Source: *ConAu 11NR, 28NR, 69; ConCaAu 1; DcLB 60; NatNAL; NotNaAm*

Johnston, Frances Benjamin
American. Photographer
Pioneer in photojournalism; took photos of White House interior, 1893.
b. Jan 15, 1864 in Grafton, West Virginia
d. May 16, 1952 in New Orleans, Louisiana
Source: *BioIn 1, 2, 3, 9, 10, 12, 14, 17, 20; DcAmB S5; GrLiveH; HanAmWH; ICPEnP; InWom, SUP; MacBEP; NorAmWA; NotAW MOD; PeoHis; WhAm 3; WhAmArt 85; WomArt*

Johnston, Frank H
[Group of Seven]
Canadian. Artist
Landscape painter, illustrator; apathetic member, Group of Seven, 1916-22.
b. Jun 19, 1888 in Toronto, Ontario, Canada
d. Jul 1, 1949 in Toronto, Ontario, Canada
Source: *ColCR; CreCan 1*

Johnston, J. Bennett, Jr.
American. Politician
Dem. senator from LA, 1972-97; member of special committee on aging.
b. Jun 10, 1932 in Shreveport, Louisiana
Source: *AlmAP 92, 96; BioIn 9, 10, 12; CngDr 77, 79, 81, 83, 85, 87, 89, 91, 93, 95; PolsAm 84; WhoAm 82, 84, 86; WhoAmL 79; WhoAmP 73; WhoGov 77; WhoSSW 75, 78, 80, 82, 84*

Johnston, Johnny
American. Actor
Radio performer who was featured in several 1940s musicals.
b. Dec 1, 1915 in Saint Louis, Missouri
d. Jan 6, 1996 in Cape Coral, Florida
Source: *BioIn 21; FilmEn; WhoHol 92, A*

Johnston, Joseph Eggleston
American. Military Leader
Left Union Army during Civil War to join Confederate Army as brigadier general; credited for victory at first battle of Bull Run, 1861.
b. Feb 3, 1807 in Prince Edward County, Virginia
d. Feb 21, 1891 in Washington, District of Columbia
Source: *Alli SUP; AmBi; BiDConf; BiDrAC; BiDrUSC 89; BiDSA; BioIn 1, 3, 4, 5, 7, 8, 9, 10, 11, 16, 17; CelCen; CivWDc; DcAmAu; DcAmB; DcAmMiB; DcNAA; EncAB-H 1974, 1996; EncSoH; HarEnMi; LinLib S; McGEWB; NatCAB 5; OxCAmH; TwCBDA; WebAB 74, 79; WebAMB; WhAm HS; WhCiWar; WhoMilH 76; WorAl; WorAlBi*

Johnston, Neil
[Donald Neil Johnston]
American. Basketball Player
Forward, Philadelphia, 1951-59; led NBA in scoring, 1953-55, in rebounding, 1955.
b. Feb 4, 1929 in Chillicothe, Ohio
d. Sep 27, 1978
Source: *BasBi; BiDAmSp BK; BioIn 11; OfNBA 87; WhoBbl 73; WhoSpor*

Johnston, Richard Malcolm
American. Author
Founder, Pen Lucy School, Baltimore, 1867; writings include *Old Mark Langston,* 1884.
b. Mar 8, 1822 in Oak Grove, Georgia
d. Sep 23, 1898 in Baltimore, Maryland
Source: *Alli SUP; AmAu; AmAu&B; AmBi; ApCAB; BenetAL 91; BibAL; BiDAmEd; BiD&SB; BiDSA; BioIn 3, 8, 12; DcAmAu; DcAmB; DcBiA; DcCathB; DcLB 74; DcLEL; DcNAA; FifSWrB; HarEnUS; NatCAB 1; OxCAmL 65, 83, 95; REnAL; SouWr; TwCBDA; WhAm HS*

Johnstone, Jay
[John William Johnstone, Jr]
American. Baseball Player
Outfielder, 1966-85; set playoff record for highest batting average in three-game series, 1976.
b. Nov 20, 1945 in Manchester, Connecticut
Source: *Ballpl 90; BaseReg 86; BioIn 13*

John the Apostle, Saint
[Saint John the Divine; Saint John the Evangelist]
Religious Figure
One of the 12 apostles of Jesus; wrote the Book of Revelations in the New Testament.
b. 1st cent.
Source: *BioIn 20; IlEncMy*

John the Baptist
Biblical Figure
Baptized Jesus in river Jordan; feast day: June 24.
b. c. 1st cent. AD, Judea
Source: *Benet 87, 96; BioIn 9, 19, 20; DcCathB; Dis&D; EncEarC; McGDA; McGEWB; OxDcByz; REn; WebBD 83*

John XXIII, Pope
[Angelo Guiseppe Roncalli]
Italian. Religious Leader
Pope, 1958-63; convened Vatican II, 1962, to effect reforms within church; promoted unity of Christians.
b. Nov 25, 1881 in Sotto il Monte, Italy
d. Jun 3, 1963 in Rome, Italy
Source: *McGEWB; NewCol 75; WebBD 83; WhAm 4; WhDW*

Joiner, Charlie
[Charles Joiner, Jr]
American. Football Player
Wide receiver, 1969-86, mostly with San Diego; set NFL records for most pass receptions, 750, in career.
b. Oct 14, 1947 in Many, Louisiana
Source: *BiDAmSp FB; FootReg 86, 87; WhoAfA 96; WhoBlA 77, 80, 85, 88, 90, 92, 94*

Jojola, Ted
American. Educator
Published *Memoirs of an American Indian House,* 1976; researched various aspects of Native American culture.
b. Nov 19, 1951 in Isleta Pueblo, New Mexico
Source: *BioIn 21; NotNaAm*

Jolas, Betsy
American. Composer
Works include "mini-opera," *O Wall,* 1976.
b. Aug 5, 1926 in Paris, France
Source: *Baker 78, 84, 92; BioIn 12, 17, 21; BriBkM 80; ConCom 92; DcCM; IntWWM 85, 90; InWom SUP; NewAmDM; NewGrDA 86; NewGrDM 80; NewGrDO; NewYTBE 73; WhoAm 94, 95, 96, 97; WhoAmM 83; WhoFr 79; WhoWor 87; WomCom*

Joliat, Aurel
Canadian. Hockey Player
Left wing, Montreal, 1922-38; won Hart Trophy, 1934; Hall of Fame, 1945.
b. Aug 29, 1901 in Ottawa, Ontario, Canada
Source: *BioIn 2; WhoHcky 73; WhoSpor*

Joliot(-Curie), (Jean) Frederic
French. Physicist
With wife Irene, won Nobel Prize in chemistry for contribution to nuclear research, 1935.
b. Mar 19, 1900 in Paris, France
d. Aug 14, 1958 in Paris, France
Source: *AsBiEn; BioIn 1, 3, 5, 6, 7, 11, 12; CamDcSc; CurBio 58; DcScB; McGEWB; NewCol 75; NobelP; WhAm 3; WorAl*

Joliot-Curie, Irene
French. Physicist
With husband, Frederic, studied artificial radioactivity; contributed to discovery of neutron.
b. Sep 12, 1897 in Paris, France
d. Mar 17, 1956 in Paris, France
Source: *AsBiEn; BiDFrPL; BiESc; BioIn 14, 15, 16, 17, 18, 19, 20; CamDcSc; ContDcW 89; CurBio 40, 56; DcScB; FacFETw; GoodHs; HerW, 84; InSci; IntDcWB; InWom, SUP; LadLa 86; LarDcSc; LegTOT; LinLib S; NobelP; NotTwCS; WhAm 3; WhoNob, 90, 95; WorAl; WorAlBi; WorScD*

Jolliet, Louis
Canadian. Explorer
First white man, with Jacques Marquette, to travel down Mississippi River, 1672.
b. 1645 in Beaupre, Quebec, Canada
d. May 1700 in Anticosti Island, Quebec, Canada
Source: *AmBi; ApCAB; BioIn 18, 20; DcAmB; DcCanB 1; EncCRAm; Expl 93; LegTOT; MacDCB 78; McGEWB; NatCAB 5; OxCAmH; OxCCan; REn; REnAW; WebAB 74, 79; WhNaAH; WhWE; WorAl; WorAlBi*

Jolson, Al
[Asa Yoelson]
American. Singer
Starred in *The Jazz Singer,* 1927, the first talking film.
b. May 26, 1886 in Saint Petersburg, Russia
d. Oct 23, 1950 in San Francisco, California
Source: *AmPS; ASCAP 66, 80; Baker 92; BiDAmM; BiDD; BiDFilm, 81, 94; BioIn 1, 12; CamGWoT; CmMov; CmpEPM; ConMus 10; CurBio 40, 50; DcAmB S4; DcArts; EncAFC; EncMT; EncVaud; EncWB; Ent; FacFETw; FamA&A; FilmEn; FilmgC; HalFC 80, 84, 88; IntDcF 1-3, 2-3; LegTOT; MotPP; MovMk; NewAmDM; NewGrDA 86; NewGrDM 80; NewYTBS 74; NotNAT A, B; OxCAmH; OxCAmT 84; OxCFilm; OxCPMus; PenEncP; PlP&P; RadStar; SaTiSS; WebAB 74, 79; WhAm 3; WhScrn 74, 77, 83; WhThe; WorAl; WorAlBi; WorEFlm*

Jommelli, Niccolo
"The Italian Gluck"
Italian. Composer
Developed more progressive, realistic Italian opera; wrote church music, opera *Armida,* 1770.
b. Sep 10, 1714 in Aversa, Italy
d. Aug 25, 1774 in Naples, Italy
Source: *Baker 78, 84, 92; BioIn 4, 7, 12; BriBkM 80; GrComp; IntDcOp; MusMk; NewAmDM; NewEOp 71; NewGrDM 80; NewGrDO; OxCMus*

Jonah
Hebrew. Biblical Figure
Hebrew prophet whose story of being swallowed by a whale is told in Old Testament, Book of Jonah.
Source: *Benet 96; BioIn 1, 2, 4, 5, 6, 7, 9, 10, 11, 12, 14, 15, 16, 17, 20; DcBiPP; EncEarC; LngCEL; UFOEn; WebBD 83*

Jonas, Franz
Austrian. Political Leader
Pres. of Republic of Austria, 1965-74.
b. Oct 4, 1899 in Vienna, Austria
d. Apr 24, 1974 in Vienna, Austria
Source: *BioIn 7, 10; DcPol; NewYTBS 74; ObitT 1971; WhAm 6; WhoGov 72; WhoWor 74*

Jonas, Hans
American. Philosopher
Pioneer in the field of biomedical ethics; gained attention in 1964 for claiming that Heidegger was pro-Hitler.
b. May 10, 1903 in Moenchengladbach, Germany
d. Feb 5, 1993 in New Rochelle, New York
Source: *AnObit 1993; BioIn 18, 19; ConAu 7NR, 23NR, 61, 140; DrAS 74P, 78P, 82P; WhoAm 74, 76, 78; WhoAmJ 80; WhoE 83*

Jonathan, Leabua, Chief
Political Leader
Prime minister of Lesotho for over 20 yrs. before ousted in coup, 1986.
b. 1914?
d. Apr 5, 1987 in Pretoria, South Africa
Source: *AfSS 78, 79, 80, 81, 82; AnObit 1987; BioIn 15, 21; DcAfHiB 86S; EncSoA; IntWW 76, 77, 78, 79, 80, 81, 82, 83; NewYTBE 70; NewYTBS 87*

Jones, Allan
American. Singer
Father of Jack Jones, famous for song "Donkey Serenade," 1937; starred in Broadway musicals during the 1930s.
b. Oct 14, 1907? in Old Forge, Pennsylvania
d. Jun 27, 1992 in New York, New York
Source: *BioIn 11, 18; CmpEPM; ConTFT 6, 11; FilmEn; FilmgC; HalFC 80, 84, 88; HolP 30; LegTOT; MotPP; MovMk; OxCFilm; VarWW 85; WhoHol A; WorAl; WorAlBi*

Jones, Anissa
American. Actor
Played Buffy in "Family Affair," 1966-71; died of drug overdose.
b. 1958 in West Lafayette, Indiana
d. 1976
Source: *LegTOT; WhoHol A; WhScrn 83*

Jones, Arthur A
American. Businessman, Inventor
Invented Nautilus exercise equipment; CEO, Nautilus Sports/Medical Industries.
b. 1924? in Arkansas
Source: *ConNews 85-3*

Jones, Barry
English. Actor
Best known for film *Brigadoon,* 1954.
b. Mar 6, 1893 in Isle of Guernsey, England
d. 1981
Source: *BiE&WWA; BioIn 4, 5; CurBio 58; FilmgC; ForYSC; HalFC 80, 84, 88; IlWWBF; IntMPA 75, 76, 77, 78, 79, 80, 81, 82, 84, 86, 88; ItaFilm; MovMk; NotNAT; PlP&P; Who 74; WhoHol A; WhoThe 77A; WhoWor 74; WhThe*

Jones, Benjamin Allyn
American. Horse Trainer
Calumet Farms leading horse trainer, 1939-58; had seven Derby winners.
b. Dec 31, 1882 in Parnell, Missouri
d. Jun 13, 1961 in Lexington, Kentucky
Source: *BiDAmSp OS; BioIn 5, 10; DcAmB S7*

Jones, Bert(ram Hays)
American. Football Player
Quarterback, 1973-82, mostly with Baltimore; led NFL in passing, 1976.
b. Sep 7, 1951 in Ruston, Louisiana
Source: *BioIn 9, 11, 12, 13; LegTOT; NewYTBE 72; WhoAm 78, 80, 82; WhoFtbl 74*

Jones, Bill T.
American. Dancer, Choreographer
Co-founder, American Dance Asylum, 1974-82; Bill T. Jones/Arnie Zane & Co., 1982.
b. Feb 15, 1952 in Bunnell, Florida
Source: *BiDD; BioIn 12, 14, 15, 16; ConBlB 1; CurBio 93; DcTwCCu 5; GayLesB; News 91; WhoAm 94, 95, 96, 97; WhoE 95, 97*

Jones, Billy
[The Happiness Boys; The Interwoven Pair; William Reese Jones]
American. Singer
Early radio star, part of team with Ernie Hare; famous for performing some of first commercial jingles for many products.
b. Mar 15, 1889 in New York, New York
d. Nov 23, 1940 in New York, New York
Source: *BioIn 5; CurBio 41; Film 2*

Jones, Bob
American. Religious Leader
Evangelist whose message was heard in every US state, 30 foreign countries; founded Bob Jones U. in SC.
b. Oct 30, 1883 in Dale County, Alabama
d. Jan 16, 1968 in Greenville, South Carolina
Source: *BioIn 9, 17, 19; ObitOF 79; PrimTiR; TwCSAPR; WhAm 4*

Jones, Bobby
[Robert Tyre Jones, Jr]
American. Golfer
Biggest name in golf, 1920s; won 13 major tournaments as amateur; only man to win "grand slam"—US, British opens and amateurs, 1930; founded Masters tournament, 1934.
b. Mar 17, 1902 in Atlanta, Georgia
d. Dec 18, 1971 in Atlanta, Georgia
Source: *AmDec 1920; BiDAmSp OS; BioIn 2, 3, 4, 5, 6, 7, 8, 9, 10, 11, 12, 13, 15, 17, 20, 21; ConAu 113; DcAmB S9; EncWB; FacFETw; LegTOT; NewYTBE 71; OxCAmH; PeoHis; WebAB 74, 79; WhAm 5; What 1; WhDW; WhoGolf; WhoSpor; WhScrn 83; WorAl; WorAlBi*

Jones, Booker T
American. Musician, Composer, Producer
Figured in "Memphis sound" mvmt. of 1960s; hits include "Green Onions," 1962.
b. Nov 12, 1944 in Memphis, Tennessee
Source: *Baker 84; BioIn 8; ConMus 8; WhoBlA 92; WhoRocM 82*

Jones, Brereton C
American. Politician
Dem. governor, KY, 1991-95.
b. Jun 27, 1939 in Point Pleasant, West Virginia
Source: *WhoAm 90; WhoAmP 91; WhoSSW 91*

Jones, Brian
[The Rolling Stones]
English. Singer, Musician
One of original Rolling Stones; found dead in swimming pool from drug overdose.
b. Feb 26, 1943 in Cheltenham, England
d. Jul 3, 1969 in London, England
Source: *BioIn 8, 14, 15, 17, 19; ConMuA 80A; LegTOT; WhAm 5; WhScrn 77, 83*

Jones, Buck
[Charles Frederick Gebhart]
American. Actor
Western hero in "Rough Rider" serials with horse "Silver."
b. Dec 4, 1891 in Vincennes, Indiana
d. Nov 30, 1942 in Boston, Massachusetts
Source: *CmMov; CurBio 43; Film 1; FilmEn; FilmgC; MovMk; OxCFilm; TwYS; WhoHol B; WhScrn 74, 77*

Jones, Candy
[Mrs. John Nebel]
American. Model, Business Executive
Cover girl, 1940s; founded Candy Jones Career Girls School, 1947; author of many books of advice on beauty, fashion, modeling.
b. Dec 31, 1925 in Wilkes-Barre, Pennsylvania
d. Jan 18, 1990 in New York, New York
Source: *BioIn 6; ConAu 107, 130; CurBio 61, 90, 90N; InWom; NewYTBS 90*

Jones, Carl
American. Fashion Designer
Co-founded, with T. J. Walker, Cross Colours, 1990.
b. c. 1955 in Tennessee
Source: *ConBlB 7*

Jones, Carolyn
American. Actor
Played Morticia on TV series "The Addams Family," 1964-66.
b. Apr 28, 1933 in Amarillo, Texas
d. Aug 3, 1983 in Los Angeles, California
Source: *BioIn 5, 7, 8, 13; ConAu 29R, 110; CurBio 83N; FilmgC; GangFlm; IntMPA 75, 76, 77, 78, 79, 80, 81, 82; InWom, SUP; MotPP; MovMk; NewYTBS 83; VarWW 85; WhAm 8; WhoAm 74, 76, 78, 80, 82; WhoHol A; WorAl; WorAlBi*

Jones, Casey
[John Luther Jones]
American. Engineer
Folk hero of songs, ballads; killed in crash of Cannon Ball Express.
b. Mar 14, 1864 in Cayce, Kentucky
d. Apr 30, 1900 in Vaughan, Mississippi
Source: *BioIn 2, 3, 4, 7; DcArts; GayN; LinLib S; NewCol 75; OxCAmH; WebAB 74, 79*

Jones, Charles A, Jr.
[The Hostages]
American. Hostage
One of 52 held by terrorists, Nov 1979-Jan 1981.
b. Jul 1, 1940 in Memphis, Tennessee
Source: *BioIn 12; NewYTBS 81*

Jones, Christopher
American. Actor
Best known for films *The Looking Glass War,* 1969; *Ryan's Daughter,* 1971.
b. Aug 18, 1941 in Jackson, Tennessee
Source: *CelR; FilmgC; HalFC 80, 84, 88; ItaFilm; MotPP; WhoAm 76; WhoHol 92, A*

Jones, Chuck
[Charles Martin Jones]
American. Cartoonist
Animation director, Warner Brothers; created characters Road Runner, Pepe Le Pew, Wile E. Coyote, Bugs Bunny, Porky Pig, Daffy Duck.
b. Sep 21, 1912 in Spokane, Washington
Source: *ASCAP 80; Au&Arts 2; BioIn 14, 16, 17, 21; ConTFT 6; CurBio 96; DcArts; DcFM; FilmEn; FilmgC; HalFC 84; IntDcF 1-2, 2-4; IntMPA 75, 76, 77, 78, 79, 80, 81, 82, 84, 86, 88, 92, 94, 96; LegTOT; LesBEnT; NewYTET; VarWW 85; WhoAm 80, 82, 84; WhoEnt 92; WhoWest 82, 84; WhoWor 78; WorEFlm*

Jones, Cleve
American. AIDS Activist
Co-founder of the San Francisco AIDS Foundation, 1982; originator of the NAMES Project AIDS Memorial Quilt, 1987.
b. 1954
Source: *GayLesB*

Jones, David
English. Author, Artist
Known for watercolor still-life, landscape, seascape; writings include *The Tribune's Visitation,* 1969.
b. Nov 1, 1895 in Brockley, England
d. Oct 28, 1974 in London, England
Source: *Benet 87, 96; CasWL; CnDBLB 7; CnE&AP; CnMWL; ConAu 9R, 28NR, 53; ConLC 2, 4, 7, 13, 42; ConPo 70, 75; DcLB 20, 100; DcNaB 1971; EncWL 2, 3; FacFETw; GrWrEL P; IntWWP 77; LngCTC; MajTwCW; McGDA; ModBrL, S1, S2; NewC; ObitT 1971; OxCEng 67; OxCLiW 86; OxDcArt; PenC ENG; PhDcTCA 77; RAdv 1, 14, 13-1; REn; RfGEnL 91; RGFMBP; TwCPaSc; TwCWr; WhAm 6; Who 74; WhoTwCL; WorAu 1950*

Jones, David Charles
American. Army Officer, Government Official
Chm., Joint Chiefs of Staff, 1978-82; commander, US Air Force, Washington, 1974-78.
b. Jul 9, 1921 in Aberdeen, South Dakota
Source: *BioIn 10, 11; CurBio 82; IntWW 75, 76, 77, 78, 79, 80, 81, 82, 83, 89, 91, 93; NewYTBS 78; WebAMB; WhoAm 80, 82, 84, 86, 88, 90, 92, 94, 95, 96, 97; WhoGov 75, 77; WhoWor 80, 82; WorDWW*

Jones, Davy
[The Monkees; David Jones]
English. Actor, Singer
Vocalist with The Monkees on popular TV series, 1966-68.
b. Dec 30, 1945 in Manchester, England
Source: *BioIn 6, 7, 9; LegTOT; WhoHol 92*

Jones, Deacon
[David Jones]
American. Football Player
Eight-time all-pro defensive end, 1961-72, mostly with LA Rams; part of Rams' "fearsome foursome" defensive line; Hall of Fame, 1980.
b. Dec 9, 1938 in Eatonville, Florida
Source: *AfrAmSG; BiDAmSp FB; BioIn 8, 9, 10, 17, 21; LegTOT; WhoBlA 80; WhoFtbl 74; WhoSpor; WorAl; WorAlBi*

Jones, Dean Carroll
American. Actor
Starred in 1960s Disney films such as *That Darn Cat,* 1965; *The Love Bug,* 1968; comedy hit *Other People's Money,* 1991.
b. Jan 25, 1936 in Morgan County, Alabama
Source: *BiE&WWA; FilmgC; HalFC 84; IntMPA 86; MotPP; VarWW 85; WhoAm 86; WhoHol A*

Jones, Edward P.
American. Author
Wrote *Lost in the City,* 1992.
b. Oct 5, 1950
Source: *BlkWr 2; ConAu 142; ConLC 76*

Jones, Edward Vason
American. Architect
Restored, redecorated White House Oval Office, State Dept. reception rooms.
b. Aug 3, 1909 in Albany, Georgia
d. Oct 1, 1980 in Albany, Georgia
Source: *BioIn 12; WhAm 7; WhoAm 78*

Jones, Elaine R.
American. Civil Rights Activist, Lawyer
First female director-counsel of the NAACP Legal Defense and Educational Fund, 1993—.
b. Mar 2, 1944 in Norfolk, Virginia
Source: *ConBlB 7; NotBlAW 2; WhoAfA 96; WhoAm 95, 96, 97; WhoAmW 97; WhoBlA 75, 77, 80, 85, 90, 92, 94*

Jones, Eli Stanley
American. Missionary
Evangelist in India; writings include *How to Be a Transformed Person,* 1951.
b. Jan 1, 1884 in Baltimore, Maryland
d. Jan 26, 1973 in Bareilly, India
Source: *AmAu&B; BioIn 1, 2, 4, 6, 9, 10, 11, 12; ConAu 93; EncWM; LuthC 75; TwCA SUP; WhAm 5, 7; WhNAA*

Jones, Elvin
American. Jazz Musician
Considered the most influential jazz drummer; member, John Coltrane Quartet, 1960-66.
b. Sep 9, 1927 in Pontiac, Michigan
Source: *AfrAmAl 6; AllMusG; Baker 84; BiDJaz; BioIn 15, 16, 18; ConMus 9; IlEncJ; LegTOT; NewAmDM; NewGrDA 86; NewGrDJ 88; PenEncP; WhoAm 86*

Jones, George (Glenn)
"The Crown Prince of Country Music"
American. Singer
Named best male vocalist by CMA, 1980, 1981; inducted into Country Music Hall of Fame, 1992.
b. Sep 12, 1931 in Saratoga, Texas
Source: *Baker 84, 92; BgBkCoM; BiDAmM; BioIn 9, 10, 11; ConMus 4; CounME 74, 74A; CurBio 95; DcArts; EncFCWM 69, 83; HarEnCM 87; HarEnR 86; IlEncCM; LegTOT; NewGrDA 86; NewYTBS 92, 95; PenEncP; WhoAm 76, 78, 82, 84, 86, 88, 90, 92, 94, 95, 96, 97; WhoEnt 92; WhoRock 81*

Jones, (Morgan) Glyn
Welsh. Author
Writings include *The Blue Bed, and Other Stories,* 1937; *The Learning Lark,* 1960.
b. Feb 28, 1905 in Merthyr Tydfil, Wales
Source: *Au&Wr 71; BioIn 10, 13; BlueB 76; CnMWL; ConAu 3NR, 9R; ConNov 72, 76, 82, 86, 91, 96; ConPo 70, 75, 80, 85, 91, 96; DcLB 15; EngPo; IntAu&W 76, 77, 82, 86, 89, 91, 93; IntWWP 77, 82; ModBrL; OxCLiW 86; OxCTwCP; RfGShF; WorAu 1950; WrDr 76, 80, 82, 84, 86, 88, 90, 92, 94, 96*

Jones, Gorilla
[William Jones]
American. Boxer
National Boxing Association middleweight champion, 1932.
b. May 12, 1906 in Memphis, Tennessee
Source: *BioIn 1; WhoBox 74*

Jones, Grace
Jamaican. Singer, Actor, Model
In James Bond film *A View to a Kill,* 1985; star of *Vamp,* 1986; hit album *Living My Life,* 1982.
b. May 19, 1952 in Spanishtown, Jamaica
Source: *Baker 92; ConMus 9; ConTFT 7, 14; CurBio 87; DrBlPA 90; EncRk 88; HarEnR 86; IlEncBM 82; IntMPA 88, 92, 94, 96; IntWW 91, 93; LegTOT; NewGrDA 86; NewWmR; NotBlAW 2; PenEncP; RolSEnR 83; VarWW 85; WhoHol 92*

Jones, Grandpa
[Louis Marshall Jones]
American. Musician, TV Personality
Known for banjo solos on TV series "Hee Haw," 1969-93.
b. Oct 20, 1913 in Henderson County, Kentucky
Source: *BgBkCoM; BiDAmM; BioIn 12, 14; CounME 74, 74A; EncFCWM 69, 83; HarEnCM 87; IlEncCM; LegTOT; NewAmDM; NewGrDA 86; PenEncP*

Jones, Gwyneth
Welsh. Opera Singer
Dramatic soprano with Covent Garden Royal Opera since 1966; noted for Verdi, Wagner roles.
b. Nov 7, 1936 in Pontnewynydd, Wales
Source: *Baker 84, 92; BioIn 7, 9, 11, 12, 15, 17; BlueB 76; CmOp; DcArts; IntDcOp; IntWW 74, 75, 76, 77, 78, 79, 80, 81, 82, 83, 89, 91, 93; IntWWM 77, 80, 85, 90; MetOEnc; MusSN; NewAmDM; NewGrDO; OxDcOp; PenDiMP; Who 74, 82, 83, 85, 88, 90, 92, 94; WhoAm 78, 80, 82, 84, 86, 88, 90, 92, 94, 95, 96, 97; WhoAmW 74, 75, 77; WhoEnt 92; WhoMus 72; WhoOp 76; WhoWor 74, 76, 78, 82, 84, 87, 89, 91, 93, 95, 96*

Jones, Gwynn
Welsh. Educator, Author
Novels include *Richard Savage,* 1935; *Times Like These,* 1936.
b. May 24, 1907 in Blackwood, Wales
Source: *ConAu 117; ConNov 72; DcLB 15; Who 85*

Jones, Hayes
American. Track Athlete
High hurdler; won gold medal, 1964 Olympics.
b. Aug 4, 1938 in Starkville, Mississippi
Source: *BioIn 6; NewYTBE 70; WhoTr&F 73*

Jones, Henry
American. Actor
Won Tony for *Sunrise at Campobello,* 1958.
b. Aug 1, 1912 in Philadelphia, Pennsylvania
Source: *BiE&WWA; BioIn 11; ConTFT 6; EncAFC; FilmEn; FilmgC; ForYSC; HalFC 80, 84, 88; IntMPA 84, 86, 88, 92, 94, 96; NotNAT; VarWW 85; WhoAm 74, 76, 78, 80, 82, 84, 86, 90, 92, 94, 95, 96, 97; WhoEnt 92; WhoHol 92, A*

Jones, Howard
English. Singer
Dance music hits include "What Is Love," 1983; "Things Can Only Get Better," 1985.
b. Feb 23, 1955 in Southampton, England
Source: *EncRk 88; EncRkSt; HarEnR 86; LegTOT; PenEncP*

Jones, Howard Mumford
American. Author
Writings include *To the Webster-Ashburton Treaty: A Study in Anglo-American Relations, 1783-1843,* 1977.
b. Apr 16, 1892 in Saginaw, Michigan
d. May 12, 1980 in Cambridge, Massachusetts
Source: *AmAu&B; AnObit 1980; Au&Wr 71; BenetAL 91; BioIn 4, 6, 12; BlueB 76; ChhPo S1, S2; CnDAL; ConAu 85, 97; DcAmB S10; DrAS 74E, 78E; IntAu&W 77, 82; IntWW 74, 75, 76, 77, 78, 79, 80; LinLib L, S; NewYTBS 80; OxCAmL 65, 83, 95; RAdv 1; REnAL; TwCA SUP; WhAm 7; WhNAA; WhoAm 74, 76, 78, 80; WhoE 74; WhoWor 74*

Jones, Inigo
English. Architect
Introduced Italian Renaissance architecture to England; restored St. Paul's Cathedral, 1634-42.
b. Jul 15, 1573 in London, England
d. Jun 21, 1652 in London, England
Source: *Alli; AtlBL; Benet 87, 96; BiDBrA; BiDD; BioIn 1, 2, 3, 5, 6, 7, 8, 10, 11, 12, 13, 14, 15, 17; BlmGEL; CamGWoT; CnThe; CroE&S; DcArts; DcBiPP; DcBrWA; DcCathB; DcD&D; DcEnL; DcNaB; EncUrb; EncWT; Ent; IntDcAr; IntDcT 3; LegTOT; LinLib S; LngCEL; MacEA; McGDA; McGEWB; NewAmDM; NewC; NewGrDM 80; NewGrDO; NotNAT A, B; OxCArt; OxCEng 85, 95; OxCLiW 86; OxCMus; OxCThe 67, 83; OxDcArt; OxDcOp; PlP&P; REn; WhDW; WhoArch; WorAl; WorAlBi*

Jones, Isham
American. Bandleader, Songwriter
Led outstanding dance band that was most popular, 1930-35; wrote "It Had to Be You," 1924.
b. Jan 31, 1894 in Coalton, Ohio
d. Oct 19, 1956 in Hollywood, California
Source: *AllMusG; AmPS; ASCAP 66, 80; BgBands 74; BiDAmM; BiDJaz; BioIn 4, 6, 9, 12, 16; CmpEPM; EncJzS; NewGrDJ 88, 94; NotNAT B; OxCPMus; PenEncP; PopAmC; WhAm 4A; WhoJazz 72*

Jones, Jack
American. Singer
Nightclub entertainer; best known for hit title song for film *Love with the Proper Stranger,* 1964.
b. Nov 11, 1938 in Los Angeles, California
Source: *BiDAmM; BioIn 7, 13; CelR; LegTOT; PenEncP; RkOn 74; VarWW 85; WhoAm 88, 90, 92; WhoEnt 92; WhoHol 92, A; WorAl; WorAlBi*

Jones, James
American. Author
Wrote *From Here To Eternity,* 1951; adapted to film, 1953.
b. Nov 6, 1921 in Robinson, Illinois
d. May 9, 1977 in Southampton, New York
Source: *AmAu&B; AuNews 1, 2; Benet 87, 96; BenetAL 91; BioIn 2, 3, 4, 7, 8, 9, 10, 11, 12, 14, 15, 16, 17, 21; BlueB 76; CamGEL; CamGLE; CamHAL; CasWL; CelR; ConAu 1NR, 1R, 6NR, 69; ConLC 1, 3, 10; ConNov 72, 76, 82A, 86A; CyWA 89; DcLB 2, 143, Y92; DcLEL 1940; DcTwCCu 1; DrAF 76; EncWL, 2, 3; FacFETw; GrWrEL N; HalFC 84, 88; IntAu&W 76, 77; IntWW 74, 75, 76, 77; LegTOT; LiExTwC; LinLib L; MajTwCW; ModAL, S1; Novels; OxCAmL 65, 83, 95; PenC AM; RAdv 1, 14, 13-1; REn; REnAL; RfGAmL 87, 94; RGTwCWr; TwCA SUP; TwCWr; WebE&AL; WhAm 7; Who 74; WhoAm 74, 76; WhoE 74; WhoWor 74; WorAl; WorAlBi; WrDr 76*

Jones, James Earl
American. Actor
Won Tonys for *The Great White Hope,* 1969; *Fences,* 1987; won 1991 Emmy for "Gabriel's Fire;" awarded Nat. Medal of Arts, 1992.
b. Jan 17, 1931 in Arkabutla, Mississippi
Source: *AfrAmAl 6; AfrAmBi 2; AmCulL; BiDFilm 94; BiE&WWA; BioIn 6, 7, 8, 10, 11, 12; BioNews 75; BkPepl; BlksAmF; CamGWoT; CelR, 90; ConAu 146; ConBlB 3; ConTFT 4, 11; CurBio 69, 94; DcTwCCu 5; DrBlPA, 90; Ebony 1; EncAFC; Ent; FacFETw; FilmEn; HalFC 80, 84, 88; InB&W 80, 85; IntDcF 1-3, 2-3; IntMPA 84, 86, 88, 92, 94, 96; ItaFilm; LegTOT; NotNAT; OxCAmT 84; OxCThe 83; PlP&P, A; VarWW 85; WhoAfA 96; WhoAm 74, 76, 78, 80, 82, 84, 86, 88, 90, 92, 94, 95, 96, 97; WhoBlA 75, 77, 80, 85, 88, 90, 92, 94; WhoEnt 92; WhoGov 72, 75; WhoHol 92, A; WhoThe 72, 77, 81; WorAl; WorAlBi*

Jones, James Robert
American. Politician, Business Executive
U.S. congressman from OK, 1973-87; chm., Budget Com., 1980-84; chm., CEO, American Stock Exchange, 1989-93; U.S. ambassador to Mexico, 1993—.
b. May 5, 1939 in Muskogee, Oklahoma
Source: *AlmAP 80; BiDrUSC 89; BioIn 12; CngDr 79; IntWW 91; NewYTBS 78, 81; WhoAm 80, 96, 97; WhoAmP 73, 75, 77, 79, 81, 83, 85, 87, 89, 91, 93, 95; WhoFI 96; WhoGov 75, 77; WhoSSW 78, 97; WhoWor 96, 97*

Jones, Jenkin Lloyd
American. Publishing Executive
Editor, *Tulsa Tribune,* 1941-88; publisher, 1963-91.
b. Nov 1, 1911 in Madison, Wisconsin
Source: *BiDAmNC; BioIn 4, 8, 19; ConAu 9R; DcLB 127; EncTwCJ; WhoAm 80, 82, 84, 86, 88, 90, 94, 95, 96, 97; WhoFI 74, 75, 89; WhoSSW 73, 88, 91; WhoWor 84, 87, 89*

Jones, Jennifer
[Phyllis Isley]
American. Actor
Won Oscar, 1943, for *The Song of Bernadette.*
b. Mar 2, 1919 in Tulsa, Oklahoma
Source: *BiDFilm, 81, 94; BiE&WWA; BioAmW; BioIn 1, 7, 9, 10, 11, 16, 18, 20; CmMov; CurBio 44; FilmEn; FilmgC; ForYSC; HalFC 80, 84, 88; IntDcF 1-3, 2-3; IntMPA 77, 80, 84, 86, 88, 92, 94, 96; InWom, SUP; ItaFilm; LegTOT; MotPP; MovMk; OxCFilm; VarWW 85; Who 85; WhoAm 86, 88, 90, 92; WhoEnt 92; WhoHol 92, A; WhoHrs 80; WorAl; WorAlBi; WorEFlm*

Jones, Jerry
[Jerral Wayne Jones]
American. Businessman, Sports Executive
Owner, Dallas Cowboys, 1989—.
b. Oct 13, 1942 in Los Angeles, California
Source: *CurBio 96; Dun&B 88; News 94; NewYTBS 94; WhoAm 94, 95, 96, 97; WhoSSW 95; WhoWor 95, 96*

Jones, Jesse Holman
American. Government Official, Real Estate Executive
Secretary of Commerce, 1940-45; built over 30 Houston, TX skyscrapers; wrote *Fifty Billion Dollars,* 1951.
b. Apr 5, 1874 in Robertson County, Tennessee
d. Jun 1, 1956 in Houston, Texas
Source: *BiDAmBL 83; BiDrUSE 71, 89; BioIn 1, 4, 7, 10, 17, 18; CurBio 40, 56; DcAmB S6; EncAB-A 26; EncAB-H 1974; EncSoH; FacFETw; WhAm 3*

Jones, Jo(nathan)
American. Jazz Musician
Drummer with Count Basie band, 1935-48; innovative swing-era techniques were major influence on jazz drummers.
b. Oct 7, 1911 in Chicago, Illinois
d. Sep 3, 1985 in New York, New York
Source: *AllMusG; AnObit 1985; ASCAP 66, 80; Baker 84, 92; BiDAfM; BiDAmM; BiDJaz; BioIn 4, 11, 14, 16; CmpEPM; EncJzS; InB&W 80; NewAmDM; NewGrDA 86; NewGrDJ 88, 94; NewGrDM 80; NewYTBS 85; OxCPMus; PenEncP; WhoJazz 72*

Jones, Joe
[Joseph John Jones]
American. Artist
Self-taught landscape painter, lithographer, muralist; did mural for ocean liner *Independence.*
b. Apr 7, 1909 in Saint Louis, Missouri
d. Apr 9, 1963 in Morristown, New Jersey
Source: *BioIn 1, 2, 6; McGDA; WhAm 4; WhAmArt 85; WhoAmA 78N, 89N, 91N, 93N*

Jones, John Paul
American. Naval Officer
Founded American naval tradition; said "I have not yet begun to fight," during Revolutionary War.
b. Jul 6, 1747 in Kirkcudbright, Scotland
d. Jul 18, 1792 in Paris, France
Source: *AmAu&B; AmRev; ApCAB; Benet 87, 96; BenetAL 91; BioIn 1, 2, 3, 4, 5, 6, 7, 8, 9, 10, 11, 12, 13, 14, 15, 16, 20; BlkwEAR; DcAmB; DcAmMiB; DcBiPP; DcNaB; Dis&D; Drake; EncAB-H 1974, 1996; EncAR; EncCRAm; GenMudB; HarEnMi; HarEnUS; HisWorL; LegTOT; LinLib S; McGEWB; MorMA; NatCAB 2; OxCAmH; OxCAmL 65, 83, 95; OxCShps; RComAH; REn; REnAL; TwCBDA; WebAB 74, 79; WebAMB; WhAm HS; WhAmRev; WhDW; WhoMilH 76; WorAl; WorAlBi*

Jones, John Paul
[Led Zeppelin; John Baldwin]
English. Musician
Keyboardist, bassist, Led Zeppelin rock group, 1968-80.
b. Jan 3, 1946 in Sidcup, England
Source: *BioIn 10, 17; LegTOT; WhoAm 80, 82, 84; WhoRocM 82*

Jones, Jonah
[Robert E Jones]
American. Musician
Trumpeter, fine showman; with Cab Calloway, 1941-51; recorded show tunes, jazz hits.
b. Dec 31, 1909 in Louisville, Kentucky
Source: *AllMusG; BioIn 5, 10, 16; CmpEPM; DrBlPA, 90; EncJzS; IlEncJ; InB&W 80; NewGrDJ 88, 94; WhoJazz 72*

Jones, KC
American. Basketball Coach
Guard, member, eight championship teams with Boston, 1958-67; coach, Boston, 1983-88; won two NBA championships; Hall of Fame, 1989.
b. May 25, 1932 in San Francisco, California
Source: *CurBio 87; InB&W 80; NewYTBE 73; OfNBA 87; WhoAm 86; WhoBbl 73*

Jones, Kenny
[The Who]
English. Musician
Joined group as drummer, 1979.
b. Sep 16, 1948 in London, England

Jones, Madison Percy, Jr.
American. Author
Novels include *The Innocent,* 1957; *A Cry of Absence,* 1971.
b. Mar 21, 1925 in Nashville, Tennessee
Source: *Au&Wr 71; ConAu 13R; ConLC 4; ConNov 72, 76; DcLEL 1940; DrAS 74E, 78E, 82E; IntAu&W 76, 77, 82, 86, 91, 93; SouWr; WhoAm 74, 76, 78, 80; WrDr 76*

Jones, Mary Harris
"Mother Jones"
American. Labor Union Official
Leader of several labor causes; spokesperson for many strikes, including 1877 PA railroad strike; Labor Hall of Fame, 1992.
b. May 1, 1830 in Cork, Ireland
d. Nov 30, 1930 in Silver Spring, Maryland
Source: *AmRef; AmSocL; AmWomWr; BiDAmL; BiDAmLf; BiDAmLL; BioIn 1, 2, 6, 8, 9, 10, 11, 15, 16, 18, 19, 20; DcAmB; DcAmImH; EncAB-H 1974, 1996; EncWB; GrLiveH; HerW, 84; InWom, SUP; LibW; NatCAB 23; NotAW; PeoHis; WebAB 74, 79; WhAm 4, HSA*

Jones, Matilda Sissieretta Joyner
"The Black Patti"
American. Singer
First Negro prima donna; star of Black Patti Troubadours, 1896-1916.
b. Jan 5, 1869 in Portsmouth, Virginia
d. Jun 24, 1933 in Providence, Rhode Island
Source: *BioIn 20; LibW; NotAW; WomFir*

Jones, Parnelli
[Rufus Parnell Jones]
American. Auto Racer
Won Indy 500, 1963; runner up, 1965.
b. Aug 12, 1933
Source: *BiDAmSp Sup; BioIn 7, 8, 9, 10; LegTOT; WhoSpor*

Jones, Peter
[Sacred Feathers]
Canadian. Native American Chief
Ojibwa Missisauga chief; Christian missionary who was baptized in 1820.
b. 1802, Canada
d. Jun 29, 1856 in Ontario, Canada
Source: *Alli SUP; BbtC; BioIn 21; DcCanB 8; DcNAA; EncNAR; EncNoAI; EncWM; MacDCB 78; NatNAL; NotNaAm; WhNaAH*

Jones, Phil(ip Howard)
American. Broadcast Journalist
CBS Capitol Hill correspondent, 1977-89; TV show "48 Hours," 1990-95; Washingto n correspondent, 1995—; won awards for Vietnam air-war coverage, 1966, 1971.
b. Apr 27, 1937 in Marion, Indiana
Source: *ConAu 102; WhoAm 76, 78, 80, 82, 84, 90, 92, 94, 95, 96, 97; WhoE 95*

Jones, Preston St. Vrain
American. Actor, Dramatist
Wrote *A Texas Trilogy,* 1974.
b. Apr 7, 1936 in Albuquerque, New Mexico
d. Sep 19, 1979 in Dallas, Texas
Source: *BioIn 10, 11, 12; ConAu 73, 89; ConLC 10; CurBio 77, 79; DcLB 7; NewYTBS 76, 79; WhAm 7; WhoAm 78; WhoThe 81*

Jones, Quincy Delight
American. Composer, Producer
Wrote scores for over 50 films including *In Cold Blood,* 1967; *The Wiz,* 1978; worked on "We Are the World," 1985; has won numerous Grammys.
b. Mar 14, 1933 in Chicago, Illinois
Source: *AfrAmBi 1; Baker 78, 84; BgBands 74; BiDAfM; BiDAmM; BiDJaz; ConAmC 76, 82; EncJzS; HarEnR 86; IlEncBM 82; InB&W 80, 85; IntMPA 86; MusMk; VarWW 85; WhoAfA 96; WhoAm 86; WhoBlA 75, 77, 80, 88, 92, 94*

Jones, R(enato) William
American. Basketball Executive
Co-founder, FIBA, 1932; director, Olympic basketball; Hall of Fame.
b. Oct 5, 1906 in Rome, Italy
Source: *BioIn 9; WhoBbl 73*

Jones, Randy
[Randall Leo Jones]
American. Baseball Player
Pitcher, 1973-82; led NL in wins, won Cy Young Award, 1976.
b. Jan 12, 1950 in Fullerton, California
Source: *Ballpl 90; BioIn 10, 11; NewYTBS 77, 78; WhoAm 78, 80, 82; WhoSpor*

Jones, Reverend Jim
[Reverend James Jones]
American. Religious Leader
Founded People's Temple; led mass suicide of nearly 1,000 followers in Guyana, 1978.
b. May 31, 1931 in Lynn, Indiana
d. Nov 18, 1978 in Jonestown, Guyana
Source: *BioIn 11; WorAlBi*

Jones, Rickie Lee
"The Duchess of Coolsville"
American. Singer, Songwriter
Combines rhythm and blues, jazz, folk music; hit single "Chuck E's in Love," 1979; won Grammy for best new artist, 1980.
b. Nov 8, 1954 in Chicago, Illinois
Source: *BioIn 12; ConMus 4; CurBio 90; EncPR&S 89; EncRk 88; EncRkSt; HarEnR 86; LegTOT; NewGrDA 86; NewWmR; PenEncP; RkOn 85; RolSEnR 83; WhoAm 95, 96, 97; WhoAmW 95; WhoEnt 92; WhoRock 81*

Jones, Robert C
American. Writer
Won Oscar for screenplay *Coming Home,* 1978.
b. Mar 30, 1930 in Los Angeles, California
Source: *VarWW 85*

Jones, Robert Edmond
American. Designer
Known for theatrical stage settings called "new stagecraft"; did several of Eugene O'Neill's plays.
b. Dec 12, 1887 in Milton, New Hampshire
d. Nov 26, 1954 in Milton, New Hampshire
Source: *BenetAL 91; BioIn 1, 3, 4, 11, 14, 17; CamGWoT; CurBio 46, 55; DancEn 78; DcAmB S5; EncWB; EncWT; IntDcT 3; LinLib L, S; MetOEnc; NewGrDO; NotNAT A, B; OxCAmL 65, 83; OxCAmT 84; OxCThe 67, 83; PlP&P; REn; REnAL; WhAm 3; WhAmArt 85; WhE&EA; WhThe*

Jones, Robert Trent
English. Architect
Designed more than 350 of world's most outstanding golf courses.
b. Jun 20, 1906 in Ince, England
Source: *BioIn 2, 3, 6, 8, 13, 15, 16, 19; NewYTBS 86; WhoAm 74, 76, 78, 80, 82, 84, 86, 88, 90, 92, 94; WhoE 74; WhoGolf; WhoSSW 95; WhoWor 74, 76, 78*

Jones, Roger W(arren)
American. Government Official
With Central Statistical Board (later Bureau of the Budget), 1933-58; 1962-68; 1969-75; head of Civil Service Commission, 1959-61.
b. Feb 3, 1908
d. May 28, 1993 in Torrington, Connecticut
Source: *BioIn 3, 5, 19; CurBio 93N; IntWW 74, 75, 76, 77, 78, 79, 80, 81, 82, 83, 89, 91, 93; WhoAm 74, 76, 78, 80, 82; WhoGov 72*

Jones, Rosie
American. Beauty Contest Winner
Miss Black America, 1990.
b. 1964 in Bridgeport, Connecticut
Source: *BioIn 16*

Jones, Rufus Matthew
American. Author
Quaker who published works on Christian mysticism; helped to establish the American Friends Service Com., 1917, became its first chm.
b. Jan 25, 1863 in South China, Maine
d. Jun 16, 1948 in Haverford, Pennsylvania
Source: *AmAu&B; AmLY; AmPeW; BiDMoPL; BioIn 1, 2, 3, 4, 5, 6, 9, 19; DcAmB S4; DcAmReB 1, 2; DcNAA; LngCTC; LuthC 75; NatCAB 38; RelLAm 91; REnAL; TwCA SUP; WebAB 74, 79; WhAm 2; WhNAA*

Jones, Sam(uel)
American. Basketball Player
Guard, Boston, 1957-69; won 10 NBA championships; Hall of Fame, 1983.
b. Jun 24, 1933 in Wilmington, North Carolina
Source: *BasBi; BiDAmSp BK; BioIn 5, 6, 11; InB&W 80; OfNBA 87; WhoAfA 96; WhoAm 74; WhoBbl 73; WhoBlA 75, 77, 80, 85, 88, 90, 92, 94; WhoSpor*

Jones, Sam(uel Pond)
"Sad Sam"
American. Baseball Player
Pitcher, 1914-35; shared record for consecutive seasons pitched in MLs, 22, until broken by Jim Kaat; three no-hitter, 1923.
b. Jul 26, 1892 in Barnesville, Ohio
d. Jul 6, 1966 in Barnesville, Ohio
Source: *BiDAmSp BB; BioIn 7, 14, 15; WhoProB 73*

Jones, Shirley
[Mrs. Marty Ingels]
American. Actor, Singer
Won Oscar, 1960, for *Elmer Gantry;* also starred in *Oklahoma,* 195 4; *Music Man,* 1962; TV includes "The Partridge Family," 1970-74.
b. Jul 31, 1934 in Smithtown, Pennsylvania
Source: *BiDAmM; BiDFilm, 81; BiE&WWA; BioIn 3, 4, 6, 9, 10, 11; BioNews 74; CmMov; ConTFT 6; CurBio 61; EncAFC; FilmEn; FilmgC; ForYSC; HalFC 80, 84, 88; IntDcF 1-3; IntMPA 77, 80, 84, 86, 88, 92, 94, 96; InWom, SUP; ItaFilm; LegTOT; MotPP; MovMk; VarWW 85; WhoAm 86, 94, 95, 96, 97; WhoAmW 95, 97; WhoHol A; WhoWor 74; WorAl; WorAlBi; WorEFlm*

Jones, Spike
[Lindley Armstrong Jones]
"King of Corn"
American. Bandleader, Musician
With City Slickers Band was noted, 1940s-60s for lampooning popular songs, using zany sound effects.
b. Dec 14, 1911 in Long Beach, California
d. May 1, 1965 in Los Angeles, California
Source: *ASCAP 66; Baker 78, 84; BioIn 1, 2, 3, 7, 12, 14, 15, 19, 20; CmpEPM; ConMus 5; DcAmB S7; EncAFC; FacFETw; FilmgC; HalFC 80, 84, 88; JoeFr; LegTOT; NewAmDM; NewGrDA 86; NewGrDM 80; OxCPMus; PenEncP; RadStar; SaTiSS; WhoCom; WhoHol B; WhScrn 74, 77, 83; WorAl; WorAlBi*

Jones, Star(let Marie)
American. Broadcast Journalist
Legal correspondent, NBC News, 1992-93; host of TV's "Jones and Jury," 1994—.
b. c. 1962
Source: *ConBlB 10; NotBlAW 2*

Jones, Stormie
American. Transplant Patient
At age six became the world's first combined heart/liver transplant recipient; died at 13.
b. 1978?
d. Nov 11, 1992 in Pittsburgh, Pennsylvania
Source: *BioIn 16*

Jones, Terry
[Monty Python's Flying Circus]
Welsh. Actor, Director, Writer
Directed film *Monty Python's Life of Brian;* wrote *Fairy Tales,* 1981; *Erik the Viking,* 1983.
b. Feb 1, 1942 in Colwyn Bay, Wales
Source: *BioIn 10, 16, 17, 18; ConAu 112, 116; ConLC 21; ConTFT 7; HalFC 88; IntMPA 92, 94, 96; MiSFD 9; ScF&FL 92; SmATA 51, 67; VarWW 85; Who 88, 90, 92, 94; WhoAm 82, 84, 86, 88, 90, 92, 94, 95, 96, 97; WhoHol 92; WhoWor 80, 82, 84, 95, 96*

Jones, Thad(deus Joseph)
American. Musician
Soloist, jazz drummer with Count Basie Orchestra, 1954-63.
b. Mar 28, 1923 in Pontiac, Michigan
d. Aug 20, 1986 in Copenhagen, Denmark
Source: *AfrAmAl 6; AllMusG; AnObit 1986; ASCAP 80; Baker 84, 92; BiDAfM; BiDAmM; BiDJaz; BioIn 4, 9, 12; BlkCond; CmpEPM; DrBlPA, 90; EncJzS; IlEncJ; InB&W 80; NewAmDM; NewGrDJ 88, 94; OxCPMus; PenEncP; WhAm 9; WhoAm 78, 80, 82*

Jones, Thom
American. Author
Wrote *The Pugilist at Rest,* a 1993 National Book Award noominee.
b. Jan 26, 1945 in Aurora, Illinois
Source: *ConLC 81*

Jones, Thomas Hudson
American. Sculptor
Best-known works include "Tomb of the Unknown Soldier," Arlington National Cemetery.
b. Jul 24, 1892 in Buffalo, New York
d. Nov 4, 1969 in Hyannis, Massachusetts
Source: *BioIn 8, 14; WhAm 5; WhAmArt 85*

Jones, Tom
American. Dramatist, Songwriter
Known for musical comedies; books, lyrics include *The Rainmaker,* 1963; plays include *The Bone Room.*
b. Feb 17, 1928 in Littlefield, Texas
Source: *AmAu&B; ASCAP 66, 80; BiE&WWA; BioIn 10, 12, 15; ConAu 6NR, 53; ConDr 73, 77D; ConTFT 6; EncMT; NewCBMT; NewGrDA 86; NotNAT; VarWW 85; WhoThe 81*

Jones, Tom
[Thomas Woodward Jones]
Welsh. Musician, Singer
Hits include "It's Not Unusual," 1964; "What's New Pussycat," 1965.
b. Jun 7, 1940 in Pontypridd, Wales
Source: *Baker 78, 84, 92; BiDAmM; BioIn 7, 8, 9, 12, 13, 14, 16, 18, 19, 20; BkPepl; CelR, 90; ConMus 11; EncFCWM 83; EncPR&S 89; EncRk 88; IntWW 76, 77, 78, 79, 80, 81, 82, 83, 89, 91, 93; LegTOT; News 93; OxCPMus; PenEncP; RkOn 78, 84; RolSEnR 83; VarWW 85; WhoAm 80, 82, 84, 86, 88, 90, 92, 94, 95, 96, 97; WhoEnt 92; WhoWor 74; WorAl; WorAlBi*

Jones, Tommy Lee
American. Actor
Films include *Coal Miner's Daughter,* 1981; *River Rat,* 1984; *The Fugitive,* 1994.
b. Sep 15, 1946 in San Saba, Texas
Source: *BiDFilm 94; ConTFT 1, 6, 13; CurBio 95; HalFC 80, 84, 88; HolBB; IntMPA 86, 88, 92, 94, 96; LegTOT; VarWW 85; WhoAm 82, 84, 86, 88, 90, 92, 94, 95, 96, 97; WhoEnt 92; WhoHol 92; WorAlBi*

Jones, Too Tall
[Edward Lee Jones]
American. Football Player
Three-time all-pro defensive end, Dallas, 1974-78, 1980-89; MVP 1982; pursued boxing career, 1979.
b. Feb 23, 1951 in Jackson, Tennessee
Source: *FootReg 87; WhoAfA 96; WhoBlA 77, 80, 85, 88, 90, 92, 94; WhoFtbl 74*

Jones, Tristan
English. Author
d. Jun 21, 1995 in Phuket, Thailand

Jones, Wallace
[Fabulous Five]
"Wah-Wah"
American. Basketball Player
Member of Fabulous Five, U of Kentucky, 1946-49; played three yrs. in pros.
b. Jul 14, 1926 in Harlan, Kentucky
Source: *BioIn 2; WhoBbl 73*

Jones, Weyman
American. Author
Books include *The Talking Leaf,* 1965; *Edge of Two Worlds,* 1968.
b. Feb 6, 1928 in Lima, Ohio
Source: *AuBYP 2, 3; ConAu 17R; SmATA 4, 11AS; WhoPubR 72*

Jones, William
American. Ethnologist
Researched and documented Algonquin religious practices; wrote several articles on the Algonquin language.
b. Mar 28, 1871 in Sac and Fox Reservation, Oklahoma
d. 1909
Source: *AmAu&B; BiInAmS; BiNAW, B, SupB; BioIn 21; DcAmB; EncNoAI; IntDcAn; NatCAB 24; NotNaAm*

Jong, Erica (Mann)
American. Author, Poet
Wrote *Fear of Flying,* 1973; *Parachutes & Kisses,* 1984; *Any Woman's Blues,* 1990.
b. Mar 26, 1942 in New York, New York
Source: *AmWomWr; ArtclWW 2; AuNews 1; Benet 87, 96; BenetAL 91; BestSel 90-2; BioIn 10, 11, 12, 13; BkPepl; BlmGWL; CamHAL; CelR 90; ConAu 26NR, 52NR, 73; ConLC 4, 6, 8, 18, 83; ConNov 82, 86, 91, 96; ConPo 75, 80, 85, 91, 96; ConPopW; ContDcW 89; CroCAP; CurBio 75; DcArts; DcLB 2, 5, 28, 152; DrAF 76; DrAP 75; DrAPF 80; EncSF 93; FacFETw; FemiCLE; FemiWr; HanAmWH; IntAu&W 82, 86, 89, 91, 93; IntDcWB; IntWW 89, 91, 93; InWom SUP; JeAmFiW; JeAmWW; LegTOT; MajTwCW; ModAL S2; ModWoWr; NewYTBS 80; Novels; OxCAmL 83, 95; OxCWoWr 95; RAdv 1; RGTwCWr; ScF&FL 92; WhoAm 76, 78, 80, 82, 84, 86, 88, 90, 92, 94, 95, 96, 97; WhoAmW 81, 83, 85, 87, 89, 91, 95, 97; WhoE 95; WhoEnt 92; WhoUSWr 88; WhoWor 80, 82, 84, 87, 91, 93; WhoWrEP 89, 92, 95; WomWMM; WorAl; WorAlBi; WorAu 1970; WrDr 76, 80, 82, 84, 86, 88, 90, 92, 94, 96*

Jongkind, Johan Barthold
Dutch. Artist
Juxtaposed strokes of unmixed colors to illustrate effects of light; helped develop Impressionism.
b. Jun 3, 1819 in Lattrop, Netherlands
d. Feb 9, 1891 in Cote-Saint-Andre, Netherlands
Source: *ArtsNiC; AtlBL; BioIn 2, 4, 5, 6, 9, 11; ClaDrA; DcArts; DcSeaP; IntDcAA 90; McGDA; OxCArt; OxDcArt; WhDW*

Jonson, Ben(jamin)
English. Dramatist, Poet
Master of dramatic satire; wrote *Volpone,* 1606.
b. Jun 11, 1572 in Westminster, England
d. Apr 6, 1637 in Westminster, England
Source: *Alli; AtlBL; BbD; BiD&SB; BlmGEL; BritAu; BritWr 1; CamGEL; CamGLE; CamGWoT; CasWL; Chambr 1; ChhPo; CnDBLB 1; CnE&AP; CnThe; CroE&S; CrtT 1, 4; CyWA 58; DcArts; DcEnA; DcEnL; DcEuL; DcLB 62, 121; DcLEL; DcPup; DramC 4; EncPaPR 91; EncWT; Ent; EvLB; GrWrEL DR, P; HisDStE; IntDcT 2; LegTOT; LitC 6, 33; LngCEL; McGEWB; McGEWD 72, 84; MouLC 1; NewC; NewCBEL; NewGrDM 80; NewGrDO; OxCEng 67, 85, 95; OxCThe 67, 83; OxDcOp; PenC ENG; PlP&P; PoLE; RAdv 1, 14, 13-1, 13-2; RComWL; REn; REnWD; RfGEnL 91; RGFBP; WebE&AL; WhDW; WorAl; WorAlBi; WorLitC*

Jonsson, John Erik
American. Business Executive, Politician
Pres. Texas Instruments, 1951-58; honorary director, 1977; mayor, Dallas, TX, 1964-71.
b. Sep 6, 1901 in New York, New York
d. Aug 31, 1995 in Dallas, Texas
Source: *AmMWSc 79, 82, 86, 89, 92, 95; BiDAmBL 83; BioIn 5, 6, 7, 10, 21; BlueB 76; CurBio 61, 95N; IntWW 74, 75, 76, 77, 79; IntYB 78, 79, 80, 81, 82; St&PR 75; WhoAm 74, 76, 78; WhoAmP*

73, 75; WhoEng 80, 88; WhoFI 74, 77; WhoGov 72; WhoSSW 73, 75, 76

Jooss, Kurt
German. Choreographer
Combined classical ballet with modern dance; known for antiwar play *The Green Table,* 1932.
b. Jan 12, 1901 in Wasseralfingen, Germany
d. May 22, 1979 in Heilbronn, Germany (West)
Source: *Baker 84; BiDD; BioIn 1, 3, 4, 8, 10, 11, 12; CnOxB; CurBio 76, 79, 79N; DancEn 78; DcArts; FacFETw; IntWW 74, 75, 76, 77, 78; NewGrDM 80; NewYTBS 75, 76, 79; OxCMus; WhoWor 74, 76, 78; WhThe; WorAl; WorAlBi*

Joplin, Janis
[Big Brother and the Holding Company]
American. Singer
Hits include "Me and Bobby McGee," 1971; died of drug overdose; life story was filmed: *The Rose,* 1979.
b. Jan 19, 1943 in Port Arthur, Texas
d. Oct 3, 1970 in Hollywood, California
Source: *AmDec 1960; ASCAP 80; Baker 78, 84; BiDAmM; BioAmW; BioIn 8, 9, 10, 11, 12, 15, 16, 17, 18, 19; BioNews 74; ConMuA 80A; ConMus 3; ContDcW 89; CurBio 70; DcArts; EncPR&S 89; EncRk 88; EncRkSt; GoodHs; GrLiveH; IlEncRk; IntDcWB; LegTOT; NewAmDM; NewGrDA 86; NewYTBE 70; OxCPMus; PenEncP; RkOn 78; RolSEnR 83; WhAm 5; WhoHol B; WhoRock 81; WhoRocM 82; WhScrn 77, 83; WorAl; WorAlBi*

Joplin, Scott
American. Musician, Composer
Developed ragtime music; wrote "The Entertainer," 1902; music revived in score of *The Sting,* 1973.
b. Nov 24, 1868 in Marshall, Texas
d. Apr 1, 1917 in New York, New York
Source: *AfrAmAl 6; AllMusG; AmCulL; AmDec 1900; ASCAP 66, 80; Baker 78, 84, 92; BiDAfM; BiDAmM; BiDD; BiDJaz; BioIn 2, 6, 8, 9, 10, 11, 12, 13, 14, 15, 16, 17, 19, 20, 21; BioNews 74; BlkAmP; BlkAWP; BlkOpe; BriBkM 80; CmpEPM; CnOxB; ConAu 123; ConBlB 6; ConMus 10; DcAmNB; DcArts; DcTwCCu 5; DrBlPA, 90; FacFETw; GayN; IlEncJ; InB&W 80, 85; IntDcOp; LegTOT; MorBAP; MorMA; MusMk; NegAl 76, 83, 89; NewAmDM; NewGrDA 86; NewGrDM 80; NewGrDO; NewOxM; NewYTBS 75; NotNAT B; OxCAmH; OxCPMus; OxDcOp; PenEncP; PopAmC; RAdv 14, 13-3; WebAB 74, 79; WhoJazz 72; WorAl; WorAlBi*

Jorda, Enrique
Spanish. Conductor
Led San Francisco Symphony, 1954-63.
b. Mar 24, 1911 in San Sebastian, Spain
d. Mar 18, 1996 in Brussels, Belgium
Source: *Baker 78, 84, 92; BioIn 3, 4, 21; IntWW 74, 75; IntWWM 77, 80, 85, 90; NewGrDM 80; PenDiMP; WhoMus 72; WhoWor 74*

Jordaens, Jacob
Flemish. Artist
Known for baroque religious, historical paintings: *Jesus Among the Doctors,* 1663.
b. May 19, 1593 in Antwerp, Belgium
d. Oct 18, 1678 in Antwerp, Belgium
Source: *AtlBL; BioIn 8, 13, 19; ClaDrA; DcArts; Dis&D; IntDcAA 90; McGDA; McGEWB; NewCol 75; OxCArt; OxDcArt; WhDW*

Jordan, Barbara C(harline)
American. Lawyer, Politician
Congresswoman from TX, 1972-78; first black to keynote Dem. National Convention, 1976.
b. Feb 21, 1936 in Houston, Texas
d. Jan 17, 1996 in Austin, Texas
Source: *AfrAmBi 1; AfrAmOr; AmPolLe; AmWomM; BiDrUSC 89; BioIn 10, 11, 12, 13; BlkAmsC; BlkWAm; CngDr 74; ConAu 151; CurBio 93; EncWB; InB&W 80, 85; NewYTBS 76; NotBlAW 1; WhoAfA 96; WhoAm 84, 86; WhoAmW 85, 87; WhoBlA 85, 88, 92, 94; WhoGov 75, 77; WomLaw; WomPO 76*

Jordan, Bobby
American. Actor
Best known for role of Bobby in Bowery Boy films.
b. 1923
d. Sep 10, 1965 in Los Angeles, California
Source: *BioIn 7; EncAFC; ForYSC; HalFC 80, 84, 88; JoeFr; WhoHol B; WhoHrs 80; WhScrn 77*

Jordan, Charles Morrell
American. Auto Executive
VP, GM design staff, 1986-92.
b. Oct 21, 1927 in Whittier, California
Source: *BioIn 11; WhoAm 74, 76, 78, 80, 82, 88, 90, 92, 94, 95, 96, 97; WhoFI 74, 75, 77, 89, 92, 94, 96; WhoWest 96; WhoWor 74, 76*

Jordan, Don
American. Boxer
Welterweight champ, defeated Akins, 1958; lost title to Paret, 1960.
b. Jun 22, 1934
Source: *BioIn 10*

Jordan, Elizabeth Garver
American. Author, Editor
Edited *Harper's Bazaar,* 1900-13; wrote *Tales of the City Room,* 1898.
b. May 9, 1865 in Milwaukeé, Wisconsin
d. Feb 24, 1947 in New York, New York
Source: *BioIn 15, 20; BriB; InWom SUP; LibW; NotAW*

Jordan, Fred
American. Religious Leader
Founder of int'l missions since 1949; noted for TV program, "Church in the Home," 1951-88.
b. 1910?
d. Apr 24, 1988 in Glendora, California

Jordan, Hamilton
[William Hamilton McWhorter Jordan]
"Ham"; "Hannibal Jerkin"
American. Presidential Aide
Chief of staff under President Carter, 1979-81; int'l. communications consultant, 1984—.
b. Sep 21, 1944 in Charlotte, North Carolina
Source: *BioIn 11, 12, 13; CurBio 77; IntWW 80, 81, 83; LegTOT; NewYTBS 76, 79, 85; PseudN 82; WhoAm 78, 80, 82, 84, 86; WhoGov 77; WhoSSW 82; WorAl; WorAlBi*

Jordan, I(rving) King
American. University Administrator
First deaf pres. of Gallaudet U, 1988—, only US institution of higher education for the deaf.
b. 1943 in Glen Riddle, Pennsylvania
Source: *BioIn 16; CurBio 91; DeafPAS; WhoAm 90*

Jordan, Jim
[James Edward Jordan]
American. Radio Performer
Played Fibber McGee in classic radio show "Fibber McGee and Molly," 1935-60.
b. Nov 16, 1896 in Peoria, Illinois
d. Apr 1, 1988 in Los Angeles, California
Source: *BioIn 1, 2, 9, 15, 16; CurBio 41, 88, 88N; FilmgC; LegTOT; RadStar; WhoHol A*

Jordan, Joseph
American. Biochemist
Expert in biochemistry and the effects of heat on chemical reactions.
b. Jun 29, 1919 in Timisoara, Romania
d. Aug 14, 1992 in State College, Pennsylvania
Source: *AmMWSc 73P, 76P, 79, 82, 86, 89, 92; BioIn 18; WhAm 10; WhoAm 74, 76, 78, 80, 82, 84, 86, 88, 90, 92; WhoE 74, 75, 77; WhoTech 89*

Jordan, June
[June Meyer]
American. Author
Books for children include *Dry Victories,* 1972; *His Own Where,* 1971.
b. Jul 9, 1936 in New York, New York
Source: *AfrAmAl 6; AfrAmW; ArtclWW 2; Au&Arts 2; AuBYP 2S, 3; BenetAL 91; BioIn 9, 12, 13, 14, 16, 17, 18, 19, 20, 21; BlkAuII, 92; BlkAWP; BlkWAm; BlkWr 1, 2; BlkWrNE; BlmGWL; ChlBkCr; ChlLR 10; ConAu 25NR, 33R; ConBlB 7; ConLC 11, 23; ConPo 80, 85, 91, 96; DcAmChF 1960; DcLB 38; DrAF 76; DrAP 75; DrAPF 80; FemiCLE; Focus; FourBJA; InB&W 80,*

85; IntAu&W 77, 91, 93; IntWWP 82; LinLib L; LivgBAA; MajAI; MajTwCW; ModWoWr; NegAl 83, 89; NotBlAW 1; OxCAmL 95; OxCChiL; OxCWoWr 95; PseudN 82; SchCGBL; SelBAAf; SelBAAu; SmATA 37; TwCChW 78, 83, 89; TwCYAW; WhoAm 84, 86; WhoAmW 77; WhoBlA 85, 88; WorAu 1975; WrDr 80, 82, 84, 86, 88, 90, 92, 94, 96

Jordan, Kathy
[Kathryn Jordan]
American. Tennis Player
Won Wimbledon, French doubles, 1980.
b. Dec 3, 1957 in Bryn Mawr, Pennsylvania
Source: *OfEnT; WhoIntT*

Jordan, Louis
"King of the Jukeboxes"
American. Jazz Musician, Singer
Alto saxist who led Tympany Five, 1940s; noted for novelty, blues recordings; starred in all-Negro movie musical, *Beware,* 1946.
b. Jul 8, 1908 in Brinkley, Arkansas
d. Feb 4, 1975 in Los Angeles, California
Source: *AllMusG; Baker 84, 92; BgBands 74; BiDAfM; BiDAmM; BiDJaz; BioIn 9, 10, 12, 15, 16; BlksB&W, C; CmpEPM; ConMus 11; DcAmB S9; DcTwCCu 5; DrBlPA, 90; EncJzS; EncRk 88; GuBlues; IlEncJ; InB&W 80; NewAmDM; NewGrDJ 88, 94; OxCPMus; PenEncP; WhoJazz 72*

Jordan, Marian Driscoll
[Mrs. Jim Jordan]
American. Radio Performer
With husband, formed one of radio's most famous comedy teams: "Fibber McGee and Molly," 1935-60.
b. Apr 15, 1897 in Peoria, Illinois
d. Apr 7, 1961 in Encino, California
Source: *CurBio 41, 61; InWom SUP; JoeFr; SaTiSS; WhAm 4; WhScrn 77*

Jordan, Michael (Jeffery)
"Air Jordan"
American. Basketball Player
Guard, Chicago Bulls, 1984-93; retired from Bulls to play baseball in Chicago White Sox org., 1994-95; rejoined Bulls, 1995—; led NBA in scoring, 1987-93, 1996—; NBA MVP, 1988, 1991-92; won two gold medals, US Olympic team 1984, 1992; starred in film *Space Jam,* 1996.
b. Feb 17, 1963 in New York, New York
Source: *AfrAmAl 6; AfrAmBi 1; AfrAmSG; AmDec 1980; BasBi; BiDAmSp BK; BioIn 13, 18; BlkOlyM; CelR 90; ConBlB 6; ConHero 2; ConNews 87-2; CurBio 87; IntWW 91, 93; LegTOT; NewYTBS 83, 84; OfNBA 87; WhoAfA 96; WhoAm 88, 90, 92, 94, 95, 96, 97; WhoBlA 85, 88, 90, 92, 94; WhoE 95; WhoMW 88, 90, 92, 96; WhoWor 95, 96, 97; WorAlBi*

Jordan, Neil
Irish. Filmmaker
Made *The Crying Game,* 1992.
b. Feb 25, 1950 in Sligo, Ireland
Source: *BiDFilm 94; BioIn 18, 19, 20; ConAu 124, 130; ConNov 86, 91, 96; ConTFT 6, 15; CurBio 93; DcIrL 96; EncEurC; IntDcF 2-2; IntMPA 92, 94, 96; IntWW 91, 93; LegTOT; MiSFD 9; News 93-3; OxCIri; RGTwCWr; WrDr 88, 90, 92, 94, 96*

Jordan, Richard
American. Actor
Starred in TV mini-series "The Captains and the Kings," 1976 which won him a Go lden Globe Award.
b. Jul 19, 1937 in New York, New York
d. Aug 30, 1993 in Los Angeles, California
Source: *AnObit 1993; BioIn 11, 19; ConTFT 12; HalFC 84; IntMPA 94; NewYTBS 93; VarWW 85; WhoHol A*

Jordan, Stanley
American. Musician, Composer
Guitarist known for innovative tapping, tuning techniques; albums include *Magic Touches,* 1985.
b. Jul 31, 1959 in Chicago, Illinois
Source: *AllMusG; BioIn 14, 15, 16; ConMus 1; NewGrDJ 88, 94; OnThGG; PenEncP; WhoAfA 96; WhoAm 88, 94, 95, 96, 97; WhoBlA 92, 94*

Jordan, Vernon Eulion, Jr.
"The Warrior of Today"
American. Civil Rights Leader
Exec. director, National Urban League, 1972-81; transition leader for Clinton administration, 1993.
b. Aug 15, 1935 in Atlanta, Georgia
Source: *AfrAmBi 1; BioIn 9, 10, 11, 12; BioNews 74; BusPN; ConBlB 3; CurBio 72, 93; EncAACR; InB&W 80, 85; NewYTBS 80; PseudN 82; WhoAm 74, 76, 78, 80, 82, 84, 86, 88, 90, 92, 94, 95, 96, 97; WhoAmL 87, 90; WhoBlA 75, 88; WhoE 75, 77, 79, 95; WhoSSW 75; WhoWor 91, 93, 97; WorAl*

Jordy, William H(enry)
American. Educator
Brown U. prof, 1948-77; wrote *American Buildings and Their Architects,* 1972.
b. Aug 31, 1917 in Poughkeepsie, New York
Source: *ConAu 1R, 25NR; DrAS 82H; WhoAm 74, 76, 78, 80, 82, 84, 86, 88, 90, 92, 94, 95, 96, 97; WrDr 82, 84, 86, 88, 90, 92, 94, 96*

Jorge Blanco, Salvador
Dominican. Political Leader
Pres. of Dominican Republic, 1982-86.
b. Jul 5, 1926 in Santiago, Dominican Republic
Source: *DcCPCAm; NewYTBS 82; WhoWor 84, 87*

Jorgensen, Anker Henrik
Danish. Political Leader
Prime minister of Denmark, 1972-82.
b. Jul 13, 1922 in Copenhagen, Denmark
Source: *BioIn 9, 11; CurBio 78; WhoWor 78, 80, 82, 84*

Jorgensen, Christine
[George Jorgensen]
American. Transsexual
Former soldier; became a woman in first public sex-change by an American, 1952.
b. May 20, 1926 in New York, New York
d. May 3, 1989 in San Clemente, California
Source: *AnObit 1989; BioIn 7, 12; ConAu 128; FacFETw; HumSex; InWom, SUP; News 89; NewYTBS 89; What 1*

Jory, Victor
American. Actor
Often cast as villain in 40-year career; among films *Gone With the Wind,* 1939.
b. Nov 23, 1902 in Dawson City, Alaska
d. Feb 12, 1982 in Santa Monica, California
Source: *BiE&WWA; BioIn 4, 11, 12, 13; ConTFT 2; FilmEn; FilmgC; ForYSC; GangFlm; HalFC 80, 84, 88; HolP 30; IntMPA 75, 76, 77, 78, 79, 80, 81, 82; LegTOT; MotPP; MovMk; NotNAT; Vers A; WhoHol A; WhoHrs 80; WhoThe 72, 77, 81; WorAl*

Josefsberg, Milt
American. Writer
Wrote comedy for Jack Benny, Lucille Ball, and Bob Hope.
b. Jun 29, 1911 in New York, New York
d. Dec 14, 1987 in Burbank, California
Source: *ConAu 29NR, 81, 124*

Joseph
Biblical Figure
Son of Jacob, who was sold into slavery by brothers; later became chief official to the Pharoah.
Source: *Benet 87, 96; BioIn 1, 2, 3, 4, 5, 6, 7, 8, 9, 10, 11, 12, 15, 16, 17, 18, 21; DcAmSR; DcBiPP; DcCathB; Dis&D; IlEncMy; IntWWP 77X; InWom SUP; LngCEL; McGDA; NotAW; OxDcByz; PenDiDA 89; PeoHis; REn; REnAW; Who 90, 92; WhoAm 88*

Joseph, Chief
American. Native American Chief
Nez Perce chief; against the 1863 Nez Perce Treaty.
b. 1790?
d. 1871
Source: *BioIn 21; NotNaAm; WhNaAH*

Joseph, Chief
"The Napoleon of the Indian Race"
American. Native American Chief
Became chief Nez Perce, 1873; refused to comply with land-cession treaty of 1855.

b. 1840 in Wallowa Valley, Washington
d. Sep 21, 1904 in Colville, Washington
Source: *AmBi; BenetAL 91; BioIn 1, 2, 3, 4, 5, 6, 7, 8, 9, 10, 11, 12, 13, 14, 15, 16, 17, 18, 19, 20, 21; DcAmB; DcAmMiB; EncAAH; EncAB-H 1996; GenMudB; HarEnMi; McGEWB; MorMA; NatNAL; NotNaAm; OxCAmH; PseudN 82; RComAH; REnAL; WebAB 74, 79; WebAMB; WhDW; WhNaAH; WorAl; WorAlBi*

Joseph, Saint
Roman. Biblical Figure
Husband of the Virgin Mary, mother of Jesus; feast day: Mar 19.
b. fl. 1st cent. BC
Source: *Benet 87, 96; BioIn 1, 2, 3, 4, 5, 6, 7, 8, 9, 10, 11, 12, 15, 16, 17, 18, 21; DcAmSR; DcBiPP; DcCathB; Dis&D; IlEncMy; IntWWP 77X; InWom SUP; LngCEL; McGDA; NewCol 75; NotAW; OxDcByz; PenDiDA 89; PeoHis; REn; REnAW; WebBD 83; Who 90, 92; WhoAm 88*

Joseph, Frederick
American. Business Executive
Chief Executive Drexel Burnham Lambert, 1974-90; presided over firm's phenomenal growth and subsequent declaration of bankruptcy; suspended by NY Stock Exchange for questionable dealings in junk bonds.
b. Apr 22, 1937 in Boston, Massachusetts
Source: *BioIn 15; Dun&B 90; St&PR 87; WhoAm 90, 92; WhoFI 89*

Joseph, Helen
South African. Author, Political Activist
Active in South African politics; charged with treason, 1956, acquitted, 1961; first S African to be put under house arrest, 1962-67, 1967-71.
b. Apr 8, 1905 in Sussex, England
d. Dec 25, 1992 in Johannesburg, South Africa
Source: *AfSS 78; AnObit 1992; BioIn 8, 11, 13, 14, 15, 16, 18, 19, 21; ConAu 128; NewYTBS 82, 92; RadHan*

Joseph, Keith (Sinjohn)
"An Architect of Thatcherism"
English. Politician
Held cabinet positions in Thatcher administration, 1979-86.
b. Jan 17, 1918
d. Dec 10, 1994 in London, England
Source: *BioIn 10, 11, 12, 13; BlueB 76; CurBio 75, 95N; IntWW 74, 75, 76, 77, 78, 79, 80, 81, 82, 83; IntYB 78, 79, 80, 81, 82; NewYTBS 94; WhAm 11; Who 74, 82, 83, 85, 88; WhoWor 74, 76, 78, 82, 87*

Joseph, Richard
American. Journalist
Specialized in travel writing; travel editor, *Esquire* mag., 1947-76; books include *Your Trip Abroad,* 1950.
b. Apr 24, 1910 in New York, New York
d. Sep 30, 1976
Source: *AmAu&B; BioIn 11; CelR; ConAu 1R, 6NR, 69; NewYTBS 76; WhAm 7; WhoAm 74, 76; WhoE 74; WhoWor 74, 76*

Joseph, Stephen (Carl)
American. Physician
NYC commissioner, 1986-89; heightened AIDS awareness by proposing that the city distribute free needles to addicts.
b. Nov 25, 1937 in New York, New York
Source: *AmMWSc 92; BioIn 14, 15, 16; CurBio 89; WhoGov 72*

Joseph I
Hungarian. Ruler
King of Hungary, 1687-1711; king of Germany, 1690-1711; Holy Roman emperor, 1705-11.
b. Jul 26, 1678 in Vienna, Austria
d. Apr 17, 1711 in Vienna, Austria
Source: *DcBiPP; DcCathB; OxCGer 76*

Joseph II
"The Hatted King"; "The Kalapos King"; "The Titus of Germany"; "The Unfortunate"
Ruler
Tried unsuccessfully to reform and unify Austrian Habsburg domains.
b. Mar 13, 1741 in Vienna, Austria
d. Feb 20, 1790 in Vienna, Austria
Source: *BioIn 9; PseudN 82*

Josephine
[Marie Josephe Rose Tascher de la Pagerie]
French. Ruler
Marriage to Napoleon, 1796, annulled 1809; played prominent part in social life of time.
b. Jun 24, 1763 in Les Trois-Ilets
d. May 29, 1814 in Malmaison, France
Source: *ApCAB; BioIn 1, 2, 3, 4, 5, 6, 7, 8, 9, 10, 11, 12, 15, 17, 20; DcBiPP; DcWomA; InWom; LegTOT; LinLib S; NewCol 75*

Joseph of Arimathea, Saint
Biblical Figure
According to the Bible, placed Jesus' body in his own tomb.
b. 1st cent. AD in Arimathea, Palestine
Source: *REn; WebBD 83*

Josephson, Brian David
Welsh. Scientist, Educator
Shared Nobel Prize in physics, 1973; worked with miniature electronics; discover ed "Josephson effects."
b. Jan 4, 1940 in Cardiff, Wales
Source: *AmMWSc 89, 92, 95; BiESc; BioIn 10, 11, 14, 15, 20, 21; BlueB 76; CamDcSc; FacFETw; IntWW 77, 78, 79, 80, 81, 82, 83, 89, 91, 93; LarDcSc; McGMS 80; RAdv 14; Who 74, 82, 83, 85, 88, 90, 92, 94; WhoAm 76, 78, 80, 82, 84; WhoNob, 90, 95; WhoScEn 94, 96; WhoWor 78, 80, 82, 84, 87, 89, 91, 93, 95, 96, 97; WhoWorJ 72, 78; WorAl; WorScD*

Josephson, Matthew
American. Author
Books include *The President Makers,* 1940; *Union House, Union Bar,* 1956.
b. Feb 15, 1899 in New York, New York
d. Mar 13, 1978 in Santa Cruz, California
Source: *AmAu&B; BenetAL 91; BioIn 1, 4, 6, 8, 11, 12, 15; ConAmA; ConAu 77, 81; DcAmB S10; DcLB 4; NewCBEL; NewYTBE 72; NewYTBS 78; OxCAmL 65, 83, 95; PenC AM; PeoHis; RAdv 13-3; REn; REnAL; TwCA, SUP; WhAm 7; WhoAm 74, 76, 78; WhoWor 74; WhoWorJ 72, 78*

Josephus, Flavius
[Yoseph ben Matatyahu; Joseph Ben Matthias]
"The Greek Livy"
Hebrew. Historian, Army Officer
Governor of Galilee; wrote *History of the Jewish War.*
b. 37? in Jerusalem, Palestine
d. 101? in Rome, Italy
Source: *AtlBL; BbD; Benet 87, 96; BiD&SB; BioIn 1, 5, 6, 7, 8, 9, 11; CasWL; ClMLC 13; DcBiPP; Grk&L; LinLib L, S; LuthC 75; NewC; OxCClL, 89; OxCEng 67, 85, 95; PenC CL; PseudN 82; RAdv 13-3; RComWL; REn; WebBD 83*

Josey, E. J.
American. Librarian
Founded Black Caucus of the American Library Association, 1970.
b. Jan 20, 1924 in Norfolk, Virginia
Source: *BiDrLUS 70; BioIn 12, 13, 14, 18; ConAu 29R; ConBlB 10; DrLC 69; Ebony 1; LivgBAA; NegAl 76, 83, 89; SchCGBL; SelBAAf; WhoAfA 96; WhoAm 76, 78, 80, 82, 84, 86, 88; WhoBlA 75, 77, 80, 85, 88, 90, 92, 94; WhoE 75, 77, 79, 81, 83, 85; WhoGov 75, 77; WhoLibI 82; WhoLibS 66; WhoWor 78, 80, 82, 89*

Joshua
Biblical Figure
In Old Testament, Book of Joshua; led Israelites' invasion of Canaan.
Source: *Benet 96; BioIn 1, 2, 3, 4, 6, 7, 8, 9, 10, 17; DcBiPP; LngCEL; McGDA*

Joslyn, Allyn Morgan
American. Actor
Performed on 3,000 radio programs; Broadway work included: *Boy Meets Girl; Arsenic and Old Lace.*
b. Jul 21, 1905 in Milford, Pennsylvania
d. Jan 21, 1981 in Woodland Hills, California
Source: *BioIn 10; FilmEn; FilmgC; IntMPA 81; MovMk; Vers A; WhoHol A; WhThe*

Joss, Addie
[Adrian Joss]
American. Baseball Player
Pitcher, Cleveland, 1902-10; fourth in MLs to throw perfect game, 1908; Hall of Fame, 1978.
b. Apr 12, 1880 in Juneau, Wisconsin
d. Apr 14, 1911 in Toledo, Ohio
Source: *Ballpl 90; BiDAmSp BB; BioIn 10, 14, 15, 17; LegTOT; WhoProB 73; WhoSpor*

Jouhaux, Leon
French. Labor Union Official
A founder of International Labor Organization; won Nobel Peace Prize, 1951.
b. Jul 1, 1879 in Paris, France
d. Apr 28, 1954 in Paris, France
Source: *BiDInt; BioIn 1, 2, 3, 9, 10, 11, 15, 17; NobelP; WhAm 3; WhoNob, 90, 95; WorAl; WorAlBi*

Joule, James Prescott
English. Physicist
Known for research in electricity, thermodynamics; introduced Joule's Law, 1840; unit of energy named for him.
b. Dec 24, 1818 in Salford, England
d. Oct 11, 1889 in Sale, England
Source: *Alli SUP; AsBiEn; BiESc; BioIn 2, 3, 4, 6, 7, 8, 9, 11, 12, 13, 14, 17; CelCen; DcBiPP; DcInv; DcNaB; DcScB; InSci; LarDcSc; LinLib S; McGEWB; WhDW; WorAl; WorScD*

Jourdan, Louis
[Louis Gendre]
French. Actor
Best known for film *Gigi,* 1958.
b. Jun 19, 1920 in Marseilles, France
Source: *BiE&WWA; ConTFT 6; CurBio 67; FilmgC; ForYSC; HalFC 84; IntMPA 86, 94; MotPP; MovMk; NotNAT; PseudN 82; WhoAm 86; WhoHol 92, A*

Journet, Marcel
French. Opera Singer
Bass with NY Met., 1900-08; repertoire included Wagner, French operas.
b. Jul 25, 1870 in Grasse, France
d. Sep 5, 1933 in Vittel, France
Source: *Baker 84; WhAm 1*

Journey
[Jonathan Cain; Aynsley Dunbar; Steve Perry; Gregg Rolie; Neil Schon; Steve Smith; Ross Valory]
American. Music Group
Progressive rock band called "America's most popular rock band," 1983; hit single "Send Her My Love," 1983.
Source: *BioIn 16, 17, 18, 19, 20, 21; ConMuA 80A; EncPR&S 89; EncRk 88; EncRkSt; HarEnR 86; IlEncRk; MiSFD 9; NewYTBE 73; PenEncP; RkOn 85; RolSEnR 83; WhoRock 81; WhoRocM 82*

Jouvet, Louis
French. Actor
Established own company, "Theatre de l'Athenee," 1934-51; improved acting, stage techniques.
b. Dec 24, 1887 in Crozon, France
d. Aug 16, 1951 in Paris, France
Source: *BiDFilm, 81, 94; BioIn 1, 2, 3, 4, 11, 14, 20; CamGWoT; ClDMEL 47, 80; CnThe; CurBio 49, 51; DcTwCCu 2; EncEurC; EncWL; EncWT; Ent; FacFETw; FilmAG WE; FilmEn; FilmgC; GrStDi; HalFC 80, 84, 88; IntDcF 1-3, 2-3; IntDcT 3; MovMk; NotNAT B; ObitOF 79; ObitT 1951; OxCAmT 84; OxCFilm; OxCFr; OxCThe 67, 83; REn; TheaDir; WhDW; WhoHol B; WhScrn 83; WhThe; WorEFlm*

Jouy, Victor (Joseph-Etienne) de
French. Dramatist
Wrote comic operas, vaudevilles, one tragedy, all set in India: *Tipposaib,* 1813.
b. 1764 in Jouy, France
d. Sep 4, 1846 in Saint-Germain-en-Laye, France
Source: *BbD; BiD&SB; NewEOp 71; OxCFr; PseudN 82*

Jovanovich, William Iliya
American. Publishing Executive
Chm., CEO, Harcourt, Brace, Jovanovich, 1970-90.
b. Feb 6, 1920 in Louisville, Colorado
Source: *BioIn 3, 6, 8, 10, 11; ConAu 107; IntWW 74, 75, 76, 77, 78, 79, 80, 81, 82, 83, 89, 91, 93; St&PR 87; WhoAm 86; WhoFI 85*

Joy, Leatrice
[Leatrice Joy Zeidler]
American. Actor
Star of Cecil B DeMille silent films; credited with popularizing bobbed hair.
b. Nov 7, 1893 in New Orleans, Louisiana
d. May 13, 1985 in Riverdale, New York
Source: *BioIn 14; Film 1; FilmEn; FilmgC; HalFC 84; MotPP; MovMk; NewYTBS 85; PseudN 82; ThFT; TwYS; VarWW 85; WhoHol A*

Joyce, Alice
"Madonna of the Screen"
American. Actor
Voted most popular actress in America, 1913-17.
b. Oct 1, 1890 in Kansas City, Missouri
d. Oct 9, 1955 in Hollywood, California
Source: *BioIn 4, 9, 11; Film 1; FilmEn; FilmgC; ForYSC; InWom; MotPP; MovMk; NotNAT B; TwYS; WhoHol A; WhScrn 74, 77, 83*

Joyce, Eileen
Australian. Pianist
Played with London Philharmonic in blitzed British towns, WW II.
b. Nov 21, 1912 in Zeehan, Australia
d. Mar 25, 1991
Source: *AnObit 1991; BioIn 1, 2, 4, 8, 18; ContDcW 89; DcArts; IntDcWB; IntWW 82; IntWWM 80, 90; InWom; MusMk; NewGrDM 80; PenDiMP*

Joyce, Elaine
[Elaine Joyce Pinchot; Mrs. Bobby Van]
American. Actor, Dancer
Host of TV show "All New Dating Game," 1986-87; films include *Motel Hell,* 1980.
b. Dec 19, 1945 in Cleveland, Ohio
Source: *VarWW 85; WhoHol 92, A*

Joyce, James Augustus Aloysius
Irish. Author, Poet
Wrote *Ulysses,* 1922; banned in US as obscene until 1933.
b. Feb 2, 1882 in Dublin, Ireland
d. Jan 13, 1941 in Zurich, Switzerland
Source: *AtlBL; CasWL; DcLEL; LngCTC; McGEWD 72; ModBrL, S1; ModWD; NewC; OxCEng 67; PenC ENG; PoIre; RAdv 1; RComWL; REn; TwCA SUP; WhoTwCL*

Joyce, Peggy Hopkins
[Margaret Upton]
"A Circle of the Cinema"
American. Actor
In Ziegfeld Follies; six marriages given wide publicity.
b. 1893 in Norfolk, Virginia
d. Jun 12, 1957 in New York, New York
Source: *BioIn 4, 16; Film 2; InWom; MotPP; NotNAT B; ObitOF 79; PseudN 82; WhoHol B; WhScrn 74, 77, 83*

Joyce, William
"Lord Haw-Haw"
German. Social Reformer
Made English language propaganda broadcasts for Nazis; hung for treason.
b. Apr 26, 1906 in New York, New York
d. Jan 3, 1946 in Wandsworth, England
Source: *BioIn 1, 2, 7, 16, 17; DcIrB 78, 88; EncTR, 91; PseudN 82; WhDW; WhWW-II*

Joyner, Al(fred, Jr.)
American. Track Athlete
Triple jumper; won gold medal, 1984 Olympics; brother of Jackie, husband of Florence Griffith.
b. Jan 19, 1960 in East Saint Louis, Illinois

Joyner, Florence Griffith
[Delores Florence Griffith]
"Flojo"
American. Track Athlete
Sprinter; set world record for 100 meters at 10.61, 1988; won 3 gold, 1 silver medal at 1988 Olympics; retired from track, 1989.
b. Dec 21, 1959 in Los Angeles, California
Source: *AfrAmAl 6; BlkWAm; FacFETw; NotBlAW 1, 2; WhoBlA 92*

Joyner, Wally
[Wallace Keith Joyner]
American. Baseball Player
Infielder, CA, 1986—.
b. Jun 16, 1962 in Atlanta, Georgia
Source: *Ballpl 90; BaseReg 86, 87; LegTOT*

Joyner-Kersee, Jackie
[Jacqueline Joyner-Kersee; Mrs. Bob Kersee]
American. Track Athlete
Won gold medals in Heptathlon and long jump, 1988 Olympics; won gold and bronze in same respective categories, 1992 Olympics; holds world record in heptathlon with over 7,000 points scored.
b. Mar 3, 1962 in East Saint Louis, Illinois
Source: *AfrAmAl 6; AfrAmBi 1; AfrAmSG; AmDec 1980; BiDAmSp OS; BlkAmWO; BlkOlyM; BlkWAm; CelR 90; ConBlB 5; ConHero 1; CurBio 87; EncWomS; FacFETw; IntWW 93; LegTOT; News 93-1; NotBlAW 1, 2; WhoAfA 96; WhoAm 90, 92, 94, 95, 96; WhoAmW 89, 91, 93, 95; WhoBlA 90, 92, 94; WhoSpor; WhoWor 95, 96; WorAlBi*

Jozsef, Attila
Hungarian. Poet
Verse volumes include *Medvetanc,* 1934.
b. Apr 11, 1905 in Budapest, Austria-Hungary
d. Dec 3, 1937 in Balatonszarszo, Hungary
Source: *Benet 87, 96; BioIn 10, 15; CasWL; ClDMEL 80; ConAu 116; EncWL 2, 3; FacFETw; PenC EUR; RAdv 14, 13-2; TwCLC 22; TwCWr; WhoTwCL; WorAu 1950*

Juan, Don
[Jaun Matus]
Mexican. Mystic
Used hallucinogenic drugs to gain power over demonic world.
b. 1891
Source: *BioIn 10*

Juana Ines de la Cruz, Sor
[Juana Ramirez de Asbaje]
Mexican. Poet, Dramatist, Religious Figure
Called the "tenth muse of Mexico;" challenged superiors who wanted her to spend less time writing and more time praying.
b. Nov 1648 in San Miguel de Nepantla, Mexico
d. Apr 17, 1695
Source: *GayLesB; HisWorL; OxCSpan; SpAmWW*

Juan Carlos, Count of Barcelona
[Don Juan de Borbon y Battenberg]
"The King Who Never Reigned"
Spanish. Prince
Father of King Juan Carlos I; helped ease nation's transition to democracy; was denied throne, backed son.
b. Jun 20, 1913 in Madrid, Spain
d. Apr 1, 1993 in Pamplona, Spain
Source: *BioIn 1, 2, 3, 4, 6, 7, 8, 10, 18, 19; CurBio 51, 93N; WhoWor 74*

Juan Carlos I
[Prince Juan Carlos Borbon y Borbon]
"Juan Carlos the Brief"
Spanish. Ruler
King of Spain, 1975—.
b. Jan 5, 1938 in Rome, Italy
Source: *BioIn 10; IntWW 83; News 93-1; NewYTBS 84; PseudN 82; WhoWor 87*

Juantorena, Alberto
Cuban. Track Athlete
Won gold medal, 1976 Olympics; set world record for 800-meter race, 1977.
b. Dec 3, 1951 in Santiago de Cuba, Cuba
Source: *NewYTBS 79; WorAl*

Juarez, Benito Pablo
"The Mexican Washington"; "The Second Washington"
Mexican. Political Leader
Pres. of Mexico, 1861-63, 1867-72; passed reform laws that reduced power of army, church.
b. Mar 21, 1806 in Oaxaca, Mexico
d. Jul 18, 1872 in Mexico City, Mexico
Source: *ApCAB; Drake; EncRev; NewCol 75; PseudN 82; REn; WhAm HS; WorAl*

Juch, Emma
American. Opera Singer, Manager
Soprano; founded Emma Juch Grand Opera Co., 1889-91; championed opera in English.
b. Jul 4, 1863 in Vienna, Austria
d. Mar 6, 1939 in New York, New York
Source: *AmBi; AmWom; Baker 78, 84; MetOEnc; NewEOp 71; NewGrDA 86; NewGrDM 80; NotAW; OxDcOp; WhAm 1; WomWWA 14*

Judah
Biblical Figure
Son of Jacob; ancestor of one of 12 tribes of Israel.
Source: *Benet 96; BioIn 5, 10; WebBD 83*

Judas Iscariot
Biblical Figure
One of 12 apostles; betrayed Jesus for 30 pieces of silver, cause of Jesus' arrest.
d. 30
Source: *Benet 87, 96; BioIn 1, 2, 3, 4, 5, 6, 8, 9, 10, 11, 17, 21; EncEarC; LngCEL; NewCol 75; WebBD 83*

Judas Priest
[K K Downing; Rob Halford; Ian Hill; Dave Holland; Glenn Tipton]
British. Music Group
Heavy metal band formed mid-1970s; album *Screaming for Vengeance,* 1982.
Source: *BiDrACP 79; BioIn 16; ConMus 10; EncPR&S 89; EncRk 88; EncRkSt; HarEnR 86; IlEncRk; PenEncP; RkOn 85; RolSEnR 83; WhoRocM 82*

Judd, Naomi (Diana)
[The Judds]
American. Singer
Mother in the country duo, The Judds, left group for health reasons in 1991; winner of seven Grammy awards.
b. Jan 11, 1946 in Ashland, Kentucky
Source: *BioIn 14, 15, 16, 20, 21; CelR 90; ConAu 146; ConMus 2; LegTOT; NewYTBS 84; WhoAm 90; WhoAmW 91*

Judd, Walter H(enry)
American. Politician
Rep. congressman from MN, 1943-60; instrumental in removing racial considerations from immigration and naturalization policies, 1952.
b. Sep 25, 1898
d. Feb 13, 1994 in Mitchellville, Maryland
Source: *BiDrAC; BiDrUSC 89; BioIn 1, 2, 5, 10, 11, 13, 17, 19, 20; CurBio 94N; InSci; PolProf E, J, K, T; WhAmP; WhoAm 74, 76, 78; WhoAmP 73, 75, 77, 79, 81, 83, 85, 87, 89, 91, 93; WhoWor 74*

Judd, Winnie Ruth McKinnell
"The Tiger Woman"
American. Murderer
Committed to insane asylum for killing, dismembering two people, 1931; escaped seven times.
b. Jan 29, 1905 in Oxford, Indiana
Source: *BioIn 9*

Judds, The
[Naomi Judd; Wynonna Judd]
American. Music Group
Mother-daughter country duo formed 1984-91; had hit album *Heart Land,* 1987.
Source: *BgBkCoM; BioIn 14, 15, 16, 21; CelR 90; ConMus 2; HarEnCM 87; NewYTBS 84; PenEncP; WhoAm 90, 92, 94, 95, 96, 97; WhoAmW 91, 93; WhoEnt 92; WhoNeCM*

Jude, Saint
[Saint Thaddeus]
Biblical Figure
One of 12 apostles; feast day: Oct 28.
b. fl. 1st cent.
Source: *Benet 87, 96; BioIn 1, 2, 3, 4, 5, 6, 8, 9, 10, 11, 14; ConAu X; DcCathB; EncEarC; REn*

Judge, Mike
American. Cartoonist
Created MTV series, "The Beavis and Butt-head Show," 1993—.
b. Oct 17, 1962 in Guayaquil, Ecuador

Judith
Biblical Figure
Heroine in the Book of Judith for killing Holofernes.
Source: *BioIn 2, 4, 6, 8, 11, 15; DcBiPP; EncAmaz 91; InWom, SUP; LngCEL; LuthC 75; OxDcOp; WebBD 83; WomWR*

Judson, Edward Zane Carroll
[Ned Buntline]
American. Adventurer
Originated dime novel, wrote 400 of them; first to give W F Cody name "Buffalo Bill."
b. Mar 20, 1823 in Stamford, New York
d. Jul 16, 1886 in Stamford, New York
Source: *Alli SUP; AmAu; AmAu&B; AmBi; ApCAB; BioIn 1, 2, 7, 9; DcAmAu; DcAmB; DcArts; DcNAA; EncAAH; EncAJ; HsB&A; LegTOT; MnBBF; OhA&B; OxCAmH; OxCAmL 65, 83, 95; PseudN 82; REn; REnAL; TwCBDA; WebAB 74, 79; WhAm HS; WorAl; WorAlBi*

Judson, Egbert Putnam
American. Inventor
Developed gentle blasting powder, 1876.
b. Aug 9, 1812 in Syracuse, New York
d. Jan 9, 1893 in San Francisco, California
Source: *DcAmB; NatCAB 24; WhAm HS*

Judson, Emily Chubbock
[Fanny Forester]
American. Author, Missionary
Missionary to Burma, 1846-47; to Rangoon, 1847; wrote *My Two Sisters,* 1854.
b. Aug 22, 1817 in Eaton, New York
d. Jun 1, 1854 in Hamilton, New York
Source: *Alli; AmAu; AmAu&B; AmBi; ApCAB; BbD; BiD&SB; CyAL 2; DcAmB; DcNAA; Drake; FemPA; NotAW; PenNWW B; PseudN 82; TwCBDA; WebAB 74, 79; WhAm HS*

Judy, Steven
American. Murderer
Executed by electrocution.
b. 1957? in Indianapolis, Indiana
d. Mar 9, 1981 in Michigan City, Indiana

Juilliard, Augustus D
American. Merchant, Philanthropist
Donated $12 million toward establishment of Juilliard School of Music, 1920.
b. Apr 19, 1836 in Canton, Ohio
d. Apr 25, 1919 in New York, New York
Source: *AmBi; Baker 84; DcAmB; NatCAB 14, 28; WhAm 1*

Juin, Alphonse Pierre
French. Soldier
Resident-general in Tunisia, 1943; in Morocco, 1947; last Marshal of France, 1953; head of NATO, 1953.
b. Dec 16, 1888 in Bone, Algeria
d. Jan 27, 1967 in Paris, France
Source: *CurBio 43, 67; WhAm 4; WhoMilH 76; WhWW-II*

Julesberg, Elizabeth Rider Montgomery
[Elizabeth Montgomery]
American. Children's Author
Wrote reading primers featuring Dick, Jane, Spot, 1940s.
b. Jul 12, 1902 in Huaras, Peru
d. Feb 19, 1985 in Seattle, Washington
Source: *AuBYP 3; BioIn 2, 3, 7, 9, 19; ConAu 42NR, 115; WhoAmW 81; WhoThe 72, 77, 81*

Julia, Raul
[Raul Rafael Carlos Julia y Arcelay]
American. Actor
Films include *Tempest,* 1982; *The Addams Family,* 1992.
b. Mar 9, 1940 in San Juan, Puerto Rico
d. Oct 24, 1994 in Manhasset, New York
Source: *BioIn 9, 11, 13, 20, 21; CamGWoT; ConTFT 1, 3, 13; CurBio 82, 95N; DcHiB; HalFC 84, 88; HispAmA; IntMPA 86, 88, 92; LegTOT; News 95, 95-1; NewYTBS 77, 94; WhoAm 86; WhoHisp 91, 92, 94; WhoHol A; WhoThe 77, 81*

Julian
[Flavius Claudius Julianus]
"The Apostate"
Roman. Ruler
General, proclaimed emperor by troops, 361; enemy of Christianity.
b. Nov 17, 331 in Constantinople, Turkey
d. Jun 26, 363 in Ctesiphon, Persia
Source: *Benet 87, 96; BioIn 5, 6, 7, 9, 10, 11, 12, 14; DcBiPP; EncEarC; LinLib L, S; LuthC 75; PseudN 82; WhDW*

Julian, Doggie
[Alvin F Julian]
American. Basketball Coach
Helped popularize basketball in New England; coached at several colleges, including Dartmouth, 1951-67; Hall of Fame.
b. Apr 5, 1901 in Reading, Pennsylvania
d. Jul 28, 1967 in Worcester, Massachusetts
Source: *BiDAmSp BK; BioIn 8, 9; ObitOF 79; WhoBbl 73*

Julian, Hubert Fauntleroy
[Huberto Fauntleroyana Juliano]
"Black Eagle"
American. Aviator
First black man to parachute from a plane over NYC, 1922; Military Governor of Ethiopia during 1939 Mussolini invasion.
b. 1897, Trinidad
Source: *BioIn 3, 7, 9; InB&W 80; NewYTBS 74*

Julian, Percy Lavon
American. Chemist
Developed synthetic cortisone for arthritis patients.
b. Apr 11, 1899 in Montgomery, Alabama
d. Apr 19, 1975 in Waukegan, Illinois
Source: *AmMWSc 73P; BioIn 1, 2, 3, 5, 6, 7, 8, 9, 10, 11, 12, 13; BlksScM; ConBlB 6; CurBio 47, 75; DcAmB S9; DcScB S2; DiAASTC; InB&W 85; InSci; McGMS 80; NatCAB 62; NegAl 83; NewYTBS 75; NotTwCS; WebAB 74, 79; WhAm 6; WhoAm 74; WhoMW 74; WhoWor 74; WorInv; WorScD*

Juliana
[Juliana Emma Maria Wilhelmina]
Dutch. Ruler
Ruled 1948-80; supported int'l efforts such as Marshall Plan, NATO; abolished the curtsy.
b. Apr 30, 1909 in The Hague, Netherlands
Source: *BioIn 1, 2, 3, 4, 5, 6, 7, 8, 10, 12, 16; ContDcW 89; CurBio 55; EncWB; GoodHs; IntDcWB; IntWW 74, 75, 82; LegTOT; WhoAmW 68, 70, 72; WhoGov 72; WhoWor 76, 78, 80, 82, 84, 95, 96; WomWR*

Julien, Isaac
English. Filmmaker
Co-founded Sankofa Film and Video, 1983; films include *Young Soul Rebels,* 1991; also has created documentaries for BBC.
b. Feb 1960 in London, England
Source: *ConBlB 3; GayLesB*

Julius II, Pope
[Giuliano della Rovere]
Italian. Religious Leader
Pope, 1503-13; noted patron of the arts; laid cornerstone of St. Peters.
b. Dec 5, 1443 in Albisola, Italy
d. Feb 21, 1513 in Rome, Italy
Source: *BioIn 19; McGEWB; NewCol 75; REn*

Julius III, Pope
[Giammaria Ciocchi del Monte]
Italian. Religious Leader
Pope, 1550-55; promoted Jesuits, began reforms, founded Collegium Germanicum, 1552.
b. Sep 10, 1487 in Rome, Italy
d. Mar 23, 1555 in Rome, Italy
Source: *PseudN 82; WebBD 83*

Jumblatt, Kamal Fouad
Lebanese. Political Leader
Powerful head of Druze sect, leader of Progressive Socialist Party, 1949-77; won Lenin Peace Prize, 1972.
b. Jan 6, 1917 in Mukhtara, Lebanon
d. Mar 16, 1977 in Beirut, Lebanon
Source: *BioIn 7, 10; CurBio 77; IntWW 75; NewYTBS 76, 77*

Jumblatt, Walid
Lebanese. Political Leader
Leader of Lebanese Druze community, pres., National Socialist Party, since father's assassination, 1977.
b. 1949?
Source: *BioIn 13; ConNews 87-4; PolLCME*

Jumel, Eliza
[Betsey Bowen; Eliza Brown]
American.
Eccentric, social climber who married Stephen Jumel, coffee planter; Aaron Burr, former US vp.
b. 1769
d. Jul 16, 1865 in New York, New York
Source: *ApCAB; BioIn 2, 3, 6, 7, 10, 12; NotAW; REnAL*

Jump, Gordon
American. Actor
Played Mr. Carlson on "WKRP in Cincinnati," 1978-82; "New WKRP in Cincinnati," 1991.
b. Apr 1, 1927? in Dayton, Ohio
Source: *HalFC 84; VarWW 85; WhoAm 84, 86*

Jumper, Betty Mae Tiger
American. Nurse
First Seminole woman to become a nurse.
b. 1923 in Indiantown, Florida
Source: *BioIn 9; NotNaAm*

Juneau, Pierre
Canadian. Broadcasting Executive
Pres., Canadian Broadcasting Corp., 1982-89.
b. Oct 17, 1922 in Verdun, Quebec, Canada
Source: *BioIn 13, 16; CanWW 31, 70, 79, 80, 81, 83, 89; IntWW 83, 89, 91, 93; News 88, 88-3; WhoAm 76, 78, 84, 86, 88, 90, 96, 97; WhoCanB 86; WhoE 85, 86, 91, 93; WhoEnt 92; WhoFI 85, 87, 89, 92; WhoMW 90; WhoWor 87, 89, 91*

Jung, Carl Gustav
"Father of Analytical Psychology"
Swiss. Psychologist, Psychiatrist
Known for classifying personalities as extroverted or introverted; wrote *Psychology of the Unconscious,* 1912.
b. Jul 26, 1875 in Basel, Switzerland
d. Jun 6, 1961 in Zurich, Switzerland
Source: *AsBiEn; Benet 87, 96; BiDPara; BiDPsy; BiESc; BioIn 1, 2, 3, 4, 5, 6, 7, 8, 9, 10, 11, 12, 13, 14, 15, 16, 17, 18, 19, 20; CasWL; CurBio 61; CyWA 89; DcScB; EncO&P 1, 2, 3; EncPaPR 91; EncSPD; EncWL, 2, 3; IlEncMy; InSci; LinLib L, S; LngCTC; LuthC 75; MakMC; McGEWB; NamesHP; OxCEng 67, 85, 95; OxCGer 76, 86; OxCMed 86; RComWL; REn; TwCA, SUP; UFOEn; WhAm 3, 4; WhDW; WhE&EA; WhoTwCL; WorAl; WorAlBi*

Junior, E(ster) J(ames, III)
American. Football Player
Two-time all-pro linebacker, St. Louis, 1981-88; Miami, 1989—; suspended by NFL for drug involvement, 1983.
b. Dec 8, 1959 in Sallsburg, North Carolina
Source: *BioIn 14; FootReg 87; NewYTBS 84*

Junkers, Hugo
German. Aircraft Designer
Built first all-metal plane to successfully fly.
b. Feb 3, 1859 in Rheydt, Prussia
d. Feb 3, 1935, Germany
Source: *EncTR 91; InSci*

Junot, Philippe
French. Banker
Married Princess Caroline of Monaco, 1978-1980.
b. 1942
Source: *BioIn 12*

Jurado, Katy
[Maria Christina Jurado Garcia]
Mexican. Actor
Oscar nominee for role of Senora Devereaux in *Broken Lance,* 1954.
b. Jan 16, 1927 in Guadalajara, Mexico
Source: *BioIn 18; FilmEn; FilmgC; ForYSC; HalFC 80, 84, 88; HispAmA; IntMPA 75, 76, 77, 78, 79, 80, 81, 82, 84, 86, 88, 92, 94, 96; MovMk; OxCFilm; PseudN 82; SweetSg D; VarWW 85; WhoAmW 74; WhoHol 92, A*

Jurgens, Curt
German. Actor
Appeared in over 150 films, including *The Enemy Below,* 1957; *The Spy Who Loved Me,* 1977.
b. Dec 12, 1915 in Munich, Germany
d. Jun 18, 1982 in Vienna, Austria
Source: *AnObit 1982; BiDFilm; BioIn 12, 13; ConAu 107; FilmgC; IntMPA 78, 79, 80, 81, 82; MotPP; MovMk; NewYTBS 82; OxCFilm; WhAm 8; WhoAm 80, 82; WhoHol A; WorEFlm*

Jurgenson, Sonny
[Christian Adolph Jurgenson, III]
American. Football Player
Five-time all-pro quarterback, 1957-74, mostly with Washington; led NFL in passing three times; Hall of Fame, 1983.
b. Aug 23, 1934 in Wilmington, North Carolina
Source: *CurBio 77; LegTOT; WhoAm 82, 84, 86; WhoFtbl 74; WorAl; WorAlBi*

Jurinac, Sena
[Srebrenka Jurinac]
Yugoslav. Opera Singer
Soprano; made US debut, San Francisco opera, 1959.
b. Oct 24, 1921 in Travnik, Yugoslavia
Source: *Baker 78, 84, 92; BioIn 3, 4, 8, 11, 14; CmOp; IntDcOp; IntWW 74, 75, 76, 77, 78, 79, 80, 81, 82, 83, 89, 91, 93; IntWWM 77, 80, 90; InWom, SUP; MetOEnc; MusSN; NewAmDM; NewEOp 71; NewGrDM 80; NewGrDO; OxDcOp; PenDiMP; PseudN 82; Who 74, 82, 83, 85, 88, 90, 92; WhoAmW 66, 68, 70, 72, 74, 75; WhoMus 72; WhoOp 76; WhoWor 74, 78*

Jussieu, Bernard de
French. Botanist
Established botanical garden, 1759; developed plant classification.
b. Aug 17, 1699 in Lyons, France
d. Dec 6, 1777? in Paris, France
Source: *DcBiPP; DcCathB; DcScB; InSci; OxCFr*

Just, Ernest Everett
American. Biologist
Harvard U zoologist noted for study of cellular biology; won Spingarn Medal, 1915.
b. Aug 14, 1883 in Charleston, South Carolina
d. Oct 27, 1941 in Washington, District of Columbia
Source: *AfrAmAl 6; BioIn 1, 6, 8, 9, 11, 13, 14, 18, 20; BlksScM; ConBlB 3; DcAmB S3; DcAmMeB 84; DcAmNB; DcNAA; DiAASTC; InB&W 80, 85; InSci; NotTwCS; ObitOF 79; SelBAAf; SelBAAu; WebAB 74, 79; WhAm 1; WhoColR; WorScD*

Just, Ward
American. Author
Novels include *A Soldier of the Revolution,* 1970; *Jack Gance,* 1989.
b. Sep 5, 1935 in Michigan City, Indiana
Source: *BenetAL 91; BioIn 15, 16; ConAu 25R, 32NR; ConLC 4, 27; ConNov 96; CurBio 89; DrAF 76; DrAPF 87; WhoAm 88, 90; WhoUSWr 88; WhoWrEP 89*

Justice, Choo Choo
[Charles Ronald Justice]
American. Football Player
Two-time All-America running back, U of NC, 1948-49; inspired song "All the Way, Choo Choo"; with Washington in NFL, 1950, 1952-54.
b. May 18, 1924 in Asheville, North Carolina
Source: *BioIn 1, 2, 8, 10; WhoFtbl 74*

Justice, Dave
American. Baseball Player
With Atlanta, 1989-96; Cleveland, 1997—; rookie of the year, 1990.
b. Apr 14, 1966 in Cincinnati, Ohio

Justice, James Robertson
English. Actor
Best known for film *Doctor in the House,* 1954, and sequels.
b. Jun 15, 1905 in Wigtown, Scotland
d. Jul 2, 1975 in Winchester, England
Source: *BioIn 10, 13; FilmEn; FilmgC; ForYSC; HalFC 80, 84, 88; IlWWBF; ItaFilm; MovMk; WhoHol C; WhScrn 77, 83*

Justice, William Wayne
American. Judge
Advocated prison reform; improved bilingual education, 1981.
b. Feb 25, 1920 in Athens, Texas
Source: *AmBench 79; BiDFedJ; BioIn 12; WhoAm 74, 76, 78, 80, 82, 84, 86, 88, 90, 92, 94, 95, 96, 97; WhoAmL 79, 87, 90, 92, 94, 96; WhoAmP 73; WhoGov 72, 75, 77; WhoSSW 73, 84, 86, 88, 91, 93, 95, 97*

Justin, John, Jr.
American. Business Executive
Chm., CEO, Justin Industries, 1974—, a manufacturer of exotic leather boots.
b. 1917 in Nocona, Texas
Source: *BioIn 19; Dun&B 90; FilmEn; FilmgC; ForYSC; HalFC 80, 84, 88; IlWWBF; IntMPA 75, 76, 77, 78, 79, 80, 81, 82, 84, 86; ItaFilm; News 92, 92-2; St&PR 91; WhoFI 83; WhoHol 92, A; WhoThe 72, 77, 81*

Justinian I
[Flavius Anicius Justinianus]
''The Great''
Byzantine. Ruler
Byzantine emperor, 527-65; completed codification of Roman law.
b. May 11, 483 in Tauresium, Illyria
d. Nov 14, 565, Byzantium
Source: *BioIn 10; NewCol 75; PseudN 82; WebBD 83*

Justiz, Manuel Jon
American. Educator
Director, National Institute of Education, 1983-85.
b. Dec 26, 1948 in Havana, Cuba
Source: *ConNews 86-4; WhoAm 86, 88, 90, 96, 97*

Justus, Roy Braxton
American. Editor, Cartoonist
Longtime syndicated, political cartoonist, Washington, DC.
b. May 16, 1901 in Avon, South Dakota
d. 1984?
Source: *WhAm 8; WhoAm 74, 76, 78, 80, 82; WhoAmA 73, 76, 78, 80, 82, 84N, 86N, 89N, 91N, 93N*

Jutra, Claude
Canadian. Director
Best known for film *Mon Oncle Antoine,* 1971.
b. Mar 11, 1930 in Montreal, Quebec, Canada
d. Apr 23, 1987 in Quebec, Quebec, Canada
Source: *AnObit 1987; BioIn 10, 15, 16; CanWW 79, 80, 81, 83; CreCan 1; DcFM; FilmEn; IntDcF 1-2, 2-2; MiSFD 9N; OxCFilm; WorEFlm; WorFDir 2*

Juvenal
[Decimus Junius Juvenalis]
''The Aquinian Sage''; ''The Last Poet of Rome''
Roman. Satirist
Attacked Roman Empire in 16 satirical poems written in five books.
b. 55? in Aquinum, Italy
d. 127?
Source: *AtlBL; BbD; BiD&SB; CasWL; ClMLC 8; CyWA 58; NewC; PenC CL; PseudN 82; RComWL; REn; WebBD 83*

K

Kaas, Patricia
French. Singer
Pop singer; albums include *Scene de Vie.*
b. 1967? in Lorraine, France

Kaat, Jim
[James Lee Kaat]
American. Baseball Player
Pitcher, 1959-83; led AL in wins. 1966.
b. Nov 7, 1938 in Zeeland, Michigan
Source: *Ballpl 90; BaseEn 88; BiDAmSp BB; BioIn 10, 12, 15; WhoAm 78, 82; WhoProB 73*

Kabalevsky, Dmitri Borisovich
Russian. Composer
Wrote piano concertos, symphonies, operas including *Colas Breugnon,* 1938.
b. Dec 30, 1904 in Saint Petersburg, Russia
d. Feb 17, 1987, Union of Soviet Socialist Republics
Source: *Baker 84; DcCM; IntWW 74; WhoMus 72; WhoWor 74*

Kabibble, Ish
[Merwyn Bogue]
American. Comedian, Musician
Comedic cornet player with Kay Kyser's "Kollege of Musical Knowledge."
d. Jun 5, 1994 in Palm Springs, California
Source: *CmpEPM; ConAu 131; JoeFr; NewYTBS 94*

Kabila, Laurent Desire
Congolese. Political Leader
Leader of The Democratic Republic of the Congo, which he renamed from Zaire, 1997—.

Kabotie, Fred
American. Artist
Painter whose works are exhibited in the permanent collections of many major museums; painted frescos at the eastern entrance to the Grand Canyon.
b. Feb 20, 1900 in Shongopavi, Arizona
Source: *BioIn 9, 11, 17, 21; ConAu 118; IlBEAAW; NotNaAm; WhAmArt 85; WhoAm 74, 76, 78, 80; WhoAmA 76, 78, 80, 82, 84, 86*

Kaczynski, Theodore (John)
American.
Suspected of sending mail bombs under the name "The Unabomer;" professor, mathematics, U of CA, Berkeley, 1967-69.
b. May 22, 1942 in Evergreen Park, Illinois

Kadar, Janos
Hungarian. Political Leader
Head of Communist Party, 1956-88; prime minister of Hungary, 1956-58, 1961-68.
b. May 26, 1912 in Fiume, Austria-Hungary
d. Jul 6, 1989 in Budapest, Hungary
Source: *AnObit 1989; BioIn 4, 5, 6, 7, 9, 10, 11, 12, 14, 15, 16, 18; ColdWar 2; CurBio 57, 89, 89N; DcTwHis; EncCW; FacFETw; HisWorL; IntWW 74, 75, 76, 77, 78, 79, 80, 81, 82, 83, 89; McGEWB; NewYTBS 89; WhAm 11; WhDW; WhoSocC 78; WhoSoCE 89; WhoWor 74, 76, 78, 80, 82, 84, 87, 89*

Kadare, Ismail
Albanian. Author
Novels have been interpreted as both pro and anti-communist: *The General of the Dead Army,* 1963; *Palace of Dreams,* 1981.
b. Jan 28, 1936 in Gjirokaster, Albania
Source: *ConLC 52; CurBio 92; IntWW 91; RAdv 14, 13-2; WhoSoCE 89; WorAu 1985*

Kael, Pauline
American. Critic, Author
New Yorker mag. movie critic, 1968-91; author of numerous books on film criticism; philosophy of film reviewing collected in *When the Lights Go Down,* 1980.
b. Jun 19, 1919 in Petaluma, California
Source: *AmAu&B; AmWomWr; ArtclWW 2; Au&Wr 71; BenetAL 91; BioIn 7, 8, 9, 10, 12, 13; BlueB 76; CelR, 90; CmCal; ConAu 6NR, 44NR, 45; ContDcW 89; ConTFT 3; CurBio 74; DcTwCCu 1; EncAJ; EncTwCJ; FemiCLE; ForWC 70; IntAu&W 76, 77, 82, 89, 91, 93; IntMPA 76, 77, 78, 79, 80, 81, 82, 84, 86, 88; IntWW 89, 91, 93; InWom SUP; LegTOT; LibW; OxCAmL 83, 95; OxCFilm; WhoAm 74, 76, 78, 80, 82, 84, 86, 88, 90, 92, 94, 95, 96, 97; WhoAmW 68A, 70, 72, 74, 75, 77, 81, 83, 85, 87, 89, 91, 93, 95, 97; WhoE 85, 86, 89, 91, 93, 95, 97; WhoEnt 92; WhoUSWr 88; WhoWrEP 89, 92, 95; WomFir; WomWMM; WorAlBi; WorAu 1970; WrDr 76, 80, 82, 84, 86, 88, 90, 92, 94, 96*

Kaempfert, Bert
German. Musician
With band, known for "easy listening" albums, 1960s-70s; had hit single "Three O'Clock in the Morning," 1965; arranged recording debut of Beatles, 1961, as ba ck-up group.
b. Oct 16, 1923 in Hamburg, Germany
Source: *Baker 84; EncPR&S 74; OxCPMus*

Kaempffert, Waldemar (Bernhard)
American. Editor, Author
NY Times science editor for 26 yrs.
b. Sep 23, 1877 in New York, New York
d. Nov 27, 1956 in New York, New York
Source: *BiDPara; BioIn 3, 4; ConAu 113; CurBio 43, 57; DcAmB S6; EncPaPR 91; InSci; ScFEYrs; WhAm 3*

Kafka, Franz
Austrian. Author, Poet
His short stories, three novels characterized by themes of loneliness; most published posthumously: *Amerika,* 1927.
b. Jul 2, 1883 in Prague, Bohemia
d. Jun 3, 1924 in Kierling, Austria
Source: *AtlBL; Benet 87, 96; BioIn 1, 2, 3, 4, 5, 6, 7, 8, 9, 10, 11, 12, 13, 14, 15, 16, 17, 18, 19, 20; CasWL; ClDMEL 47, 80; CnMD; CnMWL; ConAu 105, 126;*

CyWA 58, 89; DcArts; DcLB 81; DcTwHis; Dis&D; EncSF, 93; EncWL, 2, 3; EncWT; EuWr 9; EvEuW; FacFETw; GrFLW; HalFC 84, 88; JeHun; LegTOT; LiExTwC; LinLib L, S; LngCTC; MagSWL; MajTwCW; MakMC; McGEWB; ModGL; NewEOp 71; NewYTBS 89; Novels; OxCEng 67, 85, 95; OxCGer 76, 86; PenC EUR; PenEncH; RAdv 14, 13-2; RComWL; REn; RfGShF; RfGWoL 95; ScF&FL 1, 92; ScFSB; ShSCr 5; ShSWr; TwCA, SUP; TwCLC 2, 6, 13, 29, 47, 53; TwCSFW 91A; TwCWr; WebBD 83; WhDW; WhoHr&F; WhoTwCL; WorAl; WorAlBi; WorLitC; WrPh

Kaganovich, Lazar M(oiseevich)
Russian. Political Leader
Held various political posts, 1925-63; awarded Order of Lenin, 1943; once considered No. 2 man under Stalin.
b. Nov 22, 1893 in Kabany, Russia
d. Jul 25, 1991 in Moscow, Union of Soviet Socialist Republics
Source: *BioIn 17, 18; CurBio 42, 55; IntWW 74*

Kagel, Sam
American. Lawyer
Mediator in NFL strike, 1982.
b. Jan 24, 1909 in San Francisco, California
Source: *BioIn 13; NewYTBS 82; WhoAm 74, 76, 78; WhoLab 76*

Kahanamoku, Duke Paoa
American. Swimmer
Won Olympic gold medals in 100-meter freestyle event, 1912, 1920.
b. Aug 24, 1890 in Honolulu, Hawaii
d. Jan 22, 1968 in Honolulu, Hawaii
Source: *BiDAmSp BK; BioIn 8, 10, 12; ObitOF 79; WhAm 4A; WhoHol B; WhScrn 83; WorAlBi*

Kahane, Meir David
American. Religious Leader
Founded Jewish Defense League, 1968; tactics inspired by Black Panthers.
b. Aug 1, 1932 in New York, New York
d. Nov 5, 1990 in New York, New York
Source: *BioIn 9, 10, 12; BioNews 74; ConAu 112; CurBio 72; NewYTBE 71; WhoE 74*

Kahane, Melanie
American. Designer
Interior and industrial designer known for inventive and creative use of textures, colors, and materials; inducted into Interior Design Hall of Fame, 1985.
b. Nov 26, 1910 in New York, New York
d. Dec 22, 1988 in New York, New York
Source: *BioIn 5, 8, 9, 11, 16; CurBio 59, 89N; InWom, SUP; NewYTBS 88; WhAm 9; WhoAm 74, 76, 78, 80, 82, 84, 86, 88; WhoAmA 73, 76, 78, 80, 82, 84, 86, 89; WhoAmW 58, 61, 64, 66, 68, 70, 72, 74; WhoWor 82; WhoWorJ 72, 78*

Kahles, Charles William
American. Cartoonist
Innovative comic strips include first suspense serial; first superhero, Hairbreadth Harry, 1906.
b. Jan 12, 1878 in Lengfurt, Germany
d. Jan 21, 1931 in Great Neck, New York
Source: *EncACom; NatCAB 23; WhJnl; WorECom*

Kahlo, Frida
[Mrs. Diego Rivera]
Mexican. Artist
Majority of paintings are self-portraits; biography *Frida* written by Hay den Herrera, 1983.
b. Jul 6, 1907 in Coyoacan, Mexico
d. Jul 13, 1954 in Mexico City, Mexico
Source: *ArtLatA; Benet 96; BioIn 2, 3, 11, 12, 14, 15, 16, 17, 18, 19, 20, 21; ConAu 153; DcArts; DcHiB; DcTwCCu 4; EncWB; IntDcWB; McGDA; News 91, 91-3; NorAmWA; OxCTwCA*

Kahn, Albert
"Father of Modern Factory Design"
American. Architect
World-famous industrial designer instrumental in Allied WW II construction: Willow Run, MI bomber plant.
b. Mar 21, 1869 in Rhaunen, Germany
d. Dec 8, 1942 in Detroit, Michigan
Source: *AmDec 1920; BiDAmAr; BioIn 2, 4, 9, 10, 11, 16, 19, 20; BioNews 74; BriEAA; CurBio 42; DcAmB S3; DcTwDes; EncAAr 1, 2; EncAB-A 18; EncABHB 4; EncMA; FacFETw; InSci; IntDcAr; LegTOT; LinLib S; MacEA; McGDA; NatCAB 31; WhAm 2; WhoArch; WorAl; WorAlBi*

Kahn, Alfred Edward
American. Economist
Advised Carter on nat. inflation issues, 1978-80.
b. Oct 17, 1917 in Paterson, New Jersey
Source: *AmEA 74; AmMWSc 73S, 78S; BioIn 11, 12, 13, 16; BlueB 76; CurBio 79; IntYB 78, 79, 80, 81, 82; NewYTBS 83; WhoAm 74, 76, 78, 80, 82, 84, 86, 88, 90, 92, 94, 95, 96, 97; WhoAmP 77, 79, 81, 83, 85, 87, 89, 91, 93, 95; WhoE 74; WhoEc 81, 86; WhoGov 77; WhoWor 74*

Kahn, Ben
American. Designer
Innovative furrier whose coats were purchased by Elizabeth Taylor, Joe Namath, Joe Frazier.
b. 1887, Russia
d. Feb 5, 1976 in New York, New York
Source: *BioIn 10; NewYTBS 76; ObitOF 79*

Kahn, E(ly) J(acques), Jr.
American. Writer
Writer for *The New Yorker,* 1937-94; wrote *The Army Life,* 1942.
b. Dec 4, 1916
d. May 28, 1994 in Holyoke, Massachusetts
Source: *AmAu&B; Au&Wr 71; BioIn 2, 4, 11, 16, 19, 20; ConAu 65, 145; ConLC 86; TwCA SUP; WhAm 11; WhoAm 74, 76, 78, 80, 82, 84, 86, 88, 90, 92, 94; WhoAmJ 80; WhoE 74, 93; WhoWorJ 72, 78*

Kahn, Gus
American. Songwriter
Wrote Broadway scores, songs including "My Blue Heaven," "Mammy"; produced average of six hit songs annually for 20 yrs.
b. Nov 6, 1886 in Koblenz, Germany
d. Oct 8, 1941 in Beverly Hills, California
Source: *AmPS; AmSong; ASCAP 66, 80; BestMus; BiDAmM; BioIn 15; CmpEPM; CurBio 41; EncMT; FilmEn; HalFC 80, 84, 88; LegTOT; NewGrDA 86; NotNAT B; OxCPMus; Sw&Ld C*

Kahn, Herman
American. Physicist
Military strategist; co-founder, director, Hudson Institute think tank, 1961.
b. Feb 15, 1922 in Bayonne, New Jersey
d. Jul 7, 1983 in Chappaqua, New York
Source: *AmAu&B; AmMWSc 73P, 78S; AnObit 1983; BioIn 6, 7, 8, 10, 11, 13, 14, 15, 18; BlueB 76; CelR; ColdWar 1, 2; ConAu 44NR, 65, 110; ConIsC 1; CurBio 83, 83N; DcAmC; EncSF; FacFETw; Future; IntAu&W 77, 82; IntWW 74, 75, 76, 77, 78, 79, 80, 81, 82, 83; NatCAB 63, 63N; NewYTBS 83; PolProf K; WhAm 8; WhoAm 74, 76, 78, 80, 82; WhoWor 74, 76, 78; WrDr 80, 82, 84*

Kahn, Louis I(sadore)
American. Architect
Distinctive buildings had huge forms: Yale U Art Gallery.
b. Feb 2, 1901 in Oesel, Russia
d. Mar 17, 1974 in New York, New York
Source: *AmArch 70; AmCulL; BioNews 74; BriEAA; ConArch 87, 94; ConAu 49; CurBio 64, 74; EncAAr 1, 2; EncAB-H 1974, 1996; EncMA; NatCAB 58; NewYTBE 72; NewYTBS 74; RAdv 14; WebBD 83; WhAm 6; WhoAm 74; WhoE 74; WhoWor 74*

Kahn, Madeline Gail
American. Actor
Oscar nominee for *Paper Moon, Blazing Saddles;* star of TV series "Oh Madeline," 1983; won 1993 Tony for *Sisters Rosensweig.*
b. Sep 29, 1942 in Boston, Massachusetts
Source: *BkPepl; CurBio 77; HalFC 84; IntMPA 86; InWom SUP; MovMk; NewYTBS 74; VarWW 85; WhoAm 86; WhoHol A; WorAl*

Kahn, Otto Hermann
American. Banker, Art Patron
Business associate of Edward Harriman considered greatest art patron US has known.
b. Feb 21, 1867 in Mannheim, Germany
d. Mar 29, 1934 in New York, New York
Source: *AmBi; AmLY; ApCAB X; Baker 78, 84, 92; BioIn 3, 6, 16, 19; DcAmB S1; DcBiPP; DcNAA; LinLib S; NatCAB 14, 16, 31; NewGrDO; NotNAT B; REnAL; WebAB 74; WhAm 1; WorAl*

Kahn, Roger
American. Journalist, Author
Sports editor *Newsweek,* 1956-60; editor *Saturday Evening Post,* 1963-68.
b. Oct 31, 1927 in New York, New York
Source: *AuBYP 2, 3; Ballpl 90; BiDAmSp Sup; BioIn 4, 8, 9, 10, 11, 12, 13; ConAu 25R, 44NR; ConLC 30; Conv 3; DcLB 171; LiJour; SmATA 37; WhoAm 84, 86, 88, 90, 92, 94, 95, 96, 97; WhoE 77; WhoUSWr 88; WhoWrEP 89, 92, 95; WrDr 92, 94, 96*

Kahng, Dawon
American. Inventor, Physicist
Significant inventions in solid-state electronics include the first operative silicon MOS transistor and the floating gate memory cell.
b. May 4, 1931 in Seoul, Korea
d. May 13, 1992 in New Brunswick, New Jersey
Source: *AmMWSc 73P, 76P, 79, 82, 86, 92; BioIn 19; LElec; WhoAm 82, 84, 86, 90, 92, 95; WhoEng 80, 88; WhoTech 82, 84, 89; WhoWor 91, 93*

Kaifu Toshiki
Japanese. Political Leader
Prime minister of Japan, 1988-91; noted for being untainted in the Recruit influence-peddling scandal.
b. Jan 2, 1931 in Ichinomiya, Japan
Source: *BioIn 16; CurBio 90; EncJap; IntWW 91; WhoWor 91*

Kain, Karen Alexandria
Canadian. Dancer
Principal dancer, National Ballet of Canada, 1971—.
b. Mar 28, 1951 in Hamilton, Ontario, Canada
Source: *BiDD; BioIn 11; CanWW 83; CurBio 80; InWom SUP; WhoAm 86, 90, 92, 94, 95, 96, 97; WhoEnt 92; WhoWor 93, 95, 96, 97*

Kainen, Jacob
American. Artist
Works span four decades, range from etchings, lithographs to oils and geometric abstractions.
b. Dec 7, 1909 in Waterbury, Connecticut
Source: *BioIn 11, 12; CurBio 87; DcAmArt; WhAmArt 85; WhoAm 74, 76, 78, 80, 82, 84, 86, 88, 90, 92, 94, 95, 96, 97; WhoAmA 73, 76, 78, 80, 82, 84, 86, 89, 91, 93; WhoGov 72*

Kaiser, Edgar Fosburgh
American. Industrialist
Pres., chm., Kaiser Aluminum & Chemical Corp., Kaiser Steel Corp.
b. Jul 29, 1908 in Spokane, Washington
d. Dec 11, 1981 in San Francisco, California
Source: *BioIn 12, 13; CurBio 82; IntWW 74, 75, 76, 77, 78, 79, 80, 81; IntYB 78, 79, 80, 81, 82; NewYTBS 81; St&PR 75; WhAm 8; WhoAm 74, 76, 78, 80; WhoWest 76, 78*

Kaiser, Georg
German. Dramatist
A leader of German Expressionism; plays banned by Nazis, after 1933; wrote *Gas I,* 1918.
b. Nov 25, 1878 in Magdeburg, Germany
d. Jun 5, 1945 in Ascona, Switzerland
Source: *Benet 87, 96; BioIn 1, 4, 6, 9, 19; CamGWoT; CasWL; ClDMEL 47, 80; CnMD; CnThe; ConAu 106; DcArts; DcLB 124; EncWL, 2, 3; EncWT; Ent; EvEuW; IntDcT 2; LiExTwC; LngCTC; McGEWB; McGEWD 72, 84; ModGL; ModWD; NewC; NewEOp 71; NotNAT B; OxCEng 67, 85, 95; OxCGer 76, 86; OxCThe 67, 83; PenC EUR; PlP&P; RAdv 14, 13-2; REn; REnWD; RfGWoL 95; TwCA, SUP; TwCLC 9; WhDW; WhoTwCL; WhThe; WorAl; WorAlBi*

Kaiser, Henry John
American. Industrialist
Began Kaiser Aluminum empire, which included cement, steel, car production; WW I I "Liberty Ships" made in four days.
b. May 9, 1882 in Canajoharie, New York
d. Aug 24, 1967 in Honolulu, Hawaii
Source: *BiDAmBL 83; BioIn 1, 2, 3, 4, 5, 6, 7, 8, 11, 14, 15, 16, 17, 18; CurBio 42, 61, 67; DcAmB S8; EncAB-H 1974; EncABHB 5, 9; FacFETw; McGEWB; MorMA; REnAW; WebAB 74, 79; WebBD 83; WhAm 4A; WorAl*

Kalakaua, David
Hawaiian. Ruler
Ruled HI, 1874-91; his ideas sparked revolution, 1887; new constitution restricted his powers, 1887.
b. Nov 16, 1836
d. Jan 30, 1891 in San Francisco, California
Source: *ApCAB; BioIn 1, 2, 11; HarEnUS; LinLib S; WebBD 83*

Kalatozov, Mikhail
[Mikhail Kalatozishvili]
Russian. Director
Early films banned for negativism; won Cannes Award for *Cranes Are Flying,* 1958.
b. Dec 23, 1903 in Tiflis, Russia
d. Mar 28, 1973 in Moscow, Union of Soviet Socialist Republics
Source: *FilmEn; FilmgC; HalFC 80, 84, 88; MiSFD 9N; NewYTBE 73; ObitOF 79; OxCFilm; PseudN 82; WorEFlm*

Kalb, Bernard
American. Government Official, Author
Former TV journalist; state dept. spokesman, 1985-86; co-author with brother, Marvin: *Kissinger,* 1974.
b. Feb 5, 1932 in New York, New York
Source: *AuSpks; BioIn 12; ConAu 109; WhoTelC*

Kalb, Johann de
"Baron de Kalb"
German. Army Officer
Major general in Continental army, from 1777; died in battle.
b. Jun 29, 1721 in Huttendorf, Bavaria
d. Aug 19, 1780 in Camden, South Carolina
Source: *AmBi; AmRev; ApCAB; DcAmB; LinLib S; NatCAB 1; OxCAmH; REn; TwCBDA; WebAB 74; WhAm HS; WhAmRev*

Kalb, Marvin Leonard
American. Broadcast Journalist
Chief diplomatic correspondent, NBC News, 1980-87.
b. Jun 9, 1930 in New York, New York
Source: *AmAu&B; AuSpks; ConAu 5R; CurBio 87; IntMPA 82; WhoAm 74, 76, 78, 82, 84; WhoSSW 73; WhoTelC; WhoWor 74*

Kalber, Floyd
American. Broadcast Journalist
Newscaster on NBC's "The Today Show," 1976-79; reporter, "NBC News," 1979-84; became newscaster, Chicago, 1984.
b. Dec 23, 1924 in Omaha, Nebraska
Source: *VarWW 85; WhoAm 78, 80, 82, 84, 86*

Kalem, T(heodore) E(ustace)
[Theodoros Kalemkierides]
American. Critic
With *Time* mag., 1961-85; pres. of NY Drama Critics Circle.
b. Dec 19, 1919 in Malden, Massachusetts
d. Jul 3, 1985 in New York, New York
Source: *BiE&WWA; BioIn 6, 14; ConAmTC; ConAu 116; NewYTBS 85; NotNAT*

Kalf, Willem
Dutch. Artist
Genre, still-life painter influenced by Vermeer: *Peasant Interior.*
b. 1619? in Rotterdam, Netherlands
d. 1693 in Amsterdam, Netherlands
Source: *BioIn 19; DcArts; IntDcAA 90; McGDA; OxCArt; OxDcArt*

Kalfin, Robert
American. Director
Plays include *Yentl,* 1975; *Song for a Saturday,* 1987.
b. Apr 22, 1933 in New York, New York
Source: *ConTFT 5; NotNAT; PlP&P A; WhoThe 81*

Kalidasa
Indian. Poet, Dramatist
Acclaimed as the greatest of Sanskrit poets; wrote lyric poem *Meghaduta* and drama *Sakuntala.*
b. c. 400
Source: *Benet 96; ClMLC 9; RfGWoL 95*

Kalikow, Peter Stephen
American. Real Estate Executive, Publisher
Pres. of H.J. Kalikow and Co; purchased the *New York Post,* 1988.
b. Dec 1, 1942 in New York, New York
Source: *BioIn 14, 16; CurBio 88; WhoAm 90, 95, 96, 97; WhoE 95*

Kaline, Al(bert William)
American. Baseball Player, Sportscaster
Outfielder, Detroit, 1953-74; youngest ever to win batting title, 1955; had 3,007 career hits; Hall of Fame, 1980; TV broadcaster for Detroit Tigers, 1976—.
b. Dec 19, 1934 in Baltimore, Maryland
Source: *Ballpl 90; BiDAmSp BB; BioIn 4, 5, 6, 7, 8, 9, 10, 12, 14, 15; BioNews 74; CelR; CurBio 70; FacFETw; LegTOT; NewYTBE 73; NewYTBS 74, 75; WhoAm 74; WhoProB 73; WorAl; WorAlBi*

Kalinin, Mikhail (Ivanovich)
Russian. Political Leader
Considered "grandfather" of Russian revolution; pres., USSR, 1923-46.
b. Nov 20, 1875 in Upper Troitsa, Russia
d. Jun 3, 1946 in Moscow, Union of Soviet Socialist Republics
Source: *BiDSovU; BioIn 1, 10, 16; CurBio 42, 46; DcTwHis; EncTR 91; FacFETw; ObitOF 79; SovUn*

Kalisch, Paul
German. Opera Singer
Tenor; sang Wagnerian roles with wife Lilli Lehmann at NY Met., 1888-92.
b. Nov 6, 1855 in Berlin, Germany
d. Jan 17, 1946, Germany
Source: *Baker 78, 84, 92; NewEOp 71; NewGrDM 80; NewGrDO*

Kalish, Max
Polish. Sculptor
Commissioned, 1944, to create bronze statues of WW II personalities.
b. Mar 1, 1891 in Valojen, Poland
d. Mar 18, 1945 in New York, New York
Source: *BioIn 1, 2, 9; NatCAB 35; WhAm 2; WhAmArt 85*

Kallen, Horace M(eyer)
American. Educator, Philosopher
Co-founded, New School for Social Research, NY, 1919; advocated adult education.
b. Aug 11, 1882 in Barenstadt, Germany
d. Feb 16, 1974 in Palm Beach, Florida
Source: *AmAu&B; BioIn 1, 3, 4, 6, 10, 13, 15, 17, 19, 21; ConAu 49, 93; CurBio 53, 74, 74N; DcAmB S9; DcAmImH; DcAmReB 1, 2; EncARH; ObitOF 79; OxCAmL 65, 83; REnAL; TwCA SUP; WhAm 6; WhNAA; WorAl; WorAlBi*

Kallen, Jackie
American. Boxing Promoter
Publicist, Kronk Boxing Club, Detroit, 1978-88; manager of professional boxers, 1988—.
b. c. 1946 in Detroit, Michigan
Source: *BioIn 20; News 94, 94-1; WhoAmW 97*

Kallen, Kitty
American. Singer, Actor
Vocalist with Big Bands; had hit "Little Things Mean a Lot," 1954.
b. May 25, 1926 in Philadelphia, Pennsylvania
Source: *CmpEPM; RkOn 74; WhoHol A*

Kalmanoff, Martin
American. Composer, Conductor, Musician
Wrote works for TV, musical theater, 17 operas.
b. May 24, 1920 in New York, New York
Source: *ASCAP 66, 80; BioIn 10; ConAmC 76, 82; IntWWM 77, 80, 85; NewGrDO; WhoAm 76, 78, 80, 82, 84, 86, 88, 90, 92, 94, 95, 96, 97; WhoAmJ 80; WhoAmM 83; WhoE 75, 77, 79, 81, 83, 85, 86, 89; WhoEnt 92; WhoWorJ 72, 78*

Kalmar, Bert
American. Lyricist
With Harry Ruby wrote hit songs "Who's Sorry Now?" 1923; "Three Little Words," 1930.
b. Feb 16, 1884 in New York, New York
d. Sep 18, 1947 in Los Angeles, California
Source: *AmPS; ASCAP 66, 80; BestMus; BiDAmM; BioIn 1, 4, 10, 15; CmpEPM; EncAFC; EncMT; HalFC 80, 84, 88; LegTOT; NewCBMT; NewGrDA 86; NotNAT B; ObitOF 79; OxCAmT 84; OxCPMus; Sw&Ld C; WhThe*

Kalmbach, Herbert Warren
American. Lawyer
Personal counsel to Nixon, 1968-73; finance chm. for Nixon's presidential campaigns; linked to Watergate trail for handling secret Rep. fund.
b. Oct 19, 1921 in Port Huron, Michigan
Source: *BioIn 10, 12; NewYTBE 73; PolProf NF; WhoAm 74, 76; WhoWest 74*

Kalmus, Herbert Thomas
American. Inventor
Invented technicolor, 1929; first used in film *Becky Sharp,* 1935.
b. Nov 9, 1881 in Chelsea, Massachusetts
d. Jul 11, 1963 in Los Angeles, California
Source: *BioIn 1, 2, 6; CurBio 49, 63; DcAmB S7; DcFM; FilmEn; FilmgC; HalFC 80; InSci; WhAm 4; WorAl; WorEFlm*

Kalmus, Natalie Mabelle Dunfee
[Mrs. Herbert Kalmus]
American. Inventor
Co-inventor, technicolor film.
b. 1892
d. Nov 15, 1965 in Boston, Massachusetts
Source: *DcAmB S7; FilmgC; ObitOF 79*

Kalp, Malcolm
[The Hostages]
American. Hostage
One of 52 held by terrorists, Nov 1979-Jan 1981.
b. 1939?
Source: *NewYTBS 81*

Kaltenborn, H(ans) V(on)
American. Editor, Broadcast Journalist
Best known for series of nonstop broadcasts during Munich crisis, 1938; wrote autobiography *Fifty Fabulous Years,* 1956.
b. Jul 9, 1878 in Milwaukee, Wisconsin
d. Jun 14, 1965 in New York, New York
Source: *AmAu&B; BiDAmJo; BioIn 1, 2, 4, 5, 7, 8, 11, 16; ConAu 93; CurBio 40, 65; DcAmB S7; DcAmDH 80, 89; EncAJ; JrnUS; LinLib L, S; NatCAB 51; ObitOF 79; PseudN 82; REnAL; WebAB 74, 79; WhAm 4; WhJnl; WhNAA*

Kalthoum, Um
"The Nightingale of the Nile"
Egyptian. Singer
Arab world's most beloved songstress.
b. 1898 in Tamay-al-Zahirah, Egypt
d. Feb 3, 1975 in Cairo, Egypt
Source: *BioIn 4, 6, 7, 10; NewYTBS 75; ObitOF 79; WhScrn 77, 83*

Kamali, Norma
American. Fashion Designer
Founder and owner, OMO Norma Kamali, 1978—; known for her line of sweats; won 2 Coty Awards, 1981-82.
b. Jun 27, 1945 in New York, New York
Source: *AmDec 1980; BioIn 12, 13; CelR 90; ConFash; DcTwDes; EncFash; IntWW 93; LegTOT; News 89-1; WhoAm 82, 84, 86, 88, 90, 92, 94, 95, 96, 97; WhoAmW 85, 87, 89, 91, 93, 95, 97; WhoE 85, 86, 89; WhoFash 88; WhoWor 97*

Kamehameha I
[Kamehameha the Great]
Hawaiian. Ruler
Ruled Hawaiian Islands, 1810-19; preserved ancient customs, religious beliefs; united islands, 1795.
b. Jun 11, 1753 in Kohala, Hawaii
d. May 5, 1819 in Kailua, Hawaii
Source: *BioIn 6, 10, 11; HarEnUS; LuthC 75; McGEWB; NewCol 75; WhAm HS*

Kamehameha II
Hawaiian. Ruler
Son of Kamehameha I; ruled 1819-24; rid islands of ancient religion, taboo system.
b. 1797 in Hawaii
d. Jul 14, 1824 in London, England
Source: *BioIn 11; WebBD 83*

Kamehameha III
Hawaiian. Ruler
Reigned, 1825-54; established island independence from US, Britain, France, 1842-43; promulgated constitution, 1840.
b. Mar 7, 1813 in Keauhou, Hawaii
d. Dec 15, 1854 in Honolulu, Hawaii
Source: *BioIn 11; WebBD 83*

Kamehameha IV
[Alexander Liholiho]
Hawaiian. Ruler
Popular, efficient king, 1854-63; aimed at establishing independence.
b. Feb 9, 1834 in Ewa, Hawaii
d. Nov 30, 1863 in Honolulu, Hawaii
Source: *BioIn 11; WebBD 83*

Kamehameha V
[Lot Kamehameha]
Hawaiian. Ruler
Last of direct line of monarchs, 1863-72.
b. Dec 11, 1830 in Honolulu, Hawaii
d. Dec 11, 1872 in Honolulu, Hawaii
Source: *BioIn 11; WebBD 83*

Kamel, Hussein
[Hussein Kamel Hassan; Hussein Kamel Hassan al-Majid; Hussein Kamel Majid]
Iraqi. Military Leader
Head of Iraqi military, 1987-95; defected to Jordan, son-in-law of Saddam Hussein.
b. c. 1954, Iraq
Source: *News 96, 96-1*

Kamen, Martin David
American. Biochemist
Works in areas of photosynthesis, nuclear chemistry; professor emeritus, U of CA, 1978—.
b. Aug 27, 1913 in Toronto, Ontario, Canada
Source: *AmMWSc 73P, 76P, 79, 82, 86, 89, 92, 95; AsBiEn; BiESc; BioIn 15; CanWW 70; ConAu 118; IntWW 83; LarDcSc; WhoAm 74, 76, 78, 80, 88, 90, 92, 94, 95, 96, 97; WhoWest 94; WhoWor 74, 76, 78; WorAl*

Kamen, Milt
American. Comedian, Actor
Films include *Mother, Jugs, & Speed; WC Fields and Me,* 1976.
b. 1924 in Hurleyville, New York
d. Feb 24, 1977 in Beverly Hills, California
Source: *BioIn 6; WhoHol A*

Kamenev, Lev Borisovich
[Lev Borisovich Rosenfeld]
Russian. Revolutionary
Originally followed Lenin, later opposed him; shot to death by orders of Stalin for alleged conspiracy.
b. 1883
d. 1936
Source: *Benet 87, 96; BiDSovU; BioIn 10, 12, 16; BlkwERR; DcPol; DcTwHis; EncRev; FacFETw; McGEWB; PseudN 82; REn; SovUn; WhDW*

Kameny, Frank(lin Edward)
American. Astronomer
Initiated slogan "Gay is Good;" fired from his position with the Army Map Service for being a homosexual, 1957.
b. May 21, 1925 in New York, New York
Source: *GayLesB; LNinSix*

Kamerlingh Onnes, Heike
Dutch. Physicist
Liquefied helium, 1908; awarded 1913 Nobel Prize.
b. Sep 21, 1853 in Groningen, Netherlands
d. Feb 21, 1926 in Leiden, Netherlands
Source: *AsBiEn; BiESc; BioIn 3, 20; CamDcSc; DcScB; LarDcSc; LinLib S; NewCol 75; NobelP; NotTwCS; WhDW; WhoNob, 90, 95; WorAl; WorAlBi; WorScD*

Kaminska, Ida
Russian. Actor
Oscar nominee for *The Shop on Main Street,* 1965; founded two theaters in Warsaw, Poland.
b. Sep 4, 1899 in Odessa, Russia
d. May 21, 1980 in New York, New York
Source: *AnObit 1980; BioIn 8, 10, 12, 15; ConAu 97; CurBio 69, 80N; EncWT; Ent; FilmEn; FilmgC; HalFC 80, 84, 88; IntWW 74, 75, 76, 77, 78, 79, 80; InWom SUP; NewYTBE 73; NewYTBS 80; NotNAT A; OxCThe 83; PolBiDi; WhoAm 74; WhoAmW 70, 72, 74; WhoHol A; WhoThe 72, 77; WhScrn 83; WomFir*

Kaminsky, Max
American. Jazz Musician
Star trumpeter; peaked in 1940s with Dixieland group; led own bands, 1960s-70s.
b. Sep 7, 1908 in Brockton, Massachusetts
Source: *AllMusG; BiDAmM; BiDJaz; BioIn 6, 12, 16, 20; CmpEPM; EncJzS; IlEncJ; NewAmDM; NewGrDJ 88, 94; OxCPMus; PenEncP; WhoJazz 72*

Kamp, Irene Kittle
[Grimes Grice]
American. Editor, Author
Editor, *Glamour,* 1939-42; *Cue,* 1943-46; *Seventeen,* 1950-55.
b. Oct 28, 1910 in New York, New York
d. Jun 15, 1985 in Los Angeles, California
Source: *ConAu 116; WhoAmW 58*

Kampelman, Max M
American. Lawyer, Diplomat
Dem. named by Ronald Reagan to head US negotiating team at arms reduction talks, Geneva, 1985.
b. Nov 7, 1920 in New York, New York
Source: *ConAu 41R; CurBio 86; NewYTBS 85; WhoAm 86; WhoAmL 85; WhoAmP 85; WhoWor 84*

Kanaly, Steve(n Francis)
American. Actor
Played Ray Krebbs on TV series "Dallas," 1978-91.
b. Mar 14, 1946 in Burbank, California
Source: *BioIn 13, 15; ConTFT 3; LegTOT; VarWW 85; WhoAm 82, 84, 86, 88, 90, 92, 94, 95, 96, 97; WhoEnt 92; WhoHol 92*

Kanaris, Constantine
"The Themistocles of Modern Greece"
Greek. Statesman
War hero, 1822-28; prime minister, 1848-49, 1864-65, 1877.
b. 1790 in Psara, Greece
d. 1887 in Athens, Greece
Source: *DcBiPP, A; NewCol 75*

Kander, John
American. Composer
With Fred Ebb, wrote song "New York, New York"; won Tonys for *Cabaret,* 1967, *Woman of the Year,* 1980.
b. Mar 18, 1927 in Kansas City, Missouri
Source: *AmSong; BestMus; BiE&WWA; BioIn 9, 10, 11, 12, 15; CelR 90; ConTFT 5, 13; EncMT; HalFC 80, 84, 88; LegTOT; NewAmDM; NewCBMT; NewGrDA 86; NotNAT; OxCAmT 84; OxCPMus; PopAmC SUP; VarWW 85; WhoAm 74, 76, 78, 80, 82, 84, 86, 88; WhoThe 72, 77, 81*

Kandinsky, Wassily
Russian. Artist
A founder of modern abstract art; started Blue Rider group, 1911-14; Bauhaus teacher, 1921-33; noted for bright colors, geometric abstractions.
b. Dec 4, 1866 in Moscow, Russia
d. Dec 17, 1944 in Paris, France
Source: *AtlBL; BioIn 1, 2, 3, 4, 5, 6, 7, 8, 9, 10, 11, 12, 13, 14, 15, 16, 17, 19, 20, 21; ConArt 77, 83; ConAu 118; CurBio 45; DcArts; DcTwDes; FacFETw; IntDcAA 90; LegTOT; LinLib S; McGDA; McGEWB; ModArCr 2; NewCol 75; ObitOF 79; OxCArt; OxCTwCA; OxDcArt; REn; ThTwC 87; WhAm 4; WhDW; WorAl*

Kane, Big Daddy
American. Rapper, Songwriter
Toured with Roxanne Shante; albums include *Long Live the Kane,* 1987; *The Prince of Darkness,* 1991.
b. Sep 10, 1968 in New York, New York

Source: *ConMus 7*

Kane, Carol
American. Actor
Won two Emmys for role of Simka on TV series, "Taxi"; has appeared in numerous films.
b. Jun 18, 1952 in Cleveland, Ohio
Source: *BioIn 11, 13, 16, 17; ConTFT 2, 6, 14; EncAFC; FilmEn; HalFC 80, 84, 88; IntMPA 81, 82, 84, 86, 88, 92, 94, 96; LegTOT; VarWW 85; WhoAm 78, 80, 82, 84, 86, 88, 90, 92, 94, 95, 96, 97; WhoAmW 79, 81, 83, 87, 89, 91, 93, 95, 97; WhoEnt 92; WhoHol 92, A; WorAlBi*

Kane, Elisha Kent
American. Explorer, Physician
Searched Arctic for John Franklin; went farther than any previous expeditions, laying foundation for subsequent studies.
b. Feb 3, 1820 in Philadelphia, Pennsylvania
d. Feb 16, 1857 in Havana, Cuba
Source: *Alli; AmAu; AmBi; ApCAB; BbD; BenetAL 91; BiD&SB; BiInAmS; BioIn 1, 3, 4, 6, 7, 9, 11, 15; CyAL 2; DcAmAu; DcAmB; DcAmMeB; DcCanB 8; DcNAA; Drake; EarABI SUP; EncO&P 1, 2, 3; HarEnUS; InSci; NatCAB 3; OxCAmL 65, 83, 95; OxCCan; OxCShps; REnAL; TwCBDA; WebAB 74, 79; WebAMB; WhAm 1, HS; WhWE*

Kane, Harnett T(homas)
American. Author
Books on American South include *New Orleans Woman,* 1946.
b. Nov 8, 1910 in New Orleans, Louisiana
d. Sep 4, 1984 in New Orleans, Louisiana
Source: *AmAu&B; AmNov; BenetAL 91; BioIn 1, 2, 3, 4, 5, 14; CathA 1952; ConAu 113; CurBio 74, 84, 84N; REn; REnAL; TwCA SUP; WhAm 8; WhoSSW 73*

Kane, Helen
[Helen Schroder]
"The Boop-Boop-a-Doop Girl"
American. Singer, Actor
Baby-voiced performer, 1920s-30s; portrayed by Debbie Reynolds in *Three Little Words,* 1950.
b. Aug 4, 1908 in New York, New York
d. Sep 26, 1966 in Jackson Heights, New York
Source: *CmpEPM; EncMT; LegTOT; ThFT; WhoHol B; WhScrn 74, 77, 83*

Kane, Henry
American. Author
Mystery, crime novels include *The Little Red Phone,* 1982.
b. 1918 in New York, New York
Source: *AmAu&B; EncMys; TwCCr&M 80, 85, 91; WrDr 82, 84, 86, 88, 90*

Kane, Howie
[Jay and the Americans]
American. Singer
Part of clean-cut vocal quintet of 1960s.
b. Jun 6, 1942
Source: *WhoRocM 82*

Kane, John
American. Artist
Known for primitive landscapes of PA, cityscapes of Pittsburgh.
b. Aug 19, 1860 in West Calder, Scotland
d. Aug 10, 1934 in Pittsburgh, Pennsylvania
Source: *AmFkP; BioIn 1, 3, 4, 5, 9, 12, 13, 14, 20; BriEAA; DcAmArt; DcAmB S1; McGEWB; MusmAFA; OxCTwCA; OxDcArt; PhDcTCA 77; WhAmArt 85*

Kane, Joseph Nathan
American. Editor, Historian
Wrote of obscure items in American history: *Famous First Facts,* 1933.
b. Jan 23, 1899 in New York, New York
Source: *BioIn 1, 14; CurBio 85; WrDr 88*

Kane, Robert Joseph
American. Olympic Official
Pres., US Olympic Committee, 1976-80; sent no US athletes to summer games in Moscow to honor boycott, 1980.
b. Apr 24, 1912 in Ithaca, New York
d. May 31, 1992 in Ithaca, New York
Source: *BioIn 12, 17, 18; NewYTBS 80*

Kang, Sheng
[Chao Yun]
Chinese. Political Leader
Led communist China's intelligence agency, 1940-75.
b. 1899 in Shandong, China
d. Dec 16, 1975 in Beijing, China
Source: *DcPol; EncE 75; IntWW 74; SpyCS; WhoSocC 78A*

K'ang Yu-wei
Chinese. Scholar
Instrumental leader of China's Reform Movement, 1898, who pushed for intellectual growth; promoter of Confucianism.
b. Mar 19, 1858 in Guangdong Province, China
d. Mar 31, 1927 in Qingdao, China
Source: *BioIn 15, 18; HisWorL; IndCTCL; RAdv 14*

Kani, Karl
[Carl Williams]
American. Fashion Designer
Founded Karl Kani Infinity, a clothing company, 1994.
b. c. 1968 in New York, New York
Source: *ConBlB 10*

Kania, Stanislaw
Polish. Government Official
Communist leader, First Secretary, Polish Workers Party, 1980.
b. Mar 8, 1927 in Wrocanka, Poland
Source: *BioIn 12; CurBio 81; IntWW 74, 75, 76, 77, 78, 79, 80, 81, 82, 83, 89; NewYTBS 80, 81; WhoSocC 78; WhoSoCE 89*

Kanin, Fay
[Fay Mitchell]
American. Writer, Producer
Oscar nominee for original screenplay of *Teacher's Pet,* 1959; won Peabody for TV film *Heartsounds,* 1984.
Source: *BiE&WWA; BioIn 9, 16; ConTFT 4; EncAFC; IntMPA 75, 76, 77, 78, 79, 80, 81, 82, 84, 86, 88, 92, 94, 96; NotNAT; ReelWom; VarWW 85; WhoAm 80, 82, 84, 86, 88, 90, 92, 94, 95, 96, 97; WhoAmW 81, 83, 85, 95, 97; WhoEnt 92; WomPO 76, 78; WomWMM*

Kanin, Garson
American. Author, Director
Wrote *Tracy and Hepburn: An Intimate Memoir,* 1971; directed *Funny Girl,* 1964.
b. Nov 24, 1912 in Rochester, New York
Source: *AmAu&B; ASCAP 66; AuNews 1; BenetAL 91; BiDFilm, 81, 94; BiE&WWA; BioIn 1, 3, 8, 9, 10, 11, 12, 15, 17, 18; BlueB 76; CelR, 90; CmMov; CnMD; CnThe; ConAu 5R, 7NR; ConDr 73, 77, 82, 88, 93; ConLC 22; ConTFT 2; CurBio 41, 52; DcFM; DcLB 7; DcTwCCu 1; EncAFC; EncWT; Ent; FacFETw; FilmEn; FilmgC; HalFC 80, 84, 88; IlWWHD 1; IntAu&W 76, 77, 82, 89, 91, 93; IntDcF 1-4, 2-4; IntMPA 75, 76, 77, 78, 79, 80, 81, 82, 84, 86, 88, 92, 94, 96; IntWW 82, 83, 89, 91, 93; LegTOT; McGEWD 84; MetOEnc; MiSFD 9; ModWD; MovMk; NatPD 77, 81; NotNAT, A; OxCAmL 65, 83, 95; OxCAmT 84; OxCFilm; PenC AM; REnAL; VarWW 85; WhoAm 74, 76, 78, 80, 82, 84, 86, 88, 90, 92, 94, 95, 96, 97; WhoEnt 92; WhoThe 72, 77, 81; WhoWor 74; WorAl; WorAlBi; WorAu 1950; WorEFlm; WrDr 76, 80, 82, 84, 86, 88, 90, 92, 94, 96*

Kanner, Leo
"Father of Child Psychology"
American. Psychologist, Author
Infantile autism authority; wrote classic text *Child Psychiatry,* 1935.
b. Jun 13, 1894 in Klekotow, Austria
d. Apr 3, 1981 in Sykesville, Maryland
Source: *AnObit 1981; BiDrAPA 77; BioIn 11, 12, 13, 17; ConAu 17R, 103; EncSPD; NewYTBS 81; WhAm 7; WhoAm 74; WhoWor 74; WhoWorJ 72*

Kano, Motonobu
Japanese. Artist
Founder, Motonobu school which subordinated color to design; celebrated for exquisite landscapes, screens, murals.
b. Aug 28, 1476
d. Nov 5, 1559 in Kyoto, Japan
Source: *McGDA; NewCol 75; PriCCJL 85; WebBD 83*

Kanokogi, Rusty
[Rena Glickman]
American. Athlete
Martial arts expert; organized first US women's judo team; manager, 1976-79.
b. 1935 in New York, New York
Source: *BioIn 13; ConNews 87-1; EncWomS*

Kant, Immanuel
German. Philosopher
Best known for attempt to define rational understanding; wrote *Critique of Practical Reason.*
b. Apr 22, 1724 in Konigsberg, Germany
d. Feb 12, 1804 in Konigsberg, Germany
Source: *AsBiEn; BbD; Benet 87, 96; BiD&SB; BiDMoER 1; BiDPsy; BiESc; BioIn 1, 2, 3, 4, 5, 6, 7, 8, 9, 10, 11, 12, 13, 14, 15, 17, 18, 20, 21; BlkwCE; BlmGEL; CamDcSc; CasWL; CelCen; CyEd; CyWA 58; DcBiPP; DcEuL; DcLB 94; DcScB; Dis&D; EncEnl; EncEth; EncO&P 1, 2, 3; EncPaPR 91; EncUnb; EuAu; EvEuW; Geog 4; IlEncMy; InSci; LarDcSc; LegTOT; LinLib L, S; LngCEL; LuthC 75; McGEWB; NamesHP; NewC; NewCBEL; NinCLC 27; OxCArt; OxCEng 67, 85, 95; OxCGer 76, 86; OxCLaw; OxCPhil; OxDcArt; PenC EUR; RAdv 14, 13-4; REn; WhDW; WorAl; WorAlBi; WrPh P*

Kanter, Hal
[Henry Irving]
American. Screenwriter, Director, Producer
Co-wrote film *Pocketful of Miracles,* 1961; won 1954 Emmy for TV show "George Gobel Show," 1954-60.
b. Dec 18, 1918 in Savannah, Georgia
Source: *ConAu 81; ConTFT 2; EncAFC; FilmEn; FilmgC; HalFC 80, 84, 88; IntMPA 75, 76, 77, 78, 79, 80, 81, 82, 84, 86, 88, 92, 94, 96; MiSFD 9; NewYTET; PseudN 82; VarWW 85; WhoAm 78, 80, 82, 84, 86, 88, 90, 92, 94, 95, 96, 97; WhoEnt 92; WorEFlm*

Kanter, Rosabeth Moss
American. Consultant
Wrote *Men and Women of the Corporation,* 1977.
b. Mar 15, 1943 in Cleveland, Ohio
Source: *AmMWSc 78S; ConAu 14NR, 77; CurBio 96; IntWW 89, 91, 93; WhoAm 88, 90, 92, 94, 95, 96, 97; WhoAmW 89, 91, 93, 95, 97; WhoFI 87*

Kantner, Paul
[Jefferson Airplane; Jefferson Starship]
American. Singer, Musician
Rock 'n roll performer; with Jefferson Starship, 1972-84.
b. Mar 12, 1942 in San Francisco, California
Source: *Baker 84, 92; BioIn 9; LegTOT; WhoAm 84, 86*

Kantor, Mackinlay
American. Author, Journalist
Wrote Civil War novel *Andersonville,* 1955.
b. Feb 4, 1904 in Webster City, Iowa
d. Oct 11, 1977 in Sarasota, Florida
Source: *AmAu&B; AmNov; AuBYP 2, 3; AuSpks; Benet 87; BenetAL 91; BioIn 1, 2, 3, 4, 7, 8, 9, 10, 11, 12, 16, 17; ChhPo S1; CnDAL; ConAmA; ConAu 61, 73; ConLC 7; ConNov 72, 76; ConSFA; DcAmB S10; DcLB 9, 102; DcLEL; EncFWF; EncMys; EncSF, 93; FilmgC; HalFC 80, 84, 88; IntAu&W 76, 77; LegTOT; LinLib L, S; ModAL; Novels; OxCAmL 65, 83, 95; PenC AM; REn; REnAL; ScF&FL 1, 2; ScFSB; TwCA, SUP; TwCRHW 90, 94; TwCWr; TwCWW 82, 91; WhAm 7; WhoAm 74, 76, 78; WhScrn 83; WrDr 76*

Kantor, Mickey
[Michael Kantor]
American. Government Official
US Trade Representative, 1993-96; Secretary of Commerce, 1996-97.
b. Aug 7, 1939 in Nashville, Tennessee
Source: *CurBio 94; IntWW 93; WhoAm 94, 95, 96, 97; WhoAmL 94; WhoE 95; WhoFI 94, 96; WhoWor 96*

Kantorovich, Leonid Vital'evich
Russian. Economist
Won Nobel Prize, 1975, for theory of optimum allocation of resources.
b. Jan 19, 1912 in Saint Petersburg, Russia
d. Apr 7, 1986 in Moscow, Union of Soviet Socialist Republics
Source: *BiDSovU; BioIn 7, 10, 14, 15; IntWW 83; SovUn; Who 83; WhoNob, 90, 95; WhoSocC 78; WhoWor 82*

Kantrowitz, Adrian
American. Surgeon
Heart surgeon who developed pacemaker, 1961, artificial heart pump, 1966; performed second heart transplant operation, 1967.
b. Oct 4, 1918 in New York, New York
Source: *AmMWSc 73P, 76P, 79, 82, 86, 89, 92, 95; BioIn 7, 8; BlueB 76; CurBio 67; IntWW 74, 75, 76, 77, 78, 79, 80, 81, 82, 83, 89, 91, 93; WhoAm 74, 76, 78, 80, 82, 84, 86, 88, 90, 92, 94, 95, 96, 97; WhoE 74; WhoFrS 84; WhoMW 78, 84; WhoTech 82, 84, 89, 95; WhoWor 74, 80; WhoWorJ 72, 78*

Kantrowitz, Arnie
American. Writer
Wrote autobiography *Under the Rainbow: Growing up Gay,* 1977.
b. Nov 26, 1940 in Newark, New Jersey
Source: *ConAu 77; GayLesB*

Kapell, William
American. Pianist
Int'l concertizer, 1940s; performed modern works.
b. Sep 20, 1922 in New York, New York
d. Oct 29, 1953 in San Francisco, California
Source: *Baker 78, 84, 92; BiDAmM; BioIn 1, 2, 3, 4, 5, 7, 21; BriBkM 80; CurBio 48, 54; NewGrDA 86; NewGrDM 80; NotTwCP; PenDiMP; WhAm 3*

Kaper, Bronislau
American. Composer
Won Oscar, 1953, for score of *Lili.*
b. Feb 5, 1902 in Warsaw, Poland
d. May 1983 in Beverly Hills, California
Source: *AmPS; ASCAP 66; Baker 84; CmpEPM; ConAmC 82; FilmgC; HalFC 80, 84, 88; IntDcF 1-4, 2-4; IntMPA 75, 76, 77, 78, 80, 81, 82, 84, 86; VarWW 85; WorEFlm*

Kapitsa, Pyotr Leonidovich
Russian. Physicist
Shared 1978 Nobel Prize in physics for studies in electrical properties of matter; his work on blast furnaces changed Soviet industry; in state detention from 1934.
b. Jun 26, 1894 in Kronstadt, Russia
d. Apr 8, 1984 in Moscow, Union of Soviet Socialist Republics
Source: *AnObit 1984; CurBio 55; FacFETw; NewYTBS 84; WhoNob, 90, 95; WhoSocC 78; WorAl*

Kaplan, Gabe
[Gabriel Kaplan]
American. Actor, Comedian
Starred in TV series "Welcome Back, Kotter," 1975-79.
b. Mar 31, 1945 in New York, New York
Source: *BioIn 10, 11, 12, 20; BkPepl; ConTFT 3; IntMPA 84, 86, 88, 92, 94, 96; LegTOT; VarWW 85; WhoAm 78, 80, 82, 84, 86; WhoEnt 92; WhoHol 92; WorAl; WorAlBi*

Kaplan, Henry Seymour
American. Physician, Scientist
Pioneer in research treatment for Hodgkin's disease; invented linear accelerator.
b. Apr 24, 1918 in Chicago, Illinois
d. Feb 4, 1984 in Palo Alto, California
Source: *AmMWSc 73P, 76P, 79, 82; AnObit 1984; BioIn 11, 13; NewYTBS 84; WhAm 8; WhoAm 74, 76, 78, 80, 82; WhoAtom 77; WhoFrS 84; WhoTech 82*

Kaplan, Jacob Merrill
American. Philanthropist, Businessman
Head of Welch Grape Juice Co., 1940-58; established JM Kaplan Fund, 1947.
b. Dec 23, 1891 in Lowell, Massachusetts
d. Jul 18, 1987 in New York, New York
Source: *BioIn 1, 15; NewYTBS 87; WhAm 9; WhoAm 82, 84, 86; WhoWor 82*

Kaplan, John
American. Photographer
Won Pulitzer Prize for feature photography, 1992.
b. Aug 21, 1959 in Wilmington, Delaware
Source: *WhoAm 90, 92, 94, 95, 96, 97; WhoE 95, 97*

Kaplan, Joseph
American. Meteorologist
Known for his research on auroras and airglows during the 1920s.
b. Sep 8, 1902 in Tapolcza, Hungary
d. Oct 3, 1991 in Santa Monica, California
Source: *AmMWSc 73P, 76P, 79, 82, 86, 89, 92; BioIn 4, 17; CurBio 91N; InSci; IntWW 74, 75, 76, 77, 78, 79, 80, 81, 82, 83, 89; LinLib L, S; NewYTBS 91; WhAm 10; Who 74, 82, 83, 85, 88, 90, 92; WhoAm 74; WhoWest 74, 76*

Kaplan, Justin
American. Writer
Won Pulitzer Prize for *Mr. Clemens and Mark Twain,* 1966; editor of the sixteenth edition of *Bartlett's Familiar Quotations,* 1992.
b. Sep 5, 1925 in New York, New York
Source: *AmAu&B; Au&Wr 71; AuNews 1; BenetAL 91; BioIn 10, 12, 13; ConAu 8NR, 17R; CurBio 93; DcLB 111; DrAS 74E, 78E, 82E; IntAu&W 76; OxCAmL 83, 95; WhoAm 74, 76, 78, 80, 82, 84, 86, 88, 90, 92, 94, 95, 96, 97; WhoAmJ 80; WhoE 74; WhoUSWr 88; WhoWrEP 89, 92, 95; WorAu 1970; WrDr 76, 80, 82, 84, 86, 88, 90, 92, 94, 96*

Kaplan, Mordecai
American. Religious Leader, Author
Founded Jewish Reconstruction movement; outlined philosophy of Judaism.
b. Jun 11, 1881 in Swenziany, Lithuania
d. Nov 8, 1983 in New York, New York
Source: *AmAu&B; AmDec 1910; AnObit 1983; McGEWB; NewYTBS 83; WebAB 74; WhAm 6*

Kaplow, Herbert Elias
American. Journalist
Washington news correspondent for NBC, 1951-72; ABC, 1972-86.
b. Feb 2, 1927 in New York, New York
Source: *ConAu 119; WhoAm 76, 78, 80, 82, 84, 86, 88, 90, 92, 94, 95, 96, 97; WhoAmJ 80; WhoE 79, 81; WhoEnt 92; WhoSSW 75, 76; WhoWorJ 72*

Kapor, Mitchell
Business Executive
Founder, chm., Lotus Development Corp., 1981-86; helped create best-selling personal computer software.
b. 1951
Source: *BioIn 13*

Kapp, Joe
[Joseph Robert Kapp]
American. Football Player, Football Coach
Quarterback, Minnesota, 1967-69, New England, 1970-71; refused to sign standard contract, sued NFL, 1971, challenging reserve system, free agency; judge ruled in his favor, 1974.
b. Mar 19, 1938 in Santa Fe, New Mexico
Source: *BioIn 8, 9, 10, 13; CurBio 75; NewYTBE 72; WhoFtbl 74*

Kappel, Frederick R(ussell)
American. Business Executive
Pres., CEO, AT&T, 1956-67.
b. Jan 14, 1902
d. Nov 10, 1994 in Sarasota, Florida
Source: *BioIn 3, 4, 6, 9, 11; CurBio 95N; EncAB-A 35; LElec; WhoAm 74, 76, 78, 80; WhoFI 74; WhoGov 72, 75; WhoWor 74*

Kappel, Gertrude
German. Opera Singer
A leading Wagnerian soprano; with NY Met., 1928-36.
b. Sep 1, 1893 in Halle, Germany
d. Apr 3, 1971 in Munich, Germany (West)
Source: *Baker 84; NewYTBE 71; WhAm 5*

Kaprisky, Valerie
French. Actor
Starred in film *Breathless* with Richard Gere, 1983.
b. 1963 in Paris, France
Source: *VarWW 85; WhoHol 92*

Kaprow, Allan
American. Artist
Pioneer in performance art; known for expansionistic works called "Happenings"; "Activities."
b. Aug 23, 1927 in Atlantic City, New Jersey
Source: *AmAu&B; ConArt 77, 83, 89, 96; ConAu 105; ConDr 73; DcAmArt; DcCAA 71, 77, 88, 94; FacFETw; McGDA; OxCTwCA; PhDcTCA 77; WhoAm 74, 76, 78; WhoAmA 73, 76, 78; WhoWest 74; WorArt 1950*

Kapuscinski, Ryszard
Journalist
Writings as international foreign correspondent document life and war in the Third World; *The Emperor, The Soccer War.*
b. Mar 4, 1932 in Pinsk, Poland
Source: *ConAu 114; CurBio 92; CyWA 89; IntAu&W 89, 91, 93; IntWW 76, 77, 78, 79, 80, 81, 82, 83, 89, 91, 93; WhoSoCE 89; WhoWor 78, 84, 87, 89, 91, 93, 95, 96, 97; WorAu 1985*

Karadzic, Radovan
Bosnian. Political Leader
Leader of the Bosnian Serbs, 1992—.
b. c. 1945 in Montenegro, Yugoslavia
Source: *CurBio 95; News 95, 95-3*

Karajan, Herbert von
"The Maestro"
Austrian. Conductor
Director of the Berlin Philharmonic, 1954-89; made more than 800 recordings; criticized for Nazi past.
b. Apr 5, 1908 in Salzburg, Austria
d. Jul 16, 1989 in Anif, Austria
Source: *AnObit 1989; Baker 78, 84, 92; BioIn 1, 2, 3, 4, 5, 6, 7, 8, 9, 10, 11, 13; BriBkM 80; CelR; CmOp; CurBio 56, 86, 89, 89N; DcArts; EncTR 91; FacFETw; IntDcOp; IntWW 74, 75, 76, 77, 78, 79, 80, 81, 82, 83, 89; IntWWM 77, 80; LinLib S; MetOEnc; MusMk; MusSN; NewAmDM; NewEOp 71; NewGrDM 80; NewGrDO; NewYTBS 74, 89; OxDcOp; PenDiMP; Who 85; WorAl; WorAlBi*

Karamanlis, Constantine
[Constantinos Caramanlis]
"Costas"
Greek. Political Leader
Premier, 1955-63; pres., 1980-85, 1990-94; private law practice, 1932—.
b. Mar 8, 1907 in Prote, Greece
Source: *BioIn 9, 10, 12, 13; CurBio 56, 76; DcPol; DcTwHis; EncWB; IntWW 83; NewYTBS 74, 80; WhoWor 84; WorAl*

Karami, Rashid Abdul Hamid
Lebanese. Political Leader
Leader of Sunni Muslims, member Lebanese parliament, 1951-87; killed in bomb attack.
b. Dec 30, 1921 in Tripoli, Lebanon
d. Jun 1, 1987 in Jubayl, Lebanon
Source: *CurBio 59, 87; IntWW 76, 77, 78, 79, 80, 81, 82, 83; MidE 78, 79, 80, 81, 82; NewYTBS 84; WhAm 11; WhoWor 84, 87*

Karan, Donna Faske
"The Queen of Seventh Avenue"
American. Fashion Designer
Owner, chief designer, Donna Karan Co., NYC, 1984—; designer with Anne Klein & Co., 1974-84; won Coty, 1977, 1981; Coty Hall of Fame, 1984.
b. Oct 2, 1948 in Forest Hills, New York
Source: *BioIn 11; ConNews 88-1; WhoAm 86; WhoAmW 85, 87; WhoFash; WorFshn*

Kardiner, Abram
American. Psychoanalyst
Co-founded first US psychiatric training school, 1939; wrote *Sex and Morality,* 1954.
b. Aug 17, 1891 in New York, New York
d. Jul 20, 1981 in Easton, Connecticut
Source: *AmAu&B; AnObit 1981; BiDPsy; BiDrAPA 77; BioIn 12; ConAu 104, 107; FacFETw; IntDcAn; NewYTBS 81; WhAm 8*

Karenga, Maulana
[Ronald McKinley Everett]
American. Writer
Established holiday Kwanzaa, 1966.
b. Jul 14, 1941 in Parsonsburg, Maryland
Source: *ConBlB 10; LNinSix*

Karfiol, Bernard
American. Artist
Post-impressionist painter of children, interiors, nudes.
b. May 6, 1886 in Budapest, Austria-Hungary
d. Aug 16, 1952 in New York, New York
Source: *BioIn 1, 2, 3; CurBio 47, 52; DcAmArt; DcAmB S5; DcCAA 71, 77, 88, 94; McGDA; OxCTwCA; PhDcTCA 77; WhAm 3; WhAmArt 85; WhoAmA 78, 89N, 91N, 93N*

Karle, Jerome
American. Physicist
With Herbert A Hauptman, won Nobel Prize, 1985, for studies in molecular structure of crystals.
b. Jun 18, 1918 in New York, New York
Source: *AmMWSc 73P, 76P, 79, 82, 86, 89, 92, 95; BioIn 14, 15, 19, 20; IntWW 83, 89, 91, 93; LarDcSc; NewYTBS 85; NotTwCS; Who 90, 92, 94; WhoAm 78, 80, 82, 84, 86, 88, 90, 92, 94, 95, 96, 97; WhoE 86, 89, 91, 93, 95, 97; WhoFrS 84; WhoGov 72, 75, 77; WhoNob, 90, 95; WhoScEn 94, 96; WhoWor 87, 89, 91, 93, 95, 96, 97; WorAlBi*

Karlen, John
American. Actor
Played Harvey Lacey on TV series "Cagney and Lacey," 1982-88.
b. May 28, 1933 in New York, New York
Source: *BioIn 15; ConTFT 9; LegTOT; WhoAm 90; WhoEnt 92; WhoHol 92*

Karlfeldt, Erik Axel
Swedish. Poet
Work is purposely archaic, bases in folklore, custom; refused Nobel Prize, 1918; awarded posthumously, 1931.
b. Jul 20, 1864 in Folkarna, Sweden
d. Apr 8, 1931 in Stockholm, Sweden
Source: *Benet 87, 96; BioIn 1, 9, 15; CasWL; ClDMEL 47, 80; DcScanL; EncWL; EvEuW; FacFETw; LinLib L; PenC EUR; REn; TwCA, SUP; TwCWr; TwCWW 82; WhDW; WhoNob, 90, 95; WorAl*

Karlin, Frederick James
American. Composer, Conductor
Film scores include Oscar-winning *Lovers and Other Strangers,* 1970; won 1974 Emmy for "Autobiography of Miss Jane Pittman."
b. Jun 16, 1936 in Chicago, Illinois
Source: *ASCAP 66, 80; ConAmC 76, 82; ConTFT 9; HalFC 88; IntMPA 92*

Karloff, Boris
[William Henry Pratt]
English. Actor
In horror films *Frankenstein,* 1931; *The Mummy,* 1933.
b. Nov 23, 1887 in London, England
d. Feb 2, 1969 in Middleton, England
Source: *BiDFilm, 81, 94; BiE&WWA; BioIn 4, 6, 7, 8, 9, 10, 11, 12, 14, 15, 16, 17, 19, 21; CmMov; CurBio 41, 69; DcAmB S8; DcArts; DcNaB 1961; FacFETw; Film 1, 2; FilmEn; FilmgC; ForYSC; GangFlm; HalFC 80, 84, 88; IntDcF 1-3, 2-3; ItaFilm; LegTOT; MotPP; MovMk; NewEScF; NotNAT A, B; ObitT 1961; OxCFilm; PenEncH; PseudN 82; ScF&FL 1; TwYS; WebAB 74, 79; WhAm 5; WhoHol B; WhoHrs 80; WhScrn 74, 77, 83; WhThe; WorAl; WorAlBi; WorEFlm*

Karmal, Babrak
Afghan. Political Leader
Pro-Soviet pres. of Afghanistan, 1979-87; forced out by Soviets.
b. Jan 6, 1929 in Kabul, Afghanistan
d. Dec 1, 1996 in Moscow, Russia
Source: *BioIn 12, 13; CurBio 81; DicTyr; FarE&A 80, 81; IntWW 80, 81, 82, 83, 89, 91; MidE 80, 81, 82; NewYTBS 79; WhoWor 84, 87, 89, 91*

Karn, Richard
American. Actor
Handyman Al Borland in TV series "Home Improvement," 1991—.
Source: *BioIn 20, 21*

Karns, Roscoe
American. Comedian
Known for cynical, fast-talking roles as journalists, press agents; best-known film *20th Century,* 1934.
b. Sep 7, 1893 in San Bernardino, California
d. Feb 6, 1970 in Los Angeles, California
Source: *EncAFC; Film 2; FilmEn; FilmgC; ForYSC; HalFC 80, 84, 88; LegTOT; MotPP; MovMk; NewYTBE 70; ObitOF 79; TwYS; Vers B; WhoHol B; WhScrn 74, 77, 83*

Karolyi, Bela
American. Gymnastics Coach
Gymnastic coach; with wife Martha trained Olympians Nadia Comaneci and Mary Lou Retton; retired 1992.
b. 1942 in Transylvania, Romania
Source: *BioIn 14, 15, 16; CurBio 96; WorAlBi*

Karpin, Fred Leon
American. Journalist
Authority on contract bridge; wrote books on the game.
b. Mar 17, 1913 in New York, New York
d. Apr 11, 1986 in Washington, District of Columbia
Source: *ConAu 13R, 119*

Karpis, Alvin
[Alvin Karpowicz]
"Old Creepy"
Canadian. Criminal
Public Enemy number one, 1930s; member Ma Barker's gang; paroled after 32 yrs. in prison, 1969.
b. 1908 in Montreal, Quebec, Canada
d. Aug 12, 1979 in Torremolinos, Spain
Source: *BioIn 9, 12; DrInf; NewYTBS 79; PseudN 82*

Karpov, Anatoly Yevgenyevich
Russian. Chess Player
International Grandmaster, 1970, who was world champion, 1975-85; lost title to Kasparov, 1985.
b. May 23, 1951 in Zlatoust, Union of Soviet Socialist Republics
Source: *BioIn 10; CurBio 78; GolEC; OxCChes 84; WhoWor 82*

Karrar, Paul
Swiss. Chemist, Educator
Shared 1937 Nobel Prize for plant pigments research.
b. Apr 21, 1889 in Moscow, Russia
d. Jun 18, 1971 in Zurich, Switzerland
Source: *AsBiEn; ConAu 113; DcScB; WhAm 5; WhoNob*

Karras, Alex(ander G)
"Tippy Toes"; "The Mad Duck"
American. Football Player, Actor
Four-time all-pro defensive tackle, Detroit, 1958-70; suspended by NFL, 1963 for gambling; plays father on TV's "Webster"; married to Susan Clark.
b. Jul 15, 1935 in Gary, Indiana
Source: *BioIn 7, 9, 10, 11, 12, 13; BioNews 74; ConAu 107; ConTFT 1, 6; HalFC 84, 88; IndAu 1967; IntMPA 84, 86, 88, 92, 94, 96; LegTOT; VarWW 85; WhoAm 74, 78, 80, 82, 84, 86, 88, 90, 92, 94, 95, 96, 97; WhoEnt 92; WhoFtbl 74; WhoHol 92, A; WorAl; WorAlBi*

Karsavina, Tamara (Platonova)
"La Tamara"
Russian. Dancer
Ballerina known for highly expressive, intelligent interpretations of Mariinsky, Dyagilev.
b. Mar 9, 1885 in Saint Petersburg, Russia
d. May 26, 1978 in London, England
Source: *BiDD; BioIn 1, 2, 3, 4, 6, 8, 11, 13; ConAu 77; ContDcW 89; DcTwCCu 2; IntDcB; IntDcWB; InWom, SUP; LegTOT; MacDWB; ObitOF 79; WhDW; Who 74; WhScrn 83; WhThe*

Karsh, Yousuf
Canadian. Photographer, Journalist
Best known for photos of Winston Churchill, other famous people; wrote *Faces of Our Time,* 1971.
b. Dec 23, 1908 in Mardin, Armenia
Source: *BioIn 1, 2, 3, 4, 5, 6, 8, 10, 11, 12, 13, 14, 16; BlueB 76; CanWW 31, 79, 80, 81, 83, 89; ConAu 33R; ConPhot 82, 88, 95; CurBio 52, 80; DcArts;*

EncAJ; FacFETw; ICPEnP; IntAu&W 76, 77; IntWW 74, 75, 76, 77, 78, 79, 80, 81, 82, 83, 89, 91, 93; IntYB 78, 79, 80, 81, 82; LegTOT; LinLib L, S; MacBEP; NewYTBE 72; NewYTBS 89; Who 74, 82, 83, 85, 88, 90, 92, 94; WhoAm 84, 86, 88, 90, 92, 94, 95, 96, 97; WhoAmA 73, 76, 78, 80, 82, 84, 86, 89, 91, 93; WhoWor 74, 78, 82, 84, 89, 91, 93, 95, 96, 97

Kasavubu, Joseph
"The Father of Congo Independence"
Congolese. Political Leader
First president of Congo, 1960-65.
b. 1910 in Tshela, Belgian Congo
d. Mar 24, 1969 in Boma, Zaire
Source: *BioIn 5, 6, 7, 8, 9, 21; CurBio 61, 69; DcAfHiB 86; DcTwHis; EncRev; FacFETw; McGEWB; ObitOF 79; WhAm 5*

Kasdan, Lawrence Edward
American. Screenwriter
Co-wrote *Empire Strikes Back,* 1980; *The Big Chill,* 1983; won Clios for TV commercials.
b. Jan 14, 1949 in Miami Beach, Florida
Source: *ConAu 109; ConDr 82A; ConTFT 5; CurBio 92; HalFC 84; IntMPA 86; IntWW 89, 91, 93; NewYTBS 81; VarWW 85; WhoAm 82, 84, 86, 88, 90, 92, 94, 95, 96, 97; WhoWor 95, 96, 97*

Kasem, Casey (Kemal Amin)
[Kemal Amin Kasem]
American. Broadcaster, TV Personality
Radio Hall of Fame member; one of most recognized in radio; longtime host of syndicated TV series "America's Top 10."
b. 1933? in Detroit, Michigan
Source: *BioIn 11; CelR 90; ConNews 87-1; ConTFT 6; LegTOT; WhoAm 92, 94, 95, 96, 97*

Kashdan, Isaac
American. Chess Player, Editor
Seven times captain, US Chess Olympic team; founded *Chess Review.*
b. Nov 19, 1905 in New York, New York
d. Feb 20, 1985 in Los Angeles, California
Source: *BioIn 14; ConAu 115; GolEC; OxCChes 84; WhAm 8; WhoAm 74, 76, 78, 80, 82, 84; WhoAmJ 80*

Kaskey, Ray(mond John)
American. Sculptor, Architect
Designed massive "Portlandia" for Portland, OR municipal building, 1985; champions postmodernist style.
b. Feb 22, 1943 in Pittsburgh, Pennsylvania
Source: *ConNews 87-2; WhoAm 95, 96; WhoAmA 82, 84, 86, 89, 91, 93; WhoE 91*

Kasparov, Garry Kimovich
Russian. Chess Player
International Grandmaster, 1980; defeated Karpov, 1985, 1987; youngest champion.
b. Apr 13, 1963 in Baku, Union of Soviet Socialist Republics
Source: *CurBio 86; OxCChes 84*

Kasper, Herbert
American. Fashion Designer
Versatile dress, sportswear designer; won Cotys, 1955, 1970; Coty Hall of Fame, 1976.
b. Dec 12, 1926 in New York, New York
Source: *ConFash; EncFash; PseudN 82; WhoAm 78, 80, 82, 84, 86, 88, 90, 92; WhoFash, 88; WorFshn*

Kassebaum, Nancy Landon
[Mrs. Howard Baker]
American. Politician
Rep. senator from KS, 1979-97; daughter of Alf Landon.
b. Jul 29, 1932 in Topeka, Kansas
Source: *AlmAP 80, 82, 84, 88, 92, 96; AmPolLe; AmPolW 80; AmWomM; BiDrUSC 89; CngDr 79, 81, 83, 85, 87, 89, 91, 93, 95; CurBio 82; IntWW 89, 91, 93; InWom SUP; LegTOT; NewYTBS 83; PolsAm 84; WhoAm 80, 82, 84, 86, 88, 90, 92, 94, 95, 96, 97; WhoAmP 79, 81, 83, 85, 87, 89, 91, 93, 95; WhoAmW 81, 83, 85, 87, 89, 91, 93, 95, 97; WhoMW 80, 84, 86, 88, 90, 92, 93, 96; WhoWor 80, 82, 84, 87, 89, 91; WomCon*

Kassem, Abdul Karim (el)
Iraqi. Politician
Premier of Iraq, 1958-63; overthrown, killed by military junta.
b. Nov 21, 1914 in Baghdad, Ottoman Empire
d. Feb 9, 1963 in Baghdad, Iraq
Source: *BioIn 5, 17, 20; CurBio 59, 63; DcPol; DcTwHis; DicTyr; FacFETw*

Kassorla, Irene Chamie
American. Psychologist, Author
Psychologist to Hollywood stars; wrote best-selling sex manual *Nice Girls Do,* 1981.
b. Aug 18, 1931 in Los Angeles, California
Source: *BioIn 10; ConAu 110; NewYTBS 81; WhoWest 78, 80*

Kasten, Robert Walter, Jr.
American. Politician
Conservative Rep. senator from WI, 1981-93.
b. Jun 19, 1942 in Milwaukee, Wisconsin
Source: *AlmAP 88; BiDrUSC 89; CngDr 87; WhoAm 86; WhoAmP 87; WhoGov 77; WhoMW 78; WhoWor 82*

Kastler, Alfred
French. Physicist
Developed basic principle of laser beam; won Nobel Prize, 1966.
b. May 3, 1902 in Guebwiller, France
d. Jan 7, 1984 in Bandol, France
Source: *AnObit 1984; AsBiEn; BiESc; BioIn 7, 8, 9, 13, 14, 15, 20; CurBio 84, 84N; IntWW 74, 75, 76, 77, 78, 79, 80, 81, 82, 83; LarDcSc; McGMS 80; NewYTBS 84; NobelP; NotTwCS; Who 74, 82, 83; WhoFr 79; WhoNob, 90, 95; WhoWor 74, 80, 82*

Kastner, Erich
[Erich Kaestner]
German. Author, Poet
Wrote *Emil and the Detectives,* 1928; books burned in Germany, 1933.
b. Feb 23, 1899 in Dresden, Germany
d. Jul 24, 1974 in Munich, Germany
Source: *AuBYP 2, 3; BiDMoPL; BioIn 1, 5, 6, 8, 9, 10, 12, 16, 19; CasWL; ChlBkCr; ChlLR 4; ClDMEL 47, 80; CnMD; ConAu 40NR, 49, 73; CurBio 64, 74, 74N; DcLB 56; EncTR 91; EncWL, 2, 3; EncWT; EvEuW; HalFC 80, 84, 88; IntAu&W 76; IntWW 74; LegTOT; LinLib L; MajAI; ModGL; ModWD; ObitT 1971; OxCChiL; OxCGer 76, 86; PenC EUR; ScF&FL 92; SmATA 14; ThrBJA; WhAm 6; WhDW; WhE&EA; Who 74; WhoChL; WhoWor 74; WorAu 1950; WrChl*

Kasznar, Kurt
[Kurt Serwischer]
Austrian. Actor
Appeared in 1,000 Broadway performances of *The Sound of Music;* also appeared in *Barefoot in the Park,* 1964.
b. Aug 13, 1913 in Vienna, Austria
d. Aug 6, 1979 in Santa Monica, California
Source: *BiE&WWA; ConAu 89; EncAFC; FilmEn; FilmgC; ForYSC; HalFC 80, 84, 88; IntMPA 77, 78; MotPP; MovMk; NotNAT; PseudN 82; Vers B; WhAm 7; WhoAm 78; WhoHol A; WhoThe 77; WhScrn 83*

Katayama, Yutaka
Japanese. Businessman, Auto Executive
Pres., Nissan Motor Co., 1965-75, chm., 1975-77, in charge of US operations.
b. Sep 15, 1909 in Tokyo, Japan
Source: *BioIn 13; ConNews 87-1; WhoWest 74, 76, 78*

Katayev, Valentin Petrovich
Russian. Author
Wrote satirical novel *The Embezzlers,* 1929; play *Squaring the Circle,* 1928.
b. Jan 28, 1897 in Odessa, Russia
d. Apr 12, 1986 in Moscow, Union of Soviet Socialist Republics
Source: *Benet 87, 96; CasWL; ClDMEL 47, 80; ConAu 117; DcRusL; DcRusLS; EncWL; EncWT; EvEuW; IntWW 77, 78, 79, 80, 81, 82; McGEWD 72, 84; ModSL 1; OxCThe 67, 83; PenC EUR; REn; TwCWr*

Kath, Terry
American. Singer, Musician
Guitarist, formed group with Walter Parazaider, 1967; died of accidental self-inflicted gun wound.
b. Jan 31, 1946 in Chicago, Illinois
d. Jan 23, 1978 in Los Angeles, California
Source: *BioIn 11; OnThGG; WhoRocM 82*

Katims, Milton
American. Musician, Conductor
Led Seattle Orchestra, 1954-76; first violinist under Toscanini, NBC Symphony, 1940-54.
b. Jun 24, 1909 in New York, New York
Source: *Baker 78, 84, 92; BiDAmM; BioIn 1, 2, 3, 4, 5, 9, 11; IntWWM 90; NewAmDM; NewGrDA 86; NewGrDM 80; NewYTBS 74; PenDiMP; RadStar; WhoAm 84; WhoMus 72; WhoWest 74, 94; WhoWor 74*

Katona, George
American. Economist
Dean of "behavior" economists; believed consumer's attitudes influence economy; wrote *Psychology of Economics,* 1975.
b. Nov 6, 1901 in Budapest, Austria-Hungary
d. Jun 18, 1981 in Berlin, Germany (West)
Source: *AmEA 74; AmMWSc 73S; AnObit 1981; BioIn 11, 12, 13, 14; ConAu 104, 128; FacFETw; NewYTBS 81; WhAm 9; WhoAm 74, 76, 78, 80; WhoEc 86; WhoWor 74*

Katt, William
American. Actor
Starred in TV series "The Greatest American Hero," 1981-83.
b. Feb 16, 1955 in Los Angeles, California
Source: *ConTFT 3; HalFC 84, 88; IntMPA 86, 88, 92, 94, 96; VarWW 85; WhoHol 92*

Katz, Alex
American. Artist
Noted for new realistic paintings, cutouts and prints.
b. Jul 24, 1927 in New York, New York
Source: *AmArt; BioIn 7, 9, 10, 11, 12, 13, 14, 15, 17, 18, 19; BlueB 76; ConArt 77, 83, 89, 96; CurBio 75; DcAmArt; DcCAA 77, 88, 94; DcCAr 81; ModArCr 1; News 90, 90-3; NewYTBS 86; OxCTwCA; PrintW 83, 85; WhoAm 74, 76, 78, 80, 82, 84, 86, 88, 90, 92, 94, 95, 96, 97; WhoAmA 73, 76, 78, 80, 82, 84, 86, 89, 91, 93; WhoE 83, 85, 86, 89; WhoWorJ 72, 78; WorArt 1950*

Katz, Bernard, Sir
British. Scientist
Shared Nobel Prize in medicine, 1970, for researching the nervous system.
b. Mar 26, 1911 in Leipzig, Germany
Source: *AmMWSc 89, 92, 95; Au&Wr 71; BiESc; BioIn 9, 15, 20; BlueB 76; IntWW 74, 75, 76, 77, 78, 79, 80, 81, 82, 83, 89, 91, 93; LarDcSc; McGMS 80; NobelP; NotTwCS; Who 74, 82, 83, 85, 88, 90, 92, 94; WhoAm 88, 90; WhoMedH; WhoNob, 90, 95; WhoScEn 94, 96; WhoWor 74, 76, 78, 80, 82, 84, 87, 89, 91, 93, 95, 96, 97; WorAl; WorAlBi; WorScD*

Katz, Jonathan Ned
American. Historian
Wrote *Coming Out!: A Documentary Play about Gay Life and Liberation in the U.S.A.,* 1975; *The Invention of Heterosexuality,* 1995.
b. Feb 2, 1938 in New York, New York
Source: *GayLesB*

Katz, Lillian
American. Business Executive
Founded mail order firm, Lillian Vernon, 1951, industry's most successful retailer.
b. Mar 18, 1927 in Leipzig, Germany
Source: *ConNews 87-4; NewYTBS 85; WhoFI 83, 85*

Katz, Milton
American. Lawyer
Delegate to the Economic Cooperation Administration (Marshall Plan), 1950-51.
b. Nov 29, 1907
d. Aug 9, 1995 in Brookline, Massachusetts
Source: *Au&Wr 71; BioIn 2, 21; BlueB 76; ConAu 149, P-1; CurBio 95N; DrAS 74P, 78P, 82P; IntAu&W 76, 77; IntWW 74, 75, 76, 77, 78, 79, 80, 81, 82, 83, 89, 91, 93; IntYB 78, 79, 80, 81, 82; Who 74, 82, 83, 85, 88, 90, 92, 94; WhoAm 74, 76, 78, 80, 82, 84, 86, 88, 90, 92, 94, 95; WhoAmJ 80; WhoAmL 78, 79, 83; WhoE 86, 89; WhoWor 74; WhoWorJ 72, 78*

Katzen, Mollie
American. Author
Author of *Moosewood Cookbook,* 1977, a vegetarian cookbook.
b. Oct 13, 1950 in Rochester, New York
Source: *CurBio 96*

Katzenbach, Nicholas de Belleville
American. Lawyer
Held various govt. positions, 1961-69; with IBM since 1969, senior vp, general counsel, 1979-85.
b. Jan 17, 1922 in Philadelphia, Pennsylvania
Source: *BiDrUSE 71, 89; BlueB 76; CivR 74; CurBio 65; IntWW 83; St&PR 87; WhoAm 86; WhoAmL 85; WhoAmP 81; WhoFI 85; WhoWor 78*

Katzenberg, Jeffrey
American. Business Executive
Chm., Walt Disney Studios, 1984-1994; co-founder of DreamWorks.
b. 1950 in New York, New York
Source: *BioIn 15; ConTFT 10; CurBio 95; IntMPA 92, 94, 96; IntWW 93; LesBEnT 92; News 95, 95-3; NewYTBS 88; WhoAm 90, 92, 94, 95, 96, 97; WhoEnt 92; WhoWest 92*

Kauff, Benny
[Benjamin Michael Kauff]
American. Baseball Player
Outfielder, 1914-20; won two batting titles in Federal League; banned from MLs, 1921, for involvement in auto-theft ring.
b. Jan 5, 1890 in Pomeroy, Ohio
d. Nov 17, 1961 in Columbus, Ohio
Source: *Ballpl 90; BioIn 21; WhoProB 73*

Kauffer, Edward McKnight
American. Illustrator
Noted for posters, commercial designs including those for Great Western Railway.
b. 1891 in Great Falls, Montana
d. Oct 22, 1954 in New York, New York
Source: *BioIn 1, 3, 4, 8; IlsCB 1744; ObitOF 79; OxCEng 85; OxCTwCA*

Kauffman, Ewing Marion
American. Businessman, Baseball Executive
Owner, Marion Laboratories, Inc., 1950-89; chm. emeritus, Marion Merrell Dow Inc., 1989-93; owner, KC Royals baseball club, 1969-93.
b. Sep 21, 1916 in Garden City, Missouri
d. Aug 1, 1993 in Mission Hills, Kansas
Source: *BioIn 8, 9, 11; Dun&B 86; St&PR 87; WhAm 11; WhoAm 74, 76, 78, 80, 82, 84, 86, 88, 90, 92; WhoFI 74, 75, 77, 83, 85, 89; WhoMW 74, 76, 78, 80, 82, 84, 86, 90; WhoProB 73*

Kauffman, Jean-Paul
French. Hostage
Journalist taken hostage by Lebanese terrorists and held for 1,078 days, May 22, 1985-May 4, 1988.

Kauffmann, Angelica
[Maria Anna Catharina Angelica Kauffmann]
French. Artist
Did historical subjects, portraits, decorative wall paintings.
b. Oct 30, 1741 in Chur, Switzerland
d. Nov 5, 1807 in Rome, Papal States
Source: *BioIn 1, 3, 4, 6, 9, 10, 11, 12, 16, 17, 19; BkIE; DcArts; DcBrECP; DcCathB; DcNaB; IntDcAA 90; InWom SUP; McGDA; NewCol 75; OxCArt; OxDcArt*

Kauffmann, Stanley Jules
[Spranger Barry]
American. Critic
With *New Republic,* 1958—; *Saturday Review,* 1979-85; won criticism awards, 1972, 1982.
b. Apr 24, 1916 in New York, New York
Source: *Au&Wr 71; ConAmTC; ConAu 5R, X; LngCTC; PenC AM; PseudN 82; WhoAm 74, 76, 78, 80, 82, 84, 86, 88,*

90, 92, 94, 95, 96, 97; WhoE 74; WhoEnt 92; WhoUSWr 88; WhoWor 74, 76; WhoWrEP 89, 92, 95; WorAu 1950; WrDr 76

Kaufman, Andy
American. Actor, Comedian
Best known for appearances on "Saturday Night Live," 1975-78; played Latka Gravas on TV comedy "Taxi," 1978-83.
b. Jan 17, 1949 in New York, New York
d. May 16, 1984 in Los Angeles, California
Source: *BioIn 11, 12, 13, 14, 16, 21; ConTFT 2; LegTOT; NewYTBS 84; VarWW 85; WhAm 8; WhoAm 80, 82; WhoCom; WhoWor 82*

Kaufman, Bel
American. Author, Educator
Wrote *Up the Down Staircase,* 1965.
Source: *AmAu&B; ArtclWW 2; Au&Arts 4; BioIn 7, 12, 16; BlueB 76; ConAu 13NR, 13R; DrAF 76; DrAPF 80, 83, 85, 87, 89, 91, 93, 97; ForWC 70; IntAu&W 82, 89, 91, 93; SmATA 57; WhoAm 74, 76, 78, 80, 82, 84, 86, 88, 90, 92, 94, 95, 96, 97; WhoAmJ 80; WhoAmW 66, 68, 70, 72, 74, 75, 81, 83, 85, 87, 89; WhoE 74; WhoUSWr 88; WhoWor 74; WhoWrEP 89, 92, 95; WrDr 76, 80, 82, 84, 86, 88, 90, 92, 94*

Kaufman, Boris
Polish. Filmmaker
Noted Hollywood cameraman; won 1954 Oscar for best black-and-white cinematography for *On the Waterfront.*
b. Aug 24, 1906 in Bialystok, Poland
d. Jun 24, 1980 in New York, New York
Source: *AnObit 1980; BioIn 12; DcFM; FilmEn; FilmgC; GangFlm; HalFC 80, 84, 88; IntDcF 1-4, 2-4; IntMPA 77, 79, 80; NewYTBS 80; OxCFilm; WorEFlm*

Kaufman, Elaine
American. Restaurateur
Founder and propietor of famous NYC restaurant, Elaines, 1963—.
b. Feb 10, in New York, New York
Source: *BioIn 9, 11, 13, 16, 19; InWom SUP; News 89; NewYTBS 79, 83*

Kaufman, George S(imon)
[Kaufman and Hart]
"The Great Collaborator"
American. Dramatist, Journalist
With Moss Hart, wrote some of Broadway's most popular plays: *You Can't Take It with You,* 1936 Pulitzer winner; *The Man Who Came to Dinner,* 1939.
b. Nov 16, 1889 in Pittsburgh, Pennsylvania
d. Jun 2, 1961 in New York, New York
Source: *AmAu&B; AmCulL; Benet 96; BioIn 1, 2, 4, 5, 6, 7, 8, 9, 10, 11, 12; CasWL; ChhPo S3; CnDAL; CnMD; CnThe; ConAmA; ConAmL; ConAu 93; CurBio 41, 61; DcArts; DcLEL; EncMT; EvLB; GrWrEL DR; IntDcT 2; LngCTC; McGEWB; OxCAmL 65, 95; PenC AM; REn; REnAL; TwCA, SUP; TwCWr; WebAB 74, 79; WebE&AL; WhAm 4; WorEFlm*

Kaufman, Henry
American. Economist
Wall Street forecaster; chief economist, Salomon Bros. investment bankers, 1962-88.
b. Oct 20, 1927 in Wenings, Germany
Source: *AmEA 74; BioIn 12, 13; CurBio 81; Dun&B 86, 88, 90; IntWW 83, 89, 91, 93; NewYTBS 79, 82; St&PR 87; WhoAm 82, 84, 86, 88, 90, 92; WhoFI 87; WhoSecI 86*

Kaufman, Irving R(obert)
American. Judge
Chief judge, US Court of Appeals, 1973-80; sentenced the Rosenbergs to electric chair for espionage, 1951.
b. Jun 24, 1910 in New York, New York
d. Feb 1, 1992 in New York, New York
Source: *AmMWSc 73P; AnObit 1992; BiDFedJ; BioIn 3, 4, 5, 11, 13; CurBio 53, 92N; IntWW 83; NewYTBE 70; NewYTBS 83; PolProf T; WhAm 10; WhoAm 74, 76, 78, 80, 82, 84, 86, 88, 90; WhoAmA 73; WhoAmL 78, 79, 83, 85, 87, 90, 92; WhoE 74, 75, 79, 81, 83, 85, 86, 89; WhoFI 75; WhoGov 72, 75, 77; WhoWorJ 72, 78*

Kaufman, Joseph William
American. Lawyer, Judge
Prosecutor at WW II Nuremburg war crime trials.
b. Mar 27, 1899 in New York, New York
d. Feb 13, 1981 in Washington, District of Columbia
Source: *BioIn 12; NewYTBS 81; WhAm 7; WhoAm 80*

Kaufman, Louis
American. Violinist
Concert violinist; performed Vivaldi's "Four Seasons," 1950s.
b. May 10, 1905 in Portland, Oregon
d. Feb 9, 1994 in Los Angeles, California
Source: *Baker 78, 84, 92; BioIn 2, 9, 19; PenDiMP; WhoMus 72*

Kaufman, Murray
"Murray the K"; "The Fifth Beatle"
American. Radio Performer
Promoted The Beatles' first tour, 1964.
b. Feb 14, 1922 in New York, New York
d. Feb 21, 1982 in Los Angeles, California
Source: *AnObit 1982; BioIn 12, 13; BioNews 74; HarEnR 86; NewYTBS 82; PseudN 82*

Kaufman, Sue
[Sue Kaufman Barondess]
American. Author
Writings on life's everyday pressures include *Diary of a Mad Housewife,* 1967.
b. Aug 7, 1926? in Long Island, New York
d. Jun 25, 1977 in New York, New York
Source: *BioIn 11; ConAu 1NR, 1R, 69, X; ConLC 3, 8; DrAF 76; ForWC 70; InWom SUP; NewYTBS 77; PseudN 82; WhAm 7; WhoAm 74, 76, 78; WhoAmW 81; WrDr 76, 80*

Kaunda, Kenneth David
Zambian. Political Leader
First pres. of Zambia, 1964-91.
b. Apr 28, 1924 in Chinsali, Rhodesia
Source: *AfSS 78, 79, 80, 81, 82; BioIn 6, 7, 8, 9, 10, 11, 12, 13; ColdWar 2; ConAu 133; CurBio 66; DcAfHiB 86; EncRev; EncSoA; HisDBrE; InB&W 80, 85; IntWW 74, 75, 76, 77, 78, 79, 80, 81, 82, 83, 89, 91, 93; IntYB 78, 79, 80, 81, 82; McGEWB; NewYTBS 79; WhDW; WhoAfr; WhoGov 72, 75; WhoWor 74, 76, 78, 80, 82, 84, 87, 89, 91, 93; WorAl; WrDr 94, 96*

Kauokenen, Jorma
[Jefferson Airplane]
American. Singer, Musician
Vocalist, guitarist with Jefferson Airplane, 1965-71; with Jack Casady, formed band Hot Tuna, 1970.
b. Dec 23, 1940 in Washington, District of Columbia

Kautner, Helmut
German. Screenwriter, Director
Led revival of German cinema: *Romanze in Moll,* 1942.
b. Mar 25, 1908 in Dusseldorf, Germany
d. Apr 20, 1980 in Castellina, Italy
Source: *AnObit 1980; BiDFilm, 81, 94; BioIn 15; DcFM; EncEurC; EncTR 91; FilmEn; FilmgC; HalFC 80, 84, 88; IntDcF 2-2; IntWW 74, 75, 76, 77, 78, 79, 80; WhoWor 74; WhScrn 83; WorEFlm; WorFDir 1*

Kavan, Anna
[Helen Ferguson; Helen Emily Woods]
English. Author
Author of novels *Let Me Alone,* 1930; *Eagles' Nest,* 1957.
b. Apr 10, 1901 in Cannes, France
d. Dec 5, 1967 in London, England
Source: *ArtclWW 2; BioIn 16, 17, 18, 19; ConAu 6NR; ConLC 5, 13, 82; EncBrWW; EncSF, 93; FemiCLE; Film 1, 2; FilmEn; IntMPA 77, 80; InWom SUP; MajTwCW; MotPP; Novels; RfGEnL 91; RGTwCWr; ScFSB; SilFlmP; SweetSg B; TwCSFW 81, 86, 91; TwYS; WhoHol A; WhoSciF; WhScrn 83*

Kavanagh, Patrick
Irish. Poet
Described Irish country life in poem "The Great Hunger," 1942; novel, *Tarry Flynn,* 1948.
b. Oct 21, 1904 in Inniskeen, Ireland
d. Nov 30, 1967 in Dublin, Ireland
Source: *Benet 96; BioIn 11, 13, 17; CamGLE; CasWL; ConAu 123; ConPo 75, 80A; CyWA 89; DcIrB 78, 88;*

DclrL, 96; DcLB 15, 20; EncWL, 2, 3; GrWrEL P; MajTwCW; ModBrL S1, S2; ModIrL; OxCEng 85; OxCTwCP; PenC ENG; REn; RfGEnL 91; TwCWr; WhoTwCL; WorAu 1950

Kavanaugh, Kevin
[Southside Johnny and the Asbury Jukes]
American. Singer, Musician
Keyboardist with group since 1974.
b. Aug 27, 1951
Source: *WhoRocM 82*

Kavner, Julie Deborah
American. Actor
Played Brenda Morgenstern on TV series "Rhoda," 1974-78; won Emmy, 1978; regular on "Tracey Ullman Show," 1987-90; known as the voice of Marge on *The Simpsons,* 1990—.
b. Sep 7, 1951 in Los Angeles, California
Source: *ConTFT 2, 5; CurBio 92; News 92; VarWW 85; WhoAm 80*

Kawabata, Yasunari
Japanese. Author
First Japanese to win Nobel Prize in literature, 1968; known for impressionistic novels.
b. Jun 11, 1899 in Osaka, Japan
d. Apr 16, 1972 in Zushi, Japan
Source: *Benet 87; BiDJaL; BioIn 8, 9, 10, 12, 15, 19; CasWL; CnMWL; ConAu 33R, 93; ConLC 2, 5, 9, 18; CurBio 69, 72, 72N; CyWA 89; DcArts; DcOrL 1; EncWL, 2; FacFETw; GrFLW; LinLib L; MagSWL; MakMC; McGEWB; NewYTBE 72; NobelP; Novels; PenC CL; RComWL; REn; ShSCr 17; WhAm 5; WhDW; WhoNob, 90, 95; WhoTwCL; WorAl; WorAu 1950*

Kay, Dianne
American. Actor
Played Nancy Bradford on TV series "Eight Is Enough," 1977-81.
b. Mar 29, 1955 in Phoenix, Arizona
Source: *BioIn 12*

Kay, Hershy
American. Composer
Wrote hit scores for ballet, Broadway, screen: *Coco,* 1969; *Evita,* 1978.
b. Nov 17, 1919 in Philadelphia, Pennsylvania
d. Dec 2, 1981 in Danbury, Connecticut
Source: *AnObit 1981; ASCAP 66, 80; Baker 78, 84, 92; BiDAmM; BiDD; BiE&WWA; BioIn 6, 12, 13; BlueB 76; CnOxB; ConAmC 76, 82; CurBio 62, 82, 82N; DancEn 78; FacFETw; NewAmDM; NewGrDA 86; NewGrDM 80; NewYTBS 81; NotNAT; OxCAmT 84; OxCPMus; WhAm 9; WhoAm 74, 76, 78, 80; WhoAmJ 80*

Kay, Mary
[Mary Kay Wagner Ash]
American. Cosmetics Executive
Founder, chm., Mary Kay Cosmetics, 1963—.
b. May 12, 1917 in Hot Wells, Texas
Source: *BusPN; WhoAm 80, 82; WhoAmW 74, 77*

Kay, Ulysses Simpson
American. Composer
Compositions reflect the Neoclassical school; works included scores for TV and film, among them is *Essay on Death,* 1964, a tribute to JFK.
b. Jan 7, 1917 in Tucson, Arizona
d. May 20, 1995 in Teaneck, New Jersey
Source: *AmComp; Baker 78, 84, 92; BiDAfM; BioIn 1, 3, 6, 8, 9, 10, 11, 13, 14, 20, 21; BlkCS; BriBkM 80; ConBlAP 88; DrBlPA, 90; InB&W 80, 85; IntWWM 80, 85, 90; NewAmDM; NewGrDA 86; NewGrDM 80; NewGrDO; WebAB 74, 79; WhAm 11; WhoAm 90, 94, 95; WhoBlA 92; WhoEnt 92*

Kaye, Danny
[David Daniel Kominsky]
American. Actor, Comedian
Films include *The Secret Life of Walter Mitty,* 1947; *Hans Christian Andersen,* 1952; UNICEF ambassador-at-large, noted for comic patter-songs.
b. Jan 18, 1913 in New York, New York
d. Mar 3, 1987 in Los Angeles, California
Source: *AnObit 1987; Baker 92; BiDAmM; BiDD; BiDFilm, 81, 94; BiE&WWA; BioIn 1, 2, 3, 4, 5, 6, 7, 8, 9, 10, 11, 12, 13; BlueB 76; CelR; CmMov; CmpEPM; ConAu 121; ConNews 87-2; ConTFT 3; CurBio 41, 52, 87, 87N; DcArts; EncAFC; EncMT; FacFETw; FilmEn; FilmgC; ForYSC; Funs; HalFC 80, 84; IntDcF 1-3, 2-3; IntMPA 75, 76, 77, 78, 79, 80, 81, 82, 84, 86; IntWW 74, 75, 76, 77, 78, 79, 80, 81, 82, 83; JoeFr; LegTOT; MotPP; MovMk; NewAmDM; NewGrDA 86; NewYTBE 70; NewYTBS 87; NewYTET; NotNAT; OxCAmT 84; OxCFilm; OxCPMus; OxCThe 67; PenEncP; QDrFCA 92; RadStar; SmATA 50N; WebAB 74, 79; WhAm 9; WhoAm 74, 76, 78, 80, 82, 84, 86; WhoAmJ 80; WhoCom; WhoHol A; WhoThe 72, 77, 81; WhoUN 75; WhoWor 74, 78, 84, 87; WhoWorJ 72, 78; WorAl; WorAlBi; WorEFlm*

Kaye, Mary Margaret Mollie
[Mollie Hamilton; M M Kaye]
English. Author
Historical novels include best-seller *The Far Pavillions,* 1978.
b. Aug 21, 1908 in Simla, India
Source: *Au&Wr 71; ConAu 89; ConLC 28; NewYTBS 81; Novels; PseudN 82; SmATA 62, X; TwCRHW 90; Who 85; WrDr 86, 92*

Kaye, Nora
[Nora Koreff]
American. Dancer, Actor
With NYC Ballet, 1951-54; retired from dancing, 1961; films include *The Turning Point,* 1977; *Pennies From Heaven,* 1981.
b. Jan 17, 1920 in New York, New York
d. Feb 28, 1987 in Santa Monica, California
Source: *AnObit 1987; BiDD; BioIn 1, 2, 3, 4, 5, 7, 11, 12, 13; CnOxB; ConNews 87-4; CurBio 53, 87, 87N; DancEn 78; FacFETw; IntDcB; InWom, SUP; LibW; NewYTBS 88; PseudN 82; VarWW 85; WhAm 9; WhoAm 80, 86; WhoAmW 81*

Kaye, Sammy
American. Bandleader
Noted for "swing and sway" rhythms, 1930s-60s; star of TV show "Sammy Kaye Show," 1950-59.
b. Mar 13, 1913? in Lakewood, Ohio
d. Jun 2, 1987 in Ridgewood, New Jersey
Source: *AnObit 1987; ASCAP 66; ConNews 87-4; VarWW 85; WhAm 9; WhoAm 74, 76; WhoHol A; WorAl*

Kaye, Stubby
American. Actor, Comedian
Best known for role of Nicely-Nicely Johnson in Broadway, film *Guys and Dolls.*
b. Nov 11, 1918 in New York, New York
Source: *AmPS B; BiE&WWA; BioIn 2; EncAFC; FilmEn; FilmgC; ForYSC; HalFC 80, 84, 88; LegTOT; MotPP; NotNAT; PlP&P; QDrFCA 92; VarWW 85; WhoHol 92, A; WhoThe 77, 81*

Kaye-Smith, Sheila
English. Author
Novels, describing life in Sussex, England, include *Sussex Gorse,* 1916.
b. Feb 4, 1887 in Hastings, England
d. Jan 14, 1956 in Rye, England
Source: *BioIn 1, 2, 4, 5, 8, 14, 16; BkC 4; BlmGWL; CamGLE; CathA 1930; ChhPo S1; ConAu 118; CyWA 58; DcCathB; DcLB 36; DcLEL; EncBrWW; EvLB; FemiCLE; InWom, SUP; LngCTC; ModBrL; ModWoWr; NewC; NewCBEL; ObitT 1951; OxCEng 85, 95; PenC ENG; REn; RGTwCWr; ScF&FL 1; TwCA, SUP; TwCLC 20; TwCWr; WhAm 3*

Kayibanda, Gregoire
Rwandan. Political Leader
President of Rwanda, 1966-73.
b. May 1, 1924, Ruanda-Urundi
Source: *BioIn 21; DcAfHiB 86S; IntAu&W 77; IntWW 74, 75, 76, 77; WhoGov 72, 75; WhoWor 74*

Kayser, Heinrich Gustav Johannes
German. Physicist
Discoverer of helium in the atmosphere of the earth, 1895.
b. Mar 16, 1853 in Bingen, Germany
d. Oct 14, 1940 in Bonn, Germany
Source: *BioIn 1, 4*

Kazan, Elia
[Elia Kazanjoglou]
American. Director, Author
Won 1954 Oscar for *On the Waterfront;* co-founded Actor's Studio, 1947; has written several books.
b. Sep 7, 1909 in Constantinople, Turkey
Source: *AmCulL; AmFD; AuSpks; Benet 87, 96; BenetAL 91; BiDFilm, 81, 94; BiE&WWA; BioIn 1, 2, 3, 4, 5, 6, 7, 8, 9, 10, 11, 12; BlueB 76; CamGWoT; CelR, 90; CnThe; ConAu 21R, 32NR; ConLC 6, 16, 63; ConTFT 3; CurBio 48, 72; DcArts; DcFM; DcTwCCu 1; EncMcCE; EncWB; EncWT; Ent; FacFETw; FilmEn; FilmgC; GangFlm; GrStDi; HalFC 80, 84, 88; IlWWHD 1; IntAu&W 77, 89, 91, 93; IntDcF 1-2, 2-2; IntDcT 3; IntMPA 75, 76, 77, 78, 79, 80, 81, 82, 84, 86, 88, 92, 94, 96; IntWW 74, 75, 76, 77, 78, 79, 80, 81, 82, 83, 89, 91, 93; LegTOT; MiSFD 9; MovMk; NewYTBS 95; NotNAT, A; Novels; OxCAmL 65, 83, 95; OxCAmT 84; OxCFilm; OxCThe 67, 83; PlP&P; PolProf T; REnAL; TheaDir; WebAB 74, 79; Who 74, 82, 83, 85, 88, 90, 92, 94; WhoAm 74, 76, 78, 80, 82, 84, 86, 88, 90, 92, 94, 95, 96, 97; WhoE 74; WhoEnt 92; WhoHol 92, A; WhoThe 72; WhoWor 74, 78, 80, 82, 84, 87, 89, 95, 96, 97; WhThe; WorAl; WorAlBi; WorEFlm; WorFDir 2; WrDr 76, 80, 82, 84, 86, 88, 90, 92, 94, 96*

Kazan, Lainie
[Lainie Levine]
American. Singer, Actor
Broadway appearances include *Seesaw; The Women.*
b. May 15, 1942 in New York, New York
Source: *ConTFT 4; IntMPA 92, 94, 96; InWom SUP; LegTOT; VarWW 85; WhoAm 78, 80, 82, 84, 86, 88, 90, 92, 94, 95, 96, 97; WhoAmW 81; WhoEnt 92; WhoHol A; WorAl*

Kazantzakis, Nikos
Greek. Author
Wrote *Zorba the Greek,* 1946; epic *Odysseia,* 1938.
b. Dec 2, 1883 in Iraklion, Crete
d. Oct 26, 1957 in Freiburg, Germany (West)
Source: *AtlBL; Benet 87, 96; BioIn 14, 17; CasWL; ClDMEL 80; CnMD; ConAu 105, 132; CurBio 55, 58; CyWA 89; EncWL, 2, 3; EuWr 9; FacFETw; GrFLW; IntDcT 2; LiExTwC; LinLib L; MagSWL; MajTwCW; McGEWB; NotNAT B; Novels; OxCEng 67; PenC EUR; REn; RfGWoL 95; ScF&FL 92; TwCA SUP; TwCLC 33; TwCWr; WebBD 83; WhAm 3, 4A; WhoTwCL; WorAl; WorAlBi*

Kazee, Buell Hilton
American. Musician, Singer
Folk music performer, 1930s; recorded Rock Island Line.
b. Aug 29, 1900 in Burton Fork, Kentucky
d. Aug 31, 1976 in Winchester, Kentucky
Source: *BiDAmM; ConAu 111; CounME 74, 74A; EncFCWM 69; IlEncCM*

Kazin, Alfred
American. Critic
Best-known works: *On Native Grounds,* 1942; *The Inmost Leaf,* 1955.
b. Jun 5, 1915 in New York, New York
Source: *AmAu&B; Au&Wr 71; Benet 87, 96; BenetAL 91; BioIn 2, 4, 6, 7, 9, 11, 13, 14, 15, 16, 17, 19; BlueB 76; CasWL; CelR; ConAu 1NR, 1R, 7AS, 45NR; ConLC 38; ConLCrt 77, 82; CurBio 66; DcLB 67; DcLEL 1940; DrAS 74E, 78E, 82E; FacFETw; IntAu&W 76, 77; IntWW 74, 75, 76, 77, 78, 79, 80, 81, 82, 83, 89, 91, 93; JeAmHC; LegTOT; LinLib L; OxCAmL 65, 83, 95; PenC AM; RAdv 1, 14, 13-1; REn; REnAL; TwCA SUP; WhoAm 74, 76, 78, 80, 82, 84, 86, 88, 90, 92, 94, 95, 96; WhoAmJ 80; WhoUSWr 88; WhoWor 74, 84, 87, 89, 91, 93, 95, 96; WhoWorJ 72, 78; WhoWrEP 89, 92, 95; WorAl; WorAlBi; WrDr 80, 82, 84, 86, 88, 90, 92, 94, 96*

Kazmaier, Richard W, Jr.
"Kaz"; "Mr. Everything"; "Nassau Nugget"
American. Football Player
All-America halfback, Princeton, 1949-51; won Heisman Trophy, 1950.
b. Nov 23, 1930 in Toledo, Ohio
Source: *BioIn 2, 3, 6, 7, 8; WhoFtbl 74*

K C. and the Sunshine Band
[Oliver Brown; H(arry) W(ayne) Casey; Rick Finch; Robert Johnson; Denvil Liptrot; Jerome Smith; Ronnie Smith; James Weaver; Charles Williams]
American. Music Group
Formed 1973; hits nominated for Grammys: "That's the Way," 1975; "Shake Your Booty," 1976.
Source: *Alli, SUP; AmBench 79; AmWrBE; ArtsEM; AuBYP 3; BiAUS; BiDLA; BiDRP&D; BioIn 7, 8, 10, 11, 14, 15, 16, 17, 20, 21; BlkOpe; CivWDc; ConAu 33NR, X; DcAmC; DcBrBI; DcCathB; DcNaB; Drake; Dun&B 86; EncO&P 1, 2, 3; EncRk 88; IlEncBM 82; InB&W 80, 85; ItaFilm; LElec; LesBEnT 92; MajAI; NewCBEL; NewYHSD; NewYTBS 27; ObitOF 79; OxCMus; PeoHis; RkOn 78; RolSEnR 83; SmATA 8, 70; St&PR 96, 97; WhoAfA 96; WhoAmP 75, 77, 79, 81, 83, 85, 91, 93, 95; WhoBlA 90; WhoHol 92; WhoReal 83; WhoRock 81; WhoRocM 82; WrDr 96*

Keach, Stacy, Sr.
American. Actor, Director
Active in Hollywood since early 1940s; plays Clarence Birdseye in TV commercia ls; father of Stacy Jr.
b. May 29, 1914 in Chicago, Illinois
Source: *IntMPA 75, 76, 77, 78, 79, 80, 81, 82, 84, 86, 88, 92, 94, 96; WhoAm 74, 76, 78, 80, 82, 84, 86, 88, 90, 92, 94, 95, 96, 97; WhoEnt 92; WhoWest 74, 76, 78*

Keach, Stacy, Jr.
American. Actor
Starred in TV's "Return of Mike Hammer," 1984, 1986-87.
b. Jun 2, 1941 in Savannah, Georgia
Source: *BioIn 8, 9, 12; CamGWoT; CelR, 90; CnThe; ConTFT 4, 14; CurBio 71; FilmEn; FilmgC; HalFC 80, 84, 88; IntDcF 1-3; IntMPA 86; ItaFilm; LegTOT; MovMk; NewYTBE 72; NotNAT; VarWW 85; WhoAm 74, 76, 78, 80, 82, 84, 86, 88, 90, 92, 94, 95, 96, 97; WhoEnt 92; WhoHol 92, A; WhoThe 72, 77, 81; WorAl; WorAlBi; WorEFlm*

Kean, Edmund
English. Actor
Tragedian best known for his Shakespearean roles; career shortened by scandal, dissolute life.
b. Mar 17, 1787 in London, England
d. May 15, 1833 in London, England
Source: *BioIn 1, 2, 3, 4, 5, 6, 7, 9, 10, 11, 13, 14; BlmGEL; CelCen; CnThe; DcArts; DcBiPP; DcNaB; EncWT; Ent; FamA&A; IntDcT 3; LinLib L, S; LngCEL; NewC; NotNAT A, B; OxCAmT 84; OxCEng 85, 95; OxCThe 67; PlP&P; REn; WhAm HS; WhDW*

Kean, Thomas Howard
American. Politician, University Administrator
New Jersey Assembly rep. who succeeded Brendan Byrne as governor of NJ, 1982-89; president, Drew U., Madison, NJ, 1990—.
b. Apr 21, 1935 in New York, New York
Source: *AlmAP 88; BioIn 12; CurBio 85; NewYTBS 82; WhoAm 86; WhoAmP 87; WhoE 83; WhoWor 82*

Keane, Bil
American. Cartoonist
Creator of the "Family Circus," 1960—

b. Oct 5, 1922 in Philadelphia, Pennsylvania
Source: *BioIn 14, 15, 16; ConAu 13NR, 33R; ConGrA 1; EncTwCJ; LegTOT; SmATA 4; WhoAm 78, 80, 82, 84, 86, 88, 90, 92, 94, 95, 96, 97; WhoAmA 73, 76, 78, 80, 82, 84, 86, 89, 91, 93; WhoWest 76, 78*

Keane, John Brendon
Irish. Dramatist, Poet
Wrote most popular play in Ireland at time: *Sive,* 1959; other works include *Values,* 1973; *The Crazy Wall,* 1974.
b. Jul 21, 1928 in Listowel, Ireland
Source: *ConDr 82; DcLB 13; McGEWD 84; OxCThe 83; WhoThe 81; WrDr 86*

Keane, Mary Nesta
[M J Farrell; Molly Keane]
Irish. Author
Novel *Good Behaviour,* 1981, adapted for BBC TV production, 1982.
b. Jul 4, 1904 in County Kildare, Ireland
d. Apr 22, 1996 in Ardmore, Ireland
Source: *BlmGWL; ConAu 108, 114; ConLC 31; ConNov 91, 96; DcIrL 96; EncBrWW; FemiCLE; IntAu&W 82; TwCRHW 94; Who 82, 83, 94; WorAu 1980*

Keaney, Frank
American. Basketball Coach
Coach, Rhode Island U, 1921-48; introduced full-court press; Hall of Fame.
b. Jun 5, 1886 in Boston, Massachusetts
d. Oct 10, 1967
Source: *BioIn 1, 8, 9; WhoBbl 73*

Kearns, Doris H
American. Author, Educator
Biographer: *Lyndon Johnson and the American Dream,* 1976.
b. Jan 4, 1943 in Rockville Centre, New York
Source: *BioIn 10, 11; ConAu 103; WhoE 74*

Kearns, Jack
American. Boxing Promoter
Managed six world champions, including Jack Dempsey.
b. Aug 17, 1882 in Waterloo, Michigan
d. Jul 7, 1963 in Miami, Florida
Source: *BiDAmSp BK; BioIn 1, 2, 6, 7; BoxReg; DcAmB S7; WhoSpor*

Kearny, Stephen Watts
American. Army Officer
Led Army of the West in Mexican War, 1846-48; conquered NM, helped win CA.
b. Aug 30, 1794 in Newark, New Jersey
d. Oct 31, 1848 in Saint Louis, Missouri
Source: *AmBi; ApCAB; BioIn 2, 6, 7, 8, 9, 11, 16; CmCal; DcAmB; DcAmMiB; Drake; HarEnMi; HarEnUS; McGEWB; NatCAB 13; NewCol 75; OxCAmH; REnAW; TwCBDA; WebAB 74, 79; WebAMB; WhAm HS; WhNaAH; WhoMilH 76; WhWE; WorAl*

Keating, Charles H, Jr.
American. Financier, Real Estate Executive
Phoenix developer sentenced in 1992 to 10 yrs. in prison for defrauding depositors at the Lincoln Savings and Loan Assn.
b. 1923 in Cincinnati, Ohio
Source: *BioIn 15, 16; Dun&B 86, 88, 90; News 90; NewYTBS 89; WhoAm 84, 86; WhoWest 87, 89*

Keating, Kenneth B
American. Lawyer, Politician
Senator from NY, 1959-65; ambassador to India, 1969-73; Israel, 1973-75.
b. May 18, 1900 in Lima, New York
d. May 5, 1975 in New York, New York
Source: *BiDrAC; CurBio 50, 75N; IntWW 74; NewYTBS 75; ObitOF 79; PolProf E, K; USBiR 74; WhAm 6; WhoAm 74; WhoAmP 73; WhoE 74; WhoGov 72, 75; WhoWor 74*

Keating, Paul John
Australian. Political Leader
Succeeded Bob Hawke as prime minister, Australia, 1991-96.
b. Jan 18, 1944 in Sydney, Australia
Source: *CurBio 92; IntWW 89, 91, 93; Who 85, 88, 90, 92, 94; WhoAsAP 91*

Keaton, Buster
[Joseph Francis Keaton]
"The Great Stone Face"
American. Actor, Comedian
Perfected deadpan stare in *The Navigator,* 1924; *The General,* 1927.
b. Oct 4, 1895 in Piqua, Kansas
d. Feb 1, 1966 in Hollywood, California
Source: *AmCulL; AmFD; Benet 87; BenetAL 91; BiDFilm, 81, 94; BioIn 13, 14, 15, 16, 17, 19, 20, 21; CmCal; CmMov; ConLC 20; DcAmB S8; DcFM; EncAFC; FacFETw; Film 1, 2; FilmEn; FilmgC; Funs; HalFC 80, 84, 88; IntDcF 1-2, 2-2; ItaFilm; LegTOT; MakMC; MiSFD 9N; MotPP; MovMk; OxCFilm; PseudN 82; QDrFCA 92; SilFlmP; TwYS; WebAB 74, 79; WhAm 4; WhDW; WhoCom; WhScrn 74, 77, 83; WorAl; WorAlBi; WorEFlm; WorFDir 1*

Keaton, Diane
[Diane Hall]
American. Actor
Won 1977 Oscar for *Annie Hall;* starred in *Reds,* 1981; *The First Wives Club,* 1996.
b. Jan 5, 1946 in Los Angeles, California
Source: *BiDFilm 81, 94; BioIn 10, 11, 12; BkPepl; CelR 90; ConTFT 1, 6, 13; CurBio 78, 96; EncAFC; FilmgC; GangFlm; HalFC 84, 88; HolBB; IntDcF 1-3, 2-3; IntMPA 86, 88, 92, 94, 96; InWom SUP; LegTOT; MovMk; News 97-1; NewYTBE 72; NewYTBS 77; PseudN 82; VarWW 85; WhoAm 86, 88, 90, 92, 94, 95, 96, 97; WhoAmW 85, 95, 97; WhoCom; WhoEnt 92; WhoHol 92, A; WorAlBi*

Keaton, Michael
[Michael Douglas]
American. Actor, Comedian
Achieved superstar status for his role as Batman in *Batman,* 1989 and *Batman Returns,* 1992.
b. Sep 9, 1951 in Pittsburgh, Pennsylvania
Source: *CelR 90; ConTFT 6, 13; CurBio 92; EncAFC; GangFlm; HalFC 88; HolBB; IntMPA 88, 92, 94, 96; IntWW 93; LegTOT; News 89; QDrFCA 92; VarWW 85; WhoAm 90, 92, 94, 95, 96, 97; WhoEnt 92; WhoHol 92; WorAlBi*

Keats, Duke
[Gordon Blanchard Keats]
Canadian. Hockey Player
Center, with Detroit, Chicago, 1926-29; Hall of Fame, 1958.
b. Mar 1, 1895 in Montreal, Quebec, Canada
Source: *WhoHcky 73*

Keats, Ezra Jack
American. Illustrator, Children's Author
Known for use of collages in illustrating 32 books; won Caldecott Medal, 1963, for *The Snowy Day.*
b. Mar 11, 1916 in New York, New York
d. May 6, 1983 in New York, New York
Source: *AnObit 1983; Au&ICB; AuBYP 2; AuNews 1; BioIn 5, 6, 7, 8, 9, 10, 12, 13, 14, 16, 19, 20; BkP; ChhPo S1, S2; ChlBIID; ChlBkCr; ChlLR 1, 35; ConAu 77, 109; DcLB 61; IlsBYP; IlsCB 1946, 1957; LinLib L; MajAI; MorJA; NewbC 1956; OxCChiL; SmATA 14, 34, 34N, 57; TwCChW 78, 83, 83A, 89, 95; WhAm 8; WhoAm 74, 76, 78, 80, 82; WhoAmA 76, 78, 80, 82, 84, 86N, 89N, 91N, 93N; WrDr 76, 80, 82, 84*

Keats, John
English. Poet
Wrote *Ode on a Grecian Urn, Ode to a Nightingale.*
b. Oct 31, 1795 in London, England
d. Feb 23, 1821 in Rome, Italy
Source: *Alli; AnCL; AtlBL; Benet 87, 96; BiD&SB; BiHiMed; BioIn 1, 2, 3, 4, 5, 6, 7, 8, 9, 10, 11, 12, 13, 14, 15, 16, 17, 18, 19, 20; BlmGEL; BritAu 19; BritWr 4; CamGEL; CamGLE; CasWL; CelCen; Chambr 3; ChhPo, S1, S2, S3; CnDBLB 3; CnE&AP; CrtT 2, 4; CyWA 58; DcArts; DcBiPP; DcEnA; DcEnL; DcEuL; DcLB 96, 110; DcLEL; DcNaB; DcPup; Dis&D; EvLB; GrWrEL P; LegTOT; LinLib L, S; LngCEL; MagSWL; McGEWB; MouLC 2; NewC; NewCBEL; NewGrDM 80; NinCLC 8; OxCEng 67, 85, 95; OxCMed 86; PenC ENG; PenEncH; PoeCrit 1; RAdv 1, 14, 13-1; RComWL; REn; RfGEnL 91; RGFBP; Str&VC; WebE&AL; WhDW; WorAl; WorAlBi; WorLitC; WrPh*

Keble, John
English. Author, Educator, Clergy
Initiated Oxford Movement, 1833; wrote popular collection of sacred verse, *The Christian Year,* 1827.
b. Apr 25, 1792 in Fairford, England
d. Mar 27, 1866 in Bournemouth, England
Source: *Alli, SUP; BbD; Benet 87; BiD&SB; BioIn 1, 5, 6, 9, 10, 11, 12, 13, 14, 15, 16; BritAu 19; CamGEL; CamGLE; CasWL; CelCen; Chambr 3; ChhPo, S1, S2, S3; CyEd; DcBiPP; DcEnA; DcEnL; DcEuL; DcLB 32, 55; DcLEL; DcNaB, C; EvLB; GrWrEL P; LinLib L, S; LngCEL; LuthC 75; NewC; NewCBEL; OxCEng 67, 85, 95; PenC ENG; PoChrch; REn; RfGEnL 91; VicBrit; WebE&AL; WhDW*

Keckley, Elizabeth Hobbs
American. Slave
Born a slave, bought her freedom; became seamstress for Mary Todd Lincoln.
b. 1818 in Dinwiddie, Virginia
d. May 26, 1907 in Washington, District of Columbia
Source: *FemiCLE; InB&W 85; InWom SUP; NotBlAW 1*

Kedourie, Elie
British. Educator, Author
Noted authority on the Middle East; wrote *Politics in the Middle East,* 1992; taught at the London School of Economics.
b. Jan 25, 1926 in Baghdad, Iraq
d. Jun 29, 1992 in Washington, District of Columbia
Source: *Au&Wr 71; ConAu 10NR, 21R, 31NR, 139; IntWW 89, 91; Who 82, 83, 85, 88, 90, 92; WorAu 1975; WrDr 84, 86, 88, 90, 92, 94N*

Keefe, Barrie Colin
English. Dramatist
Wrote award-winning play *My Girl,* 1975.
b. Oct 31, 1945 in London, England
Source: *ConAu 116; DcLB 13*

Keefe, Tim(othy John)
"Sir Timothy"
American. Baseball Player
Pitcher, 1880-93; had 344 career wins; Hall of Fame, 1964.
b. Jan 1, 1857 in Cambridge, Massachusetts
d. Apr 23, 1933 in Cambridge, Massachusetts
Source: *Ballpl 90; BiDAmSp BB; LegTOT; WhoProB 73*

Keegan, John
Historian, Author
Author of classic war books including *The Face of Battle,* 1967; *The Price of Admiralty,* 1989.
b. 1934 in London, England
Source: *BestSel 90-3; BioIn 16, 17; ConAu 130; CurBio 89; IntWW 91, 93; WorAu 1980; WrDr 86, 88, 90, 92*

Keel, Howard
[Harold Clifford Leek]
American. Actor, Singer
Played Clayton Farlow on TV series, "Dallas"; singing star in *Showboat,* 1951; *Kiss Me Kate,* 1953.
b. Apr 13, 1919 in Gillespie, Illinois
Source: *BiE&WWA; CelR 90; CmMov; CmpEPM; EncMT; FilmgC; ForYSC; HalFC 84; IntMPA 86, 92, 94, 96; MGM; MovMk; NotNAT; PenEncP; PseudN 82; VarWW 85; WhoAm 74, 76; WhoHol A; WhoThe 72, 77, 81; WorAl; WorEFlm*

Keeler, Christine
English. Call Girl
Involved in 1963 British political-sex scandal known as Profumo affair.
b. 1942
Source: *BioIn 9, 10; InWom SUP; What 3*

Keeler, James Edward
American. Astronomer
Findings verified that Saturn's rings consist of many small particles.
b. Sep 10, 1857 in La Salle, Illinois
d. Aug 12, 1900 in San Francisco, California
Source: *AmBi; AsBiEn; BiDAmS; BiESc; BiInAmS; BioIn 2, 11, 13, 14; DcAmB; DcScB; HarEnUS; InSci; LarDcSc; NatCAB 10; OxCAmH; TwCBDA; WhAm 1*

Keeler, Ruby
[Ethel Hilda Keeler]
American. Dancer, Actor
Star of lavish musicals, 1930s: *42nd Street,* 1933; once wed to Al Jolson.
b. Aug 25, 1909 in Halifax, Nova Scotia, Canada
d. Feb 28, 1993 in Palm Springs, California
Source: *AnObit 1993; BiDD; BiDFilm, 81, 94; BiE&WWA; CmMov; CmpEPM; CurBio 71, 93N; EncMT; FilmEn; FilmgC; ForYSC; GoodHs; HalFC 80, 84, 88; InWom, SUP; LegTOT; MotPP; MovMk; NewAmDM; NewGrDA 86; NewYTBE 70; OxCPMus; ThFT; WhoAm 84; WhoHol 92, A; WhoThe 72, 77, 81; WorAlBi*

Keeler, Wee Willie
[William Henry Keeler]
American. Baseball Player
Outfielder, 1892-1910; had lifetime .345 batting average; coined phrase "hit 'em where they ain't"; Hall of Fame, 1939.
b. Mar 13, 1872 in New York, New York
d. Jan 1, 1923 in New York, New York
Source: *BiDAmSp BB; BioIn 3, 7, 8, 10; WhoProB 73; WhoSpor*

Keeler, William Wayne
American. Native American Leader
Appointed principal chief of the Cherokee Nation of Oklahoma, 1949; elected chief in 1971.
b. 1908
d. Aug 24, 1987 in Bartlesville, Oklahoma
Source: *BioIn 9; BlueB 76; IntWW 74, 75, 76, 77, 78, 79, 80, 81, 82, 83; NotNaAm*

Keen, Sam
American. Writer, Philosopher, Lecturer
Contributing editor to *Psychology Today;* wrote *Fire in the Belly,* 1991.
b. Nov 23, 1931 in Scranton, Pennsylvania
Source: *CurBio 95; WrDr 96*

Keen, William Williams
American. Surgeon
Pioneered in neurosurgery; first US brain surgeon; edited *Gray's Anatomy,* 1887.
b. Jan 19, 1837 in Philadelphia, Pennsylvania
d. Jun 7, 1932 in Philadelphia, Pennsylvania
Source: *Alli SUP; AmBi; AmLY; ApCAB, X; BiDAmEd; BiHiMed; BioIn 1, 3, 6, 9; DcAmAu; DcAmB S1; DcAmMeB 84; DcNAA; InSci; NatCAB 11; OxCMed 86; TwCBDA; WhAm 1*

Keenan, Brian
Irish. Hostage
Teacher taken hostage by Lebanese terrorists on Apr 11, 1986; released after 1,596 days in captivity on Aug 24, 1990.
Source: *BioIn 15; NewYTBS 92; WhoRocM 82*

Keenan, Frank
American. Actor
Stage, film actor, 1915-26; films include *The Bells; Heart's Aflame; Easy Lynne.*
b. Apr 8, 1858 in Dubuque, Iowa
d. Feb 24, 1929
Source: *EncVaud; Film 1, 2; MotPP; NotNAT B; TwYS; WhAm 1; WhoHol B; WhScrn 77, 83; WhThe*

Keenan, Mike
Canadian. Hockey Coach
Coach, Philadelphia Flyers, 1984-88; Chicago Blackhawks, 1988-92; New York Rangers, 1993-94; St. Louis Blues, 1994—.
b. Oct 21, 1949 in Toronto, Ontario, Canada
Source: *CurBio 96*

Keene, Charles Samuel
English. Artist
Illustrator for *Punch,* 1851-91; satirized middle-classes.
b. Aug 10, 1823 in Hornsey, England
d. Jan 4, 1891 in London, England
Source: *BioIn 1, 3, 5; ChhPo; ClaDrA; DcBrBI; DcBrWA; DcNaB; DcVicP, 2; McGDA; NewCBEL; OxCArt; OxDcArt*

Keene, Christopher
American. Conductor
Director, NYC Opera, 1988-95.
b. Dec 21, 1946 in Berkeley, California
d. Oct 8, 1995 in New York, New York
Source: *Baker 78, 84, 92; BioIn 16, 17, 18, 21; ConAmC 76, 82; CurBio 90, 96N; IntWW 91, 93; IntWWM 90; MetOEnc; NewAmDM; NewGrDA 86; NewGrDO; NewYTBS 95; PenDiMP; WhAm 11; WhoAm 74, 76, 78, 80, 82, 84, 86, 88, 90, 92, 94, 95, 96; WhoAmM 83; WhoE 74, 81, 83, 85, 86, 89, 91, 93, 95; WhoEnt 92*

Keene, Donald Lawrence
American. Critic, Translator
Leading US expert on Japanese literature; author of books on subject.
b. Jun 18, 1922 in New York, New York
Source: *ConAu 1R, 5NR; CurBio 88; DrAS 74F, 78F, 82F; NotNAT; WhoAm 74, 76; WrDr 86*

Keene, Laura
English. Actor
First woman theatrical producer in US, 1855-1863; at Ford's Theater starred in *Our American Cousin* the night Lincoln was assassinated.
b. Jul 20, 1820 in London, England
d. Nov 4, 1873 in Montclair, New Jersey
Source: *AmBi; ApCAB; DcAmB; Drake; FamA&A; HarEnUS; InWom, SUP; LibW; NatCAB 8; NotAW; NotNAT A, B; OxCAmH; OxCThe 67; PlP&P; TwCBDA; WebAB 74, 79; WhAm HS*

Keene, Thomas Wallace
American. Actor
Toured Shakespearean plays countrywide, 1880-98.
b. Oct 26, 1840 in New York, New York
d. Jun 1, 1898 in Tompkinsville, New York
Source: *BioIn 10; DcAmB; NatCAB 8; NotNAT B; OxCAmT 84; OxCThe 67; TwCBDA; WhAm HS*

Keener, Jefferson Ward
American. Business Executive
With BF Goodrich, 1939-74.
b. Aug 6, 1908 in Portersville, Alabama
d. Jan 2, 1981 in Akron, Ohio
Source: *BioIn 5, 7, 8, 12; BlueB 76; EncAB-A 36; IntWW 74, 75, 76, 77, 78, 79, 80; IntYB 78, 79, 80, 81, 82; NewYTBS 81; St&PR 75; WhoAm 74; WhoFI 74; WhoWor 74*

Keeshan, Bob
[Robert James Keeshan]
"Captain Kangaroo"
American. TV Personality, Author
Star of "Captain Kangaroo," 1955-81, longest-running children's program in network history.
b. Jun 27, 1927 in Lynbrook, New York
Source: *BioIn 7, 10, 12; BioNews 74; ConAu 5NR; ConTFT 4; CurBio 65; IntMPA 75, 76, 77, 78, 79, 80, 81, 82, 84, 86, 88, 92, 94, 96; LegTOT; LesBEnT; NewYTBE 72; NewYTBS 95; NewYTET; PseudN 82; SmATA 32; VarWW 85; WebAB 74, 79; WhoAm 74, 76, 78, 80, 82, 84, 86, 88, 90, 92, 94, 95, 96, 97; WhoEnt 92; WhoTelC; WhoWor 74, 76, 78; WorAlBi; WrDr 92, 94, 96*

Keesom, Willem Hendrik
Dutch. Physicist
Pioneer in cryogenics; first to turn helium unto a solid, 1926.
b. Jun 21, 1876 in Texel, Netherlands
d. Mar 24, 1956 in Oegstgeest, Netherlands
Source: *BioIn 4; DcScB*

Keeton, Kathy
[Kathryn Merle Keeton]
American. Editor, Publisher
President, General Media Publishing Group, 1991—; founded *Omni* magazine, 1978.
b. Feb 17, 1939 in Johannesburg, South Africa
Source: *BioIn 17, 19; ConAu 125; CurBio 93; EncTwCJ; WhoAm 82, 84, 86, 88; WhoAmW 81, 85, 89; WhoHol 92*

Kefauver, Estes
American. Politician
Headed televised Senate crime investigation, 1950-51; Dem. candidate for VP, 1956.
b. Jul 26, 1903 in Madisonville, Tennessee
d. Aug 10, 1963 in Bethesda, Maryland
Source: *AmAu&B; AmDec 1950; BioIn 1, 2, 3, 4, 5, 6, 7, 9, 14; CopCroC; CurBio 49, 63; DcAmB S7; DcAmSR; EncAB-A 37; LegTOT; LinLib S; NatCAB 52; ObitT 1961; OxCAmH; PolPar; PresAR; WhAm 4; WhScrn 77, 83; WorAl; WorAlBi*

Keilberth, Joseph
German. Conductor
Led Bamberg Symphony, 1949-68; noted for readings of Wagner, Strauss.
b. Apr 19, 1908 in Karlsruhe, Germany
d. Jul 7, 1968 in Munich, Germany (West)
Source: *Baker 78, 84, 92; BioIn 8; CmOp; IntDcOp; MetOEnc; NewAmDM; NewEOp 71; NewGrDM 80; NewGrDO; ObitT 1961; OxDcOp; PenDiMP; WhAm 5*

Keillor, Garrison
[Gary Edward Keillor]
American. Author, Producer
Created radio program "A Prairie Home Companion" about fictional Lake Wobegon, MN, 1974-87; wrote *Lake Wobegon Days,* 1985; radio show "American Radio Co.," 1989—.
b. Aug 7, 1942 in Anoka, Minnesota
Source: *Au&Arts 2; BenetAL 91; BestSel 89-3; BioIn 12, 13; ConAu 111; ConLC 40; ConPopW; CurBio 85; DcArts; DcLB Y87B; DrAPF 80; EncAHmr; IntAu&W 91, 93; LegTOT; MagSAmL; RGTwCWr; SmATA 58; WhoAm 86; WhoCom; WhoMW 76; WorAlBi; WorAu 1985; WrDr 88, 90, 92*

Keino, Kip
[Hezekiah Kipchoge Keino]
"The Flying Policeman"
Kenyan. Track Athlete
Long-distance runner; only man to hold Olympic records at two distances; won gold medal, 1968 Olympics.
b. Jan 17, 1940 in Kaptagunyo, British East Africa
Source: *BioIn 21; CurBio 67; WhoTr&F 73*

Keiser, Herman
American. Golfer
Touring pro, 1940s; won Masters, 1946.
b. Oct 7, 1914 in Springfield, Missouri
Source: *BioIn 1, 6; WhoGolf*

Keiser, Reinhard
German. Composer
Wrote over 120 Baroque operas, many sacred works.
b. Jan 9, 1674 in Teuchern, Germany
d. Sep 12, 1739 in Hamburg, Germany
Source: *Baker 78, 84, 92; BioIn 4, 7; BriBkM 80; GrComp; IntDcOp; MusMk; NewEOp 71; NewGrDM 80; NewGrDO; NewOxM; OxCMus; OxDcOp; PenDiMP A*

Keitel, Harvey
American. Actor, Producer
Best-known films include *Mean Streets,* 1973; *Alice Doesn't Live Here Anymore,* 1975; *Taxi Driver,* 1976; *The Piano,* 1993.
b. May 13, 1939 in New York, New York
Source: *BiDFilm 94; BioIn 20; ConTFT 5, 12; CurBio 94; HalFC 84; IntMPA 77, 86, 92, 94, 96; IntWW 93; MovMk; News 94, 94-3; VarWW 85; WhoAm 86; WhoHol 92, A*

Keitel, Wilhelm
"Lakaitel"
German. Military Leader
Chief of the high command of Nazi Armed Forces, WW II; tried, condemned by Int'l Military Tribunal for war crimes.
b. Sep 22, 1882 in Helmscherode, Germany
d. Oct 16, 1946 in Nuremberg, Germany
Source: *BioIn 1, 7, 8, 9, 11, 12, 14, 16, 17, 18; CurBio 40, 46; Dis&D; EncTR, 91; FacFETw; HarEnMi; LinLib S; ObitOF 79; PseudN 82; WhWW-II; WorAl; WorAlBi*

Keith, Benjamin Franklin
American. Entertainer
Established Vaudeville, 1800s, catering to respectable, family entertainment.
b. Jan 26, 1846 in Hillsboro, New Hampshire
d. Mar 26, 1914 in Palm Beach, Florida
Source: *BiDAmBL 83; BioIn 3, 12; DcAmB; NatCAB 15; NotNAT B; OxCThe 67, 83; WhAm 1; WhoStg 1906, 1908*

Keith, Brian
[Robert Brian Keith, Jr.]
American. Actor
Played Bill Davis on TV comedy "Family Affair," 1966-71; Milton Hardcastle on "Hardcastle and McCormick," 1983-86.
b. Nov 14, 1921 in Bayonne, New Jersey
d. Jun 24, 1997 in Malibu, California
Source: *BioIn 4, 13; ConTFT 2, 9; FilmEn; FilmgC; ForYSC; GangFlm; HalFC 80, 84, 88; IntMPA 75, 76, 77, 78, 79, 80, 81, 82, 84, 86, 88, 92, 94,*

96; LegTOT; MotPP; MovMk; PseudN 82; VarWW 85; WhoAm 86; WhoHol 92; WhoThe 81; WorAl; WorAlBi; WorEFlm

Keith, David Lemuel
American. Actor
In films *An Officer and a Gentleman,* 1982; *The Lords of Discipline,* 1983.
b. May 8, 1954 in Knoxville, Tennessee
Source: *ConTFT 4; IntMPA 86; VarWW 85; WhoEnt 92*

Keith, Ian
[Keith Ross]
American. Actor
Broadway matinee idol; supporting actor, 1924-56, in films *Abraham Lincoln,* 1930; *The Ten Commandments,* 1956.
b. Feb 27, 1899 in Boston, Massachusetts
d. Mar 26, 1960 in New York, New York
Source: *BioIn 5; Film 2; FilmEn; FilmgC; ForYSC; HalFC 80, 84, 88; MotPP; MovMk; NotNAT B; ObitOF 79; PseudN 82; SilFlmP; TwYS; WhoHol B; WhScrn 74, 77, 83; WhThe*

Keith, Louis Gerald
American. Physician
Expert on twins; founded first major center dedicated to study of multiple births, 1977.
b. Apr 24, 1935 in Chicago, Illinois
Source: *BioIn 12; News 88-2; WhoMW 82, 84*

Keith, Minor Cooper
American. Industrialist, Railroad Executive
Built railroads, developed banana plantations in Costa Rica; founded United Fruit Co., 1899.
b. Jan 19, 1848 in New York, New York
d. Jun 14, 1929
Source: *AmBi; ApCAB X; BiDAmBL 83; BioIn 1, 7, 16; DcAmB; DcAmDH 80, 89; EncLatA; McGEWB; NatCAB 14, 22; NewCol 75; WhAm 1; WorAl*

Keith, Toby
American. Singer, Songwriter, Musician
Country singer who toured the Western dance hall circuit with the Easy Money Band, 1982; released debut album *Toby Keith,* 1993, which included number one hit single "Should've Been a Coyboy;" received *Billboard* Magazine's Best New Artist Award in 1993; released album *Boomtown* in 1993.
b. Jul 8, 1961 in Clinton, Oklahoma
Source: *ConMus 17*

Keith, William
American. Artist
Prolific painter of colorful CA landscapes; 2,000 works destroyed in 1906 fire.
b. Nov 21, 1839 in Aberdeen, Scotland
d. Apr 13, 1911 in Berkeley, California
Source: *ArtsAmW 1; BioIn 2, 8, 9; ChhPo; CmCal; DcAmArt; DcAmB; EarABI, SUP; IlBEAAW; McGDA; NatCAB 13; NewYHSD; REnAW; WhAm 1; WhAmArt 85*

Kekkonen, Urho Kaleva
Finnish. Political Leader
Pres. of Finland, 1956-82, known for skilled neutrality, friendship with USSR.
b. Aug 3, 1900 in Pielavesi, Finland
d. Aug 31, 1986 in Helsinki, Finland
Source: *BioIn 2, 5, 6, 9, 10, 11, 12, 13; ConNews 86-4; CurBio 50, 86; IntWW 74, 75, 76, 77, 78, 79, 80, 81, 82, 83; IntYB 78, 79, 80, 81, 82; NewYTBS 75, 86; WhoGov 72; WhoWor 74, 76, 78, 80, 82*

Kell, George (Clyde)
American. Baseball Player, Sportscaster
Third baseman, 1943-57; won AL batting title, 1949; Hall of Fame, 1983; TV, radio broadcaster for Detroit Tigers, 1959-96.
b. Aug 23, 1922 in Swifton, Arkansas
Source: *Ballpl 90; BiDAmSp BB; BioIn 2, 3, 4, 5, 8, 14, 15, 17; LegTOT; WhoAm 84; WhoProB 73*

Kell, Reginald George
English. Musician
Principal clarinetist, British Orchestras, 1930s-40s; in US chamber music ensembles, 1950s.
b. 1918 in Newark, England
Source: *Baker 84; NewGrDM 80; WhoMus 72*

Kell, Vernon, Sir
English. Government Official
First director of MI 5, 1909-40, British equivalent of FBI.
b. 1873 in Yarmouth, England
d. 1942
Source: *BioIn 8; HisEWW; SpyCS*

Kelland, Clarence Budington
American. Author
Noted for stories about Scattergood Baines, 1920s-40s.
b. Jul 11, 1881 in Portland, Michigan
d. Feb 18, 1964 in Scottsdale, Arizona
Source: *AmAu&B; AmNov; BenetAL 91; BioIn 1, 2, 4, 6, 9; ConAu 89; DcAmB S7; OxCAmL 65, 83, 95; REn; REnAL; TwCA, SUP; TwCCr&M 80; WhAm 4; WhNAA*

Kellaway, Cecil
American. Actor
Oscar nominee: *The Luck of the Irish,* 1948; *Guess Who's Coming to Dinner,* 1967.
b. Aug 22, 1893 in Cape Town, South Africa
d. Feb 28, 1973 in Los Angeles, California
Source: *BioIn 9; EncAFC; FilmEn; FilmgC; ForYSC; MovMk; NewYTBE 73; ObitOF 79; Vers A; WhoHol B; WhScrn 77, 83; WorAl*

Kelleher, Herb(ert David)
American. Business Executive
CEO of Southwest Airlines Co., 1967—.
b. Mar 12, 1931 in Camden, New Jersey
Source: *News 95, 95-1; St&PR 84, 87, 91, 93, 96, 97; WhoAm 80, 82, 84, 88, 90, 92, 94, 95, 96, 97; WhoAmL 78, 79; WhoFI 89, 92, 94, 96; WhoScEn 96; WhoSSW 75, 76, 78, 80, 86, 88, 91, 93, 95, 97; WhoWor 80, 95*

Kellems, Vivien
American. Business Executive
Pres., Kellems Co., producer of metal clips, 1928-62; known for disputes with federal govt.
b. Jun 7, 1896 in Des Moines, Iowa
d. Jan 25, 1975 in Los Angeles, California
Source: *BioIn 1, 2, 3, 10; CurBio 48, 75, 75N; InSci; InWom, SUP; NewYTBS 75; WhAm 6; WhoAmW 58, 64*

Keller, Arthur C
American. Inventor
Invention of moving-coil playback stylus made hi-fi records possible.
b. Aug 18, 1901 in New York, New York
d. Aug 25, 1983 in Bronxville, New York
Source: *AmMWSc 79; BioIn 13, 14; LElec; NewYTBS 83; WhoEng 80, 88*

Keller, George Matthew
American. Business Executive
Chairman, Chevron Corp., 1981-88.
b. Dec 3, 1923 in Kansas City, Missouri
Source: *BioIn 13; IntWW 83; St&PR 87; WhoAm 76, 78, 80, 82, 84, 88, 90, 92, 94, 95, 96, 97; WhoFI 75, 81, 83, 85, 87, 89; WhoScEn 96; WhoWest 76, 78, 80, 82, 84, 87, 89, 92, 94; WhoWor 84, 87, 89*

Keller, Gottfried
Swiss. Author
Writer of German-speaking Swiss; short stories of Swiss provincial life included in *Seven Legends,* 1872.
b. Jul 19, 1819 in Zurich, Switzerland
d. Jul 16, 1890 in Kilchberg, Switzerland
Source: *BbD; Benet 87, 96; BiD&SB; BioIn 1, 3, 4, 5, 7, 8, 19; CasWL; ChhPo S2; ClDMEL 47; CyWA 58; DcArts; DcEuL; DcLB 129; Dis&D; EuAu; EuWr 6; EvEuW; GrFLW; LinLib L; McGEWB; NewCBEL; NewEOp 71; NewGrDO; NinCLC 2; Novels; OxCGer 76, 86; PenC EUR; RAdv 14, 13-2; REn; RfGShF; RfGWoL 95; WhDW*

Keller, Helen Adams
American. Author, Lecturer
How she learned to speak, write despite being blind, deaf told in *The Miracle Worker,* 1962.
b. Jun 27, 1880 in Tuscumbia, Alabama
d. Jun 1, 1968 in Westport, Connecticut

Source: *AmAu&B; ApCAB X; Benet 96; ConAu 89, 101; CurBio 42, 68; DcLEL; EncAB-A 6; EncWHA; HarEnUS; HerW; LngCTC; McGEWB; NatCAB 15; OxCAmL 65; REn; REnAL; WhAm 5; WhDW; WhNAA; WhoAmW 58, 61, 64, 66, 68; WomWWA 14; WorAl*

Keller, Marthe
Swiss. Actor
Films include *Marathon Man; Bobby Deerfield; Fedora.*
b. Jan 28, 1945 in Basel, Switzerland
Source: *FilmAG WE; FilmEn; HalFC 80, 84, 88; IntMPA 80, 86, 96; LegTOT; NewYTBS 77; VarWW 85; WhoAm 80, 82, 84, 86, 88; WhoEnt 92; WhoHol 92, A*

Kellerman, Annette
"The Diving Venus"; "The Million Dollar Mermaid"
Australian. Swimmer, Actor
Introduced the one-piece bathing suit; Esther Williams portrayed her in *Million Dollar Mermaid,* 1952.
b. Jul 6, 1888 in Sydney, Australia
d. Oct 30, 1975 in Southport, Australia
Source: *BioIn 6, 8, 10; Film 2; FilmgC; HalFC 80, 84, 88; InWom, SUP; PseudN 82; TwYS; What 2; WhScrn 77, 83; WomFir*

Kellerman, Sally Claire
American. Actor
Oscar nominee for role of Hot Lips Houlihan in film *M*A*S*H,* 1970.
b. Jun 2, 1937 in Long Beach, California
Source: *BioIn 12; ConTFT 5; FilmgC; HalFC 84; IntMPA 86; MovMk; NewYTBS 80; VarWW 85; WhoAm 74, 76, 78, 80, 82, 84, 86, 88, 90, 92, 94, 95, 96, 97; WhoAmW 83, 85, 87, 89, 91, 93, 95, 97; WhoEnt 92; WhoHol A; WhoWest 82, 84; WhoWor 84; WorAl*

Kelley, Clarence Marion
American. Government Official
First permanent FBI director since death of J Edgar Hoover, 1973-78.
b. Oct 24, 1911 in Kansas City, Missouri
Source: *BioIn 9, 10, 11, 12; BioNews 74; BlueB 76; CopCroC; CurBio 74; IntWW 82; IntYB 81, 82; NewYTBE 73; WhoAm 74, 76, 78, 97; WhoAmL 83, 94, 96; WhoAmP 73, 75, 77, 79; WhoGov 75, 77; WhoSSW 76; WhoWor 95, 96*

Kelley, DeForrest
American. Actor
Played Dr. McCoy in TV series, film *Star Trek,* 1967-69.
b. Jan 20, 1920 in Atlanta, Georgia
Source: *BioIn 15; ConTFT 3; Film 2; FilmgC; HalFC 80, 84; IntMPA 86; MotPP; VarWW 85; WhoHol A*

Kelley, Edgar Stillman
American. Composer
Wrote "Alice in Wonderland" suite, 1919; "Gulliver" symphony, 1936.
b. Apr 14, 1857 in Sparta, Wisconsin
d. Nov 12, 1944 in New York, New York
Source: *AmComp; AmLY; ApCAB X; ASCAP 66, 80; Baker 78, 84, 92; BiDAmM; BioIn 1; CurBio 45; DcAmB S3; DcNAA; LinLib S; NatCAB 11; NewAmDM; NewGrDA 86; NewGrDM 80; OhA&B; OxCAmT 84; REnAL; TwCBDA; WhAm 2*

Kelley, Frank Joseph
American. Government Official
Dem. attorney general of MI, 1962—.
b. Dec 31, 1924 in Detroit, Michigan
Source: *BioIn 9; WhoMW 74, 78, 80, 82, 84, 86, 88, 90, 92, 93, 96*

Kelley, Joe
[Joseph James Kelley]
American. Baseball Player
Outfielder, 1891-1908; had .319 lifetime batting average; Hall of Fame, 1971.
b. Dec 9, 1871 in Cambridge, Massachusetts
d. Aug 14, 1943 in Baltimore, Maryland
Source: *Ballpl 90; BiDAmSp BB; BioIn 3, 14, 15; WhoProB 73; WhoSpor*

Kelley, Kitty
American. Author
Wrote tell-all biographies on Jacqueline Onassis, Nancy Reagan and Frank Sinatra.
b. Apr 4, 1942 in Spokane, Washington
Source: *BioIn 11, 16; ConAu 27NR, 81; CurBio 92; LegTOT; WhoAm 80; WhoWrEP 92, 95*

Kelley, Larry
[Lawrence M Kelley]
American. Football Player
All-America end, Yale, 1934-36; won Heisman Trophy, 1936.
b. May 30, 1915 in Conneaut, Ohio
Source: *BioIn 14; WhoFtbl 74; WhoSpor*

Kelley, Sheila
American. Actor
Plays in TV drama "L.A. Law."
Source: *WhoHol 92; WhoSSW 86*

Kellin, Mike
[Myron Kellin]
American. Actor
Won 1976 Obie for *American Buffalo.*
b. Apr 26, 1922 in Hartford, Connecticut
d. Aug 26, 1983 in Nyack, New York
Source: *ASCAP 80; BiE&WWA; BioIn 13; ForYSC; HalFC 80, 84, 88; NewYTBS 83; NotNAT; PseudN 82; VarWW 85; WhAm 8; WhoAm 74, 76, 78, 80, 82; WhoHol A; WhoThe 81*

Kellner, Jamie
American. TV Executive
Pres., CEO, Fox Broadcasting Co., 1985-93, responsible for shows "The Simpsons;" "Beverly Hills 90210."
b. 1948?
Source: *WhoEnt 92*

Kellogg, Clara Louise
American. Opera Singer, Manager
Soprano who pioneered singing operas in English.
b. Jul 12, 1842 in Sumterville, South Carolina
d. May 13, 1916 in New Haven, Connecticut
Source: *AmBi; AmWom; ApCAB; DcAmB; Drake; HarEnUS; NotAW; TwCBDA; WhAm 1; WomFir; WomWWA 14*

Kellogg, Frank Billings
American. Statesman, Diplomat
Won Nobel Peace Prize, 1929, for negotiating Kellogg-Briand Pact to ban war.
b. Dec 22, 1856 in Potsdam, New York
d. Dec 21, 1937 in Saint Paul, Minnesota
Source: *AmBi; AmPeW; AmPolLe; ApCAB X; BiDInt; BiDrAC; BiDrUSC 89; BiDrUSE 71, 89; BioIn 4, 6, 7, 9, 10, 11, 15, 16; DcAmB S2; DcAmDH 80, 89; EncAB-A 11; EncAB-H 1974, 1996; FacFETw; LinLib S; McGEWB; NatCAB 12, 28; OxCAmH; OxCLaw; WebAB 74, 79; WebBD 83; WhAm 1; WhAmP; WhoNob, 90, 95; WorAl*

Kellogg, John Harvey
American. Surgeon, Inventor
Developed grain cereal flakes, late 1800s; brother of Will.
b. Feb 26, 1852 in Tyrone, New York
d. Dec 14, 1943 in Battle Creek, Michigan
Source: *Alli SUP; AmRef; AmSocL; ApCAB X; BioIn 2, 4, 9, 12, 15, 19, 21; CurBio 44; DcAmAu; DcAmB S3; DcAmMeB 84; DcAmTB; DcNAA; InSci; NatCAB 35; NewAgE 90; ObitOF 79; TwCBDA; WhAm 2, 2C; WorAl; WorAlBi*

Kellogg, Will Keith
American. Businessman
Started Battle Creek Toasted Corn Flake Co., 1906; later became W K Kellogg Co.
b. Apr 7, 1860 in Battle Creek, Michigan
d. Oct 6, 1951 in Battle Creek, Michigan
Source: *BiDAmBL 83; BioIn 2, 4, 6, 7, 21; DcAmB S5; EncAB-H 1996; FacFETw; LegTOT; NatCAB 63; NewAgE 90; WebAB 74, 79; WhAm 3; WorAl; WorAlBi*

Kelly, Bruce
American. Architect
Landscape architect; created Strawberry Fields in Central Park, 1985.
d. Jan 21, 1993 in New York, New York
Source: *BioIn 16; NewYTBS 93*

Kelly, Dan
American. Sportscaster
Hockey broadcaster; the voice of the St. Louis Blues, 1968-89; helped popularize the sport in the US.
b. 1937? in Ottawa, Ontario, Canada
d. Feb 10, 1989 in Missouri

Kelly, Ellsworth
American. Artist
Painter, sculptor known for irregular geometric forms in bright colors on huge canvases.
b. May 31, 1923 in Newburgh, New York
Source: *AmArt; Benet 87; BioIn 4, 5, 6, 7, 8, 9, 10, 12, 13, 14, 15, 17, 18, 20; BriEAA; ConArt 77, 83, 89, 96; CurBio 70; DcAmArt; DcCAA 71, 77, 88, 94; DcCAr 81; DcTwCCu 1; FacFETw; IntWW 91, 93; LegTOT; McGDA; McGEWB; News 92, 92-1; NewYTBS 80; OxCTwCA; OxDcArt; PhDcTCA 77; PrintW 83, 85; WebAB 74, 79; WhoAm 74, 76, 78, 80, 82, 84, 86, 88, 90, 92, 94, 95, 96, 97; WhoAmA 73, 76, 78, 80, 82, 84, 86, 89, 91, 93; WhoWor 74; WorAlBi; WorArt 1950*

Kelly, Emmett Lee
"Weary Willie"
American. Clown
Created character of "Weary Willie," 1931.
b. Dec 9, 1898 in Sedan, Kansas
d. Mar 28, 1979 in Sarasota, Florida
Source: *ConAu 85; CurBio 54; FilmgC; WebAB 74; WhoAm 74; WhoHol A*

Kelly, Gene
[Eugene Curran Kelly]
American. Dancer, Actor
Starred in *An American in Paris,* 1951; *Singing in the Rain,* 1952; known for energetic, innovative style; also directed, choreographed many films.
b. Aug 23, 1912 in Pittsburgh, Pennsylvania
d. Feb 2, 1996 in Beverly Hills, California
Source: *BiDAmM; BiDD; BiDFilm, 81, 94; BiE&WWA; BioIn 1, 2, 3, 4, 5, 6, 8, 9, 10, 11, 12, 14, 16, 17, 18, 19, 20, 21; BkPepl; BlueB 76; CelR, 90; CmMov; CmpEPM; CnOxB; ConTFT 3; CurBio 45, 77, 96N; DancEn 78; DcArts; DcTwCCu 1; EncAFC; EncMT; Ent; FacFETw; FilmEn; FilmgC; ForYSC; GangFlm; HalFC 80, 84, 88; IlWWHD 1A; IntDcF 1-3, 2-3; IntMPA 75, 76, 77, 78, 79, 80, 81, 82, 84, 86, 88, 92, 94, 96; LegTOT; MGM; MiSFD 9; MotPP; MovMk; NewAmDM; NewGrDA 86; News 96, 96-3; NewYTBS 27; NotNAT, A; OxCFilm; OxCPMus; PenEncP; PlP&P; VarWW 85; WhDW; WhoAm 86; WhoHol 92, A; WhThe; WorAlBi; WorEFlm; WorFDir 2*

Kelly, George Edward
American. Dramatist
Wrote 1925 Pulitzer-winner *Craig's Wife.*
b. Jan 6, 1887 in Philadelphia, Pennsylvania
d. Jun 18, 1974 in Bryn Mawr, Pennsylvania
Source: *AmAu&B; AuNews 1; BiE&WWA; CnDAL; CnMD; ConAmA; ConAmL; ConAu 49; ConDr 73; DcLEL; LngCTC; McGEWD 72; ModAL; OxCAmL 65; REnAL; TwCA; WhAm 6*

Kelly, George Lange
"Highpockets"
American. Baseball Player
First baseman, early 1900s; led NL in home runs once, RBIs twice; Hall of Fame, 1973.
b. Sep 10, 1895 in San Francisco, California
d. Oct 13, 1984 in San Francisco, California
Source: *BiDAmSp BB; WhoProB 73*

Kelly, Grace Patricia
[Princess Grace of Monaco; Princess Grace Grimaldi]
American. Actor, Princess
Won 1954 Oscar for *The Country Girl;* married Prince Rainier, 1956.
b. Nov 12, 1929 in Philadelphia, Pennsylvania
d. Sep 14, 1982 in Monte Carlo, Monaco
Source: *AmPS; AnObit 1982; BiDFilm; BiE&WWA; BioNews 74; BkPepl; ConAu 107; CurBio 55, 77, 82; GoodHs; HerW; IntMPA 82; IntWW 82; InWom; LibW; WebAB 74, 79; WhoAm 82; WorAl*

Kelly, Jack
American. Actor
Played in TV series "Maverick," 1957-62.
b. Sep 16, 1927 in Astoria, New York
d. Nov 8, 1992 in Huntington Beach, California
Source: *AnObit 1985; BioIn 4, 18; FilmEn; FilmgC; ForYSC; HalFC 80, 84, 88; LegTOT; VarWW 85; WhoAmP 87, 89, 91, 93; WhoHol 92, A*

Kelly, Jim
[James Edward Kelly]
American. Football Player
Quarterback, USFL Houston, 1984-85; signed with NFL Buffalo, 1986-97; quarterbacked losing Bills in Super Bowls XXV-XXVIII, 1990-93.
b. Feb 14, 1960 in Pittsburgh, Pennsylvania
Source: *BioIn 13; CurBio 92; FootReg 87; News 91; NewYTBS 86; WhoAm 94, 95, 96, 97; WhoE 95; WhoSpor; WhoWor 95, 96*

Kelly, John Brenden
American. Yachtsman
Father of Princess Grace; won gold medals in sculling, 1920, 1924 Olympics.
b. Oct 4, 1890 in Philadelphia, Pennsylvania
d. Jun 20, 1960 in Philadelphia, Pennsylvania
Source: *DcAmB S6; ObitOF 79*

Kelly, John Brenden, Jr.
American. Olympic Official
Brother of Princess Grace; sculling champion, pres., US Olympic Committee, 1984-85.
b. May 24, 1927 in Philadelphia, Pennsylvania
d. Mar 2, 1985 in Philadelphia, Pennsylvania
Source: *BioIn 12; CurBio 71, 85; WhAm 8; WhoAm 76, 78, 80, 82, 84; WhoAmP 73, 75, 77, 79; WhoE 74, 75*

Kelly, King
[Michael Joseph Kelly]
American. Baseball Player
Outfielder-catcher, 1878-93; credited with originating head-first slide, hit-and-run play; Hall of Fame, 1945.
b. Dec 31, 1857 in Lansingburgh, New York
d. Nov 8, 1894 in Boston, Massachusetts
Source: *Ballpl 90; BiDAmSp BB; BioIn 3, 7, 10, 12, 13; LegTOT; WhoProB 73; WhoSpor*

Kelly, Leontine Turpeau Current
American. Religious Leader
Methodist bishop; first African-American woman elected to the bishopric of a major US denomination.
b. Mar 5, 1920 in Washington, District of Columbia
Source: *BioIn 14; NotBlAW 1; PeoHis; WhoAm 90; WhoAmW 91; WhoBlA 92; WhoRel 92; WhoWest 92*

Kelly, Machine Gun
[George R Kelly; E W Moore; J C Tichenor]
American. Criminal
Public Enemy Number One, 1930s; died serving life term for 1933 kidnapping of Charles F. Urschel.
b. Jul 17, 1895 in Tennessee
d. Jul 17, 1954 in Leavenworth, Kansas
Source: *BioIn 2, 3; DcAmB S5; DrInf; ObitOF 79; WorAl*

Kelly, Michael
Irish. Opera Singer
Leading London tenor, 1787-1811.
b. Dec 25, 1762 in Dublin, Ireland
d. Oct 9, 1826 in Margate, England
Source: *Alli; Baker 78, 84, 92; BiDIrW; BioIn 1, 2, 4, 8, 9, 10, 21; CmOp; DcBiPP; DcIrW 2; IntDcOp; MetOEnc; MusMk; NewAmDM; NewEOp 71; NewGrDM 80; NewGrDO; NewOxM; OxCIri; OxCMus; OxDcOp; PenDiMP*

Kelly, Nancy
American. Actor
Won Tony for *The Bad Seed,* 1955; also played the same role in film, 1956.
b. Mar 25, 1921 in Lowell, Massachusetts
d. Jan 2, 1995 in Bel Air, California
Source: *BiE&WWA; BioIn 3, 4, 20, 21; CurBio 55, 95N; Film 2; FilmEn; FilmgC; ForYSC; HalFC 80, 84, 88; IntMPA 75, 76, 77, 78, 79, 80, 81, 82, 84, 86, 88, 92, 94; InWom, SUP; LegTOT; MotPP; MovMk; NotNAT; ThFT; VarWW 85; WhoAm 74, 76; WhoAmW 58, 66, 68, 70, 72, 74; WhoHol 92, A; WhoThe 72, 77, 81*

Kelly, Ned
[Edward Kelly]
Australian. Outlaw
Folk-hero, bankrobber, killer; hanged at 26.
b. Jun 1855 in Beveridge, Australia
d. Nov 11, 1880 in Melbourne, Australia
Source: *DrInf; OxCAusL; WhDW*

Kelly, Patrick
American. Fashion Designer
Known for "happy clothes," especially black tight tube minidresses; had international success in women's ready-to-wear, 1985; died of AIDS.
b. Sep 24, 1954 in Vicksburg, Mississippi
d. Jan 1, 1990 in Paris, France
Source: *ConBlB 3; ConFash; CurBio 89, 90, 90N; News 90, 90-2; NewYTBS 90; WhoBlA 92N*

Kelly, Patsy
[Sarah Veronica Rose Kelly]
American. Comedian
In films, 1930s-40s; won Tony for Broadway revival: *No, No, Nanette,* 1971.
b. Jan 12, 1910 in New York, New York
d. Sep 24, 1981 in Hollywood, California
Source: *AnObit 1981; BioIn 12; CelR; EncAFC; EncMT; FilmEn; FilmgC; ForYSC; Funs; HalFC 80, 84, 88; InWom SUP; JoeFr; LegTOT; MotPP; MovMk; PlP&P; PseudN 82; QDrFCA 92; ThFT; WhAm 8; What 1; WhoAm 76, 78, 80; WhoHol A; WhoThe 77, 81; WhScrn 83; WorAl*

Kelly, Paul
American. Actor
Child star, supporting actor, 1908-56, who served two years in prison for manslaughter, 1920s.
b. Aug 9, 1899 in New York, New York
d. Nov 6, 1956 in Los Angeles, California
Source: *BioIn 4, 6, 11; Film 1, 2; FilmEn; FilmgC; ForYSC; GangFlm; HalFC 80, 84, 88; HolP 30; MotPP; MovMk; NatCAB 44; NotNAT B; OxCAmT 84; TwYS; WhAm 3; WhoHol B; WhScrn 74, 77, 83; WhThe*

Kelly, Petra (Karin)
German. Politician
Spokesman, strategist for W German political party, the "Greens."
b. Nov 29, 1947 in Gunzberg, Germany
d. Oct 19, 1992 in Bonn, Germany
Source: *AnObit 1992; BioIn 13; ContDcW 89; CurBio 84, 93N; EncWB; IntWW 91; InWom SUP; LegTOT; NewYTBS 83, 92; PolLCWE; RadHan; WhAm 10; WhoWor 87, 89; WomFir*

Kelly, Red
[Leonard Patrick Kelly]
Canadian. Hockey Player
Center, Detroit, 1947-60, Toronto, 1960-67; won Norris Trophy, 1954, Lady Byng Trophy, four times; Hall of Fame, 1969.
b. Jul 9, 1927 in Simcoe, Ontario, Canada
Source: *BioIn 6, 9, 10; HocEn; NewGrDJ 88, 94; WhoE 74; WhoHcky 73; WhoSpor*

Kelly, Sharon Pratt
American. Politician
First woman Dem. mayor of Washington, DC, 1990-94.
b. Jan 30, 1944 in Washington, District of Columbia
Source: *BlkWAm; CurBio 92; NotBlAW 1; WhoAfA 96; WhoAm 92, 94, 95; WhoAmP 93, 95; WhoAmW 93, 95; WhoBlA 94; WhoE 93, 95; WomStre*

Kelly, Shipwreck
[Alvin A Kelly]
American. Eccentric
Spent total of 20,163 hrs. sitting atop flagpoles.
b. May 13, 1893
d. Oct 11, 1952 in New York, New York
Source: *BioIn 3; WebAB 74, 79*

Kelly, Stephen Eugene
American. Publisher
Publisher, *Saturday Evening Post; Holiday: McCalls* mags., 1960s-70s.
b. May 13, 1919 in New York, New York
d. Apr 6, 1978 in New York, New York
Source: *BioIn 13; ConAu 104, 110; NatCAB 61; NewYTBS 78; WhAm 7; WhoAm 76, 78*

Kelly, Thomas
American. Army Officer
Three-star general who handled Pentagon press corps during Panama, 1989, and Persian Gulf War, 1991; retired, 1991.
b. Nov 16, 1932 in Philadelphia, Pennsylvania

Kelly, Tom
[Jay Thomas Kelly]
American. Baseball Manager
Manager, Minnesota Twins, 1987—; won World Series twice, 1987, 1991.
b. Aug 15, 1950 in Graceville, Minnesota
Source: *Ballpl 90; BioIn 15, 18, 19, 21; WhoAm 88, 92, 94, 95, 96, 97; WhoMW 88, 90, 92, 93, 96*

Kelly, Walt(er Crawford)
American. Cartoonist
Created comic strip "Pogo," 1943, nationally syndicated, 1949.
b. Aug 25, 1913 in Philadelphia, Pennsylvania
d. Oct 18, 1973 in Hollywood, California
Source: *AmAu&B; ASCAP 66; BenetAL 91; BioIn 1, 2, 3, 4, 6, 10, 12; CelR; ChhPo S1; ConAu 45, 73; CurBio 56, 73, 73N; DcAmB S9; EncACom; EncAJ; EncTwCJ; IlsBYP; LegTOT; LinLib L; NewYTBE 73; REnAL; SmATA 18; WebAB 74, 79; WhAm 6; WhoAm 74; WorECom*

Kelly, Walter C
"The Virginia Judge"
American. Actor
Uncle of Grace Kelly; nickname comes from stage, film role.
b. Oct 29, 1873 in Mineville, New York
d. Jan 6, 1939 in Philadelphia, Pennsylvania
Source: *ObitOF 79; WhoHol B; WhScrn 74, 77*

Kelly, William
American. Inventor
Developed converter for changing iron into steel, 1857.
b. Aug 21, 1811 in Pittsburgh, Pennsylvania
d. Feb 11, 1888 in Louisville, Kentucky
Source: *AmBi; ApCAB; BioIn 1, 11; DcAmB; EncAB-H 1974, 1996; EncABHB 3; InSci; McGEWB; NatCAB 13; OxCAmH; TwCBDA; WebAB 74, 79; WhAm HS; WorInv*

Kelman, Charles David
American. Surgeon
Pioneer in cataract surgery who developed Kelman lenses inserted in eye following surgery.
b. May 23, 1930 in New York, New York
Source: *ConAu 110; CurBio 84; WhoAm 80; WhoWor 80*

Kelman, James
Scottish. Author
Won Booker Prize for Fiction for *How Late It Was, How Late,* 1994.
b. Jun 9, 1946 in Glasgow, Scotland
Source: *ConAu 148; ConLC 58, 86; ConNov 91, 96; DcArts; OxCEng 95; RGTwCWr*

Kelsen, Hans
Czech. Educator, Government Official
Known for doctrine on pure law, 1911; drafted Austrian constitution, 1920; professor, U of CA, 1942-52.
b. Oct 11, 1881 in Prague, Austria-Hungary
d. Apr 19, 1973 in Berkeley, California
Source: *AmPeW; BiDInt; BioIn 4, 9, 10, 14; ConAu 115; CurBio 57, 73, 73N; EncTR 91; OxCLaw; OxCPhil; ThTwC 87; WebAB 74, 79; WhAm 5*

Kelsey, Alice Geer
American. Author
Children's books include *The Thirty Gilt Pennies; Land of the Morning,* 1968.
b. Sep 21, 1896 in Danvers, Massachusetts
Source: *AnCL; Au&Wr 71; AuBYP 2; ConAu 5R; ForWC 70; IntAu&W 76, 77; MorJA; SmATA 1; WhoAmW 58, 61; WrDr 76, 80, 82, 84*

Kelsey, Linda
American. Actor
Played Billie on TV series "Lou Grant," 1977-82.

b. Jul 28, 1946 in Minneapolis, Minnesota
Source: *BioIn 12; ConTFT 7; IntMPA 92, 94, 96; VarWW 85; WhoAm 82; WhoHol 92*

Kelton, Pert
American. Actor
Stage, film comedienne who played stool pigeon in *Mary Burns-Fugitive,* 1935; played the first Alice Kramden on "The Honeymooners," when it was a comedy sketch on TV's "Cavalcade of Stars."
b. Oct 14, 1907 in Great Falls, Montana
d. Oct 30, 1968 in Ridgewood, New Jersey
Source: *BiE&WWA; BioIn 8, 11; EncAFC; EncVaud; Film 2; FilmEn; FilmgC; ForYSC; HalFC 80, 84, 88; MovMk; NotNAT B; RadStar; ThFT; WhoHol B; WhScrn 74, 77, 83*

Kelvin, William Thomson, Baron
Irish. Physicist, Mathematician
Evolved theory of electric oscillation which formed basis of wireless telegraphy.
b. Jun 26, 1824 in Belfast, Northern Ireland
d. Dec 17, 1907 in Ayrshire, Scotland
Source: *Alli, SUP; AsBiEn; BbD; BiD&SB; BiESc; BioIn 1, 2, 3, 4, 5, 6, 7, 8, 10, 11, 13, 14, 15, 16, 18, 20; BritAu 19; DcIrB 78, 88; Dis&D; InSci; LarDcSc; LinLib L; McGEWB; NewC; NewCBEL; NewCol 75; OxCEng 67; WhDW; WorAl; WorAlBi*

Kemble, Charles
English. Actor
Acted with daughter, Fanny, 1829-34; manager, Covent Garden, 1822-40; first to use historical sets, authentic costumes; noted for comic roles.
b. Nov 25, 1775 in Brecknock, Wales
d. Nov 12, 1854 in London, England
Source: *Alli, SUP; ApCAB; BiDLA; BioIn 8; CamGWoT; CelCen; DcBiPP; DcEuL; DcNaB; EncWT; FamA&A; IntDcT 3; LinLib L, S; NewC; NewCBEL; NotNAT A, B; OxCAmT 84; OxCEng 67, 85, 95; OxCLiW 86; OxCThe 67, 83; PlP&P; REn*

Kemble, Edward W(indsor)
American. Cartoonist, Illustrator
Political cartoonist, book illustrator; noted for sensitive Negro cartoons.
b. Jan 18, 1861 in Sacramento, California
d. Sep 19, 1933 in Ridgefield, Connecticut
Source: *AmBi; ArtsAmW 1; BenetAL 91; BioIn 3; ChhPo; DcBrBI; DcNAA; IlBEAAW; IlrAm 1880, A; OxCAmL 65; REnAL; TwCBDA; WhAm 1*

Kemble, Fanny
[Frances Anne Kemble]
English. Actor, Author
From English stage family; wrote *Journal,* 1835; noted for Sheridan, Shakespearian roles.
b. Nov 27, 1809 in London, England
d. Jan 15, 1893 in London, England
Source: *Alli, SUP; AmAu; AmAu&B; AmBi; AmWomWr; ApCAB; ArtclWW 2; BenetAL 91; BiD&SB; BiDSA; BioIn 1, 2, 3, 4, 5, 6, 7, 8, 9, 10, 11, 12, 14, 15, 16, 18, 19; BritAu 19; CamGLE; CamGWoT; ChhPo, S2; ContDcW 89; DcAmB; DcArts; DcEnA; DcEnL; DcEuL; DcLB 32; DcLEL; DcNaB S1; EncBrWW; EncSoH; EncWT; Ent; FamA&A; FemiCLE; GrLiveH; HanAmWH; IntDcT 3; IntDcWB; InWom, SUP; LegTOT; LibW; LinLib L, S; McGEWB; NewC; NewCBEL; NinCLC 18; NotAW; NotNAT A, B; OxCAmH; OxCAmL 65, 83, 95; OxCAmT 84; OxCEng 67, 85, 95; OxCThe 67, 83; PenNWW A; REnAL; VicBrit; WebAB 74, 79; WhAm HS*

Kemble, John Philip
English. Actor
Brother of Charles; manager, Covent Gardens, 1803-17; introduced live animals to stage; Shakespearean actor.
b. Feb 1, 1757 in Prescott, England
d. Feb 26, 1823 in Lausanne, Switzerland
Source: *Alli; BiDLA; BioIn 2, 3, 4, 8, 9, 10, 12, 13; BlmGEL; CamGWoT; CelCen; CnThe; DcBiPP; DcEuL; DcNaB; EncWT; Ent; IntDcT 3; LinLib L, S; NewC; NewCBEL; NewCol 75; NotNAT A, B; OxCEng 67, 85, 95; OxCThe 67, 83; PlP&P*

Kemelman, Harry
American. Author
Won Edgar for *Friday the Rabbi Slept Late,* 1965, first of his popular detective series on Rabbi Small.
b. Nov 24, 1908 in Boston, Massachusetts
d. Dec 15, 1996 in Marblehead, Massachusetts
Source: *AmAu&B; AuNews 1; AuSpks; BioIn 10, 11; ConAu 6NR, 9R; ConLC 2; CrtSuMy; DcLB 28; DcLEL 1940; EncMys; IntAu&W 76, 77, 82, 86, 89, 91; LegTOT; Novels; TwCCr&M 80, 85, 91; WhoAm 74, 76, 78, 80, 82, 84, 86, 88, 90, 92, 94, 95, 96, 97; WhoUSWr 88; WhoWorJ 72, 78; WhoWrEP 89, 92; WorAl; WorAlBi; WorAu 1970; WrDr 76, 82, 84, 86, 88, 90, 92, 94, 96*

Kemeny, John G(eorge)
American. Mathematician
Promoter of "new math."
b. May 31, 1926, Hungary
d. Dec 26, 1992 in Lebanon, New Hampshire
Source: *AmMWSc 73P, 76P, 79; Au&Wr 71; BioIn 5, 8, 9, 11, 12, 13; ConAu 46NR, 140; CurBio 93N; LEduc 74; NewYTBS 79; WhAm 11; WhoAm 74, 76, 78, 80, 82, 84, 86, 88, 90; WhoE 74, 75, 77, 79, 81, 85; WrDr 76, 94, 96*

Kemmis, Daniel (Orra)
American. Politician
Mayor of Missoula, MT, 1989-96; director, Center for the Rocky Mountain West, 1996—; dedicated to examining the democratic system; wrote *The Good City and the Good Life,* 1995.
b. Dec 5, 1945 in Fairview, Montana
Source: *CurBio 96; WhoAm 84, 86, 88, 90, 92, 94, 95, 96, 97; WhoAmP 75, 77, 79, 81, 83, 85; WhoWest 84, 96*

Kemp, Barry
American. Producer
Exec. producer of TV series "Newhart."
b. Dec 4, 1949 in Hannibal, Missouri
Source: *ConTFT 13; LesBEnT 92; WhoEnt 92*

Kemp, Harry (Hibbard)
"The Tramp Poet"
American. Author, Poet
His worldly travels were basis for poems, novels: *More Miles,* 1926.
b. Dec 15, 1883 in Youngstown, Ohio
d. Aug 6, 1960 in Provincetown, Massachusetts
Source: *AmAu&B; BenetAL 91; BioIn 5, 13, 15, 20; ChhPo, S2; ConAmL; ObitOF 79; OhA&B; OxCAmL 65, 83, 95; REn; REnAL; WhAm 4*

Kemp, Jack
[John French Kemp]
American. Politician, Football Player
Quarterback, 1957-70, mostly with Buffalo; Rep. con. from NY, 1970-88; secretary of Housing and Urban Development, 1989-92; vice presidential candidate, 1996.
b. Jul 13, 1935 in Los Angeles, California
Source: *BiDAmSp Sup; BiDrUSE 89; CelR 90; CngDr 74, 77, 79, 81, 83, 85, 87, 89, 91; ConAu 109; CurBio 80; EncWB; LegTOT; News 90; NewYTBS 85; WhoAm 84, 86; WhoAmP 73, 75, 77, 79, 85; WhoGov 72, 75, 77; WorAlBi*

Kemp, Jan
American. Educator
English professor; stirred academia with 1986 lawsuit against U of GA; claimed corruption in grading, treatment of athletes.
b. Mar 13, 1949 in Griffin, Georgia
Source: *BlmGWL; ConNews 87-2*

Kemp, Shawn
American. Basketball Player
Forward for Seattle Supersonics, 1989—.
b. Nov 26, 1969 in Elkhart, Indiana
Source: *BioIn 20, 21; News 95, 95-1*

Kemp, Steve(n F)
American. Baseball Player
Outfielder, 1977-86; benefitted from free agency, multi-year contracts of early 1980s; AL All-Star, 1979.
b. Aug 7, 1954 in San Angelo, Texas
Source: *Ballpl 90; BaseReg 86, 87; BioIn 10, 13*

Kempe, Rudolf
German. Conductor
Led London's Royal Philharmonic, 1961-75; conducted BBC Symphony from 1975.
b. Jun 14, 1910 in Niederpoyritz, Germany
d. May 11, 1976 in Zurich, Switzerland
Source: *Baker 78, 84, 92; BioIn 4, 8, 10, 11; BriBkM 80; CmOp; DcArts; FacFETw; IntDcOp; IntWW 74, 75, 76; MetOEnc; MusSN; NewAmDM; NewEOp 71; NewGrDM 80; NewGrDO; NewYTBS 76; ObitOF 79; OxCMus; OxDcOp; PenDiMP; WhAm 7; Who 74; WhoMus 72; WhoOp 76; WhoWor 74, 76*

Kemper, James S(cott)
American. Insurance Executive
Former head of Kemper Group, large fire, casualty co; founder, pres., Lumberman's Mutual Casualty, 1919-45.
b. Nov 18, 1886 in Van Wert, Ohio
d. Sep 17, 1981 in Chicago, Illinois
Source: *AnObit 1981; BioIn 3, 4, 7, 8, 12; CurBio 41, 81, 81N; NewYTBS 81; St&PR 75; WhAm 7; WhoAm 74, 76, 78, 80; WhoFI 74; WhoIns 75, 76, 77, 78, 79, 80, 81, 82, 84*

Kempff, (Wilhelm) Walter Friedrich
German. Pianist, Composer
Made US debut, 1964; epitomized old tradition of German pianism; considered major interpreter of Mozart, Beethoven, Schubert.
b. Nov 25, 1895 in Juterbog, Germany
d. May 23, 1991 in Positano, Italy
Source: *Baker 84; IntWW 74, 75, 76, 77, 78; IntWWM 77, 90; NewGrDM 80; Who 74, 82, 83, 85, 88, 90; WhoMus 72*

Kempner, Robert M(aximilian) W(asilii)
German. Lawyer
Chief counsel for US at Nuremberg Trials, 1945-46.
b. Oct 17, 1899
d. Aug 15, 1993 in Frankfurt, Germany
Source: *AmMWSc 73S, 78S; BioIn 2; CurBio 93N; WhoWorJ 72*

Kempson, Rachel
[Mrs. Michael Redgrave]
English. Actor
Films include *Jane Eyre,* 1971; mother of Vanessa, Lynn Redgrave.
b. May 28, 1910 in Dartmouth, England
Source: *CnThe; ConAu 130; ConTFT 7; FilmgC; HalFC 80, 84, 88; VarWW 85; Who 82, 83, 85, 88, 90, 92, 94; WhoAm 82, 84; WhoHol 92, A; WhoThe 72, 77, 81; WrDr 94, 96*

Kempthorne, Dirk Arthur
American. Politician
Rep. senator, ID, 1993—.
b. Oct 29, 1951 in San Diego, California
Source: *IntWW 93; WhoAm 88, 90, 92, 94, 95, 96, 97; WhoAmP 91; WhoWest 87, 89, 92, 94, 96*

Kemptner, Thomas
German. Hostage
Relief worker held hostage by Lebanese terrorists May 16, 1989-Jun 17, 1992.

Kempton, (James) Murray
American. Journalist
Columnist, reporter, *New York Post,* 1942-81; *New York Newsday,* 1981-97; won Pulitzer Prize, 1985.
b. Dec 16, 1917 in Baltimore, Maryland
d. May 5, 1997 in New York, New York
Source: *BioIn 6; WhoAm 97; WhoE 86*

Kendal, Felicity
English. Actor
Known for Shakespearean roles on British stage; in film *Henry VIII.*
b. Sep 25, 1946 in Olton, England
Source: *ConTFT 3, 14; IntWW 82, 83, 89, 91, 93; VarWW 85; Who 85; WhoAm 84; WhoHol 92; WhoThe 72, 77, 81; WhoWor 84, 87, 89, 91, 93, 95, 96, 97*

Kendal, Madge, Dame
English. Actor
Twenty-second child of an actor; played Shakespeare, Old English comedies with husband, William.
b. Mar 15, 1848 in Cleethorpes, England
d. Sep 14, 1935 in Chorley Wood, England
Source: *BioIn 2, 3, 4, 10; FamA&A; NewCol 75; NotNAT A, B; OxCThe 67; WhoStg 1908; WhThe*

Kendal, William Hunter
[William Hunter Grimston]
English. Actor
Acted with wife, Madge, 1869-1908; actor, manager, St. James Theater, 1879-88.
b. Dec 16, 1843 in London, England
d. Nov 6, 1917
Source: *DcNaB 1912; EncWT; NotNAT A, B; OxCThe 67, 83; PseudN 82; WhAm 1; WhoStg 1906, 1908; WhThe*

Kendall, Edward C(alvin)
American. Biochemist
Shared 1950 Nobel Prize for research in cortisone.
b. Mar 8, 1886 in South Norwalk, Connecticut
d. May 4, 1972 in Princeton, New Jersey
Source: *AmDec 1910; AmMWSc 73P; AsBiEn; BiESc; BioIn 2, 3, 4, 6, 9, 10, 11, 15, 20; CamDcSc; ConAu 111; CurBio 72; DcAmB S9; DcAmMeB, 84; DcScB S1; FacFETw; InSci; LarDcSc; McGEWB; McGMS 80; OxCMed 86; WebAB 74, 79; WebBD 83; WhAm 5; WhoNob, 90, 95; WorAl; WorScD*

Kendall, Henry Way
American. Physicist
Shared Nobel Prize in Physics, 1990, for breakthrough discoveries about the structure of matter; first to observe trace of quarks, subatomic particles.
b. Dec 9, 1926 in Boston, Massachusetts
Source: *AmMWSc 73P, 76P, 79, 82, 86, 89, 92, 95; BioIn 17, 18, 20; LarDcSc; WhoAm 92, 94, 95, 96, 97; WhoE 93, 95, 97; WhoFrS 84; WhoNob 90, 95; WhoScEn 94, 96; WhoWor 93, 95, 96, 97*

Kendall, Kay
[Justine McCarthy]
English. Actor
Married, Rex Harrison, 1957-59; starred in *Genevieve,* 1953.
b. 1926 in Hull, England
d. Sep 6, 1959 in London, England
Source: *BiDFilm, 94; CmMov; FilmEn; FilmgC; ForYSC; HalFC 80, 84, 88; MotPP; MovMk; NotNAT B; ObitT 1951; PseudN 82; WhoHol B; WhScrn 74, 77, 83; WorAl; WorEFlm*

Kendrew, John Cowdery, Sir
English. Scientist, Educator
Shared 1962 Nobel Prize in chemistry with M F Perutz; determined structure of myoglobin.
b. Mar 24, 1917 in Oxford, England
Source: *BiESc; BlueB 76; CurBio 63; IntWW 74, 75, 76, 77, 78, 79, 80, 81, 82, 83, 89; Who 85; WhoEIO 82; WhoNob, 95; WhoWor 78, 97*

Kendrick, Pearl Luella
American. Biologist
Developed standard DPT shot for diphtheria, whooping cough, tetanus.
b. Aug 24, 1890 in Wheaton, Illinois
d. Oct 8, 1980 in Grand Rapids, Michigan
Source: *AnObit 1980; BioIn 12; ContDcW 89; WhoAmW 58, 61, 64, 77; WomFir*

Kendricks, Eddie
[The Temptations]
American. Singer
Lead tenor, Temptations, 1961-71; known for hit "My Girl," 1965; successful solo career in rhythm and blues.
b. Dec 17, 1940 in Union Springs, Alabama
d. Oct 5, 1992 in Birmingham, Alabama
Source: *DrBlPA, 90; IlEncBM 82; News 93-2; RkOn 78; RolSEnR 83; WhoBlA 75, 80; WhoRocM 82*

Keniston, Kenneth
American. Psychologist
Author of *Radicals and Militants,* 1973; *All Our Children: The American Family Under Pressure,* 1977.

b. Jan 6, 1930 in Chicago, Illinois
Source: *AmAu&B; BioIn 9; ConAu 25R; WhoAm 74, 76, 78, 80, 82, 84, 97*

Kennan, George Frost
American. Historian, Diplomat
Ambassador to USSR, 1950s; won Pulitzers for *Russia Leaves the War,* 1956; *Memoirs,* 1968.
b. Feb 16, 1904 in Milwaukee, Wisconsin
Source: *AmAu&B; AmPeW; AmPolLe; Au&Wr 71; BioIn 1, 2, 3, 4, 5, 6, 7, 8, 9, 10, 11, 12, 13, 14, 15, 16, 17, 18, 19, 20; BlueB 76; ColdWar 2; ConAu 1R, 2NR, 39NR; CurBio 59; DcAmDH 80, 89; DcLEL 1940; DrAS 74H, 78H, 82H; EncAB-H 1974, 1996; EncAI&E; IntAu&W 77, 93; IntWW 74, 75, 76, 77, 78, 79, 80, 81, 82, 83, 89, 91, 93; OxCAmL 65; REnAL; WebAB 74, 79; Who 74, 82, 83, 85, 88, 90, 92, 94; WhoAm 74, 76, 78, 80, 82, 84, 86, 88, 90, 92, 94, 95, 96; WhoHol A; WhoJazz 72; WhoWor 74, 78; WorAl; WorAu 1950; WrDr 94, 96*

Kennedy, Adrienne
American. Dramatist
Off-Broadway plays include *The Owl Answers,* 1963.
b. Sep 13, 1931 in Pittsburgh, Pennsylvania
Source: *AmWomD; AmWomWr SUP; BenetAL 91; BioIn 10; BlkAmP; BlkAWP; BlkLC; BlkWr 1; BlmGWL; CamGWoT; ConAmD; ConAu 3BS, 20AS, 26NR, 103; ConBlAP 88; ConBlB 11; ConDr 73, 77, 82, 88; ConLC 66; ConTFT 13; CroCD; CrtSuDr; CyWA 89; DcLB 38; DcTwCCu 5; DramC 5; DrBlPA, 90; EncWT; FemiCLE; FemiWr; GrWomW; InB&W 80, 85; IntAu&W 91; InWom SUP; LivgBAA; MorBAP; NotNAT; NotWoAT; OxCAmL 95; OxCWoWr 95; SchCGBL; SelBAAf; SelBAAu; WhoAm 86; WhoBlA 85; WorAu 1970; WrDr 76, 80, 82, 84, 86, 88, 90, 92, 94, 96*

Kennedy, Anthony McLeod
American. Supreme Court Justice
Conservative Reagan appointee; succeeded retiring Lewis Powell, 1988.
b. Jul 23, 1936 in Sacramento, California
Source: *CurBio 88; NewYTBS 87; OxCSupC; SupCtJu; Who 90, 92, 94; WhoAm 86, 90, 92, 94, 95, 96, 97; WhoAmL 92, 94, 96; WhoAmP 89, 91, 93, 95; WhoE 91, 93; WhoWor 96*

Kennedy, Arthur
[John Arthur Kennedy]
American. Actor
Won Tony award for *Death of a Salesman,* 1949; films include *The Desperate Hours,* 1955, *The Glass Menagerie,* 1950.
b. Feb 17, 1914 in Worcester, Massachusetts
d. Jan 5, 1990 in Branford, Connecticut
Source: *AnObit 1990; BiDFilm, 81, 94; BiE&WWA; BioIn 3, 6, 10, 16, 17; CamGWoT; CmMov; ConTFT 3, 4, 10; FilmEn; FilmgC; ForYSC; GangFlm; HalFC 80, 84, 88; HolP 40; IntDcF 1-3, 2-3; IntMPA 75, 76, 77, 78, 79, 80, 81, 82, 84, 86, 88, 92; ItaFilm; LegTOT; MotPP; MovMk; NewYTBS 90; NotNAT; OxCAmT 84; PlP&P; VarWW 85; WhoAm 74, 76, 78, 80, 82; WhoHol A; WhoThe 72, 77, 81; WorAl; WorAlBi; WorEFlm*

Kennedy, Caroline Bouvier
[Mrs. Edwin Arthur Schlossberg]
American.
Daughter of John and Jacqueline Kennedy.
b. Nov 27, 1957 in New York, New York
Source: *BioNews 74; NewYTBE 70*

Kennedy, David Anthony
American.
Son of Robert and Ethel Kennedy; died of drug overdose.
b. 1955
d. Apr 25, 1984 in Palm Beach, Florida
Source: *BioIn 12, 13, 14; NewYTBS 84*

Kennedy, David M(atthew)
American. Government Official
Treasury secretary, 1969-71; ambassador to NATO, 1971-73.
b. Jul 21, 1905 in Randolph, Utah
d. May 1, 1996 in Salt Lake City, Utah
Source: *BiDrUSE 71; BioIn 5, 8, 9, 10, 12, 21; CurBio 69, 96N; IntWW 74, 75, 76, 77, 78, 79, 80, 81, 82, 83, 89, 91; IntYB 78, 79, 80, 81; PolProf NF; Who 74, 82, 83, 85, 88, 90, 92, 94; WhoAm 74; WhoAmP 73, 75, 77; WhoGov 72, 75; WhoSSW 73*

Kennedy, Edgar
American. Actor
Comedian in films since 1914, including *The Edgar Kennedy,* series, 1931-48.
b. Apr 26, 1890 in Monterey, California
d. Nov 9, 1948 in Woodland Hills, California
Source: *BioIn 1, 2; EncAFC; Film 1, 2; FilmEn; FilmgC; ForYSC; HalFC 80, 84, 88; MotPP; MovMk; NotNAT B; ObitOF 79; QDrFCA 92; TwYS; Vers A; WhoCom; WhoHol B; WhScrn 74, 77, 83*

Kennedy, Edward Moore
"Ted"
American. Politician
Dem. senator from MA, 1962—; brother of John and Robert Kennedy; involved in Chappaquiddick incident, car accident which killed Mary Jo Kopechne, 1969.
b. Feb 22, 1932 in Brookline, Massachusetts
Source: *AmOrTwC; AmPolLe; BiDrAC; BiDrUSC 89; BioIn 5, 6, 7, 8, 9, 10, 11, 12, 13, 14, 15, 16, 17, 18, 19, 20, 21; BkPepl; BlueB 76; CngDr 74, 77, 79, 81, 83, 85, 87; ConAu 110; CurBio 63, 78; IntWW 74, 75, 76, 77, 78, 79, 80, 81, 82, 83, 89, 91, 93; IntYB 78, 79, 80, 81, 82; NewYTBE 70; NewYTBS 74; PolProf J, K, NF; WebAB 74, 79; Who 82, 83, 85, 88, 90, 92, 94; WhoAm 74, 76, 78, 80, 82, 84, 86, 88, 90, 92, 94, 95, 96, 97; WhoAmP 73, 75, 77, 79, 81, 83, 85, 87, 89, 91, 93, 95; WhoE 74, 75, 77, 79, 81, 83, 85, 86, 89, 91, 93, 95, 97; WhoGov 72, 75, 77; WhoWor 74, 78, 80, 82, 84, 87, 89, 91, 93, 95, 96, 97; WorAl*

Kennedy, Ethel Skakel
[Mrs. Robert F Kennedy]
American.
Married Robert Kennedy, June 17, 1950; mother of his 11 children.
b. Apr 11, 1928 in Greenwich, Connecticut
Source: *InWom SUP; WhoAm 78, 80*

Kennedy, Florynce
American. Lawyer, Feminist
Founded Feminist Party, 1971.
b. Feb 11, 1916 in Kansas City, Missouri
Source: *BioIn 10, 11; ForWC 70; InB&W 85; InWom SUP; LivgBAA; MugS; NotBlAW 1; WhoAfA 96; WhoAm 76; WhoAmW 79; WhoBlA 77, 80, 85, 90, 92, 94*

Kennedy, George
American. Actor
Won 1967 Oscar for *Cool Hand Luke;* often in strong supporting roles: *Airport,* 1970, *Charade,* 1963.
b. Feb 18, 1925 in New York, New York
Source: *BioIn 10; CmMov; ConTFT 1; FilmEn; FilmgC; ForYSC; HalFC 80, 84, 88; IntDcF 1-3; IntMPA 84, 86, 88, 92, 94, 96; ItaFilm; LegTOT; MovMk; VarWW 85; WhoAm 86; WhoHol 92, A; WorEFlm*

Kennedy, Jayne Harrison
American. Actor
Co-hosted CBS's "NFL Today"; first black woman with network sports.
b. Oct 27, 1951 in Washington, District of Columbia
Source: *InB&W 85; VarWW 85; WhoBlA 85*

Kennedy, Joan Bennett
American., Pianist
Wife of Edward Kennedy, 1958-81; active in Joseph Kennedy Jr. Foundation for Mental Retardation.
b. Sep 5, 1936 in New York, New York
Source: *WhoAm 80; WhoAmW 74*

Kennedy, John F(itzgerald)
"JFK"; "Jack"
American. US President
First Roman Catholic pres., 1961-63; won 1957 Pulitzer for *Profiles in Courage;* assassinated while in office.
b. May 29, 1917 in Brookline, Massachusetts
d. Nov 22, 1963 in Dallas, Texas
Source: *AmAu&B; AmOrTwC; AmPolLe; AnCL; Benet 87, 96; BenetAL 91; BiDrAC; BiDrUSC 89; BiDrUSE 71, 89;*

BioIn 1, 2, 3, 4, 5, 6, 7, 8, 9, 10, 11, 12, 13; ChhPo; ColdWar 2; ConAu 1NR, 1R; ConHero 1; CurBio 50, 61, 64; DcAmB S7; DcAmSR; DcPol; DcTwHis; EncAAH; EncAB-H 1974, 1996; EncPaPR 91; FacFETw; FacPr 89, 93; HealPre; HisEAAC; HisWorL; LinLib L, S; MajTwCW; MakMC; McGEWB; NatCAB 52; OxCAmH; OxCAmL 65; PseudN 82; RAdv 13-3; REn; REnAL; SmATA 11; WebAB 74, 79; WhAm 4; WhAmP; WhDW; WhoAmP 81; WorAl

Kennedy, John F(itzgerald), Jr.
"John-John"
American. Lawyer, Editor
Son of John and Jacqueline Kennedy; as three-year-old, remembered for saluting father's casket at funeral, 1963; asst. dist. attorney, NYC 1989-93; promotes the Kennedy Library. Founded *George* magazine, 1995.
b. Nov 25, 1960 in Washington, District of Columbia
Source: *BioIn 6, 7, 8, 9, 10, 11, 12, 13; CurBio 96*

Kennedy, John Pendleton
[Mark Littleton]
American. Author, Politician
In Congress, 1838-45; secretary of Navy, 1852; wrote *Swallow Barn*, 1832.
b. Oct 25, 1795 in Baltimore, Maryland
d. Aug 18, 1870 in Newport, Rhode Island
Source: *Alli, SUP; AmAu; AmAu&B; AmBi; ApCAB; BbD; BenetAL 91; BiAUS; BibAL; BiD&SB; BiDrAC; BiDrUSC 89; BiDrUSE 71, 89; BiDSA; BioIn 1, 3, 5, 6, 7, 8, 10, 12, 13; CamGEL; CamGLE; CamHAL; CasWL; Chambr 3; CnDAL; CyAL 1; CyWA 58; DcAmAu; DcAmB; DcBiA; DcLB 3; DcLEL; DcNAA; Drake; EncSoH; EvLB; FifSWrB; GrWrEL N; HarEnUS; LinLib L; McGEWB; NatCAB 6; NinCLC 2; OxCAmL 65, 83, 95; OxCEng 67, 85, 95; PenC AM; PseudN 82; REnAL; RfGAmL 87, 94; SouWr; TwCBDA; WebE&AL; WhAm HS; WhAmP*

Kennedy, Joseph Patrick, Sr.
American. Financier, Diplomat
Self-made millionaire; US ambassador to England, 1938-40; romantically linked to actress Gloria Swanson; father of Kennedy family.
b. Sep 6, 1888 in Boston, Massachusetts
d. Nov 18, 1969 in Hyannis Port, Massachusetts
Source: *BiDAmBL 83; BioIn 1, 3, 5, 6, 7, 8, 9, 10, 11, 12; CurBio 40, 70; DcAmB S8; DcAmDH 80, 89; FacFETw; OxCFilm; WhAm 5; WhWW-II; WorAl; WorEFlm*

Kennedy, Joseph Patrick, Jr.
American.
Eldest Kennedy brother; TV movie based on his life: "Young Joe, the Forgotten Kennedy," 1977; killed in WW II plane crash.
b. Apr 19, 1915 in Chicago, Illinois
d. Aug 12, 1944 in Suffolk, England
Source: *BioIn 6, 7, 8, 9, 21; ObitOF 79*

Kennedy, Joseph Patrick, II
American. Politician
Eldest son of Robert and Ethel Kennedy; Democratic congressman from MA, 1986—.
b. Sep 24, 1952 in Brighton, Massachusetts
Source: *BiDrUSC 89; BioIn 9, 10, 11, 12; CngDr 87; CurBio 88; NewYTBE 72; WhoAm 88, 90, 92, 94, 95, 96, 97; WhoAmP 87; WhoE 83, 89, 91, 93, 95, 97*

Kennedy, Madge
American. Actor
Silent film star, 1917-26; considered last of Sam Goldwyn's original glamorous leading ladies; starred on Broadway with WC Fields in *Poppy*, 1923.
b. Apr 19, 1891 in Chicago, Illinois
d. Jun 10, 1987 in Woodland Hills, California
Source: *Film 1; FilmEn; MotPP; TwYS; VarWW 85; WhoHol A; WhoThe 77A*

Kennedy, Margaret
English. Author
Works include *The Midas Touch*, 1967.
b. Apr 23, 1896 in London, England
d. Jul 31, 1967 in Adderbury, England
Source: *Benet 87; BioIn 2, 3, 4, 8, 14, 16; BlmGWL; CamGEL; CamGLE; Chambr 3; ChhPo S2; ConAu 25R; DcLB 36; DcLEL; EvLB; FemiCLE; HalFC 80, 84, 88; InWom, SUP; LngCTC; McGEWD 72, 84; ModBrL; ModWD; ModWoWr; NewC; NewCBEL; ObitOF 79; OxCEng 67; PenC ENG; REn; TwCA, SUP; TwCRGW; TwCRHW 90; TwCWr; WhAm 4, 6; WhoAmW 68, 70, 72; WhThe*

Kennedy, Moorehead Cowell, Jr.
[The Hostages]
American. Hostage
One of 52 held by terrorists, Nov 1979-Jan 1981.
b. Nov 5, 1930 in New York
Source: *NewYTBS 81; USBiR 74*

Kennedy, Nigel Paul
English. Violinist, Conductor
Plays classical, jazz, and rock; known for unconventional behavior at classical performances; recording of Vivaldi's *The Four Seasons*, sold over 1 million copies.
b. Dec 28, 1956 in Brighton, England
Source: *BioIn 15; ConMus 8; CurBio 92; IntWW 91; IntWWM 90; PenDiMP; Who 88, 92*

Kennedy, Patrick Bouvier
American.
Third child of John F Kennedy, first born to president while in office in 68 yrs; buried next to father in Arlington National Cemetery.
b. Aug 7, 1963 in Falmouth, Massachusetts
d. Aug 9, 1963 in Boston, Massachusetts

Kennedy, Paul (Michael)
English. Historian
Wrote *The Rise and Fall of the Great Powers*, 1988; military history scholar.
b. Jun 17, 1945 in Wallsend, England
Source: *BestSel 89-1; ConAu 9NR, 30NR, 65; CurBio 93; IntAu&W 91; IntWW 89, 91, 93; WhoAm 90, 92, 94, 95, 96, 97; WrDr 80, 82, 84, 86, 88, 90, 92, 94, 96*

Kennedy, Robert Francis
"Bobby"; "RFK"
American. Politician
US Attorney General, 1961-64, appointed by brother, JFK; Dem. senator from NY, 1964-68; assassinated following victory in CA primary.
b. Nov 20, 1925 in Brookline, Massachusetts
d. Jun 6, 1968 in Los Angeles, California
Source: *AmAu&B; AmPolLe; BiDrAC; BiDrUSC 89; BiDrUSE 71, 89; BioIn 4, 5, 6, 7, 8, 9, 10, 11, 12, 13; ColdWar 2; ConAu 1NR, 1R; CopCroC; CurBio 58, 68; DcAmB S8; DcPol; EncAB-H 1974, 1996; McGEWB; WebAB 74, 79; WhAm 5; WhAmP; WorAl*

Kennedy, Rose (Fitzgerald)
[Mrs. Joseph Patrick Kennedy]
American. Author
Matriarch of politically prominent Kennedy family; wrote autobiography *Times to Remember*, 1974.
b. Jul 22, 1890 in Boston, Massachusetts
d. Jan 22, 1995 in Hyannis Port, Massachusetts
Source: *AmCath 80; BioIn 5, 6, 8, 9, 10, 11, 12, 14, 15, 17, 20, 21; CelR, 90; ConAu 53; CurBio 70, 95N; GoodHs; HerW, 84; HsB&A; InWom, SUP; LegTOT; News 95, 95-3; OhA&B; WhAm 11; WhoAm 74, 76, 78, 80, 82, 84, 86, 90, 92, 94, 95; WhoAmW 70, 72, 74, 75, 77, 79, 81, 83, 85, 87, 89; WhoE 95; WorAl; WorAlBi*

Kennedy, Ted
[Theodore Kennedy]
"Teeder"
Canadian. Hockey Player
Center, Toronto, 1942-57; won Hart Trophy, 1955; Hall of Fame, 1966.
b. Dec 12, 1925 in Humberstone, Ontario, Canada
Source: *BioIn 2; HocEn; WhoHcky 73; WhoLibS 66*

Kennedy, Tom
American. Actor
Played supporting roles in Keystone comedies, Laurel and Hardy films.
b. 1884 in New York, New York
d. Oct 6, 1965 in Woodland Hills, California
Source: *EncAFC; Film 1; FilmEn; TwYS; Vers A; WhoHol B; WhScrn 74, 77, 83*

Kennedy, Walter
American. Basketball Executive
Commissioner of NBA, 1963-75, responsible for league expansion; Hall of Fame.
b. Jun 8, 1912 in Stamford, Connecticut
d. Jun 26, 1977 in Stamford, Connecticut
Source: *BasBi; NewYTBS 77; ObitOF 79; WhoBbl 73*

Kennedy, William (Joseph)
American. Author
Won 1983 Pulitzer for *Ironweed,* third novel of Albany trilogy; adapted to film, 1987.
b. Jan 16, 1928 in Albany, New York
Source: *Au&Arts 1; Benet 87, 96; BenetAL 91; BiDConC; BioIn 13, 14, 15, 16, 17, 18, 19, 21; CelR 90; ConAu 14NR, 31NR, 85; ConLC 6, 28, 34, 53; ConNov 86, 91, 96; CurBio 85; CyWA 89; DcArts; DcLB 143, Y85B; EncWL 3; IntAu&W 89, 91, 93; IntWW 91, 93; LegTOT; MagSAmL; MajTwCW; OxCAmL 95; PostFic; RAdv 14, 13-1; RGTwCWr; ScF&FL 92; SmATA 57; WhoAm 84, 86, 88, 90, 92, 94, 95, 96, 97; WhoE 85, 86; WhoEnt 92; WhoUSWr 88; WhoWrEP 89, 92, 95; WorAlBi; WorAu 1975; WrDr 86, 88, 90, 92, 94, 96*

Kennedy, X. J
[Joseph Charles Kennedy]
American. Author
Best-known children's book: *One Winter Night in August,* 1975.
b. Aug 21, 1929 in Dover, New Jersey
Source: *AmAu&B; ConAu 1R, 4NR, 30NR, 40NR; ConLC 8; ConPo 75, 85; DcLB 5; DcLEL 1940; DrAP 75; IntAu&W 86; PenC AM; PseudN 82; SmATA 86; WhoAm 84; WhoWor 74; WorAu 1950; WrDr 86*

Kennerly, David Hume
American. Photographer
Personal photographer to Gerald Ford, 1974-77; won Pulitzer, 1972, for feature photography of Vietnam war.
b. Mar 9, 1947 in Roseburg, Oregon
Source: *AuNews 2; BioIn 10, 11, 12, 21; ConAu 101; EncTwCJ; ICPEnP A; MacBEP; WhoAm 74, 76, 78, 80, 82, 84; WhoEmL 91, 93; WhoEnt 92; WhoWor 80, 84, 87, 89, 91*

Kenneth
[Kenneth Everette Battelle]
American. Hairstylist
Owner, Kenneth Salons and Products, Inc., NYC, 1962—.
b. Apr 19, 1927 in Syracuse, New York
Source: *CelR; DcCathB; PseudN 82; WhoAm 74, 76, 78, 80, 82, 90; WorFshn*

Kenney, Bill
[William Patrick Kenney]
American. Football Player
Quarterback, KC, 1980-88; led NFL in pass completions, 1983.
b. Jan 20, 1955 in San Francisco, California
Source: *FootReg 87; WhoAmP 95; WhoMW 96*

Kenney, Douglas C
American. Editor, Screenwriter
Co-founded, edited *National Lampoon,* 1969-75; wrote film *Animal House,* 1978.
b. Dec 10, 1947 in Cleveland, Ohio
d. Aug 27, 1980 in Kauai, Hawaii
Source: *BioIn 12; ConAu 107*

Kenney, George Churchill
American. Army Officer
Commander, Allied Air Forces under MacArthur, 1942-45; participated in Japanese defeat at New Guinea.
b. Aug 6, 1889 in Yarmouth, Nova Scotia, Canada
d. Aug 9, 1977 in Miami, Florida
Source: *BiDWWGF; BioIn 1, 3, 5, 10, 11; BioNews 74; BlueB 76; ConAu P-1; CurBio 43, 77N; DcAmMiB; HarEnMi; NewYTBS 77; ObitOF 79; PolProf T; WebAMB; WhAm 8; WhoAm 74; WhWW-II; WorAl*

Kennon, Robert Floyd
American. Politician, Judge
Governor, LA, 1952-56; LA Supreme Court judge, 1945-47.
b. Aug 21, 1902 in Minden, Louisiana
d. Jan 11, 1988 in Baton Rouge, Louisiana
Source: *BiDrGov 1789; BioIn 2, 3, 10, 11, 15, 16; CurBio 88N; NewYTBS 88; PeoHis; PolProf E, T*

Kenny, Maurice (Francis)
American. Poet
Published poetry collections *Dancing Back Strong the Nation,* 1979; *Tekonwatonti/Molly Brant (1735-1795),* 1992.
b. Aug 16, 1929 in Watertown, New York
Source: *BioIn 21; ConAu 22AS, 144; ConLC 87; DcNAL; DrAPF 80; EncNAB; IntWWP 77; NatNAL; WrDr 96*

Kenny, Nick
American. Songwriter, Journalist
Hit songs include "While a Cigarette Was Burning"; pioneered early amateur radio show.
b. Feb 3, 1895 in Astoria, New York
d. Dec 1, 1975 in Sarasota, Florida
Source: *ASCAP 66; BioIn 1, 3, 4, 10; CmpEPM; ConAu 89; What 4; WhScrn 77, 83*

Kenny, Sister Elizabeth
Australian. Nurse
Developed therapy for polio victims, 1933.
b. Sep 20, 1886 in Warrialda, Australia
d. Nov 30, 1952 in Toowoomba, Australia
Source: *CurBio 42, 53; WhAm 3*

Kenny G
[Kenny Gorelick]
American. Jazz Musician
Saxophonist; hit "Songbird," 1987, is one of only two instrumentals to reach top 10 without being connected with movie or TV; Grammy for best instrumental composition for "Forever in Love," 1993.
b. Jun 5, 1956? in Seattle, Washington
Source: *BioIn 15, 16; CelR 90; CurBio 95; LegTOT*

Kenojuak
Canadian. Artist
Regarded as Canda's foremost Inuit artist; awarded the Order of Canada Medal of Service, 1967.
b. Oct 3, 1927 in Baffin Island, Northwest Territories, Canada
Source: *BioIn 11, 12, 13, 15, 21; NorAmWA; NotNaAm*

Kensett, John Frederick
American. Artist
Hudson River School painter; landscapes include *High Bank,* 1857.
b. Mar 22, 1816 in Cheshire, Connecticut
d. Dec 14, 1872 in New York, New York
Source: *AmBi; AmCulL; ApCAB; ArtsAmW 1, 3; BioIn 14, 15, 17, 19; BriEAA; DcAmArt; DcAmB; Drake; EarABI; IIBEAAW; McGDA; NatCAB 7; NewYHSD; OxCAmH; TwCBDA; WhAmArt 85; WhAm HS*

Kent, Allegra
American. Dancer
Ballerina with NYC Ballet Co., 1953-78; best-known for role in ballet, *The Seven Deadly Sins,* 1959.
b. Aug 11, 1938 in Santa Monica, California
Source: *BiDD; BioIn 8, 9, 11, 13; CnOxB; ConAu 105, 126; CurBio 70; DancEn 78; IntDcB; InWom SUP; WhoAm 74, 76, 78; WhoAmW 85; WhoHol 92; WrDr 80, 82, 84*

Kent, Arthur
"Scud Stud"
Canadian. Broadcast Journalist
Foreign correspondent noted for live coverage during the Persian Gulf War; won 2 Emmys for foreign reporting, 1989.
b. Dec 27, 1953 in Medicine Hat, Alberta, Canada
Source: *News 91*

Kent, Arthur Atwater
American. Industrialist, Inventor
First to mass-produce radio, 1926.
b. Dec 3, 1873 in Burlington, Vermont
d. Apr 4, 1949 in Bel Air, California
Source: *BiDAmBL 83; BioIn 1, 3; DcAmB S4; InSci; NatCAB 38; WhAm 2*

Kent, Corita
[Frances Kent]
American. Artist
Best known for designing "Love" postage stamp.
b. Nov 20, 1918 in Fort Dodge, Iowa
d. Sep 18, 1986 in Boston, Massachusetts
Source: *AmAu&B; AmCath 80; BioIn 8, 9, 12; ConNews 87-1; CurBio 69, 86N; InWom SUP; NewYTBS 86; NorAmWA; WhAm 9; WhoAm 78; WhoAmA 73, 76*

Kent, Jack
[John Wellington Kent]
American. Cartoonist
Drew syndicated comic strip "King Aroo," 1950-65.
b. Mar 10, 1920 in Burlington, Iowa
d. Oct 18, 1985 in San Antonio, Texas
Source: *AmAu&B; BioIn 12, 13, 14, 15; ConAu 16NR, 85, 117; ConGrA 1, 2; EncACom; FifBJA; IlsCB 1967; SmATA 24, 45N; WhoAm 74; WhoAmA 78, 80, 82, 84, 86N, 89N, 91N, 93N; WhoSSW 84; WorECom*

Kent, James
"The American Blackstone"
American. Judge
Law professor, Columbia U., 1790s-1820s; virtual creator of equity jurisdiction in US.
b. Jul 31, 1763 in Fredericksburg, New York
d. Dec 12, 1847 in New York, New York
Source: *Alli; AmAu; AmAu&B; AmBi; AmJust; ApCAB; BbD; BenetAL 91; BiAUS; BiD&SB; BioIn 3, 6, 8, 9, 11; CyAG; CyAL 1; DcAmAu; DcAmB; DcBiPP; DcEnL; DcNAA; Drake; EncAB-H 1974, 1996; HarEnUS; LinLib L; McGEWB; NatCAB 3; OxCAmH; OxCAmL 65, 83, 95; OxCLaw; PseudN 82; REnAL; TwCBDA; WebAB 74, 79; WhAm HS; WhDW*

Kent, Rockwell
[William Hogarth, Jr.]
"RK"
American. Artist
Noted for his stark dramatic lithographs, exotic landscapes.
b. Jun 21, 1882 in Tarrytown, New York
d. Mar 13, 1971 in Plattsburg, New York
Source: *AmAu&B; BenetAL 91; BioIn 1, 2, 3, 4, 5, 7, 8, 9, 10, 11, 12, 13, 14, 17, 20, 21; BriEAA; ChhPo; ConAmA; ConArt 77, 83; ConAu 4NR, 5R, 29R; CurBio 71N; DcAmArt; DcAmB S9; DcCAA 71, 77, 88, 94; GrAmP; IlrAm 1880, D; IlsBYP; IlsCB 1744; LegTOT; LinLib L; McGDA; McGEWB; NatCAB 58; OxCAmL 65, 83, 95; OxCChiL; OxCTwCA; PeoHis; PhDcTCA 77; PseudN 82; REnAL; SmATA 6; TwCA, SUP; WebAB 74, 79; WhAm 5; WhAmArt 85; What 1; WhoAmA 78N, 80N, 82N, 84N, 86N, 89N, 91N, 93N; WorAl; WorAlBi*

Kent, William
English. Architect
Built the treasury buildings in Whitehall, 1734; Horse Guards were designed from his sketches, 1750; introduced informal style of gardening.
b. 1685 in Bridlington, England
d. Apr 12, 1748 in London, England
Source: *Alli; AtlBL; BiDBrA; BkIE; ChhPo; DcBrECP; DcD&D; EncEnl; IntDcAr; MacEA; McGDA; OxCArt; OxCDecA; OxDcArt; PenDiDA 89; WhoArch*

Kentner, Louis Philip
English. Musician
Int'l concert pianist; played with Menuhin, 1950s; Liszt authority.
b. Jul 19, 1905 in Karwin, Silesia
Source: *Baker 84; DcNaB 1986; IntWW 74, 75, 76, 77, 78, 79, 80, 81, 82, 83; IntWWM 77, 80, 85; NewGrDM 80; Who 82, 83, 85; WhoMus 72; WhoWor 74, 76, 78*

Kenton, Stan(ley Newcomb)
American. Bandleader
Led outstanding jazz bands since 1941; wrote "And Her Tears Flowed Like Wine."
b. Feb 19, 1912 in Wichita, Kansas
d. Aug 25, 1979 in Hollywood, California
Source: *ASCAP 66, 80; Baker 78, 84; BgBands 74; BiDAmM; BiDJaz; BioIn 2, 3, 4, 7, 9, 10, 11, 12, 15, 16, 17, 20; BioNews 74; CmCal; CmpEPM; ConAmC 76, 82; CurBio 79; DcArts; EncJzS; IlEncJ; IntWWM 80; LegTOT; NewAmDM; NewGrDM 80; NewYTBS 79; OxCPMus; PenEncP; RadStar; WhAm 7; WhoAm 74, 76, 78; WhoWor 74; WhScrn 83; WorAl; WorAlBi*

Kentucky Headhunters
American. Music Group
"Psycho-billy" country band formed 1985; Grammy for *Pickin' on Nashville,* 1991.
Source: *Alli; BgBkCoM; BioIn 9; ConAu X; ConMus 5; St&PR 96, 97; WhoAm 95, 96, 97; WhoHol 92, A; WhoMW 93*

Kenty, Hilmer
American. Boxer
WBA lightweight champion, 1980.
b. Jul 30, 1955 in Austin, Texas

Kenyatta, Jomo
[Johnstone Kamau; Kamau Ngengi]
"Mzee"
Kenyan. Political Leader
Terrorist organizer who was first pres. of Kenya, 1964-78.
b. Oct 20, 1891 in Ichaweri, British East Africa
d. Aug 22, 1978 in Mombasa, Kenya
Source: *AfrA; AfSS 78; Au&Wr 71; BioIn 11, 12, 14, 17, 18, 19, 20, 21; BlkWr 1; ColdWar 2; ConAu 113, 124; ConBlB 5; CurBio 53, 74, 78, 78N; DcAfHiB 86; DcPol; HisWorL; IntWW 74, 75, 76, 77, 78; IntYB 78; MajTwCW; McGEWB; NewYTBS 78; ObitOF 79; PseudN 82; SchCGBL; WhDW; Who 74; WhoGov 72; WhoWor 76; WorAl*

Keogan, George
American. Basketball Coach
Coach, Notre Dame U, 1924-43, with career 327-96 record; Hall of Fame.
b. Mar 8, 1890 in Minnesota Lakes, Minnesota
d. Feb 17, 1943 in South Bend, Indiana
Source: *BasBi; BioIn 9; ObitOF 79; WhoBbl 73*

Keogh, Eugene James
American. Politician
Democratic congressman from NY, 1937-67.
b. Aug 30, 1907 in New York, New York
d. May 26, 1989 in New York, New York
Source: *BiDrAC; BiDrUSC 89; BioIn 11, 16; PolProf K; St&PR 84; WhAm 10; WhoAm 74, 76, 78, 80; WhoAmL 83; WhoAmP 73, 75, 77, 79, 81, 83, 85, 87*

Keogh, James
American. Journalist
Wrote *This is Nixon,* 1956; *President Nixon and the Press,* 1972.
b. Oct 29, 1916 in Platte County, Nebraska
Source: *BioIn 8, 9, 12; BlueB 76; ConAu 45; IntAu&W 89, 91, 93; IntWW 74, 75, 76, 77, 78, 79, 80, 81, 82, 83, 89, 91, 93; PolProf NF; USBiR 74; WhoAm 74, 76, 78, 80, 82, 84, 86, 88, 90, 92, 94, 95, 96, 97; WhoE 74; WhoGov 72, 75, 77; WrDr 80, 82, 84, 86*

Keokuk
American. Native American Chief
Sauk chief; arranged peace between Sauks, Sioux, 1837; town in IA named for him.
b. 1780 in Rock River, Illinois
d. Jun 1848 in Franklin County, Kansas
Source: *AmBi; ApCAB; BioIn 1, 6, 11; DcAmB; HarEnUS; NatCAB 9; NewCol 75; NotNaAm; OxCAmH; REnAW; WebAB 74, 79; WhAm HS*

Keon, Dave
[David Michael Keon]
Canadian. Hockey Player
Center, 1960-82, mostly with Toronto; won Calder Trophy, 1961, Lady Byng Trophy, 1962, 1963; Hall of Fame, 1986.
b. Mar 22, 1940 in Noranda, Quebec, Canada
Source: *BioIn 6, 9; HocEn; WhoHcky 73*

Keough, Danny
[Daniel Keough]
American.
Married Lisa Marie Presley, Elvis's only daughter and sole heir, Oct 3, 1988.
b. Nov 6, 1964 in Chicago, Illinois

Keough, Donald Raymond
American. Business Executive
Pres., CEO, Coca-Cola Co., 1981-93; products sold in 155 countries.
b. Sep 4, 1926 in Maurice, Iowa
Source: *BioIn 15, 18, 19; ConNews 86-1; IntWW 91, 93; St&PR 84, 87, 91, 93, 96, 97; WhoAm 76, 78, 80, 82, 84, 86, 88, 90, 92, 94, 95, 96, 97; WhoFI 77, 83, 85, 87, 89, 92, 94, 96; WhoSSW 84, 86, 88, 91, 93, 95, 97; WhoWor 87, 89, 95, 96, 97*

Keough, William Francis, Jr.
[The Hostages]
American. Hostage
One of 52 held by terrorists, Nov 1979 - Jan 1981.
b. 1931? in Waltham, Massachusetts
d. Nov 29, 1985 in Washington, District of Columbia
Source: *BioIn 12; NewYTBS 81, 85*

Kepes, Gyorgy
American. Designer, Educator
Long-time professor of visual design, MIT, very influential in his field.
b. Oct 4, 1906 in Selyp, Hungary
Source: *AmAu&B; Au&Wr 71; BioIn 1, 2, 5, 6, 9, 10, 11, 12, 13; ConAu 101; ConDes 84, 90, 97; ConPhot 82, 88, 95; CurBio 73; DcCAA 71, 77, 88, 94; DcTwDes; FacFETw; ICPEnP; MacBEP; McGDA; OxCTwCA; WhoAm 74, 76, 78, 84, 94, 97; WhoAmA 73, 76, 78, 80, 82, 84, 86, 89, 91, 93; WhoWor 84, 91, 93, 95, 96, 97*

Kepler, Johannes
[John Kepler]
"The Father of Modern Astronomy"
German. Astronomer
Described revolutions of planets around sun in Kepler's Laws, 1609.
b. Dec 27, 1571 in Weil der Stadt, Germany
d. Nov 15, 1630 in Regensburg, Germany
Source: *AstEnc; Baker 78, 84, 92; BbD; Benet 87, 96; BiD&SB; BiDPsy; BiESc; BioIn 14, 15, 16, 17, 19, 20, 21; CamDcSc; CyEd; DcInv; DcScB; Dis&D; EncEnl; EncO&P 1; EncSF, 93; InSci; LarDcSc; LegTOT; McGEWB; NamesHP; NewC; NewEOp 71; NewEScF; NewGrDM 80; PseudN 82; RAdv 14, 13-5; REn; ScFEYrs; WhDW; WorAl; WorAlBi; WorScD*

Keppard, Freddie
American. Jazz Musician
New Orleans cornetist; co-led Original Creole Orchestra, 1910s.
b. Feb 15, 1899 in New Orleans, Louisiana
d. Jul 15, 1933 in Chicago, Illinois
Source: *BiDJaz; WhoJazz 72*

Keppel, Francis
American. Educator, Government Official
Dean, Harvard U Graduate School of Education, 1948-62; US commissioner of education, 1962-66; tried to enforce Civil Rights Act, opposed racial segregation of public schools.
b. Apr 16, 1916 in New York, New York
d. Feb 19, 1990 in Cambridge, Massachusetts
Source: *AmDec 1960; BioIn 5, 6, 7, 11; BlueB 76; CurBio 63, 90, 90N; FacFETw; IntWW 76, 77, 78, 79, 80, 81, 82, 83, 89; LEduc 74; NewYTBS 90; PolProf J, K; St&PR 75; WhAm 10; WhoAm 74, 76, 78, 80, 82, 84, 86, 88*

Kerby, William Frederick
American. Businessman
Chairman, Dow Jones & Co., 1972-89.
b. Jul 28, 1908 in Washington, District of Columbia
d. Mar 17, 1989 in Bethlehem, Pennsylvania
Source: *IntWW 74, 75, 76, 77, 78, 79, 80, 81, 82, 83; St&PR 75; WhAm 10; WhoAm 74, 76, 78; WhoE 74, 75, 77, 79, 81; WhoFI 74, 75, 77, 79*

Kercheval, Ken
American. Actor
Played Cliff Barnes on TV series "Dallas," 1978-91.
b. Jul 15, 1935 in Wolcottville, Tennessee
Source: *BioIn 12, 20; ConTFT 1; VarWW 85; WhoAm 82, 84, 86, 88, 90, 92, 94, 95; WhoEnt 92; WhoHol 92*

Kerekou, Mathieu Ahmed
Beninese. Political Leader
President of Benin, 1972-91.
b. Sep 2, 1933 in Natitingou, Dahomey
Source: *WhoWor 87*

Kerensky, Alexander Fedorovitch
[Aleksandr Feodorovich Kerenski]
Russian. Political Leader
Premier, Jul-Nov 1917, whose indecisiveness enabled Bolsheviks to seize power.
b. Apr 22, 1881 in Simbirsk, Russia
d. Jun 11, 1970 in New York, New York
Source: *CurBio 66, 70; LinLib S; McGEWB; NewYTBE 70; REn; WhAm 5*

Kerkorian, Kirk
[Kerkor Kerkorian]
American. Business Executive
Began career with airlines; CEO of MGM, 1973-74; vice-chairman, 1974-79; controlling stockolder, 1979—; attempted purchase of Chrysler Corp., 1995.
b. Jun 6, 1917 in Fresno, California
Source: *BioIn 8, 10, 12; CurBio 75, 96; EncABHB 8; IntMPA 80, 81, 82, 84, 86, 88, 92, 94, 96; News 96, 96-2; WhoAm 78, 80, 82, 84, 86, 90, 92, 94, 95, 96, 97; WhoEnt 92; WhoWest 89, 92*

Kermode, (John) Frank
English. Critic
Wrote *The Genesis of Secrecy,* 1979.
b. Nov 29, 1919 in Isle of Man, England
Source: *Au&Wr 71; Benet 87, 96; BioIn 10, 13, 14, 21; BlueB 76; ConAu 1NR, 1R, 47NR; ConLCrt 77, 82; DcLEL 1940; IntAu&W 76, 77, 82, 91, 93; IntWW 75, 76, 77, 78, 79, 80, 81, 82, 83, 89, 91, 93; NewC; RAdv 13-1; Who 74, 82, 83, 85, 88, 90, 92, 94; WhoAm 86, 88, 90, 92, 94, 95, 96, 97; WhoWor 74, 76, 78, 82, 84, 87, 95, 96, 97; WorAu 1950; WrDr 76, 80, 82, 84, 86, 88, 90, 92, 94, 96*

Kern, Harold G
American. Newspaper Publisher
Published *Boston American, Boston Herald;* with Hearst Corp., 1925-75.
b. 1899
d. Feb 10, 1976 in Boston, Massachusetts
Source: *WhAm 6*

Kern, Jerome David
American. Composer
Important in transition from operettas to modern musical comedies; known for *Show Boat,* 1927; song "Ol' Man River," 1927.
b. Jan 17, 1885 in New York, New York
d. Nov 11, 1945 in New York, New York
Source: *AmMWSc 73P; ASCAP 66; CmMov; CurBio 42, 45; DcAmB S3; EncMT; McGEWB; McGEWD 72; NatCAB 34; NewCBMT; OxCAmL 65; OxCFilm; PlP&P; REn; REnAL; WebAB 74; WhAm 2*

Kerner, Otto
American. Politician, Judge
Headed Johnson's commission investigating 1960s riots; warned of racial polarization; Dem. governor of IL, 1961-68.
b. Aug 15, 1908 in Chicago, Illinois
d. May 9, 1976 in Chicago, Illinois
Source: *BiDFedJ; BiDrGov 1789; BioIn 6, 7, 9, 10, 11; BlueB 76; CurBio 61, 76N; DcAmB S10; EncAACR; IntWW 74, 75; NewYTBE 73; NewYTBS 76; PolProf J, K; WhAm 3, 6, 7; WhoAm 74, 76; WhoGov 72, 75*

Kerns, Joanna
[Joanna DeVarona]
American. Actor
Played Maggie Seaver on TV comedy "Growing Pains," 1984-92.
b. Feb 12, 1955 in San Francisco, California
Source: *BioIn 14, 15, 16; CelR 90; ConTFT 8; IntMPA 94, 96; LegTOT; WhoEnt 92; WhoHol 92; WhoWest 89; WorAlBi*

Kerouac, Jack
[Jean-Louis Incogniteau; Jean Louis Lebris de Kerouac]
American. Author, Poet
Leader of Beat Movement; wrote *On the Road,* 1957.
b. Mar 12, 1922 in Lowell, Massachusetts
d. Oct 21, 1969 in Saint Petersburg, Florida
Source: *AmAu&B; AmDec 1950; AmWr S3; AuNews 1; Benet 87, 96; BenetAL 91; BiDConC; BioIn 4, 5, 7, 8, 9, 10, 11, 12, 13, 14, 15, 16, 17, 19, 20, 21; CamGEL; CamGLE; CamHAL; CasWL; CmCal; CnMWL; ConAu 5R, X; ConLC 1, 2, 3, 5, 14, 29, 61; ConNov 76, 82A, 86A; ConPo 70; ConPopW; CurBio 59, 69; CyWA 89; DcAmB S8; DcLB 2, 16, DS3; DcLEL 1940; DcTwCCu 1; EncAB-H 1974, 1996; EncWL 2, 3; FacFETw; GayLL; GrWrEL N; HalFC 84, 88; LegTOT; LinLib L; LngCTC; MagSAmL; MakMC; ModAL, S1, S2; NewCon; NewYTBS 79; Novels; ObitT 1961; OxCAmL 65, 83, 95; OxCEng 85, 95; PenC AM; PeoHis; PolProf E; PseudN 82; RAdv 1, 14, 13-1; RComAH; REn; REnAL; RfGAmL 87, 94; RGTwCWr; TwCWr; WebAB 74, 79; WebE&AL; WhAm 5; WhDW; WhoTwCL; WorAl; WorAlBi; WorAu 1950; WorLitC*

Kerr, Alexander H
American. Manufacturer
Purchased fruit jar patent, 1902, formed co. which produced jars, lids, caps for canning.
b. Sep 4, 1862 in Philadelphia, Pennsylvania
d. Feb 9, 1925 in Riverside, California
Source: *Entr; NatCAB 30*

Kerr, Clark
American. Educator, Author
Pres., U of CA, 1958-67; cowrote *Unions, Management, and the Public,* 1948.
b. May 17, 1911 in Reading, Pennsylvania
Source: *AmAu&B; AmEA 74; AmMWSc 73S, 78S; BiDAmEd; BioIn 4, 5, 6, 7, 8, 11, 12, 13, 15; BlueB 76; CmCal; ConAu 1NR, 22NR, 45; CurBio 61; EncAB-H 1974; EncWB; IntAu&W 77; IntWW 74, 75, 76, 77, 78, 79, 80, 81, 82, 83, 89, 91, 93; LEduc 74; LinLib L, S; NewYTBE 70; PolProf E, J, K; Who 74, 82, 83, 85, 88, 90, 92, 94; WhoAm 74, 76, 78, 80, 82, 84, 86, 88, 90, 92, 94, 95, 96, 97; WhoFI 92; WhoWest 74, 76; WhoWor 74, 97; WrDr 80, 82, 84, 86, 88, 90, 92, 94, 96*

Kerr, Deborah
[Deborah Jane Kerr-Trimmer]
American. Actor
Starred in *From Here to Eternity,* 1953; *Tea and Sympathy,* 1956.
b. Sep 30, 1921 in Helensburgh, Scotland
Source: *BiDFilm, 81, 94; BiE&WWA; BioIn 1, 3, 4, 6, 7, 11, 12, 19, 20; BlueB 76; CelR, 90; ConTFT 4; CurBio 47; DcArts; EncEurC; FacFETw; FilmAG WE; FilmEn; FilmgC; ForYSC; GoodHs; HalFC 80, 84, 88; IlWWBF, A; IntDcF 1-3, 2-3; IntMPA 75, 76, 77, 78, 79, 80, 81, 82, 84, 86, 88, 92, 94, 96; IntWW 83; InWom; LegTOT; MGM; MotPP; MovMk; NotNAT; OxCFilm; PlP&P A; VarWW 85; WhoAm 74, 76, 78, 80, 82, 84, 86; WhoAmW 58, 64, 66, 68, 70, 72, 74, 83; WhoHol 92, A; WhoHrs 80; WhoThe 77, 81; WhoWor 84, 87; WorAl; WorAlBi; WorEFlm*

Kerr, Graham
English. Chef, TV Personality
Has had "how-to" cooking shows including *Galloping Gourmet,* 1969-73; "Take Kerr," 1976—.
b. Jan 22, 1934 in London, England
Source: *BioIn 9, 10, 11, 12; ConAu 108; LegTOT; WhoAm 74, 76, 78, 80; WrDr 80, 82, 84, 86, 88, 90, 92, 94, 96*

Kerr, Jean
[Bridget Jean Collins]
American. Author, Dramatist
Wrote humorous autobiographical work *Please Don't Eat the Daisies,* 1957; adapted to film, 1960; wife of Walter Francis.
b. Jul 10, 1923 in Scranton, Pennsylvania
Source: *AmAu&B; AmCath 80; ASCAP 66, 80; BenetAL 91; BiE&WWA; BioIn 12; BlueB 76; CelR; ConAu 5NR, 5R, 7NR; ConLC 22; ConTFT 1; CurBio 58; DcLEL 1940; EncAHmr; FemiCLE; HalFC 84, 88; IntAu&W 77, 89, 91, 93; IntWW 74, 75, 76, 77, 78, 79, 80, 81, 82, 83, 89, 91, 93; LegTOT; McGEWD 84; NatPD 81; NotNAT; NotWoAT; OxCAmL 65, 83; OxCAmT 84; VarWW 85; WhoAm 74, 76, 78, 80, 82, 84, 86, 88, 90, 92, 94, 95, 96, 97; WhoAmW 64, 66, 68, 70, 72, 74, 81, 83, 95, 97; WhoThe 72, 77, 81; WhoUSWr 88; WhoWor 74, 78, 80, 82, 84, 87; WhoWrEP 89, 92, 95; WorAl; WorAlBi; WorAu 1950; WrDr 76, 80, 82, 84, 86, 88, 90*

Kerr, John
American. Actor
Won Tony for *Tea and Sympathy,* 1954; also starred in film.
b. Nov 15, 1931 in New York, New York
Source: *BiE&WWA; BioIn 3, 4; FilmEn; FilmgC; ForYSC; HalFC 80, 84, 88; IntMPA 77, 80, 84, 86, 88, 92, 94, 96; MotPP; NotNAT; VarWW 85; WhoAm 74, 76, 82; WhoHol 92, A; WorAl*

Kerr, Malcolm (Hooper)
American. University Administrator
Pres., American U in Beirut; assassinated by Islamic Jihad.
b. Oct 8, 1931 in Beirut, Lebanon
d. Jan 18, 1984 in Beirut, Lebanon
Source: *AnObit 1984; ConAu 97, 111; WhAm 8; WhoAm 74, 76, 78, 80, 82; WhoWest 74, 76, 78*

Kerr, Orpheus C
[Robert Henry Newell]
American. Author, Humorist
Lampooned Civil War-era politicians; best known for five-vol. *The Orpheus C Kerr* papers, 1862-71.
b. Dec 13, 1836 in New York, New York
d. Jul 1901
Source: *Alli, SUP; AmAu; AmAu&B; AmBi; ApCAB; BbD; BenetAL 91; BibAL; BiD&SB; BioIn 13, 15; ChhPo, S1; CnDAL; ConAu 111; DcAmAu; DcAmB; DcEnL; DcLB 11; DcLEL; DcNAA; Drake; EncAHmr; EvLB; HarEnUS; NatCAB 11; OxCAmL 65, 83, 95; PseudN 82; REn; REnAL; TwCBDA; WhAm 1*

Kerr, Red
[John G Kerr]
American. Basketball Player, Basketball Coach
Forward, 1954-66, mostly with Syracuse; coach, 1966-70, with Chicago, Phoenix; coach of year, 1967.
b. Aug 17, 1932 in Chicago, Illinois
Source: *BiDAmSp BK; OfNBA 87; WhoSpor*

Kerr, Robert Samuel
American. Oilman, Politician
Dem. senator from OK, 1949-63.
b. Sep 11, 1896 in Ada, Oklahoma
d. Jan 1, 1963 in Washington, District of Columbia
Source: *BiDrAC; BiDrGov 1789; BiDrUSC 89; BioIn 1, 2, 3, 4, 5, 6, 7, 9, 11, 14, 17; ConAmBL; CurBio 50, 63; DcAmB S7; EncSoB SUP; NatCAB 53; PolProf E, K, T; REnAW; WhAm 4; WhAmP; WorAl*

Kerr, Roy Patrick
New Zealander. Mathematician
His Kerr solution solved Einstein's field equations of general relativity, 1963; formula used to describe properties of black holes.
b. May 16, 1934 in Kurow, New Zealand
Source: *LarDcSc*

Kerr, Tim(othy)
Canadian. Hockey Player
Center-right wing, Philadelphia, 1980-91, NY Rangers, 1991-92, Hartford, 1992-93; holds NHL record for most power play goals in season, 34 (1985-86).
b. Jan 5, 1960 in Windsor, Ontario, Canada
Source: *HocEn; HocReg 87; NewYTBS 85; WhoAm 90, 92, 94, 95; WhoE 86, 95*

Kerr, Walter F(rancis)
American. Critic, Author
Influential *NY Times* critic, 1966-83; won Pulitzer for criticism, 1978; entered Theater Hall of Fame, 1982.
b. Jul 8, 1913 in Evanston, Illinois
d. Oct 9, 1996 in Dobbs Ferry, New York
Source: *AmAu&B; ASCAP 66; Au&Wr 71; BiE&WWA; ConAu 5R; ConTFT 4;*

CurBio 53; IntWW 83; News 97-1; NotNAT; OxCAmL 65; REnAL; VarWW 85; WhoAm 86; WhoWor 87; WrDr 86

Kerrey, Bob
[Joseph Robert Kerrey]
American. Politician
Dem. senator from NE, 1989—; governor, 1983-87; decorated for bravery during Vietnam War.
b. Aug 27, 1943 in Lincoln, Nebraska
Source: *AlmAP 84; BiDrGov 1983; BioIn 13; ConNews 86-1; CurBio 91; IntWW 89, 91, 93; LegTOT; MedHR, 94; News 91, 91-3; NewYTBS 91; PolsAm 84; WhoAm 84, 86, 88, 90, 92, 94, 95, 96, 97; WhoAmP 83, 85, 87, 89, 91, 93, 95; WhoMW 90, 92, 93, 96; WhoWor 87, 91; WorAlBi*

Kerrigan, Nancy
American. Skater
Figure skater who won the women's Silver Medal at the 1992 Winter Olympics; struck by assailant, injuring her right knee, 1994.
b. Oct 13, 1969 in Stoneham, Massachusetts
Source: *EncWomS; News 94, 94-3; WhoAm 95, 96, 97; WhoWor 95, 96, 97*

Kerry, John F(orbes)
American. Politician
Dem. senator from MA, 1985—; lt. governor of MA, 1982-84.
b. Dec 11, 1943 in Denver, Colorado
Source: *BiDrUSC 89; BioIn 14, 15, 16, 17; CngDr 85, 87; CurBio 88; IntWW 89, 91, 93; NewYTBE 71; NewYTBS 91; WhoAm 84, 86, 88, 90, 92, 94, 95, 96, 97; WhoAmP 83, 85, 87, 89, 91, 93, 95; WhoE 83, 85, 86, 89, 91, 93, 97; WhoWor 89, 91, 93, 95, 96, 97*

Kershaw, Doug(las James)
American. Musician
Cajun fiddler, known for classic "Louisiana Man."
b. Jan 24, 1936 in Tel Ridge, Louisiana
Source: *BgBkCoM; BiDAmM; BioIn 9; ConMuA 80A; CounME 74, 74A; EncRk 88; HarEnCM 87; IlEncCM; IlEncRk; NewGrDA 86; PenEncP; RolSEnR 83; WhoAm 80; WhoRock 81; WhoWest 80*

Kerst, Donald W(illiam)
American. Physicist
Inventor of the betatron, a particle accelerator, 1940.
b. Nov 1, 1911
d. Aug 19, 1993 in Madison, Wisconsin
Source: *AmMWSc 73P, 76P, 79, 82, 86, 89, 92; AsBiEn; BiESc; BioIn 2, 8, 19, 20; CurBio 93N; InSci; IntWW 74, 75, 76, 77, 78, 79, 80, 81, 82, 83, 89, 91, 93; NewYTBS 93; WhoAm 74, 76, 78, 80, 82, 84, 86, 90, 92*

Kert, Larry
[Frederick Lawrence Kert]
American. Actor
Led the Jets gang in stage version of *West Side Story;* died of AIDS.
b. Dec 5, 1930 in Los Angeles, California
d. Jun 5, 1991 in New York, New York
Source: *AnObit 1991; BiE&WWA; BioIn 17, 18; ConTFT 4, 10; EncMT; LegTOT; NewYTBS 91; NotNAT; PlP&P A; WhoHol A; WhoThe 72, 77, 81; WorAl*

Kertesz, Andre
American. Photographer
Pioneered use of 35-mm camera in photojournalism.
b. Jul 2, 1894 in Budapest, Austria-Hungary
d. Sep 27, 1985 in New York, New York
Source: *AnObit 1985; BioIn 6, 7, 8, 9, 10, 11, 12, 13; ConAu 85, 117; ConPhot 82, 88, 95; CurBio 79, 85, 85N; DcArts; DcCAr 81; ICPEnP; IntAu&W 82; MacBEP; NewYTBS 85; PrintW 85; WhAm 9; WhAmArt 85; WhoAm 74, 76, 78, 84; WhoWor 84*

Kertesz, Istvan
Hungarian. Conductor
Made US debut with Detroit Symphony, 1961; led London Symphony, 1965-68.
b. Aug 29, 1929 in Budapest, Hungary
d. Apr 17, 1973 in Tel Aviv, Israel
Source: *Baker 78, 84, 92; BioIn 8, 9, 11; BriBkM 80; MusSN; NewAmDM; NewEOp 71; NewGrDM 80; NewGrDO; NewYTBE 73; OxDcOp; PenDiMP; WhoMus 72; WhoWor 74*

Kerwin, Joseph Peter
American. Astronaut, Physician
Member of Skylab I, II space crews.
b. Feb 19, 1932 in Oak Park, Illinois
Source: *AmMWSc 73P, 76P, 79, 95; IntWW 74; NewYTBE 73; WhoAm 74, 76, 78, 80, 82, 84, 86, 88, 90, 92, 94, 95, 96; WhoScEn 94; WhoSSW 73, 95, 97; WhoWor 78*

Kerwin, Lance
American. Actor
Played in TV series "James at 15," 1977-78; TV movie "Salem's Lot."
b. Nov 6, 1960 in Newport Beach, California
Source: *BioIn 11; LegTOT; VarWW 85; WhoHol 92*

Kesey, Ken
American. Author
Wrote *One Flew Over the Cuckoo's Nest,* 1962; adapted to film, 1975.
b. Sep 17, 1935 in La Junta, Colorado
Source: *AmAu&B; AmDec 1960; Benet 87; BenetAL 91; BioIn 8, 10, 11, 12, 13; BroV; CamGLE; CamHAL; CasWL; CmCal; ConAu 1R, 22NR; ConLC 1, 3, 6, 11, 46, 64; ConNov 72, 76, 82, 86, 91; CurBio 76; CyWA 89; DcArts; DcLB 2, 16; DcTwCCu 1; DrAF 76; DrAPF 80; EncFWF; EncWL, 2, 3; FacFETw; FifWWr; IntAu&W 76, 82; LegTOT; LinLib L; LNinSix; MagSAmL; MajTwCW; MakMC; ModAL S1; MugS; Novels; OxCAmL 83, 95; PenC AM; RAdv 1, 14, 13-1; REnAW; SmATA 66; TwCWW 82; WebE&AL; WhoAm 74, 76, 78, 80, 82, 84, 86, 88, 90, 92, 94, 95, 96, 97; WhoTwCL; WhoWest 94, 96; WhoWor 95, 96, 97; WorAl; WorAlBi; WorAu 1970; WorLitC; WrDr 76, 80, 82, 84, 86, 88, 90, 92*

Kesselring, Albert
German. Military Leader
Commanded German forces in Italy, 1943-45; led Western Front in war's closing days, 1945.
b. Nov 20, 1885 in Markstedt, Germany
d. Jul 16, 1960 in Bad Nauheim, Germany (West)
Source: *BioIn 1, 3, 5, 11, 12, 14, 16, 17; CurBio 42, 60; EncTR, 91; FacFETw; HisEWW; McGEWB; ObitT 1951; WhoMilH 76; WorAl; WorAlBi*

Kesselring, Joseph Otto
American. Dramatist
Wrote suspense comedy *Arsenic and Old Lace,* 1941; screenplay, 1944.
b. Jun 21, 1902 in New York, New York
d. Nov 5, 1967 in Kingston, New York
Source: *BioIn 8, 9, 10; McGEWD 84; NatCAB 53; WhAm 4; WhThe*

Kessler, David Aaron
"Eliot Knessler"
American. Government Official
Commissioner, FDA, 1990—; ordered the removal of misleading information from food labels.
b. May 13, 1951 in New York, New York
Source: *AmMWSc 92; BioIn 16; CurBio 91; News 92; WhoAmP 91*

Ketcham, Hank
[Henry King Ketcham]
American. Cartoonist
Created comic strip "Dennis the Menace," 1952.
b. Mar 14, 1920 in Seattle, Washington
Source: *AmAu&B; BioIn 3, 4, 5, 11, 13, 15, 17, 19; ConAu 105; CurBio 56; EncACom; EncAJ; EncTwCJ; LegTOT; LinLib L; SmATA 27, 28; WhoAm 74, 76, 78, 80, 82, 84, 86, 88, 90, 92, 94, 95, 96, 97; WhoAmA 73, 76, 78, 80, 82, 84, 86, 89, 91, 93; WhoWest 74, 76, 78, 94; WhoWor 74; WorECom*

Ketchel, Stanley
[Stanislaus Kiecal]
"Cyclone"; "The Michigan Assassin"; "The Montana Wonder"
American. Boxer
World middleweight champion, 1908; defeated by Jack Johnson, 1909.
b. Sep 14, 1887 in Grand Rapids, Michigan
d. Oct 15, 1910 in New York, New York
Source: *WhoBox 74; WhoSpor*

Ketelsen, James Lee
American. Business Executive
Chairman of Tenneco, Houston-based conglomerate, 1978—.
b. Nov 14, 1930 in Davenport, Iowa
Source: *BioIn 9, 12; IntWW 80, 81, 82, 83, 89, 91, 93; WhoAm 76, 78, 80, 82, 84, 86, 88, 90, 92, 96; WhoFI 74, 79, 81, 83, 85, 87, 89, 94; WhoMW 90; WhoSSW 84, 86, 88, 91, 93; WhoWor 82, 84, 89, 91*

Kettering, Charles Franklin
"Boss"
American. Engineer
Invented auto self-starter, 1911, replacing hand crank.
b. Aug 29, 1876 in Loudonville, Ohio
d. Nov 25, 1958 in Dayton, Ohio
Source: *BiDAmBL 83; BioIn 1, 2, 3, 4, 5, 6, 7, 9, 11, 12, 13; CurBio 40, 51, 59; DcAmB S6; DcScB; EncAB-A 36; EncABHB 5; InSci; LinLib S; NatCAB 48; NotTwCS; ObitOF 79; OxCAmH; PseudN 82; WebAB 74, 79; WhAm 3*

Kevorkian, Jack
"Dr. Death"; "Suicide Doctor"
American. Pathologist
Promotes physician-assisted suicide; inventor of the suicide machine, 1990; assisted in dozens of suicides.
b. May 26, 1928 in Pontiac, Michigan
Source: *CurBio 94; LegTOT; News 91, 91-3; WhoAm 95, 96*

Key, Francis Scott
American. Composer
Wrote "The Star-Spangled Banner," Sep 13-14, 1814; adopted by Congress as national anthem, 1931.
b. Aug 1, 1779 in Carroll County, Maryland
d. Jan 11, 1843 in Baltimore, Maryland
Source: *Alli; AmAu; AmAu&B; AmBi; Baker 78, 84, 92; BbD; Benet 87, 96; BenetAL 91; BiAUS; BibAL; BiDAmM; BiD&SB; BiDSA; BioIn 1, 3, 4, 5, 6, 7, 8, 9, 11, 19, 20, 21; ChhPo, S2; CnDAL; CyAL 1; DcAmAu; DcAmB; DcAmSR; DcArts; DcLEL; DcNAA; Drake; EncAB-H 1974, 1996; EncSoH; EvLB; LegTOT; LinLib L, S; OxCAmH; OxCAmL 65, 83, 95; OxCEng 67; PoChrch; RComAH; REn; REnAL; SouWr; WebAB 74, 79; WhAm HS; WorAl; WorAlBi*

Key, Ted
[Theodore Key]
American. Cartoonist
Created "Hazel," appeared in *Saturday Evening Post,* 1943-69; syndicated, 1969—.
b. Aug 25, 1912 in Fresno, California
Source: *AmAu&B; BioIn 3, 9, 15; ConAu 13R, X; ConGrA 1; EncTwCJ; LegTOT; ScF&FL 92; WhAmArt 85; WhoAm 74, 76, 78, 80, 82, 84, 86, 88, 90, 92, 94, 95, 96, 97; WhoE 75, 77, 86; WhoEnt 92; WhoWor 80, 82, 84, 87, 89; WhoWorJ 72, 78; WorECar*

Key, Valdimer Orlando, Jr.
American. Political Scientist, Author
Wrote *Public Opinion and American Democracy,* 1961.
b. Mar 13, 1908 in Austin, Texas
d. Oct 4, 1963 in Cambridge, Massachusetts
Source: *DcAmB S7; WebBD 83*

Keyes, Alan L(ee)
American. Politician
Candidate for US president, 1996; host of nationally syndicated radio program, "America's Wake-Up Call."
b. Aug 7, 1950 in New York, New York

Keyes, Daniel
American. Author
Books on psychological themes include *Flowers for Algernon,* 1966.
b. Aug 9, 1927 in New York, New York
Source: *BenetAL 91; BioIn 7, 15, 17; ConAu 10NR, 17R, 26NR, 54NR; ConLC 80; ConSFA; DrAPF 80, 91; DrAS 74E, 78E, 82E; EncSF, 93; IntAu&W 89, 91, 93; NewEScF; Novels; RGSF; RGTwCSF; RGTwCWr; ScF&FL 1, 2; ScFSB; SmATA 37; TwCSFW 81, 86, 91; WhoAm 82, 84, 86, 88, 90, 92, 94, 95, 96, 97; WhoMW 84, 92; WhoSciF; WhoSSW 95; WhoUSWr 88; WhoWrEP 89, 92, 95; WrDr 76, 80, 82, 84, 86, 88, 90, 92, 94, 96*

Keyes, Evelyn Louise
American. Actor
Artie Shaw's eighth wife; wrote autobiography *Scarlet O'Hara's Younger Sister,* 1977.
b. Nov 20, 1919 in Port Arthur, Texas
Source: *ConAu 85; FilmEn; FilmgC; HalFC 84; HolP 40; IntMPA 86; MotPP; MovMk; NewYTBS 77; VarWW 85; WhoHol A*

Keyes, Frances Parkinson
American. Author
Best-known novel: *Dinner at Antoine's,* 1948.
b. Jul 21, 1885 in Charlottesville, Virginia
d. Jul 3, 1970 in New Orleans, Louisiana
Source: *AmAu&B; AmNov; ArtclWW 2; Benet 87, 96; BiCAW; BioIn 1, 2, 3, 4, 5, 7, 9, 12, 14; BkC 5; CathA 1930; CelR; ConAu 5R, 7NR, 25R; DcAmB S8; EvLB; LegTOT; LngCTC; Novels; ObitT 1961; OxCAmL 95; PenC AM; REn; SouWr; TwCA, SUP; TwCRGW; TwCRHW 90, 94; TwCWr; WhAm 5; WhNAA; WhoAmW 58, 64, 66, 68, 70, 72; WomNov*

Keyes, Roger John Brownlow, Baron
English. Naval Officer
Veteran hero of WW I, WW II.
b. 1872
d. Dec 26, 1945 in Buckingham, England
Source: *BioIn 10; DcNaB 1941, C; HarEnMi; OxCShps; WhoMilH 76*

Keyhoe, Donald E(dward)
American. Writer
Former military pilot who wrote about both flight and the existence of UFOs, including the book *Aliens from Space,* 1973; served as director, Nat. Investigations Com. on Aerial Phenomena.
b. Jun 20, 1897 in Ottumwa, Iowa
d. Nov 29, 1988 in New Market, Virginia
Source: *AmAu&B; BioIn 4, 16; ConAu 127; CurBio 89N; EncO&P 3; InSci; NewYTBS 88; ScFEYrs; UFOEn; WhAm 10*

Keylor, Arthur W
American. Publisher
VP in charge of mags., Time Inc., 1972-81; brought back *Life,* 1978; introduced *People,* 1974; *Discovery,* 1980.
b. 1920?
d. Aug 17, 1981 in Manchester, Vermont
Source: *BioIn 12; ConAu 104; Dun&B 79; WhoFI 74*

Keynes, John Maynard, Baron
English. Economist, Journalist
Best known for *The General Theory of Employment, Interest, and Money,* 1936; theories of unbalanced budgets.
b. Jun 5, 1883 in Cambridge, England
d. Apr 21, 1946 in London, England
Source: *Benet 87, 96; BiDInt; BioIn 12, 13, 14, 15, 16, 17, 18, 19, 20, 21; ConAu 114; DcAmC; DcLB DS10; DcLEL; DcNaB 1941; DcScB; DcTwHis; EncABHB 7; EvLB; FacFETw; GayLesB; GrBr; GrEconB; HisEWW; LegTOT; LngCTC; MakMC; McGEWB; NewC; NewCBEL; ObitOF 79; OxCEng 67, 85, 95; OxCPhil; PseudN 82; RAdv 14, 13-3; REn; ThTwC 87; TwCA, SUP; TwCLC 64; WebE&AL; WhAm 2; WhDW; WhE&EA; WhLit; WhoEc 81, 86; WorAl; WorAlBi*

Keys, Ancel Benjamin
American. Physiologist, Author
Nutrition expert; developed WW II K-rations; researched diet, heart disease.
b. Jan 26, 1904 in Colorado Springs, Colorado
Source: *AmMWSc 73P, 82, 86; ConAu 61; CurBio 66; WhoWor 74; WrDr 86*

Keyser, Thomas De
Dutch. Artist
Outstanding Dutch portrait painter prior to Rembrandt: *Burgomasters of Amsterdam.*
b. 1596 in Amsterdam, Netherlands
d. Jun 7, 1667 in Amsterdam, Netherlands
Source: *BioIn 1, 19; McGDA; McGEWB; NewCol 75; OxCArt; OxDcArt*

Keyserling, Hermann Alexander Graf Von
German. Philosopher
Expoused intuitional "popular mysticism"; wrote *The Book of Marriage,* 1926.
b. Jul 20, 1880 in Konno, Russia
d. Apr 26, 1946 in Innsbruck, Austria
Source: *CurBio 46; EvEuW; LngCTC; OxCGer 76; PenC EUR; REn; TwCA SUP*

Keyserling, Leon Hirsch
American. Economist, Government Official
Helped establish Council of Economic Advisers; member, 1946-53, chairman, 1949-53.
b. Jan 22, 1908 in Charleston, South Carolina
d. Aug 9, 1987 in Washington, District of Columbia
Source: *BioIn 1, 2, 5, 7, 11; ConAu 61; CurBio 47, 87; PolProf E, K, T; WhoAm 86; WhoEc 86; WrDr 86*

Keyserlingk, Robert Wendelin Henry
American. Publisher
Pres., Palm Publishers; books include *Fathers of Europe,* 1972.
b. Nov 2, 1905 in Saint Petersburg, Russia
Source: *CanWW 70, 79, 80, 81, 83; CathA 1952; IntYB 78; WhoFI 74*

Keyworth, George Albert
American. Government Official
Director, US Office of Science, Technology; adviser to Reagan, 1981-86.
b. Nov 30, 1939 in Boston, Massachusetts
Source: *AmMWSc 86; CurBio 86; IntWW 82, 83, 89, 91, 93; IntWWE; WhoAm 84, 88, 90, 92, 94, 95, 96, 97; WhoAmP 85; WhoE 86; WhoFI 92; WhoMW 90; WhoTech 82*

Khachaturian, Aram
[Aram Ilych Khachaturyan]
Russian. Composer
Outstanding Soviet composer, noted for internationally popular "Saber dance," 1942.
b. Jun 6, 1903 in Tiflis, Russia
d. May 1, 1978 in Moscow, Union of Soviet Socialist Republics
Source: *Baker 78, 84; BriBkM 80; CnOxB; CurBio 48, 78, 78N; DancEn 78; DcCM; DcCom 77; DcCom&M 79; DcFM; IntDcB; IntWW 74, 75, 76; MusMk; NewGrDM 80; NewOxM; OxCMus; PenDiMP A; WhoMus 72; WorAl; WorAlBi*

Khaikin, Boris
Russian. Conductor
With Moscow's Bolshoi Theater, 1954-78; first performed many Soviet operas.
b. 1905
d. May 11, 1978 in Moscow, Union of Soviet Socialist Republics
Source: *Baker 84; BioIn 11; NewGrDM 80; WhoSocC 78*

Khalid Ibn Abdul Azia Al-Saud
Saudi. Ruler
Ruled Saudi Arabia, 1975-82, following King Faisal's assassination.
b. 1913 in Riyadh, Arabia
d. Jun 13, 1982 in Taif, Saudi Arabia
Source: *AnObit 1982; CurBio 76, 82; IntWW 80; MidE 79; NewYTBS 82; WhoGov 72; WhoWor 80; WorAl*

Khalil, Mustafa
Egyptian. Political Leader
Held many govt. positions including prime minister, 1978-80.
b. Nov 18, 1920 in El Kalyoubleh, Egypt
Source: *BioIn 11; HisEAAC; IntWW 81, 82, 83, 89, 91, 93; MidE 79, 80, 81, 82; NewYTBS 78*

Khama, Seretse M, Sir
Botswana. Political Leader
First pres. of Botswana, 1966-80.
b. Jul 1, 1921 in Serowe, Bechuanaland
d. Jul 13, 1980 in Gaborone, Botswana
Source: *CurBio 67, 80N; InB&W 85; IntWW 74; McGEWB; NewYTBS 80; Who 74; WhoWor 74*

Khambatta, Persis
Indian. Actor
Starred in *Star Trek: The Movie,* 1979; *Nighthawks,* 1982.
b. Oct 2, 1950 in Bombay, India
Source: *BioIn 11, 12; HalFC 84, 88; JohnWSW; WhoHol 92*

Khamenei, (Sayed) Ali, Hojatolislam
Iranian. Political Leader
President, Islamic Republic of Iran, 1981-89; replaced Khomeini as Iran's supreme religious leader, 1989.
b. 1939 in Khorasan, Iran
Source: *CurBio 87; NewYTBS 81, 89; WhoWor 87*

Khan, Abdul Ghaffar
"Frontier Gandhi"
Pakistani. Political Activist
Helped Gandhi gain independence for India through passive resistance; opposed Pakistani separation, 1947.
b. 1891
d. Jan 20, 1988 in Peshawar, Pakistan
Source: *BioIn 3, 8, 9, 19*

Khan, Ali Akbar
Indian. Musician, Director
Int'l tours include collaborations with Yehudi Menuhin, Duke Ellington, others.
b. Apr 14, 1922 in Shivpur, India
Source: *BioIn 9; BriBkM 80; ConAmC 76, 82; FarE&A 78, 79, 80, 81; IntWW 74, 75, 76, 77, 78, 79, 80, 81, 82, 83, 89, 91, 93; NewGrDM 80; WhoAmM 83; WhoWor 74, 76, 78*

Khan, Chaka
[Rufus; Yvette Marie Stevens]
American. Singer
Lead singer with funk-rock group Rufus, 1972-78; solo hit "I Feel for You," 1984; won several Grammys.
b. Mar 23, 1953 in Great Lakes, Illinois
Source: *ConBlB 12; ConMus 9; DrBlPA 90; EncPR&S 89; EncRk 88; EncRkSt; HarEnR 86; IlEncBM 82; InB&W 80, 85; LegTOT; NewAmDM; NewGrDA 86; PenEncP; PseudN 82; RolSEnR 83; SoulM; WhoAm 88, 90, 92, 94, 95, 96, 97; WhoAmW 91, 93; WhoBlA 85, 88; WhoEnt 92; WhoRocM 82; WorAlBi*

Khan, Fazlur Rahman
American. Architect
Designed Chicago's Sears Tower, tallest building in world, 1974.
b. Apr 3, 1929 in Dacca, India
d. Mar 27, 1982, Saudi Arabia
Source: *AnObit 1982; BioIn 11, 12, 13; ConArch 87, 94; McGMS 80; NewYTBS 82; WhAm 8; WhoAm 74, 76, 78, 80, 82; WhoTech 82; WhoWor 74*

Khan, Princess Yasmin Aga
American.
Daughter of Rita Hayworth and Prince Aly Khan; established fund-raiser in mother's name for Alzheimer's Disease research.
b. 1950?
Source: *NewYTBS 78*

Khanga, Yelena
Russian. Journalist
Wrote *Soul to Soul: The Story of a Black Russian American Family, 1865-1992,* 1992.
b. 1962 in Moscow, Union of Soviet Socialist Republics
Source: *ConBlB 6*

Kharitonov, Yevgeni
Russian. Poet, Dramatist
Attempted to form experimental literary workshop which was suppressed by Soviets, 1980; wrote *Under House Arrest.*
b. 1941?
d. Jun 29, 1981 in Moscow, Union of Soviet Socialist Republics
Source: *BioIn 12; NewYTBS 81*

Khashoggi, Adnan
Saudi. Businessman
Richest man in world, 1986.
b. Jul 25, 1935 in Mecca, Saudi Arabia
Source: *CurBio 86; LegTOT; NewYTBS 75; WhoArab 81*

Khatami, Mohammad
Iranian. Political Leader
Pres., Iran, 1997—.
b. 1943 in Ardakan, Iran

Kheel, Theodore Woodrow
American. Lawyer
Labor arbitrator who mediated many serious strikes: 1963 NYC newspaper strike, city's longest to that date.
b. May 9, 1914 in New York, New York
Source: *BioIn 7, 8, 9, 11, 12; CurBio 64; NewYTBS 80; PolProf J, K; St&PR 75; WhoAm 74, 76, 78, 80, 82, 84, 86, 88, 90, 92, 94, 95, 96, 97; WhoE 74; WhoFI 75; WhoLab 76*

Khodasevich, Vladislav
Russian. Poet
Wrote verse *Putem Zerna,* 1920.
b. May 29, 1886 in Moscow, Russia
d. Jun 14, 1939 in Paris, France
Source: *CasWL; ClDMEL 47; ConAu 115; ConLC 15; TwCLC 15*

Khomeini, Ruhollah Musavi, Ayatollah
Iranian. Religious Leader
Supreme leader of Iran, 1979-89; leader of Shite Moslems in Iran; supported taking American hostages, 1979.
b. May 17, 1900 in Khomein, Persia
d. Jun 3, 1989 in Tehran, Iran
Source: *BioIn 11; BkPepl; ColdWar 2; CurBio 79, 89; NewYTBS 89*

Khorana, Har Gobind
American. Scientist, Educator
Shared 1968 Nobel Prize in medicine for work in genetics.
b. Jan 9, 1922 in Raipur, India
Source: *AmMWSc 73P, 76P, 79, 82, 86, 89, 92, 95; AsAmAlm; AsBiEn; BiESc; BioIn 8, 9, 10, 14, 15, 20; BlueB 76; CamDcSc; CurBio 70; FarE&A 78, 79, 80, 81; IntWW 74, 75, 76, 77, 78, 79, 80, 81, 82, 83, 89, 91, 93; LarDcSc; LegTOT; McGEWB; McGMS 80; NobelP; NotAsAm; NotTwCS; WebAB 74, 79; WhDW; Who 74, 82, 83, 85, 88, 90, 92, 94; WhoAm 74, 76, 78, 80, 82, 84, 86, 88, 90, 92, 94, 95, 96, 97; WhoAsA 94; WhoE 85, 86, 89, 91, 93, 95, 97; WhoFrS 84; WhoMedH; WhoNob, 90, 95; WhoScEn 94, 96; WhoWor 74, 78, 80, 82, 84, 87, 89, 91, 93, 95, 96, 97; WorAl; WorScD*

Khrennikov, Tikhon Nikolaevich
Russian. Composer
Major spokesman for Soviet musical policy; works often based on folk music; operas include *Mother,* 1957.
b. Jun 10, 1913 in Elets, Russia
Source: *Baker 84; BiDSovU; BioIn 2, 9, 15, 21; DcCM; IntWW 83; MusMk; NewGrDM 80; OxCMus; SovUn; WhoSocC 78; WhoWor 74, 87*

Khrunov, Evgeny Vasilievich
Russian. Cosmonaut
Engineer on spacecraft *Soyuz-5,* 1969; did scientific work outside ship; awarded Red Star.
b. Sep 10, 1933
Source: *IntWW 74, 75, 76; WorDWW*

Khrushchev, Nikita Sergeyevich
Russian. Political Leader
Premier, 1958-64; favored peaceful coexistence with the West.
b. Apr 17, 1894 in Kalinovka, Ukraine
d. Sep 11, 1971 in Moscow, Union of Soviet Socialist Republics
Source: *Benet 87, 96; ColdWar 2; ConAu 112; CurBio 54, 71; DcTwHis; EncRev; FacFETw; LinLib L, S; ObitOF 79; ObitT 1971; REn; WhAm 5; WhDW; WorAl*

Khrushchev, Nina Petrovna
Russian.
Wife of Nikita Khrushchev, 1924-71; worked as teacher.
b. 1900
d. Aug 8, 1984 in Moscow, Union of Soviet Socialist Republics
Source: *AnObit 1984; BioIn 14; InWom; NewYTBS 84*

Kiam, Omar
[Alexander Kiam]
American. Fashion Designer
Championed American-designed fashions; designed clothes for Hollywood, Broadway stars.
b. 1894 in Monterrey, Mexico
d. Mar 28, 1954 in New York, New York
Source: *BioIn 3; CurBio 45, 54; DcAmB S5; EncFash; WorFshn*

Kiam, Victor Kermit, II
American. Business Executive
Pres., CEO, Remington Products, Inc., 1979—; former owner, NFL New England Patriots.
b. Dec 7, 1926 in New Orleans, Louisiana
Source: *BioIn 13; St&PR 84, 87; WhoAm 74, 76, 78, 80, 82, 84, 88, 90, 92, 96, 97; WhoE 91; WhoFI 74; WhoWor 80*

Kibbee, Guy
American. Actor
Character actor, 1931-49; played title role in *Scattergood Baines* series, 1941-42.
b. Mar 6, 1882 in El Paso, Texas
d. May 24, 1956 in East Islip, New York
Source: *BioIn 21; EncAFC; FilmEn; FilmgC; ForYSC; HalFC 80, 84, 88; HolCA; LegTOT; MotPP; MovMk; NotNAT B; OlFamFa; Vers A; WhoHol B; WhScrn 74, 77*

Kibbee, Robert Joseph
American. University Administrator
Chancellor, CUNY, NYC, 1971-82; son of actor Guy Kibbee.
b. Aug 19, 1920 in New York, New York
d. Jun 16, 1982 in New York, New York
Source: *AnObit 1982; NewYTBE 71; NewYTBS 82; WhoAm 80, 82; WhoE 74, 81*

Kicking Bird
American. Native American Leader
Kiowa tribal leader; believed that peace and accommodation with white America was necessary to the survival of the Native Americans.
b. 1835? in Oklahoma
d. May 4, 1875
Source: *BioIn 11, 21; EncNAB; NotNaAm; WhNaAH*

Kickingbird, Kirke
American. Lawyer
Executive director, Institute for the Development of Indian Law, 1971-75, 1978—.
b. 1944 in Wichita, Kansas
Source: *BioIn 21; NotNaAm*

Kicknosway, Faye
American. Poet
Self-illustrated books of poetry include *Nothing Wakes Her,* 1978.
b. Dec 16, 1936 in Detroit, Michigan
Source: *ConAu 7NR, 57; DrAPF 80; IntAu&W 86; MichAu 80; WhoUSWr 88; WhoWrEP 89, 92, 95*

Kid Chocolate
[Eligio Sardinias]
"The Cuban Bon Bon"
Cuban. Boxer
Colorful feather and junior lightweight; Hall of Fame, 1959.
b. Jan 6, 1910 in Cerro, Cuba
d. Aug 8, 1988 in Havana, Cuba
Source: *BioIn 1, 16; InB&W 80; WhoBox 74*

Kid Creole and the Coconuts
[August Darnell; Taryn Haegy; Andy Hernandez; Adriana Kaegi; Cheryl Poirier]
American. Music Group
Music is Latin based with pop-rock influences: album *Tropical Gangsters,* 1982.
Source: *BioIn 16; EncRk 88; NewGrDA 86; PenEncP; RolSEnR 83; WhoRocM 82; WhsNW 85*

Kidd, Michael
[Milton Greenwald]
American. Choreographer
Won five Tonys, 1940s-50s, including one for *Guys and Dolls,* 1957; won honorary Oscar, 1997.
b. Aug 12, 1919 in New York, New York
Source: *BiE&WWA; BioIn 1, 3, 5; CelR; CmMov; CnOxB; ConTFT 10; CurBio 60; DancEn 78; EncMT; FilmEn; FilmgC; ForYSC; HalFC 80, 84, 88; IntDcF 1-4, 2-4; IntMPA 96; LegTOT; MiSFD 9; NotNAT; OxCAmT 84; PseudN 82; VarWW 85; WhoAm 76, 86, 94, 95, 96, 97; WhoHol 92, A; WhoThe 72, 77, 81; WorAl; WorAlBi; WorEFlm*

Kidd, William
American. Skier
First American male to win a medal in Alpine skiing, 1964 Olympics.
b. Apr 13, 1943 in Burlington, Vermont
Source: *BiDAmSp OS*

Kidd, William, Captain
"The Wizard of the Sea"
Scottish. Pirate
Poe's story *The Gold Bug,* Stevenson's novel *Treasure Island* based on his exploits.
b. 1645 in Greenock, Scotland
d. May 23, 1701 in London, England
Source: *Alli; AmBi; ApCAB; Benet 87, 96; BenetAL 91; BioIn 1, 2, 3, 4, 6, 7, 8, 9, 11, 12; DcAmB; Drake; DrInf; HisDBrE; NewC; OxCAmH; OxCAmL 65, 83, 95; OxCLaw; OxCShps; PseudN 82; REn; REnAL; WebAB 74, 79; WhAm HS; WhDW; WorAl; WorAlBi*

Kidder, Alfred Vincent
American. Archaeologist
Directed Pecos pueblo project, 1915-29; won first Viking Medal, 1946.
b. Oct 29, 1885 in Marquette, Michigan
d. Jun 11, 1963 in Cambridge, Massachusetts
Source: *BioIn 1, 5, 6, 7, 8, 9, 19; DcAmB S7; McGEWB; NatCAB 50; REnAW; WhAm 4*

Kidder, Margot
American. Actor
Played Lois Lane in movies *Superman,* 1978; *Superman II,* 1981.
b. Oct 17, 1948 in Yellowknife, Northwest Territories, Canada
Source: *BioIn 20; CanWW 31, 83, 89; ConTFT 1, 6; FilmEn; HalFC 80, 84, 88; IntMPA 82, 84, 86, 88, 92, 94, 96; InWom SUP; LegTOT; VarWW 85; WhoAm 80, 82, 84, 86, 88, 90, 92, 94, 95, 96, 97; WhoAmW 87, 89, 91, 93, 95, 97; WhoEnt 92; WhoHol 92, A; WhoHrs 80; WorAlBi*

Kidjo, Anjelique
Beninese. Singer
International singer who blends various musical genres in her work, such as indigenous songs of Benin, samba, zouk, classic funk, rock-salsa, Indian and Arabic tones, and American gospel and jazz; released first album *Logozo* in 1991 and later recorded albums *Aye,* 1993 which included hit single "Agolo," and *Fifa,* 1996.
Source: *ConMus 17*

Kidman, Nicole
American. Actor
Films include *Days of Thunder,* 1990; *Far and Away,* 1992; *To Die For,* 1995; *The Portrait of a Lady,* 1996.
b. Jun 20, 1967 in Hawaii
Source: *IntMPA 94, 96; LegTOT; News 92; WhoAm 94, 95, 96, 97; WhoAmW 95, 97*

Kid 'n Play
[Christopher Martin; Christopher Reid]
American. Rap Group
Rap duo; debut album *Hype,* 1988, went gold; appeared in film *House Party,* 1990.
Source: *BioIn 15, 17; ConAu X; ConMus 5; DcCanB 1; DcLP 87B; Film 2; Law&B 89A, 92; St&PR 96, 97; WhoAfA 96; WhoBlA 94; WhoHol 92*

Kidwell, Clara Sue
American. Author, Historian
Wrote *The Choctaws: A Critical Bibliography,* 1980; asst. director for cultural resources, Smithsonian Institution's National Museum of the American Indian, 1993—.
b. Jul 8, 1941 in Tahlequah, Oklahoma
Source: *AmWomHi; ConAu 150; NotNaAm*

Kiedis, Anthony
[Red Hot Chili Peppers]
American. Singer
Won Grammy, Best Hard Rock Song, "Give it Away," (with Red Hot Chili Peppers) 1992.
b. Nov 1, 1962 in Grand Rapids, Michigan
Source: *LegTOT*

Kiefer, Anselm Karl Albert
German. Artist, Sculptor
Painter and sculptor noted for multimedia works of varied, complex subjects, including Nazism, nuclear energy.
b. Mar 8, 1945 in Donaueschingen, Germany
Source: *BioIn 13; ConArt 83; CurBio 88; WhoWor 87, 89, 91*

Kiel, Richard
American. Actor
Stands seven feet, two inches; played part of Jaws in James Bond films *The Spy Who Loved Me, Moonracker.*
b. Sep 13, 1939 in Redford, Michigan
Source: *ConTFT 9; FilmEn; ForYSC; HalFC 80, 84, 88; IntMPA 84, 86, 88, 92, 94, 96; ItaFilm; LegTOT; VarWW 85; WhoHol 92, A; WhoHrs 80*

Kiely, Benedict
American. Author
Writings focus on Ireland: *All the Way to Bantry Bay,* 1978.
b. Aug 15, 1919 in County Tyrone, Ireland
Source: *Au&Wr 71; Benet 87, 96; BioIn 3, 9, 10, 13, 14; CathA 1952; ConAu 1R, 2NR; ConLC 23, 43; ConNov 72, 76, 82, 86, 91, 96; CyWA 89; DcIrL 96; DcIrW 1, 2; DcLB 15; DcLEL 1940; IntAu&W 76, 91, 93; ModBrL S2; ModIrL; OxCIri; WhE&EA; WorAu 1950; WrDr 76, 80, 82, 84, 86, 88, 90, 92, 94, 96*

Kienholz, Edward
American. Artist
His exhibitions of 3-D art objects in life-size tableaux include *Roxy's,* 1961 and *Art in America,* 1988.
b. Oct 23, 1927 in Fairfield, Washington
d. Jun 10, 1994 in Hope, Idaho
Source: *BioIn 7, 10, 13, 14, 15, 16, 20, 21; BriEAA; ConArt 77, 83, 89, 96; CurBio 89, 94N; DcAmArt; DcCAA 71, 77, 88, 94; EncWB; IntDcAA 90; NewYTBS 94; OxCTwCA; OxDcArt; PhDcTCA 77; PrintW 85; WhAm 11; WhoAm 88; WorArt 1950*

Kienzl, Wilhelm
Austrian. Composer
A confirmed Wagnerian; wrote opera *Der Evangelimann,* 1895.
b. Jan 17, 1857 in Waizenkircen, Austria
d. Oct 3, 1941 in Vienna, Austria
Source: *Baker 78, 84, 92; MetOEnc; NewEOp 71; NewGrDM 80; NewGrDO; OxCMus; OxDcOp*

Kienzle, William X(avier)
[Mark Boyle]
American. Author
Former priest who wrote *The Rosary Murders,* 1979; *Death Wears a Red Hat,* 1980.
b. Sep 11, 1928 in Detroit, Michigan
Source: *BioIn 12, 14; ConAu 9NR, 31NR, 93; ConLC 25; IntAu&W 91; MajTwCW; PseudN 82; TwCCr&M 85, 91; WhoMW 93, 96; WrDr 92, 94, 96*

Kiepura, Jan Wiktor
"Polish Caruso"
American. Opera Singer, Actor
Popular stage, film, opera tenor; Hollywood debut, 1936, with Gladys Swarthout.
b. May 16, 1902 in Sosnowiec, Poland
d. Aug 15, 1966 in Harrison, New York
Source: *Baker 84; BiE&WWA; CurBio 43, 66; FilmgC; MovMk; NotNAT A; OxCFilm; OxCMus; WhAm 4; WhScrn 77*

Kieran, John Francis
"A Walking Encyclopedia"
American. Editor, TV Personality
Radio, TV panelist of "Information Please" from 1938; edited *Information Please Almanac.*
b. Aug 2, 1892 in New York, New York
d. Dec 10, 1981 in Rockport, Massachusetts
Source: *AmAu&B; AuBYP 2; BiDAmSp OS; BioIn 1, 2; CathA 1930; ChhPo S1; ConAu 101, 105; CurBio 40, 82; PseudN 82; REn; REnAL; WhAm 8; WhoAm 74, 76, 78; WhoE 74*

Kierkegaard, Soren Aabye
[Soren Aabye Kjerkegaard]
Danish. Philosopher, Author
Regarded as founder of existentialism; attacked organized religion.
b. May 5, 1813 in Copenhagen, Denmark
d. Nov 11, 1855 in Copenhagen, Denmark

Source: *AtlBL; Benet 87, 96; BiD&SB; BioIn 1, 2, 3, 4, 5, 6, 7, 8, 9, 10, 11, 12, 13; CasWL; ClDMEL 80; CyWA 58; DcArts; DcEuL; Dis&D; EncEth; EuAu; EvEuW; LngCTC; McGEWB; OxCEng 67, 85, 95; OxCGer 76; OxCPhil; PenC EUR; RComWL; REn; WebBD 83*

Kiernan, Walter
American. Journalist
Wrote syndicated column, "One Man's Opinion"; became radio show, 1945-69.
b. Jan 24, 1902 in New Haven, Connecticut
d. Jan 8, 1978 in Daytona Beach, Florida
Source: *BioIn 2, 11; ConAu 73; NewYTBS 78; RadStar; WhAm 7; WhoAm 74, 76*

Kiesinger, Kurt Georg
German. Politician
W Germany's third chancellor, 1966-69; controversial because of 1933 Nazi Party membership.
b. Apr 6, 1904 in Ebingen, Germany
d. Mar 9, 1988 in Frankfurt, Germany (West)
Source: *BioIn 7, 8, 15, 16, 18, 21; ColdWar 1, 2; CurBio 67, 88, 88N; DcPol; DcTwHis; EncCW; FacFETw; IntWW 74, 75, 76, 77, 78, 79, 80, 81, 82, 83; IntYB 78, 79, 80, 81, 82; NewYTBS 88; Who 74, 82, 83, 85, 88; WhoWor 74, 76, 78*

Kiesler, Frederick John
American. Architect
Noted for his "Endless House," 1960; and the Shrine of the Book, the Israeli building containing the Dead Sea Scrolls.
b. Sep 22, 1892 in Vienna, Austria
d. Dec 27, 1965 in New York, New York
Source: *BioIn 2, 3, 5, 7, 12; CamGWoT; ConArch 87; DcCAA 88; DcTwDes; FacFETw; McGDA; PenDiDA 89; WhAmArt 85; WhoAmA 91N*

Kiesling, Walt(er)
American. Football Player
Guard, 1926-38, with seven pro teams including Green Bay; Hall of Fame, 1966.
b. May 27, 1903 in Saint Paul, Minnesota
d. Mar 2, 1962
Source: *BioIn 8, 17; LegTOT; WhoFtbl 74*

Kieslowski, Krzysztof
Polish. Filmmaker
Made *Decalogue,* 1988; *Red,* 1994.
b. Jun 27, 1941 in Warsaw, Poland
d. Mar 13, 1996 in Warsaw, Poland
Source: *BiDFilm 94; BioIn 17, 20, 21; ConAu 147, 151; ConTFT 11; CurBio 95, 96N; DrEEuF; EncEurC; IntMPA 96; IntWW 93; MiSFD 9; News 96, 96-3; NewYTBS 27; WhoSoCE 89*

Kiick, Jim
[James F Kiick]
"Butch Cassidy"
American. Football Player
Running back, with Larry Csonka, in Miami backfield, 1968-74; led NFL in rushing TDs, 1969.
b. Aug 9, 1946 in Lincoln Park, New Jersey
Source: *BioIn 9, 10; WhoFtbl 74*

Kiker, Douglas
American. Broadcast Journalist, Author
Correspondent, NBC News since 1966; author of several books; won Peabody Award, 1970.
b. Jan 7, 1930 in Griffin, Georgia
d. Aug 14, 1991 in Chatham, Massachusetts
Source: *Au&Wr 71; ConAu 65, 135; LesBEnT 92; NewYTBS 91; NewYTET; WhAm 10; WhoTelC*

Kilbracken, John Raymond Godley, Baron
Irish. Author
Books include *Bring Back My Stringbag,* 1979; *Living Like a Lord,* 1955.
b. Oct 17, 1920 in London, England
Source: *Au&Wr 71; BiDIrW; BioIn 4, 6; ConAu 5R; DcIrW 2; IntAu&W 91; PseudN 82; Who 74, 85, 92; WrDr 76, 80, 86, 92*

Kilbride, Percy
American. Actor
Played Pa Kettle in film series, 1947-55.
b. Jul 16, 1888 in San Francisco, California
d. Dec 11, 1964 in Los Angeles, California
Source: *BioIn 2, 7; EncAFC; FilmEn; FilmgC; ForYSC; HalFC 80, 84, 88; MotPP; MovMk; NotNAT B; ObitOF 79; Vers A; WhoHol B; WhScrn 74, 77, 83*

Kilburn, Peter
American. Hostage
Former librarian at American U of Beirut taken hostage by Lebanese terrorist groups; after 500 days in captivity was slain, Apr 17, 1986.
b. 1925? in San Francisco, California
d. Apr 17, 1986, Lebanon
Source: *BioIn 14*

Kilenyi, Edward, Sr.
American. Musician, Composer
Hollywood music director for 30 yrs; Gershwin's teacher.
b. Jan 25, 1884 in Bekes, Austria-Hungary
d. Aug 15, 1968 in Tallahassee, Florida
Source: *ASCAP 66, 80; Baker 78, 84, 92; ConAmC 76, 82; IntWWM 90; NewGrDA 86; Who 92*

Kiley, Richard Paul
American. Actor, Singer
Won 1966 Tony Award as Don Quixote in *Man of La Mancha;* an 1988 Emmy for TV mini-series "The Thorn Birds."
b. Mar 31, 1922 in Chicago, Illinois
Source: *BiE&WWA; BioNews 75; CelR 90; ConTFT 1; CurBio 73; EncMT; FilmgC; HalFC 84, 88; IntMPA 92; NotNAT; VarWW 85; WhoAm 74, 76, 78, 80, 82, 84, 86, 88, 90, 92, 94, 95, 96, 97; WhoEnt 92; WhoHol A; WhoThe 81; WhoWor 74, 76*

Kilgallen, Dorothy
[Mrs. Richard Kollmar]
American. Journalist, TV Personality
Reporter, gossip columnist, NY *Journal-American,* beginning 1930s.
b. Jul 3, 1913 in Chicago, Illinois
d. Nov 8, 1965 in New York, New York
Source: *BioAmW; BioIn 1, 2, 3, 4, 5, 6, 7, 8, 10, 12, 15, 16; ConAu 89; CurBio 52, 66; EncAJ; EncTwCJ; InWom, SUP; LegTOT; NotNAT B; RadStar; SaTiSS; WhAm 4; WhoAmW 58, 64, 66; WhoHol B; WhScrn 74, 77, 83*

Kilgore, Al
American. Cartoonist
Drew "Bullwinkle" comic strip; co-author *Laurel and Hardy.*
b. Dec 19, 1927 in Newark, New Jersey
d. Aug 15, 1983 in New York, New York
Source: *WhoAm 74, 76; WhoAmA 76, 78, 80, 82, 84, 86, 89, 91, 93N*

Kilgore, Bernard
[Leslie Bernard Kilgore]
American. Journalist
Pres., Dow, Jones & Co., 1945-67; built *Wall Street Journal* into major newspaper.
b. Nov 9, 1908 in Albany, Indiana
d. Nov 14, 1967 in Princeton, New Jersey
Source: *BiDAmJo; BioIn 2, 5, 8, 13, 16, 19; DcLB 127; EncTwCJ; ObitOF 79; WhAm 4*

Kilgour, Joseph
Actor
Silents, 1915-26, include *Let's Get Married,* 1926; *Try and Get It,* 1924.
b. Jul 11, 1863 in Ayr, Ontario, Canada
d. Apr 20, 1933 in Bay Shore, New York
Source: *Film 1, 2; NotNAT B; TwYS; WhScrn 77*

Kilian, Victor
American. Actor
Played Grandpa Larkin, the "Fernwood Flasher," on TV series "Mary Hartman, Mary Hartman."
b. Mar 6, 1891 in Jersey City, New Jersey
d. Mar 11, 1979 in Hollywood, California
Source: *BiE&WWA; BioIn 11; EncAFC; Film 2; FilmEn; FilmgC; ForYSC; HolCA; IntMPA 79; MovMk; NewYTBS 79; NotNAT; Vers A; WhoHol A; WhoThe 81N*

Killanin, Michael Morris, Lord
Irish. Olympic Official
Pres., International Olympic Committee, 1972-80, succeeding Avery Brundage.
b. Jul 30, 1914 in London, England
Source: *BiDIrW; BioIn 9, 10, 12, 14; BlueB 76; ConAu 5NR; CurBio 73; IntAu&W 91; IntWW 74, 75, 76, 77, 78, 79, 80, 81, 82, 83, 91; NewYTBS 80; WhE&EA; Who 74, 85, 92; WhoEIO 82; WhoWor 84, 87, 91*

Killebrew, Harmon Clayton
"Killer"
American. Baseball Player
Infielder, 1954-75; had 573 home runs; led AL in home runs seven times, RBIs three times; Hall of Fame, 1984.
b. Jun 29, 1936 in Payette, Idaho
Source: *Ballpl 90; BiDAmSp BB; BioIn 5, 6, 7, 8, 9, 10, 13, 15, 16; CurBio 66; FacFETw; WhoAm 74, 76, 92; WhoProB 73; WorAl; WorAlBi*

Killian, James Rhyne, Jr.
"The Father of Public Television"
American. Government Official
Pres., MIT, 1948-58; adviser to Eisenhower on science, defense issues, 1957-59; helped develop NASA; chaired groups that created public TV, 1960s-70s.
b. Jul 24, 1904 in Blacksburg, South Carolina
d. Jan 29, 1988 in Cambridge, Massachusetts
Source: *AmMWSc 73P, 86; BioIn 1, 2, 3, 4, 5, 11, 12, 14, 15, 16; BlueB 76; ConAu 97; CurBio 59, 88; InSci; IntWW 74, 75, 76, 77, 78, 79, 80, 81, 82, 83; LesBEnT; NewYTBS 88; PseudN 82; St&PR 75; Who 74, 82, 85, 88; WhoAm 86; WhoTech 89N; WhoWor 80*

Killigrew, Thomas
English. Dramatist
Most popular play was comedy *The Parson's Wedding,* 1637; established Drury Lane Theatre, 1663.
b. Feb 7, 1612 in London, England
d. May 19, 1683 in London, England
Source: *Alli; BiD&SB; BioIn 2, 3, 12, 14, 16; BlmGEL; BritAu; CamGEL; CamGLE; CamGWoT; CasWL; Chambr 1; CnThe; DcEnA; DcEnL; DcLB 58; DcNaB, C; EncWT; Ent; EvLB; GrWrEL DR; NewC; NewCBEL; NewCol 75; NotNAT A, B; OxCEng 67, 85, 95; OxCThe 67, 83; PlP&P; REn; REnWD; RfGEnL 91*

Killy, Jean-Claude
French. Skier
Won gold medals in all three men's Alpine skiing events, 1968; co-organizer of the 1992 Winter Olympics in Albertville, France; awarded the Legion d'honneur, 1992.
b. Aug 30, 1943 in Saint-Cloud, France
Source: *BioIn 16; BioNews 74; CelR; ConAu 115; CurBio 68; FacFETw; IntWW 93; LegTOT; WhoFr 79; WhoHol 92, A; WhoWor 74; WorAl; WorAlBi*

Kilmer, Joyce
[Alfred Joyce Kilmer]
American. Poet, Essayist
Wrote poem *Trees,* 1913; killed in WW I.
b. Dec 6, 1886 in New Brunswick, New Jersey
d. Jul 30, 1918 in Seringes, France
Source: *AmAu&B; AmBi; AmLY; ApCAB X; ASCAP 66, 80; Benet 87; BenetAL 91; BibAL; BioIn 1, 5, 6, 7, 8, 15, 19, 20; ChhPo, S1, S2, S3; CnDAL; ConAmL; ConAu 120; DcAmB; DcArts; DcCathB; DcLB 45; DcLEL; DcNAA; EvLB; FacFETw; LegTOT; LinLib L, S; LngCTC; NatCAB 19; OxCAmL 65, 83; OxCTwCP; REn; REnAL; Str&VC; TwCA; WebAB 74, 79; WebAMB; WhAm 1; WorAl; WorAlBi*

Kilmer, Val
American. Actor
Played the role of Jim Morrison in *The Doors,* 1991; played Batman in *Batman Forever,* 1995.
b. Dec 31, 1959 in Los Angeles, California
Source: *BioIn 15; ConTFT 7, 14; CurBio 96; IntMPA 92, 94, 96; LegTOT; News 91; WhoAm 92, 94, 95, 96, 97; WhoHol 92*

Kilpatrick, James J(ackson), Jr.
American. Journalist
Nationally syndicated columnist; gained renown as conservative voice in commentary on "60 Minutes," 1971-79.
b. Nov 1, 1920 in Oklahoma City, Oklahoma
Source: *AmAu&B; AuNews 1, 2; BiDAmNC; BioIn 2, 5, 6, 9, 10, 11, 12, 14; CelR 90; ConAu 1NR, 1R; CurBio 80; DcAmC; EncTwCJ; WhoAm 74, 76, 78, 80, 82, 84, 86, 88, 90, 92, 94, 95, 96, 97; WhoSSW 73, 95, 97; WrDr 86, 88, 90, 92, 94, 96*

Kilroy, James, Jr.
American. Engineer
One of two people to claim responsibility for famous WW II phrase, "Kilroy was here."
b. 1925
d. Mar 11, 1987 in Boston, Massachusetts

Kim, Duk Koo
Korean. Boxer
Died of brain injuries received in title bout against Ray Mancini, Nov 6, 1982.
b. 1959?
d. Nov 13, 1982 in Las Vegas, Nevada
Source: *BioIn 13*

Kim, Willyce
American. Author
Wrote novel *Dancer Dawkins and the California Kid,* 1985.
b. 1946 in Honolulu, Hawaii
Source: *BioIn 19; GayLesB*

Kimball, Fiske
American. Museum Director, Architect
Director, Philadelphia Museum of Art, 1925-55; helped restore colonial Williamsburg, Monticello.
b. Dec 8, 1888 in Newton, Massachusetts
d. Aug 14, 1955 in Munich, Germany (West)
Source: *AmAu&B; BioIn 4, 5, 7, 10; DcAmB S5; NatCAB 47; ObitOF 79; WhAm 3; WhAmArt 85*

Kimball, Spencer Woolley
American. Religious Leader
Pres., Mormon Church, 1973-85; called America's richest, largest, fastest growing church.
b. Mar 28, 1895 in Salt Lake City, Utah
d. Nov 5, 1985 in Salt Lake City, Utah
Source: *BioIn 10, 11, 12, 13; ConAu 45; CurBio 79, 86; NewYTBS 74; WhAm 9; WhoAm 74, 76, 78, 80, 82, 84; WhoWest 76, 78, 82, 84; WhoWor 74*

Kimball, William Wallace
American. Merchant, Manufacturer
His co. became largest manufacturer of keyboard instruments in world, 1880.
b. Mar 22, 1828 in Oxford County, Maine
d. 1904 in Chicago, Illinois
Source: *Entr; NatCAB 9; WhAm 1*

Kimbro, Dennis (Paul)
American. Author
Writer of best-selling books that encourage black entrepreneurship; *Think and Grow Rich: A Black Choice,* 1991.
b. Dec 29, 1950 in Jersey City, New Jersey
Source: *ConBlB 10; WhoAfA 96; WhoBlA 94*

Kimbrough, Charles
American. Actor
Plays Jim Dial on comedy TV series "Murphy Brown," 1988—.
Source: *BioIn 16; WhoAm 92; WhoEnt 92*

Kimbrough, Emily
American. Author
With Cornelia Otis Skinner, wrote best-seller *Our Hearts Were Young and Gay,* 1942, telling of their summer vacation together in England and France.
b. Oct 23, 1899 in Muncie, Indiana
d. Feb 11, 1989 in New York, New York
Source: *AmAu&B; AmWomWr; Au&Wr 71; BenetAL 91; BioIn 1, 2, 3, 4, 9, 10, 12, 16, 17; BlueB 76; ConAu 17R, 127; CurBio 44, 89N; IndAu 1917; IntAu&W 91; InWom, SUP; OxCAmL 65; REnAL; SmATA 2, 59; WhAm 9; WhoAm 74, 76, 78, 80, 82, 84, 86, 88; WhoAmW 58, 61, 64, 66, 68, 70, 72, 74, 83, 85, 87, 89; WhoWor 74, 76; WorAu 1950; WrDr 76, 80, 82, 84, 86, 88, 90*

Kim Dae Jung
Korean. Politician
Opposition leader who has struggled to restore human rights, economic justice to S Korea.
b. Jan 6, 1924 in Hayi-do, Korea
Source: *BioIn 12, 13, 14, 15; CurBio 85; FacFETw; IntWW 89, 91, 93; NewYTBE 71; NewYTBS 89; WhoWor 91; WorAlBi*

Kim Il Sung
Korean. Political Leader
Founder, first head of state, N Korea, 1948-72, pres., 1972-94.
b. Apr 15, 1912 in Mangyongdae, Korea
d. Jul 8, 1994 in Pyongyang, Korea (North)
Source: *ColdWar 1; CurBio 51, 94; IntWW 83, 89, 93; McGEWB; NewYTBE 72; WhoGov 75; WhoWor 84, 87*

Kim Jong Il
Korean. Political Leader
Pres., N Korea, 1994—.
b. Feb 15, 1942 in Khabarovsk, Union of Soviet Socialist Republics
Source: *IntWW 89, 91, 93; News 95, 95-2; NewYTBS 89*

Kimmel, Husband Edward
"Hubby"
American. Naval Officer
Commanded naval fleet at Pearl Harbor, Feb-Dec, 1941; after Japanese attack, found guilty of "dereliction of duty"; retired from navy, 1942.
b. Feb 26, 1882 in Henderson, Kentucky
d. May 15, 1968 in Groton, Connecticut
Source: *BiDWWGF; BioIn 1, 8, 10; CurBio 42, 68; DcAmB S8; DcAmMiB; HarEnMi; NatCAB 54; ObitOF 79; OxCShps; WebAMB; WhAm 5; WhWW-II; WorAl; WorAlBi*

Kim Young Sam
Korean. Political Leader
Pres., S Korea, 1993—.
b. Dec 20, 1927 in Geoje, Korea
Source: *CurBio 95; IntWW 89, 91, 93; NewYTBS 92; WhoWor 95, 96*

Kinard, Frank M
"Bruiser"
American. Football Player
Four-time all-pro tackle, 1935-44, 1946-47; Hall of Fame, 1971.
b. Oct 23, 1914 in Pelahatchie, Mississippi
Source: *BiDAmSp FB; BioIn 14; WhoFtbl 74*

Kincaid, Jamaica
[Elaine Potter Richardson]
West Indian. Author
Known for novels dealing with mother-daughter themes; works include *At the Bottom of the River,* 1983; *Lucy,* 1990; *Autobiography of My Mother,* 1996.
b. May 25, 1949 in Saint Johns, Antigua-Barbuda
Source: *AmWomWr SUP; Au&Arts 13; Benet 96; BenetAL 91; BioIn 14; BlkLC; BlkWAm; BlkWr 1, 2; BlmGWL; ConAu 47NR, 125; ConBlB 4; ConLC 43, 68; ConNov 86, 91, 96; CurBio 91; CyWA 89; DcLB 157; DrAPF 91; FemiCLE; FemiWr; FifCWr; GrWomW; IntAu&W 91, 93; LiExTwC; ModWoWr; NewYTBS 90; NotBlAW 1; OxCWoWr 95; RAdv 14; SchCGBL; TwCYAW; WhoAfA 96; WhoAm 92; WhoAmW 93, 95, 97; WhoBlA 92, 94; WorAu 1980; WrDr 88, 90, 92, 94, 96*

Kindler, Hans
Dutch. Conductor, Musician
Internationally known cellist; organized, led Washington's National Symphony, 1931-48.
b. Jan 8, 1893 in Rotterdam, Netherlands
d. Aug 30, 1949 in Watch Hill, Rhode Island
Source: *Baker 84; BiDAmM; BioIn 1, 2; CurBio 46, 49; NatCAB 39; WhAm 2*

Kiner, Ralph McPherran
American. Baseball Player, Sportscaster
Outfielder, 1946-55; led NL in home runs seven times; Hall of Fame, 1975.
b. Oct 27, 1922 in Santa Rita, New Mexico
Source: *Ballpl 90; BiDAmSp BB; BioIn 1, 2, 3, 4, 6, 9, 11, 14, 15, 16; CurBio 54; FacFETw; NewYTBS 86; WhoAm 95, 96, 97; WhoE 95; WhoProB 73; WorAl; WorAlBi*

King, Alan
[Irwin Kniberg]
American. Comedian, Actor
Films include *Author! Author!,* 1982; *Lovesick,* 1983.
b. Dec 26, 1927 in New York, New York
Source: *AmAu&B; BioIn 4, 6, 7, 8, 9, 12, 19; CelR, 90; ConAu 89; ConTFT 3; CurBio 70; EncAFC; FilmEn; FilmgC; HalFC 88; IntMPA 84, 86, 88, 92, 94, 96; JoeFr; LegTOT; PseudN 82; WhoAm 74, 76, 78, 80, 82, 84, 86, 88, 92, 94, 95, 96, 97; WhoEnt 92; WhoHol 92, A; WorAl; WorAlBi*

King, Albert
[Albert Nelson]
American. Musician
Blues guitarist, singer; started career in 1948; had 1960s hit "Born Under a Bad Sign."
b. Apr 25, 1923 in Indianola, Mississippi
d. Dec 21, 1992 in Memphis, Tennessee
Source: *AnObit 1992; BiDAfM; BioIn 19; BluesWW; ConMuA 80A; ConMus 2; DcArts; DcLP 87A; EncPR&S 74, 89; EncRk 88; GuBlues; IlEncBM 82; IlEncRk; InB&W 80, 85; LegTOT; NewYTBS 83; OnThGG; PenEncP; PseudN 82; RolSEnR 83; SoulM; TwCWW 91; WhoBlA 94N; WhoRock 81*

King, Alberta Christine Williams
American.
Mother of Martin Luther King, Jr; shot to death.
b. 1904
d. Jun 30, 1974 in Atlanta, Georgia
Source: *InB&W 80, 85; InWom SUP; NewYTBS 74; ObitOF 79*

King, Alexander
American. Author, Editor
Best known for anecdotal autobiographies: *Mine Enemy Grows Older,* 1958; *I Should Have Kissed Her More,* 1961.
b. Nov 13, 1900 in Vienna, Austria
d. Nov 16, 1965 in New York, New York
Source: *AmAu&B; BenetAL 91; BioIn 5, 7; ConAu 110; DcAmB S7; ObitOF 79; REnAL; WhAm 4; Who 82, 83; WhoCom*

King, B. B.
[Riley B King]
"Bassman of the Blues"; "King of the Blues"; "The Beale Street Blues Boy"; "The Blues Boy"; "The Boy from Beale Street"
American. Singer, Musician
Influential blues guitarist with signature vibrato style; more than 50 albums include *Six Silver Strings,* 1985; won Grammys in 1971, 1984, 1986, 1991; won lifetime achievement Grammy, 1988.
b. Sep 16, 1925 in Itta Bena, Mississippi
Source: *AfrAmAl 6; Baker 84; BioIn 13, 14, 15, 16; BioNews 74; ConMuA 80A; ConMus 1; CurBio 70; DcArts; DcTwCCu 5; DrBlPA, 90; Ebony 1; EncFCWM 83; EncJzS; EncPR&S 89; EncRk 88; EncRkSt; HarEnR 86; IlEncJ; IlEncRk; IntWW 91; LegTOT; MusMk; NegAl 83, 89; NewAmDM; NewGrDA 86; NewGrDM 80; OxCPMus; PenEncP; PseudN 82; RkOn 74; RolSEnR 83; WhoAfA 96; WhoAm 74, 76, 78, 80, 82, 84, 86, 88, 92, 94, 95, 96, 97; WhoBlA 75, 77, 80, 85, 88, 90, 92; WhoEnt 92; WhoHol 92; WhoRock 81; WhoRocM 82; WorAl; WorAlBi*

King, Ben E
[The Drifters]
American. Musician, Singer
Lead singer with The Drifters before becoming soloist; had hit single "Stand By Me," 1961.
b. Sep 28, 1938 in Henderson, North Carolina
Source: *ConMus 7; DrBlPA 90; EncPR&S 74, 89; EncRk 88; InB&W 80; PenEncP; WhoRock 81; WhoRocM 82*

King, Bernard
American. Basketball Player
Forward, 1977—, currently Washington; led NBA in scoring, 1985.
b. Dec 4, 1956 in New York, New York
Source: *BasBi; BiDAmSp BK; BioIn 13, 14, 15, 16; InB&W 85; NewYTBS 77, 82, 83, 84, 89; OfNBA 87; WhoAfA 96; WhoAm 86, 88, 92; WhoBlA 85, 88, 90, 92, 94; WhoE 86, 89; WhoSpor*

King, Bernice Albertine
American. Clergy, Social Reformer, Lawyer
Daughter of Martin Luther King, Jr; assistant minister, Ebenezer Baptist Church, Atlanta, GA, 1990—.
b. Mar 28, 1963
Source: *BioIn 13, 16; InB&W 85*

King, Betsy
American. Golfer
Her victory at the 1992 LPGA championship was the best single tournament performance ever by a female golfer with a 17-under-par 267; won twice at both US Women's Open and at Dinah Shore's.
b. 1956? in Limekiln, Pennsylvania
Source: *BioIn 11*

King, Billie Jean
[Billie Jean Moffitt]
American. Tennis Player
Most famous woman tennis player ever; won record 20 Wimbledon titles.
b. Nov 22, 1943 in Long Beach, California
Source: *AmDec 1970; BiDAmSp OS; BioIn 7, 8, 9, 10, 11, 12, 13, 14, 15, 16; BioNews 74; BkPepl; BuCMET; CelR, 90; CmCal; ConAu 10NR, 53; ContDcW 89; CurBio 67; EncWB; EncWomS; FacFETw; GayLesB; GoodHs; GrLiveH; HanAmWH; HerW, 84; IntWW 76, 77, 78, 79, 80, 81, 82, 83, 89, 91, 93; InWom, SUP; LegTOT; LibW; NewYTBE 70; NewYTBS 75, 80; RComAH; SmATA 12; WhDW; Who 82, 83, 85, 88, 90, 92, 94; WhoAm 84, 86, 90; WhoAmW 91; WhoSpor; WomFir; WomStre; WorAl; WorAlBi; WrDr 80, 82, 84, 86, 88, 90, 92, 94, 96*

King, Bruce
American. Politician
Dem. governor, NM, 1971-75; 1979-83; 1991—.
b. Apr 6, 1924 in Stanley, New Mexico
Source: *AlmAP 80, 82, 92; BiDrGov 1789, 1978, 1988; BioIn 20; IntWW 74, 75, 76, 77, 78, 79, 80, 81, 82, 83, 89; WhoAm 74, 76, 80, 82, 92, 94, 95; WhoAmP 87; WhoWest 74, 76, 80, 82, 92, 94; WhoWor 82*

King, Cammie
American. Actor
Played Bonnie Blue Butler in *Gone with the Wind,* 1939.
b. Aug 5, 1934 in Los Angeles, California
Source: *InWom SUP; WhoHol 92, A*

King, Carole
[Carole Klein]
American. Singer, Songwriter
Won four Grammys, 1972, for album *Tapestry;* hit singles include "One Fine Day," 1980.
b. Feb 9, 1942 in New York, New York
Source: *AmSong; Baker 84; BioIn 13, 14, 15; BkPepl; ConMus 6; CurBio 74; EncFCWM 83; EncPR&S 89; EncRk 88; EncRkSt; FacFETw; GoodHs; HarEnR 86; IlEncRk; InWom SUP; LegTOT; NewAmDM; NewGrDA 86; NewYTBE 70; OxCPMus; PenEncP; PseudN 82; RolSEnR 83; VarWW 85; WhoAm 80, 82, 84, 86, 88, 92, 94, 95, 96, 97; WhoAmW 95; WhoEnt 92; WhoRock 81; WhoRocM 82; WorAl; WorAlBi*

King, Charles
American. Actor
Song, dance man in film musical *Broadway Melody,* 1929.
b. Oct 31, 1894 in New York, New York
d. Jan 11, 1944 in London, England
Source: *CmpEPM; EncMT; FilmEn; FilmgC; ForYSC; NotNAT B; TwYS; WhoHol B; WhScrn 74, 77; WhThe; WisWr*

King, Charles Glen
American. Biochemist
Discovered Vitamin C, 1932, aid in prevention of scurvy, malnutrition; on faculty of U of Pittsburgh, 1941-74.
b. Sep 22, 1896 in Entiat, Washington
d. Jan 24, 1988 in Kennett Square, Pennsylvania
Source: *AmMWSc 73P, 76P, 79, 82, 86; AsBiEn; BiESc; BioIn 2, 4, 5, 8, 15, 16; BlueB 76; CurBio 67, 88, 88N; FacFETw; IntWW 74, 75, 76, 77, 78, 79, 80, 81, 82, 83; McGMS 80; WhAm 9; WhoAm 74, 76, 78, 80, 82, 84, 86*

King, Clarence
American. Geologist
Survey of 40th parallel from CO to CA, 1866-76, was considered masterful scientific exploration; introduced use of contour lines to indicate mapped region's topography.
b. Jan 6, 1842 in Newport, Rhode Island
d. Dec 24, 1901 in Phoenix, Arizona
Source: *Alli SUP; AmAu; AmAu&B; AmBi; ApCAB; BenetAL 91; BiD&SB; BioIn 1, 2, 4, 5, 8, 10, 12, 13, 15, 16, 17; CmCal; ConAu 110; DcAmAu; DcAmB; DcLB 12; DcNAA; DcScB; EncAAH; HarEnUS; InSci; LinLib L, S; McGEWB; NatCAB 13; OxCAmH; OxCAmL 65, 83, 95; REn; REnAL; TwCBDA; WebAB 74, 79; WhAm 1; WhDW; WhNaAH; WhWE*

King, Claude
American. Musician, Singer
Country guitarist, songwriter, popular 1960s; had hit single "The Burning of Atlanta," 1962.
b. Feb 5, 1933 in Shreveport, Louisiana
Source: *BiDAmM; CounME 74, 74A; EncFCWM 69; HarEnCM 87; IlEncCM; PenEncP; RkOn 74*

King, Coretta Scott
American., Lecturer, Author
Widow of Martin Luther King, Jr; founding pres., MLK Center for Nonviolent Social Change, Atlanta, 1969—.
b. Apr 27, 1927 in Marion, Alabama
Source: *AfrAmAl 6; AfrAmBi 1; AmSocL; Au&Wr 71; BiDAfM; BioAmW; BioIn 13, 14, 15, 17, 18, 19, 20; BlkWAm; BlkWr 1; BlkWrNE; BlueB 76; CelR 90; CivR 74; CivRSt; ConAu 27NR, 29R; ConBlB 3; ContDcW 89; CurBio 69; Ebony 1; EncWB; GoodHs; HanAmWH; HerW, 84; HisWorL; InB&W 80, 85; IntAu&W 77; IntWW 83, 89, 91, 93; InWom SUP; LegTOT; LivgBAA; NegAl 76, 83, 89; NewYTBE 72; NotBlAW 1; PolProf J; RelLAm 91; SchCGBL; SelBAAf; SelBAAu; WhoAfA 96; WhoAm 74, 76, 78, 80, 82, 84, 86, 88, 90, 92, 94, 95, 96, 97; WhoAmW 70, 70A, 72, 74, 75, 77, 79, 81, 83, 85, 87, 89, 91, 93, 95, 97; WhoBlA 75, 77, 80, 85, 88, 90, 92, 94; WhoRel 77, 85; WhoSSW 73, 75, 76, 93, 95; WhoWor 74, 76; WorAl; WorAlBi*

King, Dennis
[Dennis Pratt]
American. Actor
Co-starred with Jeanette MacDonald in *The Vagabond King,* 1930.
b. Nov 2, 1897 in Coventry, England
d. May 21, 1971 in New York, New York
Source: *BiDAmM; BiE&WWA; BioIn 3, 9; CamGWoT; CmpEPM; CnThe; EncMT; FilmEn; FilmgC; ForYSC; HalFC 80, 84, 88; NewAmDM; NotNAT B; OxCAmT 84; OxCPMus; OxCThe 83; PseudN 82; WhAm 5; WhoHol B; WhoThe 72; WhScrn 74, 77, 83; WhThe*

King, Dexter (Scott)
American. Civil Rights Activist
Director of the Martin Luther King Jr. center for Nonviolent Social Change, 1995—; son of Martin Luther King, Jr.
b. 1961 in Atlanta, Georgia
Source: *ConBlB 10; InB&W 80, 85; WhoSSW 97*

King, Don(ald)
American. Boxing Promoter
Pres., CEO, Don King Productions; controversial promoter known for handling boxing champs, including Muhammad Ali and Sugar Ray Leonard; promoted over 200 championship bouts, 1970s—.
b. Aug 20, 1931 in Cleveland, Ohio
Source: *BioIn 10, 13, 14, 15, 16; CelR 90; CurBio 84; DrBlPA 90; Dun&B 90; News 89-1; ODwPR 91; WhoAfA 96; WhoAm 96, 97; WhoBlA 88, 90, 92, 94; WhoSSW 97*

King, Ernest Joseph
American. Naval Officer
Principal strategist of naval policy, WW II.
b. Nov 23, 1878 in Lorain, Ohio
d. Jun 25, 1956 in Portsmouth, New Hampshire
Source: *BiDWWGF; BioIn 1, 3, 4, 6, 7, 8, 11, 12, 17; CurBio 42, 56; DcAmB S6; DcAmMiB; EncAB-H 1974, 1996; HarEnMi; LinLib S; McGEWB; NatCAB*

46; OxCAmH; OxCShps; PseudN 82; WebAB 74, 79; WebAMB; WhAm 3; WhoMilH 76; WhWW-II; WorAl

King, Evelyn
"Champagne"
American. Singer
Recorded disco hit "Shame," 1977.
b. Jul 1, 1960 in New York, New York
Source: *BioIn 11, 12, 13; EncPR&S 89; EncRk 88; InB&W 85; InWom SUP; LegTOT; RkOn 85; RolSEnR 83; SoulM*

King, Francis Henry
[Frank Cauldwell]
Swiss. Author
Short story writer known for chilling plots: *Hard Feelings,* 1976; *The Brighton Belle,* 1968.
b. Mar 4, 1923 in Adelboden, Switzerland
Source: *Au&Wr 71; BioIn 13; ConAu 1NR, 1R, 33NR; ConLC 8; ConNov 86, 91; IntAu&W 91; IntvTCA 2; IntWW 83, 91; MajTwCW; NewC; OxCEng 85; TwCWr; Who 85, 92; WhoTwCL; WhoWor 84, 87, 91; WorAu 1950; WrDr 86, 92, 94*

King, Frank
American. Cartoonist
Creator of comic strip "Gasoline Alley."
b. Apr 9, 1883 in Cashon, Wisconsin
d. Jun 24, 1969 in Winter Park, Florida
Source: *EncACom; WebAB 74, 79; WhFla*

King, Freddy
American. Singer, Songwriter
Blues guitarist who performed with the Every Hours Blue Band, 1952; recorded with Sonny Cooper's Band, 1953; released first single, "Country Boy/That's What You Think," 1956 and instrumental hit "Hideway," 1961; appeared in the Ann Arbor Blues Festival and recorded album *Freddy King Is a Bluesmaster,* 1969.
b. Sep 3, 1934 in Gilmer, Texas
d. Dec 28, 1976 in Dallas, Texas
Source: *ConMus 17*

King, Grace Elizabeth
American. Author
Wrote local history novels: *Pleasant Ways of St. Medard,* 1916.
b. 1852 in New Orleans, Louisiana
d. Jan 12, 1932 in New Orleans, Louisiana
Source: *AmWomPl; BioIn 13, 15, 18; ConAu 116; DcLB 12; EncAHmr; InWom, SUP; NatCAB 2; OxCAmL 83; TwCBDA; WhAm 1; WomNov; WomWWA 14*

King, Henry
American. Director
Co-founder, Academy of Motion Picure Arts & Sciences; organizer of Oscars; films include *Carousel,* 1956.
b. Jan 24, 1896 in Christianburg, Virginia
d. Jun 29, 1982 in Toluca Lake, California
Source: *AnObit 1982; BiDAmM; CmMov; ConAu 89; DcFM; Film 1; FilmgC; IntMPA 75, 76, 77, 78, 79, 80, 81, 82; MovMk; NewYTBS 82; OxCFilm; WhAm 8; WorEFlm*

King, James Ambros
American. Opera Singer
Tenor who had NY Met. debut, 1966; noted for German repertory.
b. May 22, 1925 in Dodge City, Kansas
Source: *Baker 84; BioIn 15, 16; IntWWM 77, 90; MetOEnc; NewAmDM; NewGrDA 86; PenDiMP; WhoAm 74, 80, 82, 84, 86, 88; WhoAmM 83; WhoOp 76*

King, John W(illiam)
American. Politician
Governor, NH, 1963-69.
b. Oct 10, 1918
d. Aug 9, 1996 in Manchester, New Hampshire
Source: *BiDrGov 1789; BioIn 6, 7, 11; CurBio 96N; PolProf J, K; WhoAm 74, 76, 78, 80, 82, 84, 86, 88; WhoAmP 73, 75, 77, 79, 81, 83, 85, 87, 89, 91, 93, 95; WhoE 74, 77*

King, Larry
[Lawrence Harvey Zeiger]
American. Radio Performer, TV Personality
Hosts national cable TV talk show, "The Larry King Show" 1978-1985, "Larry King Live!" 1985—.
b. Nov 19, 1933 in New York, New York
Source: *BioIn 12, 13, 14, 15, 16, 17, 18, 19, 20, 21; CelR 90; ConAu 111, 139; ConTFT 10; CurBio 85; EncTwCJ; IntMPA 94, 96; IntvTCA 2; LegTOT; LesBEnT 92; News 93-1; NewYTBS 91; SaTiSS; WhoAm 88, 90, 92, 94, 95, 96, 97; WhoE 89; WhoTelC; WorAlBi*

King, Martin Luther, Sr.
[Michael Luther King, Sr.]
"Daddy King"
American. Clergy
Pastor of Ebenezer Baptist Church, Atlanta, GA who preached non-violence; father of Martin Luther King, Jr.
b. Dec 19, 1899 in Stockbridge, Georgia
d. Nov 11, 1984 in Atlanta, Georgia
Source: *AnObit 1984; BioIn 10, 11, 12, 15; BlkWr 1; ConAu 117, 125; Ebony 1; HisWorL; InB&W 80; NegAl 76, 83; NewYTBS 84; RelLAm 91; SchCGBL; SelBAAf; WhoBlA 75, 77, 80; WhoRel 77, 85*

King, Martin Luther, Jr.
[Michael Luther King, Jr.]
"The Prince of Peace"
American. Clergy, Civil Rights Leader
Led Civil Rights movement, 1950-68; won Nobel Prize, 1964; birthday is federal holiday.
b. Jan 15, 1929 in Atlanta, Georgia
d. Apr 4, 1968 in Memphis, Tennessee
Source: *AfrAmAl 6; AfrAmOr; AmAu&B; AmDec 1950, 1960; AmJust; AmOrTwC; AmPeW; AmRef; AmRef&R; AmSocL; Benet 87, 96; BenetAL 91; BiDMoPL; BiDSocW; BioIn 4, 5, 6, 7, 8, 9, 10, 11, 12, 13, 14, 15, 16, 17, 18, 19, 20, 21; BlkAWP; BlkLC; BlkWr 1, 2; BlkWrNE; CivRSt; ConAu 27NR, 44NR, P-2; ConBlB 1; ConHero 1; ConLC 83; CurBio 57, 65, 68; DcAmB S8; DcAmImH; DcAmNB; DcAmReB 1, 2; DcAmSR; DcEcMov; DcPol; DcTwCCu 1, 5; DcTwHis; EncAACR; EncAB-H 1974, 1996; EncARH; EncEth; EncRev; EncSoH; FacFETw; HeroCon; HisWorL; InB&W 80, 85; LegTOT; LinLib L; LNinSix; LuthC 75; MajTwCW; MakMC; McGEWB; NatCAB 54; NegAl 76, 83, 89; NewYTBS 74; NobelP; ObitT 1961; OxCAmH; OxCAmL 65, 83, 95; PeoHis; PolPar; PolProf E, J, K; PseudN 82; RadHan; RAdv 14, 13-4; RComAH; RelLAm 91; REnAL; SchCGBL; SelBAAf; SelBAAu; SmATA 14; TwCSAPR; WebAB 74, 79; WhAm 4A; WhAmP; WhDW; WhoNob, 90, 95; WorAl; WorAlBi*

King, Mary-Claire
American. Geneticist
Discovered that 99% of human DNA is identical to that of chimpanzees.
b. Feb 27, 1946 in Wilmette, Illinois
Source: *AmMWSc 76P, 79, 82, 86, 89, 92, 95; BioIn 20, 21; CurBio 95; WhoAm 96, 97; WhoAmW 89, 91, 93, 97; WhoScEn 94*

King, Micki
[Maxine Joyce King]
American. Diver
Won gold medal, springboard diving, 1972 Munich Olympics.
b. 1943
Source: *BiDAmSp BK; GoodHs; InWom SUP; PseudN 82*

King, Morganna
American. Actor
Played mother of Corleone family in *The Godfather I, II.*
b. Jun 4, 1930 in Pleasantville, New York
Source: *BiDJaz; InWom SUP; NewGrDJ 88; PenEncP; WhoAm 84, 88; WhoEnt 92; WhoHol A*

King, Perry
American. Actor
Played in films *Lords of Flatbush; Mandingo;* TV movies *Captains and Kings; Riptide.*
b. Apr 30, 1948 in Alliance, Ohio
Source: *BioIn 13, 14; ConTFT 2, 9; FilmEn; HalFC 80, 84, 88; HolBB; IntMPA 80, 88, 92, 94, 96; LegTOT; VarWW 85; WhoAm 90, 92; WhoBlA 90; WhoEnt 92; WhoHol 92, A*

King, Richard
American. Rancher
Owned nation's largest ranch at time of death; experimented with cattle breeding.
b. Jul 10, 1824 in Orange County, New York
d. Apr 14, 1885 in Corpus Christi, Texas
Source: *DcAmB; NatCAB 8; OxCAmH; REnAW; WebAB 74; WhAm HS; WorAl*

King, Rodney G
American. Victim, Construction Worker
Black motorist whose beating by 4 LAPD police officers was captured on videotape, Mar. 3, 1991; the acquittal of the officers sparked riots in LA that left 44 dead in 1992.
b. 1966?

King, Rufus
American. Statesman
Federalist politician; as US senator, 1789-96, 1820-26, tried to halt expansion of slavery; last Federalist candidate for pres., 1816.
b. Mar 24, 1755 in Scarboro, Maine
d. Apr 29, 1827 in Jamaica, New York
Source: *AmAu&B; AmBi; AmPolLe; ApCAB; BiAUS; BiDrAC; BiDrUSC 89; BioIn 7, 8, 15, 16; BlkwEAR; CyAG; DcAmB; DcAmDH 80, 89; DcBiPP; Drake; HarEnUS; LinLib S; McGEWB; NatCAB 6; OxCAmH; PresAR; TwCBDA; WebAB 74, 79; WhAm HS; WhAmP; WhAmRev; WorAl; WorAlBi*

King, Stephen Edwin
American. Author
Master of popular horror tales: *Carrie,* 1974; *The Shining,* 1976; *Cujo,* 1981; *It,* 1986.
b. Sep 21, 1947 in Portland, Maine
Source: *Au&Arts 1; Benet 87; BenetAL 91; BioIn 13, 14, 15, 16; CelR 90; ConAu 30NR, 61; ConLC 12, 61; ConTFT 8; CrtSuMy; CurBio 81; CyWA 89; EncSF; HalFC 88; IntAu&W 89, 91, 93; IntMPA 92; IntWW 89, 91, 93; Law&B 84; MajTwCW; NewEScF; NewYTBS 79; PenEncH; RfGAmL 94; ScF&FL 1, 2; ScFSB; SmATA 9, 65; SupFW; TwCYAW; WhoAm 78, 80, 82, 84, 86, 88, 90, 92, 94, 95, 96; WhoE 91, 93; WhoHr&F; WhoSSW 78, 91; WhoUSWr 88; WhoWor 95, 96; WhoWrEP 89, 92, 95; WorAlBi; WorAu 1980; WrDr 92*

King, Thomas
American. Author
Works attempt to abolish common Native American stereotypes; author of *Green Grass, Running Water,* 1993.
b. 1943 in Sacramento, California
Source: *BioIn 18, 21; ConAu 144; ConCaAu 1; ConLC 89; ConNov 96; DcNAL; NatNAL; NotNaAm; WrDr 96*

King, Thomas Starr
American. Author, Clergy
Unitarian minister; described beauty of American landscape in *White Hills,* 1860.
b. Dec 17, 1824 in New York, New York
d. Mar 4, 1864 in San Francisco, California
Source: *Alli SUP; AmAu&B; AmBi; ApCAB; BbD; BenetAL 91; BiD&SB; BioIn 2, 3, 12; ChhPo S1; CmCal; CyAL 2; DcAmAu; DcAmB; DcAmReB 2; DcNAA; Drake; HarEnUS; NatCAB 4; OxCAmL 65, 83, 95; REnAL; TwCBDA; WhAm HS*

King, Warren Thomas
American. Cartoonist
Editorial cartoonist, *NY Daily News,* 1955-77.
b. Jan 3, 1916 in New York, New York
d. Feb 9, 1978
Source: *EncTwCJ; WhAm 7; WhoAm 74, 76, 78; WhoAmA 73, 76, 78, 80, 82N, 84N, 86N, 89N, 91N, 93N; WhoE 74; WhoWor 74*

King, Wayne
"The Waltz King"
American. Bandleader
Led dance band, 1930s-40s; famous for waltzes, slow, dreamy style; recorded "Josephine," 1937.
b. Feb 16, 1901 in Savanna, Illinois
d. May 16, 1985 in Phoenix, Arizona
Source: *AmPS B; ASCAP 66, 80; Baker 84; BgBands 74; BiDAmM; BioIn 2, 9, 12, 14; CmpEPM; LegTOT; OxCPMus; PenEncP; RadStar; SaTiSS; WorAl*

King, William
[The Commodores]
American. Singer
Plays brass instruments, writes songs for black pop group formed 1968.
b. Jan 30, 1949 in Birmingham, Alabama
Source: *BkPepl; WhoWest 87*

King, William Lyon Mackenzie
Canadian. Political Leader
Leader of Canadian Liberal party, 1919-48; prime minister, 1921-30; 1935-48.
b. Dec 17, 1874 in Berlin, Ontario, Canada
d. Jul 22, 1950 in Kingsmere, Ontario, Canada
Source: *BiDInt; BioIn 1, 2, 3, 4, 5, 6, 7, 8, 9, 10, 11, 12, 13, 14, 15, 17, 18, 20; CurBio 40, 50; DcNaB 1941; DcPol; DcTwHis; EncPaPR 91; FacFETw; HisDBrE; HisWorL; LinLib L, S; MacDCB 78; McGEWB; OxCCan; PeoHis; WhAm 3; WhDW; WhE&EA; WhNAA; WhWW-II; WorAl; WorAlBi*

King, William Rufus de Vane
American. US Vice President
Elected with Franklin Pierce; took oath of office in Cuba where he went to find cure for TB.
b. Apr 7, 1786 in Sampson County, North Carolina
d. Apr 18, 1853 in Cahaba, Alabama
Source: *AmPolLe; BiDrUSC 89; BiDrUSE 89; DcAmDH 89; Drake; NatCAB 4; WebAB 74; WhAm HS; WhAmP*

King, Yolanda Denise
American. Actor
Daughter of Martin Luther King, Jr; formed theatre troupe, Nucleus, with Attallah Shabazz, daughter of Malcolm X.
b. Nov 17, 1955 in Montgomery, Alabama
Source: *BioIn 9, 11, 12, 13, 16; InB&W 80, 85; NotBlAW 1, 2; WhoBlA 92*

King Crimson
[Robert Fripp; Mike Giles; Greg Lake; Ian McDonald; Pete Sinfield]
English. Music Group
Heavy metal space band, 1969-74; debut album *In The Court of Crimson King,* 1969.
Source: *BioIn 9, 14, 17, 18; ConMuA 80A; ConMus 17; EncPR&S 89; EncRk 88; EncRkSt; IlEncRk; NewAmDM; RolSEnR 83; WhoHol 92; WhoRock 81; WhoRocM 82*

King Curtis
[Curtis Ousley]
American. Musician
Released first hit "Soul Twist" with the Noble Knights in 1962; later toured with Sam Cooke in the early 1960s and became Aretha Franklin's musical director in the late 1960s; released soul song "Memphis Soul Stew" in 1966.
b. Feb 7, 1934 in Fort Worth, Texas
d. Aug 14, 1971 in New York, New York
Source: *BiDAfM; EncRk 88; NewAmDM; PenEncP; RolSEnR 83; SoulM*

Kinglake, Alexander William
English. Historian
Description of Near East trip in *Eothen; or Traces of Travel Brought Home fr om the East,* 1844, considered classic travel book.
b. Aug 5, 1809 in Taunton, England
d. Jan 2, 1891 in London, England
Source: *Alli SUP; BiD&SB; BioIn 4, 9, 12, 13, 15; BritAu 19; CamGEL; CamGLE; CasWL; Chambr 3; DcEnA; DcEnL; DcLB 55, 166; DcLEL; DcNaB; EvLB; NewC; NewCBEL; OxCEng 67, 85, 95; PenC ENG; REn; WebE&AL*

Kingman, Dave
[David Arthur Kingman]
"Kong"
American. Baseball Player
Outfielder-infielder, 1971-86; had 442 career home runs; led NL in home runs twice.
b. Dec 21, 1948 in Pendleton, Oregon
Source: *Ballpl 90; BaseReg 86, 87; BiDAmSp Sup; BioIn 10, 11, 12, 13, 14, 15; CurBio 82; LegTOT; WhoAm 80, 82, 84, 86*

Kingman, Dong Moy Shu
[Tsang King-Man]
American. Artist
Watercolorist; illustrator of children's books; has contributed artwork to several films including *Lost Horizon,* 1973.
b. Mar 31, 1911 in Oakland, California
Source: *BioIn 13, 15, 16; ConAu 112; CurBio 62; IlsCB 1946; IntMPA 92; SmATA 44; WhoAm 84, 86, 90; WhoAmA 84, 91*

Kingsborough Donald
American. Business Executive
Introduced children's toy, Teddy Ruxpin, 1985; formed co., Worlds of Wonder, 1985.
b. 1947?
Source: *BioIn 15; ConNews 86-2*

Kingsbury-Smith, Joseph
American. Journalist
Nat. editor, Hearst Newspapers, 1976—; won Pulitzer for int'l reporting, 1956.
b. Feb 20, 1908 in New York, New York
Source: *BlueB 76; CelR; ConAu 133; EncTwCJ; IntAu&W 77, 89, 91; IntWW 74, 75, 76, 77, 78, 79, 80, 81, 82, 83, 89, 91, 93; St&PR 84, 87, 91, 93, 96, 97; WhoAm 74, 76, 78, 80, 82, 84, 86, 88, 92; WhoWor 74*

Kingsford-Smith, Charles Edward, Sir
Australian. Aviator
WW I flyer; commanded crew that flew first Pacific crossing, from California to Australia, 1928; lost en route to Singapore.
b. Feb 9, 1897 in Brisbane, Australia
d. Nov 8, 1935
Source: *BioIn 1, 2, 3, 4, 7, 9, 11, 12, 14; DcNaB 1931; GrBr*

King Sisters
American. Music Group
Vocal quartet sang with Big Bands, 1930s-40s; made comeback, 1960s, with "The King Family" TV series.
Source: *BiDAmM; CmpEPM; InWom SUP; PenEncP; RadStar; WhoHol A*

Kingsley, Ben
[Krishna Bhanji]
English. Actor
Won 1983 Best Actor Oscar for *Gandhi.*
b. Dec 31, 1943 in Snaiton, England
Source: *BiDFilm 94; BioIn 13, 16; CelR 90; ConTFT 1, 4, 11; CurBio 83; HalFC 88; IntMPA 86, 88, 92, 94, 96; IntWW 89, 91, 93; ItaFilm; LegTOT; NewYTBS 82, 83; VarWW 85; Who 83, 85, 88, 90, 92, 94; WhoAm 84, 86, 88, 90, 92, 94, 95, 96, 97; WhoEnt 92; WhoHol 92; WhoThe 81; WhoWor 84, 87, 89, 91, 93, 95, 96, 97; WorAlBi*

Kingsley, Charles
"CK"; "A Minute Philosopher"; "The Chariot Clergyman"; "The Chartist Parson"
English. Clergy, Author
Wrote historical romances *Hypatia,* 1853; *Westward Ho,* 1855; children's book *The Water Babies,* 1863.
b. Jun 12, 1819 in Devonshire, England
d. Jan 23, 1875 in Eversley, England
Source: *Alli, SUP; AnCL; AtlBL; AuBYP 2, 3; BbD; Benet 87, 96; BiD&SB; BioIn 1, 2, 3, 4, 5, 6, 8, 9, 10, 11, 12, 14, 15, 16; BlmGEL; BritAS; BritAu 19; CamGEL; CamGLE; CarSB; CasWL; CelCen; Chambr 3; ChhPo, S1, S2, S3; ChlBkCr; CrtT 3; CyEd; CyWA 58; DcAmSR; DcArts; DcBiA; DcBiPP; DcBrBI; DcEnA; DcEnL; DcEuL; DcLB 21, 32, 163; DcLEL; DcNaB; DcPup; Dis&D; EvLB; GrWrEL N; JBA 34; LinLib L; LngCEL; LuthC 75; McGEWB; MouLC 3; NewC; NewCBEL; NewYTBE 71; NinCLC 35; Novels; OxCChiL; OxCEng 67, 85, 95; PenC ENG; PseudAu; PseudN 82; RAdv 1, 14, 13-1; REn; RfGEnL 91; SJGFanW; StaCVF; TwCChW 83A, 89A, 95A; VicBrit; WebE&AL; WhDW; WhoChL; WrChl; YABC 2*

Kingsley, Gregory
[Shawn Russ]
American. Victim
First child to divorce his parents, 1992, for reason of abandonment.
b. 1980? in Florida

Kingsley, Henry
English. Author
Wrote romantic novels: *Geoffrey Hamlyn,* 1859; *Ravenshoe,* 1862; brother of Charles.
b. Jan 2, 1830 in Barnack, England
d. May 24, 1876 in Cuckfield, England
Source: *Alli SUP; BbD; BiD&SB; BioIn 2, 5, 9, 13, 14; BritAu 19; CamGEL; CamGLE; CarSB; CasWL; CelCen; Chambr 3; ChhPo S1, S3; CyWA 58; DcBiA; DcBiPP; DcEnA; DcEnL; DcEuL; DcLB 21; DcLEL; DcNaB, C; EvLB; GrWrEL N; HsB&A; NewC; NewCBEL; OxCAusL; OxCEng 67, 85, 95; PenC ENG; REn; RfGEnL 91; StaCVF; WebE&AL*

Kingsley, Pat(ricia)
American. Public Relations Executive
Publicist, owner; PMK, a celebrity public relations firm, 1980—.
b. May 7, 1932 in Gastonia, North Carolina
Source: *News 90, 90-2; WhoAm 92, 94, 95, 96; WhoAmW 95; WhoEnt 92; WhoWest 89*

Kingsley, Sidney
[Sidney Kieschner]
American. Dramatist
Won Pulitzer for play *Men in White,* 1934.
b. Oct 18, 1906 in New York, New York
d. Mar 20, 1995 in Oakland, New Jersey
Source: *AmAu&B; BenetAL 91; BiE&WWA; BioIn 1, 4, 10, 12, 15, 20, 21; CamGLE; CamGWoT; CamHAL; CnDAL; CnMD; CnThe; ConAmA; ConAmD; ConAu 85, 147; ConDr 73, 77, 93; ConLC 44; CroCD; CrtSuDr; CurBio 43, 95N; DcLB 7; DcLEL; EncWT; Ent; FilmgC; GangFlm; GrWrEL DR; HalFC 80, 84, 88; IntDcT 2; LegTOT; LngCTC; McGEWD 72, 84; ModAL; ModWD; NewYTBS 95; NotNAT; OxCAmL 65, 83, 95; OxCAmT 84; OxCThe 67, 83; PenC AM; PlP&P; PseudN 82; REn; REnAL; REnWD; RfGAmL 87, 94; TwCA, SUP; VarWW 85; WebE&AL; WhoAm 74, 76, 78, 80, 82, 84, 86, 88, 90, 92, 94, 95; WhoEnt 92; WhoThe 72, 77, 81; WhoWest 87; WrDr 76, 80, 82, 84, 86, 88, 90, 92, 94, 96*

Kingsolver, Barbara
American. Author
Wrote *Animal Dreams,* 1990; *Pigs in Heaven,* 1993; themes include the oppressed and the environment; won the 1993 *Los Angeles Times* Book Award for Fiction.
b. Apr 8, 1955 in Annapolis, Maryland
Source: *AmWomWr SUP; Au&Arts 15; Benet 96; ConAu 129, 134; ConLC 55, 81; ConPopW; CurBio 94; LegTOT; WorAu 1985; WrDr 94, 96*

Kingston, Maxine Hong
American. Author
Nonfiction books blend Chinese-American history, myth: *The Woman Warrior,* 1977; *China Men,* 1980; won Nat. Education Assn. Award, 1977; American Book Award, 1981.
b. Oct 27, 1940 in Stockton, California
Source: *AmWomWr, 92; ArtclWW 2; AsAmAlm; Au&Arts 8; BenetAL 91; BioIn 13, 15, 16; BlmGWL; ConAu 13NR, 69; ConLC 12, 19, 58; ConNov 96; CurBio 90; CyWA 89; DcArts; DcLB 173, Y80B; EncWHA; FemiCLE; FemiWr; GrLiveH; HanAmWH; IntAu&W 91, 93; IntWW 91, 93; InWom SUP; LegTOT; MagSAmL; MajTwCW; ModAWWr; ModWoWr; NewYTBS 77, 80, 89; NotAsAm; OxCAmL 83, 95; OxCWoWr 95; PostFic; RAdv 14; SmATA 53; TwCWW 91; WhoAm 78, 80, 82, 84, 86, 88, 90, 92, 94, 95, 96, 97; WhoAmW 83, 85, 87, 89, 91, 93, 95, 97; WhoAsA 94; WhoEmL 87; WorAu 1975; WrDr 88, 90, 92, 94, 96*

Kingston Trio, The
[Roger Gambill; George Grove; Dave Guard; Bob Shane]
American. Music Group
Rose to fame, late 1950s, with ballad "Tom Dooley."
Source: *AmPS A, B; BiDAmM; BioIn 8, 14; ConAu 134, X; ConMuA 80A; ConMus 9; EncFCWM 83; EncRk 88; NewAmDM; NewGrDA 86; NewYTBS 91; OxCEng 85; PenEncP; RkOn 74; RolSEnR 83; WhoRock 81; WhoRocM 82*

King's X
American. Music Group
Christian heavy metal rock band formed 1980; first album was *Out of the Silent Planet,* 1988.
Source: *ConMus 7*

Kinison, Sam
American. Comedian
King of shock comedy who screamed out his jokes on controversial and vulgar themes.
b. 1953 in Peoria, Illinois
d. Apr 10, 1992 in Needles, California
Source: *BioIn 15, 16; ConTFT 14; LegTOT; News 93-1; WhoCom*

Kinks, The
[Mick Avory; John Beechman; Laurie Brown; David Davies; Raymond Davies; John Gosling; Alan Holmes; Peter Quaife]
English. Music Group
British rock group, 1963—; "You Really Got Me," 1964, first big US hit.
Source: *Alli, SUP; BiDLA; BioIn 9, 15, 16, 17, 18, 20, 21; ConMuA 80A; ConMus 15; DcLEL; EncPR&S 74, 89; EncRk 88; EncRkSt; HarEnR 86; IlEncRk; LngCTC; ObitOF 79; OxCPMus; PenEncP; RkOn 78, 84; RolSEnR 83; WhoIns 90; WhoRock 81; WhoRocM 82; WhScrn 74, 77, 83*

Kinmont, Jill
[Mrs. John Boothe]
American. Skier, Teacher
Paralyzed in skiing accident; films *The Other Side of the Mountain,* parts I, II, 1975, 1978, depict her life.
b. 1936
Source: *BioIn 6, 9, 10, 11, 12; GoodHs; HerW, 84; InWom SUP*

Kinnear, Greg
American. TV Personality
Host of TV's "Talk Soup."
b. 1964 in Logansport, Indiana

Kinnear, James Wesley
American. Business Executive
President, CEO of Texaco, Inc., 1987-93.
b. Mar 21, 1928 in Pittsburgh, Pennsylvania
Source: *BioIn 15, 16; Dun&B 90; IntWW 89, 91, 93; St&PR 91; WhoAm 74, 76, 78, 80, 82, 84, 86, 88, 90, 92, 94, 95, 96, 97; WhoE 83, 85, 89, 91, 93; WhoFI 74, 85, 87, 89, 92, 94, 96; WhoWor 89*

Kinnell, Galway
American. Poet
Poems deal with life confronting death; won Pulitzer for *Selected Poems,* 1983.
b. Feb 1, 1927 in Providence, Rhode Island
Source: *AmAu&B; AmWr S3; Benet 87, 96; BenetAL 91; BiDConC; BioIn 6, 10, 12, 13, 15, 17, 20; CamGLE; CamHAL; ConAu 9R, 10NR, 34NR; ConLC 1, 2, 3, 5, 13, 29; ConPo 70, 75, 80, 85, 91, 96; CroCAP; CurBio 86; DcLB 5, Y87A; DcLEL 1940; DrAF 76; DrAP 75; DrAPF 80, 91; EncWL 2, 3; IntAu&W 82, 86, 89, 91, 93; IntvTCA 2; IntWW 77, 78, 79, 80, 81, 82, 83, 89, 91, 93; IntWWP 77, 82; LegTOT; LinLib L; MajTwCW; ModAL S1, S2; OxCAmL 65, 83, 95; OxCTwCP; PenC AM; RAdv 1, 14, 13-1; RfGAmL 94; WhoAm 74, 76, 78, 80, 82, 84, 86, 88, 94, 95, 96, 97; WhoE 85, 86, 89; WhoTwCL; WhoUSWr 88; WhoWor 74; WhoWrEP 89, 92, 95; WorAu 1950; WrDr 76, 80, 82, 84, 86, 88, 90, 92, 94, 96*

Kinney, George Romanta
American. Merchant
Started Kinney Shoes, 1894, marketing shoes for entire family at discount prices; first to apply concept of franchising.
b. 1866
d. 1919
Source: *Entr*

Kinnick, Nile
American. Football Player
All-America halfback-quarterback, U of Iowa, 1937-39; won Heisman Trophy, 1939; killed in WW II plane crash.
b. 1918? in Omaha, Nebraska
d. Jun 2, 1943, At Sea
Source: *BioIn 8; WhoFtbl 74*

Kinnock, Neil Gordon
Welsh. Politician
Succeeded Michael Foot as head of Britain's Labor Party, 1983-92.
b. Mar 28, 1942 in Tredagar, Wales
Source: *BioIn 13, 14, 15, 16; CurBio 84; EncWB; FacFETw; IntWW 83, 89, 91, 93; IntYB 78, 79, 80, 81, 82; NewYTBS 83, 90; Who 74, 82, 83, 85, 88, 90, 92, 94; WhoWor 84, 87, 89, 91, 93; WorAlBi*

Kinsey, Alfred Charles
American. Scientist
Founded Institute for Sex Research, 1942; *Kinsey Reports* shattered myths.
b. Jun 23, 1894 in Hoboken, New Jersey
d. Aug 25, 1956 in Bloomington, Indiana
Source: *AmAu&B; AmSocL; Benet 87, 96; BenetAL 91; BiDPsy; BiESc; BioIn 1, 3, 4, 5, 9, 11, 13, 14, 19, 20; CurBio 54, 56; DcAmB S6; EncAB-H 1974, 1996; IndAu 1917; InSci; LarDcSc; MorMA; NamesHP; ObitOF 79; ObitT 1951; REnAL; WebAB 74, 79; WhAm 3; WorAl; WorAlBi*

Kinski, Klaus
[Nikolaus Gunther Nakszynski]
American. Actor
Star of German, American films known for intense portrayals: *Fitzcarraldo,* 1982; father of Nastassja.
b. Oct 18, 1926 in Sopot, Poland
d. Nov 23, 1991 in Lagunitas, California
Source: *AnObit 1991; BiDFilm 94; BioIn 12, 16, 17, 18; ConNews 87-2; ConTFT 5, 10; DcArts; EncEurC; FilmAG WE; FilmEn; HalFC 80, 84, 88; IntDcF 1-3, 2-3; IntMPA 86, 92; IntWW 89, 91; ItaFilm; LegTOT; News 92, 92-2; NewYTBS 79, 91; VarWW 85; WhAm 10; WhoEnt 92; WorAlBi*

Kinski, Nastassja
[Mrs. Ibrahim Moussa; Nastassja Nakszynski]
"Nasti"
German. Actor
Starred in films *Tess,* 1978; *Unfaithfully Yours,* 1984; daughter of Klaus.
b. Jan 24, 1960 in Berlin, Germany (West)
Source: *BiDFilm 94; BioIn 13, 14; CelR 90; ConTFT 6; CurBio 84; HalFC 84, 88; IntMPA 86, 88, 92, 94, 96; IntWW 91; InWom SUP; LegTOT; NewYTBS 81; VarWW 85; WhoAm 86, 90, 95, 96, 97; WhoEnt 92; WhoHol 92*

Kinsley, Michael (E.)
American. Broadcast Journalist, Writer
Cohost of CNN's *Crossfire,* 1989—.
b. Mar 9, 1951 in Detroit, Michigan
Source: *BioIn 12, 13; CurBio 95; EncTwCJ; WhoAm 82, 86, 88, 90, 92, 94, 95, 96, 97; WhoAmP 87, 89, 91, 93, 95; WhoE 89, 93*

Kintner, Robert Edmonds
American. Radio Executive, TV Executive
Pres., ABC, 1950-56; NBC, 1958-65; televised McCarthy hearings, 1950s; criticized for violence-oriented programs.
b. Sep 12, 1909 in Stroudsburg, Pennsylvania
d. Dec 20, 1980 in Washington, District of Columbia
Source: *AnObit 1980; BioIn 2, 5, 6, 7, 9, 12; ConAu 103; CurBio 50, 81; DcAmB S10; NewYTBS 80; WhAm 7*

Kinugasa, Teinosuke
Japanese. Director
Won Oscar for best foreign film *Gate of Hell,* 1954; pioneer in the use of flashbacks.
b. Jan 1, 1896 in Mie Prefecture, Japan
d. Feb 26, 1982 in Kyoto, Japan
Source: *BiDFilm, 94; BioIn 10, 11, 12, 13, 15; FilmgC; HalFC 84, 88; IntDcF 1-2, 2-2; JapFilm; OxCFilm; WhoWor 74; WorFDir 1*

Kipling, Rudyard
[Joseph Rudyard Kipling]
English. Author, Poet
Won 1907 Nobel Prize; wrote *The Jungle Book,* 1894; *Just So Stories,* 1902.
b. Dec 30, 1865 in Bombay, India
d. Jan 18, 1936 in Burwash, England
Source: *Alli SUP; AnCL; ApCAB SUP; AtlBL; AuBYP 2, 3; BbD; Benet 87, 96; BiD&SB; BioIn 1, 2, 3, 4, 5, 6, 7, 8, 9, 10, 11, 12, 13, 14, 15, 16, 17, 18, 19, 20, 21; BlmGEL; BritWr 6; CamGEL; CamGLE; CarSB; CasWL; Chambr 3; ChhPo, S1, S2, S3; ChlBkCr; ChlLR 39; CmCal; CnDBLB 5; CnE&AP; CnMWL;*

ConAu 33NR, 105, 120; CrtT 3, 4; CyWA 58; DcAmAu; DcAmC; DcBiA; DcBrBI; DcEnA, A; DcEuL; DcInB; DcLB 19, 34, 141, 156; DcLEL; DcNaB 1931; DcPup; Dis&D; EncPaPR 91; EncSF; EncSoA; EncWL, 2, 3; EvLB; FacFETw; FamAYP; FamSYP; FilmgC; GrBr; GrWrEL N, P; HalFC 80, 84, 88; HisDBrE; JBA 34; LegTOT; LinLib L, S; LngCEL; LngCTC; MagSWL; MajTwCW; MakMC; McGEWB; MnBBF; ModBrL, S1, S2; NewC; NewCBEL; NewEScF; NobelP; Novels; OxCAmL 65, 83, 95; OxCCan; OxCChiL; OxCEng 67, 85, 95; OxCShps; OxCTwCP; PenC ENG; PenEncH; PoeCrit 3; RAdv 1, 14, 13-1; RComWL; REn; RfGEnL 91; RGFMBP; ScF&FL 1, 92; ScFEYrs; ScFSB; ShSCr 5; ShSWr; StaCVF; Str&VC; SupFW; TwCA, SUP; TwCChW 78, 83, 89; TwCLC 8, 17; TwCSFW 81, 86, 91; TwCWr; VicBrit; WebE&AL; WhDW; WhE&EA; WhLit; WhoChL; WhoHr&F; WhoLA; WhoNob, 90, 95; WhoTwCL; WorAl; WorAlBi; WorLitC; WrChl; YABC 2

Kiplinger, Austin Huntington
American. Publisher
Chm., Kiplinger Washington Editors, Inc.
b. Sep 19, 1918 in Washington, District of Columbia
Source: *AmAu&B; BioIn 3, 14; BlueB 76; ConAu 57; EncTwCJ; NatCAB 63N; St&PR 75, 84, 87, 91, 93, 96, 97; WhoAm 74, 76, 78, 80, 82, 84, 86, 88, 90, 92, 94, 95; WhoE 86; WhoSSW 73; WhoUSWr 88; WhoWor 74; WhoWrEP 89, 92, 95*

Kiplinger, Knight A
American. Publisher
Pres., Kiplinger Washington Editors, Inc; publisher, editor-in-chief *Kiplinger's Personal Finance Magazine.*

Kiplinger, W(illard) M(onroe)
American. Journalist, Publisher
Founded Kiplinger Washington Editors, Inc., 1923; publishes business newsletters, *Kiplinger's Personal Finance Magazine.*
b. Jan 8, 1891 in Bellefontaine, Ohio
d. Aug 6, 1967 in Bethesda, Maryland
Source: *AmAu&B; BioIn 1, 6, 7, 8; ConAu 89; CurBio 43, 62, 67; DcAmB S8; EncTwCJ; LinLib L; ObitOF 79; OhA&B; WhAm 4A; WorAl*

Kipnis, Alexander
American. Opera Singer
Celebrated bass; with Chicago Civic Opera, 1923-32; known for Wagner, Russian roles.
b. Feb 1, 1891 in Zhitomir, Russia
d. May 14, 1978 in Westport, Connecticut
Source: *Baker 78, 84, 92; BiDAmM; BioIn 1, 2, 3, 11, 12, 17, 21; BlueB 76; BriBkM 80; CmOp; CurBio 43, 78N; FacFETw; IntDcOp; IntWWM 77; MetOEnc; MusMk; MusSN; NewAmDM; NewEOp 71; NewGrDA 86; NewGrDM 80; NewGrDO; OxDcOp; PenDiMP; WhAm 7; WhoAm 74; WhoMus 72; WhoWor 74, 76*

Kipnis, Claude
French. Entertainer
Mime; trained with Marcel Marceau; traveled internationally; wrote *The Mime Book,* 1974.
b. Apr 22, 1938 in Paris, France
d. Feb 8, 1981 in New York, New York
Source: *AnObit 1981; BioIn 12; ConAu 103, 107; NewYTBS 81; WhAm 9; WhoAm 78, 80*

Kipnis, Igor
American. Musician
Award-winning harpsichordist; revived interest in fortepiano; son of Alexander.
b. Sep 27, 1930 in Berlin, Germany
Source: *ASCAP 80; Baker 78, 84, 92; BioIn 10, 11, 14; BriBkM 80; FacFETw; IntWWM 77, 80, 85, 90; MusSN; NewAmDM; NewGrDA 86; NewGrDM 80; PenDiMP; WhoAm 74, 76, 78, 80, 82, 84, 86, 88, 90, 92, 94, 95, 96, 97; WhoAmM 83; WhoEnt 92; WhoMus 72; WhoWor 74, 76; WhoWorJ 72, 78*

Kiptanui, Moses
Kenyan. Track Athlete
Set world record for 3,000 meters in 7 mins., 28.96 secs., in 1992.
b. 1970?, Kenya

Kiraly, Karch
American. Volleyball Player
Volleyball player on US national team; won Olympic gold medal, 1984.
b. 1961?
Source: *BioIn 14, 15, 16; ConNews 87-1; NewYTBS 84; WhoAm 94, 95, 96, 97*

Kirbo, Charles H(ughes)
American. Lawyer
Atlanta attorney; close friend, advisor to Jimmy Carter.
b. Mar 5, 1917 in Bainbridge, Georgia
d. Sep 2, 1996 in Atlanta, Georgia
Source: *BioIn 11, 12; CurBio 77, 96N; NewYTBS 76, 77, 80; WhoAm 78, 80, 82, 84, 86, 88, 90, 92; WhoAmL 79; WhoSSW 75, 76*

Kirby, Durward
American. Actor
Co-host of TV show "Candid Camera," 1961-66.
b. Aug 24, 1912 in Covington, Kentucky
Source: *LegTOT; RadStar; WhoAm 74; WhoE 74; WorAl*

Kirby, George
"Big Daddy"
American. Comedian
First black stand-up comic, known for repertoire of over 100 impersonations; starred in own TV comedy-variety show, 1972-73.
b. Jun 8, 1923 in Chicago, Illinois
d. Sep 30, 1995 in Las Vegas, Nevada
Source: *BioIn 7, 10, 11; CurBio 77; DrBlPA 90; WhoBlA 75*

Kirby, Jack
[Jacob Kurtzberg]
American. Cartoonist
Created numerous comic book heroes: *Captain America,* 1951; *Fantastic Four,* 1961.
b. Aug 28, 1917 in New York, New York
d. Feb 6, 1994 in Thousand Oaks, California
Source: *BioIn 14, 19; EncACom; EncSF, 93; FanAl; NewYTBS 94; Who 90; WorECom*

Kirby, John
American. Musician
Led sextet, "The Biggest Little Band in the Land," 1930s-40s; on "Duffy's Tavern" radio show, early 1940s.
b. Dec 31, 1908 in Baltimore, Maryland
d. Jun 14, 1952 in Hollywood, California
Source: *AllMusG; Baker 84, 92; BiDAfM; BiDAmM; BiDJaz; BioIn 10; CmpEPM; IlEncJ; InB&W 80; NewGrDA 86; NewGrDJ 88, 94; OxCPMus; PenEncP; WhoJazz 72*

Kirby, Robert Emory
American. Business Executive
Chm., Westinghouse Electric Co., 1975-83.
b. Nov 8, 1918 in Ames, Iowa
Source: *BioIn 12; CurBio 79; IntWW 78, 89; St&PR 75, 84, 87; WhoAm 76, 78, 80, 82; WhoFI 74, 79, 81, 83; WhoWor 74, 76, 78, 82*

Kirby, Rollin
American. Cartoonist
Pulitzer-winning political cartoons highlighted by attacks on establishment.
b. Sep 4, 1876 in Galva, Illinois
d. May 8, 1952 in New York, New York
Source: *AmAu&B; CurBio 44, 52; DcAmB S5; WebBD 83; WhAm 3*

Kirchhoff, Gustav Robert
German. Physicist
Credited with discovery of spectrum analysis, the spectroscope.
b. Mar 12, 1824 in Konigsberg, Prussia
d. Oct 17, 1887 in Berlin, Germany
Source: *AsBiEn; BiESc; BioIn 5, 9, 11, 12, 14; CamDcSc; DcBiPP; DcScB; InSci; LarDcSc; McGEWB; REn; WhDW; WorAl; WorAlBi; WorScD*

Kirchner, Ernst Ludwig
[L de Marsalle]
German. Artist
German expressionist; did street scenes, landscapes of vibrant color, distorted forms: "Street, Berlin," 1907.
b. May 6, 1880 in Aschaffenburg, Germany
d. Jun 15, 1938 in Davos, Switzerland

Source: *AtlBL; BioIn 2, 4, 5, 6, 7, 8, 9, 11, 12, 20; ConArt 77, 83; DcArts; FacFETw; IntDcAA 90; MakMC; McGDA; McGEWB; OxCArt; OxCGer 76, 86; OxCTwCA; OxDcArt; PhDcTCA 77; PseudN 82*

Kirchschlager, Rudolf
Austrian. Political Leader
Pres. of Austria, 1974-86.
b. Mar 20, 1915 in Niederkappel, Austria
Source: *IntWW 74, 75, 76, 77, 78, 79, 80, 81, 82, 83, 89, 91, 93; IntYB 78, 79, 80; WhoWor 76, 78, 80, 82, 84, 87*

Kirk, Alan Goodrich
American. Military Leader, Diplomat
Commanded naval task force landing troops on D-Day, 1944; foreign ambassador, 1946-62.
b. Oct 30, 1888 in Philadelphia, Pennsylvania
d. Oct 15, 1963 in New York, New York
Source: *BiDWWGF; BioIn 1, 2, 6, 8, 16; DcAmB S7; FacFETw; NatCAB 50; WebAMB; WhAm 4*

Kirk, Claude Roy, Jr.
American. Politician
First Rep. governor of FL in 94 yrs., 1967-71.
b. Jan 7, 1926 in San Bernardino, California
Source: *BiDrGov 1789; BioIn 8, 9, 11, 12; CurBio 67; NewYTBE 70; PolProf J, NF; WhoAmP 73, 75, 77, 79; WhoSSW 73*

Kirk, Grayson Louis
American. University Administrator
Replaced Dwight Eisenhower as pres., Columbia U, 1950-68.
b. Oct 12, 1903 in Jeffersonville, Ohio
Source: *AmAu&B; BioIn 2, 3, 5, 6, 8; BlueB 76; CurBio 51; IntWW 83, 91; LinLib L, S; OhA&B; St&PR 87; Who 74, 82, 83, 85, 88, 90, 92, 94; WhoAm 74, 76, 78, 80, 82, 84, 86, 88, 90, 92, 94, 95, 96, 97; WhoWor 74, 80, 82*

Kirk, Lisa
American. Singer
Featured in Broadway's *Kiss Me Kate,* 1949; in TV, nightclubs, 1950s.
b. Feb 25, 1925 in Brownsville, Pennsylvania
d. Nov 11, 1990 in New York, New York
Source: *BioIn 4, 5, 9; CmpEPM; EncMT; InWom; NewYTBS 90; NotNAT; WhoAm 74; WhoThe 77*

Kirk, Paul G(rattan), Jr.
American. Politician
Chairman, Democratic National Committee, 1985-89.
b. Jan 18, 1938 in Newton, Massachusetts
Source: *CurBio 87; IntWW 89, 91, 93; NewYTBS 85; PolPar; WhoAm 86, 88, 90, 92, 94, 95, 96, 97; WhoAmP 89, 91, 93, 95; WhoE 97; WhoFI 92; WhoWor 97*

Kirk, Phyllis
[Phyllis Kirkegaard]
American. Actor
Nora Charles on TV series "The Thin Man," 1957-59.
b. Sep 18, 1930 in Plainfield, New Jersey
Source: *FilmgC; HalFC 84, 88; IntMPA 84, 86, 88, 92; InWom; MotPP; MovMk; PseudN 82; VarWW 85; WhoAm 74, 80, 82; WhoAmW 74; WhoHol A*

Kirk, Rahsaan Roland
American. Jazz Musician
Noted for playing unusual instruments, often several at once; invented rokon whistle.
b. Aug 7, 1936 in Columbus, Ohio
d. Dec 5, 1977 in Bloomington, Indiana
Source: *AfrAmAl 6; AllMusG; BiDAfM; BioIn 11, 13, 16; ConMus 6; DcTwCCu 5; DrBlPA 90; EncJzS; IlEncJ; InB&W 80; NegAl 83, 89; NewAmDM; NewYTBS 77; OxCPMus; PenEncP*

Kirk, Ron
American. Politician
Mayor, Dallas, 1995—.
b. Jun 27, 1954 in Austin, Texas
Source: *ConBlB 11*

Kirk, Russell (Amos)
American. Journalist
Noted for works on political theory: *The Conservative Mind,* 1953; won awards for gothic, fantasy fiction.
b. Oct 19, 1918 in Plymouth, Michigan
d. Apr 29, 1994 in Mecosta, Michigan
Source: *AmAu&B; AmCath 80; Au&Wr 71; AuNews 1; BioIn 6, 10, 11, 12, 13, 14, 15; BlueB 76; ChhPo S2; ConAu 1NR, 1R, 9AS, 20NR, 145; ConIsC 1; CurBio 62, 94N; DcAmC; DrAS 74H, 78H, 82H; FacFETw; IntAu&W 77, 82, 86, 89, 91, 93; IntvTCA 2; LinLib L; MajTwCW; PenEncH; PeoHis; PolProf E; ScF&FL 1, 2, 92; TwCRGW; TwCRHW 90; WhAm 11; WhoAm 74, 76, 78, 80, 82, 84, 86, 88, 90, 92; WhoHr&F; WhoMW 74, 76, 78, 84, 93; WhoUSWr 88; WhoWor 74, 76, 80, 82, 84, 87, 89, 91; WhoWrEP 89, 92, 95; WorAu 1950; WrDr 76, 80, 82, 84, 86, 88, 90, 92, 94, 96*

Kirk, Ruth Kratz
American. Author
Wrote books on nat. parks, 1960s-70s; cowrote *Hunters of the Whale,* 1975.
b. May 7, 1925 in Los Angeles, California
Source: *AuBYP 3; ConAu 9NR; ForWC 70; SmATA 5; Who 92*

Kirkland, Caroline Matilda Stansbury
[Mrs. Mary Clavers]
American. Author
First to write realistic fiction of American frontier: *A New Home,* 1839.
b. Jan 11, 1801 in New York, New York
d. Apr 6, 1864 in New York, New York
Source: *Alli, SUP; AmAu; AmAu&B; AmWomWr; ApCAB; BbD; BibAL; BiD&SB; BlmGWL; ChhPo; CyAL 2; DcAmAu; DcAmB; DcNAA; Drake; HarEnUS; InWom, SUP; LibW; NatCAB 5; NotAW; OxCAmL 65; REn; REnAL; TwCBDA; WhAm HS; WomFir*

Kirkland, Gelsey
American. Dancer
With American Ballet Theatre, 1974-81.
b. Dec 29, 1952 in Bethlehem, Pennsylvania
Source: *BioIn 13, 15; CelR 90; CurBio 75; DcArts; IntDcB; IntWW 91; InWom SUP; NewYTBE 70; NewYTBS 75; WhoAm 86, 88; WhoAmW 85; WhoEnt 92; WorAlBi; WrDr 92*

Kirkland, Lane
[Joseph Lane Kirkland]
American. Labor Union Official
Pres., AFL-CIO, 1979-95.
b. Mar 12, 1922 in Camden, South Carolina
Source: *BiDAmL; BiDAmLL; BioIn 9, 10, 11, 12, 13; CurBio 80; EncWB; IntWW 80, 81, 82, 83, 89, 91; NewYTBS 79, 80; Who 82, 83, 85, 88, 90, 92, 94; WhoAm 74, 76, 78, 80, 82, 84, 86, 88, 90, 92, 94, 95, 96, 97; WhoAmP 87, 89, 91, 93, 95; WhoE 85, 91; WhoFI 83, 85, 96; WhoLab 76; WorAlBi*

Kirkpatrick, Jeane Duane Jordan
American. Diplomat
US permanent representative to UN, 1981; resigned, 1985.
b. Nov 19, 1926 in Duncan, Oklahoma
Source: *AmMWSc 78S; AmPolLe; AmWomM; BiDAmNC; BioIn 13, 16; CelR 90; ColdWar 2; ConAu 7NR, 53; CurBio 81; DcAmDH 89; FacFETw; IntWW 83, 91; InWom SUP; NewYTBS 81; WhoAm 86, 90, 97; WhoAmP 85, 91; WhoAmW 85, 87, 91, 97; WhoE 91; WhoUSWr 88; WhoWor 84, 87, 91, 97; WhoWrEP 89; WrDr 86, 92*

Kirkpatrick, Ralph Leonard
American. Musician
Selected to record all of Bach's keyboard music, 1956; noted harpsichordist.
b. Jan 10, 1911 in Leominster, Massachusetts
d. Apr 13, 1984 in Guilford, Connecticut
Source: *ConAu 49, 112; CurBio 71; DrAS 74H, 78H, 82H; IntWW 74; NewYTBS 84; WhAm 8; WhoAm 80, 82; WhoE 74; WhoMus 72; WhoWor 74*

Kirkus, Virginia
[Virginia Kirkus Glick]
American. Critic, Author
Founded Kirkus Service, which previews forthcoming books, 1933.
b. Dec 7, 1893 in Meadville, Pennsylvania
d. Sep 10, 1980 in Danbury, Connecticut
Source: *AmAu&B; AnObit 1980; BioIn 3, 12, 13; ConAu 101, P-2, X; CurBio 41, 54, 70, 80N; DcAmB S10; InWom, SUP; LibW; NewYTBS 80; PseudN 82; SmATA 23N; WhE&EA; WhoAmW 58, 61, 64, 72*

Kirkwood, James
American. Writer
Won Pulitzer, Tony, for musical play, *Chorus Line*, 1976.
b. Aug 22, 1930 in Los Angeles, California
d. Apr 21, 1989 in New York, New York
Source: *Au&Wr 71; AuNews 2; BioIn 13, 14, 15, 16, 17; ConAu 1R, 2NR, 6NR, 40NR, 128; ConLC 9; ConTFT 5; IntAu&W 91; NatPD 77, 81; NewYTBS 89; TwCSFW 91; VarWW 85; WhAm 10; WhoAm 76, 78, 80, 82, 84, 86, 88; WhoThe 81; WrDr 80, 82, 84, 86, 88*

Kirov, Sergei Mironovich
[Sergey Mironovich Kostrikov]
Russian. Revolutionary
One of Stalin's chief aides.
b. Mar 27, 1886 in Urzhum, Russia
d. Dec 1, 1934 in Leningrad, Union of Soviet Socialist Republics
Source: *BiDSovU; BioIn 7, 9, 10, 11, 15, 16; FacFETw; NewCol 75; REn*

Kirshner, Don
American. Music Executive
Founded Aldon Music, 1958-63, launching songwriting careers of Neil Sedaka, Neil Diamond, others.
b. Apr 17, 1934 in New York, New York
Source: *EncRk 88; IlEncRk; LesBEnT 92; NewYTET; RolSEnR 83; WhoAm 78, 80, 82, 84, 86*

Kirstein, George G
American. Publisher
Owner, publisher, *Nation*, 1955-65.
b. Dec 10, 1909 in Boston, Massachusetts
d. Apr 3, 1986 in Mamaroneck, New York
Source: *AmAu&B; NewYTBS 86; WhoAm 80*

Kirstein, Lincoln (Edward)
American. Ballet Promoter, Author
Co-founder, with George Balanchine, of New York City Ballet, 1946, and School of American Ballet, 1934.
b. May 4, 1907 in Rochester, New York
d. Jan 5, 1996 in New York, New York
Source: *AmAu&B; BiDD; BioIn 1, 3, 10, 11, 12, 13, 14, 15, 17, 18, 20, 21; CnOxB; ConAu 117, 128, 151; CurBio 52, 90, 96N; DancEn 78; FacFETw; IntAu&W 77, 91; IntDcB; IntWW 74, 75, 76, 77, 78, 79, 80, 81, 82, 83, 89, 91, 93; NewYTBS 27, 82; PeoHis; RAdv 14, 13-3; RGTwCWr; WhAm 11; WhAmArt 85; Who 74, 82, 83, 85, 88, 90, 92, 94; WhoAm 74, 76, 78, 80, 82, 84, 86, 88, 90, 92, 94, 95, 96; WhoAmA 73, 76, 78, 80, 82; WhoE 79, 81, 83, 85, 86, 91, 95; WhoMus 72; WhoWor 74; WorAlBi; WorAu 1975; WrDr 80, 82, 84, 86, 88, 90, 92, 94, 96*

Kirsten, Dorothy
American. Opera Singer
Popular soprano with NY Met., 1945-76; in film *The Great Caruso*, 1951.
b. Jul 6, 1910 in Montclair, New Jersey
d. Nov 18, 1992 in Los Angeles, California
Source: *AnObit 1992; Baker 84; BioIn 13, 14, 18, 19, 21; CurBio 48, 93N; IntWWM 90; InWom SUP; MetOEnc; NewAmDM; NewGrDA 86; NewYTBS 92; PenDiMP; RadStar; WhAm 10; WhoAm 86, 90; WhoEnt 92; WhoHol A*

Kirtley, Steven William
[The Hostages]
American. Hostage
One of 52 held by terrorists, Nov 1979-Jan 1981.
b. 1958?
Source: *NewYTBS 81*

Kisfaludy, Karoly
Hungarian. Dramatist
Founder of Hungarian drama; wrote historical play, *The Tatars in Hungary*, 1819.
b. Feb 6, 1788 in Tete, Hungary
d. Nov 21, 1830 in Pest, Hungary
Source: *BbD; BiD&SB; BioIn 7; CasWL; DcCathB; EuAu; LinLib L; McGEWD 72, 84; NewCol 75; NotNAT B; OxCThe 67; PenC EUR*

Kishi, Nobusuke
Japanese. Political Leader
Prime minister of Japan, 1956-60; resigned amid protests after he signed security treaty with US.
b. Nov 13, 1896 in Yamaguchi Prefecture, Japan
d. Aug 7, 1987 in Tokyo, Japan
Source: *AnObit 1987; BioIn 4, 5, 12, 15; CurBio 57, 87, 87N; DcPol; FarE&A 78, 79, 80, 81; IntWW 74, 75, 76, 77, 78, 79, 80, 81, 82, 83; McGEWB; WhoWor 74*

Kiss
[Eric Carr; Peter Criss; Ace Frehley; Gene Simmons; Paul Stanley]
American. Music Group
Formed 1972, known for makeup, dramatic stage shows; hit song "Beth," 1976.
Source: *BioIn 11, 12, 15, 17; BkPepl; ConMuA 80A; ConMus 5; EncPR&S 89; EncRk 88; EncRkSt; HarEnR 86; IlEncRk; MiSFD 9; NewAmDM; NewYTBS 77, 91; PenEncP; RkOn 78; RolSEnR 83; WhoRock 81; WhoRocM 82*

Kissin, Evgeny
Russian. Pianist
Child prodigy noted for romantic style, restrained power.
b. Oct 9, 1971 in Moscow, Union of Soviet Socialist Republics
Source: *Baker 92; ConMus 6*

Kissinger, Henry Alfred
"Henry the K"; "Super Kraut"; "The Drone"; "The Flying Peacemaker"; "The Iron Stomach"
American. Government Official
Secretary of State under Nixon, Ford; won Nobel Peace Prize, 1973.
b. May 27, 1923 in Fuerth, Germany
Source: *AmAu&B; AmOrTwC; AmPolLe; BiDAmNC; BiDrUSE 89; BioIn 13, 14, 15, 16; BioNews 74; BkPepl; CelR 90; CngDr 74; ColdWar 2; ConAu 1R, 2NR, 33NR; ConHero 1; CurBio 72; DcAmC; DcAmDH 89; EncAB-H 1974, 1996; EncWB; FacFETw; IntAu&W 91; IntWW 91; MajTwCW; NewYTBE 73; NewYTBS 86; NobelP; PeoHis; RComAH; WebAB 74; Who 85, 92; WhoAm 86, 90, 97; WhoAmP 91; WhoE 91, 97; WhoNob, 90, 95; WhoWor 87, 91, 97; WorAlBi; WrDr 92*

Kissinger, Nancy Maginnes
American.
Wife of Henry Kissinger.
b. 1934 in White Plains, New York
Source: *BioIn 10, 11, 12; BioNews 74; NewYTBS 74*

Kissling, Frances
American. Social Reformer
Pres., Catholics for a Free Choice, 1982—.
b. Jun 15, 1943 in New York, New York
Source: *News 89-2*

Kistiakowsky, George Bogdan
American. Chemist
Leader, explosives division, Los Alamos Project; later opposed nuclear weapons.
b. Nov 18, 1900 in Kiev, Russia
d. Dec 7, 1982 in Cambridge, Massachusetts
Source: *AmMWSc 73P, 76P, 79, 82; AnObit 1982; BiESc; BioIn 1, 4, 5, 6, 9, 11, 13; ConAu 108; CurBio 60, 83; IntWW 80, 81, 82; McGMS 80; NewYTBS 82; PolProf E; WhAm 8; Who 74, 83; WhoAm 74, 76; WhoGov 72; WhoWor 74*

Kistler, Darci Anna
American. Dancer
Star of NYC Ballet, 1980; principal dancer, 1982—; teacher, School of American Ballet, 1994—.
b. Jun 4, 1964 in Riverside, California
Source: *BioIn 12, 13, 15; CelR 90; CurBio 91; News 93-1; NewYTBS 80; WhoAm 84, 86, 88, 90, 92, 94, 95, 96, 97; WhoAmW 95, 97; WhoE 91*

Kitaen, Tawny
American. TV Personality, Model
Starred in rock band Whitesnake's music videos; co-host "America's Funniest People," 1992-94.
b. 1961?
Source: *LegTOT; WhoHol 92*

Kitagawa, Joseph Mitsuo
American. Theologian, Author
Dean, School of Divinity, U of Chicago, 1970-80; books introduced religions of Japan to the West.
b. Mar 8, 1915 in Osaka, Japan
d. Oct 7, 1992 in Chicago, Illinois
Source: *ConAu 1R, 2NR; DrAS 74P, 78P, 82P; LEduc 74; WhAm 10; WhoAm 74, 76, 78, 80; WhoAsA 94N; WhoRel 75, 77, 85, 92; WhoWor 74*

Kitaj, R(onald) B(rooks)
American. Artist
Draws large history paintings with social themes; collages of baseball stars.
b. Oct 29, 1932 in Chagrin Falls, Ohio
Source: *BioIn 13, 14, 15, 16; ConArt 83, 89, 96; CurBio 82; DcCAA 88; IntWW 83, 91; OxCTwCA; OxDcArt; PrintW 85; TwCPaSc; Who 85, 92; WhoAm 86, 90; WhoAmA 84, 91*

Kitaro
Musician, Composer
New Age artist composers on synthesizer keyboards; albums include *Asia,* 1986.
b. 1953, Japan
Source: *BioIn 16; ConMus 1; NewAgMG*

Kitasato Shibasaburo
Japanese. Bacteriologist
At approximately the same time as Yersin, discovered the bacteria responsible for bubonic plague, 1894.
b. Dec 20, 1852 in Oguni, Japan
d. Jun 13, 1931 in Nakanocho, Japan
Source: *BioIn 14; WorAlBi*

Kitchell, Iva
American. Dancer
Dance comedienne who impersonated great dancers, satirized classical ballet; featured dancer at Radio City Music Hall, NYC.
b. Mar 31, 1908 in Junction City, Kansas
d. Nov 19, 1983 in Ormond Beach, Florida
Source: *BiDD; BioIn 13, 14; CurBio 84, 84N; NewYTBS 83*

Kitchener, Horatio Herbert
English. Military Leader
Hero of victories in Africa who expanded British army as secretary of state for war, 1914.
b. Jun 14, 1850 in Ballylongford, Ireland
d. Jun 5, 1916
Source: *BioIn 10, 14, 15, 16, 21; DcAfHiB 86; DcIrB 78, 88; DcNaB 1912; DcTwHis; Dis&D; GenMudB; GrBr; HarEnMi; HisDBrE; HisWorL; LuthC 75; McGEWB; VicBrit; WebBD 83; WhDW; WhoMilH 76; WorAl; WorAlBi*

Kite, Tom
[Thomas O Kite, Jr]
American. Golfer
Turned pro, 1972; rookie of the yr., 1973; player of the yr., top career money-winner, 1989.
b. Dec 9, 1949 in Austin, Texas
Source: *BioIn 12, 13; News 90, 90-3; WhoGolf; WhoIntG; WhoSpor; WorAlBi*

Kitson, Henry Hudson
American. Sculptor
Began carving with stone tools as a child; known for award-winning busts, monuments.
b. Apr 9, 1863 in Huddersfield, New York
d. Jun 26, 1947
Source: *BioIn 1; NatCAB 12; ObitOF 79; WhAm 2; WhAmArt 85*

Kitt, Eartha Mae
American. Singer
Sang earthy songs in low-key monotone; films include *St. Louis Blues,* 1958.
b. Jan 16, 1928 in North, South Carolina
Source: *Baker 84; BiDAfM; BkPepl; ConAu 77; ConMus 9; ConTFT 3; CurBio 55; DrBlPA 90; FacFETw; FilmgC; HalFC 84, 88; InB&W 80, 85; IntMPA 92; IntWW 89, 91, 93; InWom SUP; LivgBAA; MovMk; NewAmDM; NewGrDA 86; NotBlAW 1; NotNAT; OxCPMus; PenEncP; VarWW 85; WhoAfA 96; WhoAm 74, 76, 78, 80, 82, 84, 86, 88, 90, 92, 94, 95, 96, 97; WhoAmW 58, 61, 64, 66, 68, 70, 72, 83, 95, 97; WhoBlA 75, 77, 80, 85, 88, 90, 92, 94; WhoEnt 92; WhoHol A; WhoThe 81; WorAlBi*

Kittikachorn, Thanom
Thai. Political Leader
Prime minister, 1958, 1963-71, 1972-73; aggressively opposed communism.
b. Aug 11, 1911 in Tak, Thailand
Source: *BioIn 8, 9, 10, 11; CurBio 69; DicTyr; FarE&A 78, 79, 81; IntWW 74, 75, 76, 77, 78, 79, 80, 81, 82, 83, 89, 91, 93; IntYB 78, 79, 80, 81, 82; WhoGov 72; WhoWor 74; WorDWW*

Kittle, Ron(ald Dale)
American. Baseball Player
Outfielder, Chicago White Sox, 1983-86; NY Yankees, 1986-90; Baltimore Orioles, 1990—; AL rookie of yr., 1983; All-Star, 1983.
b. Jan 5, 1958 in Gary, Indiana
Source: *Ballpl 90; BaseReg 86, 87; BioIn 13, 14, 15; NewYTBS 83, 86*

Kittredge, G(eorge) L(yman)
American. Author
Authority on English literature; wrote *Complete Works of Shakespeare,* 1936.
b. Feb 28, 1860 in Boston, Massachusetts
d. Jul 23, 1941 in Barnstable, Massachusetts
Source: *AmAu&B; Benet 87; BenetAL 91; BiDAmM; BioIn 1, 2, 4, 5, 6; ChhPo, S3; CnDAL; CurBio 41; DcAmB S3; DcLEL; DcNAA; LngCTC; NatCAB 13, 34; NewC; NotNAT B; OxCAmL 65, 83, 95; OxCAmT 84; PseudN 82; REn; REnAL; TwCA, SUP; WebAB 74, 79; WhAm 1*

Kizer, Carolyn (Ashley)
American. Poet
Published *The Ungrateful Garden,* 1961.
b. Dec 10, 1925 in Spokane, Washington
Source: *AmWomWr SUP; ArtclWW 2; BenetAL 91; BioIn 10, 12; CamGLE; CamHAL; ConAu 5AS, 7NR, 24NR, 53, 65, 111; ConLC 15, 39, 80; ConPo 70, 75, 80, 85, 91, 96; CroCAP; DcLB 5, 169; DcLEL 1940; FemiCLE; IntWWP 77; InWom SUP; LinLib L; OxCAmL 83, 95; OxCTwCP; OxCWoWr 95; PenC AM; RAdv 14; WhoAm 76, 78, 82, 84, 86, 88, 90, 92, 94, 95, 96, 97; WhoAmW 87, 89, 91, 95, 97; WhoE 86, 89; WhoUSWr 88; WhoWrEP 89, 92, 95; WorAu 1950; WrDr 86, 88, 90, 92, 94, 96*

Klafsky, Katharina
Hungarian. Opera Singer
Wagnerian soprano with Damrosch Opera Co., 1890s.
b. Sep 19, 1855 in Saint Johann, Hungary
d. Sep 22, 1896 in Hamburg, Germany
Source: *Baker 78, 84, 92; InWom, SUP; NewEOp 71; NewGrDM 80; NewGrDO; OxDcOp*

Klammer, Franz
Austrian. Skier
Won gold medal in men's downhill, 1976 Olympics.
b. 1952 in Moaswald, Austria
Source: *BioIn 10, 12, 14; FacFETw; NewYTBS 80, 84*

Klarsfeld, Beate
German. Social Reformer
Crusader to track down and bring to trial former Nazi war criminals.
b. Feb 13, 1931 in Berlin, Germany
Source: *BioIn 13; ConAu 65; News 89-1*

Klass, Perri Elizabeth
American. Physician, Writer
Boston pediatrician; writings reflect her roles as mother and pediatrician; winner of four O. Henry Awards.
b. Apr 29, 1958 in Tunapuna, Trinidad
Source: *BioIn 14, 15; IntAu&W 91, 93; News 93-2; WhoAmW 91; WrDr 92*

Klassen, Elmer Theodore
American. Government Official
Appointed first postmaster general of newly organized postal service, 1972.
b. Nov 6, 1908 in Hillsboro, Kansas
d. Mar 6, 1990 in Palm Harbor, Florida

Source: *BioIn 8, 9, 10, 16, 17; CurBio 73, 90, 90N; IntWW 74, 75, 76, 77, 78, 79, 80, 81, 82, 83; NewYTBE 71; NewYTBS 90; St&PR 75; WhAm 10; WhoAm 74, 76, 78; WhoGov 72, 75, 77; WhoSSW 73*

Kleban, Edward Lawrence
American. Lyricist
Won Tony, Pulitzer for writing lyrics for *A Chorus Line,* which opened on Broadway, 1975.
b. Apr 30, 1939 in New York, New York
d. Dec 28, 1987 in New York, New York
Source: *BioIn 12; WhAm 10; WhoAm 78, 80, 82, 84, 86, 88*

Klebe, Giselher
German. Composer
Widely diverse works include fairy-tale opera *Das Marchen von der Schonen Lilie,* 1968.
b. Jun 28, 1925 in Mannheim, Germany
Source: *Baker 78, 84; CnOxB; DancEn 78; DcCM; IntWW 74, 75, 76, 77, 78, 79, 80, 81, 82, 83, 89, 91, 93; IntWWM 77, 80, 90; MusMk; NewEOp 71; NewGrDM 80; OxDcOp; WhoWor 74, 89, 91*

Kleber, Jean Baptiste
French. Army Officer
Commanded division in Napoleon's army; recaptured Cairo from Turks; assassinated.
b. Mar 9, 1753 in Strasbourg, France
d. Jun 14, 1800 in Cairo, Egypt
Source: *CmFrR; DcBiPP; OxCFr; WebBD 83; WhoMilH 76*

Kleberg, Robert Justus, Jr.
American. Rancher, Horse Owner
Owner King Ranch, largest producer of beef cattle in US; race horse, Assault, won Triple Crown, 1946.
b. Mar 29, 1896 in Corpus Christi, Texas
d. Oct 13, 1974 in Houston, Texas
Source: *BiDAmBL 83; BioIn 1, 8, 10, 12; DcAmB S9; IntWW 74; NatCAB 58; NewYTBS 74; ObitOF 79; WhAm 6; WhoAm 74; WhoWor 74*

Klebs, Edwin
German. Bacteriologist
Co-discovered the Klebs-Loffler bacillus, the infectious agent of diphtheria, 1884.
b. Feb 6, 1834 in Konigsberg, Prussia
d. Oct 23, 1913 in Bern, Switzerland
Source: *AmBi; BiHiMed; BioIn 9; InSci; OxCMed 86*

Klee, Paul
Swiss. Artist
Abstract painter noted for fantastic shapes, exotic colors.
b. Dec 18, 1879 in Bern, Switzerland
d. Jun 29, 1940 in Muralto, Switzerland
Source: *AtlBL; Benet 87, 96; BioIn 1, 2, 3, 4, 5, 6, 7, 8, 9, 10, 11, 12, 13, 14, 15, 16, 17, 20; ConArt 77, 83; CurBio 40; CyWA 89; DcArts; DcPup; DcTwDes; EncTR, 91; FacFETw; IntDcAA 90; LegTOT; MakMC; McGDA; McGEWB; NewYTBS 87; OxCArt; OxCGer 76, 86; OxCTwCA; OxDcArt; PhDcTCA 77; REn; WhDW; WorAl; WorAlBi*

Kleiber, Carlos
German. Conductor
Conductor at major opera houses in Germany, England and US since the 1950s; son of Erich.
b. Jul 3, 1930 in Berlin, Germany
Source: *Baker 78, 84, 92; BioIn 10, 13, 16; BriBkM 80; CurBio 91; FacFETw; IntDcOp; IntWW 89, 91; MetOEnc; NewAmDM; NewGrDM 80; NewGrDO; OxDcOp; PenDiMP; WhoOp 76; WhoWor 84, 91*

Kleiber, Erich
Austrian. Conductor
Raised standards of London's Covent Garden opera, 1950s; beloved leader of Berlin State Opera, 1923-35.
b. Aug 5, 1890 in Vienna, Austria
d. Jan 27, 1956 in Zurich, Switzerland
Source: *Baker 78, 84, 92; BioIn 3, 4, 8, 10, 11, 12; BriBkM 80; CmOp; FacFETw; IntDcOp; MetOEnc; MusSN; NewAmDM; NewEOp 71; NewGrDM 80; NewGrDO; ObitT 1951; OxDcOp; PenDiMP*

Klein, Anne
American. Fashion Designer
Known for sophisticated sportswear.
b. Aug 3, 1923 in New York, New York
d. Mar 19, 1974 in New York, New York
Source: *BioIn 17, 20; BioNews 74; ConAmBL; ConDes 84, 90, 97; ConFash; DcAmB S9; FairDF US; InWom SUP; LegTOT; NewYTBS 74; WhoFash 88; WorFshn*

Klein, Calvin
[Richard Klein]
American. Fashion Designer
Designer of elegant, modern classics since 1969; jeans caused sensation due to provocative ads; controversial "kiddie-porn" ads, 1995.
b. Nov 19, 1942 in New York, New York
Source: *AmDec 1970; BioIn 13, 14, 15, 16; BkPepl; CelR 90; ConAmBL; ConDes 90; ConFash; CurBio 78, 79; DcTwDes; Dun&B 88, 90; EncFash; Entr; FacFETw; IntWW 91; LegTOT; News 96, 96-2; WhoAm 86, 90; WhoE 91; WhoFash 88; WorAlBi; WorFshn*

Klein, Chuck
[Charles Herbert Klein]
American. Baseball Player
Outfielder, 1928-44; won NL triple crown, 1933; had .320 career batting average; Hall of Fame, 1980.
b. Oct 7, 1904 in Indianapolis, Indiana
d. Mar 28, 1958 in Indianapolis, Indiana
Source: *Ballpl 90; BiDAmSp BB; DcAmB S6; LegTOT; WhoProB 73; WhoSpor*

Klein, Herbert George
American. Newspaper Editor
Managed Nixon's campaign for pres; special asst. press secretary to Nixon, 1959-61; editor-in-chief, Copley Newspapers, Inc., 1980—.
b. Apr 1, 1918 in Los Angeles, California
Source: *BioIn 8, 9, 10, 11, 12; BlueB 76; CurBio 71; IntAu&W 82, 89; IntWW 74, 75, 76, 77, 78, 79, 80, 81, 82, 83, 89, 91, 93; LesBEnT, 92; St&PR 91, 93, 96, 97; WhoAm 74, 76, 78, 80, 82, 86, 88, 90, 92, 94, 95, 96, 97; WhoAmP 73; WhoGov 72, 75; WhoSSW 73; WhoWest 89, 92, 94; WhoWor 80*

Klein, Lawrence Robert
American. Economist
Won 1980 Nobel Prize for developing econometrics.
b. Sep 14, 1920 in Omaha, Nebraska
Source: *BioIn 10, 11, 12, 14, 15; ConAu 116; GrEconS; IntWW 81, 82, 83, 89, 91, 93; NobelP; RAdv 14; ThTwC 87; Who 82, 83, 85, 88, 90, 92, 94; WhoAm 74, 76, 78, 80, 82, 84, 86, 88, 90, 92, 94, 95, 96, 97; WhoE 81, 83, 85, 86, 89, 91, 93, 95, 97; WhoEc 86; WhoFI 87, 89, 92, 94; WhoNob, 90, 95; WhoScEn 96; WhoWor 82, 84, 87, 89, 91, 93, 95, 96, 97; WorAlBi; WrDr 92*

Klein, Marty
Canadian. Agent
Talent agent; past pres., Agency for the Performing Arts.
b. 1941 in Montreal, Quebec, Canada
d. Oct 25, 1992 in West Hollywood, California

Klein, Melanie
Psychiatrist, Author
First psychoanalyst to work on child analysis.
b. Mar 30, 1882 in Vienna, Austria
d. Sep 22, 1960 in London, England
Source: *BiDPsy; BioIn 5, 7, 12, 14, 15, 17, 18, 21; ConAu 111; ContDcW 89; DcNaB 1951; IntDcWB; InWom SUP; MakMC; McGEWB; NamesHP; ObitT 1951; RAdv 14; ThTwC 87; WhAm 5; WhDW*

Klein, Robert
American. Comedian, Actor
Won Tony, 1979, for *They're Playing Our Song;* known for records, TV appearances.
b. Feb 8, 1942 in New York, New York
Source: *BioIn 11, 13, 14, 15; CelR 90; ConTFT 3; CurBio 77; EncAFC; IntMPA 92, 94, 96; JoeFr; LegTOT; VarWW 85; WhoAm 78, 80, 82, 84, 86, 88, 90, 92, 94, 95, 96, 97; WhoCom; WhoEnt 92; WhoHol 92; WhoThe 81; WorAl; WorAlBi*

Kleindienst, Richard Gordon
American. Government Official
Attorney general, 1972-73, who played key role in Richard Nixon's election, 1968.

b. Aug 5, 1923 in Winslow, Arizona
Source: *BiDrUSE 89; BioIn 8, 9, 10, 11, 12; CurBio 72; IntWW 74, 75, 76, 77, 78, 79, 80, 81, 82, 83, 89, 91, 93; NewYTBE 72; NewYTBS 74; PolProf NF; Who 74, 82, 83, 85, 88, 90, 92, 94; WhoAm 74, 76, 78, 80, 82, 84, 86, 88, 90, 92, 94, 95, 96, 97; WhoAmL 85; WhoAmP 73, 75, 77, 79, 81, 83, 85, 87, 89, 91, 93, 95; WhoGov 72*

Kleinfield, Sonny
[Nathan Richard Kleinfield]
American. Journalist, Author
Financial writer, *NY Times;* wrote *The Hidden Minority,* 1979.
b. Aug 12, 1950 in Paterson, New Jersey
Source: *ConAu 18NR, 97*

Kleist, Heinrich von
[Von Bernd Heinrich Wilhelm Kleist]
German. Author, Dramatist, Poet
Wrote novella *Michael Kohlhaas,* 1811; comedy *The Broken Jug,* 18 06.
b. Oct 18, 1777 in Frankfurt an der Oder, Germany
d. Nov 21, 1811 in Wannsee, Germany
Source: *AtlBL; Benet 87, 96; BiD&SB; BioIn 3, 4, 5, 7, 8, 9, 10, 12, 13, 15, 17, 18; CamGWoT; CasWL; CnThe; CyWA 58, 89; DcEuL; DcLB 90; DcPup; Dis&D; EncEnl; EncWT; Ent; EuAu; EuWr 5; EvEuW; GrFLW; LegTOT; McGEWB; McGEWD 72, 84; NewCBEL; NewGrDM 80; NinCLC 2, 37; NotNAT A, B; Novels; OxCGer 76, 86; OxCThe 67, 83; PenC EUR; PenEncH; RAdv 14, 13-2; RComWL; REn; REnWD; ShSCr 22; WhDW; WorAl; WorAlBi; WrPh*

Klem, Bill
[William Joseph Klem]
"The Old Arbitrator"
American. Baseball Umpire
NL umpire, 1905-41, considered best ever; first to use hand signals; with Tommy Connolly, first umpire elected to Hall of Fame, 1953.
b. Feb 22, 1874 in Rochester, New York
d. Sep 16, 1951 in Miami, Florida
Source: *Ballpl 90; BiDAmSp BB; BioIn 2, 3, 4, 5, 7, 8, 10, 12, 14, 15, 16; LegTOT; WhoProB 73*

Klemperer, Otto
German. Conductor, Composer
Led German, US symphonies; noted interpreter of German Romantics.
b. May 14, 1885 in Breslau, Germany
d. Jul 6, 1973 in Zurich, Switzerland
Source: *Baker 78, 84, 92; BiDAmM; BioIn 1, 2, 4, 6, 7, 8, 9, 10, 11, 13, 15; BriBkM 80; CmCal; CmOp; ConAu 116; CurBio 65, 73, 73N; DcArts; EncTR, 91; FacFETw; IntDcOp; IntWWM 77; LegTOT; LinLib S; MetOEnc; MusMk; MusSN; NewAmDM; NewEOp 71; NewGrDA 86; NewGrDM 80; NewGrDO; NewYTBE 72, 73; ObitT 1971; OxDcOp; PenDiMP; WhAm 5; WhDW; WhoMus 72; WorAl; WorAlBi*

Klemperer, Werner
German. Actor
Won Emmys for role of Colonel Klink on TV series "Hogan's Heroes," 1968, 1969; son of Otto.
b. Mar 22, 1920 in Cologne, Germany
Source: *CelR; ConTFT 6, 15; FilmEn; FilmgC; HalFC 84, 88; MotPP; VarWW 85; WhoHol 92, A; WorAl; WorAlBi*

Klenau, Paul von
Danish. Composer, Conductor
Wrote ballet, *Kleine Idas Blumen,* 1916.
b. Feb 11, 1883 in Copenhagen, Denmark
d. Aug 31, 1946 in Copenhagen, Denmark
Source: *Baker 78, 84; BioIn 4; NewAmDM; NewEOp 71; NewGrDM 80; OxCMus; OxDcOp*

Klepfisz, Irena
American. Poet
Published *Dreams of an Insomniac: Jewish Feminist Essays, Speeches and Diatribes,* 1990; *A Few Words in the Mother Tongue: Poems Selected and New,* 1990.
b. 1941 in Warsaw, Poland
Source: *BioIn 19, 20; BlmGWL; GayLesB; JeAmWW*

Klestil, Thomas
Austrian. Political Leader
Pres., Austria, 1992—.
b. Nov 4, 1932 in Vienna, Austria
Source: *BioIn 11; IntWW 80, 81, 82, 83, 89, 91, 93; WhoAm 86; WhoWor 74, 80, 82, 87, 93, 95, 96, 97*

Klima, Ivan
Czech. Dramatist
Began as novelist; antirealist plays are rich in symbols, myths: *The Castle,* 1964.
b. Sep 14, 1931 in Prague, Czechoslovakia
Source: *Benet 96; ConAu 17NR, 25R, 50NR; ConLC 56; ConWorW 93; EncWL 3; IntAu&W 91, 93; McGEWD 84; ModSL 2; WhoSocC 78; WhoSoCE 89; WorAu 1980*

Klima, Petr
Czech. Hockey Player
Left wing, Detroit, 1985-89; Edmonton, 1989-93; Tampa Bay, 1993—.
b. Dec 23, 1964 in Chaomutov, Czechoslovakia
Source: *BioIn 16; ConNews 87-1; HocReg 87*

Klimt, Gustav
Austrian. Artist
Founded Vienna Secession school of painting, 1897.
b. Jul 4, 1862 in Vienna, Austria
d. Feb 6, 1918 in Vienna, Austria
Source: *AtlBL; BioIn 5, 8, 9, 10, 11, 12, 13, 14, 15, 16, 18, 19; DcArts; EncFash; EncWB; FacFETw; IntDcAA 90; McGDA; OxCArt; OxCGer 76, 86; OxCTwCA; OxDcArt; PhDcTCA 77; WhDW*

Kline, Franz Joseph
American. Artist
Abstract painter, noted for huge scale black and white compositions; introduced color into later works.
b. May 23, 1919 in Wilkes-Barre, Pennsylvania
d. May 13, 1962 in New York, New York
Source: *BioIn 8, 10; McGDA; McGEWB; ObitOF 79; OxCArt; REn; WebAB 74, 79*

Kline, Kevin Delaney
American. Actor
Won Tonys for *On the Twentieth Century,* 1978; *The Pirates of Penzance,* 1981; won Oscar for *A Fish Called Wanda,* 1989; married to actress Phoebe Cates.
b. Oct 24, 1947 in Saint Louis, Missouri
Source: *BioIn 11, 13, 14, 15; CelR 90; ConTFT 3; CurBio 86; HalFC 84, 88; IntMPA 92; IntWW 89, 91, 93; NewYTBS 78, 81, 82; VarWW 85; WhoAm 84, 86, 88, 90, 92, 94, 95, 96, 97; WhoE 91; WhoEnt 92; WhoThe 81; WorAlBi*

Kline, Morris
American. Educator
Professor of mathematics, NYU, 1938-75 (with time out for WW II); critic of math teaching; wrote "Why Johnny Can't Add," 1973.
b. May 1, 1908 in New York, New York
d. Jun 10, 1992 in New York, New York
Source: *AmMWSc 73P, 76P, 79, 82, 86, 89, 92; BioIn 18; ConAu 2NR, 5R, 46NR, 139; IntAu&W 77, 82; WhAm 10; WhoAm 74, 76, 78; WhoAmJ 80; WrDr 76, 80, 82, 84, 86, 88, 90, 92, 94N*

Kline, Nathan Schellenberg
American. Psychiatrist
Developed antidepressant drugs; pioneered use of drugs in treating mental illness.
b. Mar 22, 1916 in Philadelphia, Pennsylvania
d. Feb 11, 1983 in New York, New York
Source: *AmMWSc 73P, 76P, 79, 82; BioIn 7, 8, 10, 11, 12, 13; ConAu 81; CurBio 83; IntWW 74, 75, 76, 77, 78, 79, 80, 81, 82, 83; WhAm 8; WhoAm 74, 76, 78, 80, 82; WhoE 74, 75, 77, 79, 81; WhoFrS 84; WhoWor 76, 78, 80, 82*

Kline, Otis Adelbert
American. Author
Prolific heroic-fantasy writer for *Weird Tales, Argosy* pulps.
b. 1891 in Chicago, Illinois
d. Oct 24, 1946 in New York, New York
Source: *BioIn 1; DcNAA; EncSF, 93; FanAl; NewEScF; RGSF; ScF&FL 92; ScFEYrs; ScFSB; TwCSFW 81, 86, 91; WhoHr&F; WhoSciF*

Klineberg, Otto
American. Author
His research on IQ scores of black students helped win the desegregation case, Brown vs. Board of Education, 1954.
b. Nov 2, 1899 in Quebec, Quebec, Canada
d. Mar 6, 1992 in Bethesda, Maryland
Source: *AmAu&B; AmMWSc 73S; BioIn 10, 12, 15, 17, 18, 19; IntEnSS 79; RAdv 14, 13-3*

Kling, Johnny
[John Gradwohl Kling]
"Noisy"
American. Baseball Player
Catcher, 1900-13, mostly with Cubs; known for defensive play.
b. Nov 13, 1875 in Kansas City, Missouri
d. Jan 31, 1947 in Kansas City, Missouri
Source: *Ballpl 90; BiDAmSp BB; BioIn 15; WhoProB 73*

Klinger, Max
German. Artist
Produced imaginative etchings, grandiose scale paintings, polychromatic statues.
b. Feb 18, 1857 in Leipzig, Germany
d. Jul 5, 1920 in Grossjena, Germany
Source: *AntBDN A; BioIn 9, 11; ClaDrA; Dis&D; IntDcAA 90; McGDA; NewCol 75; OxCArt; OxCTwCA; OxDcArt; PhDcTCA 77*

Klitzing, Klaus von
Polish. Physicist
Discovered that electrical resistance is quantized via the Hall effect; awarded Nobel Prize for Physics, 1985.
b. Jun 28, 1943 in Schroda, Poland
Source: *BioIn 13, 14, 15, 20; CamDcSc; NobelP; WhoNob 95; WhoScEn 94, 96; WhoWor 87, 89, 91, 93, 95, 96, 97; WorAlBi*

Klopfer, Donald Simon
American. Publisher
Co-founded Random House publishers with Bennett Cerf, 1927-75.
b. Jan 23, 1902 in New York, New York
d. May 30, 1986 in New York, New York
Source: *ConAu 119; NewYTBS 86; St&PR 75; WhAm 9; WhoAm 74, 76, 78*

Klopstock, Friedrich Gottlieb
"The Birmingham Milton"; "The Creator of Biblical Epic Poetry"; "The German Milton"; "The Milton of Germany"
German. Poet
Baroque, emotional verses include religiously inspired masterpiece, *Messias,* 1748; translated: *The Messiah,* 1826.
b. Jul 2, 1724 in Quedlinburg, Germany
d. Mar 14, 1803 in Hamburg, Germany
Source: *BbD; Benet 87, 96; BiD&SB; BioIn 3, 6, 7, 8, 14, 17; BlkwCE; CasWL; ChhPo; DcArts; DcBiPP; DcEuL; DcLB 97; EncEnl; EuAu; EuWr 4; EvEuW; LinLib L, S; LuthC 75; McGEWB; McGEWD 72, 84; NewC; NewCBEL; NewGrDM 80; NinCLC 11; OxCEng 67, 85, 95; OxCGer 76; PenC EUR; PseudN 82; RComWL; REn; RfGWoL 95; WhDW*

Klose, Margarete
German. Opera Singer
Berlin State Opera contralto, 1930s-50s; noted for Wagner, Verdi roles.
b. Aug 6, 1905 in Berlin, Germany
d. Dec 14, 1968 in Berlin, Germany (West)
Source: *Baker 84; BioIn 8; NewEOp 71*

Kluckhorn, Clyde Kay Maben
American. Anthropologist
Navajo Indian authority; wrote *Mirror for Man,* 1949.
b. Jan 11, 1905 in Le Mars, Iowa
d. Jul 29, 1960 in Santa Fe, New Mexico
Source: *AmAu&B; CurBio 51, 60; DcSoc; McGEWB; REnAL; REnWD; WhAm 4*

Klug, Aaron, Sir
British. Educator
Won Nobel Prize in chemistry, 1982, for work with microscopic techniques.
b. Aug 11, 1926 in Durban, South Africa
Source: *AmMWSc 89, 92, 95; BioIn 13, 15, 19, 20; IntWW 89, 91, 93; LarDcSc; NewYTBS 82; NobelP; NotTwCS; Who 74, 82, 83, 85, 88, 90, 92, 94; WhoAm 88, 90, 92, 94; WhoNob, 90, 95; WhoScEn 94, 96; WhoWor 84, 87, 89, 91, 93, 95, 96, 97; WorAlBi*

Kluge, John Werner
American. Broadcasting Executive
Built broadcasting and advertising empire, Metromedia; sold it for $2 billion in 1985; one of the wealthiest Americans, estimated wealth $5.6 billion in 1990.
b. Sep 21, 1914 in Chemnitz, Germany
Source: *BioIn 13, 14, 15, 16; ConAmBL; CurBio 93; Dun&B 90; IntWW 91, 93; NatCAB 63N; St&PR 75, 84, 87, 91; WhoAm 74, 76, 78, 80, 82, 84, 86, 88, 90, 92, 94, 95, 96, 97; WhoE 77, 79, 81, 83; WhoWor 91*

Klugh, Earl
American. Musician
Jazz guitarist recording since 1977; albums include *Two of a Kind,* 1982.
b. Sep 16, 1954 in Detroit, Michigan
Source: *AllMusG; BioIn 12, 13, 15; HarEnR 86; IlEncBM 82; InB&W 80, 85; NewGrDJ 88, 94; PenEncP; WhoEnt 92*

Klugman, Jack
American. Actor
Played Oscar Madison on TV comedy "The Odd Couple," 1970-75, title role in TV drama "Quincy, M.E." 1976-83; won three Emmys.
b. Apr 27, 1922 in Philadelphia, Pennsylvania
Source: *BiE&WWA; BioIn 9, 11, 12, 13, 15; BkPepl; ConTFT 1, 3; CurBio 93; EncAFC; FilmEn; FilmgC; ForYSC; HalFC 80, 84, 88; IntMPA 84, 86, 88, 92, 94, 96; ItaFilm; LegTOT; MovMk; NotNAT; VarWW 85; WhoAm 78, 80, 82, 84, 86, 88, 90, 92, 94, 95, 96, 97; WhoCom; WhoEnt 92; WhoHol 92, A; WhoTelC; WhoThe 72, 77, 81; WorAl; WorAlBi*

Kluszewski, Ted
[Theodore Bernard Kluszewski]
"Klu"
American. Baseball Player
First baseman, 1947-61; led NL in home runs, RBIs, 1954; had career .298 batting average.
b. Sep 10, 1924 in Argo, Illinois
d. Mar 29, 1988 in Cincinnati, Ohio
Source: *Ballpl 90; BiDAmSp BB; BioIn 2, 3, 4, 5, 11, 15, 16; LegTOT; NewYTBS 88; WhAm 10; WhoAm 74, 76, 78, 80, 82, 84; WhoProB 73*

Klutznick, Philip M
American. Government Official
Secretary of commerce under Carter, 1980-81.
b. Jul 9, 1907 in Kansas City, Missouri
Source: *BiDrUSE 89; BioIn 15; WhoAm 86, 90; WhoFI 75, 92; WhoMW 84; WhoWor 84, 91; WhoWorJ 72*

Knack, The
[Berton Averre; Doug Fieger; Bruce Gary; Prescott Niles]
American. Music Group
Rock band whose albums include *Get the Knack,* 1979.
Source: *EncRkSt; PenEncP; RkOn 85; RolSEnR 83; WhoRocM 82; WhsNW 85*

Knappertsbusch, Hans
German. Conductor
Prominent Wagner interpreter; led Vienna Opera, 1936-45.
b. Mar 12, 1888 in Elberfeld, Germany
d. Oct 25, 1965 in Munich, Germany (West)
Source: *Baker 78, 84, 92; BioIn 4, 7, 11; CmOp; IntDcOp; MetOEnc; MusSN; NewAmDM; NewEOp 71; NewGrDM 80; NewGrDO; ObitT 1961; OxDcOp; PenDiMP; WhAm 4*

Knaths, Karl
[Otto Karl Knaths]
American. Artist
Abstractionist with unique cubist style; known for still-lifes, Cape Cod landscapes.
b. Oct 21, 1891 in Eau Claire, Wisconsin
d. Mar 9, 1971 in Hyannis, Massachusetts
Source: *BioIn 1, 3, 4, 5, 6, 9, 16; BriEAA; CurBio 53, 71, 71N; DcAmArt; DcCAA 71, 77, 88, 94; IlBEAAW; McGDA; NewYTBE 71; OxCTwCA; PhDcTCA 77; WhAm 5; WhAmArt 85; WhoAmA 78, 78N, 80N, 82N, 84N, 86N, 89N, 91N; WorArt 1950*

Knauer, Virginia Harrington Wright
American. Government Official
Consumer affairs adviser to presidents Nixon, Reagan.
b. Mar 28, 1915 in Philadelphia, Pennsylvania
Source: *AmWomM; BioIn 8, 9, 10, 13, 14; BioNews 74; CurBio 70; InWom SUP; WhoAm 74, 76, 78, 80, 82, 84, 86, 88, 90; WhoAmP 85, 91; WhoAmW 66, 68, 70, 72, 74, 75, 77, 83, 85, 87, 89; WhoE 91; WhoGov 77*

Knebel, Fletcher
American. Author, Journalist
Washington correspondent, 1937-50; wrote *Crossing in Berlin,* 1981.
b. Oct 1, 1911 in Dayton, Ohio
d. Feb 26, 1993 in Honolulu, Hawaii
Source: *AmAu&B; AnObit 1993; Au&Wr 71; AuNews 1; BiDAmNC; BioIn 7, 10, 12, 14, 15, 18, 19; BioNews 75; ConAu 1NR, 1R, 3AS, 36NR, 140; ConLC 14, 81; ConNov 72, 76, 82, 86, 91; DcLEL 1940; DrAPF 80, 91; EncSF, 93; IntAu&W 76, 77, 82, 86, 91, 93; LegTOT; ScF&FL 1, 2; SmATA 36, 75; TwCSFW 81; WhAm 11; WhoAm 74, 76, 78, 80, 82, 84, 86, 88, 90, 92; WhoE 74; WhoWest 94; WhoWor 74; WorAu 1975; WrDr 76, 80, 82, 84, 86, 88, 90, 92, 94N*

Kneip, Richard F
American. Diplomat, Politician
Dem. governor of SD, 1971-78; US ambassador to Singapore, 1978-80.
b. Jan 7, 1933
d. Mar 9, 1987 in Sioux Falls, South Dakota
Source: *AlmAP 78; AmCath 80; BioIn 10; IntWW 74, 75, 76, 77, 78, 79, 80, 81, 82, 83*

Kneller, Godfrey, Sir
[Gottfried Kniller]
British. Artist
Became leading portraitist in England, after 1675; founded first English academy of painting, 1711; painted 10 reigning monarchs.
b. Aug 8, 1646 in Lubeck, Germany
d. Nov 7, 1723 in London, England
Source: *AtlBL; Benet 87; BioIn 1, 2, 4, 10, 15, 19; ClaDrA; DcArts; DcBrECP; DcNaB; IntDcAA 90; McGDA; OxCArt; OxCEng 67, 85, 95; OxCPMus; OxDcArt; REn*

Knerr, H(arold) H
American. Cartoonist
Drew syndicated comic strip, "Katzenjammer Kids," 1914-49.
b. Sep 4, 1882 in Bryn Mawr, Pennsylvania
d. Jul 8, 1949 in New York, New York
Source: *NatCAB 30, 47; WorECom*

Knievel, Evel
[Robert Craig Knievel]
American. Stunt Performer
Known for outrageous motorcycle stunts involving jumping over trucks, people, canyons.
b. Oct 17, 1938 in Butte, Montana
Source: *BioIn 8, 9, 10, 11, 13, 14, 16; BioNews 74; BkPepl; CelR; CurBio 72; LegTOT; NewYTBS 74; PseudN 82; VarWW 85; WhoAm 76, 78, 80, 82; WorAl*

Knievel, Robbie
American. Stunt Performer
Motorcycle stunt rider famous for jumping over cars and trucks, like his father, Evel.
b. 1963 in Butte, Missouri
Source: *BioIn 13, 16; News 90-1*

Knight, Arthur
[Arthur Rosenheimer]
American. Critic
Wrote film column for *Saturday Review* mag., 1949-73; book *The Liveliest Art,* 1957, history of cinema.
b. Sep 3, 1916 in Philadelphia, Pennsylvania
d. Jul 25, 1991 in Sydney, Australia
Source: *BioIn 9; ConAu 41R, 135; ConTFT 11; IntAu&W 89; IntMPA 75, 76, 77, 78, 79, 80, 81, 82, 84, 86, 88; OxCFilm; PseudN 82; Who 92; WhoAm 82, 88, 90*

Knight, Bobby
[Robert Montgomery Knight]
American. Basketball Coach
Coach, U.S. Military Acad., 1965-71; U.S. Olympic Gold Medal Team, 1984; Indiana U, 1971—; known for temperamental outbursts; won NCAA tournament three times with IU.
b. Oct 25, 1940 in Massillon, Ohio
Source: *BasBi; BioIn 9, 10, 11, 12, 13, 14, 15, 16; CelR 90; ConNews 85-3; CurBio 87; LegTOT; NewYTBE 71; NewYTBS 75, 84; WhoAm 82, 84, 86, 88, 90, 92, 94; WhoMW 82, 84, 86, 88, 90, 92, 93; WhoSpor*

Knight, Charles
English. Publisher, Author
Produced *Penny Magazine,* 1832-45; *Pictorial History of England,* 1837-44, inexpensive series designed to popularize learning.
b. 1791 in Windsor, England
d. Mar 9, 1873 in Addlestone, England
Source: *Alli, SUP; BbD; BiD&SB; BioIn 15, 17; BritAu 19; CasWL; Chambr 3; ChhPo; DcBiPP; DcEnA; DcEnL; DcLB 106; DcLEL; DcNaB; EvLB; LinLib L, S; NewC; NewCBEL; OxCEng 67, 85, 95*

Knight, Etheridge
American. Poet, Writer
Published *Poems from Prison,* 1968.
b. Apr 19, 1931 in Corinth, Mississippi
d. Mar 10, 1991 in Indianapolis, Indiana
Source: *Benet 96; BlkAWP; BlkLC; BlkWr 1; ConAu 21R, 23NR, 133; ConLC 40, 70; ConPo 75, 80, 85, 91; DcLB 41; DcTwCCu 5; InB&W 80; IntAu&W 91, 93; LivgBAA; OxCTwCP; PoeCrit 14; SchCGBL; SelBAAf; SelBAAu; WhoAm 76, 78, 80; WhoBlA 90, 92N; WrDr 76, 80, 82, 84, 86, 88, 90*

Knight, Frank Hyneman
American. Economist
Founded the "Chicago school" of economics; wrote *Risk, Uncertainty and Profit,* 1921.
b. Nov 7, 1885 in White Oak Township, Illinois
d. Apr 15, 1972 in Chicago, Illinois
Source: *BioIn 2, 9, 10, 11, 14, 15; DcAmB S9; GrEconS; McGEWB; RAdv 14, 13-3; ThTwC 87; WhAm 5; WhoEc 81, 86*

Knight, George Wilson
English. Author
Writings include *The Wheel of Fire,* 1930; *This Sceptered Isle,* 1940.
b. Sep 19, 1897 in Sutton, England
d. Mar 20, 1985
Source: *Au&Wr 71; BioIn 4, 14; ChhPo S1; ConAu 13R; DcLEL; IntWW 74; NewC; NewCBEL; PenC ENG; REn; REnAL; TwCA, SUP; WhE&EA; Who 74; WhoWor 74; WrDr 76*

Knight, Gladys Maria
[Gladys Knight and the Pips]
American. Singer
Lead vocalist with the Pips; member of group since 1953; won 2 Grammys, 1973, for "Midnight Train to Georgia."
b. May 28, 1944 in Atlanta, Georgia
Source: *Baker 84; BioIn 13, 15, 16; BkPepl; ConMus 1; CurBio 87; DrBlPA 90; EncPR&S 89; EncRk 88; IlEncBM 82; InB&W 80, 85; InWom SUP; NegAl 89; NewGrDA 86; OxCPMus; PenEncP; VarWW 85; WhoAfA 96; WhoAm 86, 90, 92, 94, 95, 96, 97; WhoAmW 75, 77, 85, 91, 93; WhoBlA 80, 85, 88, 90, 92, 94; WhoEnt 92; WhoRocM 82; WorAl*

Knight, Hilary
American. Illustrator, Children's Author
Illustrated *Eloise* and *Mrs. Piggle-Wiggle* books.
b. Nov 1, 1926 in Hempstead, New York
Source: *AuBYP 2, 3; BioIn 6, 8, 12, 16; ChhPo, S1, S2; ConAu 73; FourBJA; IlsCB 1957; MajAI; SmATA 15, 69; WhoAmA 84; YABC 1*

Knight, J. Z
American. Psychic
New Age channeler for 35,000 yr. old warrior, Ramtha.
b. Mar 16, 1946 in Dexter, New Mexico
Source: *BioIn 15, 16; EncO&P 3; EncPaPR 91; NewAgE 90; RelLAm 91*

Knight, James L
American. Newspaper Publisher
Co-founder, Knight-Ridder newspaper empire; chm., Knight Foundation.
d. Feb 5, 1991 in Santa Monica, California
Source: *Dun&B 86; NewYTBS 91; WhoAm 84*

Knight, John Shively, III
American. Author, Newspaper Editor
Part of Knight Newspaper family; died before becoming firmly established in newspaper operations.
b. Apr 3, 1945 in Columbus, Georgia
d. Dec 7, 1975 in Philadelphia, Pennsylvania
Source: *AuNews 2; BioIn 10, 11; ObitOF 79*

Knight, John Shivley
American. Newspaper Publisher
Founder, longtime editor, Knight-Ridder newspaper empire; won Pulitzer for column "Editor's Notebook," 1968.
b. Oct 26, 1894 in Bluefield, West Virginia
d. Jun 16, 1981 in Akron, Ohio
Source: *AuNews 2; ConAu 93, 103; CurBio 45, 81; IntWW 78; NewYTBS 81; WhAm 8; WhoAm 78; WhoSSW 78*

Knight, Philip H.
American. Business Executive
Co-founder, Nike, Inc. (originally Blue Ribbon Sports), 1967; became CEO and chairman, 1983.
b. Feb 24, 1938 in Portland, Oregon
Source: *BioIn 15, 16; ConAmBL; ConNews 85-1; Dun&B 86, 88, 90; St&PR 87, 91, 93, 96, 97; WhoAm 84, 86, 88, 90; WhoFI 83, 87, 89, 92; WhoWest 84, 87, 89, 92*

Knight, Ray
[Charles Ray Knight]
American. Baseball Player
Infielder, 1974-88; MVP, 1986 World Series with NY Mets; husband of Nancy Lopez.
b. Dec 28, 1952 in Albany, Georgia
Source: *Ballpl 90; BaseEn 88; BaseReg 87, 88; BioIn 12, 13, 14, 15; NewYTBS 85*

Knight, Shirley
American. Actor
Oscar nominee for *The Dark at the Top of the Stairs,* 1959; *Sweet Bird of Youth,* 1962; won Tony for *Kennedy's Children,* 1975.
b. Jul 5, 1937 in Goessel, Kansas
Source: *BiDFilm, 81*

Knight, Stan
[Black Oak Arkansas]
"Goober"
American. Musician
Guitarist with heavy-metal, Dixie boogie group.
b. Feb 12, 1949 in Little Rock, Arkansas
Source: *WhoRocM 82*

Knight, Suge
[Marion Knight, Jr.]
American. Record Company Executive
Cofounder and CEO, Death Row Records, 1991—.
b. Apr 19, 1966 in Los Angeles, California
Source: *ConBlB 11; ConMus 15*

Knight, Ted
[Tadeus Wladyslaw Konopka]
American. Actor
Starred in TV series "The Mary Tyler Moore Show," 1970-77; "Too Close for Comfort," 1980-86; won three Emmys.
b. Dec 7, 1923 in Terryville, Connecticut
d. Aug 26, 1986 in Pacific Palisades, California
Source: *AnObit 1986; BioIn 12, 13; BkPepl; ConNews 86-4; ConTFT 1; IntMPA 82, 84, 86; LegTOT; VarWW 85; WhAm 9; WhoAm 78, 80, 82, 84, 86; WhoCom; WhoHol A; WhoTelC; WorAl; WorAlBi*

Knight, Wayne
American. Actor
Plays Newman on "Seinfeld," 1992—; appeared in films *Jurassic Park; Space Jam.*
b. 1955?
Source: *LegTOT; News 97-1*

Knoblauch, Chuck
American. Baseball Player
Second baseman, Minnesota Twins, 1989—; Al Rookie of the Year, 1991.

Knopf, Alfred Abraham
American. Publisher
With wife Blanche founded Alfred A Knopf, Inc., 1915.
b. Sep 12, 1892 in New York, New York
d. Aug 11, 1984 in Purchase, New York
Source: *AmAu&B; ConAu 106; IntWW 74; NewYTBS 82; REnAL; St&PR 75; WebAB 74, 79; Who 83; WhoAm 84; WhoWor 82; WhoWorJ 72*

Knopfler, Mark
[Dire Straits]
Scottish. Musician, Composer
Formed rock group, 1977; hits include Grammy winner "Money for Nothing," 1986.
b. Aug 12, 1949 in Glasgow, Scotland
Source: *BioIn 11, 12, 13, 14, 15, 21; ConMus 3; ConNews 86-2; ConTFT 8; CurBio 95; LegTOT; OnThGG; WhoEnt 92*

Knorr, Nathan Homer
American. Religious Leader
Pres., Jehovah's Witnesses, 1942-77, representing over one million members.
b. Apr 23, 1905 in Bethlehem, Pennsylvania
d. Jun 15, 1977 in Wallkill, New York
Source: *BioIn 4, 5, 11; CurBio 57, 77; ObitOF 79; WhAm 7; WhoAm 74, 76; WhoRel 75, 77; WhoWor 74, 76*

Knote, Heinrich
German. Opera Singer
Famed, handsome Heldentenor; compared to Enrico Caruso; with NY Met., 1904-08.
b. Nov 26, 1870 in Munich, Germany
d. Jan 15, 1953, Germany (West)
Source: *Baker 78, 84, 92; BioIn 3; CmOp; MetOEnc; NewEOp 71; NewGrDM 80; NewGrDO; OxDcOp*

Knott, Walter
American. Businessman
Founded Knott's Berry Farm amusement park, CA, 1940; coined term "boysenberry."
b. Dec 11, 1889 in San Bernardino, California
d. Dec 3, 1981 in Buena Park, California
Source: *AnObit 1981; BioIn 4, 6, 7, 9, 10; NewYTBS 81*

Knotts, Don
American. Comedian, Actor
Won five Emmys for role of Barney Fife on TV comedy "The Andy Griffith Show," 1960-68.
b. Jul 21, 1924 in Morgantown, West Virginia
Source: *ConTFT 3; EncAFC; FilmEn; FilmgC; ForYSC; HalFC 80, 84, 88; IntMPA 82, 84, 86, 88, 92, 94, 96; JoeFr; LegTOT; MotPP; MovMk; QDrFCA 92; VarWW 85; WhoAm 74, 76, 78, 80, 82, 84, 86, 88, 90, 92, 94, 95, 96, 97; WhoCom; WhoEnt 92; WhoHol 92, A; WhoHrs 80; WhoTelC; WorAl; WorAlBi*

Knowland, William Fife
American. Politician, Newspaper Publisher
Rep. senator from CA, 1945-58; published *Oakland Tribune.*
b. Jun 26, 1908 in Alameda, California
d. Feb 23, 1974 in Oakland, California
Source: *BiDrAC; BiDrUSC 89; BioIn 1, 2, 3, 4, 5, 7, 10, 11; ConAu 89; CurBio 47, 74; DcAmB S9; LinLib L, S; NewYTBS 74; WhAm 6; Who 74; WhoAmP 73; WhoWest 74; WhoWor 74; WorAl*

Knowles, James Sheridan
English. Author
Plays include tragedy, *William Tell,* 1825; comedy, *The Hunchback,* 1832.
b. May 12, 1784 in Cork, Ireland
d. Nov 30, 1862 in Torquay, England
Source: *Alli; BbD; BiD&SB; BiDIrW; BioIn 12, 14; BritAu 19; CamGEL; CamGLE; CamGWoT; CasWL; CelCen; Chambr 3; ChhPo; CrtSuDr; DcBiPP; DcEnA; DcEnL; DcIrB 78, 88; DcIrL 96; DcIrW 1; DcLEL; DcNaB; EvLB; GrWrEL DR; LinLib L, S; McGEWD 72, 84; MouLC 3; NewC; NewCBEL; NotNAT B; OxCEng 67, 85, 95;*

OxCMed 86; OxCThe 67, 83; PoIre; REn; RfGEnL 91

Knowles, John
American. Author
Wrote *A Separate Peace,* 1960.
b. Sep 16, 1926 in Fairmont, West Virginia
Source: *AmAu&B; Au&Arts 10; Au&Wr 71; Benet 87; BenetAL 91; BioIn 7, 10, 11, 17; BlueB 76; BroV; CasWL; ConAu 17R, 40NR; ConLC 1, 4, 10, 26; ConNov 72, 76, 82, 86, 91, 96; CyWA 89; DcLB 6; DcLEL 1940; DrAF 76; DrAPF 80, 91; IntAu&W 76, 77, 82; LegTOT; LinLib L; MagSAmL; MajTwCW; Novels; OxCAmL 83, 95; RAdv 1; RfGAmL 94; RGTwCWr; SmATA 8, 89; TwCYAW; WhoAm 74, 76, 78, 80, 82, 84, 92, 94, 95, 96, 97; WhoUSWr 88; WhoWor 74; WhoWrEP 89, 92, 95; WorAl; WorAlBi; WorAu 1950; WrDr 76, 80, 82, 84, 86, 88, 90, 92, 94, 96*

Knowles, Patric
[Reginald Lawrence Knowles]
English. Actor
Films include *Adventures of Robin Hood,* 1938; *How Green Was My Valley,* 1941.
b. Nov 11, 1911 in Horsforth, England
d. Dec 23, 1995 in Woodland Hills, California
Source: *BioIn 21; EncAFC; FilmEn; FilmgC; ForYSC; GangFlm; HalFC 80, 84, 88; IntMPA 75, 76, 77, 78, 79, 80, 81, 82, 84, 86, 88, 92, 94, 96; MovMk; NewYTBS 95; VarWW 85; WhoHol 92, A; WhoHrs 80; WhoWor 74*

Knowles, Warren Perley
American. Business Executive, Politician
Rep. governor of WI, 1965-71; best-known for calling out the Nat. Guard to subdue U of WI campus protests.
b. Aug 19, 1908 in River Falls, Wisconsin
d. May 1, 1993 in Black River Falls, Wisconsin
Source: *BiDrGov 1789; Dun&B 86; IntWW 74; St&PR 84, 91; WhAm 11; WhoAm 74, 76, 78, 80, 82, 84, 92, 94; WhoAmP 85, 91; WhoFI 85; WhoWor 74*

Knox, Alexander
Canadian. Actor
Oscar nominee for *Wilson,* 1944; other films include *Gorky Park,* 1983.
b. Jan 16, 1907 in Strathroy, Ontario, Canada
d. Apr 26, 1995 in Berwick-upon-Tweed, England
Source: *BiE&WWA; BioIn 1, 2, 4, 20, 21; CanNov; ConAu 81, 148; CurBio 81; FilmEn; FilmgC; ForYSC; HalFC 80, 84, 88; IlWWBF; IntMPA 75, 76, 77, 78, 79, 80, 81, 82, 84, 86, 88, 92, 94; ItaFilm; MotPP; MovMk; NotNAT; VarWW 85; WhoAm 74; WhoHol 92, A; WhoThe 72, 77, 81*

Knox, Chuck
[Charles Robert Knox]
American. Football Coach
Head coach, LA Rams, 1973-77, Buffalo, 1978-82, Seattle, 1983-91, LA Rams, 1992-94; three-time NFL coach of year.
b. Apr 27, 1932 in Sewickley, Pennsylvania
Source: *BiDAmSp FB; BioIn 12, 16; FootReg 87; WhoAm 78, 80, 82, 84, 86, 88, 90, 94, 95; WhoE 81, 83; WhoFtbl 74; WhoSpor; WhoWest 84, 87, 89, 92, 94*

Knox, E(dmund) G(eorge) V(alpy)
English. Humorist
Editor of *Punch* mag., 1932-71.
b. May 10, 1881 in Oxford, England
d. Jan 2, 1971 in London, England
Source: *Au&Wr 71; BioIn 4, 9, 11; ChhPo, S1, S2; ConAu 29R, 112; DcLEL; DcNaB 1971; EvLB; LngCTC; NewC; NewCBEL; OxCEng 85, 95; PseudN 82; TwCA, SUP*

Knox, Frank
American. Government Official
Secretary of navy under FDR, 1940-41; Rep. nominee for VP with Landon, 1936.
b. Jan 1, 1874 in Boston, Massachusetts
d. Apr 28, 1944 in Washington, District of Columbia
Source: *CurBio 40, 44; DcAmB S3; DcLB 29; DcPol; EncAJ; JrnUS; NatCAB 37; PresAR*

Knox, Henry
American. Military Leader, Patriot, Government Official
Succeeded Washington as commander of Continental Army, 1783; US secretary of War, 1785-94.
b. Jul 25, 1750 in Boston, Massachusetts
d. Oct 25, 1806 in Thomaston, Maine
Source: *AmBi; AmPolLe; AmRev; ApCAB; BiAUS; BiDrUSE 71, 89; BioIn 1, 3, 4, 5, 6, 7, 8, 9, 10, 12, 18; BlkwEAR; CmdGen 1991; DcAmB; DcAmMiB; Drake; EncAR; EncCRAm; GenMudB; HarEnMi; HarEnUS; LinLib S; McGEWB; NatCAB 1; OxCAmH; TwCBDA; WebAB 74, 79; WebAMB; WhAm HS; WhAmRev; WhNaAH*

Knox, John
"The Apostle of Presbytery"; "The Apostle of the Scottish Reformers"; "The Reformer of a Kingdom"
Scottish. Religious Leader, Social Reformer
Chief leader of the Protestant Reformation in Scotland.
b. 1505 in Haddington, Scotland
d. Nov 24, 1572 in Edinburgh, Scotland
Source: *Alli; BbD; Benet 87, 96; BiD&SB; BioIn 1, 2, 3, 4, 5, 6, 7, 8, 9, 10, 11, 12, 13, 14, 15, 18, 20; BlmGEL; BritAu; CamGEL; CasWL; CyEd; DcBiPP; DcEnA; DcEnL; DcNaB, C; EvLB; LinLib S; LuthC 75; McGEWB; NewC; NewCBEL; OxCEng 67; OxCMus; PenC ENG; PseudN 82; RAdv 14; RComWL; REn; WebBD 83; WhDW*

Knox, Ronald Arbuthnott
"Hard Knox"
English. Author, Religious Leader
Catholic chaplain, Oxford U, 1926-39; published translation of Bible based on Vulgate text.
b. Feb 17, 1888 in Kibworth, England
d. Aug 24, 1957 in London, England
Source: *BioIn 1, 2, 4, 5, 6, 7, 11, 14; BkC 6; CathA 1930; ChhPo S2; CurBio 50, 57; DcCathB; DcLB 77; DcLEL; DcNaB 1951; EncMys; EncSF; EvLB; GrBr; LngCTC; NewC; NewCBEL; OxCEng 67, 85, 95; PseudN 82; ScFEYrs; TwCA, SUP; TwCWr; WebAB 79; WhE&EA; WhLit*

Knox, Rose Markward
American. Business Executive
Founded Knox Gelatin Co., 1890; wrote *Dainty Desserts,* 1896.
b. Nov 18, 1857
d. Sep 27, 1950
Source: *AmWomM; BiDAmBL 83; DcAmB S4; InWom, SUP; LibW; NotAW; WomFir*

Knudsen, Semon Emil
"Bunkie"
American. Auto Executive
With GM, 1939-68; chm., CEO, White Motor Corp., 1971-80.
b. Oct 2, 1912 in Buffalo, New York
Source: *BioIn 5, 7, 8, 10, 11; BusPN; CurBio 74; EncABHB 5; IntWW 74, 75, 76, 77, 78, 79, 80, 81, 82, 83, 89, 91, 93; NewYTBS 74; PseudN 82; St&PR 84, 91; Ward 77A; Who 74, 82, 83, 85, 88, 90, 92, 94; WhoAm 74, 76, 78, 80, 82, 84, 86, 88, 90, 92, 94, 95, 96, 97; WhoFI 74, 75, 77, 79, 81; WhoMW 80, 82; WhoTech 89*

Knudsen, William Signius
[Signius Wilhelm Paul Knudsen]
American. Industrialist
Helped both Ford, GM become multinational corps.
b. Mar 25, 1879 in Copenhagen, Denmark
d. Apr 27, 1948 in Detroit, Michigan
Source: *AmPolLe; BiDWWGF; BioIn 1, 5, 10; CurBio 40, 48; DcAmB S4; EncAB-H 1974; EncABHB 5; LinLib S; PseudN 82; WhAm 2*

Knudson, Tom
American. Journalist
Won Pulitzer Prize in Public Service for reporting on environmental damage to the Sierras, 1992.
b. Jul 6, 1953 in Manning, Iowa

Knussen, Oliver
[Stuart Oliver Knussen]
Scottish. Composer
Wrote fantasy opera *Where the Wild Things Are,* 1980.

b. Jun 12, 1952 in Glasgow, Scotland
Source: *Baker 78, 84; BioIn 8, 15, 17, 19, 20; ConCom 92; CurBio 94; IntDcOp; IntWW 89, 91; IntWWM 77, 80, 90; MetOEnc; NewAmDM; NewGrDM 80; NewOxM; OxDcOp; Who 85, 88, 90, 92*

Knutson, Coya
American. Politician
US rep. from MN, 1955-59; introduced first legislative measures for federal student loans.
b. Aug 23, 1912
d. Oct 10, 1996 in Edina, Minnesota
Source: *AmPolW 80; BioIn 3, 4, 5, 10, 11, 12, 17; InWom, SUP*

Kobbe, Gustav
American. Author
Writings on music include *Complete Opera Book,* 1919, which was highly successful.
b. Mar 4, 1857 in New York, New York
d. Jul 27, 1918 in Babylon, New York
Source: *Alli SUP; AmAu&B; AmLY; Baker 78, 84, 92; BiDAmM; BiD&SB; BioIn 2; ChhPo; DcAmAu; DcAmB; DcNAA; LinLib L; NatCAB 10, 35; NewEOp 71; NewGrDA 86; NewGrDO; OxDcOp; WhAm 1*

Kober, Arthur
Writer
Highly versatile; credits include over 30 films, some plays; novels include *My Dear Bella,* 1941.
b. Aug 25, 1900 in Brody, Austria
d. Jun 12, 1975 in New York, New York
Source: *AmAu&B; Au&Wr 71; Benet 87; BenetAL 91; BiE&WWA; BioIn 2, 4, 5, 10; ConAu 57, P-1; DcLB 11; IntMPA 75, 76; ModWD; NewYTBS 75; NotNAT B; ObitOF 79; OxCAmL 65, 83, 95; REn; REnAL; TwCA, SUP; WhAm 6; WhE&EA; WhoAm 74; WhoWorJ 72*

Koch, Bill
[William I Koch]
American. Yachtsman
Won 1992 America's Cup as skipper of America 3.
b. 1940? in Wichita, Kansas
Source: *News 92, 92-3*

Koch, Ed(ward Irwin)
American. Politician
Flamboyant mayor of NYC, 1978-89.
b. Dec 12, 1924 in New York, New York
Source: *BiDrAC; BiDrUSC 89; BioIn 13, 14, 15, 16, 17, 18, 19; CelR 90; CngDr 74; ConAu 113; CurBio 78; EncWB; IntWW 91; LegTOT; NewYTBS 77, 84, 89; PolProf NF; Who 92; WhoAm 86, 90; WhoAmL 85, 87; WhoAmP 87, 91; WhoE 91; WhoGov 77; WorAl; WorAlBi; WrDr 92*

Koch, Ilse
"Red Witch"; "Witch of Buchenwald"
German. Government Official
Imprisoned for life for sadistic murders, atrocities at Nazi prison camp; had lampshades made from human skin.
b. Sep 22, 1906 in Dresden, Germany
d. Sep 1, 1967 in Aichach, Germany
Source: *BioIn 14, 16; EncTR, 91; NewYTBE 71*

Koch, John
American. Artist
Prize-winning, self-taught painter of elegant Manhattan interiors, celebrities.
b. Aug 16, 1909 in Toledo, Ohio
d. Apr 19, 1978 in New York, New York
Source: *BioIn 2, 3, 4, 7, 11, 12; ConArt 77, 83, 89; CurBio 65, 78, 78N; DcCAA 71, 77, 88, 94; NatCAB 60; NewYTBS 78; WhAm 7; WhAmArt 85; WhoAm 74, 76, 78; WhoAmA 73, 76, 78, 80N, 82N, 84N, 86N, 89N, 91N, 93N*

Koch, Kenneth Jay
American. Author, Educator
Poet; began teaching children to write poetry, 1968, described in *Wishes, Lies, and Dreams,* 1970.
b. Feb 27, 1925 in Cincinnati, Ohio
Source: *Benet 87; BenetAL 91; CamGLE; CamHAL; ConAu 1R, 6NR, 36NR; ConDr 82, 88; ConLC 5, 8, 44; ConPo 85, 91; CroCAP; CurBio 78; DrAP 75; DrAPF 91; IntAu&W 91; IntvTCA 2; NewYTBE 70; PenC AM; RAdv 1, 13-1; SmATA 65; WebE&AL; WhoAm 84, 90; WhoUSWr 88; WhoWrEP 89; WorAu 1950; WrDr 86, 92*

Koch, Robert
[Heinrich Hermann Robert Koch]
German. Engineer, Scientist
Isolated bacteria that caused tuberculosis, 1882; won the Nobel Prize for Physiology or Medicine, 1905.
b. Dec 11, 1843 in Hannover, Prussia
d. May 28, 1910 in Baden-Baden, Germany
Source: *AsBiEn; BiESc; BiHiMed; BioIn 1, 2, 3, 4, 5, 6, 7, 8, 9, 10, 12, 14, 15, 16, 18, 20; CamDcSc; CelCen; DcInv; DcScB; EncSoA; InSci; LinLib S; McGEWB; NobelP; NotTwCS; OxCMed 86; RAdv 14, 13-5; REn; WhDW; WhoNob, 90, 95; WorAl; WorAlBi; WorScD*

Kocher, Emil Theodor
Swiss. Physician, Scientist
Pioneered aseptic methods, surgeries; won 1909 Nobel Prize in medicine.
b. Aug 25, 1841 in Bern, Switzerland
d. Jul 27, 1917 in Bern, Switzerland
Source: *BiESc; LarDcSc; LinLib S; OxCMed 86; WhoNob, 90, 95; WorAl*

Kodaly, Zoltan
Hungarian. Composer
His contributions to Hungarian National Opera include *Hary Janos,* 1926.
b. Dec 16, 1882 in Kecskemet, Austria-Hungary
d. Mar 6, 1967 in Budapest, Hungary
Source: *Baker 78, 84, 92; BioIn 1, 2, 3, 4, 6, 7, 8, 9, 10, 11, 12, 13, 14, 20; BriBkM 80; CmOp; CnOxB; CompSN, SUP; ConAu 112; DcArts; DcCM; DcCom 77; DcCom&M 79; DcTwCC, A; FacFETw; IntDcOp; LegTOT; MakMC; McGEWB; MetOEnc; MusMk; NewAmDM; NewEOp 71; NewGrDM 80; NewGrDO; NewOxM; ObitT 1961; OxCMus; OxDcOp; PenDiMP A; WhAm 4; WhDW; WorAl; WorAlBi*

Koehler, Georges J. F
German. Scientist
Shared 1984 Nobel Prize in medicine for work in immunology; contributions have led to progress in AIDS research, cancer treatment.
b. Apr 17, 1946 in Munich, Germany
d. Mar 1, 1995 in Freiburg, Germany
Source: *NewYTBS 84; WhoNob, 90*

Koenig, Walter
American. Actor
Played Pavel Chekov in TV's "Star Trek," 1967-69; same role in film series, 1979-86.
b. Sep 14, 1936 in Chicago, Illinois
Source: *BioIn 15, 16; ConAu 104; ConTFT 5; IntMPA 86, 92, 94, 96; ScF&FL 92; WhoEnt 92*

Koestler, Arthur
Hungarian. Author
Most famous work: *Darkness at Noon,* 1940s anti-Stalinist novel.
b. Sep 5, 1905 in Budapest, Austria-Hungary
d. Mar 3, 1983 in London, England
Source: *AnObit 1983; Au&Wr 71; AuSpks; Benet 87, 96; BioIn 1, 2, 3, 4, 5, 6, 7, 8, 9, 10, 11, 12, 13, 14, 15, 16, 17, 18; BlmGEL; BlueB 76; BritWr S1; CamGEL; CamGLE; CasWL; CnDBLB 7; CnMWL; ConAu 1NR, 1R, 33NR, 109; ConLC 1, 3, 6, 8, 15, 33; ConNov 72, 76, 82; CurBio 43, 62, 83N; CyWA 58; DcArts; DcLB Y83N; DcNaB 1981; EncGRNM; EncMcCE; EncO&P 2, 2S1, 3; EncPaPR 91; EncSF, 93; EncWB; EncWL, 2, 3; FacFETw; GrWrEL N; IntAu&W 76, 77, 82; IntWW 74, 75, 76, 77, 78, 79, 80, 81, 82; LegTOT; LiExTwC; LinLib L, S; LngCTC; MajTwCW; MakMC; ModBrL, S2; NewC; NewCBEL; NewYTBE 71; NewYTBS 83; Novels; OxCEng 67, 85, 95; PenC ENG; RAdv 13-1; REn; RfGEnL 91; RGTwCWr; ScF&FL 1, 92; ScFSB; ThTwC 87; TwCA SUP; TwCRHW 90; TwCSFW 81; TwCWr; WebE&AL; WhAm 8; WhDW; WhE&EA; Who 74, 82, 83; WhoTwCL; WhoWor 74, 76, 78, 82; WhoWorJ 72, 78; WorAl; WorAlBi; WrDr 76, 80, 82, 84*

Koffka, Kurt
German. Psychologist
Chief spokesman of Gestalt psychology; wrote *Growth of the Mind,* 1924.

b. Mar 18, 1886 in Berlin, Germany
d. Nov 22, 1941 in Northampton, Massachusetts
Source: *BiDPsy; BioIn 14; CurBio 42; DcAmB S3; DcNAA; FacFETw; GuPsyc; InSci; LuthC 75; NamesHP; ThTwC 87; WhAm 1; WhDW*

Kogan, Leonid Borisovich
Russian. Musician
Violin virtuoso; played US tours on cultural exchange program; won Lenin Prize, 1965.
b. Oct 14, 1924 in Dnepropetrovsk, Union of Soviet Socialist Republics
d. Dec 17, 1982, Union of Soviet Socialist Republics
Source: *AnObit 1982; Baker 84; BiDSovU; BriBkM 80; IntWW 74, 75, 76, 77, 78, 79, 80, 81, 82, 83N; IntWWM 77; MusSN; NewGrDM 80; NewYTBS 82; WhoMus 72; WhoSocC 78; WhoWor 74*

Kogawa, Joy (Nozomi)
Canadian. Author, Poet
Published collection of poetry *The Splintered Moon,* 1974; novel *Itsuka,* 1992.
b. Jun 6, 1935 in Toronto, Ontario, Canada
Source: *AsAmAlm; Benet 96; BenetAL 91; BlmGWL; CamGLE; CanWW 31, 83, 89; ConAu 19NR, 101; ConCaAu 1; ConLC 78; ConNov 96; ConPo 70; FemiCLE; FemiWr; IntAu&W 86, 89, 91, 93; IntWWP 77, 82; ModWoWr; OxCCanL; WhoCanL 85, 87, 92; WrDr 76, 80, 82, 84, 88, 90, 92, 94, 96*

Kohan, Buz
[Alan W Kohan]
American. Writer, Producer
TV scriptwriter for "Perry Como Specials," 1963-67; "Carol Burnett Show," 1967-73; won seven Emmys.
b. Aug 9, 1933 in New York, New York

Kohl, Helmut (Michael)
German. Political Leader
Chancellor, West Germany, 1982-91, Germany, 1991—; became longest-serving Chancellor since Bismarck, 1996.
b. Apr 3, 1930 in Ludwigshafen am Rhein, Germany
Source: *BioIn 13, 14, 15, 16, 17, 18, 19, 20, 21; ColdWar 1, 2; CurBio 77; DcTwHis; EncCW; EncWB; FacFETw; IntWW 74, 75, 76, 77, 78, 79, 80, 81, 82, 83, 89, 91, 93; IntYB 78, 79, 80, 81, 82; LegTOT; News 94, 94-1; NewYTBS 82, 90, 94; PolLCWE; Who 82, 83, 85, 88, 90, 92, 94; WhoEIO 82; WhoWor 76, 78, 80, 82, 84, 87, 89, 91, 93, 95, 96, 97; WorAlBi*

Kohl, Herbert H.
American. Politician
Dem. senator, WI, 1989—.
b. Feb 7, 1935 in Milwaukee, Wisconsin
Source: *AlmAP 92; BioIn 11, 16; CngDr 89, 91; ConAu 14NR, 65; WhoAm 90; WhoAmP 91; WhoMW 92*

Kohl, Herbert R
American. Author, Educator
Books on education include *Open Classroom: A Practical Guide to a New Way of Teaching,* 1969.
b. Aug 22, 1937 in New York, New York
Source: *AmAu&B; BioIn 14, 16; ConAu 14NR, 65; SmATA 47; WhoAm 86*

Kohler, Fred, Sir
American. Actor
Played villain in films *The Iron Horse,* 1924; *The Plainsman,* 1937; *Way of All Flesh,* 1927.
b. Apr 20, 1889 in Kansas City, Missouri
d. Oct 28, 1938 in Los Angeles, California
Source: *Film 1, 2; FilmEn; ForYSC; GangFlm; HalFC 84, 88; TwYS; WhoHol B; WhScrn 74, 77, 83*

Kohler, Kaufmann
American. Theologian
NYC rabbi; pres., Hebrew Union College, 1903-21; led reformed Judaism in US.
b. May 10, 1843 in Fuerth, Germany
d. Jan 28, 1926 in New York, New York
Source: *AmAu&B; AmBi; BioIn 7, 16, 19; DcAmB; DcAmReB 1, 2; DcNAA; EncARH; NatCAB 13; OhA&B; PeoHis; RelLAm 91; WhAm 1; WorAl; WorAlBi*

Kohler, Wolfgang
German. Psychologist
Founded Gestalt school of psychology.
b. Jan 21, 1887 in Reval, Russia
d. Jun 11, 1967 in Enfield, New Hampshire
Source: *AmAu&B; AsBiEn; BiDPsy; BioIn 4, 7, 9, 10, 11, 14, 16; DcAmB S8; DcScB S2; FacFETw; GaEncPs; GuPsyc; InSci; LuthC 75; McGMS 80; NamesHP; NatCAB 55; ThTwC 87; TwCA SUP; WhAm 4, 5; WhDW*

Kohlmeier, Louis Martin, Jr.
American. Journalist
Won Pulitzer for Washington correspondence, 1964; nat. reporting, 1965.
b. Feb 17, 1926 in Saint Louis, Missouri
Source: *BiDAmNC; ConAu 49; EncTwCJ; WhoAm 74, 76, 78, 80, 82, 84, 86, 88, 90, 92, 94, 95, 96, 97; WhoE 95; WhoSSW 73, 75, 76*

Kohner, Susan
American. Actor
Oscar nominee for role of bi-racial Sarah Jane in *Imitation of Life,* 1959.
b. Nov 11, 1936 in Los Angeles, California
Source: *BiE&WWA; FilmEn; FilmgC; ForYSC; HalFC 80, 84, 88; IntMPA 75, 76, 77, 78, 79, 80, 81, 82, 84, 86, 88, 92, 94, 96; MotPP; NotNAT; VarWW 85; WhoHol 92, A*

Kohout, Pavel
Czech. Writer
Uses fantasy, satire to enhance his politically suggestive plays, novels, TV movies.
b. Jul 2, 1928 in Prague, Czechoslovakia
Source: *BioIn 9, 11, 12, 14, 15, 16; ConAu 3NR, 45; ConLC 13; CurBio 88; EncSF 93; EncWT; IntAu&W 82; LiExTwC; McGEWD 84; NewYTBS 79; RAdv 14, 13-2; ScF&FL 92; WhoSocC 78; WhoSoCE 89; WorAu 1975*

Kohoutek, Lubos
Czech. Astronomer
Discovered "Comet of the Century," Comet Kohoutek, 1973.
b. 1935 in Moravia, Czechoslovakia
Source: *BioIn 10; BioNews 74; CurBio 74; NewYTBS 74*

Kohut, Heinz
Austrian. Psychoanalyst
Advocate of "self psychology"; edited *Psychoanalysis and Literature,* 1964.
b. May 3, 1913 in Vienna, Austria
d. Oct 8, 1981 in Chicago, Illinois
Source: *AmDec 1970; AmMWSc 73P, 76P, 79; BiDrAPA 77; BioIn 10, 11, 12, 15, 16, 20; BlueB 76; ConAu 1NR, 45, 105; NewYTBS 81; RAdv 14; WhAm 8; WhoAm 74, 76, 78, 80, 82*

Koivisto, Mauno Henrik
"Manu"
Finnish. Political Leader
First socialist president; elected Jan 1982.
b. Nov 25, 1923 in Turku, Finland
Source: *BioIn 13, 16; CurBio 82; IntWW 74, 75, 76, 77, 78, 79, 80, 81, 82, 83, 89, 91, 93; IntYB 78, 79, 80, 81, 82, 82A; NewYTBS 82; WhoWor 74, 76, 78, 80, 82, 84, 87, 89, 91, 93, 95, 96, 97*

Kokoschka, Oskar
Austrian. Artist, Author
Expressionist painter; work typified by use of symbolism, distortion; helped found German expressionist drama through melodramatic plays.
b. Mar 1, 1886 in Pochlarn, Austria
d. Feb 22, 1980 in Montreux, Switzerland
Source: *AnObit 1980; Benet 87, 96; BioIn 1, 2, 3, 4, 5, 6, 7, 8, 9, 10, 11, 12, 13, 14, 15, 16, 17, 18, 19, 20; CamGWoT; ClaDrA; ClDMEL 80; CnMD; ConArt 77, 83, 89; ConAu 93, 109; CurBio 56, 80, 80N; DcArts; DcLB 124; DcNaB 1971; EncTR, 91; EncWL; EncWT; Ent; EvEuW; FacFETw; IntAu&W 76, 77; IntDcAA 90; IntDcT 2; IntWW 74, 75, 76, 77, 78, 79; LegTOT; LiExTwC; McGDA; McGEWB; McGEWD 72, 84; ModArCr 1; ModGL; ModWD; NewYTBS 80; OxCArt; OxCGer 76, 86; OxCTwCA; OxDcArt; PhDcTCA 77; REn; REnWD; TwCPaSc;*

WhAm 9; WhDW; Who 74; WhoGrA 62; WhoWor 74, 76, 78; WorArt 1950

Kolb, Barbara Anne
American. Composer
First US woman to win Prix de Rome, 1969; wrote *Soundings*.
b. Feb 10, 1939 in Hartford, Connecticut
Source: *Baker 84; BioIn 16; ConAmC 76; ConCom 92; DcCM; InWom SUP; NewAmDM; NewGrDA 86; WhoE 74, 75; WomCom*

Kolb, Claudia
American. Swimmer
Won two gold medals, 1968 Olympics.
b. Dec 19, 1949 in Hayward, California
Source: *BiDAmSp BK; BioIn 8*

Kolbe, Maximilian Maria, Saint
[Maksymilian Kolbe]
Polish. Religious Figure
Catholic priest who chose death in place of condemned prisoner; canonized, 1982.
b. Jan 8, 1894 in Zdunska Wola, Poland
d. Aug 14, 1941 in Auschwitz, Poland
Source: *BioIn 13; EncTR; HisEWW; NewYTBE 71; NewYTBS 82*

Kolchin, Ellis Robert
American. Mathematician, Educator
Long-time Columbia U professor; known for bringing differential algebra into the mainstream of mathematics.
b. Apr 18, 1916 in New York, New York
d. Oct 30, 1991 in New York, New York
Source: *AmMWSc 73P, 76P, 79, 82, 86, 89, 92; BioIn 17; NewYTBS 91*

Kolehmainen, Hannes
"Flying Finn"
Finnish. Track Athlete
Long-distance runner; won three gold medals, 1912 Olympics, one gold, 1920 Olympics.
b. Dec 9, 1889 in Kuopio, Finland
d. Jan 11, 1966 in Helsinki, Finland
Source: *BioIn 7; ObitOF 79; WhoTr&F 73*

Kolff, Willem Johan
American. Physician
Invented the kidney dialysis machine, 1943.
b. Feb 14, 1911 in Leiden, Netherlands
Source: *AmMWSc 73P, 76P, 79, 82, 86, 89, 92, 95; BiDrACP 79; BioIn 13, 15, 16; CurBio 83; IntWW 74, 75, 76, 77, 78, 79, 80, 81, 82, 83, 89, 91, 93; LarDcSc; NotTwCS; WhoAm 74, 76, 78, 80, 82, 84, 86, 88, 90, 96, 97; WhoFrS 84; WhoMedH; WhoWest 94, 96; WhoWor 74, 76, 78*

Kollek, Teddy
[Theodore Kollek]
Israeli. Politician, Author
Mayor of Jerusalem 1965-93; headed drive to create nat. museum.
b. May 27, 1911 in Vienna, Austria
Source: *BioIn 8, 10, 11, 12, 14, 16; ConAu P-2, X; CurBio 74, 93; FacFETw; HisEAAC; IntWW 74, 75, 76, 77, 78, 79, 80, 81, 82, 83, 89, 91, 93; MidE 78, 79, 80, 81, 82; NewYTBS 85; WhoWor 74, 76, 78, 82, 95; WhoWorJ 72, 78*

Kollmar, Richard
American. Producer, Actor
Played radio detective Boston Blackie; with wife, Dorothy Kilgallen, broadcast "Dick and Dorothy," 1954-63.
b. Dec 31, 1910 in Ridgewood, New Jersey
d. Jan 7, 1971 in New York, New York
Source: *BiE&WWA; ConAu 89; CurBio 71, 71N; NewYTBE 71; NotNAT B; OxCAmT 84; RadStar; SaTiSS; WhoHol B; WhoThe 77A; WhScrn 77, 83; WhThe*

Kollsman, Paul
American. Aeronautical Engineer
Invented altimeter, measures a plane's altitude while in flight.
b. Feb 22, 1900 in Freudenstadt, Germany
d. Sep 26, 1982 in Los Angeles, California
Source: *AnObit 1982; BioIn 13; FacFETw; NewYTBS 82*

Kollwitz, Kathe Schmidt
German. Artist
Prints conveyed social justice themes: *The Peasant War.*
b. Jul 8, 1867 in Konigsberg, Germany
d. Apr 22, 1945 in Dresden, Germany
Source: *AtlBL; BiDMoPL; HerW; InWom SUP; OxCGer 76; WhAm 4*

Kolmogorov, Andrey Nikolayevich
Russian. Mathematician
Founded modern probability theory; awarded Lenin Prize, 1965.
b. Apr 23, 1903 in Tambov, Russia
d. Oct 20, 1987 in Moscow, Union of Soviet Socialist Republics
Source: *IntWW 77, 78, 79, 80, 81, 82, 83; NotTwCS*

Kolodin, Irving
American. Critic
Influential music critic with *Saturday Review* mag., 1947-82; covering jazz, classical and opera; early compiler of record guides.
b. Feb 22, 1908 in New York, New York
d. Apr 29, 1988 in New York, New York
Source: *AmAu&B; Baker 78, 84, 92; BioIn 1, 9, 12, 15, 16; ConAu 93, 125; CurBio 47, 88, 88N; NewGrDA 86; NewYTBS 88; REnAL; WhAm 9; WhoAm 74, 76, 78, 80, 82, 84; WhoAmM 83; WhoMus 72; WhoWor 74*

Kolvenbach, Peter-Hans
"The Black Pope"
Dutch. Religious Leader
Catholic priest; head of Society of Jesus, the Jesuits, 1983—.
b. 1928 in Druten, Netherlands
Source: *BioIn 13, 14; CurBio 84; IntWW 89, 91, 93; WhoRel 92; WhoWor 84, 91*

Komarov, Vladimir Mikhaylovich
Russian. Cosmonaut
Member of first three-man orbital flight, 1964; first astronaut known to have died during a mission (his chute tangled).
b. Mar 16, 1927 in Moscow, Union of Soviet Socialist Republics
d. Apr 24, 1967 in Kazakh, Union of Soviet Socialist Republics
Source: *ObitOF 79; WhAm 4*

Komer, Robert William
American. Government Official
Instrumental in American pacification efforts; directed Civil Operations and Revolutionary Development Support (CORDS) program in Vietnam.
b. Feb 23, 1922 in Chicago, Illinois
Source: *BioIn 12; ColdWar 2; EncAI&E; IntWW 74, 75, 76, 78, 79, 80, 81, 82, 83, 91, 93; WhoAm 74, 76, 78, 80, 82, 84, 86, 88, 90, 92, 94, 95, 96, 97*

Komroff, Manuel
American. Author
Historical novels include *The Magic Bow*, 1940; *The Story of Jesus*, 1955.
b. Sep 7, 1890 in New York, New York
d. Dec 10, 1974 in Woodstock, New York
Source: *AmAu&B; AmNov; AuBYP 2, 3; BenetAL 91; BioIn 2, 3, 4, 7, 9, 10, 12; CnDAL; ConAu 1R, 4NR, 53; DcLB 4; OxCAmL 65, 83, 95; REnAL; ScF&FL 1, 2; SmATA 2, 20N; TwCA, SUP; WhAm 6; WhE&EA; WhoAm 74; WhoWor 74; WrDr 76*

Komunyakaa, Yusef
[James Willie Brown, Jr.]
American. Poet
Won 1994 Pulitzer Prize for poetry with *Neon Vernacular: New and Selected Poems*, 1993.
b. 1947 in Bogalusa, Louisiana
Source: *ConAu 147; ConLC 86, 94; ConPo 96; DcLB 120; OxCTwCP; WhoAfA 96*

Kondrashin, Kiril Petrovich
Russian. Conductor
Former leader of Moscow Philharmonic; defected to West, 1978.
b. Feb 21, 1914 in Moscow, Russia
d. Mar 7, 1981 in Amsterdam, Netherlands
Source: *BioIn 11; IntWW 77, 78, 79, 80, 81; WhoMus 72; WhoOp 76; WhoSocC 78; WhoWor 74*

Konetzni, Hilde
Austrian. Opera Singer
Wagnerian soprano with Vienna Opera from 1936.
b. Mar 21, 1905 in Vienna, Austria
d. Apr 20, 1980 in Vienna, Austria
Source: *Baker 84, 92; BioIn 11, 12, 14; CmOp; IntDcOp; NewEOp 71; NewGrDM 80; NewGrDO; OxDcOp; PenDiMP; WhoMus 72*

Konev, Ivan Stepanovich
Russian. Military Leader
Supreme commander of Soviet land forces, 1946-60; founded Warsaw Pact.
b. Dec 27, 1897 in Ladeino, Russia
d. May 21, 1973 in Moscow, Union of Soviet Socialist Republics
Source: *BiDSovU; BioIn 3, 4, 6, 9, 10, 11; CurBio 43, 56, 73; GenMudB; McGEWB; NewYTBE 73; SovUn; WhoMilH 76*

Konitz, Lee
American. Jazz Musician
Alto-saxist with Stan Kenton, others, 1950s.
b. 1927
Source: *AllMusG; Baker 84, 92; BiDAmM; BiDJaz; BioIn 8, 12, 13, 16; CmpEPM; EncJzS; IlEncJ; NewAmDM; NewGrDA 86; NewGrDJ 88, 94; NewGrDM 80; PenEncP; WhoAm 80, 82*

Konoye, Fumimaro, Prince
Japanese. Political Leader
Three-time premier of Japan, 1933-41.
b. Oct 12, 1891 in Tokyo, Japan
d. Dec 15, 1945 in Tokyo, Japan
Source: *BioIn 1; CurBio 40, 46; ObitOF 79; WhWW-II*

Konrad, Gyorgy
Hungarian. Author
Wrote novels *The Case Worker*, 1974; *A Feast in the Garden*, 1992.
b. Apr 2, 1933 in Debrecen, Hungary
Source: *Benet 96; ConLC 4, 10, 73; ConWorW 93; IntWW 91, 93; WhoSoCE 89; WorAu 1975*

Konwitschny, Franz
German. Conductor
Succeeded Kleiber as director of Berlin State Opera, 1955.
b. Aug 14, 1901 in Fulnek, Germany
d. Jul 27, 1962 in Belgrade, Yugoslavia
Source: *Baker 84, 92; BioIn 6; CmOp; NewEOp 71; NewGrDM 80; NewGrDO; OxDcOp; PenDiMP*

Koo, V(i) K(yuin) Wellington
[Ku Wei-Chun]
Chinese. Statesman
Foreign minister, prime minister, Republic of China, 1926-27; ambassador to US, 1946-56.
b. 1887 in Shanghai, China
d. Nov 14, 1985 in New York, New York
Source: *BioIn 1, 4, 10, 11; ConAu 81; CurBio 41, 86; FacFETw; PseudN 82; REn; WhAm 8; Who 74; WhoLA*

Koob, Kathryn L
[The Hostages]
American. Hostage
One of 52 held by terrorists, Nov 1979 - Jan 1981.
b. 1939?
Source: *BioIn 12; NewYTBS 81*

Kool and the Gang
[Cliff Adams; "Kool" Bell; Ronald Bell; George Brown; "Spike" Mickens; Michael Ray; Claydes Smith; J T Taylor; Dennis Thomas; Rickey West; Curtis Williams]
American. Music Group
Began, 1964, as jazz group; currently rhythm and blues-pop group; had platinum single "Celebration," 1980.
Source: *Alli, SUP; BiAUS; BiDAfM; BiDBrA; BioIn 4, 10, 16; ConAu 39NR, X; CurBio 63; DcBrECP; DcNaB; DcVicP 2; EncPR&S 89; EncRk 88; HarEnR 86; IlEncBM 82; InB&W 80, 85A; IntAu&W 76X, 77X; IntMPA 78, 79, 81, 82, 84, 86; ItaFilm; NegAl 76; NewGrDA 86; NewYHSD; NewYTBE 70; PenEncP; RkOn 78; RolSEnR 83; WhAmArt 85; WhoWor 78*

Kool Moe Dee
American. Rapper
Member of Treacherous Three, early 1980s; solo hits include platinum "How Ya Like Me Now?," 1987.
b. 1963 in New York, New York
Source: *ConMus 9*

Koon, Stacey C.
American. Police Officer
LAPD Sergeant acquitted of assault in the widely-publicized videotaped beating of Rodney King in 1991.
b. 1951?

Koons, Jeff
American. Artist
Noted for his sculptures of consumer products, such as vacuums and toasters, and kitschy art forms in the early 1980s; sculpted a larger-than-life Michael Jackson and Bubbles, 1988.
b. 1955 in York, Pennsylvania
Source: *BioIn 14, 15, 16, 17, 20; CurBio 90; News 91; WorArt 1980*

Koontz, Dean R(ay)
[David Axton; Brian Coffey; Deanna Dwyer; K.R. Dwyer; Leigh Nichols; Anthony North; Richard Paige; Owen West]
American. Author
Horror novels include *Watchers*, 1987; *Midnight*, 1989; and *Hideaway*, 1992.
b. Jul 9, 1945 in Everett, Pennsylvania
Source: *BioIn 14, 15, 17, 20; ConAu 19NR, 36NR, 52NR, 108; ConLC 78; ConPopW; DcLP 87A; EncSF 93; IntAu&W 91; PenEncH; ScFSB; TwCCr&M 91; TwCSFW 86; WhoAm 90, 92, 94, 95, 96, 97; WrDr 92, 94, 96*

Koontz, Elizabeth Duncan
[Annie Elizabeth Duncan Koontz; Mrs. Harry Lee Koontz]
"Libby"
American. Educator
First black woman to head NEA; named head of the Woman's Bureau, a branch of the Labor Dept., by President Nixon, 1969.
b. Jun 3, 1919 in Salisbury, North Carolina
d. Jan 6, 1989 in Salisbury, North Carolina
Source: *BioIn 13, 16, 18, 19, 20; BlkWAm; ConAu 69; CurBio 89N; Ebony 1; InB&W 80; InWom, SUP; LEduc 74; NegAl 76, 89; NewYTBS 89; NotBlAW 1; PseudN 82; WhAm 9; WhoAm 74; WhoAmP 73, 75, 77, 79, 81, 83, 85, 87, 89; WhoAmW 64, 66, 68, 70, 72, 74, 75, 77; WhoBlA 75, 77, 80, 85, 88, 90N; WhoGov 72, 75, 77; WhoSSW 73*

Koop, C(harles) Everett
American. Government Official
Surgeon-general of the US, 1982-89; leader of public education campaign to combat AIDS epidemic.
b. Oct 14, 1916 in New York, New York
Source: *AmDec 1980; AmMWSc 73P, 76P, 79, 82, 86, 89, 92, 95; AmSocL; BioIn 12, 13, 16; CelR 90; ConHero 1; CurBio 83; IntWW 83, 91; News 89-3; WhoAm 74, 76, 78, 80, 82, 84, 88, 90, 92, 94, 95, 96, 97; WhoE 83, 85, 86, 89, 91, 95; WhoMedH; WhoScEn 94, 96; WorAlBi*

Kooper, Al
[Blood, Sweat, and Tears]
American. Musician, Producer
Rock singer, organist, guitarist, 1960s; formed Blood, Sweat, and Tears, 1968.
b. Feb 5, 1944 in New York, New York
Source: *Baker 84, 92; EncPR&S 89; EncRk 88; HarEnR 86; IlEncRk; LegTOT; OnThGG; PenEncP; RolSEnR 83; WhoAm 78, 80; WhoRock 81; WhoRocM 82; WorAl; WorAlBi*

Koopmans, Tjalling (Charles)
American. Economist
Co-winner of 1975 Nobel Prize in economics.
b. Aug 28, 1910 in Graveland, Netherlands
d. Feb 26, 1985 in New Haven, Connecticut
Source: *AmMWSc 73S; BioIn 10, 11; BlueB 76; ConAu 115; IntWW 74, 75, 76, 77, 78, 79, 80, 81, 82, 83; NewYTBS 85; WhAm 8, 11; Who 82, 83, 85; WhoAm 74, 76, 78, 80, 82, 84, 94; WhoE 77, 79, 81, 83, 85; WhoFI 94; WhoNob, 90, 95; WhoWor 74, 78, 80, 82, 84*

Kopal, Zdenek
Czech. Astronomer
Consultant to US space program; led team of astronomers in a photographic survey of the moon.
b. Apr 4, 1914
d. Jun 23, 1993 in Wilmslow, England
Source: *AmMWSc 73P, 76P, 79, 82, 86, 89, 92; AnObit 1993; BioIn 2, 8, 16, 19, 20; BlueB 76; ConAu 93, 141; CurBio 93N; IntAu&W 77; Who 74, 82, 83, 85, 88, 90, 92; WhoWor 74; WrDr 80, 82, 84, 86, 88, 90, 92, 94, 96*

Kopay, David
American. Football Player
Running back for the NFL's San Francisco 49ers, Detroit Lions, and Washington Redskins; first professional football player to come out as a gay man.
b. Jun 28, 1942 in Chicago, Illinois
Source: *GayLesB*

Kopechne, Mary Jo
American. Secretary
Died in car accident involving Edward Kennedy.
b. Jul 26, 1940
d. Jul 19, 1969 in Chappaquiddick, Massachusetts
Source: *BioIn 8, 9, 10, 11, 12*

Kopell, Bernie
[Bernard Morton Kopell]
American. Actor
Played Dr. Adam Bricker on TV series "The Love Boat," 1976-86.
b. Jun 21, 1933 in New York, New York
Source: *BioIn 12, 13, 17; ConTFT 6; LegTOT; VarWW 85; WhoAm 80, 82, 86, 90, 92; WhoEnt 92; WhoHol 92, A*

Kopit, Arthur Lee
American. Dramatist
Wrote play *Oh Dad, Poor Dad, Mama's Hung You in the Closet and I'm Feelin' So Sad,* 1960; became film, 1967.
b. May 10, 1937 in New York, New York
Source: *AmAu&B; AuNews 1; Benet 87; BenetAL 91; BiE&WWA; BioIn 13, 14; CamGLE; CamGWoT; CamHAL; CasWL; CnMD; ConAu 3BS, 81; ConDr 88; ConLC 1, 18, 33; ConTFT 4; CurBio 72; CyWA 89; IntAu&W 91; IntvTCA 2; McGEWD 84; ModAL S2; ModWD; NewYTBS 84; OxCAmT 84; PenC AM; RAdv 13-2; RfGAmL 87; WhoAm 86, 90; WhoEnt 92; WhoThe 81; WorAu 1950; WrDr 92*

Kopits, Steven E
American. Physician, Surgeon
Best known for treatment of orthopedic problems of dwarfs.
b. 1936, Austria-Hungary
Source: *BioIn 14; ConNews 87-1*

Koplovitz, Kay Smith
American. Broadcasting Executive
Pres., USA Cable Network since 1977.
b. Apr 11, 1945 in Milwaukee, Wisconsin
Source: *BioIn 12, 13, 16; ConNews 86-3; InWom SUP; LesBEnT 92; WhoAdv 90; WhoAm 90; WhoAmW 91; WhoTelC*

Koppel, Ted
[Edward James Koppel]
American. Broadcast Journalist
Anchor, ABC News "Nightline," 1980—; program started in order to cover Hostages in Iran; show won him an Emmy, 1981.
b. Feb 8, 1940 in Lancashire, England
Source: *BioIn 11, 12, 13, 14, 15, 16; CelR 90; ConAu 103; ConTFT 12; CurBio 84; EncTwCJ; IntMPA 96; IntWW 91; JrnUS; LegTOT; LesBEnT, 92; News 89-1; NewYTBS 88; VarWW 85; WhoAm 84, 86, 90, 92, 94, 95, 96, 97; WhoE 91; WhoTelC; WorAlBi*

Kops, Bernard
English. Author, Poet
Works include *Awake for Mourning,* 1958; *The World Is a Wedding,* 1963.
b. Nov 28, 1926 in London, England
Source: *BiE&WWA; BioIn 6, 10, 13; BlueB 76; ChhPo; CnMD; ConAu 5R; ConBrDr; ConDr 73, 77, 82, 88, 93; ConLC 4; ConNov 72, 76, 82, 86, 91, 96; ConPo 70, 75, 80, 85, 91, 96; CroCD; CrtSuDr; DcLB 13; DcLEL 1940; EncWT; EngPo; IntAu&W 76, 77, 82; IntWWP 77; LesBEnT; ModBrL S1; ModWD; NewC; NotNAT, A; RAdv 1; RGTwCWr; TwCWr; WhoThe 72, 77, 81; WhoWor 78; WhoWorJ 72, 78; WorAu 1950; WrDr 76, 80, 82, 84, 86, 88, 90, 92, 94, 96*

Korbut, Olga
[Mrs. Leonid Borkevich]
Russian. Gymnast
Won two gold medals, 1972 Olympics.
b. May 16, 1955 in Grodno, Union of Soviet Socialist Republics
Source: *BiDSovU; BioIn 12, 13, 16, 17, 18, 20; BioNews 74; ContDcW 89; CurBio 73; FacFETw; GoodHs; HerW, 84; IntDcWB; InWom SUP; LegTOT; LesBEnT; NewYTBE 72; WomFir; WorAl; WorAlBi*

Korda, Alexander, Sir
[Sandor Kellner; Sandor Korda]
English. Producer
Developed British film industry with London Films Co; made 112 films, including *The Third Man,* 1950.
b. Sep 16, 1893 in Turkeve, Austria-Hungary
d. Jan 23, 1956 in London, England
Source: *BiDFilm, 81, 94; BioIn 1, 4, 5, 7, 10, 12, 14, 15; CurBio 46, 56; DcArts; DcFM; DcNaB 1951; EncEurC; FacFETw; FilmEn; FilmgC; GrBr; HalFC 80, 84, 88; IlWWBF, A; IntDcF 1-2, 2-2, 2-4; MiSFD 9N; MovMk; NotNAT B; ObitOF 79; ObitT 1951; OxCFilm; PseudN 82; WhAm 3; WorAl; WorAlBi; WorEFlm; WorFDir 1*

Korda, Michael
American. Publisher
Wrote *Charmed Lives,* 1979, focusing on the life of Uncle, Alexander.
b. 1919
d. Dec 24, 1973
Source: *BioIn 10; LegTOT*

Korda, Michael Vincent
American. Editor
Editor-in-chief, Simon & Schuster, 1958—; wrote *Worldly Goods,* 1982.
b. Oct 8, 1933 in London, England
Source: *BioIn 13, 14; CelR 90; ConAu 107; CurBio 85; IntAu&W 91; IntWW 91; WhoAm 86; WhoUSWr 88; WorAlBi; WrDr 86, 92*

Kordich, Jay
"Juiceman"
American. Author
Best-selling author of *The Juiceman's Power of Juicing,* 1992; uses infomercials to promote drinking juice as the key to good health.
b. 1923? in San Pedro, California
Source: *News 93-2*

Koren, Edward Benjamin
American. Cartoonist, Educator
Known for woolly characters in *New Yorker* cartoons, 1962—; illustrator of numerous books.
b. Dec 13, 1935 in New York, New York
Source: *SmATA 5; WhoAm 80, 82, 84, 86, 88, 90, 92, 94, 95, 96, 97; WhoAmA 91; WhoE 74*

Koresh, David
American. Religious Figure
Leader of Branch Davidian cult in Waco, TX; died, along with most of his followers, in fire set after 51-day standoff with FBI agents.
b. 1959 in Houston, Texas
d. Apr 19, 1993 in Waco, Texas
Source: *LegTOT; NewYTBS 93*

Korin, Ogata
Japanese. Artist
Finest painter of decorative style started by Koetsu, Sotatso: *God of the Wind.*
b. 1658, Japan
d. 1716
Source: *McGDA; NewCol 75; OxCArt*

Korinetz, Yuri
Russian. Author
Best-known work: *There, Far Beyond the River,* 1968; translated into 10 languages.
b. Jan 14, 1923 in Moscow, Union of Soviet Socialist Republics
Source: *BioIn 11; ChlLR 4; ConAu 11NR, 61; OxCChiL; SmATA 9; TwCChW 83B, 89B*

Korjus, Miliza
Polish. Opera Singer
Appeared in film *The Great Waltz,* 1938; soprano who sang the role of the Queen of the Night in its original key.
b. 1902 in Warsaw, Poland
d. Aug 26, 1980 in Culver City, California
Source: *BioIn 12; FilmgC; NewYTBS 81; ThFT; WhoHol A; WhoMus 72*

Korman, Harvey Herschel
American. Comedian
Regular on "The Carol Burnett Show," 1967-77; won four Emmys; films include *Blazing Saddles,* 1974.
b. Feb 15, 1927 in Chicago, Illinois
Source: *ConTFT 3; CurBio 79; EncAFC; HalFC 84, 88; IntMPA 92; VarWW 85; WhoAm 74, 76, 78, 80, 82, 84, 86, 88, 90, 92, 94, 95, 96, 97; WhoEnt 92; WhoHol A; WorAlBi*

Kornberg, Arthur
American. Biochemist
Won Nobel Prize in medicine, 1959.
b. Mar 3, 1918 in New York, New York
Source: *AmDec 1950, 1960; AmMWSc 73P, 76P, 79, 82, 86, 89, 92, 95; AsBiEn; BiESc; BioIn 2, 5, 6, 8, 14, 15, 16, 17, 18, 20; CamDcSc; CurBio 68; IntWW 74, 75, 76, 77, 78, 79, 80, 81, 82, 83, 89, 91, 93; LarDcSc; McGMS 80; News 92, 92-1; NobelP; NotTwCS; WebAB 74, 79; Who 74, 82, 83, 85, 88, 90, 92, 94; WhoAm 74, 76, 78, 80, 82, 84, 86, 88, 90, 92, 94, 95, 96, 97; WhoFrS 84; WhoMedH; WhoNob, 90, 95; WhoScEn 94, 96; WhoWest 78, 80, 82, 84, 87, 89, 92, 94, 96; WhoWor 74, 78, 82, 84, 87, 89, 91, 93, 95, 96, 97; WhoWorJ 72, 78; WorScD*

Korner, Alexis
[Alexis Koerner]
"Grandfather of British Rhythm and Blues"
English. Musician
Known for discovering musicians Mick Jagger, Ginger Baker, Robert Plant, etc.
b. Apr 19, 1928 in Paris, France
d. Jan 1, 1984 in London, England
Source: *AnObit 1984; ConMuA 80A; EncPR&S 89; EncRk 88; IlEncRk; NewAmDM; NewGrDJ 88, 94; OnThGG; OxCPMus; PenEncP; RolSEnR 83; WhoRocM 82*

Korngold, Erich Wolfgang
Austrian. Composer
Won Oscars for scores of *Anthony Adverse,* 1936; *Adventures of Robin Hood,* 1938.
b. May 29, 1897 in Brunn, Austria
d. Nov 29, 1957 in Hollywood, California
Source: *AmComp; ASCAP 66, 80; Baker 78, 84, 92; BiDAmM; BioIn 1, 2, 4, 5, 10; BriBkM 80; CmMov; CmOp; CmpEPM; ConAmC 76, 82; CurBio 43, 58; DcAmB S6; DcArts; DcCom&M 79; EncEurC; FacFETw; FilmEn; FilmgC; HalFC 80, 84, 88; IntDcF 1-4, 2-4; IntDcOp; LinLib S; MusMk; NewAmDM; NewEOp 71; NewGrDA 86; NewGrDM 80; NewGrDO; OxCFilm; OxCMus; OxCPMus; PenDiMP A; WorEFlm*

Kornilov, Lavr Georgyevich
Russian. Military Leader
Commander-in-chief, Russian army, known for attempted military coup against government, 1917.
b. Jul 18, 1870 in Turkistan, Russia
d. Apr 13, 1918, Union of Soviet Socialist Republics
Source: *McGEWB; REn; WhDW; WhoMilH 76; WorAl*

Kornman, Mary
[Our Gang]
American. Actor
"Our Gang" first leading lady, 1923.
b. 1917 in Idaho Falls, Idaho
d. Jun 1, 1973 in Glendale, California
Source: *EncAFC; TwYS; WhoHol B; WhScrn 77, 83*

Korolenko, Vladimir Galaktionovich
Russian. Author
Best-known works: *Makar's Dream,* 1885; *The History of My Contemporary,* 1910.
b. Jul 27, 1853 in Zhitomir, Russia
d. Dec 25, 1921 in Polatava, Union of Soviet Socialist Republics
Source: *Benet 87, 96; BiD&SB; BiDSovU; BioIn 1, 7, 9, 13; BlkwERR; CasWL; ClDMEL 47, 80; ConAu 121; DcRusL; Dis&D; EncWL; EuAu; EvEuW; HanRL; ModSL 1; PenC EUR; REn*

Koruturk, Fahri S
[Fahri Peterson]
Turkish. Political Leader
President of Turkey, 1973-80.
b. 1903 in Istanbul, Turkey
d. Oct 12, 1987 in Istanbul, Turkey
Source: *BioIn 11; IntWW 74, 75, 76, 77, 78, 79, 80, 81, 82, 83; IntYB 79, 80, 81, 82; MidE 78, 79, 80, 81, 82; WhoWor 74, 76, 78, 80, 82, 84*

Korzybski, Alfred Habdank
American. Linguist
Originator of General Semantics; pres., Chicago's Institute of General Semantics, 1938-46.
b. Jul 3, 1879 in Warsaw, Poland
d. Mar 7, 1950 in Sharon, Connecticut
Source: *AmAu&B; EncSF; LuthC 75; REn; REnAL; TwCA SUP; WebAB 74; WhAm 2, 2A*

Kosar, Bernie, Jr.
American. Football Player
NFL Quarterback, Cleveland, 1985-93, Dallas, 1993-94, Miami, 1994—; Pro Bowl, 1987; holds NFL record for consecutive pass attempts without an interception, 308.
b. Nov 25, 1963 in Boardman, Ohio
Source: *BioIn 14, 16; FootReg 86, 87; LegTOT; NewYTBS 85; WhoAm 92, 94, 95, 96, 97; WhoMW 90, 92; WhoSSW 95*

Kosciuszko, Thaddeus
Polish. Soldier
Supporter of Americans in Revolutionary War.
b. Feb 12, 1746, Belorussia
d. Nov 15, 1817 in Solothurn, Switzerland
Source: *AmBi; ApCAB; BlkwEAR; Drake; EncAR; NatCAB 1; OxCAmH; TwCBDA; WebAB 74; WhAm HS*

Kosinski, Jerzy (Nikodem)
[Joseph Novak]
American. Author, Essayist
Wrote *Being There,* 1971, *The Hermit of 69th Street,* 1988; suicide victim.
b. Jun 14, 1933 in Lodz, Poland
d. May 3, 1991 in New York, New York
Source: *AmAu&B; AnObit 1991; AuSpks; Benet 87, 96; BenetAL 91; BioIn 13; CelR 90; ConAu 9NR, 17R, 46NR, 134; ConLC 1, 2, 3, 6, 10, 15, 53, 70; ConNov 72, 76, 82, 86; ConTFT 1; CurBio 74, 91N; CyWA 89; DcArts; DcLB Y82A; DcLEL 1940; DcLP 87A; DrAF 76; DrAPF 80, 91; EncSF, 93; EncWL, 2, 3; FacFETw; GrWrEL N; IntAu&W 76, 89, 91; IntvTCA 2; JeAmHC; LegTOT; LiExTwC; MajTwCW; ModAL S1, S2; News 91; NewYTBS 79, 82, 91; OxCAmL 83, 95; PostFic; PseudN 82; RAdv 1, 14, 13-1; RfGAmL 87, 94; RGTwCWr; ScFSB; WhAm 10; Who 82, 83, 85, 88, 90, 92N; WhoAm 74, 76, 78, 80, 82, 84, 86, 88, 90; WhoE 74, 75, 77, 79, 81, 83, 85, 86, 89, 91; WhoUSWr 88; WhoWor 74, 76, 78, 80, 82, 84, 87, 89, 91; WhoWrEP 89; WorAl; WorAlBi; WorAu 1950; WrDr 76, 80, 82, 84, 86, 88, 90*

Kossel, Karl Martin Leonhard Albrecht
German. Physician, Scientist
Separated nucleoproteins; contributed to cell research; won Nobel Prize in medicine, 1910.
b. Sep 16, 1853 in Rostock, Germany
d. Jul 5, 1927 in Heidelberg, Germany
Source: *DcScB; WhoNob, 90, 95*

Kossuth, Lajos
Hungarian. Patriot, Statesman
Principal figure in Hungarian Revolution, 1848.
b. Sep 19, 1802 in Monok, Hungary
d. Mar 20, 1894 in Turin, Italy
Source: *BioIn 1, 2, 3, 4, 7, 8, 9, 11, 17, 20; DcBiPP; HarEnUS; McGEWB; OxCGer 76, 86; PenC EUR; WhAm HS; WhDW; WorAl; WorAlBi*

Kostabi, Mark
American. Artist
His paintings, termed factory art, were sold for $50,000 apiece; opened studio, KostabiWorld, NYC, 1988.
b. 1960 in Whittier, California

Source: *BioIn 15, 16; News 89; WhoAmA 86, 89, 91, 93; WhoE 93*

Kostelanetz, Andre
American. Conductor
Led Columbia Broadcasting Orchestra, 1930s; NY Philharmonic, 1952-79; helped general audiences appreciate classics.
b. Dec 22, 1901 in Saint Petersburg, Russia
d. Jan 13, 1980 in Port-au-Prince, Haiti
Source: *AnObit 1980; Baker 78, 84, 92; BiDAmM; BioIn 1, 2, 3, 7, 9, 11, 12, 16; CmpEPM; ConAu 107; CurBio 42, 80N; DcAmB S10; IntWW 74; LegTOT; LinLib S; MusSN; NewAmDM; NewGrDA 86; NewGrDM 80; NewYTBE 72, 73; NewYTBS 80; OxCMus; OxCPMus; PenDiMP; PenEncP; RadStar; SaTiSS; Who 74; WhoAm 74; WhoMus 72; WhoWor 74; WhScrn 83; WorAl; WorAlBi*

Kosygin, Aleksei Nikolaevich
Russian. Political Leader
Prime Minister of Soviet Union, 1964-80; led Soviet effort at economic modernization, 1960s.
b. Feb 20, 1904 in Saint Petersburg, Russia
d. Dec 19, 1980 in Moscow, Union of Soviet Socialist Republics
Source: *AnObit 1980; BiDSovU; BioIn 1, 5, 6, 7, 8, 9, 11, 18; ColdWar 1; ConAu 102; CurBio 65, 81N; EncWB; IntWW 74; NewYTBS 80; Who 74, 82N; WhoGov 72; WhoSocC 78; WhoWor 80; WorAl*

Kotsching, Walter Maria
American. Government Official
Helped establish UN; permanent member, US delegation.
b. Apr 9, 1901 in Judenburg, Austria
d. Jun 23, 1985 in Newton, Pennsylvania
Source: *ConAu 117; CurBio 85*

Kottke, Leo
American. Musician
One of top acoustic guitarists, popular in Europe; recorded album *Time Step*, 1983.
b. Sep 11, 1945 in Athens, Georgia
Source: *BioIn 14; EncFCWM 83; HarEnR 86; IlEncRk; LegTOT; PenEncP; RolSEnR 83; WhoAm 84*

Kotto, Yaphet Frederick
American. Actor
Starred as Idi Amin in *Raid on Entebbe*, 1976; other films include *Alien*, 1979; *Brubaker*, 1980; appeared on Broadway in *The Great White Hope*, 1969.
b. Nov 15, 1944 in New York, New York
Source: *BlksAmF; ConTFT 5; CurBio 95; DrBlPA 90; HalFC 84, 88; InB&W 85; IntMPA 86, 92; IntWW 91; VarWW 85; WhoAm 86, 88; WhoBlA 92; WhoEnt 92; WorAlBi*

Kotzebue, August Friedrich Ferdinand von
"The Shakespeare of Germany"
German. Author
Wrote 200 plays including *The Stranger*, 1798; killed by U. student.
b. May 3, 1761 in Weimar, Germany
d. Mar 23, 1819 in Mannheim, Germany
Source: *AtlBL; BbD; BiD&SB; BioIn 6, 7; CasWL; CnThe; DcEuL; Dis&D; Ent; EuAu; EvEuW; McGEWD 72; NewC; NewCBEL; NewGrDM 80; NotNAT A, B; OxCAmT 84; OxCEng 67; OxCFr; OxCGer 76; OxCThe 67, 83; PenC EUR; REn; REnWD*

Kotzky, Alex Sylvester
American. Cartoonist
Created syndicated strip "Duke Hand," 1958-59.
b. Sep 11, 1923 in New York, New York
d. Sep 26, 1996 in New York, New York
Source: *EncACom; WhoAm 74, 76, 78, 80, 82, 84, 86; WhoAmA 76, 78, 80, 82, 84, 86, 89, 91, 93*

Kouchner, Bernard
French. Physician
Founded Medecins sans Frontieres (Doctors Without Borders), 1971, and Medecins du Monde (Doctors of the World), 1980, organizations that provide food and medical supplies to needy people throughout the world.
b. Nov 1, 1939 in Avignon, France
Source: *BioIn 19, 20; CurBio 93; IntWW 93*

Koufax, Sandy
[Sanford Koufax]
American. Baseball Player
Pitcher, Brooklyn/LA Dodgers, 1955-66; threw four no-hitters, including perfect game, 1965; won Cy Young Award three times, MVP once; youngest ever in Baseball Hall of Fame, 1971; Sports Hall of Fame, 1991.
b. Dec 30, 1935 in New York, New York
Source: *AmDec 1960; Ballpl 90; BiDAmSp BB; BioIn 4, 5, 6, 7, 8, 9, 10, 11, 12, 13, 14, 15, 16, 17, 18, 19, 20; CelR; CmCal; ConAu 89; CurBio 64; FacFETw; JeHun; LegTOT; WebAB 74, 79; WhoAm 74, 76; WhoProB 73; WhoSpor; WorAl; WorAlBi*

Kountche, Seyni
Nigerian. Political Leader
President of Niger, 1974-87; ended Niger's reliance on imports, launched politi cal reforms.
b. Jul 1, 1931 in Fandou, Niger
d. Nov 10, 1987 in Paris, France
Source: *AfSS 78, 79, 80, 81, 82; AnObit 1987; BioIn 21; DcAfHiB 86S; EncRev; IntWW 75, 76, 77, 78, 79, 80, 81, 82, 83; IntYB 79, 80, 81, 82; WhAm 11; WhoWor 78, 80, 82, 84, 87*

Kountz, Samuel L(ee)
American. Surgeon
Performed the first kidney transplant between humans who were not identical trins, 1961.
b. Oct 20, 1930 in Lexa, Arkansas
d. Dec 23, 1981 in Great Neck, New York
Source: *AmMWSc 79; BioIn 7, 11, 12; BlksScM; DiAASTC; InB&W 80; WhoBlA 77, 80*

Koussevitzky, Serge Alexandrovich
American. Conductor, Composer
Led Boston Symphony, 1924-49; founded Berkshire Music Festival, 1934; championed modern composers.
b. Jul 26, 1874 in Vyshni Volochek, Russia
d. Jun 4, 1951 in Boston, Massachusetts
Source: *AmCulL; Baker 84, 92; BiDAmM; CurBio 40, 51; DcAmB S5; MusMk; MusSN; NatCAB 39; NewGrDM 80; OxCMus*

Kovac, Michael
Czech. Political Leader
Elected by Parliament as Republic of Slovakia's first pres., 1993—.
b. Apr 1, 1936 in Hradiste, Czechoslovakia
Source: *WhoSoCE 89*

Kovacs, Ernie
American. Actor
Played Ernie in TV show "Kovacsland," 1951; "Tonight," 1956-57; married Edie Adams.
b. Jan 23, 1919 in Trenton, New Jersey
d. Jan 13, 1962 in Beverly Hills, California
Source: *AmAu&B; ASCAP 66, 80; BioIn 4, 5, 6, 11, 13, 15, 16, 19; CurBio 58, 62; DcAmB S7; EncAFC; FacFETw; FilmEn; FilmgC; Funs; HalFC 80, 84, 88; ItaFilm; JoeFr; LegTOT; MotPP; MovMk; NewYTET; NotNAT B; ObitOF 79; QDrFCA 92; WhAm 4; WhoCom; WhoHol B; WhScrn 74, 77, 83; WorAl; WorAlBi*

Kovalev, Mikhail Aleksandrovich
[Riurik Ivnev]
Russian. Author
Writings *Love Without Love, The Open House* were banned from USSR, 1930s.
b. Feb 11, 1893 in Tbilisi, Russia
d. Mar 28, 1981 in Moscow, Union of Soviet Socialist Republics
Source: *AnObit 1981; ConAu 108; DcRusL; WhoSocC 78*

Kovel, Ralph Mallory
American. Author, Antiquarian
With wife Terry wrote books on antiques regarded as "bibles" in their field.
b. Aug 20, 1920 in Milwaukee, Wisconsin
Source: *BioIn 14; BlueB 76; ConAu 8NR, 17R, 23NR; IntAu&W 91; WhoAm*

86, 90; WhoUSWr 88; WhoWrEP 89; WrDr 76, 86, 92

Kovel, Terry Horvitz
[Mrs. Ralph Kovel]
American. Author, Antiquarian
Cowriter of syndicated "Kovels Antiques" column, 1955—; on TV series "Kovels on Antiques," 1981—.
b. Oct 27, 1928 in Cleveland, Ohio
Source: *BioIn 14; ConAu 8NR, 17R, 23NR; ForWC 70; IntAu&W 89; WhoAm 74, 76, 78, 80, 82, 84, 86, 88, 90, 92; WhoAmW 66, 68, 70, 72, 74; WhoUSWr 88; WhoWrEP 89, 92, 95; WrDr 76, 80, 82, 84, 86, 88, 90, 92, 94, 96*

Kovic, Ron
American. Author, Political Activist
Vietnam vet whose autobiography *Born on the Fourth of July*, was made into an Oscar-winning movie in 1989; anti-war activist who brought attention to the plight of wounded veterans.
b. Jul 4, 1946 in Ladysmith, Wisconsin
Source: *BioIn 11, 13; ConAu 138; ConHero 2; CurBio 90; HeroCon; LegTOT; LNinSix*

Kowalski, Sharon
American. Social Reformer
Was involved in a guardianship case between her companion, Karen Thompson, and her parents.
Source: *BioIn 15, 16; GayLesB*

Kozol, Jonathan
American. Author, Educator
Wrote *Illiterate America*, 1985, and *Savage Inequalities*, 1991.
b. Sep 5, 1936 in Boston, Massachusetts
Source: *AmAu&B; AmDec 1970; BioIn 5, 8, 9, 10, 14, 15; CelR; ConAu 16NR, 45NR, 61; ConLC 17; CurBio 86; IntAu&W 89, 91, 93; IntWW 89, 91, 93; LegTOT; LNinSix; News 92, 92-1; WhoAm 74, 76, 78, 80, 82, 84, 86, 88, 90, 92, 94, 95, 96, 97; WhoE 95; WhoUSWr 88; WhoWor 95, 96, 97; WhoWrEP 89, 92, 95; WrDr 88, 90, 92, 94, 96*

Kozyrev, Andrei Y
Russian. Government Official
Helped to establish the Commonwealth of Independent States; Minister of Foreign Affairs under Yeltsin.
b. 1951?, Union of Soviet Socialist Republics
Source: *CurBio 92*

Kraenzlein, Alvin C
American. Track Athlete
Hurdler, long jumper; won four gold medals in individual events, 1900 Olympics; father of modern hurdle form.
b. Dec 12, 1876
d. Jan 6, 1928
Source: *BioIn 8; WhoTr&F 73*

Krafft-Ebing, Richard von
German. Psychiatrist
Wrote classsic collection of case histories *Psychopathia Sexualis*, 1886.
b. Aug 14, 1840 in Mannheim, Germany
d. Dec 22, 1902 in Mariagru, Austria
Source: *AsBiEn; Benet 87, 96; HumSex; InSci; OxCGer 76; OxCMed 86; REn; WhDW; WorAl*

Kraft, Chris(topher Columbus, Jr.)
American. Government Official, Engineer
Flight director, US manned space-flight program, 1959-70.
b. Feb 28, 1924 in Phoebus, Virginia
Source: *AmMWSc 82, 92; CurBio 66; FacFETw; IntWW 83, 91; WhoAm 84; WhoEng 88; WhoSSW 84; WhoWor 82; WorAl; WorAlBi*

Kraft, James Lewis
American. Manufacturer
Invented pasteurizing process for cheese.
b. Dec 11, 1874 in Stevensville, Ontario, Canada
d. Feb 16, 1953 in Chicago, Illinois
Source: *BiDAmBL 83; BioIn 1, 2, 3, 10, 13, 18; DcAmB S5; EncAB-A 25; Entr; NatCAB 62; WhAm 3*

Kraft, Joseph
American. Journalist, Author
Internationally syndicated political columnist known for non-ideological approach to world affairs.
b. Sep 4, 1924 in South Orange, New Jersey
d. Jan 10, 1986 in Washington, District of Columbia
Source: *AmAu&B; AnObit 1986; BiDAmJo; BiDAmNC; BioIn 7, 10, 12, 14, 15, 16; BlueB 76; ConAu 9R, 34NR, 118; EncTwCJ; JrnUS; NewYTBS 86; WhAm 9; WhoAm 74, 76, 78, 80, 82, 84; WhoSSW 73, 75, 76; WhoWor 76; WrDr 76, 82, 84*

Kraftwerk
[Fernando Abrantes; Fritz Hijbert; Ralf Hutter; Florian Schneider]
German. Music Group
Electronic band, formed 1970; album *Radio-Activity* was chosen as French album of the yr., 1976; current members listed above.
Source: *ConMuA 80A; ConMus 9; EncPR&S 89; EncRk 88; EncRkSt; HarEnR 86; IlEncRk; PenEncP; RkOn 85A; RolSEnR 83; WhoRock 81; WhoRocM 82*

Krag, Jens Otto
Danish. Political Leader
Social Democratic prime minister of Denmark, 1962-68, 1971-72.
b. Sep 15, 1915 in Randers, Denmark
d. Jun 22, 1978 in Frederikshavn, Denmark
Source: *CurBio 62, 78N; IntWW 74; NewYTBE 72; WhoWor 74*

Krainik, Ardis
American. Business Executive
GM, Lyric Opera of Chicago, 1981-96.
b. Mar 8, 1929 in Manitowoc, Wisconsin
d. Jan 18, 1997 in Chicago, Illinois
Source: *BioIn 12, 13; CurBio 91; IntWWM 90; MetOEnc; NewAmDM; WhoAm 80, 82, 84, 86, 88, 90, 92, 94, 95, 96, 97; WhoAmW 66, 68, 70, 77, 79, 81, 83, 85, 89, 91, 93, 95, 97; WhoEnt 92; WhoMW 82, 84, 86, 88, 90, 92, 93, 96; WhoOp 76; WhoWor 95, 96, 97*

Kramer, Jack
American. Tennis Player
US Open champion, 1946-47; Wimbledon, 1947; inducted into Int'l Tennis Hall of Fame, 1968.
b. Aug 1, 1921 in Las Vegas, Nevada
Source: *Ballpl 90; BioIn 1, 12, 14, 15, 16, 21; BioNews 74; BuCMET; CmCal; CurBio 47; FacFETw; LegTOT; WhoSpor; WorAl; WorAlBi*

Kramer, Larry
American. Screenwriter, AIDS Activist
Screenplays include *Women in Love*, 1969; founder AIDS Coalition to Unleash Power (ACT-UP), 1987.
b. Jun 25, 1935 in Bridgeport, Connecticut
Source: *Au&Wr 71; BioIn 16; ConAu 124, 126; ConGAN; ConLC 42; ConTFT 5, 13; CurBio 94; DrAPF 91; FilmgC; GayLesB; GayLL; HalFC 80, 84, 88; IntAu&W 91, 93; IntMPA 75, 76, 77, 78, 79, 80, 81, 82, 84, 86, 88, 92, 94, 96; News 91, 91-2; OxCAmL 95; RadHan; RGTwCWr; WhoAm 94, 95, 96, 97; WhoE 89*

Kramer, Stanley E
American. Director, Producer
Among his 15 Oscar-winning movies are *High Noon*, 1952, *Judgment at Nuremberg*, 1961, *Guess Who's Coming to Dinner?* 1967.
b. Sep 29, 1913 in New York, New York
Source: *BiDFilm; BioIn 15; CelR 90; ConTFT 4; CurBio 51; DcFM; FacFETw; FilmgC; HalFC 84, 88; IntDcF 2-2; IntMPA 92; IntWW 83, 91; MovMk; OxCFilm; VarWW 85; WhoAm 86, 90; WhoEnt 92; WorAl; WorAlBi; WorEFlm*

Kramm, Joseph
American. Dramatist, Actor, Director
Actor-turned-director; won 1952 Pulitzer for ninth play he wrote, first play produced, *The Shrike*.
b. Sep 30, 1907 in Philadelphia, Pennsylvania
Source: *AmAu&B; BiE&WWA; CnMD; CurBio 52; DcLEL 1940; ModWD; NotNAT; OxCAmL 83; REn; TwCA SUP; VarWW 85; WhoAm 74, 76; WhoE 74; WhoThe 72, 77; WhoWor 74*

Krantz, Judith
[Judith Tarcher]
American. Author
Wrote *Scruples,* 1978; *Princess Daisy,* 1980; *Mistral's Daughter,* 1982.
b. Jan 9, 1928 in New York, New York
Source: *ArtclWW 2; BenetAL 91; BestSel 89-1; BioIn 11, 13; BlmGWL; CelR 90; ConAu 33NR, 81; ConTFT 14; CurBio 82; IntAu&W 91; IntWW 89, 91, 93; InWom SUP; LegTOT; MajTwCW; NewYTBS 86; WhoAm 86, 90; WorAlBi; WrDr 92*

Krasna, Norman
American. Dramatist, Critic
Won Oscar for screenplay: *Princess O'Rourke,* 1943.
b. Nov 7, 1909 in New York, New York
d. Nov 1, 1984 in Los Angeles, California
Source: *AmAu&B; AnObit 1984; BiDFilm, 81, 94; BiE&WWA; BioIn 2, 3, 14, 15; CmMov; ConAu 114; CurBio 52, 83N, 85N; DcLB 26; EncAFC; EncWT; FilmEn; FilmgC; HalFC 80, 84, 88; IntDcF 1-4, 2-4; IntMPA 75, 76, 77, 78, 79, 80, 81, 82, 84; LegTOT; McGEWD 72, 84; NewYTBS 84; NotNAT; OxCAmT 84; OxCFilm; VarWW 85; WhAm 8; WhoAm 74, 76; WhoThe 72, 77, 81; WorEFlm*

Krasner, Lee
[Mrs. Jackson Pollock]
American. Artist
Abstract expressionist whose paintings were characterized by bold, outlined images.
b. Oct 27, 1908 in New York, New York
d. Jun 19, 1984 in New York, New York
Source: *AmArt; AnObit 1984; BiDWomA; BioIn 4, 7, 9, 10, 11, 12, 13, 14, 15, 16, 20; ConArt 77, 83, 89, 96; ContDcW 89; CurBio 74, 84, 84N; DcAmArt; DcCAA 88, 94; DcCAr 81; EncWB; FacFETw; GrLiveH; InWom SUP; LegTOT; NewYTBS 84; NorAmWA; WhAmArt 85; WhoAmA 82, 84, 86N, 89N, 91N, 93N; WhoAmW 83; WomArt; WorArt 1950*

Krassner, Paul
American. Journalist
Former writer for *Mad* mag; co-founded Youth International Party (Yippies), 1968; currently stand-up comic.
b. Apr 9, 1932 in New York, New York
Source: *AmAu&B; BioIn 7, 8; ConAu 11NR, 21R; WhoAm 74, 76*

Kraus, Alfredo
Spanish. Opera Singer
One of the most renowned lyric tenors of his generation; regular with NY Met. since mid-1960s.
b. Nov 24, 1927 in Las Palmas, Canary Islands, Spain
Source: *Baker 84, 92; BioIn 7, 10, 11, 15, 16; CmOp; CurBio 87; IntDcOp; IntWWM 90; MetOEnc; NewAmDM; NewGrDM 80; NewGrDO; NewYTBS 79, 88; OxDcOp; PenDiMP; WhoAm 78, 80, 90, 97; WhoEnt 92; WhoMus 72; WhoOp 76; WhoWor 97*

Kraus, Felix von
Austrian. Opera Singer
Bass; appeared annually at Wagner Festival in Bayreuth, early 1900s.
b. Oct 3, 1870 in Vienna, Austria
d. Oct 30, 1937 in Munich, Germany
Source: *Baker 78, 84, 92; NewEOp 71; NewGrDO*

Kraus, Hans Peter
American. Bookseller
Founded H.P. Kraus, 1939, one of the world's most distinguished dealers of rare books and manuscripts.
b. Oct 12, 1907 in Vienna, Austria
d. Nov 1, 1988 in Ridgefield, Connecticut
Source: *BioIn 3, 5, 11, 12, 13, 16; ChhPo S3; ConAu 127, P-2; CurBio 60, 89N; NewYTBS 88; WhAm 9; WhoAm 74, 76, 78, 80, 82*

Kraus, Lili
New Zealander. Musician
Int'l concert pianist since 1925; recorded entire Mozart, Schubert piano repertory; Japanese prisoner, WW II.
b. Mar 4, 1908 in Budapest, Austria-Hungary
d. Nov 6, 1986 in Asheville, North Carolina
Source: *Baker 84; BioIn 7; BioNews 75; CurBio 75, 87; IntWWM 85; NewGrDM 80; NewYTBE 71; WhAm 9; WhoAm 74, 76, 78, 80, 82, 84; WhoAmM 83; WhoAmW 75, 77, 83, 85, 87; WhoMus 72*

Krause, Bernie
[The Weavers; Bernard Leo Krause]
American. Singer, Songwriter
Member, folk group The Weavers, 1963-64; pres., Parasound, Inc., 1968—; sonic artist on several albums.
b. Dec 8, 1938 in Detroit, Michigan
Source: *BioIn 12, 16; WhoAm 82, 84, 86, 88, 90, 92, 94, 95, 96; WhoEnt 92; WhoRocM 82*

Kraushaar, Otto
American. Educator
Pres., Goucher College, 1949-67; oversaw the consolidation of its two campuses in 1956 resulting in a nationally ranked women's college.
b. Nov 19, 1901 in Clinton, Iowa
d. Sep 23, 1989 in Baltimore, Maryland
Source: *BioIn 2, 3, 16; ConAu 37R; CurBio 89N; DrAS 82P; NewYTBS 89; WrDr 86, 90*

Krauss, Alison (Maria)
American. Musician, Singer
Recognized as the most promising fiddlers in the Midwest by the Society for the Preservation of Bluegrass Music in America, 1983, 1984; won Grammy for *I've Got That Old Feeling,* 1990.
b. Jul 23, 1971 in Decatur, Illinois
Source: *BgBkCoM; ConMus 10; EncRkSt*

Krauss, Clemens
Austrian. Conductor
Led German operas, 1920s-40s; Wagner, Strauss interpreter; wed to singer Viorica Ursuleac.
b. Mar 31, 1893 in Vienna, Austria
d. May 16, 1954 in Mexico City, Mexico
Source: *Baker 78, 84; CmOp; IntDcOp; MetOEnc; MusSN; NewAmDM; NewEOp 71; NewGrDM 80; NewGrDO; OxDcOp; PenDiMP*

Krauss, Gabrielle
"La Rachelle Chantante"
Austrian. Opera Singer
Soprano, favorite of Paris Grand Opera, 1870s-80s.
b. Mar 24, 1842 in Vienna, Austria
d. Jan 6, 1906 in Paris, France
Source: *Baker 78, 84; CmOp; InWom; NewEOp 71; NewGrDM 80; OxDcOp*

Krauss, Ruth Ida
American. Author
Books include *A Hole Is to Dig,* 1952.
b. Jul 25, 1911 in Baltimore, Maryland
Source: *AmAu&B; Au&ICB; Au&Wr 71; AuBYP 2, 3; BkP; ConAu 1NR, 1R; ConDr 73; DrAP 75; DrAPF 91; ForWC 70; IntAu&W 91; MorJA; OxCChiL; SmATA 30; TwCChW 89; WhoAm 86; WrDr 92*

Krauss, Werner
German. Actor
Played insane doctor in silent horror classic *Cabinet of Dr. Caligari,* 1919.
b. Jul 23, 1884 in Gestungshausen, Germany
d. Oct 20, 1959 in Vienna, Austria
Source: *BiDFilm, 81, 94; BioIn 5, 14, 15; EncEurC; EncTR 91; EncWT; Ent; Film 1, 2; FilmAG WE; FilmEn; FilmgC; HalFC 80, 84, 88; IntDcF 1-3, 2-3; MotPP; ObitOF 79; OxCFilm; OxCThe 67, 83; WhoHol B; WhoHrs 80; WhScrn 74, 77, 83; WhThe; WorEFlm*

Kravchuk, Leonid Makarovich
Ukrainian. Political Leader
First democratically-elected pres. of Ukraine, 1990-94.
b. Jan 10, 1934 in Velyky Zhytyn, Ukraine
Source: *CurBio 93; IntWW 93; NewYTBS 91; WhoRus; WhoWor 95, 96, 97*

Kravis, Henry R
"Dr. No"
American. Banker
Partner in Kohlberg, Kravis, Roberts and Co. which purchased RJR Nabisco in 1988 for $25 billion, a record price for a leveraged buyout.
b. Jan 6, 1944 in Tulsa, Oklahoma
Source: *BioIn 15, 16; ConAmBL; CurBio 89; Dun&B 90; WhoAm 90*

Kravitz, Lenny
[Leonard Kravitz]
American. Singer, Songwriter
Rock and soul singer; albums include *Let Love Rule,* 1989; and *Mama Said,* 1991.
b. May 26, 1964 in New York, New York
Source: *BioIn 15, 16; ConBlB 10; ConMus 5; CurBio 96; EncRkSt; LegTOT; News 91, 91-1; OnThGG; WhoEnt 92*

Kray, Reggie
[Reginald Kray]
English. Criminal, Murderer
With brother ran "crime firm" in London's East End, 1960s; both convicted, sentenced to life in jail, 1969.
b. Oct 24, 1933 in London, England
Source: *BioIn 9, 11, 15; DrInf*

Kray, Ronnie
[Ronald Kray]
"Colonel"
English. Criminal, Murderer
With brother ran "crime firm" in London's East End, 1960s; both convicted, sentenced to life in jail, 1969.
b. Oct 24, 1933 in London, England
d. Mar 17, 1995 in Slough, England
Source: *BioIn 9, 11, 15, 20; DrInf*

Krea, Henri
Algerian. Writer, Poet
Espoused the view of a distinctively Algerian literature; wrote *Djamal,* 1961.
b. Nov 6, 1933 in Algiers, Algeria
Source: *WhoArab 81*

Krebs, Edwin Gerhard
American. Biochemist
With Edmund Fischer won 1992 Nobel Prize for the discovery of a process that regulates proteins in cells.
b. Jun 6, 1918 in Lansing, Iowa
Source: *AmMWSc 73P, 76P, 79, 82, 86, 89, 92, 95; IntWW 93; LarDcSc; Who 94; WhoAm 78, 80, 82, 84, 90, 92, 94, 95, 96, 97; WhoFrS 84; WhoMedH; WhoNob 95; WhoScEn 94, 96; WhoWest 94, 96; WhoWor 95, 96, 97*

Krebs, Hans Adolf, Sir
British. Biochemist
Won 1953 Nobel Prize for research on food cycles.
b. Aug 25, 1900 in Hildesheim, Germany
d. Nov 22, 1981 in Oxford, England
Source: *AsBiEn; BiESc; BioIn 3, 4, 5, 6, 12, 13, 14, 15, 17, 19, 20; CamDcSc; CurBio 54, 82N; DcNaB 1981; DcScB S2; FacFETw; InSci; IntWW 81; LarDcSc; McGEWB; NewYTBS 81; NotTwCS; OxCMed 86; RAdv 14; WhoNob, 90, 95; WhoWor 74, 76, 78; WorAl; WorScD*

Kredel, Fritz
American. Artist, Illustrator
Prestigious illustrator of children's classics, limited editions.
b. Feb 8, 1900 in New York, New York
d. Jun 10, 1973 in New York, New York
Source: *BioIn 1, 3, 5, 6, 8, 9, 12; ChhPo; ConAu 41R; IlsBYP; IlsCB 1744, 1946, 1957; MorJA; SmATA 17; WhAmArt 85; WhoAmA 73, 76*

Kreiner, Kathy
Canadian. Skier
Won gold medal, giant slalom, 1976 Olympics.
b. May 4, 1957 in Timmins, Ontario, Canada

Kreisler, Fritz
American. Violinist, Composer
One of most renowned virtuosos of 20th c; American debut, 1888; wrote operettas, popular violin music.
b. Feb 2, 1875 in Vienna, Austria
d. Jan 29, 1962 in New York, New York
Source: *ApCAB X; ASCAP 66, 80; Baker 78, 84, 92; BiDAmM; BioIn 1, 2, 3, 4, 6, 8, 9, 10, 11, 13, 14; BriBkM 80; CmpEPM; ConAmC 76, 82; ConAu 115; CurBio 44, 62; DcAmBC; DcAmB S7; DcArts; FacFETw; LinLib L, S; MusMk; MusSN; NatCAB 61; NewAmDM; NewGrDA 86; NewGrDM 80; NewOxM; NotNAT B; ObitT 1961; OxCAmH; OxCMus; OxCPMus; PenDiMP; REn; WebAB 74, 79; WhAm 4; WhDW; WorAl; WorAlBi*

Krementz, Jill
[Mrs. Kurt Vonnegut]
American. Photographer
Contributor to *People* mag., 1974—; known for portraits of authors.
b. Feb 19, 1940 in New York, New York
Source: *AuBYP 3; AuNews 1, 2; BioIn 8, 10, 11, 12, 13, 15; BioNews 75; ChlBkCr; ChlLR 5; ConAu 23NR, 41R, 46NR; EncTwCJ; FifBJA; ICPEnP A; InWom SUP; MacBEP; MajAI; NewYTBS 82; SmATA 8AS, 17, 71; Who 82; WhoAm 74, 76, 78, 80, 82, 84, 86, 88, 90, 92, 94, 95, 96, 97; WhoAmW 83, 85, 87, 89, 91, 93, 95, 97; WhoUSWr 88; WhoWrEP 89, 92, 95*

Kremer, Gidon
Russian. Musician
Gold medal violinist in Moscow Tchaikovsky competition, 1970; repertoire stresses contemporary composers.
b. Feb 27, 1947 in Riga, Latvia
Source: *Baker 84, 92; BioIn 11, 12, 13, 14, 15, 16; BriBkM 80; CurBio 85; IntWW 89, 91, 93; IntWWM 90; NewYTBS 87; PenDiMP; WhoAmM 83; WhoSocC 78; WhoWor 91*

Krenek, Ernst
American. Composer
Created sensation with first jazz opera, *Jonny Spielt Auf,* 1927; greatly influenced modern composers.
b. Aug 23, 1900 in Vienna, Austria
d. Dec 23, 1991 in Palm Springs, California
Source: *AmComp; AnObit 1991; Baker 78, 84, 92; BiDAmM; BiDJaz; BiGAW; BioIn 1, 2, 4, 8, 9, 10, 11, 12, 13, 14, 16, 17, 18, 19; BlueB 76; BriBkM 80; CmOp; CompSN, SUP; ConAmC 76, 82; ConAu 57, 136; ConCom 92; CpmDNM 76, 79, 80, 81; CurBio 42, 92N; DcArts; DcCM; DcCom 77; IntAu&W 77; IntDcOp; IntWW 74, 75, 76, 77, 78, 79, 80, 81, 82, 83, 89, 91; IntWWM 77, 80, 90; McGEWB; MetOEnc; MusMk; NewAmDM; NewGrDA 86; NewGrDM 80; NewGrDO; NewOxM; NewYTBS 91; OxCMus; OxDcOp; PenDiMP, A; PeoHis; WhAm 10; WhoAm 74, 76, 82, 84, 86, 88, 90; WhoEnt 92; WhoMus 72; WhoWor 74*

Krens, Thomas
American. Museum Director, Historian
Director of the Solomon R. Guggenheim Foundation, 1988—.
b. Dec 26, 1946 in New York, New York
Source: *CurBio 89, 90; IntWW 93; WhoAm 88, 90, 92, 94, 95, 96; WhoE 91, 93, 95, 97; WhoWor 91*

Krenwinkel, Patricia
American. Cultist, Murderer
Member, Charles Manson's "family"; convicted of killing Sharon Tate, six others, 1969.
b. Dec 3, 1947 in Los Angeles, California
Source: *BioIn 8, 9, 11, 12*

Krenz, Egon
German. Political Leader
Succeeded Honecker as ruler of E. Germany, 1989; during his 46-day tenure he opened all of E. Germany's borders including the Berlin Wall.
b. Mar 19, 1937 in Kolberg, Germany
Source: *BioIn 16; CurBio 90; FacFETw; IntWW 91, 93; WhoSocC 78; WhoSoCE 89; WhoWor 91*

Kreps, Juanita Morris
American. Government Official
Secretary of Commerce under Carter, 1977-79.
b. Jan 11, 1921 in Lynch, Kentucky
Source: *AmEA 74; AmMWSc 73S, 78S; AmWomM; BiDrUSE 89; BioIn 13; CngDr 77, 79; EncWB; EncWHA; HanAmWH; IntWW 77, 78, 79, 80, 81, 82, 83, 89, 91, 93; IntYB 80, 81, 82; InWom SUP; LibW; NewYTBS 76; WhoAm 74, 76, 78, 80, 82, 84, 86, 88, 90, 92, 94, 95, 96, 97; WhoAmW 74, 75, 77, 81, 83, 85, 87, 89, 91, 93, 95, 97; WhoE 77, 79; WhoFI 79, 81, 89; WhoGov 77; WhoScEn 96; WhoSSW 82, 84; WhoWor 96, 97; WomFir*

Kresge, Sebastian Spering
American. Merchant
Founder, S S Kresge's, which became K-Mart.
b. Jul 31, 1867 in Bald Mount, Pennsylvania
d. Oct 18, 1966 in Mountainhome, Pennsylvania
Source: *ApCAB X; BiDAmBL 83; BioIn 3, 4, 7, 9, 12; DcAmB S8; DcAmTB; NatCAB 52; ObitOF 79; WhAm 4*

Kresge, Stanley Sebastian
American. Business Executive
With S S Kresge Co., 1923-77; pres., 1952-66; chm., 1966-78.
b. Jun 11, 1900 in Detroit, Michigan
d. Jun 30, 1985 in Rochester, Michigan
Source: *BioIn 7, 14; EncWM; NewYTBS 85; WhAm 8; WhoAm 78, 80, 82, 84; WhoMW 82, 84*

Kreskin
[George Joseph Kresge, Jr.]
"The Amazing Kreskin"
American. Psychic, Entertainer
Uses telepathy, traditional magic; wrote *Use Your Head to Get Ahead,* 1977.
b. Jan 12, 1935 in Montclair, New Jersey
Source: *BioIn 10, 12; BioNews 74; ConAu 101; EncO&P 2S1, 3; EncPaPR 91; LegTOT; PseudN 82; VarWW 85; WhoAm 92; WhoEnt 92; WhoWor 91*

Kress, Samuel Henry
American. Merchant
Founded Kress dime store chain, 1907.
b. Jul 23, 1863 in Cherryville, Pennsylvania
d. Sep 22, 1955 in New York, New York
Source: *BiDAmBL 83; BioIn 1, 3, 4; CurBio 55; DcAmB S5; EncAB-A 29; NatCAB 41; WebAB 74, 79; WhAm 3; WorAl*

Kressy, Edmund
American. Cartoonist
With wife, created Lone Ranger comic strip, 1937.
b. 1902
d. Oct 7, 1986 in Ashburnham, Massachusetts
Source: *BioIn 15; WhAmArt 85*

Kreuger, Ivar
"Match King"
Swedish. Financier
Owned United Swedish Match Co; made 3/4 of world's matches by end of WW II.
b. Mar 2, 1880 in Kalmar, Sweden
d. Mar 12, 1932 in Paris, France
Source: *BioIn 12, 13, 21; DcAmSR; LinLib S; PseudN 82; WhDW; WorAl; WorAlBi*

Kreuger, Kurt
American. Actor
Supporting actor in 1943 films *Enemy Below; The Moon Is Down.*
b. Jul 23, 1917 in Saint Moritz, Switzerland
Source: *BioIn 18; FilmEn; FilmgC; ForYSC; HalFC 80, 84, 88; IntMPA 75, 76, 77, 78, 79, 80, 81, 82, 84, 86, 88, 92, 94, 96; MotPP; VarWW 85; WhoEnt 92; WhoHol A*

Kreutzer, Rodolphe
German. Musician, Composer
A founder of French school of violin playing; wrote 40 operas, 20 violin concertos; Beethoven wrote "Kreutzer Sonata" for him.
b. Nov 16, 1766 in Versailles, France
d. Jan 6, 1831 in Geneva, Switzerland
Source: *Baker 78, 84, 92; BioIn 2, 8, 14; BriBkM 80; DcArts; MusMk; NewAmDM; NewEOp 71; NewGrDM 80; NewGrDO; NewOxM; OxCMus; OxDcOp; PenDiMP; WebBD 83*

Kreutzmann, Bill
[The Grateful Dead; Bill Sommers]
American. Musician
Drummer with psychedelic band, formed 1965.
b. Jun 7, 1946 in Palo Alto, California
Source: *BioIn 15; WhoRocM 82*

Kreymborg, Alfred
American. Dramatist, Poet
Experimental poet; first collection, *Mushrooms,* 1916; wrote autobiography, *Troubadour,* 1925.
b. Dec 10, 1883 in New York, New York
d. Aug 14, 1966 in Milford, Connecticut
Source: *AmAu&B; ASCAP 66, 80; BenetAL 91; BioIn 4, 7, 12, 15; ChhPo, S2; CnDAL; ConAmA; ConAmL; ConAu 25R; DcLB 4, 54; DcPup; LngCTC; ModAL; NewCBEL; NotNAT A, B; ObitOF 79; OxCAmL 65, 83, 95; OxCAmT 84; OxCTwCP; PupTheA; REnAL; ScF&FL 1; SixAP; TwCA, SUP; WhAm 4*

Krick, Irving P(arkhurst)
American. Meteorologist
Head of meteorology dept., California Institute of Technology, 1938-48; worked for Air Force Weather Research Center during World War II.
b. Dec 20, 1906
d. Jun 20, 1996 in Pasadena, California
Source: *AmMWSc 79, 82, 86, 89, 92, 95; BioIn 2; CurBio 96N; InSci; WhAm 11; WhoAm 74, 76, 78, 80, 82, 84, 86, 88, 90, 92, 94, 95, 96; WhoScEn 94, 96; WhoWest 94, 96; WhoWor 74, 76, 78, 91, 93, 95, 96*

Krickstein, Aaron
American. Tennis Player
Youngest player to advance in US Open, 1983.
b. Aug 2, 1967 in Detroit, Michigan
Source: *BioIn 13, 14; NewYTBS 83; WhoAm 95, 96, 97; WhoE 95*

Krieger, Robby
[The Doors]
American. Musician
Guitarist with group, 1965-73, known for jazz innovations; had number one hit "Light My Fire," 1966.
b. Jan 8, 1946 in Los Angeles, California
Source: *LegTOT*

Krieghoff, Cornelius
German. Artist
Painted Indians, French Canadian life, landscapes in Canada, 1840-66.
b. 1815 in Amsterdam, Netherlands
d. Mar 9, 1872 in Chicago, Illinois
Source: *DcBrBI; DcCanB 10; IlBEAAW; MacDCB 78; McGDA; OxCArt; OxDcArt*

Kriek, Johann
American. Tennis Player
Won Australian Open, 1981, 1982.
b. Apr 5, 1958 in Ponogola, South Africa
Source: *BioIn 13; WhoIntT*

Krige, Alice
South African. Actor
In TV mini-series "Ellis Island," 1984; "Dream West," 1986; in film *Chariots of Fire,* 1983.
b. Jun 28, 1954 in Upington, South Africa
Source: *BioIn 14; ConTFT 7; HalFC 88; IntMPA 92, 94, 96; VarWW 85; WhoHol 92*

Krikalev, Sergei
"Space Victim"; "The Man Who Is Sick of Flying"
Russian. Cosmonaut
Cosmonaut who became stranded up in a space station 310 days due to budget problems on the ground, returned to a non-existent Soviet Union, Mar. 15, 1992.
b. 1958? in Leningrad, Union of Soviet Socialist Republics

Krim, Mathilde Galland
Italian. Geneticist, Philanthropist
Founded AIDS Medical Foundation, 1983; merged to become American Foundation for AIDS Research, co-chm., 1985—; leader in interferon research for cancer cure, 1975-85.
b. Jul 9, 1926 in Como, Italy
Source: *AmMWSc 86, 92; BioIn 12, 14, 15, 16; CelR 90; CurBio 87; News 89-2; NewYTBS 84*

Krips, Josef
Austrian. Conductor
Led San Francisco Orchestra, 1963-70; Buffalo Symphony, 1954-63.
b. Apr 8, 1902 in Vienna, Austria
d. Oct 12, 1974 in Geneva, Switzerland
Source: *Baker 78, 84, 92; BioIn 1, 2, 4, 6, 7, 10, 11; BioNews 75; BriBkM 80; CmCal; CmOp; CurBio 65, 74, 74N; FacFETw; IntDcOp; IntWW 74, 82; IntWWM 77; LinLib S; MetOEnc; MusSN; NewAmDM; NewEOp 71;*

NewGrDA 86; NewGrDM 80; NewGrDO; NewYTBS 74; ObitT 1971; OxDcOp; PenDiMP; Who 74; WhoMus 72; WhoWor 74

Krishna Menon, V(engalil) K(rishnan)
Indian. Government Official
Active in India's nationalist movement; held several diplomatic posts under Nehru including UN delegation chm., 1953-62; defense minister, 1957-62.
b. May 3, 1897 in Kozhikode, India
d. Oct 6, 1974
Source: *BioIn 3, 4, 5, 6; CurBio 53, 74, 74N; DcPol; IntWW 74; WhAm 6; Who 74; WhoWor 74*

Krishnamurti, Jiddu
Indian. Author, Philosopher
Advocate of self-knowledge; wrote books on subject: *The Future of Humanity,* 1986.
b. May 22, 1895 in Madanapelle, India
d. Feb 17, 1986 in Ojai, California
Source: *AnObit 1984, 1986; BioIn 2, 8, 9, 10, 11, 14, 15, 17, 18; ConAu 11NR, 39NR, 61, 118; CurBio 74, 86, 86N; DcLEL; DivFut; EncO&P 1, 2, 2S1, 3; FacFETw; LegTOT; McGEWB; NewYTBS 86; PopDcHi; PseudN 82; RAdv 14; RelLAm 91; WhAm 9; WhLit; Who 83, 85; WhoAm 74, 76, 78, 80, 82, 84*

Kriss Kross
[Chris Kelly; Chris Smith]
"Daddy Mack"; "Mack Daddy of Kriss Kross"
American. Rap Group
Hit songs include "Jump"; "Warm It Up;" known for kross-dresing: over-sized jeans and team shirts worn backward.
Source: *BioIn 17; FolkA 87; NewYTBS 92; WhoAfA 96; WhoAmP 83, 85; WhoBlA 94; WomPO 76, 78*

Kristel, Sylvia
Dutch. Actor
Star of erotic French film *Emmanuelle,* 1974.
b. Sep 28, 1952 in Utrecht, Netherlands
Source: *BioIn 10, 13; ConTFT 8; FilmAG WE; FilmEn; HalFC 84, 88; ItaFilm; LegTOT; NewYTBS 82; VarWW 85; WhoHol 92, A*

Kristeva, Julia
French. Author
Wrote *About Chinese Women,* 1974 (*Des chinoises*); *Black Sun,* 1987 (*Soleil noir*).
b. Jun 24, 1941 in Silven, Bulgaria
Source: *Benet 96; BiDNeoM; BioIn 14, 15, 17, 20; BlmGWL; ClDMEL 80; ConAu 154; ConLC 77; ContDcW 89; DcTwCCu 2; EncWL 3; FemiCLE; FemiWr; FrenWW; IntDcWB; OxCPhil; ThTwC 87; WhoWor 95; WorAu 1980*

Kristiansen, Kjeld Kirk
Danish. Business Executive
Pres., Interlego A/S, 1979—, a toy co. manufacturing the Lego brick.
b. 1948?, Denmark
Source: *News 88, 88-3*

Kristofferson, Kris
[Kris Carson]
American. Actor, Singer, Songwriter
Associated with progressive Nashville sound of late 60s; wrote song "Help Me Make It Through the Night"; films include *A Star Is Born,* 1976; *Heaven's Gate,* 1980.
b. Jun 22, 1936 in Brownsville, Texas
Source: *AmSong; Baker 84, 92; BgBkCoM; BioIn 12, 13, 14, 15; BioNews 74; BkPepl; CelR, 90; ConAu 104; ConLC 26; ConMus 4; ConTFT 5, 14; CounME 74, 74A; CurBio 74; EncFCWM 83; EncPR&S 89; EncRk 88; EncRkSt; FilmEn; HalFC 80, 84, 88; HarEnCM 87; HarEnR 86; IlEncCM; IlEncRk; IntMPA 84, 86, 88, 92, 94, 96; IntWW 89, 91, 93; LegTOT; MovMk; NewGrDA 86; OxCPMus; PenEncP; PseudN 82; RkOn 78; VarWW 85; WhoAm 76, 78, 80, 82, 84, 86, 88, 90, 92, 94, 95, 96, 97; WhoEnt 92; WhoHol 92, A; WhoNeCM A; WhoRock 81; WhoRocM 82; WorAl; WorAlBi*

Kristol, Irving
American. Editor
Founder, co-editor, *Public Interest,* mag., 1965—.
b. Jan 22, 1920 in New York, New York
Source: *BioIn 10, 11, 12, 13, 15; ConAu 25R, 28NR; CurBio 74; DcAmC; EncAJ; NewYTBS 81; WhoAm 82, 84, 88, 90, 92, 94, 95, 96, 97; WhoE 75, 97; WrDr 86, 88, 90, 92, 94, 96*

Kristol, William
American. Editor, Publisher
Editor and publisher of the conservative magazine *The Weekly Standard,* 1995—; chief of staff to vice president Dan Quayle.
b. Dec 23, 1952 in New York, New York
Source: *NewYTBS 92; WhoAm 92, 94, 95, 96, 97*

Kroc, Ray(mond) Albert
American. Restaurateur, Baseball Executive
Purchased original McDonald's, founded McDonald's Corp., 1955; owner, San Diego Padres, 1974-84.
b. Oct 5, 1902 in Chicago, Illinois
d. Jan 14, 1984 in San Diego, California
Source: *AnObit 1984; BioIn 9, 10, 11, 12, 13; BioNews 74; BusPN; ConAu 111; ConNews 85-1; CurBio 73, 84; EncAB-H 1996; EncWB; NewYTBS 74, 84; WhoAm 82*

Krock, Arthur Bernard
American. Journalist
Editorial commentator, *NY Times,* 1953-67; won four Pulitzers; wrote several books: *The Consent of the Governed and Other Deceits,* 1971.
b. Nov 16, 1886 in Glasgow, Kentucky
d. Apr 12, 1974 in Washington, District of Columbia
Source: *AmAu&B; AuNews 1; ConAu 49, P-2; CurBio 43, 74; EncAB-H 1974; WhAm 6; WhNAA; WhoAm 74; WhoWor 74*

Kroeber, Alfred Louis
American. Anthropologist, Author
Studied North, South American Indian cultures; wrote *Anthropology,* 1923.
b. Jun 11, 1876 in Hoboken, New Jersey
d. Oct 5, 1960 in Paris, France
Source: *AmAu&B; BioIn 5, 6, 7, 9, 14; DcAmB S6; DcSoc; InSci; McGEWB; NatCAB 49; REnAW; WebAB 74, 79; WebBD 83; WhAm 4*

Kroeber, Theodora Kracaw
[Theodora Kroeber-Quinn; Mrs. John Quinn]
American. Author, Anthropologist
Writings include *Ishi in Two Worlds,* 1961; mother of author Ursula LeGuin.
b. Mar 24, 1897 in Denver, Colorado
d. Jul 4, 1979 in Berkeley, California
Source: *AmAu&B; ConAu 5NR, 5R, 89; ForWC 70; PseudN 82; SmATA 1; WhoAmW 64; WrDr 76*

Krofft, Marty
American. Puppeteer, Producer
With brother, Sid, created various puppet, cartoon TV shows including "H R Pufnstuf," 1970s.
Source: *LesBEnT, 92; NewYTET; VarWW 85*

Krofft, Sid
American. Puppeteer, Producer
With brother, Marty, created various puppet, cartoon TV shows.
b. Jul 30, 1929 in Athens, Greece
Source: *ASCAP 80; LesBEnT, 92; NewYTET; PupTheA; VarWW 85*

Kroft, Steve
American. Broadcast Journalist
Correspondent on TV's "60 Minutes," 1989—.
b. Aug 22, 1945 in Kokomo, Indiana
Source: *BioIn 16; CurBio 96; WhoAm 94, 95, 96, 97; WhoE 95*

Kroger, Bernard Henry
American. Businessman
Founded Kroger grocery store chain, 1884.
b. Jan 24, 1860 in Cincinnati, Ohio
d. Jul 21, 1938 in Wianno, Massachusetts
Source: *BiDAmBL 83; BioIn 4; DcAmB S2; NatCAB 32; WhAm 1; WorAl*

Krogh, Egil, Jr.
''Bud''
American. Government Official
Asst. to John Erhichman, 1969-74; tried, convicted of burglary of Daniel Ellsberg's psychiatrist, 1971, receiving five-yr. sentence for conspiracy.
b. Aug 3, 1939 in Chicago, Illinois
Source: *BioIn 9, 10, 12; NewYTBS 74; PolProf NF*

Krogh, Schack August Steenberg
Danish. Scientist, Educator
Won 1920 Nobel Prize in medicine for pioneering the field of capillary control.
b. Nov 15, 1874 in Grenaa, Denmark
d. Sep 13, 1949 in Copenhagen, Denmark
Source: *BiESc; DcScB; McGEWB; NewCol 75; OxCMed 86; WhDW; WhoNob, 90, 95*

Kroker, Arthur
Canadian. Writer
Wrote *Technology and the Canadian Mind,* 1984, an examiniation of technology on the human condition.
b. 1945 in Red Rock, Ontario, Canada
Source: *ConLC 77*

Krol, John (Joseph), Cardinal
American. Religious Leader
Archbishop of Philadelphia, 1961-88; influential in the election of Pope John Paul II.
b. Oct 26, 1910 in Cleveland, Ohio
d. Mar 3, 1996 in Philadelphia, Pennsylvania
Source: *AmCath 80; BioIn 7, 8, 9, 10, 11, 14, 21; BlueB 76; CurBio 69, 96N; IntWW 74, 75, 76, 77, 78, 79, 80, 81, 82, 83, 89, 91, 93; News 96, 96-3; NewYTBE 71; NewYTBS 27; RelLAm 91; WhAm 11; WhoAm 74, 78, 80, 82, 84, 86, 88, 90, 95, 96; WhoE 74, 75, 79, 81, 83, 85, 86, 89, 91, 95; WhoPoA 96; WhoRel 75, 77, 85, 92; WhoWor 74, 82, 84, 87, 89, 91, 95, 96*

Kroll, Alexander S
American. Advertising Executive
CEO and chm., Young and Rubicam, Inc., 1982—, one of the largest advertising agencies in the US.
b. Nov 23, 1937 in Leechburg, Pennsylvania
Source: *BioIn 13, 16; Dun&B 90; IntWW 91; News 89-3; WhoAdv 90; WhoAm 90; WhoE 91; WhoFI 85*

Kroll, Leon
American. Artist
Landscape, portrait painter, known for his nudes; created mosaic dome at US Military Cemetery, Omaha Beach, France.
b. Dec 6, 1884 in New York, New York
d. Oct 25, 1974 in Gloucester, Massachusetts
Source: *ArtsAmW 1; BioIn 1, 4, 8, 10, 17; BriEAA; CurBio 43, 74, 74N; DcAmArt; DcCAA 71; IlBEAAW; IntWW 74; McGDA; NewYTBS 74; OxCTwCA; PhDcTCA 77; WhAm 6; WhAmArt 85; WhoAm 74; WhoAmA 73, 76N, 78N, 80N, 82N, 84N, 86N, 89N, 91N, 93N*

Kronberger, Petra
Austrian. Skier
Slalom skier who won 2 gold medals in the 1992 Olympics.
b. 1970?, Austria

Krone, Julie
American. Jockey
Top female jockey; was the first woman to ever compete in the Breeder's Cup races; has won over 1,600 races.
b. Jul 24, 1963 in Benton Harbor, Michigan
Source: *BioIn 15, 16; CurBio 89; EncWomS; LegTOT; News 89-2; NewYTBS 87; WhoAm 94, 95, 96, 97; WhoAmW 91, 93, 95, 97; WhoSpor; WhoWor 95, 96, 97*

Kronenberger, Louis
American. Author, Critic
Drama critic, *Time,* 1938-61; theater arts professor, Brandeis U, 1953-70; author of many novels: *The Grand Manner,* 1929.
b. Dec 9, 1904 in Cincinnati, Ohio
d. Apr 30, 1980 in Wellesley, Massachusetts
Source: *AmAu&B; AnObit 1980; Au&Wr 71; BenetAL 91; BiE&WWA; BioIn 2, 3, 4, 5, 9, 12; ChhPo; ConAu 1R, 2NR, 97; CurBio 44, 80, 80N; DcAmB S10; DrAS 74E, 78E; EncAJ; LinLib L, S; NewYTBS 80; NotNAT; OhA&B; OxCAmL 65, 83; OxCAmT 84; REnAL; TwCA SUP; WhAm 7; WhE&EA; WhoAm 74, 76, 78, 80; WhoThe 72, 77; WhoWor 74; WhoWorJ 72; WrDr 76, 80*

Kronhausen, Eberhard Wilhelm
German. Psychologist
In private practice with wife, Phyllis, since 1953; most writings deal with sexual themes: *Pornography and the Law,* 1964.
b. Sep 12, 1915 in Berlin, Germany
Source: *ConAu 6NR, 9R*

Kronhausen, Phyllis Carmen
[Mrs. Eberhard Kronhausen]
American. Psychologist
In private practice with husband since 1953; most writings deal with sexual themes, erotic art: *Sex Histories of American College Men,* 1960.
b. Jan 26, 1929 in Minnesota
Source: *ConAu 6NR, 9R*

Kronold, Selma
Polish. Opera Singer
Soprano; sang lead in American premiere of *Cavalleria Rusticana,* 1891; founded Catholic Oratorio Society.
b. 1866 in Krakow, Poland
d. Oct 9, 1920 in New York, New York
Source: *Baker 84; BiDAmM; InWom; NewEOp 71; NotAW*

Kronos Quartet, The
[Hank Dutt; David Harrington; Joan Dutcher Jeanrenaud]
American. Music Group
String quartet formed 1973; known for repertoire of works by twentieth-century composers.
Source: *AllMusG; BioIn 16; ConMus 5; NewGrDA 86; News 93-1; PenDiMP; PenEncP*

Kronstam, Henning
Danish. Dancer, Director
Director, Royal Danish Ballet, 1978-84.
b. Jun 29, 1934 in Copenhagen, Denmark
d. May 28, 1995 in Copenhagen, Denmark
Source: *BiDD; BioIn 4, 20, 21; CnOxB; DancEn 78; IntDcB; WhoWor 84*

Kropotkin, Peter Alekseyevich, Prince
Russian. Ruler
Benevolent anarchist who urged brotherhood, cooperation as way of life.
b. Dec 21, 1842 in Moscow, Russia
d. Feb 8, 1921 in Dmitrov, Union of Soviet Socialist Republics
Source: *BiD&SB; CasWL; ClDMEL 47; ConAu 119; EuAu; IntWW 80; WhDW; WorAl*

KRS-One
[Boogie Down Productions; Lawrence Parker]
American. Rapper, Producer
Reform-oriented rap artist; albums include *Criminal Minded,* 1986 and *Sex and Violence,* 1992.
b. 1965 in New York, New York
Source: *BioIn 16; ConMus 8*

Kruger, Barbara
American. Artist
Creator of black-and-white photomontages.
b. Jan 26, 1945 in Newark, New Jersey
Source: *AmDec 1980; BiDWomA; BioIn 13; ConArt 89, 96; CurBio 95; DcTwCCu 1; NorAmWA; WhoAm 97; WhoAmA 76, 78, 80, 82, 84, 86, 89, 91, 93; WorArt 1980*

Kruger, Hardy
[Eberhard Kruger]
German. Actor
Films include *The One That Got Away 1957; Wild Geese,* 1978.
b. Apr 12, 1928 in Berlin, Germany
Source: *EncEurC; FilmAG WE; FilmEn; FilmgC; ForYSC; HalFC 80, 84, 88; IntAu&W 89; IntMPA 75, 76, 77, 78, 79, 80, 81, 82, 84, 86, 88, 92, 94, 96; IntWW 89, 91, 93; ItaFilm; LegTOT; VarWW 85; WhoHol 92, A; WhoWor 74, 76*

Kruger, Otto
American. Actor
Broadway matinee idol, 1920s; film lead in *Dr. Ehrlich's Magic Bullet,* 1940.
b. Sep 6, 1885 in Toledo, Ohio
d. Sep 6, 1974 in Woodland Hills, California
Source: *BiE&WWA; BioIn 4, 9, 10, 12, 17, 21; EncAFC; Film 2; FilmEn; FilmgC; ForYSC; GangFlm; HalFC 80, 84, 88; HolCA; LegTOT; MotPP; MovMk; NatCAB 59; NewYTBS 74; NotNAT B; ObitOF 79; OlFamFa; OxCAmT 84; PlP&P; Vers A; WhAm 6; What 3; WhoHol B; WhoHrs 80; WhScrn 74, 77, 83; WhThe; WorAl*

Kruger, Paul
[Stephanus Johannes Paulus Kruger]
"Oom Paul"
South African. Political Leader
Political, military leader of Transvaal Republic; pres., 1883-1902.
b. Oct 10, 1825 in Colesberg, South Africa
d. Jul 14, 1904 in Clarens, Switzerland
Source: *BioIn 1, 3, 6, 8, 9, 10, 11, 14, 16, 17, 20, 21; DcAfHiB 86; Dis&D; EncSoA; HisDBrE; HisWorL; LinLib L, S; McGEWB; NewCol 75; WhDW; WhoMilH 76; WorAl; WorAlBi*

Kruk, John
American. Baseball Player
Outfielder and first baseman, San Diego Padres, 1986-89; first baseman, Philadelphia Phillies, 1989—.
b. Feb 9, 1961 in Charleston, West Virginia
Source: *Ballpl 90; LegTOT; News 94*

Krumgold, Joseph (Quincy)
American. Author
Won Newberys for *And Now Miguel,* 1953; *Onion John,* 1960.
b. Apr 9, 1908 in Jersey City, New Jersey
d. Jul 10, 1980 in Hope, New Jersey
Source: *AnObit 1980; AuBYP 2, 3; BioIn 12, 13, 14, 16, 19; ChlBkCr; ConAu 7NR, 9R, 101; ConLC 12; DcAmChF 1960; EncMys; LinLib L; MajAI; MorJA; NewbC 1956; NewbMB 1922; OxCChiL; SmATA 1, 23N, 48; TwCChW 78, 83, 89; TwCYAW; VarWW 85; WhAm 7; WrDr 80*

Krupa, Gene
American. Bandleader, Musician
Legendary jazz drummer; noted for virtuoso solos with Benny Goodman, 1934-38; led own band, 1940s.
b. Jan 15, 1909 in Chicago, Illinois
d. Oct 16, 1973 in Yonkers, New York
Source: *AllMusG; Baker 78, 84, 92; BgBands 74; BiDAmM; BiDJaz; BioIn 1, 2, 9, 10, 12, 15, 16; CmpEPM; ConMus 13; CurBio 47, 73, 73N; EncJzS; FacFETw; IlEncJ; LegTOT; MusMk; NewAmDM; NewGrDA 86; NewGrDJ 88, 94; NewGrDM 80; NewYTBE 73; OxCPMus; PenEncP; WhAm 6; WhoE 74; WhoHol B; WhoJazz 72; WhoMus 72; WhoPolA; WhScrn 77, 83; WorAl; WorAlBi*

Krupp, Alfred
"The Cannon King"
German. Industrialist
Famous for four-ton steel ingot and first steel cannon, 1851.
b. Apr 26, 1812 in Essen, Germany
d. Jul 14, 1887 in Essen, Germany
Source: *InSci; LegTOT; LinLib S; NewCol 75; WhDW; WorAl; WorAlBi*

Krupp von Bohlen und Halbach, Bertha
"Big Bertha"
German.
Cannon produced by Krupp Manufacturing during WW II named for her; daughter of Friedrich Krupp.
b. Mar 29, 1886 in Essen, Germany
d. Sep 21, 1957 in Essen, Germany (West)
Source: *BioIn 4; NewCol 75; ObitOF 79*

Krupskaya, Nadezhda Konstantinovna
Russian. Political Activist
Marxist revolutionary; helped found Bolsheviks; wife of Lenin.
b. Feb 26, 1869 in Saint Petersburg, Russia
d. Feb 27, 1939 in Moscow, Union of Soviet Socialist Republics
Source: *BioIn 9, 10, 12, 15, 16; BlkwERR; EncRev; FacFETw; InWom, SUP; WorAlBi*

Krutch, Joseph Wood
American. Critic
With *The Nation,* 1924-51; varied works include *The Measure of Man,* 1955.
b. Nov 25, 1893 in Knoxville, Tennessee
d. May 22, 1970 in Tucson, Arizona
Source: *AmAu&B; Au&Wr 71; Benet 87, 96; BenetAL 91; BiE&WWA; BioIn 1, 3, 4, 5, 6, 8, 9, 12, 14, 15, 16, 21; CnDAL; ConAmA; ConAmL; ConAu 1R, 4NR, 25R; ConLC 24; CurBio 59, 70; DcAmB S8; DcLB 63; DcLEL; EncAAH; EncWT; EnvEnc; EvLB; FacFETw; InSci; LinLib L; NotNAT B; OxCAmL 65, 83, 95; OxCAmT 84; OxCThe 67; PenC AM; PeoHis; RAdv 14, 13-5; REn; REnAL; ScF&FL 92; TwCA, SUP; WebAB 74, 79; WhAm 5; WhJnl; WhNAA; WhThe*

Krylov, Ivan Andreyevich
Russian. Author
His fables, published in collections beginning 1809, are classics in Russian literature.
b. Feb 14, 1768 in Moscow, Russia
d. Nov 21, 1844 in Saint Petersburg, Russia
Source: *BiD&SB; CasWL; ChhPo S1; DcEuL; DcRusL; EuAu; EvEuW; LinLib L; NewCBEL; OxCEng 85; PenC EUR; REn*

Krzyzewski, Mike
American. Basketball Coach
Duke U. coach, 1980—; teams won NCAA tournament, 1991, 1992.
b. Feb 13, 1947 in Chicago, Illinois
Source: *BioIn 19, 21; News 93-2; NewYTBS 86; WhoSpor*

Kubasov, Valery Nikolaevich
Russian. Cosmonaut
Aboard *Soyuz 6,* 1969; with *Soyuz 7, 8,* first time three spacecraft orbited earth at once.
b. Jan 7, 1935, Union of Soviet Socialist Republics
Source: *BioIn 15; IntWW 74, 75, 76; NewYTBS 75; WhoSpc; WhoWor 74*

Kubek, Tony
[Anthony Christopher Kubek]
American. Baseball Player, Sportscaster
Shortstop, NY Yankees, 1957-65; broadcaster NBC, 1966—; CTV, 1981—.
b. Oct 12, 1935 in Milwaukee, Wisconsin
Source: *Ballpl 90; BiDAmSp Sup; BioIn 4, 6, 14, 15; WhoAm 80, 82, 84, 86, 88, 90, 92, 94, 95, 96, 97; WhoE 95; WhoProB 73; WorAlBi*

Kubelik, Jan
Hungarian. Violinist
Int'l noted virtuoso; regarded as Paderewski's counterpart; active until WW I.
b. Jul 5, 1880 in Michle, Czechoslovakia
d. Dec 5, 1940 in Prague, Czechoslovakia
Source: *Baker 78, 84, 92; BioIn 2, 4, 11, 14; BriBkM 80; CurBio 41; DcArts; Dis&D; FacFETw; MusSN; NewGrDM 80; OxCMus; PenDiMP; WhAm 1*

Kubelik, Rafael (Jeronym)
Swiss. Conductor, Composer
Controversial conductor of Chicago Symphony, London's Covent Garden Opera, 1950s; music director, NY Met., 1973-74; son of Jan.
b. Jun 29, 1914 in Bychory, Austria-Hungary
d. Aug 4, 1996 in Lucerne, Switzerland
Source: *Baker 78, 84, 92; BiDAmM; BioIn 2, 4, 8, 9, 10, 11; BlueB 76; BriBkM 80; CmOp; CurBio 51, 96N; DcArts; FacFETw; IntDcOp; IntWW 74, 75, 76, 77, 78, 79, 80, 81, 82, 83, 89, 91, 93; IntWWM 77, 80, 90; MetOEnc; MusMk; MusSN; NewAmDM; NewEOp 71; NewGrDA 86; NewGrDM 80; NewGrDO; NewYTBE 71; NewYTBS 27; OxDcOp; PenDiMP; Who 74, 82, 83, 88, 90, 92, 94; WhoMus 72; WhoOp 76; WhoWor 74, 78, 89; WorAl; WorAlBi*

Kubitschek (de Oliveira), Juscelino
Brazilian. Political Leader
Pres. of Brazil, 1956-61; administration known for economic achievements including construction of new capital, Brasilia, 1957.

b. Sep 12, 1902 in Diamantina, Brazil
d. Aug 22, 1976 in Rio de Janeiro, Brazil
Source: *BiDLAmC; BioIn 4, 5, 6, 7, 9, 11, 16, 18, 20; CurBio 56, 76, 76N; DcCPSAm; DcTwHis; EncLatA; IntWW 74; McGEWB; NewYTBS 76; WhAm 7*

Kublai Khan
Mongolian. Ruler
Founded Mongol, Yuan dynasties in China; grandson of Genghis Khan; subject of poem by S T Coleridge.
b. 1216
d. 1294
Source: *Benet 87, 96; BioIn 1, 2, 3, 4, 6, 7, 8, 9, 10, 11, 13, 15, 16, 17, 20; DcBiPP; NewC; NewCol 75; REn; WebBD 83; WhDW; WorAl; WorAlBi*

Kubler-Ross, Elisabeth
American. Psychiatrist, Author
Pioneered the advancement of thanotology, the study of death; wrote best-seller *On Death and Dying,* 1969.
b. Jul 8, 1926 in Zurich, Switzerland
Source: *AmDec 1970; AmMWSc 95; AmWomWr; BenetAL 91; BioIn 12, 13, 14, 15, 16; CelR 90; ConAu 25R; ConIsC 2; CurBio 80; EncO&P 3; EncPaPR 91; GrLiveH; InWom SUP; LegTOT; WhoAm 82, 84, 86, 88, 90, 92, 94, 95, 96, 97; WhoAmW 89, 91, 93, 95, 97; WhoMedH; WhoScEn 94, 96; WhoUSWr 88; WhoWrEP 89, 92, 95; WorAl; WorAlBi; WrDr 86, 88, 90, 92, 94, 96*

Kubly, Herbert (Oswald)
American. Writer
Won National Book Award for *American in Italy,* 1955.
b. Apr 26, 1915 in New Glarus, Wisconsin
d. Aug 7, 1996 in New Glarus, Wisconsin
Source: *AmAu&B; Au&Wr 71; BioIn 5; ConAu 4NR, 5R; CurBio 96N; DrAPF 80; DrAS 74E, 78E, 82E; IntAu&W 76; REnAL; WhoAm 74, 76, 78, 80, 82, 84, 86, 88, 90, 92, 94, 95, 96, 97; WhoUSWr 88; WhoWrEP 89, 92, 95; WrDr 76, 80, 82, 84, 86, 88, 90, 92, 94, 96*

Kubrick, Stanley
American. Director
Films include *2001: A Space Odyssey,* 1968; *A Clockwork Orange,* 1971.
b. Jul 26, 1928 in New York, New York
Source: *AmDec 1960; AmFD; Benet 87, 96; BiDFilm, 81, 94; BioIn 4, 5, 6, 7, 9, 10, 11, 12, 13, 14, 15, 16; BkPepl; BlueB 76; CelR, 90; ConAu 33NR, 81; ConDr 73, 77A, 88A; ConLC 16; ConTFT 1, 7; CurBio 63; DcArts; DcFM; DcLB 26; DcTwCCu 1; EncEurC; EncSF, 93; FacFETw; FilmEn; FilmgC; GangFlm; HalFC 80, 84, 88; IlWWHD 1; IntAu&W 76, 77, 89, 91, 93; IntDcF 1-2, 2-2; IntMPA 75, 76, 77, 78, 79, 80, 81, 82, 84, 86, 88, 92, 94, 96; IntWW 74, 75, 76, 77, 78, 79, 80, 81, 82, 83, 89, 91, 93; LegTOT; MiSFD 9; MovMk; NewEScF; OxCFilm; RAdv 14, 13-3; VarWW 85; WebAB 74, 79; Who 74, 82, 83, 85, 88, 90, 92, 94; WhoAm 74, 76, 78, 80, 82, 84, 86, 88, 90, 92, 94, 95, 96, 97; WhoAmJ 80; WhoEnt 92; WhoHrs 80; WhoSciF; WhoWor 74, 76, 78, 80, 82, 84, 87, 89, 91, 93, 95; WhoWorJ 78; WomWMM; WorAl; WorAlBi; WorEFlm; WorFDir 2; WrDr 80, 82, 84, 86, 88, 90, 92, 94, 96*

Kuchel, Thomas H(enry)
American. Politician
Rep. Senator from CA, 1953-69.
b. Aug 15, 1910
d. Nov 21, 1994 in Beverly Hills, California
Source: *BiDrAC; BiDrUSC 89; BioIn 3, 5, 6, 7, 8, 11; BlueB 76; CmCal; CurBio 95N; WhoAm 74, 76, 78, 80, 82, 84; WhoAmP 79, 81, 83, 85, 87, 89, 91, 93*

Kucinich, Dennis John
American. Politician
Youngest mayor in Cleveland history, 1977-80; presided over city's default; US Representative from Ohio, 1997—

b. Oct 8, 1946 in Cleveland, Ohio
Source: *BioIn 11, 12; CurBio 79; NewYTBS 78; WhoAm 80*

Kudelka, James
Canadian. Choreographer
Choreographer for The National Ballet of Canada, 1992.
b. Sep 10, 1955 in Newmarket, Ontario, Canada
Source: *BioIn 11; CurBio 95; IntDcB*

Kudrow, Lisa
American. Actor
Plays Phoebe Buffay on TV's "Friends," 1994—.
b. Jul 30, 1963 in Encino, California
Source: *ConTFT 15; News 96, 96-1*

Kuehl, Sheila James
American. Politician, Actor
Appeared in films *Seven Brides for Seven Brothers,* 1954; *Teenage Rebel,* 1956; member of the California State Assemble, 1995—.
b. Feb 9, 1941 in Tulsa, Oklahoma
Source: *GayLesB; WhoAmL 96; WhoAmP 95; WhoEnt 92*

Kuekes, Edward Daniel
American. Artist, Cartoonist
Won Pulitzer for cartoon of irony of soldiers too young to vote fighting in Korea, 1953.
b. Feb 2, 1901 in Pittsburgh, Pennsylvania
d. Jan 13, 1987 in Oklahoma City, Oklahoma
Source: *BioIn 3; CurBio 54, 87; WhAm 9; WhoAm 74, 76, 78, 80, 82, 84, 86; WhoAmA 84*

Kuenn, Harvey Edward
American. Baseball Player
Outfielder-infielder, 1952-66; led AL in batting, 1959; had .303 lifetime batting average.
b. Dec 4, 1930 in Milwaukee, Wisconsin
d. Feb 28, 1988 in Peoria, Arizona
Source: *BaseEn 88; BiDAmSp BB; BioIn 3, 4, 5, 8, 13; NewYTBS 82; WhoProB 73*

Kuerti, Anton
Austrian. Pianist
Concert performer; founded Parry Sound; Festival of Sound.
b. Jul 21, 1938 in Vienna, Austria
Source: *Baker 84; BioIn 11, 12, 15; CanWW 31, 89; IntWWM 85, 90; NewAmDM; NewGrDA 86; WhoAm 86, 90; WhoEnt 92*

Kuhlman, Kathryn
American. Evangelist
Faith healer said to produce spontaneous cures; wrote inspirational boook *I Believe in Miracles,* 1962.
b. May 9, 1907 in Concordia, Missouri
d. Feb 20, 1976 in Tulsa, Oklahoma
Source: *BiDAmCu; BioIn 17, 19; ConAu 12NR, 57, 65; CurBio 74, 76; DcAmB S10; DcAmReB 2; EncO&P 3; EncPaPR 91; GoodHs; InWom SUP; NewYTBE 72; ObitOF 79; PrimTiR; RelLAm 91; TwCSAPR; WhAm 6, 7; WhoRel 75; WorAl; WrDr 76*

Kuhn, Bowie Kent
American. Baseball Executive
Lawyer; baseball commissioner, 1969-84, succeeded by Peter Ueberroth.
b. Oct 28, 1926 in Takoma Park, Maryland
Source: *Ballpl 90; BiDAmSp BB; BioIn 8, 9, 10, 11, 13, 15; BioNews 74; ConAu 126; CurBio 70; St&PR 87; WhoAm 86, 90; WhoE 74, 83; WhoProB 73*

Kuhn, Irene
American. Journalist
Syndicated columnist; worked for the New York *Daily News,* among others.
b. Jan 15, 1900
d. Dec 30, 1995 in Concord, Massachusetts
Source: *BioIn 1, 8, 10, 12; CurBio 96N*

Kuhn, Maggie
[Margaret E. Kuhn]
American. Social Reformer
Founded Gray Panthers, 1971.
b. Aug 3, 1905 in Buffalo, New York
d. Apr 22, 1995 in Philadelphia, Pennsylvania
Source: *AmDec 1980; BioIn 11, 13, 15, 16, 19, 20, 21; ConAu 148; ConHero 2; CurBio 78, 95N; GoodHs; InWom SUP; LegTOT; NewYTBS 95; WhoAm 86, 90; WhoAmW 87, 91; WomFir; WorAlBi*

Kuhn, Richard
German. Chemist
Won Nobel Prize, 1938, for research on carotinoids and vitamins.
b. Dec 3, 1900 in Vienna, Austria
d. Aug 1, 1967 in Heidelberg, Germany (West)
Source: *AsBiEn; BiESc; BioIn 3, 6, 8, 14, 15, 19, 20; DcScB; InSci; LarDcSc; NobelP; NotTwCS; WhoNob, 90, 95; WorScD*

Kuhn, Walt
American. Artist
Helped stage NYC's Armory Show, 1913; noted for paintings of clowns, acrobats, landscapes.
b. Oct 27, 1880 in New York, New York
d. Jul 13, 1949 in White Plains, New York
Source: *ArtsAmW 1; Benet 87; BriEAA; DcAmB S4; DcCAA 71; IlBEAAW; McGDA; ObitOF 79; OxCTwCA; PhDcTCA 77; WhAm 2; WhAmArt 85; WhoAmA 84N, 89N, 91N, 93N*

Kuiper, Gerard Peter
American. Astronomer
Founded, directed, U of AZ's Lunar Laboratory, 1960-73; first to measure mass of Pluto; discovered new satellites of Uranus, Neptune.
b. Dec 7, 1905 in Harenkarspel, Netherlands
d. Dec 23, 1973 in Mexico City, Mexico
Source: *AmMWSc 73P; AsBiEn; BiESc; BioIn 5, 10, 14, 20; CamDcSc; ConAu 45, P-2; CurBio 59, 74; DcAmB S9; LarDcSc; LuthC 75; NotTwCS; ObitOF 79; WhAm 6; Who 74; WhoWor 74; WorAl*

Kukoc, Toni
Croatian. Basketball Player
With Chicago Bulls, 1993—.
b. Sep 18, 1968 in Split, Yugoslavia
Source: *News 95*

Kulish, Mykola
Ukrainian. Dramatist
Best known for controversial tragedy, *97,* 1924.
b. 1892 in Kherson, Russia
d. 1942 in Siberia, Union of Soviet Socialist Republics
Source: *ClDMEL 80; DcRusL; ModSL 2; PenC EUR*

Kulp, Nancy Jane
American. Actor
Played Jane Hathaway on "The Beverly Hillbillies," 1962-71.
b. Aug 28, 1921 in Harrisburg, Pennsylvania
d. Feb 3, 1991 in Palm Desert, California
Source: *ConTFT 3; ForWC 70; HalFC 84, 88; News 91-3; NewYTBS 91; WhAm 10; WhoAm 74, 76, 78, 80, 82, 84, 86, 88, 90; WhoAmW 74, 89, 91; WhoHol A*

Kulwicki, Alan
American. Auto Racer
Stock car racer; won 1992 NASCAR Winston Cup.
b. 1958? in Wisconsin
d. Apr 1, 1993 in Bristol, Tennessee

Kumaratunga, Chandrika Bandaranaike
Sri Lankan. Political Leader
President, Sri Lanka, 1994—.
b. Jun 29, 1945 in Colombo, Ceylon
Source: *CurBio 96; WhoWor 96, 97*

Kume, Yutaka
Japanese. Auto Executive
President of Nissan Motor, 1985-92, chairman, 1992—.
b. May 20, 1921 in Tokyo, Japan
Source: *BioIn 15, 16; IntWW 89, 91, 93; Who 88, 90, 92, 94; WhoFI 96; WhoWor 87, 89, 95, 96, 97*

Kumin, Maxine Winokur
American. Author
Best known for pastoral poetry; won Pulitzer, 1973, for *Up Country.*
b. Jun 6, 1925 in Philadelphia, Pennsylvania
Source: *AnCL; ArtclWW 2; AuBYP 2; AuNews 2; BioIn 13, 14; CamGLE; CamHAL; ConAu 1NR, 1R, 2NR, 8AS, 21NR; ConLC 5, 13, 28; ConPo 75, 91; DrAPF 91; FemiCLE; IntvTCA 2; InWom SUP; MajTwCW; ModAWP; SmATA 12; WhoAm 86, 90, 97; WhoAmW 85, 87, 91, 97; WorAlBi; WrDr 86, 92*

Kun, Bela
Hungarian. Political Leader
Leader of Third International who tried to ignite worldwide revolution; liquidated by Stalin.
b. Feb 20, 1886 in Szilagycseh, Austria-Hungary
d. Nov 30, 1938 in Moscow, Union of Soviet Socialist Republics
Source: *BiDMarx; BiDSovU; BioIn 16, 19; DcTwHis; DicTyr; EncRev; EncTR 91; NewCol 75; WebBD 83; WhDW*

Kundera, Milan
French. Author
His books were banned in Czechoslovakia while he was in exile; wrote *The Book of Laughter and Forgetting,* 1980.
b. Apr 1, 1929 in Brno, Czechoslovakia
Source: *Au&Arts 2; Benet 87, 96; BioIn 12, 13, 14, 15, 16; CasWL; ClDMEL 80; ConAu 19NR, 52NR, 85; ConFLW 84; ConLC 4, 9, 19, 32, 68; ConWorW 93; CurBio 83; CyWA 89; DcArts; EncWL 2, 3; EuWr 13; FacFETw; IntAu&W 76, 77, 86, 89, 91, 93; IntDcT 2; IntWW 74, 75, 76, 77, 78, 79, 80, 81, 82, 83, 89, 91, 93; IntWWP 77; LegTOT; LiExTwC; MagSWL; MajTwCW; McGEWD 84; ModSL 2; NewYTBS 82, 85; OxCEng 85, 95; PenC EUR; PostFic; RAdv 14, 13-2; RfGShF; WhoAm 94, 95, 96, 97; WhoFr 79; WhoSocC 78; WhoSoCE 89; WhoWor 84, 87, 89, 91, 93, 95, 96, 97; WorAu 1970*

Kundla, John
American. Basketball Coach
Coach, Minneapolis, 1948-59; won four NBA championships.
b. Jul 3, 1916 in Star Junction, Pennsylvania
Source: *BasBi; BiDAmSp BK; OfNBA 87; WhoBbl 73*

Kunene, Mazisi (Raymond)
[Mazisi kaMdabuli Kunene]
South African. Poet
Advances traditional Zulu style in his poetry; wrote *Zulu Poems,* 1979.
b. May 12, 1930 in Durban, South Africa
Source: *AfrA; BioIn 9, 14; BlkWr 1; CamGLE; ConAu 125; ConLC 85; IntvTCA 2; IntWWP 77; LiExTwC; ModBlW; OxCTwCP; RAdv 14; SelBAAf*

Kung, Hans
[Hans Kueng]
Swiss. Religious Leader, Theologian
Roman Catholic priest; named official theologian of Second Vatican Council, 1962; wrote *The Council, Reform, and Reunion,* 1962.
b. Mar 19, 1928 in Sursee, Switzerland
Source: *BioIn 6, 8, 9, 10, 11, 12, 13, 14, 15, 17; ConAu 53; CurBio 63; DcEcMov; FacFETw; IntWW 75, 76, 77, 78, 79, 80, 81, 82, 83, 89, 91, 93; LinLib L, S; MajTwCW; McGEWB; NewYTBS 75, 79; OxCGer 76, 86; RAdv 14, 13-4; ThTwC 87; Who 82, 83, 85, 88, 90, 92, 94; WhoRel 92; WhoWor 74, 76, 78, 80, 82, 84, 87, 89, 91, 93, 95; WorAu 1975*

Kunhardt, Dorothy (Meserve)
American. Author
Children's author of the classic touch-and-feel book *Pat the Bunny,* 1940, among over 40 other books.
b. 1901 in New York, New York
d. Dec 23, 1979 in Beverly, Mississippi
Source: *AuBYP 2S; BioIn 12, 13, 16, 17; ConAu 93, 107; InWom SUP; NewYTBS 79; SmATA 22N, 53*

Kunin, Madeleine May
American. Politician
Dem. governor of VT, 1985-91, defeated by Richard Snelling; state's first female governor.
b. Sep 28, 1933 in Zurich, Switzerland
Source: *AlmAP 88; AmPolW 80; AmWomM; BiDrGov 1983, 1988; BioIn 12, 14, 15; ConAu 93; CurBio 87; IntWW 89, 91, 93; NewYTBS 85, 93; WhoAm 80, 82, 86, 88, 90, 92, 94, 95, 96, 97; WhoAmP 73, 75, 77, 79, 81, 83, 85, 87, 89, 91, 93, 95; WhoAmW 81, 83, 85, 87, 89, 91, 93, 95, 97; WhoE 79, 81, 83, 85, 86, 89, 91, 93, 95; WhoGov 75, 77; WhoWomW 91; WhoWor 89, 91; WomPO 78*

Kunitz, Stanley Jasspon
[Dilly Tante]
American. Poet
Won Pulitzer for *Selected Poems,* 1958; co-edited literary reference textbook.
b. Jul 29, 1905 in Worcester, Massachusetts
Source: *AmAu&B; Benet 87; BenetAL 91; BioIn 13, 15; CamGLE; CamHAL; CnE&AP; ConAu 26NR; ConLC 14; ConPo 85, 91; CurBio 43, 59; DcLB 48; DrAP 75; DrAPF 91; DrAS 82E; IntAu&W 91; IntvTCA 2; IntWW 83, 91; MajTwCW; ModAL S2; NewYTBS 87; OxCAmL 65; PenC AM; RAdv 13-1; REnAL; RfGAmL 87; WebE&AL; WhoAm 86, 90, 97; WorAlBi; WorAu 1950; WrDr 86, 92*

Kuniyoshi, Yasuo
American. Artist
Noted for paintings of women, figure studies, still lifes, carnival scenes.
b. Sep 1, 1893 in Okayama, Japan
d. May 14, 1953 in New York, New York
Source: *ArtsAmW 1; BioIn 1, 3, 4, 5, 11; BriEAA; ConArt 77, 83; CurBio 41, 53; DcAmArt; DcAmB S5; DcCAA 71, 77, 88, 94; FacFETw; GrAmP; IlBEAAW; McGDA; NatCAB 39; OxCTwCA; PhDcTCA 77; WhAm 3; WhAmArt 85; WhoAmA 78N, 80N, 82N, 84N, 86N, 89N, 91N, 93N*

Kunjufu, Jawanza
American. Publisher, Author
Founder, pres., African American Images, 1980—; wrote 3-vol. *Countering the Conspiracy to Destroy Black Boys,* 1982-90.
b. Jun 15, 1953 in Chicago, Illinois
Source: *ConBlB 3; SmATA 73; WhoAfA 96; WhoBlA 92, 94; WhoMW 93*

Kunstler, William M(oses)
American. Lawyer, Civil Rights Activist
Controversial defender of radicals best known for Chicago Seven trial, 1970.
b. Jul 7, 1919 in New York, New York
d. Sep 4, 1995 in New York, New York
Source: *AmAu&B; BioIn 7, 8, 9, 10, 11, 12, 18, 19; ConAu 5NR, 9R, 149; CurBio 71, 95N; IntAu&W 91; LNinSix; News 92; NewYTBE 70; WhAm 11; WhoAm 74, 76, 78, 80, 82, 84, 86, 88, 90, 92, 94, 95; WhoAmL 78, 79, 85, 90, 94; WhoE 74, 95; WhoWorJ 72; WorAlBi; WrDr 76, 86, 92*

Kunz, Erich
Austrian. Opera Singer
Bass-baritone with NY Met., 1950s; noted buffo singer.
b. May 20, 1909 in Vienna, Austria
Source: *Baker 84, 92; BioIn 4, 11, 21; CmOp; IntDcOp; IntWW 74, 75, 76, 77, 78, 79, 80, 81, 82, 83, 89, 91, 93; IntWWM 77, 80, 90; MetOEnc; MusSN; NewEOp 71; NewGrDM 80; NewGrDO; NewYTBS 95; OxDcOp; PenDiMP; WhoOp 76; WhoWor 74, 76*

Kunzel, Erich
American. Conductor
Conducted the Rhode Island Philharmonic Orchestra, 1960-1965; founder and conductor of the Cincinnati Pops including the 8 O'Clock Pops, the pops arm of the Cincinnati Synphony, 1965-1977; director of Cincinnati Pops, 1977—; recorded *Star Tracks* and *Time Warp,* 1984, *Round-Up,* 1986 and *Symphonic Star Trek,* 1996.
b. Mar 21, 1935 in New York, New York
Source: *Baker 84, 92; ConMus 17; NewAmDM; NewGrDA 86; PenDiMP; WhoAm 76, 78, 80, 82, 84, 86, 88, 90, 92, 94, 95, 96, 97; WhoAmM 83; WhoEnt 92; WhoMW 74*

Kupcinet, Irv
American. Journalist, TV Personality
Columnist, *Chicago Daily Times,* 1935-43; *Chicago Sun Times,* 1943—; hosted "Kup's Show," 1959-86.
b. Jul 31, 1912 in Chicago, Illinois
Source: *BiDAmNC; CelR, 90; EncTwCJ; VarWW 85; WhoAm 74, 76, 78, 80, 82, 84, 86, 88, 90, 92, 94, 95, 96, 97; WhoMW 74, 78, 80, 82, 84, 90, 92, 93, 96*

Kupka, Frank
[Frantisek Kupka]
Czech. Artist
Pioneer in abstract movement called Orphism; known for satirical drawings, caricatures appearing in French periodicals.
b. Sep 3, 1871 in Opocno, Bohemia
d. Jan 21, 1957 in Puteaux, France
Source: *BioIn 4, 5, 7, 8, 9, 11, 14, 17; ClaDrA; ConArt 77, 83; DcArts; EncWB; McGDA; NewCol 75; OxCTwCA; OxDcArt; PhDcTCA 77; WorECar*

Kupka, Frank
[Frantisek Kupka]
b. Sep 23, 1871
d. Jun 24, 1957
Source: *BioIn 4, 5, 7, 8, 9, 11, 14, 17; ClaDrA; ConArt 77, 83; DcArts; EncWB; McGDA; OxCTwCA; OxDcArt; PhDcTCA 77; WorECar*

Kupke, Frederick Lee
[The Hostages]
American. Hostage
One of 52 held by terrorists, Nov 1979-Jan 1981.
b. 1948? in Oklahoma
Source: *NewYTBS 81*

Kuprin, Aleksandr Ivanovich
Russian. Author
Traditionalist short story writer: *The River of Life,* 1916; *Sasha,* 1920.
b. Sep 7, 1870 in Narovchat, Russia
d. Oct 25, 1938 in Leningrad, Union of Soviet Socialist Republics
Source: *Benet 87, 96; BiDSovU; BioIn 1, 2, 11; CasWL; ClDMEL 47, 80; ConAu 104; DcRusL; DcRusLS; EncWL; EvEuW; HanRL; ModSL 1; PenC EUR; REn; TwCA, SUP; TwCWr*

Kuralt, Charles (Bishop)
American. Broadcast Journalist
Correspondent with CBS News, 1957-94; known for "On the Road" segments; TV anchor "Sunday Morning," 1979-94; won three Peabodys, 12 Emmys.
b. Sep 10, 1934 in Wilmington, North Carolina
d. Jul 4, 1997 in New York, New York
Source: *BiDAmNC; BioIn 10, 11, 12, 13, 16, 17, 18, 19, 20; CelR 90; ConAu 43NR, 89; ConTFT 5, 15; CurBio 81; EncAJ; EncTwCJ; IntMPA 86, 92, 94, 96; JrnUS; LegTOT; LesBEnT, 92; VarWW 85; WhoAm 74, 76, 78, 80, 82, 84, 86, 88, 90, 92, 94, 95, 96, 97; WhoE 91, 93; WhoEnt 92A*

Kurath, Hans
American. Linguist
Work focused on American English dialects; edited *Linguistic Atlas of New England,* 1939-43.
b. Dec 13, 1891 in Villach, Austria-Hungary
Source: *BioIn 18; ConAu 9R; DrAS 74F, 78F, 82F; WhoMW 74*

Kurchatov, Igor Vasilyevich
Russian. Physicist
Helped develop first Soviet atomic bomb; first thermonuclear bomb; first Soviet atomic electric power station.
b. Jan 12, 1903 in Sim, Russia
d. Feb 7, 1960 in Moscow, Union of Soviet Socialist Republics
Source: *BiDSovU; CurBio 60; ObitOF 79; WhAm 3; WorAlBi*

Kureishi, Hanif
English. Screenwriter, Author
Works deal with problems of immigrants in Britain, film *My Beautiful Laundrette,* 1985; *The Buddha of Suburbia,* 1990.
b. Dec 5, 1954? in Bromley, England
Source: *ConAu 139; ConBrDr; ConDr 88, 93; ConLC 64; ConNov 96; ConTFT 10; CurBio 92; DcArts; EncEurC; IntAu&W 91, 93; IntMPA 92; IntWW 91, 93; RGTwCWr; Who 92, 94; WhoAm 94, 95, 96; WhoWor 95, 96; WrDr 88, 90, 92, 94, 96*

Kurelek, William
Canadian. Artist, Illustrator
Known for realistic Canadian prairie scenes; self-illustrated children's books include *A Prairie Boy's Summer,* 1975.
b. Mar 3, 1927 in Whitford, Alberta, Canada
d. Nov 3, 1977 in Toronto, Ontario, Canada
Source: *AuBYP 2S, 3; BioIn 6, 11, 12, 13, 15, 19, 21; ChlBkCr; ChlLR 2; ConArt 77; ConAu 3NR, 49; ConCaAu 1; CreCan 1; FifBJA; IlsCB 1967; MajAI; SmATA 8, 27N; TwCChW 95;*

WhoAmA 73, 76, 78, 80N, 82N, 84N, 86N, 89N, 91N, 93N; WrDr 80

Kurland, Bob
[Robert A Kurland]
"Foothills"
American. Basketball Player
Center, first seven-footer to dominate game; first American to play on two Olympic basketball teams, 1948, 1952; Hall of Fame.
b. Dec 23, 1924 in Saint Louis, Missouri
Source: *BasBi; BiDAmSp BK; BioIn 9, 10; WhoBbl 73; WhoSpor*

Kurnitz, Harry
[Marco Page]
American. Dramatist, Screenwriter, Author
Wrote screenplay of his novel *Fast Company,* 1938; other films include *Once More with Feeling,* 1960; *Goodbye Charlie,* 1964.
b. Jan 5, 1909 in New York, New York
d. Mar 18, 1968 in Los Angeles, California
Source: *BiE&WWA; BioIn 14; ConAu 25R; EncAFC; EncMys; FilmEn; FilmgC; IntDcF 1-4; TwCCr&M 80, 85, 91; WorEFlm*

Kuron, Jacek
Polish. Political Activist, Politician
Member of Polish Parliament, 1989—; adviser to Solidarity Trade Union, 1980-1989.
b. Mar 3, 1934 in Lvov, Poland
Source: *BiDNeoM; BioIn 12; ColdWar 1, 2; IntWW 91, 93; WhoSoCE 89*

Kurosawa, Akira
Japanese. Director
Best known for action films; directed epic *Ran,* 1985; won Oscar best foreign language film, *Dersu Uzala,* 1976.
b. Mar 23, 1910 in Tokyo, Japan
Source: *Au&Arts 11; Benet 87, 96; BiDFilm, 81, 94; BioIn 6, 7, 8, 9, 10, 12, 13, 14, 15, 16, 17, 18, 19; ConAu 46NR, 101; ConLC 16; ConTFT 6, 13; CurBio 91; DcFM; EncJap; FacFETw; FarE&A 78, 79, 80, 81; FilmEn; FilmgC; HalFC 80, 84, 88; IntDcF 1-2, 2-2; IntMPA 75, 76, 77, 78, 79, 80, 81, 82, 84, 86, 88, 92, 94, 96; IntWW 74, 75, 76, 77, 78, 79, 80, 81, 82, 83, 89, 91, 93; JapFilm; LegTOT; McGEWB; MiSFD 9; MovMk; News 91, 91-1; NewYTBS 85, 89; OxCFilm; RAdv 14, 13-3; REn; VarWW 85; WhDW; Who 74, 82, 83, 85, 88, 90, 92, 94; WhoAm 94, 95, 96, 97; WhoEnt 92; WhoWor 84, 89, 91, 93, 95, 96, 97; WorEFlm; WorFDir 1*

Kurri, Jarri
Finnish. Hockey Player
Right wing, Oilers, 1980-90, Italian Hockey League, 1990-91; Kings, 1991—; first European to lead NHL in goals, set NHL record for most goals in season by right wing, 71 (1985-86); Stanly Cup teams, 1984-85, 1987-88, 1990.
b. May 18, 1960 in Helsinki, Finland
Source: *HocEn; HocReg 87; WhoAm 90; WhoSpor; WhoWest 92; WorAlBi*

Kurtis, Bill
[William Horton Kurtis]
American. Broadcast Journalist
Correspondent, co-anchor, CBS Morning News, 1982-86.
b. Sep 21, 1940 in Pensacola, Florida
Source: *BioIn 13, 14; ConAu 124, 133, X; IntMPA 86, 88, 92, 94, 96; WhoAm 80, 82, 84, 86, 88, 90, 92, 94, 95, 96, 97; WhoMW 78, 80, 82; WhoTelC; WrDr 94, 96*

Kurtz, Efrem
Russian. Conductor
Led Houston Symphony, 1948-54; NY Philharmonic recording sold over three million copies.
b. Nov 7, 1900 in Saint Petersburg, Russia
d. Jun 27, 1995 in London, England
Source: *Baker 78, 84, 92; BioIn 1, 2, 3, 4, 21; BlueB 76; CurBio 46, 95N; DancEn 78; IntWW 74, 75, 76, 77, 78, 79, 80, 81, 82, 83, 89, 91, 93; IntWWM 77, 80, 90; NewAmDM; NewGrDA 86; NewGrDM 80; NewYTBS 95; PenDiMP; WhoAmJ 80; WhoMus 72; WhoWorJ 72, 78*

Kurtz, Katherine
American. Author
Novelist, police officer; wrote two-vol. *Saint Camber,* 1978-79.
b. Oct 18, 1944 in Coral Gables, Florida
Source: *ConAu 25NR, 29R; EncSF; IntAu&W 91; NewEScF; ScF&FL 1, 2, 92; ScFSB; SJGFanW; TwCSFW 91; WhoAm 84; WhoHr&F; WrDr 76, 80, 82, 84, 86, 88, 90, 92, 94, 96*

Kurtz, Swoosie
American. Actor
Won Tony, 1980, for *Fifth of July.*
b. Sep 6, 1944 in Omaha, Nebraska
Source: *BioIn 12, 14, 15; CelR 90; ConTFT 4, 15; CurBio 87; IntMPA 86, 92, 94, 96; InWom SUP; LegTOT; NewYTBS 81; VarWW 85; WhoAm 88, 90; WhoAmW 91; WhoEnt 92; WhoHol 92, A; WhoTelC*

Kurtzman, Harvey
American. Artist, Writer
Creator of *Mad* magazine, 1952.
b. Oct 3, 1924 in New York, New York
d. Feb 21, 1993 in Mount Vernon, New York
Source: *BioIn 15, 16, 18; ConGrA 2; EncACom; WorECom*

Kurusu, Saburo
Japanese. Diplomat
Was negotiating to end tensions with US when Japanese attacked Pearl Harbor, precipitating war, Dec 7, 1941.
b. 1888 in Yokohama, Japan
d. Apr 7, 1954 in Tokyo, Japan
Source: *CurBio 42, 54; REn*

Kurz, Selma
Austrian. Opera Singer
Coloratura soprano; Vienna Opera star, 1899-1927; noted for remarkable trill.
b. Nov 15, 1875 in Bielitz, Austria
d. May 10, 1933 in Vienna, Austria
Source: *Baker 84; BioIn 6, 11; InWom; MusSN; NewEOp 71*

Kurzban, Ira Jay
American. Lawyer
Challenged US immigration policy, early 1980s; won Supreme Court decision which outlawed incarceration of aliens on basis of race, nationality, 1985.
b. May 9, 1949 in New York, New York
Source: *BioIn 16; ConNews 87-2; WhoAm 97; WhoAmL 96*

Kurzweil, Raymond C
American. Inventor
Developed reading machine for blind, 1976.
b. Feb 12, 1948 in New York, New York
Source: *BioIn 11, 13, 14, 15, 16; ConAu 134; ConNews 86-3; WhoAm 86, 90; WhoEmL 91; WhoFI 87*

Kusch, P(olycarp)
American. Physicist, Educator
Shared Nobel Prize in physics, 1955, with Willis E Lamb, Jr. for determining the magnetic moment of the electron.
b. Jan 26, 1911 in Blankenburg, Germany
d. Mar 20, 1993 in Dallas, Texas
Source: *AmMWSc 82, 92; BiESc; BioIn 15; BlueB 76; IntWW 83, 91; McGMS 80; NobelP; NotTwCS; WebAB 74; Who 92; WhoAm 84, 90; WhoNob, 90, 95; WhoSSW 91; WhoWor 74, 91*

Kushner, Harold S(amuel)
American. Religious Leader, Author
Wrote *When Bad Things Happen to Good People,* 1981, after death of young son; also wrote *How Good Do We Have to Be,* 1996.
b. Apr 3, 1935 in New York, New York
Source: *BioIn 16; ConAu 36NR, 107; Dun&B 88; IntAu&W 91; WhoAmJ 80; WhoE 86; WhoRel 92; WrDr 84, 86, 92*

Kushner, Tony
American. Dramatist
Won 1993 Pulitzer Prize for Drama for *Angels in America: Millennium Approaches;* also won the Tony Award for Best Play and the New York Drama Critics Circle Award for Best New Play.
b. c. 1956 in New York, New York
Source: *ConAmD; ConAu 144; ConDr 93; ConLC 81; ConTFT 13; GayLL; News 95, 95-2; WrDr 96*

Kuter, Laurence S(herman)
American. Army Officer, Aviator
First commander, Military Air Transport service, 1948.
b. May 28, 1905 in Rockford, Illinois
d. Nov 30, 1979
Source: *BiDWWGF; BioIn 1, 3, 4, 5, 12; ConAu 113; CurBio 48; InSci; PeoHis; WhAm 7; WhoAm 74, 76*

Kuti, Fela Anikulapo
[Fela Ransome-Kuti]
Nigerian. Musician, Political Activist
Formed band Koola lobitos early 1960s (later Afrika 70, then Egypt 80); Afro-Beat albums include *Original Sufferhead,* 1981.
b. 1938 in Lagos, Nigeria
Source: *BioIn 11, 13, 14, 15; ConBlB 1; ConMus 7; DcArts; EncRk 88; IntWW 89, 91, 93; NewYTBS 77, 86; PenEncP*

Kutner, Luis
American. Social Reformer, Lawyer
Co-founder of Amnesty Int'l.
b. Jun 9, 1909 in Chicago, Illinois
d. Mar 1, 1993 in Chicago, Illinois
Source: *ConAu 109; WhoAmL 85*

Kutschmann, Walter
[Pedro Olmo]
German. Government Official
Nazi lieutenant, accused of killing over 1,500 Jews in Poland during WW II; escaped to Argentina, never prosecuted.
b. 1914
d. Aug 30, 1986 in Buenos Aires, Argentina

Kutuzov, Mikhail Ilarionovich
Russian. Military Leader
Turned back French forces after having lost Moscow, 1812.
b. Sep 5, 1745 in Saint Petersburg, Russia
d. Apr 16, 1813 in Bunzlau, Poland
Source: *Dis&D; McGEWB; NewCol 75*

Kuwatli, Shukri al-
Syrian. Political Leader
First pres., Syria, 1943-49, 1955-59.
b. 1891 in Damascus, Syria
d. Jun 30, 1967 in Beirut, Lebanon
Source: *BioIn 4, 8; CurBio 56, 67; ObitOF 79; WhAm 4*

Kuykendall, Ralph Simpson
American. Historian
Spent 40 yrs. researching Hawaiian history.
b. Apr 12, 1885 in Linden, California
d. May 9, 1963 in Tucson, Arizona
Source: *BioIn 6; DcAmB S7; WhAm 7*

Kuznets, Simon Smith
American. Economist
Won Nobel Prize, 1971, for originating concept of gross nat. product as measure of nat. income, economic growth.
b. Apr 30, 1901 in Kharkov, Russia
d. Jul 8, 1985 in Cambridge, Massachusetts
Source: *AmMWSc 78S; AmSocL; BioIn 9, 10, 13; BlueB 76; ConAu 108; CurBio 85; EncAB-H 1974, 1996; RAdv 14; WebAB 74; WhoAm 74, 76, 78, 80, 82; WhoE 77, 79, 81, 85; WhoFI 83, 85; WhoNob, 90, 95; WhoWor 74, 80, 82, 84; WrDr 84*

Kuznetsov, Anatoli Vasilievich
[A Anatoli]
English. Author
Best known for *Babi Yar,* description of Nazi attacks on Russian Jews, 1966; defected to Britain, 1969, denouncing Soviet censorship.
b. Aug 18, 1929 in Kiev, Union of Soviet Socialist Republics
d. Jun 13, 1979 in London, England
Source: *ConAu 89; IntAu&W 76, 77; IntWW 74, 75, 76, 77; NewYTBS 79; PseudN 82; WhoWor 74; WorAu 1975*

Kuznetzov, Vassili Vasilyevich
Russian. Politician, Diplomat
First vice president of USSR, 1977-86.
b. Feb 13, 1901 in Sofilovka, Russia
d. Jun 5, 1990 in Moscow, Union of Soviet Socialist Republics
Source: *BioIn 16; CurBio 56, 90, 90N; FacFETw; IntWW 83; NewYTBS 77, 90; WhoWor 84*

Kwan, Nancy Kashen
Chinese. Actor
Starred in *The World of Suzie Wong,* 1960; *Flower Drum Song,* 1961.
b. May 19, 1939, Hong Kong
Source: *BioIn 16; ConTFT 7; FilmEn; FilmgC; HalFC 88; MotPP; MovMk; VarWW 85; WhoAsA 94; WhoHol A*

Kwoh, Yik San
Chinese. Engineer
Invented world's first robot to implement difficult brain surgery techniques, Ole, 1984.
b. 1946? in Shanghai, China
Source: *BioIn 14; News 88-2*

Ky, Nguyen Cao
Vietnamese. Political Leader
VP of S Vietnam, 1967-71; fled to US, 1975; wrote *Twenty Years and Twenty Days,* 1977.
b. Sep 8, 1930 in Son Tay, Vietnam
Source: *BioIn 14; CurBio 66; DcTwHis; FacFETw; IntWW 83, 91; NewYTBS 76*

Kyd, Thomas
English. Dramatist
Wrote day's most popular drama, revenge-play *The Spanish Tragedy,* 1587.
b. Nov 6, 1558 in London, England
d. 1594 in London, England
Source: *Alli; AtlBL; BiD&SB; BiDRP&D; BioIn 3, 5, 7, 8, 11, 12, 16, 20; BlmGEL; BritAu; BritWr 1; CamGEL; CamGLE; CamGWoT; CasWL; Chambr 1; ChhPo; CnE&AP; CnThe; CroE&S; CrtSuDr; CrtT 1, 4; CyWA 58; DcEnA; DcEnL; DcEuL; DcLB 62; DramC 3; EncWT; Ent; EvLB; GrWrEL DR; IntDcT 2; LegTOT; LitC 22; LngCEL; McGEWB; McGEWD 72, 84; MouLC 1; NewC; NewCBEL; NotNAT A, B; OxCEng 67, 85, 95; OxCThe 67, 83; PenC ENG; PlP&P; RAdv 14, 13-2; REn; REnWD; RfGEnL 91; WebE&AL; WhDW; WorAl; WorAlBi*

Kyl, Jon
American. Politician
Rep. senator from AZ, 1995—.
b. Apr 25, 1942
Source: *AlmAP 88, 92, 96; BioIn 20, 21; CngDr 89, 91, 93, 95; WhoAm 94, 95, 96, 97; WhoWest 94, 96; WhoWor 96*

Kylian, Jiri
Czech. Dancer
Director, choreographer for Netherlands Dance Theater, 1978—.
b. Mar 21, 1947 in Prague, Czechoslovakia
Source: *BiDD; BioIn 12, 13, 15; CnOxB; CurBio 82; IntDcB; WhoAm 92, 94, 95, 96, 97; WhoEnt 92; WhoWor 84, 87, 89, 91, 93, 95*

Kyne, Peter Bernard
American. Author
Known for *Cappy Ricks* stories, 1916-20s.
b. Oct 12, 1880 in San Francisco, California
d. Nov 25, 1957 in San Francisco, California
Source: *AmAu&B; BioIn 4; DcAmB S6; LinLib S; OxCAmL 65; REnAL; TwCA, SUP; TwCWW 82; WhAm 3; WhNAA*

Kyprianou, Spyros Achilles
Cypriot. Political Leader
Pres. of Cyprus, 1977-85.
b. Oct 28, 1932 in Limassol, Cyprus
Source: *BioIn 11, 12; CurBio 79; EncWB; IntWW 83, 91; NewYTBS 77; Who 85, 92; WhoWor 84, 91*

Kyser, Kay (James King Kern)
[James King Kern Kyser]
American. Musician, Bandleader
Best known as host of radio's "Kollege of Musical Knowledge," 1933-49.
b. Jun 18, 1906 in Rocky Mount, North Carolina
d. Jul 23, 1985 in Chapel Hill, North Carolina
Source: *AnObit 1985; Baker 92; BgBands 74; BiDAmM; BioIn 2, 9, 10, 12, 14, 15, 17; BioNews 74; CmpEPM; ConNews 85-3; CurBio 41, 85, 85N; FilmgC; NewGrDA 86; OxCPMus; PenEncP; PseudN 82; RadStar; SaTiSS; What 4; WhoHol A*

L

L7
[Jennifer Finch; Suzi Gardner; Dee Plakas; Donita Sparks]
American. Music Group
Female rock band; album *Bricks Are Heavy,* 1992.
Source: *ConMus 12; EncRkSt*

Laban, Rudolf von
Czech. Choreographer
Founded dance-drama; originated method of recording dance instructions similar to music scores.
b. Dec 15, 1879 in Bratislava, Austria-Hungary
d. Jul 1, 1958 in Weybridge, England
Source: *BiDD; BioIn 4, 5, 10, 12, 18; CnOxB; DancEn 78; DcArts; EncTR 91; NewGrDM 80; ObitOF 79; OxCMus; WhDW*

La Barba, Fidel
American. Boxer
Flyweight, feather champ, 1920s; Olympic gold medalist, 1924; Hall of Fame, 1973.
b. Sep 29, 1905 in New York, New York
d. Oct 2, 1981 in California
Source: *BioIn 10; WhoBox 74*

Labatt, John Kinder
Canadian. Brewer
Owned, operated brewery controlled by family, 1847-64.
b. 1803
d. 1866
Source: *DcCanB 9; Entr*

LaBelle, Patti
[Patricia Louise Holte]
American. Singer, Actor
Solo artist since 1977; 1986 album *Winner in You* went platinum; Grammy for *Burnin',* 1992; hits include: "New Attitude," 1985; "On My Own," 1986.
b. Oct 4, 1944 in Philadelphia, Pennsylvania
Source: *AfrAmBi 1; Baker 92; BiDAfM; BioIn 12, 13, 14, 15, 16; BlkWAm; CelR 90; ConBlB 13; ConMus 8; ConTFT 12; CurBio 86; DcTwCCu 5; DrBlPA 90; EncPR&S 89; EncRk 88; EncRkSt; IlEncBM 82; InB&W 80, 85; InWom SUP; LegTOT; PenEncP; SoulM; WhoAfA 96; WhoAm 88, 90, 92, 94, 95, 96, 97; WhoAmW 93, 95, 97; WhoBlA 88, 90, 92, 94; WhoEnt 92; WhoHol 92; WorAl; WorAlBi*

LaBern, Arthur Joseph
English. Author
Wrote detective fiction, popular in England: *Goodbye Piccadilly, Farewell Leicester Square,* 1967; *It Always Rains on Sunday,* 1945.
b. Feb 28, 1909 in London, England
Source: *TwCCr&M 80; WrDr 86, 90*

Lablache, Luigi
Italian. Opera Singer
Foremost bass singer of his time; Schubert, others wrote songs for him.
b. Dec 6, 1794 in Naples, Italy
d. Jan 23, 1858 in Naples, Italy
Source: *Baker 78, 84, 92; BioIn 7, 14; BriBkM 80; CmOp; DcNaB; MetOEnc; NewAmDM; NewEOp 71; NewGrDM 80; NewGrDO; OxCMus; OxDcOp; PenDiMP*

Labouisse, Henry Richardson
American. Government Official
Main organizer of Marshall Plan; head of UNICEF, 1965-79; US ambassador to Greece, 1962-65.
b. Feb 11, 1904 in New Orleans, Louisiana
d. Mar 25, 1987 in New York, New York
Source: *BioIn 4, 5, 6; CurBio 61, 87; IntWW 74, 75, 76, 77, 78, 79, 80, 81, 82, 83; IntYB 78, 79, 80, 81, 82; WhAm 9; WhoAm 74, 76, 78, 80, 82, 84, 86; WhoGov 72, 75, 77; WhoUN 75; WhoWor 74, 78, 80, 82, 84, 87*

Laboulaye, Edouard Rose
French. Author, Educator
Admired Lincoln, American form of govt; originally proposed erection of Statue of Liberty, 1865.
b. Jan 18, 1811 in Paris, France
d. May 25, 1883 in Paris, France
Source: *BbD; BiD&SB; CarSB; DcBiA; HarEnUS; ScF&FL 1*

LaBruyere, Jean de
"The Theophrastus of France"
French. Philosopher, Author
Wrote social satire on characters of Theophraste, 1688; later editions greatly enlarged.
b. Aug 16, 1645 in Paris, France
d. May 10, 1696 in Versailles, France
Source: *AtlBL; BbD; BiD&SB; CasWL; DcEuL; EuAu; EvEuW; LinLib L; OxCEng 67; OxCFr; PenC EUR; PseudN 82; REn; WhDW; WorAl*

Lacan, Jacques (Marie Emile)
French. Psychoanalyst
Wrote *Ecrits,* 1966; established the Freudian Cause, Paris.
b. Apr 13, 1901 in Paris, France
d. Sep 9, 1981 in Paris, France
Source: *AnObit 1981; Benet 96; BioIn 11, 12, 13, 14, 15, 17, 20; BlmGEL; ClDMEL 80; ConAu 104, 121; ConLC 75; CyWA 89; DcTwCCu 2; EncWL 3; FacFETw; MakMC; OxCPhil; PostFic; RAdv 14, 13-5; ThTwC 87; WhoFr 79; WorAu 1975*

Lacey, Robert
English. Author
Wrote *Majesty: Elizabeth II and the House of Windsor,* 1977; *Ford: The Men and the Machine,* 1986.
b. Jan 3, 1944 in Guildford, England
Source: *Au&Wr 71; ConAu 16NR, 33R, 43NR; IntAu&W 86, 89, 91, 93; WhoSSW 91; WhoWor 76; WrDr 76, 80, 82, 84, 86, 88, 90, 92, 94, 96*

Lach, Elmer James
Canadian. Hockey Player
Center, Montreal, 1940-54; won Hart Trophy, 1945, Art Ross Trophy, 1945, 1947; Hall of Fame, 1966.
b. Jan 22, 1918 in Nokomis, Saskatchewan, Canada
Source: *HocEn; WhoHcky 73*

Lachaise, Gaston
American. Sculptor
Noted for voluptuous female nudes, portrait busts of literary figures.
b. Mar 19, 1882 in Paris, France
d. Oct 18, 1935 in New York, New York
Source: *AtlBL; BioIn 1, 6, 8, 10, 14, 15, 18; BriEAA; ConArt 77; DcAmArt; DcAmB S1; DcCAA 71, 77, 88, 94; FacFETw; McGDA; McGEWB; NewCol 75; OxCAmH; OxCTwCA; OxDcArt; PhDcTCA 77; REn; WebAB 74, 79; WhAm 1, 4; WhAmArt 85*

Lachs, Manfred
Polish. Diplomat, Author
Prominent in development of international law after WW II; wrote *War Crimes: An Attempt to Define the Issues,* 1945.
b. Apr 21, 1914 in Stanislawow, Austria-Hungary
Source: *AnObit 1993; BioIn 2, 6; IntAu&W 77, 82; IntWW 74, 75, 76, 77, 78, 79, 80, 81, 82, 83, 89, 91; IntYB 78, 79, 80, 81, 82; OxCLaw; WhAm 11; Who 74, 82, 83, 85, 88, 90, 92; WhoEIO 82; WhoSocC 78; WhoSoCE 89; WhoUN 75, 92; WhoWor 74, 76, 78, 80, 82, 84, 87, 89, 91, 93*

Lackey, Kenneth
American. Actor
Best known as original member of Three Stooges, 1923-25.
b. 1902? in Indiana
d. Apr 16, 1976 in Columbus, North Carolina
Source: *BioIn 10; NewYTBS 76*

Laclede, Pierre
[Pierre Laclede Liguest]
French. Fur Trader
Founded St. Louis, Missouri, 1764.
b. 1724? in Bedous, France
d. Jun 20, 1778 in Kansas
Source: *DcAmB; Drake; EncCRAm; NatCAB 13; NewCol 75; REnAW; WebAB 74, 79; WhAm HS*

Laclos, Pierre (Ambroise Francois) Choderlos de
French. Author, Army Officer
Wrote novel *Les Liaisons Dangereuses,* 1782, revealing immorality of his time.
b. Oct 18, 1741 in Amiens, France
d. Nov 5, 1803 in Taranto, Italy
Source: *AtlBL; Benet 96; BiD&SB; BioIn 21; CasWL; CyWA 58; DcEuL; EncEnl; EuAu; EvEuW; LinLib L; NewCBEL; OxCFr; PenC EUR; REn*

Lacoste, Catherine
French. Golfer
Won US Women's Open, 1967, as amateur.
b. Jun 27, 1945 in Paris, France
Source: *BioIn 8; WhoFr 79; WhoGolf*

Lacoste, Rene
[The Four Musketeers; Jean Rene Lacoste]
"The Crocodile"
French. Tennis Player
French, British, US singles champion, 1920s.
b. Jul 2, 1904 in Paris, France
d. Oct 11, 1996 in Saint Jean-de-Luz, France
Source: *BioIn 10, 11, 12, 13, 14, 15, 20; EncFash; Entr; NewCol 75; NewYTBS 27; WhoFr 79*

Lacroix, Christian
French. Fashion Designer
Known for using old styles to create a "regeneration" effect on clothes.
b. May 17, 1950 in Arles, France
Source: *BioIn 15, 16; CurBio 88; IntWW 91; LegTOT; Who 92; WhoAm 90; WhoFash 88; WhoWor 91*

Ladd, Alan
American. Actor
Appeared in 150 films, including *Shane,* 1954.
b. Sep 3, 1913 in Hot Springs, Arkansas
d. Jan 29, 1964 in Palm Springs, California
Source: *BiDFilm, 81, 94; BioIn 3, 4, 5, 6, 7, 8, 9, 10, 12, 14, 20; CmMov; CurBio 43, 64; DcArts; FilmEn; FilmgC; ForYSC; GangFlm; HalFC 80, 84, 88; IntDcF 1-3, 2-3; ItaFilm; LegTOT; MotPP; MovMk; NotNAT B; ObitT 1961; OxCFilm; SaTiSS; WhAm 4; WhoHol B; WhoHrs 80; WhScrn 74, 77, 83; WorAl; WorAlBi; WorEFlm*

Ladd, Alan Walbridge, Jr.
American. Business Executive
Pres., 20th Century-Fox, 1976-79; pres., Ladd Co., 1979-83; CEO, MGM, 1983-88; pres., chm., Pathe Entertainment, LA, 1989-90; CEO, MGM, 1990-93; pres., The Ladd Co., 1993—.
b. Oct 22, 1937 in Los Angeles, California
Source: *BioIn 11, 12, 13; Dun&B 79; FilmEn; IntMPA 92; VarWW 85; WhoAm 76, 78, 80, 82, 84, 86, 88, 90, 92, 94, 95, 96, 97; WhoEnt 92; WhoFI 89, 92, 94, 96; WhoWest 87, 89, 92, 94, 96*

Ladd, Cheryl
[Mrs. Brian Russell; Cheryl Stoppelmoor]
American. Actor
Played Kris on "Charlie's Angels," 1977-81.
b. Jul 2, 1951 in Huron, South Dakota
Source: *BioIn 11, 12, 13, 14; BkPepl; CelR 90; ConTFT 2, 6; HalFC 80, 84, 88; IntMPA 81, 82, 84, 86, 88, 92, 94, 96; InWom SUP; LegTOT; PseudN 82; RkOn 85; VarWW 85; WhoAm 78, 80, 82, 86, 94, 95, 96, 97; WhoAmW 79, 81, 83; WhoEnt 92; WhoHol 92; WorAl; WorAlBi*

Ladd, Diane
[Rose Diane Ladner]
American. Actor
Oscar nominee for *Alice Doesn't Live Here Anymore,* 1975.
b. Nov 29, 1932 in Meridian, Mississippi
Source: *BioIn 16; ConTFT 7; FilmEn; HalFC 80, 84, 88; IntMPA 92; LegTOT; NewYTBS 76; VarWW 85; WhoEnt 92; WhoHol 92, A*

Ladd, George Trumbull
American. Psychologist, Philosopher
Pioneered in experimental psychology; wrote *Secret Personality,* 1918.
b. Jan 19, 1842 in Painesville, Ohio
d. Aug 8, 1921 in New Haven, Connecticut
Source: *Alli SUP; AmAu&B; AmBi; ApCAB, X; BiDAmEd; BiDAmS; BiD&SB; BiDPsy; BioIn 1, 8; DcAmAu; DcAmB; DcNAA; HarEnUS; LinLib L; NamesHP; NatCAB 13, 33; NewCol 75; OhA&B; REnAL; TwCBDA; WhAm 1; WhLit*

Ladd, William
American. Social Reformer
Founded American Peace Society, 1828.
b. May 10, 1778 in Exeter, Netherlands
d. Apr 9, 1841 in Portsmouth, Netherlands
Source: *Alli; AmBi; AmPeW; AmRef; ApCAB; BenetAL 91; BiDMoPL; BioIn 10, 15, 16; DcAmB; DcAmDH 80, 89; DcAmSR; DcNAA; Drake; HarEnUS; McGEWB; NatCAB 13; OxCAmH; OxCAmL 65, 83, 95; OxCLaw; TwCBDA; WebAB 74, 79; WhAm HS*

Ladd-Franklin, Christine
American. Psychologist
Reduced all syllogisms to single formula; developed theory of man's color sense.
b. Dec 1, 1847 in Windsor, Connecticut
d. Mar 5, 1930 in New York, New York
Source: *AmBi; AmWomSc; BiDPsy; BioIn 15, 17, 18, 20; DcAmB; DcNAA; GaEncPs; LibW; NamesHP; NatCAB 26; NewCol 75; NotAW; NotTwCS; RAdv 14; TwCBDA; WhAm 1; WhNAA; WomFir; WomMath; WomPsyc; WomSc*

Ladnier, Tommy
American. Jazz Musician
Cornetist, adept at blues; recorded jazz classics with Bechet, Mezz Mezzrow.
b. May 28, 1900 in Mandeville, Louisiana
d. Jun 4, 1939 in New York, New York
Source: *AllMusG; Baker 84, 92; BiDAmM; BiDJaz; CmpEPM; IlEncJ; LegTOT; MusMk; NewGrDJ 88, 94; NewOrJ; OxCPMus; PenEncP; WhoJazz 72; WorAl; WorAlBi*

LaDuke, Winona
American. Political Activist
Founder of White Earth Land Recovery Project.
b. 1959 in Los Angeles, California
Source: *BioIn 21; EncNAB; News 95, 95-2; WhoAmW 97*

Laemmle, Carl, Sr.
American. Film Executive
Formed IMP Co., 1909, which was first to publicize its stars including Mary Pickford; became Universal Studio, 1912; sold, 1935.
b. Jan 17, 1867 in Laupheim, Germany
d. Sep 24, 1939 in Hollywood, California
Source: *AmBi; AmCulL; BiDAmBL 83; BiDFilm 81, 94; BioIn 4, 8, 19; CmCal; DcAmB S2; DcFM; FacFETw; FilmEn; FilmgC; HalFC 80, 84, 88; IntDcF 2-4; LegTOT; NatCAB 15, 30; OxCFilm; TwYS B; WebAB 74, 79; WhAm 1; WhScrn 74, 77, 83; WorEFlm*

Laennec, Rene Theophile Hyacinthe
French. Inventor
Invented stethoscope, c. 1819; considered father of thoracic medicine.
b. Feb 17, 1781 in Quimper, France
d. Aug 13, 1826 in Kerlouanec, France
Source: *AsBiEn; BiESc; BiHiMed; BioIn 1, 2, 3, 4, 5, 6, 7, 9, 11, 16, 18; CamDcSc; DcBiPP; DcCathB; DcScB; Dis&D; InSci; LarDcSc; NewCol 75; WebBD 83*

Laeri, J(ohn) Howard
American. Financier
Director, First National City Corp., now Citicorp, 1965-71.
b. Mar 22, 1906 in Youngstown, Ohio
d. Jun 27, 1986 in Greenwich, Connecticut
Source: *BioIn 8, 15; CurBio 68, 86, 86N; St&PR 75, 84, 87; WhAm 9; WhoAm 74, 76, 78, 80*

Laettner, Christian
American. Basketball Player
Duke All-American center; NCAA Most Outstanding Player, 1991; Wooden Award, 1992; only college player in Olympics basketball team, 1992.
Source: *BioIn 17, 18, 19, 20, 21; News 93-1; NewYTBS 92*

LaFarge, Christopher
American. Architect, Author
Wrote novel in verse *Each to the Other,* 1939; prose novel *The Sudden Guest,* 1946.
b. Dec 10, 1897 in New York, New York
d. Jan 5, 1956
Source: *AmAu&B; AmNov; CnDAL; DcAmB S2; OxCAmL 65; REn; REnAL; TwCA, SUP; TwCBDA; WhE&EA*

LaFarge, John
American. Artist, Author
Noted for church murals, stained glass designs: *The Ascension,* Church of the Ascension, NYC.
b. Mar 31, 1835 in New York, New York
d. Nov 14, 1910 in Providence, Rhode Island
Source: *AmAu; AmAu&B; AmBi; ApCAB; BbD; BiD&SB; DcAmB; EarABI SUP; EncAB-H 1974; McGEWB; NewCol 75; OxCAmL 83; TwCBDA; WebAB 79; WhAm 1*

Lafarge, Marie
[Marie Fortunee Capelle]
French. Murderer
Defendant in sensational poisoning trial, 1840; first time forensic medicine decided verdict.
b. 1816 in Picardy, France
d. 1852 in Ussat, France
Source: *BioIn 11; CopCroC; DcBiPP; DrInf*

LaFarge, Oliver
American. Author, Anthropologist
American Indian authority; won 1929 Pulitzer for novel *Laughing Boy;* brother of Christopher.
b. Dec 19, 1901 in New York, New York
d. Aug 2, 1963 in Albuquerque, New Mexico
Source: *AmAu&B; AmNov; AuBYP 2; CnDAL; ConAu 81; CurBio 53, 63; DcLB 9; DcLEL; LngCTC; OxCAmL 65; PenC AM; REnAL; REnAW; SmATA 19; TwCA; WhAm 4; WhE&EA*

Lafayette, Marie Joseph Paul, Marquis
French. Army Officer, Statesman
Revolutionary war hero; negotiated French aid for American cause, 1779; close friend of George Washington.
b. Sep 6, 1757 in Chavaniac, France
d. May 20, 1834 in Paris, France
Source: *ApCAB; DcAmB; DcAmMiB; Drake; NewCol 75; OxCAmH; OxCFr; REn; REnAL; WebAB 74; WhAm HS; WorAlBi*

LaFever Minard
American. Architect, Author
Wrote building texts, including *Modern Builder's Guide,* 1833.
b. Aug 10, 1798 in Morristown, New Jersey
d. Sep 26, 1854 in Brookland, New York
Source: *Alli; DcAmB S1; MacEA; McGDA; WhAm HS; WhoArch*

Laffan, William Mackay
American. Newspaper Publisher
Started *NY Evening Sun,* 1887.
b. Jan 22, 1848 in Dublin, Ireland
d. Nov 19, 1909 in Lawrence, New York
Source: *AmAu&B; AmBi; DcAmB; DcNAA; JrnUS; NatCAB 30; WhAm 1*

Laffer, Arthur Betz
"Father of Supply-Side Economics"; "Guru of Tax Revolt"
American. Economist
Supply-side theorist who promoted Reaganomics; devised Laffer Curve.
b. Aug 14, 1940 in Youngstown, Ohio
Source: *BioIn 11, 13, 14, 15; CelR 90; CurBio 82; DcAmC; IntWW 91; NewYTBS 86; WhoAm 86, 88; WhoSSW 73*

Lafferty, Raphael Aloysius
American. Author
Science fiction works include 1973 short story Hugo winner *Eurema's Dam.*
b. Nov 7, 1914 in Neola, Iowa
Source: *Au&Wr 71; BioIn 12, 13; ConAu 32NR, 57; ConSFA; DcLB 8; EncSF; IntAu&W 91; IntvTCA 2; NewEScF; RGTwCSF; ScFnry; ScFSB; SupFW; TwCSFW 86, 91; WrDr 92*

Laffite, Jacques Henry Sabin
French. Auto Racer
Formula One racer, winner of six races, who was formerly auto mechanic.
b. Nov 21, 1943 in Magny Cours, France
Source: *BioIn 11; WhoWor 82*

Laffite, Jean
"The Pirate of the Gulf"
French. Pirate
Colorful New Orleans smuggler, privateer; fought heroically for US, War of 1812; disappeared.
b. Aug 29, 1780 in Bayonne, France
d. 1825
Source: *AmBi; BenetAL 91; BioIn 15; DcAmB; EncSoH; LegTOT; NewCol 75; OxCAmL 65, 83, 95; PseudN 82; WebAB 74, 79; WebAMB; WhAm HS; WorAl; WorAlBi*

LaFlesche, Francis
American. Ethnologist
Wrote *Dictionary of the Osage Language,* 1932.
b. Dec 25, 1857? in Omaha Indian Reservation, Nebraska
d. Sep 5, 1932 in Omaha Indian Reservation, Nebraska

LaFlesche Picotte, Susan
American. Physician
First Native American woman to become a physician, 1889.
b. Jun 17, 1865
d. 1915

LaFlesche Tibbles, Susette
[Bright Eyes]
American. Political Activist
Toured the eastern US, 1879, on a fundraising trip for Indian rights.
b. 1854 in Nebraska
d. May 26, 1903 in Omaha Indian Reservation, Nebraska
Source: *AmBi; BioAmW; BioIn 9, 10, 11, 18, 19, 20; DcAmB; NotAW; WhAm HS*

Lafleur, Guy Damien
"The Flower"
Canadian. Hockey Player
Right wing, Montreal, 1971-84; is team's all-time scoring leader; won Hart Trophy twice, Art Ross Trophy three times; Hall of Fame, 1988.
b. Sep 20, 1951 in Thurso, Quebec, Canada
Source: *BioIn 10, 11, 12, 13, 14, 15, 16; CanWW 31, 81, 83, 89; CurBio 80; HocEn; NewYTBS 84; WhoAm 80, 82, 84, 86, 90; WhoHcky 73; WorAlBi*

LaFollete, Philip Fox
American. Politician
WI governor, launched National Progressives of America, 1938-41.
b. May 18, 1897 in Madison, Wisconsin
d. Aug 18, 1965 in Madison, Wisconsin
Source: *DcAmB S7*

LaFollette, Bronson Cutting
American. Government Official
WI attorney general, 1965-69; 1974-86.
b. Feb 2, 1936 in Washington, District of Columbia
Source: *WhoAm 86; WhoAmL 85, 87; WhoAmP 85, 91; WhoGov 77; WhoMW 86*

LaFollette, Robert Marion
American. Politician
Progressive Rep. senator from WI, 1906-25; presidential candidate, 1924.
b. Jun 14, 1855 in Primrose, Wisconsin
d. Jun 18, 1925 in Washington, District of Columbia
Source: *AmBi; BiDMoPL; BiDrAC; DcAmB; EncAB-H 1974; HarEnUS; MorMA; REn; REnAL; TwCBDA; WebAB 74; WebBD 83; WhAm 1*

La Follette, Suzanne
American. Writer, Editor
Wrote *Concerning Women*, 1926; founding editor, *The National Review*, 1955.
b. 1895? in Washington
d. Apr 23, 1983 in Palo Alto, California

La Fontaine, Henri Marie
Belgian. Lawyer, Educator
Ron 1913 Nobel Peace Prize; goal was to create world bibliography to promote int'l understanding.
b. Apr 22, 1854 in Brussels, Belgium
d. May 14, 1943 in Brussels, Belgium
Source: *BiDMoPL; BioIn 9, 11, 15; CurBio 43; WhoNob, 90, 95*

LaFontaine, Jean de
French. Author
Noted for *Fables*, published in 12 books, 1668-94.
b. Jul 8, 1621 in Aisne, France
d. Apr 13, 1695 in Paris, France
Source: *AnCL; AtlBL; BbD; BiD&SB; CasWL; CyWA 58; DcEuL; EuAu; EvEuW; McGEWB; NewC; OxCEng 85; OxCFr; PenC EUR; RComWL; REn; WhoChL*

LaFontaine, Louis Hippolyte, Sir
Canadian. Statesman
Leader of French Canadians, Lower Canada; two Baldwin-LaFontaine ministries, 1840s, noted for reforms.
b. Oct 1807 in Boucherville, Quebec, Canada
d. Feb 26, 1864 in Montreal, Quebec, Canada
Source: *ApCAB; BbtC; DcNAA; Drake; HisDBrE; MacDCB 78; NewCol 75; OxCCan; WebBD 83*

Lafontaine, Oskar
"Napoleon of the Saar"
German. Politician
Prominent member of the younger generation of Germany's Social Democrats; post of minister pres. in the Saar, 1985—.
b. Sep 16, 1943 in Saarlautern, Germany (West)
Source: *BioIn 16; CurBio 90; IntWW 89, 91, 93; WhoWor 95*

La Fontaine, Pat
American. Hockey Player
Center, NY Islanders, 1984-91, Buffalo, 1991—; member US Olympic team, 1984.
b. Feb 22, 1965 in Saint Louis, Missouri
Source: *BioIn 13, 14, 15, 16; ConNews 85-1; HocReg 87; NewYTBS 84*

Lafontant-Mankarious, Jewel (Stradford)
American. Government Official, Lawyer
US coordinator for refugee affairs and ambassador at large by Pres. Bush, 1989-93.
b. Apr 22, 1922 in Chicago, Illinois
d. May 31, 1997 in Chicago, Illinois
Source: *AmWomM; BioIn 13; BlkWAm; ConBlB 3; InWom SUP; NegAl 89A; NotBlAW 1; St&PR 84; WhoAfA 96; WhoAm 90, 94, 95, 96, 97; WhoAmP 91; WhoAmW 91, 93; WhoBlA 90, 92, 94; WhoFI 89*

Laforet (Diaz), Carmen
Spanish. Author
Novel, *Nada*, 1945, won first Nadal Prize, 1944.
b. Sep 6, 1921 in Barcelona, Spain
Source: *BioIn 2, 4, 17; BlmGWL; CasWL; ClDMEL 80; ContDcW 89; ConWomW; ConWorW 93; EncCoWW; EncWL 2, 3; EvEuW; IntDcWB; IntvSpW; InWom SUP; ModSpP S; ModWoWr; OxCSpan; REn; WomWrS; WorAu 1970*

Laforgue, Jules
French. Poet, Author
One of the *Symbolist* poets in France, 1800s.
b. Aug 16, 1860 in Montevideo, Uruguay
d. Aug 20, 1887 in Paris, France
Source: *AtlBL; Benet 87, 96; BioIn 1, 2, 3, 5, 7, 8, 9, 11, 12, 13, 14, 19; CasWL; ClDMEL 47; DcArts; DcEuL; Dis&D; EuAu; EuWr 7; EvEuW; GrFLW; GuFrLit 1; LinLib L; McGEWB; NinCLC 5, 53; OxCEng 85, 95; OxCFr; PenC EUR; PoeCrit 14; REn; RfGWoL 95; ScF&FL 1; ShSCr 20; ThHElm; WhDW*

La Fosse, Charles de
French. Artist
Decorative painter; most notable works: Paris's dome of Hotel des Invalides, 1705; mythological scenes for the Trianon, 1688.
b. Jun 15, 1646 in Paris, France
d. Dec 13, 1716 in Paris, France
Source: *McGDA; NewCol 75; WebBD 83*

Lagardere, Jean-Luc
French. Business Executive
Purchased the French publisher Hachette, 1980; president, Matra Hachette et Gerant, 1992—.
b. Feb 10, 1928 in Aubiet, France
Source: *CurBio 93; IntWW 89, 91, 93; WhoFI 96; WhoFr 79; WhoWor 95, 96, 97*

Lagerfeld, Karl
German. Fashion Designer
Designer for House of Chloe; House of Chanel; led the pret-a-porter movement in the 1960s in Paris.
b. Sep 10, 1938 in Hamburg, Germany
Source: *BioIn 10, 12, 13, 14, 15, 16; BioNews 74; CelR 90; ConDes 90; ConFash; CurBio 82; DcTwDes; EncFash; FairDF FRA; IntWW 89, 91, 93; LegTOT; WhoAm 90; WhoFash, 88; WhoWor 84, 87, 89, 91; WorFshn*

Lagerkvist, Par Fabian
Swedish. Dramatist, Author, Poet
Wrote novels *Barabbas*, 1950; *The Dwarf*, 1945; won Nobel Prize, 1951.
b. May 23, 1891 in Vaxjo, Sweden
d. Jul 11, 1974 in Stockholm, Sweden
Source: *CasWL; ClDMEL 47; CnMD; CnThe; ConAu 49, 85; ConLC 13; CurBio 52, 74; CyWA 58; EncWL; EvEuW; GrFLW; IntWW 74; NewCol 75; PenC EUR; WhAm 6; WhDW; WhE&EA; WhoNob 95*

Lagerlof, Selma Ottiliana Lovisa
Swedish. Author
Wrote *Gosta Berling* saga, 1891; *Wonderful Adventures of Nils*, 1907; first woman to win Nobel Prize for literature, 1909.
b. Nov 20, 1858 in Marbacka, Sweden
d. Mar 16, 1940 in Marbacka, Sweden
Source: *CarSB; CasWL; ClDMEL 47; ConAu 108; CurBio 40; CyWA 58; EncWL; EvEuW; JBA 34; LngCTC; OxCFilm; PenC EUR; REn; TwCWr; WhoChL; WhoNob; WhoTwCL*

Lagrange, Joseph-Louis
French. Mathematician, Astronomer
Developed number theory; motion of planets; celestial mechanics.
b. Jan 25, 1736 in Turin, Italy
d. Apr 10, 1813 in Paris, France

Source: *BiD&SB; DcInv; EncEnl; NewCol 75; NewGrDM 80; OxCFr; REn*

La Guardia, Fiorello Henry
"Little Flower"
American. Politician, Lawyer
Mayor of NYC, 1934-45; airport named for him.
b. Dec 11, 1882 in New York, New York
d. Sep 20, 1947 in New York, New York
Source: *AmPolLe; BiDrAC; BiDrUSC 89; BioIn 1, 2, 3, 4, 5, 6, 7, 9, 10, 11, 12, 13, 14, 15, 16, 17, 19; ConAu 120; CurBio 40, 47; DcAmB S4; DcAmImH; EncAB-H 1974; LinLib S; McGEWB; NatCAB 36; OxCAmH; REn; WebAB 74, 79; WhAm 2; WhAmP; WhDW; WorAl*

Laguna, Ismael
Panamanian. Boxer
Won world lightweight titles, 1960s.
b. Jun 28, 1943 in Colon, Panama
Source: *BioIn 9; InB&W 80; WhoBox 74*

La Haye, Beverly
American. Social Reformer
Founder and pres. of Concerned Women for America, which emphasizes conservative women's movement, 1980—.
b. 1930?

LaHaye, Tim
American. Clergy
Head of the American Coalition for Traditional Values.
b. Apr 27, 1926 in Detroit, Michigan
Source: *BioIn 14; ConAu 9NR, 65; PrimTiR; TwCSAPR*

Lahbabi, Mohammed Aziz
Moroccan. Author, Philosopher
Muslim humanist; wrote *Le Personalisme Musulman,* 1964.
b. Dec 25, 1922 in Fez, Morocco

Lahey, Edwin A(loysius)
American. Journalist
Longtime Washington bureau chief for Knight newspapers.
b. Jan 11, 1902 in Chicago, Illinois
d. Jul 17, 1969 in Washington, District of Columbia
Source: *BioIn 1, 4, 6, 8; ConAu 115; ObitOF 79; WhAm 5; WhE&EA*

Lahey, Frank Howard
American. Surgeon
Founded Boston's Lahey Clinic, 1922.
b. Jun 1, 1880 in Haverhill, Massachusetts
d. Jun 27, 1953 in Boston, Massachusetts
Source: *BioIn 1, 3, 9; CurBio 41, 53; DcAmB S5; DcAmMeB 84; InSci; ObitOF 79; OxCMed 86; WhAm 3*

Lahr, Bert
[Irving Lahrheim]
American. Actor, Comedian
Starred as Cowardly Lion in *The Wizard of Oz,* 1939.
b. Aug 13, 1895 in New York, New York
d. Dec 4, 1967 in New York, New York
Source: *BiE&WWA; BioIn 1, 2, 3, 4, 5, 6, 7, 8, 11, 21; CamGWoT; CmpEPM; CnThe; CurBio 52, 68; DcAmB S8; EncAFC; EncMT; EncVaud; EncWB; Ent; FamA&A; FilmEn; FilmgC; ForYSC; Funs; HalFC 80, 84, 88; IntDcF 1-3; JoeFr; LegTOT; MotPP; MovMk; NotNAT A, B; OxCAmT 84; OxCPMus; OxCThe 83; PlP&P; PseudN 82; QDrFCA 92; WebAB 74, 79; WhAm 4; WhoCom; WhoHol B; WhoHrs 80; WhScrn 74, 77, 83; WhThe; WorAl; WorAlBi*

Lahr, John
American. Author, Critic
Award-winning drama critic; wrote *Automatic Vaudeville,* 1984; son of actor Bert.
b. Jul 12, 1941 in Los Angeles, California
Source: *AmAu&B; BioIn 8, 15; CamGWoT; ConAmTC; ConAu 21NR, 25R; DrAF 76; DrAPF 80, 91; IntAu&W 76, 86; LinLib L; NotNAT; WhoAm 76, 78, 80, 82, 84, 86, 88, 90, 92, 94, 95, 96, 97; WhoThe 77, 81; WhoUSWr 88; WhoWrEP 89, 92, 95; WorAu 1975; WrDr 76, 80, 82, 84, 86, 88, 90, 92*

Lahti, Christine
American. Actor
Oscar nominee for *Swing Shift,* 1984; other films include *Just Between Friends,* 1986.
b. Apr 4, 1950 in Birmingham, Michigan
Source: *BioIn 14, 15, 16; ConTFT 1, 4, 11; EncAFC; HalFC 88; HolBB; IntMPA 86, 88, 92, 94, 96; LegTOT; News 88-2; NewYTBS 86; VarWW 85; WhoAm 92, 94, 95, 96, 97; WhoAmW 91, 93, 95, 97; WhoEnt 92; WhoHol 92; WorAlBi*

Lai, Francis
French. Composer
Won Oscars for scores to *Love Story,* 1970; *Oliver's Story,* 1970.
b. 1933, France
Source: *ConTFT 2; FilmgC; HalFC 80, 88; IntMPA 84, 86, 88, 92; OxCFilm; OxCPMus; VarWW 85*

Laidler, Harry Wellington
American. Author, Economist
Founder, director of League for Industrial Democracy, 1905-57.
b. Feb 18, 1884 in New York, New York
d. Jul 14, 1970 in New York, New York
Source: *BioIn 9, 15; ConAu 5NR, 5R; CurBio 45, 70; DcAmSR; ObitOF 79; WhAm 5, 7; WhE&EA; WhNAA*

Laiken, Deirdre Susan
American. Author
Won 1987 Edgar for her first mystery novel, *Death Among Strangers.*
b. Jan 21, 1948 in New York, New York
Source: *BioIn 15, 16; ConAu 104; SmATA 40, 48*

Laimbeer, Bill
[William Laimbeer, Jr]
American. Basketball Player
Forward, 1980-93; with Detroit 1982-93; led NBA in rebounding, 1986.
b. May 19, 1957 in Boston, Massachusetts
Source: *BioIn 15, 16; OfNBA 87; WhoAm 90, 92, 94*

Laine, Cleo
[Clementina Dinah Campbell; Mrs. John Dankworth]
English. Singer, Actor
Popular jazz singer who made American debut, 1973, Carnegie Hall.
b. Oct 28, 1927 in Southall, England
Source: *Baker 84, 92; BiDAfM; BiDJaz; BioIn 9, 10, 11, 12, 14, 15; BlueB 76; CelR 90; ConMus 10; ContDcW 89; ConTFT 3, 14; CurBio 86; DcArts; DrBlPA, 90; EncJzS; InB&W 80; IntDcWB; IntWW 82, 83, 89, 91, 93; IntWWM 80, 90; InWom SUP; LegTOT; NewAmDM; NewGrDJ 88, 94; NewGrDM 80; NewOxM; OxCFilm; OxCPMus; PenDiMP; PenEncP; PseudN 82; Who 74, 82, 83, 85, 88, 90, 92, 94; WhoAfA 96; WhoAm 86, 88, 90, 92, 94, 95, 96, 97; WhoAmW 72, 74, 75, 91, 93; WhoBlA 80, 85, 90, 92, 94; WhoE 91; WhoEnt 92; WhoHol 92; WhoMus 72; WhoWor 74, 80, 82, 84, 87; WorAlBi*

Laine, Frankie
[Frank Paul LoVecchio]
American. Singer
Hit songs from 1950s include "Mule Train," 1948; "Sixteen Tons," 1956.
b. Mar 30, 1913 in Chicago, Illinois
Source: *ASCAP 66, 80; BiDAmM; BioIn 1, 2, 3, 4, 12, 19; CmpEPM; CurBio 56; EncRk 88; FilmEn; FilmgC; ForYSC; HalFC 80, 84, 88; LegTOT; NewAmDM; NewGrDA 86; OxCPMus; PenEncP; PseudN 82; RkOn 74; VarWW 85; WhoHol 92, A; WorAl; WorAlBi*

Laing, Alexander Gordon
Scottish. Soldier, Explorer
First European to reach Timbuktu; murdered there.
b. Dec 27, 1793 in Edinburgh, Scotland
d. Sep 26, 1826 in Timbuktu, Mali
Source: *BioIn 9; DcAfHiB 86; DcBiPP; DcNaB; HisDBrE; NewCBEL; WebBD 83; WhDW; WhWE*

Laing, David
Scottish. Editor, Antiquarian
Influential man of letters; secretary, Edinburgh's Bannatyne Club, 1823-61.
b. Apr 20, 1793 in Edinburgh, Scotland
d. Oct 18, 1878 in Portobelo, Panama

Source: *Alli SUP; BiDLA; BioIn 2; BritAu 19; Chambr 3; ChhPo; CmScLit; DcEnL; DcNaB; EvLB; NewCBEL*

Laing, Hugh
[Hugh Skinner]
English. Dancer
Best-known ballets written for him by Anthony Tudor, 1930s-50s; with NYC Ballet, 1950-52.
b. Jun 6, 1911, Barbados
d. May 10, 1988 in New York, New York
Source: *AnObit 1988; BiDD; BioIn 1, 3, 4, 15, 16; CnOxB; CurBio 46, 88, 88N; DancEn 78; IntDcB; NewYTBS 88*

Laing, R(onald) D(avid)
Scottish. Psychiatrist, Author
Guru of 1960s counter-culture; controversial views of schizophrenia discussed in book *The Divided Self,* 1960.
b. Oct 7, 1927 in Glasgow, Scotland
d. Aug 23, 1989 in Saint Tropez, France
Source: *Benet 87, 96; BioIn 8, 9, 10, 11, 12, 13, 14, 15, 16, 17, 20; CelR; ConAu 34NR, 107, 129; ConIsC 1; CurBio 73, 89, 89N; DcAmC; DcLEL 1940; DcNaB 1986; EncSPD; FacFETw; IntAu&W 77, 82, 86; IntWW 76, 77, 78, 79, 80, 81, 82, 83, 89; MajTwCW; MakMC; News 90-1; NewYTBE 73; NewYTBS 89; RAdv 14, 13-5; ThTwC 87; WhAm 11; Who 74, 82, 83, 85, 88; WhoAm 74, 76, 78, 80, 82, 84, 86, 88; WhoWor 78, 84, 87, 89; WorAu 1970; WrDr 76, 80, 82, 84, 86, 88*

Laingen, (Lowell) Bruce
[The Hostages]
American. Diplomat, Hostage
One of 52 held by terrorists, Nov 1979 - Jan 1981.
b. Aug 6, 1922 in Odin Township, Minnesota
Source: *BioIn 12, 20; NewYTBS 79, 81; USBiR 74; WhoAm 74, 76, 78, 80, 82, 84, 86, 88, 90, 92, 94, 95, 96, 97; WhoGov 72; WhoWor 78, 80, 82, 84*

Laird, Melvin Robert
American. Government Official
Secretary of defense under Richard Nixon, 1969-73.
b. Sep 1, 1922 in Omaha, Nebraska
Source: *BiDrAC; BiDrUSC 89; BiDrUSE 71, 89; BioIn 7, 8, 9, 10, 11, 12; ColdWar 2; ConAu 65; CurBio 64; EncWB; IntWW 74, 75, 76, 77, 78, 79, 80, 81, 82, 83, 89, 91, 93; NewYTBE 71, 73; PolProf J, K, NF; Who 85, 92; WhoAm 86, 90, 92, 94, 95, 96, 97; WhoAmP 73, 75, 77, 79, 81, 83, 85, 87, 89, 91, 93, 95; WhoSSW 73; WorAl; WorAlBi*

Laird, Rick
[The Mahavishnu Orchestra; Richard Quentin Laird]
Irish. Singer, Musician
Bassist who cofounded Mahavishnu Orchestra, 1971-73.
b. Feb 5, 1941 in Dublin, Ireland
Source: *BiDJaz; EncJzS; NewGrDJ 88, 94; WhoRocM 82*

Lajoie, Nap(oleon)
"Larry"
American. Baseball Player
Infielder, 1896-1916; had .339 lifetime batting average; Hall of Fame, 1937.
b. Sep 5, 1875 in Woonsocket, Rhode Island
d. Feb 7, 1959 in Daytona Beach, Florida
Source: *BiDAmSp BB; BioIn 2, 3, 4, 5, 6, 7, 8, 9, 10, 14, 15, 20; DcAmB S6; LegTOT; WhoProB 73; WhoSpor; WorAl; WorAlBi*

Lakatos, Imre
Hungarian. Philosopher
Developed field of scientific methodology.
b. Nov 9, 1922 in Debrecen, Hungary
d. Feb 2, 1974 in London, England
Source: *BioIn 12; ConAu 116; IntEnSS 79; MakMC; ObitT 1971; OxCPhil; ThTwC 87*

Lake, Anthony
[William Anthony Kirsopp Lake]
American. Government Official
President Clinton's national security adviser, 1993—.
b. Apr 2, 1939 in New York, New York
Source: *CurBio 94; IntWW 93; WhoAm 84*

Lake, Arthur
[Arthur Silverlake]
American. Actor
Played comic strip character Dagwood Bumstead in over two dozen *Blondie* films, 1939-50.
b. Apr 17, 1905 in Corbin, Kentucky
d. Jan 9, 1987 in Indian Wells, California
Source: *BioIn 2, 4, 8, 15; EncAFC; Film 1, 2; FilmEn; FilmgC; ForYSC; Funs; HalFC 80, 84, 88; IntMPA 77, 80; LegTOT; MotPP; MovMk; PseudN 82; QDrFCA 92; RadStar; TwYS; What 2; WhoHol A*

Lake, Greg(ory)
[Emerson, Lake, and Palmer]
English. Singer, Musician
Guitarist, bassist, vocalist with group formed 1970-79; known for acoustic ballads.
b. Nov 10, 1948 in Bournemouth, England
Source: *EncPR&S 89; LegTOT; RkOn 85; WhoRocM 82*

Lake, Ricki
[Mrs. Rob Sussman]
American. Actor, TV Personality
Appeared in *Hairspray,* 1988; host of "The Ricki Lake Show," 1993—.
b. Sep 21, 1968 in Hastings-on-Hudson, New York
Source: *IntMPA 92, 94, 96; LegTOT; News 94; WhoAmW 97; WhoHol 92*

Lake, Simon
American. Engineer, Inventor
Designed submarines, torpedo-boat used in WW I.
b. Sep 4, 1866 in Pleasantville, New Jersey
d. Jun 23, 1945 in Bridgeport, Connecticut
Source: *ApCAB X; BioIn 2, 4, 6, 8, 16; CurBio 45; DcAmB S3; InSci; NatCAB 15; OxCAmH; WebAB 74, 79; WebAMB; WhAm 2*

Lake, Veronica
[Constance Frances Marie Ockleman]
American. Actor
Popular in 1940s films; known for style-setting long, straight hair.
b. Nov 14, 1919 in New York, New York
d. Jul 7, 1973 in Burlington, Vermont
Source: *BiDFilm, 81, 94; BioAmW; BioIn 7, 8, 9, 10, 12, 13, 15; DcArts; EncAFC; FilmEn; FilmgC; ForYSC; GangFlm; HalFC 80, 84, 88; IntDcF 1-3, 2-3; InWom, SUP; LegTOT; MotPP; MovMk; NewYTBE 71, 73; ObitOF 79; ObitT 1971; OxCFilm; What 1; WhoHol B; WhoHrs 80; WhScrn 83; WomWMM; WorAl; WorAlBi; WorEFlm*

Laker, Freddie, Sir
[Frederick Alfred Laker]
English. Airline Executive
Founded Laker Airways, 1976; inexpensive, no-reservation Skytrain between London and New York.
b. Aug 6, 1922 in Canterbury, England
Source: *BioIn 13; CurBio 78; DcTwBBL; IntWW 78, 79, 80, 81, 82, 83, 89, 91, 93; NewYTBS 77, 82, 83; Who 74, 82, 83, 85, 88, 90, 92, 94*

Lalande, Joseph Jerome Lefrancais de
French. Astronomer
Popularized astronomy; established annual Lalande Prize, 1802, for year's best astronomical achievement.
b. Jul 11, 1732 in Bourg-en-Bresse, France
d. Apr 4, 1807 in Paris, France
Source: *AsBiEn; BbD; DcScB; NewCol 75*

LaLanne, Jack
American. Physical Fitness Expert, Bodybuilder
Hosted syndicated physical fitness TV series, late 1950s-70s.
b. Sep 26, 1914 in San Francisco, California
Source: *BioIn 5, 10, 11, 12, 14, 20; CurBio 94; LegTOT; LesBEnT, 92; NewYTET; WhoAm 96*

Lalas, Alexi
[Panayotis Alexander Lalas]
American. Soccer Player
Member of U.S. World Cup soccer team, 1994.
b. Jun 1, 1970 in Royal Oak, Michigan
Source: *BioIn 20, 21; News 95, 95-1*

Lalique, Rene
French. Jeweler
Created exclusive art nouveau jewelry, perfume, bottles, glass pieces.
b. Apr 6, 1860 in Ay, France
d. May 5, 1945 in Paris, France
Source: *AntBDN A; BioIn 1, 9, 10, 11, 13, 15; DcArts; DcD&D; DcNiCA; DcTwDes; EncFash; Entr; FacFETw; IlDcG; InWom SUP; LegTOT; ObitOF 79; OxCDecA; PenDiDA 89*

Lalo, Edouard Victor Antoine
French. Composer
Works include opera *LeRoi d'Ys,* 1888; ballet *Namouna,* 1882.
b. Jan 27, 1823 in Lille, France
d. Apr 22, 1892 in Paris, France
Source: *NewCol 75; WebBD 83; WorAl*

Lalonde, Marc
Canadian. Politician, Economist
Principal secretary to Pierre Trudeau, 1968-72; served in ministerial capacity, 1972-84.
b. Jul 26, 1929 in Ile Perrot, Quebec, Canada
Source: *AmCath 80; BioIn 12, 13, 15; BlueB 76; CanWW 31, 70, 79, 80, 81, 83, 89; ConNews 85-1; IntWW 74, 75, 76, 77, 78, 79, 80, 81, 82, 83, 89, 91, 93; Who 85, 88, 90, 92, 94; WhoAm 78, 80, 82, 84, 86, 88, 90, 92, 94, 95, 96, 97; WhoCan 73, 82, 84; WhoE 81, 83, 85, 86, 95; WhoWor 82*

Lalonde, Newsy
[Edward C Lalonde]
Canadian. Hockey Player
Center, 1917-22, 1926-27, mostly with Montreal; won Art Ross Trophy, 1919, 1921; Hall of Fame, 1950.
b. Dec 31, 1887 in Cornwall, Ontario, Canada
d. Nov 21, 1970 in Montreal, Quebec, Canada
Source: *BioIn 10; HocEn; WhoHcky 73; WhoSpor*

Lamantia, Philip
American. Author
Volumes of surrealist verse include *Erotic Poems,* 1946; *Becoming Visible,* 1981.
b. Oct 23, 1927 in San Francisco, California
Source: *AmAu&B; BioIn 13, 16; ConAu 111, 117; ConPo 70, 75, 80, 85, 91; DcLB 16; DcLEL 1940; DrAP 75; DrAPF 80, 87; IntAu&W 91, 93; IntvTCA 2; IntWWP 77; OxCAmL 83, 95; OxCTwCP; PenC AM; WorAu 1970; WrDr 76, 80, 82, 84, 86, 88, 90, 92, 94, 96*

Lamar, Joseph Rucker
American. Supreme Court Justice
Taft appointee who served 1910-16.
b. Oct 14, 1857 in Elbert County, Georgia
d. Jan 2, 1916 in Washington, District of Columbia
Source: *AmBi; ApCAB X; BiDFedJ; BiDSA; BioIn 1, 2, 5, 15; DcAmB; EncSoB; EncSoH; HarEnUS; NatCAB 15; OxCSupC; SupCtJu; WebAB 74, 79; WhAm 1*

Lamar, Lucius Quintus Cincinnatus
American. Politician, Supreme Court Justice
Dem. senator from MS, 1872-85; secretary of interior, 1885-88; associate justice, Supreme Court, 1888-93.
b. Sep 17, 1825 in Eatonton, Georgia
d. Jan 23, 1893 in Vineland, Georgia
Source: *AmBi; ApCAB; BiAUS; BiDConf; BiDFedJ; BiDrAC; BiDrUSC 89; BiDrUSE 71, 89; BioIn 1, 2, 4, 5, 8, 10, 11, 12, 15; CivWDc; DcAmB; EncAAH; EncSoH; EncWM; HarEnUS; LiveMA; McGEWB; OxCSupC; SupCtJu; TwCBDA; WebAB 74, 79; WhAm HS; WhAmP; WhCiWar*

Lamarck, Jean Baptiste Pierre
French. Naturalist
A forerunner of Darwin; classified animals; wrote *Philosophie Zoologique,* 1809.
b. Aug 1, 1744 in Bazentin, France
d. Dec 18, 1829 in Paris, France
Source: *BbD; BiD&SB; BiDPsy; McGEWB; NewCol 75; OxCEng 85; OxCFr; REn; WebBD 83*

LaMarr, Barbara
[Rheatha Watson]
American. Actor
Played in 22 silent movies; best known for her exotic beauty; private life was scandal plagued; died from drug overdose.
b. Jul 28, 1896 in Richard, Virginia
d. Jan 30, 1926 in Altadena, California
Source: *Film 2; FilmEn; FilmgC; MotPP; MovMk; NotNAT B; TwYS; WhoHol B; WhScrn 74, 77*

Lamarr, Hedy
[Hedwig Eva Marie Kiesler; Hedy Kieslerova]
American. Actor
Gained notoriety for her 10-minute nude sequence in film *Ecstasy,* 1933; billed as world's most beautiful woman.
b. Sep 11, 1913 in Vienna, Austria
Source: *BiDFilm, 94; BioIn 10, 11, 15; EncAFC; FilmAG WE; FilmEn; FilmgC; GangFlm; HalFC 80, 84, 88; IntMPA 92; InWom SUP; ItaFilm; LegTOT; MotPP; MovMk; NewYTBE 70; OxCFilm; PseudN 82; ThFT; VarWW 85; What 4; WhoHol 92, A; WorAl; WorAlBi; WorEFlm*

LaMarsh, Judy
[Julia Verlyn Lamarsh]
Canadian. Politician, TV Personality, Author
Canadian minister of Health and Welfare, 1963-65; only woman in Lester Pearson cabinet.
b. Dec 20, 1924 in Chatham, Ontario, Canada
d. Oct 27, 1980 in Toronto, Ontario, Canada
Source: *AnObit 1980; BlueB 76; CanWW 70, 79, 80; ConAu 13NR, 29R, 105; CurBio 81N; IntWW 74, 75, 76, 77, 78, 79, 80; InWom, SUP; NewYTBS 80; WhAm 7; WhoCan 77*

Lamartine, Alphonse Marie Louis de Prat de
"The Narcissus of France"
French. Poet, Historian
Noted for popular *Meditations poetiques,* 1820, which strongly influenced Romantic movement.
b. Oct 21, 1790 in Macon, France
d. Feb 27, 1869 in Paris, France
Source: *AtlBL; BbD; BiD&SB; CasWL; DcBiA; DcEuL; EuAu; EvEuW; NewCol 75; NinCLC 1; OxCEng 67; OxCFr; PenC EUR; PseudN 82; RComWL; REn; WorAl*

Lamas, Fernando
American. Actor, Director
Typecast as a Latin lover in 1950s films; TV series include "Falcon Crest"; married Esther Williams, Arlene Dahl.
b. Jan 9, 1925 in Buenos Aires, Argentina
d. Oct 8, 1982 in Los Angeles, California
Source: *BiE&WWA; FilmgC; IntMPA 77, 78, 79, 80, 81, 82, 84; MGM; MotPP; MovMk; NewYTBS 82; WhAm 8; WhoAm 80, 82; WhoHol A; WhoWest 78*

Lamas, Lorenzo
American. Actor
Son of Fernando Lamas, Arlene Dahl; played Lance Cumson on TV series "Falcon Crest," 1981-90.
b. Jan 20, 1958 in Santa Monica, California
Source: *BioIn 11, 12, 13, 14, 16; ConTFT 5; IntMPA 86, 88, 92, 94, 96; LegTOT; VarWW 85; WhoAm 86, 88, 90, 92, 94, 95, 96, 97; WhoEnt 92; WhoHisp 91, 92, 94; WhoHol 92; WorAlBi*

Lamaze, Fernand
Physician
Invented Lamaze Method of natural birthing.

Lamb, Brian (P.)
American. Broadcast Journalist
Host on cable television's C-SPAN, 1979—.
b. Oct 9, 1941 in Lafayette, Indiana
Source: *CurBio 95*

Lamb, Caroline Ponsonby, Lady
English. Author
Noted for affair with Lord Byron, 1812; husband later prime minister Melbourne left her, 1825.
b. Nov 13, 1785 in Roehampton, England
d. Jan 24, 1828 in London, England
Source: *Alli; BritAu 19; CasWL; Chambr 2; DcEnL; DcLEL; EvLB; NewC; OxCEng 67; REn; WebBD 83*

Lamb, Charles
[Elia; Upright Telltruth, Esq.]
"The Mitre Courtier"
English. Essayist, Author
Wrote *Essays of Elia,* 1820-25; brother of Mary Ann Lamb.
b. Feb 10, 1775 in London, England
d. Dec 27, 1834 in Edmonton, England
Source: *Alli; AtlBL; BbD; Benet 87, 96; BiD&SB; BiDLA; BioIn 1, 2, 3, 4, 5, 6, 7, 8, 9, 10, 11, 12, 13, 14, 15, 16, 17, 18, 20; BlmGEL; BritAu 19; BritWr 4; CamGEL; CamGLE; CamGWoT; CarSB; CasWL; CelCen; Chambr 3; ChhPo, S1, S2, S3; CnDBLB 3; CrtT 2; CyWA 58; DcArts; DcBiPP; DcEnA; DcEnL; DcEuL; DcInB; DcLB 93, 107, 163; DcLEL; DcNaB; Dis&D; EvLB; GrWrEL N; LinLib L, S; LngCEL; McGEWB; MouLC 3; NewC; NewCBEL; NinCLC 10; NotNAT B; OxCAusL; OxCChiL; OxCEng 67, 85, 95; OxCMus; OxCThe 67, 83; PenC ENG; PseudAu; RAdv 1, 14, 13-1; RComWL; REn; RfGEnL 91; SmATA 17; WebE&AL; WhDW; WhoChL; WorAl; WorAlBi; WorLitC*

Lamb, Gil
American. Actor
Film comedian; films include *The Fleet's In,* 1949; *The Love Bug,* 1968.
b. Jun 14, 1906 in Minneapolis, Minnesota
Source: *EncAFC; FilmgC; ForYSC; HalFC 80, 84, 88; IntMPA 75, 76, 77, 78, 79, 80, 81, 82, 84, 86, 88; VarWW 85; WhoHol 92, A*

Lamb, Harold Albert
American. Author
Wrote historical narratives *Genghis Khan,* 1927; *Tamerlane,* 1928.
b. Sep 1, 1892 in Alpine, New Jersey
d. Apr 9, 1962 in Rochester, New York
Source: *AmAu&B; AuBYP 2; ChhPo S2; ConAu 89, 101; JBA 34, 51; NatCAB 52; OxCAmL 65; REn; REnAL; ScF&FL 1; TwCA, SUP; WhAm 4; WhE&EA; WhNAA*

Lamb, Lawrence Edward
American. Physician
Noted cardiologist; writings include *Stay Youthful and Fit,* 1974.
b. Oct 13, 1926 in Fredonia, Kansas
Source: *AmMWSc 73P, 76P, 79, 82, 86; ConAu 97; WhoAm 74, 76, 78, 80, 82, 84, 86, 88, 90; WhoSSW 73*

Lamb, Mary Ann
"MB"
English. Children's Author
Killed mother in fit of insanity, 1796; sister of Charles.
b. Dec 3, 1764 in London, England
d. May 20, 1847 in London, England
Source: *Alli; ArtclWW 2; BioIn 1, 2, 6, 8, 9, 10, 11, 12; BlmGEL; CarSB; ChhPo, S2, S3; DcEnA; DcEnL; DcLEL; DcNaB; Dis&D; EncBrWW; InWom SUP; NewC; NewCBEL; OxCEng 67, 85, 95; PseudN 82; SmATA 17; WhoChL*

Lamb, Sydney MacDonald
American. Linguist
Constructed linguistics theory called stratificational grammar; wrote*Outline of Stratificational Grammar,* 1966.
b. May 4, 1929 in Denver, Colorado
Source: *ConAu 33NR; DrAS 74F, 78F; WhoAm 88, 90, 92, 94, 95, 96, 97; WhoSSW 97*

Lamb, Willis Eugene, Jr.
American. Physicist, Educator
Shared Nobel Prize in physics, 1955, for discovery of hyperfine structure of hydrogen spectrum.
b. Jul 12, 1913 in Los Angeles, California
Source: *AmMWSc 73P, 76P, 79, 82, 86, 89, 92, 95; BiESc; BioIn 3, 4, 7, 15, 20; InSci; IntWW 74, 75, 76, 77, 78, 79, 80, 81, 82, 83, 89, 91, 93; LarDcSc; McGMS 80; NobelP; RAdv 14; WebAB 74, 79; Who 92; WhoAm 74, 76, 78, 80, 82, 84, 86, 88, 90, 92, 94, 95, 96, 97; WhoFrS 84; WhoNob, 90, 95; WhoScEn 94, 96; WhoWest 80, 84, 87, 89, 92, 94, 96; WhoWor 82, 84, 87, 89, 91, 93, 95, 96, 97*

Lambeau, Curly
[Earl Louis Lambeau]
American. Football Player, Football Coach
One of founders, Green Bay Packers, 1919; Green Bay running back, 1921-29, coach, 1921-49; Hall of Fame, 1963.
b. Apr 9, 1898 in Green Bay, Wisconsin
d. Jun 1, 1965 in Sturgeon, Wisconsin
Source: *BiDAmSp FB; BioIn 6, 7, 8, 17; DcAmB S7; LegTOT; ObitOF 79; WhoFtbl 74; WhoSpor; WorAl; WorAlBi*

Lambert, Christopher
American. Actor
17th actor to play Tarzan; in 1984 film *Greystoke: The Legend of Tarzan, Lord of the Apes.*
b. Mar 29, 1957 in New York, New York
Source: *BioIn 14, 15; ConTFT 3; HalFC 88; IntMPA 86, 92, 94, 96; IntWW 93; LegTOT; WhoHol 92*

Lambert, Constant
English. Composer
Created ballet as art form in England; director, Sadler's Wells, 1931-47; composed *Romeo and Juliet,* 1926.
b. Aug 23, 1905 in London, England
d. Aug 21, 1951 in London, England
Source: *Baker 78, 84, 92; BiDD; BioIn 1, 2, 3, 4, 5, 10, 11, 14; BriBkM 80; CnOxB; DancEn 78; DcCom&M 79; DcNaB 1951; GrBr; HalFC 84, 88; IntDcB; MusMk; NewAmDM; NewGrDM 80; NewOxM; ObitT 1951; OxCEng 85, 95; OxCMus; OxDcOp; PenDiMP, A; WhE&EA; WhoThe 77; WhThe*

Lambert, Eleanor
[Mrs. Seymour Berkson]
American. Journalist
Fashion publicist who started Best Dressed polls, 1940.
Source: *BioIn 7, 9, 10, 16, 17, 19, 20; BioNews 74; ConAu 102; CurBio 49, 59; ForWC 70; InWom SUP; ObitOF 79; ODwPR 91; WhoAdv 90; WhoAm 78, 80, 82, 84, 86, 88, 90, 92, 94, 95, 96, 97; WhoAmW 61, 64, 66, 68, 70, 72, 74; WhoFI 75; WorFshn; WrDr 82, 84*

Lambert, Gerard Barnes
American. Business Executive
Successful marketing of father's invention, Listerine, 1920s, made it a household word.
b. May 15, 1886 in Saint Louis, Missouri
Source: *BioIn 4, 7, 9, 10; NatCAB 52; WhAm 4*

Lambert, J(ack) W(alter)
English. Critic
Literary, art editor, *Sunday Times,* London, 1960-76.
b. Apr 21, 1917 in London, England
Source: *Au&Wr 71; ConAu 108, 120; Who 74, 82, 83, 85; WhoThe 72, 77, 81; WrDr 80, 82, 84, 86*

Lambert, Jack
[John Harold Lambert]
American. Football Player
Nine-time all-pro linebacker, Pittsburgh, 1974-84; Hall of Fame, 1990.
b. Jul 8, 1952 in Mantua, Ohio
Source: *BiDAmSp FB; BioIn 11, 13, 14; FootReg 85; LegTOT; NewYTBS 76; WhoAm 78, 80, 82, 84; WhoSpor; WorAl*

Lambert, Piggy
[Ward L Lambert]
American. Basketball Coach
Coach, Purdue, 1916, 1918-46; pioneered fast break; Basketball Hall of Fame, 1960.
b. May 28, 1888 in Deadwood, South Dakota
Source: *BasBi; BioIn 4, 9; WhoSpor*

Lambert, Ward L
"Piggy"
American. Basketball Coach
Coach, Purdue U, 1917, 1919-46; stressed mental factor of game; introduced fast break; Hall of Fame.
b. May 28, 1888 in Deadwood, South Dakota
d. Jan 20, 1958 in Lafayette, Indiana

Source: *BioIn 4, 9; ObitOF 79; PseudN 82; WhoBbl 73*

Lamborghini, Ferruccio
Italian. Auto Executive
Founder, Lamborghini Auto Co., known for its sleek and aerodynamic sports cars.
b. 1917 in Ferrara, Italy
d. Feb 20, 1993 in Perugia, Italy

Lambsdorff, Otto
German. Government Official
Helmut Schmidt's Minister of Economic Affairs, 1977-84.
b. Dec 20, 1926 in Aachen, Germany
Source: *BioIn 13, 14; CurBio 80; EncWB; IntWW 91; NewYTBS 83; WhoEIO 82; WhoWor 82, 89*

Lamburn, Richmal Crompton
[Richmal Crompton]
English. Author
Writings include "Just William" children's series, 1920s-60s; novel *Dread Dwellings,* 1926.
b. Nov 15, 1890 in Bury, England
d. Jan 10, 1969 in Kent, England
Source: *BioIn 8, 9, 10, 14, 16; CamGLE; ConAu 25R, P-1, X; DcArts; DcLB 160; DcNaB 1961; FemiCLE; FilmgC; GrBr; HalFC 84, 88; LngCTC; MnBBF; NewC; Novels; ObitT 1961; OxCChiL; PseudN 82; RGTwCWr; ScF&FL 1, 2; SmATA 5; TwCChW 78, 83, 89, 95; WhE&EA; WhLit; WhoChL; WhoHr&F*

Lame Deer
[John Fire]
American. Native American Leader
Mission was to preserve old Sioux ways.
b. 1903 in South Dakota
d. 1976
Source: *NatNAL; NotNaAm*

Lamizana, Sangoule
Upper Voltan. Statesman
Pres., Upper Volta, 1966-80, deposed by coup.
b. 1916 in Dianra Tougan, Upper Senegal-Niger
Source: *AfSS 79, 82; DcAfHiB 86, 86S; IntWW 74, 91; NewCol 75; WhoFr 79; WhoGov 72, 75; WhoWor 74, 76, 78; WorDWW*

Lamm, Richard Douglas
"Governor Gloom"
American. Politician
Dem. governor of CO, 1974-87; wrote *The Immigration Time Bomb,* 1985.
b. Aug 3, 1935 in Madison, Wisconsin
Source: *BioIn 13, 14; CurBio 85; IntWW 83, 91; PolsAm 84; WhoAm 76, 78, 80, 82, 84, 86, 88, 90; WhoAmL 78, 79; WhoAmP 85, 91; WhoGov 77; WhoWest 87, 89, 92; WhoWor 78, 82, 87*

Lamm, Robert
American. Singer, Musician
Keyboardist, unofficial leader of group; had solo album *Skinny Boy,* 1974.
b. Oct 13, 1944 in New York, New York
Source: *WhoAm 86; WhoRocM 82*

Lamont, Corliss
American. Social Reformer
Director, ACLU, 1932-54.
b. Mar 28, 1902
d. Apr 26, 1995 in Ossining, New York
Source: *AmAu&B; Au&Wr 71; BioIn 1, 4, 9, 12, 13, 20, 21; BlueB 76; ConAu 11NR, 13R, 148; CurBio 95N; DrAS 74P, 78P, 82P; IntAu&W 76, 77, 82; IntWWP 77; NewYTBS 95; RelLAm 91; REn; REnAL; TwCA, SUP; WhAm 11; WhE&EA; WhNAA; WhoAm 74, 76, 78, 80, 82, 84, 86, 88, 90, 92; WhoUSWr 88; WhoWor 74, 76, 78, 80, 82, 89, 91, 93, 95; WhoWrEP 89, 92; WrDr 76, 80, 92, 94, 96*

Lamont, Norman
English. Government Official
Conservative chancellor of the Exchequer under John Major during recessionary early 1990s.
b. May 8, 1942 in Lerwick, Scotland
Source: *CurBio 92; IntWW 91; Who 92*

Lamont, Thomas William
American. Businessman, Philanthropist
Chm., J P Morgan bankers, 1943; noted for financing industry, loans to foreign governments.
b. Sep 30, 1870 in Claverack, New York
d. Feb 2, 1948 in Boca Grande, Florida
Source: *AmPeW; ApCAB X; BiDAmBL 83; BiDInt; BioIn 1, 2, 4, 16, 20, 21; ChhPo S1; CurBio 40, 48; DcAmB S4; DcAmDH 80, 89; DcNAA; EncABHB 9; LinLib S; NatCAB 41; WhAm 2*

LaMotta, Jake
[Jacob Lamotta]
"Bronx Bull"
American. Boxer
Robert DeNiro portrayed him in movie *Raging Bull,* 1981.
b. Jul 10, 1921 in New York, New York
Source: *BioIn 10, 15, 16; BoxReg; LegTOT; PseudN 82; WhoBox 74; WhoSpor*

Lamour, Dorothy
[Dorothy Kaumeyer]
American. Actor, Singer
Best known for 1940s "road" films with Bing Crosby, Bob Hope.
b. Dec 10, 1914 in New Orleans, Louisiana
d. Sep 22, 1996 in Los Angeles, California
Source: *BiDD; BiDFilm, 81, 94; BioIn 1, 9, 10, 12; BioNews 74; CmMov; CmpEPM; ConAu 105, 134, 153; ConTFT 11; EncAFC; EncFash; FilmEn; FilmgC; ForYSC; HalFC 80, 84, 88; IntDcF 1-3, 2-3; IntMPA 75, 76, 77, 78, 79, 80, 81, 82, 84, 86, 88, 92, 94, 96; InWom, SUP; LegTOT; MotPP; MovMk; News 97-1; NewYTBS 27; OxCFilm; OxCPMus; PseudN 82; RadStar; SaTiSS; ThFT; VarWW 85; WhoAm 74; WhoAmW 74; WhoHol 92, A; WorAl; WorAlBi; WorEFlm; WrDr 94*

L'Amour, Louis Dearborn
[Tex Burns]
American. Author
Popular writer of Western novels; wrote 101 books including *Hondo,* 1953, his first and best-selling novel.
b. Mar 22, 1908 in Jamestown, North Dakota
d. Jun 10, 1988 in Los Angeles, California
Source: *AuNews 1, 2; BioIn 10, 11, 12, 13, 14, 15, 16, 17, 18, 20; CmCal; ConAu 1R, 3NR; ConLC 25; CurBio 80, 88; NewYTBS 81, 88; REnAW; WhoAm 86, 88; WhoWest 87; WhoWor 89; WrDr 86*

Lamoureux, Charles
French. Conductor, Violinist
A pioneer Wagnerian who helped Parisians appreciate Wagner.
b. Sep 28, 1834 in Bordeaux, France
d. Dec 21, 1899 in Paris, France
Source: *Baker 78, 84, 92; BioIn 8; BriBkM 80; NewAmDM; NewEOp 71; NewGrDM 80; NewGrDO; OxCFr; OxCMus; PenDiMP*

Lampert, Zohra
American. Actor
Starred in film *Let's Scare Jessica to Death,* 1971; TV series "The Girl with Something Extra," 1973-74.
b. May 13, 1936 in New York, New York
Source: *BiE&WWA; ConTFT 1, 4; FilmEn; ForWC 70; ForYSC; HalFC 80, 84, 88; LegTOT; MotPP; NotNAT; VarWW 85; WhoHol 92, A*

Lamperti, Francesco
Italian. Teacher
Taught distinguished singers; voice professor, Milan Conservatory, 1850-75.
b. Mar 11, 1813 in Savona, Italy
d. May 1, 1892 in Como, Italy
Source: *Baker 78; NewEOp 71; NewGrDM 80*

Lampman, Archibald
Canadian. Poet
Nature writer; verse volumes include *Lyrics of Earth,* 1895.
b. Nov 17, 1861 in Morpeth, Ontario, Canada
d. Feb 10, 1899 in Ottawa, Ontario, Canada
Source: *Alli SUP; BbD; Benet 96; BenetAL 91; BiD&SB; BioIn 1, 3, 4, 5, 9, 11, 12, 17; BritAu 19; CamGEL; CamGLE; CanWr; CasWL; Chambr 3; ChhPo, S1, S2, S3; DcCanB 12; DcLB 92; DcLEL; DcNAA; GrWrEL P; LinLib L; MacDCB 78; McGEWB; NinCLC 25; OxCAmL 65; OxCCan; OxCCanL;*

OxCEng 67; PenC ENG; REnAL; RfGEnL 91; WebE&AL

Lampman, Evelyn Sibley
[Lynn Bronson]
American. Children's Author
Wrote award-winning *Treasure Mountain,* 1949; *Cayuse Courage,* 1970.
b. Apr 18, 1907 in Dallas, Oregon
d. Jun 13, 1980 in Portland, Oregon
Source: *AuBYP 2; ChlBkCr; ConAu 11NR, 13R, 101; DcAmChF 1960; MorJA; PenNWW A, B; PseudN 82; ScF&FL 92; SmATA 4, 23N, 87; TwCChW 83, 89, 95; WhoAmW 58, 61, 64, 66, 68, 70, 72, 74, 75, 77; WhoPNW*

Lamy, Jean Baptist
American. Religious Leader
Archbishop of Santa Fe, 1875-85; *Death Comes for the Archbishop,* by Willa Cather, 1927, based on his career.
b. Oct 14, 1814 in Lempdes, France
d. Feb 13, 1888 in Santa Fe, New Mexico
Source: *NatCAB 12; NewCol 75; WebAB 74; WhAm HS; WorAl*

Lancaster, Burt(on Stephen)
American. Actor
Won Oscar, 1960, for *Elmer Gantry;* in major films from 1946.
b. Nov 2, 1913 in New York, New York
d. Oct 20, 1994 in Century City, California
Source: *BiDFilm, 81, 94; BioIn 1, 3, 4, 5, 6, 7, 8, 10, 11, 12, 13, 14, 15, 16, 17, 19, 20, 21; BkPepl; BlueB 76; CelR, 90; CmMov; ConAu 116, 122, 147; ConTFT 1, 6, 14; CurBio 86, 95N; DcArts; DcTwCCu 1; FacFETw; FilmEn; FilmgC; ForYSC; GangFlm; HalFC 80, 84, 88; IntDcF 1-3, 2-3; IntMPA 75, 76, 77, 78, 79, 80, 81, 82, 84, 86, 88, 92, 94; IntWW 91; ItaFilm; LegTOT; MiSFD 9; MotPP; MovMk; News 95, 95-1; NewYTBS 94; OxCFilm; VarWW 85; WhoAm 74, 76, 78, 80, 82, 84, 86, 88, 90; WhoEnt 92; WhoHol 92, A; WhoHrs 80; WhoWor 74, 78; WorAl; WorAlBi; WorEFlm*

Lancaster, Joseph
English. Educator
Developed Lancastrian method of mass education, popular in 19th c.
b. Nov 25, 1778 in London, England
d. Oct 24, 1838 in New York, New York
Source: *Alli; ApCAB; BiDLA; BioIn 8; BritAu 19; CyEd; DcAmAu; DcCanB 7; DcNAA; DcNaB; HarEnUS; LinLib S; McGEWB; NewC; NewCBEL; OxCEng 67, 85, 95; TwCBDA; WhDW; WorAl; WorAlBi*

Lancaster, Osbert, Sir
English. Cartoonist
Created character Maudie Littlehampton for *London Daily Express,* 1939-81.
b. Aug 4, 1908 in London, England
d. Jul 27, 1986 in London, England
Source: *AnObit 1986; BioIn 3, 4, 5, 6, 7, 8, 12, 14, 15, 16, 17; BlueB 76; CnOxB; ConAu 105, 119; ConGrA 3; CurBio 64, 86N; DancEn 78; DcBrAr 1; DcNaB 1986; IlsCB 1946; IntAu&W 76, 77; IntWW 74, 75, 76, 77, 78, 79, 80, 81, 82, 83; LngCTC; NewC; NewCBEL; NewYTBS 86; OxDcOp; PhDcTCA 77; TwCA SUP; WhDW; Who 74, 82, 83, 85; WhoGrA 62, 82; WhoWor 74; WorECar; WrDr 76, 80, 82, 84, 86*

Lance, (Thomas) Bert(ram)
American. Banker, Government Official
Director, OMB, Jan-Sep, 1977.
b. Jun 3, 1931 in Gainesville, Georgia
Source: *BioIn 11, 12, 13, 14, 17; CurBio 77; WhoAm 78, 80, 82, 84, 86, 88, 90, 92, 94; WhoAmP 83, 85, 87, 89, 91, 93, 95; WhoFI 74, 75, 77, 79, 81, 83, 85; WhoGov 77; WhoSSW 73, 75, 76; WorAl; WorAlBi*

Lancetti, Pino
Italian. Fashion Designer
Known for flowing, dramatic clothes; shop opened, 1961.
b. 1932 in Perugia, Italy
Source: *ConDes 84, 90, 97; EncFash; WorFshn*

Lanchester, Elsa
[Mrs. Charles Laughton; Elizabeth Sullivan]
English. Comedian
Known for eccentric, comic roles: *The Bride of Frankenstein,* 1935.
b. Oct 28, 1902 in Lewisham, England
d. Dec 26, 1986 in Woodland Hills, California
Source: *AnObit 1986, 80, 84, 86; InWom SUP; LegTOT; MotPP; MovMk; NewYTBS 86; NotNAT; OxCFilm; PenEncH; PlP&P; PseudN 82; ThFT; VarWW 85; Vers A; WhAm 9; WhoAm 74, 76, 78, 80, 82, 84; WhoAmW 58, 70, 72, 74; WhoHol A; WhoHrs 80; WhoWor 74; WhThe; WorAl; WorAlBi*

Lancret, Nicolas
French. Artist
Rococco painter; did genre, theatrical scenes including *The Music Lesson,* 1743.
b. Jan 22, 1690 in Paris, France
d. Sep 14, 1743 in Paris, France
Source: *AtlBL; BioIn 1, 11, 15; ClaDrA; DcArts; DcBiPP; EncEnl; McGDA; NewCol 75; OxCArt; OxCFr; OxDcArt*

Land, Edwin Herbert
American. Physicist, Inventor
Founded Polaroid Corp., 1937; developed Polaroid lenses, one-step photography; had 533 patents.
b. May 7, 1909 in Norwich, Connecticut
d. Mar 1, 1991 in Cambridge, Massachusetts
Source: *AmMWSc 73P, 76P, 79, 82, 86, 89, 92; AsBiEn; BiDAmBL 83; BioIn 1, 2, 3, 5, 7, 8, 9, 11, 12, 13, 15, 16; BlueB 76; CamDcSc; CurBio 53, 81, 91N; DcArts; EncAB-H 1974, 1996; FacFETw; ICPEnP; InSci; IntWW 74, 75, 76, 77, 78, 79, 80, 81, 82, 83, 89, 91N; LarDcSc; MacBEP; McGEWB; McGMS 80; News 91-3; NewYTBE 72; NewYTBS 91; St&PR 84; WebAB 74, 79; WhAm 10; WhDW; Who 74, 82, 83, 85, 88, 90, 92N; WhoAm 74, 76, 78, 80, 82, 84, 86, 88, 90; WhoE 74, 79, 81; WhoFI 74, 75, 77, 79, 83; WhoFrS 84; WhoWor 74, 76, 78; WorAl; WorAlBi; WorInv*

Landa, Diego de
Spanish. Religious Leader
First bishop of Yucatan; helped decipher Mayan hieroglyphs.
b. Mar 17, 1524 in Cifuentes, Spain
d. Apr 29, 1579 in Yucatan, Mexico
Source: *ApCAB; BioIn 10; EncLatA; HisDcSE; WhDW*

Landau, Ely A
American. Producer
Noted for telefilms of hit plays including "Long Day's Journey into Night," 1962; founded American Film Theater, 1972.
b. Jan 20, 1920 in New York, New York
d. Nov 4, 1993 in Los Angeles, California
Source: *FilmgC; HalFC 88; IntMPA 92; LesBEnT, 92; NewYTET; WhoAm 86, 90; WhoEnt 92; WorEFlm*

Landau, Lev Davidovich
Russian. Physicist
Work with Helium III at low temperatures won him Nobel Prize in physics, 1962.
b. Jan 22, 1908 in Baku, Russia
d. Apr 2, 1968 in Moscow, Union of Soviet Socialist Republics
Source: *AsBiEn; BiESc; BioIn 5, 6, 7, 8, 11, 12, 13, 15, 16, 17, 20, 21; ConAu 113; CurBio 63, 68; DcScB; LarDcSc; McGEWB; McGMS 80; NewCol 75; NotTwCS; ObitOF 79; ObitT 1961; WhAm 5; WhDW; WhoNob, 90, 95; WorAl*

Landau, Martin
American. Actor
Starred in "Mission Impossible," 1966-69; "Space 1999," 1974-77; films include *Crimes and Misdemeanors,* 1989; won Oscar for best support ing actor in "Ed Wood," 1994.
b. Jun 20, 1933 in New York, New York
Source: *BioIn 10, 16; ConTFT 1, 7; FilmgC; HalFC 80, 84, 88; IntMPA 92; MotPP; MovMk; VarWW 85; WhoAm 86, 90; WhoEnt 92; WhoHol A; WhoWest 74*

Lander, Richard Lemon
English. Explorer
With brother John, traced course of Niger River, 1830-31.
b. Feb 8, 1804 in Truro, England
d. Feb 6, 1834 in Fernando Po, Equatorial Guinea
Source: *BioIn 6, 12, 18; DcNaB; NewCol 75; WebBD 83; WhWE*

Lander, Toni
[Toni Pihl Peterson]
Danish. Dancer
Known for unparalleled style, especially in *Etudes,* 1950.
b. Jun 19, 1931 in Copenhagen, Denmark
d. May 19, 1985 in Salt Lake City, Utah
Source: *AnObit 1985; BiDD; BioIn 5, 7, 11, 12, 14, 15, 18; CnOxB; ConNews 85-4; DancEn 78; IntDcB; WhAm 8; WhoAmW 74*

Landers, Ann
[Esther Pauline Friedman Lederer]
"Eppie"
American. Journalist
Twin sister of Dear Abby; column syndicated in over 1,000 newspapers.
b. Jul 4, 1918 in Sioux City, Iowa
Source: *AmAu&B; BioAmW; BioIn 13, 14, 15, 16; BkPepl; CelR, 90; ConAu 89; CurBio 57; EncTwCJ; ForWC 70; InWom, SUP; LegTOT; NewYTBS 74; PenNWW B; PseudN 82; WebAB 79; WhoAm 74, 76, 78, 80, 82, 84, 86, 88, 90, 92, 94, 95, 96, 97; WhoAmJ 80; WhoAmW 58, 61, 64, 66, 68, 70, 72, 74, 75, 77, 79, 81, 83, 85, 87, 89, 91, 93, 95, 97; WhoMW 74, 84, 92; WhoWor 74, 76; WhoWorJ 72, 78; WorAl; WorAlBi*

Landers, Audrey
American. Actor
Played Afton Cooper in recurring role on TV series "Dallas."
b. Jul 18, 1959 in Philadelphia, Pennsylvania
Source: *BioIn 13; ConTFT 4; LegTOT; VarWW 85; WhoEnt 92*

Landers, Harry
American. Actor
Character actor in films *The Ten Commandments,* 1956; *Rear Window,* 1954.
b. Apr 3, 1921 in New York, New York
Source: *ConTFT 9; WhoHol 92, A*

Landers, Judy
American. Actor
Starred in TV series "BJ and the Bear" and "Vegas"; sister of Audrey.
b. Oct 7, 1961 in Philadelphia, Pennsylvania
Source: *BioIn 12, 13; ConTFT 4; LegTOT*

Landes, Bertha Ethel
American. Politician
Mayor of Seattle, 1926-28; first woman to head sizable American city.
b. Oct 19, 1868 in Ware, Massachusetts
d. Nov 29, 1943 in Ann Arbor, Michigan
Source: *NotAW*

Landesberg, Steve
American. Actor, Comedian
Played Arthur Dietrich on TV series "Barney Miller," 1976-82.
b. Nov 23, 1947 in New York, New York
Source: *ConTFT 3; WhoAm 90; WhoEnt 92*

Landi, Elissa
[Elizabeth Marie Zanardi-Landi]
Italian. Actor
Best known for role in *The Sign of the Cross,* 1932.
b. Dec 6, 1904 in Venice, Italy
d. Oct 31, 1948 in Kingston, New York
Source: *AmAu&B; BioIn 1, 7, 9, 11; DcNAA; Film 2; FilmEn; FilmgC; HalFC 80, 84, 88; HolP 30; IlWWBF; InWom, SUP; MotPP; MovMk; NotNAT B; PseudN 82; ThFT; WhE&EA; WhoHol B; WhScrn 74, 77, 83; WhThe*

Landis, Carole
[Frances Lillian Mary Ridste]
American. Actor
One of favorite WW II pinups who starred in film *Four Jills in a Jeep,* 1944, based on her adventures entertaining troops.
b. Jan 1, 1919 in Fairchild, Wisconsin
d. Jul 5, 1948 in Brentwood Heights, California
Source: *BioIn 1, 15, 17; DcNAA; EncAFC; FilmEn; FilmgC; ForYSC; HalFC 80, 84, 88; MotPP; MovMk; NotNAT B; PseudN 82; WhoHol B; WhScrn 74, 77, 83*

Landis, Frederick
American. Judge
Justice on US Court of International Trade, 1965-84.
b. Jan 17, 1912 in Logansport, Indiana
d. Mar 1, 1990 in Carmel, Indiana
Source: *AmBench 79*

Landis, James McCauley
American. Educator, Government Official
Dean of Harvard Law School, 1937-46; presidential advisor; director, Office of Civilian Defense, 1942-43.
b. Sep 25, 1899 in Tokyo, Japan
d. Jul 30, 1964
Source: *BioIn 1, 5, 6, 7, 8, 11, 12, 16, 21; CurBio 42, 64; DcAmB S7; LinLib L, S; PolProf K, T; WhAm 4*

Landis, Jessie Royce
[Jessie Royse Medbury]
American. Actor
Character actress in mother roles in films *North by Northwest,* 1959; *To Catch a Thief,* 1955.
b. Nov 25, 1904 in Chicago, Illinois
d. Feb 2, 1972 in Danbury, Connecticut
Source: *BiE&WWA; BioIn 3, 9; ConAu 33R; DcAmB S9; EncAFC; FilmEn; FilmgC; ForWC 70; ForYSC; HalFC 80, 84, 88; LegTOT; MovMk; NewYTBE 72; NotNAT A; ObitOF 79; PseudN 82; Vers B; WhAm 5; WhoHol B; WhScrn 77, 83*

Landis, John David
American. Director
First success: *National Lampoon's Animal House,* 1978; acquitted, 1987, of involuntary manslaughter of Vic Morrow, others during filming *Twilight Zone—The Movie,* 1983.
b. Aug 3, 1950 in Chicago, Illinois
Source: *BioIn 13, 16; ConAu 112, 122; ConLC 26; ConTFT 7; EncAFC; HalFC 88; IntDcF 2-2; IntMPA 92; VarWW 85; WhoAm 82, 84, 86, 88, 90, 92, 94, 95, 96, 97; WhoEnt 92; WorAlBi*

Landis, Walter Savage
American. Chemist
Developed cyanamide process of nitrogen fixation.
b. Jul 5, 1881 in Pottstown, Pennsylvania
d. Sep 15, 1944 in Old Greenwich, Connecticut
Source: *BioIn 1; DcAmB S3; InSci; NatCAB 33*

Landis Kenesaw, Mountain, Judge
American. Baseball Executive
District court judge; first commissioner of baseball, 1921-44; worked to maintain game's integrity.
b. Nov 20, 1866 in Millville, Ohio
d. Nov 25, 1944 in Chicago, Illinois
Source: *ApCAB X; Ballpl 90; BiDAmSp BB; BiDFedJ; BioIn 1, 2, 3, 7, 10, 12, 14, 15, 19, 21; CurBio 44; DcAmB S3; EncAB-H 1974, 1996; FacFETw; LegTOT; LinLib S; NatCAB 33; ObitOF 79; OxCAmH; WebAB 74, 79; WhAm 2; WhoProB 73; WhoSpor; WorAlBi*

Landolfi, Tommaso
Italian. Author, Translator
Perfected the symbolic tale; wrote short story *Gogol's Wife,* 1950s.
b. Aug 9, 1908 in Pico, Italy
d. Jul 7, 1979 in Rome, Italy
Source: *ClDMEL 80; ConAu 117, 127; ConLC 11, 49; DcItL 1, 2; EncSF 93; EncWL 2, 3; ModRL; ScF&FL 1, 92; WorAu 1975*

Landon, Alf(red Mossman)
American. Businessman, Politician
Rep. presidential candidate who lost overwhelmingly to Franklin Roosevelt, 1936.
b. Sep 9, 1887 in West Middlesex, Pennsylvania
d. Oct 12, 1987 in Topeka, Kansas
Source: *AmPolLe; BiDrGov 1789; BioIn 1, 2, 3, 4, 6, 7, 8, 9, 10, 11, 21; BlueB 76; ConNews 88-1; CurBio 44, 87, 87N; EncAAH; EncAB-H 1974, 1996; EncWM; FacFETw; LegTOT; PresAR; WebAB 74, 79; WhAm 9; Who 74, 82, 83, 85, 88; WhoAm 74, 76, 78; WhoAmP 73; WhoWor 74; WorAl; WorAlBi*

Landon, Margaret (Dorothea Mortenson)
American. Author
Wrote novel *Anna and the King of Siam,* 1944, which was the inspiration for the musical *The King and I.*
b. Sep 7, 1903
d. Dec 4, 1993 in Alexandria, Virginia

Source: *AmWomWr; BioIn 16, 19, 20; ConAu 143; CurBio 94N; NewYTBS 93; PlP&P; SmATA 50; WhoAmW 58*

Landon, Michael
[Eugene Michael Orowitz]
American. Actor, Director, Writer
TV series include "Bonanza," 1959-73, "Little House on the Prairie," 1974-82, "Highway to Heaven," 1984-88.
b. Oct 31, 1937 in New York, New York
d. Jul 1, 1991 in Malibu, California
Source: *BioIn 10, 11, 12, 13, 14, 15, 16; CelR 90; ConTFT 7; CurBio 77, 91N; FilmgC; HalFC 80, 84, 88; IntMPA 77, 86; LesBEnT 92; MiSFD 9N; MotPP; News 92; NewYTBS 91; NewYTET; PseudN 82; VarWW 85; WhoAm 78, 80, 82, 84, 86, 90; WhoHol A; WhoHrs 80; WorAl; WorAlBi*

Landor, Walter Savage
English. Author, Poet
Principal prose: *Imaginary Conversations,* 1824-53.
b. Jan 30, 1775 in Rugeley, England
d. Sep 17, 1864 in Florence, Italy
Source: *Alli, SUP; AtlBL; Benet 87, 96; BiD&SB; BiDLA; BioIn 1, 3, 4, 5, 8, 9, 10, 11, 12, 13, 16, 17; BlmGEL; BritAu 19; BritWr 4; CamGEL; CamGLE; CasWL; CelCen; Chambr 3; ChhPo, S1, S3; CnE&AP; CrtT 2, 4; CyWA 58; DcArts; DcBiPP; DcEnA, A; DcEnL; DcEuL; DcLB 93, 107; DcLEL; DcNaB; EvLB; GrWrEL N, P; LinLib L, S; LngCEL; McGEWB; MouLC 3; NewC; NewCBEL; NinCLC 14; OxCEng 67, 85, 95; PenC ENG; RAdv 1, 14, 13-1; REn; RfGEnL 91; RGFBP; VicBrit; WebE&AL; WhDW*

Landowska, Wanda Louise
Polish. Musician
Harpsichordist, pianist; interpreted early keyboard music.
b. Jul 5, 1879 in Warsaw, Poland
d. Aug 16, 1959 in Lakeville, Connecticut
Source: *CurBio 45, 59; WhAm 3*

Landrieu, Mary L.
American. Politician
Dem. senator, LA, 1997—.
b. Nov 23, 1955
Source: *WhoAmW 93, 95; WhoSSW 93, 95*

Landrieu, Moon
[Maurice Edwin Landrieu]
American. Government Official
Secretary of HUD, 1979-81.
b. Jul 23, 1930 in New Orleans, Louisiana
Source: *AmCath 80; BiDrUSE 89; BioIn 9, 10, 12; CurBio 80; IntWW 80, 81, 82, 83, 89, 91, 93; LegTOT; NewYTBS 76; WhoAm 74, 76, 78, 80, 82, 84; WhoAmP 77, 79, 81; WhoGov 75, 77; WhoSSW 73, 75, 76, 78, 80, 82, 84; WhoWor 80, 82, 84; WorAl; WorAlBi*

Landru, Henri Desire
French. Murderer
French "Bluebeard" who murdered 10 women; guillotined.
b. 1869
d. Feb 25, 1922
Source: *BioIn 3, 5, 7, 9, 12; DrInf; MurCaTw; WhDW*

Landrum, Phil(lip) M(itchell)
American. Politician
Dem. rep., GA, 1953-77; co-author of Landrum-Griffith Bill, 1959, which brought labor union practices under federal scrutiny.
b. Sep 10, 1907 in Martin, Georgia
d. Nov 19, 1990 in Jasper, Georgia
Source: *BiDrAC; BiDrUSC 89; BioIn 5, 11, 12, 15; CngDr 74; CurBio 91N; NewYTBS 90; PolProf E, J, K, NF; WhoAmP 73, 75, 77, 79; WhoGov 72, 75, 77*

Landry, Tom
[Thomas Wade Landry]
American. Football Coach
First coach of Dallas, 1960-88, replaced by Jimmy Johnson; won two Super Bowls; Hall of Fame, 1990.
b. Sep 11, 1924 in Mission, Texas
Source: *BiDAmSp FB; BioIn 7, 9, 10, 11, 12, 13, 14, 16; ConAu 141; CurBio 72; FootReg 87; LegTOT; NewYTBE 71; NewYTBS 83; WhoAm 74, 76, 78, 80, 82, 84, 86, 88, 90, 92, 94, 95, 96, 97; WhoSpor; WhoSSW 73, 75, 80, 82, 86, 88, 91, 95; WorAl; WorAlBi; WrDr 96*

Landsbergis, Vytautas
Lithuanian. Political Leader
Elected pres. of Lithuania, 1990—; first non-communist pres. of a Soviet repub.
b. Oct 18, 1932 in Kaunas, Lithuania
Source: *BioIn 16; CurBio 90; IntWW 91, 93; LngBDD; News 91, 91-3; WhoWor 91; WorAlBi*

Landseer, Charles
English. Artist
Genre, historical painter; brother of Edwin: *Battle of Langside,* 1837.
b. 1799 in London, England
d. 1879
Source: *ArtsNiC; BioIn 10; DcBiPP; DcBrBI; DcBrWA; DcNaB; DcVicP, 2; OxDcArt*

Landseer, Edwin Henry, Sir
English. Artist
Popular animal painter, noted for humanized portraits of dogs.
b. Mar 7, 1802 in London, England
d. Oct 1, 1873 in London, England
Source: *Alli; AtlBL; Benet 87; BioIn 1, 2, 3, 5, 6, 9, 10, 11, 12, 13, 14, 15, 16; CelCen; ChhPo, S1, S2; ClaDrA; DcArts; DcBrBI; DcBrWA; DcNaB; DcVicP, 2; LegTOT; LinLib S; McGDA; NewC; OxCEng 85, 95; REn*

Landsteiner, Karl
American. Physician
Immunologist who won Nobel Prize for medicine, 1930.
b. Jul 14, 1868 in Vienna, Austria
d. Jun 26, 1943 in New York, New York
Source: *AmDec 1920, 1930; AsBiEn; BiESc; BioIn 3, 5, 6, 8, 11, 12, 14, 15, 20; CamDcSc; CopCroC; CurBio 43; DcAmB S3; DcAmMeB, 84; DcScB; InSci; LarDcSc; LegTOT; LinLib S; McGEWB; NewCol 75; NobelP; NotTwCS; ObitOF 79; OxCMed 86; WebAB 74, 79; WebBD 83; WhAm 2; WhDW; WhNAA; WhoNob, 90, 95; WorAl; WorAlBi; WorScD*

Landy, John
Australian. Track Athlete
Second man (Roger Bannister first) to run mile in under four minutes, 1954.
b. Apr 12, 1930 in Melbourne, Australia
Source: *BioIn 3, 4, 5, 9; ConAu 128; NewCol 75; WhoTr&F 73*

Lane, Abbe
American. Actor, Singer
Ex-wife of Xavier Cugat who starred with him in TV's "Xavier Cugat Show," 1957.
b. Dec 14, 1932 in New York, New York
Source: *BioIn 4, 5, 9, 19; ForYSC; InWom, SUP; ItaFilm; LegTOT; VarWW 85; WhoHol 92, A; WorAl*

Lane, Allen, Sir
English. Publisher
Founded Penguin Books, 1935; first British paperback publisher.
b. Sep 21, 1902 in Bristol, England
d. Jul 7, 1970 in Northwood, England
Source: *BioIn 3, 6, 9, 14, 18; ConAu 29R; CurBio 54, 70; DcNaB 1961; DcTwBBL; GrBr; LegTOT; LngCTC; OxCEng 85, 95; WhAm 5; WhDW; WhE&EA; WorAl; WorAlBi*

Lane, Burton
[Burton Levy]
American. Composer
Wrote scores for *Finian's Rainbow,* 1947; *On a Clear Day You Can See Forever,* 1965.
b. Feb 2, 1912 in New York, New York
d. Jan 5, 1997 in New York, New York
Source: *AmPS; AmSong; ASCAP 66, 80; Baker 84, 92; BestMus; BiDAmM; BiE&WWA; BioIn 5, 6, 7, 8, 9, 10, 12, 14, 15, 17; CmpEPM; CurBio 67; EncMT; FilmEn; HalFC 80, 84, 88; LegTOT; NewAmDM; NewCBMT; NewGrDA 86; NewGrDM 80; NotNAT; OxCAmT 84; OxCPMus; PlP&P; PopAmC, SUP; PseudN 82; Sw&Ld C; VarWW 85; WhoAm 76, 78, 80, 82, 84, 86, 88, 90, 92, 94, 95, 96, 97; WhoEnt 92; WhoThe 72, 77, 81*

Lane, Charles
American. Director
Films include *Sidewalk Stories,* 1989; *True Identity,* 1991; has won numerous awards.
b. Dec 5, 1953 in New York, New York
Source: *ConBlB 3; WhoAfA 96; WhoBlA 94; WhoEnt 92; WhoMW 90*

Lane, Diane
American. Actor
Films include *Rumble Fish,* 1983; *Cotton Club,* 1984.
b. Jan 22, 1965 in New York, New York
Source: *BioIn 13, 14, 16; ConTFT 2, 5; IntMPA 86, 92, 94, 96; LegTOT; WhoEnt 92; WhoHol 92*

Lane, Dick
[Richard Lane]
"Night Train"
American. Football Player
Five-time all-pro cornerback, 1952-64, mostly with Detroit; led NFL in interceptions twice; Hall of Fame, 1974; married to Dinah Washington.
b. Apr 16, 1928 in Austin, Texas
Source: *AfrAmBi 2; AfrAmSG; BiDAmSp FB; BioIn 8, 17, 21; InB&W 80; LegTOT; WhoAfA 96; WhoAmP 91; WhoBlA 77, 80, 85, 88, 90, 92, 94; WhoFtbl 74; WhoSpor*

Lane, Edward William
English. Author, Orientalist
Wrote *Customs of Modern Egyptians,* 1836; first accurate version of *Thousand and One Nights,* 1840.
b. Sep 17, 1801 in Hereford, England
d. Aug 10, 1876 in Worthing, England
Source: *Alli, SUP; BbD; BiD&SB; BioIn 1, 5, 11; BritAu 19; CamGEL; CamGLE; CelCen; Chambr 3; DcArts; DcBiPP; DcEnL; DcLEL; DcNaB; EvLB; NewC; OxCEng 67, 85, 95*

Lane, Fitz Hugh
[Nathaniel Rogers Lane]
American. Artist
Popular luminist-style marine painter, lithographer: *View of Glouster,* 1844.
b. Dec 19, 1804 in Gloucester, Massachusetts
d. Aug 13, 1865
Source: *BioIn 3, 9, 15, 17; BriEAA; DcAmArt; DcSeaP; FolkA 87; McGEWB; NewYHSD; PeoHis; WorAlBi*

Lane, Frank C
"Frantic Frankie"
American. Baseball Executive
GM for several ML teams, 1930s-50s; with Cleveland, known for unprecedented "trading" of managers with Detroit, 1957.
b. Feb 1, 1896 in Cincinnati, Ohio
d. Mar 19, 1981 in Richardson, Texas
Source: *BioIn 3, 4, 8, 10; WhoProB 73*

Lane, Kenneth Jay
American. Designer
Shoe designer, Christian Dior Shoes, 1958-63; opened own business, 1963; designs costume jewelry.
b. Apr 22, 1932 in Detroit, Michigan
Source: *BioIn 7, 10, 11; CelR, 90; ConFash; EncFash; WhoAm 74, 76, 78, 80, 82, 84, 86, 88, 90, 92, 94, 95, 96; WhoFash 88; WorFshn*

Lane, Lola
[Dorothy Mullican]
American. Actor, Singer
Co-starred with sisters Priscilla, Rosemary in sentimental films of late 1930s-40s.
b. May 21, 1906 in Macy, Indiana
d. Jun 22, 1981 in Santa Barbara, California
Source: *BioIn 10, 12; Film 2; MotPP; NewYTBS 81; PseudN 82; ThFT; WhoHol A; WhScrn 83*

Lane, Mark
American. Lawyer
Wrote *Executive Action,* 1973.
b. Feb 24, 1927 in New York, New York
Source: *BioIn 7, 11; ConAu 21NR, 61; PolProf J; WhoAm 76, 78, 80, 82, 84, 86, 88, 90, 92, 94, 95, 96, 97; WhoAmL 78, 79, 96; WhoE 95; WhoUSWr 88; WhoWor 80; WhoWrEP 89, 92, 95; WorAl; WorAlBi*

Lane, Nathan
[Joseph Lane]
American. Actor
Co-starred with Robin Williams in *The Birdcage,* 1996; won Tony Award, Best Actor in a Musical, for *A Funny Thing Happened on the Way to the Forum,* 1996.
b. Feb 3, 1956 in Jersey City, New Jersey
Source: *BioIn 21; ConTFT 10; CurBio 96; IntMPA 94, 96; News 96; WhoAm 94, 95, 96, 97*

Lane, Priscilla
[Priscilla Mullican]
American. Actor, Singer
Starred in *Brother Rat,* 1938; *Arsenic and Old Lace,* 1944.
b. Jun 12, 1917 in Indianola, Iowa
d. Apr 4, 1995 in Andover, Massachusetts
Source: *BioIn 18, 20, 21; CmpEPM; EncAFC; FilmEn; ForYSC; GangFlm; HalFC 80; InWom SUP; MotPP; MovMk; PseudN 82; ThFT; WhoHol 92, A*

Lane, Rose Wilder
American. Author
Daughter of Laura Ingalls Wilder, who was agent, editor, collaborator with mother on *Little House* books.
b. Dec 5, 1886 in De Smet, South Dakota
d. Oct 30, 1968 in Danbury, Connecticut
Source: *AmAu&B; AmWomPl; AmWomWr; ArtclWW 2; AuBYP 2S; BioIn 14, 17, 19; ConAu 102; NatCAB 54; NotAW MOD; PeoHis; REnAL; SmATA 28, 29; TwCA SUP; TwCWW 91; WhAm 5; WhNAA; WhoAmW 58A*

Lane, Rosemary
[Rosemary Mullican]
American. Singer, Actor
Co-starred in films with sisters Priscilla, Lola, late 1930s-40s.
b. Apr 4, 1914 in Indianola, Iowa
d. Nov 25, 1974 in Woodland Hills, California
Source: *FilmEn; InWom SUP; MotPP; MovMk; PseudN 82; ThFT; WhoHol B; WhScrn 77, 83*

Lane, Stewart F
American. Producer
Theatrical producer; won Tony, 1984, for *La Cage Aux Folles.*
b. May 3, 1951 in New York, New York
Source: *ConTFT 3*

Lane, Vincent
American. Business Executive
Chairman, Chicago Housing Authority, 1988—.
b. Mar 29, 1942 in West Point, Mississippi
Source: *ConBlB 5; WhoAfA 96*

Lang, Andrew
[A Huge Longway]
"A Well-Known Author"
Scottish. Author, Poet
Prolific writer of historical mysteries, folklore, mythology, fairy tales.
b. Mar 31, 1844 in Selkirk, Scotland
d. Jul 20, 1912 in Banchor, Scotland
Source: *Alli SUP; AnCL; AuBYP 2, 3; BbD; Benet 87, 96; BiD&SB; BiDPara; BioIn 1, 2, 3, 5, 6, 7, 8, 10, 12, 15, 16, 17, 19, 20; BritAu 19; CamGEL; CamGLE; CarSB; CasWL; Chambr 3; ChhPo, S1, S2, S3; ChlBkCr; CmScLit; ConAu 114, 137; DcArts; DcBiA; DcEnA, A; DcEuL; DcLB 98, 141; DcLEL; DcNaB 1912; DcPup; Dis&D; EncO&P 2, 3; EncPaPR 91; EncSF, 93; EvLB; GrWrEL P; IntDcAn; JBA 34; LinLib L; LngCTC; MajAI; ModBrL; NewC; NewCBEL; OxCChiL; OxCEng 67, 85, 95; PenC ENG; RAdv 14; REn; RfGEnL 91; ScF&FL 1; ScFEYrs; ScFSB; SJGFanW; SmATA 16; StaCVF; Str&VC; TwCChW 78A, 83A, 89A, 95A; TwCLC 16; VicBrit; WebE&AL; WhLit; WhoChL; WhoHr&F; WrChl*

Lang, Daniel
American. Author
Wrote on social, scientific problems: *Casualties of War,* 1969.
b. May 30, 1915 in New York, New York
d. Nov 17, 1981 in New York, New York
Source: *AmAu&B; ConAu 4NR, 5R, 105; WhAm 9; WhoAm 74, 76, 78, 80; WhoAmJ 80*

Lang, Eddie
[Salvatore Massaro]
American. Jazz Musician
Guitarist with Paul Whiteman, Bing Crosby, 1920s-30s.
b. Oct 25, 1902 in Philadelphia, Pennsylvania
d. Mar 26, 1933 in New York, New York
Source: *AllMusG; ASCAP 66, 80; Baker 84, 92; BiDAmM; BiDJaz; BioIn 12, 13, 15, 16; CmpEPM; IlEncJ; NewAmDM; NewGrDA 86; NewGrDJ 88, 94; NewGrDM 80; OnThGG; OxCPMus; PenEncP; PseudN 82; WhoJazz 72*

Lang, Eugene M
American. Business Executive, Philanthropist
Millionaire industrialist; founded "I Have a Dream," program for minority student education, 1981.
b. Mar 16, 1919 in New York, New York
Source: *BioIn 14, 15; News 90-3; NewYTBS 85; St&PR 91; WhoAm 90; WhoFI 85*

Lang, Fritz
Austrian. Director
Films include *The Big Heat,* 1953.
b. Dec 5, 1890 in Vienna, Austria
d. Aug 2, 1976 in Los Angeles, California
Source: *AmFD; Benet 87, 96; BiDFilm, 81, 94; BioIn 8, 9, 11, 12; BlueB 76; CmMov; ConAu 30NR, 69, 77; ConLC 20; CurBio 43, 76N; DcAmB S10; DcArts; DcFM; EncEurC; EncMys; EncSF, 93; EncWB; FacFETw; FilmEn; FilmgC; GangFlm; HalFC 80, 84, 88; IlWWHD 1; IntDcF 1-2, 2-2; IntMPA 75, 76; IntWW 74, 75, 76; ItaFilm; LegTOT; MakMC; MiSFD 9N; MovMk; NewEScF; NewYTBS 76; OxCFilm; RAdv 14; REn; TwYS, A; WhAm 7; WhDW; WhoAm 74, 76; WhoHrs 80; WhoWor 74; WhScrn 83; WomWMM; WorAl; WorAlBi; WorEFlm; WorFDir 1*

Lang, Helmut
Austrian. Fashion Designer
Creates simple, traditional works in unusual fabrics.
b. Mar 10, 1956 in Vienna, Austria
Source: *ConFash*

Lang, K(atherine) D(awn)
Canadian. Singer, Songwriter
Her music has been termed new wave country; won a Juno Award, 1987, for best country singer; Grammy, Best Pop Vocal—Female, "Constant Craving," 1992; won Grammy for female pop vocal, "Constant Craving," 1993.
b. Sep 2, 1961 in Consort, Alberta, Canada
Source: *BioIn 14, 15, 16; ConMus 4; CurBio 92; GayLesB; News 88; WhoAmW 91; WhoEnt 92; WhoNeCM; WorAlBi*

Lang, Paul Henry
American. Musicologist, Critic
Pioneer in the field of musicology; music critic.
b. Aug 28, 1901 in Budapest, Hungary
d. Sep 21, 1991 in Lakeville, Connecticut
Source: *AmAu&B; Baker 78, 84, 92; BioIn 17, 18; ConAu 103, 135; IntWW 74, 75, 76; IntWWM 77, 80, 90; NewGrDA 86; NewGrDM 80; NewGrDO; NewYTBS 91; OxCMus; REnAL; WhoMus 72*

Lang, William Cosmo Gordon, Baron
Scottish. Clergy
Archbishop of Canterbury, 1928-42; strongly opposed Edward VIII's marriage, abdication.
b. Oct 31, 1864 in Fyvie, Scotland
d. Dec 5, 1945 in London, England
Source: *CurBio 41, 46; DcNaB 1941; NewC; WhE&EA; WhLit*

Langan, Glenn
American. Actor
Appeared in dozens of films including *Margie,* 1946; *The Snake Pit,* 1948.
b. Jul 8, 1917 in Denver, Colorado
d. Jan 26, 1991 in Camarillo, California
Source: *BioIn 17; FilmEn; FilmgC; ForYSC; HalFC 80, 84, 88; IntMPA 75, 76, 77, 78, 79, 80, 81, 82, 84, 86, 88; ItaFilm; MovMk; NewYTBS 91; WhoHol A; WhoHrs 80*

Langdell, Christopher Columbus
American. Lawyer, Educator
Harvard Law School dean, 1870-95; started case method of teaching law.
b. May 22, 1826 in New Boston, New Hampshire
d. Jul 6, 1906 in Cambridge, Massachusetts
Source: *Alli SUP; AmBi; ApCAB; BiDAmEd; BioIn 3, 8; DcAmAu; DcAmB; DcNAA; HarEnUS; NatCAB 6; OxCAmH; OxCLaw; TwCBDA; WebAB 74, 79; WhAm 1*

Langdon, Harry
American. Actor
Joined Mack Sennett comedies, 1923; screen character was a baby-faced simpleton.
b. Jun 15, 1884 in Council Bluffs, Iowa
d. Dec 22, 1944 in Los Angeles, California
Source: *BiDFilm, 81, 94; BioIn 2, 6, 8, 9, 10, 11, 12, 13, 15, 18, 19; CmMov; CurBio 45; DcAmB S3; DcFM; EncAFC; EncVaud; FacFETw; Film 2; FilmEn; FilmgC; ForYSC; Funs; HalFC 80, 84, 88; IntDcF 1-3, 2-3; JoeFr; LegTOT; MotPP; MovMk; NotNAT B; ObitOF 79; OxCFilm; QDrFCA 92; SilFlmP; TwYS, A; WhoCom; WhoHol B; WhScrn 74, 77, 83; WorEFlm*

Langdon, John
American. Politician
First pro tempore pres. of US Senate, 1789.
b. Jun 26, 1741 in Portsmouth, New Hampshire
d. Sep 18, 1819 in Portsmouth, New Hampshire
Source: *AmBi; AmRev; BiDrAC; BiDrACR; BiDrGov 1789; BiDrUSC 89; BioIn 1, 6, 7, 8, 9, 12, 15, 16; DcAmB; EncAR; EncCRAm; NatCAB 1, 11; PeoHis; PresAR; TwCBDA; WhAm HS; WhAmP; WhAmRev*

Lange, Christian Louis
Norwegian. Writer, Political Activist
Shared 1921 Nobel Peace Prize for efforts to achieve int'l peace.
b. Sep 17, 1869 in Stavanger, Norway
d. Dec 11, 1938 in Oslo, Norway
Source: *BioIn 9, 11, 15; WhoNob*

Lange, David Russell
New Zealander. Political Leader
Moderate socialist head of Labour Party elected prime minister, 1984, succeeding Robert Muldoon.
b. Aug 4, 1942 in Otahuhu, New Zealand
Source: *BioIn 13, 14, 15, 16; CurBio 85; DcTwHis; FacFETw; IntWW 89, 91, 93; NewYTBS 85; Who 85, 88, 90, 92, 94; WhoAsAP 91; WhoWor 84, 87, 89, 91*

Lange, Dorothea Nutzhorn
American. Photographer
Called greatest documentary photographer in US; best known for pictures of migrant workers.
b. May 26, 1895 in Hoboken, New Jersey
d. Oct 11, 1965 in San Francisco, California
Source: *ConAu 107; InWom SUP; MacBEP; NewCol 75; NotAW MOD; ObitOF 79; WebAB 74; WhAm 4, HSA*

Lange, Hope Elise Ross
American. Actor
Oscar nominee for *Peyton Place,* 1957; star of TV's "The Ghost and Mrs. Muir," 1968-70; won two Emmys.
b. Nov 28, 1933 in Redding Ridge, Connecticut
Source: *ConTFT 5; EncAFC; FilmgC; HalFC 88; IntMPA 92; InWom SUP; MotPP; MovMk; VarWW 85; WhoAm 86, 90; WhoAmW 83; WhoEnt 92; WhoHol A; WorAlBi*

Lange, Jessica
American. Actor
Won best supporting actress Oscar for *Tootsie,* 1983; starred in *King Kong,* 1976; Oscar, Best Actress, *Blue Sky,* 1994.
b. Apr 20, 1949 in Cloquet, Minnesota
Source: *BiDFilm 94; BioIn 11, 12, 13, 14, 15, 16; CelR 90; ConTFT 2, 6, 13; CurBio 83; HalFC 84, 88; HolBB; IntDcF 1-3, 2-3; IntMPA 84, 86, 88, 92, 94, 96; IntWW 89, 91, 93; InWom SUP;*

LegTOT; News 95; NewYTBS 76, 82, 84, 85; VarWW 85; WhoAm 84, 86, 88, 90, 92, 94, 95, 96, 97; WhoAmW 87, 89, 91, 93, 95, 97; WhoEnt 92; WhoHol 92, A; WorAlBi

Lange, Ted
American. Actor
Played Isaac Washington on TV series "The Love Boat," 1977-86.
b. Jan 5, 1947 in Oakland, California
Source: *ConBlAP 88; ConTFT 3; DrBlPA, 90; IlBBlP; InB&W 85; LegTOT; VarWW 85; WhoAm 90; WhoBlA 92; WhoEnt 92*

Langella, Frank
American. Actor
Won Tony for *Seascape,* 1975; starred in film *Dracula,* 1979.
b. Jan 1, 1940 in Bayonne, New York
Source: *BioIn 11, 12, 15, 21; CelR 90; ConTFT 1, 9; CurBio 80; Ent; FilmgC; HalFC 80, 84, 88; IntMPA 84, 86, 88, 92; LegTOT; NewYTBE 70; NewYTBS 75, 80, 87; NotNAT; PlP&P A; VarWW 85; WhoAm 86, 88, 90, 92, 94, 95, 96, 97; WhoEnt 92; WhoHol 92, A; WhoThe 77, 81; WorAl; WorAlBi*

Langer, Bernhard
German. Golfer
Turned pro, 1972; won Masters, 1985, 1993.
b. Aug 27, 1957 in Anhousen, Germany (West)
Source: *BioIn 12, 14, 16; NewYTBS 81; WhoIntG; WhoWor 95, 96, 97*

Langer, Jim
[James John Langer]
American. Football Player
Center-offensive guard, Miami, 1970-79, Minnesota, 1980-81; Hall of Fame, 1987.
b. May 16, 1948 in Little Falls, Minnesota
Source: *BiDAmSp FB; BioIn 10, 11, 12, 17; FootReg 81; LegTOT; WhoAm 80; WhoSpor*

Langer, Lawrence
American. Producer, Dramatist
Founded Washington Square Players, 1914; Theatre Guild, 1919.
b. May 30, 1890 in Swansea, Wales
d. Dec 26, 1962 in New York, New York
Source: *DcAmB S7; WhAm 8*

Langer, Suzanne K
American. Philosopher
Her book *Philosophy in a New Key* was Harvard U Press' all-time best-seller.
b. Dec 20, 1895 in New York, New York
d. Jul 17, 1985 in Old Lyme, Connecticut
Source: *DrAS 82P; IntDcWB; OxCAmL 65; WebAB 79*

Langer, Walter C
American. Psychoanalyst
Wrote pioneering work of psychohistory: *Mind of Adolph Hitler,* 1943; published, 1972.
b. Feb 9, 1899 in Boston, Massachusetts
d. Jul 4, 1981 in Sarasota, Florida
Source: *BioIn 12; NewYTBS 81*

Langford, Frances
[Frances Newbern]
American. Singer, Actor
Popular 1930s-40s vocalist; co-starred with Bob Hope on WW II broadcasts.
b. Apr 4, 1913 in Lakeland, Florida
Source: *BiDAmM; BioIn 13; CmpEPM; EncAFC; FilmgC; ForYSC; HalFC 88; IntMPA 82, 84, 86, 88, 92, 94, 96; InWom SUP; MotPP; OxCPMus; PseudN 82; ThFT; VarWW 85; WhoHol 92, A*

Langford, Sam
"Boston Tar Baby"
American. Boxer
Lost Negro heavy title to Wills, 1919; fought 300 bouts, several not recorded; Hall of Fame, 1955.
b. Mar 4, 1886 in Weymouth, Nova Scotia, Canada
d. Jan 12, 1956 in Cambridge, Massachusetts
Source: *BioIn 4, 10; InB&W 80; PeoHis; WhoBox 74; WhoSpor*

Langland, William
English. Author
Credited with writing *Piers Plowman,* greatest pre-Chaucerian poem.
b. 1332 in Shropshire, England
d. 1400 in London, England
Source: *AtlBL; BiD&SB; BioIn 11, 12; BritAu; CasWL; Chambr 1; CnE&AP; CroE&S; CrtT 1; CyWA 58; DcArts; DcEnL; DcEuL; DcLEL; GrWrEL P; LinLib L, S; NewC; NewCBEL; PenC ENG; RAdv 1, 13-1; REn; RfGEnL 91; WebE&AL; WhDW*

Langley, Noel
American. Screenwriter
Wrote MGM classic screenplay *Wizard of Oz,* 1939.
b. Dec 25, 1911 in Durban, South Africa
d. Nov 4, 1980 in Desert Hot Springs, California
Source: *AnObit 1980; WhThe*

Langley, Samuel Pierpont
American. Astronomer, Inventor
Airplane pioneer, whose models were first heavier-than-air machines to fly.
b. Aug 22, 1834 in Roxbury, Massachusetts
d. Feb 27, 1906 in Aiken, South Carolina
Source: *Alli, SUP; AmBi; ApCAB; AsBiEn; BiDAmS; BiInAmS; BioIn 1, 3, 5, 6, 7, 8, 9, 12, 14; CamDcSc; DcAmAu; DcAmB; DcNAA; DcScB; FacFETw; HarEnUS; InSci; LarDcSc; LinLib L, S; McGEWB; MorMA; NatCAB 3, 15; NewCol 75; OxCAmH; REnAL; TwCBDA; WebAB 74, 79; WhAm 1; WhDW; WorAl; WorAlBi*

Langman, Claude Berel
French. Filmmaker
Awarded Grand Prize of the French National Film Academy for two-part film series *Jean de Florette* and *Manon of the Spring,* 1986.
b. Jul 1, 1934 in Paris, France
Source: *BioIn 16; ConTFT 8; CurBio 89; HalFC 88; IntMPA 92; NewYTBE 70; WhoWor 91*

Langmuir, Irving
American. Chemist
Awarded 1932 Nobel Prize, first American industrial chemist so honored; developed gas-filled incandescent lamp, high-vacuum power tube.
b. Jan 31, 1881 in New York, New York
d. Aug 16, 1957 in Falmouth, Massachusetts
Source: *AmDec 1910; AsBiEn; BiESc; BioIn 1, 2, 3, 4, 5, 6, 7, 8, 11, 13; CamDcSc; CurBio 40, 50, 57; DcAmB S6; DcScB; EncAB-A 2; EncAB-H 1974, 1996; InSci; LarDcSc; LegTOT; LinLib L, S; McGEWB; MemAm; NewCol 75; NobelP; NotTwCS; ObitT 1951; OxCAmH; RAdv 14; WebAB 74, 79; WhAm 3; WhDW; WhoNob, 90, 95; WorAl; WorAlBi; WorInv*

Langner, Nola
American. Children's Author
Wrote, illustrated *Miss Lucy,* 1969.
b. Sep 24, 1930 in New York, New York
Source: *BioIn 8, 11, 12; ConAu 15NR, 37R; IlsBYP; IlsCB 1957, 1967; SmATA 8; WhoAmA 78, 80, 82, 84*

Langsdorff, Hans
German. Naval Officer
Graf Spee commander, trapped by Royal Navy, 1939; committed suicide.
b. 1890
d. 1939
Source: *WhWW-II*

Langston, J. William
American. Physician, Educator
Parkinson's Disease research aided by discovery made treating heroin user, 1982.
Source: *BioIn 15; ConNews 86-2*

Langston, John Mercer
American. Educator, Politician
VA Rep., first black elected to US Congress; election was disputed for 2 years; served from Sept. 23, 1890 to March 3, 1891.
b. Dec 14, 1829 in Louisa County, Virginia
d. Nov 15, 1897 in Washington, District of Columbia
Source: *AfrAmAl 6; Alli SUP; ApCAB; BiDAmEd; BiDrAC; BiDrUSC 89; BiDSA; BioIn 4, 5, 6, 7, 8, 9, 10, 11, 16,*

17; BlkAmsC; DcAmAu; DcAmB; DcAmDH 80, 89; DcAmNB; DcNAA; EncAACR; EncSoH; InB&W 80, 85; McGEWB; NatCAB 3; NegAl 76, 83, 89A; OhA&B; PeoHis; SelBAAf; SelBAAu; TwCBDA; WebAB 74, 79; WhAm HS; WhAmP

Langstroth, Lorenzo Lorraine
American. Inventor, Clergy
Apiarist; invented moveable-frame beehive, 1851, which led to large scale honey production.
b. Dec 25, 1810 in Philadelphia, Pennsylvania
d. Oct 6, 1895 in Oxford, Ohio
Source: *Alli; ApCAB; BioIn 1, 2, 11; DcAmB; DcNAA; NatCAB 24; WebBD 83; WhAm HS*

Langton, Stephen
English. Religious Leader
Archbishop of Canterbury, 1207; signed Magna Carta as leader of barons against King John.
b. 1155
d. Jul 9, 1228 in Slindon, England
Source: *Alli; DcCathB; DcNaB; NewCol 75; REn*

Langtry, Lillie
[Emilie Charlotte LeBreton]
''The Jersey Lily''
American. Actor
Famed for her beauty; mistress of Edward VII; wrote autobiography *The Days I Knew,* 1925.
b. Oct 13, 1853 in Isle of Jersey, England
d. Feb 12, 1929 in Monte Carlo, Monaco
Source: *BioIn 16, 17, 21; CamGWoT; EncVaud; EncWT; Ent; Film 1; HalFC 80, 84, 88; LegTOT; OxCAmT 84; OxCThe 67; PeoHis; PseudN 82; VicBrit; WebBD 83; WhAm 2, 4; WhScrn 74, 77, 83; WhThe; WorAlBi*

Lanier, Allen
[Blue Oyster Cult]
American. Singer, Musician
Keyboardist, guitarist, vocalist with hard-rock group since 1969.
b. Jun 25, 1946 in Long Island, New York
Source: *WhoRocM 82*

Lanier, Bob
[Robert Jerry Lanier, Jr]
''Bob-A-Dob''
American. Basketball Player
Center, Detroit, 1970-80, Milwaukee, 1980-84; had career average of 20 pts. a game; Hall of Fame, 1992.
b. Sep 10, 1948 in Buffalo, New York
Source: *AfrAmSG; BasBi; BiDAmSp BK; BioIn 8, 10, 11, 12; LegTOT; NewYTBS 81; OfNBA 87; WhoAfA 96; WhoAm 74, 78, 80, 82, 95, 96, 97; WhoBbl 73; WhoBlA 77, 80, 85, 90, 92, 94; WhoSpor; WorAl; WorAlBi*

Lanier, Hal
[Harold Clifton Lanier]
American. Baseball Player, Baseball Manager
Infielder, 1964-73; manager, Houston, 1986-88.
b. Jul 4, 1942 in Denton, North Carolina
Source: *Ballpl 90; BaseReg 86, 87; BioIn 9, 15; NewYTBS 86; WhoAm 86, 88; WhoProB 73; WhoSSW 88*

Lanier, Jaron (Zepel)
American. Computer Scientist
Pioneer in virtual reality; affiliated with VPL Research Inc. until 1992.
b. May 3, 1960 in New York, New York

Lanier, Sidney
American. Poet, Musician
Best-known poems: ''Corn''; ''Song of the Chattahoochee.''
b. Feb 3, 1842 in Macon, Georgia
d. Sep 7, 1881 in Lynn, North Carolina
Source: *Alli SUP; AmAu; AmAu&B; AmBi; AmWr S1; ApCAB; AtlBL; Baker 78, 84; BbD; Benet 87, 96; BenetAL 91; BibAL; BiDAmM; BiD&SB; BiDSA; BioIn 1, 2, 3, 4, 5, 6, 8, 9, 10, 11, 12, 16, 19; CamGEL; CamGLE; CamHAL; CarSB; CasWL; Chambr 3; ChhPo, S1, S2, S3; CnDAL; CnE&AP; CrtT 3, 4; CyWA 58; DcAmAu; DcAmB; DcArts; DcEnA A; DcLB 64, DS13; DcLEL; DcNAA; Dis&D; EncAAH; EncSoH; EvLB; FifSWrB; GrWrEL P; HarEnUS; LinLib L, S; MajAI; McGEWB; MouLC 3; NatCAB 2; NewGrDA 86; NewGrDM 80; NinCLC 6; OxCAmL 65, 83, 95; OxCChiL; OxCEng 67, 85, 95; PenC AM; PeoHis; RAdv 1, 14, 13-1; REn; REnAL; RfGAmL 87, 94; SmATA 18; SouWr; TwCBDA; WebAB 74, 79; WebE&AL; WhAm HS; WhCiWar; WhFla; WorAl; WorAlBi*

Lanier, Willie E
''Contact''
American. Football Player
Linebacker, Kansas City, 1967-77; Hall of Fame, 1986.
b. Aug 21, 1945 in Clover, Virginia
Source: *BiDAmSp FB; BioIn 10, 13; WhoBlA 92; WhoFtbl 74*

Lanin, Lester
American. Bandleader
Led high-society dance bands, 1940s-60s.
b. Aug 26, 1911 in Philadelphia, Pennsylvania
Source: *BioIn 13, 15, 16; CelR 90; CmpEPM; NewYTBS 87; PenEncP; WhoAm 74, 76, 78*

Lanman, Charles Rockwell
American. Educator, Editor
Edited *Harvard Oriental Series,* from 1891.
b. Jul 8, 1850 in Norwich, Connecticut
d. Feb 20, 1941 in Boston, Massachusetts
Source: *Alli SUP; AmAu&B; ApCAB X; BiDAmEd; BiD&SB; DcAmAu; DcAmB S3; DcInB; DcNAA; NatCAB 11; TwCBDA; WebBD 83; WhAm 1*

Lanois, Daniel
Canadian. Producer
Record producer known for his ability to blend music's new technologies; produced U2's *The Unforgettable Fire,* 1984, among others.
b. 1951 in Hull, Quebec, Canada
Source: *BioIn 15, 16; ConMus 8; News 91, 91-1; WhoAm 94, 95, 96, 97*

Lansbury, Angela Brigid
[Mrs. Peter Shaw]
American. Actor, Singer
Won four Tonys; star of TV's ''Murder, She Wrote,'' 1984-97; Theatre Hall of Fame, 1982.
b. Oct 16, 1925 in London, England
Source: *BiDFilm; BiE&WWA; BioIn 13, 14, 15, 16; BkPepl; CelR 90; ConTFT 1, 7; CurBio 67; EncMT; FilmgC; HalFC 88; IntMPA 92; IntWW 91; InWom SUP; MotPP; MovMk; News 93-1; NewYTBS 75; NotNAT; NotWoAT; OxCAmT 84; OxCPMus; PeoHis; Who 74, 82, 83, 85, 88, 90, 92, 94; WhoAm 74, 76, 78, 80, 82, 84, 86, 88, 90, 92, 94, 95, 96, 97; WhoAmW 61, 66, 68, 70, 72, 74, 81, 83, 87, 89, 91, 93, 95, 97; WhoEnt 92; WhoHol A; WhoWor 74, 76; WorAl; WorAlBi*

Lansdale, Edward Geary
American. Military Leader
Counterrevolution expert whose theories had great impact on US policies in Philippines, Vietnam, 1950s-60s.
b. Feb 6, 1908 in Detroit, Michigan
d. Feb 23, 1987 in McLean, Virginia
Source: *ConAu 121; ConNews 87-2; EncAI&E*

Lansing, Joi
[Joi Loveland; Joyce Wasmansdoff]
American. Actor
Played on TV's ''Love That Bob,'' 1956-59; films include *A Hole in the Head,* 1959.
b. Apr 6, 1930 in Salt Lake City, Utah
d. Aug 7, 1972 in Santa Monica, California
Source: *FilmgC; MotPP; PseudN 82; WhoHol B; WhoHrs 80; WhScrn 77, 83*

Lansing, Robert
American. Government Official, Lawyer
Secretary of State, 1915-20; arranged purchase of Virgin Islands, 1917.
b. Oct 17, 1864 in Watertown, New York
d. Oct 30, 1928 in Washington, District of Columbia
Source: *AmAu&B; AmBi; AmDec 1910; AmLY; AmPeW; AmPolLe; ApCAB X; BiDInt; BiDrUSE 71, 89; BioIn 4, 5, 6, 7, 9, 10, 16; CopCroC; DcAmB; DcAmDH 80, 89; DcNAA; EncAB-H 1974, 1996; FacFETw; HarEnUS; LinLib L, S; McGEWB; NatCAB 20; OxCAmH; OxCLaw; PseudN 82; WebAB 74, 79; WhAm 1; WhLit; WhNAA*

Lansing, Robert
[Robert Howell Brown]
American. Actor
Played on TV's "87th Precinct," 1961-62; "Man Who Never Was," 1966-67.
b. Jun 5, 1929 in San Diego, California
Source: *BiE&WWA; ConTFT 3; FilmEn; FilmgC; ForYSC; HalFC 80, 84, 88; MotPP; NotNAT; VarWW 85; WhoAm 86, 90; WhoEnt 92; WhoHol 92, A*

Lansing, Sherry Lee
American. Film Executive
First woman in charge of production at major film studio: 20th Century Fox, 1980-82; chm., Paramount Communications Inc., 1992—.
b. Jul 31, 1944 in Chicago, Illinois
Source: *AmWomM; BioIn 13, 14, 16; ContDcW 89; ConTFT 1; CurBio 81; IntMPA 92; IntWW 91; InWom SUP; NewYTBS 80; ReelWom; VarWW 85; WhoAm 80, 82, 84, 86, 88, 90, 92, 94, 95, 96, 97; WhoAmW 81, 83, 85, 91, 93, 95, 97; WhoFI 81; WhoWest 80, 82; WomFir*

Lansky, Aaron
American.
Founder, president, National Yiddish Book Center, 1980—; organization saved 1.3 million Yiddish books, preserving the culture of Yiddish-speaking Jews of Europe.
b. Jul 17, 1955 in New Bedford, Massachusetts

Lansky, Meyer
[Maier Suchowljansky]
"Meyer the Bug"
American. Criminal
Jailed only once for two-month period on gambling conviction; called financial genius of underworld.
b. Jul 4, 1902 in Grodna, Russia
d. Jan 15, 1983 in Miami Beach, Florida
Source: *AnObit 1983; BioIn 7, 8, 9, 12, 13, 17; CopCroC; DrInf; FacFETw; LegTOT; NewYTBS 83; PseudN 82*

Lanson, Snooky
[Roy Landman]
American. Singer
Star of TV's "Hit Parade," 1950s.
b. Mar 27, 1914 in Memphis, Tennessee
d. Jul 2, 1990 in Nashville, Tennessee
Source: *BioIn 17; CmpEPM; LegTOT; NewYTBS 90; PseudN 82; RadStar; RkOn 74; What 4*

Lanston, Tolbert
American. Inventor
Patented typesetting machine, 1887.
b. Feb 3, 1844 in Troy, Ohio
d. 1913 in Washington, District of Columbia
Source: *AmBi; DcAmB; InSci; NatCAB 13; NewCol 75; WhDW*

Lanting, Frans
Dutch. Photographer
Photographs wild animals.
b. Jul 13, 1951 in Rotterdam, Netherlands
Source: *CurBio 95*

Lantz, Walter
American. Cartoonist
Created Woody Woodpecker, 1941; won Honorary Oscar, 1978.
b. Apr 27, 1900 in New Rochelle, New York
d. Mar 22, 1994 in Burbank, California
Source: *BioIn 9, 12, 15, 19, 20, 21; ConAu 108, 144; ConTFT 12; FilmEn; FilmgC; HalFC 80, 84, 88; IntDcF 1-4, 2-4; IntMPA 75, 76, 77, 78, 79, 80, 81, 82, 84, 86, 88, 92, 94; LegTOT; NewYTBS 94; SmATA 37, 79; VarWW 85; WhAm 11; WhoAm 74, 76, 78, 80, 82, 84, 86, 88, 90, 92, 94; WhoEnt 92; WorECar; WorEFlm*

Lanusse, Alejandro Agustin
Argentine. Political Leader
President, Argentina, 1971-73.
b. Aug 28, 1918
d. Aug 26, 1996 in Buenos Aires, Argentina
Source: *BiDLAmC; BioIn 9, 10; CurBio 73, 96N; IntWW 74, 75, 76, 77, 78, 79, 80, 81, 82, 83, 89, 91, 93; WhoWor 74*

Lanvin, Bernard
French. Fashion Designer
Head of Lanvin Fashions since 1963; grandnephew of Jeanne.
b. Dec 27, 1935 in Neuilly, France
Source: *BioIn 13; BusPN; WorFshn*

Lanvin, Jeanne
French. Fashion Designer
Founder, House of Lanvin, Maison de Couture, Parisian group that set world fashions.
b. 1867 in Grasse, France
d. Jul 6, 1946 in Paris, France
Source: *BioIn 1, 5, 16; CurBio 46; DcArts; DcTwDes; EncFash; FairDF FRA; InWom, SUP; LegTOT; WhoFash 88; WorAl; WorAlBi; WorFshn*

Lanyer, Aemilia
[Aemilia Bassano; Emilia Lanier]
English. Poet
Wrote *Salve deus rex judaeorum,* a small volume of poetry considered unique for its feminist recasting of Christ's Passion.
b. 1569 in Bishopsgate, England
d. 1645
Source: *BioIn 16, 19; BlmGWL; DcLB 121; DcNaB MP; FemiCLE; LitC 10, 30; OxCEng 85*

Lanza, Mario
[Alfredo Arnold Cocozza]
American. Opera Singer, Actor
Tenor who starred in MGM musical *The Great Caruso,* 1951.
b. Jan 31, 1921 in Philadelphia, Pennsylvania
d. Oct 7, 1959 in Rome, Italy
Source: *Baker 78, 84, 92; BiDAmM; BiDFilm 94; BioIn 2, 4, 5, 6, 7, 9, 11, 12, 15, 16, 21; CmMov; CmpEPM; FilmEn; FilmgC; ForYSC; HalFC 80, 84, 88; ItaFilm; LegTOT; MGM; MotPP; MovMk; NewAmDM; NewGrDA 86; NotNAT B; ObitT 1951; OxCFilm; OxCMus; OxCPMus; PenDiMP; PenEncP; PseudN 82; RadStar; RkOn 74; WhAm 3; WhoHol B; WhScrn 74, 77, 83; WorAl; WorAlBi; WorEFlm*

Laoretti, Larry
American. Golfer
Cigar-smoking golfer; won US Senior Open, 1992.
b. Jul 11, 1939 in Mahapac, New York

Lao-Tzu
[Li Erh]
Chinese. Philosopher
Founder of Taoism whose philosophy of quietism urged renunciation of desire.
b. 570BC
d. 490BC
Source: *BbD; BiD&SB; CasWL; DcOrL 1; LinLib L, S; PenC CL; PseudN 82; RComWL; REn; WhDW; WorAl*

Laparra, Raoul
French. Composer
Opera *Las Torreras,* 1929, used Spanish folk elements; killed in air raid.
b. May 13, 1876 in Bordeaux, France
d. Apr 4, 1943 in Paris, France
Source: *Baker 78, 84, 92; MetOEnc; NewEOp 71; NewGrDM 80; NewGrDO; OxCMus*

Lapchick, Joe
[Joseph Bohomiel Lapchick, Jr]
American. Basketball Player, Basketball Coach
Center with original NY Celtics, 1920s-30s; coach, St. John's U, 1936-47, 1956-65, winning over 70 percent of games; Hall of Fame, 1966.
b. Apr 12, 1900 in Yonkers, New York
d. Aug 10, 1970 in Monticello, New York
Source: *BasBi; BiDAmSp BK; BioIn 17; CurBio 65, 70; DcAmB S8; NewYTBE 70; ObitOF 79; OfNBA 87; WhoBbl 73*

Laperriere, Jacques
[Joseph Jacques Hughes Laperriere]
Canadian. Hockey Player
Defenseman, Montreal, 1962-74; won Calder Trophy, 1964, Norris Trophy, 1966; Hall of Fame, 1987.
b. Nov 22, 1941 in Rouyn, Quebec, Canada
Source: *HocEn; WhoHcky 73; WhoSpor*

Lapham, Lewis Henry
American. Editor, Writer
Editor of the highly-esteemed *Harper's Magazine,* 1975-81, 1983—; wrote

Fortune's Child, 1980; *Money and Class in America,* 1988.
b. Jan 8, 1935 in San Francisco, California
Source: *BioIn 11, 12, 13; CelR 90; ConAu 33NR; CurBio 89; WhoAm 74, 76, 78, 80, 82, 84, 86, 88, 90, 92, 94, 95, 96, 97; WhoE 83, 86, 89, 91, 95; WhoUSWr 88; WhoWrEP 89, 92, 95*

Lapidus, Morris
American. Architect
Noted for designing hospitals, shopping centers, office buildings; best known for Miami's luxury hotels.
b. Nov 25, 1902 in Odessa, Russia
Source: *AmArch 70; BioIn 4, 5, 7, 9; BlueB 76; ConArch 80, 87, 94; ConAu 77; CurBio 66; MacEA; WhoAm 74, 76, 78, 80, 82, 84, 86, 88, 90, 92, 94, 95, 96, 97; WhoAmJ 80; WhoFI 74, 96; WhoScEn 94; WhoSSW 73, 75, 95, 97; WhoWor 74, 93, 95; WhoWorJ 72, 78*

Lapidus, Ted
French. Fashion Designer
Leading French menswear designer, promoted ready-mades.
b. Jun 23, 1929 in Paris, France
Source: *ConDes 84, 90, 97; EncFash; IntWW 91; LegTOT; WhoFr 79; WorFshn*

LaPlace, Pierre-Antoine de
French. Dramatist
His eight volume *Theatre anglais,* 1745-48, contained first French translations of Shakespeare.
b. 1707
d. 1793
Source: *OxCFr*

Laplace, Pierre Simon, Marquis de
French. Astronomer, Mathematician
Developed mathematical probability theory; wrote *Exposition du systeme du Monde,* 1796.
b. Mar 23, 1749 in Beaumont-en-Auge, France
d. Mar 5, 1827 in Paris, France
Source: *AsBiEn; BbD; BiD&SB; BiESc; BioIn 1, 2, 3, 4, 8, 11, 12, 14, 15; BlkwCE; CamDcSc; CelCen; DcBiPP; DcCathB; DcScB, S1; Dis&D; InSci; LarDcSc; LinLib L, S; McGEWB; NewCol 75; OxCFr; OxCMed 86; REn; WhDW; WorAl; WorAlBi; WorScD*

LaPlante, Laura
[Irving Asher, Mrs.]
American. Actor
In silent films; films include *Meet the Wife,* 1931; *Spring Reunion,* 1957.
b. Nov 1, 1904 in Saint Louis, Missouri
d. Oct 14, 1996 in Woodland Hills, California
Source: *BioIn 8, 12, 16, 18; EncAFC; Film 2; FilmEn; FilmgC; ForYSC; HalFC 80, 84, 88; InWom SUP; SweetSg B; ThFT; TwYS; VarWW 85; What 2; WhoHol 92, A; WhoHrs 80; WhoThe 77A; WhThe*

Lapotaire, Jane
English. Actor
Won 1981 Tony for title role in *Piaf.*
b. Dec 26, 1944 in Ipswich, England
Source: *BioIn 12; ConTFT 3, 13; HalFC 88; VarWW 85; Who 82, 83, 85, 88, 90, 92, 94; WhoAmW 89; WhoHol 92; WhoThe 72, 77, 81*

Lappe, Francis Moore
American. Nutritionist, Author
Wrote controversial *Food First: Beyond the Myth of Scarcity,* 1977.
b. Feb 10, 1944 in Pendleton, Oregon
Source: *BioIn 13, 16; IntAu&W 91; InWom SUP; WhoAm 90; WhoAmW 91; WhoEmL 87; WhoUSWr 88; WhoWrEP 89; WrDr 92*

LaPread, Ronald
[The Commodores]
American. Musician
Trumpeter, bassist with black pop group; had hit singles "Sail On," "Still," 1979.
b. Sep 4, 1950 in Tuskegee, Alabama
Source: *BkPepl*

Larcom, Lucy
American. Poet, Abolitionist
Wrote simple verse of children, nature; autobiography *A New England Girlhood,* 1889.
b. Mar 5, 1824 in Beverly, Massachusetts
d. Apr 17, 1893 in Boston, Massachusetts
Source: *Alli, SUP; AmAu; AmAu&B; AmBi; AmWom; AmWomWr; ApCAB; BenetAL 91; BibAL; BiD&SB; BioAmW; BioIn 1, 3, 7, 9, 12, 13, 17, 19; BlmGWL; Chambr 3; ChhPo, S2, S3; ChrP; DcAmAu; DcAmB; DcLEL; DcNAA; FemiCLE; HanAmWH; InWom, SUP; LibW; NotAW; OxCAmL 65, 83, 95; PenNWW A; REnAL; TwCBDA; WhAm HS*

Lardner, Dionysius
Irish. Author
Scientific writer; compiled 133 volume *Cabinet Cyclopaedia,* 1829-44.
b. Apr 3, 1793 in Dublin, Ireland
d. Apr 29, 1859 in Naples, Italy
Source: *Alli; ApCAB; BbD; BiD&SB; BioIn 2; BritAu 19; CelCen; Chambr 3; DcBiPP; DcEnL; DcIrB 78, 88; DcNaB, C; EvLB; NewC; NewCBEL; OxCIri; WhoEc 81, 86*

Lardner, George, Jr.
American. Journalist
Won a 1993 Pulitzer in feature writing while on staff of the *Washington Post.*
Source: *ConAu 73*

Lardner, Ring(gold Wilmer), Sr.
American. Author, Journalist
Noted for satirical sketches, use of vernacular: *Treat 'Em Rough,* 1918.
b. Mar 6, 1885 in Niles, Michigan
d. Sep 25, 1933 in East Hampton, New York
Source: *AmAu&B; AmBi; AmCulL; AmWr; ASCAP 66; AtlBL; Ballpl 90; Benet 87; BenetAL 91; BiDAmJo; BiDAmNC; BiDAmSp OS; BioIn 12, 14, 15, 16, 17, 19, 21; CamGEL; CamGLE; CamHAL; CasWL; CnDAL; CnMWL; ConAmA; ConAmL; ConAu 104; CyWA 58; DcAmB S1; DcLB 11, 25, 86, 171; DcLEL; EncAHmr; EncAJ; EncWL; EncWT; FacFETw; GrWrEL N; JrnUS; LegTOT; LiJour; LinLib L; LngCTC; McGEWB; ModAL, S1; Novels; OxCAmL 65, 83; OxCAmT 84; PenC AM; PseudN 82; RAdv 1, 13-1; REn; REnAL; RfGAmL 87; RGTwCWr; ShSWr; Tw; TwCA, SUP; TwCLC 2, 14; TwCWr; WebAB 79; WebE&AL; WhNAA; WhoTwCL; WorAlBi*

Lardner, Ring(gold Wilmer), Jr.
[The Hollywood Ten]
American. Screenwriter
Won Oscars for *M*A*S*H,* 1970; *Woman of the Year,* 1942.
b. Aug 19, 1915 in Chicago, Illinois
Source: *BioIn 2, 6, 9, 10, 11, 14, 15, 16; ConAu 13NR, 25R, 104, 131; ConDr 88A; ConTFT 5; Conv 1; CurBio 87; DcLB 26; DrAF 76; DrAPF 80, 91; EncAFC; EncAL; EncMcCE; FacFETw; FilmEn; HalFC 84, 88; IntAu&W 91; IntDcF 1-4, 2-4; IntMPA 92; IntvTCA 2; LegTOT; MajTwCW; Novels; OxCFilm; PolProf T; SourALJ; VarWW 85; WebAB 79; WhoAm 86, 90; WhoEnt 92; WhoUSWr 88; WhoWrEP 89*

Laredo, Jaime
Bolivian. Violinist
Prize-winning virtuoso, 1950s-60s; first performed at age eight; pictured on Boli vian airmail stamp.
b. Jun 7, 1941 in Cochabamba, Bolivia
Source: *Baker 78, 84; BioIn 4, 5, 7, 8, 14; CurBio 67; IntWWM 80, 85, 90; NewAmDM; NewGrDA 86; NewGrDM 80; PenDiMP; WhoAmM 83*

Laredo, Ruth
[Ruth Meckler]
American. Pianist
Commissioned to edit works of composers; first volume, *The Preludes,* was released, 1985.
b. Nov 20, 1937 in Detroit, Michigan
Source: *Baker 84, 92; BioIn 12, 13, 14, 15, 17, 21; CurBio 87; IntWWM 90; LegTOT; NewGrDA 86; NewYTBE 73; NewYTBS 74; NotTwCP; WhoAm 78, 80, 82, 84, 86, 88; WhoAmW 79, 81, 83, 85, 87, 89; WhoMus 72*

Largent, Steve M
American. Football Player
Wide receiver, Seattle, 1976-89; holds NFL record for catching passes in 128 consecutive games, breaking Harold Carmichael's record, 1986.
b. Sep 28, 1954 in Tulsa, Oklahoma

Source: *BiDAmSp FB; BioIn 11, 16; FootReg 86, 87; WhoAm 90; WhoWest 87*

Largo Caballero, Francisco
"The Lenin of Spain"
Spanish. Political Leader
First socialist prime minister of Spanish Republic, 1936.
b. Oct 15, 1869 in Madrid, Spain
d. Mar 23, 1946 in Paris, France
Source: *BiDMarx; BioIn 1, 16; CurBio 46; DcTwHis; EncRev*

Larkin, Barry
American. Baseball Player
Shortstop, Cincinnati, 1985—; All-Star, 1989-92; U.S. Olympic team, 1984.
b. Apr 28, 1964 in Cincinnati, Ohio
Source: *Ballpl 90; BioIn 21; WhoAm 92; WhoBlA 92; WhoMW 92*

Larkin, Oliver Waterman
American. Author, Educator
Wrote 1949 Pulitzer-winner *Art and Life in America.*
b. Aug 17, 1896 in Medford, Massachusetts
d. Dec 17, 1971 in Northampton, Massachusetts
Source: *AmAu&B; Au&Wr 71; BioIn 2, 4, 9; ConAu 1R, 29R; CurBio 50, 71; NewYTBE 70; OxCAmL 65; TwCA SUP; WhAm 5*

Larkin, Patty
American. Musician, Singer
Acoustic guitar player; recordings include the successful *Tango,* 1991.
b. 1951? in Iowa
Source: *ConMus 9*

Larkin, Philip Arthur
English. Author, Librarian, Poet
Writings include *Jill,* 1940; *High Windows,* 1974.
b. Aug 9, 1922 in Coventry, England
d. Dec 2, 1985 in Kingston-upon-Hull, England
Source: *Au&Wr 71; BioIn 4, 10, 11, 12, 13; CasWL; CnE&AP; CnMWL; ConAu 5R; ConLC 18; ConPo 75; DcLEL 1940; DcNaB 1981; EncWL; IntAu&W 76, 77, 82; IntWW 74, 75, 76, 77, 78, 79, 80, 81, 82, 83; LngCTC; ModBrL, S1; NewC; Novels; OxCEng 85, 95; PenC ENG; RAdv 1; REn; WorAl; WorAu 1950*

Laroche, Guy
French. Fashion Designer
Known for chic, sophisticated styles that were classics without showy exaggeration; launched perfumes Drakkar Noir for men, Clandestine for women.
b. Jul 16, 1923 in La Rochelle, France
d. Feb 17, 1989 in Paris, France
Source: *BioIn 4, 9, 16; ConFash; DcTwDes; EncFash; LegTOT; NewYTBS 89; WhoFash, 88; WorFshn*

LaRochefoucauld, Francois, Duc de
French. Author
Wrote *Maxims,* 1665; biting observations on human conduct, desires.
b. Sep 15, 1613 in Paris, France
d. Mar 16, 1680 in Paris, France
Source: *AtlBL; BiD&SB; CasWL; CyWA 58; DcEuL; EuAu; EvEuW; NewC; OxCEng 67; OxCFr; PenC EUR; RComWL; REn; WhDW; WorAl*

Larocque, Bunny
[Michel Raymond Larocque]
Canadian. Hockey Player
Goalie, 1973-84, mostly with Montreal; shared Vezina Trophy four times.
b. Apr 6, 1952 in Hull, Quebec, Canada
d. Jul 29, 1992 in Hull, Quebec, Canada
Source: *HocEn; HocReg 85*

LaRocque, Rod
[Roderick la Rocque de la Rour]
American. Actor
Matinee idol of silent films including *Ten Commandments; Notoriety.*
b. Nov 29, 1898 in Chicago, Illinois
d. Oct 15, 1969 in Beverly Hills, California
Source: *BioIn 8, 9, 11; Film 1, 2; FilmEn; FilmgC; MotPP; MovMk; TwYS; WhoHol B; WhScrn 74, 77, 83*

LaRosa, Julius
American. Singer
Pop singer; became folk hero after Arthur Godfrey fired him on the air, 1953.
b. Jan 2, 1930 in New York, New York
Source: *AmPS A, B; BiDAmM; BioIn 15, 16; NewYTET; PenEncP; RkOn 74; VarWW 85*

LaRose, Rose
[Rosina Dapelle]
American. Entertainer
Burlesque performer, 1940s-50s, who earned $2,500 a week.
b. 1913 in New York, New York
d. Jul 27, 1972 in Toledo, Ohio
Source: *BioIn 9; NewYTBE 72; ObitOF 79*

Larouche, Lyndon Hermyle, Jr.
American. Politician
Controversial right-wing Dem. activist; founded National Democratic Policy Committee, 1985.
b. Sep 8, 1922 in Rochester, New Hampshire
Source: *BiDExR; BioIn 12, 13, 14, 15, 16; ConAu 124; WhoAm 90; WhoAmP 85, 87; WorAlBi*

Larousse, Pierre Athanase
French. Lexicographer
Noted for *Grand Dictionnaire universel du XIX siecle,* 1866-76.
b. Oct 23, 1817 in Toucy, France
d. Jan 3, 1875 in Paris, France
Source: *BiD&SB; BioIn 3; EvEuW; LinLib L; NewC; OxCEng 67; OxCFr; WhDW; WorAl*

Larrocha, Alicia de
Spanish. Pianist
Noted for renditions of Spanish composers Albeniz, Granados.
b. May 23, 1923 in Barcelona, Spain
Source: *Baker 78, 84; BioIn 8, 9, 10, 11, 12, 13, 14, 16; BriBkM 80; CurBio 68; IntWW 78, 79, 80, 81, 82, 83, 89, 91, 93; IntWWM 90; InWom, SUP; MusSN; NewAmDM; NewGrDM 80; NotTwCP; PenDiMP; WhoAm 88; WhoAmW 89; WhoWor 89*

Larroquette, John
American. Actor
Played Dan Fielding on TV show "Night Court," 1983-92; won four Emmys, 1985-88.
b. Nov 25, 1947 in New Orleans, Louisiana
Source: *BioIn 14, 15, 16; ConNews 86-2; ConTFT 3, 14; IntMPA 92, 94, 96; LegTOT; WhoAm 90; WhoHol 92; WorAlBi*

Larsen, Don(ald James)
American. Baseball Player
Pitcher, 1953-67; with Yankees, threw only perfect game in World Series history, Oct 8, 1956.
b. Aug 7, 1929 in Michigan City, Indiana
Source: *Ballpl 90; BioIn 4, 5, 7, 10, 16, 21; LegTOT; WhoProB 73; WorAl; WorAlBi*

Larsen, Emmanuel
American. Politician
Expert on China; a target of McCarthy's anti-Communist crusade, 1950.
b. 1898?
d. Apr 29, 1988 in Chevy Chase, Maryland

Larsen, Nella
[Nellie Marian Larsen]
American. Author
Wrote novels *Quicksand,* 1928; *Passing,* 1929.
b. Apr 13, 1891 in Chicago, Illinois
d. Mar 30, 1964 in New York, New York
Source: *AfrAmAl 6; AfrAmW; Benet 96; BlkLC; BlkWAm; BlkWr 1; BlmGWL; ConAu 125; ConBlB 10; CyWA 89; DcLB 51; DcTwCCu 5; EncAACR; FemiCLE; FemiWr; HarlReB; NotBlAW 1; OxCAmL 95; OxCWoWr 95; RAdv 14; RfGAmL 94; SchCGBL*

Larsen, Roy Edward
American. Publisher
Pres., Time Inc., 1939-60, succeeding Henry Luce; published *Life* magazine, 1936-46.
b. Apr 20, 1899 in Boston, Massachusetts
d. Sep 9, 1979 in Fairfield, Connecticut

Source: *BioIn 2, 5, 6, 11, 12; ConAu 89; CurBio 50, 79; EncTwCJ; IntWW 74, 75, 76, 77, 78, 79; NewYTBS 79; WhAm 7; Who 74; WhoAm 74, 76, 80; WhoFI 79; WhoGov 72; WhoWor 78*

Larsen-Todsen, Nanny
"Queen of Bayreuth"
Swedish. Opera Singer
Dramatic soprano with Swedish Royal Theater, 1907-22; NY Met., 1924-27.
b. Aug 2, 1884 in Hagby, Sweden
d. May 26, 1982 in Stockholm, Sweden
Source: *Baker 78, 84, 92; BioIn 1, 4, 13; CmOp; InWom; MetOEnc; NewEOp 71; NewGrDM 80; NewGrDO; OxDcOp*

Larson, (Lewis) Arthur
American. Government Official
Held positions in the Eisenhower administration; wrote *Eisenhower: The President Nobody Knew,* 1968.
b. Jul 4, 1910
d. Mar 27, 1993 in Durham, North Carolina
Source: *AmAu&B; AnObit 1993; BioIn 3, 4, 5, 11; BlueB 76; ConAu 1NR, 1R, 141; CurBio 93N; DrAS 74P, 78P, 82P; IntAu&W 77, 82, 86; IntWW 74, 75, 76, 77, 78, 79, 80, 81, 82, 83, 89, 91, 93; IntYB 78, 79, 80, 81, 82; WhoAmL 78, 79; WhoSSW 73; WhoWor 74; WrDr 76, 80, 82, 84, 86, 88, 90*

Larson, Gary
American. Cartoonist
Drew "The Far Side," comic feature syndicated in hundreds of newspapers, 1979-94; won the Nat. Cartoonists Society Award, 1985 and 1988, for best syndicated panel.
b. Aug 14, 1950 in Tacoma, Washington
Source: *Au&Arts 1; BioIn 14, 15, 16; ConAu 41NR, 115, 118; CurBio 91; Dun&B 88; EncACom; IntWW 93; LegTOT; SmATA, 57; WhoAm 90, 92, 94, 95, 96, 97; WorAlBi; WrDr 92, 94, 96*

Larson, John Augustus
American. Psychiatrist
Invented lie detector, 1921.
b. Dec 11, 1892 in Shelburne, Nova Scotia, Canada
d. Sep 21, 1965
Source: *AsBiEn; BioIn 7; WhAm 4; WorAl*

Larson, Nicolette
American. Singer
Has recorded songs with many other singers; hit single "I Only Want to Be With You," 1982.
b. Jul 17, 1952 in Helena, Montana
Source: *ASCAP 80; BioIn 11, 14; ConMuA 80A; InWom SUP; LegTOT; RkOn 85; WhoRocM 82*

Larson, Reed David
American. Hockey Player
Defenseman, Detroit, 1976-86, Boston, 1986—; holds NHL record for most goals, assists, pts. by American-born player.
b. Jul 30, 1956 in Minneapolis, Minnesota
Source: *BiDAmSp BK; HocEn; HocReg 87*

Larsson, Carl Olof
Swedish. Artist, Author
Wrote, illustrated *Spadarvet,* 1906; translated in 1976 as *A Farm.*
b. May 28, 1853 in Stockholm, Sweden
d. Jan 22, 1919 in Falun, Sweden
Source: *BioIn 14, 15, 19; ConAu 115*

Lartet, Edouard Armand Isidore Hippolyte
French. Paleontologist
A founder of modern paleontology; credited with discovering earliest art of man.
b. May 15, 1801 in Saint Guirauld, France
d. Jan 1871 in Seissan, France
Source: *AsBiEn; BiESc; CamDcSc; DcScB*

Lartique, Jacques-Henri Charles Auguste
French. Photographer, Artist
Known for photographs of everyday objects, sense of movement captured: *Diary of a Century,* 1970.
b. Jun 13, 1894 in Courbevoie, France
d. Sep 12, 1986 in Nice, France
Source: *ConAu 33R; IntWW 83; MacBEP; NewCol 75; NewYTBS 86; WhoWor 78*

Larue, Frederick Chaney
American. Presidential Aide
Shredded Watergate documents; spent six months in prison for obstructing justice, 1973.
b. 1928 in Mississippi
Source: *BioIn 9, 10; NewYTBE 73; PolProf NF*

LaRue, Jack
[Gaspere Biondolillo]
American. Actor
Made a career as a sneering bad guy in 200 films.
b. May 3, 1900 in New York, New York
d. Jan 11, 1984 in Santa Monica, California
Source: *FilmEn; FilmgC; ForYSC; HolCA; MotPP; MovMk; WhoHol A*

LaRussa, Tony
[Anthony Larussa, Jr]
American. Baseball Manager
Lawyer; manager, Chicago White Sox, 1979-86, Oakland, 1986-95, St. Louis, 1996—; AL manager of yr., 1983, 1988, 1992.
b. Oct 4, 1944 in Tampa, Florida
Source: *Ballpl 90; BaseReg 87; BiDAmSp Sup; BioIn 13; WhoAm 82, 84, 86, 88, 90; WhoMW 82, 84, 86; WhoSpor; WhoWest 87, 89, 92*

Lary, Frank Strong
"Bulldog"; "Mule"; "Yankee Killer"
American. Baseball Player
Pitcher, 1954-65, mostly with Detroit; known for victories over Yankees.
b. Apr 10, 1931 in Northport, Alabama
Source: *Ballpl 90; BioIn 6; WhoProB 73*

Lary, Yale
[Robert Yale Lary]
American. Football Player
Nine-time all-pro safety-punter, Detroit, 1952-53, 1956-64; led NFL in punting three times; Hall of Fame, 1979.
b. 1930 in Fort Worth, Texas
Source: *BiDAmSp FB; BioIn 7, 17; LegTOT; WhoFtbl 74; WhoSpor*

LaSalle, Eriq
American. Actor
Plays Dr. Peter Benton on TV's "ER," 1994—.
b. Jul 23, 1962 in Hartford, Connecticut
Source: *ConBlB 12; ConTFT 15; News 96*

La Salle, Rene Robert Cavelier de
French. Explorer
Traveled MS River to Gulf of Mexico, 1682; claimed land for France, naming it Louisiana; murdered by his men.
b. Nov 22, 1643 in Rouen, France
d. Mar 19, 1687 in Texas
Source: *ApCAB; BiDSA; DcAmB; Drake; NewCol 75; REn; WebAB 79; WebBD 83*

Lasch, Christopher
American. Historian
Wrote *The Culture of Narcisism,* 1979; leftist cultural theorist.
b. Jun 1, 1932
d. Feb 14, 1994 in Pittsford, New York
Source: *AmAu&B; Benet 87, 96; BiDNeoM; BlueB 76; ConAu 25NR, 73, 144; ConIsC 1; CurBio 85, 94N; DrAS 74H, 78H, 82H; MajTwCW; RadHan; WhAm 11; WhoAm 74, 82, 84, 86, 88, 90, 92, 94; WhoUSWr 88; WhoWrEP 89, 92, 95; WorAu 1975; WrDr 80, 82, 84, 86, 88, 90, 92, 94, 96*

Lasch, Robert
American. Editor
Won Pulitzer, 1966, for editorial writings; wrote *For A Free Press,* 1944.
b. Mar 26, 1907 in Lincoln, Nebraska
Source: *ConAu 102; WhoAm 74, 76, 78, 80, 82, 84, 86, 88, 90, 92, 94, 95, 96, 97; WhoWest 94, 96*

Lash, Joseph P
American. Author
Won 1971 Pulitzer for biography of the Roosevelts: *Eleanor and Franklin.*
b. Dec 2, 1909 in New York, New York
d. Aug 22, 1987 in Boston, Massachusetts
Source: *BiDAmLf; BioIn 9, 11, 14; ConAu 16NR, 17R; CurBio 72, 87; SmATA 43; WhoAm 74, 76, 78, 80, 82,*

84, 86; WhoE 74; WorAu 1970; WrDr 80, 82, 84, 86

Lasker, Albert D(avis)
American. Advertising Executive, Public Official, Philanthropist, Baseball Executive
Owner, Lord and Thomas advertising agency, 1912-42; husband of Mary.
b. May 1, 1880 in Freiburg, Germany
d. May 30, 1952 in New York, New York
Source: *BiDAmBL 83; BioIn 1, 2, 3, 4, 5, 7, 8, 10, 13; DcAmB S5; NatCAB 42; WebAB 74, 79; WhAm 3; WorAl*

Lasker, Edward
American. Chess Player, Author
Int'l master, 1963, who wrote *Chess Strategy,* 1915, first competent teaching method explaining whole game.
b. Dec 3, 1885 in Kempen, Germany
d. Mar 23, 1981 in New York, New York
Source: *AnObit 1981; Au&Wr 71; BioIn 10, 12; BlueB 76; ConAu 5NR, 5R, 103; GolEC; OxCChes 84; WhAm 7; WhNAA; WhoAm 74, 76; WhoWorJ 72, 78; WrDr 76, 80, 82*

Lasker, Emanuel
German. Chess Player
World champion, 1894-1921, known as one of greatest defensive players; author of several books on chess.
b. Dec 24, 1868 in Berlinchen, Prussia
d. Jan 11, 1941 in New York, New York
Source: *BioIn 1, 3, 4, 5, 10, 12, 14, 15, 17; CurBio 41; GolEC; ObitOF 79; OxCChes 84*

Lasker, Joe
[Joseph L Lasker]
American. Artist, Illustrator
Wrote, illustrated children's book *Merry Ever After,* 1976.
b. Jun 26, 1919 in New York, New York
Source: *ConAu 1NR, 49; FifBJA; IlsCB 1957; SmATA 9, 17AS, 83; WhAmArt 85; WhoAm 86, 90; WhoAmA 82, 84, 86, 89, 91, 93*

Lasker, Mary (Woodward)
[Mrs. Albert D(avis) Lasker]
American. Philanthropist
Pres., Albert and Mary Lasker Foundation for medical research, 1952-94.
b. Nov 30, 1900 in Watertown, Wisconsin
d. Feb 21, 1994 in Greenwich, Connecticut
Source: *BioIn 13, 14, 15, 17, 19, 20, 21; CelR; CurBio 59, 94N; InWom, SUP; NewYTBS 74, 85; WhoAm 86, 88; WhoAmW 58, 85*

Laski, Harold Joseph
English. Political Scientist, Author
Books include *American Presidency,* 1940; helped develop British Labour Party.
b. Jun 30, 1893 in Manchester, England
d. Mar 24, 1950 in London, England
Source: *BioIn 1, 2, 3, 4, 5, 6, 7, 10, 11, 12, 14, 15, 16, 19; CurBio 41, 50; DcLEL; DcNaB 1941; EvLB; GrBr; LinLib L, S; LngCTC; McGEWB; NewC; NewCBEL; REn; REnAL; TwCA, SUP; WhAm 2, 2A; WhE&EA; WorAl*

Laski, Marghanita
English. Author, Critic
Wrote books on biographical criticism and fiction, including *Little Boy Lost,* 1949; contributed to *Oxford English Dictionary,* 1951.
b. Oct 24, 1915 in London, England
d. Feb 6, 1988 in London, England
Source: *AnObit 1988; Au&Wr 71; BioIn 2, 4, 15, 16; ConAu 105, 124; CurBio 51, 88N; DcLP 87A; EncBrWW; EncSF, 93; FacFETw; FemiCLE; IntAu&W 76, 77; InWom, SUP; LngCTC; ModBrL; NewYTBS 88; PenNWW A; REn; REnAL; ScF&FL 1, 92; SmATA 55; TwCA SUP; WhE&EA; Who 74, 82, 83, 85, 88; WrDr 82, 84, 86, 88*

Laskin, Lily
French. Musician
Credited with popularizing and making harp a featured solo instrument; revived many musical scores for harp.
b. Aug 31, 1893 in Paris, France
d. Jan 5, 1988 in Paris, France
Source: *Baker 84; BioIn 15; NewGrDM 80*

Lasky, Jesse L(ouis)
American. Film Executive
With brother-in-law, Samuel Goldwyn, formed film studio, 1913, that became Paramount Studios, 1916.
b. Sep 13, 1880 in San Jose, California
d. Jan 13, 1958 in Beverly Hills, California
Source: *ApCAB X; BiDFilm; BioIn 1, 4, 5, 17; ConAu 4NR; CurBio 47, 58; DcAmB S6; DcFM; FilmgC; IntMPA 82; NatCAB 18; NotNAT B; ObitOF 79; OxCFilm; WebAB 74, 79; WhAm 3; WorEFlm*

Lasky, Jesse Louis, Jr.
[Frances Smeed]
American. Writer
Screenplays include *Samson and Delilah,* 1950; *Ten Commandments,* 1956; also wrote novels, plays; son of Hollywood film pioneer.
b. Sep 19, 1910 in New York, New York
d. Apr 11, 1988 in London, England
Source: *AmAu&B; AmNov; Au&Wr 71; AuNews 1; CmMov; ConAu 1R, 4NR, 20NR; DcFM; IntAu&W 86, 89, 91, 93; REnAL; WrDr 76, 80, 82, 84, 86, 88, 90*

Lasky, Melvin Joseph
American. Editor
Editor of anti-communist, liberal magazine, *Encounter,* 1958-1990.
b. Jan 20, 1920 in New York, New York
Source: *ColdWar 2*

Lasky, Victor
American. Journalist, Author
News columnist, critic of communism known for controversial books about John F Kennedy and Watergate scandal.
b. Jan 7, 1918 in Liberty, New York
d. Feb 22, 1990 in Washington, District of Columbia
Source: *AmAu&B; AnObit 1990; AuNews 1; BiDAmNC; BioIn 8, 10, 16, 17; BioNews 75; BlueB 76; CelR; ConAu 5R, 10NR, 131; DcAmC; FacFETw; IntAu&W 86, 91, 93; LegTOT; NewYTBS 90; WhAm 10; WhoAm 74, 76, 78, 80, 82, 84, 86, 88; WhoAmJ 80; WhoE 74; WhoWorJ 72, 78; WrDr 76, 80, 82, 84, 86, 88, 90*

Lasorda, Tommy
[Thomas Charles Lasorda]
American. Baseball Manager
Manager, LA Dodgers, 1976-96; NL manager of year, 1983, 1988; Hall of Fame, 1997.
b. Sep 22, 1927 in Norristown, Pennsylvania
Source: *AmCath 80; Ballpl 90; BiDAmSp Sup; BioIn 13, 14, 15, 16; CurBio 89; LegTOT; WhoAm 80, 82, 84, 90, 94, 95, 96, 97; WhoSpor; WhoWest 80, 82, 84, 92, 94, 96*

Lassale, Jean
French. Opera Singer
Parisian idol; baritone of Metropolitan Opera, 1890s.
b. Dec 14, 1847 in Lyons, France
d. Sep 7, 1909 in Paris, France
Source: *Baker 84; BioIn 1; NewEOp 71*

Lassalle, Ferdinand
German. Political Leader
Disciple of Karl Marx who founded German Social Democratic Party.
b. Apr 11, 1825 in Breslau, Prussia
d. Aug 28, 1864 in Geneva, Switzerland
Source: *BiD&SB; BioIn 19, 20; CelCen; DcEuL; DcLB 129; Dis&D; EncRev; LinLib L, S; McGEWB; NewCol 75; OxCGer 76, 86; REn; WhoEc 81, 86; WorAl; WorAlBi*

Lasser, Jacob Kay
American. Financier
Instrumental in simplifying tax code language, regulation; established position of certified public accountant.
b. Oct 7, 1896 in Newark, New Jersey
d. May 11, 1954 in New York, New York
Source: *BioIn 1, 2, 3, 5; CurBio 46, 54; DcAmB S5; NatCAB 42; ObitOF 79; WhAm 3*

Lasser, Louise
American. Actor
Starred in "Mary Hartman, Mary Hartman"; was married to Woody Allen.
b. Apr 11, 1939 in New York, New York
Source: *BioIn 20; BkPepl; ConTFT 3; CurBio 76; EncAFC; HalFC 84, 88; IntMPA 86, 92, 94, 96; InWom SUP; LegTOT; LesBEnT; MovMk; NewYTBE 71; NewYTBS 76; WhoAm 84, 86, 90, 94, 95; WhoCom; WhoEnt 92; WhoHol 92, A; WorAlBi*

Lasseter, John
American. Computer Animator
Works include *Toy Story,* 1995.
b. 1957 in Hollywood, California

Lassus, Orlandus de
[Roland Delattre; Orlando di Lasso]
Belgian. Composer
Ranks after Palestrina, as leading Renaissance composer; wrote over 1,500 works.
b. 1532 in Mons, Netherlands
d. Jun 14, 1594 in Munich, Germany
Source: *AtlBL; Baker 92; BioIn 20; BriBkM 80; DcCathB; GrComp; LuthC 75; NewAmDM; NewCol 75; NewGrDM 80; PseudN 82; REn*

Lasswell, Fred
American. Cartoonist
Noted for "Barney Google" comic strip since 1930s.
b. 1916 in Kennett, Missouri
Source: *BioIn 6, 15; EncACom; WhoAm 82, 84, 86, 88, 90; WorECom*

Laszlo, Magda
Hungarian. Opera Singer
Soprano who had title role in Gluck's *Alceste,* 1953; sings wide range of modern operas.
b. 1919 in Marosvasarhely, Hungary
Source: *CmOp; IntWWM 90; NewEOp 71; NewGrDM 80; NewGrDO; OxDcOp*

Lateiner, Jacob
American. Musician
Soloist in annual US, European tours since 1950; gave first concert at age eight.
b. May 31, 1928 in Havana, Cuba
Source: *Baker 84, 92; BioIn 1, 4, 7; CamGWoT; IntWWM 90; NewAmDM; NewGrDA 86; NewGrDM 80; WhoAm 74, 76, 78, 80, 82, 84; WhoAmM 83; WhoMus 72; WhoWor 74, 76*

Latham, Jean Lee
[Rose Champion; Janice Gard; Julian Lee]
American. Author
Numerous children's books include 1955 Newbery winner: *Carry On, Mr. Bowditch.*
b. Apr 19, 1902 in Buckhannon, West Virginia
Source: *AmAu&B; AmWomPl; AmWomWr; Au&Wr 71; AuBYP 2, 3; AuNews 1; BioIn 4, 6, 7, 8, 9, 10, 12, 14, 17, 19, 21; ChlBkCr; ConAu 5R, 7NR; ConLC 12; CurBio 56; DcLP 87A; IntAu&W 91; InWom; LinLib L; MajAI; MorBMP; MorJA; NewbC 1956; OxCChiL; PenNWW A; PseudN 82; SmATA 2, 68; Str&VC; TwCChW 78, 83, 89; TwCYAW; WhAm 11; WhoAm 74, 76, 78, 80, 82, 84, 86, 88, 90, 92, 94, 95, 96; WhoAmW 58, 66, 68, 70, 72, 74; WrDr 82, 84, 86, 88, 90, 92, 94, 96*

Lathen, Emma
[Martha Hennisart; Mary J Latis]
American. Authors
Their mysteries have featured John Putnam Thatcher since 1961.
Source: *AmWomWr; ArtclWW 2; BioIn 8, 11, 12, 13; CamGLE; ConAu X; ConLC 2; CorpD; CrtSuMy; DcLP 87B; DetWom; EncMys; FemiCLE; GrWomMW; IntAu&W 91; InWom SUP; Novels; PenNWW B; PseudN 82; ThrtnMM; TwCCr&M 80, 85, 91; WorAl; WorAlBi; WorAu 1970; WrDr 76, 80, 82, 84, 86, 88, 90, 92, 94, 96*

Lathrop, Rose Hawthorne
[Mother Mary Alphonsa Lathrop]
American. Philanthropist
Nathaniel Hawthorne's daughter; established homes for indigent cancer victims; wrote poetry, prose.
b. May 20, 1851 in Lenox, Massachusetts
d. Jul 9, 1926 in Hawthorne, New York
Source: *AmAu&B; AmBi; AmWom; AmWomWr; ApCAB; BbD; BenetAL 91; BiD&SB; BioAmW; BioIn 16, 17, 19; ChhPo, S1; DcAmAu; DcAmB; DcAmReB 2; DcCathB; DcNAA; HarEnUS; InWom, SUP; LibW; NatCAB 9; NewCol 75; NotAW; REn; REnAL; TwCBDA; WhAm 1; WomFir*

Latifah, Queen
[Dana Owens]
American. Rapper
Rap's hottest female star; album *All Hail the Queen,* 1989; Grammy, Best Rap Solo Performance, *U.N.I.T.Y.,* 1994.
b. Mar 18, 1970 in East Orange, New Jersey
Source: *ConBlB 1; ConMus 6; News 92, 92-2; NotBlAW 2; WhoAmW 97*

Latimer, Hugh
"The Apostle of England"
English. Religious Leader
Protestant bishop known for defending Henry VIII's divorce from Katherine of Aragon; burned at stake for heresy by Mary I.
b. 1485 in Thurcaston, England
d. Oct 16, 1555 in Oxford, England
Source: *Alli; BbD; Benet 87, 96; BiD&SB; BioIn 2, 3, 4, 5, 7, 8, 9, 11, 12, 15, 20; BritAu; CamGLE; Chambr 1; DcEnL; DcNaB; EvLB; LinLib S; LuthC 75; NewC; NewCol 75; OxCEng 67; PseudN 82; REn; WebE&AL; WhDW; WorAl; WorAlBi*

Latimer, Lewis Howard
American. Inventor
Worked with Edison; oversaw installation of first street lights in NYC; invented first incandescent electric light bulb with a carbon filament.
b. 1848
d. 1928
Source: *AfrAmAl 6; AfroAA; BioIn 9, 10, 12, 14, 17, 19, 20, 21; BlkAWP; BlksScM; BlkWrNE A; InB&W 80; NegAl 76, 83, 89; WhoColR; WorInv*

LaTouche, John
American. Lyricist
Wrote lyrics for play *Cabin in the Sky,* 1940.
b. Nov 13, 1917 in Richmond, Virginia
d. Aug 7, 1956 in Calais, Vermont
Source: *CmpEPM; CurBio 40, 56; McGEWD 72*

La Tour, Georges Dumesnil de
French. Artist
Painted daylight, candlelight scenes: *The Fortune Teller,* 1620s.
b. Mar 19, 1593 in Vic sur Seille, France
d. Jan 30, 1652 in Luneville, France
Source: *AtlBL; McGDA; McGEWB; NewCol 75; WhDW*

LaTour D'Auvergne, Theophile de
"First Grenadier of France"
French. Soldier
Noted for bravery, modesty; killed in action; until 1814 name called on soldier roster.
b. Nov 23, 1743 in Carhaix, France
d. Jun 27, 1800 in Oberhausen, Bavaria
Source: *NewCol 75*

La Tour du Pin, Patrice de
French. Poet
Wrote *Quest of Joy,* 1933; *Sum of Poetry,* 1946.
b. Mar 16, 1911 in Paris, France
d. Oct 28, 1975 in Paris, France
Source: *Benet 87, 96; BioIn 13; ClDMEL 47, 80; ConAu 115; DcTwCCu 2; EncWL 2, 3; PenC EUR*

Latrobe, Benjamin Henry
American. Architect
Considered first professional American architect; designed Philadelphia, Washington buildings; rebuilt US Capital, 1815-17.
b. May 1, 1764 in Fulneck, England
d. Sep 3, 1820 in New Orleans, Louisiana
Source: *Alli; AmBi; AmCulL; ApCAB; AtlBL; BenetAL 91; BiAUS; BiDAmAr; BiDBrA; BiDSA; BiInAmS; BioIn 1, 2, 3, 4, 5, 6, 8, 11, 12, 13, 14, 15, 16, 17, 19; BriEAA; DcAmB; DcD&D; Drake; EncAAr 1, 2; EncAB-H 1974; EncSoH; InSci; LinLib S; McGDA; McGEWB;*

NatCAB 9; NewCol 75; NewYHSD; OxCAmH; OxCAmL 65; REnAL; TwCBDA; WebAB 74, 79; WhAm HS; WhoArch; WorAl

Lattimore, Owen
American. Author
Expert on Manchuria, Mongolia, Chinese border; unjustly accused of espionage by Senator McCarthy, 1950; completely vindicated, 1955.
b. Jul 29, 1900 in Washington, District of Columbia
d. May 31, 1989 in Providence, Rhode Island
Source: *AmAu&B; AmDec 1940; AmMWSc 73S; AnObit 1989; BenetAL 91; BioIn 1, 2, 3, 4, 5, 6, 7, 9, 11, 15, 16, 17; BlueB 76; ConAu 97, 128; CurBio 45, 64, 89, 89N; EncCW; EncMcCE; FacFETw; IntWW 74, 75, 76, 77, 78, 79, 80, 81, 82, 83, 89; NewCol 75; NewYTBS 89; OxCAmL 65, 83, 95; PolProf T; REnAL; TwCA SUP; WhAm 10; WhE&EA; Who 74, 82, 83, 85, 88, 90N; WhoAm 74, 76, 78, 80, 82; WhoWor 74; WrDr 86, 88*

Lattimore, Richmond Alexander
American. Translator
Translations of Homer's Iliad, Odyssey, are standard university texts.
b. May 6, 1906 in Baodingfu, China
d. Feb 26, 1984 in Rosemont, Pennsylvania
Source: *AmAu&B; AnObit 1984; BioIn 4, 6; ConAu 1NR, 112; ConLC 3; ConPo 70, 75; DrAS 74F; ModAL, S1; NewYTBS 84; NotNAT; OxCAmL 65; RAdv 1; REnAL; TwCA SUP; WhoE 83; WrDr 76*

Lattisaw, Stacy
American. Singer
Recorded first album at age 12: *Young and In Love,* 1978.
b. Nov 25, 1966 in Washington, District of Columbia
Source: *BioIn 13; InB&W 85; LegTOT; PenEncP; RkOn 85; RolSEnR 83*

Lattner, Johnny
[John J Lattner]
American. Football Player
All-America halfback, won Heisman Trophy, 1953; had brief NFL career with Pittsburgh, 1954.
b. Oct 24, 1932 in Chicago, Illinois
Source: *BiDAmSp FB; BioIn 3, 14; WhoFtbl 74; WhoSpor*

Lattre de Tassigny, Jean de (Marie Gabriel) de
French. Army Officer
Commanded first French Army, 1944; Western Europe Land forces, 1948-50.
b. Feb 2, 1889 in Mouilleron-en-Pareds, France
d. Jan 11, 1952 in Paris, France
Source: *CurBio 45, 52; WhAm 3; WhoMilH 76*

Lattuada, Felice
Italian. Composer
Operas include *Caino,* 1957.
b. Feb 5, 1882 in Morimondo, Italy
d. Nov 2, 1962 in Milan, Italy
Source: *Baker 78, 84, 92; BioIn 6; ItaFilm; MetOEnc; NewEOp 71; NewGrDM 80; NewGrDO*

Latynina, Larisa Semyonovna
Ukrainian. Gymnast
Won 9 Olympic gold medals, 1956, 1960, 1964; first woman to do so.
b. Dec 27, 1934 in Kherson, Union of Soviet Socialist Republics
Source: *BiDSovU; BioIn 5; ContDcW 89; IntDcWB; InWom SUP*

Latzo, Pete
[Young Clancy]
American. Boxer
Won world welterweight title, 1926.
b. Aug 1, 1902 in Coloraine, Pennsylvania
d. 1968
Source: *PseudN 82; WhoBox 74*

Lau, Charlie
[Charles Richard Lau]
American. Baseball Player, Baseball Coach
Catcher, 1956-67; considered best hitting coach in baseball, 1971-83; George Brett most famous student.
b. Apr 12, 1933 in Romulus, Michigan
d. Mar 18, 1984 in Key Colony Beach, Florida
Source: *Ballpl 90; BioIn 12; ConAu 112; NewYTBS 81, 84*

Laub, Larry
American. Bowler
PBA Hall of Famer.

Laubenthal, Rudolf
German. Opera Singer
Noted Wagnerian tenor; with Metropolitan Opera, 1920s-30s.
b. Mar 10, 1886 in Dusseldorf, Germany
d. Oct 2, 1971 in Starnberg, Germany (West)
Source: *Baker 84, 92; NewEOp 71; NewGrDM 80; NewGrDO; OxDcOp; PenDiMP*

Lauck, Chester H
[Lum 'n Abner]
American. Radio Performer
Star of "Lum and Abner," 1931-55.
b. 1902
d. Feb 21, 1980 in Hot Springs, Arkansas
Source: *BioIn 1, 7, 8, 9, 12; WhoHol A*

Laud, William
English. Religious Leader
Archbishop of Canterbury, 1633-40; impeached for high treason, beheaded.
b. Oct 7, 1573 in Reading, England
d. Jan 10, 1645 in London, England
Source: *Alli; Benet 87, 96; BiD&SB; BioIn 1, 2, 3, 5, 6, 7, 8, 9, 10, 13, 14, 15, 16, 18; BlmGEL; BritAu; CamGEL; CamGLE; CyEd; DcBiPP; DcNaB; DicTyr; HisDStE; LngCEL; LuthC 75; McGEWB; NewC; OxCEng 67, 85, 95; OxCMus; PseudN 82; REn; WhDW*

Lauda, Niki
[Nikolaus-Andreas Lauda]
Austrian. Auto Racer, Author
World champion, Formula 1 Grand Prix, 1975, 1977.
b. Feb 22, 1949 in Vienna, Austria
Source: *BioIn 10, 11, 12, 13, 14, 15; CurBio 80; IntWW 81, 91; LegTOT; NewYTBS 75; WorAl; WorAlBi*

Lauder, Estee
[Josephine Esther Mentzer]
American. Cosmetics Executive
CEO, Estee Lauder Inc., 1946-82; chm. of the board, 1982—.
b. Jul 1, 1908? in New York, New York
Source: *BioAmW; BioIn 13, 14, 15, 16; BioNews 75; BusPN; CelR 90; ConAmBL; ContDcW 89; CurBio 86; IntWW 91; InWom SUP; LegTOT; News 92, 92-2; NewYTBS 85, 87; WhoAm 86, 90; WhoAmW 87, 91; WhoE 91; WhoFI 92; WorAlBi*

Lauder, Harry MacLennan, Sir
[Harry MacLennan]
"The Laird of the Halls"
Scottish. Singer
Famed music-hall comedian, noted for "Roamin' in the Gloamin'."
b. Aug 4, 1870 in Portobello, Scotland
d. Feb 26, 1950 in Strathaven, Scotland
Source: *FilmgC; HalFC 84; LinLib S; NewC; OxCThe 67; PseudN 82; WhAm 4; WhoHol B; WhScrn 74, 83*

Lauder, Joseph H
American. Business Executive
Co-founder with wife, Estee, of cosmetics firm, 1946.
b. 1910? in New York, New York
d. Jan 15, 1983 in New York, New York
Source: *NewYTBS 83*

Laue, Max Theodor Felix von
German. Physicist, Educator
Won 1914 Nobel Prize for studies in X-ray diffraction.
b. Oct 9, 1879 in Koblenz, Germany
d. Apr 24, 1960 in Berlin, Germany (West)
Source: *AsBiEn; BioIn 2, 3, 5, 12; ConAu 113; DcScB; InSci; WhAm 4; WhDW; WhoNob, 90, 95; WorScD*

Lauer, Matt
American. Broadcast Journalist
Host of NBC's "Today" show, 1997—.
b. Dec 30, 1957

Laughlin, James, IV
American. Publisher
Founder, New Directions, 1936, publishers of fine avant-garde writing; pres., 1964—.
b. Oct 30, 1914 in Pittsburgh, Pennsylvania
Source: *AmAu&B; Benet 96; BenetAL 91; BioIn 2, 7, 9, 12, 13, 16, 17, 18, 19, 21; ConAu 9NR, 21R, 22AS, 47NR; ConLC 49; ConPo 70, 75, 80, 85, 91, 96; CurBio 82; DcLB 48; IntAu&W 91; IntWWP 77; OxCTwCP; REnAL; WhoAm 74, 76, 78, 80, 82, 84, 86, 88, 90, 92, 94, 95, 96, 97; WhoWor 74; WorAu 1975; WrDr 76, 80, 82, 84, 86, 88, 90, 92, 94, 96*

Laughlin, James Laurence
American. Economist
Edited *Journal of Political Economy,* 1892-1933; helped establish Federal Reserve System.
b. Apr 2, 1850 in Deerfield, Ohio
d. Nov 28, 1933 in Jaffrey, New Hampshire
Source: *Alli SUP; AmBi; ApCAB; BiD&SB; BioIn 8, 11; DcAmAu; DcAmB S1; HarEnUS; NatCAB 11, 24; NewCol 75; OhA&B; OxCAmH; TwCBDA; WhAm 1; WhoEc 81, 86*

Laughlin, Tom
[T C Frank]
American. Actor
Known for title role in *Billy Jack* movies.
b. 1938 in Minneapolis, Minnesota
Source: *BioIn 10, 16; ConAu 116, 138; ConTFT 5; FilmEn; FilmgC; HalFC 80, 84, 88; IntMPA 84, 86, 88, 92, 94, 96; LegTOT; MiSFD 9; VarWW 85; WhoEnt 92; WhoHol 92, A*

Laughton, Charles
American. Actor
Won Oscar, 1933, for *The Private Lives of Henry VIII;* noted for *Mutiny on the Bounty,* 1935.
b. Jul 1, 1899 in Scarborough, England
d. Dec 15, 1962 in Los Angeles, California
Source: *BiDFilm, 81, 94; BioIn 1, 2, 3, 5, 6, 7, 8, 9, 10, 12, 13, 14, 15, 16, 17; CamGWoT; CmMov; CnThe; CurBio 48, 63; DcAmB S7; DcArts; DcNaB MP; EncAFC; EncEurC; EncWT; FacFETw; FamA&A; Film 2; FilmAG WE; FilmEn; FilmgC; ForYSC; HalFC 80, 84, 88; IlWWBF, A; IntDcF 1-3, 2-3; IntDcT 3; ItaFilm; LegTOT; LinLib S; MiSFD 9N; MotPP; MovMk; NotNAT A, B; ObitT 1961; OxCAmT 84; OxCFilm; OxCThe 83; PenEncH; PlP&P; WhAm 4; WhDW; WhoHol B; WhoHrs 80; WhScrn 74, 77, 83; WhThe; WorAl; WorAlBi; WorEFlm*

Lauper, Cyndi
[Cynthia Lauper; Mrs. David Thornton]
American. Singer, Actor
Five hits from first album *She's So Unusual,* broke record for most Top 10 singles from debut album; won Grammy, 1984; films include *Vibes,* 1988.
b. Jun 20, 1953 in New York, New York
Source: *Baker 92; BioIn 13, 14, 15, 16; CelR 90; ConMus 11; ConNews 85-1; CurBio 85; EncPR&S 89; EncRk 88; EncRkSt; InWom SUP; LegTOT; NewGrDA 86; NewYTBS 86; RkOn 85; WhoAm 88, 90, 92, 94, 95, 96, 97; WhoAmW 91; WhoHol 92; WhoRocM 82; WorAlBi*

Laurel, Alicia Bay
American. Author, Illustrator
Children's books include *The Goodnight Hug; The Talking Whale.*
b. May 14, 1949 in Los Angeles, California
Source: *ConAu 41R; IntAu&W 89; NewYTBE 71; WhoAmW 85, 87*

Laurel, Stan
[Laurel and Hardy; Arthur Stanley Jefferson]
American. Comedian, Actor
Joined with Oliver Hardy, 1926; made over 200 films.
b. Jun 16, 1890 in Ulverston, England
d. Feb 23, 1965 in Santa Monica, California
Source: *BiDFilm, 81, 94; BioIn 2, 5, 7, 8, 9, 10, 11, 12, 14, 15, 16, 17, 18, 20; CmCal; CmMov; DcAmB S7; DcArts; DcNaB MP; EncAFC; FacFETw; Film 1, 2; FilmEn; FilmgC; Funs; HalFC 80, 84, 88; IntDcF 1-3, 2-3; ItaFilm; JoeFr; LegTOT; MGM; MotPP; MovMk; ObitT 1961; OxCFilm; PseudN 82; QDrFCA 92; RAdv 13-3; TwYS; WebAB 74, 79; WhoHol B; WhoHrs 80; WhScrn 74, 77, 83; WorAl; WorAlBi; WorEFlm*

Lauren, Ralph
[Ralph Lifshitz]
American. Fashion Designer
Head of Polo Fashions, Inc., 1969—; won 7 Cotys; Coty Hall of Fame, 1971; created own line of paints.
b. Oct 14, 1939 in New York, New York
Source: *AmDec 1970; BioIn 10, 11, 12, 13, 14, 15, 16; CelR 90; ConAmBL; ConDes 84, 90, 97; ConFash; CurBio 80; DcArts; DcTwDes; EncFash; Entr; FacFETw; IntWW 91, 93; LegTOT; News 90, 90-1; WhoAm 82, 84, 86, 88, 90, 92, 94, 95, 96, 97; WhoE 95, 97; WhoFash, 88; WhoFI 89, 92, 94; WhoWor 97; WorAlBi; WorFshn*

Laurence, Margaret
[Jean Margaret Lauren]
Canadian. Author
Award-winning novelist, short story writer; *A Jest of God,* 1967, filmed as *Rachel, Rachel.*
b. Jul 18, 1926 in Neepawa, Manitoba, Canada
d. Jan 5, 1987 in Lakefield, Ontario, Canada
Source: *AnObit 1987; ArtclWW 2; Au&Wr 71; Benet 87; BenetAL 91; BioIn 8, 10, 11, 12, 13, 15, 16, 17, 19, 20; BlmGEL; BlueB 76; CanWr; CanWW 70, 79, 80, 81, 83; CaW; ConAu 5R, 33NR, 121; ConLC 3, 6, 13, 50, 62; ConNov 72, 76, 82, 86; ContDcW 89; CreCan 1; CyWA 89; DcArts; DcChlFi; DcLB 53; EncWB; EncWL 2, 3; FemiCLE; GrWomW; GrWrEL N; IntAu&W 76, 77; IntLitE; InWom SUP; MagSWL; MajTwCW; ModCmwL; ModWoWr; Novels; OxCCan; OxCCanL; OxCCan SUP; OxCEng 95; RAdv 14, 13-1; RfGEnL 91; ShSCr 7; SmATA 50N; TwCWW 91; WhAm 9; WhoAm 86; WhoAmW 83, 87; WhoCanL 85, 87, 92; WorAu 1970; WrDr 76, 80, 82, 84, 86*

Laurencin, Marie
French. Artist
Drew portraits of females in soft pastels; friend of Picasso, Matisse.
b. Oct 31, 1885 in Paris, France
d. Jun 8, 1956 in Paris, France
Source: *BiDD; BiDWomA; BioIn 3, 4, 5, 6, 8, 10, 11, 16, 17, 19; ClaDrA; CnOxB; DancEn 78; DcTwCCu 2; DcWomA; EncCoWW; InWom SUP; McGDA; ObitT 1951; OxCTwCA; PhDcTCA 77; WomArt*

Laurens, Henry
American. Merchant, Statesman
Pres., Continental Congress, 1777-78; captured by British off Newfoundland, exchanged for General Cornwallis, 1782.
b. Mar 26, 1724 in Charleston, South Carolina
d. Dec 8, 1792 in Charleston, South Carolina
Source: *AmBi; AmRev; ApCAB; BenetAL 91; BiAUS; BiDAmBL 83; BiDrAC; BiDrACR; BiDrUSC 89; BiDrUSE 71, 89; BioIn 8, 9, 11, 16; BlkwEAR; CyAG; DcAmB; DcAmDH 80, 89; DcBiPP; Drake; EncAB-H 1974; EncAR; EncCRAm; EncSoH; HarEnUS; McGEWB; NatCAB 3; OxCAmH; OxCAmL 65, 83, 95; REnAL; SouWr; TwCBDA; WebAB 74, 79; WhAm HS; WhAmP; WhAmRev*

Laurents, Arthur
American. Dramatist, Author
Wrote musical *West Side Story,* 1958; wrote novels, screenplays *The Way We Were,* 1972; *The Turning Point,* 1977.
b. Jul 14, 1918 in New York, New York
Source: *BenetAL 91; BestMus; BiE&WWA; BioIn 4, 9, 10, 12, 14, 15, 17; BlueB 76; CamGWoT; ConAu 8NR, 12NR; ConDr 73, 77, 82, 88; ConTFT 2, 9; CrtSuDr; CurBio 84; DcLB 26; EncMT; Ent; FilmEn; FilmgC; GrWrEL DR; HalFC 80, 84, 88; IntAu&W 89, 91; IntDcT 2; IntMPA 86, 92; IntvTCA 2; IntWW 89, 91, 93; LegTOT; McGEWD 72, 84; NatPD 81; NewCBMT; NotNAT; OxCAmL 65, 83, 95; OxCAmT 84; PenC AM; PlP&P; REnAL; RfGAmL 87, 94; TwCA SUP; VarWW 85; WhoAm 74, 76, 78, 80, 82, 84, 86, 88, 90; WhoE 74; WhoEnt 92; WhoThe 72, 77, 81; WhoWor 74, 76; WrDr 76, 80, 82, 84, 86, 88, 90, 92, 94, 96*

Lauria, Dan
American. Actor
Played Jack on TV series "The Wonder Years," 1988-93.
b. 1947
Source: *ConTFT 7; IntMPA 94, 96; WhoEnt 92; WhoHol 92*

Laurie, Annie
Scottish. Historical Figure
Subject of Scottish song written by man she rejected in marriage, c. 1700.
b. 1682
d. 1764
Source: *InWom; OxCEng 85, 95; REn*

Laurie, Joe, Jr.
American. Comedian
Vaudeville, radio, TV comic; columnist *Variety* mag.
b. 1892 in New York, New York
d. Apr 29, 1954 in New York, New York
Source: *JoeFr; NotNAT B; ObitOF 79; RadStar; WhScrn 83*

Laurie, Piper
[Rosetta Jacobs]
American. Actor
Oscar nominee for her role as mother in *Carrie,* 1976; won 1987 Emmy for "Promise."
b. Jan 22, 1932 in Detroit, Michigan
Source: *BioIn 3, 4, 14, 17; CmMov; ConTFT 3, 10; FilmEn; FilmgC; ForYSC; HalFC 80, 84, 88; IntMPA 75, 76, 77, 78, 79, 80, 81, 82, 84, 86, 88, 92, 94, 96; InWom; LegTOT; MotPP; MovMk; PseudN 82; VarWW 85; WhoAm 74, 78, 80, 82, 84, 94, 95, 96, 97; WhoAmW 66, 68, 70, 72, 83, 89, 91, 93, 95, 97; WhoEnt 92; WhoHol 92, A; WhoHrs 80; WorAlBi; WorEFlm*

Laurier, Wilfrid, Sir
Canadian. Politician
First French-Canadian to be prime minister, 1896-1911.
b. Nov 20, 1841 in Saint Lin, Quebec, Canada
d. Feb 17, 1919 in Ottawa, Ontario, Canada
Source: *ApCAB; BioIn 1, 4, 7, 8, 9, 11, 12, 13, 14, 20; DcCathB; DcNaB 1912; Dis&D; FacFETw; LinLib L, S; MacDCB 78; McGEWB; NewCol 75; OxCCan; WorAl*

Lauri-Volpi, Giacoma
Italian. Opera Singer
Tenor NY Met., 1923-34; sang in Puccini opera, age 80.
b. Dec 11, 1894 in Rome, Italy
d. Mar 17, 1979 in Valencia, Spain
Source: *Baker 84; BioIn 10; MusSN; NewEOp 71; NewGrDM 80*

Lausche, Frank John
American. Politician, Judge
Conservative Dem. senator from OH, 1956-68; five-time governor of OH, 1940s-50s.
b. Nov 14, 1895 in Cleveland, Ohio
d. Apr 21, 1990 in Cleveland, Ohio
Source: *BiDrAC; BiDrGov 1789; BiDrUSC 89; BioIn 1, 3, 4, 5, 7, 11, 16, 17; CurBio 46, 58, 90, 90N; LinLib S; NewYTBS 90; PolProf E, J, K, T; WhAm 10; WhoAmP 79, 89*

Lautenberg, Frank R
American. Politician
Dem. senator from NJ, 1982—; known for his fight to ban smoking on commercial airline flights.
b. Jan 23, 1924 in Paterson, New Jersey
Source: *AlmAP 92; BiDrUSC 89; BioIn 13, 14, 15, 16; CngDr 85, 87, 89; CurBio 91; IntWW 83, 91; PolsAm 84; WhoAm 86, 90; WhoAmP 85, 91; WhoE 91; WhoWor 87, 91*

Lauterbach, Steven
[The Hostages]
American. Hostage
One of 52 held by terrorists, Nov 1979-Jan 1981.
b. 1952?
Source: *BioIn 12; NewYTBS 81*

Lautreamont, Comte de
[Isidore Lucien Ducasse]
French. Poet
Wrote prose epic *Les Chants de Maldoror,* 1868-70.
b. Apr 4, 1846 in Montevideo, Uruguay
d. Nov 24, 1870 in Paris, France
Source: *BioIn 1, 2, 3, 7, 9, 10; CasWL; ClDMEL 47, 80; EuAu; EvEuW; NewCol 75; Novels; OxCFr; PenC EUR; PseudN 82; REn; ScF&FL 1*

Laval, Pierre
"Mossbank"
French. Political Leader
Premier of Vichy govt., 1942; collaborated with Germany, executed for treason.
b. Jun 28, 1883 in Chatelden, France
d. Oct 15, 1945 in Paris, France
Source: *BiDFrPL; BioIn 1, 2, 6, 7, 8, 14, 16, 17, 20; CurBio 45; DcTwHis; Dis&D; EncTR, 91; FacFETw; GrLGrT; HisEWW; HisWorL; LinLib S; McGEWB; PseudN 82; REn; WhDW; WhWW-II; WorAl; WorAlBi*

Lavalle, Paul
American. Conductor, Composer
Organized musical radio programs including "The Band of America," 1948.
b. Sep 6, 1908 in Beacon, New York
Source: *ASCAP 66, 80; BlueB 76; CmpEPM; IntMPA 75; RadStar; SaTiSS; WhoAm 78*

Lavater, Johann Casper
Swiss. Theologian, Author
Advocated physiognomy, judging character from facial characteristics.
b. Nov 15, 1741 in Zurich, Switzerland
d. Jan 2, 1801 in Zurich, Switzerland
Source: *CopCroC; CyEd; DcBiPP; InSci; LuthC 75; NamesHP*

Lavelle, Rita Marie
American. Government Official
Former head of EPA toxic waste clean-up program, indicted for conflict of interest, mismanagement, 1983; jailed 4.5 months.
b. Sep 8, 1947 in Portsmouth, Virginia
Source: *BioIn 13, 14; NewYTBS 83; WhoAmM 83; WhoAmW 83; WhoWest 92*

Lavelli, Dante
American. Football Player
Two-time all-pro end, Cleveland, 1946-56; Hall of Fame, 1975.
b. 1923 in Hudson, Ohio
Source: *BiDAmSp FB; LegTOT; WhoFtbl 74*

Laver, James
[Jacques Reval]
English. Author, Critic
Noted art, fashion historian; wrote *Style in Costume,* 1944.
b. Mar 14, 1899 in Liverpool, England
d. Jun 3, 1975 in London, England
Source: *Au&Wr 71; BiE&WWA; BioIn 4, 6, 10; ChhPo S3; ConAu 1R, 3NR, 57; DcNaB 1971; EvLB; IntWW 74, 75; LngCTC; ModBrL; NewC; NewCBEL; NotNAT A; ObitT 1971; OxCThe 67; PenC ENG; PseudN 82; ScF&FL 1, 2; TwCA, SUP; WhE&EA; WhLit; Who 74; WhoWor 74, 76; WhThe; WorFshn*

Laver, Rod(ney George)
"Rocket"
Australian. Tennis Player
First player to win double Grand Slam, 1962, 1969.
b. Aug 9, 1938 in Rockhampton, Australia
Source: *BioIn 6, 8, 9, 10, 11, 12, 13, 14, 15, 16; BuCMET; CelR; ConAu 112; CurBio 63; FacFETw; IntWW 83, 91; LegTOT; NewYTBE 71; NewYTBS 82; WhDW; WhoAm 78, 80, 82, 84, 90, 92; WhoWor 74, 78, 80, 82, 84, 87; WorAl; WorAlBi*

Laveran, Charles Louis Alphonse
French. Physician
Discovered basis of malaria, 1880; won 1907 Nobel Prize for protozean causes of disease.
b. Jun 18, 1845 in Paris, France
d. May 18, 1922 in Paris, France
Source: *AsBiEn; BiESc; BioIn 4, 6, 14, 15, 18, 20; DcScB; InSci; LarDcSc; LinLib S; NewCol 75; OxCMed 86; WhoNob, 90, 95*

Lavery, John, Sir
Irish. Artist
Painted interiors, landscapes, portaits of notables.
b. Mar 1856 in Belfast, Northern Ireland
d. Jan 10, 1941 in Kilmoganny, Ireland

Source: *BioIn 2, 5, 14, 17; ClaDrA; CurBio 41; DcArts; DcBrAr 1; DcIrB 78, 88; DcNaB 1941; DcVicP, 2; GrBr; McGDA; OxCArt; OxCTwCA; OxDcArt; PhDcTCA 77; TwCPaSc*

Lavigne, Kid
[George Lavigne]
"The Saginaw Kid"
American. Boxer
Noted lightweight fighter, 1890s; Hall of Fame, 1959.
b. Dec 6, 1869 in Saginaw, Michigan
d. Apr 6, 1936 in Detroit, Michigan
Source: *BiDAmSp BK; PseudN 82; WhoBox 74*

Lavin, Christine
American. Singer, Songwriter
Folk/pop/comic performer known for witty lyrics; album *Attainable Love,* include song "Sensitive New Age Guys."
b. 1952?
Source: *ConMus 6*

Lavin, Linda
American. Actor, Singer
Starred in TV series "Alice," 1976-85; won Tony for *Broadway Bound,* 1987.
b. Oct 15, 1937 in Portland, Maine
Source: *BioIn 12, 81; WorAl; WorAlBi*

Laviolette, Jack
[Jean-Baptiste Laviolette]
Canadian. Hockey Player
Defenseman, Montreal, 1917-18; career ended when lost foot in accident; Hall of Fame, 1962.
b. Jul 19, 1879 in Belleville, Ontario, Canada
d. Jan 10, 1960 in Montreal, Quebec, Canada
Source: *BioIn 10; HocEn; WhoHcky 73*

Lavis, Gilson
English. Musician
Drummer with British band Squeeze.
b. Jun 27, 1951 in Bedford, England

Lavoisier, Antoine Laurent
French. Chemist
Considered father of modern chemistry, reformed chemical nomenclature, held various government offices; guillotined during Reign of Terror.
b. Aug 13, 1743 in Paris, France
d. May 8, 1794 in Paris, France
Source: *AsBiEn; BbD; BiD&SB; BiDPsy; BiESc; BiHiMed; BioIn 1, 2, 3, 4, 5, 6, 7, 8, 9, 10, 11, 12, 13, 14, 15, 16, 17, 19, 20; CamDcSc; DcBiPP; DcCathB; DcScB; Dis&D; EncEnl; InSci; LarDcSc; LinLib L, S; McGEWB; NewCol 75; OxCFr; OxCMed 86; RAdv 14, 13-5; REn; WhDW; WorAl; WorAlBi*

Law, Andrew Bonar
English. Statesman
Conservative prime minister, 1922-23.
b. Sep 16, 1858 in Kingston, Ontario, Canada
d. Oct 30, 1923 in London, England
Source: *BioIn 2, 4, 7, 8, 9, 10, 11, 12, 13, 14, 21; DcNaB 1922; DcTwHis; FacFETw; GrBr; HisDBrE; LinLib S; NewCol 75; WorAl; WorAlBi*

Law, Bernard Francis, Cardinal
American. Religious Leader
Archbishop of Boston, 1984—; became cardinal, 1985.
b. Nov 4, 1931 in Torreon, Mexico
Source: *BioIn 13, 14; IntWW 91; NewYTBS 84, 85; RelLAm 91; WhoAm 76, 78, 82, 84, 86, 88, 90, 95, 96, 97; WhoE 86, 89, 91, 93, 95; WhoMW 80, 82, 84; WhoRel 85, 92; WhoWor 87, 89, 91, 95, 96, 97*

Law, John Phillip
American. Actor
Films include *The Russians Are Coming, the Russians Are Coming; Barbella.*
b. Sep 7, 1937 in Hollywood, California
Source: *CelR; ConTFT 7; FilmEn; FilmgC; ForYSC; HalFC 80, 84, 88; IntMPA 86, 92, 94, 96; ItaFilm; LegTOT; MotPP; WhoAm 82, 84; WhoEnt 92; WhoHol 92, A*

Law, Vern(on Sanders)
"Deacon"
American. Baseball Player
Pitcher, Pittsburgh, 1950-67; won NL Cy Young Award, 1960.
b. Mar 12, 1930 in Meridian, Idaho
Source: *Ballpl 90; BioIn 5, 6, 21; CurBio 61; WhoProB 73*

Law, William
English. Author
Best known for treatises of practical morality: *Serious Call to a Devout and Holy Life,* 1729; influenced by Jakob Boehme.
b. 1686 in King's Cliffe, England
d. 1761 in King's Cliffe, England
Source: *Alli; BioIn 1, 2, 3, 4, 5, 6, 10, 18; BlkwCE; BritAu; CamGEL; CamGLE; CasWL; Chambr 2; CyEd; DcBiPP; DcEnA; DcEnL; DcEuL; DcNaB; EncO&P 1, 2, 3; EncWM; EvLB; IlEncMy; LuthC 75; McGEWB; NewC; NewCBEL; OxCEng 67, 85, 95; REn; WebE&AL*

Lawe, John Edward
American. Labor Union Official
Pres., Transport Workers Union of America, 1985-89; VP, NY AFL-CIO, led 11-day strike of NY transit workers in 1980.
b. Feb 26, 1922 in Strokestown, Ireland
d. Jan 5, 1989 in New York, New York
Source: *BioIn 12, 13, 14, 16; CurBio 89N; NewYTBS 80, 82, 89*

Lawes, Lewis Edward
American. Criminologist
Sing Sing warden, 1919-41; wrote *Twenty Thousand Years in Sing Sing,* 1932.
b. Sep 13, 1883 in Elmira, New York
d. Apr 23, 1947 in Garrison, New York
Source: *AmAu&B; AmRef; BioIn 1, 15; CurBio 41, 47; DcAmB S4; DcNAA; WebAB 74, 79; WhAm 2; WhNAA; WhScrn 74, 77*

Lawford, Pat(ricia Kennedy)
American.
Sister of John F Kennedy; was married to Peter Lawford.
b. 1924 in Boston, Massachusetts
Source: *BioIn 17, 21; WomPO 78*

Lawford, Peter
English. Actor
Played Nick Charles in TV series "The Thin Man," 1957-59.
b. Sep 7, 1923 in London, England
d. Dec 24, 1984 in Los Angeles, California
Source: *AnObit 1984; BioIn 3, 5, 6, 10, 14, 16, 17; ConTFT 2; EncAFC; FilmAG WE; FilmEn; FilmgC; ForYSC; HalFC 80, 84, 88; IntMPA 75, 76, 77, 78, 79, 80, 81, 82, 84; ItaFilm; LegTOT; MGM; MotPP; MovMk; NewYTBS 84; OxCFilm; WhAm 8; WhoAm 74, 76, 78, 80, 82, 84; WhoHol A; WorAl; WorAlBi; WorEFlm*

Lawler, Richard Harold
American. Surgeon
Performed world's first successful kidney transplant, 1950.
b. Aug 12, 1895 in Chicago, Illinois
d. Jul 24, 1982 in Chicago, Illinois
Source: *AnObit 1982; BioIn 13*

Lawless, Theodore K(enneth)
American. Physician
Helped devise electropyrexia, a treatment for early syphilis, 1936.
b. Dec 6, 1892 in Thibodeaux, Louisiana
d. 1971
Source: *BioIn 3, 6, 8, 9, 10, 11; DcAmMeB 84; InB&W 80; NegAl 76, 83*

Lawrence, Abbott
American. Retailer, Manufacturer, Philanthropist
Manufacturing pioneer of the New England textile industry; Lawrence, MA named in his honor.
b. Dec 16, 1792 in Groton, Massachusetts
d. Aug 18, 1855 in Boston, Massachusetts
Source: *AmBi; ApCAB; BiAUS; BiDAmBL 83; BiDrAC; BiDrUSC 89; BioIn 3, 7, 16; DcAmB; DcAmDH 80, 89; DcBiPP; Drake; HarEnUS; LinLib L, S; McGEWB; NatCAB 3; TwCBDA; WebAB 74, 79; WhAm HS; WorAl; WorAlBi*

Lawrence, Andrea Mead
American. Skier
Won gold medals, women's slalom, giant slalom, 1952 Olympics.
b. 1932
Source: *BiDAmSp OS; BioIn 2, 3, 9, 11, 12, 15, 17; EncWomS; InWom SUP; WhoAm 90; WhoWest 89, 92; WomFir*

Lawrence, Bill
American. Producer, Director
Witty news correspondent, ABC national affairs advisor, 1960s.
d. 1972
Source: *BioIn 2; LesBEnT, 92; NewYTET*

Lawrence, Carol
[Carol Maria Laraia]
American. Singer, Actor
Played Maria in Broadway's *West Side Story,* 1957-60.
b. Sep 5, 1935 in Melrose Park, Illinois
Source: *BiE&WWA; BioIn 16; BioNews 74; ConTFT 4; CurBio 61; EncMT; ForYSC; InWom SUP; MotPP; PseudN 82; VarWW 85; WhoAm 74; WhoEnt 92; WhoHol A; WhoThe 77, 81*

Lawrence, D(avid) H(erbert)
English. Author
Wrote *Lady Chatterley's Lover,* 1928; banned in US, England many years.
b. Sep 11, 1885 in Eastwood, England
d. Mar 2, 1930 in Vence, France
Source: *ArtsAmW 3; AtlBL; Benet 96; BioIn 1, 2, 3, 4, 5, 6, 7, 8, 9, 10, 11, 12, 13, 14, 15, 16, 17, 18, 19, 20; CasWL; Chambr 3; ChhPo, S1, S3; CnE&AP; CnMD; CnMWL; CnThe; CyWA 58; DcArts; DcLEL; DcNaB 1922; Dis&D; EncWL, 3; EncWT; EvLB; FilmgC; GrBr; IntDcT 2; LinLib S; LngCEL; LngCTC; MakMC; McGEWB; ModBrL, S1; ModWD; NewC; NewCBEL; NotNAT B; OxCAmL 65, 95; OxCEng 67, 95; OxCTwCP; PenC ENG; RAdv 14; REn; REnAL; RfGShF; TwCA, SUP; TwCPaSc; WebE&AL; WhLit; WhoTwCL*

Lawrence, David
American. Journalist
Founder, editor, weekly *US News and World Report,* 1947.
b. Dec 25, 1888 in Philadelphia, Pennsylvania
d. Feb 11, 1973 in Sarasota, Florida
Source: *AmAu&B; BiDAmJo; BiDAmNC; BioIn 2, 3, 6, 9, 10, 11, 16; ConAu 41R, 102; CurBio 43, 73, 73N; DcAmB S9; DcLB 29; EncAJ; EncTwCJ; JrnUS; LinLib L, S; NatCAB 57; REnAL; WhAm 5; WhJnl; WhoSSW 73; WorAlBi*

Lawrence, Elliot
[Elliot Lawrence Broza]
American. Composer, Conductor
Musical director of Broadway musicals including *Bye Bye Birdie,* 1960.
b. Feb 14, 1925 in Philadelphia, Pennsylvania
Source: *AllMusG; ASCAP 66, 80; BiE&WWA; CmpEPM; NewGrDJ 88; NotNAT; OxCPMus; PseudN 82*

Lawrence, Ernest Orlando
American. Educator, Physicist
Won Nobel Prize, 1939, for invention, development of cyclotron.
b. Aug 8, 1901 in Canton, South Dakota
d. Aug 27, 1958 in Palo Alto, California
Source: *AsBiEn; BiESc; BioIn 1, 2, 3, 4, 5, 7, 8, 9, 14, 15, 16, 17, 20; CamDcSc; CurBio 40, 52, 58; DcAmB S6; DcScB; EncAB-A 32; EncAB-H 1974, 1996; FacFETw; InSci; LarDcSc; LinLib S; McGEWB; McGMS 80; MorMA; NatCAB 48; NewCol 75; NotTwCS; ObitOF 79; OxCAmH; WebAB 74, 79; WebBD 83; WhAm 3; WhDW; WhoNob, 90, 95; WorAl; WorInv*

Lawrence, Florence
"The Biograph Girl"; "The Imp Girl"
American. Actor
First film star, 1908-24, to be known by name, previously, silent stars had been anonymous.
b. Jan 2, 1886 in Hamilton, Ontario, Canada
d. Dec 27, 1938 in Beverly Hills, California
Source: *EncAFC; Film 1, 2; FilmEn; FilmgC; HalFC 80, 84, 88; IntDcF 1-3, 2-3; InWom SUP; LegTOT; LibW; MotPP; NotAW; SilFlmP*

Lawrence, Frieda
[Frieda von Richthofen]
German.
Wife of D H Lawrence, 1912-30; wrote memoir *Not I, But the Wind,* 1934; Baron Richthofen's sister.
b. Aug 11, 1879 in Melz, Germany
d. Aug 11, 1956 in Taos, New Mexico
Source: *BioIn 2, 3, 4, 5, 6, 8, 10, 12, 13, 16, 20; ContDcW 89; EncBrWW; IntDcWB; InWom SUP; LngCTC; ObitT 1951; REn*

Lawrence, Gertrude
[Gertrud Alexandra Dagmar Lawrence Klasen]
English. Actor
Associated with various Noel Coward plays in roles as stylish comedienne.
b. Jul 4, 1900 in London, England
d. Sep 6, 1952 in New York, New York
Source: *CurBio 40, 52; DcAmB S5; EncMT; FamA&A; Film 2; FilmgC; NewC; ObitOF 79; ObitT 1951; OxCFilm; OxCThe 67; PseudN 82; ThFT; WhAm 3; WhScrn 77; WorEFlm*

Lawrence, Jack
American. Composer, Lyricist, Producer
Wrote lyrics, music for "If I Didn't Care," 1939; "All or Nothing at All," 1940.
b. Apr 7, 1912 in New York, New York
Source: *ASCAP 66, 80; BiE&WWA; CmpEPM; DcLP 87B; OxCPMus; WhoE 86*

Lawrence, Jacob Armstead
American. Artist
Noted for gouache or egg tempura series on War, Harlem life, John Brown; awarded Spingarn medal, 1970.
b. Sep 7, 1917 in Atlantic City, New Jersey
Source: *AfroAA; AmArt; BioIn 13, 15, 16; BlkAull; CurBio 65, 88; DcCAA 71, 88; FacFETw; IlsBYP; InB&W 85; NegAl 89; NewYTBS 86; PrintW 85; RComAH; WhAmArt 85; WhoAm 86, 90; WhoAmA 86, 91; WhoBlA 85, 88; WhoWest 92; WhoWor 87*

Lawrence, James
American. Naval Officer
Wounded while attacking British frigate; known for crying, "Don't give up the ship," 1813.
b. Oct 1, 1781 in Burlington, New Jersey
d. Jun 1, 1813
Source: *AmBi; ApCAB; BioIn 2, 3, 7, 8, 9; DcAmB; DcAmMiB; Drake; HarEnMi; HarEnUS; LinLib S; McGEWB; NatCAB 8; OxCAmH; OxCShps; REn; TwCBDA; WebAB 74, 79; WebAMB; WhAm HS; WorAl; WorAlBi*

Lawrence, Jerome
[Jerome Lawrence Schwartz]
American. Dramatist, Author
Wrote prize-winning plays *Inherit the Wind,* 1955; *Auntie Mame,* 1956.
b. Jul 14, 1915 in Cleveland, Ohio
Source: *AmAu&B; ASCAP 66, 80; BiE&WWA; BioIn 10, 17; BlueB 76; CamGWoT; ConAmD; ConAu 41R, 44NR; ConDr 73, 77, 82, 88, 93; ConTFT 5; EncMT; IntAu&W 76, 77, 91, 93; LinLib L; ModWD; NotNAT; OhA&B; OxCAmT 84; PseudN 82; SmATA 65; WhoAm 74, 76, 78, 80, 82, 84, 86, 88, 90, 92, 94, 95, 96, 97; WhoAmJ 80; WhoEnt 92; WhoThe 72, 77, 81; WhoWest 84, 87, 89, 92, 94, 96; WhoWor 74; WhoWorJ 72, 78; WrDr 76, 80, 82, 84, 86, 88, 90, 92, 94, 96*

Lawrence, Joey
American. Actor
Played Joey in TV series "Blossom."
Source: *BioIn 18, 19, 20, 21*

Lawrence, Josephine
American. Author
Wrote popular fiction including *Under One Roof,* 1975.
b. 1897 in Newark, New Jersey
d. Feb 22, 1978 in New York, New York
Source: *AmAu&B; AmNov; AmWomWr; BioIn 1, 2, 4, 11, 12, 13; ConAu 77; OxCAmL 65; REn; REnAL; TwCA, SUP; WhNAA; WhoAm 74; WhoE 74*

Lawrence, Lawrence Shubert, Jr.
American. Business Executive
President, CEO of Shubert Theatres, 1962-72.
b. Fèb 18, 1916 in Philadelphia, Pennsylvania

d. Jul 18, 1992 in Boca Raton, Florida
Source: *BiE&WWA; BioIn 18; ConTFT 4; NotNAT*

Lawrence, Margaret
American. Actor
Starred in *Overnight,* 1911; *Tea for Three,* 1918.
b. Aug 2, 1889 in Trenton, New Jersey
d. Jun 9, 1929 in Little Rock, Arkansas
Source: *NotNAT B; WhAm 1; WhThe*

Lawrence, Marjorie Florence
Australian. Opera Singer
NY Met. soprano, 1935-41; noted Wagner interpreter.
b. Feb 17, 1909 in Deans Marsh, Australia
d. Jan 13, 1979 in Little Rock, Arkansas
Source: *Baker 84; BioNews 74; CurBio 40; MusSN; NewGrDM 80; Who 74; WhoMus 72*

Lawrence, Martin
American. Actor
Star of TV's "Martin," 1992—; banned from all NBC productions for 1994 incident on "Saturday Night Live."
b. Apr 16, 1965 in Frankfurt, Germany
Source: *ConBlB 6; DcTwCCu 5; IntMPA 96; WhoAfA 96*

Lawrence, Mary Wells
American. Advertising Executive
One of first successful female advertising executives; CEO, Wells, Rich, Green, Inc., 1966-90.
b. May 25, 1928 in Youngstown, Ohio
Source: *AmWomM; BioIn 7, 8, 10, 11, 14, 16; CelR; ContDcW 89; CurBio 67; WhoAdv 72, 80; WhoAm 84, 86; WhoAmW 85; WhoFI 83, 85; WomFir; WorAlBi*

Lawrence, Mildred Elwood
American. Author
Books for young girls include *Gateway to the Sun,* 1970; *Walk to a Rocky Road,* 1971.
b. Nov 10, 1907 in Charleston, Illinois
Source: *AuBYP 2, 3; ConAu 1R, 5NR; CurBio 53; ForWC 70; MorJA; SmATA 3*

Lawrence, Robert
American. Conductor, Critic
Radio music commentator; wrote opera adaptations and *World of Opera,* 1955.
b. Mar 18, 1912 in New York, New York
d. Aug 9, 1981
Source: *BioIn 6, 9, 12; ConAu 105; IntWWM 77, 80; NewAmDM; NewEOp 71; NewGrDA 86; WhAm 9; WhoAm 74, 76, 78, 80; WhoE 74*

Lawrence, Steve
[Sidney Liebowitz]
American. Actor, Singer
Won nine Emmys for specials with wife Eydie Gorme; the couple won a Grammy for song "We Got Us," 1960.
b. Jul 8, 1935 in New York, New York
Source: *ASCAP 66, 80; Baker 84, 92; BiDAmM; BiE&WWA; BioIn 4, 5, 6, 7, 10, 12, 18; BioNews 74; BkPepl; CelR, 90; ConTFT 11; CurBio 64; EncMT; HalFC 84; IntMPA 82, 84, 86, 88, 92, 94, 96; LegTOT; NotNAT; OxCPMus; PenEncP; PseudN 82; RkOn 74; WhoAm 74, 84, 86, 88, 90, 92, 94, 95, 96, 97; WhoEnt 92; WhoHol 92, A; WorAl; WorAlBi*

Lawrence, T(homas) E(dward)
[Thomas Edward Shaw]
"Lawrence of Arabia"
English. Author, Soldier
Spied against Turks in Arabia during WW I; wrote *The Seven Pillars of Wisdom,* 1926.
b. Aug 15, 1888 in Portmadoc, Wales
d. May 19, 1935 in Bovington Camp Hospital, England
Source: *Benet 96; BioIn 1, 2, 3, 4, 5, 6, 7, 8, 9, 10, 11, 12, 13, 14, 15, 16, 17, 18, 19, 20; CasWL; Chambr 3; DcArts; DcLEL; DcMidEa; DcNaB 1931; DcTwHis; EncPaPR 91; EncWL; EvLB; FacFETw; GayLL; GenMudB; GrBr; HarEnMi; HisDBrE; LegTOT; LinLib S; LngCEL; LngCTC; LuthC 75; MakMC; McGEWB; ModBrL; NewC; NewCBEL; NewCol 75; OxCEng 67, 85, 95; PenC ENG; PseudN 82; RAdv 14; REn; SpyCS; TwCA, SUP; TwCWr; WebE&AL; WhDW; WhoMilH 76; WhWE; WorAl*

Lawrence, Thomas, Sir
"The Wonderful Boy of Devizes"
English. Artist
Romantic portraits of English society; succeeded Reynolds as court painter, 1792.
b. May 4, 1769 in Bristol, England
d. Jan 7, 1830 in London, England
Source: *Alli; Benet 87, 96; BioIn 1, 2, 3, 4, 5, 6, 8, 9, 10, 11, 12, 13, 15, 20; BkIE; CelCen; ChhPo, S1; ClaDrA; DcArts; DcBiPP; DcBrECP; DcNaB; IntDcAA 90; LegTOT; LinLib S; McGDA; McGEWB; NewC; NewCol 75; OxCArt; OxCEng 85, 95; OxDcArt; PseudN 82; REn; TwCA SUP*

Lawrence, Vicki Ann
American. Actor
Best known for role of Mama on "The Carol Burnett Show," 1967-78; later had own series "Mama's Family," 1983-90; "Vicki!" 1992—; Emmy award winner, 1976.
b. Mar 26, 1949 in Inglewood, California
Source: *BioIn 13; IntMPA 86, 88; InWom SUP; RkOn 74; WhoAm 76, 78, 80, 82, 84, 86, 88, 90; WorAlBi*

Lawrence, William Beach
"An American Citizen"
American. Lawyer
Expert on int'l law; wrote four-volume commentary, 1880.
b. Oct 23, 1800 in New York, New York
d. Mar 26, 1881 in New York, New York
Source: *Alli, SUP; AmAu; AmBi; ApCAB; BiAUS; BioIn 5; DcAmAu; DcAmB; DcNAA; Drake; HarEnUS; NewCol 75; PseudAu; PseudN 82; TwCBDA; WhAm HS*

Lawrence-Lightfoot, Sara
American. Educator
Harvard sociology professor; wrote *I've Known Rivers,* about the black middle class.
b. Aug 22, 1944
Source: *ConBlB 10*

Lawrenson, Helen Brown
[Helen Brown Norder]
American. Editor, Author
First woman to contribute to *Esquire* 1936, with article "Latins are Lousy Lovers."
b. Oct 1, 1907 in La Fargeville, New York
d. Apr 5, 1982 in New York, New York
Source: *AnObit 1982; ConAu 106, 117; NewYTBS 82; WhoAmW 68, 70*

Lawrie, Lee
American. Artist
Architectural sculptor known for bronze Atlas in Rockefeller Center, NYC.
b. Oct 16, 1877 in Rixdorf, Germany
d. Jan 23, 1961 in Easton, Maryland
Source: *BioIn 4, 6, 8; BriEAA; DcAmArt; NatCAB 50; NewCol 75; ObitOF 79; WhAm 4; WhAmArt 85; WhoAmA 80, 82, 89N, 91N, 93N*

Lawson, Donald Elmer
American. Children's Author, Editor
Historical surveys for young people include *United States in the Korean War,* 1964.
b. May 20, 1917 in Chicago, Illinois
Source: *AuBYP 2, 3; BioIn 16; ConAu 1R, 2NR, 130; LEduc 74; SixBJA; SmATA 9; WhAm 10; WhoAm 74, 76, 78, 80, 82, 84, 86, 88; WhoMW 74, 76, 78, 80, 82, 84*

Lawson, Jennifer Karen
American. Broadcasting Executive
Exec. vp, programming, PBS, 1989-95; exec. cons., Md. Public TV, 1996—.
b. Jun 8, 1946 in Birmingham, Alabama
Source: *BioIn 7; ConBlB 1; WhoAfA 96; WhoBlA 92, 94; WhoEnt 92*

Lawson, John Howard
[The Hollywood Ten]
American. Dramatist
Co-founder, first pres., Screen Writers Guild, 1933; films include *Marching Song,* 1939.
b. Sep 25, 1895 in New York, New York
d. Aug 12, 1977 in San Francisco, California
Source: *AmAu&B; BenetAL 91; BioIn 4, 10, 11; CamGWoT; CnMD; CnThe;*

ConAmA; ConAmL; ConAu 73; EncWT; McGEWD 84; ModAL; ModWD; NotNAT; OxCAmL 65, 83, 95; OxCFilm; PenC AM; REn; REnAL; TwCA, SUP; WebE&AL; WhE&EA; WhThe; WorEFlm; WrDr 76

Lawson, Leigh
English. Actor
Films include *Tess,* 1981; TV show "Lace," 1984.
b. Jul 21, 1945 in Atherton, England
Source: *ConTFT 9; HalFC 88; JohnWSW*

Lawson, Nigel
English. Politician
British Chancellor of the Exchequer, 1983-89.
b. Mar 11, 1932 in London, England
Source: *BioIn 13, 14, 15; CurBio 87; IntWW 83, 89, 91; IntYB 82; NewYTBS 83, 86; Who 74, 82, 83, 85, 88, 90, 92; WhoWor 74, 76, 84, 87, 89, 91; WorAlBi*

Lawson, Robert
American. Illustrator, Author
Won Newbery Medal, 1945, for *Rabbit Hill.*
b. Oct 4, 1892 in New York, New York
d. May 26, 1957 in Weston, Connecticut
Source: *AmAu&B; AnCL; Au&ICB; AuBYP 2, 3; BioIn 1, 2, 3, 4, 5, 7, 8, 10, 12, 14, 19; BkCL; Cald 1938; ChhPo, S2, S3; ChlBkCr; ChlLR 2; ConAu 118, 137; DcLB 22; FamAIYP; IlBEAAW; IlsBYP; IlsCB 1744, 1946; JBA 51; LinLib L; MajAI; NewbMB 1922; OxCChiL; ScF&FL 1; Str&VC; TwCChW 78, 83, 89, 95; WhAm 3; WhAmArt 85; WhoAmA 80N, 82N, 84N, 86N, 89N, 91N, 93N; WrChl; YABC 2*

Lawson, Victor Fremont
American. Editor, Publisher
Owner, *Chicago Daily News; Chicago Record-Herald;* pres., Associated Press, 1894-1900; developed foreign news service.
b. Sep 9, 1850 in Chicago, Illinois
d. Aug 19, 1925 in Chicago, Illinois
Source: *AmAu&B; AmBi; ApCAB X; BiDAmJo; BioIn 1, 2, 8; DcAmB; NatCAB 13, 26; WebBD 83; WhAm 1*

Lawson, Yank
[John R Lausen; John R Lawson]
American. Jazz Musician
Trumpeter who was a founder of Bob Crosby band, 1935; co-led World's Greatest Jazz Band.
b. May 3, 1911 in Trenton, Missouri
d. Feb 18, 1995 in Indianapolis, Indiana
Source: *AllMusG; BiDAmM; BiDJaz; BioIn 20; CmpEPM; EncJzS; IlEncJ; NewGrDJ 88, 94; PseudN 82; WhoJazz 72*

Lawton, Henry Ware
American. Military Leader
Indian fighter who captured Geronimo, 1886.
b. Mar 17, 1843 in New York, Ohio
d. Dec 19, 1899 in San Mateo, Philippines
Source: *AmBi; ApCAB SUP; BioIn 5, 13; DcAmB; DcAmMiB; HarEnMi; HarEnUS; MedHR 94; NatCAB 10; TwCBDA; WebAMB; WhAm 1; WhNaAH*

Laxalt, Paul
American. Lawyer, Politician
Rep. senator from NV, 1974-86.
b. Aug 2, 1922 in Reno, Nevada
Source: *AlmAP 78, 80, 82, 84; AmCath 80; BiDrGov 1789; BiDrUSC 89; BioIn 10, 11, 12, 13, 14, 15; BlueB 76; CngDr 77, 79, 81, 83, 85; CurBio 79; IntWW 74, 75, 76, 77, 78, 79, 80, 81, 82, 83, 89, 91; NewYTBS 82; PolsAm 84; WhoAm 74, 76, 78, 80, 82, 84, 86, 88, 90; WhoAmL 90; WhoAmP 73, 75, 77, 79, 81, 83, 85, 87, 89, 91, 93, 95; WhoGov 75, 77; WhoWest 76, 78, 80, 82, 84, 87, 89; WhoWor 80, 82, 84, 87, 89, 91, 93, 95, 96; WorAl; WorAlBi*

Laxness, Halldor Kiljan
[Halldor Kiljan Gudjonsson]
Icelandic. Author, Dramatist
Leading modern Icelandic writer; won 1955 Noble Prize for Icelandic narratives.
b. Apr 23, 1902 in Reykjavik, Iceland
Source: *Benet 87, 96; BioIn 15; ConAu 103; ConFLW 84; CurBio 46; CyWA 58; DcScanL; EncWL 2; EvEuW; FacFETw; IntAu&W 91; IntWW 83, 91; MakMC; NewYTBE 71; Novels; OxCThe 83; PenC EUR; PseudN 82; RAdv 13-2; REn; TwCA SUP; TwCWr; Who 85, 92; WhoNob, 90, 95; WhoWor 91, 96, 97; WorAlBi*

Lay, Herman Warden
American. Business Executive
Founder, pres., Frito-Lay, Inc., 1939-65; chm., Pepsi Co. Inc., 1965-71.
b. Jun 3, 1909 in Charlotte, North Carolina
d. Dec 6, 1982 in Dallas, Texas
Source: *BioIn 8, 9, 13; IntWW 74, 75, 76, 77, 78, 79, 80, 81, 82, 83; NewYTBS 82; St&PR 84; WhAm 8; WhoAm 74, 76, 78, 80, 82; WhoFI 74; WhoWor 76, 78*

Lay, James Selden, Jr.
American. Government Official
Consultant to president's foreign intelligence advisory board, 1971-77; exec. secretary, National Security Council, 1950-61.
b. Aug 24, 1911 in Washington, District of Columbia
d. Jun 28, 1987 in Perry Point, Maryland
Source: *BioIn 2; CurBio 50, 87; WhAm 9; WhoAm 74, 76; WhoSSW 75*

Layamon
[Lawemon; Lawman]
English. Poet
Considered to be the first important writer in Middle English; wrote poems *Brut* and *Arthur.*
b. fl. 1200
Source: *BioIn 21; ClMLC 10; GrWrEL P; NewCBEL*

Layard, Austen Henry, Sir
English. Archaeologist
Excavations in Mesopotamia, 1842-51, uncovered remains of Nineveh, other ancient cities.
b. Mar 5, 1817 in Paris, France
d. Jul 5, 1894 in London, England
Source: *Alli, SUP; BbD; BiD&SB; BioIn 5, 6, 7, 8, 9, 12, 14, 20, 21; BritAu 19; CamGLE; CelCen; Chambr 3; DcEnL; DcLB 166; DcNaB S1; InSci; LinLib S; NewC; NewCBEL; OxCEng 67; WhDW*

Laybourne, Geraldine
American. TV Executive
President, Disney/ABC Cable Networks, 1995—.
b. 1947 in Plainfield, New Jersey
Source: *News 97-1; WhoAm 95, 96, 97; WhoAmW 95, 97*

Layden, Elmer Francis
[Four Horsemen of Notre Dame]
American. Football Player, Football Executive
All-American fullback, Notre Dame, 1922-24; commissioner of NFL, 1941-46, succeeded by Bert Bell.
b. May 4, 1903 in Davenport, Iowa
d. Jun 30, 1973 in Chicago, Illinois
Source: *NewYTBE 73; WhAm 6; WhoFtbl 74; WhScrn 83*

Layden, Frank
[Francis Patrick Layden]
American. Basketball Coach, Basketball Executive
GM, Utah Jazz, 1979-88; coach, 1981-88; exec., coach of yr., 1984; pres. Utah Jazz, 1989—.
b. Jan 5, 1932 in New York, New York
Source: *BasBi; BioIn 13, 14, 16; OfNBA 87; WhoAm 84, 86, 88, 90, 92, 94, 95, 96, 97; WhoWest 84, 87, 89, 92, 94, 96*

Laye, Camara
Senegalese. Author
Leading writer of French-speaking Africa: *Dark Child,* 1953.
b. Jan 1, 1928 in Kouroussa, French Guiana
d. Feb 4, 1980 in Dakar, Senegal
Source: *AfrA; AnObit 1980; Benet 87, 96; BioIn 3, 7, 8, 9, 10, 12, 13, 14, 15, 17, 21; BlkLC; BlkWr 1; CasWL; ConAu 25NR, 85, 97; ConLC 4, 38; CyWA 89; EncWL; LiExTwC; LngCTC; MajTwCW; McGEWB; Novels; PenC CL; RAdv 14, 13-2; RGAfL; SchCGBL; SelBAAf; WhoTwCL; WorAlBi; WorAu 1950*

Layne, Bobby
[Robert Lawrence Layne]
American. Football Player
Flamboyant quarterback, 1948-62; led Detroit to championships, 1952, 1953; Hall of Fame, 1967.
b. Dec 19, 1926 in Santa Anna, Texas
d. Dec 1, 1986 in Lubbock, Texas

Source: *BiDAmSp FB; BioIn 3, 7, 8, 9, 10; LegTOT; WhoFtbl 74; WhoSpor*

Layton, Joe
[Joseph Lichtman]
American. Choreographer
Won Tonys for *No Strings,* 1962; *George M!,* 1969; Emmy for "My Name Is Barbra," 1965.
b. May 3, 1931 in New York, New York
d. May 5, 1994 in Key West, Florida
Source: *BiDD; BiE&WWA; BioIn 5, 9, 19, 20; CelR, 90; CnOxB; ConTFT 5, 13; CurBio 70, 94N; DancEn 78; EncMT; MiSFD 9; NotNAT; OxCAmT 84; VarWW 85; WhAm 11; WhoAm 74, 76, 78, 80, 82, 84, 86, 88, 90, 92, 94; WhoThe 72, 77, 81; WhoWorJ 72*

Layton, Larry
[Lawrence John Layton]
American. Cultist
Member, Peoples Temple; accused of killing Congressman Leo Ryan, four others in Jonestown, Guyana, 1978.
b. Jan 1946
Source: *BioIn 11, 12; NewYTBS 78*

Lazar, Irving Paul
[Irving Paul Lazar; Samuel Paul Lazar]
"Swifty"
American. Agent
Talent and literary agent who represented theater directors, writers, since 1933; known for fabulous Oscar night gala.
b. Mar 28, 1907 in Stamford, Connecticut
d. Dec 30, 1993 in Beverly Hills, California
Source: *BiE&WWA; BioIn 13, 15; CelR 90; NewYTBS 80; WhAm 11; WhoAm 76, 78, 80, 82, 84, 86, 90, 92; WhoEnt 92; WhoWest 82*

Lazare, Kaplan
American. Merchant
One of world's best known diamond merchants; cut 726-carat Jonker diamond, 1936.
b. Jul 17, 1883 in Zabludora, Russia
d. Feb 12, 1986 in Lew Beach, New York
Source: *NewYTBS 86*

Lazarus
Biblical Figure
In New Testament, Jesus Christ raised him from the dead.
d. 30?
Source: *Benet 96; BioIn 1, 2, 3, 4, 5, 6, 7; DcCathB; McGDA; NewCol 75*

Lazarus, Charles P
American. Businessman
Chm., CEO, Toys "R" Us, 1976—.
b. 1923?
Source: *BioIn 11; ConAmBL; Dun&B 90; News 92; WhoAm 90; WhoE 91; WhoFI 87*

Lazarus, Emma
American. Poet
Wrote poem, "The New Colossus" that appears on Statue of Liberty.
b. Jul 22, 1849 in New York, New York
d. Nov 19, 1887 in New York, New York
Source: *Alli SUP; AmAu; AmAu&B; AmBi; AmWom; AmWomWr; ApCAB; ArtclWW 2; BbD; Benet 87, 96; BenetAL 91; BibAL; BiDAmM; BiD&SB; BioAmW; BioIn 1, 2, 4, 5, 6, 7, 8, 11, 12, 13, 14, 15, 16, 17, 20, 21; Chambr 3; ChhPo, S1; CnDAL; DcAmAu; DcAmB; DcAmImH; DcAmSR; DcArts; DcLEL; DcNAA; EncWHA; EvLB; FemiCLE; GoodHs; GrLiveH; HanAmWH; InWom, SUP; JeAmHC; JeAmWW; LegTOT; LibW; LinLib L; McGEWB; MouLC 4; NatCAB 3; NinCLC 8; NotAW; OxCAmL 65, 83, 95; RAdv 14; REn; REnAL; TwCBDA; WebAB 74, 79; WhAm HS; WorAl; WorAlBi*

Lazarus, Mell
American. Cartoonist
Draws, writes comics "Miss Peach," 1957—, "Momma," 1970—.
b. May 3, 1927 in New York, New York
Source: *BioIn 13, 20; ConAu 11NR, 17R; ConGrA 3; EncACom; LegTOT; WhoAm 86, 90, 95, 96, 97; WorECom*

Lazarus, Shelly
American. Advertising Executive
CEO, Ogilvy & Mather Worldwide, 1996—; joined company, 1971.
b. Sep 1, 1947 in New York, New York

Lazear, Jesse William
American. Physician
Studied Yellow Fever disease in Cuba; died from mosquito bite.
b. May 2, 1866 in Baltimore, Maryland
d. Sep 25, 1900 in Quemados, Cuba
Source: *AsBiEn; BiInAmS; DcAmB; DcAmMeB, 84; InSci; NatCAB 1, 15; WhAm HS*

Lazzari, Virgilio
American. Opera Singer
Bass; repertoire of over 50 operas, 1918-40.
b. Apr 20, 1887 in Assisi, Italy
d. Oct 4, 1953 in Castel Gandolfo, Italy
Source: *Baker 84, 92; CmOp; MetOEnc; NewEOp 71; NewGrDA 86; NewGrDM 80; NewGrDO*

Lazzeri, Tony
[Anthony Michael Lazzeri]
"Poosh 'Em Up"
American. Baseball Player
Infielder, 1926-39; had .292 career batting average, 864 stolen bases.
b. Dec 26, 1903 in San Francisco, California
d. Aug 6, 1946 in San Francisco, California
Source: *Ballpl 90; BiDAmSp BB; BioIn 1, 5, 8, 14, 15; CmCal; CurBio 46; LegTOT; WhoProB 73; WhScrn 83*

Lea, Fanny Heaslip
American. Author, Dramatist
Wrote sentimental, women-oriented stories: *Half Angel,* 1932.
b. Oct 30, 1884 in New Orleans, Louisiana
d. Jan 13, 1955 in New York, New York
Source: *AmAu&B; AmWomPl; BioIn 3, 4, 5, 12; REnAL; TwCA, SUP; WhAm 3; WhNAA; WomNov*

Lea, Homer
American. Author, Soldier
Sun Yat-sen's adviser; books predicted Japanese attack on Hawaii: *Valor of Ignorance,* 1909.
b. Nov 17, 1876 in Denver, Colorado
d. Nov 1, 1912 in Los Angeles, California
Source: *AmAu&B; AmBi; BenetAL 91; BioIn 16, 19; CmCal; DcAmB; DcAmDH 80, 89; DcAmMiB; DcNAA; EncSF 93; GayN; NatCAB 2; OxCAmL 65, 83, 95; REnAL; ScF&FL 92; WebAB 74, 79; WebAMB; WhAm 1*

Lea, Tom
American. Author
Wrote, illustrated *The Brave Bulls,* 1949; *King Ranch,* 1957.
b. Jul 11, 1907 in El Paso, Texas
Source: *AmAu&B; BenetAL 91; BioIn 1, 2, 3, 4, 8, 12, 15, 16; ConAu 115; DcLB 6; EncFWF; IlBEAAW; IntAu&W 91, 93; OxCAmL 65, 83; REnAL; REnAW; TwCA SUP; TwCWW 82, 91; WhAmArt 85; WhoAm 74, 76, 78, 80, 82, 84, 86, 88, 90; WhoAmA 73, 76, 78, 80, 82, 84, 86, 89, 91, 93; WhoEnt 92; WhoSSW 73, 75, 76; WhoWor 74, 78; WrDr 84, 86, 88, 90, 92, 94, 96*

Leach, Penelope
English. Psychologist
Child-rearing specialist who wrote *Your Baby & Child,* 1977.
b. Nov 19, 1937 in London, England
Source: *BioIn 13; ConAu 21NR, 97; CurBio 94; IntAu&W 91, 93; News 92; WrDr 76, 80, 82, 84, 86, 88, 90, 92, 94, 96*

Leach, Reggie
[Reginald Joseph Leach]
"Rifle"
Canadian. Hockey Player
First NHL player to score 80 goals in single season, including playoffs, 1975-76.
b. Apr 23, 1950 in Riverton, Manitoba, Canada
Source: *BioIn 10, 12, 13; HocEn; WhoAm 78, 80, 82, 84; WhoHcky 73*

Leach, Robin
English. TV Personality
Hosts "Lifestyles of Rich and Famous," 1983—; one of most popular syndicated TV shows in Amercia; daily show "Preview," 1990—.
b. Aug 29, 1941 in London, England

Source: *BioIn 15, 16; ConNews 85-4; ConTFT 5; CurBio 90; LegTOT; WhoAm 94, 95, 96, 97; WhoAmP 91; WhoEnt 92*

Leach, Will
[Wilford Carson Leach]
American. Director
One-time director of NY Shakespeare Festival; won Tonys, 1981, 1986; Obies, 1972, 1981.
b. Aug 26, 1934 in Petersburg, Virginia
d. Jun 20, 1988 in Rocky Point, New York
Source: *BiE&WWA; ConAu 2NR, 45; NotNAT; WhoAm 84, 86*

Leachman, Cloris
American. Actor
Won Oscar, 1971, for *The Last Picture Show;* won Emmy, 1975, for "The Mary Tyler Moore Show."
b. Apr 30, 1925 in Des Moines, Iowa
Source: *BioIn 9, 10, 15, 16; BioNews 74; BkPepl; ConTFT 4; CurBio 75; EncAFC; FilmgC; HalFC 88; IntMPA 92; InWom SUP; LesBEnT 92; MovMk; NewYTBS 75; WhoAm 86, 90; WhoAmW 85, 91; WhoEnt 92; WorAlBi*

Leacock, Stephen Butler
Canadian. Author, Educator
Economic professor noted for popular humor books, literary biographies.
b. Dec 30, 1869 in Swanmore, England
d. Mar 28, 1944 in Toronto, Ontario, Canada
Source: *Benet 96; BioIn 1, 3, 4, 5, 8, 9, 11, 14, 15, 17, 19, 21; CamGEL; CanWr; CasWL; Chambr 3; ConAmL; ConAu 141; ConCaAu 1; CurBio 44; DcArts; DcLEL; DcNAA; DcNaB 1941; EncAHmr; EncSF 93; EvLB; GrWrEL N; LinLib L, S; LngCTC; MacDCB 78; NewC; OxCAmL 65; OxCCan; OxCEng 67, 85, 95; PenC ENG; RAdv 1; REn; REnAL; RfGShF; TwCA, SUP; TwCWr; WebE&AL; WhAm 2; WhE&EA; WhLit; WhNAA*

Leadbelly
[Huddie Ledbetter]
"King of the Twelve-String Guitar"
American. Singer, Songwriter
Influential folk artist; wrote classics "Good Night, Irene," "Rock Island Line," "Take This Hammer."
b. Jan 21, 1885 in Mooringsport, Louisiana
d. Dec 6, 1949 in New York, New York
Source: *Baker 78, 84, 92; BiDAmM; BiDJaz; BioIn 2, 4, 6, 11, 14, 16, 17, 18, 19, 20; ConMuA 80A; ConMus 6; DcAmB S4; DcAmNB; DrBlPA, 90; EncFCWM 69, 83; EncRk 88; InB&W 80; LegTOT; NewAmDM; NewGrDA 86; NewGrDM 80; ObitOF 79; PenEncP; WebAB 79; WhAm 4; WhoRocM 82*

Leadon, Bernie
[The Eagles]
American. Singer, Musician
Played guitar, mandolin, banjo for Eagles, 1971-76; formed own band, recorded album *Natural Progressions,* 1977.
b. Jul 19, 1947 in Minneapolis, Minnesota
Source: *OnThGG*

Leaf, Munro
[Mun; John Calvert; Wilbur Munro Leaf]
American. Author, Illustrator
Created children's classic *The Story of Ferdinand,* 1936.
b. Dec 4, 1905 in Hamilton, Maryland
d. Dec 21, 1976 in Garrett Park, Maryland
Source: *AmAu&B; AuBYP 2, 3; BenetAL 91; BioIn 2, 4, 7, 8, 11, 12, 19; BkP; ChhPo S2; ChlBkCr; ChlLR 25; ConAu 29NR, 69, 73; DcAmB S10; JBA 51; LinLib L; LngCTC; NewYTBS 76; OxCChiL; PseudN 82; REnAL; SmATA 20; TwCA, SUP; TwCChW 78, 83, 89; WhAm 7; WhAmArt 85; WhoAm 74, 76; WhoChL*

Leah
Biblical Figure
Laban's eldest daughter; sister of Rachel; Jacob's first wife.
Source: *Benet 96; BioIn 2, 4, 5, 11, 17; InWom, SUP; NewCol 75*

Leahy, Frank
American. Football Coach
Head coach, Notre Dame, 1941-54; led team to four undefeated seasons, 1946-49; Hall of Fame, 1970.
b. Aug 27, 1908 in O'Neill, Nebraska
d. Jun 21, 1973 in Portland, Oregon
Source: *BioIn 1, 2, 3, 4, 9, 10, 19; CurBio 41, 73, 73N; NewYTBE 73; WhAm 5; WhoFtbl 74; WhoSpor*

Leahy, Patrick Joseph
American. Politician
Dem. senator from VT, 1975—.
b. Mar 31, 1940 in Montpelier, Vermont
Source: *AlmAP 80, 92; BiDrUSC 89; CngDr 85, 87, 89; CurBio 90; DrAPF 91; IntWW 75, 76, 77, 78, 79, 80, 81, 82, 83, 89, 91, 93; PolsAm 84; WhoAm 78, 80, 82, 84, 86, 88, 90, 92, 94, 95, 96, 97; WhoAmP 91; WhoE 77, 79, 81, 83, 85, 86, 89, 91, 93, 95, 97; WhoEmL 87; WhoGov 75, 77; WhoWor 80, 82, 84, 87, 89, 91*

Leahy, William Daniel
American. Naval Officer
Chief of staff for Roosevelt, Truman during WW II.
b. May 6, 1875 in Hampton, Iowa
d. Jul 20, 1959 in Bethesda, Maryland
Source: *AmAu&B; BiDWWGF; BioIn 1, 3, 5, 7, 8, 11, 13; CurBio 41, 59; DcAmB S6; DcAmDH 80, 89; DcAmMiB; LinLib S; NatCAB 61, 62; OxCShps; WebAB 74, 79; WebAMB; WhAm 3; WhWW-II; WorAl*

Leakey, Louis Seymour Bazett
[White Kikuyu]
English. Anthropologist
Discovered fossils in Africa that proved man's evolution began there.
b. Aug 7, 1903 in Kabete, East Africa Protectorate
d. Oct 1, 1972 in London, England
Source: *Au&Wr 71; BiESc; BioIn 6, 7, 8, 9, 10, 11, 14, 17, 18, 19, 20, 21; ConAu 97; CurBio 66, 72; DcNaB 1971; DcScB; EncHuEv; GrBr; LarDcSc; LinLib S; McGEWB; NewYTBE 72; ObitT 1971; WhAm 5; WhE&EA; WorAl*

Leakey, Mary (Douglas)
[Mrs. Louis Leakey]
English. Anthropologist
Discovered 3.5 million-year-old fossilized footprints in Tanzania, 1978; wrote *Disclosing the Past,* 1984.
b. Feb 6, 1913 in London, England
d. Dec 9, 1996 in Nairobi, Kenya
Source: *AfSS 81, 82; BioIn 6, 10, 11, 12, 14, 15; CamDcSc; ConAu 18NR, 97; ContDcW 89; CurBio 85; EncHuEv; FacFETw; FifIDA; IntDcWB; IntWW 77, 78, 79, 80, 81, 82, 83, 89, 91, 93; InWom SUP; LarDcSc; LegTOT; NewYTBS 27, 80; NotTwCS; Who 74, 82, 83, 85, 88, 90, 92, 94; WhoAm 82, 84, 86, 88, 90, 92; WhoScEn 94, 96; WhoWor 78, 80, 82, 84, 87, 91, 93, 95; WomFir; WorAlBi; WrDr 86, 88, 90, 92, 94, 96*

Leakey, Richard E(rskine Frere)
Kenyan. Paleontologist
Proved that three forms of humans co-existed; two became extinct, the other evolved into Homo Sapiens.
b. Dec 19, 1944 in Nairobi, British East Africa
Source: *BioIn 13, 14, 15, 16; ConAu 18NR, 93; CurBio 95; FacFETw; IntWW 83, 91; NewYTBS 90; SmATA 42; Who 85, 92; WhoAm 86, 88; WhoWor 87, 91; WorAlBi; WrDr 92*

Lean, David, Sir
English. Director
Won Oscars for *Bridge on the River Kwai,* 1957, *Lawrence of Arabia,* 1962, *Dr. Zhivago,* 1965.
b. Mar 25, 1908 in Croydon, England
d. Apr 16, 1991 in London, England
Source: *AnObit 1991; BiDFilm, 81, 94; BioIn 3, 7, 8, 10, 12, 14, 15, 16; BlueB 76; CelR, 90; ConAu 111, 134; ConTFT 6, 10; CurBio 53, 89, 91N; DcArts; DcFM; EncEurC; FacFETw; FilmEn; FilmgC; HalFC 80, 84, 88; IlWWBF, A; IntDcF 1-2, 2-2; IntMPA 75, 76, 77, 78, 79, 80, 81, 82, 84, 86, 88; IntWW 74, 75, 76, 77, 78, 79, 80, 81, 82, 83, 89, 91, 91N; LegTOT; MiSFD 9N; MovMk; NewYTBS 91; OxCFilm; WhAm 10; Who 74, 82, 83, 85, 88, 90, 92N; WhoAm 86, 88, 90; WhoWor 74, 82, 84, 87; WorAl; WorAlBi; WorEFlm; WorFDir 1*

Lear, Edward
English. Poet
Limerick writer, known for *Owl and the Pussycat,* 1871; nonsense books, 1846-72.
b. May 12, 1812 in Highgate, England
d. Jan 29, 1888 in San Remo, Italy
Source: *AnCL; AntBDN B; AtlBL; AuBYP 2, 3; Benet 87, 96; BiD&SB; BioIn 1, 2, 3, 4, 5, 6, 7, 8, 9, 10, 11, 12, 13, 14, 16, 17, 19, 20, 21; BlmGEL; BritAu 19; BritWr 5; CamGEL; CamGLE; CarSB; CasWL; Chambr 3; ChhPo, S1, S2, S3; ChlBkCr; ChlLR 1; ChrP; ClaDrA; CnE&AP; CrtT 3; DcArts; DcBrBI; DcBrWA; DcEnL; DcEuL; DcLB 32, 163, 166; DcLEL; DcNaB, C; DcVicP, 2; Dis&D; EvLB; FamAIYP; GrBIl; GrWrEL P; JBA 34; LegTOT; LinLib L; LngCEL; MajAI; McGEWB; MouLC 4; NewC; NewCBEL; NinCLC 3; OxCArt; OxCChiL; OxCEng 67, 85, 95; OxDcArt; PenC ENG; RAdv 14; REn; RfGEnL 91; SmATA 18; Str&VC; TwCChW 78A, 83A, 89A, 95A; VicBrit; WebE&AL; WhDW; WhoChL; WorECar; WrChl*

Lear, Evelyn
American. Opera Singer
Soprano with Metropolitan Opera since 1967; sang title role in Berg's *Lulu,* 1960s; won Grammy, 1965.
b. Jan 18, 1931 in New York, New York
Source: *Baker 84; BioIn 7, 8, 9, 10, 11; CurBio 73; IntWW 91; IntWWM 90; InWom SUP; MetOEnc; NewAmDM; NewGrDA 86; NewYTBE 72; PenDiMP; WhoAm 84, 90; WhoAmW 85; WhoMus 72*

Lear, Frances
American. Editor, Feminist
Founded, edited *Lear's,* 1988-94, a magazine for women over 40; ex-wife of Norman Lear.
b. Jul 14, 1923 in Hudson, New York
d. Sep 30, 1996 in New York, New York
Source: *BioIn 15, 16; CurBio 91; LegTOT; News 88, 88-3; NewYTBS 27; WhoAm 90; WhoAmW 91; WhoFI 92*

Lear, Norman Milton
American. Producer
TV comedy empire reshaped the sitcom; created "All in the Family"; "The Jeffersons"; "Maude."
b. Jul 27, 1922 in New Haven, Connecticut
Source: *BioIn 13, 14, 15; BioNews 74; CelR 90; ConAu 73; ConTFT 8; CurBio 74; Dun&B 88; EncAFC; FacFETw; FilmgC; HalFC 84, 88; IntMPA 86, 92; LesBEnT, 92; NewYTET; WhoAm 74, 76, 78, 80, 82, 84, 86, 88, 90, 92, 94, 95, 96, 97; WhoEnt 92; WhoTelC; WhoWest 84, 87, 89, 92, 94; WhoWor 80, 82, 84, 87, 89; WorAlBi*

Lear, William Powell
American. Engineer, Manufacturer
Pres. Lear Jet Corp., 1963-67, chm. 1967-69.
b. Jun 26, 1902 in Hannibal, Missouri
d. May 14, 1978 in Reno, Nevada
Source: *AmMWSc 73P; BioIn 4, 5, 6, 7, 8, 9, 10, 11, 14, 16, 19; BlueB 76; CurBio 66; DcAmB S10; FacFETw; WebAB 74, 79; WhAm 7; WhoAm 74, 76; WhoWor 74*

Learned, Michael
American. Actor
Played Olivia on "The Waltons," 1972-79; won three Emmys.
b. Apr 9, 1929 in Washington, District of Columbia
Source: *BioIn 10; ConTFT 6; HalFC 84, 88; IntMPA 86, 92; WhoAm 86, 90; WhoEnt 92; WorAlBi*

Leary, Denis
American. Actor
Films include *Gunmen, Sandlot* and *Judgement Night,* 1993.
b. 1957? in Worchester, Massachusetts
Source: *IntMPA 96*

Leary, Kathryn D.
American. Business Executive
President and CEO, Leary Group Inc., 1991—; focusses on linking black entrepreneurs to Japanese and South African markets.
b. May 31, 1952 in New York, New York
Source: *ConBlB 10*

Leary, Timothy (Francis)
American. Educator, Lecturer
Recorded "Give Peace a Chance," with John Lennon, 1969; outspoken advocate of LSD, 1960s.
b. Oct 22, 1920 in Springfield, Massachusetts
d. May 31, 1996 in Beverly Hills, California
Source: *AmAu&B; BioIn 7, 8, 9, 10, 11, 12, 13, 15, 16, 17, 21; CelR, 90; ConAu 107, 152; CurBio 96N; DcLB 16; DcTwCCu 1; EncO&P 2, 3; EncWB; FacFETw; LegTOT; LinLib L; MajTwCW; MakMC; MugS; News 96; NewYTBS 27; PenC AM; PolProf J; WhoAm 74, 76, 78, 80, 82, 84, 86, 88, 90, 92, 94, 95, 96, 97; WhoHol 92; WorAl; WorAlBi*

Least Heat Moon, William
[William Lewis Trogdon]
American. Author
Had critical, commercial success with first book *Blue Highways,* travel memoir, 1983.
b. Aug 27, 1939 in Kansas City, Missouri
Source: *BioIn 13; ConAu 115, X; ConLC 29*

Leaud, Jean-Pierre
French. Actor
Played same character in five Truffaut films, 1959-79, including *Stolen Kisses.*
b. May 5, 1944 in Paris, France
Source: *BiDFilm, 81, 94; DcTwCCu 2; EncEurC; FilmAG WE; FilmEn; HalFC 80, 84, 88; IntDcF 1-3, 2-3; IntMPA 92, 94, 96; IntWW 93; ItaFilm; MovMk; OxCFilm; WhoHol 92, A; WorEFlm*

Leavis, F(rank) R(aymond)
English. Critic, Author
One of the Cambridge Critics, edited *Scrutiny,* 1932-53; wrote *Revolution,* 1936.
b. Jul 14, 1895 in Cambridge, England
d. Apr 14, 1978 in Cambridge, England
Source: *Au&Wr 71; Benet 87, 96; BioIn 1, 4, 6, 10, 11, 12, 13, 14, 15, 17; BlmGEL; BlueB 76; BritWr 7; CamGLE; CasWL; ChhPo S1; ConAu 21R, 44NR, 77; ConLC 24; ConLCrt 77, 82; CyWA 89; DcArts; DcLEL; DcNaB 1971; EncWL, 2, 3; EvLB; FacFETw; GrBr; IntWW 74, 75, 76, 77; LngCEL; LngCTC; MajTwCW; MakMC; ModBrL, S1, S2; NewC; NewCBEL; NewYTBS 78; OxCEng 67, 85, 95; PenC ENG; PseudN 82; RAdv 1; REn; ThTwC 87; TwCA SUP; TwCWr; WebE&AL; Who 74; WhoTwCL; WhoWor 74, 76; WrDr 76*

Leavitt, Mike
American. Politician
Rep. governor, UT, 1993—.
b. Feb 11, 1951

Leavitt, Ron
American. Producer
Co-producer of TV sitcom "Married.with Children."
Source: *St&PR 91*

Lebed, Alexander
[Aleksandr Ivanovich Lebed]
Russian. Military Leader
Commander of 14th Russian army, 1992-95; led group of tanks to defend Russian Pres. Yeltsin during a coup attempt, 1991; secretary of Russian National Security Council, 1996.
b. Apr 20, 1950 in Novocherkassk, Union of Soviet Socialist Republics
Source: *LngBDD; News 97-1; WhoRel 75; WhoRus*

LeBlanc, Matt
American. Actor
Plays Joey Tribbiani on TV's "Friends," 1994—.
b. Jul 25, 1967 in Newton, Massachusetts

Leblanc, Maurice
French. Author, Dramatist
His detective fiction features Arsene Lupin.
b. Dec 19, 1864
d. Nov 6, 1941 in Perpignan, France

Source: *CasWL; ConAu 110; CorpD; CrtSuMy; CurBio 42; EncMys; EvEuW; LegTOT; LngCTC; MnBBF; OxCFr; ScF&FL 1; ScFEYrs; TwCA; TwCCr&M 80B, 85B, 91B; TwCLC 49*

LeBon, Simon
[Duran Duran]
English. Singer
Lead singer, Duran Duran since 1978, who was a popular teenage pin-up.
b. Oct 27, 1958 in Bushey, England
Source: *BioIn 13, 14*

LeBoutillier, John
"Boot"
American. Politician
Rep. con. from NY, 1980-82; wrote *Harvard Hates America,* 1978.
b. May 26, 1953 in Glen Cove, New York
Source: *AlmAP 82; BiDrUSC 89; BioIn 12, 13; CngDr 81; DcAmC; WhoAm 82, 90; WhoAmP 83, 89, 91, 93, 95; WhoE 89*

Lebowitz, Fran(ces Ann)
American. Journalist
Mag. columnist noted for satirical essays on urban life: *Social Studies,* 1981.
b. Oct 27, 1950 in Morristown, New Jersey
Source: *ArtclWW 2; BioIn 11, 12, 13, 15; CelR 90; ConAu 14NR, 81; ConLC 11, 36; CurBio 82; EncAHmr; IntvTCA 2; InWom SUP; LegTOT; MajTwCW*

Lebowsky, Stanley Richard
American. Musician, Composer
Wrote popular song "The Wayward Wind," 1956; Tony nominee for *Irma La Douche,* 1961.
b. Nov 26, 1926 in Minneapolis, Minnesota
d. Oct 19, 1986 in New York, New York
Source: *ConTFT 4; NotNAT*

Leboyer, Frederick
French. Physician, Author
Advocate of gentle birthing techniques of dimmed lights, soft voices, gentle massage; wrote *Birth without Violence,* 1974.
b. 1918 in Paris, France
Source: *BioIn 12, 13; ConAu 106; CurBio 82; WrDr 80, 82*

Lebrun, Albert
French. Political Leader
Last of the Third Republic's presidents, 1932-40; resigned when Laval assumed power.
b. Aug 29, 1871 in Mercy-le-Haut, France
d. Mar 6, 1950 in Paris, France
Source: *BioIn 2, 17; EncTR 91; HisEWW; LinLib S; ObitOF 79*

Le Brun, Charles
French. Artist
Painter to Louis XIV, 1662; head of Gobelins, 1663; designed royal furnishings; decorated Versailles, especially the Galerie de Glaces.
b. Feb 24, 1619 in Paris, France
d. Feb 22, 1690 in Paris, France
Source: *BioIn 3, 6, 11, 13, 19; ClaDrA; DcArts; DcBiPP; DcCathB; EncO&P 1, 2, 3; IntDcAA 90; IntDcAr; LinLib S; McGEWB; NewCol 75; OxCArt; OxCFr; OxDcArt; PenDiDA 89; WhDW; WhoArch*

Lebrun, Rico
[Frederico Lebrun]
American. Artist
Painted grim good-evil theme murals; did crucifixion, concentration camp series.
b. Dec 10, 1900 in Naples, Italy
d. May 10, 1964 in Malibu, California
Source: *BioIn 1, 2, 3, 4, 5, 6, 7, 8; BriEAA; CmCal; ConArt 77; CurBio 52, 64; DcAmArt; DcAmB S7; DcCAA 71, 77, 88, 94; McGDA; OxCTwCA; PhDcTCA 77; WhAm 4; WhAmArt 85; WhoAmA 78N, 89N, 91N, 93N*

LeCarre, John
[David John Moore Cornwell]
English. Author
Introduced George Smiley, antithesis of James Bond, in *Call from the Dead,* 1962; also wrote *Little Drummer Girl,* 1983; *Perfect Spy,* 1986.
b. Oct 19, 1931 in Poole, England
Source: *Au&Wr 71; Benet 87; BioIn 6, 7, 10, 11, 12, 13, 14, 15, 16, 17, 18, 19; BlueB 76; CamGLE; CelR 90; CnDBLB 8; ConAu 5R, 33NR, X; ConLC 5; ConNov 86, 91; CurBio 74; CyWA 89; DcLP 87B; EncMys; FacFETw; HalFC 88; IntAu&W 76, 77, 89, 91, 93; IntvTCA 2; IntWW 74, 75, 76, 77, 78, 79, 80, 81, 82, 83, 89, 91, 93; MajTwCW; NewC; NewYTBS 86; OxCEng 85; RfGEnL 91; SpyFic; TwCCr&M 91; TwCWr; Who 74, 82, 83, 85, 88, 90, 92, 94; WhoAm 80, 82, 84, 86, 90, 94, 95, 96, 97; WhoWor 74, 76, 78, 82, 84, 91, 93, 95, 96, 97; WorAlBi; WorAu 1950; WrDr 76, 86, 92*

Le Chatelier, Henry-Louis
French. Chemist
Best known for work on structure of alloys; developed principle of chemical equilibrium; Le Chatelier's Principle, 1884.
b. Oct 8, 1850 in Paris, France
d. Sep 7, 1936 in Paris, France
Source: *AsBiEn; DcScB; NewCol 75*

Lecky, William Edward Hartpole
Irish. Author, Historian
Published essays on Swift, Flood, Grattan, and O'Connell.
b. Mar 26, 1838 in Newton Park, Ireland
d. Oct 22, 1903 in London, England
Source: *Alli SUP; BbD; BiD&SB; BiDIrW; BioIn 1, 2; BritAu 19; CamGEL; CamGLE; CasWL; CelCen; Chambr 3; ChhPo, S1, S3; DcBiPP; DcEnA, A; DcEnL; DcEuL; DcIrB 78, 88; DcIrW 2; DcLEL; DcNaB S2; EvLB; LinLib S; McGEWB; NewC; NewCBEL; OxCEng 67, 85, 95; PenC ENG; PoIre*

LeClear, Thomas
American. Artist
Portraitist, genre painter: *Buffalo Newsboy,* 1853.
b. Mar 11, 1818 in Oswego, New York
d. Nov 26, 1882 in Rutherford, New Jersey
Source: *ApCAB; ArtsNiC; DcAmArt; DcAmB; Drake; NatCAB 8; NewYHSD; TwCBDA; WhAm HS*

Leclerc, Jacques-Philippe
French. Army Officer
Commanded French Far Eastern Forces, 1945; signed Japanese surrender document for France.
b. Nov 28, 1902 in Belloy Saint Leonard, France
d. Nov 28, 1947, Algeria
Source: *CurBio 44, 47; McGEWB; NewCol 75*

LeCorbusier
[Charles Edouard Jeanneret-Gris]
Swiss. Architect
Pioneered use of reinforced concrete; concept of house as "machine for living."
b. Oct 6, 1887, Switzerland
d. Aug 27, 1965 in Roquebrune, France
Source: *AtlBL; BioIn 11, 14, 15, 16, 17, 19, 20; CurBio 47, 66; EncMA; RAdv 13-3; REn; TwCA SUP*

Lecouvreur, Adrienne
French. Actor
Changed acting techniques by advocating natural speech, simple manner.
b. Apr 5, 1692 in Damery, France
d. Mar 20, 1730 in Paris, France
Source: *BioIn 2, 4, 5, 6, 9, 11; CamGWoT; CnThe; ContDcW 89; DcArts; DcBiPP; Dis&D; EncCoWW; EncWT; Ent; IntDcT 3; IntDcWB; InWom; NotNAT A, B; OxCFr; OxCThe 67, 83; REn*

Lederberg, Joshua
American. Educator
Shared 1958 Nobel Prize in medicine for genetics research.
b. May 23, 1925 in Montclair, New Jersey
Source: *AmMWSc 73P, 76P, 79, 82, 86, 89, 92, 95; AsBiEn; BiDrAPH 79; BiESc; BioIn 5, 6, 7, 11, 13, 14, 15, 20; BlueB 76; CamDcSc; CurBio 59; EncAB-H 1974, 1996; EncWB; InSci; IntWW 74, 75, 76, 77, 78, 79, 80, 81, 82, 83, 89, 91, 93; LarDcSc; McGMS 80; NobelP; NotTwCS; WebAB 74, 79; Who 74, 82, 83, 85, 88, 90, 92, 94; WhoAm 74, 76, 78, 80, 82, 84, 86, 88, 90, 92, 94, 95, 96, 97; WhoAmJ 80; WhoE 79, 81, 83, 85, 86, 89, 91, 93, 95, 97; WhoFrS 84; WhoMedH; WhoNob, 90, 95; WhoScEn 94, 96; WhoWest 78;*

WhoWor 74, 78, 80, 82, 84, 87, 89, 91, 93, 95, 96, 97; WhoWorJ 72, 78; WorAl; WorAlBi; WorScD

Lederer, Francis
[Frantisek Lederer; Franz Lederer]
Czech. Actor
Films include German *Pandora's Box,* 1929; *Gay Deception,* 1936.
b. Nov 6, 1906 in Prague, Bohemia
Source: *BiE&WWA; BioIn 10, 11; Film 2; FilmEn; FilmgC; ForYSC; HalFC 80, 84, 88; HolP 30; MotPP; MovMk; NotNAT; What 4; WhoAm 76, 78; WhoHol 92, A; WhoHrs 80; WhThe*

Lederer, William Julius
American. Author
Wrote *Ensign O'Toole and Me,* 1957; *The Ugly American,* 1958.
b. Mar 31, 1912 in New York, New York
Source: *AmAu&B; Au&Wr 71; BioIn 2, 5, 10; ConAu 1R, 5NR; SmATA 62; SpyFic; WhoAm 74, 76, 78, 80, 82, 84, 86, 88, 90, 92, 94, 95, 96, 97; WhoUSWr 88; WhoWor 74, 76; WhoWrEP 89, 92; WorAl; WorAu 1950*

Lederman, Leon Max
American. Physicist
Shared 1988 Nobel Prize in physics for discovering the muon neutrino, a subatomic particle.
b. Jul 15, 1922 in New York, New York
Source: *AmMWSc 73P, 76P, 79, 82, 86, 89, 92, 95; BioIn 11, 12, 13, 16; IntWW 91; LarDcSc; McGMS 80; News 89; NotTwCS; Who 90, 92, 94; WhoAm 74, 76, 78, 80, 82, 84, 86, 88, 90, 92, 94, 95, 96, 97; WhoFrS 84; WhoMW 84, 86, 90, 92, 93, 96; WhoNob 90, 95; WhoScEn 94, 96; WhoTech 89; WhoWor 91, 93, 95, 96, 97; WorAlBi*

Ledoux, Claude Nicolas
French. Architect
Built palaces, toll houses, gates around Paris; wrote influential treatise, 1804.
b. Mar 21, 1736 in Dormans, France
d. Nov 19, 1806 in Paris, France
Source: *AtlBL; BioIn 1, 3, 6, 9, 11, 13; CmFrR; DcBiPP; MacEA; McGDA; McGEWB; NewCol 75; WhoArch*

Le Duan
Vietnamese. Political Leader
Communist Party secretary-general who led Communists to victory in war for Vietnam, 1969-75.
b. Apr 7, 1908 in Quang Tri Province, Vietnam
d. Jul 10, 1986 in Hanoi, Vietnam
Source: *BiDMarx; ConAu 119; ConNews 86-4; DcMPSA; EncWB; FarE&A 78, 79, 80, 81; IntWW 74, 75, 76, 77, 78, 79, 80, 81, 82, 83; NewYTBS 86; WhoSocC 78; WhoWor 78, 80, 84*

Le Duc Tho
[Phan Dinh Khai]
Vietnamese. Government Official
First Asian and communist to win Nobel Peace Prize; shared with Henry Kissinger for work in negotiating Vietnam armistice, 1973; refused award, saying peace hadn't yet been achieved.
b. Oct 14, 1911 in Dich Le, Vietnam
d. Oct 13, 1990 in Hanoi, Vietnam
Source: *AnObit 1990; BioIn 11, 12; CurBio 75, 91N; DcMPSA; FacFETw; FarE&A 78, 79, 80, 81; IntWW 77, 78, 79, 80, 81, 82, 83, 89, 91N; News 91, 91-1; NewYTBE 73; NewYTBS 90; NobelP; WhoNob, 90; WhoWor 78, 80, 82*

Led Zeppelin
[John Bonham; John Paul Jones; Jimmy Page; Robert Plant]
English. Music Group
Heavy-metal band formed, 1968; disbanded, 1980, after death of John Bonham; wrote rock classic "Stairway to Heaven."
Source: *AmEA 74; AmMWSc 89; BiDAmM; BioIn 14, 16, 17, 18, 19; BkPepl; ConMuA 80A, 80B; ConMus 1; DcArts; DcTwCCu 1; EncPR&S 74, 89; EncRk 88; EncRkSt; FacFETw; HarEnR 86; IlEncRk; NewAmDM; NewYTBS 80, 85; OxCPMus; PenEncP; PeoHis; RkOn 78; RolSEnR 83; WhoAm 80, 84; WhoHol 92; WhoRock 81; WhoRocM 82; WorAl; WorAlBi*

Lee, Andrew Daulton
"Snowman"
American. Spy
With Christopher Boyce spied for the Soviets; sentenced to life imprisonment; nickname comes from drug use.
b. 1952 in Palos Verdes, California
Source: *NewYTBS 77; SpyCS*

Lee, Ang
Taiwanese. Director, Screenwriter
Directed *Eat Drink Man Woman,* 1994; *Sense and Sensibility,* 1995.
b. Oct 23, 1954, Taiwan
Source: *ConTFT 15; News 96, 96-3; NotAsAm*

Lee, Ann
"Ann the Word"; "Mother Ann"
American. Religious Leader
Founded first Shaker settlement in America, Watervliet, NY, 1776.
b. Feb 29, 1736 in Manchester, England
d. Sep 8, 1784 in Watervliet, New York
Source: *Alli; AmBi; AmRef; ApCAB; Benet 87, 96; BiDAmCu; BioIn 4, 5, 10, 11, 12, 14, 15, 17, 19, 21; BlkwEAR; ContDcW 89; DcAmB; DcAmReB 1, 2; DcNaB; DivFut; Drake; EncAB-H 1974, 1996; EncARH; EncCRAm; EncPaPR 91; EncWHA; GoodHs; GrLiveH; HanAmWH; HarEnUS; HerW 84; HisWorL; IlEncMy; IntDcWB; InWom, SUP; LegTOT; LibW; LuthC 75; NatCAB 5; NotAW; OxCAmH; OxCAmL 65, 83, 95; PseudAu; PseudN 82; RComAH; REn; REnAW; TwCBDA; WebAB 74, 79; WhAm HS; WhAmRev; WhDW; WomFir; WorAl; WorAlBi*

Lee, Bernard
English. Actor
Played M in James Bond films, 1962-79.
b. Jan 10, 1908 in London, England
d. Jan 16, 1981 in London, England
Source: *AnObit 1981; BioIn 13; CmMov; FilmEn; FilmgC; HalFC 80, 84, 88; IlWWBF; IntMPA 75, 76, 77, 78, 79, 80, 81; ItaFilm; NewYTBS 81; WhoHol A; WhoThe 72, 77, 81; WhScrn 83*

Lee, Brandon
American. Actor
Starred in martial arts films including *Kung Fu: The Movie,* 1986; son of Bruce.
b. Feb 1, 1965 in Oakland, California
d. Mar 31, 1993 in Wilmington, North Carolina
Source: *AnObit 1993; BioIn 14; ConTFT 13; News 93; NotAsAm; WhoHol 92*

Lee, Brenda
[Brenda Mae Tarpley]
"Little Miss Dynamite"
American. Singer
Began singing professionally at age six; 1969 Grammy nominee for "Johnny One Time"; album *Brenda Lee,* 1991.
b. Dec 11, 1944 in Atlanta, Georgia
Source: *Baker 84, 92; BgBkCoM; BiDAmM; BioIn 12, 14, 16; ConMuA 80A; ConMus 5; CounME 74, 74A; EncFCWM 83; EncRk 88; EncRkSt; HarEnCM 87; HarEnR 86; InWom, SUP; LegTOT; NewAmDM; NewGrDA 86; OxCPMus; PenEncP; PseudN 82; RkOn 74; RolSEnR 83; VarWW 85; WhoAm 74, 76, 78, 80, 82, 92, 94, 95, 96, 97; WhoAmW 68, 70, 72, 74, 89, 91, 93; WhoHol 92; WhoRock 81; WhoSSW 73*

Lee, Bruce
[Lee Yuen Kam; Lee Siu Loong]
"The Little Dragon"
American. Actor
Best known for martial arts films: *Enter the Dragon,* 1973.
b. Nov 27, 1940 in San Francisco, California
d. Jul 20, 1973, Hong Kong
Source: *BioIn 10, 11, 12, 16, 20, 21; ConTFT 15; DcAmB S9; HalFC 80, 84, 88; LegTOT; MovMk; NewYTBE 73; NotAsAm; ObitOF 79; PseudN 82; WhoHol B; WhScrn 74, 77, 83*

Lee, Canada
[Leonard Lionel Cornelius Canegata]
American. Actor, Boxer
Played in stage version of *Native Son,* 1941; film *Lifeboat,* 1944.
b. May 3, 1907 in New York, New York
d. May 9, 1952 in New York, New York
Source: *AfrAmAl 6; BioIn 2, 3, 6, 8, 12, 14, 18, 20; BlksAmF; BlksB&W C;*

CamGWoT; ConBlB 8; CurBio 44, 52; DcAmB S5; DcAmNB; DcTwCCu 5; DrBlPA, 90; Ent; FilmgC; HalFC 80, 84, 88; InB&W 80, 85; LegTOT; MotPP; MovMk; NegAl 76, 83, 89; NotNAT B; OxCAmT 84; OxCThe 83; PseudN 82; Vers A; WhAm 3; WhoHol B; WhScrn 74, 77, 83; WhThe

Lee, Charles
American. Army Officer, Author
Revolutionary War leader who gave British a plan for defeating Americans; constantly criticized Washington, dismissed from army, 1780.
b. 1731 in Dernhall, England
d. Oct 2, 1782 in Philadelphia, Pennsylvania
Source: *Alli; AmAu; AmAu&B; AmBi; AmRev; ApCAB; BenetAL 91; BioIn 1, 2, 4, 7, 8, 9, 10, 11; BlkwEAR; DcAmB; DcAmMiB; DcNaB; Drake; EncAB-H 1974, 1996; EncAR; EncSoH; HarEnMi; HarEnUS; NatCAB 1, 8; OxCAmH; REnAL; TwCBDA; WebAB 74, 79; WebAMB; WhAm HS; WhAmRev; WorAl; WorAlBi*

Lee, Christopher Frank Carandini
English. Actor
Vincent Price's rival for horror film portrayals; films include *Corridor of Mirrors,* 1947; *Dracula,* 1958; *An Eye for an Eye,* 1981.
b. May 27, 1922 in London, England
Source: *BioIn 13, 14, 15; CmMov; ConAu 73; ConTFT 6; CurBio 75; FilmgC; HalFC 84, 88; IntAu&W 89; IntMPA 86, 92; IntWW 77, 78, 79, 80, 81, 82, 83, 89, 91, 93; MotPP; MovMk; OxCFilm; PenEncH; VarWW 85; Who 82, 83, 85, 88, 90, 92, 94; WhoAm 80, 82, 84, 86, 88, 90, 92, 94, 95, 96, 97; WhoEnt 92; WhoHol A; WhoWor 80, 82, 84, 87; WorAlBi*

Lee, Dixie
[Mrs. Bing Crosby; Wilma Winifred Wyatt]
American. Actor
Ingenue in early talking films; retired after marriage, 1930.
b. Nov 4, 1911 in Harriman, Tennessee
d. Nov 1, 1952 in Holmby Hills, California
Source: *BiDD; Film 1, 2; ForYSC; HalFC 80, 84, 88; PseudN 82; TwYS; WhoHol B; WhScrn 74, 77, 83*

Lee, Doris Emrick
American. Artist
Noted for primitivistic folksy scenes: "Thanksgiving Day," 1936.
b. Feb 1, 1905 in Aledo, Illinois
d. Jun 16, 1983 in Clearwater, Florida
Source: *BioIn 13, 14, 15, 17; BriEAA; ConAu 110; CurBio 54, 86N; DcAmArt; EncAFC; GrAmP; IlsCB 1946; InWom, SUP; McGDA; NorAmWA; SmATA 35N, 44; WhAmArt 85; WhoAm 74, 76, 78; WhoAmA 78; WhoAmW 58, 64, 66, 68, 70, 72, 74*

Lee, Fitzhugh
American. Army Officer, Politician
Confederate major general, covered retreat to Appomattox; VA governor, 1886-90; nephew of Robert E Lee.
b. Nov 19, 1835 in Clermont, Virginia
d. Apr 28, 1905 in Washington, District of Columbia
Source: *AmBi; ApCAB, SUP, X; BiDConf; BiDrGov 1789; BiDSA; BioIn 5, 8, 16; CivWDc; DcAmB; DcAmDH 80, 89; DcAmMiB; DcNAA; EncSoH; GenMudB; HarEnMi; HarEnUS; NatCAB 9; NewCol 75; OxCAmH; TwCBDA; WebAB 74, 79; WebAMB; WhAm 1; WhAmP; WhCiWar*

Lee, Francis Lightfoot
American. Continental Congressman
Signed Declaration of Independence, 1776; brother of Declaration signer Richard Henry Lee.
b. Oct 14, 1734 in Westmoreland, Virginia
d. Jan 11, 1797 in Richmond County, Virginia
Source: *AmBi; ApCAB; BiAUS; BiDrAC; BiDrUSC 89; BioIn 7, 8, 9; DcAmB; Drake; EncAR; EncCRAm; EncSoH; HarEnUS; NatCAB 5; OxCAmH; TwCBDA; WhAm HS; WhAmP; WhAmRev; WorAl; WorAlBi*

Lee, Gary Earl
[The Hostages]
American. Hostage
One of 52 held by terrorists, Nov 1979-Jan 1981.
b. Feb 4, 1943 in New York, New York
Source: *BioIn 12; NewYTBS 81; USBiR 74*

Lee, Geddy
Canadian. Singer
Guitarist, bass player with progressive trio, 1974—; had many gold records; won two Junos, 1978, 1979.
b. Jul 29, 1953 in Toronto, Ontario, Canada
Source: *LegTOT; RolSEnR 83; WhoAm 82; WhoRocM 82*

Lee, Gypsy Rose
[Rose Louise Hovick]
American. Entertainer
Burlesque queen; autobiography *Gyspy,* 1957 basis for Broadway musical, 1959, movie, 1962.
b. Feb 9, 1914 in Seattle, Washington
d. Apr 26, 1970 in Los Angeles, California
Source: *AmAu&B; BiDD; BiE&WWA; BioAmW; BioIn 1, 4, 5, 7, 8, 9, 12, 13; CamGWoT; ConAu 113; ContDcW 89; CurBio 70; DcAmB S8; DcArts; EncMT; EncMys; EncVaud; Ent; FemiCLE; FilmEn; FilmgC; ForYSC; GoodHs; GrLiveH; IntDcWB; InWom, SUP; LegTOT; LibW; MotPP; MovMk; NewYTBE 70; NotAW MOD; NotNAT A, B; NotWoAT; ObitOF 79; ObitT 1961; PseudN 82; WebAB 74, 79; WhAm 5; WhoAmW 64, 66, 68, 70; WhoHol B; WhScrn 74, 77, 83; WorAl; WorAlBi; WorEFlm*

Lee, Harper
[Nelle Harper Lee]
American. Author
Won Pulitzer, 1961, for *To Kill a Mockingbird;* made into film, 1962.
b. Apr 28, 1926 in Monroeville, Alabama
Source: *AmAu&B; AmWomWr; Au&Arts 13; Benet 87; BenetAL 91; BioIn 5, 6, 8, 10, 11, 12, 15, 17; CasWL; ConAu 13R; ConLC 12, 60; CyWA 89; DcLB 6; DcTwCCu 1; DrAF 76; DrAPF 80, 91; IntvTCA 2; InWom, SUP; LegTOT; LinLib L; MagSAmL; MajTwCW; NewCon; Novels; OxCAmL 65, 83; OxCWoWr 95; REnAL; SmATA 11; SouWr; TwCWr; WhoAm 74, 76, 78, 80, 82; WhoAmW 64, 66, 68, 70, 72, 74; WhoGov 72; WorAl; WorAlBi; WorAu 1950; WorLitC*

Lee, Helen Elaine
American. Author
Wrote novel *The Serpent's Gift,* 1994.
b. Mar 13, 1959 in Detroit, Michigan
Source: *ConAu 148; ConLC 86; WhoAfA 96*

Lee, Henry
"Legion Harry"; "Light Horse Harry"
American. Politician
Eulogized Washington as "First in war, first in peace, first in hearts of his countrymen," 1779; father of Robert E.
b. Jan 29, 1756 in Dumfries, Virginia
d. Mar 25, 1818 in Cumberland Island, Georgia
Source: *Alli; AmAu&B; AmBi; AmRev; AmWrBE; ApCAB; BenetAL 91; BiAUS; BiDrAC; BiDrGov 1789; BiDrUSC 89; BiDSA; BioIn 1, 3, 7, 8, 11, 12, 13, 20, 21; CyAL 1; DcAmAu; DcAmB; DcAmMiB; DcBiPP; DcNAA; Drake; EncAR; EncCRAm; EncSoH; GenMudB; HarEnMi; HarEnUS; LinLib L, S; NatCAB 3; NewC; OxCAmH; OxCAmL 65, 83, 95; PeoHis; PseudN 82; REn; REnAL; TwCBDA; WebAB 74, 79; WebAMB; WhAm HS; WhAmP; WhAmRev; WhoMilH 76; WorAl; WorAlBi*

Lee, Henry C.
[Chang-Yuh Lee]
Chinese. Scientist
Director, Connecticut State Police Forensic Laboratory, 1980—; testified for the defense of O. J. Simpson, 1995.
b. Nov 22, 1938 in Jiangsu, China
Source: *CurBio 96; News 97-1*

Lee, Henry D
American. Merchant, Manufacturer
Produced overalls, jackets, dungarees, 1888; sold first cowboy pants with zipper fly, 1927.
b. 1849
d. 1928

Source: *Entr*

Lee, J(oseph) Bracken
American. Politician
Governor of Utah, 1949-57; mayor, Salt Lake City, 1960-72.
b. Jan 7, 1899
d. Oct 20, 1996 in Salt Lake City, Utah
Source: *BiDrGov 1789; BioIn 1, 2, 5, 6, 11, 13; BlueB 76; PolProf E; WhoAm 74, 76, 78, 80; WhoAmP 73, 75, 77, 79, 81, 83, 85, 87, 89, 91, 93, 95; WhoGov 72; WhoWest 76, 78*

Lee, James
Canadian. Politician
Progressive-Conservative Party premier of Prince Edward Island, 1982-86.
b. Mar 26, 1937 in Charlottetown, Prince Edward Island, Canada
Source: *CanWW 83, 89; IntWW 91; Who 92; WhoAm 90*

Lee, Jason
American. Missionary
Helped establish territorial government in OR, 1843; a founder, Oregon Institute, 1842.
b. Jun 23, 1803 in Stanstead, Vermont
d. Mar 12, 1845 in Stanstead, Vermont
Source: *AmBi; BioIn 1, 3, 8, 9; DcAmB; EncNAR; EncWM; LuthC 75; NatCAB 25; REnAW; WebAB 74, 79; WhAm HS; WhNaAH*

Lee, Jennie
Scottish. Politician
Member, British Parliament, 1929-31, 1945-70; played an important role in the founding of Open U, dedicated to higher education by correspondence.
b. Nov 3, 1904 in Lochgelly, Scotland
d. Nov 16, 1988 in London, England
Source: *AnObit 1988; BioIn 1, 2, 6, 7, 12, 16; ConAu 127; ContDcW 89; CurBio 89N; FacFETw; IntDcWB; InWom, SUP; NewYTBS 88; WhE&EA; WhoWor 74*

Lee, Johnny
American. Singer
Had hit song "Lookin' for Love," 1980, from film *Urban Cowboy*.
b. Jul 3, 1946 in Texas City, Texas
Source: *BioIn 12, 14; HarEnCM 87; LegTOT; PenEncP; RkOn 85; WhoEnt 92; WhoHol 92; WhoWor 96*

Lee, Joie
[Joy Lee]
American. Actor
Starred in brother Spike Lee's films, including *She's Gotta Have It*, 1986; *Do the Right Thing*, 1989; *Mo' Better Blues*, 1990.
b. 1962?
Source: *ConBlB 1; WhoHol 92*

Lee, Laurie
English. Writer
Wrote *Land at War*, 1945; *As I Walked Out One Midsummer Morning*, 1969.
b. Jun 26, 1914 in Stroud, England
d. May 14, 1997 in Gloucestershire, England
Source: *Au&Wr 71; BioIn 5, 6, 7, 8, 9, 10, 11; BlueB 76; CamGLE; CasWL; ConAu 33NR, 77; ConLC 90; ConPo 70, 75, 80, 85, 91, 96; ConPopW; DcArts; DcLB 27; DcLEL 1940; EngPo; GrWrEL P; IntAu&W 76, 89, 91, 93; IntWW 74, 75, 76, 77, 78, 79, 80, 81, 82, 83, 89, 91, 93; LngCTC; MajTwCW; ModBrL; NewC; NewCBEL; OxCEng 85, 95; OxCTwCP; PenC ENG; RAdv 1; REn; RfGEnL 91; RGTwCWr; TwCWr; WhDW; WhE&EA; Who 74; WhoWor 74, 76, 78; WorAu 1950; WrDr 76, 80, 82, 84, 86, 88, 90, 92, 94, 96*

Lee, Lila
[Augusta Appel]
American. Actor
Starred opposite Valentino in *Blood and Sand*, 1922.
b. Jul 25, 1902 in Union Hill, New Jersey
d. Nov 13, 1973 in Saranac Lake, New York
Source: *BioIn 14; Film 1; FilmgC; GangFlm; HalFC 80, 84, 88; MotPP; MovMk; ObitOF 79; PseudN 82; ThFT; TwYS; WhoHol B; WhScrn 77, 83*

Lee, Manfred B(ennington)
[Ellery Queen; Manford Lepofsky]
American. Author
With cousin Frederic Dannay wrote *Ellery Queen* mysteries, beginning 1929.
b. Jan 11, 1905 in New York, New York
d. Apr 3, 1971 in Roxbury, Connecticut
Source: *AmAu&B; ConAu 2NR, 29R; CurBio 40; DcLEL; EncMys; LngCTC; PenC AM; REn; REnAL; TwCA, SUP; WebAB 74, 79; WhAm 5*

Lee, Mark
American. Astronaut
With wife Jan Davis, first husband-and-wife team in space, 1992.
b. 1952? in Viroqua, Wisconsin
Source: *WhoSpc*

Lee, Michele
[Michele Lee Dusiak]
American. Actor, Dancer
Played Karen Fairgate MacKenzie on TV series "Knots Landing"; Tony nomination for musical *Seesaw*.
b. Jun 24, 1942 in Los Angeles, California
Source: *BiE&WWA; BioIn 13, 16; CelR 90; ConTFT 1; FilmgC; HalFC 80, 84, 88; IntMPA 84, 86, 88, 92, 94, 96; InWom SUP; LegTOT; NotNAT; PseudN 82; VarWW 85; WhoAm 84, 86, 88, 90, 92, 94, 95, 96, 97; WhoAmW 87, 89, 91, 93, 95, 97; WhoEnt 92; WhoHol 92, A; WhoTelC; WorAl; WorAlBi*

Lee, Ming Cho
American. Designer
Scenic and lighting designer; won 1983 Tony for *K2;* principal designer, NY Shakespeare Festival, 1960s-70s.
b. Oct 3, 1930 in Shanghai, China
Source: *BiE&WWA; BioIn 8, 16; CamGWoT; ConDes 84, 90, 97; ConTFT 4; CurBio 89; IntDcT 3; IntWWM 90; MetOEnc; NewYTBS 75; NotAsAm; NotNAT; WhoAm 84, 86, 88, 90, 92, 94, 95, 96, 97; WhoEnt 92; WhoOp 76; WhoThe 72, 77, 81; WhoWor 87, 89, 91, 93, 95*

Lee, Pamela
[Pamela Denice Anderson]
Canadian. Actor
Starred on TV's "Baywatch," 1993-97.
b. Jul 1, 1967 in Comox, British Columbia, Canada
Source: *News 96*

Lee, Peggy
[Norma Delores Egstrom]
American. Singer, Actor
Hits include "Fever," 1958; "Is That All There Is?," 1969.
b. May 26, 1920 in Jamestown, North Dakota
Source: *AllMusG; ASCAP 66; Baker 84, 92; BiDJaz; BioIn 2, 3, 4, 5, 6, 7, 8, 9, 10, 12, 13, 15, 16; BlueB 76; CelR, 90; CmpEPM; ConMus 8; CurBio 63; EncJzS; FilmEn; FilmgC; ForYSC; GoodHs; GrLiveH; HalFC 80, 84, 88; IntMPA 75, 76, 77, 78, 79, 80, 81, 82, 84, 86, 88, 92, 94, 96; InWom, SUP; LegTOT; NewAmDM; NewGrDA 86; NewGrDM 80; NewYTBS 88; OxCFilm; OxCPMus; PenEncP; PseudN 82; RadStar; RkOn 74; RolSEnR 83; VarWW 85; WhoAm 74, 76, 78, 80, 86, 94, 95, 96, 97; WhoAmW 58, 64, 66, 68, 70, 72, 74, 75, 81, 83; WhoEnt 92; WhoHol 92, A; WhoWor 74; WorAl; WorAlBi*

Lee, Pinky
[Pincus Leff]
American. Comedian
In vaudeville, burlesque, Broadway musicals; star of NBC's "Pinky Lee Show," 1950.
b. 1916 in Saint Paul, Minnesota
d. Apr 3, 1993 in Mission Viejo, California
Source: *BioIn 4, 8, 9; EncAFC; IntMPA 80, 82; JoeFr; LegTOT; LesBEnT 92; NewYTET; PseudN 82; What 2; WhoCom; WhoHol 92, A*

Lee, Rebecca
American. Physician
First black woman to become a doctor, 1864.
b. 1840
d. 1881
Source: *InB&W 80, 85*

Lee, Richard Henry
American. Statesman, Pamphleteer, Continental Congressman
Signed Declaration of Independence, 1776, and introduced resolution leading to it; wrote *Letters of a Federal Farmer,* 1787, opposing the Constitution; brother of Declaration signer Francis Lightfoot Lee.
b. Jan 20, 1732 in Stratford, Virginia
d. Jun 19, 1794 in Chantilly, Virginia
Source: *Alli; AmBi; AmPolLe; AmWrBE; ApCAB; BenetAL 91; BiAUS; BiDrAC; BiDrUSC 89; BiDrUSE 71, 89; BioIn 3, 7, 16; BlkwEAR; DcAmB; DcBiPP; Drake; EncAAH; EncAB-H 1974, 1996; EncAR; EncSoH; HarEnUS; LinLib L, S; McGEWB; NatCAB 3; OxCAmH; OxCAmL 65, 83, 95; REnAL; SouWr; TwCBDA; WebAB 74, 79; WhAm HS; WhAmP; WhAmRev; WorAl; WorAlBi*

Lee, Robert E(dward)
American. Army Officer
Led Army of Northern VA, 1862-65; commander, Confederate Army, 1865; pres., Washington College, 1865-70.
b. Jan 19, 1807 in Stratford, Virginia
d. Oct 12, 1870 in Lexington, Virginia
Source: *AmBi; ApCAB; Benet 96; BiDConf; BioIn 1, 2, 3, 4, 5, 6, 7, 8, 9, 10, 11, 12, 13; CelCen; CivWDc; CyAG; CyEd; DcAmB; DcAmMiB; Dis&D; EncAB-H 1974, 1996; EncSoH; GenMudB; HarEnMi; HarEnUS; LinLib S; McGEWB; NatCAB 3, 4; OxCAmL 65, 95; PseudN 82; REn; REnAL; TwCBDA; WebAB 74, 79; WebAMB; WhAm HS; WhCiWar; WhoMilH 76; WorAl*

Lee, Robert E(dwin)
American. Dramatist, Director
Cowrote plays *Inherit the Wind,* 1955; *Auntie Mame,* 1956.
b. Oct 15, 1918 in Elyria, Ohio
d. Jul 8, 1994
Source: *AmAu&B; ASCAP 66, 80; BenetAL 91; BiE&WWA; BioIn 10, 17, 20, 21; BlueB 76; ConAmD; ConAu 2NR, 45, 146; ConDr 73, 77, 82, 88, 93; ConLC 86; ConTFT 4; EncMT; IntAu&W 76, 77, 91, 93; LesBEnT 92; LinLib L; ModWD; NotNAT; OhA&B; REnAL; SmATA 65, 82; WhAm 11; WhoAm 74, 76, 78, 80, 82, 84, 86, 88, 90, 92, 94; WhoEnt 92; WhoSSW 88; WhoThe 72, 77, 81; WhoWest 76; WhoWor 74; WrDr 76, 80, 82, 84, 86, 88, 90, 92, 94, 96*

Lee, Robert E(mmet)
American. Government Official
Member, FCC, 1953-81; proponent of ultrahigh frequency (UHF).
b. Mar 31, 1912
d. Apr 5, 1993 in Arlington, Virginia
Source: *BioIn 7, 8, 12; CurBio 93N; WhoAmP 73, 75, 77, 79, 81, 83; WhoGov 72, 75*

Lee, Sidney, Sir
English. Educator, Scholar
Edited *Dictionary of National Biography;* wrote *Life of King Edward VII,* 1925-26.
b. Dec 5, 1859 in London, England
d. Mar 3, 1926 in London, England
Source: *BioIn 14, 16, 21; CamGLE; Chambr 3; DcEnA A; DcEnL; DcEuL; DcLB 149; DcLEL; DcNaB 1922; EvLB; GrBr; LinLib L; LngCTC; NewC; NewCBEL; OxCEng 67, 85, 95; PenC ENG; TwCA; WhLit*

Lee, Spike
[Shelton Jackson Lee]
American. Filmmaker, Director, Actor
Controversial black filmmaker; films include *Do the Right Thing,* 1989; *Malcolm X,* 1992.
b. Mar 20, 1957 in Atlanta, Georgia
Source: *AfrAmAl 6; AfrAmBi 1; Au&Arts 4; BioIn 15, 16, 18; BlkWr 1, 2; CelR 90; ConAu 42NR, 125, X; ConBlB 5; ConTFT 6; CurBio 89; DcArts; DcTwCCu 1, 5; DrBlPA 90; IntDcF 2-2; IntMPA 92, 94, 96; IntWW 91, 93; News 88; RAdv 14; SchCGBL; WhoAfA 96; WhoAm 90, 92, 94, 95, 96, 97; WhoBlA 90, 92, 94; WhoEnt 92; WhoHol 92; WhoWrEP 95; WrDr 92, 94, 96*

Lee, Stan
[Stanley Lieber]
American. Cartoonist
Editor, publisher, Marvel Comics empire, 1961—; created superhero Spider-Man, the Incredible Hulk, Fantastic Four.
b. Dec 28, 1922 in New York, New York
Source: *Au&Arts 5; BioIn 9, 11, 16; ConAu 108, 111; ConLC 17; CurBio 93; EncACom; EncSF, 93; FanAl; LegTOT; ScF&FL 92; WhoAm 78, 80, 82, 84, 86, 88, 92, 94, 95, 96, 97; WorECom*

Lee, Teng-Hui
Chinese. Political Leader
Succeeded Chiang Ching-Kuo as president of Republic of China, 1988; first native Taiwanese in post.
b. Jan 15, 1923 in Taipei, Taiwan
Source: *BioIn 15, 16; WhoWor 87, 89, 96*

Lee, Thomas Sim
American. Politician, Patriot
Revolutionary War leader; six-year governor of MD.
b. Oct 29, 1745 in Prince George's County, Maryland
d. Nov 9, 1819 in Frederick County, Maryland
Source: *ApCAB; BiAUS; BiDrAC; BiDrACR; BiDrGov 1789; BiDrUSC 89; BioIn 19; DcAmB; Drake; NatCAB 9; TwCBDA; WhAm HS; WhAmRev*

Lee, Tsung-Dao
American. Physicist
Co-winner, Nobel Prize, 1957, for disproving principle of parity.
b. Nov 24, 1926 in Shanghai, China
Source: *AmMWSc 86, 92; AsBiEn; BiESc; BioIn 13, 15; CurBio 58; FarE&A 80, 81; InSci; IntWW 74, 75, 76, 77, 78, 79, 80, 81, 82, 83; McGMS 80; NobelP; NotAsAm; NotTwCS; WebAB 74, 79; WhDW; Who 74, 82, 83, 85, 88, 90, 92, 94; WhoAm 74, 76, 78, 80, 84, 86, 88, 90, 92, 94, 95; WhoAsA 94; WhoAtom 77; WhoE 77, 79, 81, 83, 85, 89, 91, 93, 95, 97; WhoNob, 90, 95; WhoScEn 94; WhoWor 74, 82, 84, 87, 89, 91, 93, 95, 97; WorAl; WorAlBi*

Lee, Will
American. Actor
Played Mr. Hooper, the storekeeper, on "Sesame Street," 1969-82.
b. Aug 6, 1908 in New York, New York
d. Dec 7, 1982 in New York, New York
Source: *BiE&WWA; BioIn 13; NewYTBS 82; NotNAT; WhoHol A*

Lee, Yuan Tseh
American. Chemist
Co-winner of 1986 Nobel Prize for chemistry for research in the "crossed molecular beam technique."
b. Nov 29, 1936 in Hsin-chu, Taiwan
Source: *AmMWSc 73P, 76P, 79, 82, 86, 89, 92, 95; BioIn 13, 15; IntWW 89, 91, 93; NobelP; Who 88, 90, 92, 94; WhoAm 90, 92, 94, 95; WhoAsA 94; WhoNob 90, 95; WhoScEn 94; WhoWest 87, 92, 94; WhoWor 89, 91, 93, 95*

Leech, John
English. Cartoonist, Illustrator
Political cartoonist for *Punch,* 1841-64; illustrated works of Dickens.
b. Aug 29, 1817 in London, England
d. Oct 29, 1864 in London, England
Source: *Alli; AntBDN B; ArtsNiC; BioIn 2, 3, 8, 11, 12, 13; BritAS; CamGLE; CelCen; ChhPo, S2; ClaDrA; DcArts; DcBiPP; DcBrBI; DcBrWA; DcEnL; DcNaB; DcVicP, 2; McGDA; NewC; NewCBEL; OxCArt; OxCEng 85, 95; OxDcArt; StaCVF; WhDW; WorECar*

Leech, Margaret Kernochan
[Mrs. Ralph Pulitzer]
American. Author, Historian
Won Pulitzers for histories: *Reveille in Washington,* 1941; *In the Days of McKinley,* 1959.
b. Nov 7, 1893 in Newburgh, New York
d. Feb 24, 1974 in New York, New York
Source: *AmAu&B; ConAu 49, 93; CurBio 42, 60, 74; InWom; NewYTBS 74; OxCAmL 65; PseudN 82; REn; REnAL; TwCA SUP; WhAm 10; WhoAmW 58, 61, 64, 66, 68, 70, 72, 74*

Lee-Hamilton, Eugene Jacob
English. Poet, Translator
Wrote over 200 sonnets: *Sonnets of the Wingless Hours,* 1894.
b. Jan 6, 1845 in London, England
d. Sep 7, 1907 in Bogni di Lucca, Italy
Source: *ChhPo, S1, S3; ConAu 117; DcEnA A; DcNaB S2; NewC; NewCBEL*

Leek, Sybil
[Sybil Falk]
English. Astrologer, Author
Predicted assassinations of Kennedys, election of Nixon to presidency; wrote *Diary of a Witch,* 1968.
b. Feb 22, 1917 in Stoke-on-Trent, England
d. Oct 26, 1982 in Melbourne, Florida
Source: *AnObit 1982; BioIn 13; ConAu 102, 108; EncO&P 1; LegTOT; NewYTBS 82; ScF&FL 1, 2, 92; WhoAm 80, 82; WrDr 80, 82*

Lee Kuan Yew
Singaporean. Political Leader
Proponent of parliamentary democracy for the Republic of Singapore; became its first prime minister, 1965-90.
b. Sep 16, 1923, Singapore
Source: *BioIn 5, 7, 8, 9, 10, 11, 12, 13, 14, 15; CurBio 59, 95; DcMPSA; DcTwHis; EncWB; FacFETw; FarE&A 78, 79, 80, 81; HisDBrE; IntWW 74, 75, 76, 77, 78, 79, 80, 81, 82, 83, 89, 91, 93; IntYB 78, 79, 80, 81, 82; Who 74, 82, 83, 85, 88, 90, 92, 94; WhoAsAP 91; WhoGov 72; WhoWor 74, 76, 78, 80, 82, 84, 87, 89, 91, 93, 95, 96, 97*

Leemans, Tuffy
[Alphonse E Leemans]
American. Football Player
Halfback, NY Giants, 1936-43; led NFL in rushing, 1936; Hall of Fame, 1978.
b. 1915 in Superior, Wisconsin
d. Jan 19, 1979 in Hillsboro Beach, Florida
Source: *BioIn 9, 11; LegTOT; NewYTBS 79; WhoFtbl 74*

Lee-Smith, Hughie
American. Artist
Painted pictures depicting the isolation of black Americans.
b. Sep 20, 1915 in Eustis, Florida
Source: *AfrAmAl 6; AfroAA; BioIn 11, 19, 20; ConBlB 5; DcTwCCu 5; InB&W 80, 85; NegAl 76, 83; WhAmArt 85; WhoAfA 96; WhoAm 74, 76, 78, 80, 82, 84, 86, 88, 90, 92, 94, 95, 96, 97; WhoAmA 73, 76, 78, 80, 82, 84, 86, 89, 91, 93; WhoBlA 77, 80, 85, 88, 90, 92, 94; WhoE 74*

Leetch, Brian
American. Hockey Player
Defenseman, NY Rangers, 1988—; won Calder Trophy, 1989; Conn Smythe Trophy, 1994; Norris Trophy, 1991-92.
b. Mar 3, 1968 in Corpus Christi, Texas
Source: *BioIn 16, 21; WhoAm 92, 94, 95*

Lee Teng-hui
Taiwanese. Political Leader
Pres., Taiwan, 1988—.
b. Jan 15, 1923 in Tamsui, Taiwan
Source: *CurBio 96; FacFETw; IntWW 89, 91, 93; WhoAsAP 91; WhoWor 91, 93, 97*

Leeuwenhoek, Antonie van
Dutch. Naturalist
Pioneered in microscopy; discovered protozoa; described bacteria, 1683; studied capillary circulation.
b. Oct 24, 1632 in Delft, Netherlands
d. Aug 26, 1723
Source: *AsBiEn; BiDPsy; DcInv; DcScB; LinLib L, S; McGEWB; NewCol 75; WorAl*

Lefall, LaSalle Doheny, Jr.
American. Surgeon, Educator
Professor of surgery, dept. chm., Howard U College of Medicine, 1970—.
b. May 22, 1930 in Quincy, Florida
Source: *ConBlB 3*

LeFanu, Joseph Sheridan
Irish. Author
Eerie tales of supernatural include *House By the Churchyard,* 1863.
b. Aug 28, 1814 in Dublin, Ireland
d. Feb 7, 1873 in Dublin, Ireland
Source: *BritAu 19; CasWL; DcLB; DcLEL; DcNaB; NewCol 75; OxCEng 67; REn*

Lefebvre, Marcel Francois
French. Religious Leader
Arch-conservative Catholic archbishop opposed to Vatican II changes; excommunicated for consecrating bishops against pope's wishes, 1988.
b. Nov 29, 1905 in Tourcoing, France
d. Mar 25, 1991 in Martigny, Switzerland
Source: *BioIn 11, 13, 14, 16; CurBio 78, 91N; IntWW 83, 91N; News 88; NewYTBS 91; WorAlBi*

Lefever, Ernest Warren
American. Educator
Reagan's nominee; rejected as assistant secretary of State for Human Rights, 1981; first turned down by Senate.
b. Nov 12, 1919 in York, Pennsylvania
Source: *AmMWSc 73S, 78S; ConAu 1NR; WhoAm 86, 90*

LeFleming, Christopher Kaye
English. Composer, Educator
Wrote "Five Psalms"; orchestral suite *London River.*
b. Feb 26, 1908 in Wimborne Minster, England
d. Jun 19, 1985 in Woodbury, England
Source: *Baker 78; ConAu 117; IntWWM 77, 80; WhoMus 72*

LeFlore, Ron(ald)
American. Baseball Player
Outfielder, 1974-82, signed out of prison; only player in ML history to lead both leagues in stolen bases, AL, 1978, NL, 1980.
b. Jun 16, 1952 in Detroit, Michigan
Source: *Ballpl 90; BioIn 10, 11, 13, 16; ConAu 115; InB&W 80, 85; WhoBlA 77, 85; WorAl*

Le Gallienne, Eva
American. Actor, Author
Founded Civic Repertory Theatre, 1926-32; won special Tony, 1964; Emmy for "The Royal Family," 1978.
b. Jan 11, 1899 in London, England
d. Jun 3, 1991 in Weston, Connecticut
Source: *AmAu&B; AmCulL; AmWomWr; AnObit 1991; AuBYP 2, 3; Benet 87; BenetAL 91; BiE&WWA; BioIn 1, 2, 3, 4, 6, 7, 10, 11, 12, 13, 14, 15, 16, 17, 18, 19, 20, 21; BlueB 76; CamGWoT; CnThe; ConAu 45, 134; ConTFT 1, 10; CurBio 55, 91N; EncWT; Ent; FamA&A; FemiCLE; FilmEn; GayLesB; GrLiveH; GrStDi; HalFC 84, 88; IntAu&W 76, 77, 89; IntDcT 3; IntMPA 82, 84, 86, 88; IntWW 74, 75, 76, 77, 78, 79, 80, 81, 82, 83, 89, 91; InWom, SUP; LegTOT; LibW; LinLib L, S; NewYTBS 81, 82, 84, 91; NotNAT, A; NotWoAT; OxCAmL 83; OxCAmT 84; OxCThe 67, 83; PlP&P; REn; REnAL; SmATA 9, 68; TheaDir; VarWW 85; WebAB 74, 79; WhAm 10; Who 74, 82, 83, 85, 88, 90, 92N; WhoAm 74, 76, 78, 80, 82, 84, 86, 88, 90; WhoAmW 58, 61, 64, 66, 68, 70, 72, 74, 83, 85, 87, 89; WhoHol 92, A; WhoThe 72, 77, 81; WhoWor 74; WorAl; WorAlBi*

LeGallienne, Richard
English. Poet, Essayist
Influenced by Oscar Wilde; best known work *From a Paris Garret,* 1936.
b. Jan 20, 1866 in Liverpool, England
d. Sep 14, 1947 in Menton, France
Source: *Alli SUP; AnCL; BiD&SB; ConAu 107; EvLB; LngCTC; MouLC 4; NewC; ObitOF 79; OxCAmL 65; OxCEng 67; PenC ENG; TwCA, SUP; WebE&AL; WhAm 2; WhLit; WhNAA*

Legendre, Adrien Marie
French. Mathematician
Noted for theory of numbers published in *Theorie des Nombres,* 1830.
b. Sep 18, 1752 in Paris, France
d. Jan 10, 1833 in Paris, France
Source: *BbD; BiD&SB; BioIn 1, 2; CelCen; DcBiPP; DcScB; InSci; NewCol 75; WhDW*

Leger, Alexis St. Leger
[Marie-Rene Alexis St. Leger Leger; St. John Perse]
French. Poet
Verse collections include *Oiseaux,* 1962; won 1960 Nobel Prize.
b. May 31, 1887, Guadeloupe
d. Sep 20, 1975 in Giens, France
Source: *AnCL; ConAu 61; EncWL; IntWW 74; LinLib L, S; OxCFr; PenC EUR; PseudN 82; REn; TwCA, SUP; TwCWr; WhAm 6; Who 74; WhoNob; WhoTwCL; WhoWor 74; WorAl*

Leger, Fernand
French. Artist
Cubist; drew mechanical subjects, monumental figures; made experimental films.
b. Feb 4, 1881 in Argentan, France

d. Aug 17, 1955 in Gif-sur-Yvette, France
Source: *AtlBL; Benet 87, 96; BioIn 1, 2, 3, 4, 5, 6, 8, 9, 10, 11, 12, 13, 14, 16, 17, 21; ClaDrA; CnOxB; ConArt 77, 83; ConAu 123; CurBio 43, 55; DcArts; DcFM; DcTwCCu 2; EncWT; FacFETw; FilmEn; IntDcAA 90; LegTOT; MakMC; McGDA; McGEWB; ObitT 1951; OxCArt; OxCFilm; OxCTwCA; OxDcArt; PhDcTCA 77; PlP&P; REn; WebBD 83; WhDW; WorAl; WorAlBi; WorArt 1950; WorECar; WorEFlm*

Leger, Jules
Canadian. Statesman
Governor-general of Canada, 1974-79.
b. Apr 4, 1913 in Saint Anicet, Quebec, Canada
d. Nov 22, 1980 in Ottawa, Ontario, Canada
Source: *AmCath 80; AnObit 1980; BioIn 11, 12; BlueB 76; CanWW 70, 79, 80; CurBio 76, 81, 81N; IntWW 74, 75, 76, 77, 78, 79, 80; IntYB 78, 79, 80, 81; WhAm 7; Who 74; WhoAm 76, 78, 80; WhoCan 73, 75, 77, 80; WhoE 75, 77, 79; WhoWor 74, 76, 78, 80*

Legg, Adrian
English. Musician
Acoustic guitarist who released albums *Requiem for a Hick,* 1977, *Techno Picker,* 1984, and *High Strung Tall Tales,* 1994; named *Guitar Player* Magazine best acoustic fingerstyle guitarist, 1993-1994 and best overall guitar album of the year, 1994, for *Wine, Women and Waltz.*
b. May 16, 1948 in London, England
Source: *ConMus 17; OnThGG*

Legg, W(illiam) Dorr
American. Scholar
Involved with several gay rights organizations, including the Mattachine Society and ONE, Inc; one of the leaders who emerged from the Stonewall Riots of 1959.
b. Dec 15, 1904 in Ann Arbor, Michigan
d. Jul 26, 1994 in Los Angeles, California
Source: *GayLesB*

Leggett, William
American. Football Pioneer
With William Gummere, set up rules, organized first American football game, 1869.
b. Oct 12, 1848 in Ghent, New York
d. Oct 28, 1925
Source: *WhoFtbl 74*

Leginska
American. Conductor, Musician
One of first women symphony conductors; founded Boston Philharmonic, 1926.
b. Apr 13, 1880 in Hull, England
d. Feb 26, 1970 in Los Angeles, California
Source: *NotAW MOD*

Legrand, Michel Jean
French. Composer, Conductor
Composed scores of over 50 films including *Summer of '42,* 1971.
b. Feb 24, 1932 in Paris, France
Source: *Baker 84; BiDJaz; BioIn 14; BioNews 74; ConAu 114; ConTFT 9; DcFM; FilmgC; HalFC 88; IntMPA 86, 92, 94, 96; NewAmDM; NewGrDJ 88; OxCFilm; OxCPMus; PenEncP; VarWW 85; WhoAm 96, 97; WhoEnt 92; WhoWor 74; WorAlBi; WorEFlm*

LeGuin, Ursula K(roeber)
American. Author
Writes science fiction, fantasy: *Left Hand of Darkness,* 1969; *Malafrena,* 1979.
b. Oct 21, 1929 in Berkeley, California
Source: *AuBYP 3; Benet 87; BenetAL 91; BioAmW; BioIn 13, 14, 15, 16; BroV; CamGLE; CamHAL; CelR 90; ConAu 9NR, 21R, 32NR; ConLC 8, 13, 22, 45, 71; ConNov 86, 91; ConSFF; CurBio 83; CyWA 89; DcLB 52; DrAPF 91; FacFETw; FemiCLE; IntvTCA 2; IntWW 91; InWom SUP; MajTwCW; ModAL S2; NewEScF; OxCChiL; PostFic; RGTwCSF; ScFSB; ShSWr; SmATA 4, 52; SupFW; TwCChW 83, 89; TwCSFW 86, 91; WhoAm 86, 90; WhoAmW 87, 91; WhoUSWr 88; WhoWrEP 89; WorAlBi; WrDr 86, 92*

Lehand, Missy
[Marguerite Alice Lehand]
American. Secretary
FDR's private secretary for 20 yrs.
b. 1898?
d. Jul 31, 1944 in London, England
Source: *BioIn 9; ObitOF 79*

Lehar, Franz
Hungarian. Composer
Numerous popular operettas include *The Merry Widow,* 1905.
b. Apr 30, 1870 in Romorn, Austria-Hungary
d. Oct 24, 1948 in Bad Ischl, Austria
Source: *Baker 78, 84, 92; Benet 87, 96; BioIn 1, 3, 4, 8, 9, 12; BriBkM 80; CmOp; CmpEPM; DcArts; DcCathB; DcCom 77; DcCom&M 79; FacFETw; LegTOT; MusMk; NewAmDM; NewGrDM 80; NewOxM; NotNAT B; OxCAmT 84; OxCMus; OxCPMus; OxDcOp; PenDiMP A; PlP&P; REn; WebBD 83; WhDW; WhoStg 1908; WhThe; WorAl; WorAlBi*

Lehman, Adele Lewisohn
American. Art Collector, Philanthropist
Her prestigious art collection donated largely to Metropolitan Museum.
b. May 17, 1882 in New York, New York
d. Aug 11, 1965 in Purchase, New York
Source: *DcAmB S7*

Lehman, Herbert Henry
"The Conscience of the Senate"
American. Philanthropist, Politician
Influential Dem. governor of NY, 1932-42; senator, 1949-56; liberal spokesman.
b. Mar 28, 1878 in New York, New York
d. Dec 5, 1963 in New York, New York
Source: *ApCAB X; BiDInt; BiDrAC; BiDrGov 1789; BiDrUSC 89; BioIn 1, 2, 3, 4, 5, 6, 7, 8, 9, 10, 11, 12, 14, 17; CurBio 43, 55, 64; DcAmB S7; EncAAH; EncAB-A 2; McGEWB; NatCAB 60; OxCAmH; PolProf E, K, T; WebAB 74, 79; WhAm 4; WhAmP*

Lehman, Hughie
[Frederick Hugh Lehman]
"Old Eagle Eyes"
Canadian. Hockey Player
Goalie, Chicago, 1926-28; Hall of Fame, 1958.
b. Oct 27, 1885 in Pembroke, Ontario, Canada
d. Apr 8, 1961 in Toronto, Ontario, Canada
Source: *HocEn; WhoHcky 73*

Lehman, John Francis, Jr.
American. Government Official
Youngest secretary of Navy when appointed by Reagan, 1981-87.
b. Sep 14, 1942 in Philadelphia, Pennsylvania
Source: *BioIn 13, 14, 15, 16; CngDr 83, 85; CurBio 85; NewYTBS 85, 89; WhoAm 86, 90; WhoAmP 83; WhoE 83; WhoWor 87*

Lehmann, John Frederick
English. Journalist
Influential editor *New Writing, London Magazine,* 1954-61; associated with Hogarth Press, 1931-46.
b. Jun 2, 1907 in Bourne End, England
d. Apr 7, 1987 in London, England
Source: *Au&Wr 71; BlueB 76; CasWL; ColdWar 2; ConAu 9R; ConPo 70, 75, 85; DcLEL; EvLB; IntAu&W 76, 77, 82, 89, 91; IntWW 74, 75, 76, 77, 78, 79, 80, 81, 82, 83; IntWWP 77; LngCTC; ModBrL; NewC; OxCEng 67; PenC ENG; REn; TwCA, SUP; TwCWr; WebE&AL; WhE&EA; Who 74, 82, 83, 85; WhoAdv 90; WhoMW 88; WhoWor 74, 76, 78, 82, 84, 87; WrDr 76, 86*

Lehmann, Lilli
German. Opera Singer
Noted dramatic soprano, excelled as Wagner, Mozart heroines; sang 170 different roles.
b. Nov 24, 1848 in Wurzburg, Germany
d. May 17, 1929 in Berlin, Germany
Source: *ApCAB SUP; Baker 78, 84, 92; BiDAmM; BioIn 1, 2, 3, 7, 11, 14, 15; BriBkM 80; CmOp; ContDcW 89; FacFETw; IntDcOp; IntDcWB; InWom, SUP; LegTOT; MetOEnc; MusSN; NewAmDM; NewEOp 71; NewGrDA 86; NewGrDM 80; NewGrDO; OxDcOp; PenDiMP; WomFir; WorAl; WorAlBi*

Lehmann, Lotte
American. Opera Singer
Soprano, known for interpretation of German lieder.
b. Feb 27, 1888 in Perlberg, Germany
d. Aug 26, 1976 in Santa Barbara, California
Source: *Baker 78, 84, 92; BioIn 12, 14, 15, 16, 21; BlueB 76; BriBkM 80; CmCal; CmOp; ConAu 69, 73; ContDcW 89; CurBio 76, 76N; DcAmB S10; DcArts; FacFETw; IntDcOp; IntDcWB; IntWW 74, 75, 76; IntWWM 77; InWom; LegTOT; LibW; MetOEnc; MusMk; MusSN; NewAmDM; NewEOp 71; NewGrDA 86; NewGrDM 80; NewGrDO; NewYTBS 76; OxDcOp; PenDiMP; REn; WhAm 7, 8; What 2; Who 74; WhoAm 74, 76; WhoAmW 68, 70, 72, 74; WhoMus 72; WhoWor 74; WhScrn 83; WomFir*

Lehmann, Rosamond Nina
English. Author
Novels include *The Ballad and the Source,* 1945; *The Sea-Grape Tree,* 1976; sister of John Frederick.
b. Feb 3, 1901 in London, England
d. Mar 12, 1990 in London, England
Source: *Au&Wr 71; Benet 87, 96; BioIn 13, 14, 15, 16; CamGEL; CamGLE; CasWL; ConAu 8NR, 77, 131; ConLC 5; ConNov 76, 82, 86; ContDcW 89; CyWA 89; DcArts; DcLB 15; DcNaB 1986; EncBrWW; EncWL; EvLB; FemiCLE; GayLL; GrWrEL N; IntAu&W 77, 91; IntWW 89; InWom SUP; LngCTC; ModBrL; NewC; NewYTBS 90; Novels; OxCEng 85, 95; RAdv 1; REn; RfGEnL 91; RGTwCWr; TwCRHW 94; Who 90; WrDr 90*

Lehmann-Haupt, Christopher Charles Herbert
American. Critic
Senior book reviewer, *NY Times,* 1969—
b. Jun 14, 1934 in Edinburgh, Scotland
Source: *BioIn 15; ConAu 109; WhoAm 84, 86, 90, 92, 94, 95, 96, 97; WhoE 74, 77; WhoUSWr 88; WhoWrEP 89, 92, 95; WrDr 92*

Lehmann-Haupt, Hellmut Emil
American. Author
Authority on bibliography, book making and graphic arts; wrote *Life of the Book,* 1957.
b. Oct 4, 1903 in Berlin, Germany
d. Mar 11, 1992 in Columbia, Missouri
Source: *Au&Wr 71; BiDrLUS 70; ConAu 9R; CurBio 42, 61; DrAS 74H; LinLib L; WhoAm 74*

Lehmbruck, Wilhelm
German. Sculptor
Expressionist; did numerous nudes, exaggerated figures: *Kneeling Woman,* 1911.
b. Jan 4, 1881 in Meidereich, Germany
d. Mar 25, 1919 in Berlin, Germany
Source: *AtlBL; BioIn 1, 4, 5, 7, 8, 9, 14, 17; DcArts; McGDA; McGEWB; OxCArt; OxCTwCA; OxDcArt; PhDcTCA 77*

Lehn, Jean-Marie
French. Chemist
Shared Nobel Prize in chemistry, 1987, for research in energy technology.
b. Sep 30, 1939? in Rosheim, France
Source: *BioIn 15; IntWW 91; LarDcSc; NewYTBS 87; NobelP 91; NotTwCS; Who 90, 92, 94; WhoAm 90; WhoFr 79; WhoNob 90; WhoWor 91; WorAlBi*

Lehr, Lew
American. Actor
Did comic narration for Movietone's *Monkies Is the Kwaziest People.*
b. May 14, 1895 in Philadelphia, Pennsylvania
d. Mar 6, 1950 in Brookline, Massachusetts
Source: *BioIn 2; LegTOT; WhoHol B; WhScrn 74, 77, 83*

Lehrer, Jim
[James Charles Lehrer]
American. Broadcast Journalist
Associate editor, co-anchor "The MacNeil-Lehrer Report," 1975-83; "The MacNeil-Lehrer News Hour," 1983-95; anchor, "The NewsHouse with Jim Lehrer," 1995.
b. May 19, 1934 in Wichita, Kansas
Source: *BioIn 12, 13, 15; CelR 90; ConAu 114; ConTFT 15; CurBio 87; EncTwCJ; IntMPA 96; LegTOT; LesBEnT 92; NewYTBS 88; NewYTET; VarWW 85; WhoAm 86, 90, 97; WhoAmP 91; WhoTelC; WhoUSWr 88; WhoWrEP 89; WorAlBi; WrDr 92*

Lehrer, Tom
[Thomas Andrew Lehrer]
American. Songwriter
Satirical ditties collected in album *An Evening Wasted With Tom Lehrer,* 1959; songs popular again in "Tom Foolery" revue, 1980s.
b. Apr 9, 1928 in New York, New York
Source: *AmAu&B; ASCAP 66, 80; BioIn 3, 4, 5, 7, 12, 13, 14, 15; BlueB 76; ConAu 123, X; ConMus 7; CurBio 82; EncAHmr; EncFCWM 69; IntWWM 77, 80, 85, 90; JoeFr; LegTOT; NewAmDM; NewGrDA 86; OxCPMus; PenEncP; PeoHis; VarWW 85; Who 74, 82, 83, 85, 88, 90, 92, 94; WhoAm 74, 76, 78, 80, 82, 84, 86, 88, 90, 92, 94, 95; WhoCom; WhoEnt 92; WhoWor 74*

Leiber, Fritz (Reuter), Jr.
[Francis Lathrop]
American. Author
Popular horror, science-fiction writer, noted for "Fafhrd and Gray Mouser" series; won 6 Hugos, 3 Nebulas and 2 World Fantasy awards.
b. Dec 25, 1910 in Chicago, Illinois
d. Sep 5, 1992 in San Francisco, California
Source: *AmAu&B; AnObit 1992; BioIn 7, 12, 13, 15, 17, 18, 19; ConAu 2NR, 45; ConLC 25, 76; ConNov 76, 82, 86, 91; ConSFA; DcLB 8; DcLP 87A; DrAF 76; DrAPF 80, 91; DrmM 2; EncSF; IntvTCA 2; LegTOT; LinLib L; MajTwCW; NewEScF; Novels; PenEncH; PseudN 82; RGSF; RGTwCSF; ScF&FL 1, 2, 92; ScFSB; ScFWr; SJGFanW; SmATA 45; SupFW; TwCSFW 81, 86, 91; WhAm 10; WhoAm 82, 84, 90, 92; WhoHr&F; WhoSciF; WhoUSWr 88; WhoWrEP 89, 92; WorAu 1975; WrDr 76, 80, 82, 84, 86, 88, 90, 92*

Leiber, Judith
American. Designer
Founded Judith Leiber, Inc., 1963, a handbag manufacturer.
b. 1921, Hungary
Source: *ConFash; CurBio 96; WorFshn*

Leibman, Ron
American. Actor
Starred in film *Norma Rae,* 1979; won 1993 Tony for *Angels in America.*
b. Oct 11, 1937 in New York, New York
Source: *BioIn 12, 14; ConTFT 2, 7; EncAFC; FilmEn; HalFC 80, 84, 88; IntMPA 77, 80, 88, 92, 94, 96; LegTOT; NewYTBE 70; NotNAT; VarWW 85; WhoAm 80, 82, 84, 86, 88, 90, 92, 94, 95, 96, 97; WhoEnt 92; WhoHol 92, A; WhoThe 72, 77, 81*

Leibniz, Gottfried Wilhelm von
"A Living Dictionary"; "The First of Philosophers"
German. Philosopher, Mathematician
Developed dynamic theory of motion, 1676; invented the calculus independent of Newton, 1684; wrote *Essais de theodicee,* 1710.
b. Jul 1, 1646 in Leipzig, Germany
d. Nov 14, 1716 in Hannover, Germany
Source: *BbD; BiD&SB; BiDPsy; CasWL; CyEd; DcBiPP; DcEuL; DcInv; Dis&D; EncUnb; EuAu; EvEuW; HisDcDP; LuthC 75; NamesHP; NewC; NewCBEL; OxCEng 67; OxCGer 76, 86; OxCLaw; PseudN 82; REn*

Leibovitz, Annie
[Anna-Lou Leibovitz]
American. Photographer
Celebrity photographer; chief photographer, *Rolling Stone,* 1973-83; *Vanity Fair,* 1983—; won Clio for American Express series, 1988.
b. Oct 2, 1949 in Westbury, Connecticut
Source: *Au&Arts 11; BioIn 10, 11, 13, 14, 16; ConAu 140; CurBio 91; GrLiveH; ICPEnP A; LegTOT; News 88; NorAmWA; WhoAdv 90; WhoAm 90, 92, 94, 95, 96, 97; WhoAmW 91, 93, 95, 97; WrDr 96*

Leibowitz, Rene
French. Composer, Conductor
Used 12-tone method of composition; books include *Thinking for Orchestra,* 1958.
b. Feb 17, 1913 in Warsaw, Poland
d. Aug 28, 1972 in Paris, France

Source: *Baker 78, 84, 92; BioIn 9; ConAu 37R; DcCM; NewAmDM; NewGrDM 80; NewGrDO; NewOxM; OxCMus; PenDiMP; WhAm 5; WhoMus 72*

Leibowitz, Samuel Simon
"Sentencing Sam"
American. Lawyer
Criminal lawyer, noted for winning release of Negro defendents from death sentence in Scottsboro case, 1930s.
b. Aug 14, 1893, Romania
d. Jan 11, 1978 in New York, New York
Source: *BioIn 2, 3, 4, 5, 6, 9, 11, 12; CopCroC; CurBio 53; DcAmB S10; ObitOF 79; PseudN 82*

Leider, Frida
German. Opera Singer
Wagnerian soprano of 1920s-40s; wrote autobiography.
b. Apr 18, 1888 in Berlin, Germany
d. Jun 4, 1975 in Berlin, Germany (West)
Source: *Baker 78, 84, 92; BioIn 4, 7, 10, 11, 12, 15; BriBkM 80; CmOp; ConAu 57; IntDcOp; InWom; MetOEnc; MusSN; NewAmDM; NewEOp 71; NewGrDM 80; NewGrDO; ObitT 1971; OxDcOp; PenDiMP*

Leidy, Joseph
American. Scientist
Famed anatomist, pioneer paleontologist; wrote standard text *Treatise on Human Anatomy,* 1861; *Fossil Horse of America,* 1847.
b. Sep 9, 1823 in Philadelphia, Pennsylvania
d. Apr 30, 1891 in Philadelphia, Pennsylvania
Source: *Alli, SUP; AmBi; ApCAB; BbtC; BiDAmEd; BiDAmS; BiHiMed; BiInAmS; BioIn 8, 9, 12; CyAL 1; DcAmAu; DcAmB; DcAmMeB, 84; DcBiPP; DcNAA; DcScB; Drake; EncAB-H 1974, 1996; InSci; IntDcAn; NatCAB 5; OxCAmH; TwCBDA; WebAB 74, 79; WhAm HS*

Leigh, Carolyn
American. Songwriter
Wrote lyrics to songs "Hey, Look Me Over"; "The Best is Yet to Come"; "Young at Heart."
b. Apr 21, 1926 in New York, New York
d. Nov 19, 1983 in New York, New York
Source: *AmPS; AnObit 1983; ASCAP 66, 80; BiE&WWA; BioIn 10, 12, 13, 15, 19; ConAu 111; EncMT; InWom SUP; NewCBMT; NewYTBS 83; NotNAT; OxCPMus; WhoAmW 58, 61, 64, 66, 68*

Leigh, Janet
[Jeanette Helen Morrison]
American. Actor
Starred in *Psycho,* 1960; mother of actress Jamie Lee Curtis.
b. Jul 6, 1927 in Merced, California
Source: *BiDFilm, 81, 94; BioIn 1, 2, 3, 4, 6, 9, 12, 14, 18, 21; ConAu 134; ConTFT 3; EncAFC; FilmEn; FilmgC; ForYSC; GangFlm; HalFC 80, 84, 88; IntDcF 1-3, 2-3; IntMPA 75, 76, 77, 78, 79, 80, 81, 82, 84, 86, 88, 92, 94, 96; InWom, SUP; ItaFilm; LegTOT; MGM; MotPP; MovMk; OxCFilm; PseudN 82; VarWW 85; WhoAm 74, 82, 84, 86, 88, 90, 92, 94, 95, 96, 97; WhoAmW 58, 61, 64, 66, 68, 70, 72, 74; WhoEnt 92; WhoHol A; WhoHrs 80; WorAl; WorAlBi; WorEFlm; WrDr 94, 96*

Leigh, Jennifer Jason
[Jennifer Morrow]
American. Actor
Known for portrayals of prostitutes, abused and disturbed women, drug addicts; films include *Last Exit to Brooklyn,* 1990; *Single White Female,* 1992; *Mrs. Parker and the Vicious Circle,* 1994.
b. Feb 5, 1962 in Los Angeles, California
Source: *BioIn 12, 13, 15; ConTFT 8, 12; CurBio 92; IntMPA 92, 94, 96; News 95, 95-2; NewYTBS 82; WhoAm 94, 95, 96, 97; WhoAmW 93, 95, 97; WhoEnt 92; WhoHol 92*

Leigh, Mike
English. Director, Filmmaker
Made films *High Hopes,* 1988; *Life Is Sweet,* 1990; directed many plays including *Down Here and Up There,* 1968.
b. Feb 20, 1943 in Salford, England
Source: *BiDFilm 94; BioIn 17, 18, 19, 20; CamGWoT; ConAu 31NR, 109; ConBrDr; ConDr 82, 88, 93; ConTFT 6, 14; CurBio 94; DcArts; EncEurC; IntAu&W 89, 91, 93; IntDcT 2; IntMPA 94, 96; IntWW 91, 93; MiSFD 9; RGTwCWr; Who 82, 83, 85, 88, 90, 92, 94; WhoThe 81; WhoWor 95, 96, 97; WrDr 88, 90, 92, 94, 96*

Leigh, Mitch
[Irwins Michnick]
American. Composer
Notable works include "Man of La Mancha" featuring "The Impossible Dream," 1965.
b. Jan 30, 1928 in New York, New York
Source: *ASCAP 66, 80; Baker 84, 92; BioIn 7, 9, 10, 12, 15; ConTFT 1; EncMT; LegTOT; NewAmDM; NewCBMT; NewGrDA 86; NewGrDM 80; NewGrDO; NotNAT; OxCAmT 84; OxCPMus; PopAmC SUP; PseudN 82; VarWW 85; WhoAdv 72; WhoAm 74, 76, 78, 80*

Leigh, Vivien
[Vivian Mary Hartley]
English. Actor
Played Scarlett O'Hara in *Gone With the Wind,* 1939.
b. Nov 5, 1913 in Darjeeling, India
d. Jul 7, 1967 in London, England
Source: *BiDFilm, 81, 94; BiE&WWA; BioIn 1, 2, 3, 5, 6, 7, 8, 9, 10, 11, 12, 14, 15, 16, 18; CamGWoT; CnThe; ContDcW 89; CurBio 46, 67; DcAmB S8; DcArts; DcNaB 1961; EncEurC; EncMT; EncWT; Ent; FacFETw; FamA&A; FilmAG WE; FilmEn; FilmgC; ForYSC; GoodHs; GrBr; HalFC 80, 84, 88; IlWWBF, A; IntDcF 1-3, 2-3; IntDcWB; InWom, SUP; LegTOT; MotPP; MovMk; NotNAT A, B; ObitT 1961; OxCFilm; OxCThe 67, 83; PlP&P; PseudN 82; ThFT; WhAm 4; WhoAmW 66, 68; WhoHol B; WhScrn 74, 77, 83; WhThe; WorAl; WorAlBi; WorEFlm*

Leighton, Clare Veronica Hope
English. Illustrator, Author
Her unique wood-engravings enhance classics, modern, children's books including *Four Hedges,* 1935.
b. Apr 12, 1900 in London, England
d. Jan 1990 in Waterbury, Connecticut
Source: *AmAu&B; BiDWomA; BioIn 14, 15; ChhPo, S1; ClaDrA; ConAu 108; DcBrAr 1; GrAmP; IlsBYP; IlsCB 1946, 1957; LngCTC; NewCBEL; PeoHis; TwCA, SUP; Who 85, 90; WhoAm 88; WhoAmA 73; WhoAmW 87; WhoArt 84*

Leighton, Laura
[Laura Miller]
American. Actor
Appears on TV's "Melrose Place."
b. Jul 24, 1968 in Iowa City, Iowa

Leighton, Margaret
English. Actor
Won Tonys for *Separate Tables; Night of the Iguana.*
b. Feb 26, 1922 in Barnt Green, England
d. Jan 13, 1976 in Chichester, England
Source: *BiE&WWA; BioIn 4, 6, 7, 10, 11, 14; BlueB 76; CnThe; CurBio 57, 76N; EncWT; Ent; FacFETw; FilmAG WE; FilmEn; FilmgC; ForYSC; HalFC 80, 84, 88; IlWWBF; IntMPA 75, 76; InWom, SUP; LegTOT; MotPP; MovMk; NewYTBS 76; ObitOF 79; OxCAmT 84; OxCThe 67, 83; PlP&P; WhAm 6; Who 74; WhoAm 74; WhoAmW 64, 66, 68, 70, 72, 74, 75; WhoHol C; WhoThe 72, 77, 81N; WhoWor 74; WhScrn 83; WorAl; WorAlBi*

Leighton, Robert B(enjamin)
American. Physicist
Author of standard text *Principles of Modern Physics,* 1959; head of Mariner/Mars photointerpretation team, 1960s.
b. Sep 10, 1919
d. Mar 9, 1997 in Pasadena, California
Source: *AmMWSc 73P, 76P, 79, 82, 86, 89, 92, 95; BioIn 7; IntWW 74, 75, 76, 77, 78, 79, 80, 81, 82, 83, 89, 91, 93; WhoAm 74, 76, 78, 80, 82, 84, 88, 90, 92; WhoFrS 84; WhoScEn 96; WhoWest 89*

Leinsdorf, Erich
American. Conductor
Led Boston Symphony, 1962-69; NY Met., 1957-62; made many recordings.

b. Feb 4, 1912 in Vienna, Austria
d. Sep 11, 1993 in Zurich, Switzerland
Source: *AnObit 1993; Baker 78, 84, 92; BiDAmM; BioIn 1, 2, 4, 5, 6, 7, 8, 10, 11, 13, 14, 16, 19; BlueB 76; BriBkM 80; CelR; CmOp; ConAu 112, 119, 142; CurBio 40, 63, 93N; FacFETw; IntDcOp; IntWW 74, 75, 76, 77, 78, 79, 80, 81, 82, 83, 89, 91, 93; IntWWM 77, 80, 85, 90; LegTOT; LinLib S; MetOEnc; MusMk; MusSN; NewAmDM; NewEOp 71; NewGrDA 86; NewGrDM 80; NewGrDO; NewYTBS 93; OxDcOp; PenDiMP; VarWW 85; WhAm 11; Who 74, 82, 83, 85, 88, 90, 92; WhoAm 74, 76, 78, 80, 82, 84, 86, 88, 90, 92, 94; WhoAmM 83; WhoEnt 92; WhoMus 72; WhoOp 76; WhoWor 74, 78, 80, 82, 84, 87, 89; WorAl; WorAlBi*

Leiper, Robert Thomson
English. Scientist
Helminthologist who discovered cause of schistosomiasis.
b. Apr 17, 1881 in Kilmarnock, Scotland
d. May 21, 1969 in Saint Albans, England
Source: *BioIn 1, 9, 14; DcNaB 1961; GrBr; WhE&EA; WhLit*

Leitner, Ferdinand
German. Conductor
Music director, Stuttgart, 1947-69; Zurich, 1969-84.
b. Mar 4, 1912 in Berlin, Germany
Source: *Baker 84, 92; CmOp; IntWWM 77, 80, 90; MetOEnc; NewAmDM; NewGrDM 80; NewGrDO; OxDcOp; PenDiMP; WhoMus 72; WhoWor 84*

Leitzel, Lillian
[Mrs. Alfredo Codona; Leopoldina Alitza Pelikan]
German. Circus Performer, Gymnast
One of Ringling Brothers' top attractions, 1915-31; queen of circus aeralists; died after 29-ft. plunge.
b. 1892 in Breslau, Germany
d. Feb 15, 1931 in Copenhagen, Denmark
Source: *BioIn 4; GoodHs; LibW; NotAW; PseudN 82*

Leland, Charles Godfrey
[Hans Breitman; Mace Sloper]
American. Poet
Known for amusing dialect poems, sketches: *Hans Breitman's Barty,* 1857.
b. Aug 15, 1824 in Philadelphia, Pennsylvania
d. Mar 20, 1903 in Florence, Italy
Source: *Alli, SUP; AmAu; AmAu&B; AmBi; ApCAB; BbD; BibAL; BiD&SB; BiGAW; BioIn 5, 6, 8, 9, 14; CasWL; CelCen; Chambr 3; ChhPo, S1, S2, S3; CyAL 2; CyEd; DcAmAu; DcAmB; DcBiPP; DcEnA, A; DcEnL; DcLB 11; DcNAA; Drake; EncO&P 1, 2, 3; EncWW; EvLB; HarEnUS; LinLib L; NatCAB 5; OxCAmL 65, 83, 95; OxCEng 67; PenC AM; REn; ScF&FL 1; ScFEYrs; TwCBDA; WhAm 1*

Leland, Henry Martyn
American. Auto Manufacturer
Founded Cadillac Motor Co., 1902, Lincoln Motor Co., 1917.
b. Feb 16, 1843 in Danville, Vermont
d. Mar 26, 1932 in Detroit, Michigan
Source: *BioIn 4, 7, 10; EncABHB 4; NatCAB 40; WhAm 1; WorAl*

Leland, Mickey
[George Thomas Leland]
American. Politician, Social Reformer
Democratic congressman from TX, 1978-89; two-time chairman, Congressional Black Caucas; known for work with African famine; died in plane crash.
b. Nov 27, 1944 in Lubbock, Texas
d. Aug 7, 1989 in Gambela, Ethiopia
Source: *AfrAmAl 6; AlmAP 80, 82, 84, 88; AnObit 1989; BiDrUSC 89; BioIn 13, 16; BlkAmsC; CngDr 79, 81, 83, 85, 87, 89; ConBlB 2; NegAl 83, 89A; NewYTBS 78, 89; PolsAm 84; WhAm 10; WhoAm 80, 82, 84, 86, 88; WhoAmP 73, 75, 77, 79, 81, 83, 85, 87, 89; WhoBlA 77, 80, 85, 88, 90N; WhoSSW 80, 82, 86, 88*

Leland, Timothy
American. Editor
With *Boston Globe,* 1976-82; won Pulitzer for investigative reporting, 1972.
b. Sep 24, 1937 in Boston, Massachusetts
Source: *ConAu 102; EncTwCJ; WhoAm 74, 76, 78, 80, 82, 84, 86, 88, 90, 92, 94, 95, 96, 97*

Leloir, Luis Federico
Argentine. Chemist
Won Nobel Prize in chemistry, 1970, for discovering sugar nucleotides.
b. Sep 6, 1906 in Paris, France
d. Dec 2, 1987 in Buenos Aires, Argentina
Source: *BioIn 9, 13, 15, 16, 19, 20; IntWW 74, 75, 76, 77, 78, 79, 80, 81, 82, 83; McGMS 80; WhAm 11; Who 74, 82, 83, 85, 88; WhoNob, 90, 95; WhoWor 74, 76, 78, 80, 82, 84, 87, 89*

Lelong, Lucien
"First Gentleman of Fashion"
French. Designer
Led Paris fashions, 1919-49; perfumer; noted for lavish parties.
b. Oct 11, 1889 in Paris, France
d. May 11, 1958 in Paris, France
Source: *BioIn 4, 5; ConFash; CurBio 55, 58; DcArts; EncFash; FairDF FRA; ObitOF 79; WhAm 3; WhoFash 88; WorFshn*

LeLouch, Claude
French. Director
Won Best Foreign Film Oscar for *A Man and a Woman,* 1966.
b. Oct 30, 1937 in Paris, France
Source: *BiDFilm, 81, 94; BioIn 7, 10, 13, 16, 17; BioNews 74; ConAu 113; ConTFT 8; CurBio 82; DcFM; DcTwCCu 2; EncEurC; FilmEn; FilmgC; HalFC 80, 84, 88; IntDcF 1-2, 2-2; IntMPA 75, 76, 77, 78, 79, 80, 81, 82, 84, 86, 88, 92, 94, 96; IntWW 74, 75, 76, 77, 78, 79, 80, 81, 82, 83, 89, 91, 93; ItaFilm; LegTOT; MiSFD 9; MovMk; OxCFilm; VarWW 85; WhoAm 74; WhoFr 79; WhoHol 92; WhoWor 76, 78, 82, 84, 95, 96; WorAl; WorEFlm; WorFDir 2*

Lely, Peter, Sir
Dutch. Artist
Painted English aristocracy, ladies of Charles II's court, the "Windsor Beauties" series, 1660s.
b. Oct 14, 1618 in Soest, Germany
d. Dec 7, 1680 in London, England
Source: *AtlBL; Benet 87; BioIn 2, 4, 5, 6, 11, 15, 19; ClaDrA; DcArts; DcBiPP; DcNaB; IntDcAA 90; LegTOT; McGDA; McGEWB; NewCol 75; OxCArt; OxCEng 67, 85, 95; OxDcArt; REn; WhDW*

Lelyveld, Joseph Salem
American. Newspaper Editor
Started at *The New York Times,* 1962; managing editor, 1990-94, executive editor, 1994—.
b. Apr 5, 1937 in Cincinnati, Ohio
Source: *BlueB 76; IntAu&W 93; WhoAm 74, 76, 78, 90, 92, 94, 95, 96, 97; WhoE 93; WhoWor 74, 96, 97*

Lema, Tony
[Anthony David Lema]
"Champagne Tony"
American. Golfer
Won British Open, 1964; killed in plane crash.
b. Feb 25, 1934 in Oakland, California
d. Jul 24, 1966 in Munster, Indiana
Source: *BioIn 6, 7, 10, 13; ObitOF 79; WhoGolf*

Lemaire, Jacques Gerald
Canadian. Hockey Player
Center, Montreal, 1967-79, scoring at least 20 goals every season; won eight Stanley Cups.
b. Sep 7, 1945 in La Salle, Quebec, Canada
Source: *BioIn 13; HocEn; WhoHcky 73*

Lemaitre, Georges
Belgian. Astronomer
Devised big-bang theory that propounds a "super-atom" explosion as the beginnng of the universe.
b. Jul 17, 1894 in Charleroi, Belgium
d. Jun 20, 1966 in Louvain, Belgium
Source: *BioIn 2, 6, 7, 14, 20; DcScB S2; FacFETw; LegTOT; McGEWB; NotTwCS*

LeMay, Curtis Emerson
"Iron Eagle"
American. Air Force Officer, Politician
Air Force chief of staff; directed air assault over Japan in final days of WW II; commanded Berlin airlift after

WW II; vice presidential running mate of George Wallace, 1968.
b. Nov 15, 1906 in Columbus, Ohio
d. Oct 1, 1990 in Riverside, California
Source: *BiDWWGF; BioIn 1, 2, 3, 4, 5, 6, 7, 8, 11, 12, 15; ColdWar 2; CurBio 44, 54, 90, 90N; DcAmMiB; EncWB; FacFETw; HarEnMi; InSci; IntWW 83, 91N; NewYTBS 90; PresAR; WebAB 74, 79; WebAMB; WhoAm 74; WhoWor 74; WhWW-II; WorAl; WorAlBi*

Lembeck, Harvey
American. Actor
Comedian in 250 TV performances; with Phil Silvers in ''You'll Never Get Rich,'' 1955-59.
b. Apr 15, 1923 in New York, New York
d. Jan 5, 1982 in Los Angeles, California
Source: *BiE&WWA; BioIn 12, 13; EncAFC; ForYSC; IntMPA 75; NewYTBS 82; WhAm 8; WhoAm 74; WhoCom; WhoHol A*

Lemieux, Claude
Canadian. Hockey Player
Played for the Montreal Canadiens, 1983-90; New Jersey Devils, 1990-95; Colorado Avalanche, 1995—; won Conn Smythe Trophy, 1995.
b. Jul 16, 1965 in Buckingham, Quebec, Canada
Source: *BioIn 15, 16; News 96, 96-1; NewYTBS 86; WhoAm 96, 97*

Lemieux, Mario
Canadian. Hockey Player
Center, Pittsburgh, 1984-97; has scored over 40 goals every year in NHL; won Calder Trophy, 1985, NHL scoring championship 1987-88; Art Ross Trophy, 1988, 1989, 1992, 1993, 1996; Hart Trophy, 1988, 1993, 1996; Conn Smythe Trophy, 1991, 1992.
b. Oct 5, 1965 in Montreal, Quebec, Canada
Source: *BioIn 14, 15, 16, 18; ConNews 86-4; CurBio 88; HocReg 87; LegTOT; NewYTBS 84; WhoAm 90, 92, 94, 95, 96, 97; WhoSpor; WhoWor 95, 96; WorAlBi*

Lemmon, Jack
[John Uhler Lemmon, III]
American. Actor
Won Oscars for *Mister Roberts,* 1955; *Save the Tiger,* 1971; youngest person to receive the Life Achievement Award, 1988.
b. Feb 8, 1925 in Boston, Massachusetts
Source: *BiDFilm, 94; BiE&WWA; BioIn 3, 4, 5, 6, 7, 8, 10, 11, 12, 13, 14, 15, 16; BkPepl; BlueB 76; CelR, 90; CmMov; ConTFT 2, 7, 14; CurBio 61, 88; DcArts; DcTwCCu 1; EncAFC; FacFETw; FilmEn; FilmgC; ForYSC; Funs; HalFC 80, 84, 88; IntDcF 1-3, 2-3; IntMPA 77, 84, 86, 88, 92, 94, 96; IntWW 74, 75, 76, 77, 78, 79, 80, 81, 82, 83, 89, 91, 93; ItaFilm; LegTOT; MiSFD 9; MotPP; MovMk; OxCFilm; QDrFCA 92; VarWW 85; WhoAm 74, 76, 78, 80, 82, 84, 86, 88, 90, 92, 94, 95, 96, 97; WhoCom; WhoEnt 92; WhoHol 92, A; WhoWor 74, 76, 78, 95, 96, 97; WorAl; WorAlBi; WorEFlm*

Lemnitz, Tiana
French. Opera Singer
Leading German soprano, 1930s-50s.
b. Oct 26, 1897 in Metz, France
Source: *Baker 78, 84; BioIn 6, 7, 10, 19; CmOp; IntDcOp; IntWWM 90; InWom; MetOEnc; NewEOp 71; NewGrDM 80; OxDcOp; PenDiMP; WhoAmW 68, 70, 72*

Lemnitzer, Lyman Louis
American. Military Leader
Supreme Allied Commander in Europe, 1963-69; succeeded Maxwell Taylor as Commander of Far East Commmand, 1950s.
b. Aug 29, 1899 in Honesdale, Pennsylvania
d. Nov 12, 1988 in Washington, District of Columbia
Source: *BiDWWGF; BioIn 3, 4, 5, 6, 11, 16; BlueB 76; CmdGen 1991; CurBio 55; EncWB; IntWW 83; Who 85; WhoAm 74; WorAl*

Lemon, Bob
[Robert Granville Lemon]
American. Baseball Player, Baseball Manager
Pitcher, Cleveland, 1946-58; won at least 20 games in seven seasons; managed eight yrs. in AL; Hall of Fame, 1976.
b. Sep 22, 1920 in San Bernardino, California
Source: *Ballpl 90; BiDAmSp BB; BioIn 1, 2, 3, 4, 5, 10, 11, 12, 14, 15; FacFETw; LegTOT; NewYTBE 72; NewYTBS 78, 81; WhoAm 78, 80, 82; WhoProB 73; WhoSpor; WorAl; WorAlBi*

Lemon, Mark
English. Journalist
Co-founder, *Punch* mag; editor, 1841-70.
b. Nov 30, 1809 in London, England
d. May 23, 1870 in Cranley, England
Source: *Alli, SUP; BbD; BiD&SB; BioIn 7, 9, 16; BritAu 19; CamGLE; CasWL; CelCen; Chambr 3; ChhPo, S1; DcBiPP; DcEnA; DcEnL; DcEuL; DcLB 163; DcLEL; DcNaB; EvLB; LinLib L; NewC; NewCBEL; NotNAT B; OxCChiL; OxCEng 67, 85, 95; OxCThe 67; REn; StaCVF; VicBrit*

Lemon, Meadowlark
[Meadow George Lemon, III]
''The Clown Prince of Basketball''
American. Basketball Player
Center, star attraction, Harlem Globetrotters, 1954-78.
b. Apr 25, 1932 in Wilmington, North Carolina
Source: *LegTOT; VarWW 85; WhoAfA 96; WhoAm 74, 76, 78, 80, 82, 84, 86, 88; WhoBbl 73; WhoBlA 75, 77, 80, 88, 90, 92, 94*

Lemon, Ralph
American. Choreographer
Founded dance troupe, the Ralph Lemon Company, 1985.
b. Aug 1, 1952 in Cincinnati, Ohio

Lemon, Ted
American. Businessman
First American to head a Meursault, France vineyard, 1982—.
b. Jan 26, 1958 in Bedford, New York
Source: *ConNews 86-4*

LeMond, Greg(ory James)
American. Cyclist
First American in 83 yrs. to win Tour de France cycling race, 1986; also won in 1989, 1990.
b. Jun 26, 1961 in Los Angeles, California
Source: *BiDAmSp Sup; BioIn 13, 14, 15, 16, 17, 18, 19, 20, 21; CelR 90; ConHero 2; ConNews 86-4; CurBio 89; FacFETw; LegTOT; NewYTBS 83, 84, 89; WhoAm 90, 92, 94, 95, 96, 97; WhoWor 91, 93*

Lemonnier, Pierre Charles
French. Astronomer
Researched lunar activities for 50 yrs; recorded Uranus before recognized as a planet.
b. Nov 23, 1715 in Paris, France
d. May 31, 1799 in Bayeux, France
Source: *DcBiPP; DcScB; InSci; NewCol 75*

Lemoyne, Jean-Baptiste
French. Composer, Conductor
Wrote operas *Phedre,* 1786; *Nephte,* 1789.
b. Apr 3, 1751 in Eymet, France
d. Dec 30, 1796 in Paris, France
Source: *Baker 78, 84, 92; NewEOp 71; NewGrDM 80; NewGrDO*

Lemoyne, W(illiam) J
American. Actor
Played in first 100 productions of ''Uncle Tom's Cabin''; noted Dickens performer.
b. Apr 29, 1831 in Boston, Massachusetts
d. Nov 6, 1905 in New York, New York
Source: *DcAmB; NatCAB 5; NotNAT B; WhAm 1*

Lenard, Philipp Edward Anton
Hungarian. Scientist
Won 1905 Nobel Prize in physics; made contributions to study of atoms, falling drop theory, magnetism.
b. Jun 7, 1862 in Pressburg, Hungary
d. May 20, 1947 in Messelhausen, Germany
Source: *AsBiEn; BiESc; DcScB; Dis&D; EncTR; WhoNob*

Lenclos, Ninon de
[Anne DeLenclos]
French. Courtesan
Her beauty, wit attracted famous men of the day; wrote *La Coquette Vengee,* 1659.
b. Nov 10, 1620 in Paris, France
d. Oct 17, 1705 in Paris, France
Source: *LegTOT; NewCol 75; PenC EUR*

Lendl, Ivan
Czech. Tennis Player
Won US Open, 1985, defeating John McEnroe; won Australian Open, 1989.
b. Mar 7, 1960 in Ostrava, Czechoslovakia
Source: *BioIn 12, 13, 14, 15, 16; BuCMET; CelR 90; CurBio 84; FacFETw; IntWW 89, 91, 93; LegTOT; NewYTBS 82, 84, 86, 94; WhoAm 84, 88, 90, 92, 94; WhoSpor; WhoWor 87, 89, 91, 93, 95; WorAlBi*

L'Enfant, Pierre Charles
American. Engineer, Architect, Soldier
Designed plan for Washington, DC, 1791-92.
b. Aug 2, 1754 in Paris, France
d. Jun 14, 1825 in Green Hills, Maryland
Source: *AmBi; AmRev; AtlBL; BiDAmAr; BioIn 2, 3, 4, 6, 7, 8, 9, 11, 12, 14, 16; BriEAA; DcAmB; DcArts; DcCathB; EncAB-H 1974, 1996; EncAR; EncUrb; IntDcAr; LinLib S; MacEA; McGDA; McGEWB; NatCAB 16; OxCAmH; OxCAmL 65; PeoHis; REnAL; WebAB 74, 79; WhAm HS; WhAmRev; WhoArch; WorAl*

L'Engle, Madeleine
[Madeleine L'Engle Camp; Madeleine Franklin]
American. Author
Won 1963 Newbery for *A Wrinkle in Time.*
b. Nov 29, 1918 in New York, New York
Source: *AmAu&B; AmNov; AmWomWr; ArtclWW 2; Au&Arts 1; AuBYP 2, 3; AuNews 2; BenetAL 91; BioIn 2, 6, 7, 9, 10, 11, 12, 13, 14, 15, 16, 17, 18, 19, 21; BlmGWL; BlueB 76; ChhPo, S1, S3; ChlBkCr; ChlLR 1, 14; ConAu 1R, 3NR, 21NR; ConLC 12; ConPopW; DcAmChF 1960; DcLB 52; EncSF 93; IntAu&W 77, 86, 89, 91, 93; InWom; LegTOT; LinLib L; MajTwCW; ModWoWr; MorBMP; MorJA; NewbC 1956; NewEScF; OnHuMoP; OxCChiL; PiP; PseudN 82; RGTwCSF; ScF&FL 1, 2, 92; ScFSB; SenS; SmATA 1, 15AS, 27; TwCChW 78, 83, 89, 95; TwCSFW 81, 86, 91; TwCYAW; WhoAm 74, 76, 78, 80, 82, 84, 86, 88, 90, 92, 94, 95, 96, 97; WhoAmW 74, 75, 77, 79, 81, 83, 85, 87, 89, 91, 93, 95, 97; WhoE 74; WhoRel 85; WhoUSWr 88; WhoWor 82, 95, 96, 97; WhoWrEP 89, 92, 95; WorAlBi; WorAu 1985; WrDr 76, 80, 82, 84, 86, 88, 90, 92, 94, 96*

Lenglen, Suzanne
"Pavlova of Tennis"
French. Tennis Player
Won five consecutive Wimbledon singles titles, 1919-23, a record broken by Martina Navratilova, 1987.
b. May 24, 1899 in Compiegne, France
d. Jul 4, 1938 in Paris, France
Source: *BioIn 1, 3, 4, 5, 6, 9, 10, 11, 12, 14, 15, 16, 17; BuCMET; ContDcW 89; EncFash; GoodHs; IntDcWB; InWom, SUP; LegTOT; WhoHol B; WhoSpor; WhScrn 74, 77, 83; WomFir; WorAl; WorAlBi*

Lengyel, Emil
American. Historian
Authority on modern European politics, Nazism; wrote *Millions of Dictators,* 1936.
b. Apr 26, 1895 in Budapest, Austria-Hungary
d. Feb 12, 1985 in New York, New York
Source: *AmAu&B; AmMWSc 73S; BioIn 4, 9, 14, 15; ConAu 3NR, 9R, 115; CurBio 42, 85, 85N; DrAS 74H, 78H, 82H; REnAL; SmATA 3, 42N; TwCA, SUP; WhAm 8; WhE&EA; WhNAA; WhoAm 74, 76, 78; WhoWor 74*

Lenin, Vladimir Ilyich
[Nikolai Lenin; Joseph Richter; Vladimir Ilyich Ulyanov]
Russian. Political Leader, Author
Founder of Bolshevism; premier, 1918-24; established dictatorship of the proletariat; introduced socialist reforms.
b. Apr 22, 1870 in Simbirsk, Russia
d. Jan 21, 1924 in Gorki, Union of Soviet Socialist Republics
Source: *BiDPsy; BioIn 1, 2, 3, 4, 5, 6, 7, 8, 9, 10, 11, 12, 13; BlkwERR; CasWL; CopCroC; DcRusL; DcScB; Dis&D; EncUnb; HanRL; LinLib L, S; McGEWB; NamesHP; NewCol 75; OxCEng 67; RAdv 14, 13-3; REn; ThTwC 87; WhDW; WorAl; WorAlBi*

Lennon, Dianne
[Lennon Sisters]
American. Singer
With sisters, regulars on "The Lawrence Welk Show," 1955-71.
b. Dec 1, 1939? in Los Angeles, California
Source: *BioIn 4, 8, 9, 16; LegTOT; WorAl*

Lennon, Janet
[Lennon Sisters]
American. Singer
With sisters, had hit song "Sad Movies Make Me Cry," 1961.
b. Nov 15, 1946 in Culver City, California
Source: *BioIn 8, 9, 16; LegTOT; WorAl*

Lennon, Jimmy, Sr.
American. Boxing Ring Announcer
Ring announcer at the Olympic Auditorium, LA for many yrs., known for his eloquent style of announcing and for wearing a tuxedo; appeared in over 70 films as a ring announcer.
b. 1913?
d. Apr 20, 1992 in Santa Monica, California

Lennon, John Winston
[The Beatles]
English. Singer, Songwriter, Musician
"Love Me Do," 1962 first song written with Paul McCartney; solo career, 1970, included hit "Imagine," 1971.
b. Oct 9, 1940 in Liverpool, England
d. Dec 8, 1980 in New York, New York
Source: *Au&Wr 71; ConMus 9; CurBio 65, 81; HarEnR 86; IntWW 74; IntWWP 77; MotPP; WhoHol A; WhoWor 74; WrDr 76*

Lennon, Julian
[John Charles Julian Lennon]
English. Musician, Singer
Son of John Lennon; Paul McCartney wrote song "Hey Jude" for him; hit album *Valotte,* 1984.
b. Apr 8, 1963 in Liverpool, England
Source: *BioIn 14, 15, 16; ConMus 2; EncPR&S 89; EncRk 88; LegTOT; PenEncP; RkOn 85*

Lennon, Kathy
[Lennon Sisters]
American. Singer
With sisters, had hit song "Tonight You Belong to Me," 1956.
b. Aug 22, 1942 in Santa Monica, California
Source: *BioIn 8, 9, 16; LegTOT*

Lennon, Peggy
[Lennon Sisters]
American. Singer
With sisters, regulars on "The Lawrence Welk Show," 1955-71.
b. Apr 8, 1940 in Los Angeles, California
Source: *BioIn 8, 9, 16; LegTOT*

Lennox, Annie
Scottish. Singer
Androgynous-look singer with Eurythmics; singles include "Here Comes the Rain Again," 1984; solo album, *Diva,* 1992.
b. Dec 25, 1954 in Aberdeen, Scotland
Source: *Baker 92; BioIn 13, 14, 15, 16; ConNews 85-4; CurBio 88; EncRkSt; LegTOT; News 96; WhoAm 94, 95, 96, 97; WhoAmW 95, 97; WhoHol 92*

Leno, Jay
[James Douglas Muir Leno]
American. Comedian, TV Personality
Noted for "attitude comedy"; host of "The Tonight Show," 1992—; Emmy award winner, 1995.
b. Apr 28, 1950 in New Rochelle, New York
Source: *BioIn 14, 15, 16, 18; CelR 90; ConNews 87-1; ConTFT 6; CurBio 88; IntMPA 92, 94, 96; LegTOT; LesBEnT*

92; NewYTBS 89, 90; WhoAm 88, 90, 92, 94, 95, 96, 97; WhoCom; WhoEnt 92; WhoHol 92; WorAlBi

LeNotre, Andre
"The Father of Landscape Gardening"
French. Architect
Designed famous gardens including Versailles; The Vatican.
b. Mar 12, 1613 in Paris, France
d. Sep 15, 1700 in Paris, France
Source: *AtlBL; DcBiPP; McGDA; McGEWB; OxCFr; PseudN 82*

Lenox, Walter S
American. Manufacturer, Designer
Launched America's first fine china industry, 1894.
b. 1859
d. 1920
Source: *DcNiCA; Entr*

Lenska, Rula
[Roza-Maria Lubienska]
"The Fair One"
English. Actor
Rita Hayworth look-alike; noted for early 1980s TV commercials, "Who the hell is Rula Lenska?" fad.
b. Sep 30, 1947 in Saint Neots, England
Source: *BioIn 12; HalFC 84, 88; LegTOT; PseudN 82; WhoHol 92*

Lenski, Lois
American. Children's Author, Illustrator
Numerous books include 1946 Newbery prize-winner: *Strawberry Girl.*
b. Oct 14, 1893 in Springfield, Ohio
d. Sep 11, 1974 in Tarpon Springs, Florida
Source: *AmAu&B; AmWomWr; Au&ICB; Au&Wr 71; AuBYP 2, 3; BenetAL 91; BioIn 1, 2, 3, 4, 5, 7, 8, 9, 10, 11, 12, 13, 14, 19; BkCL; BkP; BlmGWL; CarSB; ChhPo, S1, S2; ChlBkCr; ChlLR 26; ConAu 41NR, 53, P-1; ConICB; DcLB 22; DcWomA; FamAIYP; HerW, 84; IlsCB 1744, 1946, 1957; InWom, SUP; JBA 34, 51; LinLib L; MajAI; NatCAB 63; NewbMB 1922; OhA&B; OxCChiL; REnAL; SmATA 1, 26; TwCChW 78, 83, 89; WhAm 6; WhAmArt 85; WhE&EA; WhNAA; Who 74; WhoAm 74; WhoAmA 73, 76, 78N, 80N, 82N, 84N, 86N, 89N, 91N, 93N; WhoAmW 58, 61, 64, 66, 68, 70, 72, 74*

Lenya, Lotte
[Karoline Blamauer; Mrs. Kurt Weill]
Austrian. Actor, Singer
Raspy-voiced star; won Tony for revival of *Threepenny Opera,* 1955.
b. Oct 18, 1900 in Vienna, Austria
d. Nov 27, 1981 in New York, New York
Source: *AmComp; AmPS; AmSong; ASCAP 66, 80; AtlBL; Baker 78, 84; Benet 87, 96; BenetAL 91; BestMus; BiDAmM; BiE&WWA; BioIn 1, 2, 3, 4, 5, 6, 7, 8, 9, 10, 11, 12, 13, 14, 15, 16, 18, 19, 20, 21; BriBkM 80; CamHAL; CmOp; CmpEPM; CnThe; CompSN, SUP; ConAmC 76, 82; ConMus 12; CurBio 59, 82; DancEn 78; DcAmB S4; DcCM; DcCom 77; EncMT; EncTR, 91; EncWT; FacFETw; FilmEn; FilmgC; ForYSC; HalFC 80, 84, 88; IntDcOp; IntWW 74, 75, 76, 77, 78, 79, 80, 81; LegTOT; MakMC; McGEWB; MetOEnc; MorBAP; MotPP; MusMk; NewAmDM; NewCBMT; NewEOp 71; NewGrDA 86; NewGrDM 80; NewOxM; NewYTBS 87; NotNAT, B; OxCAmT 84; OxCEng 85, 95; OxCFilm; OxCGer 76, 86; OxCMus; OxCPMus; OxDcOp; PenDiMP A; PenEncP; PlP&P; PopAmC, SUP; REn; WebAB 74, 79; WhAm 3; WhDW; WhoAmW 72; WhoHol A; WhoThe 72, 77, 81; WhThe; WorAl; WorAlBi; WorEFlm*

Lenz, Kay
American. Actor
Won Emmy, 1975, for "Heart in Hiding."
b. Mar 4, 1953 in Los Angeles, California
Source: *BioIn 10, 16; ConTFT 5, 12; HalFC 80, 84, 88; IntMPA 84, 86, 88, 92, 94, 96; LegTOT; VarWW 85; WhoAm 80, 82, 84, 86, 88, 90, 92, 94, 95; WhoAmW 83; WhoEnt 92; WhoHol 92*

Leo, Leonardo
Italian. Composer
Wrote over 60 operas; played important role in development of pre-classical symphony.
b. Aug 5, 1694 in San Vito, Italy
d. Oct 31, 1744 in Naples, Italy
Source: *Baker 78, 84, 92; BioIn 4, 7; BriBkM 80; DcBiPP; GrComp; MusMk; NewAmDM; NewEOp 71; NewGrDM 80; NewOxM; OxCMus; OxDcOp*

Leo Africanus
Arab. Traveler
Travelled widely in Africa; wrote *Description of Africa,* 1550, first book describing the Sudan.
b. 1465 in Granada, Spain
d. 1554
Source: *BiD&SB; OxCEng 67*

Leokum, Arkady
American. Author
Wrote *Tell Me Why* juvenile series.
b. 1916, Russia
Source: *BioIn 4, 15; ConAu 116; SmATA 45*

Leon, Henry Cecil
English. Author
Prolific writer of crime novels, plays, including *Cross Purposes,* 1976.
b. Sep 19, 1902 in Middlesex, England
d. May 21, 1976 in Brighton, England
Source: *BioIn 14; BlueB 76; ConAu 115; DcNaB 1971; IntAu&W 76; TwCCr&M 80; Who 74; WhoThe 77; WorAu 1950*

Leon, Kenny
American. Actor, Director
Artistic director, Alliance Theatre Company, Atlanta, GA, 1990—, the largest regional theatre in the southeast.
b. c. 1957
Source: *ConBlB 10*

Leonard
[Leonard Lewis]
English. Hairstylist
Introduced fad of brightly colored streaks in women's hairstyles.
Source: *ArtsEM; BioIn 3; DcCathB; DcWomA; EncASM; PseudN 82; Who 82, 83; WorFshn*

Leonard, Benny
[Benjamin Leiner]
"The Ghetto Wizard"; "The Mama's Boy"
American. Boxer
Great scientific boxer; lightweight winner, 1917, who made comeback as welterweight, 1931; Hall of Fame, 1955.
b. Apr 7, 1896 in New York, New York
d. Apr 18, 1947 in New York, New York
Source: *BiDAmSp BK; BioIn 1, 3, 4, 5, 7, 10, 14; BoxReg; PseudN 82; WhoBox 74; WhoSpor*

Leonard, Bill
[William Augustus Leonard, II]
American. Broadcasting Executive
Pres., CBS News, 1979-82.
b. Apr 9, 1916 in New York, New York
d. Oct 23, 1994 in Laurel, Maryland
Source: *BiDAmJo; BioIn 1, 5, 11, 15, 16, 20, 21; CurBio 95N; EncTwCJ; VarWW 85; WhoAm 74, 76, 78, 80, 82*

Leonard, Buck
[Walter Fenner Leonard]
"The Black Lou Gehrig"
American. Baseball Player
First baseman in Negro Leagues but never played in MLs; Hall of Fame, 1972.
b. Sep 8, 1907 in Rocky Mount, North Carolina
Source: *AfrAmSG; Ballpl 90; BiDAmSp BB; BioIn 10, 11, 14, 15, 21; LegTOT; WhoAfA 96; WhoBlA 77, 80, 85, 88, 90, 92, 94; WhoProB 73; WhoSpor*

Leonard, Dutch
[Hubert Benjamin Leonard]
American. Baseball Player
Lefthanded pitcher, Boston Red Sox, 1913-19, Detroit Tigers, 1919-25; accused Ty Cobb, Tris Speaker of fixing games in 1919.
b. Jul 26, 1892 in Birmingham, Ohio
d. Jul 11, 1952 in Fresno, California
Source: *BioIn 2, 3, 21; WhoProB 73*

Leonard, Dutch
[Emil John Leonard]
American. Baseball Player
Pitcher, 1933-53, known for throwing knuckleball; won 191 games in career.
b. Mar 25, 1909 in Auburn, Illinois
d. Apr 17, 1983 in Springfield, Illinois
Source: *Ballpl 90; BiDAmSp BB; BioIn 3, 13, 15*

Leonard, Eddie
[Lemuel Gordon Toney]
American. Actor
Worked in vaudeville minstrel shows for 45 yrs; composed "Ida, Sweet as Apple Cider."
b. Oct 18, 1875 in Richmond, Virginia
d. Jul 29, 1941 in New York, New York
Source: *ASCAP 66, 80; BiDAmM; BiDD; BioIn 14; CmpEPM; CurBio 41; DcNAA; Film 2; NewGrDA 86; NotNAT A, B; ObitOF 79; OxCAmT 84; OxCPMus; PseudN 82; WhoHol B; WhScrn 74, 77*

Leonard, Elmore John, Jr.
"Dutch"
American. Author
Prolific western, crime fiction writer: *City Primeval,* 1980; *La Brava,* 1983; *Glitz,* 1985; *Get Shorty,* 1990.
b. Oct 11, 1925 in New Orleans, Louisiana
Source: *BioIn 13, 14, 15, 16; ConAu 12NR, 28NR, 81; ConLC 28, 34, 71; ConNov 91; CrtSuMy; CurBio 85; EncFWF; IntAu&W 91; IntWW 91; MajTwCW; NewYTBS 84; TwCCr&M 85, 91; TwCWW 91; WhoAm 84, 86, 88, 90, 92, 94, 95, 96, 97; WhoUSWr 88; WhoWrEP 89, 92, 95; WorAlBi; WorAu 1980; WrDr 86, 92*

Leonard, Hugh
[John Keyes Byrne]
Irish. Dramatist
Won 1978 Tony for *Da.*
b. Nov 9, 1926 in Dublin, Ireland
Source: *Benet 96; BiDIrW; BioIn 10, 12, 13, 14; CamGLE; CamGWoT; ConAu 102; ConBrDr; ConDr 73, 77, 82, 88, 93; ConLC 19; ConTFT 6; CroCD; CrtSuDr; CurBio 83; DcIrL, 96; DcLB 13; DcLP 87B; FacFETw; IntAu&W 76, 82, 89, 91, 93; IntDcT 2; IntvTCA 2; IntWW 79, 80, 81, 82, 83, 89, 91, 93; IriPla; ModBrL S2; ModIrL; OxCIri; OxCThe 83; RGTwCWr; VarWW 85; Who 74, 82, 83, 85, 88, 90, 92, 94; WhoAm 80, 82, 84, 86, 88, 94, 95, 96, 97; WhoThe 72, 77, 81; WhoWor 82, 84, 87; WorAu 1970; WrDr 76, 80, 82, 84, 86, 88, 90, 92, 94, 96*

Leonard, Jack E
[Leonard Lebitsky]
"Fat Jack"
American. Comedian
Nightclub comedian whose trademark was one-line insults.
b. Apr 24, 1911 in Chicago, Illinois
d. May 9, 1973 in New York, New York
Source: *EncAFC; JoeFr; NewYTBE 73; NotNAT B; ObitOF 79; PseudN 82; WhAm 5; WhoHol B; WhScrn 77*

Leonard, John
American. Author
NY Times book review editor, 1971-76; wrote *Black Conceit,* 1973.
b. Feb 25, 1939 in Washington, District of Columbia
Source: *AmAu&B; BiDAmNC; BioIn 9, 10, 11; ConAu 12NR, 13R; DcLP 87A; DrAF 76; DrAPF 80, 91; ScF&FL 1, 2; Who 92; WhoE 74, 75*

Leonard, Sheldon
[Sheldon Leonard Bershad]
American. Actor, Producer
Produced TV shows "The Dick Van Dyke Show"; "I Spy."
b. Feb 22, 1907 in New York, New York
d. Jan 10, 1997 in Beverly Hills, California
Source: *BioIn 7, 21; BlueB 76; ConTFT 3; EncAFC; FilmEn; FilmgC; ForYSC; GangFlm; HalFC 80, 84, 88; HolCA; IntMPA 75, 76, 77, 78, 79, 80, 81, 82, 84, 86, 88, 92, 94, 96; LegTOT; LesBEnT 92; MotPP; MovMk; NewYTET; PseudN 82; RadStar; VarWW 85; Vers A; WhoAm 74, 76, 78, 80, 82, 84, 86, 88, 90, 92, 94, 95, 96, 97; WhoAmJ 80; WhoEnt 92; WhoHol 92, A; WorAl; WorAlBi*

Leonard, Sugar Ray
[Ray Charles Leonard]
American. Boxer
Won gold medal, 1976 Olympics; second boxer (Thomas Hearns first) to win championship titles in five different weight classes.
b. May 17, 1956 in Wilmington, North Carolina
Source: *AfrAmSG; BiDAmSp BK; BioIn 11, 12, 13, 14, 15, 16; BlkOlyM; CelR 90; CurBio 81; InB&W 85; IntWW 81, 82, 83, 89, 91, 93; LegTOT; NegAl 89; News 89; NewYTBS 79, 88; PseudN 82; WhoAm 82, 84, 86, 88, 90, 92, 94, 95, 96, 97; WhoBlA 92; WhoE 89, 91; WhoSpor*

Leonard, William Ellery
American. Poet
Wrote sonnet sequence *Two Lives,* 1925; verse volume *The Lynching Bee,* 1920.
b. Jan 25, 1876 in Plainfield, New Jersey
d. May 2, 1944 in Madison, Wisconsin
Source: *AmAu&B; AmLY; Benet 87; BenetAL 91; BioIn 1, 4, 5, 15; ChhPo, S1, S2, S3; CnDAL; ConAmA; ConAmL; DcAmB S3; DcLB 54; DcNAA; Dis&D; NatCAB 33; OxCAmL 65, 83, 95; REn; REnAL; SixAP; TwCA, SUP; WhAm 2; WhNAA; WisWr*

Leonardo da Vinci
[Leonardo Da Vinci; Leonardo da Vinci]
Italian. Artist
Greatest paintings: *The Last Supper,* 1498; *Mona Lisa,* 1503.
b. Apr 15, 1452 in Vinci, Italy
d. May 2, 1519 in Amboise, France
Source: *AsBiEn; AtlBL; BbD; Benet 87, 96; BiD&SB; BiHiMed; BioIn 1, 2, 3, 4, 5, 6, 7, 8, 9, 10, 11, 12, 13, 14, 15, 16, 17, 18, 19, 20; CamGWoT; CasWL; ClaDrA; DcArts; DcBiPP; DcCathB; DcInv; DcItL 1, 2; DcScB; Dis&D; EncUrb; EncWT; Ent; EuAu; GayLesB; InSci; IntDcAA 90; IntDcAr; LegTOT; LinLib L; LitC 12; LuthC 75; MacEA; McGDA; McGEWB; NewC; NewGrDM 80; OxCArt; OxCEng 67, 85, 95; OxCFr; OxCMed 86; OxDcArt; PenC EUR; RAdv 14, 13-3; REn; WhDW; WhoArch; WorAl; WorAlBi; WorInv*

Leoncavallo, Ruggiero
Italian. Composer
Best known for opera *I Pagliacci,* 1892.
b. Mar 8, 1858 in Naples, Italy
d. Aug 9, 1919 in Montecatini, Italy
Source: *AtlBL; Baker 84; BioIn 1, 2, 3, 4, 6, 7, 8, 11, 12, 14, 20; CmOp; CmpBCM; DcCom 77; GrComp; LinLib S; MusMk; NewEOp 71; OxCMus; REn; WorAl; WorAlBi*

Leone, Giovanni
Italian. Political Leader
Pres. of Italian Republic, 1971-78.
b. Nov 3, 1908 in Pamigliano, Italy
Source: *BioIn 9, 10, 11; CurBio 72; IntWW 74, 75, 76, 77, 78, 79, 80, 81, 82, 83, 89, 91, 93; IntYB 78, 79, 80, 81, 82; NewYTBE 71; Who 74; WhoGov 72; WhoWor 74, 78; WorAl*

Leone, Sergio
Italian. Director, Screenwriter
Noted for Westerns: *A Fistful of Dollars,* 1964; *For a Few Dollars More,* 1967.
b. Jan 3, 1929 in Rome, Italy
d. Apr 30, 1989 in Rome, Italy
Source: *AnObit 1989; BioIn 8, 12, 16; ConAu 123, 128; ConTFT 5; EncEurC; FacFETw; HalFC 84, 88; IntDcF 1-2, 2-2; IntMPA 86, 88; IntWW 89, 89N; ItaFilm; MiSFD 9N; News 89; NewYTBS 89; OxCFilm; VarWW 85; WorFDir 2*

Leonetti, Tommy
American. Singer
Best known as cast member in TV series "Your Hit Parade," 1957-58.
b. Sep 10, 1929 in North Bergen, New Jersey
d. Sep 15, 1979 in Houston, Texas
Source: *ASCAP 66; BioIn 4, 12; NewYTBS 79; WhScrn 83*

Leoni, Franco
Italian. Composer
Wrote operas *The Oracle,* 1905; *Rip van Winkle,* 1897.
b. Oct 24, 1864 in Milan, Italy
d. Feb 8, 1949 in London, England
Source: *Baker 78, 84, 92; MetOEnc; NewEOp 71; NewGrDM 80; NewGrDO*

Leoni, Tea
[Mrs. David Duchovny]
American. Actor
Star of TV's "The Naked Truth," 1996—.
b. Feb 25, 1966 in New York, New York

Leonidas I
"The Defender of Thermopylae"
Greek. Ruler
Ruled Sparta, 491-480 BC; known for heroic stand against Xerxes I.
d. 480BC in Thermopylae, Greece
Source: *LinLib S; NewC; PseudN 82; WhDW; WorAl*

Leonidoff, Leon
American. Producer
Produced over 600 NYC Music Hall shows, 1932-74 including many for The Rockettes.
b. Jan 2, 1895 in Bender, Romania
d. Jul 29, 1989 in North Palm Beach, Florida
Source: *BiDD; BioIn 16; CurBio 41, 89N; IntMPA 75, 76; LinLib S; NewYTBS 89*

Leonov, Alexei Arkhipovich
Russian. Cosmonaut
First man to walk in space, 1965.
b. May 30, 1934 in Listvyanka, Union of Soviet Socialist Republics
Source: *BiDSovU; BioIn 15; CurBio 65; FacFETw; IntWW 83, 91; NewYTBS 75; WhoSpc; WorAl; WorAlBi; WorDWW*

Leonov, Leonid Maximovich
Russian. Author, Dramatist
Wrote *The End of Insignificant Man,* 1922; *The Russian Forest,* 1953; won the Lenin Prize four times.
b. May 31, 1899 in Moscow, Russia
d. Aug 8, 1994
Source: *ConLC 86; EncWL 2, 3; IntAu&W 76, 77, 93; IntWW 74, 75, 76; LinLib L; OxCThe 67, 83; WhoWor 74, 76, 78*

Leonowens, Anna Harriette Crawford
Welsh. Governess
Worked for Rama IV, King of Siam; stories basis of *The King and I.*
b. Nov 5, 1834 in Carnarvon, Wales
d. Jan 19, 1914 in Montreal, Quebec, Canada
Source: *Alli, SUP; ApCAB; BbD; BiD&SB; DcAmAu; DcNAA; InWom SUP; WhAm 4*

Leontief, Wassily W
American. Economist
Developed method of input-output economic analysis; won Nobel Prize, 1973.
b. Aug 5, 1906 in Saint Petersburg, Russia
Source: *BioIn 14, 15; CurBio 67; FacFETw; GrEconS; IntWW 83, 91; NewYTBE 73; NobelP; ThTwC 87; WebAB 74; Who 85, 92; WhoAm 84, 90; WhoE 85, 91; WhoEc 86; WhoFI 92; WhoNob, 90; WhoWor 84, 91; WorAlBi; WrDr 86, 92*

Leontovich, Eugenie
American. Actor, Director
Began Broadway career in 1922; won Tony for *Anastasia,* 1959; founded Actors Workshops, 1953, 1973.
b. Mar 21, 1900 in Moscow, Russia
d. Apr 2, 1993 in New York, New York
Source: *AnObit 1993; BiE&WWA; BioIn 18, 19; FamA&A; FilmgC; HalFC 88; InWom SUP; NewYTBS 93; NotNAT; VarWW 85; WhoAmW 66, 68; WhoHol A; WhoThe 72, 77, 81; WorAl; WorAlBi*

Leopardi, Giacomo
Italian. Poet
Wrote poem "La ginestra," 1836; prose describing pessimistic philosophy, *Operette morali,* 1827.
b. Jun 29, 1798 in Recanati, Italy
d. Jun 14, 1837 in Naples, Italy
Source: *AtlBL; BbD; Benet 87, 96; BiD&SB; BioIn 3, 4, 5, 7, 10, 11, 12, 13; CasWL; CelCen; DcArts; DcBiPP; DcEuL; DcItL 1, 2; EuAu; EuWr 5; EvEuW; GrFLW; LinLib L, S; McGEWB; NewCBEL; NinCLC 22; OxCEng 67; PenC EUR; RAdv 14, 13-2; RComWL; REn; RfGWoL 95; WhDW; WorAl; WorAlBi*

Leopold, Nathan Freudenthal
[Leopold and Loeb; Morton D Ballard; George Johnson; William F Lanne; Richard A Lawrence]
"Babe"
American. Criminal, Murderer
Millionaire's son who committed murder, with Richard Loeb, to attempt the "perfect crime."
b. Nov 19, 1904 in Kenwood, Illinois
d. Aug 28, 1971 in San Juan, Puerto Rico
Source: *Au&Wr 71; BioIn 4, 5, 6, 7, 8, 9, 10, 12; ConAu 29R, P-1; DcAmB S9; MurCaTw; NewYTBE 71; PseudN 82*

Leopold II
Belgian. Ruler
Reigned 1865-1909, promoting industrial, colonial expansion.
b. Apr 9, 1835 in Brussels, Belgium
d. Dec 17, 1909 in Laeken, Belgium
Source: *DcBiPP; McGEWB*

Leopold III
Belgian. Ruler
Succeeded to throne, 1934, on death of father, Albert I; taken prisoner during German invasion, 1940; abdicated to son, Baudoin I, 1951.
b. Nov 3, 1901 in Brussels, Belgium
d. Sep 25, 1983 in Brussels, Belgium
Source: *CurBio 44, 83N; IntWW 74; LinLib S; NewYTBS 83; WhDW*

Leotard, Jules
French. Circus Performer
Trapeze artist; original "daring young man on the flying trapeze"; first to call costume leotard.
b. 1830 in Toulouse, France
d. 1870
Source: *BiDD; CnOxB; Ent; OxCThe 67, 83*

Leo XIII, Pope
[Gioacchino Vincenzo Raffaele Luigi Pecci]
Italian. Religious Leader
Known for many encyclicals: *Rerum Novarum,* 1891; his 1878-1903 pontificate perhaps century's most productive.
b. Mar 2, 1810 in Carpineto, Italy
d. Jul 20, 1903 in Rome, Italy
Source: *NewCol 75; REn; WebBD 83*

Lepage, Robert
Canadian. Actor
Actor and director noted for unconventional methods.
b. 1957 in Quebec, Quebec, Canada
Source: *ConTFT 13; CurBio 95; TheaDir; WhoAm 97*

Le Pen, Jean-Marie
French. Politician
Charismatic leader of French National Front Party, 1986—.
b. Jun 20, 1928 in La Trinite-sur-Mer, France
Source: *BiDExR; BiDFrPL; BioIn 14, 15, 16; CurBio 88; IntWW 89, 91, 93; LegTOT; NewYTBS 87; PolLCWE; WhoFr 79; WhoWor 97*

LePoer Trench, Brinsley
[Earl of Clancarty; William Francis Brinsley LePoer]
British. Banker, Politician
Flying saucer enthusiast; wrote *The Sky People,* 1960.
b. Sep 18, 1911
Source: *ConAu 116; EncO&P 2; UFOEn; Who 92*

Leppard, Raymond John
English. Conductor
Harpsichordist; director, English Chamber Orchestra, 1959-77; conductor, BBC N. Symphony, 1972-80.
b. Aug 11, 1927 in London, England
Source: *Baker 84, 92; BioIn 13; BriBkM 80; CurBio 80; IntWW 89, 91, 93; IntWWM 77, 80, 85, 90; MetOEnc; NewGrDA 86; NewGrDM 80; NewGrDO; PenDiMP; Who 74, 82, 83, 85, 88, 90, 92, 94; WhoAm 80, 82, 84, 86, 88, 90, 92, 94, 95, 96, 97; WhoE 95; WhoEnt 92; WhoMus 72; WhoMW 90, 92, 93, 96; WhoOp 76; WhoWor 80, 95, 96*

Lerdo de Tejada, Sebastian
Mexican. Political Leader
President of Mexico, 1872-76, after death of Juarez; overthrown by Diaz; exiled.
b. Apr 25, 1825 in Jalapa, Mexico
d. Apr 21, 1889 in New York, New York
Source: *ApCAB; NewCol 75; WebBD 83*

Lermontov, Mikhail
[Michael Jurevich Lermontov]
Russian. Author, Poet
Wrote first Russian novel of psychological realism, *Hero of Our Time,* 1840.
b. Oct 15, 1814 in Moscow, Russia
d. Jul 27, 1841 in Pyatigorsk, Russia
Source: *AtlBL; BbD; BiD&SB; CasWL; CyWA 58; DcEuL; DcRusL; EuAu; EvEuW; GrFLW; LegTOT; McGEWD 72; Novels; OxCEng 67; OxCThe 67; OxDcOp; PenC EUR; RAdv 14, 13-2; REn; WorAlBi*

Lerner, Alan Jay
[Lerner and Loewe]
American. Dramatist, Lyricist, Composer
Known for collaborations with Loewe; won two Tonys, two Oscars, one Grammy including film/play *Gigi,* 1958, 1974.
b. Aug 31, 1918 in New York, New York
d. Jun 14, 1986 in New York, New York
Source: *AmAu&B; AmPS; AnObit 1986; ASCAP 66; Baker 92; BenetAL 91; BestMus; BiDAmM; BiE&WWA; BioIn 4, 5, 6, 7, 9, 10, 11, 12, 14, 15, 16, 17, 18, 20; BlueB 76; CamGWoT; CelR; CmMov; CmpEPM; ConAu 31NR, 77, 119; ConDr 73, 77D; ConTFT 3; CurBio 58, 86, 86N; DcArts; DcTwCCu 1; EncMT; EncWT; Ent; FacFETw; FilmEn; FilmgC; HalFC 80, 84, 88; IntMPA 77, 80, 82; IntWW 74, 75, 76, 77, 78, 79, 80, 81, 82, 83; LegTOT; ModWD; NewCBMT; NewGrDA 86; NewGrDM 80; NewYTBS 86; NotNAT; OxCAmL 65, 83, 95; OxCAmT 84; OxCFilm; OxCPMus; PenEncP; PlP&P; REnAL; VarWW 85; WhAm 9; Who 74, 82, 83, 85; WhoAm 74, 76, 78, 80, 82, 84; WhoThe 72, 77, 81; WhoWor 78, 80, 82; WorAl; WorAlBi; WorEFlm*

Lerner, Max
American. Author, Journalist
Longtime *NY Post* syndicated columnist; his books include *Ted and the Kennedy Legend,* 1980.
b. Dec 20, 1902 in Minsk, Russia
d. Jun 5, 1992 in New York, New York
Source: *AmAu&B; AmMWSc 73S; AnObit 1992; Au&Wr 71; AuNews 1; BenetAL 91; BioIn 4, 5, 7, 10, 11, 13, 17, 18, 19; BlueB 76; CelR; ConAu 13R, 25NR; CurBio 42, 92N; DcLB 29; IntAu&W 76, 77, 82, 86, 89; IntWW 74, 75, 76, 77, 78, 79, 80, 81, 82, 83, 89, 91; IntYB 78, 79, 80, 81, 82; JrnUS; LegTOT; NewYTBS 92; OxCAmL 65, 83, 95; PenC AM; PolProf T; REnAL; TwCA, SUP; WhAm 10; Who 74, 82, 83, 85, 88, 90, 92; WhoAm 74, 76, 78, 80, 82, 84, 86, 88, 90; WhoE 74, 81, 83, 85, 86; WhoWor 74, 78, 80, 82, 84; WhoWorJ 72, 78; WorAl; WorAlBi; WrDr 76, 80, 82, 84, 86, 88, 90, 92, 94N*

Lerner, Michael
American. Philosopher, Editor
Founder and editor of the Jewish political magazine *Tikkun,* 1986.
b. 1943 in Newark, New Jersey
Source: *BioIn 20; News 94, 94-2; WhoHol 92*

LeRoux, Gaston
French. Author
Popular mystery tales, featuring detective Rouletabille include *Le Mystere d e la chambre jaune,* 1908.
b. May 6, 1868 in Paris, France
d. Apr 15, 1927 in Nice, France
Source: *BioIn 15, 17; CasWL; ConAu 108, 136; CrtSuMy; EncMys; EncSF 93; LegTOT; LngCTC; MnBBF; Novels; OxCFr; PenEncH; ScF&FL 1, 92; ScFEYrs; SmATA 65; TwCA; TwCCr&M 80B, 85B, 91B; TwCLC 25; WhoHr&F; WorAl; WorAlBi*

Leroux, Xavier
Italian. Composer
Wrote operas *Astarte,* 1901; *Les Chemineau,* 1907; songs, masses.
b. Oct 11, 1863 in Velletri, Italy
d. Feb 2, 1919 in Paris, France
Source: *Baker 78, 84; MetOEnc; NewEOp 71; NewGrDM 80*

Leroy
[Hippolyte Roy]
French. Fashion Designer
Designed for Empress Josephine, Versailles court; famed for diamond-studded gowns.
b. 1753
d. 1829
Source: *WorFshn*

Leroy, Mervyn
American. Director, Producer
Films include *The Wizard of Oz,* 1939; won Oscar for *Random Harvest,* 1942; won two special Oscars.
b. Oct 15, 1900 in San Francisco, California
d. Sep 13, 1987 in Beverly Hills, California
Source: *AmFD; AnObit 1987; BiDFilm, 81, 94; BioIn 8, 10, 11, 12, 15, 20; CmMov; ConAu 108, 123; DcFM; Dun&B 86, 88; EncAFC; Film 2; FilmEn; FilmgC; HalFC 80, 84, 88; IlWWHD 1; IntDcF 1-2, 2-2; IntMPA 75, 76, 77, 78, 79, 80, 81, 82, 84, 86; LegTOT; MiSFD 9N; MovMk; NewYTBS 87; OxCFilm; TwYS, A; VarWW 85; WhAm 9; WhoAm 74, 76, 78, 80, 82, 84, 86; WorAl; WorAlBi; WorEFlm; WorFDir 1*

Lesage, Alain-Rene
French. Author, Dramatist
Wrote classic satirical novel *Gil Blas,* 1735; comedy play *Turcaret,* 1709.
b. May 8, 1668 in Sarzeau, France
d. Nov 17, 1747 in Boulogne-sur-Mer, France
Source: *AtlBL; BbD; BiD&SB; CamGWoT; CasWL; CnThe; CyWA 58; DcArts; DcBiA; DcEuL; EncWT; EuAu; EuWr 3; EvEuW; GuFrLit 2; IntDcT 2; LitC 2, 28; McGEWB; McGEWD 72, 84; NotNAT; Novels; OxCEng 67, 85, 95; PenC EUR; REn; RfGWoL 95*

Lesage, Jean
Canadian. Statesman
Liberal party premier of Quebec, 1960-66; originated governmental religious reforms.
b. Jun 10, 1912 in Montreal, Quebec, Canada
d. Dec 11, 1980 in Quebec, Quebec, Canada
Source: *AnObit 1980; BioIn 5, 6, 7, 12, 15; BlueB 76; CanWW 70, 79, 80; CurBio 81, 81N; IntWW 74, 75, 76, 77, 78, 79, 80; IntYB 78, 79, 80, 81, 82; NewYTBS 80; WhAm 7; WhoCan 73, 75, 77, 80*

Lescaze, William
American. Architect
Functional and organic designer; head architect for NY's first low-cost housing project.
b. Mar 27, 1896 in Geneva, Switzerland
d. Feb 9, 1969 in New York, New York
Source: *BioIn 4, 8, 9, 10; ConArch 80, 87, 94; CurBio 42, 69; DcD&D; DcTwDes; EncMA; FacFETw; IntDcAr; MacEA; McGDA; WhAm 10; WhAmArt 85; WhoArch*

Lescoulie, Jack
American. TV Personality
Founding personality on NBC's "Today" show; spoke first words on show's first broadcast; played second banana to Dave Garroway, was resident jester, 1952-67.
b. May 17, 1917 in Sacramento, California
d. Jul 22, 1987 in Memphis, Tennessee
Source: *BioIn 3, 4; IntMPA 75, 76; LesBEnT; NewYTBS 87; NewYTET; WhoHol A*

Leser, Tina
[Tina Shillard Smith]
American. Fashion Designer
Specialized in exotic bathing suits, sportswear.
b. Dec 12, 1910 in Philadelphia, Pennsylvania
d. Jan 23, 1986 in Sands Point, New York
Source: *BioIn 4, 14, 15; BlueB 76; ConFash; CurBio 57, 86, 86N; EncFash; FairDF US; NewYTBS 86; PseudN 82; WhAm 9; WhoAm 74, 76, 78; WhoAmW 58, 61, 64, 66, 68, 70, 72, 74; WhoFash 88; WorFshn*

Lesh, Phil
[Grateful Dead]
American. Singer, Musician
Rock bassist, composer of electronic music; with Grateful Dead since 1965.
b. Mar 15, 1940 in Berkeley, California
Source: *EncPR&S 74; LegTOT; RkOn 74; RolSEnR 83; VarWW 85; WhoEnt 92; WhoRocM 82*

Leskov, Nikolai Semyonovich
Russian. Author
Wrote novel *Cathedral Folk,* 1872; short story *Ocharofanny srtannik,* 1873; often used "skaz" style.
b. Feb 16, 1831 in Gorokhovo, Russia
d. Mar 5, 1895 in Saint Petersburg, Russia
Source: *BbD; BiD&SB; CasWL; ClDMEL 80; DcEuL; DcRusL; EuAu; EvEuW; HanRL; LinLib L; Novels; PenC EUR; REn; WhDW*

Leslie, Edgar
American. Songwriter
Wrote songs for films; collaborated with Irving Berlin, Harry Warren, others.
b. Dec 31, 1885 in Stamford, Connecticut
d. Jan 22, 1976 in New York, New York
Source: *AmPS; ASCAP 66, 80; BiDAmM; BioIn 10; CmpEPM; OxCPMus; Sw&Ld C*

Leslie, Eliza
American. Author, Editor
Wrote on domestic economy: *Directions for Cooking,* 1837.
b. Nov 15, 1787 in Philadelphia, Pennsylvania
d. Jan 1, 1858 in Philadelphia, Pennsylvania
Source: *Alli; AmAu; AmAu&B; AmWomWr; ApCAB; BenetAL 91; BiD&SB; BioIn 2, 12, 21; ChhPo, S1, S2; CyAL 1; DcAmAu; DcAmB; DcNAA; DcWomA; Drake; EarABI; InWom, SUP; NatCAB 7; NewYHSD; NotAW; OxCAmL 65, 83, 95; PenNWW A, B; PoIre; REnAL; WhAm HS*

Leslie, Frank
[Henry Carter]
American. Illustrator, Publisher
Numerous popular publications included *Frank Leslie's Illustrated Newspaper* from 1855.
b. Mar 21, 1821 in Ipswich, England
d. Jan 10, 1880 in New York, New York
Source: *AmAu&B; AmBi; ApCAB; BenetAL 91; BiDAmJo; BioIn 1, 3, 4, 5, 7, 8, 10, 15, 16, 17; ChhPo S2; DcAmB; DcLB 43, 79; DcNaB; EncAB-H 1974; EncAJ; JrnUS; NatCAB 3; NewYHSD; OxCAmL 65, 83, 95; PseudN 82; RComAH; REnAL; TwCBDA; WebAB 74, 79; WhAm HS; WhCiWar*

Leslie, Joan
[Joan Brodell]
American. Actor
Played "the girl next door" roles for Warner Studios, 1941-46; retired to become dress designer.
b. Jan 26, 1925 in Detroit, Michigan
Source: *BiDD; BioIn 7, 10, 15, 18; CmpEPM; ConTFT 5; FilmEn; FilmgC; ForYSC; HalFC 80, 84, 88; HolP 40; IntMPA 75, 76, 77, 78, 79, 80, 81, 82, 84, 86, 88, 92, 94, 96; InWom, SUP; LegTOT; MotPP; MovMk; OxCPMus; PseudN 82; VarWW 85; What 1; WhoHol 92, A; WorAl; WorAlBi*

Leslie, Miriam Florence Folline
"Empress of Journalism"
American. Publisher
Wife of Frank Leslie, 1874-80; headed publishing empire, 1880-95.
b. 1836 in New Orleans, Louisiana
d. Sep 18, 1914
Source: *Alli SUP; AmAu; AmAu&B; AmWomWr; ApCAB; BioIn 16, 17; DcAmB; DcNAA; InWom; LibW; NatCAB 25; NotAW; REnAL; TwCBDA; WebAB 74, 79*

Lesnevich, Gus
"The Russian Lion"
American. Boxer
Light heavy weight who fought numerous title bouts; defeated by Conn, 1939, 1940.
b. Feb 22, 1915 in Cliffside Park, New Jersey
d. Feb 28, 1964 in Cliffside Park, New Jersey
Source: *BiDAmSp BK; BioIn 6; PseudN 82; WhoBox 74*

L'Esperance Quintuplets
[Alexandria L'Esperance; Danielle L'Esperance; Erica L'Esperance; Raymond L'Esperance; Veronica L'Esperance]
American. Quintuplets
First US test-tube fertilization to result in five babies; parents are Raymond and Michelle.
b. Jan 11, 1988 in Royal Oak, Michigan
Source: *BioIn 16*

Lesseps, Ferdinand Marie de
French. Engineer, Diplomat
Chief engineer for construction of Suez Canal, 1859-69.
b. Nov 19, 1805 in Versailles, France
d. Dec 7, 1894 in La Chanaie, France
Source: *ApCAB; BbD; BiD&SB; BioIn 15, 20; CelCen; Dis&D; HarEnUS; InSci; OxCFr; OxCShps; REn; WorAl*

Lesser, Sol
American. Producer
Produced serials, westerns, Tarzan movies, 1933-58.
b. Feb 17, 1890 in Spokane, Washington
d. Sep 19, 1980 in Hollywood, California
Source: *AnObit 1980; BioIn 9, 12; CmMov; FacFETw; FilmEn; FilmgC; HalFC 80, 84, 88; IntMPA 75, 76, 77, 78, 79, 80, 81; NewYTBS 80; OxCFilm; PeoHis; WhAm 7; WhoAm 74, 76, 78, 80; WhoHrs 80; WhoWest 76, 78; WhoWor 74; WorEFlm*

Lessing, Doris May
English. Author
Prize-winning works include five-volume *Children of Violence,* 1951-69; *African Stories,* 1964.
b. Oct 22, 1919 in Kermanshah, Persia
Source: *ArtclWW 2; Benet 87, 96; BioIn 5, 6, 7, 8, 9, 10, 11, 13, 14, 15, 16, 17, 18, 20, 21; BritWr S1; CamGEL; CamGLE; CnDBLB 8; CnMD; ConAu 9R, 14AS, 33NR, 54NR; ConBrDr; ConDr 73, 88, 93; ConLC 22, 40; ConNov 86, 91, 96; ContDcW 89; ConWomD; CroCD; CurBio 76, 95; CyWA 89; DcArts; DcLB Y85A; DcLEL 1940; DcLP 87A; DrAPF 91; EncBrWW; EncSF; EncWB; EncWL; EncWT; FacFETw; FemiCLE; GrWrEL N; IntAu&W 89, 91, 93; IntvTCA 2; IntWW 74, 75, 76, 77, 78, 79, 80, 81, 82, 83, 89, 91, 93; InWom SUP; LiExTwC; MajTwCW; ModBrL S2; NewEScF; NewYTBS 80; OxCEng 85; PenNWW A; RAdv 13-1; RfGEnL 91; RGTwCSF; RGTwCWr; ScFSB; ShSCr 6; TwCSFW 91; Who 85, 92, 94; WhoAm 86, 90, 95, 96, 97; WhoEnt 92; WhoWor 87, 91, 95, 96, 97; WorAlBi; WrDr 86, 92, 94, 96; WrPh*

Lessing, Gotthold Ephraim
"The Aesop of Germany"; "The Father of German Literature"; "The Frederick the Great of Thought"
German. Author
Writings include critical work: *Laocoon,* 1766; dramatic tragedy: *Emilia Galotti,* 1772; theological tract: *Education of the Human Race,* 1780.
b. Jan 22, 1729 in Kamenz, Germany
d. Feb 15, 1781 in Brunswick, Germany
Source: *AtlBL; BbD; Benet 87, 96; BiD&SB; BiDPsy; BioIn 1, 2, 4, 5, 6, 7, 9, 10, 13, 14, 17; BlkwCE; CamGWoT; CasWL; ChhPo S1; CnThe; CyEd; CyWA 58; DcArts; DcBiPP; DcEuL; DcLB 97; Dis&D; EncEnl; EncUnb; EncWT; Ent; EuAu; EuWr 4; EvEuW; GrFLW; IntDcT 2; LinLib L, S; LitC 8; LuthC 75; McGEWB; McGEWD 72, 84; NewC; NewCBEL; NotNAT A, B; OxCArt; OxCEng 67, 85, 95; OxCGer 76, 86; OxCPhil; OxCThe 67, 83; OxDcArt; PenC EUR; RAdv 14, 13-2; RComWL; REn; REnWD; RfGWoL 95; WhDW; WorAlBi; WrPh*

Les Six
[George Auric; Louis Durey; Arthur Honegger; Darius Milhaud; Francois Poulenc; Germaine Tailleferre]
French. Composers
Avant-garde group, led by Honegger, popular after WW I.
Source: *Benet 87; BioNews 74; CurBio 41, 56, 61; NewYTBS 74, 83; ObitOF 79; OxCMus; WhoHol 92*

Lester, Jerry
American. Comedian
Hosted NBC's "Broadway Open House," early 1950s.
b. 1910? in Chicago, Illinois
d. Mar 24, 1995 in Miami, Florida
Source: *BioIn 2, 3, 7, 10; LesBEnT, 92; NewYTET; WhoCom; WhoHol A*

Lester, Julius
American. Writer
Writer of fiction for young adults that addresses the black experience in America; wrote two autobiographies: *All Is Well,* 1976; *Lovesong: Becoming a Jew,* 1988.
b. Jan 27, 1939 in Saint Louis, Missouri
Source: *Au&Arts 12; BlkAuII, 92; BlkWr 1; BlkWrNE; ChlBkCr; ChlLR 41; CivR 74; ConAu 23NR; ConBlAP 88; ConBlB 9; FourBJA; InB&W 80; IntAu&W 91, 93; LNinSix; NegAl 89; SchCGBL; SelBAAf; SelBAAu; TwCChW 83, 89; WhoAfA 96; WhoBlA 90, 92, 94; WrDr 86, 88, 90, 92, 94, 96*

Lester, Mark
English. Actor
Played title role in film *Oliver,* 1968.
b. Jul 11, 1958 in Richmond, England
Source: *BioIn 15; FilmAG WE; FilmEn; FilmgC; ForYSC; HalFC 80, 84, 88; IntMPA 75, 76, 77, 78, 79, 80, 81, 82, 84, 86, 88, 92, 94, 96; ItaFilm; VarWW 85; WhoHol 92, A; WhoHrs 80*

Lester, Richard
American. Director
Films include *Superman II,* 1980; *Four Musketeers,* 1975.
b. Jan 19, 1932 in Philadelphia, Pennsylvania
Source: *BiDFilm, 81, 94; BioIn 7, 8, 10, 12, 14, 16, 19, 20; BioNews 75; BlueB 76; CelR, 90; ConLC 20; ConTFT 3; CurBio 69; DcFM; EncEurC; FacFETw; FilmEn; IntDcF 1-2, 2-2; IntMPA 75, 76, 77, 78, 79, 80, 81, 82, 84, 86, 88, 92, 94, 96; IntWW 76, 77, 78, 79, 80, 81, 82, 83, 89, 91, 93; MiSFD 9; MovMk; OxCFilm; VarWW 85; Who 74, 82, 83, 85, 88, 90, 92, 94; WhoAm 74, 76, 78, 80, 82, 84, 86, 88, 90, 92, 94, 95, 96, 97; WhoEnt 92; WhoWor 74, 76, 78, 84, 87, 89, 91, 93, 95, 96; WorAl; WorAlBi; WorEFlm; WorFDir 2*

Lesueur, Jean-Francois
French. Composer
Wrote operas *La Caverne,* 1793; *Paul et Virginie,* 1794; masses, oratorios.
b. Feb 15, 1760 in Drucat-Plessiel, France
d. Oct 6, 1837 in Paris, France
Source: *Baker 84; NewCol 75; NewEOp 71; OxCMus*

LeSueur, Percy
Canadian. Hockey Player
Forward-goalie on amateur Canadian teams, 1906-16; Hall of Fame, 1961.
b. Nov 18, 1881 in Quebec, Quebec, Canada
d. Jan 27, 1962 in Hamilton, Ontario, Canada
Source: *WhoHcky 73*

Letelier, Orlando
Chilean. Diplomat
Ambassador to US, 1971-73; killed by bomb in car.
b. Apr 13, 1932 in Temuco, Chile
d. Sep 21, 1976 in Washington, District of Columbia
Source: *BioIn 11, 12; FacFETw; IntWW 74, 75, 76; ObitOF 79; WhoGov 72; WhoWor 74*

LeTourneau, Robert Gilmour
American. Engineer, Business Executive
Founded co., 1929, which supplied most of armed forces earth-moving equipment, WW II.
b. Nov 30, 1888 in Richmond, Vermont
d. Jun 1, 1969 in Longview, Texas
Source: *BioIn 1, 2, 3, 4, 5, 8, 9; InSci; ObitOF 79; WhAm 5; WorAl*

Letterman, David
American. TV Personality
Host of "Late Night with David Letterman," 1982-1993 (NBC) and "Late Show with David Letterman," 1993— (CBS). Won six Emmys, 1981,1984-88.
b. Apr 12, 1947 in Indianapolis, Indiana
Source: *Au&Arts 10; BioIn 12, 13, 14, 15, 16; ConTFT 7, 14; CurBio 80; IntMPA 88, 92, 94, 96; IntWW 93; LegTOT; LesBEnT, 92; News 89-3; NewYTBS 86; VarWW 85; WhoAm 82, 84, 86, 88, 90, 92, 94, 95, 96, 97; WhoCom; WhoE 91, 93, 95; WhoEnt 92; WhoTelC; WorAlBi*

Lettermen, The
[Tony Butala; Gary Pike; Jim Pike]
American. Music Group
Ballad style vocalists, formed 1960; favorite of college students; nine gold albums include *Song for Young Lovers,* 1962.
Source: *EncPR&S 74, 89; PenEncP; RkOn 74; RolSEnR 83; WhoRock 81; WhoRocM 82*

Leutze, Emanuel
American. Artist
Works include *Washington Crossing the Delaware; Columbus Before the Queen.*
b. May 24, 1816 in Gumund, Germany
d. Jul 18, 1868 in Washington, District of Columbia
Source: *AmBi; ApCAB; ArtsAmW 1; BiAUS; BioIn 14; DcAmB; Drake; EarABI, SUP; HarEnUS; LegTOT; McGDA; OxCAmH; OxCAmL 65; OxCArt; PeoHis; TwCBDA; WebAB 74; WhAm HS*

Lev, Ray
American. Pianist
Concertist known for her extensive repertoire; made US debut, 1933.
b. May 8, 1912 in Rostov-on-Don, Russia
d. May 20, 1968 in New York, New York
Source: *Baker 78, 84, 92; BioIn 1, 2, 8; CurBio 49, 68; InWom; NewGrDA 86; ObitOF 79; WhAm 5*

Levant, Oscar
American. Composer, Musician
Concert pianist, caustic wit; films include *Rhapsody in Blue,* 1945; wrote autobiography *Smattering of Ignorance,* 1944.
b. Dec 27, 1906 in Pittsburgh, Pennsylvania
d. Aug 14, 1972 in Beverly Hills, California
Source: *AmAu&B; ASCAP 66, 80; Baker 78, 84, 92; BiDAmM; BioIn 1, 2, 3, 4, 5, 7, 8, 9, 10, 15, 17, 20; CmMov; CmpEPM; ConAmC 76, 82; ConAu 37R; CurBio 40, 52, 72, 72N; DcAmB S9; EncAFC; FilmEn; FilmgC; ForYSC; HalFC 80, 84, 88; HolP 40; JoeFr; LegTOT; MotPP; MovMk; NewAmDM; NewGrDA 86; NewGrDM 80; NewYTBE 72; NewYTET; OxCPMus; RadStar; REnAL; WhAm 5; WhoHol B; WhScrn 77, 83; WorAl; WorAlBi*

Levasseur, Nicolas Prosper
French. Opera Singer
Principal bass of the Paris Opera, 1828-53.
b. Mar 9, 1791 in Bresles, France
d. Dec 7, 1871 in Paris, France
Source: *NewEOp 71*

Levasseur, Rosalie
French. Opera Singer
Leading soprano, Paris Opera, 1780s.
b. Oct 8, 1749 in Valenciennes, France
d. May 6, 1826, Germany
Source: *Baker 78, 84, 92; CmOp; NewEOp 71; NewGrDM 80; NewGrDO; OxDcOp*

LeVay, Simon
English. Biologist
Neurobiologist known for his research theory that homosexuality could be biologically determined.
b. Aug 28, 1943 in Oxford, England
Source: *ConAu 142; CurBio 96; News 92, 92-2; WrDr 96*

Leveille, Norm(and)
Canadian. Hockey Player
Left wing, Boston, 1981-82; suffered career-ending cerebral hemorrhage during game, 1982.
b. Jan 10, 1963 in Montreal, Quebec, Canada
Source: *HocEn; HocReg 81*

Levene, Sam
[Samuel Levine]
American. Actor
On Broadway since 1927; hits include *Sunshine Boys,* 1972-75.
b. Aug 28, 1905, Russia

d. Dec 28, 1980 in New York, New York
Source: *AnObit 1980, 78, 79, 80, 81; LegTOT; MotPP; MovMk; NewYTBE 72; NewYTBS 80; NotNAT; OxCAmT 84; PlP&P; PseudN 82; WhAm 7; WhoAm 74, 76, 78, 80; WhoHol A; WhoThe 81; WhoWor 74; WhScrn 83; WorAl*

Levenson, Sam(uel)
American. Author
Hosted "Sam Levenson Show," 1959-64; wrote best-seller *Sex and the Single Child,* 1969.
b. Dec 28, 1911 in New York, New York
d. Aug 27, 1980 in Neponsit, New York
Source: *AnObit 1980, 80; JoeFr; NewYTBS 80; WhAm 7; WhoAm 74, 76, 78, 80; WhoAmJ 80; WhoCom; WhoWorJ 78; WorAl*

Leventhal, Albert Rice
[Albert Rice]
American. Publisher
Forty yrs. in publishing; developed Little Golden Books.
b. Oct 30, 1907 in New York, New York
d. Jan 4, 1976 in New York, New York
Source: *BioIn 10; ConAu 61, 65; ObitOF 79; WhAm 6, 7; WhoAm 74, 76*

Lever, William Hesketh
[Viscount Leverhulme]
English. Manufacturer
Founded Lever Brothers Soap Co., 1884; started model town, Port Sunlight; became Viscount, 1922.
b. 1851 in Bolton, England
d. 1925
Source: *BioIn 14, 16; DcNaB 1922; DcTwBBL; GrBr; WorAl*

LeVerrier, Urbain Jean Joseph
French. Astronomer
Credited with discovery of planet Neptune, 1846.
b. May 11, 1811 in Saint-Lo, France
d. Sep 25, 1877 in Paris, France
Source: *BiESc; CamDcSc; CelCen; DcBiPP; DcCathB; InSci; WhDW*

Leverson, Ada
[Elaine]
"Wittiest Woman in the World"
English. Author, Socialite
Close friend of Oscar Wilde; wrote novel *Love at Second Sight,* 1916.
b. 1865? in London, England
d. 1936? in London, England
Source: *BioIn 2, 4, 6, 7; CamGLE; ConAu 117; GrWrEL N; LngCTC; PenNWW A, B; REn; TwCA SUP; TwCLC 18; WomNov*

Levertov, Denise
American. Poet
Works include *The Sorrow Dance,* 1967.
b. Oct 24, 1923 in Ilford, England
Source: *AmAu&B; AmWomWr; AmWr S3; ArtclWW 2; Benet 87, 96; BenetAL 91; BioAmW; BioIn 8, 9, 10, 12, 13, 14, 16, 17, 18, 19, 20, 21; BlmGEL; BlmGWL; BlueB 76; CamGLE; CamHAL; ConAu 1R, 3NR, 19AS, 29NR, 50NR; ConLC 1, 2, 3, 5, 8, 15, 28, 66; ConPo 70, 75, 80, 85, 91, 96; CroCAP; CurBio 91; DcArts; DcLB 5, 165; DcLEL 1940; DcTwCCu 1; DrAP 75; DrAPF 80, 91; EncWL 2, 3; EngPo; FemiCLE; FemiWr; GrWomW; GrWrEL P; IntAu&W 89, 91, 93; IntvTCA 2; InWom SUP; LegTOT; LibW; LinLib L; MajTwCW; ModAL, S1, S2; ModAWP; ModBrL; ModWoWr; NewC; OxCAmL 65, 83, 95; OxCTwCP; OxCWoWr 95; PenBWP; PenC AM; PoeCrit 11; RAdv 1, 14, 13-1; REn; REnAL; RfGAmL 87, 94; RGTwCWr; WebE&AL; WhoAm 74, 76, 78, 80, 86, 88, 92, 94, 95, 96, 97; WhoAmW 66, 68, 70, 72, 74, 81, 83, 95; WhoE 74; WhoTwCL; WhoUSWr 88; WhoWor 74; WhoWrEP 89, 92, 95; WomBeaG; WorAl; WorAlBi; WorAu 1950; WrDr 76, 80, 82, 84, 86, 88, 90, 92, 94, 96*

Levesque, Rene
"Rene the Red"
Canadian. Government Official
Parti Quebecois premier of Quebec, 1976-85; sought independence for province.
b. Aug 24, 1922 in New Carlisle, Quebec, Canada
d. Nov 1, 1987 in Montreal, Quebec, Canada
Source: *AnObit 1987; BioIn 8, 9, 10, 11, 12, 13, 14, 15, 16, 18; CanWW 81, 83; ConAu 125; ConNews 88-1; CurBio 75, 88N; DcTwHis; EncWB; FacFETw; IntWW 77, 78, 79, 80, 81, 82, 83; LegTOT; NewYTBE 70; NewYTBS 76, 87; OxCCan SUP; PseudN 82; WhAm 9; Who 82, 83, 85, 88; WhoAm 76, 78, 80, 82, 84, 86; WhoCan 82, 84; WhoE 74; WhoWor 74, 80, 82, 84*

Levi, Edward Hirsch
American. Educator, Government Official
Attorney general under Gerald Ford, 1975-77; pres., U of Chicago, 1968-75.
b. Jun 26, 1911 in Chicago, Illinois
Source: *BiDrUSE 89; BioIn 8, 10, 11, 12; BlueB 76; ConAu 2NR, 49; CurBio 69; DrAS 74P, 78P, 82P; IntAu&W 82; IntWW 74, 75, 76, 77, 78, 79, 80, 81, 82, 83, 89, 91, 93; LEduc 74; NewYTBS 75; PolProf NF; Who 74, 82, 83, 85, 88, 90, 92, 94; WhoAm 74, 76, 78, 80, 82, 84, 86, 88, 90, 92, 94, 95, 96, 97; WhoAmJ 80; WhoAmL 78, 79, 83, 85, 87, 90, 92, 94, 96; WhoAmP 75, 77, 79, 81, 83, 85, 87, 89, 91, 93, 95; WhoGov 75, 77; WhoMW 74, 78, 80, 82, 88, 90, 92, 93, 96; WhoSSW 76; WhoWor 74, 78, 80, 82, 84, 87, 89; WhoWorJ 72; WrDr 76, 80, 86, 92*

Levi, Hermann
German. Conductor
Noted Wagnerian conductor; directed *Parsifal* premiere, 1882.
b. Nov 7, 1839 in Giessen, Germany
d. May 13, 1900, Germany
Source: *Baker 78, 84, 92; BioIn 2, 8, 10; BriBkM 80; IntDcOp; MetOEnc; NewAmDM; NewEOp 71; NewGrDM 80; NewGrDO; OxCMus; OxDcOp; PenDiMP*

Levi, Jonathan
American. Author
Author of *A Guide for the Perplexed,* 1992.
Source: *ConLC 76*

Levi, Julian Edwin
American. Artist
Semi-abstract painter of carefully designed landscapes.
b. Jun 20, 1900 in New York, New York
d. Feb 28, 1982 in New York, New York
Source: *BioIn 1, 2, 5, 6, 12, 13; CurBio 82; DcCAA 77; McGDA; NewYTBS 82; WhoAmA 78*

Levi, Primo
Italian. Writer, Chemist
Wrote Italian classic *Survival in Auschwitz,* 1961.
b. Jul 31, 1919 in Turin, Italy
d. Apr 11, 1987 in Turin, Italy
Source: *AnObit 1987; Benet 87, 96; BioIn 14, 15, 16, 17, 19, 21; ClDMEL 80; ConAu 12NR, 13R, 21NR, 33NR, 122; ConLC 37, 50; CurBio 87, 87N; CyWA 89; DcArts; DcItL 2; EncSF 93; EncWL 3; FacFETw; IntAu&W 86, 89, 91; LegTOT; LiExTwC; MajTwCW; NewYTBS 87; OxCEng 85, 95; RAdv 14, 13-2; RfGWoL 95; ScF&FL 92; ShSCr 12; WhoWorJ 72, 78; WorAu 1980*

Levi-Montalcini, Rita
Italian. Neurologist
With Stanley Cohen, won Nobel Prize for Physiology or Medicine, 1986, for discovery of nerve-growth factor (NGF).
b. Apr 22, 1909 in Turin, Italy
Source: *AmMWSc 73P, 76P, 79, 82, 86, 89, 92, 95; AmWomSc; BioIn 11, 15, 16, 17, 19, 20; CamDcSc; ConAu 149; ContDcW 89; CurBio 89; IntWW 89, 91, 93; InWom SUP; LarDcSc; NewYTBS 86; NobelP; NotTwCS; NotWoLS; RAdv 14; Who 90, 92, 94; WhoAm 90, 92, 94, 95; WhoNob 90, 95; WhoScEn 94, 96; WhoWor 89, 91, 93, 95, 96, 97; WomFir; WomStre; WorAlBi; WorScD*

Levin, Bernard
British. Critic, Journalist
Award-winning newspaper, mag., TV writer since 1953; books include *Enthusiasms,* 1983.
b. Aug 19, 1928
Source: *DcLP 87A; IntAu&W 89, 91; Who 83, 85, 88, 90, 92; WrDr 86, 88, 90, 92, 94, 96*

Levin, Carl Milton
American. Politician
Dem. senator from MI, 1979—.
b. Jun 28, 1934 in Detroit, Michigan

Source: *AlmAP 88, 92; BiDrUSC 89; CngDr 87, 89; IntWW 91; PolsAm 84; WhoAdv 90; WhoAm 86, 90; WhoAmP 87, 91; WhoMW 74, 76, 78, 92; WhoWor 91*

Levin, Gerald
American. Business Executive
Pres., CEO, Time Warner, Inc., 1992—.
b. May 6, 1939 in Philadelphia, Pennsylvania
Source: *Dun&B 90; News 95, 95-2; St&PR 91; WhoAm 90; WhoFI 92*

Levin, Harry Tuchman
American. Critic
Criticisms include *Memories of the Moderns,* 1980.
b. Jul 18, 1912 in Minneapolis, Minnesota
Source: *ConAu 2NR; DrAS 82E; IntAu&W 91; IntWW 83, 91; WhAm 11; WhoAm 86, 90; WhoE 85, 86; WrDr 86, 92*

Levin, Ira
American. Author
Wrote thrillers *Rosemary's Baby,* 1967; *Stepford Wives,* 1972; won Poe for *A Kiss Before Dying,* 1954.
b. Aug 27, 1929 in New York, New York
Source: *AmAu&B; ASCAP 66, 80; Au&Wr 71; AuSpks; Benet 87; BenetAL 91; BiE&WWA; BioIn 14, 15; ConAu 17NR, 21R, 44NR; ConLC 3, 6; ConNov 72, 76, 82, 86, 91, 96; ConPopW; ConTFT 2, 9; CurBio 91; EncMys; EncSF, 93; HalFC 80, 84, 88; IntAu&W 77; IntWW 93; Law&B 89A; LegTOT; MajTwCW; NatPD 81; NewEScF; NotNAT; Novels; OxCAmL 83, 95; OxCAmT 84; PenEncH; RGTwCWr; ScF&FL 1, 2, 92; ScFSB; SmATA, 66; TwCCr&M 80, 85, 91; TwCSFW 81, 86, 91; VarWW 85; WhoAm 78, 80, 82, 84, 86, 88, 90, 92, 94, 95, 96, 97; WhoHrs 80; WhoThe 81; WhoUSWr 88; WhoWrEP 89, 92, 95; WorAl; WorAlBi; WorAu 1970; WrDr 76, 80, 82, 84, 86, 88, 90, 92, 94, 96*

Levin, Jeremy
American. Hostage
CNN bureau chief, Beirut taken hostage and kept in captivity for 343 days, Mar 7, 1984-Feb 14, 1985.
Source: *BioIn 14, 15, 16*

Levin, Meyer
American. Author
Numerous works include *Compulsion,* 1956, based on 1920s Leopold-Loeb murder.
b. Oct 8, 1905 in Chicago, Illinois
d. Jul 9, 1981 in Jerusalem, Israel
Source: *AmAu&B; AmNov; AnObit 1981; Au&Wr 71; AuNews 1; Benet 87, 96; BenetAL 91; BiE&WWA; BioIn 2, 4, 7, 10, 12, 13, 14, 17, 21; BioNews 74; CelR; CnMD; ConAu 9R, 15NR, 104; ConLC 7; ConNov 72, 76, 82; CurBio 81, 81N; DcAmSR; DcLB 9, 28, Y81A; DcLEL; DrAPF 80; HalFC 84, 88; IntAu&W 76, 77, 82; JeAmFiW; JeAmHC; LegTOT; ModAL; NotNAT; Novels; OxCAmL 65, 83, 95; PenC AM; PeoHis; PupTheA; REn; REnAL; ScF&FL 1, 2, 92; SmATA 21, 27N; TwCA, SUP; WhAm 9; WhoAm 74, 76, 78, 80; WhoWorJ 72, 78; WorAl; WrDr 76, 80, 82*

Levine, Albert Norman
Canadian. Author
Novels include *The Angled Road,* 1953; *From a Seaside Town,* 1970.
b. Oct 22, 1924 in Ottawa, Ontario, Canada
Source: *Au&Wr 71; CreCan 1; DcLEL 1940; IntAu&W 76*

Levine, Beth
[Mrs. Herbert Levine]
American. Designer
Fashionable shoe designer, with husband Herbert, 1949-75.
Source: *InWom SUP; Law&B 89A; NewYTBS 91; WhoAmW 85; WorFshn*

Levine, David
American. Artist, Illustrator, Author
Illustrated award-winning juvenile books: *Fables of Aesop; The Heart of Stone,* 1964; known for caricatures of composers, performers.
b. Dec 20, 1926 in New York, New York
Source: *BioIn 8, 9, 10, 11, 12, 14, 15, 16; ConAu 113, 116; CurBio 73; EncAJ; IlrAm 1880; IlsCB 1957; IntWW 89, 91, 93; SmATA 35, 43; WhoAm 78, 80, 82, 84, 86, 88, 90, 92, 94, 95, 96; WhoAmA 76, 78, 80, 84, 86, 89, 91, 93; WhoGrA 82; WorArt 1950; WorECar*

Levine, Herbert
American. Designer
Produced fashionable shoes with wife, Beth; noted for promoting boot fashions.
d. Aug 8, 1991 in Westhampton Beach, New York
Source: *NewYTBS 91; WhoE 91; WorFshn*

Levine, Irving R(askin)
American. Broadcast Journalist
Award-winning correspondent with NBC 1950-95; wrote *Main Street, Italy,* 1963.
b. Aug 26, 1922 in Pawtucket, Rhode Island
Source: *AmAu&B; BioIn 5, 15; ConAu 13R; CurBio 59; EncAJ; EncTwCJ; LesBEnT, 92; VarWW 85; WhoAm 86, 90; WhoE 91; WhoFI 92; WhoWor 74, 84; WhoWorJ 72*

Levine, Jack
American. Artist
Expressionist noted for satirical portraits, social commentaries: *Pawnshop.*
b. Jan 3, 1915 in Boston, Massachusetts
Source: *AmArt; BioIn 1, 2, 3, 4, 5, 6, 11, 12, 14, 17; BriEAA; ConArt 77; DcAmArt; DcAmSR; DcCAA 71, 77, 88, 94; IntWW 74, 75, 76, 77, 78, 79, 80, 81, 82, 83, 89, 91, 93; McGDA; OxCTwCA; PhDcTCA 77; PrintW 83, 85; REn; WebAB 74, 79; WhAmArt 85; WhoAm 74, 76, 78, 80, 82, 84, 92, 94, 97; WhoAmA 73, 76, 78, 80, 82, 84, 86, 89, 91, 93; WhoAmJ 80; WhoWor 74, 96, 97; WhoWorJ 72, 78; WorArt 1950*

Levine, James Lawrence
American. Conductor
Artistic director, Metropolitan Opera, 1986—; frequent guest conductor, piano soloist.
b. Jun 23, 1943 in Cincinnati, Ohio
Source: *Baker 84; BioIn 13, 14, 15; CelR 90; ConMus 8; CurBio 75; EncWB; FacFETw; IntWW 83, 91; IntWWM 90; MetOEnc; NewAmDM; NewGrDA 86; News 92; NewYTBE 72; NewYTBS 85; PenDiMP; VarWW 85; WhoAm 86, 90; WhoE 91; WhoEmL 87; WhoEnt 92; WhoMW 90; WhoWor 84, 91; WorAlBi*

Levine, Joseph Edward
American. Producer
Pioneer independent producer called one of last movie moguls; films include *The Graduate,* 1967; *Carnal Knowledge,* 1971.
b. Sep 9, 1905 in Boston, Massachusetts
d. Jul 31, 1987 in Greenwich, Connecticut
Source: *BiE&WWA; BioIn 12; ConTFT 5; CurBio 79, 87; FilmgC; IntMPA 86; OxCFilm; VarWW 85; WhAm 9; WhoAm 78, 80, 82, 84, 86; WhoE 85, 86; WorEFlm*

Levine, Kathy
American. TV Personality
Founding host on cable home-shopping channel QVC, 1986—.
Source: *BioIn 18, 21*

Levine, Philip
American. Scientist
Co-discovered Rh factor in human blood and its role in hemolytic disease, 1940s.
b. Aug 10, 1900 in Kletsk, Russia
d. Oct 18, 1987 in New York, New York
Source: *AmMWSc 73P, 76P, 79, 82, 86; AnObit 1987; BiDrACP 79; BioIn 1, 7, 15; BlueB 76; CurBio 47, 87, 87N; InSci; IntWW 74, 75, 76, 77, 78, 79, 80, 81, 82, 83; McGMS 80; NewYTBS 87; WhAm 9; WhoAm 74, 76, 78, 80, 82, 84; WhoE 83, 85, 86; WhoWor 74, 76, 78, 80, 82, 87; WhoWorJ 72*

Levine, Philip
[Edgar Poe]
American. Author, Poet
Verse vols. include *Ashes,* 1979; *One For the Rose,* 1981. Pulitzer Prize for "The Simple Truth," 1994.
b. Jan 10, 1928 in Detroit, Michigan

Source: *Benet 96; BenetAL 91; BioIn 10, 12, 18, 19; CamGLE; CamHAL; ConAu 9NR, 9R, 37NR, 52NR; ConLC 2, 4, 5, 9, 14, 33; ConPo 70, 75, 80, 85, 91, 96; CroCAP; DcLB 5; DcLEL 1940; DrAP 75; DrAPF 80, 91; DrAS 74E, 78E, 82E; Focus; IntAu&W 77; IntWWP 77; LinLib L; OxCAmL 83, 95; OxCTwCP; PseudN 82; RAdv 14; WhoAm 76, 78, 80, 82, 84, 86, 88, 90, 92, 94, 95, 96, 97; WhoAmJ 80; WhoUSWr 88; WhoWest 74, 76, 78, 96; WhoWrEP 89, 92, 95; WorAu 1970; WrDr 76, 80, 82, 84, 86, 88, 90, 92, 94, 96*

Levine, Stuart R
American. Business Executive
CEO, Dale Carnegie and Associates, 1992.

Levinger, Moshe
Israeli. Religious Leader, Political Activist
Rabbi, spokesman for underground activist group that promotes the West Bank for Israeli Jews.
b. 1935 in Jerusalem, Israel
Source: *BioIn 12; HisEAAC; News 92, 92-1*

Levinsky, Battling
[Barney Lebrowitz; Barney Williams]
American. Boxer
Lost American light heavy title to Gene Tunney, 1922; Hall of Fame, 1966.
b. Jun 10, 1891 in Philadelphia, Pennsylvania
d. Feb 12, 1949 in Philadelphia, Pennsylvania
Source: *BiDAmSp BK; PseudN 82; WhoBox 74*

Levinson, Barry (Michael)
American. Director, Screenwriter
Director whose films include Oscar-winning *Rain Man,* 1988 and *Good Morning, Vietnam,* 1987; his comedy writing for "The Carol Burnett Show" earned him 3 Emmys.
b. Apr 6, 1942 in Baltimore, Maryland
Source: *BioIn 16; ConAu 149; ConTFT 6, 11; CurBio 90; IntDcF 2-2; IntMPA 92, 94, 96; IntWW 93; NewYTBS 90; WhoWrEP 92, 95; WrDr 92*

Levinson, Richard Leighton
American. Writer
Noted for creating, writing TV mystery shows including "Colombo," 1971-76; won two Emmys, one Peabody, four Edgars.
b. Aug 7, 1934 in Philadelphia, Pennsylvania
d. Mar 12, 1987 in Los Angeles, California
Source: *ConAu 13NR, 73; ConTFT 5; VarWW 85; WhoAm 80, 82, 84, 86*

Levi-Strauss, Claude Gustave
French. Anthropologist
Founder of structural anthropology who wrote several books including *From Honey to Ashes,* 1967.
b. Nov 28, 1908 in Brussels, Belgium
Source: *Au&Wr 71; Benet 87; BiDNeoM; BioIn 13, 14, 15; CamGLE; CasWL; ConAu 6NR, 32NR; ConLC 38; CurBio 72; CyWA 89; EncWL; FacFETw; IntWW 83, 91; MajTwCW; McGEWB; NewYTBS 87; OxCEng 85; RAdv 13-3; ThTwC 87; WhDW; Who 85, 92; WhoWor 84, 91; WorAl; WorAlBi; WorAu 1950*

Levitin, Sonia
American. Children's Author
Wrote award-winning *Journey to America,* 1971.
b. Aug 18, 1934 in Berlin, Germany
Source: *Au&Arts 13; AuBYP 2S, 3; BioIn 9, 15, 16, 17, 19; ConAu 14NR, 29R, 32NR; ConLC 17; DcAmChF 1960; FifBJA; SmATA 2AS, 4, 68; TwCChW 89; TwCYAW; WrDr 90, 92*

Levitt, Arthur, Jr.
American. Business Executive
Chief exec. American Stock Exchange, 1978-89; chm., Levitt Media, 1989-93; chm., NYC Economic Development Corp., 1990-93; chm., SEC, 1993—.
b. Feb 3, 1931 in New York, New York
Source: *BioIn 11, 12, 14; Dun&B 86, 88, 90; NewYTBS 77; St&PR 75, 84, 87, 91, 93, 96, 97; WhoAm 74, 76, 78, 80, 82, 84, 86, 88, 90, 92, 94, 95, 96, 97; WhoAmP 93, 95; WhoFI 79, 81, 83, 85, 87, 89, 94; WhoSecI 86; WhoWor 87*

Levitt, William J(aird)
American. Urban Planner
Postwar housing revolution leader; mass produced communities of Levittown, NJ; Levittown, NY; Levittown, PA.
b. Feb 11, 1907 in New York, New York
d. Jan 28, 1994 in Manhasset, New York
Source: *BiDAmBL 83; BioIn 1, 2, 4, 7, 8, 12, 13, 14, 15, 16; CurBio 56, 94N; NewYTBS 81, 89; WhAm 11; WhoAm 74, 76, 78, 80, 82, 84, 86, 88; WhoFI 74; WhoWor 74, 76; WorAl; WorAlBi*

Levy, Allan
American. Physician
Pioneer in sports medicine.
b. May 28, 1927
Source: *CelR 90*

Levy, Bernard-Henri
French. Philosopher
Wrote *La barbarie a visage humain,* 1977, which said that Marxism had failed to create the ideal society.
b. Nov 5, 1948 in Beni-Saf, Algeria
Source: *CurBio 93; IntWW 89, 91, 93; WhoWor 95, 96, 97*

Levy, David
Israeli. Politician
Held various Israeli government posts; resigned as foreign minister, 1992; one of first Moroccan Jews to reach cabinet rank.
b. 1938 in Rabat, French Morocco
Source: *BioIn 13, 16; ConNews 87-2; IntWW 83, 89, 91, 93; MidE 82; WhoWor 82, 87, 89, 93, 97*

Levy, David H.
American. Astronomer
Amateur astronomer, known for observing comets such as Shoemaker-Levy 9's collision with Jupiter, June 1994.
b. 1948 in Montreal, Quebec, Canada
Source: *BioIn 20, 21; CurBio 95*

Levy, David Mordecai
American. Psychiatrist
Originated concept of "sibling rivalry"; brought Rorschach test to US.
b. Apr 27, 1892 in Scranton, Pennsylvania
d. Mar 1, 1977 in New York, New York
Source: *Au&Wr 71; BioIn 11, 13; ConAu 69, 73; NatCAB 62; NewYTBS 77; WhAm 7; WhoAm 74, 76*

Levy, Florence
American. Art Director
Founder, editor, *American Art Annual,* 1898-1918.
b. Aug 13, 1870 in New York, New York
d. Nov 15, 1947 in New York, New York
Source: *NotAW; WomWWA 14*

Levy, Joseph Moses
English. Newspaper Publisher
Founded London's *Daily Telegraph,* 1855.
b. Dec 15, 1812 in London, England
d. Oct 12, 1888 in Ramsgate, England
Source: *DcNaB; NewCBEL*

Levy, Julien
"Modernist Maestro"
American. Art Historian, Author
Gallery was center for surrealist art; introduced Max Ernst, Arshile Gorky to US.
b. Jan 22, 1906 in New York, New York
d. Feb 10, 1981 in New Haven, Connecticut
Source: *AnObit 1981; BioIn 12; ConAu 103; NewYTBS 81; WhoAmA 78, 80, 82N, 84N, 86N, 89N, 91N, 93N*

Levy, Leonard Williams
American. Historian, Educator
Won Pulitzer for *Origins of the Fifth Amendment,* 1969.
b. Apr 9, 1923 in Toronto, Ontario, Canada
Source: *AmAu&B; ConAu 1NR, 1R, 20NR, 85; DrAS 74H, 78H, 82H; WhoAm 74, 76, 78, 80, 82, 84, 86, 88, 90, 92, 94, 95, 96, 97; WhoAmL 83, 85,*

87; WhoE 74, 85; WhoUSWr 88; WhoWorJ 72; WhoWrEP 89, 92, 95; WrDr 92

Levy, Raymond
French. Auto Executive
President of Renault, French state-owned carmaker, 1986—.
b. Jun 28, 1927 in Paris, France
Source: *BioIn 15; IntWW 91; WhoFr 79*

Levy, Uriah Phillips
American. Naval Officer
Purchased Monticello, 1862, expecting to give Jefferson's home to the nation, but heirs contested will.
b. Apr 22, 1792 in Philadelphia, Pennsylvania
d. Mar 22, 1862 in New York, New York
Source: *Alli SUP; ApCAB; BioIn 2, 3, 4, 5, 6, 8, 10, 11, 12; DcAmB; Drake; WebAB 74, 79; WebAMB; WhAm HS*

Levy-Bruhl, Lucien
French. Philosopher, Anthropologist
Was primarily concerned with nonrational beliefs of primitive man: *Primitive Mythology,* 1935.
b. Apr 10, 1857 in Paris, France
d. Mar 13, 1939 in Paris, France
Source: *BiDPsy; BioIn 9, 14; DcSoc; Dis&D; IntDcAn; LuthC 75; McGEWB; NamesHP; NewCol 75; OxCFr; OxCPhil; ThTwC 87; WhDW; WorAu 1970*

Lewenthal, Raymond
American. Pianist, Conductor
Soloist, recording artist; performed "Liszt Cycle," 1960s; noted for strong technique and colorful style.
b. Aug 29, 1926 in San Antonio, Texas
d. Nov 21, 1988 in Hudson, New York
Source: *Baker 78, 84, 92; BioIn 16; BlueB 76; IntWWM 77, 80; NewAmDM; NewGrDA 86; NewGrDM 80; NewYTBE 71; PenDiMP; WhAm 9; WhoAmM 83; WhoMus 72; WhoWor 74*

Lewes, George Henry
English. Critic, Philosopher
Wrote biographical classic *Life of Goethe,* 1855; common-law husband of George Eliot.
b. Apr 18, 1817 in London, England
d. Nov 28, 1878 in Surrey, England
Source: *Alli, SUP; BiD&SB; BiDPsy; BioIn 1, 2, 3, 4, 6, 7, 8, 9, 10, 11, 13, 14, 15, 16, 17, 21; BlmGEL; BritAu 19; CamGEL; CamGLE; CamGWoT; CasWL; CelCen; Chambr 3; DcBiPP; DcEnA; DcEnL; DcEuL; DcLB 55, 144; DcLEL; DcNaB; Dis&D; EncWT; EvLB; LinLib L, S; LngCEL; NamesHP; NewC; NewCBEL; NewCol 75; NinCLC 25; NotNAT B; OxCEng 67, 85; OxCThe 67, 83; PenC ENG; RAdv 14; REn; VicBrit*

Lewin, Kurt
American. Psychologist
Originated field theory of human behavior; wrote *Principles of Topological Psychology,* 1936.
b. Sep 9, 1890 in Mogilno, Prussia
d. Feb 12, 1947 in Newtonville, Massachusetts
Source: *BiDPsy; BioIn 1, 5, 8, 13, 14, 18; DcAmB S4; GuPsyc; McGEWB; NamesHP; NewCol 75; RAdv 14, 13-3; ThTwC 87; WhAm 2; WhDW*

Lewis, Allen Montgomery, Sir
British. Government Official
First governor-general of St. Lucia, 1979-80; wrote *Revised Edition of Laws of St. Lucia,* 1957.
b. Oct 26, 1909 in Castries, St. Lucia
Source: *IntWW 83, 91; IntYB 82; Who 85, 92; WhoRel 92; WhoWor 80, 91*

Lewis, Anthony
American. Journalist
Won Pulitzer for nat. reporting, 1955, 1963; wrote award-winning crime book: *Gideon's Trumpet,* 1965.
b. Mar 27, 1927 in New York, New York
Source: *BioIn 3, 4, 7, 9, 13, 16; BlueB 76; ConAu 9R; CurBio 55; EncAJ; EncTwCJ; IntAu&W 89, 91, 93; JrnUS; ScF&FL 1; SmATA 27; Who 74, 92; WhoAm 74, 76, 78, 80, 82, 84, 86, 88, 90, 92, 94, 95, 96, 97; WhoAmL 85, 87; WhoAmP 87, 89, 91, 93, 95; WhoE 89, 91, 95; WorAl; WorAlBi*

Lewis, Boyd de Wolf
American. Editor, Author
Exec. editor, Newspaper Enterprise Assoc., 1945—; published *The World Almanac,* 1966-72.
b. Aug 18, 1905 in Boston, Massachusetts
Source: *WhoAm 86, 90, 92, 94, 95, 96, 97; WhoWor 74*

Lewis, C(live) S(taples)
[N W Clerk; Clive Hamilton]
English. Author, Scholar
Wrote literary studies, science fiction, children's fantasies, Christian apologetics including *Screwtape Letters,* 1942.
b. Nov 29, 1898 in Belfast, Northern Ireland
d. Nov 22, 1963 in Heddington, England
Source: *AnCL; Au&ICB; AuBYP 2, 3; Benet 96; BiDIrW; BioIn 1, 3, 4, 6, 7, 8, 9, 10, 11, 12, 13, 14, 15, 16, 17, 18, 19, 20; CasWL; ChhPo S1, S2; ChlLR 27; ConAu 81; ConLC 14; CurBio 64; DcArts; DcIrB 78, 88; DcIrW 2; DcLEL; DcNaB 1961; EncSF 93; EncWB; EncWL, 3; EngPo; EvLB; GrBr; LngCEL; LuthC 75; MajAI; MakMC; ModBrL S1; MorJA; NewCBEL; OxCEng 67, 85, 95; OxCIri; OxCTwCP; PenC ENG; RAdv 14, 13-1; REn; RGTwCWr; SJGFanW; TwCA SUP; TwCChW 95; TwCWr; WhAm 4; WhDW; WhE&EA; WhoChL*

Lewis, Carl
[Frederick Carlton Lewis]
American. Track Athlete
Only person since Jesse Owens to win four gold medals in track and field, 1984 Olympics; won 100-meter gold medal, 1988 Olympics, when Ben Johnson was disqualified; won his 9th Olympic gold medal—for the long jump—1996.
b. Jul 1, 1961 in Birmingham, Alabama
Source: *AfrAmAl 6; AfrAmBi 2; AfrAmSG; BiDAmSp OS; BioIn 12, 13, 14, 15, 16; BlkOlyM; ConBlB 4; CurBio 84, 96; FacFETw; InB&W 85; IntWW 91, 93; LegTOT; NegAl 89; NewYTBS 84, 85, 87; WhoAfA 96; WhoAm 86, 88, 90, 92, 94, 95, 96, 97; WhoBlA 85, 88, 90, 92, 94; WhoSpor; WhoWor 95, 96, 97; WorAlBi*

Lewis, Carol
American. Track Athlete
Sister of Carl Lewis; won US title in long jump, 1982, 1983.
b. Aug 8, 1963 in Birmingham, Alabama
Source: *BioIn 12, 14; EncWomS; NewYTBS 84*

Lewis, Chris
New Zealander. Tennis Player
Won Wimbledon junior championship, 1975; lost in Wimbledon final, 1983.
b. Mar 9, 1957 in Auckland, New Zealand
Source: *BioIn 13; NewYTBS 83; WhoIntT*

Lewis, Clarence Irving
American. Philosopher, Educator
Wrote *Analysis of Knowledge and Valuation,* 1947.
b. Apr 12, 1883 in Stoneham, Massachusetts
d. Feb 3, 1964 in Menlo Park, California
Source: *BioIn 6, 8, 14; DcAmB S7; EncEth; McGEWB; OxCAmH; OxCPhil; RAdv 14, 13-4; WebBD 83; WhAm 4; WhE&EA*

Lewis, David
American. Producer
Films include *Dark Victory,* 1939; *King's Row,* 1942.
b. 1904?
d. Mar 1987 in Los Angeles, California

Lewis, David Levering
American. Writer
Won 1994 Pulitzer Prize for biography with *W. E. B. Du Bois: Biography of a Race 1868-1919..*
b. May 25, 1936 in Little Rock, Arkansas
Source: *ConAu 45; ConBlB 9; DrAS 82H; IntAu&W 77; LivgBAA; SelBAAf; SelBAAu; WhoAm 95, 96, 97; WhoE 95, 97*

Lewis, Delano (Eugene)
American. Radio Executive
President and CEO of National Public Radio (NPR), 1994—.
b. Nov 12, 1938 in Arkansas City, Kansas
Source: *ConBlB 7; WhoAfA 96; WhoAm 92, 96, 97; WhoBlA 80, 85, 88, 90, 92, 94; WhoFI 92; WhoSSW 73*

Lewis, Dominic Bevan Wyndham
English. Author
Essayist, biographer who wrote *Francois Villon,* 1928.
b. 1894 in Wales
d. Nov 23, 1969 in Altea, Spain
Source: *BioIn 1, 4; CathA 1930; ChhPo S1, S2; DcLEL; EvLB; LngCTC; ModBrL; NewC; NewCBEL; PenC ENG; REn; TwCA, SUP*

Lewis, Drew
[Andrew Lindsay Lewis, Jr]
American. Government Official
Secretary of transportation under Reagan, 1981-83.
b. Nov 3, 1931 in Philadelphia, Pennsylvania
Source: *BioIn 12, 13, 14, 15, 16; CngDr 81; CurBio 82; Dun&B 90; IntWW 81, 82, 83, 89, 91, 93; NatCAB 63N; NewYTBS 80, 81; St&PR 87, 91, 93, 96, 97; WhoAm 74, 76, 78, 80, 82, 84, 86, 88, 90, 92, 94, 95, 96, 97; WhoAmP 87; WhoE 81, 83, 85, 89, 91, 97; WhoFI 87, 89, 94, 96; WhoWor 82*

Lewis, Edmonia
[Mary Edmonia Lewis]
"Wildfire"
American. Sculptor
First black woman sculptor; *Death of Cleopatra* shown at Centennial Exposition, PA, 1876.
b. Jul 4, 1845 in Albany, New York
d. 1911? in Rome, Italy
Source: *AfrAmAl 6; AfroAA; ApCAB; BiDWomA; BioIn 3, 6, 7, 8, 9, 10, 11; ContDcW 89; DcAmArt; DcAmNB; DcWomA; GayLesB; GrLiveH; InB&W 80; IntDcWB; InWom, SUP; LibW; NatCAB 5; NegAl 76, 83, 89; NotAW; NotBlAW 1; TwCBDA; WhoColR; WomFir*

Lewis, Elizabeth Foreman
American. Children's Author
Won 1933 Newbery for *Young Fu of the Upper Yangtze.*
b. May 24, 1892 in Baltimore, Maryland
d. Aug 7, 1958 in Arnold, Maryland
Source: *AmAu&B; AmWomWr; AuBYP 2, 3; BioIn 14, 19; ChhPo S1; ConAu 137; JBA 34, 51; MajAI; NewbMB 1922; TwCChW 83, 89; TwCYAW; WhAm 3; WhE&EA; YABC 2*

Lewis, Elma Ina
American. Educator
Founder/director Elma Lewis School of Fine Arts, 1950—; founder Nat. Ctr. of Afro-American Artists, 1969, center for Black culture and art.
b. Sep 15, 1921 in Boston, Massachusetts
Source: *BiDAfM; BioIn 8, 9, 12, 13; NotBlAW 1; WhoAm 76, 90; WhoAmA 73, 76, 78, 80, 82, 84, 86, 89, 91, 93; WhoAmW 72, 74, 75; WhoBlA 92; WhoE 74, 75, 89*

Lewis, Emmanuel
American. Actor
Played title role in TV series "Webster," 1983-86.
b. Mar 9, 1971 in New York, New York
Source: *BioIn 13, 14; ConTFT 7; DrBlPA 90; InB&W 85; IntMPA 86, 88, 92, 94, 96; LegTOT; VarWW 85; WhoAfA 96; WhoBlA 94*

Lewis, Flora
American. Journalist, Author
New York Times foreign correspondent, 1942—; first woman foreign correspondent to work for the *Washington Post* 1955; has written 4 books and received numerous journalism awards.
b. 1923 in Los Angeles, California
Source: *BioIn 15; ConAu 119; CurBio 89; InWom SUP; WhoAm 90; WhoAmW 91; WhoE 89; WomStre; WrDr 92*

Lewis, Francis
American. Continental Congressman, Merchant
Member, Continental Congress, 1775-79; signed Declaration of Independence.
b. Mar 21, 1713 in Llandaff, Wales
d. Dec 30, 1802 in New York, New York
Source: *AmBi; ApCAB; BiAUS; BiDrAC; BiDrUSC 89; BioIn 3, 4, 7, 8, 9; DcAmB; Drake; EncAR; EncCRAm; HarEnUS; NatCAB 5; PeoHis; TwCBDA; WhAm HS; WhAmP; WhAmRev*

Lewis, Fulton, Jr.
American. Broadcast Journalist
Popular right-wing radio commentator who attacked New Deal, supported Joe McCarthy.
b. Apr 30, 1903 in Washington, District of Columbia
d. Aug 21, 1966 in Washington, District of Columbia
Source: *BiDAmJo; BiDAmNC; BioIn 1, 2, 3, 4, 7, 11, 16, 19; ConAu 89; CurBio 42, 66; DcAmB S8; DcAmC; DcAmDH 80, 89; EncAJ; EncTwCJ; RadStar; SaTiSS; WhAm 4*

Lewis, Henry (Jay)
American. Conductor
First black director of a US symphony orchestra; led NJ Symphony, 1968-76.
b. Oct 16, 1932 in Los Angeles, California
d. Jan 26, 1996 in New York, New York
Source: *AfrAmAl 6; Baker 78, 84, 92; BiDAfM; BioIn 7, 8, 9, 10, 11, 21; BlkCond; BlkOpe; CurBio 73, 96N; DrBlPA, 90; Ebony 1; InB&W 80, 85; IntWWM 77, 80, 90; MetOEnc; MusSN; NegAl 89; NewAmDM; NewGrDA 86; NewGrDM 80; NewGrDO; News 96, 96-3; NewYTBS 27; PenDiMP; WhAm 11; WhoAfA 96; WhoAm 74, 76, 78, 80, 82, 84, 86, 88; WhoAmM 83; WhoBlA 75, 77, 80, 85, 90, 92, 94; WhoE 74, 75, 77; WhoWor 74*

Lewis, Huey
[Huey Lewis and the News; Hugh Anthony Cregg, III]
American. Singer
Founded group, 1979; hits include "I Want a New Drug," 1983; "The Power of Love," 1984; "Hip to Be Square," 1986.
b. Jul 5, 1951 in New York, New York
Source: *BioIn 13, 14, 15, 16; CelR 90; ConMus 9; ConNews 87-3; EncPR&S 89; EncRk 88; HarEnR 86; LegTOT; PenEncP; RkOn 85; WhoAm 94, 95, 96, 97; WhoEnt 92; WorAlBi*

Lewis, Ida
American. Historical Figure
Lighthouse keeper known for numerous Atlantic rescues.
b. Feb 25, 1842 in Newport, Rhode Island
d. Oct 24, 1911 in Lime Rock, Rhode Island
Source: *BioAmW; InWom SUP; LibW; NatCAB 5; NotAW*

Lewis, Isaac Newton
American. Inventor
Invented air-cooled Lewis machine gun, 1911; used by Allies, WW I.
b. Oct 12, 1858 in New Salem, Pennsylvania
d. Nov 9, 1931 in Montclair, New Jersey
Source: *AmBi; BioIn 12; DcAmB; EncAB-A 1; InSci; NatCAB 16; WebAMB; WhAm 1*

Lewis, James W
[Robert Richardson]
American. Criminal
Accused of extorting from Johnson & Johnson during Chicago's Tylenol poisonings, 1982.
b. 1946?

Lewis, Janet
[Janet Lewis Winters]
American. Author, Poet
Novels include *The Invasion,* 1932; wife of Yvor Winters.
b. Aug 17, 1899 in Chicago, Illinois
Source: *AmAu&B; AmNov; AmWomWr; ArtclWW 2; ASCAP 66, 80; Au&Wr 71; BenetAL 91; BioIn 2, 4, 10, 12, 13, 17, 19; ChhPo, S1; CnDAL; ConAu 29NR, P-1, X; ConLC 41; ConNov 72, 76, 82, 86, 91, 96; DcLB Y87B; DcVicP 2; DrAF 76; DrAP 75; DrAPF 80, 91; FemiCLE; ForWC 70; IntAu&W 76, 77, 89, 91; IntWWP 77, 82; InWom, SUP; ModWoWr; OxCAmL 65, 83, 95; OxCTwCP; PeoHis; TwCA SUP; TwCRHW 90, 94; TwCWW 91; WhE&EA; WhoAm 74, 76, 78; WhoAmW 58, 68, 70, 72, 74, 97; WhoUSWr 88;*

WhoWrEP 89, 92; WrDr 76, 80, 82, 84, 86, 88, 90, 92, 94, 96

Lewis, Jerry
[Joseph Levitch]
American. Comedian
Zany film, TV star whose muscular dystrophy telethons have raised over $1 billion.
b. Mar 16, 1926 in Newark, New Jersey
Source: *BiDFilm, 81, 94; BioIn 6, 7, 8, 9, 10, 11, 12, 13, 14, 15, 16, 17, 19, 21; BkPepl; BlueB 76; CelR, 90; CmMov; CmpEPM; ConAu 113, 121; ConTFT 5; CurBio 62; DcArts; DcTwCCu 1; EncAFC; FacFETw; FilmEn; FilmgC; ForYSC; Funs; GrMovC; HalFC 80, 84, 88; IIWWHD 1A; IntDcF 1-2, 2-2; IntMPA 75, 76, 77, 78, 79, 80, 81, 82, 84, 86, 88, 92, 94, 96; IntWW 79, 80, 81, 82, 83, 89, 91, 93; JoeFr; LegTOT; MiSFD 9; MotPP; MovMk; NewYTBS 79; OxCFilm; QDrFCA 92; RadStar; RkOn 74; VarWW 85; WhoAm 74, 76, 78, 80, 82, 84, 86, 88, 90, 92, 94, 95, 96, 97; WhoCom; WhoEnt 92; WhoHol 92, A; WhoHrs 80; WhoWor 84, 87, 89, 91, 93, 95; WorAl; WorAlBi; WorEFlm; WorFDir 2*

Lewis, Jerry Lee
"Killer"
American. Singer, Musician
Country-rock hit singles include "Whole Lotta Shakin' Goin' On," 1957; "Breathless," 1958.
b. Sep 29, 1940 in Ferriday, Louisiana
Source: *Baker 84; BiDrAPA 89; BioIn 13, 14, 15, 16; ConMus 2; EncFCWM 83; EncPR&S 74, 89; FacFETw; HarEnCM 87; IlEncRk; IntWWM 90; NewAmDM; NewGrDA 86; OxCPMus; PeoHis; VarWW 85; WhoAm 86, 90; WhoEnt 92; WhoRocM 82; WhoSSW 88*

Lewis, Joe E
American. Actor, Comedian
Nightclub comedian whose problems with gangsters were depicted in film *The Joker Is Wild,* 1957, starring Frank Sinatra.
b. Jan 12, 1902 in New York, New York
d. Jun 4, 1971 in New York, New York
Source: *FilmgC; NewYTBE 71; ObitOF 79; WhoHol B; WhScrn 77*

Lewis, John Aaron
American. Musician
Jazz pianist, played with Dizzy Gillespie, Miles Davis, etc; formed Modern Jazz Quartet, 1952-74.
b. May 3, 1920 in La Grange, Illinois
Source: *Baker 84; BiDJaz; BioIn 13, 14, 16; DrBlPA 90; InB&W 85; NegAl 89; NewAmDM; NewGrDA 86; NewGrDJ 88; OxCPMus; PenEncP; WhoAm 84; WhoBlA 75*

Lewis, John L(lewellyn)
American. Labor Union Official
Pres., United Mine Workers, 1920-60; founded, headed CIO, 1935-40.
b. Feb 12, 1880 in Lucas, Iowa
d. Jun 11, 1969 in Washington, District of Columbia
Source: *AmOrTwC; AmSocL; BiDAmL; BiDAmLL; BioIn 1, 2, 3, 4, 5, 6, 7, 8, 9, 10, 11, 12, 13; CurBio 42, 69; DcAmB S8; DcAmSR; DcTwHis; EncAB-H 1974, 1996; LinLib S; McGEWB; NatCAB 57; ObitT 1961; OxCAmH; PeoHis; WebAB 74, 79; What 1; WhDW; WorAl*

Lewis, John Robert
American. Politician, Civil Rights Leader
Co-founder, Student Nonviolent Coordinating Com. 1960, chm., 1963-66; Dem. congressman, GA, 1987—.
b. Feb 21, 1940 in Troy, Alabama
Source: *AfrAmAl 6; AfrAmOr; AlmAP 92; AmSocL; BioIn 11, 12, 15; CngDr 87; CurBio 80; EncWB; InB&W 80, 85; WhoAfA 96; WhoAm 76, 78, 88; WhoBlA 75, 77, 80, 85, 88, 90, 92, 94; WhoSSW 73, 75, 76, 88*

Lewis, Juliette
American. Actor
Film roles in *Cape Fear,* 1991; *Husbands and Wives,* 1992.
b. Jun 21, 1973 in Los Angeles, California
Source: *CurBio 96; IntMPA 96; LegTOT; WhoAm 94, 95, 96, 97; WhoAmW 95, 97*

Lewis, Loida Nicolas
American. Business Executive
Chair and CEO, TLC Beatrice, 1994—.
b. Dec 23, 1942 in Sorsogon, Philippines
Source: *WhoAfA 96; WhoAm 96, 97; WhoWor 96, 97*

Lewis, Matthew Gregory
English. Author
Wrote sensational spine-chilling Gothic novel *The Monk.*
b. Jul 9, 1775 in London, England
d. May 14, 1818
Source: *Alli; BbD; Benet 87, 96; BiD&SB; BiDLA; BioIn 3, 5, 6, 8, 9, 12, 15; BlmGEL; BritAu 19; CasWL; CelCen; Chambr 2; ChhPo, S1, S2; CrtSuDr; CrtT 2; CyWA 58; DcArts; DcBiA; DcBiPP; DcEnA; DcEnL; DcEuL; DcLB 39, 158; DcLEL; DcNaB, C; EncO&P 1, 2, 3; Ent; EvLB; GrWrEL N; McGEWB; MnBBF; MouLC 2; NewC; NewCBEL; NinCLC 11; NotNAT B; OxCEng 67; OxCThe 67, 83; PenC ENG; PenEncH; RAdv 14; REn; RfGEnL 91; WebE&AL; WhoHr&F; WorAlBi*

Lewis, Meade Anderson Lux
"The Duke of Luxembourg"
American. Jazz Musician, Composer
Pianist who popularized boogie-woogie; wrote "Honky Tonk Train Blues," 1930s.
b. Sep 4, 1905 in Chicago, Illinois
d. Jun 7, 1964 in Minneapolis, Minnesota
Source: *ASCAP 66; Baker 84; BiDJaz; WhoHol B; WhoJazz 72; WhScrn 74, 77*

Lewis, Meriwether
[Lewis and Clark]
American. Explorer
With William Clark, commanded first expedition across America, 1804-06.
b. Aug 18, 1774 in Albemarle County, Virginia
d. Oct 11, 1809 in Nashville, Tennessee
Source: *Alli; AmAu&B; AmBi; ApCAB; BenetAL 91; BiAUS; BiDrATG; BiDSA; BilnAmS; BioIn 1, 2, 3, 4, 5, 6, 7, 8, 9, 10, 11, 12, 13, 14, 15, 16, 17, 18, 19, 20, 21; CamGEL; CamHAL; CasWL; DcAmB; DcAmMiB; Dis&D; Drake; EncAAH; EncAB-H 1974, 1996; EncSoH; Expl 93; HarEnMi; HarEnUS; LegTOT; LinLib L, S; McGEWB; NatCAB 5; OxCAmH; OxCAmL 65, 83, 95; PenC AM; PeoHis; RAdv 14, 13-3; REnAL; REnAW; TwCBDA; WebAB 74, 79; WebAMB; WhAm HS; WhDW; WhNaAH; WhWE; WorAl; WorAlBi*

Lewis, Oscar
American. Anthropologist, Author
Wrote prize-winning accounts of Mexican, Puerto Rican poor: *La Vida,* 1966.
b. Dec 25, 1914 in New York, New York
d. Dec 16, 1970 in New York, New York
Source: *AmAu&B; AmSocL; Benet 87, 96; BenetAL 91; BioIn 8, 9, 10, 14, 19; ConAu 29R, P-1; CurBio 68, 71, 71N; DcAmB S8; EncWB; IntDcAn; IntEnSS 79; LegTOT; LinLib L; RAdv 14, 13-3; ThTwC 87; WhAm 5; WhDW; WorAl; WorAlBi; WorAu 1950*

Lewis, Paul Edward
[The Hostages]
American. Hostage
One of 52 held by terrorists, Nov 1979-Jan 1981.
b. 1957?
Source: *NewYTBS 81*

Lewis, Ramsey Emanuel, Jr.
American. Musician, Composer
Hits include "The In Crowd," 1965.
b. May 27, 1935 in Chicago, Illinois
Source: *Baker 84; BiDAfM; BiDJaz; BioIn 13; CurBio 96; DrBlPA 90; EncPR&S 89; EncRk 88; InB&W 80, 85; NewAmDM; NewGrDJ 88; PenEncP; WhoAfA 96; WhoAm 74, 76, 78, 80, 82, 84, 86, 88, 90, 92, 94, 95, 96, 97; WhoBlA 75, 77, 80, 85, 88, 90, 92, 94; WhoEnt 92; WhoRock 81; WorAl; WorAlBi*

Lewis, Reggie
American. Basketball Player
Boston Celtics captain, 1993.
b. c. 1966
d. Jul 27, 1993 in Waltham, Massachusetts
Source: *News 94, 94-1*

Lewis, Reginald F.
American. Business Executive
Chm., TLC Beatrice International Holdings, Inc., largest US African-American owned business, 1987-93.
b. Dec 7, 1942 in Baltimore, Maryland
d. Jan 19, 1993 in New York, New York
Source: *AfrAmAl 6; AfrAmBi 2; AmDec 1980; AnObit 1993; BioIn 15, 16; ConAmBL; ConBlB 6; News 88; NewYTBS 91, 93; WhAm 11; WhoAm 88, 90, 92; WhoBlA 75, 77, 80, 85, 88, 90, 92, 94N; WhoFI 89, 92*

Lewis, Richard
American. Actor, Comedian
Played Marty Gold in TV series "Anything But Love," 1989-92.
b. Jun 29, 1947 in Englewood, New Jersey
Source: *CurBio 93; News 92; WhoCom*

Lewis, Robert Alvin
American. Pilot
With Paul Tibbets, co-pilot of *Enola Gay,* plane that dropped atomic bomb on Hiroshima, 1945.
b. 1918? in New York, New York
d. Jun 18, 1983 in Newport News, Virginia
Source: *NewYTBS 83*

Lewis, Robert Q
American. TV Personality
Frequent TV panelist; hosted "Robert Q Lewis Show," 1950s.
b. Apr 5, 1921 in New York, New York
d. Dec 11, 1991 in Los Angeles, California
Source: *EncAFC; LesBEnT, 92; NewYTBS 91; NewYTET; VarWW 85; WhoHol A*

Lewis, Roger
American. Business Executive
First president of Amtrak, passenger rail service, 1971-75.
b. Jan 11, 1912 in Los Angeles, California
d. Nov 12, 1987 in Washington, District of Columbia
Source: *BioIn 6, 7, 9, 10, 15, 16; BlueB 76; CurBio 73, 88, 88N; IntWW 74, 75, 76, 77, 78; ScF&FL 92; WhAm 9; WhoAm 74, 76, 78, 80; WhoE 74; WhoFI 74; WhoWor 74*

Lewis, Rosa
[Rosa Ovenden]
British. Hotel Executive
Owner, caterer of London's celebrated Cavendish Hotel; subject of BBC's "Duchess of Duke Street," 1978.
b. 1867
d. 1952
Source: *BioIn 3, 6, 7, 11, 14; DcNaB 1951; GrBr; ObitOF 79; ObitT 1951; WorAl*

Lewis, Saunders
English. Political Activist, Critic, Dramatist
Founder, pres., Welsh Nationalist Party, 1920s-30s; plays include *Esther.*
b. Oct 15, 1893 in Wallasey, England
d. Sep 1, 1985 in Cardiff, Wales
Source: *AnObit 1985; BioIn 20; CasWL; ConAu 117; EncWL 2, 3; IntAu&W 76, 77, 82; IntWW 75, 76, 77, 78, 79, 80, 81, 82, 83; IntWWP 77; OxCLiW 86; WhE&EA; WhLit; Who 74, 82, 83, 85*

Lewis, Shari
[Shari Hurwitz; Mrs. Jeremy Tarcher]
American. Ventriloquist, Author
Starred on TV with puppet Lamb Chop; won five Emmys; has PBS show "Lamb Chop's Play-a-Long."
b. Jan 17, 1934 in New York, New York
Source: *AuBYP 3; BioIn 4, 5, 13, 14; CelR 90; ConAu 19NR, 89; ConTFT 3; CurBio 58; InWom, SUP; LegTOT; News 93-1; SmATA 30, 35; VarWW 85; WhoAm 74, 76, 78, 80, 82, 84, 86, 88, 90, 92, 94, 95, 96, 97; WhoAmW 58, 61, 64, 66, 68, 70, 72, 74, 83, 95, 97; WhoEnt 92; WorAl; WorAlBi*

Lewis, Sinclair
[Harry Sinclair Lewis]
American. Author, Dramatist
First American to win Nobel Prize for literature, 1930; wrote *Babbitt,* 1922, *Arrowsmith,* 1925.
b. Feb 7, 1885 in Sauk Centre, Minnesota
d. Jan 10, 1951 in Rome, Italy
Source: *AmAu&B; AmCulL; AmNov; AmWr; AtlBL; Benet 87; BenetAL 91; BioIn 1, 2, 3, 4, 5, 6, 7, 8, 9, 10, 11, 12, 13, 14, 15, 17, 18, 19, 21; CamGEL; CamGLE; CamHAL; CasWL; Chambr 3; ChhPo; CnDAL; CnMD; CnMWL; ConAmA; ConAmL; ConAu 104, 133; CyWA 58; DcAmB S5; DcAmC; DcAmSR; DcLB 9, 102, DS1; DcLEL; Dis&D; EncAAH; EncAB-H 1974, 1996; EncSF; EncUnb; EncWL, 2, 3; EvLB; FilmgC; GrWrEL N; HalFC 80, 84, 88; LegTOT; LinLib L, S; LngCTC; MagSAmL; MajTwCW; MakMC; McGEWB; MemAm; ModAL, S1, S2; ModWD; NatCAB 57; NewEScF; NobelP; NotNAT B; Novels; ObitT 1951; OxCAmH; OxCAmL 65, 83; OxCEng 67, 85; PenC AM; RAdv 1, 14, 13-1; RComAH; RComWL; REn; REnAL; RfGAmL 87; ScF&FL 1; ScFSB; Tw; TwCA, SUP; TwCLC 3, 4, 13, 23, 39; TwCSAPR; TwCSFW 81, 86; TwCWr; WebAB 74, 79; WebE&AL; WhAm 3; WhDW; WhLit; WhNAA; WhoNob, 90, 95; WhoTwCL; WorAl; WorAlBi; WorLitC*

Lewis, Stephen Henry
Canadian. Government Official
Canadian ambassador to UN, 1984-88; advocate of organization's preservation.
b. Nov 11, 1937 in Ottawa, Ontario, Canada
Source: *CanWW 83, 89; ConNews 87-2; Dun&B 88; IntWW 89; WhoAm 86; WhoWor 87*

Lewis, Ted
[Theodore Leopold Friedman]
American. Bandleader
Cane, top-hat dance man; noted for "Me and My Shadow."
b. Jun 9, 1892 in Circleville, Ohio
d. Aug 25, 1971 in New York, New York
Source: *ASCAP 66, 80; BiDJaz; BioIn 5, 6, 8, 9, 10, 12; CmpEPM; EncJzS; FilmgC; LegTOT; NewGrDA 86; NewGrDJ 88, 94; NewYTBE 70, 71; OxCPMus; PenEncP; WhAm 5; WhoHol B; WhoJazz 72; WhScrn 74, 77; WorAl; WorAlBi*

Lewis, Ted
[Gershon Mendeloff]
"Kid"
English. Boxer
Won world feather, welter titles, 1910s; fought record-long series with welterweight Jack Britton, 1915-21; Hall of Fame, 1964.
b. Oct 24, 1894 in London, England
d. Oct 20, 1970 in London, England
Source: *BioIn 7, 9, 18; BoxReg; DcNaB MP; ObitT 1961; WhoBox 74; WhScrn 83*

Lewis, (Myrtle) Tillie
American. Business Executive
Founded Flotill Products, a food canning business; marketed pear-shaped tomatoes, 1937-70.
b. Jul 13, 1901 in New York, New York
d. Apr 30, 1977 in Stockton, California
Source: *BioIn 10*

Lewis, Tom
American. Businessman
Founded Armed Forces Radio, WW II; married to actress Loretta Young for 30 yrs.
b. 1902? in Troy, New York
d. May 20, 1988 in Los Angeles, California
Source: *IntMPA 86*

Lewis, William Arthur, Sir
British. Educator, Journalist
Won Nobel Prize in economics, 1979; first black winner in category besides peace.
b. Jan 23, 1915 in Castries, St. Lucia
d. Jun 16, 1991 in Bridgeport, Barbados
Source: *AmEA 74; Au&Wr 71; BioIn 12, 13, 15, 17, 18, 20; IntAu&W 82, 86; IntWW 74, 76, 78, 79, 80, 82, 83, 89, 91; NewYTBS 79, 91; SelBAAf; WhAm 10; Who 74, 82, 83, 85, 88, 90, 92N; WhoAm 74, 76, 78, 80, 82, 84, 86, 88, 90; WhoAmA 91; WhoBlA 80, 85, 88, 90, 92, 94N; WhoE 81, 83, 85, 86, 89, 91; WhoEc 86; WhoFI 83, 85, 89; WhoNob, 90, 95; WhoUN 75; WhoWor 80, 82, 84, 87, 89, 91*

Lewis, Wilmarth Sheldon
American. Editor, Scholar
Amassed mammoth Horace Walpole collection; edited Yale's 50-volume Walpole correspondence.
b. Nov 14, 1895 in Alameda, California
d. Oct 7, 1979 in Hartford, Connecticut
Source: *AmAu&B; BioIn 1, 2, 4, 5, 8, 9, 10, 15, 20; ChhPo; ConAu 15NR, 65, 89; CurBio 73, 80, 80N; DcLB 140; DrAS 74E, 78E; NewYTBS 79; WhAm 7, 8; WhE&EA; WhNAA; Who 74; WhoAm 74, 76, 78, 80; WhoGov 72, 75, 77*

Lewis, Wyndham
[Percy Wyndham Lewis]
English. Author, Artist
Leader, Vorticist movement, edited *Blast,* 1914; wrote satire trilogy, *The Human Age,* 1928.
b. Nov 18, 1884 in Maine
d. Mar 7, 1957 in London, England
Source: *AtlBL; BioIn 2, 3, 4, 5, 6, 8, 9, 10, 12, 13; BritWr 7; CamGEL; CasWL; CnE&AP; CnMWL; ConAu 104; CyWA 58; DcLEL; EncSF; EvLB; FacFETw; LegTOT; LngCEL; LngCTC; McGDA; ModBrL, S1; NewC; ObitT 1951; OxCArt; OxCCan; OxCEng 67; PenC ENG; RAdv 1, 14, 13-1; REn; TwCA, SUP; TwCWr; WebE&AL; WhDW; WhoTwCL; WorAl*

Lewisohn, Adolph
American. Philanthropist
Mining exec. whose endowments included Columbia U's School of Mining building.
b. 1849 in Hamburg, Germany
d. Aug 17, 1938 in New York, New York
Source: *ApCAB X; Baker 78, 84, 92; BiDAmBL 83; BioIn 1, 4; DcAmBC; DcAmB S2; NatCAB 33; NewGrDA 86; WhAm 1; WorAl; WorAlBi*

Lewisohn, Ludwig
English. Author, Artist
Wrote *The Island Within,* 1928; *This People,* 1933.
b. May 30, 1882 in Berlin, Germany
d. Dec 31, 1955 in Miami Beach, Florida
Source: *AmAu&B; AmLY; AmNov; BiDSA; BioIn 2, 4, 5, 7, 9, 11, 12, 14, 16, 17; ChhPo; CnDAL; ConAmA; ConAmL; ConAu 107; DcAmB S5; DcLB 4, 9, 28, 102; DcLEL; Dis&D; JeAmFiW; ModAL; NatCAB 42; ObitOF 79; OhA&B; OxCAmL 65, 83, 95; PenC AM; REn; REnAL; ScF&FL 1; ScFEYrs; TwCA, SUP; WhAm 3; WhNAA*

LeWitt, Sol
American. Artist
Conceptual/minimal sculptor, using square, cube, line as basic components.
b. Sep 9, 1928 in Hartford, Connecticut
Source: *AmArt; BioIn 11, 13, 14, 15, 18, 20; BriEAA; ConArt 83, 89, 96; CurBio 86; DcAmArt; DcCAA 71, 77, 88, 94; DcCAr 81; ICPEnP A; IntWW 89, 91, 93; OxCTwCA; OxDcArt; PhDcTCA 77; PrintW 83, 85; WhoAm 82, 84, 86, 88, 90, 92, 94, 95, 96, 97; WhoAmA 73, 76, 78, 80, 82, 84, 86, 89, 91, 93; WorArt 1950*

Lewton, Val Ivan
[Vladimir Ivan Leventon]
American. Producer
Specialized in low-cost horror films for RKO: *Body Snatchers,* 1945.
b. May 7, 1904 in Yalta, Russia
d. Mar 14, 1951
Source: *BiDFilm; BioIn 1, 2, 11; DcFM; FanAl; FilmEn; FilmgC; OxCFilm; WorEFlm*

Lewyt, Alexander Milton
American. Inventor, Philanthropist
Invented Lewyt vacuum cleaner; awarded French Legion of Honor for supplying equipment to Allies, WW II.
b. Dec 31, 1908 in New York, New York
d. Feb 18, 1988 in Sands Point, New York
Source: *NewYTBS 88; WhoAm 78, 80, 82, 84; WhoWor 74*

Lexcen, Ben
[Bob Miller]
Australian. Designer
Designed *Australia II* yacht, controversial winner of 1983 America's Cup race.
b. 1936 in Boggabri, Australia
d. May 1, 1988 in Sydney, Australia
Source: *BioIn 13; NewYTBS 83*

Ley, Robert
German. Political Leader
Anti-semitic head of Germany's Labor Front, 1933-45; committed suicide while awaiting trial.
b. Feb 15, 1890 in Niederbreitenbach, Germany
d. Oct 25, 1945 in Nuremberg, Germany
Source: *BiDExR; BioIn 1, 14, 16; CurBio 40, 45; Dis&D; EncTR, 91; HisEWW; LinLib S; ObitOF 79; REn*

Ley, Willy
American. Scientist, Author
Pioneer in rocket research; numerous books on space travel, rocketry include *Conquest of Space,* 1949.
b. Oct 2, 1906 in Berlin, Germany
d. Jun 24, 1969 in New York, New York
Source: *AmAu&B; AsBiEn; Au&Wr 71; AuBYP 2, 3; BenetAL 91; BioIn 2, 3, 4, 7, 8, 9, 17; ConAu 9R, 25R; CurBio 41, 53, 69; DcAmB S8; EncSF, 93; EncSUPP; FacFETw; InSci; LinLib L; NewEScF; REnAL; SmATA 2; ThrBJA; TwCA SUP; WhAm 5; WhoSciF; WorAl; WorAlBi*

Leyendecker, Joseph Christian
American. Artist
Produced over 300 covers for *Saturday Evening Post,* 1910-30s.
b. Mar 23, 1874 in Montabour, Germany
d. Jul 25, 1951 in New Rochelle, New York
Source: *BioIn 1, 2, 10; DcAmB S5; IlrAm 1880, B; ObitOF 79; WhAm 3*

Leyland, Jim
[James Richard Leyland]
American. Baseball Manager
Coach, White Sox, 1981-85; manager, Pittsburgh, 1985 —; NL manager of year, 1990.
b. Dec 15, 1944 in Toledo, Ohio
Source: *Ballpl 90; BaseEn 88; WhoAm 86, 88, 90, 92, 94, 95, 96, 97; WhoE 89, 91, 95, 97*

L'Hermitte, Leon Augustin
French. Artist
Drew realistic scenes of peasant life: *The Harvest,* 1874.
b. Jan 31, 1844 in Mont-Saint-Pere, France
d. Jul 25, 1925 in Paris, France
Source: *McGDA*

Lhevinne, Josef
American. Pianist, Teacher
Virtuoso, won Rubinstein prize, 1895; widely acclaimed in US for two-piano recitals with wife, Rosina, 1906-20s.
b. Dec 3, 1874 in Moscow, Russia
d. Dec 2, 1944 in New York, New York
Source: *Baker 78, 84, 92; BiDAmM; BioIn 2, 4, 6, 11, 12, 16, 17, 21; BriBkM 80; CurBio 45; DcAmB S3; FacFETw; MusSN; NewAmDM; NewGrDA 86; NewGrDM 80; NotTwCP; PenDiMP; WebBD 83; WhAm 2*

Lhevinne, Rosina L
[Mrs. Joseph Lhevinne]
American. Musician, Teacher
Taught at Juilliard School of Music, NYC, 1924-76; performed two-piano recitals with husband, 1906-20s.
b. Mar 29, 1880 in Moscow, Russia
d. Nov 9, 1976 in Glendale, California
Source: *Baker 78, 84; CurBio 61; InWom SUP; NewYTBE 70*

L'Hopital, Michel de
French. Statesman
Catherine de Medici's chancellor, 1560, who promoted religious tolerance; wrote judicial reforms.
b. 1507 in Aigueperse, France
d. Mar 13, 1573 in Bellebat, France
Source: *BiD&SB; CasWL; DcBiPP; DcEuL; EuAu; NewCol 75; OxCFr; OxCLaw; REn; WebBD 83*

Li, C(hoh) H(ao)
American. Biochemist
Isolated six out of eight hormones known to be secreted by pituitary gland.
b. Apr 21, 1913 in Guangzhou, China
d. Nov 28, 1987 in Berkeley, California
Source: *AmMWSc 73P, 76P, 79, 82, 86; AsBiEn; BiESc; BioIn 2, 6, 8, 9, 11; CurBio 63, 88, 88N; FacFETw; McGMS 80; NewYTBE 71; NotTwCS; WhAm 9;*

WhoAm 74, 76, 78, 80, 82, 84, 86, 88; WhoFrS 84; WhoWor 74, 80, 82, 84, 87

Liaquat Ali, Khan
Pakistani. Political Leader
Head of Moslem League, prime minister of Pakistan, 1947-51; assassinated.
b. Oct 1, 1895 in Karnal, Pakistan
d. Oct 16, 1951 in Rawalpindi, Pakistan
Source: *CurBio 48, 51; ObitT 1951*

Libby, Arthur
American. Businessman
With brother, Charles, produced first canned, compressed meats, 1868.
b. 1831
d. 1899
Source: *Entr*

Libby, Charles
American. Businessman
With brother, Arthur, founded large canned food firm, 1868.
b. 1838
d. 1895
Source: *Entr*

Libby, Willard Frank
American. Chemist, Inventor
Won Nobel Prize, 1960, for development of radioactive carbon-14.
b. Dec 17, 1908 in Grand Valley, Colorado
d. Sep 8, 1980 in Los Angeles, California
Source: *AmMWSc 73P, 76P, 79; AsBiEn; BiESc; BioIn 3, 4, 5, 6, 8, 9, 11, 12, 14, 15, 19, 20; BlueB 76; CamDcSc; ConAu 113; CurBio 54, 80; DcAmB S10; InSci; IntWW 74, 75, 76, 77, 78, 79, 80; LarDcSc; McGEWB; McGMS 80; NewYTBS 80; OxCAmH; RAdv 14; WebAB 74, 79; WhAm 7; WhDW; Who 74; WhoAm 74, 76, 78, 80; WhoNob, 90, 95; WhoWor 80; WorAl; WorScD*

Liberace
[Wladziu Valentino Liberace]
"Walter Busterkeys"
American. Musician, Entertainer
Pianist, known for elaborate costumes, flashy pianos topped by candelabras; highest paid entertainer in 1960s-70s.
b. May 16, 1919 in West Allis, Wisconsin
d. Feb 4, 1987 in Palm Springs, California
Source: *AnObit 1987; ASCAP 66; Baker 92; BioIn 3, 4, 5, 7, 10, 11, 12, 13, 14, 15, 16, 20, 21; BkPepl; CelR; ConAu 22NR, 89, 121; ConMus 9; ConNews 87-2; ConTFT 3; CurBio 54, 86, 87, 87N; DcArts; DcTwCCu 1; FacFETw; FilmEn; FilmgC; GayLesB; HalFC 80, 84, 88; IntMPA 86; IntWWM 77; LegTOT; NewAmDM; NewGrDA 86; NewYTBS 87; NewYTET; OxCPMus; PenEncP; VarWW 85; WhAm 9; WhoAm 74, 76, 78, 80, 82, 84, 86; WhoHol A; WhoWor 74; WorAl; WorAlBi*

Liberace, George J
American. Musician
Conductor, violinist; was silent, straight man for flamboyant younger brother; ran Liberace's enterprises.
b. Jul 31, 1911 in Menasha, Wisconsin
d. Oct 16, 1983 in Las Vegas, Nevada
Source: *ASCAP 66, 80; NewYTBS 83; VarWW 85; What 3*

Liberman, Alexander Semeonovitch
American. Editor, Artist, Photographer
Editorial director of Conde Nast, 1962-94; minimal painter who does geometrics, circle drawings.
b. Sep 4, 1912 in Kiev, Russia
Source: *AmArt; BioIn 13, 14, 15, 16; BriEAA; ConArt 77, 89; ConAu 113; ConPhot 82, 88; CurBio 87; DcCAA 77, 88; EncFash; EncTwCJ; ICPEnP; IntWW 91; NewYTBS 79; WhoAm 86, 90; WhoAmA 84, 91; WhoE 75*

Licavoli, Peter Joseph, Sr.
American. Criminal
Founder, leader of organized crime gang, Detroit's Purple Gang.
b. 1902?
d. Jan 11, 1984 in Tucson, Arizona
Source: *AnObit 1984; BioIn 13; NewYTBS 84*

Licavoli, Thomas
"Yonnie"
American. Criminal
Controlled much of Prohibition era crime in Detroit; sentenced to prison for murder, 1934; released, 1971.
b. 1904
d. Sep 16, 1973 in Columbus, Ohio
Source: *BioIn 10; NewYTBE 73; ObitOF 79*

Lichfield, Patrick
[Baron Soberton; Viscount Anson; Thomas Patrick John Anson Earl Lichfield]
English. Photographer
Cousin of Queen Elizabeth II; took official photos of Prince Charles' wedding, 1981.
b. Apr 25, 1939
Source: *BioIn 15; IntWW 91; NewYTBE 70; Who 85, 92*

Lichine, Alexis
American. Business Executive, Author
Wine expert; wrote *New Encyclopedia of Wines and Spirits*, 1979.
b. Dec 3, 1913 in Moscow, Russia
d. Jun 1, 1989 in Bordeaux, France
Source: *AnObit 1989; Au&Wr 71; BioIn 4, 7, 16, 17; ConAu 9R, 128; FacFETw; IntAu&W 77, 82; NewYTBS 89; WhoAm 74, 76, 78, 80; WhoFr 79; WhoWor 74, 76; WrDr 76, 80, 82, 84, 86, 88*

Lichine, David
Russian. Choreographer, Dancer
With Ballet Russe de Monte Carlo; ballets include "Graduation Ball," 1940.
b. Oct 25, 1910 in Rostov-on-Don, Russia
d. Jun 26, 1972 in Los Angeles, California
Source: *BiDD; CnOxB; DancEn 78; IntDcB; LegTOT; NewYTBE 72; WhScrn 77, 83*

Lichtenstein, Harvey
American. Businessman
President, Brooklyn Academy of Music, 1967—.
b. Apr 9, 1929 in New York, New York
Source: *BioIn 13, 14, 15, 18, 19; CurBio 87; NewYTBS 85; WhoAm 82, 84, 86, 88, 90, 92, 94, 95, 96, 97; WhoEnt 92*

Lichtenstein, Roy
American. Artist
Pioneered 1960s Pop Art movement, noted for comic strip-inspired paintings.
b. Oct 27, 1923 in New York, New York
Source: *AmArt; AmCulL; Benet 87, 96; BioIn 6, 7, 8, 9, 10, 11, 12, 13, 14, 15, 17, 19, 20; BlueB 76; BriEAA; CelR, 90; CenC; ConArt 77, 83, 89, 96; CurBio 69; DcAmArt; DcArts; DcCAA 71, 77, 88, 94; DcCAr 81; DcTwCCu 1; IntDcAA 90; IntWW 74, 75, 76, 77, 78, 79, 80, 81, 82, 83, 89, 91, 93; LegTOT; MakMC; McGDA; McGEWB; News 94, 94-1; OxCArt; OxCTwCA; OxDcArt; PhDcTCA 77; PrintW 83, 85; WebAB 74, 79; WhDW; Who 82, 83, 85, 88, 90, 92, 94; WhoAm 74, 76, 78, 80, 82, 84, 86, 88, 90, 92, 94, 95, 96, 97; WhoAmA 73, 76, 78, 80, 82, 84, 86, 89, 91, 93; WhoWor 78, 80, 82, 84; WorAl; WorAlBi; WorArt 1950*

Lichty, George
[George Maurice Lichtenstein]
American. Cartoonist
Creator of "Grin and Bear It," 1932-74.
b. May 16, 1905 in Chicago, Illinois
d. Jul 18, 1983 in Santa Rosa, California
Source: *ConAu 104, 110; EncACom; WhoAm 80, 82; WhoAmA 82, 84; WorECar*

Liddell, Eric
"The Flying Scot"
Scottish. Missionary, Track Athlete
Subject of film *Chariots of Fire*.
b. 1902, China
d. Feb 21, 1945 in Weifang, China
Source: *BioIn 7, 9, 13, 15*

Liddell Hart, Basil Henry, Sir
English. Author
Military strategist, expert on tank warfare; wrote *Revolution in Warfare*, 1946.
b. Oct 31, 1895 in London, England
d. Jan 29, 1970 in Marlow, England
Source: *Au&Wr 71; BioIn 3, 4, 7, 8, 9, 14, 17; ConAu 89, 103; CurBio 40, 70;*

DcLEL; DcNaB 1961; EvLB; GrBr; HarEnMi; LinLib L, S; LngCTC; NewC; NewCBEL; TwCA, SUP; WhoMilH 76; WhWW-II

Liddy, G(eorge) Gordon
American. Government Official
An original break-in defendant; 20-yr. sentence commuted by Jimmy Carter; released, 1977.
b. Nov 30, 1930 in New York, New York
Source: *BioIn 10, 12, 15, 16; ConAu 114; CurBio 80; NewYTBE 73; PolProf NF; WorAl; WorAlBi*

Lidz, Theodore
American. Educator, Psychiatrist
Books on psychiatry include *Schizophrenia and the Family,* 1965.
b. Apr 1, 1910 in New York, New York
Source: *AmMWSc 73S, 76P, 79, 82, 86, 89, 92, 95; BiDrAPA 77, 89; BioIn 14; BlueB 76; ConAu 29R; IntAu&W 86; NatCAB 63N; WhoAm 74, 76, 78; WhoAmJ 80; WhoWorJ 72, 78; WrDr 80, 82, 84, 86, 88, 90, 92, 94, 96*

Lie, Jonas Laurite Idemil
Norwegian. Author, Lawyer
Novels include *The Visionary,* 1874.
b. Nov 6, 1833 in Hokksund in Eiker, Norway
d. Jul 5, 1908 in Stavern, Norway
Source: *ConAu 115; EvEuW; TwCLC 5; WebBD 83*

Lie, Trygve Halvdan
Norwegian. Lawyer, Diplomat
First Secretary-General, United Nations, 1946-53.
b. Jul 16, 1896 in Oslo, Norway
d. Dec 30, 1968 in Geilo, Norway
Source: *BiDInt; CurBio 46, 69; DcTwHis; HisEWW; McGEWB; OxCLaw; REn; WhDW; WhoUN 75*

Lieber, Franz
[Francis Lieber]
American. Editor, Political Scientist, Educator
Edited *Encyclopedia Americana,* 1829-33; devised code of military law, 1863.
b. Mar 18, 1798 in Berlin, Germany
d. Oct 2, 1872 in New York, New York
Source: *AmBi; ApCAB; BiDAmEd; BiDInt; BiGAW; DcAmB; Drake; EncAB-H 1974; McGEWB; NatCAB 5; OxCAmH; OxCLaw; TwCBDA; WebAB 74; WebAMB; WhAm HS*

Lieberman, Joseph Isadore
American. Politician
Dem. senator from CT, 1989—; CT attorney general, 1983-89.
b. Feb 24, 1942 in Stamford, Connecticut
Source: *AlmAP 92; CngDr 89; ConAu 17R; CurBio 94; IntWW 91; WhoAm 86, 90; WhoAmJ 80; WhoAmL 87, 90; WhoAmP 87, 91; WhoE 91; WhoWor 91*

Lieberman, Nancy
American. Basketball Player
Starred with Dallas Diamonds of now-defunct Women's Basketball League, 1980-82; first woman to try out with NBA team.
b. Jul 1, 1958 in New York, New York
Source: *BasBi; BiDAmSp BK; BioIn 11, 12, 15; EncWomS; HerW 84; InWom SUP; NewYTBS 80, 82; WhoAmW 89; WhoEmL 87; WhoSpor; WomFir*

Liebermann, Max
German. Artist
Postimpressionist; known for genre scenes of humble people: *Women Plucking Geese,* 1872; forbidden by Nazis to paint.
b. Jul 20, 1847 in Berlin, Germany
d. Feb 8, 1935 in Berlin, Germany
Source: *AtlBL; BioIn 1, 2, 4, 6, 7, 14, 17; EncTR, 91; LegTOT; McGDA; McGEWB; NewCol 75; OxCArt; OxCGer 76, 86; OxCTwCA; OxDcArt; PhDcTCA 77; WorAl; WorAlBi*

Liebermann, Rolf
Swiss. Composer, Manager
Paris Opera Co.'s first foreign administrator, 1973-80; wrote operas *Penelope,* 1954; *Leonore,* 1952.
b. Sep 14, 1910 in Zurich, Switzerland
Source: *Baker 78, 84, 92; BioIn 6, 8, 9, 10, 11, 12; CmOp; CompSN, SUP; ConCom 92; CurBio 73; DcCM; IntWW 74, 75, 76, 77, 78, 79, 80, 81, 82, 83, 89, 91; IntWWM 77, 80, 90; MetOEnc; NewAmDM; NewEOp 71; NewGrDM 80; NewGrDO; OxCMus; OxDcOp; PenDiMP A; WhoMus 72; WhoOp 76; WhoWor 74, 76*

Liebes, Dorothy Katherine Wright
"Mother of Modern Weaving"
American. Designer
Founded Dorothy Liebes Design, Inc., 1934; revolutionized American textiles.
b. Oct 14, 1897 in Guerneville, California
d. Sep 20, 1972 in New York, New York
Source: *InWom SUP; NotAW MOD*

Liebig, Justus von
German. Chemist, Educator, Author
Regarded as founder of agricultural chemistry; founded first chemical teaching laboratory.
b. May 12, 1803 in Darmstadt, Germany
d. Apr 18, 1873 in Munich, Germany
Source: *AsBiEn; BbD; BiD&SB; BiESc; BioIn 2, 4, 5, 6, 8, 9, 10, 11, 12, 14; DcBiPP; DcScB; LarDcSc; McGEWB; NewCol 75; OxCGer 76, 86; OxCMed 86; RAdv 14; WebBD 83; WorInv; WorScD*

Liebknecht, Karl
German. Political Leader, Revolutionary
Founded Spartacus League, 1918, forerunner of German Communist party; murdered with Rosa Luxemburg.
b. Aug 13, 1871 in Leipzig, Germany
d. Jan 15, 1919 in Berlin, Germany
Source: *Benet 96; DcTwHis; EncRev; NewCol 75; OxCGer 76, 86; REn; WebBD 83; WhDW; WorAl; WorAlBi*

Liebknecht, Wilhelm
German. Politician
Co-founded Social Democratic Labor Party, 1869; father of Karl.
b. Mar 29, 1826 in Giessen, Germany
d. Aug 7, 1900 in Berlin, Germany
Source: *BbD; BiD&SB; BiDMarx; DcAmSR; EncRev; NewCol 75; OxCGer 76, 86; REn; WebBD 83*

Liebling, Abbot Joseph
American. Journalist, Author
Wrote *New Yorker* column, "Wayward Press," 1946-63; NYC histories.
b. Oct 18, 1904 in New York, New York
d. Dec 28, 1963 in New York, New York
Source: *BioIn 4, 5, 6, 8, 10, 11; ConAu 89, 104; EncAJ; OxCAmL 83; TwCA SUP*

Liebling, Estelle
American. Singer, Teacher
Soloist noted for instructing operatic stars, 1930s-50s.
b. Apr 21, 1884 in New York, New York
d. Sep 25, 1970 in New York, New York
Source: *ASCAP 66, 80; Baker 84; BiDAmM; BioIn 8; InWom; NewEOp 71; NewYTBE 70*

Liebman, Joshua Loth
American. Broadcaster, Religious Leader
Rabbi, preached popular radio sermons, 1939; wrote best-seller *Peace of Mind,* 1946.
b. Apr 7, 1907 in Hamilton, Ohio
d. Jun 9, 1948 in Brookline, Massachusetts
Source: *AmAu&B; BioIn 1, 3, 19; CurBio 46, 48; DcAmB S4; DcAmReB 2; DcNAA; NatCAB 38; OhA&B; RelLAm 91; REnAL; WhAm 2*

Liebman, Max
American. Director, Producer, Writer
Produced TV's Emmy-winning "Your Show of Shows," 1949-54; discovered Danny Kaye, other stars.
b. Aug 5, 1902 in Vienna, Austria
d. Jul 21, 1981 in New York, New York
Source: *AnObit 1981; ASCAP 66, 80; BiE&WWA; BioIn 3, 12; BlueB 76; CurBio 53, 81, 81N; IntMPA 77, 80, 82; NewYTBS 81; NewYTET; NotNAT; WhAm 8; WhoAm 74, 76, 78; WhoWorJ 72, 78*

Liebow, Averill A(braham)
Physician, Author
Noted for research on pathology of the lung.

b. Mar 31, 1911, Austria
d. May 31, 1978 in Cranberry Isles, Maine
Source: *AmMWSc 73P, 76P, 79; BioIn 11; ConAu 111; WhAm 7; WhoAm 74, 76, 78*

Liedtke, William C, Jr.
American. Businessman
Co-founder of Pennzoil, Co., one of the largest US oil companies.
b. 1924
d. Mar 1, 1991 in Houston, Texas
Source: *BioIn 8; Dun&B 86, 88, 90; NewYTBS 91*

Lifar, Serge
Russian. Dancer, Choreographer
Director, Paris Opera Ballet, 1929-58; ballets include *The Prodigal Son; Apollo.*
b. Apr 2, 1905 in Kiev, Russia
d. Dec 15, 1986 in Lausanne, Switzerland
Source: *AnObit 1986; BiDD; BioIn 1, 2, 3, 4, 5, 6, 8, 11, 12, 13, 15, 18; CnOxB; ConAu 121; ConTFT 4; DancEn 78; DcArts; DcTwCCu 2; FacFETw; IntDcB; IntWW 74, 75, 76, 77, 78, 79, 80, 81, 82, 83; NewGrDM 80; NewYTBS 86, 87; Who 74, 82, 83, 85; WhoFr 79; WhoThe 77A; WhoWor 74, 78, 82, 84; WhThe*

Lifshin, Lyn
American. Poet
Numerous vols. of verse include *Madonna Poems,* 1970s-80s.
b. 1942 in Burlington, Vermont
Source: *ArtclWW 2; BioIn 13; ConAu 10AS, 25NR; ConPo 75, 80, 85, 91; DrAP 75; DrAPF 91; IntAu&W 86; InWom SUP; WhoUSWr 88; WhoWrEP 89; WrDr 76, 82, 86, 92*

Ligachev, Yegor (Kuzmich)
Russian. Politician
High-ranking member of the Soviet Union's Politburo, 1985-90.
b. Nov 29, 1920 in Dubinkino, Union of Soviet Socialist Republics
Source: *BiDSovU; BioIn 15; CurBio 90; IntWW 89, 91, 93; SovUn; WhoRus; WhoWor 91*

Liggett, Louis Kroh
American. Merchant
Established central buying agency for retail druggists, 1901; drug store chains, Rexall, 1903, Liggett, 1909.
b. Apr 4, 1875 in Detroit, Michigan
d. Jun 5, 1946 in Washington, District of Columbia
Source: *ApCAB X; BiDAmBL 83; BioIn 1; CurBio 46; DcAmB S4; InSci; NatCAB 14; ObitOF 79; WhAm 2*

Light, Enoch Henry
American. Musician, Record Company Executive, Composer
Headed award-winning recording companies, 1950s-60s; wrote popular songs.
b. Aug 18, 1907 in Canton, Ohio
d. Jul 31, 1978 in New York, New York
Source: *ASCAP 66; NewYTBS 78; WhoAm 74, 76, 78; WhoFI 74; WhoWor 74*

Light, Judith Ellen
American. Actor
Played Karen Wolek on soap opera "One Life to Live," won two Emmys for role; played Angela Bower on TV's "Who's the Boss," 1984-92.
b. Feb 9, 1950 in Trenton, New Jersey
Source: *BioIn 14, 15, 16; ConTFT 3; VarWW 85; WhoAm 86; WhoEnt 92; WorAlBi*

Lightfoot, Gordon Meredith
Canadian. Singer, Songwriter
Folk musician has written over 400 songs including hits "If You Could Read My Mind," 1969 and "Sundown," 1974.
b. Nov 17, 1938 in Orillia, Ontario, Canada
Source: *ASCAP 66; Baker 84; BioIn 11, 14, 15; BioNews 74; BkPepl; CanWW 31, 81, 83, 89; ConAu 109; ConLC 26; CreCan 2; CurBio 78; EncFCWM 83; PenEncP; VarWW 85; WhoAm 78, 80, 82, 84, 86, 88, 90, 92, 94, 95, 96, 97; WhoEnt 92; WhoRocM 82*

Lightman, Alan (Paige)
American. Author
Wrote *Einstein's Dreams,* 1993, a novel that claims to be a record of the dreams that Einstein had in 1905.
b. Nov 28, 1948 in Memphis, Tennessee
Source: *AmMWSc 76P, 79, 82, 86, 89, 92, 95; ConLC 81; WhoAm 94, 96, 97*

Lightner, Candy
American. Social Reformer
Founded Mothers Against Drunk Driving (MADD), 1980.
b. May 30, 1946 in Pasadena, California
Source: *BioIn 14, 15, 16; ConHero 1; ConNews 85-1; WhoAm 90; WhoAmW 85, 91*

Lightner, Theodore
American. Bridge Player
Invented Lightner slam double.
b. 1893? in Grosse Pointe, Michigan
d. Nov 22, 1981 in New York, New York
Source: *BioIn 12; ConAu 113*

Lilburne, John
English. Statesman, Pamphleteer
Leader of Levelers, who opposed Cromwell; wrote pamphlet *England's Birthright,* 1645.
b. 1614 in Greenwich, England
d. Aug 29, 1657 in Eltham, England
Source: *Alli; BioIn 1, 4, 6, 10, 11, 13, 15; CasWL; DcEnL; DcNaB; NewC; NewCol 75; OxCEng 85, 95; REn; WebBD 83; WebE&AL*

Liliencron, Detlev von
[Friedrich Adolf Axel Detlev von Liliencron]
German. Author, Poet
Wrote verse vols. *Adjutantenritte,* 1883; *Poggfred,* 1896.
b. Jun 3, 1844 in Kiel, Germany
d. Jul 22, 1909 in Hamburg, Germany
Source: *Benet 87, 96; BiD&SB; CasWL; ClDMEL 47; ConAu 117; EuAu; OxCGer 76, 86; PenC EUR; REn; TwCLC 18; WebBD 83*

Lilienthal, David Eli
American. Government Official, Lawyer
Atomic Energy Commission chm., 1947-50; chaired dam, power projects, 1953-79.
b. Jul 8, 1899 in Morton, Illinois
d. Jan 14, 1981 in New York, New York
Source: *AmAu&B; AmPolLe; AnObit 1984; BiDAmBL 83; BioIn 1, 2, 5, 7, 8, 9, 10, 11, 12; BlueB 76; ConAu 3NR, 5R, 102; CurBio 44, 81N; EncAB-H 1974, 1996; IntWW 74, 75, 76, 77, 78, 79, 80; IntYB 78, 79, 80, 81; LinLib S; McGEWB; WebAB 74, 79; WhAm 7; Who 74, 82N; WhoAm 74, 76, 78, 80; WhoWor 74; WhoWorJ 72*

Lilienthal, Otto
German. Engineer, Inventor, Author
Experimented with gliders; wrote pioneering books on flying machines, 1889.
b. May 23, 1848 in Anklam, Prussia
d. Aug 10, 1896 in Berlin, Germany
Source: *AsBiEn; BioIn 5, 8, 9, 12, 14; Dis&D; InSci; NewCol 75; WhDW; WorInv*

Liliuokalani, Queen
Hawaiian. Ruler
Last ruler and only reigning queen of Islands, 1891-93; against annexation; deposed, 1893; wrote song "Aloha Oe," 1898.
b. Sep 2, 1838 in Honolulu, Hawaii
d. Nov 11, 1917 in Honolulu, Hawaii
Source: *AmBi; Baker 92; BiDAmM; BioAmW; BioIn 1, 5, 6, 9, 11, 13, 15, 19, 21; DcAmAu; DcAmDH 80; DicTyr; EncWHA; GrLiveH; HerW; LibW; McGEWB; NewAmDM; NewCol 75; NewGrDA 86; NotAW; OxCAmH; WebBD 83; WhAm 4, HSA; WomWR; WorAl*

Lillie, Beatrice Gladys
English. Comedian
Had 50-year entertainment career, beginning 1914; known for signature song, "Mad Dogs and Englishmen."
b. May 29, 1898 in Toronto, Ontario, Canada
d. Jan 20, 1989 in Henley-on-Thames, England
Source: *BioIn 15, 16; CamGWoT; ConAu 127; ContDcW 89; CurBio 45, 64, 89, 89N; EncMT; FacFETw; FamA&A; Film 2; FilmgC; FunnyW; HalFC 88; IntWW 74, 89N; InWom SUP; MovMk; NewAmDM; NewYTBS*

89; NotNAT; OxCAmT 84; OxCCanT; OxCPMus; OxCThe 83; ThFT; VarWW 85; WhAm 9; Who 83, 88, 90N; WhoHol A; WhoThe 77; WorAlBi

Lillie, Gordon William
"Pawnee Bill"
American. Circus Owner, Pioneer
Founded tent show "Historic Wild West," 1890.
b. Feb 14, 1860 in Bloomingdale, Illinois
d. Feb 3, 1942 in Pawnee, Oklahoma
Source: *BioIn 5; DcAmB S3; WhAm 1, 2*

Lilly, Bob
[Robert Lewis Lilly]
American. Football Player
Defensive tackle, first player ever drafted by Dallas, 1961-74; Hall of Fame, 1980.
b. Jul 26, 1939 in Olney, Texas
Source: *BiDAmSp FB; BioIn 10; LegTOT; NewYTBE 72; WhoAm 74; WhoFtbl 74; WhoSpor; WorAl; WorAlBi*

Lilly, Doris
American. Journalist, Author
Syndicated gossip columnist, 1977-91; wrote *How to Marry a Millionaire,* 1951 which later became a movie.
b. Dec 26, 1926 in Pasadena, California
d. Oct 9, 1991 in New York, New York
Source: *BiDAmNC; BioIn 5; CelR; ConAu 11NR, 29R, 135; InWom; NewYTBS 91; WhoAm 86; WhoAmW 75*

Lilly, Eli
American. Manufacturer
Pres., chm., Lilly Pharmaceutical Co., 1932-66; founded by his grandfather.
b. Apr 1, 1885 in Indianapolis, Indiana
d. Jan 24, 1977 in Indianapolis, Indiana
Source: *AmAu&B; BioIn 7, 11, 12, 16; BlueB 76; ConAu 69; DcAmB S10; IndAu 1917; IntDcAn; NatCAB 60; NewYTBS 77; ObitOF 79; WhAm 7; WhoAm 74, 76, 78; WhoFI 74, 75; WhoWor 74; WorAl; WorAlBi*

Lilly, John C
American. Author, Physician, Educator
Noted for studies in cerebral cortex, experiments with dolphins.
b. Jan 6, 1915 in Saint Paul, Minnesota
Source: *BioIn 14, 16; ConAu 1NR, 1R; CurBio 62; Law&B 84, 89A; NewAgE 90; WhoAm 82, 90; WhoSSW 73*

Liman, Arthur L(awrence)
American. Lawyer
Best known as chief counsel to US Senate committee during Iran-Contra scandal, 1987.
b. Nov 5, 1932 in New York, New York
d. Jul 17, 1997 in New York, New York
Source: *BioIn 15, 16; CurBio 88; News 89; NewYTBE 72; NewYTBS 87; WhoAm 86, 90, 96, 97; WhoAmL 85, 92, 96*

Limann, Hilla
Ghanaian. Political Leader
Pres. of Ghana, 1979-81.
b. Dec 12, 1934? in Gwollu, Gold Coast
Source: *AfSS 79, 80, 81, 82; BioIn 12; CurBio 81; InB&W 85; IntWW 80, 81, 82, 83, 89, 91, 93; IntYB 81, 82; Who 82, 83, 85, 88, 90, 92, 94; WhoUN 75; WhoWor 80*

Limbaugh, Rush Hudson, III
American. Radio Performer, TV Personality
Syndicated conservative talk show host of "The Rush Limbaugh Show," 1992—; radio program of same name, 1988—. Author of *The Way Things Ought to Be,* 1992 and *See, I Told You So,* 1993; publisher, monthly newsletter *The Limbaugh Letter,* 1995—.
b. Jan 12, 1951 in Cape Girardeau, Missouri
Source: *CurBio 93; News 91-3; NewYTBS 90; WhoAm 90, 94, 95, 96, 97; WhoAmP 95; WhoE 95*

Limbert, John William, Jr.
[The Hostages]
American. Hostage
One of 52 held by terrorists, Nov 1979-Jan 1981.
b. Mar 10, 1943 in Washington, District of Columbia
Source: *NewYTBS 81; USBiR 74; WhoE 91*

Limon, Jose Arcadio
American. Choreographer, Dancer
Formed modern dance company, 1945; noted for "The Moors Pavane" routine, 1949.
b. Jan 12, 1908 in Culiacan, Mexico
d. Dec 2, 1972 in Flemington, New Jersey
Source: *CurBio 53, 68, 73; DcAmB S9; MexAmB; WhAm 5; WhoE 74; WorAl*

Lin, Maya Ying
American. Architect, Sculptor
Designed Vietman War Memorial, Washington, DC, dedicated 1982; also memorial to those who have died in the civil rights movement, 1988.
b. Oct 5, 1959 in Athens, Ohio
Source: *BioIn 13, 14, 16; CurBio 93; GrLiveH; News 90; NewYTBS 81, 91; WhoAmA 91; WhoAmW 91*

Lin, Piao (Yu-Yung)
Chinese. Government Official
Defense minister, 1959-71, killed in plane crash after failing in attempt to assassinate Mao Tse-Tung.
b. Dec 5, 1907 in Huangang, China
d. Sep 13, 1971, Mongolia
Source: *CurBio 72; McGEWB; NewYTBS 74; ObitT 1971; WhAm 5; WhDW; WorAl*

Lin, Yutang
Chinese. Author, Educator, Editor
Books *My Country and My People,* 1935; *Importance of Living,* 1937, explain Chinese character to Westerners.
b. Oct 10, 1895 in Zhangzhou, China
d. Mar 26, 1976, Hong Kong
Source: *AmAu&B; Benet 87; BioIn 1, 3, 4, 5, 6, 8, 9, 10, 11; CasWL; ConAu 2NR, 45, 65; CurBio 40, 76N; DcLEL; DcOrL 1; LinLib L, S; LngCTC; RAdv 13-2; REn; REnAL; RfGAmL 94; ScF&FL 1; TwCA SUP; TwCWr; Who 74*

Linacre, Thomas
English. Author, Physician
Physician to Henry VIII, 1509; formed Royal College of Physicians, 1518.
b. 1460 in Canterbury, England
d. Oct 20, 1524 in London, England
Source: *Alli; BiESc; BiHiMed; BioIn 1, 3, 5, 6, 7, 9, 11; BlmGEL; BritAu; CamGEL; CamGLE; Chambr 1; CyEd; DcBiPP; DcCathB; DcEnL; DcEuL; DcNaB, C; DcScB; InSci; LinLib L, S; LngCEL; NewC; NewCBEL; OxCEng 67, 85, 95; OxCMed 86; REn*

Lincoln, Abbey
[Gaby Lee; Aminata Moseka; Anna Marie Woolridge]
American. Singer, Actor
Dance band vocalist; made recordings, night club appearances, 1950s; films include *For the Love of Ivy,* 1968.
b. Aug 6, 1930 in Chicago, Illinois
Source: *AllMusG; BiDAfM; BiDAmM; BiDJaz; BioIn 4, 8, 12, 15; BlkAWP; BlkWAm; CelR; ConBlAP 88; ConBlB 3; ConMus 9; DcTwCCu 5; DrBlPA, 90; EncJzS; HalFC 80, 84, 88; InB&W 80, 85; InWom SUP; NegAl 83, 89; NewGrDJ 88, 94; NotBlAW 1; PenEncP; PenNWW A, B; WhoAm 74, 94, 95, 96, 97; WhoAmW 66, 68, 70, 72, 74; WhoBlA 77, 80, 92; WhoEnt 92; WhoHol 92, A*

Lincoln, Abraham
"Abe"
American. US President
Rep., 16th pres., 1861-65; led Union during Civil War; author of Emancipation Proclamation, 1863; gave Gettysburg Address, 1863; assassinated by John W Booth.
b. Feb 12, 1809 in Hodgenville, Kentucky
d. Apr 15, 1865 in Washington, District of Columbia
Source: *AmAu&B; AmBi; AmJust; AmOrN; AmPolLe; ApCAB; AtlBL; BbD; Benet 87, 96; BenetAL 91; BiAUS; BiD&SB; BiDrAC; BiDrUSC 89; BiDrUSE 71, 89; BiDSA; BioIn 1, 2, 3, 4, 5, 6, 7, 8, 9, 10, 11, 12, 13, 14, 15, 16, 17, 18, 19, 20, 21; CelCen; Chambr 3; ChhPo S2; CivWDc; CyAG; CyWA 58; DcAmAu; DcAmB; DcAmC; DcAmMiB; DcAmReB 1, 2; DcAmSR; DcBiPP; DcLEL; DcNAA; Dis&D; Drake; EncAAH; EncAB-H 1974, 1996;*

EncARH; EncO&P 1, 2, 3; EncPaPR 91; EncSoH; EvLB; FacPr 89, 93; HalFC 80, 84, 88; HarEnMi; HarEnUS; HealPre; HisWorL; LegTOT; LinLib L; McGEWB; MemAm; NatCAB 2; NinCLC 18; OxCAmH; OxCAmL 65, 83, 95; OxCEng 67, 85, 95; OxCFilm; OxCSupC; PenC AM; PolPar; RAdv 13-3; RComAH; RComWL; REn; REnAL; REnAW; TwCBDA; TwoTYeD; WebAB 74, 79; WebE&AL; WhAm HS; WhAmP; WhCiWar; WhDW; WhNaAH; WorAl; WorAlBi; WorInv

Lincoln, Elmo
[Otto Elmo Linkenhelter]
American. Actor
First screen Tarzan in *Tarzan of the Apes,* 1918.
b. Jun 14, 1889 in Rochester, New York
d. Jun 27, 1952 in Hollywood, California
Source: *CmMov; Film 1, 2; FilmEn; FilmgC; HalFC 80, 84, 88; LegTOT; MovMk; NotNAT B; ObitOF 79; SilFlmP; TwYS; WhoHol B; WhoHrs 80; WhScrn 74, 77, 83*

Lincoln, G(eorge) Gould
"Dean of Washington Political Writers"
American. Journalist
Covered presidents from Theodore Roosevelt to Gerald Ford in 60-yr. career.
b. Jul 26, 1880 in Washington, District of Columbia
d. Dec 1, 1974 in Washington, District of Columbia
Source: *AuNews 1; BioIn 10, 12; ConAu 113; NatCAB 58; WhAm 6*

Lincoln, George A
American. Military Leader, Author
Wrote on foreign policy, national security.
b. Jul 20, 1907 in Harbor Beach, Michigan
d. May 24, 1975 in Colorado Springs, Colorado
Source: *AmMWSc 73S; ConAu 1R, 57; NewYTBE 73; WhAm 6; WhoAm 74; WhoAmP 73; WhoGov 72; WhoSSW 73*

Lincoln, Joseph C(rosby)
American. Author
Books on Cape Cod include *Cap'n Eri,* 1904.
b. Feb 13, 1870 in Brewster, Massachusetts
d. Mar 10, 1944
Source: *AmAu&B; BioIn 2, 4, 5, 12; ChhPo, S1; ConAmL; DcAmAu; DcAmB S3; DcNAA; NatCAB 14; OxCAmL 65, 95; REnAL; TwCA, SUP; WhAm 2; WhLit; WhNAA*

Lincoln, Mary Johnson Bailey
American. Educator, Author
Wrote *Boston Cook Book,* 1884.
b. Jul 8, 1844 in South Attleboro, Massachusetts
d. Dec 2, 1921 in Boston, Massachusetts
Source: *AmWomSc; BioIn 20; DcAmB; InWom, SUP; LibW; NatCAB 24; NotAW; WhAm 1; WomWWA 14*

Lincoln, Mary Todd
American. First Lady
Suffered mental instability after husband's death; ruled insane, 1875.
b. Dec 13, 1818 in Lexington, Kentucky
d. Jul 16, 1882 in Springfield, Illinois
Source: *AmBi; AmWom; ApCAB; Benet 87, 96; BioAmW; BioIn 15, 16, 17, 18, 19, 20, 21; CivWDc; DcAmB; Dis&D; EncSoH; GoodHs; HerW; InWom, SUP; LegTOT; LibW; NatCAB 2; NotAW; OxCAmH; PorAmW; REn; REnAL; TwCBDA; WhAm HS; WhCiWar; WomFir*

Lincoln, Robert Todd
American. Lawyer
First child of Abraham Lincoln; secretary of war, 1881-85; minister to Great Britain, 1889-93.
b. Aug 1, 1843 in Springfield, Illinois
d. Jul 26, 1926 in Manchester, New Hampshire
Source: *AmBi; ApCAB; BiDrUSE 71, 89; BioIn 1, 7, 8, 10, 13, 14, 16, 19, 21; CivWDc; DcAmB; DcAmDH 80, 89; EncAB-H 1974, 1996; HarEnUS; NatCAB 4, 21; OxCAmH; PeoHis; TwCBDA; WhAm 1; WhAmP; WhCiWar*

Lincoln, Victoria Endicott
American. Author
Popular novelist whose *A Private Disgrace,* 1967, concerns Lizzie Borden's trial.
b. Oct 23, 1904 in Fall River, Massachusetts
d. May 9, 1981 in Baltimore, Maryland
Source: *AmAu&B; ForWC 70; InWom SUP; OhA&B; OxCAmL 65; REnAL; TwCA SUP; WhoAm 74*

Lind, Jakov
[Heinz Landwirth]
Austrian. Author, Dramatist
Wrote short stories *Soul of Wood,* 1964; novel *Landschaft in Beton,* 1963; autobiography *Numbers,* 1972.
b. Feb 10, 1927 in Vienna, Austria
Source: *Au&Wr 71; BioIn 7, 8, 9, 10, 15; ClDMEL 80; ConAu 4AS, 7NR, 9R; ConLC 1, 2, 4, 27, 82; DcLP 87B; EncWL, 3; LiExTwC; ModGL; PenC EUR; RAdv 14, 13-2; WhoWor 74; WorAu 1950*

Lind, Jenny
[Mrs. Otto Goldschmidt; Johanna Maria Lind]
"Swedish Nightingale"
English. Opera Singer
Coloratura soprano, brought to US for concert tour, 1850-52, by P T Barnum.
b. Oct 6, 1820 in Stockholm, Sweden
d. Nov 2, 1887 in Wynd's Point, England
Source: *AmBi; Baker 78, 84, 92; BiDAmM; BioIn 1, 2, 3, 4, 5, 6, 7, 8, 9, 11, 12, 14, 15, 16, 19; BriBkM 80; CelCen; CmOp; ContDcW 89; DcArts; DcNaB; Film 1; GoodHs; HerW, 84; IntDcOp; IntDcWB; InWom, SUP; LegTOT; MetOEnc; MusMk; NatCAB 3; NewAmDM; NewEOp 71; NewGrDA 86; NewGrDM 80; NewGrDO; OxCAmH; OxCMus; OxDcOp; PenDiMP; REn; VicBrit; WhAm HS; WomFir; WorAl; WorAlBi*

Lindauer, Lois L
American. Journalist
Founder, The Diet Workshop, 1965; author of book, syndicated column *It's In To Be Thin,* 1971.
b. Feb 6, 1934 in New York, New York
Source: *ConAu 35NR, 49; WhoAmW 77, 81, 87, 91*

Lindbergh, Anne Spencer Morrow
[Mrs. Charles A. Lindbergh]
American. Author, Poet
Wrote narrative *Listen! the Wind,* 1938; best-selling essays *Gift from the Sea,* 1955.
b. Jun 22, 1907 in Englewood, New Jersey
Source: *AmAu&B; AnCL; ArtclWW 2; Benet 87; BioIn 13, 14, 15; ConAu 16NR, 17R, X; ConLC 82; CurBio 40; LngCTC; NewYTBS 77, 80; OxCAmL 65; REn; REnAL; SmATA 33, X; TwCA SUP; Who 85, 88; WhoAm 88; WhoAmW 85; WorAl; WrDr 86, 88*

Lindbergh, Charles A(ugustus)
"Lucky Lindy"
American. Aviator
Made first solo nonstop trans-Atlantic flight, NY to Paris in *Spirit of St. Louis,* May 21, 1927; became int'l. hero.
b. Feb 4, 1902 in Detroit, Michigan
d. Aug 26, 1974 in Kipahulu, Hawaii
Source: *AmAu&B; AmSocL; AsBiEn; Benet 96; BioIn 1, 2, 3, 4, 5, 6, 7, 8, 9, 10, 11, 12, 13; ConAu 53; CurBio 41, 54, 74; DcAmB S9; DcAmC; DcAmSR; DcTwHis; EncAB-H 1996; FacFETw; IntWW 74; LinLib S; McGEWB; MedHR, 94; MorMA; NatCAB 60; NewYTBE 71; NewYTBS 74; OxCAmH; OxCAmL 65, 95; RAdv 14; REn; REnAL; SmATA 33; WebAB 74, 79; WebAMB; WhAm 6; What 1; WhNAA; Who 74; WhoAm 74; WhoWor 74; WorAl*

Lindbergh, Charles Augustus
American. Politician
Progressive Rep. congressman, 1907-17; unpopular for denouncing war propaganda, 1917; father of the aviator.
b. Jan 20, 1859 in Stockholm, Sweden
d. May 24, 1924 in Crookston, Massachusetts
Source: *AmBi; BiDrAC; BiDrUSC 89; BioIn 10, 11; DcAmB; DcNAA; EncAAH; NatCAB 25; OxCAmH; WhAmP*

Lindbergh, Charles Augustus
American.
Son of Charles A, Anne Morrow; kidnapped, murdered by Bruno Hauptmann, who was electrocuted for crime.
b. Jun 22, 1930 in Hopewell, New Jersey
d. Mar 1, 1932 in Hopewell, New Jersey
Source: *BioIn 9, 10*

Lindbergh, Pelle (Per-Eric)
Swedish. Hockey Player
Goalie, Philadelphia, 1981-85; won Vezina Trophy, 1985; killed in car accident.
b. May 24, 1959 in Stockholm, Sweden
d. Nov 12, 1985 in Somerdale, New Jersey
Source: *ConNews 85-4; HocReg 85; NewYTBS 85*

Linden, Hal
[Harold Lipschitz]
American. Actor
Starred in TV series "Barney Miller," 1975-82; won Tony for musical *The Rothchilds,* 1971.
b. Mar 20, 1931 in New York, New York
Source: *BiE&WWA; BioIn 10, 15, 16; BkPepl; CelR, 90; ConTFT 3; CurBio 87; EncMT; HalFC 88; IntMPA 84, 86, 88, 92, 94, 96; LegTOT; NotNAT; VarWW 85; WhoAm 78, 80, 82, 84, 86, 92, 94, 95, 96, 97; WhoEnt 92; WhoHol 92; WhoTelC; WhoThe 72, 77, 81; WorAl; WorAlBi*

Linder, Harold Francis
American. Banker
Financial consultant, World Bank, 1970-76; ambassador to Canada, 1968.
b. Sep 13, 1900 in New York, New York
d. Jun 22, 1981 in New York, New York
Source: *AnObit 1981; BioIn 5, 12; IntWW 74, 75, 76, 77, 80, 81, 82N; IntYB 78, 79, 80, 81; NewYTBS 81; WhoAm 74, 76, 80; WhoAmP 73, 75, 79; WhoWor 80*

Lindfors, Viveca
[Elsa Viveca Torstensdotter]
American. Actor
Artistic director, founder, Berkshire Theatre Festival; wrote *Viveha, Viveca.*
b. Dec 29, 1920 in Uppsala, Sweden
d. Oct 25, 1995 in Uppsala, Sweden
Source: *BiDFilm, 81; BiE&WWA; BioIn 3, 4, 6, 10, 11, 12, 18, 21; ConAu 128; ConTFT 1, 15; CurBio 55; FilmEn; FilmgC; ForYSC; HalFC 80, 84, 88; IntMPA 75, 76, 77, 78, 79, 80, 81, 82, 84, 86, 88, 92, 94, 96; ItaFilm; LegTOT; MiSFD 9; MotPP; MovMk; NotNAT; VarWW 85; WhoAm 86, 88; WhoAmW 66, 68, 70, 72, 74, 85; WhoEnt 92; WhoHol 92, A; WhoThe 72, 77, 81; WhoUSWr 88; WhoWrEP 89, 92, 95; WorAl; WorEFlm*

Lindgren, Astrid
Swedish. Children's Author
Wrote *Pippi Longstocking* stories for children, 1950.
b. Nov 14, 1907 in Vimmerby, Sweden
Source: *Au&ICB; Au&Wr 71; AuBYP 2, 3; Benet 96; BioIn 6, 7, 8, 9, 10, 13, 15, 17, 19, 20; BlmGWL; ChlBkCr; ChlFicS; ChlLR 1, 39; ConAu 13R; CurBio 96; DcScanL; EncCoWW; IntAu&W 76; LegTOT; LinLib L; ModWoWr; MorJA; OxCChiL; RAdv 14; SmATA 2, 38; TwCChW 89B; WhoAmW 70, 72, 74, 75, 77; WhoWor 74, 76, 95, 96, 97*

Lindisfarne
[Rod Clements; Simon Cowe; Alan Hull; Ray Jackson; Ray Laidlaw]
English. Music Group
Folk-rock band, formed 1967; hits include "Run for Home," 1978.
Source: *BioIn 19; ConMuA 80A; EncRk 88; HarEnR 86; IlEncRk; PenEncP; RkOn 85A; RolSEnR 83; Who 82, 83, 85, 88, 90, 92, 94; WhoHol 92; WhoRock 81; WhoRocM 82*

Lindley, Audra
American. Actor
Played Mrs. Roper in TV series "Three's Company," 1977-79; "The Ropers," 1979-80.
b. Sep 24, 1918 in Los Angeles, California
Source: *ConTFT 3; HalFC 88; LegTOT; VarWW 85; WhoAm 88; WhoHol A; WhThe*

Lindley, David
American. Musician
Versatile guitarist; has worked with musicians ranging from Ry Cooder to Andreas Vollenweider; solo albums show reggae influence; *El Rayo-X,* 1981.
b. 1944 in San Marino, California
Source: *OnThGG; PenEncP; RolSEnR 83*

Lindner, Richard
German. Artist, Illustrator
Unique figurative painter; flat, geometric shapes combine cubism, symbolism, pop art.
b. Nov 11, 1901 in Hamburg, Germany
d. Apr 16, 1978 in New York, New York
Source: *BioIn 2, 6, 7, 8, 9, 10, 11, 12, 15; BriEAA; ConArt 77, 83, 89, 96; DcAmArt; DcCAA 71, 77, 88, 94; McGDA; NewYTBS 78; OxCTwCA; OxDcArt; PeoHis; PhDcTCA 77; PrintW 83, 85; WhAm 7; WhAmArt 85; WhoAm 74, 76, 78; WhoAmA 73, 76, 78, 80N, 82N, 84, 84N, 86N, 89N, 91N, 93N; WhoWor 74; WhoWorJ 72, 78; WorArt 1950*

Lindros, Eric (Bryan)
"The Next One"
Canadian. Hockey Player
Won silver, Canadian hockey team, 1992 Winter Olympics; center, Philadelphia Flyers, 1992—; won Hart Trophy, 1995.
b. Feb 28, 1973 in London, Ontario, Canada
Source: *BioIn 16; News 92, 92-1; WhoAm 94, 95, 96, 97*

Lindsay, David
English. Author
Wrote fantasy classic *A Voyage to Arcturus,* 1920.
b. Mar 3, 1878 in London, England
d. Jun 6, 1945 in Brighton, England
Source: *CasWL; CmScLit; ConAu 113; EncSF, 93; NewEScF; ScFEYrs; ScFSB; SupFW; TwCSFW 81; WhoHr&F*

Lindsay, Howard
American. Dramatist, Producer, Actor
Co-wrote, with Russel Crouse, *Life With Father,* 1939; *Sound of Music,* 1959; starred in *Life With Father,* 1939-46, a record run on Broadway.
b. Mar 29, 1889 in Waterford, New York
d. Feb 11, 1968 in New York, New York
Source: *AmAu&B; BenetAL 91; BestMus; BiE&WWA; BioIn 1, 2, 4, 5, 6, 7, 8, 10, 11; CamGWoT; CnThe; ConAu 25R; CurBio 42, 68; DcAmB S8; EncMT; EncWT; Film 2; FilmgC; HalFC 80, 84, 88; LegTOT; McGEWD 72, 84; ModWD; NatCAB 54; NewCBMT; NotNAT B; OxCAmL 65; OxCAmT 84; OxCPMus; OxCThe 67, 83; REn; REnAL; TwCA SUP; WhAm 4A; WhE&EA; WhoHol B; WhScrn 74, 77, 83; WhThe; WorAl; WorAlBi*

Lindsay, John Vliet
American. Politician, Lawyer
Rep. mayor, NYC, 1966-74; made unsuccessful campaign for Dem. presidential nomination, 1972.
b. Nov 24, 1921 in New York, New York
Source: *BiDrAC; BiDrUSC 89; BiE&WWA; BioNews 74; CelR 90; ConAu 101; CurBio 62; EncAB-H 1974; EncWB; IntWW 91; NewYTBE 72, 73; NewYTBS 80; PolProf J, NF; Who 85, 92; WhoAm 86, 90, 97; WhoAmL 85; WhoAmP 85, 91; WhoE 91, 97; WhoWor 84; WorAlBi*

Lindsay, Margaret
[Margaret Kies]
American. Actor
Veteran character player of over 80 films; starred in numerous *Ellery Queen* mysteries.
b. Sep 19, 1910 in Dubuque, Iowa
d. May 8, 1981 in Los Angeles, California
Source: *BioIn 11, 12; EncAFC; FilmEn; FilmgC; ForYSC; GangFlm; HalFC 80, 84, 88; HolP 30; InWom SUP; LegTOT; MotPP; MovMk; NewYTBS 81; ThFT; WhoHol A; WhScrn 83; WorAl*

Lindsay, Ted
[Robert Blake Theodore Lindsay]
Canadian. Hockey Player
Left wing, 1944-65, mostly with Detroit on Production Line with Sid Abel, Gordie Howe; known for rough play; won Art Ross Trophy, 1950; Hall of Fame, 1966.
b. Jul 29, 1925 in Renfrew, Ontario, Canada
Source: *BioIn 2, 9, 10, 11, 21; HocEn; LegTOT; WhoAm 78, 80; WhoHcky 73; WhoSpor; WorAl; WorAlBi*

Lindsay, Vachel
[Nicholas Vachel Lindsay]
American. Poet, Author, Lecturer
Wrote verse *The Cargo,* 1914; *Johnny Appleseed,* 1928; committed suicide.
b. Nov 10, 1879 in Springfield, Illinois
d. Dec 5, 1931 in Springfield, Illinois
Source: *AmAu&B; AmBi; AmLY, XR; AmWr S1; AnCL; AnMV 1926; ApCAB X; AtlBL; Benet 87; BenetAL 91; BioIn 1, 2, 4, 5, 6, 7, 8, 9, 10, 11, 12, 14, 15, 16, 17; BkCL; CamGEL; CamGLE; CamHAL; CasWL; Chambr 3; ChhPo, S2, S3; CnDAL; CnE&AP; CnMWL; ConAmA; ConAmL; ConAu 114, 135; CyWA 58; DcAmB; DcLB 54; DcLEL; DcNAA; EncWL, 2, 3; EvLB; FacFETw; GrWrEL P; LinLib L, S; LngCTC; McGEWB; ModAL; NatCAB 23; NewGrDA 86; OxCAmH; OxCAmL 65, 83; OxCEng 67; OxCTwCP; PenC AM; RAdv 1, 14, 13-1; RealN; REn; REnAL; RfGAmL 87; SixAP; SmATA 40; Str&VC; TwCA, SUP; TwCLC 17; TwCWr; WebAB 74, 79; WebE&AL; WhAm 1; WhDW; WhNAA; WhoTwCL; WorAl; WorAlBi; WorLitC*

Lindsey, Benjamin Barr
American. Judge, Social Reformer
Founded American juvenile court system, advocating treatment, not punishment, 1899.
b. Nov 25, 1869 in Jackson, Tennessee
d. Mar 26, 1943 in Los Angeles, California
Source: *AmAu&B; AmRef; AmSocL; ApCAB X; BiDSA; BiDSocW; BioIn 8, 9, 15, 19; DcAmB S3; DcAmSR; DcNAA; EncAB-H 1974, 1996; HarEnUS; LinLib L, S; LngCTC; McGEWB; NatCAB 15; NewCol 75; REnAL; WebAB 74, 79*

Lindsey, Mort
American. Composer, Conductor
Award-winning musical director of TV shows, 1960s; wrote song, "Lorna."
b. Mar 21, 1923 in Newark, New Jersey
Source: *ASCAP 66, 80; IntWWM 77, 85, 90; LegTOT; WhoEnt 92; WhoWest 78, 80, 82*

Lindstrom, Freddie
[Fred Charles Lindstrom; Frederick Anthony Lindstrom]
"Lindy"
American. Baseball Player
Infielder-outfielder, 1924-36; had .311 career batting average; Hall of Fame, 1976.
b. Nov 21, 1905 in Chicago, Illinois
d. Oct 4, 1981 in Chicago, Illinois
Source: *Ballpl 90; LegTOT; NewYTBS 75*

Lindstrom, Pia
American. Journalist
Daughter of Ingrid Bergman, who is film, theater critic in NYC.
b. Sep 20, 1938 in Stockholm, Sweden
Source: *CelR; InWom SUP; WhoAm 76, 78; WhoHol 92, A; WhoTelC*

Lindtberg, Leopold
Swiss. Director
Prominent stage, film director, 1926-84; *Last Chance,* 1945, won special Cannes Peace Prize.
b. Jun 1, 1902 in Vienna, Austria
Source: *AnObit 1984; DcFM; EncEurC; EncWT; FilmEn; FilmgC; HalFC 80, 84, 88; IntWW 74, 75, 76, 77, 78, 79, 80, 81, 82, 83; WhoWor 74, 76, 78*

Linen, James A(lexander), III
American. Publisher
Published *Time* magazine, 1945-60; pres. of Time Inc., 1960-69.
b. Jun 20, 1912 in Waverly, Pennsylvania
d. Feb 1, 1988 in Greenwich, Connecticut
Source: *BioIn 15; BlueB 76; ConAu 124; IntWW 74, 75, 76, 77, 78, 79, 80, 81, 82, 83; IntYB 78, 79, 80, 81; St&PR 75; WhAm 9; WhoAm 74, 76, 78; WhoFI 74, 75; WhoWor 74*

Ling, James J
American. Business Executive
CEO, Ling-Temco-Vought Inc., 1957-70.
b. 1922 in Hugo, Oklahoma
Source: *CurBio 70; EncAB-H 1974; IntWW 83, 91; NewYTBS 81; PeoHis; PolProf J, NF; St&PR 75, 87; WhoAm 86, 90; WhoFI 74; WhoSSW 73; WhoWor 74*

Link, Edwin Albert
American. Inventor, Aviator
Founded Link Aviation, 1935; designed "blue-box" flight simulator, and lockout submarine for divers.
b. Jul 26, 1904 in Huntington, Indiana
d. Sep 7, 1981 in Binghamton, New York
Source: *AmMWSc 79; AnObit 1981; BioIn 3, 7, 8, 9, 10, 11, 12, 13; BlueB 76; CurBio 74; IndAu 1917; IntYB 78, 79, 80, 81; NewYTBS 81; St&PR 75; WhAm 9; Who 74, 82; WhoAm 74, 76, 78, 80*

Link, O(gle) Winston
American. Photographer
Began photographing action on the Norfolk and Western Railway, 1955, as the era of steam locomotion was coming to an end.
b. Dec 16, 1914 in New York, New York
Source: *CurBio 95; WhoAm 97*

Linkletter, Art(hur Gordon)
American. TV Personality
Star of radio, TV shows "People Are Funny"; "House Party."
b. Jul 17, 1912 in Moose Jaw, Saskatchewan, Canada
Source: *AmAu&B; BioIn 1, 2, 3, 4, 5, 7, 8, 10, 12; BioNews 75; CelR, 90; ConAu 4NR, 9R; ConTFT 3; CurBio 53; IntAu&W 91, 93; IntMPA 75, 76, 77, 78, 79, 80, 81, 82, 84, 86, 88, 92, 94, 96; LegTOT; LesBEnT, 92; NewYTBS 82; NewYTET; RadStar; SaTiSS; St&PR 87; VarWW 85; WhoAm 74, 76, 78, 80, 82, 84, 86, 88, 90, 92, 94, 95, 96, 97; WhoEnt 92; WhoHol 92, A; WhoWest 76, 78, 96; WorAl; WorAlBi; WrDr 76, 80, 82, 84, 86, 88, 90, 92, 94, 96*

Linn, Bambi
American. Dancer
Noted for TV variety dance numbers with Rod Alexander, 1950s.
b. Apr 26, 1926 in New York, New York
Source: *BiDD; BiE&WWA; BioIn 1, 4; CnOxB; ConTFT 1; DancEn 78; InWom; NotNAT; WhoHol 92, A; WhoThe 72, 77A; WhThe*

Linnaeus, Carolus
Swedish. Botanist, Author
Founded modern biological system of classifying life forms giving each genus, species name.
b. May 23, 1707 in Rashult, Sweden
d. Jan 10, 1778 in Uppsala, Sweden
Source: *AsBiEn; BbD; Benet 87, 96; BiD&SB; BiDPsy; BiESc; BiHiMed; BlkwCE; EncEnl; EncPaPR 91; InSci; LarDcSc; LegTOT; LinLib L, S; NamesHP; RAdv 14, 13-5; REn; WhDW; WorAl; WorAlBi*

Linowitz, Sol Myron
American. Diplomat, Lawyer
Ambassador to Organization of American States, 1966-69; conegotiator for Panama Canal Treaties, 1977-78.
b. Dec 7, 1913 in Trenton, New Jersey
Source: *BioIn 7; WhoSSW 73; WhoWor 74, 76, 78, 80, 82, 84, 87, 89, 91, 95, 96, 97*

Linton, Ralph
American. Anthropologist, Educator, Author
Developed cultural anthropology; wrote *The Tree of Culture,* 1955.
b. Feb 27, 1893 in Philadelphia, Pennsylvania
d. Dec 24, 1953 in New Haven, Connecticut

Source: *AmAu&B; BiDPsy; BioIn 3, 4, 5, 9; DcAmB S5; InSci; IntDcAn; McGEWB; NamesHP; TwCA SUP; WebAB 74, 79; WebBD 83; WhAm 3; WhE&EA; WhNAA*

Linton, William James
English. Author, Editor, Artist
Founder, Appledore Press, New Haven, CT, 1878; well known for engravings.
b. Dec 7, 1812 in London, England
d. Dec 29, 1897 in New Haven, Connecticut
Source: *Alli SUP; AmAu&B; AmBi; ApCAB; ArtsNiC; BbD; BenetAL 91; BiD&SB; BioIn 10, 14, 16; BritAu 19; Chambr 3; ChhPo, S1, S2, S3; DcAmAu; DcAmB; DcBiPP; DcBrBI; DcBrWA; DcEnL; DcLB 32; DcNaB S1; EarABI, SUP; EncAJ; NatCAB 8; NewC; NewCBEL; REnAL; TwCBDA; VicBrit; WhAmArt 85; WhAm HS*

Linus, Saint
Italian. Religious Leader
Regarded as successor to St. Peter; pope for nearly 12 years.
d. 79?
Source: *NewCol 75; WebBD 83*

Linville, Larry Lavon
American. Actor
Played Frank Burns on TV series "M*A*S*H," 1972-77.
b. Sep 29, 1939 in Ojai, California
Source: *ConTFT 3; VarWW 85; WhoAm 78, 80, 82, 84, 86, 88, 92; WhoEnt 92*

Lionni, Leo
Dutch. Designer, Artist, Children's Author
Popular self-illustrated juvenile books include Caldecott runner-up winner, *Inch by Inch,* 1961.
b. May 5, 1910 in Amsterdam, Netherlands
Source: *AmAu&B; Au&ICB; AuBYP 2, 3; BioIn 14, 16, 17, 18, 19; BkP; ChhPo S2; ChlBIlD; ChlBkCr; ChlLR 7; ChsFB I; ConAu 53; ConDes 84, 90; DcCAr 81; DcLB 61; DcTwDes; FamAIYP; IlsCB 1957; IntAu&W 91; McGDA; OxCChiL; SmATA 8; ThrBJA; TwCChW 78, 83, 89; WhoAm 74, 76, 78, 80, 82, 90, 92, 94; WhoAmA 73, 76, 78, 80, 82, 84, 86, 89, 91, 93; WhoGrA 62, 82; WrDr 80, 82, 84, 86, 88, 90, 92, 94, 96*

Liotard, Jean-Etienne
"The Turkish Painter"
Swiss. Artist
Drew portraits, miniatures, still lifes in delicate pastels: *Lady Taking Chocolate.*
b. Dec 22, 1702 in Geneva, Switzerland
d. Jun 12, 1789 in Geneva, Switzerland
Source: *DcBrECP; McGDA; OxDcArt*

Liotta, Ray
American. Actor
Appeared in films *Something Wild,* 1986; *GoodFellas,* 1990.
b. Dec 18, 1955 in Newark, New Jersey
Source: *BioIn 19, 20; CurBio 94; IntMPA 92, 94, 96; WhoAm 92, 94, 95, 96, 97*

Lipatti, Dinu
Romanian. Pianist, Composer
Noted for his interpretations of Chopin, the Baroque masters.
b. Mar 19, 1917 in Bucharest, Romania
d. Dec 2, 1950 in Chene-Bourg, Switzerland
Source: *Baker 78, 84, 92; BioIn 2, 3, 4, 7, 18, 21; BriBkM 80; DcArts; FacFETw; MusMk; NewAmDM; NewGrDM 80; PenDiMP*

Lipchitz, Jacques
French. Sculptor
A founder, cubist school of sculpture, 1916; noted for heavy stone abstractions, monumental figures, "aerial transparencies."
b. Aug 22, 1891 in Druskinikai, Lithuania
d. May 26, 1973 in Capri, Italy
Source: *BiDSovU; BioIn 1, 2, 3, 4, 5, 6, 7, 9, 10, 11, 12, 17; BriEAA; CelR; ConArt 77, 83; CurBio 48, 62, 73, 73N; DcAmB S9; DcArts; DcCAA 71, 77, 88, 94; DcTwCCu 2; FacFETw; IntDcAA 90; LegTOT; McGDA; McGEWB; NewYTBE 73; ObitOF 79; ObitT 1971; OxCArt; OxCTwCA; OxDcArt; PhDcTCA 77; REn; WhAm 5; WhDW; WhoAmA 73, 76, 78N, 80N, 82N, 84N, 86N, 89N, 91N, 93N; WorArt 1950*

Li Peng
Chinese. Political Leader
Appointed prime minister of the People's Republic of China, 1988—.
b. Oct 1928 in Chengdu, China
Source: *BioIn 14, 15, 16, 17, 18, 19; EncCW; FacFETw; IntWW 89, 91, 93; LegTOT; NewYTBS 87, 89; WhoAsAP 91; WhoPRCh 87, 91; WhoWor 91, 93, 95, 96, 97; WorAlBi*

Lipinski, Carl
Polish. Violinist, Composer
Student of Paganini; concertmaster, Dresden orchestra, for 1839; wrote for violin, piano.
b. Nov 4, 1790 in Radzyn, Poland
d. Dec 16, 1861 in Urlow, Russia
Source: *Baker 78, 84*

Lipman, Clara
American. Actor
Writer, star of stage comedy *Julie Bon Bon: It Depends on a Woman.*
b. Dec 6, 1889 in Chicago, Illinois
d. Jun 22, 1952 in New York, New York
Source: *NotNAT B; WhAm 3; WhoStg 1906, 1908; WhoThe 77A; WhThe*

Lipman, Howard W
American. Art Collector
Folk art collector; trustee, Whitney Museum of American Art, 1968-92.
b. Jul 11, 1905 in Albany, New York
d. Oct 18, 1992 in Carefree, Arizona
Source: *WhoAm 86; WhoAmA 73, 76, 78, 80, 82, 84, 86, 89, 91*

Lipmann, Fritz Albert
American. Biochemist
Discovered coenzyme A (CoA); shared Nobel Prize for Physiology or Medicine, 1953.
b. Jun 12, 1899 in Konigsberg, Prussia
d. Jul 24, 1986 in Poughkeepsie, New York
Source: *AmMWSc 73P; AnObit 1986; AsBiEn; BiESc; BioIn 1, 3, 5, 9, 14, 15; ConAu 119; CurBio 54; InSci; IntWW 83; LarDcSc; McGMS 80; WebAB 74, 79; WhAm 9; Who 85; WhoAm 74, 76, 86; WhoE 74, 86; WhoNob, 90, 95; WhoWor 74, 84; WorAl; WorAlBi; WorScD*

Li Po
[Li T'ai Peh; Li T'ai-Pai; Li T'ai-Po]
Chinese. Poet
Considered among China's greatest poets noted for exquisite imagery, passionate lyrics.
b. 701 in Sichuan, China
d. 762 in Dangtu, China
Source: *Benet 96; BioIn 19; CasWL; DcOrL 1; LegTOT; MagSWL; PenC CL; RAdv 14; RComWL; REn; WorAlBi*

Lippi, Filippino
Italian. Artist, Religious Figure
Son of Filippo; masterpieces include *Madonna and Child Enthroned.*
b. 1459 in Prato, Italy
d. Apr 18, 1504 in Florence, Italy
Source: *DcAmB*

Lippi, Filippo, Fra
[Lippo Lippi]
Italian. Artist
Florentine monk, painted religious frescoes, canvases: *Adoration of the Magi.*
b. 1406 in Florence, Italy
d. Oct 9, 1469 in Florence, Italy
Source: *AtlBL; BioIn 1, 2, 3, 4, 5, 6, 7, 9, 11; DcArts; DcBiPP; DcCathB; IntDcAA 90; LegTOT; LinLib S; McGDA; McGEWB; OxCArt; OxDcArt; REn*

Lippincott, Joshua Ballinger
American. Publisher
Founded J B Lippincott & Co., 1836.
b. Mar 18, 1813 in Juliustown, New Jersey
d. Jan 5, 1886 in Philadelphia, Pennsylvania
Source: *AmAu&B; AmBi; ApCAB; BioIn 15; DcAmB; NatCAB 26; TwCBDA; WhAm HS*

Lippmann, Gabriel Jonas
French. Physicist
Developed color photography; won 1908 Nobel Prize in physics.
b. Aug 16, 1845 in Hallerich, Luxembourg

d. Jul 13, 1921
Source: *DcScB; LarDcSc; LinLib S; WebBD 83; WhoNob, 90, 95; WorInv*

Lippmann, Walter
American. Editor, Journalist, Author
Won Pulitzer, 1958, 1962, for syndicated column, "Today and Tomorrow."
b. Sep 23, 1889 in New York, New York
d. Dec 14, 1974 in New York, New York
Source: *ABCMeAm; AmAu&B; AmPeW; AmSocL; ApCAB X; AuNews 1; Benet 87, 96; BenetAL 91; BiDAmJo; BiDAmNC; BiDInt; BioIn 1, 2, 3, 4, 5, 6, 7, 8, 9, 10, 11, 12, 13, 14, 15, 16, 17, 18, 19; BioNews 75; CamGLE; CamHAL; CelR; ColdWar 1, 2; ConAmA; ConAu 6NR, 9R, 53; CurBio 40, 62, 75N; DcAmB S9; DcAmSR; DcArts; DcLB 29; DcLEL; DrAS 74E, 78E; EncAB-A 2; EncAB-H 1974, 1996; EncAJ; EncCW; EncTwCJ; FacFETw; IntWW 74; JeAmHC; JrnUS; LegTOT; LinLib L, S; LngCTC; MajTwCW; McGEWB; MemAm; NewYTBS 74; ObitT 1971; OxCAmH; OxCAmL 65, 83, 95; PenC AM; PolPar; PolProf E, K, T; RAdv 14, 13-3; RComAH; REn; REnAL; ThTwC 87; TwCA, SUP; TwoTYeD; WebAB 74, 79; WhAm 6; WhDW; WhJnl; WhNAA; Who 74; WhoAm 74; WhoWor 74; WorAl; WorAlBi*

Lippold, Richard
American. Sculptor
Noted for large stainless steel, wood or wire sculptural constructions.
b. May 3, 1915 in Milwaukee, Wisconsin
Source: *BioIn 2, 3, 4, 5, 6, 7, 8, 13; BriEAA; CelR; ConArt 77, 83, 89, 96; CurBio 56; DcAmArt; DcCAA 71, 77, 88, 94; DcCAr 81; EncWB; FacFETw; IntWW 91, 93; McGDA; OxCTwCA; PhDcTCA 77; REn; WhoAm 74, 76, 78, 80, 82, 84, 86, 88, 90, 92, 94, 95, 96, 97; WhoAmA 73, 76, 78, 80, 82, 84, 86, 89, 91, 93; WhoWor 74; WorAl; WorArt 1950*

Lipscomb, Eugene
"Big Daddy"
American. Football Player
Two-time all-pro defensive tackle, 1956-62, mostly with Baltimore; died of heroin overdose.
b. Nov 9, 1931 in Detroit, Michigan
d. May 10, 1963 in Pittsburgh, Pennsylvania
Source: *WhoFtbl 74*

Lipscomb, William Nunn
American. Chemist
Won Nobel Prize in chemistry, 1976.
b. Dec 9, 1919 in Cleveland, Ohio
Source: *AmMWSc 73P, 76P, 79, 82, 86, 89, 92, 95; BiESc; BioIn 5, 8, 11, 14, 15, 19, 20; BlueB 76; CamDcSc; IntAu&W 76; IntWW 74, 75, 76, 77, 78, 79, 80, 81, 82, 83, 89, 91, 93; IntWWM 77, 80; LarDcSc; McGMS 80; NobelP; NotTwCS; Who 82, 83, 85, 88, 90, 92, 94; WhoAm 74, 76, 78, 80, 82, 84, 86, 88, 90, 92, 94, 95, 96, 97; WhoE 77, 79, 81, 83, 85, 86, 89, 91, 93, 95, 97; WhoFrS 84; WhoNob, 90, 95; WhoScEn 94, 96; WhoTech 89; WhoWor 78, 80, 82, 84, 87, 89, 91, 93, 95, 96, 97; WrDr 76, 80, 82, 84, 86, 88, 90, 92, 94, 96*

Lipset, Seymour Martin
American. Sociologist, Political Scientist, Author
Known for work which explored class systems and political parties; influential books include *Agrarian Socialism,* 1950; *Political Man,* 1960.
b. Mar 18, 1922 in New York, New York
Source: *AmAu&B; AmMWSc 73S, 78S; BioIn 7, 11, 13, 14, 15; BlueB 76; ConAu 1NR, 1R; ConIsC 1; FacFETw; IntWW 89, 91, 93; LEduc 74; OxCCan, SUP; PolProf E; RAdv 14; ThTwC 87; WebAB 74, 79; WhoAm 74, 76, 78, 80, 82, 84, 86, 88, 90, 92, 94, 95, 96, 97; WhoAmJ 80; WhoSSW 95, 97; WhoUSWr 88; WhoWest 92, 94; WhoWor 74; WhoWorJ 78; WhoWrEP 89, 92, 95; WrDr 76, 80, 82, 84, 86, 88, 90, 92, 94, 96*

Lipshutz, Robert Jerome
American. Lawyer
Counsel to Jimmy Carter, 1977-79.
b. Dec 27, 1921 in Atlanta, Georgia
Source: *BioIn 11; WhoSSW 95, 97*

Lipsky, Eleazar
American. Author, Lawyer
Wrote novel *Kiss of Death,* 1947, upon which a movie was based.
b. Sep 6, 1911
d. Feb 14, 1993 in New York, New York
Source: *AmAu&B; BioIn 18, 19; ConAu 115; CurBio 93N*

Lipsyte, Robert Mitchell Michael
American. TV Personality, Writer
Hosted TV series "The Eleventh Hour," 1989-90; sports and children's fiction writer.
b. Jan 16, 1938 in New York, New York
Source: *AuBYP 3; BioIn 10, 13, 16; ChlLR 23; ConAu 8NR, 17R; ConLC 21; FifBJA; SmATA 68; TwCChW 89; WrDr 92*

Lipton, Eric
American. Journalist
Won Pulitzer Prize in explantory journalism, 1992.
Source: *WhoAm 96, 97*

Lipton, Peggy
American. Actor
Starred in TV series "The Mod Squad," 1968-73; once married to Quincy Jones.
b. Aug 30, 1947 in New York, New York
Source: *BiDAmM; BioIn 9, 15, 16; ConTFT 9; IntMPA 94, 96; InWom SUP; LegTOT; NewYTBE 72; WhoEnt 92; WhoHol A*

Lipton, Thomas Johnstone, Sir
Scottish. Merchant
Millionaire who acquired tea plantations in Ceylon, 1889; brought Lipton Tea to US, 1893.
b. May 10, 1850 in Glasgow, Scotland
d. Oct 2, 1931 in London, England
Source: *BioIn 2, 3, 6, 10, 12, 14; DcNaB 1931; DcTwBBL; Entr; GrBr; LinLib S; OxCShps; PeoHis; WhAm 3; WorAl*

LiPuma, Tommy
Record Company Executive
President of GRP Records, 1995—; senior vice president at Elektra Records, 1990-94 vice-president for jazz and progressive music at Warner Brothers Records, 1979-90; co-founder and executive of Blue Thumb Records, 1968-74.
b. c. 1940

Liquori, Marty
[Martin A Liquori]
American. Track Athlete
One of top milers, rival of Jim Ryun, late 1960s-early 1970s.
b. Sep 11, 1949 in Montclair, New Jersey
Source: *BiDAmSp OS; ConAu 130; NewYTBE 70, 72; WhoAm 86, 90; WhoTr&F 73; WorAl; WorAlBi; WrDr 96*

Lisa Ben
American. Editor
Edited journal for lesbians entitled *Vice Versa,* 1947-49.
Source: *GayLesB*

Lisagor, Peter Irvin
American. Journalist
Washington correspondent, 1959-76, who made frequent appearances on "Meet the Press."
b. Aug 5, 1915 in Keystone, West Virginia
d. Dec 10, 1976 in Arlington, Virginia
Source: *BiDAmJo; BiDAmNC; BioIn 9, 11, 16; ConAu 69; DcAmB S10; EncTwCJ; NewYTBS 76; WhAm 7; WhoAm 74, 76; WhoSSW 73*

Lisa Lisa and Cult Jam
[Mike Hughes; Alex Mosley; Lisa Velez]
American. Music Group
Latin band; had three top 40 hits including "Head to Toe," 1987.
Source: *BioIn 15, 16, 18*

Lisi, Virna
[Virna Pieralisi]
Italian. Actor
Leading lady in *Duel of the Titans,* 1963; *How to Murder Your Wife,* 1965.
b. Sep 8, 1937 in Ancona, Italy
Source: *BioIn 7, 16, 17; FilmAG WE; FilmEn; FilmgC; ForYSC; HalFC 80,*

84, 88; IntMPA 84, 86, 88, 92, 94; ItaFilm; LegTOT; MotPP; MovMk; VarWW 85; WhoHol 92, A; WhoWor 95, 96, 97

Lismer, Arthur
[Group of Seven]
Canadian. Artist
Founding member, Group of Seven, 1919; paintings depict Northern Canada.
b. Jun 27, 1885 in Sheffield, England
d. Mar 23, 1969 in Montreal, Quebec, Canada
Source: *BioIn 1, 2, 3, 4, 6, 11, 13; CreCan 2; DcBrAr 2; McGDA*

Lispector, Clarice
Brazilian. Author
Wrote *Close to the Savage Heart,* 1944.
b. Dec 10, 1925 in Chechelnik, Union of Soviet Socialist Republics
d. Dec 9, 1977 in Rio de Janeiro, Brazil
Source: *Benet 87, 3; FacFETw; FemiCLE; FemiWr; GrWomW; LatAmWr; LegTOT; PenC AM; RfGShF; RfGWoL 95; WhoWor 74; WorAlBi; WorAu 1980*

Liss, Alan R
American. Publisher
Publisher, Alan R. Liss, Inc., 1971-89; publisher of medical/scientific books and journals.
b. 1925 in New York, New York
d. Aug 20, 1992 in New York, New York
Source: *AmMWSc 92*

List, Emanuel
Austrian. Opera Singer
Bass; noted for Wagnerian roles, lieder.
b. Mar 22, 1891 in Vienna, Austria
d. Jun 21, 1967 in Vienna, Austria
Source: *Baker 78, 84; BioIn 2, 4, 11; MusSN; NewEOp 71; WhAm 4*

List, Eugene
American. Pianist
Int'l concertist; debut at age 12.
b. Jul 6, 1918 in Philadelphia, Pennsylvania
d. Mar 1, 1985 in New York, New York
Source: *Baker 78, 84, 92; BioIn 1, 2, 3, 4, 5, 7, 10, 12, 14; FacFETw; NewAmDM; NewGrDA 86; NewGrDM 80; NewYTBS 74, 85; PenDiMP; WhoAm 82*

Lister, Anne
English. Diarist
Diaries chronicle her relationships with women published as *I Know My Own Heart,* 1988.
b. Apr 3, 1791 in Yorkshire, England
d. Sep 1840, Russia
Source: *BioIn 10, 18; BlmGWL; DcNaB MP; FemiCLE; GayLesB*

Lister, Joseph
[Baron Lister of Lyme Regis]
English. Surgeon
Founded modern antiseptic surgery, 1865.
b. Apr 5, 1827 in Upton, England
d. Feb 10, 1912 in Walmer, England
Source: *Alli, SUP; AsBiEn; BbD; BiD&SB; BiESc; BiHiMed; BioIn 13, 14, 16, 18, 20; CamDcSc; DcInv; DcNaB 1912; DcScB; InSci; LarDcSc; LinLib S; McGEWB; NewC; OxCMed 86; RAdv 14; VicBrit; WhDW; WorAlBi; WorScD*

Liston, Emil
"Big Lis"
American. Basketball Coach
Organized National Assn. of Intercollegiate Basketball, 1937.
b. Aug 21, 1890 in Stockton, Missouri
d. Oct 26, 1949 in Baldwin, Kansas
Source: *WhoBbl 73*

Liston, Sonny
[Charles Liston]
American. Boxer, Actor
Heavyweight champ, 1962-64; lost title to Muhammad Ali.
b. May 8, 1932 in Little Rock, Arkansas
d. c. Dec 29, 1970 in Las Vegas, Nevada
Source: *BiDAmSp BK; BioIn 5, 6, 7, 8, 9, 10, 12, 17, 20; BoxReg; DcAmB S9; InB&W 80; LegTOT; NewYTBE 71; ObitT 1971; WhoBox 74; WhoSpor; WhScrn 77, 83*

Liszt, Franz (Ferencz)
Hungarian. Pianist, Composer
Piano virtuoso; created the symphonic poem; works include song: "Liebestraume," 1850; 20 Hungarian Rhapsodies, 1851-86.
b. Oct 22, 1811 in Raiding, Hungary
d. Jul 31, 1886 in Bayreuth, Germany
Source: *AtlBL; Baker 78, 84, 92; BbD; Benet 87, 96; BiD&SB; BioIn 1, 2, 3, 4, 5, 6, 7, 8, 9, 10, 11, 12, 13, 14, 15, 16, 17, 19, 20, 21; BriBkM 80; CelCen; CmpBCM; DancEn 78; DcArts; DcBiPP; DcCathB; DcCom 77; DcCom&M 79; GrComp; LegTOT; LinLib S; LuthC 75; McGEWB; MetOEnc; MusMk; NewAmDM; NewEOp 71; NewGrDM 80; NewGrDO; NewOxM; OxCEng 67, 85, 95; OxCFr; OxCGer 76, 86; OxDcOp; PenEncH; RAdv 14, 13-3; REn; WhDW; WorAl; WorAlBi*

Lithgow, John (Arthur)
American. Actor
Character actor who appeared in *The World According to Garp,* 1982; *Terms of Endearment,* 1983; on TV's "3rd Rock from the Sun," 1995—.
b. Oct 19, 1945 in Rochester, New York
Source: *BioIn 13, 15, 16; CelR 90; ConNews 85-2; ConTFT 1, 4, 11; CurBio 96; EncAFC; HalFC 88; IntMPA 86, 88, 92, 94, 96; LegTOT; NotNAT; VarWW 85; WhoAm 84, 86, 88, 90, 92, 94, 95, 96, 97; WhoEnt 92; WhoHol 92; WorAlBi*

Litolff, Henri Charles
French. Publisher
Pioneered in publishing inexpensive editions of classical music.
b. Feb 6, 1818 in London, England
d. Aug 6, 1891 in Paris, France
Source: *Baker 78, 84; NewOxM; OxCMus*

Little, Charles Coffin
American. Publisher
Founded Little, Brown, and Co., 1847, with James Brown; published general and legal works.
b. Jul 25, 1799 in Kennebunk, Maine
d. Aug 9, 1869 in Boston, Massachusetts
Source: *AmAu&B; ApCAB; BioIn 3; DcAmB; NatCAB 25; TwCBDA; WhAm HS*

Little, Cleavon Jake
American. Actor
Won Tony for best actor in musical *Purlie,* 1970; played black sheriff, *Blazing Saddles,* 1974; won Emmy for guest appearance on "Dear John."
b. Jun 1, 1939 in Chickasha, Oklahoma
d. Oct 22, 1992 in Sherman Oaks, California
Source: *ConTFT 4; DrBlPA 90; EncAFC; HalFC 84, 88; InB&W 85; IntMPA 92; MovMk; News 93-2; NotNAT; PlP&P A; VarWW 85; WhAm 10; WhoAm 74, 76, 78, 80, 82, 84, 86, 88, 90, 92; WhoBlA 75, 77, 80, 85, 88, 90, 92, 94N; WhoEnt 92; WhoHol A; WhoTelC; WhoThe 81; WorAl; WorAlBi*

Little, Edward Herman
American. Business Executive
Centenarian; rose from salesman to pres., Colgate-Palmolive Co., 1938.
b. Apr 10, 1881 in Charlotte, North Carolina
d. Jul 12, 1981 in Memphis, Tennessee
Source: *BioIn 4, 5, 12; DcNCBi 4; NewYTBS 81; St&PR 75; WhAm 6*

Little, (Flora) Jean
Children's Author
Works include *Stand in the Wind,* 1975; *Listen For the Singing,* 1977.
b. Jan 2, 1932 in Tainan, Taiwan
Source: *AuBYP 2, 3; BioIn 8, 9, 10, 12, 17, 19; BlmGWL; CanWW 31, 89; CaW; ChhPo S2; ChlBkCr; ChlFicS; ChlLR 4; ConAu 21R, 42NR; ConCaAu 1; DcChlFi; FemiCLE; FourBJA; IntAu&W 86, 91, 93; MajAI; OxCCanL; OxCCan SUP; Profile 1; SmATA 2, 17AS, 68; TwCChW 78, 83, 89, 95; TwCYAW; WhoAm 92; WhoCanL 85, 87, 92; WrDr 80, 82, 84, 86, 88, 90, 92, 94, 96*

Little, Joan
American. Victim
Jailed for shoplifting, 1974; while in prison gained national attention for killing white jailer who sexually abused her.
b. May 8, 1954 in Washington, North Carolina

Source: *BioIn 10, 11, 12; InB&W 80; NewYTBS 75*

Little, Lawson
[William Lawson Little, Jr]
American. Golfer
Only player to win British, US amateurs in two consecutive yrs., 1934, 1935; turned pro, 1936; won US Open, 1940.
b. Jun 23, 1910 in Newport, Rhode Island
d. Feb 1, 1968 in Pebble Beach, California
Source: *BiDAmSp OS; BioIn 8; CmCal; CurBio 40; DcAmB S8; WhoGolf*

Little, Little Jack
[John Leonard]
American. Bandleader
His band featured on radio, in nightclubs, 1920s-30s; wrote song "Shanty in Old Shanty Town."
b. May 28, 1900 in London, England
d. Apr 9, 1956 in Hollywood, California
Source: *ASCAP 66; CmpEPM; EncVaud; WhScrn 77*

Little, Lou(is)
American. Football Coach
Head coach, Columbia U, 1930-56; viewed sports within context of entire educational system.
b. Dec 6, 1893 in Leominster, Massachusetts
d. May 28, 1979 in Delray Beach, Florida
Source: *BioIn 1, 4, 5, 10, 11, 12; CurBio 45, 79, 79N; NewCol 75; NewYTBS 79; WhoFtbl 74; WhoSpor*

Little, Rich(ard Caruthers)
Canadian. Entertainer
Impressionist who can do 160 different personalities.
b. Nov 26, 1938 in Ottawa, Ontario, Canada
Source: *BioIn 10, 13, 20; BioNews 74; CanWW 81, 83, 89; CelR 90; ConTFT 3, 5; CurBio 75; IntMPA 88, 92, 94, 96; JoeFr; LegTOT; VarWW 85; WhoAm 74, 78, 80, 82, 84, 86, 88, 90, 92, 94, 95, 96, 97; WhoEnt 92; WhoHol 92; WorAl; WorAlBi*

Little, Robert Langdon
American. Social Worker
Director, Child Welfare Administration, NYC, 1990—.
b. Aug 31, 1938 in Lansing, Michigan
Source: *ConBlB 2*

Little, Royal
d. Jan 12, 1989, Bahamas

Little, Royal
American. Business Executive
Founder, past chm., Textron Inc.
b. Mar 1, 1896 in Wakefield, Massachusetts
Source: *BiDAmBL 83; BioIn 6, 7, 8, 10, 15, 16, 21; ConAu 106, 127; EncWB; FacFETw; NewYTBS 89; WhAm 9; WhoAm 74, 76, 78, 80, 82, 84, 86, 88; WhoWor 78*

Little, Sally
South African. Golfer
Turned pro, 1971; won LPGA, 1980.
b. Oct 12, 1951 in Cape Town, South Africa
Source: *BioIn 15; WhoAmW 89; WhoGolf; WhoIntG*

Little Anthony and the Imperials
[Clarence Collins; Anthony Gourdine; Tracy Lord; Glouster Rogers; Sammy Strain; Ernest Wright]
American. Music Group
Popular, 1950s-60s; hit singles include "Tears On My Pillow," 1958; "Goin' Out of My Head," 1964.
Source: *BioIn 11; DrBlPA 90; EncPR&S 74, 89; EncRk 88; IlEncBM 82; NewAmDM; NewGrDA 86; PenEncP; RolSEnR 83; WhoRock 81*

Littledale, Freya Lota
American. Children's Author
Juvenile books include *The Elves and the Shoemaker,* 1975; *The Snow Child,* 1978.
Source: *ConAu 10NR, 25NR; IntAu&W 91; SmATA 2; WhoAm 90; WhoAmW 77, 91; WhoE 91; WhoUSWr 88; WrDr 86, 92*

Little Eva
[Eva Narcissus Boyd]
American. Singer
Hits include "The Loco-Motion," 1962; words, music written by Gerry Goffin, Carole King for their babysitter.
b. Jun 29, 1945 in Bellhaven, North Carolina
Source: *AmPS A; EncRk 88; IlEncBM 82; LegTOT; PenEncP; RkOn 74; RolSEnR 83; SoulM; WhoRock 81*

Little Feat
American. Music Group
Premier blues/rock concert band formed, 1970; hits include "Dixie Chicken," "Oh Atlanta."
Source: *ConAu 69, X; ConMuA 80A; ConMus 4; DcLP 87B; EncPR&S 89; EncRk 88; EncRkSt; IlEncRk; NewGrDA 86; NewYTBS 27; OnThGG; PenEncP; RolSEnR 83; TwCCr&M 85, 91; WhE&EA; WhoHol 92; WhoRock 81; WhoRocM 82*

Littlejohn, Robert McGowan
American. Military Leader
Chief quartermaster of US Armed Forces in Europe, WW II.
b. Oct 23, 1890 in Jonesville, South Carolina
d. May 6, 1982 in Washington, District of Columbia
Source: *BiDWWGF; BioIn 1, 12, 13; CurBio 82; NewYTBS 82; WhAm 8*

Littler, Gene
[Eugene Alec Littler]
"Gene the Machine"
American. Golfer
Turned pro, 1954; has won 29 PGA events including US Open, 1961.
b. Jul 21, 1930 in San Diego, California
Source: *BiDAmSp OS; BioIn 3, 4, 5, 6, 7, 9, 11, 13; CmCal; CurBio 56; LegTOT; NewYTBS 75; WhoAm 86, 90; WhoGolf; WhoIntG*

Little Richard
[Richard Wayne Penniman]
"Georgia Peach"
American. Singer
Hits include "Tutti Frutti," 1955; "Good Golly Miss Molly," 1958; "Long Tall Sally," 1956.
b. Dec 25, 1935 in Macon, Georgia
Source: *BiDAmM; BioIn 13, 14, 15, 16; BluesWW; CelR 90; CurBio 86; DrBlPA, 90; EncPR&S 74, 89; EncRk 88; HarEnR 86; IlEncBM 82; InB&W 80, 85; LegTOT; NewAmDM; NewGrDA 86; OxCPMus; PenEncP; RolSEnR 83; SoulM; WhoAm 74, 88; WhoBlA 85, 90, 92; WhoEnt 92; WhoHol 92; WorAl; WorAlBi*

Little River Band, The
[Beeb Birtles; David Briggs; John Farnham; Rick Formosa; Graham Goble; Steve Housden; Mal Logan; George McArdle; Roger McLachan; Wayne Nelson; Derek Pellici; Glenn Shorrock]
Australian. Music Group
Vocal harmony, country-pop group begun 1975; had single "Take It Easy On Me," 1981.
Source: *BioIn 11; CabMA; ConMuA 80B; DrRegL 75; EncRk 88; EncRkSt; HarEnR 86; NewYTBS 95; PenEncP; RkOn 78; RolSEnR 83; SoulM; WhoRock 81; WhoRocM 82*

Little Tich
[Harry Relp]
English. Comedian
Popular British, Parisian music-hall comic, noted for impersonations, pantomimes; friend of Lautrec.
b. 1868, England
d. Feb 10, 1928 in London, England
Source: *EncWT; NotNAT B; OxCThe 67, 83*

Littlewood, Joan
English. Director
Founded, directed London's experimental Theatre Workshop, 1945-61; produced *O What a Lovely War,* 1963.
b. 1916 in London, England
Source: *BiE&WWA; BioIn 13; BlueB 76; CamGWoT; ConAu 116; ContDcW 89; ConTFT 4; CroCD; DcLB 13; FilmgC; HalFC 88; IntDcWB; IntWW 83, 91; InWom SUP; LngCTC; OxCFilm; OxCThe 83; PlP&P; Who 85, 92; WhoAm 74; WhoThe 81; WhoWor 74; WomWMM*

Litvak, Anatole
[Michael Anatol Litwak]
French. Director
Films include *Snake Pit; Sorry Wrong Number,* 1948.
b. May 21, 1902 in Kiev, Russia
d. Dec 15, 1974 in Neuilly, France
Source: *AmFD; BiDFilm, 81, 94; BioIn 10, 11, 15, 18; CmMov; DcFM; EncEurC; FilmEn; FilmgC; HalFC 80, 84, 88; IlWWHD 1; IntDcF 1-2, 2-2; IntWW 74; ItaFilm; LegTOT; MiSFD 9N; MovMk; NewYTBS 74; ObitOF 79; ObitT 1971; OxCFilm; WhScrn 77, 83; WorEFlm; WorFDir 1*

Litvinne, Felia
Russian. Opera Singer
Soprano who performed in US during 1880s; noted for portrayal of Gluck's *Alceste.*
b. Oct 11, 1860 in Saint Petersburg, Russia
d. Oct 12, 1936 in Paris, France
Source: *Baker 84, 92; CmOp; InWom; MetOEnc; NewEOp 71; OxDcOp*

Litvinoff, Emanuel
English. Author
Works include *Blood on the Snow,* 1975; *The Face of Terror,* 1978.
b. Jun 30, 1915 in London, England
Source: *BioIn 7; ConAu 117, 129; ConNov 72, 76, 82, 86, 91, 96; ConPo 70; DcLEL 1940; EngPo; IntAu&W 76, 77, 91, 93; IntvTCA 2; NewC; WhE&EA; WrDr 76, 80, 82, 84, 86, 88, 90, 92, 94, 96*

Litvinov, Maxim
"Old Bolshevik"
Russian. Diplomat, Statesman
Soviet foreign minister, 1929-39; ambassador to US, 1941-43; Deputy Minister of Foreign Affairs, 1946.
b. Jul 17, 1871 in Bialystok, Russia
d. Dec 31, 1951 in Moscow, Union of Soviet Socialist Republics
Source: *CurBio 41, 52; DcPol; HisEWW; ObitOF 79; WhDW*

Liu Shao-Ch'i
Chinese. Political Leader
Chm., People's Republic of China, 1959, replacing Mao Tsetung; formally purged, 1968.
b. 1898? in Ning-hsiang
d. Nov 13, 1969? in Kaifeng, China
Source: *ColdWar 1; CurBio 57, 74; DcPol; NewYTBS 74; ObitOF 79; WhAm 6; WhoPRCh 81A*

Liut, Mike
[Michael Liut]
Canadian. Hockey Player
Goalie St. Louis, 1979-85; Hartford, 1985-90; Washington, 1990-92.
b. Jan 7, 1956 in Weston, Ontario, Canada
Source: *BioIn 12, 13; HocEn; HocReg 87*

Liuzzo, Viola
American. Civil Rights Leader
Assassinated while driving marchers from Montgomery to Selma, AL.
b. 1925 in California, Pennsylvania
d. Mar 25, 1965 in Selma, Alabama
Source: *BioIn 7, 19; WhoAmW 66*

Lively, Penelope
English. Children's Author
Won British Arts Council National Book Award for *Treasures of Time,* 1980; Booker Prize for *Moon Tiger,* 1987.
b. Mar 17, 1933 in Cairo, Egypt
Source: *ArtclWW 2; Au&Wr 71; AuBYP 2S, 3; BioIn 10, 11, 13, 15, 16, 17, 19, 20, 21; BlmGWL; CamGLE; ChhPo S2; ChlBkCr; ChlLR 7; ConAu 29NR, 41R; ConLC 32, 50; ConNov 91; CurBio 94; DcLB 14, 161; FemiCLE; FourBJA; InWom SUP; MajTwCW; Novels; OxCChiL; ScF&FL 1, 2, 92; SmATA 7, 60; TwCChW 78, 83, 89; WrDr 76, 80, 82, 84, 86, 88, 90, 92, 94, 96*

Liveright, Horace Brisbin
American. Publisher, Producer
Founded Boni & Liveright, 1918, publishers of *The Modern Library* ; theater productions included *Hamlet,* 1925.
b. Dec 10, 1886 in Osceola Mills, Pennsylvania
d. Sep 24, 1933
Source: *BioIn 7, 9, 21; DcAmB S1; NotNAT B; OxCThe 67; WhAm 1; WhThe*

Livermore, Mary Ashton Rice
American. Journalist, Social Reformer, Lecturer
Edited *The Agitator,* 1869; *Woman's Journal,* 1870-72; lectured for 25 yrs. for temperance, suffrage.
b. Dec 19, 1820 in Boston, Massachusetts
d. May 23, 1905 in Melrose, Massachusetts
Source: *Alli SUP; AmAu; AmAu&B; AmBi; AmRef; AmSocL; AmWom; ApCAB; BbD; BiD&SB; BioIn 15, 16, 19; ChhPo S1; DcAmAu; DcAmB; DcNAA; Drake; InWom, SUP; LibW; NotAW; TwCBDA; WebAB 74, 79; WhAm 1; WhCiWar; WomFir*

Livesay, Dorothy (Kathleen)
Canadian. Writer
Wrote collection of poems *Day and Night,* 1944.
b. Oct 12, 1909 in Winnipeg, Manitoba, Canada
Source: *ArtclWW 2; AuNews 2; Benet 96; BenetAL 91; BioIn 1, 10, 11, 15, 16, 17, 18; BlmGWL; CamGLE; CanWr; CanWW 31, 70, 79, 80, 81, 83, 89; CasWL; ConAu 8AS, 25R, 36NR; ConCaAu 1; ConLC 4, 15, 79; ConPo 70, 75, 80, 85, 91; CreCan 2; DcLB 68; DcLEL; FemiCLE; FemiWr; GrWrEL P; IntAu&W 82, 89; IntWWP 77; MajTwCW; ModCmwL; ModWoWr; OxCCan; OxCCanL; OxCCan SUP; OxCTwCP; REnAL; RfGEnL 91; WhoCanL 85, 87, 92; WrDr 76, 80, 82, 84, 86, 88, 90, 92, 94, 96*

Livesey, Roger
Welsh. Actor
Starred in film *The Life and Death of Colonel Blimp,* 1943.
b. Jun 25, 1906 in Barry, Wales
d. Feb 5, 1976 in Watford, England
Source: *BioIn 10; Film 2; FilmAG WE; FilmEn; FilmgC; ForYSC; HalFC 80, 84, 88; IlWWBF; IntMPA 75, 76; MovMk; NewYTBS 76; PlP&P; Who 74; WhoHol C; WhoThe 72, 77, 81N; WhScrn 83*

Living Colour
American. Music Group
Hard rock album *Vivid,* 1988, included Grammy-winning "Cult of Personality."
Source: *BioIn 16, 19, 20; ConMus 7; EncRkSt; News 93-3; OnThGG*

Livingston, Barry
American. Actor
Played Ernie Douglas on TV's "My Three Sons," 1963-72.
b. Dec 17, 1953 in Los Angeles, California
Source: *WhoHol 92, A*

Livingston, Edward
American. Statesman
Jackson's secretary of State, 1831-33; minister to France, 1833-35; brother of Robert R.
b. May 26, 1764 in Columbia County, New York
d. May 23, 1836 in Rhinebeck, New York
Source: *Alli; AmAu; AmBi; AmJust; AmPolLe; ApCAB; BiAUS; BiDrAC; BiDrUSC 89; BiDrUSE 71, 89; BiDSA; BioIn 1, 3, 4, 7, 9, 10, 16; CyAG; CyAL 1; DcAmAu; DcAmB; DcAmDH 80, 89; DcBiPP; DcNAA; Drake; HarEnUS; LinLib L, S; McGEWB; NatCAB 5; OxCAmH; OxCLaw; REnAW; TwCBDA; WebAB 74, 79; WhAm HS; WhAmP*

Livingston, J(oseph) A(rnold)
American. Economist, Journalist, Author
Award-winning financial journalist; started syndicated column "Business Outlook," 1945; won Pulitzer for international reporting, 1965.
b. Feb 10, 1905 in New York, New York
d. 1989
Source: *AmEA 74; AmMWSc 73S, 78S; BioIn 16; ConAu 1R, 130; IntAu&W 77; Ward 77; WhoAm 74, 76, 78, 80, 82, 84, 88; WhoE 74; WhoUSWr 88; WhoWrEP 89*

Livingston, Jerry
[Jerry Levinson]
American. Songwriter
Wrote novelty tune "Mairzy Doats," 1943; love song "The Twelfth of Never," 1956.
b. Mar 25, 1909 in Denver, Colorado
d. Jul 2, 1987 in Los Angeles, California
Source: *AmPS; ASCAP 66, 80; BiDAmM; BioIn 9, 15; CmpEPM; NewYTBS 87; OxCPMus; PopAmC SUP; Sw&Ld C*

Livingston, M(ilton) Stanley
American. Physicist
Built cyclotron, first effective atom-smasher, with Ernest Lawrence, 1920s.
b. May 25, 1905 in Brodhead, Wisconsin
d. Aug 25, 1986 in Santa Fe, New Mexico
Source: *AmMWSc 73P, 76P, 79, 82, 86; BioIn 3, 4, 15; CurBio 55, 86, 86N; WhAm 9; WhoAm 74, 76, 86*

Livingston, Philip
American. Continental Congressman, Merchant, Philanthropist
Signed Declaration of Independence; promoted founding of Columbia U.
b. Jan 15, 1716 in Albany, New York
d. Jun 12, 1778 in New York, New York
Source: *AmBi; ApCAB; BiAUS; BiDrAC; BiDrUSC 89; BioIn 3, 7, 8, 9; DcAmB; Drake; EncAR; EncCRAm; HarEnUS; NatCAB 3; OxCAmH; TwCBDA; WhAm HS; WhAmP; WhAmRev; WorAl; WorAlBi*

Livingston, Robert R
American. Diplomat
Administered first presidential oath of office to Washington; on committee of five that drew up Declaration of Independence, 1776; first secretary of State, 1781-83.
b. Nov 27, 1746 in New York, New York
d. Feb 26, 1813 in Clermont, New York
Source: *Alli; AmBi; AmPolLe; ApCAB; BiAUS; BiDrAC; BiDrUSC 89; BioIn 1, 3, 4, 5, 8, 9, 11, 16; BlkwEAR; CyAG; DcAmAu; DcAmB; DcAmDH 80, 89; DcNAA; Drake; EncAB-H 1974; EncAR; EncCRAm; McGEWB; NatCAB 2; OxCAmH; OxCLaw; TwCBDA; WebAB 74, 79; WhAm HS; WhAmP; WorAl*

Livingston, Stanley
American. Actor
Played Chip on TV series, "My Three Sons," 1960-72.
b. Nov 24, 1950 in Los Angeles, California
Source: *WhoEnt 92; WhoHol 92, A*

Livingstone, David
Scottish. Missionary, Explorer
Discovered Victoria Falls, 1855; Henry Stanley found him, 1871, saying "Dr. Livingstone, I presume."
b. Mar 19, 1813 in Lanarkshire, Scotland
d. May 1, 1873 in Ilala, Zambia
Source: *Alli, SUP; BbD; Benet 87, 96; BiD&SB; BioIn 1, 2, 3, 4, 5, 6, 7, 8, 9, 10, 11, 12, 13, 15, 16, 17, 18, 19, 20, 21; BritAu 19; CasWL; CelCen; Chambr 3; CmScLit; DcAfHiB 86; DcBiPP, A; DcEnA; DcEnL; DcLB 166; DcLEL; DcNaB; Dis&D; EncSoA; EvLB; Expl 93; HisDBrE; LegTOT; LinLib L, S; LuthC 75; McGEWB; NewC; NewCBEL; OxCEng 67, 85, 95; OxCMed 86; RAdv 14, 13-3; REn; VicBrit; WhDW; WhWE; WorAl; WorAlBi*

Livingstone, Ken
"Red Ken"
English. Politician
Leader, Greater London Council, 1981-86 whose unorthodox policies led to the disbanding of the GLC by Thatcher in 1986; member, House of Commons, 1987—.
b. Jun 17, 1945 in London, England
Source: *BioIn 12, 14, 15, 16; IntWW 91; News 88, 88-3; Who 82, 83, 85, 88, 90, 92, 94*

Livingstone, Mary
[Mrs. Jack Benny; Sadye Marks]
American. Comedian
Played with husband, Jack Benny on radio, TV, 1930s-65.
b. Jun 22, 1908 in Seattle, Washington
d. Jun 30, 1983 in Holmby Hills, California
Source: *BioIn 10, 15; FunnyW; GoodHs; InWom SUP; LegTOT; NewYTBS 83; RadStar; SaTiSS; What 5; WhoHol A; WorAl*

Livius Andronicus
"Father of the Roman Theatre"
Roman. Poet, Dramatist, Translator
Founder of Roman epic poetry, drama; introduced Greek literature into Rome.
b. 284?BC in Tarentum, Italy
d. 204?BC
Source: *BiD&SB; CasWL; Ent; NewCol 75; OxCThe 67; PenC CL; PlP&P; REn*

Livy
[Titus Livius]
Roman. Historian
Of the 142 books which comprise his *Annals of the Roman People,* 35 are extant; remainder are in fragments.
b. 59BC in Patavium, Italy
d. 17AD in Patavium, Italy
Source: *AncWr; AtlBL; BbD; Benet 87; BiD&SB; BioIn 1, 5, 7, 9; BlmGEL; CasWL; ClMLC 11; CyWA 58; DcArts; DcBiPP; DcEnL; Grk&L; HarEnMi; LegTOT; LinLib L, S; LngCEL; NewC; NewCol 75; OxCClL, 89; OxCEng 67, 85, 95; PenC CL; RAdv 14, 13-3; RComWL; REn; WhDW; WorAl; WorAlBi*

Li Xiannian
Chinese. Political Leader
Pres., People's Republic of China, 1983-88.
b. Jun 23, 1909 in Hubei Province, China
d. Jun 21, 1992 in Beijing, China
Source: *BioIn 13; ColdWar 1, 2; EncRev; IntWW 83, 89, 91; NewYTBS 92; WhAm 10; WhoPRCh 91; WhoWor 89, 91*

Ljungberg, Gota
Swedish. Opera Singer
Soprano who sang with NY Metropolitan in 1930s.
b. Oct 4, 1893 in Sundsvall, Sweden
d. Jun 28, 1955 in Lidingo, Sweden
Source: *Baker 78, 84; BioIn 4, 10, 11; InWom; MetOEnc; MusSN; NewEOp 71; NewGrDM 80; NewGrDO; OxDcOp*

LL Cool J
[James Todd Smith]
American. Rapper
Radio, 1985, considered a rap landmark for its song-like arrangements.
b. Jan 14, 1968 in New York, New York
Source: *BioIn 15; NewYTBS 87; SoulM; WhoAm 94, 95, 96, 97*

Lleras Camargo, Alberto
Colombian. Political Leader
Liberal party president of Colombia, 1946-47, 1958-62; helped bring political peace to Colombia; head, Organization of American States, 1948-54.
b. Jul 3, 1906 in Bogota, Colombia
d. Jan 4, 1990 in Bogota, Colombia
Source: *AnObit 1990; BiDLAmC; BioIn 16, 17; CurBio 65, 90, 90N; DcTwHis; EncLatA; FacFETw; IntWW 74, 75, 76, 77, 78, 79, 80, 81, 82, 83, 89; McGEWB; NewYTBS 90*

Lleras Restrepo, Carlos
Colombian. Political Leader
Liberal party leader who served as pres., 1966-70.
b. Apr 12, 1908 in Bogota, Colombia
d. Sep 27, 1994 in Bogota, Colombia
Source: *BiDLAmC; BioIn 8, 9, 16, 20; CurBio 70, 94N; DcPol; EncLatA; IntWW 74, 75, 76, 77, 78, 79, 80, 81, 82, 83, 89, 91, 93; WhoWor 74*

Llewellyn, James Bruce
American. Business Executive
Bought Fedco food store chain, 1969; developed, headed business until 1982.
b. Jul 16, 1927 in New York, New York
Source: *ConAmBL; InB&W 80; WhoAfA 96; WhoAm 78, 84; WhoBlA 75, 77, 80, 85, 88, 90, 92, 94*

Llewellyn, Richard
[Richard David Vyvyan Llewellyn Lloyd]
Welsh. Author, Dramatist
Best known for first novel *How Green Was My Valley,* 1940.
b. Dec 8, 1906 in Saint David's, Wales
d. Nov 30, 1983 in Dublin, Ireland
Source: *AnObit 1983; BioIn 11, 13, 14, 15; ConAu 7NR, 53, X; ConLC 7, 80; CurBio 40, 84N; CyWA 58; DcLB 15; DcLEL; EvLB; HalFC 84, 88; LegTOT;*

LngCTC; NewC; NewYTBS 83; Novels; OxCLiW 86; RAdv 1; REn; SmATA 11; TwCA SUP; TwCWr; WorAlBi

Llewelyn-Davies, Richard
English. Architect, Urban Planner
Believed architecture, environment should be harmonious; best known work: research headquarters of Atlantic Richfield, PA.
b. Dec 24, 1912
d. Oct 26, 1981 in London, England
Source: *AnObit 1981; Au&Wr 71; BioIn 12; ConArch 80, 87, 94; ConAu 13R, 105; DcNaB 1981; FacFETw; MacEA; NewYTBS 81; Who 83; WhoWor 74, 76, 78*

Lloyd, Christopher
American. Actor
Played Jim on TV series "Taxi," 1978-83; won two Emmys, 1982-83 starred in three *Back to the Future* films, 1985-90.
b. Oct 22, 1938 in Stamford, Connecticut
Source: *BioIn 11, 16; ConTFT 1, 4, 11; IntMPA 92, 94, 96; IntWW 93; LegTOT; QDrFCA 92; VarWW 85; WhoAm 82, 84, 86, 88, 90, 92, 94, 95, 96, 97; WhoEnt 92; WhoHol 92; WhoTelC; WorAlBi*

Lloyd, Frank
American. Director
Directed over 100 films; won Oscars for *Divine Lady; Cavalcade.*
b. Feb 2, 1888 in Glasgow, Scotland
d. Aug 10, 1960 in Santa Monica, California
Source: *BiDFilm; CmMov; DcFM; Film 1; FilmEn; FilmgC; IlWWHD 1; LegTOT; MiSFD 9N; MovMk; NewYTBE 73; ObitOF 79; ObitT 1951; OxCFilm; TwYS; WhoHol B; WhScrn 74, 77; WorEFlm*

Lloyd, Harold
American. Comedian, Actor
Highest paid film star of 1920s; noted for thrill-comedy scenes; won special Oscar, 1952.
b. Apr 20, 1893 in Burchard, Nebraska
d. Mar 8, 1971 in Hollywood, California
Source: *BiDFilm, 81, 94; BioIn 1, 2, 3, 4, 6, 7, 8, 9, 10, 11, 12; CmCal; CmMov; CurBio 49, 71, 71N; DcArts; DcFM; EncAFC; Film 1, 2; FilmEn; FilmgC; ForYSC; Funs; HalFC 80, 84, 88; IntDcF 1-3, 2-3; JoeFr; MotPP; MovMk; NewYTBE 71; ObitOF 79; ObitT 1971; OxCFilm; QDrFCA 92; SilFlmP; TwYS; WebAB 74; WhAm 5; WhoCom; WhoHol B; WhScrn 74, 77, 83; WorAl; WorAlBi; WorEFlm*

Lloyd, John
"Legs"
English. Tennis Player
Once Britain's number one player; with Wendy Turnbull won Wimbledon mixed doubles, 1983, 1984; married to Chris Evert, 1979-87.
b. Aug 27, 1954 in Leigh-on-Sea, England
Source: *BioIn 12, 13; NewYTBS 84; WhoIntT*

Lloyd, John Henry
"Pop"; "The Black Wagner"
American. Baseball Player
Shortstop in Negro Leagues, compared to Honus Wagner; Hall of Fame, 1977.
b. Apr 15, 1884 in Florida
d. Mar 19, 1965 in Atlantic City, New Jersey
Source: *BiDAmSp BB; BioIn 14, 15, 21; DcAmNB; InB&W 80*

Lloyd, Lewis Kevin
"Black Magic"
American. Basketball Player
Guard, 1981-87, with Golden State, Houston; permanently banned from NBA for violating league's anti-drug policy, 1987.
b. Feb 22, 1959 in Philadelphia, Pennsylvania
Source: *OfNBA 87; WhoAfA 96; WhoBlA 92, 94*

Lloyd, Marie
[Matilda Alice Wood]
English. Entertainer
Legendary British music-hall idol, noted for Cockney impersonations; toured worldwide.
b. Feb 12, 1870 in London, England
d. Oct 7, 1922 in London, England
Source: *BioIn 3, 4, 9, 15, 16; CamGWoT; ContDcW 89; DcArts; DcNaB 1922; EncVaud; EncWT; Ent; IntDcWB; InWom, SUP; NotNAT A, B; OxCPMus; OxCThe 67, 83; PlP&P; VicBrit; WhScrn 83; WhThe; WorAl*

Lloyd, Robin
American. Broadcast Journalist
Correspondent, NBC News, since 1979.
b. Oct 14, 1950 in Winchester, Virginia
Source: *WhoTelC*

Lloyd, Selwyn
[John Selwyn Brooke Lloyd]
English. Politician
British Foreign Secretary, 1955-60, during the 1956 Suez Crisis.
b. Jul 28, 1904 in West Kirby, England
d. May 17, 1978 in Oxfordshire, England
Source: *BioIn 2, 3, 4, 5, 11, 14, 16; ColdWar 1; CurBio 78N; DcNaB 1971; DcPol; EncWM; GrBr; LinLib S; Who 74; WhoWor 74, 76*

Lloyd George of Dwyfor, David Lloyd George Earl
"Welsh Wizard"
English. Statesman
Liberal prime minister, 1916-22, who played principal role in formulation of Versailles Treaty.
b. Jan 7, 1863 in Manchester, England
d. Mar 26, 1945 in Llanystumdwy, Wales
Source: *Chambr 3; CurBio 44, 45; NewCol 75; ObitT 1971; OxCLiW 86; REn*

Lloyd Webber, Andrew
English. Composer, Producer
Musicals include *Jesus Christ Superstar,* 1970; *Cats,* 1981; *Phantom of the Opera,* 1986; has received numerous awards.
b. Mar 22, 1948 in London, England
Source: *Au&Arts 1; Baker 84, 92; BioIn 12, 13, 14, 15, 16, 17, 21; CamGWoT; CelR 90; ConAu 116, 149; ConMus 6; ConTFT 1, 6, 13; CurBio 82; DcArts; FacFETw; IntWW 80, 81, 82, 83, 89, 91, 93; IntWWM 90; NewAmDM; NewGrDA 86; NewGrDM 80; NewGrDO; News 89-1; OxCPMus; OxDcOp; PenEncP; RAdv 14; SmATA 56; Who 82, 83, 85, 88, 90, 92, 94; WhoAm 84, 86, 88, 90, 92, 94, 95, 96, 97; WhoEnt 92; WhoThe 77, 81; WhoWor 74, 76, 82, 84, 87, 89, 91, 93, 95, 97; WorAlBi*

Llull, Ramon
Spanish. Poet, Theologian
Determined to resolve religious differences between Christians, Muslims, and Jews; wrote *The Book of the Ordre of Chyvalry.*
b. c. 1235 in Majorca, Spain
d. 1316, At Sea
Source: *BioIn 15, 17; CasWL; ClMLC 12; DcSpL; OxCSpan; WhDW*

Loach, Ken(neth)
English. Filmmaker
Made films *Days of Hope,* 1975; *Black Jack,* 1979.
b. Jun 17, 1936 in Nuneaton, England
Source: *BiDFilm 94; BioIn 9, 12; ConTFT 12; CurBio 95; FilmgC; HalFC 80, 84, 88; IlWWBF; IntDcF 1-2; IntMPA 96; IntWW 82, 83, 89, 91, 93; MiSFD 9; OxCFilm; Who 82, 83, 85, 88, 90, 92, 94; WhoWor 95, 96, 97; WorFDir 2*

Lobel, Arnold Stark
American. Author, Illustrator
Books include *Frog and Toad Together;* won Caldecott Medal, 1971.
b. May 22, 1923 in Los Angeles, California
d. Dec 6, 1987 in New York, New York
Source: *AuNews 1; ChlLR 5; ConAu 1R, 2NR; SmATA 6; TwCChW 83; WhoAm 84; WrDr 84*

Locatelli, Pietro Antonio
Italian. Violinist, Composer
Violin virtuoso, noted for use of double stops, novel effects; wrote sonatas, concerti grossi.
b. Sep 3, 1693 in Bergamo, Italy
d. Mar 30, 1764 in Amsterdam, Netherlands
Source: *Baker 84; NewOxM; OxCMus; WebBD 83*

Locke, Alain Leroy
American. Educator, Author
First black Rhodes scholar, 1907; numerous books include *Negro in America,* 1933.
b. Sep 13, 1886 in Philadelphia, Pennsylvania
d. Jun 9, 1954 in New York, New York
Source: *AmAu&B; BiDAfM; BiDAmEd; BioIn 2, 3, 4, 5, 6, 8, 9, 10, 13, 14, 15, 17, 19, 21; BlkAWP; BlkWrNE; ConAu 106; CurBio 44, 54; DcAmB S5; DcNaB; EncAB-H 1974, 1996; InB&W 80, 85; NegAl 76, 83, 89; REnAL; SelBAAf; SelBAAu; TwCA, SUP; WebAB 74, 79; WebBD 83; WhAm 3; WhNAA; WhoColR*

Locke, Bobby
[Arthur D'Arcy Locke]
South African. Golfer
Successful foreign golfer; won British Open four times, 1940s-50s; wrote *Bobby Locke on Golf,* 1953.
b. Nov 20, 1917 in Germiston, South Africa
d. Mar 9, 1987 in Johannesburg, South Africa
Source: *AnObit 1987; BioIn 1, 2, 13, 15; EncSoA; IntWW 81, 82, 83; Who 74, 82, 83, 85; WhoGolf*

Locke, David Ross
[Petroleum V Nasby]
American. Editor, Humorist
Wrote popular satirical pieces "Nasby Letters"; collected in *The Nasby Papers,* 1864.
b. Sep 20, 1833 in Vestal, New York
d. Feb 15, 1888 in Toledo, Ohio
Source: *Alli SUP; AmAu; AmAu&B; AmBi; ApCAB; BbD; BibAL; BiDAmJo; BiD&SB; BioIn 12, 15, 16; CamGEL; CamGLE; CamHAL; CasWL; ChhPo S2; CnDAL; CyAL 2; DcAmAu; DcAmB; DcAmTB; DcLB 11, 23; DcLEL; DcNAA; Drake; EncAHmr; EvLB; GrWrEL N; JrnUS; LinLib L; NatCAB 6; OhA&B; OxCAmH; OxCAmL 65, 83, 95; PenC AM; REn; REnAL; RfGAmL 87; TwCBDA; WebAB 74, 79; WhAm HS; WhAmP; WhCiWar*

Locke, John
English. Philosopher
Wrote *Essays Concerning Human Understanding,* 1690; political theories influenced writers of US Constitution.
b. Aug 29, 1632 in Wrington, England
d. Oct 28, 1704 in Oates, England
Source: *Alli; AtlBL; BbD; Benet 87, 96; BenetAL 91; BiD&SB; BiDPsy; BiESc; BioIn 1, 2, 3, 4, 5, 6, 7, 8, 9, 10, 11, 12, 13, 14, 15, 16, 17, 20, 21; BlkwCE; BlkwEAR; BlmGEL; BritAu; CamGEL; CamGLE; CasWL; Chambr 2; ChhPo S2; CyEd; CyWA 58; DcAmC; DcAmSR; DcBiPP; DcEnA; DcEnL; DcEuL; DcInv; DcLB 31A, 101; DcLEL; DcNaB; DcScB; DcSoc; Dis&D; EncAR; EncCRAm; EncEnl; EncEth; EncUnb; EvLB; GrEconB; HarEnUS; HisDStE; InSci; IntDcAn; LarDcSc; LegTOT; LinLib L, S; LitC 7; LngCEL; LuthC 75; McGEWB; MouLC 1; NamesHP; NewC; NewCBEL; OxCAmH; OxCChiL; OxCEng 67, 85, 95; OxCLaw; OxCMed 86; OxCPhil; PenC ENG; RAdv 14, 13-3, 13-4; RComWL; REn; REnAL; RfGEnL 91; TwoTYeD; WebE&AL; WhAm HS; WhDW; WhoEc 81, 86; WorAl; WorAlBi; WrPh P*

Locke, Richard Adams
English. Journalist
Noted for "Moon Hoax," 1835, supposedly revealing Sir John Herschel's discovery of men on moon.
b. Sep 22, 1800 in East Brent, England
d. Feb 16, 1871 in New York, New York
Source: *Alli; AmAu; AmAu&B; ApCAB; BiDAmJo; BioIn 15, 16; DcAmAu; DcAmB; DcLB 43; DcNAA; EncAJ; EncSF, 93; JrnUS; NatCAB 13; OxCAmL 65; ScF&FL 1; ScFEYrs; WebBD 83; WhAm HS*

Locke, Sondra
American. Actor
Starred with Clint Eastwood in *Any Which Way You Can,* 1980.
b. May 28, 1947 in Shelbyville, Tennessee
Source: *BioIn 15, 16; ConTFT 5; ForWC 70; HalFC 80, 84, 88; IntMPA 88, 92, 94, 96; LegTOT; MiSFD 9; VarWW 85; WhoAm 80, 82, 84, 86, 88, 90, 92; WhoHol 92, A*

Locke, William John
English. Author
Popular novels include *The Beloved Vagabond,* 1906.
b. Mar 20, 1863, Barbados
d. May 15, 1930
Source: *Chambr 3; DcNaB 1922; EvLB; LinLib L, S; LngCTC; NewC; NewCBEL; NotNAT B; OxCEng 67; REn; TwCA; TwCWr; WhLit; WhScrn 83; WhThe*

Lockhart, Calvin
American. Actor
Starred in films *Cotton Comes to Harlem,* 1970; *Uptown Saturday Night,* 1974.
b. 1936, Bahamas
Source: *BioNews 74; BlksAmF; DrBlPA 90; FilmgC; HalFC 88; InB&W 80, 85; NewYTBE 70; WhoHol A*

Lockhart, Gene
[Eugene Lockhart]
American. Actor
Father of June Lockhart; character actor in over 100 films.
b. Jul 18, 1891 in London, Ontario, Canada
d. Mar 31, 1957 in Santa Monica, California
Source: *ASCAP 66, 80; BioIn 21; CurBio 50, 57; EncAFC; Film 2; FilmEn; FilmgC; ForYSC; HalFC 80, 84, 88; HolCA; MotPP; MovMk; NotNAT B; ObitOF 79; OlFamFa; Vers A; WhAm 3; WhoHol B; WhScrn 74, 77, 83; WhThe*

Lockhart, John Gibson
Scottish. Biographer, Editor
Noted for classic seven-vol. biography of his father-in-law: *Life of Sir Walter Scott,* 1838.
b. Jul 14, 1794 in Lanarkshire, Scotland
d. Nov 25, 1854 in Abbotsford, Scotland
Source: *Alli; AtlBL; BbD; Benet 87, 96; BiD&SB; BioIn 1, 3, 9, 10, 17, 18; BritAu 19; CamGLE; CasWL; CelCen; Chambr 3; ChhPo, S1, S2, S3; CmScLit; DcBiPP; DcEnA; DcEnL; DcEuL; DcLB 110, 116, 144; DcLEL; DcNaB; EvLB; LinLib L, S; MouLC 3; NewC; NewCBEL; NinCLC 6; OxCEng 67, 85, 95; PenC ENG; RAdv 1, 13-1; REn; WebE&AL*

Lockhart, June
American. Actor
Starred in TV series "Lassie," 1958-64; "Lost in Space," 1965-68.
b. Jun 25, 1925 in New York, New York
Source: *BiE&WWA; BioIn 1, 3, 5, 21; ConTFT 9; FilmEn; FilmgC; ForYSC; HalFC 80, 84, 88; IntMPA 77, 80, 84, 86, 88, 92, 94, 96; InWom, SUP; LegTOT; MotPP; MovMk; NotNAT; VarWW 85; WhoAm 82; WhoHol 92, A; WorAl*

Locklear, Arlinda Faye
American. Lawyer
First Native American woman to argue a case before the US Supreme Court, 1983.
b. 1951
Source: *BioIn 21; NotNaAm*

Locklear, Heather
American. Actor
TV series include "Dynasty," 1981-89, "T J Hooker," 1982-87, "Melrose Place," 1993—.
b. Sep 25, 1961 in Los Angeles, California
Source: *BioIn 13, 14, 15, 16; ConTFT 6, 13; IntMPA 96; LegTOT; News 94, 94-3; VarWW 85; WhoAm 95, 96, 97; WhoAmW 95, 97; WhoHol 92; WorAlBi*

Lockridge, Frances Louise
American. Author
Co-created, with husband Richard, popular sleuths, the Norths, who became subjects of film, radio, TV series.
b. Jan 10, 1896 in Kansas City, Missouri
d. Feb 17, 1963 in Norwalk, Connecticut
Source: *AmAu&B; ArtclWW 2; BioIn 2, 3, 4, 6, 7, 10, 12; ConAu 93; EncMys; NatCAB 47; REnAL; TwCA SUP; WhAm 4*

Lockridge, Richard
American. Author
With wife, Francis Louise, wrote 27 humorous detective stories featuring the Norths.
b. Sep 26, 1898 in Saint Joseph, Missouri
d. Jun 19, 1982 in Tryon, North Carolina

Source: *AmAu&B; AnObit 1982; BenetAL 91; BioIn 2, 3, 4, 6, 12, 13, 14; ConAu 85, 107; CrtSuMy; CurBio 40, 82, 82N; EncMys; LegTOT; NewYTBS 82; REnAL; ScF&FL 1, 92; TwCA, SUP; TwCCr&M 80, 85, 91; WhAm 8; WhoAm 74, 76, 78; WhThe; WorAl; WorAlBi*

Lockridge, Ross Franklin, Jr.
American. Author
Noted for sole book: *Raintree County,* 1948.
b. Apr 25, 1914 in Bloomington, Indiana
d. Mar 6, 1948
Source: *AmAu&B; BioIn 1, 4, 5, 10, 12; CyWA 58; IndAu 1917; ModAL; PenC AM; REnAL; TwCA SUP*

Lockwood, Belva Ann Bennett
American. Social Reformer, Lawyer
First woman to practice before US Supreme Court, 1879; effective women's rights advocate.
b. Oct 24, 1830 in Royalton, New York
d. May 19, 1917 in Washington, District of Columbia
Source: *AmBi; AmPeW; AmRef; AmWom; ApCAB; BiDMoPL; DcAmB; GoodHs; HarEnUS; InWom; LibW; LinLib L, S; NatCAB 2; NotAW; TwCBDA; WebAB 74, 79; WhAm 1; WhAmP; WomWWA 14*

Lockwood, Gary
[John Gary Yusolfsky]
American. Actor
In movie *2001: A Space Odyssey,* 1968.
b. Feb 21, 1937 in Van Nuys, California
Source: *ConTFT 7; FilmEn; FilmgC; ForYSC; HalFC 80, 84, 88; IntMPA 75, 76, 77, 78, 79, 80, 81, 82, 84, 86, 88, 92, 94, 96; LegTOT; MotPP; VarWW 85; WhoAm 74, 76, 78, 80, 82, 84; WhoHol 92, A; WhoHrs 80*

Lockwood, Margaret Mary
[Margaret Day]
American. Actor
Most popular actress in Britain, 1940s; films include *The Wicked Lady,* 1946; *The Man in Grey,* 1943.
b. Sep 15, 1916 in Karachi, Pakistan
d. Jul 15, 1990 in London, England
Source: *CmMov; CurBio 48, 90, 90N; DcNaB 1986; FacFETw; FilmgC; HalFC 88; IntMPA 86; InWom SUP; MotPP; MovMk; NewYTBS 90; OxCFilm; ThFT; VarWW 85; Who 74, 82, 83, 85, 88, 90; WhoHol A; WhoThe 81; WorAl; WorEFlm*

Lockwood, Robert, Jr.
American. Musician
Blues and jazz guitarist; recorded *Steady Rollin' Man,* 1973, *Mr. Blues is Back to Stay,* 1980, *Plays Robert and Robert,* 1993.
b. Mar 27, 1915 in Marvell, Arkansas
Source: *BiDAfM; BiDAmM; BluesWW; GuBlues; OnThGG*

Lockyer, Joseph Norman, Sir
English. Astronomer
Studied solar eclipses, sunspots; one of earliest to make spectroscopic examination of sun, stars.
b. May 17, 1836 in Rugby, England
d. Aug 16, 1920 in Satcombe Regis, England
Source: *Alli SUP; AsBiEn; BbD; BiD&SB; BiESc; BioIn 14; CelCen; DcBiPP; DcInv; DcNaB 1912; DcScB; InSci; LinLib L, S; NewCBEL; NewCol 75; REn; WhDW; WorAl; WorAlBi*

Loden, Barbara Ann
American. Actor
Won Tony for *After the Fall,* 1964; married Elia Kazan, 1967-80.
b. Jul 8, 1937 in Marion, North Carolina
d. Sep 5, 1980 in New York, New York
Source: *AnObit 1980; BiDFilm; BiE&WWA; ConAu 101; HalFC 84; IntDcWB; NewYTBS 80; NotNAT; OxCFilm; WhAm 7; WhoHol A; WhScrn 83; WomWMM*

Loder, John
[John Lowe]
English. Actor
Films include *Lorna Doone,* 1935; *King Solomon's Mines,* 1937.
b. Jan 3, 1898 in London, England
d. Dec 28, 1988 in Buenos Aires, Argentina
Source: *BioIn 3, 10, 12, 16; ConAu 128; Film 2; FilmEn; FilmgC; ForYSC; HalFC 80, 84, 88; IlWWBF, A; LegTOT; MotPP; MovMk; NewYTBS 89; What 4; WhoHol A*

Lodge, Henry Cabot
American. Historian, Statesman
Influential Rep. senator from MA, 1893-1924; prevented US entry into League of Nations; wrote historical biographies.
b. May 12, 1850 in Boston, Massachusetts
d. Nov 9, 1924 in Boston, Massachusetts
Source: *Alli SUP; AmAu; AmAu&B; AmBi; AmDec 1910; AmPeW; ApCAB, X; BbD; BenetAL 91; BiD&SB; BiDInt; BiDrAC; BiDrUSC 89; BioIn 1, 2, 3, 4, 7, 9, 10, 11, 12, 15, 16, 17; BritAS; Chambr 3; ChhPo S1; CyAG; DcAmAu; DcAmB; DcAmC; DcAmDH 80, 89; DcAmImH; DcAmSR; DcLB 47; DcNAA; DcTwHis; EncAB-H 1974, 1996; FacFETw; HarEnUS; LegTOT; LinLib L, S; McGEWB; NatCAB 1, 19; OxCAmH; OxCAmL 65, 83, 95; PolPar; REnAL; TwCBDA; WebAB 74, 79; WhAm 1, 8; WhAmP; WorAl; WorAlBi*

Lodge, Henry Cabot, Jr.
American. Politician, Diplomat
US delegate to UN, 1953-60; unsuccessful Rep. vice-presidential candidate, 1960.
b. Jul 5, 1902 in Nahant, Massachusetts
d. Feb 27, 1985 in Beverly, Massachusetts
Source: *AmPolLe; BiDrAC; BiDrUSC 89; BioIn 1, 2, 3, 4, 5, 6, 7, 8, 9, 11, 12, 14, 15, 16; BlueB 76; CelR; ConAu 53, 115; ConNews 85-1; CurBio 43, 54, 85, 85N; DcAmDH 80, 89; DcPol; EncCW; EncWB; FacFETw; HisDcKW; IntAu&W 82; IntWW 74, 75, 76, 77, 78, 79, 80, 81, 82, 83; LinLib S; NewYTBS 85; OxCAmH; PolPar; PolProf E, J, K, NF, T; PresAR; WebAB 74, 79; WhAm 8; WhJnl; Who 74, 82, 83, 85; WhoAm 74, 76, 78, 80, 82, 84; WhoAmP 73, 75, 77, 79, 81, 83, 85; WhoE 79, 81, 83, 85; WhoWor 74, 76, 78, 80, 82, 84; WorAl; WorAlBi*

Lodge, Oliver Joseph, Sir
English. Scientist
Eminent inventor, spiritualist, involved in psychic phenomena.
b. Jun 12, 1851 in Penkhull, England
d. Aug 22, 1940 in Amesbury, England
Source: *Alli SUP; AsBiEn; BiDPara; BiESc; BioIn 2, 5, 6, 8, 9, 10, 11, 14; Chambr 3; ChhPo S1; ConAu 117; CurBio 40; DcLEL; DcNaB 1931; DcScB; EncO&P 2; EncPaPR 91; EvLB; InSci; LarDcSc; LinLib L, S; LngCTC; NewC; OxCEng 67, 85; OxCMus; TwCA, SUP; WhLit; WhoLA; WorInv*

Lodge, Thomas
English. Author, Dramatist
Wrote romance *Rosalynde,* 1590, whose plot was later used by Shakespeare.
b. 1558? in West Ham, England
d. 1625 in London, England
Source: *Alli; BbD; Benet 87, 96; BiD&SB; BiDRP&D; BioIn 3, 5, 7, 8, 10, 11; BlmGEL; BritAu; CamGEL; CasWL; Chambr 1; ChhPo, S2; CnE&AP; CnThe; CroE&S; CrtSuDr; CrtT 1; DcArts; DcEnA; DcEnL; DcEuL; DcLB 172; DcLEL; DcNaB; Ent; EvLB; GrWrEL N; LngCEL; MouLC 1; NewC; NewCBEL; NewCol 75; OxCEng 67, 85, 95; PenC ENG; PlP&P; RAdv 14; REn; RfGEnL 91; WebE&AL*

Loeb, Gerald Martin
American. Financier, Author
Wrote syndicated weekly investment column and *Battle for Investment Survival,* 1957.
b. Jul 24, 1899 in San Francisco, California
d. 1974 in San Francisco, California
Source: *BioIn 7, 10; ConAu 49, P-1*

Loeb, Jacques
American. Biochemist
Devised tropism theory, 1888; did research on egg fertilization, regeneration of tissue.
b. Apr 7, 1859 in Mayen, Germany
d. Feb 11, 1924, Bermuda
Source: *AmBi; AmLY; AsBiEn; BiDPsy; BiESc; BioIn 15, 16, 20; DcAmAu; DcAmB; DcAmMeB, 84; DcNAA; DcScB; EncAB-H 1974, 1996; HarEnUS; InSci; LarDcSc; LinLib S; NamesHP; NatCAB 11; NotTwCS; OxCMed 86;*

REnAL; WebAB 74, 79; WhAm 1; WhDW

Loeb, James Morris
American. Banker, Philanthropist
Founded, endowed NYC's Institute of Musical Art, 1905; 350-volume Loeb Classical Library, 1910.
b. Aug 6, 1867 in New York, New York
d. May 28, 1933 in Murnau, Germany
Source: *AmBi; DcAmB S1; REnAL; WebAB 74, 79; WhAm 1*

Loeb, Richard A
[Leopold and Loeb]
American. Criminal, Murderer
With Nathan Leopold, committed "crime of century"; defended by Clarence Darrow.
b. Jun 11, 1905 in Chicago, Illinois
d. Jan 28, 1936 in Stateville, Illinois
Source: *BioIn 10*

Loeb, Sophia Irene Simon
American. Social Reformer, Journalist
First pres., Child Welfare Committee of America, 1924.
b. Jul 4, 1876 in Rovno, Russia
d. Jan 18, 1929 in New York, New York
Source: *NatCAB 24; NotAW; WhAm 1*

Loeb, William
American. Businessman, Public Official
Teddy Roosevelt's private secretary, 1899-1909; collector, port of NY, 1909-13, who instituted reforms.
b. Oct 9, 1866 in Albany, New York
d. Sep 19, 1937
Source: *AmBi; BioIn 5; CyAG; HarEnUS; NatCAB 18; WhAm 1*

Loeb, William
American. Journalist, Publisher
Influential publisher, Manchester, NH *Union Leader,* 1946-81; noted for front page right-wing editorials.
b. Dec 26, 1905 in Manchester, New Hampshire
d. Sep 13, 1981 in Burlington, Massachusetts
Source: *AnObit 1981; BioIn 4, 6, 8, 9, 10, 11, 12, 13, 19; ConAu 93, 104; CurBio 74, 81, 81N; DcLB 127; EncAJ; EncTwCJ; FacFETw; JrnUS; NewYTBS 81; PolPar; PolProf J, K, NF; St&PR 75; WhAm 8; WhoAm 74, 76, 78, 80, 82; WhoE 74, 83, 85*

Loeffler, Charles Martin Tornow
American. Violinist, Composer
Wrote orchestral works "A Pagan Poem," 1906; "Memories of My Childhood," 1925.
b. Jan 30, 1861 in Mulhouse, France
d. May 20, 1935 in Medfield, Massachusetts
Source: *AmBi; DcAmB S1; WhAm 1*

Loeffler, Ken(neth D)
American. Basketball Coach
Coached 23 yrs. at several colleges; with NBA St. Louis, 1947-49; Hall of Fame.
b. Apr 14, 1902 in Beaver Falls, Pennsylvania
d. Jan 1, 1975 in Rumson, New Jersey
Source: *BasBi; BiDAmSp BK; BioIn 9, 10; NewYTBS 75; WhoBbl 73*

Loesser, Frank Henry
American. Composer
Wrote Broadway musicals *Guys and Dolls,* 1951; *Most Happy Fella,* 1956.
b. Jun 29, 1910 in New York, New York
d. Jul 28, 1969 in New York, New York
Source: *ASCAP 66; Baker 84; BiE&WWA; CurBio 46, 69; EncMT; FilmgC; NewCBMT; OxCAmL 65; PlP&P; WebAB 79; WhAm 6; WhoHol B; WhScrn 77*

Loew, Marcus
American. Theater Owner, Producer
His vast theater chain purchased Metro, 1920; Goldwyn Pictures, 1924; later known as Metro-Goldwyn-Mayer.
b. May 7, 1870 in New York, New York
d. Sep 5, 1927 in New York, New York
Source: *BiDAmBL 83; BioIn 3, 6, 7, 10; DcAmB; DcFM; EncVaud; EncWB; FilmEn; FilmgC; HalFC 80, 84, 88; LegTOT; MGM A; NatCAB 23; NotNAT B; OxCFilm; WhAm 1; WorEFlm*

Loewe, Frederick
[Lerner and Loewe]
"Fritz"
Austrian. Composer
Noted for collaboration with lyricist Alan Lerner; hits include 1956 Tony-winner, *My Fair Lady; Camelot,* 1968.
b. Jun 10, 1901 in Vienna, Austria
d. Feb 14, 1988 in Palm Springs, California
Source: *AnObit 1988; ASCAP 66, 80; Baker 92; BiE&WWA; BlueB 76; ConTFT 6; CurBio 58, 88; DcArts; EncMT; FilmgC; HalFC 80, 84, 88; IntWW 74, 75, 76, 77, 78, 79, 80, 81, 82, 83; LegTOT; NewCBMT; NewGrDA 86; NewGrDO; News 88-2; OxCAmL 83; OxCPMus; PlP&P; REnAL; VarWW 85; WhAm 9; Who 74, 82, 83, 85, 88; WhoAm 74, 76, 78, 80, 82, 84, 86; WhoThe 77, 81; WhoWor 78; WorAl; WorAlBi*

Loewi, Otto
American. Scientist, Physician
Neurobiologist; shared 1936 Nobel Prize for medicine.
b. Jun 3, 1873 in Frankfurt am Main, Germany
d. Dec 25, 1961 in New York, New York
Source: *AsBiEn; BiESc; BioIn 3, 5, 6, 13, 14, 15, 20; DcAmB S7; DcScB; InSci; LarDcSc; McGEWB; NobelP; NotTwCS; OxCMed 86; WhAm 4; WhDW; WhoNob, 90, 95; WorAl; WorAlBi*

Loewy, Raymond Fernand
American. Designer
Industrial designer best known for designs of Coco-Cola bottle, 1960 Studebaker.
b. Nov 5, 1893 in Paris, France
d. Jul 14, 1986 in Monte Carlo, Monaco
Source: *AmCulL; BioIn 3, 5, 8, 10, 14, 15, 17, 19; ConAu 104, 119; ConDes 84, 97; CurBio 53; EncAB-H 1996; FacFETw; InSci; IntWW 83; WebAB 74, 79; Who 83; WhoAm 84; WhoWor 74*

Lofgren, Nils
[E Street Band]
"Lefty"
American. Musician, Singer, Songwriter
Pop-rock singer, guitarist; formed band Grin, 1969-74; acclaimed album *Nils Lofgren,* 1975.
b. Jun 21, 1951 in Chicago, Illinois
Source: *ASCAP 80; ConMuA 80A; HarEnR 86; IlEncRk; LegTOT; OnThGG; RolSEnR 83; WhoRock 81; WhoRocM 82*

Lofting, Hugh
American. Author
Wrote *Doctor Doolittle* series for children, 1920s-30s.
b. Jan 14, 1886 in Maidenhead, England
d. Sep 26, 1947 in Santa Monica, California
Source: *AmAu&B; AnCL; AuBYP 2, 3; BenetAL 91; BioIn 1, 2, 3, 4, 7, 8, 12, 14, 19; CamGLE; ChhPo, S1; ChlBkCr; ChlLR 19; ConAu 109; ConICB; DcArts; DcLB 160; DcLEL; DcNAA; DcPup; EngPo; EvLB; HalFC 84, 88; IlsCB 1744; JBA 34, 51; LegTOT; LinLib L; LngCTC; NewbMB 1922; NewCBEL; OxCChiL; REn; REnAL; ScF&FL 1A, 92; SmATA 15; Str&VC; TwCA, SUP; TwCChW 78, 83, 89; WhAm 2; WhAmArt 85; WhNAA; WhoChL; WorAl; WorAlBi; WrChl*

Lofts, Norah Robinson
[Juliet Astley; Peter Curtis]
English. Author
Wrote at least 50 historical romances, biographies including *Anne Boleyn,* 1979; *Day of the Butterfly,* 1979.
b. Aug 27, 1904 in Shipdham, England
d. Sep 10, 1983 in Bury Saint Edmunds, England
Source: *Au&Wr 71; AuNews 2; ConAu 5R, 6NR, 110; InWom SUP; LinLib L; LngCTC; NewYTBS 83; PenNWW B; SmATA 8; TwCA, SUP; WhAm 8; WhNAA; Who 83; WhoAm 74; WrDr 76*

Loftus, Cissie
[Marie Cecilia McCarthy]
Scottish. Actor
Best known for her impersonations of stage, film stars.
b. Oct 26, 1876 in Glasgow, Scotland
d. Jul 12, 1943 in New York, New York
Source: *CurBio 40, 43; EncVaud; NotAW; NotNAT A; OxCThe 67; REn*

Logan, Daniel
American. Psychic, TV Personality, Author, Lecturer
Wrote best-selling *Do You Have ESP?*, 1970.
b. Apr 24, 1936 in Flushing, New York
Source: *ConAu 25R; EncO&P 1, 2, 3*

Logan, Ella
[Ella Allan]
Scottish. Actor
Stage star in *Finian's Rainbow;* starred in five films.
b. Mar 6, 1913 in Glasgow, Scotland
d. May 1, 1969 in San Mateo, California
Source: *BiE&WWA; BioIn 7, 8; CmpEPM; EncMT; ForYSC; InWom; MotPP; NotNAT B; OxCAmT 84; OxCPMus; PenEncP; What 1; WhoHol B; WhScrn 74, 77, 83; WhThe*

Logan, Harlan (De Braun)
American. Publisher, Editor
Editor of *Scribner's Magazine*, 1936-39.
b. Apr 30, 1904
d. Dec 16, 1994 in Hanover, New Hampshire
Source: *BioIn 20, 21*

Logan, John
[John Burton Logan]
American. Poet, Educator
Verse volumes include *Zig-Zag Walk*, 1969; *Anonymous Lover*, 1972.
b. Jan 23, 1923 in Red Oak, Iowa
d. Nov 6, 1987 in San Francisco, California
Source: *AmAu&B; Benet 87; BenetAL 91; BiDConC; BioIn 10, 12, 15, 20; ConAu 77, 124; ConLC 5; ConPo 70, 75, 80, 85; CroCAP; DcLB 5; DrAF 76; DrAP 75; DrAPF 80; Focus; IntAu&W 77; LinLib L; OxCAmL 65, 83, 95; OxCTwCP; PenC AM; RAdv 1, 14, 13-1; WhoAm 82, 84, 86, 88; WhoUSWr 88; WorAu 1950; WrDr 76, 80, 82, 84, 86, 88*

Logan, John Alexander
American. Soldier, Politician
A founder, Grand Army of the Republic, 1865, who instituted Memorial Day, May 30, 1868.
b. Feb 9, 1826 in Murphysboro, Illinois
d. Dec 26, 1886 in Washington, District of Columbia
Source: *Alli SUP; AmAu&B; AmBi; ApCAB; BiAUS; BiD&SB; BiDrAC; BiDrUSC 89; BioIn 3, 7, 21; CivWDc; DcAmAu; DcAmB; DcNAA; Drake; HarEnMi; HarEnUS; NatCAB 4, 27; TwCBDA; WebAB 74, 79; WebAMB; WebBD 83; WhAm HS; WhAmP; WhCiWar*

Logan, Josh(ua Lockwood)
American. Director, Dramatist
Directed some of Broadway's biggest hits: *South Pacific, Annie Get Your Gun, Mister Roberts.*
b. Oct 5, 1908 in Texarkana, Texas
d. Jul 12, 1988 in New York, New York
Source: *AmAu&B; AuNews 1; BiDAmM; BiDFilm; BiE&WWA; BioIn 1, 2, 3, 5, 6, 7, 8, 10, 11; CmMov; ConAu 89; ConDr 73, 82D; ConTFT 4; DcFM; EncMT; FilmgC; HalFC 84; IntWW 83; LegTOT; LinLib L; MovMk; WhoAm 86; WhoThe 81*

Loggins, Kenny
[Loggins and Messina; Kenneth Clarke Loggins]
American. Singer, Musician, Songwriter
Won two Grammys 1980-81; wrote movie soundtracks including hits "Danger Zone," "Footloose."
b. Jan 7, 1948 in Everett, Washington
Source: *ASCAP 80; Baker 92; BioIn 11, 12, 14; BkPepl; CelR 90; ConMus 3; EncFCWM 83; EncPR&S 89; EncRkSt; IlEncRk; RkOn 82; RolSEnR 83; VarWW 85; WhoAm 86, 90; WhoEnt 92; WorAl; WorAlBi*

Loggins and Messina
[Kenny Loggins; Jim Messina]
American. Music Group
Country-rock duo, 1971-76; hit albums included single "Your Mama Don't Dance," 1972.
Source: *ASCAP 80; BioIn 16; ConMuA 80A; EncFCWM 83; EncPR&S 74, 89; EncRk 88; HarEnR 86; IlEncRk; PenEncP; RkOn 78; RolSEnR 83; WhoRock 81; WhoRocM 82*

Logroscino, Nicola
Italian. Composer
Buffo-style operas included *Ricciardo*, 1743.
b. Oct 1698 in Bitonto, Italy
d. 1765 in Palermo, Sicily, Italy
Source: *Baker 78, 84; BioIn 4; NewEOp 71; NewGrDM 80; OxDcOp*

Lohman, Ann Trow
"Madame Restell"
American. Criminal
Quack physician; notorious NYC abortionist from 1840; slit her throat.
b. 1812 in Painswick, England
d. Apr 1, 1878 in New York, New York
Source: *BiDAmBL 83; InWom SUP; NotAW*

Lolich, Mickey
[Michael Stephen Lolich]
American. Baseball Player
Pitcher, 1963-79, mostly with Detroit; last to win three games in one World Series, 1968.
b. Sep 12, 1940 in Portland, Oregon
Source: *Ballpl 90; BiDAmSp BB; BioIn 9, 10, 11, 13, 14, 15; NewYTBE 72; NewYTBS 75, 84; WhoAm 84, 86, 90; WhoProB 73*

Lollobrigida, Gina
"La Lollo"
Italian. Actor
Italy's first post-war sex-symbol; films include *Trapeze*, 1956; *Solomon and Sheba*, 1959.
b. Jul 4, 1928 in Subiaco, Italy
Source: *BiDFilm; BioIn 3, 5, 10, 11, 12, 13; ConTFT 5; CurBio 60; FilmEn; FilmgC; ForYSC; HalFC 88; IntDcF 2-3; IntMPA 75, 76, 77, 78, 79, 80, 81, 82, 92; IntWW 83, 91; InWom, SUP; MotPP; MovMk; OxCFilm; WhoHol A; WhoWor 91; WorAl; WorAlBi; WorEFlm*

Loloma, Charles
American. Artist
Jewelry designs combined traditional Hopi motifs with nontraditional materials and techniques.
b. Jan 7, 1921 in Hotevilla, Arizona
d. Jun 9, 1991
Source: *BioIn 9, 10, 11, 12, 17, 21; NotNaAm; WhoAmA 76, 78, 80, 82, 84, 86, 89, 91, 93N; WhoWest 78, 80*

Loloma, Otellie
American. Artist
Known as the single most influential Indian woman creator in clay.
b. 1922 in Second Mesa, Arizona
d. 1992 in Santa Fe, New Mexico
Source: *BioIn 21; NorAmWA; NotNaAm*

Lom, Herbert
[Herbert C Angelo Kuchacevich]
Czech. Actor
Films include *The Return of the Pink Panther*, 1974.
b. Jan 9, 1917 in Prague, Bohemia
Source: *BioIn 13, 17, 19; CmMov; ConTFT 8; FilmAG WE; FilmEn; FilmgC; ForYSC; HalFC 80, 84, 88; IlWWBF; IntDcF 2-3; IntMPA 75, 76, 77, 80, 84, 86, 88, 92, 94, 96; IntWW 91, 93; ItaFilm; LegTOT; MotPP; MovMk; VarWW 85; WhoHol 92, A; WhoHrs 80; WhThe; WorAl; WorAlBi*

Lomahaftewa, Linda
American. Artist
Work reflects Hopi spirituality and storytelling.
b. Jul 3, 1947 in Phoenix, Arizona
Source: *NorAmWA; NotNaAm; WhoAmA 73, 76, 78, 80, 82, 84, 86, 89, 91*

Lomawaima, K(imberly) Tsianina
American. Anthropologist
Specializes in the study of Native Americans; researched Native American education and federal policy regarding them.
b. Mar 30, 1955 in Kansas City, Kansas

Lomax, Alan
American. Folklorist
Son of John Lomax who recorded unknown singers in native settings; brought Huddie Ledbetter to public attention.
b. Jan 15, 1915 in Austin, Texas
Source: *AmAu&B; AmCulL; Au&Wr 71; Baker 78, 84, 92; BenetAL 91; BgBkCoM; BiDAmM; BioIn 2, 4, 5, 14, 15, 17, 19; BlueB 76; ConAu 1NR, 1R; CurBio 41; EncFCWM 69, 83; EncRk 88; IntWW 74, 75, 76, 77, 78, 79, 80,*

81, 82, 83, 89, 91, 93; LinLib L; NewAmDM; NewGrDA 86; NewGrDM 80; OxCPMus; PenEncP; PeoHis; RAdv 14; REnAL; TexWr; TwCA SUP; WebAB 74, 79; WhoAm 74, 76, 84; WhoWor 74

Lomax, John Avery
American. Folklorist
Devoted life to recording, editing, publicizing folk songs; responsible for 20,000 songs in LC.
b. Sep 23, 1867 in Goodman, Mississippi
d. Jan 26, 1948 in Greenville, Mississippi
Source: *AmAu&B; AmCulL; Baker 78, 84, 92; Benet 96; BiDSA; BioIn 2, 3, 4, 5; ChhPo S3; CnDAL; DcAmB S4; EncFCWM 69; LinLib L; LiveMA; NatCAB 38; OxCAmL 65; REn; REnAL; REnAW; Str&VC; TexWr; TwCA SUP; WebAB 74, 79; WhAm 2; WhNAA*

Lomax, Louis
American. Author, Radio Performer, Educator
Wrote award-winning *The Reluctant Negro,* 1960.
b. Aug 6, 1922 in Valdosta, Georgia
d. Jul 30, 1970 in Santa Rosa, New Mexico
Source: *AmAu&B; ConAu P-2; NewYTBE 70; WhAm 5; WhScrn 77, 83*

Lomax, Neil Vincent
American. Football Player
Quarterback, St. Louis, 1981-89; led NFL in passing, 1987; played in Pro Bowl, 1984, 1987.
b. Feb 17, 1959 in Portland, Oregon
Source: *FootReg 87; NewYTBS 81*

Lombard, Carole
[Jane Alice Peters]
American. Actor
Zany blonde comic who was married to Clark Gable at time of death in plane crash; films include *My Man Godfrey,* 1936.
b. Oct 6, 1908 in Fort Wayne, Indiana
d. Jan 16, 1942 in Las Vegas, Nevada
Source: *BiDFilm, 81, 94; BioIn 12, 13, 14, 15, 16, 17; CurBio 42; DcAmB S3; DcArts; EncAFC; FacFETw; FilmEn; FilmgC; FunnyW; GangFlm; GoodHs; HalFC 80, 84, 88; IntDcF 1-3, 2-3; InWom, SUP; LegTOT; LibW; MotPP; MovMk; NotAW; OxCFilm; ThFT; TwYS; WhAm 1; WhoCom; WhScrn 83; WorEFlm*

Lombard, Peter
Italian. Theologian
Wrote *Sententiarum Libri IV,* 1148-51; collection of teachings which became church textbook.
b. 1100? in Novara, Italy
d. 1160? in Paris, France
Source: *Benet 87, 96; NewC; OxCEng 67; REn; WebBD 83; WorAl; WorAlBi*

Lombardi, Ernie
[Ernesto Natali Lombardi]
"Bocci"; "Schnozz"
American. Baseball Player
Catcher, 1931-47; won NL batting title, 1938, 1942; NL MVP, 1938.
b. Apr 6, 1908 in Oakland, California
d. Sep 26, 1977 in Santa Cruz, California
Source: *Ballpl 90; BioIn 8, 11, 15; CmCal; WhoProB 73; WhoSpor*

Lombardi, Vince(nt Thomas)
American. Football Coach
Coach, Green Bay, 1959-68, won first two Super Bowls; Washington, 1969; played major role in NFL, AFL merger, 1966; coaching philosophy: "Winning isn't everything, it's the only thing"; Hall of Fame, 1971.
b. Jun 11, 1913 in New York, New York
d. Sep 3, 1970 in Washington, District of Columbia
Source: *AmDec 1960; BiDAmSp FB; BioIn 6, 8, 9, 10, 11, 12; CurBio 63, 70; DcAmB S8; EncWB; FacFETw; LegTOT; NewYTBE 70; WebAB 74, 79; WhAm 5; WhoFtbl 74; WhScrn 83; WorAl; WorAlBi*

Lombardo, Carmen
American. Songwriter, Musician
Saxophonist in brother, Guy's band, 1929-71; co-wrote classic "Boo Hoo."
b. Jul 16, 1903 in London, Ontario, Canada
d. Apr 17, 1971 in North Miami, Florida
Source: *ASCAP 66, 80; Baker 78, 84; BiDAmM; BioIn 9; CmpEPM; NewYTBE 71; OxCPMus; WhoHol B; WhScrn 74, 77*

Lombardo, Guy Albert
"Sweetest Music This Side of Heaven"
Canadian. Bandleader
Known for New Year's Eve performances with band, The Royal Canadians.
b. Jun 19, 1902 in London, Ontario, Canada
d. Nov 5, 1977 in Houston, Texas
Source: *Baker 84; BiE&WWA; BioIn 1, 2, 3, 4, 6, 7, 9, 10, 11, 12; CanWW 70; CreCan 1; CurBio 46, 75; NewYTBE 71; NotNAT; WebAB 74, 79; WhAm 7; WhoAm 74, 76, 78; WhoWor 74, 76*

Lombroso, Cesare
Italian. Criminologist, Physician, Educator
Founded concept of "the born criminal," but advocated humane treatment; wrote *L'uomo delinquente,* 1876.
b. Nov 6, 1836 in Venice, Italy
d. Oct 19, 1909 in Turin, Italy
Source: *BbD; BiD&SB; CopCroC; EncO&P 2, 3; InSci; LinLib S; LngCTC; McGEWB; NewCol 75; OxCLaw; WebBD 83; WhDW; WhLit*

Lomonosov, Mikhail Vasilyevich
Russian. Scientist, Scholar, Poet, Author
Established first chemical laboratory in Russia, 1748; wrote *Russian Grammar,* 1757, texts on corpuscular philosophy, physics.
b. Nov 19, 1711 in Denisovka, Russia
d. Apr 15, 1765 in Saint Petersburg, Russia
Source: *BbD; Benet 87, 96; BiD&SB; BlkwCE; CasWL; DcEuL; DcInv; DcRusL; EuAu; EvEuW; Geog 6; NewCol 75; PenC EUR; REn*

Lonborg, Jim
[James Reynold Lonborg]
American. Baseball Player
Pitcher, 1965-79; led AL in wins, won Cy Young Award, 1967.
b. Apr 16, 1942 in Santa Maria, California
Source: *Ballpl 90; BioIn 8, 10, 14; WhoAm 74, 76, 78, 80, 82, 84, 86, 88, 90, 92, 94, 95, 96, 97; WhoProB 73; WhoSpor*

London, George
[George Burnson]
American. Opera Singer
Dramatic bass-baritone who was first American to sing in Moscow's Bolshoi Theater, 1960.
b. May 30, 1920 in Montreal, Quebec, Canada
d. Mar 24, 1985 in Armonk, New York
Source: *AnObit 1985; Baker 84; BiDAmM; BioIn 2, 11, 14, 15, 19; BioNews 74; CmOp; CreCan 1; CurBio 53, 85; FacFETw; IntWWM 77, 80; MetOEnc; MusSN; NewGrDM 80; NewGrDO; NewYTBE 71; WhAm 8; WhoAm 74, 76, 78, 80, 82, 84; WhoAmM 83; WhoGov 72; WhoMus 72; WhoOp 76; WhoSSW 73; WhoWor 74, 76; WhoWorJ 72, 78*

London, Jack
American. Author
Most books deal with brutal realism: *The Call of the Wild,* 1903.
b. Jan 12, 1876 in San Francisco, California
d. Nov 22, 1916 in Glen Ellen, California
Source: *AmAu&B; AmBi; AmCulL; AmDec 1900; AmRef; AmWr; ApCAB X; AtlBL; Au&Arts 13; AuBYP 2, 3; AuNews 2; Benet 87, 96; BenetAL 91; BibAL; BiD&SB; BioIn 1, 2, 3, 4, 5, 6, 7, 8, 9, 10, 11, 12, 13, 14, 15, 16, 17, 19, 21; CamGEL; CamGLE; CamHAL; CarSB; CasWL; Chambr 3; ChlBkCr; CmCal; CnDAL; ConAmL; CyWA 58; DcAmAu; DcAmB; DcAmSR; DcArts; DcBiA; DcLB 8, 12, 78; DcLEL; DcNAA; Dis&D; EncAB-H 1974, 1996; EncAL; EncFWF; EncMys; EncPaPR 91; EncSF, 93; EncWL, 2, 3; FacFETw; FamAYP; FifWWr; FilmgC; GayN; GrWrEL N; HalFC 80, 84, 88; JBA 34; LegTOT; LiJour; LinLib L, S; LngCTC; MagSAmL; MakMC; McGEWB; MnBBF; ModAL, S1; MorMA; NatCAB 13, 57; NewEScF; NotNAT B; Novels;*

OnHuMoP; OxCAmH; OxCAmL 65, 83, 95; OxCCan; OxCChiL; OxCEng 67; PenC AM; PenEncH; PeoHis; RAdv 1, 14, 13-1; RComAH; RComWL; RealN; REn; REnAL; RfGAmL 87, 94; RfGShF; RGTwCWr; ScF&FL 1, 92; ScFEYrs; ScFSB; ShSCr 4; ShSWr; SmATA 18; Str&VC; TwCA, SUP; TwCLC 9, 15, 39; TwCSFW 81, 86, 91; TwCWr; TwCWW 82, 91; TwCYAW; WebAB 74, 79; WebE&AL; WhAm 1; WhDW; WhoHr&F; WhoTwCL; WorAl; WorAlBi; WorLitC; WrPh

London, Julie
[Julie Peck]
American. Singer, Actor
Nightclub, film, TV performer, noted for blues song "Cry Me A River."
b. Sep 26, 1926 in Santa Rosa, California
Source: *ASCAP 66, 80; BiDAmM; BioIn 1, 4, 5, 6; CmpEPM; CurBio 60; FilmEn; FilmgC; ForYSC; HalFC 80, 84, 88; IntMPA 75, 76, 77, 78, 79, 80, 81, 82, 84, 86, 88, 92, 94, 96; InWom, SUP; LegTOT; MotPP; MovMk; OxCPMus; PenEncP; WhoHol 92, A; WorAl; WorAlBi*

Lonergan, Bernard J. F
Canadian. Religious Leader
Wrote *Insight: A Study of Human Understanding.*
b. Dec 17, 1904 in Buckingham, Quebec, Canada
d. Nov 26, 1984 in Pickering, Ontario, Canada
Source: *CanWW 83; ConAu 53; CurBio 72; DrAS 74P, 78P, 82P; WrDr 84*

Long, Avon
American. Actor, Singer
Danced at Cotton Club in Harlem; appeared in *Porgy and Bess,* 1942.
b. Jun 18, 1910 in Baltimore, Maryland
d. Feb 15, 1984 in New York, New York
Source: *BiDAfM; BiDD; BiE&WWA; BioIn 13; BlkOpe; DrBlPA, 90; NewYTBS 84; NotNAT; WhAm 8; WhoAm 78; WhoHol A; WhoThe 77, 81*

Long, Crawford Williamson
American. Scientist, Physician, Engineer
First used ether anesthesia, 1842, but not publicized until after Morton's 1846 demonstration.
b. Nov 1, 1815 in Danielsville, Georgia
d. Jun 16, 1878 in Athens, Georgia
Source: *AmBi; ApCAB; AsBiEn; BiDSA; BiESc; BiHiMed; BiInAmS; BioIn 1, 2, 3, 4, 5, 6, 7, 8, 9; DcAmB; DcAmMeB, 84; InSci; LinLib S; McGEWB; NatCAB 13; NewCol 75; OxCAmH; OxCMed 86; TwCBDA; WebAB 74, 79; WhAm HS*

Long, Dale
[Richard Dale Long]
American. Baseball Player
First baseman, 1951-63; shares ML record for home runs in consecutive games (8) with Dan Mattingly.
b. Feb 6, 1926 in Springfield, Missouri
d. Jan 27, 1991 in Palm Coast, Florida
Source: *Ballpl 90; BioIn 4, 10, 15, 17; WhoProB 73*

Long, Earl Kemp
American. Politician
Governor of LA, 1939-40; 1948-52; 1956-60; brother of Huey.
b. Aug 26, 1895 in Winnfield, Louisiana
d. Sep 5, 1960 in Alexandria, Louisiana
Source: *BiDrGov 1789; BioIn 1, 2, 4, 5, 7, 8, 9, 10, 11; CurBio 50, 60; DcAmB S6; EncSoH; WhAm 4*

Long, Huey Pierce
"The Kingfish"
American. Politician
Governor of LA, 1928-32; senator, 1932-35; assassinated; noted for "Every Man a King" campaign promise.
b. Aug 30, 1893 in Winnfield, Louisiana
d. Sep 10, 1935 in Baton Rouge, Louisiana
Source: *AmBi; AmOrTwC; AmPolLe; AmRef; Benet 96; BiDExR; BiDrAC; BiDrGov 1789; BiDrUSC 89; BioIn 1, 2, 3, 4, 5, 6, 7, 8, 9, 10, 11, 12, 13, 14, 15, 17, 18, 19, 20, 21; DcAmB S1; DcNAA; DcTwHis; Dis&D; EncAAH; EncAB-H 1974, 1996; EncSoH; FacFETw; LngCTC; McGEWB; NatCAB 30; OxCAmH; OxCAmL 65; OxCFilm; REn; REnAL; REnAW; WebAB 74, 79; WhAm 1; WhAmP; WhDW; WorAl*

Long, John Luther
American. Author, Dramatist
His short story "Madame Butterfly," 1898, served as libretto for Puccini's opera, 1906.
b. Jan 1, 1861 in Hanover, Pennsylvania
d. Oct 31, 1927 in Philadelphia, Pennsylvania
Source: *AmAu&B; AmBi; BenetAL 91; BiD&SB; BioIn 7, 10, 11; CarSB; CnDAL; DcAmAu; DcAmB; DcLEL; DcNAA; LinLib L; ModWD; NewGrDO; NotNAT B; OxCAmL 65, 83; OxCAmT 84; OxCThe 67, 83; PlP&P; REnAL; WhAm 1; WhLit; WhoStg 1908; WhThe*

Long, Richard
American. Actor
Starred in TV series "Big Valley," 1965-69; "Nanny and the Professor," 1970-71.
b. Dec 17, 1927 in Chicago, Illinois
d. Dec 22, 1974 in Los Angeles, California
Source: *BioIn 10; FilmEn; FilmgC; ForYSC; HalFC 80, 84, 88; InB&W 80; IntMPA 75; MotPP; MovMk; WhoHol B; WhoHrs 80; WhScrn 77, 83*

Long, Richard
English. Artist
Creator of earth art, made with objects collected during walks in remote areas.
b. Jun 2, 1945 in Bristol, England
Source: *BioIn 15, 17, 21; ConArt 83, 89; ConBrA 79; CurBio 95; DcArts; DcCAr 81; IntWW 91, 93; TwCPaSc; WhoWor 97; WorArt 1980*

Long, Russell Billiu
American. Politician
Dem. senator from LA, 1951-86; long-time finance committee chm; son of Huey.
b. Nov 3, 1918 in Shreveport, Louisiana
Source: *BiDrAC; BiDrUSC 89; BioIn 1, 2, 4, 7, 8, 9, 10, 11, 12, 14, 15; CngDr 74, 85; CurBio 51, 65; IntWW 74, 91; PolsAm 84; WhoAm 74, 76, 78, 80, 82, 84, 86, 88, 90; WhoAmL 90; WhoAmP 73, 91; WhoE 89; WhoGov 72; WhoSSW 73, 86; WhoWor 87; WorAl; WorAlBi*

Long, Scott
American. Editor, Cartoonist
Editorial cartoonist, Minneapolis *Tribune* since 1940s.
b. Feb 24, 1917 in Evanston, Illinois
Source: *BioIn 15; ConGrA 1; WhoAm 74, 76, 78, 82, 84, 86, 88; WhoAmA 76, 78, 80, 82, 84, 86, 89, 91, 93N*

Long, Shelley
[Mrs. Bruce Tyson]
American. Actor
Played Diane Chambers on TV series "Cheers," 1982-87; won Emmy, 1983; films include *Outrageous Fortune,* 1986.
b. Aug 23, 1950 in Fort Wayne, Indiana
Source: *BioIn 13, 14, 15, 16; ConNews 85-1; ConTFT 5; EncAFC; HalFC 88; IntMPA 92; InWom SUP; VarWW 85; WhoAm 90; WhoEnt 92; WhoTelC; WorAlBi*

Long, Stephen H
American. Explorer, Naturalist
Led expeditions to Rocky Mts., 1820; Long's Peak named after him.
b. Dec 30, 1784 in Hopkinton, New Hampshire
d. Sep 4, 1864 in Alton, Illinois
Source: *Alli; AmAu&B; AmBi; ApCAB; BiAUS; DcAmB; DcNAA; Drake; TwCBDA; WhAm HS*

Longden, Johnny
American. Jockey
Triple Crown winner, 1943 on Count Fleet.
b. Feb 14, 1907 in Wakefield, England
Source: *BioIn 10, 21; CmCal; LegTOT; WorAl*

Longet, Claudine Georgette
French. Actor, Singer
Former wife of Andy Williams; convicted of manslaughter, 1977, following shooting death of lover, Spider Sabich.
b. Jan 29, 1942 in Paris, France
Source: *BioNews 74; BkPepl; InWom SUP; WhoAm 74, 76; WhoAmW 70, 72, 74, 75; WhoHol A*

Longfellow, Henry Wadsworth
American. Poet, Educator
Among his many classic works: "Paul Revere's Ride," 1863; "The Song of Hiawatha," 1855; first American to have bust in Westminster Abbey; popular verse includes *Evangeline,* 1847.
b. Feb 27, 1807 in Portland, Massachusetts
d. Mar 24, 1882 in Cambridge, Massachusetts
Source: *Alli, SUP; AmAu; AmAu&B; AmBi; AmCulL; AmWr; AnCL; ApCAB; AtlBL; AuBYP 2, 3; BbD; Benet 87, 96; BenetAL 91; BibAL; BiDAmM; BiD&SB; BiDTran; BioIn 1, 2, 3, 4, 5, 6, 7, 8, 9, 10, 11, 12, 13, 14, 16, 19, 20, 21; CamGEL; CamGLE; CamHAL; CasWL; CelCen; Chambr 3; ChhPo, S1, S2, S3; ChlBkCr; CnDAL; CnE&AP; ColARen; CrtT 3; CyAL 2; CyEd; CyWA 58; DcAmAu; DcAmB; DcAmSR; DcArts; DcBiA; DcBiPP; DcEnA; DcEnL; DcLB 1, 59; DcLEL; DcNAA; DcSpL; Drake; EncAAH; EncAB-H 1974, 1996; EvLB; FamAYP; GrWrEL P; HarEnUS; LegTOT; LinLib L, S; LuthC 75; MagSAmL; McGEWB; MemAm; MouLC 4; NatCAB 2; NewEOp 71; NewGrDA 86; NinCLC 2, 45; OxCAmH; OxCAmL 65, 83, 95; OxCEng 67, 85, 95; OxCSpan; PenC AM; PeoHis; RAdv 1, 14, 13-1; RComAH; RComWL; REn; REnAL; RfGAmL 87, 94; RGFAP; SmATA 19; Str&VC; TwCBDA; WebAB 74, 79; WebE&AL; WhAm HS; WhDW; WhNaAH; WorAl; WorAlBi*

Longley, James Bernard
American. Politician
Governor of ME, 1975-79; only independent candidate elected in any state in four decades.
b. Apr 22, 1924 in Lewiston, Maine
d. Aug 16, 1980 in Lewiston, Maine
Source: *AnObit 1980; BiDrGov 1789, 1978; BioIn 10, 11, 12; BlueB 76; NewYTBS 80; WhAm 7; WhoAm 76, 78; WhoAmL 79; WhoAmP 75, 77, 79; WhoGov 75, 77; WhoWor 78*

Longmuir, Alan
[Bay City Rollers]
Scottish. Singer, Musician
Bass player, original member of 1970s popular rock group.
b. Jun 20, 1950 in Edinburgh, Scotland
Source: *BkPepl; WhoRocM 82*

Longmuir, Derek
[Bay City Rollers]
Scottish. Singer, Musician
Drummer, original member of rock group, 1970s; brother of Alan.
b. Mar 19, 1955 in Edinburgh, Scotland
Source: *BkPepl; WhoRocM 82*

Longo, Robert
American. Artist
Pop culture artist who experiments in minimalism; noted for his life-sized charcoal drawings in Men in the Cities series during the 1980s.
b. 1953 in New York, New York
Source: *AmArt; BioIn 13, 16; CurBio 90; DcCAA 88, 94; News 90; PrintW 85; WhoAmA 86, 89, 91, 93; WorArt 1980*

Longstreet, James
American. Army Officer, Public Official, Author
Confederate general whose tardiness supposedly led to Lee's defeat at Gettysburg, 1863; wrote civil war histories.
b. Jan 8, 1821 in Edgefield District, South Carolina
d. Jan 2, 1904 in Gainesville, Georgia
Source: *AmAu&B; AmBi; ApCAB; BenetAL 91; BiDConf; BiDSA; BioIn 1, 3, 5, 7, 8, 9, 10, 12, 14, 15, 16, 17, 18, 19, 21; CivWDc; DcAmAu; DcAmB; DcAmMiB; DcBiPP; DcCathB; DcNAA; EncAB-H 1974, 1996; EncSoH; GenMudB; HarEnMi; HarEnUS; LinLib S; NatCAB 4; OxCAmH; REnAL; TwCBDA; WebAB 74, 79; WebAMB; WhAm 1; WhCiWar; WhoMilH 76; WorAl; WorAlBi*

Longus
Greek. Author
Supposedly wrote pastoral romance *Daphnis and Chloe.*
b. fl. 3rd cent., Greece
Source: *BbD; BiD&SB; BioIn 5; CasWL; ClMLC 7; CyWA 58; DcBiPP; Grk&L; LinLib L; NewCBEL; OxCClL; OxCEng 67; RAdv 14, 13-2; RComWL; WebBD 83; WorAlBi*

Longworth, Alice Roosevelt
"Washington's Other Monument"
American. Author, Socialite
Daughter of Theodore Roosevelt; noted for caustic remarks.
b. Feb 12, 1884 in Long Island, New York
d. Feb 20, 1980 in Washington, District of Columbia
Source: *AmAu&B; AnObit 1980, 1981; BioAmW; BioIn 15, 16, 21; CelR; ChhPo; ConAu 93; CurBio 43, 75, 80, 80N; FacFETw; GrLiveH; HanAmWH; InWom, SUP; LegTOT; LibW; NewYTBS 75, 80, 88; WhAm 7; WhoAm 80*

Lonsdale, Gordon Arnold
[Konon Trafimovich Molody]
Russian. Spy
Soviet spy in England, 1955-61; exchanged for English spy, 1964.
b. 1922, Union of Soviet Socialist Republics
d. Oct 9, 1970 in Moscow, Union of Soviet Socialist Republics
Source: *BioIn 7, 8, 9, 11; ConAu 104; EncE 75; NewYTBE 70; ObitOF 79; ObitT 1961; SpyCS*

Loo, Richard
American. Actor
Played villainous Japanese soldiers in WW II movies: *God Is My Co-Pilot; Tokyo Rose.*
b. 1903 in Maui, Hawaii
d. Nov 20, 1983 in Burbank, California
Source: *AnObit 1983; BioIn 13; FilmgC; ForYSC; HalFC 80, 84, 88; HolCA; MotPP; MovMk; NewYTBS 83; Vers A; WhoHol A*

Looking Glass
[Allalimya Takanin]
American. Native American Leader
One of the principal Nez Perce leaders during the 1877 Nez Perce War.
b. 1823?
d. Oct 5, 1877
Source: *BioIn 11, 21; NotNaAm; WhNaAH*

Loomis, Mahion
American. Inventor, Dentist
Pioneered in wireless telegraphy; Loomis Aerial Telegraph Co. formed, 1873, but without finances nothing developed.
b. Jul 21, 1826 in Oppenheim, New York
d. Oct 13, 1886 in Terre Alta, West Virginia
Source: *AmBi; BiDAmS; DcAmB; NatCAB 25; TwCBDA; WhAm HS*

Loos, Anita
American. Author, Dramatist
Wrote *Gentlemen Prefer Blondes,* 1925.
b. Apr 26, 1893 in Sisson, California
d. Aug 18, 1981 in New York, New York
Source: *AmAu&B; AmWomWr; AnObit 1981; ArtclWW 2; Au&Wr 71; AuNews 1; AuSpks; Benet 87, 96; BenetAL 91; BiE&WWA; BioIn 1, 2, 3, 4, 5, 6, 7, 9, 10, 11, 12, 13; BlueB 76; CelR; ConAu 21R, 26NR, 104; ConNov 76, 82; ContDcW 89; CurBio 74, 81, 81N; DcArts; DcLB 11, 26, Y81A; DcLEL; EncAFC; EvLB; FacFETw; FilmEn; FilmgC; GoodHs; HalFC 80; IntAu&W 76, 77; IntDcF 1-4; IntDcWB; IntMPA 77, 80, 82; IntWW 74, 75, 76, 77, 78, 79, 80, 81; InWom, SUP; LegTOT; LibW; LngCTC; NewYTBS 81; NotNAT, A; Novels; OxCAmL 65, 83, 95; OxCAmT 84; OxCFilm; OxCWoWr 95; PenC AM; ReelWom; REn; REnAL; TwCA, SUP; TwCWr; WhAm 9; WhoAm 74, 76, 78, 80; WhoAmW 58, 61, 64, 66, 70, 72, 74; WhoThe 72, 77, 81; WhoWor 78; WomFir; WomWMM; WorAl; WorAlBi; WorEFlm; WrDr 76, 80, 82*

Lopat, Ed(mund Walter)
[Edmund Walter Lopatynski]
"Steady Eddie"
American. Baseball Player
Pitcher, 1944-55, known for "junk" pitches; had 166 career wins.
b. Jun 21, 1918 in New York, New York
d. Jun 15, 1992 in Darien, Connecticut

Source: *Ballpl 90; BiDAmSp Sup; BioIn 2, 3, 4, 11, 14; LegTOT; WhoProB 73*

Lope de Vega
[Lope Felix de Vega Carpio]
Spanish. Dramatist, Poet
Tragic personal life; wrote 1500 plays including *The King the Greatest Mayor,* 1620-23.
b. Nov 25, 1562 in Madrid, Spain
d. Aug 27, 1635 in Madrid, Spain
Source: *BiD&SB; PenC EUR*

Loper, Don
American. Fashion Designer, Dancer
Designed fashions for Hollywood stars; professional dancer until 1940s.
b. 1906 in Toledo, Ohio
d. Nov 22, 1972 in Santa Monica, California
Source: *BiDD; BioIn 9; NewYTBE 72; ObitOF 79; WhAm 5; WhoHol B; WhScrn 77, 83*

Lopes, Davey
[David Earl Lopes]
American. Baseball Player
Infielder, 1972-87, mostly with LA; known for base stealing; four-time NL All-Star.
b. May 3, 1946 in Providence, Rhode Island
Source: *Ballpl 90; BaseReg 87, 88; BioIn 15; InB&W 80; WhoAm 76, 78, 80, 82; WhoBlA 77, 80, 85, 88, 90, 92*

Lopez, Al(fonso Ramon)
American. Baseball Player, Baseball Manager
Catcher, 1928-47; holds ML record for most games caught, 1,918; Hall of Fame, 1977.
b. Aug 20, 1908 in Tampa, Florida
Source: *Ballpl 90; BiDAmSp BB; BioIn 2, 3, 4, 5, 6, 7, 8, 14, 15, 19, 20; CurBio 60; HispAmA; LegTOT; PeoHis; WhoHisp 92, 94; WhoProB 73*

Lopez, Barry (Holstun)
American. Author
Wrote *Of Wolves and Men,* 1978; *Arctic Dreams,* 1986.
b. Jan 6, 1945 in Port Chester, New York
Source: *Au&Arts 9; BiDConC; BioIn 17, 20, 21; ConAu 7NR, 23NR, 47NR, 65; CurBio 95; DrAPF 80; IntAu&W 86, 93; MajTwCW; ScF&FL 92; SmATA 67; WhoAm 88, 90, 92, 94, 95, 96, 97; WhoUSWr 88; WhoWest 89, 92, 94; WhoWrEP 89, 92, 95; WorAu 1980*

Lopez, James Michael
[The Hostages]
"Jimmy Lopez"
American. Hostage
One of 52 held by terrorists, Nov 1979-Jan 1981.
b. 1959?
Source: *BioIn 12; NewYTBS 81*

Lopez, Josefina Maria
Mexican. Dramatist
Wrote *Simply Maria,* at age 17 which won many awards.
b. Mar 19, 1969 in Cerritos, Mexico
Source: *WhoHisp 92*

Lopez, Mario
Mexican. Actor
Co-stars on TV show "Saved By The Bell;" 1989—.
b. 1973?
Source: *BioIn 18; WhoHisp 92*

Lopez, Nancy Marie
[Mrs. Ray Knight]
American. Golfer
Turned pro, 1977; won five consecutive LPGA tournaments, 1978; her 35 tour wins automatically qualified her for LPGA Hall of Fame, 1987.
b. Jan 6, 1957 in Torrance, California
Source: *BioIn 10, 11, 13, 14, 15; ConAu 113; ContDcW 89; CurBio 78; HerW 84; MexAmB; NewYTBS 78, 82, 84, 85; WhoAm 84, 86, 90; WhoAmW 87*

Lopez, Priscilla
American. Actor
Won Tony, 1980, for *A Day in Hollywood/A Night in the Ukraine.*
b. Feb 26, 1948 in New York, New York
Source: *BioIn 10, 18; ConTFT 3; NewYTBS 75; NotHsAW 93; VarWW 85; WhoAm 82, 84, 86, 88, 90, 92; WhoAmW 87; WhoEnt 92; WhoHisp 91, 92, 94*

Lopez, Trini(dad, III)
American. Singer
Best known for "If I Had a Hammer," 1963.
b. May 15, 1937 in Dallas, Texas
Source: *BiDAmM; BioIn 8, 9, 10, 16; CelR; CurBio 68; EncRk 88; ForYSC; HalFC 88; LegTOT; MexAmB; PenEncP; RkOn 74; VarWW 85; WhoAm 74, 76, 78, 80, 82, 84, 90; WhoEnt 92; WhoHisp 91, 92, 94; WhoHol 92, A*

Lopez, Vincent
American. Bandleader, Composer
Started regular broadcasts of dance band music, 1921; popularized song "Nola"; wrote "Knock, Knock Who's There?"
b. Dec 30, 1895 in New York, New York
d. Sep 20, 1975 in Miami Beach, Florida
Source: *ASCAP 66; Baker 84; BiDAmM; BioIn 4, 5, 10, 20; ConAu 61; CurBio 60, 75N; WhScrn 77*

Lopez Bravo, Gregorio
[Gregorio Lopez-Bravo de Castro]
Spanish. Diplomat
Served in various capacities under Franco, 1963-76; foreign minister, 1969-73.
b. Dec 19, 1923 in Madrid, Spain
d. Feb 19, 1985 in Bilbao, Spain
Source: *AnObit 1985; BioIn 9, 14; CurBio 71, 85, 85N; IntWW 74, 75, 76, 77, 78, 79, 80, 81, 82, 83; WhoWor 74*

Lopez de Ayala, Pero
Spanish. Statesman, Author, Historian
Wrote historical chronicles, pub., 1780; satirical poem *Rimado del Palacio,* c. 1400.
b. 1332 in Vitoria, Spain
d. 1407 in Calahorra, Spain
Source: *Benet 87, 96; CasWL; DcSpL; EuAu; EvEuW; PenC EUR; REn*

Lopez de Legaspi, Miguel
Spanish. Conqueror
Headed expedition that conquered Philippines, 1564; founded Manila, 1571.
b. 1510
d. 1572
Source: *ApCAB; NewCol 75; WebBD 83*

Lopez de Segura Ruy
Spanish. Writer
Wrote first book of chess instructions, 1561; developed the Ruy Lopez opening in chess.
b. 1580
Source: *OxCEng 67; WebBD 83*

Lopez Mateos, Adolfo
Mexican. Political Leader
Pres. of Mexico, 1958-64.
b. May 26, 1910 in Atizapan de Zaragoza, Mexico
d. Sep 22, 1969 in Mexico City, Mexico
Source: *BiDLAmC; BioIn 4, 5, 6, 8, 9, 16; CurBio 59, 69; DcTwHis; EncLatA; EncWB; WhAm 5*

Lopez Portillo (y Pacheco), Jose
Mexican. Political Leader
Pres. of Mexico, 1976-82.
b. Jul 16, 1920 in Mexico City, Mexico
Source: *BiDLAmC; BioIn 10, 11, 12, 13, 16; ConAu 129; ConLC 46; CurBio 77; DcHiB; DcTwHis; EncWB; HispWr; IntWW 91; IntYB 78, 79, 80, 81, 82; WhoAm 78, 80, 82, 84; WhoSSW 80; WhoWor 78, 80, 82, 84; WorAl*

Lopez-Portillo y Rojas, Jose
Mexican. Author, Social Reformer
Wrote of rural life during Diaz's regime.
b. May 26, 1850 in Guadalajara, Mexico
d. May 22, 1923 in Mexico City, Mexico
Source: *AmLY; CasWL; DcSpL; PenC AM*

Lopokova, Lydia Vasilievna
[Mrs. John Maynard Keynes]
Russian. Dancer, Actor
Starred with Ballet Russe, 1920s; London ballets, 1930s.
b. Oct 21, 1892 in Saint Petersburg, Russia
d. Jun 8, 1981 in Seaford, England
Source: *AnObit 1981; BiDD; DcNaB 1981; WhThe*

Lorant, Stefan
American. Editor
As an editor, his innovative principles set standard for the field; known for presidential pictorial biographies including, *Lincoln: His Life in Photographs,* 1941.
b. Feb 22, 1901 in Budapest, Hungary
Source: *AmAu&B; Au&Wr 71; AuNews 1; BioIn 1, 8, 10, 16, 17, 18; BlueB 76; ConAu 5R, 9NR; DrAS 74H; ICPEnP; IntAu&W 76, 77, 82, 86, 89, 91; IntWW 74, 75, 76, 77, 78, 79, 80, 81, 82, 83, 89, 91, 93; WhE&EA; Who 74, 82, 83, 85, 88, 90, 92, 94; WhoAm 74, 76, 78, 80, 82, 84, 86, 88, 90, 92, 94, 95, 96; WrDr 76, 80, 82, 84, 86, 88, 90, 92, 94, 96*

Lord, Bette Bao
American. Activist, Author
Pro-democracy activist; director of Freedom House, 1993—; author of *Legacies: A Chinese Mosaic,* 1990.
b. Nov 3, 1938 in Shanghai, China
Source: *AmWomWr SUP; BestSel 90-3; ChlBkCr; ConAu 41NR, 107; ConLC 23; DcAmChF 1985; IntAu&W 89, 91, 93; News 94, 94-1; NotAsAm; OxCWoWr 95; SixBJA; SmATA 58; WhoAdv 90; WhoAmW 83, 85, 87, 89, 91, 93, 95, 97; WhoAsA 94*

Lord, Jack
[John Joseph Ryan]
American. Actor, Producer, Artist
Produced, starred in TV series "Hawaii Five-O," 1968-80.
b. Dec 30, 1930 in New York, New York
Source: *ConTFT 1; FilmgC; ForYSC; HalFC 84; IntMPA 75, 76, 77, 78, 79, 80, 81, 82, 84, 86, 88, 92, 94, 96; MotPP; MovMk; VarWW 85; WhoAm 74, 76, 78, 80, 82, 84, 86, 88, 90, 92; WhoEnt 92; WhoHol A; WhoWest 80, 82, 84, 87, 89, 92, 94; WhoWor 74, 76, 80, 82, 84, 87, 89; WorAl; WorAlBi*

Lord, Marjorie
American. Actor
Played in TV show "Make Room for Daddy," 1957-64; mother of actress Anne Archer.
b. Jul 26, 1922 in San Francisco, California
Source: *BioIn 16; FilmEn; FilmgC; HalFC 80, 84, 88; LegTOT; MovMk; VarWW 85; WhoEnt 92; WhoHol A*

Lord, Mary Pillsbury
American. Social Worker
Heir to Pillsbury fortune; chm., Advisory Committee for WAC, WW II; succeeded Eleanor Roosevelt as representative to UN commission on Human Rights, 1953-61.
b. Nov 14, 1904 in Minneapolis, Minnesota
d. Aug 21, 1978 in New York, New York
Source: *BioIn 2, 3; ConAu 85; CurBio 52; NatCAB 61; WhAm 7; WhoAm 74, 76, 78; WhoAmW 58, 64, 66, 68, 70, 72, 74*

Lord, Pauline
American. Actor
Stage performances include *Anna Christie,* 1921-25; *Ethan Frome,* 1936.
b. Aug 8, 1890 in Hanford, California
d. Oct 11, 1950 in Alamogordo, New Mexico
Source: *BioIn 2, 3, 16; CmCal; DcAmB S4; FamA&A; FilmgC; ForYSC; HalFC 80, 84, 88; InWom, SUP; LibW; NotAW; NotNAT B; NotWoAT; OxCAmT 84; ThFT; WhAm 3; WhoHol B; WhScrn 74, 77, 83; WhThe*

Lord, Phillips H
"Seth Parker"
American. Actor, Author, Producer
Radio, TV dramatist; created character Seth Parker; wrote *Seth Parker's Album,* 1930.
b. Jul 13, 1902 in Hartford, Vermont
d. Oct 19, 1975 in Ellsworth, Maine
Source: *AmAu&B; BioIn 10; REnAL; WhAm 6; WhScrn 77*

Lord, Shirley
English. Writer
Has been *Vogue* beauty director since 1980; writes fiction, as well as books on beauty.
b. Feb 28, 1934 in London, England
Source: *CelR 90; ConAu X*

Lord, Walter
American. Author, Historian
Wrote authoritative books on *Titanic* sinking: *A Night to Remember,* 1955; *The Night Lives On,* 1986.
b. Oct 8, 1917 in Baltimore, Maryland
Source: *AmAu&B; ASCAP 66, 80; BioIn 5, 9, 10; ConAu 1R, 5NR, 22NR; CurBio 72; EncAI&E; IntAu&W 76, 77, 82, 86, 89, 91, 93; REnAL; SmATA 3; WhoAm 74, 76, 78, 80, 82, 84, 86, 88, 90, 92, 94, 95, 96, 97; WhoUSWr 88; WorAu 1950; WrDr 80, 82, 84, 86, 88, 90, 92, 94, 96*

Lord, Winston
American. Diplomat
US ambassador to China, 1985-89.
b. Aug 14, 1937 in New York, New York
Source: *BioIn 9; WhoWor 89, 91*

Lorde, Audre (Geraldine)
[Gamba Adisa; Rey Domini]
American. Poet, Feminist
Poet laureate, NY, 1991; won a 1989 American Book Award for *A Burst of Light.*
b. Feb 18, 1934 in New York, New York
d. Nov 17, 1992 in Saint Croix, Virgin Islands of the United States
Source: *AfrAmAl 6; AfrAmW; AmWomWr 92, SUP; AnObit 1992; ArtclWW 2; Benet 96; BenetAL 91; BioIn 13, 16; BlkAWP; BlkLC; BlkWAm; BlkWr 1; BlkWWr; BlmGWL; BroadAu; ConAu 16NR, 25R, 26NR, 46NR, 142; ConBlB 6; ConLC 18, 71, 76; ConPo 75, 80, 85, 91; DcLB 41; DcTwCCu 5; DrAP 75; DrAPF 80, 91; FemiCLE; FemiWr; GayLesB; GayLL; GrWomW; HanAmWH; InB&W 80; InWom SUP; LivgBAA; MajTwCW; ModAWP; ModWoWr; NegAl 89; NotBlAW 1; OxCAmL 95; OxCWoWr 95; PoeCrit 12; RadHan; RAdv 14; RfGAmL 94; SchCGBL; SelBAAf; SelBAAu; WhoAmW 74; WhoBlA 77, 80, 85, 88, 90, 92, 94N; WorAu 1975; WrDr 76, 80, 82, 84, 86, 88, 90, 92*

Lords, Traci
[Nora Louise Kuzma]
American. Actor, Singer
Appeared in over 100 pornographic films; became television and film actress and recording artist.
b. 1968 in West Virginia
Source: *LegTOT; News 95; WhoAmW 97; WhoHol 92*

Loren, Sophia
[Sophia Lazarro; Mrs. Carlo Ponti; Sofia Scicolone]
Italian. Actor
Won Oscar, 1961, for *Two Women;* wrote autobiography *Sophia: Living and Loving,* 1979.
b. Sep 20, 1934 in Rome, Italy
Source: *BiDFilm, 81, 94; BioIn 4, 5, 6, 7, 8, 9, 10, 11, 12, 13, 14, 15, 16, 17, 18, 20, 21; BkPepl; CelR, 90; CmMov; ConAu 111; ContDcW 89; ConTFT 3; CurBio 59; DcArts; EncEurC; FacFETw; FilmEn; FilmgC; ForYSC; GoodHs; HalFC 80, 84, 88; IntDcF 1-3, 2-3; IntDcWB; IntMPA 75, 76, 77, 78, 79, 80, 81, 82, 84, 86, 88, 92, 94, 96; IntWW 74, 75, 76, 77, 78, 79, 80, 81, 82, 83, 89, 91, 93; InWom, SUP; ItaFilm; LegTOT; MotPP; MovMk; NewYTBE 70; OxCFilm; Who 74, 82, 83, 85, 88, 90, 92, 94; WhoAm 80, 82, 84, 86, 88, 90, 92, 94, 95, 96, 97; WhoAmW 64, 66, 68, 70, 72, 74, 75, 79, 81, 83; WhoEnt 92; WhoFr 79; WhoHol 92, A; WhoWor 74, 78, 80, 82, 84, 87, 89, 91, 93, 95, 96; WorAl; WorAlBi; WorEFlm*

Lorengar, Pilar
[Pilar Lorenca Garcia]
Spanish. Opera Singer
Dramatic soprano during 1950s-60s.
b. Jan 16, 1928 in Saragossa, Spain
d. Jun 2, 1996 in Berlin, Germany
Source: *Baker 84, 92; BioIn 15; CmOp; IntDcOp; IntWWM 80, 90; InWom SUP; MetOEnc; NewAmDM; NewGrDM 80; NewGrDO; NewYTBS 27; OxDcOp; PenDiMP; WhoOp 76*

Lorentz, Hendrick Antoon
Dutch. Physicist, Educator
Shared 1902 Nobel Prize with Pieter Zeeman; formulated Lorentz transformations leading to theory of relativity.
b. Jul 18, 1853 in Arnhem, Netherlands

d. Feb 4, 1928 in Haarlem, Netherlands
Source: *AsBiEn; BiESc; DcInv; DcScB; Dis&D; McGEWB; NewCol 75; WebBD 83; WhDW; WhoNob*

Lorentz, Pare
American. Filmmaker
Government-backed documentaries brought the misuse of human and natural resources to the attention of the American public of the 1930s.
b. Dec 11, 1905 in Clarksburg, West Virginia
Source: *AmFD; AnObit 1992; BenetAL 91; BioIn 8, 15, 19; CurBio 40, 92N; DcAmSR; DcFM; FilmEn; HalFC 80, 84, 88; IntDcF 1-2, 2-2; LinLib L; OxCFilm; REnAL; WhoE 77, 79; WorEFlm; WorFDir 1*

Lorenz, Konrad Zacharias
Austrian. Scientist
Shared Nobel Prize in medicine, 1973, for comparative studies of animal behavior.
b. Nov 7, 1903 in Vienna, Austria
d. Feb 27, 1989 in Altenburg, Austria
Source: *AmAu&B; AmMWSc 89, 92; Benet 87; BiESc; BioIn 11, 12, 13, 14, 15, 16; CamDcSc; ConAu 35NR, 61, 128; CurBio 77, 89, 89N; EncTR 91; FacFETw; InSci; IntDcAn; IntWW 89N; LarDcSc; LinLib L; MajTwCW; MakMC; McGMS 80; News 89-3; NewYTBS 89; NobelP; RAdv 13-5; ThTwC 87; WhAm 9; Who 88, 90N; WhoAm 88; WhoNob, 90, 95; WhoWor 76, 78, 80, 82, 84, 87, 89; WorAl; WorAlBi*

Lorenz, Max
German. Opera Singer
Noted Wagnerian tenor, 1930s-50s.
b. May 17, 1901 in Dusseldorf, Germany
d. Jan 11, 1975 in Salzburg, Austria
Source: *Baker 78, 84, 92; BioIn 16; CmOp; IntDcOp; MetOEnc; NewEOp 71; NewGrDM 80; NewGrDO; OxDcOp; PenDiMP; WhoMus 72*

Lorenzetti, Ambrogio
Italian. Artist
A leading early Sienese painter, noted for frescoes: *Good and Bad Government,* 1330s.
b. 1265? in Siena, Italy
d. 1348
Source: *DcBiPP; DcCathB; OxCArt; REn; WebBD 83; WhDW*

Lorenzo, Frank
[Francisco Anthony Lorenzo]
American. Business Executive
Leader of airline consolidation, cost-cutting strategies; president, Texas Air, 1980-85, Eastern Airlines, 1987-90.
b. May 19, 1940 in New York, New York
Source: *BioIn 13, 14, 15, 16; ConAmBL; CurBio 87; Dun&B 90; EncABHB 8; IntWW 91; NewYTBS 83, 85; St&PR 87, 91; WhoAm 86, 90; WhoFI 85, 92; WhoHisp 92; WhoSSW 91; WorAlBi*

Lorillard, Louis Livingston
American. Business Executive
Co-founder, Newport Jazz Festival; pres., 1954-60.
b. 1919?
d. Nov 5, 1986 in Providence, Rhode Island
Source: *NewYTBS 86*

Lorillard, Pierre
American. Merchant, Yachtsman
Tobacco exec., noted for yachting interests, breeding winning horses.
b. Oct 13, 1833 in New York, New York
d. Jul 7, 1901 in New York, New York
Source: *ApCAB; BiDAmSp OS; BioIn 5; DcAmB; WhAm HS*

Loring, Eugene
[LeRoy Kerpestein]
American. Dancer, Choreographer
Wrote ballet *Billy the Kid,* 1938.
b. 1914 in Milwaukee, Wisconsin
d. Aug 30, 1982 in Kingston, New York
Source: *BiDD; BiE&WWA; BioIn 4, 7, 8, 9, 10, 13; CnOxB; CurBio 72, 82, 82N; DancEn 78; NewYTBS 82; WhoHol A*

Loring, Gloria Jean
American. Singer, Actor
Starred in TV soap opera "Days of Our Lives," 1980-86.
b. Dec 10, 1946 in New York, New York
Source: *BioIn 15; ConTFT 3; InWom SUP; WhoAm 74, 76, 78, 80, 82, 84, 86, 88, 90, 92, 94, 95, 96, 97; WhoAmW 74, 95, 97; WhoEnt 92*

Lorjou, Bernard Joseph Pierre
French. Artist
A leader, Social Realist group, 1940s-50s; later developed strong expressionist style.
b. Sep 9, 1908 in Blois, France
d. Jan 26, 1986 in Blois, France
Source: *McGDA; OxCTwCA; PhDcTCA 77; WhoWor 74; WorArt 1950*

Lorne, Marion
American. Actor
Played Aunt Clara on TV show "Bewitched," 1964-68.
b. Aug 12, 1888 in Philadelphia, Pennsylvania
d. May 9, 1968 in New York, New York
Source: *BiE&WWA; BioIn 3, 4, 8; FilmgC; ForYSC; InWom, SUP; LegTOT; MotPP; NotNAT B; OxCThe 83; WhAm 5; WhoAmW 70; WhScrn 74, 77, 83; WhThe; WorAl*

Lorrain, Claude
[Claude Gelee; Claude Gellee]
"Le Lorrain"
French. Artist
Painted idyllic seascapes, landscapes which are noted for light, atmosphere including *Expulsion of Hagar,* 1668.
b. 1600 in Lorraine, France
d. Nov 21, 1682 in Rome, Italy
Source: *AtlBL; Benet 87, 96; BioIn 2, 4, 5, 6, 8, 9, 10, 11, 12, 13, 14, 19; ClaDrA; DcBiPP; DcSeaP; Dis&D; IntDcAA 90; McGEWB; NewC; NewCol 75; OxCArt; REn; WebBD 83; WorAlBi*

Lorre, Peter
[Laszlo Loewenstein]
American. Actor
Played sinister villain in many 1930s-40s films including *The Maltese Falcon,* 1941.
b. Jun 26, 1904 in Rosenberg, Austria-Hungary
d. Mar 24, 1964 in Hollywood, California
Source: *BiDFilm, 81, 94; BioIn 1, 6, 7, 11, 14, 15, 17, 21; CmMov; DcAmB S7; DcArts; EncEurC; EncWT; FacFETw; FilmAG WE; FilmEn; FilmgC; GangFlm; HalFC 80, 84, 88; IntDcF 1-3, 2-3; ItaFilm; LegTOT; MotPP; MovMk; NotNAT B; ObitT 1961; OlFamFa; OxCFilm; PenEncH; Vers A; WhAm 4; WhoHol B; WhoHrs 80; WhScrn 74, 77, 83; WorAl; WorAlBi; WorEFlm*

Lorring, Joan
American. Actor
Oscar nominee for *The Corn Is Green,* 1945.
b. 1931, Hong Kong
Source: *BiE&WWA; FilmgC; ForYSC; MotPP; MovMk; NotNAT; WhoHol A*

Lortel, Lucille
[Lucille Mayo]
American. Producer
Stage, film actress who founded White Barn Theatre, Westport, CT, 1947.
b. Dec 16, 1905 in New York, New York
Source: *BiE&WWA; BioIn 14, 15, 16; CamGWoT; CelR 90; ConTFT 5; CurBio 85; InWom SUP; NewYTBS 85, 88; NotNAT; NotWoAT; WhoAm 86, 88, 90, 92, 94, 95, 96, 97; WhoAmW 61, 64, 66, 68; WhoThe 81*

Lortz, Richard
American. Author, Dramatist, Editor
Wrote novel: *The Bethrothed,* 1975; drama: *The Juniper Tree,* 1972; many 1950s TV plays.
b. Jan 13, 1930 in New York, New York
d. Nov 5, 1980 in New York, New York
Source: *ConAu 11NR, 57, 102*

Lortzing, Gustav Albert
German. Composer, Conductor, Librettist
Wrote light operas *Zar und Zimmermann,* 1837; *Undine,* 1845.
b. Oct 23, 1801 in Berlin, Germany
d. Jan 21, 1851 in Berlin, Germany
Source: *Baker 84; BioIn 4, 7, 11, 12; IntDcOp; NewEOp 71; OxCMus*

Losch, Tilly
Austrian. Dancer, Artist
Glamorous ballet, dramatic dancer of 1920s-30s; painted in later yrs.

b. Nov 15, 1902 in Vienna, Austria
d. Dec 24, 1975 in New York, New York
Source: *BiDD; CurBio 44, 76N; EncMT; ForYSC; HalFC 84; ObitOF 79; ObitT 1971; WhoAmA 82N; WhoHol C; WhScrn 77, 83; WhThe*

Losey, Joseph Walton
[Victor Hanbury]
American. Director
Blacklisted for refusing to testify before House Un-American Activities Committee, 1951; films include *Don Giovanni,* 1979; *The Steaming,* 1984.
b. Jan 14, 1909 in La Crosse, Wisconsin
d. Jul 22, 1984 in London, England
Source: *BiDFilm; CurBio 69; DcFM; FilmgC; IntMPA 84; MakMC; NewYTBS 84; OxCFilm; Who 83; WhoAm 82; WorAl; WorEFlm*

Los Lobos
[Steve Berlin; David Hidalgo; Conrad Lozano; Louis Perez; Cesar Rosas]
American. Music Group
Mexican-American roots/rock band formed 1973; noted for mastery of widely diverse musical styles; contributed to *La Bamba* soundtrack, 1987; albums include *By the Light of the Moon,* 1987.
Source: *ConMus 2; EncPR&S 89; EncRk 88; EncRkSt; PenEncP; WhoHisp 92, 94*

Losonczi, Pal
Hungarian. Political Leader
Head of State, 1967-87.
b. Sep 18, 1919 in Bolho, Hungary
Source: *IntWW 74, 75, 76, 77, 78, 79, 80, 81, 82, 83, 89; IntYB 78, 79, 80, 81, 82; NewCol 75; WhoSocC 78; WhoSoCE 89; WhoWor 82, 84, 87, 89*

Lossing, Benson John
American. Author, Editor, Illustrator
Popular books on American history include *Pictorial Field Books* of Civil, Revolutionary War, 1850s-60s.
b. Feb 12, 1813 in Beekman, New York
d. Jun 3, 1891 in Dover Plains, New York
Source: *Alli, SUP; AmAu; AmAu&B; AmBi; ApCAB; BbD; BiD&SB; BioIn 2, 8, 11, 14; ChhPo; CyAL 2; DcAmAu; DcAmB; DcBiPP; DcLB 30; DcNAA; Drake; EarABI, SUP; HarEnUS; LinLib L, S; NatCAB 4; NewYHSD; TwCBDA; WhAm HS*

Lot
Biblical Figure
Nephew of Abraham who escaped Sodom and Gomorrah; his wife turned into a pillar of salt.
Source: *Benet 96; BioIn 4, 6, 10; DcBiPP; NewGrDM 80; UFOEn*

Lothrop, Harriet Mulford Stone
[Margaret Sidney]
American. Children's Author
Best-known children's book: *Five Little Peppers & How They Grew,* 1881.
b. Jun 22, 1844 in New Haven, Connecticut
d. Aug 2, 1924
Source: *Alli SUP; AmAu; AmAu&B; AmWomWr; BbD; BiD&SB; BioIn 15; BlmGWL; CarSB; ChhPo, S2; ChlBkCr; CnDAL; DcAmAu; DcAmB; DcNAA; FamSYP; InWom; JBA 34; NatCAB 8; NotAW; OxCAmL 65, 83, 95; PenNWW B; REnAL; SmATA 20; TwCBDA; TwCChW 83A, 89A, 95A; WhAm 1; WomWWA 14; WorAl*

Loti, Pierre
[Louis Marie Julien Viaud]
French. Author, Naval Officer
Noted for three novels of Breton peasant life including *An Iceland Fisherman,* 1886.
b. Jan 14, 1850 in Rochefort, France
d. Jun 10, 1923 in Hendaye, France
Source: *AtlBL; BbD; Benet 87, 96; BiD&SB; BioIn 1, 2, 4, 5, 8, 10, 13, 15, 19; CasWL; ClDMEL 47, 80; ConAu X; CyWA 58; DcArts; DcBiA; DcEuL; DcLB 123; Dis&D; EncWL; EvEuW; GuFrLit 1; LinLib L, LP, S; LngCTC; McGEWB; ModFrL; NewEOp 71; NewGrDO; Novels; OxCEng 67; OxCFr; OxCShps; PenC EUR; REn; TwCA, SUP; TwCLC 11; WhDW; WhLit*

Lott, Ronnie
[Ronald Mandel Lott]
American. Football Player
Ten-time Pro-Bowl team member; with San Francisco, 1981-90; LA Raiders, 1991-93; NY Jets, 1993-94; Kansas City, 1994—.
b. May 8, 1959 in Albuquerque, New Mexico
Source: *AfrAmSG; BioIn 12, 14, 16, 17, 18, 19, 20, 21; ConBlB 9; CurBio 94; FootReg 87; LegTOT; NewYTBS 82; WhoAfA 96; WhoAm 92, 94, 95, 96, 97; WhoBlA 85, 88, 90, 92, 94; WhoSpor*

Lott, Trent
American. Politician
Rep. senator, MS, 1989—; majority leader, 1996—.
b. Oct 9, 1941 in Grenada, Mississippi
Source: *AlmAP 78, 80, 82, 84, 88, 92, 96; BioIn 14, 16; CngDr 74, 77, 79, 81, 83, 85, 87, 89, 91, 93, 95; CurBio 96; IntWW 89, 91, 93; NewYTBS 84, 94; PolProf NF; PolsAm 84; WhoAm 74, 76, 78, 80, 82, 84, 86, 88, 90, 92, 94, 95, 96, 97; WhoAmP 83, 85, 87, 89, 91, 93, 95; WhoSSW 75, 76, 78, 80, 82, 84, 86, 88, 91, 93, 95, 97*

Lotto, Lorenzo
Italian. Artist
Did portraits, altarpieces, mystical paintings of religious subjects: *Entombment,* 1512.
b. 1480 in Venice, Italy
d. Sep 1, 1556 in Loreto, Italy
Source: *AtlBL; BioIn 2, 3, 4, 6, 13, 17; ClaDrA; DcArts; DcBiPP; DcCathB; IntDcAA 90; McGDA; McGEWB; OxCArt; OxDcArt; REn; WhDW*

Loudon, Dorothy
American. Actor
Won Tony, 1977, for role of Miss Hannigan in Broadway musical *Annie.*
b. Sep 17, 1933 in Boston, Massachusetts
Source: *BioIn 13, 14; CelR 90; ConTFT 1, 4; CurBio 84; IntMPA 92, 94, 96; InWom SUP; LegTOT; NewYTBS 77, 83; NotNAT; VarWW 85; WhoAm 78, 80, 82, 84, 86, 88, 90, 92, 94, 95, 96, 97; WhoAmW 81, 95, 97; WhoEnt 92; WhoHol 92; WhoThe 72, 77, 81; WorAl; WorAlBi*

Louganis, Greg(ory Efthimios)
American. Diver
Won gold medals in springboard, platform diving, 1984, 1988 Olympics; first man ever to win repeat gold medals in consecutive Olympics; wrote autobiography *Breaking the Surface,* 1995; Olympic Hall of Fame, 1985.
b. Jan 29, 1960 in San Diego, California
Source: *AsAmAlm; BiDAmSp BK; BioIn 13, 14, 15, 16; CelR 90; ConHero 1; CurBio 84; FacFETw; GayLesB; LegTOT; News 95, 95-3; NewYTBS 84, 88; NotAsAm; WhoAm 90; WhoHol 92; WorAlBi*

Lougheed, Peter
Canadian. Politician
Progressive-Conservative premier of Alberta, 1971-85.
b. Jul 26, 1928 in Calgary, Alberta, Canada
Source: *BioIn 11, 12, 13, 15, 16, 17; CanWW 70, 79, 80, 81, 83; CurBio 79; IntWW 76, 77, 78, 79, 80, 81, 82, 83, 89, 91; NewYTBS 80; Who 82, 83, 85, 88, 90, 92; WhoAm 78, 80, 82, 84, 86, 90, 92, 94, 95, 96, 97; WhoCan 73, 75, 77, 80, 82, 84; WhoWest 89*

Loughery, Kevin Michael
American. Basketball Coach, Basketball Player
Guard, 1962-73, mostly with Baltimore; coach Jets, 1973-77; Nets, 1977-81; Hawk s, 1981-83; Bulls, 1983-85; Bullets, 1986-88; Heat, 1988-94.
b. Mar 28, 1940 in New York, New York
Source: *OfNBA 87; WhoAm 78, 80, 82, 84, 86, 92, 94, 95; WhoBbl 73; WhoE 79, 81; WhoSSW 82, 93, 95*

Loughlin, Lori
American. Actor
Played Becky on TV series "Full House."
Source: *BioIn 12, 15; ConTFT 8*

Loughname, Lee
American. Musician
Trumpeter with group; had hit single "Does Anyone Really Know What Time It Is?" 1970.
b. Oct 21, 1946 in Chicago, Illinois
Source: *WhoAm 90*

Loughran, Tommy
American. Boxer
Light-heavyweight champion, 1927-29; Hall of Fame, 1956.
b. Nov 29, 1902 in Philadelphia, Pennsylvania
d. Jul 7, 1982 in Hollidaysburg, Pennsylvania
Source: *BioIn 10, 11, 13; BoxReg; NewYTBS 82; WhoBox 74; WhoSpor*

Louie, David Wong
American. Writer
Wrote short story collection *Pangs of Love,* 1991.
b. 1954 in Rockville Centre, New York
Source: *AsAmAlm; ConAu 139; ConLC 70; NotAsAm; WhoAsA 94; WrDr 96*

Louis, Errol T.
American. Banker
To help revitalize community, co-founded, with Mark Winston Griffith, the Central Brooklyn Federal Credit Union, 1993.
b. Aug 24, 1962 in New York, New York
Source: *BioIn 20*

Louis, Jean
French. Fashion Designer
Creator of "little Carnegie suits" for Hattie Carnegie; later, chief designer, Columbia Pictures.
b. Oct 5, 1907 in Paris, France
d. Apr 20, 1997 in Palm Springs, California
Source: *BioIn 14; CelR; EncFash; FairDF US; IntMPA 75, 76, 77, 78, 79, 80, 81, 82, 84, 86, 88, 92, 94, 96; VarWW 85; WhoAm 76; WorFshn*

Louis, Joe
[Joseph Louis Barrow]
"The Brown Bomber"
American. Boxer
Defeated James Braddock to win heavyweight crown, 1937; defended title 25 times, retiring as undefeated champ, 1949.
b. May 13, 1914 in Lexington, Alabama
d. Apr 12, 1981 in Las Vegas, Nevada
Source: *AfrAmAl 6; AfrAmSG; AmDec 1940; AnObit 1981; BiDAmSp BK; BioIn 1, 2, 3, 4, 5, 6, 7, 8, 9, 10, 11, 12, 13, 14, 15, 16, 19, 20, 21; BoxReg; CelR; ConAu 103; ConBlB 5; CurBio 40, 81, 81N; DcTwCCu 5; Ebony 1; EncAACR; EncAB-H 1974, 1996; FacFETw; InB&W 80, 85; LegTOT; McGEWB; NegAl 76, 83, 89; NewCol 75; NewYTBS 79, 81; OxCAmH; RComAH; WebAB 74, 79; WhAm 7; WhDW; WhoAm 74, 76, 78, 80; WhoBlA 75, 77, 80, 85; WhoBox 74; WhoSpor; WhScrn 83; WorAl; WorAlBi*

Louis, Morris
[Morris Louis Bernstein]
American. Artist
Abstract Expressionist; often poured paint on unsized canvas; did colored stripes in vertical patterns; *Veils* series, 1954-58.
b. Nov 28, 1912 in Baltimore, Maryland
d. Sep 7, 1962 in Washington, District of Columbia
Source: *AmCulL; BioIn 6, 7, 9, 10, 11, 13, 14, 19; BriEAA; ConArt 77, 83; DcAmArt; DcAmB S7; DcArts; DcCAA 71, 77, 88, 94; FacFETw; IntDcAA 90; McGDA; OxCTwCA; OxDcArt; PhDcTCA 77; WhAm 1; WhoAmA 78N, 80N, 82N, 84N, 86N, 89N, 91N, 93N; WorArt 1950*

Louis-Dreyfus, Julia
American. Actor
Member of "Saturday Night Live" cast, 1982-85; plays Elaine Benes on TV series "Seinfeld," 1989—.
b. Jan 13, 1961 in New York, New York
Source: *BioIn 16; ConTFT 13; CurBio 95; IntMPA 96; News 94, 94-1; WhoAm 94*

Louise, Anita
[Louise Fremault]
American. Actor
Played in TV show "My Friend Flicka," 1956-58; films from 1929-52 include *Madame DuBarry; Midsummer Night's Dream.*
b. Jan 9, 1917 in New York, New York
d. Apr 25, 1970 in West Los Angeles, California
Source: *BioIn 8; Film 2; FilmgC; HolP 30; MotPP; MovMk; NewYTBE 70; ThFT; WhoHol B; WhScrn 74, 77; WorAl*

Louise, Tina
[Tina Blacker]
American. Actor
Played Ginger Grant on TV comedy "Gilligan's Island," 1964-67.
b. Feb 11, 1938 in New York, New York
Source: *BiE&WWA; BioIn 16; ConTFT 3; FilmgC; HalFC 88; IntMPA 82, 92; MotPP; VarWW 85; WhoHol A*

Louiseboulanger
French. Fashion Designer
Known for melodramatic clothes with uneven hemlines, 1928.
b. 1900, France
Source: *EncFash; FairDF FRA; WorFshn*

Louis I
"The Pious"
Ruler
Ruled Holy Roman Empire, 814-840; son of Charlemagne; twice deposed by his sons.
b. 778
d. Jun 20, 840
Source: *CelCen; DcBiPP; DcCathB; Dis&D; LuthC 75; McGEWB; OxCFr; WebBD 83*

Louis IX
[Saint Louis]
French. Ruler
King from 1226; led two crusades, 1248-54, 1270; canonized, 1297.
b. Apr 25, 1215 in Poissy, France
d. Aug 25, 1270 in Tunis, Tunis
Source: *BioIn 1, 2, 3, 4, 5, 6, 7, 8, 11; DcBiPP; DcEuL; OxCFr; WebBD 83*

Louis Phillippe
"The Citizen King"
French. Ruler
Proclaimed king, 1830, in July revolution against Charles X; abdicated, 1848.
b. Oct 6, 1773 in Paris, France
d. Aug 26, 1850 in Claremont, England
Source: *BioIn 10; DcBiPP; WebBD 83*

Louis XI
French. Ruler
King of France, 1461-83; strengthened and consolidated country following Hundred Years War.
b. Jul 3, 1423 in Bourges, France
d. Aug 30, 1483 in Plessis-les-Tours, France

Louis XIV
"The Grand Monarch"; "The Great"; "The Sun King"
French. Ruler
Absolute monarch, ruled despotically; had longest reign in European history, 1643-1715; built Versailles.
b. Sep 16, 1638 in Saint-Germain-en-Laye, France
d. Sep 1, 1715 in Versailles, France
Source: *DcBiPP; DcCathB; Dis&D; LuthC 75; McGEWB; NewCol 75; OxCFr; WebBD 83; WhDW; WorAl*

Louis XV
"The Well Beloved"
French. Ruler
Ruled France, 1715-74; his failure to solve fiscal problems led to the Revolution; great-grandson of Louis XIV.
b. Feb 15, 1710 in Versailles, France
d. May 10, 1774 in Versailles, France
Source: *DcBiPP; DcCathB; Dis&D; LuthC 75; OxCFr; WebBD 83; WhDW*

Louis XVI
French. Ruler
Ruled from 1774; his reforms failed to stop Revolution; he and wife, Marie Antoinette, found guilty of treason, guillotined.
b. Aug 23, 1754 in Versailles, France
d. Jan 21, 1793 in Paris, France
Source: *DcBiPP; Dis&D; EncAR; HarEnUS; OxCFr; WebBD 83; WhDW; WorAl*

Loulan, JoAnn
American. Psychoanalyst
Books include *Lesbian Sex, Lesbian Passion,* 1987; *The Lesbian Erotic Dance,* 1991.
b. Jul 31, 1948 in Bath, Ohio
Source: *GayLesB*

Lousma, Jack
American. Astronaut
Crew member, *Skylab 3,* 1973, *Columbia* space shuttle, 1982.
b. Feb 29, 1936 in Grand Rapids, Michigan
Source: *BioIn 10, 13; NewYTBE 73; NewYTBS 82; WhoSpc*

Louys, Pierre
[Pierre Louis]
French. Poet, Author
Wrote verse volume *Astarte,* 1891; novel *Aphrodite,* 1896.
b. Dec 10, 1870 in Ghent, Belgium
d. Jun 4, 1925 in Paris, France
Source: *AtlBL; Benet 87, 96; BioIn 1, 2, 3, 11, 12, 19; CasWL; ClDMEL 47, 80; ConAu 105; DcLB 123; EncWL; EvEuW; GuFrLit 1; IntWW 74; LngCTC; NewEOp 71; OxCFr; REn; TwCA, SUP; WhoTwCL*

Love, Augustus Edward Hough
English. Mathematician, Scientist
Geophysicist; analysis of earthquake waves led to discovery of a major wave that was named for him.
b. Apr 17, 1863 in Weston-super-Mare, England
d. Jun 5, 1940 in Oxford, England
Source: *BiESc; BioIn 2, 6; DcNaB 1931; DcScB; LarDcSc*

Love, Bessie
[Juanita Horton]
English. Actor
Career stretched from silent films to 1980 TV; nominated for Oscar, 1929, for *Broadway Melody.*
b. Sep 19, 1898 in Midland, Texas
d. Apr 26, 1986 in London, England
Source: *AnObit 1986; BiDD; BiE&WWA; BioIn 9, 11, 12, 14; ContDcW 89; EncAFC; Film 1, 2; FilmEn; FilmgC; HalFC 80, 84, 88; IlWWBF, A; IntDcF 1-3, 2-3; IntMPA 75, 76, 77, 78, 79, 80, 81, 82, 84, 86; InWom SUP; ItaFilm; LegTOT; MotPP; MovMk; NewYTBS 86; NotNAT; OxCFilm; SilFlmP; ThFT; VarWW 85; WhoHol A; WhoThe 81*

Love, Courtney
American. Singer, Songwriter, Actor
Debuted with album *Pretty on the Inside,* 1991; in film *The People vs. Larry Flynt,* 1996.
b. Jul 9, 1965 in San Francisco, California
Source: *CurBio 96; WhoHol 92*

Love, George Hutchinson
American. Business Executive
Headed world's largest coal co., Pittsburgh Consolidated, 1945; chm., Chrysler Corp., 1961-66.
b. Sep 4, 1900 in Johnstown, Pennsylvania
d. Jul 25, 1991 in Pittsburgh, Pennsylvania
Source: *BioIn 1, 2, 6, 7, 8, 13, 17, 21; CurBio 50, 91N; IntWW 74, 75, 76, 77, 78, 79, 80, 81, 82, 83; NewYTBS 91; St&PR 75, 84; WhoAm 74; WhoFI 74*

Love, Iris Cornelia
American. Archaeologist, Art Historian
Discovered the circular temple of Aphrodite in Turkey, 1969.
b. Aug 1, 1933 in New York, New York
Source: *BioIn 13, 15, 16; CelR 90; ConAu 29R; CurBio 82; InWom SUP; WhoAmA 73, 76, 80; WhoAmW 74, 75, 77*

Love, Mike
[The Beach Boys]
American. Singer, Musician
Lead vocalist for The Beach Boys, 1961—.
b. Mar 15, 1941 in Los Angeles, California
Source: *BioIn 11, 12; BkPepl; EncPR&S 74; IlEncRk; LegTOT; RkOn 74; WhoRocM 82*

Love, Nat
"Champion of the West"; "Deadwood Dick"
American. Pioneer
One of the 5,000 black cowboys who took part in the legendary cattle drives up the Chisholm Trail.
b. Jun 1854 in Davidson County, Tennessee
d. 1921 in Los Angeles, California
Source: *BioIn 10, 11, 20; ConBlB 9; DcAmNB; InB&W 85; McGEWB; WhNaAH*

Love, Susan M(argaret)
American. Surgeon
Director of UCLA Breast Center, 1988—

b. Feb 9, 1948 in Long Branch, New Jersey
Source: *CurBio 94; GayLesB; WhoWest 96*

Lovecraft, H(oward) P(hillips)
American. Author
Noted for macabre horror stories, usually published in *Weird Tales* mag.
b. Aug 20, 1890 in Providence, Rhode Island
d. Mar 15, 1937 in Providence, Rhode Island
Source: *AmAu&B; Benet 96; BioIn 3, 4, 6, 7, 8, 9, 10, 11, 12, 13, 15, 17, 18; ChhPo, S2, S3; ConAu 104; DcArts; EncSF 93; OxCAmL 65, 95; REnAL; RfGAmL 94; RGSF; RGTwCWr; TwCA SUP; TwCLC 4; TwCSFW 86; WebAB 74, 79; WhDW; WhoHrs 80*

Lovejoy, Arthur Oncken (Schauffler)
American. Philosopher, Historian
Proponent of epistemological dualism; wrote *Great Chain of Being,* 1936.
b. Oct 10, 1873 in Berlin, Germany
d. Dec 30, 1962 in Baltimore, Maryland
Source: *AmAu&B; BioIn 1, 4, 5, 6, 11, 12, 13; DcAmB S7; DcScB; McGEWB; RAdv 14, 13-4; REnAL; TwCA SUP; WebAB 74, 79; WebBD 83; WhAm 4*

Lovejoy, Clarence Earle
American. Author, Editor
Originator, *Lovejoy's College Guide,* 1973.
b. Jun 26, 1894 in Waterville, Maine
d. Jan 16, 1974 in Red Bank, New Jersey
Source: *AmAu&B; Au&Wr 71; BioIn 6, 10; ConAu 5NR, 5R, 45; NewYTBS 75; WhAm 6; WhJnl; WhNAA*

Lovejoy, Elijah Parish
American. Journalist, Abolitionist
Newspaper editor whose presses were destroyed due to his anti-slavery editorials.
b. Nov 9, 1802 in Albion, Maine
d. Nov 7, 1837 in Alton, Illinois
Source: *AmAu; AmBi; AmRef; AmSocL; ApCAB; BiDAmJo; BioIn 3, 4, 5, 6, 7, 8, 9, 10, 11, 12, 15, 16, 18, 19, 20; DcAmB; DcAmReB 2; DcAmSR; Drake; EncAAH; EncAB-H 1974, 1996; EncAJ; HarEnUS; JrnUS; McGEWB; NatCAB 2; OxCAmH; OxCAmL 65, 83, 95; REnAL; TwCBDA; WebAB 74, 79; WhAm HS; WhAmP; WhCiWar*

Lovejoy, Frank
American. Actor
Supporting roles in films, 1948-58, include *Home of the Brave,* 1949; *House of Wax,* 1953.
b. Mar 28, 1914 in New York, New York
d. Oct 2, 1962 in New York, New York
Source: *FilmEn; FilmgC; ForYSC; MotPP; MovMk; NotNAT B; WhScrn 74, 77, 83*

Lovelace, Linda
[Linda Boreman Marciano]
American. Actor, Author
Starred in pornographic film *Deep Throat,* 1972; wrote autobiography *Ordeal,* 1984.
Source: *BioIn 12; DcLP 87B; HalFC 88; WhoHol A*

Lovelace, Richard
English. Poet, Courtier
Prototype of the dashing Cavalier; wrote verse volume *Lucasta,* 1649.
b. 1618 in Kent, England
d. 1658 in London, England
Source: *Alli; AtlBL; Benet 87, 96; BiD&SB; BiDRP&D; BioIn 1, 2, 3, 5, 9, 10, 12, 17, 19; BlmGEL; BritAu; BritWr 2; CamGEL; CamGLE; CasWL; Chambr 1; ChhPo; CnE&AP; CroE&S; CyWA 58; DcArts; DcBiPP; DcEnA; DcEnL;*

DcEuL; DcLB 131; DcLEL; DcNaB; EvLB; GrWrEL P; LitC 24; McGEWB; MouLC 1; NewC; NewCBEL; OxCEng 67, 85, 95; PenC ENG; REn; RfGEnL 91; RGFBP; WebE&AL; WhDW; WorAl; WorAlBi

Lovelace, William Randolph, II
American. Physician
NASA official, expert in space medicine; designed tests to screen astronauts.
b. Dec 30, 1907 in Springfield, Missouri
d. Dec 12, 1965
Source: *BioIn 6, 7, 9, 12; DcAmMeB 84; NatCAB 53; WhAm 4*

Loveless, Herschel C(ellel)
American. Politician
First Dem. governor in IA in 18 yrs., 1957-60; member renegotiation Board, 1961-69, which reviewed defense and space contracts.
b. May 5, 1911 in Hedrick, Iowa
d. May 3, 1989 in Winchester, Virginia
Source: *BiDrGov 1789; BioIn 4, 5, 16; BlueB 76; CurBio 89N; IntWW 74, 75, 76; St&PR 75; WhAm 10; WhoAm 74, 76, 78, 80, 82; WhoAmP 73, 75, 77, 79, 81, 83, 85, 87; WhoFI 74*

Loveless, Patty
[Patty Ramey]
American. Singer, Songwriter
Country artist known for contemporary instrumentals, traditional delivery; albums include *Patty Loveless,* 1986.
b. 1957 in Belcher Holler, Kentucky
Source: *BgBkCoM; BioIn 15, 16; ConMus 5; LegTOT; WhoAm 94, 95, 96, 97; WhoAmW 95; WhoNeCM*

Lovell, Bernard, Sir
[Alfred Charles Bernard Lovell]
English. Astronomer
Radio astronomer; investigations led to development/application of radio telescope to study of meteors.
b. Aug 31, 1913 in Oldland Common, England
Source: *AsBiEn; Au&Wr 71; BiESc; BioIn 2, 5, 7, 13, 14, 17; BlueB 76; ConAu 6NR, 13R; DcLEL 1940; FacFETw; InSci; IntAu&W 77, 82, 91; IntWW 74, 75, 76, 77, 78, 79, 80, 81, 82, 83, 89, 91; IntYB 78, 79, 80, 81, 82; LinLib L, S; McGEWB; McGMS 80; WhDW; Who 74, 82, 83, 85, 88, 90, 92; WhoWor 74, 76, 78, 82, 84, 87, 89, 91, 93, 96, 97; WorAl; WorAlBi; WrDr 76, 80, 82, 84, 86, 88, 90, 92*

Lovell, Jim
[James Arthur Lovell, Jr]
American. Astronaut
Flew Gemini 7, 12, Apollo 8, 13 space missions.
b. Mar 25, 1928 in Cleveland, Ohio
Source: *BlueB 76; CurBio 69; Dun&B 90; FacFETw; IntWW 74; St&PR 87, 91, 93, 96; WebAMB; WhoAm 84, 90; WhoGov 77; WhoSpc; WhoWor 84; WorAl; WorAlBi*

Lovelock, James
English. Scientist, Inventor, Author
Invented electron capture detector, 1957; formulated controversial Gaia hypothesis about earth's self-regulating atmosphere.
b. Jul 26, 1919 in Letchworth, England
Source: *BioIn 10, 12, 14, 15; ConAu 123; CurBio 92; IntWW 91; LegTOT; ScF&FL 92; Who 92*

Lover, Ed
[James Roberts]
American. Rapper
Co-host, with Dr. Dre, of "Yo! MTV Raps," 1989—.
b. 1960 in New York, New York

Loverboy
[Paul Dean; Matt Frenette; Doug Johnson; Mike Reno; Scott Smith]
Canadian. Music Group
Formed 1978; hits include "Queen of the Broken Hearts," 1983.
Source: *ApCAB; BioIn 16, 17; Drake; Dun&B 90; EncPR&S 89; HarEnR 86; NewYTBS 81; PenEncP; RkOn 85; RolSEnR 83; Who 74, 82, 83, 85, 85S, 88, 90, 92; WhoAm 97; WhoAmP 95; WhoPubR 72, 76; WhoRocM 82*

Lovesey, Peter Harmer
[Peter Lear]
English. Author
Historical mystery writer, created Sergeant Cribb, Constable Thackeray; wrote *Wobble to Death,* 1970.
b. Sep 10, 1936 in Whitton, England
Source: *BioIn 13, 14; ConAu 28NR, 41R; CrtSuMy; DcLB 87; DcLP 87A; EncMys; IntAu&W 77, 91; MajTwCW; ScF&FL 92; TwCCr&M 80, 85B, 91; WrDr 86, 92, 94*

Lovett, Lyle
American. Singer, Songwriter
Writes country music with blues, jazz overtones and sly lyrics; won Grammy for *Lyle Lovett and His Large Band,* 1989; married Julia Roberts, 1993.
b. Nov 1, 1957 in Klein, Texas
Source: *BioIn 16; ConMus 5; EncRkSt; LegTOT; PenEncP; WhoNeCM*

Lovett, Robert A(bercrombie)
American. Government Official
Secretary of Defense during Korean conflict, 1951-53; received Presidential Medal of Freedom, 1963.
b. Sep 14, 1895 in Huntsville, Texas
d. May 7, 1986 in Locust Valley, New York
Source: *BiDrUSE 71, 89; BioIn 1, 2, 3, 5, 7, 10, 11; CurBio 86; DcAmDH 80, 89; IntWW 74, 75, 76, 77, 78, 79, 80, 81, 82, 83; IntYB 78, 79, 80, 81, 82; NewYTBS 86; St&PR 75; WhAm 9; Who 74, 82, 83, 85; WhoAm 74, 76, 78, 80; WhoAmP 73, 75, 77, 79, 81, 83, 85*

Lovins, Amory B(loch)
American. Physicist
Energy consultant who encourages alternative forms of energy.
b. Nov 13, 1947 in Washington, District of Columbia
Source: *WhoAm 90, 92, 94, 95, 96, 97; WhoEmL 89; WhoWest 87, 89, 92, 94*

Lovin' Spoonful
[John Boone; Joe Butler; John Sebastian; Zal Yanovsky]
American. Music Group
Hit songs include "Do You Believe in Magic?," 1965.
Source: *BiDAmM; BioIn 1, 9, 14; EncPR&S 74, 89; EncRk 88; EncRkSt; HarEnR 86; IlEncRk; NewGrDA 86; NewYTBS 80; OxCPMus; PenEncP; RkOn 78; RkWW 82; RolSEnR 83; WhoHol 92, A; WhoRock 81; WhoRocM 82*

Lovitz, Jon
American. Actor, Comedian
On NBC's "Saturday Night Live," 1985-90.
b. Jul 21, 1957 in Tarzana, California
Source: *ConTFT 7, 14; IntMPA 92, 94, 96; LegTOT; WhoAm 94, 95, 96, 97; WhoEnt 92; WhoHol 92; WorAlBi*

Low, David Alexander Cecil, Sir
English. Cartoonist
Created comic character, "Colonel Blimp" satirizing the pompous British ultraconservative, 1940s.
b. Apr 7, 1891 in Dunedin, New Zealand
d. Sep 11, 1963 in London, England
Source: *ConAu 89; CurBio 40, 63; DcBrBI; DcNaB 1961; GrBr; LngCTC; ObitT 1961; WhAm 4; WhDW; WhoGrA 62*

Low, George M(ichael)
American. Scientist
Leader of Apollo spacecraft program.
b. Jun 10, 1926 in Vienna, Austria
d. Jul 17, 1984 in Troy, New York
Source: *AmMWSc 73P, 79, 82; AnObit 1984; BioIn 8, 14; BlueB 76; ConAu 113; FacFETw; IntWW 74, 75, 76, 77, 78, 79, 80, 81, 82, 83; NewYTBS 84; WhAm 9; WhoAm 74, 76, 78, 80, 82, 84; WhoE 83; WhoEng 80, 88; WhoFrS 84; WhoGov 72, 75; WhoSSW 73; WhoTech 84*

Low, Juliette Gordon
American. Social Reformer
Founded Girl Guides in US, 1912; name changed to Girl Scouts, 1913.
b. Oct 31, 1860 in Savannah, Georgia
d. Jan 18, 1927 in Savannah, Georgia
Source: *BioAmW; BioIn 15, 16, 17; BioNews 74; DcAmB; GrLiveH; HerW, 84; InWom; LibW; NatCAB 24; NotAW; PeoHis; WebAB 74, 79; WhAm 4, HSA; WomChHR; WomFir*

Lowden, Frank O(rren)
American. Politician, Lawyer
Rep. governor of IL, 1917-21; sponsored agricultural reforms.
b. Jan 26, 1861 in Sunrise City, Minnesota
d. Mar 20, 1943 in Tucson, Arizona
Source: *BiDrAC; BiDrGov 1789; BiDrUSC 89; BioIn 4, 6; CurBio 43; DcAmB S3; NatCAB 10, 31; WebAB 74, 79; WebBD 83; WhAm 2*

Lowe, Chad
American. Actor
Played Jessie on TV series "Life Goes On"; brother of Rob.
b. Jan 15, 1968 in Dayton, Ohio
Source: *BioIn 14; ConTFT 7; IntMPA 92, 94, 96; LegTOT; WhoAm 94, 95; WhoHol 92*

Lowe, Edmund Dante
American. Actor
Played opposite Victor McLaglen in *Flagg and Quirt,* film comedies, 1920s.
b. Mar 3, 1890 in San Jose, California
d. Apr 21, 1971 in Woodland Hills, California
Source: *Film 1; FilmgC; MotPP; MovMk; NewYTBE 71; TwYS; WhoHol B; WhScrn 74, 77; WorAl*

Lowe, Edward
American. Entrepreneur
Invented "Kitty Litter," 1947.
b. Jul 10, 1920 in Cassopolis, Michigan
d. Oct 4, 1995 in Sarasota, Florida
Source: *Dun&B 88; News 90-2*

Lowe, Edwin S
American. Businessman
Marketed bingo into nat. pastime; founded E S Lowe, toy co. that made bingo, Yahtzee, chess, checkers games.
b. 1910, Poland
d. Feb 25, 1986 in New York, New York
Source: *BioIn 14; NewYTBS 85, 86*

Lowe, Jack (Warren)
[Whittemore and Lowe]
American. Pianist, Composer
With Arthur Whittemore, member of two-piano team popular, 1940s-60s; wrote orchestra, chamber works.
b. Dec 25, 1917 in Aurora, Colorado
d. Jun 2, 1996 in Boynton Beach, Florida
Source: *BioIn 2, 3, 4, 7; CurBio 54, 96N; WhoAm 74, 76, 78, 80, 82; WhoMus 72*

Lowe, Nick
[Little Village; Rockpile]
English. Singer, Musician, Producer
Contributed to British New Wave Movement, 1970's; hit single "Cruel to Be Kind," came from debut solo album *Pure Pop for Now People,* 1978.
b. Mar 25, 1949 in Suffolk, England
Source: *BioIn 12, 13, 15; ConMuA 80A; ConMus 6; EncPR&S 89; EncRk 88; EncRkSt; HarEnR 86; LegTOT; PenEncP; RkOn 85; RolSEnR 83; WhoEnt 92; WhoRock 81; WhoRocM 82; WhsNW 85*

Lowe, Rob(ert Hepler)
American. Actor
Part of "Brat Pack"; films include *Masquerade,* 1988; *St. Elmo's Fire,* 1984; involved in sex scandal at the Dem. Nat. Convention, 1988.
b. Mar 17, 1964 in Charlottesville, Virginia
Source: *BioIn 13, 14, 15, 16; CelR 90; ConTFT 6, 13; HalFC 88; IntMPA 86, 88, 92, 96; News 90; VarWW 85; WhoAm 92, 94, 95, 96, 97; WhoEnt 92; WhoHol 92; WorAlBi*

Lowell, Abbott Lawrence
American. University Administrator
Pres., Harvard U, 1909-33; wrote *Conflicts of Principle,* 1932; brother of Amy.
b. Dec 13, 1856 in Boston, Massachusetts
d. Jan 6, 1943 in Boston, Massachusetts
Source: *AmAu&B; AmPeW; ApCAB X; BenetAL 91; BiDAmEd; BiDInt; BioIn 1, 3, 5, 12; CurBio 43; DcAmAu; DcAmB S3; DcNAA; EncAB-A 2; EncAB-H 1974, 1996; HarEnUS; LinLib L, S; McGEWB; NatCAB 14, 31; ObitOF 79; OxCAmH; OxCAmL 65, 83, 95; OxCLaw; REnAL; WebAB 74, 79; WhAm 2*

Lowell, Amy
American. Poet, Critic
Dominating force in Imagist movement; most known poems "Patterns"; "Lilacs."
b. Feb 9, 1874 in Brookline, Massachusetts
d. May 12, 1925 in Brookline, Massachusetts
Source: *Alli SUP; AmAu&B; AmBi; AmLY; AmWomWr; AmWr; ApCAB X; ArtclWW 2; AtlBL; Benet 87; BenetAL 91; BibAL; BioAmW; BioIn 1, 3, 5, 6, 7, 8, 9, 10, 11, 12, 15, 17, 20; BlmGWL; CamGLE; CamHAL; CasWL; Chambr 3; ChhPo, S1, S3; CnDAL; CnE&AP; ConAmA; ConAmL; ConAu 104, 151; DcAmB; DcAmBC; DcLB 54, 140; DcLEL; DcNAA; EncAB-H 1974, 1996; EncPaPR 91; EncWL 2, 3; EvLB; FacFETw; FemiCLE; GayLesB; GoodHs; GrLiveH; GrWrEL P; InWom; LibW; LinLib L, S; LngCTC; MakMC; McGEWB; ModAL; ModAWWr; ModWoWr; NatCAB 19; NewGrDA 86; NotAW; OxCAmL 65, 83; OxCEng 67; PenBWP; PenC AM; PenNWW A; PeoHis; PoeCrit 13; RAdv 1, 14, 13-1; REn; REnAL; RfGAmL 87; SixAP; Str&VC; TwCA, SUP; TwCLC 1, 8; TwCWr; WebAB 74, 79; WebE&AL; WhAm 1; WhDW; WhLit; WomFir; WomWWA 14*

Lowell, Francis Cabot
American. Industrialist
Constructed first power loom in US; founded first cotton weaving mill, 1813; MA town named after him.
b. Apr 7, 1775 in Newburyport, Massachusetts
d. Aug 10, 1817 in Boston, Massachusetts
Source: *AmBi; ApCAB; BiDAmBL 83; BiInAmS; BioIn 2, 8, 10, 11, 15; DcAmB; Drake; EncAB-H 1974, 1996; InSci; McGEWB; NatCAB 7; NewCol 75; OxCAmH; TwCBDA; WebAB 74, 79; WhAm HS*

Lowell, James Russell
American. Editor, Diplomat
First editor of *Atlantic Monthly,* 1857-61; ambassador to Spain, Great Britian, 1877-85.
b. Feb 22, 1819 in Cambridge, Massachusetts
d. Aug 12, 1891 in Cambridge, Massachusetts
Source: *Alli, SUP; AmAu; AmAu&B; AmBi; AmCulL; AmOrN; AmWr S1; ApCAB; AtlBL; BbD; Benet 87, 96; BenetAL 91; BibAL; BiDAmM; BiD&SB; BiDMoPL; BiDTran; BioIn 1, 2, 3, 4, 5, 6, 7, 8, 9, 10, 11, 12, 14, 15, 16, 17, 19; CamGEL; CamGLE; CamHAL; CasWL; CelCen; Chambr 3; ChhPo, S1, S2, S3; CnDAL; CnE&AP; ColARen; CrtT 3, 4; CyAG; CyAL 2; CyEd; CyWA 58; DcAmAu; DcAmB; DcAmC; DcAmDH 80, 89; DcAmSR; DcBiPP; DcEnA, A; DcEnL; DcLB 1, 11, 64, 79; DcLEL; DcNAA; DcSpL; Dis&D; Drake; EncAB-H 1974, 1996; EncAHmr; EvLB; GrWrEL P; HarEnUS; LegTOT; LinLib L, S; McGEWB; MouLC 4; NatCAB 1, 2; NewGrDA 86; NinCLC 2; OxCAmH; OxCAmL 65, 83, 95; OxCEng 67, 85, 95; PenC AM; RAdv 1, 14, 13-1; REn; REnAL; RfGAmL 87, 94; Str&VC; TwCBDA; WebAB 74, 79; WebE&AL; WhAm HS; WorAl; WorAlBi*

Lowell, John
American. Continental Congressman, Judge
Held major judicial posts; father of Francis Cabot, grandfather of James Russell.
b. Jun 17, 1743 in Newburyport, Massachusetts
d. May 6, 1802 in Roxbury, Massachusetts
Source: *Alli; AmBi; ApCAB; BiDFedJ; BiDrAC; BiDrUSC 89; BioIn 8; CyAL 1; DcAmB; Drake; HarEnUS; NewCol 75; TwCBDA; WhAm HS; WhAmRev*

Lowell, Josephine Shaw
American. Social Reformer, Writer
Worked to better conditions for women, the destitute; her papers provided impetus for establishment of matrons in police stations, asylums for mentally ill women, many relief organizations.
b. Dec 16, 1843 in West Roxbury, Massachusetts

d. Oct 12, 1905 in New York, New York
Source: *AmBi; AmRef; AmSocL; ApCAB; BiDSocW; BioAmW; BioIn 3, 12, 15, 17, 19, 20; ContDcW 89; DcAmB; DcAmC; DcAmImH; HarEnUS; IntDcWB; InWom, SUP; LibW; McGEWB; NatCAB 8; NotAW; OxCAmH; PeoHis; TwCBDA; WhAm 1; WomFir*

Lowell, Percival
American. Astronomer
Established Lowell Observatory, Flagstaff, AZ, 1894.
b. Mar 13, 1855 in Boston, Massachusetts
d. Nov 13, 1916 in Flagstaff, Arizona
Source: *Alli SUP; AmAu&B; AmBi; ApCAB SUP, X; ArizL; AsBiEn; BiD&SB; BiESc; BiInAmS; BioIn 4, 8, 9, 12, 13, 14, 15, 17, 20, 21; CamDcSc; DcAmAu; DcAmB; DcNAA; DcScB; FacFETw; InSci; LarDcSc; LinLib L, S; NatCAB 8; OxCAmH; RAdv 14; REnAL; TwCBDA; WebAB 74, 79; WhAm 1; WhDW; WorAl; WorAlBi*

Lowell, Robert Trail Spence, Jr.
American. Poet, Dramatist
Won Pulitzers for verse volumes *Lord Weary's Castle,* 1947; *The Dolphin,* 1974.
b. Mar 1, 1917 in Boston, Massachusetts
d. Sep 12, 1977 in New York, New York
Source: *AmAu&B; AmWr; CasWL; CnDAL; CnE&AP; CnMWL; CnThe; ConAu 9R, 73; ConDr 73; ConLC 15; ConPo 75; CroCAP; McGEWB; RAdv 1; RComWL; WrDr 76*

Lowenfels, Walter
American. Author, Poet, Editor
Works include *To An Imaginary Daughter,* 1964; verse volume *American Voices,* 1959.
b. May 10, 1897 in New York, New York
d. Jul 7, 1976 in Tarrytown, New York
Source: *AmAu&B; AuBYP 2S, 3; BioIn 11, 12, 16; BlueB 76; ConAu 1R, 3NR, 65; ConPo 70, 75; DcLB 4; DrAP 75; IntAu&W 76; IntWWP 77; PenC AM; RAdv 1; WhAm 7; WhoAm 74, 76; WrDr 76*

Lowenstein, Allard Kenneth
American. Lawyer, Political Activist, Teacher
Chm., Americans for Democratic Action, 1970s; shot by mentally deranged former protege.
b. Jan 16, 1929 in Newark, New Jersey
d. Mar 14, 1980 in New York, New York
Source: *BiDrAC; BiDrUSC 89; BioIn 9, 11, 12; CurBio 71, 80; DcAmB S10; NewYTBE 72; PolProf J, NF; WhAm 7; WhoAm 74, 76, 78, 80; WhoAmJ 80; WhoAmP 73, 75, 77, 79, 81; WhoGov 75*

Lowery, Joseph E
American. Civil Rights Leader, Clergy
Co-founded SCLC; pres., 1977—.
b. Oct 6, 1924 in Huntsville, Alabama
Source: *BioIn 13; ConBlB 2; CurBio 82; InB&W 80, 85; NegAl 89; RelLAm 91; WhoAm 86, 90; WhoBlA 88, 92; WhoRel 77, 92; WhoSSW 91*

Lowery, Robert O
American. Government Official
Former fire commissioner, NYC; first black fire administrator in major city.
b. Apr 20, 1916 in Buffalo, New York
Source: *Ebony 1; InB&W 80; NegAl 76, 89; WhoBlA 88, 92; WhoE 74*

Lowes, John Livingston
American. Scholar, Educator
Wrote *The Road to Xanadu,* 1927.
b. Dec 20, 1867 in Decatur, Indiana
d. Aug 15, 1945 in North Scituate, Massachusetts
Source: *AmAu&B; BenetAL 91; BioIn 1, 4, 5; Chambr 3; ChhPo S1; CnDAL; DcAmB S3; DcLEL; EvLB; IndAu 1917; LngCTC; OxCAmL 65, 83, 95; REn; REnAL; TwCA, SUP; WhAm 2; WhNAA*

Lowinsky, Edward Elias
American. Educator
Specialist in Renaissance music; compiled three-volume *Medici Codex of 1518.*
b. Jan 12, 1908 in Stuttgart, Germany
d. Oct 11, 1985 in Chicago, Illinois
Source: *BlueB 76; ConAu 117; DrAS 74H, 78H; WhAm 9; WhoAm 74, 76, 78, 80; WhoAmJ 80; WhoWor 74, 76*

Lowndes, Marie Adelaide Belloc
[Philip Curtin]
English. Author
Wrote *The Lodger,* 1913, novel about Jack the Ripper; later adapted into movie by Alfred Hitchcock.
b. 1868
d. Nov 11, 1947 in Eversley, England
Source: *CathA 1930; ConAu 107; DcCathB; DcLEL; EncBrWW; EncMys; EvLB; NewCBEL; ObitOF 79; PenNWW B; REn; TwCA, SUP; TwCRGW*

Lowndes, Robert A(ugustine) W(ard)
"Doc"
American. Author, Editor
Edited science fiction mags since 1940s; used 50 pen names.
b. Sep 4, 1916 in Bridgeport, Connecticut
Source: *ConAu 113, 128; ConSFA; EncSF, 93; IntAu&W 76, 91, 93; NewEScF; ScF&FL 2; ScFSB; TwCSFW 81, 86, 91; WhoHr&F; WrDr 84, 86, 88, 90, 92, 94, 96*

Lowrey, Peanuts
[Harry Lee Lowrey]
American. Baseball Player, Baseball Coach
Outfielder, 1942-43, 1945-55; led NL in pinch hits, 1952, 1953.
b. Aug 27, 1918 in Culver City, California
d. Jul 2, 1986 in Inglewood, California
Source: *BioIn 15; WhoProB 73*

Lowry, Judith Ives
American. Actor
Played Mother Dexter on TV show "Phyllis."
b. Jul 27, 1890 in Morristown, New Jersey
d. Nov 29, 1976 in New York, New York
Source: *NewYTBS 76; ObitOF 79; WhoHol A; WhoThe 81N*

Lowry, Lawrence Stephen
English. Artist
Painter, lithographer, best known for industrial scenes.
b. Nov 1, 1887 in Manchester, England
d. Feb 23, 1976 in Glossop, England
Source: *BlueB 76; ClaDrA; ConArt 77; DcBrAr 2; DcSeaP; IntWW 76; NewYTBS 76; ObitOF 79; Who 74*

Lowry, Malcolm
[Clarence Malcolm Lowry]
English. Author, Poet
Wrote *Under the Volcano,* 1947, autobiographical novel.
b. Jul 28, 1909 in Liverpool, England
d. Jun 27, 1957 in Ripe, England
Source: *AtlBL; Benet 87; BenetAL 91; BioIn 1, 4, 5, 7, 8, 9, 10, 11, 13, 14, 15, 16, 17, 18, 19, 20, 21; BlmGEL; CamGEL; CamGLE; CanWr; CasWL; ChhPo S1; CnDBLB 7; ConAu 105, 131; ConNov 76; CreCan 1; CyWA 89; DcLB 15; DcLEL, 1940; DcNaB 1951; EncWL, 2, 3; FacFETw; GrWrEL N; IntLitE; LegTOT; LiExTwC; LngCEL; LngCTC; MacDCB 78; MajTwCW; ModBrL, S1, S2; NewC; NewCBEL; Novels; OxCCan; OxCCanL; OxCCan SUP; OxCEng 67, 85; PenC ENG; RAdv 1, 14; REn; REnAL; RfGEnL 91; TwCA SUP; TwCLC 6, 40; TwCWr; WebE&AL; WhAm 4; WhDW; WhoTwCL; WorAl; WorAlBi*

Lowry, Mike
[Michael Edward Lowry]
American. Politician
Dem. governor, WA, 1993—.
b. Mar 8, 1939 in Saint John, Washington
Source: *BiDrUSC 89; BioIn 19, 20; CngDr 79, 81, 83, 85, 87; PolsAm 84; WhoAm 80, 82, 84, 86, 88, 94, 95, 96, 97; WhoAmP 79, 81, 83, 85, 87, 89, 91, 93, 95; WhoWest 80, 82, 84, 87, 89, 92, 94, 96*

Loy, Myrna
[Myrna Williams]
American. Actor
Played Nora Charles in *The Thin Man* film series, 1930s-40s; won an Honorary Oscar, 1991.
b. Aug 2, 1905 in Helena, Montana
d. Dec 14, 1993 in New York, New York
Source: *AnObit 1993; BiDFilm, 81, 94; BioIn 2, 6, 7, 8, 9, 11, 12, 14, 15, 16;*

CelR, 90; CmMov; ConTFT 3, 12; CurBio 50, 94N; DcArts; EncAFC; Film 2; FilmEn; FilmgC; ForYSC; GangFlm; GoodHs; HalFC 80, 84, 88; IntDcF 1-3, 2-3; IntMPA 75, 76, 77, 78, 79, 80, 81, 82, 84, 86, 88, 92, 94; InWom, SUP; LegTOT; MGM; MotPP; MovMk; News 94, 94-2; NewYTBS 80, 93; OxCFilm; ThFT; TwYS; VarWW 85; WhAm 11; WhoAm 74, 76, 78, 80, 82, 84, 86, 88, 90, 92, 94; WhoAmW 74, 83, 89, 91, 93; WhoCom; WhoEnt 92; WhoHol 92, A; WorAl; WorAlBi; WorEFlm

Loyd, Sam(uel)
American. Inventor
Inventor of Chess problems and challenges; created Parcheesi board game.
b. Jan 31, 1841 in Philadelphia, Pennsylvania
d. Apr 10, 1911 in New York, New York
Source: *BioIn 13; DcAmB; DcNAA; GolEC; OxCChes 84*

Lu, Yu
Chinese. Poet
Wrote nature, patriotic verse; extremely prolific; 9,000 of his 20,000 poems are extant.
b. 1125 in Shan-Yin
d. 1210, China
Source: *BioIn 10; CasWL; DcOrL 1; IndCTCL; RAdv 13-2; WebBD 83*

Lualdi, Adriano
Italian. Composer, Conductor
Operas include *La Granceola,* 1930; often wrote own librettos.
b. Mar 22, 1887 in Larino, Italy
Source: *Baker 78, 84; NewEOp 71*

Lubachivsky, Myroslav Ivan, Cardinal
American. Religious Leader
Archbishop of Lwow, UK, since 1985; head of Ukrainian Roman Catholic Church.
b. 1914 in Dolina, Ukraine
Source: *BioIn 12; IntWW 89, 91, 93; NewYTBS 80; WhoRel 92; WhoWor 87, 89, 91, 95, 96, 97*

Lubalin, Herbert Frederick
American. Designer
Called one of the world's best graphic designers; devised avant-garde typeface; redesigned *Saturday Evening Post; Reader's Digest.*
b. Mar 17, 1918 in New York, New York
d. May 24, 1981 in New York, New York
Source: *ConAu 81; ConDes 84; NewYTBS 81; WhAm 7, 9; WhoAm 78, 80, 82, 84, 86; WhoGrA 82*

Lubbers, Ruud
[Rudolphus Franciscus Maria Lubbers]
Dutch. Political Leader
Prime minister of Netherlands, 1982-94.
b. May 7, 1939 in Rotterdam, Netherlands
Source: *BioIn 16; CurBio 88; IntWW 82, 83, 91; WhoWor 84, 87, 89, 91*

Lubbock, Francis Richard
American. Politician, Soldier
Governor of TX, 1861-63, mobilizing state in support of Confederacy; captured with Jefferson Davis, 1865.
b. Oct 16, 1815 in Beaufort, South Carolina
d. 1905 in Austin, Texas
Source: *ApCAB; BiDConf; BiDrGov 1789; BioIn 8, 9, 11; CivWDc; DcAmB; DcNAA; NatCAB 9; TwCBDA; WhAm 1; WhCiWar*

Lubbock, Percy
English. Critic
Wrote *The Craft of Fiction,* 1921.
b. Jun 4, 1879 in London, England
d. 1965
Source: *BioIn 4, 12, 19, 21; CamGLE; ChhPo S2; ConAu 85; ConLCrt 77, 82; DcLB 149; DcLEL; DcNaB 1961; EvLB; LngCTC; ModBrL; NewC; NewCBEL; ObitT 1961; OxCEng 67, 85, 95; PenC ENG; REn; TwCA, SUP; TwCWr*

Lubell, Samuel
American. Pollster, Journalist
Wrote syndicated column "The People Speak," 1958-68; book *The Future of American Politics,* 1952.
b. Nov 3, 1911 in Sosnowiec, Poland
d. Aug 16, 1987 in Los Angeles, California
Source: *AmAu&B; Au&Wr 71; BiDAmJo; BiDAmNC; BioIn 3, 4, 15, 16; ConAu 13R, 123; CurBio 56, 87, 87N; WhAm 9; WhoAm 74, 76, 78; WhoSSW 73; WhoWor 74; WhoWorJ 72, 78*

Lubic, Ruth Watson
American. Nurse
Director, Maternity Center Association, 1970-95; opened the MCA's Childbearing Center, staffed by midwives, 1975.
b. Jan 18, 1927 in Bristol, Pennsylvania
Source: *AmMWSc 82, 86, 89, 92, 95; BiDrAPH 79; CurBio 96; IntMed 80; WhoAm 78, 80, 82, 84, 86, 88, 90, 92, 94, 95, 96, 97; WhoAmW 79, 81, 85, 89, 91, 93, 95, 97; WhoE 89, 95; WhoMedH; WhoWor 80, 82*

Lubin, Charles W
American. Business Executive
Pioneered in frozen baked goods; created Sara Lee cheesecake, 1949, named after his daughter.
b. 1904 in Chicago, Illinois
d. Jul 15, 1988 in Chicago, Illinois
Source: *BioIn 6, 11*

Lubin, Germaine
French. Opera Singer
Leading dramatic soprano, Paris Opera Co., 1914-44; collaboration with the Germans ended her career.
b. Feb 1, 1890 in Paris, France
d. Mar 18, 1965 in Philadelphia, Pennsylvania
Source: *Baker 84; BioIn 2, 4, 6, 7, 12, 14, 15; CmOp; IntDcOp; InWom; MetOEnc; NewEOp 71; NewGrDM 80; OxDcOp; PenDiMP*

Lubitsch, Ernst
American. Director
Noted for sophisticated comedies of manners, inventive camera work; won special Oscar, 1937.
b. Jan 28, 1892 in Berlin, Germany
d. Nov 30, 1947 in Los Angeles, California
Source: *AmCulL; AmFD; Benet 87, 96; BiDFilm, 81, 94; BioIn 1, 8, 9, 11, 12, 13, 14, 15, 17, 19; CmMov; DcAmB S4; DcArts; DcFM; EncAFC; EncEurC; FacFETw; Film 2; FilmEn; FilmgC; HalFC 80, 84, 88; IlWWHD 1; IntDcF 1-2, 2-2; LegTOT; McGEWB; MiSFD 9N; MovMk; NotNAT B; ObitOF 79; OxCFilm; TwYS, A; WhAm 2; WhoHol B; WhScrn 74, 77, 83; WorAl; WorAlBi; WorEFlm; WorFDir 1*

Lubke, Heinrich
German. Political Leader
Christian Democratic party leader; pres. Federal Republic of Germany, 1959-69.
b. Oct 11, 1894 in Enkhausen, Germany
d. Apr 6, 1972 in Bonn, Germany (West)
Source: *BioIn 5, 8, 9; CurBio 60, 72, 72N; DcPol; NewYTBE 72*

Luboff, Norman
American. Composer, Conductor
Established Norman Luboff Choir, 1963; arranged music for TV, film.
b. Apr 14, 1917 in Chicago, Illinois
d. Sep 22, 1987 in Bynum, North Carolina
Source: *ASCAP 66, 80; Baker 92; BioIn 15; ConAmC 76, 82; NewAmDM; VarWW 85; WhAm 9; WhoAm 74, 76, 78, 80, 82, 84*

Luboshutz, Pierre
Musician, Composer, Pianist
With wife, formed popular piano duo, Luboshutz and Nemenoff, from 1937.
b. Jun 22, 1894 in Odessa, Russia
d. Apr 18, 1971 in Rockport, Maine
Source: *ASCAP 66, 80; Baker 78, 84; BiDAmM; NewYTBE 71*

Lubovitch, Lar
American. Dancer, Choreographer
Modernist; known for groupings in abstract shapes; creates dances for own co. since 1963; works include *Whirligogs, Concerto Six Twenty-Two.*
b. 1943? in Chicago, Illinois

Source: *BiDD; BioIn 9, 11, 14; CmpGMD; CnOxB; CurBio 92; WhoAm 86, 90; WhoEnt 92*

Lucan
[Marcus Annaeus Lucanus]
Roman. Poet, Author
Wrote epic *Pharsalia;* conspired against Nero.
b. Jun 3, 39 in Cordoba, Spain
d. Jun 30, 65 in Rome, Italy
Source: *AncWr; BbD; Benet 87, 96; BiD&SB; BioIn 10, 14; BlmGEL; CasWL; DcArts; DcBiPP; Grk&L; LinLib L; LngCEL; NewC; NewCBEL; OxCClL, 89; OxCEng 67, 85, 95; OxDcOp; PenC CL; RAdv 14, 13-2; RComWL; REn; RfGWoL 95*

Lucas, Craig
American. Dramatist
Won 1990 Obie for *Prelude to a Kiss,* 1988, movie released, 1991.
b. Apr 30, 1951 in Atlanta, Georgia
Source: *ConAmD; ConAu 137; ConDr 93; ConLC 64; ConTFT 10; CurBio 91; IntWW 91, 93; WhoAm 92, 94, 95, 96; WhoEnt 92; WrDr 96*

Lucas, George
American. Director
Films include *Star Wars,* 1977; *The Empire Strikes Back,* 1980; *Return of the Jedi,* 1983.
b. May 14, 1944 in Modesto, California
Source: *Au&Arts 1; BenetAL 91; BiDFilm 81, 94; BioIn 11, 12, 13, 14, 15, 16; BkPepl; CelR 90; ConAu 30NR, 77; ConLC 16; ConTFT 1, 4, 11; CurBio 78; DcArts; DcTwCCu 1; DcVicP 2; EncSF, 93; FacFETw; HalFC 88; IlWWHD 1A; IntDcF 1-2, 2-2; IntMPA 92, 94, 96; IntWW 82, 83, 89, 91, 93; LegTOT; LesBEnT 92; MiSFD 9; MovMk; NewEScF; NewYTBS 81; ScF&FL 92; ScFSB; SmATA 56; TwCSFW 91; VarWW 85; Who 92, 94; WhoAm 78, 80, 82, 84, 86; WhoAmL 96; WorAlBi; WorFDir 2; WrDr 80, 82, 84, 86*

Lucas, Jerry Ray
"Luke"
American. Basketball Player
Three-time all-star forward-center, 1963-74, mostly with Cincinnati; member gold medal-winning Olympic team, 1960; Hall of Fame, 1979; lectures on memory improvement.
b. Mar 30, 1940 in Middletown, Ohio
Source: *BiDAmSp BK; BioIn 14; ConAu 108; CurBio 72; NewYTBE 72; OfNBA 87; SmATA 33; WhoBbl 73*

Lucas, Jim Griffing
American. Journalist
War correspondent; won Pulitzer for Korean War coverage, 1954.
b. Jun 22, 1914 in Checotah, Oklahoma
d. Jun 21, 1970 in Washington, District of Columbia
Source: *ConAu 104; NewYTBE 70; ObitOF 79; WhAm 5; WhoSSW 73*

Lucas, John
American. Basketball Player, Basketball Coach
Guard, 1976-88; coach, San Antonio, 1992-94; Philadelphia, 1994—.
b. Oct 31, 1953 in Durham, North Carolina
Source: *BasBi; BioIn 12, 13; ConBlB 7; CurBio 95; WhoAfA 96; WhoBlA 77, 80, 85, 88, 90, 92, 94*

Lucas, Nick
"The Singing Troubadour"
American. Entertainer
Starred in vaudeville; hit song "Tiptoe Through the Tulips with Me," 1929.
b. Aug 22, 1897 in Newark, New Jersey
d. Jul 28, 1982 in Colorado Springs, Colorado
Source: *BioIn 10; CmpEPM; EncVaud; Film 2; OnThGG; What 4; WhoHol A*

Lucas, Phil
American. Producer
Creates realistic images of Native Americans in his films to combat stereotypes; films include *Nez Perce: Portrait of a People,* 1982.
b. Jan 15, 1942 in Phoenix, Arizona
Source: *BioIn 21; NotNaAm*

Lucas, Scott Wike
American. Government Official, Politician
Dem. senator from IL, 1939-50; Senate Majority Leader, 1949-50; Dem. party whip, 1943-49.
b. Feb 19, 1892 in Chandlerville, Illinois
d. Feb 22, 1968
Source: *BiDrAC; BiDrUSC 89; BioIn 1, 2, 8, 11; CurBio 47, 68; DcAmB S8; WhAm 4A; WhoAmP 73, 75, 77, 79, 81*

Lucca, Pauline
Austrian. Opera Singer
Celebrated soprano; toured US, 1870s; star of Vienna opera, 1870s-80s.
b. Apr 25, 1841 in Vienna, Austria
d. Feb 28, 1908 in Vienna, Austria
Source: *Baker 78, 84, 92; BioIn 3; CmOp; InWom; NewEOp 71; NewGrDM 80; NewGrDO; OxDcOp; PenDiMP*

Lucchese, Thomas
"Three-Finger Brown"
American. Criminal
Worked for "Lucky" Luciano as hired killer; headed Mafia family; never arrested after 1923.
b. 1903
d. 1967

Lucci, Susan
American. Actor
Plays Erica Kane on daytime soap opera "All My Children," 1970—; nominated 17 times between 1978-97 for Daytime Emmy Award for Best Actress.
b. Dec 23, 1946 in Scarsdale, New York
Source: *BioIn 13, 14, 15, 16; CelR 90; ConTFT 7; CurBio 89; InWom SUP; WhoAm 90, 94, 95, 96, 97; WhoAmW 95, 97; WhoEnt 92; WhoHol A; WhoTelC; WorAlBi*

Luce, Charles (Franklin)
American. Business Executive
Board chm., Consolidated Edison Co., NY, 1967-82.
b. Sep 29, 1917 in Platteville, Wisconsin
Source: *BioIn 5, 7, 8, 10, 11, 12, 13, 15; BlueB 76; CurBio 68; IntWW 83, 91; NewYTBS 74, 77; St&PR 84, 87, 91, 93; WhoAm 74, 76, 78, 80, 82, 84, 86, 88, 90, 92, 94, 95, 96, 97; WhoE 74, 75, 77, 83, 85, 86; WhoFI 74, 75, 77, 79, 81, 83; WhoGov 72; WorAl*

Luce, Clare Boothe
[Mrs. Henry Luce]
American. Author, Politician, Diplomat
One of most influential women in 20th c; congresswoman, 1943-47; ambassador to Italy, 1953-57; author of hit play *The Women,* 1936.
b. Mar 10, 1903 in New York, New York
d. Oct 9, 1987 in Washington, District of Columbia
Source: *AmAu&B; AmCath 80; AmPolLe; AmPolW 80; AmWomD; AmWomM; AmWomWr; AnObit 1987; ArtclWW 2; Au&Wr 71; Benet 87, 96; BenetAL 91; BiDConC; BiDrAC; BiDrUSC 89; BiE&WWA; BioAmW; BioIn 14, 15, 16, 17, 19, 20, 21; CathA 1930; CelR; ConAu 45, 123; ConNews 88-1; CurBio 42, 53, 87, 87N; DcAmC; DcArts; EncAB-H 1996; EncCW; EncWB; EncWHA; FacFETw; GoodHs; GrLiveH; IntWW 81; IntYB 78, 79, 80, 81, 82; InWom, SUP; JrnUS; LibW; LinLib L, S; McGEWD 72; ModWD; NewYTBS 87, 88; NotNAT, A; NotWoAT; OxCAmL 65, 95; OxCWoWr 95; PolProf E, T; REn; REnAL; TwCA SUP; WebAB 74, 79; WhAm 9; WhE&EA; Who 85; WhoAm 82; WomFir; WomWMM; WorAl; WorAlBi; WrDr 80, 82, 84, 86*

Luce, Henry Robinson
American. Editor, Publisher
Founder, editor-in-chief, *Time,* 1923-64; *Fortune,* 1930-64; *Life,* 1930-64; *Sports Illustrated,* 1954-64.
b. Apr 3, 1898 in Shantung
d. Feb 28, 1967 in Phoenix, Arizona
Source: *ABCMeAm; AmAu&B; AmSocL; BiDAmBL 83; BiDAmJo; BioIn 1, 2, 3, 5, 6, 7, 8, 9, 10, 11, 12, 13, 14, 16, 17, 18, 19, 20; ColdWar 2; ConAu 89, 104; CurBio 41, 61, 67; DcAmB S8; DcAmSR; EncAB-H 1974, 1996; EncTwCJ; JrnUS; McGEWB; NatCAB 62; REn; REnAL; WebAB 74, 79; WhAm 4; WorAl*

Lucey, Patrick Joseph
American. Politician
Dem. governor, WI, 1971-79; ambassador to Mexico, 1977-80.
b. Mar 21, 1918 in La Crosse, Wisconsin
Source: *AmCath 80; BioIn 10, 12, 16; IntWW 74, 75, 76, 77, 78, 79, 80, 81, 82,*

83, 89, 91; NewYTBS 80; WhoAm 74, 76, 78, 80, 82; WhoAmP 73, 75, 77, 79, 81, 83, 85, 87, 89, 91, 93, 95; WhoGov 72, 75, 77; WhoMW 74, 76, 78; WhoWor 78

Lucian
Greek. Author
Wrote *Dialogues of the Gods; Dialogues of the Dead.*
b. 125? in Samosato, Syria
d. 200?, Egypt
Source: *AtlBL; BbD; BiD&SB; CasWL; CyWA 58; DcArts; EncSF; Grk&L; NewC; OxCEng 67; PenC CL; RComWL; REn; WorAl*

Luciano, Lucky
[Charles Luciano; Salvatore Luciano]
American. Criminal
Established national crime syndicate, 1930s; deported, 1946.
b. Nov 24, 1897 in Palermo, Sicily, Italy
d. Jan 26, 1962 in Naples, Italy
Source: *BioIn 1, 2, 3, 6, 7, 9, 10, 11, 16, 20; CopCroC; DcAmB S7; DrInf; EncACr; FacFETw*

Luciano, Ron(ald Michael)
American. Baseball Umpire
Pro football player, 1959-61; AL umpire, 1969-79; wrote *The Umpire Strikes Back,* 1982.
b. Jun 28, 1937 in Binghamton, New York
d. Jan 18, 1995 in Endicott, New York
Source: *Ballpl 90; BioIn 10, 11, 12, 13, 15; WhoAm 80, 82*

Lucid, Shannon
American. Astronaut
Spent 188 days aboard the Russian space station Mir, 1996; awarded the Space Medal of Honor, 1996.
b. 1943, China
Source: *News 97-1; WhoSpc*

Lucile
[Lady Duff-Gordon]
English. Fashion Designer
Introduced fashion parades to England; first designer with an international business; sister of novelist Elinor Glyn.
b. 1864, England
d. 1935
Source: *WorFshn*

Lucilius, Gaius
Roman. Poet
Considered founder of Latin satire; only fragments of work survive.
b. 180BC in Campania, Campania
d. 102?BC in Neapolis, Italy
Source: *BiD&SB; CasWL; NewC; NewCol 75; OxCClL, 89; PenC CL; WebBD 83*

Lucioni, Luigi
American. Artist
Noted for portraits, Vermont landscapes.
b. Nov 4, 1900 in Malnate, Italy
d. Jul 22, 1988 in New York, New York
Source: *BioIn 1, 2, 9, 16; CurBio 43, 88N; McGDA; NewYTBS 88; WhAm 9; WhAmArt 85; WhoAm 74, 76, 78, 80, 82, 84, 86, 88; WhoAmA 73, 76, 78, 80, 82, 84, 86*

Luckenbach, Edgar Frederick, Jr.
American. Shipping Executive
Chm., Luckenbach Steamship Co., Inc., 1951-74.
b. May 17, 1925 in New York, New York
d. Aug 9, 1974 in New York, New York
Source: *BiDAmBL 83; BioIn 9, 12; NatCAB 58; WhAm 6; WhoAm 74; WhoFI 74*

Luckman, Charles
American. Architect
Major projects included Madison Square Garden; Manned Space Craft Center, Houston; LA Int'l Airport.
b. May 16, 1909 in Kansas City, Missouri
Source: *AmArch 70; BioIn 1, 2, 3, 4, 5, 8, 10, 11, 13, 16; CurBio 47; IntYB 78, 79, 80, 81, 82; PolProf T; St&PR 91, 93, 96, 97; WhoAm 74, 76, 78, 80, 82, 84, 86, 88, 90, 92, 94, 95, 96, 97; WhoFI 74; WhoWest 96; WhoWor 74*

Luckman, Sid(ney)
American. Football Player
Five-time all-pro quarterback, Chicago, 1939-50; had great success in T formation; MVP, 1943; Hall of Fame.
b. Nov 21, 1916 in New York, New York
Source: *BiDAmSp FB; BioIn 1, 2, 3, 4, 5, 6, 7, 8, 9, 10, 17; LegTOT; St&PR 75; WhoFtbl 74; WhoSpor; WorAl; WorAlBi*

Luckner, Felix von, Count
"The Sea Devil"
German. Naval Officer
Exploits destroyed $25 million worth of allied shipping, WW I; Lowell Thomas wrote biography, 1927.
b. Jun 9, 1881 in Dresden, Germany
d. Apr 13, 1966 in Malmo, Sweden
Source: *NewCol 75; ObitOF 79; ObitT 1961; OxCShps*

Lucretius
[Titus Lucretius Carus]
Roman. Poet, Philosopher
Wrote six-books, unfinished didactic poem *De rerum natura* based on Epicurean doctrine.
b. 99BC
d. 55BC
Source: *AtlBL; BiESc; DcArts; DcBiPP; Dis&D; EncUnb; GrFLW; Grk&L; InSci; LinLib L, S; LuthC 75; NewC; NewCBEL; OxCEng 67, 95; PenC CL; RAdv 14, 13-2, 13-4; RComWL; REn; RfGWoL 95; WhDW; WrPh P*

Lucullus, Lucius Licinius
[Lucius Licinius Lucullus Ponticus]
Roman. Army Officer
Served in the East under Sulla; noted for banquets; term Lucullan derived from his extravagant living.
b. 110BC
d. 57BC
Source: *DcBiPP; LinLib S; NewC; NewCol 75; REn; WebBD 83*

Ludd, Ned
"King Ludd"
English. Revolutionary
Probably legendary figure; British laborers who destroyed labor-saving machines called "Luddites," 1811-16.
Source: *NewCol 75*

Ludden, Allen Ellsworth
American. TV Personality, Producer
Hosted game show "Password," 1961-67; married to Betty White.
b. Oct 5, 1918 in Mineral Point, Wisconsin
d. Jun 9, 1981 in Los Angeles, California
Source: *AnObit 1981; BioIn 12, 13; ConAu 104; NewYTBS 81; NewYTET; WhAm 7; WhoAm 80*

Luden, William H
American. Candy Manufacturer
Added menthol-flavored cough drops to candy line, 1886.
b. 1859
d. May 8, 1949 in Atlantic City, New Jersey
Source: *ApCAB X; BioIn 1; Entr; ObitOF 79*

Ludendorff, Erich Friedrich Wilhelm
German. Army Officer, Politician, Author
With Hindenburg headed German WW I war effort; later deserted Hitler; wrote books on the war.
b. Apr 9, 1865 in Kruszewnia, Prussia
d. Dec 20, 1937 in Munich, Germany
Source: *McGEWB; NewCol 75; OxCGer 76; REn; WhDW; WhoMilH 76; WorAl*

Ludikar, Pavel
Czech. Opera Singer
Bass-baritone who sang role of Figaro more than 100 times in US.
b. Mar 3, 1882 in Prague, Bohemia
d. 1970
Source: *Baker 78, 84, 92; BioIn 8; CmOp; NewEOp 71; NewGrDO*

Ludington, Sybil
[Mrs. Edward Ogden]
American. Historical Figure
Warned countryside of attack on Danbury, CT, 1777.
b. Apr 5, 1761 in Fredericksburg, New York
d. Feb 26, 1839 in Unadilla, New York
Source: *AmRev; BioIn 2, 4, 5, 10, 19; GoodHs; InWom, SUP; LibW; WebAB 74; WebAMB; WhAmRev*

Ludlam, Charles
American. Dramatist, Actor, Producer
Known for offbeat, classically comic theater co., begun, 1960; played title role in his version of *Camille,* 1973; won many Obies.
b. Apr 12, 1943 in Floral Park, New York
d. May 28, 1987 in New York, New York
Source: *AnObit 1987; BioIn 13; CamGWoT; ConAmD; ConAu 122; ConDr 77, 82, 93; ConLC 46, 50; ConTFT 3, 5; CurBio 86, 87, 87N; GayLesB; IntDcT 2; McGEWD 84; NatPD 81; NewYTBS 86, 87; NotNAT; TheaDir; WhAm 9; WhoAm 84; WhoThe 77, 81; WrDr 82*

Ludlow, Fitz Hugh
American. Author
Best known for *The Hasheesh Eater,* 1857, which was based on his own experiences.
b. Sep 11, 1836 in New York, New York
d. Sep 12, 1870 in Geneva, Switzerland
Source: *AmBi; BenetAL 91; CmCal; Dis&D; NatCAB 13; OxCAmH; OxCAmL 95; TwCBDA; WhAm HS*

Ludlum, Robert
American. Author, Actor, Producer
Wrote thrillers *The Gemini Contenders,* 1976; *The Aquitaine Progression,* 1983.
b. May 25, 1927 in New York, New York
Source: *Au&Arts 10; BestSel 89-1; BiE&WWA; BioIn 11, 12, 13, 14, 17; CelR 90; ConAu 25NR, 33R, 41NR; ConLC 22, 43; ConPopW; CrtSuMy; CurBio 82; DcLB Y82B; DcLP 87A; IntAu&W 76, 91, 93; IntWW 89, 91, 93; LegTOT; MajTwCW; NotNAT; Novels; SpyFic; TwCCr&M 80, 85, 91; WhoAm 78, 80, 82, 84, 86, 88, 90, 92, 94, 95, 96, 97; WhoE 75; WhoUSWr 88; WhoWrEP 89, 92, 95; WorAl; WorAlBi; WorAu 1980; WrDr 76, 80, 82, 84, 86, 88, 90, 92, 94, 96*

Ludwig, Christa
German. Opera Singer
Star mezzo-soprano, lieder singer; with NYC Met. Opera, 1959-93.
b. Mar 16, 1924 in Berlin, Germany
Source: *Baker 84, 92; BioIn 13; BlueB 76; CurBio 71; IntWW 74, 83, 91; IntWWM 90; InWom SUP; MetOEnc; NewAmDM; NewEOp 71; NewGrDM 80; NewYTBE 71; OxDcOp; PenDiMP; Who 74, 92; WhoAm 84, 88, 90; WhoEnt 92; WhoWor 84, 89, 91; WorAl; WorAlBi*

Ludwig, Daniel Keith
American. Business Executive, Financier
Self-made shipping tycoon; was one of America's wealthiest men; owned Nat. Bulk Carriers.
b. Jun 24, 1897 in South Haven, Michigan
d. Aug 27, 1992 in New York, New York
Source: *AnObit 1992; BiDAmBL 83; BioIn 4, 6, 9, 10, 11, 12, 13, 15, 16; BioNews 74; BusPN; CurBio 79, 92N; EncWB; NewYTBS 76; WhoAm 84*

Ludwig, Emil
[Emil Ludwig Cohn]
German. Author, Historian
Wrote *The Nile,* 1935; numerous biographies include *Napoleon,* 1924.
b. Jan 25, 1881 in Breslau, Germany
d. Sep 17, 1948 in Ascona, Switzerland
Source: *BiGAW; BioIn 1, 2, 4, 14; EncTR, 91; EvEuW; LiExTwC; LinLib L, S; LngCTC; NewCol 75; NotNAT B; ObitOF 79; OxCGer 76, 86; TwCA, SUP; WhAm 2; WhE&EA; WhLit; WhoLA*

Ludwig, Leopold
Austrian. Conductor
With Berlin orchestra, 1943-71; guest conductor, San Francisco, 1958-68.
b. Jan 12, 1908 in Witfowitz, Austria
d. 1979 in Luneberg, Germany (West)
Source: *Baker 78, 84, 92; BioIn 3, 9, 11, 12; CmOp; MetOEnc; MusSN; NewEOp 71; NewGrDM 80; NewGrDO; WhoOp 76*

Ludwig, Otto
German. Author
Early realist; wrote tragedy, *Der Erbforster,* 1850; coined term "poetic realism."
b. Feb 11, 1813 in Eisfield, Germany
d. Feb 25, 1865 in Dresden, Germany
Source: *Benet 87, 96; BiD&SB; BioIn 7, 19; CamGWoT; CasWL; CnThe; DcLB 129; Dis&D; EncWT; EuAu; EvEuW; LinLib L; McGEWD 72, 84; NinCLC 4; NotNAT B; OxCGer 76, 86; OxCThe 67, 83; PenC EUR; REn; REnWD*

Ludwig II
[Louis II]
"Mad King Ludwig"
Bavarian. Ruler, Eccentric
Patron of Wagner; built tourist-attraction castle; declared insane, committed suicide.
b. Aug 25, 1845 in Nymphenburg, Bavaria
d. Jun 13, 1886 in Lake Starnberg, Bavaria
Source: *Baker 84; DcNiCA; NewCol 75; OxCGer 76*

Luedtke, Kurt (Mamre)
American. Screenwriter
Wrote screenplays *Absence of Malice,* 1981; *Out of Africa,* 1985, won Oscar.
b. Sep 28, 1939 in Grand Rapids, Michigan
Source: *ConAu 109, 111; ConTFT 5; IntMPA 92; WhoAm 76, 78*

Luening, Otto
American. Composer
Known for pioneer work in taped electronic music solos with orchestra.
b. Jun 15, 1900 in Milwaukee, Wisconsin
d. Sep 2, 1996 in New York, New York
Source: *Baker 78, 84; BiDAmM; BioIn 1, 12, 13, 14, 15, 16; BriBkM 80; ConAmC 76, 82; ConAu 102, 153; ConCom 92; CpmDNM 78, 79, 80, 82; DcArts; DcCM; DcTwCCu 1; IntWWM 77, 80, 85, 90; NewAmDM; NewGrDA 86; NewGrDM 80; NewYTBS 80; OxCMus; WhoAm 74, 76, 78, 80, 82, 84, 86, 88, 90, 92, 94, 95, 96, 97; WhoAmM 83; WhoEnt 92; WhoWor 74, 80, 82*

Luft, Lorna
[Mrs. Colin Freeman]
American. Singer
Daughter of Judy Garland and Sid Luft; half-sister of Liza Minnelli; films include *Where the Boys Are '84,* 1984.
b. Nov 21, 1952 in Los Angeles, California
Source: *BioIn 9, 10, 12, 13, 15; BioNews 74; ConTFT 9; IntMPA 94, 96; LegTOT; NewYTBE 72; VarWW 85; WhoHol 92*

Lugar, Richard Green
American. Politician
Rep. senator from IN, 1977—.
b. Apr 4, 1932 in Indianapolis, Indiana
Source: *AlmAP 92; AmMWSc 92; BiDrUSC 89; BioIn 8, 9, 10, 11, 12, 14, 15, 16; BlueB 76; CelR 90; CngDr 87, 89; CurBio 77; DcAmDH 89; IntWW 77, 78, 79, 80, 81, 82, 83, 89, 91, 93; NewYTBS 78, 90; PolProf NF; PolsAm 84; WhoAm 74, 76, 78, 80, 82, 84, 86, 88, 90, 92, 94, 95, 96, 97; WhoAmP 73, 75, 77, 79, 81, 83, 85, 87, 89, 91, 93, 95; WhoGov 72, 75, 77; WhoMW 74, 76, 78, 80, 82, 84, 86, 88, 90, 92, 93, 96; WhoSSW 80, 95; WhoWor 74, 80, 82, 84, 87, 89, 91; WorAlBi*

Lugosi, Bela
[Bela Ferenc Blasko]
American. Actor
Master of horror films, 1930s-40s; noted for *Dracula,* 1930.
b. Oct 20, 1882 in Lugos, Hungary
d. Sep 16, 1956 in Los Angeles, California
Source: *BiDFilm 94; BioIn 12, 14, 15, 16, 17, 20; CmMov; DcAmB S6; DcArts; FacFETw; Film 1, 2; FilmEn; FilmgC; ForYSC; HalFC 80, 84, 88; IntDcF 1-3, 2-3; LegTOT; MotPP; MovMk; ObitOF 79; OxCFilm; PenEncH; TwYS; WebAB 74; WhoHol B; WhoHrs 80; WhScrn 74, 77, 83; WorAlBi; WorEFlm*

Luhan, Mabel (Ganson) Dodge
American. Author
Wrote *Lorenzo in Taos,* 1932, which is an account of her relationship with D H Lawrence.
b. Feb 26, 1879 in Buffalo, New York
d. Aug 13, 1962 in Taos, New Mexico

Source: *AmAu&B; AmWomWr; BioIn 14, 15, 17, 21; CnDAL; ConAmA; CurBio 40, 62; InWom, SUP; LibW; LngCTC; OxCAmL 65; PenC AM; REn; REnAL; TwCA, SUP; WhAm 4; WhNAA*

Luini, Bernardino
Italian. Artist
Religious painter; member, Lombard school; popular with the Victorians.
b. 1480 in Luino, Italy
d. 1532
Source: *DcBiPP; DcCathB; McGDA; NewCol 75; OxCArt*

Luisetti, Hank
[Angelo Enrico Luisetti]
American. Basketball Player
Three-time All-America forward, Stanford U., 1936-38; revolutionized game with one-handed shot; Hall of Fame.
b. Jun 16, 1916 in San Francisco, California
Source: *AmDec 1930; BiDAmSp BK; BioIn 6, 9, 10, 12, 15, 17, 21; CmCal; NewYTBS 86; WhoBbl 73; WhoSpor*

Lujack, John(ny)
American. Football Player
Two-time All-America quarterback, won Heisman Trophy, 1947; with Chicago, NFL, 1948-51; Hall of Fame.
b. Jan 4, 1925 in Connellsville, Pennsylvania
Source: *BiDAmSp FB; BioIn 14; CurBio 47; WhoFtbl 74; WhoSpor*

Lujan, Manuel, Jr.
American. Government Official
First Hispanic elected to the House of Representatives 1968, served 20 yrs; Secretary of the Interior, 1989-93.
b. May 12, 1928 in San Ildefonso, New Mexico
Source: *AlmAP 78, 80, 82, 84, 88; AmCath 80; BiDrAC; BiDrUSC 89; BiDrUSE 89; BioIn 16; CngDr 74, 77, 79, 81, 83, 85, 87, 89, 91; CurBio 89; IntWW 89, 91, 93; MexAmB; PolsAm 84; WhoAm 74, 76, 78, 80, 82, 84, 86, 88, 90, 92, 94, 95, 96, 97; WhoAmP 73, 75, 77, 79, 81, 83, 85, 87, 89, 91, 93, 95; WhoE 91, 93; WhoGov 72, 75, 77; WhoHisp 91, 92, 94; WhoWest 76, 78, 80, 84, 87; WhoWor 91, 93, 95*

Lukacs, Gyorgy
Hungarian. Philosopher
Marxist; influenced European Communist thought in the first half of the 20th century.
b. Apr 13, 1885 in Budapest, Hungary
d. Jun 4, 1971 in Budapest, Hungary
Source: *Benet 87, 96; BioIn 4, 5, 6, 7, 9, 10, 11, 12, 13, 14, 15, 17, 18; CasWL; ClDMEL 80; ColdWar 1, 2; ConAu 29R, 101; EncWL 2, 3; EuWr 10; LegTOT; LiExTwC; MajTwCW; McGEWB; NewYTBE 71; ObitOF 79; ObitT 1971; OxCGer 76; PenC EUR; RAdv 14, 13-2; WhDW; WorAu 1950*

Lukas, J(ay) Anthony
American. Author, Lecturer
Won Pulitzer for local reporting, 1968; contributing editor for leading periodicals, 1958-76.
b. Apr 25, 1933 in New York, New York
d. Jun 5, 1997 in New York, New York
Source: *AmAu&B; AuBYP 3; BioIn 13, 14, 15; ConAu 2NR, 19NR, 49; CurBio 87; IntAu&W 91; JrnUS; MajTwCW; WhoAm 86, 90; WhoE 91; WrDr 92, 94, 96*

Lukas, Paul
American. Actor
Won Oscar for *Watch on the Rhine,* 1943.
b. May 26, 1894 in Budapest, Austria-Hungary
d. Aug 15, 1971 in Tangiers, Morocco
Source: *BiE&WWA; CurBio 42, 71; FilmEn; ForYSC; GangFlm; HolP 30; MotPP; MovMk; NewYTBE 71; NotNAT B; OlFamFa; OxCFilm; TwYS; WhAm 5; WhScrn 77; WorAl; WorAlBi; WorEFlm*

Luke, Saint
Biblical Figure
Assumed author of third gospel, Acts; physician.
b. fl. 1st cent.
Source: *Alli; AmPeW; Benet 87, 96; BioIn 1, 2, 3, 4, 5, 6, 7, 8, 9, 11; DcCathB; Dis&D; EncEarC; Film 1; McGDA; McGEWB; NewC; NewCol 75; OxDcByz; REn; WebBD 83; WhDW; WhoRocM 82*

Luke, Keye
American. Actor
Appeared in 150 movies, 13 as Charlie Chan's "Number One Son."
b. Jun 18, 1904 in Guangzhou, China
d. Jan 12, 1991 in Whittier, California
Source: *AnObit 1991; BioIn 17, 18; ConTFT 8; EncAFC; FilmEn; FilmgC; HalFC 80, 84, 88; HolCA; IntMPA 77, 78, 79, 80, 81, 82, 84, 86, 88; LegTOT; MGM; MovMk; NewYTBS 91; VarWW 85; Vers A; WhoHol A; WorAl; WorAlBi*

Lukeman, Henry A
American. Sculptor
Did memorials, equestrian statues; noted for large relief of Robert E Lee on Atlanta's Stone Mountain.
b. Jan 28, 1871 in Richmond, Virginia
d. Apr 3, 1935, Norway
Source: *AmBi; DcAmB S1; NatCAB 32; WhAm 1*

Luks, George Benjamin
American. Artist, Cartoonist
Member, Ashcan school of realistic painting; created comic strip "Hogan's Alley" featuring the Yellow Kid.
b. Aug 13, 1867 in Williamsport, Pennsylvania
d. Oct 29, 1933 in New York, New York
Source: *AmBi; BioIn 1, 2, 4, 6, 12; BriEAA; DcAmB S1; McGDA; McGEWB; OxCAmL 65; OxCTwCA; REnAL; WhAm 1; WorECar*

Lully, Jean-Baptiste
[Giovanni Battista Lulli]
French. Composer
Considered father of National French Opera; head of Paris Opera, 1672-87; wrote ballets, opera *Alceste,* 1674.
b. Nov 28, 1632 in Florence, Italy
d. Mar 22, 1687 in Paris, France
Source: *AtlBL; Baker 78, 84, 92; Benet 87, 96; BriBkM 80; CamGWoT; CmpBCM; DancEn 78; DcCom 77; GrComp; IntDcB; IntDcOp; LegTOT; McGEWB; MetOEnc; MusMk; NewAmDM; NewC; NewCol 75; NewEOp 71; NewGrDM 80; NewGrDO; NewOxM; OxCFr; OxCMus; OxDcOp; PenDiMP A; REn; WhDW; WorAl; WorAlBi*

Lulu
[Marie McDonald McLaughlin]
Scottish. Singer, Actor
Best known for 1967 hit single "To Sir with Love," introduced in movie of same name.
b. Nov 3, 1948 in Glasgow, Scotland
Source: *EncRk 88; EncRkSt; FilmgC; HalFC 80, 84, 88; HarEnR 86; LegTOT; OxCPMus; PenEncP; PenNWW B; RkOn 78; RolSEnR 83; WhoAm 74; WhoHol 92, A; WhoRock 81*

Lumet, Sidney
American. Director
Films include *Network,* 1976, *The Verdict,* 1982.
b. Jun 25, 1924 in Philadelphia, Pennsylvania
Source: *AmFD; BiDFilm, 81, 94; BiE&WWA; BioIn 8, 10, 11, 12, 13, 14, 16; CelR, 90; ConTFT 1, 6, 15; CurBio 67; DcArts; DcFM; FacFETw; FilmEn; FilmgC; HalFC 80, 84, 88; IlWWHD 1; IntDcF 1-2, 2-2; IntMPA 75, 76, 77, 78, 79, 80, 81, 82, 84, 86, 88, 92, 94, 96; IntWW 74, 75, 76, 77, 78, 79, 80, 81, 82, 83, 89, 91, 93; ItaFilm; LegTOT; LesBEnT, 92; MiSFD 9; MovMk; NewYTET; NotNAT; OxCFilm; VarWW 85; Who 82, 83, 85, 88, 90, 92, 94; WhoAm 74, 76, 78, 80, 82, 84, 86, 88, 90, 92, 94, 95, 96, 97; WhoEnt 92; WhoHol 92, A; WhoWor 74, 78; WorAl; WorAlBi; WorEFlm; WorFDir 2*

Lumiere, Auguste Marie Louis
French. Scientist, Inventor, Photographer
Invented autochrome, first popular color photographic process, 1904; produced first newsreel, 1895.
b. Oct 19, 1862 in Besancon, France
d. Apr 10, 1954 in Lyons, France
Source: *BiDFilm; DcFM; Film 1; FilmEn; MacBEP; NotNAT B; OxCFilm; OxCFr; WhDW; WorEFlm*

Lumiere, Louis Jean
French. Scientist, Inventor, Photographer
Devised cinematographe, a motion picture camera, projector, 1895; produced first newsreel, 1895.
b. Oct 5, 1864 in Besancon, France
d. Jun 6, 1948 in Bandol, France
Source: *BiDFilm; DcArts; DcFM; FilmEn; FilmgC; InSci; MacBEP; NotNAT B; ObitOF 79; OxCFilm; OxCFr; TwYS; WorEFlm*

Lumley, Harry
"Apple Cheeks"
Canadian. Hockey Player
Goalie, 1943-60, with five NHL teams; won Vezina Trophy, 1954; Hall of Fame, 1980.
b. Nov 11, 1926 in Owen Sound, Ontario, Canada
Source: *HocEn; WhoHcky 73; WhoSpor*

Lummis, Charles Fletcher
American. Author, Explorer
Writings concern American southwest: *The Spanish Pioneers,* 1893.
b. 1859 in Lynn, Massachusetts
d. Nov 25, 1928
Source: *AmAu&B; AmBi; AmLY; ApCAB SUP; BiD&SB; BioIn 1, 2, 4, 5, 8, 9, 10, 12, 13, 16, 17, 20; ChhPo; CmCal; DcAmAu; DcAmB; DcAmLiB; DcNAA; HarEnUS; LinLib L, S; NatCAB 11, 42; NewGrDA 86; OhA&B; OxCAmL 65, 83, 95; REnAW; TwCBDA; WhAm 1; WhNAA; WhNaAH*

Lumumba, Patrice
Congolese. Political Leader
First prime minister of Republic of Congo, June, 1960; deposed, Sept. 1960; believed killed by Katanga Province tribesmen.
b. Jul 2, 1925 in Oualua, Belgian Congo
d. Jan 18, 1961 in Elisabethville, Zaire
Source: *BioIn 14, 18, 20, 21; ColdWar 1, 2; CurBio 60, 61; DcAfHiB 86; DcPol; EncCW; FacFETw; HisWorL; InB&W 80; LinLib S; McGEWB; ObitOF 79; ObitT 1961, 1971; WorAl; WorAlBi*

Lunardi, Vincenzo
Italian. Balloonist
First aerial traveler in England, 1784; ascent viewed by 200,000 spectators.
b. Jan 11, 1759 in Lucca, Italy
d. Jul 31, 1806 in Lisbon, Portugal
Source: *BioIn 5, 7; DcNaB; InSci*

Lunceford, Jimmy
[James Melvin Lunceford]
American. Jazz Musician, Actor
Black band leader of 1930s; members included Cy Oliver; made film *Blues in the Night,* 1941.
b. Jun 6, 1902 in Fulton, Mississippi
d. Jul 13, 1947 in Seaside, Oregon
Source: *AfrAmAl 6; ASCAP 66, 80; Baker 84; BiDAfM; BiDJaz; BioIn 1, 9, 12; BlkCond; DcAmB S4; InB&W 80, 85; NegAl 76, 83, 89; NewGrDM 80; WhoJazz 72; WhScrn 77, 83*

Lund, Art(hur Earl, Jr.)
American. Actor
Appeared on stage in *Most Happy Fella;* films include *The Molly Maguires,* 1970.
b. Apr 1, 1920 in Salt Lake City, Utah
d. Jun 6, 1990 in Holliday, Utah
Source: *BiE&WWA; BioIn 16; NewYTBS 90; NotNAT; PenEncP; VarWW 85; WhoHol A; WhoThe 72, 77, 81*

Lund, John
American. Actor
Broadway lead role in *The Hasty Heart,* 1945; films include *To Each His Own,* 1946 and string of westerns in the 1950s.
b. 1913 in Rochester, New York
d. May 10, 1992 in Los Angeles, California
Source: *BioIn 2, 10, 17, 18; EncAFC; FilmEn; FilmgC; ForYSC; HalFC 80, 84, 88; HolP 40; MotPP; MovMk; NewYTBE 71; VarWW 85; Who 74; WhoHol 92, A*

Lundahl, Arthur Charles
American. Government Official
Aerial-photography expert whose detection of missile installations in Cuba, 1962, led to the Cuban Missile Crisis.
b. 1915 in Chicago, Illinois
Source: *EncAI&E; WhoE 86*

Lundberg, Daniel
American. Business Executive
Founded Lundberg Letter, bi-weekly survey of gasoline prices; forecast 1979 gasoline shortage.
b. Oct 24, 1912 in New Britain, Connecticut
d. Aug 5, 1986 in Torrance, California
Source: *ConAu 119; NewYTBS 86; WhoWor 87*

Lunden, Joan (Elise)
[Joan Blunden]
American. Broadcast Journalist
Co-host, "Good Morning, America," 1980-97; daily syndicated talk show "Everyday with Joan Lunden," 1989.
b. Sep 19, 1950 in Fair Oaks, California
Source: *BioIn 13, 14, 15, 16; CelR 90; ConAu 145; ConTFT 10; CurBio 89; InWom SUP; VarWW 85; WhoAm 88, 90, 92, 94, 95, 96, 97; WhoAmW 87, 89, 91, 93, 95, 97; WhoE 95; WhoEmL 91; WhoTelC; WomStre*

Lundigan, William
American. Actor
Host of TV series "Climax," 1954-58.
b. Jun 12, 1914 in Syracuse, New York
d. Dec 21, 1975 in Los Angeles, California
Source: *BioIn 4, 10; FilmEn; FilmgC; ForYSC; HalFC 80, 84, 88; IntMPA 75, 76; MotPP; MovMk; NewYTBS 75; ObitOF 79; WhAm 6; What 5; WhoHol C; WhScrn 77, 83*

Lundkvist, Artur Nils
Swedish. Author
Leading figure in Swedish modernism; wrote *Agadir,* 1979.
b. Mar 3, 1906 in Oderljunga, Sweden
d. Dec 11, 1991 in Stockholm, Sweden
Source: *BioIn 10, 13; CasWL; ConAu 117; ConFLW 84; DcScanL; EncWL 2; NewYTBS 91*

Lundquist, Steve
American. Swimmer
Olympic gold medalist, 100-meter breaststroke, 1984.
b. Feb 20, 1961 in Atlanta, Georgia
Source: *BiDAmSp BK; BioIn 13, 14*

Lundy, Lamar
American. Football Player
Defensive end, member LA Rams "fearsome foursome" defensive line, 1957-69.
b. Apr 17, 1935 in Richmond, Indiana
Source: *BioIn 8; InB&W 80; WhoFtbl 74*

Lunn, Arnold Henry Moore, Sir
English. Skier
Skiing pioneer, invented modern slalom; organized first world championships, skiing events in Olympics, 1936.
b. Apr 18, 1888 in Madras, India
d. Jun 2, 1974 in London, England
Source: *BioIn 1, 2, 3, 4, 5, 8, 10, 14; BkC 4; CathA 1930; ConAu 49, 81; DcNaB 1971; GrBr; ObitOF 79; ObitT 1971; WhLit; Who 74; WhoChL; WhoLA; WhoWor 74*

Luns, Joseph Marie Antoine Hubert
Dutch. Politician, Diplomat
Secretary-general of NATO, 1971-84.
b. Aug 28, 1911 in Rotterdam, Netherlands
Source: *BioIn 4, 5, 9, 10, 12, 13; CurBio 58, 82; EncWB; IntWW 74, 75, 76, 77, 78, 79, 80, 81, 82, 83, 91, 93; IntYB 78, 79, 80, 81, 82; NewYTBE 71; Who 74, 82, 83, 85, 88, 90, 92, 94; WhoEIO 82; WhoWor 74, 80, 82, 84, 87, 89, 91, 93, 95*

Lunt, Alfred
[Lunt and Fontaine]
American. Actor
Co-starred with wife Lynn Fontaine in over 24 plays beginning in 1922 including *The Visit.*
b. Aug 19, 1892 in Milwaukee, Wisconsin
d. Aug 2, 1977 in Chicago, Illinois
Source: *BiE&WWA; BioIn 14, 15, 19, 21; BlueB 76; CamGWoT; CelR; CnThe; CurBio 41, 77N; FacFETw; FamA&A; Film 2; FilmEn; FilmgC; HalFC 80, 84, 88; IntDcT 3; IntWW 74, 77; LegTOT; MetOEnc; NotNAT; OxCAmT 84; OxCThe 67, 83; PlP&P; REn; TwYS; WebAB 79; Who 74; WhoAm 74, 76; WhoHol A; WhoThe 72, 77, 81N; WhoWor 74; WhScrn 83; WorAl*

Lupescu, Magda (Elena)
[Magda Wolff]
Romanian. Mistress
King Carol of Rumania's paramour for 22 yrs; married him in exile, 1947.
b. 1896 in Iasi, Romania
d. Jun 29, 1977 in Estoril, Portugal
Source: *BioIn 1, 4, 5, 7, 8, 11, 20; CurBio 40, 77N; InWom, SUP; NewYTBS 77; What 1*

Lupino, Ida
American. Actor, Director
Often portrayed tough, lower-class characters; films include *High Sierra,* 1941; directed many TV shows including "Alfred Hitchcock Presents."
b. Feb 4, 1918 in London, England
d. Aug 3, 1995 in Burbank, California
Source: *BiDFilm, 81, 94; BioIn 2, 4, 6, 9, 10, 11, 12, 14, 16, 20, 21; CamGWoT; ContDcW 89; CurBio 43, 95N; FilmEn; FilmgC; GangFlm; GrLiveH; HalFC 88; HanAmWH; IlWWHD 1; IntDcWB; IntMPA 75, 76, 77, 78, 79, 80, 81, 82, 84, 86, 88, 92, 94, 96; InWom, SUP; LegTOT; MiSFD 9; MotPP; MovMk; News 96, 96-1; NewYTBE 72; NewYTBS 95; OxCFilm; ReelWom; ThFT; VarWW 85; WhoAm 74, 76, 78, 80, 82, 84, 86, 88, 90, 92; WhoAmW 58, 66, 68, 70, 72, 74; WhoEnt 92; WhoHol A; WomFir; WomWMM; WorAl; WorAlBi; WorEFlm; WorFDir 2*

Lupino, Stanley
English. Actor, Dramatist, Producer
British revue, film comedian; father of Ida Lupino.
b. Jun 17, 1896 in London, England
d. Jun 10, 1942 in London, England
Source: *CurBio 42; EncMT; FilmgC; IntMPA 84; NewC; OxCThe 67; WhoHol B; WhScrn 74, 77; WhThe; WorAl*

LuPone, Patti Ann
American. Actor
Won Tony, 1980, for *Evita,*; Laurence Olivier Award, 1986, for *Les Miserables*; star in television drama "Life Goes On," 1989-93.
b. Apr 21, 1949 in Northport, New York
Source: *BioIn 12, 13, 15, 16; CamGWoT; ConMus 8; ConTFT 1, 5; CurBio 89; IntMPA 92; NewYTBS 87, 88; VarWW 85; WhoAm 86, 90; WhoAmW 91; WhoEnt 92; WhoThe 81; WorAlBi*

Lupu, Radu
Romanian. Pianist
Won first prize, Van Cliburn Piano Competition, 1966; appeared with orchestras worldwide.
b. Nov 30, 1945 in Galati, Romania
Source: *Baker 84, 92; BioIn 14, 18, 21; IntWW 74, 75, 76, 77, 78, 79, 80, 81, 82, 83, 89, 91, 93; IntWWM 77, 80, 90; NewGrDM 80; NotTwCP; PenDiMP; Who 74, 82, 83, 85, 88, 90, 92, 94; WhoAm 80, 82, 84, 86, 88, 90, 92, 94, 95, 96, 97; WhoEnt 92; WhoMus 72; WhoSoCE 89; WhoWor 78, 82, 84, 87, 89, 97*

Lupus, Peter
"Mr. Hercules"
American. Actor
Played Willie Armitage in TV series "Mission Impossible," 1966-73.
b. Jun 17, 1937 in Indianapolis, Indiana
Source: *ForYSC; ItaFilm; WhoHol 92, A*

Luque, Dolf
[Adolfo Luque]
"The Pride of Havana"
Cuban. Baseball Player
Pitcher, 1914-35; one of first successful Cubans in MLs; led NL in wins, 1923.
b. Aug 4, 1890 in Havana, Cuba
d. Jul 3, 1957 in Havana, Cuba
Source: *Ballpl 90; BiDAmSp Sup; BioIn 3, 4, 21; WhoProB 73*

Lurcat, Jean Marie
French. Artist
Responsible for revival of French tapestry after WW II.
b. Jul 1, 1892 in Bruyeres, France
d. Jan 6, 1966 in Saint-Paul-de-Vence, France
Source: *CurBio 48, 66; McGDA; ObitOF 79; WhAm 4; WhoGrA 62*

Luria, Isaac ben Solomon
Israeli. Scholar
Torah scholar whose study of the *Zohar* resulted in the founding of a school of mystical Kabbalism called Lurianic Kabbala.
b. 1534 in Jerusalem, Israel
d. Aug 5, 1572 in Safed, Syria
Source: *BioIn 7, 10, 16; CasWL; EuAu; LuthC 75; McGEWB*

Luria, Salvador Edward
American. Scientist
Shared 1969 Nobel Prize in medicine; researched viruses.
b. Aug 13, 1912 in Turin, Italy
d. Feb 6, 1991 in Lexington, Massachusetts
Source: *AmMWSc 73P, 76P, 79, 82, 86, 89, 92; BiESc; BioIn 8, 9, 13, 14, 15, 16, 17, 18, 20; ConAu 133; CurBio 70, 91N; FacFETw; IntWW 74, 75, 76, 77, 78, 79, 80, 81, 82, 83, 89, 91N; LarDcSc; McGMS 80; NewYTBS 91; NobelP; NotTwCS; ThTwC 87; WebAB 74, 79; WhAm 10; Who 74, 82, 83, 85, 88, 90, 92N; WhoAm 74, 76, 78, 80, 82, 84, 86, 88, 90; WhoE 77, 79, 81, 83, 85, 86, 89, 91; WhoFrS 84; WhoNob, 90, 95; WhoWor 74, 80, 82, 84, 87, 89, 91; WhoWorJ 72, 78; WorAl; WorAlBi; WorScD; WrDr 92, 94N*

Lurie, Alison
American. Author
Won Pulitzer, 1984, for *Foreign Affairs.*
b. Sep 3, 1926 in Chicago, Illinois
Source: *AmWomWr SUP; ArtclWW 2; Benet 87, 96; BenetAL 91; BioIn 10, 12, 13, 14, 15; BlmGWL; BlueB 76; CelR 90; ConAu 1NR, 1R, 2NR, 4NR, 17NR, 50NR; ConLC 4, 5, 18, 39; ConNov 72, 76, 82, 86, 91, 96; CurBio 86; CyWA 89; DcArts; DcLB 2; DrAF 76; DrAPF 80; DrAS 82E; FemiCLE; GrWomW; IntAu&W 76, 77, 82, 86, 89, 91; IntvTCA 2; IntWW 89, 91, 93; InWom SUP; LegTOT; MagSAmL; MajTwCW; NewYTBS 82; Novels; OxCAmL 83, 95; OxCEng 85, 95; RAdv 14; RGTwCWr; ScF&FL 92; SmATA 46; Who 88, 90, 92, 94; WhoAm 82, 84, 86, 88, 90, 92, 94, 95, 96, 97; WhoAmW 83, 87, 89, 91, 93, 95, 97; WhoE 86, 89; WhoUSWr 88; WhoWrEP 89, 92, 95; WorAlBi; WorAu 1970; WrDr 76, 80, 82, 84, 86, 88, 90, 92, 94, 96*

Lurie, Jane
American. Filmmaker
Source: *WomWMM, B*

Lurton, Horace Harmon
American. Supreme Court Justice
Conservative associate justice, appointed by Taft, 1910.
b. Feb 26, 1844 in Newport, Kentucky
d. Apr 1914 in Atlantic City, New Jersey
Source: *AmBi; ApCAB SUP, X; BiDFedJ; BioIn 2, 5, 15; DcAmB; HarEnUS; NatCAB 8; OxCSupC; SupCtJu; TwCBDA; WebAB 74, 79; WhAm 1*

Lusinchi, Jaime
Venezuelan. Political Leader
Pres. of Venezuela, 1984-89.
b. May 27, 1924 in Clarines, Venezuela
Source: *BiDLAmC; BioIn 13, 14, 16; DcCPSAm; IntWW 89, 91, 93; NewYTBS 83; WhoWor 84, 87, 89, 91, 93, 95, 97*

Lustig, Alvin
American. Designer
Student of Frank Lloyd Wright, 1935; designed chairs, houses, fabrics.
b. Feb 8, 1915 in Denver, Colorado
d. Dec 4, 1955 in New York, New York
Source: *BioIn 8; ConDes 84; DcTwDes; McGDA; WhAm 3*

Luther, Martin
German. Religious Leader
Led Protestant Reformation, 1517; Lutheran religion named for him.
b. Nov 10, 1483 in Eisleben, Germany
d. Feb 18, 1546 in Eisleben, Germany
Source: *AnCL; Baker 78, 84, 92; BbD; Benet 87, 96; BiD&SB; BioIn 1, 2, 3, 4, 5, 6, 7, 8, 9, 10, 11, 12, 13, 14, 15, 16, 17, 18, 19, 20; BlmGEL; CasWL; ChhPo, S1; CyEd; DcBiPP; DcEuL; Dis&D; EncEth; EncPaPR 91; EncRev; EuAu; EuWr 2; EvEuW; GrFLW; HisWorL; LegTOT; LinLib L; LitC 9; LngCEL; LuthC 75; McGEWB; MusMk; NewC; NewCBEL; NewGrDM 80; NewOxM; OxCEng 67, 85, 95; OxCGer 76, 86; OxCMus; OxCPhil; PenC EUR; PoChrch; RAdv 14, 13-4; RComWL; REn; RfGWoL 95; WhDW; WorAl; WorAlBi*

Luthuli, Albert John Mvumbi
South African. Political Leader, Social Reformer
Won 1960 Nobel Peace Prize for leading peaceful resistance to apartheid; pres., African National Congress (ANC).
b. 1898, Rhodesia
d. Jul 21, 1967 in Groutville, South Africa
Source: *BiDInt; CurBio 62; ObitT 1961; SelBAAf; WhAm 4; WhDW; WhoNob; WorAl*

Lutoslawski, Witold
Polish. Composer
First Government Prizewinner, 1955; works include "Concerto," 1954; "String Quartet," 1964 and 3 "Chain" pieces, 1983-86.
b. Jan 25, 1913 in Warsaw, Poland
d. Feb 7, 1994 in Warsaw, Poland
Source: *Baker 78, 84, 92; BiDAmM; BioIn 8, 12, 14, 15, 17, 19, 20, 21; BriBkM 80; CompSN, SUP; ConCom 92; CpmDNM 80; CurBio 91, 94N; DcArts; DcCM; DcCom&M 79; FacFETw; IntWW 74, 75, 76, 77, 78, 79, 80, 81, 82, 83, 89, 91, 93; IntWWM 77, 80, 90; LegTOT; McGEWB; MusMk; NewAmDM; NewGrDM 80; NewOxM; NewYTBS 94; OxCMus; PenDiMP A; PolBiDi; WhAm 11; WhDW; Who 85, 88, 90, 92, 94; WhoMus 72; WhoSocC 78; WhoSoCE 89; WhoWor 74, 76, 78, 80, 82, 84, 87, 89, 91, 93*

Lutyens, Edwin Landseer, Sir
English. Architect
Designed numerous domestic, public buildings in England, abroad.
b. Mar 29, 1869 in London, England
d. Jan 1, 1944 in London, England
Source: *BioIn 1, 2, 5, 8, 9, 12, 13, 14, 15, 16, 21; CurBio 42, 44; DcArts; DcBrAr 1; DcBrBI; DcD&D; DcNaB 1941; DcTwDes; DcVicP 2; EncUrb; FacFETw; GrBr; LinLib L, S; McGDA; OxCArt; VicBrit; WhDW; WhoArch*

Lutz, Bob
[Robert Charles Lutz]
American. Tennis Player
Won doubles with Stan Smith in US Opens, 1968, 1974, 1978. 1980.
b. Aug 29, 1947 in Lancaster, Pennsylvania
Source: *BioIn 9, 10, 12; WhoIntT*

Lutz, Robert Anthony
American. Auto Executive
Pres., COO, Chrysler Corp., 1993.
b. Feb 12, 1932 in Zurich, Switzerland
Source: *BioIn 11, 13, 16; CurBio 94; Dun&B 90; IntWW 91; News 90; St&PR 84; WhoAm 78, 80, 82, 86, 88, 90, 92, 94, 95, 96, 97; WhoFI 87, 94, 96; WhoMW 84, 88, 92; WhoWor 95, 96, 97*

Luxemburg, Rosa
"Bloody Rosa"
German. Political Leader
Leader, German Social Democratic party, Spartacus party, 1918; murdered on way to prison.
b. Mar 5, 1871 in Zamosc, Poland
d. Jan 15, 1919 in Berlin, Germany
Source: *BioIn 14, 15, 16, 17, 21; DcTwHis; EncCoWW; EncRev; FacFETw; GoodHs; HisWorL; MakMC; McGEWB; OxCGer 76; PolBiDi; REn; ThTwC 87; TwCLC 63; WomWrGe; WorAl; WorAlBi*

Luyendyk, Arie
"The Flying Dutchman"
Dutch. Auto Racer
Won Indianapolis 500, 1990, 1997.
b. 1954 in Sommelsdyk, Netherlands

Luzinski, Greg(ory Michael)
"The Bull"
American. Baseball Player
Outfielder-designated hitter, 1970-84; led NL in RBIs, 1975.
b. Nov 22, 1950 in Chicago, Illinois
Source: *Ballpl 90; BiDAmSp Sup; BioIn 10, 11, 13, 14; LegTOT; NewYTBE 72; NewYTBS 85; WhoAm 80, 82, 84; WorAl*

Lwoff, Andre Michel
French. Scientist
Shared Nobel Prize in medicine, 1965.
b. May 8, 1902 in Allier, France
Source: *AmMWSc 95; BiESc; BioIn 14, 15; IntWW 74, 75, 76, 77, 78, 79, 80, 81, 82, 83, 89, 91, 93; LarDcSc; NobelP; WhAm 11; Who 85, 88, 90, 92; WhoAm 88, 90, 92, 94; WhoFr 79; WhoNob, 90; WhoScEn 94, 96; WhoWor 80, 82, 84, 87, 89, 91, 93, 95; WorAlBi*

Lyautey, Louis Hubert Gonzalve
French. Government Official
Moroccan commissioner, 1912-25; wrote *Le Role Social de l'Officier,* 1891; became important document for French army.
b. Nov 17, 1854 in Nancy, France
d. Jul 27, 1934 in Thorey, France
Source: *BioIn 17; HarEnMi; McGEWB; NewCol 75; WhDW; WhoMilH 76*

Lydon, James
"Jimmy Lydon"
American. Actor
Played title role in *Henry Aldrich* film series, 1941-44.
b. May 30, 1923 in Harrington, New Jersey
Source: *BioIn 10; EncAFC; FilmEn; FilmgC; ForYSC; HalFC 80, 84, 88; IntMPA 75, 76, 77, 78, 79, 80, 81, 82, 84, 86, 88, 92, 94, 96; MovMk; What 4; WhoHol 92, A*

Lydon, John (Joseph)
[Johnny Rotten]
English. Singer
Vocalist for punk-rock band, Sex Pistols, 1975-78; formed group Public Image Ltd., 1978; hits include "Public Image," 1978.
b. Jan 31, 1956 in London, England
Source: *BioIn 19, 20; CurBio 96; WhoHol 92*

Lyell, Charles, Sir
Scottish. Geologist, Author
Regarded as father of modern geology, advocating uniformitarianism; wrote *Principles of Geology,* 1830-33.
b. Nov 14, 1797 in Kinnordy, Scotland
d. Feb 22, 1875 in London, England
Source: *Alli, SUP; ApCAB; AsBiEn; BbD; BbtC; BenetAL 91; BiD&SB; BiDTran; BiESc; BioIn 1, 2, 3, 5, 6, 7, 8, 9, 10, 11, 12, 13, 14, 15, 16; BlmGEL; BritAu 19; CamDcSc; CasWL; CelCen; Chambr 3; DcBiPP; DcEnL; DcNaB, C; DcScB; Drake; EncEnv; EvLB; InSci; LarDcSc; LinLib L, S; LngCEL; McGEWB; NewCBEL; NewCol 75; OxCAmH; OxCCan; OxCEng 67; RAdv 14; REnAL; VicBrit; WhDW; WorAl; WorAlBi; WorScD*

Lyle, Sandy
[Alexander Walter Barr Lyle]
English. Golfer
Turned pro, 1977; won British Open, 1985, Masters, 1988.
b. Feb 9, 1958 in Shrewsbury, England
Source: *BioIn 13, 16; Who 90, 92, 94; WhoIntG*

Lyle, Sparky
[Albert Walter Lyle]
American. Baseball Player
Relief pitcher, 1967-82; won AL Cy Young Award, 1977; wrote *The Bronx Zoo,* 1979.
b. Jul 22, 1944 in DuBois, Pennsylvania
Source: *Ballpl 90; BiDAmSp BB; BioIn 9, 11, 12, 13, 14, 15, 16, 17, 18; ConAu 117, 124, X; CurBio 78; LegTOT; NewYTBE 72; WhoAm 82; WhoProB 73; WhoSpor*

Lyly, John
English. Author
Established literary style *euphuism;* derived from his novel *Euphues,* 1578-80.
b. 1554 in Weald, England
d. 1606 in London, England
Source: *Benet 87, 96; BiD&SB; BiDRP&D; BioIn 1, 3, 5, 6, 8, 9, 11, 12, 16; BlmGEL; BritAu; BritWr 1; CamGEL; CamGLE; CasWL; Chambr 1; ChhPo; CnE&AP; CnThe; CroE&S; CrtSuDr; CrtT 1, 4; CyWA 58; DcEnA, A; DcEnL; DcEuL; DcLB 62; DcLEL; DcNaB; Dis&D; EncWT; Ent; EvLB; IntDcT 2; LngCEL; McGEWD 72, 84; MouLC 1; NewC; NewCBEL; NotNAT B; OxCEng 67, 85, 95; OxCThe 67, 83; PenC ENG; PlP&P; RAdv 14, 13-2; REn; REnWD; RfGEnL 91; WebE&AL; WhDW*

Lyman, Abe
American. Bandleader
Society band leader, 1930s; featured in film *Mr. Broadway.*
b. Aug 4, 1897 in Chicago, Illinois
d. Oct 23, 1957 in Beverly Hills, California
Source: *ASCAP 66, 80; BgBands 74; BioIn 4; CmpEPM; NotNAT B; OxCPMus; RadStar; WhoHol B; WhScrn 74, 77, 83*

Lyman, Frankie
[Frankie Lyman and the Teenagers]
American. Singer
Had top-ten hit "Why Do Fools Fall in Love?" 1956.
b. Sep 30, 1942 in Washington Heights, New York
d. Feb 28, 1968 in New York, New York
Source: *IlEncBM 82*

Lyman, Link
[William Roy Lyman]
American. Football Player
Defensive tackle, 1922-34, mostly with Chicago; Hall of Fame.
b. Nov 30, 1898 in Table Rock, Nebraska
Source: *BiDAmSp FB; BioIn 17; LegTOT; WhoFtbl 74; WhoSpor*

Lympany, Moura
English. Pianist
Int'l concertist; won Ysaya competition, 1938; championed works of British composers.
b. Aug 18, 1916 in Saltash, England
Source: *Baker 84, 92; BioIn 1, 3, 4, 18, 21; BlueB 76; IntWW 74, 75, 76, 77, 78, 79, 80, 81, 82, 83, 89, 91, 93; IntWWM 77, 80, 85, 90; NewGrDM 80; NotTwCP; PenDiMP; Who 74, 82, 83, 85, 88, 90, 92, 94; WhoMus 72; WhoWor 74, 82, 84, 87, 89, 91, 93, 95*

Lynch, Benny
Scottish. Boxer
Won world, European, British fly weight title, 1932-37.
b. Aug 6, 1946 in Glasgow, Scotland
Source: *BioIn 7; WhoBox 74*

Lynch, David
[The Platters]
American. Singer
Second tenor in vocal group founded in 1953; best known hit "Only You," 1955.
b. 1930 in Saint Louis, Missouri
d. Jan 2, 1981 in Long Beach, California
Source: *BioIn 12*

Lynch, David K
American. Director, Screenwriter
Films include *The Elephant Man,* 1980, *Blue Velvet,* 1986; TV series "Twin Peaks," 1990-91.
b. Jan 20, 1946 in Missoula, Montana
Source: *BioIn 12, 14, 15, 16; ConAu 129; ConLC 66; ConTFT 5; CurBio 87; Dun&B 90; HalFC 84, 88; IntDcF 2-2; IntMPA 86, 92; IntWW 91; News 90; NewYTBS 86, 90; VarWW 85; WorFDir 2*

Lynch, J(ohn) Joseph
American. Clergy, Educator
Directed the observatory at Fordham U, NYC, 1962-83.
b. Dec 6, 1894 in London, England
d. May 14, 1987 in New York, New York
Source: *BioIn 1, 5, 15; ConAu 123; CurBio 46, 87, 87N; InSci; WhoAm 74, 76*

Lynch, Joe
American. Boxer
World bantam weight champ, early 1920s.
b. Nov 30, 1898 in New York, New York
d. Aug 1, 1965 in New York, New York
Source: *BiDAmSp BK; BioIn 7; WhoBox 74*

Lynch, Kevin
Irish. Hunger Striker, Revolutionary
IRA member; one of 10 hunger strikers to die in prison, demanding political prisoner rather than criminal status.
b. May 25, 1956 in Dungiven, Northern Ireland
d. Aug 1, 1981 in Belfast, Northern Ireland

Lynch, Peter
American. Author
Former investment manager with Fidelity Investments; wrote *One Up On Wall Street: How to Use What You Already Know to Make Money in the Market,* 1989.
b. 1944 in Boston, Massachusetts
Source: *CurBio 94; IntWW 93; WhoWor 91*

Lynch, Thomas, Jr.
American. Continental Congressman
Planter; signed Declaration of Independence as substitute for his ill father, 1776; presumed lost at sea.
b. Aug 5, 1749 in Winyaw, South Carolina
d. 1779
Source: *AmBi; ApCAB; BiAUS; BiDrAC; BiDrUSC 89; BioIn 7, 8, 9; DcAmB; Drake; EncAR; EncCRAm; EncSoH; HarEnUS; NatCAB 10; TwCBDA; WhAm HS; WhAmP; WhAmRev*

Lynd, Helen Merrell
American. Sociologist, Author, Educator
Continued small city studies with *Update: Middletown Families: Fifty Years of Change and Continuity,* 1982.
b. Mar 17, 1896 in La Grange, Illinois
d. Jan 30, 1982 in Warren, Ohio
Source: *AmDec 1920; AmSocL; AmWomWr; AnObit 1982; BenetAL 91; BioIn 17, 19; ConAu 105; DrAS 78P; GrLiveH; InWom SUP; LinLib L; NewYTBS 82; PenC AM; REnAL; TwCA, SUP; WomSoc*

Lynd, Robert Staughton
American. Sociologist
With wife Helen wrote *Middletown,* 1929; *Middletown in Transition,* 1937, studies of small-town America.
b. Sep 26, 1892 in New Albany, Indiana
d. Nov 1, 1970 in Warren, Connecticut
Source: *AmAu&B; AmSocL; BioIn 4, 7, 9, 10, 19; DcAmB S8; DcLEL; IndAu 1917; LngCTC; McGEWB; NatCAB 55; OxCAmH; OxCAmL 65; PenC AM; REnAL; TwCA, SUP; WebAB 74, 79; WhAm 5*

Lynde, Paul Edward
American. Comedian, Actor
Known for one-liners as panelist on game show "Hollywood Squares."
b. Jun 13, 1926 in Mount Vernon, Ohio
d. Jan 9, 1982 in Beverly Hills, California
Source: *AnObit 1982; BiE&WWA; BioNews 75; BkPepl; CurBio 72, 82N; EncMT; FilmgC; IntMPA 80, 82; MotPP; MovMk; NewYTBS 82; NotNAT A; WhAm 9; WhoAm 78, 80; WhoHol A; WorAl*

Lyne, Adrian
English. Filmmaker
Made films *Flashdance,* 1983; *Fatal Attraction,* 1987
b. 1941?, England
Source: *BiDFilm 94; ConTFT 7; CurBio 94; IntMPA 94, 96; LegTOT; WhoAm 95, 96, 97*

Lynen, Feodor Felix Konrad
German. Scientist
Shared 1964 Nobel Prize in medicine for research on cholesterol.
b. Apr 6, 1911 in Munich, Germany
d. Aug 6, 1979 in Munich, Germany (West)
Source: *CurBio 67; LarDcSc; WhoNob, 90, 95*

Lynes, Joseph Russell, Jr.
American. Editor, Author
Managing editor *Harpers* mag., 1947-67; wrote *Snobs,* 1950; *The Tastemakers,* 1954.
b. Dec 2, 1910 in Great Barrington, Massachusetts
d. Sep 14, 1991 in New York, New York
Source: *BenetAL 91; BioIn 17, 18; ConAu 3NR, 135; CurBio 91N; DcLEL 1940; NewYTBS 91; OxCAmL 83; REnAL; WhoAm 74, 84, 90; WhoAmA 91; WhoWrEP 89; WrDr 92*

Lyng, Richard E
American. Government Official
Secretary of Agriculture, Reagan administration, 1986-89.
b. Jun 29, 1918 in San Francisco, California

Source: *AmCath 80; BiDrUSE 89; BioIn 8, 14, 15; CngDr 87; CurBio 86; IntWW 91; NewYTBS 86; WhoAm 84, 90; WhoAmP 83, 87, 91; WhoE 89; WhoFI 83, 89; WhoWor 80, 82, 91*

Lyngstad-Fredriksson, Annifrid
Swedish. Singer
First solo album *Something's Going On,* produced by Phil Collins, 1982.
b. Nov 15, 1945 in Stockholm, Sweden

Lynley, Carol
[Carol Ann Jones]
American. Actor
Films include *Return to Peyton Place,* 1961; *The Poseidon Adventure,* 1972.
b. Feb 13, 1942 in New York, New York
Source: *BioIn 6, 8, 12, 14, 16, 20; ConTFT 5; FilmEn; FilmgC; ForYSC; HalFC 80, 84, 88; IlsCB 1957; IntMPA 84, 86, 88, 92, 94, 96; InWom SUP; LegTOT; MotPP; MovMk; VarWW 85; WhoAm 86, 88; WhoEnt 92; WhoHol 92, A; WorAl; WorEFlm*

Lynn, Diana
[Delores Loehr]
American. Actor
Films include teenage roles in *The Major and the Minor,* 1942; *Our Hearts Were Young and Gay,* 1944.
b. Oct 7, 1926 in Los Angeles, California
d. Dec 18, 1971 in Los Angeles, California
Source: *BiE&WWA; BioIn 1, 2, 3, 9, 15; CurBio 53, 72, 72N; DcAmB S9; EncAFC; FilmEn; FilmgC; ForYSC; HalFC 80, 84, 88; InWom, SUP; LegTOT; MotPP; MovMk; NewYTBE 71; NotNAT B; WhoAmW 58; WhoHol B; WhScrn 74, 77, 83*

Lynn, Fred(ric Michael)
American. Baseball Player, Sportscaster
Outfielder, Red Sox, 1973-81; Angels, 1981-84; Orioles, 1985-88; Tigers, 1988-89, Padres, 1990; sportscaster, ESPNm 1992—; only player ever to win MVP in rookie season, 1975; won AL batting title, 1979.
b. Feb 3, 1952 in Chicago, Illinois
Source: *Ballpl 90; BaseReg 86, 87; BiDAmSp BB; BioIn 12, 13, 14, 15, 16; LegTOT; WhoAm 80, 82, 84, 86, 88, 90, 92, 94, 95, 96, 97; WhoE 89; WhoSpor; WhoWest 94, 96; WhoWor 84, 87; WorAl*

Lynn, Janet
[Janet Lynn Nowicki Salomon]
American. Skater
Five-time US champion figure skater, 1969-73; won bronze medal, 1972 Olympics.
b. Apr 6, 1953 in Chicago, Illinois
Source: *BiDAmSp BK; BioIn 9, 10, 11, 12, 13; BioNews 74; ConAu 61; HerW, 84; InWom SUP; LegTOT; NewYTBS 82; WhoAm 74, 76, 78, 80, 82, 84, 86, 88, 90, 92, 94, 95, 96, 97; WhoAmW 75, 77; WhoEmL 93; WhoEnt 92; WhoSpor*

Lynn, Loretta
[Mrs. Oliver Vanetta Lynn, Jr; Loretta Webb]
American. Singer, Songwriter
Movie *Coal Miner's Daughter,* 1977 based on her life; first woman to earn a certified gold country album.
b. Apr 14, 1935 in Butcher Hollow, Kentucky
Source: *Baker 84; BgBkCoM; BiDAmM; BioIn 9, 10, 11, 12, 13, 14, 15, 16; BioNews 74; BkPepl; CelR 90; ConAu 81; ConMus 2; ContDcW 89; CounME 74, 74A; CurBio 73; DcTwCCu 1; EncFCWM 69, 83; EncRk 88; GrLiveH; HalFC 84, 88; HarEnCM 87; HarEnR 86; HerW 84; IlEncCM; IntDcWB; InWom SUP; NewAmDM; NewGrDA 86; NewYTBE 72; OxCPMus; PenEncP; PeoHis; RolSEnR 83; VarWW 85; WhoAm 86, 90; WhoAmW 91; WhoEnt 92; WhoRock 81; WorAlBi*

Lynne, Jeff
[Electric Light Orchestra]
English. Musician
Leader of Electric Light Orchestra; solo single "Video," 1984; co-recipient of Grammy for *Traveling Wilburys, Volume I,* 1989.
b. Dec 30, 1947 in Birmingham, England
Source: *BioIn 11; BkPepl; ConMus 5; EncRk 88; LegTOT; OnThGG; RkOn 85; WhoAm 82, 90; WhoRocM 82*

Lynne, Shelby
American. Singer, Songwriter
Country torch singer; has appeared frequently on "Nashville Now;" albums include *Tough All Over,* 1990.
b. 1968 in Jackson, Alabama
Source: *ConMus 5; LegTOT*

Lynott, Phil(ip)
[Thin Lizzy]
Irish. Singer, Musician
Founded band, 1970; wrote most of group's songs which celebrate comic-book heroism.
b. Aug 20, 1951 in Dublin, Ireland
d. Jan 4, 1986 in Salisbury, England

Lynyrd Skynyrd
[Robert Burns; Allen Collins; Steve Gaines; Ed King; William Powell; Gary Rossington; Ronnie VanZant; Leon Wilkeson]
American. Music Group
Hit songs include "Free Bird," 1974.
Source: *Alli; BiDLA; BioIn 9, 16, 19; Chambr 2; ConMuA 80A; ConMus 9; CurBio 47; EncPR&S 89; EncRk 88; EncRkSt; Film 1, 2; HarEnR 86; IlBBlP; IlEncRk; InB&W 85; InWom SUP; Law&B 92; NewAmDM; NewCBEL; NewGrDA 86; NewYTBS 27, 90; OnThGG; PenEncP; RkOn 78; RolSEnR 83; WhoAmP 93; WhoGov 72; WhoHol 92; WhoOcn 78; WhoRock 81; WhoRocM 82; WhoScEu 91-1; WhScrn 77*

Lyon, Ben
American. Actor
Films include *Hell's Angels,* 1930; radio shows, "Hi Gang!"; wed to Bebe Daniels.
b. Feb 6, 1901 in Atlanta, Georgia
d. Mar 22, 1979
Source: *BioIn 3, 10, 11, 18; EncAFC; Film 1, 2; FilmEn; FilmgC; ForYSC; GangFlm; HalFC 80, 84, 88; IlWWBF, A; LegTOT; MotPP; MovMk; NewYTBS 79; OxCFilm; SilFlmP; TwYS; What 4; WhoHol A; WhoThe 81N; WhScrn 83; WhThe; WorAl*

Lyon, Mary Mason
American. Educator
Founder, pres., Mt. Holyoke College, 1837-49.
b. Feb 28, 1797 in Buckland, Massachusetts
d. Mar 5, 1849 in South Hadley, Massachusetts
Source: *AmBi; AmWom; ApCAB; BiDAmEd; DcAmB; Drake; EncAB-H 1974, 1996; HerW; InWom SUP; LibW; NatCAB 4; NotAW; TwCBDA; WebAB 74, 79; WhAm HS; WhDW*

Lyon, Nathaniel
American. Army Officer
Commanded Union forces in MO; instrumental in keeping state part of Union.
b. Jul 14, 1818 in Ashford, Connecticut
d. Aug 10, 1861 in Wilson's Creek, Missouri
Source: *Alli SUP; AmBi; ApCAB; BioIn 5, 7, 17; CivWDc; CmCal; DcAmB; Drake; HarEnMi; HarEnUS; NatCAB 4; TwCBDA; WebAMB; WhAm HS; WhCiWar*

Lyon, Phyllis Ann
American. Writer
Co-authored, with Del Martin, *Lesbian Love and Liberation,* 1973.
b. 1924 in Tulsa, Oklahoma
Source: *GayLesB; GayLL; WhoAmW 95*

Lyon, Southside Johnny
[Southside Johnny and the Asbury Jukes]
American. Singer, Musician
Harmonica player, vocalist, friend of Bruce Springsteen; group has recorded some of Springsteen's songs.
b. Dec 4, 1948 in Neptune, New Jersey

Lyons, Enid Muriel
Australian. Politician, Author
First woman in Australian House of Representatives, 1943-51; wrote autobiography *So We Take Comfort,* 1965.
b. Jul 9, 1897 in Duck River, Australia
d. Sep 2, 1981 in Sydney, Australia
Source: *AnObit 1981; BioIn 7, 10; BlueB 76; ConAu 108; FarE&A 78, 79, 80, 81;*

IntAu&W 76; IntWW 74, 75, 76; Who 74; WhoWor 74, 76; WomFir; WrDr 76

Lyons, Eugene
American. Author, Editor
Moscow correspondent for UPI, one of first Americans to report from inside Soviet Union.
b. Jul 1, 1898 in Uslian, Russia
d. Jan 7, 1985 in New York, New York
Source: *AmAu&B; BioIn 2, 4, 8, 14, 15; BlueB 76; ConAu 9R, 114; CurBio 44, 85, 85N; DcAmC; EncAJ; OxCAmL 65, 83; REn; REnAL; TwCA, SUP; WhAm 8; WhoAm 74, 76, 78; WhoWor 74; WhoWorJ 72, 78*

Lyons, Leonard
[Leonard Zucher]
American. Journalist
Broadway syndicated column "The Lyons Den" was noted for good taste in reporting gossip.
b. Sep 10, 1906 in New York, New York
d. Oct 7, 1976 in New York, New York
Source: *BiDAmNC; BioIn 2, 3, 5, 8, 10, 11; CelR; ConAu 69; DcAmB S10; NewYTBS 74, 76; WhAm 7; WhoAm 74, 76; WhoE 74; WhoWorJ 72, 78*

Lyons, Sophie Levy
"Queen of Crime"
American. Criminal
Internationally famous swindler, bank robber who later became America's first society columnist, 1897.
b. Dec 24, 1848 in New York, New York
d. May 8, 1924 in Detroit, Michigan

Lyons, Ted
[Theodore Amar Lyons]
American. Baseball Player
Pitcher, Chicago White Sox, 1923-46; had 260 career wins; Hall of Fame, 1955.
b. Dec 28, 1900 in Lake Charles, Louisiana
d. Jul 25, 1986 in Sulphur, Louisiana
Source: *Ballpl 90; BiDAmSp BB; BioIn 1, 2, 3, 7, 10, 14, 15; WhoProB 73; WhoSpor*

Lyons, William, Sir
English. Auto Executive
Founded Jaguar Cars Ltd; chairman until 1970.
b. Sep 4, 1901 in Blackpool, England
d. Feb 8, 1985 in Leamington Spa, England
Source: *AnObit 1985; BioIn 14, 19; BlueB 76; DcNaB 1981; DcTwBBL; IntWW 74, 75, 76, 77, 78, 79, 80, 81, 82, 83; IntYB 78, 79, 80, 81, 82; NewYTBS 85; Who 74, 82, 83, 85; WhoWor 74, 76, 78*

Lyot, Bernard Ferdinand
French. Astronomer, Inventor
With Meudon observatory, from 1920; invented solar coronagraph, 1930, to study sun's corona.
b. Feb 27, 1897 in Paris, France
d. Apr 2, 1952 in Cairo, Egypt
Source: *AsBiEn; BiESc; BioIn 3, 14; CamDcSc; DcScB; InSci; LarDcSc; McGMS 80; WebBD 83*

Lysenko, Trofim Denisovich
Russian. Geneticist
Made claims of man-induced hereditary changes in plants; found to be fraud.
b. Sep 29, 1898 in Karlovka, Russia
d. Nov 20, 1976, Union of Soviet Socialist Republics
Source: *AsBiEn; BiDSovU; BiESc; BioIn 2, 3, 4, 5, 6, 7, 8, 10, 11, 12; DcScB S2; FacFETw; InSci; IntWW 74, 75, 76; LarDcSc; McGEWB; NewCol 75; SovUn; WhAm 7; WhoSocC 78; WhoWor 74, 76*

Lysippus
Greek. Sculptor
Introduced new system of bodily proportions; reported to have made over 1,500 bronzes, none extant.
b. fl. 4th cent. BC
Source: *DcArts; DcBiPP; LegTOT; McGDA; NewCol 75; OxCArt; OxCClL 89; OxDcArt; WebBD 83; WhDW*

Lytell, Bert
American. Actor
Played adventurer in silent films *The Lone Wolf,* 1917-30.
b. Feb 24, 1885 in New York, New York
d. Sep 28, 1954 in New York, New York
Source: *ApCAB X; BioIn 3, 6; Film 1; FilmEn; FilmgC; MotPP; MovMk; NotNAT B; RadStar; TwYS; WhAm 3; WhoHol B; WhScrn 74, 77, 83; WhThe*

Lytle, Andrew Nelson
American. Author, Editor
Historical novels of the South include *The Long Night,* 1936.
b. Dec 26, 1902 in Murfreesboro, Tennessee
d. Dec 12, 1995 in Monteagle, Tennessee
Source: *AmAu&B; AmNov; BioIn 13, 14; ConAu 9R; ConNov 86; CyWA 58; DrAF 76; DrAPF 91; FifSWrA; IntvTCA 2; OxCAmL 65; PenC AM; RAdv 1; REnAL; RfGAmL 87; WhoAm 84; WorAu 1950; WrDr 84, 88*

Lyttleton, Oliver
[Viscount Chandos]
English. Government Official
Member, Churchill cabinet, WW II; Conservative in House of Commons, 1940-54.
b. Mar 15, 1893 in London, England
d. Jan 21, 1972 in London, England
Source: *Au&Wr 71; CurBio 41, 53, 72; DcNaB 1971; ObitT 1971*

Lytton, Edward George Earle Lytton Bulwer-Lytton, 1st Baron Lytton
[Meredith Owen]
English. Author, Poet
Best remembered historical novels: *The Last Days of Pompeii,* 1834; *Rienzi,* 1835.
b. May 15, 1803 in London, England
d. Jan 18, 1873 in Torquay, England
Source: *AtlBL; BiD&SB; BritAu 19; CasWL; CyWA 58; DcBiA; DcEnA; DcEuL; DcLEL; EvLB; HsB&A; LinLib L, S; McGEWD 72; MnBBF; MouLC 3; NewC; PenC ENG; RAdv 1; REn; ScF&FL 1*

Lytton, Edward Robert Bulwer-Lytton, Earl
[Owen Meredith]
English. Diplomat
Viceroy of India, 1875-80; ambassador to France, 1887-91; wrote epic novel *King Poppy,* 1892; son of Edward George.
b. Nov 8, 1831 in London, England
d. Nov 24, 1891 in Paris, France
Source: *Alli, SUP; BiD&SB; BritAu 19; CasWL; Chambr 3; ChhPo, S1, S2, S3; DcBiPP; DcEnA; DcEnL; DcLB 32; DcLEL; EvLB; HsB&A; NewC; NewCBEL; OxCEng 67; REn*

Lytton, Henry Alfred, Sir
[Henry Alfred Jones]
English. Actor
Appeared on stage, 1884-1934; operas include *Pirates of Penzance.*
b. Jan 3, 1867 in London, England
d. Aug 15, 1936 in London, England
Source: *DcNaB 1931; NotNAT A, B; WhThe*

Lyubimov, Yuri Petrovich
Russian. Director, Actor
Director of the Taganka Theatre, 1964-84, when he was expulsed from Russia; first exiled artist to return to USSR, 1988.
b. Sep 30, 1917 in Yaroslavl, Union of Soviet Socialist Republics
Source: *BioIn 16; CamGWoT; CurBio 88; IntWW 83, 91; OxCThe 83*

M

Ma, Yo-Yo
American. Musician
Internationally acclaimed cello virtuoso; on TV at age seven; Avery Fisher winner, 1978.
b. Oct 7, 1955 in Paris, France
Source: *AsAmAlm; Baker 84, 92; BioIn 11, 12, 13, 16, 17, 20; CelR 90; ConMus 2; CurBio 82; DcTwCCu 1; IntWW 91; IntWWM 90; NewAmDM; NewGrDA 86; NewYTBS 79; NotAsAm; PenDiMP; WhoAm 84, 86, 90, 97; WhoAmM 83; WhoAsA 94; WhoWor 91*

Maag, Peter
Swiss. Conductor
Led German operas, 1950s-60s; guest conductor for many US orchestras, 1960s-70s.
b. 1919 in Saint Gallen, Switzerland
Source: *Baker 78, 84; BioIn 14; IntWW 78, 79, 80, 81, 82, 83, 89, 91, 93; IntWWM 77, 80, 90; MetOEnc; NewAmDM; NewGrDM 80; NewYTBS 85; OxDcOp; PenDiMP; WhoEnt 92; WhoMus 72; WhoWor 74, 76, 84, 87, 89, 91, 93, 95, 96*

Maas, Peter
American. Author, Editor
Noted investigative reporter; wrote *Valachi Papers,* 1969; *Serpico,* 1973.
b. Jun 27, 1929 in New York, New York
Source: *AmAu&B; AmCath 80; Baker 84; BioIn 10, 13, 14; ConAu 93; ConLC 29; LiJour; LinLib L; WhoAm 74, 76, 78, 80, 82, 84, 86, 88, 90, 92, 94, 95, 96, 97; WhoUSWr 88; WhoWor 84; WhoWrEP 89, 92, 95; WrDr 76, 80, 82, 84, 86, 88, 90, 92, 94, 96*

Maathai, Wangari (Muta)
Kenyan. Environmentalist
Put together group of people to assist Kenyans who were being attacked in ethnic fighting, 1993; founded the Green Belt Movement, a group responsible for planting millions of trees throughout Kenya, 1977.
b. Apr 1, 1940 in Nyeri, Kenya
Source: *BioIn 19, 20, 21; CurBio 93; EnvEnDr; HeroCon; NotTwCS; RadHan; WhoWor 95; WomFir; WomStre*

Maazel, Lorin Varencove
American. Conductor, Violinist
Led major American orchestras at age nine to 11; director, Cleveland orchestra, 1972-82; guest conductor, London Philharmonia, from 1976.
b. Mar 5, 1930 in Neuilly, France
Source: *Baker 84; BioIn 13, 14, 16; CurBio 65; FacFETw; IntWW 83, 91; IntWWM 90; MetOEnc; NewAmDM; NewGrDA 86; NewYTBS 82, 89; PenDiMP; Who 85, 92; WhoAm 86, 90; WhoAmM 83; WhoE 91; WhoEnt 92; WhoMus 72; WhoMW 74; WhoWor 87, 91; WorAlBi*

Mabee, Carleton
[Fred Carleton Mabee]
American. Author
Won 1943 Pulitzer for *The American Leonardo,* concerning Samuel Morse.
b. Dec 25, 1914 in Shanghai, China
Source: *AmAu&B; BioIn 4; ConAu 1R, 21NR; DrAS 74H, 78H, 82H; OxCAmL 65; OxCCan; TwCA SUP; WhoAm 74, 76, 78, 80, 82, 84, 86, 90, 92, 94, 95, 96, 97; WhoUSWr 88; WhoWrEP 89, 92, 95; WrDr 76, 80, 82, 84, 86, 88, 90, 92, 94, 96*

Mabley, Moms
[Loretta Mary Aiken; Jackie Mabley]
American. Comedian
Noted for ''dirty old lady'' comedy routine; starred in *Amazing Grace,* 1974.
b. Mar 19, 1894 in Brevard, North Carolina
d. May 23, 1975 in White Plains, New York
Source: *BioIn 6, 10; BioNews 74; CurBio 75, 75N; DcAmB S9; InWom SUP; LegTOT; NewYTBS 87; NotBlAW 1; WhoCom; WhScrn 83*

Mabuse, Jan de
[Jan Gossaert; Jan Gossart]
Flemish. Artist
Did portraits, religious works; introduced Italian High Renaissance to the Netherlands.
b. 1478 in Maubeuge, France
d. 1533 in Antwerp, Belgium
Source: *ClaDrA; McGDA; NewCol 75; OxCArt; OxDcArt; WebBD 83*

Macapagal, Diosdado P(angan)
Philippine. Political Leader
Liberal pres. of Philippines, 1961-65; held political posts from 1946.
b. Sep 28, 1910 in Lubao, Philippines
d. Apr 21, 1997 in Manila, Philippines
Source: *BioIn 14; CurBio 62; IntWW 91; McGEWB; WhoWor 74*

MacArthur, Arthur
American. Army Officer
Military governor of Philippines, 1900-01; father of Charles.
b. Jun 2, 1845 in Springfield, Massachusetts
d. Sep 5, 1912 in Milwaukee, Wisconsin
Source: *AmBi; BioIn 1, 5, 7, 17, 20; CivWDc; DcAmB S1; DcAmMiB; GenMudB; HarEnMi; HarEnUS; MedHR 94; NatCAB 14; OxCAmH; TwCBDA; WebAB 74, 79; WebAMB; WhAm 1; WhCiWar; WhoMilH 76; WorAl; WorAlBi*

MacArthur, Charles
American. Dramatist
Wrote *The Front Page,* 1928; *Twentieth Century,* 1932, with Ben Hecht; husband of Helen Hayes.
b. Nov 5, 1895 in Scranton, Pennsylvania
d. Apr 21, 1956 in New York, New York
Source: *AmAu&B; Benet 87, 96; BenetAL 91; BioIn 1, 2, 4, 5, 7, 10, 12, 14, 15, 16, 18; CamGLE; CamHAL; CnDAL; ConAu 108; DcFM; DcLB 7, 25, 44; EncAFC; EncAJ; EncWT; FilmEn; FilmgC; GrWrEL DR; HalFC 80, 84, 88; IntDcF 1-4, 2-4; LegTOT; McGEWD 72, 84; MiSFD 9N; ModWD;*

NotNAT A, B; OxCAmL 65, 83, 95; OxCAmT 84; OxCFilm; REn; REnAL; RfGAmL 87; WhAm 3; WhoHol B; WhScrn 74, 77, 83; WhThe; WorAlBi; WorEFlm

MacArthur, Douglas
American. Army Officer
Accepted Japanese surrender, 1945; dismissed by Truman in Korea, 1951.
b. Jan 26, 1880 in Little Rock, Arkansas
d. Apr 5, 1964 in Washington, District of Columbia
Source: *AmOrTwC; BiDWWGF; BioIn 1, 2, 3, 4, 5, 6, 7, 8, 9, 10, 11, 12, 13, 14, 15, 16, 17, 18, 20, 21; ChhPo S1; CmdGen 1991; ColdWar 1, 2; ConAu 113; CurBio 41, 48, 64; DcAmB S7; DcAmC; DcAmDH 80, 89; DcAmMiB; DcPol; DcTwHis; EncAB-A 15; EncAB-H 1974, 1996; EncCW; EncJap; EncMcCE; FacFETw; GenMudB; HalFC 84, 88; HarEnMi; HisDcKW; HisEWW; HisWorL; LegTOT; LinLib S; McGEWB; MedHR 94; MemAm; NatCAB 59; ObitT 1961; OxCAmH; PolPar; PolProf T; RComAH; REn; WebAB 74, 79; WebAMB; WhAm 4; WhDW; WhoMilH 76; WhWW-II; WorAl; WorAlBi*

MacArthur, James
American. Actor
Adopted son of Helen Hayes; starred in TV series "Hawaii Five-O," 1968-80.
b. Dec 8, 1937 in Los Angeles, California
Source: *BiE&WWA; ConTFT 3; FilmEn; FilmgC; ForYSC; HalFC 80, 84, 88; IntMPA 75, 76, 77, 78, 79, 80, 81, 82, 84, 86, 88, 92, 94; LegTOT; MotPP; VarWW 85; WhoAm 80, 82, 84, 86, 88, 90, 92, 94; WhoEnt 92; WhoHol 92, A; WhoWest 94; WorAl; WorAlBi*

MacArthur, John Donald
American. Insurance Executive
Billionaire who founded Bankers Life and Casualty Co.
b. Mar 6, 1897 in Pittston, Pennsylvania
d. Jan 6, 1978 in West Palm Beach, Florida
Source: *BioIn 5, 7, 9, 10, 11, 12, 14, 15, 17; BusPN; DcAmB S10; NatCAB 63; NewYTBE 73; St&PR 75; WhoAm 74; WhoFI 74; WhoIns 75*

Macaulay, (Emilie) Rose, Dame
English. Author
Novels, written from Christian viewpoint, include satirical *Orphan Island,* 1924; adventure, comedy *Towers of Trebizond,* 1956.
b. Aug 1, 1881 in Cambridge, England
d. Oct 30, 1958 in London, England
Source: *ArtclWW 2; BiDMoPL; BioIn 15, 16, 18; BlmGWL; CamGEL; CamGLE; Chambr 3; ChhPo, S2; CnMWL; ConAu 104; ContDcW 89; CyWA 89; DcArts; DcLB 36; DcLEL; DcNaB 1951; EncBrWW; EncSF, 93; EncWL, 2, 3; EvLB; FemiCLE; GrBr; GrWrEL N; IntDcWB; InWom SUP; LngCTC; ModBrL; ModWoWr; NewC; NewCBEL; Novels; OxCEng 67, 85, 95; PenC ENG; REn; RfGEnL 91; RGTwCWr; ScF&FL 1, 92; ScFEYrs; TwCA, SUP; TwCLC 7, 44; TwCRHW 90, 94; TwCWr; WebE&AL; WomNov*

Macaulay, Thomas Babington Macaulay, Baron
English. Historian
Wrote five-volume *History of England,* 1861.
b. Oct 25, 1800 in Leicester, England
d. Dec 28, 1859 in Kensington, England
Source: *Alli; AtlBL; BbD; BiD&SB; BritAu 19; CasWL; Chambr 3; ChhPo, S1, S2; CrtT 3; CyWA 58; DcEnA; DcEuL; DcLEL; EvLB; GrWrEL N; MouLC 3; NewC; NewCBEL; OxCEng 67; PenC ENG; RAdv 1; REn; WebE&AL*

Macauley, Ed
[Charles Edward Macauley, Jr]
"Easy Ed"
American. Basketball Player
Three-time all-star center, 1949-59, mostly with Boston; Hall of Fame, 1960.
b. Mar 22, 1928 in Saint Louis, Missouri
Source: *BasBi; BiDAmSp BK; BioIn 9, 10; OfNBA 87; WhoBbl 73*

Macbeth
Scottish. Ruler
King of Scotland, 1040-57; slain by Malcolm III.
d. Aug 15, 1057 in Lumphanan, Scotland
Source: *BioIn 2, 4, 12, 17, 18; DcBiPP; DcCathB; DcNaB; McGEWB; NewCol 75; WhDW*

MacBeth, George Mann
Scottish. Poet
Impressive verse collection *The Colour of Blood,* 1967, combines violence, elegance, wit.
b. Jan 19, 1932 in Shotts, Scotland
Source: *AuBYP 3; Benet 87; BioIn 15, 16; CamGLE; ConAu 136; ConLC 2, 5, 9; ConPo 85, 91; DcLB 40; DrAPF 87; IntvTCA 2; ModBrL S1; OxCEng 95; OxCTwCP; RAdv 1; SmATA 4, 70; WorAu 1950; WrDr 86*

MacBride, Sean
Irish. Statesman
Only person to win both Nobel, 1974, and Lenin, 1977, Peace Prizes; co-founded Amnesty International.
b. Jan 26, 1904 in Paris, France
d. Jan 15, 1988 in Dublin, Ireland
Source: *AnObit 1988; BioIn 1, 2, 10, 11, 13; BlueB 76; ConAu 124; ConHero 1; CurBio 49, 88, 88N; DcIrB 88; FacFETw; HisWorL; IntWW 74, 75, 76, 77, 78, 79, 80, 81, 82, 83; IntYB 78, 79, 80, 81, 82; NewYTBS 74, 88; NobelP; Who 74, 82, 83, 85, 88; WhoNob, 90, 95; WhoUN 75; WhoWor 74, 76, 78, 80, 82, 84, 87; WorAl; WorAlBi*

Maccabees
[Eleazar Maccabees; Jochanan Maccabees; Mattathias Maccabees; Simon Maccabees]
Patriots
Jewish family who restored political, religious life from Syrian persecution; Hanukkah celebrates this event.
Source: *NewC; NewCol 75*

Maccabeus, Judas
Hebrew. Military Leader
Jewish resistance leader who defeated Seleucids to re-establish the sacred Temple of Jerusalem and to defend their religion; his heroic deeds are commemorated in Hanukka.
d. 161
Source: *BioIn 17*

MacCameron, Robert L
American. Artist
Portrait painter, popular early 1900s.
b. Jan 14, 1866 in Chicago, Illinois
d. Dec 29, 1912 in New York, New York
Source: *DcAmB; WhAm 1*

MacCarthy, Desmond Charles Otto, Sir
English. Journalist
Erudite drama/literary critic; wrote for the *New Statesman,* 1913-29.
b. May 20, 1877 in Plymouth, England
d. Jun 8, 1952 in Cambridge, England
Source: *Benet 87; BioIn 2, 3, 4, 14; CasWL; DcLEL; DcLP 87A; DcNaB 1951; GrBr; NotNAT B; ObitOF 79; OxCEng 85; REn; TwCA SUP; TwCLC 36*

Macchio, Ralph George, Jr.
American. Actor
In films *The Karate Kid,* 1984; *The Karate Kid II,* 1986.
b. Nov 4, 1962 in Long Island, New York
Source: *BioIn 13, 14, 15, 16; ConTFT 3; HalFC 88; IntMPA 92*

Maccoll, Ewan
Scottish. Singer, Songwriter
Folk singer; wrote Grammy-winning "The First Time Ever I Saw Your Face," sung by Roberta Flack.
b. Jan 25, 1915 in Auchterarder, Scotland
d. Oct 22, 1989 in London, England
Source: *AnObit 1989; BioIn 16, 17; CmScLit; ColdWar 2; DcNaB 1986; EncFCWM 69; FacFETw; NewGrDM 80; NewYTBS 89; OxCPMus; PenEncP*

MacCorkindale, Simon
English. Actor
In film *Jaws 3-D,* 1983; TV series "Falcon Crest," 1984-86.
b. Feb 12, 1953 in Cambridge, England
Source: *ConTFT 4; HalFC 88; IntMPA 88, 92; VarWW 85; WhoWest 87*

Mac Cready, Paul Beattie
American. Engineer, Inventor
Invented first human-powered aircraft to fly across English Channel, 1979; founder, pres., Meteorology Research, Inc., 1951-70.
b. Sep 29, 1925 in New Haven, Connecticut
Source: *AmMWSc 86; BioIn 12, 14, 15; ConNews 86-4; WhoAm 82, 84, 88, 90, 92, 94, 95, 96, 97; WhoFrS 84; WhoScEn 96; WhoWest 89, 92*

MacDermot, Galt
Canadian. Composer
Won Grammy for score of *Hair,* 1968.
b. Dec 19, 1928 in Montreal, Quebec, Canada
Source: *BiDAmM; BioIn 12, 14; CelR; CurBio 84; DcArts; EncMT; NotNAT; OxCPMus; PlP&P, A; WhoAm 78, 80; WhoThe 77*

MacDiarmid, Hugh
[Christopher Murray Grieve]
Scottish. Poet
Verse volumes include *A Drunk Man Looks at the Thistle,* 1926.
b. Aug 11, 1892 in Langholm, Scotland
d. Sep 9, 1978 in Edinburgh, Scotland
Source: *Au&Wr 71; Benet 87, 96; BioIn 1, 4, 6, 7, 8, 9, 11, 12, 13, 14, 16, 17, 18; BlmGEL; BlueB 76; CamGLE; CasWL; Chambr 3; ChhPo, S2, S3; CmScLit; CnDBLB 7; CnE&AP; CnMWL; ConAu 5R, X; ConLC 2, 4, 11, 19, 63; ConPo 70, 75; DcLB 20; DcLEL; DcNaB 1971; EncWL, 2, 3; EngPo; EvLB; FacFETw; GrBr; GrWrEL P; IntAu&W 76, 77; IntWW 74, 75, 76, 77, 78; IntWWP 77; LegTOT; LinLib L; LngCEL; LngCTC; MakMC; ModBrL, S1, S2; NewC; NewCBEL; OxCEng 67, 85, 95; OxCTwCP; PenC ENG; PoeCrit 9; RAdv 1, 14, 13-1; REn; RfGEnL 91; RGFMBP; RGTwCWr; TwCA, SUP; WebE&AL; WhAm 9; WhDW; WhE&EA; WhoLA; WhoTwCL; WhoWor 74; WorAl; WorAlBi; WrDr 76*

MacDonagh, Thomas
Irish. Poet, Patriot
Wrote *Of a Poet-Patriot;* executed after Easter Rebellion.
b. 1878 in Cloughjordan, Ireland
d. May 3, 1916 in Dublin, Ireland
Source: *BiDIrW; BioIn 8, 12; CamGEL; CamGLE; ChhPo, S2, S3; DcCathB; DcIrB 78, 88; DcIrL, 96; DcIrW 1; EvLB; LngCTC; ModIrL; NewC; NewCBEL; OxCIri; OxCTwCP; PoIre; REn; TwCA; TwCWr*

MacDonald, Dwight
American. Critic, Journalist
Wrote *Against the American Grain,* 1963.
b. Mar 24, 1906 in New York, New York
d. Dec 19, 1982 in New York, New York
Source: *AmAu&B; AmDec 1940; AmSocL; AnObit 1982; Benet 87, 96; BenetAL 91; BiDAmLf; BioIn 1, 4, 8, 10, 11, 13, 14, 15, 19, 20; CelR; ChhPo, S1; ConAu 29R, 108; CurBio 69, 83, 83N; DcLEL 1940; EncAB-H 1996; EncAJ; EncAL; EncTwCJ; EncWB; FacFETw; JrnUS; LinLib L; ModAL; NewYTBS 82; OxCAmL 65, 83, 95; PenC AM; PolProf J, T; RAdv 1, 13-1; SmATA 29, 33N; WhAm 8; WhoAm 74, 76, 78, 80, 82; WhoTwCL; WorAl; WorAu 1950; WrDr 76, 80, 82, 84*

MacDonald, Elizabeth G.
American. Inventor
Inventor of the powered household cleaner, Spic & Span.
b. 1894
d. May 11, 1992 in Dunedin, Florida
Source: *BioIn 16*

MacDonald, George
Scottish. Author, Poet
Wrote novel *Robert Falconer,* 1868; juvenile fantasy *At the Back of the North Wind,* 1871.
b. Dec 10, 1824 in Huntley, Scotland
d. Sep 18, 1905 in Ashstead, England
Source: *Alli, SUP; AuBYP 2, 3; BbD; Benet 87; BiD&SB; BioIn 1, 3, 4, 6, 7, 8, 9, 10, 11, 12, 13, 14, 15, 16, 19, 20; BritAu 19; CamGEL; CamGLE; CarSB; CasWL; Chambr 3; ChhPo, S1, S2, S3; ChlBkCr; CmScLit; ConAu 106, 137; DcArts; DcBiA; DcEnA, A; DcEnL; DcEuL; DcLB 18, 163; DcLEL; DcNaB S2; EncSF, 93; EvLB; FamSYP; GrWrEL N; JBA 34; LngCTC; MajAI; NewC; NewCBEL; Novels; OxCChiL; OxCEng 67, 85, 95; PenC ENG; RAdv 14; REn; RfGEnL 91; ScF&FL 1, 92; ScFSB; SJGFanW; SmATA 33; StaCVF; SupFW; TwCChW 78A, 83A, 89A, 95A; TwCLC 9; TwCSFW 91; VicBrit; WebE&AL; WhoChL; WhoHr&F; WrChl*

MacDonald, J(ames) E(dward) H(ervey)
[Group of Seven]
Canadian. Artist
Original member, Group of Seven, 1920; known for landscapes, Rocky Mountain scenes.
b. May 12, 1873 in Durham, England
d. Nov 26, 1932 in Toronto, Ontario, Canada
Source: *BioIn 1, 2, 10; CreCan 2; FacFETw; IlBEAAW; McGDA; OxCArt; OxCCan; OxCTwCA; OxDcArt*

MacDonald, James Ramsay
English. Statesman
Formed first Labour govt., 1924; prime minister, 1924, 1929-1935.
b. Oct 12, 1866 in Lossiemouth, Scotland
d. Nov 9, 1937
Source: *BiDInt; BioIn 1, 2, 3, 7, 8, 9, 11, 12, 14, 15, 16, 17, 21; ChhPo; DcAmSR; DcNaB 1931; DcPol; DcTwHis; EncSoA; EncTR 91; GrBr; LinLib L, S; McGEWB; WhDW; WhLit*

MacDonald, Jeanette
American. Singer, Actor
Soprano, noted for films with Nelson Eddy, 1930s.
b. Jun 18, 1907? in Philadelphia, Pennsylvania
d. Jan 14, 1965 in Houston, Texas
Source: *BiDAmM; BiE&WWA; BioAmW; BioIn 7, 9, 10, 11, 20, 21; CmMov; EncMT; FilmgC; GoodHs; InWom, SUP; LinLib S; MotPP; MovMk; ObitT 1961; OxCFilm; PenDiMP; ThFT; WhAm 4; WhoHol B; WhScrn 74, 77; WhThe; WorAl; WorEFlm*

MacDonald, John Alexander
Canadian. Political Leader
First prime minister of Canada, 1867-73, 1878-91; influential in passage of British N America Act, 1867.
b. Jan 11, 1815 in Glasgow, Scotland
d. Jun 6, 1891 in Ottawa, Ontario, Canada
Source: *ApCAB; BbtC; BioIn 1, 3, 4, 6, 7, 8, 9, 10, 11, 12, 13; CelCen; DcCanB 12; DcNaB, C; Drake; HisDBrE; LinLib S; MacDCB 78; McGEWB; OxCCan; WhNaAH; WorAl*

MacDonald, John Dann
American. Author
Mystery writer known for Travis McGee detective stories; wrote suspense thriller *Condominium,* 1977.
b. Jul 24, 1916 in Sharon, Pennsylvania
d. Dec 28, 1986 in Milwaukee, Wisconsin
Source: *AmAu&B; BioIn 3, 5, 7, 9, 10, 11, 12; ConAu 1NR, 1R, 19NR; ConLC 3; CorpD; CurBio 86, 87; EncMys; IntAu&W 82; SpyFic; WhAm 9; WhoAm 74, 76, 78, 80, 82, 84, 86; WhoSpyF; WorAl; WorAu 1950; WrDr 76*

MacDonald, Malcolm John
Scottish. Diplomat
Served in Labour govts., 1930s-40s; commissioner-general in Southeast Asia, 1948-55.
b. Aug 17, 1901 in Lossiemouth, Scotland
d. Jan 11, 1981 in Sevenoaks, England
Source: *Au&Wr 71; BioIn 2, 3, 4, 6, 8, 12; BlueB 76; ConAu 9R, 102; CurBio 54, 81; DcNaB 1981; IntAu&W 77, 82; IntWW 74, 75, 76, 77, 78, 79, 80; IntYB 78, 79, 80, 81; NewYTBS 81; OxCCan; WhAm 7; Who 74; WhoWor 74*

MacDonald, Peter
American. Native American Leader
Chairman of the Navajo Tribe Council, 1970-82, 1986-90.
b. Dec 16, 1928
Source: *BioIn 9, 10, 12, 13; BlueB 76; EncNAB; NewYTBS 89; NotNaAm; REnAW; WhoAm 74, 76, 88, 90; WhoWest 87, 89*

MacDonald, Ross
[Kenneth Millar]
American. Author
Wrote mysteries featuring series character Lew Archer; first novel was *The Moving Target,* 1949.
b. Dec 13, 1915 in Los Gatos, California
d. Jul 11, 1983 in Santa Barbara, California
Source: *AmAu&B; AmNov; AnObit 1983; Au&Wr 71; AuSpks; Benet 87; BenetAL 91; BioIn 2, 3, 5, 8, 9, 10, 11, 12, 13, 14, 17; BlueB 76; CmCal; ConAu 9R, 16NR, 110, X; ConLC 1, 2, 3, 14, 41; ConNov 72, 76, 82, 86A; ConPopW; CorpD; CrtSuMy; CurBio 53, 79, 83, 83N; CyWA 89; DcLB 2, DS6, Y83N; DcLEL 1940; DcTwCCu 1; DrAPF 80; EncMys; FacFETw; HalFC 80, 84, 88; IntAu&W 76; IntWW 81, 82, 83; LegTOT; LinLib L; MagSAmL; MajTwCW; ModAL, S1; NewYTBS 83; Novels; OxCAmL 83, 95; RAdv 14; RfGAmL 87, 94; TwCCr&M 80, 85, 91; WhAm 8; WhoAm 74, 76, 78, 80, 82; WhoWest 76, 78; WhoWor 74; WorAl; WorAlBi; WorAu 1950; WrDr 76, 80, 82, 84*

MacDonald-Wright, Stanton
American. Artist
Co-found, Synchromism, 1913, a style where color generates form; later turned to Oriental art.
b. Jul 8, 1890 in Charlottesville, Virginia
d. Aug 22, 1973 in Pacific Palisades, California
Source: *ArtsAmW 1; BioIn 3, 4, 7, 10; BriEAA; CmCal; ConArt 77, 83; DcAmArt; DcCAA 71, 77, 88, 94; McGDA; NewYTBE 73; OxCTwCA; OxDcArt; PhDcTCA 77; WhAm 6; WhAmArt 85; WhoAm 74; WhoAmA 73, 76N, 78N, 80N, 82N, 84N, 86N, 89N, 91N, 93N; WhoWor 74*

MacDonough, Thomas
American. Naval Officer
Captain who led one of most important battles in US navy; his victory caused British to lose claim of Great Lakes, 1814.
b. Dec 31, 1783 in New Castle County, Delaware
d. Nov 10, 1825
Source: *AmBi; ApCAB; BioIn 2, 5, 6, 8; DcAmB; DcAmMiB; Drake; HarEnMi; HarEnUS; NatCAB 7; NewCol 75; OxCAmH; OxCShps; TwCBDA; WebAB 74, 79; WebAMB; WhAm HS*

MacDougall, Curtis Daniel
American. Educator, Journalist
Advocate of interpretive journalism; wrote *Superstition and the Press,* 1983.
b. Feb 11, 1903 in Fond du Lac, Wisconsin
d. Nov 10, 1985 in Evanston, Illinois
Source: *AmMWSc 73S, 78S; Au&Wr 71; BioIn 14; ConAu 53, 117; EncAJ; WhAm 9; WhoAm 74, 76, 78, 80, 82, 84*

MacDowell, Andie
[Rosalie Anderson MacDowell]
American. Actor, Model
Debut in *Greystroke,* 1984; other films include *Sex, Lies and Videotape,* 1989.
b. Apr 21, 1958 in Gaffney, South Carolina
Source: *BioIn 14, 15, 16; CelR 90; ConTFT 9; IntMPA 92; WhoEnt 92*

MacDowell, Edward Alexander
American. Composer, Pianist
Best known for symphonic poems *Hamlet and Ophelia; Lancelot and Elaine.*
b. Dec 18, 1861 in New York, New York
d. Jan 23, 1908 in New York, New York
Source: *AmBi; ApCAB X; ASCAP 66, 80; AtlBL; Benet 87, 96; BiDAmM; BioIn 1, 2, 3, 4, 5, 6, 7, 8, 10, 12, 13, 14, 17, 19; ChhPo S1, S2; CmpBCM; DcAmB; DcCom&M 79; DcNAA; EncAAH; EncAB-A 2; EncAB-H 1974, 1996; GrComp; LinLib S; McGEWB; MusMk; NatCAB 11; OxCAmH; OxCAmL 65, 83, 95; OxCMus; REn; REnAL; TwCBDA; WebAB 74, 79; WhAm 1*

Macfadden, Bernarr Adolphus
[Bernard Adolphus Macfadden]
American. Author, Publisher
Magazines published include *True Romances; True Detective Stories,*
b. Aug 16, 1868 in Mill Spring, Missouri
d. Oct 12, 1955 in Jersey City, New Jersey
Source: *AmAu&B; AmDec 1900; BioIn 1, 2, 3, 4, 6, 10; DcAmAu; DcAmB S5; REnAL; WebAB 74; WhAm 3; WhNAA; WhScrn 77*

MacFarlane, Willie
Scottish. Golfer
Touring pro, 1920s-30s; won US Open, 1925.
b. Jun 29, 1890 in Aberdeen, Scotland
d. Aug 18, 1961 in Miami Beach, Florida
Source: *BioIn 6; WhoGolf*

Macfarren, George Alexander, Sir
English. Composer
Works include nine symphonies; opera *Robin Hood,* 1860; oratorio *The Resurrection,* 1876.
b. Mar 2, 1813 in London, England
d. Oct 31, 1887 in London, England
Source: *Alli SUP; Baker 78, 84, 92; BioIn 16; CelCen; DcBiPP; DcNaB; NewC; NewEOp 71; NewGrDM 80; NewGrDO; OxCMus; VicBrit*

MacGrath, Leueen (Emily)
English. Actor, Dramatist
Stage star in several plays including *No Exit,* 1936; collaborated with t hen-husband, George S Kaufman, on various works; including *Silk Stockings,* 1955.
b. Jul 3, 1914 in London, England
d. Mar 27, 1992 in London, England
Source: *BiE&WWA; InWom; NotNAT; WhoHol A; WhoThe 72, 77, 81*

MacGraw, Ali
American. Actor
Starred in *Love Story,* 1971; TV mini-series "Winds of War," 1983; former wife of Steve MacQueen; wrote autobiography *Moving Pictures,* 1991.
b. Apr 1, 1938 in Westchester, New York
Source: *BioIn 8, 9, 10, 11, 12, 13, 14, 15, 16; BkPepl; ConTFT 5; FilmEn; FilmgC; HalFC 80, 84, 88; IntMPA 75, 76, 77, 78, 79, 80, 81, 82, 84, 86, 88, 92; InWom SUP; LegTOT; MotPP; MovMk; NewYTBE 73; VarWW 85; WhoAm 86, 90; WhoAmW 85; WhoEnt 92; WhoHol 92, A; WorAlBi*

MacGregor, Clark
American. Business Executive
Senior vp, United Technologies, 1972-87; former politician; Nixon's campaign director, 1972.
b. Jul 12, 1922 in Minneapolis, Minnesota
Source: *BiDrAC; BiDrUSC 89; BioIn 9, 12; Dun&B 79, 86; EncAI&E; NewYTBE 70; PolProf NF; St&PR 84, 87; WhoAm 74, 76, 78, 80, 82, 84, 86, 88, 90; WhoAmP 73, 75, 77, 79, 95; WhoE 89; WhoFI 89; WhoGov 72; WhoSSW 73*

MacGregor, Ian Kinloch
American. Business Executive
Chm., Clyde Cable Vision, 1987—.
b. Sep 21, 1912 in Kinlochleven, Scotland
Source: *BioIn 13, 14; IntWW 89, 91; St&PR 87, 91; Who 82, 92; WhoAm 82; WhoFI 83*

Mach, Ernst
Austrian. Physicist
Forerunner of logical positivism known for research in ballistics.
b. Feb 18, 1838 in Chirlitz-Turas, Moravia
d. Feb 19, 1916 in Haar, Germany
Source: *AsBiEn; Baker 78, 84, 92; BiDPsy; BiESc; BioIn 1, 2, 3, 7, 8, 9, 12, 13, 14, 18; CamDcSc; DcInv; DcScB; InSci; LarDcSc; LegTOT; MacBEP; McGEWB; NamesHP; NewCol 75; OxCPhil; RAdv 14, 13-5; WorAl; WorAlBi; WorScD*

Machado (y Ruiz), Antonio
Spanish. Poet
Sensitive to social problems of Spain, verse volumes, including *Campos de Castilla,* 1917, address morality, hope, despair.
b. Jul 26, 1875 in Seville, Spain
d. Feb 22, 1939 in Collioure, France
Source: *AtlBL; Benet 87, 96; BioIn 1, 3, 5, 6, 7, 9, 10, 13, 16, 17, 19; CasWL; ClDMEL 47, 80; CnMWL; ConAu 104; DcArts; DcLB 108; DcSpL; EncWL 2, 3; EuWr 9; EvEuW; LinLib L; McGEWD 72, 84; ModRL; ModSpP S; OxCSpan; PenC EUR; RAdv 14, 13-2; REn;*

RGFMEP; TwCLC 3; TwCWr; WhDW; WhoTwCL; WorAlBi; WorAu 1950

Machado (y Ruiz), Manuel
Spanish. Author, Dramatist
Writings describe Andalusian life: *Cante Hondo*, 1912; brother of Antonio.
b. Aug 29, 1874 in Seville, Spain
d. Jan 19, 1947 in Madrid, Spain
Source: *BioIn 1, 8, 17; CasWL; ClDMEL 47, 80; DcLB 108; DcSpL; EncWL; EvEuW; McGEWD 72, 84; ModSpP S; OxCSpan; PenC EUR; REn*

Machado y Morales, Gerardo
Cuban. Political Leader
Involved in revolution against Spain, 1895-98; liberal pres. of Cuba, 1925-33; dictatorial powers caused popular revolt ending in his ousting.
b. Sep 29, 1871 in Santa Clara, Cuba
d. Mar 29, 1939 in Miami Beach, Florida
Source: *BiDLAmC; BioIn 1, 16; DicTyr; McGEWB; WebBD 83*

Machel, Samora Moises
Mozambican. Political Leader
President of newly independent Mozambique, 1975-86; never faced coup attempt; died in plane crash.
b. Sep 29, 1933 in Chilembene, Mozambique
d. Oct 19, 1986 in Muzimi, South Africa
Source: *AfSS 78, 79, 80, 81, 82; BioIn 9, 10, 12, 13; ConBlB 8; ConNews 87-1; CurBio 84, 87, 87N; DcAfHiB 86S; EncWB; IntWW 76, 77, 78, 79, 80, 81, 82, 83; NewYTBS 75; WhAm 11; WhoWor 78, 80, 82, 84, 87*

Machen, Arthur
English. Author
Macabre tales, fantasies include *Hill of Dreams*, 1907.
b. Mar 3, 1863 in Caerleon, England
d. Dec 15, 1947 in Beaconsfield, England
Source: *Alli SUP; Benet 87; BioIn 1, 2, 4, 5, 6, 7, 9, 10, 14, 15, 16, 17, 19, 21; CamGLE; CasWL; ConAu 104; CyWA 58; DcLB 156; DcLEL; DivFut; EncMys; EncO&P 1, 2, 3; EncSF, 93; EvLB; GrWrEL N; LngCTC; ModBrL; NewC; NewCBEL; Novels; OxCEng 67; OxCLiW 86; PenC ENG; PenEncH; REn; RfGEnL 91; ScF&FL 1, 92; ScFSB; ShSCr 20; StaCVF; SupFW; TwCA, SUP; TwCLC 4; TwCWr; WhDW; WhLit; WhoHr&F*

Machiavelli, Niccolo
Italian. Philosopher, Author
Wrote *The Prince*, 1513, outlining pragmatic theory of govt.
b. May 3, 1469 in Florence, Italy
d. Jun 22, 1527 in Florence, Italy
Source: *AtlBL; Benet 87, 96; BiD&SB; BioIn 1, 3, 4, 5, 6, 7, 8, 9, 10, 11, 12, 13, 14, 16, 18, 19, 20; CamGWoT; CasWL; CnThe; CyWA 58; DcArts; DcEuL; DcItL 1, 2; Dis&D; EncEth; EuAu; EuWr 2; EvEuW; GrFLW; HarEnMi; LegTOT; LinLib L, S; LitC 8; LuthC 75; McGEWB; McGEWD 72, 84; NewC; NewCBEL; NewEOp 71; OxCEng 67, 85, 95; OxCPhil; PenC EUR; RAdv 14, 13-3, 13-4; RComWL; REn; REnWD; WhDW; WorAl; WorAlBi*

Machlup, Fritz
American. Economist, Author
Challenged mainstream economic thought; considered education an economic resource; wrote over 20 books on subject.
b. Dec 15, 1902 in Wiener Neustadt, Austria
d. Jan 30, 1983 in Princeton, New Jersey
Source: *AmEA 74; AmMWSc 73S, 78S; AnObit 1983; BioIn 6, 13, 14; BlueB 76; ConAu 1R, 6NR, 109; GrEconS; IntEnSS 79; IntWW 81, 82; NewYTBS 83; WhAm 8; WhoAm 74, 76, 78, 80, 82; WhoEc 81, 86; WhoWor 74; WrDr 80, 82, 84*

MacInnes, Helen
American. Author
Writer of spy fiction: *Above Suspicion*, 1941; *Ride a Pale Horse*, 1985.
b. Oct 7, 1907 in Glasgow, Scotland
d. Sep 30, 1985 in New York, New York
Source: *AmAu&B; AnObit 1985; AuSpks; Benet 87; BenetAL 91; BioIn 1, 2, 4, 8, 10, 11, 12, 13, 14, 15, 17; BlueB 76; ConAu 1NR, 1R, 28NR, 117; ConLC 27, 39; ConNov 72, 76; CorpD; CrtSuMy; CurBio 67, 85, 85N; DcLB 87; EncMys; FacFETw; FemiCLE; ForWC 70; IntAu&W 76, 77, 82; IntWW 74, 75, 76, 77, 78, 79, 80, 81, 82, 83; LegTOT; LinLib L; MajTwCW; NewC; NewYTBS 85; Novels; REnAL; SmATA 22, 44N; TwCCr&M 80, 85, 91; WhAm 9; Who 85; WhoAm 74, 76, 78, 80, 82, 84; WhoAmW 58, 64, 66, 68, 70, 72, 74, 83, 85; WhoE 74; WhoSpyF; WhoWor 78, 80, 82, 84; WrDr 80, 82, 84*

Macintosh, Charles
Scottish. Chemist, Inventor
Developed waterproof fabric used to make raincoats, 1823.
b. Dec 29, 1766 in Glasgow, Scotland
d. Jul 25, 1843 in Glasgow, Scotland
Source: *BiESc; BioIn 3, 14; DcNaB, C; EncFash; InSci; LarDcSc; NewCol 75; WhDW; WorInv*

MacIver, Loren
American. Artist
Career as painter has spanned six decades; work doesn't fall into definite art movement or style, but sometimes called symbolic or romantic: *Winter Dunes*, 1932.
b. Feb 22, 1909 in New York, New York
Source: *BiDWomA; BioIn 1, 3, 4, 5, 6, 11, 15, 17, 19; BlueB 76; CurBio 53, 87; DcCAA 71, 77, 88, 94; IntWW 74, 75, 76, 77, 78, 79, 80, 81, 82, 83, 89, 91; McGDA; NorAmWA; OxCTwCA; PhDcTCA 77; WhAmArt 85; WhoAm 74, 76, 78, 80, 82, 84, 86, 94, 95, 96, 97; WhoAmA 73, 76, 78, 80, 82, 84, 86, 89, 91, 93; WhoAmW 58, 64, 66, 68, 70, 72, 74, 75; WhoWor 74; WomArt; WorArt 1950*

Mack, Connie
[Cornelius Alexander McGillicuddy]
"The Tall Tactician"
American. Baseball Manager
Owner, manager, Philadelphia Athletics, 1901-50; won nine pennants, five World Series; Hall of Fame, 1937.
b. Dec 22, 1862 in East Brookfield, Massachusetts
d. Feb 8, 1956 in Philadelphia, Pennsylvania
Source: *Ballpl 90; BiDAmSp BB; BioIn 14, 15, 16, 17, 19, 21; CurBio 44, 56; DcAmB S6; FacFETw; LegTOT; LinLib L, S; OxCAmH; WebAB 74, 79; WhAm 3; WhoProB 73; WhoSpor; WorAl; WorAlBi*

Mack, Connie
[Cornelius Mack, III]
American. Politician
Rep. senator, FL, 1989—.
b. Oct 29, 1940 in Philadelphia, Pennsylvania
Source: *AlmAP 88, 92, 96; BiDrUSC 89; BioIn 14, 16, 21; CngDr 83, 85, 87, 89, 91, 93, 95; IntWW 89, 91, 93; LegTOT; PolsAm 84; WhoAm 84, 86, 88, 90, 92, 94, 95, 96, 97; WhoAmP 83, 85, 87, 89, 91, 93, 95; WhoSSW 84, 86, 88, 91, 93, 95, 97; WhoWor 91, 96*

Mack, John M
American. Manufacturer
With brothers, built world's first gas-powered bus, 1900.
b. 1864
d. 1924
Source: *Entr*

Mack, Peter
American. Politician
Dem. congressman from IL, 1949-63, who flew around world, 1951-52, on goodwill tour.
b. Nov 1, 1916 in Carlinville, Illinois
d. Jul 4, 1986 in Washington, District of Columbia
Source: *WhoAmP 79*

Mack, Ted
[William E Maguiness]
American. TV Personality, Musician
Hosted amateur show on radio, TV, 1945-70; helped discover Frank Sinatra.
b. Feb 12, 1904 in Greeley, Colorado
d. Jul 12, 1976 in Tarrytown, New York
Source: *BiDAmM; BioIn 2, 4, 11; CurBio 51, 76, 76N; RadStar; WhAm 7; WhoAm 74, 76*

Mackay, Clarence Hungerford
American. Business Executive
Pres., Postal Telegraph & Cable Corp; laid the first transpacific communications cable from US to Far East; innovated uniting of radio, cable

and telegraph entities into one communications industry.
b. Apr 17, 1874 in San Francisco, California
d. Nov 12, 1938 in New York, New York
Source: *AmBi; BiDAmBL 83; BioIn 4; DcAmB S2; DcCathB; InSci; NatCAB 14, 31; WebAB 74, 79; WhAm 1*

Mackay, John Alexander
American. Clergy, University Administrator
Pres., Princeton Theological Seminary, 1936-59; wrote *Presbyterian Way of Life*, 1960.
b. May 17, 1889 in Inverness, Scotland
d. Jun 9, 1983 in Hightstown, New Jersey
Source: *AnObit 1983; Au&Wr 71; BioIn 1, 2, 3, 5, 13, 14, 18, 19; BlueB 76; ConAu 110; CurBio 52, 83N; DcAmReB 2; DcEcMov; DrAS 74P; IntWW 74; NewYTBS 83; RelLAm 91; WhAm 8, 9; Who 74, 82, 83; WhoAm 76, 78, 80; WhoRel 77; WhoWor 74*

Mackay, John William
American. Philanthropist, Businessman
Developed Comstock silver lode, 1864; with Bennett founded Commercial Cable Co., 1884; organized Postal Telegraph Co., 1886.
b. Nov 28, 1831 in Dublin, Ireland
d. Jul 20, 1902 in London, England
Source: *AmBi; ApCAB; BiDAmBL 83; BioIn 1, 2, 15; DcAmB; HarEnUS; McGEWB; NatCAB 4; NewCol 75; OxCAmH; REnAW; TwCBDA; WhAm 1*

MacKay, Mickey
[Duncan McMillan MacKay]
Canadian. Hockey Player
Played for Chicago, Boston in NHL, 1926-29; Hall of Fame, 1952.
b. May 21, 1894 in Chesley, Ontario, Canada
d. May 21, 1940 in British Columbia, Canada
Source: *WhoHcky 73*

Mackaye, James Morrison Steele
American. Designer, Inventor
Patented dozens of theatrical devices including overhead, indirect lighting; moveable stage; disappearing orchestra pit, folding chairs.
b. Jun 6, 1842 in Buffalo, New York
d. Feb 25, 1894 in Timpas, Colorado
Source: *AmAu; BioIn 20; CamGWoT; CamHAL; DcAmB; DcNAA; McGEWD 72, 84; NewCol 75; OxCAmL 65; WebAB 74, 79; WhAm HS*

MacKaye, Percy Wallace
American. Poet, Dramatist
Wrote play *Canterbury Pilgrims*, 1903; folk lore *Kentucky Mountain Fantasies*, 1928; son of Steele.
b. Mar 16, 1875 in New York, New York
d. Aug 31, 1956 in Cornish, New Hampshire
Source: *AmAu&B; CnDAL; CnThe; ConAmL; DcLEL; McGEWD 72; ModAL; ModWD; OxCAmL 65; OxCThe 67; REn; REnAL; Str&VC; TwCA, SUP; WhAm 3; WhNAA*

Macke, August
German. Artist
Member, Expressionist Blaue Reiter group.
b. Jan 3, 1887 in Meschede, Germany
d. Sep 26, 1914 in Perthes-les-Hurlus, France
Source: *BioIn 4, 17; DcArts; EncWB; FacFETw; IntDcAA 90; McGDA; NewCol 75; OxCArt; OxCGer 76, 86; OxCTwCA; OxDcArt; PhDcTCA 77*

MacKellar, William
American. Children's Author
Juvenile adventures include *Secret of the Sacred Stone*, 1970.
b. Feb 20, 1914 in Glasgow, Scotland
Source: *AuBYP 2, 3; BioIn 9; ConAu 13NR, 33R; ScF&FL 1; SmATA 4*

Mackendrick, Alexander
American. Director
Noted for *Sweet Smell of Success*, 1957; *The Ladykillers*, 1956.
b. 1912 in Boston, Massachusetts
Source: *BiDFilm; MiSFD 9; MovMk; OxCFilm; WorEFlm; WorFDir 2*

Mackenzie, Alexander
Canadian. Political Leader
First Liberal Party prime minister of Canada, 1873-78.
b. Jan 28, 1822 in Dunkeld, Scotland
d. Apr 17, 1892 in Toronto, Ontario, Canada
Source: *Alli SUP; ApCAB; BioIn 5, 7, 8; CelCen; DcCanB 12; DcNAA; DcNaB; LinLib S; MacDCB 78; McGEWB; OxCCan*

Mackenzie, Alexander, Sir
Scottish. Author, Explorer
Made first overland journey across N America north of Mexico, 1793.
b. 1755 in Lewis Island, Scotland
d. Mar 11, 1820 in Mulnain, Scotland
Source: *Alli; ApCAB; BbtC; BiDLA; BioIn 15, 16, 17, 18, 20; BritAu 19; DcLEL; DcNaB; HarEnUS; NewC; NewCBEL; OxCAmL 65; OxCCan; OxCShps; REnAL; WhDW; WorAl; WorAlBi*

Mackenzie, Alexander Campbell, Sir
Scottish. Composer
Compositions which introduce Scottish elements include "Tam o' Shanter," 1911; "Scottish Rhapsodies," 1880.
b. Aug 22, 1847 in Edinburgh, Scotland
d. Apr 28, 1935 in London, England
Source: *Baker 78, 84, 92; BioIn 2, 4, 16; BriBkM 80; DcNaB 1931; LegTOT; NewEOp 71; NewGrDM 80; NewGrDO; OxCMus; VicBrit; WorAl*

Mackenzie, Compton
[Edward Montague MacKenzie, Sir]
English. Author
Wrote *Whiskey Galore*, 1947; made into successful film *Tight Little Island*.
b. Jan 17, 1883 in West Hartlepool, England
d. Nov 30, 1972 in Edinburgh, Scotland
Source: *Au&Wr 71; AuBYP 2S, 3; Benet 87; BioIn 4, 6, 7, 8, 9, 10, 14, 16, 17; BlmGEL; CamGLE; CasWL; CathA 1930; Chambr 3; CmScLit; ConAu 37R, P-2; ConNov 72; DcArts; DcLB 34, 100; DcLEL; DcNaB 1971; EncSF; EncWL; EvLB; FacFETw; GrBr; GrWrEL N; HalFC 80, 84, 88; LegTOT; LngCEL; LngCTC; ModBrL; NewC; NewCBEL; Novels; ObitT 1971; OxCEng 67, 85; OxCMus; PenC ENG; REn; RfGEnL 91; ScF&FL 1, 2; ScFSB; SpyFic; TwCA, SUP; TwCWr; WebE&AL; WhAm 7; WhDW; WhE&EA; WhLit; WhoChL; WhoLA; WhoSpyF; WhoTwCL; WhScrn 83*

MacKenzie, Gisele
[Marie Marguerite La Fleche]
Canadian. Singer, Actor
Star of "Your Hit Parade," 1953-57; "Gisele Mackenzie Show," 1957-58.
b. Jan 10, 1927 in Winnipeg, Manitoba, Canada
Source: *ASCAP 66; BioIn 3, 4, 5; CanWW 70, 79, 80, 81, 83, 89; CmpEPM; CreCan 2; CurBio 55; InWom, SUP; PenEncP; RkOn 74; VarWW 85; WhoAm 76, 78, 80, 82, 84; WhoAmW 58, 61, 64, 66, 68, 70, 72, 74; WorAl*

Mackenzie, Henry
"Addison of the North"
Scottish. Author
Wrote popular *Man of Feeling*, 1771; *Man of the World*, 1773.
b. Aug 26, 1745 in Edinburgh, Scotland
d. Jan 14, 1831 in Edinburgh, Scotland
Source: *Alli; BiD&SB; BioIn 3, 5, 8, 11, 12, 15; BritAu; CamGEL; CamGLE; CasWL; CelCen; ChhPo S2; CmScLit; CyWA 58; DcBiA; DcBiPP; DcEnA; DcEnL; DcEuL; DcLB 39; DcLEL; DcNaB; EvLB; GrWrEL N; MouLC 3; NewC; NewCBEL; NinCLC 41; OxCEng 67, 85, 95; PenC ENG; PseudAu; REn; RfGEnL 91; WebE&AL*

MacKenzie, Warren
American. Artist
Ceramist known for functional pottery.
b. Feb 16, 1924 in Kansas City, Missouri
Source: *BioIn 12, 16, 17, 20; CenC; CurBio 94*

Mackenzie, William Lyon
Canadian. Statesman, Journalist
First mayor of Toronto, 1834; led insurgents in Toronto uprising, 1837.
b. Mar 12, 1795 in Dundee, Scotland
d. Aug 28, 1861 in Toronto, Ontario, Canada
Source: *Alli; ApCAB; BbtC; BioIn 4, 6, 7, 8, 9, 10, 12, 17; DcCanB 9; DcLEL;*

DcNAA; DcNaB; Drake; HarEnUS; HisDBrE; MacDCB 78; McGEWB; OxCCan; OxCCanL

Mackerras, Charles
[Alan Charles Mackerras, Sir]
Australian. Conductor, Composer
Acclaimed Wagner, Mozart conductor who has led symphony, opera co. orchestras on three continents.
b. Nov 17, 1925 in Schenectady, New York
Source: *Baker 78, 84; BioIn 10, 11, 12, 13, 14, 15, 21; BlueB 76; BriBkM 80; CmOp; CnOxB; CurBio 85; DancEn 78; DcArts; IntDcOp; IntMPA 75, 76, 77, 78, 79, 80, 81, 82, 88; IntWW 74, 75, 76, 77, 78, 79, 80, 81, 82, 83, 89, 91, 93; IntWWM 77, 80, 85, 90; MetOEnc; MusMk; NewAmDM; NewGrDM 80; OxDcOp; PenDiMP; Who 74, 82, 83, 85, 88, 90, 92; WhoEnt 92; WhoMus 72; WhoOp 76; WhoWor 74, 82, 84, 87, 89, 91; WorAlBi*

Mackie, Bob
[Robert Gordon Mackie]
American. Fashion Designer
Designed clothes for "The Carol Burnett Show," 1967-77; also for Cher during the 70s; won 5 Emmys.
b. Mar 24, 1940 in Monterey Park, California
Source: *BioIn 9, 10, 11, 13, 16; CelR 90; ConFash; CurBio 88; EncFash; IntWW 91, 93; LegTOT; VarWW 85; WhoAm 78, 80, 82, 84, 86, 88, 90, 92, 94, 95, 96, 97; WhoE 95; WhoEnt 92; WhoFash 88; WhoWor 91; WorFshn*

Mackin, Catherine Patricia
"Cassie"
American. Broadcast Journalist
First woman to anchor nighttime network newscast.
b. Aug 28, 1939 in Baltimore, Maryland
d. Nov 20, 1982 in Towson, Maryland
Source: *ConAu 108; ForWC 70; GoodHs; NewYTBS 82; WhoAm 78; WhoAmW 68; WhoSSW 73*

Mackinder, Halford John, Sir
English. Geographer, Educator, Public Official
Promoted geography as an academic subject; wrote *Democratic Ideals and Reality,* 1919.
b. Feb 15, 1861 in Gainsborough, England
d. Mar 6, 1947 in London, England
Source: *BioIn 1, 5, 6, 9, 10, 11, 14, 15, 17, 18; DcNaB 1941; Geog 9; NewCol 75; RAdv 14; WebBD 83; WhDW; WhE&EA; WhLit; WhoLA*

MacKinnon, Catharine A(lice)
American. Educator, Feminist, Lawyer
Professor, U of MI School of Law, 1990—; crusader for women's rights; foe of pornography.
b. Oct 7, 1946
Source: *ConAu 128, 132; CurBio 94; EncWHA; News 93-2; NewYTBS 91; WrDr 92*

Mackintosh, Cameron
English. Producer
Theatrical producer of mega-hits *Cats,* 1981; *Les Miserables,* 1985; *Phantom of the Opera,* 1989.
b. Oct 17, 1946 in Enfield, England
Source: *BioIn 11, 15, 16; ConTFT 1, 9; CurBio 91; IntWW 91; NewYTBS 86, 90; Who 92; WhoAm 90, 92, 94, 95, 96, 97; WhoEnt 92*

MacLachlan, Kyle
American. Actor
Was in *Dune,* 1984 and TV's "Twin Peaks," 1990-91.
b. Feb 22, 1959 in Yakima, Washington
Source: *ConTFT 9; CurBio 93; IntMPA 94; WhoHol 92*

MacLaine, Shirley
[Shirley MacLean Beaty]
American. Actor, Author
Won 1984 Oscar for *Terms of Endearment*; best-selling books include *Out on a Limb,* 1983.
b. Apr 24, 1934 in Richmond, Virginia
Source: *AmWomWr; BestSel 89-3; BiDD; BiDFilm, 81, 94; BioIn 3, 4, 5, 6, 7, 8, 9, 10, 11, 12, 13, 14, 15, 16; BkPepl; BlueB 76; CelR, 90; ConAu 32NR, 103; ContDcW 89; ConTFT 1, 4, 11; CurBio 59, 78; DcArts; EncAFC; EncO&P 3; EncPaPR 91; FilmEn; FilmgC; ForWC 70; ForYSC; GoodHs; HalFC 80, 84, 88; HerW; IntAu&W 77, 89; IntDcF 1-3, 2-3; IntMPA 75, 76, 77, 78, 79, 80, 81, 82, 84, 86, 88, 92, 94; IntWW 74, 75, 76, 77, 78, 79, 80, 81, 82, 83, 89, 91, 93; InWom, SUP; ItaFilm; LegTOT; MotPP; MovMk; NewAgE 90; NewGrDA 86; NewYTBS 84; OxCFilm; OxCPMus; RelLAm 91; VarWW 85; WhoAm 74, 76, 78, 80, 82, 84, 86, 88, 90, 92, 94, 95, 96; WhoAmW 61, 64, 66, 68, 70, 72, 74, 79, 81, 83, 85, 87, 89, 91, 93, 95; WhoEnt 92; WhoHol 92, A; WhoUSWr 88; WhoWor 74; WhoWrEP 89, 92, 95; WomWMM; WorAl; WorAlBi; WorEFlm; WrDr 80, 82, 84, 86, 88, 90, 92, 94, 96*

MacLane, Barton
American. Actor
Appeared in over 200 films; co-starred with Glenda Farrell in *Torchy Blane* films; TV series "The Outlaws," 1960-61.
b. Dec 25, 1900 in Columbia, South Carolina
d. Jan 1, 1969 in Santa Monica, California
Source: *Film 2; FilmgC; HalFC 80, 84, 88; LegTOT; MotPP; MovMk; Vers A; WhoHol B; WhScrn 74, 77, 83*

Maclaughlin, Don
American. Actor
Member, original cast of "As the World Turns," 1956, first US daily drama.
b. Nov 24, 1907 in Webster City, Iowa
d. May 28, 1986 in Goshen, Indiana
Source: *SaTiSS*

MacLean, Alistair (Stuart)
Scottish. Author
Wrote blood and thunder war stories that sold millions of copies: *The Guns of Navarone,* 1957.
b. Apr 28, 1922 in Glasgow, Scotland
d. Feb 2, 1987 in Munich, Germany (West)
Source: *AnObit 1987; AuBYP 2S, 3; BioIn 9, 10, 13, 14, 15, 16, 17; BlueB 76; ConAu 28NR, 57, 121; ConLC 3, 13, 50, 63; ConPopW; CrtSuMy; DcArts; DcLEL 1940; DcNaB 1986; EncSF 93; FilmgC; HalFC 80, 84, 88; IntAu&W 76, 77; IntWW 74, 75, 76, 77, 78, 79, 80, 81, 82, 83; LegTOT; MajTwCW; NewYTBS 87; Novels; SmATA 23, 50N; TwCCr&M 80, 85, 91; TwCWW 91; WhAm 9; Who 74, 82, 83, 85; WhoAm 78, 80, 82, 84, 86; WhoWor 84; WorAl; WorAlBi; WorAu 1950; WrDr 76, 80, 82, 84, 86*

Maclean, Donald Duart
English. Spy
British diplomat, Soviet spy, 1934-51; fled to USSR, 1951, with Guy Burgess during investigations by British foreign office.
b. May 25, 1913 in London, England
d. Mar 6, 1983 in Moscow, Union of Soviet Socialist Republics
Source: *BioIn 2, 4, 6, 8, 11, 12, 13, 16, 17, 18, 21; ColdWar 2; ConAu 109; DcNaB 1981; NewYTBS 83; SpyCS; WhDW*

Maclean, Norman (Fitzroy)
American. Writer
Published collection of short stories *A River Runs Through It, and Other Stories* 1976.
b. Dec 23, 1902 in Clarinda, Iowa
d. Aug 2, 1990 in Chicago, Illinois
Source: *BioIn 11, 12, 17; ConAu 49NR, 102, 132; ConLC 78; ConPopW; DrAS 74E, 78E, 82E; ShSCr 13; TwCWW 91; WhAm 10; WhoAm 74, 86, 88, 90; WorAu 1980*

MacLeish, Archibald
American. Poet, Journalist
Won Pulitzers for *Conquistador,* 1932; *Collected Poems,* 1953; verse drama: *J.B.,* 1958.
b. May 7, 1892 in Glencoe, Illinois
d. Apr 20, 1982 in Boston, Massachusetts
Source: *AmAu&B; AmCulL; AmWr; AnObit 1982; ASCAP 66, 80; Benet 87, 96; BenetAL 91; BiDAmM; BiE&WWA; BioIn 1, 2, 3, 4, 5, 7, 8, 9, 10, 11, 12, 13, 14, 15, 16, 17, 18, 19; CamGEL; CamGLE; CamGWoT; CamHAL; CasWL; CelR; ChhPo S1, S2, S3; CnDAL; CnE&AP; CnMD; CnMWL; CnThe; ConAmA; ConAmD; ConAmL; ConAu 9R, 33NR, 106; ConDr 73, 77, 82, 93; ConLC 3, 8, 14, 68; ConPo 70, 75, 80; CroCD; CrtSuDr; CurBio 40, 59,*

82, 82N; CyWA 58, 89; DancEn 78; DcAmDH 80, 89; DcAmSR; DcArts; DcLB 4, 7, 45, Y82A; DcLEL; DrAP 75; DrAPF 80; EncWL, 2, 3; EncWT; Ent; EvLB; FacFETw; Focus; GrWrEL DR, P; IntAu&W 76, 77, 82; IntWW 74, 75, 76, 77, 78, 79, 80, 81, 82, 82N; IntWWP 77, 82; LegTOT; LiExTwC; LinLib L, S; LngCTC; MajTwCW; McGEWB; McGEWD 72, 84; ModAL, S1, S2; ModWD; NewYTBS 82; NotNAT; OxCAmL 65, 83, 95; OxCEng 67, 85, 95; OxCThe 67; OxCTwCP; PenC AM; PlP&P; RAdv 1, 14, 13-1; REn; REnAL; RfGAmL 87, 94; RGFAP; RGTwCWr; SixAP; TwCA, SUP; TwCWr; WebAB 74, 79; WebE&AL; WhAm 8; WhDW; WhNAA; Who 74, 82; WhoAm 74, 76, 78, 80, 82; WhoThe 72, 77, 81; WhoWor 74, 78, 80; WorAl; WorAlBi; WrDr 76, 80, 82

MacLeish, Rod(erick)
American. Journalist
Radio, TV news commentator, 1950s-60s; wrote *City on the River,* 1972.
b. Jan 15, 1926 in Bryn Mawr, Pennsylvania
Source: *ConAu 41R; LesBEnT, 92; ScF&FL 92; WhoAm 74, 76; WhoSSW 73, 82*

MacLennan, Hugh
[John Hugh MacLennan]
Canadian. Author
Wrote nonfiction and novels, including *Two Solitudes,* 1945, whose title became a byword symbolizing tensions between French and English Canadians 1960; *Voices in Time,* 1980; winner of 5 Governor General awards.
b. Mar 20, 1907 in Glace Bay, Nova Scotia, Canada
d. Nov 7, 1990 in Montreal, Quebec, Canada
Source: *AnObit 1990; Au&Wr 71; Benet 87, 96; BenetAL 91; BioIn 1, 3, 4, 9, 10, 11, 12, 15; BlueB 76; CamGLE; CanNov; CanWr; CanWW 70, 79, 80, 81, 83, 89; CasWL; CaW; ConAu 5R, 33NR; ConLC 2, 14, 92; ConNov 72, 76, 82, 86; CreCan 2; CurBio 46, 91N; CyWA 89; DcLB 68; DcLEL 1940; EncWL, 2, 3; FacFETw; GrWrEL N; IntAu&W 76, 77, 82, 89, 91; IntvTCA 2; IntWW 77, 78, 79, 80, 81, 82, 83, 89; LinLib L; LngCTC; MagSWL; MajTwCW; McGEWB; ModCmwL; NewC; Novels; OxCAmL 65; OxCCan; OxCCanL; OxCCan SUP; PenC ENG; PeoHis; RAdv 1; REn; REnAL; RfGEnL 91; ScF&FL 92; TwCA SUP; TwCWr; WebE&AL; WhAm 10; WhDW; WhE&EA; Who 74, 82, 83, 85, 88, 90; WhoAm 74, 76, 78, 80, 82, 84, 88, 90; WhoCan 73, 75, 77; WhoCanL 85, 87, 92; WhoWor 74; WrDr 76, 80, 82, 84, 86, 88, 90*

Macleod, Colin M
Proved the existence of genetic substance DNA in all living cells.
Source: *NewYTBE 72; ObitOF 79*

MacLeod, Gavin
American. Actor
Starred in "The Mary Tyler Moore Show," 1970-77, "The Love Boat," 1977-86.
b. Feb 28, 1930 in Mount Kisco, New York
Source: *BioIn 15; IntMPA 86, 92; VarWW 85; WhoAm 86, 90; WhoEnt 92; WhoHol A; WorAlBi*

MacLeod, Iain Norman
English. Government Official
MP under Anthony Eden, Harold MacMillen.
b. Nov 11, 1913 in Skipton, England
d. Jul 20, 1970 in London, England
Source: *BioIn 2, 4, 5, 6, 8, 9, 10, 14, 18; ColdWar 2; CurBio 56, 70; DcNaB 1961; GrBr; WhAm 5*

MacLeod, John James Rickard
Scottish. Physician
Won 1923 Nobel Prize as co-discoverer of insulin, with Frederick Banting.
b. Sep 6, 1876 in Cluny, Scotland
d. Mar 16, 1935 in Aberdeen, Scotland
Source: *BiESc; BioIn 1, 2, 3, 13; DcNaB 1931; DcScB; InSci; LarDcSc; LinLib S; NotTwCS; WhAm 1; WhE&EA; WhNAA; WhoNob, 90, 95; WorAl*

MacLiammoir, Michael
Irish. Actor, Designer, Director
Co-founder of Dublin Gate Theatre, 1928; acted in and designed over 300 productions.
b. Oct 25, 1899 in Cork, Ireland
d. Mar 6, 1978 in Dublin, Ireland
Source: *CnThe; ConAu 45, 77; DcIrW 1; McGEWD 72; WhScrn 83*

Maclise, Daniel
Irish. Artist, Illustrator
Portrait painter who illustrated some of Dickens' Christmas books.
b. Jan 25, 1806 in Cork, Ireland
d. Apr 25, 1870 in London, England
Source: *BioIn 1, 8, 10, 12, 13; ChhPo S1, S2; ClaDrA; DcArts; DcBrBI; DcBrWA; DcIrB 78, 88; DcNaB; DcVicP, 2; NewCBEL; NewCol 75; OxCArt; OxCEng 85, 95; OxCIri; OxDcArt; PoIre; StaCVF*

MacMahon, Aline Laveen
American. Actor
Oscar nominee for *Dragon Seed,* 1944; role in *Trelawny of the Wells,* 1975.
b. May 3, 1899 in McKeesport, Pennsylvania
d. Oct 12, 1991 in New York, New York
Source: *BiE&WWA; EncAFC; FilmEn; FilmgC; HalFC 88; IntMPA 75, 77, 92; InWom SUP; MovMk; NewYTBS 91; NotNAT; ThFT; VarWW 85; Vers A; WhoHol A; WhoThe 77*

MacMillan, Alexander
Scottish. Publisher
Co-founded, with brother Daniel, MacMillan and Co., publishers, 1843.
b. Oct 3, 1818 in Irvine, Scotland
d. Jan 26, 1896 in London, England
Source: *CelCen; ChhPo S2; DcLB 106; NewCBEL; StaCVF*

MacMillan, Daniel
Scottish. Publisher
Established MacMillan and Co., publishers, 1843, with brother Alexander.
b. Sep 13, 1813 in Isle of Arran, Scotland
d. Jun 27, 1857 in Cambridge, England
Source: *CelCen; ChhPo, S1; DcNaB; NewC; StaCVF*

MacMillan, Donald Baxter
American. Explorer
Went with Robert Peary on expedition to N Pole, 1908-09.
b. Nov 10, 1874 in Provincetown, Massachusetts
d. Sep 7, 1970 in Provincetown, Massachusetts
Source: *AmAu&B; ApCAB X; BioIn 1, 2, 6, 7, 9, 13; CurBio 48, 70; InSci; LinLib L, S; McGEWB; OxCAmH; OxCCan; REnAL; WhAm 6; WhNAA; WorAl*

MacMillan, Ernest Campbell, Sir
"Statesman of Canadian Music"
Canadian. Conductor, Composer
Director, Toronto Symphony, 1931-56; knighted, 1935.
b. Aug 18, 1893 in Mimico, Ontario, Canada
d. May 6, 1973 in Ottawa, Ontario, Canada
Source: *Baker 78; BiDAmM; BioIn 3, 4, 9, 10, 11; BriBkM 80; CanWW 70; CreCan 1; CurBio 55, 73; IntWWM 77; MacDCB 78; NewGrDM 80; OxCMus; WhAm 5; WhoE 74; WhoMus 72*

MacMillan, Harold
[Maurice Harold MacMillan]
"Supermac"
English. Political Leader
Conservative prime minister, 1957-63; helped Britain adapt to its reduced military, economic, diplomatic power.
b. Feb 10, 1894 in London, England
d. Dec 29, 1986 in Sussex, England
Source: *BioIn 3, 4, 5, 6, 7, 8, 9, 10, 11, 12, 13, 14, 15, 16, 18, 21; BlueB 76; ColdWar 1, 2; ConAu 113, 121, 128; ConNews 87-2; CurBio 43, 55, 87, 87N; DcPol; DcTwHis; FacFETw; HisDBrE; HisEWW; HisWorL; IntAu&W 77; IntWW 74, 75, 76, 77, 78, 79, 80, 81, 82, 83; IntYB 78, 79, 80, 81, 82; LegTOT; LinLib L, S; McGEWB; NewYTBS 86; PolLCWE; RAdv 13-3; WhAm 10; WhDW; Who 74, 82, 83; WhoWor 74, 78, 80, 82, 84, 87; WorAl; WorAlBi; WrDr 76, 80, 82, 84, 86*

MacMillan, Kenneth, Sir
Scottish. Choreographer
Principal choreographer, Royal Ballet, 1977-92; director, 1970-77; knighted in 1983.
b. Dec 11, 1929 in Dumferline, Scotland

d. Oct 29, 1992 in London, England
Source: *AnObit 1992; BiDD; BioIn 4, 7, 10, 13; BlueB 76; CnOxB; ConTFT 13; DcArts; FacFETw; IntDcB; IntWW 74, 75, 76, 77, 78, 79, 80, 81, 82, 83, 89, 91; NewOxM; News 93-2; NewYTBS 92; WhAm 10; Who 74, 82, 83, 85, 88, 90, 92; WhoAm 80, 82, 84, 88, 90, 92; WhoWor 74, 76, 78, 80, 82, 84, 87, 89, 91, 93; WorAlBi*

MacMonnies, Fred W
American. Sculptor
Designed NYC's Statue of Nathan Hale; fountain at Columbian Exposition, 1893.
b. Sep 28, 1863 in New York, New York
d. Mar 22, 1937
Source: *BioIn 11; NewCol 75; WebBD 83; WhAm 1*

MacMurray, Fred(erick Martin)
American. Actor
Starred in TV series "My Three Sons," 1960-72; films include *The Shaggy Dog,* 1959 and *Double Indemnity,* 1944.
b. Aug 30, 1908 in Kankakee, Illinois
d. Nov 5, 1991 in Santa Monica, California
Source: *AnObit 1991; BiDFilm, 81, 94; BioIn 6, 7, 8, 9, 11, 17, 18; CelR; CmpEPM; ConTFT 3, 10; CurBio 67, 92N; EncAFC; Film 2; FilmEn; FilmgC; ForYSC; HalFC 88; IntDcF 1-3, 2-3; IntMPA 75, 76, 77, 78, 79, 80, 81, 82, 84, 86, 88, 92; LegTOT; MotPP; MovMk; News 92, 92-2; NewYTBS 91; OxCFilm; VarWW 85; WhAm 10; WhoAm 74, 76, 78, 80, 82, 84, 86, 88, 90; WhoHol A; WhoWor 74; WorAlBi; WorEFlm*

MacNee, Patrick
English. Actor
Played John Steed on TV's "The Avengers," 1966-69; "The New Avengers," 1978.
b. Feb 6, 1922, England
Source: *BioIn 14, 16; ConTFT 1, 7, 14; FilmgC; HalFC 80, 84, 88; LegTOT; MotPP; ScF&FL 92; VarWW 85; WhoAm 80, 82, 84, 86, 88, 90, 92, 94, 95, 96, 97; WhoEnt 92; WhoHol 92, A; WhoWor 80, 82; WorAlBi*

MacNeice, Louis
[Frederick Louis MacNeice; Louis Malone]
Irish. Poet
Wrote many poems, plays; translated some Greek classics.
b. Sep 12, 1907 in Belfast, Northern Ireland
d. Sep 3, 1963 in London, England
Source: *AtlBL; Au&Wr 71; Benet 87, 96; BiDIrW; BioIn 4, 6, 7, 8, 9, 10, 11, 12, 13, 14, 17, 21; BlmGEL; BritWr 7; CamGEL; CamGLE; CasWL; ChhPo, S1, S2, S3; CnE&AP; CnMD; CnMWL; ConAu 85; ConLC 1, 4, 10, 53; ConPo 75; DcArts; DcIrB 78, 88; DcIrL, 96; DcIrW 1; DcLB 10, 20; DcLEL; DcNaB 1961; EncWB; EncWL, 2, 3; EngPo; EvLB; FacFETw; GrBr; GrWrEL P; LinLib L; LngCEL; LngCTC; MajTwCW; ModBrL, S1, S2; ModIrL; NewC; NewCBEL; NotNAT B; ObitT 1961; OxCEng 67, 85; OxCTwCP; PenC ENG; RAdv 1, 13-1; REn; RfGEnL 91; RGFMBP; TwCA, SUP; TwCWr; WebE&AL; WhAm 4; WhDW; WhoTwCL*

MacNeil, Hermon Atkins
American. Sculptor, Designer
Designed US quarter; works depict Indians, Western life.
b. Feb 27, 1866 in Chelsea, Massachusetts
d. Oct 2, 1947 in New York, New York
Source: *ArtsAmW 1; BioIn 1, 2, 8, 14; BriEAA; DcAmB S4; IlBEAAW; LinLib S; McGEWB; NatCAB 13, 34; NewCol 75; WhAm 2*

MacNeil, Robert Breckenridge Ware
American. Broadcast Journalist
Co-anchor, PBS's "MacNeil/Lehrer Report," 1975-83; "The MacNeil-Lehrer News Hour," 1983-95.
b. Jan 19, 1931 in Montreal, Quebec, Canada
Source: *Au&Wr 71; BioIn 13, 15, 16; CanWW 31, 81, 83, 89; CelR 90; ConAu 53NR, 108, 114; ConCaAu 1; CurBio 80; EncTwCJ; IntAu&W 86, 91; LesBEnT, 92; VarWW 85; WhoAm 80, 82, 84, 86, 88, 90, 92, 94, 95, 96, 97; WhoE 95; WorAlBi*

MacNelly, Jeff(rey Kenneth)
American. Cartoonist
Draws comic strip "Shoe"; won Pulitzers, 1972, 1978.
b. Sep 17, 1947 in New York, New York
Source: *BioIn 15, 16; ConAu 102; EncACom; EncTwCJ; WhoAm 86, 90; WhoAmA 84, 91; WhoMW 92*

MacNutt, Francis, Father
American. Religious Leader
Urged prayer for healing; founding editor *Preaching,* 1950-70.
b. Apr 22, 1925 in Saint Louis, Missouri
Source: *ConAu 73*

MacPhail, Larry
[Leland Stanford MacPhail, Sr]
American. Baseball Executive
Pres., Cincinnati, 1933-37, Brooklyn, 1938-42, NY Yankees, 1945-48; introduced night baseball, 1935; Hall of Fame.
b. Feb 3, 1890 in Cass City, Michigan
d. Oct 1, 1975 in Miami, Florida
Source: *AmDec 1940; Ballpl 90; BiDAmSp BB; BioIn 1, 14, 15, 16; CurBio 45, 75, 75N; DcAmB S9; LegTOT; NewYTBE 72; NewYTBS 75; WhAm 6; WhoAm 74; WhoE 74; WhoProB 73*

MacPhail, Lee
[Leland Stanford MacPhail, Jr]
American. Baseball Executive
Succeeded Joe Cronin as pres. of AL, 1973-83; pres., ML Player Relations Com., 1983—.
b. Oct 25, 1917 in Nashville, Tennessee
Source: *Ballpl 90; BiDAmSp BB; BioIn 14, 15, 16; NewYTBS 85; WhoAm 74, 76, 78, 80, 82; WhoE 79, 81, 83; WhoProB 73*

Macpherson, Elle
[Eleanor Gow]
Australian. Model, Actor
Known for appearing on the covers of *Sports Illustrated,* swimsuit issues; was in *Sirens,* 1994.
b. 1965 in Sydney, Australia
Source: *BioIn 15, 16; CelR 90*

Macpherson, James
Scottish. Author, Historian
Noted literary forger; published *Fingal,* 1762; *Temora,* 1763, supposedly translations from Gaelic of ancient poet, Ossian.
b. Oct 27, 1736 in Ruthven, Scotland
d. Feb 17, 1796 in Ruthven, Scotland
Source: *Alli; BbD; Benet 87, 96; BiD&SB; BioIn 3, 4, 6, 8, 10, 13, 17; BlkwCE; BlmGEL; BritAu; CamGEL; CamGLE; CasWL; Chambr 2; ChhPo, S1; CmScLit; CnE&AP; DcArts; DcEnA; DcEnL; DcEuL; DcLB 109; DcLEL; DcNaB; EncEnl; EvLB; GrWrEL P; LitC 29; MouLC 2; NewC; NewCBEL; NewEOp 71; OxCEng 67, 85, 95; OxCIri; PenC ENG; RComWL; REn; RfGEnL 91; WebE&AL; WhDW*

MacRae, Gordon
American. Actor, Singer
Gained musical movie fame as baritone star of *Oklahoma,* 1955; *Carousel,* 1956.
b. Mar 12, 1921 in East Orange, New Jersey
d. Jan 24, 1986 in Lincoln, Nebraska
Source: *AnObit 1986, 78, 79, 80, 81, 82, 84, 86; LegTOT; MotPP; MovMk; NewYTBS 86; RadStar; VarWW 85; WhAm 9; WhoAm 74, 76, 78, 80, 82, 84; WhoHol A; WorAl; WorAlBi*

MacRae, Meredith
[Mrs. Greg Mullavey]
American. Actor
Daughter of Sheila and Gordon MacRae; starred in TV series "Petticoat Junction," 1966-70.
b. May 30, 1944 in Houston, Texas
Source: *BioIn 16; InWom SUP; VarWW 85; WhoHol A*

MacRae, Sheila
[Sheila Stephens]
American. Actor, Singer
In TV series "Jackie Gleason Show," 1966-70; first husband was Gordon MacRae.
b. Sep 24, 1923 in London, England

Source: *InWom SUP; LegTOT; VarWW 85; WhoAm 84*

Macready, George
American. Actor
Screen villain, 1942-71; played in *Gilda,* 1946; *Paths of Glory,* 1957.
b. Aug 29, 1909 in Providence, Rhode Island
d. Jul 2, 1973 in Los Angeles, California
Source: *CmMov; FilmEn; FilmgC; ForYSC; GangFlm; HalFC 80, 84, 88; MotPP; MovMk; NewYTBE 73; Vers A; WhoHol B; WhoHrs 80; WhScrn 77, 83*

MacSwiney, Terence
Irish. Hunger Striker, Revolutionary
Nationalist hero; died on 74th day of hunger fast; wrote *Principles of Freedom,* 1921.
b. Mar 27, 1879 in Cork, Ireland
d. Oct 24, 1920 in Brixton Prison, England
Source: *BiDIrW; BioIn 6, 7; DcIrB 78, 88; DcIrL, 96; DcIrW 1, 2; OxCIri*

MacTaggart, William, Sir
Scottish. Artist
Painted oil landscapes, still lifes; work influenced by German expressionists.
b. May 15, 1903 in Loanhead, Scotland
d. Jan 9, 1981, Scotland
Source: *AnObit 1981; BioIn 5, 10; DcBrAr 1; DcNaB 1981; PhDcTCA 77; TwCPaSc; Who 74, 82N; WhoArt 80, 82N*

Macy, Bill
[William Macy Garber]
American. Actor
Played Walter Findlay in TV series "Maude," 1972-78.
b. May 18, 1922 in Revere, Massachusetts
Source: *ConTFT 1, 4; HalFC 80, 84, 88; IntMPA 96; LegTOT; VarWW 85; WhoAm 78, 80; WhoEnt 92; WhoHol 92, A; WorAl*

Macy, George
American. Publisher
With, Limited Edition Club, 1929; Heritage Press, 1935; advocate of fine bookmaking.
b. May 12, 1900 in New York, New York
d. May 20, 1956 in New York, New York
Source: *AmAu&B; BioIn 3, 4; CurBio 54, 56; WhAm 3*

Macy, John Williams, Jr.
American. Government Official
Executive director, Civil Service Commission, 1953-58, chairman, 1961-69.
b. Apr 6, 1917 in Chicago, Illinois
d. Dec 22, 1986 in McLean, Virginia
Source: *BioIn 5, 6; BlueB 76; CurBio 62, 87; IntWW 74, 75, 76, 77, 78, 79, 80, 81, 82, 83; NewYTBS 86; WhAm 9; WhoAm 74, 76, 78, 80, 82, 84, 86; WhoAmP 73, 75, 77, 79*

Macy, Kyle Robert
American. Basketball Player
Guard, 1980-87; led NBA in free-throw percentage, 1982, 1985.
b. Apr 9, 1957 in Fort Wayne, Indiana
Source: *BioIn 11; OfNBA 87*

Macy, R(owland) H(ussey)
American. Retailer
Founder of NYC-based dept. store that bears his name.
b. 1822
d. Mar 29, 1877
Source: *BioIn 6, 7, 9, 18*

Madariaga (y Rojo), Salvador de
Spanish. Diplomat
Ambassador to U.S., France, 1928-34; self-exile during Franco regime; wrote *Spain,* 1942.
b. Jul 23, 1886 in La Coruna, Spain
d. Dec 14, 1978 in Locarno, Switzerland
Source: *Benet 87, 96; BiDInt; BioIn 1, 3, 4, 6, 7, 9, 10, 11; CasWL; ClDMEL 47, 80; ConAu 6NR, 9R, 32NR, 81; CurBio 64, 79, 79N; DcHiB; DcLEL; DcNaB 1971; DcSpL; EncSF 93; EncWL; EvEuW; HispWr; IntAu&W 77; IntWW 74, 75, 76, 77, 78; LiExTwC; LinLib L; LngCTC; NewYTBS 78; OxCSpan; REn; ScFEYrs; TwCA, SUP; TwCWr; Who 74; WhoLA*

Madden, Donald
American. Actor
Classical actor on Broadway in *Hamlet; Julius Caesar.*
b. Nov 5, 1933 in New York, New York
d. Jan 22, 1983 in Central Islip, New York
Source: *AnObit 1983; BiE&WWA; BioIn 5, 6, 13; NewYTBS 83; NotNAT; WhoThe 72, 77, 81*

Madden, John
American. Football Coach, Sportscaster
Coach, Oakland, 1969-79; has won six Emmys as analyst on CBS telecasts of NFL games 1982, 1983, 1985, 1986, 1987, 1988; lead NFL analyst, Fox TV, 1994—.
b. Apr 10, 1936 in Austin, Minnesota
Source: *BioIn 14, 15, 16; CmCal; CurBio 85; LegTOT; News 95, 95-1; VarWW 85; WhoAm 74, 76, 78, 80, 82, 84, 86, 88, 90, 92, 94, 95, 96, 97; WhoFtbl 74; WhoTelC; WhoWest 96*

Madden, Owen Victor
"Owney the Killer"
American. Criminal
Gang leader involved with Dutch Schultz, "Legs" Diamond; employed by Lindbergh to help find kidnapped son.
b. Jun 1892 in Liverpool, England
d. Apr 24, 1965 in Hot Springs, Arkansas
Source: *DcAmB S7*

Madden, Ray John
American. Politician
Dem. congressman from IN, 1943-77.
b. Feb 25, 1892 in Waseca, Minnesota
d. Sep 28, 1987 in Washington, District of Columbia
Source: *BiDrAC; WhoMW 74, 76*

Maddow, Ben
American. Screenwriter
Best known for *The Asphalt Jungle,* 1950.
b. 1909 in Passaic, New Jersey
d. Oct 9, 1992 in Los Angeles, California
Source: *BioIn 15, 16, 17, 18; DcLB 44; HalFC 88; IntDcF 2-4*

Maddox, Garry Lee
"Buggy Whip"
American. Baseball Player
Outfielder, 1972-86, known for fielding; had .285 lifetime batting average.
b. Sep 1, 1949 in Cincinnati, Ohio
Source: *Ballpl 90; BaseReg 87; BioIn 15; Dun&B 90; WhoAfA 96; WhoAm 78; WhoBlA 77, 80, 85, 88, 90, 92, 94; WhoProB 73*

Maddox, Lester Garfield
American. Politician
Segregationist Dem. governor of GA, 1967-71.
b. Sep 30, 1915 in Atlanta, Georgia
Source: *BiDrGov 1789; BioIn 7, 8, 9, 10, 11, 12; BioNews 74; ConAu 112; CurBio 67; IntWW 74, 75, 76, 77, 78, 79, 80, 81, 82, 83; NewYTBS 83; WhoAm 76, 78, 80, 82; WhoGov 72, 75, 77; WhoSSW 73, 75; WorAlBi*

Maddux, Greg(ory Alan)
American. Baseball Player
Pitcher, Chicago Cubs, 1984-92; Atlanta, 1993—; All-Star, 1988; Cy Young Award, 1992-95.
b. Apr 14, 1966 in San Angelo, Texas
Source: *Ballpl 90; BioIn 19, 20, 21; CurBio 96; News 96, 96-2; WhoAm 94, 95, 96, 97; WhoSSW 95, 97; WhoWor 95, 96, 97*

Madeira, Jean
[Jean Browning]
American. Opera Singer
Met. Opera contralto, 1948-71; noted for Carmen role.
b. Nov 14, 1918 in Centralia, Illinois
d. Jul 10, 1972 in Providence, Rhode Island
Source: *Baker 78, 84, 92; BiDAmM; BioIn 9, 11, 13; CurBio 63, 72, 72N; MetOEnc; NewGrDA 86; NewGrDM 80; NewGrDO; NewYTBE 72; PenDiMP; WhAm 5; WhoMus 72*

Madero, Francisco Indalecio
Mexican. Revolutionary, Political Leader
Liberal ruler of Mexico, 1911-13, succeeding Diaz; attempted social reforms.
b. Oct 30, 1873 in Parras, Mexico

d. Feb 22, 1913 in Mexico City, Mexico
Source: *BioIn 4, 6, 9, 10; EncRev; McGEWB; NewCol 75; REn; WebBD 83*

Madhubuti, Haki R.
[Don Luther Lee]
American. Poet
Wrote *Think Black!,* 1967; *Killing Memory, Seeking Ancestors,* 1987.
b. Feb 23, 1942 in Little Rock, Arkansas
Source: *AfrAmAl 6; BlkLC; BlkWr 1, 2; ConAu 24NR, 73; ConBlB 7; ConLC 6, 73; ConPo 96; DcLB 5, 41, DS8; DcTwCCu 5; DrAP 75; DrAPF 80; OxCTwCP; PoeCrit 5; RfGAmL 94; SchCGBL; SelBAAf; SelBAAu; WhoAfA 96; WhoBlA 90, 92, 94; WrDr 94*

Madigan, Edward R.
American. Politician
Secretary of Agriculture, 1991-93.
b. Jan 13, 1936 in Lincoln, Illinois
d. Dec 7, 1994 in Springfield, Illinois
Source: *AlmAP 78, 80, 82, 84, 88; BioIn 15, 18, 20, 21; CngDr 74, 77, 79, 81, 83, 85, 87, 89, 91; CurBio 92, 95N; IntWW 91; PolsAm 84; WhoAm 76, 78, 80, 82, 84, 86, 88, 90, 92, 94; WhoAmP 73, 75, 77, 79, 81, 83, 85, 87, 89, 91, 93; WhoE 93, 95; WhoGov 75, 77; WhoMW 74, 76, 78, 80, 82, 84, 86, 88, 90, 92*

Madison, Dolly Payne Todd
[Mrs. James Madison]
American. First Lady
Popular, influential figure in Washington society; model for several historical romances, biographies.
b. May 20, 1768 in Guilford County, North Carolina
d. Jul 12, 1849 in Orange County, Virginia
Source: *AmAu&B; AmBi; AmWomWr; DcAmB; DcAmNB; EncAR; FacPr 89; GoodHs; HerW; IntDcWB; LibW; NotAW; OxCAmL 65; REn; REnAL; WorAl*

Madison, Guy
[Robert Moseley]
American. Actor
Hero of action films and spaghetti westerns; starred in TV series "Wild Bill Hickok," 1951-58.
b. Jan 19, 1922 in Bakersfield, California
d. Feb 6, 1996 in Palm Springs, California
Source: *BioIn 1, 3, 4, 10, 13, 15, 21; FilmEn; FilmgC; ForYSC; HalFC 80, 84, 88; IntMPA 75, 76, 77, 78, 79, 80, 81, 82, 84, 86, 88, 92, 94, 96; ItaFilm; MotPP; MovMk; RadStar; VarWW 85; What 5; WhoHol 92, A*

Madison, Helene
American. Swimmer
Three-time gold medalist, 1932 Olympics; held 30 US, 12 world titles, 1930s; member of swimming Hall of Fame.
b. 1914
d. Nov 25, 1970 in Seattle, Washington
Source: *BioIn 9; NewYTBE 70; ObitOF 79*

Madison, James
American. US President
Fourth pres., 1809-17; drafted Bill of Rights.
b. Mar 16, 1751 in Port Conway, Virginia
d. Jun 28, 1836 in Orange County, Virginia
Source: *Alli; AmAu&B; AmBi; AmOrN; AmPolLe; AmRev; AmWrBE; ApCAB; BbD; Benet 87, 96; BenetAL 91; BiAUS; BiD&SB; BiDrAC; BiDrUSC 89; BiDrUSE 71, 89; BiDSA; BioIn 1, 2, 3, 4, 5, 6, 7, 8, 9, 10, 11, 12, 13, 14, 15, 16, 17, 18, 19, 20, 21; BlkwCE; BlkwEAR; CyAG; CyAL 1; CyEd; CyWA 58; DcAmAu; DcAmC; DcAmDH 80, 89; DcAmSR; DcBiPP; DcLB 37; DcLEL; DcNAA; Drake; EncAAH; EncAB-H 1974, 1996; EncAR; EncARH; EncCRAm; EncEnl; EncSoH; FacPr 89, 93; HarEnUS; HealPre; HisWorL; LegTOT; LinLib L, S; McGEWB; MemAm; NatCAB 5; OxCAmH; OxCAmL 65, 83, 95; OxCSupC; PeoHis; PolPar; RAdv 14, 13-3; RComAH; REn; REnAL; SouWr; TwCBDA; TwoTYeD; WebAB 74, 79; WhAm HS; WhAmP; WhAmRev; WhDW; WorAl; WorAlBi*

Madlock, Bill
[William Madlock, Jr]
"Mad Dog"
American. Baseball Player
Infielder, 1973-88, mostly with Pittburgh; won NL batting title four times.
b. Jan 12, 1951 in Memphis, Tennessee
Source: *Ballpl 90; BaseReg 86, 87; BiDAmSp BB; BioIn 13, 14, 15, 16, 20; LegTOT; NewYTBS 83; WhoAfA 96; WhoAm 82, 84, 86; WhoBlA 77, 80, 85, 88, 90, 92, 94; WhoSpor; WorAl; WorAlBi*

Madness
[Mike Barson; Mark Bedford; Chris Foreman; Graham "Suggs" McPherson; Carl Smyth; Lee Thompson; "Woody" Woodgate]
English. Music Group
Formed in London, 1978; hit singles include "Our House," 1983; "Yesterday's Men," 1985.
Source: *EncRk 88; EncRkSt; HarEnR 86; IlWWBF; OxCPMus; PenEncP; RkOn 85; RolSEnR 83; St&PR 97; WhoRocM 82; WhsNW 85*

Madonna
[Madonna Louise Veronica Ciccone]
"Material Girl"
American. Singer, Actor
Albums include *Like a Virgin; True Blue;* controversial work includes movie *Truth or Dare;* book *Sex;* starred in film *Evita,* 1996.
b. Aug 16, 1958 in Bay City, Michigan
Source: *AmDec 1980; Baker 92; BioIn 14, 15, 16; CelR 90; ConAu 143; ConMus 4, 16; ConNews 85-2; ConTFT 3, 9; CurBio 86; DcArts; DcTwCCu 1; EncFash; EncPR&S 89; EncRk 88; EncRkSt; HalFC 88; HarEnR 86; HolBB; IntMPA 92, 94, 96; IntWW 89, 91, 93; LegTOT; NewGrDA 86; NewYTBS 86; OxCPMus; PenEncP; RkOn 85; WhoAm 88, 90, 92, 94, 95, 96, 97; WhoAmW 93, 95, 97; WhoEnt 92; WhoHol 92; WhoWor 97; WorAlBi*

Madrid Hurtado, Miguel de la
Mexican. Political Leader
Pres. of Mexico, 1982-88.
b. Dec 12, 1934 in Colima, Mexico
Source: *BioIn 13, 14, 16; CurBio 83; IntWW 83, 91; NewYTBS 82; WhoAm 84, 86*

Maeght, Aime
French. Art Collector
Best known for Foundation Maeght, specially designed museum for display of modern art; friend of Matisse, Chagall.
b. Apr 27, 1906 in Hazebrouck, France
d. Sep 5, 1981 in Saint-Paul-de-Vence, France
Source: *AnObit 1981; BioIn 5, 6, 7, 12, 15; FacFETw; NewYTBS 81; WhoFr 79*

Maestro, Giulio
American. Children's Author, Illustrator
Prize-winning illustrator of picture books, children's readers; wrote *Who's Said Meow?* 1975.
b. May 6, 1942 in New York, New York
Source: *AuBYP 2S, 3; BioIn 11, 12, 16, 19; ChhPo S2; ConAu 8NR, 23NR, 37NR, 57; IlsBYP; IntAu&W 91, 93; MajAI; SixBJA; SmATA 8, 59; WrDr 80, 82, 84, 86, 88, 90, 92, 94, 96*

Maeterlinck, Maurice
[Mauritius Polydorus Maria Bernardus]
Belgian. Dramatist, Poet
Wrote *The Blue Bird,* 1909; won 1911 Nobel Prize.
b. Aug 29, 1862 in Ghent, Belgium
d. May 6, 1949 in Nice, France
Source: *AtlBL; BbD; Benet 87, 96; BiD&SB; BioIn 1, 2, 3, 4, 5, 6, 8, 9, 10, 11, 12, 13, 15, 17; BlmGEL; BriBkM 80; CamGWoT; CasWL; ChhPo; ClDMEL 47, 80; CnMD; CnThe; ConAu 104, 136; CyWA 58; DcArts; DcPup; DcTwCCu 2; Dis&D; EncO&P 2, 3; EncPaPR 91; EncWL, 2, 3; EncWT; Ent; EuWr 8; EvEuW; GrFLW; GuFrLit 1; HalFC 84, 88; IntDcT 2; LegTOT; LinLib L, S; LngCTC; MajMD 2; McGEWD 72, 84; ModFrL; ModRL; ModWD; NewC; NewCBEL; NewEOp 71; NewGrDM 80; NewGrDO; NobelP; NotNAT A, B; OxCAmT 84; OxCEng 67, 85, 95; OxCFr; OxCThe 67, 83; OxDcOp; PenC EUR; PlP&P; RComWL; REn; REnWD; RfGWoL 95; SmATA 66; TwCA, SUP; TwCLC 3; TwCWr; WhAm 2; WhDW; WhE&EA; WhLit; WhoLA; WhoNob; WhoTwCL; WhThe; WorAlBi*

Magana, Alvaro (Alfredo)
Salvadoran. Political Leader
Pres. of El Salvador, 1982-84.
b. Oct 8, 1925 in Ahuchapan, El Salvador
Source: *AmEA 74; BioIn 13; NewYTBS 82; WhoWor 82*

Magaziner, Ira C(harles)
American. Consultant
Adviser to President Clinton, 1993—.
b. Nov 8, 1947 in New York, New York
Source: *CurBio 95*

Magee, Harry L
American. Business Executive
Pres., Magee Carpet Co., 1920-66; introduced new method of carpet manufacture—tufting, 1952.
b. Apr 31, 1901 in Bloomsburg, Pennsylvania
d. Oct 9, 1972 in Bloomsburg, Pennsylvania
Source: *BioIn 9; NewYTBE 72*

Magee, Patrick
Irish. Actor
Won Tony, 1965, for *Marat/Sade.*
b. 1924? in Armagh, Northern Ireland
d. Aug 14, 1982 in London, England
Source: *AnObit 1982; BioIn 13; FilmgC; HalFC 80, 84, 88; IntMPA 82; ItaFilm; NewYTBS 82; NotNAT; WhoHol A; WhoHrs 80; WhoThe 72, 77*

Magellan, Ferdinand
[Fernando DeMagalhaes]
Portuguese. Navigator, Explorer
Discovered Philippines, 1521; voyage proved roundness of the Earth; explored straits which now bear his name.
b. 1480? in Sabrosa, Portugal
d. Apr 27, 1521, Philippines
Source: *AsBiEn; Benet 87, 96; BioIn 1, 2, 3, 4, 5, 6, 7, 8, 9, 10, 11, 12, 14, 15, 16, 17, 18, 19, 20; DcCathB; Dis&D; Drake; EncCRAm; EncLatA; Expl 93; HisDcSE; LegTOT; LinLib S; McGEWB; NewC; NewCol 75; OxCAmH; OxCShps; REn; WhAm HS; WhDW; WhWE; WorAl; WorAlBi*

Maginnis, Charles Donagh
Irish. Architect
Noted for ecclesiastical architecture.
b. Jan 7, 1867 in Londonderry, Northern Ireland
d. Feb 15, 1955 in Boston, Massachusetts
Source: *BioIn 3, 4, 5, 6, 13; DcAmB S5; DcCathB; NatCAB 43; WhAm 3; WhNAA*

Maginot, Andre Louis Rene
French. Politician
War minister, 1929-32 who planned system of fortifications called Maginot Line.
b. Feb 17, 1877 in Paris, France
d. Jan 7, 1932 in Paris, France
Source: *NewCol 75*

Maglich, Bogdan C
American. Physicist
Discoverer of omega-meson, 1961; noted for research in aneutronic energy process to produce a nonradioactive fuel.
b. Aug 5, 1928 in Sombor, Yugoslavia
Source: *AmMWSc 92; BioIn 11, 15; News 90-1; WhoAm 90; WhoTech 84; WhoWor 87*

Maglie, Sal(vatore Anthony)
"The Barber"
American. Baseball Player
Pitcher, 1945, 1950-58; led NL in wins, 1951.
b. Apr 26, 1917 in Niagara Falls, New York
d. Dec 28, 1992 in Niagara Falls, New York
Source: *AnObit 1992; Ballpl 90; BiDAmSp Sup; BioIn 2, 3, 4, 5, 7, 18, 19; CurBio 93N; NewYTBS 92; WhoProB 73*

Magliozzi, Ray
"Click and Clack"; "Tappet Brothers"
American. Radio Performer
Car repair expert; with brother Tom has show "Car Talk," debuted 1987 on Nat. Public Radio; also writes syndicated newspaper column.
b. Mar 30, 1949 in Cambridge, Massachusetts
Source: *BioIn 16; News 91*

Magliozzi, Tom
"Click and Clack"; "Tappet Brothers"
American. Radio Performer
Car repair expert; with brother Ray has show "Car Talk," debuted 1987 on National Public Radio; also writes syndicated newspaper column.
b. Jun 28, 1936 in Cambridge, Massachusetts
Source: *BioIn 16; News 91*

Magnani, Anna
Italian. Actor
Won 1955 Oscar for *The Red Tattoo.*
b. Mar 7, 1909 in Alexandria, Egypt
d. Sep 26, 1973 in Rome, Italy
Source: *BiDFilm; CurBio 56, 73; FilmgC; MotPP; MovMk; NewYTBE 73; OxCFilm; PlP&P; WhAm 6; WhoHol B; WhScrn 77, 83; WorEFlm*

Magnante, Charles
American. Composer, Musician
Accordionist; first to give full accordion concert, Carnegie Hall, 1939.
b. Dec 5, 1905 in New York, New York
Source: *ASCAP 66, 80*

Magnasco, Alessandro Lissandrino
Italian. Artist
Painted mystical, gloomy religious genre scenes including *Baptism of Christ.*
b. 1667 in Genoa, Italy
d. Mar 12, 1749 in Genoa, Italy
Source: *AtlBL; McGDA; McGEWB; NewCol 75*

Magnin, Cyril Isaac
"Mr. San Francisco"
American. Retailer, Business Executive
Headed specialty store, I Magnin, 1964-88.
b. Jul 6, 1899 in San Francisco, California
d. Jun 8, 1988 in San Francisco, California
Source: *BioIn 11, 12; ConAu 107; NewYTBS 88; WhoAm 84; WhoFI 83; WhoWest 76, 78, 80*

Magnin, Grover Arnold
American. Retailer
President, I Magnin, specialty store for children, women, 1944-51.
b. Dec 4, 1885 in San Francisco, California
d. Mar 17, 1969 in San Francisco, California
Source: *BioIn 8, 10; NatCAB 54*

Magnuson, Keith Arlen
Canadian. Hockey Player
Defenseman, Chicago, 1969-80, known for aggressive play.
b. Apr 27, 1947 in Saskatoon, Saskatchewan, Canada
Source: *BioIn 9, 10; ConAu 93; HocEn; WhoAm 74, 78, 80, 82; WhoHcky 73*

Magnuson, Warren Grant
American. Politician
Dem. senator, WA, 1944-81; one of the most powerful figures on Capitol Hill after he became chm., Senate Appropriations Com.
b. Apr 12, 1905 in Moorhead, Minnesota
d. May 20, 1989 in Seattle, Washington
Source: *BiDrAC; BiDrUSC 89; BioIn 1, 6, 8, 9, 10, 11, 12, 13; BlueB 76; CngDr 79; ConAu 85; CurBio 45, 89N; IntWW 74, 75, 76, 77, 78, 79, 80, 81, 82, 83, 89; IntYB 78, 79, 80, 81, 82; NewYTBS 89; PolProf E, J, K, NF, T; WhoAm 74, 76, 78, 80, 82; WhoAmP 73, 75, 77, 79, 81; WhoGov 72, 75, 77; WhoWest 76, 78, 80; WhoWor 74, 76, 78, 80; WorAlBi*

Magonigle, Harold Van Buren
American. Architect
Designed McKinley Memorial, 1904; Kansas City's Liberty War Memorial, 1923.
b. Oct 17, 1867 in Bergen Heights, New Jersey
d. Aug 29, 1935 in Vergennes, Vermont
Source: *ApCAB X; DcAmB S1; DcNAA; NatCAB 15, 27; WhAm 1*

Magritte, Rene Francois Ghislain
Belgian. Artist
Noted Surrealist painter; used iconographic images as lions, men in bowler hats.
b. Nov 21, 1898 in Lessines, Belgium
d. Aug 15, 1967 in Brussels, Belgium

Source: *ClaDrA; CurBio 66, 67; ICPEnP; NewCol 75; OxCArt; WebBD 83; WhAm 4; WorArt 1950*

Magruder, Jeb Stuart
American. Politician
Deputy director of Nixon's re-election committee, CREEP; confessed illegal involvement during Watergate trial; served about one yr. in federal prison.
b. Nov 5, 1934 in Staten Island, New York
Source: *BioIn 9, 10, 11, 12, 16, 18; ConAu 101; NewYTBE 73; NewYTBS 88; PolProf NF; WhoAm 74, 76; WorAl; WorAlBi*

Magsaysay, Ramon
Philippine. Political Leader
Led Philippines, 1953-57; arch foe of Communism.
b. Aug 31, 1907 in Iba, Philippines
d. Mar 17, 1957 in Cebu, Philippines
Source: *BioIn 2, 3, 4, 5, 7, 8, 9, 13, 19; CurBio 52, 57; DcCathB; DcMPSA; EncRev; HarEnMi; LinLib S; McGEWB; WebBD 83; WhAm 3*

Maguire, Mairead Corrigan
Irish. Social Reformer
Won Nobel Peace Prize, 1976, for promoting nonviolent women's protest in N Ireland.
b. Jan 27, 1944 in Belfast, Northern Ireland
Source: *NewYTBS 88; Who 92*

Magyar, Gabriel
Hungarian. Musician
Noted cellist who made numerous recordings.
b. Dec 5, 1914 in Budapest, Austria-Hungary
Source: *IntWWM 77, 80, 90; PenDiMP; WhoAm 74, 76, 78, 80, 82, 84, 86, 88, 90; WhoAmM 83; WhoEnt 92*

Mahaffey, John
American. Golfer
Turned pro, 1971; won PGA, 1978.
b. May 9, 1948 in Kerrville, Texas
Source: *BioIn 11, 12; WhoAm 80, 82, 84, 86, 88, 90, 92; WhoGolf*

Mahan, Alfred Thayer
American. Naval Officer, Historian
Wrote *Influence of Sea Power upon History,* 1890; greatly influenced worldwide naval buildup.
b. Sep 27, 1840 in West Point, New York
d. Dec 1, 1914 in Washington, District of Columbia
Source: *Alli SUP; AmAu; AmAu&B; AmBi; AmPeW; ApCAB SUP; BbD; BiD&SB; BiDInt; BioIn 1, 3, 8, 9, 10, 11, 13, 15, 16; Chambr 3; CyAG; DcAmAu; DcAmB; DcAmDH 80, 89; DcAmMiB; DcAmSR; DcEnA A; DcLB 47; DcNAA; EncAB-H 1974, 1996; GayN; HarEnMi; HarEnUS; LinLib L, S; McGEWB; MemAm; NatCAB 10; OxCAmH; OxCAmL 65, 83, 95; OxCShps; RAdv 14, 13-3; RComAH; REn; TwCBDA; WebAB 74, 79; WebAMB; WhAm 1; WhCiWar; WhLit; WhoMilH 76; WorAl; WorAlBi*

Mahan, Asa
American. Clergy, University Administrator
First pres., Oberlin College, 1835-50; believed in admitting students without color, sex discrimination.
b. Nov 9, 1799 in Vernon, New York
d. Apr 4, 1889 in Eastbourne, England
Source: *Alli, SUP; AmAu&B; ApCAB; BiDAmEd; BiD&SB; DcAmAu; DcAmB; DcAmReB 2; DcNAA; EncARH; LuthC 75; OhA&B; WhAm HS*

Mahan, Larry
American. Rodeo Performer
Six-time all-around rodeo champion, 1960s-70s.
b. Nov 21, 1943 in Salem, Oregon
Source: *BiDAmSp OS; BioIn 7, 8, 9, 10, 12; NewYTBS 75; WhoSpor*

Maharaj Ji, Guru
[Prem Pal Singh Rawat]
Indian. Religious Leader
Controversial messenger of God who led Divine Light Mission, 1960s-70s; followers, including some Americans, are called premies.
b. Dec 10, 1957 in Hardwar, India
Source: *BioIn 9, 10, 11, 13, 17; CurBio 74; NewYTBE 73; RelLAm 91; WhoRel 77*

Maharis, George
American. Actor
Played on TV's "Route 66," 1960-63; "Most Deadly Game," 1970-71.
b. Sep 1, 1933 in New York, New York
Source: *BiE&WWA; BioIn 13; FilmgC; HalFC 84, 88; IntMPA 88, 92; MotPP; MovMk; PlP&P; VarWW 85; WhoHol A*

Mahathir Bin Mohamad
Malaysian. Political Leader
First commoner to become prime minister in Malaysia, 1981—; aggressive leadership has many fearful of the loss of democracy.
b. Dec 20, 1925 in Alor Setar, Malaysia
Source: *BioIn 14, 15, 16; CurBio 88; IntWW 91; Who 85, 88, 92, 94; WhoWor 87, 89, 91, 93, 95, 96, 97*

Mahavira
"The Great One"
Indian. Religious Leader
Last of Jain Tirthankaras, who founded Jainism, offshoot of Hinduism.
b. 599BC in Vaardhamana, India
d. 527BC in Ksatriyakundagrama, India
Source: *BioIn 11; LegTOT; WhDW; WorAl; WorAlBi*

Mahavishnu Orchestra, The
[Billy Cogham, Jr; Jerry Goodman; Jan Hammer; Rick Laird; John McLaughlin]
American. Music Group
Name of two rock groups founded by guitar virtuoso John McLaughlin, 1970s; album *Apocalypse,* 1974.
Source: *AllMusG; BiDAmM; BiDJaz A; BioIn 14, 15, 16, 17, 18, 20; Dun&B 86, 88, 90; EncPR&S 74; EncRk 88; IlEncJ; IlEncRk; NewAgMG; NewGrDA 86; NewGrDJ 88, 94; NewYTBE 72; PoIre; RolSEnR 83; WhoAm 92, 94; WhoAmA 86N; WhoEnt 92; WhoRock 81; WhoRocM 82; WhoScEn 94*

Mahdi, Mohammed Ahmed
Sudanese. Religious Leader
Declared himself Mahdi, 1881, united Sudan in religiopolitical movement that began modern history of country.
b. 1844? in Dongola, Sudan
d. Jun 22, 1885 in Omdurman, Sudan
Source: *CelCen; McGEWB; NewCol 75*

Mahendra, Bir Bikram Shah Dev
Nepalese. Ruler
King of Nepal, 1956-72, who was world's only Hindu monarch.
b. Jun 11, 1920 in Kathmandu, Nepal
d. Jan 31, 1972 in Bharatpur, Nepal
Source: *CurBio 72; NewYTBE 72; ObitOF 79; ObitT 1971*

Maher, Bill
American. Comedian, TV Personality
Host of TV's "Politically Incorrect," 1993—.
b. Jan 20, 1956 in New York, New York
Source: *ConAu 154; ConTFT 15; News 96, 96-2; WhoAm 96, 97*

Maher, George Washington
American. Architect
Noted for original residences, early city planning.
b. Dec 25, 1864 in Mill Creek, West Virginia
d. Sep 12, 1926
Source: *WhAm 1*

Mahesh Yogi, Maharishi
Indian. Religious Leader
Founded Spiritual Regeneration Movement, 1959; proponent of TM whose early converts included The Beatles, The Rolling Stones.
b. Oct 18, 1911 in Uttar Pradesh, India
Source: *BioIn 13; BioNews 74; CurBio 72; EncO&P 1; News 91*

Mahfouz, Naguib
[Nagib Mahfuz]
Egyptian. Author
First Arab to win Nobel Prize for Literature, 1988, for *Children of Gebelaw i*; works include "The Cairo Trilogy," 1956-57.
b. Dec 11, 1911 in Cairo, Egypt
Source: *BestSel 89-2; BioIn 7, 8, 16; BlmGWL; CasWL; ConAu 128; ConFLW*

84; CurBio 89; DcArts; DcMidEa; EncWL 2; FacFETw; IntAu&W 89, 91, 93; IntWW 78, 79, 80, 81, 82, 83, 89, 91, 93; LegTOT; MajTwCW; MidE 78, 79, 80, 81, 82; NewYTBS 88, 90; NobelP 91; Who 92, 94; WhoNob 90, 95; WhoWor 91, 93, 95, 96, 97; WorAlBi

Mahin, John Lee
American. Screenwriter
Wrote script for *Dr. Jekyll and Mr. Hyde,* 1941; *Quo Vadis,* 1951.
b. 1902 in Evanston, Illinois
d. Apr 18, 1984 in Santa Monica, California
Source: *AnObit 1984; BioIn 13, 14, 15; CmMov; ConAu 112; DcLB 44; FilmEn; GangFlm; HalFC 88; IntDcF 1-4; IntMPA 84; NewYTBS 84; VarWW 85; WorEFlm*

Mahler, Fritz
Austrian. Conductor
Led Erie, PA orchestra, 1947-53; Hartford, CT orchestra, 1953-64; nephew of Gustav.
b. Jul 16, 1901 in Vienna, Austria
d. Jun 18, 1973 in New York, New York
Source: *Baker 78, 84, 92; BiDAmM; BioIn 4, 9; IntWWM 77, 80; NewGrDA 86; NewYTBE 73; WhAm 6; WhoAm 74; WhoMus 72*

Mahler, Gustav
Austrian. Composer, Conductor
Composer of nine operas; conducted NY Met., 1908-10.
b. Jul 7, 1860 in Kalischt, Bohemia
d. May 18, 1911 in Vienna, Austria
Source: *ASCAP 66, 80; AtlBL; Baker 78, 84, 92; Benet 87, 96; BiDAmM; BioIn 1, 2, 3, 4, 5, 6, 7, 8, 9, 10, 11, 12, 13, 14, 15, 16, 17, 19, 20, 21; BriBkM 80; CmOp; CmpBCM; CnOxB; DancEn 78; DcArts; DcCathB; DcCM; DcCom 77; DcCom&M 79; DcTwCC, A; Dis&D; FacFETw; GrComp; IntDcOp; JeHun; LegTOT; LinLib S; McGEWB; MetOEnc; MusMk; MusSN; NewAmDM; NewCol 75; NewEOp 71; NewGrDM 80; NewGrDO; NewOxM; OxCGer 76, 86; OxCMus; OxDcOp; PenDiMP, A; PenEncH; RAdv 14, 13-3; REn; WhAm 4, HSA; WhDW; WorAl; WorAlBi*

Mahmud of Ghazni
Afghan. Ruler, Conqueror
Founded Ghaznavid dynasty, 999-1186; staunch Muslim, who destroyed Hindu temples, forced conversion.
b. 971?
d. 1030
Source: *McGEWB; NewC; WebBD 83*

Mahone, William
American. Soldier, Railroad Executive
Major general, Confederate army, 1864; Virginia senator, 1880s.
b. Dec 1, 1826 in Southampton County, Virginia
d. Oct 8, 1895 in Washington, District of Columbia
Source: *AmBi; ApCAB; BiDConf; BiDrAC; BiDrUSC 89; BioIn 2, 5, 6; CivWDc; DcAmB; EncABHB 2; EncSoH; HarEnMi; HarEnUS; McGEWB; NatCAB 5; TwCBDA; WhAm HS; WhAmP; WhCiWar*

Mahoney, David Joseph, Jr.
American. Business Executive
CEO, Norton Simon Inc, 1969-83; received various business awards.
b. May 17, 1923 in New York, New York
Source: *BioIn 2, 9, 10, 12, 13; DcLP 87A; IntWW 74, 75, 76, 77, 83; Law&B 89A; NewYTBS 74; St&PR 84; WhoAdv 90; WhoAm 74, 76, 78, 86, 90; WhoE 77, 79; WhoFI 74, 75, 77, 83; WhoGov 72, 75*

Mahoney, James P(atrick)
Canadian. Religious Leader
Bishop of Saskatoon, 1967-95.
b. Dec 7, 1927 in Saskatoon, Saskatchewan, Canada
d. Mar 2, 1995 in Saskatoon, Saskatchewan, Canada
Source: *WhoAm 86, 90; WhoRel 85, 92; WhoWest 89*

Mahoney, Jock
[James O'Mahoney]
American. Actor
Screen's 13th Tarzan in films *Tarzan Goes to India,* 1962; *Tarzan's Three Challenges,* 1963.
b. Feb 7, 1919 in Chicago, Illinois
Source: *BioIn 8, 16; FilmEn; FilmgC; ForYSC; HalFC 80, 84, 88; IntMPA 75, 76, 77, 78, 79, 80, 81, 82, 84, 86, 88; LegTOT; MotPP; NewYTBS 89; VarWW 85; WhoHol A; WhoHrs 80*

Mahoney, Mary Eliza
American. Nurse
First African-American nurse.
b. May 7, 1845 in Boston, Massachusetts
d. Jan 4, 1926
Source: *BioIn 11, 16, 18, 21; BlksScM; BlkWAm; InB&W 80, 85; InWom, SUP; NotAW*

Mahony, Roger Michael
American. Religious Leader
Roman Catholic priest, 1962—; archbishop of Los Angeles, 1985—.
b. Feb 27, 1936 in Hollywood, California
Source: *News 88-2; RelLAm 91; WhoAm 80, 84, 88, 90, 92; WhoRel 77, 92; WhoWest 84, 87, 89, 92*

Mahovlich, Frank
[Francis William Mahovlich]
"Big M"
Canadian. Hockey Player
Left wing, 1955-78, mostly with Toronto; had 533 career goals in NHL; Hall of Fame, 1981.
b. Jan 10, 1938 in Timmins, Ontario, Canada
Source: *BioIn 6, 8, 9, 10; HocEn; WhoHcky 73*

Mahovlich, Pete(r Joseph)
"Little M"
Canadian. Hockey Player
Center, 1965-81, mostly with Montreal; won four Stanley Cups; brother of Frank.
b. Oct 10, 1946 in Timmins, Ontario, Canada
Source: *HocEn; WhoAm 74; WhoHcky 73*

Mahre, Phil(lip)
American. Skier
Won gold medal in men's slalom, 1984 Olympics; twin brother of Steve.
b. May 10, 1957 in Yakima, Washington
Source: *BiDAmSp OS; BioIn 11, 12, 13, 14, 16; NewYTBS 79, 83, 89; WhoAm 84, 86, 90, 92, 94, 95, 96, 97; WhoWest 94*

Mahre, Steve(n Irving)
American. Skier
Won silver medal in men's slalom, 1984 Olympics; twin brother of Phil.
b. May 10, 1957 in Yakima, Washington
Source: *BioIn 11, 12, 13, 14, 16; NewYTBS 79, 82, 83, 89; WhoAm 84, 86, 88*

Maier, Henry W
American. Politician
Dem. mayor of Milwaukee, 1960-68.
b. Dec 7, 1918 in Dayton, Ohio
Source: *BioIn 16; NewYTBS 88; WhoAm 84, 86, 88; WhoAmP 85, 87; WhoGov 77; WhoMW 90*

Mailer, Norman (Kingsley)
American. Author
Pearl Harbor attack inspired novel, *The Naked and the Dead,* 1948; won Pulitzers for *Armies of the Night,* 1969; *The Executioner's Song,* 1980.
b. Jan 31, 1923 in Long Branch, New Jersey
Source: *AmAu&B; AmCulL; AmNov; AmWr; Au&Wr 71; AuNews 2; AuSpks; Benet 87, 96; BenetAL 91; BioIn 1, 2, 4, 5, 6, 7, 8, 9, 10, 11, 12, 13, 14, 15, 16; BlueB 76; BroV; CamGEL; CamGLE; CamHAL; CasWL; CelR, 90; CnDAL; ConAu 1BS, 9R, 28NR; ConLC 1, 2, 3, 4, 5, 8, 11, 14, 28, 39, 74; ConNov 72, 76, 82, 86, 91, 96; ConPopW; CurBio 70; CyWA 89; DcArts; DcLB 2, 16, 28, DS3, Y80A, Y83A; DcLEL 1940; DrAF 76; DrAPF 80, 91; EncAB-H 1974, 1996; EncAJ; EncTwCJ; EncWL, 2, 3; FacFETw; FilmEn; FilmgC; GrWrEL N; HalFC 80, 84, 88; IntAu&W 76, 77, 89, 91, 93; IntvTCA 2; IntWW 74, 75, 76, 77, 78, 79, 80, 81, 82, 83, 89, 91, 93; IntWWP 77; LegTOT; LiJour; LinLib L, S; LngCTC; MagSAmL; MajTwCW; MakMC; McGEWB; MiSFD 9; ModAL, S1, S2; NewYTBS 91; Novels; OxCAmL 65, 83, 95; OxCEng 85, 95; OxCFilm; PenC AM; PeoHis; PolProf J, K, NF; RAdv 1, 14, 13-1; RComAH; REn; REnAL; RfGAmL 87, 94; RGTwCWr; ScF&FL 92; SourALJ; TwCA SUP; TwCWr; WebAB 74, 79; WebE&AL;*

WhDW; Who 74, 82, 83, 85, 88, 90, 92, 94; WhoAm 74, 76, 78, 80, 82, 84, 86, 88, 92, 94, 95, 96, 97; WhoAmJ 80; WhoE 74, 85, 86, 89, 93, 95, 97; WhoHol 92, A; WhoTwCL; WhoUSWr 88; WhoWor 74, 78, 95, 96, 97; WhoWorJ 72, 78; WhoWrEP 89, 92, 95; WorAl; WorAlBi; WrDr 76, 80, 82, 84, 86, 88, 90, 92, 94, 96

Maillol, Aristide
French. Artist
Neoclassical sculptor known for massive but graceful female nudes.
b. Dec 8, 1861 in Banyuls sur Mer, France
d. Oct 5, 1944 in Banyuls sur Mer, France
Source: *AtlBL; Benet 87; BioIn 14, 17; CurBio 42, 44; DcTwCCu 2; FacFETw; IntDcAA 90; LegTOT; McGDA; McGEWB; OxCArt; OxCTwCA; OxDcArt; PhDcTCA 77; WhDW*

Maiman, Theodore Harold
American. Physicist
Developed first working laser, 1960.
b. Jul 11, 1927 in Los Angeles, California
Source: *AmMWSc 79, 82, 86, 89, 92, 95; AsBiEn; BiESc; BioIn 14, 20; CamDcSc; LarDcSc; LElec; McGMS 80; WhDW; WhoAm 78, 80, 82, 84, 86, 88, 90, 92, 94, 95, 96; WhoFrS 84; WhoTech 84; WhoWor 80, 89, 91, 93, 95, 96, 97; WorInv*

Maimonides, Moses
Spanish. Philosopher, Religious Leader
Major intellectual of medieval Judaism; wrote *Guide of the Perplexed,* 1190.
b. Mar 30, 1135 in Cordoba, Spain
d. Dec 13, 1204 in Cairo, Egypt
Source: *BiD&SB; BiDPsy; BiESc; BioIn 14, 15, 17, 18, 19, 20; CasWL; EncO&P 1, 1S2, 2, 3; EuAu; EvEuW; NewCol 75; OxCLaw; OxCPhil; OxCSpan; RAdv 13-4; RComWL; WorAlBi*

Main, Marjorie
[Mary Tomlinson Krebs]
American. Actor
Played Ma Kettle in nine films, 1949-57, with Percy Kilbride.
b. Feb 24, 1890 in Acton, Illinois
d. Apr 10, 1975 in Los Angeles, California
Source: *BioIn 2, 8, 9, 10; CurBio 51, 75N; DcAmB S9; EncAFC; FilmEn; FilmgC; ForYSC; Funs; HalFC 80, 84, 88; HolCA; IntMPA 75; InWom, SUP; LegTOT; MGM; MotPP; MovMk; NewYTBS 75; QDrFCA 92; ThFT; Vers A; WhAm 6; What 2; WhoAm 74; WhoAmW 58, 61, 64, 66, 68, 70, 72, 74; WhoHol C; WhScrn 77, 83; WorAl; WorAlBi*

Mainbocher
[Main Rousseau Bocher]
American. Fashion Designer
Couturier whose clients include stage, screen stars; designed uniforms for Women's Marine Corps, American Red Cross.
b. Oct 24, 1890 in Chicago, Illinois
d. Dec 27, 1976 in Munich, Germany (West)
Source: *BiE&WWA; BioIn 5, 6, 7, 9, 16; ConDes 84, 90, 97; ConFash; CurBio 42, 77; IntWW 74; LegTOT; NewYTBE 71; NewYTBS 76; NotNAT; OxCAmT 84; WhAm 7; WorAl; WorFshn*

Maintenon, Francoise d'Aubigne, Marquise de
French. Consort
Second wife of King Louis XIV, 1684; author of essays, letters on education.
b. Nov 27, 1635 in Niort, France
d. Apr 15, 1719 in Saint-Cyr, France
Source: *Benet 96; BlmGWL; CyEd; DcEuL; NewCol 75; OxCEng 95; OxCFr; REn; WebBD 83*

Maison, Rene
Belgian. Opera Singer
Tenor who starred at NY Met., 1936-43.
b. Nov 24, 1895 in Traumeries, Belgium
d. Jul 15, 1962 in Mont-Dore, France
Source: *Baker 78, 84, 92; BioIn 4, 6, 11; MetOEnc; MusSN; NewEOp 71; NewGrDO*

Maitland, John
[Duke of Lauderdale]
Scottish. Statesman
Unpopular secretary of State for Scotland, 1660s; used highland troops to suppre ss the Covenanters, 1679.
b. May 24, 1616 in Lethington, Scotland
d. Aug 1682 in Tunbridge Wells, England
Source: *DcBiPP; DcNaB; HisDStE; NewCol 75*

Major, Charles
[Sir Edwin Caskoden]
American. Author
Wrote popular historical romance *When Knighthood Was in Flower,* 1898.
b. 1856 in Indianapolis, Indiana
d. Feb 13, 1913 in Shelbyville, Indiana
Source: *AmAu&B; AmBi; BenetAL 91; BibAL; BiD&SB; BioIn 2; CarSB; DcAmAu; DcAmB; DcBiA; DcLEL; DcNAA; GayN; IndAu 1816; LinLib L; LngCTC; NatCAB 13; OxCAmL 65, 83, 95; REnAL; Str&VC; TwCA; TwCBDA; WhAm 1*

Major, Clarence
American. Author
Writings focus on scenes of violence, black issues; best-known novels include *No,* 1973; *Emergency Exit,* 1979; also compiled *From Juba to Jive: A Dictionary of African-American Slang,* 1994.
b. Dec 31, 1936 in Atlanta, Georgia
Source: *BenetAL 91; BioIn 14, 16; BlkAWP; BlkLC; BlkWr 1, 2; BroadAu; ConAu 6AS, 13NR, 21R, 25NR, 53NR; ConBlB 9; ConLC 3, 19, 48; ConNov 82, 86, 91, 96; ConPo 75, 80, 85, 91, 96; DcLB 33; DrAF 76; DrAP 75; DrAPF 80, 91; DrAS 78E, 82E; InB&W 80, 85; IntAu&W 82, 86; IntWW 91, 93; IntWWP 77, 82; LinLib L; LivgBAA; NegAl 76, 83, 89; SchCGBL; SelBAAf; SelBAAu; SouBlCW; WhoAfA 96; WhoAm 76, 78, 90; WhoBlA 75, 77, 80, 85, 88, 90, 92, 94; WhoE 75; WhoUSWr 88; WhoWrEP 89; WorAu 1970; WrDr 76, 80, 82, 84, 86, 88, 90, 92, 94, 96*

Major, John (Roy)
English. Politician
Succeeded Margaret Thatcher as prime minister of Great Britain, 1990-97.
b. Mar 29, 1943 in London, England
Source: *BioIn 17, 18, 19, 20, 21; CurBio 90; FacFETw; IntWW 89, 91, 93; LegTOT; News 91, 91-2; NewYTBS 90, 92; Who 82, 83, 85, 88, 90, 92, 94; WhoWor 91, 93, 95, 96, 97*

Majorano, Gaetano
"Caffarelli"
Italian. Opera Singer
Famed male soprano, 1740s-50s; highest paid soloist of his time.
b. Apr 12, 1710 in Bitonto, Italy
d. Jan 31, 1783 in Naples, Italy
Source: *Baker 78, 84, 92; BioIn 7, 14, 15; IntDcOp; NewAmDM; NewEOp 71; NewGrDO; OxDcOp; PenDiMP*

Majors, Lee
[Harvey Lee Yeary]
American. Actor, Producer
Star of three hit TV series: "The Big Valley," 1965-69; "The Six Million Dollar Man ," 1974-78; "The Fall Guy," 1981-86.
b. Apr 23, 1940 in Wyandotte, Michigan
Source: *BioIn 11, 12; BkPepl; ConTFT 3, 15; FilmgC; HalFC 80, 84, 88; IntMPA 78, 79, 80, 81, 82, 84, 86, 88, 92; VarWW 85; WhoAm 80, 82, 84, 86, 88, 90, 92, 94, 95, 96, 97; WhoEnt 92; WhoHol 92, A; WhoTelC; WorAl; WorAlBi*

Makarios III, Archbishop
[Michael Christedoulos Mouskos]
Cypriot. Religious Leader, Politician
First pres., Republic of Cyprus, 1959-77; led political, religious life there for 25 yrs.
b. Aug 13, 1913, Cyprus
d. Aug 2, 1977 in Nicosia, Cyprus
Source: *CurBio 56, 77*

Makarova, Natalia
Russian. Dancer
Founded dance co., Makarova and Co., 1980; wrote *Defected from Russia,* 1970; won a Tony for *On Your Toes.*
b. Nov 21, 1940 in Leningrad, Union of Soviet Socialist Republics
Source: *BiDD; BiDSovU; BioIn 9, 10, 11, 12, 13, 14, 16, 17, 19; CelR, 90; ConAu 113; ContDcW 89; ConTFT 9; CurBio 72; DcArts; FacFETw; IntDcB; IntDcWB; IntWW 74, 75, 76, 77, 78, 79, 80, 81, 82, 83, 89, 91; InWom SUP; LegTOT; NewYTBS 89; VarWW 85; Who 88, 90, 92, 94; WhoAm 74, 76, 78, 80,*

82, 84, 86, 88, 92, 94; WhoAmW 74, 75, 83, 85, 89, 91; WhoE 86; WhoWor 78, 84, 87, 89, 91, 93; WorAlBi

Makeba, Miriam
"Mother Africa"
South African. Singer
Sang African melodies; often starred with Harry Belafonte, 1960s in which she won a 1965 Grammy for "An Evening with Belafonte/Makeba"; member of Paul Simon's Graceland tour, 1987.
b. Mar 4, 1932 in Prospect Township, South Africa
Source: *ASCAP 66; Baker 78, 84, 92; BioIn 5, 6, 7, 8, 9, 11, 13, 14, 15, 16, 17, 19, 21; BlkWr 1; ConAu 104; ConBlB 2; ConMus 8; ContDcW 89; CurBio 65; DrBlPA 90; EncFCWM 69; HeroCon; InB&W 80, 85; InWom, SUP; LegTOT; NewGrDA 86; News 89-2; NewYTBS 88; PenEncP; SchCGBL; WhoBlA 75, 85; WhoE 74; WhoHol 92; WomFir; WorAl*

Makem, Tommy
[The Clancy Brothers]
Irish. Singer
Recording, touring star, 1960s; his Irish folk singing with Clancy Brothers seen in several TV shows.
b. 1932 in Keady, Ireland
Source: *EncFCWM 69*

Makepeace, Chris
Canadian. Actor
Played in films *My Bodyguard,* 1980; *The Falcon and the Snowman,* 1984.
b. Apr 22, 1964 in Montreal, Quebec, Canada
Source: *BioIn 12; ConTFT 4; IntMPA 92, 94, 96; JohnWSW; NewYTBS 80; WhoEnt 92; WhoHol 92*

Makihara, (Ben) Minoru
English. Business Executive
Became pres. of Mitsubishi International Corp., 1987-90, the first non-Japanese to do so; chm., Mitsubishi International Corp., 1990-92.
b. Jan 12, 1930 in London, England
Source: *Dun&B 88, 90; IntWW 93; WhoAm 94, 95, 96; WhoE 91; WhoFI 94, 96; WhoWor 95, 96, 97*

Makins, Roger (Mellor), Sir
English. Diplomat
British ambassador to the US, 1953-56.
b. Feb 3, 1904
d. Nov 9, 1996 in Basingstoke, England
Source: *BioIn 3, 5, 7; ConAu 111*

Malamud, Bernard
American. Author
Wrote *The Natural,* 1952; adapted to film, 1984; won Pulitzer for *The Fixer,* 1967.
b. Apr 26, 1914 in New York, New York
d. Mar 18, 1986 in New York, New York
Source: *AmAu&B; AmCulL; AmWr S1; AnObit 1984, 1986; Au&Arts 16; Au&Wr 71; Benet 87, 96; BenetAL 91; BioIn 5, 6, 7, 8, 9, 10, 11, 12, 13, 14, 15, 16, 17, 19, 21; BlueB 76; CamGLE; CamHAL; CasWL; CelR; CnMWL; ConAu 1BS, 5R, 28NR, 118; ConLC 1, 2, 3, 5, 8, 9, 11, 18, 27, 44, 78, 85; ConNov 72, 76, 82, 86; ConPopW; CurBio 58, 78, 86, 86N; CyWA 89; DcArts; DcLB 2, 28, 152, Y80A, Y86N; DcLEL 1940; DcTwCCu 1; DrAF 76; DrAPF 80; EncSF 93; EncWL, 2, 3; FacFETw; GrWrEL N; IntAu&W 76, 77, 82; IntWW 74, 75, 76, 77, 78, 79, 80, 81, 82, 83; JeAmHC; LegTOT; LinLib L, S; MagSAmL; MajTwCW; ModAL, S1, S2; NewCon; NewYTBS 86; Novels; OxCAmL 65, 83, 95; OxCEng 85, 95; PenC AM; RAdv 1, 14, 13-1; REn; REnAL; RfGAmL 87, 94; RfGShF; RGTwCWr; ScF&FL 92; ShSCr 15; ShSWr; TwCWr; WebAB 74, 79; WebE&AL; WhAm 9; WhDW; Who 74, 82, 83, 85; WhoAm 74, 76, 78, 80, 82, 84; WhoE 74; WhoTwCL; WhoWor 78, 80, 82, 84; WhoWorJ 72, 78; WorAl; WorAlBi; WorAu 1950; WorLitC; WrDr 76, 80, 82, 84, 86; WrPh*

Malan, Daniel Francois
South African. Politician
Pres., Union of South Africa, 1948-54; advocated apartheid.
b. May 22, 1874 in Riebeck, South Africa
d. Feb 7, 1959 in Cape Town, South Africa
Source: *BioIn 1, 2, 3, 4, 5, 13, 15, 21; CurBio 49, 59; DcAfHiB 86; DcNaB 1951; DcPol; DcTwHis; EncSoA; McGEWB; WhAm 3; WhDW*

Malandro, Kristina
American. Actor
Plays Felicia on TV Soap, "General Hospital."
b. 1964

Malaparte, Curzio
Italian. Author
Wrote popular WW II novels *Kaputt,* 1945; *La Pelle,* 1949.
b. Jun 9, 1898 in Prato, Italy
d. Jul 19, 1957 in Rome, Italy
Source: *BiDExR; BioIn 1, 4, 13, 17; CasWL; ClDMEL 47, 80; CnMD; DcItL 1, 2; EncRev; EncWL; EvEuW; FilmEn; ItaFilm; ModRL; PenC EUR; REn; TwCA SUP; TwCLC 52; TwCWr*

Malavasi, Ray(mondo Guiseppi Giovanni Baptiste)
American. Football Coach
Coach, LA Rams, 1978-82; led team to only Super Bowl appearance to date, 1980.
b. Nov 8, 1930 in Passaic, New Jersey
d. Dec 15, 1987 in Santa Ana, California
Source: *BioIn 11, 15; FootReg 81; NewYTBS 78; WhAm 9; WhoAm 82, 84, 86; WhoWest 82*

Malbin, Elaine
American. Opera Singer
Lyric soprano who starred on TV show "Kismet," 1950s.
b. May 24, 1932 in New York, New York
Source: *BioIn 5; CurBio 59; InWom; RadStar; WhoAm 74; WhoAmW 58, 64, 66, 68, 70, 72, 74; WhoWor 74*

Malcolm, Andrew H(ogarth)
American. Journalist, Author
NY Times correspondent who wrote *The Canadians,* 1985.
b. Jun 22, 1943 in Cleveland, Ohio
Source: *BioIn 15, 16; ConAu 53; WhoAm 76, 92, 94, 95, 96, 97; WhoE 93; WhoWest 96*

Malcolm, George
English. Conductor, Pianist
Directed cathedral music, Westminister Cathedral, 1947-59.
b. Feb 28, 1917 in London, England
Source: *Baker 84; BlueB 76; BriBkM 80; IntWW 74, 75, 76, 77, 78, 79, 80, 81, 82, 83, 89, 91; IntWWM 77, 80, 85, 90; NewAmDM; NewGrDM 80; PenDiMP; Who 74, 82, 83, 85, 88, 90, 92; WhoAm 78, 80, 82, 84, 86; WhoMus 72; WhoWor 74*

Malcolm X
[El-Hajj Malik El-Shabazz; Malcolm Little]
American. Political Activist
Radical civil rights leader; formed Organization for Afro-American Unity, 1964.
b. May 19, 1925 in Omaha, Nebraska
d. Feb 21, 1965 in New York, New York
Source: *AfrAmAl 6; AmAu&B; AmJust; AmOrTwC; AmRef; AmSocL; Benet 96; BenetAL 91; BiDAmJo; BioIn 7, 8, 9, 10, 11, 12, 13, 14, 15, 16, 17, 18, 19, 20; BlkAWP; BlkLC; BlkWr 1; BlkWrNE; CivRSt; ConAu 111, 125; ConLC 82; CyWA 89; DcAmB S7; DcAmNB; DcAmReB 1, 2; DcPol; DcTwCCu 5; DcTwHis; EncAACR; EncAB-H 1974, 1996; EncARH; EncRev; FacFETw; HisWorL; LegTOT; LinLib L, S; LuthC 75; MajTwCW; MakMC; McGEWB; NegAl 76, 83, 89; OxCAmL 83, 95; RAdv 14; RComAH; RelLAm 91; SchCGBL; SelBAAf; SelBAAu; TwCSAPR; WebAB 74, 79; WhAm 4; WhAmP; WorAl; WorAlBi*

Malcuzynski, Witold
Polish. Musician
Best known for interpretations of Chopin; debuted in US at Carnegie Hall, 1942.
b. Aug 10, 1914 in Warsaw, Poland
d. Jul 17, 1977 in Majorca, Spain
Source: *Baker 78, 84, 92; BioIn 4, 11; IntWW 74, 75, 76, 77; IntWWM 77, 80; MusSN; NewGrDM 80; PenDiMP; PolBiDi; WhAm 7; WhoMus 72; WhoSocC 78; WhoWor 74*

Malden, Karl
[Mladen Sekulovich]
American. Actor
Won Oscar for *A Streetcar Named Desire,* 1951; star of TV series "Streets of San Francisco," 1972-77.
b. Mar 22, 1913 in Gary, Indiana
Source: *BiDFilm; BiE&WWA; BioIn 10, 11; BioNews 74; CelR, 90; CmMov; ConTFT 6; CurBio 57; FilmgC; GangFlm; HalFC 80, 84, 88; IntMPA 86, 92; LegTOT; MotPP; MovMk; NotNAT; OxCFilm; PlP&P; VarWW 85; WhoAm 74, 76, 78, 80, 90; WhoEnt 92; WhoHol A; WhoWor 74; WorAl; WorAlBi; WorEFlm*

Malenkov, Georgi Maximilianovich
Russian. Political Leader, Government Official
Prominent Politburo member, 1940s-50s; close to Stalin; became prime minister after Stalin's death, 1953-55.
b. Jan 8, 1901 in Orenburg, Russia
d. Jan 14, 1988
Source: *ColdWar 1; CurBio 52, 88; IntWW 74; NewYTBS 88; Who 74, 82, 83, 85, 88*

Maleska, Eugene T.
American. Editor, Puzzle Maker
Crossword puzzle editor, *NY Times,* 1978-93; puzzles known for their playful sense of humor.
b. Jan 6, 1916 in Jersey City, New Jersey
d. Aug 3, 1993 in Daytona Beach, Florida
Source: *BioIn 11; ConLC 81; LegTOT; WhoAm 86, 88, 90, 92*

Malevich, Kasimir Severinovich
Russian. Artist
Founded suprematist school of abstract art, 1913.
b. Feb 26, 1878 in Kiev, Russia
d. May 15, 1935 in Leningrad, Union of Soviet Socialist Republics
Source: *ConArt 77; EncMA; McGDA; McGEWB; OxCTwCA; WhoArch*

Malherbe, Francois de
French. Author, Poet
Court poet to Henry IV, Louis XIII; wrote *Consolation a Duperier,* 1601.
b. 1555 in Caen, France
d. Oct 16, 1628 in Paris, France
Source: *BbD; Benet 87, 96; BiD&SB; BioIn 2, 7, 9; CasWL; ChhPo; DcArts; DcCathB; DcEuL; Dis&D; EuAu; EvEuW; GuFrLit 2; LinLib L; LitC 5; McGEWB; OxCFr; PenC EUR; REn*

Malibran, Maria Felicita
[Maria Felicita Garcia]
Spanish. Opera Singer
Celebrated contralto who was popular in NY, Paris, London, 1820s-30s.
b. Mar 24, 1808 in Paris, France
d. Sep 23, 1836 in Manchester, England
Source: *ApCAB; Baker 78, 84, 92; BioIn 4, 5, 7, 10, 12, 13; BriBkM 80; CelCen; CmOp; IntDcOp; NewC; NewEOp 71; NewGrDM 80; OxCEng 67; OxCFr; REn*

Malick, Terence
[David Whitney]
"Terry Malick"
American. Director, Screenwriter
Best known for debut film *Badlands,* 1974, which took a fresh look at 1950s.
b. Nov 30, 1943 in Waco, Texas
Source: *BioIn 16; ConAu 101; ConTFT 6; FilmEn; HalFC 88; IntDcF 2-2; IntMPA 86, 88, 92, 94, 96; LegTOT; MovMk; VarWW 85; WhoAm 82; WorFDir 2*

Malik, Charles Habib
Lebanese. Government Official, Statesman
Delegate to UN, 1945-54; helped write UN Charter, 1945; pres. of UN, 1958-59.
b. Feb 11, 1906 in Bterram, Lebanon
d. Dec 28, 1987 in Beirut, Lebanon
Source: *BioIn 1, 2, 3, 5, 6, 15, 16; BlueB 76; ConAu 7NR, 45, 124; CurBio 48, 88; DrAS 74P; FacFETw; IntWW 74, 75, 76, 77, 78, 79, 80, 81, 82, 83; IntYB 78, 79, 80, 81, 82; MidE 78, 80, 81, 82; WhoAm 78, 80, 82; WhoUN 75; WhoWor 74, 84*

Malik, Yakov (Alexandrovich)
Russian. Diplomat
Outspoken, conservative Soviet ambassador to UN, 1948-75; expert on Far Eastern affairs.
b. Feb 11, 1906 in Kharkov, Russia
d. Feb 11, 1980 in Moscow, Union of Soviet Socialist Republics
Source: *AnObit 1980; IntWW 74, 75, 76; NewYTBS 80; Who 74; WhoAm 74; WhoGov 72; WhoWor 74, 76, 78*

Malina, Judith
German. Actor
Founder of the Living Theatre, 1947; won Obie, 1960.
b. Jun 4, 1926 in Kiel, Germany
Source: *BiE&WWA; BioIn 10, 14, 15, 16; CamGWoT; CelR; ConAu 18NR, 102; ContDcW 89; InWom SUP; MugS; NotNAT, A; NotWoAT; OxCThe 83; PlP&P; WhoAm 76, 78, 80, 82, 84, 86, 88, 90, 92, 94, 95, 96, 97; WhoAmW 95, 97; WhoE 95, 97; WhoEnt 92; WhoHol 92, A; WhoThe 72, 77, 81; WomFir*

Malinovsky, Rodion Yakovlevich
Russian. Military Leader
Served in Soviet army during WW I, II; minister of defense, 1957-67.
b. Nov 23, 1898 in Odessa, Ukraine
d. Mar 13, 1967 in Moscow, Union of Soviet Socialist Republics
Source: *ColdWar 1; CurBio 44, 60, 67; FacFETw; ObitT 1961; SovUn; WhAm 4; WhWW-II*

Malinowski, Bronislaw Kasper
English. Anthropologist, Educator
Founder of social anthropology; works include *Myth in Primitive Psychology,* 1926.
b. Apr 7, 1884 in Krakow, Poland
d. May 16, 1942 in New Haven, Connecticut
Source: *BiDPsy; CurBio 41, 42; DcNAA; DcNaB MP; LngCTC; NamesHP; TwCA, SUP; WhAm 2; WhoLA*

Malipiero, Gian Francesco
Italian. Composer
Works include opera trilogy: *L'Orfeide,* 1925; nocturne: *Ecuba,* 1941.
b. Mar 18, 1882 in Venice, Italy
d. Aug 1, 1973 in Treviso, Italy
Source: *Baker 78, 84, 92; BioIn 1, 2, 3, 4, 6, 8, 10, 12, 19; BriBkM 80; CmOp; CompSN, SUP; ConAu 45; DcArts; DcCM; DcCom 77; DcCom&M 79; IntDcOp; LegTOT; McGEWB; MetOEnc; MusMk; NewAmDM; NewEOp 71; NewGrDM 80; NewGrDO; NewOxM; NewYTBE 73; OxDcOp; PenDiMP A; WhoMus 72*

Malkovich, John
American. Actor
Won Obie for performance in *True West,* 1982; films include *Places in the Heart,* 1984; *Making Mr. Right,* 1987.
b. Dec 9, 1953 in Christopher, Illinois
Source: *BiDFilm 94; BioIn 14, 15, 16; CelR 90; ConTFT 5, 12; CurBio 88; HalFC 88; HolBB; IntMPA 92, 94, 96; IntWW 89, 91, 93; LegTOT; News 88-2; NewYTBS 84, 85; WhoAm 86, 88, 90, 92, 94, 95, 96, 97; WhoEnt 92; WhoHol 92; WorAlBi*

Mallarme, Stephane
French. Poet
Leading symbolist best known for poem *The Afternoon of a Faun,* 1876.
b. Mar 18, 1842 in Paris, France
d. Sep 9, 1898 in Valvins, France
Source: *AtlBL; Benet 87, 96; BioIn 1, 2, 3, 4, 5, 7, 8, 9, 11, 12, 13, 16, 17, 20, 21; CasWL; ClDMEL 47, 80; CyWA 58; DcArts; DcEuL; Dis&D; EuAu; EuWr 7; EvEuW; GrFLW; GuFrLit 1; IlEncMy; LegTOT; LinLib L; McGEWB; ModRL; NewC; NewCBEL; NewGrDM 80; NinCLC 4, 41; OxCEng 67, 85, 95; OxCFr; OxCMus; PenC EUR; PoeCrit 4; RAdv 14, 13-2; RComWL; REn; RfGWoL 95; RGFMEP; ThHElm; WhDW; WorAl; WorAlBi*

Malle, Louis
French. Director
First US-made film *Pretty Baby,* 1978; others include *Goodbye, Children,* 1988.
b. Oct 30, 1932 in Thumeries, France
d. Nov 23, 1995 in Beverly Hills, California
Source: *Benet 87, 96; BiDFilm, 81, 94; BioIn 9, 10, 11, 12, 13, 14, 16, 17, 21; CelR 90; ConAu 101, 150; ConTFT 1, 6, 13, 15; CurBio 76, 96N; DcArts; DcFM;*

DcTwCCu 2; EncEurC; FacFETw; FilmEn; FilmgC; HalFC 80, 84, 88; IntDcF 1-2, 2-2; IntMPA 76, 77, 78, 79, 80, 81, 82, 84, 86, 88, 92, 94, 96; IntWW 74, 75, 76, 77, 78, 79, 80, 81, 82, 83, 89, 91, 93; ItaFilm; LegTOT; MiSFD 9; MovMk; News 96, 96-2; NewYTBE 72; NewYTBS 85; OxCFilm; RAdv 14; VarWW 85; WhAm 11; Who 74, 82, 83, 85, 88, 90, 92, 94; WhoAm 84, 88, 90, 92, 94, 95, 96; WhoEnt 92; WhoFr 79; WhoWor 74, 76, 78, 82, 84, 87, 89, 91, 93, 95, 96; WorAl; WorAlBi; WorEFlm; WorFDir 2

Mallet-Joris, Francoise
Belgian. Author
Writes psychological love novels; works include *Into the Labyrinth,* 1953.
b. Jul 6, 1930 in Antwerp, Belgium
Source: *Au&Wr 71; Benet 87, 96; BioIn 6, 7, 9, 10, 11, 17; BlmGWL; ClDMEL 80; ConAu 17NR, 65; ConFLW 84; ConLC 11; ConWorW 93; DcLB 83; DcTwCCu 2; EncCoWW; EncWL 2, 3; FrenWW; GuFrLit 1; IntAu&W 86; InWom, SUP; ModFrL; ModRL; ModWoWr; PenC EUR; REn; WhoFr 79; WhoWor 82, 87, 91, 93, 95, 96; WorAu 1950*

Mallinckrodt, Edward
American. Manufacturer
President, Mallinckrodt Chemical Works, 1882-1928.
b. Jan 21, 1845 in Saint Louis, Missouri
d. Feb 1, 1928 in Saint Louis, Missouri
Source: *AmBi; BioIn 9; DcAmB; InSci; WhAm 1*

Mallinger, Mathilde
[Mathilde Lichtenegger]
Croatian. Opera Singer
Berlin Opera soprano, 1869-82; rival of Pauline Lucca.
b. Feb 17, 1847 in Agram, Croatia
d. Apr 19, 1920 in Berlin, Germany
Source: *Baker 78, 84, 92; CmOp; NewEOp 71; NewGrDM 80; NewGrDO; OxDcOp*

Mallock, William Hurrell
English. Author
Wrote satire on English life: *The New Republic,* 1877.
b. Feb 7, 1849 in Devonshire, England
d. Apr 5, 1923 in Wincanton, England
Source: *Alli SUP; BbD; BiD&SB; BioIn 12, 13, 16; BritAu 19; Chambr 3; DcAmC; DcCathB; DcEnA, A; DcEnL; DcLEL; DcNaB 1922; GrWrEL N; LngCTC; NewC; NewCBEL; OxCEng 67, 85, 95; PenC ENG; REn; RfGEnL 91*

Mallon, Meg
American. Golfer
In 1991 won US Women's open, LPGA, and Daikyo World Championship; first golfer to win the US Women's Sport Foundation's professional athlete of the yr. award, 1991.
b. 1963

Mallory, George Leigh
English. Mountaineer
His famous reply as to why he wanted to climb Mt. Everest was "Because it's there."
b. Jun 18, 1886 in Mobberley, England
d. Jun 8, 1924, Nepal
Source: *BioIn 14, 15; DcNaB 1922; GrBr*

Mallory, L(ester) D(ewitt)
American. Diplomat
Ambassador to Jordan, 1953-57, Guatemala, 1958-59.
b. Apr 21, 1904
d. Jun 21, 1994 in Laguna Hills, California
Source: *BioIn 5; CurBio 94N; InSci*

Mallory, Molla
Finnish. Tennis Player
Nine-time US National champion.
b. 1892?
d. Nov 22, 1959 in Stockholm, Sweden
Source: *BioIn 1, 5, 11, 12, 13; EncWomS*

Mallory, Stephen R
American. Politician
Senator from FL, 1851-61; Confederacy secretary of Navy, 1861-65.
b. 1812, Trinidad
d. Nov 19, 1873 in Pensacola, Florida
Source: *AmBi; ApCAB; BiDConf; BiDrAC; BiDSA; DcAmB; DcAmMiB; TwCBDA; WhAm HS; WhAmP*

Mallowan, Max Edgar Lucien, Sir
English. Archaeologist, Author
Wrote *Nimrud and Its Remains,* 1966, describing work, findings; married to Agatha Christie.
b. May 6, 1904 in London, England
d. Aug 19, 1978 in London, England
Source: *BioIn 7, 8, 11, 14, 21; BlueB 76; ConAu 81; DcNaB 1971; GrBr; IntAu&W 77; IntWW 74, 75, 76, 77, 78; MidE 78; WrDr 76*

Malloy, Edward Aloysius
American. University Administrator
President, U of Notre Dame, 1987—.
b. May 3, 1941 in Washington, District of Columbia
Source: *BioIn 15, 16; DrAS 78P, 82P; News 89; NewYTBS 86, 88; WhoAm 88, 90, 92, 94, 95, 96, 97; WhoMW 88, 90, 92, 93, 96; WhoRel 92; WhoWor 89, 91, 93, 95, 96, 97*

Malone, Annie Minerva Turnbo Pope
American. Businesswoman, Philanthropist
Developed line of Poro African-American beauty care products; first major African-American philanthropist in US.
b. Aug 9, 1869 in Metropolis, Illinois
d. May 10, 1957 in Chicago, Illinois
Source: *BioIn 8; HanAmWH; InB&W 85; NotAW MOD; NotBlAW 1*

Malone, Dan
American. Journalist
Won Pulitzer Prize for investigative reporting, 1992.

Malone, Dorothy
[Dorothy Maloney]
American. Actor
Won 1956 Oscar for *Written on the Wind;* played in TV series "Peyton Place," 1964-69.
b. Jan 30, 1925 in Chicago, Illinois
Source: *BiDFilm, 81, 94; BioIn 10, 12, 18; ConTFT 5; FilmEn; FilmgC; ForYSC; HalFC 80, 84, 88; HolP 40; IntDcF 1-3, 2-3; IntMPA 84, 86, 88, 92, 94, 96; InWom SUP; ItaFilm; LegTOT; MotPP; MovMk; SweetSg D; VarWW 85; WhoAm 74; WhoHol 92, A; WorAl; WorEFlm*

Malone, Dumas
American. Author
Won Pulitzer for multivolume biography of Thomas Jefferson, 1975.
b. Jan 10, 1892 in Coldwater, Mississippi
d. Dec 27, 1986 in Charlottesville, Virginia
Source: *AmAu&B; AnObit 1986; Au&Wr 71; BenetAL 91; BioIn 1, 4, 12, 13; BlueB 76; ConAu 1R, 2NR, 121; DcLB 17; DrAS 74H, 78H, 82H; EncAAH; IntAu&W 76, 77, 82; IntWW 74, 75, 76, 77, 78, 79, 80, 81, 82, 83; LiveMA; McGEWB; NewYTBS 86; OxCAmL 65, 83, 95; REnAL; TwCA SUP; WhAm 9; WhoAm 74, 76, 78, 80, 82, 84, 86; WhoSSW 73; WhoWor 74; WrDr 76, 80, 82, 84, 86*

Malone, Edmund
Irish. Author
Helped Boswell edit Johnson biography; published Shakespeare edition, 1790.
b. Oct 4, 1741 in Dublin, Ireland
d. May 25, 1812 in London, England
Source: *Alli; BbD; Benet 87, 96; BiD&SB; BiDIrW; BioIn 1, 3; BlmGEL; DcBiPP; DcEnA; DcEnL; DcEuL; DcIrB 78, 88; DcIrW 2; DcNaB; NewC; NotNAT B; OxCIri; OxCThe 83; PoIre; REn*

Malone, Joe
[Maurice Joseph Malone]
Canadian. Hockey Player
Forward, 1917-24, with three NHL teams; won Art Ross Trophy, 1918, 1920; scored NHL record seven goals in one game, 1920; Hall of Fame, 1950.
b. Feb 28, 1890 in Sillery, Quebec, Canada
d. May 15, 1969
Source: *BioIn 8; HocEn; WhoHcky 73; WhoSpor*

Malone, John Charles Custer
"King of Cable"
American. Business Executive
Pres., CEO, Tele-Communications, Inc., 1973—, one of the largest cable TV

companies in the US; chm., dir., Liberty Media Corp.
b. Mar 7, 1941 in Milford, Connecticut
Source: *CurBio 95; Dun&B 90; LesBEnT 92; WhoFI 92; WhoWest 92*

Malone, Karl
"The Mailman"
American. Basketball Player
Forward, Utah, 1985—; MVP, All-Star Game, 1989; gold medal, 1992 Summer Olympics.
b. Jul 24, 1963 in Summerfield, Louisiana
Source: *AfrAmSG; BasBi; BioIn 14, 16; CurBio 93; LegTOT; News 90, 90-1; OfNBA 87; WhoAfA 96; WhoAm 92, 94, 95, 96, 97; WhoBlA 92, 94; WhoSpor; WhoWest 92, 94, 96; WorAlBi*

Malone, Moses Eugene
American. Basketball Player
Center, 1974—; with several NBA teams, now with Milwaukee; NBA MVP three times ; led NBA in rebounding six times.
b. Mar 23, 1955 in Petersburg, Virginia
Source: *BiDAmSp BK; BioIn 13, 14, 15; CurBio 86; NewYTBS 82, 83, 86; OfNBA 87; WhoAfA 96; WhoAm 84, 86, 88; WhoBlA 85, 88, 90, 92, 94; WhoE 89; WorAlBi*

Malone, Vivian
American. Civil Rights Leader
First black woman to attend and graduate from U of AL; in 1963 was one of two black students to be admitted to the university after George Wallace backed down.
b. Jul 15, 1942 in Monroeville, Alabama
Source: *BioIn 7, 10, 11, 18; CivR 74; InWom SUP; NotBlAW 1*

Malory, Thomas, Sir
English. Author
Wrote *Morte d'Arthur,* source for later versions of King Arthur legend.
d. Mar 12, 1471? in London, England
Source: *Alli; AnCL; AtlBL; BbD; BiD&SB; BioIn 2, 3, 4, 5, 6, 7, 9, 10, 11, 12, 13, 14, 16, 17, 18, 19, 21; BlmGEL; BritAu; BritWr 1; CamGEL; CamGLE; CarSB; CasWL; Chambr 1; ChhPo S3; CrtT 1; CyWA 58; DcArts; DcCathB; DcEnA; DcEnL; DcEuL; DcLEL; DcNaB; Dis&D; EvLB; LinLib L, S; LitC 11; LngCEL; McGEWB; MouLC 1; NewC; OxCChiL; OxCEng 67, 85, 95; PenC ENG; RAdv 1, 13-1; RComWL; REn; RfGEnL 91; WebE&AL; WhDW; WorAl; WorAlBi*

Malott, Deane W(aldo)
American. Educator, University Administrator
Chancellor, Univ. of Kansas, 1939-51; pres., Cornell Univ., 1951-63.
b. Jul 10, 1898
d. Sep 11, 1996 in Ithaca, New York
Source: *AmMWSc 73S; BioIn 2, 5; BlueB 76; CurBio 96N; IntAu&W 77; IntWW 74, 75, 76, 77, 78, 79, 80, 81, 82, 83, 89, 91, 93; St&PR 75, 84, 87; Who 74, 82, 83, 85, 88, 90, 92, 94*

Malouf, David
[George Joseph David Malouf]
Australian. Author
Won 1994 *Los Angeles Times* Award for Fiction for *Remembering Babylon,* 1993.
b. Mar 20, 1934 in Brisbane, Australia
Source: *AuLitCr; Benet 96; BioIn 20; CamGLE; ConAu 124; ConLC 28, 86; ConNov 82, 86, 91, 96; ConPo 70, 80, 85, 91, 96; DcArts; IntAu&W 86, 89, 91, 93; IntWWP 77, 82; OxCAusL; OxCEng 95; OxCTwCP; RAdv 14; WhoWor 96, 97; WorAu 1975; WrDr 82, 84, 86, 88, 90, 92, 94, 96*

Malpighi, Marcello
Italian. Physician, Educator
Discovered capillaries; founded sciences of histology, embryology, plant anatomy, comparative anatomy.
b. Mar 10, 1626 in Crevalcore, Italy
d. Nov 30, 1694 in Rome, Italy
Source: *AsBiEn; McGEWB*

Malraux, Andre Georges
French. Author, Government Official
DeGaulle's minister of cultural affairs, 1958-69; wrote prize-winning novel *Man's Fate,* 1934; *Voices of Silence,* 1953.
b. Nov 3, 1901 in Paris, France
d. Nov 23, 1976 in Paris, France
Source: *Au&Wr 71; CasWL; ClDMEL 47; CnMD; CnMWL; ConAu 69, P-2; ConLC 15; CurBio 59; CyWA 58; DcFM; IntWW 74; PenC EUR; TwCA SUP; Who 74; WorEFlm*

Maltby, Richard E
American. Composer, Conductor
Songs include "Six Flats Unfurnished," "What's Your Hurry?"
b. Jun 26, 1914 in Chicago, Illinois
d. Aug 19, 1991 in Santa Monica, California
Source: *ASCAP 66, 80; ConAmC 76, 82; NewYTBS 91; PenEncP; VarWW 85*

Maltby, Richard Eldridge, Jr.
American. Director
Won 1978 Tony for *Ain't Misbehavin';* 1984 nominee for *Baby.*
b. Oct 6, 1937 in Ripon, Wisconsin
Source: *ASCAP 66; ConTFT 4; VarWW 85; WhoAm 84, 86, 88, 90, 92, 94, 95, 96, 97; WhoEnt 92; WhoThe 81*

Malthus, Thomas Robert
English. Economist
Pioneered studies in modern population; wrote *Essays on the Principle of Population,* 1798.
b. Feb 17, 1766 in Surrey, England
d. Dec 23, 1834 in Bath, England
Source: *Alli; AsBiEn; BbD; Benet 87, 96; BiD&SB; BiDLA, SUP; BiDPsy; BiESc; BioIn 1, 2, 3, 4, 7, 8, 10, 11, 12, 13, 14, 15, 16, 17, 20; BlkwCE; BlmGEL; BritAu 19; CamGEL; CamGLE; CasWL; CelCen; Chambr 2; DcBiPP; DcEnA; DcEnL; DcInB; DcLB 107, 158; DcNaB; DcScB; Dis&D; EncEnl; EncEnv; EnvEnc; EvLB; GrEconB; LarDcSc; LinLib L, S; LngCEL; LuthC 75; McGEWB; NamesHP; NewC; NewCBEL; OxCEng 67, 85, 95; PenC ENG; RAdv 14, 13-3; REn; WebE&AL; WhDW; WhoEc 81, 86; WorAl*

Maltin, Leonard
American. Critic
Has syndicated TV series, "Entertainment Tonight," 1980s; wrote *The Real Stars* , 1973.
b. Dec 18, 1950 in New York, New York
Source: *ConAu 12NR, 28NR, 29R; ConTFT 11; LegTOT; WhoAm 94, 95, 96, 97; WhoE 75; WhoEnt 92; WhoWest 94*

Maltz, Albert
[Hollywood Ten]
American. Author, Screenwriter
Wrote screenplays for several films: *Destination Tokyo,* 1944; *The Naked City,* 1948; jailed, 1950, blacklisted.
b. Oct 8, 1908 in New York, New York
d. Apr 26, 1985 in Los Angeles, California
Source: *AmAu&B; AmNov; AnObit 1985; Au&Wr 71; BenetAL 91; BiE&WWA; BioIn 2, 4, 10, 11, 14, 16, 17; CamGLE; CamHAL; CnDAL; CnMD; ConAu 41R, 115; ConDr 73, 77, 82, 93; ConNov 76, 82; ConTFT 1; CurBio 85N; DcFM; DcLB 102; EncMcCE; FilmEn; FilmgC; GangFlm; HalFC 80, 84, 88; IntAu&W 82; IntMPA 75, 76, 77, 78, 79, 80, 81, 82, 84; ModAL; ModWD; NewYTBS 85; NotNAT; Novels; OxCAmL 65, 83, 95; PenC AM; REn; REnAL; TwCA, SUP; VarWW 85; WhAm 8; WhE&EA; WhoAm 74, 76, 78, 80, 82, 84; WhoWor 74; WhoWorJ 72, 78; WrDr 76, 80, 82, 84*

Mamas and the Papas, The
[Dennis Doherty; Cass Elliot; Elaine "Spanky" McFarlane; John Phillips; Mackenzie Phillips; Michelle Gilliam Phillips]
American. Music Group
Original group formed 1965; had light CA folk-pop beat; hits include "Monday, Mon day," 1966.
Source: *Alli; BiAUS; BiDAmM; BiDLA; BiDrAC; BiDRP&D; BiDrUSC 89; BioIn 3, 4, 5, 7, 9, 10, 13, 14, 15; BioNews 74; ConMuA 80A; DcLP 87B; DcNaB; DcVicP 2; Drake; EncFCWM 69; EncPR&S 74, 89; EncRk 88; HarEnR 86; IlEncRk; InWom; NewAmDM; NewCBEL; NewGrDA 86; NewGrDM 80; NewYTBS 27, 74, 95; ObitOF 79; OxCPMus; PenEncP; RolSEnR 83; WhAm HS; WhoAtom 77; WhoHol 92, A; WhoRock 81; WhoRocM 82*

Mamet, David Alan
American. Dramatist, Director
Won Obies for *American Buffalo,* 1976; *Edmond,* 1983; Pulitzer for *Glengarry Glen Ross,* 1984.
b. Nov 30, 1947 in Chicago, Illinois
Source: *Au&Arts 3; Benet 87; BenetAL 91; BioIn 13, 14, 15, 16; CamGLE; CamGWoT; CamHAL; CelR 90; ConAu 3BS, 15NR, 81; ConBlAP 88; ConDr 82, 88; ConLC 34, 46; ConTFT 2, 8; CurBio 78; CyWA 89; DramC 4; FacFETw; IntMPA 92; IntvTCA 2; IntWW 91; MajTwCW; ModAL S2; NewYTBS 85; OxCAmL 83; OxCAmT 84; OxCThe 83; RAdv 13-2; VarWW 85; Who 92; WhoAm 86, 90; WhoE 91; WhoEmL 87; WhoEnt 92; WhoThe 81; WhoUSWr 88; WhoWrEP 89; WorAlBi; WorAu 1950, 1975; WrDr 86, 92*

Mamoulian, Rouben (Zachary)
American. Director
Films include Hollywood's first Technicolor feature *Becky Sharp,* 1935; *Silk Stockings,* 1957.
b. Oct 8, 1897 in Tiflis, Russia
d. Dec 4, 1987 in Los Angeles, California
Source: *AmFD; AnObit 1987; Baker 92; BiDFilm; BiE&WWA; BioIn 1, 2, 6, 8, 9, 10, 11, 12, 13, 15, 16, 19; BlueB 76; CamGWoT; CmMov; ConAu 25R, 124; ConTFT 6; CurBio 49, 88, 88N; DcFM; EncMT; EncWT; FilmgC; GangFlm; HalFC 80, 84, 88; IlWWHD 1; IntAu&W 89; IntDcF 1-2, 2-2; IntMPA 75, 76, 77, 78, 79, 80, 82, 84, 86, 88; IntWW 74, 75, 76, 77, 78, 79, 80, 81, 82, 83; LegTOT; MiSFD 9N; MovMk; NewYTBS 87; NotNAT; OxCAmT 84; OxCFilm; VarWW 85; WhAm 9; Who 74, 82, 83, 85, 88; WhoAm 74, 76, 78, 82, 84, 86; WhoHrs 80; WhoWor 74; WorEFlm; WorFDir 1*

Manatt, Charles Taylor
American. Politician
Chm., Dem. Nat. Com., 1981-85.
b. Jun 9, 1936 in Chicago, Illinois
Source: *BioIn 12, 13; Dun&B 90; IntWW 81, 82, 83, 89, 91, 93; NewYTBS 81; WhoAm 76, 78, 80, 82, 84, 97; WhoAmP 73, 75, 77, 79, 81, 83; WhoFI 74, 75; WhoWest 76, 78*

Manchester, Melissa Toni
American. Singer, Songwriter
Began career as back-up singer for Bette Midler; hit songs "Midnight Blue;" "Don't Cry Out Loud."
b. Feb 15, 1951 in New York, New York
Source: *Baker 84; BioIn 10, 13, 15, 16; BkPepl; CelR 90; EncPR&S 89; InWom SUP; PenEncP; VarWW 85; WhoAm 78, 80, 82, 84, 86, 88; WhoAmW 81, 83, 87, 89, 91; WorAlBi*

Manchester, William Raymond
American. Author
Best known for historical books: *American Caesar: Douglas MacArthur,* 1978; *The Death of a President,* 1967.
b. Apr 4, 1922 in Attleboro, Massachusetts
Source: *AmAu&B; Au&Wr 71; AuNews 1; BenetAL 91; BioIn 15; ConAu 1R, 3NR, 31NR; CurBio 67; IntAu&W 91; IntWW 91; MajTwCW; SmATA 65; Who 92; WhoAm 86, 90; WhoE 74; WhoEnt 92; WhoUSWr 88; WhoWor 87, 89; WhoWrEP 89; WorAu 1950; WrDr 76, 86, 92*

Mancinelli, Luigi
Italian. Conductor, Composer
Conducted in London, 1887-1905; at NY Met., 1893-1903; wrote opera *Ero e Leandro,* 1896.
b. Feb 5, 1848 in Orvieto, Italy
d. Feb 2, 1921 in Rome, Italy
Source: *Baker 78, 84, 92; BioIn 4; CmOp; MetOEnc; NewAmDM; NewEOp 71; NewGrDM 80; NewGrDO; OxDcOp; PenDiMP*

Mancini, Henry
American. Composer
Won Oscars, 1961, 1962, for songs "Moon River" and "Days of Wine and Roses;" won Oscar for *Victor/ Victoria,* 1982.
b. Apr 16, 1924 in Cleveland, Ohio
d. Jun 14, 1994 in Los Angeles, California
Source: *AmPS; AmSong; ASCAP 66, 80; Baker 78, 84, 92; BiDAmM; BioIn 6, 7, 9, 10, 11, 12, 14, 15, 16, 20; BioNews 74; CelR, 90; CmMov; CmpEPM; ConAmC 76, 82; ConMus 1; ConTFT 1, 10, 13; CurBio 64, 94N; DcTwCCu 1; FacFETw; FilmEn; FilmgC; GangFlm; HalFC 80, 84, 88; IntDcF 1-4, 2-4; IntMPA 84, 86, 88, 92, 94; IntWW 89, 91, 93; IntWWM 90; ItaFilm; LegTOT; MusMk; NewAmDM; NewGrDA 86; NewGrDM 80; News 94; NewYTBS 94; OxCFilm; OxCPMus; PenEncP; PopAmC SUP; RkOn 74; VarWW 85; WhAm 11; WhoAm 74, 76, 78, 80, 82, 84, 86, 88, 90, 92, 94; WhoAmM 83; WhoEnt 92; WhoWor 74; WorAl; WorAlBi; WorEFlm*

Mancini, Ray
"Boom Boom"
American. Boxer
Former WBA lightweight champ.
b. Mar 4, 1961 in Youngstown, Ohio
Source: *BioIn 12, 13; NewYTBS 82, 85; WhoHol 92*

Manco Capac
Legendary Figure
Supposedly the founder of Inca Dynasty in Peru.
Source: *ApCAB; DcBiPP; Drake; NewCol 75; WebBD 83; WhDW*

Mandan, Robert
American. Actor
Played Chester Tate on TV series "Soap," 1977-80.
b. Feb 2, 1932 in Clever, Missouri
Source: *VarWW 85; WhoAm 80, 82; WhoHol 92*

Mandel, Georges
French. Government Official
Held several ministry positions, 1934-42; shot by French Vichy govt. for opposition to pro-German policies.
b. Jun 5, 1885 in Chatou, France
d. Jul 7, 1944 in Fontainebleau, France
Source: *BiDFrPL; BioIn 9, 17; CurBio 40; ObitOF 79*

Mandel, Howie
Canadian. Comedian
Played Dr. Wayne Fiscus on "St. Elsewhere," 1982-88; films include *Funny Farm,* 1985.
b. Nov 29, 1955 in Toronto, Ontario, Canada
Source: *BioIn 14, 15; ConTFT 9; LegTOT; News 89-1; WhoEnt 92; WorAlBi*

Mandel, Marvin
American. Politician
Dem. governor of MD, 1969-77; found guilty of political corruption, 1977; conviction overturned, 1979.
b. Apr 19, 1920 in Baltimore, Maryland
Source: *AlmAP 78*

Mandela, Nelson (Rolihlahla)
South African. Political Activist, Political Leader
Leader, African Nat. Congress; served prison term 1964-90, for conspiracy to overthrow S African govt; pres., S Africa, 1994—.
b. Jul 18, 1918 in Umtata, South Africa
Source: *AfSS 78, 79, 80, 81, 82; BioIn 8, 11, 12, 13, 14, 15, 16, 18; BlkWr 1; ConAu 125; ConBlB 1; ConHero 1; CurBio 84, 95; DcAfHiB 86; DcCPSAf; DcTwHis; EncRev; EncSoA; FacFETw; HeroCon; IntWW 91; LegTOT; McGEWB; News 90, 90-3; NewYTBS 78, 85, 90, 91, 94; RadHan; SchCGBL; Who 92; WhoAfr; WhoNob 95; WhoWor 74, 91, 95, 96, 97; WorAlBi; WrDr 92, 94, 96*

Mandela, Winnie
[Nkosikazi Nobandle Nomzano Madikizela]
South African. Political Activist
Anti-apartheid leader with ex-husband Nelson; affiliated with African Nat. Congress since 1957; appealing 6-yr. prison term for 1988 kidnapping of 4 Soweto youths.
b. Sep 26, 1934 in Transkei, South Africa
Source: *BioIn 14, 15, 16; BlkWr 1; ConAu 125; ConBlB 2; ConHero 1; ContDcW 89; CurBio 86; EncWB; FacFETw; InB&W 80; IntDcWB; IntWW 89, 91; InWom SUP; News 89-3; NewYTBS 85; WhoWor 89; WomFir*

Mandelbaum, Fredericka
"Marm"
American. Criminal
Most successful fence in NY, 1862-84; handled over 12 million dollars in goods.
b. 1818 in New York
d. 1889
Source: *DrInf; GoodHs; InWom SUP; WorAl; WorAlBi*

Mandelli, Mariuccia Pinto
Italian. Fashion Designer
Ultramodern designer; popularized "hot pants," 1970s.
Source: *BioIn 15; ConDes 90; EncFash; WhoFash 88; WorFshn*

Mandelstam, Nadezhda Yakovlevna
[Mrs. Osip Mandelstam]
Russian. Author, Scholar
Spent most of life trying to preserve husband's work; wrote memoirs: *Hope Against Hope; Hope Abandoned* .
b. Oct 31, 1899 in Saratov, Russia
d. Dec 29, 1980 in Moscow, Union of Soviet Socialist Republics
Source: *AnObit 1980; BioIn 10; ConAu 102*

Mandelstam, Osip Emilyevich
Polish. Poet
Exiled for lampooning Stalin, 1934-37; works include *Voronezh Notebooks,*; re-arrested, disappeared, 1938.
b. Jan 15, 1891 in Warsaw, Poland
d. Dec 27, 1938 in Vtoraya Rechka, Union of Soviet Socialist Republics
Source: *AtlBL; Benet 87; BiDSovU; BioIn 1, 2, 8, 9, 10, 11, 12, 13; CasWL; ConAu 104; CyWA 89; DcRusL; EncWL 2; FacFETw; GrFLW; HanRL; LiExTwC; McGEWB; NewYTBS 74; RAdv 13-2; REn; TwCLC 6; TwCWr; WhoTwCL; WorAl; WorAlBi; WorAu 1950*

Mandelstam, Osip Emilyevich
Russian. Poet
Leader of Acheist school, known for impersonal, fatalistic poetry; died in concentration camp.
b. Jan 15, 1891? in Warsaw, Poland
d. Dec 28, 1943? in Vladivostok, Union of Soviet Socialist Republics
Source: *AtlBL; CasWL; ClDMEL 47; CnMWL; DcRusL; EncWL; McGEWB; ModSL 1; NewCol 75; PenC EUR; REn; TwCWr; WhoTwCL; WorAl; WorAu 1950*

Mandeville, John, Sir
English. Traveler
Pseudonym for unknown author of *Voyage and Travels of Sir Mandeville, Knight,* c. 1356.
b. 1300?
d. 1372
Source: *Alli; BbD; BiD&SB; CasWL; Chambr 1; ClMLC 19; DcEnA; DcEnL; DcLEL; EvLB; NewCBEL; OxCEng 67; WhNAA*

Mandlikova, Hana
Czech. Tennis Player
Won US Open, 1985, defeating Chris Evert Lloyd, Martina Navratilova.
b. Feb 19, 1963 in Prague, Czechoslovakia
Source: *BioIn 13, 14, 15; CurBio 86; LegTOT; NewYTBS 81, 85, 86; WhoIntT; WhoWor 91*

Mandrell, Barbara Ann
[Mrs. Ken Dudney]
American. Singer, Musician
Country-pop singer; first number one hit "Sleeping Single in a Double Bed," 1978; has won over 60 awards.
b. Dec 25, 1948 in Houston, Texas
Source: *Baker 84, 92; BioIn 12, 13, 14, 15, 16; CelR 90; ConAu 139; ConMus 4; CurBio 82; EncFCWM 83; HarEnCM 87; InWom SUP; OxCPMus; PenEncP; RkOn 85; VarWW 85; WhoAm 76, 78, 80, 82, 84, 86, 88, 90, 92, 94, 95, 96, 97; WhoAmW 81, 83, 85, 87, 89, 91, 93, 95, 97; WhoEnt 92; WorAlBi*

Manero, Tony
[Anthony Manero]
American. Golfer
Touring pro, 1930s; won US Open, 1936.
b. Apr 4, 1905 in New York, New York
Source: *BioIn 16; NewYTBS 89; WhoGolf*

Manessier, Alfred
French. Artist
Abstractionist whose *The Crown of Thorns* was the first non-figurative painting to win Carnegie Award, 1955.
b. Dec 5, 1911 in Saint-Ouen, France
d. Aug 1, 1993 in Orleans, France
Source: *BioIn 4, 5, 6, 10, 19; ConArt 77, 83, 89, 96; ConAu 57; CurBio 93N; IntWW 74, 75, 76, 77, 78, 79, 80, 81, 82, 83, 89, 91, 93; McGDA; OxCArt; OxCTwCA; OxDcArt; PhDcTCA 77; PrintW 85; WhoArt 80, 82, 84; WhoFr 79; WhoWor 74; WorArt 1950*

Manet, Edouard
French. Artist
Main forerunner of Impressionism; noted for *Olympia,* 1863; *Bar at the Folles Bergere,* 1882.
b. Jan 23, 1832 in Paris, France
d. Apr 20, 1883 in Paris, France
Source: *AtlBL; Benet 87, 96; BioIn 1, 2, 3, 4, 5, 6, 7, 8, 9, 10, 11, 13, 14, 15, 16, 17, 18, 19, 20, 21; ClaDrA; DcArts; IntDcAA 90; LegTOT; LinLib S; McGDA; McGEWB; OxCArt; OxCFr; OxDcArt; RAdv 14, 13-3; REn; ThHEIm; WhDW; WorAl; WorAlBi*

Manetti, Larry
American. Actor
Played Rick on "Magnum, P I," 1980-88.
b. Jul 23, 1947 in Chicago, Illinois
Source: *BioIn 12, 13*

Maney, Richard
American. Journalist
Press agent for over 300 Broadway plays, including *My Fair Lady,* 1956; *Camelot,* 1960.
b. Jun 11, 1892 in Chinook, Michigan
d. Jun 30, 1968 in Norwalk, Connecticut
Source: *BiE&WWA; CurBio 64, 68; NotNAT A; REnAL; WhAm 5*

Manfred, Frederick Feikema
[Feike Feikema]
American. Author
His novels of native area, "Siouxland," include *The Golden Bowl,* 1944; *The Wind Blows Free,* 1980.
b. Jan 6, 1912 in Doon, Iowa
Source: *AmAu&B; AmNov; Au&Wr 71; BenetAL 91; BioIn 4, 6, 7, 10, 11, 14, 20; ConAu 5NR, 9R, 25NR, 146; ConNov 72, 76, 86, 91; CurBio 50; DcLB 6; DcLP 87A; DrAF 76; DrAPF 80, 91; EncFWF; FifWWr; IntAu&W 76, 77, 82, 86, 89, 91, 93; IntvTCA 2; MinnWr; OxCAmL 65, 83; REnAL; REnAW; TwCA SUP; TwCWW 82, 91; WhoAm 74, 76, 78, 80, 82, 84, 90, 92, 94; WhoUSWr 88; WhoWrEP 89, 92; WrDr 76, 80, 82, 84, 86, 88, 92, 94, 96*

Manfred Mann
[Mike Hugg; Paul Jones; Manfred Mann; Dave Richmond; Mike Vickers]
English. Music Group
Pop hits include "Do Wah Diddy Diddy," 1964; "Blinded by the Light," 1977.
Source: *BioIn 2, 16, 17; ConMuA 80A; DrAPF 83, 85, 87, 89, 91, 93, 97; EncRk 88; EncRkSt; IlEncRk; NewYTBE 70; PenEncP; PeoHis; RkOn 78; RolSEnR 83; WhoAmP 83, 85, 87, 89, 91, 95; WhoHol 92, A; WhoRocM 82*

Mangano, Silvana
Italian. Actor
Films include *Death in Venice,* 1971; *Bitter Rice,* 1950.
b. Apr 21, 1930 in Rome, Italy
d. Dec 16, 1989 in Madrid, Spain
Source: *BiDFilm, 81, 94; BioIn 2, 3, 4, 9, 15, 16; ConTFT 5; EncEurC; FilmAG WE; FilmEn; FilmgC; HalFC 80, 84, 88; IntDcF 2-3; IntMPA 77, 82, 88; ItaFilm; LegTOT; MotPP; NewYTBS 89; OxCFilm; VarWW 85; WhoAmW 68, 70, 72, 74; WorEFlm*

Mangione, Chuck
[Charles Frank Mangione]
American. Jazz Musician, Composer
Plays flugelhorn; hit song "Feels So Good," 1978.
b. Nov 29, 1940 in Rochester, New York
Source: *AllMusG; Baker 84, 92; BiDAmM; BiDJaz; BioIn 11, 12, 15, 20; BkPepl; CurBio 80; EncJzS; EncPR&S 89; IlEncBM 82; LegTOT; NewGrDA 86; NewGrDJ 88, 94; PenEncP; RkOn 85; RolSEnR 83; TwCBrS; VarWW 85; WhoAm 78, 80, 82, 84, 86, 88, 92, 94, 95, 96, 97; WhoBlA 88; WhoEnt 92; WhoWor 80, 82, 87; WorAlBi*

Mangrum, Jim Dandy
[Black Oak Arkansas]
American. Singer
Lead singer known for long-hair, shirtless performances.
b. Mar 30, 1948 in Black Oak, Arkansas
Source: *WhoRocM 82*

Mangrum, Lloyd
American. Golfer
Turned pro, 1929; won 34 PGA tournaments including US Open, 1946; leading money winner, 1951.
b. Aug 1, 1914 in Dallas, Texas
d. Nov 17, 1973 in Apple Valley, California
Source: *BioIn 2, 3, 10; CurBio 51, 74, 74N; NewYTBE 71, 73; WhoGolf*

Manhattan Transfer
[Cheryl Bentyne; Tim Hauser; Laurel Masse; Alan Paul; Janis Siegel]
American. Music Group
Won 12 Grammys, 1980-92; albums include *Vocalese,* 1985, and *Brasil,* 1988.
Source: *AllMusG; BioIn 15, 16; CelR 90; ConMus 8; EncPR&S 89; EncRk 88; EncRkSt; HarEnR 86; IlEncRk; NewAmDM; NewGrDJ 88, 94; OxCPMus; PenEncP; RkOn 78; RolSEnR 83; WhoEnt 92; WhoRock 81; WhoRocM 82*

Manheim, Ralph
American. Translator
Translated more than 200 French and German books.
b. 1907? in New York, New York
d. Sep 26, 1992 in Cambridge, England
Source: *AnObit 1992; BioIn 14, 18, 19; ConAu 115*

Mani
[Manes; Manichaeu]
Persian. Religious Leader
Founded Manichaeism, 242; concerned with conflict between Light (goodness) and Dark (evil).
b. Apr 24, 216?, Persia
d. 276?, Persia
Source: *Benet 87, 96; CasWL; DcBiPP; DcOrL 3; LegTOT; LuthC 75; McGEWB; OxDcByz; REn; WhDW; WorAl; WorAlBi*

Manilow, Barry
[Barry Alan Pincus]
American. Singer, Songwriter
Wrote commercial jingles, accompanied Bette Midler before first hit, "Mandy," 1975 ; his 1978 *Greatest Hits* album went quadruple platinum.
b. Jun 17, 1946 in New York, New York
Source: *Baker 84, 92; BioIn 11, 12, 13, 14, 15; BkPepl; CelR 90; ConMuA 80A; ConMus 2; CurBio 78; EncPR&S 89; EncRkSt; HarEnR 86; IlEncRk; IntWW 91, 93; LegTOT; NewGrDA 86; OxCPMus; PenEncP; RkOn 78; RolSEnR 83; VarWW 85; WhoAm 76, 82, 84, 86, 88, 90, 92, 94, 95, 96, 97; WhoEnt 92; WorAl; WorAlBi*

Manion, Eddie
[Southside Johnny and the Asbury Jukes]
American. Musician
Baritone saxophonist with group since 1974.
b. Feb 28, 1952
Source: *WhoRocM 82*

Mankiewicz, Frank Fabian
American. Journalist
Press secretary to Robt. Kennedy, 1968; directed McGovern presidential campaign, 1972; wrote *Perfectly Clear: Nixon From Whittier to Watergate,* 1973.
b. May 16, 1924 in New York, New York
Source: *BiDAmNC; BioIn 8, 9, 10, 11, 12, 13; ConAu 89; EncTwCJ; IntWW 83, 91; ODwPR 91; PolProf J, NF; VarWW 85; WhoAm 74, 76, 78, 80, 82, 84, 86, 90; WhoFI 87*

Mankiewicz, Joseph (Leo)
American. Director, Producer
Won Oscars for best director, best screenplay: *A Letter to Three Wives,* 1949; *All About Eve,* 1950.
b. Feb 11, 1909 in Wilkes-Barre, Pennsylvania
d. Feb 5, 1993 in Bedford, New York
Source: *AnObit 1993; BenetAL 91; BiDFilm; BioIn 2, 3, 6, 7, 9, 11, 12, 13, 14, 15; CelR; CmMov; ConDr 77A, 88A; ConLC 81; ConTFT 5; CurBio 49, 93N; DcFM; DcLB 44; FacFETw; FilmgC; HalFC 88; IntAu&W 76, 77, 89, 91; IntMPA 77, 92; IntWW 74, 75, 76, 77, 78, 79, 80, 81, 82, 83, 89, 91, 93; MovMk; OxCFilm; REnAL; VarWW 85; WhAm 11; Who 74, 82, 83, 85, 88, 90, 92; WhoAm 74, 78, 80, 82, 84, 86, 88, 90, 92; WhoAmJ 80; WhoE 86, 89, 91; WhoEnt 92; WhoWor 74; WorAlBi; WorEFlm; WorFDir 1*

Mankiller, Wilma P(earl)
American. Native American Chief
First woman to serve as the chief of a major North American Indian tribe; principal chief, Cherokee Nation of Oklahoma, 1985-87; pres., Inter-Tribal Coun cil OK.
b. Nov 18, 1945 in Stilwell, Oklahoma
Source: *BioIn 14, 15, 16; ConAu 146; CurBio 88; NewYTBS 85; NotNaAm; WhoAm 95, 96, 97; WhoAmW 87, 89, 91, 93, 95, 97; WhoEmL 87; WhoSSW 95, 97*

Mankowitz, Wolf
English. Author, Producer, Dramatist
Films include *The Bespoke Overcoat,* 1955; books: *An Encyclopedia of English Pottery and Porcelain,* 1957.
b. Nov 7, 1924 in Whitechapel, England
Source: *Au&Wr 71; BioIn 4, 5, 6, 8, 10, 12, 13; BlueB 76; ConAu 5NR, 5R; ConDr 73, 77, 82, 88; ConNov 72, 76, 82, 86, 91; ConTFT 11; CurBio 56; DcLB 15; DcLEL 1940; FilmEn; FilmgC; HalFC 80, 84, 88; IntAu&W 76, 77, 82, 89, 91, 93; IntDcF 1-4, 2-4; IntMPA 75, 76, 77, 78, 79, 80, 81, 82, 84, 86, 88, 92, 94, 96; IntWW 74, 75, 76, 77, 78, 79, 80, 81, 82, 83, 89, 91, 93; LngCTC; NewC; NewCBEL; NewYTBS 80; NotNAT; Novels; OxCChiL; REn; ScF&FL 1, 92; TwCWr; Who 74, 82, 83, 85, 88, 90, 92, 94; WhoThe 72, 77, 81; WhoWor 74, 78, 82; WorAu 1950; WrDr 76, 80, 82, 84, 86, 88, 90, 92, 94, 96*

Manley, Dexter
American. Football Player
Defensive end, Washington, 1981-89; defensive lineman of year, 1986; banned from NFL for life, for drug abuse, 1989; currently with Ottawa, Canadian Football League.
b. Feb 2, 1959 in Houston, Texas
Source: *BioIn 15, 16; FootReg 87; LegTOT; WhoAfA 96; WhoBlA 88, 90, 92, 94*

Manley, Joan Adele Daniels
American. Publisher
With Time, Inc. since 1960; chm., Time-Life Books, Inc. 1976-80.
b. Sep 23, 1932 in San Luis Obispo, California
Source: *AmWomM; InWom SUP; NewYTBS 75; St&PR 87; WhoAm 86, 90, 92, 94, 95, 96, 97; WhoAmW 79, 81, 83, 85, 87, 89; WhoWest 94, 96*

Manley, Michael (Norman)
Jamaican. Political Leader
Prime minister of Jamaica, 1972-80, 1989-92; wrote of political philosophy in *The Politics of Change: A Jamaican Testament,* 1974.
b. Dec 10, 1924 in Kingston, Jamaica
d. Mar 6, 1997 in Kingston, Jamaica
Source: *BiDLAmC; BioIn 13, 14, 16, 17, 18, 19; ConAu 27NR, 85; CurBio 76; DcCPCAm; EncWB; InB&W 85; IntWW 83, 91, 93; IntYB 78, 79, 80, 81, 82; Who 74, 82, 83, 85, 88, 90, 92, 94; WhoWor 74, 76, 78, 80, 82, 84, 89, 91, 93*

Mann, Abby
[Abraham Goodman]
American. Screenwriter
Oscar nominee for *Judgment at Nuremberg,* 1961; *Ship of Fools,* 1965.
b. Dec 1, 1927 in Philadelphia, Pennsylvania
Source: *BioIn 15; ConAu 109; ConTFT 5; DcLB 44; FilmEn; FilmgC; HalFC 80, 84, 88; IntMPA 77, 80, 86, 92, 94, 96; InWom SUP; ItaFilm; LesBEnT, 92; MiSFD 9; NewYTET; Who 92; WhoAm 84*

Mann, Carol Ann
American. Golfer
Turned pro, 1961; won US Women's Open, 1965; leading money winner, 1969.
b. Feb 3, 1941 in Buffalo, New York
Source: *BiDAmSp OS; BiDrLUS 70; InWom SUP; NewYTBE 73; NewYTBS 76; WhoGolf; WhoLibS 66*

Mann, Erika
German. Author, Actor, Lecturer
Writings of wartime Germany include *Lights Go Down,* 1940; daughter of Thomas.
b. 1905 in Munich, Germany
d. Aug 27, 1969 in Zurich, Switzerland
Source: *BenetAL 91; BiGAW; BioIn 4, 8, 9; ConAu 25R; CurBio 40, 69; EncCoWW; EncTR, 91; EncWT; InWom, SUP; LiExTwC; LngCTC; TwCA, SUP; WhAm 5*

Mann, Heinrich Ludwig
American. Author
Novels include *Professor Unrat,* 1905; brother of Thomas.
b. Mar 27, 1871 in Lubeck, Germany
d. Mar 12, 1950 in Beverly Hills, California
Source: *CasWL; ClDMEL 47; EncWL; EvEuW; HalFC 84; LngCTC; McGEWB; ModGL; ModWD; OxCEng 67; OxCGer 76; PenC EUR; REn; TwCA SUP; TwCWr; WhAm 3; WhoLA; WhoTwCL*

Mann, Herbie
[Herbert Jay Solomon]
American. Jazz Musician
Flutist, formed afro-jazz sextet, 1959; had numerous hit albums.
b. Apr 16, 1930 in New York, New York
Source: *AllMusG; ASCAP 66; Baker 84, 92; BiDAmM; BiDJaz; BioIn 7, 10, 12; BioNews 74; ConMus 16; EncJzS; LegTOT; NewAmDM; NewGrDJ 88, 94; NewYTBE 73; OxCPMus; PenEncP; RkOn 78, 82; WhoAm 74, 76, 78, 80, 82, 84, 86, 88, 90, 92, 94, 95, 96, 97; WhoE 74; WhoEnt 92; WorAl; WorAlBi*

Mann, Horace
American. Educator, Politician
Considered father of American public education; founder, pres., Antioch College, 1852-59.
b. May 4, 1796 in Franklin, Massachusetts
d. Aug 2, 1859 in Yellow Springs, Ohio
Source: *Alli; AmAu; AmAu&B; AmBi; AmRef; AmRef&R; AmSocL; ApCAB; Benet 87, 96; BenetAL 91; BiAUS; BiDAmEd; BiD&SB; BiDMoPL; BiDrAC; BiDrUSC 89; BiDTran; BioIn 1, 2, 3, 4, 5, 6, 7, 8, 9, 10, 11, 13, 15, 19, 21; CyAG; CyAL 1; CyEd; DcAmAu; DcAmB; DcAmC; DcAmReB 1, 2; DcAmSR; DcAmTB; DcLB 1; DcNAA; Drake; EncAB-H 1974, 1996; EncARH; HarEnUS; LegTOT; LinLib L, S; LuthC 75; McGEWB; MemAm; NatCAB 3; NewCBEL; OhA&B; OxCAmH; OxCAmL 65, 83, 95; RAdv 14, 13-3; RComAH; REn; REnAL; TwCBDA; WebAB 74, 79; WhAm HS; WhAmP; WorAl; WorAlBi*

Mann, Jack
English. Hostage
Retired airline pilot taken hostage by Lebanese terrorists on May 13, 1989; after 864 days in captivity was released, Sep 24, 1991.
b. 1914?, England
d. Nov 12, 1995 in Nicosia, Cyprus

Mann, Klaus
German. Author
Lectured against fascism; wrote *Journey into Exile,* 1936; son of Thomas.
b. Nov 18, 1906 in Munich, Germany
d. May 21, 1949 in Pacific Palisades, California
Source: *BenetAL 91; BiGAW; BioIn 1, 2, 4, 11, 16, 17; ClDMEL 47; CurBio 40, 49; DcLB 56; EncGRNM; EncTR, 91; EncWL; EncWT; LiExTwC; LngCTC; ModGL; OxCGer 76, 86; ScF&FL 1; TwCA, SUP; WhAm 3; WhE&EA; WhoLA*

Mann, Michael
American. Writer, Producer
TV shows include Emmy-winning "The Jericho Mile," 1979; "Miami Vice," 1984-89; films include *The Last of the Mohicans,* 1992.
b. 1943 in Chicago, Illinois
Source: *BiDFilm 94; BioIn 12, 13, 15, 16; ConAu 120; ConTFT 5, 12; CurBio 93; IntMPA 92, 94, 96; LegTOT; NewYTBS 89; VarWW 85; Who 92*

Mann, Paul
American. Actor, Director
Founded Paul Mann Actors Workshop that trained Sidney Poitier, Faye Dunaway.
b. Dec 20, 1915 in Toronto, Ontario, Canada
d. Sep 24, 1985 in Bronxville, New York
Source: *BiE&WWA; NotNAT; WhoHol 92, A*

Mann, Theodore
American. Producer
Co-founded Circle in the Square Theatre, 1951; won Tony, Pulitzer, for co-producing *Long Day's Journey Into Night,* 1956.
b. May 13, 1924 in New York, New York
Source: *BiE&WWA; ConTFT 2; NotNAT; OxCAmT 84; VarWW 85; WhoAm 78, 80, 82, 84, 86, 88, 90, 92, 94, 95, 96, 97; WhoE 74, 75, 85, 86, 89; WhoThe 72, 77, 81; WhoWor 74, 96, 97*

Mann, Thomas
German. Author
Known for narrative psychological studies, explorations in mythology; won Nobel Prize, 1929, for *The Magic Mountain.*
b. Jun 6, 1875 in Lubeck, Germany
d. Aug 12, 1955 in Zurich, Switzerland
Source: *AtlBL; Benet 87, 96; BenetAL 91; BiGAW; BioIn 1, 2, 3, 4, 5, 6, 7, 8, 9, 10, 11, 12, 13, 14, 15, 16, 17, 18, 19, 20, 21; CasWL; ClDMEL 47, 80; CmCal; CnMWL; ConAu 104, 128; CurBio 42, 55; CyWA 58; DcArts; DcLB 66; Dis&D; EncGRNM; EncPaPR 91; EncTR, 91; EncWL, 2, 3; EncWT; EuWr 9; EvEuW; FacFETw; GrFLW; HalFC 84, 88; LegTOT; LiExTwC; LinLib L, S; LngCTC; MagSWL; MajTwCW; MakMC; McGEWB; ModGL; NewEOp 71; NewGrDM 80; NewGrDO; NobelP; Novels; ObitT 1951; OxCEng 67, 85, 95; OxCGer 76, 86; OxCMus; OxDcOp; PenC EUR; RAdv 14, 13-2; RComWL; REn; REnAL; ScF&FL 1; ShSCr 5; TwCA, SUP; TwCLC 2, 8, 14, 21, 35, 44; TwCWr; WhAm 3; WhDW; WhoTwCL; WorAl; WorAlBi; WorLitC; WrPh*

Manne, Shelly
[Sheldon Manne]
American. Jazz Musician
Hit drummer, 1940s-50s; with Woody Herman, Stan Kenton; opened own Hollywood club, 1960s.
b. Jun 11, 1920 in New York, New York
d. Sep 26, 1984 in Los Angeles, California
Source: *AllMusG; AnObit 1984; ASCAP 66, 80; Baker 92; BiDAmM; BiDJaz; BioIn 12, 14; BlueB 76; CmpEPM; EncJzS; LegTOT; NewAmDM; NewGrDA 86; NewGrDJ 88, 94; OxCPMus; PenEncP; VarWW 85; WhAm 8; WhoAm 74, 76, 78, 80, 82, 84; WhoHol A; WhoWest 76, 78; WorAl; WorAlBi*

Mannerheim, Carl Gustav Emil, Baron
Finnish. Military Leader, Political Leader
President of Finland, 1944-46; nat. hero in three wars against USSR.
b. Jun 4, 1867 in Louhissaari, Finland
d. Jan 27, 1951 in Lausanne, Switzerland
Source: *BioIn 1, 2, 3, 5, 6, 7, 8, 9, 10, 11; CurBio 40, 51; DcTwHis; FacFETw; LinLib S; REn*

Manners, Charles
English. Opera Singer, Impresario
Bass; with wife, soprano Fanny Moody, established Moody-Manners Co., 1897.
b. Dec 27, 1857 in London, England
d. May 3, 1935 in Dublin, Ireland
Source: *Baker 78, 84, 92; CmOp; NewEOp 71; NewGrDM 80; NewGrDO; OxDcOp*

Mannes, David
American. Teacher, Violinist
Founded NYC's Music School Settlement for Colored People, 1912; opened Mannes School of Music, 1916.
b. Feb 16, 1866 in New York, New York
d. Apr 25, 1959 in New York, New York
Source: *Baker 78, 84, 92; BiDAmEd; BiDAmM; BioIn 2, 4, 5, 7, 14, 15; DcAmB S6; NatCAB 47; NewAmDM; NewGrDA 86; NewGrDM 80; WhAm 3*

Mannes, Leopold Damrosch
American. Composer, Inventor
Co-invented Kodachrome color photography, 1935; longtime pres., Mannes College of Music.
b. Dec 26, 1899 in New York, New York

d. Aug 11, 1964 in Vineyard Haven, Massachusetts
Source: *DcAmB S7; WhAm 4*

Mannes, Marya
American. Author, Journalist
Mag. free-lance writer, 1930s-60s; columnist, *NY Times,* 1967-71; wrote *Uncoupling: The Art of Coming Apart,* 1973.
b. Nov 14, 1904 in New York, New York
d. Sep 13, 1990 in San Francisco, California
Source: *AmAu&B; AmWomD; AmWomPl; AmWomWr; AnObit 1990; BioIn 5, 6, 7, 9, 10, 17; CelR; ConAu 1R, 3NR, 132; ConSFA; CurBio 59; DcLEL, 1940; DcLP 87A; DrAPF 87; EncAJ; EncSF, 93; EncTwCJ; FemiCLE; ForWC 70; InWom, SUP; LibW; NewYTBE 71; NewYTBS 90; ScF&FL 1, 2, 92; WhAm 10; WhoAmW 61; WorAu 1950; WrDr 82, 84, 86*

Mannheim, Karl
Hungarian. Sociologist, Historian, Educator
Stressed science as a social organization; wrote *Ideologue und Utopie,* 1929.
b. Mar 27, 1893 in Budapest, Austria-Hungary
d. Jan 9, 1947 in London, England
Source: *BioIn 1, 2, 4, 11, 12, 13, 14, 15, 16, 21; DcSoc; EncTR; MakMC; McGEWB; NewCBEL; NewCol 75; OxCPhil; RAdv 14, 13-3; ThTwC 87; TwCA SUP; TwCLC 65; WhDW*

Manning, Archie
[Elisha Archie Manning, III]
American. Football Player
Quarterback, 1971-84, mostly with New Orleans; led NFL in pass completions, 1972.
b. May 19, 1949 in Cleveland, Mississippi
Source: *BioIn 9, 10, 12, 14, 19, 21; FootReg 81; LegTOT; NewYTBS 84; WhoAm 82; WhoFtbl 74; WhoSpor; WorAl*

Manning, Danny
American. Basketball Player
Center, LA Clippers, 1988-93; Hawks, 1994; Suns, 1994—; U.S. Olympic team, 1988; first pick in 1988 NBA draft.
b. May 17, 1966 in Hattiesburg, Mississippi
Source: *BioIn 13, 15; BlkOlyM; NewYTBS 83, 84; WhoAm 94, 95; WhoSpor*

Manning, Ernest (Charles)
Canadian. Political Leader
Premier of Province of Alberta, Canada, 1943-68.
b. Sep 20, 1908
d. Feb 19, 1996 in Calgary, Alberta, Canada
Source: *BioIn 2, 5, 21; BlueB 76; CanWW 70, 79, 80, 81, 83, 89; CurBio 96N; IntWW 74, 75, 76, 77, 78, 79, 80, 81, 82, 83, 89, 91, 93; IntYB 78, 79, 80, 81, 82; WhoWest 76, 78*

Manning, Henry Edward
English. Religious Leader
Archbishop of Westminster, 1865; cardinal, 1875; promoted English Catholicism.
b. Jul 15, 1808 in Totteridge, England
d. Jan 14, 1892 in London, England
Source: *Alli, SUP; BiD&SB; BioIn 2, 3, 5, 6, 7, 8, 9, 10, 11, 12, 14, 16, 17, 18, 19; BritAu 19; CasWL; CelCen; DcCathB; DcEnL; DcNaB; EvLB; LinLib S; LuthC 75; McGEWB; NewC; NewCBEL; OxCEng 67, 85, 95; VicBrit*

Manning, Irene
[Inez Harvout]
American. Actor, Singer, Author
Wrote column "Girl About Town;" films include *Desert Song,* 1943; *Yanke e Doodle Dandy,* 1942.
b. Jul 17, 1918 in Cincinnati, Ohio
Source: *BiE&WWA; FilmEn; FilmgC; HalFC 88; MotPP; NotNAT; WhoHol A; WhoThe 77A*

Manning, Maria
[Maria de Roux]
Swiss. Murderer
Murdered her lover with the help of her husband, 1849; Dickens profiled her in *Bleak House.*
b. 1825
d. Nov 13, 1849 in London, England
Source: *BioIn 12*

Manning, Olivia
English. Author
Wrote "Balkan Trilogy" describing WW II experiences.
b. 1915? in Portsmouth, England
d. Jul 23, 1980 in Ryde, Isle of Wight, Yugoslavia
Source: *AnObit 1980; BlmGEL; ConAu 5R, 29NR, 101; ConNov 72, 76, 82A, 86A; CyWA 89; EncWL 2, 3; EngPo; MajTwCW; ModBrL, S1, S2; ModWoWr; NewC; PenC ENG; TwCWr; WorAu 1950*

Manning, Timothy, Cardinal
American. Religious Leader
Archbishop of Los Angeles, 1970-85; made cardinal, 1973.
b. Nov 15, 1909 in Cork, Ireland
d. Jun 23, 1989 in Los Angeles, California
Source: *AmCath 80; BioIn 8, 9, 11, 13, 16; FacFETw; IntWW 74, 75, 76, 77, 78, 79, 80, 81, 82, 83, 89; NewYTBE 72, 73; NewYTBS 89; RelLAm 91; WhAm 10; WhoAm 74, 76, 78, 80, 82, 84, 86, 88; WhoRel 85; WhoWest 76, 78, 80, 82, 84; WhoWor 82, 87, 89*

Mannlicher, Ferdinand
Austrian. Inventor
Designed repeating firearms widely used in Europe; invented cartridge clip popularly used in automatic guns.
b. Jan 30, 1848 in Mainz, Germany
d. Jan 20, 1904 in Vienna, Austria

Manns, August, Sir
English. Conductor
For 45 seasons, led London's Saturday Concerts, which were started at Crystal Palace, 1856.
b. Mar 12, 1825 in Stettin, Germany
d. Mar 2, 1907 in London, England
Source: *Baker 78, 84; DcNaB S2; NewGrDM 80; OxCMus; PenDiMP*

Manoff, Dinah
American. Actor
Tony winner for *I Ought to Be in Pictures,* 1980; played Carol on TV series "Empty Nest," 1989-95.
b. Jan 25, 1958 in New York, New York
Source: *BioIn 12, 13, 16; CelR 90; ConTFT 3, 14; IntMPA 92, 94, 96; LegTOT; WhoAmW 91; WhoEnt 92; WhoHol 92; WorAlBi*

Manolete
[Manuel Laureano Rodriguez Sanchez]
Spanish. Bullfighter
One of Spain's greatest matadors; died after being gored by bull.
b. Jul 5, 1917 in Cordoba, Spain
d. Aug 29, 1947 in Linares, Spain
Source: *BioIn 1, 2, 4, 5, 6, 9; LegTOT*

Manone, Wingy
[Joseph Manone]
American. Jazz Musician
Left-handed, Louis Armstrong-style trumpeter; lost right arm, age eight; popular, 1920s-50s.
b. Feb 13, 1904 in New Orleans, Louisiana
d. Jul 9, 1982 in Las Vegas, Nevada
Source: *ASCAP 66; BiDAmM; BiDJaz; BioIn 1, 13, 16; CmpEPM; EncJzS; EncJzS; IlEncJ; NewYTBS 82; WhoJazz 72*

Manoogian, Alex
American. Business Executive, Philanthropist
Founded Masco Screw Products (later Masco Corporation), 1929; developed single-handled faucet, 1952.
b. 1901 in Smyrna, Turkey
d. Jul 10, 1996 in Detroit, Michigan
Source: *BioIn 15; Dun&B 79, 86, 88, 90; NewYTBS 27; WhoAm 78, 94, 95, 96; WhoMW 90*

Mansart, Francois
[Francois Mansard]
French. Architect
Popularized the Mansard roof.
b. Jan 23, 1598 in Paris, France
d. Sep 23, 1666 in Paris, France
Source: *AtlBL; BioIn 2, 9, 10, 12, 13; DcBiPP; DcCathB; DcD&D; IntDcAr;*

MacEA; McGDA; McGEWB; OxCArt; WhDW; WhoArch

Mansart, Jules Hardouin
[Jules Hardouin Mansard]
French. Architect
Builder for Louis XIV, from 1675; completed Versailles; grandnephew of Francois.
b. Apr 1645 in Paris, France
d. May 11, 1708 in Marly, France
Source: *AtlBL; DcBiPP; McGDA; McGEWB; OxCFr*

Mansell, Nigel
English. Auto Racer
Former Formula 1 driver, switched to Indy cars, 1993; has won nearly 30 races in his career.
b. Aug 8, 1954 in Upton-on-Severn, England
Source: *BioIn 15; IntWW 91, 93; WhoWor 93*

Mansfield, Arabella
American. Lawyer
First woman admitted to Bar in US, 1869; never practiced.
b. May 23, 1846 in Burlington, Iowa
d. Aug 2, 1911 in Aurora, Illinois
Source: *BioIn 8; LibW; NotAW*

Mansfield, Jayne
[Mrs. Mickey Hargitay; Vera Jayne Palmer]
American. Actor
Known for breathless, dizzy blonde roles in films, 1950s-60s, similar to Marilyn Monroe: *Will Success Spoil Rock Hunter?* 1957; killed in auto accident.
b. Apr 19, 1932 in Bryn Mawr, Pennsylvania
d. Jun 29, 1967 in New Orleans, Louisiana
Source: *BiDFilm; BioAmW; FilmgC; HalFC 80, 84, 88; LegTOT; MotPP; MovMk; OxCFilm; WhAm 4; WhScrn 74, 77, 83; WorAl; WorEFlm*

Mansfield, Katherine
[Kathleen Mansfield Beauchamp; Mrs. John Middleton Murry]
New Zealander. Author
Considered one of founders of modern short story; collections included in *Prelude,* 1918.
b. Oct 14, 1888 in Wellington, New Zealand
d. Jan 9, 1923 in Fontainebleau, France
Source: *ArtclWW 2; AtlBL; Benet 87, 96; BioIn 1, 2, 3, 4, 5, 6, 7, 8, 9, 10, 11, 12, 13, 14, 15, 16, 17, 20; BlmGEL; BlmGWL; BritWr 7; CamGEL; CamGLE; CasWL; Chambr 3; ChhPo S1; CnMWL; ConAu 104, 134; ContDcW 89; CyWA 58, 89; DcArts; DcEuL; DcLB 162; DcLEL; Dis&D; EncBrWW; EncWL, 2, 3; EvLB; FacFETw; FemiCLE; FemiWr; GayLL; GrBr; GrWomW; GrWrEL N; IntDcWB; IntLitE; InWom, SUP; LegTOT; LiExTwC; LinLib L; LngCEL; LngCTC; MagSWL; MakMC; ModBrL, S1, S2; ModCmwL; ModWoWr; NewC; NewCBEL; NewYTBS 88; Novels; OxCAusL; OxCEng 67, 85, 95; OxCTwCP; PenC ENG; PenNWW A, B; RAdv 1, 14, 13-1; REn; RfGEnL 91; RfGShF; RGTwCWr; ShSCr 9, 23; ShSWr; TwCA, SUP; TwCLC 2, 8, 39; TwCWr; WebE&AL; WhDW; WhoTwCL; WomFir; WorAl; WorAlBi; WorLitC*

Mansfield, Mike
[Michael Joseph Mansfield]
American. Politician
Dem. senator from MT, 1953-76; ambassador to Japan, 1977-88.
b. Mar 16, 1903 in New York, New York
Source: *BiDrAC; WhoWest 76; WhoWor 74, 76, 78, 80, 82, 84, 87, 89; WorAl; WorAlBi*

Mansfield, Richard
English. Actor
Stage roles in *Dr. Jekyll and Mr. Hyde,* 1887; *Beau Brummell,* 1890.
b. May 24, 1854 in Berlin, Germany
d. Aug 30, 1907 in New London, Connecticut
Source: *AmBi; ApCAB SUP; BenetAL 91; BioIn 1, 2, 3, 4, 5, 6, 7, 8, 9, 10, 13; CamGWoT; ChhPo; DcAmB; DcNAA; EncWT; FamA&A; IntDcT 3; NotNAT B; OxCAmL 65; OxCAmT 84; OxCThe 67, 83; PlP&P; REn; REnAL; WebAB 74, 79; WhAm 1; WhoStg 1906, 1908; WorAl*

Manship, Paul
American. Sculptor
Works include large Prometheus figure at NYC's Rockefeller Plaza.
b. Dec 25, 1885 in Saint Paul, Minnesota
d. Jan 31, 1966 in Massachusetts
Source: *BioIn 1, 7, 8, 14, 15, 17; BriEAA; CurBio 40, 66; DcAmArt; DcCAA 71, 77, 88, 94; FacFETw; LinLib S; OxCTwCA; OxDcArt; PhDcTCA 77; WhAm 4; WhAmArt 85; WhoAmA 78N, 80N, 82N, 84N, 86N, 89N, 91N, 93N*

Manso, Leo
American. Artist
Leader in the art of collage; his works are known for fluid composition and rich color.
b. Apr 15, 1914 in New York, New York
d. Feb 5, 1993 in New York, New York
Source: *AnObit 1993; BioIn 1, 15, 18, 19; DcCAA 71, 77, 88, 94; McGDA; WhoAmA 73, 76, 78, 80, 82, 84, 86, 89, 91, 93*

Manson, Charles
"No Name Maddox"
American. Murderer, Cultist
In prison for 1969 murders of actress Sharon Tate, eight others.
b. Nov 11, 1934 in Cincinnati, Ohio
Source: *AmDec 1960; BioIn 8, 9, 10, 11, 12, 14, 15, 16, 18, 19, 21; BkPepl; CmCal; DrInf; EncO&P 2S1, 3; FacFETw; LegTOT; NewYTBE 70; WorAlBi*

Manson, Patrick, Sir
Scottish. Physician
Recognized as father of tropical medicine.
b. Oct 3, 1844 in Oldmeldrum, Scotland
d. Apr 9, 1922 in London, England
Source: *AsBiEn; BiESc; BiHiMed; BioIn 4, 5, 8, 9, 14; CamDcSc; DcNaB 1922; DcScB; GrBr; HisDBrE; InSci; LarDcSc; OxCMed 86*

Mansouri, Lotfi
Canadian. Director
Succeeded Terence A. McEwen as director, San Francisco Opera, 1988— ; director of the Canadian Opera Co., 1976-1988.
b. Jun 15, 1929 in Tehran, Iran
Source: *BioIn 7, 11, 12, 13, 16; CanWW 89; CurBio 90; MetOEnc; NewGrDO; WhoAm 90; WhoAmM 83; WhoEnt 92; WhoOp 76; WhoWest 92*

Mansur, (Abu Jafar Ibn Muhammad), Al
Arab. Political Leader
Second Abbasid calyph, 754-775, who built city of Baghdad, 762.
b. 712?
d. Oct 775 in Mecca, Arabia
Source: *BioIn 12; McGEWB; WebBD 83*

Mantegna, Andrea
Italian. Artist
Historical, religious painter whose frescoes include *Triumph of Caesar.*
b. 1431 in Isola Carturo, Italy
d. Sep 13, 1506 in Mantua, Italy
Source: *AtlBL; Benet 87, 96; BioIn 1, 4, 5, 6, 7, 8, 9, 11, 13, 16, 17, 18, 19; ClaDrA; DcArts; DcBiPP; DcCathB; Dis&D; InWom SUP; LegTOT; LinLib S; LuthC 75; McGDA; McGEWB; OxCArt; OxDcArt; REn; WhDW; WorAl; WorAlBi*

Mantegna, Joe
[Joseph Anthony Mantegna]
American. Actor
Won a 1984 Tony for *Glengarry Glen Ross;* films include *Bugsy,* 1992.
b. Nov 13, 1947 in Chicago, Illinois
Source: *BioIn 12, 14, 16; ConTFT 3, 10; IntMPA 92, 94, 96; LegTOT; News 92, 92-1; NewYTBS 84; WhoAm 90; WhoEnt 92; WhoHol 92*

Mantha, Sylvio
Canadian. Hockey Player
Defenseman, 1923-37, mostly with Montreal; Hall of Fame, 1960.
b. Apr 14, 1902 in Montreal, Quebec, Canada
d. Aug 1974
Source: *HocEn; WhoHcky 73*

Mantle, (Robert) Burns
American. Critic
Dean of NYC drama critics, noted for annual compilation of *Best Plays*.
b. Dec 1873 in Watertown, New York
d. Feb 29, 1948 in Long Island, New York
Source: *AmAu&B; BioIn 1, 3, 4; CamGWoT; CurBio 44, 48; DcAmB S4; DcNAA; EncAJ; EncWT; NatCAB 37; NotNAT B; OxCAmT 84; OxCThe 67, 83; REnAL; TwCA, SUP; WhAm 2; WhNAA; WhThe*

Mantle, Mickey (Charles)
"The Arnold Palmer of Baseball"; "The Commerce Comet"
American. Baseball Player
Outfielder, NY Yankees, 1951-68; won AL triple crown, 1956, MVP, three times; had 536 career home runs; Hall of Fame, 1974.
b. Oct 20, 1931 in Spavinaw, Oklahoma
d. Aug 12, 1995 in Dallas, Texas
Source: *AmDec 1950; Ballpl 90; BiDAmSp BB; BioIn 2, 3, 4, 5, 6, 7, 8, 9, 10, 11, 12, 13, 14, 15, 16, 17, 18, 19, 20, 21; BioNews 74; ConAu 89, 149; ConHero 1; CurBio 53, 95N; FacFETw; LegTOT; News 96, 96-1; NewYTBS 74, 81, 88, 95; WebAB 74, 79; WhAm 11; WhoAm 74, 76, 78, 80, 82, 84, 86, 88, 90, 92, 94, 95; WhoHol 92; WhoProB 73; WorAl; WorAlBi*

Mantovani, Annunzio
[Annunzio Paolo]
Italian. Conductor
Noted for "Mantovani sound;" orchestral arrangements of light classics include "Donkey Serenade."
b. Nov 5, 1905 in Venice, Italy
d. Mar 30, 1980 in Tunbridge Wells, England
Source: *Baker 84; NewYTBS 80; WhAm 7; WhoWor 74; WorAlBi*

Manuel, George
Canadian. Native American Leader
Onetime leader of the National Indian Brotherhood, the Union of British Columbia Indian Chiefs, and the World Council of Indigenous Peoples.
b. Feb 17, 1921 in Neskainlith, British Columbia, Canada
d. 1989
Source: *BioIn 21; ConAu 107; NotNaAm*

Manuel I
[Emanuel the Great]
"The Fortunate"
Portuguese. Ruler
Reigned during country's golden age, 1495-1521; centralized public administration.
b. May 31, 1469 in Alcochete, Portugal
d. Dec 13, 1521 in Lisbon, Portugal
Source: *NewCol 75; WebBD 83*

Manuelito
American. Native American Leader
Tribal leader during the Navajo Wars of 1863-66; his warriors were the last to surrender after Kit Carson's scorched earth campaign to force them to relocate.
b. 1818? in Utah
d. 1894
Source: *BioIn 11; EncNAB; EncNoAI; NotNaAm; WhNaAH*

Manulis, Martin
American. Producer, Director
Won five Emmys for "Playhouse 90."
b. May 30, 1915 in New York, New York
Source: *BioIn 13; ConTFT 1; IntMPA 75, 76, 77, 78, 79, 80, 81, 82, 84, 86, 88, 92, 94, 96; LesBEnT, 92; NewYTET; VarWW 85; WhoAm 74, 76, 78, 80, 82, 84, 86, 88, 90, 92, 94, 95, 96, 97; WhoEnt 92; WhoWor 74, 80*

Manush, Heinie
[Henry Emmett]
American. Baseball Player
Outfielder, 1923-39; had .330 lifetime batting average; Hall of Fame, 1964.
b. Jul 20, 1901 in Tuscumbia, Alabama
d. May 12, 1971 in Sarasota, Florida
Source: *Ballpl 90; BioIn 14, 15; LegTOT; WhoProB 73; WhoSpor*

Manutius, Aldus
Italian. Printer, Scholar
Greatest of 16th c. printers; first to use italics.
b. 1450 in Sermoneta, Italy
d. Feb 3, 1515 in Venice, Italy
Source: *DcBiPP; DcCathB; LinLib L, S; NewC; OxCDecA; WhDW*

Manville, Tommy
[Thomas Franklin Manville, Jr]
American. Eccentric
Heir to Johns-Manville asbestos fortune, best known for marrying 11 young, blonde women.
b. Apr 9, 1894
d. Oct 8, 1967 in Chappaqua, New York
Source: *BioIn 8, 10; ObitOF 79*

Manzarek, Ray
[The Doors]
American. Singer, Musician
Formed group in 1966; keyboard player, 1966-73.
b. Feb 12, 1935 in Chicago, Illinois
Source: *EncPR&S 74; IlEncRk; LegTOT; WorAlBi*

Manzi, Jim Paul
American. Business Executive
CEO Lotus Development Corp., 1986—; highest paid executive in US, 1987.
b. Dec 22, 1951 in New York, New York
Source: *BioIn 15, 16; Dun&B 90; St&PR 91; WhoAm 86, 88, 92, 94; WhoFI 87, 89, 94*

Manzoni, Alessandro (Antonio)
Italian. Author, Poet
Noted for historical novel *I Promessi Sposi*, 1825-27.
b. Mar 7, 1785 in Milan, Italy
d. Apr 28, 1873 in Milan, Italy
Source: *AtlBL; BbD; Benet 87, 96; BiD&SB; BioIn 1, 2, 3, 4, 5, 7, 10, 11, 13, 20; CamGWoT; CasWL; CyWA 58; DcArts; DcBiA; DcCathB; DcEuL; DcItL 1, 2; EncWT; EuAu; EuWr 5; EvEuW; GrFLW; LinLib L, S; McGEWB; McGEWD 72, 84; NewC; NewCBEL; NewEOp 71; NewGrDO; NinCLC 29; NotNAT B; Novels; OxCEng 67, 85, 95; OxCFr; OxCThe 67; PenC EUR; RAdv 14, 13-2; RComWL; REn*

Manzu, Giacomo
Italian. Sculptor
Noted for bronze doors he sculptured at Salzburg Cathedral, Austria, 1958 and at St. Peter's Basilica in the Vatican, 1964.
b. Dec 22, 1908 in Bergamo, Italy
d. Jan 17, 1991 in Ardea, Italy
Source: *AnObit 1991; BioIn 2, 4, 5, 6, 7, 8, 9, 11, 16, 17, 18; ConArt 77, 83, 89; CurBio 91N; DcArts; FacFETw; IntWW 74, 75, 76, 77, 78, 79, 80, 81, 82, 83, 89, 91N; McGDA; McGEWB; NewYTBS 91; OxCArt; OxCTwCA; OxDcArt; PhDcTCA 77; Who 74, 82, 83, 85, 88, 90, 92N; WhoArt 80, 82, 84; WhoWor 74; WorArt 1950*

Mao Zedong
[Mao Tse-Tung]
Chinese. Political Leader, Author
Peasant who founded People's Republic of China, 1949; controlled until death.
b. Dec 26, 1893 in Shaeshan, China
d. Sep 9, 1976 in Beijing, China
Source: *Benet 96; BioIn 16, 17, 18, 19, 20, 21; ColdWar 1, 2; ConAu 46NR, 69, 73; CurBio 43, 62, 76N; DcOrL 1; DcTwHis; DicTyr; EncCW; EncRev; FacFETw; GrLGrT; HarEnMi; HisDcKW; HisWorL; IntWW 74; LegTOT; MajTwCW; McGEWB; NewYTBE 70, 72; NewYTBS 76; OxCEng 67; RadHan; RAdv 14; REn; WhAm 6; WorAlBi*

Maples, Marla
American. Model
Wife of real estate developer Donald Trump.
Source: *BioIn 17, 18, 19, 20; NewYTBS 92*

Maples, William R.
American. Anthropologist
Known for identifying skeletons, including those of US President Zachary Taylor, Tsar Nicholas II of Russia, and the Spanish explorer Francisco Pizzaro.
b. Aug 7, 1937 in Dallas, Texas
d. Feb 27, 1997 in Gainesville, Florida

Mapleson, James Henry
"Colonel Mapleson"
English. Impresario
Managed numerous London theaters, 1860s-90s; dominated operatic news in US, England; noted for attachments, conflicts with prima donnas.
b. May 4, 1830 in London, England
d. Nov 14, 1901 in London, England
Source: *Alli SUP; Baker 78, 84, 92; BioIn 7, 13; DcNaB S2; NewEOp 71; NewGrDA 86; NewGrDM 80; NewGrDO; OxDcOp*

Mapplethorpe, Robert
American. Photographer
His homoerotic photographs brought shock waves to art world; were subject of controversy, lawsuits.
b. Nov 4, 1946 in Floral Park, New York
d. Mar 9, 1989 in Boston, Massachusetts
Source: *AmArt; AmCulL; AnObit 1989; BioIn 13, 14, 15, 16; ConPhot 82, 88, 95; CurBio 89, 89N; DcArts; DcTwCCu 1; FacFETw; GayLesB; ICPEnP A; IntWW 89N; LegTOT; MacBEP; News 89-3; NewYTBS 89; PrintW 85; WhAm 10; WhoAm 84, 86, 88; WhoAmA 82, 84, 86, 89, 91N, 93N*

Mara, Tim(othy James)
American. Football Executive
Owner, NY Giants, 1925-59; known for building solid organization; Hall of Fame, 1963.
b. Jul 29, 1887 in New York, New York
d. Feb 16, 1959 in New York, New York
Source: *BiDAmSp FB; BioIn 5, 6, 8, 11, 17; WhoFtbl 74*

Mara, Wellington T
"Duke of Mara"; "The Duke"
American. Football Executive
Son of Tim Mara; owner, pres., NY Giants, 1965—.
b. Aug 14, 1916 in New York, New York
Source: *WhoAm 84, 86, 90; WhoE 74, 91; WhoFtbl 74*

Marable, Manning
American. Educator
Director, Institute for Research in African American Studies, Columbia University, 1993—.
b. May 13, 1950 in Dayton, Ohio
Source: *BiDAmNC; BiDNeoM; BioIn 14; ConAu 110; ConBlB 10; RadHan; WhoAm 90*

Maradona, Diego
Argentine. Soccer Player
One of the highest-paid int'l soccer stars; player on Argentina's nat. soccer team, 1978-80, as its youngest member ever; Barcelona of the Spanish League, 1980-84; Naples of the Italian League, 1984-91, Spanish Soccer Club, Seville, 1992—.
b. Oct 30, 1960 in Lanus, Argentina
Source: *BioIn 12, 15, 16; CurBio 90; DcHiB; FacFETw; IntWW 89, 91; News 91; NewYTBS 86*

Marais, Jean
[Jean Alfred Villain-Marais]
French. Actor
France's most popular leading man, 1940s-50s; many of his films directed by Jean Cocteau.
b. Dec 11, 1913 in Cherbourg, France
Source: *BiDFilm, 81, 94; BioIn 2, 6, 8, 11, 15; CurBio 62; EncEurC; EncWT; Ent; FilmAG WE; FilmEn; FilmgC; ForYSC; HalFC 80, 84, 88; IntDcF 1-3, 2-3; IntMPA 75, 76, 77, 78, 79, 80, 81, 82, 84, 86, 88, 92, 94, 96; IntWW 74, 75, 76, 77, 78, 79, 80, 81, 82, 83, 89, 91, 93; ItaFilm; MotPP; MovMk; OxCFilm; WhoFr 79; WhoHol 92, A; WhoHrs 80; WhoWor 74; WorEFlm*

Maraldo, Pamela Jean
American. Business Executive, Feminist
Pres., Planned Parenthood Federation of America, 1992—.
b. Oct 27, 1947 in Wilmington, Delaware
Source: *WhoAm 86, 88, 90, 94, 95, 96; WhoAmW 95; WhoWor 96*

Maraniss, David
American. Journalist
Won a 1993 Pulitzer for nat. reporting while on staff of the *Washington Post.*

Maranville, Rabbit
[Walter James Vincent Maranville]
American. Baseball Player
Infielder, 1912-35, known for clowning antics; Hall of Fame, 1954.
b. Nov 11, 1891 in Springfield, Massachusetts
d. Jan 5, 1954 in New York, New York
Source: *Ballpl 90; BiDAmSp BB; DcAmB S5; LegTOT; WhoProB 73; WhoSpor*

Marat, Jean Paul
French. Revolutionary, Physician
Advocated extreme violence during French Revolution; slain in bath by Charlotte Corday.
b. May 24, 1743 in Neuchatel, Switzerland
d. Jul 13, 1793 in Paris, France
Source: *Benet 87, 96; BiDMoER 1; BioIn 1, 3, 4, 7, 8, 9, 13, 15, 16, 19, 20; CmFrR; Dis&D; LinLib S; LitC 10; McGEWB; NewCol 75; OxCFr; REn; WhDW; WorAl; WorAlBi*

Maravich, Pete(r Press)
"Pistol Pete"
American. Basketball Player
Highest scoring college player ever; in NBA, 1970-80; won scoring title, 1977; Hall of Fame, 1987; died of heart attack.
b. Jun 28, 1948 in Aliquippa, Pennsylvania
d. Jan 5, 1988 in Pasadena, California
Source: *BasBi; BioIn 14, 15, 16, 17, 20; CelR; LegTOT; News 88-2; NewYTBE 70, 71; NewYTBS 84, 88; OfNBA 87; WhAm 9; WhoAm 80; WhoBbl 73*

Marble, Alice
American. Tennis Player
Winner of four US singles championships, 1936, 1938-40, Wimbledon, 1938; Lawn Tennis Hall of Fame, 1964.
b. Sep 28, 1913 in Plumas City, California
d. Dec 13, 1990 in Palm Springs, California
Source: *AnObit 1990; BiDAmSp OS; BioIn 1, 3, 6, 9, 10, 12, 14, 17; BuCMET; CmCal; CurBio 40, 91N; EncWomS; FacFETw; GoodHs; GrLiveH; InWom, SUP; LegTOT; NewYTBS 90; WhoSpor; WorAl; WorAlBi*

Marc, Franz
German. Artist
Expressionist whose paintings include *Blue Horses.*
b. Feb 8, 1880 in Munich, Germany
d. Mar 4, 1916 in Verdun, France
Source: *BioIn 4, 5, 6, 12, 15, 16, 17, 20; ConArt 83; DcArts; FacFETw; IntDcAA 90; McGDA; McGEWB; OxCArt; OxCGer 76, 86; OxCTwCA; OxDcArt; PhDcTCA 77; REn; WebBD 83*

Marcantonio, Vito Anthony
American. Politician
NY congressman, 1935-37, 1939-51; first a Rep. then American Labor party member.
b. Dec 10, 1902 in New York, New York
d. Aug 9, 1954 in New York, New York
Source: *AmRef; BiDrAC; BiDrUSC 89; CurBio 49, 54; DcAmB S5; WhAm 3; WhAmP*

Marca-Relli, Conrad
American. Artist
Abstract expressionist painter who developed the "collage technique," 1950s.
b. Jun 5, 1913 in Boston, Massachusetts
Source: *AmArt; BioIn 5, 6, 7, 8, 9, 10; BriEAA; ConArt 77, 83, 89, 96; CurBio 70; DcAmArt; DcCAA 71, 77, 88, 94; McGDA; OxCTwCA; PhDcTCA 77; PrintW 83, 85; WhoAm 84, 86, 88, 90, 92, 94, 95, 96; WhoAmA 73, 76, 78, 80, 82, 84, 86, 89, 91, 93; WorArt 1950*

Marceau, Marcel
French. Actor, Pantomimist
World's most famous mime; created character "Bip," 1947.
b. Mar 22, 1923 in Strasbourg, France
Source: *BiE&WWA; BioIn 4, 5, 7, 9, 10, 11, 12, 14, 15, 16; CamGWoT; CelR 90; CnOxB; ConAu 85; CurBio 57; DcArts; DcTwCCu 2; EncWB; EncWT; Ent; FacFETw; IntWW 74, 75, 76, 77, 78, 79, 80, 81, 82, 83, 89, 91, 93; ItaFilm; LegTOT; NewYTBE 73; NotNAT;*

OxCThe 67, 83; VarWW 85; Who 82, 83, 85, 88, 90, 92, 94; WhoAm 74, 76, 78, 80, 82, 84, 86, 88, 90, 92, 94, 95, 96, 97; WhoCom; WhoEnt 92; WhoFr 79; WhoHol 92, A; WhoWor 74, 76, 78, 80, 82, 84, 87, 89, 91, 93, 95, 96; WorAl; WorAlBi; WorEFlm

Marcel, Gabriel Honore
French. Dramatist, Philosopher
Exponent of Christian Existentialism; plays include *Le Dard,* 1936.
b. Dec 7, 1889 in Paris, France
d. Oct 9, 1973 in Paris, France
Source: *CasWL; CathA 1930; ClDMEL 47, 80; CnMD; ConAu 45, 102; ConLC 15; EncWL; Ent; EvEuW; MajTwCW; McGEWB; McGEWD 72; ModWD; NewYTBE 73; OxCFr; PenC EUR; REn; TwCWr; WhAm 6; WhoWor 74; WorAu 1950*

Marcello, Benedetto
Italian. Composer
Wrote 400 cantatas, 10 masses; known for settings of paraphrases of first 50 psalms, 1724-26.
b. Jul 24, 1686 in Venice, Italy
d. Jul 24, 1739 in Brescia, Italy
Source: *Baker 78, 84, 92; BioIn 4, 7; BriBkM 80; DcBiPP; GrComp; MusMk; NewAmDM; NewGrDM 80; NewGrDO; NewOxM; OxCMus; OxDcOp*

Marcellus II, Pope
[Marcello Cervini]
Italian. Religious Leader
First reform pope; 22-day pontificate marked by neutrality.
b. May 6, 1501 in Montepulciano, Italy
d. May 1, 1555 in Rome, Italy
Source: *DcCathB; WebBD 83*

Marcelo, (Edward) Jovy
Philippine. Auto Racer
Killed during practice at the Indianapolis Speedway in 1992—first driver fatality since 1982; won the Toyota Atlantic championship, 1991.
b. 1965?, Philippines
d. May 15, 1992 in Indianapolis, Indiana

March, Fredric
[Frederick McIntyre Bickel]
American. Actor
Won Oscars, 1932, 1946, for *Dr. Jekyll and Mr. Hyde; The Best Years of Our Lives.*
b. Aug 31, 1897 in Racine, Wisconsin
d. Apr 14, 1975 in Los Angeles, California
Source: *BiDFilm, 81, 94; BiE&WWA; BioIn 1, 14, 17; CamGWoT; CelR; CurBio 43, 75N; DcAmB S9; EncAFC; EncMcCE; Ent; FamA&A; FilmEn; FilmgC; ForYSC; GangFlm; HalFC 80, 84, 88; IntDcF 2-3; IntMPA 75; IntWW 74; ItaFilm; LegTOT; MotPP; MovMk; NewYTBE 73; NewYTBS 75; NotNAT B; ObitT 1971; OxCAmT 84; OxCFilm; REn; WhAm 6; WhoAm 74; WhoHol C; WhoHrs 80; WhoThe 72; WhScrn 77, 83; WhThe; WorAl; WorAlBi; WorEFlm*

March, Hal
American. Actor
Emcee of TV's "$64,000 Question," 1955-58.
b. Apr 22, 1920 in San Francisco, California
d. Jan 11, 1970 in Los Angeles, California
Source: *BiE&WWA; BioIn 4, 7, 8; EncAFC; ForYSC; HalFC 80, 84, 88; LegTOT; MotPP; NewYTBE 70; NotNAT B; WhAm 5; WhoHol B; WhScrn 74, 77, 83*

Marchais, Georges Rene Louis
French. Politician, Political Leader
French Communist Party leader, 1972.
b. Jun 7, 1920 in La Hoguette, France
Source: *BiDFrPL; BioIn 9, 10, 11, 12, 13; CurBio 76; IntWW 91; WhoWor 91*

Marchand, Nancy
American. Actor
Played Mrs. Pynchon on "Lou Grant," 1977-81; won two Emmys.
b. Jun 19, 1928 in Buffalo, New York
Source: *BiE&WWA; BioIn 12, 13; ConTFT 1, 7; IntMPA 84, 86, 88, 92, 94, 96; NotNAT; VarWW 85; WhoAm 80, 82, 84, 86, 88, 90, 92; WhoAmW 83, 87, 89, 91, 93, 95, 97; WhoEnt 92; WhoHol 92, A; WhoThe 72, 77, 81*

Marchetti, Gino
American. Football Player
Defensive end, 1952-64, 1966, mostly with Baltimore; voted best at position in history of NFL; Hall of Fame, 1972.
b. Jan 2, 1927 in Antioch, California
Source: *BiDAmSp FB; BioIn 8, 10, 11, 17; CmCal; LegTOT; WhoFtbl 74*

Marchetti, Victor L
American. Author
Former CIA agent whose book was censored for revealing too much about CIA activities: *The CIA and the Cult of Intelligence,* 1974.
b. 1930?
Source: *BioIn 10; ConAu 108; SpyFic; WhoSpyF*

Marciano, Rocky
[Rocco Francis Marchegiano]
American. Boxer, Actor
Undefeated heavyweight champ, 1952-56; died in plane crash.
b. Sep 1, 1923 in Brockton, Massachusetts
d. Aug 31, 1969 in Des Moines, Iowa
Source: *AmDec 1950; BiDAmSp BK; BoxReg; CurBio 52, 69; DcAmB S8; FacFETw; LegTOT; ObitT 1961; WebAB 74; WhoBox 74; WhoSpor; WhScrn 77; WorAl; WorAlBi*

Marcinkus, Paul Casimir
American. Religious Leader
Pres., Vatican Bank, 1971—; involved in monetary scandal, mid-1980s.
b. Jan 15, 1922 in Cicero, Illinois
Source: *AmCath 80; BioIn 13, 15; IntWW 83, 89, 91, 93; WhoAm 86, 88; WhoRel 92*

Marconi, Guglielmo
Italian. Inventor
Built first wireless telegraph, 1895; shared Nobel Prize in physics, 1909.
b. Apr 25, 1874 in Bologna, Italy
d. Jul 20, 1937 in Rome, Italy
Source: *AsBiEn; BiESc; BioIn 1, 2, 3, 4, 5, 6, 7, 8, 9, 10, 11, 12, 14, 15, 16, 17, 20, 21; CamDcSc; DcCathB; DcInv; DcNaB MP; DcScB; EncAJ; FacFETw; LarDcSc; LegTOT; LinLib S; McGEWB; NewCol 75; NobelP; NotTwCS; OxCCan; SaTiSS; WebBD 83; WhDW; WhoNob, 90, 95; WorAl; WorAlBi; WorInv*

Marcos, Ferdinand Edralin
Philippine. Political Leader
Pres. of Philippines, 1966-86; abandoned presidency, Feb 25, 1986.
b. Sep 11, 1917 in Sarrat, Philippines
d. Sep 28, 1989 in Honolulu, Hawaii
Source: *BioIn 7, 8, 9, 10, 11, 12, 13, 14, 15, 16; ConAu 130; CurBio 67, 89N; DcTwHis; DicTyr; EncWB; FacFETw; FarE&A 78, 79, 80, 81; IntWW 74, 75, 76, 77, 78, 79, 80, 81, 82, 83, 89; IntYB 78, 79, 80, 81, 82; McGEWB; News 90; NewYTBE 73; NewYTBS 81, 89; WhoGov 72; WhoWor 84, 87; WorAl; WorAlBi*

Marcos, Imelda Romualdez
[Mrs. Ferdinand Marcos]
"Iron Butterfly"
Philippine.
Wife of former pres. who fled country with him, 1986; known for extravagant life style.
b. Jul 2, 1931 in Tacloban, Philippines
Source: *BioIn 11, 13, 14, 15, 16; EncWB; IntWW 91; InWom, SUP; WhoWor 84; WorAlBi*

Marcosson, Isaac Frederick
American. Journalist
Leading interviewer in American journalism, 1913-36.
b. Sep 13, 1876 in Louisville, Kentucky
d. Mar 14, 1961 in New York, New York
Source: *BiDAmJo; BioIn 5, 9, 16; ConAu 89; DcAmB S7; REnAL; WhAm 4; WhE&EA*

Marcoux, Vanni
French. Opera Singer
Bass-baritone with Chicago Opera, 1913-15, 1926-32; repertory of 250 roles.
b. Jun 12, 1877 in Turin, Italy
d. Oct 22, 1962 in Paris, France
Source: *Baker 78, 84, 92; BioIn 11, 12; CmOp; IntDcOp; MusSN; NewEOp 71; OxDcOp; PenDiMP; WhAm 6*

Marcum, John Arthur
American. Author
Books include *Education, Race and Social Changes in South Africa,* 1982.
b. Aug 21, 1927 in San Jose, California
Source: *AmMWSc 73S, 78S; ConAu 14NR*

Marcus, Frank
English. Dramatist
Won Cleo Award for *The Killing of Sister George,* 1965.
b. Jun 30, 1928 in Breslau, Germany
d. Aug 5, 1996 in London, England
Source: *Au&Wr 71; BioIn 10, 13; CamGWoT; CnThe; ConAu 2NR, 45, 153; ConDr 73, 77, 82, 88; CroCD; DcLB 13; DcLEL 1940; EncWT; IntAu&W 76, 77, 82, 89; IntvTCA 2; McGEWD 72, 84; Who 88; WhoThe 72, 77, 81; WhoWor 76; WrDr 76, 80, 82, 84, 86, 88, 90, 92, 94, 96*

Marcus, Jacon R(ader)
American. Clergy, Educator
Was oldest Reform rabbi in US; wrote two-volume *Early American Jewry,* 1951, 1953.
b. Mar 5, 1896
d. Nov 14, 1995 in Cincinnati, Ohio

Marcus, Luis J
American. Inventor
Beauty-supply firm owner; invented the bobby pin, 1920s.
b. 1888?
d. Mar 1990 in Menlo Park, California

Marcus, Rudolph A
American. Educator, Scientist
Won 1992 Nobel in chemistry for theories on how electrons behave in chemical reactions.
b. Jul 21, 1923 in Montreal, Quebec, Canada
Source: *AmMWSc 92; BioIn 14, 15; IntWW 91; WhoAm 90; WhoTech 89; WhoWest 89*

Marcus, Stanley
[Harold Stanley Marcus]
American. Retailer
Neiman-Marcus founded by father, 1926; chairman, 1977—.
b. Apr 20, 1905 in Dallas, Texas
Source: *BioIn 1, 2, 3, 4, 5, 8, 9, 10, 11, 12, 14, 15, 17, 19, 21; BioNews 74; BlueB 76; BusPN; CelR; ConAmBL; ConAu 53; CurBio 49; DrAPF 91; IntWW 74, 75, 76, 77, 78, 79, 80, 81, 82, 83, 89, 91, 93; NewYTBS 79, 95; St&PR 84, 87, 91, 93, 96, 97; WhoAdv 90; WhoAm 74, 76, 78, 80, 82, 84, 86, 88, 90, 92, 94; WhoAmA 73, 76, 78, 80, 82, 84, 86, 89, 91, 93; WhoAmL 85; WhoFI 74; WhoSSW 91; WhoUSWr 88; WhoWor 74, 78, 80, 82, 84, 87, 89; WhoWrEP 89, 92; WorAl; WorFshn; WrDr 76, 80, 82, 84, 86, 88, 90, 92, 94, 96*

Marcus Aurelius Antoninus
[Marcus Annius Verus]
Roman. Ruler, Philosopher, Author
Roman emperor, A.D. 161-180; wrote *Meditations* advocating stoicism.
b. Apr 20, 121 in Rome, Italy
d. Mar 17, 180 in Vindobona, Austria
Source: *AncWr; AtlBL; BbD; BiD&SB; BioIn 14, 15, 17, 20; CasWL; CyWA 58; EncEth; LngCEL; McGEWB; NewC; NewCBEL; NewCol 75; OxCClL; OxCEng 67, 85, 95; PenC CL; REn*

Marcuse, Herbert
American. Philosopher
Best-known book, *One Dimensional Man,* 1964, expressed neo-Marxist philosophy.
b. Jul 19, 1898 in Berlin, Germany
d. Jul 29, 1979 in Starnberg, Germany (West)
Source: *AmAu&B; AmRef; AmSocL; Benet 87, 96; BenetAL 91; BiDAmLf; BiDNeoM; BioIn 8, 9, 10, 11, 12, 13, 14, 15, 19, 20; BlueB 76; CelR; ConAu 89; CurBio 69, 79N; DcAmB S10; DrAS 74P, 78P; EncAB-H 1974, 1996; EncAI&E; EncAL; EncRev; FacFETw; IntEnSS 79; IntWW 74, 75, 76, 77, 78, 79; LinLib L; LNinSix; MakMC; McGEWB; MugS; NewYTBS 79; OxCPhil; PenC AM; PolProf J; RadHan; RAdv 14, 13-4; ThTwC 87; WebAB 74, 79; WhAm 7; WhDW; Who 74; WhoAm 74, 76, 78; WhoWor 74, 78; WorAl; WorAlBi; WorAu 1950; WrDr 76, 80; WrPh P*

Marcy, William Learned
American. Politician
Secretary of war, 1845-49; secretary of state, 1853-57; coined phrase ''spoils sys tem,'' 1832.
b. Dec 12, 1786 in Sturbridge, Massachusetts
d. Jul 4, 1857 in Ballston Spa, New York
Source: *AmBi; AmPolLe; ApCAB; BiDrAC; BiDrGov 1789; BiDrUSC 89; BiDrUSE 71, 89; BioIn 4, 5, 7, 10, 16; CyAG; DcAmB; DcAmDH 80, 89; DcAmMiB; Drake; EncAB-H 1974; HarEnUS; LinLib S; McGEWB; NatCAB 6; NewCol 75; OxCAmH; TwCBDA; WebAB 74, 79; WhAm HS; WhAmP; WorAl*

Marden, Brice
American. Artist
Paintings combine both abstract and minimalist influences; works include *Grove Group,* 1973 and the *Annunciation,* series, 1978-80.
b. Oct 15, 1938 in Bronxville, New York
Source: *AmArt; BioIn 10, 13, 14, 16, 17, 20, 21; ConArt 77, 83, 89, 96; CurBio 90; DcAmArt; DcCAA 77, 88, 94; DcCAr 81; DcTwCCu 1; LegTOT; PrintW 83, 85; WhoAm 78, 80, 82, 84, 86, 88, 94; WhoAmA 73, 76, 78, 80, 82, 84, 86, 89, 91, 93; WorArt 1980*

Mardian, Robert Charles
American. Lawyer
At Nixon's request, he leaked confidential information on Daniel Ellsberg, Thomas Eagleton during Watergate hearings, 1973.
b. Oct 23, 1923 in Pasadena, California
Source: *BioIn 9, 10, 12; NewYTBE 70, 73; NewYTBS 74; St&PR 84, 87; WhoAm 74, 76; WhoAmP 73*

Marek, Kurt W
[C W Ceram]
German. Author
Books on archaelogy include *Gods, Graves, and Scholars,* 1951.
b. Jan 20, 1915 in Berlin, Germany
d. Apr 12, 1972 in Hamburg, Germany (West)
Source: *AmAu&B; Au&Wr 71; BioIn 3, 4, 9, 10; ConAu 33R, P-2, X; CurBio 57, 72, 72N; LinLib L; NewYTBE 72; REnAL; WhAm 5; WorAu 1950*

Maretzek, Max
Moroccan. Impresario
Manager, Italian Opera Co., 1849-79; wrote operas *Hamlet, Sleepy Hollow.*
b. Jun 28, 1821 in Brunn, Moravia
d. May 14, 1897 in Staten Island, New York
Source: *Alli SUP; ApCAB; Baker 78, 84, 92; BiDAmM; BioIn 1, 4, 7, 10, 19; DcAmAu; DcAmB; DcNAA; MetOEnc; NatCAB 8, 38; NewEOp 71; NewGrDA 86; NewGrDO; WhAm HS*

Margaret
[Margaret Rose]
English. Princess
Sister of Queen Elizabeth II; currently 11th in line to British throne; children are Viscount Linley and Lady Sarah Armstrong-Jones.
b. Aug 21, 1930 in Glamis, Scotland
Source: *BioIn 1, 2, 3, 4, 5, 6, 7, 8, 9, 10, 11, 12, 13, 14, 15, 17, 20; BlueB 76; CurBio 53; IntWW 74, 75, 76, 77, 78, 79, 80, 81, 82, 83, 89, 91, 93; InWom, SUP; LegTOT; NewYTBE 70; NewYTBS 82; Who 82R, 83R, 85R, 88R, 90R, 92R, 94R; WhoAmW 68, 70; WhoWor 76, 78, 80, 82, 84, 87, 89, 91, 93, 95, 96, 97*

Margaret of Anjou
French. Consort
Married Henry VI, 1445; brought on War of Roses, 1453.
b. Mar 23, 1430 in Lorraine, France
d. Apr 25, 1482 in London, England
Source: *Benet 87, 96; BioIn 1, 4, 5, 6, 9, 11, 13; BlmGEL; BlmGWL; ContDcW 89; DcCathB; DcNaB; EncAmaz 91; IntDcWB; InWom, SUP; LngCEL; McGEWB; NewC; NewCol 75; OxCEng 85, 95; REn; WebBD 83; WomFir; WomWR*

Margo
[Mrs. Eddie Albert; Maria Marguerita Boldao y Castillo]
American. Actor
Introduced the Rumba with her uncle Xavier Cugat's band; films include *From Hell to Texas,* 1958.
b. May 10, 1918 in Mexico City, Mexico
d. Jul 17, 1985 in Pacific Palisades, California
Source: *BioIn 3, 10; FilmEn; FilmgC; ForYSC; HalFC 80, 84, 88; IntMPA 75, 76, 77, 78, 79, 80, 81, 82, 84; InWom SUP; LegTOT; MotPP; MovMk; NotNAT; ThFT; VarWW 85; What 5; WhoHol A; WhoThe 77A; WorAl*

Margolin, Janet
American. Actor
Starred in *David and Lisa,* 1962; *Annie Hall,* 1977.
b. Jul 25, 1943 in New York, New York
Source: *BioIn 6, 7, 9, 12, 19; ConTFT 5, 13; EncAFC; FilmEn; FilmgC; ForYSC; HalFC 80, 84, 88; IntMPA 80, 81, 82, 84, 86, 88, 92, 94; InWom SUP; ItaFilm; LegTOT; MotPP; VarWW 85; WhoHol 92, A; WorAl*

Margolin, Stuart
American. Actor, Director
Played Angel on TV series "The Rockford Files."
b. Jan 31, 1940? in Davenport, Iowa
Source: *ConTFT 6; HalFC 80, 84, 88; IntMPA 94, 96; LegTOT; VarWW 85; WhoAm 80, 88; WhoHol A*

Margolius, Sidney Senier
American. Author
Consumer's affairs books include *Consumer's Guide to Better Buying,* 1972; *Health Foods: Facts and Fiction,* 1973.
b. May 3, 1911 in Perth Amboy, New Jersey
d. Jan 30, 1980 in Roslyn, New York
Source: *ConAu 11NR, 93; WhAm 7; WhoAm 80; WhoE 74*

Margrethe II
Danish. Ruler
First woman to rule Denmark; acceded to throne Jan 14, 1972.
b. Apr 16, 1940 in Copenhagen, Denmark
Source: *BioIn 15, 16; ContDcW 89; CurBio 72; IntDcWB; IntWW 91; InWom SUP; NewYTBE 72; WhoWor 87, 91; WomWR*

Marguerite d'Angouleme
[Margaret of Navarre]
French. Ruler, Author
Queen of Henry II of Navarre; promoted literature; wrote *Heptameron,* 1558.
b. Apr 11, 1492 in Angouleme, France
d. Dec 21, 1549
Source: *BbD; Benet 87, 96; BiD&SB; BioIn 17; CasWL; Dis&D; EuAu; GuFrLit 2; InWom; LuthC 75; NewC; NewCBEL; OxCFr; REn; WebBD 83*

Margulies, Donald
American. Dramatist
Wrote play *Sight Unseen,* 1991; won Obie Award, 1992.
Source: *BioIn 18; ConLC 76*

Margulies, Julianna
American. Actor
Plays head nurse Carol Hathaway on TV's "ER," 1994—.
b. Jun 8, 1966 in Spring Valley, New York

Margulis, Lynn
American. Biologist, Author
Formulated serial endosymbiotic theory, an alternative explanation of evolution.
b. Mar 5, 1938 in Chicago, Illinois
Source: *AmMWSc 73P, 76P, 79, 82, 86, 89, 92, 95; BiESc; BioIn 14, 16, 17, 18, 20, 21; ConAu 4NR, 53; CurBio 92; IntWW 89, 91, 93; NotTwCS; WhoAm 90, 92, 94; WhoAmW 91, 93, 95, 97; WhoThSc 1996; WomStre*

Mariamne the Hasmonaean
Ordered executed by Herod in fit of jealousy.
b. 60?BC
d. 29?BC
Source: *InWom; NewC; OxCFr*

Maria Theresa
Austrian. Ruler
Wed Francis I, Holy Roman Emperor; mother of Emperor Leopold II and Marie Antoinette.
b. May 13, 1717 in Vienna, Austria
d. Nov 29, 1780 in Vienna, Austria
Source: *Benet 87, 96; BioIn 4, 7, 8, 9, 10, 11, 13, 15, 16, 20; BlkwCE; ContDcW 89; CyEd; DcCathB; DcWomA; DicTyr; Dis&D; EncAmaz 91; HisWorL; IntDcWB; InWom, SUP; LinLib S; McGEWB; NewCol 75; REn; WebBD 83; WhDW; WomFir; WomWR; WorAl; WorAlBi*

Marichal, Juan Antonio Sanchez
"Manito"; "The Dominican Dandy"
Dominican. Baseball Player
Pitcher, 1960-75, mostly with San Francisco; led NL in wins, 1963, 1968; Hall of Fame, 1983.
b. Oct 20, 1938 in Laguana Verde, Dominican Republic
Source: *Ballpl 90; BiDAmSp BB; BioIn 14, 15; InB&W 80; WhoHisp 92; WhoProB 73*

Marie Alexandra Victoria
English. Ruler, Author
Queen of Ferdinand I, 1914-27; followed Rumanian armies as Red Cross nurse, WW I; wrote *My Country,* 1916, many Romanian fairy tales.
b. Oct 29, 1875 in London, England
d. Jul 18, 1938 in Sinaia, Romania
Source: *NewCol 75; WebBD 83*

Marie Antoinette
Austrian. Consort
Guillotined for encouraging civil war, betraying her country; known for flippant saying, "Let them eat cake."
b. Nov 2, 1755 in Vienna, Austria
d. Oct 16, 1793 in Paris, France
Source: *Benet 87, 96; BioIn 1, 2, 3, 4, 5, 6, 7, 8, 9, 10, 11, 12, 13, 14, 15, 16, 17, 19, 20; CmFrR; ContDcW 89; DcCathB; Dis&D; HerW; HisWorL; IntDcWB; InWom, SUP; McGEWB; NewCol 75; NewGrDO; OxCFr; OxCGer 76, 86; REn; WebBD 83; WhDW; WorAl; WorAlBi*

Marie de France
French. Poet
Earliest known female French writer; wrote *Lais,* a collection of twelve verse tales written in octosylabic rhyming couplets.
b. c. 12th cent.
Source: *BioIn 7, 10, 11, 14, 17; BlmGWL; CamGLE; ClMLC 8; DcCathB; EncCoWW; FemiCLE; FrenWW; InWom, SUP; LinLib L; McGEWB; MediWW; OxCEng 85*

Marie de Medicis
Italian. Consort
Queen of Henry IV of France; mother of Louis XIII; banished from France, 1631.
b. Apr 26, 1573 in Florence, Italy
d. Jul 3, 1642 in Cologne, Germany
Source: *Benet 87, 96; BioIn 6, 9, 10; Dis&D; InWom SUP; OxCFr; REn; WebBD 83; WomWR*

Marie Louise
[Maria Luigia 'Asburgo-Lorena; Marie Louise Leopoldine Francoise Therese Josephin]
French.
Second wife of Napoleon I, 1810; mother of Napoleon II.
b. Dec 12, 1791 in Vienna, Austria
d. Dec 17, 1847 in Parma, Italy
Source: *BioIn 1, 3, 4, 5, 6, 9, 10; DcWomA; Dis&D; InWom, SUP; NewCol 75; OxCGer 76, 86; WebBD 83; WomWR*

Mariens, Neal
American. Producer
TV producer of "Growing Pains;" "The Wonder Years."

Marin, John
American. Artist
Expressionist whose seascapes include *Maine Island.*
b. Dec 23, 1872 in Rutherford, New Jersey
d. Oct 1, 1953 in Addison, Maine
Source: *ArtsAmW 2; AtlBL; CurBio 49, 53; DcAmB S5; DcCAA 71; EncAAH; EncAB-H 1974; OxCAmH; REn; WebAB 74; WhAm 3*

Marin, Richard
[Cheech and Chong]
"Cheech"
American. Actor, Comedian
Teamed with Tommy Chong in counterculture records, nightclub acts, and film series: *Up in Smoke,* 1978; *Still Smokin',* 1983; *The Shrimp on the Barbie,* 1990.
b. Jul 13, 1946 in Los Angeles, California
Source: *BioIn 13; ConTFT 2; HispAmA; IntMPA 82, 84, 86, 88, 92, 94; RkOn 84; VarWW 85; WhoAm 88, 90, 92, 94, 95; WhoEnt 92; WhoHol 92*

Marina
[Duchess of Kent]
English. Consort
Married Prince George, fourth son of King George V; pres., All England Tennis Club.
b. Dec 13, 1906 in Athens, Greece
d. Aug 27, 1968 in London, England
Source: *BioIn 2, 3, 4, 5, 6, 8, 14, 16, 21; DcNaB 1961; GrBr; InWom, SUP; ObitOF 79; ObitT 1961*

Marinaro, Ed(ward Francis)
American. Actor, Football Player
All-American running back, set 17 NCAA records; in NFL, 1972-77, mostly with Min nesota; played Joe Coffey on TV's "Hill Street Blues," 1980-86.
b. Mar 3, 1950 in New York, New York
Source: *BioIn 12, 16, 21; ConTFT 7; WhoAm 86, 88, 90, 92, 94, 95, 96, 97; WhoEnt 92; WhoFtbl 74; WhoHol 92; WhoTelC*

Marinetti, Filippo Tommaso Emilio
Italian. Poet
Founded Futurism; advocate of Fascism.
b. Dec 22, 1876 in Alexandria, Egypt
d. Dec 2, 1944 in Bellagio, Italy
Source: *CasWL; ClDMEL 47; CnMD; EncWT; McGEWD 72; ModWD; NewCol 75; OxCEng 67; OxCFr; PenC EUR; REn*

Marini, Marino
Italian. Sculptor
Best known for equestrian figures.
b. Feb 27, 1901 in Pistoia, Italy
d. Aug 6, 1980 in Viareggio, Italy
Source: *AnObit 1980; BioIn 2, 3, 4, 5, 7, 9, 11, 12, 17; ConArt 77, 83, 89, 96; CurBio 54, 80, 80N; DcArts; DcCAr 81; FacFETw; IntDcAA 90; IntWW 74, 75, 76, 77, 78, 79, 80; McGDA; McGEWB; NewCol 75; OxCArt; OxCTwCA; OxDcArt; PhDcTCA 77; PrintW 85; WhDW; WhoArt 80; WhoWor 74, 76, 78; WorArt 1950*

Marino, Dan
[Daniel Constantine Marino, Jr.]
American. Football Player
Quarterback, Miami, 1983—; led NFL in passing, 1984-86.
b. Sep 15, 1961 in Pittsburgh, Pennsylvania
Source: *BiDAmSp FB; BioIn 14, 15, 16, 18; CelR, 90; CurBio 89; FootReg 86; LegTOT; NewYTBS 84, 85; WhoAm 86, 88, 90, 92, 94, 95, 96, 97; WhoSSW 86, 88, 91, 93, 95, 97; WorAlBi*

Marino, Eugene Antonio
American. Religious Leader
As archbishop of Atlanta, 1988, was highest-ranking black Catholic in US; resigned office, 1990, for violating priestly celibacy.
b. May 29, 1934 in Biloxi, Mississippi
Source: *BioIn 16; NegAl 89; NewYTBS 88; RelLAm 91; WhoAfA 96; WhoAm 80, 82, 84, 86, 88; WhoBlA 77, 80, 85, 88, 90, 92, 94; WhoE 86; WhoSSW 91*

Marinuzzi, Giuseppe (Gino)
Italian. Conductor, Composer
Led Rome Opera, 1928-34; La Scala, 1934-45; wrote three operas.
b. Mar 24, 1882 in Palermo, Sicily, Italy
d. Aug 17, 1945 in Milan, Italy
Source: *Baker 78, 84; NewEOp 71*

Mario, Giovanni Matteo
Italian. Opera Singer
Handsome tenor who was the idol of Victorian opera-goers.
b. Oct 17, 1810 in Cagliari, Sardinia, Italy
d. Dec 11, 1883 in Rome, Italy
Source: *Baker 84, 92; BioIn 3, 7, 11, 14, 19; CmOp; IntDcOp; NewAmDM; NewEOp 71; NewGrDM 80; NewGrDO*

Marion, Frances
American. Screenwriter
Won Oscars for film scripts *The Big House,* 1930; *The Champ,* 1931; used statues for doorstops.
b. Nov 18, 1888 in San Francisco, California
d. May 12, 1973 in Los Angeles, California
Source: *AmWomPl; BioIn 12; DcFM; Film 1; FilmgC; GangFlm; HalFC 80, 84, 88; NotAW MOD; TwYS A; WhScrn 77, 83; WomFir; WomWMM*

Marion, Francis
"Swamp Fox"
American. Military Leader
Earned nickname for using SC swamps as base of operations against British, 1780s.
b. 1732? in Berkeley County, South Carolina
d. Feb 27, 1795 in Berkeley County, South Carolina
Source: *AmBi; AmRev; ApCAB; Benet 87, 96; BenetAL 91; BioIn 1, 2, 3, 4, 5, 6, 7, 8, 9, 10, 11, 14, 15, 16; BlkwEAR; DcAmB; DcAmMiB; Drake; EncAR; EncCRAm; EncSoH; GenMudB; HarEnMi; HarEnUS; HisWorL; LegTOT; LinLib S; McGEWB; NatCAB 1; OxCAmH; OxCAmL 65, 83, 95; REn; REnAL; TwCBDA; WebAB 74, 79; WebAMB; WhAm HS; WhAmRev; WhoMilH 76; WorAl; WorAlBi*

Marion, Marty
[Martin Whiteford Marion]
"Mr. Shortstop"; "Slats"; "The Octopus"
American. Baseball Player
Shortstop, St. Louis, 1940-53, known for fielding; instrumental in devising player pension plan, 1946.
b. Dec 1, 1917 in Richburg, South Carolina
Source: *Ballpl 90; BiDAmSp BB; BioIn 2, 3, 4, 15, 20; LegTOT; WhoProB 73; WhoSpor*

Maris, Roger Eugene
American. Baseball Player
Outfielder, 1957-68, greatest yrs. with Yankees; holds ML record for home runs in season, 61, 1961; AL MVP, 1960, 1961.
b. Sep 10, 1934 in Hibbing, Minnesota
d. Dec 14, 1985 in Houston, Texas
Source: *BiDAmSp BB; BioIn 5, 6, 7, 8, 9, 10, 11; ConNews 86-1; CurBio 61, 86; WhoHol A; WhoProB 73*

Marisol (Escobar)
Venezuelan. Sculptor
Pop artist noted for large wooden sculptures.
b. May 22, 1930 in Paris, France
Source: *AmCulL; BiDWomA; BioIn 13, 14, 15, 16, 18, 19, 20; BriEAA; CelR, 90; ConAmWS; ConArt 77, 83, 89, 96; CurBio 68; DcCAA 71, 77, 88, 94; DcTwCCu 3; EncLatA; GoodHs; InWom, SUP; LegTOT; McGDA; NorAmWA; NotHsAW 93; OxCTwCA; PhDcTCA 77; PrintW 85; WhoAm 78, 80, 82, 84, 86, 88, 90; WhoAmA 84, 91, 93; WhoAmW 68, 70, 81, 85, 89, 91; WhoE 85, 86; WhoHisp 94; WhoWor 74; WomArt; WorArt 1950*

Maritain, Jacques
French. Philosopher
Roman Catholic convert who held that church should be involved in secular affairs; wrote *Christianity and Democracy,* 1942.
b. Nov 18, 1882 in Paris, France
d. Feb 12, 1973 in Toulouse, France
Source: *Benet 87, 96; BioIn 1, 2, 3, 4, 5, 6, 9, 10, 11, 12, 13, 14, 15, 16, 19; CasWL; CathA 1930; ChhPo S2; ClDMEL 47, 80; ConAu 41R, 85; CurBio 42, 73, 73N; DcAmC; DcTwCCu 2; EvEuW; FacFETw; LegTOT; LinLib L, S; LngCTC; McGEWB; NewYTBE 71, 73; ObitT 1971; OxCEng 67; OxCFr; OxCPhil; RAdv 14, 13-4; REn; REnAL; ThTwC 87; TwCA, SUP; WhAm 5, 7; WhE&EA; WorAl; WorAlBi; WrPh P*

Marivaux, Pierre Carlet de
French. Author, Dramatist
Among his 30 comedies still being staged in France: *The Surprise of Love,* 1722; *The Game of Love and Chance,* 1737.

b. Feb 4, 1688 in Paris, France
d. Feb 12, 1763 in Paris, France
Source: *AtlBL; BiD&SB; BlkwCE; CasWL; CnThe; CyWA 58; DcEuL; EuAu; EvEuW; McGEWB; McGEWD 84; NewC; OxCEng 85; OxCFr; OxCThe 83; PenC EUR; PlP&P; REn*

Mark, Herman Francis
American. Chemist, Educator
Pioneer in research on polymer chemistry; wrote more than 600 papers and 40 books on that topic; developed kinetic theory of rubber elasticity in the 1930s.
b. May 3, 1895 in Vienna, Austria
d. Apr 6, 1992 in Austin, Texas
Source: *AmMWSc 73P, 76P, 79, 82, 86, 89, 92; BioIn 1, 3, 5, 6, 7, 10, 12, 13, 14, 16, 17, 18, 19, 20; CurBio 61; InSci; IntWW 83, 91; McGMS 80; NewYTBS 75; WhAm 10; WhoAm 86, 90*

Mark, Mary Ellen
American. Photojournalist
Known for thought-provoking pictures.
b. Mar 20, 1940 in Philadelphia, Pennsylvania
Source: *BioIn 10, 11, 15, 16, 17; ConPhot 82, 88, 95; ICPEnP A; NewYTBS 87; NorAmWA; WhoAm 90, 92, 94, 95, 96; WhoAmA 84, 86, 89, 91, 93; WhoE 86, 91*

Mark, Norman (Barry)
American. TV Personality
Host of nationally syndicated TV show, "Breakaway," 1983-85.
b. Sep 6, 1939 in Chicago, Illinois
Source: *BioIn 16; ConAu 113; WhoAm 82, 84, 86; WhoEnt 92; WhoMW 76, 78, 80, 82, 84*

Mark, Saint
"The Evangelist"
Biblical Figure
Traditionally considered author of second Gospel.
b. 1st cent. AD in Jerusalem, Judea
Source: *Benet 87; DcCathB; NewCol 75; OxDcP 86; REn; WebBD 83; WhDW*

Markel, Lester
American. Editor
Headed Sunday edition of *NY Times*, 1923-64.
b. Jan 9, 1894 in New York, New York
d. Oct 23, 1977 in New York, New York
Source: *BioIn 1, 3, 5, 11, 14; ConAu 37R, 73; CurBio 52, 78N; EncAJ; EncTwCJ; IntWW 74, 75, 76, 77; NatCAB 63; NewYTBS 77; WhAm 7; WhoAm 74, 76; WhoWorJ 72; WrDr 76*

Marker, Chris
[Christian Francois Bouche-Villeneuve]
French. Director
Directed cinema verite documentaries: *Letter from Siberia; Cuba Si.*
b. Jul 29, 1921 in Neuilly-sur-Seine, France
Source: *BiDFilm, 81, 94; BioIn 12, 14, 16; DcFM; EncEurC; FilmEn; FilmgC; HalFC 80, 84, 88; IntDcF 1-2, 2-2; MiSFD 9; OxCFilm; WhoHrs 80; WorEFlm; WorFDir 2*

Marker, Russell Earl
American. Chemist
Co-founder of Syntex Corporation; an expert on hormones.
d. Mar 3, 1995 in Wernersville, Pennsylvania

Markert, Russell
American. Choreographer
Formed what was to become the Radio City Music Hall Rockettes, 1925; staged their dance routines for 39 years.
b. Aug 8, 1899 in Jersey City, New Jersey
d. Dec 1, 1990 in Waterbury, Connecticut
Source: *Baker 92; BiDD; BioIn 8, 9, 10, 17; FacFETw; LegTOT; NewYTBE 71; NewYTBS 90*

Markevitch, Igor
Russian. Conductor
Specialist in Russian, French, Spanish music; wrote first symphony at age 11; conducted leading orchestras for over 50 yrs.
b. Jul 27, 1912 in Kiev, Russia
d. Mar 7, 1983 in Antibes, France
Source: *AnObit 1983; Baker 78, 84, 92; BiDSovU; BioIn 4, 5, 6, 10, 11, 13; BriBkM 80; ConAu 109; IntWW 74, 75, 76, 77, 78, 79, 80, 81, 82, 83N; IntWWM 77, 80; MusSN; NewYTBS 83; PenDiMP; WhAm 8; WhoFr 79; WhoMus 72; WhoWor 74, 76, 78, 82*

Markey, Enid
American. Actor
Played Jane in *Tarzan of the Apes*, 1918.
b. Feb 22, 1886 in Dillon, Colorado
d. Nov 15, 1981 in Bay Shore, New York
Source: *BiE&WWA; BioIn 5, 12; Film 1; MotPP; NotNAT; TwYS; WhoHol A; WhoThe 72, 77*

Markey, Lucille (Parker) Wright
American. Horse Trainer
Owned Calumet Farm, 1931-82; produced seven Kentucky Derby winners including Whirlaway, Citation.
b. Dec 14, 1896 in Maysville, Kentucky
d. Jul 24, 1982 in Miami, Florida
Source: *NewYTBS 82; WhoAm 78; WhoAmW 79; WhoSSW 75; WhoWor 76*

Markham, Beryl
English. Aviator
First woman to fly solo across the Atlantic from east to west, 1936; 1940s memoir *West With the Night* reissued, 1983.
b. Oct 26, 1902 in Melton Mowbray, England
d. Aug 3, 1986 in Nairobi, Kenya
Source: *AnObit 1986; BioIn 13, 15, 16, 17, 18, 19, 20, 21; ConAu 119; ContDcW 89; CurBio 42, 86, 86N; CyWA 89; DcNaB 1986; Expl 93; FacFETw; InWom, SUP; LegTOT; WomFir*

Markham, Edwin
[Charles Edward Anson Markham]
American. Poet
Wrote popular poem "The Man with the Hoe," 1899, inspired by Millet's painting.
b. Apr 23, 1852 in Oregon City, Oregon
d. Mar 7, 1940 in New York, New York
Source: *AmAu&B; AmBi; AmLY; Benet 87; BenetAL 91; BioIn 2, 3, 4, 5, 7, 11, 12, 15; CamGLE; CamHAL; ChhPo, S1, S2, S3; CmCal; CnDAL; ConAmL; CurBio 40; DcAmB S2; DcAmSR; DcLB 54; DcLEL; DcNAA; EncAB-H 1974, 1996; EncWM; EvLB; GayN; GrWrEL P; HarEnUS; LinLib L, S; LngCTC; McGEWB; ModAL; NatCAB 9; OxCAmL 65, 83; OxCTwCP; REn; REnAL; RfGAmL 87, 94; TwCA, SUP; TwCBDA; TwCLC 47; WebAB 74, 79; WhAm 1; WhNAA; WorAlBi*

Markham, Monte
American. Actor
In TV series "The Second Hundred Years," 1967-68; "Mr. Deeds Goes to Town," 1969-70.
b. Jun 21, 1935 in Manatee, Florida
Source: *ConTFT 7; FilmgC; ForYSC; HalFC 80, 84, 88; IntMPA 77, 80, 82, 92; LegTOT; VarWW 85; WhoEnt 92; WhoHol A*

Markham, Pigmeat
[Dewey M Markham]
American. Comedian
Known for "Here come de judge" skit; appeared on "Laugh-In" TV show.
b. Apr 18, 1904 in Durham, North Carolina
d. Dec 13, 1981 in New York, New York
Source: *AnObit 1981; DrBlPA; NewYTBS 81; WhoCom*

Markie, Biz
[Marcel Hall]
"The Clown Prince of Rap"; "The Diabolical One"
American. Singer
Rap singer; received gold record for *The Biz Never Sleeps* and platinum record for single "Just a Friend" both in 1989; recorded *I Need a Haircut* in 1991 and *All Samples Cleared* in 1993.
b. Apr 8, 1964 in New York, New York

Markievicz, Constance Georgine, Countess
[Constance Gore-Booth]
Irish. Revolutionary
First woman elected to British House of Commons; refused it to sit on Dail Eireann, 1919-27.
b. Feb 4, 1868 in London, England

d. Jul 15, 1927 in Dublin, Ireland
Source: *BioIn 11; DcIrB 78; DcNaB MP; IntDcWB; NewCol 75*

Markle, C(larke) Wilson, Jr.
Canadian. Engineer
Invented computerized film colorization process hotly disputed by motion picture industry, 1970s, 1980s.
b. Sep 2, 1938 in Vancouver, British Columbia, Canada
Source: *CanWW 31, 89; ConNews 88-1*

Markle, Fletcher
Canadian. Writer, Director
Worked on TV series "Studio One," 1947-48; "Life with Father," 1953-55; films included *The Incredible Journey*, 1962.
b. Mar 27, 1921 in Winnipeg, Manitoba, Canada
d. May 23, 1991 in Pasadena, California
Source: *BioIn 1, 17, 18; CanWW 70, 79, 80, 81, 83, 89; CreCan 1; DcLB 68, Y91N; FilmgC; HalFC 80, 84, 88; IntMPA 75, 76, 77, 78, 79, 80, 81, 82, 84, 86, 88; LesBEnT 92; NewYTBS 91; NewYTET; SaTiSS*

Markova, Alicia, Dame
[Lillian Alicia Marks]
English. Dancer
First prima ballerina with the Royal Ballet, 1933-35; formed own ballet co., 1935; guest dancer in major ballets.
b. Dec 1, 1910 in London, England
Source: *BiDD; BioIn 1, 2, 3, 4, 5, 6, 7, 8, 9, 10, 11, 13, 17, 21; BlueB 76; CnOxB; ConAu P-2; ContDcW 89; CurBio 43; DancEn 78; DcArts; DcLP 87B; FacFETw; IntDcB; IntDcWB; IntWW 74, 75, 76, 77, 78, 79, 80, 81, 82, 83, 89, 91, 93; InWom, SUP; LegTOT; LinLib S; MetOEnc; NewGrDM 80; VarWW 85; WhDW; Who 74, 82, 83, 85, 88, 90, 92, 94; WhoAm 74; WhoAmW 66, 68, 70, 72, 74; WhoThe 77A; WhoWor 74, 76, 78; WhThe; WomFir; WorAl; WorAlBi*

Markova, Olga
Russian. Track Athlete
Winner of the 1992 women's Boston Marathon.

Markovic, Ante
Yugoslav. Political Leader
Prime minister, Yugoslavia, 1989-91.
b. Nov 25, 1924 in Konjic, Yugoslavia
Source: *BioIn 17; CurBio 91; IntWW 89, 91, 93; WhoWor 91*

Marks, Charles
[Smith and Dale]
American. Actor, Comedian
Teamed with Joe Smith, 1898-1960s; play *Sunshine Boys* loosely based on their lives.
b. Sep 6, 1882 in New York, New York
d. 1971
Source: *BioIn 8; JoeFr*

Marks, Johnny
[John David Marks]
American. Composer, Lyricist, Songwriter
Wrote Christmas classic "Rudolph the Red-Nosed Reindeer;" has sold over 150 million records.
b. Nov 10, 1909 in Mount Vernon, New York
d. Sep 3, 1985 in New York, New York
Source: *AnObit 1985; ASCAP 66, 80; Baker 92; BioIn 14; CmpEPM; ConAu 117; IntWWM 90; NewYTBS 85; OxCPMus; WhAm 9; WhoAm 76, 78, 80, 82, 84; WhoE 74, 75, 77, 79; WhoWor 78, 80, 82, 84, 87*

Marks, Percy
American. Author
Best known for *The Plastic Age*, 1924; *Which Way Parnassus*, 1926.
b. Sep 9, 1891 in Covelo, California
d. Dec 27, 1956
Source: *AmAu&B; AmNov; BenetAL 91; BioIn 2, 4, 6; NatCAB 46; OxCAmL 65, 83; REnAL; TwCA, SUP; WhAm 3; WhNAA*

Marks, Simon
[First Baron Marks of Broughton]
English. Retailer
Joint managing director of Marks & Spencer, Ltd., 1911-64; nat. chain stores started by father.
b. Jul 9, 1888 in Leeds, England
d. Dec 8, 1964 in London, England
Source: *BioIn 14; CurBio 62, 65; DcNaB 1961; DcTwBBL; GrBr; ObitT 1961*

Markus, Robert
American. Journalist
Baseball writer, *Chicago Tribune*, 1959—; won best columnist award, 1973.
b. Jan 30, 1934 in Chicago, Illinois
Source: *WhoAm 86, 88; WhoMW 74*

Marky Mark
[Mark Wahlberg]
American. Rapper
Albums include, *You Gotta Believe;* brother of singer Donnie Wahlberg.
b. 1971? in Boston, Massachusetts
Source: *LegTOT; News 93-3*

Marlborough, John Churchill, Duke
English. Army Officer, Statesman
Led forces against Louis XIV in War of the Spanish Succession.
b. May 26, 1650 in Ashe, England
d. Jun 16, 1722 in Windsor, England
Source: *Alli; Benet 87, 96; BioIn 1, 2, 3, 4, 5, 6, 7, 8, 9, 10, 11, 12, 14, 19, 20; BlmGEL; DcBiPP; GenMudB; HarEnMi; LinLib S; LngCEL; McGEWB; NewC; REn; WhoMilH 76*

Marley, Bob
[Bob Marley and the Wailers; Robert Nesta Marley]
Jamaican. Musician, Composer
Combined reggae music, social commentary, Rastafarian faith; sold over 20 million albums at time of death.
b. Feb 6, 1945 in Kingston, Jamaica
d. May 11, 1981 in Miami, Florida
Source: *AnObit 1981; ASCAP 80; Baker 78, 84, 92; BiDAfM; BioIn 10, 11, 12, 13; ConAu 103, 107; ConBlB 5; ConLC 17; ConMuA 80A; ConMus 3; DcArts; DcTwCCu 5; DrBlPA 90; EncPR&S 89; EncRk 88; FacFETw; HarEnR 86; IlEncBM 82; IlEncRk; InB&W 85; LegTOT; NewYTBS 77, 81; OnThGG; OxCPMus; PenEncP; RkOn 78; WhoRock 81; WhoRocM 82; WhScrn 83; WorAlBi*

Marley, John
American. Actor
Character actor nominated for Oscar for role of Phil Cavilleri in *Love Story*, 1971.
b. Oct 17, 1916 in New York, New York
d. Apr 22, 1984 in Los Angeles, California
Source: *BioIn 13, 14; FilmgC; HalFC 80, 84; VarWW 85; WhoAm 74; WhoHol A*

Marley, Rita
[Esete; Ganette; Alpharita Constantia Anderson]
Jamaican. Singer, Songwriter, Producer
Member of trio called the Soulettes that was directed by reggae artist Bob Marley, her deceased husband; member of I Threes trio in early 1970s; recorded *Harambe*, 1983 and *We Must Carry On*, 1990.
b. 1947, Cuba
Source: *ConMus 10*

Marley, Ziggy
[Melody Makers; David Marley]
"Crown Prince of Reggae"
Jamaican. Singer, Songwriter
Son of Bob Marley; lead singer and songwriter for the Melody Makers, 1979; albums include *Conscious Party*, 1988.
b. 1968, Jamaica
Source: *BioIn 15, 16; ConMus 3; EncPR&S 89; LegTOT; News 90; WhoEnt 92*

Marlowe, Christopher
English. Dramatist, Poet
Established blank verse in drama; wrote *Dr. Faustus*.
b. Feb 26, 1564 in Canterbury, England
d. May 30, 1593 in Deptford, England
Source: *Alli; AtlBL; Benet 87, 96; BiD&SB; BiDRP&D; BioIn 1, 2, 3, 4, 5, 6, 7, 8, 9, 10, 11, 12, 13, 14, 15, 16, 18, 19, 20; BlmGEL; BritAu; BritWr 1; CamGEL; CamGLE; CamGWoT; CasWL; Chambr 1; ChhPo, S1; CnDBLB 1; CnE&AP; CnThe; CroE&S; CrtSuDr;*

CrtT 1, 4; CyWA 58; DcArts; DcBiPP; DcEnA; DcEnL; DcEuL; DcLB 62; DcLEL; DcNaB; Dis&D; DramC 1; EncWT; Ent; EvLB; GayLesB; GrWrEL DR, P; IntDcT 2; LegTOT; LinLib L, S; LitC 22; LngCEL; MagSWL; McGEWB; McGEWD 72, 84; MouLC 1; NewC; NewCBEL; NewEOp 71; NotNAT A, B; OxCEng 67, 85, 95; OxCThe 67, 83; OxDcOp; PenC ENG; PlP&P; RAdv 14, 13-2; RComWL; REn; REnWD; RfGEnL 91; RGFBP; TwoTYeD; WebE&AL; WhDW; WorAl; WorLitC

Marlowe, Derek
English. Author
Books include *A Dandy in Aspic,* 1966; *Nightshade,* 1975.
b. May 21, 1938 in London, England
Source: *Au&Wr 71; BioIn 7, 14; ConAu 11NR, 17R; ConDr 88C; IntAu&W 76, 91, 93; ScF&FL 92; TwCCr&M 80, 85, 91; WrDr 76, 80, 82, 84, 86, 88, 90, 92, 94, 96*

Marlowe, Hugh
[Hugh Hipple]
American. Actor
Played Jim Matthews on TV soap "Another World," 1969-82.
b. Jan 30, 1914 in Philadelphia, Pennsylvania
d. May 2, 1982 in New York, New York
Source: *BiE&WWA; FilmgC; HalFC 80; IntMPA 75, 77; MovMk; NewYTBS 82; NotNAT; WhoHol A; WhoHrs 80; WhoThe 77; WorAl*

Marlowe, Julia
[Sarah Frances Frost]
American. Actor
Known for Shakespearean roles: *Romeo and Juliet; Twelfth Night; Hamlet.*
b. Aug 17, 1866 in Cumberland, England
d. Nov 12, 1950 in New York, New York
Source: *AmWom; BioAmW; BioIn 1, 2; CamGWoT; DcAmB S4; FamA&A; IntDcT 3; InWom SUP; LibW; NotAW; NotNAT B; NotWoAT; OxCAmH; OxCAmL 65; OxCAmT 84; OxCThe 67, 83; PlP&P; REn; TwCBDA; WhAm 3; WhoStg 1906, 1908; WhThe; WomWWA 14*

Marlowe, Marion
American. Singer, Actor
Sang on radio shows with Arthur Godfrey, Jack Paar, Perry Como, Mike Douglas, 1950s-60s.
b. Mar 7, 1930 in Saint Louis, Missouri
Source: *BiE&WWA; InWom SUP; WhoAm 74; WhoAmW 70, 72, 74*

Marlowe, Sylvia
[Mrs. Leonid Berman]
American. Musician
Harpsichordist; founded Harpsichord Music Society, 1957.
b. Sep 26, 1908 in New York, New York
d. Dec 10, 1981 in New York, New York
Source: *AnObit 1981; Baker 84, 92; BioIn 2, 6, 12, 13; IntWWM 77, 80; InWom; NewAmDM; NewGrDA 86; NewGrDM 80; NewYTBS 81; WhoAm 82; WhoAmW 74; WhoWor 74*

Marmontel, Jean Francois
French. Author, Dramatist, Librettist
Wrote tragedies; librettos for light operas; historical novel *Les Incas,* 1777.
b. Jul 11, 1723 in Bort-les-Orgues, France
d. Dec 31, 1799 in Abloville, France
Source: *BbD; BiD&SB; BioIn 2, 7, 11; CasWL; ChhPo S1; DcArts; DcBiPP; DcEuL; Dis&D; EuAu; EvEuW; NewCBEL; NewEOp 71; NewGrDM 80; NewGrDO; OxCFr; OxCThe 67; OxDcOp; PenC EUR; REn*

Marot, Clement
Poet
Introduced the elegy, epigram, sonnet into France; wrote *Temple de Cupido,* 1515.
b. 1496 in Cahors, France
d. Sep 10, 1544 in Turin, Italy
Source: *AtlBL; Benet 87, 96; BiD&SB; BioIn 9, 10; CasWL; DcArts; DcEuL; EuAu; EvEuW; GuFrLit 2; NewC; NewGrDM 80; OxCEng 67, 85, 95; OxCFr; OxCMus; PenC EUR; REn*

Marquand, John Phillips
American. Author
Wrote 1937 Pulitzer winner *The Late George Apley.*
b. Nov 10, 1893 in Wilmington, Delaware
d. Jul 16, 1960 in Newburyport, Massachusetts
Source: *AmAu&B; AmNov; AmWr; BioIn 1, 2, 3, 4, 5, 6, 7, 8, 9, 12; CasWL; CnDAL; ConAu 85; ConLC 2, 10; CyWA 58; DcAmB S6; DcLEL; DrAF 76; EncMys; EncWL; EvLB; GrWrEL N; LinLib S; LngCTC; ModAL; NatCAB 47; OxCAmL 65; PenC AM; RAdv 1; REn; REnAL; SpyFic; TwCA, SUP; TwCWr; WebAB 74, 79; WebE&AL; WhAm 4*

Marquand, Richard
English. Director
Best known for films *Return of the Jedi,* 1983; *Jagged Edge,* 1985 ; won Emmy, 1972, for "Search for the Nile."
b. Sep 22, 1938 in Cardiff, Wales
d. Sep 4, 1987 in London, England
Source: *HalFC 84, 88; LegTOT; NewYTBS 87*

Marquard, Rube
[Richard William Marquard]
American. Baseball Player
Pitcher, 1908-25; holds ML record for consecutive wins, 19, 1912; Hall of Fame, 1971.
b. Oct 9, 1889 in Cleveland, Ohio
d. Jun 1, 1980 in Baltimore, Maryland
Source: *AnObit 1980; Ballpl 90; BiDAmSp BB; BioIn 3, 7, 8, 10, 12, 14, 15, 16; DcAmB S10; LegTOT; NewYTBS 80; WhoProB 73; WhoSpor; WhScrn 83*

Marquet, Albert
French. Artist
Noted for French cityscapes.
b. Mar 27, 1875 in Bordeaux, France
d. Jun 13, 1947 in Paris, France
Source: *BioIn 1, 2, 4, 8, 11, 12, 17; DcTwCCu 2; McGDA; NewCol 75; OxCTwCA; OxDcArt; PhDcTCA 77; WebBD 83*

Marquette, Jacques, Pere
French. Explorer, Missionary
First white man, with Louis Jolliet, to travel down Mississippi River, 1673.
b. Jun 1, 1637 in Laon, France
d. May 18, 1675 in Ludington, Michigan
Source: *AmBi; Benet 87, 96; BenetAL 91; BioIn 1, 2, 3, 4, 5, 6, 7, 8, 9, 10, 11, 12, 15, 18, 19; DcAmB; DcAmReB 1, 2; DcCanB 1; DcCathB; Dis&D; Drake; EncARH; EncCRAm; EncNAR; Expl 93; HarEnUS; LinLib S; LuthC 75; MacDCB 78; McGEWB; NatCAB 12; OxCAmH; OxCAmL 65, 83, 95; OxCCan; REn; REnAW; WebAB 74, 79; WhAm HS; WhNaAH; WhWE; WorAl; WorAlBi*

Marquis, Albert Nelson
American. Publisher
Founded *Who's Who in America,* 1899.
b. Jan 12, 1854 in Brown County, Ohio
d. Dec 21, 1943 in Evanston, Illinois
Source: *AmAu&B; CurBio 44; DcAmB S5; WhAm 2*

Marquis, Don Robert Perry
[Donald Robert Perry]
American. Journalist, Poet, Dramatist
Noted for humorous works *The Old Soak,* 1921; *Archy and Mehitabel,* 1927.
b. Jul 29, 1878 in Walnut, Illinois
d. Dec 29, 1937 in Forest Hills, New York
Source: *AmAu&B; AmBi; AmLY; BiDSA; CnDAL; CnE&AP; ConAmA; ConAmL; DcAmB S2; DcNAA; GrWrEL N; LngCTC; ModAL; OxCAmL 65; PenC AM; RAdv 1; REn; REnAL; Str&VC; TwCA, SUP; TwCWr; WhAm 1; WhNAA*

Marr, Dave
[David Francis Marr]
American. Golfer
Turned pro, 1953; won PGA, 1965.
b. Dec 27, 1933 in Houston, Texas
Source: *BioIn 7, 8; WhoAm 80, 82, 84, 86, 88, 90, 92, 94, 95, 96, 97; WhoGolf; WhoSSW 82, 97*

Marriner, Neville
English. Conductor, Violinist
Founded Academy of St. Martin-in-the-Fields, 1959; music director for *Amadeus,* 1984; Grammy for *Haydn-The Creation,* 1981.
b. Apr 15, 1924 in Lincoln, England
Source: *Baker 78, 84, 92; BioIn 11, 12, 16, 19; BriBkM 80; ConMus 7; CurBio*

78; IntWW 74, 75, 76, 77, 78, 79, 80, 81, 82, 83, 89, 91, 93; IntWWM 77, 80, 90; NewAmDM; NewGrDA 86; NewGrDM 80; NewYTBS 79; PenDiMP; Who 82, 83, 85, 88, 90, 92, 94; WhoAm 80, 82, 84, 86, 88, 90, 92, 94, 95, 96, 97; WhoAmM 83; WhoMus 72; WhoMW 82, 84, 86; WhoWor 74, 82, 84, 87, 89, 91, 93, 95, 96, 97

Marriott, John Willard
American. Business Executive
Founder of Marriott hotel and restaurant chain.
b. Sep 17, 1900 in Marriott, Utah
d. Aug 13, 1985 in Wolfeboro, New Hampshire
Source: *BiDAmBL 83; BioIn 9, 11; WhAm 8, 11; WhoAm 74, 76, 78, 80, 82, 84; WhoE 83, 85; WhoFI 77, 79, 81, 83, 85; WhoSSW 75, 76; WorAl*

Marriott, John Willard, Jr.
American. Business Executive
Marriott Corp. chief executive 1972—.
b. Mar 25, 1932 in Washington, District of Columbia
Source: *BioIn 9, 11, 13, 15, 16; ConNews 85-4; Dun&B 90; St&PR 91; WhoAm 74, 76, 78, 80, 82, 84, 86, 88, 90, 94, 95, 96, 97; WhoE 83, 85, 89, 91, 95, 97; WhoFI 83, 85, 87, 89, 92, 94, 96; WhoWor 84, 87, 95, 96, 97*

Marryat, Frederick
English. Author
Among his sea adventures for boys: *Jacob Faithful,* 1834; published unflattering account of American Manners, *Diary in America,* 1839.
b. Jul 10, 1792 in London, England
d. Aug 9, 1848 in Langham, England
Source: *Alli; ApCAB; AtlBL; BbD; Benet 87, 96; BenetAL 91; BiD&SB; BioIn 1, 2, 3, 5, 6, 8, 10, 12, 14, 16; BlmGEL; BritAu 19; CamGEL; CamGLE; CarSB; CasWL; CelCen; Chambr 3; ChhPo; CyWA 58; DcArts; DcBiA; DcBiPP; DcBrBI; DcBrWA; DcCanB 7; DcEnA; DcEnL; DcLB 21, 163; DcLEL; DcNaB; Drake; EvLB; GrWrEL N; HarEnUS; HsB&A, SUP; LegTOT; LinLib L, S; LngCEL; NewC; NewCBEL; NinCLC 3; Novels; OxCAmH; OxCAmL 65, 83, 95; OxCCan; OxCChiL; OxCEng 67, 85, 95; OxCShps; PenC ENG; RAdv 1, 14, 13-1; REn; REnAL; RfGEnL 91; ScF&FL 1; ScFEYrs; StaCVF; TwCChW 83A, 89A, 95A; VicBrit; WebE&AL; WhDW; WhoChL; WhoHr&F; WrChl*

Mars, Forrest
American. Candy Manufacturer
Merged his confectionery firm with father's, 1964, to become world's largest can dy maker.
b. 1904
Source: *BioIn 7, 13; ConAmBL; Entr; WhoFI 89; WhoSSW 91*

Marsala, Joe
American. Musician, Composer
Clarinet, sax player with numerous bands, 1930s-60s; wrote "Little Sir Echo."
b. Jan 5, 1907 in Chicago, Illinois
d. Mar 3, 1978 in Santa Barbara, California
Source: *AllMusG; ASCAP 66, 80; BiDJaz; CmpEPM; IlEncJ; NewGrDJ 88, 94; WhoJazz 72*

Marsala, Marty
American. Jazz Musician
Trumpeter; led own band 1940s; brother of Joe.
b. Apr 2, 1909 in Chicago, Illinois
d. Apr 27, 1975 in Chicago, Illinois
Source: *BiDJaz; CmpEPM; EncJzS; NewGrDJ 88, 94; WhoJazz 72*

Marsalis, Branford
American. Jazz Musician, Bandleader
Jazz saxophonist who succeeded Doc Severinsen as musical director of "The Tonight Show," 1992-95.
b. Aug 26, 1960 in New Orleans, Louisiana
Source: *AfrAmAl 6; AllMusG; BioIn 13, 14, 15, 16; CelR 90; ConMus 10; ConTFT 12; CurBio 91; DcArts; DrBlPA 90; LegTOT; NewAmDM; NewGrDJ 88, 94; News 88-3; PenDiMP; PenEncP; WhoAfA 96; WhoAm 90, 92, 94, 95, 96, 97; WhoBlA 85, 88, 90, 92, 94; WhoEnt 92; WhoHol 92*

Marsalis, Wynton
American. Musician
Classical, jazz trumpeter; first artist ever to win Grammys for albums in both categories, 1983; won 1997 Pulitzer Prize for Music for "Blood on the Fields."
b. Oct 18, 1961 in New Orleans, Louisiana
Source: *AfrAmAl 6; AfrAmBi 2; AllMusG; Baker 84, 92; BiDJaz; BioIn 12, 13, 14, 15, 16, 18; CelR 90; ConMus 6; CurBio 84; DcArts; DcTwCCu 1, 5; DrBlPA 90; FacFETw; InB&W 85; IntWW 89, 91, 93; IntWWM 90; LegTOT; NegAl 89; NewAmDM; NewGrDA 86; NewGrDJ 88, 94; OxCPMus; PenDiMP; PenEncP; TwCBrS; WhoAfA 96; WhoAm 86, 88, 90, 92, 94, 95, 96, 97; WhoBlA 92, 94; WhoEnt 92; WorAlBi*

Marschner, Heinrich August
German. Composer
Operas include *Hans Heiling,* 1833.
b. Aug 16, 1795 in Zittau, Saxony
d. Dec 14, 1861 in Hannover, Hannover
Source: *Baker 84, 92; BioIn 4, 12; BriBkM 80; CmOp; MetOEnc; NewAmDM; NewEOp 71; NewGrDM 80; NewGrDO; OxCMus; PenDiMP A*

Marsden, Gerry
[Gerry and the Pacemakers]
English. Singer, Musician
Founded group, 1959; managed by Brian Epstein.
b. Sep 24, 1942 in Liverpool, England
Source: *LegTOT; WhoRocM 82*

Marsh, Edward Howard, Sir
English. Secretary, Editor, Translator
Churchill's private secretary, 1905-29; edited Rupert Brooke's poems, 1918.
b. Nov 18, 1872 in London, England
d. Jan 13, 1953 in London, England
Source: *BioIn 1, 2, 3, 4, 5, 7, 11, 13, 14; CathA 1930, 1952; ChhPo, S3; DcNaB 1951; GrBr; LngCTC; ModBrL; NewC; NewCBEL; OxCEng 67, 85, 95; PenC ENG; WhE&EA; WhoLA*

Marsh, Jean
[Jean Lyndsey Torren Marsh]
English. Actor
Starred in British series "Upstairs, Downstairs;" won Emmy, 1975.
b. Jul 1, 1934 in London, England
Source: *BioIn 11, 13; BioNews 74; ConTFT 3, 11; CurBio 77; HalFC 88; IntMPA 92, 94, 96; InWom SUP; LegTOT; NewYTBS 74; TwCRHW 90; VarWW 85; Who 82, 83, 85, 88, 90, 92, 94; WhoAm 78, 80, 82, 84, 86, 88, 90, 92, 94, 95, 96, 97; WhoAmW 83; WhoEnt 92; WhoHol 92, A; WorAlBi; WrDr 90*

Marsh, Mae
American. Actor
Starred in silent film classic *Birth of a Nation,* 1915.
b. Nov 19, 1895 in Madrid, New Mexico
d. Feb 13, 1968 in Hermosa Beach, California
Source: *BiDFilm, 81, 94; BioIn 4, 6, 8, 9, 10, 12; EncAFC; Film 1, 2; FilmEn; FilmgC; ForYSC; HalFC 80, 84, 88; IntDcF 1-3, 2-3; InWom SUP; LegTOT; MotPP; MovMk; NotAW MOD; OxCFilm; SilFlmP; ThFT; TwYS; WhAm 4A; WhoHol B; WhScrn 74, 77, 83; WorEFlm*

Marsh, Ngaio, Dame
[David Francis Marsh]
New Zealander. Author, Producer
Created character of Roderick Alleyn in over 30 mysteries, 1934-82.
b. Apr 23, 1899 in Christchurch, New Zealand
d. Feb 18, 1982 in Christchurch, New Zealand
Source: *AnObit 1982; Au&Wr 71; AuBYP 2, 3; Benet 87; BioIn 1, 4, 5, 7, 8, 11, 12, 14, 16, 17, 18, 21; BlueB 76; CamGLE; ConAu 6NR; ConLC 7, 53; ConNov 76, 82; CorpD; DcArts; DcLB 77; DcLEL; DcNaB 1981; EncBrWW; EncMys; EvLB; FacFETw; FarE&A 78, 79, 80, 81; FemiCLE; GrWrEL N; IntAu&W 76; IntWW 74, 75, 76, 77, 78, 79, 80, 81; InWom, SUP; MajTwCW; NewYTBS 82; Novels; REn; TwCCr&M 80, 85; WhE&EA; Who 74, 82;*

WhoAmW 70, 72, 75; WhoWor 74, 82; WorAl; WorAlBi; WrDr 80, 82

Marsh, Othniel Charles
American. Paleontologist
Discovered over 1000 fossil vertebrates; donated most to Yale U.
b. Oct 29, 1831 in Lockport, New York
d. Mar 18, 1899 in New Haven, Connecticut
Source: *Alli SUP; AmBi; ApCAB; AsBiEn; BiDAmS; BiD&SB; BiESc; BiInAmS; BioIn 4, 5, 7, 8, 9, 10, 13, 18, 20; CamDcSc; DcAmAu; DcAmB; DcNAA; DcRusL; DcScB; EncAB-H 1974, 1996; HarEnUS; InSci; LarDcSc; LinLib L, S; McGEWB; NatCAB 1, 9; OxCAmH; REnAL; TwCBDA; WebAB 74, 79; WhAm HS; WorAl*

Marsh, Reginald
American. Artist, Illustrator
Noted for scenes of NYC, including *The Bowery,* 1930.
b. Mar 14, 1898 in Paris, France
d. Jul 3, 1954 in Bennington, Vermont
Source: *BioIn 1, 3, 4, 5, 9, 12, 13, 14; BriEAA; CurBio 41, 54; DcAmArt; DcAmB S5; DcCAA 71, 77, 88, 94; GrAmP; IlsBYP; IlsCB 1946; McGDA; McGEWB; NatCAB 62; NewCol 75; OxCAmH; OxCTwCA; OxDcArt; PhDcTCA 77; WebAB 74, 79; WhAm 3; WhAmArt 85; WhoAmA 78N, 80N, 82N, 84N, 86N, 89N, 91N, 93N; WorArt 1950*

Marshack, Megan
American. Secretary, Journalist
With Nelson Rockefeller at his death, 1979.
b. 1953 in Sherman Oaks, California
Source: *BioIn 11, 12*

Marshak, Robert E(ugene)
American. Physicist, University Administrator
First to advance the theory of 2 types of Subatomic particles, 1947; pres., City College, NY, 1970-79.
b. Oct 11, 1916 in New York, New York
d. Dec 23, 1992 in Cancun, Mexico
Source: *AmMWSc 73P, 76P, 79, 82, 86, 89, 92; AnObit 1992; BioIn 9, 10, 12, 13, 18, 19, 21; ConAu 107, 140; CurBio 93N; IntAu&W 77; IntWW 91; LEduc 74; McGMS 80; St&PR 87; WhAm 11; WhoAm 74, 76, 78, 80, 82, 84, 86, 88, 90, 92; WhoFrS 84; WrDr 76, 80, 82, 84, 86, 88, 90, 92, 94, 96*

Marshal, Alan
Australian. Actor
Supporting actor, 1936-59; in film *The Hunchback of Notre Dame,* 1939.
b. Jan 29, 1909 in Sydney, Australia
d. Jul 9, 1961 in Chicago, Illinois
Source: *BioIn 5; FilmEn; FilmgC; ForYSC; HalFC 80, 84, 88; MotPP; VarWW 85; WhoHol B; WhScrn 74, 77, 83*

Marshall, Alan Peter
English. Producer
Films include *Midnight Express,* 1978; *Fame,* 1980; *Angel Heart,* 1986; won four Oscars.
b. Aug 12, 1938 in London, England
Source: *ConTFT 5; HalFC 88; IntMPA 92; St&PR 93*

Marshall, Alfred
English. Economist
Founder of neoclassic economics; wrote *Principles of Economics,* 1890.
b. Jul 26, 1842 in London, England
d. Jul 13, 1924 in London, England
Source: *Alli SUP; BioIn 1, 2, 3, 6, 7, 8, 13, 14, 16, 17, 21; DcNaB 1922; GrEconB; McGEWB; NewC; NewCol 75; RAdv 14, 13-3; WhDW; WhoEc 81, 86*

Marshall, Barry J(ames)
Australian. Scientist
Researcher in field of gastroenterology; hypothesis that ulcers are caused by bacteria rather than stress.
b. Sep 30, 1951 in Kalgoorlie, Australia
Source: *CurBio 96; WhoMedH; WhoScEn 96; WhoWor 89, 91*

Marshall, Brenda
[Ardis Anderson Gaines]
American. Actor
Married William Holden, 1941-71; starred opposite Errol Flynn in *The Sea Hawk,* 1940.
b. Sep 29, 1915 in Philadelphia, Pennsylvania
d. Jul 30, 1992 in Palm Springs, California
Source: *FilmEn; FilmgC; ForYSC; HalFC 80, 84, 88; MotPP; MovMk; WhoHol 92, A*

Marshall, Catherine
[Mrs. Peter Marshall]
American. Author
Inspirational books have sold more than 18 million copies: *A Man Called Peter,* 1951.
b. Sep 27, 1914 in Johnson City, Tennessee
d. Mar 18, 1983 in Boynton Beach, Florida
Source: *AmWomWr; AuBYP 2; BioIn 3, 4, 5, 7, 9, 11, 12, 13, 14, 15, 17, 19; ConAu 8NR, 17R, 109; CurBio 55, 83N; DcBiPP; IntAu&W 77; LinLib L, S; NewYTBS 83; SmATA 2, 34N; TwCSAPR; WorAl; WorAlBi; WrDr 76, 80, 82, 84*

Marshall, David (Saul)
Singaporean. Diplomat, Politician
Chief minister, Singapore, 1955-56; ambassador to France, 1978-93.
b. 1908, Singapore
d. Dec 12, 1995, Singapore
Source: *BioIn 4, 11, 12, 21; CurBio 96N; DcMPSA; FarE&A 78, 79, 80, 81; IntWW 74, 75, 76, 77, 79, 80, 81, 82, 83, 89, 91, 93; NewYTBS 95; WhAm 11; WhDW; WhoWor 74, 84, 87*

Marshall, E(dda) G(unnar)
American. Actor
Versatile film, Broadway, TV actor since late 1930s; won two Emmys for "The Defenders," 1962, 1963.
b. Jun 18, 1910 in Owatonna, Minnesota
Source: *BiE&WWA; BioIn 14, 15; CelR 90; ConTFT 3; CurBio 86; FilmEn; FilmgC; HalFC 88; IntMPA 92; MotPP; MovMk; NotNAT; PlP&P; VarWW 85; WhoAm 86, 90; WhoHol A; WhoThe 81; WorAlBi*

Marshall, Frank James
American. Chess Player
US chess champion, 1909-36.
b. Aug 10, 1877 in New York, New York
d. Nov 9, 1944 in Jersey City, New Jersey
Source: *BioIn 3, 10; DcAmB S3; GolEC; OxCChes 84; WebBD 83; WhAm 2*

Marshall, Garry Kent
American. Producer, Filmmaker
Created, produced comedy shows "Happy Days," 1974-84; "Mork and Mindy," 1978-82; films include *Nothing in Common,* 1986; *Pretty Woman,* 1990.
b. Nov 13, 1934 in New York, New York
Source: *Au&Arts 3; BioIn 13, 14, 16; CelR 90; ConAu 111; ConLC 17; ConTFT 1, 6; CurBio 92; HalFC 88; IntMPA 92; LesBEnT, 92; SmATA 60; VarWW 85; WhoAm 86, 90; WhoEnt 92; WhoTelC; WorAlBi*

Marshall, George Catlett
American. Army Officer, Government Official
Proposed Marshall Plan, to aid war-torn European countries, 1947; won Nobel Peace Prize, 1953; prominent WW II general.
b. Dec 31, 1880 in Uniontown, Pennsylvania
d. Oct 16, 1959 in Bethesda, Maryland
Source: *AmAu&B; AmPolLe; BiDInt; BiDrUSE 71, 89; BiDWWGF; BioIn 1, 2, 3, 4, 5, 6, 7, 8, 9, 10, 11, 12, 13; CmdGen 1991; ColdWar 2; CurBio 40, 47, 59; DcAmB S6; DcAmDH 80, 89; DcAmMiB; DcPol; DcTwHis; EncAB-H 1974, 1996; EncMcCE; HarEnMi; HisEWW; LinLib S; McGEWB; NatCAB 45; ObitOF 79; ObitT 1951; OxCAmH; REn; WebAB 74, 79; WebAMB; WebBD 83; WhAm 3; WhDW; WhoMilH 76; WhoNob, 90, 95; WhWW-II; WorAl*

Marshall, George Preston
American. Football Executive
Owner, Washington Redskins, 1932-63; initiated many changes in game, including halftime entertainment; Hall of Fame, 1963.
b. Oct 11, 1896 in Grafton, Virginia
d. Aug 9, 1969 in Washington, District of Columbia
Source: *BiDAmSp FB; BioIn 6, 8; WhoFtbl 74*

Marshall, Herbert
American. Actor
Leading man: *A Bill of Divorcement, 1940; The Letter, 1940.*
b. May 23, 1890 in London, England
d. Jan 22, 1966 in Beverly Hills, California
Source: *BiDFilm, 81, 94; BiE&WWA; BioIn 7, 9, 14; Film 2; FilmAG WE; FilmEn; FilmgC; HalFC 80, 84, 88; IlWWBF; IntDcF 1-3, 2-3; LegTOT; MotPP; MovMk; NotNAT B; ObitT 1961; OxCFilm; RadStar; WhAm 4; WhoHol B; WhoHrs 80; WhScrn 74, 77, 83; WhThe; WorAl; WorAlBi; WorEFlm*

Marshall, Jack
[John C Marshall]
Canadian. Hockey Player
Played amateur hockey 17 yrs., early 1900s; Hall of Fame, 1965.
b. Mar 14, 1877 in Saint Vallier, Quebec, Canada
d. Aug 7, 1965 in Montreal, Quebec, Canada
Source: *WhoHcky 73*

Marshall, James Edward
American. Children's Author, Illustrator
Best known for his George and Martha series; illustrated over 70 books.
b. Oct 10, 1942 in San Antonio, Texas
d. Oct 13, 1992 in New York, New York
Source: *AuBYP 3; BioIn 16; ChlLR 21; WhoAm 88*

Marshall, John
American. Supreme Court Justice
Fourth chief justice of Supreme Court, 1801-35.
b. Sep 24, 1755 in Germantown, Virginia
d. Jul 6, 1835 in Philadelphia, Pennsylvania
Source: *Alli; AmAu; AmAu&B; AmBi; AmJust; AmPolLe; ApCAB; Benet 87, 96; BiAUS; BiD&SB; BiDFedJ; BiDLA; BiDrAC; BiDrUSC 89; BiDrUSE 71, 89; BiDSA; BioIn 1, 2, 3, 4, 5, 6, 7, 8, 9, 10, 11, 12, 13, 14, 15, 16, 17, 18, 20; CopCroC; CyAG; CyAL 1; DcAmAu; DcAmB; DcAmC; DcAmDH 80, 89; DcAmSR; DcBiPP; DcNAA; Dis&D; Drake; EncAAH; EncAB-H 1974, 1996; EncAR; EncNAB; EncSoH; HarEnUS; HisWorL; LegTOT; LinLib L, S; McGEWB; MemAm; NatCAB 1; OxCAmH; OxCSupC; RComAH; REn; REnAL; SupCtJu; TwCBDA; WebAB 74, 79; WhAm HS; WhAmP; WhAmRev; WhDW; WorAl; WorAlBi*

Marshall, Laurence
American. Business Executive
Founded Raytheon Corp., which manufactured radio tubes, 1922; played role in development of radar, WW II.
b. 1889 in Medford, Massachusetts
d. Nov 5, 1980 in Cambridge, Massachusetts
Source: *BioIn 12; NewYTBS 80*

Marshall, Lois
Canadian. Singer
Mezzo soprano, who despite paralytic polio, made appearances with many symphonies and operas; was Mimi in *La Boheme,* 1959.
b. 1924
d. Feb 19, 1997 in Toronto, Ontario, Canada
Source: *BioIn 3, 4, 5; CanWW 70, 79, 80, 81, 83; CreCan 2; IntWWM 77, 80; InWom; WhoAm 76; WhoAmW 66, 68, 70, 72, 74, 75*

Marshall, Paule
American. Writer
Wrote *The Chosen Place, The Timeless People,* 1961; *Daughters,* 1991.
b. Apr 9, 1929 in New York, New York
Source: *AfrAmW; AmAu&B; AmWomWr, 92; ArtclWW 2; Benet 96; BenetAL 91; BioIn 13, 14, 17, 18, 19, 20, 21; BlkAWP; BlkLC; BlkWAm; BlkWr 1, 2; BlmGWL; CaribW 1; ConAu 25NR, 77; ConBlAP 88; ConBlB 7; ConLC 27, 72; ConNov 72, 76, 82, 86, 91, 96; CyWA 89; DcLB 33, 157; DcTwCCu 5; DrAF 76; DrAPF 80; EncWL 3; FemiCLE; GrWomW; InB&W 80, 85; IntAu&W 76, 77, 91, 93; InWom SUP; LivgBAA; MajTwCW; ModWoWr; NegAl 76, 83, 89; OxCAmL 95; OxCWoWr 95; RAdv 14; RfGAmL 94; SchCGBL; SelBAAf; SelBAAu; ShSCr 3; WhoAmW 70, 72; WorAu 1970; WrDr 76, 80, 82, 84, 86, 88, 90, 92, 94, 96*

Marshall, Penny
[Carole Penny Marscharelli]
American. Actor, Director
Played Laverne in TV series "Laverne and Shirley," 1976-83; directed films, *Big,* 1988; *Awakenings,* 1990; *A League of Their Own,* 1992.
b. Oct 15, 1942 in New York, New York
Source: *BiDFilm 94; BioIn 12, 13, 16; BkPepl; CelR 90; ConTFT 6; CurBio 80, 92; FilmEn; GrLiveH; HalFC 88; IntMPA 80, 86, 88, 92, 96; InWom SUP; LegTOT; LesBEnT 92; MiSFD 9; News 91, 91-3; ReelWom; WhoAm 90; WhoCom; WhoEnt 92; WhoHol 92, A; WorAlBi*

Marshall, Peter
American. Religious Leader
Senate chaplain, 1947-48; subject of *A Man Called Peter,* written by wife Catherine, 1951.
b. May 27, 1902 in Coatbridge, Scotland
d. Jan 25, 1949 in Washington, District of Columbia
Source: *BioIn 1, 2, 3, 4, 17, 21; ConAu 112; CurBio 48, 49; RelLAm 91; TwCSAPR; WhAm 2; WorAl; WorAlBi*

Marshall, Peter
[Pierre LaCock]
American. TV Personality
Best known for hosting over 5,000 shows of "The Hollywood Squares."
b. Mar 30, 1930 in Huntington, West Virginia
Source: *BioIn 13; IntMPA 82, 92; VarWW 85; Who 82, 83, 85, 88, 90, 92, 94; WhoEnt 92; WhoHol 92, A; WhoTelC*

Marshall, Ray
[F(reddie) Ray Marshall]
American. Government Official
Secretary of labor, 1977-81.
b. Aug 22, 1928 in Oak Grove, Louisiana
Source: *AmEA 74; WhoWor 80, 82, 84; WorAl*

Marshall, S(amuel) L(yman) A(twood)
American. Army Officer, Journalist
Major military historian; wrote *Pork Chop Hill* about Korean War, 1956.
b. Jul 18, 1900 in Catskill, New York
d. Dec 17, 1977 in El Paso, Texas
Source: *AmAu&B; AuBYP 2, 3; BioIn 3, 5, 8, 10, 11, 12; ConAu 73, 81; CurBio 53, 78N; DcAmB S10; DcAmMiB; NewYTBS 77; SmATA 21; WhAm 7; WhoAm 74, 76, 78; WorAu 1950*

Marshall, Thomas Riley
American. US Vice President
VP under Wilson, 1913-21; said "What this country needs is a good five-cent cigar."
b. Mar 14, 1854 in North Manchester, Indiana
d. Jun 1, 1925 in Washington, District of Columbia
Source: *AmAu&B; AmBi; AmPolLe; BiDrAC; BiDrUSC 89; BiDrUSE 71, 89; BioIn 1, 2, 4, 7, 8, 9, 10, 14; DcAmB; DcNAA; HarEnUS; IndAu 1917; NatCAB 19; VicePre; WebAB 74, 79; WhAm 1; WhAmP; WorAl*

Marshall, Thurgood
American. Supreme Court Justice
Civil rights activist; first black appointed to Supreme Court, 1967-91.
b. Jul 2, 1908 in Baltimore, Maryland
d. Jan 24, 1993 in Bethesda, Maryland
Source: *AfrAmAl 6; WhoSSW 73, 75; WhoWor 74, 78, 80, 82, 84, 87; WorAl; WorAlBi*

Marshall, Tully
[William Phillips]
American. Actor
Character actor in over 100 films, 1914-43.
b. Apr 13, 1864 in Nevada City, California
d. Mar 10, 1943 in Encino, California
Source: *BioIn 12, 17; CurBio 43; EncAFC; Film 1, 2; FilmEn; FilmgC; GangFlm; HalFC 80, 84, 88; HolCA; LegTOT; MotPP; MovMk; NotNAT B; SilFlmP; TwYS; WhAm 2; WhoHol B; WhScrn 74, 77, 83; WhThe; WorAl*

Marshall, Wilbur Buddyhia
American. Football Player
Linebacker, Chicago, 1984-87; first NFL free agent to change teams in 11 yrs., signing with Washington, 1988.
b. Apr 18, 1962 in Titusville, Florida
Source: *BioIn 16; FootReg 87; WhoBlA 85, 92*

Marshall, William
American. Actor
Vocalist with Fred Waring; had brief acting career in 1940s.
b. Oct 12, 1917 in Chicago, Illinois
Source: *FilmEn; FilmgC; InB&W 80; IntMPA 75, 76, 77, 78, 79, 80, 81, 82, 84, 86, 88; WhoHol A*

Marshall, William
American. Actor
Screen debut in *Lydia Bailey,* 1952; starred as black vampire in *Blacula,* 1972; *Scream Blacula Scream,* 1973.
b. Aug 19, 1924 in Gary, Indiana
Source: *BiE&WWA; BioIn 14, 17; BlksAmF; ConTFT 8; DrBlPA, 90; FilmEn; HalFC 84, 88; NotNAT, A; WhoBlA 80, 85, 92; WhoHol 92; WhoHrs 80*

Marshall Tucker Band, The
[Tommy Caldwell; Toy Caldwell; Jerry Eubanks; Doug Gray; George MCorkle; Paul Riddle]
American. Music Group
Dixie-rock band, formed 1972.
Source: *ConMuA 80A; EncFCWM 83; IlEncRk; PenEncP; RkOn 74, 78; RolSEnR 83; WhoRock 81; WhoRocM 82*

Marston, John
English. Author, Dramatist
Plays include *What You Will,* 1601; *Sophonisba,* 1605.
b. 1575 in Wardington, England
d. Jun 25, 1634 in London, England
Source: *Alli; AtlBL; BbD; Benet 87, 96; BiD&SB; BiDRP&D; BioIn 3, 16; BlmGEL; BritAu; CamGEL; CasWL; Chambr 1; ChhPo; CnE&AP; CroE&S; CrtT 1; CyWA 58; DcEnA; DcEnL; DcEuL; DcLEL; DcNaB; EvLB; LngCEL; McGEWD 72, 84; MouLC 1; NewC; NotNAT B; OxCEng 67, 85, 95; OxCThe 67, 83; PenC ENG; PlP&P; RAdv 14, 13-2; REn; WebE&AL*

Marston, William Moulton
[Charles Moulton]
American. Psychologist, Cartoonist
Discovered systolic blood pressure deception test (lie detector), 1915.
b. Mar 9, 1893 in Cliftondale, Massachusetts
d. Mar 2, 1947 in Rye, New York
Source: *BioIn 1, 2; DcNAA; EncAB-A 7; NatCAB 35; ObitOF 79; WhAm 2; WhNAA; WorECom*

Martell, Vincent
[Vanilla Fudge]
American. Musician
Guitarist with group, 1967-72.
b. Nov 11, 1945 in New York, New York
Source: *EncPR&S 74; IlEncRk*

Martens, Wilfried
Belgian. Political Leader
Prime minister of Belgium, 1979-92; minister of state, 1992—.
b. Apr 19, 1936 in Sleidinge, Belgium
Source: *BioIn 15, 21; CurBio 87; IntWW 79, 80, 81, 82, 83, 89, 91, 93; IntYB 82; PolLCWE; WhoEIO 82; WhoWor 80, 82, 84, 87, 89, 91, 93*

Marterie, Ralph
"The Caruso of the Trumpet"
Composer, Conductor
Trumpeter; had own radio show; made many recordings, 1950s.
b. Dec 24, 1914 in Naples, Italy
Source: *ASCAP 66; CmpEPM; PenEncP; RkOn 78*

Martha and the Vandellas
[Rosalind Ashford; Betty Kelly; Lois Reeves; Martha Reeves; Annette Sterling; Sandra Tilley]
American. Music Group
Motown group popular for dance records; hit singles "Dancing in the Streets," 1964 ; "I'm Ready for Love," 1966.
Source: *BioIn 16, 20; DcTwCCu 5; EncPR&S 74, 89; EncRk 88; EncRkSt; IlEncBM 82; InB&W 80, 85A; NewGrDA 86; OxCPMus; PenEncP; RolSEnR 83; WhoHol 92; WhoRock 81; WhoRocM 82*

Marti (y Perez), Jose Julian
Cuban. Patriot, Poet
Founded Cuban Revolutionary party, 1892; killed by Spanish while leading rebel troops.
b. Jan 28, 1853 in Havana, Cuba
d. May 19, 1895 in Dos Rios, Cuba
Source: *ApCAB SUP; Benet 96; CasWL; DcSpL; EncRev; McGEWB; NewCol 75; PenC AM; REn*

Martial
Roman. Poet
Noted for 11 books of witty epigrams describing Roman life, published, 86-98.
b. 43 in Bilbilis, Spain
d. 104 in Bilbilis, Spain
Source: *AtlBL; BbD; BiD&SB; CasWL; CyWA 58; NewC; OxCEng 67; PenC CL; RComWL; REn*

Martin, Agnes
American. Artist
Expressionist painter whose significant works were in grid paintings.
b. Mar 22, 1912 in Maklin, Saskatchewan, Canada
Source: *AmArt; BiDWomA; BioIn 13, 14, 16, 18, 20; ConArt 77, 83, 89, 96; CurBio 89; DcAmArt; DcCAA 77, 88, 94; DcCAr 81; EncWB; GrLiveH; IntWW 91, 93; NorAmWA; WhoAm 78, 80, 82, 88, 90, 94, 95, 96, 97; WhoAmA 91; WhoAmW 85; WhoE 74; WomArt; WorArt 1950*

Martin, Archer John Porter
English. Chemist
Shared Nobel Prize, 1952, for invention of partition chromatography.
b. Mar 1, 1910 in London, England
Source: *AsBiEn; BiESc; BioIn 3, 6, 9, 11, 14, 15, 19, 20; BlueB 76; CamDcSc; InSci; IntWW 74, 75, 76, 77, 78, 79, 80, 81, 82, 83, 89, 91, 93; IntYB 78, 79, 80, 81, 82; LarDcSc; McGMS 80; NobelP; WhDW; Who 74, 82, 83, 85, 88, 90, 92, 94; WhoAm 74, 76, 78, 80, 82, 84, 86, 88, 90; WhoNob, 90, 95; WhoScEn 94, 96; WhoWor 74, 82, 84, 87, 89, 91, 93, 95, 96, 97; WorAl; WorAlBi*

Martin, Billy
[Alfred Manuel Martin]
American. Baseball Player, Baseball Manager
Fiery infielder, 1950-61; managed five different teams including five stints with Yankees, 1975-88; wrote *Number 1,* 1980; killed in auto accident.
b. May 16, 1928 in Berkeley, California
d. Dec 25, 1989 in Binghampton, New York
Source: *AnObit 1989; Ballpl 90; BaseEn 88; BiDAmSp BB; BioIn 3, 4, 5, 7, 8, 9, 10, 11, 12, 13, 14, 15, 16, 17, 19, 20; CelR 90; CmCal; ConAu 108, 130; CurBio 76, 90, 90N; LegTOT; News 88, 90, 90-2; NewYTBE 72, 73; NewYTBS 74, 75, 77, 83, 85, 89; WhAm 10; WhoAm 74, 76, 78, 80, 82, 84, 86, 88; WhoProB 73; WhoSpor; WorAl; WorAlBi*

Martin, David Stone
American. Illustrator
Best known for his *Time* magazine covers and over 400 jazz album covers; illustrations for *Cross-Fire: A Vietnam Novel,* 1972.
b. Jun 13, 1913 in Chicago, Illinois
d. Mar 6, 1992 in New London, Connecticut
Source: *AnObit 1992; BioIn 15, 19; IlrAm 1880, F; IlsBYP; IlsCB 1946; SmATA 39; WhAm 10; WhAmArt 85; WhoAm 86, 88, 90; WhoGrA 62*

Martin, Dean
[Dino Crocetti]
American. Singer, Actor
Crooner best known for comedy films with Jerry Lewis, 1946-56; starred in 1960s-70s TV series.
b. Jun 17, 1917 in Steubenville, Ohio
d. Dec 25, 1995 in Beverly Hills, California
Source: *BiDAmM; BiDFilm, 81, 94; BioIn 1, 2, 4, 5, 6, 7, 8, 9, 10, 11, 16; BkPepl; BlueB 76; CelR, 90; CmMov; CmpEPM; ConMus 1; ConTFT 8, 15; CurBio 64, 96N; EncAFC; FilmEn; FilmgC; ForYSC; Funs; HalFC 80, 84,*

88; IntDcF 1-3, 2-3; IntMPA 75, 76, 77, 78, 79, 80, 81, 82, 84, 86, 88, 92, 94, 96; IntWW 79, 80, 81, 82, 83, 89, 91, 93; ItaFilm; LegTOT; LesBEnT, 92; MotPP; MovMk; NewAmDM; NewGrDA 86; News 96, 96-2; NewYTBS 95; OxCFilm; OxCPMus; PenEncP; RadStar; RkOn 74; VarWW 85; WhoAm 74, 76, 78, 80, 82, 84, 86, 88, 90, 92, 94, 95, 96; WhoEnt 92; WhoHol 92, A; WhoHrs 80; WhoWor 74; WorAl; WorAlBi; WorEFlm

Martin, Dean Paul
[Dino, Desi, and Billy]
"Dino Martin, Jr"
American. Actor
Son of Dean Martin; formed successful rock group with Desi Arnaz, Jr. as teen; in film *Players,* 1979; killed piloting Air Force jet.
b. Nov 17, 1951 in Santa Monica, California
d. Mar 21, 1987 in Riverside, California
Source: *ConNews 87-3; ForYSC; WhoHol A*

Martin, Del
American. Writer
Co-authored, with Phyllis Lyon, *Lesbian Love and Liberation,* 1973.
b. 1921
Source: *AmWomWr; BioIn 20; FemiWr; GayLesB; GayLL; LNinSix; WrDr 96*

Martin, Dick
[Rowan and Martin]
American. Comedian
Co-host of "Laugh-In," 1967-73.
b. Jan 30, 1923 in Battle Creek, Michigan
Source: *BioIn 8, 10, 16; BioNews 74; CurBio 69; Dun&B 90; FilmgC; HalFC 80, 84, 88; ScF&FL 92; VarWW 85; WhoAm 86; WhoHol 92, A; WorAl; WorAlBi*

Martin, Fletcher
American. Artist
Subject matter ranged from rodeo, baseball, racing; painted N African warfront scenes for *Life* magazine.
b. Apr 29, 1904 in Palisade, Colorado
d. May 30, 1979 in Guanajuato, Mexico
Source: *BioIn 1, 2, 3, 4, 5, 7, 11, 12; CurBio 58, 79, 79N; DcCAA 71, 77; IlBEAAW; McGDA; NewYTBS 79; WhAm 7; WhAmArt 85; WhoAm 74, 76, 78, 80; WhoAmA 73, 76, 78, 80N, 82N, 84N, 86N, 89N, 91N, 93N*

Martin, Frank
Swiss. Composer
Wrote oratorio *Le Vin Herbe,* 1941; opera *Der Sturm,* 1956.
b. Sep 15, 1890 in Geneva, Switzerland
d. Nov 21, 1974 in Naarden, Netherlands
Source: *Baker 78, 84, 92; BioIn 1, 2, 3, 4, 5, 6, 8, 9, 10, 17; BriBkM 80; CmOp; CnOxB; CompSN, SUP; DcCM; DcCom&M 79; FacFETw; IntWW 74; LegTOT; MetOEnc; MusMk; NewAmDM; NewEOp 71; NewGrDM 80; NewGrDO; NewOxM; ObitT 1971; OxCMus; OxDcOp; PenDiMP A; WhAm 6; WhDW; Who 74; WhoMus 72*

Martin, Freddy
American. Bandleader
Band leader, 1932-83; theme song was hit "Tonight We Love," 1941.
b. Dec 9, 1906 in Cleveland, Ohio
d. Sep 30, 1983 in Newport Beach, California
Source: *AnObit 1983; Baker 84; BiDAmM; BioIn 12, 13; CmpEPM; NewYTBS 83; OxCPMus; PenEncP; RadStar; VarWW 85; WhoHol A*

Martin, George
"Fifth Beatle"
English. Producer
Produced all of The Beatles' albums; scored music for film *Sgt. Pepper's Lonely Hearts Club Band.*
b. Jan 3, 1926 in London, England
Source: *AuBYP 3; BioIn 12; ConAu 3NR, 21NR; ConMuA 80A, 80B; ConMus 6; ConTFT 8; EncRk 88; HarEnR 86; IlEncRk; OxCPMus; PenEncP; RkOn 78, 84; Who 92; WhoAm 74, 78, 80, 82, 84, 86, 88; WhoUSWr 88; WhoWrEP 89*

Martin, Glenn Luther
American. Aircraft Manufacturer
Made first over-water flight in US, 1912; constructed B-10 bombers, 1932.
b. Jan 17, 1886 in Macksburg, Iowa
d. Dec 4, 1955 in Baltimore, Maryland
Source: *BiDAmBL 83; BioIn 1, 2, 4, 7, 8, 11; CurBio 43, 56; DcAmB S5; InSci; WebAB 74, 79; WhAm 3; WorAl*

Martin, Harold Eugene
American. Newspaper Publisher
Editor, publisher *Montgomery Advertiser,* 1970-78; won Pulitzer for reporting, 1970.
b. Oct 4, 1923 in Cullman, Alabama
Source: *Dun&B 88; WhoAm 74, 76, 78, 84, 86, 88, 90, 92, 94, 95, 96, 97; WhoFI 85; WhoSSW 73, 84, 86, 88; WhoWor 78, 87, 89*

Martin, Harvey Banks
American. Football Player
Four-time all-pro defensive end, Dallas, 1973-83.
b. Nov 16, 1950 in Dallas, Texas
Source: *BioIn 11, 12, 13, 15, 16; FootReg 81; InB&W 85; WhoBlA 77, 80, 85, 90*

Martin, Homer Dodge
American. Artist
Landscapes featuring aspects of Impressionism include *Normandy Farm.*
b. Nov 28, 1836 in Albany, New York
d. Feb 12, 1897 in Saint Paul, Minnesota
Source: *AmBi; ApCAB; BioIn 11; BriEAA; DcAmArt; DcAmB; EarABI; EncAAH; LinLib S; McGDA; NatCAB 9; NewYHSD; OxCAmL 65; PeoHis; TwCBDA; WebAB 74, 79; WhAmArt 85; WhAm HS*

Martin, James, Sir
English. Engineer
Military aircraft engineer who invented the ejection seat.
b. 1893 in County Down, Northern Ireland
d. Jan 5, 1981, England
Source: *AnObit 1981; BlueB 76; Who 82*

Martin, James Grubbs
American. Politician
Rep. governor of North Carolina, 1985-92.
b. Dec 11, 1935 in Savannah, Georgia
Source: *AlmAP 88; AmMWSc 73P; BiDrUSC 89; BioIn 13; IntWW 89, 91, 93; PolsAm 84; WhoAm 74, 76, 78, 80, 82, 84, 86, 88, 90, 92, 94, 95, 96, 97; WhoAmP 73, 75, 77, 79, 81, 83, 85, 87, 89, 91, 93, 95; WhoGov 75, 77; WhoSSW 76, 78, 80, 82, 84, 86, 88, 91, 93, 95, 97; WhoWor 87, 89, 91, 93, 95, 96, 97*

Martin, James Slattin, Jr.
American. Aeronautical Engineer
Directed $1 billion *Viking* project, most elaborate unmanned exploration of outer space, 1969-75.
b. Jun 21, 1920 in Washington, District of Columbia
Source: *BioIn 11; CurBio 77; NewYTBS 76; WhoGov 75, 77*

Martin, Jared
American. Actor
Played Dusty Farlow on "Dallas," 1979-81, 1985-86.
b. Dec 11, 1949? in New York, New York
Source: *VarWW 85; WhoHol A*

Martin, Jerry Lindsey
American. Baseball Player
Outfielder, 1974-84; pleaded guilty, attempted possession of cocaine, 1983.
b. May 11, 1949 in Columbia, South Carolina
Source: *Ballpl 90*

Martin, Jimmy
American. Singer, Songwriter
Traditional bluegrass performer; organized band Sunny Mountain Boys, 1955.
b. 1927 in Sneedville, Tennessee
Source: *BgBkCoM; BioIn 14; ConMus 5; HarEnCM 87; IlEncCM; PenEncP*

Martin, John
American. Journalist
Influential *NY Times* dance editor, 1927-62.
b. Jun 2, 1893 in Louisville, Kentucky
d. May 19, 1985 in Saratoga Springs, New York

Source: *AmAu&B; AnObit 1985; BioIn 6, 14; CnOxB; ConAu 116; DancEn 78; NewYTBS 85; WhoAm 78*

Martin, John
American. Broadcast Journalist
Correspondent, ABC News, since 1975.
b. Dec 3, 1938 in New York, New York
Source: *Dun&B 90; St&PR 91; Who 92; WhoAm 90; WhoAmL 92; WhoTelC*

Martin, John Bartlow
American. Journalist
Speechwriter for Democratic presidential candidates, 1950s-70s; wrote 15 books.
b. Aug 4, 1915 in Hamilton, Ohio
d. Jan 3, 1987 in Highland Park, Illinois
Source: *AmAu&B; AnObit 1987; Au&Wr 71; BioIn 3, 4, 7, 11, 15, 17; BlueB 76; ConAu 8NR, 13R, 121; CurBio 56, 87, 87N; EncAJ; IntAu&W 76; IntWW 74; LiJour; NewYTBS 87; OhA&B; PolProf K; WhAm 9; WhoAm 78, 80, 82, 84*

Martin, John C
American. Businessman
Pres., Heublein, Inc; popularized vodka in US.
b. 1906 in Coventry, England
d. May 29, 1986 in Naples, Florida
Source: *NewYTBS 86*

Martin, Joseph William, Jr.
American. Politician
Rep. representative from MA, 1925-66; chaired Republican National Convention, 1940-56.
b. Nov 3, 1884 in North Attleboro, Massachusetts
d. Mar 6, 1968 in Fort Lauderdale, Florida
Source: *AmPolLe; BiDrAC; BiDrUSC 89; BioIn 1, 3, 5, 7, 8, 11, 14, 17, 19; CurBio 40, 48, 68; DcAmB S8; FacFETw; NatCAB 57; PolProf E, T; WebAB 74, 79; WhAm 4A; WhAmP*

Martin, Judith
American. Author, Journalist
Author, syndicated newspaper column, "Miss Manners," since 1978; *Miss Manners' Guide to Excruciatingly Correct Behavior,* 1982.
b. Sep 13, 1938 in Washington, District of Columbia
Source: *ArtclWW 2; BioIn 13, 14, 15, 16, 19; CelR 90; ConAu 12NR; CurBio 86; DcLP 87A; EncTwCJ; JrnUS; WhoAm 90; WhoE 91; WhoUSWr 88; WhoWrEP 89, 92, 95; WorAlBi; WrDr 86, 88, 90, 92, 94, 96*

Martin, Kellie
American. Actor
Played Becca in TV series "Life Goes On," 1989-93.
Source: *BioIn 18, 19, 20; WhoAmW 91*

Martin, Kiel
American. Actor
Played JD LaRue on TV series "Hill Street Blues," 1981-87.
b. Jul 26, 1945? in Pittsburgh, Pennsylvania
d. Dec 28, 1990 in Rancho Mirage, California
Source: *ConTFT 7; NewYTBS 91; WhoAm 90; WhoHol A; WhoTelC*

Martin, Kingsley
English. Editor
London editor, *New Statesman,* 1930-60.
b. Jul 28, 1897 in Hertfordshire, England
d. Feb 16, 1969 in Cairo, Egypt
Source: *BioIn 2, 5, 7, 8, 9, 10, 14; ConAu 5R, 11NR, 25R; DcLEL; GrBr; LngCTC; NatCAB 36; NewC; WhAm 6*

Martin, Lynn
[Judith Lynn Morley Martin]
"The Axe"
American. Government Official
Secretary of Labor, 1991-93; congresswoman, 16th IL district, 1981-90.
b. Dec 26, 1939 in Evanston, Illinois
Source: *AlmAP 88; BiDrUSC 89; BioIn 12, 14, 16; CngDr 89, 91; CurBio 89; IntWW 91, 93; News 91; NewYTBS 80; PolsAm 84; WhoAm 90; WhoAmP 89; WhoAmW 81, 91; WhoMW 88*

Martin, Mary
American. Actor, Singer
Starred in long-running Broadway plays *South Pacific, The Sound of Music,* and *Peter Pan,* with favorite role that of Peter Pan; won Tonys for all three; mother of Larry Hagman.
b. Dec 1, 1913 in Weatherford, Texas
d. Nov 3, 1990 in Rancho Mirage, California
Source: *AnObit 1990; BiDAmM; BiE&WWA; BioIn 12, 13, 14, 15, 16, 17; BlueB 76; CamGWoT; CelR, 90; CmpEPM; CnThe; ConAu 111, 113, 132; ConTFT 11; CurBio 44, 91N; EncAFC; EncMT; EncWB; EncWT; FacFETw; FamA&A; Film 1; FilmEn; FilmgC; ForYSC; HalFC 80, 84, 88; IntMPA 88; InWom, SUP; LegTOT; LibW; LinLib S; MotPP; MovMk; NewAmDM; NewGrDA 86; News 91, 91-2; NewYTBE 71; NewYTBS 90; NewYTET; NotNAT; NotWoAT; OxCAmT 84; OxCFilm; OxCPMus; OxCThe 83; PenEncP; PlP&P; RadStar; WhAm 10; WhoAm 74, 76, 78, 80, 82, 84, 86, 88, 90; WhoAmW 58, 61, 64, 66, 68, 70, 72, 74, 83; WhoHol A; WhoThe 72, 77, 81; WhoWor 74; WorAl; WorAlBi*

Martin, Millicent
English. Singer, Actor
Broadway performances include *King of Hearts,* 1978.
b. Jun 8, 1934 in Romford, England
Source: *ConTFT 7; EncMT; FilmEn; FilmgC; ForYSC; HalFC 80, 84, 88; IlWWBF; IntMPA 77, 80, 92, 94, 96; OxCPMus; VarWW 85; WhoEnt 92; WhoHol 92, A; WhoThe 72, 77, 81*

Martin, Mungo
Canadian. Artist
Commissioned by the British Columbia government to display his artwork in Beacon Hill Park, after the government reversed its policy on the extinction of Native American art and language.
b. 1879 in Fort Ruport, British Columbia, Canada
d. Aug 16, 1962, Canada
Source: *BioIn 6, 11; MacDCB 78; NotNaAm*

Martin, Pamela Sue
American. Actor
Played Fallon Carrington Colby on TV series "Dynasty," 1981-84.
b. Jan 5, 1954 in Westport, Connecticut
Source: *BioIn 13, 14; ConTFT 6; HalFC 88; IntMPA 92; VarWW 85; WhoHol A*

Martin, Pepper
[John Leonard Roosevelt Martin]
"The Wild Hoss of the Osage"
American. Baseball Player
Outfielder-third baseman, St. Louis, 1928, 1930-40, 1944; known for defensive play, heroics in 1931 World Series.
b. Feb 29, 1904 in Temple, Oklahoma
d. Mar 5, 1965 in McAlester, Oklahoma
Source: *Ballpl 90; BioIn 15; LegTOT; WhoProB 73; WhoSpor*

Martin, Pit
[Hubert Jacques Martin]
Canadian. Hockey Player
Center, 1961-79, mostly with Chicago; won Masterton Trophy, 1970.
b. Dec 9, 1943 in Rouyn Noranda, Quebec, Canada
Source: *BioIn 10; HocEn; WhoHcky 73*

Martin, Quinn
[Martin Cohen, Jr.]
American. Producer
One of TV's most successful producers; QM Productions produced 16 network shows, including "The Fugitive;" "Streets of San Francisco;" "Cannon."
b. May 22, 1927 in Los Angeles, California
d. Sep 5, 1987 in Rancho Santa Fe, California
Source: *ConTFT 5; Dun&B 79; LesBEnT; NewYTET; VarWW 85; WhoAm 86; WhoTelC*

Martin, Rick
[Richard Lionel Martin]
Canadian. Hockey Player
Left wing, 1971-82, mostly with Buffalo on high-scoring French Connection Line with Gilbert Perreault, Rene Robert; known for hard, accurate shot.
b. Jul 26, 1951 in Montreal, Quebec, Canada

Source: *BioIn 9, 10, 11; HocEn; WhoAm 74; WhoHcky 73*

Martin, Robert Bernard
[Robert Bernard]
American. Author, Educator
Books include *The Triumph of Wit: Victorian Comic Theory*, 1974; *Tennyson: The Unique Heart*, 1980.
b. Sep 11, 1918 in La Harpe, Illinois
Source: *Au&Wr 71; ChhPo; ConAu 1R, 2NR, 25NR; DcLP 87A; DrAS 74E, 78E, 82E; IntAu&W 77, 82, 86, 89, 91, 93; WhoUSWr 88; WhoWrEP 89, 92, 95; WrDr 76, 80, 82, 84, 86, 88, 90, 92, 94, 96*

Martin, Ross
[Martin Rosenblatt]
American. Actor
Played Artemus Gordon on "The Wild, Wild West," 1965-69.
b. Mar 22, 1920 in Gradek, Poland
d. Jul 3, 1981 in Ramona, California
Source: *AnObit 1981; BioIn 12; FilmEn; FilmgC; ForYSC; HalFC 80, 84, 88; IntMPA 77, 79, 80; LegTOT; MotPP; NewYTBS 81; WhoAm 74; WhoHol A; WhoHrs 80; WhScrn 83; WorAl*

Martin, Slater
"Dugie"
American. Basketball Player
Guard, 1949-60, mostly with Minneapolis; won five NBA championships; Hall of Fame.
b. Oct 22, 1925 in Houston, Texas
Source: *BasBi; BiDAmSp BK; BioIn 5, 6, 8; OfNBA 87; WhoBbl 73*

Martin, Steve
American. Comedian, Actor
Won two Grammys for comedy albums, 1977, 1978; films include *Roxanne*, 1987; *Parentohood*, 1989; *Father of the Bride*, 1991; *Leap of Faith;* 1992 *Father of the Bride, Part II*, 1995.
b. Aug 14, 1945 in Waco, Texas
Source: *BiDFilm 94; BioIn 11, 12, 13, 14, 15, 16, 17, 18, 19, 20; BkPepl; CelR 90; ConAu 30NR, 97; ConLC 30; ConMuA 80A; ConTFT 5, 12; CurBio 78; EncAFC; FacFETw; HalFC 84, 88; IntDcF 2-3; IntMPA 82, 84, 86, 88, 92, 94, 96; IntWW 91; JoeFr; LegTOT; LesBEnT 92; MajTwCW; News 92, 92-2; QDrFCA 92; RkOn 85; VarWW 85; WhoAm 86, 90, 94, 95, 96, 97; WhoEnt 92; WhoHol 92; WorAlBi*

Martin, Strother
American. Actor
Character actor, 1950-80; films include *Harper*, 1966; *Cool Hand Luke*, 1967; *True Grit*, 1969.
b. Mar 26, 1919 in Kokomo, Indiana
d. Aug 1, 1980 in Thousand Oaks, California
Source: *BioIn 12, 13; CmMov; EncAFC; FilmEn; FilmgC; IntDcF 1-3; IntMPA 77; LegTOT; WhoAm 74; WhoHol A; WhScrn 83*

Martin, Tony
[Alfred Norris, Jr.]
American. Singer, Actor
Popular big-band era baritone; husband of Cyd Charisse.
b. Dec 25, 1913 in San Francisco, California
Source: *ASCAP 66; BioIn 3, 4, 10, 11; EncAFC; FilmgC; ForYSC; HalFC 84, 88; IntMPA 75, 76, 77, 78, 79, 80, 81, 82, 84, 86, 88, 92, 94, 96; PenEncP; RkOn 74; VarWW 85; WhoAm 74, 76, 78, 80, 82, 84, 90; WhoHol 92; WorAl; WorAlBi*

Martin, Valerie
American. Author
Author of Neo-Gothic books; wrote *Mary Reilly*, 1990.
b. Apr 14, 1948 in Sedalia, Missouri
Source: *AmWomWr SUP; BestSel 90-2; ConAu 49NR, 85; ConLC 89; ScF&FL 92; WrDr 90, 92, 94, 96*

Martin, William McChesney, Jr.
American. Government Official
Chm., Federal Reserve Board, 1951-70.
b. Dec 17, 1906 in Saint Louis, Missouri
Source: *BioIn 1, 2, 3, 4, 5, 6, 7, 8, 9, 10, 11, 12, 14, 17; BlueB 76; CurBio 51; EncABHB 7; EncWB; IntWW 74, 75, 76, 77, 78, 79, 80, 81, 82, 83; NewYTBS 85; PolProf E, J, K, NF, T; Who 74, 82, 83, 85, 88, 90, 92, 94; WhoAm 74, 76, 78, 80, 82, 84, 86; WhoGov 72; WhoSSW 73; WhoWor 74; WorAl; WorAlBi*

Martindale, Wink
[Winston Conrad Martindale]
American. TV Personality
Host of numerous game shows including "Tic Tac Dough."
b. Dec 4, 1934 in Bells, Tennessee
Source: *RkOn 74, 78; VarWW 85; WhoRock 81*

Martin du Gard, Roger
French. Author, Dramatist
Wrote long novel *Les Thibault*, 1922-40; won Nobel Prize, 1937.
b. Mar 22, 1881 in Neuilly-sur-Seine, France
d. Aug 22, 1958 in Belleme, France
Source: *AtlBL; Benet 87, 96; BiDMoPL; BioIn 1, 4, 5, 6, 7, 8, 15, 16; CasWL; ClDMEL 47, 80; CnMWL; ConAu 118; CyWA 58; DcArts; DcLB 65; DcTwCCu 2; EncWL, 2, 3; EvEuW; FacFETw; GuFrLit 1; LinLib L, S; McGEWB; McGEWD 72, 84; ModFrL; ModRL; NobelP; Novels; OxCEng 67; OxCFr; PenC EUR; REn; RfGWoL 95; TwCA, SUP; TwCLC 24; TwCWr; WhAm 3; WhDW; WhoNob, 90, 95; WhoTwCL; WorAl; WorAlBi*

Martinelli, Elsa
Italian. Actor
Discovered by Kirk Douglas; starred with him in *The Indian Fighter*, 1954; became fashion designer, 1975.
b. Aug 3, 1933 in Rome, Italy
Source: *BioIn 17; FilmgC; ForYSC; HalFC 80, 84, 88; MotPP; MovMk; WhoFI 85; WhoHol 92, A; WhoWor 84; WorEFlm*

Martinelli, Giovanni
American. Opera Singer
Sang over 50 tenor roles with NY Met., 1913-46; starred with Flagstad, 1939.
b. Oct 22, 1885 in Montagnana, Italy
d. Feb 2, 1969 in New York, New York
Source: *Baker 78, 84, 92; BiDAmM; BioIn 1, 2, 3, 4, 6, 8, 11, 12, 14, 18; CmOp; CurBio 45, 69; DcAmB S8; FacFETw; LinLib S; MetOEnc; MusSN; NewEOp 71; NewGrDA 86; NewGrDM 80; NewGrDO; OxDcOp; PenDiMP; WhAm 5; What 2; WhScrn 83*

Martinez, A(dolpe)
American. Actor
Played Cruz Castillo in TV soap "Santa Barbara," 1984-92.
b. Sep 27, 1949? in Glendale, California
Source: *DcHiB; WhoHol 92*

Martinez, Andrew
"Naked Guy"
American. Student
Attended classes nude at U of CA at Berkeley, 1992.
b. 1972
Source: *WhoHisp 92*

Martinez, Bob
[Robert Martinez]
American. Politician
Republican and first Hispanic governor of FL, 1987-91; succeeded by Lawton Chiles; director, Office of Nat. Drug Control Policy, 1991—.
b. Dec 25, 1934 in Tampa, Florida
Source: *AlmAP 88; BiDrGov 1983, 1988; BioIn 17, 18, 19, 20; CopCroC; DcHiB; HispAmA; IntWW 89, 91, 93; News 92, 92-1; WhoAm 88, 90, 92; WhoAmP 85, 87, 89, 91, 93, 95; WhoE 93; WhoHisp 91, 92, 94; WhoSSW 73, 75, 76, 82, 86, 88, 91; WhoWor 89, 91, 93*

Martinez, Eugenio R
Cuban.
Miami-based Cuban hired to break into Democratic headquarters in Watergate, 1972.
b. 1922
Source: *BioIn 10, 12, 13*

Martinez, Joseph V
American. Scientist
Research scientist, US Dept. of Energy, 1974—.

Martinez, Maria Montoya
American. Artist
Helped bring about the revival of indigenous pottery-making techniques.
b. 1887? in New Mexico
d. 1980

Source: *BioIn 15, 16, 17, 20; InWom SUP; NotNaAm*

Martinez Sierra, Gregorio
Spanish. Dramatist
Plays include *The Cradle Song,* 1917.
b. May 6, 1881 in Madrid, Spain
d. Oct 1, 1947 in Madrid, Spain
Source: *Benet 87, 96; BioIn 1, 3, 4, 5; CasWL; CathA 1952; CIDMEL 47, 80; CnMD; CnThe; ConAu 104, 115; CyWA 58; DcSpL; EncWL 2, 3; Ent; EvEuW; LinLib L; LngCTC; McGEWD 72, 84; ModRL; ModSpP S; ModWD; NotNAT B; OxCSpan; OxCThe 67, 83; PenC EUR; REn; TwCA, SUP; TwCLC 6; TwCWr*

Martini, Nino
American. Opera Singer
Tenor with NY Met., 1933-46; film appearances include *The Gay Desperado,* 1936.
b. Aug 8, 1905? in Verona, Italy
d. Dec 9, 1976 in Verona, Italy
Source: *Baker 84; BioIn 4, 11; FilmgC; RadStar*

Martini, Simone
Italian. Artist
Influential Sienese painter noted for color, decorative lines; works include *Annunciation Triptych,* 1333.
b. 1284? in Siena, Italy
d. 1344 in Avignon, Italy
Source: *AtlBL; BioIn 14; IntDcAA 90; WebBD 83; WhDW*

Martino, Al
[Alfred Cini]
American. Actor, Singer
Starred in, sang theme song, *The Godfather,* 1972.
b. Nov 7, 1927 in Philadelphia, Pennsylvania
Source: *EncPR&S 74; LegTOT; PenEncP; RkOn 74; WhoHol 92; WorAl*

Martino, Pat
[Pat Azzara]
American. Musician
Jazz guitarist who toured with Lloyd Price, 1960-1965; replaced George Benson in Jack McDuff's band, 1965; released debut album, *El Hombre,* 1967 and later *The Return,* 1989, *Interchange,* 1995 and *Nightwings,* 1996.
b. Aug 25, 1944 in Philadelphia, Pennsylvania
Source: *AllMusG; BiDJaz; BioIn 15, 16, 21; ConMus 17; EncJzS; NewGrDA 86; NewGrDJ 88, 94; OnThGG*

Martinon, Jean
French. Conductor, Composer
Directed Chicago Symphony, 1963-68; wrote opera *Hecube.*
b. Jan 10, 1910 in Lyons, France
d. Mar 1, 1976 in Paris, France
Source: *Baker 78, 84, 92; BioIn 3, 6, 7, 8, 10, 11; BriBkM 80; CompSN, SUP; DcCM; IntWW 74, 75; LinLib S; MusSN; NewAmDM; NewGrDM 80; OxCMus; PenDiMP; WhAm 6; WhoAm 74; WhoMus 72; WhoWor 74*

Martins, Peter
Danish. Dancer, Choreographer
Joined NYC Ballet, 1967; co-ballet master-in-chief, 1983-89; master-in-chief, 1989—.
b. Oct 11, 1946 in Copenhagen, Denmark
Source: *BiDD; BioIn 11, 12, 13, 14, 15; CnOxB; ConAu 113; CurBio 78; DcArts; FacFETw; IntDcB; IntWW 89, 91, 93; LegTOT; NewYTBS 83; RAdv 14; WhoAm 78, 80, 82, 84, 86, 88, 90, 92, 94, 95, 96, 97; WhoE 85, 86, 89, 91, 93, 95, 97; WhoEnt 92; WhoHol 92; WhoWor 95, 97; WorAlBi*

Martinson, Harry Edmund
Swedish. Poet
Won 1974 Nobel Prize for poetry; best-known poem is "Aniara."
b. May 6, 1905 in Jamshog, Sweden
d. Feb 11, 1978 in Stockholm, Sweden
Source: *CasWL; CIDMEL 47; ConAu 77; ConLC 14; EncWL; EvEuW; NewCol 75; PenC EUR; TwCWr; WhoNob; WhoTwCL; WorAu 1950*

Martinson, Joseph Bertram
American. Business Executive, Art Patron
Chairman, Martinson Coffee, 1950-61; founded Museum of American Folk Art, NYC.
b. Jul 24, 1911 in New York, New York
d. Oct 30, 1970, Singapore
Source: *BiE&WWA; BioIn 9; NewYTBE 70*

Martinu, Bohuslav
Czech. Composer
Wrote six symphonies, chamber music, radio operas, ballet *Istar,* 1921.
b. Dec 8, 1890 in Policka, Bohemia
d. Aug 28, 1959 in Liestal, Switzerland
Source: *AtlBL; Baker 78, 84; BiDAmM; BioIn 1, 2, 4, 5, 6, 7, 8, 10, 11, 12, 13; BriBkM 80; CmOp; CnOxB; CompSN, SUP; ConAmC 76, 82; CurBio 44, 59; DcCM; DcCom 77; DcCom&M 79; DcTwCC; FacFETw; IntDcOp; McGEWB; MetOEnc; MusMk; NewAmDM; NewEOp 71; NewGrDA 86; NewGrDM 80; NewOxM; OxCMus; OxDcOp; PenDiMP A; WhAm 3; WhDW*

Martin y Soler, Vicente
Spanish. Composer
Collaborations with librettist, Da Ponte, include opera *Una Cosa Rara,* 1786.
b. Jan 18, 1754 in Valencia, Spain
d. Jan 30, 1806 in Saint Petersburg, Russia
Source: *Baker 78, 84, 92; IntDcOp; MusMk; NewAmDM; NewEOp 71; NewGrDM 80; NewOxM; OxDcOp*

Marty, Martin
"Angel of the West"
Swiss. Missionary
Roman Catholic abbot, later bishop, known for extensive preaching to Sioux Indians in Dakotas; became vicar apostolic of Territory, 1879.
b. Jan 12, 1834 in Schwyz, Switzerland
d. Sep 19, 1896 in Saint Cloud, Minnesota
Source: *ApCAB; BioIn 12; DcAmB; DcCathB; DcNAA; NatCAB 12; WhAm HS*

Marty, Martin Emil
American. Author, Historian
Extensive works on religion include *Righteous Empire,* 1970; columnist for the *Christian Century.*
b. Feb 5, 1928 in West Point, Nebraska
Source: *BioIn 7, 8, 9, 12, 15, 16; ConAu 5R, 21NR; CurBio 68; DrAS 74H, 78H, 82H; EncTwCJ; EncWB; IntAu&W 91; IntWW 91; PeoHis; RelLAm 91; WhoAm 74, 76, 78, 80, 82, 84, 86, 88, 90, 92, 94, 95, 96, 97; WhoMW 93, 96; WhoRel 75, 77, 85, 92; WhoWor 74, 96; WorAu 1975; WrDr 86, 92*

Martyn, Bruce
American. Sportscaster
Detroit Red Wings radio sportscaster, 1964-95; Hockey Hall of Fame, 1991.

Martyn, John
Scottish. Singer, Musician
Guitarist; albums include *Sapphire,* 1984.
b. Jun 28, 1946 in Glasgow, Scotland
Source: *ConMuA 80A; EncRk 88; HarEnR 86; IlEncRk; PenEncP; RolSEnR 83; WhoRocM 82*

Marvelettes, The
[Katherine Anderson; Juanita Cowart; Gladys Horton; Georgeanna Tillman; Wanda Young]
American. Music Group
Motown rock group's hit singles include "Please Mr. Postman," 1961; "Beechwood 4-5789," 1962.
Source: *BiDAmM; EncPR&S 89; EncRk 88; InB&W 80, 85A; NewGrDA 86; PenEncP; RkOn 74, 82; RolSEnR 83; SoulM; WhoRock 81; WhoRocM 82*

Marvell, Andrew
English. Author, Poet, Politician
Great metaphysical poet; verse includes "To His Coy Mistress."
b. Mar 31, 1621 in Winestead, England
d. Aug 18, 1678 in London, England
Source: *Alli; AtlBL; BbD; Benet 87, 96; BiD&SB; BiDRP&D; BioIn 1, 2, 3, 4, 5, 7, 8, 9, 10, 11, 12, 13, 14, 15, 18, 19, 21; BlmGEL; BritAu; BritWr 2; CamGEL; CamGLE; CanWr; Chambr 1; ChhPo, S1, S2; CnDBLB 2; CnE&AP; CroE&S; CrtT 1, 4; CyWA 58; DcArts; DcEnA; DcEnL; DcEuL; DcLB 131; DcLEL; DcNaB; EvLB; GrWrEL P; LegTOT; LitC 4; LngCEL; MagSWL; McGEWB; MouLC 1; NewC; NewCBEL; NewCol 75; OxCEng 67, 85, 95; PenC*

ENG; PoeCrit 10; RAdv 1, 14, 13-1; REn; RfGEnL 91; RGFBP; WebE&AL; WhDW; WorAl; WorAlBi; WorLitC

Marvin, Lee
American. Actor
Tough-guy actor in 45 films; won Oscar, 1965, for *Cat Balou;* part of fir st "palimony" lawsuit, 1979.
b. Feb 19, 1924 in New York, New York
d. Aug 29, 1987 in Tucson, Arizona
Source: *AnObit 1987; BiDFilm, 81, 94; BioIn 7, 8, 9, 10, 11, 12, 15, 20; BkPepl; BlueB 76; CelR; CmMov; ConNews 88-1; ConTFT 3, 5; CurBio 66, 87, 87N; DcArts; FilmEn; FilmgC; ForYSC; GangFlm; HalFC 80, 84, 88; IntDcF 1-3, 2-3; IntMPA 75, 76, 77, 78, 79, 80, 81, 82, 84, 86; IntWW 79, 80, 81, 82, 83; LegTOT; MotPP; MovMk; NewYTBS 87; OxCFilm; VarWW 85; WhAm 9; WhoAm 74, 76, 78, 80, 82, 84, 86; WhoHol A; WhoWor 74; WorAl; WorAlBi; WorEFlm*

Marvin, Michelle Triola
American.
Live-in lover of Lee Marvin, responsible for first palimony case involving unmarried couples and property rights, 1979.
b. 1932?
Source: *BioIn 11, 12*

Marx, Anne Loewenstein
American. Poet
Poems include "Face Lifts for All Seasons," 1980; "45 Love Poems for 45 Years," 1982.
Source: *ConAu 12NR, 30NR; DrAPF 91; IntAu&W 86; WhoAm 74, 86, 90; WhoAmW 66, 68, 70, 72, 74*

Marx, Chico
[The Marx Brothers; Leonard Marx]
American. Comedian
Known for outrageous puns, exaggerated accent.
b. Mar 22, 1891 in New York, New York
d. Oct 11, 1961 in Hollywood, California
Source: *BioIn 1, 6, 9, 10, 11, 12, 18; CamGWoT; CmCal; CurBio 48, 61; DcAmB S7; DcFM; EncMT; EncVaud; FamA&A; Film 2; ForYSC; JoeFr; MGM; MotPP; MovMk; NotNAT B; ObitT 1961; OxCFilm; WhoHol B; WhScrn 74, 77, 83*

Marx, Groucho
[The Marx Brothers; Julius Henry Marx]
American. Comedian
Famous for ad-lib insults, radio-TV series "You Bet Your Life;" wrote autobiograph y *Groucho and Me,* 1959.
b. Oct 2, 1890 in New York, New York
d. Aug 19, 1977 in Los Angeles, California
Source: *BiDFilm 81, 94; BiE&WWA; BioIn 9, 10, 11, 12, 13; BioNews 74; BlueB 76; ConAu 73, 81; CurBio 48, 73, 77, 77N; DcAmB S10; DcArts; DcFM; EncAB-H 1996; EncMT; Ent; FacFETw; FamA&A; ForYSC; Funs; HalFC 80, 84; IntAu&W 77; IntMPA 77; IntWW 74, 75, 76, 77; JeHun; LegTOT; MotPP; NewYTBE 70; NewYTBS 77; OxCFilm; RadStar; SaTiSS; WhDW; WhoHol A; WhoWor 74; WhScrn 83*

Marx, Gummo
[The Marx Brothers; Milton Marx]
American. Agent, Comedian
Left Marx Brothers early to become business manager for act.
b. Oct 23, 1893 in New York, New York
d. Apr 21, 1977 in Palm Springs, California
Source: *BiE&WWA; DcAmB S10; FacFETw; FilmEn; HalFC 80, 84*

Marx, Harpo
[The Marx Brothers; Arthur Marx]
American. Comedian
Harp-playing, non-speaking member; autobiography *Harpo Speaks,* 1961.
b. Nov 23, 1893 in New York, New York
d. Sep 28, 1964 in Hollywood, California
Source: *ASCAP 66, 80; BiE&WWA; BioIn 1, 5, 6, 7, 9, 10, 11, 12; CamGWoT; CmCal; ConAu 113; CurBio 48, 64; DcFM; EncMT; EncVaud; FamA&A; Film 2; ForYSC; JoeFr; MGM; MotPP; MovMk; NotNAT B; ObitT 1961; OxCFilm; WhoHol B; WhScrn 74, 77, 83*

Marx, Karl Heinrich
German. Political Leader, Philosopher
Originator of idea of modern communism called Marxism; wrote *Communist Manifesto,* 1848.
b. May 5, 1818 in Treves, Prussia
d. Mar 14, 1883 in London, England
Source: *BiD&SB; BiDMarx; BiDPsy; CasWL; CyWA 58; DcScB, S1; EncEth; EuAu; LngCEL; LngCTC; LuthC 75; McGEWB; NamesHP; NewCol 75; OxCEng 85; OxCFr; OxCGer 76, 86; OxCLaw; OxCPhil; RAdv 14; RComWL; REn; WebBD 83; WhAm HS*

Marx, Richard
American. Singer
Pop singer; had hit single "Endless Summer Nights," 1988.
b. Sep 16, 1963 in Chicago, Illinois
Source: *BioIn 15, 16; CelR 90; ConMus 3; EncRkSt; LegTOT*

Marx, Zeppo
[The Marx Brothers; Herbert Marx]
American. Comedian
Romantic straight man of act; later a successful agent.
b. Feb 25, 1901 in New York, New York
d. Nov 30, 1979 in Palm Springs, California
Source: *BiE&WWA; BioIn 11, 12, 19; CamGWoT; DcAmB S10; DcArts; EncAB-H 1996; EncMT; FacFETw; FamA&A; Film 2; FilmEn; ForYSC; Funs; HalFC 80, 84; JoeFr; LegTOT; MGM; MovMk; OxCFilm; What 4; WhoHol A; WhScrn 83; WorAl; WorAlBi*

Marx Brothers, The
["Chico" (Leonard) Marx; "Groucho" (Julius) Marx; "Gummo" (Milton) Marx; "Harpo" (Arthur) Marx; "Zeppo" (Herbert) Marx]
American. Comedy Team
Starred in *Duck Soup,* 1933; *A Night at the Opera,* 1935.
Source: *AmCulL; BiDFilm; BioIn 2, 4, 6, 7, 8, 9, 10, 11, 12, 13, 14, 15, 16, 17, 19, 20, 21; CamGWoT; CmCal; CmMov; CmpEPM; ConAu X; DcFM; EncAFC; EncMT; FacFETw; FamA&A; FilmEn; FilmgC; ForYSC; Funs; GrMovC; HalFC 80, 84, 88; IntDcF 1-3, 2-3; JeAmHC; JoeFr; McGEWB; MGM; MotPP; MovMk; NotNAT A; OxCAmH; OxCAmT 84; OxCFilm; QDrFCA 92; RAdv 13-3; WhoCom; WhScrn 83; WorEFlm*

Mary
[Victoria Mary Augusta Louise Olga]
English. Consort
Married George V, 1893; mother of Edward VIII, George VI; grandmother of Queen Elizabeth II.
b. May 26, 1867 in London, England
d. Mar 24, 1953 in London, England
Source: *BioIn 1, 2, 3, 5, 9, 10, 11, 12, 14, 15, 17; DcNaB 1951; GrBr; InWom; NewCol 75; ObitT 1951; WebBD 83*

Mary, Queen of Scots
[Mary Stuart]
Scottish. Ruler
Inherited Scottish throne at age of six days; beheaded by Elizabeth I.
b. Dec 7, 1542 in Linlithgow, Scotland
d. Feb 8, 1587 in Fotheringhay Castle, England
Source: *Alli; Benet 87; BioIn 3, 4, 5, 6, 7, 8, 9, 10, 11, 12, 13, 14, 15, 16, 17, 18, 20, 21; ChhPo S1; CmScLit; ContDcW 89; DcNaB; Dis&D; EncBrWW; GoodHs; HerW, 84; HisWorL; IntDcWB; InWom, SUP; McGEWB; NewC; NewCol 75; OxCEng 95; OxCFr; OxCMus; REn; WebBD 83; WomFir; WorAl; WorAlBi*

Mary, The, Virgin Mother
"Immaculate Mary"; "Our Lady"; "The Blessed Mother"
Roman. Religious Figure
Mother of Jesus Christ; with him at Crucifixion, with apostles at Pentecost; venerated by Christians, especially Roman Catholics.
b. 1st cent. BC, Judea
Source: *Benet 87; BioIn 1, 2, 3, 4, 5, 6, 7, 8, 9, 10, 11, 12, 13, 14, 16, 17, 19, 20; BlmGWL; ChhPo, S2; ContDcW 89; DcBiPP; DcCathB; DcWomA; EncAmaz 91; EncEarC; EncPaPR 91; GoodHs; HerW; InB&W 80; IntDcWB; InWom, SUP; LngCEL; LuthC 75; MacDWB; McGEWB; NewCol 75; ObitOF 79;*

PoIre; REn; WebBD 83; WhoAmW 72; WomWR; WorAl; WorAlBi

Mary Alice
[Mary Alice Smith]
American. Actor
Appeared in film *To Sleep with Anger,* 1990; play *Having Our Say,* 1995.
b. Dec 3, 1941 in Indianola, Mississippi
Source: *BioIn 21; CurBio 95; WhoAm 92, 94, 95, 96, 97; WhoAmW 91, 93, 95, 97; WhoEnt 92*

Mary I
[Mary Tudor]
"Bloody Mary"
English. Ruler
Daughter of Henry VIII and Katharine of Aragon; first English queen to rule in own right.
b. Feb 18, 1516 in Greenwich, England
d. Nov 17, 1558 in London, England
Source: *GoodHs; McGEWB; NewC; NewCol 75; REn; WebBD 83; WomFir*

Mary Magdalene, Saint
[Mary of Magdala]
Roman. Biblical Figure
One of the women who followed, cared for Jesus in Galilee; present at his crucifixion.
Source: *Benet 96; BioIn 3, 8, 17, 20; GoodHs; InWom, SUP; LegTOT; MediFra; NewCol 75; OxDcByz; WebBD 83*

Masaccio
[Tommaso di Giovanni di Simone Cassai]
Italian. Artist
Major figure of Florentine Renaissance; only four works survive; first to use linear perspective in frescoes.
b. Dec 21, 1401 in San Giovanni Valdarno, Italy
d. 1428 in Rome, Italy
Source: *AtlBL; Benet 87, 96; BioIn 1, 2, 3, 4, 5, 7, 8, 11; DcArts; DcBiPP; IntDcAA 90; LegTOT; McGDA; McGEWB; NewCol 75; OxDcArt; REn; WhDW; WorAl*

Masaoka, Tsunenori
[Masaoka Shiki]
Japanese. Poet
Revived haiku, tanka poetic forms; considered best haiku poet of modern times.
b. Oct 14, 1867 in Matsuyama, Japan
d. Sep 19, 1902 in Tokyo, Japan
Source: *Benet 96; CasWL; ConAu 117; FacFETw; TwCLC 18*

Masaryk, Jan Garrigue
Czech. Statesman
Foreign minister in postwar government, 1940-48; son of Tomas.
b. Sep 14, 1886 in Prague, Bohemia
d. Mar 10, 1948 in Prague, Czechoslovakia
Source: *BiDInt; BioIn 1, 2, 4, 8, 11, 12, 13; CurBio 44, 48; WhAm 2; WorAl; WorAlBi*

Masaryk, Tomas Garrigue
Czech. Statesman, Philosopher
Father of modern Czechoslovakia who was first pres., 1918-35.
b. Mar 7, 1850 in Goding, Moravia
d. Sep 14, 1937 in Lany, Czechoslovakia
Source: *BioIn 1, 2, 3, 4, 5, 7, 8, 9, 10, 11, 12, 14, 15, 16, 17, 18, 20; CasWL; ClDMEL 47, 80; DcTwHis; Dis&D; EncRev; EncTR 91; EvEuW; FacFETw; McGEWB; OxCPhil; PenC EUR; REn; WorAlBi*

Mascagni, Pietro
Italian. Composer
Best known for opera *Cavalleria Rusticana,* 1890, in verismo style.
b. Dec 7, 1863 in Leghorn, Italy
d. Aug 2, 1945 in Rome, Italy
Source: *AtlBL; Baker 78, 84, 92; BioIn 1, 2, 3, 4, 6, 8, 11, 12, 17, 21; BriBkM 80; CmOp; CmpBCM; CompSN; CurBio 45; DcArts; DcCom 77; DcCom&M 79; Dis&D; IntDcOp; LegTOT; LinLib S; MetOEnc; MusMk; NewAmDM; NewEOp 71; NewGrDM 80; NewGrDO; NewOxM; OxCMus; OxDcOp; PenDiMP A; REn; WorAl; WorAlBi*

Masefield, John
English. Poet, Dramatist, Author
Poet laureate of England, 1930-67.
b. Jun 1, 1878 in Ledbury, England
d. May 12, 1967 in Berkshire, England
Source: *AnCL; AuBYP 2, 3; Benet 87, 96; BioIn 1, 2, 3, 4, 5, 6, 7, 8, 9, 10, 11, 12, 13, 14, 16, 17, 18, 19, 21; BlmGEL; BritAS; BritPl; CamGEL; CamGLE; CamGWoT; CasWL; Chambr 3; ChhPo, S1, S2, S3; CnDBLB 5; CnE&AP; CnMD; CnMWL; ConAu 25R, 33NR, P-2; ConLC 11, 47; CrtSuDr; DcArts; DcLB 10, 19, 153, 160; DcLEL; EncWL, 2, 3; EngPo; EvLB; GrWrEL P; LegTOT; LinLib L, S; LngCEL; LngCTC; MajTwCW; McGEWD 72, 84; MnBBF; ModBrL, S1; ModWD; NewC; NewCBEL; NotNAT B; Novels; ObitT 1961; OxCChiL; OxCEng 67; OxCThe 67, 83; PenC ENG; PlP&P; RAdv 1, 14, 13-1; REn; RfGEnL 91; ScF&FL 1; SmATA 19; Str&VC; TwCA, SUP; TwCChW 78, 83, 89; TwCRHW 90; TwCWr; WebE&AL; WhAm 4; WhDW; WhE&EA; WhoChL; WhoTwCL; WhThe; WorAl; WorAlBi*

Masekela, Hugh Ramapolo
South African. Musician
Trumpeter whose jazz-rock album *Grazin' in the Grass,* 1968, sold four mi llion copies; co-wrote musical play, *Sarafina!,* 1987.
b. Apr 4, 1939 in Witbank, South Africa
Source: *BioIn 14, 15; ConBlB 1; ConMus 7; CurBio 93; DrBlPA, 90; EncRk 88; IlEncBM 82; IntWW 91; NewGrDJ 88; PenEncP; RkOn 78*

Maserati, Ernesto
Italian. Auto Racer, Auto Manufacturer
Raced cars, 1920s-30s, before founding luxury car company that bears his name.
b. 1898
d. Dec 2, 1975 in Bologna, Italy
Source: *BioIn 10; Entr; LegTOT; NewYTBS 75; ObitOF 79*

Masina, Giulietta
[Mrs. Federico Fellini; Giulia Anna Masina]
Italian. Actor
Married Federico Fellini, 1943; films include *La Strada,* 1956; *Nights of Cabiria,* 1957.
b. Mar 22, 1921 in Bologna, Italy
d. Mar 23, 1994 in Rome, Italy
Source: *BioIn 5, 7, 11, 14, 17, 19, 20; ConLC 16; ContDcW 89; ConTFT 8, 13; FilmEn; FilmgC; HalFC 80, 84, 88; IntDcF 1-3, 2-3; IntMPA 92, 94; IntWW 74, 75, 76, 77, 78, 79, 80, 81, 82, 83, 89, 91, 93; InWom SUP; MovMk; NewYTBS 86; OxCFilm; VarWW 85*

Masire, Quett (Ketumile Joni)
Botswana. Political Leader
President of Botswana. 1980—.
b. Jul 23, 1925 in Kanye, Bechuanaland
Source: *AfSS 81, 82; ConBlB 5; IntWW 81, 82, 83, 89, 91, 93; Who 85, 88, 90, 92, 94; WhoAfr; WhoWor 74, 76, 78, 80, 82, 84, 87, 89, 91, 93, 95, 96, 97*

Maskell, Dan
English. Broadcaster
TV broadcaster for the BBC, 1951-92; tennis commentaries won him worldwide recognition.
b. 1909?

Maskelyne, John Nevil
English. Magician
Noted for exposing the Davenport Brothers as imposter spirtualists, 1865.
b. Dec 22, 1839 in Cheltenham, England
d. May 18, 1917 in London, England
Source: *BioIn 8, 16; CamGWoT; DcNaB MP; EncO&P 2, 3; Ent; MagIlD; NewCol 75; WebBD 83; WhThe*

Maskelyne, Nevil
English. Astronomer
Astronomer royal, from 1765; invented prismatic micrometer; wrote *British Mariner's Guide,* 1763.
b. Oct 6, 1732 in London, England
d. Feb 9, 1811 in London, England
Source: *Alli; BiESc; BioIn 14, 16; DcBiPP; DcInv; DcNaB; DcScB; LarDcSc; NewCol 75; OxCShps; WhDW*

Maslow, Abraham Harold
American. Psychologist
Founder of humanistic psychology, 1940s, emphasizing positive features of man and his capacity for personal growth, achievement.
b. Apr 1, 1908 in New York, New York
d. Jun 8, 1970 in Menlo Park, California

Source: *AmAu&B; BiDAmEd; BiDPsy; BioIn 8, 9, 10, 12, 13; ConAu 1R, 4NR; NamesHP; NewYTBE 70; WhAm 5*

Mason, Belinda
American. Political Activist
Mother who contracted AIDS after delivery from a tainted blood transfusion in 1987, became a Bush adviser on AIDS policy.
b. 1958?
d. Sep 9, 1991 in Nashville, Tennessee
Source: *BioIn 16; NewYTBS 91*

Mason, Biddy
[Bridget Mason]
American. Nurse
Skill as a nurse/midwife led to financial independence; one of the first African-American women to own property in Los Angeles.
b. Aug 15, 1818
d. Jan 15, 1891 in Los Angeles, California
Source: *BioIn 8, 11, 18; BlkWAm; InB&W 85; InWom SUP; NotBlAW 1*

Mason, Bobbie Ann
American. Author
Received the Ernest Hemingway Foundation Award for first fiction in 1983 for works *Shiloh and Other Stories* and *Love Life,* depicting life in Kentucky.
b. May 1, 1940 in Mayfield, Kentucky
Source: *AmWomWr SUP; Au&Arts 5; BenetAL 91; BioIn 14, 15, 16; BlmGWL; ConAu 11NR, 31NR, 53; ConLC 28, 43, 82; ConNov 91, 96; CurBio 89; DcArts; DcLB 173, Y87B; DrAPF 91; IntAu&W 91; LiHiK; MajTwCW; ModWoWr; NewYTBS 88; OxCAmL 95; OxCWoWr 95; RfGAmL 94; RGTwCWr; ShSCr 4; TwCYAW; WhoAm 92, 94, 95, 96, 97; WhoAmW 87, 89, 91, 93, 95, 97; WhoEmL 87, 89; WhoUSWr 88; WhoWrEP 89, 92, 95; WorAu 1980; WrDr 90, 92, 94, 96*

Mason, Charles
English. Surveyor, Astronomer
With Jeremiah Dixon, surveyed boundary between PA and MD known as Mason-Dixon Line, 1768.
b. 1730?, England
d. Feb 1787 in Philadelphia, Pennsylvania
Source: *Alli; ApCAB; BioIn 1, 2, 3, 8, 12; DcNaB; Drake; HarEnUS; NatCAB 10; WebAB 74, 79; WebBD 83; WhDW*

Mason, Daniel Gregory
American. Composer, Author, Educator
Wrote three symphonies, chamber music, piano pieces; grandson of Lowell.
b. Nov 20, 1873 in Brookline, Massachusetts
d. Dec 4, 1953 in Greenwich, Connecticut
Source: *AmAu&B; AmComp; ASCAP 66, 80; Baker 78, 84, 92; BiDAmM; BioIn 1, 3, 4, 7, 8; BriBkM 80; ConAmC 76, 82; DcAmB S5; NatCAB 15; NewAmDM; NewGrDA 86; NewGrDM 80; NewOxM; OxCAmL 65; OxCMus; REnAL; WhAm 3; WhNAA*

Mason, Dave
English. Musician
Guitarist; helped form Traffic, 1967; solo albums include *Alone Together,* 1970.
b. May 10, 1946 in Worcester, England
Source: *ConMuA 80A; EncPR&S 74, 89; EncRk 88; HarEnR 86; IlEncRk; LegTOT; OnThGG; PenEncP; RkOn 74, 78; Who 92; WhoRock 81; WhoRocM 82*

Mason, F(rancis) van Wyck
[Geoffrey Coffin; Frank W Mason; Van Wyck Mason; Ward Weaver]
American. Author
Wrote 58 novels during 40-yr. career; many mysteries contained character Hugh North, an Army intelligence officer: *Secret Mission to Bangkok,* 1960.
b. Nov 11, 1901 in Boston, Massachusetts
d. Aug 28, 1978 in Southampton, Bermuda
Source: *AuBYP 2; BenetAL 91; BioIn 7; ConAu 5R, 8NR, 81, X; DcAmB S10; EncMys; SmATA 3, 26; SpyFic; TwCCr&M 91; TwCRHW 90, 94; WhAm 7*

Mason, George
American. Colonial Figure
Member of Constitutional Convention, 1787; his criticism of document led to Bill of Rights.
b. 1725 in Fairfax County, Virginia
d. Oct 7, 1792 in Fairfax County, Virginia
Source: *AmBi; AmOrN; AmPolLe; AmWrBE; ApCAB; BiAUS; BiDSA; BioIn 3, 5, 6, 7, 8, 9, 10, 11, 12, 13, 15, 16, 17, 18, 19, 20; BlkwEAR; DcAmB; DcAmC; DcAmSR; Drake; EncAAH; EncAB-H 1974, 1996; EncAR; EncCRAm; EncSoH; HarEnUS; McGEWB; NatCAB 3; NewCol 75; OxCAmH; PolPar; RComAH; REnAL; TwCBDA; WebAB 74, 79; WhAm HS; WhAmRev*

Mason, Jackie
[Yacov Moshe Maza]
American. Comedian
Rabbi comedian, star of successful Broadway show, *The World According to Me,* 1986.
b. Jun 9, 1934 in Sheboygan, Wisconsin
Source: *BioIn 10, 15, 16; ConTFT 6; CurBio 87; IntMPA 92, 94, 96; WhoAm 92, 94, 95, 96, 97; WhoEnt 92; WhoHol 92; WorAlBi*

Mason, James Murray
American. Politician
Senator from VA, 1847-61; drafted Fugitive Slave Act, 1850; imprisoned in Trent Affair, 1861-62.
b. Nov 3, 1798 in Fairfax County, Virginia
d. Apr 28, 1871 in Alexandria, Virginia
Source: *AmBi; AmPolLe; ApCAB; BiAUS; BiDConf; BiDrAC; BiDrUSC 89; BiDSA; BioIn 7, 16; CivWDc; DcAmB; DcAmDH 80, 89; Drake; EncSoH; HarEnUS; McGEWB; NatCAB 2; NewCol 75; TwCBDA; WebAB 74, 79; WhAm HS; WhAmP; WhCiWar*

Mason, James Neville
English. Actor
Starred in *A Star is Born,* 1955; wrote *Before I Forget,* 1981.
b. May 15, 1909 in Huddersfield, England
d. Jul 27, 1984 in Lausanne, Switzerland
Source: *BiDFilm; CmMov; ConAu 113; FilmgC; IntMPA 82; IntWW 74, 75, 76, 77, 78, 79, 80, 81, 82, 83; MovMk; NewYTBS 84; OxCFilm; VarWW 85; Who 74; WhoAm 82; WhoHol A; WhoThe 81; WhoWor 78, 80, 82*

Mason, John
English. Colonizer
With land grant, founded New Hampshire, 1629; governor of Newfoundland, 1615-21.
b. 1586 in King's Lynn, England
d. Dec 1635 in London, England
Source: *AmAu&B; AmBi; ApCAB; BioIn 9; DcCanB 1; DcNaB; Drake; MacDCB 78; NewCBEL; NewCol 75; OxCCan; REnAL*

Mason, John L
American. Inventor
Patented Mason Jar, 1858, used in home canning.
Source: *AmMWSc 92; BioIn 15; Dun&B 88; St&PR 87; WhoAm 88, 90*

Mason, Lowell
American. Composer, Teacher
Established first public school music program, 1838; hymns include "Nearer, My God to Thee."
b. Jan 8, 1792 in Medfield, Massachusetts
d. Aug 11, 1872 in Orange, New Jersey
Source: *Alli; AmAu; AmAu&B; AmBi; ApCAB; Baker 78, 84, 92; BiDAmEd; BiDAmM; BioIn 1, 4, 9, 11, 13, 14, 16, 17; BriBkM 80; ChhPo, S1, S2; CyEd; DcAmAu; DcAmB; DcNAA; Drake; HarEnUS; LuthC 75; McGEWB; NatCAB 7; NewAmDM; NewGrDA 86; NewGrDM 80; OxCAmH; OxCAmL 65; OxCMus; REnAL; TwCBDA; WebAB 74, 79; WhAm HS; WorAl; WorAlBi*

Mason, Marsha
American. Actor
Starred in films *Cinderella Liberty,* 1973, *The Goodbye Girl,* 1977 *Chapter Two,* 1979; has received four Oscar nominations; former wife of Neil Simon.
b. Apr 3, 1942 in Saint Louis, Missouri
Source: *BioIn 10, 11, 12, 14, 16; CelR 90; ConTFT 1, 2, 7, 14; CurBio 81; EncAFC; FilmEn; HalFC 80, 84, 88; IntMPA 77, 80, 82, 84, 86, 88, 92, 94, 96; InWom SUP; LegTOT; MovMk;*

NotNAT; VarWW 85; WhoAm 78, 80, 82, 84, 86, 88, 90; WhoAmW 79, 81, 83, 87, 89, 91; WhoEnt 92; WhoHol 92, A; WorAl; WorAlBi

Mason, Max
American. Mathematician, Inventor
Pres., U of Chicago, 1925-28, Rockefeller Foundation, 1929-36; invented instruments for submarine detection.
b. Oct 26, 1877 in Madison, Wisconsin
d. Mar 23, 1961 in Claremont, California
Source: *BioIn 5, 6; DcAmB S7; WebBD 83; WhAm 4; WhNAA*

Mason, Nick
[Pink Floyd]
English. Singer, Musician
Drummer; oversees special audio effects in studio, concerts.
b. Jan 27, 1945 in Birmingham, England
Source: *WhoRocM 82*

Mason, Pamela Helen
English. Actor
Married to James Mason, 1940-64; host of TV, radio talk shows.
b. Mar 10, 1922 in London, England
d. Jun 29, 1996 in Beverly Hills, California
Source: *IntMPA 82; VarWW 85; WhAm 11; WhoAm 74, 76, 78, 80, 82, 84, 86, 88, 90, 92, 94, 95; WhoEnt 92; WhoHol A*

Massamba-Debat, Alphonse
Congolese. Political Leader
President of the Congo, 1963-68; ousted in coup.
b. 1921?
d. Mar 25, 1977 in Brazzaville, Congo
Source: *BioIn 11; DcAfHiB 86S; IntWW 74, 75, 76*

Massasoit
American. Native American Chief
Highly regarded Wampanoag chief who traded with Plymouth Colony Pilgrims and successfully preserved peace between the races throughout his lifetime.
b. 1590 in Bristol, Rhode Island
d. 1661 in Bristol, Rhode Island
Source: *BenetAL 91; BioIn 9, 11, 15; DcAmB; EncCRAm; OxCAmH; WebAB 74, 79; WhAm HS; WhNaAH*

Masse, Victor
[Felix-Marie Masse]
French. Composer
Operas include *Fior d' Aliza,* 1866; *Paul et Virginie,* 1876.
b. Mar 7, 1822 in Lorient, France
d. Jul 5, 1884 in Paris, France
Source: *Baker 78, 84, 92; NewEOp 71; NewGrDM 80; NewGrDO; OxCMus; OxCPMus; OxDcOp*

Masselos, William
American. Pianist
Pianist noted for contemporary music.
b. Aug 11, 1920 in Niagara Falls, New York
d. Oct 23, 1992 in New York, New York
Source: *Baker 78, 84, 92; BioIn 14; CelR; IntWWM 90; NewAmDM; NewGrDA 86; NewGrDM 80; NewYTBE 71; NewYTBS 92*

Massenet, Jules Emile Frederic
French. Composer
Best known for operas *Manon,* 1884; *Le Cid,* 1885.
b. May 12, 1842 in Montaud, France
d. Aug 13, 1912 in Paris, France
Source: *AtlBL; Benet 96; BioIn 2, 3, 4, 6, 7, 8, 9, 10, 11, 12; DcArts; Dis&D; LinLib S; LuthC 75; NewCol 75; NewEOp 71; NewGrDO; OxCFr; OxCMus; REn; WebBD 83; WhDW; WorAl*

Masserman, Jules H(oman)
American. Psychiatrist
Noted for "biodynamics" theory; wrote *Practice of Dynamic Psychiatry,* 1955.
b. Mar 10, 1905 in Chudnov, Poland
d. Nov 6, 1994 in Chicago, Illinois
Source: *AmMWSc 73P, 76P, 79, 82, 86, 89, 92, 95; BiDrAPA 77, 89; BioIn 10, 12; BlueB 76; ConAu 69; CurBio 80, 95N; WhAm 11; WhoAm 74, 76, 78, 80, 82, 84, 86, 88, 90, 92, 94; WhoWor 74, 78*

Massey, Anna
English. Actor
Daughter of Raymond Massey; TV shows include "Mayor of Casterbridge;" "Rebecca;" films include *Frenzy,* 1972.
b. Aug 11, 1937 in Thakeham, England
Source: *BiE&WWA; ConTFT 4, 14; FilmgC; HalFC 80, 84, 88; IntMPA 84, 86, 88, 92, 94, 96; VarWW 85; Who 74, 82, 83, 85, 88, 90, 92; WhoHol 92, A; WhoHrs 80; WhoThe 72, 77, 81*

Massey, D. Curtis
American. Singer, Songwriter
Had own radio, TV show; music director, "Petticoat Junction"; "Beverly Hillbillies"; won Emmy, 1961.
b. May 3, 1910 in Midland, Texas
d. Oct 20, 1991 in Rancho Mirage, California
Source: *ASCAP 66, 80*

Massey, Daniel Raymond
English. Actor
Son of Raymond Massey; Oscar nominee for *Star,* 1968.
b. Oct 10, 1933 in London, England
Source: *BiE&WWA; ConTFT 6; FilmgC; HalFC 88; IntMPA 77, 92; NotNAT; VarWW 85; Who 92; WhoHol A; WhoThe 77*

Massey, Gerald
English. Author, Poet
Verse volumes include *Lyrics of Love,* 1850.
b. May 29, 1828 in Tring, England
d. Oct 12, 1907
Source: *Alli, SUP; BbD; BiD&SB; BioIn 14; BritAu 19; Chambr 3; ChhPo, S1, S2, S3; DcBiPP; DcEnA; DcEnL; DcEuL; DcLB 32; DcLEL; DcNaB S2; EncO&P 1, 2, 3; EvLB; NewC; NewCBEL; REn; WebE&AL*

Massey, Ilona
[Ilona Hajmassy]
American. Actor
Teamed with Nelson Eddy in *Rosalie; Balaaika; Northwest Outpost.*
b. Jun 16, 1910 in Budapest, Austria-Hungary
d. Aug 10, 1974 in Bethesda, Maryland
Source: *FilmEn; FilmgC; ForYSC; MotPP; MovMk; NewYTBS 74; ThFT; WhoHol B; WhScrn 77, 83*

Massey, Raymond Hart
American. Actor, Producer
Noted for stage, film portrayals of Abraham Lincoln; starred as Dr. Gillespie on TV's "Dr. Kildare," 1961-66.
b. Aug 30, 1896 in Toronto, Ontario, Canada
d. Jul 29, 1983 in Los Angeles, California
Source: *AnObit 1983; BiDFilm; CanWW 70, 79, 80, 81, 83; CmMov; ConAu 104; CurBio 83N; FamA&A; FilmgC; IntMPA 82; MotPP; MovMk; NewYTBS 83; NotNAT; OxCFilm; OxCThe 83; PlP&P; VarWW 85; WhoAm 82; WhoThe 77*

Massey, Vincent
[Charles Vincent Massey]
Canadian. Diplomat
Canada's first minister to US, 1926-30; governor-general of Canada, 1952-59.
b. Feb 20, 1887 in Toronto, Ontario, Canada
d. Dec 30, 1967 in London, England
Source: *BioIn 2, 3, 4, 5, 6, 8, 11, 13, 16; CanWr; CurBio 51, 68; DcNaB 1961; DcTwHis; FacFETw; LinLib S; MacDCB 78; ObitT 1961; OxCCan; OxCCanT; WhAm 4*

Massey, Walter E(ugene)
American. Physicist, Educator
First black president of the Association for the Advancement of Science, 1989-91; director, National Science Foundation, 1991-93; pres., Morehouse College, 1995—.
b. Apr 5, 1938 in Hattiesburg, Mississippi
Source: *AfrAmBi 2; AmMWSc 73P, 76P, 79, 82, 86, 89, 92, 95; BlksScM; WhoAfA 96; WhoAm 78, 80, 82, 84, 86, 88, 90, 92, 94, 95, 96, 97; WhoBlA 77, 80, 85, 88, 90, 92, 94; WhoFrS 84; WhoMW 82; WhoWor 87*

Massi, Nick
[The Four Seasons; Nicholas Macioci]
American. Singer, Musician
Bass player, arranger for popular 1960s group, the Four Seasons.
b. Sep 19, 1935 in Newark, New Jersey
Source: *EncPR&S 74; RkOn 74*

Massine, Leonide Fedorovich
"Painter of the Ballet"
American. Choreographer, Dancer
Legendary name in ballet history; with Ballet Russe, Ballet Russe de Monte Carlo, American Ballet Theater, from 1920s.
b. Aug 9, 1896 in Moscow, Russia
d. Mar 16, 1979 in Cologne, Germany (West)
Source: *BioNews 75; ConAu 85, 97; CurBio 40; IntWW 74; NewCol 75; WebBD 83; Who 74; WhoWor 74; WorAl*

Massinger, Philip
English. Dramatist
Plays include *New Way to Pay Old Debts,* 1633; frequently colloborated with Fletcher.
b. 1583 in Salisbury, England
d. Mar 1640 in London, England
Source: *Alli; AtlBL; BbD; Benet 87, 96; BiD&SB; BiDRP&D; BioIn 3, 4, 5, 8, 9, 10, 12, 14, 16; BlmGEL; BritAu; CamGEL; CamGLE; CamGWoT; CasWL; Chambr 1; CnThe; CroE&S; CrtSuDr; CrtT 1; CyWA 58; DcArts; DcEnA; DcEnL; DcEuL; DcLB 58; DcLEL; DcNaB; EncWT; Ent; EvLB; GrWrEL DR; IntDcT 2; LegTOT; LngCEL; McGEWB; McGEWD 72, 84; MouLC 1; NewC; NewCBEL; NotNAT A, B; OxCEng 67, 85, 95; OxCMus; OxCThe 67, 83; PenC AM, ENG; PlP&P; RAdv 14, 13-2; REn; REnWD; RfGEnL 91; WebE&AL*

Masson, Andre (Aime Rene)
French. Artist
Pioneer of surrealism; paintings include *Death's Head,* 1927; designed sets for ballets and operas, including *Wozzeck,* 1963.
b. Jan 4, 1896 in Balaghy-sur-Therain, France
d. Oct 28, 1987 in Paris, France
Source: *AnObit 1987; BioIn 1, 4, 5, 7, 9, 10, 11, 12, 13, 15, 16, 17; ConArt 77, 83, 89; ConAu 124; CurBio 74, 88N; DcArts; DcTwCCu 2; EncWT; FacFETw; IntDcAA 90; IntWW 74, 75, 76, 77, 78, 79, 80, 81, 82, 83; McGDA; NewYTBS 87; OxCArt; OxCTwCA; OxDcArt; PhDcTCA 77; PrintW 83, 85; WhAm 9; WhDW; WhoFr 79*

Masson, Paul
American. Vintner
Built int'l reputation for his champagne, 1892.
b. 1859
d. 1940
Source: *CmCal; Entr; LegTOT*

Massys, Quentin
Flemish. Artist
Painted portraits, religious, genre subjects including *Money Changer and His Wife,* 1514.
b. 1466? in Louvain, Belgium
d. 1530 in Antwerp, Belgium
Source: *AtlBL; BioIn 1; DcCathB; LegTOT; McGEWB; NewCol 75; WebBD 83; WorAl; WorAlBi*

Masters, Edgar Lee
American. Poet, Dramatist
Wrote *Spoon River Anthology,* 1915.
b. Aug 23, 1869 in Garnett, Kansas
d. Mar 5, 1950 in Philadelphia, Pennsylvania
Source: *AmAu&B; AmLY; AtlBL; BioIn 12, 13, 14, 15; CasWL; Chambr 3; ChhPo, S1, S2, S3; CnDAL; CnE&AP; CnMWL; ConAmA; ConAmL; ConAu 104; CyWA 58; DcAmB S4; DcArts; DcLEL; EncAAH; EncUnb; EncWL; EvLB; FacFETw; LegTOT; LinLib L, S; LngCTC; MagSAmL; McGEWB; ModAL; OxCAmL 65; OxCEng 67; PenC AM; RAdv 1, 14, 13-1; REn; REnAL; RGFAP; SixAP; TwCA, SUP; TwCWr; WebAB 74, 79; WebE&AL; WhAm 2, 2A; WhoTwCL; WorAl; WorAlBi; WrPh*

Masters, John
American. Author
Wrote about the British in India: *Bhowani Junction,* 1954; *Nightrunners of Bengal,* 1951.
b. Oct 26, 1914 in Calcutta, India
d. May 6, 1983 in Albuquerque, New Mexico
Source: *AnObit 1983; Au&Wr 71; Benet 87; BioIn 3, 4, 9, 13; CamGLE; ConAu 108, 110; ConNov 72, 76, 82; DcArts; DcLEL 1940; DcNaB 1981; EncSF; IntAu&W 76, 77; LngCTC; ModBrL; NewYTBS 83; Novels; REn; RGTwCWr; ScF&FL 1, 92; TwCA SUP; TwCRHW 90, 94; TwCWr; WhAm 8; Who 74, 82, 83; WhoAm 80, 82; WrDr 76, 80, 82, 84*

Masters, William Howell
[Masters and Johnson]
American. Physician
Author with former wife, Virginia Johnson: *Human Sexual Response,* 1966.
b. Dec 27, 1915 in Cleveland, Ohio
Source: *AmMWSc 73P, 76P, 79, 82, 86, 89, 92, 95; AmSocL; AuNews 1; BioIn 7, 8, 9, 10, 11, 12, 14, 15; BioNews 74; CelR 90; ConAu 34NR; CurBio 68; EncAB-H 1974; FacFETw; HumSex; NewYTBE 70; NotTwCS; SmATA 2; WhoAm 74, 76, 78, 80, 82, 84, 86, 88, 92, 94, 95, 96, 97; WhoMW 84, 86; WhoWor 74, 82; WorAl; WorAlBi; WrDr 86, 92*

Masterson, Bat
[Bartholomew Masterson; William Barclay Masterson]
American. Lawman
Marshal of Dodge City, KS; friend of Wyatt Earp.
b. Nov 24, 1853 in Iroquois County, Illinois
d. Oct 25, 1921 in New York, New York
Source: *BioIn 4, 5, 6, 8, 9, 10, 11, 12, 13, 15, 16, 17, 18; CopCroC; DcAmB; LegTOT; REnAW; WebAB 74, 79; WebBD 83; WhAm 4, HSA; WhScrn 83*

Masterton, Bill
[William Masterton]
"Bat"
Canadian. Hockey Player
Center, Minnesota, 1967-68; first NHL player to die from injuries suffered in game; Masterton Trophy for sportsmanship, hard work named for him.
b. Aug 16, 1938 in Winnipeg, Manitoba, Canada
d. Jan 15, 1968 in Minneapolis, Minnesota
Source: *BioIn 8; HocEn; WhoHcky 73*

Mastroianni, Marcello
Italian. Actor
Films include *La Dolce Vita,* 1961; *Henry IV,* 1985; and *Dark Eyes,* 1987.
b. Sep 28, 1924 in Fontana Liri, Italy
d. Dec 19, 1996 in Paris, France
Source: *BiDFilm, 81; BioIn 6, 7, 8, 10, 11, 14, 15, 16, 17, 19, 21; BkPepl; CelR, 90; ConTFT 5, 12; CurBio 63; DcArts; FacFETw; FilmgC; ForYSC; HalFC 88; IntDcF 1-3, 2-3; IntMPA 75, 76, 77, 78, 79, 80, 81, 82, 86, 88, 92, 94, 96; IntWW 74, 75, 76, 77, 78, 79, 80, 81, 82, 83, 89, 91, 93; LegTOT; MotPP; MovMk; NewYTBE 70; NewYTBS 27, 87; OxCFilm; VarWW 85; WhoAm 92, 94, 95, 96, 97; WhoEnt 92; WhoHol A; WhoWor 74, 82, 84, 87, 89, 91, 93, 95, 96, 97; WorAl; WorAlBi; WorEFlm*

Masur, Harold Q
[Guy Fleming; Edward James]
American. Author
Mystery fiction includes *The Broker,* 1981.
b. Jan 29, 1909 in New York, New York
Source: *BioIn 14; ConAu 13NR, 77; EncMys; IntAu&W 91; TwCCr&M 80, 85, 91; WrDr 82, 84, 86, 88, 90, 92, 94, 96*

Masur, Kurt
German. Conductor
Musical director, NY Philharmonic, 1990—; director of the Gewandhaus Orchestra, 1970-90; conductor, London Philharmonic Orchestra, 1989-92.
b. Jul 18, 1927 in Brieg, Germany
Source: *Baker 84, 92; BioIn 13, 16, 17, 18, 19, 20; ConMus 11; CurBio 90; IntWW 89, 91, 93; IntWWM 90; NewAmDM; NewGrDM 80; NewGrDO; News 93; NewYTBS 82, 91; PenDiMP; WhoAm 92, 94, 95, 96, 97; WhoE 93, 97; WhoEnt 92; WhoSocC 78; WhoSoCE 89; WhoWor 91, 93, 95; WorAlBi*

Masursky, Harold
American. Geologist
Scientist, US Geological Survey, known for work on solar system; worked for NASA on Apollo, Voyager programs.
b. Dec 23, 1923 in Fort Wayne, Indiana
d. Aug 24, 1990 in Flagstaff, Arizona
Source: *AmMWSc 86, 89, 92; AnObit 1990; BioIn 14, 15, 17; CurBio 86, 90, 90N; FacFETw; IntWW 89, 91N; NewYTBS 90; WhAm 10; WhoAm 80, 82, 84, 86, 88, 90; WhoFrS 84; WhoTech 82, 84, 89, 95; WhoWest 84, 87, 89*

Mata Hari
[Margaretha Geertruida Macleod]
Dutch. Dancer, Spy
Executed by the French for being double agent for Germans.
b. Aug 7, 1876 in Leeuwarden, Netherlands
d. Oct 15, 1917 in Vincennes, France
Source: *BiDD; BioIn 1, 2, 4, 6, 7, 8, 9, 10, 11, 12, 15, 17, 19, 20; ContDcW 89; FacFETw; HalFC 84, 88; IntDcWB; LegTOT; LngCTC; NewCol 75; SpyCS; WebBD 83; WhDW; WorAl; WorAlBi*

Matalin, Mary (Joe)
[Mrs. James Carville]
American. Consultant
Chief political strategist for President George Bush's 1992 campaign.
b. Aug 19, 1953 in Chicago, Illinois
Source: *ConAu 147; CurBio 96; LegTOT; News 95, 95-2*

Mataya, Ewa
[Ewa Svensson]
Swedish. Billiards Player
Top female pool player in the world, 1990—.
b. 1964 in Gavle, Sweden

Matchabelli, Georges, Prince
American. Manufacturer
Headed internationally known perfume firm, 1923-35.
b. 1885
d. 1935
Source: *BioIn 1; Entr*

Materna, Amalia
Austrian. Opera Singer
Soprano chosen by Wagner for his *Brunhilde,* first Bayreuth Festival, 1876.
b. Jul 10, 1844 in Saint Georgen, Austria
d. Jan 18, 1918 in Vienna, Austria
Source: *Baker 78, 84; LegTOT; NewEOp 71*

Mathabane, Mark
South African. Author
Wrote memoir, *Kaffir Boy,* 1986.
b. 1960 in Alexandra, South Africa
Source: *Au&Arts 4; BlkWr 1, 2; ConAu 51NR, 125; ConBlB 5; SchCGBL; TwCYAW; WrDr 92, 94, 96*

Mather, Cotton
American. Clergy, Author
Writings contributed to hysteria of Salem witchcraft trials, 1692; helped found Yale U, 1703.
b. Feb 12, 1663 in Boston, Massachusetts
d. Feb 13, 1728 in Boston, Massachusetts
Source: *Alli; AmAu; AmAu&B; AmBi; AmSocL; AmWrBE; AmWr S2; ApCAB; AtlBL; BbD; Benet 87, 96; BenetAL 91; BiDAmM; BiD&SB; BiDSocW; BioIn 1, 2, 3, 4, 5, 6, 7, 8, 9, 10, 11, 12, 13, 14, 15, 16, 17, 19, 20, 21; CamGEL; CamGLE; CamHAL; CasWL; Chambr 3; ChhPo; CnDAL; ColARen; CopCroC; CyAL 1; CyWA 58; DcAmAu; DcAmReB 1, 2; DcArts; DcBiPP; DcLB 24, 30, 140; DcLEL; DcNAA; DcNaB; Dis&D; Drake; EncAAH; EncAB-H 1974, 1996; EncARH; EncCRAm; EncEnl; EncWW; EvLB; HarEnUS; HisWorL; InSci; LegTOT; LinLib L, S; LuthC 75; McGEWB; MouLC 2; NatCAB 4; OxCAmH; OxCAmL 65, 83, 95; OxCChiL; OxCEng 67, 85, 95; OxCMus; PenC AM; RComAH; REn; REnAL; RfGAmL 87, 94; TwCBDA; WebAB 74, 79; WebE&AL; WhAm HS; WhDW; WhNaAH; WorAl; WorAlBi; WrCNE*

Mather, Increase
American. Clergy, University Administrator
Colonial leader; pres., Harvard U, 1685-1701; father of Cotton.
b. Jun 21, 1639 in Dorchester, Massachusetts
d. Aug 23, 1723 in Boston, Massachusetts
Source: *Alli; AmAu; AmAu&B; AmBi; AmSocL; AmWrBE; ApCAB; BbD; Benet 87, 96; BenetAL 91; BiDAmEd; BiDAmS; BiD&SB; BiInAmS; BioIn 1, 6, 7, 8, 9, 14, 16, 17, 19; CamGEL; CamGLE; CamHAL; CasWL; Chambr 3; CnDAL; CyAL 1; CyEd; DcAmAu; DcAmB; DcAmBC; DcAmReB 1, 2; DcAmTB; DcLB 24; DcLEL; DcNAA; DcNaB; Drake; EncAB-H 1974, 1996; EncARH; EncCRAm; EncO&P 2, 3; EncWW; HarEnUS; HisWorL; LegTOT; LinLib L, S; LuthC 75; McGEWB; NatCAB 6; OxCAmH; OxCAmL 65, 83, 95; PenC AM; RComAH; REn; REnAL; TwCBDA; WebAB 74, 79; WhAm HS; WorAl; WorAlBi; WrCNE*

Mather, Stephen Tyng
American. Businessman, Government Official
Organized National Park Service, 1917.
b. Jul 4, 1867 in San Francisco, California
d. Jan 22, 1930 in Brookline, Massachusetts
Source: *BioIn 2, 3, 5, 7, 8, 9; DcAmB; EncAAH; NatCAB 26; NatLAC; WebAB 74, 79; WhAm 1*

Mathers, Frank
American. Hockey Coach, Hockey Executive
Coached the Hershey Bears; retired as their pres. and gm, 1991; Hockey Hall of Fame, 1992.
b. Mar 29, 1924 in Winnipeg, Manitoba, Canada

Mathers, Jerry
American. Actor, Businessman
Played the Beaver on TV series "Leave It to Beaver," 1957-63.
b. Jun 2, 1948 in Sioux City, Iowa
Source: *BioIn 4, 10, 12, 13; ConTFT 9; ForYSC; LegTOT; What 4; WhoHol 92, A*

Matheson, Murray
Australian. Actor
Films include *Twilight Zone: The Movie,* 1983; TV series "Banacek," 1972-74.
b. Jul 1, 1912 in Casterton, Australia
d. Apr 25, 1985 in Woodland Hills, California
Source: *BiE&WWA; ConTFT 1; FilmgC; HalFC 84, 88; NotNAT; WhoAm 74, 76, 78, 80; WhoHol A*

Matheson, Richard Burton
American. Screenwriter
Films include *Twilight Zone—The Movie; Jaws 3-D,* 1983.
b. Feb 20, 1926 in Allendale, New Jersey
Source: *BioIn 13, 15; CmMov; ConAu 97; ConLC 37; ConSFA; ConTFT 6; CyWA 89; DcLB 44; EncSF; FanAl; FilmgC; HalFC 88; IntAu&W 91; NewEScF; NewYTET; PenEncH; ScF&FL 1, 2; ScFSB; SupFW; TwCSFW 91; VarWW 85; WhoHrs 80; WhoSciF; WorEFlm; WrDr 92*

Matheson, Scott Milne
American. Politician
Dem. governor of UT, 1977-85; currently practicing law.
b. Jan 9, 1929 in Chicago, Illinois
Source: *BiDrGov 1789, 1978, 1983; BioIn 13; NewYTBS 90; PolsAm 84; WhAm 10; WhoAm 78, 80, 82, 84, 86, 88, 90; WhoAmP 77, 79, 81, 83, 85, 87, 89; WhoGov 77; WhoWor 82*

Matheson, Tim
American. Actor
Played in TV series "Bonanza," 1972-73; film part in *Animal House,* 1978.
b. Dec 31, 1948? in Los Angeles, California
Source: *BioIn 11, 12, 13, 14; ConTFT 3; EncAFC; HalFC 88; IntMPA 92; St&PR 91; VarWW 85; WhoEnt 92*

Mathews, Eddie
[Edwin Lee Mathews, Jr]
American. Baseball Player
Third baseman, 1952-68; had 512 career home runs; Hall of Fame, 1978.
b. Oct 13, 1931 in Texarkana, Texas

Source: *Ballpl 90; BiDAmSp BB; BioIn 3, 4, 5, 6, 8, 9, 10, 13, 14, 15, 16, 17, 20; CmCal; LegTOT; WhoAm 74, 76, 78; WhoProB 73; WhoSpor; WorAl; WorAlBi*

Mathews, Forrest David
American. Educator, Government Official
HEW secretary under Carter, 1975-76.
b. Dec 6, 1935 in Grove Hill, Alabama
Source: *BioIn 10, 11, 12; IntWW 76, 77, 78; LEduc 74; NewYTBS 75; WhoAm 74, 76, 78; WhoAmP 75, 77, 79, 81; WhoE 77; WhoSSW 73*

Mathews, Harlan
American. Politician
Dem. senator, TN, 1993—; appointed to replace US vp Gore.
b. Jan 17, 1927 in Alabama
Source: *CngDr 93; WhoAm 80, 82, 90; WhoAmP 93, 95; WhoSSW 73, 88*

Mathews, John Joseph
American. Author
Wrote novel *Sundown,* 1934; wrote tribal history *The Osages: Children of the Middle Waters,* 1961.
b. Nov 16, 1895 in Pawhuska, Oklahoma
d. Jun 11, 1979
Source: *AmAu&B; BioIn 14, 21; ConAu 142, P-2; ConLC 84; EncFWF; TwCWW 82, 91; WrDr 84, 86*

Mathews, Mitford M
American. Lexicographer
Compiled *Dictionary of Americanisms,* 1951; the first publication of its kind.
b. Feb 12, 1891 in Jackson, Alabama
d. Feb 14, 1985 in Chicago, Illinois
Source: *BioIn 14; ConAu 115; NewYTBS 85; WhAm 8*

Mathewson, Christy
[Christopher Mathewson]
"Big Six"
American. Baseball Player
Pitcher, 1900-16, mostly with NY Giants; won 37 games, 1908; had 373 career wins; one of original five elected to Hall of Fame, 1936.
b. Aug 12, 1880 in Factoryville, Pennsylvania
d. Oct 7, 1925 in Saranac Lake, New York
Source: *BiDAmSp BB; BioIn 1, 2, 3, 4, 5, 6, 7, 8, 9, 10, 11, 12, 13, 14, 15, 16, 17, 18, 19, 20; DcAmB; DcNAA; Dis&D; FacFETw; OxCAmH; WebAB 74, 79; WhAm 4, HSA; WhoProB 73; WhoSpor; WhScrn 77, 83; WorAl; WorAlBi*

Mathias, Bob
[Robert Bruce Mathias]
American. Track Athlete
First to win two gold medals in decathlon, 1948, 1952 Olympics.
b. Nov 17, 1930 in Tulare, California
Source: *BiDAmSp OS; BiDrAC; BiDrUSC 89; BioIn 2, 3, 4, 5, 6, 7, 8, 10, 12, 14, 16; CmCal; CurBio 52; FacFETw; ItaFilm; LegTOT; NewYTBE 73; WebAB 74, 79; WhoAm 74, 76; WhoAmP 73, 75, 77, 79, 81, 83, 85, 87, 89, 91, 93, 95; WhoGov 72, 75; WhoHol 92; WhoSpor; WhoTr&F 73; WhoWest 78, 89; WorAl*

Mathias, Charles McCurdy, Jr.
American. Politician
Rep. senator from MD, 1969-87.
b. Jul 24, 1922 in Frederick, Maryland
Source: *BiDrAC; BiDrUSC 89; BioIn 8, 9, 10, 11, 12; CngDr 85; CurBio 72; IntWW 83, 91; NewYTBS 86; PolsAm 84; WhoAm 74, 76, 78, 80, 82, 84, 86, 92, 94, 95, 96, 97; WhoAmL 90, 92, 94, 96; WhoAmP 85, 91; WhoE 74, 75, 77, 79, 81, 83, 85, 86, 89, 91, 95; WhoGov 72, 75, 77; WhoWor 80, 82, 87, 96*

Mathieson, Muir
Scottish. Conductor
Directed music for films: *In Which We Serve,* 1942; *Becket,* 1964.
b. Jan 24, 1911 in Stirling, Scotland
d. Aug 2, 1975 in Oxford, England
Source: *BioIn 1, 10; EncEurC; FilmEn; FilmgC; HalFC 80, 84, 88; IntDcF 1-4, 2-4; IntMPA 75; NewGrDM 80; PenDiMP; WhoHol C; WhoMus 72; WhScrn 77, 83*

Mathieu, Noel Jean
[Pierre Emmanuel]
French. Poet, Journalist
Wrote verse vol. *The Tomb of Orpheus,* 1943.
b. May 3, 1916 in Gan, France
d. Sep 22, 1984 in Paris, France
Source: *AnObit 1984; BioIn 2, 10, 13; CasWL; ClDMEL 80; ConAu 113, 130; DcTwCCu 2; EncWL, 2, 3; IntAu&W 76, 77, 82; IntWW 74, 75, 76, 77, 78, 79, 80, 81, 82, 83; IntWWP 77; LinLib L; ModFrL; OxCFr; REn; WhoFr 79; WhoWor 74, 76, 78; WorAu 1950*

Mathis, Johnny
[John Royce Mathis]
American. Singer
Smooth balladeer; recorded over 70 albums, eight gold; hits include "Wonderful! Wonderful!," 1956, "Too Much Too Little Too Late," 1978.
b. Sep 30, 1935 in San Francisco, California
Source: *Baker 84, 92; BiDAfM; BiDAmM; BioIn 4, 5, 6, 7, 10, 11, 12, 15; BioNews 75; BkPepl; CelR, 90; ConMus 2; CurBio 65, 93; DcTwCCu 5; DrBlPA, 90; EncRk 88; FacFETw; GayLesB; HarEnR 86; IlEncBM 82; InB&W 80, 85; LegTOT; NegAl 76, 83, 89; NewGrDA 86; OxCPMus; PenEncP; RkOn 74; RolSEnR 83; VarWW 85; WhoAfA 96; WhoAm 74, 76, 78, 80, 82, 84, 86, 88, 90, 92, 94, 95, 96, 97; WhoBlA 77, 80, 85, 88, 90, 92, 94; WhoEnt 92; WhoHol 92; WhoRock 81; WhoWor 74; WorAl; WorAlBi*

Mathison, Melissa
[Mrs. Harrison Ford]
American. Screenwriter
Received Oscar nomination, 1983, for screenplay of *ET.*
b. 1949?

Mathison, Richard Randolph
American. Journalist, Author
Works include *Secret Life of Howard Hughes,* 1977.
b. Oct 20, 1919 in Boise, Idaho
Source: *ConAu 1R, 3NR; WhScrn 83*

Matisse, Henri Emile Benoit
French. Artist, Author
Pioneer of modern art known for vivid female nudes, still lifes, interiors.
b. Dec 31, 1869 in Le Cateau, France
d. Nov 3, 1954 in Nice, France
Source: *AtlBL; CurBio 43, 53, 55; OxCFr; OxCTwCA; REn; WhAm 3, 4*

Matlin, Marlee
American. Actor
Deaf actress; won Oscar, Best Actress, *Children of a Lesser God,* 1987.
b. Aug 24, 1965 in Morton Grove, Illinois
Source: *BioIn 15, 16; CelR 90; ConHero 2; ConTFT 6, 9; CurBio 92; DeafPAS; IntMPA 92, 94, 96; LegTOT; News 92, 92-2; WhoAm 92, 94, 95, 96, 97; WhoAmW 91, 93, 95, 97; WhoEnt 92; WhoHol 92*

Matlock, Matty
[Julian Clifton Matlock]
American. Jazz Musician
Clarinet, sax player with Bob Crosby, 1942; 1950s-60s.
b. Apr 27, 1909 in Paducah, Kentucky
d. Jun 14, 1978 in Los Angeles, California
Source: *ASCAP 66; BiDJaz; CmpEPM; EncJzS; WhoJazz 72*

Matlovich, Leonard P., Jr.
American. Soldier
Air Force sergeant who battled against the military's anti-gay policy.
b. Jul 6, 1943 in Savannah, Georgia
d. Jun 22, 1988
Source: *GayLesB*

Matola, Sharon Rose
American. Biologist
Founder and director, Belize Zoo and Tropical Education Center, 1983—.
b. Jun 3, 1954 in Baltimore, Maryland
Source: *CurBio 93; WhoWor 95, 96, 97*

Matson, Ollie
[Oliver Genoa Matson]
American. Football Player
Running back, 1952-66, known for speed; won silver, bronze medals at Helsinki Olympics, 1952; Hall of Fame, 1972.
b. May 1, 1930 in Trinity, Texas

Source: *BiDAmSp FB; BioIn 17; BlkOlyM; CmCal; LegTOT; WhoBlA 85, 92; WhoFtbl 74; WhoSpor*

Matson, Randy
[James Randel Matson]
American. Track Athlete
First American to throw shot put over 70 ft., 1965; won gold medal, 1968 Olympics.
b. Mar 5, 1945 in Kilgore, Texas
Source: *BiDAmSp OS; BioIn 8, 9, 10; CurBio 68; WhoSpor; WhoTr&F 73*

Matsui, Robert T(akeo)
American. Politician
Dem. rep. from CA, 1979—.
b. Sep 17, 1941 in Sacramento, California
Source: *BiDrUSC 89; CurBio 94; NewYTBS 93; WhoAm 80, 82, 84, 86, 88, 90, 92, 94, 95, 96, 97; WhoAmP 79, 81, 83, 85, 87, 89, 91, 93, 95; WhoAsA 94; WhoE 95; WhoGov 75, 77; WhoWest 80, 82, 84, 87, 89, 92, 94, 96; WhoWor 96, 97*

Matsunaga, Spark Masayuki
American. Politician
Dem. senator from HI, 1977-90, representative, 1963-76; decorated Bronze Medal, Purple Heart.
b. Oct 8, 1916 in Kauai, Hawaii
d. Apr 15, 1990 in Toronto, Ontario, Canada
Source: *AlmAP 88; BiDrAC; BiDrUSC 89; BioIn 16; BlueB 76; CngDr 74, 77, 79, 81, 83, 85, 87, 89; ConAu 128, 131; IntWW 77, 78, 79, 80, 81, 82, 83, 89, 91N; IntYB 79, 80, 81, 82; NewYTBS 90; PolsAm 84; WhAm 10; WhoAm 74, 76, 78, 80, 82, 84, 86, 88; WhoAmP 73, 75, 77, 79, 81, 83, 85, 87, 89; WhoGov 72, 75, 77; WhoWest 76, 78, 80, 82, 84, 87, 89; WhoWor 80, 82, 87, 89*

Matsushita, Konosuke
Japanese. Industrialist
Founded, Matsushita Electric Housewares Manufacturing Works, 1918; president, 1961-73.
b. Nov 27, 1894 in Wasa Village, Japan
d. Apr 27, 1989 in Tokyo, Japan
Source: *AnObit 1989; BioIn 5, 6, 7, 8, 9, 10, 11, 12, 13, 14, 15, 16; ConAu 128; FacFETw; FarE&A 78, 79, 80, 81; IntAu&W 82; IntWW 74, 75, 78, 79, 80, 81, 82, 83, 89, 91; NewYTBS 89; St&PR 84, 87; WhoFI 74, 75, 77; WhoWor 74, 76, 78*

Matta, Roberto Sebastian Antonio Echaurren
Chilean. Artist
Abstract surrealist painter: *Untitled,* 1961.
b. Nov 11, 1911? in Santiago, Chile
Source: *BioIn 13, 14; ConArt 83, 89; DcTwDes; McGDA; PeoHis; PrintW 85*

Mattea, Kathy
American. Singer, Songwriter
Throaty-voiced country, folk, and blues performer; hits include "Eighteen Wheels and a Dozen Roses;" 3 CMA Awards, 1988-90.
Source: *BioIn 14, 17, 18, 19, 20; ConMus 5; WhoAm 92, 94, 95, 96, 97; WhoAmW 91, 93; WhoEnt 92; WhoNeCM*

Matteotti, Giacomo
Italian. Political Leader
Secretary-general of Socialist party, 1924; murdered after denouncing fascist party; caused int'l scandal, problems for Mussolini.
b. 1885 in Fratta Polesine, Italy
d. Jun 11, 1924
Source: *BioIn 2, 6; DcTwHis; FacFETw; HisWorL; NewCol 75; WebBD 83; WhDW*

Matter, Herbert
American. Photographer, Designer
Pioneer of photomontage posters, especially used in advertising.
b. Apr 25, 1907 in Engelberg, Switzerland
d. May 8, 1984 in Southampton, New York
Source: *AnObit 1984; BioIn 3, 4, 13, 14; ConDes 84, 90, 97; ConPhot 82, 88, 95; DcTwDes; ICPEnP A; MacBEP; NewYTBS 84; WhoGrA 62, 82*

Matteson, Tompkins Harrison
American. Artist
Pictures of American history include *The Spirit of '76.*
b. May 9, 1813 in Peterboro, New York
d. Feb 2, 1884 in Sherburne, Nevada
Source: *AmBi; ApCAB; DcAmB; Drake; EarABI, SUP; HarEnUS; NewYHSD; TwCBDA; WhAm HS*

Matthau, Walter
American. Actor
Best known for role of Oscar Madison in play, film *The Odd Couple,* 1965, 1968; won Oscar for *The Fortune Cookie,* 1972.
b. Oct 1, 1920 in New York, New York
Source: *BiDFilm, 81, 94; BiE&WWA; BioIn 3, 6, 7, 8, 9, 10, 11, 12, 14, 15, 16, 18, 19, 21; BioNews 74; CelR, 90; CmMov; CnThe; ConTFT 7, 14; CurBio 66; EncAFC; FilmEn; FilmgC; HalFC 80, 84, 88; IntDcF 1-3, 2-3; IntMPA 84, 86, 88, 92, 94, 96; IntWW 75, 76, 77, 78, 79, 80, 81, 82, 83, 89, 91, 93; ItaFilm; LegTOT; MiSFD 9; MotPP; MovMk; NewYTBE 71; NewYTBS 74; NotNAT; OxCAmT 84; OxCFilm; VarWW 85; WhoAm 74, 76, 78, 80, 82, 84, 86, 88, 90, 92, 94, 95, 96, 97; WhoCom; WhoEnt 92; WhoHol 92, A; WhoThe 72, 77, 81; WhoWor 74, 78, 80, 87; WorAl; WorAlBi; WorEFlm*

Matthes, Francois-Emile
American. Geologist, Surveyor
Renowned topographer whose work led to establishment of some US National Parks.
b. Mar 16, 1874 in Amsterdam, Netherlands
d. Jun 21, 1948 in Berkeley, California
Source: *BioIn 1, 2, 4, 12; DcAmB S4; NatCAB 36; WebAB 79; WhAm 2*

Matthes, Roland
German. Swimmer
Won two gold medals, 1968, 1972 Olympics.
b. Nov 17, 1950 in Possneck, German Democratic Republic

Matthew, Saint
Biblical Figure
One of 12 disciples of Jesus; regarded as author of the First Gospel.
Source: *Benet 87; EncEarC; NewCol 75; REn*

Matthews, Burnita S(helton)
American. Judge, Feminist
First woman to serve as federal district judge, 1949-83; noted women's rights pioneer.
b. Dec 28, 1894 in Burnell, Mississippi
d. Apr 25, 1988 in Washington, District of Columbia
Source: *AmBench 79; BiDFedJ; BioIn 15, 16; CngDr 74, 77, 79, 81, 83, 85, 87, 89; CurBio 50, 88, 88N; FacFETw; InWom; NewYTBS 88; WhAm 9; WhoAm 80, 82, 84; WhoAmL 83, 85; WhoAmW 58, 64, 66, 68, 70, 72, 74, 75, 77, 83, 85, 87; WhoE 79, 81, 83, 85; WhoGov 72, 75; WhoSSW 73; WhoWor 84; WomLaw*

Matthews, Ian
American. Composer, Singer
Guitarist; has performed with bands, solo; hits include "Woodstock," 1977.
b. Jun 16, 1945 in Lincolnshire, England
Source: *ConMuA 80A; EncPR&S 89; EncRk 88; HarEnR 86; IlEncRk; NewAgMG; PenEncP; RkOn 85; RolSEnR 83; WhoRocM 82*

Matthews, Jessie
American. Actor
Popular London musical comedy star, 1920s-30s; plays include *This Year of Grace,* 1928.
b. Mar 11, 1907 in London, England
d. Aug 19, 1981 in Pinner, England
Source: *AnObit 1981; BiDD; BiE&WWA; BioIn 7, 8, 9, 10, 12; CmpEPM; CnThe; ConAu 108; EncEurC; EncMT; Film 2; FilmAG WE; FilmEn; FilmgC; HalFC 80, 84, 88; IlWWBF, A; IntDcF 1-3, 2-3; IntMPA 75, 76, 77, 78, 79, 80, 81, 82; IntWW 77, 78, 79, 80, 81; InWom, SUP; MotPP; MovMk; NewYTBS 81; NotNAT; OxCFilm; OxCPMus; OxCThe 83; ThFT; What 2; Who 74; WhoHol A; WhoThe 72, 77, 81; WhScrn 83*

Matthews, Stanley
American. Supreme Court Justice
Nomination by Hayes, 1876, caused so much furor he was not approved until renominated by Garfield, 1881.
b. Jul 21, 1824 in Cincinnati, Ohio
d. Mar 22, 1889 in Washington, District of Columbia
Source: *Alli SUP; AmBi; ApCAB; BiDFedJ; BiDrAC; BiDrUSC 89; BioIn 2, 5, 15; DcAmAu; DcAmB; DcNAA; HarEnUS; NatCAB 2; OhA&B; SupCtJu; TwCBDA; WebAB 74, 79; WhAm HS; WhAmP*

Matthews, Stanley, Sir
English. Soccer Player
Considered one of Britain's finest soccer players; from 1934-65, played in 56 international matches.
b. Feb 1, 1915 in Stoke-on-Trent, England
Source: *BioIn 6, 7, 8; ConAu 115, 134; NewCol 75; WhDW; Who 74, 82, 83, 85, 88, 90, 92, 94; WorESoc*

Matthews, T(homas) S(tanley)
American. Editor
Succeeded Henry R. Luce as editor *Time* magazine, 1949-53 and transformed it from a joke-ridden journal to a serious one.
b. Jan 16, 1901 in Cincinnati, Ohio
d. Jan 4, 1991 in Cavendish, England
Source: *AmAu&B; Au&Wr 71; BioIn 2, 3, 5, 11, 12, 15, 17, 18; ConAu 18NR, P-1; CurBio 50; EncAJ; EncTwCJ; IntAu&W 77, 82, 86, 89, 91; OhA&B; REnAL; WhAm 10; Who 74, 82, 83, 85, 88, 90, 92N; WhoAm 74, 76, 78; WrDr 76, 80, 82, 84, 86, 88, 90*

Matthews, Vince(nt)
American. Track Athlete
Sprinter; won gold medals, 1968, 1972 Olympics; with Wayne Collett, banned from further competition for not standing at attention on victory stand, 1972.
b. Dec 16, 1947 in New York, New York
Source: *BioIn 10, 11, 21; BlkOlyM; NewYTBS 74; WhoAfA 96; WhoBlA 77, 80, 85, 90, 92, 94; WhoTr&F 73*

Matthias Corvinus
Hungarian. Ruler
During reign improved internal conditions, army, 1458-90; throne constantly challenged by uncle, Frederick III.
b. Feb 24, 1443 in Koloszvar, Transylvania
d. Apr 6, 1490 in Vienna, Austria
Source: *DcBiPP; DcEuL; NewCol 75; WebBD 83*

Matthiessen, Francis Otto
American. Author
Works on literary figures include *Notebooks of Henry James,* 1947.
b. Feb 19, 1902 in Pasadena, California
d. Apr 1, 1950
Source: *AmAu&B; BioIn 2, 4, 9, 10, 11, 12, 13, 16, 17; CasWL; ChhPo S2; DcAmB S4; EncAL; EvLB; LngCTC; ModAL; NatCAB 41; OxCAmL 65; PenC AM; REn; REnAL; TwCA, SUP; WhAm 3*

Mattingley, Garrett
English. Historian, Educator
Received special Pulitzer for book *The Armada,* 1960.
b. May 6, 1900 in Washington, District of Columbia
d. Dec 18, 1962 in Oxford, England
Source: *BioIn 13; ConAu 111; CurBio 60, 63*

Mattingly, Don(ald Arthur)
American. Baseball Player
Infielder, NY Yankees, 1982-96; won AL batting title, 1984; AL MVP, 1985; won 3 Gold Glove awards.
b. Apr 20, 1961 in Evansville, Indiana
Source: *Ballpl 90; BaseReg 86, 87; BioIn 14, 15, 16; CelR 90; ConNews 86-2; CurBio 88; LegTOT; NewYTBS 85, 86, 88; WhoAm 90, 92, 94, 95, 96, 97; WhoE 91, 95; WorAlBi*

Mattingly, Mack Francis
American. Politician
Rep. senator from GA, 1981-87.
b. Jan 7, 1931 in Anderson, Indiana
Source: *BiDrUSC 89; CngDr 85; IntWW 81, 82, 83, 89, 91, 93; PolsAm 84; WhoAm 86, 90; WhoAmP 75, 77, 79, 81, 83, 85, 87, 89, 91, 93, 95; WhoSSW 86; WhoWor 87, 91*

Mattus, Reuben
Polish. Manufacturer
Created Haagen-Dazs Ice Cream.
b. 1914?, Poland
Source: *BioIn 12, 14*

Mature, Victor
American. Actor
Leading man in films *Samson and Delilah,* 1949; *The Robe,* 1953.
b. Jan 29, 1916 in Louisville, Kentucky
Source: *BiDFilm, 81, 94; BioIn 2, 8, 11, 18; CmMov; CurBio 51; FilmgC; GangFlm; HalFC 88; IntMPA 75, 76, 77, 78, 79, 80, 81, 82, 84, 86, 88, 92; MotPP; MovMk; NewYTBE 71; OxCFilm; VarWW 85; What 2; WhoHol A; WorAl; WorAlBi; WorEFlm*

Matzeliger, Jan Ernest
American. Inventor
Patented machine that could make a shoe in one minute, 1883.
b. 1852, Suriname
d. 1889 in Lynn, Massachusetts
Source: *DcAmB; WebAB 74, 79*

Matzenauer, Margaret
Hungarian. Opera Singer
Contralto, soprano with NY Met., 1911-30.
b. Jun 1, 1881 in Temesvar, Austria-Hungary
d. May 19, 1963 in Van Nuys, California
Source: *Baker 78, 84; BiDAmM; BioIn 1, 4, 5, 6, 8, 11; IntDcOp; MetOEnc; NatCAB 51; NewEOp 71; NewGrDA 86*

Mauch, Gene William
"Skip"
American. Baseball Player, Baseball Manager
Infielder, 1947-52, 1956-57; manager, 1960-82, 1985-88; set ML record for most yrs. managed with no championships.
b. Nov 18, 1925 in Salina, Kansas
Source: *Ballpl 90; BaseReg 87; BiDAmSp Sup; BioIn 7, 10, 12, 13, 14; CurBio 74; WhoAm 82, 90; WhoProB 73; WhoWest 87*

Mauchly, John William
American. Physicist, Engineer
Co-invented ENIAC, first digital computer to handle coded material, 1946; also co-invented Binac, binary automatic computer.
b. Aug 30, 1907 in Cincinnati, Ohio
d. Jan 8, 1980 in Ambler, Pennsylvania
Source: *AmMWSc 79; AnObit 1980; BioIn 1, 6, 7, 8, 9, 12, 14, 15, 20, 21; DcAmB S10; FacFETw; HisDcDP; LarDcSc; NewYTBS 80; NotTwCS; PeoHis; PorSil; WhoAm 74, 76, 78*

Maude, Cyril
American. Actor
Actor, manager of the Haymarket, 1896-1905.
b. Apr 24, 1882 in London, England
d. Feb 20, 1951 in Torquay, England
Source: *Film 1; OxCThe 67; REn; TwYS; WhAm 3; WhoHol B; WhScrn 74, 77*

Maugham, Robin
[Robert Cecil Romer Maugham]
English. Author
Wrote *Conversations with Willie,* 1978; nephew of Somerset.
b. May 17, 1916 in London, England
d. Mar 13, 1981 in Brighton, England
Source: *AnObit 1981; Au&Wr 71; BioIn 4, 9, 10, 12; ConAu 9R, 40NR, 103, X; ConNov 72, 76; DcLEL 1940; GayLL; HalFC 84, 88; IntAu&W 76, 77, 82, 86, 89, 91; LiExTwC; LngCTC; NewC; NewCBEL; NewYTBS 81; Novels; REn; RGTwCWr; ScF&FL 1, 2, 92; TwCA SUP; TwCCr&M 80; WorAu 1970; WrDr 76, 80, 82*

Maugham, W(illiam) Somerset
English. Author
Wrote novels *Of Human Bondage,* 1915, filmed, 1934; *The Razor's Edge,* 1944, filmed, 1947.
b. Jan 25, 1874 in Paris, France
d. Dec 16, 1965 in Nice, France
Source: *AtlBL; Benet 96; BiE&WWA; BiHiMed; BioIn 1, 2, 3, 4, 5, 6, 7, 8, 9, 10, 11, 12, 13, 14, 15, 16, 17, 18, 19; BlmGEL; CasWL; Chambr 3; CnMD;*

CnMWL; CnThe; ConAu 5R, 40NR; ConLC 1, 11, 15; CyWA 58; DcBiA; DcLEL; DcNaB 1961; Dis&D; EncAl&E; EncMys; EncWL 3; EncWT; Ent; EvLB; FilmgC; IntDcT 2; LinLib S; LngCEL; LngCTC; MajTwCW; MakMC; McGEWB; McGEWD 72; ModBrL S1; ModWD; NewC; NewCBEL; NotNAT A, B; OxCEng 67, 95; OxCMed 86; OxCThe 67; PenC ENG; PlP&P; RAdv 1, 14; REn; REnWD; RfGShF; SpyFic; TwCA, SUP; TwCWr; WebE&AL; WhE&EA; WhLit; WhoTwCL; WhScrn 77; WhThe

Mauldin, Bill
[William Henry Mauldin]
American. Cartoonist
Prominent during WW II; GI characters Willie, Joe were most realistic of period.
b. Oct 29, 1921 in Mountain Park, New Mexico
Source: *AmAu&B; AmDec 1940; AmSocL; BenetAL 91; BioIn 1, 2, 3, 4, 5, 6, 7, 9, 10, 11, 13, 16, 18, 19; CelR, 90; ConAu 111, X; CurBio 45, 64; EncACom; EncAJ; EncTwCJ; EncWB; JoeFr; LegTOT; OxCAmL 65, 83, 95; REnAL; TwCA SUP; VarWW 85; WebAB 74, 79; WebAMB; WhoAm 86, 90, 97; WhoAmA 73, 76, 78, 80, 82, 84, 86, 89, 91, 93; WhoHol 92, A; WhoMW 74, 90, 96; WorECar*

Maunick, Edouard Joseph Marc
Mauritian. Poet
Wrote of social isolation, racism; works include *Shoot Me,* 1970.
b. Sep 23, 1931, Mauritius

Maupassant, Guy de
[Henri Rene Albert Guy de Maupassant]
French. Author
Recognized master of the short story who wrote *Pierre et Jean,* 1888.
b. Aug 5, 1850 in Dieppe, France
d. Jul 6, 1893 in Paris, France
Source: *AtlBL; BbD; Benet 87, 96; BiD&SB; BioIn 1, 2, 3, 4, 5, 7, 8, 9, 10, 12, 14, 15, 19; CasWL; ClDMEL 47; CrtSuMy; CyWA 58; DcArts; DcEuL; DcLB 123; Dis&D; EncWT; EuAu; EuWr 7; EvEuW; GrFLW; GuFrLit 1; LegTOT; LinLib L, S; MagSWL; McGEWB; NewC; NewCBEL; NewEOp 71; NinCLC 1, 42; Novels; OxCEng 67, 85, 95; OxCFr; PenC EUR; PenEncH; RAdv 14, 13-2; RComWL; REn; ScF&FL 1, 92; ShSCr 1; ShSWr; SupFW; WhDW; WhoHr&F; WorAl; WorAlBi; WorLitC*

Maura, Carmen
Spanish. Actor
Spanish and international star recognized for her role in Pedro Almodovar's *Women on the Verge of a Nervous Breakdown,* 1988.
b. 1946? in Madrid, Spain
Source: *BioIn 16; CurBio 92; IntMPA 92; IntWW 93; WhoWor 93*

Maurel, Victor
French. Opera Singer, Teacher
Dramatic baritone; created the first Falstaff, NY Met., 1890s.
b. Jun 17, 1848 in Marseilles, France
d. Oct 22, 1923 in New York, New York
Source: *Baker 78, 84, 92; BiDAmM; BioIn 1, 3, 6, 7, 11, 14; BriBkM 80; CmOp; IntDcOp; LegTOT; MetOEnc; NewAmDM; NewEOp 71; NewGrDM 80; NewGrDO; OxDcOp; PenDiMP*

Maurer, Alfred Henry
American. Artist
Drew elongated female figures; interested in cubism.
b. 1868 in New York, New York
d. 1932
Source: *BioIn 1, 2, 4, 5, 9, 10; BriEAA; DcAmArt; McGDA; NatCAB 25; NewCol 75*

Maurer, Emilia Sherman
American. Choreographer, Dancer
Long-time dancer and choreographer for the Radio City Music Hall's Rockettes; became director in 1971.
d. Feb 28, 1992 in Manhasset, New York
Source: *BioIn 17; NewYTBS 92*

Maurer, Ion Gheorghe
Romanian. Diplomat
Chm., Council of Ministers, 1961-74.
b. Sep 23, 1902 in Bucharest, Romania
Source: *BioIn 9; CurBio 71; IntWW 74, 75, 76, 77, 78, 79, 80, 81, 82, 83, 89, 91, 93; IntYB 78, 79, 80, 81, 82; WhoSocC 78; WhoSoCE 89; WhoWor 74*

Mauriac, Claude
French. Author
Wrote *Le Diner en ville,* (*The Dinner Party*), 1959; writer of the "new novel."
b. Apr 25, 1914 in Paris, France
Source: *Benet 87, 96; BioIn 6, 10, 12, 17, 19; CasWL; ClDMEL 80; ConAu 89, 152; ConFLW 84; ConLC 9; ConWorW 93; CurBio 93; DcLB 83; DcTwCCu 2; EncWL 2, 3; GuFrLit 1; IntAu&W 76, 77; IntWW 74, 75, 76, 77, 78, 79, 80, 81, 82, 83, 89, 91, 93; ModFrL; REn; TwCWr; WhoFr 79; WhoWor 74, 84, 87, 89, 91, 93, 95, 96; WorAu 1950*

Mauriac, Francois
French. Author, Dramatist
Won Nobel Prize in literature, 1952; psychological novels include *Le Noeud de Viperes,* 1932; *Asmodee,* 1938.
b. Oct 11, 1885 in Bordeaux, France
d. Sep 1, 1970 in Paris, France
Source: *AtlBL; Benet 87, 96; BioIn 1, 2, 3, 4, 5, 7, 8, 9, 10, 11, 12, 14, 15, 16, 17, 18, 20; CasWL; CathA 1930; ClDMEL 47, 80; CnMD; CnMWL; ConAu P-2; ConLC 4, 9, 56; CyWA 58, 89; DcArts; DcLB 65; DcTwCCu 2; Dis&D; EncWL 2, 3; EncWT; Ent; EuWr 10; EvEuW; GrFLW; GuFrLit 1; LegTOT; LinLib L, S; LngCTC; MajTwCW; MakMC; McGEWB; McGEWD 72, 84; ModFrL; ModRL; ModWD; NobelP; Novels; ObitT 1961; OxCEng 67, 85, 95; OxCFr; PenC EUR; RAdv 14, 13-2; RComWL; REn; REnWD; TwCA, SUP; TwCWr; WhAm 5; WhDW; WhoNob, 90, 95; WhoTwCL; WorAl; WorAlBi*

Maurice, Frederick Denison
[John Frederick Denison Maurice]
English. Theologian, Educator
A founder, Christian Socialism Movement, 1848; works include *Social Morality,* 1869.
b. Aug 29, 1805 in Normanston, England
d. Apr 1, 1872 in London, England
Source: *Alli, SUP; BiD&SB; BioIn 1, 2, 3, 7, 9, 10, 11, 15, 16; BritAu 19; CamGEL; CamGLE; CasWL; CelCen; Chambr 3; CyEd; DcBiPP; DcEnL; DcEuL; DcLB 55; DcNaB, C; EvLB; LuthC 75; McGEWB; NewC; NewCBEL; OxCEng 67; PenC ENG; REn; VicBrit*

Maurois, Andre
[Emile Salomon Herzog]
French. Author
Wrote biographies of Shelley, Byron, Disraeli, Washington.
b. Jul 26, 1885 in Elbeuf, France
d. Oct 9, 1967 in Paris, France
Source: *AtlBL; AuBYP 2, 3; Benet 87, 96; BioIn 1, 2, 3, 4, 5, 7, 8, 9, 12, 16, 17; CasWL; ChhPo S2; ClDMEL 47, 80; ConAu 25R, P-2; DcArts; DcLB 65; DcTwCCu 2; EncSF, 93; EncWL 2, 3; EvEuW; FacFETw; LegTOT; LinLib L, S; LngCTC; MajTwCW; ModFrL; NewC; Novels; ObitT 1961; OxCEng 67, 85, 95; OxCFr; PenC EUR; RAdv 1, 13-1; REn; ScF&FL 1, 2, 92; ScFEYrs; ScFSB; TwCA, SUP; TwCSFW 81A, 86A, 91A; TwCWr; WhAm 4; WhDW; WhE&EA; WhoHr&F; WhoLA; WhoTwCL; WorAl; WorAlBi*

Mauroy, Pierre
French. Political Leader
Premier in Francois Mitterand's Socialist govt.
b. Jul 5, 1928 in Cartignie, France
Source: *BiDFrPL; BioIn 12, 13, 14, 17; CurBio 82; IntWW 82, 83, 89, 91, 93; IntYB 82; Who 82, 83, 85, 88, 90, 92, 94; WhoEIO 82; WhoFr 79; WhoWor 82, 84, 93, 95*

Maury, Antonia Caetana De Paiua Pereira
American. Astronomer
Known for research in stellar spectroscopy.
b. Mar 21, 1866 in Cold Spring, New York
d. Jan 8, 1952 in Dobbs Ferry, New York
Source: *NotAW MOD*

Maury, Matthew Fontaine
American. Oceanographer, Naval Officer
Wrote *Physical Geography of the Sea,* 1855, first textbook of modern oceanography.

b. Jan 14, 1806 in Fredericksburg, Virginia
d. Feb 1, 1873 in Lexington, Virginia
Source: *Alli, SUP; AmAu&B; AmBi; ApCAB; AsBiEn; BbD; BiAUS; BiDAmS; BiD&SB; BiDConf; BiESc; BiInAmS; BioIn 1, 2, 3, 4, 5, 6, 7, 8, 9, 10, 12, 13, 15, 18; CamDcSc; CivWDc; CyAL 2; DcAmAu; DcAmB; DcAmMiB; DcNAA; DcScB; Drake; EncAB-H 1974, 1996; EncAI&E; EncSoH; Geog 1; HarEnUS; InSci; LinLib L, S; McGEWB; MemAm; NatCAB 6; OxCAmH; OxCShps; PeoHis; REnAL; TwCBDA; WebAB 74, 79; WebAMB; WhAm HS; WhCiWar; WhDW; WorScD*

Maury, Reuben

American. Newspaper Editor
NY Daily News editorial writer, 1926-72; known for conservative outlook.
b. Sep 2, 1899 in Butte, Montana
d. Apr 23, 1981 in Norwalk, Connecticut
Source: *AnObit 1981; BioIn 1, 9, 12; ConAu 103; EncAJ; EncTwCJ; IntYB 78, 79, 80, 81, 82; NewYTBS 81; WhAm 7; WhoAm 74, 76, 78, 80*

Mausolus

Persian. Ruler
Virtual ruler of Rhodes; enormous tomb, built for him by wife, Artemisia, Mausoleum at Halicarnassus, is one of world's wonders.
d. 353BC
Source: *DcBiPP; NewCol 75; OxCClL, 89; WebBD 83*

Maverick, Maury

American. Lawyer, Politician
Colorful Dem. representative from TX, 1930s; San Antonio mayor, 1939; wrote *A Maverick American,* 1937.
b. Oct 23, 1895 in San Antonio, Texas
d. Jun 7, 1954 in San Antonio, Texas
Source: *BioIn 1, 3, 5, 9, 15; CurBio 44, 54; DcAmB S5; EncAACR; EncSoH; NatCAB 42; PolPar; WhAm 3*

Maverick, Samuel Augustus

American. Rancher, Government Official
Helped establish Republic of Texas, 1836; term "maverick" used for unbranded cattle wandering unattended.
b. Jul 25, 1803 in Pendleton, South Carolina
d. Sep 2, 1870 in San Antonio, Texas
Source: *BioIn 6; NatCAB 6; TwCBDA; WebAB 74, 79*

Mawson, Douglas, Sir

Australian. Geologist, Explorer
Claimed over two million square miles of Antarctic territory for Australia, 1907-31.
b. May 5, 1882 in Bradford, England
d. Oct 14, 1958 in Adelaide, Australia
Source: *BioIn 4, 5, 7, 8, 9, 11, 12, 17, 18; DcNaB 1951; DcScB; Expl 93; InSci; LarDcSc; LinLib L, S; McGEWB; NewCol 75; ObitT 1951; OxCAusL; WhE&EA; WhoLA; WhWE*

Max, Peter

American. Artist, Designer
Best known for colorful, psychedelic posters, murals.
b. Oct 19, 1937 in Berlin, Germany
Source: *AmArt; AmEA 74; BioIn 10, 12, 15, 19; BioNews 74; ConAu 116; ConGrA 3; CurBio 71; IlsBYP; LegTOT; News 93-2; PrintW 83, 85; SmATA 45; WhoAm 74, 76, 78, 80, 82, 84, 88, 90, 92, 94, 95, 96; WhoAmA 73, 76, 78, 80, 82, 84, 86, 89, 91, 93; WhoSSW 73*

Maxim, Hiram Percy

American. Inventor, Manufacturer
Invented, manufactured "Maxim silencer" for guns; brother of Hudson.
b. Sep 2, 1869 in New York, New York
d. Feb 17, 1936 in La Junta, Colorado
Source: *AmBi; BioIn 4; DcAmB S2; DcNAA; EncABHB 4; NatCAB 15; OxCAmH; WebAB 74, 79; WhAm 1*

Maxim, Hiram Stevens, Sir

English. Inventor
Invented Maxim recoil-operated machine gun.
b. Feb 5, 1840 in Sangerville, Maine
d. Nov 24, 1916 in Streatham, England
Source: *AmBi; ApCAB SUP; AsBiEn; BiInAmS; BioIn 4, 5, 6, 11, 14; DcAmB; DcNaB 1912; HarEnUS; InSci; LinLib S; McGEWB; NatCAB 6; OxCAmH; TwCBDA; WebAB 74, 79; WebAMB; WhAm 1; WhDW; WorAl; WorAlBi; WorInv*

Maxim, Hudson

American. Manufacturer, Inventor
Invented smokeless explosive powders; maximite, a bursting powder more forceful than dynamite; delayed reaction detonating fuse; brother of Hiram.
b. Feb 3, 1853 in Orneville, Maine
d. May 6, 1927 in Lake Hopatcong, New Jersey
Source: *AmBi; AmLY; ApCAB X; BioIn 4, 5; ChhPo S1; DcAmB; DcNAA; HarEnUS; InSci; NatCAB 13; OxCAmH; WebAB 74, 79; WebAMB; WhAm 1; WhScrn 83*

Maximilian

[Ferdinand Maximilian Joseph]
Austrian. Ruler
Archduke of Austria, emperor of Mexico, 1864-67; empire in Mexico denounced by US; Napoleon III withdrew support.
b. Jul 6, 1832 in Vienna, Austria
d. Jun 19, 1867 in Queretaro, Mexico
Source: *ApCAB; Benet 87, 96; BioIn 1, 2, 4, 5, 6, 7, 8, 9, 10, 18, 20; CivWDc; DcBiPP; DcCathB; DicTyr; Dis&D; EncLatA; HisWorL; LegTOT; McGEWB; OxCAmH; OxCGer 76, 86; REn; WhAm HS; WhCiWar; WhDW; WorAl; WorAlBi*

Maximilian I

"The Last of the Knights"
German. Ruler
King of Germany, 1486-1519; Holly Roman Emperor, 1493-1519; laid foundation of Hapsburg greatness.
b. Mar 22, 1459 in Wiener Neustadt, Austria
d. Jan 12, 1519 in Wels, Austria
Source: *DcBiPP; DcCathB; Dis&D; LuthC 75; NewCol 75; WhDW*

Maximilian II

German. Ruler
Holy Roman Emperor, 1564-76.
b. Jul 31, 1527 in Vienna, Austria
d. Oct 12, 1576 in Regensburg, Germany
Source: *DcBiPP; DcCathB; Dis&D; NewCol 75*

Maxon, Lou Russell

American. Advertising Executive
Founder, 1927, director, Maxon Co., one of the largest US advertising firms.
b. Jul 28, 1900 in Marietta, Ohio
d. May 15, 1971
Source: *BioIn 4, 9; ConAu 116; CurBio 43, 71; NewYTBE 71; St&PR 75; WhAm 5*

Maxwell, Cedric Bryan

"Cornbread"
American. Basketball Player
Forward, 1977-88; mostly with Boston, now with Houston; led NBA in field goal percentage, 1979, 1980.
b. Nov 21, 1955 in Kinston, North Carolina
Source: *OfNBA 87; WhoBlA 85, 92*

Maxwell, Elsa

American. Journalist, Socialite
Best known for organizing parties for socially prominent people; radio show "Elsa Maxwell's Party Line," 1942.
b. May 24, 1883 in Keokuk, Iowa
d. Nov 1, 1963 in New York, New York
Source: *ASCAP 66, 80; BiDAmNC; BioIn 1, 3, 4, 6, 7; ConAu 89; CurBio 43, 64; DcAmB S7; EncAFC; FilmgC; HalFC 80, 84, 88; InWom, SUP; LegTOT; LibW; NotNAT B; ObitT 1961; WebAB 74, 79; WhAm 4; WhoAmW 58, 61, 64; WhoHol B; WhScrn 77, 83*

Maxwell, Hamish

American. Business Executive
Chm., CEO of tobacco conglomerate, Philip Morris, 1985-91.
b. 1926 in Liverpool, England
Source: *BioIn 15, 16; Dun&B 79, 86, 88, 90; News 89; St&PR 93, 96, 97; WhoAm 86, 88, 90, 92, 94, 95, 96, 97; WhoE 83, 86, 89, 91; WhoFI 87, 89, 92, 94, 96; WhoWor 87*

Maxwell, James Clerk

Scottish. Mathematician, Physicist
First physics professor at Cambridge who found light to be electromagnetic phenomenon.
b. Nov 13, 1831 in Edinburgh, Scotland

d. Nov 5, 1879 in Cambridge, England
Source: *Alli SUP; AsBiEn; BiDPsy; BiESc; BioIn 1, 2, 3, 4, 5, 6, 7, 8, 9, 10, 11, 12, 13, 14, 15, 16, 20; BritAu 19; CamDcSc; CelCen; Chambr 3; ChhPo S1; DcInv; DcNaB; DcScB; EncAJ; ICPEnP; InSci; LarDcSc; LinLib S; MacBEP; McGEWB; NamesHP; NewC; OxCEng 67; OxCMus; RAdv 14, 13-5; SaTiSS; VicBrit; WhDW; WorAl; WorAlBi; WorScD*

Maxwell, Marilyn
American. Actor
Played on TV's "Bus Stop," 1961; films include *Summer Holiday*.
b. Aug 3, 1921 in Clarinda, Iowa
d. Mar 20, 1972 in Beverly Hills, California
Source: *EncAFC; FilmEn; FilmgC; ForYSC; HalFC 80, 84, 88; MotPP; MovMk; NewYTBE 72; WhoHol B; WhScrn 77*

Maxwell, Robert Ian Charles
English. Publisher
Media tycoon; owned Mirror Group Newspapers, 1984-91; drowned under somewhat mysterious circumstances.
b. Jun 10, 1923 in Selo Slatina
d. Nov 5, 1991
Source: *BioIn 13; CurBio 88; Dun&B 90; FacFETw; IntWW 91; News 92, 90-1; WhoAm 90; WhoE 91; WhoWor 91; WorAlBi*

Maxwell, Steamer
[Fred G Maxwell]
Canadian. Hockey Player, Hockey Coach
Amateur player and coach in Winnipeg, early 1900s; Hall of Fame, 1962.
b. May 19, 1890 in Winnipeg, Manitoba, Canada
Source: *WhoHcky 73*

Maxwell, Vera (Huppe)
American. Fashion Designer
Noted for classic suits, sportswear separates; NYC Fashion Gallery dedicated, 1981.
b. Apr 22, 1901 in New York, New York
d. Jan 15, 1995 in Rincon, Puerto Rico
Source: *BiDD; BioIn 10, 11, 20, 21; CurBio 77, 95N; EncFash; InWom SUP; NewYTBS 95; WhoAm 82, 84; WhoFash, 88*

Maxwell, William
American. Author
Novels include *They Came Like Swallows*, 1937; *The Chateau*, 1961; *The Outermost Dream*, 1989.
b. Aug 16, 1908 in Lincoln, Illinois
Source: *AmAu&B; AmNov; AuBYP 2, 3; BenetAL 91; BioIn 2, 4, 7, 12, 13, 14, 15, 20; ConAu 93; ConLC 19; ConNov 72, 76, 82, 86, 91; DcLB Y80B; DrAPF 80, 91; IntAu&W 76, 77, 91; OxCAmL 65, 83, 95; REn; TwCA SUP; WhoAm 74, 76, 78, 80, 82, 84, 86, 88, 90, 92, 94, 95, 96; WhoUSWr 88; WhoWor 74; WhoWrEP 89, 92, 95; WrDr 76, 80, 82, 84, 86, 88, 90, 92, 94, 96*

May, Billy
[E William May]
American. Jazz Musician
Trumpeter, arranger with Charlie Barnet, Glenn Miller, 1940s.
b. Nov 10, 1916 in Pittsburgh, Pennsylvania
Source: *BgBands 74; BiDAmM; BiDJaz; CmpEPM; EncJzS; NewGrDJ 88, 94; OxCPMus; PenEncP; VarWW 85; WhoAm 74, 76; WhoJazz 72*

May, Brian
English. Singer, Musician
Guitarist for British rock group formed 1972; album *Night at the Opera*, 1975.
b. Jul 19, 1947 in Hampton, England
d. Apr 25, 1997 in Melbourne, Australia
Source: *BioIn 11, 13; HalFC 88; IlEncRk; LegTOT; OnThGG; RkOn 74; WhoRock 81; WhoRocM 82*

May, Edna
American. Actor
Starred in *Salvation Joan*, 1916.
b. 1879 in Syracuse, New York
d. Jan 1, 1948 in Lausanne, Switzerland
Source: *EncMT; Film 1; MotPP; WhoHol B; WhoStg 1906, 1908; WhScrn 74, 77*

May, Elaine
[Elaine Berlin]
American. Actor, Director
Appeared in revue with Mike Nichols, 1960-61; directed, acted in film *A New Leaf*, 1971.
b. Apr 21, 1932 in Philadelphia, Pennsylvania
Source: *AmWomD; BiE&WWA; BioIn 4, 5, 6, 7, 8, 9, 10, 13, 14, 15, 16; CelR; ConAmD; ConAu 124, 142; ConDr 73, 77, 82A, 88A, 93; ConLC 16; ConTFT 5; ConWomD; CurBio 61; DcLB 44; DcLP 87A; EncAFC; Ent; FacFETw; FilmEn; FilmgC; FunnyW; GoodHs; HalFC 80, 84, 88; IntDcF 2-4; IntMPA 77, 78, 79, 80, 81, 82, 84, 86, 88, 92, 94, 96; IntWW 83, 89, 91, 93; InWom, SUP; JoeFr; LegTOT; MiSFD 9; MotPP; NotNAT; NotWoAT; PlP&P; ReelWom; VarWW 85; WhoAm 74, 76, 78, 80, 82, 84, 86, 88, 90, 92, 94, 95, 96, 97; WhoAmW 64, 66, 68, 70, 72, 74, 75, 83, 85, 89, 91, 93, 97; WhoEnt 92; WhoHol 92, A; WhoThe 72, 77, 81; WhoWor 74; WomWMM; WorAl; WorAlBi; WrDr 76, 80, 82, 84, 86, 88, 90, 92, 94, 96*

May, John L.
American. Religious Leader
Archbishop of St. Louis, MO, 1980-1992; pres., Nat. Conference of Catholic Bishops, 1983-89.
b. Mar 31, 1922 in Evanston, Illinois
d. Mar 24, 1994 in Saint Louis, Missouri
Source: *AmCath 80; CurBio 91, 94N; WhoMW 90; WhoRel 85, 92*

May, Karl Friedrich
German. Author
Juvenile adventure tales usually concern desert Arabs, Indians including *Winnetou*, 1893.
b. Feb 25, 1842 in Chemnitz, Germany
d. Mar 30, 1912 in Radebeul, Germany
Source: *BioIn 1, 7, 8, 10, 15, 19; CasWL; ClDMEL 47, 80; EncFWF; EuAu; EvEuW; OxCChiL; OxCGer 76; REnAW; WhNaAH*

May, Mortimer
American. Manufacturer
Pres., chm., May Hosiery Mills, 1946-74.
b. Dec 20, 1892 in Laconia, New Hampshire
d. May 8, 1974 in Miami Beach, Florida
Source: *BioIn 6, 10; WhAm 6; WhoAm 74; WhoFI 74; WhoSSW 73; WhoWorJ 72*

May, Morton David
American. Merchant
Third, since founder/grandfather, to head May Dept. Stores Co., 1951-82; art collector.
b. 1914 in Saint Louis, Missouri
d. Apr 13, 1983 in Saint Louis, Missouri
Source: *AnObit 1983; BioIn 2, 13; NewYTBS 83; St&PR 75; WhoAm 74; WhoAmA 73, 76, 78, 80, 82, 84, 86, 89; WhoGov 72*

May, Phil(ip William)
English. Caricaturist
Illustrated *Punch* from 1896; satirized London street life, sporting events.
b. Apr 22, 1864 in Leeds, England
d. Aug 22, 1903 in London, England
Source: *AntBDN B; Benet 87; BioIn 1, 2, 6, 12, 14; ChhPo S2; DcBrAr 1; DcBrBI; DcBrWA; DcNaB S2; DcVicP 2; IlBEAAW; LegTOT; McGDA; NewCBEL; NewCol 75; OxCArt; OxCAusL; OxDcArt; REn; WhDW; WorECar*

May, Robert Lewis
American. Advertising Executive, Author
Wrote story "Rudolph the Red-Nosed Reindeer," 1939, to promote Montgomery Ward.
b. 1905
d. Aug 11, 1976 in Evanston, Illinois
Source: *BioIn 1, 2, 5, 7, 11, 13; ConAu 104; NatCAB 61; SmATA 27N*

May, Rollo (Reece)
American. Psychoanalyst
Concerned with anxiety; wrote *Man's Search for Himself*, 1952.
b. Apr 21, 1909 in Ada, Ohio
d. Oct 22, 1994 in Tiburon, California
Source: *AmAu&B; BioIn 16; BioNews 74; CelR; ConAu 111, 147; CurBio 73, 95N; FacFETw; NewYTBE 71; RAdv 14, 13-5; WhAm 11; WhoAm 74, 76, 78, 80, 82, 84, 86, 88, 90, 92, 94; WhoE 74; WhoWest 94; WorAu 1985; WrDr 90, 92, 94, 96*

Mayakovsky, Vladimir
Russian. Poet, Dramatist
Futurist writer who wrote *The Cloud in Pants,* 1915; *The Bedbug,* 1929; committed suicide.
b. Jul 19, 1893 in Bagdadi, Russia
d. Aug 14, 1930 in Moscow, Union of Soviet Socialist Republics
Source: *AtlBL; ClDMEL 47; DcArts; EncSF; EuWr 11; EvEuW; GrFLW; LinLib L; LngCTC; MajMD 2; McGEWD 72; ModSL 1; ModWD; OxCEng 67; OxCFilm; OxCThe 67; PenC EUR; PlP&P; RAdv 14, 13-2; REn; REnWD; TwCLC 4, 18; TwCSFW 86A, 91A; TwCWr; WhDW; WhoTwCL; WorAlBi; WorAu 1950*

Mayall, John Brumwell
"The Father of the British Blues"
English. Jazz Musician
Singer, organist, harmonica player; led band, The Bluesbreakers, 1960s; wrote over 200 songs.
b. Nov 29, 1933 in Manchester, England
Source: *Baker 84; BiDJaz; ConMus 7; EncJzS; EncPR&S 74, 89; EncRk 88; HarEnR 86; IlEncRk; NewYTBE 70; OxCPMus; PenEncP; RkOn 74; WhoAm 74, 76, 78, 80, 82, 84, 86, 88; WhoEnt 92*

Maybeck, Bernard Ralph
American. Architect
Eclectic builder; designed San Francisco's Palace of Fine Arts, 1915.
b. Feb 7, 1862 in New York, New York
d. Mar 2, 1957 in Glendale, California
Source: *AmCulL; BioIn 1, 2, 3, 4, 5, 6, 11, 12, 13, 19; BriEAA; ConArch 87; DcAmB S6; EncMA; McGDA; NatCAB 43; NewCol 75; PeoHis; WhAm 5; WhoArch*

Mayehoff, Eddie
American. Actor
TV shows include "The Adventures of Fenimore J. Mayehoff," 1946; "That's My Boy," 1954.
b. Jul 7, 1914 in Baltimore, Maryland
d. Nov 12, 1992
Source: *BiE&WWA; EncAFC; HalFC 88; IntMPA 82, 84, 86, 88, 92; NotNAT; WhoHol 92, A*

Mayer, Albert
American. Architect, Urban Planner
Designed Kitimat, British Columbia; Ashdod, Israel.
b. Dec 29, 1897 in New York, New York
d. Oct 14, 1981 in New York, New York
Source: *AmArch 70; AnObit 1981; BioIn 12; BlueB 76; ConAu 73, 105; EncUrb; FacFETw; IntAu&W 77, 82; IntWW 74, 75, 76, 77, 78, 79, 80, 81; MacEA; NewYTBS 81; WhAm 8; WhoAm 74, 76, 78; WhoWor 74; WhoWorJ 72, 78*

Mayer, Arthur Loeb
"Merchant of Menace"
American. Film Executive
Paramount Studios publicist, exhibitor; nickname from policy of distributing low-budget horror films.
b. May 28, 1886 in Demopolis, Alabama
d. Apr 14, 1981 in New York, New York
Source: *AmAu&B; BioIn 9, 10, 11, 12; FacFETw; IntMPA 75, 76, 77, 78, 79, 80, 81; NewYTBE 71; NewYTBS 78, 81; WhoAm 74, 76, 78; WhoWorJ 72*

Mayer, Dick
[Calvin Richard Mayer]
American. Golfer
Turned pro, 1949; won US Open, 1957.
b. Aug 29, 1924 in Stamford, Connecticut
Source: *WhoGolf*

Mayer, Edward Newton, Jr.
American. Author, Advertising Executive
Expert on direct mail marketing; wrote *How to Make Money with Your Direct Mail.*
b. 1907
d. Dec 1, 1975 in New York, New York
Source: *BioIn 10, 11; NewYTBS 75*

Mayer, Gene
[Eugene Mayer]
American. Tennis Player
Won French doubles, 1978; US doubles, 1979.
b. Apr 11, 1956 in New York, New York
Source: *BioIn 12; BuCMET; WhoAm 82, 84; WhoIntT*

Mayer, Jean
French. Nutritionist, University Administrator
Nutrition expert; pres. of Tufts U, 1976-92.
b. Feb 19, 1920 in Paris, France
d. Jan 1, 1993 in Sarasota, Florida
Source: *AmMWSc 73P, 76P, 79, 82, 86, 89, 92; AnObit 1993; BioIn 8, 9, 10, 11, 12, 15, 17, 18, 19; ConAu 117, 129, 140; CurBio 70, 93N; EncWB; IntMed 80; NewYTBS 76, 86, 93; WhAm 11; WhoAm 74, 76, 78, 80, 82, 84, 86, 88, 90, 92; WhoAmP 73, 75, 77, 79, 81, 83, 85, 87, 89, 91; WhoE 74, 86, 89, 91, 93; WhoWor 74, 76, 89, 91, 93*

Mayer, Johann Tobias
German. Astronomer
Known for lunar tables, important in determining longitude at sea.
b. Feb 17, 1723 in Esslingen, Germany
d. Feb 20, 1762 in Gottingen, Germany
Source: *BioIn 14; DcBiPP; DcScB; InSci; NewCol 75*

Mayer, L(ouis) B(urt)
American. Producer, Film Executive
Co-founded MGM Studios, 1924; founder, 1927, pres., 1931-36, Academy of Motion Picture Arts and Sciences.
b. Jul 4, 1885 in Minsk, Russia
d. Oct 29, 1957 in Los Angeles, California
Source: *BiDAmBL 83; BiDFilm; BioIn 1, 2, 3, 4, 5, 6, 7, 8, 10, 11, 12; CurBio 43, 58; DcAmB S6; DcFM; EncAB-H 1974, 1996; FilmgC; NatCAB 60; OxCAmH; OxCFilm; WebAB 74, 79; WhAm 3; WomWMM; WorEFlm*

Mayer, Maria Goeppert
German. Physicist
First woman to receive Nobel Prize in physics, 1963, for work on structure of atomic nucleus.
b. Jun 28, 1906 in Kattaivitz, Germany
d. Feb 20, 1972 in San Diego, California
Source: *BioIn 10, 11, 14, 15, 16, 17, 19, 20; CurBio 64, 72, 72N; DcAmB S9; DcScB S2; GrLiveH; InWom; LibW; McGMS 80; NatCAB 58; NobelP; NotAW MOD; ObitOF 79; WebAB 74, 79; WhAm 5; WhoAmW 58, 64, 66, 68, 70, 72; WhoNob, 90, 95*

Mayer, Martin Prager
American. Author, Critic
Works include *Fate of the Dollar,* 1980; *Money Bazaars,* 1984.
b. Jan 14, 1928 in New York, New York
Source: *AmAu&B; Au&Wr 71; BioIn 6, 8, 10; ConAu 5R; IntAu&W 77; WhoAm 74, 76, 78, 80, 82, 84, 86, 88, 90, 92, 94; WhoFI 92; WhoUSWr 88; WhoWor 96; WhoWrEP 89, 92, 95; WorAu 1950*

Mayer, Norman D
"Pops"
American. Political Activist
Held Washington Monument hostage, Dec, 1982, to protest nuclear weapons.
b. Mar 31, 1916 in El Paso, Texas
d. Dec 8, 1982 in Washington, District of Columbia

Mayer, Oscar Ferdinand
American. Meat Packer
Founded Oscar Mayer & Brother in Chicago, 1883.
b. Mar 29, 1859 in Kaesingen, Wurttemberg
d. Mar 11, 1955 in Chicago, Illinois
Source: *BiDAmBL 83; BioIn 3, 6; NatCAB 45; WhAm 3; WorAl*

Mayer, Oscar Gottfried
American. Meat Packer
Pres., Oscar Mayer Co., 1928-55, chm., 1955-65.
b. Mar 10, 1888 in Chicago, Illinois
d. Mar 5, 1965
Source: *BiDAmBL 83; BioIn 7, 10; DcAmB S7; NatCAB 54; WhAm 4*

Mayer, Oscar Gottfried, II
American. Meat Packer
Pres., Oscar Mayer Co., 1955-66; chm., 1966-77.
b. Mar 16, 1914 in Chicago, Illinois

Source: *St&PR 75; WhoAm 74; WhoFI 74; WhoMW 74*

Mayer, Robert, Sir
English. Philanthropist
Co-founded Lincoln Symphony Orchestra, 1932.
b. Jun 5, 1879 in Mannheim, Germany
d. Jan 9, 1985
Source: *AnObit 1985; Baker 92; BioIn 8, 9, 12, 14; ConAu 115; DcArts; DcNaB 1981; IntWWM 77, 80; NewGrDM 80; NewYTBS 85; WhE&EA; Who 74, 82, 83, 85; WhoMus 72*

Mayer, Sandy
[Alex Mayer]
American. Tennis Player
Teamed with brother Gene to win doubles tournaments, 1979-81; with V Gerulaitis, won Wimbledon doubles, 1975.
b. Apr 5, 1952 in Flushing, New York
Source: *BuCMET; LegTOT; WhoIntT*

Mayes, Herbert Raymond
American. Journalist
Editor *Good Housekeeping*, 1938-58; *McCall's*, 1959-62; wrote Horatio Alger's biography, 1928.
b. Aug 11, 1900 in New York, New York
d. Oct 30, 1987 in New York, New York
Source: *AmAu&B; BioIn 1, 5, 6, 10, 12; ChhPo S1; EncTwCJ; St&PR 75; WhAm 11; WhoAm 78, 80, 82, 84, 86, 88; WhoUSWr 88; WhoWrEP 89*

Mayfield, Curtis Lee
American. Singer, Songwriter
Hit soundtrack album *Superfly*, 1972.
b. Jun 3, 1942 in Chicago, Illinois
Source: *Baker 84; BioIn 16; ConBlB 2; ConMus 8; DrBlPA 90; EncPR&S 74, 89; EncRk 88; HarEnR 86; IlEncBM 82; IlEncRk; NewAmDM; NewGrDA 86; OxCPMus; PenEncP; VarWW 85; WhoAm 76, 78, 80, 82, 84, 86, 88, 92, 94, 95, 96, 97; WhoBlA 92; WhoEnt 92*

Mayhew, Jonathan
American. Clergy
Well-known, outspoken, political agitator, defender of civil liberties who pastored Boston's West Church, 1747-66; accused of inciting Stamp Act riots, 1765.
b. Oct 8, 1720 in Martha's Vineyard, Massachusetts
d. Jul 9, 1766 in Boston, Massachusetts
Source: *Alli; AmAu; AmAu&B; AmWrBE; ApCAB; BenetAL 91; BioIn 5, 7, 14, 17, 18, 19; BlkwCE; CyAL 1; DcAmAu; DcAmB; DcAmReB 1, 2; DcLB 31; DcNAA; Drake; EncARH; EncCRAm; HarEnUS; NatCAB 7; OxCAmH; OxCAmL 65, 83, 95; REnAL; TwCBDA; WebAB 74, 79; WhAm HS; WrCNE*

Mayhew, Richard
American. Artist
Award-winning painter whose works are in Brooklyn, Whitney Museums.
b. Apr 3, 1934 in Amityville, New York
Source: *AfroAA; DcCAA 77; NegAl 89; WhoAm 78, 84, 86, 88; WhoAmA 80, 82, 84, 86, 89, 91, 93; WhoBlA 77*

Mayle, Peter
English. Author
Humorist and writer of children's books; best known for his titles about southern France: *A Year in Provence*, 1989; *Toujours Provence*, 1991.
b. 1939? in Surrey, England
Source: *BioIn 16; ConAu 139; ConLC 89; CurBio 92; WhoAm 95, 96; WrDr 96*

Maynard, Don(ald)
"Sunshine"
American. Football Player
End, 1958-73, mostly with NY Titans-Jets; a favorite receiver of Joe Namath; Hall of Fame, 1987.
b. Jan 25, 1937 in Crosbyton, Texas
Source: *BiDAmSp FB; BioIn 9, 10, 17, 20; IntWWP 77; LegTOT; WhoFtbl 74*

Maynard, Ken
American. Actor
Popular cowboy star, known for riding stunts on horse, Tarzan.
b. Jul 21, 1895 in Vevay, Indiana
d. Mar 23, 1973 in Woodland Hills, California
Source: *BioIn 8, 9, 10, 12, 17; Film 2; FilmEn; FilmgC; ForYSC; HalFC 80, 84, 88; HarEnCM 87; IlEncCM; MotPP; MovMk; NewYTBE 73; TwYS; WhoHol B; WhScrn 77, 83*

Maynard, Robert Clyve
American. Newspaper Editor
First black to own controlling interest in city daily newspaper when he bought Oakland, CA *Tribune*, 1983.
b. Jun 17, 1937 in New York, New York
d. Aug 17, 1993 in Oakland, California
Source: *AmDec 1980; BiDAmNC; BioIn 13, 16; CelR 90; ConAu 110, 115; ConLC 81; CurBio 86; EncTwCJ; WhAm 11; WhoAm 80, 82, 84, 86, 88, 92, 94; WhoBlA 92; WhoUSWr 88; WhoWest 82, 84, 87, 92; WhoWor 80, 82; WhoWrEP 89, 92, 95*

Maynor, Dorothy
American. Singer
Soprano who had NY debut, 1939; founded Harlem School of Arts for Underprivileged Children, 1963.
b. Sep 3, 1910 in Norfolk, Virginia
d. Feb 19, 1996 in West Chester, Pennsylvania
Source: *Baker 78, 84; BiDAfM; BiDAmM; BioIn 2, 3, 4, 6, 8, 10, 11, 16, 18, 19, 21; BlkWAm; CurBio 40, 51, 96N; DcAfAmP; DcTwCCu 5; DrBlPA, 90; InWom, SUP; MusSN; NegAl 76, 83, 89; NewGrDA 86; NewGrDM 80; NotBlAW 1; WhoAfA 96; WhoAm 74, 76, 78, 80; WhoAmW 58, 64, 66, 68, 70, 72, 74; WhoBlA 75, 77, 80, 85, 90, 92, 94*

Mayo, Charles Horace
American. Surgeon
Co-founded Mayo Clinic, 1915.
b. Jul 19, 1865 in Rochester, Minnesota
d. May 26, 1939 in Chicago, Illinois
Source: *AmBi; AmDec 1910; ApCAB X; BioIn 1, 2, 3, 4, 5, 6, 7, 8, 9, 11, 13, 16; DcAmB S2; DcAmMeB 84; EncAB-A 11; EncAB-H 1974, 1996; InSci; LinLib S; MemAm; NatCAB 30; OxCAmH; WebAB 74, 79; WhAm 1; WorAl*

Mayo, Katherine
American. Author
Wrote popular *Mother India*, 1927.
b. Jan 24, 1867 in Ridgeway, Pennsylvania
d. Oct 9, 1940 in Bedford, Pennsylvania
Source: *AmAu&B; AmWomWr; BenetAL 91; BioIn 9; CopCroC; DcNAA; EvLB; InWom, SUP; LngCTC; NatCAB 30; NotAW; REnAL; TwCA; WhAm 1; WhNAA*

Mayo, Virginia
[Virginia Jones]
American. Actor
Glamorous star of 1940s-50s; films include *Secret Life of Walter Mitty*, 1947.
b. Nov 30, 1920 in Saint Louis, Missouri
Source: *BiDFilm; BioIn 18, 21; ConTFT 1; EncAFC; FilmEn; FilmgC; GangFlm; HalFC 80, 84, 88; IntDcF 1-3; IntMPA 84, 86, 88, 92, 94, 96; InWom SUP; ItaFilm; LegTOT; MotPP; MovMk; SweetSg D; VarWW 85; WhoEnt 92; WhoHol A; WorAl; WorAlBi; WorEFlm*

Mayo, William James
American. Surgeon
Co-founded Mayo Clinic, 1915.
b. Jun 29, 1861 in Le Sueur, Minnesota
d. Jul 28, 1939 in Rochester, Minnesota
Source: *AmBi; AmDec 1910; ApCAB X; BioIn 1, 2, 3, 4, 5, 6, 7, 8, 9, 11, 13, 16; DcAmB S2; DcAmMeB 84; EncAB-H 1974, 1996; InSci; LinLib S; MemAm; NatCAB 14, 30; OxCAmH; WebAB 74, 79; WhAm 1; WhDW; WorAl*

Mayr, Ernst Walter
American. Biologist, Educator
Influential 20th c. biologist; wrote modern classic *The Growth of Biological Thought.*
b. Jul 5, 1904 in Kempten, Germany
Source: *AmMWSc 82, 86, 92; BiESc; BioIn 13, 14; ConAu 2NR; CurBio 84; EncHuEv; EncWB; IntAu&W 77; IntWW 83, 91; LarDcSc; WhoAm 86, 90; WrDr 92*

Mayr, Richard
Austrian. Opera Singer
Bass-baritone; noted for role of Baron Ochs in *Der Rosenkavalier.*
b. Nov 18, 1877 in Henndorf, Austria
d. Dec 1, 1935 in Vienna, Austria

Source: *Baker 78, 84, 92; BioIn 11, 12; BriBkM 80; CmOp; MetOEnc; MusSN; NewEOp 71; NewGrDM 80; NewGrDO; OxDcOp; PenDiMP*

Mays, Benjamin E(lijah)
American. Educator
President, Morehouse College, 1940-67.
b. Aug 1, 1894 in Epworth, South Carolina
d. Mar 21, 1984 in Atlanta, Georgia
Source: *BioIn 20, 21; EncAACR; EncSoH; SelBAAf; SelBAAu; WhAm 8; WhoAm 82; WhoWor 82*

Mays, David John
American. Lawyer, Historian
Wrote *Business Law,* 1933; won Pulitzer, 1953 for two-volume *Edmund Pendleton.*
b. Nov 22, 1896 in Richmond, Virginia
d. Feb 17, 1971 in Richmond, Virginia
Source: *AmAu&B; BioIn 9; NewYTBE 71; OxCAmL 65; WhAm 5*

Mays, Willie
[William Howard Mays, Jr]
"Say Hey"
American. Baseball Player
Outfielder, 1951-73, mostly with Giants; had 660 career home runs; NL MVP, 1954, 1962, 1965; Hall of Fame, 1979.
b. May 6, 1931 in Fairfield, Alabama
Source: *AfrAmAl 6; AfrAmBi 2; AfrAmSG; AmDec 1950; Ballpl 90; BiDAmSp BB; BioIn 12, 13, 14, 15, 16, 17, 18, 19, 20, 21; BioNews 74; BlkAWP; CelR, 90; CmCal; ConAu 105; ConBlB 3; CurBio 55, 66; FacFETw; InB&W 80, 85; LegTOT; LinLib S; NegAl 76, 83, 89; NewYTBE 70, 73; NewYTBS 74; RComAH; WebAB 74; WhoAm 86, 90; WhoBlA 88, 92; WhoProB 73; WorAlBi*

Maysa, Ben
Kenyan. Track Athlete
Set record for 7.1-mile course in 31 mins., 52 secs. in 1992.

Maytag, Elmer Henry
American. Manufacturer
Maytag Co. produced first washing machine, 1907.
b. Sep 18, 1883 in Newton, Iowa
d. Jul 20, 1940 in Lake Geneva, Wisconsin
Source: *BiDAmBL 83; BioIn 9; NatCAB 52; WorAl*

Maywood, Augusta
American. Dancer
Prima ballerina, La Scala in Milan, 1848-62; first American ballerina to be received internationally.
b. 1825 in New York, New York
d. Nov 3, 1876 in Lvov, Austria
Source: *BiDD; BioIn 1, 3, 9, 14, 20; CnOxB; ContDcW 89; DancEn 78; IntDcB; IntDcWB; InWom, SUP; LegTOT; LibW; NotAW; WomFir*

Mazarin, Jules, Cardinal
[Giulio Mazarini]
French. Religious Leader, Statesman
Succeeded Richelieu, 1643-61; laid foundations for monarchy of Louis XIV.
b. Jul 14, 1602 in Pescina, Italy
d. Mar 9, 1661 in Vincennes, France
Source: *Benet 87, 96; BioIn 1, 4, 5, 6, 8, 9, 11, 12, 13, 20; DcBiPP; DcCathB; Dis&D; HisWorL; LinLib L, S; LuthC 75; McGEWB; NewC; NewCol 75; NewGrDM 80; NewGrDO; OxCEng 85, 95; OxDcOp; REn; WhDW; WorAl; WorAlBi*

Maze
[Frankie Beverley; Wayne "Ziggy" Linsey; Roame Lowry; Sam Porter; Wayne Thomas; Michael White]
American. Music Group
Jazz-pop group formed 1976; albums include *Joy and Pain,* 1981.
Source: *BioIn 16; HarEnR 86; InB&W 80; RkOn 85; SoulM; St&PR 97; WhoAmM 83; WhoEnt 92*

Mazel, Judy
American. Author
Wrote hugely successful *The Beverly Hills Diet,* 1981; opened weight-loss clinic catering to celebrities, 1979.
b. 1944? in Chicago, Illinois
Source: *BioIn 12; NewYTBS 81*

Mazeroski, Bill
[William Stanley Mazeroski]
"Maz"
American. Baseball Player
Second baseman, Pittsburgh, 1956-72; known for ninth inning home run that won 1960 World Series.
b. Sep 5, 1936 in Wheeling, West Virginia
Source: *Ballpl 90; BiDAmSp BB; BioIn 4, 5, 6, 7, 10, 15, 16, 18; WhoProB 73*

Mazia, Daniel
American. Biologist
Cell biologist, discovered process preparatory to and associated with cell division (mitosis) and the structures that are involved.
b. Dec 18, 1912 in Scranton, Pennsylvania
d. Jun 30, 1996 in Monterey, California
Source: *AmMWSc 73P, 76P, 79, 82, 86, 89, 92, 95; IntWW 74, 75, 76, 77, 78, 79, 80, 81, 82, 83, 89, 91; McGMS 80; NewYTBS 27; WhoAm 74, 76, 78, 80, 82, 84; WhoFrS 84*

Mazowiecki, Tadeusz
Polish. Political Leader
Elected prime minister of Poland, 1989-90; first non-Communist to head an Eastern-bloc nation since the 1940s.
b. Apr 18, 1927 in Plock, Poland
Source: *BioIn 16; ColdWar 1, 2; CurBio 90; FacFETw; IntWW 91, 93; PolBiDi; WhoSocC 78; WhoSoCE 89; WhoWor 91*

Mazurki, Mike
[Mikhail Mazurwski]
American. Actor
Appeared in adventure films, crime melodramas: *Farewell My Lovely,* 1944, *Donovan's Reef,* 1963.
b. Dec 25, 1909 in Tarnopal, Austria
d. Dec 9, 1990 in Glendale, California
Source: *BioIn 17; ConTFT 9; EncAFC; FilmEn; FilmgC; ForYSC; HalFC 80, 84, 88; HolCA; IntMPA 75, 76, 77, 78, 79, 80, 81, 82, 84, 86, 88; VarWW 85; Vers A; WhoHol A; WorAlBi*

Mazursky, Paul
American. Director
Films include *Tempest; Unmarried Woman; Bob & Carol & Ted & Alice.*
b. Apr 25, 1930 in New York, New York
Source: *BiDFilm, 81, 94; BioIn 9, 11, 12, 13, 14, 15, 16; CelR, 90; ConAu 24NR, 77; ConTFT 1, 6, 14; CurBio 80; DcLB 44; EncAFC; FacFETw; FilmEn; FilmgC; HalFC 88; IlWWHD 1; IntDcF 1-2, 2-2; IntMPA 75, 76, 77, 78, 79, 80, 81, 82, 84, 86, 88, 92, 94, 96; IntWW 91, 93; LegTOT; MiSFD 9; MovMk; VarWW 85; WhoAm 76, 78, 80, 82, 84, 86, 88, 90, 92, 94, 95, 96, 97; WhoEnt 92; WhoHol 92, A; WhoWor 95, 96; WorAl; WorAlBi; WorFDir 2*

Mazzini, Giuseppe
Italian. Revolutionary
Worked to unify Italy under a republican form of government, from 1831.
b. Jun 22, 1805 in Genoa, Italy
d. Mar 10, 1872 in Pisa, Italy
Source: *Benet 87, 96; BioIn 1, 2, 3, 4, 5, 6, 7, 8, 9, 10, 15, 17, 20, 21; CasWL; DcItL 1, 2; Dis&D; EncRev; EuAu; EvEuW; HisWorL; LinLib S; McGEWB; NewC; NewCBEL; NewCol 75; NinCLC 34; PenC EUR; REn; WhDW; WorAl; WorAlBi*

Mazzola, Anthony T
American. Editor
Editor-in-chief, *Town & Country,* 1965-72; *Bazaar,* 1972-92, creative consultant, Hearst Magazines, 1992—.
b. Jun 13, 1923 in Passaic, New Jersey
Source: *CelR 90; WhoAm 90*

Mazzoli, Romano L
American. Politician
Dem. congressman from KY, 1971-94; co-authored landmark Immigration Reform and Control Act of 1986.
b. Nov 2, 1932 in Louisville, Kentucky
Source: *AlmAP 92; BiDrUSC 89; CngDr 87, 89; PolsAm 84; WhoAm 86, 90; WhoAmP 91; WhoSSW 91*

Mboup, Souleymane
Senegalese. Biologist
One of the discoverers of the HIV-2 virus, discovering its much longer incubation period.
b. 1951 in Dakar, Senegal
Source: *ConBlB 10*

M'Bow, Mahtar-Amadou
Senegalese. Statesman
Director-general of UNESCO, 1974-87.
b. Mar 20, 1921 in Dakar, Senegal
Source: *BioIn 13, 14, 15; CurBio 87; EncWB; IntWW 91; Who 92; WhoWor 84, 87, 89*

Mboya, Tom
[Thomas Joseph Mboya]
Kenyan. Political Leader
Leader of Kenya Independence Movement, 1960s; assassination started widespread rioting.
b. Aug 15, 1930 in Rusinga Island, British East Africa
d. Jul 5, 1969 in Nairobi, Kenya
Source: *BioIn 4, 5, 6, 7, 8, 9, 18, 20, 21; CurBio 59, 69; DcAfHiB 86; DcAmSR; DcPol; FacFETw; HisWorL; InB&W 85; LinLib L, S; McGEWB; NewCol 75; ObitT 1961; WhDW; WorAl; WorAlBi*

MC 5
[Michael Davis; Wayne Kramer; Fred "Sonic" Smith; Denis Thompson; Rob Tyner]
American. Music Group
Revolutionary, high-energy rock group, 1967-72.
Source: *BiDAmM; ConMus 9; EncRk 88; Law&B 89A, 92; NewAmDM; NewYTBE 71; NewYTBS 91; PenEncP; WhoRocM 82; WhoSSW 97; WhsNW 85*

McAdam, John Loudoun
Scottish. Engineer
Invented McAdam system of road construction, c. 1815.
b. Sep 21, 1756 in Ayrshire, Scotland
d. Nov 26, 1836, Scotland
Source: *Drake*

McAdie, Alexander George
American. Meteorologist, Author
Developed modern science of meteorology.
b. Aug 4, 1863 in New York, New York
d. Nov 1, 1943 in Elizabeth City, Virginia
Source: *BioIn 2; CurBio 43; DcAmB S3; DcNAA; EncAB-A 17; InSci; NatCAB 35; WhAm 2; WhNAA*

McAdoo, Bob
[Robert Allen McAdoo]
American. Basketball Player
Center-forward, 1972-86, with seven NBA teams; led NBA in scoring three times; NBA MVP, 1975.
b. Sep 25, 1951 in Greensboro, North Carolina
Source: *BasBi; BiDAmSp BK; BioIn 13, 14; LegTOT; NewYTBS 78, 81, 85; OfNBA 87; WhoAfA 96; WhoAm 78, 80, 82, 84, 86; WhoBbl 73; WhoBlA 77, 80, 85, 88, 90, 92, 94; WhoSpor; WorAl; WorAlBi*

McAdoo, William Gibbs
American. Politician
Prominent Dem. candidate for pres., 1920, 1924; senator from CA, 1933-38.
b. Oct 31, 1863 in Marietta, Georgia
d. Feb 1, 1941 in Washington, District of Columbia
Source: *AmDec 1920; AmPolLe; ApCAB X; BiDInt; BiDrAC; BiDrUSC 89; BiDrUSE 71, 89; BioIn 5, 6, 8, 9, 10, 13; CmCal; DcAmB S3; DcNAA; EncAAH; EncAB-H 1974, 1996; EncABHB 1, 7; EncSoH; FacFETw; HarEnUS; LinLib S; McGEWB; NatCAB 14, 61, 62; NewCol 75; OxCAmH; WebAB 74, 79; WhAm 1; WhAmP; WorAl*

McAfee, George A
"One Play"
American. Football Player
Halfback, Chicago, 1940-41, 1945-50; Hall of Fame, 1966.
b. 1918
Source: *BiDAmSp FB; BioIn 8; WhoFtbl 74*

McAfee, Mildred H(elen)
American. Educator
Pres., Wellesley College, 1936-42, 1946-49.
b. May 12, 1900
d. Sep 2, 1994 in Berlin, New Hampshire
Source: *CurBio 95N; InWom, SUP; WomFir*

McArdle, Andrea
American. Singer, Actor
Original Annie, Broadway musical *Annie,* 1976.
b. Nov 4, 1963 in Philadelphia, Pennsylvania
Source: *BioIn 11, 12, 15; ConTFT 6; InWom SUP; LegTOT; NewYTBS 77; WorAl*

McArthur, Edwin Douglas
American. Conductor, Pianist
Directed St. Louis Municipal Opera for 17 yrs; hosted musical radio program for 12 yrs.
b. Sep 24, 1907 in Denver, Colorado
d. Feb 24, 1987 in New York, New York
Source: *ASCAP 66, 80; ConAu 17R, 121; WhoMus 72; WhoOp 76*

McArthur, John
American. Architect
Designed Philadelphia City Hall.
b. May 13, 1823 in Bladenock, Scotland
d. Jan 8, 1890 in Philadelphia, Pennsylvania
Source: *BiDAmAr; BioIn 9; DcAmB; MacEA; TwCBDA; WhAm HS*

McAuliffe, Anthony Clement
American. Army Officer
Noted for terse reply "Nuts" to German surrender ultimatum, 1944; commanded US for ces in Europe, 1955-56.
b. Jul 2, 1898 in Washington, District of Columbia
d. Aug 11, 1975 in Washington, District of Columbia
Source: *BiDWWGF; BioIn 1, 2, 3, 8, 10; CurBio 50, 75; DcAmB S9; WebAB 74, 79; WebAMB; WhAm 6; Who 74; WhoAm 74; WorAl*

McAuliffe, Christa
[Sharon Christa Corrigan McAuliffe]
American. Teacher
First teacher in space; died in explosion of space shuttle *Challenger.*
b. Sep 2, 1948 in Boston, Massachusetts
d. Jan 28, 1986 in Cape Canaveral, Florida
Source: *AnObit 1986; BioAmW; ConHero 1; ConNews 85-4; FacFETw; NewYTBS 86; WhoSpc; WomFir*

McAuliffe, Dick
[Richard John McAuliffe]
American. Baseball Player
Infielder, 1960-75, mostly with Detroit; known for aggressive play, unusual batting stance.
b. Nov 29, 1939 in Hartford, Connecticut
Source: *Ballpl 90; WhoProB 73*

McAuliffe, Jack B
Irish. Boxer
Lightweight fighter, 1880s; one of last bare-knuckle champs; first to retire undefeated; Hall of Fame.
b. Mar 24, 1866 in Cork, Ireland
d. Nov 5, 1937 in Forest Hills, New York
Source: *WhoBox 74*

McAvoy, May
American. Actor
Played Al Jolson's leading lady in first feature length talking picture, *The Jazz Singer,* 1927.
b. Sep 8, 1901 in New York, New York
d. Apr 26, 1984 in Sherman Oaks, California
Source: *BioIn 9, 11, 12, 13, 14; Film 1, 2; FilmEn; ForYSC; HalFC 80, 84, 88; InWom SUP; MotPP; MovMk; SilFlmP; ThFT; TwYS; What 3; WhoHol A*

MC Breed
[Eric Breed]
American. Singer
Rap artist who released his debut album, *MC Breed and DFC,* 1991 which included singles "Ain't No Future in Yo' Frontin'" and "Just Kickin' It;" later released *The New Breed,* 1993 *Funkafied,* which featured song "This Is How We Do It," and *Big Baller,* 1995.
b. 1972 in Flint, Michigan
Source: *ConMus 17*

McBride, Christian
American. Musician, Composer
Jazz bassist and member of the youthful jazz genre, the Young Lions; performed with Bobby Watson and recorded with Wallace Roney, 1989; released debut album, *Gettin' to It,* 1995 and later *Number Two Express,* 1996.
b. May 21, 1972 in Philadelphia, Pennsylvania
Source: *AllMusG; ConMus 17*

McBride, Lloyd
American. Labor Union Official
Pres., United Steelworkers of America, 1977-83.
b. Mar 8, 1916 in Farmington, Missouri
d. Nov 6, 1983 in Whitehall, Pennsylvania
Source: *AnObit 1983; BiDAmL; BioIn 11, 12, 13; CurBio 78, 84N; EncABHB 9; NewYTBS 77, 83; WhAm 8; WhoAm 78, 80, 82; WhoE 79, 81; WhoFI 83; WhoWor 80, 82*

McBride, Mary Margaret
[Martha Deane]
American. Radio Performer
Columnist, travel writer who conducted popular daytime radio show, 1934-56.
b. Nov 16, 1899 in Paris, Missouri
d. Apr 7, 1976 in West Shokun, New York
Source: *AmAu&B; AmWomWr; BioIn 1, 3, 4, 5, 9, 10, 11, 20; ConAu 65, 69; CurBio 41, 54, 76, 76N; DcAmB S10; EncTwCJ; GoodHs; InWom, SUP; LegTOT; LibW; NewYTBS 76; PenNWW A, B; RadStar; SaTiSS; WhAm 7; What 3; WhoAm 74, 76; WhoAmW 58, 61, 64, 66, 68, 70, 72, 74; WorAl; WorAlBi*

McBride, Patricia
American. Dancer
NYC Ballet star, 1959-89; made numerous TV appearances; won *Dance* mag. award, 1980.
b. Aug 23, 1942 in Teaneck, New Jersey
Source: *BiDD; BioIn 6, 7, 8, 11, 12, 13, 14, 15, 16; CnOxB; ContDcW 89; CurBio 66; IntDcB; IntDcWB; InWom, SUP; LegTOT; NewYTBS 79, 89; WhoAm 74, 76, 78, 80, 82, 84, 86, 88; WhoAmW 79, 81, 83, 85; WhoHol 92, A; WorAl; WorAlBi*

McBurney, Charles
American. Surgeon
Expert on appendicitis who devised surgical incision known by his name, 1894.
b. Feb 17, 1845 in Roxbury, Massachusetts
d. Nov 7, 1913 in Brookline, Massachusetts
Source: *AmBi; BiHiMed; BiInAmS; BioIn 1, 5, 7, 9; DcAmB; DcAmMeB, 84; InSci; LinLib S; NatCAB 13, 14, 26; OxCMed 86; WhAm 1*

McCabe, Jewell Jackson
American. Business Executive
President, National Coalition of 100 Black Women, 1977-91; chairman, 1991—; nonprofit group that provides education and mentoring services to underpriviliged women.
b. Aug 2, 1945 in Washington, District of Columbia
Source: *AfrAmBi 2; BlkWAm; ConBlB 10; WhoAfA 96; WhoBlA 80, 85, 88, 90, 92, 94*

McCabe, John
English. Composer, Pianist
Prolific composer in many genres; works include "Notturni Ed Alba," 1970, and "The Chagall Windows," 1974.
b. Apr 21, 1939 in Huyton, England
Source: *Baker 78, 84, 92; BioIn 17; CnOxB; ConCom 92; CpmDNM 80, 82; DcArts; IntWW 78, 79, 80, 81, 82, 83, 89, 91, 93; IntWWM 77, 80, 85, 90; MusMk; NewGrDM 80; NewGrDO; NewOxM; OxDcOp; PenDiMP A; Who 82, 83, 85, 88, 90, 92, 94; WhoMus 72*

McCabe, Thomas Bayard
American. Government Official
Chairman, Federal Reserve System's board of governors, 1948; pres., Scott Paper Co., 1927-67.
b. Jul 11, 1893 in Whaleyville, Maryland
d. May 27, 1982 in Swarthmore, Pennsylvania
Source: *BioIn 1, 2, 5, 7, 8, 11, 12, 13, 17; CurBio 48, 82N; IntWW 74, 75, 76, 77, 78, 79, 80, 81, 82, 83N; NewYTBS 82; WhAm 8; WhoAm 74, 76, 78, 80, 82; WhoAmP 73, 75, 77, 79; WhoE 74, 75, 77; WhoFI 74, 75, 77; WhoGov 75; WhoWor 80*

McCafferty, Don
American. Football Coach
Head coach, Baltimore, 1971-72, Detroit, 1973; won Super Bowl, 1971.
b. Mar 12, 1921 in Cleveland, Ohio
d. Jul 28, 1974 in Pontiac, Michigan
Source: *BioIn 9, 10; NewYTBE 71; NewYTBS 74; WhAm 6; WhoAm 74; WhoE 74*

McCain, John Sidney, Jr.
American. Naval Officer
Much decorated WW II submarine commander.
b. Jan 17, 1911 in Council Bluffs, Iowa
d. Mar 22, 1981
Source: *BioIn 8, 9, 12; CurBio 70, 81; FacFETw; NewYTBS 81; WhAm 7; WhoAm 74, 76; WhoWor 74*

McCain, John Sidney, III
American. Politician, Naval Officer
Son of Admiral McCain; they were the first father and son to become full admirals in navy history; Rep. senator, AZ, 1987—.
b. Aug 29, 1936, Panama Canal Zone
Source: *AlmAP 88; BiDrUSC 89; BioIn 13; CngDr 83, 85, 87; IntWW 89, 91, 93; PolsAm 84; WhoAm 84, 86, 88, 90, 92, 94, 95, 96, 97; WhoAmP 89; WhoWest 87, 89, 92, 94, 96; WhoWor 89, 91*

McCall, Dorothy Lawson
American. Author
Outspoken humanitarian who wrote *Ranch Under the Rimrock,* 1968.
b. 1888? in Boston, Massachusetts
d. Apr 2, 1982 in Portland, Oregon
Source: *BioIn 9, 10; ConAu 106, 109; InWom SUP*

McCall, Nathan
American. Journalist
Reporter, *Washington Post,* 1989—; wrote *Makes Me Wanna Holler: A Young Black Man in America,* 1994.
b. 1955 in Portsmouth, Virginia
Source: *ConAu 146; ConBlB 8; ConLC 86; News 94*

McCall, Thomas Lawson
American. Politician
Environmentalist Rep. governor of OR, 1967-74.
b. Mar 22, 1913 in Egypt, Massachusetts
d. Jan 8, 1983 in Portland, Oregon
Source: *BiDrGov 1789; BioIn 9, 10, 11, 12, 13; ConAu 108; CurBio 74, 83; IntWW 76; NewYTBS 83; PolProf J, NF; WhAm 8; WhoAm 74, 76; WhoAmP 79; WhoGov 72, 77; WhoWest 76, 82*

McCallister, Lon
[Herbert Alonzo McCallister, Jr.]
American. Actor
Juvenile actor, 1936-53; films include *Adventures of Tom Sawyer,* 1938; *Yankee Doodle Dandy,* 1942.
b. Apr 17, 1923 in Los Angeles, California
Source: *BioIn 9, 10; FilmEn; FilmgC; ForYSC; HalFC 80, 84, 88; HolP 40; LegTOT; MotPP; What 4; WhoHol 92, A*

McCallum, David
Scottish. Actor
Played Illya Kuryakin on TV series "The Man from UNCLE," 1964-67.
b. Sep 19, 1933 in Glasgow, Scotland
Source: *BioIn 7, 8; ConTFT 1, 7, 14; FilmEn; FilmgC; ForYSC; HalFC 80, 84, 88; IlWWBF; IntMPA 75, 76, 77, 78, 79, 80, 81, 82, 84, 86, 88, 92, 94, 96; ItaFilm; LegTOT; MotPP; MovMk; NotNAT; OxCFilm; WhoAm 74, 76, 78, 80, 82, 84, 86, 88, 90, 92, 94, 95, 96, 97; WhoE 74; WhoEnt 92; WhoHol 92, A; WhoWor 74, 76*

McCambridge, Mercedes
[Charlotte Mercedes McCambridge]
American. Actor
Won 1949 Oscar for *All the King's Men.*
b. Mar 17, 1918 in Joliet, Illinois
Source: *BiE&WWA; BioIn 4, 5, 6, 7, 12; ConTFT 5; CurBio 64; FilmEn; FilmgC; ForYSC; HalFC 80, 84, 88; IntDcF 1-3, 2-3; IntMPA 77, 80, 84, 86, 88, 92, 94, 96; InWom, SUP; ItaFilm; LegTOT; MotPP; MovMk; NotNAT; OxCFilm;*

RadStar; SaTiSS; WhoAm 74, 76, 78, 80, 82, 84, 86, 88, 92; WhoAmW 58, 66, 68, 70, 72, 74, 83; WhoEnt 92; WhoHol 92, A; WorAl; WorAlBi

McCandless, Bruce, II
American. Astronaut
Made first untethered spacewalk on 10th shuttle flight, Feb 1984.
b. Jun 8, 1937 in Boston, Massachusetts
Source: *BioIn 10, 14, 16; IntWW 83, 91; NewYTBS 84; WhoAm 90, 97; WhoSpc; WhoSSW 76; WorDWW*

McCann, Elizabeth Ireland
"Liz McCann"
American. Producer
Won Tonys for *The Elephant Man,* 1978; *Amadeus,* 1980.
b. Mar 31, 1932 in New York, New York
Source: *BioIn 16; NewYTBS 81; NotWoAT; WhoAm 86, 90; WhoEnt 92*

McCann, Les
American. Musician, Singer
Pianist; leads quartet Les McCann, Ltd.
b. Sep 23, 1935 in Lexington, Kentucky
Source: *AllMusG; ASCAP 66; BioIn 12; DrBlPA, 90; EncJzS; EncJzS; NewGrDJ 88; PenEncP; WhoAm 84*

McCardell, Claire
American. Fashion Designer
Leading designer of casual, popular-priced fashions, 1930s-40s; identified with "American Look."
b. May 24, 1905 in Frederick, Maryland
d. Mar 22, 1958 in New York, New York
Source: *AmCulL; AmDec 1940, 1950; BioIn 1, 3, 4, 5, 7, 12, 15, 19; ConDes 84; ConFash; CurBio 54, 58; DcAmB S6; DcTwDes; EncFash; InWom, SUP; NotAW MOD; WhAm 3; WhoAmW 58; WhoFash 88; WorFshn*

McCarey, Leo
American. Director
Won Oscars for *The Awful Truth,* 1937; *Going My Way,* 1944.
b. Oct 3, 1898 in Los Angeles, California
d. Jul 5, 1969 in Santa Monica, California
Source: *AmFD; ASCAP 66, 80; BiDFilm, 81, 94; BioIn 8, 12, 15; CurBio 46, 69; DcFM; EncAFC; FilmEn; FilmgC; HalFC 80, 84, 88; IlWWHD 1; IntDcF 1-2, 2-2; LegTOT; MiSFD 9N; MovMk; OxCFilm; TwYS, A; WhAm 5; WorAl; WorAlBi; WorEFlm; WorFDir 1*

McCarron, Chris
American. Jockey
Youngest to ride 3,000 winners; won Eclipse Award (Jockey of the Year), 1974, 1980; inducted into Racing Hall of Fame, 1989.
b. Mar 27, 1955 in Dorchester, Massachusetts
Source: *BiDAmSp OS; BioIn 13, 14, 15, 21; News 95; NewYTBS 84; WhoWor 95, 96*

McCarten, John
American. Journalist
Wrote short stories, film reviews for *New Yorker* mag.
b. Sep 10, 1916? in Philadelphia, Pennsylvania
d. Sep 26, 1974 in New York, New York
Source: *BiE&WWA; ConAu 115; NotNAT B; WhAm 6; Who 74; WhoAm 74*

McCarthy, Andrew
American. Actor
Films include *Pretty in Pink,* 1986; *Mannequin,* 1987; and *Weekend at Bernies,* 1989.
b. 1963 in Westfield, New Jersey
Source: *BioIn 14, 15; CelR 90; ConTFT 6; IntMPA 86, 88, 92*

McCarthy, Clem
American. Sportscaster
Noted for vivid radio description of Kentucky Derby, 1928-50; boxing bouts.
b. Sep 9, 1882 in Rochester, New York
d. Jun 4, 1962 in New York, New York
Source: *BioIn 6, 9, 21; CurBio 41, 62; RadStar*

McCarthy, Eugene Joseph
American. Politician
Dem. senator from MN, 1958-70; Dem. presidential candidate, 1968, 1972.
b. Mar 29, 1916 in Watkins, Minnesota
Source: *AmAu&B; BiDAmNC; BiDrAC; BiDrUSC 89; BioIn 13, 14, 15, 16; ColdWar 2; ConAu 1R, 2NR; EncAB-H 1974; IntAu&W 89; IntWW 91; IntYB 81; McGEWB; MinnWr; NewYTBS 87; PolProf NF; WebAB 79; Who 92; WhoAm 86, 90, 97; WhoAmP 87, 91; WhoUSWr 88; WhoWrEP 89; WrDr 86, 92*

McCarthy, Frank
American. Producer
Films include *Patton,* 1970; *MacArthur,* 1977.
b. Jul 8, 1912 in Richmond, Virginia
d. Dec 1, 1986 in Los Angeles, California
Source: *AnObit 1986; BioIn 15; ConTFT 4; CurBio 45, 87, 87N; FilmgC; HalFC 80, 84, 88; IntMPA 75, 76, 77, 78, 79, 80, 81, 82, 84, 86; St&PR 75; WhAm 9; WhoAm 74, 76, 78, 80, 82, 84, 86; WhoWest 76, 78*

McCarthy, J(oseph) P(riestley)
American. Radio Performer
One of most respected interviewers in US; considered king of Detroit radio, with WJR-AM 760 1958-63 and 1965-95; Nat. Radio Hall of Fame, 1992; Marconi Award, 1994.
b. Mar 22, 1933 in New York, New York
d. Aug 16, 1995 in New York, New York
Source: *BioIn 10*

McCarthy, Jenny
American. Actor, TV Personality
Host of MTV's "Singled Out."
b. Nov 1, 1972 in Chicago, Illinois

McCarthy, Joe
[Joseph Vincent McCarthy]
American. Baseball Manager
Managed 24 yrs., including Yankees, 1931-46; first to win pennant in both leagues; has highest winning percentage in ML history; Hall of Fame, 1957.
b. Apr 21, 1887 in Philadelphia, Pennsylvania
d. Jan 13, 1978 in Buffalo, New York
Source: *Ballpl 90; BiDAmSp BB; BioIn 1, 2, 5, 6, 7, 8, 9, 11, 14, 15, 16, 18, 19; CurBio 48, 78, 78N; DcAmB S10; FacFETw; LegTOT; WhoProB 73; WhScrn 83*

McCarthy, Joe
[Joseph Raymond McCarthy]
American. Politician
Rep. senator from WI, 1947-57; best known for early-1950s subcommittee investiga tions of alleged communist activities; censured by Senate, derided for "witch hunt" tactics, 1954.
b. Nov 14, 1908 in Grand Chute, Wisconsin
d. May 2, 1957 in Bethesda, Maryland
Source: *AmOrTwC; AmPolLe; BiDrAC; BiDrUSC 89; BioIn 4, 5, 6, 7, 8, 9, 10, 11; ColdWar 2; ConAu 111; CurBio 50, 57; DcAmB S6; DcTwHis; EncAAH; EncAB-H 1974, 1996; McGEWB; NewCol 75; PolProf E, T; REn; WebAB 74, 79; WebBD 83; WhAm 3; WhAmP; WorAl*

McCarthy, John
English. Hostage
Journalist taken hostage by Lebanese terrorists; held captive for 1,939 days; Apr 17, 1986-Aug 8, 1991.
Source: *BioIn 14, 15, 17; IntWWM 90; NewYTBS 85; PoIre; WhoRocM 82*

McCarthy, John
American. Scientist
Co-founder of the field of artificial intelligence.
b. Sep 4, 1927 in Boston, Massachusetts
Source: *AmMWSc 73P, 76P, 79, 82, 86, 89, 92, 95; BioIn 13, 14, 15, 20; HisDcDP; NotTwCS; WhoAm 82, 84, 86, 88, 90, 92, 94, 95, 96, 97; WhoFrS 84; WhoScEn 94, 96; WhoTech 84, 89, 95; WhoWor 82*

McCarthy, Justin Huntly
English. Politician, Author
A leader, Irish Home Rule Party, 1880s-90s; novels include *Lady Judith.*

b. 1860
d. Mar 21, 1936
Source: *BiD&SB; ChhPo, S1; DcEnA A; EvLB; HarEnUS; LngCTC; ModWD; NotNAT B; OxClri; Polre; ScF&FL 1; WhLit*

McCarthy, Kevin
American. Actor
Film debut in *Death of a Salesman*, 1951; TV shows include "Flamingo Road."
b. Feb 15, 1914 in Seattle, Washington
Source: *BiE&WWA; ConTFT 4; FilmEn; FilmgC; ForYSC; HalFC 80, 84, 88; IntMPA 77, 80, 92, 94, 96; ItaFilm; LegTOT; MovMk; NotNAT; WhoHol 92, A; WhoHrs 80; WhoThe 72, 77, 81; WorAlBi*

McCarthy, Mary Therese
American. Author, Critic
One of America's pre-eminent literary figures, 1930s-1970s; wrote autobiographical novels *Memories of a Catholic Girlhood*, 1957, *The Group*, 1963.
b. Jun 21, 1912 in Seattle, Washington
d. Oct 25, 1989 in New York, New York
Source: *AmAu&B; AmWomWr; AmWr; Au&Wr 71; BenetAL 91; BiDConC; BiE&WWA; BioAmW; BioIn 3, 4, 6, 7, 8, 9, 10, 11, 12, 13, 16; CasWL; CelR 90; ConAu 5R, 129; ConLC 24; CurBio 90N; CyWA 89; DcLEL 1940; DrAPF 89; EncWB; FemiCLE; IntAu&W 91; IntWW 89; InWom, SUP; LibW; MajTwCW; ModAL S1; NewYTBS 79, 89; PenC AM; RAdv 1; REn; REnAL; WebAB 74, 79; Who 90; WhoAm 86; WhoTwCL; WorAl; WorAlBi; WrDr 86, 90*

McCarthy, Tommy
[Thomas Francis Michael McCarthy]
"Little Mack"; "The Kid"
American. Baseball Player
Outfielder, 1884-96, known for defensive play; Hall of Fame, 1946.
b. Jul 24, 1864 in South Boston, Massachusetts
d. Aug 5, 1922 in Boston, Massachusetts
Source: *BiDAmSp BB; BioIn 3, 7, 14, 15; WhoProB 73; WhoSpor*

McCarthy, William J
American. Labor Union Official
Succeeded Jackie Presser as Teamsters' pres., 1988-91.
b. 1918?
Source: *BioIn 16; NewYTBS 88; WhoAm 90; WhoE 91; WhoFI 92*

McCartney, Bill
American. Football Coach
Head football coach at University of Colorado, 1982-94; founded Promise Keepers Christian men's group, 1990.
b. Aug 22, 1940 in Riverview, Michigan
Source: *News 95, 95-3*

McCartney, Linda
[Wings; Louise Eastman McCartney; Mrs. Paul McCartney]
American. Musician, Photographer
Married Paul McCartney, 1969; keyboardist, vocalist for Wings, formed 1971 by husband.
b. Sep 24, 1942 in New York, New York
Source: *Baker 92; BioIn 6, 7, 8, 9, 10, 11, 12, 13, 14; BlueB 76; CelR, 90; ConLC 35; ConMuA 80A, 80B; ConMus 4; CurBio 86; DcArts; EncPR&S 89; EncRk 88; EncRkSt; FacFETw; FilmEn; ForYSC; IlEncRk; IntMPA 92, 94, 96; IntWW 74, 75, 76, 77, 78, 79, 80, 81, 82, 83, 89, 91; IntWWM 77, 90; LegTOT; MotPP; NewAmDM; NewGrDM 80; NewOxM; OnThGG; OxCPMus; RolSEnR 83; Who 82, 83, 85, 88, 90, 92; WhoAm 88, 90, 92, 94, 95, 96, 97; WhoEnt 92; WhoHol 92, A; WhoRocM 82; WhoWor 78, 80, 82, 84, 87, 89, 91, 93, 95, 97; WorAl; WorAlBi*

McCartney, Paul
[Wings; The Beatles; James Paul McCartney]
English. Singer, Songwriter
Most successful of the Beatles, best-selling composer, recording artist of all time; greatest hit: "Yesterday."
b. Jun 18, 1942 in Liverpool, England
Source: *Baker 92; BioIn 6, 7, 8, 9, 10, 11, 12, 13, 14, 15, 16; BkPepl; BlueB 76; CelR, 90; ConLC 35; ConMuA 80A, 80B; ConMus 4; CurBio 66, 86; DcArts; EncPR&S 89; EncRk 88; EncRkSt; FacFETw; FilmEn; ForYSC; HarEnR 86; IlEncRk; IntMPA 92, 94, 96; IntWW 74, 75, 76, 77, 78, 79, 80, 81, 82, 83, 89, 91; IntWWM 77, 90; LegTOT; MotPP; NewAmDM; NewGrDM 80; NewOxM; OnThGG; OxCPMus; PenEncP; RkOn 78; RolSEnR 83; Who 82, 83, 85, 88, 90, 92; WhoAm 78, 80, 82, 84, 86, 88, 90, 92, 94, 95, 96, 97; WhoEnt 92; WhoHol 92, A; WhoRocM 82; WhoWor 74, 78, 80, 82, 84, 87, 89, 91, 93, 95, 97; WorAl; WorAlBi*

McCarty, Kelli
American. Beauty Contest Winner
Miss USA, 1991.

McCarty, Maclyn
American. Biologist
With Avery and MacLeod provided proof that the genetic substance, DNA, is found in all living cells.
b. Jun 9, 1911 in South Bend, Indiana
Source: *AmMWSc 73P, 76P, 79, 82, 86, 89, 92, 95; BiESc; ConAu 120; IntWW 89, 91, 93; McGMS 80; NotTwCS; WhoAm 74, 76, 78, 80, 82, 84, 86, 88, 90, 92, 94, 95, 96, 97; WhoFrS 84; WhoMedH; WhoScEn 94, 96*

McCarty, Mary
American. Actor
Nurse Starch on TV series "Trapper John, MD."
b. 1923 in Winfield, Kansas
d. Apr 5, 1980 in Westwood, California
Source: *BioIn 1, 11, 12; WhoHol A; WhoThe 72, 77, 81; WhScrn 83*

McCashin, Constance Broman
American. Actor
Played Laura Avery on TV series "Knots Landing."
b. Jun 18, 1947 in Chicago, Illinois
Source: *VarWW 85*

McCay, Winsor
American. Cartoonist
Best known for "Little Nemo" cartoons.
b. Sep 26, 1869 in Spring Lake, Michigan
d. Jul 26, 1934 in Sheepshead Bay, New York
Source: *EncACom; LegTOT; SmATA 41; WorECar; WorECom*

McClanahan, Rob
American. Hockey Player
Left wing in NHL, 1980-84; member US Olympic gold medal-winning team, 1980.
b. Jan 9, 1958 in Saint Paul, Minnesota
Source: *HocEn; HocReg 81*

McClanahan, Rue
[Eddi-Rue McClanahan]
American. Actor
Starred in TV shows "Maude," 1972-78; "Golden Girls," 1986-92; "The Golden Palace," 1992—; won an Emmy, 1987.
b. Feb 21, 1936 in Healdton, Oklahoma
Source: *BioIn 14, 15, 16; CelR 90; ConTFT 4; CurBio 89; IntMPA 92; LegTOT; WhoAm 86, 90; WhoAmW 91; WhoEnt 92; WhoHol A; WhoThe 81; WhoWor 91; WorAlBi*

McClellan, George Brinton
American. Military Leader
Indecisive Union general who was Dem. presidential candidate against Lincoln, 1864.
b. Dec 3, 1826 in Philadelphia, Pennsylvania
d. Oct 29, 1885 in Orange, New Jersey
Source: *AmAu&B; AmBi; AmPolLe; ApCAB; BiAUS; BiD&SB; BioIn 1, 2, 3, 4, 6, 7, 8, 9, 10, 11, 15, 16, 17, 20; CivWDc; CmdGen 1991; DcAmAu; DcAmB; DcAmMiB; DcNAA; Drake; EncAB-H 1974, 1996; HarEnMi; HarEnUS; LinLib S; McGEWB; NatCAB 4; OxCAmH; REn; REnAL; TwCBDA; WebAB 74, 79; WebAMB; WhAm HS; WhCiWar; WhoMilH 76; WorAl*

McClellan, John Little
American. Politician
Dem. senator from AR, 1943-77; second-longest serving senator; known for heading crime investigations, 1960s.
b. Feb 25, 1896 in Sheridan, Arkansas
d. Nov 27, 1977 in Little Rock, Arkansas
Source: *BiDrAC; BiDrUSC 89; BioIn 2, 3, 4, 5, 9, 10, 11, 12; CngDr 74; CurBio 50; DcAmB S10; EncWB; IntWW 74, 75,*

76, 77; WhAm 7; WhoAm 74, 76, 78; WhoAmP 73; WhoGov 72, 75, 77; WhoSSW 73, 75, 76, 82; WhoWor 74; WorAl

McClintic, Guthrie
American. Producer
Produced, directed over 90 stage plays, many of which starred wife, Katherine Cornell.
b. Aug 6, 1893 in Seattle, Washington
d. Oct 29, 1961 in Sneden's Landing, New York
Source: *BioIn 1, 4, 6, 13, 20; CamGWoT; CurBio 43, 62; DcAmB S7; EncWT; GrStDi; IntDcT 3; NotNAT A, B; OxCAmT 84; OxCThe 67, 83; TheaDir; WhAm 4; WhThe*

McClintock, Barbara
American. Geneticist
Won Nobel Prize in medicine, 1983, for genetic research.
b. Jun 16, 1902 in Hartford, Connecticut
d. Sep 2, 1992 in Long Island, New York
Source: *AmDec 1980; AmMWSc 73P, 76P, 79, 82, 86, 89, 92; AmWomSc; AnObit 1992; BioAmW; BioIn 11, 12, 13, 14, 15, 16; CamDcSc; ContDcW 89; CurBio 84, 92N; EncWB; EncWHA; GrLiveH; IntWW 74, 75, 76, 77, 78, 79, 80, 81, 82, 83, 89, 91; InWom SUP; LadLa 86; LarDcSc; LegTOT; NewYTBS 83, 92; NobelP; NotTwCS; NotWoLS; RAdv 14, 13-5; WhAm 10; WhoAm 84, 88, 90, 92; WhoAmW 58, 64, 66, 68, 70, 72, 74, 75, 77, 81, 83, 85, 87, 91; WhoE 85, 86, 89, 91; WhoFrS 84; WhoNob, 90, 95; WhoTech 89; WhoWor 84, 87, 89, 91; WomFir; WomStre; WorAlBi; WorScD*

McClintock, Francis Leopold, Sir
English. Explorer
Led Arctic expeditions in search of Sir John Franklin, 1850-59; wrote *Voyage of the Fox in the Arctic Seas.*
b. Jul 8, 1819 in Dundalk, Ireland
d. Nov 17, 1907 in London, England
Source: *ApCAB; BiDIrW; BioIn 2, 11, 18; BritAu 19; DcCanB 13; DcIrB 78, 88; DcIrW 2; DcNaB S2; Drake; Expl 93; McGEWB; NewCBEL; OxCCan; OxCShps; WhWE*

McClinton, Delbert
American. Singer
Rhythm and blues performer highlighted in NBC's "Saturday Night Live," 1980s.
b. Nov 4, 1940 in Lubbock, Texas
Source: *BioIn 11, 12, 14; ConMus 14; EncFCWM 83; LegTOT; OnThGG; PenEncP; RkOn 85; RolSEnR 83; SoulM; WhoRock 81*

McCloskey, James
American. Detective
Uncovered evidence in 1986 that freed Nathaniel Walker from kidnap and rape charges; founded Centurion Ministries, 1983 to aid falsely accused prioners.
Source: *BioIn 15, 17, 18, 19; Dun&B 88; Law&B 84; News 93-1; NewYTBS 86, 92; OxCAmT 84; PoIre; St&PR 91; WhoAm 86; WhoE 86*

McCloskey, John
American. Clergy
First American cardinal, 1875; principal builder of NYC's St. Patrick's Cathedral.
b. Mar 10, 1810 in New York, New York
d. Oct 10, 1885 in New York, New York
Source: *AmBi; ApCAB; BioIn 1, 6, 8, 19; DcAmB; DcBiPP; DcCathB; HarEnUS; LinLib S; McGEWB; NatCAB 1; RelLAm 91; TwCBDA; WebAB 74, 79; WhAm HS*

McCloskey, John Michael
American. Businessman
Environmentalist; chairman of oldest environmental agency, Sierra Club, 1985—.
b. Apr 26, 1934 in Eugene, Oregon
Source: *BioIn 16; NatLAC; News 88-2; WhoAm 74, 76, 78, 86, 90, 92, 94, 95, 96, 97; WhoWest 76, 78, 82*

McCloskey, Paul Norton, Jr.
American. Politician
Moderate Rep. con. from CA, 1967-83.
b. Sep 29, 1927 in San Bernardino, California
Source: *BiDrAC; BiDrUSC 89; BioIn 8, 9, 10, 12, 13, 16; CngDr 81; CurBio 71; IntWW 83; NewYTBE 71; PolProf NF; WhoAm 86, 90; WhoAmP 73, 75, 77, 79, 81, 83, 85, 87, 89, 91; WhoGov 77; WorAlBi*

McCloskey, Robert
American. Children's Author, Illustrator
Won 1942, 1948 Caldecott Medals for *Make Way for Ducklings; Time of Wonder.*
b. Sep 15, 1914 in Hamilton, Ohio
Source: *AmAu&B; AnCL; Au&ICB; AuBYP 2, 3; BenetAL 91; BioIn 1, 2, 4, 5, 7, 8, 9, 10, 12, 14, 15, 19; BkP; Cald 1938; ChlBkCr; ChlLR 7; ConAu 9R; DcLB 22; FamAIYP; IlsBYP; IlsCB 1744, 1946, 1957; JBA 51; LinLib L; NewbC 1956; OhA&B; OxCChiL; REnAL; SmATA 2, 39; Str&VC; TwCChW 78, 83, 89; WhoAm 74, 76, 78, 80, 82, 84, 86, 88, 90, 92, 94, 95, 96; WhoAmA 73, 76, 78, 80, 82, 84, 86; WrDr 80, 82, 84, 86, 88, 90, 92, 94, 96*

McCloskey, Robert James
American. Diplomat
In US foreign service since 1955; served as ambassador to Netherlands, 1976-78, Greece, 1978-81.
b. Nov 25, 1922 in Philadelphia, Pennsylvania
d. Nov 28, 1996 in Chevy Chase, Maryland
Source: *IntWW 91; WhoAm 90; WhoAmP 91; WhoE 91; WhoWor 84*

McCloy, John Jay
American. Government Official
Asst. secretary of war, WW II; served as general policy advisor to Presidents Eisenhower, Kennedy, Johnson.
b. Mar 31, 1895 in Philadelphia, Pennsylvania
d. Mar 11, 1989 in Stamford, Connecticut
Source: *AmPolLe; AnObit 1989; BiDAmBL 83; BioIn 1, 2, 3, 4, 5, 6, 11, 12, 13, 15, 16, 17, 18, 21; ColdWar 2; CurBio 47, 61, 89, 89N; FacFETw; IntWW 74, 75, 76, 77, 78, 79, 80, 81, 82, 83, 89N; News 89-3; NewYTBS 75; PolProf E, J, K, NF, T; St&PR 87; WhAm 10; Who 74, 82, 83, 85, 88, 90N; WhoAm 74, 76, 78, 80, 82, 84, 86, 88; WhoAmL 78, 79; WhoE 74; WhoFI 74; WhoWor 74*

McClung, Nellie Letitia Mooney
Canadian. Author
Women's rights champion who wrote of life in W Canada.
b. Oct 20, 1873 in Chatsworth, Ontario, Canada
d. Sep 1, 1951 in Victoria, British Columbia, Canada
Source: *BioIn 17, 18, 20; CanNov; CanWr; ChhPo; MacDCB 78; ObitOF 79; OxCCan; WhLit; WhNAA; WomWWA 14*

McClure, Doug
American. Actor
Played Trampas in TV series "The Virginian," 1962-71.
b. May 11, 1935 in Glendale, California
d. Feb 5, 1995 in Sherman Oaks, California
Source: *BioIn 20, 21; ConTFT 5, 14; FilmEn; HalFC 80, 84, 88; IntMPA 84, 86, 88, 92, 94; LegTOT; MotPP; VarWW 85; WhoAm 88, 90, 92; WhoHol 92, A*

McClure, James A
American. Politician
Republican senator from ID, 1973-91.
b. Dec 27, 1924 in Payette, Idaho
Source: *AlmAP 78, 80, 82, 84, 88; BiDrAC; BiDrUSC 89; BioIn 9, 10, 12; BlueB 76; CngDr 74, 77, 79, 81, 83, 85, 87, 89; IntWW 75, 76, 77, 78, 79, 80, 81, 82, 83, 89, 91, 93; IntYB 81, 82; PolsAm 84; St&PR 87; WhoAm 74, 76, 78, 80, 82, 84, 86, 88, 90; WhoAmP 73, 75, 77, 79, 81, 83, 85, 87, 89, 91, 93, 95; WhoGov 77; WhoWest 76, 78, 80, 84, 87, 89, 92, 94, 96; WhoWor 80, 84, 87, 89, 91*

McClure, Michael Thomas
American. Poet, Dramatist
One of San Francisco Beat poets, 1950s, influenced by ideas in biology, mysticism; *Josephine, the Mouse Singer* won 1980 Obie.
b. Oct 20, 1932 in Marysville, Kansas
Source: *AmAu&B; Benet 87; BenetAL 91; BioIn 13; ConAu 17NR; ConDr 82; ConLC 6; ConPo 85, 91; CroCAP; DrAPF 91; IntAu&W 89; IntvTCA 2;*

McGEWD 84; NatPD 77; PenC AM; RAdv 1, 13-1; WhoAm 86, 88; WhoUSWr 88; WrDr 86, 92

McClure, Samuel Sidney
American. Newspaper Publisher
Founded McClure Syndicate, first newspaper syndicate in US, 1884.
b. Feb 17, 1857 in Antrim, Northern Ireland
d. Mar 21, 1949 in New York, New York
Source: *ABCMeAm; AmAu&B; AmRef; AmSocL; BiDAmJo; BioIn 1, 2, 5, 6, 7, 13; DcAmB S4; DcNAA; EncAB-H 1974, 1996; JrnUS; LinLib L; McGEWB; MorMA; NatCAB 12; REn; REnAL; WebAB 74, 79; WebBD 83; WhAm 2; WhNAA; WorAl*

McCobb, Paul Winthrop
American. Designer
Used natural wood, metal in furniture design; introduced room dividers.
b. 1917 in Boston, Massachusetts
d. Mar 10, 1969 in New York, New York
Source: *CurBio 58, 69; WhAm 5*

McColgan, Liz
British. Track Athlete
Set world indoor 5,000-meter record of 15 mins., 3.17 secs. in 1992.
Source: *BioIn 17*

McCollum, Elmer Verner
American. Chemist, Nutritionist
Discovered vitamins A, B, D, E, 1913-22; popularized use of white rat for experimental purposes.
b. Mar 3, 1879 in Fort Scott, Kansas
d. Nov 15, 1967 in Baltimore, Maryland
Source: *AmDec 1920; AsBiEn; BiESc; BioIn 1, 2, 3, 5, 7, 8, 9, 11, 12, 14, 20; ConAu P-1; DcAmMeB 84; DcScB; EncAB-H 1974, 1996; InSci; LarDcSc; LinLib S; NotTwCS; WhAm 4; WhNAA; WorScD*

McColough, C(harles Peter)
American. Business Executive
Pres., Xerox Corp., 1966-71; chm., 1971-85; chm., exec. com., 1985—.
b. Aug 1, 1922 in Halifax, Nova Scotia, Canada
Source: *BioIn 9, 12; CanWW 70, 79, 80, 81, 83, 89; CurBio 81; Dun&B 79, 86; IntWW 74, 75, 76, 77, 78, 79, 80, 81, 82, 83, 89, 91, 93; IntYB 79; LElec; St&PR 87; Who 74, 85, 88; WhoAm 74, 76, 78, 80, 82, 84, 86, 90; WhoAmP 73, 77, 79, 81, 83, 85, 87, 89, 91, 93, 95; WhoE 74, 81, 83, 85; WhoFI 74, 75, 77, 79, 81, 83, 85, 87; WhoWor 74, 82, 84, 87*

McConaughey, Matthew (David)
American. Actor
Starred in *A Time to Kill*, 1996.
b. Nov 4, 1969 in Uvalde, Texas
Source: *News 97-1*

McCone, John Alex
American. Business Executive
Founded Bechtel-McCone, 1937, which modified bombers, WW II; chm., Atomic Energy Commission, 1958-61; director, CIA, 1961-65.
b. Jan 4, 1902 in San Francisco, California
d. Feb 14, 1991 in Pebble Beach, California
Source: *AmCath 80; BioIn 4, 5, 6, 11; BlueB 76; ColdWar 2; CurBio 59, 91N; EncAI&E; IntWW 83; NewYTBS 91; PolProf E, J, K, T; Who 85, 90, 92N*

McConnell, Joseph H(oward)
American. Broadcasting Executive
President, NBC, 1949-52; devised television code including standards for commercials, children's programming.
b. May 13, 1906
d. Mar 3, 1997 in Atlanta, Georgia
Source: *BioIn 2; BlueB 76; IntWW 74, 75, 76, 77, 78, 79, 80, 81; IntYB 78, 79, 80, 81; LElec; WhoAm 74, 76, 78; WhoFI 74; WhoSSW 73*

McConnell, Mitch
American. Politician
Rep. senator from KY, 1985—.
b. Feb 20, 1942 in Colbert County, Alabama
Source: *AlmAP 88, 92, 96; BioIn 14; CngDr 85, 87, 89, 91, 93, 95; WhoSSW 86*

McCoo, Marilyn
[The Fifth Dimension; Mrs. Billy Davis, Jr.]
American. Singer, Actor
With Fifth Dimension, 1966-73; co-host of "Solid Gold."
b. Sep 3, 1943 in Jersey City, New Jersey
Source: *BioIn 8, 13, 14, 15, 16; DrBlPA 90; EncPR&S 74; IlEncRk; InB&W 85; LegTOT; WhoBlA 92*

McCord, David (Thompson Watson)
American. Poet
Wrote verse volume *On Occasion*, 1943; essays *About Boston*, 1948.
b. Nov 15, 1897 in New York, New York
d. Apr 13, 1997 in Boston, Massachusetts
Source: *AmAu&B; AnCL; AuBYP 3; BenetAL 91; BioIn 6, 9, 11, 12, 13, 16, 19; BkCL; BkP; ChhPo, S1, S2; ChlBkCr; ChlLR 9; ConAu 38NR, 73; DcLB, 61; IntAu&W 91; MajAI; OxCAmL 65, 83, 95; OxCChiL; REnAL; SmATA 18; Str&VC; ThrBJA; TwCChW 78, 83, 89, 95; WhE&EA; WhNAA; WhoAm 74, 76, 78, 80, 82, 84, 86; WhoWor 74, 76, 78, 80, 82; WrDr 80, 82, 84, 86, 88, 90*

McCord, James Walter
American. Government Official
CIA officer; with six others, found guilty of Watergate break-in, 1973; served time in prison, 1975.
b. 1918 in Waurika, Oklahoma
Source: *AuNews 1; BioIn 9, 10, 11, 12; BioNews 74; NewYTBE 73; PolProf NF*

McCord, Kent
American. Actor
Starred in TV series "Adam-12," 1968-75.
b. Sep 26, 1942 in Los Angeles, California
Source: *LegTOT; WhoAm 74; WhoEnt 92; WhoHol 92, A; WorAl*

McCormach, Mark Hume
American. Lawyer, Businessman
Owner, International Management Group; wrote *What They Don't Teach You at Harvard Business School*, 1985.
b. Nov 6, 1930 in Chicago, Illinois
Source: *ConAu 17NR; Who 83; WhoGolf; WhoMW 78*

McCormack, John
American. Opera Singer
Tenor noted for Irish folksongs, ballads; concert performer honored by US, Irish stamps, 1984.
b. Jun 14, 1884 in Athlone, Ireland
d. Sep 16, 1945 in Dublin, Ireland
Source: *Baker 78, 84, 92; BiDAmM; BioIn 1, 2, 3, 4, 6, 7, 10, 11, 12, 14, 17, 18; BriBkM 80; CmOp; CmpEPM; CurBio 45; DcCathB; DcIrB 78, 88; FacFETw; FilmgC; HalFC 80, 84, 88; IntDcOp; LegTOT; MetOEnc; MusMk; MusSN; NewAmDM; NewEOp 71; NewGrDA 86; NewGrDM 80; NewGrDO; NotNAT B; OxDcOp; PenDiMP; PeoHis; REn; WhAm 2; WhDW; WhoHol B; WhScrn 74, 77, 83; WorAl; WorAlBi*

McCormack, John William
American. Lawyer, Politician
Speaker of the House, 1962-71.
b. Dec 21, 1891 in Boston, Massachusetts
d. Nov 22, 1980 in Dedham, Massachusetts
Source: *AmPolLe; BiDrAC; BiDrUSC 89; BioIn 3, 5, 6, 7, 8, 9, 11, 12, 14; CurBio 43, 62; DcAmB S10; EncWB; IntWW 74, 75, 76, 77, 78, 79, 80; WebAB 74, 79; Who 74; WhoAm 74*

McCormack, Mike
American. Football Player
Tackle, 1951, 1954-62, mostly with Cleveland; Hall of Fame, 1984.
b. Jun 21, 1930 in Chicago, Illinois
Source: *BiDAmSp FB; BioIn 10, 17; LegTOT; WhoFtbl 74; WhoSpor*

McCormack, Patty
American. Actor
Murderous child of stage, film versions of *Bad Seed.*
b. Aug 21, 1945 in New York, New York
Source: *BiE&WWA; BioIn 3, 9, 12, 15; ConTFT 8; FilmEn; FilmgC; ForYSC; HalFC 80, 84, 88; InWom SUP; MotPP; MovMk; NotNAT; WhoHol 92, A; WhoHrs 80*

McCormick, Anne (Elizabeth) O'Hare
American. Journalist
With *NY Times,* 1922-54; best known as foreign correspondent; first woman to receive Pulitzer for journalism, 1937.
b. May 16, 1881 in Wakefield, England
d. May 29, 1954 in New York, New York
Source: *AmAu&B; CathA 1930; ConAu 118; CurBio 40, 54; DcAmB S5; InWom SUP; OhA&B; REn; REnAL; TwCA SUP; WhAm 3*

McCormick, Carolyn
American. Actor
Plays Elizabeth Olivet on TV's "Law and Order."
Source: *BioIn 15; WhoHol 92*

McCormick, Cyrus Hall
American. Inventor, Manufacturer
Invented the reaper, 1834.
b. Feb 15, 1809 in Rockbridge County, Virginia
d. May 13, 1884 in Chicago, Illinois
Source: *AmBi; ApCAB, X; BiDAmBL 83; BioIn 1, 3, 4, 5, 6, 8, 9, 10, 11, 12, 13, 14, 15, 17, 18, 21; DcAmB; Drake; EncAAH; EncAB-H 1974, 1996; HarEnUS; InSci; LegTOT; LinLib S; McGEWB; MemAm; NatCAB 5, 21; OxCAmH; TwCBDA; WebAB 74, 79; WhAm HS; WhDW; WorAl*

McCormick, Cyrus Hall
American. Manufacturer
Entered family business, International Harvester Co., 1914.
b. Sep 22, 1890 in Chicago, Illinois
d. Mar 30, 1970 in Hartford, Connecticut
Source: *NatCAB 54; WhAm 5*

McCormick, Joseph Medill
American. Journalist, Politician
Chicago Tribune publisher, from 1908; Rep. senator from IL, 1919-25; son of Robert.
b. May 16, 1877 in Chicago, Illinois
d. Feb 25, 1925 in Washington, District of Columbia
Source: *AmAu&B; AmBi; BiDrUSC 89; DcAmB; JrnUS; LinLib L, S; NatCAB 19; OxCAmH; WhAmP*

McCormick, Maureen
American. Actor
Played Marcia on TV's "The Brady Bunch," 1969-74; "The Bradys," 1990.

McCormick, Myron
American. Actor
Stage: *South Pacific,* 1949-54; *No Time for Sergeants,* 1955-57; film: *No Time For Sergeants,* 1958; *The Hustler,* 1961.
b. Feb 8, 1908 in Albany, Indiana
d. Jul 30, 1962 in New York, New York
Source: *BioIn 3, 6; CurBio 54, 62; FilmgC; ForYSC; HalFC 80, 84, 88; NotNAT B; SaTiSS; WhAm 4; WhoHol B; WhScrn 74, 77, 83*

McCormick, Patricia Keller
American. Swimmer
First diver to win gold medals in platform, springboard diving in two consecutive Olympics, 1952, 1956.
b. 1930
Source: *BiDAmSp BK; BioIn 3, 4, 9, 11, 17; EncAmaz 91; InWom SUP*

McCormick, Robert K
American. Broadcast Journalist
Member, NBC's first TV news team to cover nat. political event, 1948.
b. Aug 11, 1911 in Danville, Kentucky
d. Sep 4, 1985 in New York, New York
Source: *BioIn 14; ConAu 117*

McCormick, Robert Rutherford
American. Newspaper Publisher
Publisher, *Chicago Tribune,* 1910; *NY Daily News,* 1919; isolationist, foe of New Deal, Roosevelt; championed freedom of press.
b. Jul 30, 1880 in Chicago, Illinois
d. Apr 1, 1955 in Wheaton, Illinois
Source: *AmAu&B; BiDAmBL 83; BiDAmJo; BioIn 1, 2, 3, 4, 7, 12, 13, 15, 16; CurBio 42, 55; DcAmB S5; LinLib L, S; McGEWB; NatCAB 41; ObitT 1951; OxCAmH; REnAL; WebAB 74, 79; WhAm 3; WhJnl; WorAlBi*

McCourt, Dale Allen
Canadian. Hockey Player
Center, 1977-84; with Detroit, involved in controversial free agent compensation case with Rogie Vachon, 1978-79.
b. Jan 26, 1957 in Falconbridge, Ontario, Canada
Source: *BioIn 11; HocEn; HocReg 81*

McCovey, Willie Lee
"Stretch"
American. Baseball Player
First baseman, 1959-80, mostly with San Francisco; had 521 career home runs; Hall of Fame, 1986.
b. Jan 10, 1938 in Mobile, Alabama
Source: *Ballpl 90; BiDAmSp BB; BioIn 13, 14, 15, 16; CurBio 70; FacFETw; InB&W 85; NewYTBS 86; WhoAm 86, 90; WhoBlA 92; WhoProB 73; WhoWor 84; WorAlBi*

McCowen, Alec
[Alexander Duncan McCowen]
English. Actor
Originated stage role of Equus, 1973; films include *Frenzy, Never Say Never Again.*
b. May 26, 1926 in Tunbridge Wells, England
Source: *CamGWoT; CelR 90; ConAu 129; ConTFT 8; CurBio 69; FilmgC; HalFC 84, 88; IntMPA 92; IntWW 91; MovMk; NotNAT; OxCThe 83; VarWW 85; Who 85, 92; WhoAm 74; WhoHol A; WhoThe 81; WhoWor 84, 91*

McCoy, Charles
[Norman Selby]
"Kid"; "The Corkscrew Kid"
American. Boxer, Actor
Light-heavyweight fighter, 1900-16; term "the real McCoy" supposedly originated with him; Hall of Famer.
b. Oct 13, 1873 in Rush County, Indiana
d. Apr 18, 1940 in Detroit, Michigan
Source: *BiDAmSp BK; BioIn 6, 9; WhoBox 74; WhScrn 77, 83*

McCoy, Charles B(relsford)
American. Business Executive
Pres., E. I. du Pont Nemours & Co., 1967-71; chm., 1971-73; board member until 1987.
b. Apr 16, 1909
d. Jan 16, 1995 in Greenville, Delaware
Source: *BioIn 8, 9; CurBio 95N; Dun&B 79; IntWW 74, 75, 76, 77, 78, 79, 80, 81, 82, 83; St&PR 75; WhoAm 74, 76; WhoE 74; WhoFI 74, 75*

McCoy, Clyde
American. Jazz Musician
Trumpeter who led band, 1930s-60s; theme song: "Sugar Blues."
b. Dec 29, 1903 in Ashland, Kentucky
d. Jan 11, 1990
Source: *BgBands 74; BioIn 5; CmpEPM; OxCPMus; PenEncP*

McCoy, Elijah
American. Inventor
Invented automatic lubricator, used to automatically drip oil into the moving parts of a locomotive, 1872.
b. May 2, 1844 in Colchester, Ontario, Canada
d. 1929 in Eloise, Michigan
Source: *BioIn 18, 19, 20, 21; BlksScM; ConBlB 8; NegAl 76, 83, 89*

McCoy, Horace
American. Author, Screenwriter
Wrote novels *They Shoot Horses, Don't They?* 1935, filmed, 1969; *Scalpel,* 1952.
b. Apr 14, 1897 in Pegram, Tennessee
d. Dec 17, 1955 in Beverly Hills, California
Source: *AmAu&B; AmNov; BenetAL 91; BioIn 1, 2, 4, 10, 12, 13, 14; ConAu 108; DcLB 9; OxCAmL 65, 83, 95; REnAL; TexWr; TwCCr&M 80, 85, 91; TwCLC 28; WhJnl; WhNAA; WorAu 1950*

McCoy, Tim(othy John Fitzgerald)
American. Actor
Popular western star; hero of Universal's first sound serial *The Indians Are Coming,* 1930.
b. Apr 10, 1891 in Saginaw, Michigan
d. Jan 29, 1978 in Nogales, Arizona
Source: *BioIn 8, 78; MotPP; NewYTBS 78; SilFlmP; TwYS; WhAm 7; WhoAm 74; WhoHol A; WhScrn 83*

McCoy, Van
American. Composer, Musician
Recorded disco hit "The Hustle," 1975.
b. Jan 6, 1944 in Washington, District of Columbia
d. Jul 6, 1979 in Englewood, New Jersey
Source: *BioIn 10; ConMuA 80A; DrBlPA, 90; EncRk 88; LegTOT; RolSEnR 83; WhScrn 83*

McCracken, Branch
American. Basketball Coach
Coach, Indiana U, 1939-43, 1947-65, compiling 364-174 record; won two NCAA titles; Hall of Fame.
b. Jun 9, 1908 in Monrovia, Indiana
d. Jun 4, 1970 in Bloomington, Indiana
Source: *BasBi; IndAu 1917; NewYTBE 70; WhoBbl 73; WhoSpor*

McCracken, James (Eugene)
American. Opera Singer
Leading tenor, popular performer with NY Met., 1950s-60s.
b. Dec 16, 1926 in Gary, Indiana
d. Apr 30, 1988 in New York, New York
Source: *AnObit 1988; Baker 84; BioIn 6, 9, 11, 13, 15, 16; BriBkM 80; CmOp; ConAu 126; CurBio 63, 88, 88N; FacFETw; LegTOT; MetOEnc; MusSN; NewAmDM; NewGrDA 86; NewGrDM 80; NewGrDO; NewYTBE 72; NewYTBS 88; OxDcOp; PenDiMP; WhoAm 86; WhoAmM 83; WhoMus 72; WhoOp 76; WorAl; WorAlBi*

McCracken, Joan
American. Actor, Singer
Starred in *Bloomer Girl,* 1944; *Billion Dollar Baby,* 1945.
b. Dec 31, 1922 in Philadelphia, Pennsylvania
d. Nov 1, 1961 in New York, New York
Source: *BiDD; BioIn 1, 3, 6; CmpEPM; DcAmB S7; EncMT; InWom; NotNAT B; WhThe*

McCrae, John
Canadian. Physician, Poet
Best known for nostalgic poem, "In Flanders Fields," 1915.
b. Nov 30, 1872 in Guelph, Ontario, Canada
d. Jan 28, 1918 in Wimereux, France
Source: *Benet 87, 96; BenetAL 91; BioIn 5, 12, 17; CanWr; CasWL; ChhPo, S1; ConAu 109; CreCan 2; DcAmMeB; DcLB 92; DcLEL; DcNAA; Dis&D; EvLB; LegTOT; LinLib L; LngCTC; MacDCB 78; NewC; OxCAmL 65; OxCCan; OxCCanL; OxCMed 86; REn; REnAL; TwCA; TwCLC 12*

McCrary, Tex
[Tex and Jinx; John Reagan McCrary]
American. Journalist
With wife Jinx hosted early morning radio breakfast show, 1946-52.
b. Oct 13, 1910 in Calvert, Texas
Source: *BiDAmNC; BioIn 1, 2, 3; BlueB 76; CurBio 53; IntMPA 75, 76, 77, 78, 79, 80, 81, 82, 84, 86; LegTOT; RadStar; WorAl*

McCrea, Joel
American. Actor
Appeared in nearly 90 films, best known for Westerns: *Sullivan's Travels,* 1941, *Buffalo Bill,* 1944.
b. Nov 5, 1905 in South Pasadena, California
d. Oct 20, 1990 in Woodland Hills, California
Source: *AnObit 1990; BiDFilm, 81, 94; BioIn 2, 3, 8, 9, 10, 12, 14, 17, 18, 20; CmMov; DcArts; EncAFC; FacFETw; Film 2; FilmEn; FilmgC; ForYSC; GangFlm; HalFC 80, 84, 88; IntDcF 1-3, 2-3; IntMPA 75, 76, 77, 78, 79, 80, 81, 82, 84, 86, 88; LegTOT; MotPP; MovMk; News 91, 91-1; NewYTBS 90, 91; OxCFilm; VarWW 85; What 3; WhoHol A; WorAl; WorAlBi; WorEFlm*

McCree, Wade Hampton, Jr.
American. Government Official
US Solicitor General, 1977-81.
b. Jul 3, 1920 in Des Moines, Iowa
d. Aug 30, 1987 in Detroit, Michigan
Source: *AfrAmAl 6; BiDFedJ; Ebony 1; InB&W 80; NegAl 83; NewYTBS 77; WhAm 9; WhoAm 74, 76, 78, 80, 82, 84, 86; WhoAmL 78, 79, 83, 85; WhoAmP 77, 79, 81, 83, 85, 87; WhoBlA 80; WhoGov 72, 75, 77; WhoMW 74, 76*

McCreesh, Raymond
Irish. Hunger Striker, Revolutionary
IRA member; one of 10 hunger strikers to die in prison, demanding political prisoner rather than criminal status.
b. Feb 25, 1957 in Camlough, Northern Ireland
d. May 21, 1981 in Belfast, Northern Ireland

McCrory, Milton
"Iceman"
American. Boxer
Defeated Colin Jones, 1983, to earn WBC welterweight title.
b. Feb 7, 1962 in Detroit, Michigan

McCullers, Carson (Smith)
American. Author
Best known for first novel, *The Heart Is a Lonely Hunter,* 1940.
b. Feb 19, 1917 in Columbus, Georgia
d. Sep 29, 1967 in Nyack, New York
Source: *AmAu&B; AmDec 1940; AmNov; AmWomD; AmWomWr 92; AmWr; ArtclWW 2; Benet 87, 96; BenetAL 91; BiE&WWA; BioIn 2, 4, 5, 6, 7, 8, 9, 10, 11, 12, 13, 15, 16, 17, 19, 20; BlmGWL; CamGEL; CamGLE; CamHAL; CasWL; CnDAL; CnMD; CnMWL; ConAu 1BS, 3BS, 5R, 18NR, 25R; ConLC 1, 4, 10, 12, 48; ConNov 76, 82A, 86A; ContDcW 89; CrtSuDr; CyWA 58, 89; DcAmB S8; DcArts; DcLB 2, 7, 173; DcLEL 1940; EncSoH; EncWL, 2, 3; EncWT; FacFETw; FemiCLE; FifSWrA; GayLesB; GayLL; GoodHs; GrLiveH; GrWomW; GrWrEL N; HalFC 80, 84, 88; HanAmWH; IntDcWB; InWom, SUP; LegTOT; LibW; LinLib L; LngCTC; MagSAmL; MajTwCW; McGEWD 72, 84; ModAL, S1, S2; ModAWWr; ModWD; ModWoWr; NewCon; NotAWMOD; NotNAT B; NotWoAT; Novels; ObitT 1961; OxCAmL 65, 83, 95; OxCEng 85, 95; OxCWoWr 95; PenC AM; RAdv 1, 14, 13-1; REn; REnAL; RfGAmL 87; ShSCr 9; ShSWr; SmATA 27; SouWr; TwCA, SUP; TwCWr; WebAB 74, 79; WebE&AL; WhAm 4; WhDW; WhoAmW 64, 66, 68, 70; WhoTwCL; WorAl; WorAlBi; WorLitC; WrPh*

McCulley, Johnston
[Raley Brien; George Drayne; Rowena Raley; Harrington Strong]
American. Author
Wrote *Zorro* adventure novels, 1924-58.
b. Feb 2, 1883 in Ottawa, Illinois
d. Nov 23, 1958 in Glendale, Ohio
Source: *AmAu&B; BenetAL 91; BioIn 5; ConAu 115; EncFWF; MnBBF; REnAL; ScFEYrs; TwCWW 82, 91; WhAm 3; WhE&EA; WhNAA*

McCullin, Donald
English. Photographer
Free-lance photographer known for war photography in Cyprus, 1964.
b. Oct 9, 1935 in London, England
Source: *BioIn 12; ConAu 106; ConPhot 88; DcCAr 81; ICPEnP; IntWW 75, 76, 77, 78, 79, 80, 81, 82, 83, 89, 91, 93; MacBEP; Who 88, 90, 92, 94; WhoWor 78*

McCulloch, Robert P
American. Oilman
Best known for buying, shipping the London Bridge to AZ for reconstruction.
b. 1912? in Saint Louis, Missouri
d. Feb 25, 1977 in Los Angeles, California
Source: *BioIn 2, 4, 8, 9, 11; NewYTBS 77; ObitOF 79*

McCullough, Colleen
Australian. Author
Wrote *The Thorn Birds,* 1977.
b. Jun 1, 1937 in Wellington, Australia
Source: *AmWomWr; ArtclWW 2; AuWomWr; Benet 87; BioIn 11, 12, 13, 14, 17; BlmGWL; ConAu 81; CurBio 82; EncSF 93; FemiCLE; IntWW 91, 93; InWom SUP; LegTOT; MajTwCW; NewYTBS 81; OxCAusL; ScF&FL 92; TwCRHW 90, 94; WhoAm 90, 95, 96,*

97; WhoWor 95; WorAl; WorAlBi; WorAu 1975; WrDr 90, 92, 94, 96

McCullough, David Gaub
American. Author, TV Personality
Won a 1993 Pulitzer Prize in Biography for *Truman,* 1992; host of TV series "Smithsonian World," 1983-88.
b. Jul 7, 1933 in Pittsburgh, Pennsylvania
Source: *CurBio 93*

McCullough, Paul
American. Actor
Partner with Bobby Clark in comedy serials of 1920s-30s.
b. 1883 in Springfield, Ohio
d. Mar 25, 1936 in Boston, Massachusetts
Source: *FilmgC; WhoHol B; WhScrn 74, 77; WhThe*

McCurdy, Ed
American. Singer
Ballad singer; has recorded folk, sacred, children's songs.
b. Jan 11, 1919 in Willow Hill, Pennsylvania
Source: *ASCAP 66, 80; BiDAmM; EncFCWM 69; PenEncP*

McCurry, Michael D(emaree)
American. Government Official
White House press secretary, 1995—.
b. Oct 27, 1954 in Charleston, South Carolina
Source: *CurBio 96; WhoAm 94, 95, 96, 97*

McCutcheon, George Barr
American. Author, Editor
Popular novels include *Graustark,* 1901; *Brewster's Millions,* 1902; brother of John Tinney McCutcheon.
b. Jul 26, 1866 in South Raub, Indiana
d. Oct 23, 1928 in New York, New York
Source: *AmAu&B; AmBi; BenetAL 91; BibAL; BiD&SB; BioIn 2, 12, 14; CnDAL; DcAmAu; DcAmB; DcAmBC; DcBiA; DcLEL; DcNAA; EncMys; EvLB; GayN; IndAu 1816; LinLib L, S; LngCTC; NatCAB 14; OxCAmL 65, 83, 95; REn; REnAL; ScF&FL 1; TwCA, SUP; TwCRGW; TwCRHW 90, 94; WebBD 83; WhAm 1; WhNAA; WhScrn 77, 83*

McCutcheon, John Tinney
American. Cartoonist
Chicago Tribune political cartoonist, 1903-45; won Pulitzer, 1932.
b. May 6, 1870 in South Raub, Indiana
d. Jun 10, 1949 in Lake Forest, Illinois
Source: *AmAu&B; BiDAmJo; BioIn 1, 2, 16; ChhPo, S1, S2; IndAu 1816; LinLib L, S; NewCol 75; REnAL; WebAB 74, 79; WhAm 2; WhE&EA; WorECar*

McDaniel, Hattie
American. Actor
Won 1939 Oscar for *Gone With The Wind.*
b. Jun 10, 1895 in Wichita, Kansas
d. Oct 26, 1952 in Hollywood, California
Source: *BiDAfM; BioIn 20, 21; BlksAmF; BlkWAm; BluesWW; ConBlB 5; CurBio 40, 52; DcAmB S5; DcAmNB; DcTwCCu 5; DrBlPA, 90; EncAFC; FilmEn; FilmgC; ForYSC; HalFC 80, 84, 88; InB&W 85; IntDcF 1-3, 2-3; InWom SUP; LegTOT; MotPP; MovMk; NotAW MOD; NotBlAW 1; NotNAT B; OlFamFa; OxCFilm; PenEncP; RadStar; SaTiSS; ThFT; Vers A; WhoHol B; WhScrn 74, 77, 83; WorAl; WorAlBi*

McDaniel, Mildred
American. Track Athlete
High jumper; won gold medal, 1956 Olympics.
b. Nov 4, 1933 in Atlanta, Georgia
Source: *BiDAmSp OS; BioIn 17; BlkOlyM; WhoTr&F 73*

McDaniel, Xavier Maurice
American. Basketball Player
Forward, Seattle, 1985—; with Wichita State U, only player in NCAA history to lead nation in scoring, rebounding in same yr., 1985.
b. Jun 4, 1963 in Columbia, South Carolina
Source: *BioIn 14; OfNBA 87; WhoAfA 96; WhoBlA 94*

McDermott, Alice
American. Author
Novels tell simple suburban stories in rich detail, utilize complex time structures: *That Night,* 1987; *At Weddings and Wakes,* 1992.
b. Jun 27, 1953 in New York, New York
Source: *AmWomWr SUP; BioIn 15; ConAu 40NR, 109; ConLC 90; CurBio 92; DrAPF 91; NewYTBS 87*

McDermott, Johnny
[John J McDermott]
American. Golfer
Touring pro, early 1900s; won US Open, 1911, 1912; charter member, Hall of Fame, 1940.
b. Aug 12, 1891 in Philadelphia, Pennsylvania
d. Aug 1, 1971 in Yeadon, Pennsylvania
Source: *BiDAmSp OS; NewYTBE 71; WhoGolf*

McDermott, Terry
American. Skater
Won speed skating gold medal, 1964 Olympics.

McDevitt, Ruth
American. Actor
TV shows include "Mr. Peepers," 1953-55; "Pistols 'n' Petticoats," 1966-67.
b. Sep 13, 1895 in Coldwater, Michigan
d. May 27, 1976 in Hollywood, California
Source: *BiE&WWA; BioIn 10; ForYSC; HalFC 80, 84, 88; NewYTBS 76; NotNAT; WhoAm 74; WhoHol A; WhoSpc; WhoTech 89; WhoThe 72, 77; WhScrn 83*

McDivitt, Jim
[James Alton McDivitt]
American. Astronaut, Businessman
Flew on Gemini 4, 1965; Apollo 9, 1969.
b. Jun 10, 1929 in Chicago, Illinois
Source: *AmCath 80; AmMWSc 73P, 95; BioIn 6, 7, 8, 9, 10; BlueB 76; CurBio 65; IntWW 74, 75, 76, 77; St&PR 75; WhoAm 74, 76, 78, 80, 82, 90, 92; WhoFI 92; WhoScEn 94; WhoSSW 73, 95; WhoWor 74; WorAl*

McDonald, Country Joe
American. Singer, Songwriter, Musician
Member of best known political rock group of mid-1960s; convicted in MA for chanting obscenities.
b. Jan 1, 1942 in El Monte, California
Source: *BioIn 10, 14; ConMuA 80A; EncFCWM 83; EncPR&S 74; IlEncRk; LegTOT; LNinSix; PenEncP; WhoRock 81; WhoRocM 82; WorAl; WorAlBi*

McDonald, David John
American. Labor Union Official
Pres., United Steelworkers of America, 1952-65.
b. Nov 22, 1902 in Pittsburgh, Pennsylvania
d. Aug 8, 1979 in Palm Springs, California
Source: *BiDAmL; BiDAmLL; BioIn 1, 3, 4, 5, 8, 11, 12, 17; BlueB 76; ConAu 45; CurBio 53, 79; DcAmB S10; NewYTBS 77; PolProf E, J, K; WhAm 7; WhoAm 74, 76; WhoLab 76*

McDonald, Erroll
American. Publishing Executive
In several positions at Random House, 1978—; currently exec. editor, Pantheon, 1990—.
b. 1954 in Limon, Costa Rica
Source: *BioIn 15; ConBlB 1*

McDonald, Harl
American. Composer
Works stressing themes of Americana include symphony, *Santa Fe Trail,* 1934.
b. Jul 27, 1899 in Boulder, Colorado
d. Feb 10, 1955 in Philadelphia, Pennsylvania
Source: *AmComp; ASCAP 66, 80; Baker 78, 84, 92; BiDAmM; BioIn 1; ConAmC 76, 82; LegTOT; NatCAB 44; NewAmDM; NewGrDA 86; NewGrDM 80; OxCAmL 65; OxCMus; REnAL; WhAm 3*

McDonald, Lanny
[Larry King McDonald]
Canadian. Hockey Player
Right wing with three NHL teams, 1973-89; first recipient of Clancy Trophy, 1988 ; Hockey Hall of Fame, 1992.
b. Feb 16, 1953 in Hanna, Alberta, Canada
Source: *HocEn; HocReg 87; WhoAm 86, 88*

McDonald, Larry
[Lawrence Patton McDonald]
American. Politician
Archconservative Dem. congressman from GA, 1974-83; died aboard Korean jetliner shot down by Soviet Union.
b. Apr 1, 1935 in Atlanta, Georgia
d. Sep 1, 1983
Source: *AlmAP 78, 80; BiDrUSC 89; BioIn 11, 13; CngDr 81, 83; NewYTBS 83; WhoAm 80, 82; WhoAmP 75, 77, 79, 81, 83; WhoSSW 80, 82*

McDonald, Marie
[Mrs. Vic Orsett]
"The Body"
American. Actor
Married seven times-better known in gossip columns than movies; had brief film career.
b. Jul 6, 1923 in Burgin, Kentucky
d. Oct 21, 1965 in Hidden Hills, California
Source: *BioIn 1, 7; FilmEn; FilmgC; ForYSC; HalFC 80, 84, 88; MotPP; WhoHol B; WhScrn 74, 77, 83*

McDonald, Maurice James
American. Restaurateur
Brother of Richard, original owners of hamburger restaurant.
b. 1902?
d. 1971
Source: *BioIn 9, 10; NewYTBE 71*

McDonald, Michael
[Doobie Brothers]
American. Singer, Songwriter
Has successful solo career including hit single with Patti LaBelle "On My Own," 1986.
b. Dec 2, 1952 in Saint Louis, Missouri
Source: *EncRkSt; LegTOT; RkOn 85; WhoRocM 82*

McDonald, Richard
American. Restaurateur
Owned original hamburger restaurant, San Bernardino, CA, purchased by Ray Croc, 1955.
Source: *BioIn 10, 18; Dun&B 90; Law&B 89A; St&PR 91*

McDonnell, James Smith
American. Aircraft Manufacturer
Co-founder, McDonnell-Douglas Corp., 1967.
b. Apr 9, 1899 in Denver, Colorado
d. Aug 22, 1980 in Saint Louis, Missouri
Source: *AmMWSc 73P; BiDAmBL 83; BioIn 1, 2, 3, 5, 6, 7, 8, 9, 12, 15; DcAmB S10; IntWW 74, 75, 76, 77, 78, 79, 80; NewYTBS 80; WhAm 7; WhoAm 74, 76, 78, 80; WhoFI 74, 75, 77; WhoMW 74, 76; WhoWor 74*

McDonnell, Joe
[Joseph McDonnell]
Irish. Hunger Striker, Revolutionary
IRA member; one of 10 hunger strikers to die in prison, demanding political prisoner rather than criminal status.
b. 1951 in Belfast, Northern Ireland
d. Jul 8, 1981 in Belfast, Northern Ireland
Source: *BioIn 12*

McDonnell, John Finney
American. Aircraft Manufacturer
Chm., CEO, McDonnell Douglas Corp., 1988—; son of James.
b. Mar 18, 1938 in Baltimore, Maryland
Source: *BioIn 15; Dun&B 79, 90; St&PR 93, 96, 97; WhoAm 88, 90, 92, 94, 95, 96, 97; WhoFI 87, 89, 92, 94, 96; WhoMW 84, 86, 88, 90, 92, 93, 96; WhoWor 89, 91, 95, 96, 97*

McDonnell, Mary
American. Actor
Nominated for an Oscar for her performance in *Dances with Wolves,* 1990; appeared in *Independence Day,* 1996.
b. 1952 in Wilkes-Barre, Pennsylvania
Source: *IntMPA 92, 94, 96; WhoAm 94, 95, 96, 97*

McDonnell, Sanford N
American. Business Executive
Chm., McDonnell-Douglas Corp., 1980-88; nephew of James Smith McDonnell.
b. Oct 12, 1922 in Little Rock, Arkansas
Source: *BioIn 11, 13, 15; Dun&B 88; IntWW 83; News 88; St&PR 84; WhoAm 84; WhoWor 84*

McDonough, Mary Elizabeth
American. Actor
Played Erin on TV series "The Waltons," 1972-81.
b. May 4, 1961 in Los Angeles, California
Source: *BioIn 12*

McDougald, Gil(bert James)
American. Baseball Player
Infielder, NY Yankees, 1951-60; AL rookie of year, first rookie to hit grand slam in World Series, 1951.
b. May 19, 1928 in San Francisco, California
Source: *Ballpl 90; BioIn 2, 3, 4, 5, 14, 21; St&PR 84, 87; WhoProB 73*

McDougall, Alexander
American. Army Officer
Organized Bank of New York; commanded Hudson Highlands, 1778, to keep river secure.
b. 1732 in Islay, Scotland
d. Jun 9, 1786 in New York, New York
Source: *AmBi; AmRev; BiAUS; BiDrAC; BioIn 10, 11; BlkwEAR; DcAmB; DcAmMiB; Drake; EncAR; NatCAB 11; WebAMB; WhAm HS; WhAmP; WhAmRev*

McDougall, Gay J.
American. Civil Rights Activist, Lawyer
Executive director, International Human Rights Law Group, 1994—.
b. Aug 13, 1947 in Atlanta, Georgia
Source: *ConBlB 11*

McDougall, Walt(er)
American. Cartoonist
Introduced cartooning, news illustration to daily newspaper, 1884.
b. Feb 10, 1858 in Newark, New Jersey
d. Mar 4, 1938 in Waterford, Connecticut
Source: *WhAm 4; WorECom*

McDougall, William
American. Psychologist, Educator
Developed hormic theory of psychology; wrote *Body and Mind,* 1911.
b. Jun 22, 1871 in Chadderton, England
d. Nov 28, 1938 in Durham, North Carolina
Source: *AmAu&B; AmBi; BiDAmEd; BiDPara; BiDPsy; BioIn 2, 4, 9, 14, 15; DcAmB S2; DcNAA; DcNaB 1931; DcNCBi 4; EncO&P 1, 2, 3; EncPaPR 91; GuPsyc; LiveLet; LngCTC; NamesHP; NewCBEL; OxCAmH; REnAL; ThTwC 87; WebAB 74, 79; WebBD 83; WhAm 1; WhNAA*

McDowall, Roddy
[Roderick Andrew McDowall]
English. Actor
Starred in *My Friend Flicka,* 1943; *Planet of the Apes,* film, TV series.
b. Sep 17, 1928 in London, England
Source: *BiE&WWA; BioIn 15, 16; ConTFT 2, 8; FilmgC; HalFC 88; IntMPA 92, 96; IntWW 91; MotPP; MovMk; NotNAT; OxCFilm; VarWW 85; WhoAm 86, 90, 97; WhoEnt 92; WhoWor 91, 97; WorAlBi*

McDowell, Ephraim
American. Surgeon
Pioneered in abdominal surgery; performed first ovarian operation in US, 1809.
b. Nov 11, 1771 in Rockbridge County, Virginia
d. Jun 25, 1830 in Danville, Kentucky
Source: *ApCAB; BiHiMed; BioIn 1, 3, 4, 5, 6, 8, 9; DcAmB; DcAmMeB, 84; Drake; InSci; NatCAB 5; NewCol 75; OxCAmH; OxCMed 86; REnAW; TwCBDA; WebAB 74, 79; WhAm HS*

McDowell, Irvin
American. Army Officer
Union general, relieved of command after second battle of Bull Run, 1862; later exonerated.
b. Oct 15, 1818 in Columbus, Ohio
d. May 4, 1885 in San Francisco, California
Source: *AmBi; ApCAB; BioIn 1, 6, 7; CivWDc; DcAmB; DcAmMiB; Drake; HarEnMi; HarEnUS; TwCBDA; WebAMB; WhAm HS; WhCiWar; WhoMilH 76*

McDowell, Katharine Sherwood Bonner
[Sherwood Bonner]
American. Author
Wrote novels of Southern life: *Volcanic Interlude,* 1880.
b. Feb 26, 1849 in Holly Springs, Mississippi
d. Jul 22, 1883 in Holly Springs, Mississippi
Source: *Alli SUP; AmAu; AmAu&B; BiD&SB; BiDSA; BioAmW; DcAmAu; DcNAA; FemiCLE; InWom SUP; NotAW; OxCAmL 65; PenNWW B; REnAL; SouWr; TwCBDA*

McDowell, Malcolm
English. Actor
Films include *Clockwork Orange,* 1971; *Cat People,* 1982.
b. Jun 13, 1943 in Leeds, England
Source: *BioIn 8, 9, 10, 12, 13, 21; ConTFT 5; CurBio 73; DcArts; EncEurC; FilmEn; FilmgC; HalFC 84, 88; IntDcF 1-3, 2-3; IntMPA 86, 88, 92, 94, 96; IntWW 79, 80, 81, 82, 83, 89, 91, 93; ItaFilm; LegTOT; MovMk; NewYTBE 72; VarWW 85; Who 90, 92, 94; WhoAm 86, 88, 92, 94, 95, 96, 97; WhoEnt 92; WhoHol 92, A; WhoWor 82, 84, 87; WorAl; WorAlBi*

McDowell, Sam(uel Edward)
"Sudden Sam"
American. Baseball Player
Pitcher, 1961-75, mostly with Cleveland; led AL in strikeouts five times.
b. Sep 21, 1942 in Pittsburgh, Pennsylvania
Source: *Ballpl 90; BioIn 7, 9, 10; WhoProB 73*

McDuffie, Robert
American. Violinist
Classical violinist known for his solo performances throughout the world.
b. 1958 in Macon, Georgia
Source: *News 90, 90-2*

McEachin, James Elton
American. Actor
Played title role on TV's "Tenafly," 1973-74; films include *Play Misty for Me,* 1971.
b. May 20, 1930 in Pennert, North Carolina
Source: *DrBlPA 90; HalFC 88; WhoBlA 75, 77, 85, 92; WhoHol A*

McElhenny, Hugh
"King"
American. Football Player
Six-time all-pro halfback, 1952-64, mostly with San Francisco; known for open field running; Hall of Fame, 1970.
b. Dec 31, 1928 in Los Angeles, California
Source: *BiDAmSp FB; BioIn 8, 10, 17; CmCal; LegTOT; WhoFtbl 74*

McElligott, Thomas J
American. Advertising Executive
Cofounded Fallon, McElligott, Minneapolis, 1981; firm has won over 600 industry awards.
b. Jul 25, 1943 in Bemidji, Minnesota
Source: *BioIn 16; ConNews 87-4; WhoAm 90; WhoFI 92*

McElroy, Neil Hosler
American. Business Executive, Government Official
Chm. of Procter and Gamble, 1959-72; secretary of Defense under Dwight Eisenhower, 1957-59.
b. Oct 30, 1904 in Berea, Ohio
d. Nov 30, 1972 in Cincinnati, Ohio
Source: *BiDrUSE 71, 89; BioIn 2, 3, 4, 5, 6, 7, 9, 10, 11, 12; CurBio 51, 73; DcAmB S9; NatCAB 58; NewYTBE 72; WhAm 5; WorAl*

McEnroe, John Patrick, Jr.
"Superbrat"
American. Tennis Player
Won US Open, 1979-81, 1984; Wimbledon, 1981, 1983-84.
b. Feb 16, 1959 in Wiesbaden, Germany (West)
Source: *BiDAmSp OS; BioIn 12, 13, 14, 15, 16; CelR 90; CurBio 80; FacFETw; IntWW 81, 82, 83, 89, 91, 93; NewYTBS 79, 83, 85, 89; WhoAm 80, 82, 84, 86, 88, 90, 92, 94, 95, 96, 97; WhoE 95; WhoIntT; WhoWor 82, 84, 87, 89, 91, 93, 95, 96*

McEntee, Peter Donovan
English. Political Leader
Governor, commander-in-chief, Belize, 1976-80.
b. Jun 27, 1920
Source: *IntWW 77, 78, 79, 80, 81, 82, 83, 89, 91, 93; Who 74, 82, 83, 85, 88, 90, 92, 94; WhoWor 78, 80, 82, 84*

McEntire, Reba
American. Singer
Country singer named CMAs Entertainer of Year four times, 1984-87; won Grammy, 1986; albums include *For My Broken Heart,* 1991.
b. Mar 28, 1954 in McAlester, Oklahoma
Source: *BioIn 14, 15, 16; ConMus 11; ConNews 87-3; CurBio 94; EncFCWM 83; EncRkSt; HarEnCM 87; LegTOT; News 94, 94-2; PenEncP; WhoAm 90; WhoAmW 91; WhoEnt 92; WhoNeCM; WorAlBi*

McEwan, Ian (Russell)
English. Author
Novels include *The Innocent,* 1990; *Black Dogs,* 1992.
b. Jun 21, 1948 in Aldershot, England
Source: *BestSel 90-4; BioIn 13; BlmGEL; CamGLE; ConAu 14NR, 41NR, 61; ConLC 13, 66; ConNov 82, 86, 91, 96; ConTFT 14; CurBio 93; DcArts; DcLB 14; EncSF 93; IntAu&W 89, 91, 93; IntWW 89, 91, 93; LegTOT; MajTwCW; Novels; OxCEng 95; PostFic; RGTwCWr; ScF&FL 92; Who 82, 83, 85, 88, 90, 92, 94; WorAu 1975; WrDr 80, 82, 84, 86, 88, 90, 92, 94, 96*

McEwen, Mark
American. Broadcast Journalist
Weather reporter, "CBS This Morning," 1987—.
b. Sep 16, 1954 in San Antonio, Texas
Source: *BioIn 19; ConBlB 5; WhoAfA 96; WhoBlA 92, 94*

McEwen, Terence Alexander
"Terry McEwen"
Canadian. Director
Succeeded Kurt Herbert Adler as director, San Francisco Opera, 1982-88.
b. Apr 13, 1929 in Thunder Bay, Ontario, Canada
Source: *BioIn 13, 14; CurBio 85, 86; MetOEnc; NewYTBS 83; WhoAm 88; WhoEnt 92; WhoWest 87*

McFadden, Mary Josephine
[Mrs. Vasilis Calitsis]
American. Fashion Designer
Clothes have distinctive dramatic look, include vibrant colors, fine pleating.
b. Oct 1, 1938 in New York, New York
Source: *BioIn 13, 16; CelR 90; ConDes 90; CurBio 83; DcTwDes; EncFash; IntWW 91; InWom SUP; NewYTBS 79; St&PR 91, 93, 96, 97; WhoAm 76, 78, 80, 82, 84, 86, 88, 90, 92, 94, 95, 96, 97; WhoAmA 84, 91; WhoAmW 77, 79, 81, 83, 85, 87, 89, 91, 93, 95, 97; WhoE 95, 97; WhoFash, 88*

McFarland, Ernest William
American. Politician
Majority leader of Senate during Truman administration who lost Senate seat to Barry Goldwater, 1952.
b. Oct 9, 1894 in Earlsboro, Oklahoma
d. Jun 8, 1984 in Phoenix, Arizona
Source: *BiDrAC; BiDrUSC 89; BioIn 2, 3, 7, 11, 12, 14, 21; CurBio 51; WhoAm 74; WhoAmP 73, 75, 77, 79, 81, 83*

McFarland, Spanky
[Our Gang; George Emmett McFarland]
American. Actor
Fat boy in "Our Gang" series, 1931-45.
b. Oct 2, 1928 in Fort Worth, Texas
Source: *BioIn 9, 15, 16, 19; EncAFC; FilmEn; FilmgC; ForYSC; HalFC 80, 84, 88; LegTOT; MovMk; What 3; WhoCom; WhoHol 92, A; WorAl*

McFarlane, Robert Carl
"Bud"
American. Government Official
Nat. security adviser to Ronald Reagan, 1983-85.
b. Jul 12, 1937 in Washington, District of Columbia
Source: *BioIn 13, 14, 15, 16; CurBio 84; DcAmDH 89; IntWW 89, 91, 93; NewYTBS 82, 83, 85, 89; WhoAm 84; WhoAmP 81, 83, 85, 87, 89, 91, 93, 95; WhoE 85, 86*

McFee, Henry Lee
American. Artist
Painted landscapes, still-lifes; influenced by Cezanne, cubism.
b. Apr 14, 1886 in Saint Louis, Missouri
d. Mar 19, 1953 in Claremont, California
Source: *ArtsAmW 3; BioIn 2, 3; BriEAA; DcCAA 71, 77, 88, 94; McGDA; ObitOF 79; PhDcTCA 77; WhAm 3; WhAmArt 85; WhoAmA 89N, 91N, 93N*

McFee, William
[pseud. Morley Punshon]
American. Author
Nautical writings include *Casuals of the Sea,* 1916; *Harbourmaster,* 1932.
b. Jun 15, 1881 in London, England
d. Jul 2, 1966 in New Milford, Connecticut
Source: *AmAu&B; AmNov; BenetAL 91; BioIn 1, 2, 4, 5, 7, 9, 21; CnDAL; ConAmA; ConAu 116; CyWA 58; DcAmB S8; DcLB 153; DcLEL; EvLB; LngCTC; NatCAB 52; NewCBEL; ObitT 1961; OxCAmL 65, 83; REn; REnAL; TwCA, SUP; TwCWr; WhAm 4; WhE&EA; WhLit; WhNAA*

McFerrin, Bobby
American. Singer
A capella singer; won three Grammys, 1989, for calypso-style "Don't Worry, Be Happy"; two 1986 Grammys for "Another Night in Tunisia"; 1987 Grammy for "Round Midnight."
b. Mar 11, 1950 in New York, New York
Source: *AllMusG; Baker 92; BioIn 14, 15, 16; CelR 90; ConMus 3; ConTFT 12; CurBio 89; DcTwCCu 5; DrBlPA 90; LegTOT; NewGrDJ 88, 94; News 89-1; PenEncP; WhoAfA 96; WhoBlA 92, 94; WhoEnt 92; WorAlBi*

McGarity, Lou
[Robert Louis McGarity]
American. Jazz Musician
Trombonist with Bob Crosby, Eddie Condon.
b. Jul 22, 1917 in Athens, Georgia
d. Aug 28, 1971 in Alexandria, Virginia
Source: *BiDAmM; BiDJaz; BioIn 9; CmpEPM; EncJzS; NewGrDJ 88; NewYTBE 71; WhoJazz 72*

McGavin, Darren
American. Actor
Starred in TV series "The Night Stalker," 1974-75.
b. May 7, 1922 in Spokane, Washington
Source: *BiE&WWA; ConTFT 5; FilmEn; FilmgC; ForYSC; HalFC 80, 84, 88; IntMPA 77, 78, 79, 80, 81, 82, 84, 86, 88, 92, 94, 96; LegTOT; MiSFD 9; MotPP; MovMk; NotNAT; VarWW 85; WhoAm 86, 90, 92, 94, 95, 96, 97; WhoEnt 92; WhoHol 92, A; WorAl; WorAlBi*

McGee, Charles
American. Artist
Created charcoal drawings of black urban life since the late 1950s; also created minimalist sculptures with mixed media and other avant-garde works.
b. Dec 15, 1924 in Clemson, South Carolina
Source: *AfroAA; ConBlB 10; InB&W 80*

McGee, Frank
[Francis McGee]
Canadian. Hockey Player
Amateur center, Ottawa, early 1900s; scored 14 goals in one game, 1905; Hall of Fame, 1945; killed in action, WW I.
b. 1880?
d. Sep 16, 1916, France
Source: *WhoHcky 73*

McGee, Frank
American. Broadcast Journalist
Correspondent for NBC News.
b. Sep 12, 1921 in Monroe, Louisiana
d. Apr 17, 1975 in New York, New York
Source: *BiDAmJo; BioIn 6, 7, 10, 16; CelR; ConAu 89, 105; CurBio 64, 74, 74N; EncAJ; EncTwCJ; NewYTBS 74; NewYTET; WhAm 6; WhoAm 74*

McGee, Gale William
American. Historian, Politician
Dem. senator from WY, 1959-77; served as OAS ambassador, backing Panama Canal Treaty.
b. Mar 17, 1915 in Lincoln, Nebraska
d. Apr 9, 1992 in Bethesda, Maryland
Source: *BiDrAC; BiDrUSC 89; BioIn 5, 6, 8, 9, 10, 11, 12, 17, 18, 19; BlueB 76; CngDr 74; CurBio 61, 92N; DrAS 74H, 78H; IntWW 74, 75, 76, 77, 78, 79, 80, 81, 82, 83, 89, 91; PolProf J, K, NF; WhoAm 82, 84, 86, 90; WhoAmP 73, 75, 77, 79, 81, 83, 85, 87, 89, 91; WhoE 79, 81, 83, 85, 86; WhoGov 72, 75, 77*

McGee, Thomas D'Arcy
Canadian. Editor, Public Official
Founded newspapers *The Nation* (NYC), *The New Era* (Montreal); helped establish Dominion of Canada, served in Parliament, assassinated.
b. Apr 13, 1825 in Carlingford, Ireland
d. Apr 7, 1868 in Ottawa, Ontario, Canada
Source: *ApCAB; BbtC; BioIn 2, 8, 9, 17, 20; BritAu 19; CamGLE; CanWr; ChhPo, S1; DcCanB 9; DcCathB; DcIrB 78, 88; DcIrL, 96; DcLB 99; DcNAA; DcNaB; Drake; HarEnUS; HisDBrE; LinLib L; MacDCB 78; NewC; OxCCan; OxCCanL; OxCIri; PoIre; REn; REnAL; WhAm HS*

McGee, Willie Dean
American. Baseball Player
Outfielder, New York 1977-81, St. Louis, 1981-90, Oakland, 1990; San Francisco, 1991—; won NL batting titles, 1985, 1990; NL MVP, 1985; Golden Glove, 1983, 85-86.
b. Nov 2, 1958 in San Francisco, California
Source: *Ballpl 90; BaseReg 86, 87; BioIn 14; NewYTBS 85; WhoAfA 96; WhoAm 88; WhoBlA 85, 88, 90, 92, 94; WhoMW 90*

McGill, James
Canadian. Fur Trader, Philanthropist
Left bulk of estate to found McGill U, Montreal, 1829.
b. Oct 6, 1744 in Glasgow, Scotland
d. Dec 19, 1813 in Montreal, Quebec, Canada
Source: *ApCAB; DcCanB 5; Drake; LinLib S; MacDCB 78; WorAl; WorAlBi*

McGill, Ralph Emerson
American. Journalist
Editor, *Atlanta Constitution,* 1942-60, known for pro-civil rights editorials; won Pulitzer, 1959, Presidential Medal of Freedom, 1964.
b. Feb 5, 1898 in Soddy, Tennessee
d. Feb 3, 1969 in Atlanta, Georgia
Source: *BiDAmJo; BioIn 1, 2, 5, 8, 9, 10; ConAu 5R; CurBio 47, 69; DcAmB S8; DcLEL 1940; EncSoH; EncWB; ObitOF 79; WhAm 5*

McGill, William James
American. University Administrator
Pres., Columbia U, 1970-80.
b. Feb 27, 1922 in New York, New York
Source: *BioIn 8, 9; BlueB 76; CurBio 71; IntWW 74, 75, 76, 77, 78, 79, 80, 81, 82, 83, 89, 91; LEduc 74; NewYTBE 70; St&PR 91; WhoAm 74, 76, 78, 80, 82, 84, 90; WhoE 74, 75, 79; WhoWest 82*

McGillis, Kelly
American. Actor
Starred in *Top Gun,* 1986 and *The Accused,* 1988.
b. Jul 9, 1957 in Newport, California
Source: *BioIn 16; CelR 90; ConTFT 9; HalFC 88; HolBB; IntMPA 92, 94, 96; IntWW 91; News 89-3; WhoAm 95, 96, 97; WhoAmW 95, 97; WhoHol 92; WorAlBi*

McGimsie, Billy
[William George McGimsie]
Canadian. Hockey Player
Amateur center in Kenora, Ontario, early 1900s; Hall of Fame, 1962.
b. Jun 7, 1880 in Woodsville, Ontario, Canada
d. Oct 28, 1968 in Calgary, Alberta, Canada

Source: *WhoHcky 73*

McGinley, Phyllis
American. Poet, Author
Light verse volumes include 1960 Pulitzer winner *Times Three.*
b. Mar 21, 1905 in Ontario, Oregon
d. Feb 22, 1978 in New York, New York
Source: *AmAu&B; AmWomWr; ArtclWW 2; Au&Wr 71; AuBYP 2; Benet 87, 96; BenetAL 91; BioAmW; BioIn 1, 2, 3, 4, 5, 6, 7, 8, 9, 10, 11, 13, 15; BkP; BlueB 76; CelR; ChhPo, S1, S2, S3; CnE&AP; CnMWL; ConAu 9R, 19NR, 77; ConLC 14; ConPo 70, 75; CurBio 41, 61, 78N; DcAmB S10; DcArts; DcLB 11, 48; EncAHmr; EvLB; FemiCLE; IntAu&W 77; IntWW 74, 75, 76, 77; IntWWP 77; InWom, SUP; JBA 51; LegTOT; LibW; LinLib L; LngCTC; ModAL; NewYTBS 78; OxCAmL 65, 83, 95; PenC AM; RAdv 1; REn; REnAL; SmATA 2, 24N, 44; TwCA SUP; TwCChW 78, 83, 89; TwCWr; WhAm 7; WhoAm 74, 76, 78; WhoAmW 58, 61, 64, 66, 68, 70, 72, 74, 75, 77; WhoTwCL; WhoWor 74; WorAl; WorAlBi; WrDr 76*

McGinnis, George
American. Basketball Player
Forward, Indiana, ABA, 1971-75; 1975-82 with three NBA teams; led ABA in scoring, 1975.
b. Aug 12, 1950 in Indianapolis, Indiana
Source: *BasBi; BiDAmSp BK; BioIn 8, 10, 11, 12; LegTOT; OfNBA 87; WhoAm 80, 82; WhoBbl 73; WhoBlA 85, 92; WorAl*

McGinnis, Scott
American. Actor
Starred in 1980s films *Racing with the Moon; Star Trek III.*
b. Nov 19, 1958 in Glendale, California
Source: *ConTFT 7; WhoHol 92*

McGinniss, Joe
American. Author
Wrote *The Selling of the President 1968;* described mass market techniques of presidential campaign.
b. Dec 9, 1942 in New York, New York
Source: *AmAu&B; AuNews 2; BestSel 89-2; BiDConC; BioIn 13, 14, 16; ConAu 25R, 26NR; ConLC 32; ConPopW; CurBio 84; IntAu&W 91, 93; LiJour; NewYTBS 80; WhoAm 82, 84, 86, 88, 90, 92, 94, 95, 96; WhoUSWr 88; WhoWrEP 89, 92, 95; WrDr 76, 80, 82, 84, 86, 88, 90, 92, 94, 96*

McGinnity, Joe
[Joseph Jerome McGinnity]
"Iron Man"
American. Baseball Player
Pitcher, 1899-1908; had 247 career wins; known for pitching both games of doubleheaders; Hall of Fame, 1946.
b. Mar 19, 1871 in Rock Island, Illinois
d. Nov 14, 1929 in New York, New York
Source: *Ballpl 90; BiDAmSp BB; BioIn 2, 3, 7, 8, 10, 14, 15, 16; LegTOT; WhoProB 73*

McGiver, John
American. Actor
Played in TV shows, 1967-72; charactor actor in films, 1956-75, including *Breakfast at Tiffany's.*
b. Nov 5, 1913 in New York, New York
d. Sep 9, 1975 in West Fulton, New York
Source: *BiE&WWA; BioIn 10; EncAFC; FilmgC; ForYSC; HalFC 80, 84, 88; MotPP; MovMk; NotNAT B; WhoHol C; WhoThe 72, 77; WhScrn 77, 83; WorAl*

McGivern, William Peter
American. Author
Wrote 23 mystery novels: *The Big Heat,* 1952; *Night of the Juggler,* 1974.
b. Dec 6, 1922 in Chicago, Illinois
d. Nov 18, 1982 in Palm Desert, California
Source: *AmAu&B; AnObit 1982; BioIn 13; ConAu 49; EncMys; NewYTBS 82; WhAm 8; WhoAm 80, 82; WhoWor 80, 82; WorAu 1950*

McGivney, Michael Joseph
American. Clergy
Founded Knights of Columbus, 1882.
b. Aug 12, 1852 in Waterbury, Connecticut
d. Aug 14, 1890 in Thomaston, Connecticut
Source: *BioIn 19; DcAmB; DcAmReB 2; DcCathB; WebBD 83; WhAm HS*

McGoohan, Patrick (Joseph)
American. Actor
Played in TV series, Disney films; won Emmy for "Columbo," 1975.
b. Mar 19, 1928 in New York, New York
Source: *BioIn 11; ConTFT 5; FilmAG WE; FilmEn; FilmgC; ForYSC; HalFC 80, 84, 88; IlWWBF; IntMPA 77, 80, 84, 86, 88, 92, 94, 96; ItaFilm; LegTOT; MiSFD 9; MotPP; WhoAm 78, 80, 82, 84, 88, 90, 92, 96, 97; WhoHol 92, A; WhoThe 77A; WhThe; WorAl; WorAlBi*

McGovern, Arthur F
American. Philosopher
Prominent scholar of Marxism and Christianity; wrote *Marxism and Christianity: An American Christian Perspective,* 1980.
b. Dec 4, 1929 in Columbus, Ohio
Source: *ConAu 116; DrAS 82P*

McGovern, Elizabeth
American. Actor
Played in films *Ordinary People,* 1980 Oscar winner; *Ragtime,* 1981; *She's Having a Baby,* 1987.
b. Jul 18, 1961 in Evanston, Illinois
Source: *BioIn 12, 13, 16; CelR 90; ConTFT 2, 3, 6, 13; HalFC 84, 88; IntMPA 86, 88, 92, 94, 96; LegTOT; NewYTBS 81; VarWW 85; WhoAm 90; WhoEnt 92; WorAlBi*

McGovern, George Stanley
American. Politician
Liberal senator from SD, 1963-81; Dem. presidential candidate, 1972; lost to Richard Nixon in huge landslide.
b. Jul 19, 1922 in Avon, South Dakota
Source: *AmPolLe; BiDrAC; BiDrUSC 89; BioIn 13, 14, 15; CngDr 79; ColdWar 2; ConAu 8NR; CurBio 67; DrAS 82H; EncAB-H 1974; FacFETw; IntWW 91; McGEWB; NewYTBE 71, 73; PolProf J, NF; PresAR; WebAB 79; Who 92; WhoAm 86, 90; WhoAmP 91; WorAlBi*

McGovern, Maureen Therese
"Disaster Queen"
American. Singer, Actor
Known for singing film themes of disaster movies: *The Morning After,* 1973; *We May Never Love Like This Again,* 1974; co-starred in Broadway's *The Pirates of Penzance,* 1981.
b. Jul 27, 1949 in Youngstown, Ohio
Source: *BioIn 14, 16; CelR 90; ConTFT 6; CurBio 90; NewYTBS 84; PenEncP; RkOn 84; WhoAm 86, 88; WhoAmW 85, 91; WhoEnt 92; WhoRocM 82; WorAlBi*

McGovern, Terry
[John Terrence McGovern]
American. Boxer
Early bantam, featherweight champion; Hall of Fame, 1955.
b. Mar 9, 1880 in Johnstown, Pennsylvania
d. Feb 26, 1918 in New York, New York
Source: *BoxReg; WhoBox 74; WhoSpor*

McGowan, William George
American. Business Executive
Chm., CEO, MCI Communications Corp., 1968-92; led challenge to AT&T which caused Bell's breakup in the mid-80s.
b. Dec 10, 1927 in Ashley, Pennsylvania
d. Jun 8, 1992 in Washington, District of Columbia
Source: *BioIn 12, 13, 14, 15; ConAmBL; Dun&B 90; LElec; News 93-1; St&PR 84, 91; WhoAm 82, 84, 86, 88; WhoE 89; WhoFI 83, 85, 87, 92*

McGraw, Donald Cushing
American. Publisher
McGraw-Hill Publishing Co., pres., 1953-56, chm., 1966-74.
b. May 21, 1897 in Madison, New Jersey
d. Feb 7, 1974 in Boynton Beach, Florida
Source: *BiDrLUS 70; BioIn 3, 10; DcAmB S9; NewYTBS 74; WhAm 6; WhoFI 74; WhoWor 74*

McGraw, Harold Whittlesey, Jr.
American. Publisher
With McGraw-Hill Book Co. since 1947; chm., 1976-88; chm. emeritus, 1988—.
b. Jan 10, 1918 in New York, New York
Source: *BioIn 11, 14; Dun&B 88; NewYTBS 79; St&PR 84, 87, 91; WhoAm 74, 76, 78, 80, 82, 84, 86, 88, 90, 92, 94, 95, 96, 97; WhoE 83, 85, 86, 89, 91, 95; WhoFI 74, 77, 79, 81, 83, 85, 87, 89, 92, 94, 96; WhoWor 84*

McGraw, John Joseph
"Little Napoleon"
American. Baseball Player, Baseball Manager
Infielder, 1891-1916; had career .334 batting average; won 10 pennants in 33 yrs. as manager; Hall of Fame, 1937.
b. Apr 7, 1873 in Truxton, New York
d. Feb 25, 1934 in New Rochelle, New York
Source: *BiDAmSp BB; BioIn 9, 10, 12, 13; DcAmB S1; DcNAA; EncAB-A 4; OxCAmH; WebAB 74, 79; WhAm 4, HSA; WhoProB 73; WorAl*

McGraw, Mike
American. Journalist
Won Pulitzer Prize for National reporting, 1992.

McGraw, Tim
American. Singer
Country singer who released debut album *Tim McGraw* in 1993 and later released albums *Not a Moment Too Soon* which featured number one hits "Indian Outlaw" and "Don't Take the Girl" and *All I Want* which included single "I Like It, I Love It;" received Country Radio Music Award and American Music Award for best new country artist, 1994; received American Country Music album of the year award for *Not a Moment Too Soon,* 1994.
b. May 1, 1966 in Jacksonville, Florida
Source: *ConMus 17*

McGraw, Tug
[Frank Edwin McGraw]
American. Baseball Player
Relief pitcher, 1965-84, known for throwing effective screwball; had 180 career saves.
b. Aug 30, 1944 in Martinez, California
Source: *Ballpl 90; BiDAmSp Sup; BioIn 10, 12, 13, 14, 17; LegTOT; NewYTBS 74, 85; WhoAm 82, 84; WhoProB 73; WorAl*

McGriff, Fred(erick Stanley)
American. Baseball Player
First baseman, New York Yankees, 1981-82; Toronto, 1986-91; San Diego Padres, 1990-93; Atlanta Braves, 1993—; led AL in home runs, 1989; led NL in home runs, 1992.
b. Oct 31, 1963 in Tampa, Florida
Source: *Ballpl 90; BaseEn 88; BioIn 16, 19, 21; WhoAfA 96; WhoAm 92, 94, 95, 96, 97; WhoBlA 92, 94; WhoSSW 95, 97*

McGrory, Mary
American. Writer
Syndicated columist; won Pulitzer Prize for Commentary, 1975.
b. Aug 22, 1918 in Boston, Massachusetts
Source: *AmWomWr; BiDAmNC; BioIn 5, 8, 10, 11; ConAu 106; InWom SUP; WhoAm 84, 97; WhoAmW 85, 97; WomFir*

McGuane, Thomas Francis
American. Author, Screenwriter
Best known for novels *Ninety-Two in the Shade,* 1973; *Nobody's Angel,* 1982.
b. Dec 11, 1939 in Wyandotte, Michigan
Source: *Benet 87; BenetAL 91; BioIn 15, 16; CamGLE; CamHAL; ConAu 5NR, 24NR; ConLC 45; ConTFT 8; CurBio 87; CyWA 89; DcLB 2; EncAHmr; HalFC 88; MajTwCW; PostFic; TwCWW 91; WhoAm 74, 76, 78, 80, 82, 84, 86, 90, 92, 94, 95, 96; WhoUSWr 88; WhoWest 94; WhoWrEP 89, 92, 95; WrDr 92*

McGuffey, William Holmes
American. Educator, Author
Famous for six school books, *Eclectic Readers,* 1836-57, that had great influence on 19th-c. youth; over 122,000,000 sold.
b. Sep 23, 1800 in Washington, Pennsylvania
d. May 4, 1873 in Charlottesville, Virginia
Source: *AmAu; AmAu&B; AmBi; ApCAB; Benet 87, 96; BenetAL 91; BiDAmEd; BioIn 1, 2, 3, 4, 5, 6, 7, 8, 9, 10, 11, 13, 15, 17, 18, 19; ChhPo, S1, S2, S3; CyEd; DcAmB; DcAmC; DcLB 42; DcLEL; DcNAA; EncAAH; EncAB-H 1974, 1996; McGEWB; MemAm; NatCAB 4; OhA&B; OxCAmH; OxCAmL 65, 83, 95; PenC AM; REn; REnAL; SmATA 60; TwCBDA; WebAB 74, 79; WhAm HS; WorAl; WorAlBi*

McGuinn, Roger
[The Byrds]
American. Musician
Banjoist, lead vocalist; founded The Byrds, 1965-72.
b. Jul 13, 1942 in Chicago, Illinois
Source: *BioIn 13, 14, 17; ConMuA 80A; EncFCWM 83; EncRk 88; IlEncRk; LegTOT; OnThGG; WhoRock 81; WhoRocM 82*

McGuinness, Martin
Irish. Politician, Political Activist
IRA leader currently an elected member of N Ireland Assembly.
b. 1950?
Source: *BioIn 15, 20; ConNews 85-4*

McGuire, Al
American. Basketball Coach
Coach, Marquette U, 1964-77; won NCAA championship, 1977; basketball Hall of Fame, 1992.
b. Sep 7, 1928 in New York, New York
Source: *BasBi; BioIn 8, 9, 11; NewYTBS 76; WhoBbl 73; WorAl*

McGuire, Biff
American. Actor
Stage debut, 1946: *The Moon Is Blue;* films include *The Heart Is a Lonely Hunter,* 1968; *Serpico,* 1973.
b. Oct 25, 1926 in New Haven, Connecticut
Source: *BiE&WWA; HalFC 84, 88; NotNAT; VarWW 85; WhoHol 92, A; WhoThe 72, 77, 81*

McGuire, Dick
[Richard J McGuire]
American. Basketball Player
Guard, New York, 1949-57, Detroit, 1957-60; led NBA in assists, 1950.
b. Jan 25, 1926 in Huntington, New York
Source: *BasBi; BiDAmSp BK; BioIn 3; OfNBA 87; WhoSpor*

McGuire, Dorothy Hackett
American. Actor
Star of stage, film *Claudia,* 1941; won Drama Critics Circle Award, 1941; TV show "Rich Man, Poor Man."
b. Jun 14, 1918 in Omaha, Nebraska
Source: *BiDFilm; BiE&WWA; ConTFT 3; CurBio 41; FilmgC; HalFC 88; IntMPA 92; InWom SUP; MotPP; MovMk; NotNAT; OxCFilm; VarWW 85; WhoAm 78, 80, 82, 84, 86, 88, 90; WhoEnt 92; WhoHol A; WhoThe 81; WorAlBi; WorEFlm*

McGuire Sisters
[Christine McGuire; Dorothy McGuire; Phyllis McGuire]
American. Music Group
Popular vocal group, 1950s; had hit single "Sincerely," 1954.
Source: *AmPS A, B; BiDAmM; BioIn 3; CurBio 41; DetWom; InWom, SUP; MotPP; PenEncP; RkOn 74, 82; WhoAmW 64; WhoHol A; WorAl*

McGwire, Mark David
American. Baseball Player
First baseman, Oakland, 1986—; broke 57-yr.-old ML record for home runs by rookie, led AL in home runs, 1987; AL rookie of yr., 1987; All-Star, 1987-89; Golden Glove Award, 1990.
b. Oct 1, 1963 in Claremont, California
Source: *Ballpl 90; BaseEn 88; BaseReg 87, 88; BioIn 15, 16; WhoAm 96, 97; WhoWest 96; WorAlBi*

McHale, John Joseph
American. Baseball Executive
Infielder in 64 games with Detroit, 1940s; Montreal Expos, pres., 1968-87; CEO, 1987—.

b. Sep 21, 1921 in Detroit, Michigan
Source: *AmCath 80; BiDAmSp BB; BioIn 15; CanWW 83, 89; WhoAm 74, 76, 78, 80, 82, 84, 86, 88; WhoE 74, 75, 77, 79, 81, 83, 85, 86, 91; WhoProB 73; WhoRel 92*

McHale, Kevin (Edward)
American. Basketball Player
Forward, Boston, 1980-93; led NBA in field goal percentage, 1987, 1988; won three NBA championships, 1981, 1984, 1986.
b. Dec 19, 1957 in Hibbing, Minnesota
Source: *BasBi; BiDAmSp Sup; BioIn 13, 14, 15; NewYTBS 84; OfNBA 87; WhoAm 88, 90, 92, 94, 95, 96, 97; WhoE 89, 95; WorAlBi*

McHale, Tom
American. Author
Wrote of conflicts between Italian, Irish Catholics: *School Spirit,* 1976.
b. 1942? in Scranton, Pennsylvania
d. Mar 30, 1982 in Pembroke Pines, Florida
Source: *AuNews 1; ConAu 77, 106; ConLC 3, 5; ConNov 72, 76; DrAPF 80; IntAu&W 76, 77; WrDr 80*

McHenry, Donald Franchot
American. Government Official
US ambassador to the United Nations, 1979-81.
b. Oct 13, 1938 in Saint Louis, Missouri
Source: *BioIn 13, 14; CurBio 80; InB&W 85; IntWW 91; NegAl 89A; NewYTBS 78, 80; Who 85, 92; WhoAm 84, 88; WhoAmP 73; WhoBlA 88, 92; WhoGov 77*

McHugh, Frank
[Francis Curray McHugh]
American. Actor
Character actor with Warner Bros., 1930-42, generally as the hero's best-friend in over 150 films.
b. May 23, 1898 in Homestead, Pennsylvania
d. Sep 11, 1981 in Greenwich, Connecticut
Source: *BiE&WWA; EncAFC; Film 2; FilmEn; FilmgC; ForYSC; HolCA; IntMPA 82; MotPP; MovMk; NewYTBS 81; NotNAT; OlFamFa; Vers A; WhoHol A*

McHugh, Jimmy
[James McHugh]
American. Songwriter
Hits include "I Can't Give You Anything But Love," 1928; "On the Sunny Side of the Street," 1930.
b. Jul 10, 1894? in Boston, Massachusetts
d. May 23, 1969 in Beverly Hills, California
Source: *ASCAP 66, 80; Baker 78, 84, 92; BestMus; BiDAmM; BiE&WWA; BioIn 1, 4, 5, 6, 8, 9, 14, 15, 16; CmpEPM; ConAmC 76, 82; EncMT; FilmEn; FilmgC; LegTOT; NewAmDM; NewCBMT; NewGrDA 86; NewGrDM 80; OxCAmT 84; OxCPMus; PenEncP; Sw&Ld C; WhAm 5; WhoHol B; WhScrn 74, 77, 83; WorAl; WorAlBi*

McIlhenny, Walter S
American. Business Executive
Chm., family-owned co. that invented Tabasco sauce, 1848.
b. 1911 in Washington, District of Columbia
d. Jun 23, 1985 in Lafayette, Indiana
Source: *NewYTBS 85*

McIlwain, Charles Howard
American. Educator, Historian
Wrote 1923 Pulitzer winner *The American Revolution.*
b. Mar 15, 1871 in Saltsburg, Pennsylvania
d. 1968
Source: *AmAu&B; BioIn 4, 14; ConAu 102; OxCAmL 65; TwCA, SUP; WhAm 6; WhNAA; Who 74*

McIlwee, Thomas
Irish. Hunger Striker, Revolutionary
IRA member; one of 10 hunger strikers to die in prison, demanding political prisoner rather than criminal status.
b. Nov 30, 1957 in Bellaghy, Northern Ireland
d. Aug 8, 1981 in Belfast, Northern Ireland

McInerney, Jay
American. Author
Wrote *Bright Lights, Big City,* 1984; *Ransom,* 1985.
b. Jan 13, 1955 in Hartford, Connecticut
Source: *Au&Arts 18; BenetAL 91; BioIn 14, 15, 16; CelR 90; ConAu 45NR, 116, 123; ConLC 34; ConNov 91, 96; ConPopW; CurBio 87; DcArts; LegTOT; OxCAmL 95; WhoAm 92, 94, 95, 96, 97; WorAlBi; WrDr 92, 94, 96*

McIntire, Carl
American. Evangelist
Founder, Bible Presbyterian Church, 1936, Int'l. Council of Christian Churches, 1948; daily radio program, "20th C. Reformation Hour," combines fundamentalist Christianity, hawkish patriotism.
b. May 17, 1906 in Ypsilanti, Michigan
Source: *BioIn 9, 10, 11, 12, 17, 18; CurBio 71; LuthC 75; NewYTBE 70; PeoHis; PolProf J; PrimTiR; RelLAm 91; TwCSAPR*

McIntire, John
American. Actor
Played wagon master on long-running TV series "Wagon Train," 1961-64; often appear ed with wife Jeannette Nolan.
b. Jun 27, 1907 in Spokane, Washington
d. Jan 30, 1991 in Laguna Beach, California
Source: *BiDFilm, 81; BioIn 17; ConTFT 15; FilmEn; FilmgC; ForYSC; GangFlm; HalFC 80, 84, 88; IntMPA 75, 76, 77, 78, 79, 80, 81, 82, 84, 86, 88; LesBEnT 92; MotPP; RadStar; SaTiSS; VarWW 85; WhoHol A; WorEFlm*

McIntyre, Frank J
Actor
Silent screen comedian in *Too Fat to Fight,* 1917; *Traveling Salesman,* 1918.
b. 1879
d. Jun 8, 1949 in Ann Arbor, Michigan
Source: *Film 1; MotPP; WhoHol B; WhScrn 74, 77*

McIntyre, Hal
[Harold W McIntyre]
American. Jazz Musician
Altoist with Glenn Miller, 1937-41; led own band, 1940s-50s.
b. Nov 29, 1914 in Cromwell, Connecticut
d. May 5, 1959 in Hollywood, California
Source: *BgBands 74; BiDAmM; BiDJaz; BioIn 9, 12, 16; CmpEPM; NewGrDJ 88, 94; PenEncP*

McIntyre, James
American. Actor
With partner Thomas Heath appeared in minstrel shows as blackface comedian for over 50 years, beginning 1874.
b. Aug 8, 1857 in Kenosha, Wisconsin
d. Aug 18, 1937 in Southampton, New York
Source: *BioIn 4; DcAmB S2; EncVaud; OxCAmT 84; WhoStg 1908*

McIntyre, James Francis Aloysius, Cardinal
American. Religious Leader
Archbishop of Los Angeles, 1948-70; appointed cardinal, 1953.
b. Jun 25, 1886 in New York, New York
d. Jul 16, 1979 in Los Angeles, California
Source: *BioIn 12, 19; CurBio 53; DcAmB S10; DcAmReB 2; IntWW 74; LinLib S; RelLAm 91; WebBD 83; WhAm 7; Who 74; WhoAm 74, 76; WhoRel 77; WhoWest 76*

McIntyre, James Talmadge, Jr.
American. Government Official, Lawyer
Director of Carter's Office of Management and Budget, late 1970s, after Lance's resignation.
b. Dec 17, 1940 in Vidalia, Georgia
Source: *BioIn 11, 12; CurBio 79; IntWW 91; NewYTBS 77; WhoAm 78, 80, 82, 84, 86; WhoAmP 91; WhoE 79*

McIntyre, John Thomas
American. Author, Dramatist
Wrote realistic novels *Slag,* 1927; *Steps Going Down,* 1936.
b. Nov 26, 1871 in Philadelphia, Pennsylvania
d. May 21, 1951 in Philadelphia, Pennsylvania
Source: *AmAu&B; BioIn 2, 3, 4; DcAmAu; OxCAmL 65; REnAL; TwCA, SUP*

McIntyre, O(scar) O(dd)
American. Journalist
Wrote daily column "New York Day by Day," syndicated in over 500 newspapers, from 1912.
b. Feb 18, 1884 in Plattsburg, Missouri
d. Feb 13, 1938
Source: *AmAu&B; AmBi; BiDAmJo; BioIn 2, 4, 10, 14, 16; DcAmB S2; DcNAA; NatCAB 36; OhA&B; REnAL; TwCA; WhAm 1; WhNAA*

McKay, Claude
American. Author
Wrote *Home to Harlem,* 1928, first best-seller written by a black.
b. Sep 15, 1889 in Sunny Ville, Jamaica
d. May 22, 1948 in Chicago, Illinois
Source: *Benet 96; BenetAL 91; BiDConC; BlkLC; CaribW 1; ConBlB 6; CyWA 89; DcAmB S4; DcAmNB; DcLB 4, 45, 51, 117; DcTwCCu 5; EncAACR; EncWL 2, 3; FifCWr; GrWrEL P; LiExTwC; McGEWB; ModBlW; NewCol 75; OxCAmL 65; OxCTwCP; PeoHis; PoeCrit 2; RAdv 14; REn; REnAL; RfGAmL 87, 94; SchCGBL; SelBAAf; SelBAAu; TwCLC 7, 41; WebAB 74, 79; WhAm HS; WorLitC*

McKay, David O
"The Missionary President"
American. Religious Leader
Led Church of Jesus Christ of Latter-Day Saints, since 1951.
b. Sep 8, 1873 in Huntsville, Utah
d. Jan 18, 1970 in Salt Lake City, Utah
Source: *CurBio 51, 70; NewYTBE 70; WhAm 5*

McKay, Donald
American. Designer, Shipbuilder
Designed, built large, fast clipper ships, 1845-69, including famed *Flying Cloud.*
b. Sep 4, 1810 in Shelburne County, Nova Scotia, Canada
d. Sep 20, 1880 in Hamilton, Massachusetts
Source: *AmBi; ApCAB; BioIn 5, 6, 7, 9, 17; DcAmB; EncAB-H 1974, 1996; McGEWB; NatCAB 2; NewCol 75; OxCAmH; TwCBDA; WebAB 74, 79; WhAm HS*

McKay, Festus Claudius
Jamaican. Author, Poet
Books of poetry include *Songs of Jamaica,* 1912; novels include *Banana Bottom,* 1933.
b. Sep 15, 1889 in Clarendon, Jamaica
Source: *BlkWr 1; ConAu 124; MajTwCW*

McKay, Jim
[James Kenneth McManus]
American. Sportscaster
Host, ABC's "Wide World of Sports," beginning in 1961; has won 12 Emmys, covered Olympics 1960-88.
b. Sep 24, 1921 in Philadelphia, Pennsylvania
Source: *BiDAmSp FB; BioIn 13; ConAu 85, 115; CurBio 73; LesBEnT; VarWW 85; WhoAm 86*

McKay, John Harvey
American. Football Coach
Head coach, USC, 1960-75, with 121-37-8 record; in NFL with Tampa Bay, 1976-84.
b. Jul 5, 1923 in Everettville, West Virginia
Source: *BiDAmSp FB; ConAu 115; WhoAm 80, 82, 84; WhoSSW 78, 80, 82; WhoWest 76*

McKay, Scott
[Carl Chester Gose]
American. Actor
Made stage debut, 1937; appeared on Broadway in *Absurd Person Singular,* 1975-76.
b. May 28, 1915 in Pleasantville, Iowa
Source: *BiE&WWA; BioIn 15; NewYTBS 87; NotNAT; VarWW 85; WhoHol A; WhoThe 77, 81*

McKean, Michael
American. Actor
Played Lenny on TV series "Laverne & Shirley," 1976-83.
b. Oct 17, 1947? in New York, New York
Source: *BioIn 11; ConTFT 3, 14; IntMPA 92, 94, 96; VarWW 85; WhoAm 90, 95, 96, 97; WhoEnt 92; WhoHol 92*

McKean, Thomas
American. Lawyer
Signed Declaration of Independence, 1776, as DE delegate; PA governor for three terms, eventually charged with nepotism.
b. Mar 30, 1735 in New London, Pennsylvania
d. Jun 24, 1817 in Philadelphia, Pennsylvania
Source: *AmBi; DcAmB; Drake; WebAB 74; WhAm HS; WhAmP*

McKechnie, Bill
[William Boyd McKechnie]
"Deacon Bill"
American. Baseball Player, Baseball Manager
Infielder, early 1900s; only manager to win pennants with three different NL teams; Hall of Fame, 1962.
b. Aug 7, 1887 in Wilkinsburg, Pennsylvania
d. Oct 29, 1965 in Bradenton, Florida
Source: *BioIn 2, 5, 7, 14, 15, 19; WhoProB 73*

McKechnie, Donna
American. Dancer, Actor
Won Tony, 1975, for *A Chorus Line.*
b. Nov 16, 1942 in Pontiac, Michigan
Source: *BiDD; BioIn 15; ConTFT 7; InWom SUP; VarWW 85; WhoAm 84; WhoHol A; WhoThe 81; WorAlBi*

McKee, Lonette
American. Actor, Singer
Appeared in *The Cotton Club,* 1984; *Jungle Fever,* 1991; *Malcolm X,* 1992.
b. c. 1952 in Detroit, Michigan
Source: *ConBlB 12; News 96, 96-1*

McKee, Lonette
American. Actor, Singer
Films include *The Cotton Club,* 1984; *Brewster's Millions,* 1985; on stage in *Lady Day at Emerson's Bar and Grill.*
b. Jul 21, 1954 in Detroit, Michigan
Source: *BioIn 11, 13, 14, 15; BlksAmF; ConTFT 6, 14; DrBlPA 90; IntMPA 86, 88; NewYTBS 78, 83; WhoBlA 92; WhoHol 92*

McKeel, Johnny
[The Hostages; John D McKeel, Jr]
American. Hostage
One of 52 held by terrorists, Nov 1979 - Jan 1981.
b. 1954?
Source: *BioIn 12; NewYTBS 81*

McKeen, John Elmer
American. Business Executive
Pres., chm., Pfizer Drug Co., 1949-68, which manufactured penicillin.
b. Jun 4, 1903 in New York, New York
d. Feb 23, 1978 in Palm Beach, Florida
Source: *AmMWSc 73P, 79; BioIn 2, 11; CurBio 61, 78; St&PR 75; WhoAm 74, 76; WhoFI 74*

McKegney, Tony
Canadian. Hockey Player
One of few black NHL players, 1979-91; with several teams; including Buffalo Sabres, 1979-84.
b. Feb 15, 1958 in Montreal, Quebec, Canada
Source: *BioIn 16, 18; ConBlB 3*

McKellar, Danica
American. Actor
Played Winnie Cooper on TV series "The Wonder Years," 1988-93.
Source: *BioIn 16*

McKellen, Ian (Murray), Sir
English. Actor, Director
Won 1981 Tony for his role, Salieri, in *Amadeus;* played title role in *Richard III,* 1995.
b. May 25, 1939 in Burnley, England
Source: *BioIn 12, 13, 14, 15, 16; CamGWoT; CelR 90; CnThe; ConTFT 1, 4, 11; CurBio 84; DcArts; GayLesB; HalFC 88; IntDcT 3; IntMPA 88, 92, 94, 96; IntWW 78, 79, 80, 81, 82, 83, 89, 91, 93; News 94, 94-1; NewYTBS 81; OxCThe 83; VarWW 85; Who 83, 85, 88, 90, 92, 94; WhoAm 94, 95, 96, 97; WhoHol 92; WhoThe 81; WhoWor 82, 84, 87, 89, 91, 93, 95, 96, 97*

McKelway, St. Clair
American. Author, Screenwriter
Contributor to the *New Yorker* mag. for over 30 yrs; sketches collected in *Edinburgh Caper*, 1962.
b. Feb 13, 1905 in Charlotte, North Carolina
d. 1976 in Washington, District of Columbia
Source: *AmAu&B; BioIn 12; BlueB 76; ConAu 5R, 93; LiJour; NewYTBS 80; WhAm 7; WhoAm 74, 76; WhoWor 74*

McKenna, Frank
Canadian. Politician
Liberal premier of New Brunswick, 1987—.
b. Jan 19, 1948 in Apolaqui, New Brunswick, Canada
Source: *BioIn 15; CanWW 89; IntWW 91; Who 92; WhoAm 90; WhoE 91*

McKenna, Siobhan
Irish. Actor
Stage debut, 1940; films include *Doctor Zhivago*, 1965.
b. May 24, 1922 in Belfast, Northern Ireland
d. Nov 16, 1986 in Dublin, Ireland
Source: *BiE&WWA; ConTFT 4; CurBio 56, 87; EncWT; FilmgC; ForYSC; IntMPA 86; IntWW 83; InWom SUP; MotPP; NewC; NewYTBS 86; NotNAT; OxCThe 83; PlP&P; VarWW 85; WhoAm 84, 86; WhoEnt 92; WhoHol A; WhoThe 77; WorAl*

McKenna, Virginia
English. Actor
Played Joy Adamson in *Born Free*, 1965.
b. Jun 7, 1931 in London, England
Source: *BioIn 4, 81*

McKenney, Ruth
American. Author
Wrote humorous sketches in *New Yorker* mag. published as *My Sister Eileen*, 1938.
b. Nov 18, 1911 in Mishawaka, Indiana
d. Jun 25, 1972 in Columbus, Ohio
Source: *AmAu&B; AmDec 1930; AmWomWr; Benet 87, 96; BenetAL 91; BioIn 1, 2, 3, 4, 9, 15; ConAu 37R, 93; CurBio 42, 72, 72N; EncAHmr; EncAL; InWom; LngCTC; NewYTBE 72; NotNAT B; OhA&B; OxCAmL 65, 83, 95; REn; REnAL; TwCA, SUP; WhAm 5; WhoAmW 61, 64, 66, 68, 70, 72*

McKenzie, Kevin
American. Dancer
Principal dancer, American Ballet Theater, 1979-91; artistic director, 1992—.
b. Apr 29, 1954 in Burlington, Vermont
Source: *BiDD; IntDcB; WhoAm 82, 84, 86; WhoEnt 92*

McKenzie, Red
[William McKenzie]
American. Singer
Vocalist, kazoo player; led novelty act *Mound City Blue Blowers*, 1920s.
b. Oct 14, 1907 in Saint Louis, Missouri
d. Feb 7, 1948 in New York, New York
Source: *BiDAmM; BiDJaz; WhoJazz 72*

McKeon, Doug
[Douglas Jude McKeon]
American. Actor
Played Jane Fonda's son in *On Golden Pond*, 1981.
b. Jun 10, 1966 in Pompton Plains, New Jersey
Source: *BioIn 12; ConTFT 4; IntMPA 88, 92, 94, 96; JohnWSW; WhoHol 92*

McKeon, Nancy
American. Actor
Played Jo on TV series "Facts of Life," 1980-88.
b. Apr 4, 1966 in Westbury, New York
Source: *BioIn 12, 13; ConTFT 8, 15; IntMPA 96; LegTOT; VarWW 85*

McKeon, Philip
American. Actor
Played Tommy on TV series, "Alice."
b. Nov 11, 1964 in Westbury, New York
Source: *BioIn 11, 12, 14; VarWW 85; WhoHol 92*

McKern, Leo
[Reginald McKern]
English. Actor
Films include *A Man for All Seasons*, 1952.
b. Mar 16, 1920 in Sydney, Australia
Source: *BioIn 12; CamGWoT; CnThe; ConAu 134; ConTFT 2, 8; FilmEn; FilmgC; HalFC 80, 84, 88; IlWWBF; IntMPA 84, 86, 88, 92, 94, 96; IntWW 91; ItaFilm; MovMk; OxCAusL; VarWW 85; Who 82, 83, 85, 88, 90, 92, 94; WhoHol 92, A; WhoThe 72, 77, 81; WrDr 94, 96*

McKernan, John Rettie, Jr.
American. Politician
Rep. governor of Maine, 1987—.
b. May 20, 1948 in Bangor, Maine
Source: *AlmAP 88, 92; BiDrUSC 89; CngDr 83, 85; IntWW 89, 91, 93; PolsAm 84; WhoAm 84, 86, 88, 90, 92, 94, 95; WhoAmP 73, 75, 77, 85, 87, 91; WhoE 89, 91, 93, 95; WhoGov 75; WhoWor 89, 91, 93, 95*

McKernan, Ron
[The Grateful Dead]
"Pigpen"
American. Singer, Musician
Vocalist; harmonica, percussion player; original member, Grateful Dead, 1967-73.
b. Sep 8, 1946 in San Bruno, California
d. Mar 8, 1973 in Corte Madera, California
Source: *BioIn 9; EncPR&S 74; IlEncRk; WhoRocM 82*

McKerrow, Amanda
American. Dancer
Won gold prize, Moscow International Ballet Competition, 1981, highest honor ever given to American.
b. Nov 7, 1964 in New Mexico
Source: *BioIn 15; NewYTBS 81; WhoAm 90; WhoEnt 92*

McKim, Charles Follen
American. Architect
Founded prestigious firm McKim, Mead, and White, 1879-1908; designed Boston Public Library, 1887.
b. Aug 24, 1847 in Chester County, Pennsylvania
d. Sep 14, 1909 in Saint James, New York
Source: *AmBi; AmCulL; ApCAB, X; BiDAmAr; BioIn 2, 8, 9, 13, 14, 16, 19; BriEAA; DcAmB; DcAmLiB; EncAAr 1; EncMA; HarEnUS; IntDcAr; LinLib S; MacEA; McGDA; McGEWB; NatCAB 11, 23; OxCAmH; OxCAmL 65; TwCBDA; WebAB 74, 79; WhAm 1; WhAmArt 85; WhoAmA 84; WhoArch*

McKinley, Chuck
[Charles Robert McKinley]
American. Tennis Player
Won Wimbledon men's singles, 1963; leading US player, 1960s.
b. Jan 5, 1941 in Saint Louis, Missouri
d. Aug 11, 1986 in Dallas, Texas
Source: *AnObit 1986; BiDAmSp Sup; BuCMET; CurBio 63; LegTOT*

McKinley, Ida Saxton
[Mrs. William McKinley]
American. First Lady
After tragic deaths of two children, she developed epilepsy; husband was devoted, caring.
b. Jun 8, 1847 in Canton, Ohio
d. May 26, 1907 in Canton, Ohio
Source: *AmWom; BioAmW; BioIn 16, 17; FacPr 89; GoodHs; InWom SUP; NatCAB 11; NotAW; TwCBDA; WhAm 1*

McKinley, Ray
American. Singer, Musician, Bandleader
Drummer, vocalist who led new Glenn Miller Band, 1956-66.
b. Jun 18, 1910 in Fort Worth, Texas
d. May 7, 1995 in Largo, Florida
Source: *AllMusG; ASCAP 66; BgBands 74; BiDAmM; BiDJaz; BioIn 2, 9, 12, 16, 18, 20, 21; CmpEPM; EncJzS; NewAmDM; NewGrDJ 88; OxCPMus; PenEncP; WhoJazz 72*

McKinley, William
American. US President
Rep., 25th president, 1897-1901; led US through Spanish-American War; assassinated.
b. Jan 29, 1843 in Niles, Ohio
d. Sep 14, 1901 in Buffalo, New York
Source: *AmAu&B; AmBi; AmPolLe; ApCAB SUP; Benet 87, 96; BenetAL 91; BiDrAC; BiDrGov 1789; BiDrUSC 89; BiDrUSE 71, 89; BioIn 1, 2, 3, 4, 5, 6, 7, 8, 9, 10, 11, 12, 13, 14, 15, 16, 17,*

18, 19, 20; CivWDc; CyAG; DcAmB; Dis&D; EncAAH; EncAB-H 1974, 1996; EncWM; FacFETw; FacPr 89, 93; GayN; HarEnUS; HealPre; HisWorL; LegTOT; LinLib L, S; McGEWB; NatCAB 11; OhA&B; OxCAmH; OxCAmL 65, 83; PolPar; RComAH; REn; REnAL; TwCBDA; WebAB 74, 79; WhAm 1; WhAmP; WhCiWar; WhDW; WorAl; WorAlBi

McKinney, Bill
[William McKinney]
American. Musician
Drummer for jazz band called McKinney's Cotton Pickers, 1920s.
b. Sep 17, 1894 in Paducah, Kentucky
d. Oct 14, 1969 in Cynthiana, Kentucky
Source: *BiDJaz; InB&W 80; WhoJazz 72*

McKinney, Cynthia A(nn)
American. Politician
First black female rep. from GA, 1993—.
b. Mar 17, 1955 in Atlanta, Georgia
Source: *ConBlB 11; CurBio 96; News 97-1; WhoAfA 96; WhoAm 96, 97; WhoAmP 93, 95; WhoAmW 95, 97; WhoBlA 94; WhoSSW 97*

McKinney, Stewart Brett
American. Politician
Rep. congressman from CT, 1971-87; championed liberal causes.
b. Jan 30, 1931 in Pittsburgh, Pennsylvania
d. May 7, 1987 in Washington, District of Columbia
Source: *BiDrUSC 89; BioIn 11; CngDr 87; ConNews 87-4; WhoAm 86; WhoAmP 73, 75, 77, 79, 81, 83, 85; WhoGov 77*

Mc Kinney, Tamara
American. Skier
Only American woman to win World Cup Alpine championship, 1983.
b. 1963
Source: *BioIn 12, 13; NewYTBS 80*

McKinnon, Isaiah
"Ike"
American. Police Chief
Cheif of Police, Detroit, 1994—.
b. Jun 21, 1943 in Montgomery, Alabama
Source: *ConBlB 9; WhoAfA 96; WhoAm 95, 96, 97*

McKissick, Floyd Bixler
American. Civil Rights Leader
Nat. director, CORE, 1966-67, succeeded by Roy Innis; as lawyer, involved in civil rights cases.
b. Mar 9, 1922 in Asheville, North Carolina
d. Apr 28, 1991 in Durham, North Carolina
Source: *AfrAmBi 1; BioIn 14; ConAu 49, 134; ConBlB 3; CurBio 68, 91N; InB&W 80; IntWW 74, 75, 76, 77, 78, 79, 80, 81, 82, 83, 89, 91, 91N; NegAl 89; NewYTBS 91; PolProf J; SelBAAf; SelBAAu; WhAm 10; WhoAm 74, 76, 78; WhoBlA 85, 90, 92N; WhoWor 74*

McKuen, Rod Marvin
American. Poet, Singer
Wrote pop song, "Jean" for film *The Prime of Miss Jean Brodie,* 1969.
b. Apr 23, 1933 in San Francisco, California
Source: *AmAu&B; AuNews 1; Baker 84; BenetAL 91; BioIn 13; BioNews 74; BkPepl; CelR 90; ConLC 3; ConPo 70; CurBio 70; EncFCWM 69; IntAu&W 91; IntWW 91; IntWWM 90; NewAmDM; NewGrDA 86; NewYTBE 71; OxCPMus; VarWW 85; Who 92; WhoAm 86, 88; WhoHol A; WhoWrEP 89; WorAlBi; WrDr 86, 92*

McLaglen, Victor
American. Actor
Former boxer promoted as "great white hope" against black boxer Jack Johnson to wh om he lost; Oscar winner for *The Informer,* 1935.
b. Dec 11, 1886 in Tunbridge Wells, England
d. Nov 7, 1959 in Newport Beach, California
Source: *BiDFilm, 81, 94; BioIn 5, 7, 9, 17, 21; CmMov; DcAmB S6; EncAFC; Film 2; FilmEn; FilmgC; ForYSC; IntDcF 1-3, 2-3; ItaFilm; LegTOT; MotPP; MovMk; NotNAT B; ObitT 1951; OlFamFa; OxCFilm; TwYS; WhAm 3; WhoHol B; WhScrn 74, 77, 83; WorEFlm*

McLain, Denny
[Dennis Dale McLain]
American. Baseball Player
Pitcher, 1963-72, mostly with Detroit; last to win 30 games in one season, 1968; won AL Cy Young Award, 1968, 1969, MVP, 1968; jailed for extortion, 1984.
b. Mar 29, 1944 in Chicago, Illinois
Source: *Ballpl 90; BiDAmSp Sup; BioIn 7, 8, 9, 10, 14, 15, 16, 19, 20; BioNews 74; CurBio 69; LegTOT; NewYTBE 70, 72; NewYTBS 84, 85, 89; WhoProB 73; WhoSpor*

McLaren, Bruce Leslie
New Zealander. Auto Racer, Auto Manufacturer
Grand Prix driver who designed formula I, II sports cars bearing his name; killed in crash.
b. Aug 30, 1937 in Auckland, New Zealand
d. Jun 2, 1970 in Sussex, England
Source: *BioIn 7, 8, 9, 10, 12; NewYTBE 72; ObitT 1961*

McLaren, Norman
Canadian. Filmmaker
Innovator in animation who won Academy Award for short *Neighbors,* 1952.
b. Apr 11, 1914 in Stirling, Scotland
d. Jan 26, 1987 in Montreal, Quebec, Canada
Source: *AnObit 1987; BioIn 5, 6, 11, 12, 15, 16, 19; BlueB 76; CanWW 70, 79, 80, 81, 83; ConArt 77; ConGrA 2; ConNews 87-2; CreCan 1; DcFM; EncEurC; FacFETw; FilmEn; FilmgC; HalFC 80, 84, 88; IntDcF 1-2, 2-4; IntWW 74, 75, 76, 77, 78, 79, 80, 81, 82, 83; OxCFilm; St&PR 75; VarWW 85; WhAm 9; WhoAm 84, 86; WhoAmA 73, 76, 78, 80, 82, 84, 86; WhoE 75, 77; WhoGrA 62, 82; WhoHrs 80; WhoWor 74; WorECar; WorEFlm*

McLaren, Wayne
American. Model
Modeled as the Marlboro Man for Philip Morris' cigarette campaign.
b. 1941? in Lake Charles, Louisiana
d. Jul 22, 1991 in Newport Beach, California

McLarnin, Jimmy
"Baby Face"
Irish. Boxer
Welter-, lightweight champ, 1930s; great box office draw; Hall of Famer.
b. Dec 17, 1905 in Belfast, Northern Ireland
Source: *BiDAmSp BK; BioIn 10; WhoBox 74; WhoSpor*

McLarty, Thomas F, III
"Mack"
American. Government Official
US Chief of Staff, 1993-94; senior advisor to the pres., 1994—.
b. Jun 14, 1946 in Hope, Arkansas
Source: *Dun&B 90; WhoAm 90; WhoFI 89; WhoSSW 91*

McLaughlin, Ann Dore
American. Government Official
Succeeded William Brock as labor secretary under Reagan, 1987-89; Pres. and CEO, New American Schools Development Corp. 1992-93.
b. Nov 16, 1941 in Newark, New Jersey
Source: *BiDrUSE 89; BioIn 15, 16; CurBio 88; IntWW 89, 91, 93; NewYTBS 87; WhoAm 82, 84, 86, 88, 90; WhoAmW 83, 85, 87, 89, 91; WhoE 89; WhoEmL 87; WhoFI 89; WhoWor 89*

McLaughlin, Audrey
Canadian. Politician
Leader, New Dem. Party, 1989-94; first woman in N America to head a nat. political party.
b. Nov 7, 1936 in Dutton, Ontario, Canada
Source: *BioIn 16; CanWW 31; CurBio 90; News 90, 90-3; WhoAm 92, 95, 97; WhoAmW 91, 93; WhoWomW 91; WhoWor 96*

McLaughlin, Frederic
American. Hockey Executive
Founded Chicago Blackhawks, 1926; won Stanley Cup, 1934, 1938; Hall of Fame, 1963.

b. Jun 27, 1877 in Chicago, Illinois
d. Dec 17, 1944 in Chicago, Illinois
Source: *BioIn 10; WhoHcky 73*

McLaughlin, John
[Mahavishnu Orchestra]
English. Singer, Musician
First jazz-rock group to attain fame in both types of music, 1972-74.
b. Jan 4, 1942 in Yorkshire, England
Source: *AllMusG; Baker 84, 92; BiDJaz; BioIn 9, 11, 13; ConMuA 80A; ConMus 12; EncJzS; EncPR&S 74; EncRk 88; HarEnR 86; IlEncRk; NewAmDM; NewGrDA 86; NewGrDJ 88, 94; OnThGG; OxCPMus; PenEncP; RkWW 82; WhoAm 86; WhoEnt 92; WhoRock 81*

McLaughlin, John J
Canadian. Chemist
Patented Canada Dry ginger ale, 1907.
d. 1924

McLaughlin, John (Joseph)
American. Presidential Aide, Editor
Roman Catholic priest, who was a Nixon speechwriter, strong Watergate defender, 1971-74; editor and columnist the *National Review,* 1981-89.
b. Mar 3, 1927 in Providence, Rhode Island
Source: *BioIn 10; BioNews 74; ConAu 129; CurBio 87; WhoAm 88, 90, 92, 94, 95, 96, 97; WhoAmP 95; WhoEnt 92*

McLaughlin, Leo (Plowden)
American. Clergy
Pres., Fordham U., 1965-69; introduced nontraditional curricula.
b. Jul 30, 1912
d. Aug 15, 1996 in New York, New York
Source: *BioIn 8, 9; CurBio 96N; WhoAm 74; WhoSSW 73*

McLean, Don
American. Singer, Songwriter
Hit songs "American Pie," 1971; "Vincent," 1972; four Grammy nominations.
b. Oct 2, 1945 in New Rochelle, New York
Source: *BioIn 14; ConMus 7; CurBio 73; EncPR&S 74, 89; EncRk 88; EncRkSt; HarEnR 86; IlEncRk; IntWW 91; IntWWM 90; NewYTBE 72; PenEncP; RkOn 74; WhoAm 86, 90, 97; WhoE 91; WhoEnt 92; WorAlBi*

McLean, Evalyn Walsh
American. Socialite
Owned famed Hope diamond; gave lavish Washington parties.
b. Aug 1, 1886 in Denver, Colorado
d. Apr 26, 1947 in Washington, District of Columbia
Source: *CurBio 43, 47; InWom, SUP; LibW; NotAW*

McLean, Robert
American. Newspaper Publisher
Director, 1924-68, pres., 1938-57, Associated Press; publisher *Sunday Philadelphia Bulletin,* 1931-64.
b. Oct 1, 1891 in Philadelphia, Pennsylvania
d. Dec 5, 1980 in Montecito, California
Source: *BioIn 2, 5, 12; ConAu 103; CurBio 51, 81, 81N; DcAmB S10; IntWW 74; NewYTBS 80; St&PR 75; WhAm 7; WhoE 74, 75; WhoWor 74*

McLellan, Diana
English. Journalist
Gossip columnist; writes "Diana's Washington," in *Washington* magazine, 1985—.
b. Sep 22, 1937 in Leicester, England
Source: *BioIn 10; CelR 90; ConAu 114; InWom SUP*

McLeod, Fred(erick)
Scottish. Golfer
Touring pro, early 1900s; won US Open, 1908; charter member, Hall of Fame, 1940.
b. Apr 25, 1882 in North Berwick, Scotland
d. May 8, 1976 in Augusta, Georgia
Source: *BioIn 10; NewYTBS 76; WhoGolf*

McLerie, Allyn Ann
Canadian. Actor
Played on TV show "Tony Randall Show," 1976-78.
b. Dec 1, 1926 in Grand Mere, Quebec, Canada
Source: *BiDD; BiE&WWA; ConTFT 5; FilmgC; ForYSC; HalFC 80, 88; IntMPA 77, 80, 82, 88, 92, 94, 96; NotNAT; VarWW 85; WhoAm 84, 86; WhoHol 92, A; WhoThe 72, 77, 81*

McLish, Rachel Elizondo
American. Bodybuilder
Miss Olympia, 1980, 1982.
b. 1958 in Harlingen, Texas
Source: *HispAmA; WhoHisp 91, 92, 94*

McLoughlin, John
"Father of Oregon"
Canadian. Fur Trader
Headed Hudson Bay Co., which established Ft. Vancouver, 1825; helped to open Oregon to permanent settlement.
b. Oct 19, 1784 in Riviere du Loup, Quebec, Canada
d. Sep 3, 1857 in Oregon City, Oregon
Source: *AmBi; BioIn 1, 3, 5, 7, 9, 10, 11, 15, 16; DcAmB; DcAmMeB; DcCanB 8; DcCathB; MacDCB 78; McGEWB; NatCAB 6; OxCCan; REnAW; WebAB 74, 79; WhAm HS; WhWE*

McLuhan, (Herbert) Marshall
Canadian. Author, Educator
Mass communications expert; wrote *Understanding Media,* 1964; coined term "medium is the message," stressed importance of changing technology.
b. Jul 21, 1911 in Edmonton, Alberta, Canada
d. Dec 31, 1980 in Toronto, Ontario, Canada
Source: *AmAu&B; AmDec 1960; AnObit 1980; Benet 87, 96; BenetAL 91; BioIn 7, 8, 9, 10, 11, 12, 13, 14, 16, 17; BlueB 76; CanWr; CanWW 70, 79, 80; CasWL; CelR; ConAu 9R, 12NR, 34NR, 102; ConCaAu 1; ConLC 37, 83; CurBio 67, 81, 81N; CyWA 89; DcLB 88; DcLEL 1940; DcTwDes; DcTwHis; DrAS 74E, 78E, 82E; EncAJ; EncWB; FacFETw; Future; IntAu&W 77, 82; IntWW 74, 75, 76, 77, 78, 79, 80; LegTOT; LinLib L; MajTwCW; MakMC; MugS; NewC; NewYTBS 81; NewYTET; OxCCan; OxCCanL; OxCCan SUP; PenC AM; RAdv 14; ThTwC 87; WhAm 7; Who 74; WhoAm 74, 76, 78, 80; WhoTwCL; WhoWor 74, 78; WorAl; WorAlBi; WorAu 1950; WrDr 76, 80, 82*

MC Lyte
[Lana Moorer]
American. Rapper
Albums include *Eyes on This,* 1989; *Act Like You Know,* 1991; her "Cha Cha Cha" first Number One rap single, 1989.
b. 1971? in New York, New York
Source: *ConMus 8*

McMahon, Brien
[James O'Brien McMahon]
American. Politician
Dem. senator from CT, from 1944; author of McMahon Act for control of atomic energy, 1945.
b. Oct 6, 1903 in Norwalk, Connecticut
d. Jul 28, 1952 in Washington, District of Columbia
Source: *BiDrAC; BiDrUSC 89; BioIn 2, 3, 4, 11; CurBio 45, 52; DcAmB S5; DcCathB; EncCW; FacFETw; NatCAB 40; NewCol 75; ObitOF 79; PolProf T; WhAm 3; WorAl; WorAlBi*

McMahon, Don(ald John)
American. Baseball Player
Relief pitcher, 1957-74; led NL in saves, 1959.
b. Jan 4, 1930 in New York, New York
d. Jul 22, 1987 in Los Angeles, California
Source: *AnObit 1987; Ballpl 90; BaseEn 88; WhoProB 73*

McMahon, Ed(ward Lee)
American. Entertainer
Best known as Johnny Carson's right-hand man on "The Tonight Show," 1962-92; host of syndicated "Star Search," 1983—.
b. Mar 6, 1923 in Detroit, Michigan
Source: *BioIn 15, 16; BioNews 74; BkPepl; CelR 90; IntMPA 92, 96; LesBEnT 92; VarWW 85; WhoAm 86, 90, 97; WhoEnt 92; WhoHol A; WhoTelC; WorAlBi*

McMahon, Horace
American. Actor
Character actor in over 125 films, 1937-68; played in TV series ''Naked City,'' 1959 -63.
b. May 17, 1907 in Norwalk, Connecticut
d. Aug 17, 1971 in Norwalk, Connecticut
Source: *BiE&WWA; BioIn 9; FilmEn; ForYSC; MotPP; MovMk; NewYTBE 73; NotNAT B; WhoHol B; WhScrn 74, 77, 83*

McMahon, Jim
[James Robert McMahon]
American. Football Player
Quarterback, Chicago, 1982-89; San Diego, 1989-90; Philadelphia, 1990-92; Minnesota, 1993-94; Phoenix, 1994—.
b. Aug 21, 1959 in Jersey City, New Jersey
Source: *BiDAmSp FB; BioIn 14, 15; ConNews 85-4; FootReg 87; LegTOT; LesBEnT; NewYTBS 81, 85, 86; WhoAm 90, 92, 94; WhoMW 88, 90, 93*

McMahon, William
Australian. Politician
Prime minister, Australia, 1971-72; retained seat in Parliament until 1982; knighted by Queen Elizabeth II.
b. Feb 23, 1908 in Sydney
d. Mar 31, 1988 in Sydney, Australia
Source: *AmMWSc 73P; AnObit 1988; BioIn 9, 10, 15, 16; BlueB 76; CurBio 71, 88N; FarE&A 78, 79, 80, 81; IntWW 74, 75, 76, 77, 78, 79, 80, 81, 82, 83; IntYB 78, 79, 80, 81, 82; Who 74, 82, 83, 85, 88; WhoWor 74*

McManus, George
American. Cartoonist
Created popular comic strip ''Life With Father,'' 1913.
b. Jan 23, 1884 in Saint Louis, Missouri
d. Oct 22, 1954 in Santa Monica, California
Source: *ArtsAmW 2; BenetAL 91; BioIn 2, 3, 6, 15; DcAmB S5; EncACom; EncAJ; EncTwCJ; FacFETw; LegTOT; REnAL; WhAm 3; WhScrn 77; WorECom*

McManus, Jason Donald
American. Journalist, Editor
Editor-in-chief, Time, Inc., 1987-95.
b. Mar 3, 1934 in Mission, Kansas
Source: *BioIn 15; ConAu 125; IntWW 89, 91, 93; St&PR 91, 93, 96; WhoAm 84, 86, 88, 90, 92, 94, 95, 96, 97; WhoE 91; WhoFI 92, 94*

McManus, Sean
American. Broadcasting Executive
VP, NBC Sports; youngest vp in network sports TV history.
b. Feb 16, 1955 in New York, New York
Source: *WhoAm 84; WhoTelC*

McMaster, John Bach
American. Historian
Wrote nine-volume *History of the People of the United States,* 1883-1927.
b. Jun 29, 1852 in New York, New York
d. May 24, 1932 in Darien, Connecticut
Source: *AmAu&B; AmBi; ApCAB; Benet 87; BiDAmEd; BiD&SB; BioIn 1, 7, 9, 11, 15; DcAmAu; DcAmB; DcAmC; DcAmSR; DcLB 47; DcNAA; EncAAH; HarEnUS; LinLib L, S; McGEWB; NatCAB 11; OxCAmH; REn; REnAL; TwCBDA; WebAB 74, 79; WhAm 1*

McMillan, Edwin Mattison
American. Chemist
Shared 1951 Nobel Prize as co-discoverer of elements 93-94, neptunium and plutonium; awarded Atoms for Peace Award, 1963.
b. Sep 12, 1907 in Redondo Beach, California
d. Sep 7, 1991 in El Cerrito, California
Source: *AmMWSc 73P, 76P, 79, 82, 86, 89, 92; AsBiEn; BiESc; BioIn 2, 3, 6, 15, 17, 18, 19, 20; CamDcSc; CmCal; CurBio 91N; FacFETw; InSci; IntWW 83, 91; LarDcSc; LinLib S; McGMS 80; NewYTBS 91; NobelP; OxCAmH; WebAB 74, 79; WhAm 10; WhDW; Who 74, 82, 83, 85, 88, 90, 92N; WhoAm 74, 76, 78, 80, 82, 84, 86, 88, 90; WhoFrS 84; WhoNob, 90, 95; WhoWest 80, 82, 84, 87, 89; WhoWor 74, 76, 78, 82, 84, 87, 89, 91; WorAl; WorAlBi; WorInv; WorScD*

McMillan, Terry
American. Author
Wrote *Disappearing Acts,* 1989; *Waiting to Exhale,* 1992; *How Stella Got Her Groove Back,* 1996.
b. Oct 18, 1951 in Port Huron, Michigan
Source: *AfrAmAl 6; AmWomWr SUP; BlkWAm; ConBlB 4; ConLC 50, 61; ConPopW; CurBio 93; DcTwCCu 5; DrAPF 91; LegTOT; News 93-2; NewYTBS 92; RfGAmL 94; SchCGBL; TwCYAW; WhoAm 94, 95; WhoBlA 92; WrDr 92, 94, 96*

McMillen, Thomas
[Charles Thomas McMillen]
''Slaprock''
American. Politician, Basketball Player
Professional basketball player, 1975-85, mostly with Atlanta Hawks; Dem. congressman, MD, 1987-93.
b. May 26, 1952 in Mansfield, Pennsylvania
Source: *AlmAP 88; BiDrUSC 89; CngDr 87; CurBio 93; WhoAm 88, 90, 92, 94, 95, 96; WhoBbl 73; WhoE 89, 91, 93, 95*

McMullen, Mary
[Mary Reilly]
American. Author, Fashion Designer
Suspense, mystery novelist; wrote *Better Off Dead,* 1982.
b. 1920 in Yonkers, New York
Source: *BioIn 2, 14; ConAu 114, 128, X; EncMys; IntAu&W 91, 93; PenNWW A; TwCCr&M 80, 85, 91; WrDr 82, 84, 86, 88, 90, 92, 94, 96*

McMurrin, Sterling M(oss)
American. Educator, Government Official
Faculty member of several universities, including U of Utah, 1948-60; US commissioner of education, 1961-62.
b. Jan 12, 1914
d. Apr 6, 1996 in Saint George, Utah
Source: *ConAu 29R, 152; CurBio 96N; PolProf K*

McMurtrie, Douglas C
American. Type Designer, Bibliographer
Graphics arts expert; wrote *The Golden Book,* 1927.
b. Jul 20, 1888 in Belmar, New Jersey
d. Sep 29, 1944 in Evanston, Illinois
Source: *CurBio 44; DcAmB S3; WhAm 2*

McMurtry, James Lawrence
American. Singer, Songwriter
Folksinger; debut album *Too Long in the Wasteland,* 1989; son of novelist Larry.
b. Mar 18, 1962 in Fort Worth, Texas
Source: *News 90-2*

McMurtry, Larry Jeff
American. Author
Writings portray Texas, the West; 1986 Pulitzer winner, *Lonesome Dove,* was filmed as TV miniseries, 1989.
b. Jun 3, 1936 in Wichita Falls, Texas
Source: *Benet 87; BenetAL 91; BioIn 13, 14, 15, 16; BroV; ConAu 5NR, 19NR; ConLC 11, 27, 44; ConNov 86, 91; CurBio 84; CyWA 89; DcLB Y87A; DrAPF 91; EncFWF; EncWL; MajTwCW; REnAW; TwCWW 91; WhoAm 90; WorAlBi; WorAu 1975; WrDr 86, 92*

McNair, Barbara
American. Singer, Actor
Nightclub singer-turned-actress; starred in Broadway musical *No Strings,* 1963, film *They Call Me Mister Tibbs,* 1970.
b. Mar 4, 1939 in Racine, Wisconsin
Source: *Baker 84, 92; BiDAfM; BiE&WWA; BioIn 9; CurBio 71; DrBlPA; ForYSC; HalFC 88; InB&W 85; InWom SUP; ItaFilm; LegTOT; VarWW 85; WhoAm 78, 80, 82; WhoBlA 80, 85, 90, 92; WhoHol A*

McNair, Malcolm Perrine
''Mr. Retailing''
American. Economist, Educator, Author
Known for system of tracking retail inventory and calculating projected profits; author of many books about retailing including *The Retail Method of Inventory,* 1925.
b. Oct 6, 1894 in West Sparta, New York
d. Sep 9, 1985 in North Conway, New Hampshire
Source: *BioIn 1, 4, 14; ConAu 117; St&PR 75; WhoAm 74, 76, 78*

McNair, Robert Evander
American. Politician
Democratic governor of SC, 1965-71.
b. Dec 14, 1923 in Cades, South Carolina
Source: *BiDrGov 1789; BioIn 7; BlueB 76; St&PR 84, 87; WhoAm 74, 76, 78, 80, 82, 84, 86; WhoAmL 78, 79, 83; WhoAmP 73, 75, 77, 79, 81, 83, 85, 87, 89, 91, 93, 95; WhoSSW 73*

McNair, Ronald Ervin
American. Astronaut
Crew member who died in explosion of space shuttle *Challenger.*
b. Oct 12, 1950 in Lake City, South Carolina
d. Jan 28, 1986 in Cape Canaveral, Florida
Source: *ConBlB 3; NewYTBS 86; WhoAm 86*

McNally, Andrew, III
American. Publisher
Rand-McNally, pres., 1948-74, chm., 1974-93.
b. Aug 17, 1909 in Chicago, Illinois
Source: *BioIn 4, 7; CurBio 56; Dun&B 79, 86, 90; St&PR 75, 84, 87, 91, 93, 96, 97; WhoAm 74, 76, 78, 80, 82, 84, 86, 88, 90, 92, 94, 95, 96, 97; WhoFI 74, 79, 81, 83, 92; WhoMW 74, 76, 82, 84, 86, 88*

McNally, Dave
[David Arthur McNally]
American. Baseball Player
Pitcher, 1962-75, mostly with Baltimore; won 20 games four straight seasons; part of arbitrator free agent decision with Andy Messersmith, 1973.
b. Oct 31, 1942 in Billings, Montana
Source: *Ballpl 90; BiDAmSp BB; BioIn 8, 15; LegTOT; WhoAm 74; WhoProB 73*

McNally, John Victor
"Johnny Blood"
American. Football Player
Flamboyant halfback, 1925-33, 1935-38, including four world championships with Green Bay; Hall of Fame, 1963.
b. Nov 27, 1904 in New Richmond, Wisconsin
d. Nov 28, 1985 in Palm Springs, California
Source: *BiDAmSp FB; BioIn 6, 7, 8, 9, 10, 14, 17; WhoFtbl 74*

McNally, T. M.
American. Author
Won 1990 Flannery O'Connor Award for Short Fiction; author of short story collection *Low Flying Aircraft,* 1991; novel *Until Your Heart Stops,* 1993.
b. 1961
Source: *ConLC 82*

McNally, Terrence
American. Dramatist
Known for satires on society; won Obie for *Bad Habits,* 1974; New York Drama Critics' Circle Award for *Love! Valour! Compassion!,* 1995.
b. Nov 3, 1939 in Saint Petersburg, Florida
Source: *Benet 96; BenetAL 91; BioIn 10, 12, 14, 15, 16, 17, 19, 21; CamGWoT; CelR, 90; ConAmD; ConAu 2NR, 45; ConDr 73, 77, 82, 88, 93; ConLC 4, 7, 41, 91; ConTFT 1, 4; CrtSuDr; CurBio 88; DcLB 7; DcTwCCu 1; GayLL; IntAu&W 77, 91, 93; LegTOT; McGEWD 72, 84; NatPD 77, 81; NotNAT; OxCAmT 84; PlP&P; RAdv 14; VarWW 85; WhoAm 74, 76, 78, 80, 82, 84, 86, 88, 90, 92, 94, 95, 96, 97; WhoE 93, 95; WhoEnt 92; WhoSSW 86; WhoThe 72, 77, 81; WhoWor 95, 96, 97; WorAu 1970; WrDr 76, 80, 82, 84, 86, 88, 90, 92, 94, 96*

McNamara, George
Canadian. Hockey Player
Played for several amateur teams, early 1900s; Hall of Fame, 1958.
b. Aug 26, 1886 in Sault Sainte Marie, Ontario, Canada
d. Mar 10, 1952
Source: *WhoHcky 73*

McNamara, John Francis
American. Baseball Manager
Minor league catcher, 1951-67; manager, Boston, 1985-88.
b. Jun 4, 1932 in Sacramento, California
Source: *Ballpl 90; BaseEn 88; BaseReg 87, 88; WhoAm 82, 86, 90; WhoE 86; WhoMW 82; WhoProB 73*

McNamara, Margaret Craig
[Mrs. Robert S McNamara]
American. Educator
Developed Reading Is Fundamental (RIF) to encourage poor children to read, 1966.
b. Aug 22, 1915 in Seattle, Washington
d. Feb 3, 1981 in Washington, District of Columbia
Source: *BioIn 11; NewYTBS 81; SmATA 24N*

McNamara, Robert S(trange)
American. Banker, Government Official
President, Ford Motor Co., 1960-61; Defense Secretary, 1961-68; President, World Bank, 1968-81.
b. Jun 9, 1916 in San Francisco, California
Source: *BiDrUSE 71, 89; BioIn 13, 14, 15; ConAu 129; CurBio 61, 87; Dun&B 90; EncAB-H 1974, 1996; EncABHB 7; EncWB; IntWW 91; NewYTBE 73; NewYTBS 75; PeoHis; PolProf J, K; St&PR 75, 87; Ward 77G; Who 92; WhoAm 86, 97; WhoGov 77; WhoUSWr 88; WhoWor 87, 91, 97; WhoWrEP 89; WrDr 92*

McNamee, Graham
"The Father of Sportscasting"
American. Broadcaster
Introduced many sportscasting techniques, expressions still in use.
b. Jul 10, 1888 in Washington, District of Columbia
d. May 9, 1942 in New York, New York
Source: *BiDAmJo; BiDAmSp OS; BioIn 7, 16; CurBio 42; DcAmB S3; EncAJ; NatCAB 31; WhAm 2; WhScrn 83*

McNamer, Deirdre
American. Author
Wrote *Rima in the Weeds,* 1991.
b. 1950
Source: *ConLC 70*

McNary, Charles Linza
American. Statesman
Rep. senator from OR, from 1917; advocated farm aid.
b. Jun 12, 1874 in Salem, Oregon
d. Feb 25, 1944 in Fort Lauderdale, Florida
Source: *ApCAB X; BiDrAC; BiDrUSC 89; BioIn 1, 17; CurBio 40, 44; DcAmB S3; EncAAH; InB&W 85; NatCAB 32; NatLAC; WhAm 2; WhAmP; WhoAm 86; WhoBlA 92*

McNaughton, F(oye) F(isk)
American. Publisher, Editor
Editor, publisher of Pekin (IL) *Daily Times,* 1927-81.
b. May 15, 1890 in Ray, Indiana
d. Dec 29, 1981 in Effingham, Illinois
Source: *WhJnl; WhoFI 75, 77*

McNealy, Scott (G.)
American. Business Executive
President, Sun Microsystems, 1984—.
b. Nov 13, 1954 in Columbus, Indiana
Source: *CurBio 96; St&PR 93, 96, 97; WhoAm 97*

McNeil, Claudia Mae
American. Actor
Emmy-winner for "The Nurses," 1963; Tony nomination for *Tiger, Tiger Burning B right,* 1962.
b. Aug 13, 1917 in Baltimore, Maryland
Source: *BiDAfM; BiE&WWA; NotNAT; WhoAfA 96; WhoAm 74, 76, 78, 80, 82, 84, 86; WhoAmW 66, 68, 70, 72, 74; WhoBlA 75, 77, 80, 85, 90, 92, 94; WhoHol A; WhoThe 81; WhoWor 74*

McNeil, Lori
American. Tennis Player
In 1987, became first black woman since 1958 to reach US Open semi-finals.
b. Dec 18, 1963 in San Diego, California
Source: *BioIn 16; ConBlB 1; WhoBlA 92*

McNeile, Herman Cyril
English. Author
Created detective hero *Bull-Dog Drummond,* 1920.
b. Sep 28, 1888 in Bodmin, England
d. Aug 14, 1937 in Pulborough, England
Source: *BioIn 2, 14; DcLB 77; DcLEL; EncMys; EvLB; LngCTC; NewC; NewCBEL; REn; SpyFic; TwCA, SUP; TwCCr&M 85; WorAl; WorAlBi*

McNeill, Don(ald Thomas)
American. Radio Performer
Hosted "Breakfast Club," longest-running morning show on radio, 1933-68.
b. Dec 3, 1907 in Galena, Illinois
d. May 7, 1996 in Evanston, Illinois
Source: *BioIn 1, 2, 3, 4, 6, 13, 14, 21; CurBio 49, 96N; NewYTBS 27; RadStar; SaTiSS; VarWW 85*

McNeill, Robert Edward, Jr.
American. Banker
Chm., Manufacturers Hanover Trust Co., 1963-71; played major role in controversial merger of the two banks.
b. Jan 20, 1906 in Live Oak, Florida
d. May 4, 1981 in Orlando, Florida
Source: *NewYTBS 81; WhoAm 74, 76*

McNeill, William Hardy
Canadian. Historian
Wrote *The Rise of the West,* 1963 which posits the theory that cultures rise and fall due to their interactions and not their internal structure.
b. Oct 31, 1917 in Vancouver, British Columbia, Canada
Source: *BioIn 6, 14, 15, 17; BlueB 76; ConAu 5R; DrAS 74H, 78H, 82H; IntAu&W 86; WhoAm 74, 76, 78, 80, 82, 84, 86, 88, 90, 92, 94, 95, 96; WhoE 95; WhoUSWr 88; WhoWor 74, 91, 93; WhoWrEP 89, 92, 95; WrDr 76, 80, 82, 84, 86, 88, 90, 92, 94, 96*

McNellis, Maggi
[Margaret Eleanor Roche]
American. TV Personality
Hosted radio, TV shows, 1940s-50s; often on 10 best-dressed women list.
b. Jun 1, 1917 in Chicago, Illinois
d. May 24, 1989 in New York, New York
Source: *BioIn 3, 4, 16; CurBio 55, 89, 89N; IntMPA 82; InWom; NewYTBS 89; WhoAmW 58*

McNerney, Walter James
American. Business Executive
Pres., Blue Cross and Blue Shield, 1977-81; award-winning health policy educator, consultant.
b. Jun 8, 1925 in New Haven, Connecticut
Source: *IntWW 91; St&PR 91; WhoAm 86, 88; WhoFI 89; WhoMW 74, 84*

McNichol, Jimmy
[James Vincent McNichol]
American. Actor, Singer
Starred with sister Kristy in TV movie *Blinded by the Light.*
b. Jul 2, 1961 in Los Angeles, California
Source: *BioIn 12; ConTFT 3; LegTOT; VarWW 85; WhoHol 92*

McNichol, Kristy
American. Actor
Played Buddy Lawrence on TV series "Family," 1976-80; won Emmys, 1977, 1979; plays Barbara Weston on TV comedy "Empty Nest," 1988—.
b. Sep 9, 1962 in Los Angeles, California
Source: *BioIn 11, 12, 13, 14, 16; BkPepl; ConTFT 3; HalFC 88; IntMPA 86, 88, 92, 94, 96; InWom SUP; LegTOT; NewYTBS 81; VarWW 85; WhoAm 86, 88, 90, 92; WhoEnt 92; WhoHol 92*

McNickle, D'Arcy
[William D'Arcy McNickle]
American. Author
One of the originators of modern Native American literature and ethnohistory; wrote novel *The Surrounded,* 1936.
b. Jan 18, 1904 in Saint Ignatius, Montana
d. Dec 1977 in Albuquerque, New Mexico
Source: *AmMWSc 73S; AmSocL; BenetAL 91; BioIn 9, 12, 13, 18, 19, 21; CamGLE; CamHAL; ConAu 5NR, 9R, 85; ConIsC 1; ConLC 89; EncFWF; EncNAB; EncNoAI; IntAu&W 77; NatNAL; NotNaAm; SmATA 22N; TwCWW 82, 91; WhoPNW; WrDr 76, 80*

McNutt, Paul Vories
American. Government Official, Politician
Dem. governor, IN, 1933; held New Deal posts including Commissioner to Philippines, 1937.
b. Jul 18, 1891 in Franklin, Indiana
d. Mar 24, 1955 in New York, New York
Source: *BioIn 1, 3, 4, 7, 11; CurBio 40, 55; DcAmB S5; EncAB-A 2; IndAu 1917; WhAm 3*

McPartland, Jimmy
[James Duigald McPartland]
American. Jazz Musician, Bandleader
Dixieland cornetist; led own band, 1940s-50s; architect of Chicago-style jazz.
b. Mar 15, 1907 in Chicago, Illinois
d. Mar 13, 1991 in New York, New York
Source: *AllMusG; AnObit 1991; Baker 84, 92; BiDJaz; BioIn 9, 11, 16, 17, 18; CmpEPM; Conv 2; DcArts; EncJzS; LegTOT; NewAmDM; NewGrDJ 88, 94; NewYTBS 91; OxCPMus; PenEncP; WhoAm 74; WhoJazz 72; WorAl; WorAlBi*

McPartland, Margaret Marian
[Mrs. Jimmy McPartland]
English. Pianist, Songwriter
Had own jazz trio, 1950s-60s; founded Halcyon record label; once married to James.
b. Mar 20, 1918 in Slough, England
Source: *Baker 84; BiDJaz; BioIn 13, 14, 16; CmpEPM; InWom SUP; NewAmDM; NewGrDA 86; NewGrDJ 88; OxCPMus; PenEncP; PeoHis; WhoAm 74, 88; WhoE 74; WorAlBi*

McPhail, Sharon
American. Lawyer
Pres., Nat. Bar Assn., 1991-92.
b. Nov 6, 1948 in Cambridge, Massachusetts
Source: *ConBlB 2; WhoBlA 92*

McPhatter, Clyde
[The Drifters]
American. Singer
Former lead tenor in group, 1953-56; began solo career, 1956.
b. Nov 15, 1933 in Durham, North Carolina
d. Jun 13, 1972 in New York, New York
Source: *Baker 84, 92; BioIn 10, 12; DcTwCCu 5; EncPR&S 74; EncRk 88; IlEncBM 82; LegTOT; OxCPMus; PenEncP; RkWW 82; SoulM*

McPhee, John (Angus)
American. Author
Staff writer, *New Yorker,* 1965—; wrote best-sellers *Coming into the Country,* 1977; *Assembling California,* 1993.
b. Mar 8, 1931 in Princeton, New Jersey
Source: *Benet 87; BenetAL 91; BioIn 13, 14, 16; ConAu 20NR, 65; ConLC 36; CurBio 82; CyWA 89; IntAu&W 91; MajTwCW; OxCAmL 83; SourALJ; WhoAm 86, 90; WrDr 86, 92*

McPherson, Aimee Semple
"Sister Aimee"
American. Evangelist
Founded International Church of Foursquare Gospel, 1918; ministry characterized by spectacle, optimistic Fundamentalism.
b. Oct 9, 1890 in Ingersoll, Ontario, Canada
d. Sep 27, 1944 in Oakland, California
Source: *AmDec 1920; AmWomWr; BiDAmCu; BioIn 1, 2, 4, 5, 7, 8, 9, 10, 11, 12, 15, 16, 17, 18, 19, 20; BioNews 74; CmCal; ContDcW 89; CurBio 44; DcAmB S3, S5; DcAmReB 1, 2; EncAAH; EncARH; FacFETw; GoodHs; HanAmWH; HeroCon; HisWorL; IntDcWB; InWom, SUP; LegTOT; LibW; LuthC 75; McGEWB; NatCAB 35; NotAW; OxCWoWr 95; PrimTiR; RelLAm 91; TwCSAPR; WebAB 74, 79; WhAm 2, 4A, HSA; WomFir; WorAl; WorAlBi*

McPherson, James Alan
American. Author
Won Pulitzer Prize for *Elbow Room,* 1977.
b. Sep 16, 1943 in Savannah, Georgia
Source: *AfrAmAl 6; AmAu&B; BenetAL 91; BioIn 12, 13, 14, 15, 17, 19, 21; BlkAWP; BlkWr 1; BlkWrNE; ConAu 24NR, 25R; ConLC 19, 77; CurBio 96; CyWA 89; DcLB 38; DrAF 76; DrAPF 80; InB&W 80, 85; LivgBAA; MajTwCW; NegAl 89; OxCAmL 83, 95; RfGAmL 94; SchCGBL; SelBAAf; SelBAAu; ShSWr; WhoAfA 96; WhoAm 74, 76, 80, 82, 84, 86, 88, 90, 92, 94, 95, 96, 97; WhoBlA 88, 90, 92, 94;*

WhoE 83, 85, 86; WhoEmL 87; WhoMW 86, 90, 93; WorAu 1985

McPherson, James Birdseye
American. Military Leader
Union general, 1862; led army of the Tennessee, 1864; killed in action.
b. Nov 14, 1828 in Green Creek, Ohio
d. Jun 22, 1864 in Atlanta, Georgia
Source: *AmBi; ApCAB; BioIn 1, 3, 4, 7; CivWDc; DcAmB; DcAmMiB; Drake; HarEnMi; HarEnUS; NatCAB 4; NewCol 75; TwCBDA; WebAMB; WhAm HS; WhCiWar*

McQueen, Butterfly
[Thelma McQueen]
American. Actor
Played Prissy in *Gone With the Wind,* 1939; other films include *Mildred Pierce,* 1945; *The Mosquito Coast,* 1986.
b. Jan 7, 1911 in Tampa, Florida
d. Dec 23, 1995 in Augusta, Georgia
Source: *AfrAmAl 6; BioIn 8, 11, 15, 20, 21; BlksAmF; BlksB&W C; BlkWAm; ConBlB 6; DrBlPA, 90; EncAFC; FilmEn; FilmgC; ForYSC; HalFC 80, 84, 88; InB&W 80, 85; IntDcF 1-3, 2-3; InWom SUP; LegTOT; MotPP; MovMk; NewYTBE 70; NotBlAW 1; ThFT; VarWW 85; What 2; WhoAfA 96; WhoBlA 77, 80, 85, 88, 90, 92, 94; WhoHol 92, A; WhoThe 72, 77, 81; WorAl; WorAlBi*

McQueen, Steve
[Terence Stephen McQueen]
American. Actor
Starred in *Bullitt,* 1968; *The Getaway,* 1973; *The Towering Inferno,* 1974.
b. Mar 24, 1930 in Indianapolis, Indiana
d. Nov 7, 1980 in Juarez, Mexico
Source: *AnObit 1980, 78, 79, 80, 81; IntWW 74, 75, 76, 77, 78, 79, 80; LegTOT; MotPP; MovMk; NewYTBS 80; OxCFilm; WhoAm 74; WhoHol A; WhoHrs 80; WhoWor 74; WhScrn 83; WorAl; WorAlBi; WorEFlm*

McRae, Carmen
American. Singer
Jazz singer, who cut first album, 1954.
b. Apr 8, 1922 in New York, New York
d. Nov 10, 1994 in Beverly Hills, California
Source: *AfrAmAl 6; Baker 84, 92; BiDAfM; BiDAmM; BiDJaz; BioIn 8, 12, 13, 15, 16; BlkWAm; ConMus 9; CurBio 83, 95N; DcTwCCu 5; DrBlPA, 90; EncJzS; InB&W 80; InWom SUP; LegTOT; NegAl 89; NewAmDM; NewGrDA 86; NewGrDJ 88, 94; NotBlAW 1; OxCPMus; PenEncP; WhoAfA 96; WhoAm 74, 76, 82, 84; WhoAmW 70, 72, 81, 83; WhoBlA 75, 77, 80, 85, 88, 90, 92, 94; WhoE 74; WhoEnt 92; WhoHol 92*

McRaney, Gerald
American. Actor
Played Rick Simon on TV series "Simon and Simon, 1981-88;" "Major Dad," 1989-93.
b. Aug 19, 1948 in Collins, Mississippi
Source: *BioIn 13, 16; ConTFT 8; IntMPA 92, 94, 96; LesBEnT 92; VarWW 85; WhoAm 88; WhoEnt 92; WorAlBi*

McShane, Ian
English. Actor
Films include *Last of Sheila,* 1963.
b. Sep 29, 1942 in Blackburn, England
Source: *ConTFT 2; FilmgC; HalFC 80, 84, 88; IntMPA 88, 92, 94, 96; ItaFilm; VarWW 85; WhoHol 92, A; WhoThe 72, 77, 81*

McSpaden, Byron
[Gold Dust Twins]
"Jug"
American. Golfer
Won several PGA tournaments, 1940s; formed Gold Dust Twins with Byron Nelson.
b. May 21, 1908 in Rosedale, Kansas
Source: *WhoGolf*

McTaggart, David
Canadian. Social Reformer
Chm. of the Board, Greenpeace International, an environmental organization, 1979—.
b. 1932 in Vancouver, British Columbia, Canada
Source: *News 89*

McTear, Houston
American. Track Athlete
Set US men's 60-meter indoor run record, 1978.
b. 1956?
Source: *BioIn 10*

McVie, Christine Perfect
[Fleetwood Mac]
English. Singer, Songwriter
First solo album, *Christine McVie,* contained hit single "Got a Hold on Me," 1984.
b. Jul 12, 1943 in Birmingham, England
Source: *BioIn 13, 14; RkOn 85; WhoAm 86, 90; WhoAmW 81; WhoEnt 92; WhoRocM 82; WhoWest 92*

McVie, John
[Fleetwood Mac]
English. Musician
Bass guitarist with Fleetwood Mac, 1967—; albums include *Mr. Wonderful,* 1969.
b. Nov 26, 1946 in London, England
Source: *BioIn 13; LegTOT; WhoAm 78, 80, 82, 84; WhoRocM 82*

McWherter, Ned Ray
American. Politician
Dem. governor of Tennessee, 1987-95.
b. Oct 15, 1930 in Palmersville, Tennessee
Source: *AlmAP 88, 92; IntWW 91; WhoAm 86, 88, 90, 92, 94, 95; WhoAmP 85, 87, 91; WhoSSW 88, 91, 93, 95; WhoWor 89, 91, 93, 95*

McWhirter, A(lan) Ross
English. Author, Publisher
Editor *The Guinness Book of World Records,* first edition, 1955.
b. Aug 12, 1925 in London, England
d. Nov 27, 1975 in London, England
Source: *ConAu 17R, 46NR, 61; SmATA 31N*

McWhirter, Norris Dewar
English. Author, Publisher
Twin brother of Alan; editor *The Guinness Book of World Records.*
b. Aug 12, 1925 in London, England
Source: *Au&Wr 71; BioIn 12, 15; ConAu 13R, 50NR; IntAu&W 86, 89, 91, 93; IntWW 81, 82, 83, 89, 91, 93; Who 82, 83, 85, 88, 90, 92, 94; WhoFI 96; WhoWor 84, 87, 89, 91, 93, 95, 96, 97; WorAl; WorAlBi*

McWilliams, Alden S
American. Cartoonist
Known for comic strips "Twin Earths," 1953-63; "Dateline: Danger!," 1968-74.
b. 1916 in Greenwich, Connecticut
d. Mar 19, 1993 in Stamford, Connecticut
Source: *EncACom; WorECom*

McWilliams, Carey
American. Author
Sociological analyses of minorities in CA include *Mask for Privilege,* 1948.
b. Dec 13, 1905 in Steamboat Springs, Colorado
d. Jun 27, 1980 in New York, New York
Source: *AmAu&B; AnObit 1980; BenetAL 91; BiDAmJo; BioIn 4, 8, 10, 12, 15, 16, 20; CelR; ChiSch; CmCal; ConAu 2NR, 45, 101; CurBio 43, 80N; DcAmB S10; DcLB 137; EncAJ; EncTwCJ; OxCAmL 65, 83, 95; PeoHis; REnAL; ScF&FL 92; TwCA SUP; WhAm 7, 8; WhoAm 74, 76, 78, 80; WhoE 75, 77; WhoWor 74*

Mead, George Herbert
American. Psychologist, Philosopher
Developed American pragmatism; wrote *Philosophy of the Present,* 1932.
b. Feb 27, 1863 in South Hadley, Massachusetts
d. Apr 26, 1931 in Chicago, Illinois
Source: *BiDPsy; BioIn 7, 8, 9, 11, 12, 13, 14, 15, 16, 19; DcAmB S1; DcNAA; McGEWB; NamesHP; OhA&B; OxCPhil; RAdv 14, 13-3, 13-4; ThTwC 87; WebAB 74, 79; WhAm 1*

Mead, George Houk
American. Business Executive
Organized Mead Corp., 1905.
b. Nov 5, 1877 in Dayton, Ohio

d. Jan 1, 1963 in Dayton, Ohio
Source: *BiDAmBL 83; BioIn 1, 2, 6, 9; NatCAB 53; WhAm 4*

Mead, Margaret
[Margaret Beteson]
American. Anthropologist, Author
Studied primitive cultures; wrote *Cooperation and Competition among Primitive Peoples*, 1937.
b. Dec 16, 1901 in Philadelphia, Pennsylvania
d. Nov 15, 1978 in New York, New York
Source: *AmAu&B; AmDec 1920; AmMWSc 73S, 76P; AmSocL; AmWomSc; AmWomWr; Au&Wr 71; AuBYP 2, 3; AuNews 1; Benet 87, 96; BenetAL 91; BioAmW; BioIn 2, 3, 4, 5, 6, 7, 8, 9, 10, 11, 12, 13, 14, 15, 16, 17, 18, 19, 20, 21; BioNews 74; BlueB 76; CamDcSc; CelR; ConAu 1R, 4NR, 81; ConHero 1; ConIsC 1; ConLC 37; ContDcW 89; CurBio 40, 51, 79N; DcAmB S10; DcLEL; EncAB-H 1974, 1996; EncEnv; EncPaPR 91; EncWHA; EvLB; FacFETw; FemiCLE; FemiWr; FifIDA; GaEncPs; GoodHs; GrLiveH; HanAmWH; HerW, 84; InSci; IntAu&W 77; IntDcAn; IntDcWB; IntWW 74, 75, 76, 77, 78; InWom, SUP; LegTOT; LibW; LinLib L, S; LngCTC; MajTwCW; MakMC; McGEWB; McGMS 80; NewYTBE 72; NewYTBS 78; OxCAmL 65, 83, 95; OxCWoWr 95; PenC AM; PorAmW; RAdv 14, 13-3; RComAH; REn; REnAL; SmATA 20N; ThTwC 87; TwCA, SUP; WebAB 74, 79; WhAm 7; WhDW; WhNAA; Who 74; WhoAm 74, 76, 78; WhoAmW 58, 61, 64, 66, 68, 70, 72, 74, 79; WhoWor 74, 76, 78; WomFir; WomStre; WorAl; WorAlBi; WrDr 76*

Mead, William Rutherford
American. Architect
Partner, McKim, Mead, and White, largest architectural firm of its day; promoted classic styles.
b. Aug 20, 1846 in Brattleboro, Vermont
d. Jun 20, 1928 in Paris, France
Source: *AmBi; AmCulL; ApCAB, X; BiDAmAr; BioIn 2, 8, 13, 19; DcAmB; EncAAr 1; LinLib S; MacEA; NatCAB 23; TwCBDA; WhAm 1; WhAmArt 85; WhoAmA 84; WhoArch*

Meade, George Gordon
American. Military Leader
Union general who commanded army of the Potomac, 1863-65; repulsed Lee at Gettysburg.
b. Dec 31, 1815 in Cadiz, Spain
d. Nov 6, 1872 in Philadelphia, Pennsylvania
Source: *AmBi; ApCAB; BioIn 1, 3, 5, 6, 7, 9, 12, 17; CivWDc; DcAmB; DcAmMiB; DcBiPP; EncAB-H 1974, 1996; GenMudB; HarEnMi; HarEnUS; LinLib S; McGEWB; NatCAB 4; NewCol 75; OxCAmH; TwCBDA; WebAB 74, 79; WebAMB; WhAm HS; WhCiWar; WhFla; WhoMilH 76; WorAl*

Meade, James Edward
English. Economist
Won Nobel Prize, 1977, for pioneering work on macroeconomics.
b. Jun 23, 1907 in Swanage, England
d. Dec 22, 1995 in Cambridge, England
Source: *BioIn 15; BlueB 76; ConAu 2NR, 150; GrEconS; IntWW 83; NobelP; WhAm 11; Who 83, 88; WhoEc 81, 86; WhoNob, 95; WhoWor 82, 89; WrDr 86, 88*

Meade, Julia
"Miss Lady of Television"
American. Actor
Longtime commercial spokesperson on "The Ed Sullivan Show."
b. Dec 17, 1930 in Boston, Massachusetts
Source: *BioIn 4, 5; CelR, 90; ConTFT 3; InWom; NotNAT*

Meader, Vaughn
American. Actor
Did impersonations of JFK; album *The First Family*, 1962, sold 2 1/2 million copies; career ended when Kennedy died.
b. Mar 20, 1936 in Boston, Massachusetts
Source: *BioIn 9, 10; What 5; WhoCom*

Meadows, Audrey
American. Actor
Played Alice Kramden on TV series "The Honeymooners."
b. Feb 8, 1924 in Wuchang, China
d. Feb 3, 1996 in Los Angeles, California
Source: *BioIn 19, 20, 21; ConTFT 2; CurBio 58; EncAFC; ForYSC; InWom SUP; LegTOT; LesBEnT, 92; MotPP; VarWW 85; WhoAm 74, 86, 88; WhoCom; WhoEnt 92; WhoHol A; WorAl; WorAlBi*

Meadows, Earle
[Heavenly Twins]
American. Track Athlete
Pole vaulter; with Bill Sefton, known for great vaults; won gold medal, 1936 Olympics.
b. Jun 29, 1913 in Corinth, Mississippi
Source: *WhoTr&F 73*

Meadows, Jayne Cotter
[Mrs. Steve Allen]
American. Actor
Married Steve Allen, 1954—; TV shows include "I've Got a Secret," 1952-58; "Medical Center," 1969-72.
b. Sep 27, 1926 in Wuchang, China
Source: *BiE&WWA; BioNews 75; CurBio 58; InWom SUP; MotPP; VarWW 85; WhoAm 82; WhoHol A*

Meagher, Mary T
American. Swimmer
Won 1984 Olympic gold medal for 200-meter butterfly; broke world records.
b. Oct 27, 1964? in Louisville, Kentucky
Source: *BioIn 12, 14, 15, 16; NewYTBS 84*

Means, Marianne Hansen
American. Journalist
Political columnist, 1965—; wrote *The Woman in the White House*, 1963.
b. Jun 13, 1934 in Sioux City, Iowa
Source: *BiDAmNC; ConAu 9R; EncTwCJ; ForWC 70; IntAu&W 76, 77; InWom SUP; WhoAm 74, 76, 78, 80, 86, 90; WhoAmW 66, 68, 70, 72, 74, 75, 89; WhoSSW 73*

Means, Russell
American. Political Activist, Actor
Active in the American Indian Movement since the late 1960s; film debut as Chingachgook in *The Last of the Mohicans*, 1992.
b. 1940 in Pine Ridge, South Dakota
Source: *BioIn 10, 16; FacFETw*

Means, Russell C(harles)
American. Political Activist
Co-founded AIM, 1960s; retired from group, 1988; led 71-day takeover of Wounded Knee, SD, 1973.
b. Nov 10, 1940 in Pine Ridge, South Dakota
Source: *BioIn 10, 16; BioNews 74; CurBio 78; FacFETw; PolProf NF*

Meany, George
American. Labor Union Official
Pres., AFL-CIO, 1955-79.
b. Aug 16, 1894 in New York, New York
d. Jan 10, 1980 in Washington, District of Columbia
Source: *AmCath 80; AmDec 1950; AmSocL; AnObit 1980; BiDAmL; BiDAmLL; BioIn 2, 3, 4, 5, 6, 7, 8, 9, 10, 11, 12, 14, 15, 17, 18, 19; BioNews 74; BlueB 76; BusPN; CelR; ColdWar 1, 2; ConAu 97; CurBio 42, 54, 80N; DcPol; EncAB-H 1974, 1996; FacFETw; IntWW 74, 75, 76, 77, 78, 79; LinLib S; McGEWB; NewYTBE 72; NewYTBS 80; PolProf E, J, K, NF, T; WebAB 74, 79; WhAm 7; Who 74; WhoAm 74, 76, 78; WhoE 79; WhoFI 75; WhoGov 72, 75; WhoLab 76; WhoSSW 73, 75, 76, 82; WhoWor 74, 78; WorAl; WorAlBi*

Meara, Anne
[Stiller and Meara; Mrs. Jerry Stiller]
American. Comedian
Played Veronica Rooney on TV series "Archie Bunker's Place," 1979-82.
b. Sep 20, 1924 in New York, New York
Source: *BioIn 15; BioNews 75; EncAFC; FunnyW; HalFC 88; IntMPA 92; InWom SUP; VarWW 85; WhoAm 82, 90; WhoAmW 91; WhoEnt 92; WhoHol A; WorAlBi*

Mearns, David Chambers
American. Librarian
With Library of Congress, 1940s-60s; edited *The Lincoln Papers*, 1948.

b. Dec 31, 1899 in Washington, District of Columbia
d. May 21, 1981 in Alexandria, Virginia
Source: *AmAu&B; BiDrLUS 70; BioIn 5, 6, 12, 13, 17; ConAu 1R, 104; CurBio 61, 81; NewYTBS 81; WhAm 7; WhoAm 74, 76; WhoLibS 66*

Mears, Rick Ravon
American. Auto Racer
One of three drivers to win Indianapolis 500 four times: 1979, 1984, 1988, 1991.
b. Dec 3, 1951 in Wichita, Kansas
Source: *BiDAmSp OS; BioIn 12; ConAu 113; EncTwCJ; EngPo; St&PR 91; WhoAm 82, 84, 86, 88, 90, 92, 94; WhoE 86; WhoWest 94*

Mears, Walter Robert
American. Editor, Journalist, Author
Exec. editor, AP, 1984-88; vp, columnist, 1989—; won Pulitzer, 1977.
b. Jan 11, 1935 in Lynn, Massachusetts
Source: *ConAu 111, 113; St&PR 87, 91, 93, 96, 97; WhoAm 76, 78, 80, 82, 84, 86, 90, 92, 94, 95, 96, 97; WhoE 79, 81, 83, 85, 86*

Meat Loaf
[Marvin Lee Aday]
American. Musician, Actor
Sang with Amboy Dukes; Grammy, Best Solo Rock Vocal, "I'd Do Anything for Love, (But I Won't Do That)," 1993.
b. Sep 27, 1948? in Dallas, Texas
Source: *BioIn 11, 12, 14, 15; BkPepl; EncRk 88; HarEnR 86; NewGrDA 86; RkOn 74; WhoAm 95*

Mecham, Evan
American. Politician
Rep. governor of AZ, 1987-88; his impeachment, 1988, was state's first, first in US since 1929.
b. May 12, 1924 in Duchesne, Utah
Source: *AlmAP 88; BiDAmNC; BiDrGov 1983; BioIn 15, 16; NewYTBS 88; WhoAm 88, 90; WhoAmP 87, 89, 91, 93; WhoWest 87, 89, 92*

Meciar, Vladimir
Slovak. Political Leader
Prime minister of Slovakia, 1994—.
b. Jul 26, 1942 in Zvolen, Slovakia
Source: *CurBio 94; IntWW 91, 93; WhoWor 93, 95, 96, 97*

Mecom, John Whitfield
American. Oilman
One of world's largest independent oil operators.
b. Jan 13, 1911 in Liberty, Texas
d. Oct 12, 1981 in Houston, Texas
Source: *AnObit 1981; BioIn 4, 7, 11, 12; NewYTBS 81; WhAm 8; WhoSSW 73*

Medary, Milton B
American. Architect
Gothic-style designer who did the Valley Forge Memorial Chapel.
b. Feb 6, 1874 in Philadelphia, Pennsylvania
d. Aug 7, 1929 in Philadelphia, Pennsylvania
Source: *BiDAmAr; DcAmB; WhAm 1*

Medawar, Peter Brian, Sir
English. Zoologist
Shared 1960 Nobel Prize in medicine for work on immunology, skin grafts.
b. Feb 28, 1915 in Rio de Janeiro, Brazil
d. Oct 2, 1987 in London, England
Source: *AsBiEn; Au&Wr 71; BiESc; BioIn 1, 5, 6, 8, 11, 13, 14, 15, 17, 18, 20; CamDcSc; ConAu 97, 123; CurBio 61, 87, 87N; DcLEL 1940; DcNaB 1986; FacFETw; InSci; IntWW 74, 75, 76, 77, 78, 79, 80, 81, 82, 83; LarDcSc; McGEWB; McGMS 80; NotTwCS; RAdv 14, 13-5; WhAm 9; Who 85; WhoNob, 90, 95; WhoWor 74, 78, 80, 82, 84, 87; WorAl; WorScD*

Medeiros, Humberto, Cardinal
American. Religious Leader
Spiritual leader of Boston's Roman Catholics, 1970-83.
b. Oct 15, 1915, Azores
d. Sep 17, 1983 in Boston, Massachusetts
Source: *CurBio 71, 83; NewYTBE 70, 73; NewYTBS 83; WhoAm 80, 82; WhoE 81, 83*

Medford, Kay
American. Actor
Oscar nominee for *Funny Girl,* 1968.
b. Sep 14, 1920 in New York, New York
d. Apr 10, 1980 in New York, New York
Source: *AnObit 1980; BiE&WWA; BioIn 12; ForWC 70; ForYSC; NotNAT; WhoHol A; WhoThe 72, 77, 81; WhScrn 83*

Medici, Cosimo de
[Cosimo the Elder]
Italian. Ruler
First of Medici family to rule Florence, 1433; known chiefly for genorosity to scholars, artists.
b. Sep 27, 1389 in Florence, Italy
d. Aug 1, 1464 in Florence, Italy
Source: *Benet 96; DcBiPP A; McGEWB; OxCArt; WebBD 83*

Medici, Francesco de
Italian. Ruler
Successor as Grand Duke of Tuscany, 1574-87.
b. Mar 25, 1541
d. Oct 19, 1587
Source: *BioIn 10; WebBD 83*

Medici, Lorenzo de
[Lorenzo the Magnificent]
Italian. Poet, Ruler, Art Patron
Virtual Florentine ruler from 1470s; tyrannical, but made Florence prosperous, center of culture.
b. Jan 1, 1449 in Florence, Italy
d. Apr 8, 1492 in Florence, Italy
Source: *BbD; Benet 87, 96; BiD&SB; BioIn 12, 14, 17, 18, 19, 20, 21; CasWL; DcCathB; DcItL 1, 2; DicTyr; EuAu; EvEuW; HisWorL; LegTOT; LinLib L, S; McGEWB; NewCol 75; OxCThe 83; OxDcArt; PenC EUR; WhDW*

Medicine, Beatrice A.
American. Anthropologist
One of a few Native American women to hold an advanced degree in anthropology; wrote *Native American Women: A Perspective,* 1978.
b. Aug 1, 1924 in Wakpala, South Dakota
Source: *NotNaAm*

Medill, Joseph
American. Journalist, Politician, Editor
A founder, Rep. party, 1854; edited *Chicago Tribune,* from 1855; Chicago mayor who reorganized city government.
b. Apr 6, 1823 in Saint John, New Brunswick, Canada
d. Mar 16, 1899 in San Antonio, Texas
Source: *AmAu&B; AmBi; ApCAB; BiDAmJo; BioIn 1, 2, 15, 16, 21; DcAmB; DcLB 43; EncAJ; JrnUS; McGEWB; NatCAB 1; OxCAmH; OxCAmL 65, 83, 95; TwCBDA; WebAB 74, 79; WhAm HS; WhAmP*

Medina, Ernest L
American. Army Officer
Stood trial for ordering murder of Vietnamese civilians in My Lai, 1968.
b. 1936
Source: *BioIn 8, 9; NewYTBE 71*

Medina, Harold Raymond
American. Judge
Best known for trial of 11 communists charged with conspiracy, 1949; books on law include *The Anatomy of Freedom,* 1959.
b. Feb 16, 1888 in New York, New York
d. Mar 14, 1990 in Westwood, New Jersey
Source: *AmAu&B; AnObit 1990; Au&Wr 71; BioIn 1, 2, 3, 5, 6, 10, 11, 16; CurBio 49, 90N; FacFETw; MexAmB; NewYTBS 90; PolProf T; WhoAm 84; WhoAmL 85; WhoE 74, 86; WhoHisp 91N*

Medina, Patricia
American. Actor
Married Joseph Cotten, 1960—; heroine of swashbucklers *The Three Musketeers,* 1948; *Fortunes of Captain Blood,* 1950; *Black Knight,* 1954.
b. Jul 19, 1920 in London, England

Source: *BiE&WWA; BioIn 10; BioNews 74; FilmEn; FilmgC; ForYSC; HalFC 88; IntMPA 92, 96; MotPP; MovMk; VarWW 85; WhoHol A*

Medley, Bill
[Righteous Brothers; William Thomas Medley]
American. Singer
With Bobby Hatfield had hit "Soul and Inspiration," 1966; solo hit "Brown-Eyed Woman," 1968; recorded Grammy-winning "Time of My Life," with Jennifer Warnes, 1987.
b. Sep 19, 1940 in Santa Ana, California
Source: *BioIn 12; ConMus 3; EncPR&S 89; IntMPA 75, 76, 77, 78, 79, 80, 82, 84, 86; LegTOT; RkOn 78; WhoRocM 82*

Medoff, Mark Howard
American. Dramatist
Wrote award-winning play *Children of a Lesser God,* 1981.
b. Mar 18, 1940 in Mount Carmel, Illinois
Source: *AuNews 1; BioIn 15; CamGWoT; ConAu 5NR; ConDr 88; ConLC 23; ConTFT 4; CyWA 89; DcLB 7; IntAu&W 91; NotNAT; OxCAmT 84; WhoAm 86, 90, 97; WrDr 86, 92*

Medtner, Nicholas
German. Composer, Pianist
Wrote mainly for piano, voice; noted for fairy tale sonatas, 1912.
b. Dec 24, 1880 in Moscow, Russia
d. Nov 13, 1951 in London, England
Source: *Baker 84; DcCom&M 79; OxCMus; WebBD 83*

Medvedev, Zhores Aleksandrovich
Russian. Biologist
Books include *Soviet Science,* 1978.
b. Nov 14, 1925 in Tiflis, Union of Soviet Socialist Republics
Source: *BiDSovU; BioIn 9, 10, 13; ConAu 69; CurBio 73; IntAu&W 91; IntWW 74, 77, 78, 79, 80, 81, 82, 83, 89, 91, 93; NewYTBE 70, 71, 73; SovUn; WhoWor 84, 89; WrDr 86, 92*

Medwick, Joe
[Joseph Michael Medwick]
"Ducky"
American. Baseball Player
Outfielder, 1932-48; won NL triple crown, MVP, 1937; Hall of Fame, 1968.
b. Nov 4, 1911 in Carteret, New Jersey
d. Mar 21, 1975 in Saint Petersburg, Florida
Source: *Ballpl 90; BiDAmSp BB; BioIn 3, 8, 10, 14, 15; DcAmB S9; LegTOT; NewYTBS 75; WhoProB 73; WorAl; WorAlBi*

Meehan, Thomas Edward
American. Writer
Wrote *Annie;* basis for Broadway smash hit; won Tony, 1977.
b. Aug 14, 1932 in Ossining, New York
Source: *ConAu 28NR, 29R; ConDr 82D, 88D; NewYTBS 81*

Meek, Carrie
American. Politician
Became first black to represent Florida in Congress since Reconstruction, 1993—.
b. Apr 29, 1926 in Tallahassee, Florida
Source: *BioIn 19, 20, 21; ConBlB 6; NotBlAW 2*

Meek, Donald
Scottish. Actor
Character actor 1929-46; *Stagecoach,* 1939; *My Little Chickadee,* 1940; *Top Hat,* 1935.
b. Jul 14, 1880 in Glasgow, Scotland
d. Nov 18, 1946 in Los Angeles, California
Source: *BioIn 1, 21; EncAFC; Film 2; FilmEn; FilmgC; ForYSC; HalFC 80, 84, 88; HolCA; IntDcF 1-3; MotPP; MovMk; NotNAT B; OlFamFa; Vers A; WhoHol B; WhScrn 74, 77, 83; WhThe*

Meek, Samuel Williams
American. Advertising Executive
With J Walter Thompson agency, 1925-63; director, Time Inc., 1922-70.
b. Sep 22, 1895 in Nashville, Tennessee
d. Aug 15, 1981 in Greenwich, Connecticut
Source: *BioIn 7, 12; NewYTBS 81; St&PR 75, 84; WhAm 8; WhoAm 74, 76, 78, 80, 82*

Meeker, Howie
[Howard William Meeker]
Canadian. Hockey Player, Sportscaster
Right wing, Toronto, 1946-54; won Calder Trophy, 1947; long-time commentator on CBC's "Hockey Night in Canada."
b. Nov 4, 1924 in Kitchener, Ontario, Canada
Source: *HocEn; LegTOT; WhoHcky 73*

Meeker, Ralph
[Ralph Rathgeber]
American. Actor
Known for roles in action, adventure films; played Mike Hammer in *Kiss Me Deadly,* 1955.
b. Nov 21, 1920 in Minneapolis, Minnesota
d. Aug 5, 1988 in Los Angeles, California
Source: *BiDFilm, 81; BiE&WWA; BioIn 16; CmMov; ConTFT 7; FilmEn; FilmgC; ForYSC; GangFlm; HalFC 80, 84, 88; IntMPA 75, 76, 77, 78, 79, 80, 81, 82, 84, 86, 88; LegTOT; MotPP; MovMk; NewYTBS 88; NotNAT; VarWW 85; WhoHol A; WhoHrs 80; WhoThe 72, 77, 81; WorAl; WorEFlm*

Meer, Jan van der
Dutch. Artist
Painted landscapes of the Netherlands in browns, greens.
b. 1628 in Haarlem, Netherlands
d. 1691
Source: *ClaDrA; WebBD 83*

Meer, Simon van der
Dutch. Engineer
Physical engineer, won, with Carlo Rubbia, Nobel Prize for Physics, 1984; work contributed to keeping particles in colliding-beam apparatus on course.
b. Nov 24, 1925 in The Hague, Netherlands
Source: *WorScD*

Meese, Edwin, III
American. Government Official, Presidential Aide
US Attorney General, 1985-88.
b. Dec 2, 1931 in Oakland, California
Source: *AmDec 1980; BiDrUSE 89; BioIn 12, 13, 14, 15, 16; CngDr 87; CurBio 81; IntWW 81, 82, 83, 89, 91, 93; IntYB 82; LegTOT; NewYTBS 81, 84; Who 82, 83, 85, 88, 90, 92, 94; WhoAm 82, 84, 86, 88; WhoAmL 85, 87, 90; WhoAmP 85, 87, 89, 91, 93, 95; WhoE 86, 89, 91; WhoWor 87, 89, 91, 93, 95; WorAlBi*

Megadeth
American. Music Group
Music described as thrash- or death-metal rock; gold records include "Peace Sells.But Who's Buying?" 1986.
Source: *ConMus 9; EncRkSt; OnThGG*

Meggendorfer, Lothar
German. Cartoonist, Illustrator
Master of moveable, toy books, 1880s-1900.
b. Nov 6, 1847 in Munich, Germany
d. 1925 in Munich, Germany
Source: *BioIn 13; ChhPo S3; ConAu 115; SmATA 36; WorECar*

Mehta, Ved Parkash
Indian. Author, Journalist
Wrote five memoirs about battling blindness: *Sound-Shadows of the New World,* 1986.
b. Mar 21, 1934 in Lahore, India
Source: *Au&Wr 71; Benet 87; BenetAL 91; BioIn 4, 6, 9, 10, 11, 12, 13, 14, 15, 16; CamGLE; ConAu 1R, 2NR, 23NR; ConLC 37; CurBio 75; CyWA 89; DcLEL 1940; DrAPF 91; IntAu&W 76, 77, 82, 86, 89, 91; LiExTwC; MajTwCW; NewYTBE 72; NewYTBS 78; OxCEng 85, 95; Who 74, 82, 83, 85, 92, 94; WhoAm 92, 94, 95, 96; WhoUSWr 88; WhoWor 74, 76; WhoWrEP 89, 92, 95; WorAu 1950; WrDr 76, 80, 86, 92, 94, 96*

Mehta, Zubin
Indian. Conductor
Conductor, LA Philharmonic, 1962-78; NY Philharmonic, 1978-91.
b. Apr 29, 1936 in Bombay, India
Source: *AsAmAlm; Baker 78, 84, 92; BiDAmM; BioIn 7, 8, 9, 10, 11, 12, 13, 14, 15; BlueB 76; BriBkM 80; CelR, 90;*

CmCal; CmOp; ConAu 2NR; ConMus 11; CurBio 69; DcArts; DcTwCCu 1; IntWW 74, 75, 76, 77, 78, 79, 80, 81, 82, 83, 89, 91, 93; IntWWM 77, 80, 85, 90; LegTOT; LinLib S; MetOEnc; MusMk; MusSN; NewAmDM; NewEOp 71; NewGrDA 86; NewGrDM 80; NewGrDO; NewYTBE 70; NewYTBS 76, 78; NotAsAm; OxDcOp; PenDiMP; VarWW 85; Who 74, 82, 83, 85, 88, 90, 92, 94; WhoAm 74, 76, 78, 80, 82, 84, 86, 88, 90, 92, 94, 95, 96, 97; WhoAmM 83; WhoAsA 94; WhoE 81, 83, 85, 86, 89, 91; WhoEnt 92; WhoMus 72; WhoOp 76; WhoWest 96; WhoWor 74, 78, 80, 82, 84, 87, 89, 91, 93, 95, 96, 97; WorAl; WorAlBi

Mehul, Etienne Nicolas
French. Composer
Wrote over 40 operas including *Ariodant,* 1799; *Joseph,* 1807.
b. Jun 22, 1763 in Givet, France
d. Oct 18, 1817 in Paris, France
Source: *Baker 84; BioIn 2, 4, 7, 9; BriBkM 80; CmOp; Dis&D; GrComp; MusMk; NewCol 75; NewEOp 71; NewGrDM 80; OxCFr; OxCMus; WebBD 83*

Meier, Richard Alan
American. Architect
Designed L A Getty Trust arts complex; won 1984 Pritzger; member of ''NY Five'' group of postmodernistic architects.
b. Oct 12, 1934 in Newark, New Jersey
Source: *BioIn 13, 14, 15, 16; CelR 90; ConArch 87; ConDes 97; CurBio 85; DcTwDes; EncWB; IntWW 91; WhoAm 84, 90, 97; WhoAmA 84, 91*

Meier-Graefe, Julius
German. Critic, Author
Wrote over 50 books on art, travel; founded four art mags; favored Egyptian art.
b. Jun 10, 1867 in Resitza, Germany
d. Jul 1935
Source: *BioIn 8, 10, 20; DcTwDes; FacFETw; TwCA; WhoLA*

Meighan, Thomas
American. Actor
Star of Paramount, 1915-32, in over 80 films including *Miracle Man,* 1932.
b. Apr 9, 1879 in Pittsburgh, Pennsylvania
d. Jul 8, 1936 in Great Neck, New York
Source: *BioIn 10, 17; EncAFC; Film 1, 2; FilmEn; FilmgC; ForYSC; GangFlm; HalFC 80, 84, 88; MotPP; MovMk; NotNAT B; SilFlmP; TwYS; WhAm 1; WhoHol B; WhScrn 74, 77, 83; WhThe*

Meighen, Arthur
Canadian. Political Leader
Conservative prime minister of Canada, 1920-21, 1926.
b. Jun 16, 1874 in Anderson, Ontario, Canada
d. Aug 5, 1960 in Toronto, Ontario, Canada
Source: *BioIn 1, 2, 5, 7, 8, 11; DcNaB 1951; FacFETw; LinLib S; MacDCB 78; McGEWB; ObitOF 79; ObitT 1951; OxCCan; WhAm 4*

Meigs, Montgomery Cunningham
American. Army Officer
Noted for saving Fort Pickens, winning harbor Pensacola for US, 1861; served in Civil War.
b. May 3, 1816 in Augusta, Georgia
d. Jan 2, 1892 in Washington, District of Columbia
Source: *AmBi; ApCAB; BilnAmS; BioIn 5, 7, 10, 12; CivWDc; DcAmB; Drake; HarEnUS; MacEA; NatCAB 4; TwCBDA; WebAMB; WhAm HS; WhCiWar*

Meiklejohn, Alexander
American. Educator, University Administrator
Books on progressive education include *Liberal College,* 1920; pres., Amherst, 1912-24.
b. Feb 3, 1872 in Rochdale, England
d. Sep 16, 1964 in Berkeley, California
Source: *AmAu&B; ApCAB X; BiDAmEd; BioIn 4, 7, 8, 11, 12, 13, 14; ConAu 111; DcAmB S7; EncMcCE; NatCAB 51; OxCAmL 65, 83, 95; PeoHis; REnAL; WebAB 74, 79; WhAm 4*

Meilhac, Henri
French. Dramatist
Collaborated with Ludovic Halevy on light comedies, libretti for Offenbach's operas: *La Vie Parisienne,* 1866.
b. Feb 23, 1831 in Paris, France
d. Jul 6, 1897 in Paris, France
Source: *BiD&SB; BioIn 6, 7; CamGWoT; CasWL; DcEuL; Dis&D; EncWT; EuAu; EvEuW; IntDcOp; McGEWD 72, 84; MetOEnc; NewGrDO; NotNAT B; OxCFr; OxCThe 67, 83; OxDcOp; PenC EUR; PlP&P; REn; WebBD 83*

Mein, John Gordon
American. Diplomat
Traveled world to serve at several US embassies, including last post as ambassador to Guatemala, 1965-68; first US ambassador assassinated.
b. Sep 10, 1913 in Cadiz, Kentucky
d. Aug 28, 1968
Source: *BioIn 8, 10, 16; DcAmDH 80, 89; NatCAB 54; WhAm 5*

Meinhof, Ulrike Marie
German. Terrorist, Revolutionary
Co-leader of Baader-Meinhof Gang, W German terrorists in 1970s; committed suicide in prison.
b. Oct 7, 1934 in Oldenburg, Germany
d. May 9, 1976 in Stuttgart, Germany (West)
Source: *BiDNeoM; BioIn 9, 10, 11; EncCoWW*

Meinhold, Keith
American. Naval Officer
Petty Officer 1st Class; disclosed sexual orientation on ''ABC World News Tonight;'' discharged May 1992; first of gays fired to win back his job; reinstated Nov 1992.
b. 1962?

Meir, Golda
[Golda Myerson]
Israeli. Political Leader
Prime minister of Israel, 1969-74; wrote *My Life,* 1975.
b. May 3, 1898 in Kiev, Russia
d. Dec 8, 1978 in Jerusalem, Israel
Source: *BioIn 4, 8, 9, 10, 11, 12, 13, 14, 16, 17, 18, 20, 21; CelR; ColdWar 1, 2; ConAu 81, 89; ConHero 1; ContDcW 89; CurBio 70, 79N; DcAmImH; DcMidEa; DcPol; DcTwHis; FacFETw; GoodHs; HerW, 84; HisEAAC; HisWorL; IntDcWB; IntWW 74, 75, 76, 77, 78; IntYB 78, 79; InWom; JeHun; LegTOT; LinLib S; McGEWB; MidE 78; NewYTBS 74, 78; PolLCME; WhAm 7; WhDW; Who 74; WhoAmW 66, 68, 70, 72, 74, 75; WhoGov 72; WhoWor 74; WhoWorJ 72, 78; WomFir; WomWR; WorAl; WorAlBi*

Meisner, Randy
[The Eagles]
American. Singer, Musician
Bass player with Eagles, 1971-77; left to pursue solo career.
b. Mar 8, 1946 in Scotts Bluff, Nebraska
Source: *ASCAP 80; BioIn 12; LegTOT; RkOn 85*

Meisner, Sanford
American. Actor, Director
Appeared in numerous theatrical performances; starred in *Tender Is the Night,* 1962; director of New York's Neighborhood Playhouse, 1936-59, 1964-ca. 1988; wrote *Sanford Meisner on Acting,* 1987.
b. Aug 31, 1905 in New York, New York
d. Feb 2, 1997 in Sherman Oaks, California
Source: *BiE&WWA; BioIn 11, 17; CurBio 91; NotNAT; PlP&P; WhoHol 92*

Meissonier, Jean Louis Ernest
French. Artist
Noted for genre scenes, military subjects.
b. Feb 21, 1815 in Lyons, France
d. Jan 31, 1891 in Paris, France
Source: *BioIn 2, 5; CelCen; ClaDrA; DcCathB; Dis&D; LinLib S; NewC; NewCol 75; WebBD 83*

Meitner, Lise
Austrian. Physicist
Noted for work in nuclear fission, 1938; co-winner, Fermi award, 1966; research helped usher in Atomic Age, 1945.
b. Nov 7, 1878 in Vienna, Austria
d. Oct 28, 1968 in Cambridge, England

Source: *AsBiEn; BiESc; BioIn 1, 3, 4, 5, 6, 8, 9, 11, 12, 13, 14, 15, 16, 19, 20, 21; CamDcSc; ContDcW 89; CurBio 45, 68; DcScB; EncTR; FacFETw; GoodHs; HerW, 84; InSci; IntDcWB; InWom, SUP; LarDcSc; LegTOT; LinLib S; McGMS 80; NotTwCS; ObitT 1961; REn; WhAm 5; WhDW; WhoAmW 68; WomFir; WorAl; WorAlBi; WorScD*

Mejia Victores, Oscar Humberto
Guatemalan. Political Leader
Seized presidency in Aug 1983 coup.
b. Dec 9, 1930 in Guatemala City, Guatemala
Source: *BioIn 13; DicTyr; NewYTBS 83; WhoWor 84, 87*

Mekka, Eddie
American. Actor
Played Carmine on TV show "Laverne and Shirley," 1976-83.
b. Jun 14, 1952 in Worcester, Massachusetts
Source: *ConTFT 2; LegTOT; VarWW 85; WhoHol 92*

Melachrino, George Miltiades
English. Bandleader
Formed group, Melachrino Strings, known for unique smooth sound; played every instrument except harp, piano.
b. May 1, 1909 in London, England
d. Jun 18, 1965 in London, England
Source: *Baker 78, 84; BioIn 7; ObitOF 79; WhoMus 72; WhScrn 74, 77*

Melanchthon, Philipp
German. Religious Leader, Social Reformer
Wrote guidelines for churches, schools which led to first modern public school system in Saxony; tried to unite Catholics, Protestants.
b. Feb 16, 1497 in Bretten, Germany
d. Apr 19, 1560 in Wittenberg, Saxony
Source: *BbD; Benet 87, 96; BiD&SB; BioIn 2, 4, 5, 6, 7, 8, 9, 10, 11, 12, 14, 19; CasWL; DcEuL; EuAu; EvEuW; Geog 3; LinLib S; LuthC 75; NewC; NewCBEL; NewCol 75; NewGrDM 80; OxCEng 67; OxCGer 76, 86; PenC EUR; REn; WebBD 83; WhDW*

Melanie
[Melanie Safka]
American. Singer, Songwriter
Singer, guitarist, often in folk vein; hit song "Brand New Key," 1971.
b. Feb 3, 1948 in New York, New York
Source: *BioIn 14; EncFCWM 83; EncPR&S 74; EncRk 88; IlEncRk; InWom SUP; PenEncP; WorAl; WorAlBi*

Melba, Nellie, Dame
[Helen Porter Mitchell Armstrong]
Australian. Opera Singer
Outstanding coloratura of her day; star of London's Covent Garden, NY Met. from 1890s; made Dame, 1918; dessert, "peaches melba" was created in her honor.
b. May 19, 1859 in Melbourne, Australia
d. Feb 23, 1931 in Sydney, Australia
Source: *Baker 78, 84; BiDAmM; BriBkM 80; FacFETw; InWom, SUP; LngCTC; MusSN; NewC; NewEOp 71; OxCAusL; REn; WhAm 1*

Melbourne, William Lamb, Viscount
English. Political Leader
Prime Minister, 1834; 1835-41; favored adviser of Queen Victoria; husband of Lady Caroline Lamb.
b. Mar 15, 1779 in Hertfordshire, England
d. Nov 24, 1848 in Hertfordshire, England
Source: *BioIn 1, 3, 5, 6, 7, 8, 10, 11, 12, 13, 16, 21; CelCen; McGEWB; NewCol 75; WebBD 83; WhDW*

Melcher, Frederic Gershon
American. Publisher
R.R. Bowker exec; established Newbery Medal for children's tales, 1921; Caldecott Medal for illustrations, 1937.
b. Apr 12, 1879 in Malden, Massachusetts
d. Mar 9, 1963 in Montclair, New Jersey
Source: *AmAu&B; ChhPo, S1, S2; CurBio 45, 63; WhAm 4*

Melcher, John
American. Politician
Dem. senator from MT, 1977-89; mayor of Forsyth, MY, 1955-61.
b. Sep 6, 1924 in Sioux City, Iowa
Source: *AlmAP 78, 80, 82, 84, 88; AmCath 80; BiDrAC; BiDrUSC 89; BioIn 11, 12, 13; CngDr 74, 77, 79, 81, 83, 85, 87; IntWW 77, 78, 79, 80, 81, 82, 83, 89, 91, 93; PolsAm 84; WhoAm 74, 76, 78, 80, 82, 84, 86, 88, 90; WhoAmP 73, 75, 77, 79, 81, 83, 85, 87, 89, 91, 93, 95; WhoGov 72, 75, 77; WhoWest 76, 78, 80, 82, 84, 87, 89; WhoWor 80, 82, 87, 89*

Melchers, Gari
[Julius Gari Melchers]
American. Artist
Did portraits, landscapes, sacred scenes, murals for Library of Congress.
b. Aug 11, 1860 in Detroit, Michigan
d. Nov 30, 1932 in Fredericksburg, Virginia
Source: *AmBi; ApCAB X; ArtsEM; BioIn 11, 14; BriEAA; DcAmArt; DcAmB; LegTOT; McGDA; NatCAB 13; PeoHis; WhAm 1*

Melchior, Lauritz
American. Opera Singer
Famed Wagnerian tenor with NY Met., 1926-50; considered finest heldentenor of the day.
b. Mar 20, 1890 in Copenhagen, Denmark
d. Mar 18, 1973 in Santa Monica, California
Source: *Baker 78, 84, 92; BioIn 1, 2, 3, 4, 5, 6, 8, 9, 10, 11, 12, 14, 16, 17, 21; BriBkM 80; CmOp; CurBio 41, 73, 73N; FacFETw; FilmEn; FilmgC; ForYSC; HalFC 80, 84, 88; IntDcOp; LegTOT; MetOEnc; MGM; MovMk; MusMk; MusSN; NewAmDM; NewEOp 71; NewGrDA 86; NewGrDM 80; NewGrDO; NewYTBE 73; ObitT 1971; OxDcOp; PenDiMP; WhAm 5; WhoHol B; WhoMus 72; WhScrn 77, 83; WorAlBi*

Meles Zenawi
Ethiopian. Political Leader
Pres., Ethiopia, 1991-95; prime minister, Ethiopia, 1995.
b. May 9, 1955 in Adua, Ethiopia
Source: *ConBlB 3; NewYTBS 91; WhoWor 96, 97*

Melford, Austin
[Alfred Austin Melford]
English. Actor, Director, Producer
London stage performer since 1904.
b. Aug 24, 1884 in Alverstoke, England
d. Aug 19, 1971
Source: *ConAu 115; IntMPA 75, 76, 77, 78, 79, 80, 81, 82, 84, 86, 88; WhoThe 77; WhThe*

Melies, Georges
French. Director, Producer
Originator of fiction and fantasy film; best known film *A Trip to the Moon,* 1902.
b. Dec 8, 1861 in Paris, France
d. Jan 21, 1938 in Paris, France
Source: *BiDFilm, 81, 94; BioIn 9, 10, 12, 15; CamGWoT; DcArts; DcFM; DcTwCCu 2; EncEurC; EncSF, 93; FacFETw; Film 1; FilmEn; FilmgC; HalFC 80, 84, 88; IntDcF 1-2, 2-2; MiSFD 9N; MovMk; NewEScF; OxCFilm; TwYS; WhoHrs 80; WhScrn 77, 83; WorEFlm; WorFDir 1*

Melis, Jose
Cuban. Bandleader, Pianist
Music director for Jack Paar's "Tonight Show" who made several recordings.
b. Feb 27, 1920 in Havana, Cuba
Source: *ASCAP 66, 80*

Mellencamp, John
[John Cougar Mellencamp]
American. Singer, Songwriter
First American rock singer to have two hits in the Top Five simultaneously with "Hurt So Good" and "Jack and Diane," 1982.
b. Oct 7, 1951 in Seymour, Indiana
Source: *Baker 92; BioIn 14, 15, 16; CelR 90; ConMus 2; CurBio 86, 88; EncPR&S 89; EncRkSt; HarEnR 86; LegTOT; NewYTBS 87; PenEncP; RkOn 85; WhoAm 90, 92, 94, 95, 96, 97; WhoEnt 92; WhoHol 92; WorAlBi*

Mellinger, Frederick
American. Businessman
Introduced mail order business selling racy lingerie to postwar America,

1946; became Frederick's of Hollywood, 1947.
b. 1914 in New York, New York
d. Jun 2, 1990 in Los Angeles, California
Source: *AnObit 1990; BioIn 9, 10, 16; News 90; NewYTBS 90*

Mello, Dawn
American. Business Executive
Fashion exec; vp, B. Altman, 1971-75; vp, Bergdorf Goodman, 1975-89; director, Gucci International, 1989—.
b. 1938?
Source: *News 92, 92-2*

Mellon, Andrew William
American. Financier, Government Official
Secretary of Treasury, 1921-32; ambassador to Great Britain, 1932-33; endowed Washington's National Gallery of Art.
b. Mar 24, 1855 in Pittsburgh, Pennsylvania
d. Aug 26, 1937 in Southampton, New York
Source: *AmBi; AmDec 1900; AmPolLe; ApCAB X; BiDAmBL 83; BiDrUSE 71, 89; BioIn 1, 3, 4, 9, 10, 11, 12, 13, 15, 16; DcAmB S2; DcAmDH 80, 89; DcArts; DcNAA; DcTwHis; EncAB-H 1974, 1996; FacFETw; LinLib S; McGEWB; MemAm; NatCAB 28; OxCAmH; WebAB 74, 79; WhAm 1; WhAmArt 85; WorAl*

Mellon, Paul
American. Business Executive, Philanthropist
Board chm., Nat. Gallery of Art, Washington, 1979-85; established Bollinger Foundation; wrote memoirs *Reflections in a Silver Spoon,* 1992; son of Andrew.
b. Jun 11, 1907 in Pittsburgh, Pennsylvania
Source: *BioIn 4, 6, 7, 8, 10, 11, 13, 15, 16; BlueB 76; CelR; CurBio 66; IntWW 74, 75, 76, 77, 78, 79, 80, 81, 82, 83, 89, 91, 93; IntYB 78, 79, 80, 81, 82; NewYTBS 91; OxDcArt; PeoHis; ThHElm; Who 74, 82, 83, 85, 88, 90, 92, 94; WhoAm 74, 76, 78, 80, 82, 84, 86, 88, 90, 92, 94, 95, 96, 97; WhoAmA 73, 76, 78, 80, 82, 84, 86, 89, 91, 93; WhoE 85; WhoFI 74; WhoGov 72, 75, 77; WhoSSW 75, 76; WhoWor 74; WorAl; WorAlBi*

Mellon, Richard King
American. Banker
Led Mellon Bank, 1946-67; controlled one of history's largest family fortunes; nephew of Andrew.
b. Jun 19, 1899 in Pittsburgh, Pennsylvania
d. Jun 3, 1970 in Pittsburgh, Pennsylvania
Source: *BiDAmBL 83; BioIn 1, 2, 7, 8, 9; CurBio 65, 70; NewYTBE 70; WhAm 5*

Mellon, William Larimer, Jr.
American. Physician
Influenced by Albert Schweitzer; began mission in Haiti by establishing hospital in Schweitzer's honor.
b. Jun 26, 1910 in Pittsburgh, Pennsylvania
d. Aug 3, 1989 in Deschapelles
Source: *BioIn 3, 4, 5, 6, 7, 16; CurBio 65, 89, 89N; NewYTBS 89; WhoWor 74*

Mellor, Walter
American. Architect
Designed WW I American Battle Monument, Ypres, BE.
b. Apr 25, 1880 in Philadelphia, Pennsylvania
d. Jan 11, 1940
Source: *BiDAmAr; CurBio 40; WhAm 1*

Melnick, Daniel
American. Film Executive, Producer
Films include *All That Jazz,* 1979; *Altered States,* 1980; won Emm ys for "Death of a Salesman," 1951; "Ages of Man."
b. Apr 21, 1932 in New York, New York
Source: *BioIn 13, 15; ConTFT 3; IntMPA 92; LesBEnT; Who 82; WhoAm 78, 80, 82, 84, 86, 88, 90, 92, 94, 95, 96, 97*

Meloy, Francis Edward, Jr.
American. Diplomat
Ambassador to Dominican Republic, 1969-73; Guatemala, 1973-75; Lebanon, 1975-76.
b. Mar 28, 1917 in Washington, District of Columbia
d. Jun 16, 1976 in Beirut, Lebanon
Source: *BioIn 10, 11, 16; BlueB 76; DcAmDH 80, 89; USBiR 74; WhAm 7; WhoAm 74, 76, 78; WhoAmP 73, 75; WhoGov 72, 75*

Melton, James
American. Opera Singer
Lyric tenor with NY Met., 1942-50; concert, radio, film star.
b. Jan 2, 1904 in Moultrie, Georgia
d. Apr 21, 1961 in New York, New York
Source: *Baker 78, 84, 92; BiDAmM; BioIn 2, 3, 4, 5, 6; CmpEPM; CurBio 45, 61; DcAmB S7; FilmgC; ForYSC; HalFC 80, 84, 88; MetOEnc; NewGrDA 86; NewGrDO; RadStar; SaTiSS; WhAm 4; WhScrn 74, 77*

Melville, Herman
American. Author
Wrote *Moby Dick,* 1851.
b. Aug 1, 1819 in New York, New York
d. Sep 28, 1891 in New York, New York
Source: *Alli, SUP; AmAu; AmAu&B; AmBi; AmCulL; AmWr; ApCAB; AtlBL; BbD; Benet 87, 96; BenetAL 91; BibAL; BiD&SB; BiDTran; BioIn 1, 2, 3, 4, 5, 6, 7, 8, 9, 10, 11, 12, 13, 14, 15, 16, 17, 18, 19, 20, 21; CamGEL; CamGLE; CamHAL; CasWL; Chambr 3; ChhPo, S2; CnDAL; CnE&AP; ColARen; CrtT 3, 4; CyAL 2; CyWA 58; DcAmAu; DcAmB; DcArts; DcBiA; DcEnA; DcEnL; DcLB 3, 74; DcLEL; DcNAA; Dis&D; Drake; EncAB-H 1974, 1996; EncSF, 93; EvLB; GayLesB; GrWrEL N; InSci; LegTOT; LinLib L, S; LuthC 75; MagSAmL; McGEWB; MemAm; MouLC 4; NatCAB 4; NewEOp 71; NewGrDA 86; NewGrDO; NinCLC 3, 12, 29; Novels; OxCAmH; OxCAmL 65, 83, 95; OxCEng 67, 85, 95; OxCShps; PenC AM; PenEncH; PeoHis; RAdv 1, 14, 13-1; RComAH; RComWL; REn; REnAL; RfGAmL 87, 94; RfGShF; RGFAP; ShSCr 1; SmATA 59; TwCBDA; WebAB 74, 79; WebE&AL; WhAm HS; WhDW; WorAl; WorAlBi; WorLitC; WrPh*

Melville, Jean-Pierre
[Jean-Pierre Grumbach]
French. Director
Pseud. is from favorite novelist, Herman Melville; films include *Les Enfants Terribles,* 1949.
b. Oct 20, 1917 in Paris, France
d. Aug 2, 1973 in Paris, France
Source: *BiDFilm, 81, 94; BioIn 16, 20; DcFM; DcTwCCu 2; EncEurC; FilmEn; FilmgC; GangFlm; HalFC 80, 84, 88; IntDcF 1-2, 2-2; ItaFilm; MiSFD 9N; NewYTBE 72; ObitT 1971; OxCFilm; WhoWor 74; WorEFlm; WorFDir 2*

Memling, Hans
Flemish. Artist
Portraitist, religious painter; noted for color, detail; works include *Last Judgement Altarpiece.*
b. 1430 in Seligenstadt, Belgium
d. Aug 11, 1494 in Bruges, Belgium
Source: *AtlBL; Benet 87; BioIn 5, 6, 7, 9, 20; ClaDrA; DcArts; DcCathB; LegTOT; LuthC 75; NewC; OxCArt; OxDcArt; REn; WhDW; WorAl; WorAlBi*

Memmi, Albert
Tunisian. Author
Writes about oppression of women, blacks; works include *The Pillar of Salt,* 1953.
b. 1920 in Tunis, Tunisia
Source: *Au&Wr 71; BioIn 10; ClDMEL 80; ConAu 14NR, 32NR, 81; ConWorW 93; DcOrL 3; EncWL 3; IntAu&W 76, 77, 82, 89; IntWW 74, 75, 76, 77, 78, 79, 80, 81, 82, 83, 89, 91, 93; LiExTwC; MidE 78, 79, 80, 81, 82; ModFrL; REn; TwCWr; WhoFr 79; WhoWor 74, 76, 78, 80; WhoWorJ 78; WorAu 1950*

Memphis Slim
[Peter Chatman]
American. Pianist, Singer
Int'l. blues performer; hits include "Beer Drinking Woman."
b. Sep 3, 1916 in Memphis, Tennessee
d. Feb 24, 1988 in Paris, France
Source: *BioIn 7, 11; EncRk 88; WhoRocM 82*

Menander
Greek. Dramatist
Has been called the greatest representative of Greek New Comedy; wrote *The Shearing of Glycera* and *The Sikyonion.*
b. c. 342BC in Athens, Greece
d. c. 292BC in Athens, Greece
Source: *AncWr; AtlBL; Benet 87, 96; BiD&SB; BioIn 5, 10, 11; BlmGEL; CamGWoT; CasWL; ClMLC 9; CnThe; CyWA 58; DcArts; DramC 3; EncWT; Ent; GrFLW; Grk&L; IntDcT 2; LegTOT; LinLib L, S; McGEWB; NewC; NewGrDM 80; NotNAT B; OxCClL, 89; OxCEng 67, 85, 95; OxCThe 67, 83; PenC CL; RAdv 14, 13-2; RComWL; REn; REnWD; RfGWoL 95; WhDW; WorAl; WorAlBi*

Menard, H. William
American. Geologist
First to use aqua-lung for studying sea floor; won Bowie Medal, 1985.
b. Dec 10, 1920 in Fresno, California
d. Feb 9, 1986 in La Jolla, California
Source: *AmMWSc 82; BioIn 14, 15; BlueB 76; ConAu 37R, 118; IntWW 83; NewYTBS 86; WhoAm 84; WhoFrS 84; WhoOcn 78; WrDr 84*

Men at Work
[Greg Ham; Colin Hay; John Rees; Jerry Speiser; Ron Strykert]
Australian. Music Group
Album *Business As Usual,* 1982, included hits "Who Can It be Now?;" "Down Under."
Source: *Alli; DcVicP, 2; EncPR&S 89; EncRk 88; EncRkSt; HarEnR 86; PenEncP; PeoHis; RkOn 85; RolSEnR 83; WhE&EA; Who 94; WhoHol 92*

Menchik-Stevenson, Vera Francevna
English. Chess Player
Women's world champion chess player, 1927-44.
b. Feb 16, 1906 in Moscow, Russia
d. Jun 27, 1944 in London, England
Source: *InWom SUP; OxCChes 84*

Menchu, Rigoberta
Guatemalan. Social Reformer, Author
Guatemalan indian rights activist; wrote of civil rights abuses in *I, Rigoberta Menchu,* 1983; won 1992 Nobel Peace Prize.
b. 1959 in Chimel, Guatemala
Source: *BioIn 18; ContDcW 89; CurBio 93; DcHiB; HeroCon; ModWoWr; News 93-2; WhoAm 94, 95; WhoWor 95, 96, 97; WomFir; WomStre*

Mencius
Chinese. Philosopher
Urged adoption of principles of Confucius; believed in natural goodness of man.
b. 371BC in Shandong, China
d. 289BC, China
Source: *BbD; BiD&SB; CasWL; CyEd; DcOrL 1; LegTOT; McGEWB; WorAl; WorAlBi*

Mencken, H(enry) L(ouis)
"The Sage of Baltimore"
American. Editor, Satirist
Known for biting satire, insult, debunking in *The American Mercury,* 1924-33; traced development of American English in *The American Language,* 1918.
b. Sep 12, 1880 in Baltimore, Maryland
d. Jan 29, 1956 in Baltimore, Maryland
Source: *ABCMeAm; AmAu&B; AmLY; AmSocL; AmWr; AtlBL; Benet 96; BiDAmJo; BiDAmNC; BioIn 1, 2, 3, 4, 5, 6, 7, 8, 9, 10, 11, 12, 13, 14, 15, 16, 17, 18, 19, 20; CasWL; Chambr 3; ChhPo, S2; CnDAL; CnMWL; ConAmA; CyWA 58; DcAmB S6; DcAmC; DcAmReB 1, 2; DcArts; DcLEL; DcTwHis; EncAAH; EncAB-H 1974, 1996; EncARH; EncUnb; EncWL, 3; EvLB; FacFETw; JrnUS; LinLib S; McGEWB; ModAL S1; NotNAT B; OxCAmL 95; OxCEng 67, 95; PenC AM; RAdv 14; RfGAmL 94; SouWr; TwCA, SUP; WebAB 74, 79; WebE&AL; WhAm 3; WhDW; WhE&EA; WhJnl; WhLit*

Mendel, Gregor Johann
Austrian. Botanist, Geneticist
Experiments with garden peas were basis of modern theory of heredity.
b. Jul 22, 1822 in Heinzendorf, Silesia
d. Jan 6, 1884 in Brunn, Bohemia
Source: *AsBiEn; BiDPsy; BiESc; BioIn 1, 2, 3, 4, 5, 6, 7, 8, 9, 10, 11, 12, 13; DcCathB; Dis&D; EncAAH; EncSPD; InSci; LarDcSc; LinLib S; LuthC 75; OxCGer 76, 86; RAdv 14, 13-5; REn; WorAl; WorAlBi*

Mendeleev, Dmitri Ivanovich
Russian. Chemist
Classified chemical elements by atomic weight; invented the periodic table.
b. Feb 7, 1834 in Tobolsk, Russia
d. Feb 2, 1907 in Saint Petersburg, Russia
Source: *AsBiEn; BiESc; Dis&D; McGEWB; NewCol 75; WebBD 83; WorAl*

Mendelsohn, Eric
German. Architect
Noted for art nouveau structure, Einstein Tower, Potsdam, East Germany, 1919-21.
b. Mar 21, 1887 in Allenskin, Germany
d. Sep 15, 1953 in San Francisco, California
Source: *AtlBL; BioIn 1, 3, 4, 5, 6, 7, 9, 11; ConArch 80, 87; CurBio 53; DcD&D; DcNaB 1951; MacEA; McGDA*

Mendelssohn, Felix
[Felix Mendelssohn-Bartholdy]
German. Composer, Conductor, Musician
Works include five symphonies; wrote famed overture to *Midsummer Night's Dream,* 1826.
b. Feb 3, 1809 in Hamburg, Germany
d. Nov 4, 1847 in Leipzig, Germany
Source: *AtlBL; Baker 78, 84; BbD; Benet 87; BiD&SB; BioIn 1, 2, 3, 4, 5, 6, 7, 8, 9, 10, 11, 12, 13, 14, 15, 16, 17, 20; BriBkM 80; CelCen; CmpBCM; CnOxB; DcBiPP; DcCom 77; DcCom&M 79; GrComp; JeHun; LegTOT; LinLib S; MetOEnc; MusMk; NewAmDM; NewC; NewCol 75; NewEOp 71; NewGrDM 80; NewOxM; NotNAT B; OxCEng 85; OxCGer 76, 86; OxCMus; OxDcOp; PenDiMP A; RAdv 14, 13-3; REn; WhDW; WorAl; WorAlBi*

Mendes, Catulle
[Abraham Catulle Mendes]
French. Author, Critic
Founded Parnassian school of poetry; wrote *Legende du Parnasse Contemporain,* 1884.
b. May 22, 1841 in Bordeaux, France
d. Feb 8, 1909 in Saint-Germain-en-Laye, France
Source: *BbD; BiD&SB; BioIn 1, 7, 8; CasWL; ChhPo; ClDMEL 47; Dis&D; EuAu; EvEuW; LngCTC; NewCol 75; NewEOp 71; NewGrDM 80; OxCFr; PenC EUR; REn; ScF&FL 1; WhLit*

Mendes, Chico
"The Amazonian Gandhi"
Brazilian. Political Activist
Through nonviolent resistance, saved almost 3 million acres of rain forest; assassinated for his activism; became symbol of environmental movemwent.
b. Dec 15, 1944 in Xapuri, Brazil
d. Dec 11, 1944 in Xapuri, Brazil
Source: *AnObit 1988; BioIn 16; ConHero 2; DcTwHis; EnvEnc; RadHan*

Mendes, Sergio
[Sergio Mendes and Brasil '66]
Brazilian. Musician, Bandleader
Hits include "The Look of Love," "Never Gonna Let You Go."
b. Feb 11, 1941 in Niteroi, Brazil
Source: *BiDAmM; BiDJaz; EncJzS; EncPR&S 74; LegTOT; PenEncP; RkOn 74; VarWW 85; WorAl; WorAlBi*

Mendes-France, Pierre
French. Statesman
Socialist premier, 1954-55; ended France's war in Indochina.
b. Jan 11, 1907 in Paris, France
d. Oct 18, 1982 in Paris, France
Source: *AnObit 1982; Au&Wr 71; BioIn 1, 3, 4, 7, 8, 13, 14, 17, 18, 21; ColdWar 1, 2; ConAu 43NR, 81, 108; CurBio 54, 83, 83N; DcPol; DcTwHis; EncWB; FacFETw; HisEWW; IntWW 74, 75, 76, 77, 78, 79, 80, 81, 82; IntYB 78, 79, 80, 81, 82; LinLib S; NewYTBS 82; PolLCWE; WhAm 8; Who 74, 82; WhoFr 79; WhoWor 74, 78, 80, 82; WhoWorJ 72, 78; WorAl; WorAlBi*

Mendez, Aparicio
Uruguayan. Political Leader
Pres., Uruguay, 1976-81.
b. Aug 24, 1904 in Rivera, Uruguay

d. Jun 1988 in Montevideo, Uruguay
Source: *BioIn 16; DcCPSAm; IntWW 77, 78, 79, 80, 81; IntYB 78, 79, 80, 81, 82; NewYTBS 88*

Mendl, Lady Elsie de Wolfe
American. Interior Decorator
America's first woman decorator; wrote trend-setting *The House in Good Taste,* 1913.
b. Dec 20, 1865 in New York, New York
d. Jul 12, 1950 in Versailles, France
Source: *BiCAW; DcAmB S4; NotAW; WhAm 4; WhoStg 1906, 1908; WomWWA 14*

Mendoza, Mark
[Twisted Sister]
"The Animal"
American. Musician
Bassist with heavy metal group, formed 1976.
b. Jul 13, 1954
Source: *WhoRocM 82*

Menelik II
[Sahle Mariam]
Ethiopian. Ruler
Emperor, 1889-1913; expanded realm; established country's independence; succeeded by regency due to illness, 1910.
b. Aug 17, 1844 in Ankober, Ethiopia
d. Dec 12, 1913 in Addis Ababa, Ethiopia
Source: *NewCol 75; WebBD 83*

Menem, Carlos Saul
Argentine. Political Leader
First Peronist, besides Juan Peron, to be elected to pres. of Argentina, 1989—.
b. Jul 1, 1930 in Anillaco, Argentina
Source: *BioIn 16; CurBio 89; DcCPSAm; IntWW 91; NewYTBS 89; WhoWor 91*

Menendez de Aviles, Pedro
Spanish. Naval Officer, Colonizer
Founded St. Augustine, Florida, 1500s; attempted to establish Spanish rule in Florida.
b. Feb 15, 1519 in Aviles, Spain
d. Sep 17, 1574 in Santander, Spain
Source: *AmBi; BioIn 6, 7, 11, 17, 18, 20; DcAmB; Drake; EncCRAm; EncSoH; HarEnUS; McGEWB; NatCAB 11; NewCol 75; OxCAmH; REnAW; WebAB 74, 79; WhAm HS; WhDW; WhFla; WhNaAH; WhWE*

Menendez Pidal, Ramon
Spanish. Linguist, Historian
Expert on origins of Spanish language.
b. Mar 13, 1869 in La Coruna, Spain
d. Nov 14, 1968 in Madrid, Spain
Source: *Benet 87, 96; BioIn 1, 8, 16; CasWL; ClDMEL 47, 80; ConAu 116, 153; DcSpL; EvEuW; HispWr; OxCSpan; REn; WhDW*

Menes
Egyptian. Ruler
Credited with uniting Egypt, its first king; founder of first dynasty; ruled 62 yrs.
b. fl. 3400BC
Source: *NewCol 75; WebBD 83; WorAlBi*

Meng, John Joseph
American. Educator, Historian
Authority on late 18th-century Franco-American relations; taught at Catholic U, 1931-38; Queen's College, 1938-49 and Hunter College, 1949-52; following decades were spent in educational administration.
b. Dec 12, 1906 in Cleveland, Ohio
d. Feb 15, 1988 in Jackson, Mississippi
Source: *AmCath 80; BioIn 6, 7, 16; CurBio 61; DrAS 74H, 78H; LEduc 74; WhAm 9; WhoAm 74, 76, 78, 80, 82, 84, 86, 88; WhoE 74*

Mengelberg, Willem
[Josef Willem Mengelberg]
Dutch. Conductor
Noted for leading Amsterdam's Concertgebouw for 50 yrs; often led NY Philharmonic, 1920s.
b. Mar 28, 1871 in Utrecht, Netherlands
d. Mar 22, 1951 in Zuort, Switzerland
Source: *Baker 78, 84; BioIn 1, 2, 4, 8, 11; BriBkM 80; FacFETw; MusMk; MusSN; NewAmDM; NewGrDM 80; PenDiMP; WebBD 83*

Mengele, Josef
"The Angel of Extermination"
German. Physician
Doctor at Auschwitz concentration camp; known for medical experimentation; subject of intense manhunt for alleged war crimes.
b. Mar 16, 1911 in Gunzburg, Bavaria
d. Feb 7, 1979 in Bertioga, Brazil
Source: *BioIn 9, 11; ConNews 85-2; EncTR, 91; EncWB; FacFETw; LegTOT*

Mengers, Sue
American. Agent
Talent agent who represents movie stars.
b. Sep 2, 1938 in Hamburg, Germany
Source: *BioIn 15, 19; ConNews 85-3; IntMPA 84, 92; VarWW 85; WhoAm 80, 82, 84; WhoWest 87*

Mengs, Anton Raphael
German. Artist
Historical, portrait painter; neoclassicist; wrote treatise on taste in painting, 1762.
b. Mar 22, 1728 in Aussig, Bohemia
d. Jun 29, 1779 in Rome, Italy
Source: *BioIn 1, 10, 11, 12, 14, 18; EncEnl; IntDcAA 90; LuthC 75; McGDA; McGEWB; NewCol 75*

Menguistu Haile Mariam
Ethiopian. Political Leader
Marxist Ethiopian head of state, 1977-91.
b. 1937 in Wollamo, Ethiopia
Source: *BioIn 14, 15; ColdWar 1; CurBio 81; EncWB; IntWW 91; WhoWor 84, 89, 91*

Menjou, Adolphe Jean
American. Actor
Starred in Chaplin's *A Woman of Paris,* 1923; Oscar nominee for *The Front Page,* 1931.
b. Feb 8, 1890 in Pittsburgh, Pennsylvania
d. Oct 29, 1963 in Beverly Hills, California
Source: *BiDFilm; CurBio 48, 64; DcAmB S7; Film 1; FilmgC; MotPP; MovMk; OxCFilm; TwYS; WhAm 4; WhoHol B; WhScrn 77; WorEFlm*

Menken, Adah Isaacs
American. Actor, Poet
Starred in stage melodrama *Mazeppa.*
b. Jun 15, 1835? in New Orleans, Louisiana
d. Aug 10, 1868 in Paris, France
Source: *Alli SUP; AmAu; AmAu&B; AmBi; AmWomWr; ApCAB; BbD; BenetAL 91; BiD&SB; BiDSA; BioAmW; BioIn 1, 3, 4, 5, 6, 7, 9, 11, 12, 14, 15, 16, 17, 18, 20; BlkAWP; BlkWAm; CamGWoT; ChhPo, S1; CmCal; CnDAL; ContDcW 89; DcAmAu; DcAmB; DcNAA; DcNaB; Drake; EncAmaz 91; Ent; FamA&A; InB&W 80, 85; IntDcWB; InWom, SUP; LibW; NatCAB 5; NotAW; NotBlAW 1; NotNAT A, B; NotWoAT; OxCAmH; OxCAmL 65, 83, 95; OxCAmT 84; OxCThe 67, 83; PenNWW A; REn; REnAL; WebAB 74, 79; WhAm HS*

Menken, Alan
American. Composer
Composed musical scores for Disney movie *The Little Mermaid, Beauty and the Beast,* and *Aladdin.*
b. 1949 in New Rochelle, New York
Source: *ConMus 10; ConTFT 11; IntMPA 96; WhoAm 97*

Menken, Helen
American. Actor
First wife of Humphrey Bogart; produced *Stage Door Canteen,* 1942-46; *Second Husband,* 1937-46.
b. Dec 12, 1901 in New York, New York
d. Mar 27, 1966 in New York, New York
Source: *BiE&WWA; BioIn 7; InWom; NotNAT B; OxCAmT 84; PlP&P; SaTiSS; WhAm 4; WhoAmW 58, 64, 66; WhScrn 77; WhThe*

Mennen, Frederick
American. Inventor
Inventor and founder of Jiffy Pop Popcorn business.
b. 1929?
d. Mar 19, 1991 in LaPorte, Indiana
Source: *NewYTBS 91*

Mennen, William Gerhard
American. Philanthropist, Merchant
Talcum powder first sold in sifter-top tin cans, 1890.
b. Dec 20, 1884 in Newark, New Jersey
d. Feb 17, 1968 in Montclair, New Jersey
Source: *BioIn 8; Entr; WhAm 4*

Mennin, Peter
American. Composer, Educator
Pres., Julliard School, 1962-83; wrote nine symphonies.
b. May 17, 1923 in Erie, Pennsylvania
d. Jun 17, 1983 in New York, New York
Source: *AmComp; ASCAP 66, 80; Baker 78, 84, 92; BiDAmM; BiE&WWA; BioIn 1, 4, 6, 7, 8, 9, 12, 13; BlueB 76; BriBkM 80; CelR; CompSN, SUP; ConAmC 76, 82; CurBio 64, 83N; DcCM; DcCom&M 79; FacFETw; IntWW 74, 75, 76, 77, 78, 79, 80, 81, 82, 83; IntWWM 80; MusMk; NewAmDM; NewGrDA 86; NewGrDM 80; NewOxM; NewYTBE 72; NewYTBS 83; OxCMus; PenDiMP A; WhAm 8; WhoAm 74, 76, 78, 80, 82; WhoE 74, 77, 79, 81, 83; WhoMus 72; WhoWor 74, 76, 78*

Menninger, Karl Augustus
American. Psychiatrist
Pioneered popularization of psychiatry; co-founded Menninger Clinic and Foundation, 1941, using group practice methods.
b. Jul 23, 1893 in Topeka, Kansas
d. Jul 18, 1990 in Topeka, Kansas
Source: *AmAu&B; AmMWSc 73P, 76P, 79, 82, 86, 89, 92; AnObit 1990; Au&Wr 71; BiDrAPA 77, 89; BioIn 1, 4, 5, 7, 10, 11, 16; ConAu 17R, 29NR, 132; CurBio 48, 90, 90N; FacFETw; InSci; IntWW 74, 75, 76, 77, 78, 79, 80, 81, 82, 83, 89, 91N; MajTwCW; News 91-1; NewYTBS 90; PeoHis; RAdv 14, 13-5; REnAL; TwCA, SUP; WebAB 74, 79; WhAm 10; WhNAA; WhoAm 74, 76, 78, 80, 82, 84, 86, 88; WhoMW 74, 76, 78; WhoWor 74; WorAl; WorAlBi*

Menninger, William C
American. Scientist, Physician
Co-founded Menninger Clinic, 1920; pres., Menninger Foundation, from 1957; brother of Karl.
b. Oct 15, 1899 in Topeka, Kansas
d. Sep 6, 1966 in Topeka, Kansas
Source: *AmAu&B; ConAu 25R; CurBio 45, 66; REnAL; WhAm 4*

Menno Simonsz(con)
Dutch. Clergy
One of the leaders of the Dutch Anabaptism; followers later founded the Mennonite church.
b. 1496 in Witmarsum, Germany
d. Jan 31, 1561 in Lubeck, Netherlands

Menotti, Gian Carlo
Italian. Composer
Foremost composer-librettist of modern opera; wrote Pulitzer Prize-winning operas *The Consul,* 1950, *The Saint of Bleecker Street,* 1955; also wrote Christmas opera *Amahl and the Night Visitors,* 1954.
b. Jul 7, 1911 in Cadigliano, Italy
Source: *AmComp; AmCulL; ASCAP 66; AuBYP 2S, 3; Baker 78, 84, 92; Benet 87; BenetAL 91; BiE&WWA; BioIn 12, 13, 14, 15, 16, 17, 19, 20; BlueB 76; CelR 90; ChhPo S2; CompSN SUP; ConAmC 76, 82; ConAu 104; ConCom 92; CurBio 47, 79; DcArts; DcCM; DcTwCCu 1; FacFETw; GayLesB; IntDcOp; IntWW 74, 75, 76, 77, 78, 79, 80, 81, 82, 83, 89, 91, 93; IntWWM 90; LegTOT; LinLib L, S; McGEWB; McGEWD 72; MetOEnc; NewAmDM; NewEOp 71; NewGrDA 86; NewGrDO; NewOxM; NewYTBS 74, 85; NotNAT; OxCAmL 65; OxCAmT 84; OxCMus; OxDcOp; PenDiMP A; REn; REnAL; SmATA 29; WebAB 74; Who 74, 82, 83, 85, 88, 90, 92, 94; WhoAm 74, 76, 78, 80, 82, 84, 86, 88, 92, 94, 95, 96, 97; WhoAmM 83; WhoEnt 92; WhoMus 72; WhoWor 74, 76, 78, 87, 89, 91, 93, 95; WorAl; WorAlBi*

Menuhin, Hephzibah
American. Pianist
Played numerous sonata recitals with brother, Yehudi.
b. May 20, 1920 in San Francisco, California
d. Jan 1, 1981 in London, England
Source: *AnObit 1981; Baker 78, 84, 92; BioIn 12, 14; ConAu 108; IntWWM 77, 80; NewGrDM 80; NewYTBS 81; PenDiMP; WhoMus 72*

Menuhin, Yehudi
American. Violinist
Child prodigy, debut with San Francisco Symphony at age seven.
b. Apr 22, 1916 in New York, New York
Source: *Baker 78, 84, 92; BioIn 1, 2, 3, 4, 5, 6, 7, 8, 9, 10, 11, 12, 13, 14, 15, 18; BlueB 76; BriBkM 80; CelR, 90; CmCal; ConAu 2NR, 45; ConMus 11; CurBio 41, 73; DcArts; DcTwCCu 1; FacFETw; IntWW 74, 75, 76, 77, 78, 79, 80, 81, 82, 83, 89, 91, 93; IntWWM 77, 80, 85, 90; LegTOT; LinLib S; MusMk; MusSN; NewAmDM; NewGrDA 86; NewGrDM 80; NewYTBS 76, 81; OxCMus; PenDiMP; SmATA 40; VarWW 85; WebAB 74, 79; Who 74, 82, 83, 85, 88, 90, 92; WhoAm 74, 76, 78, 80, 82, 84, 86, 88, 92, 94, 95, 96, 97; WhoAmJ 80; WhoAmM 83; WhoEnt 92; WhoFr 79; WhoHol 92, A; WhoMus 72; WhoWor 74, 78, 80, 82, 84, 87, 89, 91, 93, 95; WhoWorJ 78; WorAl; WorAlBi; WrDr 80, 82, 84, 86, 88, 90, 92, 94, 96*

Menzel, Jiri
Czech. Director
Won Oscar for best foreign language film *Closely Watched Trains,* 1966.
b. Feb 23, 1938 in Prague
Source: *BioIn 8, 16; ConTFT 12; DcFM; DrEEuF; EncEurC; FilmEn; FilmgC; HalFC 80, 84, 88; IntDcF 1-2, 2-2; IntWW 91, 93; LegTOT; MiSFD 9; OxCFilm; VarWW 85; WhoHol 92; WhoSoCE 89; WhoWor 74, 95, 96, 97; WorEFlm; WorFDir 2*

Menzies, Robert Gordon, Sir
Australian. Politician
Served longest continuous term as Australia's prime minister, 1939-66.
b. Dec 20, 1894 in Jeparit, Australia
d. May 14, 1978 in Melbourne, Australia
Source: *BioIn 1, 2, 4, 5, 6, 7, 8, 9, 11, 12, 13, 20; ConAu 77, 81; CurBio 41, 50; DcNaB 1971; FacFETw; HisWorL; IntWW 74, 75, 76, 77, 78; LinLib S; McGEWB; WhWW-II*

Menzies, William Cameron
American. Designer
Set designer; won Oscars as production designer of *Gone With the Wind,* 1939.
b. Jul 29, 1896 in New Haven, Connecticut
d. Mar 5, 1957 in Beverly Hills, California
Source: *BiDFilm, 81, 94; BioIn 4, 11, 20; ConDes 84; DcArts; DcFM; FilmEn; FilmgC; GangFlm; HalFC 80, 84, 88; IlWWHD 1A; IntDcF 1-4, 2-4; MiSFD 9N; NewEScF; NotNAT B; OxCFilm; WhoHrs 80; WorEFlm*

Mercadante, Saverio
Italian. Composer
Wrote nearly 60 operas including *Elisa e Claudio,* 1821; *Il Giuramento,* 1837.
b. Sep 17, 1795 in Altamura, Italy
d. Dec 17, 1870 in Naples, Italy
Source: *Baker 78, 84; CmOp; DcCom 77; IntDcOp; MetOEnc; NewAmDM; NewEOp 71; NewGrDM 80; OxDcOp; PenDiMP A*

Mercader, Ramon
[Frank Jacson]
Cuban. Assassin
Assassinated Russian leader Leon Trotsky, 1940.
b. 1914
d. Oct 18, 1978 in Havana, Cuba
Source: *BioIn 4, 5, 6, 11; FacFETw; ObitOF 79*

Mercator, Gerhardus
[Gerhard Kremer]
Flemish. Cartographer
Noted for device called mercator projection, 1569; started great *Atlas,* 1578.
b. Mar 5, 1512 in Rupelmonde, Flanders
d. Dec 2, 1594 in Duisburg, Germany
Source: *AsBiEn; McGEWB; NewC; OxCEng 85; REn; WhDW*

Mercer, Beryl
American. Actor
Typically played someone's mother in films 1922-39.
b. Aug 13, 1882 in Seville, Spain
d. Jul 28, 1939 in Santa Monica, California

Source: *EncAFC; Film 2; FilmEn; FilmgC; ForYSC; HalFC 80, 84, 88; HolCA; InWom SUP; MotPP; MovMk; NotNAT B; ThFT; WhoHol B; WhScrn 74, 77, 83; WhThe*

Mercer, David
English. Dramatist, Screenwriter
Won French Film Academy's "Caesar" for screenplay of *Providence,* 1977.
b. Jun 27, 1928 in Wakefield, England
d. Aug 8, 1980 in Haifa, Israel
Source: *AnObit 1980; Au&Wr 71; BioIn 7, 9, 10, 12, 13; BlmGEL; BlueB 76; CamGLE; CamGWoT; CnThe; ConAu 9R, 23NR, 102; ConBrDr; ConDr 73, 77, 82E, 88E, 93; ConLC 5; CroCD; DcArts; DcLB 13; DcLEL 1940; EncWT; Ent; GrWrEL DR; IntDcT 2; MajTwCW; McGEWD 84; NewYTBS 80; OxCEng 85, 95; OxCThe 83; RfGEnL 91; RGTwCWr; Who 74; WhoThe 72, 77, 81; WrDr 76, 80*

Mercer, Henry Chapman
American. Anthropologist
Used ancient findings in unique ways: invented process of printing large designs in color on fabrics, paper, 1904.
b. Jun 24, 1856 in Doylestown, Pennsylvania
d. Mar 9, 1930 in Doylestown, Pennsylvania
Source: *Alli SUP; AmBi; AmLY; ApCAB X; BioIn 10, 11, 13, 15, 16; CenC; DcAmAu; DcAmB; DcNAA; DcTwDes; NatCAB 21; PenDiDA 89; TwCBDA; WhAm 1; WhAmArt 85; WhNAA; WhoAm 74*

Mercer, Johnny
[John H Mercer]
American. Singer, Songwriter
Won Oscars for the lyrics to "On the Atchison," 1946; "Moon River," 1961; wrote "That Old Black Magic," 1942.
b. Nov 18, 1909 in Savannah, Georgia
d. Jun 25, 1976 in Bel Air, California
Source: *AllMusG; AmPS; AmSong; ASCAP 66, 80; Baker 78, 84; BestMus; BiDAmM; BiDJaz; BiE&WWA; BioIn 1, 4, 7, 9, 10, 11, 12, 14, 15, 16, 20; CelR; CmpEPM; ConMus 13; CurBio 48, 76N; EncMT; FilmEn; FilmgC; HalFC 80, 84, 88; IntDcF 1-4, 2-4; IntMPA 75, 76; LegTOT; NewAmDM; NewGrDA 86; NewGrDJ 88, 94; NewYTBS 76; OxCPMus; PenEncP; RadStar; WhAm 7, 8; WhoAm 74, 76, 78, 80; WhoHol A; WhoThe 72, 77; WhScrn 83; WorAl; WorAlBi*

Mercer, Mabel
American. Singer
Gravel-voiced cabaret performer at NYC nightclubs, 1940s-60s; annual Stereo Review award named for her.
b. Feb 1, 1900 in Burton-on-Trent, England
d. Apr 21, 1984 in Pittsfield, Massachusetts
Source: *AnObit 1984; Baker 84, 92; BiDAfM; BiDJaz; BioAmW; BioIn 7, 9, 10, 11, 13, 14, 15; BlkWAm; CelR; CmpEPM; CurBio 73, 84, 84N; DrBlPA, 90; FacFETw; InB&W 80, 85; InWom SUP; LegTOT; NewGrDA 86; NewYTBS 84; NotBlAW 2; OxCPMus; PenEncP; WhoAm 76; WhoAmW 68, 70, 72, 74*

Merchant, Ismail
Indian. Producer
With James Ivory and Ruth Prawer Jhabvala, form the longest creative partnership in film history—over 25 yrs; films include *The Guru, The Europeans, A Room with a View.*
b. Dec 25, 1936 in Bombay, India
Source: *BioIn 15, 16; CelR 90; ConTFT 1, 6, 13; CurBio 93; DcArts; EncEurC; GayLesB; HalFC 88; IntMPA 86, 88, 92, 94, 96; IntWW 89, 91, 93; LegTOT; NotAsAm; Who 82, 83, 85, 88, 90, 92, 94; WhoWor 91*

Merchant, Natalie
[10,000 Maniacs]
American. Singer, Songwriter
Was with 10,000 Maniacs; debut album (with 10,000 Maniacs) *Human Conflict No. 5,* 1982; solo album, *Tigerlily,* 1995.
b. Oct 26, 1963 in Jamestown, New York
Source: *EncRkSt; LegTOT; News 96, 96-3; WhoAmW 97*

Merchant, Vivien
[Ada Thomson]
English. Actor
Starred in *The Homecoming,* 1967; written by ex-husband Harold Pinter.
b. Jul 22, 1929 in Manchester, England
d. Oct 3, 1982 in London, England
Source: *AnObit 1982; BioIn 7, 10, 13, 15; FilmEn; FilmgC; HalFC 80, 84, 88; LegTOT; MotPP; NewYTBS 82; OxCFilm; PlP&P; Who 74, 82; WhoHol A; WhoThe 72, 77, 81*

Mercouri, Melina
[Mrs. Jules Dassin; Maria Amalia Mercouri]
Greek. Actor, Politician
Starred in *Never on Sunday,* 1960; Greece's minister of culture during the 1980s.
b. Oct 18, 1925 in Athens, Greece
d. Mar 6, 1994 in New York, New York
Source: *BioIn 5, 6, 7, 8, 9, 13, 14, 15, 16; BkPepl; CelR, 90; ConAu 106, 144; ContDcW 89; ConTFT 5, 13; CurBio 65, 88, 94N; FilmgC; ForYSC; GoodHs; HalFC 88; IntDcF 1-3, 2-3; IntMPA 84, 86, 88, 92, 94; IntWW 74, 75, 76, 77, 78, 79, 80, 81, 82, 83, 89, 91, 93; InWom, SUP; MotPP; MovMk; NewYTBE 71; NewYTBS 94; OxCFilm; VarWW 85; WhoAm 76, 78, 80, 82; WhoEIO 82; WhoHol A; WhoWor 84, 87, 89, 91; WomFir; WorAl; WorAlBi; WorEFlm*

Mercury, Freddie
[Queen; Frederick Bulsara]
English. Singer, Musician
Formed popular rock group Queen, 1971; hits include "Bohemian Rhapsody," "Another One Bites the Dust."
b. Sep 8, 1946 in Zanzibar, Zanzibar
d. Nov 24, 1991 in Kensington, England
Source: *AnObit 1991; BkPepl; IlEncRk; LegTOT; News 92, 92-2; NewYTBS 91; RkOn 74; WhoRock 81; WhoRocM 82*

Meredith, Burgess
[Oliver Burgess Meredith]
American. Actor
Best known for role in *Rocky* films, 1977-81; played on Broadway in *The Playboy of the Western World,* 1946.
b. Nov 16, 1907 in Cleveland, Ohio
Source: *BiDFilm; BiE&WWA; BioIn 14; ConTFT 4; CurBio 40; EncAFC; EncWT; FilmgC; HalFC 88; HolP 30; IntMPA 92, 96; MotPP; MovMk; NotNAT; OxCAmT 84; OxCFilm; PlP&P; VarWW 85; WhoAm 86, 90; WhoEnt 92; WhoHol A; WhoThe 81; WorAlBi; WorEFlm*

Meredith, Don
[Joseph Donald Meredith]
"Dandy Don"
American. Football Player, Sportscaster
Quarterback, Dallas, 1960-68; with "ABC Monday Night Football," 1970-73, 1977—; w on Emmy, 1972.
b. Apr 10, 1938 in Mount Vernon, Texas
Source: *ConAu 102; ConTFT 1; DrAPF 91; LegTOT; LesBEnT 92; NewYTBS 77; VarWW 85; WhoAm 76, 78, 80, 82, 84, 86; WhoFtbl 74; WorAl; WorAlBi*

Meredith, George
English. Author, Poet
Wrote novel *Ordeal of Richard Feverel,* 1859; tragic poem *Modern Love,* 1862.
b. Feb 2, 1828 in Portsmouth, England
d. May 18, 1909 in Boxhill, England
Source: *Alli, SUP; AtlBL; BbD; Benet 87, 96; BiD&SB; BioIn 1, 2, 3, 4, 5, 7, 8, 9, 10, 11, 12, 13, 14, 16, 18; BlmGEL; BritAu 19; BritWr 5; CamGEL; CamGLE; CasWL; CelCen; Chambr 3; ChhPo, S1, S3; CnDBLB 4; CnE&AP; ConAu 117, 153; CrtT 3, 4; CyEd; CyWA 58; DcArts; DcBiA; DcBiPP; DcEnA, A; DcEnL; DcEuL; DcLB 18, 35, 57, 159; DcLEL; DcNaB S2; Dis&D; EvLB; GrWrEL N, P; LegTOT; LinLib L, S; LngCEL; LngCTC; McGEWB; MouLC 4; NewC; NewCBEL; Novels; OxCEng 67, 85, 95; PenC ENG; RAdv 1, 14, 13-1; REn; RfGEnL 91; ScF&FL 1; StaCVF; TwCLC 17, 43; VicBrit; WebE&AL; WhDW; WhLit; WorAl; WorAlBi*

Meredith, James Howard
American. Civil Rights Leader
Involved in peaceful desegregation of public schools, registering blacks to vote; wrote *Three Years in Mississippi,* 1966.

b. Jun 25, 1933 in Kosciusko, Mississippi
Source: *AmSocL; BioIn 6, 7, 8, 9, 11; ConAu 77; ConHero 1; EncAACR; FacFETw; InB&W 80, 85; LiveMA; WebAB 74, 79; WhoAfA 96; WhoAm 74, 76, 78, 80, 82, 84, 86, 88, 92, 94, 95, 96; WhoBlA 88, 90, 92, 94; WhoWor 74*

Meredith, Scott
American. Businessman
Founded, Scott Meredith Literary Agency, 1946.
b. Nov 24, 1923 in New York, New York
d. Feb 11, 1993 in New York, New York
Source: *AmAu&B; AnObit 1993; BioIn 10, 13; ConAu 3NR, 9R, 140; LesBEnT; NewYTBS 93; WhAm 11; WhoAm 74, 76, 78, 80, 82, 84, 86, 88; WhoE 74, 75, 77, 79, 81; WhoUSWr 88; WhoWor 84, 87, 89; WhoWrEP 89, 92; WrDr 76, 80, 82, 84, 86, 88, 90, 92, 94, 96*

Meredith, Sidney
American. Businessman
Co-founded, Scott Meredith Literary Agency, 1946-82; brother of Scott.
b. 1919? in New York, New York
d. Jul 1, 1992 in Rockville Centre, New York

Merejkowski, Dmitri Sergeyevich
[Dmitry Sergeyevich Merezhovsky]
Russian. Author
Best known for trilogy of novels, *Christ and AntiChrist,* 1895-1905.
b. Aug 14, 1865 in Saint Petersburg, Russia
d. Dec 9, 1941 in Paris, France
Source: *CyWA 58*

Meres, Francis
English. Historian, Critic
Wrote *Palladis Tamia, Wit's Treasury,* 1598, a review of all literary works from Chaucer to his time.
b. Jan 29, 1565 in Kirton, England
d. Jan 29, 1647 in Wing, England
Source: *Alli; BioIn 3; BlmGEL; BritAu; CamGEL; CamGLE; CasWL; Chambr 1; DcEnL; DcEuL; DcLEL; DcNaB; EvLB; LngCEL; NewC; NewCBEL; OxCEng 67, 85, 95; PenC ENG; REn*

Merezhkovsky, Dmitry Sergeyevich
Russian. Author
Wrote *Tolstoy as Man and Artist,* 1902; attacked Bolshevism in *Kingdom of Anti-Christ,* 1922.
b. Aug 2, 1865 in Saint Petersburg, Russia
d. Dec 2, 1941 in Paris, France
Source: *Benet 87, 96; CasWL; ClDMEL 80; DcRusLS; EvEuW; LiExTwC; LngCTC; McGEWB; NewCol 75; PenC EUR; REn; TwCA, SUP; TwCLC 29*

Mergenthaler, Ottmar
American. Inventor
Invented the linotype, 1884.
b. May 11, 1854 in Hachtel, Germany
d. Oct 28, 1899 in Baltimore, Maryland
Source: *AmBi; BioIn 1, 3, 4, 5, 6, 7, 8, 11, 12; DcAmB; EncAB-H 1974, 1996; EncAJ; HarEnUS; InSci; LegTOT; LinLib L, S; McGEWB; NatCAB 9; NewCol 75; OxCAmH; OxCAmL 65, 83, 95; TwCBDA; WebAB 74, 79; WhAm HS; WhDW; WorAl; WorAlBi; WorInv*

Merida, Carlos
Mexican. Artist
Leading abstract expressionist of Mexico; his murals, bas-reliefs, mosaics adorn many important buildings in Mexico City.
b. Dec 2, 1891 in Guatemala City, Guatemala
d. Dec 22, 1984 in Mexico City, Mexico
Source: *ArtLatA; BioIn 5, 9; CurBio 60; DcCAr 81; DcTwCCu 4; IlsBYP; IlsCB 1946; McGDA; OxCTwCA; WhoAmA 73, 76, 78, 80; WhoGrA 62*

Merimee, Prosper
French. Author, Historian, Critic
Wrote *Carmen,* 1846, later made into the famous opera by Bizet.
b. Sep 28, 1803 in Paris, France
d. Sep 23, 1870 in Cannes, France
Source: *AtlBL; BbD; Benet 87, 96; BiD&SB; BioIn 1, 3, 4, 5, 7, 8, 9, 10, 15, 19; CasWL; CelCen; CyWA 58; DcArts; DcBiA; DcBiPP; DcEuL; DcLB 119; Dis&D; EncWT; EuAu; EuWr 6; EvEuW; GuFrLit 1; LegTOT; LinLib L, S; McGEWB; NewC; NewCBEL; NewEOp 71; NewGrDM 80; NewGrDO; NinCLC 6; NotNAT B; Novels; OxCEng 67, 85, 95; OxCFr; OxDcOp; PenC EUR; PenEncH; REn; RfGShF; RfGWoL 95; ShSCr 7; SupFW; WhDW; WorAl; WorAlBi*

Merivale, Philip
English. Actor
Played title role in *Death Takes a Holiday,* 1929.
b. Nov 2, 1880 in Rehutia, India
d. Mar 13, 1946 in Los Angeles, California
Source: *CurBio 46; FilmgC; ForYSC; PlP&P; REn; WhAm 2; WhoHol B; WhScrn 74, 77, 83*

Meriwether, Lee
American. Author
Wrote 1887 best-seller *A Tramp Trip: How to See Europe on Fifty Cents a Day.*
b. Dec 25, 1862 in Columbus, Mississippi
d. Mar 12, 1966 in Saint Louis, Missouri
Source: *Alli SUP; AmAu&B; ApCAB; BiD&SB; BiDSA; BioIn 7; ConAu 116; DcAmAu; LiveMA; NatCAB 10; ScFEYrs; TwCBDA; WhAm 4; WhNAA*

Meriwether, Lee
American. Actor, Beauty Contest Winner
Miss America, 1955; co-star, "Barnaby Jones," 1973-80.
b. May 27, 1935 in Los Angeles, California
Source: *BioIn 12; ConTFT 2; ForYSC; HalFC 80, 84, 88; InWom SUP; LegTOT; VarWW 85; WhoAm 78, 80, 82, 84, 86; WhoEnt 92; WhoHol 92, A; WorAl*

Meriwether, W(ilhelm) Delano
American. Physician
Clinical, research hematologist; NAAU sprinting champ, 1971-72.
b. Apr 23, 1943 in Nashville, Tennessee
Source: *CurBio 78; InB&W 80; NegAl 89; NewYTBS 76; WhoAm 80, 82; WhoBlA 77*

Merkel, Una
American. Actor
Career began in silent films with W C Fields; won Tony for *The Ponder Heart,* 1956.
b. Dec 10, 1903 in Covington, Kentucky
d. Jan 4, 1986 in Los Angeles, California
Source: *AnObit 1986; BiE&WWA; BioIn 9, 14, 21; EncAFC; Film 2; FilmEn; FilmgC; ForYSC; HalFC 80, 84, 88; HolCA; IntDcF 1-3; IntMPA 75, 76, 77, 78, 79, 80, 81, 82, 84, 86; InWom SUP; LegTOT; MGM; MotPP; MovMk; NewYTBS 86; NotNAT; OlFamFa; QDrFCA 92; ThFT; VarWW 85; Vers A; What 3; WhoHol A; WhoThe 77A; WhThe*

Merman, Ethel
[Ethel Agnes Zimmerman]
American. Singer, Actor
Starred on Broadway in *Annie Get Your Gun,* 1946; *Hello, Dolly,* 1970.
b. Jan 16, 1909 in Astoria, New York
d. Feb 15, 1984 in New York, New York
Source: *BiDAmM; BiE&WWA; BioIn 1, 2, 3, 4, 5, 6, 7, 9, 10, 11, 12, 13; BioNews 75; CamGWoT; CelR; CmMov; CmpEPM; CnThe; ConTFT 1; CurBio 41, 55, 84N; EncAFC; EncMT; EncWT; Ent; FacFETw; FamA&A; FilmEn; FilmgC; ForYSC; GoodHs; IntMPA 75, 76, 77, 78, 79, 80, 81, 82, 84; LibW; MovMk; NewAmDM; NotNAT, A; NotWoAT; OxCPMus; OxCThe 83; PenEncP; RadStar; VarWW 85; WebAB 74, 79; WhAm 8; WhoAm 74, 76, 78, 80, 82; WhoAmW 58, 64, 66, 68, 70, 72, 74, 83; WhoHol A; WhoThe 72, 77, 81; WhoWor 74; WorAl; WorAlBi*

Merola, Gaetano
Italian. Conductor
Founder, director, San Francisco Opera, 1923-53.
b. Jan 4, 1881 in Naples, Italy
d. Aug 30, 1953 in San Francisco, California
Source: *Baker 78, 84, 92; BiDAmM; BioIn 3, 9; CmCal; MetOEnc;*

NewAmDM; NewEOp 71; NewGrDA 86; NewGrDO; OxDcOp; WhAm 6

Merriam, Charles
American. Publisher
With brother George founded G & C Merriam Co., 1832; published first Merriam-Webster dictionary, 1847.
b. Nov 1806 in West Brookfield, Massachusetts
d. Jul 9, 1887 in Springfield, Massachusetts
Source: *AmAu&B; ApCAB; DcAmB; TwCBDA; WebAB 74, 79; WhAm HS*

Merriam, Clinton Hart
American. Naturalist, Author
Founder, chief of US Biological Service, 1885-1910.
b. Feb 5, 1855 in New York, New York
d. Mar 19, 1942 in Berkeley, California
Source: *Alli SUP; AmAu&B; ApCAB SUP; BioIn 1, 3, 10; CurBio 42; DcAmAu; DcAmB S3; DcNAA; DcScB; InSci; NatCAB 13; NatLAC; TwCBDA; WebBD 83; WhAm 2*

Merriam, Eve
American. Author, Poet
Wrote books for children and adults; poetry books include *It Doesn't Always Have to Rhyme,* 1964; won an Obie, 1976.
b. Jul 19, 1916 in Philadelphia, Pennsylvania
d. Apr 11, 1992 in Cartagena, Colombia
Source: *AmAu&B; AmWomD; AmWomWr SUP; AnObit 1992; ArtclWW 2; AuBYP 2, 3; BioIn 1, 8, 9, 12, 13, 15, 16, 17, 18, 19; BkP; BlkAmP; ChhPo, S1, S2, S3; ChlBkCr; ChlLR 14; ConAu 5R, 29NR, 137; ConTFT 1; DcLB 61; DrAP 75; DrAPF 80; ForWC 70; InWom SUP; MajAI; OxCChiL; ScF&FL 92; SmATA 3, 40, 73; ThrBJA; TwCChW 78, 83, 89; TwCYAW; WhoAm 74, 76, 78, 80, 82, 84; WhoAmW 66, 68, 70, 72, 74, 75, 77, 81; WhoE 74; WhoUSWr 88; WhoWrEP 89, 92, 95; WrDr 80, 82, 84, 86, 88, 90, 92, 94N*

Merriam, Frank Finley
American. Politician
Defeated Upton Sinclair in nasty battle for governorship of CA, 1934-38.
b. Dec 22, 1865 in Delaware County, Iowa
d. Apr 25, 1955 in Long Beach, California
Source: *BiDrGov 1789; BioIn 1, 3, 5, 7; CmCal; NatCAB 42; ObitOF 79; WhAm 3*

Merrick, David
[David Margulois]
American. Producer
Plays include *Fanny,* 1954; *Gypsy,* 1958; *Promises, Promises,* 1969; and *Oh, Kay!,* 1990.
b. Nov 27, 1912 in Saint Louis, Missouri
Source: *BiE&WWA; BioIn 13, 15, 17, 18, 19; BioNews 74; CamGWoT; CelR, 90; ConTFT 6; CurBio 61; EncMT; HalFC 88; IntMPA 84, 86, 88, 92, 94, 96; IntWW 74, 77, 78, 79, 80, 81, 82, 83, 89, 91, 93; LegTOT; NewYTBE 70, 73; NewYTBS 86; OxCAmT 84; VarWW 85; WebAB 74, 79; WhoAm 76, 78, 80, 82, 84, 86, 88, 92, 94, 95, 96, 97; WhoE 85, 86, 89, 91; WhoEnt 92; WhoThe 77, 81; WhoWor 74, 78; WorAl; WorAlBi*

Merrick, Joseph Carey
"Elephant Man"
English.
Grotesquely disfigured man whose life was basis for play, movie *The Elephant Man.*
b. Aug 5, 1862 in Leicester, England
d. Apr 11, 1890 in London, England
Source: *BioIn 15, 19; DcNaB MP; OxCMed 86*

Merrifield, R(obert) Bruce
American. Biochemist
Won Nobel Prize for new method of manufacturing proteins in lab, 1984.
b. Jul 5, 1921 in Fort Worth, Texas
Source: *AmMWSc 73P, 76P, 79, 82, 86, 89, 92, 95; BioIn 9, 14, 15; CurBio 85; NewYTBS 84; NobelP; Who 88, 90, 92, 94; WhoAm 74, 76, 78, 80, 82, 84, 86, 88, 90, 92, 94, 95, 96, 97; WhoE 86, 89, 91, 93, 95, 97; WhoFrS 84; WhoNob, 90, 95; WhoScEn 94, 96; WhoWor 87, 89, 91, 93, 95, 96, 97; WorAlBi*

Merrill, Charles Edward
American. Business Executive
Founded Merrill, Lynch, Pierce, Fenner & Beane (now Smith), 1914.
b. Oct 19, 1885 in Green Cove, Florida
d. Oct 6, 1956 in Southampton, New York
Source: *BiDAmBL 83; BioIn 1, 2, 3, 4, 9, 10, 17, 21; CurBio 56; DcAmB S6; NatCAB 53; WhAm 3; WorAl*

Merrill, Dina
[Nedinia Hutton]
American. Actor
Daughter of E F Hutton and Marjorie Merriweather Post; made film debut, 1957.
b. Dec 29, 1925 in New York, New York
Source: *BioIn 14; CelR 90; ConTFT 8, 15; EncAFC; FilmEn; FilmgC; HalFC 88; IntMPA 77, 78, 79, 80, 81, 82, 84, 86, 88, 92; InWom, SUP; LegTOT; MotPP; MovMk; VarWW 85; WhoAm 86; WhoAmW 85; WhoEnt 92; WhoHol 92; WorAl*

Merrill, Frank Dow
American. Army Officer
Organized WW II volunteer regiment, "Merrill's Marauders," designed for jungle combat, 1943.
b. Dec 4, 1903
d. Dec 11, 1955 in Fernandina, Florida
Source: *BiDWWGF; BioIn 1, 4, 6, 13; DcAmB S5; HarEnMi; NatCAB 46; ObitOF 79; WebAMB; WhAm 3*

Merrill, Gary Franklin
American. Actor
Acting career spanned 50 years; best known for marriage to Bette Davis, 1950-60; starred with her in *All About Eve,* 1950.
b. Aug 2, 1914 in Hartford, Connecticut
d. Mar 6, 1990 in Falmouth, Maine
Source: *AnObit 1990; BiE&WWA; BioIn 16; ConAu 131; FilmgC; HalFC 88; IntMPA 82, 88; MotPP; MovMk; NewYTBS 90; NotNAT; VarWW 85; WhoAm 82; WhoHol A; WorAlBi*

Merrill, Henry Tindall
"Dick"
American. Pilot
Made first round-trip trans-Atlantic flight, 1936.
b. 1894? in Iuka, Mississippi
d. Nov 30, 1982 in Lake Elsinore, California
Source: *InSci; NewYTBS 82*

Merrill, James (Ingram)
American. Poet
Won Pulitzer for *Divine Comedies,* 1976; son of Charles.
b. Mar 3, 1926 in New York, New York
d. Feb 6, 1995 in Tucson, Arizona
Source: *AmAu&B; AmMWSc 92; AmWr S3; Benet 87, 96; BenetAL 91; BioIn 4, 8, 9, 10, 11, 12, 13; CamGLE; CamHAL; ConAu 10NR, 13R, 49NR, 147; ConGAN; ConLC 2, 3, 6, 8, 13, 18, 34, 91; ConPo 70, 75, 80, 85, 91; CroCAP; CurBio 81, 95N; DcLB 5, 165, Y85A; DcLEL 1940; DrAF 76; DrAP 75; DrAPF 89; EncWL 2, 3; FacFETw; GayLL; GrWrEL P; IntWW 89, 91, 93; IntWWP 77; LegTOT; MagSAmL; MajTwCW; ModAL, S1, S2; News 95, 95-3; NewYTBS 95; OxCAmL 65, 83, 95; OxCTwCP; PenC AM; PeoHis; REnAL; RfGAmL 87, 94; RGTwCWr; WhoAm 74, 76, 78, 80, 82, 84, 86, 88, 90, 92, 94, 95; WhoE 74, 79, 81, 83, 85, 86, 89; WhoUSWr 88; WhoWor 74; WhoWrEP 89, 92, 95; WorAu 1950; WrDr 76, 80, 82, 84, 86, 88, 90, 92, 94, 96*

Merrill, John Putnam
American. Physician, Surgeon
Led 1954 medical team which did first successful organ transplant from one human to another.
b. Mar 10, 1917 in Hartford, Connecticut
d. Apr 4, 1984, Bahamas
Source: *AmMWSc 73P, 76P, 79, 82, 86, 89, 92; BiDrACP 79; BioIn 13, 14; NewYTBS 84; WhAm 8; WhoAm 82; WhoE 74, 75; WhoWor 82*

Merrill, Robert
American. Opera Singer
Baritone who became first American to sing 500 performances at NY Met., 1973.
b. Jun 4, 1919 in New York, New York
Source: *Baker 84; BiDAmM; BioIn 1, 2, 3, 4, 5, 7, 9, 10, 11, 13; BlueB 76; CelR, 90; CmpEPM; ConAu 81; IntWW 74, 75, 76, 77, 78, 79, 80, 81, 82, 83, 89, 91,*

93; IntWWM 77, 80, 90; MetOEnc; NewAmDM; NewEOp 71; NewGrDA 86; NewGrDM 80; PenDiMP; RadStar; VarWW 85; WhoAm 74, 76, 78, 80, 82, 84, 86, 88, 90, 92, 94, 95, 96, 97; WhoAmM 83; WhoEnt 92; WhoGov 72, 75, 77; WhoHol 92; WhoMus 72; WhoOp 76; WhoWor 74, 78, 80, 82, 84, 87, 89; WorAl; WorAlBi

Merrill, Steve
[Steven Merrill]
American. Politician
Rep. governor, NH, 1993-96.
b. Jun 21, 1946 in Connecticut
Source: *AlmAP 96; WhoAmP 89, 91, 93*

Merriman, Nan
American. Opera Singer
Mezzo-soprano; soloed with Toscanini on broadcasts, recordings, 1940s.
b. Apr 28, 1920 in Pittsburgh, Pennsylvania
Source: *Baker 78, 84, 92; CmOp; IntDcOp; IntWWM 77, 80, 90; MetOEnc; NewAmDM; NewGrDA 86; NewGrDM 80; NewGrDO; OxDcOp; RadStar; WhoAmW 66, 68, 70, 72, 74*

Merritt, Abraham
American. Author
Edited *The American Weekly,* 1937-43.
b. Jan 20, 1884 in Beverly, New Jersey
d. Aug 30, 1943 in Clearwater, Florida
Source: *AmAu&B; BioIn 7, 10, 12; ConAu 120; DcNAA; FacFETw; NatCAB 32; Novels; REnAL; ScFSB; WhAm 2; WhE&EA; WhoSciF; WorAu 1950*

Merritt, Hiram Houston
American. Neurologist
Co-developed Dilantin, anti-epilepsy drug.
b. Jan 2, 1902 in Wilmington, North Carolina
d. Jan 9, 1979 in New York, New York
Source: *BiDrAPA 77; BioIn 7, 11, 13; DcNCBi 4; WhAm 7, 8; WhoAm 74, 76, 78, 80*

Merritt, Wesley
American. Military Leader
Led first US Philippine expedition; occupied Manila in Spanish-American War, 1898.
b. Jun 16, 1836 in New York, New York
d. Dec 3, 1910 in Natural Bridge, Virginia
Source: *AmBi; ApCAB; DcAmB; DcAmMiB; Drake; HarEnUS; NatCAB 9; TwCBDA; WebAMB; WhAm 1*

Merton, Robert King
American. Sociologist
Noted for work in the sociology of science and theory; books include *Social Theory and Social Structure,* 1949.
b. Jul 5, 1910 in Philadelphia, Pennsylvania
Source: *AmAu&B; AmMWSc 92; BioIn 5, 7, 14, 15, 16; ConAu 31NR; EncAB-H 1974, 1996; EncWB; IntAu&W 91; IntWW 91; RAdv 13-3; ThTwC 87; WebAB 74, 79; WhoAm 90; WhoUSWr 88; WhoWrEP 89; WrDr 92*

Merton, Thomas
[Father M Louis]
American. Poet, Author
Celebrated Trappist monk; wrote autobiography *Seven Storey Mountain,* 1948.
b. Jan 31, 1915 in Prades, France
d. Dec 10, 1968 in Bangkok, Thailand
Source: *AmAu&B; AmPeW; Benet 87, 96; BenetAL 91; BiDConC; BiDMoPL; BioIn 1, 2, 3, 4, 5, 8, 9, 10, 11, 12, 13, 14, 15, 16, 17, 18, 19, 20, 21; CathA 1930; ConAu 5R, 22NR, 25R, 53NR; ConLC 1, 3, 11, 34, 83; CyWA 89; DcAmB S8; DcAmReB 1, 2; DcLB 48, Y81B; EncARH; EncWB; FacFETw; IlEncMy; LegTOT; LinLib L, S; LngCTC; MajTwCW; MakMC; ModAL; OxCAmL 65, 83, 95; OxCTwCP; PenC AM; PoeCrit 10; RadHan; RAdv 14, 13-4; REnAL; TwCA SUP; WebAB 74, 79; WhAm 5; WrPh*

Mertz, Barbara Louise Gross
[Barbara Michaels; Elizabeth Peters]
American. Author
Writes Gothic romances: *Patriot's Dream,* 1976.
b. Sep 29, 1927 in Canton, Illinois
Source: *Au&Wr 71; BestSel 90-4; BioIn 11, 14, 15, 16, 21; ConAu 11NR, 21R, 36NR, 57; CrtSuMy; DcLP 87A; DrAS 74H; GrWomMW; IntAu&W 91, 93; LegTOT; PenNWW A; ScF&FL 1, 2, 92; SmATA 49; TwCCr&M 80, 85, 91; TwCRGW; TwCRHW 90, 94; WrDr 76, 80, 84, 86, 88, 90, 92, 94, 96*

Merwin, W(illiam) S(tanley)
American. Poet
Won Pulitzer for collection, *The Carrier of the Ladders,* 1971.
b. Sep 30, 1927 in New York, New York
Source: *AmAu&B; Benet 87, 96; BenetAL 91; BioIn 8, 10, 12, 13, 15, 16, 17, 19, 20; CamGLE; CamHAL; CasWL; ChhPo S2; CnE&AP; ConAu 13R, 15NR, 51NR; ConLC 1, 2, 3, 5, 8, 13, 18, 45, 88; ConPo 70, 75, 85, 91, 96; CroCAP; CurBio 88; CyWA 89; DcLB 5; DcLEL 1940; DrAF 76; DrAP 75; DrAPF 91; EncWL 3; IntvTCA 2; MajTwCW; ModAL, S1, S2; OxCAmL 65, 95; OxCTwCP; PenC AM; RAdv 1, 14, 13-1; RfGAmL 87, 94; RGTwCWr; WebE&AL; WhoAm 74, 76, 78, 80, 82, 84, 86, 88, 94, 95, 96; WhoE 74; WhoTwCL; WorAu 1950; WrDr 76, 86, 92, 94, 96*

Meselson, Matthew Stanley
American. Biologist
Molecular biologist known for his research on the Watson-Crick theory of DNA structure.
b. May 24, 1930 in Denver, Colorado
Source: *AmMWSc 73P, 76P, 79, 82, 86, 89, 92; BiESc; BioIn 13, 14, 15; IntWW 74, 75, 76, 77, 78, 79, 80, 81, 82, 83, 89, 91, 93; LarDcSc; McGMS 80; WhoAm 74, 76, 78, 80, 82, 84, 86, 88, 90, 92, 94, 95, 96; WhoE 74, 93; WhoFrS 84; WhoScEn 94, 96; WhoTech 89; WhoWor 74; WorScD*

Me'Shell Ndegeocello
[Michelle Johnson]
German. Singer, Songwriter
Funk and R & B singer; released first album in 1993, *Plantation Lullabies,* which included song "If That's Your Boyfriend (He Wasn't Last Night);" later recorded *Peace Beyond Passion,* 1996; received Gibson Guitar Award for best bass player, 1996.
b. Aug 29, 1968 in Berlin, Germany

Meskill, Thomas J
American. Judge, Politician
First Rep. elected governor in 16 yrs., 1971-75; US Circuit Court judge, 1975—; chief judge, 1992-93.
b. Jan 30, 1928 in New Britain, Connecticut
Source: *BiDrUSC 89; BioIn 10; CurBio 74; IntWW 83, 91; WhoAm 86, 90; WhoAmL 92; WhoAmP 85, 91; WhoE 89*

Mesmer, Franz Anton
German. Physician
Used magnetism and hypnotism in treating diseases.
b. May 23, 1734 in Baden-Baden, Germany
d. Mar 5, 1815 in Merseburg, Germany
Source: *AsBiEn; BiDPara; BiDPsy; BiESc; BioIn 19; BlkwCE; DcScB; DrInf; EncEnl; McGEWB; NamesHP; OxCGer 76, 86; OxCMed 86; REn; WorAl; WorAlBi*

Messager, Andre Charles Prosper
French. Composer, Conductor
Director, Paris Opera-Comique, early 1900s; noted Wagnerian conductor; wrote operas including *Beatrice,* 1914.
b. Dec 30, 1853 in Montlucon, France
d. Feb 24, 1929 in Paris, France
Source: *Baker 84, 92; BioIn 4; DcArts; NewEOp 71; NewGrDO; OxCMus*

Messel, Oliver
English. Designer, Artist
Designed for films including *The Sleeping Beauty,* 1946; *The Magic Flute,* 1947.
b. Jan 13, 1905 in London, England
d. Jul 14, 1978 in Bridgetown, Barbados
Source: *BiDD; BioIn 6, 11, 12; CamGWoT; CnOxB; CnThe; DancEn 78; EncWT; Ent; IntDcB; MetOEnc; NewYTBS 78; NotNAT; ObitOF 79; OxCThe 67; WhoOp 76; WhoThe 72, 77*

Messerschmitt, Willy
[Wilhelm Messerschmitt]
German. Aircraft Designer
Developed Me-109 fighter plane used during WW II; Me-262, first jet liner used in military.

b. Jun 26, 1898 in Augsburg, Germany
d. Sep 15, 1978 in Munich, Germany
Source: *BioIn 2, 3, 10, 11, 14; CurBio 40, 78, 78N; EncTR, 91; FacFETw; HisEWW; InSci; IntWW 74, 75, 76, 77, 78; LegTOT; LinLib S; ObitOF 79; WhoWor 74; WorAl; WorAlBi*

Messersmith, Andy
[John Alexander Messersmith]
American. Baseball Player
Pitcher, 1968-79; part of arbitrator rule, 1973 (with Dave McNally), that allowed players who perform one season without a signed contract to become free agent, sell services to highest bidder.
b. Aug 6, 1945 in Toms River, New Jersey
Source: *Ballpl 90; BiDAmSp Sup; BioIn 8; NewYTBE 73; WhoAm 78, 80; WhoProB 73*

Messiaen, Olivier (Eugene Prosper Charles)
French. Composer, Musician
His music glorifying beauty of UT resulting in mountain named for him, 1978; studies bird songs.
b. Dec 10, 1908 in Avignon, France
d. Apr 28, 1992 in Paris, France
Source: *AnObit 1992; Baker 78, 84, 92; Benet 96; BioIn 1, 2, 3, 4, 7, 8, 9, 10, 11, 12, 14, 15; BriBkM 80; CnOxB; CompSN, SUP; ConCom 92; CurBio 74, 92N; DcArts; DcCM; DcCom 77; DcCom&M 79; DcTwCCu 2; FacFETw; IlEncMy; IntDcOp; IntWW 74, 75, 76, 77, 78, 79, 80, 81, 82, 83, 89, 91; IntWWM 77, 80, 90; LegTOT; MakMC; McGEWB; MetOEnc; MusMk; NewAmDM; NewGrDM 80; NewGrDO; NewOxM; NewYTBS 92; OxCMus; OxDcOp; PenDiMP A; PenEncH; WhAm 10; WhDW; Who 82, 83, 85, 88, 90, 92; WhoFr 79; WhoMus 72; WhoWor 76, 78, 82, 84, 87, 89, 91*

Messick, Dale
American. Cartoonist
Created popular comic strip "Brenda Starr, Reporter," 1940.
b. 1906 in South Bend, Indiana
Source: *BioIn 5, 6, 10, 16, 17; CurBio 61; EncACom; EncTwCJ; InWom, SUP; LegTOT; LibW; SmATA 48, 64; WhoAm 74, 76, 78, 80, 82, 84; WhoAmA 76, 78, 80, 82, 84, 86, 89, 91, 93; WhoAmW 64, 66, 68, 72, 81, 83; WomFir; WorECom*

Messick, Henry Hicks
American. Journalist, Author
Investigative reporter specializing in organized crime; wrote *Of Grass & Snow: The Secret Criminal Life,* 1979.
b. Aug 14, 1922 in Happy Valley, North Carolina
Source: *BiDAmNC; ConAu 2NR, 45*

Messier, Mark (Douglas)
"Mess"; "Moose"; "The Terminator"
Canadian. Hockey Player
Left wing, Edmonton, 1979-91; NY Rangers, 1991-97; Vancouver, 1997— ; won Conn Smythe Trophy, 1984, Hart Trophy as MVP, 1989-90, 1991-92; played on six Stanley Cup teams.
b. Jan 18, 1961 in Edmonton, Alberta, Canada
Source: *BioIn 13, 16, 20, 21; CurBio 95; HocEn; HocReg 87; News 93-1; NewYTBS 92; WhoAm 90, 92, 94, 95, 96, 97; WhoWest 92; WhoWor 96*

Messina, Jim
[Buffalo Springfield; Loggins and Messina; Poco]
American. Singer, Songwriter
Bass player, vocalist; directed Buffalo Springfield at age 19; part of Loggins and Messina, 1972-77.
b. Dec 5, 1947 in Maywood, California
Source: *ASCAP 80; BioIn 12, 16; LegTOT; WorAl; WorAlBi*

Messing, Shep
American. Soccer Player
Goalie in NASL, 1973-79; had goals against average of under two per game.
b. Oct 9, 1949 in New York, New York
Source: *BioIn 11; ConAu 111; NewYTBE 72*

Messmer, Otto
American. Cartoonist
Created "Felix the Cat," 1919; featured in over 300 shorts, 1920s-30s.
b. Aug 16, 1892 in Union City, New Jersey
d. Oct 28, 1983 in Teaneck, New Jersey
Source: *ConAu 111; EncACom; IntDcF 2-4; NewYTBS 83; SmATA 37; WorECar*

Messner, Reinhold
Italian. Mountaineer, Author
First person to reach summit of Mt. Everest without artificial oxygen, May, 1978.
b. Sep 17, 1944 in Bressanone, Italy
Source: *BioIn 11, 12, 15, 17, 19; ConAu 15NR, 35NR, 81; CurBio 80; IntAu&W 77, 82*

Messner, Tammy Faye
American. Evangelist
Was married to evangelist Jim Bakker. Both were forced out as a result of a scandal involving their PTL ministry, 1987.
b. Mar 7, 1942? in International Falls, Minnesota
Source: *BioIn 15, 16; ConAu 128; PrimTiR; RelLAm 91; TwCSAPR*

Mesta, Perle Skirvin
American. Diplomat
Ambassador to Luxembourg, 1949-53; known for parties given for political leaders.
b. Oct 12, 1891 in Sturgis, Michigan
d. Mar 16, 1975 in Oklahoma City, Oklahoma
Source: *BioNews 74; ConAu 57; DcAmDH 80, 89; WhAm 6; WhoAm 74; WhoWor 74*

Mestrovic, Ivan
American. Sculptor
First living artist to have one-man show at NYC's Met. Museum, 1947.
b. Aug 15, 1883 in Vrpolje, Croatia
d. Jan 16, 1962 in South Bend, Indiana
Source: *BioIn 1, 2, 3, 4, 5, 6, 9, 10, 15; ConArt 77, 83; CurBio 40, 62; DcAmB S7; DcArts; DcCAA 71, 77; LegTOT; LinLib S; McGDA; ObitT 1961; OxCTwCA; OxDcArt; PhDcTCA 77; WhAm 4*

Metalious, Grace de Repentigny
American. Author
Wrote *Peyton Place,* 1956; adapted into movie and TV series.
b. Sep 8, 1924 in Manchester, New Hampshire
d. Feb 25, 1964 in Boston, Massachusetts
Source: *AmAu&B; ConAu P-2; LngCTC; TwCWr*

Metallica
American. Music Group
Formed, 1981; heavy metal albums include *.And Justice for All,* 1988; have won 2 Grammys.
Source: *ConMus 7; EncRkSt*

Metastasio, Pietro
[Pietro Armando Dominico Trapassi]
Italian. Dramatist, Poet, Librettist
Viennese court poet, from 1729; wrote librettos for many operas, melodramas including *Attilio Regolo,* 1750.
b. Jan 3, 1698 in Rome, Italy
d. Apr 12, 1782 in Vienna, Austria
Source: *AtlBL; Baker 84, 92; Benet 96; BiD&SB; BlkwCE; BriBkM 80; CamGWoT; CasWL; CmOp; CnThe; DcEuL; DcItL 1, 2; Ent; EuAu; EvEuW; IntDcOp; McGEWD 72, 84; MetOEnc; NewAmDM; NewC; NewCBEL; NewEOp 71; NewGrDM 80; NewOxM; OxCEng 67; OxDcOp; PenC EUR; REn; REnWD; RfGWoL 95*

Metaxas, John
[Ioannis Metaxas]
Greek. Political Leader
Dictator of Greece, 1936-41, who led country into WW II against Germany, Italy.
b. Apr 12, 1871 in Cephalonia, Greece
d. Jan 29, 1941 in Athens, Greece
Source: *BiDExR; BioIn 1; CurBio 40, 41; DcTwHis; DicTyr; EncTR 91; HisEWW; LinLib S; WhWW-II; WorAlBi*

Metcalf, Laurie
American. Actor
Film debut in *Desperately Seeking Susan,* 1985; played Jackie in TV

series "Roseanne," 1988-97; Emmy award winner, 1993, 1994.
b. Jun 15, 1955 in Edwardsville, Illinois
Source: *BioIn 14, 15, 16; ConTFT 7, 15; IntMPA 92, 94, 96; LegTOT; NewYTBS 87; WhoAm 94, 95, 96, 97; WhoAmW 95, 97; WhoHol 92*

Metcalf, Lee
American. Politician
Dem. senator from MT, 1961-78; advocated conservation.
b. Jan 28, 1911 in Stevensville, Montana
d. Jan 12, 1978 in Helena, Montana
Source: *AlmAP 78; AuSpks; BiDrAC; BioIn 5, 7, 8, 9, 10, 11, 12; BlueB 76; CngDr 74, 77; CurBio 70, 78, 78N; IntWW 74, 75, 76, 77; NewYTBS 78; PolProf E, J, K, NF; WhAm 7; WhoAm 74, 76, 78; WhoAmP 73, 75, 77; WhoGov 72, 75, 77; WhoWest 76, 78*

Metcalf, Willard Leroy
American. Artist
Landscape, figure painter; *Family of Birches.*
b. Jul 1, 1858 in Lowell, Massachusetts
d. Mar 9, 1925 in New York, New York
Source: *AmBi; ArtsAmW 1; BioIn 14, 16, 19, 20; DcAmArt; DcAmB; IlBEAAW; NatCAB 13, 31; WhAm 1*

Metcalfe, Ralph H
American. Track Athlete, Politician
Dem. congressman from IL, 1970-78; founding member, Congressional Black Caucus; finished second behind Jesse Owens in 100-meters, 1936 Olympics.
b. May 30, 1910 in Atlanta, Georgia
d. Oct 10, 1978 in Chicago, Illinois
Source: *AlmAP 78; BioIn 11; CivR 74; CngDr 74, 77; Ebony 1; NewYTBS 78; ObitOF 79; WhAm 7; WhoAm 74, 76, 78; WhoAmP 73; WhoBlA 75, 77; WhoGov 72, 75, 77; WhoMW 74, 76, 78; WhoTr&F 73*

Metchnikoff, Elie
[Ilya Ilyich Mechnikov]
Russian. Biologist
Discovered white blood cells destroyed harmful bacteria in bloodstream; won Nobel Prize, 1908.
b. May 15, 1845 in Ivanovka, Russia
d. Jul 16, 1916 in Paris, France
Source: *AsBiEn; BiESc; BiHiMed; BioIn 17, 18, 20, 21; DcScB; InSci; InWom SUP; LarDcSc; LngCTC; McGEWB; NewCol 75; NotTwCS; OxCMed 86; WhoNob, 90, 95; WorAl; WorAlBi; WorScD*

Meters, The
[Joseph Modeliste; Art Neville; Leo Nocentelli; George Porter]
American. Music Group
Off-beat funk hits include "Sophisticated Sissy," 1968.
Source: *Alli SUP; BioIn 3, 16, 17; ConMus 14; DcNaB; DcTwCCu 5; EncPR&S 89; EncRk 88; HarEnR 86; IlEncRk; IlsBYP; NewGrDA 86; RkOn 78, 84; RolSEnR 83; SoulM; WhoAm 92, 94, 95, 96, 97; WhoEnt 92; WhoRock 81; WhoRocM 82; WhoScEu 91-1*

Metheny, Pat(rick Bruce)
American. Jazz Musician
Innovative fusion-style guitarist; characteristic melodic approach, exotic rhythms apparent in Grammy-winning *Offramp,* 1982.
b. Aug 12, 1954 in Lee's Summit, Missouri
Source: *AllMusG; Baker 92; BioIn 11, 12, 13, 14, 15, 16; ConMus 2; ConTFT 12; CurBio 96; NewAgMG; NewAmDM; NewGrDA 86; NewGrDJ 88, 94; OnThGG; PenEncP; WhoAm 82, 84, 86, 88, 90, 92, 94, 95, 96, 97; WhoEnt 92*

Methuselah
Biblical Figure
According to Old Testament, lived 969 yrs; descendant of Seth, son of Enoch; name mentioned to suggest great age.
Source: *Benet 96; Dis&D; LngCEL; NewCol 75*

Metrano, Art
American. Actor
Played Lieutenant Mauser in two *Police Academy* films, 1985, 1986; star of one-man play *Twice Blessed,* based on own story of breaking his neck in 1989.
b. Sep 22, 1937 in New York, New York
Source: *BioIn 9; ConTFT 5; HalFC 88; WhoEnt 92; WhoHol 92*

Metrinko, Michael John
[The Hostages]
American. Hostage
One of 52 held by terrorists, Nov 1979-Jan 1981.
b. Nov 11, 1946 in Pennsylvania
Source: *BioIn 12; NewYTBS 81; USBiR 74*

Metternich-Winneburg, Clemens
Austrian. Statesman
Austrian foreign minister, 1809-48, forced into exile by revolution.
b. May 15, 1773 in Koblenz, Germany
d. Jun 11, 1859 in Vienna, Austria
Source: *BioIn 1, 2, 3, 4, 5, 6, 7, 8, 9, 10, 12, 13; DcEuL; OxCFr; SpyCS*

Metzenbaum, Howard M(orton)
American. Politician
Dem. senator from OH, 1974, 1977-95.
b. Jun 4, 1917 in Cleveland, Ohio
Source: *AlmAP 88, 92; BiDrUSC 89; BioIn 13, 14, 15; CngDr 89; CurBio 80; IntWW 77, 78, 79, 80, 81, 82, 83, 89, 91, 93; NewYTBS 91; PolsAm 84; St&PR 75; WhoAm 74, 76, 78, 80, 82, 84, 86, 88, 90, 92, 94, 95, 96, 97; WhoAmJ 80; WhoAmP 73, 75, 77, 79, 81, 83, 85, 87, 89, 91, 93, 95; WhoMW 80, 82, 84, 86, 88, 90, 92, 93, 96; WhoWor 80, 82, 84, 87, 89, 91*

Metzinger, Jean
French. Artist
Early cubist who co-wrote text: *Du cubisme,* 1912.
b. 1883 in Nantes, France
d. Nov 3, 1956 in Paris, France
Source: *BioIn 4, 5, 14, 17; ClaDrA; ConArt 77; DcTwCCu 2; McGDA; NewCol 75; OxCArt; OxCTwCA; OxDcArt; PhDcTCA 77*

Mew, Charlotte Mary
English. Poet
Wrote verse volumes *The Farmer's Bride,* 1916; *The Rambling Sailor,* 1929.
b. Nov 15, 1869 in London, England
d. Mar 24, 1928 in London, England
Source: *ArtclWW 2; BioIn 1, 2, 5, 9, 12, 13, 14, 16, 18, 20, 21; Chambr 3; ChhPo, S1; ContDcW 89; DcLB 19; DcLEL; DcNaB, 1922; EvLB; GrWrEL P; IntDcWB; InWom SUP; LngCTC; ModBrL; NewC; NewCBEL; OxCEng 85, 95; PenC ENG; REn; RGTwCWr; TwCA, SUP; TwCLC 8*

Meyer, Debbie
[Deborah Meyer]
American. Swimmer
First to win three gold medals in individual events in Olympics, 1968.
b. Aug 14, 1952 in Annapolis, Maryland
Source: *BiDAmSp BK; BioIn 8, 9, 10, 11; CmCal; EncWomS; GoodHs; InWom SUP; LegTOT; WhoSpor; WorAl; WorAlBi*

Meyer, Joseph
American. Composer
Wrote songs "If You Knew Susie," 1925; "Crazy Rhythm," 1928.
b. Mar 12, 1894 in Modesto, California
d. Sep 24, 1987 in New York, New York
Source: *AmPS; ASCAP 66, 80; BiDAmM; BioIn 11, 15, 16; CmpEPM; EncMT; NewAmDM; OxCPMus; PopAmC; Sw&Ld C*

Meyer, Nicholas
American. Screenwriter, Director
Wrote *Seven-Per-Cent Solution,* 1974; directed *Star Trek II,* 1982.
b. Dec 24, 1945 in New York, New York
Source: *BioIn 13, 14; ConAu 7NR, 49; ConTFT 1, 14; HalFC 84, 88; IntAu&W 76, 77, 91, 93; IntMPA 86, 88, 92, 94, 96; LegTOT; MiSFD 9; ScF&FL 92; TwCCr&M 80, 85, 91; VarWW 85; WhoAm 76, 78, 80, 82, 84, 86, 88, 95, 96, 97; WhoEnt 92; WorAu 1975; WrDr 76, 80, 82, 84, 86, 88, 90, 92, 94, 96*

Meyer, Ray(mond Joseph)
American. Basketball Coach
Coach, DePaul U, 1942-86; Hall of Fame, 1979.
b. Dec 18, 1913 in Chicago, Illinois
Source: *AmCath 80; BiDAmSp BK; BioIn 11, 12, 13, 16; NewYTBS 81; WhoAm 76, 78, 80, 82, 84, 86, 88, 90, 92, 94,*

95, 96, 97; WhoBbl 73; WhoMW 80, 82, 84

Meyer, Ron
American. Business Executive
Co-founded Creative Artists Agency, 1975; pres., MCA, 1995—.
b. 1944
Source: *WhoAm 94, 95, 96, 97*

Meyer, Russ
"King of the Nudies"
American. Director
Noted for sexploitation films: *Vixen*, 1969; *Fanny Hill.*
b. Mar 21, 1922 in Oakland, California
Source: *BioIn 8, 10, 16; FilmEn; FilmgC; HalFC 88; IntMPA 81, 92, 94, 96; LegTOT; MiSFD 9; VarWW 85; WhoAm 74, 76, 78, 80, 82, 84, 86, 88; WhoWest 78*

Meyerbeer, Giacomo
[Jakob Liebmann Beer]
German. Composer
Very popular in his day; wrote spectacular French operas *Les Huguenots*, 1836; *Le Prophete*, 1849.
b. Sep 5, 1791 in Berlin, Germany
d. May 2, 1864 in Paris, France
Source: *AtlBL; Baker 78, 84, 92; Benet 87; BioIn 1, 2, 3, 4, 5, 6, 7, 8, 9, 11, 12, 16, 17, 20; BriBkM 80; CmOp; CmpBCM; CnOxB; DcArts; DcCom 77; DcCom&M 79; Dis&D; GrComp; IntDcOp; JeHun; LegTOT; LinLib S; McGEWB; MetOEnc; MusMk; NewAmDM; NewC; NewEOp 71; NewGrDM 80; NewGrDO; NewOxM; OxCFr; OxCMus; OxDcOp; PenDiMP A; REn; WhDW; WorAl; WorAlBi*

Meyerhof, Otto Fritz
American. Physiologist
Won 1922 Nobel Prize for work on consumption of oxygen, chemical pathways.
b. Apr 12, 1884 in Hannover, Germany
d. Oct 6, 1951 in Philadelphia, Pennsylvania
Source: *AsBiEn; BiESc; BiHiMed; CamDcSc; DcAmB S5; DcScB; FacFETw; InSci; LarDcSc; McGEWB; WhAm 3; WhoNob, 90, 95*

Meyerhoff, Joseph
American. Real Estate Executive, Philanthropist
Headed property co. that built thousands of homes in US, 1933-78; gave generously to art, music, Jewish causes.
b. Apr 8, 1899, Russia
d. Feb 2, 1985 in Baltimore, Maryland
Source: *BioIn 5, 14; NewYTBS 85; St&PR 75; WhAm 8; WhoAm 74, 76, 78, 80, 82, 84; WhoWor 74, 82; WhoWorJ 72*

Meyerowitz, Jan
American. Composer
Operas include *The Barrier*, 1950.
b. Apr 23, 1913 in Breslau, Germany
Source: *Baker 78, 84, 92; BiDAmM; ConAmC 76, 82; DcCM; IntAu&W 77; IntWWM 85; NewAmDM; NewEOp 71; NewGrDA 86; NewGrDM 80; NewGrDO; OxCMus; WhoAmM 83*

Meyers, Ari(adne)
American. Actor
Played Emma McArdle on TV series "Kate & Allie."
b. 1970 in New York, New York
Source: *BioIn 14, 15, 16; ConTFT 4; WhoHisp 92; WhoHol 92*

Meynell, Alice Christina Gertrude
English. Poet, Essayist
Prose essays collected in *Colour of Life*, 1896; befriended poet Francis Thompson.
b. Sep 22, 1847 in Barnes, England
d. Nov 27, 1922 in London, England
Source: *Alli SUP; BbD; BiD&SB; Chambr 3; CnE&AP; DcEnA A; DcEuL; DcLEL; EvLB; LngCTC; ModBrL; NewC; PenC ENG; REn; TwCA SUP*

Mezzrow, Mezz
[Milton Mezzrow]
American. Jazz Musician
Saxophonist-clarinetist; led Harlem's first mixed band, 1937; wrote "Really the Blues," 1946.
b. Nov 9, 1899 in Chicago, Illinois
d. Aug 5, 1972 in Paris, France
Source: *AllMusG; BiDAmM; BiDJaz; BioIn 1, 9; CmpEPM; EncJzS; NewGrDA 86; NewGrDJ 88, 94; NewYTBE 72; OxCPMus; PenEncP; WhAm 5; WhoJazz 72*

Mfume, Kweisi
[Frizzell Gray]
American. Politician, Civil Rights Leader
Democratic Congressman from Maryland, 1987-96; president of the National Association for Advancement of Colored People (NAACP) 1996—.
b. Oct 24, 1948 in Baltimore, Maryland
Source: *AfrAmAl 6; AfrAmBi 2; AlmAP 88, 92, 96; BiDrUSC 89; BioIn 17, 19, 20, 21; BlkAmsC; CngDr 87, 89, 91, 93, 95; ConBlB 6; CurBio 96; NegAl 89A; News 96, 96-3; NewYTBS 27, 95; WhoAm 88, 90, 92, 94, 95, 96, 97; WhoAmP 87, 89, 91, 93, 95; WhoE 89, 91, 93, 95, 97*

Michael, George
[Wham!; Georgios Kyriaku Panayiotou; George Michael Panos]
English. Singer
Hits with Wham! include "Wake Me Up Before You Go-Go," 1984; solo hits include "Faith," 1987; won 1987 grammy for "I Knew You Were Waiting (For Me);" 1988 Grammy for album of the yr., *Faith.*
b. Jun 25, 1963 in London, England
Source: *BioIn 14, 15, 16; CelR 90; ConMus 9; CurBio 88; EncPR&S 89; EncRkSt; IntWW 89, 91, 93; LegTOT; News 89-2; OxCPMus; WhoAm 94, 95, 96, 97; WhoEnt 92; WorAlBi*

Michael, Moina Belle
"The Poppy Lady"
American. Social Reformer
Originated Poppy Day, 1918, to raise money for war veterans.
b. Aug 15, 1869 in Good Hope, Georgia
d. May 10, 1944 in Athens, Georgia
Source: *CurBio 44; ObitOF 79; WhAm 2*

Michaels, Al
American. Sportscaster
Three-time winner of Sportscaster of the Year Award; "Monday Night Football" announcer, 1986—.
b. Jun 18, 1935 in New York, New York
Source: *Ballpl 90; BioIn 13, 15, 16; LesBEnT 92; WhoAm 90*

Michaels, Lorne
[Lorne Lipowitz]
Canadian. Producer, Writer
Emmy-award winning producer of "Saturday Night Live" TV show.
b. Nov 17, 1944 in Toronto, Ontario, Canada
Source: *Au&Arts 12; BioIn 13, 16; ConAu 142; ConCaAu 1; ConTFT 2, 9; IntMPA 92, 94, 96; LegTOT; LesBEnT 92; VarWW 85; WhoAm 86, 90; WhoEnt 92*

Michael the Archangel, Saint
Biblical Figure
Supposed to have battled Satan, driving him to Hell; one of three archangels in Hebrew tradition; feast day Sep 29.
Source: *BioIn 1, 2, 3, 4, 5, 6, 11; NewCol 75; REn*

Michael V
Romanian. Ruler
Preceded (1927-30) and succeeded (1940-47) father, Carol II, to throne; lives in exile in Switzerland.
b. Oct 25, 1921 in Sinaia, Romania
Source: *BioIn 10; CurBio 44; NewCol 75; WhWW-II*

Michalowski, Kazimierz
Polish. Archaeologist
Best known for discovering seventh-century Faras Basilica in Sudan, 1960s; Byzantine-Coptic murals.
b. Dec 14, 1901 in Ternopol, Poland
d. Jan 1, 1981 in Warsaw, Poland
Source: *AnObit 1981; BioIn 12; ConAu 108; IntWW 74, 75, 76, 77, 78, 79, 80; MidE 78, 79, 80; PolBiDi; WhoSocC 78; WhoWor 74, 76, 78*

Michals, Duane Steven
American. Photographer
Member sharp focus school of photography, with fanatical devotion to realism, technical perfection.
b. Feb 18, 1932 in McKeesport, Pennsylvania

Source: *BioIn 13, 14, 15, 16; ConPhot 82, 88; CurBio 81; ICPEnP; PrintW 85; WhoAm 78, 80, 82, 84, 86, 88, 90; WhoAmA 84, 91*

Michalske, Mike
[August Michalske]
American. Football Player
Guard, 1926-28, 1929-35, 1937, mostly with Green Bay; first to use blitz; Hall of Fame, 1964.
b. Apr 24, 1903 in Cleveland, Ohio
Source: *BiDAmSp FB; BioIn 6, 8, 17; WhoFtbl 74; WhoSpor*

Michaux, Henri
French. Artist
Paintings focused on subconscious mind, effects of drugs; wrote several critically acclaimed poems.
b. May 24, 1899 in Namur, Belgium
d. Oct 17, 1984 in Paris, France
Source: *AnObit 1984; Benet 87, 96; BioIn 1, 3, 4, 5, 8, 9, 10, 11, 13, 14, 15, 20; CasWL; ClDMEL 80; CnMWL; ConArt 77, 83, 89, 96; ConAu 85, 114; ConFLW 84; ConLC 8, 19; DcCAr 81; DcTwCCu 2; EncWL, 2, 3; EvEuW; GuFrLit 1; LinLib L; ModFrL; ModRL; OxCFr; OxCTwCA; PenC EUR; PhDcTCA 77; REn; RfGWoL 95; TwCA SUP; TwCWr; WhAm 8; WhoFr 79; WhoTwCL; WorAlBi; WorArt 1950*

Micheaux, Oscar
[Oscar Devereaux Michaux]
American. Director, Filmmaker
The only black film director who was able to sustain a career through the 1920s, 1930s, and 1940s; made *The Homesteader,* 1919.
b. Jan 2, 1884 in Metropolis, Illinois
d. Mar 26, 1951 in Charlotte, North Carolina
Source: *AmAu&B; BioIn 12, 14, 15, 16, 17, 20, 21; BlkAWP; BlksAmF; ConBlB 7; DcAmB S5; DcAmNB; DcLB 50; DcTwCCu 5; DrBlPA, 90; IntDcF 1-2, 2-2; MorBAP; PeoHis; RAdv 14; SchCGBL; SelBAAf; TwCWW 91; WorFDir 1*

Michel, Hartmut
German. Scientist
Shared Nobel Prize in chemistry, 1988, for work with plant protein structures and photosynthesis.
b. Jul 18, 1948 in Ludwigsburg, Germany (West)
Source: *AmMWSc 92, 95; BioIn 16, 18, 19, 20; LarDcSc; NobelP 91; NotTwCS; Who 90, 92, 94; WhoNob 90, 95; WhoScEn 94, 96; WhoWor 91, 93, 95, 96, 97; WorAlBi*

Michel, Robert H(enry)
American. Politician
Rep. congressman from IL, 1957—; House minority leader, 1981—.
b. Mar 2, 1923 in Peoria, Illinois
Source: *AlmAP 80, 88, 92; BiDrAC; BiDrUSC 89; BioIn 12, 13, 14, 16; CngDr 87, 89; CurBio 81; IntWW 89, 91, 93; NewYTBS 80; PolsAm 84; WhoAm 74, 76, 78, 80, 82, 84, 86, 88, 90, 92, 94, 95; WhoAmP 73, 75, 77, 79, 81, 83, 85, 87, 89, 91, 93, 95; WhoE 95; WhoGov 72, 75, 77; WhoMW 74, 76, 78, 80, 82, 84, 86, 88, 90, 92, 93*

Michelangeli, Arturo Benedetti
Italian. Musician
Piano virtuoso who toured US, 1950, 1966; noted for love of dangerous sports, idiosyncrasies.
b. Jan 5, 1920 in Brescia, Italy
Source: *Baker 78, 84, 92; BioIn 5, 7, 9, 11, 21; BriBkM 80; IntWW 91; IntWWM 77, 80, 90; MusMk; MusSN; NewAmDM; NewGrDM 80; News 88-2; NotTwCP; PenDiMP; WhoWor 78*

Michelangelo (Buonarroti)
[Michelangelo di Lodovico Buonarroti Simoni]
Italian. Artist, Poet
Leader of High Renaissance; works include marble sculpture *David,* 1504; paintings of Sistine Chapel, 1508-12.
b. Mar 6, 1475 in Caprese, Italy
d. Feb 18, 1564 in Rome, Italy
Source: *AtlBL; BbD; Benet 87; BiD&SB; BioIn 1, 2, 3, 4, 5, 6, 7, 8, 9, 10, 11, 12, 13, 14, 15, 16, 17, 18, 19, 20, 21; CasWL; ClaDrA; DcArts; DcCathB; DcEuL; Dis&D; EuAu; EvEuW; GayLesB; IntDcAA 90; IntDcAr; LegTOT; LitC 12; LuthC 75; MacEA; McGDA; McGEWB; NewCBEL; NewCol 75; OxCArt; OxCEng 67, 85, 95; OxDcArt; PenC EUR; RAdv 14, 13-3; REn; WebBD 83; WhoArch; WorAl; WorAlBi*

Michelin, Andre
French. Manufacturer
With brother Edouard, first to make rubber tires for motorcars, 1895.
b. 1853
d. 1931
Source: *BioIn 3, 4; WebBD 83; WhDW*

Michelin, Edouard
French. Manufacturer
With brother, Andre, first to make rubber tires for cars, 1895.
b. 1856, France
d. Aug 25, 1940
Source: *BioIn 3, 4; CurBio 40*

Michelin, Francois
French. Industrialist
With Michelin & Co. since 1959; managing director, 1966—.
b. Jul 3, 1926 in Clermont-Ferrand, France
Source: *BioIn 8, 10, 13; IntWW 74, 75, 76, 77, 78, 79, 80, 81, 82, 83, 89, 91, 93; WhoFI 96; WhoFr 79; WhoWor 95, 96*

Michell, John
English. Geologist, Astronomer
Leading pioneer in the field of seismology; made important contributions to astronomy.
b. 1724 in Nottinghamshire, England
d. Apr 21, 1793 in Thornhill, England
Source: *AsBiEn; BiESc; BioIn 8, 14; CamDcSc; DcNaB; DcScB; InSci; LarDcSc; NewCBEL; WorAl; WorAlBi; WorScD*

Michell, Keith
Australian. Actor
Played Henry on PBS "Six Wives of Henry VIII;" on stage played Abelard in *Abel ard and Heloise.*
b. Dec 1, 1928 in Adelaide, Australia
Source: *BiE&WWA; CamGWoT; CnThe; ConTFT 2, 8; EncMT; FilmgC; HalFC 88; IlWWBF; IntMPA 82, 92; IntWW 89, 91, 93; MovMk; NotNAT; OxCAusL; OxCThe 83; VarWW 85; Who 74, 92; WhoHol A; WhoThe 72, 77, 81; WhoWor 74*

Michelson, Albert Abraham
American. Physicist
Known for measuring speed of light; first American to receive Nobel Prize in physics, 1907.
b. Dec 19, 1852 in Strelno, Germany
d. May 9, 1931 in Pasadena, California
Source: *AmBi; AmDec 1900; ApCAB; AsBiEn; BiDAmS; BiESc; BioIn 1, 2, 3, 4, 5, 7, 8, 10, 11, 12, 13, 14, 15, 16, 20; CamDcSc; CmCal; DcAmB; DcInv; DcNAA; DcScB; Dis&D; EncAB-H 1974, 1996; InSci; LarDcSc; LinLib S; McGEWB; MemAm; NatCAB 12, 33; NewCol 75; OxCAmH; OxCAmL 65; RAdv 13-5; REnAL; TwCBDA; WebAB 74, 79; WebBD 83; WhAm 1; WhDW; WhoNob, 90, 95; WorAl; WorAlBi; WorScD*

Michener, James A(lbert)
American. Author
Wrote *Tales of the South Pacific,* 1947; *Centennial,* 1974.
b. Feb 3, 1907 in New York, New York
Source: *AmAu&B; AmNov; Au&Wr 71; AuNews 1; Benet 87, 96; BenetAL 91; BioIn 1, 2, 3, 4, 5, 6, 7, 8, 9, 10, 11, 12, 13, 14, 15; BioNews 74; CelR 90; ConAu 5R, 21NR, 45NR; ConLC 1, 5, 11, 60; ConNov 72, 76, 86, 91, 96; ConPopW; CurBio 48; CyWA 89; DcLEL, 1940; EncSF 93; FacFETw; FilmgC; HalFC 88; IntAu&W 76, 77, 89, 91, 93; IntvTCA 2; IntWW 74, 75, 76, 77, 78, 79, 80, 81, 82, 83, 89, 91, 93; LinLib S; LngCTC; ModAL; NewYTBS 85; OxCAmL 65, 83, 95; PenC AM; PlP&P; RAdv 1, 14; REnAL; TwCA SUP; TwCRHW 90, 94; TwCWW 82, 91; WebAB 74, 79; Who 74, 82, 83, 85, 88, 90, 92, 94; WhoAm 74, 76, 78, 80, 82, 84, 86, 88, 90, 92, 94, 95, 96, 97; WhoUSWr 88; WhoWor 74, 78; WhoWrEP 89, 92, 95; WorAl; WorAlBi; WrDr 76, 86, 92, 94, 96*

Michener, Roland
[Daniel Roland Michener]
Canadian. Politician
Governor General, Canada, 1967-74.
b. Apr 19, 1900 in Lacombe, Alberta, Canada
d. Aug 6, 1991 in Ottawa, Ontario, Canada
Source: *BioIn 8, 17; BlueB 76; CanWW 70, 79, 80, 81, 83, 89; CurBio 91N; IntWW 74, 76, 77, 78, 79, 80, 81, 82, 83, 89, 91; IntYB 78, 79, 80, 81, 82; LinLib S; St&PR 84, 87, 91; WhAm 10; Who 74, 82, 83, 85, 88, 90, 92N; WhoAm 74, 76, 78, 80, 82, 84, 86, 88, 90; WhoCan 73, 75, 77, 80, 82, 84; WhoGov 72; WhoWor 74*

Michnik, Adam
Polish. Political Activist, Politician
Dissident, 1965-89; adviser to Solidarity Trade Union, 1980-81; member of Polish Parliament, 1989—.
b. Oct 17, 1946 in Warsaw, Poland
Source: *BioIn 13, 14, 15, 16; ColdWar 1, 2; CurBio 90; EncRev; NewYTBS 87; WhoSocC 78; WhoSoCE 89*

Mickelson, George Speaker
American. Politician
Rep. governor of South Dakota, 1987-93; died in a plane crash.
b. Jan 31, 1941 in Mobridge, South Dakota
d. Apr 19, 1993 in Dubuque, Iowa
Source: *AlmAP 88, 92; BiDrGov 1988; IntWW 91; WhoAm 80, 82, 90; WhoAmP 75, 77, 79, 81, 83, 85, 87, 89, 91; WhoMW 74, 76, 78, 80, 92; WhoWor 91*

Mickens, Spike
[Kool and the Gang; Robert Mickens]
American. Musician
Trumpeter with Kool and the Gang.

Micombero, Michel
Political Leader
Pres. of Burundi, 1966-76; led coup to establish republic, 1966.
b. 1940
d. Jul 16, 1983 in Mogadishu, Somalia
Source: *AfSS 78, 79, 80, 81, 82; AnObit 1983; BioIn 11, 13, 21; DcAfHiB 86S; IntWW 74, 75, 76, 77, 78, 79, 80, 81, 82, 83; NewYTBS 83; WhoGov 72; WhoWor 74, 76*

Middendorf, John William, II
American. Diplomat, Government Official
US ambassador to Netherlands, 1967-73; secretary of Navy, 1974-77.
b. Sep 22, 1924 in Baltimore, Maryland
Source: *ASCAP 80; BioIn 10, 11, 12; ConAmC 76, 82; IntWW 83, 91; St&PR 84; WhoAm 74, 84, 90; WhoAmP 75, 77, 79, 81, 83, 85, 87, 89, 91, 93, 95; WhoGov 72, 75, 77; WhoWor 74*

Middlecoff, Cary
"Doc"
American. Golfer
Turned pro, 1947; won US Open, 1949, 1956, Masters, 1955.
b. Jan 6, 1921 in Halls, Tennessee
Source: *BiDAmSp OS; BioIn 2, 3, 4, 5, 9, 10, 13; CurBio 52; WhoGolf; WhoSpor*

Middleton, Arthur
American. Continental Congressman
Signed Declaration of Independence, 1776; ardent patriot, aristocrat.
b. Jun 26, 1742 in Charleston, South Carolina
d. Jan 1, 1787 in Goose Creek, South Carolina
Source: *AmBi; ApCAB; BiDrAC; BiDrUSC 89; BiDSA; BioIn 3, 7, 8, 9; DcAmB; EncAR; EncCRAm; HarEnUS; NatCAB 5; TwCBDA; WhAm HS; WhAmP; WhAmRev*

Middleton, Ray
American. Actor
Played on stage in *Annie Get Your Gun; South Pacific.*
b. Feb 8, 1907 in Chicago, Illinois
d. Apr 10, 1984 in Panorama City, California
Source: *BiE&WWA; BioIn 13, 14; CmpEPM; EncMT; FilmgC; IntMPA 77, 82, 84; NewYTBS 84; NotNAT; OxCPMus; PlP&P; VarWW 85; WhAm 8; WhoHol A; WhoThe 77, 81*

Middleton, Thomas
English. Dramatist
Satirical comedies include *A Chast Mayd in Cheape-side,* published 1630; often collaborated with Dekker, Rowley.
b. Apr 18, 1580 in London, England
d. Jul 4, 1627 in Newington Butts, England
Source: *Alli; AtlBL; BbD; Benet 87, 96; BiD&SB; BiDRP&D; BioIn 4, 5, 9, 10, 12; BlmGEL; BritAu; BritWr 2; CamGEL; CamGLE; CamGWoT; CasWL; Chambr 1; CnE&AP; CnThe; CrtSuDr; CrtT 4; DcLB 58; DcLEL; DramC 5; Ent; EvLB; GrWrEL DR; IntDcT 2; LitC 33; LngCEL; McGEWB; McGEWD 72, 84; NewC; NewCBEL; OxCEng 85, 95; PenC ENG; RAdv 14, 13-2; REn; REnWD; RfGEnL 91; WebE&AL*

Midgeley, Thomas
American. Inventor, Chemist
Developed antiknock gasoline, 1921; exec., Ethyl Corp. from 1923.
b. May 18, 1889 in Beaver Falls, Pennsylvania
d. Nov 2, 1944 in New York, New York
Source: *DcAmB S3; WebBD 83*

Midler, Bette
[Mrs. Harry Kipper]
"The Divine Miss M"; "The Last of the Tacky Ladies"
American. Singer, Actor
Concert, recording, film star; Oscar nominee for *The Rose,* 1979 and *For The Boys,* 1992; other films include *Beaches,* 1988 and *The First Wives Club,* 1996; won two Grammys, 1973, 1980; a Tony, 1973; an Emmy, 1978.
b. Dec 1, 1945 in Honolulu, Hawaii
Source: *Baker 92; BiDFilm 94; BioIn 9, 10, 11, 12, 13, 14, 15, 16; BioNews 75; BkPepl; CelR 90; ConAu 106; ConMus 8; ContDcW 89; ConTFT 4, 11; CurBio 73; EncAFC; EncPR&S 89; EncRk 88; FunnyW; GoodHs; HalFC 88; HarEnR 86; IlEncRk; IntDcF 2-3; IntDcWB; IntMPA 82, 84, 86, 88, 92, 94, 96; IntWW 91, 93; InWom SUP; LegTOT; NewGrDA 86; News 89; NewWmR; NewYTBE 73; NewYTBS 80, 86; OxCPMus; PenEncP; RkOn 78; RolSEnR 83; VarWW 85; WhoAm 74, 76, 78, 80, 82, 84, 86, 88, 90, 92, 94, 95, 96, 97; WhoAmW 81, 83, 85, 87, 89, 91, 93, 95, 97; WhoCom; WhoEnt 92; WhoHol 92, A; WhoRock 81; WhoThe 81; WorAl; WorAlBi*

Midnight Oil
[Peter Garrett; Peter Gifford; Rob Hurst; Jim Moginie; Martin Rotsey]
Australian. Music Group
Debut US album *10, 9, 8, 7, 6, 5, 4, 3, 2, 1,* 1983.
Source: *BioIn 16, 17; ConMus 11; EncRkSt; EnvEnDr; OnThGG*

Midori
Japanese. Violinist
Child prodigy; has appeared as a guest soloist with many of the world's top orchestras.
b. Oct 25, 1971 in Osaka, Japan
Source: *AsAmAlm; Baker 92; BioIn 15, 16, 17, 18, 19, 20; ConMus 7; CurBio 90; IntWW 93; NewYTBS 86, 91; NotAsAm; WhoAm 94, 95, 96, 97; WhoAmW 95, 97; WhoAsA 94*

Miele, Jerry J
[The Hostages]
American. Hostage
One of 52 held by terrorists, Nov 1979-Jan 1981.
b. 1939?
Source: *NewYTBS 81*

Mielke, Erich
German. Government Official
Head of East Germany's former Stasi Secret police; first East German govt. official to go on trial in United Germany, 1992.
b. Dec 28, 1908 in Berlin, Germany
Source: *IntWW 74, 75, 76, 77, 91; WhoSoCE 89*

Mielziner, Jo
American. Designer
Created sets, lighting for over 300 productions including *A Street Car Named Desire.*
b. Mar 19, 1901 in Paris, France
d. Mar 15, 1976 in New York, New York
Source: *BiE&WWA; BioIn 1, 2, 4, 7, 10, 11, 13; BlueB 76; CamGWoT; CelR; CnThe; ConAu 45, 65; ConDes 84, 90, 97; CurBio 46, 76, 76N; DcAmB S10; EncWT; Ent; IntDcT 3; IntWW 74, 75; LegTOT; McGDA; MetOEnc; NewYTBS 76; NotNAT, B; OxCAmT 84; OxCThe 67, 83; PlP&P; WhAm 6; WhAmArt 85; WhoAm 74, 76; WhoAmA 73, 76, 78N, 80N, 82N, 84N, 86N, 89N, 91N, 93N; WhoThe 72, 77; WhoWor 74; WorAl; WorAlBi*

Mies van der Rohe, Ludwig
American. Architect
Master of 20th-c. architecture; built first steel and glass skyscrapers: Seagram Bldg., NYC, 1956.
b. Mar 27, 1886 in Aachen, Germany
d. Aug 18, 1969 in Chicago, Illinois
Source: *AmCulL; AtlBL; Benet 87, 96; BiDAmEd; BioIn 1, 2, 3, 4, 5, 7, 8, 9, 10, 11, 12, 13, 14, 15, 16, 17, 19, 20; BriEAA; ConArch 80, 87, 94; ConDes 84, 97; CurBio 51, 69; DcAmB S8; DcArts; DcD&D; DcNiCA; DcTwDes; EncAAr 1, 2; EncAB-H 1974, 1996; IntDcAr; LinLib S; MacEA; MakMC; McGEWB; ObitT 1961; OxCArt; OxDcArt; PenDiDA 89; RAdv 14, 13-3; REn; WebAB 74, 79; WhAm 5; WhDW; WhoAmA 78N, 80N, 82N, 84N, 86N, 89N, 91N, 93N; WhoArch; WorAl; WorAlBi*

Mifflin, George Harrison
American. Publisher
With Hurd and Houghton from 1867; pres., Houghton-Mifflin, 1908-21.
b. May 1, 1845 in Boston, Massachusetts
d. Apr 5, 1921
Source: *AmAu&B; ApCAB X; BioIn 3; WhAm 1*

Mifune, Toshiro
Japanese. Actor
Played in TV's "Shogun," 1981; films include *Inchon,* 1982.
b. Apr 1, 1920 in Qingdao, China
Source: *BiDFilm 94; BioIn 7, 11, 12, 14; ConTFT 5; CurBio 81; DcArts; EncJap; FacFETw; FarE&A 78, 79, 80, 81; FilmEn; FilmgC; ForYSC; HalFC 80, 84, 88; IntDcF 1-3, 2-3; IntMPA 75, 76, 77, 78, 79, 80, 81, 82, 84, 86, 88, 92, 94, 96; IntWW 74, 75, 76, 77, 78, 79, 80, 81, 82, 83, 89, 91, 93; ItaFilm; JapFilm; LegTOT; MotPP; MovMk; OxCFilm; VarWW 85; WhoHol 92, A; WhoHrs 80; WhoWor 74, 76, 78, 82, 84, 87, 89, 91, 93, 95, 96; WorEFlm*

Migenes, Julia
American. Actor, Opera Singer
Starred in original Broadway version of *Fiddler on the Roof,* 1964-67; ha d NY Met. debut, 1980; films include *Carmen,* 1984.
b. 1945
Source: *BioIn 12; CelR 90; IntWWM 90; LegTOT; MetOEnc; NewGrDO; NewYTBS 81; WhoHisp 92, 94*

Mihajlov, Mihajlo
Yugoslav. Political Activist, Author
Dissident, jailed for 13 years, unable to publish in native country; wrote *Underground Notes,* 1976.
b. Sep 26, 1934 in Pancevo, Yugoslavia
Source: *BioIn 7, 11, 12; ConAu 105, 130; CurBio 79; IntAu&W 86, 89, 93; IntWW 81, 82, 83, 89, 91, 93; LiExTwC; WhoSoCE 89; WhoWor 91; WrDr 94, 96*

Mihajlovic, Dragoliub
Yugoslav. Soldier
Organized *chetniks,* guerrillas to fight Nazi invasion of Yugoslavia, 1941; war minister, 1942-44; captured by Tito, executed for treason.
b. Mar 27, 1893 in Ivanjica, Serbia
d. Jul 17, 1946 in Belgrade, Yugoslavia
Source: *CurBio 42, 46; NewCol 75*

Mikan, George Lawrence, Jr.
American. Basketball Player
Forward, 1946-56, mostly with Minneapolis; led NBA in scoring three times, in rebounding once; Hall of Fame, 1959.
b. Jun 18, 1924 in Joliet, Illinois
Source: *BiDAmSp BK; BioIn 1, 2, 3, 5, 6, 7, 8, 9, 10, 12, 16; OfNBA 87; WhoBbl 73; WorAl; WorAlBi*

Mikhail-Ashrawi, Hanan
Lebanese. Political Activist
Advocate for the Palestinian cause.
b. 1947 in Ramallah, Lebanon

Mikhalkov, Nikita
Russian. Filmmaker
Made films *An Unfinished Piece for Player Piano,* 1976; *Close to Eden,* 1992.
b. Oct 21, 1945 in Moscow, Union of Soviet Socialist Republics
Source: *CurBio 95; IntMPA 88, 92; MiSFD 9*

Mikhalkov, Sergei Vladimirovich
Russian. Author
Award-winning Soviet children's writer: *Krasny Galstuk,* 1947.
b. Mar 12, 1913 in Moscow, Russia
Source: *BiDSovU; CasWL; ConAu 116; DcRusLS; IntAu&W 76, 77, 91; IntWW 74, 75, 76, 83, 91; IntWWP 77; OxCThe 67; WhoSocC 78; WhoWor 74, 84, 91*

Mikita, Stan(ley)
[Stanley Gvoth]
"Stosh"
American. Hockey Player
Center, Chicago, 1958-80; scored 541 career goals; won Art Ross Trophy four times; Hall of Fame, 1983.
b. May 20, 1940 in Sokolce, Czechoslovakia
Source: *BioIn 10, 20; CurBio 70; HocEn; LegTOT; WhoAm 74, 76, 78, 80; WhoHcky 73; WhoSpor; WorAl; WorAlBi*

Miki Takeo
Japanese. Politician
Prime minister, 1974-76.
b. Mar 17, 1907 in Donari, Japan
d. Nov 13, 1988 in Tokyo, Japan
Source: *BioNews 75; CurBio 75, 89; IntWW 83; NewYTBS 74; WhoWor 74*

Mikkelsen, Henning Dahl
American. Cartoonist
Created comic strip "Ferd'nand," 1937-82.
b. Jan 9, 1915 in Skive, Denmark
d. Jun 1, 1982 in Hemet, California
Source: *BioIn 1; WhAm 8; WhoAm 78, 80, 82; WorECom*

Mikkelsen, Vern
[Arild Verner Agerskov Mikkelsen]
American. Basketball Player
Forward, Minneapolis, 1945-59; won four NBA championships.
b. Oct 21, 1928 in Fresno, California
Source: *BasBi; BiDAmSp BK; OfNBA 87; WhoBbl 73*

Mikoyan, Anastas Ivanovich
Russian. Politician
Soviet official for three decades; nominal chief of state, 1964-65.
b. Nov 25, 1895 in Sanain
d. Oct 22, 1978 in Moscow, Union of Soviet Socialist Republics
Source: *BioIn 1, 2, 3, 13; CurBio 55, 79; DcTwHis; EncCW; EncRev; IntWW 74, 75, 76, 77, 78; IntYB 78; SovUn; WhDW; Who 74; WhoWor 74, 76*

Mikoyan, Artem Ivanovich
Russian. Scientist
Co-designed Soviet MiG jet; brother of Anastas.
b. 1905, Armenia
d. Dec 9, 1970 in Moscow, Union of Soviet Socialist Republics
Source: *BioIn 2, 3, 9; ColdWar 1; ObitOF 79; SovUn*

Mikulski, Barbara Ann
American. Politician
Dem. senator, MD, 1987—.
b. Jul 20, 1936 in Baltimore, Maryland
Source: *AlmAP 84, 92; AmPolW 80; AmWomM; BiDrUSC 89; BioIn 10, 11, 12, 14, 15, 16; CngDr 77, 79, 81, 83, 85, 87, 89; CurBio 85; IntWW 89, 91, 93; InWom SUP; News 92; PolsAm 84; WhoAm 78, 80, 82, 86, 88, 90, 92, 94, 95, 96, 97; WhoAmP 75, 77, 79, 81, 83,*

85, 87, 89, 91, 93, 95; WhoAmW 74, 75, 77, 79, 81, 83, 85, 87, 89, 91, 93, 95, 97; WhoE 77, 79, 81, 83, 85, 86, 89, 91, 93, 95, 97; WhoGov 75, 77; WhoPoA 96; WhoWomW 91; WhoWor 89, 91; WomPO 78

Mikva, Abner Joseph
American. Politician, Judge
Dem. congressman from IL, 1968-79; US Court of Appeals judge, 1979-91; chief ju stice US Court of Appeals, 1991-94; counsel to the US Pres., 1994—.
b. Jan 21, 1926 in Milwaukee, Wisconsin
Source: *BiDrAC; BiDrUSC 89; BioIn 12; CngDr 87, 89; CurBio 80; WhoAm 74, 76, 78, 80, 82, 84, 86, 88, 90, 92, 94, 95, 96, 97; WhoAmL 83, 85, 87, 90, 92, 94, 96; WhoAmP 85, 91; WhoE 83, 85, 86, 89, 91, 93, 95, 97; WhoGov 72, 75, 77; WhoMW 76, 78, 80, 82; WhoWorJ 72*

Milano, Alyssa
American. Actor
Played Samantha Micelli on TV show "Who's the Boss?" 1984-92.
b. Dec 19, 1972 in New York, New York
Source: *BioIn 15, 16; ConTFT 4, 14; LegTOT; WhoHol 92*

Milano, Fred
[Dion and the Belmonts]
American. Singer
Tenor with group formed 1958; had hit single "Teenager in Love," 1959.
b. Aug 22, 1939 in New York, New York
Source: *EncPR&S 74; IlEncRk; RkOn 74*

Milanov, Zinka Kunc
American. Opera Singer
Dramatic soprano, NY Met., 1937-66; noted for Verdi roles.
b. May 17, 1906 in Zagreb, Yugoslavia
d. May 30, 1989 in New York, New York
Source: *AnObit 1989; Baker 84; BioIn 13, 14, 15, 16; CurBio 44, 89, 89N; InWom; MetOEnc; NewAmDM; NewGrDA 86; NewYTBS 89; PenDiMP; WhoMus 72; WhoWor 74*

Mildenburg, Anna von
[Anna von Bahr-Mildenburg]
Austrian. Opera Singer
A leading Wagnerian soprano, 1890s-1920s.
b. Nov 29, 1872 in Vienna, Austria
d. Jan 27, 1947 in Vienna, Austria
Source: *Baker 78, 84; InWom; NewEOp 71; NewGrDM 80*

Milder-Hauptmann, Pauline Anna
Turkish. Opera Singer
Soprano noted for Gluck roles.
b. Dec 13, 1785 in Constantinople, Turkey
d. May 29, 1838 in Berlin, Germany
Source: *Baker 78, 84; InWom; NewEOp 71; OxDcOp*

Mildmay, Audrey
English. Opera Singer
Soprano who, with Rudolf Bing, instigated Edinburgh Festival, 1947.
b. Dec 19, 1900 in Hurstmonceaux, England
d. May 31, 1953 in London, England
Source: *CmOp; NewEOp 71; NewGrDM 80; OxDcOp*

Miles, Bernard, Sir
English. Actor, Author
Founder of the London Mermaid Theater 1959; starred in many plays including *Richard III,* and *Treasure Island,* as well as films, knighted in 1969, life peer, 1979.
b. 1907, England
d. Jun 14, 1991 in Yorkshire, England
Source: *BioIn 5, 17, 18, 19; CamGWoT; CnThe; ConAu 133; DcArts; EncWT; FilmAG WE; FilmEn; FilmgC; HalFC 80, 84, 88; IlWWBF; IntMPA 75, 76, 77, 78, 79, 80; IntWW 74, 75, 76, 77, 78; NewYTBS 91; OxCThe 67, 83; PlP&P; WhAm 10; Who 74; WhoHol A; WhoThe 72, 77, 81; WrDr 94, 96*

Miles, Buddy
American. Singer, Musician
Drummer, known for husky voice; albums include *Sneak Attack,* 1981.
b. Sep 5, 1946 in Omaha, Nebraska
Source: *BiDJaz A; ConMuA 80A; EncRk 88; HarEnR 86; IlEncRk; LegTOT; RkOn 78, 84; RolSEnR 83; WhoRocM 82*

Miles, Elaine
American. Actor
Plays Marilyn on TV series "Northern Exposure," 1990—.

Miles, Josephine
American. Educator, Poet
Books on poetry, literature include *Poetry and Change,* 1974.
b. Jun 11, 1911 in Chicago, Illinois
d. May 12, 1985 in Berkeley, California
Source: *AmAu&B; AmWomWr; ArtclWW 2; Benet 87; BenetAL 91; BioIn 4, 14, 15; BlueB 76; ChhPo S2; CmCal; ConAu 1R, 2NR, 116; ConLC 1, 2, 14, 34, 39; ConLCrt 77, 82; ConPo 70, 75, 80, 85; DcLB 48; DrAP 75; DrAPF 80; DrAS 74E, 78E, 82E; FemiCLE; IntAu&W 77, 82; IntWW 74, 75, 76, 77, 78, 79, 80, 81, 82, 83; IntWWP 77, 82; InWom SUP; ModAL; ModWoWr; NewYTBS 85; OxCAmL 65, 83, 95; OxCTwCP; PenC AM; RAdv 1; TwCA SUP; WhAm 8; WhoAm 74, 76, 78, 80, 82, 84; WhoAmW 58, 66, 68, 70, 72, 74, 81, 83, 85; WomBeaG; WrDr 76, 80, 82, 84*

Miles, Nelson Appleton
American. Military Leader
General; helped crush Indians in West, capturing Geronimo, 1886; commanded forces at Wounded Knee massacre, 1890.
b. Aug 8, 1839 in Westminster, Massachusetts
d. May 15, 1925 in Washington, District of Columbia
Source: *AmAu&B; AmBi; ApCAB; BioIn 5, 6, 7, 8, 9, 15, 16, 17, 18, 19; CivWDc; CmdGen 1991; DcAmAu; DcAmB; DcAmMiB; DcNAA; Drake; HarEnMi; HarEnUS; LinLib S; McGEWB; MedHR 94; NatCAB 4, 9; NewCol 75; REnAW; TwCBDA; WebAB 74, 79; WebAMB; WhAm 1; WhNaAH; WhoMilH 76; WhScrn 77, 83; WorAl; WorAlBi*

Miles, Sarah
[Mrs. Robert Bolt]
English. Actor
Oscar nominee for *Ryan's Daughter,* 1970; other films include *Hope and Glory,* 1987.
b. Dec 31, 1943 in Igatestone, England
Source: *BiDFilm; BioIn 6, 15, 16; BkPepl; CelR; ConTFT 3; DrAPF 91; FilmgC; HalFC 84, 88; IntMPA 86, 92; IntWW 91; InWom SUP; MotPP; MovMk; VarWW 85; WhoAm 76, 78, 80; WhoHol A; WhoThe 81; WorAl; WorAlBi*

Miles, Sylvia
American. Comedian
Oscar nominee for *Midnight Cowboy; Farewell My Lovely.*
b. Sep 9, 1932 in New York, New York
Source: *BiE&WWA; CelR; ConTFT 7; FilmEn; IntMPA 92; LegTOT; NewYTBE 72; NotNAT; WhoHol 92, A*

Miles, Tichi Wilkerson
American. Publisher
Publisher, editor-in-chief of *Hollywood Reporter* since 1962.
b. May 10, 1932 in Los Angeles, California
Source: *InWom SUP; WhoAm 74, 78, 80; WhoWest 76, 78; WhoWor 80, 84*

Miles, Vera
American. Actor
Films include *The Searchers,* 1956; *Psycho,* 1960; *Psycho II,* 1983.
b. Aug 23, 1930 in Boise City, Oklahoma
Source: *BiDFilm, 81, 94; BioIn 4, 10; ConTFT 5; FilmgC; ForWC 70; HalFC 84, 88; IntMPA 77, 78, 79, 80, 81, 82, 84, 86, 88, 92; InWom SUP; MotPP; MovMk; VarWW 85; WhoAm 76, 78, 80, 82, 84, 86, 88, 90, 92, 94, 95; WhoAmW 74, 75, 95; WhoEnt 92; WhoHol A; WorAl; WorEFlm*

Milestone, Lewis
American. Director
Won Oscars for *Two Arabian Knights; All Quiet on the Western Front.*
b. Sep 30, 1895 in Chisinau, Russia
d. Sep 25, 1980 in Los Angeles, California
Source: *AmFD; AnObit 1980; BiDFilm, 81, 94; BioIn 5, 9, 10, 11, 12, 14, 15;*

CmMov; ConAu 101; DcFM; EncAFC; FacFETw; FilmEn; FilmgC; GangFlm; HalFC 80, 84, 88; IlWWHD 1; IntDcF 1-2, 2-2; IntMPA 75, 76, 77, 78, 79, 80, 81; ItaFilm; LegTOT; MiSFD 9N; MovMk; NewYTBS 80; OxCFilm; TwYS, A; WhScrn 83; WorEFlm; WorFDir 1

Milford, Penny
[Penelope Milford]
American. Actor
Oscar nominee for *Coming Home,* 1978; played on TV's "Seizure: The Story of Kathy Morris," 1980.
b. 1949 in Winnetka, Illinois
Source: *BioIn 12; JohnWSW; VarWW 85; WhoHol 92*

Milhaud, Darius
[Les Six]
French. Composer, Actor
Member of jazz group Les Six, 1920s; 400 works include ballet *La Creacion du Monde,* 1923, first use of blues, jazz in symphonic score.
b. Sep 4, 1892 in Aix-en-Provence, France
d. Jun 22, 1974 in Geneva, Switzerland
Source: *Baker 78, 84, 92; Benet 87, 96; BiDD; BioIn 1, 2, 3, 4, 5, 6, 7, 8, 9, 10, 11, 12; BioNews 74; BriBkM 80; CelR; CmCal; CmOp; CnOxB; CompSN, SUP; ConAu 49; CurBio 41, 61, 74, 74N; DancEn 78; DcArts; DcCM; DcCom 77; DcCom&M 79; DcFM; DcTwCCu 2; FacFETw; FilmEn; IntDcB; IntDcF 2-4; IntDcOp; LegTOT; LinLib S; McGEWB; MetOEnc; MusMk; NewAmDM; NewEOp 71; NewGrDA 86; NewGrDM 80; NewGrDO; NewOxM; NewYTBS 74; ObitT 1971; OxCFilm; OxCMus; OxDcOp; PenDiMP A; REn; WhAm 6; WhDW; Who 74; WhoMus 72; WhoWor 74; WhoWorJ 72; WhScrn 77; WorEFlm*

Mili, Gjon
American. Photographer
Worked for *Life* magazine 45 yrs; pioneered use of high-speed flash, multi-exposure prints.
b. Nov 28, 1904 in Kerce, Albania
d. Feb 14, 1984 in Stamford, Connecticut
Source: *AnObit 1984; BioIn 12, 13, 14; ConAu 112; ConPhot 82, 88, 95; ICPEnP; InB&W 80; NewYTBS 84*

Milk, Harvey
American. Politician
Supervisor, City of San Francisco, 1977-78; assassinated along with Mayor George Moscone.
b. May 22, 1930 in Woodmere, New York
d. Nov 27, 1978 in San Francisco, California
Source: *AmRef&R; BioIn 11, 13; GayLesB; PolPar*

Milken, Michael
American. Business Executive
High-risk venture capitalist with Drexel Burnham Lambert; holds record for most money earned in single year, $550 million, 1987; indicted for racketeering, securities fraud, 1989; sentenced to 10 years in prison, 1990, served 22 mos, released, 1993.
b. 1946 in Van Nuys, California
Source: *AmDec 1980; BioIn 11, 13, 15, 16; ConAmBL; EncAB-H 1996; EncABHB 7; NewYTBS 78*

Mill, James
Scottish. Philosopher, Historian
Spent 10 yrs. researching three-vol. *History of British India,* 1817.
b. Apr 6, 1773 in Northwater Bridge, Scotland
d. Jun 23, 1836 in London, England
Source: *Alli; BbD; BiD&SB; BiDLA; BiDPsy; BioIn 1, 6, 7, 8, 9, 10, 17; BritAu 19; CamGEL; CamGLE; CasWL; CelCen; Chambr 2; CmScLit; CyEd; DcBiPP; DcEnA; DcEnL; DcEuL; DcInB; DcLB 107, 158; DcLEL; DcNaB; EncEth; EvLB; HisDBrE; LinLib L, S; McGEWB; NamesHP; NewC; NewCBEL; NewCol 75; OxCEng 67, 85, 95; OxCPhil; PenC ENG; WhoEc 81, 86*

Mill, John Stuart
English. Philosopher, Economist
Wrote *A System of Logic,* 1843; *On Liberty,* 1859.
b. May 20, 1806 in London, England
d. May 8, 1873 in Avignon, France
Source: *Alli, SUP; AtlBL; BbD; Benet 87, 96; BiD&SB; BiDBrF 1; BiDPsy; BioIn 1, 2, 3, 4, 5, 6, 7, 8, 9, 10, 11, 12, 13, 14, 15, 16, 17, 18, 19, 20; BlmGEL; BritAu 19; CamGEL; CamGLE; CasWL; CelCen; Chambr 3; CnDBLB 4; CrtT 3, 4; CyEd; CyWA 58; DcAmC; DcAmSR; DcArts; DcBiPP; DcEnA; DcEnL; DcEuL; DcInB; DcLB 55; DcLEL; DcNaB; DcScB; DcSoc; Dis&D; EncEth; EncUnb; EvLB; FemiWr; GrEconB; LegTOT; LinLib L, S; LngCEL; LuthC 75; McGEWB; MouLC 3; NamesHP; NewC; NewCBEL; NinCLC 11; OxCEng 67, 85, 95; OxCLaw; OxCMus; OxCPhil; PenC ENG; RadHan; RAdv 14, 13-3, 13-4; REn; RfGEnL 91; TwoTYeD; VicBrit; WebE&AL; WhDW; WhoEc 81, 86; WorAl; WorAlBi; WrPh P*

Milla, Roger
Cameroonian. Soccer Player
Forward, Cameroon World Cup team, 1982, 1990; oldest man ever to score in the World Cup at 38 yrs.
b. 1952, Cameroon
Source: *ConBlB 2*

Millais, John Everett, Sir
English. Artist
A founder, pre-Raphaelite Brotherhood, 1848; works included controversial *Christ in House of His Parents,* 1850.
b. Jun 8, 1829 in Southampton, England
d. Aug 13, 1896 in London, England
Source: *ArtsNiC; AtlBL; Benet 87, 96; BioIn 1, 2, 3, 4, 5, 6, 7, 8, 9, 10, 11, 12, 14, 16; CelCen; ChhPo, S1, S2; ClaDrA; DcArts; DcBiPP; DcBrBI; DcBrWA; DcNaB S1; DcVicP, 2; IntDcAA 90; LinLib S; LuthC 75; McGDA; McGEWB; NewC; NewCBEL; OxCArt; OxCEng 85, 95; OxDcArt; REn; VicBrit; WorAl; WorAlBi*

Milland, Ray(mond Alton)
[Reginald Alfred John Truscott-Jones]
American. Actor, Director
Debonair leading man who made more than 120 movies; won Oscar, 1945, for *The Lost Weekend.*
b. Jan 3, 1905 in Neath, Wales
d. Mar 10, 1986 in Torrance, California
Source: *AnObit 1986; BiDFilm, 81, 94; BioIn 14, 15, 17; CmMov; ConTFT 3; CurBio 46, 86; EncAFC; FacFETw; FilmEn; FilmgC; ForYSC; GangFlm; HalFC 80, 84, 88; IlWWBF, A; IntMPA 82; ItaFilm; LegTOT; MiSFD 9N; MotPP; MovMk; NewYTBE 72; NewYTBS 86; OxCFilm; VarWW 85; WhoAm 84; WhoHrs 80; WorAlBi*

Millar, Jeff(rey) Lynn
American. Journalist, Critic, Cartoonist
Created syndicated comic strip "Tank McNamera," 1974—.
b. Jul 10, 1942 in Houston, Texas
Source: *BioIn 10; ConAu 11NR, 69; WhoAdv 90; WhoAm 86, 90; WhoEnt 92*

Millar, Margaret (Ellis)
[Mrs. Kenneth Millar]
Canadian. Author
Mystery novels include 1956 Edgar-winner, *Beast in View.*
b. Feb 5, 1915 in Kitchener, Ontario, Canada
d. Mar 26, 1994 in Santa Barbara, California
Source: *AmAu&B; AmNov; AmWomWr; Au&Wr 71; BenetAL 91; BioIn 1, 2, 3, 5, 8, 9, 10, 11, 12, 13, 14, 17, 19, 20; BlueB 76; CanWW 70, 79, 80, 81, 83, 89; ConAu 9R, 13R, 16NR, 110; ConNov 76, 82, 86, 91; CrtSuMy; CurBio 46, 94N; DcLB 2, Y83N; DcLEL 1940; DetWom; DrAPF 80; EncMys; FemiCLE; GrWomMW; IntAu&W 76, 91, 93; IntWW 81, 82, 83; InWom SUP; MajTwCW; Novels; OxCCanL; REnAL; SmATA 61; ThrtnMM; TwCCr&M 80, 85, 91; TwCRGW; TwCRHW 90; WhAm 8, 11; WhoAm 74, 76, 78, 80, 82, 84, 86, 88, 90, 92, 94; WhoAmW 70, 72, 89, 91, 93; WhoWest 76, 78; WhoWor 74, 76; WorAu 1950; WrDr 76, 80, 82, 84, 86, 88, 90, 92, 94, 96*

Millay, Edna St. Vincent
[Nancy Boyd]
American. Author, Poet
Won Pulitzer for *The Ballad of the Harp Weaver,* 1922.
b. Feb 22, 1892 in Rockland, Maine
d. Oct 19, 1950 in Austerlitz, New York
Source: *AmAu&B; AmCulL; AmWomD; AmWomPl; AmWomWr; AmWr; ApCAB X; ArtclWW 2; ASCAP 66, 80; AtlBL; Benet 87, 96; BenetAL 91; BioAmW; BioIn 1, 2, 3, 4, 5, 6, 8, 9, 10, 11, 12, 15, 16, 17, 18, 19, 20, 21; CamGLE;*

CamHAL; CasWL; Chambr 3; ChhPo, S1, S2, S3; CnDAL; CnE&AP; CnMD; CnMWL; ConAmA; ConAmL; ConAu 104, 130; ContDcW 89; CyWA 58; DcAmB S4; DcArts; DcLB 45; DcLEL; EncWL 2, 3; EvLB; FacFETw; FemiCLE; GayLesB; GayLL; GoodHs; GrLiveH; GrWomW; GrWrEL P; HanAmWH; HerW, 84; IntDcWB; InWom, SUP; LegTOT; LibW; LinLib L, S; LngCTC; MajTwCW; McGEWB; McGEWD 72, 84; ModAL; ModAWWr; ModWD; ModWoWr; NatCAB 38; NewGrDA 86; NotAW; NotNAT B; NotWoAT; OxCAmL 65, 83, 95; OxCEng 67, 85, 95; OxCTwCP; OxCWoWr 95; PenBWP; PenC AM; PenNWW A, B; PoeCrit 6; RAdv 1, 14, 13-1; REn; REnAL; RfGAmL 87, 94; RGTwCWr; SixAP; Str&VC; Tw; TwCA, SUP; TwCLC 3, 4, 49; TwCWr; WebAB 74, 79; WhAm 3; WhDW; WhNAA; WomFir; WorAl; WorAlBi

Miller, Alfred Jacob
American. Artist
Sketched Native Americans; works long forgotten; rediscovered, 1930s.
b. Jan 2, 1810 in Baltimore, Maryland
d. Jun 26, 1874 in Baltimore, Maryland
Source: *ApCAB; ArtsAmW 1; BioIn 1, 2, 3, 4, 7, 8, 9, 10, 13; DcAmArt; IlBEAAW; McGDA; NewYHSD; OxCAmH; PeoHis; REnAW; WhAm HS; WhNaAH; WhWE*

Miller, Alice Duer
American. Author
Wrote *White Cliffs of Dover,* 1941.
b. Jul 28, 1874 in Staten Island, New York
d. Aug 22, 1942 in New York, New York
Source: *AmAu&B; AmWomD; AmWomPl; AmWomWr; BenetAL 91; ChhPo, S1; DcAmAu; DcNAA; InWom, SUP; LibW; LngCTC; NotAW; NotNAT B; ObitOF 79; REn; REnAL; TwCA, SUP; WhAm 2; WhLit; WhNAA; WhoHol A, B; WomWWA 14*

Miller, Ann
[Lucille Ann Collier]
American. Dancer, Actor, Singer
Star of *Sugar Babies,* 1979-86; known for MGM musicals: *On the Town,* 1949.
b. Apr 12, 1923? in Cherino, Texas
Source: *BioIn 9, 10, 11, 12, 16, 17; CelR 90; CmMov; ConTFT 4; CurBio 80; HalFC 88; IntDcF 1-3, 2-3; IntMPA 75, 76, 77, 78, 79, 80, 81, 82, 84, 86, 88, 92, 96; InWom SUP; MovMk; NewYTBS 79; NotWoAT; ThFT; VarWW 85; WhoAm 86, 90; WhoAmW 74; WhoEnt 92; WhoHol 92, A; WhoThe 81; WhoTwCL; WorAl; WorAlBi*

Miller, Arjay Ray
American. Business Executive
Dean of Stanford U graduate business school, 1969-79.
b. Mar 4, 1916 in Shelby, Nebraska
Source: *BioIn 7, 8, 11, 12; CurBio 67; EncABHB 5; IntWW 74, 75, 76, 77, 78, 91; St&PR 87; Who 92; WhoAm 86, 90; WhoFI 74; WhoWest 92*

Miller, Arnold Ray
American. Labor Union Official
Pres., UMW, 1972-79.
b. Apr 25, 1923 in Leewood, West Virginia
d. Jul 12, 1985 in Charleston, West Virginia
Source: *BiDAmL; BioNews 75; CurBio 74; NewYTBE 72; NewYTBS 74; WhAm 8; WhoAm 74, 76, 78, 80; WhoLab 76; WorAl*

Miller, Arthur
American. Dramatist
Wrote *Death of a Salesman,* 1949; *The Crucible,* 1953; married Marilyn Monroe, 1956-61; won Pulitzer, 1949; Tonys, 1947, 1949, 1953; Emmys, 1976, 1981.
b. Oct 17, 1915 in New York, New York
Source: *AmAu&B; AmCulL; AmNov; AmWr; Au&Arts 15; Au&Wr 71; AuNews 1; Benet 87, 96; BenetAL 91; BiE&WWA; BioIn 1, 2, 4, 5, 7, 8, 9, 10, 11, 12, 13, 14, 15, 16, 17, 18, 19, 20, 21; BlueB 76; CamGEL; CamGLE; CamGWoT; CamHAL; CasWL; CelR, 90; CnDAL; CnMD; CnMWL; CnThe; ConAmD; ConAu 1R, 2NR, 3BS, 30NR, 54NR; ConDr 73, 77, 82, 88, 93; ConLC 1, 2, 6, 10, 15, 26, 47, 78; ConTFT 1, 11; CroCD; CrtSuDr; CurBio 47, 73; CyWA 58, 89; DcArts; DcFM; DcLB 7; DcLEL 1940; DcTwCCu 1; DrAF 76; DramC 1; DrAPF 80, 91; EncAB-H 1974, 1996; EncMcCE; EncWL 2, 3; EncWT; Ent; FacFETw; FilmEn; FilmgC; GrWrEL DR; HalFC 80, 84, 88; IntAu&W 76, 77, 89, 91, 93; IntDcT 2; IntMPA 84, 86, 88, 92, 94, 96; IntWW 74, 75, 76, 77, 78, 79, 80, 81, 82, 83, 89, 91, 93; JeAmHC; JeHun; LegTOT; LinLib L, S; LngCTC; MagSAmL; MajMD 1; MajTwCW; MakMC; McGEWB; McGEWD 72, 84; ModAL, S1, S2; ModWD; NatPD 77, 81; NewCon; NewEOp 71; NewGrDO; NotNAT, A; OxCAmL 65, 83, 95; OxCAmT 84; OxCEng 67, 85, 95; OxCFilm; OxCThe 67, 83; PenC AM; PlP&P; PolProf E, T; RAdv 14, 13-2; RComAH; RComWL; REn; REnAL; REnWD; RfGAmL 87, 94; TwCA SUP; TwCWr; VarWW 85; WebAB 74, 79; WebE&AL; WhDW; Who 74, 82, 83, 85, 88, 90, 92, 94; WhoAm 74, 76, 78, 80, 82, 84, 86, 88, 90, 92, 94, 95, 96, 97; WhoAmJ 80; WhoE 85, 86, 89, 91; WhoEnt 92; WhoThe 72, 77, 81; WhoTwCL; WhoUSWr 88; WhoWor 74, 78, 80, 82, 84, 87, 89, 93, 95, 96, 97; WhoWorJ 72, 78; WhoWrEP 89, 92, 95; WorAl; WorAlBi; WorEFlm; WorLitC; WrDr 76, 80, 82, 84, 86, 88, 90, 92, 94, 96; WrPh*

Miller, Barry
American. Actor
Won Tony, 1985, for *Biloxi Blues;* in movie *Fame.*
b. Feb 8, 1958 in Los Angeles, California
Source: *ConTFT 2, 10; IntMPA 92, 94, 96; VarWW 85; WhoHol 92*

Miller, Bebe
American. Choreographer, Dancer
Artist director, Bebe Miller Co., 1984—; commissioned performances include *The Hendrix Project,* 1991.
b. Sep 1950 in New York, New York
Source: *BioIn 16; ConBlB 3*

Miller, Bob
[Robert Joseph Miller]
American. Politician
Dem. governor, NV, 1989—.
b. Mar 30, 1945 in Evanston, Illinois
Source: *AlmAP 92, 96; BiDrGov 1988; BioIn 20; LegTOT; WhoAm 88, 90, 92, 94, 95, 96, 97; WhoAmL 78, 79; WhoAmP 87, 89; WhoWest 87, 89, 92, 94, 96*

Miller, Carl S
American. Inventor
Invented first copying machine, making carbon paper obsolete, 1950.
b. Jul 23, 1912 in Edmonton, Alberta, Canada
d. Apr 20, 1986 in Saint Paul, Minnesota
Source: *AmMWSc 79; BioIn 14; NewYTBS 86*

Miller, Caroline
American. Author
Wrote 1933 Pulitzer-winning novel *Lamb in His Bosom.*
b. Aug 26, 1903 in Waycross, Georgia
d. Jul 12, 1992 in Waynesville, North Carolina
Source: *AmNov; BioIn 2, 4, 12; ChhPo; DcLB 9; DcLEL; FemiCLE; InWom; OxCAmL 65, 83; REnAL; SouWr; TwCA, SUP*

Miller, Cheryl
American. Basketball Coach, Basketball Player
Member of the gold-medal winning women's basketball team, 1984 Olympics; head women's basketball coach, University of Southern California, 1993—.
b. 1964 in Riverside, California
Source: *AfrAmSG; AmDec 1980; BasBi; BioIn 13; ConBlB 10; EncWomS; InB&W 85; LegTOT*

Miller, Dennis
American. Comedian, TV Personality
Comic anchorman for "Saturday Night Live" weekend update segments 1985-91; talk show host, "The Dennis Miller Show," 1992; "Dennis Miller Live," 1996.
b. Nov 3, 1953 in Pittsburgh, Pennsylvania

Source: *BioIn 16; ConTFT 10; IntMPA 96; LegTOT; News 92; WhoAm 94, 95, 96, 97; WhoCom*

Miller, Don
[Four Horsemen of Notre Dame]
American. Football Player
Member, Notre Dame backfield, 1923-24; in film *Spirit of Notre Dame,* 1931.
b. 1902? in Defiance, Ohio
d. Jul 28, 1979 in Cleveland, Ohio
Source: *NewYTBS 79; WhoFtbl 74; WhScrn 83*

Miller, Dorie
American. Laborer
Navy messman who won Navy Cross for downing 4 enemy planes, USS *Arizona,* Pearl Harbor.
b. Oct 12, 1919 in Waco, Texas
d. Dec 1943, At Sea
Source: *AfrAmAl 6; BioIn 4, 8; BlksScM; DcAmNB; NegAl 76, 83, 89*

Miller, Elizabeth Smith
American. Social Reformer, Suffragist
Originated "Bloomer costume," 1851, made popular by Amelia Bloomer.
b. Sep 20, 1822 in Hampton, New York
d. May 22, 1911 in Geneva, New York
Source: *AmRef; DcNAA; InWom SUP; LibW; NotAW; WhAm 1; WomFir*

Miller, Frankie
Scottish. Singer
Rhythm and blues, rock songs include "Darlin'," 1978.
b. 1950? in Glasgow, Scotland
Source: *BiDAmM; ConMuA 80A; EncRk 88; HarEnR 86; IlEncRk; PenEncP; RkOn 85; RolSEnR 83; WhoRocM 82*

Miller, Frederic
American. Brewer
Brewery is second largest in industry due to introduction of "Lite" beer, 1973.
b. 1824
d. 1888
Source: *Entr*

Miller, G(eorge) William
American. Government Official
Succeeded Arthur Burns as Federal Reserve Board chm., 1978-79; treasury secretary under Carter, 1979-81.
b. Mar 9, 1925 in Sapulpa, Oklahoma
Source: *BioIn 11, 17; BlueB 76; CurBio 78; Dun&B 90; IntWW 74, 75, 76, 77, 78, 79, 80, 82; IntYB 81; NewYTBS 77, 79; St&PR 87; Who 82, 83, 88, 94; WhoAm 74, 76, 78, 84, 86, 88, 90, 92, 94, 95, 96, 97; WhoE 74, 75, 77, 83, 89; WhoFI 77, 92, 94; WhoWor 74*

Miller, Gilbert Heron
American. Producer
Broadway, London stage productions noted for elegant staging; best known for *Victoria Regina,* 1935.
b. Jul 3, 1884 in New York, New York
d. Jan 2, 1969 in New York, New York
Source: *BiE&WWA; BioIn 4, 5, 8, 10; CamGWoT; CurBio 58, 69; DcAmB S8; NatCAB 54; NotNAT B; ObitOF 79; OxCThe 67; PlP&P; WhAm 5; WhThe*

Miller, Glenn
American. Bandleader
Leading figure of Big Band era, 1930s-42; hits include "In the Mood"; "Chattanooga Choo-Choo."
b. Mar 1, 1904 in Clarinda, Iowa
d. Dec 15, 1944? in English Channel
Source: *AllMusG; ASCAP 66, 80; Baker 78, 84; BgBands 74; BiDAmM; BiDJaz; BioIn 3, 4, 8, 9, 10, 11, 12; CmpEPM; CurBio 42; DcAmB S3; DcArts; FacFETw; FilmgC; HalFC 80, 84, 88; LegTOT; NewAmDM; NewGrDA 86; NewGrDJ 88; NewGrDM 80; OxCPMus; PenEncP; PeoHis; RadStar; WebAB 74, 79; WhAm 2; WhoHol B; WhoJazz 72; WhScrn 74, 77, 83; WorAl; WorAlBi*

Miller, Henry John
American. Actor, Manager
Influenced by Dion Boucicault; acted on Broadway, 1899-1906.
b. Feb 1, 1860 in London, England
d. Apr 9, 1926 in New York, New York
Source: *AmBi; DcAmB; FamA&A; NatCAB 38; WebAB 74, 79; WhAm 1*

Miller, Henry (Valentine)
American. Author
Books *Tropic of Cancer,* 1934; *Tropic of Capricorn,* 1939, banned in US until 1960s.
b. Dec 26, 1891 in New York, New York
d. Jun 7, 1980 in Pacific Palisades, California
Source: *AgeMat; AmAu&B; AmCulL; AmNov; AmWr; AnObit 1980; Benet 87, 96; BenetAL 91; BioIn 1, 2, 3, 4, 5, 6, 7, 8, 9, 10, 11, 12, 13, 14, 15, 16, 17, 18, 19, 20, 21; BlueB 76; CamGEL; CamGLE; CamHAL; CasWL; CelR; CmCal; CnDAL; CnMWL; ConAu 9R, 33NR, 97; ConLC 1, 2, 4, 9, 14, 43, 84; ConNov 72, 76; CurBio 80N; CyWA 89; DcAmB S10; DcArts; DcLB 4, 9, Y80A; DcLEL; DrAF 76; DrAPF 80; EncWL 2, 3; FacFETw; GrWrEL N; IntAu&W 76, 77; IntWW 74, 75, 76, 77, 78, 79, 80; LiExTwC; LinLib L; LngCTC; MagSAmL; MajTwCW; MakMC; McGEWB; ModAL, S1, S2; NewCBEL; NewYTBS 80; Novels; OxCAmL 65, 83, 95; OxCEng 85, 95; PenC AM; RAdv 1, 14, 13-1; REn; REnAL; RfGAmL 87, 94; RGTwCWr; TwCA, SUP; TwCWr; WebAB 74, 79; WebE&AL; WhAm 7; WhDW; Who 74; WhoAm 74, 76, 78, 80; WhoTwCL; WhoWor 74, 78, 80; WhScrn 83; WorAl; WorAlBi; WorLitC; WrDr 76, 80; WrPh*

Miller, Howard
American. Manufacturer
With father, founded Miller Clock Co., 1926, known for grandfather clocks.
b. 1905 in Michigan
Source: *Entr*

Miller, James Clifford, III
American. Government Official
Succeeded David Stockman as director, OMB, 1985.
b. Jun 25, 1942 in Atlanta, Georgia
Source: *AmMWSc 73S; BioIn 12, 13, 14, 15; CurBio 86; IntWW 89, 91, 93; NewYTBS 81, 84, 85; WhoAm 82, 84, 86, 88, 90, 92, 94, 95, 96, 97; WhoAmP 91; WhoE 97; WhoEmL 87; WhoFI 83, 85, 87, 89, 92, 94, 96; WhoScEn 96; WhoWor 96, 97*

Miller, Jason
American. Dramatist, Actor
Won Tony, Pulitzer, for writing *That Championship Season,* 1973.
b. Apr 22, 1939 in Scranton, Pennsylvania
Source: *AuNews 1; BiDrAPA 89; BioIn 12; BioNews 74; CelR; ConAmD; ConAu 73; ConDr 82, 88, 93; ConLC 2; ConTFT 4; CurBio 74; DcLB 7; HalFC 80, 84, 88; IntMPA 92, 94, 96; ItaFilm; LegTOT; MiSFD 9; NatPD 77; NewYTBE 72; NotNAT; OxCAmL 83, 95; PlP&P A; WhoAm 78, 80, 82, 84, 86, 88, 92, 94, 95, 96, 97; WhoEnt 92; WhoHol 92, A; WhoThe 77, 81; WorAl; WorAu 1970; WrDr 86, 92*

Miller, Joaquin
[Cincinnatus Hiner Miller]
"The Frontier Post"
American. Poet, Adventurer
Wrote verse volumes *Specimens,* 1868; *Pacific Poems,* 1870.
b. Sep 8, 1837 in Liberty, Indiana
d. Feb 17, 1913 in Oakland, California
Source: *Alli SUP; AmBi; ApCAB SUP; Benet 87, 96; BenetAL 91; BibAL; BioIn 12, 14, 18; CmCal; CnDAL; DcAmB; DcNAA; FifWWr; GayN; LegTOT; LinLib L, S; LngCTC; McGEWB; MouLC 4; NotNAT B; OxCAmL 65; OxCEng 67; PenC AM; REn; REnAL; Str&VC; TwCBDA; WebAB 74, 79; WhAm 1; WorAl; WorAlBi*

Miller, Joe
"Father of Jests"
English. Actor
Popular Drury Lane comedian, from 1709; name used unfairly after death in *Joe Miller's Jest-Book,* collection of coarse jokes.
b. 1684
d. 1738 in London, England
Source: *BioIn 1; DcBiPP; DcEnL; NewC; WebBD 83*

Miller, Johnny Laurence
American. Golfer
Turned pro, 1969; won US Open, 1973, British Open, 1976.
b. Apr 29, 1947 in San Francisco, California
Source: *BiDAmSp OS; BioNews 74; ConAu 93; CurBio 74; NewYTBS 75; WhoAm 76, 78, 80, 82, 84, 86, 90; WhoIntG*

Miller, Jonathan (Wolfe)
English. Author
Wrote *Darwin for Beginners,* 1982; directed *Long Day's Journey Into Night,* 1985.
b. Jul 21, 1934 in London, England
Source: *BiE&WWA; BioIn 6, 7, 9, 11, 13, 14, 15, 16, 17, 18, 20; BlueB 76; CamGWoT; CelR 90; ConAu 110, 115; ConTFT 5, 12; CurBio 70, 86; EncWT; Ent; FacFETw; FilmgC; GrStDi; HalFC 88; IntAu&W 91, 93; IntDcOp; IntDcT 3; IntvTCA 2; IntWW 74, 75, 76, 77, 78, 79, 80, 81, 82, 83, 89, 91, 93; IntWWM 90; MetOEnc; MiSFD 9; NewGrDO; NewYTBS 84; NotNAT; OxCThe 83; OxDcOp; TheaDir; Who 74, 82, 83, 85, 88, 90, 92, 94; WhoAm 90, 92, 94, 95, 96, 97; WhoEnt 92; WhoHol 92, A; WhoOp 76; WhoThe 72, 77, 81; WhoWor 84, 87, 89, 91, 93, 95, 96, 97; WorAl; WorAlBi; WrDr 80, 82, 84, 86, 88, 90, 92, 94, 96*

Miller, Marilyn
American. Actor
Sang "Easter Parade" in film *As Thousands Cheer,* 1933.
b. Sep 1, 1898 in Findlay, Ohio
d. Apr 7, 1936 in Evansville, Indiana
Source: *AmBi; BiDAmM; BiDD; BioAmW; BioIn 3, 8, 14, 16; CamGWoT; CmpEPM; EncMT; EncWT; Ent; Film 2; FilmEn; FilmgC; HalFC 80, 84, 88; InWom, SUP; LegTOT; LibW; MovMk; NewAmDM; NotAW; NotNAT B; NotWoAT; OxCAmT 84; OxCPMus; PlP&P; ThFT; WhoHol B; WhScrn 74, 77, 83; WorAl; WorAlBi*

Miller, Marvin Julian
American. Baseball Executive
Exec. director, ML Baseball Players Assn., 1966-83; led 13-day strike, 1972.
b. Apr 14, 1917 in New York, New York
Source: *Ballpl 90; BiDAmL; BiDAmLL; BiDAmSp BB; BioIn 9, 10, 12, 13; CurBio 73; WhoAm 74, 76, 78, 80, 82*

Miller, Max
American. Director
Directed original "Today" show, 1950s; produced documentary films.
b. Jan 28, 1911 in New York, New York
d. Oct 24, 1992 in Studio City, California
Source: *WhoE 74, 75, 77, 79, 81, 83, 85, 86*

Miller, Max (Carlton)
American. Author
Best-known book based on experiences as a reporter: *I Cover the Waterfront,* 1932.
b. Feb 9, 1899 in Traverse City, Michigan
d. Dec 27, 1967 in La Jolla, California
Source: *AmAu&B; Au&Wr 71; ConAu 1R, 16NR, 25R; CurBio 40, 68; NewYTBE 73; REnAL; TwCA, SUP; WhAm 4, 5; WhNAA*

Miller, Merle
American. Author, Journalist
Wrote presidential biographies: *Plain Speaking: An Oral Biography of Harry Truman,* 1974.
b. May 17, 1919 in Montour, Iowa
d. Jun 10, 1986 in Danbury, Connecticut
Source: *AmAu&B; AmNov; Au&Wr 71; AuNews 1; AuSpks; BenetAL 91; BioIn 10, 15; CelR; ConAu 4NR, 9R, 119; CurBio 86, 86N; LinLib L; REn; REnAL; WhAm 9; WhoAm 76, 78, 80, 82, 84; WhoWor 74; WorAu 1950; WrDr 76, 80, 82, 84, 86*

Miller, Mitch(ell William)
American. Conductor
Host of TV series "Sing Along with Mitch," 1961-66; hit single "Yellow Rose of Texas," 1955.
b. Jul 4, 1911 in Rochester, New York
Source: *Baker 84, 92; BiDAmM; BioIn 2, 3, 4, 5, 6, 7, 10, 12, 17; CelR, 90; CmpEPM; ConMus 11; CurBio 56; LegTOT; NewAmDM; NewGrDA 86; OxCPMus; PenEncP; RkOn 74; VarWW 85; WhoAm 74, 76, 78, 80, 82, 84; WhoAmA 73; WhoHol 92; WorAlBi*

Miller, Nicole (Jacqueline)
[Mrs. Kim Taipale]
American. Fashion Designer
Founder of Nicole Miller Inc., 1982.
b. Mar 20, 1951 in Fort Worth, Texas
Source: *CurBio 95; News 95; WhoAm 94, 95, 96, 97; WhoAmW 95, 97*

Miller, Nolan
American. Fashion Designer
Designed fashion for TV series "Dynasty."
b. 1935 in Texas
Source: *BioIn 13, 14; ConTFT 8*

Miller, Olive Beaupre
American. Author
Edited six-vol. children's classic, *My Bookhouse,* 1920-35.
b. Sep 11, 1883 in Aurora, Illinois
d. Mar 25, 1968 in Tucson, Arizona
Source: *AmAu&B; BioIn 10; NatCAB 54; WhoAmW 58, 61*

Miller, Olive Thorne
[Harriet Mann Miller]
American. Children's Author
Ornithologist; wrote children's books on birds: *Nesting Time,* 1888.
b. Jun 25, 1831 in Auburn, New York
d. Dec 25, 1918 in Los Angeles, California
Source: *Alli SUP; AmAu; AmAu&B; AmLY; AmWom; AmWomSc; AmWomWr; BbD; BiD&SB; BiInAmS; BioIn 15, 20; CarSB; ChhPo, S1; DcAmAu; DcAmB; DcNAA; InWom, SUP; LibW; NatCAB 9; NotAW; OhA&B; PenNWW A, B; TwCBDA; WhAm 1; WomSc; WomWWA 14*

Miller, Otto Neil
American. Business Executive
Chairman of Chevron Corp., 1967-74.
b. Jan 9, 1909? in Harlan, Iowa
d. Feb 4, 1988 in San Francisco, California
Source: *AmMWSc 82; IntWW 74, 75, 76, 77, 78, 79, 80, 81, 82, 83; WhoWest 76, 78*

Miller, Paul
American. Journalist, Business Executive
Pres., CEO of Gannett Co., 1957-70, chm. 1970-78; pres. of The Associated Press, 1963-72, chm. 1972-77.
b. Sep 28, 1906 in Diamond, Missouri
d. Aug 21, 1991 in West Palm Beach, Florida
Source: *BioIn 1, 4, 11, 12, 17, 19; BlueB 76; DcLB 127; EncTwCJ; NewYTBS 91; WhAm 10; WhoAm 74, 76, 78, 80, 82, 84, 86, 88, 90; WhoE 74, 75; WhoFI 74, 75; WhoWor 74, 76*

Miller, Perry Gilbert Eddy
American. Historian, Critic
Wrote on Puritanism: *The New England Mind,* 1939.
b. Feb 25, 1905 in Chicago, Illinois
d. Dec 9, 1963 in Cambridge, Massachusetts
Source: *AmAu&B; Benet 96; BioIn 3, 4, 6, 7, 8; DcAmB S7; DcAmReB 2; EncAB-H 1996; NewCol 75; PenC AM; REn; REnAL; TwCA SUP; WebAB 74; WhAm 4*

Miller, Reggie
[Reginald Wayne Miller]
American. Basketball Player
With Indiana Pacers, 1987—; member of US Olympic men's basketball team, 1996.
b. Aug 24, 1965 in Riverside, California
Source: *BioIn 13; CurBio 96; News 94; WhoAfA 96; WhoAm 95, 96, 97; WhoBlA 92, 94*

Miller, Roger Dean
American. Singer, Songwriter
Country-pop singer who won 11 Grammys; hit single "King of the Road," 1965.
b. Jan 2, 1936 in Fort Worth, Texas
d. Oct 25, 1992 in Los Angeles, California
Source: *AmSong; Baker 84, 92; BiDAmM; BioIn 14, 15; ConMus 4; CurBio 86; EncFCWM 83; EncRk 88; HarEnCM 87; NewAmDM; NewGrDA 86; OxCPMus; PenEncP; VarWW 85; WhAm 10; WhoAm 74, 76, 78, 80, 82, 84, 86, 88, 90, 92; WhoEnt 92; WorAl*

Miller, Shannon (Lee)
American. Gymnast
Won five gold medals, 1992 Olympics.
b. Mar 10, 1977 in Rolla, Missouri
Source: *CurBio 96; EncWomS; WhoAmW 93, 95, 97; WhoSpor; WhoWor 95, 96, 97*

Miller, Steve
[The Steve Miller Band]
American. Musician, Singer
Hit songs include "Heart Like a Wheel," 1981; "Abracadabra," 1982.
b. Oct 5, 1943 in Los Angeles, California
Source: *BioIn 11, 12, 13, 16; BkPepl; ConMuA 80A; ConMus 2; EncPR&S 74, 89; EncRk 88; IlEncRk; LegTOT; NewAmDM; NewGrDA 86; OnThGG; PenEncP; RkOn 74, 78; VarWW 85; WhoRock 81; WhoRocM 82*

Miller, Thomas
American. Producer
TV producer of sitcoms including "Happy Days" and "Full House."
Source: *Alli, SUP; BiDrACR; BioIn 5; DcNCBi 4; ItaFilm; NewYHSD; WhoHol 92*

Miller, Walter Dale
American. Politician
After Mickelson's death became Rep. governor of SD, 1993—.
b. Oct 5, 1925 in New Underwood, South Dakota
Source: *BiDrGov 1988; BioIn 20; WhoAm 92, 94, 95; WhoAmP 91; WhoMW 88, 90, 92, 93; WhoWor 93, 95*

Miller, William
American. Religious Leader
Prophesied second coming of Christ, 1843, 1844; followers called Millerites, then Adventists; Seventh-Day Adventists founded, based on his teachings, 1860s.
b. Feb 15, 1782 in Pittsfield, Massachusetts
d. Dec 20, 1849 in Hampton, New York
Source: *AmBi; AmSocL; ApCAB; BenetAL 91; BiDAmCu; BioIn 1, 3, 5, 6, 7, 9, 10, 11, 19, 20; DcAmB; DcAmReB 1, 2; DcNAA; Dis&D; EncARH; HarEnUS; LuthC 75; McGEWB; NatCAB 6; REnAL; TwCBDA; WebAB 74, 79; WhAm HS; WhDW*

Miller, William E
American. Politician
Rep. congressman from NY who was Barry Goldwater's running mate in 1964 presidential election.
b. Mar 22, 1914 in Lockport, New York
d. Jun 24, 1983 in Buffalo, New York
Source: *CurBio 83; IntWW 74, 75, 76; LinLib S; NewYTBS 83; PolProf J, K; PresAR*

Miller, William Ernest
American. Judge
Served on US Appeals Court, 1970-76.
b. Feb 3, 1908 in Johnson City, Tennessee
d. Apr 12, 1976 in Cincinnati, Ohio
Source: *BiDFedJ A; BioIn 10; WhAm 7; WhoAm 74, 76; WhoAmP 73; WhoGov 72, 75, 77; WhoSSW 73, 75*

Miller, William Mosley
"Fish Bait"
American. Government Official
Doorkeeper, US House of Representaives, 1948-76.
b. Jul 20, 1909 in Pascagoula, Mississippi
d. Sep 12, 1989 in Pascagoula, Mississippi
Source: *BioIn 11, 16; BioNews 75; WhoAmP 73, 77; WhoGov 72*

Miller, Zell (Bryan)
American. Politician
Dem. governor, GA, 1990—.
b. Feb 24, 1932 in Young Harris, Georgia
Source: *AlmAP 92, 96; BiDrGov 1988; BioIn 20; CurBio 96; IntWW 91, 93; LegTOT; PolsAm 84; WhoAm 76, 78, 80, 82, 86, 88, 90, 92, 94, 95, 96, 97; WhoAmP 73, 75, 77, 79, 81, 83, 85, 87, 89, 91, 93, 95; WhoGov 75, 77; WhoSSW 76, 78, 80, 82, 84, 86, 88, 91, 93, 95, 97; WhoWor 93, 95*

Milles, Carl Wilhelm Emil
American. Sculptor
Famous for huge sculptures, fountains at Chicago Exhibition, NY World's Fair, 1930s.
b. Jun 23, 1875 in Lagga, Sweden
d. Sep 19, 1955 in Stockholm, Sweden
Source: *BriEAA; CurBio 40, 52, 55; McGDA; NatCAB 43; OxCArt; REn; WhAm 3*

Millet, Jean Francois
French. Artist
Paintings on pleasant subjects include *The Gleaners,* 1857; *Man With the Hoe,* 1863.
b. Oct 4, 1814 in Gruchy, France
d. Jan 20, 1875 in Barbizon, France
Source: *AtlBL; BioIn 1, 2, 3, 5, 6, 7, 8, 9, 10, 11, 13, 14, 15, 16, 19; CelCen; ChhPo, S3; ClaDrA; DcArts; DcCathB; IlBEAAW; LinLib S; McGEWB; NewCol 75; OxCArt; OxCFr; REn*

Millett, John D(avid)
American. University Administrator
President of Miami University OH, 1953-64.
b. Mar 14, 1912
d. Nov 14, 1993 in Cincinnati, Ohio
Source: *AmMWSc 73S; BioIn 3, 19, 20; ConAu 104, 143; CurBio 94N; IndAu 1917; LEduc 74; WhoAm 74, 76, 78, 80, 82, 84, 86, 88; WhoWor 78, 80*

Millett, Kate
[Katherine Murray Millett]
American. Political Activist, Sculptor, Artist, Writer
Supports many women's issues groups; member of CORE, 1965—; books include *Sexual Politics,* 1970.
b. Sep 14, 1934 in Saint Paul, Minnesota
Source: *AmAu&B; AmWomWr; ArtclWW 2; AuNews 1; BenetAL 91; BioIn 9, 10, 11, 12, 16; BlmGWL; CelR; ConAu 32NR, 53NR, 73; ConLC 67; ContDcW 89; CurBio 71, 95; EncWB; FemiCLE; FemiWr; ForWC 70; GayLL; GrLiveH; IntAu&W 91, 93; IntDcWB; IntvTCA 2; InWom SUP; LegTOT; MajTwCW; MakMC; MugS; OxCAmL 83, 95; OxCWoWr 95; PolProf NF; RadHan; WhoAm 74, 76, 78, 80, 82, 84, 86, 88, 90, 92, 94, 95, 96, 97; WhoAmW 79, 81, 83, 85, 87, 89, 91, 93, 95, 97; WhoUSWr 88; WhoWrEP 89, 92, 95; WomWMM A, B; WorAlBi; WorAu 1985; WrDr 76, 80, 82, 84, 86, 88, 90, 92, 94, 96*

Milligan, Spike
British. Director, Author
Best known for "The Goon Show" with Peter Sellers, Harry Secombe on BBC, 1950s.
b. Apr 16, 1918 in Ahmadnagar, India
Source: *Au&Wr 71; BioIn 13, 15, 16, 17, 18; BlueB 76; ChhPo S1, S2; ConAu 4NR, 33NR, X; ConTFT 6; DcIrL, 96; EncSF 93; EncWT; EngPo; FacFETw; FilmgC; HalFC 80, 84, 88; IlWWBF, A; IntAu&W 91; IntWW 82, 83, 89, 91, 93; LegTOT; MajTwCW; OxCChiL; QDrFCA 92; VarWW 85; Who 92; WhoCom; WhoHol 92, A; WhoThe 72, 77; WrDr 76, 80, 82, 84, 86, 88, 90, 92, 94, 96*

Millikan, Clark Blanchard
American. Educator
Early force in growth of jet aircraft, guided missiles.
b. Aug 23, 1903 in Chicago, Illinois
d. Jan 2, 1966 in Pasadena, California
Source: *AmMWSc 73P; BioIn 7, 8; DcAmB S8; ObitOF 79; WhAm 4*

Millikan, Robert Andrews
American. Physicist
Studied elementary electronic charge, photoelectric effect; won Nobel Prize, 1923.
b. Mar 22, 1868 in Morrison, Illinois
d. Dec 19, 1953 in San Marino, California
Source: *AmAu&B; AmLY; AsBiEn; BiDAmEd; BiESc; BioIn 1, 2, 3, 4, 5, 7, 8, 11, 12, 13; CamDcSc; CurBio 40, 52, 54; DcAmB S5; DcInv; DcScB; EncAB-H 1974, 1996; FacFETw; InSci; LarDcSc; LinLib L, S; McGEWB; NatCAB 42; OxCAmH; RAdv 14, 13-5; REnAL; WebAB 74, 79; WhAm 3; WhDW; WhE&EA; WhNAA; WhoNob, 90, 95; WorAl; WorScD*

Milliken, William Grawn
American. Politician
Moderate Rep. governor of MI, 1969-82; served longer than any governor in state history.
b. Mar 26, 1922 in Traverse City, Michigan
Source: *BioIn 8, 9, 10, 12, 16; BioNews 75; IntWW 74, 75, 76, 77, 78, 79, 80, 81, 82, 83; WhoAm 74, 76, 78, 80, 82, 84, 86; WhoAmP 73, 77, 79, 81, 83, 85, 87, 89, 91, 93, 95; WhoGov 72, 75, 77; WhoMW 74, 76, 78, 80, 82; WhoWor 78, 82*

Millington, June
American. Musician
Leader of group Fanny; albums include *Mothers Pride.*
b. 1949, Philippines
Source: *GayLesB; OnThGG*

Millis, Walter
American. Author, Journalist
Books on American military history include *Arms and Men,* 1956.
b. Mar 16, 1899 in Atlanta, Georgia
d. Mar 17, 1968 in New York, New York
Source: *AmAu&B; BioIn 4, 8, 16; ConAu 37R, P-1; DcAmB S8; DcAmDH 80, 89; OxCAmL 65; RAdv 13-3; REn; REnAL; TwCA, SUP; WhAm 5; WhE&EA*

Milli Vanilli
[Fabrice Morvan; Rob Pilatus]
German. Music Group
Eurodisco duo, known for dancing and long cornrow hair; debut album *Girl You Know It's True,* 1989, sold 7 million copies; revealed that group never sang, only lip-synced songs; stripped of Grammy, 1990.
Source: *BioIn 17; ConMus 4*

Millner, Wayne E
American. Football Player
End, 1936-41, 1945, mostly with Washington; Hall of Fame, 1968.
b. Jan 13, 1913 in Roxbury, Massachusetts
d. Nov 20, 1976 in Falls Church, Virginia
Source: *BioIn 8, 11; NewYTBS 76; WhoFtbl 74*

Millo, Aprile
American. Opera Singer
Verdian soprano with credited roles in *Don Carlo,* 1985-86; *Turandot,* 1986-87; and *Il Trovatore,* 1988-89 at the Metropolitan Opera.
b. Apr 14, 1958 in New York, New York
Source: *BioIn 16; ConTFT 13; CurBio 88; IntWWM 90; MetOEnc; NewGrDO; NewYTBS 88; OxDcOp; PenDiMP; WhoAm 90; WhoEnt 92*

Mills, Alley
American. Actor
Played Norma on TV series "The Wonder Years," 1988-93.
Source: *BioIn 19; ConTFT 10; WhoEnt 92*

Mills, Billy
American. Track Athlete
Won gold medal in the 10,000-meter race, setting a then-Olympic record of 28:24.4.
b. 1938 in Pine Ridge Reservation, South Dakota
Source: *BioIn 7, 8, 9, 12, 21; EncNAB; NotNaAm; WhoSpor; WhoTr&F 73*

Mills, Darius Ogden
American. Businessman, Philanthropist
Founder, pres., Bank of California, 1860-70s; established Mills Hotels, NYC, to help house lower-income men, 1988.
b. Sep 5, 1825 in North Salem, New York
d. Sep 25, 1910 in New York, New York
Source: *AmBi; ApCAB, X; BiDAmBL 83; BioIn 13, 16; DcAmB; NatCAB 1, 18; TwCBDA; WhAm 1*

Mills, Donald
[The Mills Brothers]
American. Singer
Member of the family vocal group, 1930s-70s; often on Bing Crosby radio shows; hits include "Lazy River," 1931.
b. Apr 29, 1915 in Piqua, Ohio
Source: *BioIn 10, 12, 17; BioNews 74; InB&W 80; OxCPMus; WhoAfA 96; WhoBlA 88, 90, 92, 94; WhoHol 92*

Mills, Donna
[Donna Jean Miller]
American. Actor
Played Abby Ewing on TV series "Knots Landing," 1980-91.
b. Dec 11, 1943 in Chicago, Illinois
Source: *BioIn 12, 14, 15; CelR 90; ConTFT 3; HalFC 84, 88; IntMPA 86, 92; InWom SUP; LegTOT; VarWW 85; WhoAm 90; WhoEnt 92; WhoHol A; WhoTelC; WorAlBi*

Mills, Florence
American. Entertainer
Starred in black musical revues on Broadway, 1920s: *Blackbirds of 1926.*
b. Jan 25, 1895 in Washington, District of Columbia
d. Nov 1, 1927 in New York, New York
Source: *AfrAmAl 6; BiDAfM; BiDAmM; BiDD; BiDJaz; BioIn 9, 16, 18; DcAmNB; DrBlPA, 90; EncMT; EncVaud; Ent; InWom, SUP; NegAl 76, 83, 89; NotAW; NotNAT B; NotWoAT; OxCAmT 84; OxCPMus; OxCThe 83; WhoHol B*

Mills, Harry
[The Mills Brothers]
American. Singer
Member of vocal group, popular 1930s-70s; noted for stage presence, pleasing personalities.
b. Aug 19, 1913 in Piqua, Ohio
d. Jun 28, 1982 in Los Angeles, California
Source: *BioNews 74; InB&W 80, 85; NewYTBS 82; OxCPMus*

Mills, Hayley
[Hayley Catherine Rose Vivian Mills]
English. Actor
Known for child, adolescent roles in Walt Disney films; won Oscar for *Polyanna,* 1960.
b. Apr 18, 1946 in London, England
Source: *BioIn 5, 6, 7, 8, 9, 10, 11, 15, 16; CelR; ConTFT 3; CurBio 63; FilmAG WE; FilmEn; FilmgC; HalFC 80, 84, 88; IlWWBF; IntMPA 75, 76, 77, 78, 79, 80, 81, 82, 84, 86, 88, 92, 94, 96; IntWW 83, 91; InWom, SUP; LegTOT; MotPP; MovMk; NotNAT A; RkOn 74; VarWW 85; WhoAmW 66, 68, 70, 72, 74; WhoEmL 91; WhoEnt 92; WhoHol 92, A; WhoThe 77, 81; WhoWor 74, 91; WorAl; WorAlBi; WorEFlm*

Mills, Herbert
[The Mills Brothers]
American. Singer
Member of family vocal group; hits include "Glow Worm," 1952.
b. Apr 2, 1912 in Piqua, Ohio
d. Apr 12, 1989 in Las Vegas, Nevada
Source: *AnObit 1989; BioIn 10, 12, 16, 17; BioNews 74; InB&W 80; NewYTBS 89; OxCPMus; WhoBlA 92*

Mills, Irving
American. Musician, Composer
Discovered, managed Duke Ellington, 1926; wrote "Minnie the Moocher."
b. Jan 16, 1894 in New York, New York
d. Apr 21, 1985 in Palm Springs, California
Source: *AmPS; AnObit 1985; ASCAP 66, 80; BiDAmM; BioIn 4, 12, 14; CmpEPM; ConAu 115; FacFETw; PenEncP; Sw&Ld C*

Mills, John
[The Mills Brothers]
American. Singer
Replaced son in family vocal group, 1936-56.
b. Feb 11, 1889 in Bellefonte, Pennsylvania
d. Dec 8, 1967 in Bellefonte, Pennsylvania
Source: *WhScrn 77, 83*

Mills, John, Sir
[Lewis Ernest Watts Mills]
English. Actor
Won Oscar for *Ryan's Daughter,* 1970; father of Hayley, Juliet Mills.
b. Feb 22, 1908 in Felixstowe, England
Source: *BiDFilm, 81, 94; BiE&WWA; BioIn 2, 6, 7, 9, 11, 12, 13, 15, 19; BlueB 76; CamGWoT; CelR; CmMov; ConAu 108; ConTFT 11; CurBio 63; DcArts; EncEurC; EncMT; FacFETw; FilmAG WE; FilmEn; FilmgC; ForYSC; HalFC 80, 84, 88; IlWWBF, A; IntDcF 1-3, 2-3; IntMPA 75, 76, 77, 78, 79, 80, 81, 82, 84, 86, 88, 92, 94, 96; IntWW 74, 75, 76, 77, 78, 79, 80, 81, 82, 83, 89, 91, 93; ItaFilm; LegTOT; MotPP; MovMk; NotNAT A; OxCFilm; OxCPMus; PlP&P; VarWW 85; Who 88, 90, 92; WhoAm 90, 92; WhoEnt 92; WhoHol 92, A; WhoThe 72, 77, 81; WhoWor 74; WorAl; WorAlBi; WorEFlm*

Mills, Juliet
[Mrs. Maxwell Caulfield]
English. Actor
Starred in "Nanny and the Professor," 1970-71; daughter of John Mills.
b. Nov 21, 1941 in London, England

Source: *BiE&WWA; BioIn 6, 14, 21; ConTFT 3; FilmEn; FilmgC; ForYSC; HalFC 80, 84, 88; IlWWBF; IntMPA 84, 86, 88, 92, 94, 96; InWom; ItaFilm; LegTOT; MotPP; NotNAT A; VarWW 85; WhoHol 92, A; WhoThe 72, 77, 81; WhoWor 74; WorAlBi*

Mills, Mary
American. Golfer
Turned pro, 1962; won US Women's Open, 1963, LPGA, 1964, 1973.
b. Jan 19, 1940 in Laurel, Mississippi
Source: *WhoGolf*

Mills, Ogden Livingston
American. Government Official
Secretary of Treasury under Hoover, 1932-33.
b. Aug 23, 1884 in Newport, Rhode Island
d. Oct 11, 1937 in New York, New York
Source: *AmBi; BiDrAC; BiDrUSC 89; BiDrUSE 71, 89; BioIn 4, 10; DcAmB S2; DcNAA; NatCAB 32; WhAm 1; WhAmP*

Mills, Robert
American. Architect, Engineer
Designed Washington Monument, Treasury Building, Post Office, Washington, DC.
b. Aug 12, 1781 in Charleston, South Carolina
d. Mar 3, 1855 in Washington, District of Columbia
Source: *Alli; AmBi; ApCAB; BiAUS; BiDAmAr; BiDSA; BioIn 1, 2, 10, 11, 13, 14, 15, 16, 20; BriEAA; DcAmAu; DcAmB; DcD&D; DcNAA; Drake; EncAAr 1, 2; HarEnUS; IntDcAr; LegTOT; MacEA; McGDA; McGEWB; NatCAB 18; NewYHSD; OxCAmH; OxCAmL 65; OxCArt; TwCBDA; WebAB 74, 79; WhAm HS; WhoArch; WorAl; WorAlBi*

Mills, Stephanie
American. Actor, Singer
Made Broadway debut in *The Wiz,* 1975, revival, 1984; hit songs include "You're Putting a Rush on Me," 1987; won Grammy, 1980.
b. Mar 22, 1957 in New York, New York
Source: *BioIn 16; DrBlPA, 90; IlEncBM 82; InB&W 85; LegTOT; NotBlAW 2; RkOn 85; WhoAm 90; WhoAmW 87; WhoBlA 80, 85, 90, 92; WhoEnt 92*

Mills, Wilbur Daigh
American. Politician
Dem. con. from AR, 1939-77; chaired Ways and Means Committee, 1958-74; career ruined by 1974 sex scandal.
b. May 24, 1909 in Kensett, Arkansas
d. May 2, 1992 in Searcy, Arkansas
Source: *AlmAP 82; BiDrAC; BiDrUSC 89; BioIn 4, 5, 6, 7, 8, 9, 10, 11, 12; CngDr 74; CurBio 56; FacFETw; IntWW 74, 75, 76, 77, 78, 79, 80, 81, 82, 83, 89, 91; News 92; NewYTBE 71; PolProf E, J, K, NF; WhAm 10; Who 74, 82, 83, 85, 90, 92; WhoAm 74, 76, 78, 80, 82, 84, 86, 88, 90; WhoAmL 85; WhoAmP 87, 91; WhoGov 72; WhoSSW 75, 76, 82; WhoWor 74*

Mills Brothers, The
[Donald Mills; Harry Mills; Herbert Mills; John Mills]
American. Music Group
First black vocal group to break the color barrier, 1930s; hits include million- seller "Paper Doll," 1943; noted for radio, TV, club appearances.
Source: *Alli, SUP; AllMusG; AmPS A, B; BiDAfM; BiDAmM; BiDBrA; BioIn 2, 5, 10; BioNews 74; CmpEPM; ConMus 14; CurBio 63; DcArts; DcBiPP; DcNaB; DcTwCCu 5; DcVicP 2; DrBlPA 90; EncVaud; InB&W 80, 85, 85A; NatCAB 12; NewCBEL; NewGrDA 86; NewGrDJ 88, 94; NewYTBS 82, 89; OxCCan SUP; OxCPMus; PenEncP; RadStar; RkOn 74, 82; ScFEYrs; StaCVF; VarWW 85; Who 82, 83, 85, 88, 90, 92, 94; WhoHol 92, A; WhoRock 81*

Milne, A(lan) A(lexander)
English. Author
Wrote *Winnie-the-Pooh,* 1926; *The House at Pooh Corner,* 1928.
b. Jan 18, 1882 in London, England
d. Jan 31, 1956 in Hartfield, England
Source: *AnCL; AuBYP 2, 3; Benet 96; BiDMoPL; BioIn 1, 2, 3, 4, 5, 6, 7, 8, 9, 10, 11, 12, 13, 14, 15, 17, 19; BkCL; CarSB; CasWL; Chambr 3; ChhPo, S1, S2; ChlLR 1; CnMD; DcArts; DcLEL; DcNaB 1951; EncMys; EngPo; Ent; EvLB; GrBr; JBA 34, 51; LngCTC; MajAI; McGEWD 72; ModBrL; ModWD; NewC; NewCBEL; NotNAT B; OxCEng 67, 95; OxCTwCP; PenC ENG; RAdv 1, 14; REn; RGTwCWr; SJGFanW; Str&VC; TwCA, SUP; TwCChW 78, 95; TwCWr; WhAm 3; WhDW; WhE&EA; WhLit; WhoChL; WhoLA; WhThe; YABC 1*

Milne, Christopher Robin
English. Author
The original Christopher Robin of his father's classic tale, *Winnie the Pooh,* 1926.
b. Aug 21, 1920 in London, England
d. Apr 20, 1996 in London, England
Source: *AuNews 2; BioIn 7, 10, 11; ConAu 11NR, 27NR, 61, 152; IntAu&W 89, 91, 93; News 96; NewYTBS 27; WrDr 76, 80, 82, 84, 86, 88, 90, 92, 94, 96*

Milne, David Brown
Canadian. Artist
Painter of rural Ontario landscapes; pioneered post-impressionism in Canada.
b. Jan 8, 1882 in Paisley, Ontario, Canada
d. Dec 26, 1953 in Toronto, Ontario, Canada
Source: *CreCan 1; McGDA; McGEWB; NewCol 75; OxCArt; OxCTwCA; OxDcArt*

Milne, George Francis, Baron
British. Military Leader
WW I general who led campaign into Turkey, occupying Constantinople until 1920.
b. Nov 5, 1866 in Aberdeen, Scotland
d. Mar 23, 1948 in London, England
Source: *BioIn 1, 5, 11; DcNaB 1941*

Milner, Alfred, Viscount
British. Statesman
Colonial-secretary, 1919-21; recommended Egypt's independence, 1921.
b. Mar 23, 1854 in Giessen, Germany
d. May 13, 1925 in Canterbury, England
Source: *BioIn 16; DcAfHiB 86; DcEuL; DcNaB 1922; DcTwHis; Dis&D; GrBr; HisDBrE; LngCTC; McGEWB; VicBrit*

Milner, Martin Sam
American. Actor
Played Pete Malloy in "Adam-12," 1968-75.
b. Dec 28, 1931 in Detroit, Michigan
Source: *ConTFT 7; FilmgC; HalFC 84, 88; IntMPA 86, 92; MotPP; VarWW 85; WhoAm 76, 78, 80; WhoHol A*

Milnes, Sherrill Eustace
American. Opera Singer
Outstanding Verdi baritone; joined NY Met., 1965 in debut *Faust*; one of the most recorded opera stars.
b. Jan 10, 1935 in Downers Grove, Illinois
Source: *Baker 84, 92; BioIn 13, 14, 15; CelR 90; CurBio 70; IntWW 83, 91; IntWWM 90; InWom SUP; MetOEnc; NewAmDM; NewGrDA 86; NewGrDO; NewYTBS 79; PenDiMP; WhoAm 74, 76, 78, 80, 82, 84, 86, 88, 90, 92, 94, 95, 96, 97; WhoEnt 92; WhoOp 76; WhoWor 74; WorAl; WorAlBi*

Milosevic, Slobodan
Serbian. Political Leader
Pres., Serbia, 1989—; held a number of posts within the Communist Party, including pres., 1986-1989.
b. Aug 29, 1941 in Pozarevac, Yugoslavia
Source: *BioIn 16; CurBio 90; IntWW 91, 93; News 93-2; NewYTBS 88, 91; WhoSoCE 89; WhoWor 91, 93, 95, 96, 97*

Milosz, Czeslaw
[J. Syruc]
American. Author, Educator
Founded catastrophist school of Polish poetry; won Nobel Prize, 1980.
b. Jun 30, 1911 in Sateiniai, Lithuania
Source: *Benet 87, 96; BenetAL 91; BioIn 10, 11, 12, 13, 14, 15, 16; CasWL; ClDMEL 80; ConAu 23NR, 51NR, 81; ConFLW 84; ConLC 5, 11, 22, 31, 56, 82; ConWorW 93; CurBio 81; CyWA 89;*

DcArts; DrAS 74F, 78F; EncWL, 2, 3; EuWr 13; IntAu&W 89, 91, 93; IntWW 81, 82, 83, 89, 91, 93; IntWWP 77; LegTOT; LiExTwC; MagSWL; MajTwCW; ModSL 2; NewYTBS 80, 90; NobelP; OxCAmL 83, 95; OxCEng 85, 95; PenC EUR; PoeCrit 8; PolBiDi; RAdv 14, 13-2; RfGWoL 95; Who 82, 83, 85, 88, 90, 92, 94; WhoAm 80, 82, 84, 86, 88, 90, 92, 94, 95, 96, 97; WhoNob, 90, 95; WhoSoCE 89; WhoTwCL; WhoUSWr 88; WhoWest 82, 84, 87, 89, 92, 94, 96; WhoWor 82, 84, 87, 89, 91, 93, 95, 96, 97; WhoWrEP 89, 92, 95; WorAl; WorAlBi; WorAu 1950

Milsap, Ronnie
American. Singer
Blind country singer whose hits include "Any Day Now," 1982.
b. Jan 16, 1944 in Robinsville, North Carolina
Source: *Baker 84, 92; BgBkCoM; BioIn 14, 17; CelR 90; ConMus 2; EncFCWM 83; HarEnCM 87; HarEnR 86; PenEncP; RkOn 85; WhoAm 86, 90; WhoEnt 92; WorAlBi*

Milstein, Cesar
British. Biologist
Shared 1984 Nobel Prize in medicine for immunological research with antibodies.
b. Oct 8, 1927 in Bahia Blanca, Argentina
Source: *AmMWSc 89, 92, 95; BiESc; BioIn 12, 14, 15; CamDcSc; IntWW 89, 91, 93; LarDcSc; NewYTBS 84; NobelP; NotTwCS; Who 82, 83, 85, 88, 90, 92, 94; WhoAm 88, 90, 92, 94, 95; WhoMedH; WhoNob, 90, 95; WhoScEn 94, 96; WhoWor 87, 89, 91, 93, 95, 96, 97; WorAlBi*

Milstein, Nathan
American. Violinist
Violin Virtuoso, noted concertist; toured with Horowitz in Russia; made US debut, 1929; won Grammy, 1975.
b. Dec 31, 1904 in Odessa, Russia
d. Dec 21, 1992 in London, England
Source: *Baker 78, 84; BiDAmM; BiDSovU; BioIn 1, 2, 3, 4, 5, 9, 10, 11, 14, 17, 18, 19; BlueB 76; BriBkM 80; CelR, 90; CurBio 50, 93N; FacFETw; IntWW 74, 89, 91; IntWWM 77, 80, 90; LegTOT; MusMk; MusSN; NewAmDM; NewGrDA 86; NewGrDM 80; PenDiMP; WhAm 11; Who 74, 82, 83, 85, 88, 90, 92; WhoAm 78, 80, 82, 84, 86, 88, 92; WhoAmM 83; WhoEnt 92; WhoMus 72; WhoWor 78, 80, 82, 84, 87, 89, 91, 93*

Milton, John
English. Poet
Wrote in four languages; known for masterpiece, written after losing eyesight, *Paradise Lost,* 1667.
b. Dec 9, 1608 in London, England
d. Nov 8, 1674 in London, England
Source: *Alli; AtlBL; BbD; Benet 87, 96; BiD&SB; BiDRP&D; BioIn 1, 2, 3, 4, 5, 6, 7, 8, 9, 10, 11, 12, 13, 14, 15, 17, 18, 19, 20, 21; BlmGEL; BritAu; BritWr 2; CamGEL; CamGLE; CasWL; ChhPo, S1, S2, S3; CnDBLB 2; CnE&AP; CnThe; CroE&S; CrtT 2, 4; CyEd; CyWA 58; DcArts; DcBiPP; DcEnA, A; DcEnL; DcEuL; DcLB 131, 151; DcLEL; DcNaB; Dis&D; EncWT; Ent; EvLB; GrWrEL P; HisDStE; HsB&A; LegTOT; LinLib L, S; LitC 9; LngCEL; LuthC 75; MagSWL; McGEWB; MouLC 1; NewC; NewCBEL; NewEOp 71; NotNAT B; OxCEng 67, 85, 95; OxCMus; OxDcOp; PenC ENG; PlP&P; PoChrch; RAdv 1, 14, 13-1; RComWL; REn; REnWD; RfGEnL 91; RGFBP; WebE&AL; WhDW; WorAl; WorAlBi; WorLitC; WrPh*

Mimieux, Yvette Carmen M
American. Actor
Films include *The Black Hole,* 1979; appeared in many TV movies.
b. Jan 8, 1939 in Los Angeles, California
Source: *BioIn 16; ConTFT 5; FilmgC; HalFC 84, 88; IntMPA 86, 92; InWom SUP; MotPP; MovMk; WhoAm 74; WhoHol A*

Min, Anchee
Chinese. Writer
Author of *Red Azalea,* 1994.
b. Jan 14, 1957 in Shanghai, China
Source: *AsAmAlm; BioIn 20; ConAu 146; ConLC 86; NotAsAm*

Minamoto Yoritomo
Japanese. Military Leader, Ruler
Devised the system of bakufu, or rule by feudal lords; became Shogun, 1192.
b. 1147, Japan
d. Feb 9, 1199 in Kamakura, Japan
Source: *EncJap; HisWorL; McGEWB*

Mindszenty, Jozsef, Cardinal
Hungarian. Religious Leader
Regarded in West as symbol of resistance to totalitarian regimes; imprisoned by Nazis, Communists.
b. Mar 29, 1892 in Csehimindszent, Austria-Hungary
d. May 6, 1975 in Vienna, Austria
Source: *BioIn 1, 2, 3, 4, 5, 6, 8, 9, 10, 11, 12, 18; ColdWar 1, 2; ConAu 57, 65; CurBio 57, 75N; DcTwHis; EncCW; EncWB; FacFETw; IntWW 74; NewYTBE 71; NewYTBS 75; ObitT 1971; WhAm 6; WorAl; WorAlBi*

Mineo, Sal(vatore)
"The Switchblade Kid"
American. Actor, Singer
Oscar nominations for *Rebel Without a Cause,* 1955; *Exodus,* 1960.
b. Jan 10, 1939 in New York, New York
d. Feb 12, 1976 in Los Angeles, California
Source: *BioIn 4, 5, 10, 11, 12, 15, 18; ConTFT 2; FilmEn; FilmgC; ForYSC; HalFC 80, 84, 88; IntDcF 1-3, 2-3; IntMPA 75, 76; LegTOT; MotPP; MovMk; NewYTBS 76; RkOn 74; WhAm 6; WhoHol C; WhScrn 83; WorAl*

Miner, Jack
[John Thomas Miner]
American. Ornithologist
Established bird sanctuary, 1904, for study of migratory birds; foundation continues today.
b. Apr 10, 1865 in Dover Centre, Ohio
d. Nov 3, 1944 in Kingsville, Ontario, Canada
Source: *BioIn 2; DcNAA; MacDCB 78; ObitOF 79; OhA&B; OxCCan; WhAm 4; WhNAA*

Miner, Worthington C
"Tony"
American. Producer
Created "The Ed Sullivan Show," 1948-71.
b. Nov 13, 1900 in Buffalo, New York
d. Dec 11, 1982 in New York, New York
Source: *BiE&WWA; BioIn 14; CurBio 53, 83; IntMPA 77, 80, 82; NewYTBS 82; NewYTET; NotNAT; WhAm 8; WhoAm 74, 76, 78, 80, 82; WhoThe 77A; WhoWor 82; WhThe*

Ming, T'ai-Tsu
[Yuan-Chang Chu; Hung Wu]
Chinese. Ruler
Founder, first emperor of Ming dynasty, 1368-98; ended Yuan dynasty by capturing Peking; drove out Mongols, united China.
b. 1328 in Anhui Province, China
d. 1398
Source: *BioIn 14; Dis&D; WebBD 83; WhDW*

Mingus, Charles
"Jazz's Angry Man"
American. Jazz Musician, Bandleader
Bass virtuoso who elevated bass to melody carrier; led sextet, 1960s.
b. Apr 22, 1922 in Nogales, Arizona
d. Jan 5, 1979 in Cuernavaca, Mexico
Source: *AfrAmAl 6; AllMusG; Baker 78, 84, 92; BiDAfM; BiDAmM; BiDJaz; BioIn 5, 6, 7, 9, 11, 12, 13, 14, 15, 16, 17, 19; CmpEPM; ConAmC 76, 82; ConAu 85, 93; ConMus 9; CurBio 71, 79, 79N; DcAmB S10; DcArts; DcTwCCu 5; DrBlPA, 90; EncJzS; FacFETw; IlEncJ; InB&W 80, 85; IntWWM 77; LegTOT; MusMk; NegAl 83, 89; NewAmDM; NewGrDA 86; NewGrDJ 88, 94; NewGrDM 80; NewYTBS 79; OxCPMus; PenEncP; WhAm 7; WhoAm 74, 76, 78; WhoBlA 75, 77; WhoWor 74; WhScrn 83; WorAl; WorAlBi*

Mingxia, Fu
Chinese. Diver
Youngest world champion diver in the history of int'l aquatic competition at age 12.
b. Aug 16, 1977, China

Mink, Patsy Takemoto
American. Politician
Liberal Dem. representative from HI, 1965-77.

b. Dec 6, 1927 in Paia, Hawaii
Source: *AlmAP 92; AmPolW 80; AmWomM; AsAmAlm; BiDrAC; BiDrUSC 89; CngDr 74; CurBio 68; InWom, SUP; NotAsAm; PolProf J, NF; WhoAm 74, 76, 78, 80, 82, 84, 92, 94, 95, 96, 97; WhoAmP 73, 75, 77, 79, 81, 83, 85, 87, 89, 91, 93, 95; WhoAmW 61, 64, 66, 68, 70, 72, 74, 75, 77, 79, 81, 83, 85, 91, 93, 95, 97; WhoAsA 94; WhoE 95; WhoGov 77; WhoWest 76, 92, 94, 96; WomPO 78*

Minkowski, Oskar
German. Physiologist, Pathologist
First to put forth the theory that diabetes was caused by the suppression of a fluid of the pancreas—later discovered as insulin.
b. Jan 13, 1858 in Aleksotas, Russia
d. Jul 18, 1931 in Furstenberg an der Havel, Germany
Source: *BiHiMed; BioIn 9; DcScB S2*

Minnelli, Liza
American. Actor, Singer
Daughter of Judy Garland, Vincente Minnelli; won Oscar for *Cabaret,* 1972; other films include *Arthur,* 1981.
b. Mar 12, 1946 in Los Angeles, California
Source: *Baker 92; BiDAmM; BiDD; BiDFilm, 81, 94; BiE&WWA; BioAmW; BioIn 8, 9, 10, 11, 12, 13, 14, 15, 16; BkPepl; BlueB 76; CelR, 90; ContDcW 89; ConTFT 8; CurBio 70, 88; DcArts; EncMT; FilmEn; FilmgC; GoodHs; HalFC 80, 84, 88; IntDcF 1-3, 2-3; IntMPA 75, 76, 77, 78, 79, 80, 81, 82, 84, 86, 88, 92, 94, 96; IntWW 74, 75, 76, 77, 78, 79, 80, 81, 82, 83, 89, 91, 93; InWom SUP; ItaFilm; LegTOT; MotPP; MovMk; NewAmDM; NewGrDA 86; NotNAT; OxCAmT 84; OxCPMus; PenEncP; VarWW 85; WhoAm 76, 78, 80, 82, 84, 86, 88, 90, 92, 94, 95, 96, 97; WhoAmW 74, 79, 81, 83, 85, 87, 89, 91, 93, 95, 97; WhoE 93, 95; WhoEnt 92; WhoHol 92, A; WhoThe 77, 81; WhoWor 78; WorAl; WorAlBi*

Minnelli, Vincente
American. Director
Won Oscar for *Gigi,* 1958; married Judy Garland, 1945-50; father of Liza Minnelli.
b. Feb 28, 1913 in Chicago, Illinois
d. Jul 25, 1986 in Beverly Hills, California
Source: *AnObit 1986; BiDD; BiDFilm, 81; CelR; CmMov; ConAu 117, 119, 153; CurBio 75, 86N; DcFM; EncMT; FilmgC; HalFC 84; IntMPA 86; IntWW 74, 75, 76, 77, 78, 79, 80, 81, 82, 83; MovMk; NewYTBS 86; NotNAT; OxCFilm; VarWW 85; WhoAm 86; WhoWor 74; WorEFlm*

Minnesota Fats
[Rudolf Walter Wanderone]
American. Billiards Player
Legendary figure portrayed by Jackie Gleason in *The Hustler,* 1961.
b. 1913? in New York, New York
d. Jan 17, 1996 in Nashville, Tennessee
Source: *BiDAmSp BK; BioIn 7, 8; LegTOT; WhoAm 76, 78, 80, 82*

Minoso, Minnie
[Saturnino Orestes Arrieta Armas Minoso]
Cuban. Baseball Player
Outfielder, 1949, 1951-64, 1976, 1980; led AL in hits, 1960; only player in ML's five decades.
b. Nov 29, 1922 in Havana, Cuba
Source: *Ballpl 90; BaseEn 88; BioIn 18, 20, 21; WhoHisp 91, 92, 94; WhoSpor*

Minot, George Richards
American. Physician, Educator
Shared Nobel Prize, 1934, for discoveries of effects of liver therapy on anemia.
b. Dec 2, 1885 in Boston, Massachusetts
d. Feb 25, 1950 in Brookline, Massachusetts
Source: *AmDec 1920; AsBiEn; BiESc; BiHiMed; BioIn 1, 2, 3, 4, 5, 6, 9, 11, 15, 20; DcAmB S4; DcAmMeB 84; DcScB; HarEnUS; InSci; LarDcSc; NatCAB 38; NotTwCS; ObitOF 79; OxCAmL 83; OxCMed 86; WebAB 74, 79; WebBD 83; WhAm 2; WhNAA; WhoNob, 90, 95*

Minow, Newton Norman
American. Broadcasting Executive, Lawyer
Known for stiff license renewal policy while FCC chm., 1961-63; won Peabody, 1961; chm., PBS, 1978.
b. Jan 17, 1926 in Milwaukee, Wisconsin
Source: *BioIn 5, 6, 7, 8, 11, 12, 14; ConAu 13R; CurBio 61; IntWW 83, 91; LesBEnT 92; NatCAB 63N; St&PR 87, 91; VarWW 85; WhoAm 74, 76, 78, 80, 82, 84, 86, 88, 90, 92, 94, 95, 96; WhoAmJ 80; WhoAmL 78, 79, 83, 85, 87, 90, 92; WhoAmP 73, 75, 77, 79, 81, 83, 85, 87, 89, 91, 93, 95; WhoMW 84, 92; WhoWor 74, 78, 80, 82, 84; WrDr 86, 92*

Minsky, Abraham Bennett
[The Minsky Brothers]
American. Producer
With brothers, owned chain of burlesque houses; helped sponsor Bert Lahr, Abbott and Costello.
b. Mar 1, 1881 in New York, New York
d. Sep 5, 1949 in New York, New York
Source: *BioIn 2, 3; NatCAB 37; ObitOF 79*

Minsky, Harold
[The Minsky Brothers]
American. Producer
Diehard supporter of old-time striptease burlesque; ran show around US; son of Abraham.
b. 1915?
d. Dec 28, 1977 in Las Vegas, Nevada
Source: *BioIn 11; NewYTBS 77*

Minsky, Marvin Lee
American. Scientist, Educator
Pioneer in the field of artificial intelligence; cofounder of MIT's Artificial Intelligence Laboratory, 1964; wrote *The Society of Mind,* 1986.
b. Aug 9, 1927 in New York, New York
Source: *AmMWSc 73P, 76P, 79, 82, 86, 89, 92, 95; BioIn 12, 15, 16, 18, 20; ConAu 21R; HisDcDP; IntWW 91; WhoAm 74, 76, 78, 80, 82, 84, 86, 88, 90, 95, 96; WhoFrS 84; WhoScEn 94, 96; WhoWrEP 89*

Minsky, Morton
[The Minsky Brothers]
American. Producer
Dominated burlesque shows, NYC, until 1937; theaters shut down due to public disapproval.
b. Jan 10, 1902 in New York, New York
d. Mar 23, 1987 in New York, New York
Source: *BioIn 15; ConAu 122, 135; EncVaud; NewYTBS 87*

Minton, Sherman
American. Supreme Court Justice
Conservative who served 1949-56; supported landmark school desegregation decision, 1954.
b. Oct 20, 1890 in Georgetown, Indiana
d. Apr 9, 1965 in New Albany, Indiana
Source: *BiDFedJ; BiDrAC; BiDrUSC 89; BioIn 2, 3, 4, 5, 7, 9, 11, 15; CurBio 41, 49, 65; DcAmB S7; FacFETw; IndAu 1967; LegTOT; NatCAB 53; OxCSupC; PolProf E, T; SupCtJu; WebAB 74, 79; WhAm 4*

Mintz, Shlomo
Israeli. Musician
Famed violinist who has toured world, recorded over ten works.
b. Oct 30, 1957? in Moscow, Union of Soviet Socialist Republics
Source: *Baker 84, 92; BioIn 14, 15; ConNews 86-2; IntWW 89, 91, 93; IntWWM 80, 90; NewYTBE 73; PenDiMP; WhoAm 86, 88, 90, 92, 94, 95, 96, 97; WhoAmM 83; WhoEnt 92*

Minuit, Peter
Dutch. Colonial Figure
Director, Dutch colony of New Netherland, 1626-31; bought Manhattan from Indians for trinkets valued at $24.
b. 1580 in Wesel, Germany
d. Jun 1638
Source: *AmBi; ApCAB; BenetAL 91; BioIn 1, 3, 8; DcAmB; Drake; EncAAH; EncCRAm; HarEnUS; McGEWB; NatCAB 12; OxCAmH; REn; REnAL; WebAB 74, 79; WhAm HS; WhDW; WhNaAH; WorAl; WorAlBi*

Mirabeau, Honore Gabriel Riquetti
French. Revolutionary, Statesman, Orator
Leader for first two yrs. of French Revolution; moderate who advocated constitutional monarchy.
b. Mar 9, 1749 in Bignon, France
d. Apr 2, 1791 in Paris, France
Source: *DcEuL; OxCFr; REn*

Mirabella, Grace
American. Fashion Editor, Publishing Executive
Editor in chief, *Vogue,* 1971-88; founder, *Mirabella* magazine, 1988—.
b. Jun 10, 1930 in Maplewood, New Jersey
Source: *BioIn 9, 16; CelR 90; CurBio 91; InWom SUP; WhoAm 74, 76, 78, 80, 82, 84, 86, 88, 90, 92, 95, 96; WhoAmW 79, 81, 83, 85, 89, 91, 93, 95; WhoE 93; WhoUSWr 88; WhoWrEP 89, 92, 95*

Miranda, Carmen
[Maria Do Carmo Miranda Da Cunha Sebastian]
"The Brazilian Bombshell"
Brazilian. Singer, Dancer, Actor
Flamboyant musical comedy star, 1940s; noted for fast-tempo songs, elaborate hats; films include *Down Argentine Way,* 1940.
b. Feb 9, 1915 in Marco Canavezes, Portugal
d. Aug 5, 1955 in Beverly Hills, California
Source: *BiDAmM; CmpEPM; CurBio 41, 55; DcAmB S5; FilmgC; MotPP; MovMk; OxCFilm; WhoHol B; WhScrn 77; WorEFlm*

Miranda, Ernesto
American. Criminal
US Supreme Court ruling, 1966, that an individual must be advised of rights at time of arrest was the result of his case.
b. 1940?
d. Jan 31, 1976 in Phoenix, Arizona
Source: *BioIn 8, 10; CopCroC; EncACr*

Miranda, Francisco de
Venezuelan. Soldier, Revolutionary
Patriot who surrendered to Spain while pres. of Venezuela, 1812.
b. Mar 28, 1750 in Caracas, Venezuela
d. Jul 14, 1816 in Cadiz, Spain
Source: *ApCAB; BiDLAmC; BioIn 2, 3, 5, 6, 7, 8, 11, 13, 16, 20; Drake; EncLatA; HisDcSE; HisWorL; McGEWB; NewCol 75; OxCAmH; REnAL; WhAm HS; WhoMilH 76*

Miriam
Hebrew. Biblical Figure
Sister of Moses, who guarded him until he was found by the Pharaoh's daughter.
b. fl. 1575BC
Source: *BioIn 11; CasWL; InWom SUP*

Mirisch, Walter Mortimer
American. Director, Producer
Films include *In the Heat of the Night,* 1967; *Same Time, Next Year,* 1978.
b. Nov 8, 1921 in New York, New York
Source: *ConTFT 8; DcFM; FilmgC; HalFC 84, 88; IntMPA 86, 92; VarWW 85; WhoAm 74, 76, 78, 80, 82, 84, 86, 88, 90, 92, 94, 95, 96, 97; WhoEnt 92; WhoWest 76, 78; WhoWor 74*

Mirkin, Gabe
"Dr. Sport"
American. Physician
Authority on sports medicine; wrote *The Sportsmedicine Book.*
b. Jun 18, 1935 in Brookline, Massachusetts
Source: *BioIn 11; ConAu 129; WhoE 81, 83*

Miro, Joan
Spanish. Artist
Member, French school of surrealist painters, 1930s; works express nightmare, horror.
b. Apr 20, 1893 in Barcelona, Spain
d. Dec 25, 1983 in Palma de Majorca, Spain
Source: *AnObit 1983; Benet 87, 96; BioIn 1, 2, 4, 5, 6, 7, 8, 9, 10, 11, 12, 13, 14, 15, 16, 17, 18, 19, 20; CelR; ClaDrA; CnOxB; ConArt 77, 83, 89, 96; ConAu 111, 121; ConNews 85-1; CurBio 40, 73, 84, 84N; DancEn 78; DcArts; DcCAr 81; DcHiB; FacFETw; IntDcAA 90; IntWW 74, 75, 76, 77, 78, 79, 80, 81, 82, 83; LegTOT; MakMC; McGDA; McGEWB; NewYTBS 80, 83; OxCArt; OxCTwCA; OxDcArt; PhDcTCA 77; PrintW 83, 85; REn; WhAm 8; WhDW; Who 82, 83; WhoAm 74; WhoArt 80, 82; WhoFr 79; WhoGrA 62; WhoWor 74, 76, 78, 82; WorArt 1950*

Mirren, Helen
[Ilynea Lydia Mironoff]
English. Actor
Films include *O Lucky Man,* 1973; *Excalibur,* 1981.
b. Jul 26, 1946 in London, England
Source: *BiDFilm 94; CamGWoT; ConTFT 2, 10; CurBio 95; DcArts; Ent; HalFC 88; IntMPA 88, 92, 94, 96; IntWW 82, 83, 91; InWom SUP; LegTOT; OxCThe 83; VarWW 85; WhoAm 95, 96, 97; WhoAmW 95, 97; WhoHol 92, A; WhoThe 72, 77, 81; WhoWor 84, 87, 91, 93, 95, 96, 97*

Mirvish, Edwin
"Honest Ed"
Canadian. Businessman
Founder, Honest Ed's Famous Bargain House, 1948, the first discount house in N America.
b. Jul 24, 1914 in Colonial Beach, Virginia
Source: *BioIn 9, 16; CanWW 31, 80, 81, 83, 89; CurBio 89; OxCCanT; Who 85, 88, 92, 94*

Mischakoff, Mischa
[Mischa Fischberg]
American. Violinist
Concertmaster, NBC Symphony Orchestra under Toscanini, 1937-51; Detroit Symphony, 1951-68.
b. Apr 3, 1895 in Proskurov, Russia
d. Feb 1, 1981 in Petoskey, Michigan
Source: *AnObit 1981; Baker 78, 84, 92; BioIn 2, 4, 8, 12; NewYTBS 81; RadStar; WhoAm 80; WhoWorJ 72*

Mishima, Yukio
[Kimitake Hiraoka]
Japanese. Author
Wrote modern Kabuki, no dramas; tetralogy *The Sea of Fertility;* committed public hara-kiri protesting Japan's westernization.
b. Jan 14, 1925 in Tokyo, Japan
d. Nov 25, 1970 in Tokyo, Japan
Source: *Au&Wr 71; Benet 87, 96; BiDExR; BiDJaL; BioIn 5, 7, 8, 9, 10, 12, 14, 15, 17, 20, 21; CasWL; CnMD; ConAu 29R, 97; ConLC 2, 4, 6, 9, 27; CyWA 89; DcArts; DcOrL 1; DramC 1; EncWB; EncWL, 2; EncWT; FacFETw; GayLesB; GayLL; GrFLW; LegTOT; LinLib L; MagSWL; MajAI; MajTwCW; MakMC; McGEWD 84; ModWD; NewCol 75; NewYTBE 70; Novels; PenC CL; RAdv 13-2; RComWL; REn; RfGWoL 95; ShSCr 4; WhAm 5; WhDW; WhoTwCL; WorAl; WorAlBi; WorAu 1950*

Misrach, Richard
American. Photographer
Nature photographer; specializes in swamps, forests and deserts; works collected in *Desert Cantos,* 1987.
b. Jul 11, 1949 in Los Angeles, California
Source: *ConPhot 82, 88; DcCAr 81; ICPEnP A; News 91, 91-2; PrintW 83, 85; WhoAdv 90; WhoAm 90; WhoAmA 91; WhoWor 91*

Missing Persons
[Dale Bozzio; Terry Bozzio; Warren Cuccurullo; Patrick O'Hearn]
American. Music Group
New wave group who had gold debut album *Spring Session M,* 1983.
Source: *HarEnR 86; NewAgMG; RkOn 85; WhoRocM 82*

Mistinguett
[Jeanne-Marie Bourgeois]
French. Entertainer
Vivacious Parisian nightclub star noted for beautiful legs, song "Mon Homme," 1920s.
b. Apr 5, 1875 in Enghien-les-Bains, France
d. Jan 5, 1956 in Bougival, France
Source: *BioIn 2, 3, 4; NotNAT A, B; OxCThe 67, 83; WebBD 83; WhThe*

Mistral, Frederic
French. Poet
As member of Le Felibrige, influenced language, literature of Provence; wrote

pastoral *Mireio,* 1859; won Nobel Prize, 1904.
b. Sep 8, 1830 in Maillane, France
d. Mar 25, 1914 in Maillane, France
Source: *AtlBL; BbD; Benet 87, 96; BiD&SB; BioIn 1, 4, 5, 7, 9, 15; CasWL; ChhPo S1; ClDMEL 47, 80; ConAu 122; DcEuL; EuAu; GuFrLit 1; LegTOT; LinLib L, S; ModRL; NewC; NewEOp 71; NobelP; OxCEng 67; OxCFr; PenC EUR; REn; TwCLC 51; TwCWr; WhDW; WhoNob, 90, 95; WorAl; WorAlBi*

Mistral, Gabriela
[Lucila Godoy y Alcayaga]
Chilean. Poet, Diplomat
Verse volumes include *Lager,* 1954; *Sonnets of Death;* won 1945 Nobel Prize.
b. Apr 7, 1899 in Vicuna, Chile
d. Jan 10, 1957 in New York, New York
Source: *AtlBL; BiDMoPL; CasWL; DcCathB; DcSpL; EncWL; IntDcWB; LinLib L; ObitOF 79; PenC AM; PenNWW B; REn; TwCA, SUP; WhAm 3; WhoNob; WhoTwCL; WorAl*

Mistry, Rohinton
Canadian. Author
Won Canada's 1991 Governor General's Award for *Such a Long Journey.*
b. 1952 in Bombay, India
Source: *BioIn 19; CanWW 89; ConAu 141; ConCaAu 1; ConLC 71; ConNov 96; LiExTwC; RAdv 14; WhoCanL 87, 92*

Mita, Katsushige
Japanese. Business Executive
President, Hitachi, the Japanese electrical, electronic equipment firm, since 1981.
b. Apr 6, 1924 in Tokyo, Japan
Source: *BioIn 15; IntWW 82, 83, 89, 91, 93; WhoFI 96; WhoWor 82, 84, 87, 89, 91, 95, 96, 97*

Mitchel, John Purroy
American. Politician
Mayor of NY, 1914-18; noted for civic reforms.
b. Jul 19, 1879 in New York, New York
d. Jul 6, 1918 in Lake Charles, Louisiana
Source: *AmBi; AmRef; BioIn 3, 7, 15; DcAmB; DcAmImH; DcCathB; NatCAB 18; WhAm 1*

Mitchell, Arthur Adam
"Pied Piper of Dance"
American. Dancer, Choreographer
First black man to achieve prominence in classical dance; with NYC Ballet, 1952-69; founder, director of Dance Theater of Harlem, 1969—.
b. Mar 27, 1934 in New York, New York
Source: *BiDD; BioIn 16; ConBlB 2; CurBio 66; DrBlPA 90; InB&W 80, 85; IntWW 91; NewYTBS 74; WhoAm 86, 90; WhoBlA 85, 88, 92; WhoE 91; WhoEnt 92; WhoWor 74*

Mitchell, Billy
[William Mitchell]
American. Air Force Officer
Commander, WW I air forces; vocal proponent of supremacy of air power; court-martialed for criticizing management of military air service, 1925.
b. Dec 29, 1879 in Nice, France
d. Feb 19, 1936 in New York, New York
Source: *AmBi; BioIn 1, 2, 3, 4, 5, 6, 7, 8, 9, 10, 11, 12, 13, 14; DcAmB S2; DcAmMiB; DcNAA; EncAB-A 14; EncAB-H 1974, 1996; FacFETw; HarEnMi; HisEWW; HisWorL; LinLib S; NatCAB 26; NewCol 75; WebAB 74, 79; WebAMB; WhAm 1; WhoMilH 76; WorAl; WorAlBi*

Mitchell, Bobby
[Robert C Mitchell]
American. Football Player
End, Cleveland, 1958-61, Washington, 1962-68; led NFL in receiving, 1962; Hall of Fame, 1983.
b. Jun 6, 1935 in Hot Springs, Arkansas
Source: *BiDAmSp FB; BioIn 6, 10, 17; InB&W 80; LegTOT; Who 92; WhoBlA 85, 92; WhoFtbl 74; WhoSpor*

Mitchell, Cameron
[Cameron Mizell]
American. Actor
On stage, in film *Death of a Salesman;* in TV show "High Chaparral," 1967-71.
b. Nov 4, 1918 in Dallastown, Pennsylvania
Source: *BiE&WWA; BioIn 16, 17, 20; ConTFT 5, 13; FilmEn; FilmgC; ForYSC; GangFlm; HalFC 80, 84, 88; IntMPA 75, 76, 77, 78, 79, 80, 81, 82, 84, 86, 88, 92, 94; ItaFilm; LegTOT; MotPP; MovMk; PlP&P; WhoAm 80, 82; WhoHol 92, A; WhoHrs 80; WorAl*

Mitchell, Chad
[Chad Mitchell Trio; William Chad Mitchell]
American. Singer
Founded trio, 1959; biggest hit "Lizzie Borden," 1962; replaced in group by John Denver, 1965-69.
b. Dec 5, 1936 in Portland, Oregon
Source: *PenEncP; RkOn 74; WhoAm 74*

Mitchell, Clarence M
American. Diplomat, Civil Rights Leader
Chief Washington lobbyist for NAACP; played prominent role in passage of Fair Housing Act of 1968.
b. Mar 8, 1911 in Baltimore, Maryland
d. Mar 18, 1984 in Baltimore, Maryland
Source: *BioIn 10, 11, 12, 13; CivR 74; CivRSt; Ebony 1; FacFETw; InB&W 80, 85; NegAl 76, 83; NewYTBS 84; PolProf E, J, K, NF; WhAm 8; WhoAm 74, 76, 78, 80, 82; WhoBlA 80; WhoSSW 73*

Mitchell, Corinne
American. Painter
Painter who became the first black to have a solo exhibit at the National Museum of Women, Washington, D.C., 1992.
b. Mar 10, 1914 in Mecklenburg, Virginia
d. Apr 21, 1993 in Washington, District of Columbia
Source: *BioIn 20; ConBlB 8; WhoBlA 75, 77, 80*

Mitchell, David
American. Designer
Won Tony for scene designs in *Annie,* 1977; also active in films, operas, ballets.
b. May 12, 1932 in Honesdale, Pennsylvania
Source: *ConTFT 4; WhoAm 86, 88; WhoThe 81*

Mitchell, Edgar Dean
American. Astronaut
Lunar module pilot, *Apollo 14,* 1971; sixth man to walk on moon.
b. Sep 17, 1930 in Hereford, Texas
Source: *AmMWSc 73P, 79, 82, 86; BioIn 14; BlueB 76; ConAu 53; EncO&P 2, 3; EncPaPR 91; FacFETw; NewAgE 90; NewYTBE 71; WhoSpc; WhoSSW 73, 75; WorDWW*

Mitchell, George John
American. Politician, Lawyer
Dem. senator from ME, 1980—; elected senate majority leader, 1988.
b. Aug 20, 1933 in Waterville, Maine
Source: *AlmAP 88, 92; BiDrUSC 89; BioIn 15, 16; CngDr 81, 83, 85, 87, 89; CurBio 89; IntWW 89, 91, 93; News 89-3; PolsAm 84; WhoAm 78, 80, 82, 84, 86, 88, 90, 92, 94, 95; WhoAmL 79, 87; WhoAmP 73, 75, 77, 79, 81, 83, 85, 87, 89, 91, 93, 95; WhoE 74, 75, 77, 81, 83, 85, 86, 89, 91, 93, 95; WhoGov 77; WhoWor 80, 82, 84, 87, 89, 91; WorAlBi*

Mitchell, Grant
American. Actor
Starred in over 80 films including *Mr. Smith Goes to Washington.*
b. Jun 17, 1875 in Columbus, Ohio
d. May 1, 1957 in Los Angeles, California
Source: *FilmgC; ForYSC; MotPP; MovMk; Vers A; WhoHol B; WhScrn 74, 77*

Mitchell, Guy
[Al Cernik]
American. Singer
Hits include "My Heart Cries for You," 1950; "Heartaches by the Number," 1959.
b. Feb 27, 1927, Yugoslavia
Source: *BioIn 2, 3, 4; CmpEPM; EncRk 88; FilmgC; HalFC 84, 88; IntMPA 75, 76, 77, 78, 79, 80, 81, 82, 84, 86, 88; OxCPMus; PenEncP; RkOn 74, 82; WhoHol A; WhoSSW 91*

Mitchell, Howard (Bundy)
American. Conductor
Cellist; conducted National Symphony, Washington, DC, 1949-69.
b. Mar 11, 1911 in Lyons, Nebraska
d. Jun 22, 1988 in Ormond Beach, Florida
Source: *AmCath 80; Baker 78, 84, 92; BiE&WWA; BioIn 2, 3, 4, 16; CurBio 88N; NewAmDM; NewGrDA 86; NewGrDM 80; WhAm 9; WhoAm 74, 76, 78, 80, 82; WhoMus 72; WhoWor 74*

Mitchell, Joan
American. Artist
One of finest painters of second generation of abstract expressionists; large, c olorful works called "metaphors of natural world."
b. Feb 12, 1926 in Chicago, Illinois
d. Oct 30, 1992 in Paris, France
Source: *AmArt; AnObit 1992; BiDWomA; BioIn 4, 5, 6, 10, 12, 13, 14, 15; BriEAA; ConArt 77, 83, 89, 96; CurBio 86, 93N; DcAmArt; DcCAA 71, 77, 88, 94; DcCAr 81; FacFETw; IntWW 89, 91; InWom SUP; NewYTBS 91, 92; NorAmWA; OxCTwCA; PhDcTCA 77; PrintW 85; WhAm 10; WhoAm 78, 80, 82, 84, 86, 88, 90, 92; WhoAmA 73, 76, 78, 80, 82, 84, 86, 89, 91, 93N; WhoAmW 81, 83, 85, 87, 89; WomArt; WorArt 1950*

Mitchell, John
American. Labor Union Official
VP, AFL, 1899-1914; wrote *The Wage Earner and His Problems,* 1913.
b. Feb 4, 1870 in Braidwood, Illinois
d. Sep 9, 1919 in New York, New York
Source: *AmBi; AmDec 1910; BiDAmL; BiDAmLL; BioIn 2, 6, 9, 15, 20; CyAG; DcAmB; DcAmSR; DcCathB; DcNAA; EncAB-H 1974, 1996; HarEnUS; LinLib S; McGEWB; NatCAB 15, 24; OxCAmH; REnAL; WhAm 1; WorAl; WorAlBi*

Mitchell, John Newton
American. Government Official
Attorney General, 1969-72; convicted in Watergate scandal, Jan 1, 1975.
b. Sep 15, 1913 in Detroit, Michigan
d. Nov 9, 1988 in Washington, District of Columbia
Source: *AmPolLe; BiDrUSE 71, 89; BioIn 8, 9, 10, 11, 12, 13, 14, 16; BlueB 76; CurBio 69, 89; FacFETw; IntWW 74, 75, 76, 77, 78, 79, 80, 81, 82, 83; LinLib S; NewYTBS 74, 75; PolProf NF; WhAm 9; WhDW; Who 74, 82; WhoAm 74, 76, 78, 80; WhoAmP 73; WhoSSW 73; WorAl*

Mitchell, Joni
[Roberta Joan Anderson]
American. Singer, Songwriter
Wrote, recorded first hit, "Chelsea Morning," 1962; won 1970 Grammy for *Clouds,* 1969; other albums include *Night Ride Home,* 1991.
b. Nov 7, 1943 in Fort Macleod, Alberta, Canada
Source: *Baker 84, 92; BioIn 11, 12, 14, 15, 16; BioNews 74; BkPepl; CanWW 81, 83, 89; CelR, 90; ConAu 112; ConCaAu 1; ConLC 12; ConMuA 80A; ConMus 2, 17; ContDcW 89; CurBio 76; DcArts; EncFCWM 83; EncPR&S 89; EncRk 88; EncRkSt; FacFETw; GoodHs; GrLiveH; HarEnR 86; IlEncRk; IntDcWB; IntWW 89, 91, 93; InWom SUP; LegTOT; NewAmDM; NewGrDA 86; News 91; OnThGG; OxCPMus; PenEncP; RkOn 78; RolSEnR 83; WhoAm 74, 76, 78, 80, 82, 84, 86, 88, 90, 92, 94, 95, 96, 97; WhoAmW 72, 75, 77, 79, 81, 83, 85, 87, 89, 91, 93, 95; WhoEnt 92; WhoHol 92; WhoRock 81; WhoRocM 82; WorAl; WorAlBi*

Mitchell, Joseph
American. Writer
Staff writer, *The New Yorker,* 1938-96; published collections of writings, *McSorley's Wonderful Saloon,* 1943; *The Botton of the Harbor,* 1960; *Up in the Old Hotel,* 1993.
b. Jul 27, 1908 in Fairmont, North Carolina
d. May 24, 1996
Source: *BioIn 3, 13, 15, 18, 21; ConAu 77; ConLC 98; ConNov 72, 76, 82, 86, 91; EncTwCJ; IntAu&W 76, 77; IntWW 89, 91; LiJour; News 97-1; NewYTBS 27; SourALJ; SouWr; WhoAm 76, 80, 82, 88, 90; WhoWor 80, 82; WrDr 76, 80, 82, 84, 86, 88, 90, 92, 94, 96*

Mitchell, Kevin Darrell
"Boogie Bear"; "Mitch"; "World"
American. Baseball Player
Third baseman, New York Mets, 1984-86; San Diego Padres, 1987; San Francisco Giants, 1987-91; Seattle Mariners, 1992; currently with Cincinnati, 1992—; led NL in home runs, RBIs, 1989; NL MVP, 1989.
b. Jan 13, 1962 in San Diego, California
Source: *Ballpl 90; BaseEn 88; BioIn 16; WhoAm 92, 94, 95; WhoMW 93; WhoWest 94; WorAlBi*

Mitchell, Margaret
American. Author
Won Pulitzer for her only book *Gone With the Wind,* 1936.
b. Nov 8, 1900 in Atlanta, Georgia
d. Aug 16, 1949 in Atlanta, Georgia
Source: *AmAu&B; AmWomWr; ArtclWW 2; Benet 87; BenetAL 91; BioAmW; BioIn 1, 2, 3, 4, 5, 6, 7, 8, 10, 11, 12, 13, 14, 15, 16, 17, 18, 19, 21; BlmGWL; CasWL; Chambr 3; CnDAL; ConAu 109, 125; CyWA 58; DcAmB S4; DcArts; DcLB 9; DcLEL; DcNAA; EvLB; FacFETw; FemiCLE; FifSWrA; FilmgC; GrWrEL N; HalFC 80, 84, 88; InWom; LegTOT; LinLib L, S; LngCTC; MajTwCW; ModAL; NotAW; Novels; OxCAmL 65, 83, 95; OxCEng 85, 95; OxCWoWr 95; PenC AM; PenNWW B; RAdv 14; REn; REnAL; RfGAmL 87; SouWr; TwCA, SUP; TwCLC 11; TwCRGW; TwCRHW 90; TwCWr; WebAB 74, 79; WebE&AL; WhAm 2; WhNAA; WomChHR; WorAl; WorAlBi*

Mitchell, Margaret Julia
"Maggie"
American. Actor
Comedy star of play *Fanchon the Cricket,* 1861.
b. Jun 14, 1832 in New York, New York
d. Mar 22, 1918 in New York, New York
Source: *ApCAB; BioIn 16; InWom; NotAW; TwCBDA; WebBD 83*

Mitchell, Maria
American. Astronomer
Discovered comet, 1847; one of original teachers at Vassar College.
b. Aug 1, 1818 in Nantucket, Massachusetts
d. Jun 28, 1889 in Lynn, Massachusetts
Source: *Alli; AmBi; AmWom; AmWomSc; ApCAB; BiDAmEd; BiDAmS; BiESc; BiInAmS; BioAmW; BioIn 1, 2, 3, 4, 5, 6, 7, 8, 9, 10, 11, 12, 15, 17, 18, 20, 21; CamDcSc; ContDcW 89; CyAL 2; CyEd; DcAmAu; DcAmB; DcBiPP; DcScB; Drake; EncAB-H 1974, 1996; EncWHA; GoodHs; GrLiveH; HanAmWH; HerW, 84; InSci; IntDcWB; InWom, SUP; LarDcSc; LibW; LinLib S; McGEWB; NatCAB 5; NotAW; OxCAmH; PeoHis; RAdv 14; TwCBDA; WebAB 74, 79; WhAm HS; WomFir; WomSc; WorScD*

Mitchell, Martha Elizabeth Beall
[Mrs. John Mitchell]
American.
Known for calling reporters in middle of night with Washington gossip.
b. Sep 2, 1918 in Pine Bluff, Arkansas
d. May 31, 1976 in New York, New York
Source: *BioNews 74; DcAmB S10; NewYTBE 70; WhAm 6; WhoAm 74*

Mitchell, Millard
American. Actor
Character actor, 1940-53; films include *Singin' in the Rain,* 1952.
b. 1900 in Havana, Cuba
d. Oct 12, 1953 in Santa Monica, California
Source: *EncAFC; FilmEn; FilmgC; GangFlm; HalFC 80, 84, 88; MotPP; WhoHol B; WhScrn 74, 77, 83*

Mitchell, Peter Dennis
English. Chemist
Won 1978 Nobel Prize in chemistry.
b. Sep 20, 1920 in Mitcham, England
d. Apr 10, 1992
Source: *AmMWSc 92; BiESc; BioIn 11, 12, 14, 15, 18, 19, 20; IntWW 79, 80, 81, 82, 83, 89, 91; LarDcSc; NobelP; WhAm 10; Who 82, 83, 85, 88, 90, 92; WhoAm 88, 90; WhoNob, 90; WhoWor 80, 82, 84, 87, 89, 91*

Mitchell, Reginald Joseph
English. Aircraft Designer
Built eight-gun Spitfire fighter plane, which contributed to victory in Battle of Britain, 1940.
b. 1895
d. 1937

Source: *BioIn 2, 3, 4; DcNaB 1931; HisEWW; WhDW*

Mitchell, Silas Weir
American. Neurologist, Author
Wrote historical novel *Hugh Wynne, Free Quaker,* 1898.
b. Feb 15, 1829 in Philadelphia, Pennsylvania
d. Jan 4, 1914 in Philadelphia, Pennsylvania
Source: *Alli SUP; AmAu; AmAu&B; AmBi; ApCAB, X; BbD; BibAL; BiDAmS; BiD&SB; BiHiMed; BiInAmS; BioIn 1, 2, 5, 6, 7, 8, 9, 12, 13, 20; Chambr 3; ChhPo, S1, S2, S3; CnDAL; CyWA 58; DcAmAu; DcAmB; DcAmMeB; DcLEL; DcNAA; DcScB; Dis&D; EncSF, 93; HarEnUS; InSci; LinLib L, S; NatCAB 9; OxCAmH; OxCAmL 65; OxCMed 86; REn; REnAL; TwCBDA; WebAB 74, 79; WhAm 1*

Mitchell, Thomas
American. Actor
Won Oscar for *Stagecoach,* 1939; played Scarlett O'Hara's father in *Gone With the Wind.*
b. Jul 11, 1892 in Elizabeth, New Jersey
d. Dec 17, 1962 in Beverly Hills, California
Source: *BiDFilm, 81, 94; BioIn 21; CmMov; Film 2; FilmEn; FilmgC; HalFC 80, 84, 88; HolCA; LegTOT; MovMk; NatCAB 51; OlFamFa; OxCFilm; Vers A; WhAm 4; WhoHol B; WhScrn 74, 77; WorAl; WorAlBi; WorEFlm*

Mitchell, W(illiam) O(rmond)
Canadian. Author
Works deal with nostalgia, humor of small-town life in Canada: *Who Has Seen the Wind,* 1947.
b. Mar 13, 1914 in Weyburn, Saskatchewan, Canada
Source: *Benet 96; BenetAL 91; BioIn 3, 13; CamGLE; CanWr; CanWW 31, 70, 79, 80, 81, 83, 89; CasWL; CaW; ConAu 15NR, 43NR, 77; ConCaAu 1; ConLC 25; ConNov 72, 76, 82, 86, 91, 96; CreCan 1; DcLB 88; DcLEL 1940; IntAu&W 76, 77, 91, 93; IntvTCA 2; OxCCan; OxCCanL; OxCCanT; TwCWr; WhoCanL 85, 87, 92; WrDr 76, 80, 82, 84, 86, 88, 90, 92, 94, 96*

Mitchell, William Leroy
American. Auto Executive
Chief designer of Cadillac, 1935-77; originator of famous 1948 Cadillac tail fins.
b. Jul 2, 1912 in Cleveland, Ohio
d. Sep 18, 1989 in Royal Oak, Michigan
Source: *BioIn 11, 16; CurBio 59; Ward 77; WhAm 10; WhoAm 74, 76, 78, 80, 82, 84, 86, 88*

Mitchell, Willie
American. Musician
Trumpeter, keyboard player; rhythm and blues/soul albums include *Best Of.,* 1980.
b. 1928 in Ashland, Mississippi
Source: *EncRk 88; HarEnR 86; IlEncRk; RkOn 84; RolSEnR 83; SoulM; WhoRocM 82*

Mitchelson, Marvin M(orris)
American. Lawyer
Known for palimony trial involving Lee Marvin and Michelle Triola Marvin and the Joan Collins-Peter Holm divorce.
b. May 7, 1928 in Detroit, Michigan
Source: *BioIn 11, 13, 15, 16; ConAu 104; News 89-2; NewYTBS 80; WhoAm 82, 84, 90, 92, 97; WhoAmL 92*

Mitchison, Naomi Margaret (Haldane)
Scottish. Author
Numerous works include historical novel *The Conquered,* 1923; children's book *Snake,* 1976.
b. Nov 1, 1897 in Edinburgh, Scotland
Source: *Benet 87; BioIn 13, 15; CamGEL; CamGLE; CasWL; Chambr 3; CmScLit; ConAu 15NR, 77; ConNov 86, 91; DcLB 160; DcLEL; EncBrWW; EngPo; EvLB; FemiCLE; IntvTCA 2; IntWW 83, 91; InWom, SUP; LngCTC; NewC; OxCChiL; OxCEng 85; PenC ENG; REn; ScFSB; SmATA 24; TwCA SUP; TwCChW 89; TwCRHW 90; TwCSFW 91; Who 85S, 92; WhoLA; WrDr 86, 92*

Mitch Ryder and the Detroit Wheels
[John Badenjek; Joe Cubert; Earl Eliot; Jimmy McCartney; Mitch Ryder]
American. Music Group
Leading teenage blue-eyed soul band of mid-1960s; first hit "Jenny Take a Ride," 1965.
Source: *ConMuA 80A; EncRk 88; PenEncP; WhoRock 81; WhoRocM 82*

Mitchum, Robert
[Robert Charles Duran Mitchum]
American. Actor
One of the first anti-hero actors; more than 100 films include *The Story of G I Joe,* 1945; *Crossfire,* 1947; *Cape Fear,* 1962.
b. Aug 6, 1917 in Bridgeport, Connecticut
d. Jul 1, 1997 in Santa Barbara, California
Source: *ASCAP 66, 80; BiDFilm, 81, 94; BioIn 1, 4, 5, 6, 8, 9, 10, 11, 13, 14, 16; BkPepl; CelR, 90; CmMov; ConTFT 3; CurBio 70; DcArts; FacFETw; FilmEn; FilmgC; ForYSC; GangFlm; HalFC 80, 84, 88; IntDcF 2-3; IntMPA 75, 76, 77, 78, 79, 80, 81, 82, 84, 86, 88, 92, 94, 96; IntWW 74, 75, 76, 77, 78, 79, 80, 81, 82, 83, 89, 91, 93; ItaFilm; LegTOT; MotPP; MovMk; OxCFilm; RkOn 74; VarWW 85; WhoAm 74, 76, 78, 80, 82, 84, 86, 88, 90, 92, 94; WhoEnt 92; WhoHol 92, A; WhoRock 81; WhoWor 78; WorAl; WorAlBi; WorEFlm*

Mitford, Jessica
English. Author, Journalist
Wrote best-seller *American Way of Death,* 1963.
b. Sep 11, 1917 in Gloucester, England
d. Jul 23, 1996 in Oakland, California
Source: *AmAu&B; AmWomWr; ArtclWW 2; AuSpks; Benet 87; BioIn 8, 9, 10, 11, 12, 17, 18, 20, 21; BlueB 76; ConAu 1NR, 1R, 17AS, 152; ConLC 12; ContDcW 89; CurBio 74; DcArts; FacFETw; IntAu&W 76, 89, 91, 93; IntDcWB; IntvTCA 2; IntWW 74, 75, 76, 77, 78, 79, 80, 81, 82, 83, 89, 91, 93; InWom SUP; LegTOT; NewC; NewYTBS 27, 77; Who 92; WhoAm 76, 78, 80, 82, 84, 86, 88, 90, 92, 94, 95, 96; WhoAmW 66, 68, 70, 72, 74, 75, 83, 85; WhoUSWr 88; WhoWor 74, 76, 78; WhoWrEP 89, 92, 95; WorAu 1950; WrDr 76, 80, 82, 84, 86, 88, 90, 92, 94, 96*

Mitford, Mary Russell
English. Author
Known for sketches of country life: *Our Village,* 1824-32.
b. Dec 16, 1787 in Alresford, England
d. Jan 10, 1855 in Swallowfield, England
Source: *Alli; ArtclWW 2; BbD; Benet 87, 96; BiD&SB; BiDLA; BioIn 2, 3, 4, 5, 7, 9, 10, 13, 16, 17, 18; BlmGWL; BritAu 19; CamGEL; CamGLE; CasWL; Chambr 3; ChhPo, S1, S2; CyWA 58; DcArts; DcEnA; DcEnL; DcEuL; DcLB 110, 116; DcLEL; DcNaB, C; EncBrWW; EvLB; InWom, SUP; NewC; NewCBEL; NinCLC 4; Novels; OxCEng 67, 85, 95; PenC ENG; PenNWW A; REn; RfGEnL 91; StaCVF; WebE&AL*

Mitford, Nancy Freeman
English. Author
Satirical novels include *Love in a Cold Climate,* 1949.
b. Nov 28, 1904 in Chelsea, England
d. Jun 30, 1973 in Versailles, France
Source: *Au&Wr 71; ConAu 9R; ConNov 72; DcLEL; DcNaB 1971; EvLB; GrBr; GrWrEL N; LngCTC; ModBrL; NewC; NewCBEL; NewYTBE 73; OxCEng 85, 95; PenC ENG; RAdv 1; REn; RGTwCWr; TwCA SUP; TwCWr; WhAm 6; WomFir*

Mitropoulos, Dimitri
Greek. Conductor, Composer
Conducted NY Philharmonic, 1949-58; Met. Opera, 1954-60; introduced modern composers.
b. Feb 18, 1896 in Athens, Greece
d. Nov 2, 1960 in Milan, Italy
Source: *Baker 84, 92; BioIn 2, 3, 4, 5, 6, 7, 11, 12; BriBkM 80; CmOp; CurBio 41, 52, 61; DcAmB S6; DcTwCCu 1; LegTOT; LinLib S; MetOEnc; NewAmDM; NewEOp 71; NewGrDA 86; NewGrDM 80; NewGrDO; ObitT 1951; PenDiMP; WhAm 4*

Mitscher, Marc Andrew
"Pete"
American. Military Leader
Naval aviator; commander-in-chief of Atlantic Fleet, 1946-47; commanded aircraft carrier *Hornet,* WW II; known as doer, preferring the offensive tactic.
b. Jan 26, 1887 in Hillsboro, Wisconsin
d. Feb 3, 1947 in Norfolk, Virginia
Source: *BioIn 1, 2, 3, 7, 17, 19; CurBio 44, 47; DcAmB S4; DcAmMiB; HarEnMi; InSci; NatCAB 36; ObitOF 79; WebAMB; WhAm 2; WhoMilH 76; WhWW-II; WorAl*

Mitscherlich, Alexander
German. Psychoanalyst
Founded Sigmund Freud Institute, Frankfurt, 1959.
b. Sep 20, 1908 in Munich, Germany
d. Jun 26, 1982 in Frankfurt, Germany (West)
Source: *AnObit 1981, 1982; BioIn 12, 13; ConAu 107; IntWW 74, 75, 76, 77, 78, 79, 80, 81, 82, 83; NewYTBS 83*

Mitscherlich, Eilhardt
German. Chemist
Discovered principle of isomorphism, permanganic, selenic acids; named benzene, 1834.
b. Jan 7, 1794 in Neuende, Germany
d. Aug 28, 1863 in Berlin, Germany
Source: *AsBiEn; BiESc; CamDcSc; DcScB; InSci; NewCol 75*

Mitsotakis, Constantine
Greek. Political Leader, Lawyer
Prime minister of Greece, 1990—, succeeding Andreas Papandreou.
b. Oct 18, 1918 in Chania, Greece
Source: *BioIn 16, 17, 21; CurBio 90; IntWW 74, 75, 76, 91, 93; IntYB 82; WhoWor 91*

Mittermaier, Rosi
German. Skier
Won gold medals in women's downhill, slalom, 1976 Olympics.
b. Aug 5, 1950 in Reit im Winkl, Germany (West)
Source: *BioIn 10, 11, 17; GoodHs; InWom SUP; WorAl*

Mittermeier, Russell A
"Russell of the Apes"
American. Scientist, Writer
Noted primatologist, herpetologist, and biopolitician helps lead world effort to save tropical rainforests.
b. Nov 8, 1949 in New York, New York
Source: *BioIn 14; CurBio 92*

Mitterrand, Francois (Maurice Marie)
French. Political Leader
Pres., France, 1981-1995.
b. Oct 26, 1916 in Jarnac, France
d. Jan 8, 1996 in Paris, France
Source: *BiDFrPL; BioIn 5, 7, 8, 9, 10, 11, 12, 13, 14, 15, 16, 17, 18, 20, 21; ColdWar 1, 2; CurBio 68, 82; DcPol; DcTwHis; EncCW; EncWB; FacFETw; IntWW 74, 75, 76, 77, 78, 79, 80, 81, 82, 83, 89, 91, 93; LegTOT; News 96, 96-2; NewYTBS 27, 81; PolLCWE; WhAm 11; Who 82, 83, 85, 88, 90, 92, 94; WhoFr 79; WhoWor 80, 82, 84, 87, 89, 91, 93, 95, 96; WorAlBi*

Mix, Ron(ald J)
"Intellectual Assassin"
American. Football Player
Tackle, 1960-72, mostly with San Diego; Hall of Fame, 1979.
b. Mar 10, 1938 in Los Angeles, California
Source: *BiDAmSp FB; BioIn 5, 17; LegTOT; WhoFtbl 74*

Mix, Tom
American. Actor
Starred in over 400 westerns, usually with his horse, Tony.
b. Jan 6, 1880 in Mix Run, Pennsylvania
d. Oct 12, 1940 in Florence, Arizona
Source: *BiDFilm 94; BioIn 4, 6, 7, 8, 9, 10, 11, 12, 13, 16, 17, 18, 20; CmCal; CmMov; CurBio 40; DcAmB S2; DcArts; EncACom; FacFETw; Film 1, 2; FilmEn; FilmgC; HalFC 80, 84, 88; IntDcF 1-3, 2-3; LegTOT; MnBBF; MotPP; MovMk; NotNAT B; OxCFilm; SilFlmP; TwYS; WebAB 74, 79; WhAm 1; WhoHol B; WhScrn 74, 77, 83; WorAl; WorAlBi; WorEFlm*

Miyake, Issey
American. Fashion Designer
Designs clothes with a blend of Oriental and Western influence.
b. Apr 22, 1938 in Hiroshima, Japan
Source: *BioIn 12, 13, 14, 15; CelR 90; ConDes 90; ConFash; DcArts; EncFash; IntWW 89, 91; LegTOT; WhoAm 88, 90, 92, 94, 95, 96, 97; WhoFash 88; WhoWor 87, 91*

Miyazawa, Kiichi
Japanese. Political Leader
Became prime minister of Japan, 1991-93; former diplomat.
b. Oct 8, 1919 in Tokyo, Japan
Source: *BioIn 11, 12, 15, 17, 18, 19; CurBio 92; FarE&A 78, 79, 80, 81; IntWW 74, 75, 76, 77, 78, 79, 80, 81, 82, 83, 89, 91, 93; News 92, 92-2; NewYTBS 91; WhoAsAP 91; WhoWor 87, 89, 91, 93, 95*

Mize, Johnny
"John Robert Mize"
American. Baseball Player
First baseman, 1936-53; led NL in home runs four times, in RBIs three times; Hall of Fame, 1981.
b. Jan 7, 1913 in Demorest, Georgia
d. Jun 2, 1993 in Demorest, Georgia
Source: *AnObit 1993; Ballpl 90; BiDAmSp BB; BioIn 2, 3, 4, 6, 7, 8, 9, 10, 14, 15, 17, 18, 19; LegTOT; NewYTBS 93; WhoProB 73; WhoSpor*

Mize, Larry
American. Golfer
Touring pro, 1980s; won Masters, 1987.
b. Sep 23, 1958 in Augusta, Georgia
Source: *BioIn 15*

Mizener, Arthur Moore
American. Author
Noted for biographies of F Scott Fitzgerald: *The Far Side of Paradise,* 1951; Ford Maddox Ford: *The Saddest Story,* 1971.
b. Sep 3, 1907 in Erie, Pennsylvania
d. Feb 11, 1988 in Bristol, Rhode Island
Source: *AmAu&B; BioIn 2, 4; ConAu 5NR, 5R; DrAS 74E, 78E, 82E; IntWW 83; REnAL; TwCA SUP; WhAm 9; WhoAm 74, 76, 78, 80; WhoE 74; WhoWor 74; WrDr 76, 86*

Mizner, Addison
American. Architect
Noted for creating look of Palm Beach, FL with Spanish architecture.
b. 1872 in Benicia, California
d. Feb 5, 1933 in Palm Beach, Florida
Source: *AmDec 1920; BiDAmAr; BioIn 3, 12, 14, 15, 17; ChhPo; DcAmB S1; DcNAA; LegTOT; MacEA; WebAB 74, 79; WhFla*

Mizoguchi, Kenji
Japanese. Director
Films created realistic, unified universe; *The Life of Oharu,* 1952, considered masterpiece.
b. May 16, 1898 in Tokyo, Japan
d. Aug 24, 1956 in Kyoto, Japan
Source: *BiDFilm, 81, 94; BioIn 12, 15; DcArts; DcFM; FacFETw; FilmEn; FilmgC; HalFC 80, 84, 88; IntDcF 1-2, 2-2; JapFilm; MiSFD 9N; MovMk; OxCFilm; WorEFlm; WorFDir 1*

Mizrahi, Isaac
American. Fashion Designer
Noted for his "place mat" skirt and cowl-back evening dress; won Perry Ellis Award, 1989.
b. Oct 14, 1961 in New York, New York
Source: *BioIn 16; ConFash; CurBio 91; IntWW 93; News 91, 91-1; WhoAm 94, 95, 96, 97; WhoWor 97*

Mkapa, Benjamin William
Tanzanian. Political Leader
Pres., Tanzania, 1995—.
b. Nov 12, 1938 in Ndanda, Tanganyika
Source: *AfSS 80, 81, 82; IntWW 80, 81, 82, 83, 89, 91, 93; WhoAfr; WhoWor 87, 89, 91*

Mnouchkine, Ariane
French. Director
Helped establish avant-garde Theatre du Soleil, 1964; productions marked by unconventionality, multi-culturalism; *Les Atrides,* 1991.
b. 1939? in Boulogne-sur-Seine, France
Source: *CamGWoT; ContDcW 89; CurBio 93; DcArts; DcTwCCu 2;*

EncWT; GrStDi; IntDcT 3; OxCThe 83; TheaDir; WomFir

Moats, Alice-Leone
American. Author, Journalist
Wrote sassy etiquette book *No Nice Girl Swears,* 1933, reissued, 1983.
b. Mar 12, 1911? in Mexico City, Mexico
d. May 14, 1989 in Philadelphia, Pennsylvania
Source: *BioIn 13, 16; ConAu 128, P-1; CurBio 43, 89, 89N; NewYTBS 84*

Moberg, Vihelm
[Carl Artur Vilhelm Moberg]
Swedish. Author
Novels of Swedish life, emigration to America include *The Emigrants,* 1949.
b. Aug 20, 1898 in Algutsboda, Sweden
d. Aug 9, 1973 in Stockholm, Sweden
Source: *CasWL; ClDMEL 47; ConAu 45, 97; DcScanL; EvEuW; OxCEng 67; WorAu 1950*

Mobius, August Ferdinand
German. Mathematician, Astronomer
Noted for discovery of geometric phenomenon the one-sided Mobius strip, 1858.
b. Nov 17, 1790 in Schulpforte, Germany
d. Sep 26, 1868 in Leipzig, Germany
Source: *AsBiEn; BiESc; BioIn 20; CamDcSc; DcInv; DcScB; Dis&D; LarDcSc; WebBD 83; WhDW; WorAl; WorAlBi*

Mobley, Mary Ann
[Mrs. Gary Collins]
American. Actor, Beauty Contest Winner
Miss America, 1959; in movie *Smokey and the Bandit, Part II,* 1980.
b. Feb 17, 1937 in Mississippi
Source: *BioIn 12, 16; ConTFT 3; FilmgC; HalFC 88; LegTOT; MotPP; VarWW 85; WhoHol A*

Mobutu Sese Seko
[Joseph D(esire) Mobutu]
Congolese. Political Leader
Dictatorial pres. of Zaire, coming to power in coup, 1965-97; exiled.
b. Oct 14, 1930 in Lisala, Belgian Congo
Source: *AfSS 78, 79, 80, 81, 82; BioIn 5, 7, 8, 9, 10, 11, 13, 14, 17, 18, 19, 20, 21; ColdWar 1, 2; ConBlB 1; CurBio 66; DcAfHiB 86S; DicTyr; EncRev; FacFETw; IntWW 75, 76, 77, 78, 79, 80, 81, 82, 83, 91; LinLib S; McGEWB; News 93; WhoWor 87, 89, 91, 93, 95, 96, 97*

Moby
[Richard Melville Hall]
American. Composer
Techno music performer and disc jockey; played in bands the Vatican Commandos and AWOL, 1983-1984; worked as a disc jockey at Club Mars in NYC, 1980; worked under the nicknames Barracuda, Mindstorm, and Voodoo Child and recorded songs "Mobility" and "Go;" released album *Move,* 1993 and *Everything Is Wrong,* 1995.
b. Sep 11, 1965 in Darien, Connecticut
Source: *ConMus 17*

Moczar, Mieczyslaw
Polish. Political Activist
Member, Communist Party, 1937-71; noted for leading the underground resistance against the German secret police during WW II.
b. Dec 25, 1913 in Lodz, Poland
d. Nov 1, 1986 in Warsaw, Poland
Source: *AnObit 1986; BioIn 8, 9, 12, 15; IntWW 74, 75, 76, 77, 78, 79, 80, 81, 82, 83; NewYTBS 80, 86; WhoSocC 78; WhoSoCE 89*

Modell, Art(hur B)
American. Football Executive
Owner, Cleveland Browns, 1961—; president, NFL, 1967-70.
b. Jun 23, 1925 in New York, New York
Source: *WhoAm 82, 84, 86, 88; WhoMW 74, 82, 92*

Modernaires, The
[Ralph Brewster; Bill Conway; Hal Dickinson; Chuck Goldstein]
American. Music Group
Vocal quartet; introduced by Charlie Barnet, 1936; recorded "Chattanooga Choo Choo" with Glenn Miller.
Source: *CmpEPM; OxCPMus; WhoHol 92*

Modern Jazz Quartet, The
[Kenny Clarke; Percy Heath; Milt Jackson; John Lewis]
American. Music Group
Black group founded by Jackson, Lewis, 1952.
Source: *Alli, SUP; AllMusG; BiDAfM; BiDAmM; BiDJaz A; BiDLA; BiDSA; BioIn 12, 14, 15, 16, 17; ChhPo S3; CivR 74; CurBio 62; DcBrECP; DcVicP 2; EncJzS; EncJzS; IlEncJ; InB&W 80, 85A; NegAl 76, 83, 89; NewAmDM; NewGrDA 86; NewGrDJ 88, 94; NewYTBS 86; ObitT 1961; OxCCan; OxCLiW 86; OxCPMus; PenEncP; WhoAmW 61; WhoRocM 82*

Modigliani, Amedeo
Italian. Artist
Noted for elongated portraits, nudes.
b. Jul 12, 1884 in Leghorn, Italy
d. Jan 25, 1920 in Paris, France
Source: *AtlBL; BioIn 1, 2, 3, 4, 5, 6, 7, 8, 9, 11, 12, 15, 16, 17; ClaDrA; DcArts; FacFETw; IntDcAA 90; LegTOT; McGDA; McGEWB; OxCArt; OxCTwCA; OxDcArt; PhDcTCA 77; WebAB 74; WhDW; WorAl; WorAlBi*

Modigliani, Franco
American. Economist
Won Nobel Prize, 1985, for theories of savings, corporate finance.
b. Jun 18, 1918 in Rome, Italy
Source: *AmEA 74; AmMWSc 73S; BioIn 13, 14, 15; GrEconS; IntWW 81, 82, 83, 89, 91, 93; NewYTBS 85; NobelP; Who 88, 90, 92, 94; WhoAm 74, 76, 78, 80, 82, 84, 86, 88, 90, 92, 94, 95, 96, 97; WhoE 86, 89, 91, 93, 95, 97; WhoEc 81, 86; WhoFI 85, 87, 89, 92, 94, 96; WhoNob, 90, 95; WhoScEn 96; WhoWor 87, 89, 91, 93, 95, 96, 97; WorAlBi; WrDr 92, 94, 96*

Modine, Matthew
American. Actor
Films include *Vision Quest,* 1985; *Full Metal Jacket,* 1987.
b. Mar 22, 1959 in Loma Linda, California
Source: *BioIn 14, 15, 16; CelR 90; ConTFT 6, 13; HalFC 88; IntMPA 92, 94, 96; LegTOT; NewYTBS 87; WhoAm 94*

Modjeska, Helena
[Helena Opid]
Polish. Actor
Introduced Ibsen to American theater in *A Doll's House.*
b. Oct 12, 1840 in Krakow, Poland
d. Apr 9, 1909 in Bay Island, California
Source: *AmBi; AmWom; ApCAB; BioIn 2, 4, 6, 7, 8, 9, 10, 12, 13, 16, 17, 19; CmCal; DcAmB; DcAmImH; EncWT; Ent; FamA&A; IntDcT 3; InWom, SUP; LegTOT; LibW; NatCAB 10; NotAW; NotNAT A; NotWoAT; OxCAmL 65; OxCAmT 84; OxCThe 67, 83; PolBiDi; REnAL; WhAm 1*

Modjeski, Ralph
American. Engineer
Chief engineer for American bridges: Manhattan Bridge, NYC; son of actress Helena Modjeska.
b. Jan 27, 1861 in Krakow, Poland
d. Jun 26, 1940 in Los Angeles, California
Source: *BioIn 4; CurBio 40; DcAmB S2; DcTwDes; FacFETw; InSci; LinLib S; NatCAB 15; PolBiDi; WhAm 1; WhoPolA*

Modl, Martha
German. Opera Singer
Noted Wagnerian soprano; starred at Bayreuth, 1951-67.
b. Mar 22, 1912 in Nuremberg, Germany
Source: *Baker 84, 92; BioIn 4, 13, 14; CmOp; IntDcOp; IntWW 74, 91; IntWWM 80, 90; InWom, SUP; MetOEnc; NewEOp 71; NewGrDM 80; NewGrDO; OxDcOp; PenDiMP; WhoOp 76; WhoWor 74*

Moe, Doug(las Edwin)
American. Basketball Player, Basketball Coach
ABA All-Star player 1968-70; coach, San Antonio, 1976-80, Denver, 1980-90; Philadelphia 76ers, 1992-93; NBA coach of year, 1988.
b. Sep 21, 1938 in New York, New York

Source: *BasBi; BiDAmSp Sup; BioIn 16; OfNBA 87; WhoAm 86, 88, 90, 92; WhoBbl 73; WhoWest 84, 87, 89*

Moe, Tommy
[Thomas Sven Moe]
American. Skier
Won 1994 silver and gold olympic medals in downhill skiing; first American to win two Alpine skiing gold medals in one olympic event.
b. Feb 14, 1970 in Missoula, Montana
Source: *WhoAm 95, 96, 97; WhoWor 95, 96*

Moeller, Michael E
[The Hostages]
American. Hostage
One of 52 held by terrorists, Nov 1979-Jan 1981.
b. 1950? in Loup City, Nebraska
Source: *BioIn 12; NewYTBS 81*

Moeller, Philip
American. Dramatist
New York playwright; wrote *Madame Sand,* 1917.
b. Aug 26, 1880 in New York, New York
d. Nov 23, 1958 in Detroit, Michigan
Source: *AmAu&B; BenetAL 91; BioIn 4, 20; CamGWoT; EncWT; GrStDi; ModWD; NotNAT B; OxCAmL 65, 83, 95; OxCAmT 84; PlP&P; REnAL; TheaDir; WhAm 3; WhNAA; WhThe*

Moffat, Donald
English. Actor
Films include *Rachel, Rachel; Eleanor and Franklin; Popeye.*
b. Dec 26, 1930 in Plymouth, England
Source: *BiE&WWA; BioIn 14; ConTFT 4, 14; IntMPA 92, 94, 96; NotNAT; VarWW 85; WhAm 3; WhoAm 74, 76, 78, 80, 82, 84, 86, 88, 90, 92, 96, 97; WhoHol 92, A; WhoThe 72, 77, 81*

Moffatt, James
American. Theologian, Translator
Noted for biblical translations, 1913-20s.
b. Jul 4, 1870 in Glasgow, Scotland
d. Jun 27, 1944 in New York, New York
Source: *AmAu&B; BioIn 1, 3, 5, 14; CurBio 44; DcAmB S3; DcLEL; DcNaB 1941; EvLB; GrBr; LuthC 75; NewCBEL; RAdv 14; WhAm 2; WhLit*

Moffatt, Katy
American. Singer
Folk-country vocalist; released debut album, *Katy,* in 1976; contributed to album *A Town South of Bakersfield,* 1986; later recorded *Walking on the Moon,* 1989, *Hearts Gone Wild,* 1994 and *Midmight Radio,* 1996.
b. Nov 19, 1950 in Fort Worth, Texas
Source: *BioIn 11; WhoAm 82, 84, 86, 88, 90, 92, 94, 95, 96, 97; WhoAmW 95, 97; WhoEnt 92; WhoSSW 82, 84; WhoWest 89*

Moffett, Anthony Toby
American. Politician
Resigned congressional seat to run for Senate; lost to Lowell Weicker, 1982.
b. Aug 18, 1944 in Holyoke, Massachusetts
Source: *AlmAP 78*

Moffett, Ken(neth Elwood)
American. Public Official, Baseball Executive
Federal mediator, 1962-83; succeeded Marvin Miller as executive director, ML Baseball Players Assn., 1983.
b. Sep 11, 1931 in Lykens, Pennsylvania
Source: *BioIn 13; NewYTBS 81; WhoAm 84; WhoGov 72, 75; WhoLab 76*

Moffo, Anna
American. Opera Singer
Soprano who made debut at Met., 1959; made numerous recordings, films, TV appearances.
b. Jun 27, 1934 in Wayne, Pennsylvania
Source: *Baker 84; BioIn 13; BioNews 74; CelR 90; CurBio 61; IntWW 91; IntWWM 90; InWom SUP; ItaFilm; LegTOT; MetOEnc; NewEOp 71; NewGrDA 86; NewYTBE 72; PenDiMP; WhoAm 86; WhoAmW 85; WhoEnt 92; WhoHol 92, A; WhoMus 72; WorAl; WorAlBi*

Mofford, Rose
American. Politician
Dem. governor, AZ, 1988-90; became governor on impeachment of Evan Mecham.
b. Jun 10, 1922 in Globe, Arizona
Source: *BioIn 15, 16, 20; IntWW 89, 91, 93; NewYTBS 88; PolsAm 84; WhoAm 80, 82, 84, 86, 88, 90; WhoAmP 85, 87, 89, 91, 93, 95; WhoAmW 83, 85, 87, 89, 91, 93; WhoWest 82, 84, 87, 89, 92; WhoWor 91*

Mohammed
[Mahomet; Muhammad]
"Prophet of Allah"
Arab. Religious Leader
Prophet who founded Islam, 622; wrote *The Koran;* considered by most Muslims to have been sinless.
b. Jan 30, 570 in Mecca, Arabia
d. Jun 8, 632 in Medina, Saudi Arabia
Source: *BioIn 1, 2, 3, 4, 5, 6, 7, 8, 9, 10, 11, 12, 13; BlmGEL; Dis&D; HisWorL; IlEncMy; LegTOT; LinLib L, S; LngCEL; LuthC 75; McGEWB; NewC; OxCEng 85, 95; OxDcByz; RAdv 14, 13-4; RComWL; REn; WhDW; WorAl; WorAlBi*

Mohammed V
[Sidi Mohammed Ben Moulay Youssef]
Moroccan. Ruler
Ruled, 1957-61, after France recognized country's independence.
b. Aug 10, 1910 in Fez, Morocco
d. Feb 26, 1961 in Rabat, Morocco
Source: *CurBio 51, 61*

Mohammed Zahir Shah
Afghan. Ruler
Crowned King, 1933; abdicated, 1973.
b. Oct 30, 1914 in Kabul, Afghanistan
Source: *BioIn 15, 16, 17; CurBio 56; FarE&A 78, 79, 81; IntWW 74, 77, 78, 79, 80, 81, 82, 83, 89, 91, 93; MidE 78, 79, 80, 81, 82; WhoGov 72; WhoWor 74*

Mohieddin, Ahmed Faud
[Fouad Mohie Al'din]
Egyptian. Political Leader
Prime minister of Egypt, 1982-84.
b. Feb 16, 1926
d. Jun 5, 1984 in Cairo, Egypt
Source: *IntWW 82, 83; MidE 81, 82; NewYTBS 84; WhoArab 81; WhoWor 82*

Moholy-Nagy, Laszlo
American. Artist, Photographer, Designer
Noted constructivist; developed "photogram" technique; organized Chicago's New Bauhaus, 1937.
b. Jul 20, 1895 in Bacsbarsod, Austria-Hungary
d. Nov 24, 1946 in Chicago, Illinois
Source: *BioIn 1, 2, 4, 8, 9, 11, 12, 13, 14, 15, 20, 21; ConArt 77, 83; ConDes 84; ConPhot 82, 88; DcAmB S4; DcArts; DcCAA 88, 94; DcTwDes; EncWT; ICPEnP; MacBEP; MacEA; McGDA; OxCAmH; OxCArt; OxCDecA; OxCFilm; OxCTwCA; OxDcArt; PhDcTCA 77; TheaDir; WebAB 74, 79; WhAmArt 85*

Mohs, Friedrich
German. Mineralogist
Introduced Mohs scale of hardness, 1812.
b. Jan 29, 1773 in Gernrode, Germany
d. Sep 29, 1839 in Agardo, Italy
Source: *AsBiEn; BiESc; CamDcSc; DcBiPP; DcScB; InSci; LarDcSc; WorAl; WorAlBi*

Moi, Daniel arap
Kenyan. Political Leader
Succeeded Jomo Kenyatta as pres. of Kenya, 1978—.
b. Sep 2, 1924 in Sacho, Kenya
Source: *AfSS 78, 79, 80, 81, 82; BioIn 13, 14, 15; ConBlB 1; CurBio 79; DcAfHiB 86S; DcTwHis; InB&W 80, 85; IntWW 74, 75, 76, 77, 78, 79, 80, 81, 82, 83, 89, 91, 93; IntYB 79, 81, 82; News 93-2; NewYTBS 78, 82; Who 82, 83, 85, 88, 90, 92, 94; WhoGov 72; WhoWor 74, 76, 78, 80, 82, 84, 87, 89, 91, 95*

Moiseyev, Igor Alexandrovich
Russian. Choreographer
Founded Moiseyev Dance Company, a folk-dance troupe, 1937; first performed in US, 1958, under newly established American-Soviet cultural exchange program.
b. Jan 21, 1906 in Kiev, Russia
Source: *BioNews 74; CnOxB; CurBio 58; DancEn 78; FacFETw; IntWW 83, 91; WhoWor 74, 89; WorAl; WorAlBi*

Moissan, Ferdinand Frederick Henri
French. Chemist
Won Nobel Prize, 1906; noted for isolation of fluorine element; produced artificial diamonds.
b. Sep 28, 1852 in Paris, France
d. Feb 20, 1907 in Paris, France
Source: *AsBiEn; BiESc; DcScB; WhoNob, 90, 95*

Moisseiff, Leon Solomon
Engineer
Bridge engineer who developed suspension bridges.
b. Nov 10, 1872 in Riga, Latvia
d. Sep 3, 1943 in Belmar, New Jersey
Source: *BioIn 4; CurBio 43; DcAmB S3; InSci; NatCAB 40; WhAm 2*

Moley, Raymond Charles
American. Political Scientist, Government Official
Advisor to FDR; originated term "New Deal."
b. Sep 27, 1886 in Berea, Ohio
d. Feb 18, 1975 in Phoenix, Arizona
Source: *AmAu&B; ConAu 61; CurBio 45, 75; DcAmB S9; DcTwHis; OhA&B; REn; REnAL; WhAm 6; WhNAA; WhoAm 74*

Moliere
[Jean Baptiste Poquelin]
French. Dramatist, Actor
Wrote *The School for Wives,* 1662; *The Imaginary Invalid,* 1673.
b. Jan 15, 1622 in Paris, France
d. Feb 17, 1673 in Paris, France
Source: *AtlBL; BbD; Benet 87, 96; BiD&SB; BioIn 14, 15, 19, 20, 21; BlmGEL; CamGWoT; CasWL; ChhPo; CnOxB; CnThe; CyWA 58; DcArts; DcCathB; DcEnL; DcEuL; Dis&D; EncWT; Ent; EuAu; EuWr 3; EvEuW; GrFLW; IntDcT 2; LegTOT; LinLib L, S; LitC 10, 28; LngCEL; MagSWL; McGEWB; McGEWD 72, 84; NewC; NewEOp 71; NewGrDM 80; NewGrDO; NotNAT A, B; OxCEng 67, 85, 95; OxCFr; OxCMus; OxCThe 67, 83; PenC EUR; PlP&P, A; RAdv 14, 13-2; RComWL; REn; REnWD; RfGWoL 95; WorAl; WorAlBi; WorLitC*

Molina, Gloria
American. Politician
Member, LA City Council, 1988—; cofounder of many organizations, including Hispanic American Democrats.
b. May 31, 1948 in Los Angeles, California
Source: *BioIn 16; DcHiB; HispAmA; MexAmB; NewYTBS 91; NotHsAW 93; WhoAmP 83, 85, 87, 89, 91, 93, 95; WhoAmW 93; WhoHisp 91, 92, 94*

Molinari, Alberto
Italian. Hostage
Italian businessman held hostage by Lebanese terrorists Sep 11, 1985-Nov 18, 1991.

Molinari, Susan
American. Politician
Republican congresswoman from NY, 1991-97; keynote speaker, Republican National Convention, 1996; anchor, CBS, 1997—.
b. Mar 27, 1958 in New York, New York
Source: *AlmAP 92, 96; BioIn 17, 18, 19, 21; CngDr 91, 93, 95; CurBio 96; News 96; WhoAm 97; WhoAmP 87, 89, 91, 93, 95; WhoAmW 97; WhoE 97; WhoWomW 91*

Molinaro, Al
American. Actor
Played Murray the Cop on "The Odd Couple," Al on "Happy Days."
b. Jun 24, 1919 in Kenosha, Wisconsin
Source: *ConTFT 8; LegTOT; VarWW 85*

Molitor, Paul Leo
American. Baseball Player
Infielder, Milwaukee, 1978-92; Toronto Blue Jays, 1992—; had 39-game hitting streak, 1987.
b. Aug 22, 1956 in Saint Paul, Minnesota
Source: *Ballpl 90; BaseEn 88; BaseReg 87, 88; BiDAmSp Sup; BioIn 15; WhoAm 92, 94, 95, 96, 97; WhoE 95, 97; WhoWor 95, 96*

Mollenhoff, Clark Raymond
American. Journalist
Won Pulitzer for labor racketeering investigation, 1958, that ultimately led to Congressional probe; wrote of corruption in almost every presidential administration: *The President Who Failed: Carter Out of Control,* 1980.
b. Apr 16, 1921 in Burnside, Iowa
d. Mar 2, 1991 in Lexington, Virginia
Source: *AmAu&B; AmMWSc 78S; ConAu 13NR, 17R, 133; CurBio 58, 91N; EncTwCJ; IntAu&W 76, 77, 82; NewYTBE 70; NewYTBS 91; WhAm 10; WhoAm 74, 76, 78, 80, 82, 84, 86, 88, 90; WhoAmL 90; WhoSSW 78, 80, 82, 84; WhoUSWr 88; WhoWor 74, 80, 82, 84, 87, 89; WhoWrEP 89, 92; WrDr 86, 90*

Mollet, Guy
French. Political Leader
Premier of France, 1956-57; secretary-general of French Socialists, 1946-69.
b. Dec 31, 1905 in Orne, France
d. Oct 3, 1975 in Paris, France
Source: *BiDInt; BioIn 1, 2, 4, 5, 10, 17; CurBio 50, 75N; DcPol; DcTwHis; FacFETw; IntWW 74, 75; NewYTBS 75; ObitT 1971; WhAm 6; WhoWor 74*

Molloy, John T
American. Author, Journalist, Critic, Businessman
"Wardrobe engineer;" author of *Dress for Success,* 1975; syndicated column.
b. 1937?
Source: *ConAu 81*

Molly Hatchet
[Barry Borden; Danny Joe Brown; Bruce Crump; Jimmy Farrar; Dave Hlubek; Steve Holland; Duane Rolland; Banner Thomas; Riff West]
American. Music Group
Southern blues-boogie, heavy-metal band formed 1975; album *Beating the Odds* sold over two million copies.
Source: *ConMuA 80A; HarEnR 86; PenEncP; RkOn 85; RolSEnR 83; WhoRocM 82*

Molnar, Ferenc
Hungarian. Dramatist, Author, Journalist
Noted for light sophisticated plays including *Liliom,* 1909; source for Broadway's *Carousel,* 1945.
b. Jan 12, 1878 in Budapest, Austria-Hungary
d. Apr 1, 1952 in New York, New York
Source: *AtlBL; Benet 87, 96; BioIn 1, 2, 3, 4, 5, 7; CamGWoT; CasWL; ClDMEL 47, 80; CnMD; CnThe; ConAu 109, 153; CyWA 58; DcArts; EncWL, 2, 3; EncWT; Ent; EvEuW; HalFC 80, 84, 88; IntDcT 2; LegTOT; LiExTwC; LngCTC; MajMD 2; McGEWD 72, 84; ModWD; NotNAT A, B; OxCAmT 84; OxCThe 67, 83; PenC EUR; PlP&P; REn; REnWD; RfGWoL 95; TwCA, SUP; TwCLC 20; WhAm 3; WhDW; WhScrn 77, 83; WorAl; WorAlBi*

Molotov, Vyacheslav Mikhaylovich
[Vyacheslav Mikhaylovich Skryabin]
Russian. Political Leader
Prime minister, USSR, 1930-41; Molotov cocktail named after him.
b. Mar 9, 1890 in Kukarka, Russia
d. Nov 8, 1986 in Moscow, Union of Soviet Socialist Republics
Source: *BioIn 1, 2, 3, 4, 5, 6, 10, 12, 13, 15, 16; ColdWar 1; ConAu 121; CurBio 40, 54, 87N; EncCW; EncRev; EncTR 91; FacFETw; IntWW 83; McGEWB; NewYTBS 86; SovUn; WhAm 9; Who 85, 88N; WorAlBi*

Molson, Hartland de Montarville
Canadian. Hockey Executive
Pres., Montreal Canadiens, till 1964; Hall of Fame, 1973.
b. May 29, 1907 in Montreal, Quebec, Canada
Source: *CanWW 31, 89*

Molson, John
Canadian. Brewer
Man of diverse talents who founded brewery, 1785.
b. 1764 in Lincolnshire, England
d. Jan 11, 1836 in Montreal, Quebec, Canada
Source: *ApCAB; Entr; MacDCB 78*

Moltke, Helmuth James, Graf von
German. Social Reformer
Opposed Nazi regime; organized group to plan post-Hitler order; executed in prison.

b. Mar 11, 1907 in Kreisau, Silesia
d. Jan 23, 1945 in Plotzensee Prison, Germany
Source: *BioIn 10, 14, 17, 20; EncTR, 91; HisEWW; OxCGer 76*

Moltke, Helmuth Karl Bernhard von
German. Statesman, Soldier
Reorganized Prussian Army, 1858-63, with Bismarck's aid; field marshal, 1871.
b. Oct 26, 1800 in Parchim, Silesia
d. Apr 24, 1891 in Berlin, Germany
Source: *HarEnMi; OxCGer 76; REn*

Molyneux, Edward H
English. Fashion Designer, Art Collector
Designed feminine clothes with English influence worn by Gertrude Lawrence, Adele Astaire.
b. Sep 5, 1891 in London, England
d. Mar 23, 1974 in Monte Carlo, Monaco
Source: *CurBio 42, 74; NewYTBS 74; WorFshn*

Momaday, N(avarre) Scott
American. Poet, Author
Pulitzer Prize-winning Kiowa Native American novelist of *The House of Dawn,* 1968.
b. Feb 27, 1934 in Lawton, Oklahoma
Source: *Benet 96; BenetAL 91; BioIn 10, 11, 12, 16; ConAu 14NR, 25R, 34NR; ConLC 2, 19, 85; ConNov 91, 96; ConPopW; CurBio 75; CyWA 89; DcArts; DcNAL; DrAPF 91; DrAS 74E, 78E, 82E; EncNAB; IntAu&W 89, 91, 93; MajTwCW; OxCAmL 83, 95; REnAW; RfGAmL 94; SmATA 30; TwCWW 91; TwCYAW; WhoAm 74, 76, 78, 80, 82, 84, 86, 88, 92, 94, 95, 96; WhoUSWr 88; WhoWest 92, 94; WhoWrEP 89, 92, 95; WrDr 92, 94, 96*

Mommsen, Theodor
[Christian Matthias Theodor Mommsen]
German. Historian
Wrote classic *History of Rome,* 1854-56; shared Nobel Prize, 1902.
b. Nov 30, 1817 in Garding, Germany
d. Nov 1, 1903 in Charlottenburg, Germany
Source: *BbD; Benet 87, 96; BiD&SB; BioIn 3, 7, 9, 13, 15, 17; CelCen; DcEuL; Dis&D; LinLib L, S; LngCTC; LuthC 75; McGEWB; NewC; NewCol 75; NobelP; OxCClL; OxCEng 67; OxCGer 76, 86; OxCLaw; REn; WhoNob, 90, 95*

Mompou, Federico
Spanish. Composer
Wrote over 200 piano works, mostly in unique folklike idiom.
b. Apr 10, 1893 in Barcelona, Spain
d. Jun 30, 1987 in Barcelona, Spain
Source: *Baker 78, 84, 92; BioIn 11, 15; DcCM; NewGrDM 80; NewOxM; NewYTBS 87; OxCMus; WhoMus 72*

Monaghan, (James) Jay, (IV)
American. Author, Historian
Americana writings include *Overland Trail,* 1947.
b. Mar 19, 1891 in Philadelphia, Pennsylvania
d. 1981 in Santa Barbara, California
Source: *AmAu&B; BioIn 11; ConAu 41R, 103; DrAS 74H, 78H; PeoHis; REnAL; REnAW*

Monaghan, Tom
[Thomas S Monaghan]
American. Businessman, Baseball Executive
Founded Domino's Pizza, 1960; owner, Detroit Tigers, 1983-92.
b. Mar 25, 1937 in Ann Arbor, Michigan
Source: *BioIn 16; ConAmBL; ConNews 85-1; CurBio 90; Dun&B 90; NewYTBS 84, 91; WhoAm 86, 90; WhoFI 92; WhoMW 92*

Monash, Paul
American. Producer, Writer
Produced TV show, "Peyton Place," 1964-69.
b. Jun 14, 1917 in New York, New York
Source: *ConTFT 5; HalFC 84, 88; IntMPA 86, 92, 94, 96; LesBEnT*

Monck, Charles Stanley, Sir
Irish. Politician
First governor general, Dominion of Canada, 1866-68.
b. Oct 10, 1819 in Templemore, Ireland
d. Nov 29, 1894 in Enniskerry, Ireland
Source: *ApCAB; DcBiPP; DcCanB 12; DcNaB S1; Drake; MacDCB 78*

Moncreiffe, Jain
[Rupert Jain Moncreiffe]
English. Diplomat, Author
Genealogist, pres., Burke's Peerage from 1983; wrote *Simple Heraldry.*
b. Apr 9, 1919
d. Feb 27, 1985 in London, England
Source: *ConAu 115*

Moncrief, Sidney A
American. Basketball Player
Guard, Milwaukee, 1979-89, Atlanta, 1990-91; NBA defensive player of year, 1983, 1984.
b. Sep 21, 1957 in Little Rock, Arkansas
Source: *BiDAmSp BK; BioIn 14; OfNBA 87; WhoAm 86; WhoBlA 88, 92*

Mondale, Joan Adams
[Mrs. Walter Mondale]
"Joan of Art"
American., Author
VP's wife, who wrote *Politics in Art,* 1972.
b. Aug 8, 1930 in Eugene, Oregon
Source: *BioIn 12, 13, 14; ConAu 41R; CurBio 80; InWom SUP; NewYTBS 76, 78; WhoAm 78, 80, 82, 84, 86, 88, 90, 92, 94, 95, 96, 97; WhoAmA 78, 80, 82, 84, 86, 89, 91, 93; WhoAmW 77, 79, 81, 95, 97; WhoE 77, 79, 81, 83, 86; WhoMW 93, 96*

Mondale, Walter Frederick
"Fritz"
American. US Vice President
Dem. senator from MN, 1964-77; VP, 1977-80, under Carter; unsuccessful presidential candidate against Reagan, 1980.
b. Jan 5, 1928 in Ceylon, Minnesota
Source: *AmPolLe; WhoMW 74, 76, 78, 80, 93, 96; WhoWor 78, 80, 84, 87, 89, 91, 93, 95, 96, 97; WorAl; WorAlBi*

Mondavi, Robert Gerald
American. Businessman
Founder, Robert Mondavi Winery, 1967; helped popularize oak-barrel aging and brought CA's Napa Valley wine region to world prominence.
b. Jun 18, 1913 in Virginia, Minnesota
Source: *BioIn 12, 16; NewYTBS 79; WhoAm 74, 90; WhoWest 89, 92*

Mondrian, Piet(er Cornelis)
Dutch. Artist
Abstract painter influenced by cubism; developed geometric style called neoplasticism.
b. Mar 7, 1872 in Amersfoort, Netherlands
d. Feb 1, 1944 in New York, New York
Source: *AtlBL; Benet 87; BioIn 10, 14, 15, 16, 17, 20, 21; ConArt 77, 83; CurBio 44; DcArts; DcTwDes; EncFash; FacFETw; IlEncMy; IntDcAA 90; LegTOT; LinLib L; MakMC; McGDA; McGEWB; ModArCr 4; NewCol 75; OxCArt; OxCTwCA; OxDcArt; PhDcTCA 77; REn; WhAm 4; WhDW; WorAl; WorAlBi*

Moneo, Jose Rafael
[Jose Rafael Moneo Valles]
Spanish. Architect
Winner of Pritzker Architecture Prize, 1996.
b. May 9, 1937 in Tudela, Spain
Source: *BioIn 15, 16, 20; ConArch 80, 87, 94; News 96; WhoAm 90, 92, 95, 96, 97; WhoE 95, 97*

Monet, Claude-Oscar
French. Artist
Leader of impressionists whose painting *Impression: Sunrise* gave group its name.
b. Nov 14, 1840 in Paris, France
d. Dec 5, 1926 in Giverny, France
Source: *AtlBL; McGDA; McGEWB; NewCol 75; OxCArt; OxCFr; REn*

Moneta, Ernesto Teodora
Italian. Political Leader
Shared 1907 Nobel Peace Prize for founding Lombard Peace Union, 1887.
b. Sep 20, 1833 in Milan, Italy
d. Feb 10, 1918 in Milan, Italy
Source: *BioIn 9, 11; LinLib L; WhoNob*

Monette, Paul
American. Writer
Author of *Becoming a Man: Half a Life Story,*1992 about homosexuality and AIDS.
b. Oct 16, 1945 in Lawrence, Massachusetts
d. Feb 10, 1995 in West Hollywood, California
Source: *ConAu 139, 147; ConGAN; ConLC 82; ConNov 96; GayLL; NewYTBS 95*

Monge, Gaspard
French. Mathematician
Known for geometrical research, which led to development of modern descriptive geometry; friend of Napoleon; stripped of positions after restoration.
b. May 10, 1746 in Beaune, France
d. Jul 28, 1818 in Paris, France
Source: *BiDMoER 1; BiESc; BioIn 1, 7, 8, 16; CamDcSc; CmFrR; CyEd; DcBiPP; DcCathB; DcScB; InSci; LarDcSc; NewCol 75; OxCFr; WhDW; WorScD*

Mongella, Gertrude
Tanzanian. Diplomat
Tanzania's high commissioner to India, 1991—; secretary-general, Fourth World Conference on Women, 1992.
b. Sep 13, 1945 in Ukerewe, United Republic of Tanzania
Source: *ConBlB 11*

Mongkut
[Rama IV]
Thai. Ruler
Ruled, 1851-68; began modernizing Siam.
b. Oct 18, 1804 in Bangkok, Thailand
d. Oct 15, 1868 in Bangkok, Thailand
Source: *BioIn 1, 5, 6, 8, 9, 11, 12, 13, 14; McGEWB; NewCol 75*

Monicelli, Mario
Italian. Director
Directed *The Big Deal on Madonna Street,* 1960; wrote *Crackers,* 1984.
b. May 15, 1915 in Rome, Italy
Source: *BioIn 16; DcFM; EncEurC; FilmEn; FilmgC; HalFC 80, 84, 88; IntDcF 1-2, 2-2; IntMPA 75, 76, 77, 78, 79, 80, 81, 82, 84, 86, 88, 92, 94, 96; IntWW 74, 75, 76, 77, 78, 79, 80, 81, 82, 83, 89, 91, 93; ItaFilm; MiSFD 9; VarWW 85; WhoWor 74; WorEFlm; WorFDir 2*

Moninari-Pradelli, Francesco
Italian. Conductor
A principal conductor, San Francisco Opera, NYC Met., 1950s-60s.
b. Jul 4, 1911 in Bologna, Italy
Source: *NewEOp 71*

Moniuszko, Stanislaus
Polish. Composer
Composed operas, sacred music, songs in *Spiewnik Domowy,* 1843-59.
b. May 5, 1819 in Ubiel, Poland
d. Jun 4, 1872 in Warsaw, Poland
Source: *GrComp; NewEOp 71; OxCMus*

Monk, Allan James
Canadian. Opera Singer
Baritone who sang title role in *Wozzeck,* 1970s-80s.
b. Aug 19, 1942 in Mission City, British Columbia, Canada
Source: *IntWWM 90; MetOEnc; WhoAm 78, 80, 82, 84, 88, 90, 92, 94, 95, 96, 97; WhoEnt 92; WhoOp 76*

Monk, Art
[James Arthur Monk]
American. Football Player
Wide receiver, Washington Redskins, 1980-94; New York Jets, 1994-95; holds NFL record for career receptions, 1992.
b. Dec 5, 1957 in White Plains, New York
Source: *AfrAmSG; BioIn 19, 20, 21; CurBio 95; News 93-2; WhoAfA 96; WhoAm 92, 94, 95, 96, 97; WhoBlA 85, 88, 90, 92, 94*

Monk, Maria
American. Author
Imposter; claimed scandalous nunnery practices in *Awful Disclosures by Maria Monk,* 1836.
b. Jun 1, 1816 in Saint John's, Quebec, Canada
d. Sep 4, 1849 in New York, New York
Source: *DcCanB 7; InWom SUP; LibW; NotAW; WebBD 83*

Monk, Meredith Jane
American. Choreographer, Singer
"Next Wave" choreographer known for Obie-winning *Vessel,* 1971; founded dance troupe, The House, 1969.
b. Nov 20, 1942 in Lima, Peru
Source: *Baker 92; BiDD; BioIn 12, 14, 16; CamGWoT; CelR 90; ConAmC 82; ConCom 92; ConMus 1; ConTFT 3; CurBio 85; IntWWM 85, 90; InWom SUP; NewAmDM; NewGrDA 86; NewYTBS 91; NotWoAT; WhoAm 80, 82, 90, 92, 94, 95, 96, 97; WhoAmA 89, 91; WhoAmM 83; WhoAmW 81, 83, 85, 95, 97; WhoE 91, 95; WhoEnt 92*

Monk, Thelonious Sphere, Jr.
American. Songwriter, Musician
Leading jazz pianist who helped develop "bop," 1940s; known for chord structures, active into 1970s.
b. Oct 17, 1917 in Rocky Mount, North Carolina
d. Feb 17, 1982 in Englewood, New Jersey
Source: *AnObit 1982; Baker 84; BiDAfM; BiDAmM; CmpEPM; ConAmC 82; CurBio 64, 82; DrBlPA; EncJzS; IlEncJ; InB&W 85; NewYTBS 82; WhoAm 80; WhoBlA 77; WhoE 74; WhoWor 74*

Monkees, The
[Mickey Dolenz; Davy Jones; Mike Nesmith; Peter Tork]
American. Music Group
Prefabricated 1960s pop group formed by TV executives; had hit TV series, 1966-68, hit singles "Last Train to Clarksville," 1966, "I'm a Believer," 1967; disbanded in early 1970s; reunion tour, 1986.
Source: *BiDAmM; BioIn 9, 14, 18; ConMuA 80A; ConMus 7; EncPR&S 74, 89; EncRk 88; EncRkSt; FilmgC; HalFC 80, 84, 88; HarEnR 86; IlEncRk; NewGrDA 86; NewYTBE 72; ObitOF 79; OxCPMus; PenEncP; RkOn 74, 78; RolSEnR 83; VarWW 85; WhoHol 92, A; WhoNeCM A; WhoRock 81; WhoRocM 82; WorAl; WorAlBi*

Monmouth, James Scott, Duke
[James Crofts; James Fitzroy]
English. Imposter
Led unsuccessful uprising against James II; beheaded.
b. Apr 9, 1649 in Rotterdam, Netherlands
d. Jul 25, 1685 in London, England
Source: *Benet 87, 96; BioIn 3, 5, 6, 8, 9, 10, 11, 12, 16; BlmGEL; DcBiPP; DcNaB; HarEnMi; LngCEL; McGEWB; REn; WhDW; WhoMilH 76*

Monnet, Jean Omer Marie Gabriel
French. Economist, Diplomat
Father of European Economic Community; helped reconstruction of France after WW II.
b. Nov 9, 1888 in Cognac, France
d. Mar 16, 1979 in Rambouillet, France
Source: *BiDInt; ColdWar 2; CurBio 47; IntWW 74; NewYTBS 79; WebBD 83; Who 74; WorAl*

Monnoyer, Jean-Baptiste
French. Artist
Noted floral painter; decorated Versailles.
b. Jul 19, 1636 in Lille, France
d. Feb 16, 1699 in London, England
Source: *BioIn 19; McGDA*

Monod, Jacques Lucien
French. Biochemist
Awarded Nobel Prize in medicine with Jacob, Lwoff; director, Pasteur Institute, 1970s.
b. Feb 9, 1910 in Paris, France
d. May 31, 1976 in Cannes, France
Source: *AsBiEn; BiESc; BioIn 7, 9, 10, 11; CamDcSc; ConAu 69; CurBio 71; DcScB S2; FacFETw; IntWW 74; LarDcSc; NotTwCS; WhAm 7; Who 74; WhoAm 74; WhoNob, 90, 95; WhoWor 74, 76; WorAl*

Monro, Harold Edward
English. Author, Businessman
Opened London's Poetry Bookshop, 1913; founded *Poetry Review,* 1912.
b. Mar 14, 1879 in Brussels, Belgium
d. Mar 16, 1932 in Broadstairs, England

Source: *AnCL; BioIn 2, 7, 13; ChhPo, S1, S2, S3; DcLEL; DcNaB 1931; EvLB; GrWrEL P; LngCTC; ModBrL; NewC; NewCBEL; OxCEng 67; PenC ENG; REn; TwCA, SUP; WebE&AL; WhoLA; WhoTwCL*

Monroe, Bill
[William Smith Monroe]
"Father of Bluegrass"
American. Singer, Songwriter
Wrote Elvis Presley hit "Blue Moon of Kentucky," 1947.
b. Sep 13, 1911 in Rosine, Kentucky
d. Sep 9, 1996 in Springfield, Tennessee
Source: *Baker 84, 92; BgBkCoM; BioIn 8, 9, 10, 12, 14, 15, 16, 20; CmpEPM; ConMus 1; CounME 74, 74A; EncFCWM 83; HarEnR 86; LegTOT; LesBEnT 92; NewAmDM; NewGrDA 86; NewGrDM 80; News 97-1; NewYTET; OxCPMus; PenEncP; WhoAm 74, 80, 82, 84, 86, 88, 92, 94, 95, 96, 97; WhoNeCM C*

Monroe, Bill
[William Blanc Monroe, Jr]
American. Broadcast Journalist
Moderator, exec. producer, NBC's "Meet the Press," 1975-84.
b. Jul 17, 1920 in New Orleans, Louisiana
Source: *BioIn 10; ConAu 108; VarWW 85; WhoAm 80, 82, 84; WhoTelC*

Monroe, Earl
[Vernon Earl Monroe]
"The Pearl"
American. Basketball Player
Guard, 1967-80, with Baltimore, NY Knicks; rookie of year, 1968; Hall of Fame, 1990.
b. Nov 21, 1944 in Philadelphia, Pennsylvania
Source: *BasBi; BiDAmSp BK; BioIn 10, 11, 12, 15; CurBio 78; InB&W 80, 85; LegTOT; NewYTBE 71; NewYTBS 74; OfNBA 87; WhoAfA 96; WhoAm 78, 80, 82, 84, 86, 88, 92, 94, 95, 96, 97; WhoBbl 73; WhoBlA 77, 80, 85, 88, 90, 92, 94; WhoE 95; WhoSpor; WorAl; WorAlBi*

Monroe, Elizabeth Kortright
[Mrs. James Monroe]
American. First Lady
Introduced more formal ways of White House entertaining.
b. Jun 30, 1768 in New York, New York
d. Sep 23, 1830 in Loudoun County, Virginia
Source: *AmBi; AmWom; ApCAB; BioIn 16, 17, 19; FacPr 89; GoodHs; HarEnUS; InWom SUP; NatCAB 6; NotAW; TwCBDA*

Monroe, Harriet
American. Poet, Editor
Founded, edited *Poetry: A Magazine of Verse*, 1912-36, which championed new verse.
b. Dec 23, 1860 in Chicago, Illinois
d. Sep 26, 1936 in Arequipa, Peru
Source: *AmAu&B; AmBi; AmLY; AmWomPl; AmWomWr; ArtclWW 2; Benet 87, 96; BenetAL 91; BiD&SB; BioAmW; BioIn 1, 4, 5, 6, 8, 10, 11, 13, 14, 15, 17; CamGEL; CamGLE; CamHAL; CasWL; ChhPo, S2; CnDAL; ConAmL; ConAu 109; DcAmAu; DcAmB S2; DcLB 54, 91; DcNAA; EvLB; FacFETw; FemiCLE; HarEnUS; InWom, SUP; JrnUS; LibW; LinLib L; LngCTC; NatCAB 28; NotAW; OxCAmL 65, 83, 95; OxCWoWr 95; PenC AM; REn; REnAL; RGTwCWr; TwCA, SUP; TwCLC 12; WebAB 74, 79; WhAm 1; WhNAA; WomFir; WomWWA 14*

Monroe, James
American. US President
Fifth in office, 1817-25; declared Monroe Doctrine, 1823; term called "era of good feeling."
b. Apr 28, 1758 in Westmoreland, Virginia
d. Jul 4, 1831 in New York, New York
Source: *Alli; AmAu&B; AmBi; AmPolLe; AmRev; ApCAB; BenetAL 91; BiAUS; BiD&SB; BiDLA; BiDrAC; BiDrGov 1789; BiDrUSC 89; BiDrUSE 71, 89; BiDSA; BioIn 1, 2, 3, 4, 5, 6, 7, 8, 9, 10, 11, 12, 13, 14, 15, 16, 17, 18, 19, 20; CelCen; CyAG; DcAmAu; DcAmB; DcAmDH 80, 89; DcBiPP; DcNAA; Dis&D; Drake; EncAAH; EncAB-H 1974, 1996; EncAR; EncSoH; FacPr 89, 93; HarEnMi; HealPre; HisWorL; LegTOT; LinLib L, S; McGEWB; MemAm; NatCAB 6; OxCAmH; OxCAmL 65, 83, 95; PolPar; RComAH; REnAL; TwCBDA; WebAB 74, 79; WebBD 83; WhAm HS; WhAmP; WhAmRev; WhDW; WorAl; WorAlBi*

Monroe, Lucy
American. Singer
Called "star-spangled soprano," for her rendition of national anthem in over 5,000 performances.
b. Oct 23, 1906 in New York, New York
d. Oct 13, 1987 in New York, New York
Source: *BioIn 15; CurBio 42, 87, 87N; NewYTBS 87; RadStar*

Monroe, Marilyn
[Norma Jean (Mortenson) Baker]
American. Actor
Ultimate pin-up girl, cult figure; starred in *Some Like It Hot*, 1959; *Bus Stop*, 1956; died of drug overdose.
b. Jun 1, 1926 in Los Angeles, California
d. Aug 5, 1962 in Hollywood, California
Source: *AmDec 1950; BiDFilm, 81, 94; BioAmW; BioIn 2, 3, 4, 5, 6, 7, 8, 9, 10, 11, 12, 13, 14, 15, 16, 17, 18, 19, 20, 21; CmCal; CmMov; CmpEPM; ConAu 113, 129; ContDcW 89; CurBio 59, 62; DcAmB S7; DcArts; DcTwCCu 1; EncAB-H 1996; EncAFC; EncWB; FacFETw; FilmEn; FilmgC; GangFlm; HalFC 80, 84, 88; HanAmWH; IntDcF 1-3, 2-3; IntDcWB; InWom, SUP; LegTOT; LibW; MotPP; MovMk; NotAW MOD; NotNAT B; ObitT 1961; OxCFilm; RAdv 13-3; RComAH; WebAB 74, 79; WebBD 83; WhAm 4; WhDW; WhoHol B; WhScrn 74, 77, 83; WorAl; WorAlBi; WorEFlm*

Monroe, Marion
American. Psychologist
Co-author of *Dick and Jane* school books, 1940s-70s.
b. Feb 4, 1898 in Mount Vernon, Indiana
d. Jun 25, 1983 in Long Beach, California
Source: *AnObit 1983; BioIn 13, 14; ConAu 110; FacFETw; NewYTBS 83; SmATA 34, 34N; WhoAmW 58, 61, 64, 68*

Monroe, Phil
American. Cartoonist
Created cartoon characters the Road Runner, Tony the Tiger, Charley Tuna, and others.
b. 1917?
d. Jul 14, 1988 in Los Angeles, California

Monroe, Vaughn
American. Singer, Bandleader
Noted for songs "Racing with the Moon," "Ballerina."
b. Oct 7, 1911 in Akron, Ohio
d. May 21, 1973 in Stuart, Florida
Source: *ASCAP 66, 80; BgBands 74; BiDAmM; BioIn 1, 2, 4, 6, 9, 10, 12; CmpEPM; CurBio 42, 73N; FilmgC; HalFC 84; NewYTBE 73; OxCPMus; PenEncP; RadStar; RkOn 74; WhAm 6; What 4; WhoHol B; WhScrn 77, 83; WorAl; WorAlBi*

Monroney, Mike (Aimer Stillwell)
American. Politician
Dem. senator from OK, 1951-69; opposed Joe McCarthy.
b. Mar 2, 1902 in Oklahoma City, Oklahoma
d. Feb 13, 1980 in Rockville, Maryland
Source: *AnObit 1980; BioIn 2, 3; CurBio 51; St&PR 75; WhoAm 74; WhoAmP 73*

Monsarrat, Nicholas John Turney
English. Author
Wrote *The Cruel Sea*, 1951.
b. Mar 22, 1910 in Liverpool, England
d. Aug 7, 1979 in London, England
Source: *Au&Wr 71; CanWr; CanWW 70, 79; ConAu 1R, 3NR; ConNov 72, 76; ConSFA; CurBio 79; DcLEL; DcNaB 1971; EncSF; EvLB; IntAu&W 76, 77; IntWW 74, 75, 76, 77, 78, 79; LinLib L; LngCTC; ModBrL; NewCBEL; NewYTBS 79; OxCEng 85, 95; REn; TwCA SUP; TwCWr; Who 74; WrDr 76, 80*

Monsigny, Pierre-Alexandre
French. Composer
Noted French comic opera writer: *Les Aveux Indiscrets*, 1759.
b. Oct 17, 1729 in Fauquembergue, France
d. Jan 14, 1817 in Paris, France
Source: *Baker 78, 84, 92; GrComp; MusMk; NewEOp 71; NewGrDM 80;*

NewGrDO; NewOxM; OxCMus; OxDcOp

Montagnier, Luc
French. Scientist
Co-discovered the AIDS virus, 1984.
b. Aug 8, 1932 in Chabris, France
Source: *BioIn 16; CamDcSc; CurBio 88; IntMed 80; IntWW 89, 91, 93; LarDcSc; NotTwCS; Who 92, 94; WhoFr 79; WhoWor 80, 91*

Montagu, Ashley Montague Francis
American. Anthropologist, Educator
Numerous works include *Fallacy of Race,* 1942; *Natural Superiority of Women,* 1953.
b. Jun 28, 1905 in London, England
Source: *AmAu&B; AmMWSc 73S; ConAu 5NR, 5R; LesBEnT; TwCA SUP; WebAB 74; Who 92; WhoAm 84, 90; WhoE 74; WhoWorJ 72; WrDr 92*

Montagu, Ewen
[Edward Samuel Montagu]
English. Lawyer
Judge advocate of British fleet, 1945-73; largely responsible for "operation mincemeat," which deceived Germany about Sicily invasion, WW II.
b. Mar 29, 1901 in London, England
d. Jul 19, 1985 in London, England
Source: *AnObit 1985; BioIn 14, 17, 18; ConAu 77, 116; CurBio 56, 85, 85N; FacFETw; WrDr 80, 82, 84, 86*

Montagu, Mary Wortley, Lady
English. Author
Wrote witty, descriptive letters of Middle Eastern life; published posthumously, 1763.
b. May 26, 1689 in London, England
d. Aug 21, 1762 in London, England
Source: *Alli; ArtclWW 2; AtlBL; BbD; Benet 87, 96; BiD&SB; BiDEWW; BioIn 1, 2, 3, 4, 5, 6, 7, 8, 9, 10, 11, 12, 13; BlkwCE; BlmGEL; BlmGWL; BritAu; CamGEL; CamGLE; Chambr 2; ChhPo; ContDcW 89; DcArts; DcBrAmW; DcEnA; DcEnL; DcEuL; DcLB 95, 101; DcLEL; DcNaB; Dis&D; EncBrWW; EncEnl; EvLB; FemiCLE; GrWrEL P; IntDcWB; InWom, SUP; LinLib L, S; LitC 9; LngCEL; MouLC 2; NewC; NewCBEL; OxCEng 67, 85; PenBWP; PenC ENG; PoeCrit 16; RAdv 1, 14, 13-1; REn; RfGEnL 91; WomFir*

Montaigne, Michel Eyquem de
French. Essayist, Courtier
Introduced the essay as a literary form, often using quotations from classical writers.
b. Feb 28, 1533 in Bordeaux, France
d. Sep 13, 1592 in Bordeaux, France
Source: *AtlBL; BbD; BiD&SB; BioIn 1, 2, 3, 4, 5, 6, 7, 8, 9, 10, 12, 13; CasWL; CroE&S; CyEd; CyWA 58; DcArts; DcBiPP; DcEnL; DcEuL; Dis&D; EuAu; EvEuW; GuFrLit 2; LuthC 75; McGEWB; NewC; NewCBEL; OxCEng 67, 85, 95; OxCFr; OxCPhil; PenC EUR; RAdv 14, 13-2, 13-4; RComWL; REn; WorAl*

Montalban, Ricardo
Mexican. Actor
Played Mr. Rourke on TV series "Fantasy Island," 1978-83.
b. Nov 25, 1920 in Mexico City, Mexico
Source: *BiE&WWA; BioIn 5, 9, 11, 12, 16, 20; CelR 90; CmpEPM; ConTFT 3; DcHiB; FilmEn; FilmgC; ForYSC; HalFC 80, 84, 88; HispAmA; IntMPA 77, 78, 79, 80, 81, 82, 84, 86, 88, 92, 94, 96; ItaFilm; LegTOT; MexAmB; MGM; MotPP; MovMk; VarWW 85; WhoAm 78, 80, 82, 84, 86, 88, 90, 92, 94, 95, 96, 97; WhoEnt 92; WhoHisp 91, 92, 94; WhoHol 92, A; WhoTelC; WorAl; WorAlBi; WorEFlm*

Montale, Eugenio
Italian. Poet, Critic
Won 1975 Nobel Prize; wrote *The Occasions,* 1939; *Satura,* 1963.
b. Oct 12, 1896 in Genoa, Italy
d. Sep 12, 1981 in Milan, Italy
Source: *AnObit 1981; Benet 87, 96; BioIn 1, 7, 8, 9, 10, 11, 12, 13, 15, 17, 18; CasWL; ClDMEL 47, 80; CnMWL; ConAu 17R, 30NR, 104; ConLC 7, 9, 18; CurBio 76, 81, 81N; DcArts; DcItL 1, 2; DcLB 114; EncWL, 2, 3; EuWr 11; EvEuW; FacFETw; GrFLW; IntWW 74, 75, 76, 77, 78, 79, 80, 81; IntWWP 77; LegTOT; LinLib L; MajTwCW; MakMC; McGEWB; ModRL; NewYTBS 75, 81; NobelP; OxCEng 85, 95; PenC EUR; PoeCrit 13; RAdv 14, 13-2; REn; RfGWoL 95; RGFMEP; TwCWr; WhoNob, 90, 95; WhoTwCL; WhoWor 78, 80; WorAl; WorAlBi; WorAu 1950*

Montana, Bob
American. Cartoonist
Created syndicated comic strip "Archie," 1942.
b. Oct 23, 1920 in Stockton, California
d. Jan 4, 1975 in Meredith, New Hampshire
Source: *BioIn 10, 12; ConAu 89; EncACom; LegTOT; SmATA 21N; WhAm 6; WhoAm 74; WhoAmA 73, 76N, 78N, 80N, 82N, 84N, 86N, 89N, 91N, 93N; WhoE 74; WhoWor 74; WorECom*

Montana, Bull
[Luigi Montagna; Louis Montana]
American. Actor
Former professional wrestler; character actor, 1919-43.
b. May 16, 1887 in Vogliera, Italy
d. Jan 24, 1950 in Los Angeles, California
Source: *BioIn 2; EncAFC; Film 1, 2; FilmgC; HalFC 80, 84, 88; TwYS; WhoHol B; WhoHrs 80; WhScrn 74, 77, 83*

Montana, Claude
French. Fashion Designer
Helped popularize shoulder pads in '80s women's styles; abandoned tough leather look in favor of elegant simplicity.
b. Jun 29, 1949 in Paris, France
Source: *BioIn 16; CelR 90; ConDes 84, 90, 97; ConFash; CurBio 92; DcArts; EncFash; IntWW 91; WhoFash 88; WhoWor 95*

Montana, Joe
[Joseph C Montana, Jr]
"Big Sky"; "Golden Joe"
American. Football Player
Quarterback, San Francisco, 1979-93; Kansas City, 1993-95; set several NFL records for passing; Super Bowl MVP, 1982, 1985, 1990; NFL MVP, 1989-90.
b. Jun 11, 1956 in New Eagle, Pennsylvania
Source: *AmDec 1980; BioIn 12, 13, 14, 15, 16, 20; CelR 90; CurBio 83; FacFETw; FootReg 87; LegTOT; News 89-2; NewYTBS 81, 82, 89; WhoAm 84, 86, 88; WhoWest 87; WorAlBi*

Montana, Patsy
American. Singer, Composer
Called Queen of Country Western Music, 1973; wrote over 200 songs.
b. Oct 30, 1914 in Hot Springs, Arkansas
d. May 4, 1996 in San Jacinto, California
Source: *ASCAP 66, 80; BgBkCoM; BiDAmM; BioIn 11, 14, 19, 21; CmpEPM; CounME 74, 74A; EncFCWM 69, 83; HarEnCM 87; IlEncCM; InWom, SUP; PenEncP; WhoAm 86; WhoEnt 92; WhoNeCM C*

Montand, Yves
[Ivo Livi]
French. Singer, Actor
Vocalist, int'l film star whose films include *Let's Make Love,* 1960; husband of Simone Signoret; first pop singer to give a solo performance at the Met, 1982.
b. Oct 13, 1921 in Monsummano Alto, Italy
d. Nov 9, 1991 in Senlis, France
Source: *AnObit 1991; BiDAmM; BiDFilm, 81, 94; BioIn 5, 9, 11, 13, 15, 16; CelR, 90; ConMus 12; ConTFT 6, 10; CurBio 60, 88, 92N; DcArts; DcTwCCu 2; EncEurC; FacFETw; FilmAG WE; FilmEn; FilmgC; ForYSC; HalFC 80, 84, 88; IntDcF 1-3, 2-3; IntMPA 77, 80, 84, 86, 88, 92; IntWW 74, 75, 76, 77, 78, 79, 80, 81, 82, 83, 89, 91; ItaFilm; LegTOT; MotPP; MovMk; News 92, 92-2; NewYTBS 87, 91; OxCFilm; OxCPMus; VarWW 85; WhAm 10; WhoAm 74; WhoFr 79; WhoHol 92, A; WhoWor 74, 76, 78, 84, 87, 89, 91; WorAl; WorAlBi; WorEFlm*

Montcalm, Louis Joseph de
French. Military Leader
Commander French forces in Canada; killed in defense of Quebec.
b. Feb 29, 1712 in Nimes, France
d. Sep 14, 1759 in Quebec, Quebec, Canada

Source: *BbtC; Drake; NewCol 75; OxCCan; OxCFr; WorAl*

Montefiore, Moses Haim, Sir
English. Philanthropist
Banking exec. who devoted life to political, civil emancipation of English Jews.
b. Oct 24, 1784 in Leghorn, Italy
d. Jul 28, 1885 in Ramsgate, England
Source: *BioIn 3, 5, 7, 9, 12; DcNaB; Dis&D; NewCol 75; WebBD 83*

Monteilhet, Hubert
French. Author
Wrote award-winning suspense novel *The Praying Mantises,* 1962.
b. 1928 in Paris, France
Source: *Au&Wr 71; ConAu 117; TwCCr&M 80B, 85B, 91B; WhoSpyF*

Monteleone, Thomas F(rancis)
[Brian T LoMedico; Mario Martin, Jr.]
American. Author, Dramatist
Writer of short stories, plays, novels: *The Time-Swept City,* 1977.
b. Apr 14, 1946 in Baltimore, Maryland
Source: *ConAu 50NR, 113; EncSF 93; IntAu&W 89, 91, 93; NewEScF; PenEncH; ScFSB; TwCSFW 91; WrDr 92*

Montemezzi, Italo
Italian. Composer
Wrote operas *Giovanni Gallurese,* 1905; *L'Amore Dei Tre Re,* 1913.
b. Aug 4, 1875 in Vigasio, Italy
d. May 15, 1952 in Verona, Italy
Source: *Baker 78, 84, 92; BioIn 1, 2, 3, 6, 8; BriBkM 80; CmOp; CompSN; IntDcOp; MetOEnc; NewAmDM; NewEOp 71; NewGrDM 80; NewGrDO; OxCMus; OxDcOp*

Montenegro, Hugh
"The Quadfather"
American. Composer
TV and film soundtrack composer; pioneered quadrasonic recording; released the soundtracks *Original Music from "The Man From Uncle,"* 1966 and *The Good, The Bad, and The Ugly,* 1968; released first quadrasonic pop album, *Love Theme from the Godfather,* 1972.
b. 1925 in New York, New York
d. Feb 6, 1981 in Palm Springs, California

Montesquieu, Charles Louis de Secondat, Baron
French. Philosopher, Jurist
Wrote *Lettres Persanes,* 1721; *De L'Esprit des Lois,* 1748.
b. Jan 18, 1689 in Bordeaux, France
d. Feb 10, 1755 in Paris, France
Source: *AtlBL; BbD; Benet 96; BiD&SB; CasWL; CyWA 58; DcEuL; EuAu; EvEuW; NewC; OxCEng 67; OxCFr; PenC EUR; RComWL; REn*

Montessori, Maria
Italian. Educator, Social Reformer
Opened first Montessori school for children, Rome, 1907; wrote *The Montessori Method,* 1912.
b. Aug 31, 1870 in Chiaravalle, Italy
d. May 6, 1952 in Noordwijk, Netherlands
Source: *BiDMoPL; BiDPsy; BioIn 1, 2, 3, 4, 5, 6, 7, 8, 9, 10, 11, 12, 13, 14, 16, 17, 18, 19, 20, 21; CathA 1930; ConAu 115, 147; ContDcW 89; CurBio 40, 52; DcCathB; DcTwHis; FacFETw; GoodHs; HerW 84; InSci; IntDcWB; InWom, SUP; LegTOT; LinLib L, S; LngCTC; LuthC 75; McGEWB; NamesHP; ObitT 1951; OxCChiL; OxCMed 86; RadHan; RAdv 14, 13-3; REn; ThTwC 87; WebBD 83; WhDW; WomFir; WomPsyc; WorAl; WorAlBi*

Monteux, Claude
American. Musician, Conductor
Flutist; led Columbus, OH orchestra, 1950s; son of Pierre.
b. Oct 15, 1920 in Brookline, Massachusetts
Source: *Baker 84; BioIn 6; IntWWM 90; NewAmDM; NewGrDA 86; NewGrDM 80; PenDiMP; WhoAm 74, 76, 78; WhoAmM 83; WhoMus 72*

Monteux, Pierre
American. Conductor
Conducted 60 orchestras including the one in San Francisco, 1935-52.
b. Apr 4, 1875 in Paris, France
d. Jul 1, 1964 in Hancock, Maine
Source: *Baker 78, 84, 92; BiDAmM; BioIn 1, 2, 3, 4, 6, 7, 8, 11, 13; BriBkM 80; CmCal; CnOxB; CurBio 46, 64; DcArts; DcTwCCu 2; FacFETw; IntDcOp; LegTOT; MetOEnc; MusMk; MusSN; NewAmDM; NewEOp 71; NewGrDA 86; NewGrDM 80; NewGrDO; NotNAT B; ObitT 1961; PenDiMP; WhAm 4; WorAl; WorAlBi*

Monteverdi, Claudio
Italian. Composer
Wrote opera *Orfeo,* 1607; considered greatest composer of his day.
b. May 15, 1567 in Cremona, Italy
d. Nov 29, 1643 in Venice, Italy
Source: *AtlBL; Baker 78, 84; Benet 87, 96; BioIn 1, 2, 3, 4, 5, 6, 7, 8, 9, 10, 11, 12, 13, 14, 16, 17, 20; BriBkM 80; CmOp; CmpBCM; DcCom 77; DcCom&M 79; GrComp; IntDcOp; LegTOT; LinLib S; MetOEnc; MusMk; NewAmDM; NewEOp 71; NewGrDM 80; NewOxM; OxCMus; OxDcOp; PenDiMP A; RAdv 14, 13-3; REn; WhDW; WorAlBi*

Montez, Lola
[Countess Lansfeld; Marie Dolores Eliza Rosanna Gilbert; Lola Montes]
Irish. Dancer
Mistress of Louis I of Bavaria, 1847-48; virtually controlled govt.
b. 1818 in Limerick, Ireland
d. Jan 17, 1861 in Astoria, New York
Source: *AmAu&B; BiDD; BiDIrW; BioIn 1, 2, 3, 4, 7, 8, 9, 10, 11, 13, 17, 21; CamGWoT; CmCal; CnOxB; ContDcW 89; DancEn 78; DcArts; DcIrB 78, 88; DcIrW 2; DcNAA; DcNaB; Drake; FamA&A; FilmgC; GoodHs; HalFC 80, 84, 88; IntDcWB; InWom, SUP; LegTOT; LibW; NewC; NewCol 75; NotAW; NotNAT A, B; OxCAmH; OxCAmL 65; OxCAmT 84; OxCAusL; OxCGer 76, 86; PenNWW B; REnAL; REnAW; WebAB 74, 79; WhAm HS; WorAl*

Montez, Maria
[Maria Antonia Garcia Vidal de Santo Silas]
"The Queen of Technicolor"
Spanish. Actor
Starred in adventure films, 1940s: *Arabian Nights; Tangier.*
b. Jun 6, 1918 in Barahona, Dominican Republic
d. Sep 7, 1951 in Paris, France
Source: *CmMov; FilmEn; FilmgC; ForYSC; LegTOT; MotPP; MovMk; WhoHol B; WhoHrs 80; WhScrn 74, 77; WorEFlm*

Montezuma, Carlos
American. Political Activist, Physician
Proponent of Native American independence from reservations and assimilation into the mainstream culture.
b. 1867? in Arizona
d. Jan 31, 1923
Source: *BiNAW, B; DcAmMeB; EncNAB; NotNaAm; WhAm 1; WhNaAH*

Montezuma I
Aztec. Ruler
Emperor, 1440-64; rebuilt Tenochtitlan, 1446, following flood, plague; issued Draconian code of laws.
b. 1390 in Tenochtitlan, Mexico
d. 1464 in Tenochtitlan, Mexico
Source: *ApCAB; Drake; WebBD 83*

Montezuma II
Aztec. Ruler
Emperor, 1502-19; conquered by Cortes.
b. 1480 in Tenochtitlan, Mexico
d. Jun 30, 1520 in Tenochtitlan, Mexico
Source: *Drake; McGEWB; NewCol 75; WebBD 83; WhAm HS*

Montfort, Simon de
"Simon the Righteous"
English. Political Leader
Led revolt against Britain's Henry III; became virtual ruler; called Great Parliament, 1265.
b. 1208 in Normandy, France
d. Aug 4, 1265 in Evesham, England
Source: *BioIn 17, 19, 20; McGEWB; NewCol 75; WebBD 83; WhDW*

Montgolfier, Jacques Etienne
French. Balloonist, Inventor
Invented first practical hot air balloon, 1783 with Joseph Montgolfier.

b. Jan 7, 1745 in Vidalon les Annonay, France
d. Aug 2, 1799 in Serrieres, France
Source: *AsBiEn; BioIn 1, 4, 6, 8, 12, 13; DcBiPP; DcCathB; DcScB; InSci; LarDcSc; LinLib S; McGEWB; NewCol 75; WebE&AL; WhDW; WorAl; WorAlBi*

Montgolfier, Joseph Michel
French. Balloonist, Inventor
Invented first practical hot air balloon, 1783 with Jacques Montgolfier.
b. Aug 26, 1740 in Vidalon les Annonay, France
d. Jun 26, 1810 in Balaruc les Bains, France
Source: *AsBiEn; BioIn 1, 4, 12, 13; DcBiPP; DcCathB; DcScB; LarDcSc; LinLib S; McGEWB; OxCFr; REn; WhDW; WorAl; WorAlBi*

Montgomery, Belinda
American. Actor
Doogie's mom in TV series "Doogie Howser, M.D.," 1989-93.
b. 1950
Source: *HalFC 84, 88; WhoAm 88*

Montgomery, Elizabeth
American. Actor
Played Samantha on "Bewitched," 1964-72; daughter of Robert Montgomery.
b. Apr 15, 1933 in Los Angeles, California
d. May 18, 1995 in Los Angeles, California
Source: *BioIn 3, 8, 12, 14; ConAu X; ConTFT 3, 14; FilmgC; ForYSC; HalFC 80, 84, 88; IntMPA 84, 86, 88, 92, 94, 96; InWom, SUP; LegTOT; News 95; VarWW 85; WhoAm 86, 88, 90; WhoHol 92, A; WorAl; WorAlBi*

Montgomery, George
[George Montgomery Letz]
American. Actor
Western hero in films *Riders of the Purple Sage; Texas Rangers;* TV show "Cimarron City," 1958-60.
b. Aug 29, 1916 in Brady, Montana
Source: *BioIn 4, 8, 10, 12; FilmEn; FilmgC; ForYSC; HalFC 80, 84, 88; HolP 40; IntMPA 75, 76, 77, 78, 79, 80, 81, 82, 84, 86, 88, 92, 94, 96; LegTOT; MotPP; MovMk; WhoHol 92, A*

Montgomery, Lucy Maud
Canadian. Author
Wrote popular girls stories: *Anne of Green Gables,* 1908.
b. Nov 30, 1874 in Clifton, Prince Edward Island, Canada
d. Apr 24, 1942 in Toronto, Ontario, Canada
Source: *AmWomPl; ArtclWW 2; BioIn 1, 3, 4, 6, 7, 10, 11, 12, 14, 15, 16, 17, 18, 19; BlmGWL; CanWr; CarSB; CasWL; Chambr 3; ChhPo, S1, S2, S3; ChlBkCr; CreCan 2; DcLB 92; DcLEL; DcNAA; EvLB; InWom; JBA 34; LegTOT; LinLib L; LngCTC; MacDCB 78; OnHuMoP; OxCAmL 65; OxCCan; PenNWW A; REn; REnAL; TwCA; TwCChW 78; TwCWr; WhNAA; YABC 1*

Montgomery, Melba
American. Singer, Songwriter
Country singer; paired with George Jones, 1963-67.
b. Oct 14, 1938 in Iron City, Tennessee
Source: *BgBkCoM; BiDAmM; BioIn 14; EncFCWM 69, 83; HarEnCM 87; IlEncCM; InWom SUP; PenEncP*

Montgomery, Richard
American. Army Officer
Revolutionary War officer; captured Montreal, 1775; killed in assault on Quebec.
b. Dec 2, 1736 in Swords, Ireland
d. Dec 31, 1775 in Quebec, Canada
Source: *AmBi; ApCAB; BioIn 12; DcAmB; DcAmMiB; DcCanB 4; DcNaB; Drake; HarEnUS; MacDCB 78; McGEWB; NatCAB 1; OxCAmH; OxCCan; TwCBDA; WhAm HS*

Montgomery, Robert Henry
[Henry Montgomery, Jr.]
American. Actor, Director
Starred in *Here Comes Mr. Jordan,* 1941; TV adviser to Eisenhower; father of Elizabeth Montgomery.
b. May 21, 1904 in Beacon, New York
d. Sep 27, 1981 in New York, New York
Source: *ApCAB; BiDFilm; BiE&WWA; CmMov; ConAu 108; CurBio 48, 81; Film 2; FilmgC; IntMPA 82; NewYTBE 71; NewYTET; NotNAT A; OxCFilm; WhoAm 80; WhoHol A; WorEFlm*

Montgomery, Ruth Shick
American. Journalist, Author
Syndicated political columnist, 1958-68; wrote *Threshold of Tomorrow,* 1983; *Aliens Among Us,* 1985.
b. Jun 11, 1912 in Sumner, Illinois
Source: *AmWomWr; AuNews 1; BioIn 15; ConAu 1R, 2NR, 17NR; InWom; NewAgE 90; WhoAm 86, 90; WhoUSWr 88; WhoWrEP 89; WrDr 82*

Montgomery, Wes
[John Leslie Montgomery]
American. Jazz Musician
Virtuoso guitar soloist who used thumb as plectrum; recorded *A Day in the Life,* one of all-time best-selling jazz albums.
b. Mar 6, 1925 in Indianapolis, Indiana
d. Jun 15, 1968 in Indianapolis, Indiana
Source: *AllMusG; Baker 84; BiDAfM; BiDAmM; BiDJaz; BioIn 6, 12, 13, 15, 16, 19, 21; EncJzS; IlEncJ; InB&W 80, 85; LegTOT; NewAmDM; OnThGG; OxCPMus; PenEncP; WorAl; WorAlBi*

Montgomery of Alamein, Bernard Law Montgomery, Viscount
English. Military Leader
Field marshal during WW II who defeated Germans at El Alamein, 1942; led Allied landings in Normandy, 1944.
b. Nov 17, 1887 in Kennington Oval, England
d. Mar 25, 1976 in Islington, England
Source: *Au&Wr 71; BioIn 11; ConAu 65, 69; CurBio 42, 76; IntWW 76; WhE&EA; Who 74; WhoMilH 76; WhoWor 74; WhWW-II; WorAl*

Montor, Henry
American. Philanthropist
Helped found United Jewish Appeal, 1938; founded Israel Bond Organization, 1950.
b. 1906 in Nova Scotia, Canada
d. Apr 15, 1982 in Jerusalem, Israel
Source: *BioIn 12, 13; NewYTBS 82*

Montoya, Carlos
American. Musician
Internationally renowned flamenco guitarist, soloist.
b. Dec 13, 1903 in Madrid, Spain
d. Mar 3, 1993 in Wainscott, New York
Source: *AnObit 1993; ASCAP 66, 80; Baker 84, 92; BioIn 2, 7, 8, 10, 18, 19; BriBkM 80; CelR; CurBio 68; NewAmDM; News 93; NewYTBE 71; NewYTBS 93; OnThGG; USBiR 74; WhoAm 86, 90; WhoE 74, 91; WhoEnt 92; WhoMus 72; WhoWor 74*

Montoya, Joseph Manuel
American. Politician
Dem. senator from NM, 1965-77; on Senate Watergate Committee, 1973.
b. Sep 24, 1915 in Pena Blanca, New Mexico
d. Jun 5, 1978 in Washington, District of Columbia
Source: *BiDrAC; BiDrUSC 89; BioIn 9, 10, 11, 12; CngDr 74; CurBio 75, 78N; DcAmB S10; IntWW 74; NewYTBS 78; ObitOF 79; WhAm 7; WhoAm 74; WhoAmP 73; WhoGov 77*

Monty, Gloria
[Gloria Montemuro]
American. Producer
Known for turning daytime drama "General Hospital" into top-rated show; won Emmys 1981, 1984.
b. Aug 12, 1921 in Union Hill, New Jersey
Source: *BioIn 12; ConTFT 10; InWom SUP; VarWW 85; WhoAm 90; WhoAmW 68, 70, 72, 91; WhoEnt 92; WhoTelC*

Monty Python's Flying Circus
[Graham Chapman; John Cleese; Terry Gilliam; Eric Idle; Terry Jones; Michael Palin]
English. Comedy Team
Zany comedy group, starred in TV series, movies, 1969-83; at one time, highest-rated comedy show in Britain, US.
Source: *Au&Arts 7; BioIn 10, 11, 13, 14, 15, 16, 17, 18, 19; ConAu 35NR, 107, 111, 129, X; ConLC 21; HalFC 84, 88; IntMPA 92; LElec; NewYTBS 77, 89;*

SmATA 67; VarWW 85; WhoCom; WhoHol 92; WhoRocM 82

Moodie, Susanna
Canadian. Author
Best known for *Roughing It in the Bush,* 1852.
b. Dec 6, 1803 in Suffolk, England
d. Apr 8, 1885 in Toronto, Ontario, Canada
Source: *Alli, SUP; ApCAB; ArtclWW 2; BbtC; Benet 87; BenetAL 91; BiD&SB; BioIn 7, 8, 10, 13; BlmGWL; BritAu 19; CamGLE; CanWr; Chambr 3; ChhPo; ContDcW 89; DcEnL; DcLB 99; DcLEL; DcNAA; DcWomA; FemiCLE; LinLib L; McGEWB; NinCLC 14; OxCCan; OxCCanL; RAdv 14, 13-1; REn; REnAL*

Moody, Dwight Lyman
American. Evangelist
With Ira Sankey, promoted Evangelism in US, Britain; published *Gospel Hymns,* 1875.
b. Feb 5, 1837 in East Northfield, Massachusetts
d. Dec 22, 1899 in Northfield, Massachusetts
Source: *Alli SUP; AmAu&B; AmBi; AmSocL; ApCAB; BbD; BenetAL 91; BiD&SB; BioIn 1, 2, 3, 4, 5, 6, 8, 9, 11, 12, 13, 14, 16, 19; CelCen; DcAmAu; DcAmB; DcAmReB 1, 2; DcAmTB; DcBiPP; DcNAA; EncAAH; EncAB-H 1974, 1996; EncARH; HarEnUS; LinLib L, S; LngCTC; LuthC 75; McGEWB; NatCAB 7; NewYTBE 72; OxCAmH; OxCAmL 65, 83, 95; REn; REnAL; TwCBDA; WebAB 74, 79; WhAm 1; WorAl*

Moody, Helen Wills
[Helen Newington Wills Moody Roark]
"Queen of the Nets"; "Miss Poker Face"
American. Tennis Player
US women's singles champ, 1923-25, 1927-29, 1931.
b. Oct 6, 1905 in Berkeley, California
Source: *AmDec 1930; BiDAmSp OS; BioIn 14, 15, 16, 17; BuCMET; ContDcW 89; GoodHs; GrLiveH; InWom SUP; WebAB 74; Who 74, 92; WomFir*

Moody, Orville
American. Golfer
Turned pro, 1967; won US Open, 1969.
b. Dec 9, 1933 in Chickasha, Oklahoma
Source: *BioIn 13; NewYTBS 83; WhoGolf; WhoIntG*

Moody, Ron
[Ronald Moodnick]
English. Actor
Played in stage, film versions of *Oliver!;* TV show "Nobody's Perfect."
b. Jan 8, 1924 in London, England
Source: *BioIn 12; ConAu 108; ConTFT 2, 8; EncMT; FilmEn; FilmgC; HalFC 80, 84, 88; IntAu&W 86; IntMPA 96; ItaFilm; LegTOT; VarWW 85; WhoAm 80; WhoEnt 92; WhoHol 92; WhoMus 72; WhoThe 72, 77, 81; WhoWor 80, 82, 84, 87, 89, 91, 93, 95, 96, 97*

Moody, William Vaughn
American. Dramatist, Poet, Educator
Works include play *The Great Divide,* 1907.
b. Jul 8, 1869 in Spencer, Indiana
d. Oct 17, 1910 in Colorado Springs, Colorado
Source: *AmAu&B; AmBi; BenetAL 91; BibAL; BiD&SB; BioIn 1, 2, 7, 8, 9, 11, 12, 13, 15, 20; CamGEL; CamGLE; CamGWoT; CamHAL; CasWL; ChhPo, S1, S3; CnDAL; CnThe; ConAu 110; DcAmAu; DcAmB; DcLB 7, 54; DcLEL; DcNAA; EncWT; Ent; EvLB; GayN; GrWrEL DR; IndAu 1816; IntDcT 2; LinLib L, S; LngCTC; McGEWD 72, 84; ModAL; ModWD; NotNAT A; OxCAmL 65, 83, 95; OxCAmT 84; OxCThe 67, 83; OxCTwCP; PenC AM; PlP&P; RAdv 14, 13-1; REn; REnAL; REnWD; RfGAmL 87, 94; TwCA, SUP; TwCBDA; WebAB 74, 79; WebE&AL; WhAm 1*

Moody Blues
[Graeme Edge; Justin Hayward; Denny Laine; John Lodge; Patrick Moraz; Michael Pinder; Thomas Ray; Clint Warwick]
English. Music Group
Single hits include "Nights in White Satin," 1967; "The Voice," 1981; albums include *Sur La Mer,* 1988.
Source: *Alli; BiDLA; BioIn 14; BkIE; CelR 90; ConMuA 80A; DcLP 87B; EncPR&S 74, 89; EncRk 88; EncRkSt; FacFETw; HarEnR 86; IlEncRk; NewAgMG; NewAmDM; OxCPMus; PenEncP; RkOn 78; RolSEnR 83; WhoHol 92; WhoRock 81; WhoRocM 82*

Moog, Robert A
American. Inventor
Created instrument called "The Moog Synthesizer," electronic musical instrument which revolutionized popular, classical music.
b. May 23, 1934 in Flushing, New York
Source: *Baker 84; BioIn 13, 16; NewAmDM; NewGrDA 86; WhoE 74; WhoEnt 92*

Moon, Keith
[The Who]
English. Musician
Drummer who helped create rock opera *Tommy.*
b. Aug 23, 1946 in Wembley, England
d. Sep 7, 1978 in London, England
Source: *BioIn 18; HarEnR 86; IlEncRk; LegTOT; WhoRock 81*

Moon, Sung Myung
[Yong Myung Moon]
Korean. Religious Leader
Head of Unification Church, reported to have 3,000,000 members worldwide; conver ts called "Moonies."
b. Jan 6, 1920 in Kwangju Sangsa Ri, Korea
Source: *BioIn 13, 14, 15, 16; BioNews 74; CurBio 83; EncO&P 2S1, 3; EncWB; NewYTBS 74; RelLAm 91; WhoRel 85; WorAlBi*

Moon, Warren (Harold)
American. Football Player
Quarterback, Edmonton, in CFL, 1978-83; Houston, 1984-94; Minnesota, 1994—; NFL Pro Bowl starting quarterback, 1988-90.
b. Nov 18, 1956 in Los Angeles, California
Source: *AfrAmBi 1; AfrAmSG; BioIn 13; ConBlB 8; CurBio 91; FootReg 87; News 91, 91-3; NewYTBS 83; WhoAfA 96; WhoAm 92, 94, 95; WhoBlA 85, 88, 90, 92, 94; WhoSpor*

Mooney, Tom
[Thomas Joseph Mooney]
American. Labor Union Official
Convicted of killing nine persons in bomb explosion, 1916; pardoned after 22 yrs. in 1939.
b. Dec 8, 1892? in Chicago, Illinois
d. Mar 6, 1942 in San Francisco, California
Source: *CurBio 42*

Moore, Arch Alfred, Jr.
American. Politician
Rep. governor of WV, 1969-77, 1985-89.
b. Apr 16, 1923 in Molinosville, West Virginia
Source: *AlmAP 88; BiDrAC; BiDrGov 1789; BiDrUSC 89; BioIn 8, 9, 11; IntWW 74, 75, 76, 77, 78, 79, 80, 81, 82, 83, 89, 91, 93; WhoAm 74, 76, 86, 88; WhoAmP 73, 89; WhoE 74, 75, 77; WhoGov 72, 75, 77; WhoSSW 88; WhoWor 91; WomPO 76*

Moore, Archie
[Archibald Lee Wright]
"Ol' Man River"
American. Boxer
World light-heavyweight champ, 1952-62; has KO'd more men in ring than any other fighter.
b. Dec 13, 1916? in Benoit, Mississippi
Source: *BiDAmSp BK; BioIn 3, 4, 15, 16; CurBio 60; DrBlPA, 90; Ebony 1; FacFETw; InB&W 85; NewYTBS 87; Who 74; WhoBlA 75, 77; WhoBox 74; WhoHol A; WorAlBi*

Moore, Audley
"Queen Mother"
American. Political Activist
Campaigner for civil rights, women's rights and Pan African nationalism.
b. 1898 in New Iberia, Louisiana
d. May 2, 1997 in New York, New York
Source: *BioIn 15; BlkWAm; NotBlAW 1*

Moore, Bert C
[The Hostages]
American. Hostage
One of 52 held by terrorists, Nov 1979 - Jan 1981.
b. Mar 3, 1935 in Kentucky

Source: *NewYTBS 81*

Moore, Brian
[Michael Bryan; Bernard Mara]
Canadian. Author
Novels attempt to come to terms with N Irish past: *The Lonely Passion of Judith Hearne,* 1956.
b. Aug 25, 1921 in Belfast, Northern Ireland
Source: *Au&Wr 71; AuSpks; Benet 87, 96; BenetAL 91; BiDConC; BiDIrW; BioIn 6, 8, 9, 10, 11, 12, 14, 15, 17; BlueB 76; CamGLE; CanWr; CanWW 31, 70, 79, 80, 81, 83, 89; CasWL; CaW; ConAu 1NR, 1R, 11NR, 25NR, 42NR; ConCaAu 1; ConLC 1, 3, 5, 7, 8, 19, 32, 90; ConNov 72, 76, 82, 86, 91, 96; CreCan 2; CurBio 86, 91; CyWA 89; DcArts; DcIrL, 96; DcIrW 1; DcLEL 1940; DrAF 76; DrAPF 80, 91; EncSF, 93; EncWL 2, 3; FacFETw; GrWrEL N; IntAu&W 76, 77, 82, 86, 89, 91, 93; IntvTCA 2; IntWW 76, 77, 78, 79, 80, 81, 82, 83, 89, 91, 93; LegTOT; LiExTwC; MajTwCW; ModBrL S1, S2; ModIrL; NewC; Novels; OxCCan; OxCCanL; OxCCan SUP; OxCEng 85, 95; OxCIri; PenC ENG; RAdv 1; REn; REnAL; RfGEnL 91; RGTwCWr; ScF&FL 1, 2, 92; ScFSB; SJGFanW; TwCSFW 81; TwCWr; WebE&AL; Who 74, 82, 83, 85, 88, 90, 92, 94; WhoAm 78, 80, 82, 84, 86, 88, 90, 92, 94, 95, 96, 97; WhoCanL 85, 87, 92; WhoE 75; WhoUSWr 88; WhoWor 84, 87, 89, 91, 93, 95, 96, 97; WhoWrEP 89, 92, 95; WorAl; WorAu 1950; WrDr 76, 80, 82, 84, 86, 88, 90, 92, 94, 96*

Moore, Clayton
American. Actor
Starred in "The Lone Ranger," 1949-56.
b. Sep 14, 1914 in Chicago, Illinois
Source: *FilmEn; HalFC 88; VarWW 85; WhoHol 92, A*

Moore, Clement Clarke
American. Scholar, Poet
Wrote *A Visit from St. Nicholas,* 1823.
b. Jul 15, 1779 in New York, New York
d. Jul 10, 1863 in Newport, Rhode Island
Source: *Alli; AmAu; AmAu&B; AmBi; AnCL; ApCAB; BenetAL 91; BibAL; BiDAmM; BiD&SB; BioIn 2, 3, 4, 6, 9, 12, 15, 17, 19, 20, 21; BkCL; CarSB; ChhPo, S1, S2; ChlBkCr; CnDAL; CyAL 1; DcAmAu; DcAmB; DcLB 42; DcLEL; DcNAA; Drake; EvLB; HarEnUS; MajAI; NatCAB 7; OxCAmL 65, 83, 95; OxCChiL; REn; REnAL; SmATA 18; Str&VC; TwCBDA; WebAB 74, 79; WhAm HS; WorAl*

Moore, Colleen
[Kathleen Morrison]
American. Actor
Bobbed-haired flapper star of numerous 1920s films; wrote *Silent Star,* an autobiography.
b. Aug 19, 1902 in Port Huron, Michigan
d. Jan 25, 1988 in Paso Robles, California
Source: *AnObit 1988; BioIn 8, 14; ConAu 124; FacFETw; Film 1; FilmEn; FilmgC; IntDcF 1-3, 2-3; InWom, SUP; MotPP; MovMk; NewYTBE 72; NewYTBS 88; ThFT; TwYS; VarWW 85; What 2; WhoAmW 61, 64, 74; WhoHol A*

Moore, Constance
American. Actor
Played on TV show "Widow on Main Street," 1961-62.
b. Jan 18, 1922 in Sioux City, Iowa
Source: *BiDrAPA 89, 78, 79, 80, 81, 82, 84, 86, 88, 92, 94, 96; InWom SUP; MotPP; VarWW 85; WhoHol A*

Moore, Demi
[Demetria Guynes; Mrs. Bruce Willis]
American. Actor
Films include *St. Elmo's Fire,* 1985, *Ghost,* 1990; noted for posing nude for *Vanity Fair,* during late pregnancy, 1991.
b. Nov 11, 1962 in Roswell, New Mexico
Source: *BiDFilm 94; BioIn 13, 14, 15, 16; ConTFT 3, 10; CurBio 93; IntMPA 88, 92, 94, 96; LegTOT; News 91; VarWW 85; WhoAm 92, 94, 95, 96, 97; WhoAmW 93, 95, 97; WhoEnt 92; WhoHol 92; WorAlBi*

Moore, Dick(ie)
[Our Gang; John Richard Moore, Jr.]
American. Actor
Child actor who appeared in many "Our Gang" episodes; gave Shirley Temple first screen kiss in *Miss Andy Rooney,* 1942.
b. Sep 12, 1925 in Los Angeles, California
Source: *Au&Wr 71; BiE&WWA; BioIn 7, 9, 11, 15, 18; ConAu 17R, X; EncAFC; Film 2; FilmEn; FilmgC; ForYSC; HalFC 80, 84, 88; HolP 30; IntMPA 75, 76, 77, 78, 79, 80, 81, 82, 84, 86, 88, 92, 94, 96; MotPP; MovMk; NotNAT; What 3; WhoE 91; WhoHol 92, A*

Moore, Dickie
[Richard Winston Moore]
Canadian. Hockey Player
Right wing, 1951-65, 1967-68, mostly with Montreal; won Art Ross Trophy, 1958, 1959; Hall of Fame, 1974.
b. Jan 6, 1931 in Montreal, Quebec, Canada
Source: *BioIn 10; HocEn; WhoHcky 73; WhoSpor*

Moore, Don W
American. Cartoonist
Drew "Flash Gordon" comic strip, 1934-54; wrote TV show "Captain Video," 1949.
b. 1901?
d. Apr 7, 1986 in Venice, Florida
Source: *NewYTBS 86*

Moore, Douglas Stuart
American. Composer
Wrote 1951 Pulitzer-winning opera *Giants in the Earth;* folk opera *Ballad of Baby Doe,* 1956.
b. Aug 10, 1893 in Cutchogue, New York
d. Jul 25, 1969 in Greenport, New York
Source: *AmAu&B; AmComp; ASCAP 66, 80; Baker 78, 84, 92; BiDAmM; BioIn 1, 3, 6, 7, 8, 9; BriBkM 80; CompSN; ConAmC 76, 82; ConAu P-1; CurBio 47, 69; DcCM; DcCom&M 79; IntDcOp; NewGrDM 80; OxCAmL 65; OxCMus; REn; REnAL; WhAm 5*

Moore, Dudley Stuart John
English. Actor, Musician
Starred in *10,* 1979; *Arthur,* 1981; won Grammy, 1974; special Tonys, 1969, 1974.
b. Apr 19, 1935 in Dagenham, England
Source: *BiE&WWA; BioIn 13, 16; CelR 90; ConTFT 8; CurBio 82; EncAFC; FacFETw; FilmgC; HalFC 88; IntMPA 92; IntWW 82, 83, 89, 91, 93; NewGrDJ 88; NewYTBE 73; NewYTBS 74; NotNAT; OxCPMus; Who 82, 83, 85, 88, 90, 92, 94; WhoAm 80, 82, 84, 86, 88, 90, 92, 94, 95, 96, 97; WhoEnt 92; WhoHol A; WhoThe 77; WhoWor 84, 87, 91, 93, 95, 96, 97; WorAlBi*

Moore, Garry
[Thomas Garrison Morfit]
American. TV Personality
Writer, "Jimmy Durante-Garry Moore Show," 1943-48; star, "Garry Moore Show," 1950-54, 1966-67; moderator, "To Tell The Truth," 1969-77.
b. Jan 31, 1915 in Baltimore, Maryland
d. Nov 28, 1993 in Hilton Head Island, South Carolina
Source: *AnObit 1993; BioIn 1, 2, 3, 4, 5, 7, 13, 15, 19, 20; CelR; CurBio 54, 94N; IntMPA 75, 76, 77, 78, 79, 80, 81, 82, 84, 86, 88, 92, 94; LegTOT; LesBEnT 92; NewYTBS 93; NewYTET; RadStar; SaTiSS; VarWW 85; WhoAm 74, 76, 78, 80, 82, 84, 86; WhoCom; WhoE 74; WhoEnt 92; WorAl; WorAlBi*

Moore, George Augustus
Irish. Author, Poet, Dramatist
Wrote realistic novel, *Sister Teresa,* 1901; reminiscences, *Memoirs of My Dead Life,* 1906.
b. Feb 24, 1852 in County Mayo, Ireland
d. Jan 21, 1933 in London, England
Source: *Alli, SUP; AtlBL; BbD; BiD&SB; BiDIrW; BiDLA; CamGEL; CasWL; Chambr 3; ChhPo; ConAu 104; CyWA 58; DcArts; DcBiA; DcEnA A; DcIrB 78, 88; DcIrW 1; DcLEL; DcNaB 1931; EncWL; EvLB; FacFETw; GrBr; GrWrEL N; LngCTC; ModBrL; ModWD; NewC; NewCBEL; NotNAT B; OxCCan; OxCEng 67, 85, 95; OxCThe 67; PenC ENG; PoIre; RAdv 1; REn; REnWD; RfGShF; TwCA, SUP; TwCWr; VicBrit; WebE&AL; WhoTwCL; WhThe; WorAl*

Moore, George Edward
English. Philosopher
Known for *Principia Ethica,* 1903, closely reasoned investigation of nature of good.
b. Nov 4, 1873 in Surrey, England
d. Oct 24, 1958 in Cambridge, England
Source: *BioIn 4, 5, 6, 9, 11, 12, 14; Chambr 3; DcNaB 1951; EvLB; GrBr; LngCTC; MakMC; McGEWB; NewCBEL; OxCEng 67, 85; OxCPhil; RAdv 14, 13-4; REn; TwCA SUP; WhAm 4; WhE&EA; WhoLA*

Moore, George Stevens
American. Business Executive, Banker
Pres., chm., First National Bank of NY, 1959-70.
b. Apr 1, 1905 in Hannibal, Missouri
Source: *BioIn 8, 9, 10, 12, 15; CurBio 70; Dun&B 88; IntWW 74, 75, 76, 77, 78, 79, 80, 81, 82, 83; St&PR 75, 91; WhoAm 74, 76, 78; WhoE 74*

Moore, Gerald
English. Musician, Author
Pianist best known for accompaning singers; wrote *Am I Too Loud,* 1962; retired after 50 yrs., 1967.
b. Jul 30, 1899 in Watford, England
d. Mar 13, 1987 in Buckinghamshire, England
Source: *AnObit 1987; Au&Wr 71; Baker 78, 84, 92; BioIn 6, 7, 8, 10, 11, 15; BlueB 76; ConAu 1R, 5NR, 122; CurBio 67, 87, 87N; DcArts; DcNaB 1986; FacFETw; IntAu&W 76, 77, 82; IntWW 74, 75, 76, 77, 78, 79, 80, 81, 82, 83; IntWWM 77, 80, 85; MusMk; NewAmDM; NewGrDM 80; NewYTBS 87; PenDiMP; WhE&EA; Who 74, 82, 83, 85; WhoAm 74, 76, 78; WhoMus 72; WhoWor 76, 78; WhScrn 83; WrDr 76, 80, 82, 84, 86*

Moore, Grace
American. Singer
Popular opera, film soprano, 1930s; hosted own radio show; killed in plane crash; 1953 film based on her life.
b. Dec 1, 1901 in Tennessee
d. Jan 26, 1947 in Copenhagen, Denmark
Source: *BiDAmM; BioAmW; BioIn 1, 2, 3, 4, 5, 6, 8, 9, 10, 11, 13; CmpEPM; CurBio 44, 47; DcAmB S4; EncMT; FilmEn; FilmgC; HalFC 80, 84, 88; InWom; LegTOT; MovMk; MusSN; NatCAB 38; NewEOp 71; NewGrDM 80; NotAW; NotNAT A, B; OxCAmT 84; OxCFilm; OxCPMus; PlP&P; RadStar; REnAL; ThFT; WhAm 2; WhoHol B; WhScrn 74, 77, 83; WhThe*

Moore, Harry Thornton
American. Author, Critic
Works on D H Lawrence include *The Price of Love.*
b. Aug 2, 1908 in Oakland, California
d. Apr 11, 1981 in Carbondale, Illinois
Source: *AmAu&B; Au&Wr 71; BioIn 10, 12; ConAu 5R, 103; DrAS 78E; IntAu&W 76; Who 74; WhoAm 80; WhoWor 78; WorAu 1950; WrDr 80*

Moore, Henry Spencer
"The Father of the Hole"
English. Sculptor
Sculptures fused abstract, distorted figures with traditional concepts; known for *Reclining Figure,* 1929.
b. Jul 30, 1898 in Castleford, England
d. Aug 31, 1986 in London, England
Source: *Benet 96; ConNews 86-4; DcBrAr 1; DcNaB 1986; IntWW 83; NewYTBS 86; RAdv 14; REn; Who 85; WhoArt 84; WhoWor 84*

Moore, John Bassett
American. Lawyer, Educator
International law expert; judge of the World Court, 1921-28.
b. Dec 3, 1860 in Smyrna, Delaware
d. Nov 12, 1947 in New York, New York
Source: *AmAu&B; ApCAB SUP, X; BiDInt; BioIn 1, 16; DcAmAu; DcAmB S4; DcAmDH 80, 89; DcNAA; HarEnUS; LinLib S; NewCol 75; ObitOF 79; OxCLaw; REnAL; TwCBDA; WhAm 2*

Moore, Julia A. Davis
"Sweet Singer of Michigan"
American. Poet
Popular during her day; now known as hilariously bad poet.
b. Dec 1, 1847 in Kent County, Michigan
d. Jun 5, 1920 in Manton, Michigan
Source: *ConAu 116; OxCAmL 83; PenC AM; REnAL*

Moore, Lenny
[Leonard Edward Moore]
American. Football Player
Running back-receiver, Baltimore, 1956-67; NFL MVP, 1964; Hall of Fame, 1975.
b. Nov 25, 1933 in Reading, Pennsylvania
Source: *AfrAmSG; BiDAmSp FB; BioIn 6, 7, 8, 10, 11, 17, 21; InB&W 80; LegTOT; WhoBlA 85, 92; WhoFtbl 74; WhoSpor*

Moore, Marianne Craig
American. Poet, Editor
Verse volumes include *Observations,* 1924, won Pulitzer for *Collected Poems,* 1951.
b. Nov 15, 1887 in Saint Louis, Missouri
d. Feb 5, 1972 in New York, New York
Source: *AmAu&B; AmWr; AnCL; AnMV 1926; Benet 96; CasWL; CnDAL; CnE&AP; CnMWL; ConAmA; ConAmL; ConAu 1R, 3NR; CurBio 68, 72; EncAB-H 1996; EncWHA; ForWC 70; IntWWP 77; InWom; PenC AM; RGTwCWr; WhAm 5; WhE&EA; WhoAmW 58, 61, 64, 66, 68, 70, 72; WomFir*

Moore, Mary Tyler
American. Actor
Starred in "The Dick Van Dyke Show," 1961-66, "Mary Tyler Moore Show," 1970-77; Oscar nominee for *Ordinary People,* 1981.
b. Dec 29, 1936 in New York, New York
Source: *BioIn 13, 14, 15, 16; BkPepl; CelR 90; ConTFT 6; CurBio 71; EncAFC; FilmgC; FunnyW; HalFC 80, 84, 88; IntMPA 75, 76, 77, 78, 79, 80, 81, 82, 84, 86, 88, 92, 94, 96; InWom SUP; JoeFr; LegTOT; LesBEnT, 92; MotPP; MovMk; News 96, 96-2; NewYTBS 74, 85; VarWW 85; WhoAm 86, 88, 90, 92, 94, 95, 96, 97; WhoAmW 89, 91, 93, 95; WhoCom; WhoEnt 92; WhoHol 92, A; WorAlBi*

Moore, Melba
[Beatrice Hill]
American. Singer, Actor
Won Tony for *Purlie,* 1971.
b. Oct 29, 1945 in New York, New York
Source: *AfrAmBi 1; Baker 84, 92; BiDAfM; BioIn 9, 10, 11, 12, 14, 15; BlkWAm; CelR; ConMus 7; ConTFT 4; CurBio 73; DrBlPA, 90; IlEncBM 82; InB&W 80, 85; InWom SUP; LegTOT; NegAl 89; NewYTBS 78; NotBlAW 1; PlP&P, A; RkOn 85; VarWW 85; WhoAfA 96; WhoAm 76, 78, 80, 82, 84, 86, 88, 90; WhoAmW 81, 83; WhoBlA 80, 85, 88, 90, 92, 94; WhoEnt 92; WhoHol 92, A; WorAl; WorAlBi*

Moore, Michael
American. Filmmaker
Creator, controversial documentary, *Roger and Me,* about ex-GM chm. Roger Smith, 1989.
b. 1954? in Flint, Michigan
Source: *ConTFT 14; IntMPA 96; LegTOT; News 90, 90-3*

Moore, Roger George
English. Actor
Starred in "The Saint," 1967-69; movie role as James Bond, Agent 007, 1973-85.
b. Oct 14, 1928 in London, England
Source: *BioIn 14, 15; CelR 90; ConTFT 5; CurBio 75; FilmgC; HalFC 88; IntMPA 92; IntWW 91; MotPP; MovMk; NewYTBE 70; NewYTBS 85; VarWW 85; Who 92; WhoAm 86, 88; WhoHol A; WorAlBi*

Moore, Roy W
American. Business Executive
With Canada Dry Corp., 1934-71; chairman, 1960-66.
b. Feb 27, 1891 in Macon, Georgia
d. Sep 29, 1971 in Bridgeport, Connecticut
Source: *BioIn 4, 9; NewYTBE 71; WhAm 5*

Moore, Sam(uel David)
[Sam and Dave]
American. Singer
With Dave Prater, one of leading soul acts, 1960s; hit song "Soul Man," 1967, popularized again, late 1970s, by Dan Aykroyd, John Belushi as Blues Brothers.
b. Oct 12, 1935 in Miami, Florida

Source: *BioIn 12, 13; LegTOT; WhoAfA 96; WhoBlA 94; WhoRocM 82*

Moore, Sara Jane
American. Attempted Assassin
Tried to kill Gerald Ford, Sep 22, 1975; sentenced to life in prison.
b. Feb 15, 1930 in Charleston, West Virginia
Source: *BioIn 10, 11, 13; InWom SUP; WorAl; WorAlBi*

Moore, Stanford
American. Biochemist
Shared Nobel Prize in chemistry, 1972, with William Stein.
b. Sep 4, 1913 in Chicago, Illinois
d. Aug 23, 1982 in New York, New York
Source: *AmMWSc 73P, 76P, 79, 82; AnObit 1982; BiESc; BioIn 9, 10, 13, 15, 19, 20; BlueB 76; CamDcSc; IntWW 74, 75, 76, 77, 78, 79, 80, 81, 82; LarDcSc; LegTOT; McGMS 80; NewYTBS 82; NobelP; NotTwCS; WebAB 74, 79; WhAm 8; Who 74, 82; WhoAm 74, 76, 78, 80, 82; WhoE 77, 79, 81; WhoNob, 90, 95; WhoTech 82; WhoWor 74, 80; WorAl; WorAlBi*

Moore, Terry
[Helen Koford]
American. Actor
After seven-year legal battle was recognized as widow of Howard Hughes and inherited part of his estate; married, 1949.
b. Jan 1, 1932 in Los Angeles, California
Source: *BusPN; FilmgC; IntMPA 75, 76, 77, 78, 79, 80, 81, 82, 84, 86, 88, 92; MotPP; VarWW 85; WhoHol A*

Moore, Thomas
Irish. Poet
Noted for *Irish Melodies,* 1807-35; *Lalla Rookh,* 1817.
b. May 28, 1779 in Dublin, Ireland
d. Feb 25, 1852 in Bromham, England
Source: *Alli; AtlBL; Baker 78, 84, 92; BbD; Benet 87, 96; BiD&SB; BiDIrW; BiDrAC; BioIn 1, 2, 3, 4, 5, 7, 9, 10, 11, 12, 14, 15, 16, 17, 19, 21; BlmGEL; BritAu 19; CamGEL; CamGLE; CasWL; CelCen; ChhPo, S1, S2, S3; CnE&AP; CrtT 2, 4; CyWA 58; DcArts; DcBiA; DcBiPP; DcCathB; DcEnA, A; DcEnL; DcEuL; DcIrB 78, 88; DcIrL, 96; DcIrW 1; DcLB 96, 144; DcLEL; DcNaB; EvLB; GrWrEL P; HsB&A; LinLib L, S; LngCEL; LuthC 75; MouLC 3; NewC; NewCBEL; NewEOp 71; NewGrDM 80; NewGrDO; NinCLC 6; OxCCan; OxCEng 67, 85, 95; OxCIri; OxCMus; OxCPMus; OxDcOp; PenC ENG; PoChrch; PoIre; REn; RfGEnL 91; ScF&FL 1; WebE&AL; WhDW*

Moore, Tom
American. Actor
Leading man in silent films, early talkies; character actor in *Cinderella Man.*
b. 1885 in County Meath, Ireland
d. Feb 12, 1955 in Santa Monica, California
Source: *BioIn 3; Film 1; FilmEn; ForYSC; MotPP; MovMk; TwYS; WhoHol B; WhScrn 74, 77, 83*

Moore, Victor
American. Actor
Vaudeville comedian in films, 1915-55.
b. Feb 24, 1876 in Hammonton, New Jersey
d. Jul 23, 1962 in Long Island, New York
Source: *CmpEPM; EncAFC; EncMT; EncVaud; Film 1, 2; FilmEn; FilmgC; ForYSC; HalFC 80, 84, 88; JoeFr; LegTOT; MotPP; MovMk; NotNAT B; OxCAmT 84; OxCPMus; PlP&P; QDrFCA 92; TwYS; Vers A; WhAm 4; WhoHol B; WhoStg 1908; WhScrn 74, 77, 83; WhThe; WorAl*

Moore, William
American. Critic
Black dance critic; founder journal *Dance Herald,* 1975-79; frequent lecturer.
b. 1933 in New York, New York
d. Oct 24, 1992 in New York, New York

Moorehead, Agnes
American. Actor
Played Endora on "Bewitched," 1964-72; starred in original radio version of "Sorry, Wrong Number," 1943.
b. Dec 6, 1906 in Clinton, Massachusetts
d. Apr 30, 1974 in Rochester, Minnesota
Source: *BiDFilm, 81, 94; BiE&WWA; BioAmW; BioIn 1, 2, 3, 10, 11; CamGWoT; CelR; CmMov; ConAu 49; CurBio 52, 72, 74N; DcAmB S9; FilmEn; FilmgC; ForWC 70; ForYSC; GayLesB; HalFC 80, 84, 88; IntDcF 1-3, 2-3; InWom, SUP; ItaFilm; LegTOT; MGM; MotPP; MovMk; NewYTBS 74; NotNAT B; OxCFilm; RadStar; SaTiSS; Vers A; WhAm 6; WhoHol B; WhoHrs 80; WhoThe 72, 77; WhScrn 77, 83; WorAl; WorAlBi; WorEFlm*

Moorehead, Alan
Australian. Author, Journalist
Distinguished war correspondent, WW II; wrote *Cooper's Creek,* 1963.
b. Jul 22, 1910 in Melbourne, Australia
d. Sep 30, 1983 in London, England
Source: *AnObit 1983; Au&Wr 71; Benet 87; BioIn 4, 6, 9, 13, 17; BlueB 76; ConAu 5R, 6NR, 110; FarE&A 78, 79, 80, 81; IntAu&W 76, 77, 82; IntWW 74, 75, 76, 77, 78, 79, 80, 81, 82, 83; LngCTC; NewC; NewCBEL; NewYTBS 83; OxCAusL; REn; TwCA SUP; WhAm 8; WhE&EA; WhoWor 74; WrDr 76, 80, 82, 84*

Moorer, Thomas H(inman)
American. Naval Officer
Much-decorated chm., US Joint Chiefs of Staff, 1970-74; Chief of Naval Operations, 1967-70.
b. Feb 9, 1912 in Mount Willing, Alabama
Source: *BioIn 7, 8, 9, 10, 11, 12; BlueB 76; CurBio 71; Dun&B 86; IntWW 74, 75, 76, 77, 78, 79, 80, 81, 82, 83, 89, 91; St&PR 84, 87, 91; WebAMB; Who 74, 82, 83, 85, 88, 90, 92, 94; WhoAm 82, 84, 86, 88, 90, 92, 94, 95, 96, 97; WhoGov 72, 75; WorAl; WorAlBi; WorDWW*

Moores, Dick
[Richard Arnold Moores]
American. Cartoonist
Drew syndicated comic strip "Gasoline Alley," after death of creator Frank King.
b. Dec 12, 1909 in Lincoln, Nebraska
d. Apr 22, 1986 in Asheville, North Carolina
Source: *BioIn 16; ConAu 69; ConGrA 2; EncACom; EncTwCJ; WhoAm 76, 78, 80, 82, 84; WhoSSW 82, 84; WhoWor 78, 80; WorECar*

Moorhead, William Singer
American. Politician
Dem. congressman from PA, 1959-81.
b. Apr 8, 1923 in Pittsburgh, Pennsylvania
d. Aug 3, 1987 in Baltimore, Maryland
Source: *AlmAP 82*

Moos, Malcolm Charles
American. Author, Educator
Drafted speeches for D D Eisenhower, changing his image into a tougher, more aggressive leader; pres., U of MN, 1967-82.
b. Apr 19, 1916 in Saint Paul, Minnesota
d. 1982 in Ten Mile Lake, Minnesota
Source: *AmAu&B; AmMWSc 73S, 78S; BioIn 5, 8, 12; ConAu 37R; CurBio 68; IntWW 82N; LEduc 74; WhAm 8; WhoAm 74, 76, 78, 80; WhoMW 74, 76, 78; WhoWor 74, 78*

Mora, Jim
[James Ernest Mora]
American. Football Coach
Head coach, Philadelphia and Baltimore, USFL, 1983-86, New Orleans, NFL, 1986—; named coach of yr., 1984, 1987; first coach ever to win award in two leagues.
b. May 24, 1935 in Glendale, California
Source: *BiDAmSp Sup; BioIn 14; FootReg 87; NewYTBS 84; WhoAm 86, 88, 90, 92, 94, 95, 96, 97; WhoSpor; WhoSSW 88, 91, 93, 95*

Moraes, Vinicius de
Brazilian. Author, Diplomat, Lyricist
Wrote *Oredu da Conceicao,* which was basis for film *Black Orpheus.*
b. 1913
d. 1980 in Rio de Janeiro, Brazil
Source: *BioIn 10, 12, 13; ConAu 101; DcBrazL; IntAu&W 77; IntWW 74, 75, 76, 77, 78, 79, 80; ModLAL; PenC AM; WhoWor 74; WorAu 1970*

Moraga, Cherrie
American. Writer
Edited *This Bridge Called My Back: Writings by Radical Women of Color,* 1981; poetry collection *Loving in the War Years,* 1983.
b. Sep 25, 1952 in Whittier, California
Source: *AmWomWr 92, SUP; BioIn 19, 20; BlmGWL; ConAu 131; DcHiB; DcLB 82; FemiWr; GayLesB; GayLL; HispAmA; HispWr; NotHsAW 93; OxCAmL 95; OxCWoWr 95; RfGAmL 94; WhoHisp 91, 92, 94*

Morales, Esai
American. Actor
Films include *Bad Boys,* 1983; *La Bamba,* 1987.
b. Oct 1, 1962 in New York, New York
Source: *BioIn 14, 16; CelR 90; ConTFT 5; LegTOT; WhoEnt 92; WhoHisp 92; WhoHol 92*

Morales Bermudez, Francisco
Peruvian. Political Leader
Pres. of Peru, 1975-80.
b. Oct 4, 1921 in Lima, Peru
Source: *BiDLAmC; BioIn 16; EncWB; IntWW 76, 77, 78, 79, 80, 81, 82, 83, 89, 91, 93; IntYB 79, 80, 81, 82; WhoWor 78, 80*

Moran, Bugs
[George C Moran]
American. Criminal
Gangster who rivaled Al Capone for control of Chicago crime, 1920s; target of St. Valentine's Day Massacre, 1929.
b. 1893 in Minnesota
d. Feb 25, 1957 in Leavenworth, Kansas
Source: *EncACr; LegTOT; ObitOF 79*

Moran, Edward
American. Artist
Noted for large scenes of American history; brother of Thomas.
b. Aug 19, 1829 in Bolton, England
d. Jun 9, 1901 in New York, New York
Source: *AmBi; ApCAB; ArtsAmW 1; ArtsNiC; BioIn 7; DcAmB; DcSeaP; EarABI; IlBEAAW; NatCAB 11; NewYHSD; TwCBDA; WhAmArt 85; WhAm HS*

Moran, Erin
American. Actor
Played Joanie on "Happy Days," 1974-83.
b. Oct 18, 1961 in Burbank, California
Source: *LegTOT; VarWW 85; WhoHol A*

Moran, George
American. Actor
Moran & Mack comedy team in vaudeville appeared in films with W C Fields: *My Little Chickadee,* 1940.
b. 1882 in Elwood, Kansas
d. Aug 1, 1949 in Oakland, California
Source: *BiDD; BioIn 2; EncVaud; Film 2; WhoHol B; WhScrn 74, 77, 83*

Moran, Paddy
[Patrick Joseph Moran]
Canadian. Hockey Player
Goalie; played 16 yrs., mostly with Quebec, early 1900s; Hall of Fame, 1958.
b. Mar 11, 1887 in Quebec, Quebec, Canada
d. Jan 14, 1966 in Quebec, Quebec, Canada
Source: *WhoHcky 73*

Moran, Polly
American. Comedian
Teamed with Marie Dressler in movies: *The Passionate Plumber,* 1932.
b. Jun 28, 1883 in Chicago, Illinois
d. Jan 25, 1952 in Los Angeles, California
Source: *Film 1; FilmgC; Funs; HalFC 84; MotPP; MovMk; QDrFCA 92; ThFT; TwYS; WhoCom; WhScrn 74, 77, 83*

Moran, Thomas
American. Artist, Illustrator
Landscapes include panoramic views of the West; the Teton's Mt. Moran named after him.
b. Jan 22, 1837 in Bolton, England
d. Aug 25, 1926 in Santa Barbara, California
Source: *AmBi; ApCAB; ArtsAmW 1; ArtsNiC; BioIn 3, 5, 7, 8, 9, 11, 12, 14, 15; ChhPo; DcAmArt; DcAmB; DcSeaP; EarABI, SUP; EncAAH; HarEnUS; IlBEAAW; LegTOT; LinLib S; McGDA; McGEWB; NatCAB 3, 22; NewYHSD; REnAW; TwCBDA; WhAm 1, 4; WhAmArt 85; WhAm HSA; WhNaAH*

Morandi, Giorgio
Italian. Artist
Surrealist known for landscapes, pastel still lifes.
b. Jul 20, 1890 in Bologna, Italy
d. Jun 18, 1964 in Bologna, Italy
Source: *BioIn 1, 4, 6, 7, 9, 11, 15, 16, 17; ConArt 77, 83, 89; DcArts; EncWB; FacFETw; IntDcAA 90; McGDA; ObitOF 79; OxCArt; OxCTwCA; OxDcArt; PhDcTCA 77; WhAm 4; WorAl; WorArt 1950*

Morano, Albert Paul
American. Politician
Rep. representative from CT, 1951-59.
b. Jan 18, 1908 in Paterson, New Jersey
d. Dec 16, 1987 in Greenwich, Connecticut
Source: *BiDrAC; BiDrUSC 89; BioIn 2, 3; CurBio 52, 88, 88N; WhoAmP 73, 75, 77, 79*

Morath, Max Edward
American. Entertainer, Musician
Ragtime pianist who revived vintage music on TV, Broadway, national tours, 1960s-70s.
b. Oct 1, 1926 in Colorado Springs, Colorado
Source: *BioIn 6, 15; CurBio 63; NewAmDM; NewGrDA 86; OxCPMus; PenEncP; WhoAm 78, 80, 82, 84, 86, 88, 90, 92, 94, 95, 96, 97; WhoEnt 92*

Moravia, Alberto
[Alberto Pincherle]
Italian. Author, Journalist
Italy's best-known contemporary novelist; wrote about women, sex, and the moral foibles of middle class Rome society; international reputation established with *Woman of Rome,* 1947.
b. Nov 28, 1907 in Rome, Italy
d. Sep 26, 1990 in Rome, Italy
Source: *AnObit 1990; Au&Wr 71; Benet 87, 96; BioIn 1, 2, 3, 4, 5, 6, 7, 8, 9, 10, 12, 13, 16, 17; CasWL; ClDMEL 47, 80; CnMD; CnMWL; ConAu 25R, 33NR, 132, X; ConFLW 84; ConLC 2, 7, 11, 18, 27, 46; CurBio 70, 90N; CyWA 58, 89; DcArts; DcItL 1, 2; EncWL 2, 3; EuWr 12; EvEuW; FacFETw; FilmEn; HalFC 84, 88; IntAu&W 76, 77, 89; IntWW 74, 75, 76, 77, 78, 79, 80, 81, 82, 83, 89, 91N; ItaFilm; LegTOT; LiExTwC; LinLib L; LngCTC; MajTwCW; McGEWB; McGEWD 84; ModRL; NewYTBS 90; Novels; OxCEng 67, 85, 95; PenC EUR; RAdv 14, 13-2; REn; RfGShF; RfGWoL 95; ScF&FL 1, 92; TwCA SUP; TwCWr; WhDW; Who 74, 82, 83, 85, 88, 90, 92N; WhoTwCL; WhoWor 74, 78, 80, 82, 84, 87, 89, 91; WomWMM; WorAl; WorAlBi*

Morceli, Noureddine
Algerian. Track Athlete
Set a world indoor 1,000-meter record of 2 mins., 15.26 secs. in 1992.
b. 1970?, Algeria

More, Kenneth Gilbert
English. Actor
Played title role in "Father Brown series," 1974; wrote autobiographies *Happy Go Lucky,* 1959; *More of Less,* 1978.
b. Sep 20, 1914 in Gerrards Cross, England
d. Jul 12, 1982 in London, England
Source: *AnObit 1982; CmMov; CnThe; ConAu 107; FilmgC; IntMPA 82; IntWW 78; NewYTBS 82; Who 74; WhoHol A; WhoThe 81; WhoWor 74*

More, Paul Elmer
American. Philosopher, Editor, Critic
Editor *The Nation,* 1909-14; leader in New Humanism; works include *Platonism,* 1917.
b. Dec 12, 1864 in Saint Louis, Missouri
d. Mar 9, 1937 in Princeton, New Jersey
Source: *AmAu&B; AmBi; AmLY; BenetAL 91; BiD&SB; BiDSA; BioIn 1, 2, 3, 4, 5, 7; CasWL; Chambr 3; CnDAL; ConAmA; ConAmL; DcAmAu; DcAmB S2; DcAmC; DcLEL; DcNAA; EvLB; LinLib L, S; LngCTC; LuthC 75; ModAL; NatCAB 27; OxCAmH; OxCAmL 65, 83, 95; PenC AM; REn; REnAL; TwCA, SUP; TwCBDA; WebAB 74, 79; WhAm 1; WhLit; WhNAA*

More, Thomas, Sir
English. Author, Statesman
Leading figure of English humanism, defender of Roman Catholicism; best-known work: *Utopia,* 1516.
b. Feb 7, 1478 in London, England
d. Jul 6, 1535 in London, England
Source: *Alli; AtlBL; BbD; Benet 87, 96; BiD&SB; BioIn 1, 2, 3, 4, 5, 6, 7, 8, 9, 10, 11, 12, 13, 14, 15, 17, 20, 21; BlmGEL; BritAu; CamGEL; CasWL; Chambr 1; ChhPo, S2; CopCroC; CroE&S; CrtT 1, 4; CyEd; CyWA 58; DcCathB; DcEnA; DcEnL; DcEuL; DcLEL; DcNaB, C; Dis&D; EncSF, 93; EncUrb; EvLB; HisWorL; LegTOT; LinLib L, S; LitC 10; LngCEL; LuthC 75; McGEWB; MouLC 1; NewC; NewCBEL; NewEScF; OxCEng 67; PenC ENG; RAdv 1, 14, 13-1, 13-4; REn; RfGEnL 91; ScFEYrs; WebE&AL; WhDW*

Moreau, Gustave
French. Artist
Symbolist who left paintings, including *Dance of Salome,* to form Moreau Museum; noted for violent scenes.
b. Apr 6, 1826 in Paris, France
d. Apr 18, 1898 in Paris, France
Source: *AtlBL; BioIn 4, 5, 6, 7, 8, 9, 10, 11, 12, 16; ClaDrA; DcArts; Dis&D; IntDcAA 90; McGDA; OxCArt; OxCFr; OxCTwCA; OxDcArt; PhDcTCA 77; ThHEIm; WhDW*

Moreau, Jeanne
French. Actor
Films include *Frantic; Lovers.*
b. Jan 23, 1928 in Paris, France
Source: *BiDFilm, 81, 94; BioIn 7, 9, 11, 14, 16; CelR, 90; ContDcW 89; ConTFT 8; CurBio 66; DcArts; DcTwCCu 2; EncEurC; FacFETw; FilmAG WE; FilmEn; FilmgC; ForYSC; GoodHs; HalFC 80, 84, 88; IntDcF 1-3, 2-3; IntDcWB; IntMPA 79, 80, 81, 82, 84, 86, 88, 92, 94, 96; IntWW 74, 75, 76, 77, 78, 79, 80, 81, 82, 83, 89, 91, 93; InWom SUP; ItaFilm; LegTOT; MiSFD 9; MotPP; MovMk; OxCFilm; VarWW 85; Who 74, 82, 85, 88, 90, 92, 94; WhoFr 79; WhoHol 92, A; WhoWor 74, 82, 84, 87, 89, 91, 93, 95, 96; WorAlBi; WorEFlm*

Morefield, Richard H
[The Hostages]
American. Hostage
One of 52 held by terrorists, Nov 1979-Jan 1981.
b. Sep 9, 1930 in Los Angeles, California
Source: *BioIn 12; NewYTBS 81; WhoAm 88*

Morehouse, Ward
American. Critic, Dramatist
Wrote syndicated column "Broadway After Dark," 1926-66.
b. Nov 24, 1899 in Savannah, Georgia
d. Dec 7, 1966 in New York, New York
Source: *AmAu&B; ConAu 25R; CurBio 40, 67; DcAmB S8; NotNAT B; OxCAmT 84; OxCThe 67; REnAL; WhAm 4; WhThe*

Morello, Joseph A
American. Jazz Musician
Drummer with Dave Brubeck quartet, 1950s-60s.
b. Jul 17, 1928 in Springfield, Massachusetts
Source: *BiDAmM; BiDJaz; BioIn 16; CmpEPM; EncJzS; NewAmDM; NewGrDJ 88; WhoAm 74; WhoEnt 92*

Morelos y Pavon, Jose Maria
Mexican. Clergy, Military Leader
Led revolution against Spain after Hidalgo's execution, 1813; shot by royalists.
b. Sep 30, 1765 in Valladolid, Mexico
d. Dec 22, 1815 in San Cristobal, Mexico
Source: *BioIn 1, 3, 5, 8, 9, 10; EncLatA; EncRev; HisDcSE; NewCol 75; WebBD 83*

Moreno, Rita
[Rosita Dolores Alverio; Mrs. Leonard Gordon]
American. Actor, Singer
Only woman to win show business' four top awards: Oscar, Grammy, Tony, Emmy; starred in *West Side Story,* 1961.
b. Dec 11, 1931 in Humacao, Puerto Rico
Source: *BioIn 3, 4, 6, 7, 10, 13, 14, 17, 18, 20; BlueB 76; CelR, 90; ConTFT 1, 3, 14; CurBio 85; DcHiB; FilmEn; FilmgC; ForYSC; HalFC 80, 84, 88; HispAmA; IntMPA 75, 76, 77, 78, 79, 80, 81, 82, 84, 86, 88, 92, 94, 96; InWom, SUP; LegTOT; MotPP; MovMk; NewYTBS 75; NotHsAW 93; NotNAT; ReelWom; SweetSg D; VarWW 85; WhoAm 74, 76, 78, 80, 82, 84, 86, 88, 90, 92, 94, 95, 96, 97; WhoAmW 66, 68, 70, 72, 74, 75, 77, 79, 81, 95, 97; WhoEnt 92; WhoHisp 91, 92, 94; WhoHol 92, A; WhoThe 77, 81; WorAl; WorAlBi*

Morenz, Howie
[Howarth William Morenz]
"Babe Ruth of Hockey"; "Meteor"; "Stratford Flash"
Canadian. Hockey Player
Center, 1923-37, mostly with Montreal; won Hart Trophy three times, Art Ross Trophy twice; Hall of Fame, 1945; died of complications after breaking leg in game.
b. Jun 21, 1902 in Mitchell, Ontario, Canada
d. Mar 8, 1937 in Montreal, Quebec, Canada
Source: *BioIn 9, 10, 13, 21; HocEn; LegTOT; WhoHcky 73; WhoSpor; WorAl; WorAlBi*

Morey, Walt(er Nelson)
American. Children's Author
Wrote best-seller *Gentle Ben,* 1965; later adapted to film and became a TV series.
b. Feb 3, 1907 in Hoquiam, Washington
d. Jan 12, 1992 in Wilsonville, Oregon
Source: *AnObit 1992; Au&Wr 71; AuBYP 2, 3; BioIn 9, 16, 17, 18, 19; ConAu 29R, 31NR, 136; DcAmChF 1960; IntAu&W 91; MajAI; OxCChiL; SmATA 3, 9AS, 51, 70; ThrBJA; TwCChW 78, 83, 89, 95; WhAm 10; WhoAm 74, 76, 78, 80, 82; WrDr 80, 82, 84, 86, 88, 90, 92, 94N*

Morgagni, Giovanni Battista
Italian. Scientist
Founded pathologic anatomy, 1760s.
b. Feb 25, 1682 in Forli, Italy
d. Dec 6, 1771 in Padua, Italy
Source: *AsBiEn; BiHiMed; BioIn 7, 9, 16; CamDcSc; CopCroC; DcBiPP; DcCathB; DcScB; InSci; LarDcSc; McGEWB; NewCol 75; OxCMed 86; WebBD 83; WorAl; WorAlBi*

Morgan, Arthur
American. Engineer, Educator
Pres. of Antioch College, 1920-36; first chm., Tennessee Valley Authority (TVA), 1933.
b. Jun 20, 1878 in Cincinnati, Ohio
d. Nov 12, 1975 in Xenia, Ohio
Source: *AmAu&B; AmMWSc 73P; Au&Wr 71; ConAu 3NR, 5R, 61; CurBio 56; OhA&B; WhAm 6; WhNAA*

Morgan, C(onwy) Lloyd
English. Psychologist, Zoologist
Considered one of the founders, if not the founder of the field of animal psychology.
b. Feb 6, 1852 in London, England
d. Mar 6, 1936 in Hastings, England
Source: *Alli SUP; BiDPsy; BioIn 2; DcNaB 1931; DcScB; NamesHP; WhE&EA; WhLit; WhoLA*

Morgan, Charles Langbridge
English. Author, Critic
London *Times* drama critic, 1926-39; books include *The Fountain,* 1932.
b. Jan 22, 1894 in Kent, England
d. Feb 6, 1958 in London, England
Source: *BioIn 14; CasWL; CnMD; CnThe; CroCD; DcLEL; DcNaB 1951; EvLB; GrBr; GrWrEL N; LngCTC; ModBrL; ModWD; NewC; NewCBEL; NotNAT B; OxCEng 67, 85, 95; OxCThe 67, 83; PenC ENG; PlP&P; REn; TwCA, SUP; TwCWr; WebE&AL; WhoLA; WhThe*

Morgan, Daniel
American. Politician, Army Officer
Best known for defeating Banastre Tarleton, 1781; helped suppress Whiskey Rebelli on, 1794.
b. 1736 in Bucks County, Pennsylvania
d. Jul 6, 1802 in Winchester, Virginia
Source: *Alli; AmBi; AmRev; ApCAB; BiAUS; BiDrAC; BiDrUSC 89; BioIn 2,*

3, 5, 6, 7, 8, 10, 14; DcAmB; Drake; EncAR; EncCRAm; EncSoH; GenMudB; HarEnMi; HarEnUS; NatCAB 1; OxCAmH; TwCBDA; WebAB 74, 79; WebAMB; WhAm HS; WhAmRev; WhoMilH 76; WorAl; WorAlBi

Morgan, Dennis
[Stanley Morner]
American. Actor, Singer
Musicals, comedies include *Desert Song,* 1943; *Christmas in Connecticut,* 1945; *My Wild Irish Rose,* 1947.
b. Dec 10, 1920 in Prentice, Wisconsin
Source: *FilmEn; FilmgC; IntMPA 75, 76, 77, 78, 79, 80, 81, 82; MotPP; MovMk; VarWW 85; WhoHol A; WorAl*

Morgan, Edward P
American. Journalist
ABC News commentator whose "Voice of Labor" won Peabody, 1956; wrote *Clearing the Air,* 1963.
b. Jun 23, 1910 in Walla Walla, Washington
Source: *AmAu&B; BiDAmJo; BioIn 16; ConAu P-1; CurBio 51, 64; EncTwCJ; LesBEnT, 92; LinLib L; WhoAm 74, 76, 78, 80, 82; WhoSSW 73, 75, 76; WhoWor 74*

Morgan, Edwin George
Scottish. Author, Poet
Poems include "The Vision of Cathkin Braes," 1952; "The Cape of Good Hope," 1955.
b. Apr 27, 1920 in Glasgow, Scotland
Source: *Au&Wr 71; BioIn 14; CasWL; ConAu 5R; ConPo 75; ConTFT 3; DcLEL 1940; HalFC 88; IntMPA 92; IntvTCA 2; OxCEng 85; Who 85; WorAlBi; WrDr 82*

Morgan, Frank
[Francis Phillip Wupperman]
American. Actor
Played title role in *The Wizard of Oz,* 1939.
b. Jul 1, 1890 in New York, New York
d. Sep 18, 1949 in Beverly Hills, California
Source: *BioIn 2, 7, 9, 11, 21; EncAFC; EncMT; Film 1, 2; FilmEn; FilmgC; ForYSC; HalFC 80, 84, 88; HolCA; LegTOT; MGM; MotPP; MovMk; NatCAB 57; NotNAT B; OlFamFa; OxCAmT 84; PlP&P; RadStar; SaTiSS; TwYS; WhAm 3; WhoHol B; WhoHrs 80; WhScrn 74, 77, 83; WhThe; WorAl; WorAlBi*

Morgan, Frank
American. Jazz Musician
Virtuoso jazz saxophonist; debut album *Intoducing Frank Morgan,* 1955.
b. Dec 23, 1933 in Minneapolis, Minnesota
Source: *AllMusG; ConMus 9; NewGrDJ 88, 94; ODwPR 91*

Morgan, Frederick, Sir
English. Army Officer
Chief planner, Allied invasion of Europe, WW II; acted as Britain's controller of atomic energy.
b. Feb 5, 1894 in Paddock Wood, England
d. Mar 20, 1967 in Northwood, England
Source: *CurBio 46, 67; NewC; ObitT 1961; WhWW-II*

Morgan, Garrett Augustus
American. Inventor
Invented gas mask, 1912; human hair straightener, 1913; automatic traffic signal, 1922.
b. Mar 4, 1877 in Paris, Kentucky
d. Jul 27, 1963 in Cleveland, Ohio
Source: *BioIn 6, 8, 9, 10, 11, 16; BlksScM; ConBlB 1; DcAmNB; NegAl 89*

Morgan, Harry
[Harry Bratsburg]
American. Actor
Starred in TV series "Dragnet," 1967-70; "M*A*S*H," 1975-83.
b. Apr 10, 1915 in Detroit, Michigan
Source: *BioIn 4, 13; ConTFT 3; FilmEn; FilmgC; GangFlm; HalFC 80, 84, 88; IntMPA 75, 76, 77, 78, 79, 80, 81, 82, 84, 86, 88, 92, 94, 96; LegTOT; MotPP; NewYTBE 71; VarWW 85; WhoAm 94; WhoCom; WhoHol 92, A; WorAl; WorAlBi*

Morgan, Helen Riggins
American. Singer, Actor
Broadway, nightclub star, 1920s-30s; the original "torch singer;" noted for "My Bill."
b. Aug 2, 1900 in Danville, Illinois
d. Oct 9, 1941 in Chicago, Illinois
Source: *BiDAmM; CmpEPM; DcAmB S3; EncMT; FamA&A; FilmEn; FilmgC; NotAW; PlP&P; ThFT; WhoHol B; WhScrn 74, 77*

Morgan, Henry
American. TV Personality
Appeared on TV quiz show, "I've Got a Secret," 1952-76.
b. Mar 31, 1915 in New York, New York
d. May 19, 1994 in New York, New York
Source: *BioIn 1, 2, 4, 6, 19, 20; CurBio 47, 94N; ForYSC; HolCA; JoeFr; NewYTBS 94; RadStar; SaTiSS; WhoAm 80, 82, 84, 86, 88, 92, 94; WhoCom; WhoEnt 92; WhoHol 92, A; WorAl; WorAlBi*

Morgan, Henry, Sir
Welsh. Pirate, Statesman
Led buccaneers, 1660s; captured Panama City, 1671, becoming English hero; governor of JA, 1674.
b. 1635 in Llanrhymney, Wales
d. Aug 25, 1688 in Lawrencefield, Jamaica
Source: *Alli; ApCAB; Benet 87; BenetAL 91; BioIn 1, 2, 3, 4, 5, 6, 7, 8, 11, 14, 15, 18, 19; DcNaB; Dis&D; Drake; DrInf; GenMudB; HisDBrE; LinLib S; NewCol 75; OxCAmH; OxCAmL 65, 83, 95; OxCLiW 86; OxCShps; REn; REnAL; WebBD 83; WhDW*

Morgan, J(ohn) P(ierpont)
American. Financier
Formed US Steel Corp., 1901, first billion-dollar corp. in world; known for industrial consolidations, philanthropy.
b. Apr 17, 1837 in Hartford, Connecticut
d. Mar 31, 1913 in Rome, Italy
Source: *AmBi; ApCAB, X; BiDAmBL 83; BioIn 1, 2, 3, 4, 5, 6, 7, 8, 9, 10, 12, 13, 15, 16, 20; DcAmB; DcAmBC; DcAmC; DcAmSR; DcLB 140; EncAB-H 1974, 1996; EncABHB 2, 6, 9; GayN; HarEnUS; LinLib S; McGEWB; MemAm; NatCAB 10, 14; OxCAmH; OxDcArt; REn; REnAL; TwCBDA; WebAB 74, 79; WebBD 83; WhAm 1; WhDW; WorAl; WorAlBi*

Morgan, J(ohn) P(ierpont), Jr.
American. Philanthropist
Headed J P Morgan Co. from 1913; floated huge loans for WW I construction.
b. Sep 7, 1867 in Irvington, New York
d. Mar 13, 1943 in New York, New York
Source: *ApCAB X; BiDAmBL 83; BioIn 1, 4, 6, 7, 12, 15, 16, 20; CurBio 43; DcAmBC; DcAmB S3; DcLB 140; EncAB-H 1974, 1996; EncABHB 7; FacFETw; LinLib S; McGEWB; NatCAB 15; NewCol 75; OxCAmH; OxDcArt; WebBD 83; WhAm 2*

Morgan, Jane
American. Singer
Popular vocalist, 1940s-50s; hit ballad "Fascination," 1957.
b. 1920 in Boston, Massachusetts
d. 1974?
Source: *BiDAmM; InWom SUP; LegTOT; WhoAm 74; WorAl*

Morgan, Jaye P
American. Singer
Husky-voiced popular vocalist, 1950s-70s; frequent TV guest.
b. Dec 3, 1932 in Denver, Colorado
Source: *BiDAmM; PenEncP; RkOn 74; VarWW 85; WhoAm 82; WhoHol A*

Morgan, Joe (Leonard)
American. Baseball Player
Second baseman, 1963-84; NL MVP, 1975, 1976; considered NL's most complete player during his peak; Hall of Fame, 1990.
b. Sep 19, 1943 in Bonham, Texas
Source: *AfrAmSG; Ballpl 90; BiDAmSp BB; BioIn 10, 11, 12, 13, 14, 15, 16; ConBlB 9; CurBio 84; LegTOT; NewYTBS 83; WhoAfA 96; WhoAm 78, 80, 82, 84, 86, 88, 90, 92, 94, 95, 96; WhoBlA 77, 80, 85, 92, 94; WhoProB 73; WhoWest 94, 96; WorAl; WorAlBi*

Morgan, Julia
American. Architect
Most prolific woman architect in US; designed William Randolph Hearst's San Simeon estate, CA, 1919-47.
b. Jan 26, 1872 in San Francisco, California
d. Feb 2, 1957 in San Francisco, California
Source: *AmCulL; BioAmW; BioIn 1, 4, 10, 11, 12; CmCal; DcAmB S6; EncAAr 2; EncWHA; GrLiveH; IntDcAr; InWom SUP; LegTOT; MacEA; NotAW MOD; WomArt; WomFir*

Morgan, Lewis Henry
American. Ethnologist
Through his studies of kinship and social evolution, he contributed to the field of scientific anthropology.
b. Nov 21, 1818 in Aurora, New York
d. Dec 17, 1881 in Rochester, New York
Source: *Alli, SUP; AmAu; AmAu&B; AmBi; AmSocL; ApCAB; BbD; BiDAmEd; BiD&SB; BiInAmS; BioIn 1, 2, 3, 5, 7, 11, 13, 14, 17, 18, 19, 20; DcAmAu; DcAmB; DcAmSR; DcNAA; DcSoc; EncAAH; EncAB-H 1974, 1996; EncAL; EncNAB; HarEnUS; InSci; IntDcAn; McGEWB; NatCAB 6; OxCAmH; OxCAmL 65, 83, 95; OxCCan; RAdv 14, 13-3; REnAW; TwCBDA; WebAB 74, 79; WhAm HS; WhNaAH*

Morgan, Lorrie
[Loretta Lynn Morgan]
American. Singer
Country singer who performed with the George Jones band, 1981-1983 and sang regularly at the Grand Ole Opry; recorded *Leave the Light On,* 1989, *Something in Red,* 1991 and *Watch Me,* 1992.
b. Jun 27, 1959
Source: *BgBkCoM; BioIn 20, 21; ConMus 10; LegTOT; WhoAm 94, 95, 96, 97; WhoAmW 95, 97*

Morgan, Marabel
American. Anti-Feminist, Author
Developed concept of "Total Woman," which advises women to improve their marriages through submission to husbands.
b. Jun 25, 1937 in Crestline, Ohio
Source: *AmWomWr; ASCAP 80; AuNews 1; BioIn 10, 11; ConAu 2NR, 49; IntAu&W 76, 77; InWom SUP; LegTOT; WhoAm 78, 80, 82, 84, 86, 88, 90, 92, 94, 95, 96, 97; WhoAmW 79, 81, 95, 97; WhoUSWr 88; WhoWrEP 89, 92, 95; WorAl; WrDr 76, 86, 90*

Morgan, Michele
[Simone Roussel]
French. Actor
Won best actress award at Cannes festival for *Symphonie Pastorale,* 1946.
b. Feb 29, 1920 in Neuilly, France
Source: *BiDFilm, 81, 94; BioIn 11, 12; DcTwCCu 2; EncEurC; FilmAG WE; FilmEn; FilmgC; ForYSC; GangFlm; HalFC 80, 84, 88; IntDcF 1-3, 2-3; IntMPA 75, 76, 77, 78, 79, 80, 81, 82, 84, 86, 88, 92, 94, 96; IntWW 74, 75, 76, 77, 78, 79, 80, 81, 82, 83, 89, 91, 93; InWom, SUP; ItaFilm; MotPP; MovMk; OxCFilm; VarWW 85; WhoFr 79; WhoHol 92, A; WhoWor 74; WorEFlm*

Morgan, Ralph
[Raphael Kuhner Wupperman]
American. Actor
Brother of Frank Morgan; character actor in over 100 films, 1923-53, including *Gang Busters; Power and the Glory.*
b. Jul 6, 1883 in New York, New York
d. Jun 11, 1956 in New York, New York
Source: *FilmEn; FilmgC; HolCA; MotPP; MovMk; NatCAB 58; NotNAT B; OxCAmT 84; Vers A; WhoHol B; WhScrn 74, 77, 83*

Morgan, Robert Burren
American. Politician
Dem. senator from NC, 1974-81.
b. Oct 5, 1925 in Lillington, North Carolina
Source: *BiDrUSC 89; WhoSSW 73, 78, 80; WhoWor 80*

Morgan, Robin
American. Editor, Author
Editor in chief, *Ms.* magazine, 1989-93; wrote *Sisterhood Is Powerful,* 1970.
b. Jan 29, 1941 in Lake Worth, Florida
Source: *AmWomWr SUP; ArtclWW 2; ConAu 29NR, 69; ConLC 2; ContDcW 89; DrAPF 80; EncWB; EncWHA; FemiCLE; FemiWr; InWom SUP; JeAmWW; MajTwCW; News 91, 91-1; RadHan; WhoAm 90; WhoAmW 79, 81, 83, 85, 91; WhoHol 92*

Morgan, Rose Meta
American. Entrepreneur
Opened House of Beauty, Harlem, 1943; called the number one establishment of its kind in the world by *Ebony.*
b. c. 1912 in Shelby, Mississippi
Source: *ConBlB 11*

Morgan, Russ
American. Songwriter, Bandleader
Trombonist, arranger, who led band, 1930s-40s; known for sweet, sentimental soun d; wrote "You're Nobody Till Somebody Loves You," 1944.
b. Apr 29, 1904 in Scranton, Pennsylvania
d. Aug 7, 1969 in Las Vegas, Nevada
Source: *ASCAP 66, 80; Baker 78, 84; BgBands 74; BiDAmM; BiDJaz; BioIn 2, 8, 9, 12; CmpEPM; NewGrDJ 88, 94; OxCPMus; PenEncP; RadStar; WhoHol B; WhoJazz 72; WhScrn 74, 77, 83*

Morgan, Russell H(edley)
American. Physician
Pioneer in radiology.
b. Oct 9, 1911 in London, Ontario, Canada
d. Feb 24, 1986 in Baltimore, Maryland
Source: *AmMWSc 73P, 76P, 79, 82, 86; BioIn 7, 14; NewYTBS 86; WhAm 9; WhoAm 74, 76, 78; WhoE 74*

Morgan, Terence
English. Actor
Leading man in British films *Captain Horatio Hornblower,* 1951; *It Started in Paradise,* 1952.
b. Dec 8, 1921 in London, England
Source: *FilmEn; FilmgC; ForYSC; HalFC 80, 84, 88; IlWWBF; IntMPA 75, 76, 77, 78, 79, 80, 81, 82, 84, 86, 88, 92; ItaFilm; WhoHol 92, A*

Morgan, Thomas E(llsworth)
American. Politician
Dem. rep. from PA, 1945-77; chm., House Int'l Relations Com., 1958-76.
b. Oct 13, 1906
d. Jul 31, 1995 in Waynesburg, Pennsylvania
Source: *BiDrAC; BiDrUSC 89; BioIn 5, 11, 12; BlueB 76; CngDr 74; CurBio 95N; InSci; IntWW 74, 75, 76, 77, 78; PolProf J, K, NF; WhoAm 74, 76, 78; WhoAmP 73, 75, 77, 79, 81, 83, 85, 87, 89, 91, 93, 95; WhoE 74, 75, 77; WhoGov 72, 75, 77*

Morgan, Thomas Hunt
"The Twentieth Century Mendel"
American. Scientist, Zoologist
Genetics expert best known for establishing chromosome theory of heredity; won Nobel Prize in medicine, 1933; wrote *Theory of the Gene,* 1928.
b. Sep 25, 1866 in Lexington, Kentucky
d. Dec 4, 1945 in Pasadena, California
Source: *AmDec 1910; AsBiEn; BiESc; BioIn 1, 2, 3, 4, 5, 6, 8, 11, 12, 14, 15, 20; CamDcSc; CurBio 46; DcAmAu; DcAmB S3; DcAmMeB 84; DcScB; EncAAH; EncAB-H 1974, 1996; FacFETw; InSci; LarDcSc; LinLib L, S; McGEWB; NatCAB 12, 35; NewCol 75; NobelP; NotTwCS; ObitOF 79; OxCMed 86; RAdv 14, 13-5; ThTwC 87; WebAB 74, 79; WhAm 2; WhLit; WhoNob, 90, 95; WorAl; WorScD*

Morgan, Vicki
American. Mistress
Mistress of Alfred Bloomingdale; unsuccessfully sued estate for $10 million.
b. Aug 9, 1952 in Colorado
d. Jul 7, 1983 in North Hollywood, California
Source: *BioIn 13*

Morgana, Nina
American. Singer
Soprano with Met. Opera, 1920-35.
b. 1895 in Buffalo, New York
d. Jul 8, 1986 in Ithaca, New York
Source: *EncAB-A 10; NewYTBS 86*

Morganweck, Frank
"Connie Mack of Pro Basketball"; "Pop"
American. Basketball Executive
Promoted, managed, financed basketball for 32 yrs; Hall of Fame.
b. Jul 15, 1875 in Egg Harbor, New Jersey
d. Dec 8, 1941
Source: *BioIn 9; WhoBbl 73*

Morgenthau, Hans Joachim
American. Political Scientist, Author, Educator
Opposed US involvement in Vietnam; taught at US universities; writings include *Politics Among Nations,* 1946.
b. Feb 17, 1904 in Coburg, Germany
d. Jul 19, 1980 in New York, New York
Source: *AmAu&B; AmMWSc 73S, 78S; AmPeW; BiDInt; BioIn 4, 6, 11, 12, 13, 18, 20; ConAu 9R, 101; CurBio 63, 80; DcAmB S10; FacFETw; NewYTBS 80; TwCA SUP; WhAm 7; WhoAm 74, 76, 78, 80; WhoAmJ 80; WhoWor 74; WhoWorJ 72, 78*

Morgenthau, Henry
American. Diplomat
Made fortune in real estate, banking; ambassador to Turkey, 1913-16, Mexico, 1920.
b. Apr 26, 1856 in Mannheim, Germany
d. Nov 25, 1946 in New York, New York
Source: *AmAu&B; ApCAB X; BioIn 1, 2, 4, 7, 9, 11, 17; DcAmB S4; DcNAA; LinLib L, S; NatCAB 15, 36; NewCol 75; WebAB 74, 79; WebBD 83; WhAm 2; WhNAA*

Morgenthau, Henry, Jr.
American. Government Official
Secretary of Treasury, 1934-45.
b. May 11, 1891 in New York, New York
d. Feb 6, 1967 in Poughkeepsie, New York
Source: *AmPolLe; BiDrUSE 71, 89; BioIn 1, 2, 4, 5, 7, 8, 10, 11, 16, 17, 18; ColdWar 1, 2; ConAu 116; CurBio 40, 67; DcAmB S8; EncAB-A 2; EncAB-H 1974, 1996; EncABHB 7; EncCW; EncTR 91; FacFETw; HisEWW; LegTOT; LinLib L, S; McGEWB; NewCol 75; ObitT 1961; OxCAmH; PolProf T; WebAB 74, 79; WebBD 83; WhAm 4; WhJnl; WhWW-II; WorAl; WorAlBi*

Morgenthau, Robert Morris
American. Lawyer
District attorney, NY County since 1975, who introduced revolutionary prosecution system.
b. Jul 31, 1919 in New York, New York
Source: *BioIn 6, 8, 12, 13, 14, 15; ColdWar 2; CurBio 86; IntWW 89, 91, 93; WhoAm 74, 76, 78, 80, 82, 84, 86, 88, 90, 94, 95, 96, 97; WhoAmL 79, 87, 90, 92, 94, 96; WhoE 74; WhoGov 72; WhoWorJ 72*

Mori, Hanae
Japanese. Designer
Japanese heritage evident in textile designs; designed skiwear for 1972 Olympics.
b. Jan 8, 1926 in Kyoto, Japan
Source: *BioIn 15, 16; BioNews 74; ConDes 84, 90, 97; ConFash; EncFash; InWom SUP; WhoAm 90, 92, 94, 95, 96, 97; WhoAmW 91, 93, 95, 97; WhoFash, 88; WorFshn*

Morial, Ernest Nathan
"Dutch"
American. Politician
Dem., first black mayor of New Orleans, 1978-86.
b. Oct 9, 1929 in New Orleans, Louisiana
d. Dec 24, 1989 in New Orleans, Louisiana
Source: *AmCath 80; BioIn 11, 13, 14, 15, 16; InB&W 80, 85; NewYTBS 77, 89; WhAm 10; WhoAm 76, 78, 80, 82, 84, 86; WhoAmP 73, 79, 81, 83, 85, 87, 89, 91; WhoBlA 75, 77, 80, 85, 88, 90, 92N; WhoFash; WhoSSW 78, 80, 84*

Moriarty, Cathy
American. Actor
Starred in *Raging Bull,* 1981; *Neighbors,* 1982.
b. Nov 29, 1960 in New York, New York
Source: *BioIn 19, 21; IntMPA 92, 94, 96; NewYTBS 81; WhoAm 96, 97*

Moriarty, Erin
American. Broadcast Journalist
Regular in TV series "48 Hours."

Moriarty, Michael
American. Actor
Won Tony for *Find Your Way Home,* 1974; Emmy for *The Glass Menagerie,* 1974; TV show "Law and Order," 1990-94.
b. Apr 5, 1941 in Detroit, Michigan
Source: *BioIn 10, 11, 12; ConTFT 1, 4, 13; CurBio 76; FilmEn; HalFC 80, 84, 88; IntMPA 81, 86, 88, 92, 94, 96; LegTOT; MovMk; NewYTBS 74; NotNAT; PlP&P A; VarWW 85; WhoAm 78, 80, 82, 84, 86, 88, 90, 92, 94, 95, 96, 97; WhoEnt 92; WhoHol 92, A; WhoThe 77, 81; WorAl; WorAlBi*

Morike, Eduard Friedrich
German. Poet, Author
Works include verse volume *Gedichte,* 1838; sentimental novel *Maler Nolten,* 1832.
b. Sep 8, 1804 in Ludwigsburg, Wurttemberg
d. Jun 4, 1875 in Stuttgart, Wurttemberg
Source: *AtlBL; BiD&SB; BioIn 3, 4, 5, 7, 8, 9, 10, 11, 20; CasWL; EuAu; EvEuW; OxCGer 76, 86; PenC EUR; RComWL; REn; RfGWoL 95*

Morini, Erica
Austrian. Musician
International concert violinist; made US debut, 1921.
b. Jan 5, 1904 in Vienna, Austria
d. Oct 30, 1995 in New York, New York
Source: *Baker 78, 84, 92; BioIn 14, 21; CurBio 46, 96N; InWom SUP; MusSN; NewGrDA 86; NewGrDM 80; NewYTBS 95; Who 85; WhoAm 84; WhoAmM 83; WhoMus 72; WhoWorJ 72*

Morison, Patricia
American. Actor
Starred on stage *Kiss Me Kate,* 1948; films include *Song of Bernadette,* 1943.
b. Mar 19, 1914 in New York, New York
Source: *BiE&WWA; BioIn 10; EncMT; FilmEn; FilmgC; HalFC 88; HolP 40; InWom SUP; MotPP; NotNAT; ThFT; VarWW 85; WhoHol 92, A; WhoThe 77A*

Morison, Samuel Eliot
American. Historian
Won Pulitzers for *Admiral of the Ocean Sea: A Life of Christopher Columbus,* 1943; *John Paul Jones: A Sailor's Biography,* 1960.
b. Jul 9, 1887 in Boston, Massachusetts
d. May 15, 1976 in Boston, Massachusetts
Source: *AmAu&B; AmWr S1; Au&Wr 71; AuBYP 2, 3; AuSpks; Benet 87, 96; BenetAL 91; BioIn 2, 3, 4, 5, 6, 7, 8, 10, 11, 12, 13, 14, 16; BlueB 76; CelR; ConAu 1R, 4NR, 65; CurBio 51, 62, 76N; DcAmB S10; DcAmMiB; DcLB 17; DcLEL; DrAS 74H; EncAB-H 1974, 1996; FacFETw; IntAu&W 76, 77; IntWW 74, 75, 76; LegTOT; LinLib L, S; LngCTC; McGEWB; NatCAB 61; NewYTBS 76; OxCAmH; OxCAmL 65, 83, 95; OxCCan SUP; OxCShps; PenC AM; PeoHis; RAdv 14, 13-3; REn; REnAL; ThTwC 87; TwCA SUP; WebAB 74, 79; WebAMB; WhAm 6, 7; WhLit; Who 74; WhoAm 74, 76; WhoWor 74; WorAl; WorAlBi; WrDr 76*

Morisot, Berthe
French. Artist
Impressionist, noted for soft-colored landscapes, portraits; often modelled for brother-in-law, Edouard Manet.
b. Jan 14, 1841 in Bourges, France
d. Mar 2, 1895 in Paris, France
Source: *AtlBL; BiDWomA; BioIn 2, 3, 4, 5, 6, 8, 9, 10, 11, 15, 16, 17, 18; ContDcW 89; DcArts; DcWomA; GoodHs; IntDcAA 90; IntDcWB; LegTOT; McGDA; NewCol 75; OxCArt; OxDcArt; ThHElm; WebBD 83; WomArt; WorAl; WorAlBi*

Morissette, Alanis
Canadian. Singer, Songwriter
Won two Grammys for *Jagged Little Pill,* 1995; two Grammys for "You Oughta Know," 1995.
b. Jun 1, 1974 in Ottawa, Ontario, Canada

Source: *EncRkSt; News 96, 96-2*

Morita, Akio
Japanese. Businessman
Co-founded Sony Corp., 1946; chm., 1976-94; CEO 1976-89.
b. Jan 26, 1921 in Nagoya, Japan
Source: *BioIn 9, 10, 12, 13, 14, 15, 16; CurBio 72; EncJap; FarE&A 78, 79, 80, 81; IntWW 74, 75, 76, 77, 78, 79, 80, 81, 82, 83, 89, 91, 93; LegTOT; LElec; News 89; NewYTBE 70; Who 82, 83, 85, 88, 90, 92, 94; WhoAm 74, 76, 78, 80, 82, 84, 86, 88, 90, 92, 94, 95; WhoEnt 92; WhoFI 74, 92; WhoScEn 96; WhoWor 74, 76, 78, 80, 84, 89, 91, 95, 97*

Morita, Pat
[Noriyuki Morita]
American. Actor, Comedian
TV shows include "Happy Days," 1975-76, 1982-83; films include *The Karate Kid* series, 1984, 1986 and 1989.
b. Jun 28, 1932 in Isleton, California
Source: *BioIn 15, 16; ConNews 87-3; ConTFT 3; HalFC 88; IntMPA 92, 94, 96; VarWW 85; WhoAm 95, 96, 97; WhoAsA 94; WhoEnt 92; WhoHol 92; WorAlBi*

Moritz, Charles Worthington
American. Business Executive
Chm., CEO, Dun and Bradstreet, 1985-93; chm. 1994—.
b. Aug 22, 1936 in Washington, District of Columbia
Source: *Dun&B 90; St&PR 84, 87, 91, 93; WhoAm 78, 80, 82, 84, 86, 88, 90, 92, 94, 95, 96; WhoE 86, 89, 91, 95; WhoFI 85, 87, 89, 92, 94, 96; WhoWor 82*

Morland, George
English. Artist
Engraver who produced over 400 works including moralities series after Hogarth, 1786.
b. Jun 26, 1763 in London, England
d. Oct 29, 1804 in London, England
Source: *BioIn 1, 3, 4, 13, 15; CelCen; ClaDrA; DcBiPP; DcBrWA; DcNaB; McGDA; NewC; NewCol 75; OxCArt; OxCEng 85, 95; WebBD 83*

Morley, Christopher (Darlington)
"Kit"
American. Author, Journalist
Works include best-selling novel *Kitty Foyle,* 1939; books on bookselling *Parnassus on Wheels,* 1917.
b. May 5, 1890 in Haverford, Pennsylvania
d. Mar 28, 1957 in Roslyn Heights, New York
Source: *AmAu&B; AmNov; ApCAB X; Benet 87, 96; BenetAL 91; BiDAmNC; BioIn 1, 2, 3, 4, 5, 8, 9, 11, 12, 17; CarSB; CasWL; ChhPo, S1, S2, S3; CnDAL; ConAmA; ConAmL; ConAu 112; DcAmB S6; DcLB 9; DcLEL; EncSF 93; EvLB; FacFETw; GrWrEL N; LegTOT; LinLib L, S; LngCTC; ModAL; Novels; ObitT 1951; OxCAmL 65, 83, 95; OxCEng 67; PenC AM; REn; REnAL; RfGAmL 87, 94; ScF&FL 1; Str&VC; TwCA, SUP; WhAm 3; WhNAA*

Morley, Eric Douglas
English. Impresario
Founded Miss World beauty pageant, 1951.
b. Sep 26, 1918 in London, England
Source: *Who 74, 82, 85, 92; WhoWor 74, 76, 78, 80, 82*

Morley, John, Viscount
English. Journalist, Politician, Historian
MP, 1880s-90s; editor *Fortnightly Review,* 1867-82; books include *Voltaire,* 1872.
b. Dec 24, 1838 in Blackburn, England
d. Sep 23, 1923 in London, England
Source: *Alli SUP; BbD; BiD&SB; BioIn 14, 16, 17, 21; BritAu 19; CamGEL; CamGLE; CasWL; CelCen; DcBiPP; DcEnA; DcEnL; DcEuL; DcLB 57, 144; DcLEL; DcNaB 1922; GrBr; HisDBrE; LinLib L; LngCTC; McGEWB; NewC; NewCBEL; OxCEng 67, 85, 95; PenC ENG; VicBrit; WhLit*

Morley, Robert
English. Actor, Dramatist
Known for his jovial roles on stage and screen; spokesman for British Airways, 1970s-1980s; starred in *Oscar Wilde,* 1960 among many others.
b. May 26, 1908 in Semley, England
d. Jun 3, 1992 in Reading, England
Source: *AnObit 1992; Au&Wr 71; BiE&WWA; BioIn 2, 5, 6, 7, 11, 12, 13, 17, 18, 19; BlueB 76; CamGWoT; CelR 90; CnThe; ConAu 113, 130; ConTFT 7, 11; CurBio 63, 92N; DcArts; EncWT; Ent; FilmAG WE; FilmEn; FilmgC; ForYSC; HalFC 80, 84, 88; IlWWBF, A; IntAu&W 76; IntMPA 75, 76, 77, 78, 79, 80, 81, 82, 84, 86, 88, 92; IntWW 74, 75, 76, 77, 78, 79, 80, 81, 82, 83, 89, 91; ItaFilm; LegTOT; MotPP; MovMk; NewYTBS 92; NotNAT, A; OxCFilm; OxCThe 67, 83; PlP&P; Vers A; Who 74, 82, 83, 85, 88, 90, 92; WhoAm 80, 82, 84; WhoHol 92, A; WhoHrs 80; WhoThe 72, 77, 81; WhoWor 74; WorAl; WorAlBi*

Moro, Aldo
Italian. Politician
Leader, Christian Democratic Party; kidnapped, killed by Red Brigade terrorists.
b. Sep 23, 1916 in Maglie, Italy
d. May 9, 1978 in Rome, Italy
Source: *BioIn 6, 7, 10, 11, 12, 13, 21; CurBio 64, 78, 78N; DcTwHis; EncWB; FacFETw; IntWW 74, 75, 76, 77, 78; IntYB 78; LegTOT; NewCol 75; NewYTBS 78; PolLCWE; Who 74; WorAl; WorAlBi*

Moroni, Giovanni Battista
[Giambattista]
Italian. Artist
Portrait painter of Brescian school.
b. 1525 in Albino, Italy
d. Feb 5, 1578 in Bergamo, Italy
Source: *BioIn 12; DcCathB; McGDA; NewCol 75; WebBD 83*

Moronobu, Hishikawa
Japanese. Artist
Designer of the Ukiyoe school; wrote 130 illustrated books on subject, only a few of his genre scenes remain.
b. 1618
d. 1703
Source: *BioIn 10; NewCol 75*

Morphy, Paul Charles
American. Chess Player
At age 21, acknowledged as greatest chess player in world.
b. Jun 22, 1837 in New Orleans, Louisiana
d. Jul 10, 1884 in New Orleans, Louisiana
Source: *AmBi; ApCAB; BioIn 3, 4, 5, 9, 10, 11, 12; DcAmB; Dis&D; Drake; GolEC; NatCAB 13; NewCol 75; OxCChes 84; WebAB 74, 79; WhAm HS*

Morrall, Earl E
American. Football Player
Quarterback, 1956-76; led Baltimore, Miami to Super Bowls, 1968, 1972; NFL MVP, 1968.
b. May 17, 1934 in Muskegon, Michigan
Source: *BiDAmSp FB; NewYTBE 71; WhoFtbl 74*

Morrice, James Wilson
Canadian. Artist
Landscape painter who greatly influenced young Canadian artists; works include *The Ferry.*
b. Aug 10, 1865 in Montreal, Quebec, Canada
d. Jan 23, 1924 in Tunis, Tunisia
Source: *BioIn 1, 2, 3, 4, 8, 15, 19; CreCan 2; DcBrAr 2; MacDCB 78; McGDA; McGEWB; NewCol 75; OxCArt; OxCTwCA; OxDcArt; PhDcTCA 77*

Morrill, Justin Smith
American. Politician
Congressman, later senator, who sponsored Morrill Act, 1857; provided land for land-grant colleges, early state universities.
b. Apr 14, 1810 in Strafford, Vermont
d. Dec 28, 1898 in Washington, District of Columbia
Source: *Alli SUP; AmBi; ApCAB; BiAUS; BiDrAC; BiDrUSC 89; BioIn 1, 2, 3, 5, 7, 8, 14, 16; CyAG; DcAmAu; DcAmB; DcNAA; Drake; EncAAH; EncAB-H 1974, 1996; HarEnUS; LinLib S; McGEWB; NatCAB 1; NewCol 75; OxCAmH; TwCBDA; WebAB 74, 79; WebBD 83; WhAm HS; WhAmP; WhCiWar*

Morris, Bill
American. Author
Wrote *Motor City*, 1992, a novel of American society and the automobile industry during the 1950s.
b. 1952
Source: *ConLC 76*

Morris, Chester
American. Actor
Oscar nominee for *Alibi*, 1929; played Boston Blackie in 13 films, 1941-49.
b. Feb 16, 1901 in New York, New York
d. Sep 11, 1970 in New Hope, Pennsylvania
Source: *BiE&WWA; BioIn 9, 11; EncAFC; Film 1, 2; FilmEn; FilmgC; ForYSC; GangFlm; HalFC 80, 84, 88; HolP 30; LegTOT; MotPP; MovMk; NotNAT B; WhAm 5; WhoHol B; WhoHrs 80; WhScrn 74, 77, 83; WhThe; WorAl*

Morris, Clara
American. Actor, Author
With Augustin Daly Co., 1871-73; wrote autobiography *Silent Singer.*
b. Mar 17, 1848 in Toronto, Ontario, Canada
d. Nov 20, 1925 in New Canaan, Connecticut
Source: *AmAu&B; AmBi; AmWom; ApCAB; BiD&SB; BioIn 2, 3, 4, 7, 10, 13, 16; DcAmAu; DcAmB; DcNAA; FamA&A; NatCAB 11; NotAW; OhA&B; OxCAmT 84; OxCCanT; OxCThe 67; PlP&P; TwCBDA; WhAm 1; WhoHol B; WhScrn 77; WomWWA 14*

Morris, Desmond
English. Zoologist, Author
Pioneer in study of new science, comparative ethology; wrote best-selling *The Naked Ape*, 1967; other books include *The Human Zoo*, 1969; *Bodywatching*, 1985.
b. Jan 24, 1928 in Purton, England
Source: *Au&Wr 71; BioIn 6, 8, 10, 11, 12, 14; CelR; ConAu 2NR, 18NR, 45; CurBio 74; DcLEL 1940; IntAu&W 76, 77, 82, 86, 89, 91; IntWW 91; LinLib L; MajTwCW; SmATA 14; TwCPaSc; Who 92; WhoAm 86, 90; WhoWor 87; WorAu 1975; WrDr 76, 80, 82, 84, 86, 88, 90, 92, 94, 96*

Morris, Edmund
American. Historian, Biographer
His biography *The Rise of Theodore Roosevelt* won a Pulitzer Prize in 1980.
b. May 27, 1940 in Nairobi, Kenya
Source: *BioIn 13, 16; ConAu 89; CurBio 89; WhoAm 82, 84; WhoE 85, 86; WhoUSWr 88; WhoWrEP 89, 92, 95; WrDr 82, 84, 86, 88, 90, 92, 94, 96*

Morris, Ernest Brougham
American. Businessman
Owner of the Saratoga Raceway harness track, NY, 1963-87; Hall of Fame, 1987.
b. May 11, 1908 in Rensselaer, New York
d. Dec 22, 1991 in Manchester, New Hampshire
Source: *NewYTBS 91; WhAm 10; WhoAm 74, 76, 78, 80, 82, 84, 86; WhoE 74, 75, 77, 79, 81; WhoWor 78, 80*

Morris, Gary
American. Singer
Hit country singles in the 1980s include "Baby Bye Bye;" "Lasso the Moon."
Source: *BioIn 14; CelR 90; HarEnCM 87*

Morris, Glenn
American. Track Athlete
Won decathlon, 1936 Olympics; played title role in film *Tarzan's Revenge*, 1938.
b. Jun 18, 1912 in Simla, Colorado
d. Jan 31, 1974 in Palo Alto, California
Source: *BioIn 10; NewYTBS 74; ObitOF 79; WhoTr&F 73; WhScrn 83*

Morris, Gouverneur
American. Statesman
Member, Constitutional Convention, 1787; minister to France, 1792-94; senator, 1800-03.
b. Jan 31, 1752 in Morrisania, New York
d. Nov 6, 1816 in Morrisania, New York
Source: *Alli; AmAu&B; AmBi; AmRev; AmWrBE; ApCAB; BenetAL 91; BiAUS; BiD&SB; BiDrAC; BiDrUSC 89; BioIn 2, 3, 5, 6, 7, 8, 9, 10, 15, 16, 18; BlkwEAR; CyAG; CyAL 1; DcAmAu; DcAmB; DcAmDH 80, 89; DcNAA; Drake; EncAB-H 1974, 1996; EncAR; EncCRAm; HarEnUS; LinLib L, S; McGEWB; NatCAB 2; OxCAmH; OxCAmL 65, 83, 95; RComAH; REn; REnAL; TwCBDA; WebAB 74, 79; WhAm HS; WhAmP; WhAmRev; WorAl; WorAlBi*

Morris, Greg
American. Actor
Starred in TV series "Mission Impossible," 1966-73.
b. Sep 26, 1934 in Cleveland, Ohio
d. Aug 27, 1996 in Las Vegas, Nevada
Source: *BlksAmF; DrBlPA, 90; HalFC 84, 88; InB&W 85; LegTOT; VarWW 85; WhoAm 82; WhoBlA 85, 88, 92; WhoHol 92, A; WorAl*

Morris, Howard
American. Actor, Director
Directed comedies *Who's Minding the Mint?*, 1967; *With Six You Get Eggroll*, 1968.
b. Sep 4, 1919 in New York, New York
Source: *EncAFC; FilmEn; FilmgC; ForYSC; HalFC 80, 84, 88; IntMPA 75, 76, 77, 78, 79, 80, 81, 82, 84, 86, 88, 92, 94, 96; JoeFr; MiSFD 9; VarWW 85; WhoAm 86; WhoCom; WhoHol 92, A*

Morris, Jack
[John Scott Morris]
American. Baseball Player
Pitcher, Detroit, 1977-90, Minnesota, 1990-91—; Toronto, 1991; threw no-hitter, Apr 7, 1984; MVP World Series, 1991.
b. May 16, 1956 in Saint Paul, Minnesota
Source: *Ballpl 90; BaseReg 86, 87; WhoSSW 88; WorAlBi*

Morris, James Peppler
American. Opera Singer
Bass-baritone known for role of Wotan in *Ring* cycle.
b. Jan 10, 1947 in Baltimore, Maryland
Source: *Baker 84, 92; BioIn 14, 15; CurBio 86; IntWW 93; MetOEnc; WhoAm 78, 80, 82, 84, 86, 88, 90, 92, 94, 95, 96, 97; WhoAmM 83*

Morris, Jan
[James Humphrey Morris]
English. Journalist
Foreign correspondent known for account of British conquest of Mt. Everest in London *Times*, 1953.
b. Oct 2, 1926 in Clevedon, England
Source: *AuSpks; Benet 87, 96; BioIn 10, 11, 14, 15, 16, 17; BlueB 76; ConAu 1NR, 53; ContDcW 89; CurBio 64, 86; DcArts; DcLEL 1940; IntAu&W 76, 77, 86, 89, 91, 93; IntWW 74, 75, 76, 77, 78, 79, 80, 81, 82, 83, 89, 91, 93; InWom SUP; MajTwCW; NewYTBS 74; OxCLiW 86; ScF&FL 92; Who 85, 88, 90, 92, 94; WhoWor 84, 87, 89, 91, 93, 95, 96, 97; WomFir; WrDr 76, 80, 82, 84, 86, 88, 90, 92, 94, 96*

Morris, Joe
[Joseph Morris]
American. Football Player
Running back, NY Giants, 1982-90; led NFL in TDs with 21, 1985.
b. Sep 15, 1960 in Fort Bragg, North Carolina
Source: *BioIn 13, 15; FootReg 86, 87; InB&W 85; WhoAfA 96; WhoBlA 88, 90, 92, 94*

Morris, Lewis
American. Continental Congressman
Signed Declaration of Independence, 1776; half-brother of Gouverneur.
b. Apr 8, 1726 in Morrisania, New York
d. Jan 22, 1798 in Morrisania, New York
Source: *AmBi; ApCAB; BiAUS; BiDrAC; BiDrUSC 89; BioIn 3, 7, 8, 9; DcAmB; Drake; EncAR; EncCRAm; HarEnUS; NatCAB 3; NewCol 75; TwCBDA; WebBD 83; WhAm HS; WhAmP; WhAmRev*

Morris, Mark
American. Choreographer
Modern dance choreographer of works ranging from baroque to punk rock music; founded the Mark Morris Dance Group, 1981.
b. Aug 29, 1956 in Seattle, Washington

Source: *CurBio 88; DcArts; IntDcB; News 91, 91-1; NewYTBS 89; RAdv 14; WhoWor 91*

Morris, Mercury
[Eugene Morris]
American. Football Player
Halfback, 1969-76, mostly with Miami, in backfield with Larry Csonka; jailed, 1983-86, for drug trafficking.
b. Jan 5, 1947 in Pittsburgh, Pennsylvania
Source: *BioIn 8, 10, 13, 14, 16; NewYTBS 82; WhoFtbl 74*

Morris, Newbold
American. Politician
Liberal Rep; reform candidate for NYC mayor, 1945, 1949.
b. Feb 2, 1902 in New York, New York
d. Mar 30, 1966 in New York, New York
Source: *BioIn 2, 3, 5, 7, 11; CurBio 52, 66; PolProf T; WhAm 4*

Morris, Richard Brandon
American. Historian, Author
Considerable expertise in America's colonial history; works include *The Peacemakers,* 1965.
b. Jul 24, 1904 in New York, New York
d. Mar 3, 1989 in New York, New York
Source: *AmAu&B; AuBYP 2, 3; BioIn 7, 13, 16, 17; ConAu 49, 128; DrAS 74H, 78H, 82H; NewYTBS 89; WhAm 10; WhoAm 74, 76, 78, 80, 82; WorAu 1980*

Morris, Robert
"The Financier"
American. Continental Congressman, Merchant
Signed Declaration of Independence, 1776; superintendent of finance, 1781-84; founded national bank; later, imprisoned for debt.
b. Jan 31, 1734 in Liverpool, England
d. May 7, 1806 in Philadelphia, Pennsylvania
Source: *Alli, SUP; AmBi; AmRev; ApCAB; BiAUS; BiDAmBL 83; BiDLA; BiDrAC; BiDrUSC 89; BioIn 2, 3, 4, 7, 8, 9, 10, 11, 12, 14, 15, 16; BlkwEAR; CurBio 71; CyAG; DcAmB; DcBiPP; DcNAA; Drake; EncAB-H 1974, 1996; EncABHB 6; EncAR; EncCRAm; HarEnUS; LinLib S; McGEWB; NatCAB 2; OxCAmH; RComAH; REnAL; TwCBDA; WebAB 74, 79; WhAm HS; WhAmP; WhAmRev; WorAl; WorAlBi*

Morris, Robert
American. Sculptor
Minimalist; works in gray painted plywood and plastic cubes, pyramids, and polyhedreon forms.
b. Feb 9, 1931 in Kansas City, Missouri
Source: *AmArt; BioIn 8, 9, 12, 13, 14, 15, 16, 20, 21; BriEAA; ConArt 77, 83, 89, 96; CurBio 71; DcAmArt; DcCAA 71, 77, 88, 94; DcCAr 81; LegTOT; MakMC; McGDA; OxCTwCA; OxDcArt; PhDcTCA 77; PrintW 85; WhoAm 74, 76, 78, 82, 84, 86, 88, 90, 92, 94, 95, 96; WhoAmA 73, 76, 78, 80, 82, 84, 86, 89, 91, 93; WorArt 1950*

Morris, Wayne
American. Actor
Hero in action films *Kid Galahad,* 1937; *Brother Rat,* 1938.
b. Feb 17, 1914 in Los Angeles, California
d. Sep 14, 1959 in Oakland, California
Source: *BioIn 5, 8, 11; FilmEn; FilmgC; ForYSC; HalFC 80, 84, 88; HolP 30; LegTOT; MotPP; MovMk; NotNAT B; WhoHol B; WhScrn 74, 77, 83; WorAl*

Morris, William
English. Designer, Poet
Designer of furniture, wallpaper and stained glass; wrote *The Life and Death of Jason,* 1867.
b. Mar 24, 1834 in Walthamstow, England
d. Oct 3, 1896 in Hammersmith, England
Source: *Alli SUP; AtlBL; BbD; Benet 87, 96; BiD&SB; BiDNeoM; BioIn 1, 2, 3, 4, 5, 6, 7, 8, 9, 10, 11, 12, 13, 14, 15, 16, 17, 18, 21; BlmGEL; BritAu 19; BritWr 5; CamGEL; CamGLE; CasWL; CelCen; ChhPo, S1, S2, S3; CnDBLB 4; CnE&AP; CrtT 3, 4; DcAmSR; DcArts; DcBiA; DcBrBI; DcBrWA; DcD&D; DcEnA, A; DcEnL; DcEuL; DcLB 18, 35, 57, 156; DcNaB S1; DcNiCA; DcTwDes; EncMA; EncSF, 93; EncUrb; EvLB; GrWrEL P; IntDcAr; LegTOT; LinLib L, S; LngCEL; MacEA; McGDA; McGEWB; MouLC 4; NewC; NewCBEL; NinCLC 4; Novels; OxCArt; OxCChiL; OxCDecA; OxCEng 67, 85, 95; OxDcArt; PenC ENG; PenDiDA 89; RadHan; RAdv 1, 14, 13-1; RComWL; REn; RfGEnL 91; ScF&FL 1, 92; ScFEYrs; ScFSB; SJGFanW; StaCVF; Str&VC; SupFW; TwCSFW 81B, 86B, 91; VicBrit; WebE&AL; WhDW; WhoHr&F; WorAl; WorAlBi; WorFshn*

Morris, William, Jr.
American. Agent
Talent agent; partner, pres., William Morris Agency, 1915-50.
b. Oct 22, 1899 in New York, New York
d. 1989
Source: *BiE&WWA; BioIn 16; BlueB 76; IntMPA 76, 77, 78, 79, 80, 81, 82, 84, 86, 88; NotNAT; WhoAm 74, 76, 78*

Morris, William Richard
[Viscount Nuffield]
English. Industrialist, Philanthropist
Founded Morris Motors, 1919; merged with Austin Motors, 1952, to form British Motor Corp.
b. Oct 10, 1877 in Worcester, England
d. Aug 22, 1963
Source: *BioIn 14; CurBio 63; DcNaB 1961; DcTwBBL; GrBr; ObitT 1961; OxCMed 86; WhAm 4; WhDW*

Morris, Willie
American. Author, Editor
Editor of *Harpers* mag, 1967-71; wrote award-winning autobiography *North Toward Home,* 1967.
b. Nov 29, 1934 in Jackson, Mississippi
Source: *AmDec 1960; AuBYP 2S, 3; AuNews 2; AuSpks; BioIn 7, 8, 9, 10, 11, 12, 13; BlueB 76; CelR; ConAu 13NR, 17R; CurBio 76; DcLB Y80B; DrAF 76; DrAPF 80; EncAJ; EncTwCJ; IntAu&W 77, 89, 91, 93; IntvTCA 2; IntWW 74, 75, 76, 77, 78, 79, 80, 81, 82, 83, 89, 91, 93; LegTOT; LiJour; LiveMA; SouWr; WhoAm 74, 76, 78, 80, 82, 84, 86, 88, 90, 92, 94, 95, 96, 97; WhoE 74; WhoWor 74; WorAl; WorAlBi; WorAu 1975; WrDr 80, 82, 84, 86, 88, 90, 92, 94, 96*

Morris, Wright Marion
American. Author
Novels include *Love Among the Cannibals,* 1957; *A Life,* 1973.
b. Jan 6, 1910 in Central City, Nebraska
Source: *AmAu&B; AmNov; AmWr; Au&Wr 71; Benet 87; BenetAL 91; BioIn 13, 14; CamGLE; CamHAL; CasWL; ConAu 9R, 21NR; ConLC 18, 37; ConNov 86, 91; ConPhot 88; CurBio 82; CyWA 89; DrAPF 91; ICPEnP; IntvTCA 2; MajTwCW; ModAL S2; OxCAmL 65; PenC AM; RAdv 13-1; RfGAmL 87; TwCA SUP; TwCWW 91; WebE&AL; WhAmArt 85; WhoAm 86, 90; WhoAmA 91; WhoUSWr 88; WhoWrEP 89; WorAlBi; WrDr 86, 92*

Morrison, Cameron
American. Politician
Dem. governor of NC, 1921-25; US senator, 1930-32, congressman, 1943-45.
b. Oct 5, 1869 in Richmond County, North Carolina
d. Aug 20, 1953 in Quebec, Canada
Source: *BiDrAC; BiDrGov 1789; BioIn 7; DcNCBi 4; NatCAB 3; WhAm 3*

Morrison, Hobe
American. Critic
Former editor, critic for *Variety.*
b. Mar 24, 1904 in Philadelphia, Pennsylvania
Source: *BiE&WWA; ConAmTC; ConAu 77; NotNAT; OxCAmT 84; WhoThe 72, 77, 81*

Morrison, Jim
[The Doors; James Douglas Morrison]
"Lizard King"
American. Singer, Songwriter
Known for poetic rock lyrics; best-selling albums include *Waiting for the Sun,* 1969; *An American Prayer,* 1978.
b. Dec 8, 1943 in Melbourne, Florida
d. Jul 3, 1971 in Paris, France
Source: *ASCAP 80; Baker 84, 92; BioIn 12, 15, 16, 17, 18, 19; ConAu 40NR, 73; ConLC 17; ConMus 3; DcAmB S9; LegTOT; NewYTBE 71; WhAm 5; WhoRocM 82; WhScrn 77; WorAl; WorAlBi*

Morrison, Philip
American. Physicist, Educator
Published first scientific paper on methods of communication with extraterrestrials, 1959.
b. Nov 7, 1915 in Somerville, New Jersey
Source: *AmMWSc 73P, 76P, 79, 82, 86, 89, 92, 95; BioIn 5, 7, 12, 13; ConAu 106; CurBio 81; NotTwCS; WhoAm 84, 86, 88, 90; WhoFrS 84*

Morrison, Sterling
[The Velvet Underground]
American. Musician, Songwriter
Influenced rock and roll's evolution; Rock and Roll Hall of Fame, 1995.
b. Aug 29, 1942 in East Meadow, New York
d. Sep 2, 1996 in Poughkeepsie, New York
Source: *BioIn 21; News 96, 96-1*

Morrison, Theodore
American. Author
Wrote four novels, four books of poetry; edited *The Portable Chaucer,* modern version of Chaucer's principal work, that has become a standard reference.
b. Nov 4, 1901 in Concord, New Hampshire
d. Nov 27, 1988 in Northampton, Massachusetts
Source: *AmAu&B; BioIn 3, 4, 16; BlueB 76; ConAu 1NR, 1R, 127; DrAS 74E, 78E, 82E; IntAu&W 91; OxCAmL 65, 83, 95; REnAL; TwCA SUP; WhAm 9; WhoAm 74, 76, 78; WrDr 76, 80, 82, 84, 86, 88, 90*

Morrison, Toni
[Chloe Anthony Wofford]
American. Author
Wrote *Song of Solomon,* 1977; *Tar Baby,* 1981; awarded 1988 Pulitzer for *Beloved;* won Nobel Prize for Literature, 1993.
b. Feb 18, 1931 in Lorain, Ohio
Source: *AfrAmAl 6; AfrAmW; AmDec 1970; AmWomWr, 92; AmWr S3; ArtclWW 2; Au&Arts 1; Benet 87, 96; BenetAL 91; BioIn 11, 12, 13, 14, 15, 16, 17, 18, 19, 20, 21; BlkAWP; BlkLC; BlkWAm; BlkWr 1, 2; BlkWWr; BlmGWL; BroV; CamGLE; CamHAL; CelR 90; ConAu 27NR, 29R, 42NR; ConBlAP 88; ConBlB 2; ConHero 2; ConLC 4, 10, 22, 55, 81, 87; ConNov 82, 86, 91, 96; ConPopW; ContDcW 89; CurBio 79; CyWA 89; DcArts; DcLB 6, 33, 143, Y81A, Y93; DcTwCCu 1, 5; DrAF 76; DrAPF 80, 85, 91; EncAB-H 1996; EncWB; EncWHA; EncWL 2, 3; FacFETw; FemiCLE; FemiWr; GrLiveH; GrWomW; HanAmWH; InB&W 80, 85; IntDcWB; IntvTCA 2; IntWW 91, 93; InWom SUP; LegTOT; LivgBAA; MagSAmL; MajTwCW; ModAL S2; ModAWWr; ModBlW; ModWoWr; NegAl 83, 89; NewYTBS 81; NotBlAW 1; OxCAmL 83, 95; OxCWoWr 95; PenNWW A, B; PostFic; RadHan; RAdv 14, 13-1; RfGAmL 94; RGTwCWr; ScF&FL 92; SchCGBL; SelBAAf; SelBAAu; SmATA 57; TwCRHW 94; TwCYAW; WhoAfA 96; WhoAm 84, 86, 88, 90, 92, 94, 95, 96, 97; WhoAmW 89, 91, 93, 95, 97; WhoBlA 85, 88, 90, 92, 94; WhoE 95, 97; WhoNob 95; WhoUSWr 88; WhoWor 95, 96, 97; WhoWrEP 89, 92, 95; WomFir; WorAlBi; WorAu 1975; WorLitC; WrDr 84, 86, 88, 90, 92, 94, 96*

Morrison, Trudi Michelle
American. Lawyer
First black, woman appointed deputy sergeant-at-arms of US Senate, 1985.
b. 1950? in Denver, Colorado
Source: *BioIn 14, 15; ConNews 86-2; WhoAfA 96; WhoBlA 88, 90, 92, 94*

Morrison, Van
[Them; George Ivan Morrison]
Irish. Singer, Songwriter
Talented rock musician, lyricist combines genres from r&b to Celtic melodies; first solo US hit, 1967, ''Brown-Eyed Girl;'' albums include *Moondance,* 1970; *Hymns to the Silence,* 1991.
b. Aug 31, 1945 in Belfast, Northern Ireland
Source: *Baker 84, 92; BioIn 12, 14; ConAu 116; ConLC 21; ConMuA 80A; ConMus 3; CurBio 96; DcArts; EncPR&S 74, 89; EncRk 88; EncRkSt; HarEnR 86; IlEncRk; LegTOT; NewAmDM; NewGrDA 86; OxCPMus; PenEncP; RkOn 78; RkWW 82; RolSEnR 83; SoulM; WhoAm 80, 82, 88, 90, 92, 94, 95, 96, 97; WhoEnt 92; WhoRock 81; WhoRocM 82*

Morrison of Lambeth, Herbert Stanley Morrison, Baron
English. Statesman
Labor party leader, House of Commons, 1945-51; foreign secretary, 1951; created baron, 1959.
b. Jan 3, 1888 in Brixton, England
d. Mar 6, 1965 in London, England
Source: *CurBio 40, 51, 65; NewCol 75; WebBD 83*

Morrisseau, Norval
Canadian. Artist
Ojibwa artist whose pictographs and other works were influenced by rock paintings found along the northern shores of Lake Superior and by the birch bark scrolls of the Midewiwin.
b. Mar 14, 1932 in Sand Point Reserve, Ontario, Canada
Source: *BioIn 6, 11, 12, 13, 21; NotNaAm*

Morrissey
[Steven Patrick Morrissey]
English. Singer
Rock singer; albums include *Kill Uncle,* 1991; *Your Arsenal,* 1992.
b. 1959 in Manchester, England
Source: *ConMus 10; DcArts; EncRkSt; LegTOT*

Morrow, Bobby
American. Track Athlete
Sprinter; won 100-meter, 200-meter, 400-meter relay, 1956 Olympics.
b. Oct 15, 1935 in Harlingen, Texas
Source: *BioIn 4; WhoTr&F 73*

Morrow, Buddy
American. Musician
Trombonist noted for tone, range; led big band, 1950s.
b. Feb 8, 1919 in New Haven, Connecticut
Source: *ASCAP 66, 80; BgBands 74; BiDJaz; BioIn 2, 18; CmpEPM; NewGrDJ 88, 94; PenEncP; WhoJazz 72*

Morrow, Dwight Whitney
American. Diplomat
Ambassador to Mexico, 1927-30; senator, 1930-31; daughter married Charles Lindbergh.
b. Jan 11, 1873 in Huntington, West Virginia
d. Oct 5, 1931 in Englewood, New Jersey
Source: *AmBi; AmPeW; AmPolLe; BiDInt; BiDrAC; BiDrUSC 89; BioIn 1, 3, 4, 5, 10, 11, 16, 17; DcAmB; DcAmDH 80, 89; DcNAA; EncAB-H 1974; LinLib S; McGEWB; NatCAB 23; NewCol 75; WebAB 74, 79; WebBD 83; WhAm 1*

Morrow, Ken(neth)
American. Hockey Player
Defenseman, NY Islanders, 1980-89; member US Olympic gold medal-winning team, 1980; first ever to win gold medal, Stanley Cup in same season.
b. Oct 17, 1956 in Flint, Michigan
Source: *HocEn; HocReg 87*

Morrow, Richard Martin
American. Business Executive
Chairman of Amoco, petroleum retailer, since 1983.
b. 1926 in Wheeling, West Virginia
Source: *AmMWSc 92; BioIn 15; Dun&B 90; St&PR 75, 84, 87, 91, 93, 96; WhoAm 84, 86, 88, 90, 92, 94, 95, 96, 97; WhoFI 81, 83, 85, 87, 89, 92, 94; WhoMW 86, 88, 90, 92, 93, 96; WhoWor 82, 84, 91*

Morrow, Rob
American. Actor
Played Fleischmann in TV series ''Northern Exposure.''
b. Sep 21, 1962 in New Rochelle, New York
Source: *BioIn 20; IntMPA 94, 96; LegTOT; WhoAm 92, 94, 95, 96, 97; WhoEnt 92; WhoHol 92*

Morrow, Vic
American. Actor
Starred in ''Combat,'' 1962-67; died in helicopter crash making movie.
b. Feb 14, 1929 in New York, New York

d. Jul 23, 1982 in Castaic, California
Source: *AnObit 1982; FilmEn; FilmgC; IntMPA 82; MotPP; WhoHol A*

Morse, Barry
Canadian. Actor
Played in TV shows "Golden Bowl;" "Space 1999;" "Fugitive."
b. Jun 10, 1918 in London, England
Source: *BioIn 15; CanWW 31, 70, 79, 80, 81, 83, 89; CreCan 1; FilmgC; HalFC 88; NotNAT; VarWW 85; WhoHol A; WhoThe 77A*

Morse, Ella Mae
American. Singer
Jazz-style vocalist, 1940s; had comeback, early 1950s, with "The Blacksmith Blues."
b. Sep 12, 1924 in Mansfield, Texas
Source: *CmpEPM; InWom SUP; OxCPMus; PenEncP; WhoHol A*

Morse, Philip McCord
American. Physicist
First director, Atomic Energy Commission's Brookhaven Lab, 1946-49.
b. Aug 6, 1903 in Shreveport, Louisiana
d. Sep 5, 1985 in Concord, Massachusetts
Source: *AmMWSc 73P, 76P, 79, 82; BioIn 1, 5, 11, 14, 15; BlueB 76; ConAu 117; CurBio 48, 85; InSci; IntWW 74, 75, 76, 77, 78, 79, 80, 81, 82, 83; McGMS 80; NewYTBS 85; St&PR 75; WhAm 9; WhoAm 74, 76, 78, 80, 82, 84; WhoE 74; WhoFrS 84*

Morse, Robert Alan
American. Actor
Won 1961 Tony for *How to Succeed in Business without Really Trying;* starred in film version, 1967; played Truman Capote in *Tru.*
b. May 18, 1931 in Newton, Massachusetts
Source: *BiE&WWA; BioIn 16; ConTFT 7; EncAFC; EncMT; FilmgC; HalFC 84, 88; IntMPA 86, 92; NotNAT; OxCAmT 84; VarWW 85; WhoAm 74, 76, 78, 80, 82, 90, 92, 94, 95, 96, 97; WhoE 91; WhoEnt 92; WhoThe 81; WorAl*

Morse, Samuel Finley Breese
American. Inventor, Artist
Invented Morse code; founded National Academy of Design.
b. Apr 27, 1791 in Charlestown, Massachusetts
d. Apr 2, 1872 in New York, New York
Source: *Alli, SUP; AmBi; ApCAB; AsBiEn; BiD&SB; BiInAmS; BioIn 1, 2, 3, 4, 5, 6, 7, 8, 9, 10, 11, 12, 13, 14, 15, 16, 17, 19, 21; BriEAA; CamDcSc; DcAmArt; DcAmAu; DcAmB; DcBiPP; DcNAA; Drake; EncAB-H 1974, 1996; FolkA 87; HarEnUS; ICPEnP; InSci; LinLib S; MacBEP; McGDA; McGEWB; NatCAB 4; NewYHSD; OxCAmH; OxCAmL 65; OxDcArt; TwCBDA; WebAB 74, 79; WhAm HS; WhDW; WorAl; WorInv*

Morse, Wayne Lyman
American. Politician
Senator from OR, 1945-69; switched from liberal Rep. to Dem., 1956; championed labor, farmers.
b. Oct 20, 1900 in Madison, Wisconsin
d. Jul 22, 1974 in Portland, Oregon
Source: *AmPolLe; BiDMoPL; BiDrAC; BiDrUSC 89; BioIn 1, 3, 4, 5, 6, 7, 8, 9, 10, 11, 12; BioNews 74; ConAu 49; CurBio 42, 54, 74; DcAmB S9; EncAB-H 1974; IntWW 74; NatCAB 58; NewYTBS 74; WhAm 6; WhoAm 74; WhoAmP 73*

Mortier, Gerard
Belgian. Director
Director, Opera Nationale de la Monnaie, Brussels, 1981-92; Salzburg Music Festival, 1992—.
b. Nov 25, 1943 in Ghent, Belgium
Source: *BioIn 12; CurBio 91; IntWW 91, 93; IntWWM 90; NewGrDO; WhoEnt 92; WhoWor 84, 87, 89, 91, 93, 95, 96, 97*

Mortimer, Charles Greenough
American. Business Executive
CEO, General Foods, 1954-65; helped develop Maxim freeze dried coffee, Gravy Train dog food.
b. Jul 26, 1900 in New York, New York
d. Dec 25, 1978 in Orleans, Massachusetts
Source: *BioIn 3, 4, 5, 11, 12; CurBio 55, 79; DcAmB S10; IntWW 74, 75, 76, 78; ObitOF 79; WhoAm 76; WhoFI 74*

Mortimer, John Clifford
English. Author, Lawyer
Wrote *Rumple of the Bailey,* 1978; adapted *Brideshead Revisited* as PBS series.
b. Apr 21, 1923 in Hampstead, England
Source: *Au&Wr 71; BioIn 13, 14, 16, 17, 18, 20, 21; CamGLE; CnDBLB 8; CnMD; CnThe; ConAu 13R, 21NR; ConBrDr; ConDr 73, 77, 88, 93; ConLC 43; ConNov 91, 96; ConPopW; ConTFT 9; CroCD; CrtSuMy; CyWA 89; DcLEL 1940; Ent; FacFETw; FilmgC; GrWrEL DR; HalFC 80, 88; IntAu&W 76, 77, 86, 89, 91, 93; IntDcT 2; IntWW 81, 82, 83, 89, 91, 93; LngCTC; McGEWD 72; ModWD; NewC; OxCEng 85, 95; OxCThe 83; REnWD; RfGEnL 91; RGTwCWr; TwCA; TwCCr&M 85, 91; TwCWr; Who 74, 82, 83, 85, 88, 92, 94; WhoThe 77; WorAu 1950; WrDr 76, 92, 94, 96*

Morton, Arthur
American. Composer
Composer with film companies since 1948; scores include *Superman,* 1978; *Poltergeist II,* 1986.
b. Aug 8, 1908 in Duluth, Minnesota
Source: *ConTFT 5; IntMPA 75, 76, 77, 78, 79, 80, 81, 82, 84, 86, 88, 92, 94, 96*

Morton, Bruce Alexander
American. Journalist
CBS News Washington anchorman since 1975.
b. Oct 28, 1930 in Norwalk, Connecticut
Source: *VarWW 85; WrDr 76*

Morton, Craig
[Larry Craig Morton]
American. Football Player
Quarterback, 1965-82, mostly with Dallas as back-up to Don Meredith; led Denver to Super Bowl, 1977.
b. Feb 5, 1943 in Flint, Michigan
Source: *BiDAmSp Sup; BioIn 9, 10, 11; CurBio 78; NewYTBE 71; NewYTBS 74, 75; WhoAm 78, 80, 82; WhoFtbl 74; WhoSpor*

Morton, Digby
[Henry Digby Morton]
Irish. Designer
Opened own couture house in London, 1930; best known for his traditionally tailored clothes.
b. Nov 27, 1906 in Dublin, Ireland
d. Dec 5, 1983 in London, England
Source: *ConFash; EncFash; FairDF ENG; Who 74, 82, 83; WorFshn*

Morton, Frederic
American. Author
Novels include *An Unknown Woman,* 1976; non-fiction: *The Rothschilds,* 1962.
b. Oct 5, 1924 in Vienna, Austria
Source: *AmAu&B; AmNov; BiGAW; BioIn 2, 10, 15; ConAu 1R, 3NR, 20NR, 43NR; IntAu&W 86; LiExTwC; ModAL; WhoAm 74, 76, 78, 80, 82, 84, 86, 88, 90, 92, 94, 95, 96, 97; WhoUSWr 88; WhoWrEP 89, 92, 95; WorAu 1950*

Morton, Jelly Roll
American. Jazz Musician, Songwriter
Pianist considered inventor of orchestral jazz, early 1900s; wrote "Jelly Roll Blues," 1917.
b. Sep 20, 1885 in Gulfport, Louisiana
d. Jul 10, 1941 in Los Angeles, California
Source: *AmCulL; Baker 78, 84; BiDAmM; BiDJaz; CmpEPM; ConMus 7; DcAmB S3; DcAmNB; DcArts; DrBlPA, 90; IlEncJ; LegTOT; NewCol 75; NewGrDM 80; NewOxM; OxCAmH; WebAB 74, 79; WhoJazz 72; WorAl; WorAlBi*

Morton, John
American. Continental Congressman, Farmer
Signed Declaration of Independence, 1776; first among the signers to die.
b. 1724 in Ridley Park, Pennsylvania
d. 1777 in Ridley Park, Pennsylvania
Source: *AmBi; ApCAB; BiAUS; BiDrAC; BiDrUSC 89; BioIn 1, 7, 8, 9; DcAmB; Drake; EncAR; EncCRAm; HarEnUS; NatCAB 10; NewCol 75; TwCBDA; WebBD 83; WhAm HS; WhAmP; WhAmRev*

Morton, Joy
American. Manufacturer
Built nation's largest salt co., 1885.

b. Sep 27, 1855 in Detroit, Michigan
d. May 9, 1934 in Lisle, Illinois
Source: *BiDAmBL 83; EncAB-A 5; Entr; NatCAB 17; PeoHis; WhAm 1; WorAl; WorAlBi*

Morton, Julius Sterling
American. Journalist, Government Official
Founded Arbor Day; first observed Apr 22, 1872.
b. Apr 22, 1832 in Adams, New York
d. Apr 27, 1902 in Lake Forest, Illinois
Source: *AmBi; ApCAB SUP; BiDrUSE 71, 89; BioIn 1, 3, 4, 6, 9, 10, 13; DcAmB; DcNAA; EncAAH; HarEnUS; InSci; NatCAB 6; NatLAC; NewCol 75; REnAW; TwCBDA; WebAB 74, 79; WhAm 1*

Morton, Levi Parsons
American. US Vice President
VP under Benjamin Harrison, 1889-93; governor of NY, 1895-97.
b. May 16, 1824 in Shoreham, Vermont
d. May 16, 1920 in Rhinebeck, New York
Source: *AmBi; AmPolLe; ApCAB, X; BiDAmBL 83; BiDrAC; BiDrGov 1789; BiDrUSC 89; BiDrUSE 71, 89; BioIn 1, 4, 7, 8, 9, 10, 14, 16; DcAmB; DcAmDH 80, 89; HarEnUS; NatCAB 1; TwCBDA; VicePre; WebAB 74, 79; WhAm 1; WhAmP*

Morton, Oliver Hazard Perry Throck
American. Politician
Rep. senator from IN, 1867-77; played major role in passage of 15th Amendment, 1870, which enfranchised blacks.
b. Aug 4, 1823 in Salisbury, Indiana
d. Nov 1, 1877 in Indianapolis, Indiana
Source: *AmBi; ApCAB; BiAUS; BiDrAC; BiDrGov 1789; BiDrUSC 89; DcAmB; Drake; McGEWB; NatCAB 13; TwCBDA; WebAB 74, 79; WhAm HS; WhAmP*

Morton, Rogers Clark Ballard
American. Government Official
Secretary of Interior, 1971-75; secretary of Commerce, 1975-76.
b. Sep 19, 1914 in Louisville, Kentucky
d. Apr 19, 1979 in Easton, Maryland
Source: *BiDrAC; BiDrUSC 89; BiDrUSE 71, 89; BioIn 8, 9, 10, 11, 12; BlueB 76; CngDr 74; CurBio 71; DcAmB S10; IntWW 74, 75, 76, 77, 78; NewYTBE 70; NewYTBS 79; WhAm 7; WhoAm 74, 76, 78; WhoAmP 73, 75, 77; WhoGov 72, 75, 77; WhoSSW 75, 76; WhoWor 74*

Morton, Thruston Ballard
American. Politician
Rep. senator from KY, 1957-69; congressman, 1947-53.
b. Aug 19, 1907 in Louisville, Kentucky
d. Aug 14, 1982 in Louisville, Kentucky
Source: *BiDrAC; BiDrUSC 89; BioIn 3, 4, 5, 6, 11, 13, 17; CurBio 57, 82; IntWW 74, 75, 76, 77, 78, 79, 80, 81, 82; NewYTBS 82; PolProf E, J, K; WhAm 8; WhoAm 74, 76, 78, 80, 82; WhoFI 74; WhoSSW 73; WorAl*

Morton, William Thomas Green
American. Dentist
First to use ether as anesthetic, 1846.
b. Aug 9, 1819 in Charlton, Massachusetts
d. Jul 15, 1868 in New York, New York
Source: *Alli; AmBi; ApCAB, X; AsBiEn; BiESc; BiHiMed; BiInAmS; BioIn 1, 3, 4, 5, 6, 7, 9, 14; DcAmB; DcAmMeB, 84; DcNAA; Drake; HarEnUS; InSci; LinLib S; McGEWB; NatCAB 8; NewCol 75; OxCAmH; OxCMed 86; TwCBDA; WebAB 74, 79; WebBD 83; WhAm HS; WhDW; WorAl*

Mosbacher, Dee
American. Filmmaker
Film about conservative parents speaking about homophobia, *Straight from the Heart,* 1995, was nominated for Best Documentary Short Subject Oscar.
b. 1949
Source: *GayLesB*

Mosbacher, Georgette
American. Socialite, Business Owner
Formed Exclusives by Georgette Mosbacher, a cosmetics company, 1991.
b. c. 1947 in Highland, Illinois
Source: *LegTOT; News 94, 94-2*

Mosbacher, Robert Adam
American. Government Official
Secretary of Commerce, 1987-92.
b. Mar 11, 1927 in Mount Vernon, New York
Source: *BiDrUSE 89; BioIn 13; CngDr 89; CurBio 89; IntWW 89, 91, 93; NewYTBS 75, 88; WhoAm 80, 82, 84, 86, 88, 90, 92, 94, 95, 96; WhoAmP 91; WhoE 91; WhoFI 89, 92, 96; WhoWor 91, 93, 95, 96, 97*

Mosby, John Singleton
American. Soldier
Best known for raids on Union outposts with group called "Mosby's Rangers," 1863-65.
b. Dec 6, 1833 in Edgemont, Virginia
d. May 30, 1916 in Washington, District of Columbia
Source: *Alli SUP; AmBi; ApCAB; Benet 87; BenetAL 91; BiD&SB; BiDSA; BioIn 5, 7, 13; CivWDc; DcAmAu; DcAmB; DcNAA; EncSoH; GenMudB; HarEnUS; NatCAB 4; OxCAmH; REn; TwCBDA; WebAB 74, 79; WebAMB; WebBD 83; WhAm 1; WhCiWar*

Moscheles, Ignaz
Czech. Composer, Musician
Pianist, child prodigy; renowned for his teaching, piano improvisation; invented "singing tone."
b. May 30, 1794 in Prague, Bohemia
d. Mar 10, 1870 in Leipzig, Germany
Source: *Baker 78, 84, 92; BioIn 1, 2, 4, 7, 9, 16, 17; BriBkM 80; DcBiPP; MusMk; NewAmDM; NewCol 75; NewGrDM 80; NewOxM; OxCMus; PenDiMP, A*

Moscona, Nicola
Greek. Opera Singer
Bass; with NY Met., 1937-62.
b. Sep 23, 1907 in Athens, Greece
d. Sep 17, 1975 in Philadelphia, Pennsylvania
Source: *Baker 78, 84, 92; BioIn 10, 11; MetOEnc; NewEOp 71; NewGrDO; NewYTBS 75; WhAm 6*

Moscone, George Richard
American. Government Official
Mayor of San Francisco, 1976-78; murdered by Daniel White.
b. Nov 24, 1929 in San Francisco, California
d. Nov 27, 1978 in San Francisco, California
Source: *BioIn 11; DcAmB S10; NewYTBS 75, 78; WhAm 7; WhoAm 78; WhoAmP 73; WhoGov 77*

Mosconi, Willie
[William Joseph Mosconi]
American. Billiards Player
Twelve-time world pool champ between 1941-57.
b. Jun 21, 1913 in Philadelphia, Pennsylvania
Source: *AnObit 1993; BiDAmSp BK; BioIn 1, 6, 18, 19; BioNews 74; CelR; CurBio 63, 93N; NewCol 75; NewYTBS 93; WhoAm 76, 78, 80, 82; WhoEnt 92; WhoSpor; WorAl; WorAlBi*

Mosel, Tad
American. Dramatist
Won Pulitzer for play *All the Way Home,* 1961; wrote screenplay for *Up the Down Staircase,* 1967.
b. May 1, 1922 in Steubenville, Ohio
Source: *BenetAL 91; BiE&WWA; BioIn 6, 10; ConAmD; ConAu 73; ConDr 77, 82, 88, 93; CurBio 61; DcLEL 1940; LegTOT; LesBEnT 92; McGEWD 72, 84; ModWD; NewYTET; NotNAT; OxCAmL 65, 83, 95; OxCAmT 84; REnAL; WhoAm 74, 76, 78, 80, 82; WrDr 76, 80, 82, 84, 86, 88, 90, 92, 94, 96*

Moseley-Braun, Carol
American. Politician
Dem. senator, IL, 1993—; first black female senator in US.
b. Aug 16, 1947 in Chicago, Illinois
Source: *AlmAP 96; BioIn 18, 19, 20, 21; CngDr 93, 95; CurBio 94; WhoAm 94, 95, 96, 97; WhoAmW 95, 97; WhoBlA 92; WhoMW 93, 96*

Mosely, Mark DeWayne
American. Football Player
Kicker, 1970-80, mostly with Washington; set several NFL records for field goal kicking.
b. Mar 12, 1948 in Lanesville, Texas

Source: *BioIn 13, 14; FootReg 87; WhoAm 84, 86, 90*

Mosenthal, Salomon Hermann von
German. Author, Dramatist, Librettist
Best known for libretto, *Merry Wives of Windsor,* 1849.
b. Jan 14, 1821 in Cassel, Germany
d. Feb 17, 1877 in Vienna, Austria
Source: *BiD&SB; NewEOp 71; NotNAT B; OxCGer 76*

Moser, Barry
American. Publisher, Engraver
Noted wood engraver; publisher of prestigious Pennyroyal Press, 1970—.
b. Oct 15, 1940 in Chattanooga, Tennessee
Source: *BioIn 12, 13, 14, 15, 16; ChlBkCr; MajAI; SixBJA; SmATA 15AS, 56, 79; WhoAm 82, 84, 86; WhoAmA 78, 80, 82, 84, 86, 89, 91, 93; WhoGrA 82*

Moses
Biblical Figure
Hebrew leader who delivered Ten Commandments to Israelites on Mount Sinai, precepts form foundation of Judaism, Christianity.
b. 1392?BC, Egypt
d. 1272?BC in Moab, Syria
Source: *BioIn 11; DcOrL 3; McGEWB; NewCol 75; REn*

Moses, Edwin Corley
American. Track Athlete
Hurdler; won gold medals in 400-meter hurdles, 1976, 1984 Olympics, bronze medal, 1988 Olympics.
b. Aug 31, 1955 in Dayton, Ohio
Source: *BiDAmSp OS; BioIn 13, 14, 15, 16; BlkOlyM; CurBio 86; DrAPF 91; InB&W 85; IntWW 83; NewYTBS 84, 85; WhoAm 86, 90; WhoBlA 85, 88, 92*

Moses, Gilbert, III
American. Director
Won Obies for *Slaveship,* 1973; *The Taking of Miss Janie,* 1977.
b. Aug 20, 1942 in Cleveland, Ohio
d. Apr 14, 1995 in New York, New York
Source: *BioIn 15, 20, 21; BlkAmP; BlkAWP; ConBlAP 88; ConBlB 12; ConTFT 5, 14; DrBlPA, 90; InB&W 80, 85; IntMPA 84, 86, 88, 92, 94; MiSFD 9; MorBAP; NewYTBE 72; NotNAT; WhoAfA 96; WhoAm 80, 82, 84, 86, 88, 90, 92, 94, 95, 96; WhoBlA 90, 92, 94; WhoThe 77, 81*

Moses, Grandma
[Anna Mary Robertson Moses]
American. Artist
Started painting in her late 70s; subjects are rural life, including *Black Horses,* 1941.
b. Aug 7, 1860 in Greenwich, New York
d. Dec 13, 1961 in Hoosick Falls, New York
Source: *AuBYP 2; Benet 87, 96; BioAmW; BioIn 14, 15, 16, 17, 18, 20; BriEAA; ConAu 93; ConHero 2; CurBio 49, 62; DcAmArt; DcAmB S7; DcTwCCu 1; EncAAH; FolkA 87; GrLiveH; HerW, 84; InWom, SUP; LegTOT; LibW; LinLib S; McGDA; McGEWB; MusmAFA; NatCAB 46; NorAmWA; NotAW MOD; OxCArt; OxCTwCA; OxDcArt; PhDcTCA 77; REn; WebAB 74, 79; WhAm 4; WhAmArt 85; WhoAmA 80N, 82N, 84N, 86N, 89N, 91N, 93N; WhoAmW 58, 61; WomArt; WorAl; WorAlBi; WorArt 1950*

Moses, Robert
American. Government Official
N.Y. city parks commissioner, 1934-60; developed bridges, playgrounds, state parks, highways, Jones Beach, Shea Stadium etc.
b. Dec 18, 1888 in New Haven, Connecticut
d. Jul 29, 1981 in West Islip, New York
Source: *AmDec 1940; AmRef; AmSocL; AnObit 1981; BiE&WWA; BioIn 2, 3, 4, 5, 6, 7, 10, 11, 12, 13, 15, 16, 19; BlueB 76; CelR; ConAu 45, 104; CurBio 40, 54, 81, 81N; EncAB-A 31; EncAB-H 1996; EncWB; FacFETw; IntWW 74, 75, 76, 77, 78, 79, 80, 81; LinLib L, S; NewCol 75; NewYTBS 81; PolPar; PolProf J, K, T; WebAB 74, 79; WhAm 8; WhoAm 74, 76, 78, 80; WhoAmP 73, 75, 77, 79; WhoWorJ 72, 78; WorAl; WorAlBi*

Moses, Robert Parris
American. Educator
Director, Algebra Project, Cambridge, MA, 1982—.
b. Jan 23, 1935 in New York, New York
Source: *AfrAmOr; BiDAmLf; BioIn 7, 11; ConBlB 11; LNinSix*

Moshoeshoe II
[Constantine Bereng Seeiso]
Ruler
King, upon restoration of Lesotho's independence, 1966-90 when he was dethroned; exiled from country, 1970; returned as head of state, 1970.
b. May 2, 1938 in Mokhotlong, Lesotho
d. Jan 15, 1996 in Maseru, Lesotho
Source: *DcAfHiB 86S; DcCPSAf; IntWW 83, 91; NewCol 75; WhoWor 87, 91*

Mosienko, Bill
[William Mosienco]
"Mosi"
Canadian. Hockey Player
Right wing, Chicago, 1941-55; won Lady Byng Trophy, 1945; scored three goals in 21 seconds, 1952; Hall of Fame, 1965.
b. Nov 2, 1921 in Winnipeg, Manitoba, Canada
Source: *BioIn 20; HocEn; WhoHcky 73*

Moskowitz, J(ay)
American. Government Official
Succeeded Healy as head of Nat. Institutes of Health, 1993—.
b. Jan 9, 1943 in New York, New York
Source: *WhoAm 80, 82, 84, 86, 88, 90, 92, 94, 95, 96, 97*

Mosley, J(ohn) Brooke
American. Religious Leader
Assistant Episcopal bishop of PA, 1975-82; pres., Union Theological Seminary, 1970-74.
b. Oct 18, 1915 in Philadelphia, Pennsylvania
d. Mar 4, 1988 in New York, New York
Source: *BioIn 8, 9, 16; BlueB 76; NewYTBS 88; WhAm 9; WhoAm 74, 76, 78, 80, 82, 84, 86; WhoE 74, 75, 77; WhoRel 75, 77; WhoWor 74*

Mosley, Leonard O(swald)
English. Author
Best known for biographies of Charles Lindbergh, Dulles, the Du Pont family.
b. Feb 11, 1913 in Manchester, England
Source: *Au&Wr 71; ConAu 108, 109, 139; WrDr 86, 92*

Mosley, Nicholas
English. Author
Won Whitbread Award for *Hopeful Monsters,* 1990.
b. Jun 25, 1923 in London, England
Source: *Au&Wr 71; Benet 96; BioIn 13, 17, 21; CamGLE; ConAu 41NR, 69; ConLC 43, 70; ConNov 72, 76, 82, 86, 91, 96; DcLB 14; IntAu&W 76, 77, 82, 91, 93; ModBrL S1, S2; Novels; OxCEng 85, 95; RGTwCWr; WhoWor 76; WorAu 1970; WrDr 76, 80, 82, 84, 86, 88, 90, 92, 94, 96*

Mosley, Oswald Ernald, Sir
English. Politician
One-time potential candidate for prime minister; completely reversed loyalties to found British Union of Fascists, 1932-43.
b. Nov 16, 1896 in Staffordshire, England
d. Dec 2, 1980 in Orsay, France
Source: *BiDExR; BioIn 1, 2, 6, 8, 10, 11, 12, 13; ConAu 102, P-2; CurBio 40, 81N; DcNaB 1971; DcTwHis; GrBr; IntWW 74, 75, 76, 77, 78, 79, 80; IntYB 78, 79, 80, 81; NewCol 75; NewYTBS 80; WebBD 83; WhDW; Who 74; WhoWor 74, 76, 78*

Mosley, Walter
American. Author
Wrote novels, *Devil in a Blue Dress,* 1990; *White Butterfly,* 1992.
b. Jan 12, 1952 in Los Angeles, California
Source: *Au&Arts 17; BlkWr 2; ConAu 142; ConBlB 5; ConLC 97; ConPopW; CurBio 94; SchCGBL; WhoAm 96*

Mosley, Zack Terrell
American. Cartoonist
Created nationally syndicated cartoon, "Smilin' Jack," 1933-73.
b. Dec 12, 1906 in Hickory, Oklahoma

Source: *BioIn 15; ConGrA 2; EncACom; WhAmArt 85; WhoAm 74, 76, 78, 80, 82, 84, 86, 88, 90, 92, 94, 95, 96, 97; WhoAmA 84, 91; WhoSSW 86*

Moss, Arnold
American. Actor, Director
Acclaimed classical actor; known for Shakespearean roles on stage, villains in films.
b. Jan 28, 1911 in New York, New York
d. Dec 15, 1989 in New York, New York
Source: *BiE&WWA; BioIn 16; FilmgC; HalFC 84, 88; IntMPA 84, 86, 88; MovMk; NewYTBS 89; NotNAT; VarWW 85; Vers A; WhoAm 74, 76, 78, 84, 88; WhoHol A; WhoThe 81*

Moss, Cynthia Jane
American. Biologist
By observing and writing about elephants in Kenya for over 25 yrs., has contributed to knowledge of their social behavior.
b. Jul 24, 1940 in Ossining, New York
Source: *ConAu 12NR, 65; CurBio 93; WrDr 92*

Moss, Frank Edward
American. Politician
Dem. senator from UT, 1959-77.
b. Sep 23, 1911 in Salt Lake City, Utah
Source: *BiDrAC; BiDrUSC 89; BioIn 5, 6, 8, 9, 10, 11, 12, 13; BlueB 76; CngDr 74; ConAu 13NR, 61; CurBio 71; IntWW 74, 75, 76, 77, 78, 79, 80, 81, 82, 83; WhoAm 74, 76; WhoAmL 79, 85; WhoAmP 73, 75, 77, 79, 81, 83, 85, 87, 89, 91, 93, 95; WhoGov 72, 75, 77; WhoWest 76*

Moss, Geoffrey
American. Cartoonist, Illustrator
Syndicated political cartoonist with *Washington Post,* 1974—; first to be featured without captions.
b. Jun 30, 1938 in New York, New York
Source: *BioIn 11; WhoAm 78, 80, 82, 84, 86, 88, 90*

Moss, Howard
American. Editor
Poetry editor, *The New Yorker,* 1948-87.
b. Jan 22, 1922 in New York, New York
d. Sep 16, 1987 in New York, New York
Source: *AmAu&B; AnObit 1987; Au&Wr 71; BenetAL 91; BioIn 10, 12, 15, 16; ChhPo S3; ConAu 1NR, 1R, 44NR, 123; ConLC 7, 14, 45, 50; ConPo 70, 75, 80, 85; CroCAP; DcLB 5; DcLEL 1940; DrAP 75; DrAPF 80; IntAu&W 76, 77, 82; IntWWP 77, 82; LinLib L; NewYTBS 87; OxCAmL 83, 95; OxCTwCP; PenC AM; RAdv 1; St&PR 84; WhAm 9; WhoAm 74, 76, 78, 80, 82, 84, 86; WhoWor 74; WorAu 1950; WrDr 76, 80, 82, 84, 86*

Moss, Jerry
[Jerome Sheldon Moss]
American. Music Executive
Co-founder, A & M Records, Inc; hits include *Taste of Honey,* 1965.
b. 1935 in New York, New York
Source: *BioIn 9, 11; HarEnR 86; WhoAm 86*

Moss, Kate
English. Model
Model known for her very slight figure.
b. Jan 16, 1974 in London, England
Source: *News 95, 95-3; WhoAm 95, 96, 97; WhoWor 97*

Moss, Stirling Crauford
English. Auto Racer
Six-time Grand Prix winner, 1956-61; retired after accident, 1962; wrote *How to Watch Motor Racing,* 1975.
b. Sep 17, 1929 in London, England
Source: *Au&Wr 71; BioIn 3, 5, 6, 7, 8, 9, 10, 11, 12, 13, 14, 15, 16; ConAu 5R; IntWW 83, 91; Who 85, 92; WrDr 86, 92*

Mossadegh, Mohammed
Iranian. Political Leader
Premier of Iran, 1951-53; nationalized Britain's oil holdings.
b. 1880? in Tehran, Persia
d. Mar 5, 1967 in Tehran, Iran
Source: *BioIn 2, 3, 4, 7, 8; ColdWar 1; CurBio 51, 67; WhAm 4*

Mossbauer, Rudolf Ludwig
German. Physicist
Shared Nobel Prize in physics, 1961, with R Hofstadter.
b. Jan 31, 1929 in Munich, Germany
Source: *AsBiEn; BiESc; BioIn 6, 8, 14, 15; IntWW 83, 91; LarDcSc; McGMS 80; NobelP; RAdv 14; WhDW; Who 83, 92; WhoAm 90, 92; WhoNob, 95; WhoScEn 94, 96; WhoWor 74, 82, 84, 91, 93, 95, 96, 97; WorAl; WorAlBi*

Most, Donny
American. Actor
Played Ralph Malph on TV series "Happy Days," 1974-80.
b. Aug 8, 1953 in New York, New York
Source: *BioIn 12; ConTFT 7; LegTOT; VarWW 85; WhoEnt 92*

Most, Johnny
American. Sportscaster
Gravelly-voiced broadcaster for the Boston Celtics, 1952-90.
b. 1924?
d. Jan 3, 1993 in Hyannis, Massachusetts

Mostel, Zero
[Samuel Joel Mostel]
American. Actor
Played Tevye in *Fiddler on the Roof;* won three Tonys.
b. Feb 28, 1915 in New York, New York
d. Sep 8, 1977 in Philadelphia, Pennsylvania
Source: *BiE&WWA; IntWW 74, 75, 76, 77; JoeFr; LegTOT; MotPP; MovMk; NewYTBS 77; NotNAT; OxCAmT 84; OxCPMus; OxCThe 83; PlP&P; QDrFCA 92; WhAm 7; WhoAm 74, 76, 78; WhoCom; WhoHol A; WhoThe 72, 77, 81; WhoWor 74; WhScrn 83; WorAl; WorAlBi*

Moszkowski, Moritz
German. Composer, Pianist
Wrote etudes, symphonic poems, two books of Spanish dances.
b. Aug 23, 1854 in Breslau, Germany
d. Mar 4, 1925 in Paris, France
Source: *Baker 78, 84, 92; BioIn 2, 4, 7, 13; BriBkM 80; GrComp; MusMk; NewGrDM 80; NewGrDO; OxCMus*

Motels, The
[Martha Davis; Brian Glascock; Michael Goodroe; Marty Jourard; Guy Perry]
American. Music Group
Songs they popularized include "Only the Lonely," 1982; "Remember the Night," 1983.
Source: *BioIn 16; EncPR&S 89; EncRkSt; FolkA 87; HarEnR 86; InB&W 80; NewWmR; PenEncP; RkOn 85; RolSEnR 83; WhoRocM 82; WhsNW 85*

Moten, Bennie
American. Bandleader
Led swinging Kansas City band, 1920s; Count Basie's band patterned after his.
b. Nov 13, 1894 in Kansas City, Missouri
d. Apr 2, 1935 in Kansas City, Missouri
Source: *AllMusG; Baker 84, 92; BgBands 74; BiDAfM; BiDAmM; BiDJaz; BioIn 13; BlkCond; CmpEPM; DrBlPA, 90; IlEncJ; InB&W 80; NewAmDM; NewGrDA 86; NewGrDJ 88, 94; NewGrDM 80; OxCPMus; PenEncP; WhAm 4; WhoJazz 72*

Mothers of Invention, The
[Jimmy Carl Black; Ray Collins; Roy Estrada; Bunk Gardner; Don Preston; James Sherwood; Ian Underwood; Frank Zappa]
American. Music Group
Backup group for Frank Zappa, often changed by him.
Source: *Alli; BiDAmM; BiDJaz A; BioIn 14, 15, 16, 17, 18, 19, 20, 21; BioNews 74; CelR; ConAu 143, X; ConMuA 80A; EncPR&S 74, 89; EncRk 88; EncRkSt; MotPP; NewAmDM; NewGrDA 86; NewYTBE 70; RolSEnR 83; WhoAmP 91; WhoHol 92, A, B; WhoRock 81; WhoRocM 82*

Motherwell, Robert Burns
American. Artist
One of founders of Abstract Expressionism, 1940s; best-known series is *Elegies to the Spanish Republic,* 1949-76; awarded Nat. Medal of Arts, 1989.
b. Jan 24, 1915 in Aberdeen, Washington
d. Jul 16, 1991 in Provincetown, Massachusetts

Source: *AmArt; Benet 87; BioIn 1, 2, 3, 4, 6, 7, 9, 10, 11, 12, 13, 14, 15; BriEAA; CelR 90; ConArt 83, 89; CurBio 62, 91N; DcCAA 71, 88; EncAB-H 1974, 1996; FacFETw; IntWW 83, 91; McGEWB; NewCol 75; NewYTBS 76, 84, 91; OxDcArt; PrintW 85; WhAmArt 85; WhoAm 86, 90; WhoAmA 84, 91; WorAlBi*

Motherwell, William
Scottish. Poet, Editor
Wrote *Minstrelsy, Ancient and Modern,* 1827.
b. Oct 13, 1797 in Glasgow, Scotland
d. Nov 1, 1835 in Glasgow, Scotland
Source: *Alli; BiD&SB; BioIn 5; BritAu 19; CamGEL; CamGLE; Chambr 3; ChhPo, S1, S3; CmScLit; DcEnA; DcEnL; DcLEL; DcNaB; EvLB; NewC; NewCBEL; OxCEng 67, 85, 95; REn*

Motley, Arthur Harrison
"Red"
American. Publisher
President, publisher of *Parade* mag., 1946-78.
b. Aug 22, 1900 in Minneapolis, Minnesota
d. May 29, 1984 in Palm Springs, California
Source: *AuNews 2; BioIn 1, 3, 4, 5, 6, 7, 10, 11; BioNews 74; ConAu 112; CurBio 61; NewYTBS 84; St&PR 75; WhAm 8; WhoAdv 72; WhoAm 74, 76, 78; WhoE 74, 75*

Motley, Constance Baker
American. Judge
First African American woman elected to NY Senate, 1964-65; appointed federal judge 1966—.
b. Sep 14, 1921 in New Haven, Connecticut
Source: *AfrAmAl 6; AmBench 79; AmWomM; BiDFedJ; BioIn 13, 15, 17, 18, 19, 20; BlkWAm; CivR 74; ConBlB 10; CurBio 64; Ebony 1; EncAACR; InB&W 80, 85; InWom, SUP; NegAl 89; NewYTBS 77; NotBlAW 1; PolProf J; WhoAfA 96; WhoAm 74, 76, 80, 82, 84, 86, 88, 90, 92, 94, 95, 96, 97; WhoAmL 83, 85, 90, 92, 94, 96; WhoAmW 58, 61, 64, 66, 68, 70, 72, 74, 79, 81, 85, 89, 95, 97; WhoBlA 75, 77, 80, 85, 88, 90, 92, 94; WhoE 74, 75, 77, 85, 86, 89, 91, 93, 95; WomFir; WomLaw*

Motley, John Lothrop
American. Historian, Diplomat
Writings on Holland include *Rise of the Dutch Republic,* 1856; minister to Austria, England.
b. Apr 15, 1814 in Dorchester, Massachusetts
d. May 29, 1877 in Dorchester, England
Source: *Alli, SUP; AmAu; AmAu&B; AmBi; ApCAB; BbD; Benet 87; BenetAL 91; BiAUS; BibAL; BiD&SB; BioIn 2, 3, 6, 9, 10, 11, 14, 16; CamGEL; CelCen; Chambr 3; CyAL 2; DcAmAu; DcAmB; DcAmDH 80, 89; DcBiPP, A; DcEnA; DcEnL; DcLB 1, 30, 59; DcLEL; DcNAA; Drake; EvLB; HarEnUS; LinLib L; McGEWB; NatCAB 5; NewCol 75; OxCAmH; OxCAmL 65, 83, 95; OxCEng 67, 85, 95; PenC AM; REn; REnAL; TwCBDA; WebAB 74, 79; WebBD 83; WhAm HS*

Motley, Marion
American. Football Player
Fullback, Cleveland, 1946-53, often compared to Jim Brown; led NFL in rushing, 1950; Hall of Fame, 1968.
b. Jun 5, 1920 in Leesburg, Georgia
Source: *AfrAmSG; BiDAmSp FB; BioIn 7, 8, 9, 10, 12, 17, 21; InB&W 85; LegTOT; NewYTBS 82; WhoFtbl 74; WhoSpor*

Motley, Willard Francis
American. Author
Naturalistic novels include *Knock On Any Door,* 1947.
b. Jul 14, 1912 in Chicago, Illinois
d. Mar 5, 1965 in Mexico City, Mexico
Source: *AmAu&B; AmNov; BioIn 11, 12; BlkAWP; ConAu 106; GrWrEL N; OxCAmL 65; PenC AM; REn; REnAL; TwCA SUP; WhAm 4*

Motley Crue
[Tommy Lee; Mick Mars; Vince Neil; Nikki Sixx]
American. Music Group
Heavy metal band; albums include *Shout at the Devil,* 1983.
Source: *BioIn 15, 21; ConMus 1; EncPR&S 89; EncRkSt; PenEncP; RkOn 85; WhoHol 92, A*

Mott, Charles Stewart
American. Industrialist
Founded Mott Foundation, 1926; chm., US Sugar Corp.
b. Jun 2, 1875 in Newark, New Jersey
d. Feb 18, 1973 in Flint, Michigan
Source: *BiDAmBL 83; BioIn 5, 6, 7, 8, 9, 10, 11, 12, 15; BusPN; DcAmB S9; EncABHB 4; NatCAB 58; WhAm 5; WhoFI 74, 81*

Mott, Frank Luther
American. Author, Educator
Won 1939 Pulitzer for four-volume *History of American Magazines,* 1930-57.
b. Apr 4, 1886 in Keokuk County, Iowa
d. Oct 23, 1964
Source: *AmAu&B; BenetAL 91; BioIn 2, 4, 6, 7, 8, 9, 12; ConAu 1R; CurBio 41, 64; DcAmB S7; EncAB-A 36; EncAJ; NatCAB 52; NewCol 75; OxCAmL 65, 83, 95; REn; REnAL; TwCA SUP; WhAm 4; WhE&EA; WhNAA*

Mott, John Raleigh
American. Evangelist
Won Nobel Peace Prize, 1946, as leader in founding World Council of Churchs.
b. May 25, 1865 in Livingston Manor, New York
d. Jan 31, 1955 in Orlando, Florida
Source: *AmPeW; BiDInt; BioIn 1, 3, 4, 6, 7, 9, 11, 12, 15, 17, 19; DcAmB S5; DcAmReB 1, 2; DcAmSR; EncARH; EncWM; LuthC 75; McGEWB; NatCAB 44; ObitOF 79; WebAB 74, 79; WhAm 3; WhoNob; WorAl; WorAlBi*

Mott, Lucretia Coffin
American. Social Reformer
Co-founded women's rights movement in US, 1848.
b. Jan 3, 1793 in Nantucket, Massachusetts
d. Nov 11, 1880 in Philadelphia, Pennsylvania
Source: *Alli; AmBi; AmPeW; AmRef; AmSocL; AmWom; AmWomWr; ApCAB; BenetAL 91; BiDMoPL; BioAmW; BioIn 15, 18, 19, 21; DcAmB; DcAmReB 1, 2; DcAmSR; DcAmTB; Drake; EncAB-H 1974, 1996; EncWHA; FemiWr; GoodHs; HanAmWH; HerW; InWom SUP; LibW; McGEWB; NatCAB 2; NewCol 75; NotAW; TwCBDA; WebAB 74, 79; WhAm HS; WhAmP; WomFir*

Mott, Nevill Francis, Sir
English. Physicist
Shared Nobel Prize, 1977, for investigations of electronic structure of magnetic system.
b. Sep 30, 1905 in Leeds, England
d. Aug 8, 1996 in Milton Keynes, England
Source: *AmMWSc 92, 95; Au&Wr 71; BiESc; BioIn 2, 3, 11, 14, 15, 20; CamDcSc; ConAu 129; FacFETw; IntAu&W 76, 77, 82; IntWW 74, 75, 76, 77, 78, 79, 80, 81, 82, 83, 89, 91, 93; LarDcSc; NewYTBS 27; NobelP; NotTwCS; RAdv 14; WhE&EA; Who 92, 94; WhoAm 90; WhoNob, 90, 95; WhoWor 87, 91; WorAl; WorAlBi*

Mott, Stewart Rawlings
American. Philanthropist, Businessman
Son of Charles Mott; inherited $20 million trust fund; director, US Sugar Corp., 1965—.
b. Dec 4, 1937 in Flint, Michigan
Source: *BioIn 9, 10, 11, 12; BusPN; NewYTBE 72; WhoAm 74, 76, 78, 80, 82, 84, 86, 88, 90, 92, 94, 95, 96, 97; WhoE 74; WhoFI 89; WhoWor 78*

Mott (the Hoople)
[Verden Allen; Ariel Bender; Nigel Benjamin; Morgan Fisher; Dale "Buffin" Griffin; Ian Hunter; Ray Major; Mick Ralphs; Rick Ronson; Stan Tippens; Pete Watts]
English. Music Group
Hard rock group formed 1969 in Hereford, England; had success with David Bowie-produced albums.
Source: *ConMuA 80A; DcWomA; EncPR&S 74, 89; EncRk 88; EncRkSt; HarEnR 86; IlEncRk; OnThGG; PenEncP; RkOn 78; RolSEnR 83; WhoHol 92; WhoRock 81; WhoRocM 82*

Mott, William Penn, Jr.
American. Government Official
Director, National Park Service, 1985-93.
b. Oct 19, 1909 in New York, New York
d. 1993
Source: *AnObit 1992; BioIn 14, 15, 16; ConNews 86-1; NatLAC; NewYTBS 86*

Motta, Dick
[John Richard Motta]
American. Basketball Coach
Coach, Chicago, 1968-76, Washington, 1976-80, Dallas, 1980-87; coach of year, 1971.
b. Sep 3, 1931 in Salt Lake City, Utah
Source: *BasBi; BiDAmSp BK; BioIn 10, 11; ConAu 111, 134; LegTOT; OfNBA 87; WhoAm 74, 76, 78, 80, 82, 84, 86, 90, 92; WhoBbl 73; WhoE 79; WhoSSW 86; WhoWest 92; WrDr 94*

Mottelson, Benjamin Roy
Danish. Physicist
Shared Nobel Prize in physics for developing theories on atomic nucleus, 1975.
b. Jul 9, 1926 in Chicago, Illinois
Source: *BiESc; BioIn 14, 15; LarDcSc; NobelP; Who 92; WhoAm 90; WhoNob, 90, 95; WhoWor 87, 91; WorAlBi*

Mottl, Felix
Austrian. Conductor
Protege of Wagner; conducted at Bayreuth, from 1886.
b. Aug 24, 1856 in Unter Saint Veit, Austria
d. Jul 2, 1911 in Munich, Germany
Source: *Baker 78, 84; BioIn 7, 8, 11; BriBkM 80; CmOp; IntDcOp; MetOEnc; MusSN; NewAmDM; NewCol 75; NewEOp 71; NewGrDM 80; OxCMus; OxDcOp; PenDiMP; WebBD 83*

Mottley, John
English. Author
Noted for publishing *Joe Miller's Jest-book,* 1739.
b. 1692 in London, England
d. Oct 3, 1750 in London, England
Source: *Alli; BioIn 3; BritAu; DcBiPP; DcEnL; DcLEL; DcNaB; NewC; NewCBEL; OxCEng 67, 85, 95*

Mottola, Tommy
American. Business Executive
Pres., CBS Records, Inc.
b. Jul 14, in New York, New York
Source: *CelR 90; ConMuA 80B*

Mould, Bob
American. Singer, Songwriter, Musician
Alternative rock artist; co-founding member of band Husker Du, 1979-1988, which released debut album, *Land Speed Record,* in 1981; solo album recordings include *Workbook,* 1989 and *Copper Blue,* 1992.
b. 1961 in Malone, New York
Source: *ConMus 10*

Mould, Jacob Wrey
English. Architect
Designed many NYC churches, homes; assistant architect to Olmsted in Central Park plans, 1850s-60s.
b. Aug 8, 1825 in Chislehurst, England
d. Jun 14, 1886 in New York, New York
Source: *ApCAB, X; BioIn 8; MacEA; NatCAB 3; WhAm HS*

Moultrie, William
American. Army Officer, Politician
Revolutionary war leader; defended Charleston, 1779; twice governor of SC.
b. Dec 4, 1730 in Charleston, South Carolina
d. Sep 27, 1805 in Charleston, South Carolina
Source: *Alli; AmBi; ApCAB; BiAUS; BiDrACR; BiDrGov 1789; BiDSA; BioIn 4, 8, 9, 10; DcAmAu; DcAmB; DcNAA; Drake; EncAR; EncCRAm; EncSoH; HarEnMi; NewCol 75; TwCBDA; WebAB 74, 79; WebAMB; WebBD 83; WhAm HS; WhAmRev; WhoMilH 76; WorAl; WorAlBi*

Mount, William Sidney
American. Artist
Portrait, genre painter, known for scenes of black life.
b. Nov 26, 1807 in Setauket, New York
d. Nov 19, 1868 in Setauket, New York
Source: *AmBi; ApCAB; ArtsAmW 1; BioIn 1, 4, 5, 8, 9, 10, 11, 12, 14; BriEAA; ChhPo; DcAmArt; DcAmB; Drake; EncAB-H 1974, 1996; McGDA; McGEWB; NatCAB 14; NewCol 75; NewGrDA 86; NewYHSD; OxCAmH; TwCBDA; WebAB 74, 79; WebBD 83; WhAm HS*

Mountain
[Corky Laing; Felix Pappalardi; David Perry; Leslie West]
American. Music Group
Heavy-metal group formed, 1969; albums include *Twin Peaks,* 1977.
Source: *BioIn 17; ConMuA 80A; Dun&B 86; EncRk 88; HarEnR 86; IlEncRk; InSci; PenEncP; RolSEnR 83; WhoAm 95, 96, 97; WhoE 95, 97; WhoRel 92; WhoRock 81; WhoRocM 82*

Mountain Wolf Woman
American. Writer
Wrote autobiography *Mountain Wolf Woman, Sister of Crashing Thunder,* 1958.
b. 1884
d. Nov 9, 1960 in Black River Falls, Wisconsin
Source: *BioIn 7, 10, 11, 21; ConAu 144; ConLC 92; EncNAB; EncNAR; FemiCLE; InWom SUP; NatNAL; NotNaAm; RelLAm 91*

Mountbatten, Edwina
[Countess Mountbatten of Burma]
English.
Colorful, charming wife of Louis Mountbatten, last viceroy of India.
b. Nov 28, 1901 in London, England
d. Feb 21, 1960 in Jesselton, North Borneo
Source: *DcNaB 1951*

Mountbatten of Burma, Louis Mountbatten, Earl
English. Naval Officer
Great-grandson of Queen Victoria; killed in bomb explosion credited to IRA.
b. Jun 25, 1900 in Windsor, England
d. Aug 27, 1979 in Mullaghmore, Ireland
Source: *CurBio 42, 79; IntWW 79; NewCol 75; WebBD 83; Who 74; WhoWor 74; WhWW-II*

Moure, Erin
Canadian. Poet
Published poetry collections *Empire, York Street,* 1979; *Domestic Fuel,* 1985.
b. Apr 17, 1955 in Calgary, Alberta, Canada
Source: *BioIn 16; BlmGWL; CanWW 31, 89; ConAu 113; ConLC 88; ConPo 91, 96; DcLB 60; IntAu&W 86; OxCTwCP; WhoCanL 85, 87, 92*

Mourning, Alonzo
American. Basketball Player
With the Charlotte Hornets, 1992-95, Miami Heat, 1995—.
b. Feb 8, 1970 in Chesapeake, Virginia
Source: *BioIn 20, 21; News 94, 94-2; WhoAfA 96; WhoAm 95, 96, 97; WhoSpor; WhoSSW 95*

Mourning Dove
[Christine Quintasket]
American. Author
Considered the first Native American female novelist; first novel, *Co-Ge-We-A, the Half-Blood,* 1927.
b. 1885? in Idaho
d. Aug 8, 1936
Source: *NotNaAm; RfGAmL 94*

Moussa, Ibrahim
Egyptian. Producer
Talent agent and producer; former husband of Nastassja Kinski.
b. Sep 30, 1946 in Alexandria, Egypt
Source: *VarWW 85*

Moutoussamy-Ashe, Jeanne
American. Photographer
Published *Daddy and Me: A Photo Story of Arthur Ashe and His Daughter, Camera,* 1993; wife of Arthur Ashe.
b. 1951 in Chicago, Illinois
Source: *BioIn 15, 17, 19, 20; BlkWAm; ConBlB 7; IlBBlP; NotBlAW 2; WhoAfA 96*

Mowat, Farley McGill
Canadian. Author
Known for books about Northern Canada Eskimos; works in 60 languages have sold seven million copies.
b. May 12, 1921 in Belleville, Ontario, Canada

Source: *AmAu&B; Au&Arts 1; AuBYP 2, 3; Benet 87; BenetAL 91; BioIn 13, 14, 15, 16; CamGLE; CanWr; CanWW 83, 89; CasWL; ChlLR 20; ConAu 1R, 4NR, 24NR; ConLC 26; CreCan 2; CurBio 86; DcLB 68; IntAu&W 91; IntWW 83, 91; MajTwCW; OxCCan; OxCCanL; OxCCan SUP; OxCChiL; SmATA 23, 55; ThrBJA; TwCChW 89; WhoAm 86, 90; WhoCanL 87; WhoWor 91; WhoWrEP 89; WorAu 1950; WrDr 86, 92*

Mowbray, Alan
English. Actor
Character actor in 200 films, 1931-62, including *My Man Godfrey.*
b. Aug 18, 1897 in London, England
d. Mar 25, 1969 in Hollywood, California
Source: *BiE&WWA; FilmgC; MotPP; MovMk; NotNAT B; Vers A; WhoHol B; WhScrn 74, 77*

Mowrer, Edgar Ansel
American. Journalist
Chicago Daily News correspondent; won 1933 Pulitzer for describing Hitler's rise.
b. Mar 8, 1892 in Bloomington, Illinois
d. Mar 2, 1977 in Madeira, Portugal
Source: *AmAu&B; AmPeW; Au&Wr 71; BiDAmJo; BiDAmNC; BiDInt; BioIn 1, 4, 6, 8, 11, 16; BlueB 76; ConAu 69, P-1; CurBio 41, 62, 77N; DcAmB S10; DcLB 29; DrAS 74P; EncAJ; EncTwCJ; IntAu&W 76; IntWW 74; JrnUS; LinLib L; NewYTBS 77; REnAL; TwCA, SUP; WhAm 7; WhNAA; Who 74; WhoAm 74, 76; WhoE 74*

Mowrer, Lilian Thomson
American. Author
Wrote *Journalist's Wife,* 1937; wife of Edgar.
b. 1889? in London, England
d. Sep 30, 1990 in Chicago, Illinois
Source: *ConAu 65, 132; CurBio 91N; NewYTBS 90; WhoAmW 85; WrDr 90*

Mowrer, Paul Scott
American. Journalist, Poet
Won 1928 Pulitzer for foreign reporting; verse volumes include *Teeming Earth,* 1965; brother of Edgar.
b. Jul 14, 1887 in Bloomington, Illinois
d. Apr 5, 1971 in Beaufort, South Carolina
Source: *AmAu&B; AmPeW; BenetAL 91; BiDAmJo; BiDInt; BioIn 1, 3, 9, 16; ChhPo; ConAu 4NR, 5R, 29R; DcLB 29; EncTwCJ; JrnUS; REnAL; WhAm 5; WhNAA*

Mowry, Jess
American. Author
Wrote *Way Past Cool,* 1992; *Six Out Seven,* 1993.
b. Mar 27, 1960 in Mississippi
Source: *BioIn 18, 20; ConAu 133; ConBlB 7; WrDr 94, 96*

Moye, Michael
American. Producer
Co-producer of TV sitcom "Married.with Children."

Moyers, Bill
[William Don Moyers]
American. Journalist
Correspondent, CBS News, 1981-86; TV show "A World of Ideas with Bill Moyers;" wrote *Listening to America,* 1971; won several Emmys.
b. Jun 5, 1934 in Hugo, Oklahoma
Source: *AuNews 1; BioIn 6, 7, 8, 9, 10, 11, 12, 13, 14, 16; CelR 90; ConAu 31NR, 52NR, 61; ConLC 74; ConTFT 7, 15; CurBio 66, 76; IntAu&W 89; IntMPA 88, 92, 94, 96; IntWW 83, 91; LegTOT; LesBEnT, 92; LiJour; News 91; PolPar; PolProf J; VarWW 85; Who 85, 92; WhoAm 86, 90; WhoTelC; WhoWor 84, 91; WorAlBi*

Moyes, Patricia
[Mrs. John S. Haszard]
Irish. Author
Won Edgar Allan Poe Award for *Many Deadly Returns,* 1970.
b. Jan 19, 1923 in Bray, Ireland
Source: *Au&Wr 71; BiE&WWA; BioIn 14; ConAu 13NR, 17R, 29NR, 54NR, X; CrtSuMy; EncMys; FemiCLE; GrWomMW; IntAu&W 89; InWom SUP; Novels; SmATA 63; TwCCr&M 80, 85, 91; TwCYAW; WrDr 76, 80, 82, 84, 86, 88, 90, 92, 94, 96*

Moynihan, Daniel Patrick
American. Politician, Diplomat
Dem. senator from NY, 1977—; outspoken proponent of arms control.
b. Mar 16, 1927 in Tulsa, Oklahoma
Source: *AlmAP 78, 80, 82, 84, 88, 92, 96; AmAu&B; AmCath 80; AmMWSc 73S; AmPolLe; BiDrUSC 89; BioIn 7, 8, 9, 10, 11, 12, 13, 14, 15, 16; BlueB 76; CelR, 90; CngDr 77, 79, 81, 83, 85, 87, 89, 91, 93, 95; ConAu 5R; CurBio 68, 86; DcAmDH 80, 89; DcLEL 1940; FacFETw; IntAu&W 91, 93; IntWW 74, 75, 76, 77, 78, 79, 80, 81, 82, 83, 89, 91, 93; IntYB 78, 79, 80, 81, 82; LesBEnT; LinLib S; NewYTBS 76, 90, 93; PolProf J, NF; PolsAm 84; USBiR 74; Who 83, 85, 88, 90, 92, 94; WhoAm 74, 76, 78, 80, 82, 84, 86, 88, 90, 92, 94, 95, 96, 97; WhoAmP 73, 75, 77, 79, 81, 83, 85, 87, 89, 91, 93, 95; WhoE 74, 77, 79, 81, 83, 85, 86, 89, 91, 93, 95, 97; WhoGov 72, 77; WhoScEn 96; WhoWor 74, 76, 78, 80, 82, 84, 87, 89, 91; WorAl; WorAlBi; WrDr 80, 82, 84, 86, 88, 90, 92, 94, 96*

Mozart, Leopold
[Johann Georg Leopold Mozart]
Austrian. Musician, Composer
Court composer, 1757; devised violin technique; father of Wolfgang.
b. Nov 14, 1719 in Augsburg, Germany
d. May 28, 1787 in Salzburg, Germany
Source: *Baker 78, 84; BioIn 4, 5, 7, 9, 12, 14, 16, 18, 20, 21; NewAmDM; NewGrDM 80; NewOxM; OxCMus; WebBD 83*

Mozart, Wolfgang Amadeus
[Johannes Chrysostomus Wolfgangus Theophilus Mozart]
Austrian. Composer
Composed over 600 works, including *The Marriage of Figaro,* 1786.
b. Jan 27, 1756 in Salzburg, Austria
d. Dec 5, 1791 in Vienna, Austria
Source: *AtlBL; Baker 78, 84, 92; Benet 87, 96; BioIn 13, 14, 15, 16, 17, 18, 19, 20, 21; BlkwCE; BriBkM 80; CmOp; CmpBCM; CnOxB; DcArts; DcCom 77; DcCom&M 79; DcPup; Dis&D; EncEnl; EncPaPR 91; GrComp; IntDcOp; LegTOT; LuthC 75; McGEWB; MetOEnc; MusMk; NewAmDM; NewCol 75; NewEOp 71; NewGrDM 80; NewOxM; OxCEng 85, 95; OxCGer 76, 86; OxCMus; OxDcOp; PenDiMP A; RAdv 14, 13-3; REn; WebBD 83; WhDW; WorAl; WorAlBi*

Mr. Big
American. Music Group
Hard-rock band; number one hit "To Be with You," 1992.
Source: *WhE&EA; WhoHol 92; WhoRocM 82*

Mr. Mister
[Steve Farris; Steve George; Pat Mastelotto; Richard Page]
American. Music Group
Rugged rock band; albums include *I Wear the Face,* 1982; *Welcome to the Real World,* 1985.
Source: *Alli; MnBBF; RkOn 85; WhoRocM 82*

Mravinsky, Eugene
[Evgeni]
Russian. Conductor
Led Leningrad Philharmonic; noted for performances of Tchaikovsky.
b. Jun 4, 1903 in Saint Petersburg, Russia
d. Jan 20, 1988 in Leningrad, Union of Soviet Socialist Republics
Source: *Baker 84; BiDSovU; WhoMus 72*

Mubarak, (Mohammed) Hosni
Egyptian. Political Leader
Pres., Egypt, 1981—; succeeded Anwar Sadat.
b. May 4, 1928 in Kafr-El Meselha, Egypt
Source: *BioIn 12, 13, 14, 15; CurBio 82; DcMidEa; EncWB; FacFETw; HisEAAC; IntWW 82, 83, 89, 91; LegTOT; MidE 79, 82; News 91; NewYTBS 78, 81, 90; PolLCME; WhoWor 84, 87, 91*

Muccio, John Joseph
American. Diplomat
First American ambassador to Republic of S Korea, 1949-52; served 40 yrs. in foreign service in the Far East and Latin America.

b. Mar 19, 1900 in Valle Agricola, Italy
d. May 19, 1989 in Washington, District of Columbia
Source: *BioIn 2, 3, 11, 16; CurBio 89N; NewYTBS 89; PolProf T; WhAm 10*

Mucha, Alphonse Marie
Czech. Artist
Specialized in designing posters in art nouveau style.
b. Jul 24, 1860 in Ivancice, Moravia
d. Jul 14, 1939 in Prague, Czechoslovakia
Source: *AntBDN A; BioIn 6, 7, 9, 10, 12; DcNiCA; ICPEnP A; MacBEP; NewCol 75; PhDcTCA 77*

Mucha, Jiri
Czech. Author, Screenwriter
Books include *The Fireflies,* 1962; screenplays: *The King of Kings,* 1959.
b. Mar 12, 1915 in Prague, Bohemia
Source: *BioIn 8, 16; CasWL; ConAu 11NR, 21R, 26NR, 134; IntAu&W 82, 91, 93; ModSL 2; PenC EUR; TwCWr; WhE&EA; WhoSoCE 89; WrDr 76, 80, 82, 84, 86, 88, 90, 92, 94, 96*

Muck, Karl
German. Conductor
Led Berlin Royal Opera, 1892-1912; Boston Symphony, 1912-18.
b. Oct 22, 1859 in Darmstadt, Germany
d. Mar 3, 1940 in Stuttgart, Germany
Source: *Baker 78, 84, 92; BioIn 8, 9, 11; BriBkM 80; CmOp; CurBio 40; IntDcOp; MetOEnc; MusMk; MusSN; NewAmDM; NewEOp 71; WebBD 83*

Muczynski, Robert
American. Composer, Musician
Works, influenced by Russian modern school, include *Dovetail Overture,* 1960.
b. Mar 19, 1929 in Chicago, Illinois
Source: *ASCAP 66, 80; Baker 78, 84, 92; BioIn 7, 9; ConAmC 76, 82; CpmDNM 78, 79, 81, 82; IntWWM 90; NewGrDA 86; WhoAmM 83*

Mudd, Roger Harrison
American. Broadcast Journalist
Newscaster, CBS, 1961-80; NBC, 1980-86; PBS, 1987—; won several Emmys.
b. Feb 9, 1928 in Washington, District of Columbia
Source: *BioIn 12, 13, 14; ConTFT 5; EncTwCJ; IntMPA 92; IntWW 89, 91, 93; LesBEnT; VarWW 85; WhoAm 74, 76, 78, 80, 82, 84, 86, 88, 90, 92, 94, 95, 96, 97; WhoSSW 73; WorAlBi*

Mudd, Samuel Alexander
American. Physician
Treated broken leg of John Wilkes Booth; convicted in Lincoln assassination plot.
b. Dec 20, 1833 in Bryantown, Maryland
d. Jan 10, 1883
Source: *BioIn 5, 6, 7, 10, 12, 13, 21; EncSoH*

Mudgett, Herman Webster
[Dr. Harry Holmes]
American. Murderer
Owned home known as "Murder Castle in Chicago" where he killed more than 200 women.
b. May 14, 1860 in Gilmanton, New Hampshire
d. May 7, 1896 in Philadelphia, Pennsylvania
Source: *BioIn 10*

Mueller, Christian F
American. Manufacturer
Established one of America's leading noodle companies, 1867.
b. Jun 23, 1839 in Wurttemberg, Germany
d. Jan 7, 1926 in Irvington, New Jersey
Source: *Entr; NatCAB 34*

Mueller, Erwin Wilhelm
American. Physicist
Invented field ion microscope; first to see an atom through it.
b. Jun 13, 1911 in Berlin, Germany
d. May 17, 1977 in Washington, District of Columbia
Source: *AsBiEn; BiESc; BioIn 11; CamDcSc; ConAu 69; LarDcSc; NewYTBS 77; WhAm 7; WhoAm 74, 76*

Mueller, Peter
American. Skater
Won speed skating gold medal, 1976 Olympics.
b. 1954?
Source: *BioIn 10*

Mueller, Reuben Herbert
American. Religious Leader
Methodist bishop who founded National Council of Churches, 1950; pres., 1963-66.
b. Jun 2, 1897 in Saint Paul, Minnesota
d. Jul 5, 1982 in Franklin, Indiana
Source: *BioIn 6, 7; ConAu 107; CurBio 64, 82N; EncWM; IndAu 1917; IntWW 74, 75, 76, 77, 78, 79, 80, 81, 82; NewYTBS 82; RelLAm 91; WhoAm 74*

Mugabe, Robert (Gabriel)
Zimbabwean. Political Leader
Exec. pres., Zimbabwe, 1988—; prime minister, 1980-87; co-founder, Zimbabwe African Nat. Union, 1963, pres., 1977-80.
b. Feb 21, 1924 in Kutama, Rhodesia
Source: *AfSS 78, 79, 80, 81, 82; BioIn 11, 13, 14, 15, 16, 17, 18, 20, 21; ColdWar 1, 2; CurBio 79; DcAfHiB 86, 86S; DcCPSAf; DcTwHis; EncRev; EncWB; FacFETw; InB&W 85; IntWW 81, 82, 83, 89, 91, 93; IntYB 82; LegTOT; News 88; NewYTBS 80, 84; RadHan; Who 82, 83, 85, 88, 90, 92, 94; WhoAfr; WhoWor 82, 84, 87, 89, 91, 93, 95, 96, 97*

Muggeridge, Malcolm
"St. Mugg"
English. Author, Broadcaster
WW II counterintelligence spy; prolific writer of religious, political, personal themes; known for caustic commentaries on British royal family.
b. Mar 24, 1903 in Sanderstead, England
d. Nov 14, 1990 in London, England
Source: *AnObit 1990; Au&Wr 71; AuNews 1; Benet 87; BioIn 3, 4, 7, 8, 9, 10, 11, 12, 13, 14, 15, 16, 17, 21; BlueB 76; ChhPo S2; ConAu 33NR, 101; CurBio 55, 75, 91N; DcAmC; FacFETw; IntAu&W 76, 89; IntMPA 75, 76, 77, 78, 79, 80, 81, 82; IntvTCA 2; IntWW 74, 75, 76, 77, 78, 79, 80, 81, 82, 83, 89, 91N; LegTOT; MajTwCW; NewC; NewYTBS 76, 90; ScF&FL 1, 92; WhAm 10; WhE&EA; Who 74, 82, 83, 85, 88, 90, 92N; WhoAm 74, 76, 78, 80, 82, 84, 86; WhoWor 74, 78, 80, 82, 84, 87, 89, 91; WorAu 1950; WrDr 76, 80, 82, 84, 86, 88, 90*

Mugnone, Leopoldo
Italian. Conductor
Conducted first performances of *Cavalleria Rusticana; Tosca;* wrote opera's, light music.
b. Sep 29, 1858 in Naples, Italy
d. Dec 22, 1941 in Naples, Italy
Source: *Baker 78, 84, 92; BioIn 11; CmOp; IntDcOp; MetOEnc; NewEOp 71; NewGrDM 80; NewGrDO; OxDcOp*

Muhammad, Elijah
[Elijah Poole]
American. Religious Leader
Follower of Wali Farad; leader of Black Muslims, 1934.
b. Oct 10, 1897 in Sandersville, Georgia
d. Feb 25, 1975 in Chicago, Illinois
Source: *AfrAmAl 6; AfrAmBi 2; AmJust; AmSocL; BiDAmCu; BioIn 5, 9, 10, 11, 12, 17, 19; CelR; CivR 74; ConBlB 4; CurBio 71, 75N; DcAmB S9; DcAmReB 1, 2; Ebony 1; EncAACR; EncAB-H 1974, 1996; EncARH; EncWB; FacFETw; InB&W 80, 85; LegTOT; MakMC; NegAl 76, 83, 89; ObitT 1971; PolProf J; RelLAm 91; SelBAAf; SelBAAu; WebAB 74, 79; WhoRel 75; WorAl; WorAlBi*

Muhammad, Wallace D
American. Religious Leader
Leader, American Muslim Mission, 1975-85; won numerous humanitarian awards; wrote *Religion on the Line,* 1983.
b. Oct 30, 1933 in Detroit, Michigan
Source: *BioIn 13; WhoAm 86, 88; WhoBlA 92; WhoMW 90; WhoRel 92*

Muhlenberg, Heinrich Melchior
American. Religious Leader
Organized the Lutheran Church in America.
b. Sep 6, 1711 in Einbeck, Germany
d. Oct 7, 1786 in New Providence, Pennsylvania

Source: *BiGAW; LinLib S; McGEWB; NewCol 75; WorAl*

Muir, Edwin
Scottish. Author, Critic
Wrote *Latitudes,* 1924; introduced Franz Kafka to English readers.
b. May 15, 1887 in Deerness, Scotland
d. Jan 3, 1959 in Cambridge, England
Source: *AnCL; AtlBL; Benet 87, 96; BioIn 3, 4, 5, 6, 7, 8, 10, 11, 12, 13, 14, 17; BlmGEL; CamGEL; CamGLE; CasWL; ChhPo, S1, S3; CmScLit; CnE&AP; CnMWL; ConAu 104; ConLCrt 77, 82; DcArts; DcLB 20, 100; DcLEL; DcNaB 1951; EncWL, 2, 3; EngPo; EvLB; FacFETw; GrBr; GrWrEL P; LegTOT; LinLib L; LngCEL; LngCTC; ModBrL, S1, S2; NewC; NewCBEL; ObitT 1951; OxCEng 67, 85, 95; OxCTwCP; PenC ENG; RAdv 1, 14, 13-1; RComWL; REn; RfGEnL 91; RGFMBP; RGTwCWr; TwCA, SUP; TwCLC 2; TwCWr; WebE&AL; WhDW; WhoTwCL*

Muir, Jean
"Miss Muir"
English. Fashion Designer
Designer known for classic designs.
d. May 28, 1995 in London, England
Source: *Alli SUP; BioIn 15, 16, 20, 21; FairDF ENG; ForWC 70; InWom SUP; NewYTBS 27, 95; WorFshn*

Muir, Jean
American. Actor
Hired to play in TV series "The Aldrich Family," 1950 blacklisted as a communist sympathizer, career virtually destroyed.
b. Feb 13, 1911 in New York, New York
d. Jul 23, 1996 in Mesa, Arizona
Source: *BioIn 2, 15, 16; EncAFC; FilmEn; FilmgC; ForYSC; HalFC 80, 84, 88; InWom SUP; ThFT; WhoHol 92, A; WhThe*

Muir, John
American. Naturalist, Author
Conservationist who helped establish Yosemite National Park.
b. Jul 21, 1838 in Dunbar, Scotland
d. Dec 24, 1914 in Los Angeles, California
Source: *AmAu&B; AmBi; AmDec 1900; AmSocL; ApCAB SUP, X; Benet 87, 96; BenetAL 91; BibAL; BiDAmS; BiD&SB; BiDTran; BiInAmS; BioIn 1, 2, 3, 4, 5, 6, 7, 8, 9, 10, 11, 12, 13, 14, 15, 16, 17, 18, 19, 20, 21; CmCal; DcAmAu; DcAmB; DcAmImH; DcLEL; DcNAA; EncAAH; EncAB-H 1996; EncARH; EncEnv; EncPaPR 91; EnvEnc; EvLB; FacFETw; GayN; HarEnUS; InSci; JBA 34; LegTOT; LinLib L, S; McGEWB; MorMA; NatCAB 9; NatLAC; OxCAmH; OxCAmL 65, 83, 95; RAdv 14, 13-5; REn; REnAL; REnAW; TwCA, SUP; TwCBDA; TwCLC 28; WebAB 74, 79; WhAm 1; WisWr; WorAl; WorAlBi*

Muir, Malcolm
American. Publisher
Pres., editor-in-chief, *Newsweek,* 1937-61; pres., McGraw-Hill, 1928-37; founder, *Business Week,* 1929.
b. Jul 19, 1885 in Glen Ridge, New Jersey
d. Jan 30, 1979 in New York, New York
Source: *AmAu&B; BioIn 3, 8, 11, 12; ConAu 85, 93; CurBio 79, 79N; EncAJ; IntWW 74, 75, 76, 77, 78; NewYTBS 79; WhAm 7; WhJnl; WhoAm 74, 76, 78; WorAl; WorAlBi*

Mukerji, Dham Gopal
Indian. Author
Won 1928 Newbery for *Gay-Neck: The Story of a Pigeon.*
b. Jul 6, 1890 in Calcutta, India
d. Jul 14, 1936 in New York, New York
Source: *DcLEL; LngCTC; SmATA 40; TwCA; TwCChW 83*

Mukherjee, Bharati
American.
Novels, short stories showcase lives of Third World immigrants in America:*The Tiger's Daughter,* 1972; *The Middleman and Other Stories,* 1988.
b. Jul 27, 1940 in Calcutta, India
Source: *AsAmAlm; Benet 96; BenetAL 91; BestSel 89-2; BioIn 16; ConAu 45NR, 107; ConLC 53; ConNov 91, 96; CurBio 92; CyWA 89; DcLB 60; EncWL 3; FemiCLE; FemiWr; IntAu&W 91, 93; IntLitE; IntWW 91; MagSAmL; MajTwCW; NotAsAm; OxCWoWr 95; RfGAmL 94; RGTwCWr; WhoAm 90; WhoAmW 91, 93, 95, 97; WhoAsA 94; WhoCanL 87; WorAu 1985; WrDr 76, 80, 82, 84, 86, 88, 90, 92, 94, 96*

Muldaur, Diana Charlton
[Mrs. James Mitchell Vickery]
American. Actor
Played in TV shows "Survivors," 1970-71; "McCloud," 1971-73; "Born Free," 1974.
b. Aug 10, 1938 in New York, New York
Source: *ConTFT 8; FilmgC; HalFC 84, 88; IntMPA 86, 92; VarWW 85; WhoAm 74, 76, 78, 80, 82, 84, 86, 88, 90, 92, 94, 95, 96, 97; WhoAmW 87, 89, 91, 93, 95, 97; WhoEnt 92; WhoHol A*

Muldaur, Maria
American. Singer
Noted for hit "Midnight at the Oasis," 1974; nominated for Grammys.
b. Sep 12, 1943 in New York, New York
Source: *ConMuA 80A; EncRk 88; IlEncRk; LegTOT; NewGrDJ 88; NewYTBS 74; PenEncP; RkOn 74, 78; RolSEnR 83; WhoAm 86; WhoRock 81*

Muldoon, Paul
Irish. Poet
Wrote *Why Brownlee Left,* 1980.
b. Jun 20, 1951 in County Armagh, Northern Ireland
Source: *Benet 96; BiDIrW; BioIn 13; BlmGEL; CamGLE; ConAu 52NR, 113, 129; ConLC 32, 72; ConPo 75, 80, 85, 91, 96; DcIrL, 96; DcLB 40; IntAu&W 91, 93; ModIrL; OxCEng 95; OxCTwCP; RGTwCWr; WhoAm 97; WorAu 1985; WrDr 76, 80, 82, 84, 86, 88, 90, 92, 94, 96*

Muldoon, Robert David, Sir
New Zealander. Political Leader
Prime minister, 1975-84.
b. Sep 25, 1921 in Auckland, New Zealand
d. Aug 5, 1992 in Auckland. New Zealand
Source: *BioIn 10, 11, 12, 13; BlueB 76; CurBio 78; FarE&A 78, 79, 80, 81; IntWW 74, 75, 77, 78, 79, 80, 81, 82, 83, 89, 91; IntYB 78, 79, 80, 81, 82; NewYTBS 75; WhAm 10; Who 74, 82, 83; WhoWor 74, 78, 80, 82, 84, 87*

Muldowney, Shirley
"Cha Cha"
American. Auto Racer
Professional drag racer since 1959; won Nat. Hot Rod Assn. world championship, 1977, 1980, 1982.
b. 1940 in Burlington, Vermont
Source: *BioIn 10, 11, 12, 13; ConNews 86-1; EncWomS; GrLiveH; InWom SUP; LegTOT; WhoSpor*

Mulford, Clarence Edward
American. Author
Wrote popular Westerners including *Hopalong Cassidy,* 1910.
b. Feb 3, 1883 in Streator, Illinois
d. May 10, 1956 in Portland, Maine
Source: *AmAu&B; BioIn 2, 4, 17, 19; DcAmB S6; EvLB; FilmgC; LngCTC; MnBBF; OxCAmL 65; REnAL; TwCA, SUP; TwCWW 82; WhAm 3; WhE&EA; WhNAA*

Mulhall, Jack
[John Joseph Francis]
American. Actor
Joined D W Griffith Stock Co., 1913, appeared in over 100 films.
b. Oct 7, 1894 in Wappingers Falls, New York
d. Jun 1, 1979 in Woodland Hills, California
Source: *Film 1; FilmEn; FilmgC; ForYSC; MotPP; MovMk; NewYTBS 79; TwYS; WhoHol A*

Mulhare, Edward
Irish. Actor
Played on TV shows "The Ghost and Mrs. Muir;" "Knight Rider."
b. Apr 8, 1923 in County Cork, Ireland
d. May 24, 1997 in Van Nuys, California
Source: *BiE&WWA; ConTFT 10; FilmEn; FilmgC; ForYSC; HalFC 80, 84, 88; LegTOT; MotPP; NotNAT; WhoHol A; WorAl; WorAlBi*

Mulhern, Matt
American. Actor
Played the Lieutenant on TV series "Major Dad."
b. Jul 21, 1960 in Philadelphia, Pennsylvania
Source: *ConTFT 2; IntMPA 92, 94, 96*

Mull, Martin
American. Actor, Comedian
Played on TV shows "Mary Hartman, Mary Hartman;" "Fernwood 2-Night."
b. Aug 18, 1943 in Chicago, Illinois
Source: *BioNews 74; ConAu 105; ConLC 17; ConTFT 3, 15; IntMPA 88, 92, 94, 96; LegTOT; LesBEnT; RolSEnR 83; VarWW 85; WhoAm 78, 80, 82, 84, 86, 88, 90, 92, 94, 95, 96, 97; WhoCom; WhoEnt 92; WhoHol 92; WorAlBi*

Mullavey, Greg
American. Actor
Husband of Meredith MacRae; starred in TV series "Mary Hartman, Mary Hartman."
b. Sep 10, 1939 in Buffalo, New York
Source: *ConTFT 7, 15; VarWW 85; WhoEnt 92; WhoHol 92*

Mullen, Joe
American. Hockey Player
Right wing, St. Louis, 1979-86, Calgary, 1986-90; Pittsburgh, 1990—; first player to have 20-goal year in minors and NHL in same season (1981-82); won Lady Byng Trophy, 1987, 1989.
b. Feb 26, 1957 in New York, New York
Source: *BiDAmSp BK; BioIn 12*

Muller, Hermann Joseph
American. Scientist, Educator
Won Nobel Prize in physiology for work on mutations, 1946.
b. Dec 21, 1890 in New York, New York
d. Apr 5, 1967 in Indianapolis, Indiana
Source: *AsBiEn; BiESc; BioIn 1, 2, 3, 4, 5, 7, 8, 9, 12, 14, 15, 20; CamDcSc; DcAmB S8; DcAmMeB 84; DcScB; FacFETw; InSci; LarDcSc; McGEWB; McGMS 80; NewCol 75; NotTwCS; ObitOF 79; ObitT 1961; RAdv 14, 13-5; TexWr; ThTwC 87; WebAB 74, 79; WhAm 4; WhE&EA; WhNAA; WhoNob, 90, 95; WorAl; WorScD*

Muller, Hilgard
South African. Government Official
S African minister of foreign affairs, 1964-77.
b. May 4, 1914 in Potchefstroom, South Africa
d. Jul 10, 1985, South Africa
Source: *AfSS 78, 79, 80, 81, 82; ConAu 117; EncSoA; IntWW 74, 75, 76, 77, 78, 79, 80, 81, 82, 83; IntYB 78, 79, 80, 81, 82; WhAm 9; Who 74, 82, 83, 85; WhoWor 74, 76, 84*

Muller, Johannes Peter
German. Scientist
Founded modern science of physiology.
b. Jul 14, 1801 in Koblenz, Prussia
d. Apr 28, 1858 in Berlin, Germany
Source: *AsBiEn; BiDPsy; BiESc; BiHiMed; CamDcSc; DcScB; InSci; LarDcSc; McGEWB; McGEWD 72; NamesHP; OxCMed 86*

Muller, Karl Alex(ander)
Swiss. Physicist
Shared 1987 Nobel Prize in physics for co-discovery of superconductivity in some substances at temperatures once thought too high.
b. Apr 20, 1927 in Basel, Switzerland
Source: *BioIn 15; IntWW 91; Law&B 89A; NewYTBS 87; PenDiDA 89; Who 90, 92; WhoAm 90, 92; WhoNob 90, 95; WhoScEn 94, 96; WhoWor 91, 93, 95, 96, 97; WorAlBi; WorScD*

Muller, Maria
Bohemian. Opera Singer
Lyric soprano; with NY Met., 1924-35; noted for Wagnerian roles.
b. Jan 29, 1898 in Leitmoritz, Bohemia
d. Mar 13, 1958 in Bayreuth, Germany (West)
Source: *Baker 78, 84, 92; BioIn 1, 14; CmOp; InWom SUP; MetOEnc; NewEOp 71; NewGrDM 80; NewGrDO; OxDcOp*

Muller, Paul Hermann
Swiss. Chemist
Received 1948 Nobel Prize for his findings concerning the toxic effects on insects of the insecticide, DDT.
b. Jan 12, 1899 in Olsten, Switzerland
d. Oct 12, 1965 in Basel, Switzerland
Source: *AsBiEn; BiESc; BioIn 14, 15, 20; CamDcSc; DcLP 87B; DcScB; IntWWM 85; LarDcSc; McGEWB; McGMS 80; NobelP; WhoNob, 90, 95*

Muller-Munk, Peter
American. Designer
One of best known industrial designers in US who designed Bell and Howell's 16 mm movie camera, 1967.
b. Jun 25, 1904 in Berlin, Germany
d. Mar 12, 1967 in Pittsburgh, Pennsylvania
Source: *BioIn 1, 7, 8; ConDes 84; DcTwDes; McGDA*

Mullien, Chris
American. Basketball Player
Guard, Golden State Warriors, 1985—; on Olympic Dream Team, 1992.

Mulligan, Gerry
[Gerald Joseph Mulligan]
American. Jazz Musician, Composer
Noted baritone saxophonist, arranger; formed own pianoless quartet, 1950s; developed "cool" jazz.
b. Apr 6, 1927 in New York, New York
d. Jan 20, 1996 in Darien, Connecticut
Source: *AllMusG; ASCAP 66, 80; Baker 84, 92; BgBands 74; BiDAmM; BiDJaz; BioIn 3, 5, 7, 11, 12; CmpEPM; ConMus 16; CurBio 60, 96N; DcArts; EncJzS; IlEncJ; LegTOT; NewAmDM; NewGrDA 86; NewGrDJ 88, 94; NewGrDM 80; NewYTBS 27; OxCPMus; PenEncP; WhAm 11; WhoAm 74, 78, 80, 82, 84, 86, 88, 90, 92, 94, 95, 96; WhoE 74; WhoEnt 92; WhoHol 92, A; WorAl; WorAlBi*

Mulligan, Richard
American. Actor
Played Burt Campbell on TV comedy "Soap", 1977-81, Harry Weston on "Empty Nest," 1988-95; won Emmys, 1980, 1989.
b. Nov 13, 1932 in New York, New York
Source: *BioIn 19; CelR 90; ConTFT 4, 13; EncAFC; FilmgC; HalFC 80, 84, 88; IntMPA 84, 86, 88, 92, 94, 96; LegTOT; VarWW 85; WhoAm 78, 80, 82, 84, 86; WhoCom; WhoHol 92, A; WhoThe 77, 81; WorAlBi*

Mulliken, Robert Sanderson
American. Chemist
Won 1966 Nobel Prize in chemistry for work with chemical bonds, structure of molecules.
b. Jun 7, 1896 in Newburyport, Massachusetts
d. Oct 31, 1986 in Arlington, Virginia
Source: *AmMWSc 73P, 76P, 79, 82, 86; AsBiEn; BiESc; BioIn 6, 7, 8, 13, 15, 16, 19, 20; CamDcSc; ConAu 109, 120; CurBio 67, 87; IntWW 74, 75, 76, 77, 78, 79, 80, 81, 82, 83; IntYB 78, 79, 80, 81, 82; LarDcSc; McGMS 80; WebAB 74, 79; WhAm 9; Who 85; WhoAm 74, 76, 78, 80, 82, 84, 86; WhoFrS 84; WhoMW 78, 80, 82, 84; WhoNob, 90, 95; WhoWor 74, 80, 82, 84, 87*

Mullin, Willard
American. Cartoonist
Noted sports cartoonist; created the Brooklyn Dodger Bum; drawings appeared in hundreds of mags.
b. Sep 14, 1902 in Franklin, Ohio
d. Dec 21, 1978 in Corpus Christi, Texas
Source: *Ballpl 90; BioIn 4, 9, 11; ConAu 89; FacFETw; NewYTBE 71; NewYTBS 78; ObitOF 79; WhAm 7; WhoAmA 80N, 82N, 84N, 86N, 89N, 91N, 93N*

Mullis, Kary B(anks)
American. Biochemist
Won Nobel Prize for chemistry, 1993; invented technique for synthesizing copies of any given fragment of DNA.
b. Dec 28, 1944 in Lenoir, North Carolina
Source: *CamDcSc; CurBio 96; LarDcSc; WhoAm 92, 94, 95, 96, 97; WhoNob 95; WhoScEn 94, 96; WhoWest 87, 89, 92, 94, 96; WhoWor 95, 96, 97*

Mulroney, Brian
[Martin Brian Mulroney]
Canadian. Political Leader
Millionaire Conservative Party leader who defeated John Turner's Liberal

Party to become prime minister, Sep 1984; resigned 1993.
b. Mar 20, 1939 in Baie Comeau, Quebec, Canada
Source: *CanWW 81, 83; CelR 90; CurBio 84; DcTwHis; FacFETw; IntWW 89, 91; LegTOT; News 89-2; NewYTBS 84; Who 85, 88, 90, 92; WhoAm 84, 86, 88, 90, 92, 94, 95, 96, 97; WhoCan 84; WhoE 85, 86, 89, 91, 93, 95, 97; WhoWor 84, 87, 89, 91, 93, 95, 96, 97; WorAlBi*

Mumford, Lawrence Quincy
American. Librarian
Librarian of Congress, 1954-74.
b. Dec 11, 1903 in Ayden, North Carolina
d. Aug 15, 1982 in Washington, District of Columbia
Source: *AnObit 1982; BiDrLUS 70; BioIn 2, 3, 7, 10, 11, 13, 15, 17; CurBio 54, 83; DcNCBi 4; IntWW 78; LinLib L, S; WhAm 8; Who 74; WhoAm 82; WhoGov 72, 75; WhoSSW 73, 75; WhoWor 74*

Mumford, Lewis
American. Author, Architect
Works interpret American life in terms of architecture: *The City in History,* 1961.
b. Oct 19, 1895 in Flushing, New York
d. Jan 26, 1990 in Amenia, New York
Source: *AmAu&B; AmWr S2; AnObit 1990; Au&Wr 71; Benet 87, 96; BenetAL 91; BiDAmLf; BioIn 3, 4, 5, 6, 8, 9, 10, 11, 12, 13, 14, 15, 16, 17, 18, 19, 21; BlueB 76; CasWL; CelR; CnDAL; ConAmA; ConAmL; ConAu 1R, 5NR, 130; CurBio 63, 90, 90N; DcAmSR; DcArts; DcLB 63; DcLEL; DcTwDes; DrAS 74H, 78H, 82H; EncAB-H 1974, 1996; EncEnv; EncUrb; EvLB; FacFETw; IntAu&W 76, 77, 89, 91; IntEnSS 79; IntWW 74, 75, 76, 77, 78, 79, 80, 81, 82, 83, 89; LegTOT; LinLib L, S; LngCTC; McGDA; McGEWB; ModAL, S1; News 90, 90-2; NewYTBS 85, 90; OxCAmH; OxCAmL 65, 83, 95; PenC AM; RadHan; RAdv 14, 13-5; REn; REnAL; ThTwC 87; TwCA, SUP; WebAB 74, 79; WebE&AL; WhAm 10; WhDW; WhE&EA; WhLit; Who 74, 82, 83, 85, 88, 90; WhoAm 74, 76, 78, 80, 82, 84, 86, 88; WhoArt 80, 82, 84; WhoWor 74, 78, 80, 82, 84; WorAl; WorAlBi; WrDr 76, 80, 86, 88, 90*

Mumtaz Mahal
[Arjumamd Bano Begum]
Hindu. Ruler
Favorite wife of Mogul emperor Shah Jahan, who built Taj Mahal as her mausoleum, 1648.
b. 1593? in Agra, India
d. 1631? in Burhanpur, India
Source: *BioIn 4, 8; NewCol 75*

Muncey, Bill
[William Muncey]
American. Boat Racer
Powerboat racer of Unlimited hydroplanes; drove over Atlas Van Lines racing team; killed in blow-over accident on water.
b. Nov 12, 1928 in Royal Oak, Michigan
d. Oct 18, 1981 in Acapulco, Mexico
Source: *BioIn 6, 9, 10, 11, 12*

Munch, Charles
French. Conductor
Led Boston Symphony, 1949-62; founded Paris Philharmonic, 1930s.
b. Sep 26, 1891 in Strasbourg, France
d. Nov 6, 1968 in Richmond, Virginia
Source: *Baker 78, 84, 92; BiDAmM; BioIn 1, 2, 3, 4, 7, 8, 11; BriBkM 80; CurBio 47, 68; DcAmB S8; FacFETw; LegTOT; LinLib S; MusSN; NewAmDM; NewGrDA 86; NewGrDM 80; PenDiMP; REnAL; WorAl; WorAlBi*

Munch, Edvard
Norwegian. Artist
Early expressionist noted for lithographs, woodcuts, macabre paintings including *Vampire,* 1894.
b. Dec 12, 1863 in Loyten, Norway
d. Jan 23, 1944 in Oslo, Norway
Source: *AtlBL; Benet 87, 96; BioIn 1, 2, 3, 4, 5, 6, 7, 8, 9, 10, 11, 12, 13, 14, 15, 16, 17, 19, 20; ConArt 77; CurBio 40, 44; DcArts; EncWT; FacFETw; IntDcAA 90; LegTOT; MakMC; McGDA; McGEWB; NewCol 75; OxCArt; OxCTwCA; OxDcArt; PenEncH; PhDcTCA 77; REn; WebBD 83; WhAm 4; WhDW; WorAl; WorAlBi*

Munchhausen, Hieronymus Karl Friedrich von, Baron
[Karl Friedrich Hieronymus von Munchausen]
German. Soldier
His name is associated with exaggerated tales.
b. May 11, 1720 in Hannover, Germany
d. Feb 22, 1797
Source: *Alli; BiD&SB; ClDMEL 47; EncWL; LinLib L, S; LngCEL; OxCGer 76*

Munchinger, Karl
German. Conductor
Founded Stuttgart Chamber Orchestra, 1945; the "Klassische Philharmonie," 1966.
b. May 29, 1915 in Stuttgart, Germany
d. Mar 13, 1990 in Stuttgart, Germany
Source: *Baker 78, 84, 92; BriBkM 80; IntWW 74, 75, 76, 77, 78, 79, 80, 81, 82, 83, 89; IntWWM 90; NewAmDM; NewGrDM 80; PenDiMP; WhoMus 72; WhoWor 74, 76, 78*

Mundt, Karl Earl
American. Educator, Politician
Rep. senator from SD, 1949-72; chaired Senate's Army-McCarthy hearings, 1954.
b. Jun 3, 1900 in Humboldt, South Dakota
d. Aug 16, 1974 in Washington, District of Columbia
Source: *BiDrAC; BiDrUSC 89; BioIn 1, 2, 3, 5, 9, 10, 11, 12; BioNews 74; CurBio 48, 74; DcAmB S9; IntWW 74; NewYTBS 74; WhAm 6; WhoAm 74; WhoAmP 73; WhoGov 72; WhoMW 74*

Mungo, Raymond
American. Writer
Wrote nonfiction works *Famous Long Ago,* 1970; *Return to Sender,* 1975.
b. Feb 21, 1946 in Lawrence, Massachusetts
Source: *BioIn 10, 13; ConAu 2NR, 49; ConLC 72*

Muni, Paul
[Muni Weisenfreund]
American. Actor
Won Oscar for *The Story of Louis Pasteur,* 1936.
b. Sep 22, 1895 in Lemberg, Austria
d. Aug 25, 1967 in Montecito, California
Source: *BiDFilm, 81, 94; BiE&WWA; BioIn 1, 2, 3, 4, 6, 7, 8, 9, 10, 11, 17; BioNews 74; CurBio 44, 67; DcAmB S8; EncWT; Ent; FamA&A; Film 2; FilmEn; FilmgC; ForYSC; IntDcF 1-3, 2-3; ItaFilm; LegTOT; MotPP; MovMk; NotNAT A, B; ObitT 1961; OxCAmT 84; OxCFilm; PlP&P; WhoHol B; WhScrn 74, 77, 83; WhThe; WorAl; WorAlBi; WorEFlm*

Munn, Frank
"Golden Voice of Radio"
American. Singer
Popular radio tenor from 1923.
b. 1894 in New York, New York
d. Oct 1, 1953 in New York, New York
Source: *BioIn 20; CurBio 44, 53; RadStar*

Munnings, Alfred James, Sir
English. Artist
Finest painter of animals of his time.
b. Oct 8, 1878 in Suffolk, England
d. Jul 17, 1959 in Dedham, England
Source: *BioIn 1, 2, 3, 4, 5, 6, 12, 14, 21; BritAS; ChhPo S1; ClaDrA; DcBrAr 1; DcBrBI; DcNaB 1951; GrBr; OxCArt; PhDcTCA 77*

Munoz Marin, Luis
Puerto Rican. Politician
First elected governor of Puerto Rico, 1948-64.
b. Feb 18, 1898 in San Juan, Puerto Rico
d. Apr 30, 1980 in San Juan, Puerto Rico
Source: *BiDLAmC; BioIn 1, 3, 4, 5, 6, 7, 8, 10, 11, 12, 16, 20; CaribW 4; ConAu 97; CurBio 42, 53, 80N; DcAmB S10; DcCPCAm; DcHiB; DcPol; DcTwHis; EncLatA; FacFETw; HispWr; LinLib L, S; NewYTBS 80; PolProf K; PueRA; RComAH; WebAB 74, 79; WhAm 7; WhNAA; WhoAmP 73, 75, 77, 79, 81, 83, 85; WhoSSW 73; WorAl; WorAlBi*

Munro, Alice
Canadian. Writer
Novelist and short story writer; books include *Dance of Happy Shades,* 1968; *Friend of My Youth,* 1990.
b. Jul 10, 1931 in Wingham, Ontario, Canada
Source: *ArtclWW 2; AuNews 2; Benet 87, 96; BenetAL 91; BioIn 13; BlmGWL; CamGLE; CanWW 31, 70, 79, 80, 81, 83, 89; ConAu 33NR, 33R, 53NR; ConCaAu 1; ConLC 6, 10, 19, 50, 95; ConNov 72, 76, 82, 86, 91; CurBio 90; CyWA 89; DcArts; DcLB 53; DcLEL 1940; EncWL 3; FemiCLE; GrWomW; IntAu&W 76, 77, 91, 93; IntLitE; IntWW 93; InWom SUP; MagSWL; MajTwCW; ModWoWr; News 97-1; OxCCan; OxCCanL; OxCCan SUP; RAdv 14, 13-1; RfGEnL 91; RfGShF; RGTwCWr; ShSCr 3; SmATA 29; WhoAm 80, 82, 86, 88, 90, 92, 94, 95, 96, 97; WhoAmW 83, 85, 89, 91, 93, 95, 97; WhoCanL 85, 87, 92; WhoWor 95, 96; WhoWrEP 92, 95; WorAlBi; WorAu 1980; WrDr 76, 80, 82, 84, 86, 88, 90, 92, 94, 96*

Munroe, Charles Edward
American. Chemist
Pioneer in chemical engineering, expert on explosives; discovered smokeless gunp owder, "Munroe Effect."
b. May 24, 1849 in Cambridge, Massachusetts
d. Dec 7, 1938
Source: *ApCAB; BiDAmS; BioIn 2, 4; DcAmB S2; DcNAA; InSci; NatCAB 9, 29; TwCBDA; WhAm 1*

Munsel, Patrice Beverly
American. Singer
Soprano who at 18, was youngest singer ever accepted at NY Met; in films, Broadway musicals.
b. May 14, 1925 in Spokane, Washington
Source: *Baker 84; BiE&WWA; CurBio 45; FilmgC; HalFC 84; MusSN; WhoAm 74; WhoE 74; WhoHol A; WhoMus 72*

Munsey, Frank Andrew
American. Publisher, Author
Owned 18 newspapers, *Munsey's Weekly* magazine, from 1888.
b. Aug 21, 1854 in Mercer, Maine
d. Dec 22, 1925 in New York, New York
Source: *ABCMeAm; Alli SUP; AmAu&B; AmBi; ApCAB X; BiDAmBL 83; BiDAmJo; BioIn 3, 4, 9; CarSB; ConAu 116; DcAmAu; DcAmB; DcLB 25; DcNAA; EncAB-H 1974, 1996; FacFETw; LinLib L, S; McGEWB; NatCAB 20; OxCAmH; OxCAmL 83; REnAL; TwCBDA; WebAB 74, 79; WhAm 1; WhJnl, SUP*

Munshin, Jules
American. Actor
Broadway star of *Call Me Mister,* 1946.
b. Feb 22, 1915 in New York, New York
d. Feb 19, 1970 in New York, New York
Source: *BiE&WWA; CmMov; CmpEPM; EncAFC; FilmEn; FilmgC; ForYSC; HalFC 80, 84, 88; MotPP; NewYTBE 70; NotNAT B; WhoHol B; WhScrn 74, 77, 83*

Munson, Gorham B(ert)
American. Author, Editor
Books include *Robert Frost: A Study in Sensibility and Good Sense,* 1927; *Twelve Decisive Battles of the Mind,* 1942.
b. May 26, 1896 in Amityville, New York
d. Aug 15, 1969 in Middletown, Connecticut
Source: *AmAu&B; AuBYP 2; BioIn 4, 7, 8; CnDAL; ConAu P-1; OxCAmL 65, 83; PenC AM; REnAL; TwCA, SUP; WhAm 5*

Munson, Ona
American. Actor
Played Belle Watling in *Gone With the Wind,* 1939.
b. Jun 16, 1906 in Portland, Oregon
d. Feb 11, 1955 in New York, New York
Source: *BioIn 3; FilmEn; FilmgC; HalFC 80, 84, 88; InWom SUP; LegTOT; MotPP; MovMk; NotNAT B; ThFT; Vers A; WhoHol B; WhScrn 74, 77; WhThe*

Munson, Thurman Lee
"Squatty"
American. Baseball Player
Catcher, NY Yankees, 1969-79; AL MVP, 1976; killed in plane crash.
b. Jun 7, 1947 in Akron, Ohio
d. Aug 2, 1979 in Canton, Ohio
Source: *BiDAmSp Sup; ConAu 89, 108; CurBio 77, 79; DcAmB S10; NewYTBS 75, 79; WhoAm 78; WhoBlA 77; WhoProB 73*

Muntzer, Thomas
German. Social Reformer
During Protestant Reformation, led movement that propounded inner experience, not scripture, as religiously-authoritative, empowering common man to transform society.
b. 1490 in Stolberg, Thuringia
d. May 27, 1525 in Muhlhausen, Germany
Source: *BioIn 7, 8, 10, 13, 16, 17, 20; OxCGer 76, 86*

Muoi, Do
Vietnamese. Political Leader
Prime minister of Vietnam, 1988-91; general secretary, Communist Party, 1991—.
b. 1917?

Murasaki, Shikibu, Lady
Japanese. Author
Wrote one of earliest novels *Tale of the Genji,* c. 1020.
b. 978? in Kyoto, Japan
d. 1031? in Kyoto, Japan
Source: *Benet 87; BiDJaL; BioIn 3, 5, 13; CasWL; ContDcW 89; CyWA 58; DcArts; DcOrL 1; GrFLW; IntDcWB; LinLib L; McGEWB; Novels; PenC CL; REn; WhDW; WomFir; WorAl; WorAlBi*

Murat, Joachim
French. Military Leader, Politician
Brother-in-law of Napoleon I; king of Naples, 1808-15.
b. Mar 25, 1767 in La Baslide-Fortumiere, France
d. Oct 13, 1815 in Pizzo, Italy
Source: *BenetAL 91; BioIn 1, 9; CmFrR; Dis&D; HarEnMi; LinLib S; McGEWB; NewCol 75; OxCFr; REn; REnAL; WhoMilH 76; WorAl; WorAlBi*

Muratore, Lucien
French. Opera Singer
Tenor; starred with US opera companies, 1913-22; created over 30 roles.
b. Aug 29, 1876 in Marseilles, France
d. Jul 16, 1954 in Paris, France
Source: *Baker 78, 84, 92; MetOEnc; MusSN; NewEOp 71; NewGrDM 80; NewGrDO; WhAm 3; WhScrn 77*

Muratori, Lodovico Antonio
"Father of Italian History"
Italian. Historian
Researched sources of medieval Italian history, archaeology.
b. Oct 21, 1672 in Vignola, Italy
d. Jan 23, 1750
Source: *DcItL 1, 2; EncEnl; McGEWB; NewCBEL; NewCol 75; WebBD 83*

Murcer, Bobby Ray
"Okie"
American. Baseball Player
Outfielder, 1965-66, 1969-83, mostly with Yankees; often touted as next Mickey Mantle; had lifetime .277 batting average.
b. May 20, 1946 in Oklahoma City, Oklahoma
Source: *BiDAmSp Sup; BioIn 10; NewYTBE 73; NewYTBS 74; WhoAm 74, 76, 78, 80; WhoProB 73*

Murchison, Clint(on Williams, Jr.)
American. Football Executive
Founder, owner, Dallas Cowboys, 1960-84.
b. 1924 in Texas
d. Mar 30, 1987 in Dallas, Texas
Source: *BioIn 5, 6, 11, 12; NewYTBS 85; WhoAm 84*

Murchison, Clint(on Williams, Sr.)
American. Financier
His successful oil drillings in 1920s resulted in a $560 million empire and ownership of 115 companies.
b. Apr 11, 1895 in Tyler, Texas
d. Jun 20, 1969 in Athens, Texas

Source: *BioIn 1, 3, 4, 6, 8, 11, 12; NatCAB 58; ObitOF 79; WhAm 5*

Murchison, Kenneth MacKenzie
American. Architect
Designed several public buildings, particularly rail stations: Baltimore Union Station.
b. Sep 29, 1872 in New York, New York
d. Dec 16, 1938
Source: *BioIn 5; NatCAB 42; WhAm 1*

Murdoch, Iris
[Jean Iris Murdoch]
Irish. Author
Wrote 22 thought-provoking novels: *Black Prince,* 1973; *The Good Apprentice,* 1985.
b. Jul 15, 1919 in Dublin, Ireland
Source: *ArtclWW 2; Au&Wr 71; Benet 87, 96; BioIn 3, 4, 5, 7, 8, 10, 11, 12, 13; BlmGEL; BlmGWL; BlueB 76; BritWr S1; CamGEL; CamGLE; CasWL; CnDBLB 8; ConAu 8NR, 13R; ConDr 73, 77, 82, 88; ConLC 1, 2, 3, 4, 6, 8, 11, 15, 22, 31, 51; ConNov 72, 76, 82, 86, 91; ContDcW 89; ConTFT 15; CurBio 58, 80; CyWA 89; DcArts; DcIrL 96; DcLB 14; DcLEL 1940; EncBrWW; EncWL, 2, 3; FemiCLE; GrWomW; GrWrEL N; IntAu&W 76, 77, 89, 91; IntDcWB; IntWW 74, 75, 76, 77, 78, 79, 80, 81, 82, 83, 89, 91; InWom; LegTOT; LinLib L; LngCEL; LngCTC; MagSWL; MajTwCW; MakMC; McGEWB; ModBrL, S1, S2; ModIrL; ModWoWr; NewC; Novels; OxCPhil; PenC ENG; PlP&P; RAdv 1, 14, 13-1; REn; RfGEnL 91; ThTwC 87; TwCWr; WebE&AL; Who 74, 82, 83, 85, 88, 90, 92; WhoAm 80, 82, 84, 86, 88, 90, 92, 94, 95, 96, 97; WhoAmW 66, 68, 70, 72, 74; WhoTwCL; WhoWor 74, 76, 78, 80, 82, 84, 87, 91, 95, 96, 97; WorAl; WorAlBi; WorAu 1950; WrDr 76, 80, 82, 84, 86, 88, 90, 92, 94, 96; WrPh*

Murdoch, Rupert
[Keith Rupert Murdoch]
American. Publisher
Founder, News Corp. Ltd., a global empire; owned the *Star, London Times,* and Fox Television Network.
b. Mar 11, 1931 in Melbourne, Australia
Source: *ABCMeAm; AmDec 1980; BioIn 9, 10, 11, 12, 13; BlueB 76; CelR 90; ConAu 111; ConTFT 5; CurBio 77; EncAJ; EncTwCJ; EncWB; FacFETw; FarE&A 78, 79, 80, 81; IntAu&W 89, 91; IntMPA 86, 88, 92, 94, 96; IntWW 74, 75, 76, 77, 78, 79, 80, 81, 82, 83, 89, 91; LegTOT; News 88; NewYTBS 76, 90; Who 74, 82, 83, 85, 88, 90, 92; WhoAm 78, 80, 82, 84, 86, 88, 90, 92, 94, 95, 96, 97; WhoE 79, 81, 89; WhoFI 79, 81, 89, 92, 94, 96; WhoWor 74, 78, 80, 82, 84, 87, 89, 91, 93, 95, 96, 97; WorAlBi*

Muren, Dennis
American. Special Effects Technician
Worked on films *ET,* 1982; *The Abyss,* 1989; *Jurassic Park,* 1993.
b. Nov 1, 1946 in Glendale, California
Source: *ConTFT 13*

Murfree, Mary Noailles
[Charles Egbert Craddock]
American. Author
Wrote novels of southern history, TN mountains.
b. Jan 24, 1850 in Murfreesboro, Tennessee
d. Jul 31, 1922 in Murfreesboro, Tennessee
Source: *Alli SUP; AmAu; AmAu&B; AmBi; AmWom; AmWomWr; ApCAB, SUP; ArtclWW 2; BbD; Benet 87, 96; BenetAL 91; BibAL; BiD&SB; BiDSA; BioIn 1, 8, 9, 12, 13; BlmGWL; CarSB; Chambr 3; CnDAL; ConAu 122; DcAmAu; DcAmB; DcLEL; DcNAA; EncSoH; FemiCLE; FifSWrB; GrWrEL N; HarEnUS; InWom SUP; LibW; LinLib L; NatCAB 2; NotAW; OxCAmL 65, 83, 95; PenNWW A, B; REn; REnAL; RfGAmL 87, 94; ScF&FL 1; SouWr; TwCBDA; WhAm 1; WomNov; WomWWA 14*

Murillo, Bartolome Esteban
Spanish. Artist
Painter of sentimental Baroque religious scenes: *Vision of St. Anthony.*
b. Jan 1, 1618 in Seville, Spain
d. Apr 3, 1682 in Cadiz, Spain
Source: *AtlBL; McGDA; McGEWB; NewCol 75; OxCArt; REn; WorAl*

Murkowski, Frank Hughes
American. Politician
Rep. senator from AK, 1981—; senate amb., UN Gen. Assembly, 1994-95.
b. Mar 28, 1933 in Seattle, Washington
Source: *BiDrUSC 89; CngDr 81, 83, 85, 87; IntWW 81, 82, 83, 89, 91, 93; St&PR 75, 84; WhoAm 78, 80, 82, 84, 86, 88, 90, 92, 94, 95, 96, 97; WhoAmP 87; WhoFI 75, 77; WhoWest 82, 84, 87, 89, 92, 94, 96; WhoWor 82, 84, 87, 89, 91*

Murnau, Friedrich W
[Friedrich Wilhelm Plumpe]
German. Director
Made German, American films, 1920s; used novel camera techniques.
b. Dec 28, 1899 in Bielefeld, Germany
d. Mar 11, 1931 in California
Source: *BiDFilm; DcFM; FilmEn; HalFC 84; MovMk; OxCFilm*

Murphey, Michael Martin
American. Singer, Songwriter
Pop and country performer; songwriter for The Monkees in the late 1960s; solo hits include "Wildfire," 1975.
b. Mar 14, 1945 in Texas
Source: *BgBkCoM; ConMus 9; WhoAm 94, 95, 96, 97*

Murphy, Arthur Richard, Jr.
American. Publisher, Business Executive
Publisher, *Sports Illustrated,* 1959-65; pres., McCall Corp., 1965-67; publisher *Quest* mag., 1977-78.
b. Aug 26, 1915 in Boston, Massachusetts
d. Aug 29, 1987 in Jupiter, Florida
Source: *BioIn 15; ConAu 123; NewYTBS 87; WhAm 9; WhoAm 74, 76, 78, 80, 82, 84*

Murphy, Audie
American. Actor
Received 24 decorations to become WW II's most decorated soldier; most film roles in low-budget Westerns.
b. Jun 20, 1924 in Kingston, Texas
d. May 28, 1971 in Roanoke, Virginia
Source: *BiDFilm, 81, 94; BioIn 1, 3, 4, 7, 8, 9, 10, 12, 13; CmMov; DcAmMiB; DcArts; FacFETw; FilmEn; FilmgC; ForYSC; HalFC 80, 84, 88; IntDcF 1-3, 2-3; LegTOT; MotPP; MovMk; NewYTBE 71; WebAB 74, 79; WebAMB; WhoHol B; WhScrn 74, 77, 83; WorAl; WorEFlm*

Murphy, Ben(jamin Edward)
American. Actor
In TV mini-series "The Winds of War," 1983.
b. Mar 6, 1942 in Jonesboro, Arkansas
Source: *BioIn 13; ConTFT 3; IntMPA 84, 86, 88, 92, 94, 96; VarWW 85; WhoAm 74, 76, 78, 80, 82, 84, 86, 88, 90, 92, 94, 95, 96, 97; WhoEnt 92; WhoHol 92*

Murphy, Calvin Jerome
American. Basketball Player
Guard, 1970-83, mostly with Houston; led NBA in free-throw percentage, 1981, 1983.
b. May 9, 1948 in Norwalk, Connecticut
Source: *BiDAmSp BK; OfNBA 87; WhoAfA 96; WhoAm 82; WhoBbl 73; WhoBlA 92, 94*

Murphy, Charles
"Stretch"
American. Basketball Player
Collegiate center, 1928-30, known as one of sport's first good big men; Hall of Fame, 1960.
b. Apr 10, 1907 in Marion, Indiana
Source: *BiDAmSp BK; BioIn 9; WhoBbl 73*

Murphy, Dale Bryan
American. Baseball Player
Outfielder, Atlanta, 1976-90, Philadelphia, 1990-92; led NL in home runs, RBIs twice; MVP, 1982, 1983.
b. Mar 12, 1956 in Portland, Oregon
Source: *Ballpl 90; BaseReg 86, 87; BiDAmSp BB; BioIn 16; CelR 90; NewYTBS 82, 85; WhoAm 84, 86, 88, 90, 92; WhoSSW 86; WorAlBi*

Murphy, Eddie
[Edward Regan Murphy]
American. Comedian, Actor
Regular, "Saturday Night Live," 1980-84; films include *Beverly Hills Cop,* 1984 and its sequel *Beverly Hills Cop II,* 1987; won a Grammy, 1982, for comedy album, *Eddie Murphy.*
b. Apr 3, 1961 in Hempstead, New York
Source: *AfrAmAl 6; AfrAmBi 1; BiDFilm 94; BioIn 12, 13; BlksAmF; CelR 90; ConBlB 4; ConTFT 2, 6, 13; CurBio 83; DcArts; DcTwCCu 5; DrBlPA 90; EncAFC; HalFC 88; IntDcF 2-3; IntMPA 84, 86, 88, 92, 94, 96; LegTOT; MiSFD 9; NegAl 89; News 89-2; NewYTBS 81; QDrFCA 92; VarWW 85; WhoAfA 96; WhoAm 84, 86, 88, 90, 92, 94, 95, 96, 97; WhoBlA 85, 88, 90, 92, 94; WhoCom; WhoEnt 92; WhoHol 92; WhoTelC; WorAlBi*

Murphy, Frank
[William Francis Murphy]
American. Supreme Court Justice, Politician
Dem. governor of MI, 1936-38; attorney general, 1939-40; supreme court justice, 1940-49.
b. Apr 23, 1890 in Harbor Beach, Michigan
d. Jul 17, 1949 in Detroit, Michigan
Source: *BiDFedJ; BiDrGov 1789; BiDrUSE 71, 89; BioIn 1, 2, 3, 5, 6, 7, 8, 10, 11, 12, 15; CurBio 40, 49; DcAmB S4; DcCathB; EncAB-H 1974, 1996; FacFETw; McGEWB; NatCAB 37; NewCol 75; OxCSupC; PolPar; PolProf T; WebAB 74, 79; WebBD 83; WhAm 2*

Murphy, Franklin D(avid)
American. University Administrator
Chancellor, UCLA, 1960-68.
b. Jan 29, 1916
d. Jun 16, 1994 in Los Angeles, California
Source: *BioIn 2, 3, 5, 7, 8, 9; BlueB 76; CurBio 71, 94N; Dun&B 79, 86; IntWW 74, 75, 76, 77, 78, 79, 80, 81, 82, 83, 89, 91, 93; IntYB 78, 79, 80, 81, 82; St&PR 75, 84, 87; Ward 77; WhAm 11; WhoAm 74, 76, 78, 80, 82, 84, 86, 88, 90, 92, 94; WhoFI 74, 75, 77, 79, 81, 85; WhoGov 72; WhoWest 76, 84, 87, 89, 92, 94; WhoWor 74, 76, 78, 80, 82, 84, 87, 89, 91*

Murphy, George Lloyd
American. Actor, Politician
Tap-dancing star of numerous 1930-40s musicals; won special Oscar, 1950; senator from CA, 1964-70.
b. Jul 4, 1902 in New Haven, Connecticut
d. May 3, 1992 in Palm Beach, Florida
Source: *BiDrAC; BiDrUSC 89; BioIn 11; BlueB 76; ConAu 45; CurBio 65; FilmgC; IntMPA 82; IntWW 74, 75, 76, 77, 78, 79, 80, 81, 82, 83; MotPP; MovMk; VarWW 85; WhoAm 74, 76; WhoAmP 73, 75, 77, 79, 81; WorEFlm*

Murphy, Jack R
"Murph the Surf"
American. Criminal
Convicted murderer, jewel thief; stole Star of India sapphire from American Institute of Natural History, NYC, 1964; paroled, 1986.
b. May 26, 1937 in Los Angeles, California
Source: *BioNews 74*

Murphy, Jimmy
[James Edward Murphy]
American. Cartoonist
Created "Toots and Casper" syndicated comic strip.
b. Nov 20, 1891 in Chicago, Illinois
d. Mar 9, 1965 in Beverly Hills, California
Source: *ArtsAmW 2; BioIn 9; WhAm 4; WhoHol A; WorECom*

Murphy, John Michael
American. Politician
Dem. representative from NY, 1963-81; convicted in Abscam scandal, 1980.
b. Aug 3, 1926 in Staten Island, New York
Source: *AlmAP 80*

Murphy, Johnny (John Joseph)
[John Joseph Murphy]
"Fireman"; "Fordham Johnny"; "Grandma"
American. Baseball Player
Relief pitcher, 1932-43, 1946-47, mostly with Yankees; led AL in saves four times; helped organize ML Players Assn.
b. Jul 14, 1908 in New York, New York
d. Jan 14, 1970 in New York, New York
Source: *Ballpl 90; BiDAmSp Sup; BioIn 8, 13, 14; WhoProB 73*

Murphy, Larry
[Lawrence Thomas Murphy]
Canadian. Hockey Player
Defenseman, Los Angeles 1980-83; Washington, 1983-89; Minnesota, 1989-90; Pittsburgh, 1990-; set NHL record for most assists, 60, points, 76 by rookie defenseman; Max Kaminsky trophy, 1979-80.
b. Mar 8, 1961 in Scarborough, Ontario, Canada
Source: *HocReg 86, 87; WhoAm 94, 95, 96, 97*

Murphy, Patrick Vincent
American. Business Executive
NY police commissioner, 1970-73; pres. of Police Foundation, 1973-85.
b. May 12, 1920 in New York, New York
Source: *BioIn 9, 11, 13; ConAu 105; CurBio 72; NewYTBE 70, 71; NewYTBS 82; WhoAm 74, 76, 78, 80, 82, 84, 86, 92, 95, 96, 97*

Murphy, Reg
[John Reginald Murphy]
American. Journalist
Publisher of *Baltimore Sun,* 1981-90; exec. v.p., Nat. Geographic Soc., 1993—.
b. Jan 7, 1934 in Hoschton, Georgia
Source: *ConAu 33R; EncTwCJ; WhoAm 74, 76, 78, 80, 82, 84, 86, 94, 95, 96, 97; WhoSSW 73; WhoWest 82*

Murphy, Robert Daniel
American. Statesman
US ambassador to Belgium, 1949.
b. Oct 28, 1894 in Milwaukee, Wisconsin
d. Jun 9, 1978 in New York, New York
Source: *BioIn 1, 2, 3, 5, 6, 8, 10, 11, 12; ConAu P-1; CurBio 43, 58; DcAmB S10; DcAmDH 80, 89; EncAI&E; HisEWW; IntWW 74, 75, 76; NatCAB 60; St&PR 75; WhAm 7; Who 74; WhoAm 74, 76, 78; WhoWor 74*

Murphy, Rosemary
American. Actor
Won Emmy for "Eleanor and Franklin," 1976; three-time Tony nominee.
b. Jan 13, 1927 in Munich, Germany
Source: *BiE&WWA; ConTFT 7; FilmgC; ForWC 70; HalFC 84; NotNAT; WhoAm 86; WhoAmW 77; WhoHol 92, A; WhoThe 72, 77, 81*

Murphy, Thomas Aquinas
American. Auto Executive
Chm. of GM, 1974-80.
b. Dec 10, 1915 in Hornell, New York
Source: *BioIn 11, 12; BusPN; EncABHB 5; IntWW 83, 89, 91, 93; St&PR 84, 87; Ward 77; Who 85; WhoAm 76, 78, 80, 82, 84, 86, 88, 90, 92, 94, 95, 96, 97; WhoFI 74, 79, 81; WhoMW 80, 82, 84*

Murphy, Thomas F(rancis)
American. Judge, Lawyer, Police Chief
Police commissioner, New York, 1950-51; chief prosecutor in Alger Hiss trials, 1949-50.
b. Dec 3, 1905
d. Oct 26, 1995 in Salisbury, Connecticut
Source: *BiDFedJ; BioIn 2; CurBio 96N; WhoAm 74, 76, 78, 80, 82, 84, 86, 88, 90, 92, 94, 96; WhoAmL 90, 92; WhoE 93; WhoGov 72, 75, 77*

Murphy, Turk
[Melvin Murphy]
American. Jazz Musician, Bandleader
Traditional jazz trombonist, noted for reviving earlier jazz, ragtime hits.
b. Dec 16, 1915 in Palermo, California
d. May 30, 1987 in San Francisco, California
Source: *AllMusG; AnObit 1987; Baker 84, 92; BioIn 15; CmpEPM; EncJzS; NewAmDM; NewGrDA 86; NewGrDJ 88, 94; OxCPMus; PenEncP; WhAm 9; WhoAm 74*

Murphy, W(illiam) B(everly)
American. Business Executive
Pres., Campbell Soup Co., 1953-72.
b. Jun 17, 1907
d. May 29, 1994 in Bryn Mawr, Pennsylvania
Source: *BioIn 3, 4, 5, 20; CurBio 94N; IntWW 74, 75, 76, 77, 78, 79, 80, 81, 82, 83, 89, 91; WhAm 11; WhoAm 74, 76, 78, 80, 82, 84, 86, 88, 90, 92, 94; WhoE 74; WhoFI 74; WhoWor 74, 76, 78, 80, 82, 84, 87, 89*

Murphy, Warren B
American. Author, Screenwriter
Thrillers include co-authored "The Destroyer" series, 1971—.
b. Sep 13, 1933 in Jersey City, New Jersey
Source: *ConAu 13NR; TwCCr&M 85*

Murphy, William Parry
American. Physician
Shared Nobel Prize in medicine, 1934, with George Minot, George Whipple.
b. Feb 6, 1892 in Stoughton, Wisconsin
d. Oct 9, 1987
Source: *AmMWSc 73P, 82; AsBiEn; BiESc; BioIn 1, 3, 6; BlueB 76; InSci; IntWW 74, 75, 76, 77, 78, 79, 80, 81, 82, 83; LarDcSc; LinLib S; WebAB 74, 79; WhAm 9; Who 74, 82, 83, 85, 88; WhoAm 74, 76, 78, 80, 82, 84, 86; WhoE 79, 81, 83, 85, 86; WhoNob, 90, 95; WhoWor 82, 84, 87*

Murray, Albert L(ee)
American. Writer
Wrote race relations book *The Omni-Americans,* 1970.
b. May 12, 1916 in Nokomis, Alabama
Source: *BioIn 9; ConAu 26NR, 49; ConLC 73; CurBio 94; WhoAm 74*

Murray, Allen Edward
American. Business Executive
Chairman of Mobil Corp., 1986—.
b. Mar 5, 1929 in New York, New York
Source: *BioIn 13; IntWW 89, 91, 93; St&PR 84, 87, 91, 93; WhoAm 78, 80, 82, 84, 86, 88, 90, 92, 94, 95, 96, 97; WhoE 86, 89, 91; WhoFI 83, 85, 87, 89, 92, 94; WhoSSW 93; WhoWor 84, 87, 89, 91*

Murray, Anne
[Morna Anne]
Canadian. Singer
First gold record "Snowbird," 1970; won three Grammys including one for "You Needed Me," 1978.
b. Jun 20, 1945 in Springhill, Nova Scotia, Canada
Source: *Baker 84; BioIn 10, 11, 12, 13; BkPepl; CanWW 31, 70, 79, 80, 81, 83, 89; CelR 90; ConMus 4; CurBio 82; EncFCWM 83; InWom SUP; LegTOT; VarWW 85; WhoAm 80, 82, 84, 86, 88, 90, 92, 94, 95, 96, 97; WhoAmW 81, 83, 85, 87, 89, 91, 93, 95, 97; WhoEmL 87; WhoEnt 92; WorAlBi*

Murray, Arthur
[Arthur Murray Teichman]
American. Dancer
Began Arthur Murray School of Dancing; over 450 schools throughout US.
b. Apr 4, 1895 in New York, New York
d. Mar 3, 1991 in Honolulu, Hawaii
Source: *AnObit 1991; BiDD; BioIn 1, 3, 5, 6, 9, 12, 13, 17, 18; CurBio 43, 91N; LegTOT; News 91, 91-3; NewYTBS 80, 91; WhAm 10; What 3; WhoAm 74, 76, 78, 80, 82, 84, 86, 88, 90; WorAl; WorAlBi*

Murray, Bill
American. Actor, Comedian
Cast member on "Saturday Night Live," 1977-80; films include two *Ghostbusters* films, 1984, 1989; *Groundhog Day,* 1993.
b. Sep 21, 1950 in Evanston, Illinois
Source: *BiDFilm 94; CelR 90; ConTFT 1, 6, 13; CurBio 85; EncAFC; HalFC 88; HolBB; IntMPA 84, 86, 88, 92, 94, 96; IntWW 91, 93; LegTOT; MiSFD 9; QDrFCA 92; VarWW 85; WhoAm 82, 84, 86, 88, 90, 92, 94, 95, 96, 97; WhoCom; WhoEnt 92; WhoHol 92*

Murray, Charles Alan
American. Sociologist, Author
Wrote *Losing Ground,* 1984, influential work of social policy, poverty in America.
b. Jan 8, 1943 in Newton, Iowa
Source: *CurBio 86*

Murray, Don(ald Patrick)
American. Actor
Oscar nominee for *Bus Stop,* 1956; played on TV's "Knot's Landing."
b. Jul 31, 1929 in Hollywood, California
Source: *BiDFilm, 81; BiE&WWA; BioIn 4, 5; ConTFT 1, 15; FilmEn; FilmgC; ForYSC; HalFC 80, 84, 88; IntMPA 75, 76, 77, 78, 79, 80, 81, 82, 84, 86, 88, 92, 94, 96; LegTOT; MiSFD 9; MotPP; MovMk; VarWW 85; WhoAm 74, 76, 78, 80, 82, 84, 86, 88, 90, 92; WhoHol 92, A; WhoWor 80; WorAl; WorAlBi; WorEFlm*

Murray, Eddie Clarence
American. Baseball Player
First baseman, Orioles, 1977-88, Dodgers, 1989-91, NY Mets, 1991-93; Cleveland Indians, 1993—; won three Gold Glove Awards; had 733 RBIs in the 1980s.
b. Feb 24, 1956 in Los Angeles, California
Source: *BaseReg 86, 87; BiDAmSp BB; WhoAfA 96; WhoAm 90, 92, 94, 95, 96, 97; WhoBlA 85, 88, 90, 92, 94; WhoE 85, 86, 89; WhoMW 96*

Murray, Elizabeth
American. Artist
Artist who combines several kinds of twentieth-century art, namely, cubism, fauvism, surrealism.
b. 1940 in Chicago, Illinois
Source: *AmArt; BiDWomA; BioIn 13; ConArt 83, 89, 96; CurBio 95; DcCAA 88, 94; NewYTBS 91; NorAmWA; PrintW 83, 85; WhoAm 82, 84, 86, 88, 90, 92, 94, 95, 96; WhoAmA 76, 78, 80, 82, 84, 86, 89, 91, 93; WorArt 1980*

Murray, Gilbert
[George Gilbert Aime Murray]
English. Author, Translator
Among most influential translators of Greek drama, wrote on public affairs.
b. Jan 2, 1866 in Sydney, Australia
d. May 20, 1957 in London, England
Source: *Benet 87; BiDInt; BiDPara; BioIn 1, 2, 3, 4, 5, 8, 9, 12, 13, 14, 19; CasWL; ChhPo, S1, S2, S3; ConAu 110; DcCathB; DcEnA, A; DcLB 10; DcLEL; DcNaB 1951; EncO&P 1, 2, 3; EncPaPR 91; EvLB; LinLib L, S; LngCTC; ModBrL; NewC; NewCBEL; ObitOF 79; ObitT 1951; OxCEng 67, 85; PenC ENG; REn; TwCA, SUP; WhAm 3; WhE&EA; WhLit; WhThe*

Murray, James Augustus Henry, Sir
Scottish. Lexicographer
First editor of *Oxford English Dictionary,* from 1879.
b. Feb 7, 1837 in Hawick, Scotland
d. Jul 26, 1915 in Oxford, England
Source: *Alli SUP; BiD&SB; BioIn 4, 10, 11, 12, 14, 20; BritAu 19; Chambr 3; DcEnA A; DcLEL; DcNaB 1912; EvLB; GrBr; LinLib L, S; NewC; NewCBEL; NewCol 75; OxCEng 67, 85, 95*

Murray, Jan
[Murray Janofsky]
American. Comedian
Vaudeville, nightclub entertainer; films include *The Busybody,* 1967.
b. Oct 4, 1917 in New York, New York
Source: *BioIn 2, 3; EncAFC; ForYSC; IntMPA 80, 84, 86, 88, 92, 94, 96; JoeFr; LegTOT; RadStar; VarWW 85; WhoAm 82; WhoCom; WhoHol 92, A; WorAl*

Murray, Jim
American. Journalist
Sports Illustrated cofounder, writer, 1954-61.
b. Dec 29, 1919 in Hartford, Connecticut
Source: *BioIn 10, 11; ConAu 65; IntAu&W 76*

Murray, John
American. Religious Leader
Regarded as father of American Universalism; established first Universalist church in US, 1779.
b. Dec 10, 1741 in Alton, England
d. Sep 3, 1815 in Boston, Massachusetts
Source: *Alli; AmAu&B; AmBi; ApCAB; BioIn 1, 3, 5, 14; DcAmB; DcNAA; Drake; EncCRAm; LuthC 75; NatCAB 13; OxCAmL 65, 83, 95; TwCBDA; WhAm HS; WhAmRev*

Murray, John, Sir
Canadian. Oceanographer
Co-founded the field of oceanography; organized the underwater *Challenger* Expedition, 1872-76.
b. Mar 3, 1841 in Cobourg, Ontario, Canada
d. Mar 16, 1914 in Kirkliston, Scotland
Source: *BiESc; BioIn 6; BritAu 19; DcNaB 1912; DcScB; InSci; LarDcSc; MacDCB 78; OxCShps; WhLit*

Murray, Joseph
American. Physician
Won Nobel Prize in medicine, 1990, for work in transplanting human organs and bone marrow.
b. Apr 1, 1919 in Milford, Massachusetts
Source: *AmMWSc 92; IntWW 91; WhoAm 90; WhoNob 90*

Murray, Kathryn Hazel
[Mrs. Arthur Murray]
American. Dancer
Was mistress of ceremonies for TV's "Arthur Murray Party," 1950-60.
b. Sep 15, 1906 in Jersey City, New Jersey
Source: *WhoAm 74, 76, 78, 80, 82, 84, 86, 88, 92, 94, 95; WhoAmW 74; WhoEnt 92*

Murray, Ken
[Don Court]
American. Actor
Won special Oscar for fantasy film *Bill and Coo,* 1947, which he starred in, produced.
b. Jul 14, 1903 in New York, New York
d. Oct 12, 1988 in Burbank, California
Source: *BioIn 2, 5, 10, 16; ConAu 126; EncAFC; EncVaud; FilmEn; FilmgC; ForYSC; HalFC 80, 84, 88; IntMPA 84, 86, 88; LegTOT; LesBEnT; NewYTBS 88; NotNAT A; RadStar; SaTiSS; VarWW 85; WhoHol A; WorAl*

Murray, Lenda
American. Bodybuilder
Winner of Ms. Olympia competition, 1990, 1991, 1992, 1993, 1994.
b. c. 1962 in Detroit, Michigan
Source: *ConBlB 10*

Murray, Mae
[Marie Koenig]
American. Dancer, Actor
Appeared in dozens of films, 1916-31: *The Merry Widow,* 1925; subject of biography, *The Self-Enchanted,* 1965.
b. Apr 10, 1889 in Portsmouth, Virginia
d. Mar 23, 1965 in Woodland Hills, California
Source: *BiDD; BioIn 5, 6, 7, 9, 10, 19; CmpEPM; DcAmB S7; Film 1, 2; FilmgC; HalFC 80, 84, 88; InWom SUP; LegTOT; MotPP; MovMk; NotNAT B; OxCFilm; ThFT; TwYS; WhoHol B; WhScrn 74, 77*

Murray, Margaret Alice
English. Archaeologist
First woman Egyptologist; published over 80 books on ancient Egypt.
b. Jul 13, 1863 in Calcutta, India
d. Nov 13, 1963 in London, England
Source: *BioIn 6, 7, 14; ConAu 5R; DcLEL; DcNaB 1961; EncWW; GrBr; IntDcAn; InWom, SUP; WhE&EA; WhoLA*

Murray, Patty
American. Politician
Dem. senator, WA, 1993—.
b. Oct 11, 1950 in Seattle, Washington
Source: *AlmAP 96; BioIn 18, 19, 20; CngDr 93, 95; CurBio 94; IntWW 93; WhoAm 94, 95, 96, 97; WhoAmP 91; WhoAmW 91, 93, 95, 97; WhoWest 94, 96*

Murray, Pauli
American. Lawyer, Civil Rights Leader
One of the founders of NOW, 1966; first African-American to receive a Doctor of Judicial Science degree from Yale.
b. Nov 20, 1910 in Baltimore, Maryland
d. Jul 1, 1985 in Pittsburgh, Pennsylvania
Source: *AmWomWr; AmWomWr; BioIn 9, 11, 12, 14, 15, 16, 17, 18, 20, 21; BlkAWP; BlkWAm; BlkWr 1; BlkWrNE; ConAu 116, 125; DcLB 41; Ebony 1; FemiCLE; HarlReB; InB&W 80, 85; InWom SUP; NewYTBS 74, 85, 87; PeoHis; SchCGBL; SelBAAf; SelBAAu; WhAm 8; WhoAm 76, 78, 82, 84; WhoAmW 58, 61, 64, 66, 77; WhoBlA 75, 77, 80, 85; WomPubS 1925*

Murray, Philip
American. Labor Union Official
Pres., United Steelworkers of America, 1942-52.
b. May 25, 1886 in Lanarkshire, Scotland
d. Oct 9, 1952 in San Francisco, California
Source: *AmDec 1940; AmSocL; BiDAmL; BiDAmLL; BioIn 1, 2, 3, 5, 6, 7, 8, 9, 11, 14, 15, 19; CurBio 41, 49, 52; DcAmB S5; DcCathB; EncAB-H 1974, 1996; EncABHB 9; EncMcCE; McGEWB; MorMA; ObitT 1951; OxCAmH; PolProf T; WebAB 74, 79; WhAm 3; WorAl; WorAlBi*

Murray, Troy
Canadian. Hockey Player
Center, Chicago, 1981—; won Selke Trophy, 1986.
b. Jul 31, 1962 in Winnipeg, Manitoba, Canada
Source: *HocReg 87*

Murrow, Edward R
[Edward Egbert Roscoe Murrow]
American. Broadcast Journalist
TV moderator, "See It Now," 1951-58; director, US Information Agency, 1961-64.
b. Apr 25, 1908 in Greensboro, North Carolina
d. Apr 27, 1965 in Pawling, New York
Source: *ConAu 89, 103; CurBio 42, 53, 65; EncAB-H 1974; REnAL; WebAB 74; WhAm 4; WhoHol A; WhScrn 74, 77*

Murry, John Middleton
English. Author
Editor *The Adelphi,* 1923-48; wrote *Pencillings,* 1923; wed to Katherine Mansfield.
b. Aug 6, 1889 in London, England
d. May 13, 1957 in Bury Saint Edmunds, England
Source: *Benet 87, 96; BiDMoPL; BioIn 1, 2, 4, 5, 6, 7, 8, 11, 12, 13, 14, 15, 16, 17, 21; BlmGEL; CamGLE; CasWL; ChhPo, S1; ConAu 118; DcArts; DcLB 149; DcLEL; DcNaB 1951; EvLB; FacFETw; GrBr; LngCEL; LngCTC; MakMC; ModBrL; NewC; NewCBEL; ObitT 1951; OxCEng 67, 85, 95; PenC ENG; REn; TwCA, SUP; TwCLC 6, 16; TwCWr; WebE&AL; WhAm 3; WhE&EA; WhLit; WhoLA; WhoTwCL*

Murtha, John Patrick
American. Politician
Dem. rep. from PA, 1974—; first Vietnam veteran elected to Congress; named, not indicted, in Abscam scandal.
b. Jun 17, 1932 in New Martinsville, West Virginia
Source: *AlmAP 88*

Musburger, Brent Woody
American. Sportscaster
With CBS Sports, 1974-90; hosted "NFL Today."
b. May 26, 1939 in Portland, Oregon
Source: *BiDAmSp Sup; VarWW 85; WhoAm 76, 78, 80, 82, 84, 86, 88, 90, 92, 94, 95, 96, 97*

Muses, Charles Arthur
American. Mathematician, Author
Parapsychologist, editor, *Journal for Study of Consciousness.*
b. Apr 28, 1919 in New Jersey
Source: *AmMWSc 73P, 76P; ConAu 115, 135; WrDr 94*

Museveni, Yoweri Kaguta
Ugandan. Political Leader
Succeeded Milton Obote as president of Uganda, 1986—; cofounded the Front for Nat. Salvation in the early 1970s.
b. 1944 in Ntungamo, Uganda
Source: *IntWW 89, 91, 93; NewYTBS 86; WhoAfr; WhoWor 87, 89, 91, 93, 95, 96, 97*

Musgrave, Thea
Scottish. Composer
Operas include *The Decision,* 1967; *Mary, Queen of Scots,* 1977.
b. May 27, 1928 in Edinburgh, Scotland
Source: *Baker 78, 84, 92; BioIn 10, 11, 12; BlueB 76; BriBkM 80; CmOp; CompSN SUP; ConAmC 76, 82; ConCom 92; ContDcW 89; CpmDNM 79, 80; CurBio 78; DcArts; DcCM;*

DcCom&M 79; EncWB; IntDcWB; IntWW 81, 82, 83, 89, 91, 93; IntWWM 80, 90; InWom SUP; MetOEnc; MusMk; NewAmDM; NewGrDA 86; NewGrDM 80; NewGrDO; NewOxM; OxCMus; OxDcOp; PenDiMP A; Who 74, 82, 83, 85, 88, 90, 92, 94; WhoAm 86, 94, 95, 96, 97; WhoAmM 83; WhoAmW 85, 87, 95, 97; WhoMus 72; WhoWor 74, 76, 78, 84, 95, 96, 97; WomCom

Musial, Joe
American. Cartoonist
Drew "Katzenjammer Kids," 1952-77; ghost artist for major comic strips; introduced comics for educational use.
b. 1905?
d. Jun 6, 1977 in Manhasset, New York
Source: *BioIn 11, 12; ConAu 69; EncACom; NatCAB 60*

Musial, Stan(ley Frank)
"Stan the Man"
American. Baseball Player
Outfielder-infielder, St. Louis, 1941-44, 1946-63; won NL batting title five times; had 3,630 lifetime hits; Hall of Fame, 1969.
b. Nov 21, 1920 in Donora, Pennsylvania
Source: *Ballpl 90; BiDAmSp BB; BioIn 1, 2, 3, 4, 5, 6, 7, 8, 9, 10, 13, 14, 15, 17, 18, 20; ConAu 93; CurBio 48; FacFETw; LegTOT; WebAB 74, 79; WhoAm 74, 76, 78, 80, 82, 84, 86, 88; WhoMW 88, 90; WhoProB 73; WorAl; WorAlBi*

Music, Antonio Zoran
Italian. Artist
Multifaceted painter; works reflect Dalmatian background; won Prix de Paris, 1951.
b. 1909 in Gorizia, Italy
Source: *BioIn 4; McGDA*

Muske, Carol (Anne)
[Carol Muske-Dukes]
American. Poet
Published poetry collections *Camouflage*, 1975; *Red Trousseau*, 1993.
b. Dec 17, 1945 in Saint Paul, Minnesota
Source: *BioIn 13, 14; ConAu 32NR, 65; ConLC 90; DrAPF 80; IntAu&W 86; IntWWP 77; ModAWP; OxCTwCP; WhoUSWr 88; WhoWrEP 89, 92, 95*

Muskie, Edmund S(ixtus)
American. Politician
Secretary of State under Carter, 1980-81; Dem. senator from ME, 1959-80; governor of ME, 1955-59.
b. Mar 28, 1914 in Rumford, Maine
d. Mar 26, 1996 in Washington, District of Columbia
Source: *AmCath 80; AmPolLe; BiDrAC; BiDrUSC 89; BiDrUSE 89; BioIn 3, 4, 5, 6, 8, 9, 10, 11, 12; CngDr 74; ConAu 2NR, 151; CurBio 55, 68, 96N; DcAmDH 89; EncWB; FacFETw; IntWW 74, 75, 76, 77, 78, 79, 80, 81, 82, 83, 89, 91, 93; IntYB 78, 79, 80, 81, 82; LinLib S; NewYTBE 70, 72; NewYTBS 80; PresAR; WhAm 11; Who 74, 82, 83, 85, 88, 90, 92, 94; WhoAm 74, 76, 78, 80, 82, 84, 86, 88, 90, 92, 94, 95, 96; WhoAmL 79; WhoAmP 73, 75, 77, 79, 81, 83, 85, 87, 89, 91, 93, 95; WhoE 74, 75, 77, 79, 81, 83, 85, 86, 91, 93, 95; WhoGov 72, 75, 77; WhoWor 74, 78, 80, 82, 84; WorAl*

Musset, Alfred de
[Louis Charles Alfred de Musset]
French. Writer
Wrote lyric verse *Les Nuites*, 1835-37; play *Andrea del Sarto*, 1833; had love affair with George Sand, 1833-39.
b. Dec 11, 1810 in Paris, France
d. May 2, 1857 in Paris, France
Source: *AtlBL; Benet 87, 96; BioIn 1, 4, 5, 7, 8, 9, 13; CamGWoT; CelCen; CnThe; CyWA 58; DcArts; DcBiPP; DcEuL; Dis&D; EncWT; Ent; EuAu; EuWr 6; GrFLW; GuFrLit 1; LegTOT; LinLib L, S; McGEWB; McGEWD 72, 84; NewC; NewCBEL; NewEOp 71; NewGrDM 80; NinCLC 7; NotNAT B; OxCEng 67, 85, 95; OxCFr; OxCThe 67, 83; PenC EUR; RComWL; REn; REnWD; ScF&FL 1; WhDW; WorAl; WorAlBi*

Musso, George Francis
"Moose"
American. Football Player
Tackle-guard, Chicago, 1933-44; Hall of Fame, 1982.
b. 1911 in Edwardsville, Illinois
Source: *BioIn 6; WhoFtbl 74*

Musso, Vido
American. Jazz Musician
Played tenor sax, clarinet with Big Bands, 1930s-40s.
b. Jan 17, 1913 in Carrini, Sicily, Italy
d. Jan 9, 1982 in Los Angeles, California
Source: *BiDJaz; BioIn 13; CmpEPM; WhoJazz 72*

Mussolini, Benito Amilcare Andrea
"Il Duce"
Italian. Political Leader
Founded Italian Fascist Party, 1919; prime minister, 1922-43; allied with Hitler, 1939.
b. Jul 29, 1883 in Predappio, Italy
d. Apr 28, 1945 in Milan, Italy
Source: *BiDExR; CasWL; CurBio 42, 45; EvEuW; REn; WhAm 4; WhoLA*

Mussolini, Rachele Guidi
Italian.
Widow of Benito Mussolini; wrote autobiography *My Life with Mussolini.*
b. 1890 in Forli, Italy
d. Oct 30, 1979 in Forli, Italy
Source: *BioIn 7, 10; ConAu 111; NewYTBS 79*

Mussorgsky, Modest Petrovich
Russian. Composer
Known for opera *Boris Godunov*, based on Pushkin's play.
b. Mar 21, 1839 in Karevo, Russia
d. Mar 28, 1881 in Saint Petersburg, Russia
Source: *AtlBL; Baker 92; BioIn 14, 15, 16, 17, 20; DcArts; McGEWB; NewAmDM; REn; WhDW*

Muster, Thomas
Austrian. Tennis Player
Won French Open, 1995.
b. Oct 2, 1967 in Leibnitz, Austria

Mutesa I
Ugandan. Ruler
Ruled Buganda, now Uganda, c. 1857-84; expanded trade, let Europeans into country.
b. 1838?
d. Oct 1884 in Nabulagala, Buganda
Source: *McGEWB; NewCol 75*

Mutesa II
[Sir Edward Frederick William Mutesa]
"King Freddie"
English. Ruler
King, Buganda, 1939-53, 1955-66; went into exile when deposed by Uganda's Pres. Obote.
b. Nov 19, 1924
d. Nov 21, 1969 in London, England
Source: *DcAfHiB 86*

Muti, Riccardo
Italian. Conductor
Music director, Philadelphia Orchestra, 1980-92.
b. Jul 28, 1941 in Naples, Italy
Source: *Baker 78, 84, 92; BioIn 9, 11, 12, 13; BriBkM 80; CelR 90; CurBio 80; DcArts; IntDcOp; IntWW 81, 82, 83, 89, 91, 93; IntWWM 80, 85, 90; LegTOT; MetOEnc; MusSN; NewAmDM; NewGrDA 86; NewGrDM 80; NewGrDO; OxDcOp; PenDiMP; Who 74, 82, 83, 85, 88, 90, 92, 94; WhoAm 82, 84, 86, 88, 90, 92, 94, 95, 96, 97; WhoAmM 83; WhoE 89, 91, 93, 95; WhoEnt 92; WhoOp 76; WhoWor 87, 89, 91, 93, 95; WorAlBi*

Mutombo, Dikembe
Zairean. Basketball Player
Center, Denver Nuggets, 1991—.
b. Jun 25, 1966 in Kinshasa, Zaire
Source: *BioIn 20, 21; ConBlB 7; WhoAfA 96; WhoAm 94, 95, 96, 97; WhoBlA 94; WhoWest 94, 96; WhoWor 95, 96*

Mutsuhito
Japanese. Ruler
Reign, 1867-1912, marked end of feudalism, birth of modern Japan.
b. Nov 3, 1852 in Kyoto, Japan
d. Jul 30, 1912 in Tokyo, Japan
Source: *DcBiPP; HisWorL; LegTOT; LinLib S; WhDW; WorAl; WorAlBi*

Mutter, Anne-Sophie
German. Musician
Child prodigy violinist; soloist performing with orchestras worldwide,

known for technical command, accurate intonation, and rich sound; won classical music Bambi Award, 1987.
b. Jun 29, 1963 in Rheinfelden, Germany (West)
Source: *Baker 84, 92; BioIn 15, 16, 17; CurBio 90; IntWW 89, 91, 93; IntWWM 90; News 90, 90-3; PenDiMP*

Muybridge, Eadweard
[Edward James Muggeridge]
English. Photographer
Took first pictures of objects in rapid motion; proved that horse is completely off ground during part of stride, circa 1877.
b. Apr 9, 1830 in Kingston, England
d. May 8, 1904 in Kingston, England
Source: *AmBi; BenetAL 91; BioIn 7, 9, 10, 12, 13, 14, 15; BriEAA; CmCal; DcAmArt; DcAmB; DcArts; DcFM; DcNAA; DcNaB S2; FilmEn; GayN; HalFC 84, 88; ICPEnP; InSci; LarDcSc; LegTOT; MacBEP; NatCAB 19; OxCAmL 65, 83, 95; OxCFilm; OxDcArt; PeoHis; REnAL; WebAB 74, 79; WhAmArt 85; WhAm HS; WhDW; WorAlBi; WorEFlm*

Muzio, Claudia
Italian. Opera Singer
Soprano with NY Met., 1916-22; Chicago Opera until 1932.
b. Feb 7, 1889 in Pavia, Italy
d. May 24, 1936 in Rome, Italy
Source: *Baker 78, 84, 92; BioIn 12, 14, 15, 18, 20; CmOp; IntDcOp; InWom SUP; MetOEnc; MusSN; NewAmDM; NewEOp 71; NewGrDA 86; NewGrDM 80; NewGrDO; OxDcOp; PenDiMP; WhAm 1*

Muzorewa, Abel Tendekai
Rhodesian. Political Leader, Clergy
Pres., African Nat. Council, 1971-85; first black prime minister of Zimbabwe, Rhodesia, Jun-Dec, 1979.
b. Apr 14, 1925 in Umtali, Rhodesia
Source: *AfSS 78, 79; BioIn 14, 21; CurBio 79; InB&W 85; NewYTBS 79; WhoWor 84, 87*

Mwinyi, Ali Hassan
Tanzanian. Political Leader
Succeeded Julius Nyerere to become second pres., Tanzania, 1985-95.
b. May 8, 1925 in Dar es Salaam, Tanzania
Source: *BioIn 16; ConBlB 1; CurBio 95; DcCPSAf; IntWW 89, 91, 93; Who 92; WhoAfr; WhoWor 84, 87, 89, 91, 93, 95, 96*

Mydans, Carl M
American. Photographer
On staff of *Life,* 1936-72; author, *China: A Visual Adventure,* 1979.
b. May 20, 1907 in Boston, Massachusetts
Source: *ConAu 97; ConPhot 82; CurBio 45; LinLib L; MacBEP; WhoAm 74; WhoE 74*

Myer, Buddy
[Charles Solomon Myer]
American. Baseball Player
Second baseman, 1925-41; led AL in batting, 1935; had lifetime .303 batting average.
b. Mar 16, 1904 in Ellisville, Mississippi
d. Oct 31, 1974 in Baton Rouge, Louisiana
Source: *Ballpl 90; BiDAmSp BB; BioIn 1, 4, 5, 10, 15; WhoProB 73*

Myers, Dee Dee
[Margaret Jane Myers; Mrs. Todd Purdum]
American. Government Official
White House press secretary, 1993-94.
b. Sep 1, 1961 in Quonset Point, Rhode Island
Source: *CurBio 94; WhoAm 94, 95, 96, 97; WomFir*

Myers, Garry Cleveland
American. Psychologist
Expert on child care; wrote *Your Child and You,* 1969.
b. Jul 15, 1884 in Sylvan, Pennsylvania
d. Jul 19, 1971
Source: *BiDAmEd; ConAu P-2; OhA&B; WhAm 5; WhE&EA; WhNAA*

Myers, Jerome
American. Artist
Depicted NYC street scenes; an initiator of 1913 Armory Show.
b. Mar 20, 1867 in Petersburg, Virginia
d. Jun 19, 1940 in New York, New York
Source: *AmAu&B; BioIn 4, 6, 8, 11; BriEAA; CurBio 40; DcAmArt; DcAmB S2; DcNAA; GrAmP; McGDA; NatCAB 46; PhDcTCA 77; WhAm 1; WhAmArt 85*

Myers, Mike
Canadian. Comedian, Actor
Creator of character Wayne Campbell in skits on "Saturday Night Live;" evolved into hit movie, *Wayne's World,* 1992; starred in *Austin Powers,* 1997.
b. 1964 in Scarborough, Ontario, Canada
Source: *ConTFT 11; News 92, 92-3*

Myers, Norman
English. Author, Environmentalist
Environmental consultant who has carried out projects in more than 90 countries over 20 yrs. for such clients as the UN, the World Bank, and the World Wildlife Fund.
b. Aug 24, 1934 in Whitewell, England
Source: *ConAu 1NR, 20NR, 49; CurBio 93; EnvEnDr; WhoWor 89, 95, 96, 97*

Myers, Russell
American. Cartoonist
Created comic strip "Broom Hilda," 1970—; also created "Herb and Jamal."
b. Oct 9, 1938 in Pittsburg, Kansas
Source: *EncACom; LegTOT; Ward 77; WhoAm 86, 90; WorECom*

Myers, Walter Dean
American. Author
Wrote *Where Does the Day Go?,* 1969.
b. Aug 12, 1937 in Martinsburg, West Virginia
Source: *Au&Arts 4; AuBYP 2S, 3; BioIn 13, 14, 15, 16, 17, 18, 19, 20; BlkAuII, 92; BlkAWP; BlkLC; BlkWr 1, 2; ChlBkCr; ChlLR 4, 16, 35; ConAu 20NR, 33R, 42NR; ConBlB 8; ConLC 35; DcAmChF 1960, 1985; DcLB 33; FifBJA; LivgBAA; MajAI; OnHuMoP; ScF&FL 92; SchCGBL; SelBAAf; SelBAAu; SmATA 2AS, 27, 41, 71; TwCChW 89; TwCYAW; WhoAfA 96; WhoAm 76, 95, 96, 97; WhoBlA 90, 92, 94; WrDr 90, 92, 94, 96*

Myerson, Bess
American. Government Official, Beauty Contest Winner
First Jewish Miss America, 1945; commissioner of cultural affairs, NYC, 1982-87.
b. Jul 16, 1924 in New York, New York
Source: *AmWomM; BioAmW; BioIn 3, 8, 9, 10, 11, 12; BioNews 74; CelR; ConAu 108; ContDcW 89; IntMPA 77, 80, 82; InWom SUP; LegTOT; NewYTBE 72; WhoAm 76, 78, 80, 82, 84, 86; WhoAmJ 80; WhoAmW 68, 70, 72, 74, 75, 79, 83; WhoWorJ 78; WorAl*

Myles, Alannah
Canadian. Singer, Songwriter
Had solo No. 1 hit "Black Velvet," 1989; debut album, *Alannah Myles,* went quadruple platinum in Canada.
Source: *BioIn 17; ConMus 4*

Myrdal, Alva Reimer
[Mrs. Karl Gunnar Myrdal]
Swedish. Sociologist, Diplomat
Swedish ambassador to India, 1956-61; won Nobel Peace Prize, 1982, for advocating nuclear disarmament.
b. Jan 31, 1902 in Uppsala, Sweden
d. Feb 1, 1986 in Stockholm, Sweden
Source: *BioIn 14, 15, 17, 20; ConAu 69, 118; CurBio 86; Future; IntDcWB; IntWW 83; IntYB 82; InWom SUP; NewYTBS 82, 86; Who 83; WhoNob, 90, 95; WhoWor 82*

Myrdal, Jan
Swedish. Author, Journalist
Books on Orient include *China Notebook,* 1979.
b. Jul 19, 1927 in Stockholm, Sweden
Source: *BioIn 8; ConAu 17R, 117, 132; ConWorW 93; DcScanL; IntAu&W 76, 77, 89; IntWW 74, 75, 76, 77, 78, 79, 80, 81, 82, 83, 89, 91, 93; WhoWor 84, 87, 89, 91, 93, 95, 96*

Myrdal, Karl Gunnar
Swedish. Sociologist
Shared Nobel Prize in economics, 1974; writings include *An American Dilemma,* which helped destroy "separate but equal" racial policy in US; husband of Alva.
b. Dec 6, 1898 in Gustafs, Sweden

d. May 17, 1987 in Stockholm, Sweden
Source: *BioIn 1, 6, 8, 10, 11, 12, 14; ConAu 4NR, 9R; CurBio 75, 87; IntAu&W 77, 82; IntWW 74, 75, 76, 78, 80, 82, 83; IntYB 78, 79, 80, 81, 82; McGEWB; WhAm 10; Who 85; WhoNob, 90, 95; WhoWor 78, 80, 82, 84, 87*

Myricks, Larry
American. Track Athlete
Long jumper; won gold medal, 1979 World Cup.
b. Mar 10, 1956 in Jackson, Mississippi
Source: *BioIn 12; BlkOlyM*

Myron
Greek. Sculptor
Considered one of the greatest Attic sculptors of time; works include *Discus Thrower.*
b. fl. 480BC
d. 440BC
Source: *DcBiPP; LegTOT; McGDA; McGEWB; NewCol 75; OxCArt; WebBD 83*

N

Naber, John
American. Swimmer
Won four gold medals, one silver medal, 1976 Olympics.
b. Jan 20, 1956 in Evanston, Illinois
Source: *BioIn 10*

Nabokov, Nicolas
Russian. Composer
Wrote ballet *Union Pacific,* 1934; opera about Rasputin, *The Holy Devil,* 1958.
b. Apr 4, 1903 in Minsk, Russia
d. Apr 6, 1978 in New York, New York
Source: *AmComp; Baker 78, 84, 92; BioIn 2, 8, 9, 10, 11; CnOxB; CompSN, SUP; ConAmC 76, 82; ConAu 65, 77, 85; DancEn 78; DcAmB S10; DcCM; IntWWM 77; MusMk; NewGrDA 86; NewGrDM 80; NewGrDO; OxCMus; WhAm 7; WhoAm 74, 76, 78*

Nabokov, Vladimir
[Vladimir Sirin]
American. Author, Translator
Wrote *Lolita,* 1955, *Pale Fire,* 1962, and critical works; translated Russian authors.
b. Apr 23, 1899 in Saint Petersburg, Russia
d. Jul 2, 1977 in Montreux, Switzerland
Source: *AmAu&B; AmCulL; AmNov; AmWr; Au&Wr 71; Benet 87; BenetAL 91; BioIn 13; BlueB 76; CamGEL; CamGLE; CamHAL; CasWL; CelR; ClDMEL 47, 80; CnMWL; ConAu 5R, 20NR, 69; ConLC 1, 2, 3, 6, 8, 11, 15, 23, 46, 64; ConNov 72, 76; ConPo 75; CurBio 77N; CyWA 89; DcArts; DcLB 2, DS3, Y80A; DcLEL; DcRusL; DcTwCCu 1; DrAF 76; EncSF, 93; EncWL, 2, 3; EvEuW; GrWrEL N; HalFC 84, 88; IntAu&W 76, 77; IntWW 74, 75, 76, 77; IntWWP 77, 82; LegTOT; LinLib L; LngCTC; MagSAmL; MagSWL; MajTwCW; ModAL, S1, S2; ModSL 1; NewCon; NewEScF; NewYTBS 77; Novels; OxCAmL 65, 83, 95; OxCEng 67; OxCTwCP; PenC AM; RAdv 14, 13-2; REn; REnAL; RfGAmL 87, 94; RfGShF; ScF&FL 1, 2, 92; ScFSB; ShSCr 11; TwCA SUP; TwCWr; WebE&AL; WhAm 7; WhDW; Who 74; WhoAm 74, 76, 78; WhoTwCL; WhoWor 74; WorAl; WorAlBi; WorLitC; WrDr 76*

Nabors, Jim
[James Thurston Nabors]
American. Actor, Singer
Played Gomer Pyle on TV comedies "The Andy Griffith Show," 1963-64, "Gomer Pyle, USMC," 1964-69; has several gold albums as singer.
b. Jun 12, 1932 in Sylacauga, Alabama
Source: *BioIn 8; BkPepl; CelR; ConTFT 3; CurBio 69; IntMPA 88, 92, 94, 96; LegTOT; VarWW 85; WhoAm 86; WhoCom*

Nachbaur, Franz
German. Opera Singer
Tenor known for Wagnerian roles; with Munich Opera until 1890.
b. Mar 25, 1835 in Weiler Giessen, Germany
d. Mar 21, 1902 in Munich, Germany
Source: *Baker 84; NewEOp 71; NewGrDM 80*

Nachman, Gerald Weil
American. Journalist, Author
Critic, columnist, *San Francisco Chronicle,* 1979-93; wrote book *Out on a Whim,* 1983.
b. Jan 13, 1938 in Oakland, California
Source: *BiDAmNC; ConAu 16NR, 65; WhoAm 74, 76, 78, 80, 82, 84, 86, 88, 90, 92, 94, 95, 96, 97; WhoWest 96*

Nadar
[Gaspard-Felix Tournachon]
French. Balloonist, Photographer
Known for mapmaking by surveying from a balloon; invented the photo-essay.
b. Apr 5, 1820 in Paris, France
d. Mar 21, 1910 in Paris, France
Source: *BioIn 4, 5, 7, 10, 11, 12, 13, 16, 20; DcArts; DcBiPP; Dis&D; GuFrLit 1; ICPEnP; MacBEP; NewCol 75; OxCFr; PseudAu; ThHEIm; WorECar*

Nader, George
American. Actor
Leading man in action pictures, 1950s; did series of thrillers in Germany playing an FBI agent.
b. Oct 9, 1921 in Pasadena, California
Source: *ConAu 109; FilmEn; FilmgC; ForYSC; HalFC 80, 84, 88; IntMPA 77, 80, 86, 88, 92, 94, 96; ItaFilm; MotPP; VarWW 85; WhoHol 92, A; WhoHrs 80*

Nader, Michael
American. Actor
Played Dex Dexter on TV soap opera "Dynasty," 1983-89.
b. Feb 18, 1945 in Saint Louis, Missouri
Source: *BioIn 14; ConTFT 8; WhoHol 92*

Nader, Ralph
American. Political Activist, Author
Founder of consumer rights movement in US, who wrote *Unsafe at Any Speed,* 1965.
b. Feb 27, 1934 in Winsted, Connecticut
Source: *AmAu&B; AmDec 1960, 1970; AmJust; AmRef&R; AmSocL; BioIn 7, 8, 9, 10, 11, 12, 13; BkPepl; BlueB 76; CelR, 90; ConAu 77; ConHero 1; CurBio 68, 86; DcTwDes; EncAB-H 1974, 1996; EncABHB 5; EnvEnc; EnvEnDr; FacFETw; HeroCon; IntAu&W 77; IntWW 74, 75, 76, 77, 78, 79, 80, 81, 82, 83, 89, 91, 93; LegTOT; LinLib L, S; LNinSix; MakMC; McGEWB; MugS; News 89; NewYTBS 90; PolPar; PolProf J, NF; RComAH; WebAB 74, 79; WhDW; Who 74, 82, 83, 85, 88, 90, 92, 94; WhoAm 74, 76, 78, 80, 82, 84, 86, 88, 90, 92, 94, 95, 96, 97; WhoAmL 78, 79; WhoUSWr 88; WhoWor 74, 78; WhoWrEP 89, 92, 95; WorAl; WorAlBi; WrDr 82, 84, 86, 88, 90, 92, 94, 96*

Nadir Shah
[Tahmasp Qoli Khan; Nadr Shah Qoli Beg]
Persian. Ruler
Ruled, 1736-47; deposed Tahmasp II in Afghanistan; made Sunni sect of Islam nat. religion.

b. Oct 22, 1688 in Khurasan, Persia
d. Jun 19, 1747 in Fathabad, Iran
Source: *DcBiPP; DicTyr; HisWorL; WebBD 83; WhoMilH 76*

Nagai, Sokichi
Japanese. Author, Educator
Novels described bygone days in Tokyo: *The River Sumida,* 1909.
b. Dec 3, 1879 in Tokyo, Japan
d. Apr 30, 1959 in Ichikawa, Japan
Source: *CasWL; ConAu 117; PenC CL*

Nagako, Empress
Japanese. Consort
Princess who married Emperor Hirohito of Japan, Jan 26, 1924.
b. 1903
Source: *BioIn 9, 10*

Nagano, Osami
Japanese. Naval Officer
Planned and launched attack on Pearl Harbor, Dec 7, 1941.
b. Jun 15, 1880 in Kochi, Japan
d. Jan 5, 1947 in Tokyo, Japan
Source: *BioIn 1; HisEWW; WorAl; WorAlBi*

Nagel, Conrad
American. Actor
Matinee idol, 1920-35; received special Oscar for work on Motion Picture Relief Fund, 1947.
b. Mar 16, 1897 in Keokuk, Iowa
d. Feb 21, 1970 in New York, New York
Source: *BiE&WWA; BioIn 4, 8, 9, 12, 17; DcAmB S8; Film 1; FilmEn; FilmgC; ForYSC; MotPP; MovMk; NewYTBE 70; NotNAT B; RadStar; SilFlmP; TwYS; WhAm 5; WhoHol B; WhScrn 74, 77, 83; WhThe*

Nagle, Kel(vin David George)
Australian. Golfer
Turned pro, 1946; won British Open, 1960.
b. Dec 21, 1920 in Sydney, Australia
Source: *LegTOT; WhoGolf*

Nagler, Eric
Canadian. Entertainer
Children's performer known for inventive musical instruments; host of TV show "Eric's World," 1991—.
b. Jun 1, 1942 in New York, New York
Source: *BioIn 16; ConMus 8*

Naguib, Mohammed
Egyptian. Political Leader
Became first pres. of Egypt, 1952, after military coup; removed from office, 1954.
b. Feb 20, 1901 in Khartoum, Sudan
d. Aug 28, 1984 in Cairo, Egypt
Source: *BioIn 3, 4, 6, 14; CurBio 52; NewYTBS 84*

Nagurski, Bronko
[Bronislaw Nagurski]
American. Football Player
Fullback, Chicago, 1930-37, 1943; Hall of Fame, 1963.
b. Nov 3, 1908 in Rainy River, Ontario, Canada
d. Jan 7, 1990 in International Falls, Minnesota
Source: *AmDec 1930; AnObit 1990; BiDAmSp FB; BioIn 3, 5, 6, 7, 8, 10, 12, 13, 15, 16, 17; LegTOT; NewYTBE 72; NewYTBS 84, 90; WebAB 79; WhoFtbl 74; WorAl; WorAlBi*

Nagy, Imre
Hungarian. Statesman
Minister of agriculture, 1944; of interior, 1945; prime minister, 1953-56; executed.
b. Jun 7, 1896 in Kaposvar, Austria-Hungary
d. Jun 17, 1958 in Budapest, Hungary
Source: *BioIn 13; ColdWar 1, 2; ConAu 118; DcTwHis; EncCW; EncRev; EncWB; FacFETw; HisWorL; LegTOT; ObitT 1951; WhAm 3; WorAl; WorAlBi*

Nahayan, Zayed bin al-, Sultan
Arab. Political Leader
Pres., United Arab Emirates, 1971—; emir of Abu Dhabi, 1966—.
b. 1918? in Abu Dhabi, United Arab Emirates
Source: *BioIn 13; IntWW 91*

Naidu, Sarojini
"The Nightingale of India"
Indian. Poet, Politician, Feminist
First Indian woman pres. of Indian National Congress, 1925; wrote sentimental verse *The Bird of Time,* 1912.
b. Feb 13, 1879 in Hyderabad, India
d. Mar 2, 1949 in Lucknow, India
Source: *ArtclWW 2; Benet 87, 96; BioIn 1, 2, 3, 7, 8, 10, 11; BlmGWL; CasWL; ChhPo, S2; ContDcW 89; CurBio 43, 49; DcLEL; EncWL 2, 3; EvLB; FemiCLE; GrWrEL P; IntDcWB; InWom; LegTOT; LngCTC; McGEWB; ModWoWr; OxCTwCP; PenBWP; PenC ENG; RadHan; REn; RfGEnL 91; TwCWr; WebE&AL; WomFir*

Naipaul, V(idiahar) S(urajprasad)
Author
Wrote *Among the Believers,* 1981.
b. Aug 17, 1932, Trinidad and Tobago
Source: *CasWL; ConAu 1NR; ConLC 18, 37; ConNov 86; CurBio 77; EncWL SUP; IntWW 83; LngCEL; NewC; NewYTBS 80; PenC ENG; REn; Who 85; WhoAm 86; WhoWor 87; WrDr 86*

Nair, Mira
Indian. Filmmaker
Filmmaker whose movies portray immigrants struggling in society; movies include *Salaam Bombay!,* 1988 and *India Cabaret,* 1983.
b. 1957 in Bhubaneswar, India
Source: *AsAmAlm; BioIn 16; ConTFT 12; CurBio 93; DrIndFM; IntMPA 96; LegTOT; MiSFD 9; NotAsAm; WhoAsA 94*

Naisbitt, John
American. Author
Wrote *Megatrends;* one of most sought-after interpreters of contemporary scene.
b. 1929 in Salt Lake City, Utah
Source: *BioIn 13; ConAu 113, 128; CurBio 84; WhoAm 84; WhoWrEP 92, 95; WrDr 88, 90, 92, 94, 96*

Naish, J(oseph) Carrol
American. Actor
Character actor in over 200 films; Oscar nominee for *Sahara; A Medal for Benny.*
b. Jan 21, 1900 in New York, New York
d. Jan 24, 1973 in La Jolla, California
Source: *BiE&WWA; CurBio 57, 73; FilmgC; MotPP; MovMk; NewYTBE 73; Vers A; WhoHol B; WhScrn 77*

Naismith, James A
American. Basketball Pioneer
Invented basketball, 1891; original member, Hall of Fame, named in his honor, 1959.
b. Nov 6, 1861 in Almonte, Ontario, Canada
d. Nov 28, 1939 in Lawrence, Kansas
Source: *ConAu 118; DcAmB S2; NatCAB 33; WebAB 74; WhAm 1; WhoBbl 73*

Najib Ahmadzi
[Ahmadzi Najibullah]
Pakistani. Political Leader
President of Afghanistan, 1986-92; installed by Soviets after forcing out Karmal.
b. 1947 in Paktia, Pakistan
d. Sep 27, 1996 in Kabul, Pakistan
Source: *CurBio 88*

Nakai, Raymond
American. Native American Leader
Helped to modernize the Navajo nation; emphasized the production of the reservation's natural resources; served as Navajo Council chair, 1963-71.
b. 1918 in Lukachukai, Arizona
Source: *BioIn 21; NotNaAm; REnAW*

Nakasone, Yasuhiro
Japanese. Political Leader
Prime minister, 1982-87; introduced Western-style leadership through candor, aggressiveness.
b. May 27, 1918 in Takasaki, Japan
Source: *BioIn 9, 11, 12, 13; CurBio 83; EncWB; FacFETw; FarE&A 78, 79, 80, 81; IntWW 74, 75, 76, 77, 78, 79, 80, 81; NewYTBE 70; NewYTBS 82, 85; Who 88, 90, 92, 94; WhoAsAP 91; WhoWor 74, 84, 87, 89, 91, 93*

Nakian, Reuben
"Grand Old Man of American Sculpture"
American. Artist
Sculptor, known for works dealing with Greek, Roman mythology.
b. Aug 10, 1897 in College Park, New York
d. Dec 4, 1986 in Stamford, Connecticut
Source: *AmArt; BioIn 2, 5, 7, 10, 12, 14, 15; BriEAA; CenC; CurBio 85, 87, 87N; DcAmArt; DcArts; DcCAA 71, 77, 88, 94; McGDA; NewYTBS 86; OxCTwCA; PhDcTCA 77; WhAm 9; WhAmArt 85; WhoAm 74, 86; WhoAmA 73, 76, 78, 80, 82, 84, 86; WhoWor 74; WorArt 1950*

Naldi, Nita
[Anita Anne Dooley]
American. Actor
The temptress opposite Valentino in *Blood and Sand,* 1922.
b. Apr 1, 1899 in New York, New York
d. Feb 17, 1961 in New York, New York
Source: *Film 1; FilmEn; FilmgC; HalFC 80, 84, 88; LegTOT; MotPP; SilFlmP; TwYS; WhoHol B; WhScrn 74, 77, 83*

Nall, Anita
[Nadia Anita Nall]
American. Swimmer
Winner of 1992 Olympic gold, silver and bronze medals; set world record in 400 medley relay.
b. Jul 21, 1976

Namath, Joe
[Joseph William Namath]
"Broadway Joe"
American. Football Player, Sportscaster
Quarterback, 1965-77, mostly with NY Jets; best known for passing, upset Super B owl victory, 1969; Pro Football Hall of Fame, 1985.
b. May 31, 1943 in Beaver Falls, Pennsylvania
Source: *BiDAmSp FB; BkPepl; BlueB 76; CelR, 90; ConAu 89; ConTFT 3; CurBio 66; FacFETw; FilmgC; HalFC 80, 84, 88; IntMPA 84, 86, 88, 92, 94, 96; ItaFilm; LegTOT; NewYTBE 70, 71, 72; NewYTBS 81, 85; VarWW 85; WebAB 74, 79; WhoAm 78, 80, 82, 84, 86, 88, 90, 92, 94, 95, 96, 97; WhoFtbl 74; WhoHol 92, A; WhoSpor; WorAl; WorAlBi*

Namgyal, Palden Thondup
Indian. Ruler
King of Sikkim, 1963-75; deposed by India which annexed country.
b. May 22, 1923 in Gangtok, Sikkim
d. Jan 29, 1982 in New York, New York
Source: *AnObit 1982; NewYTBS 74, 82; WhoWor 74, 76, 78, 80, 82, 84*

Nampeyo
American. Artist
Reintroduced ancient designs to Hopi pottery; led the Sityatki Revival Movement which changed the nature of Hopi pottery.
b. 1860? in Hano, Arizona
d. Jul 20, 1942
Source: *MusmAFA; NorAmWA; NotNaAm; WhNaAH*

Namphy, Henri
Haitian. Political Leader
Succeeded Duvalier as pres. of Haiti in 1986; a coup ousted him in 1988 and sent him into exile.
b. Nov 2, 1932 in Cap Haitien, Haiti
Source: *BioIn 14, 16; CurBio 88; DcCPCAm; IntWW 91; NewYTBS 86; WhoWor 87, 89, 91*

Nanak
Indian. Religious Figure
First Sikh Guru; poems are in Sikh bible *Adi Granth.*
b. Apr 15, 1469 in Rai Bhoi di Talvandi, India
d. Oct 10, 1538 in Kartarpur, India
Source: *Benet 87; BioIn 4, 5, 8, 9, 10, 11, 16, 20; CasWL; DcOrL 2; LegTOT; McGEWB; PopDcHi; WhDW*

Nanne, Lou(is Vincent)
"Sweet Lou from the Soo"
Canadian. Hockey Player, Hockey Executive
Defenseman, Minnesota, 1967-78, general manager, 1978-88.
b. Jun 2, 1941 in Sault Ste. Marie, Ontario, Canada
Source: *BioIn 12; HocEn; WhoAm 80, 82, 84, 86, 88, 90, 92, 94, 95, 97; WhoEmL 87; WhoHcky 73; WhoMW 80, 82, 84, 86, 88, 90*

Nansen, Fridtjof
Norwegian. Explorer, Statesman
Led first expedition across ice fields of Greenland, 1888; won Nobel Peace Prize, 1922, for refugee work.
b. Oct 10, 1861 in Christiania, Norway
d. May 30, 1930 in Lysaker, Norway
Source: *BiD&SB; BiDInt; BiESc; BioIn 1, 2, 3, 4, 5, 6, 8, 9, 10, 11, 12, 15, 18, 20; CamDcSc; DcScB, S1; Expl 93; FacFETw; HisWorL; InSci; LarDcSc; LinLib L, S; LngCTC; McGEWB; NewC; NobelP; OxCCan; OxCEng 67; OxCShps; REn; WhDW; WhoNob, 90, 95; WhWE; WorAlBi*

Napier, Charles James, Sir
English. Army Officer
Successful admiral who fell into disgrace after declining to attack in a major battle.
b. Aug 10, 1782 in London, England
d. Aug 29, 1853 in Portsmouth, England
Source: *Alli; BiD&SB; BioIn 3, 6, 7; CelCen; CopCroC; DcBiPP; DcBrWA; DcInB; DcNaB; GenMudB; HarEnMi; HisDBrE; LinLib S; WhoMilH 76*

Napier, John
Scottish. Mathematician
Invented logarithms, 1614; calculated abbreviated method of multiplication using numbered rods, "Napier's bones."
b. 1550 in Edinburgh, Scotland
d. Apr 4, 1617 in Edinburgh, Scotland
Source: *Alli; AsBiEn; BiESc; BioIn 1, 2, 3, 4, 8, 9, 15, 21; BritAu; CamDcSc; CmScLit; CyEd; DcBiPP; DcInv; DcNaB; DcScB; HisDcDP; InSci; LarDcSc; LinLib S; McGEWB; NewC; NewCol 75; OxCEng 67, 85, 95; RAdv 14; REn; WorAl; WorAlBi; WorScD*

Napier, John
English. Designer
Won Best Set and Costume Design Tonys for *The Life and Adventures of Nicholas Nickleby,* 1981; *Cats,* 1982.
b. Mar 1, 1944 in London, England
Source: *BioIn 13; CamGWoT; ConDes 84, 90, 97; ConTFT 5, 14; IntDcT 3; NewYTBS 83; Who 85, 88, 90, 92, 94; WhoAm 96, 97; WhoHol A; WhoThe 77, 81*

Napier, Robert Cornelis
English. Army Officer
Used engineering skills to build roads to battles; commander-in-chief in India, 1870-76; governor of Gibraltar, 1876-82.
b. Dec 6, 1810 in Colombo, Ceylon
d. Jan 14, 1890 in London, England
Source: *DcNaB; HarEnMi; WebBD 83; WhoMilH 76; WorAl; WorAlBi*

Napoleon I
[Napoleon Bonaparte]
French. Ruler
Formed Napoleonic Code, 1804-10; overthrown at Waterloo, 1815.
b. Aug 15, 1769 in Ajaccio, Corsica, France
d. May 5, 1821, St. Helena
Source: *BioIn 14, 15, 16, 17, 18, 19, 20; DcBiPP; FilmgC; HisDcSE; LegTOT; NewC; REn; TwoTYeD; WebBD 83; WhAm HS; WhDW*

Napoleon III
[Charles Louis Napoleon Bonaparte]
"Napoleon le Petit"
French. Ruler
Proclaimed himself emperor, 1852; deposed in bloodless revolution, 1871; preceeded Bismarck.
b. Apr 20, 1808 in Paris, France
d. Jan 9, 1873 in Chislehurst, England
Source: *CelCen; DcBiPP; DcCathB; Dis&D; HarEnUS; NewC; WebBD 83; WhDW*

Napolitano, Janet
American. Lawyer
U.S. Attorney, Phoenix AZ District, 1993—; member of legal team that represented Anita Hill, 1991.
b. Nov 29, 1957
Source: *News 97-1*

Napravnik, Eduard
Russian. Conductor, Composer
Led St. Petersburg Opera House; introduced over 80 renowned Russian works.
b. Aug 24, 1839 in Beischt, Bohemia
d. Nov 23, 1916 in Saint Petersburg, Russia
Source: *Baker 78, 84; BioIn 7; BriBkM 80; CmOp; NewEOp 71; NewGrDM 80; NewOxM; OxCMus; OxDcOp; PenDiMP*

Naranjo-Morse, Nora
American. Artist, Poet
Pueblo potter who works in clay and metal; published *Mud Woman: Poems from the Clay,* 1992.
b. 1953
Source: *BioIn 21; NorAmWA; NotNaAm*

Narayan, R(asipuram) K(rishnaswami)
Indian. Author
Best known for books set in fictional Indian city, including *Swami and Friends,* 1935.
b. Oct 10, 1906 in Madras, India
Source: *Au&Wr 71; Benet 87, 96; BioIn 4, 6, 7, 9, 10, 11, 12, 13, 16; CamGLE; CasWL; ConAu 33NR; ConLC 47; ConNov 91; CurBio 87; CyWA 89; DcLEL; DcOrL 2; FacFETw; IntAu&W 76, 77, 89; IntvTCA 2; IntWW 91; LngCTC; MajTwCW; OxCEng 85, 95; RAdv 13-2; REn; RfGEnL 91; RGTwCWr; ShSWr; SmATA 62; TwCA SUP; Who 92; WrDr 92*

Naruse, Mikio
Japanese. Filmmaker
Directed film *Late Chrysanthemums,* 1954; at first considered culturally alien to W audiences.
b. Aug 20, 1905 in Tokyo, Japan
d. 1969 in Tokyo, Japan
Source: *BiDFilm 94; BioIn 12; ConAu 118; DcFM; FilmEn; IntDcF 1-2, 2-2; JapFilm; MiSFD 9N; WorEFlm; WorFDir 1*

Nascimento, Milton
Brazilian. Singer, Songwriter, Musician
Sings original pop in sophisticated folk style; has recorded over 25 albums, several available in US, including *Miltons,* 1989.
b. 1942 in Rio de Janeiro, Brazil
Source: *ConBlB 2; ConMus 6; NewGrDJ 88, 94*

Nash, Clarence
"Ducky"
American. Entertainer
Voice of Donald Duck since cartoon character's inception, 1934.
b. Dec 7, 1905 in Independence, Missouri
d. Feb 20, 1985 in Burbank, California
Source: *BioIn 1, 10*

Nash, George Frederick
American. Actor
Films include *Oliver Twist,* 1933; silent films: *The Great Gatsby,* 1926.
b. 1873 in Philadelphia, Pennsylvania
d. Dec 31, 1944 in Amityville, New York
Source: *NotNAT B; WhoHol B; WhScrn 74, 77, 83; WhThe*

Nash, Graham
[Crosby, Stills, Nash, and Young; The Hollies]
English. Musician, Singer
Member of two well-known groups, 1960s-70s; solo career spent helping antinuclear power movement; helped define soft CA sound, 1960s.
b. Feb 2, 1942 in Blackpool, England
Source: *ASCAP 80; BioIn 13; BkPepl; ConMuA 80A; EncRk 88; IlEncRk; LegTOT; RkOn 78; WhoAm 78, 86; WhoRock 81; WhoRocM 82; WorAl; WorAlBi*

Nash, John
English. Architect
Designed London's Regent Park, 1812-20; redesigned Buckingham Palace, 1820s.
b. 1752 in London, England
d. May 13, 1835 in Cowes, Isle of Wight, England
Source: *AtlBL; BiDBrA; BioIn 2, 3, 4, 5, 7, 10, 12; DcArts; DcBiPP; DcD&D; DcNaB; EncMA; EncUrb; IntDcAr; MacEA; McGDA; McGEWB; NewC; OxCArt; WhDW; WhoArch*

Nash, Johnny
American. Singer
Brought reggae to attention of American public with number one hit "I Can See Clearly Now," 1972.
b. Aug 19, 1940 in Houston, Texas
Source: *ASCAP 66; ConBlAP 88; DrBlPA, 90; EncRk 88; HarEnR 86; IlEncRk; LegTOT; OxCPMus; PenEncP; RkOn 74; RolSEnR 83; SoulM; WhoAm 76, 78, 80, 82; WhoHol 92; WhoRock 81*

Nash, N Richard
[Nathan Richard Nusbaum]
American. Writer
Award-winning plays include *The Rainmaker,* 1957; wrote screenplay for *Porgy and Bess,* 1959.
b. Jun 7, 1913 in Philadelphia, Pennsylvania
Source: *CnMD; ConAu 14NR, 85; IntMPA 86; McGEWD 72; ModWD; NotNAT; VarWW 85; WhoThe 81*

Nash, Ogden Frederick
American. Author
Wrote poem, "Candy Is Dandy, But Liquor Is Quicker."
b. Aug 19, 1902 in Rye, New York
d. May 19, 1971 in Baltimore, Maryland
Source: *CnMWL; CurBio 41, 71; EncWL; LngCTC; ModAL; OxCAmL 65; PenC AM; RAdv 1; REn; REnAL; SmATA 2; TwCA, SUP; WhAm 5; WhoTwCL*

Nash, Paul
English. Artist, Designer
Official artist during both world wars; noted for finding unusual scenes to paint.
b. May 11, 1889 in London, England
d. Jul 11, 1946 in London, England
Source: *BioIn 1, 2, 3, 4, 5, 6, 7, 10, 12, 14; ChhPo S1; ClaDrA; ConArt 77, 83; ConPhot 82, 88; CurBio 46; DcArts; DcBrAr 1; DcBrBI; DcNaB 1941; DcTwDes; FacFETw; GrBr; ICPEnP A; McGDA; ObitOF 79; OxCArt; OxCTwCA; OxDcArt; PhDcTCA 77; TwCPaSc*

Nash, Philleo
American. Government Official
Commissioner of US Bureau of Indian Affairs, 1961-66; special assistant for minority affairs under Truman, 1946-52.
b. Oct 25, 1909 in Wisconsin Rapids, Wisconsin
d. Oct 12, 1987 in Marshfield, Wisconsin
Source: *AmMWSc 73S, 76P; BioIn 6, 15, 16; BlueB 76; CurBio 62, 88, 88N; FifIDA; IntDcAn; IntWW 74, 75, 76, 77, 78, 79, 80, 81, 82, 83; NewYTBS 87; WhAm 9; WhoAm 74, 76, 78; WhoAmP 73, 75, 77, 79; WhoSSW 73, 75*

Nash, Thomas
English. Author, Dramatist
Only surviving play is satirical masterpiece *Summer's Last Will and Testament,* 1593.
b. 1567 in Lowestoft, England
d. 1601 in Yarmouth, England
Source: *Alli; AtlBL; BbD; BiD&SB; BioIn 1, 2, 3, 5, 6, 8, 10, 11, 15; BritAu; Chambr 1; CyWA 58; DcBiPP; DcEnA; DcEnL; DcEuL; DcNaB; Dis&D; EvLB; LinLib L; NewC; OxCEng 67; REn*

Nasland, Mats
Swedish. Hockey Player
Left wing, Montreal, 1982-90; currently playing in Europe; won Lady Byng Trophy, 1988.
b. Oct 31, 1959 in Timra, Sweden
Source: *HocReg 87*

Nasrin, Taslima
Bangladeshi. Author
Object of several fatwas, or religious sanctions, resulting in death threats by fundamentalist Muslim leaders.
b. Aug 25, 1962 in Mymensingh, Pakistan
Source: *HeroCon; News 95, 95-1; RadHan*

Nasser, Gamal Abdel
Egyptian. Political Leader
Led coup that deposed King Farouk, 1952; pres. of Egypt, 1956-70.
b. Jan 15, 1918 in Beni Mor, Egypt
d. Sep 28, 1970 in Cairo, Egypt

Source: *BioIn 3, 4, 5, 6, 7, 8, 9, 10, 11, 12, 13, 16, 17, 18, 19, 20, 21; ColdWar 1; ConAu 113; CurBio 54, 70; DcPol; FacFETw; LegTOT; LinLib S; McGEWB; NewYTBE 71; ObitT 1961; WhAm 5; WhDW; WorAl; WorAlBi*

Nast, Conde
American. Publisher
Pres., publisher, *Vogue; House and Garden; Glamour* mags.
b. Mar 26, 1874 in New York, New York
d. Jan 11, 1942 in New York, New York
Source: *AmAu&B; BioIn 7, 9, 12, 13; CurBio 42; EncTwCJ; WhAm 2; WorAl; WorAlBi; WorFshn*

Nast, Thomas
American. Cartoonist, Illustrator
Political cartoonist; originated elephant, donkey as symbols of Rep., Dem. part ies; biting style popularized term "nasty."
b. Sep 27, 1840 in Landau, Germany
d. Dec 7, 1902 in Guayaquil, Ecuador
Source: *AmBi; AmRef; AmSocL; ApCAB; ArtsNiC; Benet 87, 96; BenetAL 91; BiDAmJo; BioIn 3, 4, 7, 8, 9, 10, 11, 12, 13, 14, 15, 16, 19; ChhPo; CivWDc; ConAu 112; ConGrA 1; DcAmB; DcAmSR; DcArts; Drake; EarABI, SUP; EncAB-H 1974, 1996; EncAJ; HarEnUS; IlBEAAW; IlrAm 1880; JrnUS; LegTOT; LinLib L; McGDA; McGEWB; MemAm; NatCAB 7; NewYHSD; OxCAmH; OxCAmL 65, 83, 95; PolPar; RComAH; REn; REnAL; SmATA 33, 51; TwCBDA; WebAB 74, 79; WhAm 1, 4A; WhAmArt 85; WhAm HSA; WhAmP; WhCiWar; WhDW; WorAl; WorAlBi; WorECar*

Nastase, Ilie
Romanian. Tennis Player
Won US Opens, 1972, 1975, French Open, 1973, Italian Opens, 1970, 1973; won doubles with J Connors, Wimbledon, 1973.
b. Jul 19, 1946 in Bucharest, Romania
Source: *BioIn 9, 10, 11, 12, 13; BkPepl; BuCMET; CurBio 74; IntWW 81, 82, 83, 89, 91, 93; LegTOT; NewYTBE 73; WhoAm 76, 78, 80, 82, 84, 88, 92, 94; WhoIntT; WhoWor 78; WorAl; WorAlBi*

Nathan, George Jean
American. Editor, Critic
Co-founded, edited, *American Mercury,* 1924-30; wrote on contemporary theater.
b. Feb 14, 1882 in Fort Wayne, Indiana
d. Apr 8, 1958 in New York, New York
Source: *AmAu&B; Benet 87; BenetAL 91; BioIn 1, 2, 3, 4, 5, 6, 9, 13, 14, 15, 19, 20; CamGLE; CamGWoT; CamHAL; ChhPo S3; CnDAL; ConAmA; ConAmL; ConAu 114; CurBio 45, 58; DcAmB S6; DcCathB; DcLB 137; DcLEL; EncAJ; EncWT; IndAu 1816; LegTOT; LinLib L; LngCTC; ModAL; NatCAB 61; NotNAT A, B; ObitT 1951; OxCAmL 65, 83, 95; OxCAmT 84; OxCEng 67, 85, 95; OxCThe 67, 83; PenC AM; REn; REnAL; TwCA, SUP; TwCLC 18; WebAB 74, 79; WhAm 3; WhE&EA; WhLit; WhThe*

Nathan, Robert
American. Author, Composer
Wrote romantic poetry, wry prose, including *Portrait of Jennie,* 1940.
b. Jan 2, 1894 in New York, New York
d. May 25, 1985 in Los Angeles, California
Source: *AmAu&B; AmNov; ASCAP 66, 80; Au&Wr 71; BenetAL 91; BioIn 1, 2, 4, 5, 6, 8, 10, 12, 14, 15; BlueB 76; ChhPo, S1, S3; CnDAL; ConAmA; ConAmC 76A, 82; ConAmL; ConAu 6NR, 13R, 116; ConNov 72, 76, 82; DcLB 9; EncSF; HalFC 88; IntAu&W 77, 82; IntWW 74, 75, 76, 77, 78, 79, 80, 81, 82, 83; JeAmFiW; LinLib L; LngCTC; NewYTBS 85; OxCAmL 65, 83; REn; REnAL; ScF&FL 1, 2, 92; SmATA 6, 43N; SupFW; TwCA, SUP; WhAm 8; WhE&EA; WhoAm 74, 76, 78; WhoAmJ 80; WhoWest 74; WhoWorJ 72, 78; WrDr 76, 80, 82, 84*

Nathans, Daniel
American. Biologist
Shared Nobel Prize in medicine, 1978, for work with DNA.
b. Oct 30, 1928 in Wilmington, Delaware
Source: *AmMWSc 73P, 76P, 79, 82, 86, 89, 92, 95; BiESc; BioIn 11, 12, 14, 15, 20; IntMed 80; IntWW 79, 80, 81, 82, 83, 89, 91, 93; LarDcSc; LegTOT; McGMS 80; NobelP; NotTwCS; Who 82, 83, 85, 88, 90, 92, 94; WhoAm 74, 76, 78, 80, 82, 84, 86, 88, 90, 92, 94, 95, 96, 97; WhoE 79, 81, 83, 85, 86, 89, 91, 93, 95, 97; WhoFrS 84; WhoMedH; WhoNob, 90, 95; WhoScEn 94, 96; WhoTech 84, 89, 95; WhoWor 80, 82, 84, 87, 89, 91, 93, 95, 96, 97; WorAl; WorAlBi*

Nation, Carry A(melia Moore)
American. Social Reformer
Proponent of temperance; known for using hatchet to smash saloons.
b. Nov 25, 1846 in Garrard County, Kentucky
d. Jun 9, 1911 in Leavenworth, Kansas
Source: *AmAu&B; AmBi; AmWomWr; BioIn 15, 16, 17, 19, 21; DcAmB; DcAmSR; DcAmTB; DcNAA; EncAAH; EncVaud; EncWHA; InWom, SUP; LibW; LngCTC; McGEWB; NotAW; OxCAmH; OxCAmL 65; WebAB 74, 79; WebBD 83; WhAm 4, HSA*

Natori, Josie
Philippine. Fashion Designer
President, The Natori Company, 1977— .
b. May 9, 1947 in Manila, Philippines
Source: *AsAmAlm; News 94, 94-3; NotAsAm*

Natta, Giulio
Italian. Chemist, Educator
Pioneer in plastics, substance chemistry; shared Nobel Prize with Karl Ziegler, 1963.
b. Feb 26, 1903 in Imperia, Italy
d. May 2, 1979 in Bergamo, Italy
Source: *AsBiEn; BiESc; BioIn 6, 7, 11, 12, 13, 14, 15, 19, 20; CamDcSc; ConAu 113; CurBio 64, 79; DcScB S2; IntWW 74, 75, 76, 77, 78; LarDcSc; McGMS 80; NobelP; NotTwCS; WhAm 7; Who 74; WhoNob, 90, 95; WhoWor 74, 76, 78; WorInv*

Nattier, Jean Marc
French. Artist
Often painted royalty, nobility in guise of mythological characters: *Portrait of a Lady as Diana,* 1756.
b. Mar 17, 1685 in Paris, France
d. Nov 7, 1766 in Paris, France
Source: *BioIn 11; ClaDrA; DcBiPP; McGDA; NewCol 75; OxCFr*

Natwick, Mildred
American. Actor
Oscar nominee for *Barefoot in the Park,* 1967.
b. Jun 19, 1908 in Baltimore, Maryland
d. Oct 25, 1994
Source: *BiE&WWA; BioIn 15, 20; ConTFT 7, 14; EncAFC; Ent; FilmEn; FilmgC; ForYSC; HalFC 80, 84, 88; HolCA; IntMPA 75, 76, 77, 78, 79, 80, 81, 82, 84, 86, 88, 92, 94; InWom SUP; LegTOT; MotPP; MovMk; NotNAT; OxCAmT 84; VarWW 85; Vers A; WhoAm 76; WhoAmW 66, 68, 70, 72, 74; WhoHol 92, A; WhoThe 72, 77, 81; WorAl; WorAlBi*

Naudin, Emilio
Italian. Opera Singer
Tenor; Meyerbeer created role of Vasco da.Gama in *Africaine* for him, 1865.
b. Oct 23, 1823 in Parma, Italy
d. May 5, 1890 in Bologna, Italy
Source: *Baker 78, 84, 92; NewEOp 71; NewGrDO*

Naughton, David
American. Actor, Singer
Noted for Dr. Pepper commercials; star of *American Werewolf in London,* 1981.
b. 1951? in West Hartford, Connecticut
Source: *BioIn 12; ConTFT 6, 13; IntMPA 88, 92, 94, 96; ItaFilm; LegTOT; VarWW 85*

Nauman, Bruce
American. Artist
Artist who has been dabbling in an array of media, including body art, neon tubing, fiberglass and photography since the 1960s.
b. Dec 6, 1941 in Fort Wayne, Indiana
Source: *AmArt; BioIn 7, 9, 10, 13, 14, 16, 17, 19, 20, 21; BriEAA; ConArt 77, 83, 89, 96; CurBio 90; DcAmArt; DcCAA 77, 88, 94; DcCAr 81; IntWW 91, 93; News 95; OxCTwCA; PrintW 83,*

85; WhoAm 82, 84, 86, 88; WhoAmA 78, 80, 82, 84, 86, 89, 91, 93

Navarro, Fats
[Theodore Navarro]
American. Jazz Musician
Bop trumpeter, active in 1940s; recorded with Goodman, Eckstine.
b. Sep 24, 1923 in Key West, Florida
d. Jul 7, 1950 in New York, New York
Source: *AfrAmAl 6; AllMusG; Baker 84, 92; BiDAfM; BiDAmM; BiDJaz; BioIn 5, 11, 16, 20; CmpEPM; IlEncJ; InB&W 80; LegTOT; NegAl 83, 89; NewAmDM; NewGrDA 86; NewGrDJ 88, 94; NewGrDM 80; OxCPMus; PenEncP; TwCBrS; WorAl; WorAlBi*

Navasky, Victor Saul
American. Author, Editor
Political journalist, editor of *Nation* since 1977; wrote *Kennedy Justice,* 1971.
b. Jul 5, 1932 in New York, New York
Source: *BioIn 12, 13; ConAu 10NR; CurBio 86; EncTwCJ; IntAu&W 89; IntWW 89, 91, 93; ScF&FL 1, 2; WhoAm 80, 82, 84, 86, 88, 90, 92, 94, 95, 96, 97; WhoE 74, 93, 95, 97; WhoUSWr 88; WhoWrEP 89, 92, 95*

Navon, Yitzhak
Israeli. Political Leader
Labor party member, 1968—; pres. of Israel, 1978-83.
b. Apr 19, 1921 in Jerusalem, Palestine
Source: *BioIn 11, 12, 13; CurBio 82; DcMidEa; IntWW 78, 79, 80, 81, 82, 83; IntYB 79, 80, 81, 82; MidE 78, 79, 80, 81, 82; NewYTBS 78; WhoWor 80, 82, 84, 87, 89, 91*

Navratilova, Martina
American. Tennis Player
Number one female tennis player, 1978-79, 1982-86; won 17 Grand Slam titles; broke record for total victories (158) in 1992.
b. Oct 18, 1956 in Prague, Czechoslovakia
Source: *AmDec 1980; BiDAmSp OS; BioIn 10, 11, 12, 13, 14, 15, 16, 17, 18, 19, 20, 21; BuCMET; CelR 90; CurBio 77; EncWomS; FacFETw; GayLesB; GrLiveH; HerW 84; IntWW 81, 82, 83, 89, 91, 93; InWom SUP; LegTOT; News 89-1; NewYTBS 75, 77, 78, 83, 85; Who 94; WhoAm 78, 80, 82, 84, 86, 88, 90, 92, 94, 95, 96, 97; WhoAmW 83, 85, 87, 89, 91, 93, 95, 97; WhoIntT; WhoSpor; WhoWor 78, 80, 82, 84, 87, 89, 91, 93, 95, 96, 97; WorAl; WorAlBi*

Naylor, Gloria
American. Author
Writes about the black female experience in America: *The Women of Brewster Place,* 1982; *Bailey's Cafe,* 1992.
b. Jan 25, 1950 in New York, New York
Source: *AfrAmAl 6; AfrAmW; AmWomWr SUP; Au&Arts 6; Benet 96; BenetAL 91; BioIn 13, 16; BlkLC; BlkWAm; BlkWr 1, 2; BlkWrNE; BlmGWL; ConAu 27NR, 51NR, 107; ConBlB 10; ConLC 28, 52; ConNov 86, 91, 96; ConPopW; CurBio 93; CyWA 89; DcLB 173; DcTwCCu 5; FemiCLE; FemiWr; GrWomW; HanAmWH; InB&W 85; IntAu&W 91, 93; MagSAmL; MajTwCW; ModWoWr; NegAl 89; NotBlAW 2; OxCWoWr 95; RAdv 14; RfGAmL 94; SchCGBL; WhoAfA 96; WhoBlA 90, 92, 94; WorAu 1980; WrDr 88, 90, 92, 94, 96*

Nazareth
[Peter Agnew; Manny Charlton; Dan McCafferty; Darrell Sweet]
Scottish. Music Group
Hard rock group formed, 1969; known for making quiet versions of other artists music close to heavy-metal.
Source: *ConMuA 80A; EncRk 88; HarEnR 86; IlEncRk; NewAmDM; OnThGG; PenEncP; RkOn 78; RolSEnR 83; WhoRock 81; WhoRocM 82*

Nazimova, Alla
[Alla Leventon]
Russian. Actor
Known for her expressive pantomime in silent films, 1916-25; also bold acting style in *Camille; A Doll's House.*
b. Jun 4, 1879 in Yalta, Russia
d. Jul 13, 1945 in Hollywood, California
Source: *BioIn 1, 2, 3, 4, 5, 10, 11, 15, 16, 17; CamGWoT; CnThe; ContDcW 89; CurBio 45; DcAmB S3; EncVaud; EncWT; Ent; FamA&A; Film 1, 2; FilmEn; FilmgC; ForYSC; HalFC 80, 84, 88; IntDcF 1-3, 2-3; IntDcWB; InWom, SUP; LinLib L; MotPP; MovMk; NatCAB 36; NotAW; NotNAT B; OxCAmT 84; OxCFilm; OxCThe 67, 83; PlP&P; TwYS; WhAm 2; WhoHol B; WhoStg 1908; WhScrn 74, 77, 83; WhThe; WomFir; WorAl; WorAlBi; WorEFlm*

Ndadaye, Melchior
Burundian. Political Leader
President of Burundi, 1993; assassinated.
b. 1953, Burundi
d. Oct 21, 1993 in Bujumbura, Burundi
Source: *AnObit 1993; ConBlB 7*

Ndour, Youssou
Senegalese. Musician
Singer, drummer; Afro-pop style termed "mbalax;" albums include *Set,* 1990.
b. Oct 1, 1959 in Dakar, Senegal
Source: *BioIn 16; ConBlB 1; ConMus 6; CurBio 96; PenEncP*

Neagle, Anna, Dame
[Florence Marjorie Robertson]
English. Actor, Producer
First lady of British screen, 1930s-40s; set West End record with 2,062 performances in *Charlie Girl,* 1965-71.
b. Oct 20, 1904 in London, England
d. Jun 3, 1986 in London, England
Source: *AnObit 1986; BiDD; BiDFilm, 81, 94; BiE&WWA; BioIn 2, 4, 9, 10, 13, 14, 15; BlueB 76; ConAu 119; ConTFT 4; CurBio 86, 86N; DcArts; DcNaB 1986; EncEurC; EncMT; EncWT; FacFETw; FilmAG WE; FilmEn; FilmgC; ForYSC; HalFC 80, 84, 88; IlWWBF, A; IntDcF 1-3, 2-3; IntMPA 75, 76, 77, 78, 79, 80, 81, 82, 84, 86; IntWW 75, 76, 77, 78, 79, 80, 81, 82, 83; InWom, SUP; LegTOT; MotPP; MovMk; NewYTBS 86; NotNAT, A; OxCFilm; OxCPMus; ThFT; VarWW 85; Who 85; WhoHol A; WhoThe 72, 77, 81; WorEFlm*

Neal, James Foster
American. Lawyer
Successful in winning difficult, controversial cases, including Jimmy Hoffa, Watergate trials.
b. Sep 7, 1929 in Summer County, Tennessee
Source: *BioIn 12; ConNews 86-2; WhoAm 82*

Neal, Larry
[Lawrence P Neal]
American. Poet, Dramatist
Major influence in black arts movement; editor, *Liberator* art mag., 1960s; co-founded, Black Arts Theater, NYC, 1965.
b. Sep 5, 1937 in Atlanta, Georgia
d. Jan 6, 1981 in Hamilton, New York
Source: *AnObit 1981; BioIn 12, 14, 17; BlkAmP; BlkAWP; BlkWr 1; BlkWrNE; ConAu 81, 102; ConBlAP 88; ConPo 75, 80; DcLB 38; DcTwCCu 5; DrAP 75; DrAPF 80; DrBlPA 90; InB&W 80, 85; LivgBAA; MorBAP; NewYTBS 81; SchCGBL; SelBAAf; SelBAAu; WhoBlA 77, 80; WorAu 1975; WrDr 76, 80, 82*

Neal, Patricia
[Patsy Lou Neal]
American. Actor
Won Tony for *Another Part of the Forest,* 1947; Oscar for *Hud,* 1963.
b. Jan 20, 1926 in Packard, Kentucky
Source: *BiDFilm, 81, 94; BiE&WWA; BioIn 1, 6, 7, 8, 9, 10, 11, 12, 13; BioNews 74; BlueB 76; CelR, 90; ConHero 1; ConTFT 3; CurBio 64; FilmEn; FilmgC; ForYSC; GoodHs; HalFC 80, 84, 88; IntDcF 1-3, 2-3; IntMPA 75, 76, 77, 78, 79, 80, 81, 82, 84, 86, 88, 92, 94, 96; IntWW 74, 75, 76, 77, 78, 79, 80, 81, 82, 83, 89, 91, 93; InWom, SUP; ItaFilm; LegTOT; MotPP; MovMk; NotNAT, A; OxCFilm; VarWW 85; WhoAm 74, 76, 78, 80, 82, 84, 86, 90, 92; WhoAmW 66, 68, 70, 72, 74; WhoEnt 92; WhoHol 92, A; WhoHrs 80; WhoThe 77A; WhoWor 74, 78, 82, 87, 89, 91, 93, 95; WhThe; WorAl; WorAlBi; WorEFlm*

Neale, Greasy
[Alfred Earl Neale]
American. Football Player
Baseball outfielder, Cincinnati, 1916-24; coach, Philadelphia, 1941-50, known for several innovations, including five-man defensive line; Football Hall of Fame, 1969.
b. Nov 5, 1891 in Parkersburg, West Virginia
d. Nov 2, 1973 in Lake Worth, Florida

Source: *Ballpl 90; BioIn 2, 9, 10; WhoFtbl 74; WhoSpor*

Nealon, Kevin
American. Comedian
Comedian on "Saturday Night Live," 1986—, whose acts include bodybuilder Pump You Up Franz and Weekend Update; films include *All I Want for Christmas,* 1991.
b. 1954?

Near, Holly
American. Singer, Songwriter
Feminist folksinger; established own label, Redwood Records.
b. Jun 6, 1949 in Ukiah, California
Source: *Baker 92; BioIn 11, 12, 13, 14, 16; ConAu 143; ConMus 1; ConTFT 6; EncFCWM 83; GayLesB; LegTOT; PenEncP; RadHan; WrDr 96*

Nearing, Scott
American. Sociologist
Father of the modern ecology movement; wrote *Living the Good Life,* 1954.
b. Aug 6, 1883 in Morris Run, Pennsylvania
d. Aug 24, 1983 in Harborside, Maine
Source: *AmAu&B; AmLY; AmMWSc 73S, 78S; AmPeW; AnObit 1983; BenetAL 91; BiDAmLf; BioIn 9, 10, 11, 12, 13, 17, 18, 20; ChhPo; ConAu 11NR, 41R, 110; CurBio 71, 83N; DcAmSR; EncAACR; EncAL; EnvEnc; FacFETw; NewYTBE 72, 73; NewYTBS 83; OxCAmL 95; RadHan; REnAL; WhAm 7, 8; WhE&EA; WhoAm 74, 76, 78, 80, 82; WorAl; WorAlBi*

Nebel, Long John
American. Radio Performer
Hosted various radio programs, 1956-78; author, *The Way-Out World of Long John Nebel,* 1961.
b. Jun 11, 1911 in Chicago, Illinois
d. Apr 10, 1978 in New York, New York
Source: *WhAm 7; WhoAm 76*

Nebuchadnezzar I
Babylonian. Ruler
Ruled most of Mesopotamia, c. 1124-1103 B.C.
b. 1146BC
d. 1123BC
Source: *NewC; WebBD 83*

Nebuchadnezzar II
Babylonian. Ruler
King, 605-562 BC; destroyed city, temple of Jerusalem, 586 BC.
b. 630?BC
d. 562?BC
Source: *DcBiPP; Dis&D; LinLib S; McGEWB; NewC; REn; WhDW; WorAl*

Nechita, Alexandra
American. Artist
Had nineteen gallery exhibitions by age eleven; published *Outside the Lines: Paintings by Alexandra Nechita,* 1996.
b. Aug 27, 1985, Romania
Source: *News 96*

Necker, Jacques
French. Financier, Statesman
Helped reform France financially during Louis XVI's reign.
b. Sep 30, 1732 in Geneva, Switzerland
d. Apr 4, 1804, Switzerland
Source: *Benet 87, 96; BioIn 12, 15, 16; CmFrR; DcBiPP; DcEuL; Dis&D; EncEnl; LinLib S; McGEWB; NewCBEL; OxCFr; REn; WhoEc 81; WorAl; WorAlBi*

Neddermeyer, Seth H
American. Physicist
Won Enrico Fermi Award, 1983; developed trigger for the atomic bomb.
b. Sep 7, 1907 in Richmond, Michigan
d. Jan 30, 1988 in Seattle, Washington
Source: *AmMWSc 76P; BioIn 13*

Nederlander, James Morton
American. Producer, Theater Owner
Owns theatres nationwide; has produced *Annie; Hello Dolly; Woman of the Year.*
b. Mar 21, 1922 in Detroit, Michigan
Source: *BiE&WWA; BioIn 12, 17; ConTFT 2; IntWW 93; NewYTBS 81; NotNAT; VarWW 85; WhoAm 76, 78, 80, 82, 84, 86, 88, 90, 92, 94, 95, 96, 97; WhoE 91, 93, 95, 97; WhoEnt 92; WhoThe 81; WhoWest 74; WhoWor 84, 89, 91*

Needham, Hal
American. Director, Stunt Performer
Directed five films starring Bert Reynolds: *Smokey and the Bandit,* 1977; *Cannonball Run,* 1981.
b. Mar 6, 1931 in Memphis, Tennessee
Source: *BioIn 12; ConTFT 6; HalFC 84, 88; IntDcF 1-4; IntMPA 84, 86, 92, 94, 96; MiSFD 9; VarWW 85; WhoAm 82, 84, 86, 88, 90, 92, 94, 95, 96, 97; WhoHol 92; WhoWor 80, 82*

Needham, Joseph
English. Historian, Author
Scholar who wrote *Science and Civilisation in China,* a 7 volume opus which he began in the late 1930s; did pioneering research in chemical embryology and Chinese science.
b. Dec 9, 1900 in London, England
d. Mar 24, 1995, England
Source: *Au&Wr 71; BiESc; BioIn 9, 10, 11, 12, 14, 16, 18, 20, 21; BlueB 76; ConAu 5NR, 9R, 34NR; FarE&A 78, 79, 80, 81; InSci; IntAu&W 76, 77, 82, 86, 89, 91; IntWW 74, 75, 76, 77, 78, 79, 80, 81, 82, 83, 89, 91, 93; LarDcSc; LinLib L, S; NewCBEL; NewYTBS 95; WhAm 11; WhE&EA; Who 74, 82, 83, 85, 88, 90, 92, 94; WhoAm 88, 90, 92, 94, 95; WhoScEn 94; WhoWor 74, 82, 84, 87; WorAu 1950*

Needham, Paul M, Jr.
[The Hostages]
American. Hostage
One of 52 held by terrorists, Nov 1979-Jan 1981.
b. 1951?
Source: *NewYTBS 81*

Neel, Alice Hartley
"Quintessential Bohemian"
American. Artist
Representational painter known for portraits; first to have major exhibit in Moscow, 1981.
b. Jan 28, 1900 in Merion Square, Pennsylvania
d. Oct 13, 1984 in New York, New York
Source: *CurBio 76, 85N; DcAmArt; InWom SUP; NewYTBS 84; WhAm 8; WhoAm 78; WhoAmA 84; WhoAmW 85; WomArt*

Neel, (Louis) Boyd
English. Conductor
Organized internationally known String Orchestra, 1933; wrote *Story of an Orchestra,* 1950.
b. Jul 19, 1905 in London, England
d. Sep 30, 1981 in Toronto, Ontario, Canada
Source: *AnObit 1981; Baker 78, 84, 92; BioIn 1, 2, 3, 12; BlueB 76; CanWW 70, 79, 80, 81; ConAu 108; CreCan 1; DcNaB 1981; IntWW 74, 75, 76, 77, 78, 79, 80, 81; IntWWM 77, 80; NewAmDM; NewGrDM 80; NewYTBE 70; PenDiMP; WhAm 8; Who 74; WhoAm 76, 78, 80, 82; WhoWor 74*

Neel, Louis Eugene Felix
French. Physicist, Educator
Co-winner of 1970 Nobel Prize in physics; conducted early research in magnetic properties of solids, minerals.
b. Nov 22, 1904 in Lyons, France
Source: *AmMWSc 92, 95; BiESc; CamDcSc; IntWW 74, 75, 76, 77, 78, 79, 80, 81, 82, 83, 89, 91, 93; LarDcSc; McGMS 80; NewYTBE 70; Who 74, 82, 83, 85, 88, 90, 92, 94; WhoNob, 90, 95; WhoScEn 94, 96; WhoWor 74, 76, 78, 80, 82, 84, 87, 89, 91, 93, 95, 96, 97; WorAl*

Neely, Mark E., Jr.
American. Author
Won Pulitzer Prize for *The Fate of Liberty,* 1992.
b. Nov 10, 1944 in Amarillo, Texas
Source: *ConAu 25NR, 106; DrAS 82H; WhoAm 94, 95; WhoE 95*

Neeson, Liam
Irish. Actor
Stage and movie star; Broadway hit *Anna Christie;* films include *Ethan Frome,* 1993 *Schindler's List,* 1993, *Michael Collins,* 1996.

b. Jun 7, 1952 in Balleymena, Northern Ireland
Source: *BioIn 16; ConTFT 7; CurBio 94; IntMPA 92, 94, 96; LegTOT; News 93; WhoAm 95, 96, 97; WhoHol 92*

Nefertiti
Egyptian. Ruler
Probably shared power of throne with pharoah husband Akhenaton; often shown wearing a pharoah's crown.
b. 1390BC
d. 1360BC
Source: *InWom, SUP; LegTOT; NewCol 75; WebBD 83*

Neff, Hildegarde
[Hildegarde Knef]
German. Actor, Author
Wrote autobiographies *Gift Horse; Verdict.*
b. Dec 28, 1925 in Ulm, Germany
Source: *BiDAmM; BioIn 3, 7, 9, 10, 11; CelR; ConAu 4NR, 45; FilmEn; FilmgC; ForYSC; IntMPA 75, 76, 77, 78, 79, 80, 81, 82, 84, 86, 88, 92, 94, 96; InWom SUP; ItaFilm; LegTOT; MotPP; MovMk; OxCFilm; WhoHol 92, A; WorAl*

Neff, Wallace
American. Architect
Designed "Pickfair," built for Mary Pickford, Douglas Fairbanks, Sr.
b. 1895 in La Mirada, California
d. Jun 8, 1982 in Pasadena, California
Source: *AmArch 70; AmCath 80; BioIn 12, 15, 17, 21; ConArch 80, 87; WhAm 8; WhoAm 74, 76, 78; WhoWest 74*

Negri, Pola
[Barbara Appolonia Chalupiec]
American. Actor
Star of silent German films, 1917-22; known for Hollywood vamp role, off-screen affair with Rudolph Valentino.
b. Dec 31, 1894 in Janowa, Poland
d. Aug 1, 1987 in San Antonio, Texas
Source: *AnObit 1987; BiDFilm, 81, 94; ContDcW 89; EncEurC; Film 1, 2; FilmAG WE; FilmEn; FilmgC; IntDcF 1-3, 2-3; IntDcWB; InWom SUP; MotPP; MovMk; NewYTBE 70; NewYTBS 87; OxCFilm; SilFlmP; ThFT; TwYS; VarWW 85; WhoHol A; WomFir; WorEFlm*

Negrin, Juan
Spanish. Physician, Politician
Last premier, Second Republic, 1937-39; leader of Loyalists in Spanish Civil War until 1939.
b. Feb 3, 1894 in Las Palmas, Canary Islands, Spain
d. Nov 14, 1956 in Paris, France
Source: *CurBio 45, 57; ObitOF 79*

Negulesco, Jean
American. Director
Films include *Daddy Long Legs,* 1955; *Johnny Belinda,* 1948.
b. Feb 29, 1900 in Craiova, Romania
Source: *AnObit 1993; BiDFilm, 81; BioIn 9, 10, 11, 19; CmMov; FilmEn; FilmgC; HalFC 80, 84, 88; IlWWHD 1; IntDcF 1-2, 2-2; IntMPA 75, 76, 77, 78, 79, 80, 81, 82, 84, 86, 88, 92, 94; ItaFilm; MiSFD 9; MovMk; NewYTBS 93; OxCFilm; WomWMM; WorEFlm; WorFDir 1*

Nehemiah
Hebrew. Biblical Figure
Central figure in Book of Nehemiah; governor of Judea, 445 BC; rebuilt Jerusalem.
b. 400BC
Source: *DcOrL 3; NewCol 75; WebBD 83*

Neher, Erwin
German. Scientist
Won Nobel Prize in physiology for research on living cells that has shed new light on heart disease, diabetes and epilepsy, 1991.
b. Mar 20, 1944 in Landberg, Germany
Source: *AmMWSc 92, 95; BioIn 17, 18, 20; IntWW 91, 93; LarDcSc; NobelP 91; NotTwCS; Who 94; WhoMedH; WhoNob 95; WhoScEn 94, 96; WhoScEu 91-3; WhoWor 93, 95, 96, 97*

Neher, Fred
American. Cartoonist
Draws cartoon "Life's Like That," 1934-77.
b. Sep 29, 1903 in Nappanee, Indiana
Source: *WhAmArt 85; WhoAmA 73, 76, 78, 80, 82, 84, 86, 89, 91, 93*

Nehru, Jawaharlal
Indian. Political Leader
Father of Indira Gandhi; India's first prime minister, 1947-64.
b. Nov 14, 1889 in Allahabad, India
d. May 27, 1964 in Delhi, India
Source: *Benet 87, 96; BiDMoPL; BioIn 1, 2, 3, 4, 5, 6, 7, 8, 9, 10, 11, 12, 13, 14, 15, 16, 17, 18, 19, 20; CasWL; ConAu 34NR, 85; CurBio 41, 48, 64; DcLEL; DcNaB 1961; DcPol; DcTwHis; EncRev; FacFETw; HisDBrE; HisDcKW; HisWorL; LegTOT; LngCTC; MajTwCW; McGEWB; ObitT 1961; OxCEng 67, 85, 95; RAdv 14, 13-3; REn; WhAm 4; WorAl; WorAlBi*

Neihardt, John Gneisenau
American. Author
Wrote verse, fiction on Native Americans: *Song of the Messiah,* 1935.
b. Jan 8, 1881 in Sharpsburg, Illinois
d. Nov 3, 1973 in Columbia, Missouri
Source: *AmAu&B; AmLY; AnMV 1926; BioIn 3, 4, 11, 12, 14, 15, 17, 21; ChhPo, S2, S3; CnDAL; ConAmA; ConAmL; ConAu P-1; ConLC 32; EncPaPR 91; IntAu&W 76, 77; IntWW 74, 75; IntWWP 77; LinLib S; OxCAmL 65; REn; REnAL; TwCA, SUP; WebAB 74, 79; WhAm 6; WhoMW 74*

Neill, A(lexander) S(utherland)
Scottish. Educator, Author
Co-founder, Int'l School in Dresden, 1921; wrote *The Free Child,* 1953.
b. Oct 17, 1883 in Forfar, Scotland
d. Sep 24, 1973 in Suffolk, England
Source: *BioIn 1, 5, 6, 8, 9, 10, 12, 13, 14, 16, 17, 18; ConAu 45, 101; CurBio 61, 73, 73N; DcNaB 1971; EncSF 93; EvLB; FacFETw; LngCTC; McGEWB; NewYTBE 73; ObitT 1971; ScF&FL 1; ThTwC 87; WhAm 6; WhDW; WhE&EA; WhoWor 74*

Neilson, William A(llan)
American. University Administrator
Pres., Smith College, 1917-39; noted for progressive, innovative administration, financially successful.
b. Mar 29, 1869 in Doune, Scotland
d. Feb 13, 1946 in Falls Village, Connecticut
Source: *AmAu&B; AmLY; BiDAmEd; BioIn 1, 4, 5; CurBio 46; DcAmB S4; DcNAA; LinLib L; NatCAB 33; REnAL; TwCA, SUP; WhAm 2*

Neiman, LeRoy
American. Artist
Known for paintings of athletes; collected in *Leroy Neiman Posters,* 1980.
b. Jun 8, 1927 in Saint Paul, Minnesota
Source: *AmArt; BioIn 14, 19; CurBio 96; News 93-3; WhoAm 86, 88, 90, 92, 94, 95, 96, 97; WhoAmA 84, 86, 89, 91, 93; WhoE 74, 85, 86, 89, 91, 93, 95, 97; WhoWor 87, 89, 91, 93, 95, 96, 97*

Nekrasov, Nikolay Alexeyevich
Russian. Author
Influential in radical wing of literature, using popular, social concerns rather than literary values; best-known poem: *The Pedlars,* 1861.
b. Dec 10, 1821 in Greshnevo, Russia
d. Jul 27, 1877? in Saint Petersburg, Russia
Source: *BiD&SB; CasWL; ChhPo S1; DcRusL; EuAu; EvEuW; PenC EUR; REn*

Nelligan, Kate
[Kate Nelligan]
Canadian. Actor
Starred in "Therese Raquin;" film roles *Dracula; Eye of the Needle; Other People's Money,* 1991.
b. Mar 16, 1951 in London, Ontario, Canada
Source: *BioIn 13; CelR 90; ConTFT 1, 7, 14; CurBio 83; HalFC 84, 88; IntMPA 84, 86, 88, 92, 94, 96; IntWW 82, 83, 89, 91, 93; InWom SUP; LegTOT; NewYTBS 82; OxCCanT; VarWW 85; WhoAm 86, 88, 90, 92, 94, 95, 96, 97; WhoAmW 97; WhoEnt 92; WhoHol 92; WhoThe 77, 81; WhoWor 84, 87, 89, 91, 93, 95, 96, 97; WorAlBi*

Nelson, Baby Face
[Lester N Gillis; George Nelson]
American. Criminal
Member of John Dillinger's outlaw gang, 1930s.
b. Dec 6, 1908 in Chicago, Illinois
d. Nov 27, 1934 in Fox River Grove, Illinois
Source: *BioIn 5, 10, 12, 14, 15, 18, 20; BriEAA; ConArch 80, 87, 94; ConAu 81, 118; ConDes 84, 90, 97; DcD&D; DcTwDes; DrInf; EncMA; FacFETw; LegTOT; McGDA; WhoAm 74, 76, 78, 80, 82, 84; WhoCon 73; WorAl; WorAlBi*

Nelson, Barry
[Robert Haakon Nielson]
American. Actor
Star of Broadway's *Rat Race; Cactus Flower;* appeared on TV show "The Hunter."
b. Apr 16, 1920 in San Francisco, California
Source: *BiE&WWA; ConTFT 5; FilmEn; FilmgC; ForYSC; HalFC 80, 84, 88; IntMPA 84, 86, 88, 96; LegTOT; MotPP; MovMk; NotNAT; OxCAmT 84; PlP&P A; VarWW 85; WhoAm 86; WhoHol 92, A; WhoThe 81; WorAl; WorAlBi*

Nelson, Battling
[Oscar Nielson]
"Durable Dane"
American. Boxer
Lightweight champion, 1908-10; Hall of Fame, 1957; known for tireless fights.
b. Jun 5, 1882 in Copenhagen, Denmark
d. Feb 7, 1954 in Chicago, Illinois
Source: *BiDAmSp BK; BioIn 1, 3; BoxReg; WhoBox 74; WhoSpor*

Nelson, Ben
[E Benjamin Nelson]
American. Politician
Dem. governor, NE, 1991—.
b. May 17, 1941 in McCook, Nebraska

Nelson, Byron
[Gold Dust Twins; John Byron Nelson, Jr]
American. Golfer
Turned pro, 1932; won 49 PGA tournaments including Masters, 1937, 1942, PGA, 1940, 1945, US Open, 1939; Hall of Fame, 1953.
b. Feb 4, 1912 in Fort Worth, Texas
Source: *BiDAmSp OS; BioIn 2, 4, 6, 11, 13, 14, 15, 18, 19, 21; CurBio 45; LegTOT; NewYTBS 85, 93; WhoGolf; WhoSpor; WorAl; WorAlBi*

Nelson, Christian
American. Inventor
Confectioner who created the Eskimo Pie a chocolate-covered ice cream bar in Onawa, IA.
b. 1896?
d. Mar 8, 1992 in Laguna Hills, California
Source: *St&PR 84*

Nelson, Craig T
American. Actor
Films include two *Poltergeist* movies, 1982, 1986; star of TV series "Coach," 1989—; Emmy award winner, 1992.
b. Apr 4, 1944 in Spokane, Washington
Source: *BioIn 16; ConTFT 3; HalFC 84, 88; IntMPA 92; WhoAm 90; WhoEnt 92; WorAlBi*

Nelson, David
American. Actor
Son of Ozzie and Harriet; appeared on their TV show, 1952-65.
b. Oct 24, 1936 in New York, New York
Source: *BioIn 4, 10; ConTFT 5; ForYSC; IntMPA 75, 76, 77, 78, 79, 80, 81, 82, 84, 86, 88, 92, 94, 96; MiSFD 9; MotPP; VarWW 85; What 5; WhoHol 92, A*

Nelson, Don(ald Arvid)
American. Basketball Coach, Basketball Player
Forward, 1962-73, mostly with Boston; led NBA in field-goal percentage; coach, Milwaukee, 1976-87; NBA coach of yr., 1983, 1985.
b. May 15, 1940 in Muskegon, Michigan
Source: *BasBi; BiDAmSp Sup; BioIn 11; OfNBA 87; WhoAm 84, 86, 88, 90, 92, 94, 95, 96; WhoBbl 73; WhoE 97; WhoMW 82; WhoWest 87, 89, 92, 94*

Nelson, Ed(win Stafford)
American. Actor
Played on TV shows "Peyton Place," 1965-70; "Silent Force," 1971-72.
b. Dec 21, 1928 in New Orleans, Louisiana
Source: *BioIn 20; FilmgC; ForYSC; HalFC 80, 84, 88; VarWW 85; WhoAm 74, 76, 78, 80, 82, 84, 86, 88, 90, 92; WhoEnt 92; WhoHol 92, A; WhoHrs 80; WhoWor 78*

Nelson, Erik Henning
Swedish. Aviator
With others, made first around the world flight, flying two planes in 57 hops from Seattle, Apr-Sep 1924.
b. 1888, Sweden
d. May 9, 1970 in Honolulu, Hawaii
Source: *BioIn 2, 6, 8; InSci; NewYTBE 70; ObitOF 79*

Nelson, Gaylord Anton
American. Politician
US Dem. senator, WI, 1963-80; originator of Earth Day, 1970.
b. Jun 4, 1916 in Clear Lake, Wisconsin
Source: *BiDrAC; BiDrGov 1789; BiDrUSC 89; BioIn 5, 7, 8, 9, 10, 11, 12, 13; EncAAH; IntWW 74, 75, 76, 77, 78, 79, 80, 81, 82, 83, 89, 91, 93; NatLAC; WhoAm 74, 76, 78, 80, 82, 84, 86, 88, 90, 92, 94, 95, 96, 97; WhoAmP 73, 75, 77, 79, 81, 83, 85, 87, 89, 91, 93, 95; WhoE 95; WhoGov 72, 75, 77; WhoMW 74, 76, 78, 80; WhoWor 74, 78, 80, 82; WorAlBi*

Nelson, Gene
[Eugene Leander Berg]
American. Actor, Dancer
Films include *Tea For Two,* 1950; *Three Sailors and a Girl,* 1953; appeared in Broadway production of *Oklahoma!,* 1955.
b. Mar 24, 1920 in Seattle, Washington
d. Sep 16, 1996 in Calabasas, California
Source: *BiDD; BioIn 2, 9, 17; CmMov; CmpEPM; ConTFT 7; EncAFC; FilmEn; FilmgC; ForYSC; HalFC 80, 84, 88; IntMPA 75, 76, 77, 78, 79, 80, 81, 82, 84, 86, 88, 92, 94, 96; MiSFD 9; MotPP; MovMk; NewYTET; PlP&P, A; VarWW 85; WhoHol 92, A; WhoThe 77, 81*

Nelson, George H
American. Architect, Designer
Best known for modernistic furniture, storage systems, clocks.
b. 1908 in Hartford, Connecticut
d. Mar 5, 1986 in New York, New York
Source: *BioIn 10; BriEAA; ConAu 81; EncMA; McGDA; NewYTBS 86; WhoAm 74, 76, 78, 80, 82; WhoCon 73*

Nelson, Harriet
[Harriet Hilliard; Mrs. Ozzie Nelson; Peggy Lou Snyder]
American. Actor, Singer
Began career as singer in Ozzie Nelson's orchestra; starred on TV, 1952-65.
b. Jul 18, 1912 in Des Moines, Iowa
d. Oct 2, 1994 in Laguna Beach, California
Source: *CmpEPM; ConTFT 3; CurBio 49; FilmgC; IntMPA 86; MotPP; News 95-1; ThFT; VarWW 85; WhoAm 86; WhoHol A*

Nelson, Horatio Nelson, Viscount
English. Naval Officer
Defeated French fleet at Trafalgar, 1805; killed in battle.
b. Sep 29, 1758 in Burnham Thorpe, England
d. Oct 21, 1805
Source: *BioIn 1, 2, 3, 4, 5, 6, 7, 8, 9, 10, 11, 13, 21; NewC; REn*

Nelson, Jill
American. Journalist
Staff writer, *Washington Post,* 1986-90; contributing editor, *Essence.*
b. 1952 in New York, New York
Source: *ConBlB 6*

Nelson, Judd
American. Actor
Films include *The Breakfast Club,* 1985; member of young actors known as "brat pack."
b. Nov 27, 1960 in Portland, Maine
Source: *ConTFT 4*

Nelson, Larry Gene
American. Golfer
Turned pro, 1971; won PGA, 1981, 1987, US Open, 1983.
b. Sep 10, 1947 in Fort Payne, Alabama

Source: *BioIn 12, 13; WhoAm 82, 84, 86, 88; WhoIntG*

Nelson, Ozzie
[Oswald George Nelson]
American. Actor, Bandleader
Starred in TV series "The Adventures of Ozzie and Harriet," 1952-65.
b. Mar 20, 1906 in Jersey City, New Jersey
d. Jun 3, 1975 in Hollywood, California
Source: *ASCAP 66, 80; BiDAmM; BioIn 1, 2, 3, 4, 7, 9, 10, 12; CmpEPM; ConAu 57, 93; CurBio 49, 75; DcAmB S9; FilmgC; HalFC 80, 84, 88; IntMPA 75; LegTOT; MotPP; PenEncP; SaTiSS; WhAm 6; WhoAm 74; WhScrn 77, 83*

Nelson, Ralph
American. Director
Films include *Requiem for a Heavyweight,* 1962; *Lillies of the Field,* 1963; also directed TV shows.
b. Aug 12, 1916 in New York, New York
d. Dec 21, 1987 in Santa Monica, California
Source: *AnObit 1987; BiDFilm, 81, 94; BioIn 15; ConAu 49, 124; ConTFT 1; FilmEn; FilmgC; HalFC 80, 84, 88; IlWWHD 1A; IntMPA 75, 77, 80, 84; LesBEnT; MiSFD 9N; MovMk; NewYTBS 87; NewYTET; WhAm 9; WhoAm 74, 76, 78, 80, 82, 84; WhoWest 76, 78, 84; WhoWor 74, 76, 82; WorEFlm*

Nelson, Rick
[Stone Canyon Band; Eric Hilliard Nelson]
American. Singer, Actor
Sold 35 million records before age 21; son of Ozzie, Harriet; killed in plane crash.
b. May 8, 1940 in Teaneck, New Jersey
d. Dec 31, 1985 in Dekalb, Texas
Source: *AnObit 1985; BiDAmM; BioIn 14, 15, 17, 18, 21; BkPepl; ConAu 118; ConMuA 80A; ConMus 2; ConNews 86-1; ConTFT 3; CounME 74, 74A; EncFCWM 83; EncPR&S 89; EncRk 88; EncRkSt; FilmgC; HalFC 80, 84, 88; HarEnCM 87; HarEnR 86; IlEncCM; IlEncRk; IntMPA 75, 76, 77, 78, 79, 80, 81, 82, 84, 86; MotPP; NewGrDA 86; OxCPMus; PenEncP; RkOn 74; RolSEnR 83; VarWW 85; WhAm 9; WhoAm 74, 76, 78, 80, 82, 84; WhoHol A; WhoRock 81; WorAl; WorAlBi*

Nelson, Thomas, Jr.
American. Soldier, Continental Congressman
Staunch patriot; signed Declaration of Independence, 1776; succeeded Jefferson as governor of VA, 1781.
b. Dec 26, 1738 in Yorktown, Virginia
d. Jan 4, 1789 in Hanover County, Virginia
Source: *AmBi; ApCAB; BiAUS; BiDrAC; BiDrACR; BiDrUSC 89; BioIn 3, 7, 8, 9, 10, 16; DcAmB; Drake; EncCRAm; EncSoH; HarEnUS; NatCAB 7; TwCBDA; WhAm HS; WhAmP; WhAmRev*

Nelson, Tracy
[Mrs. William Moses]
American. Actor
Daughter of Rick, Kris Nelson, niece of Mark Harmon; appeared on TV show "Square Pegs," 1982-83.
b. Oct 25, 1963 in Santa Monica, California
Source: *BioIn 13; ConTFT 10; IntMPA 94, 96; LegTOT*

Nelson, William Rockhill
American. Newspaper Editor
Joined *Salt Lake Tribune,* 1881, editor-in-chief, 1907-15.
b. Mar 7, 1841 in Fort Wayne, Indiana
d. Apr 13, 1915 in Kansas City, Missouri
Source: *BiDAmJo; BioIn 1, 2, 3, 10, 16; DcAmB; DcLB 23; EncAJ; JrnUS; NatCAB 4; WhAm 1*

Nelson, Willie
American. Singer, Songwriter, Musician
Won Grammys for country songs "Blue Eyes Crying in the Rain," 1975; "Georgia on My Mind," 1978.
b. Apr 30, 1933 in Abbott, Texas
Source: *Baker 84; BgBkCoM; BiDAmM; BioIn 11, 12, 13; CelR 90; ConAu 107; ConLC 17; ConMuA 80A; ConMus 1, 11; ConTFT 5; CounME 74, 74A; CurBio 79; DcArts; EncFCWM 69, 83; EncRk 88; EncRkSt; HalFC 84, 88; HarEnCM 87; HarEnR 86; IlEncCM; IlEncRk; IntMPA 84, 86, 88, 92, 94, 96; LegTOT; NewAmDM; NewGrDA 86; News 93; OnThGG; OxCPMus; PenEncP; RkOn 85; RolSEnR 83; VarWW 85; WhoAm 78, 80, 82, 84, 86, 88, 90, 92, 94, 95, 96, 97; WhoEnt 92; WhoHol 92; WhoRock 81; WorAlBi*

Nemec, Jan
Czech. Director
Films include *Diamonds of the Night.*
b. Jul 2, 1936 in Prague, Czechoslovakia
Source: *BioIn 16; DcFM; DrEEuF; EncEurC; FilmEn; FilmgC; HalFC 80, 84, 88; IntDcF 1-2, 2-2; MiSFD 9; OxCFilm; WhoWor 74; WorEFlm; WorFDir 2*

Nemerov, Howard (Stanley)
American. Poet
Verse volumes include *Mirrors and Windows,* 1958; among many awards is 1978 Pulitzer; US poet laureate, 1988-90.
b. Mar 1, 1920 in New York, New York
d. Jul 5, 1991 in University City, Missouri
Source: *AmAu&B; AmWr; AnObit 1991; Au&Wr 71; Benet 87, 96; BenetAL 91; BioIn 4, 5, 7, 8, 10, 12; BlueB 76; CamGLE; CamHAL; CasWL; ChhPo S1; CnE&AP; ConAu 1NR, 1R, 2BS, 27NR, 53NR, 134; ConLC 2, 6, 9, 36, 70; ConNov 72, 76, 82; ConPo 70, 75, 80, 85, 91; CroCAP; CurBio 64, 91N; CyWA 89; DcArts; DcLB 5, 6, Y83A; DcLEL 1940; DrAF 76; DrAP 75; DrAPF 80; EncWL 2, 3; FacFETw; GrWrEL P; IntAu&W 76, 82, 89, 91, 93; IntWW 74, 75, 76, 77, 78, 79, 80, 81, 82, 83, 89, 91; IntWWP 77; LegTOT; LinLib L; MajTwCW; ModAL, S1, S2; NatCAB 63N; News 92, 92-1; NewYTBS 91; Novels; OxCAmL 65, 83, 95; OxCTwCP; PenC AM; RAdv 1, 14, 13-1; REn; REnAL; RfGAmL 87, 94; RGTwCWr; TwCA SUP; WhAm 10; WhoAm 74, 76, 78, 80, 82, 84, 86, 88, 90; WhoTwCL; WhoUSWr 88; WhoWor 74, 80, 82, 84; WhoWorJ 72, 78; WhoWrEP 89; WorAl; WorAlBi; WrDr 76, 80, 82, 84, 86, 88, 90, 92, 94N*

Nemirovich-Danchenko, Vladimir I
Russian. Author, Dramatist, Producer
Co-founder, Moscow Art Theatre; author, *My Life in the Russian Theatre,* 1937.
b. Dec 23, 1858 in Tiflis, Russia
d. Apr 25, 1943 in Moscow, Union of Soviet Socialist Republics
Source: *CasWL; DcRusL; ModWD; OxCThe 67; PlP&P; REn*

Nenni, Pietro Sandro
Italian. Political Leader, Journalist
Leader of Italian Socialist Party, 1949-69.
b. Feb 9, 1891 in Faenza, Italy
d. Jan 1, 1980 in Rome, Italy
Source: *CurBio 47; IntWW 74*

Nepela, Ondrej
Czech. Skater
Three-time world champion figure skater, 1971-73; won gold medal, 1972 Olympics.
Source: *BioIn 16*

Nernst, Walther Hermann
German. Chemist
Won Nobel Prize, 1920; studied electrochemistry; developed theory of galvanic cells.
b. Jun 25, 1864 in Briesen, Germany
d. Nov 18, 1941 in Muskau, Germany
Source: *AsBiEn; BiESc; CamDcSc; DcInv; DcScB S1; InSci; LarDcSc; ObitOF 79; WhDW; WhoNob, 90, 95; WorAl*

Nero
[Nero Claudius Caesar Germanicus]
Roman. Ruler
Known for persecuting Christians; started fire that destroyed Rome.
b. Dec 15, 37 in Antium, Latinum
d. Jun 9, 68 in Rome, Italy
Source: *Benet 87, 96; BioIn 1, 2, 3, 4, 7, 8, 9, 10, 11, 12, 14, 15, 16, 17, 18, 19, 20; BlmGEL; DicTyr; Dis&D; EncEarC; HisWorL; LegTOT; LngCEL; LuthC 75; NewC; NewGrDM 80; OxCClL, 89; OxCThe 67; OxDcOp; PenC CL; PlP&P; REn; WhDW*

Nero, Franco
Italian. Actor
Played the role of Lancelot in 1967 film *Camelot.*
b. Nov 23, 1941 in Parma, Italy
Source: *ConTFT 6, 13; FilmAG WE; FilmEn; FilmgC; IntMPA 92, 94; IntWW 91, 93; LegTOT; VarWW 85; WhoHol 92, A*

Nero, Peter
American. Pianist, Conductor
Known for nightclub, pop concert performances; leader of over 150 orchestras since 1971; with Philadelphia Pops since 1979.
b. May 22, 1934 in New York, New York
Source: *Baker 84; BiDAmM; BioIn 13; CelR, 90; ConAmC 76; LegTOT; PenEncP; WhoAm 74, 76, 78, 80, 82, 84, 86, 88, 92, 94, 95, 96, 97; WhoAmM 83; WhoE 74, 91, 93; WhoEnt 92; WhoWest 87, 89; WorAl; WorAlBi*

Neruda, Pablo
[Neftali Ricardo Reyes Basualto]
Chilean. Author, Diplomat
Won 1971 Nobel Prize in literature for surrealist poetry.
b. Jul 12, 1904 in Parral, Chile
d. Sep 23, 1973 in Santiago, Chile
Source: *Benet 87, 96; BenetAL 91; BioIn 2, 4, 7, 8, 9, 10, 11, 12, 15, 16, 17, 18, 19; CasWL; CelR; CnMWL; ConAu 45, P-2; ConLC 1, 2, 5, 7, 9, 28, 62; CurBio 70, 73, 73N; CyWA 89; DcArts; DcHiB; DcSpL; DcTwCCu 3; EncLatA; EncWB; EncWL, 2, 3; FacFETw; GrFLW; HispLC; HispWr; LatAmWr; LegTOT; LiExTwC; LinLib L, S; MajTwCW; MakMC; ModLAL; NewYTBE 71; NobelP; ObitT 1971; OxCEng 85, 95; OxCSpan; PenC AM; PoeCrit 4; RadHan; RAdv 14, 13-2; REn; RfGWoL 95; RGFMEP; SpAmA; TwCA SUP; TwCWr; WhAm 6; WhDW; WhoNob, 90, 95; WhoTwCL; WhoWor 74, 78; WorAl; WorAlBi; WorLitC*

Nerval, Gerard de
[Gerard Labrunie]
French. Poet, Translator, Author
Major influence on symbolists, surrealists through his use of fantasy in works: *Sylvie,* 1853.
b. May 22, 1808 in Paris, France
d. Jan 25, 1855 in Paris, France
Source: *AtlBL; BbD; BiD&SB; BioIn 11, 13, 15; CasWL; DcArts; DcEuL; Dis&D; EuAu; EuWr 6; EvEuW; GrFLW; GuFrLit 1; LinLib L; McGEWB; NewEOp 71; NewGrDM 80; NewGrDO; NinCLC 1; OxCEng 85, 95; OxCFr; PenC EUR; PoeCrit 13; RfGShF; RfGWoL 95; ShSCr 18; WhDW*

Nervi, Pier Luigi
Italian. Engineer, Architect
First to use reinforced concrete; designed, built UNESCO's Paris headquarters.
b. Jun 21, 1891 in Sondrio, Italy
d. Jan 9, 1979 in Rome, Italy
Source: *BioIn 4, 5, 6, 8, 11, 12, 13; ConArch 80, 87, 94; ConAu 113; CurBio 58, 79, 79N; DcArts; DcD&D; DcTwDes; EncMA; FacFETw; InSci; IntDcAr; IntWW 74, 75, 76, 77, 78; LinLib S; MacEA; McGDA; McGEWB; NewYTBS 79; OxCArt; WhAm 9; WhDW; Who 74; WhoArch; WhoWor 74; WorAl; WorAlBi*

Nesbit, Edith
[Mrs. Hubert Bland]
English. Children's Author
Wrote popular tales of the "Bastable Children": *The Treasure Seekers,* 1899.
b. Aug 19, 1858 in London, England
d. May 4, 1924
Source: *ArtclWW 2; AtlBL; AuBYP 2; BioIn 15, 16, 19, 20; BlmGWL; CarSB; CasWL; ChhPo; ContDcW 89; DcLEL; DcNaB 1922; EncBrWW; EvLB; FamSYP; InWom, SUP; JBA 34; LngCTC; MorJA; NewC; NewCBEL; OxCEng 67; PenC ENG; PenNWW A; ScFEYrs; TwCA, SUP; TwCChW 78; VicBrit; WhoChL; WomFir; YABC 1*

Nesbit, Evelyn
[Evelyn Nesbit Thaw]
"The Girl on the Red Velvet Swing"
American. Actor
Showgirl, whose husband, Harry Thaw, killed Stanford White in jealousy over her, 1906.
b. Dec 25, 1885 in Tarentum, Pennsylvania
d. Jan 18, 1967 in Santa Monica, California
Source: *BioAmW; BioIn 7, 8, 9, 11; Film 1, 2; InWom; NotNAT A, B; TwYS; WhoHol B; WhScrn 74, 77, 83*

Nesbitt, Cathleen Mary
English. Actor
Originated stage role of Mrs. Higgins in *My Fair Lady,* 1956.
b. Nov 24, 1889 in Liskeard, England
d. Aug 2, 1982 in London, England
Source: *AnObit 1982; BioIn 10, 11; ConAu 107; CurBio 56, 82; FilmgC; InWom; MotPP; MovMk; NewYTBS 82; NotNAT, A; Who 74; WhoAmW 58; WhoHol A; WhoThe 72, 77*

Nesmith, Mike
[The Monkees; Michael Nesmith]
American. Singer, Songwriter
Vocalist with The Monkees on popular TV series, 1966-68; known for trademark wool cap.
b. Dec 30, 1942 in Houston, Texas
Source: *BgBkCoM; BioIn 7, 9, 14; ConMuA 80A; ConTFT 5; EncFCWM 83; EncPR&S 74, 89; EncRk 88; HarEnCM 87; IlEncCM; IlEncRk; IntMPA 92, 94, 96; LegTOT; OnThGG; PenEncP; VarWW 85; WhoAm 84, 86, 88, 90, 92, 94, 95, 96, 97; WhoHol 92; WhoRock 81*

Ness, Eliot
[The Untouchables]
American. Government Official
FBI special agent who headed investigation of Al Capone's gangsterism in Chicago, 1929-32; exploits popularized in books, films, TV series.
b. Apr 19, 1903 in Chicago, Illinois
d. May 7, 1957 in Cleveland, Ohio
Source: *BioIn 1, 15, 16; CopCroC; EncACr; LegTOT; WhAm 3; WorAl; WorAlBi*

Nessen, Ron(ald Harold)
American. Journalist, Presidential Aide
Press secretary, under Pres. Ford, 1974-76.
b. May 25, 1934 in Rockville, Maryland
Source: *BioIn 10, 11, 12; ConAu 106; CurBio 76; PolProf NF; WhoAm 76, 78, 82, 84, 86, 90, 92, 94, 95, 96, 97; WhoAmP 75, 77, 79, 81, 83; WhoE 89*

Nessler, Victor E
German. Composer
Wrote popular opera *Der Trompeter von Sackingen,* 1884.
b. Jan 28, 1841 in Baldenheim, Germany
d. May 28, 1890 in Strassburg, Germany
Source: *Baker 78, 84; NewEOp 71*

Nestingen, Ivan Arnold
American. Government Official
Dem. mayor of Madison, WI, 1956-61; under secretary, HEW, 1961-65.
b. Sep 23, 1921 in Sparta, Wisconsin
d. Apr 24, 1978 in Washington, District of Columbia
Source: *BioIn 5, 6, 11; CurBio 62, 78; IntWW 74, 75, 76; WhoAm 74*

Nestle, Henri
Swiss. Candy Manufacturer
Original chocolate factory in Vevey, Switzerland.
b. 1814, Germany
d. 1890
Source: *Entr; WebBD 83*

Nestle, Joan
American. Writer
Wrote *A Restricted Country,* 1987.
b. May 12, 1940 in New York, New York
Source: *BioIn 16, 19; GayLesB; GayLL; OxCWoWr 95; WhoUSWr 88; WhoWrEP 89, 92, 95*

Nestorius
Syrian. Religious Leader
Patriarch of Constantinople, 428-431, who believed in both divine, human nature of Christ.
b. 389? in Germanicia, Syria
d. 451 in Oasis, Egypt
Source: *BioIn 4; LinLib S; McGEWB*

Netanyahu, Benjamin
[Binyamin Netanyahu]
"Bibi"
Israeli. Political Leader
Israel's ambassador to the United Nations, 1984-88; prime minister of Israel, 1996—.
b. Oct 21, 1949 in Tel Aviv, Israel
Source: *ConAu 152; CurBio 96; HisEAAC; IntWW 89, 91, 93; News 96; WhoWor 87, 89, 96, 97*

Netanyahu, Yonatan
[Johnathan Netaniahu]
"Yoni"
Israeli. Army Officer
Lt. colonel, youngest tank commander in Israeli army; led rescue of hijacked plane at Entebbe Airport; only member of strike force killed.
b. 1946 in New York
d. Jul 3, 1976 in Entebbe, Uganda
Source: *BioIn 12, 21; ConAu 114*

Nethersole, Olga
English. Actor
Arrested in NY for alleged indecency in play *Sapho*, 1900; acquitted; symbol to younger generation of revolt against prudery.
b. Jan 18, 1870 in London, England
d. Jan 9, 1951 in Bournemouth, England
Source: *BioIn 2; CamGWoT; FamA&A; OxCThe 67; PeoHis; WhAm 3; WhoStg 1906, 1908*

Neto, Agostinho
Angolan. Political Leader
First pres. of People's Republic of Angola, 1975-79.
b. Sep 17, 1922 in Icolo e Bengo, Angola
d. Sep 10, 1979 in Moscow, Union of Soviet Socialist Republics
Source: *AfrA; AfSS 78, 79; BiDMarx; BioIn 6, 7, 10; ColdWar 1; ConAu 89, 101; IntWW 78, 79; IntYB 79; NewYTBS 75, 79; PenC CL*

Netsch, Walter Andrew, Jr.
American. Architect
Worked to establish "field theory" of design since 1960; functional, beautiful buildings include U libraries.
b. Feb 23, 1920 in Chicago, Illinois
Source: *BioIn 9, 12; ConArch 80, 87, 94; WhoAm 74, 76, 78, 80, 82, 84; WhoWor 74*

Nettles, Graig
American. Baseball Player
Third baseman, 1967-86, mostly with Yankees; led AL in home runs, 1976.
b. Aug 20, 1944 in San Diego, California
Source: *Ballpl 90; BaseReg 86, 87; BiDAmSp Sup; BioIn 9, 11, 12, 13; CurBio 84; LegTOT; WhoProB 73; WorAl*

Nettleton, Lois June
American. Actor
Won Clarence Derwent for stage role in *God and Kate Murphy*, 1959.
b. Aug 16, 1931 in Oak Park, Illinois
Source: *BiE&WWA; IntMPA 82; NotNAT; VarWW 85; WhoAm 86; WhoHol A; WhoThe 77*

Neuendorff, Adolf
German. Conductor
Conducted first American performances of *Lohengrin*, 1871; led Boston's Music Hall Concerts, 1880s.
b. Jun 13, 1843 in Hamburg, Germany
d. Dec 4, 1897 in New York, New York
Source: *Baker 78, 84; NewEOp 71*

Neuharth, Allen Harold
American. Publisher, Business Executive
With Gannett Co., 1973-91; chm., Freedom Forum, 1991—.
b. Mar 22, 1924 in Eureka, South Dakota
Source: *BioIn 10, 11, 12, 13; ConAmBL; ConNews 86-1; CurBio 86; Dun&B 79; NatCAB 63, 63N; WhoAm 74, 76, 78, 80, 82, 84, 86, 88, 90, 92, 94, 95, 96, 97; WhoE 75, 77, 81, 83, 85, 86, 89; WhoFI 74, 75, 77, 79, 81, 83, 85, 87, 89; WhoSSW 82, 84, 91; WhoUSWr 88; WhoWor 78, 82; WhoWrEP 89, 92, 95*

Neuhaus, Richard John
Canadian. Author
Lutheran pastor; writings include *The Naked Public Square: Religion and Democracy in America*, 1984.
b. May 14, 1936 in Pembroke, Ontario, Canada
Source: *BioIn 10, 13; CurBio 88; IntAu&W 77, 82; WhoAmP 73, 75, 77, 79; WhoE 89; WhoRel 75, 77, 85, 92; WrDr 76, 80, 82, 84, 86*

Neumann, Angelo
Austrian. Opera Singer, Manager
Tenor who produced travelling Wagnerian opera co. in Europe, 1880s.
b. Aug 18, 1838 in Vienna, Austria
d. Dec 20, 1910 in Prague, Czechoslovakia
Source: *Baker 78, 84, 92; MetOEnc; NewEOp 71; NewGrDO; OxDcOp*

Neumann, John Nepomucene, Saint
American. Religious Figure
Roman Catholic bishop, Philadelphia, 1852-60; in 1977 was canonized as first US male Saint.
b. Mar 28, 1811 in Prachatice, Bohemia
d. Jan 5, 1860 in Philadelphia, Pennsylvania
Source: *ApCAB; BiDAmEd; BioIn 6, 7, 8, 11, 12; DcAmB; DcAmReB 2; DcCathB; HarEnUS; NatCAB 5; NewYTBS 77; PeoHis; TwCBDA; WebAB 74, 79; WhAm HS; WorAlBi*

Neumann, Robert Gerhard
American. Diplomat
Ambassador to Afghanistan, 1966-73, to Morocco, 1973-76, to Saudi Arabia, 1981; expert on Middle East affairs.
b. Jan 2, 1916 in Vienna, Austria
Source: *AmMWSc 73S, 78S; BioIn 12; ConAu 5R; IntWW 75, 76, 77, 78, 79, 80, 81, 82, 83, 89, 91, 93; IntYB 78, 79, 80, 81, 82; USBiR 74; WhoAm 74, 76, 78, 80, 82, 84, 86, 88, 90, 92, 94, 95, 96, 97; WhoAmP 73, 75, 77, 79, 81, 83, 85, 87, 89, 91, 93, 95; WhoE 79, 95; WhoGov 72, 75, 77; WhoUSWr 88; WhoWest 74, 76; WhoWor 74, 76, 91, 93; WhoWrEP 89, 92, 95*

Neumeier, John
American. Choreographer, Dancer
Dancer with the Stuttgart Ballet in the 1960s; director, Hamburg Ballet since 1973.
b. Feb 24, 1942 in Milwaukee, Wisconsin
Source: *BiDD; BioIn 9, 11, 12, 13; CnOxB; CurBio 91; IntDcB; IntWW 89, 91, 93; NewYTBS 77; WhoAm 80, 82, 84, 86, 88, 90, 92, 94, 95, 96, 97; WhoEnt 92; WhoWor 82, 84, 91, 93, 95, 96, 97*

Neurath, Konstantin von
German. Diplomat
Appointed "protector" of Czechs, 1939; considered too lenient, later replaced; tried, sentenced in Nuremberg trial for war crimes, 1946.
b. Feb 2, 1873 in Klein Glattbach, Germany
d. Aug 14, 1956 in Enzweihingen, Germany (West)
Source: *BioIn 1, 3, 4; DcPol; Dis&D; EncTR; HisEWW; NewCol 75; ObitOF 79; WhWW-II*

Neurath, Otto
Austrian. Educator
Invented isotypes, pictograph symbols used to visualize statistics, 1923.
b. Dec 10, 1882 in Vienna, Austria
d. Dec 22, 1945 in Oxford, England
Source: *BioIn 1, 14; ConAu 117; ConDes 84; CurBio 46; OxCPhil; ThTwC 87*

Neutra, Richard Joseph
American. Architect
Designed five public housing units; known for postwar housing project with full traffic segregation, 1943.
b. Apr 8, 1892 in Vienna, Austria
d. Apr 16, 1970 in Wuppertal, Germany (West)
Source: *AmAu&B; BioIn 1, 2, 3, 4, 5, 6, 7, 8, 9, 10, 11, 12, 13, 14, 17, 19, 20; ConAu 5NR, 5R, 29R; DcAmB S8; DcArts; EncAAr 1, 2; EncAB-H 1974; EncMA; IntAu&W 77; McGEWB; NatCAB 57; WebAB 74; WhAm 5; WhAmArt 85*

Neuwirth, Bebe
American. Actor
Played Lilith on TV sitcom "Cheers," 1982-93; won Emmy, 1990; won Tony for *Chicago,* 1997.
b. Dec 31, in Newark, New Jersey
Source: *BioIn 15, 16, 17, 20; ConTFT 10; IntMPA 96; WhoAm 92, 94, 95, 96, 97; WhoAmW 89, 91, 93, 95, 97; WhoEnt 92; WhoHol 92*

Nevada, Emma
[Emma Wixom]
American. Opera Singer
Internationally renowned coloratura soprano, 1880s-1905.
b. Feb 7, 1859 in Alpha, California
d. Jun 20, 1940 in Liverpool, England
Source: *AmWom; ApCAB; Baker 78, 84, 92; BiDAmM; BioIn 4, 9, 11; CmCal; CmOp; DcAmB S2; LibW; MetOEnc; MusSN; NewAmDM; NewEOp 71; NewGrDA 86; NewGrDM 80; NewGrDO; NotAW; OxDcOp; PenDiMP; TwCBDA; WhAm 5*

Nevelson, Louise Berliawsky
American. Artist
Pioneer creator of large wall, environmental sculpture: *Sky Gate, New York,* 1978.
b. Sep 23, 1899 in Kiev, Russia
d. Apr 17, 1988 in New York, New York
Source: *ConArt 83; CurBio 67, 88; DcCAA 71; DcWomA; EncAB-H 1974; IntDcWB; NewYTBE 71; WhoAm 86; WhoAmA 84; WhoAmW 87*

Nevers, Ernie
[Ernest Alonzo Nevers]
American. Football Player, Baseball Player
Fullback, 1926-31; scored record 40 pts. in one game, 1929; pitcher, St. Louis, 1925-27; football Hall of Fame, 1963.
b. Jun 11, 1903 in Willow River, Minnesota
d. May 3, 1976 in San Rafael, California
Source: *Ballpl 90; BiDAmSp FB; BioIn 17; CmCal; DcAmB S10; LegTOT; NewYTBS 76; WhoFtbl 74; WhoSpor; WorAl*

Neville, Aaron
[Neville Brothers]
"Wild Tchoupitoulas"
American. Singer
Pop hits include "Tell It Like It Is;" sang duets with Linda Ronstadt on *Cry Like a Rainstorm, Howl Like the Wind.*
b. Jan 24, 1941 in New Orleans, Louisiana
Source: *BioIn 16; ConMus 5; EncPR&S 89; EncRkSt; LegTOT; PenEncP; WhoEnt 92*

Neville, John
English. Actor, Director
English matinee idol, 1950s; artistic director, Canada's Stratford Festival, 1985-89.
b. May 2, 1925 in London, England
Source: *BiE&WWA; BioIn 5; BlueB 76; CamGWoT; CanWW 31, 79, 80, 81, 83, 89; CnThe; ConTFT 4, 14; FilmgC; HalFC 80, 84, 88; IntDcT 3; IntWW 74, 75, 76, 77, 78, 79, 80, 81, 82, 83, 89, 91, 93; MotPP; NotNAT, A; OxCCanT; OxCThe 83; Who 74, 82, 83, 85, 88, 90, 92, 94; WhoAm 88, 90, 92, 94, 95; WhoEnt 92; WhoHol 92, A; WhoMW 88, 90; WhoThe 72, 77, 81; WhoWor 84, 87, 89, 91, 93, 95, 96, 97*

Neville, Kris Ottman
American. Author, Editor
Known for science fiction novels: *The Unearth People; Invaders on the Moon.*
b. May 9, 1925 in Carthage, Missouri
d. Dec 24, 1980
Source: *ConAu 117; TwCSFW 81; WrDr 84*

Neville Brothers, The
American. Music Group
Formed, 1977; R&B/soul performers capture the "New Orleans sound"; albums include *Wild Tchoupitoulas; Yellow Moon.*
Source: *BioIn 15, 16, 17; ConAu X; ConMus 4; DcArts; DcTwCCu 5; EncPR&S 89; EncRkSt; NewYTBS 87; PenEncP; RkOn 78; RolSEnR 83; SoulM; St&PR 96, 97; WhoAfA 96; WhoAm 92, 94, 95, 96, 97; WhoBlA 94; WhoEnt 92; WhoRocM 82; WrDr 96*

Nevin, Ethelbert Woodbridge
American. Composer
Piano pieces included "Narcissus;" wrote music for "The Rosary;" "Mighty Lak a Rose."
b. Nov 25, 1862 in Edgeworth, Pennsylvania
d. Feb 17, 1901 in New Haven, Connecticut
Source: *AmBi; ASCAP 66; Baker 84; DcAmB; OxCAmL 65; REnAL; TwCBDA; WhAm 1*

Nevins, Allan
American. Journalist, Historian
Won Pulitzers for books on American history: *Grover Cleveland,* 1932.
b. May 20, 1890 in Camp Point, Illinois
d. Mar 5, 1971 in Menlo Park, California
Source: *AmAu&B; Benet 87, 96; BenetAL 91; BiDAmEd; BioIn 1, 2, 4, 5, 8, 9, 10, 11, 13, 19; ConAu 5R, 29R, 30NR; CurBio 68, 71, 71N; DcAmC; DcLB 17; EncAAH; EncAB-H 1974, 1996; EncWB; FacFETw; LegTOT; LinLib L, S; LngCTC; NewYTBE 71; OxCAmH; OxCAmL 65, 83, 95; PenC AM; RAdv 14, 13-3; REn; REnAL; TwCA, SUP; WebAB 74, 79; WhAm 5, 8; WorAl; WorAlBi*

Nevski, Alexander, Saint
Russian. Soldier
Kept Russia intact by defeating several outside invaders, circa 1240; Grand Duke of Kiev, Novgorod, 1252.
b. 1220?
d. 1263
Source: *BioIn 4; WhDW*

New, Lloyd Kiva
American. Artist
Cherokee fabric designer; worked with several government and private organizations for the support of Native American art.
b. Feb 18, 1916 in Fairland, Oklahoma
Source: *BioIn 21; NotNaAm*

Neway, Patricia
American. Opera Singer
Soprano who created title role in *Maria Golovin,* 1958.
b. Sep 30, 1919 in New York, New York
Source: *Baker 78, 84, 92; BiE&WWA; CmOp; IntWWM 90; MetOEnc; NewEOp 71; NewGrDA 86; NewGrDM 80; NewGrDO; NotNAT; OxDcOp; VarWW 85; WhoMus 72; WhoThe 72, 77, 81*

Newberry, John Stoughton
American. Railroad Executive
Founder, pres., MI Car Co., which made railroad cars for Union Army, 1863-80.
b. Nov 18, 1826 in Sangerfield, New York
d. Jan 2, 1887 in Detroit, Michigan
Source: *Alli SUP; ApCAB; BiDAmBL 83; BiDrAC; BiDrUSC 89; BioIn 4; DcAmB; DcNAA; NatCAB 12, 41; WhAm HS*

Newbery, John
English. Publisher
Pioneer publisher of children's books: *Mother Goose's Nursery Rhymes,* c. 1760; Newbery Award for excellence in juvenile literature given in his honor since 1922.
b. 1713 in Berkshire, England
d. Dec 22, 1767 in London, England
Source: *Alli; Benet 87, 96; BenetAL 91; BioIn 3, 4, 7, 8, 9, 11, 12, 19, 21; BlkwCE; BritAu; CamGLE; ChhPo, S1; DcLB 154; DcLEL; DcNaB; FacFETw; LegTOT; LinLib L; MajAI; NewC; NewCBEL; OxCChiL; OxCEng 85, 95; REn; REnAL; SmATA 20; WhoChL*

Newcomb, Simon
American. Astronomer
Wrote *Popular Astronomy,* 1878; *The Stars,* 1901.
b. Mar 12, 1835 in Wallace, Nova Scotia, Canada
d. Jul 11, 1909 in Washington, District of Columbia
Source: *Alli SUP; AmAu; AmAu&B; AmBi; ApCAB; AsBiEn; BbD; BiAUS; BiDAmS; BiD&SB; BiDPara; BiESc; BiInAmS; BioIn 3, 4, 5, 6, 8, 11, 12, 14, 16, 18; ConAu 108; DcAmAu; DcAmB; DcCanB 13; DcNAA; DcScB; EncO&P 1, 2, 3; EncPaPR 91; EncSF, 93; GrEconB; HarEnUS; InSci; LinLib L, S; McGEWB; NatCAB 7; OxCAmH; OxCShps; PeoHis; REnAL; ScF&FL 1; ScFEYrs; TwCBDA; TwCSFW 81;*

WebAB 74, 79; WebAMB; WhAm 1; WhDW; WhLit; WhoEc 81, 86

Newcombe, Don(ald)
"Newk"
American. Baseball Player
One of first black pitchers in MLs, mostly with Brooklyn, 1949-51, 1954-60; first recipient of Cy Young Award, 1956, NL MVP, 1956.
b. Jun 14, 1926 in Madison, New Jersey
Source: *Ballpl 90; BiDAmSp BB; BioIn 2, 3, 4, 6, 7, 10, 11, 15, 16, 20; CurBio 57; InB&W 80; WhoProB 73; WhoSpor*

Newcombe, John
"Newk"
Australian. Tennis Player
Won Wimbledon championship, 1967, 1970, 1971.
b. May 23, 1944 in Sydney, Australia
Source: *BioIn 8, 10, 11, 12; BuCMET; ConAu 25NR, 69; CurBio 77; WhoWor 74*

Newcomen, Thomas
English. Inventor
Developed first practical steam engine.
b. Feb 24, 1663 in Dartmouth, England
d. Aug 5, 1729 in London, England
Source: *AsBiEn; BiESc; BioIn 3, 6, 7, 9, 12, 14; DcAmB; DcInv; DcNaB; DcScB; EncEnl; InSci; McGEWB; WhDW; WorInv*

Newell, Allen
American. Scientist
Co-founder of the field of artificial intelligence; founding pres., American Assn. for Artificial Intelligence.
b. Mar 17, 1927 in San Francisco, California
d. Jul 19, 1992 in Pittsburgh, Pennsylvania
Source: *AmMWSc 73S, 76P, 78S, 79, 82, 86, 89, 92; BioIn 15, 18, 19, 20; ConAu 104; HisDcDP; NotTwCS; WhAm 10; WhoAm 74, 76, 78, 80, 82, 84, 86, 88, 90, 92; WhoE 75; WhoEng 80, 88; WhoFrS 84*

Newell, Edward Theodore
American. Scholar
Numismatist expert on hellenistic coins.
b. Jan 15, 1886 in Kenosha, Wisconsin
d. Feb 18, 1941 in New York, New York
Source: *BioIn 2, 4; CurBio 41; DcAmB S3; DcNAA; NatCAB 41; WhAm 1*

Newell, Pete
American. Basketball Coach
Coach, US Olympic team that won gold medal, 1960.
b. Aug 13, 1913 in Vancouver, British Columbia, Canada
Source: *BioIn 5; CmCal; WhoBbl 73*

New Grass Revival, The
American. Music Group
Progressive bluegrass band formed in 1971; plays traditional instruments but incorporates rock, jazz, reggae, R&B influences; albums include *When the Storm Is Over,* 1979.
Source: *Alli SUP; AmMWSc 86; BgBkCoM; BioIn 9, 16; ConMus 4; EncFCWM 83; HarEnCM 87; IlEncCM; OxCCan; WhoAm 97; WhoNeCM; WhoScEu 91-1*

Newhall, Beaumont
American. Historian, Photographer
Pioneered in writing books on history of photography.
d. Feb 26, 1993 in Santa Fe, New Mexico
Source: *BioIn 13; ConAu 9R; DcCAr 81; WhoAm 86; WhoAmA 84*

Newhall, Nancy Wynne
American. Critic, Editor
Photography critic; one of the first to produce books in the oversize format; book with Ansel Adams, *This is the American Earth,* is a classic work in conservationism.
b. May 9, 1908 in Lynn, Massachusetts
d. Jul 7, 1974 in Jackson, Wyoming
Source: *BioIn 10; ConAu 49; NewYTBS 74; WhAm 6*

Newhart, Bob
[George Robert Newhart]
American. Comedian
Known for low-key, dry humor; starred in TV comedies "The Bob Newhart Show," 1972-78; "Newhart," 1982-90; "Bob," 1992-93.
b. Sep 29, 1929 in Oak Park, Illinois
Source: *BioIn 5, 6, 10, 11, 13; BkPepl; CelR, 90; ConTFT 2, 9; CurBio 62; FilmgC; ForYSC; HalFC 84; IntMPA 77, 78, 79, 80, 81, 82, 84, 86, 88, 92, 94, 96; JoeFr; LegTOT; VarWW 85; WhoAm 74, 76, 78, 80, 82, 84, 86, 88, 90, 92, 94, 95, 96, 97; WhoCom; WhoEnt 92; WhoHol 92, A; WhoTelC; WhoWest 89, 92, 94, 96; WhoWor 74; WorAl; WorAlBi*

Newhouse, S(amuel) I(rving), Jr.
"Si"
American. Publishing Executive
Member of Newhouse media empire; in charge of the book and magazine division.
b. Nov 8, 1927 in New York, New York
Source: *BioIn 10, 14, 15, 16; IntWW 91; News 97-1; NewYTBS 89; WhoAm 88; WhoE 91; WhoWor 91; WorAlBi*

Newhouse, Samuel Irving
American. Newspaper Publisher
Owned 31 newspapers; bought Booth Newspapers, Inc. for $305 million.
b. May 24, 1895 in New York, New York
d. Aug 29, 1979 in New York, New York
Source: *ABCMeAm; BioIn 2, 3, 5, 6, 7, 10, 11, 12, 13; ConAu 89; CurBio 61, 79; DcAmB S10; IntWW 74; WhAm 7; WhoAm 74; WorAl*

Newhouser, Hal
[Harold Newhouser]
"Prince Hal"
American. Baseball Player
Pitcher, 1939-55, mostly with Detroit; led AL in wins four times; AL MVP, 1944, 1945—first player to do so consecutively; Hall of Fame, 1992.
b. May 20, 1921 in Detroit, Michigan
Source: *Ballpl 90; BiDAmSp BB; BioIn 1, 2, 4, 5, 6, 15, 17, 18; LegTOT; WhoProB 73; WhoSpor*

Ne Win, U
[Maung Shu Maung]
Burmese. Political Leader
Pres. of Burma, 1974-81; chm., Burma Socialist Party, 1973-88.
b. May 24, 1911 in Paungdale, Burma
Source: *CurBio 71; McGEWB; NewCol 75*

New Kids on the Block
[Jon Knight; Jordan Knight; Joe McIntyre; Donnie Wahlberg; Danny Wood]
American. Music Group
Teen pop group formed in Boston, 1985; albums include *Hangin' Tough,* 1988; *Step By Step,* 1990.
Source: *ConMus 3; EncRkSt; News 91, 91-2*

Newkirk, Ingrid
English. Social Reformer
Animal activist; co-founded People for the Ethical Treatment of Animals, 1980.
b. 1949
Source: *BioIn 16; News 92, 92-3; WhoAm 96; WhoAmW 95*

Newley, Anthony George
English. Actor, Singer, Songwriter
Stage productions include *Stop the World, I Want to Get Off,* 1961-63; wo n Grammy for "What Kind of Fool Am I?" 1962.
b. Sep 24, 1931 in London, England
Source: *BiE&WWA; ConAu 105; ConDr 82D; ConTFT 5; CurBio 66; EncMT; FilmgC; HalFC 84; MotPP; MovMk; NotNAT; OxCFilm; OxCThe 83; VarWW 85; WhoAm 86*

Newman, Alfred
American. Composer, Conductor
Among his nine Oscar-winning scores: *Alexander's Ragtime Band,* 1938; *Song of Bernadette,* 1943; wrote for over 250 films.
b. Mar 17, 1901 in New Haven, Connecticut
d. Feb 17, 1970 in Hollywood, California
Source: *AmPS; ASCAP 66, 80; Baker 78, 84; BiDAmM; BioIn 1, 2, 6, 8, 9; CmMov; CmpEPM; ConAmC 76, 82;*

CurBio 43, 70; DcFM; FilmEn; FilmgC; GangFlm; HalFC 80, 84, 88; IntDcF 1-4, 2-4; LegTOT; NewGrDM 80; NewYTBE 70; OxCFilm; PopAmC, SUP; WhAm 5; WhoHol B; WhScrn 74, 77, 83; WorEFlm

Newman, Arnold Abner
American. Photographer
Best known for environmental symbolic portraiture, especially portraits of famous artists.
b. Mar 3, 1918 in New York, New York
Source: *BioIn 11; ConPhot 82; CurBio 80; MacBEP; News 93-1; WhoAm 86; WhoAmA 84*

Newman, Barnett
American. Artist
Abstract expressionist best known for *Stations of the Cross* series, 1958-66.
b. Jan 29, 1905 in New York, New York
d. Jul 3, 1970 in New York, New York
Source: *AmCulL; BioIn 5, 7, 8, 9, 10, 11, 12, 13, 14, 17, 19, 20; BriEAA; ConArt 77, 83, 89, 96; CurBio 69, 70; DcAmArt; DcAmB S8; DcArts; DcCAA 71, 77, 88, 94; DcTwCCu 1; EncAB-H 1974, 1996; FacFETw; IntDcAA 90; LegTOT; McGDA; McGEWB; NatCAB 53; NewCol 75; OxCTwCA; OxDcArt; PhDcTCA 77; WhAm 4, 5; WhAmArt 85; WhoAmA 78N, 80N, 82N, 84, 84N, 86N, 89N, 91N, 93N; WorAl; WorAlBi; WorArt 1950*

Newman, Barry Foster
American. Actor
Starred in TV series "Petrocelli," 1974-76.
b. Nov 7, 1938 in Boston, Massachusetts
Source: *FilmgC; HalFC 84; VarWW 85; WhoAm 76, 78, 80, 82, 84, 86, 88; WhoEnt 92; WhoHol A; WorAl*

Newman, David
American. Screenwriter
Films include *Bonnie and Clyde,* 1967; *Superman,* 1978.
b. Feb 4, 1937 in New York, New York
Source: *BioIn 8, 12, 15; ConAu 102; ConDr 77A; ConTFT 5; FilmEn; HalFC 84, 88; IntMPA 75, 76, 77, 78, 79, 80, 81, 82, 84, 86, 88, 92, 94, 96; WhoAm 74, 76, 78, 80, 82, 84, 86, 88*

Newman, Edwin Harold
American. Author, Broadcast Journalist
Won six Emmys; wrote *Strictly Speaking,* 1974; *Sunday Punch,* 1979.
b. Jan 25, 1919 in New York, New York
Source: *ConAu 5NR, 69; ConLC 14; ConTFT 5; CurBio 67; IntMPA 86; LesBEnT; VarWW 85; WhoAm 86, 97; WhoTelC*

Newman, Ernest
[William Roberts]
English. Critic, Biographer
Renowned columnist with major English papers including London *Sunday Times,* 1923-59.
b. Nov 30, 1868 in Liverpool, England
d. Jul 7, 1959 in Tadworth, England
Source: *Baker 78, 84, 92; BioIn 4, 5, 6; ConAu 122; DancEn 78; DcLEL; DcNaB 1951; LngCTC; NewC; NewCBEL; NewGrDM 80; NewGrDO; NewOxM; ObitOF 79; OxCMus; OxDcOp; REn; ScFEYrs; TwCA, SUP; WhAm 3; WhE&EA; WhLit*

Newman, Joe Dwight
American. Jazz Musician
Trumpeter who bridged swing and bebop music; played with the Count Basie Orchestra during the 1940-50s.
b. Sep 27, 1922 in New Orleans, Louisiana
d. Jul 4, 1992 in New York, New York
Source: *BiDJaz; CmpEPM; EncJzS; NewAmDM; PenEncP*

Newman, John Henry, Cardinal
English. Theologian, Author
Catholic convert, cofounded Oxford Movement; *Apologia Pro Vita Sua,* 1864, considered masterpiece; helped define liberal arts education.
b. Feb 21, 1801 in London, England
d. Aug 11, 1890 in Birmingham, England
Source: *Alli, SUP; AtlBL; BbD; Benet 87, 96; BiD&SB; BioIn 1, 2, 3, 4, 5, 6, 7, 8, 9, 10, 11, 12, 13, 14, 15, 16, 17, 18, 19, 20, 21; BlmGEL; BritAu 19; CamGEL; CamGLE; CasWL; CelCen; Chambr 3; ChhPo, S1, S3; CrtT 3, 4; CyEd; CyWA 58; DcAmC; DcArts; DcBiPP; DcCathB; DcEnA; DcEnL; DcEuL; DcLB 18, 32, 55; DcLEL; DcNaB; EvLB; GrWrEL N; HisWorL; LinLib L; LngCEL; LuthC 75; McGEWB; MouLC 4; NewC; NewCBEL; NewCol 75; NinCLC 38; OxCEng 67, 85, 95; OxCIri; PenC ENG; PoChrch; RAdv 14, 13-4; REn; RfGEnL 91; VicBrit; WebBD 83; WebE&AL; WhDW; WorAl*

Newman, Joseph Westley
American. Inventor, Businessman
Head of Newman Energy Products; patents include automobile windshield rain deflectors.
b. Jul 2, 1936 in Mobile, Alabama
Source: *BioIn 13; ConNews 87-1*

Newman, Paul
American. Actor, Director, Producer, Auto Racer
Starred in *The Hustler,* 1961; *The Verdict,* 1982; won Oscar for *The Color of Money,* 1987; races Formula One cars.
b. Jan 26, 1925 in Cleveland, Ohio
Source: *BiDFilm, 81, 94; BiE&WWA; BioIn 4, 5, 6, 7, 8, 9, 10, 11, 12, 13, 14, 15, 16, 17, 20, 21; BkPepl; BlueB 76; CelR, 90; CmMov; ConTFT 1, 3, 14; CurBio 59, 85; DcArts; DcTwCCu 1; EncAFC; FacFETw; FilmEn; FilmgC; ForYSC; GangFlm; HalFC 80, 84, 88; IlWWHD 1A; IntDcF 1-3, 2-3; IntMPA 77, 78, 79, 80, 81, 82, 84, 86, 88, 92, 94, 96; IntWW 74, 75, 76, 77, 78, 79, 80, 81, 82, 83, 89, 91, 93; LegTOT; MiSFD 9; MotPP; MovMk; NewCol 75; News 95, 95-3; NewYTBE 71; NewYTBS 86; NotNAT A; OxCFilm; Who 90, 92, 94; WhoAm 74, 76, 78, 80, 82, 84, 86, 88, 90, 92, 94, 95, 96, 97; WhoEnt 92; WhoHol 92, A; WhoThe 72; WhoWor 74, 78, 95, 96; WhThe; WorAl; WorAlBi; WorEFlm*

Newman, Peter Charles
Canadian. Author, Editor
Author of books on Canadian business: *The Canadian Establishment,* 1975; editor, *Maclean's* mag., 1971-82.
b. May 10, 1929 in Vienna, Austria
Source: *CanWW 31, 83; ConAu 3NR, 9NR; WhoAm 84, 86, 97*

Newman, Phyllis
American. Actor, Singer
Won Tony, 1962, for *Subways are for Sleeping.*
b. Mar 19, 1935 in Jersey City, New Jersey
Source: *BiE&WWA; ForYSC; InWom SUP; NotNAT; VarWW 85; WhoHol 92, A; WhoThe 77, 81; WorAl*

Newman, Randy
American. Singer, Songwriter
Known for sarcastic hit single, "Short People," from 1978 album *Little Criminals.*
b. Nov 28, 1943 in Los Angeles, California
Source: *AmSong; Baker 84, 92; BiDAmM; BioIn 12, 13; BkPepl; ConMuA 80A; ConMus 4; ConTFT 9; CurBio 82; EncPR&S 74, 89; EncRk 88; EncRkSt; IlEncRk; IntMPA 94, 96; LegTOT; NewGrDA 86; RkOn 78; VarWW 85; WhoAm 78, 80, 82, 84, 86, 88, 90, 92, 94, 95, 96, 97; WhoEnt 92; WhoRock 81; WhoRocM 82; WorAl; WorAlBi*

Newmar, Julie
[Julia Charlene Newmeyer]
American. Dancer, Actor
Played Catwoman on TV series "Batman," 1966-67; won Tony, 1959, for *Marriage Go 'Round.*
b. Aug 16, 1935 in Los Angeles, California
Source: *BiDD; BiE&WWA; BioIn 15, 18, 21; EncAFC; FilmEn; ForYSC; InWom; ItaFilm; LegTOT; NotNAT; VarWW 85; WhoAm 74; WhoHol 92*

New Order
[Bernard Albrecht; Joy Division; Peter Hook; Stephen Morris]
American. Music Group
New wave, dance music hits include "Blue Monday," 1983.
Source: *BioIn 19; ConMus 11; EncRk 88; EncRkSt; HarEnR 86; NewYTBS 93; OnThGG; RolSEnR 83; WhoHol 92; WhoRocM 82; WhScrn 83; WhsNW 85*

Newquist, Roy
American. Editor
With *Chicago's American,* 1963—; critic, *NY Post,* 1963—.
b. Jul 25, 1925 in Ashland, Wisconsin
Source: *AmAu&B; ConAu 13R; LiJour*

Newsom, Bobo
[Norman Louis Newsom]
"Buck"
American. Baseball Player
Pitcher, 1929-53, with at least 18 clubs; known for storytelling; had 211-222 career wins-losses.
b. Aug 11, 1907 in Hartsville, South Carolina
d. Dec 7, 1962 in Orlando, Florida
Source: *Ballpl 90; BioIn 18; WhoProB 73*

Newton, Christopher
English. Actor
Artistic director of the Shaw Festival, Niagara-on-the-Lake, Ontario, 1980—.
b. Jun 11, 1936 in Deal, England
Source: *BioIn 20, 21; CanWW 31; ConTFT 12; CurBio 95; IntAu&W 89; IntWW 89, 91, 93; IntWWM 90; OxCCanT*

Newton, Helmut
Australian. Photographer
Known for his erotic and provocative photographs.
b. Oct 31, 1920 in Berlin, Germany
Source: *BioIn 16; ConPhot 82, 88, 95; CurBio 91; EncFash; ICPEnP; IntWW 93; LegTOT*

Newton, Huey P(ercy)
American. Political Activist
Founded Black Panther Party with Bobby Seale, 1966; shot to death outside "crack" cocaine house.
b. Feb 17, 1942 in New Orleans, Louisiana
d. Aug 22, 1989 in Oakland, California
Source: *AmSocL; CurBio 73, 89; InB&W 85; LivgBAA; NewYTBE 70; NewYTBS 89; WhoBlA 85*

Newton, Isaac, Sir
English. Philosopher, Mathematician
Developed reflecting telescope, 1668; law of universal gravitation.
b. Dec 25, 1642 in Woolsthorpe, England
d. Mar 20, 1727 in Kensington, England
Source: *Alli; AsBiEn; AstEnc; BbD; Benet 87, 96; BiD&SB; BiDPsy; BiESc; BioIn 1, 2, 3, 4, 5, 6, 7, 8, 9, 10, 11, 12, 13, 14, 15, 16, 17, 18, 20, 21; BlkwCE; BlmGEL; BritAu; CamDcSc; CamGEL; CamGLE; CasWL; Chambr 2; CyEd; CyWA 58; DcBiPP; DcEnA; DcEnL; DcInv; DcLEL; DcNaB; DcScB; Dis&D; EncEnl; EvLB; InSci; LarDcSc; LegTOT; LinLib L; LitC 35; LngCEL; LuthC 75; McGEWB; NamesHP; NatCAB 5; NewC; NewCBEL; NewGrDM 80; OxCEng 67, 85, 95; OxCMed 86; OxCMus; OxCPhil; RAdv 14, 13-4, 13-5; REn; WhDW; WorAl; WorAlBi; WorScD*

Newton, John
English. Clergy, Songwriter
Wrote gospel hymns; with William Cowper published *Onley Hymns,* 1779.
b. Jul 24, 1725 in London, England
d. Dec 21, 1807 in London, England
Source: *Alli; BiD&SB; BioIn 1, 2, 4, 5, 6, 7, 8, 10, 11, 12, 13, 14, 15, 16, 17; CasWL; Chambr 2; ChhPo, S2, S3; DcAfL; DcBiPP; DcEnL; DcEuL; DcNaB; EvLB; LuthC 75; NewC; NewCBEL; OxCEng 67, 85, 95; OxCMus; PoChrch; WebE&AL; WhDW*

Newton, Juice
[Judy Cohen]
American. Singer
Country-pop singer; hit singles include "Angel of the Morning," 1981; "Break It to Me Gently," 1982.
b. Feb 18, 1952 in Virginia Beach, Virginia
Source: *BgBkCoM; BioIn 12, 13, 14; EncFCWM 83; LegTOT; RkOn 85; WhoAm 86; WhoRocM 82*

Newton, Robert
English. Actor
Character actor in British films of the 1930s-40s; films include *Treasure Island,* 1950.
b. Jun 1, 1905 in Shaftesbury, England
d. Mar 25, 1956 in Beverly Hills, California
Source: *BiDFilm, 81, 94; BioIn 4; EncEurC; FilmAG WE; FilmEn; FilmgC; ForYSC; HalFC 80, 84, 88; IlWWBF; IntDcF 2-3; LegTOT; MotPP; MovMk; NotNAT B; OxCFilm; Vers A; WhoHol B; WhScrn 74, 77, 83; WhThe; WorAl; WorEFlm*

Newton, Wayne
"The Midnight Idol"
American. Singer
Hit singles include "Danke Schoen," 1963; "Daddy Don't You Walk So Fast," 1972; highly successful nightclub performer, 1970s—.
b. Apr 3, 1942 in Norfolk, Virginia
Source: *Baker 84, 92; BioIn 10, 11, 12, 13; BkPepl; CelR 90; ConMus 2; ConTFT 11; CurBio 90; LegTOT; PenEncP; RkOn 74, 82; VarWW 85; WhoAm 74, 76, 78, 80, 82, 84, 86, 88, 92, 94, 95, 96, 97; WhoEnt 92; WhoHol 92, A; WhoRock 81; WhoWest 82, 92, 94; WorAl; WorAlBi*

Newton-John, Olivia
English. Singer, Actor
Hit songs include "Physical," 1981; "Heart Attack," 1982; winner of 3 Grammys, 2 CMA awards; starred in *Grease; Xanadu.*
b. Sep 26, 1948 in Cambridge, England
Source: *ASCAP 80; Baker 84, 92; BioIn 11, 12, 13; BioNews 74; BkPepl; CelR 90; ConMus 8; ConTFT 5; CurBio 78; EncRk 88; EncRkSt; HalFC 80, 84, 88; HarEnCM 87; HarEnR 86; HerW, 84; IlEncCM; IlEncRk; IntMPA 86, 88, 92, 94, 96; IntWW 89, 91, 93; InWom SUP; LegTOT; NewGrDA 86; OxCPMus; PenEncP; RolSEnR 83; VarWW 85; WhoAm 76, 78, 80, 82, 84, 86, 88, 90, 92, 94, 95, 96, 97; WhoAmW 81; WhoEnt 92; WhoHol 92; WhoRock 81; WhoWor 76; WorAl; WorAlBi*

Ney, Michel de la Moskova, Prince
French. Military Leader
Known for defense in retreat from Moscow, 1812; commanded Napoleon's Waterloo campaign, 1815.
b. Jan 10, 1769 in Saarlouis, France
d. Dec 7, 1815 in Paris, France
Source: *OxCFr; REn*

Ney, Richard
American. Actor
Starred in *Mrs. Miniver* with Greer Garson, 1942; later became businessman, author: *The Wall Street Jungle.*
b. 1918 in New York, New York
Source: *AuNews 1; FilmEn; FilmgC; ForYSC; HalFC 84; IntMPA 82; VarWW 85*

Neyland, Robert Reese
American. Football Coach
Considered one of footballs greatest coaches; at U. of TN 21 yrs., 1920s-50s.
b. Feb 17, 1892 in Greenville, Texas
d. Mar 28, 1962 in New Orleans, Louisiana
Source: *BiDAmSp FB; BiDWWGF; BioIn 3, 4, 6, 8, 9, 10, 18; DcAmB S7; NatCAB 50; WhAm 4; WhoFtbl 74*

Neyman, Jerzy
American. Mathematician
Principal founder of the field of modern theoretical statistics; won Nat. Medal of Science, 1968.
b. Apr 16, 1899 in Bendery, Russia
d. Aug 5, 1981 in Oakland, California
Source: *AnObit 1981; BioIn 13, 14; ConAu 108; DcScB S2; WhAm 8*

Ng, Fae Myenne
American. Author
Wrote *Bone,* 1993, which focuses on the affects of cultural assimilation on Chinese Americans.
b. 1957?
Source: *ConAu 146; ConLC 81*

Ngau, Harrison
Malaysian. Environmentalist
Environmental activist known since the 1970s for his opposition to the deforestation of Malaysia.
Source: *News 91, 91-3*

Ngo-Dinh-Diem
Vietnamese. Political Leader
Pres., Repub. of Vietnam, 1954-63.
b. Jan 3, 1901 in Hue, Vietnam
d. Nov 3, 1963 in Saigon, Vietnam (South)

Source: *Bioln 3, 4, 5, 6, 13; ColdWar 2; CurBio 64; FacFETw; McGEWB; ObitOF 79; WorAlBi*

Ngo dinh Nhu, Madame
Vietnamese. Politician
Sister-in-law of Ngo dinh Diem; served as his official hostess, 1955-63.
b. 1924

Ngor, Haing S
American. Actor
Won Oscar for Best Supporting Actor, *The Killing Fields,* 1984.
d. Feb 25, 1996 in Los Angeles, California
Source: *Bioln 15, 16; HalFC 88*

Ngugi, James Thiong'o
Kenyan. Author
E Africa's foremost novelist; author of the region's first major English-language novel, *Weep Not, Child,* 1964.
b. Jan 5, 1938 in Limuru, Kenya
Source: *AfrA; AfSS 78, 79, 80, 81, 82; Benet 87, 96; Bioln 13, 14, 15, 17, 18, 19, 21; BlkLC; BlkWr 1, 2; CamGLE; CamGWoT; CasWL; ConAu 27NR, X; ConDr 73, 77, 82, 88; ConLC 3, 36; ConNov 72, 76, 82, 86, 91, 96; CrtSuDr; CyWA 89; DcArts; DcLB 125; DcLEL 1940; DcLP 87A, 87B; DcTwHis; EncWB; EncWL 2, 3; IntAu&W 91; IntDcT 2; IntLitE; IntvWPC; LiExTwC; MajTwCW; ModBlW; ModCmwL; PenC CL; RAdv 14, 13-2; RfGEnL 91; RGAfL; RGTwCWr; SchCGBL; SelBAAf; TwCWr; WebE&AL; WhoWor 89, 96; WorAlBi; WorAu 1970; WrDr 76, 92, 94*

Nguyen Huu Tho
Vietnamese. Revolutionary, Politician
Pres. of the Nat. Liberation Front; a guerrilla movement opposed to the US supported S Vietnamese government; was Vietnam's vp, 1976-80.
b. Jul 10, 1910 in Cho Lon, Vietnam
Source: *Bioln 10; FarE&A 78, 79, 80, 81; IntWW 74, 75, 76, 77, 78, 79, 80, 81, 82, 89, 91, 93; WhoAsAP 91; WhoSocC 78; WhoWor 80, 82, 84, 87, 89, 91, 93, 96*

Nguyen Khanh
Vietnamese. Military Leader, Political Leader
Military official involved in a coup against S. Vietnamese pres. Diem, 1963; served as pres., Jan-Oct 1964.
b. 1927
Source: *Bioln 6, 7, 9; IntWW 75, 76, 77, 78, 79, 80, 81, 82, 83, 89, 91, 93; WhoAsAP 91*

Nguyen thi Binh, Madame
Vietnamese. Politician
Minister of Education, 1976—; member, Council of State, 1981—; vp Vietnam, 1992-93, 95—.
b. 1927, Vietnam
Source: *CurBio 76; IntDcWB; WhoWor 74*

Nguyen Van Thieu
Vietnamese. Statesman
Pres., Republic of Vietnam, 1967-75.
b. Apr 5, 1923 in Tri Thuy, Vietnam
Source: *Bioln 8, 9, 10, 11, 12, 14, 18; ColdWar 1, 2; CurBio 68; FarE&A 78, 79, 80, 81; IntWW 74, 75, 76, 77, 78, 79, 80, 81, 82, 83, 89, 91, 93; NewYTBE 72; WhoGov 72; WhoWor 74, 89*

Niarchos, Stavros (Spyros)
Greek. Shipping Executive
Founded Niarchos Group, 1939, world's largest privately owned fleet of tankers.
b. Jul 3, 1909 in Athens, Greece
d. Apr 15, 1996 in Zurich, Switzerland
Source: *Bioln 18, 21; CelR; CurBio 58, 96N; IntWW 74, 75, 76, 77, 78, 79, 80, 81, 82, 83, 89, 91, 93; IntYB 78, 79, 80, 81, 82; NewYTBE 70; Who 74, 82, 85, 88, 90, 92, 94; WhoFI 74, 77; WhoFr 79; WhoWor 74, 76, 78; WorAl*

Niatum, Duane
[Duane McGinness]
American. Poet
Edited two important anthologies of Native American poetry, *Carriers of the Dream Wheel,* 1975; *Harper's Book of Twentieth Century Native American Poetry,* 1986.
b. 1938 in Seattle, Washington
Source: *Bioln 21; ConAu 21NR, 41R, 45NR; DrAPF 80; IntWWP 77; NatNAL; NotNaAm; WhoUSWr 88; WhoWrEP 89, 92, 95*

Niblo, Fred
[Federico Nobile]
American. Director
Directed Valentino in films *Mark of Zorro; Three Musketeers; Blood and Sand.*
b. Jan 6, 1874 in York, Nebraska
d. Nov 11, 1948 in New Orleans, Louisiana
Source: *BiDFilm 81, 94; Bioln 1, 3, 11; CmMov; DcFM; EncVaud; FilmEn; FilmgC; HalFC 80, 84, 88; IntDcF 1-2, 2-2; MiSFD 9N; MovMk; NatCAB 38; NotNAT B; OxCFilm; TwYS; WhoHol B; WhScrn 74, 77, 83; WorEFlm*

Nicholas, Saint
[Nicholas of Myra]
Roman. Religious Leader
Bishop who is patron saint of children; "Santa Claus" derived from Dutch form of name "Sinte Klaas."
b. 4th cent. in Lycia, Asia Minor
d. Dec 6, 345
Source: *Benet 87, 96; BiB N; Bioln 1, 2, 3, 4, 5, 6, 7, 8, 9, 10, 11, 12, 14, 15; BlmGEL; CasWL; DcBiPP; DcCanB 3; DcCathB; DcNaB; Dis&D; EncEarC; IntWWP 82X; LngCEL; LuthC 75; NewC; OxDcByz; OxDcP 86; REn; WhoRel 92*

Nicholas, Cindy
Canadian. Swimmer
Marathon swimmer; first woman to complete two-way English Channel swim.
b. Aug 20, 1957 in Toronto, Ontario, Canada
Source: *Bioln 11, 12; CanWW 31, 89; WhoAmW 91*

Nicholas, Denise
American. Actor
Played in TV series "Room 222," 1969-74; also had roles in feature films.
b. Jul 12, 1944 in Detroit, Michigan
Source: *BlksAmF; DrBlPA, 90; InB&W 85; WhoAfA 96; WhoBlA 88, 92, 94; WhoHol A*

Nicholas, Nicholas John, Jr.
American. Business Executive
Pres., chief operating officer, Time, Inc., 1986-92.
b. Sep 3, 1939 in Portsmouth, New Hampshire
Source: *IntWW 91, 93; St&PR 84; WhoAm 82, 90, 92; WhoE 81, 89, 91; WhoFI 85, 87, 89, 92; WhoWor 89*

Nicholas Brothers
[Fayard Nicholas; Harold Nicholas]
American.
Tap dance team famous for impossible jumps into splits, late 1920s-40s; regularly performed at Cotton Club; in films *Sun Valley Serenade,* 1941; *Stormy Weather,* 1943.
Source: *BiDD; Bioln 14, 17, 18, 21; DcTwCCu 5; DrBlPA 90; HalFC 84; InB&W 80, 85B; NewGrDJ 88, 94*

Nicholas I
Russian. Ruler
Ruled Russia, 1825-55; during reign Turkey declared war on Russia, 1853, which led to the Crimean War.
b. Jul 6, 1796 in Tsarkoe Selo, Russia
d. Mar 2, 1855 in Saint Petersburg, Russia
Source: *NewCol 75; WebBD 83; WhDW*

Nicholas II
[Nikolai Aleksandrovich Romanov]
Russian. Ruler
Last czar of Russia, 1894-1917, whose disorganization led to revolution of 1917; executed with family.
b. May 18, 1868 in Tsarskoe Selo, Russia
d. Jul 16, 1918 in Ekaterinburg, Union of Soviet Socialist Republics
Source: *NewCol 75; WebBD 83; WhDW*

Nicholas of Cusa
German. Religious Leader, Scientist
Cardinal, 1448-64; believed earth revolved on axis around sun before Newton, Copernicus.
b. 1401? in Cusa, Germany
d. Aug 11, 1464 in Todi, Italy
Source: *AsBiEn; BiESc; Bioln 18; DcLB 115; DcScB; IlEncMy; InSci; LuthC 75;*

McGEWB; NewCol 75; OxCLaw; OxCMed 86; OxCPhil; RAdv 14, 13-4; WorAl; WorAlBi

Nichols, Anne
American. Dramatist, Architect
Best known for *Abie's Irish Rose,* 1922.
b. Nov 26, 1891? in Dales Mill, Georgia
d. Sep 15, 1966 in Englewood Cliffs, New Jersey
Source: *AmAu&B; AmWomD; AmWomPl; AmWomWr; BiE&WWA; BioIn 7, 16; CamGWoT; EvLB; InWom; LegTOT; LngCTC; McGEWD 72; ModWD; NotNAT B; NotWoAT; OxCAmT 84; REn; REnAL; TwCWr; WhAm 4; WhScrn 83; WhThe*

Nichols, Beverley
[John Beverley Nichols]
English. Writer
Successful, witty works include novels, plays, nonfiction; best known for scandalous autobiography *Father Figure,* 1972.
b. Sep 9, 1898 in Bristol, England
d. Sep 15, 1983 in Kingston-upon-Thames, England
Source: *AnObit 1983; ConAu 17NR, 93, 110; DcLEL; DcNaB 1981; EvLB; IntAu&W 77; NewC; OxCChiL; ScF&FL 92; TwCA SUP; TwCChW 78; TwCCr&M 80, 85, 91; WhAm 8; WhE&EA; Who 83; WhThe; WrDr 82, 84*

Nichols, Bobby
[Robert Nichols]
American. Golfer
Turned pro, 1959; won PGA, 1964.
b. Apr 14, 1936 in Louisville, Kentucky
Source: *BioIn 10; LegTOT; WhoGolf; WhoIntG*

Nichols, Kid
[Charles Augustus Nichols]
American. Baseball Player
Pitcher, 1890-1901, 1904-06, mostly with Boston; had 360 career wins; Hall of Fame, 1949.
b. Sep 14, 1869 in Madison, Wisconsin
d. Apr 11, 1953 in Kansas City, Missouri
Source: *Ballpl 90; BiDAmSp BB; BioIn 3, 7, 14, 15; LegTOT; WhoProB 73; WhoSpor*

Nichols, Mike
[Michael Igor Peschkowsky]
American. Director
Noted for works on Broadway, film; won many Tonys, including one for *The Odd Couple,* 1965; won Oscar for *The Graduate,* 1967.
b. Nov 6, 1931 in Berlin, Germany
Source: *AmFD; BenetAL 91; BiDFilm 81, 94; BiE&WWA; BioIn 4, 5, 6, 7, 8, 9, 10, 11, 13; BkPepl; BlueB 76; CamGWoT; CelR, 90; ConTFT 1, 8; CurBio 61, 92; DcFM; DcTwCCu 1; EncAFC; EncWT; Ent; FacFETw; FilmEn; FilmgC; GrStDi; HalFC 80, 84, 88; IlWWHD 1; IntDcF 1-2, 2-2; IntMPA 75, 76, 77, 78, 79, 80, 81, 82, 84, 86, 88, 92, 94, 96; IntWW 74, 75, 76, 77, 78, 79, 80, 81, 82, 83, 89, 91; LegTOT; MiSFD 9; MovMk; News 94; NewYTBS 84; NewYTET; NotNAT; OxCAmT 84; OxCFilm; OxCThe 83; TheaDir; VarWW 85; WebAB 74, 79; WhoAm 78, 80, 82, 84, 86, 88, 90, 92, 94, 95, 96, 97; WhoE 74; WhoEnt 92; WhoHol 92, A; WhoThe 72, 77, 81; WhoWest 96; WhoWor 74, 78, 80, 82, 95; WomWMM; WorAl; WorAlBi; WorEFlm; WorFDir 2*

Nichols, Nichelle
American. Actor
Was Lieut. Uhura on "Star Trek," 1966-69.
b. c. 1933 in Robbins, Illinois
Source: *ConBlB 11; InB&W 80, 85; WhoHol 92*

Nichols, Peter
English. Dramatist
Published play *A Day in the Death of Joe Egg,* 1967; wrote screenplay for *Georgy Girl,* 1966.
b. Jul 31, 1927 in Bristol, England
Source: *Au&Wr 71; Benet 87, 96; BioIn 10, 12, 13, 14, 15, 16, 17; BlmGEL; BlueB 76; CamGLE; CamGWoT; CnThe; ConAu 33NR, 104; ConDr 73, 77, 82, 88; ConLC 5, 36, 65; ConTFT 4; CrtSuDr; CyWA 89; DcArts; DcLB 13; DcLEL 1940; EncWT; Ent; LegTOT; MajTwCW; McGEWD 72; ModBrL S1, S2; NewYTBS 74; VarWW 85; WhoThe 72, 77, 81; WorAu 1950, 1970; WrDr 76, 80, 82, 84, 86, 88, 90, 92*

Nichols, Red
[The Five Pennies; Ernest Loring Nichols]
American. Musician, Radio Performer
Popular 1920s-30s jazz trumpeter; biographical film, *The Five Pennies,* 1959.
b. May 8, 1905 in Ogden, Utah
d. Jun 28, 1965 in Las Vegas, Nevada
Source: *AllMusG; ASCAP 66, 80; Baker 78, 84; BiDAmM; BiDJaz; BioIn 4, 7, 9, 12; CmpEPM; IlEncJ; LegTOT; NewAmDM; NewGrDA 86; NewGrDJ 88, 94; NewGrDM 80; OxCPMus; PenEncP; WhoHol B; WhoJazz 72; WhScrn 74, 77, 83; WorAl; WorAlBi*

Nichols, Ruth Rowland
American. Aviator
Held over 35 firsts in women's aviation categories; co-founded the Ninety-Nines with Amelia Earhart.
b. Feb 23, 1901 in New York, New York
d. Sep 25, 1960 in New York, New York
Source: *DcAmB S6; InSci; InWom; NotAW MOD; WhAm 4; WhoAmW 58, 61*

Nicholson, Ben
English. Artist
Abstract painter who won Guggenheim International Award, 1956.
b. Apr 10, 1894 in Uxbridge, England
d. Feb 6, 1982 in London, England
Source: *AnObit 1982; BioIn 1, 2, 4, 5, 6, 8, 9, 11, 12, 13, 17; BlueB 76; ConArt 77, 83, 89, 96; ConAu 110; ConBrA 79; CurBio 58, 82, 82N; DcArts; DcBrAr 1; DcCAr 81; FacFETw; IntDcAA 90; IntWW 74, 75, 76, 77, 78, 79, 80, 81; MakMC; McGDA; McGEWB; NewYTBS 82; OxCArt; OxCTwCA; OxDcArt; PhDcTCA 77; TwCPaSc; WhAm 8; WhDW; Who 74, 82; WhoAm 74, 76, 78, 80, 82; WhoAmA 76, 78, 80, 82, 84N, 86N, 89N, 91N, 93N; WhoWor 74, 76; WorArt 1950*

Nicholson, Jack
[John Joseph Nicholson]
American. Actor, Director
Won Oscars for *One Flew Over the Cuckoo's Nest,* 1975; *Terms of Endearment,* 1983; played Joker in mega-hit, *Batman,* 1989.
b. Apr 22, 1937 in Neptune, New Jersey
Source: *BiDFilm 81, 94; BioIn 8, 9, 10, 11, 12, 13; BioNews 74; BkPepl; CelR, 90; ConAu 116, 143; ConTFT 1, 3, 11; CurBio 74, 95; DcArts; DcTwCCu 1; FacFETw; FilmEn; FilmgC; GangFlm; HalFC 80, 84, 88; IntDcF 1-3, 2-3; IntMPA 82, 92, 94, 96; IntWW 75, 76, 77, 78, 79, 80, 81, 82, 83, 89, 91, 93; ItaFilm; LegTOT; MiSFD 9; MotPP; MovMk; News 89-2; NewYTBS 74; OxCFilm; VarWW 85; Who 90, 92, 94; WhoAm 76, 78, 80, 82, 84, 86, 88, 90, 92, 94, 95, 96, 97; WhoEnt 92; WhoHol 92, A; WhoHrs 80; WhoWor 78, 95, 96, 97; WorAl; WorAlBi*

Nicholson, Seth Barnes
American. Astronomer
Discovered four satellites of Jupiter, 1914-51.
b. Nov 12, 1891 in Springfield, Illinois
d. Jul 2, 1963 in Los Angeles, California
Source: *AsBiEn; BiESc; BioIn 4, 6, 8, 9; DcAmB S7; DcScB; InSci; WebBD 83; WhAm 4*

Nickerson, Albert L(indsay)
American. Business Executive
Began career as service station attendent, 1933; director of Socony-Vacuum, 1946; CEO, Mobil Oil, 1958-69.
b. Jan 17, 1911 in Dedham, Massachusetts
d. Aug 7, 1994 in Cambridge, Massachusetts
Source: *BioIn 4, 5; CurBio 59, 94N; IntWW 74, 75, 76, 77, 78, 79, 80, 81, 82, 83, 89, 91, 93; IntYB 78, 79, 80, 81, 82; WhAm 11; Who 74, 82, 83, 85, 88, 90, 92, 94; WhoAm 74, 76, 78, 80, 82, 84, 86, 88, 90, 92, 94*

Nicklaus, Jack William
"Golden Bear"
American. Golfer
Turned pro, 1961; has won more major tournaments, 17, than any golfer; has written several books on golf

technique, strategy; has designed several golf courses in US.
b. Jan 21, 1940 in Columbus, Ohio
Source: *BiDAmSp OS; BusPN; ConAu 16NR, 39NR, 89; CurBio 62; FacFETw; IntWW 81, 82, 83, 89, 91, 93; NewYTBE 72, 73; NewYTBS 74, 75, 79, 86; WebAB 74, 79; Who 82, 83, 85, 88, 90, 92, 94; WhoAm 74, 76, 78, 80, 82, 84, 86, 88, 92, 94, 95, 96, 97; WhoGolf; WhoIntG; WhoWor 97*

Nickles, Donald Lee
American. Politician
Rep. senator from OK, 1981—.
b. Dec 6, 1948 in Ponca City, Oklahoma
Source: *BiDrUSC 89; CngDr 81, 83, 85, 87; IntWW 81, 82, 83, 89, 91, 93; WhoAmP 79, 81, 83, 85, 87, 89, 91, 93, 95*

Nicks, Stevie
[Fleetwood Mac; Stephanie Nicks]
American. Singer, Songwriter
First solo album was *Bella Donna,* 1981.
b. May 26, 1948 in Phoenix, Arizona
Source: *BioIn 12, 13; BkPepl; ConMus 2; EncPR&S 89; IntWW 93; InWom SUP; LegTOT; RkOn 85; VarWW 85; WhoAm 80, 82, 84, 86, 88, 90, 92, 94, 95, 96, 97; WhoAmW 81, 83; WhoEnt 92; WhoRocM 82*

Nick the Greek
[Nicholas Andrea Dandolos]
American. Gambler
Gained fame as fastest craps shooter in US; estimated he won, lost $500 million.
b. 1896 in Rethymon, Crete
d. Dec 25, 1966 in Los Angeles, California
Source: *BioIn 7, 8; ObitOF 79*

Nicodemus
Biblical Figure
Helped Joseph of Arimathea bury Jesus.
Source: *Benet 96; BioIn 2, 4, 5, 9; DcCathB; DcLP 87B; NewCol 75; WebBD 83; WhoHol 92*

Nicolai, Carl Otto Ehrenfried
German. Composer
Wrote popular opera *Merry Wives of Windsor,* 1849.
b. Jun 9, 1810 in Konigsberg, Germany
d. May 11, 1849 in Berlin, Germany
Source: *Baker 84; Dis&D; NewEOp 71; OxCMus; WebBD 83*

Nicolay, John George
American. Author
Private secretary to Lincoln, 1861-65; with John Hay, wrote first authoritative biography *Abraham Lincoln: A History,* published serially, 1886-90.
b. Feb 26, 1832 in Essingen, Bavaria
d. Sep 26, 1901 in Washington, District of Columbia
Source: *Alli SUP; AmAu; AmAu&B; AmBi; ApCAB; BbD; BiD&SB; BioIn 1, 7, 9, 15; CamGEL; CivWDc; DcAmAu; DcAmB; DcNAA; HarEnUS; NatCAB 8; OhA&B; OxCAmL 65, 83, 95; REnAL; TwCBDA; WebBD 83; WhAm 1; WhAmP; WhCiWar*

Nicolet, Jean
French. Explorer
First European to discover Lake Michigan and area of WI and MI, 1634.
b. 1598 in Cherbourg, France
d. Nov 1, 1642 in Sillery, Quebec, Canada
Source: *AmBi; ApCAB; BioIn 1, 4, 5, 18; DcAmB; EncCRAm; InSci; LegTOT; OxCAmH; REnAW; WebAB 74, 79; WhAm HS; WhNaAH; WhWE; WorAl; WorAlBi*

Nicolini
[Nicola Grimaldi]
Italian. Opera Singer
Celebrated male contralto, formerly soprano; renowned for his acting.
b. Apr 1673 in Naples, Italy
d. Jan 1, 1732 in Naples, Italy
Source: *Baker 84, 92; NewAmDM; NewEOp 71; NewGrDM 80; NewGrDO; OxDcOp; PenDiMP*

Nicoll, (John Ramsay) Allardyce
American. Critic
Theater historian; master of dramatic research.
b. Jun 28, 1894 in Glasgow, Scotland
d. Apr 17, 1976, England
Source: *Au&Wr 71; BiE&WWA; BioIn 4, 10, 11; BlueB 76; ChhPo; ConAu 5NR, 9R, 65; DcLEL; DcNaB 1971; EncWT; EvLB; IntAu&W 76; IntWW 74, 75, 76; LngCTC; NewCBEL; NotNAT; OxCThe 67, 83; REn; TwCA, SUP; WhE&EA; WhLit; Who 74; WhoAm 74; WhoThe 72, 77, 81; WhoWor 74; WrDr 76*

Nicolle, Charles Jules Henri
French. Physician
Won 1928 Nobel Prize in medicine for work on typhus.
b. Sep 21, 1866 in Rouen, France
d. Feb 28, 1936 in Tunis, Tunisia
Source: *AsBiEn; BiESc; BiHiMed; CamDcSc; DcAmB S1; DcScB, S1; InSci; LarDcSc; WhoNob, 90, 95*

Nicolson, Harold George, Sir
English. Statesman, Author
MP, 1935-45; *Diaries and Letters,* Vols. I-III, 1930-62, cover historic events.
b. Nov 21, 1886 in Tehran, Persia
d. May 1, 1968 in Cranbrook, England
Source: *BioIn 14, 15, 16, 17, 18, 20, 21; ConAu P-1; DcLEL; DcNaB 1961; EncSF 93; EncWB; EvLB; GrBr; LngCTC; ModBrL; NewC; NewCBEL; OxCEng 85, 95; PenC ENG; REn; TwCA, SUP; TwCWr; WhAm 7; WhoLA; WorAl*

Nicolson, Nigel
English. Author
Wrote *Portrait of a Marriage,* 1973, about 50-yr. union of his father and mother.
b. Jan 19, 1917 in London, England
Source: *BioIn 13, 21; BlueB 76; ConAu 101; DcLB 155; IntAu&W 77, 89, 91, 93; IntYB 78, 79, 80, 81, 82; Who 74, 82, 83, 85, 88, 90, 92, 94; WorAu 1975; WrDr 76, 80, 82, 84, 86, 88, 90, 92, 94, 96*

Nicot, Jean
French. Diplomat
Ambassador to Portugal; best known for tobacco, Nicotiana, named in his honor; used as a cure all.
b. 1530 in Nimes, France
d. May 5, 1600 in Paris, France
Source: *DcBiPP; DcScB; Dis&D; OxCFr*

Nidal, Abu
[Sabri Khalil al-Banna]
Palestinian. Terrorist
Founder, leader, Fatah-Revolutionary Council, 1973—.
b. May 1937 in Jaffa, Palestine
d. 1984 in Baghdad, Iraq
Source: *ConNews 87-1*

Nidetch, Jean
American. Business Executive
Founded Weight Watchers International, 1963; wrote *Weight Watchers Cookbook,* 1966.
b. Oct 12, 1923 in New York, New York
Source: *BioIn 9, 10, 12, 13; ConAu 89; CurBio 73; GoodHs; GrLiveH; LegTOT; St&PR 75, 84, 87; WhoAm 74, 76, 78, 80, 82, 84, 86, 88, 96; WhoAmW 74, 75, 77, 79, 83, 85, 87, 89; WhoWor 76; WorAlBi*

Niebuhr, Helmut Richard
American. Theologian
Wrote on theology, Christian ethics; professor of Christian ethics at Yale U for 30 yrs.
b. Sep 3, 1894 in Wright City, Missouri
d. Jul 5, 1962 in Greenfield, Massachusetts
Source: *AmAu&B; BioIn 6, 7, 8, 11, 12, 13, 14, 19, 20; ConAu 116; DcAmB S7; DcAmReB 1, 2; EncARH; IntEnSS 79; LuthC 75; McGEWB; NatCAB 47; ObitOF 79; RelLAm 91; ThTwC 87; WhAm 4*

Niebuhr, Reinhold
American. Theologian, Author
Pioneered philosophy of "Christian realism;" wrote *Nature and Destiny of Man,* 1943; received Presidential Medal of Freedom, 1964.
b. Jun 21, 1892 in Wright City, Missouri
d. Jun 1, 1971 in Stockbridge, Massachusetts
Source: *AmAu&B; AmDec 1940, 1950; AmPeW; AmSocL; AmWr; Benet 87, 96; BenetAL 91; BiDMoPL; BioIn 1, 2, 3, 4, 5, 6, 7, 8, 9, 10, 11, 12, 13, 14, 15, 16, 17, 18, 19, 20, 21; CasWL; ColdWar 1;*

ConAu 29R, 41R; CurBio 41, 51, 71, 71N; DcEcMov; DcLB 17; EncAB-H 1974, 1996; EncARH; EncEth; FacFETw; IntEnSS 79; LegTOT; LinLib L; LngCTC; LuthC 75; MakMC; McGEWB; ModAL; MorMA; NewYTBE 71; ObitT 1971; OxCAmH; OxCAmL 65, 83, 95; PeoHis; PolPar; PolProf E, K, T; RAdv 14, 13-4; RComAH; RelLAm 91; REn; REnAL; ThTwC 87; TwCA, SUP; WebAB 74, 79; WhAm 5; WhE&EA; WorAl; WorAlBi; WrPh P

Niekisch, Ernest
German. Political Activist, Revolutionary
Socialist leader active in several socialist parties; promoted nationalism and revolutionary ideals; wrote for several newspapers; started his own journal; imprisoned for "literary high treason," 1937-39.
b. May 23, 1889 in Trebnitz, Silesia
d. May 23, 1967 in Berlin, Germany (West)
Source: *BiDExR; BioIn 14; EncTR 91*

Niekro, Joe
[Joseph Franklin Niekro]
American. Baseball Player
Pitcher, 1967-88; with brother Phil, holds ML record for wins by brother combination; most winning pitcher in Astros' history.
b. Nov 4, 1944 in Martins Ferry, Ohio
Source: *Ballpl 90; BaseEn 88; BaseReg 87, 88; BiDAmSp BB; BioIn 12, 15, 16, 17; LegTOT; WhoAm 82, 84, 86; WhoProB 73*

Niekro, Phil(ip Henry)
American. Baseball Player
Pitcher, 1964-87; first knuckleball pitcher, 18th in ML history to win 300 games, 1985; Hall of Fame, 1997.
b. Apr 1, 1939 in Blaine, Ohio
Source: *Ballpl 90; BaseReg 86, 87; BiDAmSp BB; BioIn 8, 11, 12, 13; LegTOT; NewYTBS 82, 84, 85; WhoAm 82, 84, 86; WhoProB 73*

Nielsen, Alice
American. Opera Singer
Grand, light opera soprano featured in Victor Herbert operettas, 1920s-30s.
b. Jun 7, 1876 in Nashville, Tennessee
d. Mar 8, 1943 in New York, New York
Source: *Baker 78, 84; BiDAmM; CurBio 43; DcAmB S3; InWom, SUP; NewEOp 71; NewGrDO; NotAW; NotNAT B; ObitOF 79; OxCAmT 84; WhAm 2; WhoStg 1906, 1908; WhThe; WomWWA 14*

Nielsen, Arthur Charles
American. Businessman
Founded market research firm that conducts Nielsen TV ratings, 1923.
b. Sep 5, 1897 in Chicago, Illinois
d. Jun 1, 1980 in Chicago, Illinois
Source: *BiDAmBL 83; BioIn 2, 5, 7, 8, 11, 12; BlueB 76; CurBio 51; DcAmB S10; InSci; IntYB 78, 79, 80, 81; NewYTBS 80; St&PR 75; WhAm 7; WhoAm 74, 76, 78, 80, 84; WhoFI 74, 75, 83; WhoMW 76, 78; WorAl*

Nielsen, Carl August
Danish. Composer, Conductor
Led Copenhagen music functions, 1915-27; wrote symphonies, operas including *Maskerade,* 1906.
b. Jun 9, 1864 in Norre-Lyndelse, Denmark
d. Oct 2, 1931 in Copenhagen, Denmark
Source: *Baker 84; DcCM; McGEWB; NewOxM; WebBD 83*

Nielsen, Leslie
Canadian. Actor
Starred in *The Poseidon Adventure,* 1972; *Airplane,* 1980.
b. Feb 11, 1926 in Regina, Saskatchewan, Canada
Source: *BioIn 13; CanWW 31; ConTFT 3, 11; FilmEn; FilmgC; ForYSC; IntMPA 82, 84, 86, 88, 92, 94, 96; MotPP; MovMk; VarWW 85; WhoAm 82, 90, 92, 94, 95, 96, 97; WhoEnt 92; WhoHol A; WorAl*

Nielson, Brigitte
Danish. Actor
Films include *Beverly Hills Cop II,* 1987; once married to Sylvester Stallone.
Source: *BioIn 14, 15*

Nieman, Lucius William
American. Newspaper Publisher
Founded *Milwaukee Journal,* 1882; newspaper won Pulitzer, 1919.
b. Dec 13, 1857 in Bear Creek, Wisconsin
d. Oct 1, 1935
Source: *BiDAmJo; BioIn 5; DcAmB S1; DcLB 25; EncAB-A 6; NatCAB 1, 27; WhAm 1*

Niemann, Albert
German. Opera Singer
Tenor; starred in Wagnerian premiers, 1860s-80s.
b. Jan 15, 1831 in Erxleben, Germany
d. Jan 13, 1917 in Berlin, Germany
Source: *Baker 78, 84, 92; BioIn 1, 16; CmOp; MetOEnc; NewEOp 71; NewGrDM 80; NewGrDO; OxDcOp; PenDiMP*

Niemann, Gunda
German. Skater
Won 2 gold medals in speedskating in the 3,000 and 5,000 meters at the 1992 Winter Olympics; won a silver medal in the 1,500 meter race.

Niemeyer, Oscar
[Soares Filho Oscar Niemeyer]
Brazilian. Architect
Designs were considered flamboyant compared to minimal standards used during depressed times in Europe; won Lenin Peace Prize, 1963; Pritzger, 1988.
b. Dec 15, 1907 in Rio de Janeiro, Brazil
Source: *BioIn 1, 5, 7, 9, 10, 12, 16, 18; ConArch 80, 87, 94; CurBio 60; DcArts; DcD&D; EncLatA; EncMA; IntDcAr; IntWW 74, 75, 76, 77, 78, 79, 80, 81, 82, 83, 89, 91, 93; MacEA; MakMC; McGDA; McGEWB; OxCArt; Who 74, 82, 83, 85, 88, 90, 92, 94; WhoArch; WhoWor 74, 89*

Nieminen, Toni
Finnish. Skier
Became the youngest male, at 16, in Olympic history to win an inividual gold medal at the 1992 Winter Olympics in ski jumping; also won a team gold medal and a bronze.
b. 1976? in Lahti, Finland

Niemoller, Martin
[Friedrich Gustav Emil Martin Niemoller]
German. Theologian
Protestant who led church's opposition to Hitler; became prominent pacifist; pres., World Council of Churches, 1961-68.
b. Jan 14, 1892 in Lippstadt, Germany
d. Mar 6, 1984 in Wiesbaden, Germany
Source: *AnObit 1984; BioIn 1, 2, 5, 6, 7, 9, 12, 13, 14, 15, 16; CurBio 65, 84, 84N; DcEcMov; DcTwHis; EncGRNM; EncTR 91; IntWW 74, 75, 76, 77, 78, 79, 80, 81, 82, 83; LngCTC; LuthC 75; NewYTBS 84; OxCGer 76, 86; REn; WhDW; Who 82, 83, 85N*

Niepce, Joseph Nicephore
French. Physician, Scientist
Photographic discoveries include first negative on paper, 1816; first known photograph on metal, 1827.
b. Mar 7, 1765 in Chalon-sur-Saore, France
d. Apr 5, 1833 in Chalon-sur-Saone, France
Source: *AsBiEn; BioIn 2, 8, 12, 13; CamDcSc; DcBiPP; DcFM; DcInv; DcScB; ICPEnP; InSci; LarDcSc; MacBEP; NewCol 75; OxCFr; WorInv*

Nietzsche, Friedrich Wilhelm
German. Philosopher, Poet
Glorified the "super man," denouncing Christianity; among most influential works: *Thus Spake Zarathustra,* 1891.
b. Oct 15, 1844 in Rocken, Saxony
d. Aug 25, 1900 in Weimar, Germany
Source: *AtlBL; Baker 92; BiD&SB; BiDPsy; BioIn 1, 2, 3, 4, 5, 6, 7, 8, 9, 10, 11, 12, 13, 14, 15, 16, 17, 18, 19, 20, 21; BlmGEL; CasWL; ClDMEL 47, 80; ConAu 107; CyEd; CyWA 58; DcArts; DcEuL; Dis&D; EncPaPR 91; EncRev; EncUnb; EncWL; EuAu; EvEuW; LinLib L, S; LuthC 75; NamesHP; NewC; NewCBEL; NewCol 75; NewGrDO; OxCEng 67, 85, 95; OxCGer 76; OxCPhil; OxDcOp; PenC EUR; RAdv 14, 13-4; RComWL; REn; RfGWoL 95*

Nieuwendyk, Joe
Canadian. Hockey Player
Center, Calgary, 1987—; won Calder Trophy, 1988-89; rookie of the yr., 1988.
b. Sep 10, 1966 in Oshawa, Ontario, Canada
Source: *HocReg 87; WorAlBi*

Niezabitowska, Malgorzata
Polish. Government Official, Journalist
Official spokeswoman of Poland's Solidarity-run govt., 1989—; active in Poland's underground press, 1980s.
b. Nov 25, 1948 in Warsaw, Poland
Source: *BioIn 16; IntWW 91; News 91-3*

Nighbor, Frank
"Dutch"
Canadian. Hockey Player
Center, 1917-30, mostly with Ottawa; won Hart Trophy, 1924, Lady Byng Trophy, 1925, 1926; Hall of Fame, 1945.
b. Jan 26, 1893 in Pembroke, Ontario, Canada
d. Apr 13, 1966 in Pembroke, Ontario, Canada
Source: *HocEn; WhoHcky 73; WhoSpor*

Nightingale, Florence
"Lady with a Lamp"
English. Nurse, Social Reformer
Introduced improved nursing practices in Crimean War; made nursing respected medical profession.
b. May 15, 1820 in Florence, Italy
d. Aug 13, 1910 in London, England
Source: *Alli, SUP; Benet 87, 96; BiDBrF 1; BiDMoPL; BiHiMed; BioIn 1, 2, 3, 4, 5, 6, 7, 8, 9, 10, 11, 12, 13, 14, 15, 16, 17, 18, 19, 20, 21; CelCen; ContDcW 89; DcBiPP; DcLB 166; DcNaB S2; EncBrWW; FemiCLE; FilmgC; GayLesB; GoodHs; HalFC 80, 84, 88; HerW, 84; HisDBrE; HisWorL; IntDcWB; InWom, SUP; LegTOT; LinLib S; LngCTC; LuthC 75; McGEWB; NewC; OxCEng 85, 95; OxCMed 86; RAdv 14; REn; VicBrit; WhDW; WomFir; WorAl; WorAlBi*

Night Ranger
[Jack Blades; Alan "Fitz" Fitzgerald; Brad Gillis; Kelly Keagy; Jeff Watson]
American. Music Group
Album *Midnight Madness,* 1983, produced hit single "Sister Christian."
Source: *EncPR&S 89; RkOn 85; WhoRocM 82*

Nijinska, Bronislava
Russian. Dancer, Choreographer
Began career with Imperial Ballet in Russia, 1908-11; established own ballet studio in Hollywood, 1940-50.
b. Jan 8, 1891 in Minsk, Russia
d. Feb 21, 1972 in Pacific Palisades, California
Source: *BiDD; BioIn 1, 3, 4, 6, 9, 10, 12, 13, 14, 15, 16, 17, 18; ConAu 117; ContDcW 89; DcTwCCu 2; FacFETw; IntDcWB; InWom, SUP; NewYTBE 72; ObitOF 79; ObitT 1971; RAdv 14; WhThe; WomFir*

Nijinsky, Vaslav
[Waslaw Nijinsky]
Russian. Dancer
One of world's greatest dancers, 1909-19, known for performances of *The Rite of Spring.*
b. Feb 28, 1890 in Kiev, Russia
d. Apr 8, 1950 in London, England
Source: *BiDD; BioIn 1, 2, 3, 4, 5, 6, 7, 8, 9, 10, 11, 12, 13, 14, 16, 17, 20, 21; ConAu 115; CurBio 40, 50; DancEn 78; DcArts; Dis&D; EncWB; FacFETw; LegTOT; LinLib L, S; LngCTC; NotNAT A, B; OxCMus; RAdv 14, 13-3; WhAm 4; WhDW; WhThe; WorAl; WorAlBi*

Nikisch, Arthur
Hungarian. Conductor
Internationally acclaimed Leipzig conductor; often led without score.
b. Oct 12, 1855 in Lebenyi Szent, Hungary
d. Jan 23, 1922 in Leipzig, Germany
Source: *Baker 78, 84, 92; BioIn 2, 8, 11; BriBkM 80; FacFETw; IntDcOp; MusMk; MusSN; NewAmDM; NewEOp 71; NewGrDA 86; NewGrDM 80; OxCMus; PenDiMP*

Nikolais, Alwin
American. Choreographer, Composer
Wrote electronic ballet scores, won acclaim for portrayal of extraterrestrial creatures in Monetti's opera, *Help! Help! the Globolinks.*
b. Nov 25, 1912 in Southington, Connecticut
d. May 8, 1993 in New York, New York
Source: *Baker 78, 84; BiDD; BioIn 8, 9, 11, 12; CelR, 90; CmpGMD; CnOxB; ConAmC 76; ConDr 77E; CurBio 68; DancEn 78; DcCM; DcTwCCu 1; NewYTBE 70; WhoAm 74, 76, 78, 80, 82, 84, 86, 88*

Nikolayev, Andriyan Grigoryevich
Russian. Cosmonaut
Crew member on *Vostok 3;* first to make group flight with *Vostok 4,* 1962.
b. Sep 5, 1929 in Shorshely, Union of Soviet Socialist Republics
Source: *CurBio 64; IntWW 74; WhoWor 74*

Niles, John Jacob
American. Singer, Songwriter
Folklorist who collected, performed American songs, ballads and carols.
b. Apr 28, 1892 in Louisville, Kentucky
d. Mar 1, 1980 in Lexington, Kentucky
Source: *AmAu&B; AnObit 1980; ASCAP 66; Baker 78, 84, 92; BiDAmM; BioIn 1, 2, 5, 8, 12, 14; BlueB 76; ChhPo, S1; ConAmC 76, 82; ConAu 33NR, 41R, 97; CpmDNM 82; CurBio 59, 80, 80N; DcAmB S10; DrAS 74E, 78E; EncFCWM 69, 83; FacFETw; IntWWM 77, 80; LiHiK; NewAmDM; NewGrDA 86; NewYTBS 80; OxCPMus; PenEncP; WhAm 7, 8; WhoAm 74, 76, 78, 80; WhoMus 72; WhoWor 74*

Nilsson
[Harry Edward Nelson, III]
American. Singer, Songwriter
Singer who won Grammy Award for best contemporary vocal performance, male, for "Everybody's Talkin'," 1969; received platinum album for *Nilsson Schmilsson,,* gold album for *Son of Schmilsson,* 1972 and a gold single for "Without You," 1972; recorded *Without Her-Without You,* 1990.
b. Jun 15, 1941 in New York, New York
Source: *EncRkSt*

Nilsson, Anna Q(uerentia)
Swedish. Actor
Silent screen star, 1911-28; fall ended her leading roles but she was able to appear as character actress.
b. Mar 30, 1888 in Ystad, Sweden
d. Feb 11, 1974 in Hemet, California
Source: *BioIn 10, 11; Film 1; FilmEn; FilmgC; InWom SUP; MotPP; MovMk; NewYTBS 74; SilFlmP; TwYS; WhoHol B; WhScrn 77, 83*

Nilsson, Birgit
Swedish. Opera Singer
Considered one of finest Wagnerian sopranos of all time, 1950s-60s.
b. May 17, 1918 in West Karup, Sweden
Source: *Baker 78, 84, 92; BiDAmM; BioIn 4, 5, 6, 7, 8, 9, 10, 11, 12, 13; BriBkM 80; CelR; CmOp; ConAu 129; CurBio 60; FacFETw; IntDcOp; IntWW 74, 75, 76, 77, 78, 79, 80, 81, 82, 83, 89, 91, 93; IntWWM 77, 80, 90; InWom, SUP; LegTOT; MetOEnc; MusMk; MusSN; NewAmDM; NewGrDA 86; NewGrDM 80; NewYTBE 71, 72; NewYTBS 79; OxDcOp; PenDiMP; WhoAm 86, 88, 92, 94, 95, 96, 97; WhoEnt 92; WhoHol 92, A; WhoMus 72; WhoOp 76; WhoWor 89, 91, 93, 95, 96, 97; WorAl; WorAlBi*

Nilsson, Christine
Swedish. Opera Singer
Soprano who had NY Met. debut, 1883; noted as Marguerite in *Faust.*
b. Aug 20, 1843 in Wexio, Sweden
d. Nov 22, 1921 in Stockholm, Sweden
Source: *ApCAB; Baker 84, 92; BiDAmM; BioIn 1, 3, 13; CelCen; CmOp; IntDcOp; InWom, SUP; MetOEnc; NewEOp 71; NewGrDM 80; NewGrDO; OxCMus; OxDcOp; PenDiMP*

Nimeiry, Gaafar Mohammed al
Sudanese. Political Leader
Former revolutionary; arrested for suspicion of overthrowing govt; pres. of Sudan, 1971-85, overthrown in coup.
b. Jan 1, 1930 in Wad Nubawi, Sudan
Source: *AfSS 78, 79; BioIn 10; CurBio 77; IntYB 79; MidE 79; NewYTBE 73; NewYTBS 78; WhoWor 84; WorDWW*

Nimitz, Chester William
American. Naval Officer
Commander of Pacific Fleet, 1941-45, who planned strategy that defeated Japanese, WW II.
b. Feb 24, 1885 in Fredericksburg, Texas
d. Feb 20, 1966 in San Francisco, California
Source: *BiDWWGF; BioIn 1, 2, 3, 6, 7, 9, 10, 11, 13; DcAmB S8; DcAmMiB; DcTwHis; EncAB-H 1974, 1996; FacFETw; HarEnMi; LinLib S; McGEWB; MorMA; OxCAmH; OxCShps; WebAB 74, 79; WebAMB; WhAm 4; WhDW; WorAl*

Nimoy, Leonard
American. Actor, Producer
Played Mr. Spock on TV series "Star Trek," 1966-69; also in film series.
b. Mar 26, 1931 in Boston, Massachusetts
Source: *BioIn 10, 11; CelR 90; ConAu 25NR, 57; ConTFT 1, 7, 14; CurBio 77; FilmEn; FilmgC; HalFC 80, 84, 88; IntMPA 80, 81, 82, 84, 86, 88, 92, 94, 96; IntWW 91, 93; LegTOT; MiSFD 9; ScF&FL 92; VarWW 85; WhoAm 74, 76, 78, 80, 82, 84, 86, 88, 90, 92, 94, 95, 96, 97; WhoEnt 92; WhoHol 92, A; WorAl; WorAlBi*

Nin, Anais
American. Author
Best known for diaries; wrote *A Spy in the House of Love,* 1954; *Delta of Venus,* 1977.
b. Feb 21, 1903 in Paris, France
d. Oct 14, 1977 in Los Angeles, California
Source: *AmAu&B; AmWomWr; ArtclWW 2; Au&Wr 71; AuNews 2; Benet 87, 96; BenetAL 91; BioAmW; BioIn 1, 2, 4, 7, 8, 9, 10, 11, 12, 13, 14, 15, 16, 17, 18, 19, 20, 21; BlmGWL; BlueB 76; CamGEL; CamGLE; CamHAL; ConAu 13R, 22NR, 53NR, 69; ConLC 1, 4, 8, 11, 14, 60; ConNov 72, 76; ContDcW 89; CurBio 75, 77N; CyWA 89; DcAmB S10; DcArts; DcLB 2, 4, 152; DrAF 76; EncWL 2, 3; FacFETw; FemiCLE; GrWomW; GrWrEL N; HanAmWH; IntAu&W 76; IntDcWB; InWom, SUP; LegTOT; LiExTwC; LinLib L; MagSAmL; MajTwCW; ModAL, S1, S2; ModAWWr; ModWoWr; NewYTBS 77; OxCAmL 65, 83, 95; OxCWoWr 95; RAdv 1, 14, 13-1; RfGAmL 87, 94; RfGShF; RGTwCWr; ScF&FL 1; ShSCr 10; TwCA SUP; WorAl; WorAlBi; WrDr 76*

Nino, Pedro Alonzo
Spanish. Navigator
Navigator of the *Nina,* one of three ships of Columbus' 1492 voyage to discover New World.
b. 1468 in Monguer, Spain
d. 1505? in Galicia, Spain
Source: *ApCAB; Drake*

Nipon, Albert
American. Fashion Designer
Head of Albert Nipon, Inc., 1971-78; arrested for tax fraud, 1978.
b. Sep 11, 1927 in Philadelphia, Pennsylvania
Source: *ConNews 86-4; WhoAm 84, 90, 92, 94*

Nirenberg, Marshall Warren
American. Chemist
Shared Nobel Prize, 1968, for researching the genetic code.
b. Apr 10, 1927 in New York, New York
Source: *AmMWSc 73P, 76P, 79, 82, 86, 89, 92, 95; AsBiEn; BiESc; BioIn 7, 8, 14, 15, 20; BlueB 76; CurBio 65; FacFETw; IntWW 74, 75, 76, 77, 78, 79, 80, 81, 82, 83, 89, 91, 93; LarDcSc; McGMS 80; NotTwCS; WebAB 74, 79; Who 74, 82, 83, 85, 88, 90, 92, 94; WhoAm 74, 76, 78, 80, 82, 84, 86, 88, 90, 92, 94, 95, 96, 97; WhoE 74, 77, 79, 81, 83, 85, 86, 89, 91, 95, 97; WhoFrS 84; WhoGov 72; WhoMedH; WhoNob, 90, 95; WhoScEn 94, 96; WhoWor 74, 80, 82, 84, 87, 89, 91, 93, 95, 96, 97; WorScD*

Nirvana
American. Music Group
Formed, 1987; grunge rock albums include *Bleach,* 1989; *Nevermind,* 1991, went triple platinum.
Source: *BioIn 18, 20; ConMus 8; DcArts; EncRk 88; EncRkSt; News 92; NewYTBS 94; PenEncP*

Nitschke, Ray(mond E)
American. Football Player
Middle linebacker, Green Bay, 1958-72; Hall of Fame, 1978.
b. Dec 29, 1936 in Elmwood Park, Illinois
Source: *BioIn 8, 10, 15, 17; LegTOT; WhoFtbl 74*

Nitti, Francesco Saverio
Italian. Political Leader
Anti-fascist premier of Italy, 1919-20; exiled to France by Mussolini; retired to aid in postwar reconstruction, 1945.
b. Jul 19, 1868 in Melfi, Italy
d. Feb 20, 1953 in Rome, Italy
Source: *BiDInt; BioIn 3; ObitOF 79*

Nitty Gritty Dirt Band, The
[Ralph Barr; Chris Darrow; Jimmie Fadden; Jeff Hanna; Jim Ibbotson; Bruce Kunkel; John McEuen; Leslie Thompson]
American. Music Group
Group formed in 1960s; plays blue grass to hard rock; had triple album, *Dirt, Silver and Gold,* 1976.
Source: *AmMWSc 89; BgBkCoM; BiDAmM; ChhPo; ConMuA 80A; ConMus 6; CounME 74, 74A; EncPR&S 74; EncRk 88; HarEnCM 87; HarEnR 86; IlEncCM; IlEncRk; NewAmDM; NewGrDA 86; OxCPMus; PenEncP; RkOn 78; RolSEnR 83; WhoNeCM; WhoRock 81; WhoRocM 82*

Nitze, Paul Henry
American.
Leading arms control expert and negotiator; co-writer of the Nat. Security Council Memorandum-68.
b. Jan 15, 1907 in Amherst, Massachusetts
Source: *BioIn 2, 5, 6, 7, 8, 11, 12, 13, 14, 15, 16; BlueB 76; ColdWar 2; CurBio 62; DcAmDH 89; IntWW 74, 75, 76, 77, 78, 79, 80, 81, 82, 83, 89, 91, 93; NewYTBS 81; PolProf J, K, T; WhoAm 74, 76, 78, 80, 82, 84, 86, 88, 90, 92, 96, 97; WhoAmP 73, 75, 77, 79, 81, 83, 85, 87, 89, 91, 93, 95; WhoE 95, 97; WhoWor 74, 82, 84, 87, 89, 96*

Niven, David
[James David Graham Niven]
Scottish. Actor, Author
Won 1958 Oscar for *Separate Tables;* book *The Moon's A Balloon,* 1972, sold over four million copies.
b. Mar 1, 1910 in Kirriemuir, Scotland
d. Jul 29, 1983 in Chateau D'Oex, Switzerland
Source: *AnObit 1983; AuSpks; BiDFilm 81, 94; BioIn 4, 5, 7, 8, 9, 10, 11, 13, 14, 18, 20; BkPepl; BlueB 76; CelR; ConAu 31NR, 77, 110; ConTFT 1; CurBio 57, 83N; DcNaB 1981; EncEurC; FilmEn; ForYSC; IntAu&W 76, 77; IntDcF 1-3, 2-3; IntMPA 82; MotPP; MovMk; NewYTBS 83; OxCFilm; VarWW 85; WhAm 8; Who 74, 82; WhoAm 74, 76, 78, 80, 82; WhoHol A; WhoWor 74; WorAl; WorAlBi; WorEFlm; WrDr 76, 80, 82, 84*

Nix, Robert N(elson) C(ornelius), Sr.
American. Politician
First black Dem. congressman from PA, 1958-79.
b. Aug 9, 1905 in Orangeburg, South Carolina
d. Jun 22, 1987 in Philadelphia, Pennsylvania
Source: *BiDrAC; BiDrUSC 89; BlkAmsC; CngDr 77; InB&W 80; WhoBlA 85; WhoGov 77*

Nixon, E(dgar) D(aniel)
American. Civil Rights Leader
Organized Brotherhood of Sleeping Car Porters, the first successful black union.
b. Jul 12, 1899 in Montgomery, Alabama
d. Feb 25, 1987 in Montgomery, Alabama
Source: *EncAACR; InB&W 85; WhoBlA 77, 80, 85, 90N*

Nixon, Marni
American. Opera Singer
"Ghost-sang" for film stars including Audrey Hepburn, Natalie Wood, others.
b. Feb 22, 1929 in Altadena, California

Source: *FilmgC; HalFC 80, 84, 88; LegTOT; MotPP; VarWW 85; WhoAm 86; WhoAmL 83; WhoHol A*

Nixon, Patricia
[Mrs. Richard M. Nixon; Thelma Catherine Patricia Ryan]
American. First Lady
High school teacher before marriage to Richard Nixon, Jun 21, 1940; biography written by daughter Julie, 1986.
b. Mar 16, 1912 in Ely, Nevada
d. Jun 22, 1993 in Park Ridge, New Jersey
Source: *BioIn 5, 8, 9, 10, 11, 12, 13, 18, 19, 20; CurBio 70, 93N; LegTOT; NewYTBE 70; WorAl; WorAlBi*

Nixon, Richard M(ilhous)
American. US President, Politician, Author
37th pres., Rep., 1969-74, first pres. to resign; ended US involvement in Vietnam, repaired relations with People's Republic of China, initiated detente with USSR; administration marred by Watergate scandal.
b. Jan 9, 1913 in Yorba Linda, California
d. Apr 22, 1994 in New York, New York
Source: *AmAu&B; AmOrTwC; AmPolLe; Benet 96; BiDrAC; BiDrUSC 89; BiDrUSE 71, 89; BioIn 1, 2, 3, 4, 5, 6, 7, 8, 9, 10, 11, 12, 13; BioNews 74; BkPepl; ConAu 73, 147; ConLC 86; CopCroC; CurBio 48, 58, 69, 94; DcTwHis; EncAAH; EncAB-H 1974, 1996; EncSoH; EncWB; FacPr 89, 93; HealPre; HisEAAC; IntAu&W 93; IntWW 74, 75, 76, 77, 78, 79, 80, 81, 82, 83, 89, 91, 93; LegTOT; McGEWB; VicePre; WebAB 74, 79; WhAm 11; WhDW; WhoAm 74, 76, 78, 80, 82, 84, 86, 88, 90, 92, 94; WhoE 74, 81, 83, 85, 91; WhoGov 72, 75, 77; WhoSSW 73; WhoWest 74, 76, 78; WhoWor 74, 78, 80, 82, 84, 87, 89, 91, 93; WorAl; WrDr 86, 94*

Nixon, Tricia
[Mrs. Edward Cox; Patricia Nixon]
American.
Elder daughter of Richard Nixon.
b. Feb 21, 1946 in San Francisco, California
Source: *BioIn 14; LegTOT; NewYTBE 71*

Nizer, Louis
American. Lawyer, Author
Special counsel to Motion Picture Assn. of America; wrote autobiography *Reflections Without Mirrors,* 1978.
b. Feb 6, 1902 in London, England
d. Nov 10, 1994 in New York, New York
Source: *ASCAP 66, 80; BiE&WWA; BioIn 4, 6, 9, 11, 13, 20, 21; CelR; ConAu 53, 147; CurBio 55, 95N; EncMcCE; IntMPA 75, 76, 77, 78, 79, 80, 81, 82, 84, 86, 88, 92, 94; LegTOT; LinLib L; NewYTBE 71; NewYTBS 77, 94; NotNAT; St&PR 75, 84, 87, 91, 93; VarWW 85; WebAB 74, 79; WhoAm 74, 76, 78, 80, 82, 86; WhoAmJ 80; WhoAmL 78, 79; WhoE 74; WhoWor 74, 76; WhoWorJ 72, 78; WorAl; WorAlBi; WrDr 76, 80, 82, 84, 86, 88*

Nkoli, Simon
[Tseko Simon Nkoli]
South African. Social Reformer
Member of South Africa's United Democratic Front; leader during the Soweto uprising of 1976.
b. 1957 in Phiri, South Africa
Source: *BioIn 21; GayLesB*

Nkomo, Joshua (Mqabuko Nyongolo)
South African. Politician
Minister of Home Affairs, 1980-82; sr. minister in pres. office, 1988-90; vp, 1990—.
b. 1917 in Matabeleland, Rhodesia
Source: *AfSS 78, 79, 80, 81, 82; BioIn 6, 10, 11, 12, 13; ConBlB 4; CurBio 76; DcAfHiB 86; DcTwHis; FacFETw; HisWorL; InB&W 80, 85; IntWW 74, 75, 76, 77, 78, 79, 80, 81, 82, 83, 89, 91, 93; IntYB 81, 82; NewYTBS 78; WhoAfr; WhoWor 80, 82, 84, 87, 89, 91, 93, 95, 96, 97*

Nkrumah, Kwame
Ghanaian. Political Leader
Dictator; first pres. of Ghana, 1960-66.
b. Sep 21, 1909 in Nkroful, Gold Coast
d. Apr 27, 1972 in Bucharest, Romania
Source: *BiDInt; BiDMoPL; BioIn 2, 3, 4, 5, 6, 7, 8, 9, 10, 11, 12, 13, 14, 15, 16, 17, 18, 19, 20, 21; BlkWr 2; ColdWar 1, 2; ConAu 113, 132; ConBlB 3; CurBio 53, 72, 72N; DcLEL 1940; DcNaB 1971; DcPol; DicTyr; EncRev; FacFETw; GrLGrT; HisWorL; InB&W 80; McGEWB; NewYTBE 72; ObitT 1971; OxCPhil; RadHan; RAdv 14; SchCGBL; SelBAAf; WhAm 5; WhDW; WorAl; WorAlBi*

Noah
Commanded by God to build ark to save humans, animals from flood.
Source: *Benet 96; BioIn 1, 2, 4, 5, 6, 7, 8, 9, 10, 11, 13, 14, 17, 20; EncEarC; InWom; NewCol 75*

Noah, Yannick Simon Camille
French. Tennis Player
Won French Open, 1983; Davis Cup, 1991.
b. May 16, 1960 in Sedan, France
Source: *CurBio 87; InB&W 85; NewYTBS 82, 84; WhoIntT*

Nobel, Alfred Bernhard
Swedish. Inventor, Philanthropist
Left $9.2 million for annual Nobel Prizes, first awarded 1901; invented dynamite, 1866.
b. Oct 21, 1833 in Stockholm, Sweden
d. Dec 10, 1896 in San Remo, Italy
Source: *AsBiEn; Benet 87, 96; BiESc; BioIn 1, 2, 3, 4, 5, 6, 7, 8, 9, 10, 11, 14, 15, 16, 17, 19, 20; CamDcSc; DcScB; Dis&D; InSci; LinLib L, S; McGEWB; NewC; NewCol 75; REn; WebBD 83; WorAl*

Nobile, Umberto
Italian. Explorer, Army Officer
One of first men to fly over N Pole, in dirigible *Norge,* 1926.
b. Jan 21, 1885 in Naples, Italy
d. Jul 29, 1978 in Rome, Italy
Source: *BioIn 4, 8, 11, 12, 18; ConAu 81; Expl 93; FacFETw; InSci; McGEWB; NewYTBS 78; WhAm 7; WhWE; WorAl; WorAlBi*

Noble, Elaine
American. Politician
Member, MA House of Representatives, 1975-77.
b. Jan 22, 1944 in New Kensington, Pennsylvania
Source: *GayLesB; InWom SUP*

Noble, Ray
English. Bandleader
Led dance bands, 1930s-40s; wrote "Cherokee," 1938; popular radio actor, 1940s-50s.
b. Dec 17, 1903 in Brighton, England
d. Apr 2, 1978 in London, England
Source: *Baker 78, 84; BgBands 74; BiDAmM; BioIn 10, 11, 12, 14; CmpEPM; FacFETw; NewAmDM; NewGrDA 86; NewGrDJ 88; NewGrDM 80; OxCPMus; PenEncP; What 5; WhoHol A*

Noble, Reg
[Edward Reginald Noble]
Canadian. Hockey Player
Left wing, 1917-33, with three NHL teams; Hall of Fame, 1962.
b. Jun 23, 1895 in Collingwood, Ontario, Canada
d. Jan 19, 1962 in Alliston, Ontario, Canada
Source: *HocEn; WhoHcky 73*

Noel-Baker, Philip John
[Baron Noel-Baker of Derby]
English. Diplomat, Author
Won Nobel Peace Prize, 1959, for working toward world disarmament; Labor MP, 1929-70.
b. Nov 1, 1889 in London, England
d. Oct 8, 1982 in London, England
Source: *AnObit 1982; Au&Wr 71; BiDMoPL; BioIn 1, 5, 9, 11, 13, 15, 17, 18; BlueB 76; ConAu 108; CurBio 46, 83N; DcNaB 1981; IntWW 82, 83N; IntYB 81; NewYTBS 82; WhAm 8; WhLit; Who 82; WhoLA; WhoNob, 90, 95; WhoWor 82*

Nofziger, Lyn
[Franklyn Curran Nofziger]
American. Presidential Aide
Conservative Rep. known for harsh words, unkempt appearance; served as press secretary for Nixon, Reagan.
b. Jun 8, 1924 in Bakersfield, California

Source: *BioIn 10, 11, 12, 13; CurBio 83; JrnUS; PolProf NF; WhoAmP 73, 75, 77*

Noguchi, Isamu
American. Sculptor, Designer
Works contributed to modern abstract art movement; also designed stage sets during the 1950s.
b. Nov 17, 1904 in Los Angeles, California
d. Dec 30, 1988 in New York, New York
Source: *AmArt; AmCulL; AnObit 1988; AsAmAlm; BiDD; BioIn 1, 2, 3, 4, 5, 6, 7, 8, 10, 11, 12, 13, 14, 15, 16, 17, 18, 19, 20, 21; BlueB 76; BriEAA; CamGWoT; CelR; CenC; CnOxB; ConArt 77, 83, 89, 96; CurBio 43, 89, 89N; DancEn 78; DcAmArt; DcArts; DcCAA 71, 77, 88, 94; DcCAr 81; DcTwDes; EncJap; FacFETw; IntWW 74, 75, 76, 77, 78, 79, 80, 81, 82, 83; LegTOT; McGDA; McGEWB; NewYTBS 88; NotAsAm; OxCArt; OxCTwCA; OxDcArt; PenDiDA 89; PhDcTCA 77; RComAH; WebAB 74, 79; WhAm 9; WhAmArt 85; WhoAm 74, 76, 78, 80, 82, 84, 86, 88; WhoAmA 73, 76, 78, 80, 82, 84, 86, 89, 89N, 91N, 93N; WhoWor 74; WomWMM; WorAl; WorAlBi; WorArt 1950*

Nol, Lon
Cambodian. Political Leader
Deposed Prince Sihanouk, ending 1,100-year old Cambodian monarchy, 1970-75.
b. Nov 13, 1913 in Preyveng, Cambodia
d. Nov 17, 1985 in Fullerton, California
Source: *BioIn 9, 14, 15; ConNews 86-1; WhoGov 72; WorDWW*

Nolan, Bob
[Sons of the Pioneers]
American. Songwriter, Singer
Credited with performing, writing over 1,000 gospel, country, western songs including "Cool Water," 1936.
b. 1908?, Canada
d. Jun 16, 1980 in Costa Mesa, California
Source: *BioIn 12, 14; ConAu 101; DcAmB S10; NewAmDM; NewGrDA 86; PeoHis; WhScrn 83*

Nolan, Christopher
Irish. Author
Severely handicapped writer who won Great Britain's Whitbread Book of the Year Award in 1988 for his autobiography *Under the Eye of the Clock.*
b. Sep 5, 1965 in Mullingar, Ireland
Source: *BiDIrW; BioIn 15, 16; ConAu 111; ConLC 58; CurBio 88; DcIrL 96; WrDr 90, 92, 94, 96*

Nolan, Jeannette
American. Actor
Married John McIntire; played in TV shows "The Virginian," 1967-68; "Dirty Sally," 1974.
b. Dec 30, 1911 in Los Angeles, California
Source: *FilmgC; VarWW 85; WhoHol A*

Nolan, Jeannette Covert
American. Children's Author
Writings include *The Story of Joan of Arc,* 1954.
b. Mar 31, 1896 in Evansville, Indiana
d. Oct 12, 1974 in Indianapolis, Indiana
Source: *AmAu&B; Au&Wr 71; AuBYP 2; ConAu 4NR, 5R; FilmEn; IndAu 1917; JBA 51; SmATA 2; WhAm 6; WhoAm 74*

Nolan, Kathy
[Kathleen Nolan]
American. Actor
Former pres., Screen Actors Guild; starred in "The Real McCoys," 1957-63.
b. Sep 27, 1933 in Saint Louis, Missouri
Source: *BioIn 5; InWom SUP; LegTOT; VarWW 85; WhoAm 80, 82, 84, 86, 88, 90, 92; WhoHol 92, A; WomFir*

Nolan, Lloyd
American. Actor
Character actor known for gangster and cop roles; co-starred in "Julia," 1968-71.
b. Aug 11, 1902 in San Francisco, California
d. Sep 27, 1985 in Brentwood, California
Source: *BiE&WWA; BioIn 4, 11, 14, 15; CmMov; ConNews 85-4; ConTFT 1; CurBio 56, 85, 85N; EncAFC; FilmEn; FilmgC; ForYSC; GangFlm; HalFC 80, 84, 88; HolP 30; IntMPA 82, 84, 86; LegTOT; MotPP; MovMk; NewYTBS 85; NotNAT; VarWW 85; WhAm 9; WhoAm 74; WhoHol A; WhoThe 77A; WhoWor 74; WhThe; WorAl; WorAlBi; WorEFlm*

Nolan, Sidney, Sir
Australian. Painter
Influential post-war artist; known for his Ned Kelly series, 1940s-50s.
b. Apr 22, 1917 in Melbourne, Australia
d. Nov 27, 1992 in London, England
Source: *AnObit 1992; BioIn 15, 18, 19, 20; ConArt 77, 83, 89; DcArts; IntWW 91; McGDA; NewYTBS 92; OxCArt; OxCAusL; OxCTwCA; OxDcArt; PhDcTCA 77; WhDW; Who 82, 83, 85, 88, 90, 92*

Nolan, Thomas Brennan
American. Geologist
Helped shaped the mission of the US Geologic Survey.
b. May 21, 1901 in Greenfield, Massachusetts
d. Aug 2, 1992 in Washington, District of Columbia
Source: *AmMWSc 73P, 76P, 79, 82, 86, 89, 92; BlueB 76; IntWW 74, 75, 76, 77, 78, 79, 80, 81, 82, 83, 89, 91; WhAm 10; WhoAm 74, 76, 78, 80, 82, 84, 86, 88; WhoGov 72, 75, 77*

Noland, Kenneth Clifton
American. Artist
Paintings emphasized pure color, made color the subject; experimented with bull's eye, chevron motifs.
b. Apr 10, 1924 in Asheville, North Carolina
Source: *BriEAA; ConArt 83; CurBio 72; DcAmArt; IntWW 83; McGDA; McGEWB; NewCol 75; WhoAm 74, 76, 78, 80, 82, 84, 90, 92, 94, 97; WhoAmA 84; WhoWor 74*

Nolde, Emil
[Emil Hansen]
German. Artist
Expressionist, influenced by primitive art; forbidden to paint by Nazis, but con tinued to do landscapes, seascapes.
b. Aug 7, 1867 in Nolde, Germany
d. Apr 15, 1956 in Seebull, Sweden
Source: *AtlBL; Benet 87, 96; BioIn 4, 5, 6, 7, 8, 9, 10, 12, 13, 14, 17; ConArt 77, 83; DcArts; Dis&D; EncTR, 91; FacFETw; IntDcAA 90; LegTOT; MakMC; McGDA; McGEWB; OxCArt; OxCGer 76, 86; OxCTwCA; OxDcArt; PhDcTCA 77; WhAm 4*

Noll, Chuck
[Charles Henry Noll]
American. Football Coach
Head coach, Pittsburgh, 1969-92; led Steelers to four Super Bowl wins, 1975-76, 1979-80; Hall of Fame, 1993.
b. Jan 5, 1932 in Cleveland, Ohio
Source: *BiDAmSp FB; FootReg 87; LegTOT; WhoAm 84, 86, 96, 97; WhoFtbl 74; WhoSpor*

Nolte, Henry R, Jr.
American. Auto Executive, Lawyer
VP, general counsel, Ford Motor Co., 1974-89.
b. Mar 3, 1924 in New York, New York
Source: *AutoN 79; St&PR 84, 87; Ward 77; WhoAm 84, 86; WhoAmL 85; WhoFI 85*

Nolte, Nick
American. Actor
Star of TV mini-series "Rich Man, Poor Man," 1976; films include *48 Hours,* 1982; *Cape Fear; The Prince of Tides,* 1991.
b. Feb 8, 1942 in Omaha, Nebraska
Source: *BioIn 12; BkPepl; CelR 90; ConTFT 1, 6; CurBio 80; HalFC 84; IntMPA 78, 79, 80, 81, 82, 84, 86; IntWW 91, 93; News 92; NewYTBS 82; VarWW 85; WhoAm 86, 88, 90, 92, 94, 95, 96; WhoEnt 92*

Nomelleni, Leo Joseph
American. Football Player
Six-time all-pro defensive tackle, 1950-63; Hall of Fame, 1969.
b. Jun 19, 1924 in Lucca, Italy
Source: *BioIn 2, 6; WhoFtbl 74*

Nomo, Hideo
Japanese. Baseball Player
Pitcher, Los Angeles Dodgers, 1995—.
b. Aug 31, 1968 in Osaka, Japan
Source: *News 96, 96-2*

Nomura, Kichisaburo
Japanese. Diplomat
Ambassador to US at time of Pearl Harbor attack, 1940-41; the attack ended his negotiations.
b. Dec 1877 in Wakayama-Ken, Japan
d. May 8, 1964 in Tokyo, Japan
Source: *BioIn 3, 6, 7, 9, 10; CurBio 41, 64; HisEWW; ObitOF 79; REn*

Nono, Luigi
Italian. Composer
Avant-garde works include *Intolleranza,* 1960, which provoked neo-Fascist riot, 1961.
b. Jan 29, 1924 in Venice, Italy
d. May 9, 1990 in Venice, Italy
Source: *AnObit 1990; Baker 78, 84, 92; BioIn 6, 7, 8, 9; BriBkM 80; CnOxB; CompSN, SUP; ConCom 92; DcArts; DcCM; FacFETw; IntDcOp; IntWW 74, 75, 76, 77, 78, 79, 80, 81, 82, 83, 89; IntWWM 77, 80; McGEWB; MetOEnc; MusMk; NewAmDM; NewEOp 71; NewGrDM 80; NewGrDO; NewOxM; NewYTBS 90; OxCMus; OxDcOp; PenDiMP A; WhDW; WhoWor 74*

Noonan, Peggy
American. Writer
Presidential speechwriter, 1984-86; responsible for phrases "a kinder, gentler nation," "read my lips," "a thousand points of light."
b. Sep 7, 1950 in New York, New York
Source: *BestSel 90-3; BioIn 16; ConAu 132; CurBio 90; News 90, 90-3; NewYTBS 89; WomStre; WrDr 94, 96*

Noone, Jimmie
American. Jazz Musician
Early jazz clarinetist who led his own band, 1920s-30s.
b. Apr 23, 1895 in Cut Off, Louisiana
d. Apr 19, 1944 in Los Angeles, California
Source: *AllMusG; Baker 84; BiDAfM; BiDAmM; BiDJaz; CmpEPM; IlEncJ; InB&W 80, 85; LegTOT; NewAmDM; NewGrDJ 88, 94; NewGrDM 80; NewOrJ; OxCPMus; PenEncP; WhoJazz 72; WorAl; WorAlBi*

Noone, Kathleen
American. Actor
Emmy award-winning actress, TV soap "All My Children;" played Claudia Whittaker on "Knots Landing," 1991-93.
Source: *BioIn 17*

Noone, Peter
[Herman's Hermits]
English. Singer, Musician
Herman of Herman's Hermits, 1963-71; number one hit "I'm Henry the Eighth, I Am," 1965.
b. Nov 5, 1947 in Manchester, England
Source: *BioIn 12; EncPR&S 89; LegTOT; VarWW 85*

Noor, Queen
[Lisa Najeeb Halaby]
American. Consort
Wife of King Hussein of Jordan; has played major role in education, social welfare, arts in Jordan.
b. Aug 23, 1951 in Washington, District of Columbia
Source: *BioIn 11*

Norden, Carl Lukas
Dutch. Inventor, Engineer
Developed airplane instruments; the Norden bombsight, 1921-31.
b. Apr 23, 1880 in Semarang, Dutch East Indies
d. Jun 15, 1965 in Zurich, Switzerland
Source: *BioIn 7, 9; DcAmB S7; InSci; WebAMB*

Nordenskiold, Nils Adolph Erik, Baron
Swedish. Geologist, Explorer
First to navigate Northwest Passage, 1878-80; made six trips to Spitsbergen; wrote *Voyage of the Vega,* 1881.
b. Nov 18, 1832 in Helsinki, Finland
d. Aug 12, 1901 in Dalbyo, Sweden
Source: *DcScB; NewCol 75*

Nordhoff, Charles Bernard
American. Author, Traveler
Co-wrote with James Hall popular S Seas adventures: *Mutiny on the Bounty,* 1932; *Pitcairn's Island,* 1934.
b. Feb 1, 1887 in London, England
d. Apr 11, 1947 in Santa Barbara, California
Source: *AmAu&B; AmNov; AuBYP 2, 3; Benet 87; BenetAL 91; BioIn 1, 2, 4, 5, 7, 8, 12, 13; CnDAL; CyWA 58; DcAmB S5; DcLEL; DcNAA; LngCTC; MnBBF; OxCAmL 65, 83, 95; PenC AM; REn; REnAL; TwCA, SUP; WhAm 2; WorAl; WorAlBi*

Nordica, Lillian
[Lillian Norton]
"The Lily of the North"
American. Opera Singer
Celebrated Wagnerian soprano with NY Met., 1896-1907; first American singer widely acclaimed in Europe.
b. May 12, 1859 in Farmington, Maine
d. May 10, 1914 in Batavia, Dutch East Indies
Source: *AmBi; ApCAB SUP, X; Baker 84; BiDAmM; BioAmW; BioIn 1, 3, 4, 5, 6, 7, 8, 9; DcAmB; LinLib S; MusSN; NewGrDM 80; NotAW; TwCBDA; WebAB 74; WhAm 1; WhoStg 1906, 1908; WomWWA 14*

Nordli, Odvar
Norwegian. Political Leader
Held various political posts since 1952 including prime minister, 1976-81.
b. Nov 3, 1927 in Stange, Norway
Source: *IntWW 74, 75, 76, 77, 78, 79, 80, 81, 82, 83, 89, 91, 93; IntYB 82; WhoWor 74, 80, 82, 84*

Norell, Norman
[Norman Levinson]
American. Fashion Designer
Dramatic clothes for women were widely copied; influenced Paris fashion; created many styles.
b. Apr 20, 1900 in Noblesville, Indiana
d. Oct 25, 1972 in New York, New York
Source: *AmDec 1950; BioIn 4, 6, 7, 9, 10; ConDes 84, 90, 97; ConFash; CurBio 64, 72, 72N; DcAmB S9; DcTwDes; EncFash; FairDF US; LegTOT; NewYTBE 72; WhAm 5; WhoFash 88; WorAl; WorAlBi; WorFshn*

Norena, Eide
[Kaja Hansen Eide]
Norwegian. Opera Singer
Soprano with Chicago Civic Opera, NY Met., 1930s; noted for Italian roles.
b. Apr 26, 1884 in Horten, Norway
d. Nov 19, 1968 in Lausanne, Switzerland
Source: *Baker 78, 84, 92; BiDAmM; BioIn 4; CmOp; InWom; MetOEnc; NewEOp 71; NewGrDM 80; NewGrDO; OxDcOp; PenDiMP*

Norfolk, Lawrence
English. Author
Wrote *Lempriere's Dictionary,* 1992.
b. 1963 in London, England
Source: *ConAu 144; ConLC 76; WrDr 96*

Noriega (Moreno), Manuel Antonio
Panamanian. Political Leader
Leader, Panamanian army, virtual dictator, 1983-89; overthrown in US invasion, 1989; convicted in US on eight counts including cocaine trafficking and racketeering, 1992; sentenced to 40 years in prison.
b. Feb 11, 1940 in Panama City, Panama
Source: *ColdWar 1; CurBio 88; WhoWor 89*

Norman, Greg
"Great White Shark"
Australian. Golfer
Turned pro, 1976; won British Open, 1986; leading money winner, 1986.
b. Feb 10, 1955 in Queensland, Australia
Source: *BioIn 12, 13, 14, 15, 16, 17, 19, 20, 21; ConAu 133; CurBio 89; LegTOT; News 88-3; NewYTBS 81, 84; WhoAm 92, 94, 95, 96; WhoIntG; WhoWor 91, 95, 96; WorAlBi*

Norman, Jessye
American. Opera Singer
"A soprano of magnificent presence," with Metropolitan Opera Co., 1983—; 3 Grammys, 1980, 1982, 1985.
b. Sep 15, 1945 in Augusta, Georgia
Source: *AfrAmAl 6; Baker 84, 92; BiDAfM; BioIn 9, 10, 11, 13; BlkOpe; BlkWAm; BriBkM 80; CelR 90; ConBlB 5; ConMus 7; ContDcW 89; CurBio 76; DcArts; DcTwCCu 5; DrBlPA, 90; EncWB; FacFETw; GrLiveH; InB&W 80, 85; IntDcOp; IntWW 78, 79, 80, 81, 82, 83, 89, 91, 93; IntWWM 90; InWom SUP; LegTOT; MetOEnc; MusSN; NewAmDM; NewGrDA 86; NewGrDM 80; NewGrDO; NotBlAW 1; OxDcOp; PenDiMP; Who 82, 83, 85, 88, 90, 92, 94; WhoAfA 96; WhoAm 76, 78, 80, 82, 84, 86, 88, 90, 92, 94, 95, 96, 97; WhoAmM 83; WhoAmW 91, 93; WhoBlA 77, 80, 85, 88, 90, 92, 94; WhoEnt 92; WhoOp 76; WhoWor 84, 87, 89, 91, 93, 95, 96, 97; WorAlBi*

Norman, Marsha Williams
American. Dramatist
Won Pulitzer, 1983 for play *'Night Mother;* work characterized by honesty, natural dialogue, broken dramas; filmed, 1986.
b. Sep 21, 1947 in Louisville, Kentucky
Source: *ConAu 105; ConLC 28; CurBio 84; DcLB Y84B; InWom SUP; NewYTBS 79, 83; VarWW 85; WhoAmW 87*

Norman, Pat
American. Social Reformer
Executive director, Institute for Community Health Outreach, San Francisco, 1990—; involved in gay and lesbian rights.
b. Jan 21, 1939 in New York, New York
Source: *ConBlB 10; InB&W 85*

Normand, Mabel
American. Actor
Silent screen comedienne; co-star with Chaplin in *Tillie's Punctured Romance,* 1914; credited with throwing first custard pie, ca. 1913.
b. Nov 10, 1894 in Boston, Massachusetts
d. Feb 23, 1930 in Monrovia, California
Source: *BiDFilm 81, 94; BioAmW; BioIn 15, 18, 21; Film 1, 2; FilmEn; FilmgC; FunnyW; HalFC 80, 84, 88; LegTOT; MotPP; MovMk; NotAW; NotNAT B; OxCFilm; ReelWom; SilFlmP; TwYS, A; WhoHol B; WhScrn 74, 77, 83; WomWMM; WorEFlm*

Normandin, Jean-Louis
French. Hostage
French TV crew member taken hostage by Lebanese terrorists on Mar 8, 1986 for 629 days, Nov 27, 1987.
b. 1951?, France

Norrington, Roger Arthur Carver
English. Conductor
Conductor, Bournemouth Sinfonietta, 1985-89; founded Schutz Choir, 1962; London Classical Players, 1977; staged "weekend experiences" of noted composers during the 1980s.
b. Mar 16, 1934 in Oxford, England
Source: *BioIn 16; CurBio 90; IntWW 91; NewAmDM; News 89; PenDiMP; Who 92; WhoEnt 92; WhoWor 91*

Norris, Bruce A
American. Hockey Executive
Owner, president, Detroit Red Wings, 1945-82; sold team to Mike Ilitch; Hall of Fame, 1969.
b. Feb 19, 1924 in Chicago, Illinois
Source: *NewYTBS 86; WhoHcky 73*

Norris, Christopher
American. Actor
Played Nurse Gloria Brancusi in TV series "Trapper John, MD," 1979-86.
b. Oct 7, 1953 in New York, New York
Source: *VarWW 85; WhoHol 92, A*

Norris, Chuck
[Carlos Ray Norris]
"Blond Bruce Lee"
American. Actor
World middleweight champion in karate, 1968-74; his action movies include a trio of *Missing in Action* films, 1984-87 and *The Delta Force,* 1986.
b. Mar 10, 1940 in Ryan, Oklahoma
Source: *BioIn 12; CelR 90; ConTFT 13; CurBio 89; HalFC 84; IntMPA 86, 92, 94, 96; NewYTBS 84; VarWW 85; WhoAm 86, 95, 96, 97*

Norris, Frank(lin)
American. Author
Wrote *McTeague,* 1899; *The Pit,* 1903.
b. Mar 5, 1870 in Chicago, Illinois
d. Oct 25, 1902 in San Francisco, California
Source: *AmAu&B; AmBi; AmWr; AtlBL; BbD; Benet 87; BenetAL 91; BiD&SB; BioIn 1, 2, 3, 4, 5, 6, 8, 9, 10, 11, 12, 13, 14, 15, 16, 18, 19; CamGEL; CamGLE; CamHAL; CasWL; Chambr 3; CmCal; CnDAL; CrtT 3, 4; CyWA 58; DcAmAu; DcAmB; DcArts; DcBiA; DcLB 12, 71; DcLEL; DcNAA; EncAAH; EvLB; FifWWr; GayN; GrWrEL N; HalFC 84, 88; LegTOT; LinLib L; LngCTC; MagSAmL; ModAL; NatCAB 14, 15; Novels; OxCAmH; OxCAmL 65, 83, 95; OxCEng 67, 85, 95; PenC AM; RAdv 1, 13-1; RealN; REn; REnAL; REnAW; RfGAmL 87; ScF&FL 1; TwCA, SUP; TwCBDA; TwCLC 24; TwCWr; TwCWW 82, 91; WebAB 74, 79; WebE&AL; WhAm 1; WhDW; WhoHr&F; WorAl; WorAlBi*

Norris, George William
American. Politician
Rep. con. from NE, 1903-13, senator, 1913-43; supported Anti-Injunction Act, Muscle Shoals Act, 20th Amendment to Constitution.
b. Jul 11, 1861 in Sandusky, Ohio
d. Sep 3, 1944 in McCook, Nebraska
Source: *AmDec 1910; AmPolLe; AmRef; ApCAB X; BiDrAC; BiDrUSC 89; BioIn 1, 2, 3, 4, 5, 6, 7, 8, 9, 10, 11, 12, 14, 15, 16, 18; DcAmB S3; EncAAH; EncAB-A 7; EncAB-H 1974, 1996; FacFETw; LinLib S; McGEWB; MorMA; NatCAB 33; OhA&B; OxCAmH; REnAW; WebAB 74, 79; WhAm 2; WhAmP; WorAl*

Norris, James, Sr.
Canadian. Hockey Executive
Owner, Detroit Falcons, 1933-52, changing name to Red Wings; Hall of Fame, 1958.
b. Dec 10, 1879 in Saint Catharines, Ontario, Canada
d. Dec 4, 1952
Source: *EncAB-A 25; WhoHcky 73*

Norris, James D
American. Hockey Executive
Son of James, Sr; with Arthur Wirtz, co-owner, Chicago Blackhawks, 1946-66; Hall of Fame, 1962.
b. Nov 6, 1906 in Chicago, Illinois
d. Feb 25, 1966 in Chicago, Illinois
Source: *WhoHcky 73*

Norris, Kathleen Thompson
American. Author
Wrote *Mother,* 1911; her 82 novels sold 10 million copies.
b. Jul 16, 1880 in San Francisco, California
d. Jun 18, 1960 in San Francisco, California
Source: *NotAW MOD; TwCA*

Norrish, Ronald George Wreyford
English. Educator
Shared 1967 Nobel Prize in chemistry for studying effects of energy pulses on rapid chemical reactions.
b. Nov 9, 1897 in Cambridge, England
d. Jun 7, 1978 in Cambridge, England
Source: *AsBiEn; BiESc; BioIn 8, 11, 13, 14, 15, 19, 20; BlueB 76; DcNaB 1971; FacFETw; IntWW 74, 75, 76, 77, 78; LarDcSc; McGMS 80; Who 74; WhoNob, 90, 95; WhoWor 74; WorAl*

Norstad, Lauris
American. Air Force Officer
Supreme commander of NATO, 1956-63.
b. Mar 24, 1907 in Minneapolis, Minnesota
d. Sep 12, 1988 in Tucson, Arizona
Source: *AnObit 1988; BiDWWGF; BioIn 1, 2, 3, 4, 5, 6, 11, 16; BlueB 76; CurBio 48, 59, 88N; EncCW; FacFETw; HarEnMi; HisDcKW; InSci; IntWW 74, 75, 76, 77, 78, 79, 80, 81, 82, 83; IntYB 78, 79, 80, 81, 82; LinLib S; PolProf E, K; St&PR 75, 84; WebAMB; WhAm 9; Who 74, 82, 83, 85, 88; WhoAm 74, 76, 78, 80, 82, 84; WhoFI 74; WhoWor 74*

North, Alex
American. Composer, Conductor
Scored films including *Prizzi's Honor,* 1985; won Emmy for theme to "Rich

Man, Poor Man,'' 1976; lifetime achievement Oscar, 1986.
b. Dec 4, 1910 in Chester, Pennsylvania
d. Sep 8, 1991 in Los Angeles, California
Source: *AnObit 1991; ASCAP 66, 80; Baker 78, 84, 92; BiDD; BiE&WWA; BioIn 1, 3, 17, 18; CmpEPM; ConAmC 76, 82; ConNews 86-3; ConTFT 2, 12; DancEn 78; DcCM; FilmEn; FilmgC; HalFC 80, 84, 88; IntDcF 1-4, 2-4; IntMPA 75, 76, 77, 78, 79, 80, 81, 82, 84, 86, 88; IntWW 89, 91; IntWWM 90; NewAmDM; NewGrDA 86; NewGrDM 80; NewYTBS 86; NotNAT; OxCPMus; VarWW 85; WhAm 10; WhoAm 78, 80, 82, 84, 86, 88, 90; WhoAmM 83; WorEFlm*

North, Andy
American. Golfer
Turned pro, 1972; won US Open, 1978, 1985.
b. Mar 9, 1950 in Thorp, Wisconsin
Source: *BioIn 11; WhoIntG; WhoSpor*

North, Frederick North, Baron
English. Political Leader
Prime minister, 1770-82, known for reforms; his rigid colonial policies led Americans to revolt.
b. Apr 13, 1732 in London, England
d. Aug 5, 1792 in London, England
Source: *BioIn 8, 9, 10; DcNaB; LinLib S; McGEWB; NewCol 75; OxCAmH*

North, Jay
American. Actor
Played Dennis the Menace in TV series, 1959-63.
b. Aug 3, 1952 in North Hollywood, California
Source: *BioIn 5, 9, 11; FilmgC; HalFC 80, 84, 88; LegTOT; WhoHol 92, A*

North, John Ringling
American. Circus Owner
Ringling Brothers, Barnum & Bailey combined shows, pres., 1947-67, chm., 1955-67.
b. Aug 14, 1903 in Baraboo, Wisconsin
d. Jun 4, 1985 in Brussels, Belgium
Source: *AnObit 1985; ASCAP 66, 80; BiDAmBL 83; BioIn 2, 3, 4, 8, 14, 20; CurBio 51, 85N; NewYTBS 85; WhoAm 74, 76, 78, 80, 82*

North, Oliver Laurence, Jr.
''Larry''; ''Ollie''
American. Presidential Aide
Marine colonel; his White House operations sparked Iran-Contra controversy, 1986.
b. Oct 7, 1943 in San Antonio, Texas
Source: *BiDAmNC; ConNews 87-4; CurBio 92; NewYTBS 87*

North, Sheree
[Dawn Bethel]
American. Actor
Groomed by Fox Studios as sexpot substitute for Monroe but film career was limited; had lots of TV appearences.
b. Jan 17, 1933 in Los Angeles, California
Source: *BioIn 15; ConTFT 6; EncAFC; FilmEn; FilmgC; HalFC 80, 84, 88; IntMPA 80, 81, 82, 84, 86, 88, 92, 94, 96; LegTOT; MotPP; VarWW 85; WhoHol 92, A*

North, Sterling
American. Writer, Critic
Literary editor, *Chicago Daily News,* 1933-43; *NY Post,* 1943-49; noted for children's books: *Rascal,* 1963, filmed by Disney.
b. Nov 4, 1906 in Edgerton, Wisconsin
d. Dec 21, 1974 in Whippany, New Jersey
Source: *AmAu&B; AmNov; Au&Wr 71; AuBYP 2, 3; BenetAL 91; BioIn 2, 4, 6, 7, 9, 10, 13, 14, 15, 19; ConAu 5R, 40NR, 53; CurBio 43, 75, 75N; DcAmChF 1960; LinLib L, S; MajAI; NewYTBS 74; REnAL; ScF&FL 1, 2; SmATA 1, 26N, 45; ThrBJA; TwCA, SUP; TwCChW 78, 83, 89, 95; TwCYAW; WhAm 6; WhE&EA; WhoAm 74; WhoE 74*

Northcliffe, Alfred Charles William Harmsworth, Viscount
English. Newspaper Publisher
Began career with popular newspaper, *Answers to Correspondents,* 1888; later published *Daily Mirror,* 1903; *The Times,* 1908.
b. Jul 15, 1865 in Chapelizod, Ireland
d. Aug 14, 1922 in London, England
Source: *DcLEL; LngCTC; MnBBF; NewC; OxCEng 67*

Northrop, John Howard
American. Biochemist
Co-winner of Nobel Prize for work on crystallization, purification of enzymes, 1946.
b. Jul 5, 1891 in Yonkers, New York
d. May 27, 1987 in Wickenberg, Arizona
Source: *AmMWSc 73P, 76P, 79, 82, 86; AsBiEn; BiESc; BioIn 1, 3, 6; BlueB 76; CamDcSc; CurBio 47, 87, 87N; FacFETw; InSci; IntWW 74, 75, 76, 77, 78, 79, 80, 81, 82, 83; LarDcSc; McGEWB; McGMS 80; NewYTBS 87; NotTwCS; WebAB 74, 79; WhAm 9; Who 74, 82, 83, 85; WhoAm 74, 76, 78, 80, 82, 84, 86; WhoNob, 90, 95; WhoWest 78, 80, 82, 84, 87; WhoWor 74, 82, 84, 87; WorAl; WorAlBi; WorScD*

Northrop, John Knudsen
American. Aircraft Manufacturer
Founded Lockheed Aircraft, 1927; Northrop Aircraft, 1939.
b. Nov 10, 1895 in Newark, New Jersey
d. Feb 18, 1981 in Glendale, California
Source: *BiDAmBL 83; BioIn 1, 2, 11, 12, 17; CurBio 49, 81; FacFETw; InSci; IntYB 78, 79; LegTOT; NewYTBS 81; WebAB 74; WebAMB; WhAm 7; WhoAm 74*

Northrup, Jim
[James Thomas Northrup]
American. Baseball Player
Outfielder, 1964-75, mostly with Detroit; known for grand slam home runs, 1968.
b. Nov 24, 1939 in Breckenridge, Michigan
Source: *Ballpl 90; BaseEn 88; WhoProB 73*

Norton, Andre
[Alice Mary Norton]
American. Author
Noted for original, complex fantasy, science fiction books; award-winning works include *Iron Butterflies,* 1980.
b. Feb 17, 1912 in Cleveland, Ohio
Source: *AmAu&B; ArtclWW 2; Au&Arts 14; AuBYP 2, 3; BioIn 12, 15, 17, 19, 21; ChlBkCr; ConAu 1R, 2NR, 31NR, X; ConLC 12; ConSFA; CurBio 57; DcLB 8, 52; EncSF, 93; IntAu&W 91, 93; InWom SUP; LegTOT; LinLib L; MajAI; MajTwCW; MorJA; NewEScF; Novels; OhA&B; OnHuMoP; OxCChiL; PenNWW A, B; RGSF; RGTwCSF; ScF&FL 1, 2, 92; ScFSB; SenS; SJGFanW; SmATA 1, 43, 91; SupFW; TwCChW 83, 89; TwCSFW 81, 86, 91; TwCYAW; WhoAm 86; WhoHr&F; WhoSciF; WorAu 1950; WrDr 76, 86, 88, 90, 92*

Norton, Charles Eliot
American. Author, Educator
Influential Fine Arts professor, Harvard U, 1873-98; founded *The Nation,* 1865; friend of literary giants.
b. Nov 16, 1827 in Cambridge, Massachusetts
d. Oct 21, 1908 in Cambridge, Massachusetts
Source: *Alli, SUP; AmAu; AmAu&B; AmBi; ApCAB; BbD; Benet 87, 96; BenetAL 91; BiDAmEd; BiD&SB; BiDTran; BioIn 1, 3, 4, 5, 7, 8, 10, 11, 15, 16; CamGEL; CamGLE; CamHAL; CarSB; Chambr 3; ChhPo S1; CyAL 2; DcAmAu; DcAmB; DcLB 1, 64; DcNAA; EncAB-H 1974, 1996; EvLB; GayN; HarEnUS; LinLib L, S; LngCTC; NatCAB 6; OxCAmH; OxCAmL 65, 83, 95; OxCEng 67, 85, 95; PenC AM; REn; TwCBDA; WebAB 74, 79; WhAm 1; WhAmArt 85*

Norton, Eleanor Holmes
American. Government Official, Lawyer
Asst. legal director, ACLU, 1965-70; chm., EEOC, 1977-83; professor of Law, Georgetown U, 1982—; delagate to Congress from DC, 1990—.
b. Apr 8, 1938 in Washington, District of Columbia
Source: *AfrAmAl 6; BioNews 75; CurBio 76; InB&W 85; NewYTBE 71; NotBlAW 1; WhoAfA 96; WhoAm 86; WhoAmW 85; WhoBlA 77, 80, 85, 88, 90, 92, 94; WhoGov 77; WomLaw*

Norton, Elliot
[William Elliot Norton]
American. Critic, Lecturer
With *Boston Herald America,* 1973-82; star of TV program, 1958-82; won special Tony for Broadway reviews, 1971.
b. May 17, 1903 in Boston, Massachusetts
Source: *BiE&WWA; BioIn 4, 7; CamGWoT; CelR; ConAmTC; ConAu 109; NotNAT; OxCAmT 84; WhoAm 74, 76, 78, 80, 82, 84; WhoE 74, 83, 85, 86, 95, 97; WhoEnt 92; WhoThe 72, 77, 81*

Norton, Jack
American. Actor
Character actor whose speciality was the amiable drunk, 1934-48.
b. 1889 in New York, New York
d. Oct 15, 1958 in Saranac Lake, New York
Source: *BioIn 5; EncAFC; FilmEn; FilmgC; ForYSC; HalFC 80, 84, 88; HolCA; MotPP; MovMk; NotNAT B; QDrFCA 92; Vers A; WhoHol B; WhScrn 74, 77, 83*

Norton, Ken(neth Howard)
American. Boxer
Defeated Muhammad Ali, 1973, then lost in re-match bout; total career record: 32 bouts, 22 KOs.
b. Aug 9, 1945 in Jacksonville, Illinois
Source: *BioIn 9, 10, 15, 21; InB&W 80, 85; LegTOT; NewYTBS 81; WhoAm 74, 78, 80, 82; WhoBox 74; WhoHol 92; WorAl*

Norton, Mary
English. Children's Author
Best known for *The Borrowers,* series—fantasy stories of six-inch people written in the 1950s-60s.
b. Dec 10, 1903 in London, England
d. Aug 29, 1992 in Hartland, England
Source: *AnCL; AnObit 1992; Au&ICB; Au&Wr 71; AuBYP 2, 3; BioIn 5, 6, 8, 9, 12, 16, 17, 18, 19; BkCL; CamGLE; CasWL; ChlBkCr; ChlLR 6; ConAu 97, 139; DcLB 160; IntAu&W 89, 91; LegTOT; MajAI; NewCBEL; NewYTBS 92; OxCChiL; ScF&FL 1, 92; SJGFanW; SmATA 18, 60, 72; ThrBJA; TwCChW 78, 83, 89, 95; Who 85, 88, 90, 92; WrDr 76, 80, 82, 84, 86, 88, 90, 92, 94N*

Norton-Taylor, Judy
American. Actor
Played Mary Ellen on "The Waltons," 1972-81.
b. Jan 29, 1958 in Santa Monica, California
Source: *BioIn 11; ConTFT 3; InWom SUP; LegTOT; WhoAm 82, 86, 88; WhoHol A; WorAl*

Norville, Deborah (Anne)
[Mrs. Karl Wellner]
American. Broadcast Journalist
Co-anchor of "Today" show, 1990-91; host of "Inside Edition," 1994—.
b. Aug 8, 1958 in Dalton, Georgia
Source: *BioIn 16; ConTFT 15; CurBio 90; LegTOT; LesBEnT 92; News 90, 90-3; WhoAm 94, 95, 96, 97; WhoAmW 95, 97*

Norvo, Red
[Kenneth Norvo]
American. Jazz Musician
Vibraphonist who led own band, 1930s-40s; once wed to his vocalist, Mildred Bailey.
b. Mar 31, 1908 in Beardstown, Illinois
Source: *AllMusG; ASCAP 66, 80; Baker 84, 92; BgBands 74; BiDAmM; BiDJaz; BioIn 4, 8, 9, 10, 12, 16; CmpEPM; ConMus 12; EncJzS; EncJzS; LegTOT; NewAmDM; NewGrDA 86; NewGrDJ 88, 94; NewGrDM 80; OxCPMus; PenEncP; VarWW 85; WhoAm 74; WhoHol 92; WhoJazz 72; WorAl; WorAlBi*

Norwich, Alfred Duff Cooper, Viscount
English. Statesman, Author
Held various political posts including secretary of State for War, 1935-37; writings include *Old Men Forget,* 1953.
b. Feb 22, 1890 in London, England
d. Jan 1, 1954 in Vigo, Spain
Source: *BioIn 3, 5; CurBio 40, 54; DcLEL; EvLB; LngCTC; NewC; NewCBEL; WhAm 3*

Norwich, Diana (Manners) Cooper, Viscountess
[Diana Olivia Winifred Maud Manners]
English. Socialite, Actor
Eccentric beauty who inspired poetry, comedy; immortalized by Hilaire Belloc, Evelyn Waugh; played the Madonna in *The Miracle,* for 12 yrs.
b. Aug 29, 1892 in London, England
d. Jun 16, 1986 in London, England
Source: *Au&Wr 71; DcLEL 1940; LngCTC; NewC; Who 82*

Norwich, William
American. Journalist
Society columnist, NY *Daily News,* 1985—.
b. Jul 18, 1954 in Norwich, Connecticut
Source: *BioIn 16; CelR 90*

Norworth, Jack
American. Songwriter, Actor
Composed "Shine On, Harvest Moon" and "Take Me Out to the Ball Game;" appeared in vaudeville as blackface comedian.
b. Jan 5, 1879 in Philadelphia, Pennsylvania
d. Sep 1, 1959 in Beverly Hills, California
Source: *ASCAP 66, 80; BiDAmM; BioIn 2, 4, 5, 7; CmpEPM; EncAFC; EncMT; Film 2; NatCAB 48; NewGrDA 86; NotNAT B; OxCAmT 84; OxCPMus; OxCThe 67, 83; WhoHol B; WhScrn 74, 77, 83; WhThe*

Nossiter, Bernard Daniel
American. Journalist
Chief, *New York Times* UN bureau, 1979-83; wrote "Fat Years and Lean," 1990.
b. Apr 10, 1926 in New York, New York
d. Jun 24, 1992 in New York, New York
Source: *ConAu 41R; EncTwCJ; IntAu&W 89, 91, 93; WhAm 10; Who 82, 83, 85, 88, 90, 92; WhoAm 74, 76, 78, 80, 82, 84, 88, 90, 92; WhoE 91; WhoFI 92; WhoWor 74*

Nostradamus
[Michel de Notredame]
French. Astrologer, Physician
Wrote rhymed astrological predictions.
b. Dec 14, 1503 in Saint-Remy, France
d. Jul 2, 1566 in Salon, France
Source: *Benet 87; BioIn 4, 6, 10, 13, 14, 17; DcArts; DivFut; EncO&P 1, 2, 3; EncPaPR 91; EncWW; LegTOT; LinLib L, S; LitC 27; NewC; OxCEng 85, 95; OxCFr; OxCGer 76, 86; REn; WhDW*

Nott, John William Frederic, Sir
English. Government Official
Defense minister responsible for British Military operations in Falkland Islands, 1982.
b. Feb 1, 1932 in London, England
Source: *BioIn 13; BlueB 76; IntWW 83, 89, 91, 93; IntYB 78, 79, 80, 81, 82; NewYTBS 82; Who 74, 82, 83, 85, 94; WhoEIO 82*

Nougues, Jean
French. Composer
Wrote popular opera *Quo Vadis,* 1909.
b. Apr 25, 1875 in Bordeaux, France
d. Aug 28, 1932 in Paris, France
Source: *Baker 78, 84, 92; NewEOp 71; OxDcOp*

Nouri, Michael
American. Actor
Films include *Flashdance,* 1983; stars in numerous TV movies.
b. Dec 9, 1945 in Washington, District of Columbia
Source: *ASCAP 80; BioIn 13; ConTFT 1, 7; IntMPA 86, 88, 92, 94, 96; WhoHol 92*

Nourrit, Adolphe
French. Opera Singer
Celebrated tenor of Parisian, Italian opera, 1830s.
b. Mar 3, 1802 in Paris, France
d. Mar 8, 1839 in Naples, Italy
Source: *Baker 78, 84, 92; BioIn 6, 7, 14, 20, 21; BriBkM 80; CmOp; IntDcOp; MetOEnc; NewAmDM; NewEOp 71; NewGrDM 80; NewGrDO; OxDcOp; PenDiMP*

Novaes (Pinto), Guiomar
Brazilian. Musician
Outstanding pianist; noted for deep concentration, colorful performances; had US debut, 1915.

b. Feb 28, 1895 in Sao Paulo, Brazil
d. Mar 7, 1979 in Sao Paulo, Brazil
Source: *Baker 84, 92; BiDAmM; BioIn 3, 4, 11, 16, 17; BriBkM 80; CurBio 53, 79; InWom SUP; MusSN; NewYTBS 79; NotTwCP; PenDiMP; WhAm 7; WhoAm 74; WhoAmW 74; WhoWor 74*

Novak, Kim
[Marilyn Pauline Novak]
American. Actor
Starred in *Vertigo,* 1959; played Kit Marlowe on TV series "Falcon Crest," 1986-87.
b. Feb 18, 1933 in Chicago, Illinois
Source: *BiDFilm 81, 94; BioIn 3, 4, 5, 6, 7, 10, 11, 12, 13; ConTFT 2, 7, 15; CurBio 57; DcArts; FilmEn; FilmgC; ForYSC; HalFC 80, 84, 88; IntDcF 1-3, 2-3; IntMPA 77, 78, 79, 80, 81, 82, 84, 86, 88, 92, 94, 96; InWom, SUP; LegTOT; MotPP; MovMk; OxCFilm; VarWW 85; WhoAm 74, 76, 78, 80, 82, 84, 86, 88, 90, 92, 94, 95, 96, 97; WhoAmW 58, 95, 97; WhoEnt 92; WhoHol 92, A; WhoHrs 80; WorAl; WorAlBi; WorEFlm*

Novak, Robert
[Evans and Novak]
American. Journalist
Syndicated columnist since 1963; books include *The Reagan Revolution,* 1981, with Rowland Evans, Jr.
b. Feb 26, 1931 in Joliet, Illinois
Source: *CelR; ConAu 13R; EncAJ; LegTOT; WhoAm 84*

Novak, Vitezslav
Czech. Composer
Patriotic operas include *Karlstejn,* 1916.
b. Dec 5, 1870 in Kamenitz, Bohemia
d. Jul 18, 1949 in Skutec, Czechoslovakia
Source: *Baker 78, 84; BioIn 1, 2, 3, 4, 8; BriBkM 80; CompSN; DcCM; NewAmDM; NewGrDM 80; NewGrDO; NewOxM; OxCMus; OxDcOp*

Novalis
[Friedrich von Hardenberg]
German. Poet
Influenced *le romantisme* movement in France, which later developed into Romantic Movement; prose poems include *Hymns to the Night,* 1800.
b. May 2, 1772 in Halle, Germany
d. Mar 25, 1801 in Weissenfels, Germany
Source: *BbD; Benet 87, 96; BiD&SB; BioIn 14, 17, 21; BlkwCE; CasWL; DcArts; DcBiPP; DcEnL; DcLB 90; Dis&D; EuAu; EuWr 5; EvEuW; GrFLW; IlEncMy; LinLib L; LuthC 75; McGEWB; NewCBEL; NinCLC 13; OxCEng 67; OxCFr; OxCGer 76, 86; PenC EUR; PseudAu; RAdv 14, 13-2; REn; RfGWoL 95; WhDW*

Novarro, Ramon
[Ramon Samaniegos]
Mexican. Actor
Silent screen leading man best known for title role in *Ben Hur,* 1926.
b. Feb 6, 1899 in Durango, Mexico
d. Oct 31, 1968 in Los Angeles, California
Source: *BiDFilm 81, 94; BioIn 7, 8, 9, 10, 11, 14, 16, 20; CmMov; CmpEPM; DcAmB S8; Film 1, 2; FilmEn; FilmgC; ForYSC; HalFC 80, 84, 88; HispAmA; IntDcF 1-3, 2-3; LegTOT; MexAmB; MotPP; MovMk; ObitT 1961; OxCFilm; SilFlmP; TwYS; WhAm 5; What 1; WhoHol B; WhScrn 74, 77, 83; WorAl; WorAlBi; WorEFlm*

Novello, Antonia Coello
American. Physician, Government Official
Succeeded C Everett Koop as surgeon general, 1990-93; first woman, first Hispanic to hold post.
b. Aug 23, 1944 in Fajardo, Puerto Rico
Source: *AmMWSc 89, 92, 95; CurBio 92; HispAmA; WhoAm 88, 90, 92, 94, 95, 96, 97; WhoAmW 89, 91, 93, 95, 97; WhoHisp 91, 92, 94; WhoScEn 94, 96; WhoSSW 84*

Novello, Don
American. Comedian
Best known as Father Guido Sarducci on TV's "Saturday Night Live," 1978-80, 1985-86.
b. Jan 1, 1943 in Ashtabula, Ohio
Source: *ConAu 44NR, 107; ConTFT 3; IntMPA 92, 94, 96; LegTOT; VarWW 85; WhoAm 82, 84, 86, 88, 90, 92, 94, 95, 96, 97; WhoEnt 92; WhoHol 92; WhoUSWr 88; WhoWrEP 89, 92, 95*

Novello, Ivor
[David Ivor Davies]
Welsh. Songwriter, Actor
Wrote song "Keep the Home Fires Burning;" appeared in film *Once a Lady,* 1932.
b. Jan 15, 1893 in Cardiff, Wales
d. Mar 6, 1951 in London, England
Source: *BestMus; BioIn 1, 2, 3, 4, 10, 14, 15; CnThe; DcArts; DcLEL; DcNaB 1951; EncEurC; EncMT; EncWT; Ent; EvLB; FacFETw; Film 2; FilmEn; FilmgC; ForYSC; GrBr; HalFC 80, 84, 88; IlWWBF, A; IntDcF 1-3, 2-3; LngCTC; McGEWD 72, 84; ModWD; MotPP; MusMk; NewAmDM; NewC; NewCBEL; NewGrDM 80; NewGrDO; NewOxM; NotNAT A, B; ObitT 1951; OxCLiW 86; OxCMus; OxCPMus; OxCThe 67, 83; PenDiMP; REn; TwCA SUP; TwCWr; WhAm 4; WhE&EA; WhoHol B; WhScrn 74, 77, 83; WhThe; WorAl*

Novi, Carlo
[Southside Johnny and the Asbury Jukes]
Mexican. Musician
Tenor saxophonist with group since 1974.
b. Aug 7, 1949 in Mexico City, Mexico

Novotna, Jarmila
Czech. Opera Singer
Aristocratic soprano with NY Met., 1939-54.
b. Sep 23, 1907 in Prague, Czech Republic
d. Feb 9, 1994 in New York, New York
Source: *Baker 84, 92; BioIn 14, 16, 19, 20; CmOp; CurBio 40, 94N; IntDcOp; IntWWM 90; MetOEnc; MusSN; NewEOp 71; NewGrDM 80; NewGrDO; OxDcOp; PenDiMP; WhoAm 74; WhoHol 92; WhoMus 72; WhoWor 74*

Novotny, Antonin
Czech. Political Leader
Communist party leader; pres. of Czechoslovakia, 1957-68.
b. Dec 10, 1904 in Letnany, Czechoslovakia
d. Jan 28, 1975 in Prague, Czechoslovakia
Source: *BioIn 4, 5, 8, 10, 18; ColdWar 1, 2; CurBio 58, 75N; DicTyr; EncCW; EncRev; FacFETw; IntWW 74; LegTOT; NewYTBS 75; ObitT 1971; WhAm 6*

Nowicki, Matthew
[Maciej Nowicki]
Polish. Architect
Considered "ahead of his time;" works express love for drawing; died, in plane crash, before completing urban project in India.
b. Jun 26, 1910 in Chitai, Russia
d. Aug 31, 1951
Source: *BioIn 2, 3, 8, 10; ConArch 80, 87; DcNCBi 4; EncMA; IntDcAr; MacEA; McGDA*

Nowlan, Phil
[Frank Phillips]
American. Cartoonist
Best known for creating comic strip character, Buck Rogers, 1929.
b. 1888 in Philadelphia, Pennsylvania
d. Feb 1, 1940 in Philadelphia, Pennsylvania
Source: *LegTOT; WorECom*

Noyce, Robert Norton
American. Business Executive, Scientist
Invented integrated circuit and microchip, which helped to usher in computer age and revolutionized the electronics industry; founded Intel Corp., 1968.
b. Dec 12, 1927 in Burlington, Iowa
d. Jun 3, 1990 in Austin, Texas
Source: *AmMWSc 73P, 76P, 79, 82, 86, 89, 92; BioIn 12, 13; ConNews 85-4; FacFETw; HisDcDP; IntWW 89; LarDcSc; LElec; St&PR 87; WhAm 10; WhoAm 76, 78, 80, 82, 84, 86, 88; WhoEng 80; WhoFI 89; WhoFrS 84; WhoWest 74, 76, 87, 89*

Noyes, Alfred
English. Poet, Author
Noted for narrative verse based on English history; best-known poem, "The Highwayman."

b. Sep 16, 1880 in Wolverhampton, England
d. Jun 28, 1958 in Isle of Wight, England
Source: *AuBYP 2S, 3; Benet 87, 96; BioIn 1, 2, 3, 4, 5, 6, 13, 14; BkC 6; CamGLE; CathA 1930; Chambr 3; ChhPo, S1, S2, S3; ConAu 104; DcArts; DcCathB; DcLB 20; DcLEL; DcNaB 1951; EncSF, 93; EngPo; EvLB; FacFETw; GrBr; GrWrEL P; LegTOT; LinLib L, S; LngCTC; ModBrL; NewC; NewCBEL; ObitOF 79; ObitT 1951; OxCEng 67, 85, 95; OxCShps; PenC ENG; REn; RfGEnL 91; RGTwCWr; ScF&FL 1; SJGFanW; TwCA, SUP; TwCLC 7; TwCWr; WhAm 3; WhE&EA; WhLit; WhoHr&F; WhoLA*

Noyes, Blanche Wilcox
American. Aviator, Actor
Co-designed twin motored plane, 1933.
b. Jun 23, 1900 in Cleveland, Ohio
d. 1981 in Washington, District of Columbia
Source: *InWom, SUP; WhoAm 74, 76; WhoAmW 72, 74*

Noyes, Frank B(rett)
American. Newspaper Executive
Last surviving founder of AP, pres., 1900-38; chm., *Washington Evening Star.*
b. Jul 7, 1863 in Washington, District of Columbia
d. Dec 1, 1948 in Washington, District of Columbia
Source: *ApCAB X; BiDAmJo; BioIn 1, 2, 16; DcAmB S4; EncAJ; NatCAB 13; ObitOF 79; WhAm 2; WhJnl*

Noyes, John Humphrey
American. Social Reformer
Perfectionist; established utopistic Oneida Community, 1848; noted for starting leading flatware co.
b. Sep 3, 1811 in Brattleboro, Vermont
d. Apr 13, 1886 in Niagara Falls, Ontario, Canada
Source: *Alli SUP; AmAu; AmAu&B; AmBi; AmPeW; AmRef; AmSocL; ApCAB; BbD; Benet 87, 96; BenetAL 91; BiDAmCu; BiDAmLf; BiD&SB; BiDMoPL; BioIn 1, 2, 4, 8, 9, 11, 12, 15, 19; DcAmAu; DcAmB; DcAmReB 1, 2; DcAmSR; EncAAH; EncAB-H 1974, 1996; EncARH; HarEnUS; LinLib S; LuthC 75; McGEWB; NatCAB 11; OxCAmH; OxCAmL 65, 83, 95; PeoHis; REn; REnAL; WebAB 74, 79; WhAm HS*

Nozick, Robert
American. Philosopher, Author
Controversial Harvard philosophy professor, 1969-85; wrote award-winning: *Anarchy, State and Utopia,* 1975.
b. Nov 16, 1938 in New York, New York
Source: *BioIn 10, 11, 12, 13; ConAu 61; CurBio 82; DcAmC; DrAS 74P, 78P, 82P; EncWB; IntWW 91, 93; MakMC; OxCPhil; RAdv 14; WhoAm 74, 76, 78, 80, 82, 84, 86, 88, 90, 92, 94, 95, 96, 97; WhoAmJ 80; WorAu 1975; WrDr 92, 94, 96*

Noziere, Violette
French. Murderer
Murdered her father and attempted to poison her mother in order to obtain their savings; sentenced to life imprisonment.
b. 1915

Nsubuga, Emmanuel, Cardinal
Ugandan. Religious Leader
Became Uganda's only Cardinal in 1976; opponent of human rights abuses under Idi Amin's rule.
b. Nov 5, 1914 in Kisule, Uganda
d. Apr 20, 1991 in Cologne, Germany
Source: *AfSS 78, 79, 80, 81, 82; BioIn 11, 17; IntWW 79, 80, 81, 82, 83, 89, 91; NewYTBS 91; WhAm 10; WhoWor 82, 84, 87, 89, 91*

Ntaryamira, Cyprien
Burundian. Political Leader
President of Burundi, 1994; killed in a plane crash.
b. c. 1955, Burundi
d. Apr 6, 1994
Source: *ConBlB 8*

Nu, U
[Thakin Nu]
Burmese. Political Leader
First prime minister of Burmese Republic, 1948-56, 1957-58; led revolution against opposing govt., 1970.
b. May 25, 1907 in Wakema, Burma
d. Feb 14, 1995 in Rangoon, Myanmar
Source: *BioIn 2, 12, 20, 21; CurBio 51, 95N; DcMPSA; DcOrL 2; DcPol; FarE&A 78, 79, 80, 81; IntWW 74, 75, 76, 77, 78, 79, 80, 81, 82, 83, 89, 91, 93; McGEWB; PenC CL; WhoWor 74*

Nuffield, William Richard Morris
English. Auto Manufacturer
Founded Morris Motors Ltd., 1919; produced the first MG; as the result of a merger, 1952, became British Motor Corp.
b. Oct 10, 1877 in Worcestershire, England
d. Aug 22, 1963 in Huntercombe, England
Source: *BioIn 12, 14; DcTwHis; GrBr*

Nugent, Edward
American. Actor
Ten-year film career in supporting roles, 1928-38, included films *42nd Street,* 1933; *Ah, Wilderness!,* 1935.
b. Feb 7, 1904 in New York, New York
Source: *FilmEn; ForYSC; TwYS; WhoHol 92, A*

Nugent, Elliott
American. Dramatist, Director, Producer
Co-authored *Male Animal* with James Thurber, 1940; co-produced *The Seven Year Itch* on Broadway.
b. Sep 20, 1899 in Dover, Ohio
d. Aug 9, 1980 in New York, New York
Source: *AmAu&B; BiE&WWA; BioIn 3, 5, 7, 9, 10; CnMD; ConAu 5R, 101, 103; ConDr 77; CurBio 44, 80; EncAFC; Film 2; FilmEn; FilmgC; ForYSC; GangFlm; HalFC 80, 84, 88; IlWWHD 1A; IntMPA 79; McGEWB; McGEWD 72, 84; MiSFD 9N; ModWD; MovMk; NotNAT, A; OxCAmT 84; WhAm 7; WhoAm 74, 76; WhoHol A; WhoThe 72, 77A; WhoWor 74; WhThe; WorEFlm; WrDr 80, 82*

Nugent, Nelle
American. Producer
Partner of Elizabeth McCann; stage productions include *The Dresser; Mass Appeal;* won five Tonys.
b. Mar 24, 1939 in Jersey City, New Jersey
Source: *BioIn 12, 16; ConTFT 1; NewYTBS 81; NotWoAT; VarWW 85; WhoAm 82, 84, 86, 88, 90, 92, 94, 95, 96, 97; WhoAmW 81, 83, 85, 87, 89, 91; WhoE 95, 97; WhoEnt 92; WhoWor 96, 97*

Nugent, Ted
[The Amboy Dukes; Theodore Anthony Nugent]
"Motor City Mad Man"
American. Singer
Known for wild antics, wearing earplugs while performing; songs include Journey to the "Centre of the Mind," 1967.
b. Dec 13, 1948 in Detroit, Michigan
Source: *ASCAP 80; BkPepl; EncPR&S 89; EncRk 88; EncRkSt; HarEnR 86; LegTOT; OnThGG; PenEncP; RolSEnR 83; VarWW 85; WhoAm 82, 84, 86, 94, 95, 96, 97; WhoEnt 92*

Nuitter, Charles Louis
[Charles Louis Truinet]
French. Author, Musician, Librettist
Wrote librettos for stage productions including Delibe's *Coppelia.*
b. Apr 24, 1828 in Paris, France
d. Feb 24, 1899 in Paris, France
Source: *Baker 84; NewEOp 71*

Nujoma, Samuel Shafiihuma
Namibian. Political Leader
Elected first pres. of Namibia after 74 yrs. of S African colonial rule, 1990— .
b. May 12, 1929 in Owambo, Namibia
Source: *BioIn 16; CurBio 90; DcCPSAf; IntWW 89; News 90; NewYTBS 76, 81; WhoWor 91*

Numan, Eppo
Dutch. Pilot, Artist
First to fly an ultralight aircraft across the Atlantic, 1992.
b. 1943?

Source: *InWom SUP; WhoAmW 85*

Numan, Gary
[Gary Anthony James Webb]
English. Singer, Musician
Considered first superstar of the synthesiser; albums include *She's Got Claws,* 1981.
b. Mar 8, 1958 in London, England
Source: *BioIn 12; EncRk 88; EncRkSt; HarEnR 86; LegTOT; PenEncP; RkOn 85; RolSEnR 83; WhoRocM 82*

Nungesser, Charles Eugene Jules Marie
French. Aviator
One of France's leading pilots, WW I; destroyed 45 German planes; lost at sea during attempted transatlantic flight to NYC.
b. 1892 in Paris, France
d. May 1927
Source: *BioIn 5, 8, 11; WhoMilH 76*

Nunn, Bobby
American. Musician
Bass player; original member of pop group the Coasters, 1955-58; hits include "Yakety Yak," 1958.
b. 1925?
d. Nov 5, 1986 in Los Angeles, California
Source: *NewYTBS 86*

Nunn, Sam(uel Augustus, Jr.)
American. Politician
Dem. senator from GA, 1972-97; chm., Senate Armed Forces Com., 1984-95.
b. Sep 8, 1938 in Perry, Georgia
Source: *AlmAP 78, 80, 82, 84, 88, 92, 96; BioIn 9, 10, 11, 12, 13; CngDr 74, 77, 79, 81, 83, 85, 87, 89, 91, 93, 95; CurBio 80; EncWB; IntWW 74, 75, 76, 77, 78, 79, 80, 81, 82, 83, 89, 91, 93; LegTOT; News 90, 90-2; NewYTBS 86, 93; PolsAm 84; WhoAm 76, 78, 80, 82, 84, 86, 88, 90, 92; WhoAmL 78; WhoAmP 73, 75, 77, 79, 81, 83, 85, 87, 89, 91, 93, 95; WhoGov 75, 77; WhoSSW 78, 80, 82, 86, 88, 91; WhoWor 80, 82, 87, 89, 91; WorAlBi*

Nunn, Trevor Robert
English. Director
Master of London stage, Broadway; noted for running four hits at one time; won three Tonys.
b. Jan 14, 1940 in Ipswich, England
Source: *BioIn 12; CnThe; CurBio 80; IntDcT 3; IntWW 77, 78, 79, 80, 81, 82, 83, 89, 91, 93; OxCThe 83; VarWW 85; Who 74, 82, 83, 85, 88, 90, 92, 94; WhoAm 90, 92, 94, 95, 96, 97; WhoEnt 92; WhoThe 81; WhoWor 82, 84, 87, 89, 91, 93, 95, 96, 97*

Nureyev, Rudolf (Hametovich)
Austrian. Dancer
Defected from Soviet Union, 1961; partnered with Margot Fonteyn, 1962-79; directed Paris Opera Ballet, 1983-89.
b. Mar 17, 1938 in Irkutsk, Union of Soviet Socialist Republics
d. Jan 6, 1993 in Paris, France
Source: *BiDD; BioIn 14, 15, 17, 18, 19, 20, 21; BioNews 74; BkPepl; CelR, 90; CnOxB; ConTFT 5, 12; CurBio 63, 93N; DancEn 78; DcArts; GayLesB; HalFC 80, 84, 88; IntDcB; IntMPA 84, 86, 88, 92, 94; IntWW 74, 75, 76, 77, 78, 79, 80, 81, 82, 83, 89, 91; LegTOT; LinLib S; News 93-2; NewYTBE 70; NewYTBS 74, 93; SovUn; VarWW 85; WhAm 10; Who 74, 88, 90, 92; WhoAm 74, 76, 78, 80, 82, 84, 86, 88, 90, 92; WhoEnt 92; WhoHol 92, A; WhoWor 74, 76, 78, 80, 82, 84, 87, 89, 91, 93; WorAl; WorAlBi*

Nuridsany, Claude
French. Filmmaker
With Marie Perennou, made *Microcosmos,* winner of the 1996 Cannes Film Festival grand prize for technical achievement.
b. Apr 11, 1946 in Paris, France

Nurmi, Paavo Johannes
Finnish. Track Athlete
Distance runner; won seven gold medals in Olympics; set 20 world records.
b. Jun 13, 1897 in Turku, Finland
d. Oct 2, 1973 in Helsinki, Finland
Source: *BioIn 10; NewYTBE 73; ObitOF 79; WhoTr&F 73*

Nussbaum, Karen
American. Labor Union Official, Government Official
Co-founder, exec. director, 9 to 5, Nat. Assn. of Working Women; and pres., District 925, a secretarial and clerical union, 1981—; pres. Service Employees International Union, 1975-93; dir. Women's Bureau, US Department of Labor, 1993—.
b. Apr 25, 1950 in Chicago, Illinois
Source: *InWom SUP; News 88-3; WhoAm 96, 97; WhoAmW 95, 97*

Nu Thakin
Burmese. Political Leader
Prime minister, Burma, 1947-62.
b. May 25, 1903
d. Feb 14, 1995 in Yangon, Myanmar

Nuttall, Zelia Maria Magdalena
American. Author, Archaeologist
Wrote on ancient Mexico; noted for unearthing paintings on deerskin, 1890.
b. Sep 6, 1857 in San Francisco, California
d. Apr 12, 1933 in Casa Alvaredo, Mexico
Source: *AmWomSc; InWom SUP; LibW; NotAW; WhAm 1; WomFir*

Nutting, Wallace
American. Author, Photographer
Wrote *Furniture Treasury,* 1928-33, descriptive books on Eastern states.
b. Nov 17, 1861 in Marlborough, Massachusetts
d. Jul 19, 1941 in Framingham, Massachusetts
Source: *AmAu&B; BioIn 6, 11, 12, 13, 14, 16; CurBio 41; DcAmB S3; DcNAA; ICPEnP A; MacBEP; NatCAB 30; REnAL; WhAm 1; WhAmArt 85; WhLit*

Nuyen, France
[France Nguyen Vannga]
American. Actor
Starred on stage in *The World of Suzie Wong,* 1958; films include *South Pacific,* 1958; starred on TV's "St. Elsewhere," 1985-88.
b. Jul 31, 1939 in Marseilles, France
Source: *BiE&WWA; BioIn 5, 6; ConTFT 1; FilmEn; FilmgC; ForYSC; HalFC 80, 84, 88; InWom; LegTOT; MotPP; VarWW 85; WhoAm 74; WhoHol 92, A*

N.W.A.
"Dr. Dre"; "Eazy-E"; "Ice Cube"; "M.C. Ren"; "Yella"
American. Rap Group
Formed c. 1988; controversial performers of "gangsta" rap; released debut album *Straight Outta Compton,* 1989.
Source: *AfrAmAl 6; BioIn 17, 19, 20; ConMus 6; NewYTBS 94, 95; WhoAm 96, 97*

Nyad, Diana
American. Swimmer
First to swim from Bahamas to US, 1979.
b. Aug 22, 1949 in New York, New York
Source: *BioIn 9, 10, 11, 12; ConAu 111, 136; CurBio 79; LegTOT; WhoAmW 85; WhoSpor; WomFir; WrDr 94*

Nye, Edgar Wilson
[Bill Nye]
American. Author
Comic works include *Bill Nye and Boomerang,* 1881; used puns, misquotes, scrambled sentences.
b. Aug 25, 1850 in Shirley, Maine
d. Feb 22, 1896 in Arden, North Carolina
Source: *Alli SUP; AmAu; AmAu&B; AmBi; ApCAB; BbD; BenetAL 91; BibAL; BiDAmJo; BiDAmNC; BiD&SB; BioIn 2, 5, 9, 11, 12, 13, 15, 16; ChhPo S1, S2; CnDAL; DcAmAu; DcAmB; DcLB 11, 23; DcLEL; DcNAA; DcNCBi 4; EncAHmr; EncAJ; LinLib L, S; NatCAB 6; OxCAmL 65, 83, 95; REnAL; ScFEYrs; TwCBDA; WhAm HS; WisWr*

Nye, Gerald Prentice
American. Politician, Editor
Leading isolationist; Rep. senator from ND, 1925-44; helped expose Teapot Dome oil scandals.
b. Dec 19, 1892 in Hortonville, Wisconsin
d. Jul 17, 1971 in Washington, District of Columbia
Source: *AmPolLe; AmRef; BiDrAC; BiDrUSC 89; BioIn 1, 6, 7, 9, 12, 15; CurBio 41, 71; DcAmB S9; EncAB-H*

1974, 1996; NewYTBE 71; ObitOF 79; REnAW; WhAm 5

Nye, Russel Blaine
American. Historian, Educator
Wrote 1944 Pulitzer-winner *George Bancroft: Brahmin Rebel.*
b. Feb 17, 1913 in Viola, Wisconsin
Source: *AmAu&B; Au&Wr 71; BioIn 19, 20, 21; ConAu 1R, 4NR; CurBio 45; DcLEL 1940; DrAS 82E; OxCAmL 65; REnAL; TwCA SUP; WhoAm 84; WrDr 86, 96*

Nyerere, Julius Kambarage
Tanzanian. Political Leader
Son of tribal chief who became first pres. of Tanzania, 1964-85.
b. Mar 1922 in Butiama, Tanganyika
Source: *AfrA; AfSS 78, 79, 80, 81, 82; BioIn 12; ColdWar 1; ConAu 105; CurBio 63; DcAfHiB 86; DcPol; DcTwHis; FacFETw; GrLGrT; IntWW 74, 75, 76, 77, 78, 79, 80, 81, 82, 83, 89, 91, 93; IntYB 78, 79, 80, 81, 82; NewYTBS 76; SelBAAf; Who 74, 82, 83, 85, 88, 90, 92, 94; WhoAfr; WhoGov 72; WhoWor 74, 76, 78, 80, 82, 84, 87*

Nyiregyhazi, Ervin
American. Pianist
Held first piano concert at age six; wrote over 100 works for piano.
b. Jan 19, 1903 in Budapest, Austria-Hungary
d. Apr 13, 1987 in Los Angeles, California
Source: *AnObit 1987; Baker 84; BioIn 11; ConAmC 82; NewGrDA 86; NewGrDM 80; NewYTBS 78*

Nykvist, Sven Vilhem
Swedish. Filmmaker
Best known as Ingmar Bergman's cameraman, 1960s; won Oscars for *Cries and Wh ispers,* 1973; *Fanny and Alexander,* 1983.
b. Dec 3, 1922 in Moheda, Sweden
Source: *ConTFT 5; DcFM; FilmEn; FilmgC; HalFC 84; IntMPA 86; NewYTBS 83; OxCFilm; VarWW 85; WhoAm 82, 84, 86, 88, 90, 92, 94, 95, 96, 97; WhoEnt 92; WorEFlm*

Nylons, The
Canadian. Music Group
Formed, 1979; a capella quartet performs 50s-60s classics, along with original compositions; albums include *Rockapella,* 1989.
Source: *BioIn 11; ConMus 6; WhoGov 72, 75*

Nype, Russell
American. Actor
Won Tonys for *Call Me Madam,* 1951; *Goldilocks,* 1959.
b. Apr 26, 1924 in Zion, Illinois
Source: *BiE&WWA; BioIn 2; EncMT; NotNAT; VarWW 85; WhoHol 92, A; WhoThe 72, 77, 81*

Nyro, Laura
American. Singer, Songwriter
Best known for writing pop music, 1960s-70s, with poetic lyrics; albums include *NY Tendaberry,* 1969.
b. Oct 18, 1947 in New York, New York
d. Apr 8, 1997 in Danbury, Connecticut
Source: *BiDAmM; BioIn 10, 14; CelR; ConLC 17; ConMuA 80A; ConMus 12; EncFCWM 83; EncPR&S 89; EncRk 88; IlEncRk; LegTOT; NewAmDM; NewGrDA 86; NewYTBS 76; OxCPMus; PenEncP; RkOn 74, 78, 82; RolSEnR 83; SoulM; WhoAm 76, 78, 80, 82, 84; WhoAmW 81; WhoRock 81; WhoRocM 82; WorAl; WorAlBi*

Nystrom, Bob
[Thor Robert Nystrom]
Swedish. Hockey Player
Right wing, NY Islanders, 1972-86; won four Stanley Cups.
b. Oct 10, 1952 in Stockholm, Sweden
Source: *HocEn; HocReg 85; NewYTBS 75, 82*

O

Oakes, Richard
American. Political Activist
Involved with the Indians of All Tribes organization, which took over Alcatraz Island in 1969; involved in the Red River Indians' efforts to regain tribal land.
b. 1942 in Saint Regis Reservation, New York
d. Sep 20, 1972 in Santa Clara, California
Source: *BioIn 21; EncNAB; NotNaAm*

Oakeshott, Michael Joseph
English. Author
Books include *Experience and Its Modes,* 1933; *Rationalism in Politics and Other Essays,* 1962.
b. Dec 11, 1901 in Kent, England
Source: *BioIn 11, 17, 20, 21; DcNaB 1986; IntWW 74, 75, 76, 77, 78, 79, 80, 81, 82, 83, 89; Who 74, 82, 83, 85, 88, 90*

Oakie, Jack
American. Actor
Known for comic roles in over 100 films, 1930s-40s; Oscar nominee for *The Great Dictator,* 1940.
b. Nov 12, 1903 in Sedalia, Missouri
d. Jan 23, 1978 in Los Angeles, California
Source: *BiDD, 78; JoeFr; LegTOT; MotPP; MovMk; NewYTBS 78; OlFamFa; QDrFCA 92; RadStar; TwYS; What 2; WhoCom; WhoHol A; WhScrn 83; WorAl; WorAlBi*

Oakland, Simon
American. Actor
TV shows include "Toma," 1973-74; "Black Sheep Squadron," 1977-78.
b. Aug 28, 1922 in New York, New York
d. Aug 29, 1983 in Cathedral City, California
Source: *BioIn 13; ConTFT 1; FilmEn; FilmgC; ForYSC; HalFC 80, 84, 88; IntMPA 75, 76, 77, 78, 79, 80, 81, 82, 84, 86; LegTOT; NewYTBS 83; VarWW 85; WhAm 8; WhoAm 78, 80, 82; WhoHol A*

Oakley, Annie
[Mrs. Frank E Butler; Phoebe Anne Oakley Moses; Phoebe Anne Oakley Mozee]
American. Pioneer
Performed in Buffalo Bill's Wild West Show, 1885-1902.
b. Aug 13, 1860 in Darke County, Ohio
d. Nov 2, 1926 in Greenville, Ohio
Source: *BioAmW; BioIn 1, 3, 4, 5, 6, 7, 10, 11, 12, 15, 16, 17, 18, 19, 20, 21; ContDcW 89; DcAmB; EncAAH; EncWomS; Ent; Film 1; FilmgC; GoodHs; GrLiveH; HerW, 84; IntDcWB; InWom, SUP; LegTOT; LibW; LinLib S; McGEWB; NotAW; OxCAmH; OxCAmT 84; REnAL; REnAW; WebAB 74, 79; WhAm 4, HSA; WhoHol B; WhoSpor; WhScrn 77, 83; WomFir; WorAl; WorAlBi*

Oak Ridge Boys, The
[Duane Allen; Joe Bonsall; Bill Golden; Richard Sterban]
American. Music Group
Country-pop group known for four-part harmonies; hit single "Elvira," 1981.
Source: *BgBkCoM; BioIn 16, 17; CelR 90; ConMus 4; EncFCWM 83; HarEnCM 87; HarEnR 86; IlEncCM; LesBEnT, 92; NewYTET; PenEncP; RkOn 85; VarWW 85; WhoRock 81*

Oasis
[Paul Arthurs; Liam Gallagher; Noel Gallagher; Tony McCarroll; Paul McGuigan; Alan White]
English. Music Group
Released albums *Definitely Maybe,* 1994; *(What's the Story) Morning Glory?,* 1995.
Source: *Au&Wr 71; ConAu 3NR, 45; ConMus 16; DcLEL 1940; DcLP 87A; EncRkSt; MotPP; News 96, 96-3; WhoHol 92; WrDr 76, 80, 82, 84, 86, 88*

Oates, John William
[Hall and Oates]
American. Singer, Songwriter
Recorded 3 gold albums with Daryl Hall; hits include "Rich Girl," "Say It Isn't So," and "Maneater."
b. Apr 7, 1948 in New York, New York
Source: *IlEncRk; RkWW 82; WhoAm 80, 82, 84, 86, 88; WhoRock 81*

Oates, Joyce Carol
American. Author
Prolific novelist, short story writer; wrote award-winning *Them,* 1969; *Bellefleur,* 1980.
b. Jun 16, 1938 in Lockport, New York
Source: *AmAu&B; AmWomD; AmWomWr; AmWr S2; ArtclWW 2; Au&Arts 15; AuNews 1; Benet 87, 96; BestSel 89-2; BiDConC; BioAmW; BioIn 8, 9, 10, 11, 12, 13, 15, 16, 17, 19, 20, 21; BioNews 74; BlmGWL; BlueB 76; BroV; CamGLE; CamHAL; CelR, 90; ConAu 5R, 25NR, 45NR; ConLC 1, 2, 3, 6, 9, 11, 15, 19, 33, 52; ConNov 72, 76, 82, 86, 96; ConPo 96; ConPopW; ContDcW 89; CurBio 70, 94; CyWA 89; DcArts; DcLB 2, 5, 130, Y81A; DcLEL 1940; DrAF 76; DrAPF 80; EncWL 2, 3; FemiCLE; FemiWr; ForWC 70; GrWomW; IntAu&W 76, 77, 82; IntDcWB; IntWW 89, 93; InWom SUP; LegTOT; LibW; LinLib L; MagSAmL; MajTwCW; ModAL S1, S2; ModWoWr; NewYTBS 82; Novels; OxCAmL 83, 95; OxCEng 85, 95; OxCTwCP; OxCWoWr 95; PenEncH; PenNWW A; RAdv 1, 14, 13-1; RfGAmL 94; RfGShF; RGTwCWr; ShSCr 6; ShSWr; TwCRHW 90; WhoAm 74, 76, 78, 80, 82, 84, 86, 88, 90, 92, 94, 95, 96, 97; WhoAmW 70, 72, 74, 81, 83, 85, 87, 91, 93, 95, 97; WhoUSWr 88; WhoWor 74, 80, 82, 95, 96, 97; WhoWrEP 89, 92, 95; WorAl; WorAlBi; WorAu 1970, 1975; WorLitC; WrDr 76, 80, 82, 84, 86, 88, 90, 94, 96*

Oates, Titus
English. Clergy
With Israel Tonge, invented Popish Plot, 1678, a plan to assassinate Charles, II, replace with brother James.
b. Sep 15, 1649 in Oakham, England
d. Jul 12, 1705 in London, England
Source: *Alli; Benet 87, 96; BioIn 2, 5, 9; BlmGEL; LngCEL; LuthC 75; McGEWB; NewC; OxCEng 85, 95; REn; WhDW*

Oates, Warren
American. Actor
Starred in *In the Heat of the Night,* 1967; *Stripes,* 1981.
b. Jul 5, 1928 in Depoy, Kentucky
d. Apr 3, 1982 in Hollywood Hills, California
Source: *AnObit 1982; BiDFilm 94; CmMov; ConTFT 1; FilmEn; FilmgC; GangFlm; HalFC 84, 88; IntDcF 1-3, 2-3; ItaFilm; LegTOT; NewYTBS 82; WhAm 8; WhoAm 82; WhoHol A*

Obando (y Bravo), Miguel
Nicaraguan. Religious Leader
Cardinal since 1985; played leading role in ousting Somoza, 1979; vocal critic of Sandinistas.
b. Feb 2, 1926 in La Libertad, Nicaragua
Source: *BioIn 13; ConNews 86-4; CurBio 88; DcCPCAm; IntWW 93; NewYTBS 83, 84, 85; WhoWor 87*

Obasanjo, Olusegun
Nigerian. Political Leader
Head of federal military govt., commander-in-chief of armed forces, 1976-79.
b. May 5, 1937 in Abeokuta, Nigeria
Source: *AfSS 78, 79, 80, 81, 82; BioIn 11, 15, 16, 18, 19, 21; ConBlB 5; DcAfHiB 86S; InB&W 80; IntWW 76, 77, 78, 79, 80, 81, 82, 83, 89, 93; IntYB 78, 79, 80, 81, 82; Who 82, 83, 85, 88, 90, 94; WhoAfr; WhoWor 78*

Obata, Gyo
American. Architect
Designs include the Dallas-Fort Worth Airport.
b. Feb 28, 1923 in San Francisco, California
Source: *AmArch 70; AsAmAlm; BioIn 16, 20; BlueB 76; ConArch 80, 87, 94; EncAAr 2; MacEA; NotAsAm; WhoAm 74, 76, 78, 82, 88, 90, 95, 96; WhoAsA 94; WhoFI 74, 87, 89; WhoTech 89; WhoWor 74*

Ober, Philip (Nott)
American. Actor
Made Broadway debut in *The Animal Kingdom,* 1932; films include *Torpedo Run,* 1958; appeared on many TV shows.
b. Mar 23, 1902 in Fort Payne, Alabama
d. Sep 13, 1982 in Santa Monica, California
Source: *BiE&WWA; BioIn 13; EncAFC; FilmgC; ForYSC; HalFC 80, 84, 88; IntMPA 75, 76, 77, 78, 79, 80, 81, 82, 84, 86; NewYTBS 82; NotNAT; Vers A; WhoHol A; WhThe*

Oberlin, Johann Friedrich
Alsatian. Clergy, Educator
Lutheran pastor noted for improving education, agricultural methods; Oberlin College, Ohio named for him.
b. Aug 31, 1740 in Strasbourg, France
d. Jun 1, 1826 in Ban-de-la-Roche, France
Source: *NewCol 75; OxCGer 76, 86*

Oberon, Merle
[Estelle Merle O'Brien Thompson]
American. Actor
Films include *Divorce of Lady X; Wuthering Heights,* 1930s-40s.
b. Feb 19, 1911 in Bombay, India
d. Nov 23, 1979 in Los Angeles, California
Source: *BiDFilm 81, 94; BioIn 9, 10, 12, 13, 16, 17; CmMov; CurBio 41, 80N; DcAmB S10; DcArts; EncEurC; FilmAG WE; FilmEn; FilmgC; ForYSC; HalFC 80, 84, 88; IlWWBF; IntDcF 1-3, 2-3; IntMPA 75, 77; IntWW 79; InWom, SUP; LegTOT; MotPP; MovMk; NewYTBS 79; OxCFilm; ThFT; WhAm 7; Who 74; WhoAm 74, 76, 78, 80; WhoHol A; WhScrn 83; WomWMM; WorAl; WorAlBi; WorEFlm*

Oberth, Hermann Julius
German. Scientist
His book *Die Rakete zu den Planetenraumen* 1923 on rockets gained him recognition in modern astronautics.
b. Jun 25, 1894 in Nagyszeben, Austria-Hungary
d. Dec 29, 1989 in Nuremberg, Germany
Source: *BiESc; BioIn 4, 6, 8, 10, 12, 16; ConAu 113; CurBio 90N; FacFETw; InSci; IntWW 74, 75, 76, 77, 78; NewYTBS 89; WhDW; WhoWor 74, 76, 78*

Obolensky, Serge
Russian. Businessman, Socialite
Distant relative of Czar Nicholas II; with Hilton Hotels, 1940s; later had own consulting firm.
b. Oct 3, 1890 in Tsarskoe Selo, Russia
d. Sep 29, 1978 in Grosse Pointe, Michigan
Source: *BioIn 5, 6, 10, 11; BusPN; CelR; CurBio 59, 78, 78N; EncAI&E; NewYTBE 70; WhoAm 74, 76, 78*

Oboler, Arch
American. Dramatist
Radio shows include "Lights Out," 1940s; directed, wrote film *Strange Holiday,* 1948.
b. Dec 6, 1909 in Chicago, Illinois
d. Mar 19, 1987 in Westlake Village, California
Source: *AmAu&B; AnObit 1987; BiE&WWA; BioIn 11, 15; CnMD; ConAu 105, 122; CurBio 40, 87, 87N; DcFM; FilmEn; FilmgC; HalFC 80, 84, 88; IntMPA 82; MiSFD 9N; ModWD; NotNAT; REnAL; TwCA SUP; VarWW 85; WhE&EA; WhoAm 74, 76, 78; WhoHrs 80; WorEFlm*

Obomsawin, Alanis
Canadian. Filmmaker
Documentary filmmaker of Native life; made *Christmas at Moose Factory,* 1971.
b. 1932 in Lebanon, New Hampshire
Source: *BioIn 21; NotNaAm; WhoAm 96, 97; WhoAmW 93*

Obote, Milton
[Apollo Milton Obote]
Ugandan. Political Leader
President of Uganda, 1966-71, deposed in military coup led by Idi Amin; succeeded Amin, 1980-86.
b. Dec 28, 1924 in Akokoro, Uganda
Source: *AfSS 78, 79, 80, 81, 82; BioIn 6, 7, 8, 9, 12, 13, 14, 18; CurBio 81; DcPol; DcTwHis; InB&W 85; IntWW 74, 75, 76, 77, 78, 79, 80, 81, 82, 83, 89; IntYB 81, 82; McGEWB; Who 74, 83, 85, 88, 90; WhoWor 87*

O'Boyle, Patrick Aloysius, Cardinal
American. Religious Leader
First Roman Catholic archbishop of Washington, DC, 1948-73; championed civil rights, defended church orthodoxy.
b. Jul 18, 1896 in Scranton, Pennsylvania
d. Aug 10, 1987 in Washington, District of Columbia
Source: *BioIn 1, 8, 9, 10, 11; CurBio 73, 87; IntWW 83; PolProf J; WhAm 9; WhoAm 76, 80, 82, 84, 86; WhoWor 84, 87*

Obraztsova, Elena
Russian. Opera Singer
Principal mezzo-soprano, Bolshoi Opera, since 1965; NY Met. debut, 1975; Lenin award, 1976.
b. Jul 7, 1939 in Leningrad, Union of Soviet Socialist Republics
Source: *Baker 84; BioIn 13; CurBio 83; InWom SUP*

Obregon, Alejandro
Colombian. Painter
His paintings depicted the violence of his country.
b. Jun 4, 1920, Colombia
d. Apr 11, 1992 in Cartagena, Colombia
Source: *BioIn 13; DcCAr 81; DcTwCCu 3; IntWW 74, 75, 76, 77, 78, 79, 80, 81, 82, 83, 89, 91, 93; McGDA; OxCTwCA; WhoWor 74, 78, 84, 87, 89, 91*

Obregon, Alvaro
Mexican. Statesman, Soldier
Pres. of Mexico, 1920-24, 1928; assassinated.
b. Feb 17, 1880 in Alamos, Mexico
d. Jul 17, 1928 in San Angel, Mexico
Source: *BiDLAmC; BioIn 9, 10, 12, 16; DcTwHis; EncLatA; EncPaPR 91; EncRev; HisWorL; LinLib S; McGEWB; NewCol 75; REn; WhDW*

O'Brian, Hugh
[Hugh J Krampe]
American. Actor
Best known for TV show "Life and Legend of Wyatt Earp," 1955-61.
b. Apr 19, 1930 in Rochester, New York
Source: *ASCAP 66; BiE&WWA; ConTFT 2; CurBio 58; FilmgC; IntMPA 75, 76, 77, 78, 79, 80, 81, 82, 84, 86, 88, 94; MotPP; MovMk; VarWW 85; WhoAm 74, 76, 78, 80, 82, 84, 86, 88, 92; WhoHol A; WhoThe 81; WorAl; WorAlBi*

O'Brian, Jack
American. Journalist, Critic
Noted for syndicated column "Voice of Broadway," 1967—; host, NYC radio show "Critics Circle."
b. Aug 16, 1921 in Buffalo, New York
Source: *BiDAmNC; ConAu 103; EncTwCJ; IntAu&W 76; IntMPA 82; WhoAm 76, 78, 80, 82, 84, 86, 88, 90, 92, 94, 95, 96, 97*

O'Brian, Patrick
Irish. Author
Writer of fiction set during the Napoleonic Wars; books include *The Letter of Marque,* 1990.
b. 1914, Ireland
Source: *ConAu 144; ConPopW; CurBio 95; NewYTBS 93; WhoWor 97; WorAu 1985; WrDr 96*

O'Brien, Conan
American. Comedian, TV Personality
Host of NBC's "Late Night with Conan O'Brien," 1993—; comic writer, "Saturday Night Live" and "The Simpsons."
b. Apr 18, 1963 in Brookline, Massachusetts
Source: *ConTFT 14; CurBio 96; IntMPA 96; LegTOT; News 94, 94-1; WhoAm 94, 95, 96, 97; WhoE 95; WhoWor 96*

O'Brien, Conor Cruise
[Donat O'Donnell]
Irish. Author, Diplomat
Writings on Irish politics, the Third World, the UN, int'l politics include *States of Ireland,* 1972.
b. Nov 3, 1917 in Dublin, Ireland
Source: *Benet 87, 96; BiDIrW; BioIn 7, 8, 10, 11, 18, 20, 21; BlueB 76; ConAu 47NR, 65; CurBio 67; DcIrL, 96; DcIrW 2; DcLEL 1940; IntAu&W 89, 93; IntWW 74, 75, 76, 77, 78, 79, 80, 81, 82, 83, 89, 93; LegTOT; LinLib L; ModIrL; OxCIri; Who 74, 82, 83, 85, 88, 90, 94; WhoWor 74, 82, 84, 87, 89, 91, 93, 95, 96; WorAu 1950; WrDr 76, 80, 82, 84, 86, 88, 90, 94, 96*

O'Brien, Dan
American. Track Athlete
Won gold medal in the decathlon, 1996 Olympics.
b. Jul 18, 1966
Source: *AfrAmSG; CurBio 96*

O'Brien, Davey
[Robert David O'Brien]
American. Football Player
All-America quarterback, won Heisman Trophy, 1938; had brief NFL career, Philadelphia, 1939-40.
b. Jun 22, 1917 in Dallas, Texas
d. Nov 18, 1977 in Fort Worth, Texas
Source: *BiDAmSp FB; BioIn 11, 14; DcAmB S10; NewYTBS 77; WhoFtbl 74; WhoSpor*

O'Brien, Edmond
American. Actor
Won Oscar for *The Barefoot Contessa,* 1954.
b. Sep 10, 1915 in New York, New York
d. May 8, 1985 in Inglewood, California
Source: *AnObit 1985; BiDFilm 81, 94; BioIn 14, 15; ConTFT 2; FilmEn; FilmgC; ForYSC; GangFlm; HalFC 80, 84, 88; IntDcF 1-3, 2-3; IntMPA 75, 76, 77, 78, 79, 80, 81, 82, 84; ItaFilm; LegTOT; MotPP; MovMk; NewYTBS 85; OxCFilm; RadStar; VarWW 85; WhAm 8; WhoAm 74, 76, 78, 80, 82, 84; WhoHol A; WhoHrs 80; WorAl; WorAlBi; WorEFlm*

O'Brien, Edna
Irish. Author
Writings include *The Country Girls,* 1960; *Some Irish Loving,* 1979.
b. Dec 15, 1931 in Tuamgraney, Ireland
Source: *CasWL; ConAu 1R; ConLC 13; ConNov 86; CurBio 80; IntWW 83; NewC; TwCWr; Who 85; WhoAmW 87; WorAu 1950; WrDr 86*

O'Brien, George
"The Chest"
American. Actor
Starred in *The Iron Horse,* 1924; Western hero in 1930s films.
b. Apr 19, 1900 in San Francisco, California
d. Sep 4, 1985 in Broken Arrow, Oklahoma
Source: *BioIn 8, 10, 14, 21; CmMov; Film 2; FilmEn; FilmgC; ForYSC; HalFC 80, 84, 88; IntMPA 75, 76, 77, 78, 79, 80, 81, 82, 84; MotPP; MovMk; SilFlmP; TwYS; What 4; WhoHol A; WorEFlm*

O'Brien, John J
American. Basketball Referee, Basketball Executive
Organized several pro leagues, early 1900s; founder, 1921, first president, 1921-47, American Basketball League; Hall of Fame.
b. Nov 4, 1888 in New York, New York
d. Dec 9, 1967 in Rockville Centre, New York
Source: *BioIn 8, 9; WhAm 8; WhoBbl 73*

O'Brien, Larry
[Lawrence Francis O'Brien, Jr]
American. Basketball Executive, Government Official
Chairman, Democratic National Committee, 1968-69, 1970-72; directed John F Kennedy's presidential campaign; commissioner of NBA, 1975-84; Hall of Fame, 1984.
b. Jul 7, 1917 in Springfield, Massachusetts
d. Sep 27, 1990 in New York, New York
Source: *AmCath 80; BiDAmSp BK; BiDrUSE 71, 89; BioIn 5, 6, 7, 8, 9, 10, 11, 12; ConAu 57; CurBio 61, 77, 90; IntAu&W 86, 89; IntWW 74, 75, 76, 77, 78, 79, 80, 81, 82, 83, 89; LinLib S; NewYTBE 70; NewYTBS 90; PolProf J, K, NF; WhAm 10; WhoAm 74, 76, 78, 80, 82, 84, 86, 88, 90; WhoAmP 73, 75, 77, 79; WhoE 81, 83, 85, 86; WhoSSW 73; WhoWor 78, 80, 82; WrDr 76, 86*

O'Brien, Leo W
American. Politician
Democratic congressman from NY, 1952-66; led legislation granting statehood to Alaska, Hawaii.
b. Sep 21, 1900 in Buffalo, New York
d. May 4, 1982 in Albany, New York
Source: *BiDrAC; CurBio 59, 82, 82N; NewYTBS 82; WhAm 8*

O'Brien, Margaret
[Angela Maxine O'Brien]
American. Actor
Child actress; made film debut at age four; won special Oscar for *Babes on Broadway,* 1944.
b. Jan 15, 1937 in San Diego, California
Source: *BiDFilm 81, 94; BioIn 1, 2, 3, 4, 5, 6, 8, 9, 15; ConTFT 3; EncAFC; FilmEn; FilmgC; ForYSC; HalFC 80, 84, 88; IntDcF 1-3, 2-3; IntMPA 75, 76, 77, 78, 79, 80, 81, 82, 84, 86, 88; InWom, SUP; LegTOT; MGM; MotPP; MovMk; VarWW 85; What 2; WhoAm 74, 76, 78, 80, 82, 84, 86, 88, 92; WhoAmW 58, 68, 70, 72, 74; WhoHol 92, A; WorAl; WorAlBi; WorEFlm*

O'Brien, Parry
[William Parry O'Brien]
American. Track Athlete
Shot putter; developed style used today; won gold medals, 1952, 1956 Olympics.
b. Jan 28, 1932 in Santa Monica, California
Source: *BiDAmSp OS; BioIn 3, 4, 5, 7, 10; CmCal; WhoSpor; WhoTr&F 73*

O'Brien, Pat
[William Joseph Patrick O'Brien]
American. Actor
Starred in *Knute Rockne-All American,* 1940; won two Emmys for "The Other Woman," 1974; often portrayed priests, Irish cops.
b. Nov 11, 1899 in Milwaukee, Wisconsin
d. Oct 15, 1983 in Santa Monica, California
Source: *AnObit 1983; BiDFilm 81, 94; BiE&WWA; BioIn 5, 7, 14; ConAu 111; CurBio 66, 84, 84N; EncAFC; Film 2; FilmEn; FilmgC; ForYSC; GangFlm; HalFC 80, 84, 88; IntDcF 1-3; IntMPA 75, 76, 77, 78, 79, 80, 81, 82, 84; LegTOT; MotPP; MovMk; NewYTBS 83; NotNAT, A; OxCFilm; TwYS; VarWW 85; WhoHol A; WorAl; WorAlBi*

O'Brien, Tim
[William Timothy O'Brien]
American. Author, Journalist
Wrote *Northern Lights,* 1975; *Going After Cacciato,* 1978.
b. Oct 1, 1946 in Austin, Minnesota

Source: *Au&Arts 16; BiDConC; BioIn 12, 13, 16, 17, 19, 20, 21; ConAu 40NR, 85; ConLC 7, 19, 40; ConNov 96; ConPopW; CurBio 95; DcLB 152, Y80B; PostFic; ScF&FL 92; WhoAm 92; WorAu 1980; WrDr 90, 94, 96*

O'Brien, Willis Harold
American. Special Effects Technician, Cartoonist
Best known for special effects in *King Kong,* 1933; won Oscar for *Mighty Joe Young,* 1949.
b. Mar 2, 1886 in Oakland, California
d. Nov 8, 1962 in Hollywood, California
Source: *BioIn 6; CmMov; DcAmB S7; EncSF; FanAl; FilmgC; ObitOF 79*

O'Brien-Moore, Erin
American. Actor
Starred on stage in *Street Scene,* 1929; played Nurse Choate in TV's ''Peyton Place,'' 1965-68.
b. May 2, 1908 in Los Angeles, California
d. May 3, 1979 in Los Angeles, California
Source: *BioIn 11; ForYSC; InWom SUP; NewYTBS 79; ThFT; WhoHol A; WhThe*

O'Callahan, Jack
American. Hockey Player
Defenseman, Chicago, 1982-87; member US Olympic gold medal-winning team, 1980.
b. Jul 24, 1957 in Charlestown, Massachusetts
Source: *HocEn; HocReg 87*

O'Callahan, Joseph Timothy
American. Clergy, Educator
Awarded Congressional Medal of Honor, 1945, for bravery at aircraft carrier *Franklin* disaster.
b. May 14, 1905 in Roxbury, Massachusetts
d. Mar 18, 1964 in Worcester, Massachusetts
Source: *BioIn 6, 7, 9; DcAmB S7*

Ocasek, Ric
American. Singer, Songwriter
New Wave/rock performer with The Cars, c. 1976-88; solo hit single ''Emotion in Motion.''
b. 1949 in Baltimore, Maryland
Source: *BioIn 12; ConMus 5; LegTOT; WhoEnt 92; WhoHol 92; WhoRocM 82*

O'Casey, Sean
[John O'Casey; Sean O'Cathasaigh]
Irish. Dramatist
Plays center on Irish slum life, struggle for independence: *The Plough and the Stars,* 1926.
b. Mar 30, 1880 in Dublin, Ireland
d. Sep 18, 1964 in Torquay, England
Source: *AtlBL; BiE&WWA; BioIn 6, 7, 8, 9, 10, 11, 12, 13, 14, 15, 16, 17, 18; BlmGEL; BritWr 7; CamGEL; CamGLE; CamGWoT; CasWL; Chambr 3; CnMD; CnMWL; CnThe; ConAu 89; ConBrDr; ConLC 1, 5, 9, 11, 15, 88; CroCD; CrtSuDr; CurBio 62, 64; CyWA 58, 89; DcIrB 78, 88; DcIrL 96; DcLB 10; DcLEL; DcNaB 1961; EncWL 2, 3; EncWT; Ent; EvLB; FilmgC; GrBr; GrWrEL DR; HalFC 80, 84, 88; IntDcT 2; IriPla; LegTOT; LngCTC; MagSWL; MajMD 1; MajTwCW; McGEWB; McGEWD 72, 84; ModBrL, S1, S2; ModIrL; ModWD; NewC; NewCBEL; NotNAT A, B; ObitT 1961; OxCAmT 84; OxCEng 67, 85, 95; OxCIri; OxCThe 67, 83; PenC ENG; PlP&P; RAdv 14, 13-2; RComWL; REn; REnWD; RGTwCWr; TwCA, SUP; TwCWr; WebE&AL; WhAm 4; WhDW; WhoTwCL; WhThe; WorAl; WorAlBi*

Occom, Samson
American. Clergy
First Native American to publish a text in the English language, *Sermons,* 1772.
b. 1723
d. Jul 14, 1792
Source: *Alli; AmAu&B; AmWrBE; ApCAB; BiNAW, B, SupB; BioIn 11, 13, 17, 19, 21; CyAL 1; DcAmB; DcAmReB 1, 2; DcNAA; DcNAL; EncCRAm; EncNAR; EncNoAI; HarEnUS; LuthC 75; NatNAL; NotNaAm; OxCAmH; OxCAmL 65, 83, 95; PoChrch; WhAm HS*

Ocean, Billy
[Leslie Sebastian Charles]
English. Singer
Co-wrote Grammy winning single, ''Caribbean Queen,'' 1984; hits include ''Loverboy.''
b. Jan 21, 1950 in Fyzabad, Trinidad
Source: *ConMus 4; EncRkSt; HarEnR 86; LegTOT; PenEncP; RkOn 85; SoulM*

Ochoa, Severo
Spanish. Biochemist
Shared Nobel Prize in medicine, 1959.
b. Sep 24, 1905 in Luarca, Spain
d. Nov 1, 1993 in Madrid, Spain
Source: *AmMWSc 73P, 76P, 79, 82, 86, 89; AnObit 1993; AsBiEn; BiESc; BioIn 2, 5, 6, 7, 9, 12, 14, 15, 19, 20; BlueB 76; CurBio 62, 94N; DcHiB; IntWW 74, 75, 76, 77, 78, 79, 80, 81, 82, 83, 89, 93; LarDcSc; LegTOT; McGMS 80; NewYTBS 93; NobelP; NotTwCS; WebAB 74, 79; WhAm 11; Who 74, 82, 83, 85, 88, 90, 94; WhoAm 74, 76, 78, 80, 82, 84, 86, 88, 90, 92; WhoE 74, 77, 79, 81, 83, 85, 86, 89; WhoFrS 84; WhoNob, 95; WhoScEn 94; WhoWor 74, 76, 78, 82, 84, 87, 89, 91, 93; WorAl; WorAlBi; WorScD*

Ochs, Adolph Shelby, II
American. Newspaper Executive
Managing editor, *Chattanooga Times,* 1922-74.
b. Apr 14, 1885 in Chattanooga, Tennessee
d. May 29, 1974 in Chattanooga, Tennessee
Source: *BioIn 10; NewYTBS 74; WhJnl*

Ochs, Adolph Simon
American. Newspaper Publisher
Published *NY Times,* 1896-1935; director, AP, 1900-35; introduced rotogravure illustrations, book review supplements.
b. Mar 12, 1858 in Cincinnati, Ohio
d. Apr 8, 1935 in Chattanooga, Tennessee
Source: *AmAu&B; AmBi; ApCAB X; Benet 87, 96; BiDAmBL 83; BiDAmJo; BioIn 1, 2, 3, 4, 5, 6, 7, 8, 9, 10, 11, 12, 14, 15, 16; DcAmB S1; EncAB-A 2; EncAB-H 1974, 1996; GayN; JrnUS; LinLib L, S; McGEWB; MorMA; NatCAB 1; OxCAmH; OxCAmL 65; REn; REnAL; TwCBDA; WebAB 74, 79; WhAm 1; WhDW*

Ochs, Phil(ip David)
American. Singer, Political Activist
Song ''I Ain't Marching Anymore,'' 1963, protested Vietnam War.
b. Dec 19, 1940 in El Paso, Texas
d. Apr 9, 1976 in Far Rockaway, New York
Source: *ASCAP 66, 80; BiDAmM; BioIn 8, 10, 11, 14, 17, 20; ConAu 65; ConLC 17; ConMuA 80A; DcAmB S10; EncFCWM 69, 83; EncRk 88; HarEnR 86; IlEncRk; LegTOT; LNinSix; NewGrDA 86; NewYTBE 71; OxCPMus; PenEncP; RolSEnR 83; WhoRock 81*

Ochsner, Alton
[Edward William Alton Ochsner]
American. Surgeon, Teacher
Among the first to link cigarette smoking with cancer, 1940s; wrote *Smoking and Cancer,* 1954.
b. May 4, 1896 in Kimball, South Dakota
d. Sep 24, 1981 in New Orleans, Louisiana
Source: *AmMWSc 73P, 79; AnObit 1981; BioIn 1, 2, 3, 4, 7, 8, 12, 18; ConAu 17R, 105; CurBio 66, 81, 81N; IntWW 76, 77, 78, 79, 80, 81; NewYTBS 81; OxCMed 86; WhAm 8; WhoAm 74, 76, 78, 80; WhoSSW 73, 75, 76*

Ochterveldt, Jacob Lucasz
Dutch. Artist
Paintings include ''Hunting Party with a Shepherd,'' 1652.
b. 1634
d. 1708
Source: *McGDA; OxCArt*

O'Connell, Arthur
American. Actor
Oscar nominee for *Picnic; Anatomy of a Murder.*
b. Mar 29, 1908 in New York, New York
d. May 19, 1981 in Los Angeles, California
Source: *BiE&WWA; BioIn 12; EncAFC; FilmEn; FilmgC; ForYSC; HalFC 80, 84, 88; IntMPA 75, 76, 77, 78, 79, 80, 81; LegTOT; MovMk; NewYTBS 81; NotNAT; WhAm 7; WhoAm 74, 76, 78, 80; WhoHol A; WhoHrs 80; WhoThe 77, 81; WhScrn 83; WorAl*

O'Connell, Daniel
"The Liberator"
Irish. Political Leader
Elected to Parliament, 1828; mayor of Dublin, 1841; convicted for establishing the Catholic Association, conspiracy.
b. Aug 6, 1775 in Cahirsiveen, Ireland
d. May 15, 1847 in Genoa, Italy
Source: *Alli; Benet 87, 96; BiD&SB; BioIn 1, 2, 6, 7, 9, 10, 11, 12, 13; CelCen; DcAmSR; DcBiPP; DcCathB; DcIrB 78, 88; DcNaB; EncRev; HisDBrE; HisWorL; LinLib S; McGEWB; NewYTBS 88; OxCIri; REn; VicBrit; WorAl; WorAlBi*

O'Connell, Helen
American. Singer
Popular vocalist with Jimmy Dorsey, 1939-43; made comeback, 1950s.
b. May 23, 1921 in Lima, Ohio
d. Sep 10, 1993 in San Diego, California
Source: *BioIn 3, 4, 9; CmpEPM; VarWW 85; What 3; WhoHol A*

O'Connell, Hugh
American. Actor
Character actor, 1929-41; films include *My Favorite Wife,* 1940.
b. Aug 4, 1898 in New York, New York
d. Jan 19, 1943 in Hollywood, California
Source: *CurBio 43; NotNAT B; WhoHol B; WhScrn 74, 77, 83; WhThe*

O'Connor, Basil
American. Lawyer
Had law firm partnership with FDR, 1925-33; pres., American National Red Cross, 1944-49; recipient of several awards.
b. Jan 8, 1892 in Taunton, Massachusetts
d. Mar 9, 1972 in Phoenix, Arizona
Source: *BioIn 1, 3, 4, 9; CurBio 44, 72, 72N; NewYTBE 72; WhAm 5*

O'Connor, Buddy
[Herbert William O'Connor]
Canadian. Hockey Player
Defenseman, Montreal, 1941-47, NY Rangers, 1947-51; won Hart, Lady Byng trophies, 1948; Hall of Fame, 1988.
b. Jun 21, 1916 in Montreal, Quebec, Canada
Source: *HocEn; WhoHcky 73; WhoSpor*

O'Connor, Carroll
American. Actor, Writer, Producer
Played Archie Bunker in "All in the Family," 1971-79; earned more awards than any other actor for a single characterization; played Chief Bill Gillespie on TV series "In the Heat of the Night," 1987-94.
b. Aug 2, 1924 in New York, New York
Source: *ASCAP 80; BioIn 12, 13; BioNews 74; BkPepl; CelR 90; ConTFT 1; CurBio 72; FilmgC; HalFC 84; IntMPA 94, 96; LegTOT; MovMk; NewYTBE 71; VarWW 85; WhoAm 76, 78, 80, 82, 84, 86, 88, 90, 92, 94, 95, 96, 97; WhoCom; WhoHol A; WhoTelC; WorAl; WorAlBi*

O'Connor, Donald
American. Dancer, Singer
Best known for 1940s-50s Hollywood musicals: *Singin' in the Rain,* 1952.
b. Aug 28, 1925 in Chicago, Illinois
Source: *ASCAP 66, 80; BiDD; BioIn 2, 3, 4, 10, 15, 17, 18; CmMov; CmpEPM; ConTFT 3; CurBio 55; EncAFC; FilmEn; FilmgC; ForYSC; HalFC 80, 84, 88; HolP 40; IntDcF 1-3, 2-3; IntMPA 75, 76, 77, 78, 79, 80, 81, 82, 84, 86, 88, 94, 96; ItaFilm; LegTOT; MotPP; MovMk; OxCFilm; OxCPMus; QDrFCA 92; VarWW 85; WhoAm 74, 76, 78, 80, 82, 84; WhoHol 92, A; WhoHrs 80; WorAl; WorAlBi; WorEFlm*

O'Connor, Edwin Greene
American. Author
Won Pulitzer, 1962, for *The Edge of Sadness.*
b. Jul 29, 1918 in Providence, Rhode Island
d. Mar 23, 1968 in Boston, Massachusetts
Source: *AmAu&B; ConAu 93; ConLC 14; CurBio 63, 68; DcAmB S8; ModAL; OxCAmL 65; PenC AM; REnAL; WhAm 5; WorAl; WorAu 1950*

O'Connor, Flannery
American. Author
Stories have Southern locales, originality, power; wrote collection of short stories *A Good Man Is Hard to Find,* 1955.
b. Mar 25, 1925 in Savannah, Georgia
d. Aug 3, 1964 in Milledgeville, Georgia
Source: *AmAu&B; AmWomWr, 92; AmWr; ArtclWW 2; Benet 87; BiDConC; BioAmW; BioIn 3, 4, 5; BlmGWL; ConAu 1R, 3NR; ConLC 15; ConNov 76; CurBio 58, 65; CyWA 89; DcArts; DcLB 152, DS12; DcTwCCu 1; EncWB; EncWHA; EncWL, 2, 3; FemiCLE; FifSWrA; GrLiveH; GrWomW; GrWrEL N; IntDcWB; InWom, SUP; LegTOT; LibW; LinLib L; MagSAmL; MajTwCW; ModAL, S1, S2; NatCAB 55; NewCon; NotAW MOD; Novels; OxCAmL 65, 83, 95; OxCEng 85, 95; OxCWoWr 95; PenC AM; PeoHis; RAdv 1, 14, 13-1; REn; REnAL; RfGAmL 87; ShSCr 1, 23; ShSWr; SouWr; TwCWr; WebE&AL; WhAm 4; WhoAmW 58, 61, 64, 66; WhoTwCL; WorAl; WorAlBi; WorAu 1950; WorLitC; WrPh*

O'Connor, Frank
[Michael O'Donovan]
Irish. Author
Stories record realities of life in Ireland.
b. 1903 in Cork, Ireland
d. Mar 10, 1966 in Dublin, Ireland
Source: *AmAu&B; AtlBL; Benet 87, 96; BiDIrW, B; BioIn 2, 3, 4, 5, 7, 8, 11, 12, 13, 15, 16, 17; BlmGEL; CamGEL; CamGLE; CasWL; CnMD; ConAu 25R, 93; ConLC 14, 23; CyWA 89; DcIrB 78, 88; DcIrL, 96; DcIrW 1, 2, 3; DcLB 162; DcLEL; EncWL 2, 3; EvLB; GrWrEL N; LinLib L; LngCEL; LngCTC; ModBrL, S1, S2; ModIrL; NewC; NewCBEL; NotNAT B; Novels; OxCEng 67, 85, 95; OxCIri; OxCTwCP; PenC ENG; RAdv 1, 14, 13-1; REn; RfGShF; RGTwCWr; ShSCr 5; ShSWr; TwCA SUP; WhAm 4; WhDW; WhE&EA; WorAlBi*

O'Connor, John Joseph, Cardinal
American. Religious Leader
Succeeded Terence Cardinal Cooke as archbishop of NY, 1984.
b. Jan 15, 1920 in Philadelphia, Pennsylvania
Source: *BioIn 14, 15, 16, 17; CurBio 84; NewYTBS 84, 85; WhoAm 78, 80, 82, 84, 95, 96, 97; WhoE 86, 93, 95; WhoRel 85; WhoWor 87, 95, 96, 97; WorAlBi*

O'Connor, Kevin
American. Actor, Producer
Stage actor; starred in *Tom Paine,* 1968 and *Warren Harding;* produced *Nuts,* 1974 among others.
b. May 7, 1938 in Honolulu, Hawaii
d. Jun 22, 1991
Source: *ConTFT 4, 10; NewYTBS 91; NotNAT; Who 92; WhoHol 92, A; WhoThe 77, 81*

O'Connor, Mark
American. Musician
Eclectic violinist's albums include *The Nashville Cats;* won CMA Musician of the Year, 1991, 1992.
Source: *BioIn 19; NewAgMG; WhoNeCM*

O'Connor, Sandra Day
American. Supreme Court Justice
First woman Supreme Court justice; nominated by Reagan, 1981.
b. Mar 26, 1930 in El Paso, Texas
Source: *AmBench 79; AmDec 1980; AmWomM; BioIn 13, 18; CelR 90; CngDr 83, 85, 87, 89, 91, 93, 95; ConHero 1; CurBio 82; DrAS 82P; EncAB-H 1996; EncWB; EncWHA; GrLiveH; HerW 84; IntWW 83, 89, 93; InWom SUP; LegTOT; NatCAB 63N; News 91-1; OxCSupC; SupCtJu; Who 85, 88, 90, 94; WhoAm 82, 84, 86, 88, 90, 92, 94, 95, 96, 97; WhoAmL 78, 79, 83, 85, 87, 90, 94, 96; WhoAmP 73, 75, 77, 79, 81, 83, 85, 87, 89, 93, 95; WhoAmW 74, 75, 79, 81, 83, 85, 87, 89, 91, 93, 95, 97; WhoE 83, 85, 86, 89, 91, 93; WhoWest 78; WhoWomW 91; WhoWor 89, 91, 96, 97; WomFir; WomLaw; WomStre*

O'Connor, Sinead
Irish. Singer, Songwriter
Pop singer; combines pop, jazz, Celtic sounds; hit single "Nothing Compares to You," 1990; known for clean-shaven head and controversial antics.
b. Dec 8, 1966 in Dublin, Ireland
Source: *ConTFT 12; EncRkSt; LegTOT; WhoAm 94, 95, 96, 97*

O'Connor, Thomas Power
"Tay Pay O'Connor"
Irish. Journalist
Held longest record of unbroken parliamentary service in his time, 1880-1929; wrote *The Parnell Movement,* 1886.
b. Oct 5, 1848 in Athlone, Ireland
d. Nov 18, 1929 in London, England
Source: *Alli SUP; BiDIrW; BioIn 2; DcIrB 78, 88; DcIrW 2; DcLEL; DcNaB 1922; LinLib L, S; LngCTC; NewC; NewCBEL; OxCEng 67, 85, 95; WhLit*

O'Connor, Una
[Agnes Teresa McGlade]
Irish. Actor
Horror films include *The Bride of Frankenstein; The Invisible Man.*
b. Oct 23, 1881 in Belfast, Northern Ireland
d. Feb 4, 1959 in New York, New York
Source: *FilmEn; FilmgC; ForYSC; MotPP; MovMk; ThFT; Vers A; WhoHol B; WhScrn 74, 77*

Octavia
[Octavia Minor]
Roman.
Roman empress divorced by Mark Anthony so he could marry Cleopatra.
b. 69BC
d. 11BC
Source: *InWom, SUP; LegTOT; REn*

O'Dalaigh, Cearbhall
Irish. Judge
Pres. of Ireland, 1974-76; resigned.
b. Feb 12, 1911 in Bray, Ireland
d. Mar 21, 1978 in Sneem, Ireland
Source: *WhoWor 74*

O'Day, Anita
[Anita Belle Colton]
American. Singer
Popular jazz singer who uses scat style; hits include "And Her Tears Flowed Like Wine," 1944.
b. Oct 18, 1919 in Chicago, Illinois
Source: *Baker 84; WhoHol 92, A; WorAlBi*

O'Day, Dawn
[Anne Shirley]
American. Actor
In films, 1923-45, including *Stella Dallas,* 1934.
b. 1918
Source: *AnObit 1993; BioIn 10, 15, 19; EncAFC; Film 2; FilmEn; FilmgC; ForYSC; GangFlm; HalFC 80, 84, 88; InWom SUP; LegTOT; MotPP; MovMk; ThFT; TwYS; WhoHol 92, A*

Ode, Robert C
[The Hostages]
American. Hostage
One of 52 held by terrorists, Nov 1979 - Jan 1981.
b. Dec 10, 1915 in Illinois
d. Sep 8, 1995 in Sun City West, Arizona
Source: *NewYTBS 81; USBiR 74*

O'Dell, Scott
American. Author
Wrote *Island of the Blue Dolphins,* 1960, *The Black Pearl,* 1967, and 24 other children's books; won three Newbery prizes.
b. May 23, 1903 in Los Angeles, California
d. Oct 15, 1989 in Mount Kisco, New York
Source: *AmAu&B; AmNov; AnCL; Au&ICB; AuBYP 2, 3; BioIn 1, 2, 5, 6, 7, 9, 10, 11, 14, 15, 16; BkCL; CamGLE; ChlLR 1; ConAu 12NR, 61; ConLC 30; DcAmChF 1960, 1985; DcLB 52; LinLib L; MorJA; OxCChiL; PiP; SenS; SmATA 12; Str&VC; TwCChW 78, 83; WhoAm 74, 76, 78, 80, 82, 84, 86; WhoWor 74, 78; WrDr 80, 82, 84*

Odets, Clifford
American. Dramatist
Wrote *The Country Girl,* 1950; best known for plays of social protest.
b. Jul 18, 1906 in Philadelphia, Pennsylvania
d. Aug 14, 1963 in Los Angeles, California
Source: *AmAu&B; AmCulL; AmWr S2; Benet 87, 96; BioIn 1, 2, 3, 4, 5, 6, 7, 8, 9, 11, 12, 13, 14, 15, 16, 17, 18, 19, 20; CamGEL; CamGLE; CamGWoT; CamHAL; CasWL; CmCal; CnDAL; CnMD; CnMWL; CnThe; ConAmA; ConAmD; ConAu 85; ConLC 2, 28, 98; CroCD; CrtSuDr; CurBio 41, 63; CyWA 58, 89; DcAmB S7; DcFM; DcLB 7, 26; DcLEL; DramC 6; EncAL; EncMcCE; EncWL 2, 3; EncWT; Ent; EvLB; FilmEn; GrWrEL DR; IntDcT 2; JeAmHC; LegTOT; LinLib L; LngCTC; MajMD 1; MajTwCW; MakMC; McGEWB; McGEWD 72, 84; ModAL, S2; ModWD; NatCAB 62; NotNAT A, B; OxCAmL 65, 83, 95; OxCAmT 84; OxCEng 67, 85, 95; OxCFilm; OxCThe 67, 83; PenC AM; PlP&P; PolProf T; RAdv 14, 13-2; REn; REnAL; REnWD; RfGAmL 87, 94; RGTwCWr; TwCA, SUP; TwCWr; WebAB 74, 79; WebE&AL; WhAm 4; WhoTwCL; WhThe; WorAl; WorAlBi; WorEFlm*

Odetta
[Odetta Felious]
American. Singer, Musician
Folksinger who has also performed blues and gospel; TV appearances include "The Autobiography of Miss Jane Pittman" and "Dinner with the President," 1963.
b. Dec 31, 1930 in Birmingham, Alabama
Source: *Baker 84, 92; BiDAmM; BioIn 5, 8, 12, 14, 18, 21; BlkWAm; CurBio 60; DrBlPA, 90; EncFCWM 69; InB&W 80, 85; ItaFilm; LegTOT; NewGrDA 86; OnThGG; PenEncP; RolSEnR 83; VarWW 85; WhoAm 74, 76; WhoAmW 61, 64, 66, 68, 70, 72, 74, 75; WhoE 74; WhoHol 92, A; WhoRock 81; WhoRocM 82; WhoWor 74; WorAl; WorAlBi*

Odlum, Floyd Bostwick
American. Financier
Chm., RKO Radio Pictures, 1937-48; chief exec. officer, Atlas Corp., 1923-60.
b. Mar 30, 1892 in Union City, Michigan
d. Jun 17, 1976 in Indio, California
Source: *BioIn 2, 3, 4, 5, 10, 11, 12; CurBio 41, 76; IntWW 74; St&PR 75; WhoAm 74*

O'Doherty, Brian
[Patrick Ireland]
Irish. Artist, Author
Director, visual arts programs, National Endowment for the Arts, 1969-76; wrote *The Strange Case of Mademoiselle P.,* 1992.
b. 1934 in Ballaghaderin, Ireland
Source: *ConAu 105; ConLC 76; TwCPaSc; WhoAmA 73, 76, 78, 80, 82*

O'Donnell, Cathy
[Ann Steely]
American. Actor
Played opposite Harold Russell in *Best Years of Our Lives,* 1946.
b. Jul 6, 1925 in Siluria, Alabama
d. Apr 11, 1970 in Los Angeles, California
Source: *FilmEn; FilmgC; ForYSC; HalFC 84; MotPP; WhScrn 74, 77, 83*

O'Donnell, Chris
American. Actor
Appeared in *Men Don't Leave,* 1990.
b. 1970 in Chicago, Illinois
Source: *IntMPA 94, 96; LegTOT; WhoAm 96, 97*

O'Donnell, Emmett, Jr.
"Rosie"
American. Military Leader
Joined military, 1928; made general, 1959; director of information for US Air Forces, 1946-47.
b. Sep 15, 1906 in New York, New York
d. Dec 26, 1971 in McLean, Virginia
Source: *BioIn 1, 2, 3, 4, 9, 15; CurBio 48, 71, 72N; DcAmB S9; HisDcKW; InSci; WhAm 5*

O'Donnell, Kenneth P
American. Government Official
Best friend of John F Kennedy; wrote *Johnny We Hardly Knew Ye.*
b. Mar 4, 1924 in Worchester, Massachusetts
d. Sep 9, 1977 in Boston, Massachusetts
Source: *ConAu 73, 81; PolProf J*

O'Donnell, Peadar
Irish. Author, Political Activist
IRA member; wrote *The Big Window,* 1954.
b. Feb 22, 1893 in County Meenmore, Ireland
d. May 13, 1986 in Dublin, Ireland
Source: *AnObit 1986; BiDIrW; BioIn 1, 4, 9, 10, 12, 17; ConAu 119; DcIrB 88; DcIrL, 96; DcIrW 1, 2; IntWW 77;*

ModIrL; NewCBEL; OxCIri; TwCA, SUP; WhE&EA; Who 85

O'Donnell, Peter
English. Author
Crime novels with Modesty Blaise series character include *Dragon's Claw,* 1978.
b. Apr 11, 1920 in London, England
Source: *ConAu 114, 117; DcLB 87; IntAu&W 93; ScF&FL 1, 92; SpyFic; TwCCr&M 80, 85, 91; WrDr 82, 84, 86, 88, 90, 94, 96*

O'Donnell, Rosie
[Roseanne O'Donnell]
American. Actor, Comedian
Appeared on Broadway in *Grease,* 1994; host of "The Rosie O'Donnell Show," 1996—.
b. 1962 in Commack, New York
Source: *CurBio 95; News 94, 94-3; WhoAm 94, 95, 96, 97; WhoAmW 95*

O'Donoghue, Michael
American. Writer
One of the original writers on TV's "Saturday Night Live;" wrote screenplay for *Scrooged,* 1988.
b. Jan 5, 1940
d. Nov 9, 1994
Source: *BioIn 12; ConAu 128, 147; ConLC 86; ConTFT 15*

O'Driscoll, Martha
American. Actor
On screen for 11 yrs; made 37 films including *Carnegie Hall,* 1947.
b. Mar 4, 1922 in Tulsa, Oklahoma
Source: *EncAFC; FilmEn; FilmgC; ForYSC; HalFC 80, 84, 88; WhoHol 92, A*

Oduber (Quiros), Daniel
Costa Rican. Political Leader
Liberal pres. of Costa Rica, 1974-78.
b. Aug 25, 1921 in San Jose, Costa Rica
Source: *BiDLAmC; BioIn 11, 16; CurBio 77; DcCPCAm; IntWW 74, 75, 76, 77, 78, 79, 80, 81, 82, 83, 89, 93; WhoWor 76, 78*

Odum, Howard Washington
American. Sociologist, Educator
Wrote on American black, social problems of the South: *Southern Regions of the US,* 1936.
b. May 24, 1884 in Bethlehem, Georgia
d. Nov 8, 1954 in Chapel Hill, North Carolina
Source: *AmAu&B; BiDAmEd; BioIn 3, 4, 6, 7, 10, 14; DcAmB S5; EncAACR; EncSoH; EncWB; NatCAB 44; OxCMus; REnAL; SouWr; TwCA SUP; WhAm 3; WhNAA*

O'Dwyer, Paul
[Peter Paul O'Dwyer]
American. Lawyer, Politician
Liberal Dem. opposed to Vietnam involvement; lost senate race to Javits, 1968; brother of William.
b. Jun 29, 1907 in Bohola, Ireland
Source: *BioIn 8, 11, 12; ConAu 97; CurBio 69; NewYTBE 70; PolProf J*

O'Dwyer, William
American. Politician, Diplomat
Mayor of NYC, 1946-50; resigned over racketeering scandal; ambassador to Mexico, 1950-52.
b. Jul 11, 1890 in Bohola, Ireland
d. Nov 24, 1964 in New York, New York
Source: *BiDWWGF; BioIn 1, 2, 4, 5, 6, 7, 11, 12, 15, 16; CurBio 41, 47, 65; DcAmB S7; DcAmDH 80, 89; PolProf T; WhAm 4*

Oe, Kenzaburo
Japanese. Author
Won 1994 Nobel Prize for Literature; wrote *The Catch,* 1958; *The Crazy Iris and Other Stories of the Atomic Aftermath,* 1984.
b. Jan 31, 1935 in Ose, Japan
Source: *Benet 87, 96; CasWL; ConAu 50NR, 97; ConFLW 84; ConLC 10, 36, 86; CurBio 96; CyWA 89; DcLB Y94; DcOrL 1; EncWL 2; FarE&A 78, 79, 80, 81; IntAu&W 76, 77, 89; IntWW 74, 75, 76, 77, 78, 79, 80, 81, 82, 83, 89, 93; MajTwCW; News 97-1; RAdv 13-2; ShSCr 20; WhoNob 95; WhoWor 74, 96, 97; WrDr 96*

Oenslager, Donald Mitchell
American. Designer
Set designs for operas, ballets, plays include *The Irregular Verb To Love.*
b. Mar 7, 1902 in Harrisburg, Pennsylvania
d. Jun 21, 1975 in Bedford, New York
Source: *BiE&WWA; BioIn 1, 10, 12; ConAu 57, 61; CurBio 46; NotNAT B; OxCThe 67, 83; PlP&P; WhAm 6; WhoAm 74; WhoAmA 73, 76, 78, 80, 82, 84, 86, 89N, 91N, 93N; WhoWor 74; WhThe*

Oersted, Hans Christian
Danish. Physicist, Chemist
First to realize the interaction between electric current, magnetic needle: electromagnetism.
b. Aug 14, 1777 in Rudkobing, Denmark
d. Mar 9, 1851 in Copenhagen, Denmark
Source: *AsBiEn; BiESc; BioIn 2, 3, 8, 9, 14; CamDcSc; CelCen; DcBiPP; DcInv; DcScB; InSci; LarDcSc; LinLib S; McGEWB; WhDW; WorAl; WorAlBi; WorScD*

Oerter, Al(fred A)
American. Track Athlete
Discus thrower; won gold medals in four straight Olympics, 1956-68.
b. Aug 19, 1936 in Astoria, New York
Source: *AmDec 1960; IntWW 83; LegTOT; WhoTr&F 73; WorAl; WorAlBi*

O'Faolain, Sean
[John Whelan]
"Irish Chekhov"
Irish. Author
Writings include *Come Back to Erin,* 1940, *The Talking Trees,* 1970; known for carefully crafted short stories.
b. Feb 22, 1900 in Cork, Ireland
d. Apr 20, 1991 in Dublin, Ireland
Source: *AnObit 1991; Benet 87, 96; BiDIrW; BioIn 1, 3, 4, 5, 6, 7, 8, 11, 13, 15, 16, 17, 18; BlmGEL; BlueB 76; CamGLE; CasWL; CathA 1930; ConAu 12NR, 61; ConLC 1, 7, 14, 32, 70; ConNov 72, 76, 82, 86; CurBio 90; CyWA 58, 89; DcArts; DcIrL, 96; DcIrW 1, 2; DcLB 15, 162; DcLEL; EncWL; EvLB; GrWrEL N; IntAu&W 76, 77, 89; IntWW 74, 75, 76, 77, 78, 79, 80, 81, 82, 83, 89; LegTOT; LinLib L; LngCEL; LngCTC; MajTwCW; ModBrL, S1, S2; ModIrL; NewC; NewCBEL; Novels; OxCEng 85, 95; OxCIri; PenC ENG; RAdv 1, 14, 13-1; REn; RfGShF; RGTwCWr; ScF&FL 92; ShSCr 13; ShSWr; TwCA, SUP; TwCWr; WhAm 10; WhE&EA; WhLit; WhoAm 74; WhoWor 74, 76, 78, 84, 87, 89, 91; WorAl; WorAlBi; WrDr 76, 80, 82, 84, 86, 88, 90, 94N*

Offenbach, Jacques
[Jacques Eberst]
French. Musician, Composer
Best known for four-act opera *The Tales of Hoffmann;* credited with creating the French operetta.
b. Jun 20, 1819 in Cologne, Germany
d. Oct 4, 1880 in Paris, France
Source: *AtlBL; Baker 78, 84, 92; Benet 87, 96; BiDD; BioIn 1, 2, 3, 4, 5, 6, 7, 8, 9, 10, 11, 12, 13, 19; BriBkM 80; CelCen; CmOp; CmpBCM; CnOxB; DancEn 78; DcArts; DcCom 77; DcCom&M 79; Dis&D; GrComp; IntDcOp; LegTOT; LinLib S; McGEWB; MetOEnc; MusMk; NewEOp 71; NewGrDM 80; NewGrDO; NewOxM; NotNAT B; OxCAmT 84; OxCFr; OxCMus; OxCPMus; OxDcOp; PenDiMP A; PlP&P; REn; WhDW; WorAl; WorAlBi*

O'Flaherty, Liam
Irish. Author
Best known for novel *The Informer,* 1926; became classic film, 1935.
b. Aug 28, 1896 in County Galway, Ireland
d. Sep 7, 1984 in Dublin, Ireland
Source: *AnObit 1984; Benet 87, 96; BioIn 4, 5, 9, 10, 11, 14, 17, 19; CasWL; Chambr 3; ConAu 101, 113; ConLC 5, 34; ConNov 72, 76, 82; CyWA 58, 89; DcIrB 88; DcIrL, 96; DcLB 36, 162, Y84N; DcLEL; EncWL; EvLB; GrWrEL N; HalFC 84, 88; IntAu&W 76, 77, 82; IntWW 74, 75, 76, 77, 78, 79, 80, 81, 82, 83; LegTOT; MajTwCW; ModBrL, S1, S2; ModIrL; NewC; Novels; OxCIri; PenC ENG; REn;*

RfGShF; ScF&FL 92; ShSCr 6; ShSWr; Who 85N; WhoWor 74; WorAl; WorAlBi; WrDr 76, 80, 82, 84

Ogarkov, Nikolai
Russian. Military Leader
Chief of the Soviet General Staff, 1977-84.
b. Oct 30, 1917 in Kalinin District, Union of Soviet Socialist Republics
Source: *BiDSovU; BioIn 13, 14; ColdWar 1, 2; IntWW 91; NewYTBS 84*

Ogilvie, Richard Buell
American. Politician
Rep. governor of IL, 1968-73.
b. Feb 22, 1923 in Kansas City, Missouri
d. May 10, 1988 in Chicago, Illinois
Source: *BiDrGov 1789; BioIn 8, 9, 15, 16; BlueB 76; IntWW 74, 75, 76, 77, 78, 79, 80, 81, 82, 83; St&PR 84, 87; WhAm 9; WhoAm 74, 76, 78, 80, 82, 84, 86; WhoAmP 73, 75, 77, 79, 81, 83, 85, 87; WhoGov 72, 75, 77; WhoMW 74, 76, 80, 82, 84; WhoWor 78*

Ogilvy, David Mackenzie
English. Advertising Executive
Founded Ogilvy, Benson & Mather, 1948; wrote *Confessions of an Advertising Man,* 1963.
b. Jun 23, 1911 in West Horsley, England
Source: *BioIn 5, 6, 7, 8, 10, 11, 12, 13; ConAmBL; ConAu 105; CurBio 61; IntWW 74, 75, 76, 77, 78, 79, 80, 81, 82, 83, 89, 93; IntYB 78, 79, 80, 81, 82; Who 74, 82, 83, 85, 90, 94; WhoAdv 80, 90; WhoAm 76, 78, 80, 82, 84, 86, 88, 90, 92, 94, 95, 96, 97; WorAl*

Ogilvy, Ian
English. Actor
Played in PBS TV series "Upstairs, Downstairs;" "Return of the Saint."
b. Sep 30, 1943 in Woking, England
Source: *FilmgC; HalFC 80, 84, 88; IlWWBF; ItaFilm; WhoHol 92, A; WhoHrs 80*

Oglethorpe, James Edward
English. Colonizer
MP, 1722-54; founded GA, 1733.
b. Dec 22, 1696 in London, England
d. Jun 30, 1785 in Essex, England
Source: *AmBi; AmWrBE; ApCAB; BiDrACR; BiDSA; BioIn 3, 4, 5, 6, 8, 9, 10, 11, 13, 16, 20; DcAmB; DcAmMiB; DcNaB; Drake; EncAAH; EncCRAm; EncSoH; EncWM; HisDBrE; LinLib S; McGEWB; NewCBEL; OxCAmH; OxCAmL 65, 83, 95; REnAL; TwCBDA; WebAB 74, 79; WhAm HS; WhNaAH; WorAl*

O'Grady, Sean
American. Boxer
WBA lightweight champion, 1987.
b. Feb 10, 1959 in Oklahoma City, Oklahoma
Source: *BioIn 12; NewYTBS 77*

Ogrodnick, John Alexander
Canadian. Hockey Player
Left wing, 1979—, currently with Detroit; member first All-Star team, 1984.
b. Jun 20, 1959 in Ottawa, Ontario, Canada
Source: *HocEn; HocReg 87*

Oh, Sadaharu
Japanese. Baseball Player
Often called the "Babe Ruth of Japan;" had 868 home runs in career that ended in 1980.
b. May 5, 1940 in Tokyo, Japan
Source: *Ballpl 90; BioIn 11, 12, 14; LegTOT; NewYTBS 85; WhoWor 78; WorAl; WorAlBi*

O'Hair, Madalyn Murray
American. Atheist, Lawyer
Founded American Atheists, 1965; challenged Bible reading in public schools, won Supreme Court case, 1963.
b. Apr 13, 1919 in Pittsburgh, Pennsylvania
Source: *AmDec 1960; BioIn 10, 11, 12, 13, 14, 18; BioNews 75; ConAu 12NR; CurBio 77; EncARH; EncUnb; InWom SUP; LibW; WhoAm 86; WhoAmW 87; WhoWor 87; WorAlBi*

O'Hanlon, Virginia
[Laura Virginia O'Hanlon Douglas]
American. Student
Wrote to NY *Sun,* 1897, asking if Santa Claus existed; editor responded with now-famous essay, "Yes Virginia, there is a Santa Claus."
b. 1889
d. May 13, 1971 in Valatie, New York
Source: *BioIn 2, 5, 9; GoodHs; InWom*

O'Hara, Frank
[Francis Russell O'Hara]
American. Poet
Published collection of poetry *A City Winter, and Other Poems,* 1952; applied techniques of abstract expressionism and French surrealism.
b. Jun 27, 1926 in Baltimore, Maryland
d. Jul 25, 1966 in New York, New York
Source: *AmAu&B; Benet 87, 96; BiDConC; BioIn 7, 8, 9, 10, 12, 13, 17, 19, 20; CamGLE; CamHAL; ConAu 9R, 25R, 33NR; ConLC 2, 5, 13, 78; ConPo 75, 80A, 85A; CroCAP; DcArts; DcLB 5, 16; DcLEL 1940; EncWL 2, 3; GayLL; GrWrEL P; LegTOT; LinLib L; MajTwCW; ModAL S1, S2; OxCAmL 83, 95; OxCTwCP; PenC AM; RAdv 1, 14, 13-1; RfGAmL 87, 94; RGTwCWr; WebE&AL; WhAm 4; WorAu 1950*

O'Hara, Jill
American. Actor
Appeared on stage in *Hair; Promises, Promises.*
b. Aug 23, 1947 in Warren, Pennsylvania
Source: *EncMT; WhoHol 92, A*

O'Hara, John Henry
American. Author
Writings include *Butterfield 8, From the Terrace;* both filmed, 1960.
b. Jan 31, 1905 in Pottsville, Pennsylvania
d. Apr 11, 1970 in Princeton, New Jersey
Source: *AmAu&B; AmNov; AmWr; Benet 96; BiDAmNC; BiE&WWA; CasWL; CnDAL; CnMD; ConAmA; ConLC 11; CurBio 41, 70; CyWA 58; ModAL S1; PenC AM; RGTwCWr; TwCA SUP; WhAm 5*

O'Hara, Mary
[Mary O'Hara Alsop; Mary Sture-Vasa]
American. Author
Wrote *My Friend Flicka,* 1941.
b. Jul 10, 1885 in Cape May, New Jersey
d. Oct 15, 1980 in Chevy Chase, Maryland
Source: *AmAu&B; WorAl; WrDr 80, 82*

O'Hara, Maureen
[Maureen Fitzsimmons]
American. Actor
Star of films, 1939-71: *How Green Was My Valley,* 1941; *Miracle on 34th Street,* 1947.
b. Aug 17, 1921 in Milltown, Ireland
Source: *BioIn 3, 10, 11, 12; CmMov; ConTFT 8; CurBio 53; FilmgC; HalFC 84; IntDcF 1-3, 2-3; IntMPA 84, 86, 88, 94, 96; InWom; MotPP; MovMk; OxCFilm; ThFT; VarWW 85; WhoAm 74; WhoHol A; WomWMM; WorAl; WorAlBi; WorEFlm*

O'Hara, Patrick
"Patsy"
Irish. Hunger Striker, Revolutionary
IRA member; one of 10 hunger strikers to die in prison, demanding political prisoner rather than criminal status.
b. 1957 in Londonderry, Northern Ireland
d. May 21, 1981 in Belfast, Northern Ireland
Source: *BioIn 12*

O'Hearn, Robert Raymond
American. Designer
Broadway stage designs include *My Fair Lady,* 1956; *West Side Story,* 1958; production designer with NY Met., 1960-85.
b. Jul 19, 1921 in Elkhart, Indiana
Source: *BioIn 6, 7; ConTFT 5; NotNAT; WhoAm 74, 76, 78, 80, 82, 84, 86, 88, 90, 92, 94, 95, 96, 97; WhoE 74, 75, 77; WhoWor 74*

OhEithir, Breandan
Irish. Author
Wrote first Irish-language novel Lig Sinn I Gcathu (Lead Us into Temptation) to head bestseller list in Ireland, 1987; nephew of Liam O'Flaherty.
b. Jan 18, 1930 in Aran Island, Ireland
d. Oct 26, 1990 in Dublin, Ireland

Source: *BiDIrW B; ConAu 132; IntAu&W 82, 86; NewYTBS 90*

O'Herlihy, Dan
[Daniel Peter O'Herlihy]
Irish. Actor
Oscar nominee for *The Adventures of Robinson Crusoe,* 1952.
b. May 1, 1919 in Wexford, Ireland
Source: *ConTFT 6; FilmEn; FilmgC; HalFC 80, 84, 88; IntMPA 77, 84, 86, 88, 94, 96; ItaFilm; LegTOT; MovMk; WhoHol 92, A; WorAl; WorAlBi*

O'Higgins, Bernardo
"Liberator of Chile"
Chilean. Soldier, Statesman
Dictator, 1817-23; deposed by revolution.
b. Aug 20, 1778 in Chillan, Chile
d. Oct 24, 1842 in Lima, Peru
Source: *ApCAB; BiDLAmC; BioIn 2, 3, 4, 5, 7, 8, 16, 17; DcHiB; DcIrB 78, 88; EncLatA; EncRev; HisWorL; McGEWB; REn; WhAm HS*

Ohlin, Bertil Gotthard
Swedish. Economist
Won Nobel Prize in economics, 1977, for studies done on int'l trade and capital movements.
b. Apr 23, 1899 in Klipan, Sweden
d. Aug 3, 1979 in Valadalen, Sweden
Source: *BioIn 15; IntEnSS 79; IntWW 79; WhE&EA; WhoEc 81, 86; WhoNob, 95*

Ohm, Georg Simon
German. Physicist
Practical unit of electrical resistance is named in his honor.
b. Mar 16, 1787 in Erlangen, Germany
d. Jul 7, 1854 in Munich, Germany
Source: *AsBiEn; BiESc; BioIn 3, 5, 8, 9, 11, 12; CelCen; DcBiPP; LarDcSc; LinLib S; McGEWB; REn; WorAl; WorScD*

O'Horgan, Tom
American. Director
Won Obie Award for *Futz,* 1967; Tony nominee for *Hair,* 1968.
b. May 3, 1926 in Chicago, Illinois
Source: *BioIn 9, 11, 13; CelR; CurBio 70; EncMT; EncWT; IntMPA 94, 96; NewYTBE 72; NotNAT, A; OxCAmT 84; WhoAm 78, 80, 82, 84, 86; WhoThe 81*

Ohrbach, Nathan M
American. Merchant
Opened first store in Brooklyn, NY, 1911; chm. of Ohrbach's Inc. until 1965.
b. Aug 31, 1885 in Vienna, Austria
d. Nov 19, 1972 in New York, New York
Source: *NewYTBE 72; WhAm 5, 7*

Oistrakh, David Fyodorovich
Russian. Violinist
Toured US from 1955; noted for phenomenal technique, tone.
b. Oct 23, 1908 in Odessa, Russia
d. Oct 24, 1974 in Amsterdam, Netherlands
Source: *Baker 84, 92; CurBio 56, 74; DcArts; IntWW 74; NewYTBS 74; WhAm 6; Who 74*

Oistrakh, Igor Davidovich
Russian. Violinist
Virtuoso; made numerous concert tours with father, David.
b. Apr 27, 1931 in Odessa, Union of Soviet Socialist Republics
Source: *Baker 84; BiDSovU; BriBkM 80; IntWW 74, 75, 76, 77, 78, 79, 80, 81, 82, 83, 89, 93; IntWWM 77, 80, 90; NewGrDM 80; Who 74, 82, 83, 85, 88, 90, 94; WhoMus 72; WhoSocC 78; WhoWor 74*

O'Jays, The
[Edward Levert; Sam Strain; Walter Williams]
American. Music Group
Hits include "Use Ta Be My Girl," 1977; "Girl, Don't Let It Get You Down," 1980.
Source: *Alli; BiDAfM; BioIn 11, 20, 21; ConAu X; ConMuA 80A; ConMus 13; DcVicP 2; DcWomA; EncPR&S 74, 89; EncRk 88; EncRkSt; HarEnR 86; IlEncBM 82; IlEncRk; InB&W 80, 85, 85A; ItaFilm; Law&B 89A, 92; NewGrDA 86; ObitOF 79; PenEncP; RkOn 74, 78; RolSEnR 83; SoulM; WhoHol 92; WhoRock 81; WhoRocM 82*

Ojeda, Eddie
[Twisted Sister]
American. Musician
Guitarist with heavy metal group formed 1976.
b. Aug 5, 1954 in New York, New York

Ojukwu, Chukwuemeka Odumegwu
Nigerian. Political Leader
Head of state of Republic of Biafra (Nigeria), 1967-70; fled to Ivory Coast, 1970-82; arrested, 1984.
b. Nov 4, 1933 in Nnewi, Nigeria
Source: *AfSS 78, 79, 80, 81; BioIn 8, 9, 21; CurBio 69; DcAfHiB 86S; DcPol; DcTwHis; EncRev; IntWW 74, 75, 76, 77, 78, 79, 80, 81, 82, 83, 89, 93; WhoAfr; WhoWor 74*

Okada, Kenzo
American. Artist
Works reflect Japanese landscapes.
b. Sep 28, 1902 in Yokohama, Japan
d. Jul 25, 1982 in Tokyo, Japan
Source: *AnObit 1982; BioIn 3, 4, 6, 7, 13; DcCAA 71, 77, 88, 94; FarE&A 78; IntWW 74, 75, 76, 77, 78, 79, 80, 81, 82; McGDA; NewYTBS 82; OxCTwCA; PhDcTCA 77; PrintW 83, 85; WhAm 8; WhoAm 74, 80, 82; WhoAmA 73, 76, 78, 80, 82, 84, 84N, 86N, 89N, 91N, 93N; WhoE 74; WorArt 1950*

Okamura, Arthur
American. Artist, Educator, Writer
Professor of arts, CA College of Arts and Crafts, 1966—; wrote *Passionate Journey,* 1984.
b. Feb 24, 1932 in Long Beach, California
Source: *BioIn 5, 6; DcCAA 71, 77, 88, 94; WhoAm 74, 76, 78, 80, 82, 84, 86, 88, 90, 92, 94, 95, 96, 97; WhoAmA 73, 76, 78, 80, 82, 84, 86, 89, 91, 93; WhoWor 74*

O'Keefe, Dennis
[Edward Vanes Flanagan, Jr.]
American. Actor
Played Hal Towne in TV's "The Dennis O'Keefe Show," 1959-60.
b. Mar 28, 1910 in Fort Madison, Iowa
d. Aug 31, 1968 in Santa Monica, California
Source: *FilmgC; HolP 40; MotPP; MovMk; WhAm 5; WhoHol B; WhScrn 74, 77*

O'Keefe, Walter
American. Author, Actor
Host of 1940s radio quiz show "Double or Nothing;" popularized song "The Man on the Flying Trapeze," 1930s.
b. Aug 18, 1900 in Hartford, Connecticut
d. Jun 26, 1983 in Torrance, California
Source: *ASCAP 66; RadStar*

O'Keeffe, Georgia
[Mrs. Alfred Stieglitz]
American. Artist
One of founders of Modernism known for brilliant paintings of flowers, bleached skulls, Western terrain.
b. Nov 15, 1887 in Sun Prairie, Wisconsin
d. Mar 6, 1986 in Santa Fe, New Mexico
Source: *AmArt; AnObit 1986; ArtsAmW 1, 2; Benet 87, 96; BioAmW; BioIn 1, 2, 4, 5, 6, 7, 8, 9, 10, 11, 12, 13, 14, 15, 16, 17, 18, 19, 20, 21; BlueB 76; BriEAA; CelR; ConArt 77, 83, 89, 96; ConAu 110, 118; ConHero 1; ContDcW 89; CurBio 41, 64, 86, 86N; DcAmArt; DcArts; DcCAA 71, 77, 88, 94; DcCAr 81; DcTwCCu 1; EncAB-H 1974, 1996; EncWHA; GoodHs; GrLiveH; IlBEAAW; IntDcAA 90; IntDcWB; InWom, SUP; LegTOT; LibW; LinLib S; McGDA; McGEWB; ModArCr 1; NewYTBS 86; NorAmWA; OxCArt; OxCTwCA; OxDcArt; PhDcTCA 77; RAdv 14; REn; WebAB 74, 79; WhAm 9; WhAmArt 85; Who 74, 82, 83, 85; WhoAm 74, 76, 78, 80, 82, 84; WhoAmA 73, 76, 78, 80, 82, 84, 86N, 89N, 91N, 93N; WhoAmW 58, 64, 66, 68, 70, 72, 74, 75, 83, 85; WhoWest 74; WhoWor 74; WomArt; WomFir; WorAl; WorAlBi; WorArt 1950*

O'Keeffe, John
Irish. Dramatist
Comedies, farces include *Wild Oats,* 1791.
b. Jun 24, 1747 in Dublin, Ireland
d. Feb 4, 1833 in Southampton, England

Source: *BiD&SB; BioIn 12, 13, 14, 17; BlmGEL; BritAu 19; CamGLE; CamGWoT; DcBrWA; DcIrB 88; DcIrL, 96; DcLB 89; DcLEL; DcNaB; Ent; GrWrEL DR; IntDcT 2; NewC; NewCBEL; NewGrDO; NotNAT A, B; OxCEng 67, 85, 95; OxCIri; OxCThe 67, 83; PoIre*

Okigbo, Christopher (Ifenayichukwu)
Nigerian. Poet
Published poetry collections *Heavensgate,* 1962; *Limits,* 1962; poetry combined traditional African culture with Christianity and Western poetics.
b. 1932 in Ojoto, Nigeria
d. 1967
Source: *AfrA; Benet 87, 96; BioIn 9, 14, 17, 19; BlkWr 1; CamGLE; CasWL; ConAu 77; ConLC 25, 84; ConPo 75, 80A; DcLB 125; DcLEL 1940; EncWL 2, 3; GrWrEL P; MajTwCW; ModBlW; ModCmwL; OxCTwCP; PenC CL; PoeCrit 7; RAdv 14, 13-2; RGAfL; SelBAAf; TwCWr; WebE&AL; WorAu 1970*

O'Konski, Alvin E(dward)
American. Politician
Rep. congressman from WI, 1943-73; co-wrote GI Bill of Rights.
b. May 26, 1904 in Kewaunee, Wisconsin
d. Jul 8, 1987 in Kewaunee, Wisconsin
Source: *AmCath 80; BiDrAC; BiDrUSC 89; BioIn 4; CurBio 55, 87; WhoAm 86; WhoAmP 85*

Okoye, Christian
Nigerian. Football Player
Running back, Kansas City Chiefs, 1987—; led NFL in rushing yardage, 1989.
b. Aug 16, 1961 in Enugu, Nigeria
Source: *BioIn 16; News 90, 90-2; WhoAm 92, 94; WhoBlA 92*

Okri, Ben
Nigerian. Author
Won 1991 Booker Prize for *The Famished Road.*
b. Mar 15, 1959 in Minna, Nigeria
Source: *Benet 96; BlkWr 2; CamGLE; ConAu 130, 138; ConLC 87; ConNov 91, 96; DcArts; DcLB 157; IntWW 91, 93; LiExTwC; RGTwCWr; ScF&FL 92; SchCGBL; WorAu 1985; WrDr 96*

Okun, Arthur Melvin
American. Economist
Best known for "Okun's Law;" chm., Council of Economic Advisers, 1968-69.
b. Nov 28, 1928 in Jersey City, New Jersey
d. Mar 23, 1980 in Washington, District of Columbia
Source: *AmEA 74; AmMWSc 78S; AnObit 1980; BioIn 8, 9, 10, 11, 12; ConAu 61, 97; CurBio 70, 80; IntWW 78; PolProf J; WhAm 7*

Okun, Milton Theodore
American. Composer
Songs include "Sinner Man"; "Odds Against Tomorrow."
b. Dec 23, 1923 in New York, New York
Source: *ASCAP 66, 80; ConMuA 80B; VarWW 85; WhoAm 76, 78, 80, 82, 84; WhoE 74*

Olaf, Pierre
[Pierre-Olaf Trivier]
French. Actor
Supporting actor in films *Three Women; Camelot; Art of Love.*
b. Jul 14, 1928 in Cauderan, France
Source: *BiE&WWA; NotNAT; WhoHol 92, A; WhoThe 72, 77, 81*

Olajuwon, Hakeem
[Akeem Abdul Ajibola Olajuwon]
"The Dream"
American. Basketball Player
Seven-foot forward, Houston Rockets, 1984—; formed team's "Twin Towers" combination with Ralph Sampson, 1984-87; NBA Rookie of the Year, 1984; MVP, 1993-94, 1995 NBA Finals.
b. Jan 21, 1963 in Lagos, Nigeria
Source: *ConNews 85-1; CurBio 93; LegTOT; NewYTBS 83, 86; OfNBA 87; WhoBlA 85*

Oland, Warner
Swedish. Actor
Played Charlie Chan in films, 1931-38.
b. Oct 3, 1880 in Umea, Sweden
d. Aug 5, 1938 in Stockholm, Sweden
Source: *BioIn 17, 21; CmMov; Film 1, 2; FilmEn; FilmgC; ForYSC; HalFC 80, 84, 88; IntDcF 1-3; LegTOT; MotPP; MovMk; NotNAT B; OlFamFa; SilFlmP; TwYS; WhoHol B; WhoHrs 80; WhScrn 74, 77, 83; WhThe; WorAl; WorAlBi*

Olatunji, Michael Babatunde
Nigerian. Author, Musician
Books on music include *Musical Instruments of Africa,* 1965.
Source: *AuBYP 2, 2S, 3; BioIn 8, 9; DrBlPA, 90*

Olav V
[Olaf V]
Norwegian. Ruler
Succeeded father, King Haakon VII, Sep 21, 1957; role is mainly ceremonial, but is symbol of national unity; succeeded by son, Prince Harald.
b. Jul 2, 1903 in Sandringham, England
d. Jan 17, 1991 in Oslo, Norway
Source: *BioIn 4, 6, 8, 10; CurBio 62*

Olbers, Heinrich Wilhelm Matthaus
German. Astronomer, Physician
Developed means for calculating orbits of comets, 1779; discovered five comets including Olbers Comet, 1815.
b. Oct 11, 1758 in Arbergen, Germany
d. Mar 2, 1840 in Bremen, Germany
Source: *AsBiEn; BioIn 14; DcScB; InSci; LarDcSc; NewCol 75*

Olcott, Chauncey
[Chancellor Olcott]
American. Singer, Songwriter
Popular tenor; wrote Irish songs including "When Irish Eyes Are Smiling," 1913; film *My Wild Irish Rose,* 1947, portrays life.
b. Jul 21, 1860 in Buffalo, New York
d. Mar 18, 1932 in Monte Carlo, Monaco
Source: *AmAu&B; AmBi; ASCAP 66; BioIn 3, 6, 9, 10; DcAmB; NotNAT A; OxCAmT 84; REnAL; WhAm 1; WhoStg 1906, 1908; WhThe*

Olcott, Henry Steel
American. Author, Teacher
Writings include *The Olcott Family,* 1874; helped establish school system in Ceylon, 1880.
b. Aug 2, 1832 in Orange, New Jersey
d. Feb 17, 1907 in Adyar, India
Source: *Alli, SUP; AmAu&B; AmBi; BiDAmCu; BiDPara; BioIn 4, 8, 9, 19, 21; ConAu 118; DcAmB; DcAmReB 1, 2; DcNAA; DivFut; EncARH; EncO&P 1, 2, 3; EncPaPR 91; NatCAB 8; NewCBEL; OhA&B; WhAm 1; WorAl; WorAlBi*

Olczewska, Maria
[Marie Berchtenbreitner]
German. Opera Singer
Mezzo-soprano, noted for Wagnerian roles; with NY Met., 1930s.
b. Aug 12, 1892 in Augsburg, Germany
d. May 17, 1969 in Baden-Baden, Germany (West)
Source: *Baker 78, 84, 92; BioIn 8; CmOp; MetOEnc; NewEOp 71; NewGrDM 80; OxDcOp*

Old Coyote, Barney
American. Educator
Professor, director of American Indian Studies, Montana State University, 1970—; received a Distinguished Service Award from the US Department of the Interior, 1968, for his efforts as the coordinator fo a job coprs training program.
b. Apr 10, 1923 in Saint Xavier, Montana
Source: *BioIn 9, 10, 21; NotNaAm*

Oldenbourg, Zoe
French. Author
Novels include *The Awakened,* 1956; *The Chains of Love,* 1958.
b. Mar 31, 1916 in Saint Petersburg, Russia
Source: *Benet 87, 96; BioIn 5, 9, 10; EncCoWW; EncWL; IntAu&W 76, 77, 89; IntWW 74, 75, 76, 77, 78, 79, 80, 81, 82, 83, 89, 93; InWom; LinLib L; ModWoWr; REn; TwCWr; WhoAm 82; WhoFr 79; WhoWor 74, 82; WorAu 1950*

Oldenburg, Claes Thure
American. Artist, Sculptor
Known for "soft" sculptures of ice cream cones, hamburgers, etc.
b. Jan 28, 1929 in Stockholm, Sweden
Source: *AmAu&B; ConArt 83; ConAu 117; CurBio 70; DcCAA 71; OxCArt; WebAB 79; WhoAm 86, 97; WhoAmA 84; WhoWor 87, 97*

Oldenburg, Richard
American. Museum Director
Director of New York's Museum of Modern Art (MOMA), 1972-94; chm. of Sotheby's N.Am. N.Y.C., 1995—; brother of Claes.
b. Sep 21, 1933 in Stockholm, Sweden
Source: *CelR, 90*

Olderman, Murray
American. Cartoonist, Journalist
Football writings include *The Pro Quarterback,* 1966; *The Defenders,* 1973.
b. Mar 27, 1922 in New York, New York
Source: *ConAu 1NR, 45*

Oldfield, Barney
[Berna Eli Oldfield]
American. Auto Racer
First to travel a mile a minute, 1903.
b. Jan 29, 1878 in Wauseon, Ohio
d. Oct 4, 1946 in Beverly Hills, California
Source: *BiDAmSp OS; BioIn 1, 3, 5, 6, 10, 11, 12, 13, 17; CurBio 46; DcAmB S4; Film 1; FilmgC; HalFC 80, 84, 88; LegTOT; WebAB 74, 79; WhoHol B; WhoSpor; WhScrn 74, 77, 83; WorAl; WorAlBi*

Oldfield, Brian
American. Track Athlete
Shot putter; rival of Randy Matson on 1972 Olympic team.
b. Jun 1, 1945 in Elgin, Illinois
Source: *BioIn 10, 11, 12; NewYTBE 73; WhoTr&F 73*

Oldfield, Maurice, Sir
English. Government Official
Chief of British Secret Intelligence Service, 1973-79; inspiration of John LeCarre, Ian Fleming spy novels.
b. Nov 6, 1915 in Bakewell, England
d. Mar 10, 1981, England
Source: *AnObit 1981; BioIn 10, 11, 12, 15; DcNaB 1981; NewYTBS 81; Who 74*

Oldfield, Mike
English. Composer
Wrote song that was used for theme to film *The Exorcist,* 1973: "Tubular Bells."
b. May 15, 1953 in Reading, England
Source: *BioIn 13; ConMuA 80A; EncRk 88; EncRkSt; HarEnR 86; IlEncRk; LegTOT; OnThGG; OxCPMus; PenEncP; RkOn 78, 84; RolSEnR 83*

Oldham, Todd
American. Designer
Fashion designer; designs include hand-beaded and embroidered outfits; his collections include Times 7, a line of women's shirts, and Garage Sale—the outrageous. Host of "House of Style," MTV.
b. 1961 in Corpus Christi, Texas
Source: *ConDes 97; ConFash; News 95*

Oldman, Gary
English. Actor
Played Lee Harvey Oswald in *JFK,* 1991; also in *Bram Stoker's Dracula,* 1992; *Immortal Beloved,* 1994.
b. Mar 21, 1958 in London, England
Source: *BiDFilm 94; CurBio 96; IntMPA 94, 96; IntWW 93; LegTOT; WhoAm 94, 95, 96, 97; WhoHol 92*

Old Person, Earl
American. Native American Leader
Chief of the Blackfeet Nation, 1978—.
b. Apr 13, 1929 in Browning, Montana
Source: *BioIn 12, 21; NotNaAm; WhoGov 72, 75*

Olds, Irving S
American. Business Executive
Chairman, US Steel, 1940-52.
b. Jan 22, 1887 in Erie, Pennsylvania
d. Mar 4, 1963 in New York, New York
Source: *CurBio 48, 63; WhAm 4*

Olds, Ranson E(li)
American. Inventor
Built three-wheeled horseless carriage, 1886; founded Olds Motor Vehicle Co., 1896.
b. Jun 3, 1864 in Geneva, Ohio
d. Aug 26, 1950 in Lansing, Michigan
Source: *WebAB 74; WhAm 3; WorAl*

Olds, Sharon
American. Poet
Published collections of poetry *Satan Says,* 1980; *The Gold Cell,* 1987.
b. Nov 19, 1942 in San Francisco, California
Source: *AmWomWr SUP; Benet 96; ConAu 18NR, 41NR, 101; ConLC 32, 39, 85; ConPo 96; ConPopW; DcLB 120; DrAPF 80; FemiCLE; IntAu&W 86; OxCAmL 95; OxCTwCP; WhoAm 96; WhoAmW 91, 93, 95; WhoUSWr 88; WhoWrEP 89, 92, 95; WorAu 1980; WrDr 94, 96*

O'Leary, Hazel R(eid)
American. Government Official
Secretary of Energy, 1993-97.
b. May 17, 1937 in Newport News, Virginia
Source: *CurBio 94; St&PR 91; WhoAmW 91; WhoFI 92*

O'Leary, Jean
American. Social Reformer
Former nun; member of several gay rights organizations including National Gay Rights Advocates.
b. 1948 in Cleveland, Ohio
Source: *AmSocL; BioIn 19; GayLesB*

Olga
[Olga Erteszek]
American. Fashion Designer
Designed intimate apparel for women; when she sold Olga Co., 1984, annual sales were $67 million.
d. Sep 15, 1989 in Los Angeles, California
Source: *BioIn 11, 16, 21; DcBiPP; DcLP 87B; IntAu&W 76X, 77X; InWom SUP; NewYTBS 89; ObitOF 79; WhoAmW 68; WhScrn 83; WomWR; WorFshn*

Olin, Ken
American. Actor, Director
Played Michael Steadman on Emmy Award-winning TV series "Thirtysomething," 1987-91.
b. Jul 30, 1954 in Chicago, Illinois
Source: *IntMPA 94, 96; LegTOT; News 92; WhoHol 92*

Olin, Lena
Swedish.
Films include *The Unbearable Lightness of Being,* 1988; Oscar-nomination for *Enemies: A Love Story,* 1990.
b. Mar 22, 1956 in Stockholm, Sweden
Source: *ConTFT 11; IntMPA 92; News 91-2; WhoEnt 92*

Oliphant, Laurence
English. Author
Best known for *Piccadilly,* 1866.
b. 1829 in Cape Town, South Africa
d. Dec 23, 1888 in Twickenham, England
Source: *Alli, SUP; ApCAB; BbD; BiD&SB; BioIn 4, 11, 12, 13; BritAu 19; CamGEL; CamGLE; CasWL; Chambr 3; DcBiA; DcBrBI; DcEnA; DcEnL; DcEuL; DcLB 18, 166; DcLEL; DcNaB; EvLB; HarEnUS; NatCAB 6; NewC; NewCBEL; NinCLC 47; OxCEng 67, 85, 95; PenC ENG; REn; StaCVF*

Oliphant, Margaret
English. Author
Books on English society include *Salem Chapel,* 1876.
b. Apr 4, 1828 in Musselburgh, Scotland
d. Jun 25, 1897 in Eton, England
Source: *Alli SUP; ArtclWW 2; BbD; BiD&SB; BioIn 15, 16, 17, 21; BlmGEL; BlmGWL; BritAu 19; CamGEL; CamGLE; CasWL; CmScLit; ContDcW 89; DcArts; DcBiA; DcEnA A; DcEnL; DcEuL; DcLB 18, 159; DcLEL; EncBrWW; EvLB; FemiCLE; IntDcWB; LinLib L; NewC; NinCLC 11; Novels; OxCEng 67, 85; PenC ENG; PenEncH; RAdv 14; REn; RfGShF; WhoHr&F*

Oliphant, Patrick Bruce
American. Cartoonist
Syndicated cartoonist for *Washington Star,* 1975-81; now in over 500 int'l newspapers and magazines; won Pulitzer for editorial cartooning, 1967.
b. Jul 24, 1935 in Adelaide, Australia
Source: *BioIn 7, 8, 9, 10, 12; ConAu 101; WhoAm 74, 76, 86; WhoAmA 76, 78, 84*

Olitski, Jules
American. Artist
Noted for misty color-fields, spraying paint directly on canvas; first living American to have one-man show at NYC's Met. Museum, 1969.
b. Mar 27, 1922 in Snovsk, Union of Soviet Socialist Republics
Source: *AmArt; BioIn 10, 12, 13, 14, 17; BriEAA; CenC; ConArt 77, 83, 89, 96; CurBio 69; DcAmArt; DcCAA 71, 77, 88, 94; DcCAr 81; IntWW 74, 75, 76, 77, 78, 79, 80, 81, 82, 83, 89, 93; McGDA; OxCTwCA; OxDcArt; PhDcTCA 77; WhoAm 74, 76, 78, 80, 82, 84, 86, 88, 90, 92, 94, 95, 96, 97; WhoAmA 73, 76, 78, 80, 82, 84, 86, 89, 91, 93; WhoE 75, 77, 79, 91, 93; WhoWor 74; WorArt 1950*

Oliva, Tony
[Antonio Pedro Oliva, Jr]
Cuban. Baseball Player
Outfielder, Minnesota, 1962-76; won AL batting title three times.
b. Jul 20, 1940 in Pinar del Rio, Cuba
Source: *Ballpl 90; BioIn 13, 18; HispAmA; LegTOT; NewYTBE 73; WhoHisp 91, 94; WhoProB 73; WhoSpor; WorAl; WorAlBi*

Oliver, Daniel
American. Government Official
Controversial chairman of Federal Trade Commission, 1986-89.
b. Apr 10, 1939 in New York, New York
Source: *News 88-2; WhoAm 82, 84, 86, 88, 90, 92, 94, 95, 96, 97; WhoAmL 83, 85; WhoAmP 83, 85, 87, 89, 93, 95; WhoFI 89*

Oliver, Edith
American. Critic
On *New Yorker* mag.'s editorial staff, 1947-94; off-Broadway reviewer, 1961-94.
b. Aug 11, 1913 in New York, New York
Source: *BiE&WWA; ConAmTC; NotNAT; NotWoAT; WhoAm 74, 76, 78, 80, 82, 84, 86, 88; WhoAmW 68, 70, 72, 74, 75; WhoThe 72, 77, 81*

Oliver, Edna May
[Edna May Cox Nutter]
American. Actor
Films include *Little Women,* 1933; *David Copperfield,* 1935.
b. Nov 9, 1883 in Malden, Massachusetts
d. Nov 9, 1942 in Hollywood, California
Source: *BioIn 21; CurBio 43; EncAFC; FilmEn; FilmgC; ForYSC; Funs; HalFC 80, 84, 88; HolCA; InWom, SUP; LegTOT; MotPP; MovMk; OlFamFa; OxCFilm; QDrFCA 92; ThFT; TwYS; Vers A; WhAm 2; WhScrn 74, 77, 83; WorAl; WorAlBi; WorEFlm*

Oliver, Harry
[Harold Oliver]
Canadian. Hockey Player
Right wing, 1926-37, mostly with Boston; Hall of Fame, 1967.
b. Oct 26, 1898 in Selkirk, Manitoba, Canada
Source: *WhoHcky 73*

Oliver, James A(rthur)
American. Zoologist
Director, NY Zoological Society, 1958-59; herpetologist, helped plan, manage Bronx Zoo's famed reptile house, 1950s.
b. Jan 1, 1914 in Caruthersville, Missouri
d. Dec 2, 1981 in New York, New York
Source: *BioIn 3, 5, 7, 12, 13; ConAu 106; CurBio 66, 82, 82N; NewYTBS 81; WhAm 8; WhoAm 74, 76, 78, 80; WhoE 74; WhoWor 74*

Oliver, Joe
[Joseph Oliver]
"King"
American. Musician, Bandleader
Jazz pioneer whose band featured Louis Armstrong, Johnny Dodds; hits include "Dixieland Blues;" first black jazz band to record, 1923.
b. May 11, 1885 in Abend, Louisiana
d. Apr 8, 1938 in Savannah, Georgia
Source: *AfrAmAl 6; Baker 78, 84; BiDAfM; BiDAmM; BiDJaz; BioIn 1, 4, 5, 6, 7, 10, 11, 12, 15, 16; DcAmB S2; DcArts; InB&W 80, 85; NegAl 76, 83, 89; NewGrDM 80; NewOrJ; OxCPMus; WebAB 74, 79; WhAm 4, HSA*

Oliver, Stephanie Stokes
American. Editor
Editor, *Essence,* 1986-94, editor-in-chief *Heart & Soul* magazine, 1994—.
b. Jan 13, 1952 in Seattle, Washington

Oliver, Sy
[Melvin James Oliver]
American. Musician
Trumpeter, vocalist, bandleader; composer, arranger for Jimmy Lunceford, 1930s; Tommy Dorsey, 1940s.
b. Dec 17, 1910 in Battle Creek, Michigan
d. May 27, 1988 in New York, New York
Source: *AllMusG; AnObit 1988; BgBands 74; BiDAfM; BiDAmM; BiDJaz; BioIn 8, 10, 12, 15, 16; CmpEPM; DrBlPA, 90; EncJzS; InB&W 80, 85; LegTOT; NewGrDA 86; NewGrDJ 88, 94; NewYTBS 88; OxCPMus; PenEncP; WhoJazz 72*

Olivero, Magda
[Maria Maddalena Olivero]
Italian. Opera Singer
Soprano who had NY Met. debut at age 63—an unprecedented occurrence.
b. Mar 25, 1914 in Saluzzo, Italy
Source: *Baker 84; BiDAmM; BioIn 11, 20, 21; CmOp; CurBio 80; IntDcOp; MusSN; NewEOp 71; NewGrDM 80; NewYTBE 71; WhoAm 82; WhoOp 76*

Olivetti, Adriano
Italian. Manufacturer, Businessman
Pres., Olivetti and Co., 1938-60.
b. Apr 11, 1901 in Ivrea, Italy
d. Feb 28, 1960
Source: *BioIn 4, 5, 6, 11; CurBio 59, 60; EncWB; ObitT 1951; WhAm 4*

Olivetti, Camillo
Italian. Businessman, Manufacturer
Founded Olivetti & C. SpA office equipment and information systems co; began manufacturing typewriters, 1908.
b. 1868, Italy
d. Dec 4, 1943 in Biella, Italy
Source: *BioIn 11; Entr*

Olivier, Laurence Kerr, Sir
[Baron Olivier of Brighton]
"Sir Larry"
English. Actor, Producer, Director
The English-speaking world's most revered actor; won Oscar for *Hamlet,* 1948; once wed to Vivien Leigh.
b. May 22, 1907 in Dorking, England
d. Jul 11, 1989 in Amhurst, England
Source: *BioIn 1, 2, 3, 4, 5, 6, 7, 8, 12, 13; CmMov; ConAu 150; ConTFT 1; CurBio 46, 89; DcFM; DcNaB 1986; EncWT; FamA&A; LinLib S; MotPP; MovMk; NewYTBS 86, 89; NotNAT; OxCFilm; OxCThe 83; WhoAm 80, 82, 84, 86, 88; WhoWor 74, 78, 80, 82, 84, 87, 89; WorAl*

Olmert, Ehud
Israeli. Politician
Mayor of Jerusalem, 1993—.
b. 1946?

Olmos, Edward James
American. Actor
Played role of Lt. Martin Castillo, "Miami Vice," 1984-89, which won him an Emmy, 1985; films include *Blade Runner,* 1982.
b. Feb 24, 1947 in Boyle Heights, California
Source: *BioIn 12; ConTFT 14; CurBio 92; DcHiB; HispAmA; IntMPA 92, 94, 96; LegTOT; MexAmB; MiSFD 9; News 90, 90-1; WhoAm 90, 94, 95, 96, 97; WhoEnt 92; WhoHisp 91, 92, 94; WhoHol 92*

Olmstead, Bert
[Murray Bert Olmstead]
"Dirtie Bertie"
Canadian. Hockey Player
Left wing, 1948-62, mostly with Montreal; Hall of Fame, 1985.
b. Sep 4, 1926 in Scepter, Saskatchewan, Canada
Source: *HocEn; WhoHcky 73*

Olmsted, Frederick Law
"Father of American Parks"
American. Landscape Architect
Planned, supervised laying out of Central Park, NYC, other city parks.
b. Apr 27, 1822 in Hartford, Connecticut
d. Aug 28, 1903 in Brookline, Massachusetts
Source: *Alli, SUP; AmAu; AmAu&B; AmBi; AmCulL; ApCAB; AtlBL; BbD; BiD&SB; BioIn 2, 3, 4, 6, 7, 8, 9, 10, 11, 12, 13, 14, 15, 17, 18, 19, 20, 21; BriEAA; CmCal; ConAu 120; CyAL 2; DcAmAu; DcAmB; DcArts; DcBiPP; DcNAA; Drake; EncAAH; EncAAr 1, 2; EncAB-H 1974, 1996; EncEnv; EncSoH; EncUrb; HarEnUS; IntDcAr; LinLib S; MacEA; McGDA; McGEWB; MemAm; NatCAB 2; NatLAC; NewYTBE 72; OxCAmH; OxCAmL 65, 83, 95; REnAL; REnAW; TwCBDA; WebAB 74, 79; WhAm 1, 3; WhCiWar; WhoArch; WorAl; WorAlBi*

Olsen, Ashley Fuller
American. Actor
Played Michelle on TV's "Full House;" shares role with twin sister Mary Kate Olsen.
b. Jun 13, 1986

Olsen, Harold G
"Ole"
American. Basketball Coach
Coached at five colleges, including OH State, 1922-46; one of founders of NCAA tournament; Hall of Fame.
b. May 12, 1895 in Rice Lake, Wisconsin
d. Oct 29, 1953 in Evanston, Illinois
Source: *BiDAmSp BK; BioIn 3, 9; ObitOF 79; WhoBbl 73*

Olsen, Kenneth Harry
American. Business Executive
Founder, pres., Digital Equipment Corp., 1957-92.
b. Feb 20, 1926 in Bridgeport, Connecticut
Source: *ConNews 86-4; CurBio 87; HisDcDP; LarDcSc; LElec; WhoAm 74, 76, 78, 80, 82, 84, 88, 90, 92, 94, 95, 96, 97; WhoE 83, 85, 86, 89, 91, 93; WhoFI 74, 77, 79, 81, 83, 85, 87, 89; WhoFrS 84; WhoWor 84, 89*

Olsen, Mary Kate
American. Actor
Played Michelle on TV series "Full House;" shares role with twin sister Ashley Olsen.
b. Jun 13, 1986
Source: *BioIn 21*

Olsen, Merlin Jay
American. Football Player, Sportscaster, Actor
Twelve-time all-pro defensive tackle, member LA Rams' "fearsome foursome," 1962-73; Hall of Fame, 1982; analyst, NBC Sports, 1977-93.
b. Sep 15, 1940 in Logan, Utah
Source: *BiDAmSp FB; BioIn 12, 13; VarWW 85; WhoAm 74, 76, 78, 82, 84, 86, 88, 92, 94, 95, 96, 97; WhoE 95; WhoFtbl 74; WhoTelC; WorAl*

Olsen, Ole
[Olsen and Johnson]
American. Comedian
Starred in over 1,400 performances of *Hellzapoppin,* 1938-41.
b. Nov 6, 1892 in Peru, Indiana
d. Jan 26, 1963 in Albuquerque, New Mexico
Source: *BioIn 2, 6, 16; DcAmB S7; EncMT; EncVaud; FilmEn; FilmgC; HalFC 80, 84, 88; JoeFr; LegTOT; MovMk; NotNAT B; OxCAmT 84; QDrFCA 92; WhoHol B; WhScrn 74, 77, 83; WhThe; WorAl; WorEFlm*

Olsen, Tillie
American. Author
Wrote *Tell Me a Riddle,* 1962 which won an O'Henry Award.
b. Jan 14, 1912 in Omaha, Nebraska
Source: *AmWomWr; ArtclWW 2; BenetAL 91; BioIn 11, 12, 13; ConAu 1NR; ConLC 13; ConNov 91, 96; CyWA 89; DcLB 28, Y80B; DrAPF 91; EncWL 3; FemiCLE; IntDcWB; InWom SUP; JeAmWW; MajTwCW; ModAL S2; OxCAmL 83; RfGAmL 94; RfGShF; TwCWW 91; WhoAm 82, 84, 86, 88, 90, 92, 94, 95, 96, 97; WhoAmW 83, 95, 97; WhoUSWr 88; WhoWor 95, 96, 97; WhoWrEP 89, 92, 95; WorAu 1970; WrDr 92*

Olson, Billy Richard
American. Track Athlete
Pole vaulter; broke world record 11 times, 1982-86.
b. Jul 19, 1958 in Abilene, Texas
Source: *BioIn 13; ConNews 86-3; NewYTBS 86*

Olson, Charles John
American. Poet
Co-founded Black Mountain school of poetry; wrote *Call Me Ishmael,* 1947.
b. Dec 27, 1910 in Worcester, Massachusetts
d. Jan 10, 1970 in New York, New York
Source: *AmAu&B; CasWL; ConAu P-1; ConLC 11; ConPo 70, 75; CroCAP; DcLEL 1940; ModAL S1; OxCAmL 83; PenC AM; RAdv 1; TwCA SUP; WebE&AL; WhAm 5; WhoTwCL*

Olson, Gregg William
American. Baseball Player
Relief pitcher, Baltimore, 1989—; AL rookie of year, 1989.
b. Oct 11, 1966 in Omaha, Nebraska

Olson, James E(lias)
American. Business Executive
Pres., CEO of A T & T, 1985-88; credited with making co. more aggressive, confident.
b. Dec 3, 1925 in Devils Lake, North Dakota
d. Apr 18, 1988 in New York, New York
Source: *BioIn 14; Dun&B 79, 86, 88; St&PR 84, 87; WhoAm 74, 76, 78, 80, 82, 84, 86; WhoE 85, 86; WhoFI 75, 87; WhoWor 87*

Olson, Johnny
American. TV Personality
TV announcer whose cry "Come on down!" was trademark of game show "The Price Is Right."
b. 1910
d. Oct 12, 1985 in Santa Monica, California
Source: *ConNews 85-4*

Olson, Nancy
American. Actor
Oscar nominee for *Sunset Boulevard,* 1950.
b. Jul 14, 1928 in Milwaukee, Wisconsin
Source: *BiE&WWA, 80, 88; NotNAT; VarWW 85; WhoAmW 61; WhoHol 92, A*

O'Malley, J. Pat
American. Actor
TV shows include "My Favorite Martian," 1963-64.
b. Mar 15, 1904 in Burnley, England
d. Feb 27, 1985 in San Juan Capistrano, California
Source: *BiE&WWA; FilmgC; MovMk; NotNAT; WhoHol A*

O'Malley, Susan
American. Sports Executive
President of the Washington Bullets basketball team, 1991—.
b. c. 1962
Source: *News 95, 95-2*

O'Malley, Walter Francis
American. Baseball Executive
Owner, Brooklyn/LA Dodgers, 1950-79; moved team to LA, 1957, where they were first team with three million attendance, 1978.
b. Oct 9, 1903 in New York, New York
d. Aug 9, 1979 in Rochester, Minnesota
Source: *BiDAmBL 83; BiDAmSp BB; BioIn 3, 4, 5, 6, 8, 11, 12, 15, 21; CurBio 54, 79; DcAmB S10; NewYTBS 79; WhoAm 78; WhoProB 73*

Omar I
[Omar ibn al-Khattab]
Arab. Religious Leader
Succeeded Abu Bakr as second caliph; made Islam an imperial power; founded Cairo, c. 642.
b. 581?
d. 644 in Medina, Arabia
Source: *BioIn 5, 8; NewC; NewCol 75*

Omar Khayyam
Persian. Poet, Astronomer
Best known for poems translated by Edward FitzGerald.
b. 1048 in Nishapur, Persia
d. 1131 in Nishapur, Persia
Source: *BbD; BiD&SB; BiESc; ClMLC 11; DcOrL 3; GrFLW; McGEWB; NewC; WorAl; WorAlBi*

Omarr, Sydney
American. Astrologer, Journalist
Astrology columns appear in over 200 newspapers.
b. Aug 5, 1926 in Philadelphia, Pennsylvania
Source: *ConAu 116; DivFut*

O'Meara, Mark
American. Golfer
Won a record four AT&T Pebble Beach Nat. Pro-Am golf tournaments, 1985, 1989, 1990, and 1992.
b. Jan 13, 1957 in Goldsboro, North Carolina
Source: *BioIn 12*

O'Meara, Walter (Andrew)
American. Author
Wrote historical novels, *The Grand Partage,* 1951 *The Spanish Bride,* 1954.
b. Jan 29, 1897 in Minneapolis, Minnesota
d. Sep 29, 1989 in Cohasset, Massachusetts
Source: *AmAu&B; Au&Wr 71; BioIn 1, 4, 5, 6, 10, 16, 17; ConAu 13R, 129; CurBio 89N; MinnWr; NewYTBS 89; ScF&FL 1, 2, 92; WhAm 10; WhoAm 74, 76*

Omlie, Phoebe Jane Fairgrave
American. Aviator
Her many firsts for women include record parachute jump, 1922; establishment of flying school, 1923.
b. Nov 21, 1902 in Des Moines, Iowa
d. Jul 17, 1975 in Indianapolis, Indiana
Source: *InWom SUP; NotAW MOD*

Onassis, Aristotle Socrates
Greek. Shipping Executive
Founded oil tanker business, 1932; Olympic Airways, 1957; married Jackie Kennedy, 1968.
b. Jan 15, 1906 in Smyrna, Turkey
d. Mar 15, 1975 in Paris, France
Source: *BioIn 3, 4, 5, 6, 7, 8, 9, 15, 20; BusPN; CurBio 63; IntWW 74; WhAm 6; Who 74; WhoAm 74; WhoWor 74; WorAl*

Onassis, Christina
"Chryso Mou"
Greek. Business Executive
Inherited multi-million dollar shipping and real estate interests from father, Aristotle Onassis; daughter Athena is sole heir; died of apparent heart attack.
b. Dec 11, 1950 in New York, New York
d. Nov 19, 1988 in Buenos Aires, Argentina
Source: *AnObit 1988; BioIn 9, 10, 11, 12, 13; BkPepl; CurBio 76, 89, 89N; InWom SUP; NewYTBS 78, 88*

Onassis, Jacqueline (Lee Bouvier Kennedy)
[Mrs. Aristotle Onassis]
American. Editor, First Lady
Newspaper photographer before marriage to John Kennedy, 1953; married Aristotle Onassis, 1968; editor at Doubleday.
b. Jul 28, 1929 in Southampton, New York
d. May 19, 1994 in New York, New York
Source: *BkPepl; CelR, 90; ContDcW 89; CurBio 61; EncFash; HerW; LegTOT; LibW; NewYTBE 70; NewYTBS 76; WhoAm 86; WhoAmW 70, 72, 74, 87; WhoWor 74*

Ondaatje, Michael
Canadian. Author
Won Booker Prize for *The English Patient,* 1992; the first Canadian ever to win a Booker.
b. Dec 9, 1943 in Ceylon, Sri Lanka
Source: *BenetAL 91; BioIn 11, 13, 16, 17, 18, 19, 20, 21; CamGLE; CanWW 31, 70, 79, 80, 81, 83, 89; CaW; ConAu 77; ConLC 14, 29, 51, 76; ConNov 91; ConPo 70, 75, 80, 85, 91; CurBio 93; DcLB 60; EncWL 3; IntAu&W 82, 91, 93; IntWW 89, 91, 93; LiExTwC; OxCCanL; OxCCan SUP; OxCEng 95; OxCTwCP; RAdv 14, 13-1; WhoAm 82, 84, 86, 88, 94, 95, 96; WhoCanL 85, 87, 92; WhoWrEP 89; WorAu 1975; WrDr 76, 80, 82, 84, 86, 88, 90, 92, 94, 96*

O'Neal, Frederick
American. Actor
Film and stage actor in the 1940s; first African-American pres., Actor's Equity Assn., 1964-73.
b. 1905 in Brooksville, Mississippi
d. Aug 25, 1992 in New York, New York
Source: *AfrAmAl 6; AfrAmBi 2; AmCath 80; AnObit 1992; BiE&WWA; BioIn 1, 3, 6, 10, 19; BlueB 76; DcTwCCu 5; DrBlPA, 90; Ebony 1; FilmgC; HalFC 80, 84, 88; InB&W 85; IntMPA 75, 76, 77, 78, 79, 80, 81, 82, 84, 86, 88, 92; MotPP; MovMk; NegAl 89; NewYTBS 92; NotNAT; WhAm 10; WhoAm 74, 76, 78, 80, 82, 84, 86, 88, 90, 92; WhoBlA 92; WhoE 89; WhoEnt 92; WhoHol 92, A; WhoThe 72, 77, 81; WhoWor 74, 76*

O'Neal, Patrick
American. Actor
TV shows include "Emerald Point," 1983; films include *The Way We Were,* 1973.
b. Sep 26, 1927 in Ocala, Florida
Source: *BioIn 11, 20; ConTFT 4; FilmEn; FilmgC; ForYSC; HalFC 80, 84, 88; IntMPA 75, 76, 77, 78, 79, 80, 81, 82, 84, 86, 88, 94; ItaFilm; LegTOT; NotNAT; VarWW 85; WhoHol 92, A; WhoHrs 80; WhoThe 72, 77, 81; WorAl*

O'Neal, Ron
American. Actor
Films include *Superfly,* 1972; *Superfly TNT,* 1973.
b. Sep 1, 1937 in Utica, New York
Source: *BlksAmF; ConTFT 6, 13; DcTwCCu 5; DrBlPA, 90; FilmEn; HalFC 80, 84, 88; IntMPA 80, 81, 82, 88, 94, 96; MiSFD 9; NewYTBE 72; VarWW 85; WhoHol 92, A*

O'Neal, Ryan
[Patrick Ryan O'Neal]
American. Actor
Starred in film *Love Story,* 1970; TV series "Peyton Place," 1960s.
b. Apr 20, 1941 in Los Angeles, California
Source: *BioIn 9, 10, 13; BkPepl; CelR, 90; ConTFT 1, 6, 13; CurBio 73; EncAFC; FilmEn; FilmgC; ForYSC; HalFC 80, 84, 88; IntMPA 75, 76, 77, 78, 79, 80, 81, 82, 84, 86, 88, 94, 96; IntWW 89, 93; LegTOT; MovMk; NewYTBE 71; VarWW 85; WhoAm 74, 76, 78, 80, 82, 84, 86, 88, 90, 92, 94, 95, 96, 97; WhoHol 92, A; WorAl; WorAlBi*

O'Neal, Shaquille
[Shaquille Rashaun O'Neal]
"Shaq"; "The Shack"
American. Basketball Player
Center, LSU, 1989-92; Orlando Magic, 1992-96, LA Lakers, 1996—; won 1993 NBA Rookie of the Year award.
b. Mar 6, 1972 in Newark, New York
Source: *AfrAmSG; ConBlB 8; CurBio 96; LegTOT; News 92, 92-1; WhoAfA 96; WhoAm 94, 95, 96, 97; WhoBlA 94; WhoSSW 95*

O'Neal, Tatum
American. Actor
Youngest Oscar winner in history for *Paper Moon,* 1973.
b. Nov 5, 1963 in Los Angeles, California
Source: *BkPepl; CelR 90; ConTFT 3; EncAFC; FilmEn; IntMPA 82, 88, 94, 96; IntWW 89, 93; InWom SUP; LegTOT; MovMk; VarWW 85; WhoAm 78, 80, 82, 84, 86, 88, 90, 94, 95, 96, 97; WhoHol 92, A; WorAl; WorAlBi*

Onegin, Sigrid
[Sigrid Hoffman]
Swedish. Opera Singer
Contralto, noted for Lady Macbeth role, NY Met., 1922-24.
b. Jun 1, 1891 in Stockholm, Sweden
d. Jun 16, 1943 in Magliasco, Switzerland
Source: *Baker 78, 84; BioIn 4, 10; CmOp; NewEOp 71*

O'Neil, James F(rancis)
American. Publisher
Published *American Legion,* 1950-78.

b. Jun 13, 1898 in Manchester, New Hampshire
d. Jul 28, 1981 in New York, New York
Source: *AmCath 80; BioIn 1, 8, 12; CurBio 47, 81, 81N; WhAm 8; WhoAm 74, 76, 78, 80, 82; WhoFI 74, 75, 77, 79, 81*

O'Neil, Roger
American. Broadcast Journalist
Correspondent, NBC News, since 1979.
b. Apr 17, 1945 in Chicago, Illinois
Source: *WhoTelC*

O'Neill, Cherry Boone
American. Author
Oldest daughter of Pat Boone; wrote *Starving for Attention,* about her battles with anorexia nervosa.
b. Jul 7, 1954 in Denton, Texas
Source: *ConAu 112*

O'Neill, Ed
American. Actor
Plays Al Bundy in controversial TV series "Married.with Children," 1987-97; films include *Little Giants.*
b. Apr 12, 1946 in Youngstown, Ohio
Source: *ConTFT 5, 13; IntMPA 94, 96; LegTOT*

O'Neill, Eugene Gladstone
American. Dramatist
Considered America's finest playwright; won Pulitzer's for many works, including *The Iceman Cometh,* 1946; awarded 1936 Nobel Prize.
b. Oct 16, 1888 in New York, New York
d. Nov 27, 1953 in Boston, Massachusetts
Source: *AmAu&B; AmWr; AtlBL; AuNews 1; Benet 96; Chambr 3; CnDAL; CnMD; CnMWL; CnThe; ConAmA; ConAmL; Dis&D; EncAB-H 1996; OxCAmL 83; RGTwCWr; WebAB 74; WebE&AL; WhAm 3; WhoNob, 95; WhoTwCL*

O'Neill, Gerard Kitchen
American. Physicist
Inventor of the colliding-beam storage ring.
b. Feb 6, 1927 in New York, New York
d. Apr 27, 1992 in Redwood, California
Source: *AmMWSc 76P, 79, 82, 86, 89; BioIn 11, 12, 13, 14, 15; ConAu 21NR, 93; Future; IntAu&W 82; SmATA 65; WhAm 10; WhoAm 74, 76, 78, 80, 82, 84, 86, 88; WhoE 91; WhoWor 80, 82, 84, 87, 91; WhoWrEP 92, 95*

O'Neill, James
American. Actor
Best known for 1913 film *The Count of Monte Cristo;* made int'l tour in stage version; father of playwright Eugene.
b. Oct 14, 1847 in County Kilkenny, Ireland
d. Aug 10, 1920 in New London, Connecticut
Source: *BioIn 4, 9, 14, 19; DcAmB; FamA&A; Film 1; FilmgC; HalFC 80, 84, 88; NatCAB 11, 28; NotNAT B; OxCAmH; OxCAmL 65; OxCAmT 84; OxCThe 83; PlP&P; REnAL; WhoStg 1906, 1908; WhScrn 77, 83*

O'Neill, Jennifer
American. Actor, Model
Starred in *The Summer of '42,* 1971.
b. Feb 20, 1949 in Rio de Janeiro, Brazil
Source: *ConTFT 6; IntMPA 84, 86, 88, 94, 96; MovMk; NewYTBE 71; VarWW 85; WhoAm 82; WhoHol 92, A*

O'Neill, Rose Cecil
American. Illustrator, Author
Created Kewpie doll, 1909; wrote several Kewpie books.
b. Jun 25, 1874 in Wilkes-Barre, Pennsylvania
d. Apr 6, 1944 in Springfield, Missouri
Source: *AmAu&B; AmWomWr; BioAmW; BioIn 1, 2, 4, 5, 6, 7, 8; ChhPo, S2; DcAmB S3; DcNAA; DcWomA; InWom SUP; LibW; NotAW; TwCA, SUP; WebAB 74, 79; WomNov; WorECom*

O'Neill, Steve
[Stephen Francis O'Neil]
American. Baseball Player, Baseball Manager
Catcher, 1911-28; mostly with Cleveland; managed for 14 yrs., including world championship, 1945, with Detroit.
b. Jul 6, 1891 in Minooka, Pennsylvania
d. Jan 26, 1962 in Cleveland, Ohio
Source: *Ballpl 90; WhoProB 73*

O'Neill, Terence Marne
Irish. Political Leader
Prime minister of N Ireland, 1963-69.
b. Sep 10, 1914 in London, England
d. Jun 13, 1990, England
Source: *BioIn 8, 16, 17; ConAu 108; CurBio 90N; DcNaB 1986; FacFETw; NewYTBS 90*

O'Neill, Thomas P(hilip), Jr.
"Tip"
American. Politician
Dem. congressman from MA, 1952-87; Speaker of House, 1976-87.
b. Dec 9, 1912 in Cambridge, Massachusetts
d. Jan 5, 1994 in Boston, Massachusetts
Source: *BiDrAC; BioIn 9, 10, 11; CngDr 85; CurBio 74, 94N; IntWW 77, 78, 79, 80, 81, 82, 83, 89, 93; NewYTBE 71; NewYTBS 76; WebAB 79; Who 94; WhoAm 86; WhoAmP 87*

O'Neill, William Atchison
American. Politician
Democratic governor of CT, 1979-91, succeeded by Lowell Weicker.
b. Aug 11, 1930 in Hartford, Connecticut
Source: *AlmAP 88; BioIn 12; CurBio 85; IntWW 82, 83, 89, 93; NewYTBS 80; WhoAm 86, 90; WhoAmP 85, 87; WhoE 91; WhoWor 84, 87, 91*

Onetti, Juan Carlos
Spanish. Author
Wrote *A Brief Life,* 1950; *The Shipyard,* 1961.
b. Jul 1, 1909 in Montevideo, Uruguay
d. May 30, 1994
Source: *Benet 87, 96; BioIn 7, 16, 17, 18, 20; CasWL; ConAu 32NR, 85, 145; ConFLW 84; ConLC 7, 10, 86; ConWorW 93; DcCLAA; DcHiB; DcTwCCu 3; EncLatA; EncWL 2, 3; HispWr; IntAu&W 76, 77; IntvLAW; IntWW 74, 75, 76, 77, 78, 79, 80, 81, 82, 83, 89, 93; LatAmWr; MajTwCW; ModLAL; OxCSpan; PenC AM; RAdv 14, 13-2; RfGShF; ShSCr 23; SpAmA; WhoTwCL; WhoWor 74; WorAu 1970*

Ongala, Remmy
[Ramadhani Mtoro Ongala]
Zairean. Singer, Musician
Leader, Orchestre Super Matimila, 1981—.
b. 1947 in Kivu, Belgian Congo
Source: *BioIn 18, 21; ConBlB 9*

Ongania, Juan Carlos
Argentine. Political Leader
Pres., Argentina, 1966-70.
b. May 17, 1914
d. Jun 8, 1995 in Buenos Aires, Argentina
Source: *BiDLAmC; BioIn 7, 8, 16, 21; CurBio 95N; DcPol; EncLatA; IntWW 74, 75, 76, 77, 78, 79, 80, 81, 82, 83, 89, 93*

Onions, Charles Talbut
English. Author
Compiled *Oxford Dictionary of English Etymology,* 1966.
b. Sep 10, 1873 in Birmingham, England
d. Jan 8, 1965 in Oxford, England
Source: *BioIn 7, 14; ConAu 107; DcLEL; DcNaB 1961; GrBr; LngCTC; NewC; ObitT 1961; WhE&EA*

Onizuka, Ellison
American. Astronaut
Crew member who died in explosion of space shuttle *Challenger.*
b. Jun 24, 1946 in Kealakekua, Hawaii
d. Jan 28, 1986 in Cape Canaveral, Florida
Source: *NewYTBS 86; NotAsAm; WhoSpc*

Ono, Yoko
[Mrs. John Lennon]
American. Artist, Musician
Married John Lennon, 1969; recorded, with husband, *Double Fantasy,* 1980.
b. Feb 18, 1933 in Tokyo, Japan
Source: *AsAmAlm; Baker 92; BioIn 8, 9, 10, 11, 12, 13; CelR, 90; ConArt 77; ConMuA 80A; ConMus 11; CurBio 72; DcTwCCu 1; EncRk 88; HarEnR 86; IlEncRk; InWom SUP; LegTOT; NewGrDA 86; News 89-2; NorAmWA; NotAsAm; PenEncP; VarWW 85; WhoAm 74, 86; WhoAmA 78, 80, 82, 84, 86, 89, 91, 93; WhoAmW 74, 87, 89, 91, 93, 95; WhoAsA 94; WhoHol 92; WhoRocM 82; WomWMM A, B*

Onoda, Hiroo
Japanese. Soldier
Surrendered, 1974; wrote *My 30 Year War in Luband Island,* 1975.
b. 1922? in Kinan, Japan
Source: *BioIn 10; ConAu 108; NewYTBS 74*

Onsager, Lars
Norwegian. Educator
Won 1968 Nobel Prize in chemistry for discovering reciprocal relations named after him.
b. Nov 20, 1903 in Oslo, Norway
d. Oct 5, 1976 in Coral Gables, Florida
Source: *AmMWSc 73P, 76P; AsBiEn; BiESc; BioIn 3, 4, 5, 6, 7, 8, 11, 14, 15, 19, 20; BlueB 76; CurBio 58, 77N; DcAmB S10; DcScB S2; InSci; IntWW 74, 75, 76; LarDcSc; McGMS 80; NewYTBS 76; NobelP; NotTwCS; ThTwC 87; WebAB 74, 79; WhAm 7; Who 74; WhoAm 74, 76; WhoNob, 95; WhoSSW 75, 76, 78; WhoWor 74*

Ontkean, Michael
Canadian. Actor
In TV series "The Rookies," 1972-74; films include *Slap Shot,* 1984.
b. Jan 24, 1946, Canada
Source: *ConTFT 3, 10; HalFC 84, 88; IntMPA 96; LegTOT; VarWW 85; WhoHol A*

Oparin, Aleksandr Ivanovich
Russian. Biochemist
Noted for his studies on the origin of life; won numerous awards.
b. Mar 2, 1894 in Uglich, Russia
d. Apr 21, 1980
Source: *AnObit 1981; BiESc; BioIn 14; ConAu 108; DcScB S2; FacFETw; IntWW 77, 78, 79, 80; NotTwCS; ThTwC 87; WhoSocC 78; WhoWor 74, 76, 78*

Opatoshu, David
American. Actor
Began career in Yiddish theater; films include *Exodus,* 1960; won 1991 Emmy for "Gabriel's Fire."
b. Jan 30, 1918 in New York, New York
d. Apr 30, 1996 in Los Angeles, California
Source: *BiE&WWA; BioIn 21; ConTFT 7; FilmEn; FilmgC; ForYSC; HalFC 80, 84, 88; IntMPA 81, 82, 84, 86, 88, 94, 96; ItaFilm; NotNAT; VarWW 85; WhoHol 92; WhoThe 77, 81*

Opechancanough
American. Native American Leader
Became "werowance" of Pamunkey, ca. 1607; led two rebellions against the English settlers in Virginia, 1622 and 1644.
b. 1556?
d. 1646
Source: *NotNaAm*

Opel, John Roberts
American. Business Executive
With IBM from 1949; pres., 1974-83; chief exec., 1981-85; chm., 1983-86; chm., exec. com., 1986-93.
b. Jan 5, 1925 in Kansas City, Missouri
Source: *BioIn 12, 13; CurBio 86; IntWW 75, 76, 77, 78, 79, 80, 81, 82, 83, 89, 93; LElec; NewYTBS 82; WhoAm 74, 76, 78, 80, 82, 86; WhoE 79, 81, 83, 85; WhoFI 79, 81, 83, 85; WhoWor 82, 84*

Ophuls, Marcel
American. Director
Son of Max Ophuls; made controversial documentary *The Sorrow and the Pity* about France under German occupation.
b. Nov 1, 1927 in Frankfurt am Main, Germany
Source: *BiDFilm 81, 94; BioIn 10, 11, 12, 13, 15, 16; ConTFT 8; CurBio 77; DcTwCCu 2; FilmEn; HalFC 80, 84, 88; IntDcF 1-2; IntMPA 94, 96; ItaFilm; LegTOT; MiSFD 9; OxCFilm; VarWW 85; WhoAm 78, 80, 82, 84, 86, 88, 90, 92, 94, 95, 96, 97; WhoWor 82; WorAl; WorFDir 2*

Ophuls, Max
[Max Oppenheimer]
French. Director
Known for fluid motion camera technique: *Caught; Reckless Movement.*
b. May 6, 1902 in Saarbrucken, Germany
d. Mar 26, 1957 in Hamburg, Germany (West)
Source: *Benet 87, 96; BiDFilm 81, 94; BiGAW; BioIn 4, 8, 12, 15; ConAu 113; DcArts; DcFM; DcTwCCu 2; EncEurC; EncWT; FilmEn; FilmgC; HalFC 80, 84, 88; IntDcF 1-2; ItaFilm; LegTOT; MiSFD 9N; MovMk; ObitT 1951; OxCFilm; WorEFlm; WorFDir 1*

Opie, Peter Mason
English. Editor, Author
Collected British folklore: *Oxford Book of Children's Verse,* 1973.
b. Nov 25, 1918 in Cairo, Egypt
d. Feb 5, 1982 in West Liss, England
Source: *AnCL; AnObit 1982; Au&Wr 71; DcArts; DcNaB 1981; OxCEng 85, 95; Who 82; WhoWor 78*

Oppen, George
American. Poet
Won 1969 Pulitzer for *On Being Numerous.*
b. Apr 24, 1908 in New Rochelle, New York
d. Jul 7, 1984 in Sunnyvale, California
Source: *AmAu&B; AnObit 1984; Benet 96; BioIn 8, 11, 12, 14, 17; CamGLE; CamHAL; CmCal; ConAu 8NR, 13R, 113; ConLC 7, 13, 34; ConPo 70, 75, 80; DcLB 5, 165; DrAP 75; DrAPF 80; IntWWP 77; NewYTBS 84; OxCAmL 65, 83, 95; OxCTwCP; PenC AM; RAdv 1, 13-1; WhAm 8; WhoAm 74, 76, 78, 80, 82; WhoWest 74, 76, 78; WhoWor 74, 78; WorAu 1970; WrDr 76, 80, 82, 84*

Oppenheim, James
American. Poet, Author
Poem volumes include *The Sea,* 1923; books include *Behind Your Front,* 1928.
b. May 24, 1882 in Saint Paul, Minnesota
d. Aug 4, 1932 in New York, New York
Source: *AmAu&B; BioIn 14; CasWL; ChhPo, S1, S2; ConAmL; DcAmB; DcLB 28; DcNAA; LinLib L; OxCAmL 65, 83, 95; REn; REnAL; TwCA, SUP; WhAm 1; WhNAA*

Oppenheimer, Frank F
American. Physicist
Worked in fields of radioactive elements, electromagnetic uranium, cosmic radiation, social effects of science.
b. Aug 14, 1912 in New York, New York
d. Feb 3, 1985 in Sausalito, California
Source: *AmMWSc 73P; BioIn 5, 9, 10, 12; WhoTech 82, 84*

Oppenheimer, Harry Frederick
South African. Industrialist, University Administrator
Chm., Consolidated Diamond Mines of SW Africa; Chancellor, Cape Town U., since 1 957-82.
b. Oct 28, 1908 in Kimberley, South Africa
Source: *AfSS 78, 79, 80, 81, 82; BioIn 4, 5, 6, 9, 10, 12, 13, 14, 16, 21; EncSoA; IntWW 74, 75, 76, 77, 78, 79, 80, 81, 82, 83, 89, 93; IntYB 78, 79, 80, 81, 82; NewYTBS 83; St&PR 84; Who 74, 82, 83, 85, 88, 90, 94; WhoAm 74, 76, 78; WhoWor 74, 76, 78, 82, 84, 87, 91, 93, 95, 96, 97*

Oppenheimer, J(ulius) Robert
"Father of the Atom Bomb"
American. Physicist
Headed Los Alamos, NM, lab during development of first atomic bombs; declared security risk for previous communist affiliations, 1954; name cleared, 1963.
b. Apr 22, 1904 in New York, New York
d. Feb 18, 1967 in Princeton, New Jersey
Source: *AmSocL; BioIn 5, 6, 7, 8, 9, 11, 12, 13; ColdWar 2; CurBio 45, 64, 67; DcAmB S8; EncAB-H 1974, 1996; InSci; OxCAmH; REnAL; WebAB 74*

Opper, Frederick Burr
American. Cartoonist
Best known for "Happy Hooligan" cartoon.
b. Jan 2, 1857 in Madison, Ohio
d. Aug 28, 1937 in New Rochelle, New York
Source: *Alli SUP; AmAu&B; AmBi; AuNews 1; BioIn 4, 6, 10, 12, 13, 15; ChhPo; DcAmB S2; DcNAA; EncACom; NatCAB 6, 44; OhA&B; REnAL; TwCBDA; WhAm 1; WhAmArt 85; WhJnl; WhNAA; WorECom*

Orange, Walter
[The Commodores]
"Clyde"
American. Musician, Singer
Drummer with group since 1968; albums include *In the Pocket,* 1981.
b. 1947 in Florida
Source: *BkPepl; RolSEnR 83*

Orantes, Manuel
Spanish. Tennis Player
Won US Open, 1975; Italian Open, 1972.
b. Feb 6, 1949 in Granada, Spain
Source: *WhoIntT; WhoWor 78, 80, 82*

Orbach, Jerry
American. Actor
Leading man in films since 1961, including *Prince of the City,* 1981; won Tony for *Promises, Promises,* 1969.
b. Oct 20, 1935 in New York, New York
Source: *BiE&WWA; BioIn 8, 9; CelR, 90; ConTFT 1, 7, 14; CurBio 70; EncMT; HalFC 84, 88; IntMPA 86, 88, 94, 96; LegTOT; NotNAT; OxCAmT 84; OxCPMus; VarWW 85; WhoAm 74, 76, 78, 80, 82, 84, 86, 88, 90, 92, 94, 95, 96, 97; WhoHol 92, A; WhoThe 72, 77, 81; WorAl; WorAlBi*

Orbison, Roy
American. Singer, Musician
Ballad rock singer often compared with Elvis Presley; best-selling song "Oh, Pretty Woman," 1964; known for trademark dark glasses.
b. Apr 23, 1936 in Vernon, Texas
d. Dec 6, 1988 in Hendersonville, Tennessee
Source: *AnObit 1988; Baker 84, 92; BgBkCoM; BiDAmM; BioIn 9, 12, 14, 15, 16, 17, 18, 19, 21; ConMuA 80A; ConMus 2; CounME 74, 74A; DcArts; EncFCWM 69, 83; EncPR&S 89; EncRk 88; EncRkSt; HarEnCM 87; HarEnR 86; IlEncCM; IlEncRk; LegTOT; NewGrDA 86; News 89-2; NewYTBS 88; OnThGG; OxCPMus; PenEncP; PopAmC SUP; RkOn 74; RolSEnR 83; VarWW 85; WhAm 9; WhoHol A; WhoRock 81; WhoRocM 82; WorAl; WorAlBi*

Orczy, Emmuska, Baroness
[Emma Madgalena Rosalia Maria Josefa Barbara Orczy]
English. Author
Best known for *The Scarlet Pimpernel,* 1905.
b. Sep 23, 1865 in Tarna-Ors, Hungary
d. Nov 12, 1947 in London, England
Source: *ArtclWW 2; AuBYP 2, 3; BioIn 1, 4, 5, 8, 14, 15, 16; DcLEL; DcVicP 2; EncMys; EvLB; GrWomMW; InWom, SUP; LegTOT; LngCTC; NewC; NotNAT B; REn; SmATA 40; TwCA, SUP; TwCWr; WhE&EA; WhLit; WhoLA; WhoSpyF; WhThe*

Ord, Edward Otho Cresap
American. Army Officer
Led attack against Confederate Army, Dranesville, VA, 1861.
b. Oct 18, 1818 in Cumberland, Maryland
d. Jul 22, 1883 in Havana, Cuba
Source: *AmBi; ApCAB; BioIn 3, 7, 12; CivWDc; DcAmB; Drake; EncSoH; HarEnMi; HarEnUS; NatCAB 4; TwCBDA; WebAMB; WhAm HS; WhCiWar*

O'Ree, Willie
[William Eldon O'Ree]
Canadian. Hockey Player
Forward, first black in NHL, with Boston, 1957-58, 1960-61.
b. Oct 15, 1935 in Fredericton, New Brunswick, Canada
Source: *AfrAmAl 6; BioIn 19; ConBlB 5; InB&W 80; WhoHcky 73*

O'Reilly, Anthony John Francis
Irish. Business Executive
Chm. of H.J. Heinz Co. since 1979; he is the highest paid US CEO, 1991.
b. May 7, 1936 in Dublin, Ireland
Source: *BioIn 9, 10, 11, 12; NewYTBE 73; Who 82, 83, 85, 88, 90, 94; WhoAm 74, 76, 78, 80, 82, 84, 86, 88, 90, 92, 94, 95, 96, 97; WhoE 83, 85, 86, 89, 91, 93, 95, 97; WhoFI 81, 83, 85, 87, 89, 94, 96; WhoWor 84, 87, 89*

Orff, Carl
German. Composer
Known for innovative three-part oratorio *Carmina Burana,* 1937.
b. Jul 10, 1895 in Munich, Germany
d. Mar 29, 1982 in Munich, Germany (West)
Source: *AnObit 1982; Baker 78, 84, 92; BioIn 2, 3, 4, 7, 8, 9, 11, 12, 13, 14, 21; BriBkM 80; CmOp; CnOxB; CompSN, SUP; ConAu 106; CurBio 76, 82, 82N; DancEn 78; DcArts; DcCM; DcCom 77; DcCom&M 79; IntDcOp; IntWW 74, 75, 76, 77, 78, 79, 80, 81; IntWWM 77, 80; LegTOT; MetOEnc; MusMk; NewEOp 71; NewGrDM 80; NewGrDO; NewOxM; NewYTBS 82; OxCGer 76, 86; OxCMus; OxDcOp; PenDiMP A; WhAm 8; WhDW; WhoMus 72; WhoWor 74, 76, 78, 82*

Orfilo, Alejandro
[Washington Alejandro Orfilo]
Argentine. Diplomat
Secretary-general, Organization of American States, 1975-84.
b. Mar 9, 1925 in Mendoza, Argentina
Source: *BioIn 13; IntWW 91*

Origen Adamantius
Greek. Religious Figure, Philosopher
Most influential theologian before St. Augustine; tried to prove Christian view of universe compatible with Greek thought.
b. c. 185 in Alexandria, Egypt
d. 254 in Tyre
Source: *BbD; BiD&SB; CasWL; ClMLC 19; OxCEng 67; PenC CL; REn*

Orkin, Ruth
American. Photographer
Her black and white photographs of American street life are in permanent museum collections.
b. Sep 3, 1921 in Boston, Massachusetts
d. Jan 16, 1985 in New York, New York
Source: *ConAu 114, 119; ConPhot 82, 88, 95; ICPEnP A; MacBEP; NewYTBS 85; NorAmWA; WhoAmA 82, 84, 86N, 89N, 91N, 93N*

Orlando, Tony
[Tony Orlando and Dawn; Michael Anthony Orlando Cassavitis]
American. Singer
With Dawn, had biggest selling single, 1973, "Tie a Yellow Ribbon Round the Old Oak Tree."
b. Apr 3, 1944 in New York, New York
Source: *BioIn 10, 11, 12; BioNews 74; BkPepl; ConMus 15; ConTFT 6; EncRk 88; LegTOT; PenEncP; RkOn 74; VarWW 85; WhoAm 78, 80, 82; WhoHisp 94; WorAl; WorAlBi*

Orlando, Vittorio Emanuele
Italian. Judge, Political Leader
Prime minister, 1917-19; represented Italy at Versailles Peace Conference, 1919.
b. May 19, 1860 in Palermo, Sicily, Italy
d. Dec 1, 1952 in Rome, Italy
Source: *BioIn 1, 3; CurBio 44, 53; DcTwHis; LinLib S; REn*

Orleans
American. Music Group
Pop singles include "Love Takes Time," 1979.
Source: *BioIn 1; ConMuA 80A; EncO&P 1; HarEnUS; IlEncRk; InWom; OxCFr; PenEncP; REn; RkOn 78; RolSEnR 83; WhoRock 81; WhoRocM 82*

Orley, Bernard van
Flemish. Artist
Paintings include *Holy Family;* designed stained glass, tapestries.
b. 1491 in Brussels, Belgium
d. Jan 6, 1542 in Brussels, Belgium
Source: *NewCol 75*

Ormandy, Eugene
[Jeno Ormandy Blau]
American. Conductor
One of world's greatest conductors, who led Philadelphia Orchestra 44 yrs., longest of any conductor in US history; won Grammy, 1967.
b. Nov 18, 1899 in Budapest, Austria-Hungary
d. Mar 12, 1985 in Philadelphia, Pennsylvania
Source: *AnObit 1985; ASCAP 66, 80; Baker 78, 84, 92; BiDAmM; BioIn 1, 2, 3, 4, 5, 7, 8, 10, 11, 12, 13, 14, 15, 18; BioNews 74; BlueB 76; BriBkM 80; ConNews 85-2; CurBio 41, 85, 85N;*

DcArts; DcTwCCu 1; IntWW 74, 75, 76, 77, 78, 79, 80, 81, 82, 83; IntWWM 77, 80; LegTOT; LinLib S; MetOEnc; MusMk; MusSN; NewGrDA 86; NewGrDM 80; NewYTBS 85; PenDiMP; RadStar; VarWW 85; WebAB 74, 79; WhAm 8; Who 74, 82, 83, 85; WhoAm 74, 76, 78, 80, 82, 84; WhoAmM 83; WhoE 74, 75, 77, 79, 81, 83; WhoMus 72; WhoWor 74, 78, 80, 82, 84; WorAl; WorAlBi

Ormond, Julia
English. Actor
Played title role in *Sabrina,* 1995.
b. 1965 in Epsom, England
Source: *ConTFT 15; IntMPA 96*

Ornish, Dean
American. Physician
Developed diet program for reversing heart disease, 1988.
b. Jul 16, 1953 in Dallas, Texas
Source: *ConAu 142; CurBio 94; WrDr 96*

Ornitz, Samuel
[The Hollywood Ten]
American. Editor, Author
One of group of screenwriters jailed, 1950, for suspected Communist Party membership.
b. Nov 15, 1890 in New York, New York
d. Mar 11, 1957 in Los Angeles, California
Source: *AmAu&B; BioIn 14, 15, 16; ConAu 117; DcLB 28, 44; EncAL; WhAm 3; WhNAA*

O'Rourke, Jim
[James Henry O'Rourke]
"Orator Jim"
American. Baseball Player
Outfielder, 1876-93, 1904; oldest player ever in NL game; had .310 lifetime batting average; Hall of Fame, 1945.
b. Aug 24, 1852 in Bridgeport, Connecticut
d. Jan 8, 1919 in Bridgeport, Connecticut
Source: *Ballpl 90; BiDAmSp BB; BioIn 3, 7, 14, 15, 16; WhoProB 73*

O'Rourke, P. J
American. Humorist, Editor
Editor, *Nat. Lampoon,* 1973-81; wrote *Parliament of Whores,* 1991.
b. Nov 14, 1947 in Toledo, Ohio
Source: *BioIn 16; ConAu 13NR, 77; IntAu&W 91; WhoAm 88; WhoWest 87; WrDr 92*

Orozco, Jose Clemente
Mexican. Artist
A leader of the Mexican muralist movement; frescoes include *Quetzalcoatl,* 1930s.
b. Nov 23, 1883 in Zapotlan, Mexico
d. Sep 7, 1949 in Mexico City, Mexico
Source: *AtlBL; Benet 87, 96; BioIn 1, 2, 3, 4, 5, 6, 7, 8, 9, 10, 12, 16, 20; ConArt 77, 83; CurBio 40, 49; DcArts; DcHiB; DcTwCCu 4; EncLatA; IntDcAA 90; McGDA; McGEWB; OxCArt; OxCTwCA; OxDcArt; PhDcTCA 77; REn; WhAm 2*

Orpen, William Newneham, Sir
English. Artist
Known for exhibition of war pictures, 1918, in London; wrote *An Onlooker in France,* 1921.
b. Nov 27, 1878 in Stillorgan, Ireland
d. Sep 29, 1931 in London, England
Source: *WhoLA*

Orr, Bobby
[Robert Gordon Orr]
Canadian. Hockey Player
Defenseman, 1966-77, mostly with Boston; revolutionized play of defensemen to more offensive; won Art Ross Trophy twice, Hart Trophy three times, Norris Trophy eight times; Hall of Fame, 1969.
b. Mar 20, 1948 in Parry Sound, Ontario, Canada
Source: *BioIn 7, 8, 9, 10, 11, 12, 14, 15, 16, 17, 20, 21; CanWW 31, 81, 83, 89; CelR; ConAu 112; CurBio 69; HocEn; LegTOT; NewYTBE 71; NewYTBS 76; WhoAm 78, 80, 82, 84, 86, 88, 92, 94, 95, 96, 97; WhoHcky 73; WhoSpor; WorAl; WorAlBi*

Orr, Douglas William
American. Architect
Designed Taft Memorial Tower, Washington, DC; helped renovate White House, 1949-50; pres., American Institute of Architects, 1947-49.
b. Mar 25, 1892 in Meriden, Connecticut
d. Apr 29, 1966 in Stony Creek, Connecticut
Source: *BioIn 7, 10; NatCAB 54; ObitOF 79; WhAm 5*

Orr, Kay Avonne
American. Politician
Rep. governor of Nebraska, 1987-91, defeated by Ben Nelson; first elected Rep. woman governor in US history.
b. Jan 2, 1939 in Burlington, Iowa
Source: *AlmAP 88; ConNews 87-4; NewYTBS 88; WhoAm 84, 86; WhoAmP 87; WhoAmW 85, 87; WhoMW 84*

Orr, Robert Dunkerson
American. Politician
Republican governor of IN, 1981-89.
b. Nov 17, 1917 in Ann Arbor, Michigan
Source: *AlmAP 88; BioIn 13; IntWW 81, 82, 83, 89, 93; WhoAm 76, 78, 80, 82, 84, 86, 88, 90, 92, 96; WhoAmP 73, 75, 77, 79, 81, 83, 85, 87, 89, 93, 95; WhoGov 75, 77; WhoMW 80, 82, 84, 86, 88, 90; WhoWor 82, 87, 89, 91, 93*

Orry-Kelly
American. Fashion Designer
Won Oscars for costumes in *An American in Paris,* 1951; *Some Like It Hot,* 1959.
b. Dec 31, 1897 in Kiama, Australia
d. Feb 26, 1964 in Hollywood, California
Source: *BioIn 6; CmMov; ConDes 84; DcAmB S7; EncFash; FilmEn; FilmgC; HalFC 80, 84, 88; IntDcF 1-4, 2-4; NotNAT B; WhAm 4*

Orser, Brian
Canadian. Skater
Won silver medals, 1984, 1988 Olympics.
b. Dec 18, 1961 in Penetanguishene, Ontario, Canada
Source: *CelR 90*

Ortega, Katherine Davalos
American. Government Official
Thirty-eighth US treasurer, 1983-89.
b. Jul 16, 1934 in Tularosa, New Mexico
Source: *BioIn 13; GrLiveH; NewYTBS 83, 84*

Ortega, Santos
American. Actor
Played in TV soap opera "As the World Turns," 1956-76.
b. 1899 in New York, New York
d. Apr 10, 1976 in Fort Lauderdale, Florida
Source: *BioIn 10*

Ortega Saavedra, Daniel
[Jose Daniel Ortega]
Nicaraguan. Political Leader
Leader of Sandinista revolutionaries; head of State, pres., Nicaragua, 1979-90; succeeded by Violeta Chamorro.
b. Nov 11, 1945 in La Libertad, Nicaragua
Source: *BiDLAmC; BiDMarx; ColdWar 1, 2; CurBio 84; DcCPCAm; DcTwHis; DicTyr; IntWW 89, 93; NewYTBS 84; WhoWor 89, 91, 93, 95*

Ortega y Gasset, Jose
Spanish. Philosopher
Best known for analysis of Western society, *The Revolt of the Masses,* 1930.
b. May 9, 1883 in Madrid, Spain
d. Oct 18, 1955 in Madrid, Spain
Source: *AtlBL; Benet 87, 96; BioIn 1, 2, 3, 4, 5, 7, 9, 11, 12, 13, 14, 15, 16, 17, 18; CasWL; ClDMEL 47, 80; CnMWL; ConAu 106, 130; CyWA 58; DcHiB; DcSpL; EncWL 2, 3; EuWr 9; EvEuW; HispLC; HispWr; LegTOT; LinLib L; LngCTC; MajTwCW; MakMC; McGEWB; ModRL; ModSpP S; ObitT 1951; OxCEng 67, 85, 95; OxCPhil; OxCSpan; PenC EUR; RAdv 14, 13-4; REn; ThTwC 87; TwCA, SUP; TwCLC 9; TwCWr; WhAm 3, 4; WhDW; WorAl; WorAlBi*

Ortelius, Abraham
Flemish. Cartographer
Developed first modern atlas, 1570.
b. Apr 4, 1527 in Antwerp, Belgium
d. Jun 28, 1598 in Antwerp, Belgium
Source: *AntBDN I; BiESc; BioIn 2, 4, 13, 14; DcBiPP; DcNaB; DcScB; InSci;*

McGEWB; NewCol 75; OxCEng 85, 95; OxCShps; WhWE

Ortese, Anna Maria
Italian. Author
Works combine realism and fantasy; author of *The Iguana,* 1965.
b. 1914 in Rome, Italy
Source: *BlmGWL; ConLC 89; DcItL 2*

Ortiz, Alfonso
American. Anthropologist, Educator
Wrote *The Tewa World: Space, Time, Being and Becoming in a Pueblo Society,* 1969.
b. Apr 30, 1939 in San Juan Pueblo, New Mexico
Source: *BioIn 9; NotNaAm*

Ortiz, Peter J(ulien)
American. Military Leader
Marine officer during WW II; subject of films *13 Rue Madeleine,* 1946; *Operation Secret,* 1952.
b. 1913?
d. May 16, 1988 in Prescott, Arizona
Source: *BioIn 7, 8, 12*

Ortiz, Simon
American. Poet
Published collection of verse *Going for the Rain,* 1976.
b. May 27, 1941
Source: *CamGLE; CamHAL; EncNAB; NatNAL; OxCAmL 95*

Orton, Arthur
"Tichborne Claimant"
English. Imposter
Claimed to be heir to Lady Tichborne, 1868; imprisoned, 1870-84.
b. Mar 20, 1834 in London, England
d. Apr 1, 1898 in London, England
Source: *BioIn 2, 4, 9, 10; DcNaB S1; Dis&D; NewC*

Orton, Joe
[John Kingsley Orton]
English. Dramatist
Writings include *Mr. Sloane,* 1964; *What the Butler Saw,* produced in 1969.
b. Jan 1, 1933 in Leicester, England
d. Aug 9, 1967 in London, England
Source: *Benet 87; BioIn 8, 9, 11, 12, 13; BlmGEL; CamGLE; CamGWoT; CnThe; ConAu 25R, 85; ConBrDr; ConDr 77F, 82E, 88E; ConLC 4, 13, 43; CroCD; CrtSuDr; CyWA 89; DcArts; DcLB 13; DcLEL 1940; DcNaB 1961; DramC 3; EncWT; Ent; GayLL; GrBr; GrWrEL DR; IntDcT 2; LegTOT; LngCEL; LngCTC; MajTwCW; MakMC; McGEWD 72, 84; ModBrL S1, S2; ModWD; NotNAT B; OxCEng 85, 95; OxCThe 83; RAdv 14, 13-2; REnWD; RGTwCWr; ScF&FL 92; WebE&AL; WorAl; WorAlBi; WorAu 1970*

Orwell, George
[Eric Arthur Blair]
English. Author, Critic
Wrote *Animal Farm,* 1946; *1984,* 1949.
b. Jun 25, 1903 in Motihari, India
d. Jan 21, 1950 in London, England
Source: *AtlBL; Au&Arts 15; Benet 87, 96; BioIn 1, 2, 3, 4, 5, 6, 7, 8, 9, 10, 11, 12, 13, 14, 15, 17, 18, 19, 21; BlmGEL; BritWr 7; CamGEL; CamGLE; CasWL; CnMWL; CopCroC; CyWA 58, 89; DcAmC; DcAmSR; DcArts; DcLB 15, 98; DcLEL; DcNaB 1941; DcTwHis; EncSF, 93; EncWL, 2, 3; EvLB; GrBr; GrWrEL N; HalFC 80, 84, 88; LegTOT; LiJour; LinLib L; LngCEL; LngCTC; MagSWL; MakMC; McGEWB; ModBrL, S1, S2; NewC; NewCBEL; NewEScF; Novels; OxCEng 67, 85, 95; PenC ENG; RadHan; RAdv 1, 14, 13-1; REn; RGTwCSF; RGTwCWr; ScF&FL 1, 92; ScFSB; ScFWr; SmATA 29; ThTwC 87; TwCA, SUP; TwCLC 2, 6, 15, 31, 51; TwCSFW 81, 86; TwCWr; TwCYAW; WebE&AL; WhAm 4; WhDW; WhoSciF; WhoTwCL; WorAl; WorAlBi; WorLitC*

Orwell, Sonia
[Mrs. George Orwell]
English. Editor, Translator
Translated French play *Days in the Trees;* essayist for *Horizon* mag.
b. 1919?
d. Dec 11, 1980 in London, England
Source: *BioIn 12; ConAu 102*

Ory, Kid
[Edward Ory]
American. Jazz Musician
Noted "tailgate" trombonist; wrote "Muskrat Ramble."
b. Dec 25, 1886 in La Place, Louisiana
d. Jan 23, 1973 in Honolulu, Hawaii
Source: *AfrAmAl 6; AllMusG; ASCAP 66, 80; Baker 84; BiDAfM; BiDAmM; BiDJaz; BioIn 5, 7, 9, 16; CmCal; CmpEPM; ConAu 41R; DcAmB S9; DrBlPA, 90; EncJzS; IlEncJ; InB&W 80, 85; LegTOT; MusMk; NegAl 83, 89; NewGrDA 86; NewGrDM 80; NewOrJ; NewYTBE 73; OxCPMus; PenEncP; WhAm 5; WhoHol B; WhoJazz 72; WhScrn 77; WorAl; WorAlBi*

Osborn, Henry Fairfield
American. Paleontologist
Curator, then president, American Museum of Natural History, NYC, 1891-1933; made "dinosaur" a household word.
b. Aug 8, 1857 in Fairfield, Connecticut
d. Nov 6, 1935 in Garrison, New York
Source: *AmAu&B; AmBi; ApCAB X; BiDAmEd; BiDAmS; BiESc; BioIn 1, 2, 13, 20; ChhPo S1; DcAmAu; DcAmB S1; DcNAA; DcScB; InSci; LarDcSc; LinLib L, S; NatCAB 11, 26; REn; REnAL; TwCBDA; WebAB 74, 79; WhAm 1; WhNAA*

Osborn, Paul
American. Dramatist, Screenwriter
Won Tony for *Morning's at Seven,* 1980; films include *The Yearling,* 1947; *South Pacific,* 1958.
b. Sep 4, 1901 in Evansville, Indiana
d. May 12, 1988 in New York, New York
Source: *AmAu&B; AnObit 1988; BiE&WWA; BioIn 12; BlueB 76; CamGWoT; CnMD; ConAu 108, 112, 125; ConTFT 7; EncWT; FilmEn; IndAu 1917; McGEWD 72, 84; ModWD; NewYTBS 80, 85, 88; NotNAT; OxCAmT 84; WhAm 9; WhNAA; WhoAm 74, 76, 78, 80, 82, 84, 86; WhoThe 72; WhThe; WorAu 1980; WorEFlm*

Osborn, Robert C(hesley)
American. Cartoonist, Caricaturist
Drawings appeared in *Harper's, Fortune, Look,* and others; art reflected social consciousness.
b. Oct 26, 1904
d. Dec 20, 1994 in Salisbury, Connecticut
Source: *AmAu&B; BioIn 1, 3, 5, 7, 8, 12; ConAu 13R; CurBio 95N; IlsBYP; IlsCB 1957; WhAm 11; WhAmArt 85; WhoAm 74, 76, 78, 80, 82, 86, 88, 90, 92, 94, 95; WhoE 86, 93; WhoGrA 62, 82*

Osborne, Adam
American. Computer Executive
Produced Osborne 1 personal computer; wrote *An Introduction to Microcomputers,* 1976.
b. Mar 6, 1939 in Bangkok, Thailand
Source: *AmMWSc 73P; ConAu 109; HisDcDP; LElec; PorSil; WhoFrS 84; WhoTech 84, 89*

Osborne, Joan
American. Singer, Songwriter
Released albums *Soul Show,* 1991; *Blue Million Miles,* 1993; *Relish,* 1995.
b. Jul 8, 1962 in Anchorage, Kentucky
Source: *News 96*

Osborne, John Franklin
American. Editor, Journalist
Columnist, senior editor: *New Republic,* 1968-81; wrote column "Nixon Watch."
b. Mar 15, 1907 in Corinth, Mississippi
d. May 2, 1981 in Washington, District of Columbia
Source: *ConAu 61, 108; WhAm 7; WhoAm 78*

Osborne, John (James)
English. Dramatist, Author
Won 1963 Tony for *Luther;* Oscar for *Tom Jones,* 1978.
b. Dec 12, 1929 in London, England
d. Dec 24, 1994 in Shropshire, England
Source: *Au&Wr 71; Benet 87, 96; BiE&WWA; BioIn 4, 5, 6, 7, 8, 9, 10, 11, 12, 13, 15, 17, 18, 20, 21; BlmGEL; BlueB 76; BritWr S1; CamGEL; CamGLE; CamGWoT; CasWL; CelR; CnMD; CnMWL; CnThe; ConAu 13R,*

21NR, 147; ConBrDr; ConDr 73, 77, 82, 88, 93; ConLC 1, 2, 5, 11, 45, 86; ConTFT 5, 14; CroCD; CrtSuDr; CurBio 95N; CyWA 89; DcArts; DcLB 13; DcLEL 1940; EncWL 2, 3; EncWT; Ent; FilmEn; FilmgC; GrWrEL DR; HalFC 80, 84, 88; IntAu&W 76, 77, 82, 89, 93; IntDcT 2; IntMPA 75, 76, 77, 78, 79, 80, 81, 82, 84, 86, 88, 94; IntWW 74, 75, 76, 77, 78, 79, 80, 81, 82, 83, 89, 93; LegTOT; LinLib L; LngCEL; LngCTC; MagSWL; MajMD 1; MajTwCW; MakMC; McGEWB; McGEWD 72, 84; ModBrL, S1, S2; ModWD; NewC; News 95, 95-2; NewYTBS 94; NotNAT, A; OxCAmT 84; OxCEng 67, 85, 95; OxCFilm; OxCThe 67, 83; PenC ENG; PlP&P; RAdv 14, 13-2; REn; REnWD; RGTwCWr; TwCWr; VarWW 85; WebE&AL; WhAm 11; WhDW; Who 74, 82, 83, 85, 88, 90, 94; WhoAm 74, 76, 78, 80, 82, 84, 86, 88; WhoHol 92, A; WhoThe 72, 77, 81; WhoTwCL; WhoWor 74, 76, 78, 80, 82, 84, 87, 91, 93, 95; WorAl; WorAlBi; WorAu 1950; WorEFlm; WorLitC; WrDr 76, 80, 82, 84, 86, 88, 90, 94, 96

Osborne, Leone Neal
American. Children's Author
Writings include *Than Hoa of Viet-Nam,* 1966.
b. Sep 25, 1914 in Toledo, Oregon
Source: *BioIn 9; ConAu 21R; SmATA 2*

Osborne Brothers, The
American. Music Group
Progressive bluegrass band formed, 1953; hit songs include "Ruby," 1956; "Rocky Top," 1969.
Source: *Baker 84; BgBkCoM; BioIn 7, 11; ConMus 8; CounME 74, 74A; EncFCWM 69, 83; HarEnCM 87; IlEncCM; NewAmDM; NewGrDA 86; NewGrDJ 88, 94; PenEncP; WhoAm 84*

Osbourne, Jeffrey
American. Singer
Had hit single "On the Wings of Love," 1982.
b. Oct 9, 1948 in Providence, Rhode Island
Source: *RkOn 85*

Osbourne, Ozzy
[Black Sabbath; John Michael Osbourne]
English. Singer
Lead singer in heavy-metal band Black Sabbath; known for occult lyrics, bizarre onstage acts.
b. Dec 3, 1948 in Ashton, England
Source: *BioIn 12; ConMus 3; EncRk 88; EncRkSt; HarEnR 86; LegTOT; RolSEnR 83; WhoAm 95, 96, 97; WhoHol 92; WorAlBi*

Osceola
[Osceola Nickanochee; Billy Powell]
American. Native American Leader
Leader during Seminole Wars; attacted US troops successfully for two yrs; tricked, arrested by Gen. Thomas S Jesup.
b. 1804 in Georgia
d. Jan 30, 1838 in Fort Moultrie, South Carolina
Source: *AmBi; ApCAB; BioIn 3, 4, 5, 6, 7, 8, 9, 10, 11, 12, 14, 16, 17, 18, 19, 20; DcAmB; DcAmMiB; EncNoAI; EncSoH; HarEnMi; HarEnUS; HisWorL; LegTOT; NatCAB 9; NotNaAm; WebAB 74, 79; WebAMB; WhAm HS*

Osgood, Charles
[Charles Osgood Wood, III]
American. Broadcast Journalist, Author
CBS News TV, radio correspondent since 1972; host of radio show "The Osgood File," 1981—; co-anchor of the "Morning News;" host of "Sunday Morning," 1994—.
b. Jan 8, 1933 in New York, New York
Source: *BiDAmNC; BioIn 12, 13; ConAu 109; EncTwCJ; News 96, 96-2; VarWW 85; WhoAm 80, 82, 84, 86, 88, 90, 92, 94, 95, 96, 97; WhoE 91; WhoTelC*

Osgood, Frances Sargent Locke
American. Poet
Closely associated with Edgar Allan Poe; wrote *Casket of Fate,* 1840.
b. Jun 18, 1811 in Boston, Massachusetts
d. May 12, 1850 in New York, New York
Source: *AmAu; AmAu&B; AmBi; ApCAB; BbD; BiD&SB; CnDAL; CyAL 2; DcLEL; Drake; NotAW; OxCAmL 83; REnAL; TwCBDA; WhAm HS*

O'Shea, Michael
American. Actor
TV shows include "It's a Great Life," 1954-56; films include *Jack London,* 1943; *Last of the Redmen,* 1947.
b. Mar 17, 1906 in Hartford, Connecticut
d. Dec 1973 in Dallas, Texas
Source: *AmBi; BiE&WWA; BioIn 4, 10; DcAmB; FilmEn; FilmgC; ForYSC; HalFC 80, 84, 88; MotPP; NewYTBE 73; WhAm 1; WhoHol B; WhScrn 77, 83*

O'Shea, Milo
Irish. Actor
Nominated for Tony, 1982, for *Mass Appeal.*
b. Jun 2, 1926 in Dublin, Ireland
Source: *BioIn 12, 13; ConTFT 6; CurBio 82; FilmgC; HalFC 80, 84, 88; IntMPA 88, 94, 96; LegTOT; MovMk; NotNAT; VarWW 85; WhoHol A*

O'Shea, Tessie
English. Comedian
Character actress; films include *Bedknobs and Broomsticks,* 1971.
b. Mar 13, 1918 in Cardiff, Wales
d. Apr 21, 1995 in Leesburg, Florida
Source: *FilmgC; VarWW 85; WhoAm 74; WhoAmW 68, 70, 72; WhoHol A*

O'Sheel, Shaemas
[Shaemas Shields]
American. Author
Best known for poem "They Went Forth to Battle, But They Always Fell."
b. Sep 19, 1886 in New York, New York
d. Apr 2, 1954 in North Tarrytown, New York
Source: *AmAu&B; BioIn 3; ChhPo, S3; CnDAL; OxCAmL 65, 83, 95; REnAL; ScF&FL 1; WhAm 7*

Oshima, Nagisa
Japanese. Film Executive, Director
Produced erotic film *In the Realm of the Senses,* 1976.
b. Mar 31, 1932 in Kyoto, Japan
Source: *BiDFilm, 81, 94; BioIn 10, 12, 13, 15, 16, 21; ConAu 116, 121; ConLC 20; DcArts; DcFM; FarE&A 78, 79, 80, 81; FilmEn; HalFC 88; IntDcF 1-2; IntMPA 94, 96; IntWW 74, 75, 76, 77, 78, 79, 80, 81, 82, 83, 89, 93; JapFilm; MiSFD 9; OxCFilm; VarWW 85; WhoWor 74, 82, 84, 87, 89, 91, 93, 95, 96; WorEFlm; WorFDir 2*

Oshkosh
American. Native American Chief
Chief of the Menominee Tribe, 1827-58; tried to hold ancestral lands and preserve the unity of his tribe.
b. 1795 in Wisconsin
d. Aug 20, 1858 in Keshena, Wisconsin
Source: *BioIn 5, 11; EncNAB; NotNaAm; WhNaAH*

Osler, William, Sir
Canadian. Physician, Educator
Helped develop modern medical practice; wrote *The Principles and Practice of Medicine,* 1882.
b. Jul 12, 1849 in Bondhead, Ontario, Canada
d. Dec 29, 1919 in Oxford, England
Source: *AmAu&B; AmBi; ApCAB; BiESc; BiHiMed; BioIn 1, 2, 3, 4, 5, 6, 7, 8, 9, 11, 13, 14, 16, 17, 18, 20; DcAmAu; DcAmB; DcAmMeB, 84; DcLEL; DcNAA; DcNaB 1912; GrBr; InSci; LarDcSc; LinLib L, S; MacDCB 78; McGEWB; OxCAmH; OxCEng 67, 85, 95; OxCMed 86; PeoHis; RAdv 14; REnAL; VicBrit; WebAB 74, 79; WhAm 1*

Oslin, K(ay) T(oinette)
American. Singer
Country singer; had hit single, gold debut album *80's Ladies,* 1987; won Grammy, 1988.
b. 1942 in Crossett, Arkansas

Osman I
[Othman I]
Turkish. Political Leader
Founded dynasty that ruled Ottoman Empire.
b. 1259, Bithynia
d. 1326 in Sogut, Ottoman Empire
Source: *NewCol 75; WebBD 83*

Osmena, Sergio, Jr.
Philippine. Politician
Served as pres. of the Philippines, 1944-46, after Quezon's death.

b. Sep 9, 1878 in Cebu, Philippines
d. Oct 19, 1961 in Manila, Philippines
Source: *BioIn 1, 2, 6, 9, 12; CurBio 44, 61; LinLib S; McGEWB; WhAm 4; WhWW-II*

Osmond, Donny
[The Osmonds; Donald Clark Osmond]
American. Singer
Co-starred with sister on "Donny & Marie Show," 1976-79; performed with family since age four; launched solo career with album *Donny Osmond,* 1989.
b. Dec 9, 1957 in Ogden, Utah
Source: *BioIn 12, 13; BkPepl; CelR 90; ConMus 3; EncPR&S 74, 89; IntMPA 84, 86, 88, 94, 96; LegTOT; OxCPMus; RkOn 74; VarWW 85; WhoAm 78, 80, 82, 84, 86, 88, 92, 94; WhoHol 92; WorAl; WorAlBi*

Osmond, Ken
American. Actor
Played Eddie Haskell on "Leave It to Beaver," 1957-63.
b. Jun 7, 1943 in Los Angeles, California

Osmond, Marie
[The Osmonds; Olive Marive Osmond]
American. Singer
Co-starred with brother on "Donny & Marie Show," 1976-79; performed with family since age seven; solo albums include *Paper Roses.*
b. Oct 13, 1959 in Ogden, Utah
Source: *BgBkCoM; BioIn 11, 12, 13, 14, 15, 16, 17; BkPepl; CelR 90; ConAu 112; ConTFT 6; EncFCWM 83; EncPR&S 74, 89; IntMPA 79, 80, 81, 82, 84, 86, 88, 94, 96; InWom SUP; LegTOT; OxCPMus; RkOn 74; VarWW 85; WhoAm 78, 80, 82, 84, 86, 88, 90, 92, 94; WhoAmW 89, 91, 93; WhoHol 92; WorAl; WorAlBi; WrDr 94*

Osmonds, The
[Alan Osmond; Donny Osmond; Jay Osmond; Jimmy Osmond; Marie Osmond; Merrill Osmond; Wayne Osmond]
American. Music Group
Vocal, instrumental family group formed, 1959; hits include "Down by the Lazy River," 1972.
Source: *BioIn 10, 16, 17; ConMuA 80A; EncPR&S 74, 89; EncRk 88; EncRkSt; HarEnR 86; LesBEnT; OxCPMus; PenEncP; RkOn 74, 78; RolSEnR 83*

Ospina Perez, Mariano
Colombian. Political Leader
President of Colombia, 1946-50; led Conservatives for 30 years.
b. Nov 24, 1891 in Medellin, Colombia
d. Apr 14, 1976 in Bogota, Colombia
Source: *BiDLAmC; BioIn 2, 10, 11, 16; CurBio 50, 76, 76N; EncLatA; NewYTBS 76*

Ossietzky, Carl von
German. Journalist
Won Nobel Peace Prize, 1935; prevented from accepting it by Hitler's decree.
b. Oct 3, 1889 in Hamburg, Germany
d. May 4, 1938 in Berlin, Germany
Source: *BiDMoPL; BioIn 1, 3, 5, 9, 11, 14, 15; EncGRNM; EncTR; NobelP; OxCGer 76, 86; PenC EUR; WhDW; WhoNob, 95*

Ostade, Adriaen van
Dutch. Artist
Genre painter of peasant life; among 1000 oils: *Cottage Dooryard,* 1640s.
b. Dec 10, 1610 in Haarlem, Netherlands
d. May 2, 1685 in Haarlem, Netherlands
Source: *AtlBL; BioIn 19; ClaDrA; DcArts; McGDA; NewCol 75; OxCArt; OxDcArt*

Ostenso, Martha
American. Author
Writings include *A Far Land,* 1924; *A Man Had Tall Sons,* 1958.
b. Sep 17, 1900 in Bergen, Norway
d. Nov 24, 1963
Source: *AmAu&B; AmNov; AmWomWr SUP; ArtclWW 2; BioIn 1, 2, 4, 6, 13, 17; BlmGWL; CanNov; CanWr; ChhPo S1; CnDAL; ConAmL; ConAu P-1; ConCaAu 1; CreCan 1; DcLB 92; FemiCLE; InWom, SUP; LinLib L; MinnWr; OxCAmL 65, 83, 95; OxCCan; OxCCanL; PeoHis; REnAL; TwCA, SUP; TwCWW 82; WhAm 4; WhE&EA; WhNAA; WhoAmW 58*

Osterwald, Bibi
[Margaret Virginia Osterwald]
American. Actor
Played in TV series "Bridget Loves Bernie," 1972; films include *Tiger Makes Out,* 1967.
b. Feb 3, 1920 in New Brunswick, New Jersey
Source: *BiE&WWA; ConTFT 6; ForWC 70; LegTOT; NotNAT; VarWW 85; WhoAm 74, 76, 78, 80, 82, 84, 86; WhoAmW 74; WhoHol 92, A; WhoThe 72, 77, 81*

Ostin, Mo
[Morris Meyer Ostrofsky]
American. Record Company Executive
Chairman/CEO, Warner Bros. Reprise Records, 1969-94; head of DreamWorks SKG Records, 1995—.
b. Mar 27, 1927 in New York, New York
Source: *ConMus 17; News 96, 96-2*

Ostrovsky, Aleksandr Nikolaevich
Russian. Dramatist
Satirical, realistic plays include *The Forest,* 1871; *The Snow Maiden,* 1800s.
b. Apr 12, 1823 in Moscow, Russia
d. May 28, 1886 in Moscow, Russia
Source: *BiD&SB; CamGWoT; CasWL; CnThe; EuAu; EvEuW; HanRL; McGEWD 72; PenC EUR; REnWD*

Ostwald, Friedrich Wilhelm
German. Chemist
One of the founders of physical chemistry; won 1909 Nobel Prize for work on catalysis.
b. Sep 2, 1853 in Riga, Russia
d. Apr 4, 1932 in Leipzig, Germany
Source: *AsBiEn; BiESc; BioIn 6, 9, 14, 15, 19, 20; CamDcSc; DcScB, S1; NotTwCS; WhoNob, 95; WorAl; WorScD*

O'Sullivan, Gilbert
[Raymond Edward O'Sullivan]
Irish. Singer
Had two hits, 1972: "Alone Again (Naturally);" "Clair."
b. Dec 1, 1946 in Waterford, Ireland
Source: *BioIn 14; EncRk 88; EncRkSt; LegTOT; PenEncP; RkOn 78, 84; RolSEnR 83*

O'Sullivan, John
English. Business Executive, Editor
Editor, US conservative magazine *National Review,* 1988—.
b. Apr 25, 1942 in Liverpool, England
Source: *AmMWSc 79, 82, 86, 89, 95; ConAu 132; IntWW 89, 93; Who 92; WhoAm 92, 97*

O'Sullivan, Maureen
American. Actor
Played Jane in Johnny Weissmuller's Tarzan films; appeared in *Hannah and Her Sisters,* 1986; mother of Mia Farrow.
b. May 17, 1911 in Boyle, Ireland
Source: *BiE&WWA; CmMov; ConTFT 3; EncAFC; FilmEn; FilmgC; ForYSC; HalFC 80, 84, 88; IntDcF 1-3, 2-3; IntMPA 77, 82, 84, 86, 88, 94, 96; InWom, SUP; LegTOT; MGM; MotPP; MovMk; OxCFilm; ThFT; WhoAm 84, 92; WhoHol 92, A; WhoHrs 80; WorAl; WorAlBi; WorEFlm*

O'Sullivan, Timothy H
American. Photographer
Student of Mathew Brady, known for Civil War, western landscape photographs.
b. 1840 in New York, New York
d. Jan 14, 1882 in Staten Island, New York
Source: *BriEAA; DcAmArt; MacBEP; NewCol 75; WebAB 74*

Oswald, Lee Harvey
American. Assassin
Allegedly shot John Kennedy, Nov 22, 1963; killed two days later by Jack Ruby.
b. Oct 18, 1939 in New Orleans, Louisiana
d. Nov 24, 1963 in Dallas, Texas
Source: *BioIn 6, 7, 8, 9, 10, 11, 12, 13; DcAmB S7; EncAB-H 1996; LegTOT; NewCol 75; PeoHis; PolProf K; WorAl; WorAlBi*

Oswald, Marina Nikolaevna
[Mrs. Ken Porter; Marina Nikolaevna Pruskova]
Russian.
Wife of Lee Harvey Oswald at time he allegedly killed John Kennedy.
b. Jul 17, 1941 in Moltovsk, Russia
Source: *BioIn 6, 7, 8, 9, 10, 11; InWom*

Otis, Elisha Graves
American. Inventor, Manufacturer
Developed first passenger elevator, 1857.
b. Aug 3, 1811 in Halifax, Vermont
d. Apr 8, 1861 in Yonkers, New York
Source: *AmBi; ApCAB; AsBiEn; BiDAmBL 83; BioIn 3, 6, 7, 9, 11, 15, 18, 21; DcAmB; LinLib S; MacEA; McGEWB; NatCAB 11; NewCol 75; OxCAmH; WebAB 74, 79; WhAm HS; WhDW; WorAl; WorAlBi; WorInv*

Otis, James
American. Colonial Figure, Author
Wrote pamphlets which set basis for US political theory on national law: *In a Letter to a Noble Lord.*
b. Feb 5, 1725 in West Barnstable, Massachusetts
d. May 23, 1783 in Andover, Massachusetts
Source: *Alli; AmAu; AmAu&B; AmBi; AmOrN; AmWrBE; ApCAB; BiAUS; BiD&SB; BioIn 5, 7, 8, 9, 10, 12, 14, 15, 19; CyAG; CyAL 1; DcAmAu; DcAmB; DcAmSR; DcLB 31; DcLEL; DcNAA; Drake; EncAB-H 1974, 1996; EncAR; EncCRAm; EncPaPR 91; EncRev; HarEnUS; LinLib L, S; McGEWB; NatCAB 1; OxCAmH; OxCAmL 65, 83, 95; REnAL; TwCBDA; WebAB 74, 79; WhAm HS; WhAmRev; WhDW; WorAl; WorAlBi*

O'Toole, Peter Seamus
Irish. Actor
Won international fame for portrayal of T E Lawrence in award-winning film *Lawrence of Arabia,* 1962.
b. Aug 2, 1932 in County Galway, Ireland
Source: *BkPepl; ConTFT 4; CurBio 68; FilmgC; IntWW 76, 77, 78, 79, 80, 81, 82, 83, 89, 93; MotPP; MovMk; NewC; NewYTBS 83; VarWW 85; Who 94; WhoAm 86; WhoHol A; WhoThe 81; WorEFlm*

Ott, David Lee
American. Composer
Orchestral, choral pieces exhibit strong melodies: *DodecaCelli,* 1988; honors include several Pulitzer Prize nominations.
b. Jul 5, 1947 in Crystal Falls, Michigan
Source: *WhoEnt 92*

Ott, Mel(vin Thomas)
"Master Melvin"
American. Baseball Player
Outfielder, NY Giants, 1926-47; led NL in home runs six times; had 511 career home runs; Hall of Fame, 1951.
b. Mar 2, 1909 in Gretna, Louisiana
d. Nov 21, 1958 in New Orleans, Louisiana
Source: *Ballpl 90; BiDAmSp BB; BioIn 2, 3, 5, 6, 7, 8, 9, 10, 14, 15, 16, 17; CurBio 41, 59; DcAmB S6; LegTOT; NewYTBE 70; WhoProB 73; WorAl; WorAlBi*

Ottaviani, Alfredo, Cardinal
Italian. Religious Leader
Spokesman for ultra-orthodox wing of church during Vatican II Council, 1962-65.
b. Oct 29, 1890 in Rome, Italy
d. Aug 3, 1979, Vatican City
Source: *BioIn 3, 6, 7, 8, 12, 14; CurBio 64, 79, 79N; IntWW 74, 75, 76, 77, 78, 79; NewYTBS 79*

Otter, Anne Sofie von
Swedish. Singer
Played Octavian in Wagner's *Der Rosenkavalier,* and Cherubino in Mozart's *The Marriage of Figaro,.*
b. May 9, 1955 in Stockholm, Sweden
Source: *Baker 92; BioIn 21; CurBio 95; IntWWM 90*

Ottey, Merlene
Jamaican. Track Athlete
Set a world record of 6.96 seconds for the women's 60 meters on Feb 14, 1992.

Otto, Jim
[James Otto]
American. Football Player
Center, Oakland, 1959-74; Hall of Fame, 1980.
b. Jan 5, 1938 in Wausau, Wisconsin
Source: *BioIn 6, 12, 17; CmCal; LegTOT; NewYTBS 81; WhoFtbl 74; WhoSpor*

Otto, Kristin
German. Swimmer
Won six gold medals, 1988 Olympics, more than any other female swimmer.
b. Feb 7, 1965 in Leipzig, German Democratic Republic

Otto, Nikolaus August
German. Engineer
Co-inventor of first practical internal combustion engine that ran on coal gas, 1867.
b. Jun 10, 1832 in Holzhausen, Germany
d. Jan 26, 1891 in Cologne, Germany
Source: *AsBiEn; BioIn 6, 8, 12, 13; CamDcSc; InSci; LarDcSc; NewCol 75; WebBD 83; WhDW; WorAl; WorAlBi; WorInv*

Otto, Whitney
American. Author
Wrote *How to Make an American Quilt,* 1990.
b. Mar 5, 1955 in Burbank, California
Source: *ConAu 140; ConLC 70; WrDr 96*

Otway, Thomas
English. Poet, Dramatist
One of the first creators of sentimental drama.
b. Mar 3, 1652 in Trotton, England
d. Apr 14, 1685 in London, England
Source: *Alli; BbD; Benet 87, 96; BiD&SB; BioIn 3, 5, 8, 9, 12, 13; BlmGEL; BritAu; CamGEL; CamGLE; CamGWoT; CasWL; Chambr 2; ChhPo, S1; CnThe; CrtSuDr; CrtT 2; CyWA 58; DcArts; DcEnA; DcEnL; DcEuL; DcLB 80; DcLEL; DcNaB; EncWT; Ent; EvLB; GrWrEL DR; IntDcT 2; LinLib L; LngCEL; McGEWD 72, 84; MouLC 1; NewC; NewCBEL; NotNAT B; OxCEng 67, 85, 95; OxCThe 67, 83; PenC ENG; PlP&P; RAdv 14, 13-2; REn; REnWD; RfGEnL 91; WebE&AL; WhDW*

Oudry, Jean-Baptiste
French. Artist
One of the foremost 18th c. animal painters; also known for his tapestry designs.
b. Mar 17, 1686 in Paris, France
d. Apr 30, 1755 in Beauvais, France
Source: *BioIn 11, 12, 13, 14; ClaDrA; EncEnl; McGDA; OxCArt; OxCDecA; OxDcArt; PenDiDA 89*

Ouedraogo, Idrissa
Burkinabe. Filmmaker
Films realistically portray life in Burkina Faso, have been commercially released in U.S.: *Yaaba,* 1989; *Tilai,* 1990.
b. 1954? in Banfora, Upper Volta
Source: *CurBio 93; MiSFD 9; WhoWor 95, 96, 97*

Oughtred, William
English. Inventor, Mathematician
Invented slide rule, 1622; introduced multiplication sign, 1631.
b. Mar 5, 1575 in Eton, England
d. Jun 30, 1660 in Albury, England
Source: *Alli; AsBiEn; BiESc; BioIn 2, 3; CyEd; DcNaB; DcScB; LarDcSc; WebBD 83; WhDW; WorAl; WorAlBi*

Ouida
[Marie Louise de la Ramee]
English. Author
Novels are noted for romance, fashionable life: *A Dog of Flanders,* 1872.
b. Jan 1, 1839 in Bury Saint Edmunds, England
d. Jan 25, 1908 in Viareggio, Italy
Source: *ArtclWW 2; BbD; BiD&SB; BlmGEL; BlmGWL; BritAu 19; CamGEL; CamGLE; CasWL; Chambr 3; ContDcW 89; CyWA 58; DcArts; DcBiA; DcEnA, A; DcEnL; DcEuL; DcLB 18, 156; DcLEL; EncBrWW; EvLB; FemiCLE; GrWrEL N; HalFC 84, 88; HsB&A; IntDcWB; InWom, SUP; JBA 34; LegTOT; LngCTC; NewC; NewCBEL; Novels; OxCChiL; OxCEng 67, 85, 95; PenC ENG; PenNWW B; REn; StaCVF; VicBrit*

Ouimet, Francis de Sales
American. Golfer
Won US Open as amateur, 1913, known for putting; helped make golf popular in US.
b. May 8, 1893 in Brookline, Massachusetts
d. Sep 2, 1967 in Newton, Massachusetts
Source: *NatCAB 53; WhoGolf*

Ouray
American. Native American Leader
Known for his treaty negotiating skills; negotiated several treaties including on which relocated the White River and Uncompahgre Utes to Utah, 1880.
b. 1833? in Taos, New Mexico
d. Aug 27, 1880 in Utah
Source: *BioIn 3, 11, 13, 15, 21; DcAmB; NotNaAm; WhAm HS*

Our Gang
[The Little Rascals; Matthew (Stymie) Beard; Tommy (Butch) Bond; Norman (Chubby) Chaney; Joe (Fat Joe; Wheezer) Cobb; Jackie Condon; Jackie Cooper; Mickey Daniels; Mickey Gubitosi; Scott Hastings; Darla Jean Hood; Allen Clayton (Farina) Hoskins; Bobby (Wheezer) Hutchins; Mary Ann Jackson; Dearwood (Waldo) Kaye; Mary Kornman; Eugene (Porky) Lee; "Spanky" (George Emmett) McFarland; Dickie Moore; Carl (Alfalfa) Switzer; Billy (Buckwheat) Thomas]
Americans. Child Actors
Highly popular children's film comedy group, 1930s-40s; syndicated TV reruns continue today.
Source: *BioIn 12, 19; EncAFC; Film 1, 2; HalFC 80, 88; InWom SUP; LesBEnT, 92; MotPP; NewYTBS 80, 81; NewYTET; NotNAT; WhoCom; WhoHol 92, A*

Oursler, (Charles) Fulton
[Anthony Abbott]
American. Journalist, Author, Dramatist
Wrote religious novel *The Greatest Story Ever Told,* 1949; filmed, 1965.
b. Jan 22, 1893 in Baltimore, Maryland
d. May 24, 1952 in New York, New York
Source: *AmAu&B; AuBYP 2, 3; BioIn 1, 2, 3, 4, 6, 7, 8, 14, 17; CathA 1930; ConAu 108; CurBio 42, 52; DcAmB S5; DcAmC; DcCathB; DcSpL; EncAJ; EncPaPR 91; NatCAB 45; NotNAT B; REn; REnAL; ScF&FL 1; TwCA SUP; TwCCr&M 80; TwCSAPR; WhAm 3; WhE&EA; WhNAA*

Oursler, Will(iam Charles)
[Gale Gallager; Nick Marine]
American. Author
Writings include *The Trail of Vincent Doon,* 1941; *One Way Street,* 1952.
b. Jul 12, 1913 in Baltimore, Maryland
d. Jan 7, 1985 in New York, New York
Source: *AmAu&B; BiDPara; BioIn 5, 7, 14; ConAu 2NR, 5R, 115; EncO&P 1, 2, 3; NewYTBS 85; WhAm 8; WhoAm 74, 76, 78, 80, 82, 84; WhoWor 74, 76, 78, 80, 82*

Ouspenskaya, Maria
Russian. Actor
Oscar nominee for *Dodsworth,* 1936; *Love Affair,* 1939.
b. Jul 29, 1876 in Tula, Russia
d. Dec 3, 1949 in Los Angeles, California
Source: *BioIn 2, 21; Film 1, 2; FilmEn; FilmgC; ForYSC; HalFC 80, 84, 88; HolCA; IntDcF 1-3; InWom SUP; LegTOT; MotPP; MovMk; NotNAT B; OlFamFa; PlP&P; ThFT; Vers A; WhoHol B; WhoHrs 80; WhScrn 74, 77, 83; WhThe; WorAl; WorAlBi; WorEFlm*

Outcault, Richard Felton
American. Cartoonist
Best known for characters "Yellow Kid"; "Buster Brown."
b. Jan 14, 1863 in Lancaster, Ohio
d. Sep 25, 1928 in Flushing, New York
Source: *AmAu&B; BioIn 3, 15, 16, 21; DcAmB; DcNAA; JrnUS; LinLib L; NatCAB 22; OhA&B; REnAL; WebAB 74, 79; WhAm 1; WorECom*

Outlaws, The
[Harvey Dalton Arnold; Rick Cua; David Dix; Billy Jones; Henry Paul; Hughie Thomasson; Monte Yoho]
American. Music Group
Merged country rock with Southern rock; hit single "(Ghost) Riders in the Sky," 1980.
Source: *BioIn 5; ConMuA 80A; CurBio 41; HarEnR 86; IlEncRk; OnThGG; PenEncP; RkOn 85, 85A; RolSEnR 83; WhoAmP 87, 89, 91; WhoHol 92; WhoRocM 82*

Ovando Candia, Alfredo
Bolivian. Political Leader
Organized 1967 military offensive against Che Guevara's forces; pres. of Bolivia, 1969-70.
b. Apr 6, 1918 in Coboja, Bolivia
d. Jan 24, 1982 in La Paz, Bolivia
Source: *BioIn 8, 9, 12, 13, 16; CurBio 82; EncLatA; IntWW 74, 75, 76, 77, 78, 79, 80, 81, 82; WhoWor 74*

Overman, Lynne
American. Actor
Character actor in films *Midnight,* 1934; *Reap the Wild Wind,* 1942.
b. Sep 19, 1887 in Maryville, Missouri
d. Feb 19, 1943 in Santa Monica, California
Source: *CmMov; CurBio 43; EncAFC; FilmEn; FilmgC; ForYSC; HalFC 80, 84, 88; HolCA; MovMk; NotNAT B; Vers B; WhoHol B; WhoThe 81; WhScrn 74, 77, 83; WhThe*

Overstreet, Bonaro Wilkinson
American. Author
Writings include *Search for a Self,* 1938; *The Iron Curtain,* 1963.
b. Oct 30, 1902 in Geyserville, California
d. Sep 10, 1985 in Arlington, Virginia
Source: *AmAu&B; Au&Wr 71; WhNAA; WhoAm 74, 76, 78, 80, 82, 84; WhoAmW 61, 64, 66, 68, 70, 72, 74, 75, 77, 81, 83; WhoSSW 73, 75, 76; WhoWor 74, 78*

Ovett, Steve
English. Track Athlete
Held world record in mile, 1981; broken by Sebastian Coe two days later.
b. Aug 9, 1955 in Brighton, England
Source: *BioIn 12*

Ovid
[Publius Ovidius Naso]
Roman. Poet
Noted works include *The Art of Love; Metamorphoses.*
b. Mar 20, 43BC in Sulmona, Italy
d. Jan 2, 17AD in Tomi, Dacia
Source: *AncWr; AtlBL; BbD; Benet 87; BiD&SB; BioIn 4, 5, 6, 7, 9, 10, 11, 13, 15, 20; BlmGEL; CasWL; DcArts; DcEnL; DcEuL; Dis&D; GrFLW; Grk&L; LegTOT; LinLib L, S; LngCEL; MagSWL; McGEWB; NewC; NewGrDM 80; NewGrDO; OxCClL, 89; OxCEng 67, 85, 95; OxDcByz; PenC CL; PoeCrit 2; RAdv 14, 13-2; RComWL; REn; RfGWoL 95; WhDW; WorAl; WorAlBi*

Ovington, Mary White
American. Social Reformer
White social worker, a founder of NAACP, 1908; board chm., 1919-32.
b. Apr 11, 1865 in New York, New York
d. Jul 15, 1951 in Newton Highlands, Massachusetts
Source: *AmAu&B; AmWomPl; AmWomWr; BiDAmLf; BiDSocW; BioIn 1, 2, 12, 21; BlkWrNE; EncAACR; EncWB; InWom SUP; NotAW MOD; WhAm 3; WomNov*

Ovitz, Michael S.
American. Agent, Business Executive
Co-founder, Creative Arts Agency, 1975-95; talent agency that caters to an elite celebrity clientele; helped create "Tele-TV," 1994; president, Walt Disney Co., 1995-96.
b. Dec 14, 1946 in Encino, California
Source: *BioIn 16; CurBio 95; IntWW 91; News 90-1; NewYTBS 89; WhoAm 90, 94, 95, 96, 97; WhoEnt 92*

Owado, Masako
Japanese.
Married Crown Prince Naruhito of Japan, 1993.
b. 1964, Japan

Owen, David Anthony Llewellyn
English. Politician
Britain's foreign secretary, 1977-79; co-founder, British Social Dem. Party, 1981.
b. Jul 2, 1938 in Plympton, England

Source: *BioIn 11, 13; ColdWar 2; IntWW 91; NewYTBS 77; Who 90, 92; WhoWor 91, 97*

Owen, Guy, Jr.
American. Author
Writings include *The Flim-Flam Man and Other Stories,* 1980.
b. Feb 24, 1925 in Clarkton, North Carolina
d. Jul 23, 1981 in Raleigh, North Carolina
Source: *AnObit 1981; BioIn 12, 13, 20; ConAu 1R, 3NR, 104; ConNov 76, 82; DcLB 5; DrAF 76; DrAP 75; DrAPF 80; DrAS 74E, 78E, 82E; IntAu&W 82; SouWr; WhAm 8; WhoAm 82; WhoSSW 73, 80; WrDr 76, 80, 82, 84*

Owen, Lewis James
American. Educator
Writings on stock market include *Washington's Final Victory,* 1967.
b. Apr 2, 1925 in Nanjing, China
Source: *Alli; DrAS 74E; WhoAm 74, 76, 78, 80, 82, 84, 86*

Owen, Mickey
[Arnold Malcolm Owen]
American. Baseball Player
Catcher, 1937-45, 1949-51, 1954; set NL record by not committing error in 100 straight games, 1941, but remembered for mistake that cost Brooklyn 1941 World Series.
b. Apr 4, 1916 in Nixa, Missouri
Source: *Ballpl 90; LegTOT; WhoProB 73*

Owen, (John) Reginald
English. Actor
Only actor to play both Dr. Watson in *Sherlock Holmes,* 1932, Sherlock Holmes in *A Study in Scarlet,* 1933.
b. Aug 5, 1887 in Wheathampstead, England
d. Nov 5, 1972 in Boise, Idaho
Source: *BiE&WWA; BioIn 9, 16, 21; ConAu 37R; EncAFC; Film 2; FilmEn; FilmgC; ForYSC; HalFC 80, 84, 88; HolCA; LegTOT; MGM; MotPP; MovMk; NewYTBE 72; NotNAT B; OlFamFa; PlP&P; Vers A; WhoHol B; WhScrn 77, 83; WhThe; WorAl*

Owen, Richard, Sir
English. Zoologist
Headed British Museum's natural history dept., 1856-84; opposed Darwin; wrote *On Anatomy of Vertebrates,* 1868.
b. Jul 20, 1804 in Lancaster, England
d. Dec 18, 1891 in London, England
Source: *Alli, SUP; AsBiEn; BiD&SB; BiESc; BioIn 3, 7, 8, 14, 20; BritAu 19; CelCen; Chambr 3; DcBiPP; DcEnL; DcNaB; DcScB; InSci; LarDcSc; LinLib S; McGEWB; NewCol 75; OxCEng 67, 85, 95; OxCMed 86; WhDW; WorAlBi*

Owen, Richard Lee, II
American. Criminal
Self-taught lawyer who publishes *Criminal Law Review.*
b. 1946?
Source: *BioIn 12*

Owen, Robert
Welsh. Manufacturer, Social Reformer
Wrote *New View of Society,* 1813; founded co-operative community of New Harmony, IN, 1825.
b. May 14, 1771 in Newtown, Wales
d. Nov 17, 1858 in Newtown, Wales
Source: *Alli, SUP; AmRef; ApCAB; Benet 87, 96; BiDAmLf; BiD&SB; BiDLA SUP; BiDTran; BioIn 2, 3, 4, 5, 6, 7, 8, 9, 10, 11, 14, 15, 16, 17, 20, 21; BlmGEL; BritAu 19; CamGLE; CasWL; CelCen; CyEd; DcAmSR; DcBiPP; DcEnL; DcLB 158; DcLEL; DcNaB; Drake; EncO&P 1, 2, 3; EncUnb; EncUrb; EvLB; GrEconB; HarEnUS; LinLib L, S; LngCEL; LuthC 75; NewC; NewCBEL; OxCAmH; OxCAmL 65, 83, 95; OxCEng 67, 85, 95; OxCLiW 86; RadHan; REn; WhDW; WhoEc 81, 86; WorAl; WorAlBi*

Owen, Robert Dale
American. Social Reformer, Author
Sponsored bill founding Smithsonian Institute; son of Robert.
b. Nov 8, 1801 in Glasgow, Scotland
d. Jun 24, 1877 in Lake George, New York
Source: *Alli, SUP; AmAu; AmAu&B; AmBi; AmSocL; BbD; BiAUS; BiDAmCu; BiDAmL; BiDAmLf; BiDAmLL; BiD&SB; BiDrUSC 89; BioIn 2, 6, 10, 11, 14, 19; ChhPo S2; CyAL 2; DcAmAu; DcAmB; DcAmSR; DcEnL; DcNAA; DcNaB; Drake; EncARH; EncO&P 1, 2, 3; EncPaPR 91; EncUnb; HarEnUS; IndAu 1816; LuthC 75; McGEWB; NewCBEL; OxCAmH; OxCAmL 83; REnAL; TwCBDA; WebAB 74, 79; WhAm HS; WorAl; WorAlBi*

Owen, Steve
[Stephen Joseph Owen]
"Stout Steve"
American. Football Coach
Head coach, NY Giants, 1933-53, with 151-100-17 record; pioneered many coaching strategies including A-formation, umbrella defense; Hall of Fame, 1966.
b. Apr 21, 1898 in Cleo Springs, Oklahoma
d. May 17, 1964 in Oneida, New York
Source: *BiDAmSp FB; BioIn 1, 6, 7, 8, 17; CurBio 46, 64; DcAmB S7; LegTOT; ObitOF 79; WhoSpor*

Owen, Tobias Chant
American. Physicist
With NASA during outer planet probes, 1970s: *Voyager* to outer planets, 1972.
b. Mar 20, 1936 in Oshkosh, Wisconsin
Source: *AmMWSc 73P, 76P, 79, 82, 86, 89, 95; ConAu 29NR, 111; WhoAm 84, 86, 88, 90; WhoE 83, 85, 86; WhoFrS 84*

Owen, Wilfred
English. Poet
Wrote about his hatred of war; best-known poem: *Strange Meeting.*
b. Mar 18, 1893 in Oswestry, England
d. Nov 4, 1918 in Landrecies, France
Source: *AtlBL; Benet 87, 96; BioIn 2, 3, 4, 5, 6, 7, 8, 9, 10, 11, 12, 13; BlmGEL; BritWr 6; CamGEL; CamGLE; ChhPo, S1, S2; CnE&AP; CnMWL; ConAu 104; DcArts; DcLB 20; DcLEL; EncWL 2, 3; EvLB; GrWrEL P; LinLib L; LngCEL; LngCTC; MagSWL; MakMC; ModBrL, S1, S2; NewC; NewCBEL; OxCEng 67, 95; PenC ENG; RAdv 1, 14, 13-1; REn; RGFMBP; TwCA, SUP; TwCLC 5, 27; TwCWr; WebE&AL; WhDW; WhoTwCL; WorAl; WorAlBi; WorLitC*

Owens, Buck
[Alvis Edgar Owens, Jr]
American. Singer, Musician
Co-hosted long-running country music variety TV show "Hee Haw," 1969-85; proponent of "honky-tonk Bakersfield Sound."
b. Aug 12, 1929 in Sherman, Texas
Source: *Baker 84, 92; BgBkCoM; BioIn 12, 14, 15, 16; CelR; ConMus 2; CounME 74, 74A; EncFCWM 69, 83; HarEnCM 87; IlEncCM; LegTOT; NewGrDA 86; PenEncP; WhoAm 76, 78, 80, 82, 84, 86, 88, 90, 92, 94, 95, 96, 97; WhoWest 76, 78, 89; WorAl; WorAlBi*

Owens, Gary
American. Actor
Featured in TV series "Laugh-In," 1968-73.
b. May 10, 1935 in Mitchell, South Dakota
Source: *VarWW 85*

Owens, Harry
American. Bandleader
Known for radio show, 1930s; song "Sweet Leilani," 1934, won two Oscars.
b. Apr 18, 1902 in O'Neill, Nebraska
d. Dec 12, 1986 in Eugene, Oregon
Source: *ASCAP 66; BgBands 74; BioIn 9, 15; CmpEPM; NewYTBS 86; OxCPMus; RadStar*

Owens, Jesse
[James Cleveland Owens]
American. Track Athlete
Won four gold medals, 1936 Olympics; has received numerous awards.
b. Sep 12, 1913 in Danville, Alabama
d. Mar 31, 1980 in Tucson, Arizona
Source: *AfrAmAl 6; AfrAmBi 1; AfrAmSG; AmDec 1930; AnObit 1980; BiDAmSp OS; BioIn 3, 4, 5, 6, 7, 8, 9, 10, 11, 12, 13, 14, 15, 16, 17, 18, 21; BioNews 74; ConAu 97, 110; ConHero 2; CurBio 56, 80, 80N; DcAmB S10; DcTwCCu 5; Ebony 1; EncAACR; EncAB-H 1996; HeroCon; InB&W 80,*

85; LegTOT; McGEWB; NegAl 76, 83, 89; NewYTBS 80; SelBAAf; SelBAAu; St&PR 75; WebAB 74, 79; WhAm 7; What 1; WhDW; WhoAm 76, 78, 80; WhoBlA 75, 77; WhoSpor; WhScrn 83; WorAl; WorAlBi

Owens, Major (Robert)
American. Librarian, Politician, Writer
Became first librarian to serve in the U.S. House of Representatives, representing New York, 1983—.
b. Jun 28, 1936 in Memphis, Tennessee
Source: *AfrAmBi 1; ConBlB 6; NegAl 89A*

Owens, Michael Joseph
American. Manufacturer
Revolutionized glass industry with invention of Owens automatic bottling machine, 1895.
b. Jan 1, 1859 in Mason County, Virginia
d. Dec 27, 1923 in Toledo, Ohio
Source: *ApCAB X; BioIn 1, 7, 8; DcAmB; NatCAB 13, 28; WhAm 1*

Owens, Rochelle
[Rochelle Bass]
American. Dramatist, Poet
Writings include *The String Game,* 1965; *He Wants Shih,* 1972; won Obie for *Futz,* 1968.
b. Apr 2, 1936 in New York, New York
Source: *AmWomD; AmWomWr, SUP; ASCAP 80; BioIn 9, 10, 15, 16; CamGWoT; ConAmD; ConAu 2AS, 17R, 39NR; ConDr 73, 77, 82, 88, 93; ConLC 8; ConPo 70, 75, 80, 85, 96; ConTFT 5; ConWomD; CroCD; CrtSuDr; DrAP 75; DrAPF 80; EncWT; FemiCLE; ForWC 70; IntAu&W 76, 77, 82; IntWWP 82; InWom SUP; McGEWD 84; ModWoWr; MugS; NatPD 77, 81; NotNAT; NotWoAT; PlP&P; WhoAm 74, 76, 78, 80, 82, 84, 86, 88, 90, 92, 94, 95, 96, 97; WhoAmW 83; WhoThe 72, 77, 81; WhoUSWr 88; WhoWrEP 89, 92, 95; WorAu 1970; WrDr 76, 80, 82, 84, 86, 88, 90, 94, 96*

Owens, Steve E
American. Football Player
Fullback, won Heisman Trophy, 1969; in NFL with Detroit, 1970-75.
b. Dec 9, 1947 in Gore, Oklahoma
Source: *WhoAm 76; WhoFtbl 74*

Owings, Nathaniel Alexander
American. Architect
His Lever House in Manhattan set style for office building, 1960s; also designed Sears Tower, Chicago, 1975.
b. Feb 5, 1903 in Indianapolis, Indiana
d. Jun 13, 1984 in Jacona, New Mexico
Source: *AmCulL; BioIn 8, 9, 12, 13, 14, 19; BlueB 76; ConArch 87, 94; ConAu 61, 113; CurBio 71; IndAu 1967; IntWW 74, 75, 76, 77, 78, 79, 80, 81, 82, 83; St&PR 75; WhAm 9; WhoAm 74, 76, 78, 80, 82; WhoFI 74; WhoGov 72; WhoWest 74, 76, 78; WhoWor 74*

Owsley, Frank Lawrence
American. Historian
Wrote Confederate American history: *Plain Folks of the Old South,* 1949.
b. Jan 20, 1890 in Montgomery County, Alabama
d. Oct 21, 1956 in Winchester, England
Source: *AmAu&B; BioIn 4, 13; ConAu 116; CurBio 56; DcAmB S6; DcLB 17; EncSoH; WhAm 3; WhNAA*

Oxenberg, Catherine
American. Actor
Played Amanda Carrington on "Dynasty," 1984-86.
b. Sep 21, 1961 in New York, New York
Source: *BioIn 16; ConTFT 7, 14; IntMPA 92, 94, 96; LegTOT; WhoHol 92*

Oxnam, G(arfield) Bromley
American. Religious Leader
Pres. of De Pauw U, IN, 1928-36; wrote *A Testament of Faith,* 1958.
b. Aug 14, 1891 in Sonora, California
d. Mar 12, 1963 in White Plains, New York
Source: *AmAu&B; BiDInt; BioIn 1, 2, 3, 6, 11, 17, 19; CurBio 44, 63; DcAmB S7; DcAmReB 2; EncMcCE; EncWM; Meth; PolProf T; WebAB 74, 79; WhAm 4; WhE&EA; WhNAA*

Oz, Amos
[Amos Klausner]
Israeli. Author
Work often documents Israeli society; best-known novel: *My Michael,* 1972.
b. May 4, 1939 in Jerusalem, Palestine
Source: *AuSpks; Benet 87, 96; BioIn 9, 10, 11, 13; CasWL; ConAu 27NR, 47NR, 53; ConLC 5, 8, 11, 27, 33, 54; ConWorW 93; CurBio 83; CyWA 89; DcMidEa; EncWB; EncWL 2, 3; IntAu&W 77, 82, 86, 93; IntWW 89, 93; LegTOT; MajTwCW; Novels; RAdv 14, 13-2; RfGShF; WhoWor 84, 87, 89, 91, 93, 95, 96, 97; WhoWorJ 72, 78; WorAu 1970; WrDr 76, 80, 82, 84, 86, 88, 90*

Oz, Frank
[Frank Richard Oznowicz]
American. Puppeteer
Performs voices of many of Muppet, Sesame Street characters; won three Emmys.
b. May 24, 1944? in Hereford, England
Source: *BioIn 12; ConTFT 7, 15; IntMPA 94, 96; LegTOT; MiSFD 9; SmATA 60; VarWW 85; WhoAm 86, 94, 95, 96, 97; WhoHol 92*

Ozaki, Koyo
[Ozaki Tokutaro]
Japanese. Author
Very popular during his time; known for unfinished masterpiece *Konjikiyasha.*
b. Oct 1, 1868 in Tokyo, Japan
d. Oct 30, 1903 in Tokyo, Japan
Source: *BiDJaL; CasWL; DcOrL 1*

Ozal, Turgut
Turkish. Political Leader
Prime minister, 1983-93; major objectives were industrial growth, track expansion.
b. Oct 13, 1927 in Malatya, Turkey
d. Apr 17, 1993 in Ankara, Turkey
Source: *AnObit 1993; BioIn 13; CurBio 85, 93N; IntWW 82, 83, 89; MidE 80, 81, 82; NewYTBS 83; PolLCME; WhAm 11; WhoWor 82, 84, 87, 89, 91, 93*

Ozanam, (Antoine) Frederic
French. Critic
Known for writings on foreign literature; intended to show impact of religion on history.
b. Apr 23, 1813 in Milan, Italy
d. Sep 8, 1853 in Marseilles, France
Source: *BiD&SB; BioIn 1, 2, 3, 4, 5, 6, 7, 12; DcBiPP; DcCathB; DcEuL; OxCFr*

Ozawa, Seiji
Japanese. Conductor
Music director, Boston Symphony Orchestra, 1973—; won Emmy for musical direction of "Central Park in the Dark/A Hero's Life," 1976.
b. Sep 1, 1935 in Shenyang, China
Source: *AsAmAlm; Baker 78, 84, 92; BiDAmM; BioIn 6, 8, 9, 11, 12, 13; BriBkM 80; CmCal; CurBio 68; FarE&A 80, 81; IntWW 74, 75, 76, 77, 78, 79, 80, 81, 82, 83, 89, 93; IntWWM 77, 80, 85, 90; LegTOT; MusMk; MusSN; NewGrDA 86; NewGrDM 80; NewGrDO; NewYTBE 70; NotAsAm; OxDcOp; PenDiMP; VarWW 85; Who 83, 85, 88, 90, 94; WhoAm 74, 76, 78, 80, 82, 84, 86, 88, 90, 92, 94, 95, 96, 97; WhoAmM 83; WhoAsA 94; WhoE 77, 79, 81, 83, 85, 86, 89, 91, 93, 95, 97; WhoWest 74, 76; WhoWor 74, 76, 78, 80, 82, 84, 87, 89, 91, 93, 95, 96, 97; WorAl; WorAlBi*

Ozenfant, Amedee
French. Artist
Cofounder, with Le Corbusier, of the Purism art movement.
b. Apr 15, 1886 in Saint-Quentin, France
d. May 4, 1966 in Cannes, France
Source: *BioIn 1, 4, 7, 17; ClaDrA; ConArt 83; DcTwCCu 2; DcTwDes; MacEA; McGDA; ObitOF 79; ObitT 1961; OxCArt; OxCTwCA; OxDcArt; PhDcTCA 77; WhAm 4; WhoAmA 86N, 89N, 91N; WorArt 1950*

P

Paar, Jack
American. Entertainer
Pioneer talk show host; star of ''Tonight Show,'' 1957-62; ''Jack Paar Show,'' 1962-65, 1973.
b. May 1, 1918 in Canton, Ohio
Source: *AmAu&B; BioIn 1, 3, 4, 5, 6, 7, 8, 9, 12, 13; CelR; ConTFT 6; CurBio 59; ForYSC; IntMPA 75, 76, 77, 78, 79, 80, 81, 82, 84, 86, 88, 92, 94, 96; IntWW 74, 75, 76, 77, 78, 79, 80, 81, 82, 83, 89, 91, 93; JoeFr; LegTOT; LesBEnT, 92; NewYTBE 73; NewYTET; RadStar; VarWW 85; WhoAm 74, 76, 78; WhoCom; WhoHol 92, A; WhoWor 74; WorAl; WorAlBi*

Paasikivi, Juho Kusti
Finnish. Political Leader
In his positions as prime minister and pres. of Finland he strengthened relations with the Soviet Union to prevent Soviet aggression.
b. Nov 27, 1870 in Tampere, Finland
d. Dec 14, 1956 in Helsinki, Finland
Source: *BiDMoPL; BioIn 1, 4, 5, 8, 9, 21; CurBio 44, 57; ObitOF 79; ObitT 1951; PolLCWE; WhAm 3; WhDW*

Paasio, Rafael
Finnish. Political Leader
Prime minister of Finland, leader of Social Democratic Party, 1966-68.
b. Jun 6, 1903 in Uskela, Finland
d. Apr 21, 1980 in Turku, Finland
Source: *AnObit 1980; IntWW 77, 78, 79; IntYB 78, 79, 80; NewYTBS 80*

Pablo Cruise
[Bud Cockrell; David Jenkins; Cory Lerios; Steve Price]
American. Music Group
Band formed in 1973 with a mellow rock sound; songs include ''Cool Love,'' 1981.
Source: *ConMuA 80A; Dun&B 86, 88, 90; HarEnR 86; IlEncRk; NotNAT; RkOn 74, 78, 82; RolSEnR 83; WhoFI 85; WhoRock 81; WhoRocM 82*

Pabst, Frederick
American. Brewer
Pres., Pabst Brewing, 1889-1904.
b. Mar 28, 1836 in Saxony, Germany
d. Jan 1, 1904 in Milwaukee, Wisconsin
Source: *BioIn 5; Entr; NatCAB 3; WhAm 1*

Pabst, Georg Wilhelm
Austrian. Director
Used Pessimistic realism in his films *Pandora's Box; Diary of a Lost Girl.*
b. Aug 27, 1885 in Raudnitz, Bohemia
d. May 29, 1967 in Vienna, Austria
Source: *BiDFilm 94; BioIn 12, 15; DcFM; EncEurC; FilmEn; FilmgC; MovMk; OxCFilm; TwYS, A; WhScrn 77, 83*

Paca, William
American. Continental Congressman
Signed the Declaration of Independence, governor of Maryland, 1782-85.
b. Oct 31, 1740 in Abingdon, Maryland
d. Oct 13, 1799 in Abingdon, Maryland
Source: *AmBi; ApCAB; BiAUS; BiDFedJ; BiDrAC; BiDrACR; BiDrUSC 89; BioIn 3, 7, 8, 9, 11; DcAmB; Drake; EncAR; EncCRAm; EncSoH; HarEnUS; NatCAB 9; NewCol 75; TwCBDA; WhAm HS; WhAmP; WhAmRev*

Pacchierotti, Gasparo
Italian. Opera Singer
Male soprano popular in London, 1770s; among greatest castrati of day.
b. May 1740 in Fabriano, Italy
d. Oct 28, 1821 in Padua, Italy
Source: *Baker 84; CmOp; NewEOp 71; NewGrDM 80; NewGrDO; OxCMus*

Pacciardi, Randolfo
Italian. Political Activist, Journalist
Anti-Fascist who organized Free Italy movement against Mussolini's Black Shirts, 1923.
b. Jan 1, 1899 in Grosetto, Italy
d. Apr 14, 1991 in Rome, Italy
Source: *BioIn 1, 17; CurBio 91N; NewYTBS 91*

Pace, Frank, Jr.
American. Government Official, Business Executive
Held various govt. posts, 1946-82; CEO, General Dynamics Corp; founded, chaired, International Executive Service Corps, 1964-82.
b. Jul 5, 1912 in Little Rock, Arkansas
d. Jan 8, 1988 in Greenwich, Connecticut
Source: *BioIn 2, 3, 4, 6, 11, 15, 16; BlueB 76; CurBio 50, 88, 88N; HisDcKW; IntWW 74, 75, 76, 77, 78, 79, 80, 81, 82, 83; IntYB 78, 79, 80, 81, 82; NewYTBS 88; PolProf E, T; St&PR 75, 84, 87; WhAm 9; WhoAm 74, 76, 78, 80, 82, 84, 86, 88; WhoWor 76, 78*

Pacheco, Francisco
Spanish. Artist, Author
Authored influential study of Spanish Art of the 17th c.
b. 1564 in Sanlucar de Barrameda, Spain
d. 1654 in Seville, Spain
Source: *BioIn 12, 17, 19, 21; ClaDrA; McGDA; OxCSpan; OxDcArt*

Pachelbel, Johann
German. Composer, Organist
Wrote ''Hexachordum Apollinis,'' 1699.
b. Sep 1, 1653 in Nuremberg, Germany
d. Mar 3, 1706 in Nuremberg, Germany
Source: *Baker 78, 84, 92; BioIn 4, 7, 20; BriBkM 80; GrComp; LuthC 75; McGEWB; MusMk; NewAmDM; NewGrDM 80; NewOxM; OxCMus*

Pacini, Giovanni
Italian. Composer
Wrote oratorios, chamber music, operas including *Medea,* 1843.
b. Feb 17, 1796 in Catania, Sicily, Italy
d. Dec 6, 1867 in Pescia, Italy
Source: *Baker 78, 84, 92; CmOp; DcBiPP; IntDcOp; MetOEnc; NewAmDM; NewEOp 71; NewGrDM 80; NewGrDO; NewOxM; OxCMus; OxDcOp*

Pacino, Al(fredo James)
American. Actor
Starred in *The Godfather,* 1972; *Scent of a Woman,* 1993; won Oscar for both performances; won two Tonys.
b. Apr 25, 1940 in New York, New York
Source: *AmDec 1970; BiDFilm 81, 94; BioIn 9, 10, 11, 12, 13; BioNews 74; BkPepl; CamGWoT; CelR, 90; ConTFT 1, 6, 13; CurBio 74; DcTwCCu 1; Ent; FilmEn; FilmgC; HalFC 88; IntDcF 1-3, 2-3; IntMPA 84, 86, 88, 92, 94, 96; IntWW 79, 80, 81, 82, 83, 89, 91, 93; LegTOT; MovMk; News 93; NewYTBE 72; NewYTBS 77; VarWW 85; WhoAm 76, 78, 80, 82, 84, 86, 88, 90, 92, 94, 95, 96, 97; WhoEnt 92; WhoHol 92, A; WhoThe 77, 81; WorAl; WorAlBi*

Packard, David
American. Business Executive
Founded Hewlett-Packard with William Hewlett, 1939; served in Nixon administration, 1969-71.
b. Sep 7, 1912 in Pueblo, Colorado
d. Mar 26, 1996 in San Francisco, California
Source: *AmMWSc 73P, 79, 82, 86, 89, 92, 95; BioIn 8, 9, 10, 12, 13, 15, 16; BlueB 76; CmCal; ConAmBL; CurBio 96N; Dun&B 79, 86, 88, 90; EncWB; Entr; HisDcDP; IntWW 74, 75, 76, 77, 78, 79, 80, 81, 82, 83, 89, 91, 93; IntYB 78, 79, 80, 81, 82; LegTOT; LElec; News 96, 96-3; NotTwCS; PolProf NF; St&PR 84, 87, 91, 93; WhAm 11; WhoAm 74, 76, 78, 80, 82, 84, 86, 88, 90, 92, 94, 95, 96; WhoAmP 73, 75, 77, 79; WhoEng 80, 88; WhoFI 74, 75, 77, 79, 81, 83, 85, 87, 89, 92, 94, 96; WhoFrS 84; WhoScEn 94, 96; WhoWest 74, 76, 82, 84, 87, 89, 92, 94, 96; WhoWor 74, 76, 78, 87, 91*

Packard, Elizabeth Parsons Ware
American. Social Reformer, Author
Crusaded for married women's rights, legislation for insane.
b. Dec 28, 1816 in Ware, Massachusetts
d. Jul 25, 1897 in Chicago, Illinois
Source: *AmRef; BioIn 15, 17, 21; InWom SUP; NotAW*

Packard, Vance (Oakley)
American. Author, Journalist
Social critic, wrote *Status Seekers,* 1959; *Waste Makers,* 1960.
b. May 22, 1914 in Granville Summit, Pennsylvania
d. Dec 12, 1996 in Vineyard Haven, Massachusetts
Source: *AmAu&B; AuNews 1; AuSpks; BenetAL 91; BiDAmNC; BioIn 4, 5, 6, 7, 8, 10, 11, 20; BioNews 74; BlueB 76; CelR; ConAu 7NR, 9R; CurBio 58; DcLEL 1940; EncTwCJ; IntAu&W 76, 77, 82, 86, 89, 91, 93; IntWW 74, 75, 76, 77, 78, 79, 80, 81, 82, 83, 89, 91, 93; LegTOT; LinLib L, S; LngCTC; NewYTBS 27; PolProf E; REnAL; Who 74, 82, 83, 85, 88, 90, 92, 94; WhoAm 74, 76, 78, 80, 82, 84, 86, 88, 90, 92, 94, 95, 96, 97; WhoE 74; WhoUSWr 88; WhoWor 74, 78, 80, 82, 84, 87, 89, 91; 93, 95, 96, 97; WhoWrEP 89, 92; WorAl; WorAlBi; WorAu 1950; WrDr 76, 80, 82, 84, 86, 88, 90, 92, 94, 96*

Packer, Alfred G
American. Murderer
Murdered and ate five prospectors, 1873.
b. Nov 21, 1842 in Allegheny County, Pennsylvania
d. Apr 24, 1907 in Denver, Colorado
Source: *BioIn 2, 8, 11*

Packwood, Bob
[Robert William Packwood]
American. Politician
Rep. senator from OR, 1969-95; resigned after being accused of sexual misconduct.
b. Sep 11, 1932 in Portland, Oregon
Source: *AlmAP 78, 80, 92, 96; BiDrAC; BiDrUSC 89; BioIn 9, 10, 11, 12, 13, 14, 15; BlueB 76; CelR 90; CngDr 74, 77, 79, 81, 83, 85, 87, 89, 91, 93, 95; CurBio 81; IntWW 75, 76, 77, 78, 79, 80, 81, 82, 83, 89, 91, 93; LegTOT; NewYTBS 82, 84, 86; PolsAm 84; WhoAm 74, 76, 78, 80, 82, 84, 86, 88, 90, 92, 94, 95, 96, 97; WhoAmL 85; WhoAmP 73, 75, 77, 79, 81, 83, 85, 87, 89, 91, 93, 95; WhoGov 72, 75, 77; WhoWest 74, 76, 78, 80, 82, 84, 87, 89, 92, 94, 96; WhoWor 80, 82, 84, 87, 89, 91*

Paddleford, Clementine Haskin
American. Editor, Journalist
Called "best known food editor" in America, 1953; 12-million estimated weekly readers; known for vivid descriptions of food.
b. Sep 27, 1900 in Stockdale, Kansas
d. Nov 13, 1967 in New York, New York
Source: *BioIn 3, 4, 5, 8; ConAu 89; CurBio 58, 68; InWom, SUP; WhAm 4; WhoAmW 58, 64, 66, 68*

Paderewski, Ignace Jan
Polish. Pianist, Statesman
Popular pianist who was foremost interpreter of Chopin; pres. of Poland, 1919.
b. Nov 18, 1860 in Kurilovka, Poland
d. Jun 29, 1941 in New York, New York
Source: *ApCAB X; Baker 78; BiDAmM; BioIn 14, 16, 17, 21; CurBio 41; DcCathB; FacFETw; FilmgC; HalFC 80; HisWorL; LinLib S; McGEWB; MusSN; NewAmDM; NotTwCP; REn; WhAm 1; WhoHol B; WhoPolA; WhScrn 74, 77, 83; WorAl*

Padover, Saul Kussiel
American. Educator, Historian
Authority on Thomas Jefferson; wrote the *Complete Jefferson,* 1943.
b. Apr 13, 1905 in Vienna, Austria
d. Feb 22, 1981 in New York, New York
Source: *AmAu&B; AmMWSc 73S, 78S; BioIn 3, 12; ConAu 49, 103; CurBio 52, 81; EncAI&E; IntAu&W 77; REnAL; WhE&EA; WhNAA; WhoAm 74, 76, 78; WhoWor 74; WhoWorJ 72*

Paer, Ferdinando
Italian. Composer
Best known of 43 operas include *La Griselda,* 1796; *Agnes,* 1819.
b. Jun 1, 1771 in Parma, Italy
d. May 3, 1839 in Paris, France
Source: *Baker 78, 84, 92; BioIn 4; BriBkM 80; CmOp; DcBiPP; IntDcOp; MetOEnc; NewAmDM; NewEOp 71; NewGrDM 80; NewGrDO; NewOxM; OxCMus; OxDcOp*

Paganini, Niccolo
Italian. Violinist, Composer
Revolutionized violin technique, fingering methods.
b. Oct 27, 1782 in Genoa, Italy
d. May 27, 1840 in Nice, France
Source: *AtlBL; Baker 78, 84, 92; BioIn 1, 2, 3, 4, 5, 6, 7, 8, 9, 10, 11, 12, 13; BriBkM 80; CmpBCM; DancEn 78; DcArts; DcCom 77; GrComp; LegTOT; LinLib S; McGEWB; MusMk; NewAmDM; NewOxM; OxCMus; PenDiMP, A; WhDW; WorAl; WorAlBi*

Page, Alan Cedric
American. Football Player
Eight-time all-pro defensive tackle, 1967-81; member Minnesota's "purple people eaters" defense; Hall of Fame, 1988; first black elected to MN Supreme Court, 1992.
b. Aug 7, 1945 in Canton, Ohio
Source: *NewYTBS 81; WhoAfA 96; WhoAm 74, 76, 78, 80, 82, 84, 86, 96, 97; WhoAmL 87, 94, 96; WhoBlA 77, 80, 85, 88, 90, 92, 94; WhoEmL 89; WhoFtbl 74; WhoMW 93, 96*

Page, Charles Grafton
American. Inventor
Researcher in electromagnetism; developed electric locomotive.
b. Jan 25, 1812 in Salem, Massachusetts
d. May 5, 1868 in Washington, District of Columbia
Source: *Alli; ApCAB; BiDAmS; BiInAmS; BioIn 1, 6, 11; DcAmAu; DcAmB; DcNAA; Drake; NatCAB 1, 5; WhAm HS*

Page, Clarence
American. Journalist
Syndicated columnist; Pulitzer Prize winner.
b. Jun 2, 1947 in Dayton, Ohio
Source: *BioIn 1, 16; ConAu 145; ConBlB 4; WhoAm 90; WhoMW 90*

Page, Frederick Handley, Sir
English. Aircraft Manufacturer
Started first private aircraft manufacturing co., 1909; built first two-engined bomber, WW I.
b. Nov 15, 1885 in Cheltenham, England
d. Apr 21, 1962 in London, England
Source: *BioIn 6, 7, 12, 14; DcNaB 1961; GrBr; InSci; ObitOF 79; ObitT 1961*

Page, Geraldine
"Gerry"
American. Actor
Stage actress best known for playing Tennessee Williams' heroines; won Oscar, 1986, for *A Trip to Bountiful.*
b. Nov 22, 1924 in Kirksville, Missouri
d. Jun 13, 1987 in New York, New York
Source: *AnObit 1987; BiDFilm 81, 94; BiE&WWA; BioIn 3, 5, 6, 11, 12, 14, 15, 16; CamGWoT; CelR; CnThe; ConNews 87-4; ConTFT 1, 4, 5; CurBio 53, 87, 87N; Ent; FamA&A; FilmEn; FilmgC; ForYSC; GrLiveH; HalFC 80, 84, 88; IntDcF 1-3, 2-3; IntMPA 77, 80, 84, 86; InWom, SUP; LegTOT; MotPP; MovMk; NewYTBS 85, 87; NotNAT; NotWoAT; OxCAmT 84; OxCThe 83; PlP&P; VarWW 85; WhAm 9; WhoAm 74, 76, 78, 80, 82, 84, 86; WhoAmW 58, 61, 64, 66, 68, 70, 72, 74, 75, 77; WhoE 74; WhoHol A; WhoThe 72, 77, 81; WhoWor 74, 76; WorAl; WorAlBi; WorEFlm*

Page, Hot Lips
[Oran Thaddeus Page]
American. Jazz Musician
Jazz, blues trumpeter; blues singer with Artie Shaw, early 1940s.
b. Jan 27, 1908 in Dallas, Texas
d. Nov 5, 1954 in New York, New York
Source: *AllMusG; Baker 84; CmpEPM; DcAmB S5; DrBlPA, 90; IlEncJ; NewAmDM; NewGrDA 86; NewGrDJ 88, 94; OxCPMus; WhoJazz 72*

Page, Irvine H
American. Physician
Leader in fight against cardiovascular disease; identified compounds that affect blood pressure and developed therapies to reverse the disorder.
b. Jan 7, 1901 in Indianapolis, Indiana
d. Jun 10, 1991 in Hyannis Port, Massachusetts
Source: *AmMWSc 73P, 92; CurBio 91N; IntWW 91; NewYTBS 91; WhoAm 90*

Page, Jimmy
[Honeydrippers; Led Zeppelin; Yardbirds; James Patrick Page]
English. Musician
Guitarist with heavy-metal groups; best known for Led Zeppelin tours, albums: *Led Zeppelin III,* 1970.
b. Jan 9, 1944 in Helston, England
Source: *ASCAP 80; Baker 84; BioIn 10, 11, 13, 14; ConLC 12; ConMus 4; EncPR&S 89; EncRk 88; LegTOT; OnThGG; WhoAm 80, 82, 84; WhoRocM 82*

Page, Joe
[Joseph Francis Page]
"Fireman"; "The Gay Reliever"
American. Baseball Player
Relief pitcher, NY Yankess, 1944-50; had 76 career saves; known for heroics, 1947 World Series; inspired MLs to train pitchers for relief.
b. Oct 28, 1917 in Cherry Valley, Pennsylvania
d. Apr 21, 1980 in Latrobe, Pennsylvania
Source: *Ballpl 90; BioIn 1, 2, 7, 12, 14, 16; CurBio 50, 80, 80N; DcAmB S10; WhoProB 73*

Page, Patti
[Clara Ann Fowler]
"The Singing Rage"
American. Singer
Popular vocalist, 1950s; hits include "Confess," 1948.
b. Nov 8, 1927 in Clarence, Oklahoma
Source: *Baker 84, 92; BiDAmM; BioIn 2, 3, 4, 7, 10, 12, 14; BioNews 74; CelR; CmpEPM; ConMus 11; CurBio 65; EncFCWM 83; FilmgC; ForYSC; HalFC 80, 84, 88; HarEnCM 87, 87A; IntMPA 75, 76, 77, 78, 79, 80, 81, 82, 84, 86, 88, 92, 94, 96; InWom, SUP; LegTOT; NewAmDM; NewGrDA 86; OxCPMus; PenEncP; RkOn 74; VarWW 85; WhoAm 74, 76, 78, 80, 82; WhoAmW 58, 66, 68, 70, 72, 74; WhoHol 92, A; WhoRock 81; WorAl; WorAlBi*

Page, Ruth
American. Dancer
Led the movement in using American themes in ballet and translating operas into ballet.
b. Mar 22, 1899 in Indianapolis, Indiana
d. Apr 7, 1991 in Chicago, Illinois
Source: *AnObit 1991; BioAmW; BioIn 11, 12; CurBio 91N; FacFETw; IntDcB; InWom SUP; NewYTBS 91; WhAm 10; WhoAm 86; WhoAmW 89, 91*

Page, Thomas Nelson
American. Author, Diplomat
Wrote of Aristocratic Old South: *The Old Dominion,* 1908.
b. Apr 23, 1853 in Hanover County, Virginia
d. Nov 1, 1922 in Hanover County, Virginia
Source: *Alli SUP; AmAu; AmAu&B; AmBi; AmLY; ApCAB, X; BbD; Benet 87; BenetAL 91; BibAL; BiD&SB; BiDSA; BioIn 1, 3, 5, 6, 8, 9, 12, 13, 16; CamGEL; CamGLE; CamHAL; CarSB; CasWL; Chambr 3; ChhPo; CnDAL; ConAu 118; CyWA 58; DcAmAu; DcAmB; DcAmDH 80, 89; DcBiA; DcLB 12, 78, DS13; DcLEL; DcNAA; EncSoH; FifSWrB; GayN; GrWrEL N; HarEnUS; JBA 34; LinLib L, S; McGEWB; NatCAB 1, 19; Novels; OxCAmL 65, 83, 95; OxCChiL; PenC AM; REn; REnAL; RfGAmL 87, 94; ShSCr 23; SouWr; Str&VC; TwCBDA; WebE&AL; WhAm 1; WhLit*

Page, Walter Hines
American. Diplomat
U.S. ambassador to Great Britain; urged U.S. intervention in WW I.
b. Aug 15, 1855 in Cary, North Carolina
d. Dec 21, 1918 in Pinehurst, North Carolina
Source: *AmAu&B; AmBi; ApCAB X; BenetAL 91; BiDSA; BioIn 1, 3, 5, 8, 9, 11, 12, 13, 16, 17; ChhPo, S2; CnDAL; DcAmAu; DcAmB; DcAmDH 80, 89; DcLB 71, 91; DcLP 87A; DcNAA; EncAAH; EncAB-H 1974, 1996; EncAJ; EncSoH; FacFETw; GayN; HarEnUS; LinLib L, S; McGEWB; NatCAB 3, 19; OxCAmH; OxCAmL 65, 83, 95; PeoHis; REnAL; SouWr; TwCBDA; WebAB 74, 79; WhAm 1; WhoAm 86; WhoE 86*

Pagels, Elaine
American. Historian
Studies early history of Christianity; wrote *The Gnostic Gospels,* 1977; *Adam, Eve, and the Serpent,* 1987.
b. Feb 13, 1943 in Palo Alto, California
Source: *BioIn 12; CurBio 96; News 97-1*

Paget, James, Sir
British. Surgeon
A founder modern pathology; discovered cause of Trichinosis.
b. Jan 11, 1814
d. Dec 30, 1899
Source: *BiHiMed; BioIn 1, 2, 5, 9, 14, 16; CelCen; DcBiPP, A; DcNaB S1; InSci; OxCMed 86; VicBrit*

Pagett, Nicola
[Nicola Scott]
English. Actor
Played in TV shows "Upstairs, Downstairs"; "Anna Karenina."
b. Jun 15, 1945 in Cairo, Egypt
Source: *BioIn 11; ConTFT 5; HalFC 88; IntMPA 92, 94, 96; VarWW 85; WhoHol 92; WhoThe 77, 81*

Paglia, Camille
American. Author
Author of *Sexual Personae,* 1990; controversial in her critique of feminism.
b. Apr 2, 1947 in Endicott, New York
Source: *BioIn 17, 18, 20, 21; ConLC 68; CurBio 92; IntWW 93; LegTOT; News 92, 92-3; OxCAmL 95; WhoAm 94, 95, 96, 97; WhoAmW 93, 95, 97; WrDr 96*

Pagnol, Marcel Paul
French. Dramatist, Producer
Wrote Marseilles trilogy: *Marius,* 1929; *Fanny,* 1931; *Cesar,* 1936.
b. Apr 18, 1895 in Aubagne, France
d. Apr 18, 1974 in Paris, France
Source: *BiE&WWA; CasWL; ConAu 49; CurBio 56, 74; McGEWD 72; ModWD; MovMk; NewYTBS 74; OxCFilm; OxCFr; PenC EUR; REn; TwCWr; WhAm 6; Who 74; WorEFlm*

Pahlevi, Farah Diba
Iranian. Ruler
Descendant of Mohammed, who married Shah of Iran, Dec 21, 1959.
b. Oct 14, 1938 in Tehran, Iran
Source: *CurBio 76; IntWW 76, 80, 91; WhoWor 76, 78*

Pahlevi, Mohammed Riza
[Shah of Iran]
Iranian. Ruler
Headed Iran, 1941-79; overthrown by Ayatollah Khomeini; died in exile.

b. Oct 26, 1919 in Tehran, Persia
d. Jul 27, 1980 in Cairo, Egypt
Source: *AnObit 1980; ConAu 106; CurBio 50, 80; IntWW 74; NewYTBS 74, 78, 80; WhoGov 72*

Pahlevi, Riza
Persian. Ruler
Founder, modern Iran who encouraged westernization, industrialization; Shah, 1925-41.
b. Mar 16, 1877 in Alasht, South Africa
d. Jul 26, 1944 in Johannesburg, South Africa
Source: *BioIn 10*

Pahlevi, Riza Cyrus
Iranian.
Son of Shah of Iran who proclaimed himself shah following father's death, 1980.
b. Oct 31, 1960
Source: *BioIn 12, 16*

Pahlmann, William Carroll
American. Interior Decorator
Known for model rooms shown in dept. stores, Scandinavian furniture, "Pahlmann eclectic look"; designed Four Seasons restaurant, NYC.
b. Dec 12, 1906 in Pleasant Mound, Illinois
d. Nov 6, 1987 in Guadalajara, Mexico
Source: *BioIn 4, 7, 14; CurBio 64, 88*

Paige, Emmett, Jr.
American. Military Leader
First black soldier to become a general, 1976; head of Information Systems Comma nd, 1984-88.
b. Feb 20, 1931 in Jacksonville, Florida
Source: *AfrAmBi 1; AfrAmG; BioIn 15, 16; BlksScM; ConNews 86-4; InB&W 85; NegAl 89; WhoAfA 96; WhoAm 82, 84, 86; WhoBlA 80, 85, 88, 90, 92, 94*

Paige, Janis
[Donna Mae Jaden]
American. Singer, Actor
Stage, film musical comedy star, 1940s-60s; trained as opera singer.
b. Sep 16, 1923 in Tacoma, Washington
Source: *BiE&WWA; BioIn 1, 2, 4, 5, 6, 9, 10, 17, 18; CmpEPM; ConTFT 2; CurBio 59; EncAFC; EncMT; FilmgC; ForYSC; HalFC 80, 88; HolP 40; IntMPA 75, 76, 77, 78, 79, 80, 81, 82, 84, 86, 88, 92, 94, 96; InWom; MotPP; MovMk; NotNAT; OxCPMus; VarWW 85; WhoAmW 74; WhoEnt 92; WhoHol A; WhoThe 77*

Paige, Robert (John Arthur)
American. Actor
Leading man in B rated comedies including *Tangier.*
b. Dec 2, 1910 in Indianapolis, Indiana
d. 1988
Source: *BioIn 4, 10, 15; EncAFC; Film 2; FilmEn; FilmgC; ForYSC; HalFC 80, 84, 88; HolP 40; MotPP; WhoHol A*

Paige, Satchel
[Leroy Robert Paige]
American. Baseball Player
Pitcher in Negro Leagues before coming to MLs, 1948-53, 1965; known for "hesitation pitch," numerous shutouts; Hall of Fame, 1971.
b. Jul 7, 1906 in Mobile, Alabama
d. Jun 8, 1982 in Kansas City, Missouri
Source: *AfrAmAl 6; AfrAmBi 1; AfrAmSG; AmDec 1930; AnObit 1982; Ballpl 90; BiDAmSp BB; BioIn 18, 19, 20, 21; BioNews 74; ConAu 107; ConBlB 7; CurBio 52, 82; LegTOT; NewYTBS 76, 81, 82; WebAB 74, 79; WhAm 8; WhoAm 76, 78, 80, 82; WhoBlA 77, 80, 85; WhoProB 73; WhoSpor*

Paik, Nam June
American. Artist
Known for creating scenes on multiple TV screens which together create electronic paintings.
b. Jul 20, 1932 in Seoul, Korea
Source: *AmArt; Baker 78, 84, 92; BioIn 9, 10, 11, 12, 13, 14; CelR 90; ConAmC 76, 82; ConArt 77, 83, 89, 96; CurBio 83; DcCAA 88, 94; DcCM; IntWW 93; IntWWM 90; LesBEnT 92; ModArCr 4; NewAmDM; NewYTBS 82; PrintW 85; WhoAm 82; WhoAmA 78, 80, 82, 84, 86, 89, 91, 93; WhoWor 74; WorArt 1980*

Paine, Albert Bigelow
American. Author
Wrote three-volume biography of *Mark Twain,* 1912.
b. Jul 10, 1861 in New Bedford, Massachusetts
d. Apr 9, 1937 in New Smyrna, Florida
Source: *AmAu&B; AmBi; BenetAL 91; BiD&SB; BioIn 4; CarSB; ChhPo, S1, S2; CnDAL; ConAu 108; DcAmAu; DcAmB S2; DcNAA; EncPaPR 91; JBA 34; LinLib L; NatCAB 13, 28; OxCAmL 65, 83, 95; OxCChiL; REn; REnAL; ScF&FL 1; ScFEYrs; TwCA; TwCBDA; TwCSFW 81; WhAm 1; WhNAA*

Paine, Robert Treat
American. Government Official
Delegate to first Continental Congress, 1774; one of few to sign both Olive Branch Petition, 1775, Declaration of Independence.
b. Mar 11, 1731 in Boston, Massachusetts
d. May 12, 1814 in Boston, Massachusetts
Source: *Alli; AmAu; AmAu&B; AmBi; AmRev; ApCAB, SUP; BbD; BenetAL 91; BiAUS; BiD&SB; BiDrAC; BiDrUSC 89; BioIn 6, 7, 8, 9; DcAmB; Drake; EncCRAm; HarEnUS; NatCAB 5; OxCAmL 65; REnAL; TwCBDA; WebAB 74, 79; WhAm HS; WhAmP; WhAmRev; WhoWest 74*

Paine, Thomas
American. Philosopher, Author
Advocated colonial independence in *Common Sense,* Jan 1776.
b. Jan 29, 1737 in Thetford, England
d. Jun 8, 1809 in New York, New York
Source: *ABCMeAm; Alli; AmAu; AmAu&B; AmBi; AmPolLe; AmRef; AmRev; AmWrBE; AmWr S1; ApCAB; AtlBL; BbD; Benet 87, 96; BenetAL 91; BiDAmJo; BiD&SB; BioIn 1, 2, 3, 4, 5, 6, 7, 8, 9, 10, 11, 12, 13, 14, 15, 16, 17, 18, 19, 20, 21; BlkwCE; BlkwEAR; BlmGEL; CamGEL; CamGLE; CamHAL; CasWL; CmFrR; CnDAL; ColARen; CrtT 3; CyAG; CyAL 1; CyWA 58; DcAmAu; DcAmB; DcAmC; DcAmReB 1, 2; DcAmSR; DcArts; DcBiPP; DcEnA; DcEnL; DcEuL; DcLB 31, 43, 73, 158; DcNAA; DcNaB; Dis&D; Drake; EncAB-H 1974, 1996; EncAJ; EncAR; EncARH; EncCRAm; EncEnl; EncEth; EncNAB; EncUnb; EvLB; HarEnUS; HisDBrE; HisWorL; JrnUS; LegTOT; LinLib L, S; LngCEL; LuthC 75; McGEWB; MemAm; MouLC 2; NatCAB 5; NewCBEL; OxCAmH; OxCAmL 65, 83, 95; OxCEng 67, 85, 95; OxCLaw; OxCPhil; PenC AM, ENG; PeoHis; RAdv 14, 13-3; RComAH; RComWL; REn; REnAL; RfGAmL 87, 94; RfGEnL 91; TwCBDA; TwoTYeD; WebAB 74, 79; WebE&AL; WhAm HS; WhAmP; WhAmRev; WhDW; WorAl; WorAlBi*

Paine, Thomas Otten
American. Engineer, Government Official
Supervised first manned space flight, *Apollo 7,* as Deputy Administrator of NASA, 1968-70.
b. Nov 9, 1921 in Berkeley, California
d. May 4, 1992 in Brentwood, California
Source: *AmMWSc 73P; BioIn 8, 9, 11, 17, 18, 19; BlueB 76; CurBio 70, 92N; IntWW 74, 75, 76, 77, 78, 79, 80, 81, 82, 83, 89, 91; LElec; St&PR 75, 84, 87, 91, 93; WhAm 10; Who 74, 82, 83, 85, 88, 90, 92; WhoAm 74, 76, 78, 80, 82, 84, 86, 88; WhoAmP 73, 75, 77; WhoEng 88; WhoFI 81, 83; WhoFrS 84; WhoTech 89; WhoWest 82, 84, 87, 89, 92*

Pais, Abraham
American. Physicist
Wrote *Subtle Is the Lord . . .,* 1983, a biography of his colleague Albert Einstein; one of the founding fathers of particle physics.
b. May 19, 1918 in Amsterdam, Netherlands
Source: *AmMWSc 76P, 79, 82, 86, 89, 92, 95; BioIn 19, 20; ConAu 109; CurBio 94; IntWW 74, 75, 76, 77, 78, 79, 80, 81, 82, 83, 89, 91, 93; WhoAm 74, 76, 78, 80, 82, 84, 86, 88, 90, 92, 94, 95, 96, 97; WhoAmJ 80; WhoE 95; WhoFrS 84; WhoScEn 94, 96; WhoWor 97; WhoWorJ 72, 78*

Paisiello, Giovanni
Italian. Composer
Wrote over 100 operas including *Il Barbiere di Siviglia,* 1782, a rival to Rossini's later masterpiece.
b. May 8, 1740 in Taranto, Italy
d. Jun 5, 1816 in Naples, Italy

Source: *Baker 78, 84, 92; BioIn 4, 6, 7, 11, 12; BlkwCE; BriBkM 80; CmOp; DcCom 77; GrComp; IntDcOp; MetOEnc; MusMk; NewAmDM; NewEOp 71; NewGrDM 80; NewGrDO; NewOxM; OxDcOp*

Paisley, Ian Richard Kyle
Irish. Clergy, Political Leader
Protestant minister who is most influential representative against Catholics in Ulster.
b. Apr 6, 1926 in Armagh, Northern Ireland
Source: *BioIn 12, 14, 15, 16; CurBio 71, 86; DcTwHis; EncWB; FacFETw; HisDBrE; IntWW 74, 75, 76, 77, 78, 79, 80, 81, 82, 83, 89, 91, 93; IntYB 78, 79, 80, 81, 82; NewYTBE 70; Who 74, 82, 83, 85, 88, 90, 92; WhoEIO 82; WhoWor 74, 80, 82, 84, 87, 89, 91, 93, 95, 96, 97*

Pakula, Alan Jay
American. Director
Films include *Klute,* 1971; *All the President's Men,* 1976; *Sophie's Choice,* 1982.
b. Apr 7, 1928 in New York, New York
Source: *BioIn 12, 13, 14, 16; CelR 90; ConAu 124, 130; CurBio 80; HalFC 84, 88; IntDcF 2-2; IntMPA 86, 92; IntWW 91; NewYTBS 82; OxCFilm; VarWW 85; WhoAm 86, 88, 90; WhoE 89, 91; WhoEnt 92; WorFDir 2*

Pal, George
American. Producer, Director
Won Oscars for special effects for *When Worlds Collide,* 1951; *War of the Worlds,* 1952; *The Time Machine,* 1960.
b. Feb 1, 1908 in Cegled, Austria-Hungary
d. May 2, 1980 in Beverly Hills, California
Source: *AnObit 1980; BioIn 12; CmMov; DcAmB S10; EncSF, 93; FacFETw; FilmEn; FilmgC; HalFC 80, 84, 88; IlWWHD 1A; IntDcF 1-2, 2-4; MiSFD 9N; NewEScF; ScF&FL 92; WhoHrs 80; WorECar; WorEFlm*

Palacio Valdes, Armando
Spanish. Author
Popular 19th-century Spanish novelist known for his optimistic, simple outlook.
b. Oct 4, 1853 in Entralgo, Spain
d. Feb 3, 1938 in Madrid, Spain
Source: *BioIn 1; CasWL; ClDMEL 47, 80; DcSpL; EncWL, 3; EvEuW; ModRL; NewCBEL; Novels; OxCSpan; PenC EUR; WhE&EA; WhoLA*

Palade, George Emil
American. Biologist, Educator
Shared 1974 Nobel Prize in medicine for research on internal components of cells.
b. Nov 19, 1912 in Iasi, Romania
Source: *AmMWSc 92; AsBiEn; BiESc; BioIn 7, 8, 10, 15, 20; CamDcSc; FacFETw; IntWW 75, 76, 77, 78, 79, 80, 81, 82, 83, 89, 91, 93; LarDcSc; McGMS 80; NobelP; Who 82, 83, 85, 88, 90, 92, 94; WhoAm 76, 78, 80, 82, 84, 86, 88, 90, 92, 94, 95, 96, 97; WhoE 77, 79, 81, 83, 85, 86, 89; WhoFrS 84; WhoMedH; WhoNob, 90, 95; WhoScEn 94, 96; WhoWest 92, 94, 96; WhoWor 78, 80, 82, 84, 87, 89, 91, 93, 95, 96, 97; WorAl; WorAlBi*

Palamas, Gregory, Saint
"Father and Doctor of the Orthodox Church"
Byzantine. Religious Figure
Greek Orthodox monk, named Saint, 1368; leader of Hesychasm.
b. Nov 1296 in Constantinople, Byzantine Empire
d. 1359 in Thessalonia, Byzantine Empire
Source: *CasWL; IlEncMy; OxDcByz; PenC CL*

Palance, Jack
[Walter Jack Palahnuik]
American. Actor
Oscar nominee for *Sudden Fear,* 1952; *Shane,* 1953; won Oscar for *City Slickers,* 1992.
b. Feb 18, 1920 in Lattimore Mines, Pennsylvania
Source: *BiDFilm 81; BioIn 3, 10, 13, 17, 18, 20; CmMov; ConTFT 5, 12; CurBio 92; DcArts; FilmgC; ForYSC; HalFC 80, 84, 88; IntDcF 2-3; IntMPA 75, 76, 77, 78, 79, 80, 81, 82, 84, 86, 88, 92, 94, 96; MovMk; OxCFilm; VarWW 85; WhoAm 74, 76, 78, 80, 82, 90; WhoEnt 92; WhoHol 92, A; WhoHrs 80; WhoWor 74; WorAl; WorAlBi; WorEFlm*

Pales Matos, Luis
Puerto Rican. Poet
Known for his African and African-American influenced Spanish poetry.
b. Mar 20, 1898 in Guayama, Puerto Rico
d. Feb 23, 1959 in San Juan, Puerto Rico
Source: *Benet 96; BiDHisL; BioIn 5, 10, 16, 18; CaribW 4; CasWL; DcHiB; DcTwCCu 4; EncLatA; EncWL; HispWr; LatAmWr; ModLAL; OxCSpan; PenC AM; PueRA; SpAmA*

Palestrina, Giovanni
Italian. Composer
Among greatest Renaissance composers noted for Motets, Masses including *Missa Papae Marcelli.*
b. Dec 27, 1525 in Palestrina, Italy
d. Feb 2, 1594 in Rome, Italy
Source: *AtlBL; REn*

Paley, Barbara Cushing
[Mrs. William S Paley]
"Babe"
American. Socialite
Described as one of world's great beauties, who was perennially on best-dressed lists.
b. Jul 5, 1915 in Boston, Massachusetts
d. Jul 6, 1978 in New York, New York
Source: *DcAmB S10; NewYTBS 78; ObitOF 79*

Paley, William Samuel
American. Radio Executive, TV Executive
Bought United Independent Broadcasting Co., 1928, which later became CBS.
b. Sep 28, 1901 in Chicago, Illinois
d. Oct 26, 1990 in New York, New York
Source: *BiDAmBL 83; BiDAmJo; BioIn 1, 2, 4, 6, 10, 11, 12, 13, 14, 15, 16; ConAu 132; ConTFT 5; CurBio 40, 51, 91N; Dun&B 90; EncTwCJ; EncWB; FacFETw; IntMPA 86, 88; IntWW 83, 91N; LesBEnT, 92; News 91-2; NewYTBS 80, 90; St&PR 84, 87, 91N; VarWW 85; WhoAm 86, 90; WhoAmA 84, 91N; WhoE 91; WhoFI 89; WhoTelC; WhoWor 84, 87, 91; WorAlBi*

Palillo, Ron
American. Actor
Played a Sweathog on "Welcome Back, Kotter," 1975-79.
b. Apr 2, 1954 in New Haven, Connecticut
Source: *BioIn 11; LegTOT; WhoHol 92*

Palin, Michael
[Monty Python's Flying Circus]
English. Actor, Author
Zany films include *The Missionary,* 1982; *The Meaning of Life,* 1983.
b. May 5, 1943 in Sheffield, England
Source: *BioIn 11, 13; ConAu 35NR; ConLC 21; ConTFT 5; HalFC 84, 88; IntAu&W 91; IntMPA 88, 92, 94, 96; IntWW 91; LegTOT; QDrFCA 92; ScF&FL 92; SmATA 67; VarWW 85; Who 92; WhoCom; WhoHol 92; WhoWor 89; WrDr 92*

Palladio, Andrea
Italian. Architect
Developed neoclassic architectural style, popular in 18th c; published influential textbook, 1570.
b. Nov 30, 1508 in Padua, Italy
d. Aug 19, 1580
Source: *AtlBL; Benet 87, 96; BioIn 14, 16, 17; BlmGEL; DcD&D; EncWT; Ent; IntDcAr; MacEA; McGDA; McGEWB; OxCArt; OxCEng 85, 95; OxCThe 67; OxDcArt; PenDiDA 89; PlP&P; RAdv 14; REn; WhDW; WhoArch; WorAl; WorAlBi*

Pallette, Eugene
American. Actor
Popular, 1913-46; films include *Topper,* 1937; *My Man Godfrey,* 1936.
b. Jul 8, 1889 in Winfield, Kansas
d. Sep 3, 1943 in Los Angeles, California
Source: *BioIn 3, 12, 17, 21; Film 1, 2; FilmEn; FilmgC; ForYSC; HalFC 80, 84, 88; LegTOT; MotPP; MovMk; NotNAT B; OlFamFa; OxCFilm; TwYS; Vers A; WhoHol B; WhScrn 74, 77, 83*

Palligrosi, Tony
[Southside Johnny and the Asbury Jukes]
American. Musician
Trumpeter with group since 1974.
b. May 9, 1954

Palme, Olof
[Sven Olof Joachim Palme]
Swedish. Government Official
Leader of Sweden's socialist party; prime minister, 1969-76, 1982; assassinated.
b. Jan 30, 1927 in Stockholm, Sweden
d. Feb 28, 1986 in Stockholm, Sweden
Source: *BioIn 8, 9, 10, 11, 13, 14, 15, 17, 21; ConNews 86-2; CurBio 70, 86, 86N; FacFETw; IntWW 83; IntYB 79, 80, 81, 82; PolLCWE; Who 85; WhoGov 72; WhoWor 74, 76, 84*

Palmer, Alexander Mitchell
American. Government Official
US attorney general, 1919-20; his crusade against radicals became known as the Red Scare.
b. May 4, 1872 in Moosehead, Pennsylvania
d. May 11, 1936 in Washington, District of Columbia
Source: *AmPolLe; ApCAB X; BiDrAC; BiDrUSC 89; BiDrUSE 71, 89; BioIn 1, 2, 4, 6, 8, 10, 15; DcAmB S2; EncAB-H 1974, 1996; McGEWB; NatCAB 27; WebAB 74, 79; WhAm 1, 4A, HSA; WhAmP*

Palmer, Alice Elvira Freeman
American. Educator
Pres., Wellesley College, 1882; co-founded, American Assn. of U. Women, 1882.
b. Feb 21, 1855 in Colesville, New York
d. Dec 6, 1902 in Paris, France
Source: *AmAu&B; AmBi; AmWom; AmWomM; BiDAmEd; ChhPo, S1; DcAmB; DcNAA; HerW; InWom SUP; LibW; NatCAB 7; NotAW; REnAL; TwCBDA; WebAB 74, 79; WhAm 1; WomFir*

Palmer, Arnold Daniel
American. Golfer
Turned pro, 1954; won seven major tournaments including four Masters; first to win $1 million on tour.
b. Sep 10, 1929 in Youngstown, Pennsylvania
Source: *BiDAmSp OS; BioIn 13, 14, 15; CelR 90; ConAu 85; CurBio 60; FacFETw; IntWW 76, 77, 78, 79, 80, 81, 82, 83, 89, 91, 93; NewYTBS 77, 81, 83; WebAB 74, 79; Who 82, 83, 85, 88, 90, 92, 94; WhoAm 74, 76, 78, 80, 82, 84, 86, 88, 90, 92, 94, 95, 96, 97; WhoE 74, 75, 77, 89, 93, 95; WhoEnt 92; WhoGolf; WhoIntG; WhoWor 84; WorAlBi*

Palmer, Austin Norman
American. Educator
Originated method of penmanship taught in US schools.
b. 1859
d. 1927
Source: *WebBD 83*

Palmer, Betsy
[Patricia Hrunek]
American. Actor
Panelist on "I've Got a Secret," 1957-67.
b. Nov 1, 1926 in East Chicago, Indiana
Source: *BiE&WWA; BioIn 4, 5, 10; ConTFT 2; FilmgC; HalFC 84, 88; IntMPA 86, 92, 94, 96; InWom; LegTOT; LesBEnT, 92; MotPP; NotNAT; VarWW 85; WhoHol A; WhoThe 81*

Palmer, Carl
[Asia; Emerson, Lake, and Palmer]
English. Musician
Drummer with Emerson, Lake, and Palmer, 1970-79; formed group Asia, 1981.
b. Mar 20, 1951 in Birmingham, England
Source: *LegTOT; WhoRocM 82*

Palmer, Daniel David
American. Physician
Founded Palmer School of Chiropractic, Davenport, IA, 1898.
b. Mar 7, 1845 in Toronto, Ontario, Canada
d. Oct 20, 1913 in Los Angeles, California
Source: *AmBi; BioIn 5, 13; DcAmB; DcAmMeB 84; DcNAA; NatCAB 18; NewAgE 90; WebAB 74, 79; WhAm 4, HSA; WhoMW 74*

Palmer, Erastus Dow
American. Sculptor
His most famous work in marble, *The White Captive,* 1858, in Metropolitan Museum, NYC.
b. Apr 2, 1817 in Pompey, New York
d. Mar 9, 1904 in Albany, New York
Source: *AmBi; ApCAB; BioIn 7, 9; BriEAA; DcAmArt; DcAmB; Drake; HarEnUS; McGDA; NatCAB 5; NewYHSD; OxCAmH; OxCArt; OxDcArt; TwCBDA; WhAm 1; WhAmArt 85*

Palmer, Frances Flora Bond
"Fanny Palmer"
American. Artist
Produced over 200 lithographs for Currier and Ives, 1849-59.
b. Jun 26, 1812 in Leicester, England
d. Aug 20, 1876 in New York, New York
Source: *BioIn 7; IlBEAAW; InWom SUP; NotAW; PeoHis; WhAm HS; WomFir*

Palmer, Frederick
American. Author, Journalist
Covered all major world events, 1895-1945; author *My Year of the War,* 1915.
b. Jan 29, 1873 in Pleasantville, Pennsylvania
d. Sep 2, 1958 in Charlottesville, Virginia
Source: *AmAu&B; ApCAB X; BioIn 4, 5, 6; DcAmAu; NatCAB 46; OxCCan; REnAL; ScF&FL 1; TwCA, SUP; WhAm 3; WhLit; WhNAA*

Palmer, Jim
[James Alvin Palmer]
American. Baseball Player, Sportscaster
Pitcher, Baltimore, 1966-84; only pitcher in AL to win Cy Young Award three times; ABC sports network broadcaster, 1984—.
b. Oct 15, 1945 in New York, New York
Source: *Ballpl 90; BiDAmSp BB; BioIn 10, 11, 12, 13, 14, 15, 17, 20; CurBio 80; LegTOT; News 91, 91-2; WhoAm 78, 80, 82, 84, 86, 88, 92, 94, 95, 96, 97; WhoE 95; WhoProB 73; WhoSpor; WorAl; WorAlBi*

Palmer, Lilli
[Lilli Marie Peiser; Mrs. Carlos Thompson]
German. Actor, Author
Married to Rex Harrison, 1943-57; films include *Body and Soul,* 1948; *The Boys from Brazil,* 1978.
b. May 24, 1914 in Posen, Germany
d. Jan 27, 1986 in Los Angeles, California
Source: *AnObit 1986; BiDFilm 81, 94; BioIn 2, 9, 10, 11, 14, 15; ConTFT 3; CurBio 51, 86, 86N; FilmAG WE; FilmEn; FilmgC; ForYSC; GangFlm; HalFC 80; IntMPA 77, 82, 86; IntWW 83; InWom, SUP; MotPP; MovMk; NewYTBS 86; NotNAT A; OxCFilm; VarWW 85; WhAm 9; WhoAm 74, 76, 78, 80, 82, 84; WhoAmW 83; WhoHol A; WhoThe 72, 77, 81; WhoWor 74; WorAl; WorAlBi; WorEFlm*

Palmer, Nathaniel Brown
American. Explorer
Discovered Palmer Land in Antarctic, 1820; improved design of clipper ships.
b. Aug 8, 1799 in Stonington, Connecticut
d. Jun 21, 1877 in San Francisco, California
Source: *AmBi; BioIn 1, 3, 4, 6, 8, 9; DcAmB; McGEWB; NatCAB 25; OxCShps; TwCBDA; WhAm HS; WhWE; WorAl; WorAlBi*

Palmer, Peter
American. Actor, Singer
Played title role in film *Lil' Abner,* 1959.
b. Sep 20, 1931 in Milwaukee, Wisconsin
Source: *BiE&WWA; FilmgC; ForYSC; HalFC 80, 84, 88; NotNAT; WhoHol 92, A*

Palmer, Potter
American. Business Executive
Chicago real estate entrepreneur, once partner of Marshall Field; opened Palmer House Hotel, 1870s.
b. May 20, 1826 in Albany County, New York
d. May 4, 1902 in Chicago, Illinois
Source: *ApCAB SUP; BiDAmBL 83; BioIn 3, 4, 15; DcAmB; GayN; NatCAB*

12; TwCBDA; WebAB 74, 79; WhAm 1, 2; WorAl; WorAlBi

Palmer, Robert
English. Singer, Musician
Hit singles "Bad Case of Loving You," 1979; "Some Like It Hot," 1985.
b. Jan 19, 1949 in Batley, England
Source: *BioIn 12, 16; ConAu 121; ConMuA 80A; ConMus 2; EncRk 88; EncRkSt; IlEncRk; LegTOT; NewGrDA 86; NewGrDJ 88; PenEncP; RkOn 85; RolSEnR 83; SoulM; WhoHol 92; WhoRock 81*

Palmer, William
English. Murderer, Physician
Hanged for poisoning three, suspected of killing 13; case led to "Palmer Act" which allowed change of venue to London for sensational trials.
b. 1824
d. 1856 in London, England
Source: *BioIn 2, 3, 4, 8, 9; DcNaB; OxCMed 86*

Palmerston, Henry John Temple, Viscount
"Pam"
English. Statesman
Frequent foreign minister, 1830-51; prime minister, 1855-58, 1859-65; rescued Turkey from Russia.
b. Oct 20, 1784 in Broadlands, England
d. Oct 18, 1865 in Hertfordshire, England
Source: *Alli; Benet 87, 96; BioIn 1, 2, 3, 4, 5, 6, 7, 8, 9, 10, 11, 12, 13; CelCen; DcBiPP; LinLib S; McGEWB; NewCBEL; REn; WhAm HS; WhCiWar; WhDW*

Palmieri, Eddie
[Eduardo Palmieri]
American. Pianist
First Latin musician to win a Grammy award, 1976.
b. Dec 15, 1936 in New York, New York
Source: *AllMusG; BioIn 13, 17, 18, 20; ConMus 15; CurBio 92; NewGrDA 86; PenEncP; WhoHisp 94*

Palminteri, Chazz
[Calogero Lorenzo Palminteri]
American. Actor
Appeared in *A Bronx Tale.*
b. May 15, 1951 in New York, New York
Source: *IntMPA 96; WhoAm 96, 97*

Paltrow, Bruce
American. Director, Producer
Exec. producer-director of TV series "St. Elsewhere," 1982-88.
b. Nov 26, 1943 in New York, New York
Source: *BioIn 15; ConTFT 9; IntMPA 88, 92, 94, 96; MiSFD 9; NewYTBS 81; VarWW 85*

Paltrow, Gwyneth
American. Actor
Played title role in *Emma,* 1996.
b. Sep 28, 1973 in Los Angeles, California
Source: *News 97-1*

Paludan, Jacob
[Stig Henning Jacob Puggard Paludan]
Danish. Author, Journalist
Wrote two-vol. novel *Joergen Stein,* 1966.
b. Feb 7, 1896 in Copenhagen, Denmark
d. Sep 26, 1975 in Copenhagen, Denmark
Source: *BioIn 1, 3; ClDMEL 80; ConAu 115; DcScanL; EncWL 2, 3; Novels; PenC EUR; RAdv 13-2; REn; WhE&EA; WhoLA*

Paludan-Muller, Frederik
Danish. Poet
Romantic poet known for *The Danseuse,* 1833.
b. Feb 7, 1809 in Kerteminde, Denmark
d. Dec 28, 1876 in Copenhagen, Denmark
Source: *BbD; BiD&SB; BioIn 7; CasWL; DcEuL; DcScanL; EuAu; EvEuW; LinLib L; PenC EUR; ScF&FL 1*

Pan, Hermes
American. Choreographer
Known for choreography films that paired Fred Astaire, Ginger Rogers: *Flying Down to Rio,* 1933; won Oscar for *A Damsel in Distress,* 1937.
b. Dec 10, 1911 in Memphis, Tennessee
d. Sep 19, 1990 in Beverly Hills, California
Source: *BioIn 5, 14; ConTFT 9; FacFETw; HalFC 88; IntMPA 88; WhoAm 90; WhoWest 89*

Panama, Norman
American. Screenwriter
Films include *My Favorite Blonde,* 1942; *White Christmas,* 1954.
b. Apr 21, 1914 in Chicago, Illinois
Source: *BiE&WWA; BioIn 14; CmMov; ConAu 104; ConDr 88A; EncAFC; FilmEn; FilmgC; HalFC 80, 84, 88; IntMPA 75, 76, 77, 78, 79, 80, 81, 86, 92, 96; MiSFD 9; NotNAT; VarWW 85; WorEFlm*

Panchen Lama
[Panchen Erdeni; Bainqen Erdini Qoigyu Gyaincain]
Tibetan. Religious Leader, Political Leader
Was not accepted in Tibet when installed as Panchen Lama, 1944; first visited Ti bet, 1952; honorary chairman of Chinese Buddhist Assn., 1953-1989.
b. 1937 in Qinghai, China
d. Jan 28, 1989 in Xigaze, China
Source: *BioIn 5, 11, 16, 19; IntWW 83, 89N; NewYTBS 78, 89*

Pandit, Vijaya Lakshmi (Nehru)
Indian. Politician, Diplomat
First female pres., UN, 1953-54; wrote autobiography *The Scope of Happiness: A Personal Memoir,* 1979; sister of Jawahari.
b. Aug 18, 1900 in Allahabad, India
d. Dec 1, 1990 in New Delhi, India
Source: *BioIn 1, 2, 3, 5, 6, 7, 8, 11, 12, 17; ConAu 104; ContDcW 89; CurBio 46, 91N; FacFETw; FarE&A 78, 80, 81; HerW, 84; HisDcKW; IntDcWB; IntWW 74, 75, 76, 77, 78, 79, 80, 81, 82, 83, 89, 91N; InWom, SUP; McGEWB; NewYTBS 90; Who 74, 82, 83, 85, 88, 90, 92N; WhoUN 75; WomFir; WomWR*

Panek, LeRoy Lad
American. Author
Pioneer in sensational fiction; won Edgars for *Watteau's Shepherds: The Detective Novel in Britain, 1914-40,* 1979; *Introduction to the Detective Story,* 1987.
b. Jan 26, 1943 in Cleveland, Ohio
Source: *ConAu 32NR, 113*

Paneth, Friedrich Adolf
Austrian. Chemist
Co-invented radioactive tracer techniques.
b. Aug 31, 1887 in Vienna, Austria
d. Sep 17, 1958 in Vienna, Austria
Source: *BiESc; BioIn 3, 5, 14; DcNaB 1951; DcScB; LarDcSc; ObitT 1951; WhE&EA*

Panetta, Leon E(dward)
American. Government Official
Director, Office of Management & Budget, 1993; White House Chief of Staff, 1994-97.
b. Jun 28, 1938 in Monterey, California
Source: *AlmAP 92; BiDrUSC 89; BioIn 8, 13, 16; CngDr 77, 79, 81, 83, 85, 87, 89; ConAu 101; CurBio 93; NewYTBS 92; PolsAm 84; WhoAm 78, 80, 82, 84, 86, 88, 90, 92, 94, 95, 96; WhoAmL 79; WhoAmP 77, 79, 81, 83, 85, 87, 89, 91, 93, 95; WhoE 89; WhoFI 92, 94; WhoGov 77; WhoWest 78, 80, 82, 84, 87, 89, 92, 94*

Pang, May
American. Secretary
Friend, mistress of John Lennon; wrote *Loving John,* 1983.
b. 1950?
Source: *ConAu 118; WhoAmW 89; WhoRocM 82*

Pangborn, Clyde Edward
American. Aviator
With Hugh Herndon, flew first non-stop Pacific crossing, from Japan to Washington, Oct 1931.
b. Oct 28, 1894 in Bridgeport, Washington
d. Mar 29, 1958 in New York, New York
Source: *BioIn 4, 5, 11; DcAmB S6; ObitOF 79*

Pangborn, Franklin
American. Actor
Known for roles in over 150 films as prissy hotel manager, bank clerk, including *A Star Is Born,* 1937.
b. Jan 23, 1893 in Newark, New Jersey
d. Jul 20, 1958 in Santa Monica, California
Source: *BioIn 21; EncAFC; FilmEn; FilmgC; HolCA; IntDcF 2-3; LegTOT; MovMk; OlFamFa; QDrFCA 92; Vers A; WhoCom; WhoHol B; WhScrn 74, 77, 83*

Panic, Milan
Yugoslav. Business Executive, Political Leader
Prime minister, Yugoslavia, 1992; founded ICN Pharmaceuticals, 1960.
b. Dec 20, 1929 in Belgrade, Serbia
Source: *BioIn 9, 10, 18, 19; CurBio 93; Dun&B 88, 90; IntWW 93; St&PR 75, 84, 87, 91, 93, 96, 97; WhoAm 74, 76, 78, 82, 84, 86, 88, 92, 96; WhoFI 96; WhoWor 93, 95, 96, 97*

Panizza, Ettore
Argentine. Conductor, Composer
Led Buenos Aires' Teatro Colon until retirement, 1950s; Toscanini's assistant, Milan, 1920s.
b. Aug 12, 1875 in Buenos Aires, Argentina
d. Nov 29, 1967 in Milan, Italy
Source: *Baker 78, 84, 92; BiDAmM; BioIn 4, 8, 10; CmOp; MetOEnc; NewEOp 71; NewGrDM 80; OxDcOp*

Panizzi, Anthony, Sir
English. Librarian
Celebrated principal librarian of British Museum, 1856-66; pioneered its catalog, designed reading room.
b. Sep 16, 1797 in Brescello, Italy
d. Apr 8, 1879 in London, England
Source: *Alli; BioIn 6, 8, 14, 15; CasWL; CelCen; DcEnL; DcNaB; NewCol 75; OxCEng 85; OxCFr*

Pankhurst, Christabel Harriette, Dame
English. Suffragist
Daughter of woman-suffrage advocate, Emmeline; published mother's biography, 1935.
b. Sep 22, 1880 in Manchester, England
d. Feb 14, 1958 in Santa Monica, California
Source: *DcNaB 1951; DcTwHis; GrBr; HerW; IntDcWB; LngCTC; ObitOF 79; OxCEng 85; WhoLA*

Pankhurst, Emmeline Goulden
English. Suffragist
Militant reformer known for hunger strikes, bombings; wrote first British woman-suffrage bill, 1860s.
b. Jul 14, 1858 in Manchester, England
d. Jun 14, 1928 in London, England
Source: *ConAu 116; DcNaB 1922; EncBrWW; FacFETw; HerW; IntDcWB; InWom, SUP; LngCTC; McGEWB; OxCEng 85; VicBrit; WomFir*

Pankhurst, Sylvia
[Estelle Sylvia Pankhurst]
English. Suffragist
With daughters, launched British feminist movement; forerunner of the US version; won women's voting rights, 1918.
b. May 5, 1882 in Manchester, England
d. Sep 27, 1960 in Addis Ababa, Ethiopia
Source: *BiDBrF 1; BiDWomA; BioIn 5, 8, 9, 11, 12, 14, 15, 16; ContDcW 89; DcWomA; FemiCLE; HerW, 84; HisWorL; IntDcWB; InWom, SUP; LngCTC; NewC; ObitT 1951; RadHan; TwCPaSc; WhE&EA; WhoLA; WomFir*

Pankow, James
American. Musician
Trombonist with group; hit single "Wishing You Were Here," 1974.
b. Aug 20, 1947 in Chicago, Illinois

Pan Ku
Chinese. Historian
One of the most influential Chinese historians; wrote *The History of the Former Han Dynasty,* a work that has influenced generations of later historians.
b. 32? in Xi'an, China
d. 92

Pannenberg, Wolfhart Ulrich
German. Theologian
Theological writings include *Theology and Philosophy of Science,* 1976; *Ethics,* 1981.
b. Oct 2, 1928 in Stettin, Germany
Source: *BioIn 16; ConAu 11NR; EncWB; IntWW 91; WhoRel 85*

Pannini, Giovanni Paolo
[Giovanni Paolo Panini]
Italian. Artist
Drew cityscapes, ancient Roman landmarks: *View of Roman Forum,* 1735.
b. 1691? in Piacenza, Italy
d. 1765 in Rome, Italy
Source: *BioIn 1, 2, 4; ClaDrA; McGDA; NewCol 75; OxDcArt*

Panofsky, Erwin
American. Art Historian, Educator
Noted exponent of iconology; wrote *Meaning in the Visual Arts,* 1955.
b. Mar 30, 1892 in Hannover, Germany
d. Mar 14, 1968 in Princeton, New Jersey
Source: *AmAu&B; BiDAmEd; BioIn 4, 8, 9, 13, 14, 20; ConAu 113, 117; DcAmB S8; DcArts; FacFETw; OxCArt; OxDcArt; ThTwC 87; WebAB 74, 79; WhAm 4A; WorAu 1970*

Panov, Valery
Israeli. Dancer
Principal dancer, Maly Theatre of Opera and Ballet, 1957-63; wrote *To Dance,* 1978.
b. Mar 12, 1938 in Vilna, Union of Soviet Socialist Republics
Source: *BiDD; BiDSovU; BioIn 10, 11, 12, 13, 14; BioNews 74; ConAu 102; CurBio 74; IntDcB; IntWW 91; WhoAm 82; WhoWor 84, 87*

Pantaleoni, Helenka (Tradeusa Adamowski)
American. Government Official
Headed UNICEF, 1955-87.
b. Nov 22, 1900 in Brookline, Massachusetts
d. Jan 5, 1987 in New York, New York
Source: *BioIn 4; CurBio 56, 87, 87N; InWom; WhoAm 74, 76, 78; WhoAmW 58, 64, 66, 68, 70, 72, 74; WhoUN 75; WhoWor 78*

Panter-Downes, Mollie
English. Author, Journalist
Wrote *New Yorker* mag. column, "Letter from London," 1939-84; books include *One Fine Day,* 1947.
b. Aug 25, 1906 in London, England
d. Jan 22, 1997 in Surrey, England
Source: *BioIn 1, 4, 16; ConAu 101; FemiCLE; LngCTC; NewC; TwCA, SUP; WhE&EA; Who 85, 92; WhoAmW 68, 70, 72, 74; WhoWor 74*

Pao, Y(ue) K(ong), Sir
Chinese. Shipping Executive
Chm. of World-Wide Shipping and Wharf Holdings, 1974-86.
b. 1918 in Chekiang
d. Sep 23, 1991, Hong Kong
Source: *BioIn 11, 14, 15; FarE&A 78, 79; IntWW 83, 91; NewYTBS 76; Who 85, 92*

Papadopoulos, George
Greek. Political Leader
Headed a group of colonels that seized control of Greek government; premier, 1967-81.
b. May 5, 1919 in Eleochorian, Greece
Source: *BioIn 8, 9, 10; CurBio 70; FacFETw; IntWW 83, 91; IntYB 78, 79, 80, 81, 82; NewYTBE 73; WhoGov 72; WhoWor 74; WorDWW*

Papandreou, Andreas (George)
Greek. Political Leader
First Socialist prime minister of Greece, 1981-90; defeated by Constantine Mitsotakis; son of George.
b. Feb 5, 1919 in Chios, Greece
d. Jun 23, 1996 in Athens, Greece
Source: *BioIn 7, 8, 9, 11, 12, 13, 14, 15, 16; CurBio 70, 83, 96N; DcPol; EncWB; FacFETw; IntWW 74, 75, 76, 77, 78, 79, 80, 81, 82, 83, 89, 91, 93; IntYB 82; LegTOT; News 97-1; NewYTBS 81, 82, 85; PolLCWE; WhAm 11; Who 90, 92, 94; WhoAm 74; WhoEIO 82; WhoWor 74, 76, 78, 82, 84, 87, 89, 91, 93, 95, 96*

Papandreou, George
Greek. Political Leader
Organized Democratic Socialist Party, 1935; premier, 1944-45; father of Andreas.
b. Feb 13, 1888 in Patras, Greece
d. Nov 1, 1968 in Athens, Greece
Source: *BioIn 1, 7, 8, 21; CurBio 44, 68; DcPol; DcTwHis; FacFETw; HisEWW; ObitT 1961; PolLCWE*

Papanicolaou, George Nicholas
American. Physician
Developed "Pap" test, 1943, to detect uterine cancer.
b. May 13, 1883 in Comi, Greece
d. Feb 19, 1962 in Miami, Florida
Source: *BioIn 2, 4, 5, 6, 8, 10, 13, 20; DcAmB S7; DcAmMeB 84; DcScB; LarDcSc; NatCAB 50; OxCMed 86; WhAm 4; WorAl*

Papanin, Ivan D
Russian. Explorer
Commanded first Russian ice floe station, 1937; headed polar research stations.
b. Nov 26, 1894 in Sevastopol, Russia
d. Jan 30, 1980 in Moscow, Union of Soviet Socialist Republics
Source: *IntWW 76, 77; NewYTBS 86; WhoOcn 78; WhoSocC 78; WhoWor 78*

Papas, Irene
Greek. Actor
Films include *Zorba the Greek,* 1964; *The Trojan Women,* 1971.
b. Sep 3, 1926 in Chiliomondion, Greece
Source: *BioIn 17; CelR; ConTFT 2, 8; EncEurC; FilmEn; FilmgC; ForYSC; HalFC 80, 84, 88; IntDcF 1-3, 2-3; IntMPA 77, 80, 84, 86, 88, 92, 94, 96; InWom SUP; ItaFilm; LegTOT; MotPP; MovMk; OxCFilm; VarWW 85; WhoAm 76, 78, 80, 82, 84, 86, 88, 92; WhoEnt 92; WhoHol A; WhoWor 82, 84; WorAl; WorAlBi*

Papashvily, George
American. Author, Sculptor
Wrote *Anything Can Happen,* 1945; books on Soviet Georgian folklore.
b. Aug 23, 1898 in Kobiankari, Russia
d. Mar 29, 1978 in Cambria, California
Source: *AmAu&B; BioIn 4, 10, 11, 12; ConAu 77, 81; CurBio 45, 78; REnAL; SmATA 17; TwCA, SUP; WhoAmA 73, 76, 78N, 80N, 82N, 84N, 86N, 89N, 91N, 93N*

Papen, Franz von
German. Diplomat, Politician
Hitler's foreign ambassador to Austria, Turkey; acquitted at Nuremberg.
b. Oct 29, 1879 in Werl, Germany
d. May 2, 1969 in Obersabach, Germany (West)
Source: *BiDExR; BioIn 1, 2, 3, 8, 9; CurBio 41, 69; DcTwHis; Dis&D; EncAI&E; EncTR, 91; FacFETw; HisEWW; ObitT 1961; REn; SpyCS*

Papi, Genarro
Italian. Conductor
Led Chicago Civic Opera, 1925-32; assisted Toscanini at Met., 1916-25.
b. Dec 21, 1886 in Naples, Italy
d. Nov 29, 1941 in New York, New York
Source: *Baker 84; NewEOp 71*

Papineau, Louis-Joseph
Canadian. Political Leader
Led movement for political reform in Canada.
b. Oct 7, 1786 in Montreal, Quebec, Canada
d. Sep 25, 1871 in Montebello, Quebec, Canada
Source: *BbtC; DcCanB 10; DcNaB; Drake; HarEnUS; MacDCB 78; McGEWB; OxCCan*

Papini, Giovanni
Italian. Author
Wrote popular *Life of Christ,* 1921; *Gog,* a satire on modern society, 1931.
b. Jan 9, 1881 in Florence, Italy
d. Jul 8, 1956 in Florence, Italy
Source: *BiDExR; BioIn 1, 2, 4; CasWL; CathA 1930; ClDMEL 47, 80; CnMWL; ConAu 121; DcCathB; DcItL 1, 2; EncWL; EvEuW; LinLib L, S; LngCTC; PenC EUR; RAdv 14, 13-2; REn; TwCA, SUP; TwCLC 22; TwCWr; WhE&EA; WhoLA*

Papp, Joseph
[Joseph Papirofsky]
American. Director, Producer
Founded NY Shakespeare Festival, 1956; won over 20 Tonys, six Obies, three Pulitzers; his *A Chorus Line* was longest-running show on Broadway, 1975-90.
b. Jun 22, 1921 in New York, New York
d. Oct 31, 1991 in New York, New York
Source: *AmCulL; BiE&WWA; BioIn 5, 7, 8, 9, 10, 11, 12, 13, 14, 16; BlueB 76; CamGWoT; CelR, 90; CnThe; ConTFT 1, 12; CurBio 65, 92N; DcArts; DcTwCCu 1; EncMcCE; EncMT; EncWT; Ent; FacFETw; IntWW 79, 80, 81, 82, 83, 89, 91; LegTOT; LesBEnT, 92; News 92, 92-2; NewYTBE 71, 72; NewYTBS 91, 92; NewYTET; NotNAT, A; OxCAmT 84; OxCThe 67, 83; PlP&P, A; VarWW 85; WhoAm 74, 76, 78, 80, 82, 84, 86, 90; WhoE 77, 79, 81, 83, 85, 86, 91; WhoThe 72, 77, 81; WhoWor 74; WorAl; WorAlBi*

Papp, Laszlo
Hungarian. Boxer
Undefeated amateur, pro middleweight, light-middleweight; first man to win three consecutive Olympic boxing gold medals, 1948-56.
b. Mar 25, 1926, Hungary
Source: *BioIn 6; IntWW 81, 82, 83, 89, 91, 93; NewYTBS 74; WhoAm 88; WhoBox 74; WhoE 86, 89; WhoFI 87; WhoSoCE 89; WhoTech 89; WhoWor 89*

Pappas, Ike
American. Broadcast Journalist
Correspondent, CBS News since 1965.
b. Apr 16, 1933 in New York, New York
Source: *WhoTelC*

Pappas, Milt(on Steven)
"Gimpy"; "The Golden Greek"
American. Baseball Player
Pitcher, 1957-73; threw no-hitter, 1972; had 209 career wins.
b. May 11, 1939 in Detroit, Michigan
Source: *Ballpl 90; BaseEn 88; BiDAmSp BB; BioIn 6, 13, 15; WhoAm 74, 76; WhoProB 73*

Paracelsus, Philippus Aureolus
[Theophrastus B Von Hohenheim]
Swiss. Physician
Controversial Renaissance thinker who abandoned medieval medical tradition to seek answers in nature.
b. Nov 10, 1493 in Einsiedeln, Switzerland
d. Sep 24, 1541 in Salzburg, Austria
Source: *AsBiEn; BiESc; BiHiMed; CasWL; DcCathB; EuAu; EvEuW; InSci; LuthC 75; McGEWB; NewC; RAdv 14, 13-4, 13-5*

Paray, Paul
French. Conductor
Director, Detroit Symphony, 1952-63.
b. May 24, 1886 in Treport, France
d. Oct 10, 1979 in Monte Carlo, Monaco
Source: *Baker 78, 84, 92; BiDAmM; BioIn 2, 4, 11, 12; MusSN; NewAmDM; NewGrDA 86; NewGrDM 80; NewYTBS 79; OxCMus; PenDiMP; WhAm 7; WhoAm 74, 76, 78; WhoFr 79*

Parazaider, Walter
American. Musician
With Terry Kath, formed group, 1967; hits include "Saturday in the Park," 1972.
b. Mar 14, 1945 in Chicago, Illinois

Parcells, Bill
[Duane Charles Parcells]
American. Football Coach, Sportscaster
Head coach, NY Giants, 1983-1991; won Super Bowl, 1987, 1991; sports commentator for NBC 1991-96; head coach, New England, 1996-97; NY Jets, 1997—.
b. Aug 22, 1941 in Englewood, New Jersey
Source: *BioIn 13, 15; CelR 90; CurBio 91; FootReg 87; NewYTBS 82; WhoAm 86, 90, 94, 95, 96, 97; WhoE 85, 86, 89, 91, 93, 95, 97; WhoSpor*

Pare, Ambroise
"Father of Modern Surgery"
French. Surgeon
Introduced more humane medical treatment; surgeon to four French kings.
b. 1510? in Laval, France
d. Dec 22, 1590 in Paris, France

Source: *AsBiEn; BiESc; BiHiMed; BioIn 1, 2, 3, 4, 5, 6, 7, 8, 9, 13, 16, 18, 19; DcEuL; DcScB; InSci; McGEWB; NewCol 75; OxCFr; OxCMed 86; REn; WhDW; WorAl; WorAlBi*

Parent, Bernie
[Bernard Marcel Parent]
Canadian. Hockey Player
Goalie, 1965-79, mostly with Philadelphia; won Vezina, Conn Smythe trophies twice; Hall of Fame, 1984.
b. Apr 3, 1945 in Montreal, Quebec, Canada
Source: *BioIn 10, 12; HocEn; NewYTBS 74; WhoHcky 73; WhoSpor*

Parent, Elizabeth Anne
American. Educator
Editor, *Harvard Educational Review,* 1973-74; taught at several colleges and universities in the field of Native American Studies, 1976—.
b. 1941 in Bethel, Alaska
Source: *BioIn 21; NotNaAm; WhoWest 92, 94*

Pareto, Vilfredo
Italian. Economist
Known for hatred of democracy; called creator of facist ideology by Mussolini.
b. Aug 15, 1848 in Paris, France
d. Aug 19, 1923 in Celigny, Switzerland
Source: *BioIn 1, 2, 7, 8, 11, 12, 13, 14, 16; ClDMEL 47; GrEconB; LuthC 75; MakMC; McGEWB; RAdv 14, 13-3; REn; ThTwC 87; TwCA, SUP; WhDW; WhoEc 81, 86; WorAl; WorAlBi*

Paretsky, Sara
American. Author
Creator of the female detective V.I. Warshawski.
b. Jun 8, 1947 in Ames, Iowa
Source: *BestSel 90-3; BioIn 16; ConAu 125, 129; ConPopW; CrtSuMy; CurBio 92; FemiCLE; GrWomMW; RAdv 14; RGTwCWr; TwCCr&M 91; WhoAm 90; WhoAmW 91; WhoMW 92; WorAu 1985; WrDr 92, 94, 96*

Paris, Jerry
American. Actor, Director
Directed, played the neighbor in "The Dick Van Dyke Show," 1961-66.
b. Jul 25, 1925 in San Francisco, California
d. Mar 31, 1986 in Los Angeles, California
Source: *BioIn 14; ConTFT 3; EncAFC; FilmEn; FilmgC; ForYSC; HalFC 80, 84, 88; IntMPA 88; LesBEnT; MiSFD 9N; NewYTBS 86; NewYTET; VarWW 85; WhoAm 74, 78, 80, 82, 84; WhoHol A*

Parish, Mitchell
American. Lyricist
Wrote the lyrics for more than 600 songs including "Star Dust" and "Volare."
b. Jul 10, 1900, Lithuania
d. Mar 31, 1993 in New York, New York
Source: *AmPS; AmSong; AnObit 1993; ASCAP 66, 80; BiDAmM; BioIn 4, 15, 16, 18, 19; CmpEPM; NewYTBS 93; Sw&Ld C*

Parish, Peggy
[Margaret Cecile Parish]
American. Children's Author
Wrote more than 30 books, many of which featured her best-known character, Amelia Bedelia.
b. Jul 14, 1927 in Manning, South Carolina
d. Nov 18, 1988 in Manning, South Carolina
Source: *AuBYP 3; BioIn 12, 16, 19; ChlBkCr; ChlLR 22; ConAu 18NR, 38NR, 73, 127; ForWC 70; FourBJA; LegTOT; MajAI; SmATA 17, 59, 73; TwCChW 83, 89, 95; WhAm 9; WhoAm 82, 84, 86, 88; WhoAmW 66, 68, 70; WhoWor 84, 87, 89*

Parish, Robert L
American. Basketball Player
Center, Golden State, 1976-80, Boston, 1980-94, Charlotte, 1994—; won three NBA championships.
b. Aug 30, 1953 in Shreveport, Louisiana
Source: *BioIn 14; NewYTBS 85; OfNBA 87; WhoAm 84, 86, 88; WhoBlA 92; WhoE 89; WorAlBi*

Parizeau, Jacques
Canadian. Political Leader
Premier of Quebec, 1994—.
b. Aug 9, 1930 in Montreal, Quebec, Canada
Source: *BioIn 11, 17, 19, 20, 21; CanWW 31, 70, 79, 80, 81, 83, 89; CurBio 93; IntWW 93; News 95, 95-1; NewYTBS 94; WhoAm 96, 97; WhoCan 80; WhoWor 95, 96*

Park, Brad
[Douglas Bradford Park]
Canadian. Hockey Player
Defenseman, 1968-85, mostly with NY Rangers, Boston; second to Denis Potvin in career assists by defenseman; Hall of Fame, 1988.
b. Jul 6, 1948 in Toronto, Ontario, Canada
Source: *BioIn 9, 10, 11; CurBio 76; HocEn; LegTOT; WhoAm 78, 80, 82, 84, 86; WhoHcky 73; WorAl*

Park, Chung Hee
Korean. Army Officer, Political Leader
Pres., 1963-79; assassinated.
b. Sep 30, 1917 in Sosan Gun, Korea
d. Oct 26, 1979 in Seoul, Korea (South)
Source: *BioIn 8, 9, 10, 11, 12, 13; ConAu 10NR, 61, 97; CurBio 69, 80, 80N; DcTwHis; DicTyr; FarE&A 78, 79; IntWW 74, 75, 76, 77, 78, 79; IntYB 78, 79; McGEWB; NewYTBS 79; WhoGov 72; WhoWor 74, 76, 78; WorAl*

Park, Maud May Wood
American. Suffragist
First pres., League of Women Voters, 1919.
b. Jan 25, 1871 in Boston, Massachusetts
d. May 8, 1955 in Reading, Massachusetts
Source: *DcAmB S5; NotAW MOD; WhAm 3*

Park, Mungo
Scottish. Explorer
Explored Niger River; wrote *Travels in Interior of Africa,* 1799.
b. Sep 10, 1771, Scotland
d. 1806?
Source: *Alli; BbD; BiD&SB; BioIn 2, 3, 4, 6, 7, 8, 9, 10, 11, 12, 18, 20, 21; BritAu; CelCen; Chambr 2; CmScLit; DcAfHiB 86; DcBiPP; DcLEL; DcNaB, C; EvLB; Expl 93; HisDBrE; InSci; LegTOT; LinLib L, S; NewC; NewCBEL; NewCol 75; OxCEng 67, 85, 95; OxCMed 86; RAdv 14, 13-3; WhDW; WhWE*

Park, Robert Ezra
American. Sociologist
Important member of the "Chicago School"; known for his studies on human ecology and ethnic minorities.
b. Feb 14, 1864 in Harveyville, Pennsylvania
d. Feb 7, 1944 in Nashville, Tennessee
Source: *AmSocL; BioIn 3, 10, 11, 12, 13, 14, 17, 19; DcAmB S3; DcAmImH; DcNAA; DcSoc; MakMC; NatCAB 37; PeoHis; RAdv 14, 13-3; WebAB 74, 79; WhAm 2; WhNAA*

Park, Thomas
American. Zoologist
Specialized in population ecology; helped to transform ecology from a natural history based on field observations into a science with contolled experiments.
b. Nov 17, 1908 in Danville, Illinois
d. Mar 30, 1992 in Chicago, Illinois
Source: *AmMWSc 73P, 76P, 79, 82, 86, 89, 92; AuBYP 3; BioIn 5, 6, 17, 18; CurBio 92N; WhAm 10; WhoAm 74, 76, 78, 80, 82, 84, 86, 88, 90*

Park, Tongsun
[Park Tong Sun]
"Onassis of the Orient"
Korean. Businessman
Indicted on 36 counts of influence buying on behalf of Korea, 1978.
b. Mar 16, 1935? in Pyongyang, Korea
Source: *BioIn 11, 12; NewYTBS 78*

Parkening, Christopher William
American. Musician
Classical guitarist, began playing as a child; noted for int'l. concert tours.
b. Dec 14, 1947 in Los Angeles, California
Source: *Baker 84; BioIn 10, 15; ConMus 7; CurBio 87; IntWWM 90; NewYTBS 74; PenDiMP; WhoAm 84; WhoAmM 83*

Parker, Ace
[Clarence Parker]
American. Football Player
Quarterback, 1937-41, 1945-46, mostly with Brooklyn; MVP, 1940; Hall of Fame, 1972.
b. May 17, 1913 in Portsmouth, Virginia
Source: *Ballpl 90; BiDAmSp FB; BioIn 17; LegTOT; NewYTBE 71; WhoFtbl 74*

Parker, Alan William
English. Director
Films include *Midnight Express,* 1978; *Fame,* 1980.
b. Feb 14, 1944 in London, England
Source: *ConTFT 5; CurBio 94; IntAu&W 89; IntWW 89, 91, 93; VarWW 85; Who 82, 83, 85, 88, 90, 92, 94; WhoAm 82, 84, 86, 88, 90, 92, 94, 95, 96, 97; WhoEnt 92; WhoWor 95, 96, 97*

Parker, Albert
American. Business Executive, Baker
Owner of Claxton Bakery, one of the world's largest fruitcake producers.
d. May 21, 1995 in Claxton, Georgia
Source: *BioIn 19; NewYTBS 83; St&PR 75, 84; WhoHol 92; WhoWorJ 72, 78*

Parker, Alton Brooks
American. Judge, Politician
Dem. presidential candidate, 1904; lost to Theodore Roosevelt.
b. May 14, 1852 in Cortland, New York
d. May 10, 1926 in New York, New York
Source: *AmBi; AmDec 1900; AmPolLe; ApCAB X; BioIn 7, 8; CyAG; DcAmB; HarEnUS; NatCAB 10, 27; NewCol 75; PeoHis; PresAR; TwCBDA; WhAm 1; WhAmP*

Parker, Arthur C(aswell)
American. Anthropologist
Director, Rochester Museum, ca. 1914-1955.
b. 1881 in Cattaraugus Indian ReservaNew York
d. Jan 1, 1955
Source: *AmAu&B; BenetAL 91; BiNAW, B, SupB; BioIn 3, 4, 11, 12; DcAmB S5; REnAL; WhAm 3*

Parker, Bonnie
[Bonnie and Clyde]
American. Criminal
Two-year crime spree in southwest included 12 murders, numerous robberies.
b. Oct 1, 1910 in Rowena, Texas
d. May 23, 1934 in Gibsland, Louisiana
Source: *BioIn 8, 9, 12, 18, 21; EncACr; HanAmWH; InWom SUP; LegTOT; WorAl; WorAlBi*

Parker, Brant (Julian)
American. Cartoonist
Created nat. syndicated comic strips, "Wizard of Id," 1964; "Crock," 1975; "Goosemeyer," 1980.
b. Aug 26, 1920 in Los Angeles, California
Source: *ConAu 114; EncACom; EncTwCJ; WhoAm 78, 80, 82, 84, 86, 88; WorECom*

Parker, Buddy
[Raymond Parker]
American. Football Coach
Head coach, St. Louis, 1949, Detroit, 1951-56, Pittsburgh, 1957-64; won NFL championships, 1952-53; introduced two-minute offense.
b. Dec 16, 1913 in Kemp, Texas
d. Mar 22, 1982 in Kaufman, Texas
Source: *BioIn 3, 4, 12, 13; CurBio 55, 82, 82N; NewYTBS 82; WhoFtbl 74*

Parker, Cecil
English. Actor
Character actor of ten British films, 1929-69, including *The Lady Vanishes.*
b. Sep 3, 1898 in Hastings, England
d. Apr 21, 1971 in Brighton, England
Source: *FilmgC; MovMk; NewYTBE 71; Vers B; WhoHol B; WhScrn 74, 77*

Parker, Charlie
[Charles Christopher Parker]
"Bird"; "Yardbird"
American. Jazz Musician
Alto-saxophonist; co-creator of bebop.
b. Aug 29, 1920 in Kansas City, Kansas
d. Mar 12, 1955 in New York, New York
Source: *AfrAmAl 6; AllMusG; AmCulL; AmDec 1950; Baker 78, 84, 92; BiDAfM; BiDAmM; BiDJaz; BioIn 12, 13, 14, 15, 16, 17, 18, 19, 20, 21; CmpEPM; ConAmC 76, 82; ConMus 5; DcAmB S5; DcAmNB; DcArts; DcTwCCu 1, 5; DrBlPA, 90; FacFETw; IlEncJ; InB&W 85; LegTOT; MakMC; McGEWB; MusMk; NegAl 76, 83, 89; NewAmDM; NewGrDA 86; NewGrDJ 88, 94; NewGrDM 80; NewOxM; OxCAmH; OxCPMus; PenEncP; RAdv 14, 13-3; WebAB 74, 79; WhAm 4, HSA; WorAl; WorAlBi*

Parker, Daniel Francis
American. Editor
Won George Polk Award for sports column, "NY Mirror," 1955.
b. Jul 1, 1893 in Waterbury, Connecticut
d. May 20, 1967 in Waterbury, Connecticut
Source: *BioIn 2, 4, 6, 7; WhAm 4*

Parker, Dave
[David Gene Parker]
"The Cobra"
American. Baseball Player
Outfielder, Pittsburgh, 1973-83, Cincinnati, 1984-87; four-time NL MVP.
b. Jun 9, 1951 in Jackson, Mississippi
Source: *Ballpl 90; BaseEn 88; BaseReg 87, 88; BiDAmSp BB; BioIn 11, 12, 13, 14, 15, 16, 17; InB&W 80, 85; LegTOT; WhoAfA 96; WhoAm 78, 80, 82, 84, 86, 88; WhoBlA 77, 80, 85, 88, 90, 92, 94; WhoMW 88; WhoSpor; WhoWest 89; WorAl; WorAlBi*

Parker, Dorothy Rothschild
American. Author, Poet, Journalist
Mag. writer known for caustic wit; wrote verse *Death and Taxes,* 1931.
b. Aug 22, 1893 in West Bend, New Jersey
d. Jun 7, 1967 in New York, New York
Source: *BiE&WWA; ConLC 15; DcLEL; EvLB; LngCTC; ModAL; OxCAmL 65; PenC AM; RAdv 1; REn; REnAL; TwCA; TwCWr; WhAm 4; WhoAmW 58, 61, 64, 66, 68*

Parker, Eleanor
American. Actor
Films include *Return to Peyton Place,* 1961; *The Sound of Music,* 1965.
b. Jun 26, 1922 in Cedarville, Ohio
Source: *BiDFilm 81, 94; BioIn 10; ConTFT 5; FilmEn; FilmgC; ForYSC; HalFC 80, 84, 88; IntMPA 75, 76, 77, 78, 79, 80, 81, 82, 84, 86, 88, 92, 94, 96; InWom SUP; ItaFilm; LegTOT; MotPP; MovMk; VarWW 85; WhoHol 92, A; WorAl; WorAlBi; WorEFlm*

Parker, Ely Samuel
American. Military Leader
Military secretary to Gen. Ulysses S. Grant; penned final copies of terms of surrender that ended the Civil War.
b. 1828 in Indian Falls, New York
d. Aug 31, 1895 in Fairfield, Connecticut
Source: *ApCAB; BiNAW, B; BioIn 10, 11, 12, 16, 21; CivWDc; DcAmB; HarEnUS; NatCAB 5; NotNaAm; TwCBDA; WebAMB; WhAm HS; WhCiWar; WhNaAH*

Parker, Fess
American. Actor
Played Davy Crockett and Daniel Boone in movies, on TV.
b. Aug 16, 1927 in Fort Worth, Texas
Source: *ASCAP 66; BioIn 16; FilmgC; HalFC 84; IntMPA 86, 92; MotPP; RkOn 74; VarWW 85; WhoHol A; WorAlBi*

Parker, Francis Wayland
American. Educator
Leading proponent of progressive elementary education; introduced innovative educational concepts.
b. Oct 9, 1837 in Bedford, New Hampshire
d. Mar 2, 1902 in Chicago, Illinois
Source: *Alli SUP; AmAu&B; AmBi; ApCAB; BiDAmEd; BioIn 1, 8, 14, 15; DcAmAu; DcAmB; DcNAA; EncAB-A 8; OxCAmH; TwCBDA; WebAB 74, 79; WhAm 1*

Parker, Frank
American. Tennis Player
US Open singles champion, 1944-45, doubles champion, 1943.
b. Jan 31, 1916 in Milwaukee, Wisconsin
d. Jul 24, 1997 in San Diego, California
Source: *BiDAmSp OS; BioIn 1; BuCMET; CurBio 48; WhoAm 74, 76, 78*

Parker, George Safford
American. Manufacturer
Designed fountain pen, 1887.
b. Nov 1, 1863 in Shullsburg, Wisconsin
d. Apr 19, 1937 in Chicago, Illinois
Source: *BioIn 5, 14, 18; Entr; NatCAB 63*

Parker, George Swinnerton
American. Businessman
With brothers, built board game industry which produced such classics as Monopoly, Clue, Risk.
b. Dec 12, 1866 in Salem, Massachusetts
d. Sep 26, 1952 in Boston, Massachusetts
Source: *BiDAmBL 83; BioIn 4, 18; EncAB-A 26; Entr; NatCAB 40; WhAm 3; WorAl*

Parker, Gilbert, Sir
Canadian. Author
Portrayed Canadian life in short stories *Pierre and His People,* 1892; novel, *The Weavers,* 1907.
b. Nov 23, 1862 in Addington, Ontario, Canada
d. Sep 6, 1932 in London, England
Source: *BbD; Benet 87; BenetAL 91; BiD&SB; BioIn 1, 2, 12, 14, 17; CanWr; Chambr 3; DcAmAu; DcBiA; DcEnA A; DcNAA; DcNaB 1931; LinLib L; LngCTC; NewC; NewCol 75; OxCAmL 65; OxCCan; OxCCanL; REn; REnAL; StaCVF; TwCA, SUP; WhLit*

Parker, Graham
[Graham Parker and the Rumour]
English. Singer, Songwriter
Punk-rock musician often compared to Bob Dylan, Elvis Costello, Bruce Springsteen for angry, eloquent songs.
b. Nov 18, 1950 in London, England
Source: *BioIn 11, 12, 14, 16; ConMuA 80A; ConMus 10; EncPR&S 89; EncRk 88; HarEnR 86; IlEncRk; LegTOT; PenEncP; RkOn 85; RolSEnR 83; WhoEnt 92*

Parker, Jameson
American. Actor
Played A J Simon on TV series "Simon & Simon," 1982—.
b. Nov 18, 1950 in Baltimore, Maryland
Source: *BioIn 12, 13, 14; ConTFT 6; HalFC 84, 88; IntMPA 86; VarWW 85*

Parker, Jean
[Mae Green; Luise Stephanie Zelinska]
American. Actor
Played hard-boiled characters in 1940s films including *Little Women,* 1949.
b. Aug 11, 1912 in Butte, Montana
Source: *EncAFC; FilmEn; FilmgC; GangFlm; HalFC 80, 84, 88; IntMPA 75; InWom SUP; MGM; MotPP; MovMk; ThFT; VarWW 85; Who 92; WhoHol 92, A; WhoUSWr 88*

Parker, Jim
[James Parker]
American. Football Player
Seven-time all-pro offensive guard, Baltimore, 1957-67; Hall of Fame, 1973.
b. Apr 3, 1934 in Macon, Pennsylvania
Source: *AfrAmSG; BiDAmSp FB; BioIn 17, 20, 21; InB&W 80; IntWWM 90; LegTOT; Who 92; WhoBlA 92; WhoFtbl 74; WhoSpor; WhoWor 96*

Parker, Maceo
American. Musician
Saxophonist; album *Roots Revisited* gained him solo recognition.
Source: *BioIn 17, 19, 20; ConMus 7; WhoAm 92, 94, 95, 96, 97; WhoEnt 92*

Parker, Pat
American. Poet
Poetry collections include *Child of Myself,* 1972; *WomanSlaughter,* 1978.
b. Jan 20, 1944 in Houston, Texas
d. Jun 4, 1989
Source: *ArtclWW 2; BioIn 17, 19; BlkWr 2; ConAu 42NR, 57; DrAP 75; DrAPF 80; FemiCLE; GayLesB; IntWWP 77; OxCWoWr 95; SchCGBL; WhoUSWr 88; WhoWrEP 89, 92*

Parker, Quanah
American. Native American Leader
Principal chief of the Comanches, 1878-1911; led Native Americans in raids against white settlements in Texas, 1867-75.
b. 1952? in Cedar Lake, Texas
d. Feb 25, 1911

Parker, Ray, Jr.
American. Singer
Versatile performer, record producer; had number one hit "Ghostbusters," 1984.
b. May 1, 1954 in Detroit, Michigan
Source: *BioIn 12, 13, 15, 16; DrBlPA 90; EncPR&S 89; EncRkSt; InB&W 85; LegTOT; OnThGG; RolSEnR 83; SoulM; WhoAfA 96; WhoBlA 85, 88, 90, 92, 94; WhoRocM 82*

Parker, Robert B(rown)
American. Author
Writer and creator of the Spenser mystery novels.
b. Sep 17, 1932 in Springfield, Massachusetts
Source: *ConAu 52NR; ConPopW; CurBio 93; IntAu&W 93; WhoAm 80, 82, 84, 86, 88, 90, 92, 94, 95, 96, 97; WhoEnt 92; WorAu 1985; WrDr 94, 96*

Parker, Sarah Jessica
[Mrs. Matthew Broderick]
American. Actor
Starred in Broadway hit *Annie;* TV shows include "Square Pegs," 1982-83; "A Year in the Life," 1987-88; "Equal Justice," 1990-91; films include, *LA Story,* 1991; *Ed Wood,* 1994.
b. Mar 25, 1965 in Nelsonville, Ohio
Source: *BioIn 13, 14; ConTFT 7, 15; IntMPA 92, 94, 96; LegTOT; WhoAm 96, 97; WhoAmW 97; WhoHol 92*

Parker, Suzy
[Cecelia Parker]
American. Model
Highest-paid fashion model, cover girl in US, 1950s; unsuccessful movie career.
b. Oct 28, 1933 in San Antonio, Texas
Source: *BioIn 4, 5, 6, 21; FilmEn; FilmgC; HalFC 84; IntMPA 84, 86, 88, 92, 94, 96; InWom, SUP; MovMk; VarWW 85; WhoAm 82; WhoHol 92, A*

Parker, Theodore
American. Religious Leader, Social Reformer
Liberal Unitarian minister; transcendentalist, friend of Emerson; antislavery leader.
b. Aug 24, 1810 in Lexington, Massachusetts
d. May 10, 1860 in Florence, Italy
Source: *Alli; AmAu; AmAu&B; AmBi; AmOrN; AmPeW; AmRef; ApCAB; BbD; Benet 87, 96; BenetAL 91; BiDAmM; BiD&SB; BiDMoPL; BiDTran; BioIn 1, 2, 3, 5, 6, 8, 9, 10, 11, 15, 19, 21; CamGLE; CamHAL; CasWL; CelCen; Chambr 3; CyAL 2; DcAmAu; DcAmB; DcAmReB 1, 2; DcAmSR; DcBiPP; DcEnL; DcLB 1; DcLEL; DcNAA; Drake; EncAB-H 1974, 1996; EncARH; EvLB; HarEnUS; LinLib L, S; LuthC 75; McGEWB; NatCAB 2; OxCAmH; OxCAmL 65, 83, 95; REn; REnAL; TwCBDA; WebAB 74, 79; WhAm HS; WhCiWar*

Parker, Thomas
English. Clergy
Calvinist minister who advocated Presbyterian ecclesiastical policy.
b. Jun 8, 1595 in Wiltshire, England
d. Apr 24, 1677 in Newbury, Massachusetts
Source: *Alli; AmAu&B; AmWrBE; ApCAB; BenetAL 91; DcAmAu; DcAmB; DcNaB; Drake; NatCAB 12; OxCAmL 65, 83, 95; WhAm HS*

Parker, Tom, Colonel
[Andreas Cornelius Van Kuijk; Thomas Andrew Parker]
American. Manager
Managed career of Elvis Presley, 1956-77; controlled rights to merchandise all "Elvis" products.
b. 1910? in Breda, Netherlands
d. Jan 21, 1997 in Las Vegas, Nevada
Source: *ArtsEM; BioIn 5, 12, 13; EncRk 88; LegTOT*

Parkerson, Michelle
American. Writer, Filmmaker
Made documentary *A Litany for Survival: The Life and Work of Audre Lorde,* 1987.
b. 1953 in Washington, District of Columbia
Source: *GayLesB*

Parkes, Henry, Sir
"The Father of Australian Federation"
English. Politician
Premier of New South Wales, 1872-91; preeminent advocate of Australian Social and educational reform.
b. May 27, 1815 in Stoneleigh, England
d. Apr 27, 1896 in Sydney, Australia
Source: *Alli SUP; BioIn 1, 2, 3, 12, 20; CamGEL; CamGLE; DcLEL; DcNaB S1; HisDBrE; HisWorL; LinLib L; McGEWB; OxCAusL*

Parkhurst, Charles Henry
American. Clergy
Pres. Society for Prevention of Crime, 1892, that helped defeat Tammany.
b. Apr 17, 1842 in Framingham, Massachusetts
d. Sep 8, 1933
Source: *Alli SUP; AmAu&B; AmBi; AmRef; AmSocL; ApCAB, X; BbD; BiD&SB; BioIn 1, 2, 4, 12, 15, 19; CyAG; DcAmAu; DcAmB; DcAmReB 1, 2; DcAmSR; DcNAA; HarEnUS; LinLib L; NatCAB 4; TwCBDA; WhAm 1*

Parkhurst, Helen
American. Educator
Founded progressive Dalton Plan of education, 1920.
b. Mar 7, 1887 in Durand, Wisconsin
d. Jun 1, 1973 in New Milford, Connecticut
Source: *AmWomM; BiDAmEd; BioIn 9, 12; ConAu 41R; EncWHA; InWom SUP; NewYTBE 73; NotAW MOD; ObitOF 79; WhAm 6*

Parkhurst, Michael Hus
American. Labor Union Official
Founder, pres., Independent Truckers Assn; led strike, 1962.
b. Apr 13, 1942
Source: *BioIn 13; NewYTBS 83*

Parkins, Barbara
Canadian. Actor
Starred in *Valley of the Dolls*, 1961; TV series "Peyton Place," 1963-67.
b. May 22, 1942 in Vancouver, British Columbia, Canada
Source: *FilmEn; FilmgC; HalFC 80, 84, 88; IntMPA 86, 92; LegTOT; VarWW 85; WhoAm 78, 80, 82; WhoHol 92, A*

Parkinson, C(yril) Northcote
English. Political Scientist
Wrote *Parkinson's Law*, 1957, humorous essays on managerial bureaucracy.
b. Jul 30, 1909 in Durham, England
d. Mar 9, 1993 in Canterbury, England
Source: *Au&Wr 71; BioIn 4, 5, 6, 7, 10, 11, 12, 15, 18, 19; BlueB 76; ConAu 5NR, 5R, 140; CurBio 60, 93N; IntAu&W 76, 77, 82, 89, 91; IntWW 74, 75, 76, 77, 78, 79, 80, 83, 91; LinLib L, S; LngCTC; NewYTBE 71; NewYTBS 87; RAdv 1; TwCRHW 94; WhE&EA; Who 74, 82, 83, 85, 88, 90, 92; WhoAm 74, 76, 78, 80, 82, 84; WhoWor 74, 76, 78; WorAu 1950; WrDr 76, 80, 82, 84, 86, 88, 90, 92, 94N*

Parkinson, James
English. Surgeon
Described Parkinson's disease, 1817; wrote first text on appendicitis.
b. Apr 11, 1755 in London, England
d. Dec 21, 1824 in London, England
Source: *BiESc; BiHiMed; BioIn 3, 4, 7, 9, 16; DcNaB, C; DcScB; EncSPD; InSci; NewCBEL; WhDW*

Parkinson, Norman
[Ronald Smith]
English. Photographer
Known for fashion, celebrity portraits; has photographed British royalty since 1931.
b. Apr 21, 1913 in Roehampton, England
d. Feb 15, 1990, Singapore
Source: *AnObit 1990; BioIn 4, 13, 14, 16, 17; ConPhot 82, 88, 95; DcArts; DcNaB 1986; EncFash; ICPEnP A; IntWW 89; LegTOT; NewYTBS 83, 90; Who 82, 83, 85, 88, 90*

Parkman, Francis
American. Historian, Author
Explored West; best known work, *The Oregon Trail*, 1849.
b. Sep 16, 1823 in Boston, Massachusetts
d. Nov 8, 1893 in Boston, Massachusetts
Source: *Alli, SUP; AmAu; AmAu&B; AmBi; AmWr S2; ApCAB; AtlBL; BbD; BbtC; Benet 87, 96; BenetAL 91; BibAL; BiD&SB; BiInAmS; BioIn 1, 2, 3, 4, 5, 6, 7, 8, 9, 10, 11, 13, 14, 15, 16, 17, 18, 20; CamGEL; CamGLE; CamHAL; CasWL; CyAL 2; CyWA 58; DcAmAu; DcAmB; DcAmC; DcArts; DcCanB 12; DcLB 1, 30; DcLEL; DcNAA; Dis&D; Drake; EncAAH; EncAB-H 1974, 1996; EncFWF; EvLB; HarEnUS; LegTOT; LiJour; LinLib L, S; McGEWB; MemAm; MouLC 4; NatCAB 1; NinCLC 12; OxCAmH; OxCAmL 65, 83, 95; OxCCan; OxCEng 67, 85, 95; PenC AM; RAdv 14, 13-3; REn; REnAL; REnAW; RfGAmL 87, 94; TwCBDA; WebAB 74, 79; WebE&AL; WhAm HS; WhDW; WhNaAH*

Parks, Bert
[Bert Jacobson]
American. Actor
Radio and TV host during the 1940-50s; hosted Miss America Pageant, 1954-79.
b. Dec 30, 1914 in Atlanta, Georgia
d. Feb 2, 1992 in La Jolla, California
Source: *AnObit 1992; BioIn 9, 10, 12, 13, 19; ConTFT 5, 10; CurBio 73, 92N; IntMPA 84, 86, 88, 92; LegTOT; LesBEnT, 92; News 92, 92-3; RadStar; VarWW 85; WhAm 10; WhoAm 74, 76, 78, 80, 82, 84, 86; WhoEnt 92; WhoHol 92, A; WorAl; WorAlBi*

Parks, Floyd Lavinius
American. Military Leader
Commanded US sector of Berlin when American troops entered, Jul-Oct, 1945.
b. Feb 9, 1896 in Louisville, Kentucky
d. Mar 10, 1959 in Washington, District of Columbia
Source: *BiDWWGF; BioIn 3, 5; WhAm 3*

Parks, Gordon Alexander Buchanan
American. Director
Photographer for *Life* mag., 1948-72; directed film *Shaft*, 1972; won Spingarn, 1972.
b. Oct 30, 1912 in Fort Scott, Kansas
Source: *AmAu&B; AuNews 2; BioIn 16; BlkAWP; BlkLC; BlksAmF; BlksScM; ConBlB 1; ConLC 16; ConPhot 82; CurBio 68, 92; DcLB 33; DrBlPA 90; FacFETw; HalFC 88; InB&W 85; IntMPA 86, 92; LivgBAA; MacBEP; NegAl 89; NewYTBS 74; SelBAAf; SmATA 8; VarWW 85; WhoAm 86, 88, 90; WhoBlA 92; WhoEnt 92; WrDr 86, 92*

Parks, Larry
[Samuel Klausman]
American. Actor
Played Al Jolson in *The Jolson Story*, 1946; *Jolson Sings Again*, 1949; victim of 1950s Communist witch-hunts.
b. Dec 3, 1914 in Olathe, Kansas
d. Apr 13, 1975 in Studio City, California
Source: *BiE&WWA; BioIn 10; CmMov; DcAmB S9; EncAFC; EncMcCE; FilmEn; FilmgC; ForYSC; HalFC 80, 84, 88; HolP 40; IntMPA 75; LegTOT; MotPP; MovMk; NewYTBS 75; What 1; WhoHol C; WhoThe 72; WhScrn 77, 83; WhThe; WorAl*

Parks, Lillian Rogers
American. Author
Wrote *My Thirty Years Backstairs at the White House*, 1961; TV mini-series, 1979.
b. 1897?
Source: *BioIn 5, 8, 11*

Parks, Michael
American. Actor
Played in TV show "Then Came Bronson," 1969-70; also played in some films.
b. Apr 4, 1938 in Corona, California
Source: *ConTFT 7; FilmEn; FilmgC; ForYSC; HalFC 80, 84, 88; IntMPA 75, 76, 77, 78, 79, 80, 81, 82, 84, 86, 88, 92, 94, 96; ItaFilm; MiSFD 9; MotPP; VarWW 85; WhoHol 92, A*

Parks, Rosa Lee McCauley
American. Civil Rights Leader
Refusal to give up bus seat to a white man on Dec 1, 1955 in Montgomery, AL, initiated a bus boycott sparking the civil rights movement; won Spingarn, 1978.
b. Feb 4, 1913 in Tuskegee, Alabama
Source: *BioIn 14, 15, 16; ConBlB 1; ConHero 1; CurBio 89; FacFETw; HanAmWH; HerW, 84; InB&W 80, 85; InWom SUP; NewYTBS 88; NotBlAW 1; WhoBlA 88, 92; WorAlBi*

Parks, Sam(uel McLaughlin)
American. Golfer
Turned pro, 1933; won US Open, 1935.
b. Jun 23, 1909 in Hopedale, Ohio
Source: *BioIn 15, 21; WhoGolf*

Parks, Van Dyke
American. Songwriter, Composer, Producer
Sang with the NY Metropolitan Opera, 1951; collaborated with Brian Wilson on songs for the *Smile* album, 1965; released debut album *Song Cycle,* 1968; scored films *Goin' South,* 1980 and *The Two Jakes,* 1990; released *Orange Crate Art,* 1995 with Brian Wilson.
b. 1942 in Hattiesburg, Mississippi
Source: *ConMus 17*

Parliament
[George Clinton; Raymond "Tiki" Fulwood; Eddie Hazel; Junie Morrison; Gary Shider; Bernie Worrell]
American. Music Group
Rock/funk hits include "One Nation under a Groove," 1978.
Source: *Alli SUP; BiDBrA; BioIn 17, 19, 20; ConMuA 80A; DcTwCCu 5; EncPR&S 89; HarEnUS; NewAmDM; NewGrDA 86; PenEncP; PeoHis; RkOn 84; RolSEnR 83; SoulM*

Parmar, Pratibha
Indian. Filmmaker
Films include *Khush,* 1991; essay "Queer Looks," 1993.
Source: *GayLesB*

Parmenides
Greek. Philosopher
Eleatic philosopher who maintained that nothing changes, nothing passes away.
b. 515BC, Italy
Source: *BbD; Benet 87; BiD&SB; BioIn 14; CasWL; Grk&L; LegTOT; NewC; OxCClL 89; PenC CL; REn; WorAlBi; WrPh P*

Parmigano
[Francesco Mazzola]
Italian. Artist
Mannerist painter noted for *Mystic Marriage of St. Catherine,* c. 1521; influenced by Correggio.
b. Jan 11, 1503 in Parma, Italy
d. Aug 24, 1540 in Casalmaggiore, Italy
Source: *AtlBL; BioIn 1, 2, 6, 9, 10, 12; ClaDrA; NewCol 75*

Parnell, Charles Stewart
Irish. Political Leader
Promoted Irish independence by uniting Irish factions, introducing first Home Rule bill in Parliament, 1886.
b. Jun 27, 1846 in Avondale, Ireland
d. Oct 6, 1891 in Brighton, England
Source: *Benet 87, 96; BioIn 1, 3, 4, 5, 7, 8, 9, 10, 11, 12, 14, 16, 17, 18, 19, 20, 21; BlmGEL; CelCen; DcIrB 78, 88; DcNaB; HarEnUS; HisDBrE; HisWorL; LinLib S; LngCEL; LngCTC; McGEWB; NewC; OxCEng 85, 95; OxCIri; REn; VicBrit; WhDW; WorAl; WorAlBi*

Parnis, Mollie
American. Fashion Designer
Designed understated, conservative clothes, from 1937.
b. Mar 18, 1905 in New York, New York
d. Jul 18, 1992 in New York, New York
Source: *AnObit 1992; BioIn 4, 7, 9, 11, 14, 18, 19; CelR; CurBio 56, 92N; EncFash; FairDF US; InWom SUP; LegTOT; NewYTBS 92; WhoAm 74; WhoFash 88; WorAl; WorAlBi; WorFshn*

Parr, A(lbert) E(ide)
American. Zoologist
Director of American Museum of Natural History, 1942-59.
b. Aug 15, 1900 in Bergen, Norway
d. Jul 17, 1991 in Wilder, Vermont
Source: *AmMWSc 73P, 76P; BioIn 1, 5, 17; BlueB 76; CurBio 42; InSci; IntWW 74, 75, 76, 77, 78, 79, 80, 81, 82, 83, 89, 91; NewYTBS 91; WhAm 10; WhoAm 74*

Parr, Catherine
English. Consort
Sixth wife of Henry VIII, 1543; survived him.
b. 1512
d. 1548
Source: *Alli; Benet 87, 96; BiDLA; BlmGWL; ContDcW 89; DcEnL; DcNaB; IntDcWB; InWom, SUP; LegTOT; NewCBEL; REn; WebBD 83*

Parra, Nicanor
American. Poet
Important Spanish language poet; known as the creator of anti-poetry.
b. Sep 5, 1914 in San Fabian, Chile
Source: *Benet 87, 96; BenetAL 91; BioIn 16, 17, 18; ConAu 32NR, 85; ConFLW 84; ConLC 2; ConSpAP; ConWorW 93; DcCLAA; DcHiB; DcTwCCu 3; EncLatA; EncWL 2, 3; FacFETw; HispLC; HispWr; IntAu&W 89; IntvLAW; IntWW 74, 75, 76, 77, 78, 79, 80, 81, 82, 83, 89, 91, 93; IntWWP 77; LatAmWr; LiExTwC; MajTwCW; ModLAL; OxCSpan; PenC AM; RAdv 14, 13-2; SpAmA; WhoWor 74, 82, 84; WorAlBi; WorAu 1970*

Parrhasius
Greek. Artist
Representative of the Ionic School; the master of outline drawing.
b. fl. 4th cent. ?BC in Ephesus, Asia Minor
Source: *DcBiPP; LinLib S; McGDA; NewC; OxCArt; OxCClL, 89; OxDcArt*

Parrington, Vernon L(ouis)
American. Historian, Educator, Author
Won 1927 Pulitzer for *The Colonial Mind.*
b. Aug 3, 1871 in Aurora, Illinois
d. Jun 16, 1929 in Winchcomb, England
Source: *AmAu&B; AmBi; Benet 96; BioIn 3, 7, 8, 11, 12, 13, 16, 19, 20; ConAu 113; DcAmB; EncAAH; McGEWB; NatCAB 25; OxCAmH; OxCAmL 83, 95; REnAW; WebAB 74, 79; WhAm 1*

Parrish, Anne
American. Author
Novels include *Sea Level,* 1934; *Poor Child,* 1945.
b. Nov 12, 1888 in Colorado Springs, Colorado
d. Sep 5, 1957 in Danbury, Connecticut
Source: *AmAu&B; AmNov; BenetAL 91; BioIn 1, 2, 4, 5, 13, 14; CnDAL; ConAmL; ConAu 115; EvLB; IlsBYP; IlsCB 1744, 1946; InWom, SUP; LngCTC; ObitT 1951; OxCAmL 65, 83, 95; REnAL; ScF&FL 1; SmATA 27; TwCA, SUP; TwCChW 83, 89, 95; TwCWr; WhAm 3; WhE&EA; WhNAA*

Parrish, Lance Michael
American. Baseball Player
Catcher, Detroit, 1977-86, Philadelphia, 1987-88; CA Angels, 1988—; six-time AL All-Star.
b. Jun 15, 1956 in McKeesport, Pennsylvania
Source: *Ballpl 90; BaseReg 86, 87; BioIn 13, 14*

Parrish, Maxfield
American. Artist
Student of Howard Pyle; known for original posters, book illustrations.
b. Jul 25, 1870 in Philadelphia, Pennsylvania
d. Mar 30, 1966 in Plainfield, New Hampshire
Source: *AmAu&B; ArtsAmW 1; BenetAL 91; BioIn 1, 2, 3, 5, 6, 7, 9, 10, 12, 19; ChhPo; ChlBkCr; ConICB; CurBio 65, 66; DcAmB S8; DcBrBI; FacFETw; IlrAm 1880, B; IlsBYP; IlsCB 1744; JBA 34, 51; LegTOT; OxCAmL 65; OxCChiL; PeoHis; REnAL; SmATA 14; TwCBDA; WebAB 74; WhAm 4; WhAmArt 85; WhoAmA 89N, 91N, 93N*

Parry, Albert
American. Educator, Author
Chaired Dept. of Russian studies, Colgate Un., 1947-1969; wrote books on history of Bohemianism in US.
b. Feb 24, 1901 in Rostov-on-Don, Russia
d. May 4, 1992 in Los Angeles, California
Source: *AmAu&B; BioIn 5, 6, 17, 18; ConAu 1R, 6NR; CurBio 92N; DrAS 74H, 78H; IntAu&W 91; WhAm 10; WhoAm 74, 76, 78, 80, 82, 84, 86, 88, 90; WhoWor 74, 76, 89, 91; WrDr 76, 80, 82, 84, 86, 88, 90, 92, 94*

Parry, Charles Hubert Hastings, Sir
English. Composer, Musicologist
Works included choral composition *Jerusalem,* 1916; oratorio *King Saul,* 1894.
b. Feb 27, 1848 in Bournemouth, England
d. Oct 7, 1918 in Littlehampton, England
Source: *Alli SUP; Baker 78, 84; BioIn 3, 4, 5, 16, 18; CelCen; DcArts; DcNaB 1912; LinLib L, S; LngCTC; LuthC 75; NewCBEL; TwCA; VicBrit*

Parry, William Edward, Sir
English. Explorer, Naval Officer
Discovered, named Melville Island, Barrow Strait.
b. Dec 19, 1790 in Bath, England
d. Jul 8, 1855 in Ems, Germany
Source: *Alli; ApCAB; BioIn 3, 5, 6, 11, 18, 20; BritAu 19; CelCen; DcBiPP; DcCanB 8; DcLEL; DcNaB; Drake; HarEnUS; MacDCB 78; NewCBEL; OxCEng 67, 85, 95; OxCShps; WhDW; WhoStg 1908; WhWE*

Parseghian, Ara (Raoul)
American. Football Coach, Sportscaster
Head coach at several universities, including Notre Dame, 1964-75; won national championships, 1966, 1973.
b. May 10, 1923 in Akron, Ohio
Source: *BiDAmSp FB; BioIn 7, 8, 9, 10, 11, 16, 19, 21; BioNews 74; ConAu 105; CurBio 68; LegTOT; NewYTBE 71; NewYTBS 75; WhoAm 76, 78, 80, 82, 84, 86, 88, 92; WhoFash; WhoFtbl 74; WorAl; WorAlBi*

Parsons, Benny
American. Auto Racer
Won Daytona 500, 1975.
b. Jul 12, 1941
Source: *BioIn 10, 21; WhoSpor*

Parsons, Betty Pierson
American. Artist
Pioneer dealer in American art; director, Betty Parsons Gallery, 1946-82, showed work of all major American modern artists.
b. Jan 31, 1900 in New York, New York
d. Jul 23, 1982 in Southold, New York
Source: *AnObit 1982*

Parsons, Charles Algernon, Sir
English. Inventor
Produced first practical steam turbine, 1884.
b. Jun 13, 1854 in London, England
d. Feb 11, 1931 in Kingston, Jamaica
Source: *AsBiEn; BiESc; BioIn 1, 2, 3, 4, 5, 6, 7, 8, 9, 12, 14, 20; CamDcSc; DcInv; DcIrB 88; DcNaB 1931; GrBr; InSci; LarDcSc; LinLib S; McGEWB; NewCol 75; OxCShps; WhDW; WorAl; WorAlBi*

Parsons, Elsie Clews
[Elsie Worthington Clews Parson]
American. Sociologist
Her studies of American Indians, including the Pueblo, are classics.
b. Nov 27, 1875 in New York, New York
d. Dec 19, 1941 in New York, New York
Source: *AmPeW; AmWomWr; BenetAL 91; BioAmW; BioIn 2, 16; CurBio 42; DcAmB S3; GrLiveH; InWom, SUP; NotAW; ObitOF 79; REnAL; REnAW; WebAB 79; WomSoc*

Parsons, Estelle
American. Actor
Won 1967 Oscar for role of Blanche Barrow in *Bonnie and Clyde.*
b. Nov 20, 1927 in Lynn, Massachusetts
Source: *BiE&WWA; BioIn 10, 11, 12, 13; CamGWoT; CelR, 90; ConTFT 3; CurBio 75; Ent; FilmEn; FilmgC; HalFC 80, 84, 88; IntMPA 77, 84, 86, 88, 92, 94, 96; InWom SUP; LegTOT; MovMk; NotNAT; OxCAmT 84; VarWW 85; WhoAm 74, 76, 78, 80, 82, 84, 86, 88, 90, 92, 94, 95, 96, 97; WhoAmW 81, 83, 95, 97; WhoE 91, 93; WhoEnt 92; WhoHol 92, A; WhoThe 72, 77, 81; WorAl; WorAlBi*

Parsons, Gram
[The Byrds; The Flying Burrito Brothers; Cecil Connor]
American. Singer, Songwriter
Tried to blend country, rock styles; compositions later recorded by Emmylou Harris; died of drug overdose.
b. Nov 5, 1946 in Winter Haven, Florida
d. Sep 19, 1973 in Joshua Tree, California
Source: *Baker 92; BgBkCoM; BioIn 10, 12, 14, 17; ConMuA 80A; ConMus 7; CounME 74, 74A; EncFCWM 83; EncPR&S 74, 89; EncRk 88; EncRkSt; HarEnCM 87; IlEncCM; IlEncRk; LegTOT; NewGrDA 86; OxCPMus; PenEncP; RolSEnR 83; WhoRock 81; WhoRocM 82; WhScrn 77, 83*

Parsons, Louella Oettinger
American. Journalist
Influential Hollywood syndicated gossip columnist, 1922-65; rival of Hedda Hopper.
b. Aug 6, 1881 in Freeport, Illinois
d. Dec 9, 1972 in Santa Monica, California
Source: *BiDAmJo; ConAu 93; CurBio 40, 73; FilmgC; InWom SUP; NotAW MOD; OxCFilm; REnAL; WebAB 74; WhAm 5; WhoHol B; WhScrn 77; WorEFlm*

Parsons, Richard Dean
American. Business Executive
President, Time Warner, 1995—.
b. Apr 4, 1948 in New York, New York
Source: *ConBlB 11; WhoAm 92, 94, 95, 96, 97; WhoE 95; WhoFI 94*

Parsons, Talcott
American. Sociologist
Emphasized analysis of society over narrower empirical studies.
b. Dec 13, 1902 in Colorado Springs, Colorado
d. May 8, 1979 in Munich, Germany (West)
Source: *AmAu&B; AmMWSc 73S, 78S; Au&Wr 71; BioIn 5, 6, 11, 12, 13, 14, 17; BlueB 76; ConAu 4NR, 5R, 35NR, 85; CurBio 79N; DcAmB S10; EncAB-H 1974, 1996; FacFETw; IntAu&W 77; IntEnSS 79; IntWW 74, 75, 76, 77, 78; LegTOT; LinLib L; MajTwCW; MakMC; McGEWB; NewYTBS 79; PolProf E; RAdv 14, 13-3; ThTwC 87; WebAB 74, 79; WhAm 7; WhDW; WhoAm 74, 76, 78; WhoWor 74; WorAl; WorAlBi; WorAu 1975; WrDr 76, 80, 82*

Parsons, William
[Third Earl of Rosse]
Irish. Astronomer
Built 72-inch reflecting telescope, "Leviathan," 1845; named Crab Nebulae, 1848.
b. Jun 17, 1800 in York, England
d. Oct 13, 1867 in Monkstown, Ireland
Source: *AsBiEn; BioIn 8, 14; DcIrB 78, 88; DcNaB; DcScB; InSci; NewCol 75*

Part, Arvo
Estonian. Composer
Classical composer, popular since the 1980s.
b. Sep 11, 1935 in Paide, Estonia
Source: *Baker 78, 84, 92; BioIn 14, 17, 20, 21; ConCom 92; CurBio 95; DcCM; IntWW 91, 93; IntWWM 90; NewGrDM 80; PenDiMP A; SovUn*

Partch, Harry
American. Composer
Formulated 43 microtonal scale; invented unusual instruments; avante-garde works included *Oedipus,* 1952.
b. Jun 24, 1901 in Oakland, California
d. Sep 3, 1974 in San Diego, California
Source: *AmComp; Baker 78, 84, 92; BiDAmM; BioIn 1, 2, 6, 7, 8, 9, 10, 17; BriBkM 80; CmCal; CompSN SUP; ConAmC 76, 82; CurBio 65, 74, 74N; DcCM; NewAmDM; NewGrDA 86; NewGrDM 80; NewGrDO; NewOxM; NewYTBS 74; PenEncP; WhAm 6; WhoAm 74; WhoWest 74*

Partch, Virgil Franklin, II
American. Cartoonist
Created comic strip "Big George."
b. Oct 17, 1916 in Saint Paul Island, Alaska
d. Aug 10, 1984 in Newhall, California
Source: *Au&Wr 71; BioIn 1, 14, 15; ConAu 108, 113; ConGrA 1; CurBio 46; SmATA 39N, 45; WhAm 9; WhoAm 74, 76, 78, 80, 82, 84, 86, 88; WhoAmA 73, 76, 78, 80, 82, 84, 86N, 89N, 91N, 93N; WorECar*

Parton, Dolly Rebecca
[Mrs. Carl Dean]
American. Singer, Songwriter, Actor
First gold record, 1978, for "Here You Come Again"; movie debut in *Nine to Five,* 1980; Grammy award winner.
b. Jan 19, 1946 in Sevierville, Tennessee
Source: *Baker 84; BiDAmM; BioIn 13, 14, 15, 16; BkPepl; ConAu 150; ContDcW 89; ConTFT 5; EncAFC; HalFC 88; HarEnR 86; HerW 84; IntMPA 82, 88; IntWW 89, 91, 93; InWom SUP; VarWW 85; WhoAm 80, 82, 84, 86, 88, 90, 92, 94, 95, 96, 97; WhoAmW 87, 89, 91, 93, 95; WhoEnt 92*

Parton, James
American. Author
Noteworthy biographies include *Andrew Jackson,* 1860.
b. Feb 9, 1822 in Canterbury, England
d. Oct 17, 1891 in Newburyport, Massachusetts
Source: *Alli, SUP; AmAu; AmAu&B; AmBi; ApCAB; BbD; BenetAL 91; BiD&SB; BioIn 2, 4, 8, 14; ChhPo, S1; DcAmAu; DcAmB; DcLB 30; DcNAA; Drake; EncAJ; HarEnUS; NatCAB 1; OxCAmH; OxCAmL 65, 83, 95; REnAL; TwCBDA; WebAB 74, 79; WhAm HS*

Parton, Sara Payson Willis
[Mrs. James Parton]
"Fanny Fern"
American. Author, Journalist
Wrote popular *Fern Leaves* series, 1853-57.
b. Jul 9, 1811 in Portland, Maine
d. Oct 10, 1872 in New York, New York
Source: *Alli; AmAu; AmAu&B; AmBi; AmWom; AmWomWr; ApCAB; BbD; BiDAmNC; BiD&SB; BioIn 15, 16, 18; BlmGWL; CyAL 2; DcAmB; DcLB 43, 74; DcNAA; Drake; EncAB-H 1974; JrnUS; LibW; NatCAB 1; NotAW; PseudAu; REnAL; TwCBDA; WebAB 74, 79; WhAm HS*

Partridge, Bellamy
American. Biographer, Author
Numerous light, popular books included *Country Lawyer,* 1939.
b. Jul 10, 1878 in Phelps, New York
d. Jul 5, 1960 in Bridgeport, Connecticut
Source: *AmAu&B; AmNov; BenetAL 91; BioIn 2, 3, 4, 5, 7; REn; REnAL; TwCA, SUP; WhAm 4; WhNAA*

Partridge, Eric Honeywood
"Word King"
New Zealander. Lexicographer, Author
His popular guides to English language included *Dictionary of Catch Phrases,* 1977.
b. Feb 6, 1894 in Gisborne, New Zealand
d. Jun 1, 1979 in Devonshire, England
Source: *Au&Wr 71; BioIn 10, 11, 12; BlueB 76; ChhPo; ConAu 1R, 3NR, 85; CurBio 63, 79; DcLEL; DcNaB 1971; EvLB; IntAu&W 76, 77; IntWW 74, 75, 76, 77, 78; LngCTC; NewC; NewCBEL; OxCAusL; TwCA SUP; Who 74; WhoE 74; WhoWor 74, 76, 78; WorAl; WrDr 76*

Pascal, Blaise
French. Mathematician, Theologian
Formulated Pascal's law which states fluids transmit equal pressure in all directions.
b. Jun 19, 1623 in Clermont, France
d. Aug 19, 1662 in Paris, France
Source: *AsBiEn; AtlBL; BbD; Benet 87, 96; BiD&SB; BiDPsy; BiESc; BioIn 1, 2, 3, 4, 5, 6, 7, 8, 9, 10, 11, 12, 13, 14, 15, 16, 17, 20, 21; BlkwCE; BlmGEL; CamDcSc; CasWL; CyWA 58; DcAmC; DcBiPP; DcCathB; DcEuL; DcInv; DcScB; Dis&D; EncEth; EuAu; EuWr 3; EvEuW; GuFrLit 2; HisDcDP; IlEncMy; InSci; LarDcSc; LegTOT; LinLib L, S; LitC 35; LngCEL; LuthC 75; McGEWB; NamesHP; NewC; NewCBEL; OxCEng 67, 85, 95; OxCFr; PenC EUR; RAdv 14, 13-4; RComWL; REn; RfGWoL 95; WhDW; WorAl; WorAlBi; WorScD; WrPh P*

Pascal, Gabriel
Hungarian. Producer
Persuaded GB Shaw to sell film rights to his plays; productions include *Pygmalion,* 1938; *Major Barbara,* 1941; *Caesar and Cleopatra,* 1945.
b. Jun 4, 1894, Austria-Hungary
d. Jul 6, 1954 in New York, New York
Source: *BioIn 3, 7, 9; CurBio 42, 54; FilmEn; FilmgC; HalFC 80, 84, 88; IlWWBF A; MiSFD 9N; NotNAT A, B; ObitT 1951; OxCFilm; WorEFlm*

Pascoli, Giovanni
Italian. Poet
Verse vols. include *Myricae,* 1891-1905; *Canti di Castelvecchio,* 1903.
b. Dec 31, 1855 in San Mauro, Italy
d. Apr 6, 1912 in Castelvecchio, Italy
Source: *Benet 87, 96; BioIn 1, 7, 14; CasWL; ClDMEL 47, 80; DcItL 1, 2; EncWL 2, 3; EuAu; EuWr 7; EvEuW; LinLib L; OxCEng 67, 85, 95; PenC EUR; REn; TwCLC 45; TwCWr; WhDW; WhoTwCL*

Pasdeloup, Jules Etienne
French. Conductor
Organized popular weekly concerts, 1861-84, which introduced Parisians to fine music; later revived.
b. Sep 15, 1819 in Paris, France
d. Aug 13, 1887 in Fontainebleau, France
Source: *Baker 84; BioIn 8; BriBkM 80; NewGrDM 80; OxCFr; OxCMus*

Pasero, Tancredi
Italian. Opera Singer
Leading bass, Milan Opera, 1926-51; noted for Verdi roles.
b. Jan 11, 1893 in Turin, Italy
d. Feb 17, 1983 in Milan, Italy
Source: *Baker 84, 92; BioIn 11; CmOp; IntDcOp; MetOEnc; NewEOp 71; NewGrDM 80; NewGrDO; OxDcOp; PenDiMP*

Pasolini, Pier Paolo
Italian. Director
Clashed frequently with authorities over contents of films because of sex, violence including *Canterbury Tale,* 1944.
b. Mar 5, 1922 in Bologna, Italy
d. Nov 2, 1975 in Ostia, Italy
Source: *Benet 87, 96; BiDFilm 81, 94; BioIn 8, 9, 10, 11, 12, 13, 14, 15, 16, 17, 18, 19, 20, 21; CasWL; ClDMEL 80; ConAu 61, 93; ConLC 20, 37; CurBio 70, 76N; DcArts; DcItL 1, 2; DcLB 128; EncEurC; EncWL 2, 3; FacFETw; FilmEn; FilmgC; GayLL; GrFLW; HalFC 80, 84, 88; IntAu&W 76; IntDcF 1-2, 2-2; IntWW 74, 75; ItaFilm; LegTOT; MajTwCW; MakMC; MiSFD 9N; MovMk; Novels; OxCEng 85, 95; OxCFilm; PenC EUR; RAdv 14, 13-2; REn; RfGWoL 95; TwCWr; WhAm 6; WhoWor 74; WhScrn 77; WorAu 1950; WorEFlm; WorFDir 2*

Pass, Joe
[Joseph Anthony Passalaqua]
American. Jazz Musician
Jazz guitarist; teamed with Oscar Peterson, Ella Fitzgerald.
b. Jan 13, 1929 in New Brunswick, New Jersey
d. May 23, 1994 in Los Angeles, California
Source: *AllMusG; Baker 92; BiDAmM; BiDJaz; BioIn 12, 13, 15, 16, 19, 20; ConMus 15; EncJzS; IlEncJ; LegTOT; NewAmDM; NewGrDA 86; NewGrDJ 88, 94; News 94; OnThGG; PenEncP; WhAm 11; WhoAm 80, 82, 92*

Passarella, Art
American. Baseball Umpire
AL umpire, 1945-53; appeared in film *Damn Yankees,* 1958.
b. 1910
d. Oct 1981 in Hemet, California
Source: *BioIn 11, 12; NewYTBS 81; WhScrn 83*

Passy, Frederic
French. Government Official
Held positions in French legislature, 1847-49, 1881-89; shared first Nobel Peace Prize, 1901.
b. May 20, 1822 in Paris, France
d. Jun 12, 1912 in Neuilly-sur-Seine, France
Source: *BiDMoPL; BioIn 5, 9, 11, 15; LinLib L, S; NobelP; OxCLaw; WhoNob, 90, 95; WorAl; WorAlBi*

Pasta, Giuditta Negri
Italian. Opera Singer
Legendary soprano with amazing range; noted for Rossini roles, 1820s-30s.
b. Apr 9, 1798 in Saronno, Italy
d. Apr 1, 1865 in Como, Italy
Source: *Baker 84; InWom SUP; NewEOp 71*

Pasternak, Boris Leonidovich
Russian. Author
Forced to refuse Nobel Prize for literature, 1958; wrote *Doctor Zhivago,* 1957.
b. Feb 11, 1890 in Moscow, Russia
d. May 29, 1960 in Moscow, Union of Soviet Socialist Republics
Source: *AtlBL; Benet 87, 96; BiDSovU; BioIn 1, 2, 4, 5, 6, 7, 8, 9, 10, 11, 12, 13, 14, 15, 16, 17, 20; CasWL; ChhPo S1; ClDMEL 47, 80; CnMWL; ConLC 10, 18; CurBio 59, 60; DcArts; DcRusL; DcRusLS; EncWL; EvEuW; HanRL; LngCTC; MakMC; McGEWB; ModSL 1; OxCEng 67, 85, 95; PenC EUR; RComWL; REn; RfGShF; RfGWoL 95; RGFMEP; SovUn; TwCA, SUP; TwCWr; WhAm 4; WhoNob, 90, 95; WhoTwCL; WorAl*

Pasternak, Joe
[Joseph Vincent Pasternak]
American. Producer
Saved Universal from bankruptcy by producing successful Deanna Durbin musicals; films include *Destry Rides Again,; Anchors Aweigh,* 1945.
b. Sep 19, 1901 in Szilagy-Smoloyn, Romania
d. Sep 13, 1991 in Beverly Hills, California
Source: *AnObit 1991; ASCAP 66; BioIn 14, 15, 17, 18; CmMov; ConTFT 11; FilmEn; FilmgC; GangFlm; HalFC 80, 84, 88; IntDcF 1-4, 2-4; IntMPA 75, 76, 77, 78, 79, 80, 81, 82, 84, 86, 88, 92; NewYTBS 91; VarWW 85; WhoAm 82; WhoWor 74; WorAlBi; WorEFlm*

Pasteur, Louis
French. Chemist, Bacteriologist
Developed process of food sterilization—pasteurization.
b. Dec 27, 1822 in Dole, France
d. Sep 28, 1895 in Saint-Cloud, France
Source: *AsBiEn; Benet 87, 96; BiESc; BiHiMed; BioIn 1, 2, 3, 4, 5, 6, 7, 8, 9, 10, 11, 12, 13, 14, 15, 16, 17, 18, 20, 21; CamDcSc; CelCen; DcBiPP; DcCathB; DcInv; DcScB; EncEnv; InSci; LarDcSc; LegTOT; LinLib L; LngCEL; McGEWB; NewCol 75; OxCFr; OxCMed 86; RAdv 14, 13-5; REn; WebBD 83; WhDW; WorAl; WorAlBi; WorScD*

Pastor, Tony
[Antonio Pastor]
American. Actor, Manager
Pioneer developer of vaudeville; managed Fourteenth Street Theatre, 1881-1908.
b. May 28, 1837 in New York, New York
d. Aug 26, 1908 in Elmhurst, New York
Source: *Alli; AmAu&B; BiDAmM; BioIn 3, 5, 16; CamGWoT; DcAmB; DcNAA; FamA&A; NewGrDA 86; NotNAT A, B; OxCAmL 65; OxCAmT 84; OxCPMus; OxCThe 67, 83; REn; REnAL; WebAB 74, 79; WhoStg 1906, 1908*

Pastor, Tony
[Antonio Pestritto]
American. Bandleader
Saxist, singer with Artie Shaw, 1930s; led band, 1940s; noted for rhythm vocals.
b. Oct 26, 1907 in Middletown, Connecticut
d. Oct 31, 1969 in New London, Connecticut
Source: *BgBands 74; BiDAmM; BiDJaz; BioIn 8, 9, 12; CmpEPM; EncJzS; NewGrDA 86; NewGrDJ 88, 94; PenEncP; WhoHol B; WhoJazz 72*

Pastora (Gomez), Eden
"Commander Zero"
Nicaraguan. Political Leader
Hero of 1979 revolution that toppled Anastasio Somoza.
b. Jan 22, 1937 in Dario, Nicaragua
Source: *BioIn 12, 13, 15; CurBio 86; DcCPCAm*

Pastore, John Orlando
American. Politician
Dem. senator from RI, 1950-76; best known for war on sex, violence on TV which resulted in "family viewing time," 1975.
b. Mar 17, 1907 in Providence, Rhode Island
Source: *AlmAP 82; BiDrAC; BiDrGov 1789; BiDrUSC 89; BioIn 2, 3, 5, 6, 9, 10, 11, 12, 16, 17; CngDr 74; CurBio 53; IntWW 83; LesBEnT, 92; WhoAm 86; WhoAmP 85; WhoE 74; WhoGov 72, 75, 77; WhoWor 74*

Pastorini, Dan(te Anthony, Jr.)
American. Football Player
Quarterback, 1971-83, mostly with Houston.
b. Dec 25, 1949 in Sonora, California
Source: *BioIn 12; FootReg 81; WhoFtbl 74*

Pastorius, Jaco
[Blood, Sweat, and Tears; John Francis Anthony Pastorius, III]
American. Musician
Jazz-rock bass guitarist known for rapid-fire fingering techniques.
b. Dec 1, 1951 in Norristown, Pennsylvania
d. Sep 21, 1987 in Fort Lauderdale, Florida
Source: *AllMusG; AnObit 1987; BioIn 12, 13; ConNews 88-1; LegTOT; NewGrDA 86; NewGrDJ 88, 94; PenEncP; WhAm 9; WhoAm 82, 84, 86; WhoRocM 82*

Pataki, George E(lmer)
American. Politician
New York State Assemblyman, 1985-92; New York State Senator, 1993-95; Governor of New York, 1995—.
b. Jun 24, 1945 in Peekskill, New York
Source: *CurBio 96*

Patch, Alexander M(c Carrell)
American. Military Leader
Commanded American Division in Guadalcanal area, WW II.
b. Nov 23, 1889 in Fort Huachuca, Arizona
d. Nov 21, 1945 in San Antonio, Texas
Source: *CurBio 43, 46; DcAmB S3*

Patchen, Kenneth
American. Poet, Author
His surrealistic poems included in *Hurrah for Anything,* 1957; popular on college campuses.
b. Dec 13, 1911 in Niles, Ohio
d. Jan 8, 1972 in Palo Alto, California
Source: *AmAu&B; AmNov; Au&Wr 71; Benet 87, 96; BenetAL 91; BioIn 1, 2, 4, 5, 8, 9, 12, 13, 15, 17; CamGEL; CamGLE; CamHAL; CasWL; ChhPo, S1; CnDAL; ConAu 1R, 3NR, 33R, 35NR; ConLC 1, 2, 18; ConNov 72; ConPo 70, 75, 80A; DcAmB S9; DcLB 16, 48; DcLEL; EncWB; GrWrEL P; LegTOT; LinLib L; MajTwCW; ModAL; Novels; OhA&B; OxCAmL 65, 83, 95; OxCTwCP; PenC AM; RAdv 1, 14, 13-1; REn; REnAL; RfGAmL 87, 94; TwCA, SUP; WebE&AL; WhAm 5; WhoTwCL*

Pate, Jerry
[Jerome Kendrick Pate]
American. Golfer
Turned pro, 1975; won US Open, 1976; youngest to win $1 million on tour.
b. Sep 16, 1953 in Macon, Georgia
Source: *BioIn 11, 12; LegTOT; NewYTBS 81; WhoAm 78, 80, 82, 84, 86, 88; WhoGolf; WhoIntG*

Pate, Maurice
American. Government Official, Businessman
First director, UN International Children's Relief Fund (UNICEF), 1947-65.
b. Oct 14, 1894 in Pender, Nebraska
d. Jan 19, 1965 in New York, New York
Source: *BioIn 2, 5, 6, 7, 8, 11; DcAmB S7; NatCAB 51; WhAm 4*

Pater, Jean-Baptiste
French. Artist
Painted genre scenes in style of Watteau.
b. 1695 in Valenciennes, France
d. 1736 in Paris, France
Source: *McGDA*

Pater, Walter (Horatio)
English. Author, Critic
Wrote *Studies in History of the Renaissance,* 1873; his masterpiece, *Marius the Epicurian,* 1885.
b. Aug 5, 1839 in Shadwell, England
d. Jul 30, 1894 in Oxford, England
Source: *Alli SUP; AtlBL; BbD; Benet 87, 96; BiD&SB; BioIn 1, 2, 4, 5, 6, 7, 8, 9, 10, 11, 12, 13, 14, 16, 18, 20, 21; BlmGEL; BritAu 19; BritWr 5; CamGEL; CamGLE; CasWL; Chambr 3; ChhPo S1; CnDBLB 4; CrtT 3, 4; CyWA 58; DcArts; DcBiA; DcEnA, A; DcEuL; DcLB 57, 156; DcLEL; DcNaB; EvLB;*

GayLesB; GrWrEL N; LegTOT; LinLib L, S; LngCEL; McGEWB; MouLC 4; NewC; NewCBEL; NinCLC 7; Novels; OxCArt; OxCEng 67, 85, 95; OxDcArt; PenC ENG; RAdv 1, 14, 13-1; REn; RfGEnL 91; StaCVF; VicBrit; WebE&AL; WhDW

Paterno, Joe
[Joseph Vincent Paterno]
American. Football Coach
Assistant football coach, Pennsylvania State University, 1950-66, head football coach, 1966—; won national championship, 1982, 1986.
b. Dec 21, 1926 in New York, New York
Source: *BiDAmSp FB; BioIn 9, 10, 11, 12, 13, 14, 15, 16; CelR 90; CurBio 84; LegTOT; News 95; WhoAm 76, 78, 80, 82, 84, 86, 88, 92, 94, 95, 96, 97; WhoE 74; WhoFtbl 74; WorAl; WorAlBi*

Paterson, Basil Alexander
American. Politician
Senator from NY, 1965-70; secretary of State, 1979-82.
b. Apr 27, 1926 in New York, New York
Source: *BioIn 11; NegAl 89A; NewYTBS 78; WhoAfA 96; WhoAm 80, 82, 84, 86, 88, 90, 92, 94, 95, 96, 97; WhoAmL 96; WhoAmP 73, 75, 77, 79, 91, 93, 95; WhoBlA 80, 85, 88, 90, 92, 94; WhoE 95*

Paterson, William
American. Politician, Supreme Court Justice
Delegate to Constitutional Convention whose plan of equal votes for every state led to compromise of bicameral legislature; Paterson, NJ named after him.
b. Dec 24, 1745 in County Antrim, Ireland
d. Sep 9, 1806 in Albany, New York
Source: *AmBi; AmPolLe; ApCAB; BiAUS; BiDFedJ; BiDrAC; BiDrGov 1789; BiDrUSC 89; BioIn 1, 2, 5, 7, 8, 11, 12, 15, 16; BlkwEAR; CyAG; DcAmB; HarEnUS; McGEWB; NatCAB 1; OxCAmH; OxCSupC; SupCtJu; TwCBDA; WebAB 74, 79; WhAm HS; WhAmP; WhAmRev*

Pathe, Charles
French. Filmmaker
Introduced the newsreel, 1909 in France, 1910 in US.
b. Dec 25, 1863 in Chevry Cossigny, France
d. Dec 25, 1957 in Monte Carlo, Monaco
Source: *BioIn 4, 5, 21; DcArts; DcFM; DcTwCCu 2; EncEurC; FilmEn; FilmgC; HalFC 80, 84, 88; IntDcF 2-4; NotNAT B; OxCFilm; WorEFlm*

Patinkin, Mandy
[Mandel Patinkin]
American. Actor
Won Tony for *Evita,* 1980; films include *Ragtime,* 1981; *Yentl,* 1983.
b. Nov 30, 1952 in Chicago, Illinois
Source: *Baker 92; BioIn 14, 15, 16; CelR 90; ConMus 3; ConTFT 3, 10; HolBB; IntMPA 92, 94, 96; VarWW 85; WhoAm 82, 84, 86, 88, 90, 92, 94, 95, 96, 97; WhoE 93; WhoEnt 92; WhoHol 92; WorAlBi*

Patino, Simon Iturri
"Tin King"
Bolivian. Industrialist, Diplomat
Peasant who became one of world's richest men when his property was found to have rich tin vein, 1894.
b. Jun 1, 1862 in Cochabamba, Bolivia
d. Apr 20, 1947 in Buenos Aires, Argentina
Source: *BioIn 1, 4, 9, 19; CurBio 42, 47; McGEWB; NatCAB 40; WhAm 2; WorAl; WorAlBi*

Patman, (John Williams) Wright
American. Lawyer
Liberal Dem., held fourth longest congressional career, 1929-76.
b. Aug 6, 1893 in Hughes Springs, Texas
d. Mar 7, 1976 in Bethesda, Maryland
Source: *BiDrAC; BioIn 1, 6, 7, 8, 9, 10, 11, 12, 18; BioNews 74; CelR; CngDr 74; ConAu 107, 109; CurBio 46, 76N; EncABHB 7; NewYTBS 76; PolProf E, J, K, NF, T; WhAm 6; WhoAm 74; WhoAmP 73, 75, 77; WhoGov 72, 75; WhoSSW 73, 75; WorAl; WorAlBi*

Patmore, Coventry Kersey Dighton
English. Poet, Librarian
Wrote long work on married love, *The Angel in the House,* 1854-62.
b. Jul 23, 1823 in Woodford, England
d. Nov 26, 1896 in Lymington, England
Source: *Alli SUP; AtlBL; BbD; BiD&SB; BioIn 1, 2, 4, 5, 8, 10, 14, 17, 18; BlmGEL; BritAu 19; CamGEL; CasWL; Chambr 3; ChhPo S3; CnE&AP; CrtT 3; DcCathB; DcEnL; DcEuL; DcNaB S1; EvLB; GrWrEL P; IlEncMy; LngCEL; MouLC 4; NewC; NewCBEL; NinCLC 9; OxCEng 85, 95; PenC ENG; REn; VicBrit; WebE&AL*

Paton, Alan Stewart
South African. Author, Political Activist
Writings depict racial conflict in S Africa: *Cry, the Beloved Country,* 1948; founded doomed Liberal Party, 1950s.
b. Jan 11, 1903 in Pietermaritzburg, South Africa
d. Apr 12, 1988 in Durban, South Africa
Source: *AfSS 78, 79, 80, 81, 82; Au&Wr 71; AuBYP 2; CamGEL; CasWL; ConAu P-1; ConLC 4, 10, 25; ConNov 72, 76, 86; CurBio 52, 88; CyWA 58; DcAfHiB 86; DcLEL 1940; EncSoA; EncWL; GrWrEL N; IntAu&W 76, 77, 82, 86, 89; IntWW 74, 75, 76, 77, 78, 79, 80, 81, 82, 83; LngCTC; McGEWB; NewC; PenC ENG; REn; SmATA 11; TwCA SUP; TwCWr; WebE&AL; Who 85; WhoTwCL; WhoWor 74, 84, 87; WorAl; WrDr 76*

Paton, Richard
American. Physician
Conceived idea for Eye Bank, 1940s; pres., medical director, 1974-76.
b. Apr 7, 1901 in Baltimore, Maryland
d. Feb 27, 1984 in Southampton, New York
Source: *AnObit 1984*

Patou, Jean
French. Fashion Designer
His sudden drop of hemline, 1929, fostered belief in relationshipo between skirt lengths, financial unrest: hemline theory; known for world's most expensive perfume: Joy.
b. 1887
d. Mar 1936 in Paris, France
Source: *BioIn 13; ConFash; FairDF FRA; LegTOT; WhoFash, 88; WorFshn*

Patrick, Frank A
Canadian. Hockey Executive
With brother Lester, pioneered hockey in western Canada; introduced 22 rules used in NHL; Hall of Fame, 1958.
b. Dec 21, 1885 in Ottawa, Ontario, Canada
d. Jun 29, 1960 in Vancouver, British Columbia, Canada
Source: *WhoHcky 73*

Patrick, Gail
[Margaret Fitzpatrick]
American. Producer, Actor
Exec. producer of "Perry Mason" TV series, 1957-66.
b. Jun 20, 1911 in Birmingham, Alabama
d. Jul 6, 1980 in Hollywood, California
Source: *AnObit 1980; BioIn 10, 11, 12, 21; EncAFC; FilmEn; FilmgC; GangFlm; HalFC 80, 84, 88; HolP 30; InWom SUP; MotPP; MovMk; OlFamFa; ThFT; WhoHol A; WhScrn 83*

Patrick, John
[John Patrick Goggan]
American. Dramatist
Plays include *The Hasty Heart,* 1945; Pulitzer-winner *Teahouse of the August Moon,* 1954.
b. May 17, 1905 in Louisville, Kentucky
d. Nov 7, 1995 in Delray Beach, Florida
Source: *AmAu&B; BenetAL 91; BioIn 3, 4, 10, 12, 21; CamGWoT; ConAmD; ConAu 89, 150; ConDr 88, 93; CrtSuDr; EncAFC; FilmEn; GangFlm; HalFC 84, 88; IntAu&W 76, 77, 89, 91, 93; IntWW 74, 75, 76, 77, 78, 79, 80, 81, 82, 83, 89, 91; LegTOT; NewYTBS 95; OxCAmL 65, 83, 95; PenC AM; REn; REnAL; VarWW 85; WhoAm 74, 76, 78, 80, 82, 84, 88; WhoWor 74, 80, 82, 84, 87, 89, 91; WorAl; WrDr 92*

Patrick, Lee
American. Actor
Played Mrs. Topper in TV series "Topper"; Effie in *The Maltese Falcon.*
b. Nov 22, 1906 in New York, New York

d. Nov 21, 1982 in Laguna Hills, California
Source: *BiE&WWA; BioIn 10; FilmgC; HalFC 80, 84, 88; HolCA; MotPP; MovMk; NewYTBS 82; NotNAT; Vers A; WhoHol A*

Patrick, Lester B
"Silver Fox"
Canadian. Hockey Coach, Hockey Executive
Instrumental in organizing pro hockey, establishing rules, playoff system; coach, NY Rangers, 1926-39; Patrick Trophy named for him, 1966; NHL division named for him, 1974; Hall of Fame, 1945.
b. Dec 30, 1883 in Drummondville, Quebec, Canada
d. Jun 1, 1960 in Victoria, British Columbia, Canada
Source: *HocEn; ObitOF 79; WhoHcky 73*

Patrick, Lynn
Canadian. Hockey Player, Hockey Executive
Left wing, NY Rangers, 1934-46; served as coach/GM, 1949-67; son of Lester; Hall of Fame, 1980.
b. Feb 3, 1912 in Victoria, British Columbia, Canada
d. Jan 26, 1980 in Saint Louis, Missouri
Source: *BioIn 1, 12; HocEn; NewYTBS 80*

Patrick, Saint
Irish. Religious Figure
Patron saint of Ireland; called one of most successful missionaries in history; brought organized church to Ireland.
b. 385 in Bannavem Taberniae, England
d. 461 in Saul, Ireland
Source: *Alli; CasWL; EvLB; NewC; NewCol 75; REn*

Patrick, Ted
"Black Lightning"
American. Social Reformer
Crusader against religious cults who has deprogrammed nearly 2,000 members since 1972.
b. 1930
Source: *BioIn 10, 11, 12, 13; InB&W 80*

Patsayev, Viktor Ivanovich
Russian. Cosmonaut
With 2 others was in space for a record 24 days; after landing, all were found dead.
b. Jun 19, 1933 in Aktyubinsk, Union of Soviet Socialist Republics
d. Jun 29, 1971
Source: *BioIn 9, 10, 15; FacFETw; WhoSpc*

Pattee, Fred Lewis
American. Educator, Historian
Works include *New American Literature,* 1930.
b. Mar 22, 1863 in Bristol, New Hampshire
d. May 6, 1950 in Winter Park, Florida
Source: *AmAu&B; BenetAL 91; BioIn 2, 3, 4, 9; CnDAL; DcAmAu; DcLB 71; NatCAB 39; OxCAmL 65, 83, 95; REn; REnAL; TwCA, SUP; TwCBDA; WhAm 3; WhNAA*

Patten, Chris(topher Francis)
English. Political Leader
Governor of Hong Kong, 1992-97.
b. May 12, 1944 in Blackpool, England
Source: *BioIn 15, 17, 18, 19; CurBio 93; Who 82, 83, 85, 88, 94; WhoWor 96, 97*

Patten, Gilbert
[Burt L Standish]
American. Author
His adventure books include the 200-vol. *Frank Merriwell* series, from 1896.
b. Oct 25, 1866 in Corinna, Maine
d. Jan 16, 1945 in Vista, California
Source: *AmAu&B; BioIn 1, 2, 3, 4, 5, 7, 10, 12; CurBio 45; DcAmB S3; DcNAA; NatCAB 34; OxCAmL 65; REnAL; ScFEYrs; TwCA, SUP; WebAB 74, 79; WhAm 2*

Patterson, Alicia
[Mrs. Harry F Guggenheim]
American. Editor, Publisher
Founded *Newsday* magazine with husband, 1940.
b. Oct 15, 1909 in Chicago, Illinois
d. Jul 2, 1963 in New York, New York
Source: *AmAu&B; ConAu 89; CurBio 55, 63; WhAm 4*

Patterson, Eleanor Medill
"Cissy"
American. Publisher
Editor, publisher, *Washington Times-Herald,* 1939-48.
b. Nov 7, 1884 in Chicago, Illinois
d. Jul 24, 1948 in Marlboro, Maryland
Source: *AmAu&B; BioIn 1; ConAu 118; CurBio 40, 48; DcAmB S4; DcLB 29; EncAJ; InWom; NotAW; OxCAmH; WebAB 74, 79; WhAm 2*

Patterson, Floyd
American. Boxer
Won Olympic gold medal, 1952; youngest ever to win heavyweight title, 1956.
b. Jan 4, 1935 in Waco, North Carolina
Source: *AfrAmSG; BiDAmSp BK; BioIn 4, 5, 6, 7, 8, 9, 10, 11, 13, 14, 15; BlkOlyM; BoxReg; CurBio 60; FacFETw; InB&W 80, 85; LegTOT; NewYTBE 70; WhoAm 84, 86, 88, 92; WhoBlA 92; WhoBox 74; WhoSpor; WorAl; WorAlBi*

Patterson, Frederick Douglass
American. University Administrator, Educator
President, Tuskegee Institute, 1935-53; founded United Negro College Fund, largest independent source of money for black colleges in US, 1943.
b. Oct 10, 1901 in Washington, District of Columbia
d. Apr 26, 1988 in New Rochelle, New York
Source: *BioIn 13; CurBio 47, 88; InB&W 80, 85; NewYTBS 88; NotTwCS; WhAm 9; WhoAm 74, 76, 78, 80, 82, 84, 86; WhoBlA 85*

Patterson, Joseph Medill
American. Publisher
With cousin Robert McCormick founded first US tabloid, *NY Daily News,* 1919; sole owner, from 1925; brother of Eleanor.
b. Jan 6, 1879 in Chicago, Illinois
d. May 26, 1946 in New York, New York
Source: *AmAu&B; AmDec 1920; BiDAmBL 83; BiDAmJo; BioIn 1, 2, 13, 16; ConAu 118; CurBio 42, 46; DcAmB S4; DcAmSR; DcLB 29; EncACom; EncAJ; EncTwCJ; JrnUS; LinLib L, S; NatCAB 36; NotNAT B; OxCAmH; WhAm 2; WhJnl; WorAlBi*

Patterson, Lorna
American. Actor
Star of TV series "Private Benjamin"; films include *Airplane!* 1980.
b. Jul 1, 1957 in Whittier, California
Source: *BioIn 12; VarWW 85*

Patterson, Melody
American. Actor
Played Wrangler Jane on TV series, "F Troop," 1965-67.
b. 1947 in Los Angeles, California
Source: *WhoHol A*

Patterson, Neva
American. Actor
TV shows include "Governor and J.J.," 1969-72; "Doc Elliott," 1974.
b. Feb 10, 1922 in Nevada, Iowa
Source: *BiE&WWA; BioIn 2; ForYSC; HalFC 88; NotNAT; WhoHol 92, A; WhoThe 77A; WhThe*

Patterson, Orlando
Jamaican. Author, Educator
Wrote *Freedom in the Making of Western Culture,* which won the National Book Award for nonfiction, 1991.
b. Jun 5, 1940 in Westmoreland, Jamaica
Source: *Benet 87; BenetAL 91; BioIn 9, 14, 17, 18, 19; BlkAWP; BlkWr 1; BlkWrNE; ConAu 27NR, 65; ConBlB 4; ConNov 72, 76, 82, 86, 91; FifCWr; InB&W 80; LegTOT; SchCGBL; WhoAm 92, 94, 95, 96, 97; WhoBlA 92; WhoE 95; WorAu 1980; WrDr 76, 80, 82, 84, 86, 88, 90, 92*

Patterson, P(ercival Noel) J(ames)
Jamaican. Politician
Prime Minister of Jamaica, 1992—.
b. Apr 10, 1935 in Saint Andrew, Jamaica
Source: *CurBio 95*

Patterson, Tom
[Harry Thomas Patterson]
Canadian. Journalist
Founded Stratford Shakespearean Festival, Stratford, ON, 1952.
b. Jun 11, 1920 in Stratford, Ontario, Canada
Source: *BioIn 11; CanWW 70, 79, 80, 81, 83; ConAu 128; CreCan 2; OxCThe 83; WhoAm 84; WhoThe 72, 77, 81*

Patterson, William Allan
American. Airline Executive
With United Airlines, 1931-66; introduced instrument-controlled flight, female flight attendants.
b. Oct 1, 1899 in Honolulu, Hawaii
d. Mar 7, 1980 in Glenview, Illinois
Source: *AnObit 1980; BioIn 1, 2, 8, 12; CurBio 46, 80; DcAmB S10; EncAB-A 12; EncABHB 8; NewYTBS 80; WhAm 7*

Patti, Adelina Juana Maria
Italian. Opera Singer
Famed coloratura; most popular, best paid singer of her day.
b. Feb 19, 1843 in Madrid, Spain
d. Sep 27, 1919 in Brecknock, Wales
Source: *AmWom; ApCAB; Baker 84; Drake; NewC; NotAW; OxCLiW 86; TwCBDA; WhAm 1; WhoStg 1908*

Patti, Carlotta
Italian. Singer
Popular concert soprano; US debut, 1861; sister of Adelina.
b. Oct 30, 1835 in Florence, Italy
d. Jun 27, 1889 in Paris, France
Source: *ApCAB; Baker 78, 84, 92; DcNaB; Drake; NewGrDM 80; OxCMus*

Patti, Sandi
American. Singer
"The Voice" of contemporary Christian music; award winning albums include *Morning Like This,* 1986.
b. Jul 12, 1956 in Oklahoma City, Oklahoma
Source: *BioIn 15, 16; ConMus 7; WhoAmW 91*

Patton, Edward L
American. Engineer
Led construction of the 800-mile-long trans-Alaska oil pipeline, 1974.
b. 1917? in Newport News, Virginia
d. Mar 5, 1982 in Bellevue, Washington
Source: *AnObit 1982; NewYTBS 82*

Patton, George Smith, Jr.
"Old Blood and Guts"
American. Army Officer
Commanded 3rd Army, WW II; leader in "Battle of The Bulge," 1944; portrayed by George C Scott in Oscar-winning film *Patton,* 1970.
b. Nov 11, 1885 in San Gabriel, California
d. Dec 21, 1945 in Heidelberg, Germany
Source: *BiDWWGF; BioIn 1, 2, 3, 4, 5, 6, 7, 8, 9, 10, 11, 12, 13; CurBio 43, 46; DcAmB S3; DcAmMiB; DcTwHis; EncAB-H 1974, 1996; HarEnMi; HisEWW; LinLib S; McGEWB; MorMA; NatCAB 37; OxCAmH; REnAL; WebAB 74, 79; WebAMB; WhAm 2; WhDW; WhoMilH 76; WhWW-II; WorAl*

Patzak, Julius
Austrian. Opera Singer
Outstanding tenor; appeared over 1,000 times, Munich State Opera, 1928-45.
b. Apr 9, 1898 in Vienna, Austria
d. Jan 26, 1974 in Rottach-Egern, German Democratic Republic
Source: *Baker 78, 84, 92; BioIn 10; BriBkM 80; CmOp; IntDcOp; MetOEnc; NewAmDM; NewEOp 71; NewGrDM 80; NewGrDO; NewYTBS 74; ObitT 1971; OxDcOp; PenDiMP; WhoMus 72*

Pauker, Ana
[Ana Rabinsohn]
Romanian. Political Leader
Foreign minister, 1947-52, ousted by Communists from Politiburo during purge of Jewish officials.
b. 1894 in Bucharest, Romania
d. Jun 1960 in Bucharest, Romania
Source: *BioIn 1, 2, 3, 5; CurBio 48; InWom; WhAm 4*

Paul, Saint
[Paulus; Saul of Tarsus]
"The Apostle to the Gentiles"
Roman. Biblical Figure
One of the founders of the Christian religion; opposed it until conversion after a vision; ministered to Gentiles, presumably wrote Pauline epistles, suffered martyrdom.
d. 64? in Rome, Italy
Source: *Benet 87, 96; BioIn 1, 2, 3, 4, 5, 6, 7, 8, 9, 10, 11, 12, 13, 14, 15, 16, 20; CurBio 41, 47, 63, 64; DcBiPP; DcCanB 4; DcCathB; DcNaB; Dis&D; EncEarC; HisWorL; IlEncMy; IntWW 79N; LegTOT; LinLib L, S; McGDA; McGEWB; MnBBF; NewC; NewCol 75; NewYTBE 71; NewYTBS 77; ObitOF 79; OxDcByz; OxDcP 86; REn; UFOEn; WebBD 83; WhAmArt 85; WhDW; WhoHol 92; WhoRocM 82; WorAl; WorAlBi*

Paul, Alice
American. Lawyer
Founded Nat. Woman's Party, 1913; author of proposed ERA.
b. Jan 11, 1885 in Moorestown, New Jersey
d. Jul 9, 1977 in Moorestown, New Jersey
Source: *AmDec 1910; AmRef; AmSocL; BiCAW; BioAmW; BioIn 1, 6, 8, 9, 10, 11, 14, 15, 18, 19, 21; ContDcW 89; CurBio 47, 77N; DcAmB S10; EncAB-H 1996; EncWHA; GoodHs; GrLiveH; HanAmWH; HerW, 84; IntDcWB; InWom, SUP; LibW; NewYTBS 77; PolPar; PorAmW; RComAH; WebAB 74, 79; WhAm 7; WhoAmW 77; WomFir; WomWWA 14; WorAl; WorAlBi*

Paul, Bob
[Robert Paul]
Canadian. Skater
Figure skater; with partner Barbara Wagner, won gold medal, pairs skating, 1960 Olympics.
b. Jun 2, 1937 in Toronto, Ontario, Canada
Source: *BioIn 10; Dun&B 90; St&PR 91; WhoAm 90; WhoE 91; WhoFI 92; WhoWor 89*

Paul, Elliot Harold
American. Journalist, Author
Works include *Last Time I Saw Paris,* 1942, concerning Parisians, expatriates.
b. Feb 13, 1891 in Malden, Massachusetts
d. Apr 7, 1958 in Providence, Rhode Island
Source: *AmAu&B; BioIn 1, 2, 3; CnDAL; ConAmL; CurBio 40, 58; EncMys; LngCTC; OxCAmL 65; PenC AM; REn; REnAL; TwCA, SUP; WhAm 3*

Paul, Gabe
[Gabriel Paul]
American. Baseball Executive
Pres., NY Yankees, 1973-77, Cleveland, 1978-84.
b. Jan 4, 1910 in Rochester, New York
Source: *Ballpl 90; BiDAmSp BB; BioIn 15; WhoAm 76, 78, 80, 82, 84, 86, 88, 90, 92, 94, 95, 97; WhoE 75, 77; WhoMW 78, 80, 82, 84; WhoProB 73; WhoSSW 86, 95, 97; WhoWor 78, 80, 89, 91, 93, 95*

Paul, Les
[Les Paul and Mary Ford; Lester William Polfus]
American. Musician, Inventor
Jazz guitarist; duo with wife, 1950s; developed eight-track tape recorder; credited with inventing electric guitar, 1941; Hall of Fame, 1988.
b. Jun 9, 1916 in Waukesha, Wisconsin
Source: *BioIn 2, 3, 4, 5, 10, 11, 12, 14, 15, 16; CmpEPM; ConMus 2; CurBio 87; EncFCWM 83; EncRk 88; HarEnCM 87; HarEnR 86; LegTOT; NewAmDM; NewGrDA 86; OxCPMus; PenEncP; WhoAm 86, 88; WhoEnt 92; WhoHol A; WhoRock 81*

Paul, Prince of Yugoslavia
Yugoslav. Ruler
Ruled Yugoslavia as regent for nephew, Peter II, 1934-41; forced into exile after signing secret pact with Hitler.
b. Apr 15, 1893 in Saint Petersburg, Russia
d. Sep 14, 1976 in Paris, France
Source: *BioIn 11; CurBio 41, 76N; ObitOF 79*

Paul, Wolfgang
German. Physicist
Won Nobel Prize in physics, 1989, for development of methods to isolate

atoms and subatomic particles for study.
b. Aug 10, 1913 in Lorenzkirch, Germany
Source: *AmMWSc 92; BioIn 19, 20; IntWW 91, 93; LarDcSc; NewYTBS 93; NobelP 91; NotTwCS; WhAm 11; Who 92, 94; WhoAtom 77; WhoNob 90, 95; WhoScEn 94; WhoWor 91, 93; WorAlBi*

Paul-Boncour, Joseph
French. Statesman
Represented France at formation of UN, 1945; premier, 1932.
b. Aug 4, 1873 in Saint-Aignan, France
d. Mar 28, 1972
Source: *BiDInt; BioIn 9, 17; CurBio 45, 72, 72N; HisEWW; NewYTBE 72; ObitT 1971*

Pauley, Edwin Wendell
American. Oilman
Founded Petrol Corp., 1928, now Standard Oil; advised presidents, Truman, JFK, Johnson.
b. Jan 7, 1903 in Indianapolis, Indiana
d. Jul 28, 1981 in Beverly Hills, California
Source: *AnObit 1981; BioIn 1, 5, 11, 12; CurBio 45, 81; EncAB-A 35; IntWW 78; IntYB 78, 79, 80, 81, 82; PolProf T; WhAm 8; WhoAm 74, 76, 78, 80; WhoAmP 73, 75, 77, 79; WhoWest 74, 76*

Pauley, Jane
[Margaret Jane Pauley; Mrs. Garry Trudeau]
American. Broadcast Journalist
Was co-host of NBC's "Today" show, 1976-89; co-host of "Dateline NBC," 1992—.
b. Oct 31, 1950 in Indianapolis, Indiana
Source: *BioIn 11, 12, 13, 14, 15, 16, 18; BkPepl; CelR 90; ConAu 106; ConTFT 5; CurBio 80; EncAJ; EncTwCJ; GoodHs; GrLiveH; HerW 84; IntMPA 79, 80, 81, 82, 84, 86, 88, 92, 94, 96; InWom SUP; JrnUS; LegTOT; LesBEnT 92; NewYTBS 90; VarWW 85; WhoAm 78, 80, 82, 84, 86, 88, 90, 92, 94, 95, 96, 97; WhoAmW 79, 81, 83, 85, 87, 89, 91, 93, 95, 97; WhoE 95; WorAlBi*

Paul I
Greek. Ruler
Sixth monarch of Greece, 1947-64; succeeded by son, Constantine.
b. Dec 14, 1901 in Athens, Greece
d. Mar 6, 1964 in Tatoi, Greece
Source: *CurBio 47, 64; WhAm 4*

Pauli, Wolfgang Ernst
Swiss. Physicist, Educator
Won Nobel Prize in physics, 1945 for contributions to new law of nature—exclusion principle.
b. Apr 25, 1900 in Vienna, Austria
d. Dec 15, 1958 in Zurich, Switzerland
Source: *AsBiEn; BiESc; DcScB; InSci; McGEWB; McGMS 80; ObitOF 79; WhAm 3; WhDW; WhoNob, 90, 95; WorAl*

Paul III, Pope
[Alessandro Farnese]
Italian. Religious Leader
His pontificate, 1534-49, marked first stages of Counter-Reformation; convened Council of Trent, 1545; gave approval to Jesuits, 1540.
b. Feb 29, 1468 in Canino, Italy
d. Nov 10, 1549 in Rome, Italy
Source: *DcCathB; McGEWB; NewCol 75; OxCArt; OxDcArt; WebBD 83*

Pauling, Linus C(arl)
American. Chemist, Physicist
First to receive two unshared Nobel Prizes in two separate fields; in chemistry for work with chemical bonds, 1954; Peace Prize for warning of dangers of radioactivity in weapons, 1962.
b. Feb 28, 1901 in Portland, Oregon
d. Aug 19, 1994 in Big Sur, California
Source: *AmAu&B; AmMWSc 76P, 79, 82, 86, 89, 92; AmPeW; AmSocL; AsBiEn; BiESc; BioIn 1, 2, 3, 4, 5, 6, 7, 8, 9, 10, 11, 12, 13, 14, 15, 16; BlueB 76; CamDcSc; ConAu 116; CurBio 49, 64, 94; EncAB-H 1974, 1996; FacFETw; InSci; IntAu&W 77, 82; IntWW 74, 75, 76, 77, 78, 79, 80, 81, 82, 83, 89, 91, 93; LarDcSc; MajTwCW; McGEWB; McGMS 80; News 95-1; NobelP; OxCAmH; PeoHis; RAdv 13-5; ThTwC 87; WebAB 74, 79; WhAm 11; WhDW; Who 92, 94; WhoAm 74, 76, 78, 80, 82, 84, 86, 88, 90, 92, 94; WhoFrS 84; WhoNob, 90, 95; WhoScEn 94; WhoWest 78, 80, 82, 84, 87, 89, 92, 94; WhoWor 74, 78, 80, 82, 84, 87, 89, 91, 93; WorAl; WorAlBi; WrDr 76, 86, 92, 94*

Paul Revere and the Raiders
[Charlie Coe; Joe Correro; Mark Lindsay; Paul Revere; Freddy Weller]
American. Music Group
Late 1960s-early 1970s pop hits include "Indian Reservation," 1971.
Source: *BioIn 9, 16; EncPR&S 74, 89; EncRk 88; OxCMus; PenEncP; RolSEnR 83; WhoRocM 82*

Paulsen, Pat
American. Comedian
Regular on "The Smothers Brothers Show," 1966-68; ran for pres., 1968.
b. Jul 6, 1927 in South Bend, Washington
d. Apr 25, 1997 in Tijuana, Mexico
Source: *ConTFT 3; LegTOT; WhoAm 84, 88, 90; WhoCom; WhoEnt 92; WhoHol A*

Paulucci, Jeno Francisco
American. Business Executive
Started several food processing businesses, including Chun King (canned Chinese food), 1947, Jeno's, Inc. (frozen pizzas, snacks), 1967, Pizza Kwik, 1980s.
b. Jul 7, 1918 in Aurora, Minnesota
Source: *BioIn 14, 15, 16; ConAmBL; ConNews 86-3; Entr; St&PR 87, 91; WhoAm 74, 76, 78, 80, 82, 84, 86, 88*

Paulus, Friedrich von
German. Military Leader
Led German army which fell to Russians at Stalingrad, Feb 1943.
b. Sep 23, 1890 in Breitenau, Germany
d. Feb 1, 1957 in Dresden, German Democratic Republic
Source: *BioIn 1, 2, 4, 6, 10, 14, 17; DcTwHis; EncGRNM; EncTR; HarEnMi; HisEWW*

Paul VI, Pope
[Giovanni Battista Montini]
Italian. Religious Leader
Carried through Vatican II reforms in 1963-78 pontificate; issued controversial encyclical, *Humanae Vitae,* which condemned birth control.
b. Sep 26, 1897 in Concesio, Italy
d. Aug 6, 1978 in Castel Gandolfo, Italy
Source: *BioIn 3, 4, 5, 6, 14, 16, 17, 18, 19; CurBio 56, 63; WebBD 83; WhoWor 74*

Pavan, Marisa
[Marisa Pierangeli]
Italian. Actor
Oscar nominee for her role in *Rose Tattoo,* 1955.
b. Jun 19, 1932 in Cagliari, Sardinia, Italy
Source: *BioIn 3; FilmEn; FilmgC; ForYSC; HalFC 80, 84, 88; IntMPA 75, 76, 77, 78, 79, 80, 81, 82, 84, 86, 88, 92, 94, 96; InWom SUP; ItaFilm; LegTOT; MotPP; VarWW 85; WhoAm 74; WhoAmW 74; WhoHol 92, A; WorAl*

Pavarotti, Luciano
Italian. Opera Singer, Actor
Best selling classical vocalist; starred in *Yes, Giorgio,* 1982; won five Grammys, one Emmy.
b. Oct 12, 1935 in Modena, Italy
Source: *Baker 84, 92; BiDAmM; BioIn 8, 9, 10, 11, 12, 13, 14, 15, 16; BriBkM 80; CelR 90; CmOp; ConAu 112; ConMus 1; CurBio 73; DcArts; DcTwCCu 1; EncWB; FacFETw; HalFC 84, 88; IntDcOp; IntWW 79, 80, 81, 82, 83, 89, 91, 93; IntWWM 85, 90; LegTOT; MetOEnc; MusSN; NewAmDM; NewEOp 71; NewGrDA 86; NewGrDM 80; NewGrDO; OxDcOp; PenDiMP; RAdv 14; VarWW 85; Who 92, 94; WhoAm 74, 76, 78, 80, 82, 84, 86, 88, 90, 92, 94, 95, 96, 97; WhoAmM 83; WhoEnt 92; WhoHol 92; WhoMus 72; WhoOp 76; WhoWor 78, 80, 82, 84, 87, 89, 91, 93, 95, 96, 97; WorAl; WorAlBi*

Pavelich, Mark
American. Hockey Player
Center, 1981—; first American-born player to score five goals in one NHL game (1983); member US Olympic gold medal-winning team, 1980.
b. Feb 28, 1958 in Eveleth, Minnesota
Source: *BiDAmSp BK; BioIn 14; HocEn; HocReg 87; NewYTBS 86*

Pavese, Cesare
Italian. Author
Imprisoned by Fascists, 1935; novels reflect his escapist attitudes: *The House on the Hill,* 1939.
b. Sep 9, 1908 in Cuneo, Italy
d. Aug 1950 in Turin, Italy
Source: *Benet 87, 96; BioIn 4, 6, 8, 12; CasWL; ClDMEL 80; CnMWL; ConAu 104; CyWA 89; DcArts; DcItL 1, 2; DcLB 128; EncWL, 2, 3; EuWr 12; EvEuW; FacFETw; GrFLW; LiExTwC; MakMC; McGEWB; ModRL; Novels; OxCEng 67, 85, 95; PenC EUR; PoeCrit 13; RAdv 14, 13-2; REn; RfGShF; RfGWoL 95; RGFMEP; ShSCr 19; TwCA SUP; TwCLC 3; TwCWr; WhDW; WhoTwCL; WorAl; WorAlBi*

Pavin, Corey
American. Golfer
Professional golfer, 1982—; PGA America Player of Year, 1991; won US Open, 1995.
b. Nov 16, 1959 in Oxnard, California
Source: *News 96*

Pavlov, Ivan Petrovich
Russian. Physiologist
Discovered conditioned reflex with experiments on dogs; won Nobel Prize, 1904.
b. Sep 14, 1849 in Ryazan, Russia
d. Feb 27, 1936 in Leningrad, Union of Soviet Socialist Republics
Source: *AsBiEn; BiDPsy; BiDSovU; BiESc; BiHiMed; BioIn 1, 2, 3, 4, 5, 6, 7, 9, 10, 11, 12, 14, 15, 20; CamDcSc; ConAu 118; DcScB; FacFETw; InSci; LarDcSc; LngCTC; McGEWB; NamesHP; NewCol 75; NotTwCS; OxCMed 86; RAdv 14, 13-3; SovUn; WebBD 83; WhoNob, 90, 95; WorAl*

Pavlova, Anna
Russian. Dancer
Most celebrated dancer of her time who performed in Paris, New York.
b. Jan 31, 1885 in Saint Petersburg, Russia
d. Jan 23, 1931, Netherlands
Source: *Benet 87; BioIn 1, 2, 3, 4, 5, 6, 7; HerW; LinLib S; REn; WhDW; WhoHol B; WhScrn 74, 77, 83; WhThe; WorAl*

Pawley, Howard Russell
Canadian. Politician
New Dem. Party premier of Manitoba, 1981-88.
b. Nov 21, 1934 in Brampton, Ontario, Canada
Source: *BioIn 12; CanWW 31, 83, 89; WhoAm 84, 88; WhoAmL 78; WhoMW 74, 76, 84, 86, 88*

Paxinou, Katina
Greek. Actor
Won Oscar for her role in *For Whom the Bell Tolls,* 1943.
b. Dec 17, 1900 in Piraeus, Greece
d. Feb 22, 1973 in Athens, Greece
Source: *BiE&WWA; BioIn 9, 10; CnThe; ContDcW 89; CurBio 43, 73, 73N; EncEurC; EncWT; Ent; FilmEn; FilmgC; ForYSC; HalFC 80, 84, 88; IntDcWB; InWom SUP; LegTOT; MotPP; MovMk; NewYTBE 73; OxCFilm; OxCThe 67, 83; WhoHol B; WhoThe 72; WhScrn 74, 77, 83; WhThe; WorAl; WorEFlm*

Paxton, Bill
American. Actor
Starred in *Twister,* 1996.
b. May 17, 1955 in Fort Worth, Texas
Source: *ConTFT 5; IntMPA 94, 96; LegTOT; WhoAm 96, 97*

Paxton, Joseph, Sir
English. Architect
Designed Crystal Palace for London Exhibition, 1851.
b. Aug 3, 1803 in Woburn, England
d. Jun 8, 1865 in Sydenham, England
Source: *Alli; BioIn 13; CelCen; DcBiPP; DcD&D; EncMA; MacEA; McGDA; OxCArt; VicBrit; WhoArch*

Paxton, Tom
[Thomas R Paxton]
American. Singer, Musician, Songwriter
Albums include *Outward Bound,* 1966; *In the Orchard,* 1985.
b. Oct 31, 1937 in Chicago, Illinois
Source: *ASCAP 80; BiDAmM; BioIn 8, 13, 14, 18; ConMuA 80A; ConMus 5; CurBio 82; EncFCWM 69, 83; EncRk 88; HarEnR 86; IlEncRk; NewGrDA 86; OxCPMus; PenEncP; RolSEnR 83; SmATA 70; WhoAm 74, 76, 82, 84, 86, 88, 90, 92, 94, 95, 96, 97; WhoEnt 92; WhoRock 81; WhoRocM 82*

Paycheck, Johnny
[Don Lytle]
American. Singer
Best known for hit country single "Take This Job and Shove It," 1978.
b. May 31, 1941 in Greenfield, Ohio
Source: *BgBkCoM; BiDAmM; BioIn 14; CounME 74, 74A; EncFCWM 69, 83; HarEnCM 87; IlEncCM; LegTOT; NewGrDA 86; PenEncP; VarWW 85; WhoAm 78, 80, 82, 84, 94, 95, 96, 97; WhoRock 81; WorAlBi*

Payen, Anselme
French. Chemist
Discovered cellulose.
b. Jan 6, 1795 in Paris, France
d. May 12, 1871 in Paris, France
Source: *AsBiEn; BiESc; BioIn 6, 7; DcBiPP; DcScB; WorInv*

Payne, Donald M
American. Politician
Dem. US congressman representing NJ, 1989—.
b. Jul 16, 1934 in Newark, New Jersey
Source: *AlmAP 92; BioIn 16; BlkAmsC; CngDr 89; ConBlB 2; NegAl 89A; WhoBlA 92*

Payne, Freda
American. Singer
Hits include "Band of Gold," 1970.
b. Sep 19, 1945 in Detroit, Michigan
Source: *BioIn 13; DrBlPA 90; EncRk 88; IlEncBM 82; InB&W 80, 85; LegTOT; PenEncP; RkOn 74, 78; RolSEnR 83; WhoBlA 85, 92*

Payne, John
American. Actor
Leading man in 1940s-50s films; portrayed Kris Kringle's lawyer in Christmas classic *Miracle on 34th Street,* 1947.
b. May 23, 1912 in Roanoke, Virginia
d. Dec 5, 1989 in Malibu, California
Source: *AnObit 1989; BioIn 9, 16, 17; CmMov; CmpEPM; ConTFT 8; FilmEn; FilmgC; ForYSC; HalFC 80, 84, 88; IntMPA 77, 80, 82, 84, 86, 88; MotPP; MovMk; NewYTBS 89; VarWW 85; What 3; WhoHol A; WorAl; WorAlBi; WorEFlm*

Payne, John Howard
American. Actor, Dramatist
Wrote, adapted at least 60 plays; wrote lyrics for "Home Sweet Home," 1823.
b. Jun 9, 1791 in New York, New York
d. Apr 9, 1852 in Tunis, Tunis
Source: *Alli; AmAu; AmAu&B; AmBi; BbD; Benet 87, 96; BenetAL 91; BibAL; BiDAmM; BiD&SB; BioIn 1, 2, 3, 4, 8, 9, 10, 12, 13, 14; CamGEL; CamGLE; CamGWoT; CamHAL; CasWL; Chambr 3; ChhPo, S2, S3; CnDAL; CrtSuDr; CyAL 1; DcAmAu; DcAmB; DcEnL; DcLB 37; DcLEL; DcNAA; GrWrEL DR; LinLib L, S; McGEWB; NatCAB 2; NotNAT A, B; OxCAmL 65, 83, 95; OxCAmT 84; OxCEng 67, 85, 95; OxCMus; OxCThe 67, 83; PenC AM; PlP&P; REn; REnAL; RfGAmL 87, 94; ScF&FL 92; TwCBDA; WebAB 74, 79; WhAm HS*

Payne, Leon
American. Songwriter
Singer, one-man band, 1920s-30s; blind from childhood.
b. Jun 15, 1917 in Alba, Texas
d. Sep 11, 1969 in San Antonio, Texas
Source: *BgBkCoM; BiDAmM; CounME 74; EncFCWM 69; HarEnCM 87; IlEncCM; PenEncP*

Payne, Robert
[Pierre Stephen Robert Payne]
American. Author
Published over 100 books; known for biographies.
b. Dec 4, 1911 in Saltash, England
d. Feb 18, 1983 in Hamilton, Bermuda
Source: *AmAu&B; AnObit 1983; Au&Wr 71; BioIn 1, 2, 4, 5, 6, 7, 8, 9, 11, 13; ChhPo; ConAu 25R, 31NR, 109; CurBio 83N; EngPo; NewYTBS 83; ScF&FL 1, 2, 92; TwCA SUP; WhAm 8; WhoE 74; WhoWor 74, 76*

Payne, Roger S.
American. Biologist, Conservationist
Studied the musical sounds of the humpback whale.
b. Jan 29, 1935 in New York, New York
Source: *CurBio 95; WhoAm 97; WhoTech 95*

Payson, Joan Whitney
American. Baseball Executive
Philanthropist; principal owner, NY Mets, 1962-75.
b. Feb 5, 1903 in New York, New York
d. Oct 4, 1975 in New York, New York
Source: *BiDAmBL 83; CurBio 72, 75, 75N; InWom SUP; LegTOT; NatCAB 58; NewYTBS 75; WhAm 6; WhoAm 74; WhoAmW 58, 70, 72, 74, 75; WhoE 74, 75; WhoProB 73; WorAl; WorAlBi*

Payton, Lawrence
[The Four Tops]
American. Singer
With group, 1954-97; first hit "Baby I Need Your Loving," 1964.
b. 1938? in Detroit, Michigan
d. Jun 20, 1997 in Southfield, Michigan
Source: *IlEncRk; WhoRock 81*

Payton, Walter
"Sweetness"
American. Football Player
Halfback, Chicago, 1975-87; holds NFL career record in rushing.
b. Jul 25, 1954 in Columbia, Mississippi
Source: *AfrAmAl 6; AfrAmSG; BiDAmSp FB; BioIn 11, 12, 13, 14, 15, 16, 19, 20, 21; ConBlB 11; CurBio 85; FacFETw; InB&W 80, 85; LegTOT; NegAl 89; NewYTBS 84, 86; WhoAm 78, 80, 82, 84, 86, 88, 92, 94, 95, 96, 97; WhoBlA 85, 92; WhoMW 88, 90, 92, 93; WorAl; WorAlBi*

Payton-Wright, Pamela
American. Actor
Won Obies for *Effect of Gamma Rays on Man-in-the-Moon Marigolds; Jessie and the Bandit Queen,* 1976.
b. Nov 1, 1941 in Pittsburgh, Pennsylvania
Source: *ConTFT 5; PlP&P A; WhoAm 78, 80, 82, 84, 86, 88; WhoHol 92, A; WhoThe 77, 81*

Paz, Octavio
Mexican. Poet, Critic
Lyrical poetry uses rich imagery of Mexico's landscape to explore love, death, loneliness; poem "Sun Stone," 1957, inspired by a huge Aztec calendar stone; won Nobel Prize, 1990.
b. Mar 31, 1914 in Mexico City, Mexico
Source: *Benet 87, 96; BenetAL 91; BioIn 6, 9, 10, 12, 13, 14, 15, 16, 17, 18, 19, 20, 21; CasWL; CnMWL; ConAu 32NR, 73; ConFLW 84; ConLC 3, 4, 6, 10, 19, 51, 65; ConSpAP; ConWorW 93; CurBio 74; CyWA 89; DcArts; DcCLAA; DcHiB; DcLB Y90; DcMexL; DcTwCCu 4; EncLatA; EncWL 2, 3; FacFETw; GrFLW; HispLC; HispWr; IntAu&W 76, 77, 89, 91, 93; IntWW 74, 75, 76, 77, 78, 79, 80, 81, 82, 83, 89, 91, 93; IntWWP 77; LatAmWr; LegTOT; LiExTwC; LinLib L; MagSWL; MajTwCW; ModLAL; News 91, 91-2; NewYTBS 94; NobelP 91; OxCSpan; PenC AM; PoeCrit 1; RAdv 14, 13-2; RfGWoL 95; RGFMEP; SpAmA; TwCWr; Who 74, 82, 83, 85, 88, 90, 92, 94; WhoAm 74, 76, 78, 84, 88, 90, 92, 94, 95, 96, 97; WhoNob 90, 95; WhoSSW 91, 93, 95; WhoTwCL; WhoWor 74, 78, 80, 82, 84, 87, 89, 91, 93, 95, 96, 97; WorAl; WorAlBi; WorAu 1950; WorLitC*

Peabody, Eddie
"The Banjo King"
American. Musician
Most famous banjoist during, 1930s-40s.
b. Feb 19, 1902 in Reading, Massachusetts
d. Nov 7, 1970 in Covington, Kentucky
Source: *BioIn 9; CmpEPM; EncVaud; RadStar; WhoHol B*

Peabody, Elizabeth Palmer
American. Educator
Founded first kindergarten in US, 1861, in Boston; sister-in-law of Nathaniel Hawthorne.
b. May 16, 1804 in Billerica, Massachusetts
d. Jan 3, 1894 in Jamaica Plain, Massachusetts
Source: *Alli, SUP; AmAu; AmAu&B; AmBi; AmRef; AmSocL; AmWom; AmWomWr; ApCAB; BenetAL 91; BiDAmEd; BiD&SB; BiDTran; BioIn 2, 4, 5, 6, 7, 8, 10, 11, 12, 15, 17, 19, 21; ChhPo, S1; CnDAL; ContDcW 89; CyEd; DcAmAu; DcAmB; DcLB 1; DcNAA; Drake; FemiCLE; GrLiveH; HanAmWH; IntDcWB; InWom, SUP; LibW; McGEWB; NatCAB 12; NotAW; OxCAmH; OxCAmL 65, 83, 95; REnAL; TwCBDA; WebAB 74, 79; WhAm HS; WomFir; WorAl; WorAlBi*

Peabody, Endicott
American. Clergy, Educator
Founder, headmaster of Groton School, 1884-1940.
b. May 30, 1857 in Salem, Massachusetts
d. Nov 17, 1944 in Groton, Massachusetts
Source: *BiDAmEd; BioIn 8, 12; CurBio 45; DcAmB S3; PeoHis; WhAm 2*

Peabody, George
American. Philanthropist, Merchant
Founded, endowed Peabody Institute, Baltimore; Peabody Museum, Yale, Harvard; Peabody Education Fund.
b. Feb 18, 1795 in Peabody, Massachusetts
d. Nov 4, 1869 in London, England
Source: *AmBi; AmSocL; ApCAB; Baker 92; BiDAmBL 83; BiInAmS; BioIn 3, 4, 5, 6, 7, 8, 9, 12, 13, 16, 17, 19, 20, 21; CelCen; CyEd; DcAmB; DcBiPP; DcNaB; Drake; EncAB-H 1974, 1996; EncABHB 6; HarEnUS; LinLib L, S; McGEWB; NatCAB 5; NewGrDA 86; OxCAmH; TwCBDA; WebAB 74, 79; WhAm HS; WorAl; WorAlBi*

Peabody, Josephine Preston
American. Poet, Dramatist
Wrote plays *The Piper,* 1910; *Marlowe,* 1901.
b. May 30, 1874 in New York, New York
d. Dec 4, 1922 in Cambridge, Massachusetts
Source: *AmAu&B; AmBi; AmWomD; AmWomPl; AmWomWr; ApCAB X; BenetAL 91; BiCAW; BiD&SB; BioIn 16; CarSB; ChhPo, S1; CnDAL; ConAmL; DcAmAu; DcAmB; DcNAA; EvLB; InWom SUP; LibW; LinLib L; LngCTC; ModWD; NatCAB 13, 19; NotAW; NotWoAT; OxCAmL 65, 83, 95; OxCAmT 84; REnAL; TwCA; TwCBDA; WhAm 1; WomWWA 14*

Peach, Charles William
English. Naturalist
His study of fossils yielded many valuable contributions to the knowledge of marine life.
b. Sep 30, 1800 in Wansford, England
d. Feb 28, 1886 in Edinburgh, Scotland
Source: *DcNaB*

Peacock, Thomas Love
English. Author, Poet
Works include satirical novel *Nightmare Alley,* 1818; Shelley's close friend.
b. Oct 18, 1785 in Weymouth, England
d. Jan 23, 1866 in Halliford, England
Source: *Alli; AtlBL; BbD; Benet 87, 96; BiD&SB; BiDLA; BioIn 1, 2, 3, 4, 5, 6, 7, 8, 9, 10, 12, 13, 16, 17, 18; BlmGEL; BritAu 19; BritWr 4; CamGEL; CamGLE; CasWL; CelCen; Chambr 3; ChhPo, S1, S2; CrtT 2, 4; CyWA 58; DcArts; DcBiA; DcBiPP; DcEnA; DcEnL; DcEuL; DcInB; DcLB 96, 116; DcLEL; DcNaB; EvLB; GrWrEL N; LngCEL; McGEWB; MouLC 3; NewC; NewCBEL; NinCLC 22; Novels; OxCEng 67, 85, 95; OxCLiW 86; PenC ENG; RAdv 1, 14, 13-1; REn; RfGEnL 91; RfGShF; ScF&FL 1; WebE&AL; WhDW*

Peake, Mervyn Laurence
English. Illustrator, Author
Wrote *Titus* trilogy novels, 1946-59; illustrated books by Lewis Carroll, R L Stevenson.
b. Jul 9, 1911 in Kuling, China
d. Nov 17, 1968 in Burcot, England
Source: *BioIn 10, 11, 12, 13, 14, 15, 17; ConAu 3NR; DcBrAr 2; DcLB 15, 160; DcNaB 1961; EncSF 93; GrBr; MakMC; NewCBEL; Novels; ObitOF 79; OxCEng 85, 95; OxCTwCA; SmATA 23*

Peale, Charles Willson
American. Artist, Naturalist
Best known for painting portraits of Revolutionary War figures; founded Peale Museum, 1786.

b. Apr 15, 1741 in Queen Annes County, Maryland
d. Feb 22, 1827 in Philadelphia, Pennsylvania
Source: *Alli; AmBi; AmCulL; AmRev; AntBDN J, O; ApCAB; AtlBL; BbD; Benet 87, 96; BenetAL 91; BiD&SB; BiInAmS; BioIn 1, 2, 3, 4, 5, 7, 8, 9, 10, 11, 12, 13, 14, 17, 18, 19; BlkwEAR; BriEAA; DcAmArt; DcAmB; DcScB; Dis&D; Drake; EncAB-H 1974, 1996; EncAR; EncCRAm; IlBEAAW; InSci; LinLib S; McGDA; McGEWB; MorMA; NewYHSD; OxCAmH; OxCAmL 65; OxCArt; OxDcArt; REn; TwCBDA; WebAB 74, 79; WhAm HS; WhAmRev*

Peale, James
American. Artist
Noted for miniatures of George, Martha Washington; brother of Charles Willson Peale.
b. 1749 in Chestertown, Maryland
d. May 24, 1831 in Philadelphia, Pennsylvania
Source: *AntBDN J; ApCAB; BioIn 1, 2, 3, 13; BriEAA; DcAmArt; DcAmB; FolkA 87; McGDA; NewYHSD; OxCAmH; OxDcArt; TwCBDA; WhAm HS; WhAmRev*

Peale, Norman Vincent
American. Clergy
Wrote *The Power of Positive Thinking,* 1952.
b. May 31, 1898 in Bowersville, Ohio
d. Dec 24, 1993 in Pawling, New York
Source: *AmAu&B; AmDec 1940, 1950; AnObit 1993; Au&Wr 71; AuBYP 2, 3; AuNews 1; BenetAL 91; BioIn 1, 2, 3, 4, 5, 7, 8, 10, 11, 12, 13, 14, 16; BioNews 74; CelR; ConAu 29NR, 55NR, 81, 143; ConLC 81; CurBio 46, 74, 94N; EncTwCJ; EncWB; LegTOT; LinLib L, S; MajTwCW; NewYTBS 93; OhA&B; PolProf E; PrimTiR; RadStar; RelLAm 91; REnAL; SmATA 20, 78; St&PR 93; TwCSAPR; WebAB 74, 79; WhAm 11; WhoAm 74, 76, 78, 80, 82, 84, 86, 88, 90, 92, 94; WhoE 86, 89, 91, 93; WhoRel 77, 85, 92; WhoWor 74, 78, 80, 82, 84, 87, 89, 91, 93; WorAl; WorAlBi; WrDr 76, 80, 82, 84, 86, 88, 90, 92, 94, 96*

Peale, Raphael
American. Artist
Miniaturist; established portrait gallery of distinguished persons with brother, Rembrandt; son of Charles Willson.
b. Feb 17, 1774 in Annapolis, Maryland
d. Mar 4, 1825 in Philadelphia, Pennsylvania
Source: *BioIn 1, 3, 4, 13; DcAmB; Drake; McGDA; OxCAmH; OxCArt; WhAm HS*

Peale, Rembrandt
American. Artist
Historical painter noted for portraits of Washington, Jefferson; son of Charles Willson.
b. Feb 22, 1778 in Richboro, Pennsylvania
d. Oct 3, 1860 in Philadelphia, Pennsylvania
Source: *Alli; AmAu&B; AmBi; ApCAB; ArtsNiC; BenetAL 91; BiD&SB; BiInAmS; BioIn 1, 2, 3, 4, 5, 8, 10, 11, 13, 14, 15, 17, 19, 20; BriEAA; DcAmArt; DcAmAu; DcAmB; DcNAA; DcScB, S1; Drake; HarEnUS; LegTOT; McGDA; McGEWB; NatCAB 5; NewYHSD; OxCAmH; OxCAmL 65, 83, 95; OxDcArt; TwCBDA; WhAm HS*

Peale, Titian Ramsay
American. Artist
Member of first party to climb Pike's Peak; did many paintings of animals seen on expedition.
b. Nov 17, 1799 in Philadelphia, Pennsylvania
d. Mar 13, 1885 in Philadelphia, Pennsylvania
Source: *ApCAB; BiDAmS; BiInAmS; BioIn 12, 14; BriEAA; DcAmB; DcNAA; DcScB; IlBEAAW; McGDA; NatCAB 21; NewYHSD; OxDcArt; WhAm HS*

Peano, Giuseppe
Italian. Mathematician
Helped to establish the theory of symbolic logic.
b. Aug 27, 1858 in Cuneo, Sardinia
d. Apr 20, 1932 in Turin, Italy
Source: *AsBiEn; BiESc; BioIn 10, 12, 20; CamDcSc; DcScB; LarDcSc; NotTwCS; OxCPhil*

Pearce, Alice
American. Actor
Played Gladys Kravitz on TV's "Bewitched," 1964-66.
b. Oct 16, 1919 in New York, New York
d. Mar 3, 1966 in Los Angeles, California
Source: *BiE&WWA; FilmEn; FilmgC; ForYSC; MotPP; WhScrn 74, 77, 83*

Pearl, Jack
American. Radio Performer
Popularized expression "Vas you dere, Sharlie?" on radio program, 1932-47.
b. Oct 29, 1895 in New York, New York
d. Dec 25, 1982 in New York, New York
Source: *BiE&WWA; EncMT; EncVaud; JoeFr; NewYTBS 82; SaTiSS; What 1; WhoCom; WhoHol A; WhoThe 77A; WhThe*

Pearl, Minnie
[Sarah Ophelia Colley Cannon]
American. Comedian
Trademark was straw hat with price tag hanging on it; appeared on TV's "Hee Haw;" Country Hall of Fame, 1975.
b. Oct 25, 1912 in Centerville, Tennessee
d. Mar 4, 1996 in Nashville, Tennessee
Source: *BgBkCoM; BiDAmM; BioIn 12, 14, 15, 16, 18, 21; ConAu 129, 151; ConMus 3; CounME 74, 74A; CurBio 92, 96N; EncFCWM 69, 83; FunnyW; GoodHs; HarEnCM 87; IlEncCM; InWom SUP; LegTOT; NewAmDM; NewGrDA 86; News 96, 96-3; PenEncP; RadStar; SaTiSS; VarWW 85; WhoAm 74, 76, 78, 80, 82, 84, 86, 88, 92, 94, 95, 96; WhoCom; WhoEnt 92; WhoHol 92, A; WorAl; WorAlBi*

Pearl Jam
[Dave Abbruzzese; Jeff Ament; Stone Gossard; Mike McCready; Eddie Vedder]
American. Music Group
Formed in Seattle, 1991; debut album *Ten,* 1991.
Source: *BioIn 19; ConMus 12; EncRkSt; News 94, 94-2; OnThGG*

Pearlroth, Norbert
American. Journalist
Only researcher for "Ripley's Believe It or Not" newspaper feature, 1923-83.
b. May 1893, Poland
d. Apr 14, 1983 in New York, New York
Source: *AnObit 1983; BioIn 13; NewYTBS 83*

Pears, Charles
English. Artist, Illustrator, Author
Naval artist, illustrated his writings.
b. Sep 9, 1870 in Pontefract, England
d. Jan 1958, England
Source: *BiDLA; DcBrBI; WhE&EA*

Pears, Peter, Sir
English. Opera Singer
Tenor, who was definitive interpreter of works of Benjamin Britten.
b. Jun 22, 1910 in Farnham, England
d. Apr 3, 1986 in Aldeburgh, England
Source: *AnObit 1986; Baker 78, 84; BioIn 3, 8, 10, 11, 14, 15, 18, 19; BlueB 76; BriBkM 80; CmOp; CurBio 75, 86, 86N; DcArts; FacFETw; IntDcOp; IntWW 74, 75, 76, 77, 83; IntWWM 77, 80; LegTOT; MetOEnc; MusMk; MusSN; NewAmDM; NewEOp 71; NewGrDM 80; NewYTBS 74, 75, 86; OxCMus; OxDcOp; PenDiMP; Who 74, 82, 83, 85; WhoMus 72; WhoOp 76; WhoWor 74*

Pearse, Padraic
[Patrick Henry Pearse]
Irish. Poet, Patriot
Shot by British firing squad because of his part in the Easter Week rebellion, 1916; wrote *Collected Works,* 1916.
b. Nov 10, 1879 in Dublin, Ireland
d. May 3, 1916 in Dublin, Ireland
Source: *BiDIrW B; BioIn 1, 4, 11, 12, 14, 17; CasWL; ChhPo; DcArts; DcIrB 78, 88; DcIrW 2, 3; DcNaB MP; FacFETw; LngCTC; McGEWB; NewC; PenC ENG; REn; TwCA, SUP*

Pearson, Cyril Arthur, Sir
English. Publisher, Philanthropist
Founded mag *Pearson's Weekly;* newspapers *Daily Express,* 1900.
b. Feb 24, 1866 in Wells, England
d. Dec 9, 1921 in London, England

Source: *DcNaB 1912; NewCol 75*

Pearson, David
American. Auto Racer
Won Daytona 500, 1976.
b. Dec 22, 1934
Source: *BiDAmSp OS; BioIn 8, 9, 10, 11, 15; LegTOT; WhoAmL 85; WhoWor 87; WorAl*

Pearson, Drew
American. Journalist
With Robert S. Allen wrote daily column "Washington Merry Go-Round," 1932-69.
b. Dec 13, 1897 in Evanston, Illinois
d. Sep 1, 1969 in Washington, District of Columbia
Source: *AmAu&B; BioIn 1, 2, 4, 6, 7, 8, 9, 10, 11, 12, 15, 16, 17; ConAu 5R, 25R; CurBio 41, 69; DcAmB S8; DcAmSR; EncAJ; EncMcCE; EncTwCJ; JrnUS; LegTOT; LinLib L, S; ObitT 1961; PolProf E; REnAL; SaTiSS; ScF&FL 1, 2; TwCA SUP; WebAB 74, 79; WhAm 5; WhE&EA; WhScrn 77, 83; WorAlBi*

Pearson, Drew
American. Football Player
Three-time all-pro wide receiver, Dallas, 1973-83; led NFL in receiving, 1977.
b. Jan 12, 1951 in Newark, New Jersey
Source: *AfrAmBi 2; BiDAmSp FB; FootReg 81; WhoAfA 96; WhoAm 78, 80, 82; WhoBlA 77, 80, 85, 90, 92, 94*

Pearson, Lester B(owles)
Canadian. Political Leader, Author
Liberal prime minister of Canada, 1963-68; won Nobel Peace Prize, 1957, for helping to resolve Arab-Israeli War.
b. Apr 23, 1897 in Newtonbrook, Ontario, Canada
d. Dec 27, 1972 in Ottawa, Ontario, Canada
Source: *BiDInt; BioIn 1, 2, 3, 4, 5, 6, 7, 8, 9, 10, 11, 12, 13, 15, 19; CanWW 70; CurBio 47, 63, 73, 73N; DcNaB 1971; DcTwHis; LinLib L, S; MacDCB 78; McGEWB; NewYTBE 72; ObitT 1971; OxCCan SUP; WhAm 5; WhDW; WhoNob, 90, 95; WorAl*

Peary, Harold
"Great Gildersleeve"
American. Actor
Played the Great Gildersleeve in movies, radio for 16 years.
b. Jul 25, 1908? in San Leandro, California
d. Mar 30, 1985 in Torrance, California
Source: *BioIn 10, 14; ForYSC; HalFC 80, 88; WhoCom; WhoHol A*

Peary, Robert Edwin
American. Explorer
First man to reach N Pole, Apr 6, 1909.
b. May 6, 1856 in Cresson, Pennsylvania
d. Feb 20, 1920 in Washington, District of Columbia
Source: *AmAu&B; AmBi; AmDec 1900; AsBiEn; BenetAL 91; BiD&SB; BiInAmS; BioIn 1, 2, 3, 4, 5, 6, 7, 8, 9, 10, 11, 12, 13, 15, 16, 17, 18, 19, 20, 21; Chambr 3; DcAmAu; DcAmB; DcNAA; FacFETw; GayN; HarEnUS; InSci; LinLib L, S; LngCTC; McGEWB; MemAm; NatCAB 14, 37; OxCAmH; OxCCan; OxCShps; REn; REnAL; TwCBDA; WebAB 74, 79; WebAMB; WhAm 1; WhDW; WhWE; WorAl*

Pease-Windy Boy, Jeanine
American. Educator
Appointed president of Little Big Horn College, 1982.
b. 1949 in Nespelem, Washington
Source: *NotNaAm*

Peattie, Donald Culross
American. Author, Naturalist
Best known for nature writings: *The Road of a Naturalist,* 1944.
b. Jun 21, 1898 in Chicago, Illinois
d. Nov 16, 1964 in Santa Barbara, California
Source: *AmAu&B; AuBYP 2, 3; BenetAL 91; BioIn 2, 3, 4, 7, 16; ConAmA; ConAu 102; CurBio 40, 65; DcAmB S7; DcLEL; InSci; LinLib L; MnBBF; OxCAmL 65, 83, 95; REnAL; TwCA, SUP; WhAm 4; WhE&EA; WhNAA*

Pechstein, Max
German. Artist
Founder of Die Brucke (The Bridge) a group of German expressionist painters.
b. Dec 31, 1881 in Zwickau, Germany
d. Jun 29, 1955 in Berlin, Germany
Source: *BioIn 2, 3, 4, 14, 17, 20; ConArt 77, 83; EncWB; FacFETw; McGDA; ObitOF 79; OxCArt; OxCTwCA; OxDcArt; PhDcTCA 77*

Peck, Dale
American. Author
Author of *Martin and John,* 1993, about a gay male coping with the death of his companion.
b. Jul 13, 1967 in Bay Shore, New York
Source: *ConAu 146; ConLC 81*

Peck, George Wilbur
American. Journalist
Wrote humorous Peck's Bad Boy stories, 1880s; governor of WI, 1891-95.
b. Sep 28, 1840 in Henderson, New York
d. Apr 16, 1916
Source: *AmAu; AmAu&B; BbD; BenetAL 91; BiD&SB; BioIn 5, 8, 15; CarSB; CnDAL; DcAmAu; DcAmB; DcLB 42; DcNAA; JrnUS; NatCAB 12; OxCAmL 65, 83, 95; OxCChiL; PenC AM; REn; REnAL; TwCBDA; WhAm 1; WhAmP; WhoChL; WisWr*

Peck, Gregory
[Eldred Gregory Peck]
American. Actor
Won Oscar, 1962, for *To Kill a Mockingbird;* other films include *The Omen,* 1976; *Gentleman's Agreement,* 1947.
b. Apr 5, 1916 in La Jolla, California
Source: *BiDFilm 81, 94; BiE&WWA; BioIn 1, 2, 3, 4, 5, 6, 7, 10, 11, 12, 13, 14, 15, 16, 17, 18, 21; BkPepl; BlueB 76; CelR, 90; CmCal; CmMov; ConTFT 1, 6; CurBio 47, 92; DcTwCCu 1; FilmEn; FilmgC; ForYSC; HalFC 80, 84, 88; IntDcF 1-3, 2-3; IntMPA 75, 76, 77, 78, 79, 80, 81, 82, 84, 86, 88, 92, 94, 96; IntWW 74, 75, 76, 77, 78, 79, 80, 81, 82, 83, 89, 91, 93; LegTOT; MotPP; MovMk; NewYTBS 89, 92; OxCFilm; VarWW 85; Who 74, 82, 83, 85, 88, 90, 92, 94; WhoAm 74, 76, 78, 80, 82, 84, 86, 88, 90, 92, 94, 95, 96, 97; WhoEnt 92; WhoGov 72, 75; WhoHol 92, A; WhoHrs 80; WhoWor 74, 78, 80, 82, 84, 87, 89, 91, 93, 95, 96, 97; WhThe; WorAl; WorAlBi; WorEFlm*

Peck, M. Scott
American. Psychiatrist, Author
Wrote *The Road Less Traveled,* 1978, which appeared on the New York Times list of bestsellers for 8 years, holding a nonfiction record.
b. May 22, 1936 in New York, New York
Source: *BioIn 14, 15, 16; ConAu 20NR, 89; CurBio 91; WrDr 92*

Peckford, Brian
[Alfred Brian Peckford]
Canadian. Politician
Progressive-conservative party premier of Newfoundland, 1979-89.
b. Aug 27, 1942 in Whitbourne, Newfoundland, Canada
Source: *BioIn 12, 13; CanWW 31, 81, 83, 89; IntWW 80, 81, 82, 83, 89, 91; IntYB 80, 81, 82; News 89-1; Who 82, 83, 85, 88, 90, 92; WhoAm 80, 82, 84, 88, 90; WhoCan 80, 82, 84; WhoE 83, 85, 86, 89*

Peckinpah, Sam
[David Samuel Peckinpah]
"Bloody Sam"
American. Director
Best known for glorifying anti-hero in violent Westerns: *The Wild Bunch,* 1969.
b. Feb 21, 1925 in Fresno, California
d. Dec 28, 1984 in Inglewood, California
Source: *AnObit 1984; BiDFilm 94; BioIn 9, 10, 12, 13, 15, 16, 17, 20, 21; BlueB 76; CelR; CmMov; ConAu 109, 114; ConLC 20; ConTFT 1; CurBio 73, 85N; DcArts; DcFM; DcTwCCu 1; FilmEn; FilmgC; IlWWHD 1; IntDcF 1-2, 2-2; IntMPA 75, 76, 77, 78, 79, 80, 81, 82, 84; IntWW 74, 75, 76, 77, 78, 79, 80, 81, 82, 83; ItaFilm; LegTOT; LesBEnT; MiSFD 9N; MovMk; NewYTBE 70; NewYTBS 84; OxCFilm; VarWW 85; WhAm 8; WhoAm 74, 76, 78, 80, 82, 84;*

WhoWor 78; WorAl; WorAlBi; WorEFlm; WorFDir 2

Pecora, Ferdinand
American. Judge
Headed Senate banking investigation into 1929 Wall Street crash; later gave birth to Securities and Exchange Commission.
b. Jan 6, 1882 in Nicosia, Sicily, Italy
d. Dec 7, 1971 in New York, New York
Source: *BioIn 2, 9, 16; DcAmB S9; NewYTBE 71; WhAm 5*

Pedersen, Charles J
American. Chemist
Shared Nobel Prize in chemistry, 1987, for research in energy technology.
b. 1904? in Pusan, Korea
d. Oct 26, 1989 in Salem, New Jersey
Source: *AmMWSc 92; BioIn 15, 16; NewYTBS 89; Who 90; WhoAm 88; WhoE 89; WhoNob 90; WhoWor 89; WorAlBi*

Pedersen, Christiern
"Father of Danish Literature"
Danish. Theologian, Historian, Translator
Translated Bible into Danish, published 1550.
b. 1480?
d. 1554
Source: *BiD&SB; CasWL; LuthC 75; NewCBEL; WebBD 83*

Pedro I
[Antonio Pedro de Alcantara Bourbon]
Brazilian. Ruler
Fled to Brazil, 1807; later declared independence from Portugal, crowned emperor, 1822; abdicated, 1831.
b. Oct 12, 1798 in Lisbon, Portugal
d. Sep 24, 1834 in Lisbon, Portugal
Source: *NewCol 75; WebBD 83*

Pedro II
[Pedro de Alcantara]
Brazilian. Ruler
Crowned after abdication of father, Pedro I, 1841; forced to abdicate after Brazil became a republic, Nov 15, 1889.
b. Dec 2, 1825 in Rio de Janeiro, Brazil
d. Dec 5, 1891 in Paris, France
Source: *NewCol 75; WebBD 83*

Peel, Robert, Sir
English. Statesman
Started Irish police force known as Peelers; later reorganized London's police force known as "Bobbies."
b. Feb 5, 1788 in Lancashire, England
d. Jan 2, 1850 in London, England
Source: *Alli; BioIn 1, 2, 3, 4, 5, 6, 7, 8, 9, 11, 12, 13, 15, 16, 17, 18, 21; CelCen; CopCroC; DcBiPP; DcNaB; HisDBrE; HisWorL; LinLib S; McGEWB; REn; VicBrit; WhDW; WorAl; WorAlBi*

Peel, Ronald Francis (Edward Waite)
English. Geographer, Editor
Expert on world's desert areas; edited *Geographical Journal,* 1978-80.
b. Aug 22, 1912 in Yorkshire, England
d. Sep 21, 1985 in Cambridge, England
Source: *BioIn 2, 4, 15; BlueB 76; ConAu 117; Who 74, 82, 83, 85*

Peele, George
English. Dramatist, Poet
Wrote play *The Old Wives' Tale,* 1595; verse *Polyhymnia,* 1590.
b. 1558 in London, England
d. 1597 in London, England
Source: *Alli; AtlBL; Benet 87, 96; BiD&SB; BiDRP&D; BioIn 3, 5, 8, 9, 10, 11, 12, 16; BritAu; CamGEL; CamGLE; CamGWoT; CasWL; Chambr 1; ChhPo S1; CnE&AP; CnThe; CroE&S; CrtT 1; CyWA 58; DcArts; DcEnA; DcEnL; DcLEL; DcNaB; EncWT; Ent; EvLB; GrWrEL DR; LngCEL; MouLC 1; NewC; NotNAT A, B; OxCEng 67; OxCThe 67, 83; PenC ENG; RAdv 13-2; REn; WebE&AL*

Peerce, Jan
[Jacob Pincus Perelmuth]
American. Opera Singer
Leading tenor, NY Met., 1941-66; wrote *Bluebird of Happiness,* 1976.
b. Jun 3, 1904 in New York, New York
d. Dec 15, 1984 in New York, New York
Source: *AnObit 1984; Baker 78, 84, 92; BioIn 1, 2, 3, 4, 7, 9, 11, 13, 14, 18; BriBkM 80; CelR; CmOp; CmpEPM; ConAu 101, 114; CurBio 42, 85N; FacFETw; HalFC 88; IntDcOp; LegTOT; MetOEnc; MusSN; NewAmDM; NewEOp 71; NewGrDA 86; NewGrDM 80; NewGrDO; NewYTBS 84; OxDcOp; PenDiMP; RadStar; VarWW 85; WhoAm 82; WhoHol A; WhoMus 72; WhoWor 74; WhoWorJ 72; WorAl; WorAlBi*

Peers, William Raymond
American. Military Leader, Author
Combat commander who led investigation of 1968 My Lai massacre.
b. Jun 14, 1914 in Stuart, Iowa
d. Apr 6, 1984 in San Francisco, California
Source: *ConAu 112; EncAI&E; NewYTBE 70; NewYTBS 84; WhAm 8; WhoAm 74, 76, 78; WhoGov 72; WhoWor 74; WorDWW*

Peete, Calvin
American. Golfer
Turned pro, 1971; has 10 career PGA wins; first black to win $1 million on tour.
b. Jul 18, 1943 in Detroit, Michigan
Source: *AfrAmSG; BioIn 12, 13, 14, 15; ConBlB 11; ConNews 85-4; InB&W 85; LegTOT; NewYTBS 82, 83, 90; WhoAfA 96; WhoAm 84, 86, 88, 94, 95, 96, 97; WhoBlA 85, 90, 92, 94; WhoIntG*

Peeters, Pete(r)
Canadian. Hockey Player
Goalie, 1978-1991, currently with Washington; won Vezina Trophy, 1983.
b. Aug 1, 1957 in Edmonton, Alberta, Canada
Source: *BioIn 13; HocEn; HocReg 87; NewYTBS 83; WhoE 85*

Pegler, Westbrook
[Francis Pegler; James Westbrook Pegler]
American. Journalist
Outspoken, controversial reporter; won Pulitzer for reporting on racketeering in labor union, 1941.
b. Aug 2, 1894 in Minneapolis, Minnesota
d. Jun 24, 1969 in Tucson, Arizona
Source: *AmAu&B; Ballpl 90; BiDAmSp OS; BioIn 1, 3, 4, 6, 7, 8, 9, 10, 16; ConAu 89, 103; CurBio 40, 69; DcAmB S8; DcAmC; DcLB 171; EncAJ; EncMcCE; EncTwCJ; FacFETw; JrnUS; LegTOT; LiJour; OxCAmL 65, 83, 95; REnAL; WebAB 74, 79; WhAm 5; WhScrn 77, 83*

Pei, I(eoh) M(ing)
American. Architect
Int'l designs include the annex to the Nat. Gallery of Art in Washington, DC, 1978; the glass pyramid at the Louvre, 1984; won Pritzker Award, 1983.
b. Apr 26, 1917 in Guangzhou, China
Source: *AmArch 70; AmCulL; BioIn 4, 5, 6, 7, 8, 11, 12, 13, 14, 15, 16; CelR 90; ConArch 87, 94; CurBio 69, 90; DcArts; DcD&D; EncAAr 2; EncAB-H 1996; EncWB; FacFETw; IntWW 75, 78, 79, 80, 81, 82, 83; News 90; Who 94; WhoAm 74, 76, 78, 80, 82, 84, 86, 88, 90, 92, 94, 95, 96, 97; WhoAmA 91; WhoArch; WhoE 74, 95; WhoWor 74, 84, 87, 89, 91, 93, 95, 96, 97*

Pei, Mario Andrew
Italian. Educator
Philology professor who regarded language as "mankind's most important invention;" devoted life to making linguistics interesting, enjoyable.
b. Feb 16, 1901 in Rome, Italy
d. Mar 2, 1978 in Glen Ridge, New Jersey
Source: *BiDInt; BioIn 3, 4, 8, 9, 11, 12; ConAu 5NR, 5R, 77; CurBio 68, 78; DcAmB S10; DrAS 74H; NatCAB 60; REnAL; TwCA SUP; WhAm 7; WhoAm 74, 76, 78; WhoWor 74; WrDr 76*

Peirce, Benjamin
American. Astronomer, Mathematician
Noted for researching rings of Saturn; wrote math book *Linear Associative Algebra,* 1870.
b. Apr 4, 1809 in Salem, Massachusetts
d. Oct 6, 1880 in Cambridge, Massachusetts

Source: *Alli, SUP; AmAu; AmBi; ApCAB; BiDAmEd; BiDAmS; BiInAmS; BioIn 5, 8; CyEd; DcAmAu; DcAmB; DcBiPP; DcNAA; DcScB; Drake; EncAB-H 1974, 1996; HarEnUS; InSci; LinLib S; NatCAB 8; NewCol 75; OxCAmH; REnAL; TwCBDA; WebAB 74, 79; WhAm HS*

Peirce, Charles Sanders
"Father of Pragmatism"
American. Philosopher
First used term "pragmatism" in magazine article, 1878.
b. Sep 10, 1839 in Cambridge, Massachusetts
d. Apr 19, 1914 in Milford, Pennsylvania
Source: *Alli SUP; AmAu; AmAu&B; AmBi; ApCAB; Benet 87; BiDAmS; BiInAmS; DcAmAu; DcAmB; DcNAA; EncAB-H 1974; EncWB; InSci; LarDcSc; LinLib L, S; LngCTC; OxCAmH; OxCAmL 65, 83, 95; OxCPhil; PenC AM; RAdv 14, 13-4; REn; REnAL; ThTwC 87; TwCBDA; WebAB 74, 79; WebE&AL; WhAm 1*

Peirce, Waldo
American. Illustrator, Artist
Works include *Maine Swimming Hole,* 1944; illustrated juvenile poetry book *The Children's Hour,* 1944.
b. Dec 17, 1884 in Bangor, Maine
d. Mar 8, 1970 in Searsport, Maine
Source: *BioIn 1, 2, 4, 8, 9, 10, 13; CurBio 44, 70; DcCAA 71, 77, 88, 94; IlsCB 1744; NatCAB 55; SmATA 28; WhAm 5; WhAmArt 85; WhoAmA 78N, 80N, 82N, 84N, 86N, 89N, 91N, 93N*

Peiresc, Nicholas-Claude Fabri de
French. Archaeologist, Naturalist
Discovered Orion Nebula, 1610.
b. Dec 1, 1580 in Beaugensier, France
d. Jun 24, 1637 in Aix-en-Provence, France
Source: *DcScB*

Pele
[Edson Arantes do Nascimento]
"Perola Negra"
Brazilian. Soccer Player
Scored 1,281 career goals; played with NY Cosmos, 1974-77, for $4.7 million; took on cabinet post of special minister for sports in Brazil, 1995.
b. Oct 23, 1940 in Tres Coracoes, Brazil
Source: *BioIn 13, 15, 16, 17, 19, 20, 21; BkPepl; CelR; ConBlB 7; CurBio 67; EncLatA; EncWB; FacFETw; InB&W 80, 85; IntWW 81, 82, 83, 89, 91, 93; LegTOT; NegAl 76, 83, 89; NewYTBE 71; NewYTBS 75; WhDW; WhoAm 78, 80, 82, 84, 86, 88, 90, 92, 94, 95, 96, 97; WhoHol 92; WhoSpor; WhoWor 78; WorAl; WorAlBi; WorESoc*

Pelikan, Jaroslav
[Jan Pelikan, Jr]
American. Clergy, Historian
Wrote five-vol. history of church doctrine: *The Christian Tradition,* 1969.
b. Dec 17, 1923 in Akron, Ohio
Source: *BioIn 13, 15; ConAu 1NR, 1R; CurBio 87; DrAS 74P, 78P, 82P; IntAu&W 77; IntWW 91, 93; LinLib L; RelLAm 91; WhoAm 86, 90; WhoE 86, 89; WhoRel 92; WorAu 1975; WrDr 80, 82, 84, 86, 88, 90, 92, 94, 96*

Pelkey, Edward
"Fast Eddie"
American. Billiards Player
Portrayed by Paul Newman in *The Hustler,* 1961.
b. 1898
d. 1983 in San Jose, California
Source: *BioIn 13*

Pell, Claiborne DeBorda
American. Politician
Dem. senator from RI, 1961-97.
b. Nov 22, 1918 in New York, New York
Source: *AlmAP 92; BiDrAC; BioIn 13, 14, 15; BlueB 76; CngDr 87, 89; ConAu 49; CurBio 72; IntWW 74, 75, 76, 77, 78, 79, 80, 81, 82, 83; IntYB 78, 79, 80, 81, 82; NewYTBS 87; PolProf J, K, NF; PolsAm 84; WhoAm 86, 90; WhoAmP 87, 95*

Pella, Giuseppe
Italian. Economist
Italy's budget minister, 1960-62; served 22 yrs. in Chamber of Deputies.
b. Apr 18, 1902 in Rome, Italy
d. May 31, 1981 in Rome, Italy
Source: *AnObit 1981; BioIn 3, 12; CurBio 53, 81, 81N; IntWW 74, 75, 76, 77, 78, 79, 80, 81; IntYB 78, 79, 80, 81; NewYTBS 81; WhAm 8*

Peller, Clara
American. Actor
Famous for "Where's the beef," Wendy's hamburgers TV commercial.
b. 1901
d. Aug 11, 1987 in Chicago, Illinois
Source: *AnObit 1987; BioIn 13, 14, 15; NewYTBS 87*

Pelletier, Wilfrid
Canadian. Conductor
Founder, director, Metropolitan Opera Auditions of the Air, 1934-46; founder, Montreal Symphony Orchestra, 1935.
b. Jun 20, 1896 in Montreal, Quebec, Canada
d. Apr 9, 1982 in New York, New York
Source: *AnObit 1982; Baker 78; BiDAmM; BioIn 4, 7, 12; CanWW 70, 79, 80, 81; CreCan 2; CurBio 44, 82, 82N; IntWWM 77, 80; MetOEnc; NewGrDA 86; NewGrDM 80; NewGrDO; WhAm 8, 10; Who 74, 82; WhoAm 74, 76, 78, 80, 82; WhoWor 74*

Pelli, Cesar
American. Architect
One of first to use glass as nonstructural outer walls; works include US Embassy in Tokyo, extension to Museum of Modern Art, NYC.
b. Oct 12, 1926 in Tucuman, Argentina
Source: *AmCulL; BioIn 9, 13, 15; ConArch 80, 87, 94; CurBio 83; DcHiB; EncAAr 2; FacFETw; IntDcAr; IntWW 89, 91, 93; MacEA; News 91; WhoAm 76, 78, 80, 82, 84, 86, 88, 90, 92, 94, 95, 96, 97; WhoAmA 78, 80, 82, 84, 86, 89, 91, 93; WhoE 81, 83, 91; WhoScEn 96; WhoWor 74, 97*

Pellico, Silvio
Italian. Author, Dramatist
Wrote major romantic tragedy *Francesca da Rimini,* 1814.
b. Jun 25, 1788 in Saluzzo, Italy
d. Jan 31, 1854 in Turin, Italy
Source: *BiD&SB; BioIn 7; CasWL; CelCen; DcCathB; DcEuL; EuAu; EvEuW; LinLib L; McGEWD 84; OxCThe 83; PenC EUR; REn*

Pelopidas
Military Leader
General who helped liberate Thebes from Sparta, 379 B.C.
d. 364BC
Source: *BioIn 11; DcBiPP; LinLib S; NewCol 75; OxCClL*

Peltier, Leonard
American. Political Activist
Convicted in the shooting deaths of two FBI agents at the Pine Ridge Indian Reservation, 1975.
b. Sep 12, 1944 in Grand Forks, North Dakota
Source: *BioIn 12, 13; EncNAB; LNinSix; News 95, 95-1; NotNaAm*

Pemberton, Brock
American. Director, Producer
Plays include *Enter Madame; Harvey; Miss Lulu Bett.*
b. Dec 14, 1885 in Leavenworth, Kansas
d. Mar 11, 1950 in New York, New York
Source: *BioIn 2, 10, 20; CurBio 45, 50; DcAmB S4; NotNAT B; OxCAmT 84; WhAm 2; WhoHol B; WhScrn 83; WhThe*

Pemberton, John Clifford
American. Military Leader
Although born in the North, served as officer in confederate army; surrendered to Grant at Vicksburg.
b. Aug 10, 1814 in Philadelphia, Pennsylvania
d. Jul 13, 1881 in Penllyn, Pennsylvania
Source: *ApCAB; BiDConf; BioIn 1, 5, 17; CivWDc; DcAmB; EncSoH; HarEnUS; NatCAB 10; TwCBDA; WebAMB; WhAm HS; WhCiWar; WhoMilH 76*

Pena, Elizabeth
American. Actor
Films include *La Bamba,* 1986; star of "I Married Dora," 1987.
b. Sep 23, in Elizabeth, New Jersey
Source: *BioIn 17, 18, 20; ConTFT 5; IntMPA 92; WhoEnt 92; WhoHisp 92*

Pena, Federico F.
American. Government Official
Secretary of Transportation, 1993-96; Secretary of Energy, 1996—.
b. Mar 15, 1947 in Laredo, Texas
Source: *BioIn 13, 14, 15, 16; CngDr 93, 95; CurBio 93; MexAmB; WhoAm 90; WhoAmP 89, 93, 95; WhoHisp 92; WhoWest 92*

Pender, Mel(vin)
American. Track Athlete
Only US sprinter in both 1964, 1968 Olympics; won gold medal in 400-meter relay, 1968.
b. Oct 31, 1937 in Atlanta, Georgia
Source: *BlkOlyM; NewYTBS 74, 76; WhoBlA 77, 80, 85, 90, 92; WhoTr&F 73*

Penderecki, Krzysztof
Polish. Composer
Wrote controversial avant-garde opera *Devils of Loudun,* 1969; won many awards, including Grammys.
b. Nov 23, 1933 in Debica, Poland
Source: *Baker 78, 84, 92; BioIn 8, 9, 10, 11, 12, 14, 15; BriBkM 80; CnOxB; CompSN SUP; ConCom 92; CpmDNM 78; CurBio 71; DcCM; DcCom&M 79; FacFETw; IntDcOp; IntWW 74, 75, 76, 77, 78, 79, 80, 81, 82, 83, 89, 91, 93; IntWWM 77, 80, 90; LegTOT; McGEWB; MetOEnc; MusMk; NewAmDM; NewGrDM 80; NewGrDO; NewOxM; NewYTBS 86; OxDcOp; PenDiMP A; PenEncH; PolBiDi; Who 82, 83, 85, 88, 90, 92, 94; WhoAm 76, 78, 80, 82, 84, 86, 88, 90, 92, 94, 95, 96, 97; WhoAmM 83; WhoSocC 78; WhoSoCE 89; WhoWor 74, 76, 78, 80, 82, 84, 87, 89, 91, 93, 95, 96, 97*

Pendergast, Thomas Joseph
American. Political Leader
Dem. political boss in Kansas City, 1920s-1930s; one of strongest political bosses in US.
b. Jul 22, 1872 in Saint Joseph, Missouri
d. Jan 26, 1945 in Kansas City, Missouri
Source: *CurBio 45; DcAmB S3; FacFETw*

Pendergrass, Teddy
[Theodore D Pendergrass]
"Teddy Bear"
American. Singer
Album *Life Is a Song Worth Singing,* 1978, was double platinum; paralyzed in car accident.
b. Mar 26, 1950 in Philadelphia, Pennsylvania
Source: *BioIn 11, 12, 14, 15, 16; ConMus 3; DrBlPA 90; EncPR&S 89; EncRk 88; EncRkSt; HarEnR 86; LegTOT; NewAmDM; NewGrDA 86; PenEncP; RkOn 85; RolSEnR 83; SoulM; VarWW 85; WhoAm 80, 82, 86, 90, 92, 94, 95, 96, 97; WhoBlA 88, 92; WhoEnt 92; WhoHol 92*

Pendleton, Austin
American. Actor, Director
Won Obie, Drama Desk Award for *The Last Sweet Days of Isaac,* 1970.
b. Mar 27, 1940 in Warren, Ohio
Source: *ConTFT 4; HalFC 80, 84, 88; IntMPA 92, 94, 96; NewYTBE 70; WhoAm 80, 82, 84, 86, 88; WhoHol 92, A; WhoThe 77, 81*

Pendleton, Clarence McLane, Jr.
American. Government Official
Chairman, US Civil Rights Commission, 1981-88.
b. Nov 10, 1930 in Louisville, Kentucky
d. Jun 5, 1988 in San Diego, California
Source: *CurBio 84, 88; InB&W 80; NewYTBS 88; WhAm 9; WhoAm 84, 86; WhoAmP 83, 85, 87; WhoGov 75*

Pendleton, Don
[Donald Eugene Pendleton]
American. Author
Author of the "Executioner" novels.
b. 1927 in Little Rock, Arkansas
d. Oct 23, 1995 in Sedona, Arizona
Source: *BioIn 14, 19, 21; ConAu 33R; IntAu&W 91; Novels; ScF&FL 1, 2, 92; TwCCr&M 80, 85, 91; WhoMW 74, 76, 78, 80; WrDr 82, 84, 86, 88, 90, 92*

Pendleton, George Hunt
American. Politician
As senator from OH, 1879-85 he sponsored bill which is the basis of US present day civil service system.
b. Jul 29, 1825 in Cincinnati, Ohio
d. Nov 24, 1889 in Brussels, Belgium
Source: *AmBi; ApCAB; BiAUS; BiDrAC; BiDrUSC 89; BioIn 16; DcAmB; DcAmDH 80, 89; Drake; EncAAH; HarEnUS; McGEWB; NatCAB 3; OhA&B; TwCBDA; WhAm HS; WhAmP; WhCiWar*

Pendleton, Moses Robert Andrew
American. Choreographer, Dancer
Co-founder of the Pilobolus Dance Theatre, 1971, and Momix, 1980—; dance troupes noted for their mixture of acrobatics and surrealism.
b. Mar 28, 1949 in Saint Johnsbury, Vermont
Source: *BiDD; BioIn 2, 4, 12, 16; CurBio 89; WhAm 3; Who 92; WhoAm 78, 80, 82, 84, 86, 88, 90, 92, 94, 95, 96, 97; WhoEnt 92*

Pendleton, Nat
American. Actor
Character actor in over 150 films including eight *Dr. Kildare* pictures, 1934-44.
b. Aug 9, 1899 in Davenport, Iowa
d. Oct 11, 1967 in San Diego, California
Source: *Film 2; FilmEn; FilmgC; ForYSC; MotPP; MovMk; Vers A; WhoHol B; WhScrn 74, 77, 83*

Penfield, Wilder Graves
American. Physician
Founded Montreal Neurological Institute, 1934-60; known for neurosurgical treatment of brain injuries, particularly epilepsy.
b. Jan 26, 1891 in Spokane, Washington
d. Apr 5, 1976 in Montreal, Quebec, Canada
Source: *BiDPsy; BioIn 2, 4, 5, 7, 8, 10, 11, 12, 13; BlueB 76; CanWW 70; ConAu 3NR, 5R; CurBio 55, 68, 76N; InSci; IntWW 74, 75, 76; LarDcSc; McGEWB; McGMS 80; NewYTBS 76; OxCCan; OxCMed 86; WhAm 7; Who 74; WhoAm 74, 76; WhoCan 73, 75; WhoWor 74*

Penn, Arthur Hiller
American. Director
Films include *The Miracle Worker,* 1962; *Bonnie and Clyde,* 1967.
b. Sep 27, 1922 in Philadelphia, Pennsylvania
Source: *Benet 87; BiE&WWA; BioIn 13, 14, 15, 16; ConAu 112, 130; ConTFT 2; CurBio 72; DcFM; FilmgC; HalFC 88; IntDcF 2-2; IntMPA 92; IntWW 91; MovMk; NotNAT; OxCAmT 84; OxCFilm; VarWW 85; WhoAm 74, 76, 82, 84, 86, 88, 90, 92, 94, 95, 96, 97; WhoEnt 92; WhoThe 81; WhoWest 96; WhoWor 74; WorAlBi; WorEFlm; WorFDir 2; WrDr 94*

Penn, Irving
American. Photographer
Known for fashion photographs in *Vogue,* often compared to paintings.
b. Jun 16, 1917 in Plainfield, Pennsylvania
Source: *AmArt; BioIn 4, 5, 6, 7, 10, 12, 14; BriEAA; ConPhot 82, 88, 95; CurBio 80; DcArts; DcTwCCu 1; DcTwDes; EncFash; FacFETw; ICPEnP; IntWW 91, 93; MacBEP; WhoAm 74, 76, 78, 80, 82, 84, 86, 88, 90, 92, 94, 95, 96; WhoAmA 76, 78, 80, 82, 84, 86, 89, 91, 93*

Penn, John
American. Continental Congressman, Lawyer
Signed Declaration of Independence as NC delegate, 1776.
b. May 17, 1741 in Caroline County, Virginia
d. Sep 14, 1788 in Williamsburg, North Carolina
Source: *AmBi; ApCAB; BiAUS; BiDrAC; BiDrUSC 89; BioIn 7, 8, 9; DcAmB; Drake; NatCAB 7; TwCBDA; WhAm HS; WhAmP*

Penn, Michael
American. Singer, Songwriter
Album *March,* contains singles "No Myth," "Brave New World" and "Battle Room."

Source: *BioIn 17; ConMus 4*

Penn, Sean
American. Actor, Director
Films include *Fast Times at Ridgemont High,* 1982; *At Close Range,* 1985; *State of Grace,* 1989.
b. Aug 17, 1960 in Burbank, California
Source: *BioIn 13, 14, 15, 16; CelR 90; ConNews 87-2; ConTFT 2, 3, 10; CurBio 93; HalFC 88; HolBB; IntMPA 84, 86, 88, 92, 94, 96; LegTOT; MiSFD 9; NewYTBS 91; VarWW 85; WhoAm 86, 88, 90, 92, 94, 95, 96, 97; WhoEnt 92; WhoHol 92; WorAlBi*

Penn, William
English. Colonizer
Quaker who founded PA, 1682, based on religious, political freedom.
b. Oct 14, 1644 in London, England
d. Jul 30, 1718 in Ruscombe, England
Source: *Alli; AmAu&B; AmBi; AmRef; AmSocL; AmWrBE; ApCAB; BbD; Benet 87, 96; BenetAL 91; BiD&SB; BiDrACR; BioIn 1, 2, 3, 4, 5, 6, 7, 8, 9, 10, 11, 12, 13, 14, 15, 19, 20; BritAu; CamGEL; CamGLE; CasWL; Chambr 2; CopCroC; CyAG; CyEd; DcAmB; DcAmReB 1, 2; DcAmSR; DcBiPP; DcEnL; DcEuL; DcLB 24; DcLEL; DcNaB; Dis&D; Drake; EncAAH; EncAB-H 1974, 1996; EncARH; EncCRAm; EvLB; HarEnUS; HisDBrE; HisWorL; LinLib S; LitC 25; LuthC 75; McGEWB; NatCAB 2; NewCBEL; OxCAmH; OxCAmL 65, 83, 95; OxCEng 67, 85, 95; PenC AM; REn; REnAL; TwCBDA; WebAB 74, 79; WhAm HS; WhAmP; WhDW; WhNaAH; WhoMilH 76; WorAl; WorAlBi*

Penn & Teller
American. Entertainers
Duo's stage act combines drama, music, satire and philosophy, 1975—.
Source: *BioIn 14, 15, 16, 18, 19; News 92, 92-1*

Pennario, Leonard
American. Musician, Composer
Soloed with LA Orchestra, age 15; played with Heifetz, Piatigorsky in trio concerts.
b. Jul 9, 1924 in Buffalo, New York
Source: *ASCAP 66, 80; Baker 78, 84, 92; BioIn 4, 5, 7, 11; ConAmC 76, 82; CurBio 59; IntWWM 85; MusSN; NewAmDM; NewGrDA 86; NewGrDM 80; WhoAm 74, 76, 78, 80, 82, 84, 86, 88, 90, 92, 94, 95, 96, 97; WhoAmM 83; WhoE 74; WhoMus 72; WhoWor 74*

Pennel, John (Thomas)
American. Track Athlete
Pole vaulter; first person to vault 17 feet, 1963.
b. Jul 25, 1940 in Memphis, Tennessee
d. Sep 26, 1993 in Santa Monica, California
Source: *BioIn 6, 7, 8, 19, 20; CurBio 63, 94N; WhoSpor; WhoTr&F 73*

Pennell, Joseph Stanley
American. Artist, Illustrator
Produced etchings for wife's travel books including *Italian Pilgrimage,* 1886; lithographer; leading graphic artist of his time.
b. Jul 4, 1860? in Philadelphia, Pennsylvania
d. Apr 23, 1926 in New York, New York
Source: *GrAmP; McGDA; NatCAB 10; OxCAmL 83; REnAL; TwCBDA; WebAB 79; WhAm 1; WhAmArt 85*

Pennell, Joseph Stanley
American. Author
Wrote Civil War story, *History of Rome Hanks,* 1944.
b. Jul 4, 1908 in Junction City, Kansas
d. Sep 26, 1963 in Seaside, Oregon
Source: *AmAu&B; BenetAL 91; BioIn 2, 4; CurBio 44; OxCAmL 65, 83, 95; REnAL; TwCA SUP; WhAm HS*

Penner, Fred
Canadian. Singer, Songwriter
Children's music entertainer; released first album, *The Cat Came Back,* 1980; received Juno Award for best children's recording for *Fred Penner's Place,* 1989; recorded *The Season,* 1990 and *Happy Feet,* 1992.
b. Nov 6, 1946 in Winnipeg, Manitoba, Canada
Source: *ConMus 10; SmATA 67*

Penner, Joe
[Joseph Pinter]
American. Comedian
Famous for phrase ''Wanna buy a duck?;'' in films, 1934-40.
b. Nov 11, 1904 in Budapest, Austria-Hungary
d. Jan 10, 1941 in Philadelphia, Pennsylvania
Source: *BioIn 2; CurBio 41; EncVaud; FilmgC; ForYSC; HalFC 80, 84, 88; MotPP; QDrFCA 92; RadStar; SaTiSS; WhoCom; WhoHol B; WhScrn 74, 77*

Penner, Rudolph Gerhard
American. Economist
Director, Congressional Budget Office, 1983-87.
b. Jul 15, 1936 in Windsor, Ontario, Canada
Source: *AmMWSc 73S, 78S; BioIn 13, 14; NewYTBS 83; WhoAm 84, 86, 88, 90, 92, 94, 95; WhoE 74, 93; WhoFI 85, 87, 92; WhoGov 77*

Penney, J(ames) C(ash)
American. Merchant
Founded dept. store chain, 1902; grew to one of nation's largest.
b. Sep 16, 1875 in Hamilton, Missouri
d. Feb 12, 1971 in New York, New York
Source: *AmDec 1900; BiDAmBL 83; BioIn 1, 2, 3, 4, 5, 6, 7, 8, 9, 10, 14, 17, 18, 19; CurBio 47, 71; DcAmB S9; LinLib S; NatCAB 63; NewYTBE 71; WebAB 74, 79; WhAm 5; WorAl*

Penney, William George
English. Physicist, Mathematician
Led British team in the development of the atomic bomb in Los Alamos, New Mexico, 1944 and 1945.
b. Jun 24, 1901 in Gibraltar, England
d. Mar 6, 1991 in East Hendred, England
Source: *CurBio 91N; FacFETw; NewYTBS 91*

Pennington, Ann
American. Actor
Dancer who introduced ''Black Bottom,'' 1926.
b. 1893 in Camden, New Jersey
d. Nov 4, 1971 in New York, New York
Source: *BiE&WWA; BioIn 8, 9; EncMT; Film 1; InWom SUP; NewYTBE 71; NotNAT B; TwYS; What 2; WhoHol B; WhScrn 74, 77*

Pennington, John Selman
American. Journalist
Credited with helping launch Jimmy Carter's political career by exposing a vote fraud in state senate race, 1962.
b. 1924? in Andersonville, Georgia
d. Nov 23, 1980 in Saint Petersburg, Florida
Source: *ConAu 102*

Pennock, Herb(ert Jefferis)
''The Knight of Kennett Square''
American. Baseball Player
Pitcher, 1912-34; had 240 career wins; Hall of Fame, 1948.
b. Feb 10, 1894 in Kennett Square, Pennsylvania
d. Jan 30, 1948 in New York, New York
Source: *Ballpl 90; BioIn 14, 15; LegTOT; WhoProB 73*

Penrose, Roger
English. Physicist, Author
Author of *The Emperor's New Mind,* 1989, which sparked controversy on the subject of the interrelationship between artificial intelligence and the human mind.
b. Aug 8, 1931 in Colchester, England
Source: *BestSel 90-2; BiESc; BioIn 14, 15, 16; BlueB 76; CamDcSc; ConAu 139; IntWW 91, 93; LarDcSc; McGMS 80; News 91; NotTwCS; RAdv 14; Who 74, 82, 83, 85, 88, 90, 92, 94; WhoScEn 94; WhoWor 89; WrDr 92, 94, 96*

Penske, Roger
American. Auto Racer, Business Executive
Former racing champion who founded Penske Corp., late 1960s; racers include Mario Andretti.
b. 1937? in Shaker Heights, Ohio
Source: *BiDAmSp OS; BioIn 6, 11, 12, 15, 16; Dun&B 86, 88, 90; News 88-3; NewYTBS 77; WhoSpor*

Pentifallo, Kenny
[Southside Johnny and the Asbury Jukes]
American. Musician
Drummer with group since 1974.

b. Dec 30, 1940
Source: *WhoRocM 82*

Penzias, Arno Allan
American. Physicist
Astrophysicist who proved "big bang" theory of creation; shared Nobel Prize in physics, 1978.
b. Apr 26, 1933 in Munich, Germany
Source: *AmMWSc 92; BiESc; BioIn 13, 14, 15, 16; CamDcSc; CurBio 85; Dun&B 88; IntWW 79, 80, 81, 82, 83, 89, 91, 93; LarDcSc; LElec; NobelP; St&PR 84, 87, 91, 93, 96, 97; Who 82, 83, 85, 88, 90, 92, 94; WhoAm 76, 78, 82, 84, 86, 88, 90, 92, 94, 95, 96, 97; WhoAmJ 80; WhoE 79, 81, 83, 85, 86, 89, 91, 93, 95, 97; WhoEng 88; WhoFI 92, 94, 96; WhoFrS 84; WhoNob, 90; WhoScEn 94, 96; WhoTech 89; WhoWor 80, 82, 84, 87, 89, 91, 93, 95, 96, 97; WorAl; WorAlBi; WorScD*

Pep, Willie
[William Papaleo]
"Will o' the Wisp"
American. Boxer
World featherweight champ, 1942-48, 1949-50; Hall of fame, 1963.
b. Sep 19, 1922 in Middletown, Connecticut
Source: *BiDAmSp BK; BioIn 1, 3, 4, 7, 10, 16; BoxReg; WhoBox 74; WhoSpor*

Pepa
[Salt-N-Pepa; Sandra Denton]
American. Rapper
Grammy, Best Rap Performance by a Group or Duo, "None of Your Business," 1994.
b. Sep 9, 1969 in New York, New York

Pepin III
[Pepin le Bref; Pepin the Short]
French. Ruler
First Carolingian king of Franks, 751-68; son of Charles Martel; father of Charlemagne.
b. 715
d. 768
Source: *OxCFr*

Pepitone, Joe
[Joseph Anthony Pepitone]
"Pepi"
American. Baseball Player
First baseman-outfielder, 1962-73, mostly with Yankees; known for fielding, off-field life-style.
b. Oct 9, 1940 in New York, New York
Source: *Ballpl 90; BioIn 9, 10, 12, 14, 15, 19; ConAu 109; CurBio 73; NewYTBE 70, 71, 72; NewYTBS 74, 85; WhoProB 73*

Peppard, George
American. Actor
Star of TV shows "Banacek," 1972-74; "The A-Team," 1983-87; in *Breakfast at Tiffany's.*
b. Oct 1, 1928 in Detroit, Michigan
d. May 8, 1994 in Los Angeles, California
Source: *BioIn 14, 19, 20; CelR, 90; ConTFT 3, 13; CurBio 65, 94N; FilmEn; FilmgC; HalFC 88; IntMPA 84, 86, 88, 92, 94; IntWW 91, 93; ItaFilm; LegTOT; MiSFD 9; MotPP; MovMk; VarWW 85; WhAm 11; WhoAm 74, 76, 78, 80, 82, 84, 86, 88, 90, 92, 94; WhoEnt 92; WhoHol 92; WorAl; WorAlBi*

Pepper, Art(hur Edward)
American. Jazz Musician
Top altoist; with Stan Kenton, 1948-52; received long jail sentences for narcotics violations.
b. Sep 1, 1925 in Gardena, California
d. Jun 15, 1982 in Los Angeles, California
Source: *AllMusG; AnObit 1982, 1984; Baker 84, 92; BiDAmM; BiDJaz; BioIn 12, 13, 16, 20, 21; CmpEPM; ConAu 107; EncJzS; IlEncJ; LegTOT; NewAmDM; NewGrDA 86; NewGrDJ 88; NewGrDM 80; NewYTBS 82; OxCPMus; PenEncP*

Pepper, Claude Denson
American. Politician
Dem. senator from FL, 1936-51; congressman, 1963-89; oldest member of Congress; instrumental in passage of law against mandatory retirement based only on age, 1 989.
b. Sep 8, 1900 in Dudleyville, Alabama
d. May 30, 1989 in Washington, District of Columbia
Source: *AlmAP 88; AmPolLe; BiDrAC; BiDrUSC 89; BioIn 1, 2, 6, 10, 11, 12, 13, 14, 15, 16; CngDr 74, 77, 79, 81, 83, 85, 87, 89; ConAu 128; CurBio 41, 83, 89, 89N; DcAmC; EncAACR; EncSoH; EncWB; FacFETw; IntWW 74, 75, 76, 77, 78, 79, 80, 81, 82, 83; News 89; NewYTBS 80, 81, 89; PolProf NF, T; PolsAm 84; WhAm 10; Who 74, 82, 83, 85, 88, 90N; WhoAm 74, 76, 78, 80, 82, 84, 86, 88; WhoAmP 87; WhoGov 72, 75, 77; WhoSSW 73, 75, 76, 78, 80, 82, 86, 88; WhoWor 78, 80*

Pepperell, William, Sir
American. Army Officer
Led land forces that captured French fortress at Louisburg, 1745; first native American created baronet, 1746.
b. Jun 27, 1696 in Kittery, Maine
d. Jul 6, 1759 in Kittery, Maine
Source: *Alli; BbtC; BenetAL 91; BiDAmBL 83; DcAmB; DcAmMiB; DcNaB; EncCRAm; HarEnMi; HarEnUS; McGEWB; NatCAB 3; NewCBEL; OxCCan; REnAL; TwCBDA; WebAB 79; WhAm HS*

Pepusch, Johann Christoph
[John Pepusch]
German. Composer
Arranged music for ballad-operas: *The Beggar's Opera,* 1728.
b. 1667 in Berlin, Germany
d. Jul 20, 1752 in London, England
Source: *Baker 84; BriBkM 80; DcArts; DcBiPP; IntDcOp; MetOEnc; MusMk; NewAmDM; NewEOp 71; NewGrDM 80; NewGrDO; NewOxM; OxCMus*

Pepys, Samuel
English. Diarist, Naval Officer
Kept diary, 1660-69, detailing social, daily conditions of Restoration life.
b. Feb 23, 1633 in London, England
d. May 26, 1703 in Clapham, England
Source: *Alli; AtlBL; BbD; Benet 87, 96; BiD&SB; BioIn 1, 2, 3, 4, 5, 6, 7, 8, 9, 10, 11, 12, 13, 14, 15, 16, 17, 18, 20; BlmGEL; BritAu; BritWr 2; CamGEL; CamGLE; CamGWoT; CasWL; Chambr 1; CnDBLB 2; CroE&S; CrtT 2, 4; CyWA 58; DcArts; DcLB 101; DcNaB, C; DcPup; Dis&D; HisDStE; LegTOT; LinLib L, S; LitC 11; LngCEL; LngCTC; MagSWL; McGEWB; NewCBEL; NewGrDM 80; NotNAT B; OxCEng 85, 95; OxCMus; OxCShps; OxCThe 67, 83; OxDcOp; PenC ENG; PlP&P; RAdv 1, 13-1; REn; RfGEnL 91; WhDW; WorAl; WorAlBi; WorLitC*

Perahia, Murray
American. Pianist, Conductor
Won many awards for performing complete Mozart concertos; won first Avery Fisher Award, 1975.
b. Apr 19, 1947 in New York, New York
Source: *Baker 78, 84, 92; BiDAmM; BioIn 9, 10, 12, 13, 14, 15, 16, 17, 20, 21; ConMus 10; CurBio 82; DcArts; IntWW 89, 91, 93; IntWWM 77, 80, 85, 90; NewAmDM; NewGrDA 86; NewGrDM 80; NotTwCP; PenDiMP; Who 85, 88, 90, 92, 94; WhoAm 78, 80, 82, 84, 86, 88, 90, 92, 94, 95, 96, 97; WhoAmM 83; WhoEnt 92; WhoWor 80, 82, 84, 87, 89, 91, 93, 95, 96, 97*

Percy, Charles Harting
American. Politician
Moderate Rep. senator from IL, 1967-85.
b. Sep 27, 1919 in Pensacola, Florida
Source: *AuBYP 2S, 3; BiDrAC; BiDrUSC 89; BioIn 2, 3, 5, 6, 7, 8, 9, 10, 11, 12, 14, 16; BioNews 74; BlueB 76; CngDr 74, 77, 79, 81, 83; ConAu 65; CurBio 59; IntWW 74, 75, 76, 77, 78, 79, 80, 81, 82, 83, 89, 91, 93; NatCAB 63N; PolsAm 84; WhoAm 74, 76, 78, 80, 82, 84, 86, 88, 90, 92, 94; WhoAmP 73, 75, 77, 79, 81, 83, 85, 87, 89, 91, 93, 95; WhoGov 72, 75, 77; WhoMW 74, 76, 78, 80, 82, 84; WhoWor 74, 78, 80, 82, 84; WorAl; WorAlBi*

Percy, Henry, Sir
English. Revolutionary
Led rebellions against King Henry IV; Shakespeares *Henry IV* was based on his life.
b. May 20, 1364
d. Jul 21, 1403 in Shrewsbury, England
Source: *Benet 87, 96; BioIn 4, 10; DcBiPP; DcNaB; LegTOT; NewC; REn; WhDW*

Percy, Walker
American. Author
Southern author; wrote about search for faith and love in chaotic modern world: *Love in the Ruins,* 1971.
b. May 28, 1916 in Birmingham, Alabama
d. May 10, 1990 in Covington, Louisiana
Source: *AmAu&B; AmCath 80; AmWr S3; AnObit 1990; Benet 87, 96; BenetAL 91; BiDConC; BioIn 9, 10, 11, 12, 13, 14, 15, 16, 17, 18, 19, 20; CamGLE; CamHAL; ConAu 1NR, 1R, 23NR, 131; ConLC 2, 3, 6, 8, 14, 18, 47, 65; ConNov 72, 76, 82, 86; ConPopW; CurBio 76, 90, 90N; CyWA 89; DcLB 2, Y80A, Y90N; DcLEL 1940; DrAF 76; DrAPF 80, 89; EncSoH; EncWL 2, 3; FacFETw; FifSWrA; GrWrEL N; IntAu&W 76, 77, 91; IntvTCA 2; LegTOT; LinLib L; LiveMA; MagSAmL; MajTwCW; ModAL, S1, S2; News 90; NewYTBS 90; Novels; OxCAmL 65, 83, 95; PeoHis; RAdv 1, 14, 13-1; RfGAmL 87, 94; RGTwCWr; ScF&FL 1, 2, 92; SouWr; TwCSFW 81, 86; WebE&AL; WhAm 10; WhoAm 74, 76, 78, 80, 82, 84, 86, 88; WhoSSW 73, 75, 88; WhoWor 74; WorAl; WorAlBi; WorAu 1950; WrDr 76, 80, 82, 84, 86, 88, 90*

Perdue, Frank
American. Businessman
Chm. of Perdue Farms, Inc., one of the largest poultry processors in the US.
b. 1920 in Salisbury, Massachusetts
Source: *BioIn 9, 11, 12, 13; CelR 90; ConAmBL; CurBio 79; NewYTBS 76; WhoAm 90; WhoFI 92*

Pereda, Jose Marie de
Spanish. Author
Wrote Spanish regional novels: *Mountain Scenes,* 1864; *Sotileza,* 1884.
b. Feb 6, 1833 in Polanco, Spain
d. Mar 1, 1906 in Santander, Spain
Source: *CasWL; ConAu 117; CyWA 58; TwCLC 16*

Pereira, Aristides
Cape Verdean. Political Leader
Pres. of Republic of Cape Verde, 1975-1991.
b. Nov 17, 1924 in Boa Vista, Cape Verde
Source: *BioIn 14; DcAfHiB 86; IntWW 83, 91; WhoWor 84, 91*

Pereira, William Leonard
American. Architect, Urban Planner
Designed San Francisco's Transamerica Corp. pyramid; Cape Canaveral.
b. Apr 25, 1909 in Chicago, Illinois
d. Nov 13, 1985 in Los Angeles, California
Source: *AmArch 70; BioIn 1, 5, 6, 11, 12, 14, 15; ConArch 87, 94; CurBio 79, 86; IntWW 74, 75, 76, 77, 78, 79, 80, 81, 82, 83; NewYTBS 85; WhoAm 84*

Perelman, Ronald O
American. Businessman
Financial empire includes Revlon; named the richest man in the United States in 1989.
b. 1943 in Greensboro, North Carolina
Source: *BioIn 15, 16; CurBio 91; Dun&B 86, 88, 90; IntWW 91; St&PR 91; WhoAm 90; WhoE 91; WhoFI 92*

Perelman, S(idney) J(oseph)
American. Author
Won 1956 Oscar for screenplay, *Around the World in Eighty Days.*
b. Feb 1, 1904 in New York, New York
d. Oct 17, 1979 in New York, New York
Source: *AmAu&B; Au&Wr 71; AuNews 1, 2; Benet 96; BiE&WWA; BioIn 3, 4, 5, 6, 7, 8, 9, 10, 11, 12, 13, 14, 15, 17; BioNews 75; BlueB 76; CelR; CnDAL; ConAu 73, 89; ConDr 73, 77, 93; ConLC 3, 5, 9, 15; CurBio 71; DcAmB S10; DcArts; DcLEL; FilmgC; IntAu&W 76, 77; IntWW 74, 75, 76, 77, 78, 79; LngCTC; McGEWD 72; NewYTBE 70, 72; NotNAT; OxCAmL 65, 95; PenC AM; RAdv 1, 14; REn; REnAL; RfGAmL 94; TwCA, SUP; TwCWr; WebAB 74, 79; WebE&AL; WhAm 7; WhDW; Who 74; WhoAm 74, 76, 78, 80; WhoWor 74, 78; WorECar; WrDr 76, 80*

Perennou, Marie
French. Filmmaker
With Claude Nuridsany, made *Microcosmos,* winner of the 1996 Cannes Film Festival grand prize for technical achievement.
b. 1946? in Paris, France

Peres, Shimon
Israeli. Political Leader
Prime minister of Israel, 1984-86 and 1995-96; vice prime minister, 1986-90; foreign minister, 1992-95.
b. Aug 16, 1923 in Wolozyn, Poland
Source: *BioIn 10, 11, 12, 13, 14, 15, 16, 17, 20, 21; ConAu 85; CurBio 76, 95; DcMidEa; EncWB; FacFETw; HisEAAC; IntWW 74, 75, 76, 77, 78, 79, 80, 81, 82, 83, 89, 91, 93; IntYB 79, 80, 81, 82; LegTOT; MidE 78, 79, 80, 81, 82; News 96, 96-3; NewYTBS 77, 84, 86; PolLCME; Who 90, 92, 94; WhoNob 95; WhoWor 74, 78, 80, 82, 84, 87, 89, 91, 93, 95, 96, 97; WhoWorJ 72, 78*

Peret, Benjamin
French. Author, Poet
One of first surrealist poets; collections include *Four Years After the Dog,* 1974.
b. 1899 in Nantes, France
d. 1959 in Paris, France
Source: *BioIn 10; ClDMEL 80; ConAu 117; DcTwCCu 2; GuFrLit 1; ModFrL; OxCFr; PenC EUR; TwCLC 20*

Peretti, Elsa
American. Model, Designer
European fashion model, who also designs jewelry.
b. May 1, 1940 in Florence, Italy
Source: *BioIn 13, 14, 15, 16; ConFash; EncFash; InWom SUP; LegTOT; NewYTBS 74; WhoAm 80, 82, 84, 86; WhoAmW 79, 81, 83, 91, 93, 95; WhoFash 88; WorFshn*

Peretz, Isaac Loeb
Polish. Author
Major force behind Yiddish literary movement, Jewish theater; plays include *The Golden Chain,* 1907; *The Hunchback,* 1414.
b. May 18, 1851 in Zamosc, Poland
d. Apr 3, 1915 in Warsaw, Poland
Source: *BioIn 1, 2, 5, 6, 7, 11; CnMD; ConAu 109; EuAu; McGEWB; McGEWD 84; OxCThe 83; PenC EUR*

Perez, Anna
American. Government Official
Press secretary for First Lady Barbara Bush, 1989-92.
b. 1951 in New York, New York
Source: *AfrAmBi 1; BioIn 16; ConBlB 1; NegAl 89A; WhoAmW 91; WhoBlA 92*

Perez, Carlos Andres
Venezuelan. Political Leader
Pres., Venezuela, 1974-79, 1989-94.
b. Oct 27, 1922 in La Vega de La Pipa, Venezuela
Source: *BiDLAmC; BioIn 10, 11, 13, 14, 16; CurBio 76; DcCPSAm; EncLatA; EncWB; News 90, 90-2; NewYTBS 88; WhoWor 91, 93*

Perez, Rosie
American. Actor
Appeared in *Do the Right Thing,* 1989, *Fearless,* 1994.
b. 1964 in New York, New York
Source: *CurBio 95; IntMPA 96*

Perez, Tony
[Ananasio Rigal Perez]
Cuban. Baseball Player
Infielder, 1964-86, mostly with Cincinnati; known for fielding; seven-time NL All-Star.
b. May 14, 1942 in Camaguey, Cuba
Source: *Ballpl 90; BaseReg 86, 87; BioIn 9, 11, 15, 16, 19, 20; Dun&B 90; InB&W 80; WhoAm 82; WhoHisp 91, 92, 94; WhoProB 73*

Perez de Cuellar, Javier
Peruvian. Statesman
Secretary-general of UN, 1982-91.
b. Jan 19, 1920 in Lima, Peru
Source: *BioIn 11, 12, 13, 14, 15; CurBio 82; DcHiB; DcTwHis; EncWB; FacFETw; IntWW 74, 75, 76, 77, 78, 79, 80, 81, 82, 83, 89, 91, 93; IntYB 78, 79, 80, 81, 82; LegTOT; News 91, 91-3; NewYTBS 81, 86; Who 83, 85, 88, 90, 92, 94; WhoAm 94; WhoGov 72; WhoUN 75, 92; WhoWor 78, 80, 82, 84, 87, 89, 91, 93, 95, 96; WorAlBi*

Perez Esquivel, Adolfo
Argentine. Political Activist
Surprise winner of 1980 Nobel Peace Prize; human rights activist jailed, abused by own govt; Catholic lay leader.
b. Nov 26, 1931 in Buenos Aires, Argentina
Source: *BioIn 12, 14, 15; CurBio 81; DcHiB; IntWW 81, 82, 83, 91, 93; NewYTBS 80; NobelP; Who 82, 83, 85, 88, 90, 92, 94; WhoNob, 90; WhoWor 82, 84, 87, 89, 91, 93, 95, 96, 97*

Perez Galdos, Benito
Spanish. Author
Father of modern Spanish novel; wrote 46-vol. *Episodios Nacionales*, 1873-1912, historical fiction of 19th c. Spain.
b. May 10, 1843 in Las Palmas, Canary Islands, Spain
d. Jan 4, 1920 in Madrid, Spain
Source: *AtlBL; Benet 87, 96; BiD&SB; BioIn 4, 5, 8, 9, 10, 15, 16; CasWL; ClDMEL 47, 80; CnMD; ConAu 125, 153; CyWA 58; DcArts; DcHiB; DcSpL; EncWL, 2, 3; EvEuW; GrFLW; HispWr; LinLib L, S; McGEWD 72, 84; ModRL; ModSpP S; ModWD; NewCBEL; Novels; OxCSpan; OxCThe 67, 83; PenC EUR; RAdv 14, 13-2; REn; RfGWoL 95; TwCA, SUP; TwCLC 27; WhDW*

Perez Jimenez, Marcos
Venezuelan. Politician
Pres. of Venezuela, 1952-58.
b. Apr 25, 1914 in Tachira, Venezuela
Source: *BiDLAmC; BioIn 3, 4, 5, 6, 7, 11, 12, 16; CurBio 54; DcCPSAm; DcPol; EncLatA; EncWB; IntWW 74, 75, 76, 77, 78, 79, 80, 81, 82, 83, 89, 91, 93*

Pergolesi, Giovanni Battista
Italian. Composer
Noted for intermezzos, comic operas: *La Serva Padrona,* 1733.
b. Jan 4, 1710 in Jesi, Italy
d. Mar 16, 1736 in Pozzuoli, Italy
Source: *AtlBL; Baker 78, 84, 92; BioIn 1, 2, 3, 4, 7, 17; BlkwCE; BriBkM 80; CmOp; CmpBCM; DcBiPP; DcCathB; DcCom&M 79; DcPup; EncEnl; GrComp; IntDcOp; LuthC 75; McGEWB; MusMk; NewAmDM; NewEOp 71; NewGrDM 80; NewGrDO; NewOxM; OxCMus; OxDcOp; PenDiMP A; REn; WhDW*

Peri, Jacopo
Italian. Composer
Wrote *Dafne,* 1597, considered the first opera.
b. Aug 20, 1561 in Rome, Italy
d. Aug 12, 1633 in Florence, Italy
Source: *Baker 78, 84, 92; BioIn 1, 3, 4, 5, 7, 12, 13; BriBkM 80; CmOp; CmpBCM; GrComp; IntDcOp; LinLib S; MetOEnc; MusMk; NewAmDM; NewEOp 71; NewGrDM 80; NewGrDO; NewOxM; OxCMus; OxDcOp; PenDiMP A*

Pericles
Greek. Statesman
Led democratic party, 460-429 BC; called "The Periclean Age"; instrumental in building of Parthenon.
b. 495?BC in Athens, Greece
d. 429?BC in Athens, Greece
Source: *DicTyr; HarEnMi; HisWorL; LegTOT; McGEWB; NewC; OxCClL 89; REn; WhDW*

Perkin, William Henry, Sir
English. Chemist
Produced first synthetic dye, mauve, 1856.
b. Mar 12, 1838 in London, England
d. Jul 14, 1907 in Sudbury, England
Source: *AsBiEn; BiESc; BioIn 2, 3, 4, 5, 6, 8, 9, 12, 14, 19; CamDcSc; DcInv; DcNaB, S2; DcScB; Dis&D; InSci; LarDcSc; LinLib S; RAdv 14; WebBD 83; WhDW; WorAl; WorAlBi; WorInv*

Perkins, Anthony
American. Actor
Best known for role of Norman Bates in *Psycho* films, 1960, 1983, 1986; son of Osgood.
b. Apr 14, 1932 in New York, New York
d. Sep 12, 1992 in Hollywood, California
Source: *AnObit 1992; BiDFilm 81, 94; BiE&WWA; BioIn 5, 6, 10, 11, 13, 14, 15, 16; BkPepl; BlueB 76; CelR 90; ConTFT 2, 6, 11, 13; CurBio 60, 92N; DcArts; FilmEn; FilmgC; ForYSC; HalFC 80, 84, 88; IntDcF 1-3, 2-3; IntMPA 75, 76, 77, 78, 79, 80, 81, 82, 84, 86, 88, 92; ItaFilm; LegTOT; MiSFD 9; MotPP; MovMk; News 93-2; NewYTBE 72; NewYTBS 92; NotNAT; OxCAmT 84; OxCFilm; VarWW 85; WhAm 10; WhoAm 74, 76, 78, 80, 82, 84, 86, 88, 90, 92; WhoEnt 92; WhoHol 92, A; WhoHrs 80; WhoThe 72, 77, 81; WorAl; WorAlBi; WorEFlm*

Perkins, Carl Dewey
American. Politician
Dem. congressman from KY, 1949-84; chairman, House Education and Labor Committee, 1967-84.
b. Oct 15, 1912 in Hindman, Kentucky
d. Aug 3, 1984 in Lexington, Kentucky
Source: *AnObit 1984; BiDrAC; BiDrUSC 89; BioIn 7, 8, 10, 11; CngDr 83; NewYTBS 84; WhoAm 84; WhoGov 72, 75, 77*

Perkins, Carl Lee
American. Songwriter, Singer
Wrote hit song "Blue Suede Shoes," 1955; sung by Elvis Presley, 1956.
b. Apr 9, 1932 in Jackson, Tennessee
Source: *Baker 84; BiDAmM; BioIn 11, 13, 14, 15; ConAu 102; ConMus 9; EncFCWM 83; EncPR&S 89; EncRk 88; HarEnCM 87; HarEnR 86; NewAmDM; NewGrDA 86; NewGrDJ 88; OxCPMus; PenEncP; WhoAm 82; WhoEnt 92; WhoHol A*

Perkins, Edward Joseph
American. Diplomat
First black American ambassador to serve in S Africa, 1986-89; ambassador to Liberia, 1983-85.
b. Jun 8, 1928 in Sterlington, Louisiana
Source: *BioIn 15; IntWW 91; USBiR 74; WhoAfA 96; WhoAm 86, 90; WhoAmP 87, 89, 91, 93, 95; WhoBlA 88, 90, 92, 94; WhoWor 87, 91*

Perkins, Frances
American. Government Official
First woman to serve in cabinet position: FDR's secretary of Labor, 1933-45.
b. Apr 10, 1882 in Boston, Massachusetts
d. May 14, 1965 in New York, New York
Source: *AmDec 1930, 1940; AmPolLe; AmPolW 80; BiDrUSE 71, 89; BioAmW; BioIn 1, 2, 3, 5, 7, 8, 9, 10, 11, 15, 16, 17, 19, 20, 21; ContDcW 89; CurBio 40, 65; DcAmSR; DcTwHis; EncAB-A 1; EncAB-H 1974; FacFETw; GoodHs; HerW, 84; IntDcWB; InWom, SUP; LibW; LinLib S; McGEWB; ObitT 1961; OxCAmH; PolPar; WebAB 74, 79; WhAm 4; WhAmP; WhLit; WhoAmW 58, 64, 66; WomStre; WomWWA 14; WorAl; WorAlBi*

Perkins, Jacob
American. Inventor
Inventions include machine for cutting, heading nails in one operation.
b. Jul 9, 1766 in Newburyport, Massachusetts
d. Jul 30, 1849 in London, England
Source: *Alli; AmBi; ApCAB; BiInAmS; BioIn 5, 7, 12, 14; DcAmB; DcBiPP; DcInv; Drake; HarEnUS; NatCAB 10; NewYHSD; WhAm HS; WhDW; WorInv*

Perkins, Kieren
Australian. Swimmer
World record-holder of the 800-meters freestyle swimming; set record 1,500-meters freestyle, 1992.
Source: *WhoWor 95, 96*

Perkins, Marlin
[Richard Marlin Perkins]
American. TV Personality, Adventurer
Pioneer in filming wild animals in natural surroundings; host, "Wild Kingdom," 1963-85.
b. Mar 28, 1905 in Carthage, Missouri
d. Jun 14, 1986 in Saint Louis, Missouri
Source: *AnObit 1986; BioIn 2, 3, 6, 7, 12, 13, 15, 16; ConAu 103, 119; InSci; LinLib L, S; SmATA 21, 48N; WebAB 74, 79; WhoAm 74, 78, 80, 84*

Perkins, Maxwell Evarts
American. Editor
Scribner's editor who discovered Fitzgerald, Hemingway, Thomas Wolfe.
b. Sep 20, 1884 in New York, New York
d. Jun 17, 1947 in Stamford, Connecticut

Source: *AmAu&B; BenetAL 91; BioIn 1, 2, 3, 6, 9, 11, 12; DcAmB S4; NatCAB 37; REnAL; WebAB 74, 79; WhAm 2; WhE&EA; WorAl*

Perkins, Millie
American. Actor
Films include title role in *Diary of Anne Frank,* 1959.
b. May 12, 1940 in Passaic, New Jersey
Source: *FilmEn; FilmgC; HalFC 88; IntMPA 92; InWom SUP; MotPP; VarWW 85; WhoHol A*

Perkins, Milo Randolph
American. Government Official
Executive director, Board of Economic Warfare, 1941.
b. Jan 28, 1900 in Milwaukee, Wisconsin
d. Oct 26, 1972
Source: *BioIn 1; CurBio 42; WhAm 5*

Perkins, Osgood
[James Ridley Osgood Perkins]
American. Actor
Films include *Scarface,* 1932; *The Front Page,* 1931; father of Anthony.
b. May 16, 1892 in West Newton, Massachusetts
d. Sep 23, 1937 in Washington, District of Columbia
Source: *BioIn 17; CamGWoT; EncAFC; FamA&A; FilmgC; ForYSC; HalFC 80, 84, 88; NotNAT B; OxCAmT 84; OxCThe 83; PlP&P; WhoHol B; WhScrn 74, 77, 83; WhThe*

Perkins, Ray
[Walter Ray Perkins]
American. Football Coach
Head coach, NY Giants, 1979-82, Tampa Bay, 1987-90.
b. Dec 6, 1941 in Olive Branch, Mississippi
Source: *BioIn 12, 13, 14, 15; FootReg 87; NewYTBS 85; WhoAm 84, 86, 88, 90, 92, 94; WhoSSW 86, 88, 91*

Perkoff, Stuart Z
American. Poet, Artist
Beat poet whose books of poetry include *Suicide Room,* 1956.
b. Jul 29, 1930 in Saint Louis, Missouri
d. Jun 14, 1974
Source: *BioIn 13; ConAu 113; ConPo 70; DcLB 10, 16*

Perky, Henry D
American. Manufacturer, Inventor
Devised machine for shredding wheat kernels for cereal.
b. Dec 7, 1843 in Mount Holmes, Ohio
d. Jun 29, 1906 in Glencoe, Maryland
Source: *NatCAB 13, 24*

Perle, Richard Norman
American. Government Official
Assistant US Secretary of Defense, 1981-87.
b. Sep 16, 1941 in New York, New York
Source: *BioIn 12, 13, 18; ColdWar 2; WhoAm 82, 84, 86, 88, 90, 92, 94, 95, 96, 97; WhoAmP 91*

Perlea, Jonel
American. Conductor, Educator
Led Connecticut Symphony, 1955-70; Bucharest, Romania Orchestra, 1930s-40s.
b. Dec 13, 1901 in Ograda, Romania
d. Jul 30, 1970 in New York, New York
Source: *Baker 84; BioIn 4, 9; CmOp; NewGrDM 80; NewYTBE 70*

Perlman, Itzhak
Israeli. Violinist
Concert performer; winner of 13 Grammys.
b. Aug 31, 1945 in Tel Aviv, Palestine
Source: *Baker 78, 84, 92; BioIn 7, 9, 10, 11, 12, 14, 16, 18, 20, 21; BriBkM 80; CelR 90; ConHero 1; ConMus 2; CurBio 75; DcTwCCu 1; FacFETw; IntWW 75, 76, 77, 78, 79, 80, 81, 82, 83, 89, 91, 93; IntWWM 77, 80, 90; LegTOT; MidE 78, 79, 80, 81, 82; MusSN; NewAmDM; NewGrDA 86; NewGrDM 80; PenDiMP; VarWW 85; Who 82, 83, 85, 88, 90, 92, 94; WhoAm 78, 80, 82, 84, 86, 88, 90, 92, 94, 95, 96, 97; WhoAmM 83; WhoE 89, 91, 93, 95, 97; WhoEnt 92A; WhoMus 72; WhoWor 82, 84, 87, 89, 91, 93, 95, 96*

Perlman, Rhea
[Mrs. Danny DeVito]
American. Actor
Played Carla Tortelli on TV comedy "Cheers," 1982-93; won Emmys, 1984, 1985, 1986.
b. Mar 31, 1948 in New York, New York
Source: *BioIn 13, 15, 16; ConTFT 6; IntMPA 92, 94, 96; LegTOT; VarWW 85; WhoAm 90; WhoAmW 91; WhoEnt 92; WhoHol 92; WorAlBi*

Perlman, Ron
American. Actor
Played Vincent on TV series "Beauty and the Beast," 1987-89.
b. Apr 13, 1950 in New York, New York
Source: *BioIn 16; CelR 90; ConTFT 8, 15; IntMPA 92, 94, 96; LegTOT*

Perlmutter, Nathan
American. Civil Rights Leader
Director, Anti-Defamation League of B'nai B'rith, 1979-87; awarded Presidential Medal of Freedom, 1987.
b. Mar 2, 1923 in New York, New York
d. Jul 12, 1987 in New York, New York
Source: *AnObit 1987; ConAu 13R, 49NR, 123; NewYTBS 87; WhoAm 86; WhoAmJ 80; WhoE 83, 85, 86; WhoRel 85; WhoWor 84, 87; WhoWorJ 72, 78*

Perls, Frederick Salomon
German. Psychiatrist
Founded Gestalt school of therapy, 1952.
b. 1894, Germany
d. Mar 14, 1970 in Chicago, Illinois
Source: *BioIn 9, 10; ConAu 101; NewYTBE 70*

Pero, A. J
[Twisted Sister]
American. Musician
Drummer with heavy metal group, formed 1976.
b. Oct 14, 1959 in Staten Island, New York

Peron, Eva Duarte
[Mrs. Juan Peron]
"Evita"
Argentine. Political Leader
Co-governed with husband; play *Evita* based on her life.
b. May 7, 1919 in Los Toldos, Argentina
d. Jul 26, 1952 in Buenos Aires, Argentina
Source: *BioIn 9, 10, 11; CurBio 49, 52*

Peron, Isabel Martinez de
[Mrs. Juan Peron]
Argentine. Political Leader
First female president of Argentina; succeeded husband, 1974-76; ousted in military coup.
b. Feb 4, 1931 in Las Rioja, Argentina
Source: *BioIn 13, 16; BioNews 74; ContDcW 89; CurBio 75; DcCPSAm; EncWB; IntDcWB; IntWW 74; InWom SUP; NewYTBE 73; NewYTBS 74; WhoWor 84; WomWR; WorAlBi*

Peron, Juan
Argentine. Political Leader
Pres. of Argentina, 1946-55, 1973-74.
b. Oct 8, 1895 in Lobos, Argentina
d. Jul 1, 1974 in Buenos Aires, Argentina
Source: *BioNews 74; ConAu 49; CurBio 44, 74, 74N; DcTwHis; DicTyr; EncRev; LegTOT; NewYTBS 74; WhAm 6; WhoWor 74*

Perot, H(enry) Ross
American. Philanthropist, Businessman
Self-made billionaire; founder, owner, Electronics Data Systems, 1962-84; candidate for US presidency, 1992; candidate for US presidency with Reform Party, 1996.
b. Jun 27, 1930 in Texarkana, Texas
Source: *BioIn 8, 9, 10, 11, 12, 13, 14, 15, 16; BusPN; CelR 90; ConAmBL; ConAu 142; CurBio 71, 96; Dun&B 88; LElec; NewYTBE 71, 73; NewYTBS 27, 86; PolProf NF; PorSil; WhoAm 86, 90; WhoFI 92; WhoSSW 91; WhoWor 91; WrDr 96*

Perpich, Rudy George
American. Politician
Democratic governor of MN, 1977-79, 1983-91, defeated by Arne Carlson.
b. Jun 27, 1928 in Carson Lake, Minnesota
d. Sep 21, 1995 in Saint Paul, Minnesota
Source: *AlmAP 88; AmCath 80; BiDrAC; BiDrGov 1789; BioIn 14, 16; IntWW 91;*

NewYTBS 76; PolsAm 84; WhAm 11; WhoAm 74, 76, 78, 80, 84, 86, 88, 90; WhoAmP 73, 75, 77, 79, 81, 83, 85, 87, 89, 91, 93, 95; WhoGov 75, 77; WhoMW 74, 76, 84, 86, 88, 90; WhoWor 87, 89, 91

Perranoski, Ron(ald Peter)
American. Baseball Player
Relief pitcher, 1961-73, mostly with Dodgers; had 179 career saves.
b. Apr 1, 1936 in Paterson, New Jersey
Source: *Ballpl 90; BiDAmSp Sup; BioIn 7; WhoProB 73*

Perrault, Charles
French. Author, Poet
Known for his collection of fairy tales, including *Cinderella,* 1697.
b. Jan 12, 1628 in Paris, France
d. May 16, 1703 in Paris, France
Source: *AnCL; AuBYP 2S, 3; BbD; Benet 87, 96; BiD&SB; BioIn 1, 2, 3, 5, 7, 8, 12, 13, 16; BlmGEL; CarSB; CasWL; ChhPo, S3; ChlBkCr; DcArts; DcBiPP; DcCathB; DcEuL; DcPup; EuAu; EvEuW; GuFrLit 2; LegTOT; LinLib L, S; LitC 2; LngCEL; MajAI; NewC; NewCBEL; NewEOp 71; NewGrDM 80; Novels; OxCChiL; OxCEng 67, 85, 95; OxCFr; OxDcOp; PenC EUR; REn; RfGWoL 95; SJGFanW; SmATA 25; Str&VC; WhDW; WhoChL; WorAlBi; WrChl*

Perrault, Claude
French. Architect
Designed east, front colonnade of the Louvre, 1667-70; Paris Observatory, 1668-72 ; brother of Charles.
b. Sep 25, 1613 in Paris, France
d. Oct 9, 1688 in Paris, France
Source: *BiESc; BioIn 2, 10; DcBiPP; DcCathB; DcD&D; DcScB; InSci; IntDcAr; MacEA; McGDA; McGEWB; NewCol 75; NewGrDM 80; OxCArt; WhDW; WhoArch*

Perreault, Gilbert
Canadian. Hockey Player
Center, Buffalo, 1970-87; 12th player in NHL history to score 500 goals (1986).
b. Nov 13, 1950 in Victoriaville, Quebec, Canada
Source: *BioIn 9, 10, 11, 13; HocEn; HocReg 87; WhoAm 86; WhoHcky 73*

Perret, Auguste
French. Architect
Known for his valuable contributions to reinforced concrete construction.
b. Feb 12, 1874 in Brussels, Belgium
d. Feb 25, 1954 in Paris, France
Source: *BioIn 1, 2, 3, 4, 5, 10, 13, 14; ConArch 80, 87; DcArts; DcD&D; DcTwDes; EncMA; EncUrb; FacFETw; IntDcAr; MacEA; McGDA; McGEWB; WhAm 3; WhDW; WhoArch*

Perret, Gene
American. Writer
TV scriptwriter; won Emmys for "Carol Burnett Show," 1974, 1975, 1978.
b. Apr 3, 1937 in Philadelphia, Pennsylvania
Source: *BioIn 16; ConAu 114, 117; SmATA 76; WhoEnt 92*

Perrin, Jean Baptiste
French. Scientist
Won 1926 Nobel Prize in physics; discovered sedimentation equilibrium.
b. Sep 30, 1870 in Lille, France
d. Apr 17, 1942 in New York, New York
Source: *AsBiEn; BiESc; BioIn 3, 8, 9, 14, 15, 20; CamDcSc; DcNaB; DcScB; InSci; LarDcSc; NotTwCS; WhoNob, 90, 95; WorScD*

Perrine, Charles Dillon
American. Astronomer
Discoverer of Jupiter's sixth and seventh moons.
b. Jul 28, 1867 in Steubenville, Ohio
d. Jun 21, 1951 in Villa General Mitre, Argentina
Source: *BioIn 2; DcAmB S5; DcScB; NatCAB 13; WhAm 4*

Perrine, Valerie
American. Actor
Films include *Lenny,* 1974; *Superman II,* 1981.
b. Sep 3, 1943 in Galveston, Texas
Source: *BioIn 10, 11, 15, 16; ConTFT 3; CurBio 75; HalFC 88; IntMPA 88, 92, 94, 96; InWom SUP; LegTOT; NewYTBS 74; VarWW 85; WhoAm 76, 78, 80, 82, 84, 86, 88, 90, 92, 94, 96, 97; WhoEnt 92; WhoHol 92, A; WhoWor 95, 96; WorAl; WorAlBi*

Perry, Anne
[Juliet Marion Hulme]
English. Author
Author of books featuring the detective Thomas Pitt; wrote *The Cater Street Hangman,* 1979; *Pentecost Alley,* 1996.
b. Oct 28, 1938 in London, England
Source: *BioIn 20, 21; ConAu 22NR, 50NR, 101; ConNov 96; ConPopW; CurBio 96; GrWomMW; TwCCr&M 91; WorAu 1985; WrDr 92, 94, 96*

Perry, Antoinette
American. Actor, Director
Tony Award is named for her; prominent in American Theater Wing, other welfare groups.
b. Jun 27, 1888 in Denver, Colorado
d. Jun 28, 1946 in New York, New York
Source: *BioIn 1, 3, 16; CurBio 46; DcAmB S4; InWom, SUP; LegTOT; LibW; NatCAB 37; NotAW; NotNAT B; NotWoAT; OxCAmT 84; WhAm 2; WhoHol B; WhScrn 74, 77, 83; WhThe*

Perry, Bliss
American. Author, Educator
Editor, *Atlantic Monthly,* 1899-1909; wrote *American Mind,* 1912.
b. Nov 25, 1860 in Williamstown, Massachusetts
d. Feb 13, 1954 in Exeter, New Hampshire
Source: *AmAu&B; ApCAB SUP; BbD; BiD&SB; BioIn 1, 2, 3, 4, 5, 6; CnDAL; ConAmL; DcAmAu; DcAmB S5; DcLB 71; LinLib L, S; LngCTC; NatCAB 10, 46; ObitT 1951; OxCAmL 65, 83, 95; REn; REnAL; TwCA, SUP; TwCBDA; WhAm 3; WhLit*

Perry, Carrie Saxon
American. Politician
First African-American woman Dem. mayor of Hartford, CT, 1987-93.
b. Aug 10, 1931 in Hartford, Connecticut
Source: *BioIn 16; BlkWAm; NegAl 89A; News 89-2; NotBlAW 1; WhoAm 90; WhoAmP 91; WhoAmW 91; WhoBlA 92; WhoE 91*

Perry, Eleanor Bayer
[Oliver Weld Bayer]
American. Screenwriter, Author
Oscar nominee for *David and Lisa,* 1962; other films include *The Man Who Loved Cat Dancing,* 1973.
b. 1915? in Cleveland, Ohio
d. Mar 14, 1981 in New York, New York
Source: *AnObit 1981; ConAu 103, 111; ConDr 77A, 82A; DcLB 34; HalFC 84; IntMPA 81; WhAm 7, 8; WhoAm 80; WhoAmW 74; WomWMM, B*

Perry, Frank
American. Director
Films include *David and Lisa,* 1962; *Diary of a Mad Housewife,* 1970.
b. Aug 21, 1930 in New York, New York
d. Aug 29, 1995 in New York, New York
Source: *BioIn 9, 12, 13, 16; BlueB 76; ConTFT 9, 15; CurBio 72, 95N; FilmEn; FilmgC; HalFC 80, 84, 88; IIWWHD 1A; IntMPA 92, 94, 96; MiSFD 9; MovMk; NewYTBS 95; VarWW 85; WhoAdv 72; WhoAm 78, 80, 82, 84, 86, 88, 90, 92, 94, 95, 96, 97; WhoEnt 92; WhoHol 92, A; WhoWor 82*

Perry, Gaylord Jackson
American. Baseball Player
Pitcher, 1962-83, known for throwing spitball; had 314 career wins, 3,534 strikeouts; only pitcher to win Cy Young Award in both leagues; Hall of Fame, 1991.
b. Sep 15, 1938 in Williamston, North Carolina
Source: *Ballpl 90; BiDAmSp BB; BioIn 7, 10, 12, 13, 14, 15; BioNews 74; ConAu 113; CurBio 82; NewYTBE 72, 73; NewYTBS 74; WhoAm 74, 76, 78, 80, 82, 92, 94, 95, 96, 97; WhoProB 73; WorAlBi*

Perry, Harold R
American. Religious Leader
Second black bishop in American Catholic history, 1965.
b. Oct 9, 1916 in Lake Charles, Louisiana
d. Jul 17, 1991 in Marrero, Louisiana
Source: *BioIn 7; CurBio 91N; InB&W 85; NewYTBS 91; WhoAm 88; WhoBlA 92N*

Perry, Jim
[James Evan Perry]
American. Baseball Player
Pitcher, 1959-75; with brother Gaylord, held ML record for wins by brother combination, 529, until broken by Phil and Joe Niekro, 1987.
b. Oct 3, 1936 in Williamston, North Carolina
Source: *Ballpl 90; BaseEn 88; BiDAmSp BB; BioIn 6, 15; WhoProB 73; WhoSpor*

Perry, Joe
[Fletcher Perry]
American. Football Player
Fullback, San Francisco, 1948-60, 1963, Baltimore, 1961-62; led NFL in rushing twice; Hall of Fame, 1969.
b. Jan 27, 1927 in Stephens, Arkansas
Source: *AfrAmSG; BiDAmSp FB; BioIn 10, 17, 21; CmCal; InB&W 80; LegTOT; WhoFtbl 74*

Perry, Luke
American. Actor
Teen sweetheart who played rebel Dylan McKay on TV's "Beverly Hills, 90210," 1990—; played on soap "Loving," 1987-88.
b. Oct 11, 1966 in Fredericktown, Ohio
Source: *ConTFT 11; IntMPA 94, 96; LegTOT; News 92, 92-3; WhoAm 95, 96, 97*

Perry, Matthew
American. Actor
Plays Chandler Bing on TV's "Friends," 1994—.
b. Aug 19, 1969 in Williamstown, Massachusetts
Source: *ConTFT 15; WhoHol 92*

Perry, Matthew Calbraith, Commodore
American. Naval Officer
Noted for opening Japan to US trade, 1854; brother of Oliver Hazard.
b. Apr 10, 1794 in Newport, Rhode Island
d. Mar 4, 1858 in New York, New York
Source: *Alli; AmBi; ApCAB; Benet 87, 96; BenetAL 91; BiAUS; BioIn 1, 2, 3, 4, 6, 7, 8, 9, 11, 14, 15, 16, 17, 20; DcAmB; DcAmDH 80, 89; DcAmMiB; DcNAA; EncAB-H 1974, 1996; EncJap; HarEnMi; HarEnUS; HisWorL; LegTOT; LinLib S; McGEWB; MorMA; NatCAB 4; OxCAmH; OxCAmL 65, 83, 95; OxCShps; REn; REnAL; TwCBDA; WebAB 74, 79; WebAMB; WhAm HS; WhoMilH 76; WorAl*

Perry, Nancy Ling
[S(ymbionese) L(iberation) A(rmy)]
"Fahizah"
American. Revolutionary
Involved in Patty Hearst kidnapping, 1974; killed in gun battle with police.
b. Sep 19, 1947 in Santa Rosa, California
d. May 24, 1974 in Los Angeles, California
Source: *BioIn 10; InWom SUP; WorAl; WorAlBi*

Perry, Oliver Hazard, Admiral
American. Naval Officer
National hero who defeated British on Lake Erie, 1813; dispatched, "Have met the enemy and they are ours."
b. Aug 20, 1785 in South Kingstown, Rhode Island
d. Aug 23, 1819 in Angostura, Venezuela
Source: *Alli; AmBi; ApCAB; BbtC; BenetAL 91; BioIn 1, 2, 3, 4, 5, 6, 7, 8, 9, 10, 11, 17, 19, 20, 21; DcAmB; DcAmMiB; Drake; EncAB-H 1974, 1996; GenMudB; HarEnMi; HarEnUS; HisWorL; LegTOT; LinLib S; McGEWB; NatCAB 4; OxCAmH; OxCAmL 65, 83, 95; OxCShps; REn; REnAL; REnAW; TwCBDA; WebAB 74, 79; WebAMB; WhAm HS; WhoMilH 76; WorAl; WorAlBi*

Perry, Ralph Barton
American. Author
Won 1935 Pulitzer for *The Thought and Character of William James.*
b. Jul 3, 1876 in Poultney, Vermont
d. Jan 22, 1957 in Boston, Massachusetts
Source: *AmAu&B; BenetAL 91; BioIn 2, 3, 4, 6; ConAu 123; DcAmB S6; LinLib L; McGEWB; NatCAB 43; OxCAmH; OxCAmL 65, 83, 95; OxCPhil; REnAL; TwCA, SUP; WhAm 3; WhE&EA; WhNAA*

Perry, Steve
American. Singer
Had hit single "Foolish Heart," on first solo album *Street Talk,* 1984.
b. Jan 22, 1949 in Hanford, California
Source: *LegTOT; RkOn 85*

Perry, Troy D.
American. Religious Leader
Founder of the Universal Fellowship of Metropolitan Community Churches, 1968, the largest Christian church for gays and lesbians.
b. Jul 27, 1940 in Tallahassee, Florida
Source: *GayLesB*

Perry, Walt
American. Musician
Plays brass instruments for group Chicago.
b. Mar 14, 1945 in Chicago, Illinois

Perry, William
"The Refrigerator"
American. Football Player
Huge defensive tackle, Chicago, 1985—; known for offensive plays as runner, receiver.
b. Dec 16, 1962 in Aiken, South Carolina
Source: *BioIn 14, 15, 16; FootReg 87; LegTOT; NewYTBS 85; WhoBlA 92; WorAlBi*

Perry, William J(ames)
American. Government Official
U.S. Secretary of Defense, 1994-97.
b. Oct 11, 1927 in Vandergrift, Pennsylvania
Source: *AmMWSc 73P, 76P, 79, 82, 86, 89, 92, 95; BioIn 11, 12, 15, 19, 20, 21; CurBio 95; WhoAm 78, 80, 82, 84, 86, 88, 90, 92, 94, 95, 96, 97; WhoAmP 77, 79, 81; WhoGov 77; WhoSSW 95; WhoWest 74, 87; WhoWor 96, 97*

Perryman, Jill
Australian. Actor
Award-winning stage performances include *No, No, Nanette,* 1972; *Palace of Dreams,* 1980.
b. May 30, 1933 in Melbourne, Australia
Source: *ConTFT 5; WhoHol 92; WhoThe 77, 81*

Pershing, John J(oseph)
"Black Jack"
American. Army Officer
Commander of American Expeditionary Force in Europe, 1917-19; won Pulitzer, 1932 for memoirs.
b. Sep 13, 1860 in Linn City, Missouri
d. Jul 15, 1948 in Washington, District of Columbia
Source: *AmAu&B; ApCAB X; Benet 96; BioIn 1, 2, 3, 4, 5, 6, 7, 8, 9, 10, 11, 13; CmdGen 1991; DcAmB S4; DcAmMiB; DcNAA; DcTwHis; EncAB-H 1974, 1996; FacFETw; HarEnMi; LinLib L, S; McGEWB; NatCAB 35; OxCAmH; OxCAmL 65, 95; REn; REnAL; REnAW; WebAB 74, 79; WebAMB; WhAm 2; WhDW; WhoMilH 76; WorAl*

Persiani, Fanny
[Fanny Tacchinardi]
Italian. Opera Singer
Brilliant soprano popular in Paris, 1837-50.
b. Oct 4, 1812 in Rome, Italy
d. Nov 3, 1867 in Neuilly, France
Source: *Baker 78, 84, 92; BioIn 15; CmOp; NewEOp 71; NewGrDM 80; OxDcOp; PenDiMP*

Persichetti, Vincent
American. Composer
Wrote over 150 pieces including nine symphonies: *The Creation,* 1970; taught at Juilliard, NYC, for 40 yrs.
b. Jun 6, 1915 in Philadelphia, Pennsylvania
d. Aug 14, 1987 in Philadelphia, Pennsylvania

Source: *AmComp; AnObit 1987; ASCAP 66, 80; Baker 78, 84; BiDAmM; BioIn 1, 4, 8, 9, 14, 15, 16; BlueB 76; BriBkM 80; CompSN, SUP; ConAmC 76, 82; ConAu 124; CpmDNM 72, 74, 75, 77, 78, 81, 82; DcCM; FacFETw; IntWWM 77, 80, 85; MusMk; NewAmDM; NewCol 75; NewGrDA 86; NewGrDM 80; NewGrDO; NewOxM; NewYTBS 87; OxCMus; WhAm 9; WhoAm 74, 76, 78, 80, 82, 84, 86; WhoAmM 83*

Persinger, Gregory A
[The Hostages]
American. Hostage
One of 52 held by terrorists, Nov 1979-Jan 1981.
b. Dec 25, 1957
Source: *NewYTBS 81*

Persinger, Louis
American. Musician, Conductor
Concert master, San Francisco Symphony, 1916-28; violinist, taught Menuhin.
b. Feb 11, 1888 in Rochester, Illinois
d. Dec 31, 1966 in New York, New York
Source: *Baker 84; BiDAmM; WhAm 4*

Persius
Roman. Satirist
Wrote six satires explaining stoicism.
b. Dec 4, 34? in Volaterrae, Italy
d. Nov 24, 62?
Source: *AncWr; Benet 87, 96; CasWL; Grk&L; LegTOT; NewC; NewCBEL; OxCEng 67, 85, 95; RAdv 14, 13-2; REn; RfGWoL 95*

Persoff, Nehemiah
American. Actor
Films include *On the Waterfront,* 1954; *Some Like It Hot,* 1959; *Yentyl,* 1983.
b. Aug 14, 1920 in Jerusalem, Palestine
Source: *BiE&WWA; ConTFT 7; FilmEn; FilmgC; ForYSC; HalFC 80, 84, 88; IntMPA 75, 76, 77, 78, 79, 80, 81, 82, 84, 86, 88, 92; ItaFilm; MotPP; NotNAT; VarWW 85; WhoAm 74, 76, 78, 80, 82, 84; WhoEnt 92; WhoHol 92, A; WhoThe 72, 77, 81; WhoWor 74, 76; WorAl; WorAlBi*

Person, Chuck Connors
American. Basketball Player
Forward, Indiana, 1986-92, Minnesota, 1992-94; NBA rookie of year, 1987.
b. Jun 27, 1964 in Brantley, Alabama
Source: *BioIn 15; OfNBA 87; WhoAfA 96; WhoBlA 92, 94; WhoMW 92*

Person, Waverly
American. Geologist
Director, US Geological Survey, 1977—.
b. May 1, 1927 in Blackridge, Virginia
Source: *ConBlB 9*

Pertini, Sandro
[Allessandro Pertini]
Italian. Political Leader
President of Italy, 1978-86; considered one of the nation's most beloved leaders.
b. Sep 25, 1896 in Stella, Italy
d. Feb 24, 1990 in Rome, Italy
Source: *AnObit 1990; BioIn 11, 13, 14, 16, 17; FacFETw; NewYTBS 78, 83, 85, 90; WhAm 10; WhoWor 82, 84, 87*

Perugino
Italian. Artist
Painted Sistine Chapel fresco "Christ Delivering Keys to St. Peter," 1500; Raphael's teacher.
b. 1445 in Perugia, Italy
d. 1523 in Perugia, Italy
Source: *AtlBL; NewC*

Perutz, M(ax) F(erdinand)
British. Scientist
Shared Nobel Prize in chemistry, 1962, with John Cowdery Kendrew; determined structure of hemoglobin.
b. May 19, 1914 in Vienna, Austria
Source: *BiESc; BioIn 14, 15; CamDcSc; CurBio 63; FacFETw; NobelP; ThTwC 87; Who 85, 92; WhoAm 90; WhoNob, 90, 95; WhoWor 91, 97; WorAlBi; WrDr 92*

Pesci, Joe
American. Actor
Starred in box office hit *Home Alone,* 1990; won Oscar for best supporting actor in *GoodFellas,* 1991.
b. Feb 9, 1943 in Newark, New Jersey
Source: *ConTFT 8; CurBio 94; GangFlm; IntMPA 92, 94, 96; LegTOT; News 92; WhoAm 92, 94, 95, 96, 97; WhoEnt 92; WhoHol 92*

Pescow, Donna
American. Actor
Star of TV series "Angie"; in film *Saturday Night Fever,* 1977.
b. Mar 24, 1954 in New York, New York
Source: *BioIn 11; ConTFT 3; IntMPA 92, 94, 96; LegTOT; VarWW 85; WhoHol 92*

Pestalozzi, Johann Heinrich
Swiss. Educator
His theories, practices of education laid foundation of modern primary school.
b. Jan 12, 1746 in Zurich, Switzerland
d. Feb 17, 1827 in Brugg, Switzerland
Source: *BbD; BiD&SB; BiDPsy; BioIn 1, 3, 4, 5, 6, 7, 8, 10, 13, 17, 20; BlkwCE; CasWL; CelCen; CyEd; DcEuL; DcLB 94; Dis&D; EncEnl; EuAu; EvEuW; LinLib L, S; LuthC 75; McGEWB; NamesHP; OxCGer 76, 86; PenC EUR; REn; WhDW; WorAl; WorAlBi*

Petacci, Claretta
Italian. Mistress
Benito Mussolini's mistress.
b. Feb 28, 1912 in Rome, Italy
d. Apr 29, 1945 in Milan, Italy
Source: *BioIn 1, 2, 6*

Petain, Henri Philippe
French. Military Leader, Statesman
Hero of Battle of Verdun, 1916; surrendered to Hitler, 1940, later headed Vichy govt.
b. Apr 24, 1856 in Cauchy a la Tour, France
d. Jul 23, 1951 in Ile d'Yeu, France
Source: *BioIn 1, 2, 3, 5, 6, 7, 8, 9, 10, 11, 12, 14, 16, 17, 20; CurBio 40, 51; DcCathB; DcPol; DicTyr; FacFETw; HarEnMi; LinLib S; LngCTC; OxCFr; REn; WhDW; WorAlBi*

Petalesharo
American. Native American Leader
Opposed Morning Star Ritual, a Native American ceremony which included human sacrifice.
b. 1797? in Nebraska
d. 1832?
Source: *EncNAB; NotNaAm*

Peter, Saint
Biblical Figure
One of twelve Apostles; leader of Christians after crucifixion.
d. 64?
Source: *Benet 87, 96; BioIn 1, 2, 3, 4, 5, 6, 7, 8, 9, 10, 11, 12, 13, 14, 15, 16, 20; ConAu X; ConMus 4; CurBio 43, 70; DcAfHiB 86; DcBiPP; DcCanB 4; DcCathB; DcNaB; DcPol; EncEarC; EuAu; FacFETw; IntAu&W 82X, 86X; LegTOT; MajAI; McGDA; McGEWB; NewAmDM; NewC; NewCol 75; NewYTBE 70; ObitOF 79; OxCPMus; OxDcByz; OxDcP 86; REn; WhDW; WhoPolA*

Peter, Laurence Johnston
American. Author
Wrote best-seller on subject of human imcompetence: *The Peter Principle,* 1969.
b. Sep 16, 1919 in Vancouver, British Columbia, Canada
d. Jan 12, 1990 in Los Angeles, California
Source: *AmMWSc 73S; BioIn 8, 10, 15, 16; ConAu 17NR, 130; DcLB 53; IntAu&W 76, 77, 82; LEduc 74; NewYTBS 90; WhAm 10; WhoAm 74, 76, 78, 80, 82, 84, 86, 88; WhoUSWr 88; WhoWrEP 89; WorAlBi; WrDr 86, 90*

Peter, Valentine J
American. Religious Leader
Roman Catholic priest, 1959—; exec. director, Father Flanagan's Boy's Home, Boys Town, NE, 1984—.
b. Nov 20, 1934 in Omaha, Nebraska
Source: *AmCath 80; News 88-2; WhoRel 92*

Peter and Gordon
[Peter Asher; Gordon Waller]
English. Music Group
Folk-pop duo, 1961-68; hits include "World without Love," 1964, written by Paul McCartney; Lady Godiva, 1966.
Source: *BioIn 11; ConMuA 80A, 80B; EncPR&S 89; EncRk 88; IlEncRk; ItaFilm; PenEncP; RkOn 78; RolSEnR 83; Who 74; WhoRock 81; WhoRocM 82*

Peter II
[Peter Karageorgeovitch; Petar Petrovic]
Yugoslav. Ruler
Succeeded throne on death of father, Alexander, 1934; reign ended, 1945, when country became a republic.
b. Sep 6, 1923 in Belgrade, Yugoslavia
d. Nov 4, 1970 in Los Angeles, California
Source: *CurBio 43, 70; WebBD 83*

Peterkin, Julia Mood
American. Author
Books about South Carolina include 1928 Pulitzer winner *Scarlet Sister Mary.*
b. Oct 31, 1880 in Laurens County, South Carolina
d. Aug 10, 1961 in Orangeburg, South Carolina
Source: *AmAu&B; BioIn 21; CnDAL; ConAmA; ConAu 102; LngCTC; OxCAmL 65; REn; REnAL; TwCA, SUP; WhAm 4*

Peter, Paul, and Mary
[Noel Paul Stookey; Mary Travers; Peter Yarrow]
American. Music Group
Won Grammy, 1963, for "Blowin' in the Wind;" group disbanded, 1971; reunited 1978—.
Source: *BioIn 6, 8, 11, 12; ConMus 4; EncFCWM 69, 83; EncRk 88; FacFETw; HarEnR 86; IlEncRk; NewAmDM; NewGrDA 86; OxCPMus; PenEncP; VarWW 85; WhoRocM 82*

Peters, Bernadette
[Bernadette Lazzara]
American. Actor, Singer
Won Tony for *Song and Dance,* 1986; films include *The Jerk,* 1979; *Pennies from Heaven,* 1981.
b. Feb 28, 1948 in New York, New York
Source: *BioIn 14, 15, 16; BkPepl; CelR 90; ConMus 7; ConTFT 1, 3, 10; CurBio 84; EncMT; HalFC 80, 84, 88; IntMPA 86, 92, 94, 96; InWom SUP; LegTOT; NotNAT; RkOn 85; VarWW 85; WhoAm 78, 80, 82, 84, 86, 88, 90, 92, 94, 95, 96, 97; WhoAmW 79, 81, 83, 85, 87, 89, 91, 93, 95, 97; WhoEmL 87; WhoEnt 92; WhoHol 92, A; WhoThe 72, 77, 81; WorAl; WorAlBi*

Peters, Brandon
American. Actor
Stage actor, 1924-56; appearances include *Life With Father; Love on the Dole.*
b. 1893 in Troy, New York
d. Feb 27, 1956 in New York, New York
Source: *BioIn 4; NotNAT B; WhScrn 83*

Peters, Brock
[Brock Fisher]
American. Actor, Singer
Award-winning star of stage, screen; films include *To Kill a Mockingbird,* 1962.
b. Jul 27, 1927 in New York, New York
Source: *BiDAfM; BiE&WWA; BlksAmF; ConTFT 6; DcTwCCu 5; DrBlPA, 90; Ebony 1; FilmEn; FilmgC; ForYSC; HalFC 80, 84, 88; InB&W 85; IntMPA 77, 80, 86, 88, 92, 94, 96; ItaFilm; LegTOT; MotPP; MovMk; NotNAT; VarWW 85; WhoAm 74, 76, 78, 80, 82, 84, 86, 88, 90, 92; WhoBlA 75, 77, 80, 85, 88, 92; WhoEnt 92; WhoHol 92, A; WomWMM; WorAl; WorAlBi*

Peters, C(larence) J(ames), (Jr.)
American. Scientist
Virologist; wrote *Virus Hunter,* 1997.
b. Sep 23, 1940 in Midland, Texas
Source: *BiDrACP 79*

Peters, Charles
American. Editor
Founder and editor of magazine, *The Washington Monthly,* 1968—.
b. Dec 22, 1926 in Charleston, West Virginia
Source: *BioIn 13, 14, 15, 16, 17; ConAu 122; CurBio 90*

Peters, Ellis
[Edith Mary Pargeter]
English. Author
Won 1963 Edgar for *Death and the Joyful Woman.* Creator of the medieval sleuth Brother Cadfael.
b. Sep 28, 1913 in Horsehay, England
d. Oct 15, 1995 in Shropshire, England
Source: *Au&Wr 71; BioIn 10, 14, 17, 20, 21; ConAu 149, X; CrtSuMy; DcLP 87B; DetWom; GrWomMW; IntAu&W 91; IntWW 91; InWom SUP; LngCTC; MajTwCW; PenNWW B; RAdv 14; TwCCr&M 80, 85, 91; TwCRHW 90; WhE&EA; Who 92; WhoWor 95, 96; WorAu 1950; WrDr 86, 92, 94*

Peters, Jean
American. Actor
Screen debut, 1947, with Tyrone Power in *Captain from Castile;* married to Howard Hughes, 1957-71.
b. Oct 15, 1926 in Canton, Ohio
Source: *BiDFilm 81; FilmEn; FilmgC; ForYSC; HalFC 80, 84, 88; IntMPA 75, 82; InWom SUP; LegTOT; MotPP; MovMk; VarWW 85; WhoHol 92, A; WorAl; WorEFlm*

Peters, Jon
American. Producer, Business Executive
Produced films *A Star Is Born,* 1976; *The Color Purple,* 1985; turned his hairstyling business into major production co.
b. 1945 in Van Nuys, California
Source: *BioIn 10, 11, 16; ConTFT 3; HalFC 88; IntMPA 82, 92; IntWW 91; NewYTBS 89; VarWW 85; WhoAm 90; WhoEnt 92*

Peters, Roberta
[Roberta Peterman]
American. Opera Singer
Outstanding soprano; had NY Met. debut, age 20, 1950.
b. May 4, 1930 in New York, New York
Source: *Baker 78, 84, 92; BiDAmM; BioIn 2, 3, 4, 7, 8, 9, 10, 11, 12, 13, 14; BlueB 76; CelR, 90; CmOp; ConTFT 4; CurBio 54; FacFETw; IntDcOp; IntWWM 80, 90; InWom, SUP; MetOEnc; MusSN; NewAmDM; NewEOp 71; NewGrDA 86; NewGrDM 80; NewGrDO; VarWW 85; WhoAm 74, 76, 78, 80, 82, 84, 86, 88, 90, 92, 94, 95, 96, 97; WhoAmJ 80; WhoAmM 83; WhoAmW 58, 61, 64, 66, 68, 70, 83, 85, 87, 89, 91, 93, 95, 97; WhoE 74; WhoEnt 92; WhoHol 92, A; WhoOp 76; WhoWor 74, 76; WhoWorJ 72, 78; WorAl; WorAlBi*

Peters, Susan
[Suzanne Carnahan]
American. Actor
Oscar nominee for *Random Harvest,* 1942; paralyzed in accident, 1944.
b. Jul 3, 1921 in Spokane, Washington
d. Oct 23, 1952 in Visalia, California
Source: *BioIn 1, 3; FilmEn; FilmgC; ForYSC; HalFC 80, 84, 88; MGM; MotPP; MovMk; NotNAT B; WhoHol B; WhScrn 74, 77, 83*

Peters, Tom
[Thomas J. Peters]
American. Consultant, Author
Wrote *In Search of Excellence: Lessons from America's Best-Run Companies,* 1982; *Liberation Management: Necessary Disorganization for the Nanosecond Nineties,* 1992.
b. Nov 7, 1942 in Baltimore, Maryland
Source: *BestSel 89-1; ConAu 123, 135; CurBio 94; WhoWest 82; WrDr 94, 96*

Petersen, Donald Eugene
American. Auto Executive
President of Ford Motor Co., 1980-85; CEO 1985-90.
b. Sep 4, 1926 in Pipestone, Minnesota
Source: *AmMWSc 92; BioIn 12, 13, 14, 15, 16; ConAmBL; ConNews 85-1; CurBio 88; DrAPF 91; Dun&B 90; EncABHB 5; IntWW 89, 91, 93; St&PR 87; WhoAm 78, 80, 82, 84, 86, 90; WhoFI 74, 75, 85, 89; WhoMW 74, 76, 78, 82, 84, 86, 90; WhoWor 82, 84, 87, 91; WorAlBi*

Petersen, Paul
American. Actor, Singer
Played Jeff on TV series "The Donna Reed Show," 1958-66; brief recording career included song "My Dad," 1962.
b. Sep 23, 1945 in Glendale, California
Source: *IntMPA 88, 92, 94, 96; RkOn 82; WhoHol 92*

Petersen, Wolfgang
German. Director
Nominated for best director Oscar for *Das Boot* (The Boat), 1983.
b. Mar 14, 1941 in Emden, Germany
Source: *BioIn 14; ConTFT 8; EncEurC; HalFC 88; IntMPA 86, 88, 92, 94, 96; MiSFD 9; VarWW 85; WhoAm 95, 96, 97; WhoEnt 92; WhoWor 95, 96, 97*

Petersham, Maud
[Mrs. Miska Petersham]
American. Children's Author, Illustrator
With husband, won 1946 Caldecott Medal for *The Rooster Crows.*
b. Aug 5, 1890 in Kingston, New York
d. Nov 29, 1971 in Ravenna, Ohio
Source: *AuBYP 2, 3; BioIn 1, 2, 12, 19; ConAu 29NR, 33R, 73; DcLB 22; JBA 51; OxCChiL; REnAL; SmATA 17; TwCChW 83*

Petersham, Miska
American. Children's Author, Illustrator
Numerous self-illustrated juvenile books include *Story Book of* series, 1930s.
b. Sep 20, 1888 in Budapest, Austria-Hungary
d. May 15, 1960
Source: *AuBYP 3; BenetAL 91; BioIn 1, 2, 4, 5, 7, 12, 14, 19; ChhPo S3; ChlBkCr; ChlLR 24; ConAu 29NR, 73; DcLB 22; InWom; MajAI; OxCChiL; SmATA 17; TwCChW 78, 83, 89, 95; WhAmArt 85; WhoAmA 80N, 82N, 84, 84N, 86N, 89N, 91N, 93N*

Peterson, David Robert
Canadian. Politician
Liberal Party premier of Ontario, 1985-92.
b. Dec 28, 1943 in Toronto, Ontario, Canada
Source: *BioIn 14, 15, 16; CanWW 31, 83, 89; ConNews 87-1; CurBio 88; NewYTBS 85; Who 88, 90, 92, 94; WhoAm 86, 88, 90, 92, 94, 95, 96, 97; WhoCan 84; WhoE 86, 89, 91; WhoWor 91*

Peterson, Helen White
American. Native American Leader
Executive director, National Congress of American Indians, 1953-61.
b. Aug 3, 1915 in Pine Ridge Reservation, South Dakota
Source: *BioIn 21; NotNaAm*

Peterson, Lorraine Collett
American. Model
Was model for Sun-Maid raisin logo, 1915; still used today.
b. 1893 in Kansas City, Missouri
d. Mar 30, 1983 in Fresno, California
Source: *NewYTBS 83*

Peterson, Oscar Emanuel
Canadian. Jazz Musician
Classically trained jazz pianist known for ability to play at fast speed; most recorded pianist of all time; best known composition is "Canadian Suite."
b. Aug 15, 1925 in Montreal, Quebec, Canada
Source: *Baker 84; BioIn 13, 14, 15, 16; CanWW 83, 89; CelR 90; CmpEPM; CreCan 1; CurBio 83; DrBlPA 90; InB&W 85; IntWW 91; NegAl 89; NewAmDM; OxCPMus; PenEncP; PeoHis; VarWW 85; Who 92; WhoAm 86, 90; WhoBlA 85, 92; WhoEnt 92; WhoWor 87, 91; WorAl; WorAlBi*

Peterson, Roger Tory
American. Ornithologist
Award-winning ornithology books include *Field Guide to Birds,* 1934.
b. Aug 28, 1908 in Jamestown, New York
d. Jul 28, 1996 in Old Lyme, Connecticut
Source: *AmArt; AmAu&B; AmMWSc 76P, 79, 82; BenetAL 91; BioIn 4, 5, 6, 7, 8, 10, 11, 12, 14, 15, 18, 19, 21; BlueB 76; CelR; ConAu 1NR, 1R, 152; CurBio 59, 96N; InSci; IntAu&W 77, 82; IntWW 74, 75, 76, 77, 78, 79, 80, 81, 82, 83, 89, 91, 93; LinLib L; NatLAC; News 97-1; NewYTBS 27, 74, 80; REnAL; TwCA SUP; WebAB 74, 79; WhAmArt 85; WhoAm 74, 76, 78, 80, 82, 84, 86, 88, 90, 92, 94, 95, 96; WhoAmA 76, 78, 80, 82, 84, 86, 89, 91, 93; WhoWor 74*

Peterson, Virgilia
American. Critic
Moderator for radio program "The Author Meets the Critic," 1950s; won Peabody for radio show "Books in Profile," 1956.
b. May 16, 1904 in New York, New York
d. Dec 24, 1966 in Sharon, Connecticut
Source: *AmAu&B; BioIn 3, 6, 7, 8, 10; ConAu 25R; CurBio 53, 67; InWom; WhAm 4; WhoAmW 58, 61, 64, 66; WorAu 1950*

Peter the Great
[Peter I]
Russian. Ruler
Introduced Western civilization into Russia; created regular Army, Navy; founded capital, St. Petersburg, 1703.
b. May 30, 1672 in Moscow, Russia
d. Jan 28, 1725 in Saint Petersburg, Russia
Source: *Benet 87, 96; BlkwCE; CasWL; DcBiPP; DcRusL; GrLGrT; HarEnMi; HisWorL; LinLib S; NewCol 75; REn; WebBD 83; WhDW; WhoMilH 76*

Petipa, Marius
French. Dancer, Choreographer
Developed classical ballet in Russia; founded Bolshoi and Kirov ballets.
b. Mar 11, 1822 in Marseilles, France
d. Jun 2, 1910 in Gurzuf, Russia
Source: *BiDD; BioIn 4, 5, 8, 9, 11; DcBiPP; NewOxM; NotNAT B; WhDW*

Petit, Philippe
French. Stunt Performer
Aerialist who walked across a tightrope between the towers of the World Trade Center, 1974.
b. Aug 13, 1949 in Nemours, France
Source: *BioIn 11, 15, 16; CurBio 88*

Petit, Roland
French. Dancer, Choreographer
Founded Les Ballets de Paris, 1948; noted for *An American in Paris,* 1944.
b. Jan 13, 1924 in Villemomble, France
Source: *BiDD; BioIn 2, 3, 4, 9; CnOxB; CurBio 52; DancEn 78; DcTwCCu 2; IntDcB; IntWW 74, 75, 76, 77, 78, 79, 80, 81, 82, 83, 89, 91, 93; LegTOT; VarWW 85; Who 74, 82, 83, 85, 88, 90, 92, 94; WhoFr 79; WhoHol 92, A; WhoThe 77A; WhoWor 74, 82, 84, 87, 89, 91, 93, 95, 97; WhThe*

Petitpierre, Max
Swiss. Government Official, Statesman
Instrumental in modifying the Swiss policy of neutrality during the Cold War.
b. Feb 26, 1899
d. Mar 25, 1994 in Neuchatel, Switzerland
Source: *BioIn 3, 19, 20; CurBio 94N; IntWW 74, 75, 76, 77, 78, 79, 80, 81, 82, 83; WhoFI 74; WhoWor 74*

Peto, John Frederick
American. Artist
Self-taught *trompe l'oeil* painter, noted for realistic still lifes of books, guns.
b. May 21, 1854 in Philadelphia, Pennsylvania
d. Nov 23, 1907 in Island Heights, New Jersey
Source: *AmCulL; BioIn 2, 5, 13; BriEAA; DcAmArt; McGDA; McGEWB; NewCol 75; OxCArt; OxDcArt; WhAmArt 85*

Petra
American. Music Group
Christian rock band formed in 1972; became "overnight success" after ten years of struggle.
Source: *ConMus 3*

Petrarch, Francesco
Italian. Poet
Wrote *Canzoniere,* lyrics, love sonnets; crowned poet lauraete, Rome, 1341.
b. Jul 20, 1304 in Arezzo, Italy
d. Jul 19, 1374 in Arqua, Italy
Source: *AtlBL; BbD; BiD&SB; BioIn 1, 2, 3, 4, 5, 6, 7, 8, 9, 10, 11, 12, 13; CasWL; CroE&S; CyEd; CyWA 58;*

DcArts; EuAu; EvEuW; LinLib L, S; McGEWB; NewC; NewCBEL; OxCEng 67; PenC EUR; RComWL; REn

Petri, Angelo
American. Vintner
Headed Petri Wine Co., 1933-56; renamed United Vintners, 1949.
b. Sep 5, 1883 in Marseilles, France
d. Oct 4, 1961 in San Francisco, California
Source: *BioIn 6; DcAmB S7*

Petri, Elio
Italian. Director
Won Oscar, 1970, for *Investigation of a Citizen above Suspicion.*
b. Jan 29, 1929 in Rome, Italy
d. Nov 10, 1982 in Rome, Italy
Source: *AnObit 1982; BiDFilm 81, 94; BioIn 13, 16; DcFM; EncEurC; FacFETw; FilmEn; FilmgC; HalFC 80, 84, 88; IntDcF 1-2, 2-2; ItaFilm; LegTOT; MiSFD 9N; NewYTBS 82; WorEFlm; WorFDir 2*

Petrie, Charles Alexander, Sir
English. Historian
English history books include *A Drift to World War 1900-1914,* 1968.
b. Sep 28, 1895 in Liverpool, England
d. Dec 13, 1977 in London, England
Source: *Au&Wr 71; ConAu 8NR, 17R; DcLEL; IntAu&W 76, 77; IntWW 74; NewCBEL; TwCA SUP; Who 74; WhoWor 74*

Petrie, (William Matthew) Flinders, Sir
English. Archaeologist, Egyptologist
Revolutionized excavating by introducing systematic examination, sequence dating.
b. Jun 3, 1853 in Charlton, England
d. Jul 28, 1942 in Jerusalem, Palestine
Source: *Benet 87, 96; BioIn 5, 6, 7, 8, 9, 14, 15; DcLEL; DcNaB 1941; DcScB; EvLB; GrBr; InSci; IntDcAn; LegTOT; LinLib L, S; LngCTC; LuthC 75; McGEWB; REn; TwCA, SUP; WhE&EA; WhLit; WhoLA*

Petrillo, James Caesar
American. Labor Union Official
Pres., American Federation of Musicians, 1940-58; believed music crucial to morale during WW II.
b. Mar 16, 1892 in Chicago, Illinois
d. Oct 23, 1984 in Chicago, Illinois
Source: *AnObit 1984; BiDAmL; BiDAmLL; BioIn 1, 3, 4, 6, 11; CurBio 40, 85N; WhoFI 74*

Petrocelli, Rico (Americo Peter)
[Americo Peter Petrocelli]
American. Baseball Player
Shortstop, Boston, 1963, 1965-76; set AL record for home runs by shortstop, 40, 1969.
b. Jun 27, 1943 in New York, New York
Source: *Ballpl 90; BioIn 9, 18, 21; WhoAm 74; WhoProB 73*

Petronius, Gaius
[Petronius Arbiter]
Roman. Author
Reputed to be author of satire *Satyricon,* sometimes considerd first Western European novel.
Source: *AtlBL; BbD; Benet 87, 96; BiD&SB; BioIn 2, 5, 9, 14, 20; CasWL; DcArts; Dis&D; GrFLW; LegTOT; McGEWB; OxCClL 89; OxCEng 67, 85; RComWL; WorAlBi*

Petrosian, Tigran Vartanovich
Russian. Chess Player
World chess champion, 1963-69; member, Soviet team that took first place, Chess Olympics, 1958-74.
b. Jun 17, 1929 in Tbilisi, Union of Soviet Socialist Republics
d. Aug 13, 1984 in Moscow, Union of Soviet Socialist Republics
Source: *AnObit 1984; BiDSovU; BioIn 8, 9, 10; GolEC; IntWW 74, 75, 76, 77, 78, 79, 80, 81, 82, 83; WhoSocC 78; WhoWor 78*

Petrov, Ossip
Russian. Opera Singer
One of greatest Russian basses; popular, 1830s-70s.
b. Nov 15, 1807 in Elisavetgrad, Russia
d. Mar 14, 1878 in Saint Petersburg, Russia
Source: *Baker 84; CmOp; NewEOp 71; NewGrDM 80*

Pet Shop Boys
English. Music Group
British pop duo; debut album *Please,* 1986, featured chart-topping dance hits "West End Girls" and "(Opportunities) Let's Make Lots of Money."
Source: *BioIn 16, 20; ConMus 5; EncRkSt*

Pett, Saul
American. Journalist
Worked 45 years as a feature writer for AP; won the 1982 Pulitzer Prize for feature writing.
b. Mar 18, 1918 in Passaic, New Jersey
d. Jun 14, 1993 in McLean, Virginia
Source: *BioIn 19; WhoAm 84; WhoE 85; WhoUSWr 88; WhoWrEP 89, 92, 95*

Pettet, Joanna
American. Actor
Films include *The Group; Casino Royale;* appeared on TV series "Knots Landing," 1983.
b. Nov 16, 1944 in London, England
Source: *ConTFT 7, 14; FilmEn; FilmgC; HalFC 80, 84, 88; IntMPA 96; VarWW 85; WhoHol 92, A*

Pettiford, Oscar
American. Jazz Musician, Songwriter
Bass player; developed pizzicato jazz cello.
b. Sep 30, 1922 in Okmulgee, Oklahoma
d. Sep 8, 1960 in Copenhagen, Denmark
Source: *AfrAmAl 6; AllMusG; Baker 84, 92; BiDAfM; BiDAmM; BiDJaz; BioIn 5, 8, 11, 16; CmpEPM; InB&W 80, 85; LegTOT; NegAl 76, 83, 89; NewAmDM; NewGrDA 86; NewGrDJ 88, 94; PenEncP; WhoJazz 72; WorAl; WorAlBi*

Pettit, Bob
[Robert Lee Pettit, Jr]
American. Basketball Player
Ten-time all-star center-forward, 1954-65, mostly with St. Louis; led NBA in scoring, 1956, 1959, in rebounding, 1956; MVP, 1956, 1959; Hall of Fame, 1970.
b. Dec 12, 1932 in Baton Rouge, Louisiana
Source: *BasBi; BiDAmSp BK; BioIn 4, 21; CurBio 61; Dun&B 86; LegTOT; OfNBA 87; WhoBbl 73; WhoFI 75; WhoSpor; WorAl; WorAlBi*

Pettit, William Thomas
American. Broadcast Journalist
Reporter with NBC News since 1968; chief national affairs correspondent, 1985-89; London correspondent, 1989-95; has won three Emmys.
b. Apr 23, 1931 in Cincinnati, Ohio
d. Dec 22, 1995 in New York, New York
Source: *WhAm 11; WhoAm 74, 76, 78, 80, 82, 84, 86, 88, 90, 92, 94, 95, 96*

Petty, Richard
American. Auto Racer
Has won more grand national stock car races than any other racer.
b. Jul 2, 1938 in Level Cross, North Carolina
Source: *BiDAmSp OS; BioIn 7, 8, 9, 10, 13, 15; BioNews 74; CelR, 90; CurBio 80; NewYTBS 75, 88; WhoAm 74, 86, 88; WhoSSW 84; WorAlBi*

Petty, Tom
[Tom Petty and the Heartbreakers]
American. Musician, Singer, Songwriter
Hit songs include "Refugee," 1980; "Don't Do Me Like That," 1979; founded The Heartbreakers rock group, 1975; recorded two albums with The Traveling Wilburys, 1988 and 1990.
b. Oct 20, 1952 in Gainesville, Florida
Source: *ConMus 9; ConNews 88-1; CurBio 91; EncPR&S 89; EncRk 88; IlEncRk; NewAmDM; NewGrDA 86; PenEncP; RkOn 85; WhoAm 90, 92, 94, 95; WhoEnt 92*

Petty, William, Sir
English. Economist, Educator, Physician
Cowrote first book on vital statistics, 1662.
b. May 26, 1623 in Romsey, England
d. Dec 16, 1687 in London, England
Source: *Alli; AntBDN I; BioIn 2, 3, 7, 10, 12, 15, 16; BritAu; CyEd; DcBiPP; DcEnL; DcNaB; DcScB; GrEconB; InSci; NewC; NewCol 75; OxCEng 67, 85, 95; OxCIri; OxCMed 86; REn; WebBD 83*

Peugeot, Rodolphe
French. Auto Executive
Former pres., now director of Societe Peugeot et Cie.
b. Apr 2, 1902 in Selancourt, France
Source: *IntWW 74, 75, 76, 77, 78, 79, 80, 81; WhoFI 74; WhoFr 79; WhoWor 74*

Pevsner, Antoine
French. Artist, Sculptor
Founded Constructivist school, which applies cubism principles to sculpture.
b. Jan 18, 1886 in Orel, Russia
d. Apr 12, 1962 in Paris, France
Source: *BioIn 4, 5, 6, 14, 15; ConArt 77, 83; CurBio 59, 62; DcArts; IntDcAA 90; McGDA; McGEWB; OxCArt; OxCTwCA; OxDcArt; PhDcTCA 77; WhAm 4; WhDW; WorArt 1950*

Pevsner, Nikolaus Bernhard Leon, Sir
English. Architect, Art Historian
Best known for 46-volume series *The Buildings of England,* 1951-74.
b. Jan 30, 1902 in Leipzig, Germany
d. Aug 18, 1983 in London, England
Source: *Au&Wr 71; ConAu 7NR, 9R, 110; DcLEL; DcNaB 1981; IntWW 83; LngCTC; NewYTBS 83; OxCEng 85, 95; WhoWor 74; WorAu 1950*

Pew, J(ohn) Howard
American. Industrialist
Pres., Sun Oil, 1912-1947; experimented with new oil refining techniques.
b. Jan 27, 1882 in Bradford, Pennsylvania
d. Nov 27, 1971 in Ardmore, Pennsylvania
Source: *BiDAmBL 83; BioIn 2, 9, 11, 12; DcAmB S9; ObitOF 79; WhAm 5, 7*

Peyre, Henri Maurice
American. Author
Critical works include *The Contemporary French Novel,* 1955.
b. Feb 21, 1901 in Paris, France
d. Dec 9, 1988 in Norwalk, Connecticut
Source: *AmAu&B; Au&Wr 71; BioIn 5; ConAu 3NR, 5R; DrAS 74F; WhAm 9; WhoAm 78, 80, 82, 84, 86; WhoUSWr 88; WhoWor 74, 76; WhoWrEP 89*

Peyrefitte, Roger
[Pierre Roger Peyrefitte]
French. Author
Wrote best-seller, biography of Germaine Germain, *Manouche,* 1972.
b. Aug 17, 1907 in Castres, France
Source: *Au&Wr 71; Benet 87, 96; BioIn 7, 10; ClDMEL 80; ConAu 65; EncWL; EvEuW; IntAu&W 76, 77, 82, 89, 91; IntWW 74, 75, 76, 77, 78, 79, 80, 81, 82, 83, 89, 91; LinLib L; Novels; PenC EUR; REn; TwCWr; Who 74, 82, 83, 85, 88, 90, 92; WhoFr 79; WhoWor 74; WorAu 1950*

Pfeiffer, Jane Cahill
American. Business Executive
With IBM, 1955-78; board chairman, NBC, Inc., 1978-80.
b. Sep 29, 1932 in Washington, District of Columbia
Source: *AmWomM; BioIn 11; CurBio 80; GrLiveH; InWom SUP; LesBEnT 92; WhoAm 76, 78, 80, 82, 84, 88, 90, 92, 94, 95, 96, 97; WhoAmW 79, 81, 83, 85, 87, 89, 91, 93, 95, 97; WhoE 89, 95, 97; WhoEnt 92; WhoFI 79, 81; WhoWor 80, 82, 91, 93; WomFir*

Pfeiffer, Michelle
American. Actor
Sultry actress; starred in films *The Fabulous Baker Boys,* 1989, *Dangerous Liaisons,* 1989, *Married to the Mob,* 1988, *One Fine Day,* 1996.
b. Apr 29, 1957 in Santa Ana, California
Source: *BiDFilm 94; BioIn 14, 15, 16; ConTFT 8, 15; CurBio 90; GangFlm; HalFC 88; HolBB; IntDcF 2-3; IntMPA 86, 88, 92, 94, 96; IntWW 91; LegTOT; News 90, 90-2; WhoAm 94, 95, 96, 97; WhoEnt 92; WhoHol 92; WorAlBi*

Pfitzner, Hans
German. Composer
Wrote choral works, operas including *Palestrina,* 1917.
b. May 5, 1869 in Moscow, Russia
d. May 22, 1949 in Salzburg, Austria
Source: *Baker 78; BioIn 3, 4, 8, 10, 12; BriBkM 80; CmOp; CompSN, SUP; DcCM; DcCom 77; EncTR 91; MetOEnc; MusMk; NewAmDM; NewEOp 71; NewGrDM 80; NewOxM; OxCGer 76, 86; OxCMus; OxDcOp; PenDiMP A*

Pfizer, Charles
Manufacturer

Phaedrus
Roman. Author
Wrote fables in verse based on Aesop.
b. 15BC
d. 50AD
Source: *BiD&SB; CasWL; DcArts; Grk&L; LegTOT; LinLib L; NewC; NewCol 75; OxCClL; OxCEng 67; PenC CL; RAdv 13-2*

Phair, Liz
[Elizabeth Clark Phair]
American. Singer, Songwriter
Debut album *Exile in Guyville,* 1993.
b. Apr 17, 1967 in Cincinnati, Ohio
Source: *ConMus 14; News 95, 95-3; WhoAmW 97*

Pham Hung
[Pham Van Thien]
Vietnamese. Political Leader
Prime minister of Vietnam, 1987-88; instrumental in defeat of US in Vietnam War.
b. Jun 11, 1912 in Vinh Long Province, Vietnam
d. Mar 10, 1988 in Ho Chi Minh City, Vietnam
Source: *BioIn 11; FarE&A 78, 79, 80, 81; IntWW 76, 77, 78, 79, 80, 81, 82, 83*

Pham van Dong
Vietnamese. Political Leader
Prime minister of Vietnam, 1976-87.
b. Mar 1, 1906 in Quang Nam, Vietnam
Source: *BiDMarx; BioIn 8, 10, 13, 14; CurBio 75; DcMPSA; FacFETw; FarE&A 78, 79, 80, 81; IntWW 74, 75, 76, 77, 78, 79, 80, 81, 82, 83, 89, 91, 93; IntYB 78, 79, 80, 81, 82; WhoSocC 78; WhoWor 74, 76, 78, 80, 82, 84, 87, 89, 91*

Phelan, John Joseph
American. Business Executive
Chm., chief exec., NY Stock Exchange, 1984-91.
b. May 7, 1931 in New York, New York
Source: *BioIn 12, 14, 15; ConNews 85-4; Dun&B 90; IntWW 83, 89, 91, 93; NewYTBS 87; St&PR 91; WhoAm 82, 90; WhoE 86; WhoFI 81, 83, 85, 89; WhoSecI 86; WhoWor 87*

Phelps, Digger
[Richard Frederick Phelps]
American. Basketball Coach
Coach, Notre Dame, 1971-91.
b. Jul 4, 1941 in Beacon, New York
Source: *BiDAmSp Sup; BioIn 10, 12, 13, 19; ConAu 103; WhoAm 76, 78, 80, 82, 84, 86, 88; WhoMW 80, 82*

Phelps, Elizabeth Stuart Ward
American. Children's Author
Wrote popular religious tales, including *The Sunny Side,* 1851.
b. Aug 13, 1815 in Andover, Massachusetts
d. Nov 30, 1852
Source: *Alli; AmAu; AmAu&B; AmBi; ApCAB; CarSB; Chambr 3; CyAL 1; Drake; OxCAmL 83; REnAL; TwCBDA*

Phelps, John Wolcott
American. Army Officer
Organized escaped slaves into first black Union troops, 1862.
b. Nov 13, 1813 in Guilford, Vermont
d. Feb 2, 1885 in Brattleboro, Vermont
Source: *Alli SUP; AmAu&B; AmBi; ApCAB; BioIn 7; CivWDc; DcAmAu; DcAmB; DcNAA; Drake; HarEnUS; TwCBDA; WhCiWar*

Phelps, William Lyon
American. Educator, Journalist
Yale U English professor, 1892-1933; popularized the arts through his lectures, essays.
b. Jan 2, 1865 in New Haven, Connecticut
d. Aug 21, 1943 in New Haven, Connecticut
Source: *AmAu&B; ApCAB X; BenetAL 91; BiDAmEd; BioIn 2, 4, 5; ChhPo, S1, S3; CnDAL; ConAmL; CurBio 43; DcAmAu; DcAmB S3; DcNAA; EvLB; LinLib L; LngCTC; LuthC 75; NatCAB 32; OxCAmL 65, 83, 95; REnAL;*

ScF&FL 1; TwCA, SUP; WhAm 2; WhLit

Phidias
Greek. Sculptor
Member of Periclean circle who designed sculptures for Parthenon.
b. 500BC in Athens, Greece
d. 432BC
Source: *AtlBL; BioIn 1, 4, 20; OxCClL; REn; WorAl; WorAlBi*

Philbin, Regis (Francis Xavier)
American. TV Personality
Co-host, "Morning Show," WABC New York, 1983-88; co-host, "Live with Regis and Kathie Lee," 1988—.
b. Aug 25, 1933 in New York, New York
Source: *BioIn 8; CelR 90; CurBio 94; IntMPA 96*

Philbrick, Herbert Arthur
American. Advertising Executive, Author
Described triple life led for nine years as "Citizen, communist, counterspy," in *I Led Three Lives,* 1952.
b. May 11, 1915
d. Aug 16, 1993 in North Hampton, New Hampshire
Source: *BioIn 1, 2, 3, 9, 10; CurBio 53; DcAmC*

Philby, Harold St. John Bridger
British. Explorer, Author
Adviser to King Ibn Saud of Saudi Arabia for 30 years.
b. 1885
d. Sep 30, 1960 in Beirut, Lebanon
Source: *NewCol 75; WebBD 83*

Philby, Kim
[Harold Adrian Russell Philby]
English. Traitor
Agent for Soviets, 1933-63; defected to Moscow, 1963.
b. Jan 1, 1912 in Ambala, India
d. May 11, 1988 in Moscow, Russia
Source: *AnObit 1988; BiDSovU; BioIn 6, 7, 8, 10, 11, 12, 13, 15, 16, 17, 18, 20, 21; ColdWar 1, 2; ConAu 125; DcNaB 1986; EncAI&E; HisEWW; LegTOT; NewCol 75; News 88-3; NewYTBS 88; SpyCS*

Philidor, Francois Andre Danican
[Francois Danican]
French. Composer, Chess Player
Comic opera composer; wrote first description of chess strategy: *L'analyse du Jeu des Eches,* 1749.
b. Sep 7, 1726 in Dreux, France
d. Aug 24, 1795 in London, England
Source: *Baker 78; BioIn 14; DcBiPP; DcNaB; GrComp; MusMk; NewEOp 71; NewGrDM 80; OxCChes 84; OxCFr*

Philip, Prince
[Duke of Edinburgh]
English. Consort
Married Elizabeth II, 1947; became British citizen, renouncing Greek, Danish ties same year.
b. Jun 10, 1921 in Corfu, Greece
Source: *BioIn 1, 2, 3, 5, 6, 7, 8, 9, 10, 11, 12, 13, 14, 15, 16, 17; CurBio 47; IntWW 74; LegTOT; WhoWor 74, 76, 78, 80, 82, 84, 87, 89, 91, 95, 96, 97*

Philip, Saint
Biblical Figure
One of the twelve apostles.
Source: *NewCol 75; WebBD 83*

Philipe, Gerard
French. Actor, Director
France's leading romantic star of post-war years; starred in *Devil in the Flesh,* 1947.
b. Dec 4, 1922 in Cannes, France
d. Nov 27, 1959 in Paris, France
Source: *BiDFilm 81; BioIn 3, 5, 7, 11, 14; CamGWoT; DcTwCCu 2; EncEurC; EncWT; Ent; FilmAG WE; FilmEn; FilmgC; HalFC 80, 84, 88; IntDcF 1-3, 2-3; IntDcT 3; ItaFilm; MotPP; MovMk; NotNAT, B; ObitT 1951; OxCFilm; OxCThe 67, 83; WhoHol A, B; WhScrn 74, 77, 83; WorEFlm*

Philip II
[Philip of Macedon]
Macedonian. Ruler
Established federal system of Greek states; father of Alexander the Great.
b. 382BC, Macedonia
d. 336BC
Source: *NewCol 75; OxCClL; WebBD 83*

Philip II
[Philip Augustus]
French. Ruler
Ruled, 1179-1223; son of Louis VII; increased kingdom through various wars, 1181-85.
b. Jul 21, 1165 in Gonesse, France
d. Jul 14, 1223 in Mantes, France
Source: *Dis&D; HarEnMi; HisWorL; NewCol 75; WebBD 83*

Philip II
Spanish. Ruler
Ruled, 1556-98; married four times, including Mary I of England; conquered Portu gal, 1580-81.
b. 1527
d. 1598
Source: *BioIn 10; DcBiPP; NewCol 75; WebBD 83*

Philips, David Graham
[John Graham]
American. Journalist, Author
Critic of Victorianism; best-known novel *Susan Lenox: Her Fall and Rise,* 1917.
b. Oct 31, 1867 in Madison, Indiana
d. Jan 24, 1911 in New York, New York
Source: *AmAu&B; BioIn 15, 16; CnDAL; DcLEL; DcNAA; IndAu 1816; LngCTC; OxCAmL 65; REnAL*

Philips, Katherine
[Orinda; Katherine Fowler]
English. Poet
Acclaimed for her translations of French poetry and drama.
b. 1632 in London, England
d. 1664 in London, England
Source: *BiDEWW; BlmGWL; CamGEL; CamGLE; DcLB 131; EncBrWW; FemiCLE; LitC 30; NewCBEL*

Philip V
Macedonian. Ruler
Reign marked by wars with Rome, Balkans, 221-179 B.C; attempted to rebuild kingdom.
b. 237BC
d. 179BC
Source: *NewCol 75; WebBD 83*

Philip VI
[Philip of Valois]
French. Ruler
First to rule from house of Valois, 1328-50; conflicts with Edward III led to Hundred Years' War, 1337.
b. 1293
d. 1350
Source: *NewCol 75; WebBD 83*

Phillip, Andy
[Andrew Michael Phillip]
American. Basketball Player
Guard, 1947-58, with several pro teams; led NBA in assists, 1951-52; Hall of Fame.
b. Mar 7, 1922 in Granite City, Illinois
Source: *BasBi; BiDAmSp BK; BioIn 9; OfNBA 87; WhoBbl 73; WhoSpor*

Phillip, Arthur
English. Naval Officer, Colonizer
Established first British convict settlement at New South Wales in 1786.
b. Oct 11, 1738 in London, England
d. Aug 31, 1814 in Bath, England
Source: *Alli; BiDLA SUP; BioIn 2, 7, 8; DcBiPP; DcNaB; HisWorL; McGEWB; NewCBEL; OxCAusL*

Phillips, Bum
[Oail Andres Phillips]
American. Football Coach
Head coach, Houston, 1975-80, New Orleans, 1981-85.
b. Sep 29, 1923 in Orange, Texas
Source: *BioIn 12, 14, 17; WhoAm 80, 82, 84*

Phillips, Caryl
English. Author, Dramatist
Wrote *The Final Passage,* 1985, winner of the Malcolm X Prize for Literature.
b. Mar 13, 1958 in Saint Kitts, British West Indies

Source: *BlkWr 2; ConAu 141; ConBrDr; ConDr 88, 93; ConLC 96; ConNov 91, 96; CurBio 94; DcLB 157; RGTwCWr; WhoWor 95, 96, 97; WorAu 1985; WrDr 88, 90, 92, 94, 96*

Phillips, Channing Emery
American. Clergy
First black man nominated for pres. by major party, at 1968 Dem. convention.
b. Mar 23, 1928 in New York, New York
d. Nov 11, 1987 in New York, New York
Source: *BioIn 9; InB&W 80, 85; WhAm 9; WhoAm 74, 76, 78, 80, 82, 84, 86; WhoAmP 73, 75, 77, 79, 81; WhoRel 75; WhoSSW 73*

Phillips, Charles
American. Manufacturer
Created product which made him nation's largest producer of milk of magnesia, 1873.
b. 1820
d. 1882
Source: *Entr*

Phillips, Chynna
American. Singer, Actor
Member of pop group Wilson Phillips; daughter of John and Michelle.
b. 1968 in Los Angeles, California
Source: *BioIn 15; LegTOT*

Phillips, Esther
[Esther Mae Jones]
"Little Esther"
American. Singer
Best known for album *From a Whisper to a Scream,* 1972.
b. Dec 23, 1935 in Galveston, Texas
d. Aug 7, 1984 in Los Angeles, California
Source: *AnObit 1984; BiDAfM; BiDJaz; BluesWW; DrBlPA, 90; EncPR&S 89; EncRk 88; InB&W 85; LegTOT; NewGrDA 86; PenEncP; SoulM; WhoRock 81*

Phillips, Harry Irving
American. Journalist
Created WW II rookie Private Oscar Purkey; wrote *Private Purkey's Private Peace,* 1945.
b. Nov 26, 1889 in New Haven, Connecticut
d. Mar 15, 1965 in Milford, Connecticut
Source: *DcAmB S7; WhAm 4*

Phillips, Harvey Gene
American. Musician
Tuba player; responsible for present-day renaissance of interest in tuba performance.
b. Dec 2, 1929 in Aurora, Missouri
Source: *Baker 84, 92; ConMus 3; IntWWM 90; NewAmDM; NewGrDA 86; TwCBrS; WhoAm 82, 84, 86, 88, 90; WhoAmM 83; WhoE 74, 75; WhoEnt 92*

Phillips, Irna
"Queen of the Soaps"
American. Writer
Scriptwriter for TV's longest-running soap opera, "Guiding Light," 1938-73.
b. Jul 1, 1901, Germany
d. Dec 22, 1973 in Chicago, Illinois
Source: *AmWomWr; BioIn 5, 6, 10, 12; NotAW MOD; SaTiSS; WhAm 6; WhoAmW 64, 66, 68, 70, 72*

Phillips, John
[The Mamas and the Papas]
American. Singer
Formed "goodtime rock 'n' roll" group, 1965; hits include "Monday, Monday," 1966; re-organized band, 1980s.
b. Aug 30, 1935 in Parris Island, South Carolina
Source: *Baker 84, 92; BioIn 7, 9, 11, 12; Dun&B 86, 88; LegTOT; WhoAm 90; WhoMW 84*

Phillips, Julia
American. Author, Filmmaker
Wrote scathing Hollywood tell-all *You'll Never Eat Lunch in This Town Again,* 1991; first woman to win best-picture Oscar for co-producing *The Sting.*
b. Apr 7, 1944 in New York, New York
Source: *BioIn 10; HalFC 88; IntMPA 92, 94, 96; LegTOT; News 92, 92-1; WhoAm 78, 80, 82, 84, 86; WhoWor 82, 84, 87*

Phillips, Kevin (Price)
American. Political Scientist
Wrote *Boiling Point: Democrats, Republicans, and the Decline of Middle-Class Prosperity,* 1993.
b. Nov 30, 1940 in New York, New York
Source: *BiDAmNC; ConAu 40NR, 65; CurBio 94; EncTwCJ; WhoAm 74, 76, 78, 80, 82, 84, 86, 88, 90, 92, 94, 95, 96, 97; WhoAmP 73; WhoUSWr 88; WhoWrEP 89, 92, 95*

Phillips, Lena Madesin
American. Feminist, Lawyer
Founded National Federation of Business and Professional Women's Clubs, 1919.
b. Sep 15, 1881 in Nicholasville, Kentucky
d. May 21, 1955 in Marseilles, France
Source: *AmWomM; BioIn 1, 3, 4, 9, 10, 12; DcAmB S5; InWom, SUP; LibW; NotAW MOD; WhAm 3*

Phillips, Lou Diamond
[Lou Upchurch]
American. Actor
Starred in films *La Bamba,* 1987, *Young Guns,* 1988.
b. Feb 17, 1962, Philippines
Source: *BioIn 15, 16; CelR 90; ConTFT 7, 14; IntMPA 92, 94, 96; LegTOT; NewYTBS 87; WhoHol 92*

Phillips, MacKenzie
[Laura Mackenzie Phillips]
American. Actor
Daughter of John Phillips; starred in TV series "One Day at a Time," 1975-80, 1981-83.
b. Nov 10, 1959 in Alexandria, Virginia
Source: *BioIn 11, 15, 20; ConTFT 7; HalFC 88; LegTOT; MovMk; VarWW 85; WhoHol 92*

Phillips, Marjorie Acker
American. Artist, Art Patron
Established first major modern art museum in US, 1921.
b. Oct 25, 1894 in Bourbon, Indiana
d. Jun 19, 1985 in Washington, District of Columbia
Source: *AnObit 1985; BioIn 14; DcWomA; IndAu 1967; NewYTBS 84; WhoAm 78; WhoAmA 78; WhoWor 78*

Phillips, Mark Anthony Peter
English.
Married Princess Anne, Nov 14, 1973; divorced 1992.
b. Sep 22, 1948, England
Source: *BioIn 13, 16; NewYTBE 73; Who 74, 82, 83, 85, 88, 90, 92, 94; WhoAm 82; WhoWor 84, 87, 89, 91, 93, 95, 96, 97*

Phillips, Michelle Gillam
[The Mamas and the Papas]
American. Actor, Singer
Hits with group include "California Dreamin'," 1966; married to John Phillips, 1962-70.
b. Apr 6, 1944 in Long Beach, California
Source: *BioIn 9, 11, 13, 14, 15, 16; ConTFT 5; IntMPA 92; WhoEnt 92; WhoRocM 82*

Phillips, Robin
English. Actor, Director
Director of Canada's Stratford Shakespeare Festival, 1975-80; London, ON Grand Theater, 1983.
b. Feb 28, 1942 in Haslemere, England
Source: *BioIn 10, 13, 20; CanWW 31, 79, 80, 81, 83, 89; ConTFT 5; OxCCanT; OxCThe 83; Who 82, 83, 85, 88, 90, 92, 94; WhoAm 78, 80, 82; WhoHol 92; WhoThe 72, 77, 81; WhoWest 92, 94*

Phillips, Sam
American. Music Executive
Began Sun Records, 1952; first recorded Elvis Presley, Carl Perkins.
b. Jan 5, 1923 in Florence, Alabama
Source: *BgBkCoM; BioIn 12, 15, 16; ConMuA 80B; ConMus 5; IlEncRk; NewGrDA 86; RkWW 82; RolSEnR 83; WhoRock 81*

Phillips, Sian
Welsh. Actor
Starred on TV in "How Green Was My Valley;" "I, Claudius."
b. May 14, 1934 in Bettws y Coed, Wales

Source: *BioIn 14; ConTFT 8; FilmgC; HalFC 80, 84, 88; IntMPA 96; IntWW 82, 91; Who 92; WhoHol 92, A; WhoThe 77, 81; WhoWor 91*

Phillips, Tommy
[Thomas Phillips]
Canadian. Hockey Player
Played on amateur teams, early 1900s; Hall of Fame, 1945.
b. May 22, 1880 in Kenora, Ontario, Canada
d. Dec 5, 1923
Source: *WhoHcky 73*

Phillips, Wendell
American. Author, Abolitionist, Orator
b. Nov 29, 1811 in Boston, Massachusetts
d. Feb 2, 1884 in Boston, Massachusetts
Source: *Alli; AmAu; AmAu&B; AmBi; AmOrN; AmRef; AmSocL; ApCAB; Benet 87, 96; BenetAL 91; BiDAmLf; BiD&SB; BiDTran; BioIn 1, 2, 4, 5, 6, 7, 8, 10, 12, 15, 16, 19; CelCen; Chambr 3; ChhPo; CivWDc; CyAG; CyAL 2; DcAmAu; DcAmB; DcAmSR; DcAmTB; DcBiPP; DcNAA; Drake; EncAB-H 1974, 1996; HarEnUS; LegTOT; LinLib L, S; McGEWB; NatCAB 2; OxCAmH; OxCAmL 65, 83, 95; RComAH; REn; REnAL; TwCBDA; WebAB 74, 79; WhAm HS; WhCiWar; WhNaAH*

Phillpotts, Eden
English. Author
His more than 250 works depict rural life, environment of west England.
b. Nov 4, 1862 in Mount Aber, India
d. Dec 29, 1960 in Exeter, England
Source: *BbD; BiD&SB; BioIn 2, 4, 5, 8, 13, 14, 15, 20, 21; CamGLE; CarSB; Chambr 3; ChhPo, S1, S2, S3; ConAu 93, 102; CrtSuMy; DcBiA; DcEnA A; DcLB 10, 70, 135, 153; DcLEL; DcNaB 1951; EncMys; EncSF, 93; EncWT; EngPo; EvLB; InWom SUP; LegTOT; LinLib L, S; LngCTC; ModBrL; NewC; NewCBEL; NotNAT B; ObitT 1951; OxCEng 85, 95; OxCThe 67, 83; PenEncH; REn; ScF&FL 1, 92; ScFEYrs; ScFSB; SJGFanW; SmATA 24; StaCVF; SupFW; TwCA, SUP; TwCCr&M 80, 85, 91; TwCWr; WhAm 4; WhE&EA; WhLit; WhoChL; WhoHr&F; WhoLA; WhThe*

Philo Judaeus
"The Jewish Plato"
Alexandrian. Philosopher
Pled with Caligula not to demand divine honors from Jews; regarded as forerunner of Christian theology.
b. 20BC
d. 50AD
Source: *BioIn 5, 11; CyEd; Grk&L; JeHun; McGEWB; NewCol 75; RAdv 13-4*

Phinney, Archie
American. Anthropologist
Preserved the language and folklore of the Nez Perce; awarded the Indian Council Fire Award, 1946.
b. 1903 in Idaho
d. 1949
Source: *BioIn 21; NotNaAm*

Phips, William, Sir
American. Colonial Figure
First royal governor of MA, 1692-94; recalled to England for negligent administr ation of Salem witchcraft trials.
b. Feb 2, 1651 in Woolwich, Maine
d. Feb 18, 1695 in London, England
Source: *AmBi; ApCAB; BenetAL 91; BiDrACR; BioIn 4, 5, 9, 11; DcAmMiB; Drake; HarEnMi; MacDCB 78; McGEWB; NatCAB 6; NewCol 75; OxCAmH; OxCAmL 65, 83, 95; OxCCan; OxCShps; PeoHis; REn; REnAL; WebAB 74, 79; WebAMB; WhAm HS*

Phoenix, River
American. Actor
Appeared in films *Stand By Me,* 1986, *I Love You to Death,* 1990; received Oscar nomination, 1988, for *Running on Empty.*
b. Aug 23, 1970 in Madras, Oregon
d. Oct 31, 1993 in Los Angeles, California
Source: *AnObit 1993; BioIn 15, 16; ConTFT 6, 9, 12; IntMPA 92, 94; LegTOT; News 90, 94, 90-2, 94-2; NewYTBS 91; WhAm 11; WhoAm 94; WhoHol 92; WorAlBi*

Phryne
Greek. Courtesan
Model for Apelle's *Aphrodite Emerging;* Praxitele's *Aphrodite.*
b. 300BC in Athens, Greece
Source: *IntDcWB; InWom SUP; NewC; OxCClL 89; REn*

Phyfe, Duncan
Scottish. Cabinetmaker, Furniture Designer
Called finest American furniture maker of his day, especially in use of mahogany.
b. 1768 in Inverness, Scotland
d. Aug 16, 1854 in New York, New York
Source: *AmBi; AmCulL; AntBDN G; BioIn 2, 3, 4, 11, 15, 19; BriEAA; CabMA; DcAmB; DcArts; DcD&D; DcNiCA; LegTOT; McGDA; McGEWB; NatCAB 19; OxCAmH; OxCAmL 65; OxCDecA; PenDiDA 89; WebAB 74, 79; WhAm HS; WorAl; WorAlBi*

Piaf, Edith
[Edith Gassion]
French. Singer
Known for tragic love songs: "La Vie en Rose."
b. Dec 1915 in Paris, France
d. Oct 11, 1963 in Paris, France
Source: *Baker 78, 84, 92; BioIn 2, 3, 5, 6, 7, 9, 12, 14, 15, 16, 17; CamGWoT; CmpEPM; ConAu 113; ConMus 8; ContDcW 89; CurBio 50, 63; DcArts; DcTwCCu 2; FacFETw; GoodHs; IntDcWB; InWom, SUP; ItaFilm; LegTOT; MusMk; NewAmDM; NewGrDM 80; NewYTBS 81; NotNAT B; ObitT 1961; OxCPMus; OxCThe 67, 83; PenEncP; WhAm 4; WhoHol B; WhScrn 74, 77; WorAl; WorAlBi*

Piaget, Jean
Swiss. Psychologist
Known for contributions to child psychology, intellectual development.
b. Aug 9, 1896 in Neuchatel, Switzerland
d. Sep 16, 1980 in Vienna, Austria
Source: *AnObit 1980; Benet 87, 96; BiDPsy; BioIn 4, 5, 7, 8, 9, 10, 11, 12, 13, 14, 15, 17, 20; ConAu 21R, 31NR, 101; CurBio 58, 80, 80N; DcTwHis; FacFETw; GaEncPs; GuPsyc; InSci; IntEnSS 79; IntWW 74, 75, 76, 77, 78, 79, 80; LegTOT; LinLib L, S; MajTwCW; MakMC; McGEWB; McGMS 80; NewYTBS 80; RAdv 14, 13-3; SmATA 23N; ThTwC 87; WhAm 7; WhDW; Who 74; WhoWor 74, 78, 80; WorAl; WorAlBi*

Piastro, Michel
Russian. Conductor, Violinist
Concertmaster with NY Philharmonic under Toscanini, 1931-43; led radio's "Longines Symphonette."
b. Sep 1892 in Keatz, Russia
d. Apr 10, 1970 in New York, New York
Source: *Baker 84; ConAmC 76; NewYTBE 70; WhAm 5*

Piatigorsky, Gregor
American. Musician
Cellist who debuted in US, 1929; with Berlin Philharmonic, 1924-28; often duoed with Heifetz.
b. Apr 17, 1903 in Ekaterinoslav, Russia
d. Aug 6, 1976 in Los Angeles, California
Source: *Baker 78, 84, 92; BiDAmM; BiDSovU; BioIn 2, 3, 4, 5, 6, 7, 8, 9, 10, 11; BlueB 76; BriBkM 80; CelR; ConAu 69; CurBio 45, 76, 76N; DcAmB S10; IntWWM 77; LegTOT; MusMk; MusSN; NewAmDM; NewGrDA 86; NewGrDM 80; NewYTBS 76; OxCChes 84; PenDiMP; WhAm 7; Who 74; WhoAm 74, 76; WhoMus 72; WhoWor 74; WhScrn 83; WorAl; WorAlBi*

Piave, Francesco Maria
Italian. Librettist
Wrote over 70 librettos, including Verdi's *Rigoletto,* 1832; *La Traviata,* 1852.
b. May 18, 1810 in Mureno, Italy
d. Mar 5, 1876 in Milan, Italy
Source: *BioIn 6, 20; IntDcOp; MetOEnc; NewEOp 71; NewGrDO; OxDcOp*

Piazza, Marguerite
American. Opera Singer, Actor
Soprano who had NY Met. debut, 1950; starred on TV's "Show of Shows," 1950-54.
b. May 6, 1926 in New Orleans, Louisiana
Source: *AmCath 80; BioIn 8, 10; BioNews 74; BlueB 76; WhoAm 74, 76, 78, 80, 82, 84, 86, 88, 90, 92, 94, 95, 96, 97; WhoAmW 61, 64, 66, 68, 70, 72, 74, 75, 83, 85, 87, 89, 91, 93, 95, 97; WhoEnt 92*

Piazzola, Astor
Argentine. Bandleader, Composer
Argentinean bandeneon master who created the nuevo tango; played with Anibal Troilo's Orquesta Tipica in Buenos Aires, 1936-1944; formed own band, Orquesta del 46, 1946; received first prize in Fabien Sevitsky Competition for *Sinfonia Buenos Aires*, 1954; released *Five Tango Sensations* in 1991.
b. 1921 in Mar del Plata, Argentina
d. Jul 4, 1992, Argentina
Source: *DcTwCCu 3; PenEncP*

Picabia, Francis
French. Artist
Early cubist, surrealist; introduced DaDa movement to Paris, NYC, 1918; known for machinist works, human figure paintings.
b. Jan 22, 1879 in Paris, France
d. Nov 30, 1953 in Paris, France
Source: *AtlBL; BioIn 2, 3, 4, 9, 11, 12, 13, 14, 15; ClaDrA; ConArt 77, 83; DcArts; DcTwCCu 2; EncWB; IntDcAA 90; McGDA; NewCol 75; OxCArt; OxCTwCA; OxDcArt*

Picard, Charles Emile
French. Mathematician
Proved Picard theorem worked on algebraic surfaces, 1879.
b. Jul 24, 1856 in Paris, France
d. Dec 11, 1941 in Paris, France
Source: *CamDcSc; DcScB; InSci; WebBD 83*

Picard, Henry
American. Golfer
Touring pro, 1930s; won Masters, 1938, PGA, 1939; Hall of Fame, 1961.
b. Nov 28, 1907 in Plymouth, Massachusetts
d. Apr 30, 1997 in Charleston, South Carolina
Source: *BiDAmSp OS; BioIn 6, 15; WhoGolf*

Picard, Jean
French. Astronomer
First used telescopic sights, computed size of the Earth, 1668-70, made recorded observations of barometric lights, 1675.
b. Jul 21, 1620 in La Fleche, France
d. Oct 12, 1682 in Paris, France
Source: *AsBiEn; BiESc; BioIn 12; DcBiPP; DcCathB; DcInv; DcScB; InSci; WebBD 83; WhDW*

Picasso, Pablo Ruiz y
Spanish. Artist
Profoundly influenced 20th c. art; masterpiece, *Guernica*, 1937, denounced war.
b. Oct 25, 1881 in Malaga, Spain
d. Apr 8, 1973 in Mougins, France
Source: *BioNews 74; CurBio 43, 62, 73; DcArts; DcFM; DcTwHis; NewYTBE 71, 73; OxCEng 85, 95; OxCFr; REn; WebBD 83; WhAm 5; WhoGrA 62; WhScrn 77*

Picasso, Paloma
French. Designer
Daughter of Pablo Picasso; designs jewelry for Tiffany and Co.
b. Apr 19, 1949 in Paris, France
Source: *BioIn 7, 9, 10, 11, 12, 13, 14, 15, 16; CelR 90; ConFash; CurBio 86; DcHiB; EncFash; IntWW 89, 91, 93; LegTOT; News 91, 91-1; NewYTBS 78, 80; NotHsAW 93; WhoHisp 91, 92, 94; WhoWor 95*

Piccard, Auguste
Swiss. Physicist
Set altitude records for free balloons in airtight gondola with hydrogen filled Balloon he invented, 1932; invented diving bell used in deep-sea diving, 1962.
b. Jan 28, 1884 in Basel, Switzerland
d. Mar 1, 1962 in Lausanne, Switzerland
Source: *AsBiEn; BiESc; BioIn 1, 3, 4, 5, 6, 7, 8, 12, 18, 20; ConAu 113; CurBio 47, 62; DcScB; Expl 93; FacFETw; InSci; LinLib L, S; McGEWB; NotTwCS; ObitT 1961; WhDW; WorAl; WorAlBi; WorInv*

Piccard, Jacques Ernest Jean
Swiss. Inventor, Explorer
Built bathyscaphe, which made deepest dive ever, 1960, to 35,800 feet.
b. Jul 28, 1922 in Brussels, Belgium
Source: *Au&Wr 71; BioIn 7, 8, 9; ConAu 65; CurBio 65; IntWW 74, 75, 76, 77, 78, 79, 80, 81, 82, 83, 89, 91, 93; Who 92; WhoWor 84, 87, 89, 91, 93, 95, 96, 97*

Piccard, Jean Felix
Swiss. Scientist
Known for stratospheric balloon flights, cosmic ray research.
b. Jan 28, 1884 in Basel, Switzerland
d. Jan 28, 1963 in Minneapolis, Minnesota
Source: *BioIn 1, 4, 5, 6, 7, 8; CurBio 63; DcAmB S7; InSci; NatCAB 47; WebAB 74, 79; WhAm 4*

Piccard, Jeannette Ridlon
[Mrs. Jean Piccard]
American. Balloonist, Religious Leader
Piloted balloon to record 57,559 ft., 1934; consultant to NASA, 1963; ordained Episcopal priest, 1973.
b. Jan 5, 1895 in Chicago, Illinois
d. May 17, 1981 in Minneapolis, Minnesota
Source: *AnObit 1981; WhoRel 75, 77*

Piccinni, Nicola
[Nicola Piccini]
Italian. Composer
Wrote 139 operas including comic opera, *La Buona Figliuola*, 1760.
b. Jan 16, 1725 in Bari, Italy
d. May 7, 1800 in Passy, France
Source: *Baker 84; MusMk; NewCol 75; NewEOp 71; NewGrDM 80; OxCMus*

Piccolo, Brian
"Pic"
American. Football Player
Running back, Chicago, 1965-69; film *Brian's Song*, 1973, based on his life; cancer victim.
b. Oct 21, 1943 in Pittsfield, Massachusetts
d. Jun 16, 1970 in New York, New York
Source: *BioIn 8, 9, 21; LegTOT; NewYTBE 70; ObitOF 79; WhoFtbl 74*

Pickard, Greenleaf Whittier
American. Engineer
Radio communicatons pioneer; invented the crystal detector.
b. Feb 4, 1877 in Portland, Maine
d. Jan 8, 1956 in Newton, Massachusetts
Source: *BioIn 4, 6; InSci; NatCAB 45; WhAm 3*

Pickens, Slim
[Louis Bert Lindley, Jr.]
American. Actor
Best known for role in *Dr. Strangelove*, 1964; Cowboy Hall of Fame, 1984.
b. Jun 29, 1919 in Kingsberg, California
d. Dec 8, 1983 in Modesto, California
Source: *AnObit 1983; BioIn 13; ConTFT 2; EncAFC; FilmEn; FilmgC; ForYSC; HalFC 80, 84, 88; HolCA; IntMPA 75, 76, 77, 78, 79, 80, 81, 82, 84; ItaFilm; LegTOT; MovMk; NewYTBS 83; VarWW 85; Vers A; WhAm 8; WhoAm 80, 82; WhoHol A; WorAl*

Pickens, T(homas) Boone, Jr.
American. Business Executive
Founded Mesa Petroleum Co., 1964; gained control of Gulf, Unocal, 1982.
b. May 22, 1928 in Holdenville, Oklahoma
Source: *BioIn 13, 14, 15, 16; CelR 90; ConAmBL; CurBio 85; Dun&B 88, 90; IntWW 91, 93; NewYTBS 87; St&PR 84, 87, 91; WhoAm 76, 78, 80, 82, 84, 88, 90, 92, 94, 95, 96; WhoFI 85, 87, 89, 92, 94; WhoSSW 84, 88, 95; WorAlBi*

Pickering, Edward Charles
American. Astronomer
Directed Harvard Observatory, 1877-1919; devised meridian photometer.
b. Jul 19, 1846 in Boston, Massachusetts
d. Feb 3, 1919 in Cambridge, Massachusetts
Source: *Alli SUP; AmBi; ApCAB, X; AsBiEn; BiDAmEd; BiDAmS; BiDPara; BiESc; BiInAmS; BioIn 3, 11, 14, 17; DcAmAu; DcAmB; DcNAA; DcScB; EncO&P 1, 2, 3; EncPaPR 91; HarEnUS; InSci; LarDcSc; LinLib L, S; McGEWB; NatCAB 6; TwCBDA; WebAB 74, 79; WhAm 1; WhDW*

Pickering, Thomas (Reeve)
American. Diplomat
Chief delegate to UN 1989-92; ambassador to Russia 1993-97.
b. Nov 5, 1931 in Orange, New Jersey
Source: *BioIn 13, 14, 16; BlueB 76; DcAmDH 80, 89; IntWW 75, 76, 77, 78, 79, 80, 81, 82, 83, 89, 91, 93; MidE 78, 79, 80, 81; NewYTBS 84, 88; USBiR 74; Who 90, 92, 94; WhoAm 74, 76, 78, 80, 82, 84, 86, 88, 90, 92, 94, 95, 96, 97; WhoAmP 75, 77, 79, 81, 83, 85, 87, 89, 91, 93, 95; WhoGov 72, 75, 77; WhoUN 92; WhoWor 74, 76, 78, 82, 87, 89, 91, 93, 95, 96, 97*

Pickering, Timothy
American. Politician
Federalist leader; secretary of state, 1795-1800, dismissed by Adams; in US Congress, 1803-17.
b. Jul 17, 1745 in Salem, Massachusetts
d. Jan 29, 1829 in Salem, Massachusetts
Source: *Alli; AmAu&B; AmBi; AmPolLe; AmRev; ApCAB; BenetAL 91; BiAUS; BiDrAC; BiDrUSC 89; BiDrUSE 71, 89; BioIn 3, 4, 5, 7, 8, 9, 10, 12, 16; CyAG; CyAL 1; DcAmB; DcAmDH 80, 89; DcBiPP; DcNAA; Drake; EncAB-H 1974, 1996; EncAR; EncCRAm; HarEnUS; McGEWB; NatCAB 1; OxCAmH; REnAL; TwCBDA; WebAB 74, 79; WebAMB; WhAm HS; WhAmP; WhAmRev*

Pickering, William
English. Publisher
Improved printing standards; issued 53-vol. Aldine edition of *English Poets.*
b. Apr 2, 1796 in London, England
d. Apr 27, 1854 in London, England
Source: *AntBDN B; BioIn 9, 15, 16, 17; DcLB 106; DcNaB; NewC; NewCBEL; OxCDecA; OxCEng 67, 85, 95*

Pickering, William Henry
American. Astronomer
Predicted existence, location of ninth planet, 1919.
b. Feb 15, 1858 in Boston, Massachusetts
d. Jan 16, 1938, Jamaica
Source: *Alli SUP; AmBi; ApCAB, X; AsBiEn; BiDAmS; BiESc; BioIn 1, 11; DcAmAu; DcNAA; DcScB; InSci; NatCAB 33; TwCBDA; WebAB 74, 79; WhAm 1; WhNAA*

Pickett, Bill
American. Rodeo Performer
Responsible for introducing the bulldogging event.
b. Dec 5, 1870 in Williamson County, Texas
d. Apr 21, 1932 in Tulsa, Oklahoma
Source: *BioIn 16; ConBlB 11; DcAmNB; InB&W 85*

Pickett, Cindy
American. Actor
Played Dr. Carol Novino on TV series "St. Elsewhere," 1985-88; first film: *Hot to Trot,* 1988.
Source: *ConTFT 7*

Pickett, George Edward
American. Military Leader
Confederate general; led "Pickett's charge" at Gettysburg, 1863.
b. Jan 25, 1825 in Richmond, Virginia
d. Jul 30, 1875 in Norfolk, Virginia
Source: *AmBi; ApCAB; BiDConf; BioIn 5, 9, 21; CivWDc; DcAmB; DcAmMiB; Drake; EncPaPR 91; EncSoH; HarEnMi; HarEnUS; LinLib S; NatCAB 5; TwCBDA; WebAB 74, 79; WebAMB; WhAm HS; WhCiWar; WhoMilH 76; WorAl*

Pickett, Wilson
"The Wicked Picket"
American. Singer, Songwriter
Hits include "In the Midnight Hour," 1965; "Funky Broadway," 1967.
b. Mar 18, 1941 in Prattville, Alabama
Source: *BiDAfM; BiDAmM; BioIn 8, 11, 15, 17, 19; ConMuA 80A; ConMus 10; DcArts; DrBlPA, 90; EncPR&S 74, 89; EncRk 88; EncRkSt; GuBlues; HarEnR 86; IlEncBM 82; IlEncRk; InB&W 80, 85; LegTOT; NewAmDM; NewGrDA 86; OxCPMus; PenEncP; RkOn 74; RolSEnR 83; SoulM; WhoEnt 92; WhoRock 81; WhoRocM 82; WorAl; WorAlBi*

Pickford, Jack
[Jack Smith]
Canadian. Actor
Child star, romantic lead, 1910-28; Mary Pickford's brother.
b. Aug 18, 1896 in Toronto, Ontario, Canada
d. Jan 3, 1933 in Paris, France
Source: *BioIn 15; Film 1, 2; FilmEn; FilmgC; HalFC 80, 84, 88; NotNAT B; SilFlmP; TwYS; WhoHol B; WhScrn 74, 77, 83*

Pickford, Mary
[Gladys Mary Smith]
"America's Sweetheart"
Canadian. Actor
Won Oscar, 1929, for *Coquette;* married to Douglas Fairbanks, Sr. and Buddy Rogers.
b. Apr 8, 1894 in Toronto, Ontario, Canada
d. May 29, 1979 in Santa Monica, California
Source: *BiDFilm; BioAmW; BlueB 76; CanWW 70; CurBio 45; Film 1; FilmgC; IntWW 74, 75; MotPP; MovMk; NewYTBE 71; OxCFilm; PlP&P; ThFT; WhoAm 74, 76, 78; WhoAmW 61, 64, 66, 68, 70, 72, 74; WhoHol A; WhoThe 77A; WhoWor 74; WomWMM*

Pico della Mirandola, Giovanni
Italian. Philosopher
Prominent Renaissance Humanist; stressed free will, dignity: *De hominis dignitate Oratio,* 1486.
b. 1463 in Modena, Italy
d. 1494 in Florence, Italy
Source: *AtlBL; Benet 87, 96; BioIn 1, 7, 13; CasWL; DcBiPP; DcCathB; DcEuL; EncO&P 2, 3; EuAu; EvEuW; IlEncMy; LitC 15; McGEWB; NewC; NewCBEL; NewCol 75; OxCEng 67, 85, 95; OxCPhil; PenC EUR; RAdv 14, 13-4; RComWL; REn; WebBD 83; WorAl; WorAlBi*

Picon, Molly
American. Actor
Comedic actress in Yiddish theater starting in 1923, hits include *Milk and Honey,* 1961; films include *Come Blow Your Horn,* 1963.
b. Jun 1, 1898 in New York, New York
d. Apr 6, 1992 in Lancaster, Pennsylvania
Source: *ASCAP 66; BiE&WWA; BioIn 1, 2, 6, 12, 16, 17, 18, 19; CamGWoT; ConAu 104; ConTFT 12; CurBio 51, 92N; EncAFC; EncVaud; HalFC 80, 84, 88; InWom, SUP; LegTOT; NewGrDA 86; NewYTBS 92; NotNAT, A; NotWoAT; OxCAmT 84; VarWW 85; WhoAm 74; WhoAmW 58, 61, 70, 72, 74; WhoHol 92, A; WhoThe 72, 77, 81; WhoWor 74; WorAl; WorAlBi*

Pictet, Raoul-Pierre
Swiss. Chemist
Discovered liquefaction of oxygen; developed early refrigeration system.
b. Apr 4, 1846 in Geneva, Switzerland
d. Jul 27, 1929 in Paris, France
Source: *AsBiEn; DcScB*

Pidgeon, Walter
American. Actor
Films from, 1925-77 include *Mrs. Miniver; Madame Curie.*
b. Sep 23, 1898 in Saint John, New Brunswick, Canada
d. Sep 25, 1984 in Santa Monica, California
Source: *AnObit 1984; BiDFilm; BiE&WWA; BioIn 5, 9, 14; CanWW 70; CmMov; CurBio 42, 84N; FilmgC; ForYSC; IntMPA 75, 76, 77, 78, 79, 80, 81, 82, 84; MotPP; MovMk; OxCFilm; TwYS; VarWW 85; WhAm 8; WhoAm 74, 76; WhoHol A; WhoThe 77; WorAl; WorAlBi; WorEFlm*

Piech, Ferdinand
Austrian. Business Executive
CEO of Volkswagen, 1993—.
b. Apr 17, 1937 in Vienna, Austria
Source: *BioIn 13, 16; Who 92, 94; WhoFI 96; WhoWor 95, 96, 97*

Pieck, Wilhelm
German. Political Leader
President of East Germany from 1949.
b. Jan 3, 1876 in Guben, Germany
d. Sep 7, 1960 in Berlin, German Democratic Republic
Source: *BioIn 1, 2, 3, 5, 11; CurBio 49, 60; EncGRNM; EncTR 91; HisEWW; ObitT 1951; WhAm 4; WorAl; WorAlBi*

Pierce, Charles
American. Entertainer
Female impersonator for more than four decades; made impressions of Bette Davis and Mae West, among others.
b. 1926 in Watertown, New York
Source: *GayLesB*

Pierce, David Hyde
American. Actor
Plays Niles Crane on "Frasier," 1993—.
b. Apr 3, 1959 in Saratoga Springs, New York
Source: *IntMPA 96; LegTOT; News 96, 96-3; WhoAm 95, 96*

Pierce, Edward Allen
American. Financier
Original member of brokerage house, Merrill, Lynch, Pierce, Fenner & Smith; early supporter of federal regulation of stockbrokers.
b. Aug 31, 1874 in Orrington, Maine
d. Dec 16, 1974 in New York, New York
Source: *BioIn 3, 10; DcAmB S9; NewYTBS 74; WhAm 6*

Pierce, Franklin
American. US President
Dem., 14th pres., 1853-57; tried unsuccessfully to end sectional controversy over slavery.
b. Nov 23, 1804 in Hillsboro, New Hampshire
d. Oct 8, 1869 in Concord, New Hampshire
Source: *AmAu&B; AmBi; AmPolLe; ApCAB; BenetAL 91; BiAUS; BiDrAC; BiDrUSC 89; BiDrUSE 71, 89; BioIn 1, 2, 3, 4, 5, 6, 7, 8, 9, 10, 11, 12, 13, 14, 15, 16, 17, 18, 19, 20; CelCen; CyAG; DcAmB; DcBiPP; Drake; EncAAH; EncAB-H 1974, 1996; EncSoH; FacPr 89, 93; HarEnUS; HealPre; LegTOT; LinLib L, S; McGEWB; NatCAB 4; OxCAmH; OxCAmL 65, 83; PolPar; RComAH; REnAL; TwCBDA; WebAB 74, 79; WhAm HS; WhAmP; WhCiWar; WhDW; WorAl; WorAlBi*

Pierce, Frederick S
American. TV Executive
Exec. VP of ABC-TV since 1980; when pres., 1974-80, brought network to top in ratings.
b. 1934? in New York, New York
Source: *BioIn 13, 14, 15; ConNews 85-3; Dun&B 86; EncTwCJ; LesBEnT, 92; VarWW 85; WhoAm 86; WhoE 83, 86*

Pierce, George Washington
American. Inventor
Invented the Pierce oscillator which provided more accurate radio transmission and reception.
b. Jan 11, 1872 in Webberville, Texas
d. Aug 25, 1956 in Franklin, New Hampshire
Source: *BioIn 5, 17; DcScB; InSci; WhAm 3; WhNAA*

Pierce, Jane Means
[Mrs. Franklin Pierce]
American. First Lady
Always wore black in White House due to death of last surviving child, 1853.
b. Mar 12, 1806 in Hampton, New Hampshire
d. Dec 2, 1863 in Andover, Massachusetts
Source: *AmWom; ApCAB; BioIn 1, 2, 3, 4, 5, 6, 7, 8, 9, 13; FacPr 89; NotAW; TwCBDA*

Pierce, John Davis
American. Educator
Helped establish the University of Michigan.
b. Feb 18, 1797 in Chesterfield, New Hampshire
d. Apr 5, 1882 in Medford, Massachusetts
Source: *ApCAB; BiDAmEd; DcAmB; WhAm HS*

Pierce, John Robinson
American. Engineer
His theories, experiments led to the development of satellite communications.
b. Mar 27, 1910 in Des Moines, Iowa
Source: *AmMWSc 73P, 79, 82, 86, 89, 92, 95; AsBiEn; BiESc; BioIn 3, 5, 6, 8, 17; BlueB 76; IntWW 74, 75, 76, 77, 78, 79, 80, 81, 82, 83, 89, 91, 93; LarDcSc; McGMS 80; WhoAm 74, 76, 78, 80, 86, 88, 90, 92, 94, 95, 96, 97; WhoEng 88; WhoScEn 96; WhoTech 89; WhoWor 74, 87; WrDr 76, 86*

Pierce, Mary
American. Tennis Player
Started playing professionally at age 14; competed as an amateur at the 1992 Olympic Summer Games.
b. 1975 in Montreal, Quebec, Canada
Source: *News 94; WhoAmW 93, 97*

Pierce, Samuel Riley, Jr.
American. Government Official
Reagan's secretary of HUD.
b. Sep 8, 1922 in Glen Cove, New York
Source: *AmDec 1980; BiDrUSE 89; BioIn 5, 9, 11, 12, 13, 14, 16; CngDr 87; CurBio 82; InB&W 80, 85; IntWW 81, 82, 83, 89, 91, 93; IntYB 78, 79, 80, 81, 82; NegAl 76, 83, 89A; NewYTBS 78, 80; WhoAm 74, 76, 78, 80, 82, 84, 86, 88, 90, 92, 94, 95, 96, 97; WhoAmP 87, 91; WhoBlA 88, 92; WhoE 74, 75, 77, 79, 81, 83, 85, 86, 89, 91, 93, 95, 97; WhoFI 74, 75, 77, 79, 81, 83, 85, 87, 89, 92, 94; WhoLab 76; WhoWor 76, 78, 80, 82, 84, 87, 89, 91, 93, 95, 96, 97*

Pierce, Webb
American. Singer
Country recording star, 1950s-60s; hits include "Slowly," 1954.
b. Aug 8, 1926 in West Monroe, Louisiana
d. Feb 24, 1991 in Nashville, Tennessee
Source: *ASCAP 80; Baker 92; BgBkCoM; BiDAmM; BioIn 14, 17; CmpEPM; CounME 74, 74A; DcArts; EncFCWM 69, 83; HarEnCM 87; IlEncCM; NewAmDM; NewGrDA 86; NewYTBS 91; PenEncP; RkOn 74*

Piercy, Marge
American. Author
Wrote *Woman on the Edge of Time,* 1976; *Mars and Her Children,* 1992.
b. Mar 31, 1936 in Detroit, Michigan
Source: *AmAu&B; AmWomWr; ArtclWW 2; Benet 87, 96; BenetAL 91; BioIn 12; BlmGWL; ConAu 1AS, 13NR, 21R, 43NR; ConLC 3, 6, 14, 18, 27, 62; ConNov 82, 86, 91, 96; ConPo 70, 75, 80, 85, 91, 96; CurBio 94; CyWA 89; DcLB 120; DrAF 76; DrAP 75; EncSF 93; FemiCLE; FemiWr; GrLiveH; IntAu&W 77; IntWWP 77, 82; InWom SUP; JeAmWW; LegTOT; MajTwCW; MichAu 80; ModAL S2; ModAWP; ModWoWr; NewEScF; OxCAmL 95; OxCTwCP; OxCWoWr 95; RadHan; ScF&FL 1, 92; ScFSB; TwCSFW 81, 86, 91; WhoAm 76, 78, 80, 82, 84, 86, 88, 90, 92, 94, 95, 96, 97; WhoAmW 81, 83, 91, 93, 95, 97; WhoE 91, 93, 95, 97; WhoUSWr 88; WhoWrEP 89, 92, 95; WorAlBi; WorAu 1970; WrDr 76, 80, 82, 84, 86, 88, 90, 92, 94, 96*

Pierne, Gabriel
French. Composer
His eight operas included *Sophie Arnould,* 1927.
b. Aug 16, 1863 in Metz, France
d. Jul 17, 1937 in Ploujean, France
Source: *Baker 78, 84; BioIn 3, 4, 8; CompSN; DcCom&M 79; LegTOT; MusMk; NewAmDM; NewEOp 71; NewGrDM 80; NewOxM; OxCMus; OxDcOp; PenDiMP*

Piero della Francesca
[Pietro di Benedetto dei Franceschi]
Italian. Artist
Major Renaissance painter who developed perspective; court portraits, altarpieces include *Resurrection,* c. 1463.
b. 1420 in Borgo San Sepolcro, Italy
d. Oct 12, 1492 in Borgo San Sepolcro, Italy
Source: *AtlBL; DcArts; DcScB; McGDA; McGEWB; NewCol 75; OxCArt; WhDW*

Pierpoint, Robert Charles
American. Broadcast Journalist
Sunday morning correspondent, CBS News, 1982—; wrote *At the White House,* 1981.

b. May 16, 1925 in Redondo Beach, California
Source: *ConAu 107; EncTwCJ; LesBEnT, 92; WhoAm 76, 78, 80, 82, 84, 86, 88, 90, 92*

Piersall, Jimmy
[James Anthony Piersall]
American. Baseball Player
Outfielder, 1950, 1952-67; wrote of mental breakdown in *Fear Strikes Out,* also made into movie.
b. Nov 14, 1929 in Waterbury, Connecticut
Source: *Ballpl 90; BaseEn 88; BioIn 3, 4, 5, 6, 10, 12, 21; LegTOT; What 5; WhoProB 73*

Pierson, Frank R(omer)
American. Screenwriter
Won Oscar for *Dog Day Afternoon,* 1975.
b. May 12, 1925 in Chappaqua, New York
Source: *ConAu 114, 123, X; FilmgC; IntMPA 77, 84, 92; LesBEnT; NewYTET; VarWW 85; WhoAm 78, 80, 82, 84, 86, 88, 95, 96, 97; WhoEnt 92*

Pihos, Pete(r L)
"Big Dog"
American. Football Player
Five-time all-pro end, Philadelphia, 1947-55; led NFL in receiving three times; Hall of Fame, 1970.
b. Oct 22, 1923 in Orlando, Florida
Source: *BiDAmSp FB; BioIn 17; LegTOT; WhoFtbl 74*

Pike, Gary
[The Lettermen]
American. Singer
Joined group as replacement, late 1960s; younger brother of Jim.
Source: *EncPR&S 74, 89; PenEncP; RkOn 74; RolSEnR 83; WhoRock 81; WhoRocM 82; WhoWest 89*

Pike, James Albert, Bishop
American. Religious Leader, Author
Wrote *Faith of the Church,* 1952, book on Episcopal church teaching.
b. Feb 14, 1913 in Oklahoma City, Oklahoma
d. Sep 2, 1969, Israel
Source: *AmAu&B; Au&Wr 71; BioIn 2, 4, 6, 7, 8, 9, 10, 11, 19; ConAu 1R, 4NR; CurBio 57, 69; DcAmReB 1, 2; EncPaPR 91; LuthC 75; NatCAB 56; RelLAm 91; WhAm 5; WorAl*

Pike, Jim
[The Lettermen]
American. Singer
A founder of group, got its name from his high school football experience; first big hit single: "The Way You Look Tonight," 1961.
b. Nov 6, 1938 in Saint Louis, Missouri
Source: *EncPR&S 74; WhoRock 81; WhoRocM 82*

Pike, Otis Grey
American. Politician
Dem. congressman from NY, 1961-79.
b. Aug 31, 1921 in Riverhead, New York
Source: *BiDrAC; BiDrUSC 89; BioIn 10, 11, 12; BlueB 76; CngDr 77; CurBio 76; NewYTBS 75; PolProf NF; WhoAm 74, 76, 78; WhoAmP 73, 75, 77, 79; WhoE 74, 75, 77; WhoGov 72, 75, 77*

Pike, Zebulon Montgomery
American. Army Officer, Explorer
Led expedition through Southwest, sighting peak in CO named for him, 1806-07.
b. Feb 5, 1779 in Lamberton, New Jersey
d. Apr 27, 1813 in York, Ontario, Canada
Source: *Alli; AmAu&B; AmBi; ApCAB; BenetAL 91; BiAUS; BiDLA; BioIn 1, 2, 3, 4, 5, 6, 7, 8, 9, 15, 17, 18, 19, 20; CyAL 1; DcAmB; DcAmMiB; DcNAA; Drake; EncAAH; EncSoH; HarEnMi; HarEnUS; LinLib S; McGEWB; NatCAB 2; OxCAmH; OxCAmL 65, 83, 95; PenC AM; REnAL; REnAW; TwCBDA; WebAB 74, 79; WebAMB; WhAm HS; WhNaAH; WhWE; WorAl; WorAlBi*

Pilate, Pontius
Roman. Political Leader
Procurator of Judaea, who tried to evade responsibility in trial of Jesus; died after AD 36.
b. fl. 26AD
Source: *Benet 87; BioIn 15; NewCol 75; REn; WorAlBi*

Pile, Frederick Alfred
English. Army Officer
Worked in British War Office 1928-32; directed defense of Suez Canal 1932-1946; renowned for allowing tired infantry men to ride on large guns during WWI.
b. Sep 14, 1884, England
d. Nov 14, 1976 in London, England
Source: *BioIn 11, 17; CurBio 91N; DcNaB 1971; Who 74*

Pilkington, Francis Meredyth
Irish. Children's Author
Noted for Irish fairy tales, legends: *The Three Sorrowful Tales of Erin,* 1965.
b. Jun 16, 1907 in Dublin, Ireland
Source: *Alli; BioIn 9; ConAu P-2; SmATA 4; WrDr 76, 80, 82, 84, 86, 88, 90*

Pillsbury, Charles Alfred
American. Manufacturer
Miller whose new process produced 10,000 barrels of flour a day, 1889, making Pillsbury largest flour mill in world.
b. Dec 3, 1842 in Warner, New Hampshire
d. Sep 17, 1899 in Minneapolis, Minnesota
Source: *ApCAB SUP; BiDAmBL 83; BioIn 18; DcAmB; EncAAH; Entr; McGEWB; WebAB 74, 79; WhAm 1, HS, HSA; WorAl*

Pillsbury, John Sargent
American. Manufacturer, Politician
Miller, who was partner with nephew in C A Pillsbury Co; governor of MN, 1876-82.
b. Jul 29, 1828 in Sutton, New Hampshire
d. Oct 18, 1901 in Minneapolis, Minnesota
Source: *AmBi; ApCAB SUP; BiDrGov 1789; BioIn 1, 4; DcAmB; NatCAB 10, 54; NewCol 75; TwCBDA; WhAm 1, 5; WhAmP*

Pillsbury, John Sargent
American. Manufacturer
Son of Charles A Pillsbury; joined Pillsbury Mills, Inc., 1900; chm., 1932.
b. Dec 6, 1878 in Minneapolis, Minnesota
d. Jan 31, 1968 in West Palm Beach, Florida
Source: *BiDAmBL 83; BioIn 1, 8, 10; NatCAB 54; WhAm 5*

Pillsbury, Philip Winston
American. Manufacturer
Pres., Pillsbury Co., 1940-52; chm., 1952-65.
b. Apr 16, 1903 in Minneapolis, Minnesota
d. Jun 14, 1984 in Minneapolis, Minnesota
Source: *AnObit 1984; BiDAmBL 83; BioIn 7; IntWW 74, 75, 76, 77, 78, 79, 80, 81, 82, 83; NewYTBS 84; St&PR 75; WhAm 8; WhoAm 74, 76, 78, 80, 82, 84*

Pilote, Pierre Paul
Canadian. Hockey Player
Defenseman, 1955-69, mostly with Chicago; won Norris Trophy three times; Hall of Fame, 1975.
b. Dec 11, 1931 in Kenogami, Quebec, Canada
Source: *BioIn 9; HocEn; WhoHcky 73*

Pilou, Jeannette
Egyptian. Opera Singer
Soprano, NY Met. debut, 1967.
Source: *BioIn 8; IntWWM 90; MetOEnc; NewEOp 71; NewGrDM 80*

Pilsudski, Jozef
Polish. Army Officer, Statesman
Overthrew government, exercised supreme power, 1926-35.
b. Dec 5, 1867 in Wilno, Poland
d. May 12, 1935
Source: *BioIn 2, 8, 9, 12, 13, 16, 20, 21; DicTyr; Dis&D; EncTR 91; FacFETw; HisWorL; NewCol 75; PolBiDi; WebBD 83; WhDW; WorAlBi*

Pinay, Antoine
French. Political Leader, Statesman
Mayor, Saint-Chamond, 1929-77; prime minister of France, 1952.
b. Dec 30, 1891
d. Dec 13, 1994 in Saint-Chamond, France
Source: *BiDFrPL; BioIn 2, 3, 4, 5, 7, 9, 17, 20, 21; CurBio 95N; IntWW 74, 75, 76, 77, 78, 79, 80, 81, 82, 83, 89, 91, 93; NewYTBS 94; WhAm 9; Who 74, 82, 83, 85, 88, 90, 92, 94; WhoFr 79; WhoWor 74*

Pincay, Laffit, Jr.
American. Jockey
Won KY Derby, 1984; biggest money winner in thoroughbred racing, 1970-74, 1979.
b. Dec 29, 1946 in Panama City, Panama
Source: *BioIn 9, 10, 12, 13, 14, 15, 21; BioNews 75; ConNews 86-3; LegTOT; NewYTBS 74, 79, 82, 85; WhoAm 84, 86, 88, 90, 92, 94, 95, 96, 97; WhoHisp 92, 94; WhoSpor; WorAl; WorAlBi*

Pinchback, P(inckney) B(enton) S(tewart)
American. Politician, Lawyer
Black acting governor of LA, 1872-73; appointed US senator, 1873, but seat denied him; first black governor in US history.
b. May 10, 1837 in Macon, Georgia
d. Dec 21, 1921 in Washington, District of Columbia
Source: *AmPolLe; ApCAB; BiDrGov 1789; BioIn 5, 6, 8, 9, 10, 12, 13, 20; DcAmB; EncAACR; EncSoH; HarEnUS; InB&W 85; TwCBDA; WhAm 1*

Pinchot, Bronson Alcott
American. Actor
Films include *Beverly Hills Cop,* 1984; star of TV comedy "Perfect Strangers," 1986-93.
b. May 20, 1959 in New York, New York
Source: *BioIn 14, 15, 16; ConTFT 5, 9; IntMPA 92; WhoAm 90; WhoEnt 92; WorAlBi*

Pinchot, Gifford
American. Politician
Reformer governor of PA, 1923-27, 1931-35; forestry, conservation expert, head of Forest Service, 1898-1910.
b. Aug 11, 1865 in Simsbury, Connecticut
d. Oct 4, 1946 in New York, New York
Source: *AmAu&B; AmDec 1900; AmLY; AmPolLe; AmRef; ApCAB X; BiDrGov 1789; BioIn 1, 2, 3, 4, 5, 6, 7, 8, 9, 10, 11, 12, 13, 14, 15, 17, 19, 20; CopCroC; CurBio 46; CyAG; DcAmB S4; DcAmSR; DcAmTB; DcNAA; EncAAH; EncAB-H 1974, 1996; EncEnv; EnvEnc; GayN; HarEnUS; InSci; LegTOT; LinLib S; McGEWB; MorMA; NatCAB 11, 14, 36; NatLAC; NotTwCS; OxCAmH; PolPar; REnAL; REnAW; TwCBDA; WebAB 74, 79; WhAm 2; WhLit; WhNAA*

Pinckney, Charles Cotesworth
American. Statesman
Minister to France, 1796; refused bribe of French officials in XYZ Affair.
b. Feb 25, 1746 in Charleston, South Carolina
d. Aug 16, 1825 in Charleston, South Carolina
Source: *AmBi; AmPolLe; AmRev; ApCAB; BiAUS; BiDSA; BioIn 3, 6, 7, 8, 9, 11, 15, 16; BlkwEAR; CyAG; DcAmB; Drake; EncAR; EncCRAm; EncSoH; HarEnUS; LinLib L, S; NatCAB 2; OxCAmH; PresAR; REn; REnAL; TwCBDA; WebAB 74, 79; WhAm HS; WhAmP; WhAmRev; WorAl*

Pinckney, Darryl
American. Author
Wrote *High Cotton,* 1992.
b. 1953 in Indianapolis, Indiana
Source: *BlkWr 2; ConAu 143; ConLC 76; SchCGBL; WhoAm 96*

Pincus, Gregory
American. Scientist, Physician, Engineer
With John Rock, experimented with progesterone as means of birth control, 1950s; discovered birth control pill, 1954.
b. Apr 9, 1903 in Woodbine, New Jersey
d. Aug 22, 1967 in Boston, Massachusetts
Source: *BioIn 7, 8, 9, 11, 17, 20; CurBio 66, 67; InSci; JeHun; LegTOT; McGMS 80; OxCMed 86; WhAm 4; WorAl; WorAlBi; WorInv*

Pindar
Greek. Poet
Chief medium was choral lyric; set standard for triumphal ode.
b. Sep 4, 518?BC in Thebes, Greece
d. 442?BC
Source: *AncWr; AtlBL; BbD; Benet 87; BiD&SB; CasWL; ClMLC 12; CyWA 58; DcArts; DcEnL; Grk&L; NewC; OxCClL 89; OxCEng 67; PenC CL; RAdv 14, 13-2; RComWL; REn; RfGWoL 95; WhDW; WorAl; WorAlBi*

Pindling, Lynden Oscar
Bahamian. Government Official
First black prime minister of Bahamas, 1967-92.
b. Mar 22, 1930 in Nassau, Bahamas
Source: *BiDLAmC; BioIn 7, 8, 9, 10, 13, 16; CurBio 68; InB&W 80, 85; IntWW 74, 75, 76, 77, 78, 79, 80, 81, 82, 83, 89, 91, 93; NewYTBE 73; Who 74, 82, 83, 85, 88, 90, 92, 94; WhoWor 74, 76, 78, 80, 82, 84, 87, 89, 91, 93, 96*

Pineau, Christian (Paul Francis)
French. Government Official
Hero of French Resistance, World War II; foreign minister, 1956-58.
b. Oct 14, 1904
d. Apr 5, 1995 in Paris, France
Source: *BiDFrPL; BioIn 4, 7, 17, 20, 21; CurBio 95N; HisEWW; IntWW 74, 75, 76, 77, 78, 79, 80, 81, 82, 83, 89, 91, 93; Who 74, 82, 83, 85, 88, 90, 92, 94; WhoFr 79; WhoWor 74, 78*

Pinel, Philippe
French. Physician, Social Reformer
Pioneered humane treatment of insane; established psychiatry as medical field.
b. Apr 20, 1745 in Saint-Andre, France
d. Oct 26, 1826 in Paris, France
Source: *AsBiEn; BiDPsy; BiESc; BiHiMed; BioIn 1, 3, 5, 6, 7, 8, 9, 12, 17, 18; BlkwCE; CopCroC; DcBiPP; DcScB; EncSPD; GaEncPs; InSci; McGEWB; NamesHP; NewCol 75; OxCMed 86; WorAl; WorAlBi*

Pinero, Arthur Wing, Sir
English. Dramatist
Best known for "problem plays:" *The Second Mrs. Tanqueray,* 1896.
b. May 25, 1855 in Islington, England
d. Nov 23, 1934 in London, England
Source: *BbD; Benet 87, 96; BiD&SB; BioIn 1, 2, 4, 5, 8, 9, 10, 11, 13, 14, 16, 17, 20; BlmGEL; BritAu 19; BritPl; CamGEL; CamGLE; CamGWoT; CasWL; CelCen; Chambr 3; CnThe; ConAu 110, 153; CrtSuDr; CyWA 58; DcArts; DcEnA, A; DcLB 10; DcLEL; DcNaB 1931; EncWT; Ent; EvLB; GrBr; GrWrEL DR; HalFC 80, 84, 88; IntDcT 2; LegTOT; LinLib L, S; LngCTC; McGEWD 72, 84; ModBrL; ModWD; NewC; NewCBEL; NotNAT, A, B; OxCAmT 84; OxCEng 67, 85, 95; OxCThe 67, 83; PenC ENG; PlP&P; RAdv 14, 13-2; REn; REnWD; RfGEnL 91; TwCLC 32; VicBrit; WebE&AL; WhDW; WhE&EA; WhLit; WhoLA; WhoStg 1906, 1908; WhScrn 77, 83; WhThe; WorAl; WorAlBi*

Pinero, Miguel
"Mickey"
Puerto Rican. Dramatist, Actor
While in prison for armed robbery, wrote award-winning play *Short Eyes,* 1974.
b. Dec 19, 1946 in Gurabo, Puerto Rico
d. Jun 16, 1988 in New York, New York
Source: *AnObit 1988; BiDHisL; BioIn 13; ConAu 29NR, 61, 125; ConDr 82, 88; ConLC 4, 55; CurBio 83, 88N; DcHiB; HispAmA; HispWr; NewYTBS 74; PlP&P A; WrDr 84, 86, 88*

Piniella, Lou(is Victor)
"Piney"; "Sweet Lou"
American. Baseball Player, Baseball Manager
Outfielder, 1964, 1968-84; had .291 career batting average; manager of NY Yankees, Cincinnati Reds and Seattle Mariners.
b. Aug 28, 1943 in Tampa, Florida
Source: *Ballpl 90; BaseEn 88; BaseReg 87; BiDAmSp Sup; BioIn 12, 13, 14, 15, 17, 19; CurBio 86; NewYTBS 74, 87; WhoAm 86, 88, 92, 94, 95, 96, 97; WhoE 89; WhoMW 92; WhoProB 73; WhoWest 94, 96*

Pinkerton, Allan
American. Detective
Founded Pinkerton Detective Agency, 1850; secret service for US govt., 1861.
b. Aug 25, 1819 in Glasgow, Scotland
d. Jul 1, 1884 in Chicago, Illinois
Source: *Alli SUP; AmAu&B; AmBi; AmJust; ApCAB; BenetAL 91; BiDAmBL 83; BiD&SB; BioIn 1, 6, 7, 8, 9, 10, 11, 12, 17, 18, 21; CivWDc; DcAmAu; DcAmB; DcAmSR; DcNAA; EncAB-H 1974, 1996; EncAI&E; EncMys; HarEnUS; LegTOT; LinLib S; McGEWB; NatCAB 3; OxCAmH; OxCAmL 65, 83, 95; OxCLaw; REnAL; TwCBDA; WebAB 74, 79; WhAm HS; WhCiWar; WhDW; WorAl; WorAlBi*

Pinkett, Jada
American. Actor
Appeared on TV's "A Different World," 1992-93; movies include *Menace II Society,* 1993.
b. c. 1971 in Baltimore, Maryland
Source: *ConBlB 10; WhoAfA 96*

Pink Floyd
[Syd Barrett; Jon Carin; Rachel Furay; Dave Gilmour; Nick Mason; Scott Page; Guy Pratt; Tim Renwick; Margret Taylor; Gary Wallis; Roger Waters; Rick Wright]
English. Music Group
Album *Dark Side of the Moon,* 1973, was on *Billboard* list of top LPs for over 500 weeks.
Source: *BioIn 17, 18; ConLC 35; ConMuA 80A; ConMus 2; DcArts; EncPR&S 89; EncRk 88; EncRkSt; FacFETw; HarEnR 86; IlEncRk; NewAmDM; OxCPMus; PenEncP; RkOn 78, 84; RolSEnR 83; WhoRock 81; WhoRocM 82*

Pinkham, Lydia Estes
American. Manufacturer
Invented home remedy "Vegetable Compound," 1876.
b. Feb 19, 1819 in Lynn, Massachusetts
d. May 17, 1883 in Lynn, Massachusetts
Source: *AmBi; BiDAmBL 83; BioIn 15; DcAmB; DcAmMeB 84; EncAB-H 1996; GrLiveH; InWom SUP; LibW; NotAW; WebAB 74, 79; WhAm HS; WomFir; WorAl*

Pinkney, William
American. Diplomat
Influential in passage of Missouri Compromise, 1820; senator from MD, 1819-22, renowned for eloquence.
b. Mar 17, 1764 in Annapolis, Maryland
d. Dec 25, 1822 in Washington, District of Columbia
Source: *Alli; AmBi; ApCAB; BiAUS; BiDrAC; BiDrUSC 89; BiDrUSE 71, 89; BiDSA; BioIn 1, 7, 8, 10, 15, 16; CyAG; CyAL 1; DcAmB; DcAmDH 80, 89; Drake; EncSoH; HarEnUS; NatCAB 5; OxCAmH; OxCSupC; TwCBDA; WebAB 74, 79; WhAm HS; WhAmP*

Pinkwater, Daniel Manus
American. Children's Author, Illustrator
Books include *I Was a Second Grade Werewolf,* 1983; *Attila the Pun,* 1981.
b. Nov 15, 1941 in Memphis, Tennessee
Source: *Au&Arts 1; AuBYP 3; BioIn 11, 15, 17, 19; ConAu 12NR, 29R, 38NR, X; ConLC 4, 35; FifBJA; IntAu&W 77; MajAI; SJGFanW; SmATA 3, 3AS, 8, 46, 76; TwCChW 89; TwCSFW 91; TwCYAW; WhoAm 86, 88, 90, 92; WhoE 77; WrDr 90, 92, 94, 96*

Pinnock, Trevor David
English. Conductor, Musician
Founder, conductor and soloist of the English Concert, Britain's leading baroque ensemble; group's prominent recording *The Four Seasons,* 1979; established NYC's Classical Band, 1989.
b. Dec 16, 1946 in Canterbury, England
Source: *Baker 84; BioIn 16; CanWW 31; IntWW 91; IntWWM 90; NewAmDM; PenDiMP; Who 92; WhoEnt 92; WhoWor 91*

Pinochet Ugarte, Augusto
Chilean. Political Leader
President of Chile, 1973-90; ousted Allende in bloody coup; succeeded by Patrici o Aylwin.
b. Nov 25, 1915 in Valparaiso, Chile
Source: *BiDLAmC; BioIn 10, 11, 12, 13, 14, 15, 16; ColdWar 1, 2; CurBio 74; DcCPSAm; EncWB; FacFETw; IntWW 74, 76, 77, 78, 79, 80, 81, 82, 83, 89, 91, 93; IntYB 78, 79, 80, 81, 82; NewYTBE 73; NewYTBS 78; WhoWor 78, 80, 82, 84, 87, 89, 91, 93, 95, 96, 97; WorAl; WorAlBi*

Pinsent, Gordon Edward
Canadian. Actor, Writer
Wrote, starred in film *The Rowdyman,* 1969.
b. Jul 12, 1930 in Grand Falls, Newfoundland, Canada
Source: *BioIn 12, 15; CanWW 31, 70, 79, 80, 81, 83, 89; FilmgC; HalFC 88; IntvTCA 2; OxCCanT; WhoCanL 87; WhoHol A*

Pinson, Vada Edward
American. Baseball Player
Outfielder, 1958-75, mostly with Cincinnati; had .286 lifetime batting average, 2,757 hits.
b. Aug 8, 1938 in Memphis, Tennessee
d. Oct 21, 1995 in Oakland, California
Source: *Ballpl 90; BaseEn 88; BiDAmSp BB; BioIn 5, 6, 15, 16; InB&W 80; WhoAfA 96; WhoAm 74; WhoBlA 77, 80, 85, 90, 92, 94; WhoProB 73*

Pinter, Harold
English. Dramatist
Wrote *The Dumb Waiter,* 1957; screenplay *The French Lieutenant's Woman,* 1981.
b. Oct 10, 1930 in London, England
Source: *Au&Wr 71; Benet 87, 96; BiDFilm 94; BiE&WWA; BioIn 6, 7, 8, 9, 10, 11, 12, 13, 15, 16, 17, 18, 19, 20; BlmGEL; BlueB 76; BritWr S1; CamGEL; CamGLE; CamGWoT; CasWL; CelR; CnDBLB 8; CnThe; ConAu 5R, 33NR; ConBrDr; ConDr 73, 77, 82, 88, 93; ConLC 1, 3, 6, 9, 11, 15, 27, 58, 73; ConPo 70; ConTFT 2, 11; CroCD; CrtSuDr; CurBio 63; CyWA 89; DcArts; DcFM; DcLB 13; DcLEL 1940; EncEurC; EncWL, 2, 3; EncWT; Ent; FacFETw; FilmEn; FilmgC; GrWrEL DR; HalFC 80, 84, 88; IntAu&W 76, 77, 86, 89, 91, 93; IntDcF 1-4, 2-4; IntDcT 2; IntMPA 84, 86, 88, 92, 94, 96; IntvTCA 2; IntWW 74, 75, 76, 77, 78, 79, 80, 81, 82, 83, 89, 91, 93; IntWWP 77; LegTOT; LinLib L; LngCEL; LngCTC; MagSWL; MajMD 1; MajTwCW; MakMC; McGEWB; McGEWD 72, 84; MiSFD 9; ModBrL, S1, S2; ModWD; NewC; NewYTBE 71; NewYTBS 79; NotNAT; OxCAmT 84; OxCEng 85, 95; OxCFilm; OxCThe 67, 83; OxCTwCP; PenC ENG; PlP&P; RAdv 14, 13-2; RComWL; REn; REnWD; RfGEnL 91; RGTwCWr; TwCWr; WebE&AL; WhDW; Who 74, 82, 83, 85, 88, 90, 92, 94; WhoAm 80, 82, 84, 86, 88, 90, 92, 94, 95, 96, 97; WhoEnt 92; WhoHol 92; WhoThe 72, 77, 81; WhoTwCL; WhoWor 74, 78, 80, 82, 84, 87, 89, 91, 93, 95, 96, 97; WorAl; WorAlBi; WorAu 1950; WorEFlm; WorLitC; WrDr 76, 80, 82, 84, 86, 88, 90, 92, 94, 96*

Pintuicchio
[Betto di Biago]
Italian. Artist
Umbrian school historical painter; did Sistine Chapel frescoes with Perugino.
b. 1454 in Perugia, Italy
d. Dec 11, 1513 in Siena, Italy
Source: *AtlBL; McGDA; NewCol 75; OxCArt*

Pinza, Ezio
[Fortunato Pinza]
American. Opera Singer
Celebrated bass; NY Met., 1926-48; starred in Broadway's *South Pacific,* 1949.
b. May 18, 1892 in Rome, Italy
d. May 9, 1957 in Stamford, Connecticut
Source: *Baker 78, 84, 92; BiDAmM; BioIn 1, 2, 3, 4, 5, 6, 8, 10, 11, 14, 18, 21; BriBkM 80; CmOp; CmpEPM; CurBio 41, 53, 57; DcAmB S6; EncMT; FacFETw; FilmEn; FilmgC; ForYSC; IntDcOp; LegTOT; MetOEnc; MusSN; NatCAB 46; NewAmDM; NewEOp 71; NewGrDA 86; NewGrDM 80; NotNAT B; OxCAmT 84; OxCPMus; OxDcOp; PenDiMP; PlP&P; WhAm 3; WhoHol B; WhScrn 74, 77, 83; WorAl; WorAlBi*

Pio da Pietrelcina, Francesco Forgione, Father
[Padre Pio]
Italian. Religious Figure
Capuchin monk believed to have been marked by *stigmata,* or stains of crucified Christ, 1918.
b. May 25, 1887 in Pietrelcina, Italy

d. Sep 23, 1968 in San Giovanni Rotondo, Italy
Source: *BioIn 8, 11; EncO&P 1, 2, 3; EncPaPR 91*

Pious, Minerva
American. Actor
Played Mrs. Nussbaum on radio show "Allen's Alley," 1933-49.
b. 1909 in Odessa, Russia
d. Mar 16, 1979 in New York, New York
Source: *BioIn 8, 11, 15; EncAFC; FunnyW; HalFC 80, 84, 88; InWom SUP; LegTOT*

Piozzi, Hester Lynch Salisbury
[Hester Thrale]
English. Diarist
Close friend of Samuel Johnson; published their correspondence in *Anecdotes of the Late Samuel Johnson,* 1786.
b. Jan 16, 1741 in Bodvel, Wales
d. May 2, 1821 in Clifton, England
Source: *Alli; BiD&SB; BiDLA; BioIn 17, 18, 19, 20; BritAu; CasWL; ChhPo, S2; DcEnA; DcEnL; DcEuL; EvLB; NewC; OxCEng 67; PenC ENG*

Piper, H(enry) Beam
American. Author
Wrote science fiction tales: *Little Fuzzy,* 1962; *Space Viking,* 1963.
b. 1904 in Altoona, Pennsylvania
d. Nov 11, 1964
Source: *ConAu 117; DcLB 8*

Piper, William Thomas
American. Aircraft Manufacturer
Designed Piper Cub airplane, 1931.
b. Jan 8, 1881 in Knapps Creek, New York
d. Jan 15, 1970 in Lock Haven, Pennsylvania
Source: *BioIn 1, 2, 5, 7, 8, 9, 11; CurBio 46, 70; DcAmB S8; EncAB-A 36; InSci; LegTOT; NatCAB 56; WhAm 5; WorAl*

Pipher, Mary
American. Author, Psychologist
Author of *Reviving Ophelia,* 1994; *The Shelter of Each Other,* 1996.
b. c. 1948 in Beaver City, Nebraska
Source: *News 96*

Pipp, Wally
[Walter Clement Pipp]
American. Baseball Player
First baseman, 1913-28; led league in home runs, 1916, 1917; best known as player Lou Gehrig replaced in NY lineup, 1925.
b. Feb 17, 1893 in Chicago, Illinois
d. Jan 11, 1965 in Grand Rapids, Michigan
Source: *Ballpl 90; BaseEn 88; BioIn 4, 7, 21; WhoProB 73*

Pippen, Scottie
American. Basketball Player
Chicago Bulls forward, 1987—; member of US Olympic Dream Team, 1992.
b. Sep 25, 1965 in Hamburg, Arkansas
Source: *BioIn 15, 18; CurBio 94; LegTOT; News 92, 92-2; WhoAm 92, 94, 95, 96, 97; WhoBlA 92; WhoMW 92, 93, 96; WhoSpor; WhoWor 95, 96, 97*

Pippin, Horace
American. Artist
Self-taught primitive painter, one of America's leading black artists; did *The End of the War: Starting Home,* 1931.
b. Feb 22, 1888 in West Chester, Pennsylvania
d. Jul 6, 1946 in West Chester, Pennsylvania
Source: *AfrAmAl 6; AfroAA; AmFkP; BioIn 1, 2, 4, 6, 8, 9, 11, 12, 13, 14, 19, 20, 21; CurBio 45, 47; DcAmArt; DcAmB S4; DcAmNB; DcTwCCu 5; FolkA 87; InB&W 80, 85; McGDA; McGEWB; MusmAFA; NegAl 76, 83, 89; OxCTwCA; WhAmArt 85*

Piquet, Nelson
Brazilian. Auto Racer
Formula One racer; world champion, 1981.
b. Aug 17, 1952 in Brasilia, Brazil
Source: *BioIn 12, 15, 16; IntWW 91, 93; WhoWor 82*

Pirandello, Luigi
Italian. Author, Dramatist
Awarded Nobel Prize in literature, 1934; created "theater within the theater."
b. Jun 28, 1867 in Agrigento, Sicily, Italy
d. Dec 10, 1936 in Rome, Italy
Source: *AtlBL; Benet 87, 96; BioIn 1, 2, 4, 5, 7, 8, 9, 10, 12, 14, 15, 20; CamGWoT; CasWL; ClDMEL 47, 80; CnMD; CnMWL; CnThe; ConAu 104, 153; CyWA 58; DcArts; DcEuL; DcItL 1, 2; Dis&D; DramC 5; EncWL 2, 3; EncWT; Ent; EuWr 8; EvEuW; FacFETw; GrFLW; IntDcT 2; ItaFilm; LegTOT; LinLib L; LngCTC; MagSWL; MajMD 2; MakMC; McGEWB; McGEWD 72, 84; ModRL; ModWD; NewC; NobelP; NotNAT A, B; Novels; OxCAmT 84; OxCEng 67, 85, 95; OxCThe 67, 83; PenC EUR; PlP&P, A; RAdv 14, 13-2; RComWL; REn; REnWD; RfGShF; RfGWoL 95; ShSCr 22; TheaDir; TwCA, SUP; TwCLC 4, 29; TwCWr; WhDW; WhE&EA; WhoNob, 90, 95; WhoTwCL; WhThe; WorAl; WorAlBi; WorLitC*

Piranesi, Giovanni Battista
Italian. Engraver
Imaginary Prisons, 16 large plates, 1745, considered his masterpieces.
b. Oct 4, 1720 in Venice, Italy
d. Nov 1, 1778 in Rome, Italy
Source: *AntBDN G; AtlBL; Benet 87, 96; BioIn 1, 2, 6, 8, 9, 10, 11, 13; BlkwCE; DcCathB; DcD&D; EncEnl; IntDcAA 90; IntDcAr; LinLib S; MacEA; McGDA; McGEWB; NotNAT B; OxCArt; OxCEng 85, 95; OxDcArt; PenDiDA 89; WhoArch*

Pire, Dominique
Belgian. Clergy
Won Nobel Peace Prize, 1958, for work with European refugees.
b. Feb 10, 1910 in Dinant, Belgium
d. Jan 30, 1969 in Louvain, Belgium
Source: *LinLib S; WhoNob, 90, 95*

Piret, Edgar L
American. Scientist
Chemical engineer, developed process for quick-dried portable food used by army's K-Combat Rations, WW II.
b. Jul 1, 1910 in Winnipeg, Manitoba, Canada
d. Oct 2, 1987 in Cambridge, Massachusetts
Source: *AmMWSc 73P, 79, 82, 86; USBiR 74; WhoAm 82; WhoGov 72, 75; WhoTech 82, 84, 89*

Pirner, Dave
[Soul Asylum]
American. Singer, Songwriter, Musician
Debut album *Say What You Will,* 1984.
b. Apr 16, 1964 in Green Bay, Wisconsin

Pirsig, Robert M(aynard)
American. Philosopher
Wrote *Zen and the Art of Motorcycle Maintenance,* 1974, rev. 1984; *Lila: An Inquiry into Morals,* 1991.
b. Sep 6, 1928 in Minneapolis, Minnesota
Source: *ConAu 42NR, 53; ConLC 4, 6, 73; ConPopW; IntAu&W 77; OxCAmL 95; WhoAm 76, 78, 80, 82, 84, 86, 88, 90, 92, 94, 95, 96, 97; WhoUSWr 88; WhoWrEP 89, 92, 95; WorAu 1985*

Pisano, Andrea
[Andrea da Pontedera]
Italian. Architect, Sculptor
Noted for famed bronze doors on baptistery, Florence Cathedral, 1330-36.
b. 1290 in Pisa, Italy
d. 1348 in Orvieto, Papal States
Source: *AtlBL; BioIn 14, 15; DcArts; IntDcAA 90; McGDA; NewCol 75; OxCArt; OxDcArt; REn*

Pisano, Antonio
Italian. Artist
Int'l. Gothic-style painter, medalist; with da Fabriano executed frescoes of Venice's Doge's Palace.
b. 1395 in Pisa, Italy
d. 1455 in Rome, Italy
Source: *BioIn 9, 10; OxCArt; OxCDecA*

Pisano, Giovanni
Italian. Architect
Founded Italian Gothic sculpture; chief architect, Pisa, Sienna cathedrals; son of Nicola.
b. 1250 in Pisa, Italy
d. 1314
Source: *AtlBL; MacEA; McGDA; OxCArt*

Pisano, Nicola
Italian. Sculptor
Earliest great Italian sculptor; executed hexagonal marble pulpit, Pisa Baptistery.
b. 1220
d. 1283
Source: *AtlBL; BioIn 15; McGDA; OxCArt*

Piscopo, Joe
[Joseph Charles Piscopo]
American. Comedian
Repertory player, ''Saturday Night Live,'' 1980-84; in film *Johnny Dangerously*, 1984.
b. Jun 17, 1951 in Passaic, New Jersey
Source: *BioIn 13, 19, 20; CelR 90; ConTFT 3; IntMPA 92, 94, 96; LegTOT; WhoAm 84, 86, 88, 90, 92; WhoCom; WhoEnt 92; WhoHol 92; WhoTelC*

Pisier, Marie-France
French. Actor
Films include *Other Side of Midnight*, 1977; *Cousin Cousine*, 1976.
b. May 10, 1946 in Da Lat, Vietnam
Source: *BioIn 11, 17; ConTFT 8; FilmEn; HalFC 84, 88; IntMPA 92*

Pisis, Filippo Tibertelli de
Italian. Artist
Painted architecture, landscapes, still lifes; influenced by French impressionism.
b. May 11, 1896 in Ferrara, Italy
d. Apr 2, 1956 in Milan, Italy
Source: *BioIn 2, 4; McGDA; OxCTwCA*

Pissaro, Lucien
English. Artist
One of most original book designers of all time; painted modified form of *pointillisme*.
b. Feb 20, 1863 in Paris, France
d. Jul 10, 1944 in Chard, England
Source: *DcBrAr 1; DcNaB 1941; OxCArt; OxCTwCA; PhDcTCA 77*

Pissarro, Camille Jacob
French. Artist
Impressionist painter known for Parisian street scenes, views of Normandy countryside, sunlit village road scenes.
b. Jul 10, 1831 in Saint Thomas, Danish West Indies
d. Nov 13, 1903 in Paris, France
Source: *AtlBL; BioIn 1, 2, 3, 4, 5, 6, 7, 9, 10, 11; REn*

Piston, Walter
American. Musician, Composer
Won Pulitzers, 1948, 1961 for symphonies.
b. Jan 20, 1894 in Rockland, Maine
d. Nov 12, 1976 in Belmont, Massachusetts
Source: *Baker 78, 84; BiDAmM; BioIn 1, 2, 3, 4, 5, 6, 7, 8, 10, 11, 12, 14; BriBkM 80; CelR; CompSN, SUP; ConAu 69; CurBio 48, 61, 77N; DcCM; DcCom&M 79; FacFETw; IntWW 74, 75, 76; IntWWM 77; LegTOT; MusMk; NewAmDM; NewGrDA 86; NewGrDM 80; NewOxM; NewYTBS 76; OxCAmL 65; OxCMus; PenDiMP A; REnAL; WebAB 74; WhAm 7; Who 74; WhoAm 74, 76; WhoMus 72; WhoWor 74; WorAl; WorAlBi*

Pitcher, Molly
[Mary Ludwig Hays McCauley]
American. Historical Figure
Earned nickname carrying water for soldiers in Battle of Monmouth, 1778.
b. Oct 13, 1750 in Trenton, New Jersey
d. Jan 22, 1832 in Carlisle, Pennsylvania
Source: *AmBi; DcAmB; InWom; NotAW; OxCAmL 65; REn; TwCBDA; WebAB 74; WhAm HS*

Pitkin, Walter Boughton
American. Author, Educator
Wrote best seller *Life Begins at Forty*, 1932.
b. Feb 6, 1878 in Ypsilanti, Michigan
d. Jan 25, 1953 in Palo Alto, California
Source: *AmAu&B; BioIn 3, 4; CurBio 41, 53; DcAmB S5; InSci; OxCAmL 65; REnAL; TwCA, SUP; WebAB 74, 79; WhAm 3; WorAl*

Pitlik, Noam
American. Director
Won Emmy, 1979, for directing ''Barney Miller.''
b. Nov 4, 1932 in Philadelphia, Pennsylvania
Source: *VarWW 85; WhoAm 80, 82; WhoHol 92; WhoWest 82*

Pitman, Isaac
English. Inventor
Invented phonographic shorthand, 1837.
b. Jan 4, 1813 in Trowbridge, England
d. Jan 12, 1897 in Somerset, England
Source: *Alli; BioIn 6, 8, 12; DcBiPP; DcEnL; DcNaB S1; InSci; LegTOT; LinLib L, S; LngCTC; NewCBEL; OxCEng 67, 85, 95; WhDW*

Pitman, James
[Isaac James Pitman]
English. Politician, Business Executive
Developed 42-character phonetic alphabet for teaching children to read.
b. Aug 14, 1901 in London, England
d. Sep 1, 1985
Source: *AnObit 1985; BioIn 15; BlueB 76; ConAu 117, P-2; DcNaB 1981; IntAu&W 91; IntWW 74, 75, 76, 77, 78, 79, 80, 81, 82, 83; IntYB 78, 79, 80, 81, 82; SmATA 46N; WhE&EA; Who 74, 82, 83, 85; WhoWor 74, 76, 78; WrDr 76, 80, 82, 84, 86, 88*

Pitney, Arthur
American. Inventor
Invented postage meter; with Walter Bowes formed co. to manufacture them, 1920.
b. 1871
d. 1933
Source: *Entr*

Pitney, Gene
American. Singer, Songwriter
Pop, rock balladeer; wrote ''Hello Mary Lou,'' for Rick Nelson, 1961; had number two hit single''Only Love Can Break a Heart,'' 1962.
b. Feb 17, 1941 in Rockville, Connecticut
Source: *AmPS A; EncPR&S 89; EncRk 88; EncRkSt; HarEnR 86; LegTOT; NewGrDA 86; OxCPMus; PenEncP; RkOn 74; RolSEnR 83; WhoRock 81; WhoRocM 82; WorAl; WorAlBi*

Pitre, Didier
''Cannonball''; ''Flying Frenchman''; ''Pit''
Canadian. Hockey Player
Defenseman, Montreal, 1917-23; Hall of Fame, 1962.
b. 1884 in Sault Ste. Marie, Ontario, Canada
d. Jul 29, 1934
Source: *HocEn; WhoHcky 73*

Pitrone, Jean Maddern
American. Author
Books include *The Touch of His Hand*, 1970; *The Dodges: Auto Family Fortune and Misfortune*, 1981.
b. Dec 20, 1920 in Ishpeming, Michigan
Source: *AuBYP 2S, 3; BioIn 9; ConAu 8NR, 17R; ForWC 70; SmATA 4; WhoAmW 74, 75, 83, 91; WhoMW 84; WrDr 76, 80, 82, 84, 86, 88, 90, 92, 94, 96*

Pitseolak, Peter
Canadian. Photographer
Photographed his people, the Inuk, from the 1930s to the 1970s.
b. 1902
d. 1973
Source: *BioIn 19, 21; ConAu 93; NotNaAm*

Pitt, Brad
[William Bradley Pitt]
American. Actor
Appeared in *Interview with the Vampire*, 1994 and *Legends of the Fall*, 1995.
b. Dec 18, 1964 in Shawnee, Oklahoma
Source: *ConTFT 10; CurBio 96; LegTOT; News 95, 95-2; WhoAm 94, 95*

Pitt, David Thomas
English. Politician, Physician
One of the earliest campaigners for civil rights in Britain; president, British

Medical Associaiton, 1985-86; member of House of Lords, 1975-94.
b. Oct 3, 1913 in Saint David's, Grenada
d. Dec 18, 1994 in London, England
Source: *BioIn 20; ConBlB 10; Who 74*

Pitt, Percy
English. Conductor
Led British Grand Opera syndicate, 1907-28.
b. Jan 4, 1870 in London, England
d. Nov 23, 1932 in London, England
Source: *Baker 78, 84, 92; CmOp; NewEOp 71; OxDcOp; PenDiMP*

Pitt, William, the Younger
"The Younger Pitt"
English. Political Leader, Author
Often considered Britain's greatest prime minister, 1783-1801, 1804-06; led England during French aggression.
b. May 28, 1759 in Hayes, England
d. Jan 23, 1806 in Putney, England
Source: *Alli; ApCAB; McGEWB; NewC; NewCol 75; REn*

Pittman, Robert W(arren)
American. TV Executive
Responsible for planning, developing MTV, cable music network.
b. Dec 28, 1953 in Jackson, Mississippi
Source: *ConNews 85-1; LesBEnT 92; WhoAm 84, 86, 88, 90, 92, 94, 95, 96; WhoE 89, 93, 95, 97; WhoEmL 87, 91; WhoEnt 92; WhoFI 85, 87, 92, 94*

Pitts, Zasu
[Eliza Susan Pitts]
American. Actor
Comedienne in over 100 films, 1917-63, including *Life With Father,* 1947.
b. Jan 3, 1900 in Parsons, Kansas
d. Jun 7, 1963 in Hollywood, California
Source: *BiDFilm; BioIn 3, 4, 6; Film 1; FilmgC; ForYSC; IntDcF 1-3; InWom, SUP; JoeFr; MotPP; MovMk; OxCFilm; ThFT; TwYS; Vers A; WhoHol B; WhScrn 74, 77; WhThe; WorEFlm*

Pitz, Henry Clarence
American. Illustrator
Illustrated over 160 books: *Treasyre Island,* 1954.
b. Jun 16, 1895 in Philadelphia, Pennsylvania
d. Nov 26, 1976 in Philadelphia, Pennsylvania
Source: *AmAu&B; BioIn 1, 2, 3, 4, 5, 6, 8, 9, 11, 12, 13; ChhPo, S1, S3; ConAu 9R, 69; ConICB; IlrAm 1880, E; IlsBYP; IlsCB 1744, 1946, 1957; MorJA; NewYTBS 76; OxCChiL; SmATA 4, 24N; WhAm 7; WhAmArt 85; WhoAm 74, 76; WhoAmA 73, 76, 78N, 80N, 82N, 84N, 86N, 89N, 91N, 93N; WrDr 76, 80*

Pius IX, Pope
[Giovanni Maria Mastai-Ferretti]
"Pio Nono"
Italian. Religious Leader
In longest pontificate (1846-78), convened First Vatican Council, defined dogma of Immaculate Conception, centralized authority in Vatican.
b. May 13, 1792 in Senigallia, Italy
d. Feb 7, 1878 in Rome, Italy
Source: *BioIn 14, 17, 20; DcCathB; McGEWB; NewCol 75; WebBD 83*

Pius X, Pope
[Giuseppe Melchiorre Sarto]
Italian. Religious Leader
Widely venerated pope, 1903-14; known for staunch opposition to Modernism, pioneering liturgical changes.
b. Jun 2, 1835 in Riese, Italy
d. Aug 20, 1914 in Rome, Italy
Source: *McGEWB; NewCol 75; WebBD 83*

Pius XI, Pope
[Ambrogio Damiano Achille Ratti]
Italian. Religious Leader
Pope, 1922-39; best known for negotiating Lateran Treaty, 1929, which established Vatican's independence from Italy; also condemned communism, Nazism, promoted missions.
b. May 31, 1857 in Desio, Italy
d. Feb 10, 1939 in Rome, Italy
Source: *DcCathB; McGEWB; WebBD 83*

Pius XII, Pope
[Eugenio Maria Giuseppi Giovanni Pacelli]
Italian. Religious Leader
During 1939-58 pontificate, opposed communism, defined dogma of Assumption; maintained neutrality in WW II.
b. Mar 2, 1876 in Rome, Italy
d. Oct 9, 1958 in Rome, Italy
Source: *BioIn 10; CurBio 41, 50, 58; DcCathB; HisEWW; McGEWB; WebBD 83*

Pivot, Bernard
French. Journalist, TV Personality
TV host of the French literary talk show "Apostrophes," 1975-90.
b. May 5, 1935 in Lyons, France
Source: *BioIn 15; CurBio 90; IntAu&W 89, 91, 93; IntWW 89, 91, 93; WhoFr 79*

Pizarro, Francisco
Spanish. Conqueror
Defeated Incas; founded capital of Lima, Peru, 1535.
b. 1470 in Trujilo, Spain
d. Jun 26, 1541 in Lima, Peru
Source: *ApCAB; Benet 87, 96; BioIn 1, 3, 4, 5, 6, 7, 8; Dis&D; Drake; EncCRAm; EncLatA; GenMudB; LinLib S; REn; WebBD 83; WhAm HS; WhDW*

Pizzetti, Ildebrando
Italian. Composer
Operas include *Fra Gherardo,* 1928.
b. Sep 20, 1880 in Parma, Italy
d. Feb 13, 1968 in Rome, Italy
Source: *Baker 78, 84, 92; BioIn 2, 3, 4, 6, 8, 13; CmOp; CompSN; DcCM; DcCom&M 79; DcFM; IntDcOp; LegTOT; MetOEnc; NewAmDM; NewEOp 71; NewGrDM 80; NewGrDO; NewOxM; OxCFilm; OxCMus; OxDcOp; PenDiMP A; WhAm 4A; WorEFlm*

Pizzolato, Orlando
Italian. Track Athlete
Won NY Marathon, 1984, 1985.
b. 1958?
Source: *BioIn 14, 15; NewYTBS 85, 86*

Place, Francis
English. Political Activist
Influential, radical reformer; early advocate of birth control; instrumental in passage of Reform Bill, 1832, legalization of labor unions.
b. Oct 3, 1771 in London, England
d. Jan 1, 1854 in London, England
Source: *Alli; BioIn 4, 9, 10, 16; BritAu 19; CyEd; DcNaB; LuthC 75; NewCBEL; VicBrit*

Place, Mary Kay
American. Actor
Starred in *The Big Chill,* 1983; won Emmy for "Mary Hartman, Mary Hartman," 1977.
b. Sep 23, 1947 in Tulsa, Oklahoma
Source: *ASCAP 80; BioIn 14; ConTFT 3; EncFCWM 83; HarEnCM 87; IntMPA 86, 88, 92, 94, 96; LegTOT; VarWW 85; WhoAm 86, 90; WhoEnt 92; WhoHol 92*

Placzek, Adolf K(urt)
American. Editor
Books on architecture include *The Macmillan Encyclopedia of Architects,* 1982; *The Buildings of the United States,* 1986.
b. Mar 9, 1913 in Vienna, Austria
Source: *BiDrLUS 70; BioIn 5; ConAu 112; DrAS 74H, 78H, 82H; WhoAm 74, 76, 78, 80, 82, 84, 86, 88, 90, 92, 94, 95, 96, 97; WhoAmA 78, 80, 82, 84, 86, 89, 91, 93; WhoE 86; WhoLibS 66*

Plage, Dieter
German. Filmmaker
Wildlife filmmaker; brought attention to African conservation issues.
d. Apr 3, 1993
Source: *BioIn 18, 19; NewYTBS 93*

Plain, Belva
American. Author
Wrote *Evergreen,* 1978; *Random Winds,* 1980.
b. Oct 9, 1919 in New York, New York
Source: *BestSel 89-4; ConAu 14NR, 29NR, 53NR, 81; ConPopW; DrAPF 91; IntAu&W 91; LegTOT; SmATA 62; WhoAm 95, 96, 97; WhoAmW 95, 97; WrDr 82, 86, 92*

Planck, Max Karl Ernst Ludwig
German. Physicist
Pioneer of modern physics who developed quantum theory, 1900-01; won 1918 Nobel Prize.

b. Apr 23, 1858 in Kiel, Germany
d. Oct 4, 1947 in Gottingen, Germany
Source: *AsBiEn; BiESc; CamDcSc; ConAu 115; DcScB; Dis&D; FacFETw; LarDcSc; McGEWB; OxCGer 76; REn; WhAm 4; WhDW; WhoNob, 90, 95; WorAl*

Plancon, Pol-Henri
French. Opera Singer
Celebrated bass, NY Met., 1893-1908; noted as Mephistopheles.
b. Jun 12, 1854 in Fumay, France
d. Aug 11, 1914 in Paris, France
Source: *Baker 84; NewEOp 71*

Planinc, Milka
Yugoslav. Political Leader
First female prime minister of Yugoslavia, May 1982-83; received many decorations for yrs. of political service.
b. Nov 21, 1924 in Drnis, Yugoslavia
Source: *BioIn 18; IntDcWB; IntWW 83, 89, 91, 93; WhoSocC 78; WhoSoCE 89; WhoWor 82, 84, 87*

Plank, Eddie
[Edward Stewart Plank]
"Gettysburg Eddie"
American. Baseball Player
Pitcher, 1901-17, mostly with Philadelphia; had 327 career wins, 69 shutouts; Hall of Fame, 1946.
b. Aug 31, 1875 in Gettysburg, Pennsylvania
d. Feb 24, 1926 in Gettysburg, Pennsylvania
Source: *Ballpl 90; BiDAmSp BB; BioIn 2, 3, 7, 14, 15, 17; LegTOT; WhoProB 73; WhoSpor*

Planquette, Jean(-Robert)
French. Composer
Noted for operetta *The Chimes of Normandy,* 1877.
b. Jul 31, 1848 in Paris, France
d. Jan 28, 1903 in Paris, France
Source: *Baker 78, 84; NewEOp 71*

Plant, Robert Anthony
[Honeydrippers; Led Zeppelin]
English. Singer, Songwriter
With hard-rock group Led Zeppelin since 1968; solo albums include *Shaken 'n' Stirred,* 1985; *Now and Zen,* 1988.
b. Aug 20, 1948 in Bromwich, England
Source: *ASCAP 80; BioIn 10, 13, 14, 16; BkPepl; ConMus 2; EncPR&S 89; NewYTBS 85; RkOn 85; WhoAm 80, 82, 84, 86, 88, 92, 94; WhoEnt 92; WhoRocM 82*

Plante, Jacques
[Joseph Jacques Omer Plante]
"Jake the Snake"
Canadian. Hockey Player
Goalie, 1952-75, mostly with Montreal; first to wear mask in game, 1959; won Vezina Trophy seven times; Hall of Fame, 1978.
b. Feb 17, 1929 in Shawinigan, Quebec, Canada
d. Feb 27, 1986 in Geneva, Switzerland
Source: *BioIn 5, 8, 9, 10, 11, 12, 14, 21; ConAu 108, 118; FacFETw; HocEn; LegTOT; NewYTBS 86; WhoHcky 73; WhoSpor; WorAl; WorAlBi*

Plantin, Christophe
French. Printer, Publisher
Noted for *Polyglot Bible,* 1569-72; books famed for accuracy, typography.
b. 1514
d. 1589
Source: *BioIn 5, 6, 11; ChhPo; DcBiPP; DcCathB; InSci; NewCol 75; NewOxM; OxCFr; WebBD 83; WhDW*

Plasmatics, The
[Jean Beauvoir; Wes Beech; Stu Deutsch; Richie Stotts; Wendy O(rlean) Williams]
American. Music Group
Punk band with theatrical antics; albums include *Coup d'Etat,* 1982.
Source: *HarEnR 86; InB&W 85; RolSEnR 83; WhoRocM 82; WhsNW 85*

Plater-Zyberk, Elizabeth
American. Architect
Helped design prototype neighborhoods to prevent environmental and traffic problems in suburbia.
b. 1950 in Bryn Mawr, Pennsylvania
Source: *BioIn 15, 17; WomArch*

Plath, Sylvia
[Mrs. Ted Hughes; Victoria Lucas]
American. Author, Poet
Confessional verse collected in *Ariel,* 1965; wrote autobiographical novel, *The Bell Jar,* 1962; suicide victim.
b. Oct 27, 1932 in Boston, Massachusetts
d. Feb 11, 1963 in London, England
Source: *AmAu&B; AmCulL; AmWomWr; AmWr S1; ArtclWW 2; Au&Arts 13; AuBYP 2S, 3; Benet 87, 96; BenetAL 91; BioAmW; BioIn 7, 8, 9, 10, 11, 12, 13; BlmGEL; BlmGWL; CamGEL; CamGLE; CamHAL; CasWL; ChhPo S1; ConAu 34NR, P-2; ConLC 1, 2, 3, 5, 9, 11, 14, 17, 51, 62; ConPo 75, 80A, 85A; ContDcW 89; CroCAP; CyWA 89; DcAmB S7; DcArts; DcLB 5, 6, 152; DcLEL 1940; DcNaB MP; DcTwCCu 1; EncWB; EncWHA; EncWL, 2, 3; FacFETw; FemiCLE; FemiWr; GoodHs; GrLiveH; GrWomW; GrWrEL P; HanAmWH; IntDcWB; InWom SUP; LegTOT; LibW; LinLib L; LngCEL; LngCTC; MagSAmL; MajTwCW; MakMC; ModAL S1, S2; ModAWP; ModAWWr; ModWoWr; NewCon; NewYTBS 74; NotAW MOD; Novels; OxCAmL 65, 83, 95; OxCEng 85, 95; OxCTwCP; OxCWoWr 95; PenBWP; PenC AM; PenNWW A, B; PoeCrit 1; RAdv 1, 14, 13-1; RfGAmL 87, 94; RGFAP; RGTwCWr; TwCWr; TwCYAW; WebE&AL; WhAm 4; WhDW; WhoAmW 61; WhoTwCL; WorAl; WorAlBi; WorAu 1950; WorLitC; WrPh*

Plato
Greek. Philosopher, Author
Student of Socrates who founded the Academy, 387 BC; called world's most influential philosopher.
b. May 21, 427BC in Athens, Greece
d. Jan 14, 347BC in Athens, Greece
Source: *AsBiEn; AstEnc; AtlBL; Baker 78, 84; BbD; Benet 87, 96; BiD&SB; BioIn 4, 5, 6, 7, 8, 9, 10, 11, 12, 13; CasWL; ChhPo S1; CyWA 58; DcAmC; DcAmSR; DcEnL; DcEuL; DcScB; Dis&D; EncPaPR 91; GayLesB; IlEncMy; InSci; MagSWL; NewC; OxCClL, 89; OxCEng 67; OxCThe 67, 83; PenC CL; RAdv 13-3, 13-4; RComWL; REn; ScFEYrs; WhDW; WorAl; WorAlBi*

Platt, Harry
[Henry Barstow Platt]
American. Business Executive
Great-great grandson of Charles Tiffany; joined firm, 1947, chm., 1981—.
Source: *BioIn 12, 14, 15; NewYTBS 81; Who 88N; WhoAm 88*

Platt, Lewis E
American. Business Executive
President, CEO, Hewlett-Packard Co., electronics and computer firm, 1993—
b. Apr 11, 1941 in Johnson City, New York
Source: *Dun&B 86, 88, 90; WhoAm 88; WhoFI 89*

Platters, The
[David Lynch; Herb Reed; Paul Robi; Zola Taylor; Tony Williams]
American. Music Group
Formed 1953, hits include "Only You," 1955; "Smoke Gets in Your Eyes," 1958.
Source: *AmPS A, B; BiDAfM; BiDAmM; BiDJaz A; BioIn 14, 15, 16, 17, 18, 21; DcTwCCu 5; EncPR&S 74, 89; EncRk 88; EncRkSt; HalFC 84; HarEnR 86; IlEncBM 82; InB&W 80; NewAmDM; NewGrDA 86; NewYTBS 86, 92; OxCPMus; PenEncP; RkOn 74; RolSEnR 83; SoulM; WhoBlA 94N; WhoHol 92; WhoRock 81; WhoRocM 82*

Plautus, Titus Maccius
Roman. Dramatist
Wrote comedies from original Greek: *Asinaria.*
b. c. 254BC in Sarsina, Italy
d. c. 184BC in Rome, Italy
Source: *AtlBL; BbD; Benet 87, 96; BiD&SB; BioIn 5, 11; BlmGEL; CasWL; CyWA 58; DcBiPP; Dis&D; DramC 6; Grk&L; IntDcT 2; LinLib L, S; LngCEL; LuthC 75; McGEWB; McGEWD 84; NewC; NewGrDM 80; NotNAT B; OxCClL; OxCEng 67, 85, 95; OxCThe 83; PenC CL; PlP&P; RComWL; REn; REnWD*

Player, Gary Jim
South African. Golfer
Turned pro, 1953; has won nine major tournaments; third in golf history to win all four major events.
b. Nov 1, 1935 in Johannesburg, South Africa
Source: *BioIn 13, 14, 15; ConAu 101; CurBio 61; EncSoA; FacFETw; IntWW 83, 91, 93; NewYTBS 74, 78, 86; Who 85, 92, 94; WhoAm 82, 84, 86, 88, 90, 92, 94, 95, 96, 97; WhoIntG; WhoWor 74, 78, 80, 82, 84, 87, 89, 91, 93, 95, 96; WorAlBi*

Plaza Lasso, Galo
Ecuadorean. Political Leader
Pres., Ecuador, 1948-52; sec. gen., Organization of American States, 1968-75.
b. Feb 17, 1906 in New York, New York
d. Jan 28, 1987 in Quito, Ecuador
Source: *AnObit 1987; BiDLAmC; BioIn 1, 2, 5, 8, 15, 16; CurBio 69, 87; DcCPSAm; McGEWB; WhoUN 75*

Pleasant, Mary Ellen
American. Entrepreneur, Madam
Ran several laundries in San Francisco, 1850s; played key role in repealing law banning black testimony in California courts, 1863.
b. Aug 19, 1814 in Philadelphia, Pennsylvania
d. Jan 11, 1904 in San Francisco, California
Source: *BioIn 3, 6, 8, 11, 18, 19; BlkWAm; ConBlB 9; DcAmNB; InWom SUP; NotAW; NotBlAW 1*

Pleasence, Donald
English. Actor
Made stage debut, 1939; appeared in *Oh God,* 1977; *Halloween,* 1978.
b. Oct 5, 1919 in Worksop, England
d. Feb 2, 1995 in Saint Paul de Vence, France
Source: *BiE&WWA; BioIn 6, 7, 8, 13, 14, 17, 20, 21; BlueB 76; CamGWoT; ConTFT 2, 7, 14; CurBio 69, 95N; DcArts; EncEurC; Ent; ForYSC; HalFC 80, 84, 88; IntDcF 2-3; IntMPA 75, 76, 77, 78, 79, 80, 81, 82, 84, 86, 88, 92, 94, 96; IntWW 74, 75, 76, 77, 78, 79, 80, 81, 82, 83, 89, 91, 93; LegTOT; MotPP; MovMk; News 95, 95-3; NotNAT; OxCFilm; Who 74, 82, 83, 85, 88, 90, 92, 94; WhoAm 74, 76, 78, 80, 82, 84, 86, 88, 90, 92, 94, 95; WhoEnt 92; WhoHol A; WhoHrs 80; WhoThe 81; WhoWor 76, 78, 80, 82, 84, 87, 91, 93, 95*

Plekhanov, Georgi Valentinovich
Russian. Philosopher
Founder of Russian philosophic Marxism who disagreed with Bolshevik policy, rejected terrorism.
b. Nov 26, 1857 in Tambov, Russia
d. May 30, 1918 in Leningrad, Union of Soviet Socialist Republics
Source: *CasWL; DcRusL; DcTwHis; EncRev; FacFETw; WhDW*

Plenty Coups
American. Native American Chief
Recognized by the US government as the head chief of the Crow, 1890; negotiated land concessions by the Crow, 1880-1921.
b. 1848? in Montana
d. Mar 4, 1932
Source: *BioIn 1, 9, 11, 17, 21; EncNAB; EncNoAI; NotNaAm; RelLAm 91; REnAW; WhNaAH*

Pleshette, John
American. Actor
Played Richard Avery in TV series "Knots Landing," 1979-83.
b. Jul 27, 1942 in New York, New York
Source: *ConTFT 8; WhoHol A*

Pleshette, Suzanne
[Mrs. Thomas Gallagher, III]
American. Actor
Played Emily Hartley on TV series "The Bob Newhart Show," 1972-78.
b. Jan 31, 1937 in New York, New York
Source: *BioIn 16, 17, 20; CelR 90; ConTFT 7, 14; EncAFC; FilmEn; FilmgC; ForYSC; HalFC 80, 84, 88; IntMPA 77, 80, 84, 86, 88, 92, 94, 96; InWom, SUP; LegTOT; MotPP; MovMk; WhoAm 84, 86, 90; WhoAmW 85, 87, 91; WhoEnt 92; WhoHol 92, A; WorAl; WorAlBi; WorEFlm*

Pletcher, Stew
[Stuart Pletcher]
American. Jazz Musician
Trumpeter with Red Norvo, 1930s.
b. Feb 21, 1907 in Chicago, Illinois
Source: *CmpEPM; NewGrDJ 88; WhoJazz 72*

Pleven, Rene Jean
French. Statesman
Staunch advocate of European unity; held various government posts, 1940-1973.
b. Apr 15, 1901
d. Jan 13, 1993 in Paris, France
Source: *BiDFrPL; BioIn 2, 3, 8; CurBio 50; IntWW 91; Who 74, 82, 83, 85, 88, 90, 92*

Plimpton, Francis Taylor Pearson
American. Lawyer, Diplomat
Founded one of NYC's largest law firms; pres., American Bar Association, 1968-70.
b. Dec 7, 1900 in New York, New York
d. Jul 30, 1983 in Huntington, New York
Source: *BioIn 5, 9, 11; IntWW 74; NewYTBE 70; NewYTBS 83; St&PR 75; WhAm 8; WhoAm 80, 82; WhoE 74; WhoUN 75; WhoWor 74*

Plimpton, George Ames
American. Author
America's participatory journalist; wrote of experiences in several books including *Out of My League,* 1961, *Paper Lion,* 1966; founded *Paris Review,* 1953.
b. Mar 18, 1927 in New York, New York
Source: *AuNews 1; BioIn 13, 14, 15; CelR 90; ConAu 32NR; ConLC 36; CurBio 69; EncTwCJ; IntvTCA 2; IntWW 91; MajTwCW; NewYTBE 70; SmATA 10; WebAB 74; WhoAm 86, 90, 97; WhoE 91; WhoHol A; WhoUSWr 88; WhoWrEP 89; WorAu 1980; WrDr 86, 92*

Plimsoll, Samuel
English. Politician, Social Reformer
The "Plimsoll Line," the load line amidship on cargo ships, is result of his campaigning for safe shipping, 1876.
b. Feb 10, 1824 in Bristol, England
d. Jun 3, 1898 in London, England
Source: *Alli SUP; BioIn 2, 4, 8, 11, 16, 17; DcBiPP; DcNaB C, S1; OxCLaw; OxCShps; VicBrit; WhDW*

Pliny the Elder
[Gaius Plinius Secundus]
Roman. Scholar
Known for one surviving work, 37-vol. *Natural History;* died observing eruption of Mt. Vesuvius.
b. 23 in Como, Italy
d. Aug 24, 79 in Stabiae, Italy
Source: *AtlBL; BbD; Benet 87, 96; BiD&SB; BioIn 20; CasWL; DcArts; DcInv; DcScB; EncO&P 1S2, 2, 3; Grk&L; LegTOT; LinLib L, S; McGDA; NewC; OxCArt; OxCClL, 89; OxCEng 67, 85, 95; OxCMed 86; PenC CL; RAdv 14, 13-5; RComWL; REn; WhDW; WhWE; WorAlBi*

Pliny the Younger
[Gaius Plinius Caecilius Secundus]
Roman. Orator, Statesman
Wrote letters describing his time; made early reference to "Christians"; nephew of Pliny the Elder.
b. 62 in Como, Italy
d. 114, Bithynia
Source: *AtlBL; BbD; Benet 87, 96; BiD&SB; CasWL; Grk&L; McGDA; NewC; OxCEng 67, 85, 95; PenC CL; RComWL; REn; WhDW*

Plisetskaya, Maya Mikhailovna
Russian. Dancer
Prima ballerina with Bolshoi Ballet, 1960s; leading roles include *Swan Lake, Sleeping Beauty, Don Quixote.*
b. Nov 20, 1925 in Moscow, Union of Soviet Socialist Republics
Source: *BiDD; BioIn 13, 14, 15, 16; CurBio 63; FacFETw; IntWW 91; InWom, SUP; NewYTBS 74; WhoHol A; WorAlBi*

Plishka, Paul Peter
American. Opera Singer
Bass; NY Met. debut, 1967.
b. Aug 28, 1941 in Old Forge, Pennsylvania
Source: *Baker 84; BioIn 9, 11, 13; MetOEnc; NewAmDM; NewGrDA 86; NewGrDM 80; WhoAm 74; WhoOp 76*

Plomer, William Charles Franklyn
South African. Author
His opera *Gloriana* was performed during coronation of Queen Elizabeth II, 1953.
b. Dec 10, 1903 in Pietersburg, South Africa
d. Sep 21, 1973 in London, England
Source: *Au&Wr 71; BioIn 4, 8, 10, 13; BlkAWP; CamGEL; CasWL; Chambr 3; ChhPo, S2; CnE&AP; ConAu P-2; ConLC 4, 8; ConNov 72; ConPo 70, 75; DcLEL; DcNaB 1971; EncSoA; EncWL; EvLB; IntWWP 77; LngCTC; ModBrL, S1; NewC; NewCBEL; NewGrDO; OxCEng 85, 95; OxCTwCP; PenC ENG; REn; RfGShF; SmATA 8; TwCA, SUP; TwCWr; WebE&AL; WhoTwCL; WhoWor 74*

Plomley, Roy
English. Dramatist, Radio Performer
Creator, host of world's longest-running radio show "Desert Island Discs," 1942-85.
b. Jan 20, 1914 in Kingston-upon-Thames, England
d. May 29, 1985 in London, England
Source: *AnObit 1985; Au&Wr 71; ConAu 107, 116; DcNaB 1981; FacFETw; Who 85; WhoWor 76; WrDr 76*

Plotinus
Egyptian. Philosopher
Most famous of neo-Platonists; philosophy combines mysticism, dialectics, is historically important.
b. 204 in Lycopolis, Egypt
d. 270 in Minturnae, Campania
Source: *Benet 87, 96; BiD&SB; BioIn 2, 3, 7, 11, 13; CasWL; DcScB; NewC; OxCEng 67; OxCPhil; PenC CL; RComWL; REn*

Plotkin, Jerry
[The Hostages]
American. Hostage
One of 52 held by terrorists, Nov 1979-Jan 1981.
b. 1934? in New York, New York
d. Jun 6, 1996 in Los Angeles, California
Source: *NewYTBS 81*

Plotkin, Mark
American. Botanist
Vice President for plant conservation, Conservation International, 1993—.
b. c. 1955 in New Orleans, Louisiana
Source: *News 94, 94-3*

Plotkin, Mark J.
American. Botanist
Researched the Amazon rain forests; wrote *Tales of a Shaman's Apprentice,* 1993; studied the medicinal uses of tropical plants.
b. May 21, 1955 in New Orleans, Louisiana

Plotnik, Arthur
American. Author, Editor
Wrote *The Elements of Editing: A Modern Guide for Editors & Journalists,* 1982.
b. Aug 1, 1937 in White Plains, New York
Source: *BiDrLUS 70; BioIn 10; ConAu 20NR, 69; JrnUS; WhoAm 78, 80, 82, 84, 86, 88, 90, 92, 94, 95, 96, 97; WhoAmJ 80; WhoLibI 82; WhoUSWr 88; WhoWrEP 89, 92, 95*

Plowden, David
American. Photographer
Photographer of scenes such as barns, mills, and railroads; published *Farewell to Steam,* 1966; *Small Town America,* 1994.
b. Oct 9, 1932 in Boston, Massachusetts
Source: *BioIn 11; ConAu 33R; ConPhot 82, 88, 95; CurBio 96; ICPEnP A; MacBEP; SmATA 52; WhoAm 94, 95, 96, 97; WhoAmA 86, 89, 91, 93; WrDr 90, 92, 94, 96*

Plowright, Joan Anne
[Mrs. Laurence Olivier]
English. Actor
Won NY Drama Critics Award for *A Taste of Honey,* 1961.
b. Oct 28, 1929 in Scunthorpe, England
Source: *BiE&WWA; BioIn 16; CamGWoT; ConTFT 4; CurBio 64; HalFC 88; IntMPA 92; IntWW 83, 91; InWom SUP; NotNAT; OxCThe 83; PlP&P; Who 85, 92; WhoAm 97; WhoEnt 92; WhoHol A; WhoThe 81; WhoWor 84, 87, 91, 97*

Plucker, Julius
German. Mathematician, Physicist
Known for work in analytical geometry, spectroscopy; originated line geometry.
b. Jun 16, 1801 in Elberfeld, Germany
d. May 22, 1868 in Bonn, Germany
Source: *AsBiEn; BiESc; BioIn 1, 2, 3, 14; DcBiPP; DcScB; InSci; LarDcSc; NewCol 75*

Plumb, Charles
American. Cartoonist
Creator of comic strip Ella Cinders.
b. 1900 in San Gabriel, California
d. Jan 19, 1982
Source: *WorECom*

Plummer, Amanda
American. Actor
Daughter of Tammy Grimes and Christopher Plummer; won Tony, 1982, for *Agnes of God.*
b. Mar 23, 1957 in New York
Source: *BioIn 13, 14, 15; CelR 90; ConTFT 6, 15; IntMPA 86, 88, 92, 94, 96; LegTOT; NewYTBS 81; VarWW 85; WhoAm 86, 88, 92, 94, 95, 96, 97; WhoEnt 92; WhoHol 92*

Plummer, (Arthur) Christopher
Canadian. Actor
Played Baron von Trapp in *The Sound of Music,* 1965; noted Shakespearean actor; won Tony, 1974; Tony for *Barrymore,* 1997.
b. Dec 13, 1929 in Toronto, Ontario, Canada
Source: *BiE&WWA; BioIn 4, 5, 7, 11, 12, 13, 16; CamGWoT; CanWW 31, 70, 79, 80, 81, 83, 89; CelR 90; CnThe; ConTFT 4; CreCan 2; CurBio 56, 88; EncWT; FilmAG WE; FilmgC; HalFC 88; IntMPA 84, 86, 92; IntWW 74, 75, 76, 77, 78, 79, 80, 81, 82, 83, 89, 91; MotPP; MovMk; NotNAT; OxCAmT 84; OxCCanT; PlP&P; VarWW 85; Who 82, 83, 85, 88, 90, 92; WhoAm 74, 76, 78, 80, 82, 84, 86, 88, 90; WhoHol 92, A; WhoThe 72; WhoWor 84, 87, 89, 91; WorAl; WorAlBi; WorEFlm*

Plunkett, Jim
[James William Plunkett, JR]
American. Football Player
Quarterback; won Heisman Trophy, 1970; in NFL, 1971-88, mostly with Oakland/LA Raiders; won Super Bowl, 1981.
b. Dec 5, 1947 in San Jose, California
Source: *BiDAmSp FB; BioIn 9, 10, 11, 12, 13, 14, 16, 20; CelR; CmCal; CurBio 71, 82; LegTOT; NewYTBE 70, 71; NewYTBS 81, 84; WhoAm 74, 78, 80, 82, 84, 86, 88, 92; WhoFtbl 74; WhoHisp 91, 92, 94; WhoSpor*

Plutarch
Greek. Author
Wrote hundreds of short pieces, especially biographies comparing Greek, Roman figures; has influenced philosophers, writers for hundreds of years.
b. 46 in Chaeronea, Greece
d. 120 in Chaeronea, Greece
Source: *AtlBL; Baker 84, 92; BbD; Benet 87, 96; BiD&SB; BioIn 1, 2, 4, 5, 7, 8, 9, 11, 16, 20; BlmGEL; CasWL; CyEd; CyWA 58; DcArts; DcEnL; Dis&D; GrFLW; Grk&L; LegTOT; LngCEL; LuthC 75; MagSWL; McGEWB; NewC; OxCClL, 89; OxCEng 67; OxDcByz; PenC CL; RAdv 13-3; RComWL; REn; RfGWoL 95; WhDW; WorAl; WorAlBi*

Poage, W(illiam) R(obert)
American. Politician
Dem. congressman from TX, 1937-79; chaired agriculture committee, 1967-74.
b. Dec 28, 1899 in Waco, Texas
d. Jan 3, 1987 in Temple, Texas
Source: *AlmAP 78; BiDrAC; BiDrUSC 89; BioIn 8, 11, 12, 15; CngDr 74, 77; CurBio 69, 87, 87N; EncAAH; NewYTBS*

87; PolProf J, NF; WhAm 9; WhoAm 74, 76, 78, 80, 82, 84, 86; WhoAmL 78, 79; WhoAmP 73, 75, 77, 79, 81, 83, 85, 87, 89; WhoGov 72, 75, 77; WhoSSW 73, 75, 76, 78

Pocahontas
[Matoaka; Mrs. John Rolfe]
American. Princess
Daughter of Powhatan; supposedly saved life of Captain John Smith.
b. 1595 in Virginia
d. Mar 1617 in Gravesend, England
Source: *AmBi; Benet 87, 96; BenetAL 91; BioAmW; BioIn 2, 3, 4, 5, 6, 7, 8, 9, 10, 11, 12, 13; DcAmB; DcNAA; DcNaB; Drake; EncAAH; EncAB-H 1974; EncCRAm; EncNAB; EncSoH; EncWHA; HerW, 84; InWom, SUP; LegTOT; LibW; LinLib S; LuthC 75; McGEWB; NewC; NotAW; NotNaAm; OxCAmH; OxCAmL 65, 83, 95; OxCEng 85, 95; REn; REnAL; WebAB 74, 79; WhAm HS; WhDW; WhNaAH; WorAl; WorAlBi*

Pocklington, Peter H
"Peter Puck"
Canadian. Businessman, Hockey Executive
Owner, Edmonton Oilers, 1976—; chairman, Pocklington Financial Corp.
b. Nov 18, 1941 in Regina, Saskatchewan, Canada
Source: *BioIn 13, 15; CanWW 83, 89; ConNews 85-2; NewYTBS 83; St&PR 91; WhoAm 84, 86, 88; WhoCan 80; WhoWest 92*

Poco
[Paul Cotton; Richie Furay; George Grantham; Randy Meisner; Jim Messina; Tim Schmit; Rusty Young]
American. Music Group
Albums include *Deliverin'*, 1970; *Crazy Eyes*, 1973; *Ghost Town*, 1982.
Source: *BgBkCoM; BioIn 16; ConMuA 80A; EncPR&S 89; EncRk 88; EncRkSt; HarEnCM 87; HarEnR 86; IlEncCM; IlEncRk; PenEncP; RkOn 78; RolSEnR 83; WhoNeCM A; WhoRock 81; WhoRocM 82*

Podesta, Rossana
Italian. Actor
Films include *Helen of Troy*, 1956.
b. Jun 20, 1934 in Tripoli, Libya
Source: *BioIn 3; FilmAG WE; FilmEn; FilmgC; ForYSC; HalFC 80, 84, 88; IntMPA 75, 76, 77, 78, 79, 80, 81, 82, 84, 86, 88; ItaFilm; VarWW 85; WhoHol 92, A*

Podgorny, Nikolai Viktorovich
Russian. Politician
Pres., USSR, 1965-77.
b. Feb 18, 1903 in Karlovka, Russia
d. Jan 11, 1983 in Kiev, Union of Soviet Socialist Republics
Source: *BioIn 6, 7, 8, 9, 11, 13; CurBio 66, 83; IntWW 74, 75, 76, 80, 81; IntYB 78, 79, 80, 81, 82; NewYTBS 83; WhoGov 72; WhoSocC 78; WhoWor 76*

Podhoretz, Norman
American. Author
Books include *Why We Were in Vietnam*, 1982; *The Bloody Crossroads*, 1986.
b. Jan 16, 1930 in New York, New York
Source: *AmAu&B; AmSocL; Au&Wr 71; Benet 87; BenetAL 91; BioIn 8, 9, 10, 11, 12, 13, 15; BlueB 76; CelR; ColdWar 1, 2; ConAu 7NR, 9R; CurBio 68; CyWA 89; DcAmC; EncAJ; EncTwCJ; IntAu&W 76, 77, 86; IntWW 89, 91, 93; JeAmHC; LegTOT; LinLib L; NewYTBE 72; OxCAmL 83, 95; PenC AM; PolProf J, K; WhoAm 74, 76, 78, 80, 82, 84, 86, 88, 90, 92, 94, 95, 96, 97; WhoAmJ 80; WhoE 91, 93, 95; WhoRel 92; WhoUSWr 88; WhoWor 74; WhoWorJ 72; WhoWrEP 89, 92, 95; WorAu 1950; WrDr 82, 84, 86, 88, 90, 92, 94, 96*

Podoloff, Maurice
American. Basketball Executive
First commissioner of NBA, 1949-63; Hall of Fame.
b. Aug 18, 1890 in Elizabethgrad, Russia
d. Nov 25, 1985 in New Haven, Connecticut
Source: *BasBi; BiDAmSp BK; BioIn 11, 14; FacFETw; NewYTBS 77, 85; WhoBbl 73*

Podres, Johnny
[John Joseph Podres]
American. Baseball Player
Pitcher, 1953-55, 1957-67, 1969, mostly with Brooklyn/LA; led NL in ERA, 1957.
b. Sep 30, 1932 in Witherbee, New York
Source: *Ballpl 90; BioIn 4, 5, 11, 13, 19; WhoProB 73*

Poe, Edgar Allan
American. Poet, Author, Journalist
Invented modern detective story; noted for macabre themes in poems, short stories: *The Raven*, 1845; *The Gold Bug*, 1843.
b. Jan 19, 1809 in Boston, Massachusetts
d. Oct 7, 1849 in Baltimore, Maryland
Source: *Alli; AmAu; AmAu&B; AmBi; AmCulL; AmWr; AnCL; ApCAB; AtlBL; Au&Arts 14; BbD; Benet 87, 96; BenetAL 91; BibAL; BiD&SB; BiDSA; BiDTran; BioIn 1, 2, 3, 4, 5, 6, 7, 8, 9, 10, 11, 12, 13, 14, 15, 16, 17, 18, 19, 20, 21; BlmGEL; CamGEL; CamGLE; CamHAL; CasWL; CelCen; Chambr 3; ChhPo, S1, S2, S3; CnDAL; CnE&AP; ColARen; CopCroC; CrtSuMy; CrtT 3, 4; CyAL 2; CyWA 58; DancEn 78; DcAmAu; DcAmB; DcAmC; DcArts; DcBiA; DcEnA; DcEnL; DcLB 3, 59, 73, 74; DcLEL; DcNAA; DcPup; Dis&D; EncAB-H 1974, 1996; EncAJ; EncMys; EncSF, 93; EncSoH; EvLB; FifSWrB; FilmgC; GrWrEL N, P; HalFC 80, 84, 88; HarEnUS; LinLib L, S; MagSAmL; McGEWB; MemAm; MnBBF; MorMA; MouLC 3; NatCAB 1; NewEOp 71; NewEScF; NewGrDA 86; NewGrDM 80; NewGrDO; NinCLC 1, 16, 55; NotNAT B; Novels; OxCAmH; OxCAmL 65, 83, 95; OxCAmT 84; OxCEng 67, 85, 95; PenC AM; PenEncH; PeoHis; PoeCrit 1; RAdv 1, 14, 13-1; RComAH; RComWL; REn; REnAL; RfGAmL 87, 94; RfGShF; RGFAP; ScF&FL 1, 92; ScFEYrs; ScFSB; ScFWr; ShSCr 1, 22; ShSWr; SmATA 23; SouWr; SpyFic; Str&VC; SupFW; TwCBDA; TwCCr&M 80A, 85A, 91A; WebAB 74, 79; WebE&AL; WhAm HS; WhDW; WhoHr&F; WhoHrs 80; WhoSciF; WhoSpyF; WorAl; WorAlBi; WorLitC*

Poe, James
American. Screenwriter
Won Oscar for *Around the World in Eighty Days*, 1957.
b. Oct 4, 1921 in Dobbs Ferry, New York
d. Jan 24, 1980 in Malibu, California
Source: *BioIn 15; ConAu 93, 113; DcLB 44; FilmEn; HalFC 84; NewYTBS 80; WhAm 7; WhoAm 74, 76, 78, 80; WhScrn 83*

Pogany, Willy
Hungarian. Illustrator
Worked on over 150 books, including children's classics.
b. Aug 24, 1882 in Szeged, Hungary
d. Jul 30, 1955 in New York, New York
Source: *BioIn 1, 2, 3, 4, 6, 12, 14, 15; ChhPo, S1, S2; ConICB; DcBrBI; IlrAm 1880; IlsCB 1744; JBA 34, 51; NatCAB 44; OxCChiL; REn; SmATA 30, 44; WhAm 3*

Pogorelich, Ivo
Yugoslav. Pianist
Int'l pianist who turned star overnight when he was barred from the Int'l Chopin Piano Competition because of his attire, 1980; noted for his unorthodox piano interpretation.
b. Oct 20, 1958 in Belgrade, Yugoslavia
Source: *Baker 84, 92; BioIn 12, 14, 15, 16; ConNews 86-4; CurBio 88; IntWW 89, 91, 93; IntWWM 90; NewYTBS 86; NotTwCP; PenDiMP; WhoSoCE 89*

Pogue, William R(eid)
American. Astronaut
With NASA 1966-75; piloted third Skylab mission.
b. Jan 23, 1930 in Okemah, Oklahoma
Source: *AmMWSc 95; NewYTBE 73; NotTwCS; WhoAm 74, 76, 78, 80, 82, 84, 86, 88, 90, 92, 94, 95, 96, 97; WhoScEn 94, 96; WhoSpc; WhoSSW 73, 75, 76, 95, 97; WorDWW*

Pogues, The
English. Music Group
Folk-rock band formed in 1982; million-selling album *If I Should Fall from Grace with God*, 1988.
Source: *BioIn 21; ConMus 6; EncRk 88; EncRkSt; OnThGG; PenEncP; WhoHol 92; WhoRocM 82*

Pohl, Dan(ny Joe)
American. Golfer
Turned pro, 1977; known for long drives off tee.
b. Apr 1, 1955 in Mount Pleasant, Michigan
Source: *WhoIntG*

Pohl, Frederik
American. Editor, Author
Science fiction books include *The Abominable Snowman,* 1963; *Man Plus,* 1977.
b. Nov 26, 1919 in New York, New York
Source: *Benet 87, 96; BioIn 10, 11, 12, 13, 14, 15, 17; ConAu 1AS, 11NR, 37NR; ConLC 18; ConNov 72, 76, 82, 86, 91, 96; ConSFA; CyWA 89; DcLB 8; DcLP 87A; DrAF 76; DrAPF 80, 91; DrmM 1; EncSF, 93; Future; IntAu&W 77, 82, 91, 93; IntvTCA 2; LegTOT; MajTwCW; NewEScF; Novels; PenC AM; RGSF; RGTwCSF; ScF&FL 1, 2, 92; ScFSB; ScFWr; SmATA 24; TwCSFW 81, 86, 91; WhoAm 74, 76, 78, 80, 86, 88, 90, 92, 94, 95, 96, 97; WhoSciF; WhoUSWr 88; WhoWrEP 89, 92, 95; WorAl; WorAlBi; WorAu 1950; WrDr 76, 80, 82, 84, 86, 88, 90, 92, 94, 96*

Poincare, Jules Henri
French. Mathematician
Made major contributions to cosmology, relativity, topology.
b. Apr 29, 1854 in Nancy, France
d. Jul 17, 1912 in Paris, France
Source: *AsBiEn; BioIn 3; CamDcSc; DcScB; Dis&D; InSci; LarDcSc; McGEWB; NewCol 75; NotTwCS; OxCPhil; RAdv 14, 13-5; WorAl*

Poincare, Raymond
French. Statesman, Author
Wartime pres., 1913-20, known for eloquent oratory.
b. Aug 20, 1860 in Bar-le-Duc, France
d. Oct 15, 1934 in Paris, France
Source: *BiDFrPL; BioIn 1, 2, 10, 13, 17; DcTwHis; EncTR 91; FacFETw; LegTOT; LinLib L, S; LngCTC; McGEWB; OxCFr; REn; WhDW; WorAl; WorAlBi*

Poindexter, John Marlan
American. Presidential Aide
Reagan's nat. security adviser, 1985-86; resigned amid controversy over his part in directing Iran-Contra operation.
b. Aug 12, 1936 in Washington, District of Columbia
Source: *BioIn 13, 14, 15, 16; CurBio 87; DcAmDH 89; IntWW 91; NewYTBS 85; WhoAm 82*

Poinsett, Joel Roberts
American. Government Official
Secretary of War, 1837-40; amateur botanist whose name was given the poinsettia, traditional Christmas flower.
b. Mar 2, 1779 in Charleston, South Carolina
d. Dec 12, 1851 in Statesburg, South Carolina
Source: *Alli; AmBi; ApCAB; BiAUS; BiDrAC; BiDrUSC 89; BiDrUSE 71, 89; BiDSA; BioIn 1, 3, 6, 8, 10, 16; CyAL 1; DcAmAu; DcAmB; DcAmDH 80, 89; DcNAA; Drake; EncAB-H 1974; EncSoH; HarEnUS; NatCAB 6; NewCol 75; TwCBDA; WebAB 74, 79; WhAm HS; WhAmP*

Pointer, Anita
[The Pointer Sisters]
American. Singer
With sisters, first black woman to perform at Grand Ole Opry, Nashville.
b. Jan 23, 1948 in East Oakland, California
Source: *BiDJaz; BioIn 15; EncJzS; EncPR&S 89; InB&W 85; LegTOT; WhoHol 92*

Pointer, Bonnie
[The Pointer Sisters]
American. Singer
Left sister group, 1978, to pursue solo career; hit single "I Can't Help Myself," 1979.
b. Jul 11, 1951 in East Oakland, California
Source: *EncPR&S 89; InB&W 85; LegTOT; RkOn 85*

Pointer, June
[The Pointer Sisters]
American. Singer
With sisters, hits include "He's So Shy," 1980; "I'm So Excited," 1982.
b. Nov 30, 1954 in East Oakland, California
Source: *BiDJaz; BioIn 15; EncPR&S 89; InB&W 85; LegTOT; WhoHol 92*

Pointer, Ruth
[The Pointer Sisters]
American. Singer
With sisters, first pop act to perform at San Francisco Opera House.
b. Mar 19, 1946 in East Oakland, California
Source: *BiDJaz; BioIn 15, 19; EncJzS; EncPR&S 89; InB&W 85; LegTOT; WhoHol 92*

Pointer Sisters, The
[Anita Pointer; Bonnie Pointer; June Pointer; Ruth Pointer]
American. Music Group
Pop, rhythm and blues group; hit singles include "Fire," 1979; "Break Out," 1984.
Source: *BiDJaz; BioIn 10, 12; BioNews 74; ConMus 9; DcTwCCu 5; DrBlPA 90; EncPR&S 89; EncRk 88; EncRkSt; HarEnR 86; IlEncBM 82; InB&W 80, 85A; InWom SUP; NewAmDM; NewGrDA 86; PenEncP; RkWW 82; RolSEnR 83; SoulM; WhoRocM 82*

Poiret, Paul
French. Fashion Designer
Exotic, artistic clothes influenced by Persian coloring, Oriental shapes, 1903-14.
b. Apr 20, 1879 in Paris, France
d. Apr 30, 1944 in Paris, France
Source: *BioIn 5, 9, 10, 12, 16, 21; CurBio 44; DcArts; DcTwDes; EncFash; MakMC; ObitOF 79; WhoFash 88; WorFshn*

Poirier, Richard
American. Critic
Writings include *Norman Mailer,* 1972; *Robert Frost: The Work of Knowing,* 1977.
b. Sep 9, 1925 in Gloucester, Massachusetts
Source: *AmAu&B; BlueB 76; ConAu 1R, 3NR, 40NR; ConLCrt 77, 82; DcLEL 1940; DrAS 74E, 78E, 82E; IntAu&W 86, 89, 91, 93; WhoAm 74, 76, 78, 80, 82, 84, 86, 88, 90, 92, 94, 95, 96; WhoE 74, 89; WhoUSWr 88; WhoWrEP 89, 92, 95; WorAu 1970; WrDr 80, 82, 84, 86, 88, 90, 92*

Poiseuille, Jean Louis Marie
French. Physician
One of the discoverers of the mathematical expression now know as the Hagen-Poiseuille equation.
b. Apr 22, 1799 in Paris, France
d. Dec 26, 1869 in Paris, France
Source: *BioIn 12; DcScB; OxCMed 86*

Poitier, Sidney
American. Actor, Director
First black man to win Oscar for best actor: *Lilies of the Field,* 1963; and first black to win a lifetime achievement award from the American Film Institute.
b. Feb 20, 1924 in Miami, Florida
Source: *AfrAmBi 1; BiDFilm, 81, 94; BiE&WWA; BioIn 4, 5, 6, 7, 8, 9, 10, 11, 12, 14, 15, 16; BioNews 74; BkPepl; BlksAmF; BlkWr 1; BlueB 76; CelR, 90; ConAu 117; ConLC 26; ConTFT 7; CurBio 59; DcArts; DrBlPA 90; EncAFC; FacFETw; FilmEn; FilmgC; ForYSC; HalFC 80, 84, 88; IlWWHD 1A; InB&W 85; IntDcF 1-3, 2-3; IntMPA 75, 76, 77, 78, 79, 80, 81, 82, 84, 86, 88, 92; IntWW 74, 75, 76, 77, 78, 79, 80, 81, 82, 83, 89, 91, 93; LegTOT; MiSFD 9; MotPP; MovMk; NegAl 89; News 90-3; NewYTBS 89; NotNAT; OxCFilm; SelBAAf; VarWW 85; Who 74, 82, 92; WhoAfA 96; WhoAm 86, 90; WhoBlA 92, 94; WhoEnt 92; WhoHol 92, A; WhoThe 72, 77, 81; WhoWor 74; WorAlBi*

Polacco, Giorgio
Italian. Conductor
Led Italian repertory, Chicago Opera, 1918-30.
b. Apr 12, 1875 in Venice, Italy
d. Apr 30, 1960 in New York, New York

Source: *Baker 84; BiDAmM; BioIn 2, 5; CmOp; MetOEnc; NewEOp 71; NewGrDM 80*

Polanski, Roman
Polish. Director
Received critical acclaim for *Rosemary's Baby,* 1968; *Chinatown,* 1974.
b. Aug 18, 1933 in Paris, France
Source: *BiDFilm, 81; BioIn 7, 8, 9, 10, 11, 12, 13, 14, 15, 16; CelR, 90; ConAu 77; ConLC 16; ConTFT 1, 6, 13; CurBio 69; DcArts; DcFM; EncEurC; FacFETw; FilmEn; FilmgC; HalFC 80, 84, 88; HorFD; IntDcF 1-2, 2-2; IntMPA 75, 76, 77, 78, 79, 80, 81, 82, 84, 86, 88, 92, 94, 96; IntWW 74, 75, 76, 77, 78, 79, 80, 81, 82, 83, 89, 91, 93; ItaFilm; LegTOT; MakMC; MiSFD 9; MovMk; NewYTBE 73; NewYTBS 76, 88; OxCFilm; PenEncH; PolBiDi; RAdv 14; VarWW 85; WhoAm 74, 76, 78, 80, 82, 84, 86, 88, 90, 92, 94, 95, 96, 97; WhoEnt 92; WhoHol 92; WhoHrs 80; WhoSoCE 89; WhoWest 74; WhoWor 74, 80, 82, 84, 87, 89, 91, 93, 95, 96, 97; WorAl; WorAlBi; WorEFlm; WorFDir 2*

Polanyi, John C
Canadian. Chemist
Co-winner of 1986 Nobel Prize for Chemistry for research in "crossed molecular beam technique."
b. Jan 23, 1929 in Berlin, Germany

Polgar, Judit
Hungarian. Chess Player
At 15, youngest person to achieve the title of Grandmaster.
Source: *BioIn 16, 18; NewYTBS 89*

Polhill, Robert
American. Hostage
Business professor in Lebanon seized by Islamic Jihad Jan 24, 1987 and held captive 1,184 days; released Apr 22, 1990.
b. 1934 in Fishkill, New York

Poli, Robert E
American. Labor Union Official
Pres. of PATCO, who led air controllers strike, 1981.
b. Feb 27, 1936 in Pittsburgh, Pennsylvania
Source: *BioIn 14; NewYTBS 81*

Police, The
[Stewart Copeland; Andy Summers; Gordon "Sting" Sumner]
British. Music Group
Group blended New Wave rock, Jamaican, int'l rhythms, melodic pop, 1977-83; hit song "Every Breath You Take," from *Synchronicity,* 1983.
Source: *BioIn 12, 15, 16; ConLC 26; ConMuA 80A; EncPR&S 89; EncRk 88; EncRkSt; FacFETw; HarEnR 86; IlEncRk; NewAmDM; NewYTBS 89; OxCPMus; PenEncP; RkOn 85; RolSEnR 83; WhoRock 81; WhoRocM 82; WhsNW 85*

Poling, Daniel A
American. Evangelist
Leading temperance leader; editor, *Christian Herald,* 1926-66.
b. Nov 30, 1884 in Portland, Oregon
d. Feb 7, 1968 in Philadelphia, Pennsylvania
Source: *AmAu&B; CurBio 43, 68; NatCAB 54; OhA&B; WhAm 5*

Poling, Harold Arthur
"Red"
American. Auto Executive
Succeeded Donald Petersen as president of Ford Motor Co., 1990-93.
b. Oct 14, 1925 in Troy, Michigan
Source: *BioIn 15, 16; Dun&B 90; IntWW 91, 93; St&PR 91; WhoAm 78, 80, 82, 84, 86, 88, 90, 92, 94, 95, 96, 97; WhoFI 87, 89, 92, 94; WhoMW 90, 92; WhoWor 87, 89, 91*

Politi, Leo
American. Author, Illustrator
Won 1950 Caldecott for *Song of the Swallows.*
b. Nov 21, 1908 in Fresno, California
d. Mar 25, 1996 in Los Angeles, California
Source: *Au&ICB; AuBYP 2, 3; BioIn 1, 2, 3, 4, 5, 7, 8, 9, 12, 14, 16, 19; BkP; Cald 1938; CathA 1952; ChlBkCr; ChlLR 29; ConAu 13NR, 17R, 47NR, 151; IlBEAAW; IlsBYP; IlsCB 1744, 1946, 1957; JBA 51; MajAI; OxCChiL; SmATA 1, 47, 88; Str&VC; TwCChW 78; WhAmArt 85; WrDr 80, 82, 84, 86, 88, 90*

Politz, Alfred
American. Business Executive
Founded research co., 1943; pres., 1947-64; noted for developing marketing research techniques.
b. 1902 in Berlin, Germany
d. Nov 8, 1982 in Odessa, Florida
Source: *BioIn 1, 4, 11, 13; NewYTBS 82; WhAm 8; WhoAm 74*

Polk, James Knox
American. US President
Dem., 11th pres., 1845-49; led US in war against Mexico, resulting in annexation of Southwest.
b. Nov 2, 1795 in Mecklenburg County, North Carolina
d. Jun 15, 1849 in Nashville, Tennessee
Source: *Alli; AmAu&B; AmBi; AmPolLe; ApCAB; BenetAL 91; BiAUS; BiDrAC; BiDrGov 1789; BiDrUSC 89; BiDrUSE 71, 89; BiDSA; BioIn 1, 2, 3, 4, 5, 6, 7, 8, 9, 10, 11, 12, 13; CelCen; CyAG; DcAmB; DcBiPP; Drake; EncAAH; EncAB-H 1974, 1996; EncSoH; EncWM; FacPr 89, 93; HarEnUS; LegTOT; LinLib L, S; McGEWB; MorMA; NatCAB 6; OxCAmH; OxCAmL 65, 83; REn; REnAL; TwCBDA; WebAB 74, 79; WhAm HS; WhAmP; WhDW; WorAl*

Polk, Ralph Lane
American. Publisher
Pres., R L Polk, 1949-63; chm., 1963-83.
b. Jul 21, 1911 in Detroit, Michigan
d. Feb 9, 1984 in Bloomfield Hills, Michigan
Source: *St&PR 75, 84; WhoAm 74, 76, 78*

Polk, Sarah Childress
[Mrs. James Polk]
American. First Lady
Served as husband's official secretary; banned dancing, liquor from White House.
b. Sep 4, 1803 in Murfreesboro, Tennessee
d. Aug 14, 1891 in Nashville, Tennessee
Source: *AmWom; ApCAB; BioIn 16, 17; GoodHs; InWom, SUP; NatCAB 6; NotAW; TwCBDA; WhAm HS*

Polk, Willis Jefferson
American. Architect
Designed one of first glass, non-loadbearing outer walls for Hallidie Bldg., San Francisco, 1918.
b. 1867 in Frankfort, Kentucky
d. 1924 in San Mateo, California
Source: *BiDAmAr; DcAmB; EncMA; MacEA*

Polke, Sigmar
German. Artist
Painter who experimented in a variety of styles and themes; known for German themes.
b. Feb 13, 1941, Germany
Source: *ConArt 77, 83, 89, 96; DcCAr 81; WhoAm 94, 95, 96; WhoWor 97; WorArt 1980*

Pollack, Egon
[Egon Pollak]
Czech. Conductor
Led Hamburg Opera, 1917-31; noted R Strauss interpreter; died on stage.
b. May 3, 1879 in Prague, Bohemia
d. Jun 14, 1933 in Prague, Czechoslovakia
Source: *Baker 78, 84, 92; NewEOp 71; NewGrDO; OxDcOp; WhAm 6*

Pollack, Sydney
American. Director
Films include *They Shoot Horses, Don't They?,* 1969; *Absence of Malice,* 1981; won Emmy for "The Game," 1966.
b. Jul 1, 1934 in South Bend, Indiana
Source: *BiDFilm, 81, 94; BioIn 10, 14, 15, 16, 21; ConTFT 1, 2, 7, 15; CurBio 86; FilmEn; FilmgC; GangFlm; HalFC 84, 88; IntDcF 1-2, 2-2; IntMPA 86, 88, 92, 94, 96; IntWW 89, 91, 93; LegTOT; MiSFD 9; MovMk; NewYTBE 70; NewYTBS 82; WhoAm 76, 78, 80, 82, 84, 86, 88, 90, 92, 94, 95, 96, 97; WhoEnt 92; WhoHol 92; WhoWor 78, 80, 82, 84, 87; WorEFlm; WorFDir 2*

Pollaiuolo, Antonio
Italian. Artist
Best-known works include *Tobias and the Angel.*
b. 1431 in Florence, Italy

d. 1498 in Rome, Italy
Source: *AtlBL; McGDA; McGEWB; OxCArt; REn*

Pollard, Fritz
[Frederick Douglass Pollard]
American. Football Player, Football Coach
Running back, played in first modern Rose Bowl, 1916; only black head coach in NFL, with Hammond, 1923-25.
b. Jan 27, 1894 in Chicago, Illinois
d. May 11, 1986 in Silver Spring, Maryland
Source: *AfrAmSG; BioIn 3, 9, 11, 14, 15, 21; FacFETw; InB&W 80, 85; LegTOT; NewYTBE 70; NewYTBS 78, 86; WhoBlA 85; WhoSpor*

Pollard, Jim
[James C Pollard]
"Kangaroo Kid"
American. Basketball Player
Forward, Minneapolis Lakers, 1948-55; won five NBA championships; Hall of Fame, 1977.
b. Jul 9, 1922 in Oakland, California
d. Jan 22, 1993 in Stockton, California
Source: *BasBi; BiDAmSp BK; BioIn 18; OfNBA 87; WhoBbl 73; WhoSpor*

Pollard, Michael J
American. Actor
Oscar nominee for *Bonnie and Clyde,* 1967; other films include *Melvin and Howard,* 1980.
b. May 30, 1939 in Passaic, New Jersey
Source: *BiE&WWA; ConTFT 7; EncAFC; FilmgC; HalFC 88; IntMPA 92; MotPP; MovMk; VarWW 85; WhoAm 74; WhoHol A*

Pollitt, Harry
English. Political Leader
Chm., British Communist party, 1956-60; ran unsuccessfully for House of Commons, eight times.
b. Nov 22, 1890 in Droylesden, England
d. Jun 27, 1960
Source: *BioIn 1, 4, 5, 10, 11, 14, 19, 21; CurBio 48, 60; DcNaB 1951; GrBr; ObitOF 79; ObitT 1951; WhE&EA*

Pollock, Channing
American. Author, Dramatist
Wrote over 30 plays including *Harvest of My Years,* 1943; wrote song made famous by Fannie Brice, "My Man," 1920.
b. Mar 4, 1880 in Washington, District of Columbia
d. Aug 17, 1946 in New York, New York
Source: *AmAu&B; AmLY; ASCAP 66, 80; BenetAL 91; BioIn 1, 2, 4; CnDAL; CurBio 46; DcAmB S4; DcNAA; MagIlD; ModWD; NatCAB 34; NotNAT A, B; OxCAmL 65, 83, 95; OxCAmT 84; REn; REnAL; TwCA, SUP; WhAm 2; WhLit; WhNAA; WhoStg 1908; WhThe*

Pollock, Charles
American. Artist
Known for geometric abstract paintings; brother of Jackson.
b. 1902?
d. May 8, 1988 in Paris, France
Source: *BioIn 13; NewYTBS 82, 88*

Pollock, Jackson
American. Artist, Author
Founded "action painting" and Abstract Expressionism movement.
b. Jan 28, 1912 in Cody, Wyoming
d. Aug 11, 1956 in East Hampton, New York
Source: *AmDec 1950; AtlBL; Benet 87, 96; BioIn 2, 3, 4, 5, 6, 7, 8, 9, 10, 11, 12, 13, 14, 15, 16, 17, 18, 19, 20; BioNews 74; BriEAA; ConArt 77; CurBio 56; DcAmArt; DcAmB S6; DcArts; DcCAA 71, 77, 88, 94; DcTwCCu 1; EncAB-H 1974, 1996; FacFETw; IntDcAA 90; LegTOT; MakMC; McGDA; McGEWB; ModArCr 3; OxCArt; OxCTwCA; OxDcArt; PhDcTCA 77; RAdv 14; RComAH; REn; WebAB 74, 79; WhAm 4; WhAmArt 85; WhAm HSA; WhDW; WhoAmA 78N, 80N, 82N, 84N, 86N, 89N, 91N, 93N; WorAl; WorAlBi; WorArt 1950*

Pollock, Sam
Canadian. Hockey Executive
GM, Montreal, 1964-78; known for shrewd trading; considered most successful in modern hockey.
b. Dec 15, 1925 in Montreal, Quebec, Canada
Source: *BioIn 11; FolkA 87; WhoAm 74, 76, 78; WhoHcky 73*

Polo, Marco
Italian. Traveler, Author
Medieval account of Asian travels was chief source of knowledge of East.
b. 1254 in Venice, Italy
d. Jan 9, 1324 in Venice, Italy
Source: *AsBiEn; BbD; Benet 87, 96; BiD&SB; BioIn 1, 2, 3, 4, 5, 6, 7, 8, 9, 10, 11, 12, 13, 14, 15, 16, 17, 18, 19, 20, 21; BlmGEL; CasWL; ClMLC 15; CyWA 58; DcCathB; DcEuL; DcItL 1, 2; Dis&D; EuAu; EvEuW; Expl 93; LegTOT; LinLib L, S; LngCEL; McGEWB; NewC; NewCBEL; OxCEng 67, 85, 95; OxCGer 76; OxCShps; PenC EUR; RAdv 14, 13-3; RComWL; REn; WhDW; WhWE; WorAl; WorAlBi*

Pol Pot
[Saloth Sar]
Cambodian. Political Leader
Prime minister of Cambodia, 1975-79, whose efforts to create agrarian society resulted in disease, starvation.
b. May 19, 1928 in Memot, Cambodia
Source: *BiDMarx; BioIn 11, 12; ColdWar 1, 2; CurBio 80; DcMPSA; DcTwHis; DicTyr; EncRev; EncWB; FacFETw; FarE&A 79; IntWW 78, 79, 80, 81, 82, 83, 89, 91, 93; LegTOT; WhoSocC 78; WhoWor 87, 91*

Polshek, James Stewart
Architect
One of the most respected uncelebrated architects of the late 20th-century.
b. Feb 11, 1930 in Akron, Ohio
Source: *AmArch 70; BioIn 13; ConArch 80, 87, 94; MacEA; WhoAm 76, 78, 82, 84, 86, 88, 92, 95, 96; WhoWor 95*

Polya, George
American. Mathematician
His mathematical text *How to Solve It,* sold over one million copies.
b. Dec 13, 1887 in Budapest, Austria-Hungary
d. Sep 7, 1985 in Palo Alto, California
Source: *AmMWSc 73P, 76P, 79, 82; BioIn 11, 14, 15, 20; ConAu 117; FacFETw; NewYTBS 85; NotTwCS; WhAm 9; WhoAm 78, 86*

Polybius
Greek. Historian
Greek historian of the second century B.C. whose *Histories* provides the most detailed contemporary account of the rise of the Roman Empire.
b. c. 200BC in Megalopolis, Greece
d. c. 118BC in Megalopolis, Greece
Source: *ClMLC 17; Grk&L; LegTOT; OxCClL 89; RAdv 14, 13-3; RfGWoL 95; WhDW*

Polycletus the Elder
Greek. Sculptor
Greatest Greek sculptor of his time; greatest achievement was figure of Hera in temple near Argos.
b. fl. 5th cent. ?BC in Argos, Greece
Source: *Benet 87; NewCol 75; OxCClL 89; OxDcArt*

Polygnotus
Greek. Artist
Greatest Greek painter of his time, taking subject matter from epic poetry; first to draw open mouth with teeth showing, facial expressions.
b. 490BC in Thaos, Greece
d. 425?BC in Athens, Greece
Source: *DcBiPP; NewCol 75*

Pomerantz, Fred P
American. Business Executive
Founded Leslie Fay, Inc., makers of women's apparel.
b. 1902 in New York, New York
d. Feb 21, 1986 in West Palm Beach, Florida
Source: *Dun&B 79; NewYTBS 86*

Pompadour, Jeanne Antoinette Poisson
French. Mistress
Influential mistress of Louis XV from 1745; patronized authors, artists; hair style named for her.
b. Dec 29, 1721 in Paris, France
d. Apr 15, 1764 in Versailles, France
Source: *Benet 96; NewCol 75; OxCEng 67; OxCFr; WebBD 83*

Pompey the Great
[Pompeius Magnus]
Roman. Army Officer, Statesman
Rival of father-in-law, Julius Caesar; formed first Triumvirate, rulers of Rome, 60 BC.
b. Sep 30, 106BC in Rome, Italy
d. Sep 29, 48BC in Alexandria, Egypt
Source: *Benet 87, 96; BioIn 1, 2, 5, 6, 9, 11, 12, 13, 20; DcBiPP; DicTyr; LegTOT; McGEWB; NewC; OxCClL; REn; WhDW*

Pompidou, Georges Jean Raymond
French. Political Leader
Prime minister, 1962-68; pres., 1969-74.
b. Jul 5, 1911 in Cantal, France
d. Apr 2, 1974 in Paris, France
Source: *BiDInt; BioIn 6, 7, 8, 9, 10, 12, 13; ConAu 49; CurBio 62, 74; DcTwHis; NewYTBE 71, 73; WhAm 6; Who 74; WhoGov 72; WhoWor 74*

Ponce de Leon, Juan
Spanish. Explorer
Discovered FL, 1513, searching for legendary fountain of youth.
b. Apr 8, 1460 in Leon, Spain
d. 1521 in Havana, Cuba
Source: *AmBi; ApCAB; Benet 87, 96; BenetAL 91; BioIn 1, 3, 4, 5, 6, 7, 8, 11, 15, 18, 19, 20, 21; DcAmB; DcBiPP; DcCathB; DcHiB; Drake; EncCRAm; EncLatA; EncSoH; HarEnUS; HisDcSE; LinLib S; McGEWB; NatCAB 11; OxCAmH; REn; REnAW; WebAB 74, 79; WhAm HS; WhDW; WhNaAH; WhWE; WorAl; WorAlBi*

Ponchielli, Amilcare
Italian. Composer
Wrote opera *La Gioconda,* 1876, featuring "Dance of the Hours."
b. Aug 31, 1834 in Paderno, Italy
d. Jan 16, 1886 in Milan, Italy
Source: *Baker 78, 84, 92; BioIn 3, 4, 6, 7, 10, 12; BriBkM 80; CmOp; CmpBCM; DcCom 77; DcCom&M 79; GrComp; IntDcOp; LegTOT; MetOEnc; MusMk; NewAmDM; NewCol 75; NewEOp 71; NewGrDM 80; NewGrDO; NewOxM; OxCMus; OxDcOp; PenDiMP A*

Ponnamperuma, Cyril (Andrew)
American. Chemist
Professor of chemistry at U of MD, 1971-94; wrote book *Origins of Life.*
b. Oct 16, 1923
d. Dec 20, 1994 in Washington, District of Columbia
Source: *AmMWSc 73P, 76P, 79, 82, 86, 89, 92, 95; AsBiEn; BiESc; BioIn 13, 14, 20, 21; CurBio 84, 95N; IntWW 89, 91, 93; NotTwCS; WhAm 11; WhoAm 82, 84, 90, 92, 94; WhoE 86, 95; WhoFrS 84; WhoGov 72; WhoScEn 94; WorScD*

Pons, Lily
French. Opera Singer
Coloratura soprano, reigning diva, NY Met., 1928-53; wife of Andre Kostelanetz.
b. Apr 12, 1904 in Cannes, France
d. Feb 13, 1976 in Dallas, Texas
Source: *Baker 84; BiDAmM; BioIn 1, 2, 3, 4, 5, 7, 8, 9, 10, 11, 14; CmOp; CmpEPM; CurBio 44, 76, 76N; FilmgC; ForYSC; HalFC 80, 84, 88; InWom, SUP; LegTOT; LibW; LinLib S; MusMk; MusSN; NewCol 75; NewEOp 71; RadStar; ThFT; What 2; Who 74; WhScrn 83; WorAl; WorAlBi*

Ponselle, Carmela
[Carmela Ponzillo]
American. Opera Singer
Mezzo-soprano, NY Met., 1920s-30s; sister of Rosa.
b. Jun 7, 1892 in Schenectady, New York
d. 1977
Source: *Baker 78, 84, 92; BioIn 11; InWom; NewAmDM; NewEOp 71*

Ponselle, Rosa
[Rose Ponzillo]
American. Opera Singer
Outstanding NY Met. soprano, 1918-37; debuted with Caruso, made several recordings.
b. Jan 22, 1894 in Meriden, Connecticut
d. May 25, 1981 in Stevenson, Maryland
Source: *Baker 84; BiDAmM; LibW; LinLib S; MusSN; NewCol 75; NewEOp 71; NewYTBE 72; NewYTBS 81; WhAm 8; WhoAmW 75; WhoMus 72*

Ponsonby, Sarah
[Ladies of Llangollen]
Irish. Writer
Eloped with fellow nobelwoman Lady Eleanor Butler.
b. 1755
d. 1831
Source: *GayLesB*

Pontecorvo, Gillo
[Gilberto Pontecorvo]
Italian. Director
Films include *Kapo; Battle of Algiers; Burn.*
b. Nov 19, 1919 in Pisa, Italy
Source: *BiDFilm, 81, 94; BioIn 9, 13, 16; DcFM; EncEurC; FilmEn; FilmgC; HalFC 80, 84, 88; IntDcF 1-2, 2-2; IntMPA 92, 94, 96; IntWW 89, 91, 93; ItaFilm; LegTOT; MiSFD 9; MovMk; OxCFilm; WorEFlm; WorFDir 2*

Ponti, Carlo
Italian. Producer
Credited with discovering Sophia Loren, whom he later married; won Oscar for *La Strada,* 1956.
b. Dec 11, 1913 in Milan, Italy
Source: *BioIn 7, 8, 9, 11; CelR; ConTFT 3; DcFM; FilmgC; HalFC 80, 84, 88; IntMPA 75, 76, 77, 78, 79, 80, 81, 82, 84, 86, 88, 92, 94, 96; IntWW 74, 75, 76, 77, 78, 79, 80, 81, 82, 83, 89, 91, 93; OxCFilm; VarWW 85; Who 85, 92; WhoWor 74, 76, 78, 80, 82, 84, 87, 89, 91, 93, 95; WorAl; WorAlBi; WorEFlm*

Ponti, Gio(vanni)
Italian. Architect, Designer
Created frescos at Padua, scenography for La Scala; marine decorator for Andrea Doria.
b. Nov 18, 1891 in Milan, Italy
d. Sep 15, 1979 in Milan, Italy
Source: *BioIn 3, 4, 8, 12, 13, 14; ConArch 80, 87, 94; ConDes 84, 90, 97; DcArts; DcD&D; DcTwDes; EncMA; IntDcAr; IntWW 74, 75, 76, 77, 78, 79; MacEA; McGDA; PenDiDA 89; WhAm 7; WhoArch; WhoWor 74*

Pontiac
American. Native American Chief
Ottawa chief who became symbol of Indian resistance; attacked British command in Detroit, 1763.
b. 1720 in Ohio
d. Apr 20, 1769 in Missouri
Source: *AmBi; ApCAB; BenetAL 91; BioIn 4, 5, 6, 7, 8, 9, 10, 11, 12; BlkwEAR; DcAmB; DcAmMiB; Drake; EncAAH; EncAB-H 1974, 1996; EncCRAm; EncNAB; EncNoAI; GenMudB; HarEnMi; HarEnUS; HisWorL; LegTOT; LinLib S; McGEWB; NatCAB 10; NotNaAm; OxCAmH; OxCAmL 65, 83, 95; OxCCan; RComAH; REn; REnAL; WebAB 74, 79; WebAMB; WebBD 83; WhAm HS; WhDW; WhNaAH; WhoMilH 76; WorAl; WorAlBi*

Pontian, Saint
Roman. Religious Leader
Pope, 230-235; first to abdicate.
d. 236?
Source: *BioIn 5, 7; DcCathB; OxDcP 86; WebBD 83*

Pontoppidan, Henrik
Danish. Author
Novels, short stories describe Denmark in realistic style; shared Nobel Prize, 1917.
b. Jul 24, 1857 in Fredericia, Denmark
d. Aug 21, 1943 in Copenhagen, Denmark
Source: *Benet 87, 96; BioIn 1, 3, 4, 5, 9, 12, 15; CasWL; ClDMEL 47, 80; CyWA 58; DcScanL; EncWL; EvEuW; FacFETw; LegTOT; LinLib L, S; NewCBEL; NobelP; Novels; PenC EUR; REn; TwCA, SUP; TwCLC 29; WhDW; WhE&EA; WhLit; WhoLA; WhoNob, 90, 95; WhoTwCL; WorAl*

Pontormo, Jacopo da
[Jacopo Carrucci]
Italian. Artist
Disciple of Michelangelo, Florentine School; best known for frescoes.
b. 1494 in Pontormo, Italy
d. Dec 1556 in Florence, Italy
Source: *DcArts; LegTOT; McGDA; McGEWB; OxCArt; REn; WorAl; WorAlBi*

Ponty, Jean-Luc
French. Violinist
Former classical, now jazz, rock, and fusion violinist credited with increased popularity of jazz violin.
b. Sep 29, 1942 in Avranches, France
Source: *Baker 84, 92; BiDJaz; BioIn 13, 15, 16, 17; ConMuA 80A; ConMus 8; ConNews 85-4; EncJzS; IlEncJ; IlEncRk; LegTOT; NewAgMG; NewAmDM; NewGrDJ 88, 94; NewGrDM 80; PenEncP; RolSEnR 83; WhoAm 78, 80, 82, 84, 86, 88, 90, 92, 94, 95, 96, 97; WhoEnt 92; WhoRock 81; WhoWor 74*

Pool, David de Sola
American. Religious Leader
Founded several Jewish organizations including Synagogue Council of America, 1938; wrote *Why I Am a Jew,* 1957.
b. May 16, 1885 in London, England
d. Dec 1, 1970 in New York, New York
Source: *AmAu&B; JeAmHC; NewYTBE 70; WhAm 5; WhNAA*

Poole, Ernest
American. Journalist, Author
Won Pulitzer for *His Family,* 1917.
b. Jan 23, 1880 in Chicago, Illinois
d. Jan 10, 1950 in Franconia, New Hampshire
Source: *AmAu&B; AmLY; AmNov; BenetAL 91; BioIn 2, 4, 7, 9, 12; CnDAL; ConAmA; ConAmL; ConAu 109; DcAmB S4; DcLB 9; DcLEL; LinLib L; NatCAB 18; OxCAmL 65, 83, 95; REn; REnAL; TwCA, SUP; WhAm 2; WhLit; WhNAA*

Poole, William Frederick
American. Librarian
Published *Poor's Index,* first index to periodicals in US, 1848; organized Cincinnati Public Library, 1869, Chicago Public Library, 1874.
b. Dec 24, 1821 in Salem, Massachusetts
d. Mar 1, 1894 in Evanston, Illinois
Source: *Alli, SUP; AmAu; AmAu&B; AmBi; ApCAB; BbD; BenetAL 91; BiD&SB; BioIn 1, 2, 3, 6, 10, 11, 15; CyEd; DcAmAu; DcAmB; DcAmLiB; DcNAA; Drake; HarEnUS; NatCAB 6, 22; OhA&B; OxCAmL 65, 83, 95; REn; REnAL; TwCBDA; WhAm HS*

Poons, Lawrence
[Larry Poons]
American. Artist
Op art painter; prominent member of Colour Field school of art.
b. Oct 1, 1937 in Tokyo, Japan
Source: *AmArt; BioIn 8, 9; BriEAA; CenC; ConArt 77, 83, 89, 96; DcCAA 71, 77, 88; DcCAr 81; McGDA; OxCTwCA; PhDcTCA 77; PrintW 85; WhoAm 82, 84, 86, 88, 94, 95, 96, 97; WhoAmA 73, 76, 78, 80, 82, 84, 86, 89, 91, 93; WorArt 1950*

Poor, Henry Varnum, III
American. Artist
Landscape painter; did 12 panel fresco in Dept. of Justice, Washington, DC; founded art school, 1946.
b. Sep 30, 1888 in Chapman, Kansas
d. Dec 8, 1970 in New York, New York
Source: *ArtsAmW 1; BioIn 1, 3, 7, 9; BriEAA; CenC; CurBio 42, 71, 71N; DcAmArt; DcAmB; DcCAA 71, 77, 88; IlBEAAW; McGDA; WhAm 5; WhAmArt 85; WhoAmA 78N, 80N, 82N, 84N, 86N, 89N, 91N, 93N*

Pop, Iggy
[James Newell Osterberg]
"Iggy Stooge"
American. Singer
Early proponent of punk rock known for primitive sound, outlandish stage antics; albums include *Instinct,* 1988.
b. Apr 21, 1947 in Ann Arbor, Michigan
Source: *BioIn 14, 15, 17, 19, 20, 21; ConMuA 80A; ConMus 1; CurBio 95; DcArts; EncPR&S 89; EncRk 88; EncRkSt; HarEnR 86; IlEncRk; LegTOT; NewAmDM; NewGrDA 86; RolSEnR 83; WhoAm 84, 86, 88, 90, 92, 94, 95, 96, 97; WhoRock 81; WhoRocM 82*

Popa, Vasko
Yugoslav. Poet
Contemporary poet inspired by Serbian folk tradition: *Earth Erect,* 1973.
b. Jul 29, 1922 in Grebenac, Yugoslavia
Source: *Benet 96; BioIn 17; CasWL; ClDMEL 80; ConAu 112, 148; ConFLW 84; ConLC 19; EncWL 2, 3; ModSL 2; NewYTBS 91; PenC EUR; RAdv 14, 13-2; RfGWoL 95; RGFMEP; TwCA; TwCWr; WhoSocC 78; WhoSoCE 89; WhoTwCL; WorAlBi; WorAu 1970*

Popcorn, Faith
American. Consultant
Trend analyst; predicts new areas of consumer interest; predicted Coke's "New Coke" flavor would fail.
b. May 11, 1947? in New York, New York
Source: *BioIn 15; ConNews 88-1; CurBio 93; NewYTBS 91*

Pope, Alexander
English. Poet
Verse satirist; wrote *The Rape of the Lock,* 1714; *Moral Essays,* 1731-35.
b. May 21, 1688 in London, England
d. May 30, 1744 in Twickenham, England
Source: *Alli; AtlBL; BbD; Benet 87, 96; BiD&SB; BioIn 1, 2, 3, 4, 5, 6, 7, 8, 9, 10, 11, 12, 13, 14, 15, 16, 17, 18, 20; BlkwCE; BlmGEL; BritAu; BritWr 3; CamGEL; CamGLE; CasWL; Chambr 2; ChhPo, S1, S3; CnDBLB 2; CnE&AP; CrtT 2, 4; CyWA 58; DcArts; DcBiPP; DcCathB; DcEnA; DcEnL; DcEuL; DcLB 95, 101; DcLEL; DcNaB, C; Dis&D; EncEnl; EvLB; GrWrEL P; LegTOT; LinLib L, S; LitC 3; LngCEL; LuthC 75; MagSWL; McGEWB; MouLC 2; NewC; NewCBEL; NewGrDM 80; OxCEng 67, 85, 95; OxCMus; PenC ENG; RAdv 1, 14, 13-1; RComWL; REn; RfGEnL 91; RGFBP; WebE&AL; WhDW; WorAl; WorAlBi; WorLitC; WrPh*

Pope, Generoso
American. Publisher
Owner and publisher of *The National Enquirer* and *Weekly World News,* 1952-88.
b. Jan 13, 1927 in New York, New York
d. Oct 2, 1988 in Lantana, Florida
Source: *BioIn 8, 9, 16; ConAmBL; ConAu 126; EncTwCJ; News 88; NewYTBS 88; WhoAm 88, 92; WhoSSW 88*

Pope, John Russell
American. Architect
Designs include the National Gallery.
b. Apr 24, 1874 in New York, New York
d. Aug 27, 1937 in New York, New York
Source: *AmBi; BiDAmAr; BioIn 1, 4, 13, 17; DcAmB S2; DcD&D; EncAAr 1, 2; EncWB; IntDcAr; LinLib S; MacEA; McGDA; NatCAB 28; WhAm 1*

Popov, Aleksandr Stepanovich
Russian. Inventor
Independent of Marconi, he built a radio; the Soviets claimed that he was the first.
b. Mar 16, 1859 in Turinskiye Rudniki, Russia
d. Jan 13, 1906 in Saint Petersburg, Russia
Source: *BiESc; BioIn 2, 5, 6, 18; CamDcSc; DcScB; InSci; LarDcSc; WorInv*

Popov, Dusko
"Tricycle"
British. Spy
Double agent for Britain, WW II; model for Ian Fleming's James Bond.
b. 1912 in Dubrovnik, Yugoslavia
d. Aug 21, 1981 in Opio, France
Source: *AnObit 1981; AuSpks; BioIn 10, 11, 12, 13, 17; BioNews 74; ConAu 105; FacFETw*

Popov, Oleg Konstantinovich
Russian. Clown
Russia's "Chaplin"; much-loved entertainer with Moscow's State Circus, 1955—.
b. Aug 3, 1930 in Moscow, Union of Soviet Socialist Republics
Source: *BiDSovU; CamGWoT; CurBio 64; EncWT; Ent; IntWW 74, 75, 83, 89, 91, 93; WhoWor 74*

Popovich, Pavel Romanovich
Russian. Cosmonaut
Crew member, *Vostok 4;* first to make group flight with *Vostok 3,* 1962.
b. Oct 5, 1930

Source: *BioIn 6, 7, 15; IntWW 74, 75, 76, 77; WhoSocC 78; WhoSpc; WhoWor 74; WorDWW*

Popovi Da
American. Artist
Parents were credited with reviving the art of Pueblo pottery; graduated from the Santa Fe Indian School, where he studied art, 1939.
b. Apr 10, 1923
d. Oct 17, 1971 in Santa Fe, New Mexico
Source: *BioIn 11; EncNAB; NotNaAm*

Popper, Hans
Austrian. Pathologist
Founded the study of liver and its diseases: hepatology.
b. Nov 24, 1903 in Vienna, Austria
d. May 6, 1988 in New York, New York
Source: *AmMWSc 73P, 76P, 79, 82, 86; AnObit 1988; BiDrACP 79; BlueB 76; FacFETw; NewYTBS 88; WhAm 9; WhoAm 74, 76, 78, 80, 82, 84, 86; WhoWorJ 72, 78*

Popper, Karl R(aimund), Sir
English. Philosopher
Wrote *The Open Society and Its Enemies,* 1945; *The Poverty of Historicism,* 1957; known for ideas on Marxism.
b. Jul 28, 1902 in Vienna, Austria
d. Sep 17, 1994 in Croydon, England
Source: *Au&Wr 71; Benet 87, 96; BiESc; BioIn 4, 6, 10, 11, 12, 13, 14, 17, 18, 20, 21; ConAu 3NR, 5R, 20NR, 146; ConLC 86; CurBio 94N; FacFETw; IntAu&W 76, 77, 82, 89; IntEnSS 79; IntWW 93; LinLib L; MajTwCW; MakMC; McGEWB; NewCBEL; OxCEng 85, 95; RAdv 14, 13-4, 13-5; TwCA SUP; WhAm 11; WhDW; WhE&EA; Who 94; WhoScEn 94; WrDr 76, 94, 96*

Porizkova, Paulina
American. Model, Actor
Popular model represents Estee Lauder Company; films include *Anna,* 1987; *Her Alibi,* 1988.
b. Apr 9, 1965 in Protejov, Czechoslovakia
Source: *BioIn 14, 15, 16; ConNews 86-4; LegTOT; WhoAm 94, 95, 96, 97; WhoEnt 92; WhoHol 92*

Porpora, Niccolo
Italian. Composer
Wrote over 40 operas including *Mitridate,* 1736; famed singing teacher.
b. Aug 19, 1686 in Naples, Italy
d. Feb 1766 in Naples, Italy
Source: *Baker 84; BioIn 14; NewCol 75; NewEOp 71; OxCMus*

Porritt, Arthur Espie, Sir
New Zealander. Government Official
Member, Royal Medical Household, 1936-67; vp, governor-general of New Zealand, 1967-72.
b. Aug 10, 1900 in Wanganui, New Zealand
Source: *BioIn 14; IntMed 80; IntWW 83; WhE&EA; Who 85, 92*

Porsche, Ferdinand
Austrian. Auto Manufacturer, Inventor
Invented German Volkswagon.
b. Sep 3, 1875 in Maffersdorf, Bohemia
d. Jan 30, 1951 in Stuttgart, Germany (West)
Source: *BioIn 2, 5, 8, 11, 19; DcTwDes; EncTR 91; Entr; FacFETw; LegTOT; ObitOF 79*

Porsche, Ferdinand
Austrian. Auto Manufacturer
Pres., F Porsche K G, Stuttgart, 1972—; wrote *We at Porsche,* 1976; son of Ferdinand.
b. Sep 19, 1909 in Wiener Neustadt, Austria
Source: *BioIn 5, 8, 9, 11, 14; ConAu 89; WhoFI 74; WhoWor 74*

Portales, Diego (Jose Victor)
Chilean. Politician
Chief minister of the Conservative Party and virtual dictator of Chile, 1830-1837; leader in the defeat of the Peru-Bolivian confederation, 1836.
b. Jun 26, 1793 in Santiago, Chile
d. Jun 6, 1837 in Valparaiso, Chile
Source: *ApCAB; BioIn 16; DcHiB; DicTyr; EncLatA; HisWorL*

Porter, Bernard H
American. Author
English history books include *British Imperialism 1850-1970,* 1976.
b. Feb 14, 1911 in Porter, Maine
Source: *BioIn 16; ConAu 24NR, 107; DrAPF 91; IntAu&W 91; WhoE 89; WhoTech 89; WhoUSWr 88; WhoWrEP 89; WrDr 86, 90*

Porter, Bill
[William Porter]
American. Track Athlete
Hurdler; won gold medal, 110-meter hurdles, 1948 Olympics.
b. Mar 24, 1926 in Jackson, Michigan
Source: *WhoTr&F 73*

Porter, Cole
American. Composer, Lyricist
Wrote musicals *Kiss Me, Kate; Can-Can; Silk Stockings;* song "Night and Day."
b. Jun 9, 1892 in Peru, Indiana
d. Oct 15, 1964 in Santa Monica, California
Source: *ASCAP 66; Baker 84; BiDAmM; CamHAL; CmMov; CmpEPM; ConAmC 76, 82; ConAu 93; DancEn 78; EncAB-H 1974; EncMT; EncWT; Ent; FilmEn; FilmgC; IndAu 1917; LngCTC; McGEWB; McGEWD 72; MnPM; MusMk; NewCBMT; OxCAmL 95; OxCFilm; PopAmC SUP; REnAL; WebAB 74; WhAm 4; WorAl*

Porter, Connie
American. Writer
Author of *All-Bright Court,* 1991, a novel of the sufferings of black Americans in a northern inductrial community.
b. 1959? in New York
Source: *ConLC 70*

Porter, Darrell Ray
American. Baseball Player
Catcher, 1971-87; MVP, 1982 World Series.
b. Jan 17, 1952 in Joplin, Missouri
Source: *Ballpl 90; BaseReg 86, 87; BioIn 12, 13, 14, 16; WhoAm 82, 84, 86, 88*

Porter, David Dixon
American. Military Leader
Commanded Civil War fleet; wrote book on experiences, 1887.
b. Jun 8, 1813 in Chester, Pennsylvania
d. Feb 13, 1891 in Washington, District of Columbia
Source: *Alli SUP; AmAu&B; AmBi; ApCAB; BenetAL 91; BiD&SB; BioIn 4, 7, 8, 9, 10; CivWDc; DcAmAu; DcAmB; DcAmMiB; DcNAA; Drake; GenMudB; HarEnMi; HarEnUS; LinLib S; NatCAB 2; OxCAmH; OxCShps; REnAL; TwCBDA; WebAB 74, 79; WebAMB; WhAm HS; WhCiWar; WhoMilH 76; WorAl; WorAlBi*

Porter, Don
American. Actor
Played Ann Sothern's boss on "Private Secretary," 1953-57, and on "The Ann Sothern Show," 1958-61; played Gidget's father on "Gidget," 1965; film *The Candidate,* 1972.
b. 1912 in Oklahoma
d. Feb 11, 1997 in Los Angeles, California
Source: *FilmEn; FilmgC; ForYSC; HalFC 80, 84, 88; IntMPA 77, 80, 92, 94, 96; NotNAT; WhoHol 92, A; WhoThe 72, 77, 81*

Porter, Edwin
American. Director
Films include *Great Train Robbery; Uncle Tom's Cabin,* 1903.
b. Apr 21, 1870 in Connellsville, Pennsylvania
d. Apr 30, 1941 in New York, New York
Source: *CmMov; CurBio 41; DcAmB S3; DcFM; FilmgC; LegTOT; OxCFilm; REnAL; TwYS; WomWMM; WorEFlm*

Porter, Eleanor H
American. Author
Best known for children's *Polyanna* books, 1913-18.
b. Dec 19, 1868 in Littleton, New Hampshire
d. May 21, 1920 in Cambridge, Massachusetts
Source: *AmAu&B; AmLY; BenetAL 91; BioIn 14; CarSB; ConAu 108; DcLB 9; DcLEL; DcNAA; EvLB; LngCEL;*

OxCAmL 65; REn; REnAL; TwCA, SUP; TwCChW 83, 89; TwCRHW 90; TwCWr

Porter, Eliot Furness
American. Photographer
Wildlife photographer; concentrated on the minute elements in nature to convey its greatness; publications include *Birds of North America,* 1972.
b. Dec 6, 1901 in Winnetka, Illinois
d. Nov 2, 1990 in Santa Fe, New Mexico
Source: *AmArt; BioIn 7, 8, 10, 11, 12, 13; MacBEP; WhoAm 74, 76, 78, 80, 82, 84, 86, 88, 90; WhoAmA 76, 78, 80, 82, 84, 86, 89*

Porter, Eric Richard
English. Actor
Played Soames on TV's "The Forsyte Saga."
b. Apr 8, 1928 in London, England
d. May 15, 1995 in London, England
Source: *ConTFT 3; FilmEn; FilmgC; HalFC 84, 88; IntWW 74, 75, 76, 77, 78, 79, 80, 81, 82, 83, 89, 91, 93; OxCThe 83; VarWW 85; WhAm 11; Who 85, 92, 94; WhoThe 81; WhoWor 84, 87, 91, 93, 95*

Porter, Fairfield
American. Artist
Representative painter; had several one-man shows, 1950s-70s.
b. Jun 10, 1907 in Winnetka, Illinois
d. Sep 18, 1975 in Southampton, New York
Source: *BioIn 3, 4, 6, 10, 11, 13, 14, 18, 19; BlueB 76; BriEAA; ConAu 61; DcAmArt; DcCAA 71, 77, 88, 94; DcTwCCu 1; NewYTBS 75; ObitOF 79; OxCTwCA; PeoHis; PhDcTCA 77; PrintW 83, 85; WhAm 6; WhoAm 74, 78; WhoAmA 73, 76N, 78N, 80N, 84N, 86N, 89N, 91N, 93N; WhoE 74*

Porter, Gene Stratton
American. Author, Naturalist
Wrote sentimental novels including *Freckles,* 1904; *Laddie,* 1913 ; noted now as nature photographer.
b. Aug 17, 1868 in Wabash County, Indiana
d. Dec 6, 1924 in Los Angeles, California
Source: *AmAu&B; AmBi; AmLY; CarSB; ChhPo; CnDAL; DcAmB S1; DcLEL; DcNAA; EvLB; IndAu 1816; InWom; LinLib L, S; LngCTC; NatCAB 15; NotAW; OxCAmL 65; PenC AM; PenNWW B; REn; REnAL; TwCA, SUP; TwCWr; WebAB 74; WhAm 1; WhoChL*

Porter, George, Sir
English. Educator
Shared 1967 Nobel Prize in chemistry for researching rapid chemical reactions.
b. Dec 6, 1920 in Stainforth, England
Source: *AsBiEn; BiESc; BioIn 4, 8, 9, 14, 15, 19, 20; BlueB 76; CamDcSc; ConAu 107; IntAu&W 77, 82, 91; IntWW 74, 75, 76, 77, 78, 79, 80, 81, 82, 83, 89; IntYB 78, 79, 80, 81, 82; LarDcSc; McGMS 80; NobelP; NotTwCS; Who 74, 82, 83, 85, 88, 90; WhoAm 88, 90, 92, 94, 95; WhoNob, 90, 95; WhoScEn 94, 96; WhoWor 74, 76, 78, 80, 82, 84, 87, 89, 91, 93, 95, 96, 97; WorAl; WorAlBi; WrDr 76, 80, 82, 84, 86, 88, 90, 92, 94, 96*

Porter, Hal
Australian. Author
Best-known novel *The Tilted Cross,* 1961, considered an Australian classic.
b. Feb 16, 1911 in Victoria Park, Australia
d. Sep 29, 1984, Australia
Source: *AnObit 1984; Au&Wr 71; AuLitCr; Benet 87; BlueB 76; CamGLE; CasWL; ConAu 3NR, 9R, 114; ConDr 73, 77, 82, 93; ConNov 72, 76, 82; ConPo 70, 75, 80; DcLEL 1940; FarE&A 78, 79, 80, 81; GrWrEL N; IntAu&W 76, 82; IntWW 78, 79, 80, 81, 82, 83; IntWWP 77, 82; LegTOT; ModCmwL; NewC; OxCAusL; OxCThe 83; OxCTwCP; RAdv 13-1; RfGEnL 91; RfGShF; TwCRHW 90, 94; WhAm 11; WhoWor 74, 78, 84, 87; WorAu 1985; WrDr 76, 80, 82, 84*

Porter, James A(mos)
American. Painter
Art professor, Howard University, 1927-70; researched early black artists, bringing much art out of obscurity.
b. Dec 22, 1905 in Baltimore, Maryland
d. Feb 28, 1970
Source: *BioIn 3, 8; InB&W 80, 85; SelBAAf; WhAmArt 85*

Porter, Katherine Anne
"The Angel of Malignity"
American. Author
Won Pulitzer, 1966, for her only full-length novel, *Ship of Fools.*
b. May 15, 1894 in Indian Creek, Texas
d. Sep 18, 1980 in Silver Spring, Maryland
Source: *AmAu&B; AmWomWr 92; BioIn 1, 3, 4, 5; CasWL; CnDAL; CnMWL; ConAmA; ConAu 1NR, 101; ConLC 15; ConNov 76; CurBio 40, 63; CyWA 58; DcLEL; DrAF 76; EncWL; EvLB; ForWC 70; LinLib L; LngCTC; MakMC; ModAL, S1; OxCAmL 65; PenC AM; RAdv 1, 13-1; REn; TwCA, SUP; TwCWr; WhE&EA; WhoAmW 58*

Porter, Nyree Dawn
New Zealander. Actor
Horror films include *Beyond the Grave.*
b. 1940
Source: *FilmgC; HalFC 80, 84, 88; VarWW 85; WhoHol A*

Porter, Quincy
American. Composer
Won Pulitzer for Concerto for "Two Pianos & Orchestra," 1954.
b. Feb 7, 1897 in New Haven, Connecticut
d. Nov 12, 1966 in New Haven, Connecticut
Source: *AmComp; Baker 78, 84; BioIn 1, 3, 6, 7, 8; CompSN; ConAmC 76, 82; DcCM; IntWWM 77, 80; LegTOT; NewAmDM; NewGrDA 86; NewGrDM 80; NotNAT B; OxCMus; WhAm 4*

Porter, Richard William
American. Engineer
Appointed project engineer of the guided missile program for General Electric, 1945; became manager of GE's guided missile program, 1952.
b. Mar 24, 1913
d. Oct 6, 1996 in Cheverly, Maryland
Source: *BioIn 5; InSci; IntWW 74, 75, 76, 77, 78, 79, 80, 81, 82, 83; IntYB 78, 79, 80, 81, 82; WhoAm 74, 76, 78, 80, 82, 84*

Porter, Rodney Robert
English. Chemist
Shared Nobel Prize in medicine, 1972, for studying the chemical structure of antibodies.
b. Oct 8, 1917 in Liverpool, England
d. Sep 6, 1985 in Winchester, England
Source: *BiESc; BioIn 9, 10, 14, 15, 20; BlueB 76; CamDcSc; DcNaB 1981; IntWW 74, 75, 76, 77, 78, 79, 80, 81, 82, 83; LarDcSc; McGMS 80; NewYTBE 72; WhAm 9; Who 74, 82, 83, 85; WhoNob, 90, 95; WhoWor 74, 78, 80, 82, 84; WorAl*

Porter, Sylvia Field
American. Journalist, Author
Syndicated financial columnist; wrote *Sylvia Porter's Your Finances in the 1990s,* 1990.
b. Jun 18, 1913 in Patchogue, New York
d. Jun 5, 1991 in Pound Ridge, New York
Source: *AmWomWr; BioIn 13, 17, 18; ConAu 81, 134; CurBio 80, 91N; EncTwCJ; InWom SUP; LibW; News 91; NewYTBS 80, 91; PenNWW A; WhoAm 74, 76, 78, 80, 82, 86, 90; WhoAmW 87, 91; WhoE 74, 89; WhoFI 83, 85; WhoUSWr 88; WhoWrEP 89; WorAl; WrDr 86, 90*

Porter, William James
American. Diplomat
Chief US negotiator at Paris peace talks to end Vietnam War, 1971, 1972; ambassador to four countries in 40-yr. foreign service career.
b. Sep 1, 1914 in Staleybridge, England
d. Mar 15, 1988 in Fall River, Massachusetts
Source: *BioIn 9, 10, 11, 15, 16; BlueB 76; CurBio 74, 88; IntWW 74, 75, 76, 77, 78, 79, 80, 81, 82, 83; MidE 78; USBiR 74; WhoAmP 73, 75, 77, 79; WhoGov 72, 75, 77; WhoWor 76, 78, 80, 82, 84*

Porter, William Trotter
American. Journalist
Founded racy journal, *Spirit of the Times,* 1831; noted for tales of Southwest.
b. Dec 24, 1809 in Newburg, Vermont

d. Jul 19, 1858 in New York, New York
Source: *Alli; AmAu&B; ApCAB; BenetAL 91; BiDAmSp OS; BioIn 4, 9, 12, 15; DcAmB; DcLB 3, 43; DcNAA; JrnUS; OxCAmL 65; REnAL; TwCBDA; WhAm HS*

Portis, Charles
American. Author
Best-known work, *True Grit,* 1968; John Wayne won Oscar in film, 1969.
b. Dec 28, 1933 in El Dorado, Arkansas
Source: *AmAu&B; ConAu 1NR, 45; DcLB 6; EncFWF; IntAu&W 91; MagSAmL; TwCWW 82, 91; WorAu 1980; WrDr 84, 86, 88, 90, 92*

Portman, Eric
English. Actor
Character actor, 1934-69; films include *Mark of Cain; Prince and the Pauper.*
b. Jul 13, 1903 in Halifax, England
d. Dec 7, 1969 in Saint Veep, England
Source: *BiE&WWA; BioIn 4, 8, 9; CnThe; CurBio 57, 70; FilmAG WE; FilmEn; FilmgC; ForYSC; HalFC 80, 84, 88; IlWWBF, A; MotPP; NotNAT B; ObitT 1961; OxCThe 83; PlP&P; WhoHol B; WhScrn 74, 77, 83; WhThe*

Portman, John Calvin, Jr.
American. Architect
Urban developments include Peachtree Center, Atlanta; Renaissance Center, Detroit.
b. Dec 4, 1924 in Walhalla, South Carolina
Source: *BioIn 9, 10, 11, 12, 13, 14, 15; ConArch 87, 94; EncAAr 2; News 88-2; NewYTBE 73; St&PR 91; WhoAm 74, 76, 78, 80, 82, 84, 86, 88, 92, 94; WhoSSW 73, 75; WorAl; WorAlBi*

Posey, Alexander Lawrence
[Fux Fixico; Chinnubbie Harjo]
American. Writer
Bought *Indian Journal,* 1902; poems collected and published, 1910.
b. Aug 3, 1873 in Oklahoma
d. May 27, 1908
Source: *AmAu&B; BenetAL 91; BiNAW, B, SupB; BioIn 11; ConAu 144; DcAmB; DcNAA; DcNAL; EncNAB; NatCAB 19; NotNaAm; REnAL; REnAW; WhNaAH*

Posner, Richard Allen
American. Judge
Federal judge, US Court of Appeals, Chicago, 1981-93, chief judge, 1993.
b. Jan 11, 1939 in New York, New York
Source: *BioIn 14; ConAu 135; CurBio 93; GrEconS; WhoAm 84, 86, 88, 90, 92, 94, 95, 96, 97; WhoAmL 87, 90, 92, 94, 96; WhoAmP 87, 89, 91, 93, 95; WhoEc 81, 86; WhoMW 88, 90, 93*

Posner, Vladimir
Russian. TV Personality
Popular TV host in Soviet Union; co-hosted with Phil Donahue, 1985.
b. Apr 1, 1934 in Paris, France
Source: *BioIn 14; NewYTBS 85*

Post, Charles William
American. Businessman
Founded Postum Cereal Co., 1897; created Grape-Nuts cereal.
b. Oct 26, 1854 in Springfield, Illinois
d. May 9, 1914 in Santa Barbara, California
Source: *BiDAmBL 83; BioIn 4, 7, 18; DcAmB; NatCAB 14, 25; WebAB 74, 79; WhAm 1; WorAl*

Post, Elizabeth Lindley
American. Author
Continues editing work of Emily Post, her husband's grandmother.
b. May 7, 1920 in Englewood, New Jersey
Source: *ArtclWW 2; ConAu 49; WhoAm 76, 78, 80, 82, 84, 86, 88, 90, 92; WhoAmW 72, 74, 75*

Post, Emily (Price)
American. Author, Journalist
Wrote definitive work on proper social behavior, *Etiquette,* 1922.
b. Oct 3, 1873 in Baltimore, Maryland
d. Sep 25, 1960 in New York, New York
Source: *AmAu&B; AmWomWr; BenetAL 91; BiDAmNC; BioAmW; BioIn 1, 14; ConAu 89, 103; ContDcW 89; CurBio 41, 60; DcAmB S6; EncAJ; EncWB; EvLB; IntDcWB; InWom, SUP; JrnUS; MorMA; OxCAmL 65, 83, 95; RadStar; REn; REnAL; WebAB 74, 79; WhAm 4; WhE&EA; WomFir; WomNov; WorAlBi*

Post, Marjorie Merriweather
American. Business Executive, Philanthropist
Post cereal heiress; wife of E F Hutton, Joseph Davies; mother of Dina Merrill.
b. Mar 15, 1887 in Springfield, Illinois
d. Sep 12, 1973 in Hollywood, California
Source: *BiDAmBL 83*

Post, Sandra
Canadian. Golfer
Turned pro, 1968; won LPGA, 1968.
b. Jun 4, 1948 in Oakville, Ontario, Canada
Source: *BioIn 11, 13; WhoGolf; WhoIntG*

Post, Wiley
American. Aviator
Solo round the world flight, 1933; killed in crash with Will Rogers.
b. Nov 22, 1900 in Grand Saline, Texas
d. Aug 15, 1935 in Point Barrow, Alaska
Source: *AmBi; BioIn 2, 6, 12; DcAmB S1; DcNAA; WebAB 74; WhAm 1; WhoHol B; WhScrn 74, 77*

Poston, Tom
American. Comedian, Actor
Broadway, stage actor; played George Utley on TV comedy ''Newhart,'' 1982-90.
b. Oct 17, 1927 in Columbus, Ohio
Source: *BiE&WWA; BioIn 5, 6, 12, 16, 21; ConTFT 4; CurBio 61; EncAFC; FilmgC; ForYSC; HalFC 80, 84, 88; IntMPA 88, 92, 94, 96; LegTOT; NotNAT; VarWW 85; WhoAm 74, 80, 82, 86, 88, 90, 92, 94, 95, 96, 97; WhoEnt 92; WhoHol A; WhoTelC; WhoThe 77; WorAl; WorAlBi*

Potemkin, Grigori Alexsandrovich
Russian. Military Leader
Conspirator in plot against Peter III, 1762; favored by Catherine III, 1774; created Prince of Tauris, 1787.
b. Sep 13, 1739 in Chizhovo, Russia
d. Oct 5, 1791 in Iasi, Romania
Source: *McGEWB; NewCol 75; REn; WebBD 83*

Potofsky, Jacob Samuel
American. Labor Union Official
President of Amalgamated Clothing Workers of America (ACWA), 1946-72.
b. Nov 16, 1894 in Radomisl, Russia
d. Aug 5, 1979 in New York, New York
Source: *BiDAmL; BiDAmLL; BioIn 1, 11, 12; CurBio 46, 79; NewYTBE 70, 72; NewYTBS 79; PolProf T; WhAm 7; WhoAm 74; WhoLab 76; WhoWor 74; WhoWorJ 72; WorAl*

Potok, Anna Maximilian Apfelbaum
American. Designer
Pres., Maximilian Furs, 1953-72; cons., Maximilian Furs, 1972-87.
b. Jun 4, 1904 in Warsaw, Poland
d. Apr 22, 1987 in New York, New York
Source: *BioIn 15; ConNews 85-2; InWom SUP; NewYTBS 82, 87; WhAm 9; WorFshn*

Potok, Chaim
American. Author
Best-sellers include, *The Chosen,* 1967, filmed, 1982; *The Promise,* 1969.
b. Feb 17, 1929 in New York, New York
Source: *AmAu&B; Au&Arts 15; Au&Wr 71; AuNews 1, 2; AuSpks; Benet 87, 96; BenetAL 91; BioIn 10, 11, 13, 14, 15, 16, 17, 21; BioNews 74; ConAu 17R, 19NR, 35NR; ConLC 2, 7, 14, 26; ConNov 86, 91, 96; CurBio 83; CyWA 89; DcLB 28, 152; DrAF 76; DrAPF 80, 91; IntAu&W 76, 77, 86; JeAmFiW; JeAmHC; LegTOT; LinLib L; MagSAmL; MajTwCW; Novels; RAdv 14; SmATA 33; TwCYAW; WhoAm 74, 76, 78, 80, 82, 84, 86, 88, 90, 92, 94, 95, 96, 97; WhoAmJ 80; WhoE 74, 86; WhoUSWr 88; WhoWor 74; WhoWorJ 72, 78; WhoWrEP 89, 92, 95; WorAl; WorAlBi; WorAu 1975; WrDr 76, 80, 82, 84, 86, 88, 90, 92, 94, 96*

Potter, Beatrix
[Helen Beatrix Potter]
English. Illustrator, Author
Wrote *The Tale of Peter Rabbit,* 1902.
b. Jul 6, 1866 in London, England

d. Dec 22, 1943 in Sawrey, England
Source: *AnCL; AuBYP 2, 3; Benet 87, 96; BioIn 1, 2, 3, 4, 5, 6, 7, 8, 9, 10, 11, 12, 13, 14, 15, 16, 17, 19, 20, 21; CamGLE; CarSB; CasWL; ChhPo, S1, S2; ChlBkCr; ChlLR 1, 19; ConAu 108; CurBio 44; DcArts; DcBrAr 1; DcBrBI; DcBrWA; DcLB 141; DcLEL; DcNaB 1941; DcVicP 2; DcWomA; EncBrWW; EvLB; FacFETw; FamAIYP; FemiCLE; GrBr; HerW, 84; InWom, SUP; JBA 34, 51; LegTOT; LinLib L; LngCTC; ModWoWr; NewC; NewCBEL; NewYTBS 88; OxCChiL; OxCEng 67, 85; PenC ENG; PenNWW B; RAdv 14; REn; Str&VC; TwCChW 78, 83, 89; TwCPaSc; VicBrit; WhDW; WhoChL; WorAl; WorAlBi; WrChl; YABC 1*

Potter, Dennis (Christopher George)
English. Dramatist
Wrote screenplays *Pennies from Heaven,* 1978; *The Singing Detective,* 1986.
b. May 17, 1935 in Berry Hill, England
d. Jun 7, 1994 in Ross-on-Wye, England
Source: *Au&Wr 71; BiDFilm 94; BioIn 10; CamGLE; CamGWoT; ConAu 33NR, 107, 145; ConBrDr; ConDr 73, 77, 82, 88, 93; ConLC 58, 86; ConTFT 3; CurBio 94, 94N; DcArts; DcLEL 1940; FacFETw; IntAu&W 89, 91, 93; IntMPA 92, 94; IntWW 89, 91, 93; LegTOT; MajTwCW; MiSFD 9; OxCEng 85, 95; RAdv 14; RGTwCWr; WhAm 11; Who 74, 82, 83, 85, 88, 90, 92, 94; WhoThe 77, 81; WhoWor 91, 93; WorAu 1985; WrDr 76, 80, 82, 84, 86, 88, 90, 92, 94, 96*

Potter, Henry Codman
American. Religious Leader, Social Reformer
Episcopal bishop of NYC, 1887-1908; initiated building of still-unfinished Cathedral of St. John the Divine, 1892; outspoken critic of civic corruption.
b. Jun 25, 1834 in Schenectady, New York
d. Jul 21, 1908 in Cooperstown, New York
Source: *Alli SUP; AmAu&B; AmBi; ApCAB, X; BiD&SB; DcAmB; NatCAB 1, 14; TwCBDA; WebAB 79; WhAm 1*

Potter, Stephen
English. Author
Introduced new word to language with series of books: *One Upmanship,* 1952.
b. Feb 1, 1900 in London, England
d. Dec 2, 1969 in London, England
Source: *AuBYP 2, 3; BioIn 2, 3, 4, 5, 8, 9, 13, 17; ConAu 25R, 101; DcArts; DcLEL; DcNaB 1961; EvLB; LngCTC; MajTwCW; ModBrL; NewC; NewCBEL; ObitOF 79; ObitT 1961; PenC ENG; RAdv 1; REn; TwCA SUP; TwCWr; WhAm 5; WhDW*

Potthast, Edward Henry
American. Artist
Ambidextrous painter who excelled at watercolors: *The Water's Fine.*
b. Jun 10, 1857 in Cincinnati, Ohio
d. Mar 9, 1927 in New York, New York
Source: *ArtsAmW 1, 3; BioIn 9; IIBEAAW; IlrAm 1880; NatCAB 22; WhAm 1*

Potts, Annie
American. Actor
Appeared in *Jumpin' Jack Flash,* 1985; TV series "Designing Women," 1986-93.
b. Oct 28, 1952 in Franklin, Kentucky
Source: *BioIn 19, 20; ConTFT 15; IntMPA 92, 94, 96; LegTOT; News 94, 94-1; WhoAm 92, 94, 95, 96, 97; WhoAmW 95, 97; WhoEnt 92*

Potts, Nadia
English. Dancer
With Toronto's National Ballet of Canada, 1966—.
b. Apr 20, 1948 in London, England
Source: *BiDD; BioIn 11; CanWW 83, 89; CnOxB; WhoAm 78, 80, 82, 84; WhoE 81, 83*

Potvin, Denis Charles
"Bear"
Canadian. Hockey Player
Defenseman, NY Islanders, 1973-88; won Norris Trophy three times.
b. Oct 29, 1953 in Hull, Quebec, Canada
Source: *BioIn 10, 11, 12, 14, 15; ConAu 113; CurBio 86; HocEn; HocReg 87; NewYTBE 73; NewYTBS 77, 84; WhoAm 78, 80, 82, 84; WhoE 85, 86; WorAlBi*

Potzsch, Anett
German. Skater
World champion figure skater, 1978, 1980; won gold medal, 1980 Olympics.
b. 1961, German Democratic Republic

Poulenc, Francis
[Les Six]
French. Composer
Best known for *Dialogues des Carmelites.*
b. Jan 7, 1899 in Paris, France
d. Jan 30, 1963 in Paris, France
Source: *AtlBL; Baker 78, 84; Benet 87; BioIn 1, 2, 3, 4, 5, 6, 7, 8, 11, 12, 13, 14, 16, 17, 18, 20; BriBkM 80; CmOp; CnOxB; CompSN, SUP; DancEn 78; DcCM; DcCom 77; DcCom&M 79; DcFM; DcTwCC, A; DcTwCCu 2; FacFETw; FilmEn; IntDcB; IntDcOp; LegTOT; MakMC; McGEWB; MetOEnc; MusMk; NewAmDM; NewEOp 71; NewGrDM 80; NewOxM; ObitT 1961; OxCMus; OxDcOp; PenDiMP A; REn; WhAm 4; WorAl; WorAlBi*

Poulin, Dave
[David Poulin]
Canadian. Hockey Player
Center, Philadelphia, 1982-89; Boston, 1989—; won Frank Selke award for best defensive forward, 1987.
b. Dec 17, 1958 in Mississauga, Ontario, Canada
Source: *HocReg 86, 87*

Poulson, Norris
American. Politician
Mayor of LA, 1953-61.
b. Jul 23, 1895 in Baker County, Oregon
d. Sep 25, 1982 in Orange, California
Source: *BioIn 5, 8, 11, 13; NewYTBS 82; PolProf E; WhAm 8*

Poulter, Thomas Charles
American. Explorer
Geophysicist known for travels in Antarctica; second in command on Byrd's second Antarctic expedition, 1933-35; honored by Congress, National Geographic Society.
b. Mar 3, 1897 in Salem, Massachusetts
d. Jun 14, 1978 in Menlo Park, California
Source: *AmMWSc 73P; BioIn 1, 11; WhAm 7; WhoAm 74, 76, 78; WhoWor 74*

Pound, Ezra Loomis
American. Poet, Critic
Indicted for treason, WW II; wrote *Cantos,* 1925-60.
b. Oct 30, 1885 in Hailey, Idaho
d. Nov 1, 1972 in Venice, Italy
Source: *AmAu&B; AmLY; AmWr; Au&Wr 71; Baker 92; Benet 96; BioIn 1, 2, 3, 4, 5, 6, 7, 8, 9, 10, 11, 12, 13; CasWL; Chambr 3; CnDAL; CnE&AP; CnMD; CnMWL; ConAu 5R; ConLC 18; CurBio 42, 63; DcAmB S9; EncAB-H 1974, 1996; LiExTwC; MakMC; McGEWB; NewGrDO; OxCTwCP; REnAL; WebAB 74, 79; WhAm 5, 7*

Pound, Louise
American. Educator, Scholar
Developed scholarly study of American speech, folklore.
b. Jun 30, 1872 in Lincoln, Nebraska
d. Jun 17, 1958 in Lincoln, Nebraska
Source: *AmAu&B; BenetAL 91; BiDAmEd; BioIn 3, 4, 5, 6, 12; FemiCLE; InWom SUP; NatCAB 46; NotAW MOD; OxCAmL 65, 83; OxCWoWr 95; PeoHis; REnAL; WhAm 3; WhNAA; WhoAmW 58; WomWWA 14*

Pound, Roscoe
American. Educator
Dean, Harvard Law School, 1916-37; wrote on law philosophy, practice.
b. Oct 27, 1870 in Lincoln, Nebraska
d. Jul 1, 1964 in Cambridge, Massachusetts
Source: *AmAu&B; AmDec 1900; AmJust; BenetAL 91; BiDAmEd; BioIn 1, 3, 5, 7, 8, 10, 12, 14; ConAu 111; CopCroC; CurBio 47, 64; DcAmB S7; EncAB-H 1996; InSci; LinLib S; McGEWB; ObitT*

1961; OxCAmH; OxCAmL 65, 83, 95; OxCLaw; REnAL; ThTwC 87; WebAB 74, 79; WhAm 4; WhNAA

Poundmaker
Canadian. Native American Chief
Chief of the Cree; had leading role in the Riel Rebellion, 1885.
b. 1842? in Saskatchewan, Canada
d. Jul 4, 1886
Source: *BioIn 11; EncNAB; NotNaAm; WhNaAH*

Poundstone, Paula
American. Comedian
Popular stand-up comedienne.
b. 1959
Source: *LegTOT*

Poussaint, Alvin F.
American. Psychiatrist, Educator
Associate professor of psychiatry, Harvard Medical School, 1969—; production consultant, "The Cosby Show," 1984-92.
b. May 15, 1923 in New York, New York

Poussin, Nicolas
French. Artist
Baroque pictorial classicism paintings include *St. John on Patmos.*
b. Jun 1594 in Villers, France
d. Nov 19, 1665 in Rome, Italy
Source: *AtlBL; Benet 87, 96; BioIn 1, 3, 4, 5, 6, 7, 11, 12, 13, 16, 19, 20, 21; ClaDrA; DcArts; DcBiPP; DcCathB; IntDcAA 90; LegTOT; LinLib S; McGDA; McGEWB; OxCFr; RAdv 13-3; REn; WhDW*

Povich, Maury
American. TV Personality
Hosted TVs "A Current Affair," 1986-91; "The Maury Povich Show," 1991—; married to Connie Chung.
b. Jan 7, 1939 in Washington, District of Columbia
Source: *BioIn 14, 16; CelR 90; ConAu 138; ConTFT 11; LegTOT; News 94, 94-3*

Powdermaker, Hortense
American. Anthropologist, Author
Books like *Hollywood: The Dream Factory,* 1950, are based on her findings in many US areas.
b. Dec 24, 1896 in Philadelphia, Pennsylvania
d. Jun 15, 1970 in Berkeley, California
Source: *BioIn 12, 18, 19, 21; CurBio 61, 70; DcAmB S8; IntDcAn; NatCAB 55; NewYTBE 70; NotAW MOD; ObitOF 79; WhAm 5*

Powell, Adam Clayton, Jr.
American. Politician, Clergy
Dem. congressman from 1945; expelled, 1967, for misuse of funds but re-elected the same year.
b. Nov 29, 1908 in New Haven, Connecticut
d. Apr 4, 1972 in Miami, Florida
Source: *AfrAmAl 6; AfrAmOr; AmAu&B; AmPolLe; AmRef; BiDrAC; BiDrUSC 89; BioIn 2, 3, 4, 5, 6, 7, 8, 10, 11, 12, 15, 16, 17, 18, 21; BlkAmsC; BlkLC; BlkWr 1; BlkWrNE; CivRSt; ConAu 33R, 102; ConBlB 3; ConLC 89; CurBio 42, 72, 72N; DcAmB S5, S9; DcPol; DcTwCCu 5; EncAACR; EncAB-H 1974, 1996; EncARH; EncWB; FacFETw; InB&W 80, 85; LegTOT; NegAl 76, 83, 89A; NewYTBE 72; ObitT 1971; PolPar; PolProf E, J, K; RelLAm 91; SchCGBL; SelBAAf; SelBAAu; WebAB 74, 79; WhAm 5; WhAmP; WorAl; WorAlBi*

Powell, Anthony Dymoke
English. Author
Known for social satire in long series of novels, *A Dance to the Music of Time.*
b. Dec 21, 1905 in London, England
Source: *Benet 87; BioIn 13, 14, 15, 16; BritWr 7; CamGEL; CamGLE; CnDBLB 7; ConAu 1NR, 1R, 32NR; ConLC 1; ConNov 86, 91; CurBio 77; CyWA 89; DcLEL; EncWL; EvLB; IntAu&W 91; IntvTCA 2; IntWW 91; MajTwCW; McGEWB; ModBrL S1, S2; OxCEng 85; PenC ENG; RAdv 13-1; REn; RfGEnL 91; TwCA SUP; Who 92; WhoTwCL; WhoWor 91; WrDr 86, 92*

Powell, Boog
[John Wesley Powell]
American. Baseball Player
First baseman, 1961-77, mostly with Baltimore; had 339 career home runs; AL MVP, 1970.
b. Aug 17, 1941 in Lakeland, Florida
Source: *Ballpl 90; BaseEn 88; BiDAmSp BB; BioIn 6, 10, 15, 16; CurBio 88; FacFETw; InB&W 85; IntWW 91; LegTOT; NegAl 89; NewYTBS 91; Who 92; WhoAm 90; WhoAmP 91; WhoBlA 92; WhoProB 73; WhoSpor*

Powell, Cecil Frank
English. Physicist, Educator
Won Nobel Prize for discovery of pi-mesons, 1950.
b. Dec 5, 1903 in Tonbridge, England
d. Aug 9, 1969 in Belluno, Italy
Source: *AsBiEn; BiESc; BioIn 2, 3, 6, 8, 9, 10, 14, 15, 20; CamDcSc; ConAu 113; DcNaB 1961; DcScB; GrBr; InSci; LarDcSc; McGMS 80; NotTwCS; WhAm 5; WhoNob, 90, 95; WorAl; WorScD*

Powell, Colin (Luther)
American. Military Leader
Chm. Joint Chiefs of Staff, 1989-92; key leader of Gulf War.
b. Apr 5, 1937 in New York, New York
Source: *AfrAmOr; CurBio 88; HarEnMi; InB&W 85; IntWW 89, 91, 93; NewYTBS 89, 90, 91; Who 92, 94; WhoAm 82, 84, 86, 88, 90, 92, 94, 95, 96, 97; WhoBlA 85*

Powell, Dick
American. Actor
Starred in 1930s musicals, 1940s thrillers; TV series, 1956-62.
b. Nov 24, 1904 in Mountain View, Arkansas
d. Jan 2, 1963 in Hollywood, California
Source: *BiDAmM; BiDFilm, 81, 94; BioIn 1, 3, 4, 5, 6, 7, 9; CmMov; CmpEPM; CurBio 48, 63; FilmEn; FilmgC; ForYSC; HalFC 80, 84, 88; IntDcF 1-3, 2-3; LegTOT; MiSFD 9N; MotPP; MovMk; NewYTET; NotNAT B; OxCPMus; RadStar; WhAm 4; WhoHol B; WhScrn 74, 77, 83; WorAl; WorAlBi; WorEFlm*

Powell, Earl
"Bud"
American. Jazz Musician
Early bop pianist; with Cootie Williams band, 1940s.
b. Sep 27, 1924 in New York, New York
d. Aug 1, 1966 in New York, New York
Source: *BiDAfM; BiDAmM; BiDJaz; BioIn 7, 8, 11, 15, 16; DrBlPA, 90; InB&W 80, 85; NewGrDM 80; WhAm 4*

Powell, Earl A, III
American. Art Director
Succeeded J. Carter Brown as director of the Nat. Gallery of Art, 1992—.
b. Oct 24, 1943 in Spartanburg, South Carolina
Source: *BioIn 12; WhoAm 88; WhoAmA 91; WhoWest 89*

Powell, Eleanor
American. Dancer, Actor
Billed as "world's greatest tap dancer" while with MGM.
b. Nov 21, 1912 in Springfield, Massachusetts
d. Feb 11, 1982 in Beverly Hills, California
Source: *AnObit 1982; BiDD; BiDFilm 94; BiE&WWA; BioIn 8, 9, 12, 13, 14, 20; CmMov; CmpEPM; EncAFC; EncMT; FilmEn; FilmgC; ForYSC; GoodHs; IntDcF 1-3, 2-3; MGM; MotPP; MovMk; NewYTBS 82; OxCFilm; ThFT; WhoHol A; WhoThe 77A; WhThe; WorAl; WorAlBi*

Powell, Enoch
[John Enoch Powell]
English. Politician, Author
Conservative, later Ulster Unionist MP, 1950-87; writings on history, politics in clude *A Nation or No Nation,* 1978.
b. Jun 16, 1912 in Birmingham, England
Source: *Au&Wr 71; BioIn 5, 7, 8, 9, 10, 11, 12, 13, 14, 15, 17, 21; BlueB 76; DcPol; DcTwHis; EngPo; FacFETw; IntAu&W 77, 82, 91; IntWW 74, 75, 76, 77, 78, 79, 80, 81, 82, 83, 89, 91; IntWWP 77, 82; IntYB 78, 79, 80, 81, 82; WhDW; WhE&EA; Who 74, 82, 83, 85, 88, 90, 92; WhoWor 74; WrDr 76, 80, 82, 84, 86, 88, 90, 92*

Powell, Gordon George
Australian. Author
Former Presbyterian minister whose books include *The Secret of Serenity*, 1957.
b. Jan 22, 1911 in Warrnambool, Australia
Source: *Au&Wr 71; BioIn 5, 7; ConAu 1R; WrDr 76, 80, 84, 86, 88, 90, 92, 94, 96*

Powell, Jane
[Suzanne Burce]
American. Singer, Actor
In MGM musicals, 1940s-50s, including *Seven Brides for Seven Brothers*, 1954.
b. Apr 1, 1928 in Portland, Oregon
Source: *BioIn 15, 16; CelR 90; CmMov; CmpEPM; ConTFT 7; CurBio 74; EncAFC; FacFETw; FilmgC; HalFC 84, 88; IntMPA 86, 92; InWom, SUP; MotPP; MovMk; OxCPMus; VarWW 85; WhoAm 82; WhoAmW 77; WhoHol 92, A; WorEFlm*

Powell, Jody
[Joseph Lester Powell]
American. Presidential Aide, Journalist
Press secretary for Carter, 1976-81; nationally syndicated columnist.
b. Sep 30, 1943 in Vienna, Georgia
Source: *BioIn 10; WorAl*

Powell, John Wesley
American. Anthropologist, Geologist
Indian authority who made govt.-sponsored exploratory trips to Rocky Mt. region, classified Indian languages.
b. Mar 24, 1834 in Mount Morris, New York
d. Sep 23, 1902 in Haven, Maine
Source: *Alli SUP; AmAu&B; AmBi; AmSocL; ApCAB; BbD; BenetAL 91; BiDAmS; BiD&SB; BiInAmS; BioIn 1, 2, 3, 4, 5, 6, 8, 9, 11, 12, 13, 14, 15, 17, 18, 19, 20; DcAmAu; DcAmB; DcNAA; DcScB; EncAAH; EncAB-H 1974, 1996; EnvEnc; GayN; Geog 3; HarEnUS; InSci; IntDcAn; LarDcSc; LinLib L, S; McGEWB; MemAm; NatCAB 3; NatLAC; OhA&B; OxCAmH; OxCAmL 65, 83, 95; RAdv 14; REnAL; REnAW; TwCBDA; WebAB 74, 79; WhAm 1; WhNaAH; WhWE*

Powell, Lawrence Clark
American. Author, Educator
Bibliophile known for variety of writings: *A Passion for Books*, 1959; founded UCLA School of Library Service, 1960-66.
b. Sep 3, 1906 in Washington
Source: *AmAu&B; AmEA 74; BiDAmEd; BiDrLUS 70; BioIn 2, 3, 5, 7, 8, 10, 13, 15, 16, 19, 20; ChhPo, S3; CmCal; ConAu 8NR, 21R, 25NR; CurBio 60; LinLib L; OxCAmL 83; ScF&FL 92; WhoAm 74, 76; WhoLibI 82; WhoLibS 55, 66; WorAu 1950*

Powell, Lewis Franklin, Jr.
American. Supreme Court Justice
Served on court, 1971-87; known for casting swing vote on most significant, bitterly contested cases.
b. Sep 19, 1907 in Suffolk, Virginia
Source: *BiDFedJ A; BioIn 7, 9, 10, 11, 12, 13, 14, 15; CelR 90; CngDr 87, 89, 91, 93, 95; CurBio 65; DrAS 74P, 78P, 82P; EncAB-A 36; EncWB; FacFETw; IntWW 74, 75, 76, 77, 78, 79, 80, 81, 82, 83, 89, 91; IntYB 78, 79, 80, 81, 82; NatCAB 63N; NewYTBS 76, 87; OxCSupC; PeoHis; St&PR 75; SupCtJu; WebAB 74, 79; Who 74, 82, 83, 85, 88, 90, 92, 94; WhoAm 74, 76, 78, 80, 82, 84, 86, 88, 90, 92, 94, 95, 96, 97; WhoAmL 78, 79, 83, 85, 87, 90, 92, 94, 96; WhoAmP 85, 91; WhoE 79, 81, 83, 85, 86, 89, 91, 93; WhoGov 72, 75, 77; WhoSSW 75, 76; WhoWor 78, 80; WorAlBi*

Powell, Maud
American. Violinist
One of the few female violinists of her time; brought classical music to small to wns, outposts in US by touring.
b. Aug 22, 1867 in Peru, Illinois
d. Jan 2, 1920 in Uniontown, Pennsylvania
Source: *AmBi; AmWom; Baker 84; DcAmB; GrLiveH; NatCAB 13; NewGrDA 86; NotAW; WhAm 1; WomWWA 14*

Powell, Maxine
American. Educator, Fashion Designer
Founder, Maxine Powell Finishing and Modeling School, 1951; finishing instructor, Motown Records, Detroit, 1964-69.
b. May 30, 1924 in Texarkana, Texas
Source: *BioIn 20; ConBlB 8*

Powell, Michael Latham
"Mickey"
English. Director, Producer
Innovative filmmaker; films include *Life and Death of Colonel Blimp*, 1943, *The Red Shoes*, 1948, and 30 others.
b. Sep 30, 1905 in Canterbury, England
d. Feb 19, 1990 in Avening, England
Source: *BiDFilm; BioIn 15; CmMov; ConAu 150; ConDr 82A, 88A; CurBio 87, 90; DcFM; DcNaB 1986; FilmEn; HalFC 84; IntMPA 86, 88; IntWW 83, 89; MovMk; NewYTBS 80, 90; OxCFilm; VarWW 85; WhE&EA; Who 85, 88, 90; WorEFlm; WorFDir 1*

Powell, Mike
[Michael Anthony Powell]
American. Track Athlete
Long jumper; broke Bob Beamon's 23-year long jump record, 1991.
b. Nov 10, 1963 in Philadelphia, Pennsylvania
Source: *AfrAmSG; BlkOlyM; ConBlB 7; CurBio 93; NewYTBS 91; WhoAfA 96; WhoBlA 94; WhoSpor*

Powell, Robert
English. Actor
Starred in TV epic "Jesus of Nazareth."
b. Jun 1, 1944 in Salford, England
Source: *BioIn 13, 15; ConTFT 5; HalFC 88; InB&W 85; IntMPA 96; IntWW 89, 91, 93; ItaFilm; VarWW 85; Who 88; WhoHol 92; WhoReal 83; WhoThe 77, 81*

Powell, Teddy
American. Bandleader, Musician
Violinist, vocalist, arranger, who led dance bands, 1940s; wrote "Bewildered."
b. Mar 1, 1906 in Oakland, California
Source: *ASCAP 66, 80; BiDJaz; WhoJazz 72*

Powell, William
American. Actor
Starred with Myrna Loy in six *Thin Man* films, 1934-47.
b. Jul 29, 1892 in Pittsburgh, Pennsylvania
d. Mar 5, 1984 in Palm Springs, California
Source: *AnObit 1984; BiDFilm, 81, 94; BioIn 1, 6, 8, 9, 11, 13, 14, 17, 19; CmMov; CurBio 47, 84N; DcArts; EncAFC; Film 1, 2; FilmEn; FilmgC; ForYSC; GangFlm; HalFC 80, 84, 88; IntDcF 1-3, 2-3; IntMPA 75, 76, 77, 78, 79, 80, 81, 82, 84; LegTOT; MGM; MotPP; MovMk; NewYTBS 84; OxCFilm; TwYS; VarWW 85; WhAm 8; What 2; WhoCom; WhoHol A; WhoThe 77A; WhThe; WorAl; WorAlBi; WorEFlm*

Powell, William Henry
American. Artist
Large-scale paintings include *The Discovery of the Mississippi by DeSoto*, 1853, in Capitol rotunda, Washington, DC.
b. Feb 14, 1823 in New York, New York
d. Oct 6, 1879 in New York, New York
Source: *ApCAB; BiAUS; DcAmB; HarEnUS; NatCAB 19; NewYHSD; TwCBDA; WhAm HS*

Power, Donald Clinton
American. Lawyer, Business Executive
Helped form General Telephone and Electronics (GTE), 1950s; chm., CEO, 1959-66.
b. Dec 25, 1899 in Paine Station, Ohio
d. Mar 11, 1979 in Galloway, Ohio
Source: *BioIn 3, 5, 10, 11, 12; BlueB 76; CurBio 60, 79; IntWW 74, 79; IntYB 78, 79, 80, 81, 82; NewYTBS 79; WhAm 7; WhoWor 74, 76*

Power, Eugene Barnum
American. Photographer
Pioneer in microphotography who arranged first major microfilming effort for libraries; founded University Microfilms, Ann Arbor, MI, 1938-70.
b. Jun 4, 1905 in Traverse City, Michigan

Source: *BioIn 8; St&PR 75; WhAm 11; Who 82, 83, 85, 88, 90, 92, 94; WhoAm 74, 76, 78, 80, 82, 84, 86, 88, 90, 92, 94; WhoGov 72; WhoWor 78*

Power, Jules
American. Producer
TV productions include ABC's "AM America," PBS's "Over Easy;" winner of Emmy, Peabody awards.
b. Oct 19, 1921 in Hammond, Indiana
Source: *Film 1; IndAu 1917; WhoAm 74, 76, 78, 80, 82, 84, 86, 88, 90, 92, 94, 95, 96, 97; WhoEnt 92*

Power, Thomas S(arsfield)
American. Military Leader
Commander of Strategic Air Command, 1957-64.
b. Jun 18, 1905 in New York, New York
d. Dec 7, 1970 in Palm Springs, California
Source: *BiDWWGF; BioIn 3, 4, 5, 6, 9; CurBio 58, 71, 71N; InSci; NewYTBE 70; WhAm 6*

Power, Tyrone
[Frederick Tyrone Edmond Power]
American. Actor
Broadway matinee idol; films, 1914-30; father of Tyrone, Jr.
b. May 2, 1869 in London, England
d. Dec 30, 1931 in Hollywood, California
Source: *AmBi; BioIn 9, 10; CamGWoT; DcAmB; Film 1, 2; FilmEn; FilmgC; HalFC 80, 84, 88; NotNAT A, B; OxCAmT 84; TwYS; WhoHol B; WhoStg 1908; WhScrn 74, 77*

Power, Tyrone, Jr.
American. Actor
Handsome leading man better known for his looks than his talent.
b. May 5, 1914 in Cincinnati, Ohio
d. Nov 15, 1958 in Madrid, Spain
Source: *BiDFilm; CamGWoT; CmMov; CurBio 50, 59; DcAmB S6; EncWT; FilmgC; ForYSC; IntDcF 1-3, 2-3; MotPP; MovMk; ObitT 1951; OxCFilm; OxCThe 67, 83; WhAm 3; WhoHol B; WhScrn 74, 77; WhThe; WorEFlm*

Power, Tyrone William Grattan
Irish. Actor
Drury Lane comedian; toured America, wrote *Impressions of America,* 1836; lost at sea en route from NY to Liverpool; grandfather of actor, Tyrone Power.
b. Nov 2, 1797 in Kilmacthomas, Ireland
d. Mar 1841
Source: *NatCAB 13; OxCThe 83; WebBD 83*

Powers, Anne
[Anne Powers Schwartz]
American. Author
Books include *The Gallant Years,* 1946; *Eleanor, the Passionate Queen,* 1981.
b. May 7, 1913 in Cloquet, Minnesota
Source: *AmAu&B; AmCath 80; Au&Wr 71; BioIn 6, 11; ConAu 1NR, 1R, X; IntAu&W 77, 82, 86; MinnWr; SmATA 10, X; WhAm 9; WhoAm 74, 76, 78, 80, 82, 84, 86; WhoAmW 58, 70, 72, 74, 75; WhoUSWr 88; WrDr 76, 80, 82, 84, 86, 88, 90, 92, 94N*

Powers, Brian M
American. Business Executive
First US tai-pan (big boss) for Hong Kong's oldest trading firm, 1988—; story told in Clavell's novel *Noble House.*
b. 1950 in Massapequa, New York
Source: *BioIn 15; NewYTBS 87*

Powers, Francis Gary
American. Pilot
Plane shot down over USSR, 1960; exchanged for Soviet spy, Rudolf Abel, 1962.
b. Aug 17, 1929 in Pound, Virginia
d. Aug 1, 1977 in Encino, California
Source: *BioIn 5, 6, 7, 8, 9, 10, 11, 12, 17, 18; ColdWar 1, 2; ConAu 109; DcAmB S10; EncAI&E; EncCW; EncE 75; LegTOT; NewYTBS 77; PolProf E, K; SpyCS; What 5; WhDW; WorAl; WorAlBi*

Powers, Hiram
American. Sculptor
Noted for famed neoclassic marble: *The Greek Slave,* 1843.
b. Jul 29, 1805 in Woodstock, Vermont
d. Jun 27, 1873 in Florence, Italy
Source: *AmBi; AmCulL; ApCAB; ArtsNiC; BiAUS; BiDTran; BioIn 2, 5, 7, 9, 11, 13, 17, 19; BriEAA; DcAmArt; DcAmB; DcBiPP; Drake; EncAB-H 1974, 1996; HarEnUS; IlBEAAW; LegTOT; LinLib S; McGDA; McGEWB; NatCAB 3; NewYHSD; OxCAmH; OxCAmL 65; OxCArt; OxDcArt; REnAL; TwCBDA; WebAB 74, 79; WhAm HS; WorAlBi*

Powers, James Farl
American. Author
Short stories include *Prince of Darkness and Other Stories,* 1947; won Nat. Book Award for *Morte d'Urban,* 1962.
b. Jul 8, 1917 in Jacksonville, Illinois
Source: *AmAu&B; AmCath 80; Au&Wr 71; BioIn 3, 4, 6, 8, 12, 15, 16, 17, 19; CathA 1952; ConAu 1R, 2NR; ConLC 1, 4, 8; ConNov 72, 76; DrAF 76; ModAL; OxCAmL 65; PenC AM; RAdv 1; REnAL; TwCA SUP; WebE&AL; WhoAm 74, 76, 78, 80, 82, 84, 90, 92, 94, 97; WhoTwCL; WhoUSWr 88; WhoWrEP 89, 92, 95; WrDr 76, 86*

Powers, John Robert
American. Business Executive
Founded model agency, 1921; modeling schools, 1929.
b. Sep 14, 1896 in Easton, Pennsylvania
d. Aug 19, 1977 in Glendale, California
Source: *BioIn 11; CurBio 45, 77N; WhoAm 74, 76; WorAl*

Powers, Stefanie
[Stefania Zofia Ferderkievicz]
American. Actor
Played Jennifer Hart on TV series "Hart to Hart," 1979-84.
b. Nov 12, 1945 in Hollywood, California
Source: *BioIn 13, 14, 15, 16; CelR 90; ConTFT 6; FilmgC; HalFC 84, 88; IntMPA 86, 92; InWom SUP; MotPP; MovMk; VarWW 85; WhoAm 86, 90, 92, 94, 95, 96, 97; WhoAmW 95, 97; WhoEnt 92; WhoHol A; WhoTelC; WorAlBi*

Powhatan
American. Native American Chief
Maintained friendly relations with colonists after daughter Pocahontas married John Rolfe, 1614.
b. 1550?
d. Apr 1618
Source: *AmBi; ApCAB; BioIn 2, 4, 8, 9, 11, 18, 21; DcAmB; Drake; EncCRAm; EncSoH; HarEnUS; LegTOT; McGEWB; NatCAB 10; REnAW; WebAB 74, 79; WhAm HS*

Powolny, Frank
American. Photographer
Best known for pinup of Betty Grable that GI's carried to battle, WW II.
b. 1902
d. Jan 9, 1986 in Valencia, California

Powter, Susan
Australian. TV Personality, Author
Author of *Stop the Insanity!,* 1993.
b. 1957 in Sydney, Australia
Source: *News 94, 94-3*

Powys, John Cowper
English. Author
Wrote *Meaning of Culture;* novel, *Wolf Solent,* 1929.
b. Oct 8, 1872 in Shirley, England
d. Jun 17, 1963 in Merionethshire, Wales
Source: *BioIn 1, 4, 5, 6, 7, 8, 9, 10, 11, 12, 13, 14, 15, 17, 21; BlmGEL; CamGEL; CamGLE; CasWL; ConAu 85; ConLC 7, 9, 15, 46; CyWA 58; DcArts; DcLB 15; DcLEL; DcNaB 1961; EncSF, 93; EncWL 2, 3; EvLB; FacFETw; GrBr; GrWrEL N; LinLib L, S; LngCEL; LngCTC; MajTwCW; ModBrL, S1, S2; NewC; NewCBEL; Novels; ObitT 1961; OxCEng 67, 85, 95; OxCLiW 86; OxCTwCP; PenC ENG; REn; RfGEnL 91; RGTwCWr; ScF&FL 1, 92; ScFSB; SJGFanW; SupFW; TwCA, SUP; TwCRHW 90; TwCSFW 81; TwCWr; WebE&AL; WhAm 4; WhDW; WhE&EA; WhNAA; WhoHr&F; WhoLA; WhoTwCL*

Powys, Llewelyn
English. Author, Essayist
Novels include *Black Laughter,* 1924; brother of John, Theodore.
b. Aug 13, 1884 in Dorchester, England
d. Dec 2, 1939 in Davos, Switzerland
Source: *BioIn 1, 2, 3, 5, 6, 8, 9, 10, 12, 13, 17; ChhPo S1; CyWA 58; DcLB 98; DcLEL; EvLB; FacFETw; LngCTC;*

NewC; NewCBEL; OxCEng 67, 85, 95; PenC ENG; REn; TwCA, SUP; TwCWr; WebE&AL; WhAm 2; WhE&EA; WhLit; WhNAA; WhoLA; WhoTwCL

Powys, Theodore Francis
English. Author
Allegorical novels with Dorsetshire settings include *Unclay,* 1931.
b. Dec 20, 1875 in Shirley, England
d. Nov 27, 1953 in Sturminster, England
Source: *BioIn 1, 3, 4, 5, 6, 8, 12, 13; BlmGEL; CasWL; CyWA 58; DcLEL; EncWL; EvLB; LngCEL; LngCTC; ModBrL; NewC; NewCBEL; OxCEng 67; PenC ENG; REn; TwCA, SUP; TwCWr; WebE&AL; WhE&EA; WhoTwCL*

Poynting, John Henry
English. Physicist
Developed Poynting's vector concerning flow of electromagnetic radiation in space, 1880s.
b. Sep 9, 1852 in Manchester, England
d. Mar 30, 1914 in Birmingham, England
Source: *BiESc; BioIn 2, 14; CamDcSc; DcNaB 1912; DcScB; InSci; LarDcSc; NewCol 75*

Pozsgay, Imre
Hungarian. Politician
Minister of state, member of the Presidium of Hungary, 1989—; advocated reforms that led to the country's first free election since WW II.
b. Nov 26, 1933 in Kony, Hungary
Source: *BioIn 16; ColdWar 1, 2; CurBio 90; IntWW 77, 78, 79, 80, 81, 82, 83, 89, 91; WhoSoCE 89*

Pozzi, Lucio
American. Artist
Works defy categorization; painting, drawing, print making, performances, word works, still and video photography, installations and set design.
b. Nov 29, 1935 in Milan, Italy
Source: *ConArt 77, 83, 89, 96; DcCAr 81; News 90, 90-2; WhoAmA 76, 78, 80, 82, 84, 86, 89, 91, 93; WhoE 89*

Prada, Miuccia
Italian. Business Executive, Fashion Designer
CEO and director of design, Fratelli Prada.
b. c. 1950 in Milan, Italy
Source: *News 96, 96-1*

Prado Ugarteche, Manuel
Peruvian. Statesman
Pres. of Peru, 1939-45, 1956-62; ousted by military junta; exiled in Paris, 1962-67.
b. Apr 21, 1889
d. Aug 14, 1967
Source: *BiDLAmC; BioIn 4, 8, 16; CurBio 42, 67; McGEWB; WhAm 4*

Praeger, Frederick A(mos)
American. Publisher
Founded Frederick A. Praeger Inc., publishing firm, 1950.
b. Sep 16, 1915 in Vienna, Austria
d. May 28, 1994 in Boulder, Colorado
Source: *AmAu&B; BioIn 5, 11, 14; CurBio 59, 94N; EncAI&E; IntWW 91, 93; St&PR 91; WhAm 11; WhoAm 74, 76, 78, 80, 84, 86, 88, 90, 92; WhoAmA 84, 91; WhoLibI 82; WhoWor 74*

Praetorius, Michael
[Michael Schultheiss]
German. Composer, Author
Noted for treatise *Syntagma Musicum,* 1614-20, describing ancient instruments, ecclesiastical music.
b. Feb 15, 1571 in Kreuzberg, Germany
d. Feb 15, 1621 in Wolfenbuttel, Germany
Source: *AtlBL; Baker 78, 84, 92; BioIn 4; BriBkM 80; LuthC 75; McGEWB; NewAmDM; NewCol 75; NewGrDM 80; NewOxM; WhDW*

Prang, Louis
American. Lithographer
Developed color printing; marketed first Christmas cards in England, US, 1875.
b. Mar 12, 1824 in Breslau, Germany
d. Jun 14, 1909 in Los Angeles, California
Source: *BiInAmS; BioIn 2, 3, 4, 9, 11, 12, 16; DcAmArt; DcAmB; DcNAA; NatCAB 11; NewYHSD; TwCBDA; WhAm 1; WhAmArt 85*

Prasad, Rajendra
Indian. Politician
First president of India, 1950-62.
b. Dec 3, 1884 in Bihar, India
d. Feb 28, 1963 in Patna, India
Source: *BioIn 2, 3, 4, 5, 6, 9, 10, 12; CurBio 50, 63; DcPol; DcTwHis; McGEWB; ObitT 1961; WhAm 4; WhDW*

Pratella, Francesco Balilla
Italian. Composer
Used "futurist" mode; wrote opera, *Lilia,* 1903.
b. Feb 1, 1880 in Lugo di Romagna, Italy
d. May 18, 1955 in Ravenna, Italy
Source: *Baker 78, 84, 92; DcCM; NewGrDM 80; NewGrDO*

Prater, Dave
[Sam and Dave; David Prater]
American. Singer
With Sam Moore, one of leading soul acts, 1960s; "hit song Soul Man," 1967, popularized again, late 1970s, by Dan Aykroyd, John Belushi as Blues Brothers.
b. May 9, 1937 in Ocilla, Georgia
d. Apr 9, 1988 in Sycamore, Georgia
Source: *BioIn 8, 12, 15, 16; LegTOT; WhoRocM 82*

Prather, Richard Scott
American. Author
Mystery books include *Dead Man's Walk,* 1965; *The Kubla Kan Caper,* 1966.
b. Sep 9, 1921 in Santa Ana, California
Source: *BioIn 14; BlueB 76; ConAu 1R, 5NR; CorpD; DcLP 87A; IntAu&W 91; TwCCr&M 85, 91; WhoWest 74, 76; WrDr 80, 82, 84, 86, 88, 90, 92, 94, 96*

Pratt, Babe
[Walter Pratt]
Canadian. Hockey Player
Defenseman, 1935-47, mostly with NY Rangers; won Hart Trophy, 1944; Hall of Fame, 1966.
b. Jan 7, 1916 in Stony Mountain, Manitoba, Canada
d. Dec 16, 1988 in Vancouver, British Columbia, Canada
Source: *BioIn 1, 8, 10, 16; HocEn; WhoHcky 73; WhoSpor*

Pratt, Bela Lyon
American. Sculptor
Best-known work *Peace Restraining War.*
b. Dec 11, 1867 in Norwich, Connecticut
d. May 18, 1917 in Jamaica Plain, Massachusetts
Source: *AmBi; ApCAB X; DcAmB; McGDA; NatCAB 14; WhAm 1*

Pratt, Charles
American. Oilman, Philanthropist
Established Pratt Institute, Brooklyn, 1887; first free Public Library in NYC, 1888.
b. Oct 2, 1830 in Watertown, Massachusetts
d. May 4, 1891 in New York, New York
Source: *AmBi; ApCAB, X; BiDAmBL 83; DcAmB; NatCAB 9, 26; TwCBDA; WhAm HS; WorAl; WorAlBi*

Pratt, Edwin John
Canadian. Poet
Best-known heroic narrative: *Behind the Log,* 1947.
b. Feb 4, 1883 in Western Bay, Newfoundland, Canada
d. Apr 26, 1964 in Toronto, Ontario, Canada
Source: *BioIn 1, 3, 4, 5, 6, 7, 9; CanWr; CasWL; ChhPo, S1; ConAu 93; CreCan 2; DcLEL; EvLB; LngCTC; NewC; OxCCan, SUP; OxCEng 67; PenC ENG; REn; REnAL; TwCA SUP; WebE&AL; WhDW; WhE&EA; WhLit; WhNAA*

Pratt, Fletcher
American. Author
Prolific writer on military history, science fiction: *Alien Planet,* 1962; *Fleet Against Japan,* 1946.
b. Apr 25, 1897 in Buffalo, New York
d. Jun 10, 1956 in Long Branch, New Jersey
Source: *AmAu&B; AuBYP 2; BioIn 1, 2, 4, 6, 7; ConAu 113; CurBio 42, 56; EncSF; NatCAB 46; NewEScF; REnAL; RGSF; ScF&FL 1, 2, 92; ScFSB;*

SupFW; TwCA SUP; TwCSFW 81, 86, 91; WhAm 3; WhE&EA; WhNAA; WhoHr&F; WhoSciF

Praxiteles
Greek. Sculptor
Second only in reputation to Phidias; lone surviving work: *Hermes with the Infant Dionysus.*
b. 370?BC in Athens, Greece
d. 330?BC
Source: *AtlBL; LegTOT; NewC*

Praz, Mario
Italian. Scholar, Critic
Wrote *The Romantic Agony,* 1933.
b. Sep 6, 1896 in Rome, Italy
d. Mar 23, 1982 in Rome, Italy
Source: *AnObit 1982; Au&Wr 71; BioIn 4, 7, 10, 12, 13, 14; CasWL; ClDMEL 80; ConAu 101, 106; IntWW 74, 75, 76, 77, 78, 79, 80, 81; LinLib L; LngCTC; NewCBEL; NewYTBS 82; OxCEng 85, 95; RAdv 13-2; ThTwC 87; TwCA SUP; WhE&EA; Who 74, 82; WhoWor 74, 76, 78*

Predock, Antoine Samuel
American. Architect
Architectural style dubbed ''cosmic modernism;'' creates building sensitive to environment and space.
b. Jun 24, 1936 in Lebanon, Missouri
Source: *BioIn 15; News 93-2; WhoAm 84, 86, 88, 90*

Prefontaine, Steve Roland
American. Track Athlete
Long-distance runner; finished fourth in 5,000 meters, 1972 Olympics; held every US outdoor distance record above 2,000 meters.
b. Jan 25, 1951 in Coos Bay, Oregon
d. May 30, 1975 in Eugene, Oregon
Source: *BiDAmSp OS; BioIn 9, 10, 12; DcAmB S9; WhoTr&F 73*

Pregl, Fritz
Austrian. Chemist
Invented method of micro-analysis of organic substances; won 1923 Nobel Prize.
b. Sep 3, 1859 in Laibach, Austria
d. Dec 13, 1930 in Graz, Austria
Source: *AsBiEn; BiESc; DcInv; DcScB; Dis&D; McGEWB; WhoNob, 90, 95; WorAl*

Prelog, Vladimir
Swiss. Chemist
Won Nobel Prize in chemistry, 1975.
b. Jul 23, 1906 in Sarajevo, Yugoslavia
Source: *AmMWSc 89, 92, 95; BiESc; BioIn 2, 10, 14, 15, 17, 19, 20; IntWW 74, 75, 76, 77, 78, 79, 80, 81, 82, 83, 89, 91, 93; LarDcSc; McGMS 80; NobelP; NotTwCS; Who 74, 82, 83, 85, 88, 90, 92, 94; WhoAm 88, 90, 92; WhoNob, 90, 95; WhoScEn 94, 96; WhoSoCE 89; WhoWor 74, 76, 78, 80, 82, 84, 87, 89, 91, 93, 95, 96, 97*

Premice, Josephine
American. Actor, Singer, Dancer
Tony nominee for *A Hand Is on the Gate,* 1967.
b. Jul 21, 1926 in New York, New York
Source: *BiE&WWA; DrBlPA, 90; InB&W 85; NotNAT*

Preminger, Otto Ludwig
American. Director, Producer
Films include *Laura,* 1944; *Anatomy of a Murder,* 1959; *Exodus,* 1960.
b. Dec 5, 1906 in Vienna, Austria
d. Apr 23, 1986 in New York, New York
Source: *BiDFilm; BiE&WWA; BioNews 74; CmMov; ConNews 86-3; CurBio 59; FilmgC; IntMPA 82; IntWW 74, 75, 76, 77, 78, 79, 80, 81, 82, 83; NotNAT; OxCFilm; VarWW 85; WebAB 74, 79; Who 82; WhoAm 84; WhoHol A; WorEFlm*

Prendergast, Maurice Brazil
[The Eight]
American. Artist
Post-impressionist watercolorist; paintings include *Umbrellas in the Rain.*
b. Oct 1861 in Boston, Massachusetts
d. Feb 1, 1924 in New York, New York
Source: *DcAmB; NatCAB 30; OxCAmL 65; WhAm 1*

Prentice, George Denison
American. Journalist
First editor, *New England Review;* editor, *Louisville Courier-Journal,* 1830-68.
b. Dec 18, 1802 in New London, Connecticut
d. Jan 22, 1870
Source: *Alli; AmAu; ApCAB; BbD; BiD&SB; BiDSA; ChhPo, S1; CyAL 2; DcAmAu; DcLB 43; DcNAA; Drake; EncSoH; HarEnUS; NatCAB 3; OxCAmL 65, 83; REnAL; TwCBDA; WhAm HS*

Prentiss, Paula
[Mrs. Richard Benjamin; Paula Ragusa]
American. Actor
Starred in *What's New, Pussycat?,* 1965; TV series with husband, ''He and She,'' 1967-68.
b. Mar 4, 1939 in San Antonio, Texas
Source: *BiDFilm; BioIn 8, 9, 16; ConTFT 7; EncAFC; FilmEn; FilmgC; ForYSC; HalFC 80, 84, 88; IntMPA 75, 76, 77, 78, 79, 80, 81, 82, 84, 86, 88, 92, 94, 96; InWom, SUP; LegTOT; MotPP; MovMk; NewYTBE 71; VarWW 85; WhoHol 92, A; WorAl; WorAlBi*

Prescott, Orville
American. Critic
Book critic, *NY Times,* 1942-66.
b. Sep 8, 1906
d. Apr 28, 1996 in New Canaan, Connecticut
Source: *AmAu&B; AuBYP 2, 3; AuSpks; BioIn 4, 8, 11, 21; ConAu 41R, 152; CurBio 96N; LinLib L, S; REnAL; WhoAm 74, 76, 78, 80, 82, 84, 86, 88, 90*

Prescott, Peter Sherwin
American. Journalist
Book critic, *Newsweek,* 1971-91, senior writer, 1978-91; won Polk award, 1 978.
b. Jul 15, 1935 in New York, New York
Source: *BioIn 15, 16; ConAu 14NR; ConTFT 7; HalFC 88; IntMPA 92; InWom SUP; WhoAm 76, 78, 80, 82, 84, 86, 88, 90, 92, 94, 95, 96, 97; WhoE 75, 77; WhoWor 78; WorAlBi*

Prescott, Samuel
American. Patriot
Captured with Paul Revere on his famous ride; escaped, rode on to warn Concord; captured by British, 1777.
b. Aug 19, 1751 in Concord, Massachusetts
d. 1777 in Halifax, Nova Scotia, Canada
Source: *DcAmB; EncAR; EncCRAm; WebAB 74, 79; WebAMB; WhAm HS; WhAmRev*

Prescott, William Hickling
American. Historian
Best-known dramatic, exciting narrative: *History of the Conquest of Peru,* 1847.
b. May 4, 1796 in Salem, Massachusetts
d. Jan 28, 1859 in Boston, Massachusetts
Source: *Alli; AmAu; AmAu&B; AmBi; ApCAB; AtlBL; BbD; Benet 87, 96; BenetAL 91; BibAL; BiD&SB; BioIn 1, 3, 4, 5, 6, 7, 8, 9, 11, 13, 14, 16, 18; CamGEL; CamGLE; CamHAL; CelCen; Chambr 3; CyAL 1; CyWA 58; DcAmAu; DcAmB; DcBiPP; DcEnA; DcEnL; DcLB 1, 30, 59; DcLEL; DcNAA; DcSpL; Drake; EncAAH; EvLB; HarEnUS; LinLib S; McGEWB; MemAm; NatCAB 6; OxCAmH; OxCAmL 65, 83, 95; OxCEng 67, 85, 95; OxCSpan; PenC AM; RAdv 13-3; REn; REnAL; TwCBDA; WebAB 74, 79; WhAm HS*

Presle, Micheline
[Micheline Chassagne]
French. Actor
In films since 1938, including *Devil in the Flesh,* 1947.
b. Aug 22, 1922 in Paris, France
Source: *BiDFilm, 81; EncEurC; FilmAG WE; FilmEn; FilmgC; ForYSC; HalFC 80, 84, 88; IntDcF 1-3, 2-3; IntMPA 75, 76, 77, 78, 79, 80, 81, 82, 84, 86, 88, 92, 94, 96; ItaFilm; MotPP; MovMk; OxCFilm; WhoFr 79; WhoHol 92, A; WorEFlm*

Presley, Elvis Aaron
''Elvis the Pelvis''; ''The King''
American. Singer, Actor
Rock 'n roll idol; hit songs include ''Hound Dog,'' 1956; ''All Shook Up,'' 1957.
b. Jan 8, 1935 in Tupelo, Mississippi
d. Aug 16, 1977 in Memphis, Tennessee
Source: *AmCulL; BiDAmM; BiDFilm; CmMov; CurBio 59, 77; EncFCWM 69; FilmgC; HarEnR 86; MakMC; MotPP; MovMk; NewYTBS 77; OxCFilm; WebAB 74; WhoAm 74, 78; WhoHol A; WhoWor 76; WorEFlm*

Presley, Lisa Marie
American.
Only child of Elvis and Priscilla Presley.
b. Feb 1, 1968 in Memphis, Tennessee
Source: *BioIn 10, 14, 15, 16; LegTOT*

Presley, Priscilla Ann Beaulieu
American. Actor
Married to Elvis Presley, 1967-73; wrote autobiography *Elvis and Me,* 1985; starred in *Naked Gun* films.
b. May 24, 1945 in New York, New York
Source: *BioIn 10, 13, 14, 15, 16; CelR 90; ConTFT 8; CurBio 90; IntMPA 92; WhoEnt 92; WorAlBi*

Presnell, Harve
American. Actor, Opera Singer
Films include *Unsinkable Molly Brown,* 1964; *Paint Your Wagon,* 1969.
b. Sep 14, 1933 in Modesto, California
Source: *ConTFT 8; FilmEn; FilmgC; ForYSC; HalFC 80, 84, 88; LegTOT; MotPP; VarWW 85; WhoHol 92, A*

Press, Irina Natanovna
Russian. Track Athlete
Won gold medals, 80-meter hurdles, 1960 Olympics, pentathlon, 1964 Olympics; sister of Tamara.
b. Mar 10, 1939, Union of Soviet Socialist Republics
Source: *BiDSovU; IntDcWB; WhoTr&F 73*

Press, Tamara
Russian. Track Athlete
Shot putter, discus thrower; won one gold medal, 1960 Olympics, two gold medals, 1964 Olympics.
b. May 10, 1937, Union of Soviet Socialist Republics
Source: *BiDSovU; ContDcW 89; IntDcWB; IntWW 91; WhoTr&F 73*

Presser, Jackie
American. Labor Union Official
Succeeded Roy Williams as president of Teamsters, 1983-88.
b. Aug 6, 1926 in Cleveland, Ohio
d. Jul 9, 1988 in Lakewood, Ohio
Source: *BioIn 13; BusPN; CurBio 83, 88, 88N; FacFETw; News 88; NewYTBS 83, 88; WhAm 9; WhoAm 84, 86, 88; WhoE 86; WhoFI 87*

Presser, Theodore
American. Publisher
Founded music monthly, *Etude,* 1883; published sheet music.
b. Jul 3, 1848 in Pittsburgh, Pennsylvania
d. Oct 27, 1925 in Philadelphia, Pennsylvania
Source: *Baker 78, 84, 92; BiDAmM; BioIn 1, 2, 5, 7; DcAmB; DcNAA; NatCAB 20; NewAmDM; NewGrDA 86; NewGrDM 80; WhAm 1*

Pressler, Larry
American. Politician
Rep. senator, SD, 1979-97; target of "Abscam," 1980; rebuffed bribery overtures from FBI sting operation.
b. Mar 29, 1942 in Humboldt, South Dakota
Source: *AlmAP 78, 80, 82, 84, 88, 92, 96; BiDrUSC 89; BioIn 12, 13; CngDr 77, 79, 81, 83, 85, 87, 89, 91, 93, 95; CurBio 83; IntWW 82, 83, 89, 91, 93; IntYB 82; NewYTBS 95; PolsAm 84; WhoAm 78, 80, 82, 84, 86, 88, 90, 92, 94, 95, 96, 97; WhoAmP 75, 77, 79, 81, 83, 85, 87, 89, 91, 93, 95; WhoGov 75, 77; WhoMW 76, 78, 80, 82, 84, 86, 88, 90, 92, 93, 96; WhoWor 80, 82, 87, 89, 91*

Pressman, David
American. Actor
Appeared on TV soap opera "One Life to Live" since 1970; won four Emmys.
b. Oct 10, 1913 in Tiflis, Russia
Source: *BiE&WWA; NotNAT; VarWW 85; WhoEnt 92*

Preston, Billy
[William Everett Preston]
American. Singer
Hits include "You Are So Beautiful," 1975; "With You I'm Born Again," 1979.
b. Sep 9, 1946 in Houston, Texas
Source: *BiDAfM; DrBlPA 90; EncPR&S 74; EncRk 88; HarEnR 86; IlEncBM 82; IlEncRk; InB&W 80, 85; LegTOT; PenEncP; RkOn 78; RolSEnR 83; SoulM; WhoAfA 96; WhoAm 80, 82; WhoBlA 77, 80, 85, 88, 90, 92, 94; WhoEnt 92; WhoRock 81; WhoRocM 82; WorAlBi*

Preston, Frances Williams
American. Business Executive
Pres. and CEO B.M.I. (Broadcast Music, Inc.).
Source: *BioIn 15; WhoAm 88; WhoAmW 89, 91; WhoEnt 92*

Preston, John
American. Author
Editor of *The Advocate,* 1975-76; edited *Dispatches: Writers Confront AIDS,* 1989.
b. Dec 11, 1945 in Framingham, Massachusetts
d. Apr 27, 1994 in Portland, Maine
Source: *ConAu 130, 145; ConGAN; ConLC 86; GayLL; WhoUSWr 88; WhoWrEP 89, 92; WrDr 94, 96*

Preston, Robert
[Robert Preston Meservey]
American. Actor
Best known for role of Professor Harold Hill in Broadway (1,375 performances), film (1962) versions of *The Music Man.*
b. Jun 8, 1918 in Newton Highlands, Massachusetts
d. Mar 21, 1987 in Santa Barbara, California
Source: *AnObit 1987; BiE&WWA; BioIn 4, 5, 6, 7, 10, 11, 13, 14, 15, 16; CelR; CmMov; ConNews 87-3; ConTFT 2, 5; CurBio 58, 87, 87N; EncAFC; EncMT; FamA&A; FilmEn; GangFlm; HolP 40; IntDcF 1-3, 2-3; IntMPA 84, 86; LegTOT; MovMk; NewYTBS 87; NotNAT; OxCAmT 84; OxCPMus; VarWW 85; WhAm 9; WhoAm 74, 76, 78, 80, 82, 84, 86; WhoE 74; WhoHol A; WhoThe 72, 77, 81; WhoWor 74; WorAl; WorAlBi; WorEFlm*

Prestopino, Gregorio
American. Artist
Expressionist; used oils, watercolors to paint Manhattan, Harlem subjects; later turned to impressionist rural scenes.
b. Jun 21, 1907 in New York, New York
d. Dec 16, 1984 in Princeton, New Jersey
Source: *BioIn 1, 4, 6, 7, 14; CurBio 64, 85, 85N; DcCAA 71, 77, 88, 94; McGDA; WhAm 9; WhAmArt 85; WhoAm 74, 76, 78, 80, 82, 84; WhoAmA 73, 76, 78, 80, 82, 84, 86N, 89N, 91N, 93N; WhoE 74*

Pretenders, The
[Martin Chambers; Pete Farndon; Malcolm Foster; James Honeyman-Scott; Chrissie Hynde; Robbie McIntosh]
English. Music Group
Early 1980s English rock band best known for hit album *The Pretenders,* 1980.
Source: *BioIn 15, 16, 18, 19, 20; ConMus 8; DcBiPP; EncPR&S 89; EncRk 88; EncRkSt; HarEnR 86; IlEncRk; NewAmDM; NewGrDA 86; NewWmR; ObitOF 79; OnThGG; PenEncP; RkOn 85; RolSEnR 83; WhoRock 81; WhoRocM 82; WhsNW 85*

Pretorius, Marthinus Wessel
South African. Politician
First pres. of S African Republic, 1857-60, 1864-71; Pretoria named after him.
b. Sep 17, 1819 in Graaff Reinet, South Africa
d. May 19, 1901 in Potchefstroom, South Africa
Source: *BioIn 21; DcAfHiB 86; EncSoA; HarEnMi*

Preus, Jacob A(all) O(ttesen)
American. Clergy
President, Lutheran Missouri Synod, 1969-81.
b. Jan 8, 1920
d. Aug 13, 1994 in Burnsville, Minnesota
Source: *BioIn 10, 11, 12; ConAu 33R; CurBio 75, 94N; RelLAm 91; WhoAm 74, 76, 78, 80, 82, 84, 86, 88, 90, 92, 94, 95; WhoMW 74, 76, 78; WhoRel 75, 77, 92*

Preval, Rene
Haitian. Political Leader
Pres., Haiti, 1996—.
b. Jan 17, 1943, Haiti
Source: *IntWW 93*

Previn, Andre
American. Composer, Pianist, Conductor
Won two Oscars, seven Grammys; conductor, Pittsburgh Symphony, 1976-84; music director, LA Philharmonic, 1984—.
b. Apr 6, 1929 in Berlin, Germany
Source: *AllMusG; AmPS; ASCAP 66, 80; Baker 78, 84; BiDAmM; BioIn 1, 5, 6, 7, 8, 9, 10, 11, 12, 13, 14, 15, 16, 17, 21; BriBkM 80; CelR, 90; CmMov; CmpEPM; ConAmC 76; ConAu 115; ConMus 15; CpmDNM 80; CurBio 72; DcCom&M 79; DcTwCCu 1; EncJzS; EncJzS; FacFETw; FilmEn; FilmgC; HalFC 80, 84, 88; IntDcF 1-4, 2-4; IntMPA 75, 76, 77, 78, 79, 80, 81, 82, 84, 86, 88, 92, 94, 96; IntWW 76, 83, 91; IntWWM 90; LegTOT; MusSN; NewAmDM; NewGrDA 86; NewGrDJ 88; NewGrDM 80; NewOxM; NewYTBS 76, 86; OxCFilm; OxCPMus; PenDiMP, A; PenEncP; PlP&P; PopAmC, SUP; Who 74, 82, 83, 85, 88, 90, 92; WhoAm 74, 76, 78, 80, 82, 84, 86, 88, 90, 92, 94, 95; WhoAmM 83; WhoE 79, 81, 83; WhoEnt 92; WhoHol 92, A; WhoMus 72; WhoWest 87, 89; WhoWor 74, 78, 80, 82, 84, 87, 89, 91, 93, 95; WorAl; WorAlBi; WorEFlm; WrDr 86, 88, 90, 92*

Previn, Dory Langdon
American. Lyricist, Singer
Wrote, sang sad pop songs; once wed to Andre.
b. Oct 22, 1925 in Rahway, New Jersey
Source: *ASCAP 66; IlEncRk; InWom SUP; PenEncP; VarWW 85; WhoAm 82*

Previtali, Fernando
Italian. Conductor
Led Italian Radio Orchestra, 1936-53; premiered noted modern works.
b. Feb 16, 1907 in Adria, Italy
Source: *Baker 78, 84, 92; CmOp; MetOEnc; NewEOp 71; NewGrDM 80; NewGrDO; PenDiMP; WhoMus 72; WhoOp 76*

Prevost, Marcel
French. Author, Dramatist
Prolific writer of feminist fiction: *Cousin Laura,* 1890.
b. May 1, 1862 in Paris, France
d. Apr 8, 1941 in Vianne, France
Source: *BioIn 1; CasWL; ClDMEL 47; ConAu 116; CurBio 41; EncWL; NotNAT B; OxCFr; TwCA, SUP; WhLit; WhThe*

Prevost d'Exiles, Antoine Francois, Abbe
"The Abbe Prevost"
French. Author, Translator
Noted for *Historie du Chevalier des Grieux et de Manon Lescaut,* 1731.
b. Apr 1, 1697 in Hesdin, France
d. Nov 23, 1763 in Chantilly, France
Source: *Alli; AtlBL; BbD; Benet 87; BiD&SB; CasWL; CyWA 58; DcBiA; DcBiPP; DcEuL; Dis&D; EuAu; EvEuW; NewC; NewCBEL; OxCEng 67; OxCFr; PenC EUR; RComWL; REn*

Prey, Hermann
"Europe's Leonard Bernstein"
German. Opera Singer
Concert baritone, TV star noted for Mozart, R. Strauss roles.
b. Jul 11, 1929 in Berlin, Germany
Source: *Baker 78, 84, 92; BioIn 7, 9, 10, 11, 13, 15; BriBkM 80; CmOp; CurBio 75; IntDcOp; IntWW 74, 75, 76, 77, 78, 79, 80, 81, 82, 83, 89, 91, 93; IntWWM 77, 80, 90; MetOEnc; MusSN; NewAmDM; NewEOp 71; NewGrDM 80; NewGrDO; NewYTBE 70; OxDcOp; PenDiMP; Who 82, 83, 85, 88, 90, 92, 94; WhoAm 84; WhoMus 72; WhoOp 76; WhoWor 74*

Price, Alan
[The Animals]
English. Singer, Songwriter
Left The Animals, 1965; solo albums include *Travellin' Man,* 1986.
b. Apr 19, 1942 in Fairfield, England
Source: *BioIn 12; ConMuA 80A; EncPR&S 74; EncRk 88; HarEnR 86; IlEncRk; OxCPMus; RolSEnR 83; WhoHol 92; WhoRocM 82*

Price, Byron
American. Editor, Government Official
US director of censorship during WW II; UN official, 1947-54.
b. Mar 25, 1891 in Clearspring, Indiana
d. Aug 6, 1981 in Hendersonville, North Carolina
Source: *BiDAmJo; BioIn 1, 6, 12, 16; BlueB 76; ConAu 104; CurBio 42, 81, 81N; EncAJ; IntWW 74, 75, 76, 77, 78, 79, 80, 81; WhAm 8; Who 74; WhoUN 75*

Price, Deb(orah Jane)
American. Journalist
Writes syndicated column on gay and lesbian issues, 1992—.
b. Feb 27, 1958 in Lubbock, Texas
Source: *BiDAmNC; ConAu 152; GayLesB*

Price, Dennis
[Dennistoun Frankly John Rose-Price]
English. Actor
Leading man in British films including *Kind Hearts and Coronets; Theatre of Blood.*
b. Jun 23, 1915 in Twyford, England
d. Oct 7, 1973 in Isle of Guernsey, England
Source: *BiE&WWA; BioIn 10, 13, 17; DcNaB MP; FilmAG WE; FilmEn; FilmgC; ForYSC; HalFC 80, 84, 88; IlWWBF; ItaFilm; MovMk; NewYTBE 73; NotNAT B; ObitT 1971; OxCFilm; WhoHol B; WhoThe 72; WhScrn 77, 83; WhThe*

Price, Don K.
[Don Krasher Price, Jr.]
American. Political Scientist
Studied science and technology's impact on political institutions and public policy; wrote *The Scientific Estate,* 1965.
b. Jan 23, 1910
d. Jul 10, 1995 in Wellesley, Massachusetts
Source: *AmMWSc 73S, 78S; BioIn 5, 7, 8; BlueB 76; ConAu 73; IntWW 74, 75, 76, 77, 78, 79, 80, 81, 82, 83, 89, 91, 93; LEduc 74; NewYTBS 95; WhAm 11; WhoAm 76, 78, 80, 82, 84, 86, 88, 90, 92, 94, 95*

Price, Florence Beatrice Smith
American. Composer
First black woman symphonic composer in US; work performed 1933.
b. Apr 8, 1888 in Little Rock, Arkansas
d. Jun 3, 1953 in Chicago, Illinois
Source: *BiDAfM; EncWHA; FacFETw; InB&W 80, 85; InWom SUP; NotAW MOD*

Price, Garrett
American. Illustrator, Cartoonist
Best known for cover work for *New Yorker; Colliers* mags.
b. 1896 in Bucyrus, Kansas
d. Apr 8, 1979 in Norwalk, Connecticut
Source: *ArtsAmW 3; BioIn 8, 11, 13; ChhPo; ConAu 85; IlrAm 1880, D; IlsBYP; IlsCB 1957; SmATA 22N; WorECar*

Price, George
American. Cartoonist
Regular contributor, *New Yorker,* 1926-95. Collection of works, *People's Zoo,* 1971.
b. Jun 9, 1901 in Coytesville, New Jersey
d. Jan 12, 1995 in Englewood, New Jersey
Source: *AmAu&B; BioIn 1, 20; ConAu 103, 147; NewYTBE 71; NewYTBS 95; WhAmArt 85; WhoAm 74, 76, 78, 80, 82, 84, 86, 88, 90; WhoAmA 73, 76, 78, 80, 82, 84, 86, 89, 91, 93; WhoWor 74; WorECar*

Price, Gwilym Alexander
American. Business Executive
Pres., chm., Westinghouse Electric Co., 1946-63; promoted work in atomic energy.
b. Jun 20, 1895 in Canonsburg, Pennsylvania
d. Jun 1, 1985
Source: *BioIn 1, 2, 3, 5; CurBio 49, 85; WhAm 8*

Price, H(enry) Ryan
British. Horse Trainer
Won Schweppes Gold Trophy four times.
b. Aug 16, 1912
d. Aug 16, 1986
Source: *FacFETw; Who 82, 83, 85*

Price, Hugh B.
American. Business Executive
President and CEO, National Urban League, 1994—.
b. Nov 22, 1941 in Washington, District of Columbia
Source: *ConBlB 9; WhoAm 94, 95, 96; WhoE 95*

Price, Irving L
American. Manufacturer
With Herman Fischer, started Fischer-Price Toys, 1930.
b. Sep 21, 1884 in Worcester, Massachusetts
d. Nov 23, 1976 in East Aurora, New York
Source: *Entr; NatCAB 60*

Price, Kenny
American. Singer, Musician
Country music guitar player; appeared on "Hee Haw," 1974-84.
b. May 27, 1931 in Florence, Kentucky
d. Aug 4, 1987 in Florence, Kentucky
Source: *BiDAmM; BioIn 14; CounME 74, 74A; EncFCWM 69, 83; HarEnCM 87; IlEncCM; PenEncP*

Price, Leontyne
American. Opera Singer
Soprano star in *Porgy and Bess,* 1952-54; with NY Met. since 1960-1985; won Spingarn, 1964.
b. Feb 10, 1927 in Laurel, Mississippi
Source: *AfrAmAl 6; Baker 78, 84; BiDAfM; BiDAmM; BiE&WWA; BioIn 5, 6, 7, 8, 9, 10, 11, 12, 13, 14, 15, 16; BioNews 74; BlkOpe; BlkWAm; BlueB 76; BriBkM 80; CelR, 90; CmOp; ConBlB 1; ConMus 6; ContDcW 89; CurBio 61, 78; DcArts; DcTwCCu 1, 5; DrBlPA, 90; Ebony 1; EncAACR; EncWB; FacFETw; GoodHs; GrLiveH; HanAmWH; IntDcOp; IntWW 74, 75, 76, 77, 78, 79, 80, 81, 82, 83, 89, 91, 93; IntWWM 77, 80, 90; InWom, SUP; LegTOT; LibW; LinLib S; MetOEnc; MusMk; MusSN; NegAl 76, 83, 89; NewAmDM; NewEOp 71; NewGrDA 86; NewGrDM 80; NewYTBS 82; NotBlAW 1; OxDcOp; PenDiMP; PlP&P; RAdv 14; VarWW 85; WebAB 74, 79; Who 85, 88, 90, 92, 94; WhoAfA 96; WhoAm 74, 76, 78, 80, 82, 84, 86, 88, 90, 92, 94, 95, 96, 97; WhoAmM 83; WhoAmW 61, 64, 66, 68, 70, 72, 74, 75, 77, 81, 83, 85, 95, 97; WhoBlA 75, 77, 80, 85, 88, 90, 92, 94; WhoEnt 92; WhoMus 72; WhoOp 76; WhoWor 74, 78, 80, 82, 84, 87, 89, 91, 93, 95, 96, 97; WomFir; WorAl; WorAlBi*

Price, Margaret Berenice
Welsh. Opera Singer
Soprano, known for Mozart roles 1960s, Verdi roles, 1970s.
b. Apr 13, 1941 in Blackwood, Wales
Source: *Baker 84; BioIn 14, 15; CurBio 86; IntWW 91; IntWWM 90; MetOEnc; Who 85, 92; WhoWor 84*

Price, Melvin
American. Politician
Dem. congressman from IL, 1945-88; first chm. of House Ethics committee, known for support of military.
b. Jan 1, 1905 in East Saint Louis, Illinois
d. Apr 22, 1988 in Washington, District of Columbia
Source: *AlmAP 78, 80, 82, 84, 88; AmCath 80; BioIn 10, 15, 16; NewYTBS 88; PolsAm 84; WhAm 9; WhoAm 74, 76, 78, 80, 82, 84, 86; WhoAmP 73, 75, 77, 79, 81, 83, 85, 87; WhoMW 74, 76, 84, 86, 88*

Price, Nancy
[Lillian Nancy Bache Price]
English. Actor, Producer
Founded People's National Theatre, 1939.
b. Feb 3, 1880 in Kinver, England
d. Mar 31, 1970, England
Source: *BioIn 3; ChhPo S3; ConAu 111; EngPo; Film 2; FilmgC; HalFC 80, 84, 88; ObitT 1961; OxCThe 67; PenNWW B; PlP&P; WhoHol B; WhScrn 74, 77, 83; WhThe*

Price, Nick
[Nicholas Raymond Leige Price]
South African. Golfer
Won 1983 World Series of Golf; 1992 PGA Championship; 1994 British Open.
b. Jan 28, 1957 in Durban, South Africa
Source: *BioIn 13; CurBio 96; WhoAm 95, 96, 97; WhoWor 95, 96*

Price, Ray
[Noble Ray Price]
"The Cherokee Cowboy"
American. Musician, Singer
Pop-country hits include "For the Good Times," 1970, nominated for Grammy.
b. Jan 12, 1926 in Perryville, Texas
Source: *Baker 84; BgBkCoM; BioIn 14, 15; ConMus 11; CounME 74, 74A; EncFCWM 69, 83; HarEnCM 87; IlEncCM; LegTOT; NewAmDM; NewGrDA 86; NewGrDJ 88; PenEncP; RkOn 74; VarWW 85; WhoAm 76, 78, 80, 82, 84, 86, 88, 90, 92, 94; WhoEnt 92; WorAl; WorAlBi*

Price, Reynolds
[Edward Reynolds Price]
American. Author, Educator
Best known for *A Long and Happy Life,* 1962.
b. Feb 1, 1933 in Macon, North Carolina
Source: *AmAu&B; Benet 87; BenetAL 91; BioIn 6, 8, 10, 11, 13, 15, 16, 17, 18, 19, 20, 21; ConAu 1NR, 1R; ConLC 3, 6, 13, 43, 50, 63; ConNov 72, 76, 82, 86, 91; CurBio 87; CyWA 89; DcLB 2; DcLEL 1940; DrAF 76; DrAPF 80, 91; FifSWrA; IntAu&W 76, 77, 91; IntvTCA 2; LegTOT; MagSAmL; ModAL S2; NewYTBS 87, 89; Novels; OxCAmL 83, 95; PenC AM; RAdv 1; ShSCr 22; SouWr; WhoAm 74, 76, 78, 80, 82, 84, 86, 88, 90, 92, 94, 95, 96, 97; WhoUSWr 88; WhoWor 74; WhoWrEP 89, 92, 95; WorAlBi; WorAu 1950; WrDr 76, 80, 82, 84, 86, 88, 90, 92*

Price, Richard
American. Writer
Wrote scripts for *The Color of Money,* 1986; *Sea of Love,* 1989.
b. Oct 12, 1949 in New York, New York
Source: *BioIn 10, 12, 13, 15, 16, 17, 18, 19, 20, 21; ConAu 3NR, 49; ConLC 6, 12; ConTFT 12; CurBio 94; DcLB Y81B; DrAF 76; DrAPF 80; IntMPA 96; WhoUSWr 88; WhoWrEP 89, 92, 95; WorAu 1985*

Price, Roger Taylor
American. Publisher
Founded Price-Stern-Sloan Publishers, Inc., 1960; stand-up comedian, 1950-63.
b. Mar 6, 1920 in Charleston, West Virginia
d. Oct 31, 1990 in North Hollywood, California
Source: *ConAu 9R; IntMPA 86, 88; VarWW 85; WhoAm 86*

Price, Sammy
"King of Boogie Woogie"
American. Jazz Musician
Pianist who influenced many musicians during his seventy year career.
b. Oct 6, 1908 in Honey Grove, Texas
d. Apr 14, 1992 in New York, New York
Source: *AllMusG; BiDJaz; BioIn 16, 17, 18; IlEncJ; NewGrDJ 88, 94*

Price, Sterling
American. Military Leader
Confederate major general, defeated at Westport, MO, 1864.
b. Sep 11, 1809 in Prince Edward County, Virginia
d. Sep 29, 1867 in Saint Louis, Missouri
Source: *AmBi; ApCAB; BiAUS; BiDConf; BiDrAC; BiDrGov 1789; BiDrUSC 89; BioIn 5, 8, 9, 17, 18; CivWDc; DcAmB; Drake; EncSoH; HarEnMi; HarEnUS; NatCAB 12; NewCol 75; REnAW; TwCBDA; WebAMB; WebBD 83; WhAm HS; WhCiWar; WhNaAH*

Price, Steve
[Pablo Cruise]
American. Musician, Singer
Hit song "Love Will Find a Way," 1978.
Source: *ConAu 16NR; IlEncRk; RkOn 78; WhoAm 86; WhoE 91; WhoEmL 91; WhoFI 92; WhoRock 81*

Price, Vincent
"Master of Menace"
American. Actor
Starred in horror films *House of Wax,* 1953; *Theatre of Blood,* 1973.
b. May 27, 1911 in Saint Louis, Missouri

d. Oct 25, 1993 in Los Angeles, California
Source: *AnObit 1993; BiDFilm, 81, 94; BiE&WWA; BioIn 4, 5, 6, 9, 10, 11, 14, 15, 16, 17, 19, 20, 21; CelR, 90; CmMov; ConAu 89; ConTFT 4, 12; CurBio 56, 94N; DcArts; FilmEn; FilmgC; ForYSC; GangFlm; HalFC 80, 84, 88; IntDcF 1-3, 2-3; IntMPA 75, 76, 77, 78, 79, 80, 81, 82, 84, 86, 88, 92, 94; IntWW 78, 79, 80, 81, 82, 83, 89, 91, 93; ItaFilm; LegTOT; MotPP; MovMk; NewEScF; News 94, 94-2; NewYTBS 93; NotNAT; OxCFilm; PenEncH; RadStar; SaTiSS; VarWW 85; WhoAm 74, 76, 78, 80, 82, 84, 86, 88, 90; WhoAmA 73, 76, 78, 80, 82, 84, 86, 89, 91, 93; WhoEnt 92; WhoGov 72; WhoHol 92, A; WhoHrs 80; WhoThe 72, 77, 81; WorAl; WorAlBi; WorEFlm*

Pride, Charley
"Country Charley"
American. Singer
Won Grammy for "Kiss an Angel Good Morning," 1972; first black country music star.
b. Mar 18, 1938 in Sledge, Mississippi
Source: *Baker 84, 92; BgBkCoM; BiDAmM; BioIn 9, 10, 12, 13, 14, 15, 16; BioNews 74; CelR 90; ConMuA 80A; ConMus 4; CounME 74, 74A; CurBio 75; DcTwCCu 5; DrBlPA, 90; EncFCWM 69, 83; HarEnCM 87; IlEncCM; InB&W 85; NegAl 89; NewGrDA 86; ODwPR 91; OxCPMus; PenEncP; RkOn 78; VarWW 85; WhoAfA 96; WhoAm 74, 76, 84, 86, 88; WhoBlA 85, 88, 92, 94; WhoEnt 92; WhoRock 81; WorAlBi*

Priesand, Sally Jane
American. Religious Leader
First ordained female rabbi, 1972; wrote *Judaism and the New Woman,* 1975.
b. Jun 27, 1946 in Cleveland, Ohio
Source: *CurBio 65; InWom SUP; NewYTBE 71; WhoAm 74, 76, 78, 80, 82, 84, 86, 88, 90, 92, 94, 95, 96, 97; WhoAmW 83, 85, 87, 89, 97; WhoEmL 87; WhoRel 75, 77, 92; WorAlBi*

Priest, Ivy (Maude) Baker
American. Government Official
US treasurer under Dwight Eisenhower, 1953-61.
b. Sep 7, 1905 in Kimberley, Utah
d. Jun 23, 1975 in Santa Monica, California
Source: *AmWomM; CurBio 52; DcAmB S9; EncWB; InWom SUP; NotAW MOD; WhAm 6; WhoAm 74; WhoAmP 73; WhoAmW 58, 61; WhoGov 72; WhoWest 74*

Priestley, Joseph
English. Chemist
Discovered what is now called oxygen, 1774; wrote *Essay on First Principles of Government,* 1768.
b. Mar 13, 1733 in Fieldhead, England
d. Feb 6, 1804 in Northumberland, Pennsylvania
Source: *Alli; AmAu&B; AmBi; AmRef; ApCAB; AsBiEn; BenetAL 91; BiDAmS; BiD&SB; BiDPsy; BiESc; BiHiMed; BilnAmS; BioIn 1, 2, 3, 4, 5, 6, 7, 8, 9, 10, 11, 12, 13, 14, 15, 16, 19, 20, 21; BlkwCE; BlmGEL; BritAu; CamDcSc; CamGEL; CamGLE; CasWL; Chambr 2; CmFrR; CyAL 2; CyEd; DcAmAu; DcAmB; DcAmReB 1, 2; DcAmSR; DcBiPP; DcEnL; DcEuL; DcLEL; DcNAA; DcNaB; DcScB; Dis&D; Drake; EncEnl; EvLB; HarEnUS; InSci; LarDcSc; LinLib L, S; LngCEL; LuthC 75; McGEWB; NamesHP; NatCAB 6; NewC; NewCBEL; OxCAmH; OxCAmL 65, 83, 95; OxCEng 67, 85, 95; OxCMed 86; OxCPhil; RAdv 14, 13-5; REn; TwCBDA; WhAm HS; WorAl; WorAlBi; WorScD*

Priestley, (J)ohn (B)oynton
English. Author, Dramatist
Wrote *Angel Pavement; Literature and Western Man; The Edwardians.*
b. Sep 13, 1894 in Bradford, England
d. Aug 14, 1984 in Stratford-upon-Avon, England
Source: *Au&Wr 71; BiE&WWA; BioIn 1, 2, 3, 4, 5, 6, 7, 9, 10, 11, 12, 13, 14, 15, 17, 18, 20; CasWL; Chambr 3; ChhPo; CnMD; CnThe; ConAu 9NR; ConLC 9; DcLEL; DcNaB 1981; EncWL; EncWT; Ent; EvLB; IntAu&W 76, 77, 82; IntWW 74, 75, 76, 77, 78, 79, 80, 81, 82, 83; LinLib S; NewCBEL; NotNAT A; OxCEng 67; OxCThe 67; PenC ENG; TwCA, SUP; VarWW 85; WhAm 8; WhDW; WhE&EA; WhLit; Who 74, 82, 83, 85N; WhoLA; WhoThe 77; WhoWor 74, 78, 80, 82, 84*

Priestly, Jack
American. Filmmaker
Award-winning cinematographer; winner of two Emmys for "Naked City" series as director of photography.
b. Jul 27, 1926 in New York, New York
d. May 26, 1993 in Los Angeles, California
Source: *HalFC 88; NewYTBS 93*

Priestly, Jason
American. Actor
Plays Brandon Walsh on TV series "Beverly Hills 90210," 1991—.
b. Aug 28, 1969 in Vancouver, British Columbia, Canada
Source: *ConTFT 15*

Prigogine, Ilya
"The Poet of Thermodynamics"
Russian. Chemist
Won 1977 Nobel Prize in chemistry.
b. Jan 25, 1917 in Moscow, Russia
Source: *AmMWSc 89, 92, 95; BioIn 11, 12; CamDcSc; ConAu 131; CurBio 87; FacFETw; IntAu&W 77; IntWW 74, 75, 76, 77, 78, 79, 80, 81, 82, 83, 91, 93; LarDcSc; McGMS 80; NewYTBS 77; NobelP; NotTwCS; Who 82, 83, 85, 88, 90, 92, 94; WhoAm 80, 82, 84, 86, 88, 90; WhoFrS 84; WhoNob, 90, 95; WhoScEu 91-2; WhoSSW 80, 82, 86, 88, 91; WhoThSc 1996; WhoUSWr 88; WhoWor 74, 76, 78, 80, 82, 84, 87, 89, 91; WhoWrEP 89, 92, 95; WrDr 94, 96*

Prima, Louis
American. Musician
Popular bandleader, jazz trumpeter, 1940s-50s; known for zany singing in films.
b. Dec 7, 1912 in New Orleans, Louisiana
d. Aug 24, 1978 in New Orleans, Louisiana
Source: *ASCAP 66; RkOn 74; WhAm 7; WhoAm 74, 76, 78; WhoHol A; WhoJazz 72; WorAl; WorAlBi*

Primaticcio, Francesco
Italian. Artist, Architect
Head artist at Fontainebleau, 1540.
b. 1503 in Bologna, Italy
d. Sep 1570 in Paris, France
Source: *REn*

Prime, Geoffrey Arthur
English. Spy
Convicted of spying for Soviets, 1968-81; sentenced to 35 years.
b. 1938? in Alton, England
Source: *BioIn 13, 14; NewYTBS 82*

Primeau, Joe
[A Joseph Primeau]
Canadian. Hockey Player
Center, Toronto, 1927-36; won Lady Byng Trophy, 1932; Hall of Fame, 1963.
b. Jan 24, 1906 in Lindsay, Ontario, Canada
d. May 15, 1989 in Toronto, Ontario, Canada
Source: *BioIn 10; HocEn; WhoHcky 73; WhoSpor*

Primo de Rivera, Jose A
Spanish. Revolutionary
Founded Spanish fascist movement, Falange.
b. 1903
d. 1936
Source: *BioIn 13; WhoMilH 76*

Primo de Rivera (y Orbaneja), Miguel
Spanish. Political Leader, Military Leader
Dictator of Spain, 1923-30; nationalistic regime held as its motto, "Country, Religion, Monarchy."
b. Jan 8, 1870 in Cadiz, Spain
d. Mar 16, 1930 in Paris, France
Source: *BioIn 16; DcTwHis; DicTyr; EncRev; FacFETw*

Primrose, William
American. Violinist
Organized Primrose Quartet, 1938; wrote autobiography, 1978.
b. Aug 23, 1904 in Glasgow, Scotland
d. May 1, 1982 in Provo, Utah

Source: *AnObit 1982; Baker 84; BioIn 1, 3, 4, 5, 9, 12; BriBkM 80; ConAu 102, 106, 116; CurBio 46, 82N; MusSN; NewGrDA 86; NewYTBS 82; Who 74, 82; WhoAm 74; WhoMus 72*

Primus, Pearl
American. Dancer
Choreographer who based her work on African and West Indian music.
b. Nov 29, 1919, Trinidad
d. Oct 29, 1994 in New Rochelle, New York
Source: *AfrAmAl 6; BiDD; BioIn 1, 2, 6, 8, 11, 13, 16, 17, 18, 20, 21; BlkWAm; CmpGMD; CnOxB; ConBlB 6; ContDcW 89; CurBio 95N; DancEn 78; DcTwCCu 5; DrBlPA, 90; GrLiveH; IntDcWB; InWom, SUP; NegAl 76; NotBlAW 1; WhAm 11; WhoAm 74, 76, 78, 94; WhoBlA 75, 77, 80, 85, 90, 92; WomFir*

Prince, Faith
American. Actor
Tony Award winner for Miss Adelaide in *Guys and Dolls,* 1992.
b. 1959 in Augusta, Georgia
Source: *ConTFT 8; News 93-2*

Prince, Hal
[Harold Smith Prince]
American. Producer, Director
Plays include *Damn Yankees, West Side Story, Fiddler on the Roof, Phantom of the Opera;* has won over 16 Tonys.
b. Jan 30, 1928 in New York, New York
Source: *BiE&WWA; BioIn 7, 8, 9, 10, 12, 13, 14, 15; BioNews 75; ConTFT 2, 8; CurBio 71; DcArts; EncMT; HalFC 84; IntMPA 88; IntWW 83; LegTOT; NewYTBE 73; NotNAT; OxCAmT 84; PeoHis; VarWW 85; Who 82, 83, 85, 88, 90, 92, 94; WhoAm 86; WhoE 74; WhoThe 81*

Prince, Prairie
[The Tubes]
American. Musician
Drummer with The Tubes since late 1960s.
b. May 7, 1950 in Charlotte, North Carolina

Prince, William
American. Actor
Character actor since 1943; films include *Destination: Tokyo,* 1944; *The Soldier,* 1982.
b. Jan 26, 1913 in Nichols, New York
d. Oct 8, 1996 in Tarrytown, New York
Source: *BiE&WWA; ConTFT 7; FilmEn; FilmgC; HalFC 80, 84, 88; IntMPA 75, 76, 77, 78, 79, 80, 81, 82, 84, 86, 88, 92, 94, 96; ItaFilm; NotNAT; VarWW 85; WhoHol 92, A; WhoThe 72, 77, 81*

Princip, Gavrilo
Serbian. Assassin
Assassinated Archduke Ferdinand and wife, 1914; sparked WW I.
b. Jul 25, 1895 in Bosnia, Austria-Hungary
d. Apr 30, 1918 in Prague, Czechoslovakia
Source: *REn; SpyCS*

Principal, Victoria
[Mrs. Harry Glassman]
American. Actor
Played Pamela Ewing on TV series "Dallas," 1978-87.
b. Jan 3, 1950 in Fukuoka, Japan
Source: *BioIn 14, 15, 16; ConTFT 5; HalFC 88; IntAu&W 91; IntMPA 92, 94, 96; InWom SUP; VarWW 85; WhoAm 86, 90, 92, 94, 95, 96, 97; WhoAmW 91, 93, 95, 97; WhoEnt 92; WhoHol 92, A; WorAlBi*

Prine, John
American. Singer, Songwriter
Gifted storytelling songwriter; albums include *Bruised Orange,* 1978 and *John Prine Live,* 1989; his compositions recorded by numerous other artists.
b. Oct 10, 1946 in Maywood, Illinois
Source: *BioIn 14, 18, 21; ConMuA 80A; ConMus 7; EncFCWM 83; EncRk 88; EncRkSt; IlEncCM; IlEncRk; LegTOT; NewGrDA 86; OnThGG; PenEncP; RolSEnR 83; WhoAm 82, 84, 86, 88, 90, 92, 94, 95, 96, 97; WhoEnt 92; WhoRock 81*

Pringle, Aileen
American. Actor
Silent movie leading lady known for exotic siren roles in *Three Weeks, Souls for Sale.*
b. Jul 23, 1895 in San Francisco, California
d. Dec 16, 1989 in New York, New York
Source: *BioIn 8, 9, 16, 17; Film 1, 2; FilmEn; FilmgC; HalFC 80, 84, 88; InWom SUP; LegTOT; MotPP; MovMk; NewYTBS 89; SilFlmP; ThFT; TwYS; What 2; WhoHol A*

Pringle, Laurence
[Sean Edmund]
American. Children's Author
Nature tales include *From Pond to Prairie,* 1972.
b. Nov 26, 1935 in Rochester, New York
Source: *AuBYP 3; BiE&WWA; BioIn 9; ChlBkCr; ChlLR 4; ConAu 29R; EncMT; FourBJA; OxCFilm; OxCThe 67; SmATA 4, 6AS, 68; WhoHol A; WhoThe 77A*

Printemps, Yvonne
[Yvonne Wigniolle]
French. Actor, Singer
Former Folies Bergere performer, graduated to theater; played first title role appearence in *Mozart,* 1926.
b. Jul 25, 1898 in Ermont, France
d. Jan 18, 1977 in Paris, France
Source: *BiE&WWA; BioIn 11; CnThe; EncMT; HalFC 84; NewYTBS 77; OxCFilm; OxCThe 83; WhoHol A; WhThe*

Prinze, Freddie
American. Actor, Comedian
Starred in TV series *Chico and the Man,* 1974-77; suicide ruled accidental, 1983.
b. Jun 22, 1954 in New York, New York
d. Jan 29, 1977 in Los Angeles, California
Source: *BioIn 10; LegTOT; WhoCom; WorAl; WorAlBi*

Prior, Matthew
English. Poet, Diplomat
Noted epigrammist; co-wrote *Country Mouse and the City Mouse,* 1687, and philosophical prose.
b. Jul 21, 1664 in Winborne, England
d. Sep 18, 1721 in Cambridge, England
Source: *Alli; AtlBL; BbD; Benet 87, 96; BiD&SB; BioIn 3, 4, 5, 6, 9, 10, 13, 15, 17; BlkwCE; BlmGEL; BritAu; CamGEL; CamGLE; CasWL; Chambr 2; ChhPo, S1; CnE&AP; CrtT 2; DcBiPP; DcEnA; DcEnL; DcEuL; DcLB 95; DcLEL; DcNaB, C; EvLB; GrWrEL P; LegTOT; LitC 4; LngCEL; NewC; NewCBEL; OxCEng 67, 85, 95; PenC ENG; REn; RfGEnL 91; WebE&AL; WhDW*

Prio Socarras, Carlos
Cuban. Political Leader
President of Cuba, 1948-52; overthrown by Batista.
b. Jul 14, 1903 in Bahia Honda, Cuba
d. Apr 5, 1977 in Miami Beach, Florida
Source: *BiDLAmC; BioIn 1, 2, 5, 11, 16; CurBio 49, 77, 77N*

Priscilla of Boston
[Priscilla Kidder]
American. Fashion Designer
Best known for designing bridal gowns.
b. Dec 14, 1916 in Quincy, Massachusetts
Source: *InWom SUP; WhoAm 80, 82, 84; WhoAmW 81; WorFshn*

Pritchard, John Michael, Sir
English. Conductor
Chief conductor, BBC's Symphony Orchestra, 1982-89.
b. Feb 5, 1921 in London, England
d. Dec 4, 1989 in San Francisco, California
Source: *Baker 84; BioIn 9, 12, 15, 16; BlueB 76; CmOp; DcNaB 1986; FacFETw; IntWW 74, 75, 76, 77, 78, 79, 80, 81, 82, 83, 89; IntWWM 77, 80, 90; MetOEnc; NewAmDM; NewGrDM 80; NewYTBS 89; PenDiMP; Who 74, 82, 83, 90; WhoAm 88; WhoMus 72; WhoOp 76; WhoWor 74, 89*

Pritchett, Henry S
American. Educator, Astronomer
President, MIT, 1900-06, Carnegie Foundation of Advanced Teaching, 1906-30.
b. Apr 16, 1857 in Fayette, Missouri
d. Aug 28, 1939 in Santa Barbara, California

Source: *AmBi; BiDAmEd; BiDAmS; DcAmB S2; NatCAB 10, 29; WhAm 1*

Pritchett, V(ictor) S(awdon), Sir
English. Author
Fiction combines subtle pessimism, irony; wrote travel nonfiction *The Spanish Temper,* 1954.
b. Dec 16, 1900 in Ipswich, England
d. Mar 20, 1997 in London, England
Source: *Au&Wr 71; Benet 87, 96; BioIn 3, 4, 8, 9, 10, 11, 12, 13, 14, 15, 17, 20; BlueB 76; CamGEL; CamGLE; CasWL; ConAu 31NR, 61; ConLC 5, 15, 41; ConLCrt 77; ConNov 72, 76, 86, 91, 96; CurBio 74; CyWA 89; DcArts; DcLB 15; DcLEL; EncWB; EncWL 3; FacFETw; IntAu&W 76, 77, 82, 89, 91, 93; IntvTCA 2; IntWW 74, 75, 76, 77, 78, 79, 80, 81, 82, 83, 89, 91, 93; LngCTC; MajTwCW; ModBrL, S1, S2; NewC; NewCBEL; NewYTBS 80, 85; Novels; OxCEng 67, 85, 95; PenC ENG; RAdv 1, 13-1; REn; RfGEnL 91; RfGShF; RGTwCWr; ShSWr; TwCA SUP; TwCWr; Who 74, 85, 92, 94; WhoAm 82, 84, 86, 88, 90, 92, 94, 95, 96, 97; WhoTwCL; WhoWor 74, 76, 78, 84, 87, 89, 91, 93, 95, 96, 97; WrDr 76, 86, 92, 94, 96*

Pritikin, Nathan
American. Nutritionist
Director, Longevity Research Institute, 1976-85; author of diet, exercise, cookbooks.
b. Aug 29, 1915 in Chicago, Illinois
d. Feb 21, 1985 in Albany, New York
Source: *AnObit 1985; BioIn 12; ConAu 27NR, 89, 114; FacFETw; NewYTBS 79, 85; WhAm 8; WhoAm 82, 84; WrDr 82, 84*

Pritzker, Abram Nicholas
American. Financier
Owned Braniff Airways; *McCall's* mag; estimated fortune: $1.5 billion.
b. Jan 6, 1896 in Chicago, Illinois
d. Feb 9, 1986 in Chicago, Illinois
Source: *BioIn 14, 15, 17; ConAmBL; ConNews 86-2; Dun&B 79; NewYTBS 86; WhoAm 82, 84; WhoMW 78; WhoWorJ 72*

Procol Harum
[Gary Brooker; Matthew Fisher; Robert Harrison; David Knights; Keith Reid; Ray Royer; Robin Trower; Barry Wilson]
English. Music Group
British classical rock band, late 1960s; had biggest hit song with "A Whiter Shade of Pale," 1967.
Source: *Alli, SUP; BiDBrA; ConMuA 80A; DcNaB; EncPR&S 74, 89; EncRk 88; EncRkSt; FolkA 87; HarEnR 86; IlEncRk; NewCBEL; NewYTBS 78; NotNAT B; ObitOF 79; PenEncP; RkOn 78; RolSEnR 83; WhoRock 81; WhoRocM 82*

Procope, Ernesta Gertrude Foster Bowman
American. Insurance Executive
Founder and pres., EG Bowman Co. Inc., 1953—.
b. Feb 9, in New York, New York
Source: *AmWomM; BioIn 16; InB&W 85; InWom SUP; NotBlAW 1; WhoAmW 91; WhoBlA 92*

Procter, Bryan Waller
[Barry Cornwall]
English. Poet, Lawyer
Wrote verse vol. *Dramatic Scenes,* 1819.
b. Nov 21, 1787
d. Oct 4, 1874
Source: *Alli, SUP; BbD; BiD&SB; BioIn 2, 17, 21; BritAu 19; CamGEL; CamGLE; CasWL; CelCen; Chambr 3; ChhPo, S1; DcEnA; DcEnL; DcEuL; DcLB 96, 144; DcLEL; DcNaB; EvLB; LinLib L; NewC; NewCBEL; OxCEng 67, 85, 95; REn*

Procter, William Cooper
American. Manufacturer, Philanthropist
Pres., Procter and Gamble, 1907-30; instituted profit-sharing.
b. Aug 25, 1862 in Glendale, Ohio
d. May 2, 1934
Source: *BiDAmBL 83; BioIn 1, 3, 10, 15; DcAmB S1; EncAB-A 7; NatCAB 25; WhAm 1; WorAl*

Proctor, Barbara Gardner
American. Advertising Executive
Founder, creative director, CEO, Proctor and Gardner Advertising, Chicago, 1971- -.
b. Nov 30, 1933 in Black Mountain, North Carolina
Source: *AmWomM; BioIn 13, 15; ConNews 85-3; Ebony 1; InB&W 85; InWom SUP; NotBlAW 1; WhoAdv 80, 90; WhoAm 82, 90; WhoAmW 85, 87; WhoBlA 85, 88, 92; WhoFI 81; WhoMW 90*

Prodi, Romano
Italian. Business Executive, Political Leader
Chairman, IRI, largest company in Italy; prime minister of Italy, 1996—.
b. Aug 9, 1939 in Emilia-Romagna, Italy
Source: *BioIn 15; WhoWor 89, 97*

Proell Moser, Annemarie
Austrian. Skier
World Cup Alpine champion, 1971-75, 1979; won gold medal, women's downhill, 1980 Olympics.
b. Mar 27, 1953 in Kleinarl, Austria
Source: *BioIn 9, 11; CurBio 76; GoodHs; HerW, 84; IntDcWB; InWom SUP; WorAl; WorAlBi*

Profaci, Joe
[Joseph Profact]
Criminal
One of the original five Mafia families in NY.
b. Oct 2, 1898? in Palermo, Sicily, Italy
d. Jun 6, 1962 in Bay Shore, New York

Professor Longhair
American. Pianist
Energetic piano playing style inspired New Orleans rock and roll musicians of the 1950s and 60s.
b. Dec 19, 1918 in Bogalusa, Louisiana
d. Jan 30, 1980 in New Orleans, Louisiana
Source: *AnObit 1980; Baker 84, 92; BiDAfM; BioIn 12, 18; ConMus 6; DcTwCCu 5; EncRk 88; InB&W 85; NewAmDM; NewGrDA 86; NewYTBS 80; PenEncP; RolSEnR 83; SoulM*

Profet, Margie
American. Biologist
Developed many hypotheses, including several on reproduction.
b. 1958 in Berkeley, California
Source: *AmMWSc 95; News 94; NotWoLS; WhoAmW 97; WhoScEn 94, 96*

Profumo, John Dennis
English. Government Official
Foreign affairs minister, 1959-60; secretary of War, 1960-63; resigned due to involvement in political-sex scandal known as Profumo affair.
b. Jan 30, 1915
Source: *BioIn 5, 6, 7, 8, 9, 10, 16; CurBio 59; IntWW 89, 91, 93; SpyCS; Who 74, 82, 83, 85, 88, 90, 92, 94*

Prokhorov, Alexander Mikhailovich
Russian. Physicist
Shared 1964 Nobel Prize in physics with Basov; explored new method for generating electromagnetic waves.
b. Jul 11, 1916 in Atherton, Australia
Source: *AsBiEn; BiDSovU; BioIn 15; IntWW 91; LarDcSc; NobelP; Who 74, 82, 83, 85, 88, 90, 92, 94; WhoNob, 90, 95; WhoWor 91; WorAlBi*

Prokofiev, Sergei Sergeevich
Russian. Composer
Concert pianist best known for composing fairy tale for narrator, orchestra, *Peter and the Wolf,* 1936.
b. Apr 23, 1891 in Sontsovka, Russia
d. Mar 5, 1953 in Moscow, Union of Soviet Socialist Republics
Source: *AnCL; AtlBL; CurBio 41, 53; DcCM; DcFM; McGEWB; OxCFilm; REn; WhAm 3; WorEFlm*

Prokosch, Frederic
American. Author, Poet
Had 60-year career that included his best-selling novel *The Asians,* 1935.
b. May 17, 1908 in Madison, Wisconsin
d. Jun 2, 1989 in Plan de Grasse, France
Source: *AmNov; AnObit 1989; BenetAL 91; BioIn 2, 3, 4, 5, 7, 13, 15, 16; BlueB 76; CasWL; ConAu 73, 128; ConLC 4, 48; ConNov 72, 76, 82, 86; ConPo 70, 75, 80, 85; CyWA 89; DcLB 48; DrAF 76; DrAPF 87; EngPo; FacFETw;*

IntAu&W 89, 91; IntWW 74, 75, 76, 77, 78, 79, 80, 81, 82, 83, 89; IntWWP 77; LngCTC; NewYTBS 89; Novels; OxCAmL 65, 83, 95; PenC AM; REn; REnAL; SixAP; TwCA, SUP; Who 74, 82, 83, 85, 88, 90N; WrDr 76, 80, 82, 84, 86, 88

Pronovost, Marcel
[Rene Marcel Pronovost]
Canadian. Hockey Player
Defenseman, Detroit, 1950-65, Toronto, 1965-70; Hall of Fame, 1978.
b. Jun 15, 1930 in Lac-la-Tortue, Quebec, Canada
Source: *HocEn; WhoHcky 73*

Propertius, Sextus
Roman. Poet
Popular elegaic poet; works valued for charm, eloquence; best known work *Cynthia,* 29 B.C.
b. 55BC in Assisi, Italy
d. 16BC in Rome, Italy
Source: *Benet 87; BioIn 4, 14; CasWL; Grk&L; OxCClL 89; OxCEng 85; REn*

Prosky, Robert Joseph
American. Actor
Played Sgt. Jablonski on "Hill Street Blues," 1984-87.
b. Dec 13, 1930 in Philadelphia, Pennsylvania
Source: *BioIn 14; ConTFT 3; IntMPA 86, 92; VarWW 85; WhoAm 86, 88, 90, 92, 94, 95, 96, 97; WhoEnt 92; WorAlBi*

Prost, Alain Marie Pascal
French. Auto Racer
Formula One racer; has won more races than any other driver, passing previous record set by Jackie Stewart; Grand Prix champion, 1985, 1986.
b. Feb 24, 1955 in Lorette, France
Source: *BioIn 14, 15; ConNews 88-1; IntWW 91, 93; NewYTBS 87; WhoWor 82, 89, 91, 95, 96*

Protagoras
Greek. Philosopher
Most famous Sophist who said "Man is the measure of all things."
b. 490?BC in Abdera, Greece
d. 421?BC
Source: *BiDPsy; Grk&L; NewCol 75; OxCPhil; WebBD 83*

Prothrow-Stith, Deborah
American. Physician
First female public health commissioner, Massachusetts, 1987-89; expanded treatment programs for patients with AIDS; earned the Secretary of Health and Human Services Award, 1989.
b. Feb 6, 1954 in Marshall, Texas
Source: *ConBlB 10; NotBlAW 2*

Protopopov, Ludmilla Evgenievna Belousova
[Mrs. Oleg Protopopov]
Russian. Skater
With husband, won gold medals in pairs figure skating, 1964, 1968 Olympics.
b. Nov 22, 1935 in Ulyanousk, Union of Soviet Socialist Republics
Source: *BioIn 8, 12*

Protopopov, Oleg Alekseevich
Russian. Skater
With wife Ludmilla, won gold medals in pairs figure skating, 1964, 1968 Olympics.
b. Jul 16, 1932 in Leningrad, Union of Soviet Socialist Republics
Source: *BioIn 8, 12*

Proudhon, Pierre Joseph
French. Anarchist, Journalist
Regarded as father of anarchism, wrote *What Is Property?,* 1840; influenced European revolutionists.
b. Jan 15, 1809 in Besancon, France
d. Jan 16, 1865 in Paris, France
Source: *AtlBL; BbD; Benet 87, 96; BiD&SB; BioIn 1, 2, 4, 7, 8, 11, 12, 13; CasWL; CelCen; DcAmSR; DcBiPP; DcEuL; Dis&D; EuAu; McGEWB; OxCFr; REn; WhoEc 81; WorAl; WorAlBi*

Proulx, E(dna) Annie
American. Author
Wrote novels *Postcards,* 1992; *The Shipping News,* 1993; won 1993 National Book Award for Fiction.
b. Aug 22, 1935 in Norwich, Connecticut
Source: *ConAu 145; ConLC 81; ConNov 96; ConPopW; CurBio 95; RGTwCWr; WhoAm 94, 95, 96, 97; WhoAmW 93, 95, 97; WhoE 95; WrDr 96*

Proust, Joseph Louis
French. Chemist
Established law of definite proportions, called Proust's law; discovered grape sugar, leucine in cheese, 1818.
b. Sep 26, 1754 in Angers, France
d. Jul 5, 1826 in Angers, France
Source: *AsBiEn; BiESc; BioIn 3, 6, 14, 15; DcInv; DcScB; InSci; LarDcSc; NewCol 75; WorScD*

Proust, Marcel
French. Author
Wrote lengthy autobiography: *Remembrance of Things Past,* 1922-32.
b. Jul 10, 1871 in Paris, France
d. Nov 18, 1922 in Paris, France
Source: *AtlBL; Benet 87, 96; BioIn 1, 2, 3, 4, 5, 7, 8, 9, 10, 11, 12, 13, 14, 15, 16, 17, 18, 19, 20; BlmGEL; CasWL; ClDMEL 47, 80; CnMWL; ConAu 104, 120; CyWA 58; DcArts; DcEuL; DcLB 65; DcTwCCu 2; DcTwHis; Dis&D; EncWL 2, 3; EuWr 8; EvEuW; FacFETw; GayLesB; GrFLW; GuFrLit 1; JeHun; LegTOT; LinLib L, S; LngCEL; LngCTC; MagSWL; MajTwCW; MakMC; McGEWB; ModFrL; ModRL; NewC; Novels; OxCEng 67, 85, 95; OxCFr; PenC EUR; RAdv 14, 13-2; RComWL; REn; RfGWoL 95; TwCA, SUP; TwCLC 7, 13, 33; TwCWr; WhDW; WhoTwCL; WorAl; WorAlBi; WorLitC*

Prouty, Jed
American. Actor
Character actor in over 100 films including *Jones Family* comedies, 1930s.
b. Apr 6, 1879 in Boston, Massachusetts
d. May 10, 1956 in New York, New York
Source: *EncAFC; Film 2; FilmEn; FilmgC; ForYSC; HalFC 80, 84, 88; HolCA; MotPP; MovMk; NotNAT B; TwYS; Vers A; WhoHol B; WhScrn 74, 77, 83*

Provensen, Alice Rose Twitchell
American. Illustrator, Children's Author
With husband Martin produced colorful self-illustrated children's books, including *Year at Maple Hill,* 1978.
b. Aug 14, 1918 in Chicago, Illinois
Source: *ChlLR 11; ConAu 5NR, 53; IlsCB 1946, 1957; SmATA 9; ThrBJA; WhoAm 86, 90; WhoAmW 89; WhoChL; WhoE 74*

Provensen, Martin
American. Illustrator, Children's Author
Self-illustrated books include *Who's in the Egg,* 1968; *Our Animal Friends,* 1974.
b. Jul 10, 1916 in Chicago, Illinois
d. Mar 27, 1987 in Clinton Corners, New York
Source: *BioIn 5, 8, 9, 11, 12, 15, 16, 18, 19; ChlBkCr; ChlLR 11; ConAu 5NR, 53, 122; ConGrA 3; IlsBYP; IlsCB 1946, 1957; NewYTBS 87; SmATA 9, 51N; ThrBJA; WhoAm 86; WhoChL; WhoGrA 62, 82*

Provine, Dorothy Michele
American. Actor
Played in TV show "Roaring Twenties," 1960-62; played title role in film *Bonnie Parker Story,* 1958.
b. Jan 20, 1937 in Deadwood, South Dakota
Source: *EncAFC; FilmgC; HalFC 84, 88; IntMPA 86, 92; InWom SUP; MotPP; MovMk; VarWW 85; WhoAm 74, 76; WhoHol A*

Prowse, Juliet
American. Dancer, Actor
Had film debut in *Can-Can,* 1960; TV series "Mona McClusky," 1966.
b. Sep 25, 1936 in Bombay, India
d. Sep 14, 1996 in Los Angeles, California
Source: *BiDD; BioIn 13; ConTFT 9; FilmEn; FilmgC; ForYSC; HalFC 84, 88; InWom, SUP; MotPP; News 97-1; VarWW 85; WhoAm 82; WhoHol 92, A; WorAlBi*

Proxmire, William
American. Politician
Dem. senator from WI, 1959-89; awarded "Golden Fleece" for bureaucratic waste.
b. Nov 11, 1915 in Lake Forest, Illinois
Source: *AlmAP 78, 80, 82, 84, 88; BiDrAC; BiDrUSC 89; BioIn 4, 5, 6, 8, 9, 10, 11, 12, 13, 15, 16; BlueB 76; CelR; CngDr 87; ConAu 29R, 31NR; CurBio 78; EncABHB 7; EncWB; IntWW 74, 75, 76, 77, 78, 79, 80, 81, 82, 83, 89, 91, 93; IntYB 78, 79, 80, 81, 82; LegTOT; NewYTBE 71, 73; NewYTBS 75, 88; PolPar; PolProf E, J, K, NF; PolsAm 84; WhoAm 74, 76, 78, 80, 82, 84, 86, 88, 92, 94, 95, 96, 97; WhoAmP 73, 75, 77, 79, 81, 83, 85, 87, 89, 91, 93, 95; WhoGov 72, 75, 77; WhoMW 74, 76, 78, 80, 82, 84, 86, 88, 90; WhoWor 74, 78, 80, 82, 87, 89, 91; WorAl; WorAlBi; WrDr 76, 80, 82, 84*

Prudden, Bonnie
American. Physical Fitness Expert
Director, Institute for Physical Fitness, 1950—; author of numerous fitness books.
b. Jan 29, 1914 in New York, New York
Source: *BioIn 5, 12; ConAu 14NR, 77; WhoAmW 58, 61, 85*

Prudhomme, Paul
American. Chef
Cajun chef; author of *Chef Paul Prudhomme's Louisiana Kitchen,* 1984.
b. Jul 13, 1940 in Opelousas, Louisiana
Source: *BioIn 14; CelR 90*

Prudhon, Pierre-Paul
French. Artist
Romanticist whose paintings include *Crime Pursued by Vengeance and Justice,* 1808.
b. Apr 4, 1758 in Cluny, France
d. Feb 16, 1823 in Paris, France
Source: *McGEWB; NewCol 75; WebBD 83*

Pruitt, Greg(ory Donald)
American. Football Player
Four-time all-pro halfback, 1973-84, mostly with Cleveland.
b. Aug 18, 1951 in Houston, Texas
Source: *BiDAmSp FB; BioIn 10, 11, 12, 13; LegTOT; NewYTBS 84; WhoAfA 96; WhoAm 78, 80, 82, 84; WhoBlA 75, 77, 80, 85, 90, 92, 94; WhoFtbl 74*

Prusiner, Stanley (Ben)
American. Neurologist
Discovered that bovine spongiform encephalopathy (aka "mad cow" disease) is caused by a protein called a "prion," 1982.
b. May 28, 1942 in Des Moines, Iowa
Source: *AmMWSc 82, 86, 89, 92, 95; WhoAm 90, 92, 94, 95, 96, 97; WhoMedH; WhoScEn 94, 96; WhoWest 92, 94, 96*

Pryor, Arthur W
"The Paganini of the Trombone"
American. Musician
Trombone soloist; formed Pryor's Band, 1903.
b. Sep 22, 1870 in Saint Joseph, Missouri
d. Jun 18, 1942 in West Long Branch, New Jersey
Source: *Baker 84; BioIn 2; CurBio 42; DcAmB S3; NatCAB 40; NotNAT B; ObitOF 79; WhAm 2*

Pryor, David Hampton
American. Politician
Dem. senator from AR, 1979-97; governor of AR, 1975-79.
b. Aug 29, 1934 in Camden, Arkansas
Source: *AlmAP 82, 92; BiDrAC; BiDrGov 1978; BiDrUSC 89; BioIn 11; CngDr 89; IntWW 79, 80, 81, 82, 83, 89, 91, 93; PolsAm 84; WhoAm 76, 78, 80, 82, 84, 86, 88, 90, 92, 94, 95, 96, 97; WhoAmL 79; WhoAmP 73, 75, 77, 79, 81, 83, 85, 87, 89, 91, 93, 95; WhoSSW 86, 88, 91, 93, 95; WhoWor 80, 82, 87, 89, 91*

Pryor, Nicholas
[Nicholas David Probst]
American. Actor
Films include *Smile,* 1975; *Risky Business,* 1983.
b. Jan 28, 1935 in Baltimore, Maryland
Source: *BiE&WWA; ConTFT 5; HalFC 88; NotNAT; VarWW 85; WhoHol 92, A*

Pryor, Richard Franklin Lennox Thomas
American. Actor, Comedian
Stand-up comic; films include *Stir Crazy,* 1980; semi-autobiographical *Jo Jo Dancer,* 1986; won five Grammys for comic albums.
b. Dec 1, 1940 in Peoria, Illinois
Source: *BioIn 13, 16; BkPepl; BlksAmF; CelR 90; ConAu 122; ConBlAP 88; ConBlB 3; ConTFT 3; DrBlPA 90; EncAFC; FilmgC; HalFC 88; InB&W 85; IntMPA 86, 92; IntWW 91; MovMk; NegAl 89; VarWW 85; WhoAm 86, 90; WhoBlA 92; WhoEnt 92; WhoHol A; WorAlBi*

Pryor, Roger
American. Actor
Hosted numerous radio programs, 1940s; wed to Ann Sothern, 1936-42.
b. Aug 27, 1901 in New York, New York
d. Jan 31, 1974 in Puerto Vallarta, Mexico
Source: *BioIn 2, 10, 11; CmpEPM; EncAFC; FilmEn; FilmgC; HalFC 80, 84, 88; HolP 30; RadStar; Vers A; WhAm 6; What 4; WhScrn 74, 77, 83; WhThe*

Przhevalsky, Nikolai Mikhailovich
Russian. Geographer, Explorer
Traveled to Central China, 1870; Gobi Desert, 1884.
b. Apr 6, 1839 in Smolensk, Russia
d. Nov 1, 1888 in Karakol, Russia
Source: *McGEWB; NewCol 75; WebBD 83*

Psalmanazar, George
French. Imposter
Posed as Formosan Christian; sent to Oxford to teach fictitious language, 1704.
b. 1679? in Languedoc, France
d. May 3, 1763 in London, England
Source: *Alli; BbD; BiD&SB; BioIn 4, 7, 8, 18; BlkwCE; CasWL; Chambr 2; DcBiPP; DcEnL; DcLEL; DcNaB; Dis&D; EvLB; OxCEng 67, 85, 95*

Ptolemy
[Claudius Ptolemeaus]
Greek. Mathematician, Astronomer
Devised astronomical system whereby sun, planets revolved around Earth.
b. 150 in Alexandria, Egypt
Source: *BbD; Benet 87; BiD&SB; BioIn 14, 15; NewC; OxCClL 89; OxCEng 67, 85; PenC CL; REn*

Public Enemy
American. Rap Group
Rap group; "Fight the Power" was featured in Spike Lee film *Do the Right Thing.*
Source: *AfrAmAl 6; BiAUS; BioIn 18, 19; ConMus 4; DcTwCCu 5; EncRkSt; News 92, 92-1; WhFla; WhoAmP 85, 87*

Pucci, Emilio Marchese di Barsento
Italian. Designer
Noted for jersey print dresses, colorful sportswear, status-symbol accessories; business started, 1950.
b. Nov 20, 1914 in Naples, Italy
d. Nov 29, 1992 in Florence, Italy
Source: *BioNews 74; ConDes 90; CurBio 61; DcTwDes; EncFash; IntWW 83, 91; WhoFash 88; WhoWor 84, 87, 91; WorAlBi; WorFshn*

Puccini, Giacomo
Italian. Composer
Wrote many operas with exotic settings including *La Boheme,* 1896; *Madame Butterfly,* 1904.
b. Dec 22, 1858 in Lucca, Italy
d. Nov 29, 1924 in Brussels, Belgium
Source: *AtlBL; Baker 78, 84, 92; Benet 87, 96; BioIn 2, 3, 4, 5, 6, 7, 8, 9, 10, 11, 12, 13, 14, 16, 17, 19, 20; BriBkM 80; CamGWoT; CmOp; CmpBCM; CompSN, SUP; DcCom 77; DcCom&M 79; DcTwCC, A; FacFETw; IntDcOp; LegTOT; LinLib S; McGEWB; MetOEnc; MusMk; NewAmDM; NewEOp 71; NewGrDM 80; NewOxM; OxCAmL 65, 83, 95; OxCEng 85, 95; OxCMus; OxDcOp; PenDiMP A; PlP&P; RAdv 14, 13-3; REn; WhDW; WorAl; WorAlBi*

Puccio, Thomas Philip
American. Lawyer
Known for organized crime cases.

b. Sep 12, 1944 in New York, New York
Source: *BioIn 14, 15; ConNews 86-4; NewYTBS 85*

Puck, Wolfgang
Austrian. Chef, Restaurateur
Celebrity chef; owner of several restaurants in California; regular on "Good Morning, America."
b. Jan 8, 1949 in Saint Veit, Austria
Source: *BioIn 13; ConAu 124; LegTOT; News 90, 90-1; NewYTBS 91*

Puckett, Kirby
American. Baseball Player
Outfielder, Minnesota, 1984-96; tied ML record with four hits in first ML game; won AL batting title, 1989.
b. Mar 14, 1961 in Chicago, Illinois
Source: *AfrAmSG; Ballpl 90; BaseEn 88; BaseReg 87, 88; BioIn 15; ConBlB 4; LegTOT; WhoAfA 96; WhoAm 90, 92, 94, 95, 96, 97; WhoBlA 88, 90, 92, 94; WhoMW 92, 93; WhoSpor; WorAlBi*

Pudney, John Sleigh
English. Author, Dramatist
Wrote *Jacobson's Ladder,* 1938.
b. Jan 19, 1909 in Langley, England
d. Nov 10, 1977, England
Source: *Au&Wr 71; BioIn 10, 12; ChhPo, S1, S2, S3; ConAu 5NR, 9R, 77; ConNov 72, 76; ConPo 70, 75; IntWW 74, 75, 76, 77; LngCTC; ModBrL; NewC; PenC ENG; SmATA 24; Who 74; WhoChL; WhoWor 74; WorAu 1950; WrDr 76*

Pudovkin, Vsevolod
Russian. Director
Pioneer of Soviet cinema; films include *Mother,* 1926; *End of St. Petersburg,* 1927.
b. Feb 6, 1893 in Penza, Russia
d. Jun 30, 1953 in Riga, Union of Soviet Socialist Republics
Source: *BiDFilm; DcFM; IntDcF 1-2, 2-2; MovMk; OxCFilm; REn; WhoHol B; WhScrn 74, 77, 83; WorEFlm*

Puente, Tito
American. Bandleader
Led dance band, 1950s; often named musician of month; won Grammys, 1978, 1983.
b. Apr 20, 1923 in New York, New York
Source: *AllMusG; BioIn 11, 13, 20, 21; CurBio 77; DcHiB; DcTwCCu 4; FacFETw; IntWWM 90; LegTOT; NewGrDA 86; OxCPMus; PenEncP; WhoAm 86, 88; WhoEnt 92; WhoHisp 91, 92, 94; WhoWor 84*

Pugachev, Yemelyan I
Russian. Imposter
Cossack soldier, posed as Peter III; led army, peasants rebellion against Catherine II; defeated, captured, executed.
b. 1741
d. 1775
Source: *BioIn 9; McGEWB; NewCol 75; REn; WebBD 83*

Puget, Pierre
French. Sculptor
Baroque sculptor; works include *Milo of Crotona.*
b. Oct 16, 1620 in Marseilles, France
d. Dec 2, 1694 in Marseilles, France
Source: *DcArts; DcSeaP; IntDcAA 90; McGDA; McGEWD 84; OxCArt; OxDcArt*

Puig, Manuel
Argentine. Author
Best known for all-dialogue novel, *Kiss of the Spider Woman,* 1979; filmed, 1985.
b. Dec 28, 1932 in General Villegas, Argentina
d. Jul 22, 1990 in Cuernavaca, Mexico
Source: *AnObit 1990, 3; FacFETw; GayLesB; GayLL; HispLC; HispWr; IntAu&W 76, 77; IntvLAW; LatAmWr; LegTOT; LiExTwC; MajTwCW; NewYTBS 90; OxCSpan; PostFic; RAdv 14, 13-2; RfGWoL 95; SpAmA; WorAlBi; WorAu 1975*

Pulaski, Kazimierz
Polish. Nobleman, Army Officer
Revolutionary War hero, organized Pulaski cavalry corps, 1778; mortally wounded at Savannah.
b. Mar 4, 1747 in Winiary, Poland
d. Oct 11, 1779 in Savannah, Georgia
Source: *AmBi; ApCAB; BioIn 20, 21; DcAmB; Drake; HarEnMi; PolBiDi; TwCBDA; WebAB 74, 79; WebAMB; WhAm HS*

Pulci, Luigi
Italian. Author
Wrote comic masterpiece *The Morgante Maggiore,* 1483.
b. Aug 15, 1432 in Florence, Italy
d. Nov 1484 in Padua, Italy
Source: *Benet 96; BiD&SB; BioIn 7; CasWL; DcCathB; DcEuL; DcItL 1, 2; EuAu; EvEuW; LinLib L; McGEWB; NewCBEL; OxCEng 67, 85, 95; PenC EUR; REn; WhDW*

Pulford, Harvey
Canadian. Hockey Player
Defenseman, Ottawa Silver Sevens, 1893-1908; Hall of Fame, 1945.
b. 1875 in Toronto, Ontario, Canada
d. Oct 31, 1940 in Ottawa, Ontario, Canada
Source: *WhoHcky 73*

Pulitzer, Joseph
American. Editor, Publisher
Founded newspaper empire based on sensationalism, pro-labor policies; established Pulitzer Prizes, 1917.
b. Apr 10, 1847 in Mako, Hungary
d. Oct 29, 1911 in Charleston, South Carolina
Source: *ABCMeAm; AmAu&B; AmBi; AmDec 1900; AmSocL; ApCAB, X; Benet 87, 96; BenetAL 91; BiDAmBL 83; BiDAmJo; BiDrAC; BiDrUSC 89; BioIn 1, 2, 3, 4, 5, 6, 7, 8, 9, 10, 11, 12, 13, 14, 15, 16, 17, 18, 19; CasWL; ConAu 114; DcAmB; DcAmSR; DcArts; DcLB 23; DcLEL; EncAB-H 1974, 1996; EncAJ; EvLB; GayN; HarEnUS; JrnUS; LegTOT; LinLib L, S; McGEWB; MemAm; NatCAB 1; OxCAmH; OxCAmL 65, 83, 95; PolPar; RAdv 14; RComAH; REn; REnAL; WebAB 74, 79; WhAm 1; WhDW; WorAl; WorAlBi*

Pulitzer, Joseph, II
American. Journalist
Editor, publisher, *St. Louis Post-Dispatch,* 1912-55.
b. Mar 21, 1885 in New York, New York
d. Mar 30, 1955 in Saint Louis, Missouri
Source: *AmAu&B; BiDAmJo; BioIn 3, 4, 16; CurBio 54, 55; DcAmB S5; DcLB 29; EncAJ; JrnUS; WhAm 3*

Pulitzer, Lilly
[Lillian McKim Rousseau]
American. Designer
Created cotton chintz shifts, skirts; became a fashion craze, 1950s-60s.
Source: *BioIn 13, 15; ConFash; EncFash; InWom SUP; WorFshn*

Pulitzer, Peter
[Herbert Pulitzer, Jr]
American. Publisher
Grandson of Joseph Pulitzer; involved in divorce scandal with ex-wife, Roxanne, 1982.
b. 1930?
Source: *BioIn 13, 16; ConAu 128; LegTOT*

Pulitzer, Ralph
American. Publisher
Pres., Press Publishing Co., 1911-30; vp, Pulitzer Publishing, 1906-39; son of Joseph.
b. Jun 11, 1879 in Saint Louis, Missouri
d. Jun 14, 1939 in New York, New York
Source: *AmAu&B; BioIn 3, 4, 7; DcAmB S2; DcNAA; NatCAB 37; WhAm 1; WhJnl; WhNAA*

Pulitzer, Roxanne
American.
Ex-wife of Peter Pulitzer; granted headline-making divorce, 1982.
b. Feb 10, 1952? in Glendale, California
Source: *BioIn 13*

Pullein-Thompson, Diana
[Diana Pullein-Thompson Farr]
American. Children's Author
Books include *Ponies on the Trail,* 1978; *Ponies in Peril,* 1979.
b. Oct 30, 1930 in Wimbledon, England
Source: *Au&Wr 71; BioIn 21; ConAu X; IntAu&W 86; OxCChiL; SmATA 3; TwCChW 83, 89, 95; WhoChL; WrDr 86, 92*

Puller, Lewis B., Jr.
American. Author
Winner of Pulitzer Prize for autobiography, *Fortunate Son: The Healing of a Vietnam Vet,* 1992.
b. 1946
Source: *PeoHis*

Pulliam, Keisha Knight
American. Actor
Played Rudy, ''The Bill Cosby Show,'' 1984-92.
b. Apr 9, 1979 in Newark, New Jersey
Source: *CelR 90; DrBlPA 90; WhoEnt 92*

Pullman, George Mortimer
American. Inventor
Developed railroad sleeping car, 1864.
b. Mar 3, 1831 in Brocton, New York
d. Oct 19, 1897 in Chicago, Illinois
Source: *AmBi; ApCAB; BiDAmBL 83; BioIn 2, 3, 5, 6, 7, 15, 20, 21; DcAmB; EncAB-H 1974, 1996; EncABHB 2; InSci; LinLib S; McGEWB; NatCAB 11; OxCAmH; REnAW; TwCBDA; WebAB 74, 79; WhAm HS; WhDW; WorAl*

Pully, B. S
Comedian, Actor
Films include *Nob Hill,* 1945; *The Bellboy,* 1960.
b. May 14, 1910 in Newark, New Jersey
d. Jan 6, 1972 in Philadelphia, Pennsylvania
Source: *BioIn 9; WhoHol B; WhScrn 77*

Pupin, Michael Idvorsky
American. Physicist, Inventor
Developed x-ray photography; won 1924 Pulitzer for *From Immigrant to Inventor.*
b. Oct 4, 1858 in Idvor, Hungary
d. Mar 12, 1935 in New York, New York
Source: *AmAu&B; AmBi; ApCAB X; AsBiEn; BioIn 1, 4, 5, 6, 8, 16, 21; DcAmAu; DcAmB S1; DcInv; DcNAA; DcScB; HarEnUS; LinLib S; McGEWB; NatCAB 13, 26; NewCol 75; OxCAmL 65, 83; REnAL; WebAB 74, 79; WhAm 1*

Purcell, Edward M(ills)
American. Physicist, Educator
Shared Nobel Prize in physics, 1952, with Felix Bloch.
b. Aug 30, 1912 in Taylorville, Tennessee
d. Mar 7, 1997 in Cambridge, Massachusetts
Source: *AmMWSc 76P, 79, 82, 86, 89, 92, 95; AsBiEn; BiESc; BioIn 3, 5, 8, 15; BlueB 76; CamDcSc; InSci; IntWW 74, 75, 76, 77, 78, 79, 80, 81, 82, 83, 89; LarDcSc; LegTOT; McGMS 80; NobelP; NotTwCS; WebAB 74, 79; Who 74, 82, 83, 85, 88, 90, 92, 94; WhoAm 74, 78, 80, 82, 84, 86, 88, 90, 92, 94, 95, 96, 97; WhoE 74, 77, 79, 81, 83, 85, 89, 91, 93, 95, 97; WhoFrS 84; WhoNob, 90, 95; WhoScEn 94, 96; WhoWor 74, 82, 84, 87, 89, 91, 93, 95, 96, 97; WorAl; WorAlBi; WorScD*

Purcell, Henry
English. Composer
Noted Baroque composer; ''English Operas'' include *Fairy Queen,* 1692.
b. 1658 in London, England
d. Nov 21, 1695 in Westminster, England
Source: *Alli; AtlBL; Baker 84; BioIn 1, 2, 3, 4, 5, 6, 7, 8; BlmGEL; DcBiPP; DcNaB; LngCEL; LuthC 75; NewC; NewGrDO; OxCMus; REn; WorAl*

Purcell, Lee
American. Actor
Films include *Stir Crazy,* 1980; *Valley Girl,* 1983.
b. Jun 15, 1953 in North Carolina
Source: *ConTFT 4; WhoAm 95, 96, 97; WhoAmW 95, 97; WhoEnt 92*

Purcell, Sarah
[Sarah Pentecost]
American. TV Personality
Co-host of TV series ''Real People,'' 1979-84.
b. Oct 8, 1948 in Richmond, Indiana
Source: *BioIn 12, 18; VarWW 85*

Purdie, Bernard
American. Musician
Session drummer for Aretha Franklin, Steely Dan, others; albums include *Shaft,* 1976.
b. Jun 11, 1939 in Elkton, Maryland
Source: *BiDJaz; BioIn 8; EncJzS; EncRk 88; HarEnR 86; NewGrDJ 88, 94; WhoRocM 82*

Purdom, Edmund
English. Actor
1953 films include *The Student Prince; The Egyptian.*
b. Dec 19, 1926 in Welwyn Garden City, England
Source: *BioIn 3; FilmgC; HalFC 84, 88; IntMPA 86, 92; MotPP; VarWW 85; WhoHol A*

Purdy, James
American. Author
Wrote *In a Shallow Grave,* 1975; *Sleepers in Moon-Crowned Valleys* trilogy, 1970-81.
b. Jul 17, 1923 in Fremont, Ohio
Source: *AmAu&B; Au&Wr 71; Benet 87, 96; BenetAL 91; BioIn 6, 9, 10, 11, 12, 13, 14, 17, 18; BlueB 76; CamGLE; CamHAL; CasWL; ConAu 1AS, 19NR, 33R; ConLC 2, 4, 10, 28, 52; ConNov 72, 76, 82, 86, 91; CyWA 89; DcArts; DcLB 2; DrAF 76; DrAP 75; DrAPF 80, 91; EncWL 2, 3; GrWrEL N; IntAu&W 76, 77, 82, 86, 89, 91; IntWW 74, 75, 76, 77, 78, 79, 80, 81, 82, 83, 89, 91, 93; IntWWP 77, 82; LegTOT; MajTwCW; ModAL S1, S2; Novels; OxCAmL 65, 83, 95; PenC AM; RAdv 1, 14, 13-1; REn; REnAL; RfGAmL 87; TwCWr; WebE&AL; WhoAm 74, 76, 78, 80, 82, 84, 86, 88, 90, 92, 94, 95, 96, 97; WhoE 74, 95, 97; WhoTwCL; WhoUSWr 88; WhoWor 74; WhoWrEP 89, 92, 95; WorAu 1950; WrDr 76, 80, 82, 84, 86, 88, 90, 92, 94, 96*

Purdy, Susan Gold
American. Author, Illustrator
Self-illustrated children's books include *Costumes for You to Make,* 1971; *Books for You to Make,* 1973.
b. May 17, 1939 in New York, New York
Source: *AuBYP 2, 3; BioIn 8; ChhPo, S1; ConAu 10NR, 13R; ForWC 70; IlsCB 1957; SmATA 8; WhoAmW 72, 74, 75, 77, 79; WhoE 77, 79; WhoUSWr 88; WhoWrEP 89*

Pure Prairie League
[Michael Connor; Billy Hands; Michael Reilly; Jeff Wilson]
American. Music Group
Country-rock band formed 1971; albums include *Something in the Night,* 1981.
Source: *BgBkCoM; ConMuA 80A; DrRegL 75; EncFCWM 83; HarEnCM 87; HarEnR 86; IlEncCM; IlEncRk; NewYTBE 73; RkOn 85; St&PR 91, 93; WhoRocM 82*

Purim, Flora
Brazilian. Singer
Leading jazz interpreter, 1970s; albums include *Butterfly Dreams,* 1973.
b. Mar 6, 1942 in Rio de Janeiro, Brazil
Source: *AllMusG; BiDJaz; BioIn 10, 13; EncJzS; InWom SUP; NewGrDJ 88, 94; PenEncP; WhoAm 76, 78, 80, 82, 84, 86, 88; WhoAmW 81, 83; WhoEnt 92; WhoRocM 82*

Purl, Linda
American. Actor
Appears in TV movies, shows, including ''Happy Days,'' 1982-83.
b. Sep 2, 1955 in Greenwich, Connecticut
Source: *BioIn 11, 12, 13, 15; ConTFT 5; HalFC 84, 88; IntMPA 88, 92, 94, 96; LegTOT; VarWW 85; WhoHol 92*

Purtell, William Arthur
American. Politician
Rep. senator from CT, 1952-59; ardent Eisenhower supporter.
b. May 6, 1897 in Hartford, Connecticut
d. May 31, 1978 in Hartford, Connecticut
Source: *BiDrAC; BiDrUSC 89; BioIn 4, 11; CurBio 56, 78; DcAmB S10; NewYTBS 78; ObitOF 79; WhAm 7; WhoAmP 73, 75, 77*

Purviance, Edna
American. Actor
Starred in Chaplin films, 1915-23, including *The Tramp,* 1915; made one talking film, 1947.
b. Oct 21, 1894 in Reno, Nevada
d. Jan 13, 1958 in Woodland Hills, California
Source: *EncAFC; Film 1, 2; FilmEn; FilmgC; HalFC 80, 84, 88; IntDcF 1-3, 2-3; LegTOT; MotPP; MovMk;*

OxCFilm; TwYS; WhoCom; WhoHol B; WhScrn 74, 77, 83; WorEFlm

Purvis, Melvin
American. Government Official
FBI agent credited with capturing or killing John Dillinger, Pretty Boy Floyd, 1930s.
b. Oct 24, 1903 in Timmonsville, South Carolina
d. Feb 29, 1960 in Florence, South Carolina
Source: *BioIn 5, 12; CopCroC; FacFETw*

Pusey, Edward Bouverie
English. Author, Clergy
Leader of Oxford Movement, co-writer *Tracts for the Times,* 1834.
b. Mar 22, 1800 in Pusey, England
d. Sep 14, 1882 in Ascot Priory, England
Source: *Alli, SUP; BbD; BiD&SB; BioIn 6, 13, 14, 15, 16; BritAu 19; CamGEL; CamGLE; CasWL; CelCen; Chambr 3; DcBiPP; DcEnL; DcEuL; DcLB 55; DcLEL; DcNaB; EvLB; LuthC 75; McGEWB; NewC; NewCBEL; OxCEng 67, 85, 95; REn; VicBrit*

Pusey, Merlo John
American. Author, Editor
Won Pulitzer 1952, for two-vol. biography of Charles Evans Hughes.
b. Feb 3, 1902 in Woodruff, Utah
d. Nov 25, 1985 in Washington, District of Columbia
Source: *AmAu&B; AmMWSc 73S, 78S; Au&Wr 71; BioIn 2, 3, 4, 10; BlueB 76; ConAu 9NR, 9R, 117; CurBio 52, 86; DrAS 74H, 78H, 82H; EncTwCJ; IntAu&W 76, 82, 86; LinLib L; NewYTBS 85; OxCAmL 65; REnAL; TwCA SUP; WhoAm 74, 76, 78; WhoE 74; WrDr 76, 80, 82, 84, 86*

Pusey, Nathan Marsh
American. Educator
Twenty-fourth pres. of Harvard, 1953-71.
b. Apr 4, 1907 in Council Bluffs, Iowa
Source: *BioIn 3, 4, 5, 6, 8, 9, 11; BlueB 76; ConAu 109; CurBio 53; DrAS 74H, 78H, 82H; IntWW 74, 75, 76, 77, 78, 79, 80, 81, 82, 83, 89, 91, 93; LEduc 74; Who 74, 82, 83, 85, 88, 90, 92, 94; WhoAm 74; WhoE 74; WhoWor 74*

Pushkin, Aleksandr Sergeyevich
Russian. Author, Poet
Introduced Russian Romanticism; wrote *Boris Godunov,* 1831.
b. Jun 6, 1799 in Moscow, Russia
d. Feb 10, 1837 in Saint Petersburg, Russia
Source: *AtlBL; BbD; Benet 87, 96; BiD&SB; CasWL; ChhPo S1; CnThe; CyWA 58; DcBiA; DcEuL; DcRusL; EuAu; EvEuW; McGEWD 72, 84; NewC; OxCEng 67; PenC EUR; RComWL; REn; WhDW*

Pushmataha
American. Native American Chief
Choctaw chief, 1805-1824; negotiator in several treaties with the US government.
b. 1764? in Mississippi
d. Dec 23, 1824
Source: *BioIn 14; EncNAB; NotNaAm; REnAW; WhNaAH*

Pusser, Buford
American. Lawman
TN sheriff whose exploits were basis for movie *Walking Tall,* 1973.
b. 1937
d. Aug 21, 1974 in Adamsville, Tennessee
Source: *BioIn 9, 10, 14; NewYTBS 74*

Putch, William Henry
American. Director
Producer, director, Totem Pole Playhouse, Fayettesville, PA, 1954-83; married to Jean Stapleton.
b. Apr 22, 1924 in Pittsburgh, Pennsylvania
d. Nov 23, 1983 in Syracuse, New York
Source: *WhoE 74, 75; WhoFI 74, 75, 77; WhoSSW 80*

Putnam, Israel
American. Army Officer
Commander of American Revolutionary Army during battle of Long Island, 1776; was inspiration for Guiterman's poem, "Death and General Putnam," 1935.
b. Jan 7, 1718 in Salem, Massachusetts
d. May 29, 1790 in Brooklyn, Connecticut
Source: *AmBi; AmRev; ApCAB; BenetAL 91; BioIn 1, 2, 4, 5, 7, 9, 10, 16; BlkwEAR; DcAmB; DcAmMiB; Drake; EncAR; EncCRAm; HarEnMi; HarEnUS; LegTOT; LinLib S; McGEWB; NatCAB 1, 21; OxCAmH; OxCAmL 65, 83, 95; REn; REnAL; TwCBDA; WebAB 74, 79; WebAMB; WhAm HS; WhAmRev; WorAl; WorAlBi*

Puttnam, David Terence
English. Producer
Films include Oscar-winner *Chariots of Fire,* 1981; chm. of Columbia Pictures, Aug-Nov 1987.
b. Feb 25, 1941 in London, England
Source: *BioIn 14, 15, 16; CurBio 89; DcArts; HalFC 88; IntMPA 86, 92; IntWW 83, 89, 91, 93; VarWW 85; Who 85, 88, 90, 92, 94; WhoAm 88, 90, 92, 94, 95, 96, 97; WhoEnt 92; WhoWor 84, 87, 89, 91, 93, 95, 96, 97*

Puvis de Chavannes, Pierre Cecile
French. Artist
Painted pale murals for French, American public buildings.
b. Dec 14, 1824 in Lyons, France
d. Oct 10, 1898 in Paris, France
Source: *AtlBL; DcArts; OxCFr*

Pu-Yi, Henry
[P'ui; Hsuan T'ung]
Chinese. Ruler
Became last imperial emperor of China at age three; puppet emperor Kang Teh of Manchukuo, 1934-45; life story film, *The Last Emperor,* 1987, won many Oscars.
b. Feb 11, 1906 in Beijing, China
d. Oct 17, 1967 in Beijing, China
Source: *BioIn 7, 8, 10; ObitOF 79*

Puzo, Mario
American. Author
Won Oscars for screenplays of *The Godfather I, II,* 1972, 1974.
b. Oct 15, 1920 in New York, New York
Source: *AmAu&B; Benet 87; BenetAL 91; BiDConC; BioIn 3, 9, 10, 11, 13, 14, 15, 17; ConAu 4NR, 42NR, 65; ConLC 1, 2, 6, 36; ConNov 72, 76, 82, 86, 91, 96; ConPopW; ConTFT 10; CurBio 75; DcLB 6; DcLEL 1940; DrAF 76; DrAPF 80, 91; GangFlm; HalFC 84, 88; IntAu&W 76, 77; LegTOT; MajTwCW; Novels; RfGAmL 94; ScF&FL 92; VarWW 85; WhoAm 76, 78, 80, 82, 84, 86, 88, 92, 94, 95, 96, 97; WhoUSWr 88; WhoWor 87, 89, 91, 93, 95, 96, 97; WhoWrEP 89, 92, 95; WorAl; WorAlBi; WorAu 1970; WrDr 76, 80, 82, 84, 86, 88, 90, 92, 94, 96*

Pye, Henry
English. Poet
Poet laureate, 1790; wrote epic *Alfred,* 1801.
b. Feb 20, 1745 in London, England
d. Aug 11, 1813 in Westminster, England
Source: *Alli; BritAS; BritAu; Chambr 2; DcEnA; DcEnL; DcEuL; DcLEL; EvLB; NewC; OxCEng 67; PoLE; REn*

Pyle, Denver
American. Actor
TV shows include "Dukes of Hazzard," 1979-85.
b. May 11, 1920 in Bethune, Colorado
Source: *ConTFT 9; FilmEn; FilmgC; ForYSC; HalFC 80, 84, 88; LegTOT; MovMk; VarWW 85; WhoAm 82, 84; WhoHol 92, A; WhoWest 74; WhoWor 82*

Pyle, Ernie
[Ernest Taylor Pyle]
American. Journalist
Won Pulitzer 1944 for WW II stories; killed by Japanese machine gun.
b. Aug 3, 1900 in Dana, Indiana
d. Apr 18, 1945 in Ie Shima, Okinawa, Japan
Source: *AmAu&B; AmDec 1940; BenetAL 91; BiDAmJo; BiDAmNC; BioIn 1, 2, 3, 4, 5, 6, 7, 8, 9, 10, 12, 14, 15, 16, 17, 21; ConAu 115; CurBio 41, 45; DcAmB S3; DcLB 29; DcNAA; EncAJ; EncTwCJ; EncWB; FacFETw; IndAu 1917; JrnUS; LegTOT; LinLib L; NatCAB 33; OxCAmL 65, 83, 95; REn; REnAL; TwCA SUP; WebAB 74, 79; WebAMB; WhAm 2; WhWW-II; WorAlBi*

Pyle, Howard
American. Author, Illustrator
Known for juvenile tales: *Story of King Arthur and His Knights*, 1903.
b. Mar 5, 1853 in Wilmington, Delaware
d. Nov 9, 1911 in Florence, Italy
Source: *Alli SUP; AmAu; AmAu&B; AmBi; AnCL; AntBDN B; ApCAB; AuBYP 2, 3; BbD; BenetAL 91; BibAL; BiD&SB; BioIn 1, 2, 3, 5, 7, 8, 10, 12, 13, 14, 15, 19; CamGLE; CarSB; ChhPo, S1, S2, S3; ChlBkCr; ChlLR 22; ClaDrA; ConAu 109, 137; ConGrA 2; DcAmAu; DcAmB; DcBrBI; DcLB 42, DS13; DcLEL; DcNAA; FamSYP; GayN; HarEnUS; IlBEAAW; IlrAm 1880, A; IlsBYP; JBA 34; LinLib L, S; MajAI; NatCAB 9, 29; OxCAmL 65, 83, 95; OxCChiL; RAdv 14; REnAL; ScF&FL 1; SmATA 16; TwCBDA; TwCChW 78A, 83A, 89A, 95A; TwCYAW; WebAB 74, 79; WhAm 1; WhAmArt 85; WhoChL; WrChl*

Pyle, Howard
[John Howard Pyle]
American. Politician
Rep. governor of AZ, 1951-55; known for ordering raid on polygamous AZ community, Short Creek, 1953.
b. Mar 25, 1906 in Sheridan, Wyoming
d. Nov 29, 1987 in Tempe, Arizona
Source: *BiDrGov 1789; BioIn 4, 5, 7, 8; CurBio 55, 88, 88N; WhoAm 74, 76, 78; WhoMW 74*

Pym, Barbara Mary Crampton
English. Author
Wrote seven novels including *Quartet in Autumn; Unsuitable Attachment.*
b. Jun 2, 1913 in Oswestry, England
d. Jan 11, 1980 in Oxford, England
Source: *AnObit 1982; ArtclWW 2; Au&Wr 71; BioIn 12; ConAu 97, P-1; ConLC 13; DcNaB 1971; OxCEng 85, 95; WorAu 1970; WrDr 76, 80*

Pym, Francis Leslie
Welsh. Government Official
Succeeded Lord Carrington as British foreign secretary during Falkland Islands War, 1982.
b. Feb 13, 1922 in Abergavenny, Wales
Source: *BioIn 11, 13; BlueB 76; CurBio 82; EncWB; IntWW 79, 80, 81, 82, 83, 91, 93; IntYB 78, 79, 80, 81, 82; NewYTBS 82; Who 74, 82, 83, 85, 88, 92; WhoEIO 82; WhoWor 82, 84, 87, 91*

Pynchon, Thomas
[Thomas Ruggles Pynchon, Jr.]
American. Author
Challenging novels include prize-winning *V*, 1963; *The Crying of Lot 49*, 1966; *Rainbow*, 1973; *Vineland*, 1990.
b. May 8, 1937 in Glen Cove, New York
Source: *AmAu&B; AmDec 1960; AmWr S2; Benet 87, 96; BenetAL 91; BestSel 90-2; BioIn 8, 9, 10, 11, 12, 13, 15, 16; BlueB 76; CamGEL; CamGLE; CamHAL; CasWL; ConAu 13R, 22NR; ConLC 2, 3, 6, 9, 11, 18, 33, 62, 72; ConNov 72, 76, 82, 86, 91, 96; ConPopW; CurBio 87; CyWA 89; DcArts; DcLB 2, 173; DcLEL 1940; DcTwCCu 1; DrAF 76; DrAPF 91; EncSF, 93; EncWB; EncWL, 2, 3; FacFETw; GrWrEL N; IntAu&W 76, 77, 91, 93; IntWW 91, 93; LegTOT; MagSAmL; MajTwCW; MakMC; ModAL S2; NewEScF; Novels; OxCAmL 83, 95; OxCEng 85, 95; PenC AM; PostFic; RAdv 1, 14, 13-1; RfGAmL 87, 94; ScF&FL 92; ScFSB; ShSCr 14; TwCSFW 81, 86, 91; WebE&AL; WhoAm 74, 76, 78, 80, 82, 84, 86, 88, 92, 94, 95, 96, 97; WhoUSWr 88; WhoWor 95, 96, 97; WhoWrEP 89, 92, 95; WorAl; WorAlBi; WorAu 1950; WorLitC; WrDr 76, 80, 82, 84, 86, 88, 90, 92, 94, 96*

Pyne, Joe
Entertainer
Talk show interviewer known for aggressive style.
b. 1925 in Chester, Pennsylvania
d. Mar 23, 1970 in Hollywood, California
Source: *BioIn 7, 8; WhoHol B; WhScrn 74, 77, 83*

Pythagoras
"The Samian Sage"
Greek. Philosopher, Mathematician
Discovered principles of musical pitch.
b. 582BC in Samos, Greece
d. 507BC
Source: *AsBiEn; Baker 78, 84; BbD; BiD&SB; BioIn 12; CasWL; DivFut; LinLib L, S; NewAmDM; NewC; NewGrDM 80; PenC CL; REn; WebBD 83; WhDW; WorAl; WorAlBi*

Pytheas
Greek. Navigator, Geographer
Only fragments survive about voyages to Britain, N Europe.
Source: *BioIn 5, 7, 11, 16, 18; DcBiPP; Grk&L; InSci; NewC; OxCClL, 89; OxCShps; PenC CL; WhDW; WorAl; WorAlBi*

Q

Qadhafi, Muammar al-
[Moamar al-Gaddafi; Muammar Muhammed Gadhafi; Moammar Khadafy]
Libyan. Political Leader
Led military coup against monarchy, 1969; head of state, 1969—.
b. 1942 in Sirta, Libya
Source: *BioIn 14, 15, 17, 18, 19, 20; CurBio 73; DcTwHis; IntWW 80, 81; IntYB 80, 81; MidE 80; WhoGov 72; WhoWor 84, 87, 89, 91, 93, 95*

Qoboza, Percy
South African. Publisher
Influential black publisher of several papers shut down by apartheid.
b. Jan 17, 1938 in Johannesburg, South Africa
d. Jan 17, 1988 in Johannesburg, South Africa
Source: *AnObit 1988; BioIn 11, 12; ConAu 124; NewYTBS 77, 88*

Quabus bin Saud
[Qaboos bin Said]
Ruler
Sultan of Oman, 1970—; deposed father, Said bin Taimur.
b. Nov 18, 1940 in Salalah, Oman
Source: *BioIn 10, 11, 12, 13; CurBio 78; IntWW 74, 75, 76, 77, 78, 79, 80, 81, 82, 83, 89, 91, 93; MidE 78, 79, 80, 81, 82; WhoWor 80, 82, 84, 87, 89, 95*

Quackenbush, Bill
[Hubert George Quackenbush]
Canadian. Hockey Player
Defenseman, Detroit, 1942-49, Boston, 1949-56; won Lady Byng Trophy, 1949; Hall of Fame, 1976.
b. Mar 2, 1922 in Toronto, Ontario, Canada
Source: *HocEn*

Quad, M
[Charles Bertrand Lewis]
American. Journalist
Humorous sketches collected in *Brother Gardner's Lime Kiln Club,* 1882.
b. Feb 15, 1842 in Liverpool, Ohio
d. Sep 21, 1924
Source: *Alli, SUP; AmAu; AmAu&B; BbD; BenetAL 91; BiDAmNC; BiD&SB; BioIn 15; ConAu 114; DcAmAu; DcAmB; DcNAA; EncAHmr; HarEnUS; HsB&A; NatCAB 6; OhA&B; OxCAmL 65, 83, 95; REnAL; ScF&FL 1; TwCBDA; WhAm 1*

Quaid, Dennis William
American. Actor
Starred in film *The Right Stuff,* 1983; *Wyatt Earp,* 1994.
b. Apr 9, 1954 in Houston, Texas
Source: *BioIn 13, 15, 16; CelR 90; ConTFT 6; HalFC 84, 88; IntMPA 86, 92; IntWW 91; News 89; NewYTBS 88; VarWW 85; WhoAm 82, 84, 86, 88, 90, 92, 94, 95; WorAlBi*

Quaid, Randy
American. Actor
Oscar nominee for *The Last Detail,* 1973; other films include *Nationa l Lampoon's Vacation,* 1983; TV comedy "Davis Rules," 1991-92.
b. May 11, 1950 in Houston, Texas
Source: *BioIn 14, 16; ConTFT 6, 13; EncAFC; HalFC 84, 88; IntMPA 84, 86, 88, 92, 94, 96; LegTOT; MovMk; NewYTBS 84; VarWW 85; WhoAm 84, 86, 88, 90, 92, 94, 95, 96, 97; WhoEnt 92A; WhoHol 92, A; WorAlBi*

Quaison-Sackey, Alex(ander)
Ghanaian. Diplomat
First black African to preside over UN General Assembly, 1964-65.
b. Aug 9, 1924 in Winneba, Gold Coast
d. Dec 28, 1992 in Accra, Ghana
Source: *AfSS 78, 79, 80, 81, 82; BioIn 6, 7, 18, 19, 21; CurBio 66, 93N; IntWW 74, 75, 76, 77, 78, 79, 80, 81, 82, 83, 89, 91; WhoUN 75*

Qualen, John Mandt
Canadian. Actor
Films include *Anatomy of a Murder,* 1959; *A Patch of Blue,* 1966.
b. Dec 8, 1899 in Vancouver, British Columbia, Canada
d. Sep 12, 1987 in Torrance, California
Source: *FilmgC; IntMPA 82; MovMk; VarWW 85; Vers A; WhoHol A; WhoWest 74, 76, 78, 80, 82*

Quanah
[Quannah Parker]
American. Native American Chief
Comanche chief who convinced Indians about benefits of white civilization, education, 1875, following defeat at Adobe Walls.
b. 1845 in Wichita Falls, Texas
d. Feb 23, 1911 in Fort Sill, Oklahoma
Source: *AmBi; DcAmB; NewCol 75; WebAB 74, 79; WebAMB; WhAm 4, HSA*

Quant, Mary
English. Cosmetics Executive, Fashion Designer
Credited with starting Mod Look in London; also hot pants, body stockings.
b. Feb 11, 1934 in London, England
Source: *AmDec 1950; BioIn 7, 8, 10, 15, 16, 17, 21; BlueB 76; ConDes 84, 90, 97; ConFash; ContDcW 89; CurBio 68; DcArts; DcTwDes; EncFash; FacFETw; FairDF ENG; IntDcWB; IntWW 74, 75, 76, 77, 78, 79, 80, 81, 82, 83, 89, 91, 93; InWom, SUP; LegTOT; Who 74, 82, 83, 85, 88, 90, 92, 94; WhoFash 88; WhoWor 74, 84, 87, 89, 91, 93, 95, 96, 97; WomFir; WorAl; WorAlBi; WorFshn*

Quantrill, William Clarke
[Charley Hart]
American. Soldier, Outlaw
Confederate sympathizer who killed 180 citizens in Lawrence, KS, 1863; called "bloodiest man in American history."
b. Jul 31, 1837 in Canal Dover, Ohio
d. Jun 6, 1865 in Louisville, Kentucky
Source: *AmAu&B; BioIn 4, 5, 6, 7, 8, 9, 11, 15, 18, 21; CivWDc; DcAmB; DrInf; EncSoH; HarEnMi; REnAL; WebAB 74, 79; WebAMB; WhAm HS; WhCiWar*

Quaritch, Bernard
English. Bookseller, Publisher
Most famous antiquarian book dealer, active in London, 1850s-90s.
b. Apr 23, 1819 in Worbis, Saxony
d. Dec 17, 1899 in Hampstead, England
Source: *BioIn 1, 10, 12; DcLEL; DcNaB S1; LngCEL; LngCTC; NewCBEL; OxCEng 67, 85, 95*

Quarry, Jerry
American. Boxer
Prominent heavyweight fighter, 1970s.
b. May 18, 1945 in Los Angeles, California
Source: *BioIn 7, 8, 9, 10; NewYTBS 74; WhoBox 74*

Quarterflash
[Jack Charles; Rick DiGiallonardo; Rich Gooch; Marv Ross; Rindy Ross; Brian David Willis]
American. Music Group
Had 1981 hit single ''Harden My Heart.''
Source: *HarEnR 86; PenEncP; RkOn 85; RolSEnR 83; WhoRocM 82*

Quarterman, Lloyd Albert
American. Chemist
One of six African-American scientists to work on the Manhattan Project, 1943-46.
b. May 31, 1918 in Philadelphia, Pennsylvania
d. 1982 in Chicago, Illinois
Source: *BioIn 13, 19, 20; ConBlB 4; NotTwCS*

Quasimodo, Salvatore
Italian. Poet
Won Nobel Prize for literature, 1959; poems noted for delicate phrases, tight structure.
b. Aug 20, 1901 in Syracuse, Sicily, Italy
d. Jun 14, 1968 in Naples, Italy
Source: *Benet 87, 96; BioIn 5, 8, 9, 10, 15, 17, 18; CasWL; ClDMEL 80; CnMWL; ConAu 25R, P-1; ConLC 10; CurBio 60, 68; DcArts; DcItL 1, 2; DcLB 114; EncWL, 2, 3; EuWr 12; EvEuW; FacFETw; ItaFilm; LegTOT; LinLib S; LngCTC; MajTwCW; McGEWB; ModRL; NobelP; ObitT 1961; OxCEng 85, 95; PenC EUR; RAdv 14, 13-2; REn; RfGWoL 95; RGFMEP; TwCWr; WebBD 83; WhAm 5; WhoNob, 90, 95; WhoTwCL; WorAl; WorAlBi; WorAu 1950*

Quatro, Suzi
[Suzi Soul; The Pleasure Seekers; Cradle]
American. Singer
Promoted as the first raunchy female rock star; songs include ''The Wild One,'' 1974.
b. Jun 3, 1950 in Detroit, Michigan
Source: *BioIn 12; BioNews 74; ConMuA 80A; EncPR&S 89; EncRk 88; EncRkSt; HarEnR 86; IlEncRk; InWom SUP; LegTOT; PenEncP; RkOn 85; RolSEnR 83; WhoRock 81; WhoRocM 82*

Quayle, Anna
English. Actor
Won Tony for *Stop the World I Want to Get Off,* 1962.
b. Oct 6, 1936 in Birmingham, England
Source: *BiE&WWA; ConTFT 4; HalFC 84, 88; NotNAT; VarWW 85; WhoHol A; WhoThe 81*

Quayle, (John) Anthony, Sir
English. Actor, Director
Versatile actor; built Stratford-upon-Avon into a center of British theater; received Oscar nomination for *Anne of a Thousand Days,* 1969.
b. Sep 7, 1913 in Ainsdale, England
d. Oct 20, 1989 in London, England
Source: *AnObit 1989; BiE&WWA; BioIn 2, 9, 14, 16, 17; BlueB 76; CamGWoT; CelR; CnThe; ConAu 130; ConTFT 5; CurBio 71, 90N; DcArts; DcNaB 1986; Ent; FacFETw; FilmAG WE; FilmEn; FilmgC; ForYSC; HalFC 80, 84, 88; IlWWBF; IntDcF 1-3, 2-3; IntDcT 3; IntMPA 75, 76, 77, 78, 79, 80, 81, 82, 84, 86, 88; IntWW 74, 75, 76, 77, 78, 79, 80, 81, 82, 83, 89; ItaFilm; LegTOT; MovMk; NewYTBE 71; NewYTBS 89; NotNAT; OxCThe 67, 83; PlP&P; VarWW 85; WhAm 10; WhE&EA; Who 74, 82, 83, 85, 85S, 88, 90; WhoHol A; WhoThe 72, 77, 81; WhoWor 74, 76, 78, 82, 84, 87, 89; WorAl; WorAlBi*

Quayle, Dan
[James Danforth Quayle]
American. Politician
Bush's vp, 1989-92; Rep. senator from IN, 1981-89.
b. Feb 4, 1947 in Indianapolis, Indiana
Source: *AlmAP 80; AmPolLe; BiDrUSC 89; CelR 90; CngDr 77, 79, 81, 83, 85, 87, 89, 91; CurBio 89; IntWW 81, 82, 83, 89, 91, 93; LegTOT; News 89-2; NewYTBS 88; PolsAm 84; VicePre; Who 90, 92, 94; WhoAm 78, 80, 82, 84, 86, 88, 90, 92, 94, 95, 96, 97; WhoAmP 77, 79, 81, 83, 85, 87, 89, 91; WhoE 91, 93; WhoEmL 87, 93; WhoMW 78, 80, 82, 84, 86, 88, 90, 93, 96; WhoWor 82, 87, 89, 91, 93, 95, 96, 97*

Quayle, Marilyn Tucker
[Mrs. Dan Quayle]
American.
Lawyer; married Dan Quayle, 1972; wrote *Embrace the Serpent,* 1992.
b. Jul 29, 1949 in Indianapolis, Indiana
Source: *BioIn 16; CelR 90; NewYTBS 89, 92; WhoAm 90, 94, 95, 96, 97; WhoAmL 94, 96; WhoAmW 91, 95, 97; WhoE 91; WhoMW 92, 93, 96*

Queen
[John Deacon; Brian May; Freddie Mercury; Roger Taylor]
English. Music Group
Hard-rock band formed in 1972; hit singles ''Bohemian Rhapsody,'' 1976 and ''Another One Bites the Dust,'' 1980.
Source: *BiDLA; BioIn 17, 18, 20; ConMuA 80A; ConMus 6; DcArts; EncPR&S 89; EncRk 88; EncRkSt; HalFC 84, 88; HarEnR 86; IlEncRk; NewCBEL; NewYTBS 91; OxCPMus; PenEncP; RkOn 78; RolSEnR 83; ScF&FL 92; SJGFanW; VarWW 85; WhoAmP 95; WhoRock 81; WhoRocM 82*

Queen, Ellery
[Frederic Dannay; Manfred B. Lee]
American. Author
Fictitious detective used as pseudonym for popular mystery novels.
Source: *AmAu&B; ConLC 3, 11; CorpD; CrtSuMy; CurBio 40; DcLEL; DcLP 87A, 87B; EncMys; EvLB; FacFETw; GrWrEL N; IntAu&W 76, 76X, 77, 77X, 93; IntvTCA 2; IntWW 74, 75, 76, 77, 78, 79, 80, 81, 82, 83N; LegTOT; LinLib LP; LngCTC; MajTwCW; NewYTBE 71; NewYTBS 82; Novels; OxCAmL 65, 83, 95; PenC AM; RAdv 14; REn; REnAL; RfGAmL 87, 94; ScF&FL 1, 92; SmATA 3; TwCA, SUP; TwCCr&M 80, 85, 91; TwCWr; WebAB 74, 79; WhAm 8; Who 74, 82, 83N; WhoAm 74, 76, 78, 80, 82; WhoWor 74; WorAlBi; WrDr 76, 80, 82, 84, 86, 88, 90, 96*

Queen, Richard I
[The Hostages]
American. Hostage
Held with 52 other Americans by terrorists; the only hostage released early (mid-1980) due to illness.
b. 1952?
Source: *BioIn 12*

Queen Ida
American. Singer, Musician
Zydeco singer and accordionist since early 1970s; won 1982 Grammy for album *Queen Ida on Tour.*
b. Jan 15, 1929 in Lake Charles, Louisiana
Source: *ConMus 9*

Queensberry, John Sholto Douglas
[Marquis of Queensberry]
English. Nobleman
Drafted rules for boxing, 1865; some provisions still govern sport today; major figure in Oscar Wilde's downfall.
b. Jul 20, 1844, England
d. Jan 31, 1900 in London, England
Source: *NewC; NewCol 75; WhDW*

Queensberry, William Douglas, Duke
''Old Q''
English. Statesman
Developed horse racing; known for extravagances, escapades.
b. 1724 in London, England
d. Dec 23, 1810
Source: *BioIn 8, 9; DcBiPP; NewC; NewCol 75; OxCEng 85; WebBD 83*

Queensryche
American. Music Group
Heavy metal band formed in 1981; hit albums include *Operation: Mindcrime* and *Empire.*
Source: *BioIn 17; ConMus 8; EncRkSt; NewYTBS 80; WhoHol 92*

Queeny, Edgar Monsanto
American. Business Executive
Monsanto Chemical Co. pres., 1928-43; chm., 1943-60.
b. Sep 29, 1897 in Saint Louis, Missouri
d. Jul 7, 1968 in Saint Louis, Missouri
Source: *BiDAmBL 83; BioIn 1, 2, 5, 8, 9; ObitOF 79; WhAm 5*

Queler, Eve Rabin
American. Conductor
Founder, music director, Opera Orchestra, NY, 1968; conductor, Shaw Concerts, NYC, 1971-72.
b. Jan 1, 1936 in New York, New York
Source: *Baker 84; BioIn 9; IntWW 91; IntWWM 90; InWom SUP; MetOEnc; NewAmDM; PenDiMP; WhoAm 86, 88; WhoE 89; WhoEnt 92*

Quennell, Peter (Courtney)
English. Editor, Critic
Biographer, literary historian; co-edited *History Today,* 1951-79.
b. Mar 9, 1905 in London, England
d. Oct 27, 1993 in London, England
Source: *Au&Wr 71; Benet 87, 96; BioIn 4, 5, 11, 12, 13, 14, 18, 19, 20, 21; BlueB 76; CamGLE; ChhPo S2, S3; ConAu 113, 115, 143; ConPo 70; CurBio 84, 94N; DcArts; DcLB 155; DcLEL; EvLB; IntAu&W 76, 77, 89; IntWW 74, 75, 76, 77, 78, 79, 80, 81, 82, 83, 89, 91, 93; IntWWP 77; LegTOT; LinLib L; LngCTC; ModBrL; NewC; NewCBEL; OxCEng 85, 95; OxCTwCP; PenC ENG; RAdv 1, 13-1; REn; RGTwCWr; TwCA, SUP; TwCWr; WhAm 11; Who 74, 82, 83, 85, 88, 90, 92, 94; WhoWor 84, 87, 89, 91, 93; WrDr 76, 80, 82, 84, 86, 88, 90, 92*

Quercia, Jacopo della
Italian. Sculptor
Master of Quattrocento Sienese School.
b. 1374
d. 1438
Source: *BioIn 15; DcArts; DcCathB; IntDcAA 90; McGDA; McGEWB; NewCol 75; OxCArt; OxDcArt; WebBD 83; WhDW*

Quesnay, Francois
French. Economist, Physician
Physician to Louis XV of France; writings on economics include *Tableau economique,* 1758.
b. Jun 4, 1694 in Merey, France
d. Dec 16, 1774 in Versailles, France
Source: *BbD; BiD&SB; BioIn 1, 7, 8, 14, 16; BlkwCE; CasWL; DcAmC; DcBiPP; DcEuL; Dis&D; EncEnl; EuAu; GrEconB; LinLib L, S; NewCBEL; NewCol 75; OxCFr; REn; WhoEc 81, 86*

Quevado y Villegas, Francisco Gomez de
Spanish. Poet
The most respected satirist in Spanish literature.
b. Sep 17, 1580 in Madrid, Spain
d. Sep 8, 1645 in Villanueva de los Infantes, Spain
Source: *BioIn 13; OxCEng 85; RAdv 13-2; REn; WhDW; WorAlBi*

Quezon (y Molina), Manuel Luis
Philippine. Political Leader
First pres. of Philippines, 1935-42.
b. Aug 19, 1878 in Baler, Philippines
d. Aug 1, 1944 in Saranac Lake, New York
Source: *BiDrAC; BiDrUSC 89; BioIn 1, 2, 8, 10, 13, 20; CurBio 44; DcAmB S3; EncRev; LinLib L, S; McGEWB; OxCAmH; WhAm 2; WhAmP; WhWW-II; WorAl; WorAlBi*

Quicksilver Messenger Service
[John Cipollina; Gary Duncan; Gregory Elmore; David Freiberg; Nicky Hopkins; Dino Valenti]
American. Music Group
Formed in 1965; albums include *Happy Trails,* 1969.
Source: *BiDAmM; ConMuA 80A; EncRk 88; EncRkSt; HarEnR 86; IlEncRk; NewAmDM; NewGrDA 86; NewYTBS 94; PenEncP; RkOn 74, 78; RolSEnR 83; WhoRock 81; WhoRocM 82*

Quidde, Ludwig
German. Historian
Pres., German Peace Society, 1914-29; won Nobel Peace Prize, 1927.
b. Mar 23, 1858 in Bremen, Germany
d. Mar 5, 1941 in Munich, Germany
Source: *BiDMoPL; BioIn 9, 11, 15; CurBio 41; LinLib L; NobelP; WhE&EA; WhoLA; WhoNob, 90, 95; WorAl; WorAlBi*

Quidor, John
American. Artist
Painted Washington Irving scenes, Hudson River landscapes.
b. Jan 26, 1801 in Tappan, New York
d. Dec 13, 1881 in Jersey City, New Jersey
Source: *AmBi; BioIn 4, 9, 11; BriEAA; DcAmArt; DcAmB; FolkA 87; McGDA; NewYHSD; OxCAmH; WhAm HS*

Quiet Riot
[Frankie Banal; Carlos Cavazo; Kevin DuBrow; Rudy Sarzo]
American. Music Group
Heavy metal band whose debut album *Mental Health,* 1983, sold over four million copies.
Source: *EncPR&S 89; PenEncP; RkOn 85*

Quilico, Louis
Canadian. Opera Singer
Dramatic baritone; NY Met. debut, 1972.
b. Jan 14, 1929 in Montreal, Quebec, Canada
Source: *Baker 84; BioIn 13, 15, 16; CanWW 31, 79, 80, 81, 83, 89; CreCan 2; IntWWM 90; MetOEnc; NewAmDM; NewGrDM 80; NewGrDO; OxDcOp; WhoAm 86, 90; WhoWor 87*

Quill, Mike
[Michael J. Quill]
Irish. Labor Union Official
Organizer, pres., Transport Workers Union, 1934-66.
b. Sep 8, 1905
d. Jan 28, 1966 in New York, New York
Source: *BiDAmLf; CurBio 41, 53, 66; EncAL; WhAm 4*

Quillan, Eddie
American. Actor
Appeared in over 150 films in 60-year career including *Grapes of Wrath,* 1940, *Brigadoon,* 1954.
b. Mar 31, 1907 in Philadelphia, Pennsylvania
d. Jul 19, 1990 in Burbank, California
Source: *BioIn 10, 17, 19; ConTFT 9; EncAFC; Film 2; FilmEn; FilmgC; ForYSC; HalFC 80, 84, 88; IntMPA 75, 76, 77, 78, 79, 80, 81, 82, 84, 86, 88; MovMk; TwYS; VarWW 85; Vers A; What 4; WhoE 91; WhoHol A*

Quiller-Couch, Arthur Thomas, Sir
English. Critic, Educator, Author
Edited Oxford Books of Verse, 1900-39.
b. Nov 21, 1863 in Bodmin, England
d. May 12, 1944 in Fowey, England
Source: *BbD; Benet 96; BiD&SB; BioIn 1, 4, 5, 12, 14, 15, 20, 21; CasWL; Chambr 3; ChhPo, S1, S2; ConAu 118; DcBiA; DcEnA, A; DcLB 153; DcLEL; DcNaB 1941; EvLB; GrBr; GrWrEL N; JBA 34; LngCTC; MnBBF; ModBrL; NewC; NewCBEL; OxCEng 67, 85, 95; PenC ENG; RAdv 1; REn; TwCA, SUP; TwCWr; WhAm 2; WhE&EA*

Quimby, Harriet
"Dresden-China Aviatrix"
American. Aviator, Journalist
First woman to fly English Channel, Apr 16, 1912.
b. May 1, 1884 in Arroyo Grande, California
d. Jul 1, 1912 in Boston, Massachusetts
Source: *BioIn 1, 10, 13, 17, 19; InSci; InWom, SUP; LibW; WhAm 1; WomWWA 14*

Quindlen, Anna
American. Journalist, Author
Winner of the 1992 Pulitzer Prize for commentary; author of novel, *Object Lessons,* 1991; writes syndicated Op-Ed column, 1989-94.
b. Jul 8, 1953 in Philadelphia, Pennsylvania
Source: *BioIn 15, 16; ConAu 138; CurBio 93; News 93-1; WhoAm 94, 95, 96; WhoAmW 93, 95, 97; WhoE 93, 95; WomStre; WorAu 1985*

Quine, Richard
American. Actor, Director
Child performer in vaudeville; directed *Sex and the Single Girl,* 1964, *How to Murder Your Wife,* 1965; suicide victim.
b. Nov 12, 1920 in Detroit, Michigan
d. Jun 10, 1989 in Los Angeles, California
Source: *AnObit 1989; ASCAP 66, 80; BiDFilm, 81, 94; BioIn 13, 16; CmMov; ConTFT 8; DcFM; EncAFC; FilmEn; FilmgC; ForYSC; HalFC 80, 84, 88; IlWWHD 1A; IntMPA 75, 76, 77, 78, 79, 80, 81, 82, 84, 86, 88; MiSFD 9N; MotPP; MovMk; NewYTBS 89; OxCFilm; VarWW 85; WhoHol A; WorEFlm; WorFDir 2*

Quinlan, Karen Ann
American. Victim
Comatose since 1975; parents won landmark court decision to remove life-support systems.
b. Mar 29, 1954 in Scranton, Pennsylvania
d. Jun 11, 1985 in Morris Plains, New Jersey
Source: *BioIn 10, 11, 12; ConNews 85-2; NewYTBS 85*

Quinlan, Kathleen
American. Actor
Films include *I Never Promised You a Rose Garden,* 1977; *The Promise,* 1979.
b. Nov 19, 1954 in Pasadena, California
Source: *BioIn 11, 13; ConTFT 5; HalFC 84, 88; IntMPA 84, 86, 88, 92, 94, 96; ItaFilm; LegTOT; NewYTBS 77; VarWW 85; WhoAm 96, 97; WhoAmW 97; WhoEnt 92; WhoHol 92*

Quinn, Anthony Rudolph Oaxaca
American. Actor
Won Oscars for *Viva Zapata,* 1952; *Lust for Life,* 1956.
b. Apr 21, 1916 in Chihuahua, Mexico
Source: *BioIn 13, 14, 15, 16; CelR 90; ChiLit A; ChiSch; CmMov; ConTFT 7; CurBio 57; FilmgC; HalFC 84, 88; HispWr; IntMPA 86, 92; IntWW 74, 75, 76, 77, 78, 79, 80, 81, 82, 83, 89, 91; MexAmB; MotPP; NewYTBS 83, 86; OxCFilm; VarWW 85; WhoAm 74, 76, 86, 90; WhoEnt 92; WhoHisp 92; WhoHol A; WhoThe 81; WhoWor 74, 87, 91; WorAlBi; WorEFlm*

Quinn, Arthur Hobson
American. Teacher, Author
Professor of history, English literature, 1939-45; writings include *Pennsylvania Stories,* 1899.
b. 1875 in Philadelphia, Pennsylvania
d. Oct 16, 1960 in Bala-Cynwyd, Pennsylvania
Source: *AmAu&B; BenetAL 91; BioIn 1, 4, 5; CathA 1930; DcAmAu; DcAmB S6; NotNAT B; OxCAmL 65, 83; OxCAmT 84; PenC AM; REnAL; TwCA, SUP; WhAm 4; WhE&EA; WhNAA*

Quinn, Edmond T
American. Sculptor
Works include bronze statue of Edwin Booth as "Hamlet" in NYC.
b. Dec 20, 1868 in Philadelphia, Pennsylvania
d. Sep 9, 1929 in New York, New York
Source: *AmBi; DcAmB; WhAm 1; WhAmArt 85*

Quinn, Jane Bryant
American. Journalist
Financial business columnist, *Newsweek;* wrote *Everyone's Money Book.*
b. Feb 5, 1939 in Niagara Falls, New York
Source: *BioIn 12, 13, 16; ConAu 93; EncTwCJ; IntAu&W 89; InWom SUP; News 93; WhoAm 76, 78, 80, 82, 84, 86, 88, 90, 92, 94, 95, 96, 97; WhoAmW 74, 75, 81, 83, 85, 87, 89, 91, 93, 95, 97; WhoFI 83, 85, 87, 89, 92; WhoTelC; WorAlBi*

Quinn, John
American. Lawyer, Art Collector
Major collector books, modern art; subject of 1968 Pulitzer-winner *Man From New York.*
b. Apr 24, 1870 in Tiffin, Ohio
d. 1924
Source: *BioIn 5, 8, 10, 11, 14, 17; DcAmBC; NatCAB 18; OhA&B; OxCAmL 83, 95; WhAm 1; WhAmArt 85*

Quinn, Martha
American. TV Personality
Video Jockey for MTV, 1981-1991.
b. May 11, 1959 in Albany, New York
Source: *BioIn 13, 14, 15; ConNews 86-4; ConTFT 14; InWom SUP; LegTOT*

Quinn, Pat
[John Brian Patrick Quinn]
Canadian. Hockey Player, Hockey Coach
Defenseman, Toronto Maple Leafs, 1968-70; Vancouver Canucks, 1970-72; Atlanta Flames, 1972-77; coach, Philadelphia flyers, 1977-82; LA Kings, 1984-86, Team C Canada, 1986; pres. & gm. Vancouver Canucks, 1987, head coach, Vancouver Canuck s, 1990—.
b. Jan 29, 1943 in Hamilton, Ontario, Canada
Source: *HocEn; WhoAm 86, 88, 90, 92, 94, 95, 96, 97; WhoHcky 73; WhoWest 87, 89, 92, 94, 96*

Quinn, Sally
[Mrs. Ben Bradlee]
American. Journalist
Co-anchorperson, "CBS Morning News," 1973-74; reporter *Washington Post,* 1969-73, 1974-80.
b. Jul 1, 1941 in Savannah, Georgia
Source: *AuNews 2; BioIn 10, 11, 13, 15, 16; ConAu 27NR, 65; CurBio 88; EncTwCJ; InWom SUP; WhoAm 74, 76, 78, 80, 82, 84, 86, 88, 90, 92, 94, 95, 96; WhoAmP 95; WhoAmW 81, 83, 85, 89, 91, 93, 95, 97; WhoE 95; WhoUSWr 88; WhoWrEP 89, 92, 95*

Quint, Bert
American. Broadcast Journalist
Roving correspondent who covered India-Pakistan Wars, 1965, 1971; Mid-East War, 1973.
b. Sep 22, 1930 in New York, New York
Source: *ConAu 69; WhoAm 97; WhoWest 96; WhoWor 97*

Quintero, Jose Benjamin
Panamanian. Director
Won Tony, 1973, for *A Moon for the Misbegotten.*
b. Oct 15, 1924 in Panama City, Panama
Source: *BiE&WWA; CamGWoT; ConTFT 8; CurBio 54; HispWr; MetOEnc; NewYTBS 74, 77; NotNAT; OxCAmT 84; OxCThe 83; PlP&P, A; VarWW 85; WhoAm 86, 90; WhoEnt 92; WhoHisp 92; WhoThe 81; WhoWor 74*

Quintilian Marcus Fabius
Roman. Orator
Wrote book on principles of rhetoric; taught oratory in Rome, 68-88.
b. 35 in Calagurris, Spain
d. 95
Source: *BbD; BiD&SB; CasWL; NewC; OxCEng 67; RComWL; REn; WebBD 83*

Quiroga, Horacio
Uruguayan. Author
Known for short stories; wrote jungle tales *Anaconda,* 1921.
b. Dec 31, 1878 in Salto, Uruguay
d. Feb 9, 1937 in Buenos Aires, Argentina
Source: *Benet 87, 96; BenetAL 91; BioIn 15, 16, 17; CasWL; ConAu 117, 131; DcHiB; DcSpL; DcTwCCu 3; EncWB; EncWL, 2, 3; HispLC; HispWr; LatAmWr; MajTwCW; ModLAL; OxCSpan; PenC AM; PenEncH; RAdv 14, 13-2; REn; TwCLC 20*

Quisenberry, Dan(iel Raymond)
American. Baseball Player
Relief pitcher, 1979-90, mostly with KC; holds AL record for career saves, 238.
b. Feb 7, 1953 in Santa Monica, California
Source: *Ballpl 90; BaseEn 88; BaseReg 87, 88; BiDAmSp BB; BioIn 12, 13, 14, 15; LegTOT; WhoAm 84, 90*

Quisling, Vidkun Abraham
Norwegian. Government Official, Traitor
Minister of Defense, 1931-33; founded political party similar to Nazis, 1931; helped Hitler invade Norway, 1940; executed for treason; name became synonymous with "traitor."
b. Jul 18, 1887 in Fryesdal, Norway
d. Oct 24, 1945 in Oslo, Norway
Source: *CurBio 40, 46; LngCTC; NewCol 75; REn; WebBD 83*

Quivers, Robin
American. Radio Performer, TV Personality
On Howard Stern Show, early 1980s—.

b. c. 1953
Source: *News 95; WhoAmW 97*

R

Raab, Selwyn
American. Journalist, Author
Reporter, *NY Times,* 1974—; news editor, NBC News, 1966-71; won many awards in field.
b. Jun 26, 1934 in New York, New York
Source: *BioIn 9, 10; ConAu 73; WhoAm 76, 78, 80, 82, 84, 86, 88, 90, 92, 94, 95, 96, 97*

Rabaud, Henri
French. Composer, Conductor
Composed opera *Antoine et Cleopatre,* 1917; oratorio *Job,* 1900.
b. Nov 10, 1873 in Paris, France
d. Sep 11, 1949 in Paris, France
Source: *Baker 78, 84; BioIn 2, 3, 8; CompSN; MetOEnc; NewEOp 71; NewGrDM 80; NewGrDO; OxCMus; OxDcOp*

Rabbitt, Eddie
[Edward Thomas Rabbit]
American. Singer, Songwriter
Wrote over 300 songs including "Kentucky Rain;" hit single "I Love a Rainy Night."
b. Nov 27, 1941 in New York, New York
Source: *BioIn 14, 16; ConMuA 80A; ConMus 5; HarEnCM 87; IlEncCM; LegTOT; PenEncP; RkOn 85; VarWW 85; WhoAm 86, 90; WhoEnt 92; WhoRock 81*

Rabe, David William
American. Dramatist
Won 1971 Obie for *Basic Training of Pavlo Hummel.*
b. Mar 10, 1940 in Dubuque, Iowa
Source: *Benet 87, 96; BenetAL 91; BioIn 13, 14, 15; CamHAL; CelR 90; ConAu 3BS, 85; ConDr 88; ConLC 8, 33; ConTFT 3; CurBio 73; CyWA 89; DcLB 7, Y91; DcLEL 1940; IntMPA 92, 96; IntvTCA 2; McGEWD 84; ModAL S2; NewYTBE 71; OxCAmL 83; OxCAmT 84; OxCThe 83; RAdv 13-2; VarWW 85; WhoAm 86, 90, 97; WhoEnt 92; WorAlBi; WrDr 86, 92*

Rabelais, Francois
[Alcofribas Nasier]
French. Author
Noted for ribald humor; wrote *Gargantua and Pantagruel.*
b. 1494 in Chinon, France
d. 1553 in Paris, France
Source: *AtlBL; BbD; Benet 87, 96; BiD&SB; CasWL; CyWA 58; DcEnL; DcEuL; DcScB; Dis&D; EncSF, 93; EuAu; EuWr 2; EvEuW; GuFrLit 2; InSci; LitC 5; MagSWL; McGEWB; NewC; NewEOp 71; NewGrDM 80; Novels; OxCEng 67, 85, 95; OxCFr; OxCMed 86; OxDcOp; PenC EUR; RAdv 14, 13-2; RComWL; REn; WhDW; WorLitC*

Rabi, Isidor Isaac
Austrian. Physicist
Pioneer in exploring atom; won Nobel Prize, 1944, for developing method of measuring magnetic properties of atoms.
b. Jul 29, 1898 in Rymahow, Austria
d. Jan 11, 1988 in New York, New York
Source: *AmMWSc 76P, 79, 82, 86; AsBiEn; BiESc; BioIn 1, 3, 4, 5, 6, 7, 10, 13; BlueB 76; CamDcSc; CurBio 48, 88; InSci; IntWW 74, 75, 76, 77, 78, 79, 80, 81, 82, 83; JeAmHC; LarDcSc; LinLib S; McGEWB; McGMS 80; NewYTBS 85, 88; OxCAmH; WebAB 74, 79; WhAm 9; Who 74, 82, 83, 85, 88; WhoAm 74, 76, 78, 80, 82, 84; WhoE 77, 79, 81, 83, 85; WhoFrS 84; WhoNob, 90, 95; WhoWor 74, 82, 84, 87; WhoWorJ 72; WorAl; WorAlBi; WorScD*

Rabin, Michael
American. Violinist
Internationally known virtuoso; debuted at age fourteen.
b. May 2, 1936 in New York, New York
d. Jan 19, 1972 in New York, New York
Source: *Baker 78, 84, 92; BiDAmM; BioIn 2, 3, 4, 5, 9, 14; NewAmDM; NewGrDA 86; NewYTBE 71, 72; WhAm 5*

Rabin, Yehuda L
Airline Executive
One of founders of Israeli Air Force.
b. 1917?, Russia
d. Jan 4, 1981 in New York, New York
Source: *NewYTBS 81*

Rabin, Yitzhak
Israeli. Statesman, Political Leader
Ambassador to US, 1968-73; Israeli prime minister, 1974-77, 1992-95; first Israeli PM to be assassinated.
b. Mar 1, 1922 in Jerusalem, Palestine
d. Nov 4, 1995 in Tel Aviv, Israel
Source: *BioIn 9, 10, 11, 12, 14, 17, 18, 19, 20, 21; ColdWar 1, 2; ConAu 111, 149; CurBio 74, 95, 96N; DcMidEa; FacFETw; HarEnMi; HeroCon; HisEAAC; IntWW 76, 77, 78, 79, 80, 81, 82, 83, 93; IntYB 78, 79, 80, 81, 82; MidE 78, 79, 80, 81, 82; NewCol 75; News 96, 93-1, 96-2; NewYTBS 75, 93, 95; PolLCME; WhAm 11; Who 94; WhoAm 74, 76; WhoGov 72; WhoNob 95; WhoWor 74, 76, 78, 87, 89, 91, 93, 95, 96; WhoWorJ 72, 78*

Rachel
Hebrew. Biblical Figure
Along with three other women, mothered twelve sons chosen to head the twelve tribes of Israel.
b. 1753BC
Source: *LegTOT; NewCol 75*

Rachel
[Elisa(beth) Rachel Felix]
French. Actor
Entered Comedie-Francaise, 1838; noted tragedienne of Corneille, Racine plays.
b. Feb 28, 1820 in Mumpf, Switzerland
d. Jan 3, 1858 in Cannes, France
Source: *BioIn 18, 19, 20; CamGWoT; CnThe; DcEuL; Dis&D; EncWT; FamA&A; NewCol 75; NotNAT A, B; OxCAmT 84; OxCFr; OxCThe 67, 83; PlP&P; REn; WhDW*

Rachmaninoff, Sergei Vasilyevich
Russian. Composer
Last of romantic composers; best known for *Second Piano Concerto,* 1901.
b. Apr 1, 1873 in Oneg, Russia
d. Mar 28, 1943 in Beverly Hills, California
Source: *ASCAP 66; AtlBL; CurBio 43; DcAmB S3; FacFETw; NewCol 75; REn; WebBD 83; WhAm 2; WorAl*

Racicot, Marc F
American. Politician
Rep. governor, MT, 1993—.
b. Jul 24, 1948 in Thompson Falls, Montana
Source: *WhoAm 90; WhoAmL 92; WhoAmP 91; WhoWest 92*

Racine, Jean Baptiste
French. Dramatist
Plays include tragedy *Andromaque,* 1667; comedy *Les Plaideurs,* 1668.
b. Dec 1639 in Laferte-Milon, France
d. Apr 26, 1699 in Paris, France
Source: *AtlBL; BbD; BiD&SB; BioIn 1, 2, 5, 7, 8, 9, 10, 11, 12; CasWL; CnThe; CyWA 58; DcEuL; Dis&D; EncWT; EuAu; EvEuW; LinLib L, S; McGEWB; McGEWD 72; NewC; NewCBEL; NewEOp 71; OxCEng 67; OxCFr; OxCThe 67; PenC EUR; RComWL; REn*

Rackham, Arthur
English. Illustrator
Noted for imaginative, delicate pen drawings for children's books.
b. Sep 19, 1867
d. Sep 1939
Source: *AntBDN B; BioIn 1, 2, 3, 5, 8, 9, 10, 12, 14, 15, 17, 19, 20; CamGLE; CarSB; ChhPo, S1, S2, S3; ChlBkCr; ClaDrA; ConICB; DcBrAr 1; DcBrBI; DcBrWA; DcLB 141; DcNaB 1931; DcPup; DcVicP, 2; FacFETw; JBA 34, 51; LngCTC; MajAI; McGDA; NewCBEL; OxCChiL; OxCEng 85, 95; OxDcArt; PenEncH; SmATA 15; StaCVF; Str&VC; TwCPaSc; WhE&EA; WhoChL*

Radbourn, Old Hoss
[Charles Gardner Radbourn]
American. Baseball Player
Pitcher, 1880-91; won 60 games, 1884; had 308 career wins; Hall of Fame, 1939.
b. Dec 11, 1854 in Rochester, New York
d. Feb 5, 1897 in Bloomington, Illinois
Source: *Ballpl 90; LegTOT; WhoProB 73*

Radcliffe, Ann
English. Author
Gothic romances include *Mysteries of Udolpho,* 1794.
b. Jul 9, 1764 in London, England
d. Feb 7, 1823 in London, England
Source: *ArtclWW 2; BbD; Benet 87, 96; BioIn 1, 2, 3, 5, 7, 9, 12; BlmGEL; BlmGWL; BritAu; CamGEL; CamGLE; CasWL; CrtSuMy; CrtT 2; DcArts; DcBiPP; DcBrAmW; DcEnA; DcEuL; DcLB 39; DcLEL; DcNaB; EncMys; EvLB; FemiCLE; GrWomW; LegTOT; LngCEL; MouLC 2; NewC; NinCLC 6; OxCEng 67, 85, 95; PenC ENG; PenEncH; PenNWW A; RAdv 1, 14, 13-1; REn; RfGEnL 91; SupFW; WebE&AL; WhoHr&F; WorAl; WorAlBi*

Radecki, Thomas
American. Psychiatrist
Chm., National Coalition on TV Violence, 1980—.
Source: *BiDrAPA 89; BioIn 15; ConNews 86-2*

Radek, Karl Bernhardovich
Russian. Political Leader
One of co-authors of new Soviet Constitution, 1936; arrested, imprisoned for treason, 1937.
b. 1885 in Lvov, Poland
d. 1939?
Source: *BiDSovU; McGEWB; NewCol 75; WebBD 83*

Rader, Dotson
American. Author
Novels include *Miracle,* 1978; *Beau Monde,* 1981.
b. Jul 25, 1942 in Evanston, Illinois
Source: *BioIn 10, 11, 13; CelR; ConAu 11NR, 61; DrAPF 80, 91; LiJour; MugS; WhoAm 86, 90*

Rader, Doug(las Lee)
"Rojo"; "The Red Rooster"
American. Baseball Player, Baseball Manager
Infielder, 1967-77, mostly with Houston; manager, Texas, 1983-85.
b. Jul 30, 1944 in Chicago, Illinois
Source: *Ballpl 90; BioIn 9, 11, 13, 16; WhoAm 74, 84, 86, 90; WhoProB 73; WhoSSW 84; WhoWest 89, 92*

Radford, Arthur William
American. Naval Officer
Chm., Joint Chiefs of Staff, 1953-57, under Eisenhower.
b. Feb 27, 1896 in Chicago, Illinois
d. Aug 17, 1973 in Washington, District of Columbia
Source: *BiDWWGF; BioIn 2, 3, 4, 10, 11; CurBio 49, 73; DcAmB S9; DcAmMiB; HarEnMi; InSci; NewYTBE 73; OxCShps; WebAMB; WhAm 6; WorAl*

Radisson, Pierre Espirit
French. Explorer
Hudson Bay explorations led to formation of Hudson Bay Co. by English, 1670.
b. 1636 in Lyons, France
d. 1710
Source: *McGEWB; NewCol 75; WebAB 74; WhAm HS*

Radner, Gilda
[Mrs. Gene Wilder]
American. Comedian
Original cast member of TV series "Saturday Night Live," 1975-80; won Emmy, 1978; autobiography *It's Always Something,* 1989, details her fight against cancer.
b. Jun 28, 1946 in Detroit, Michigan
d. May 20, 1989 in Los Angeles, California
Source: *AnObit 1989; BestSel 89-4; BioIn 11, 12, 15, 16, 17, 18, 19, 20; BkPepl; ConAu 128, 129; ConTFT 3, 8; CurBio 80, 89, 89N; EncAFC; FunnyW; IntMPA 86, 88; InWom SUP; LegTOT; News 89; NewYTBS 77, 80, 89; VarWW 85; WhAm 10; WhoAm 84, 86; WhoCom; WhoRocM 82*

Radziwill, Lee Bouvier
[Caroline Lee Bouvier Radziwill]
American.
Wrote childhood memoir, *One Special Summer,* with sister, Jacqueline Onassis.
b. Mar 3, 1933 in New York, New York
Source: *BioIn 16; BkPepl; CurBio 77; InWom SUP; NewYTBS 74; WhoAm 74, 76, 78, 80; WhoAmW 74*

Rae, Bob
Canadian. Politician
Member, New Democratic Party (NDP); first socialist premier of Ontario, 1990-95.
b. Aug 2, 1948 in Ottawa, Ontario, Canada
Source: *CanWW 83; CurBio 91; NewYTBS 90; Who 92; WhoCan 82, 84*

Rae, Charlotte
[Charlotte Rae Lubotsky]
American. Actor
Starred on TV shows "Diff'rent Strokes," 1978-79; "Facts of Life," 1980-86.
b. Apr 22, 1926 in Milwaukee, Wisconsin
Source: *BiE&WWA; ConTFT 2; InWom SUP; LegTOT; NotNAT; VarWW 85; WhoAm 80, 82, 84, 86, 88, 90, 92; WhoHol 92, A; WhoTelC; WhoThe 72, 77, 81*

Raeburn, Henry, Sir
"The Scottish Reynolds"
Scottish. Artist
Noted portrait painter from 1787.
b. Mar 4, 1756 in Stockbridge, Scotland
d. Jul 8, 1823 in Edinburgh, Scotland
Source: *AtlBL; Benet 87, 96; BioIn 1, 3, 4, 7, 10, 15; CelCen; CmScLit; DcArts; DcBiPP; DcBrECP; DcNaB; IntDcAA 90; LegTOT; LinLib S; McGDA; NewC; OxCArt; OxDcArt; REn*

Raeder, Erich
German. Naval Officer
Commander-in-chief, German Navy; tried at Nuremberg, sentenced to Spandau.
b. Apr 24, 1876 in Wandsbek, Germany

d. Nov 6, 1960 in Kiel, Germany (West)
Source: *BioIn 1, 3, 4, 5, 6, 12, 14, 18; CurBio 41, 61; Dis&D; EncTR, 91; HarEnMi; HisEWW; ObitT 1951; OxCShps; WhoMilH 76; WhWW-II; WorAl; WorAlBi*

Raedler, Dorothy (Florence)
American. Producer
Produced Gilbert and Sullivan operettas beginning in 1936.
b. Feb 24, 1917
d. Dec 11, 1993 in Saint Croix, Virgin Islands of the United States
Source: *BiE&WWA; BioIn 3, 19, 20; CurBio 94N; InWom; NotNAT; WhAm 11; WhoAm 84, 86, 88, 90, 92, 94; WhoEnt 92; WhoThe 72, 77, 81*

Raemaekers, Louis
Dutch. Cartoonist
His WWI anti-German cartoons won him fame.
b. Apr 6, 1869 in Roermond, Netherlands
d. Jul 26, 1956 in Scheveninaen, Netherlands
Source: *BiDMoPL; BioIn 4, 12; ObitOF 79; ObitT 1951; WhAm 3; WhLit; WorECar*

Rafferty, Chips
[John Goffage]
Australian. Actor
Best-known Australian films include *The Rat of Tobruk; The Overlanders; Outback.*
b. Mar 26, 1909, Australia
d. May 27, 1971 in Sydney, Australia
Source: *FilmEn; FilmgC; ForYSC; HalFC 80, 84, 88; IntDcF 1-3, 2-3; MovMk; NewYTBE 71; ObitT 1971; OxCAusL; OxCFilm; WhoHol B; WhScrn 74, 77, 83*

Rafferty, Gerry
Scottish. Singer, Songwriter
Had hit single "Baker Street," 1978; albums include *Sleepwalking,* 1982.
b. Apr 16, 1947 in Paisley, Scotland
Source: *EncRk 88; EncRkSt; HarEnR 86; IlEncRk; PenEncP; RkOn 85*

Rafferty, Max(well Lewis, Jr.)
American. Educator, Author
CA Superintendent of Public Instruction; opposed to progressive education; wrote *Suffer, Little Children,* 1962.
b. May 7, 1917 in New Orleans, Louisiana
d. Jun 13, 1982 in Troy, Alabama
Source: *AmAu&B; ConAu 1NR, 1R, 107; CurBio 69, 82, 82N; DcAmC; LEduc 74; NewYTBS 82; PolProf J; WhAm 8; WhoAm 74, 76, 78, 80, 82*

Raffi
[Raffi Cavoukian]
Canadian. Singer, Songwriter
Popular children's performer since 1974; albums include *Singable Songs for the Very Young,* 1976; *Everything Grows,* 1987.
b. Jul 8, 1948 in Cairo, Egypt
Source: *BioIn 15, 16; CelR 90; ChlBkCr; ConAu 136; ConMus 8; ConNews 88-1; SixBJA; SmATA 68; WhoAm 94, 95, 96, 97; WrDr 94, 96*

Raffin, Deborah
American. Actor
Films include *Once is Not Enough,* 1975; *Touched by Love,* 1980.
b. Mar 13, 1953 in Los Angeles, California
Source: *BioIn 10, 11, 12, 13, 16; CelR 90; ConTFT 5, 12; FilmEn; HalFC 80, 84, 88; IntMPA 75, 76, 77, 78, 79, 80, 81, 82, 84, 86, 88, 92, 94, 96; LegTOT; VarWW 85; WhoEnt 92; WhoHol 92, A*

Raffles, Thomas Stamford, Sir
English. Statesman
Founded Singapore, 1819; lt. governor of Java, 1811-16; lt. governor of Bengkulu, 1818-23.
b. Jul 5, 1781, Jamaica
d. Jul 5, 1826 in London, England
Source: *Alli; BiDLA SUP; BioIn 1, 3, 4, 6, 7, 8, 9, 10, 13, 15, 16, 18; CelCen; DcBiPP; DcInB; DcNaB; DcPup; NewCol 75; WebBD 83; WhDW*

Rafsanjani, Hashemi
[Ali Akbar Hashemi Rafsanjani]
Iranian. Political Leader
Pres., Iran, 1989-97; founding member of the Islamic Rep. party, 1979.
b. 1934 in Rafsanjan, India
Source: *BioIn 12, 15, 16; ConNews 87-3; CurBio 89; EncRev; IntWW 91; LegTOT*

Rafshoon, Gerald Monroe
American. Presidential Aide
Media director, Jimmy Carter's re-election campaign, 1980.
b. Jan 11, 1934 in New York, New York
Source: *BioIn 13, 14; CurBio 79; WhoAdv 90; WhoAm 80, 82, 84, 86, 88, 90, 92, 94, 95, 96, 97; WhoAmP 79; WhoE 86; WhoFI 75*

Raft, George
[George Ranft]
American. Actor
Played gangsters in *Scarface,* 1932; *Each Dawn I Die,* 1939.
b. Sep 26, 1895 in New York, New York
d. Nov 24, 1980 in Hollywood, California
Source: *AnObit 1980; BiDFilm; BioIn 4, 9, 10, 11, 12, 13, 14; BioNews 74; CmMov; DcAmB S10; DcArts; FacFETw; FilmEn; FilmgC; GangFlm; HalFC 80, 84, 88; IntDcF 1-3, 2-3; IntMPA 75, 77; ItaFilm; LegTOT; MotPP; MovMk; NewYTBS 80; OxCFilm; What 3; WhoHol A; WhScrn 83; WorAl; WorAlBi; WorEFlm*

Ragan, Regis
[The Hostages]
American. Hostage
One of 52 held by terrorists, Nov 1979-Jan 1981.
b. 1942?
Source: *NewYTBS 81*

Raglan, Fitzroy James Henry Somerset, Baron
English. Military Leader
Led British forces in Crimean War, lost arm in battle; raglan sleeves named for him.
b. Sep 30, 1788 in Badminton, England
d. Jun 28, 1855 in Sevastopol, Russia
Source: *BioIn 20; HarEnMi; NewCol 75; VicBrit; WebBD 83; WhoMilH 76; WorAlBi*

Ragland, Rags
[John Lee Mortgan Beauregard Ragland]
American. Actor
1940s films include *Anchors Aweigh; Whistling in the Dark.*
b. Aug 23, 1906 in Louisville, Kentucky
d. Aug 20, 1946 in Hollywood, California
Source: *CurBio 46; FilmgC; ForYSC; MotPP; MovMk; Vers A; WhoHol B; WhScrn 74, 77*

Rahal, Bobby
American. Auto Racer
Won Indianapolis 500, 1986.
b. 1953?
Source: *BioIn 12, 13, 15, 16; NewYTBS 89; WhoSpor*

Rahman, Abdul, Prince
Indian. Political Leader
First king of Malaya, 1957-60.
b. Feb 8, 1903 in Alor Star, Kedah
d. Dec 6, 1990 in Kuala Lumpur, Malaysia
Source: *AnObit 1990; BioIn 4, 5, 6, 7, 8, 9, 10, 12, 13, 17; CurBio 57, 60, 91N; DcMPSA; FacFETw; IntWW 89; NewYTBS 90; WhAm 3; WhDW*

Rahman, Mujibur, Sheik
Bangladeshi. Political Leader
Founding pres. of Bangladesh, 1975; prime minister, 1972-75; killed in military coup.
b. Mar 17, 1920 in Tungipara, India
d. Aug 15, 1975 in Dacca, Bangladesh
Source: *BioIn 10; CurBio 73, 75, 75N; DcTwHis; EncRev; FacFETw; IntWW 74; NewYTBE 70, 71; NewYTBS 75; Who 74; WhoWor 74*

Rahner, Karl
Austrian. Theologian
Proponent of theology of liberation, applying theology to social, political problems; over 30 books, 1938-82.
b. Mar 5, 1904 in Freiburg, Germany
d. Mar 30, 1984 in Innsbruck, Austria
Source: *AnObit 1984; BioIn 6, 7, 8, 9, 10, 11, 12, 13, 14, 15, 17, 19; ConAu 109, 112; CurBio 70, 84, 84N;*

DcEcMov; FacFETw; LinLib L, S; McGEWB; NewYTBS 79, 84; OxCGer 76, 86; RAdv 14; ThTwC 87; WorAu 1975

Raikes, Robert
English. Printer, Educator
Helped establish first Sunday school for children, 1780.
b. 1735
d. 1811
Source: *Alli; BioIn 1, 3, 5, 6, 10, 14, 16; CyEd; DcBiPP; DcNaB; EncWM; LinLib L; LuthC 75; OxCChiL; WebBD 83; WhDW; WorAlBi*

Raimu
[Jules Muraire]
French. Actor
Character star of French stage, films including *Fanny.*
b. Dec 17, 1883 in Toulon, France
d. Sep 20, 1946 in Paris, France
Source: *BioIn 1, 11; CnThe; EncEurC; EncWT; Ent; FilmAG WE; FilmEn; FilmgC; HalFC 80, 84, 88; IntDcF 1-3, 2-3; MotPP; MovMk; OxCFilm; WhoHol B; WhScrn 74, 77; WorEFlm*

Raine, William MacLeod
Author
Wrote over 80 Western novels, including *Dry Bones in the Valley,* 1953.
b. Jun 22, 1871 in London, England
d. Jul 25, 1954 in Denver, Colorado
Source: *AmAu&B; AmLY; BenetAL 91; EncFWF; EvLB; MnBBF; PeoHis; REnAL; TwCA, SUP; TwCWW 82, 91; WhAm 3; WhE&EA; WhLit; WhNAA*

Rainer, Luise
Austrian. Actor
Won Oscars for *The Great Ziegfeld,* 1936; *The Good Earth,* 1937.
b. Jan 12, 1912 in Vienna, Austria
Source: *BiDFilm, 81, 94; BioIn 6, 7, 9, 11, 16; FilmgC; HalFC 84, 88; InWom, SUP; MotPP; MovMk; OxCFilm; ThFT; VarWW 85; Who 85, 92; WhoHol A; WhoThe 77A; WhThe; WorAl; WorAlBi; WorEFlm*

Raines, Cristina
American. Actor
Played on TV show "Flamingo Road," 1981-82.
b. Feb 28, 1953 in Manila, Philippines
Source: *BioIn 11; HalFC 88; NewYTBS 78; VarWW 85; WhoHol 92, A*

Raines, Ella
[Ella Wallace Raubes]
American. Actor
Best known role in *Phantom Lady,* 1944.
b. Aug 6, 1921 in Snoquaimie, Massachusetts
d. May 30, 1988 in Sherman Oaks, California
Source: *BioIn 4, 10, 15, 16; FilmEn; FilmgC; ForYSC; GangFlm; HalFC 80, 84, 88; HolP 40; IntMPA 75, 76, 77, 78, 79, 80, 81, 82, 84, 86, 88; InWom; LegTOT; MotPP; MovMk; VarWW 85; WhoHol A*

Raines, Tim(othy)
"Rock"
American. Baseball Player
Outfielder, Montreal, 1979-90, Chicago White Sox 1990—; led NL in stolen bases four times; won NL batting title, 1986.
b. Sep 16, 1959 in Sanford, Florida
Source: *Ballpl 90; BaseReg 86, 87; BiDAmSp Sup; BioIn 12, 13, 14, 15, 16; InB&W 85; WhoAfA 96; WhoAm 92, 94, 95, 96, 97; WhoBlA 85, 88, 90, 92, 94; WhoMW 93; WhoSpor; WorAlBi*

Rainey, Gertrude
[Gertrude Malissa Nix Pridgett]
"Ma Rainey"
American. Singer
Blues pioneer who recorded in 1920s-30s; Bessie Smith was her protege.
b. Apr 26, 1886 in Columbus, Georgia
d. Dec 22, 1939 in Columbus, Georgia
Source: *AfrAmAl 6; Baker 84, 92; BiDJaz; BioAmW; BioIn 15, 16, 17, 18, 19, 20, 21; BlkWAm; BluesWW; CmpEPM; ContDcW 89; DcAmB S2; DcAmNB; DcTwCCu 5; DrBlPA, 90; GayLesB; IlEncJ; IntDcWB; LegTOT; MusMk; NegAl 89; NewAmDM; NewGrDA 86; NewGrDJ 88, 94; NewGrDM 80; NotAW; NotBlAW 1; OxCPMus; PenEncP; WhAm 4, HSA; WhoJazz 72; WhoRocM 82; WomFir; WorAl; WorAlBi*

Rainey, Joseph Hayne
American. Politician
First black man elected to House of Representatives from SC, 1870-79.
b. Jun 21, 1832 in Georgetown, South Carolina
d. Aug 2, 1887 in Georgetown, South Carolina
Source: *ApCAB; BiAUS; BiDrAC; BiDrUSC 89; BioIn 5, 7, 9, 17; BlkAmsC; BlkCO; DcAmB; DcAmNB; EncSoH; InB&W 80, 85; NatCAB 11; TwCBDA; WhAm HS; WhAmP; WorAl*

Rainey, Melanie
American.
First Miss Black USA.
d. Apr 24, 1995 in Chicago, Illinois

Rainier III, Prince
[Louis Henri Maxence Bertrand; Prince of Monaco]
Monacan. Ruler
Succeeded grandfather, 1949—; family is oldest reigning dynasty in Europe; founded Monaco Red Cross, 1948.
b. May 31, 1923, Monaco
Source: *BioIn 10, 13, 15, 16; CurBio 55; IntWW 91; WhoFr 79; WhoWor 87, 91*

Rain-in-the-Face
American. Native American Leader
Leading warrior in the defeat of Gen. Custer at Little Big Horn, 1876.
b. 1835? in North Dakota
d. Sep 14, 1905 in Standing Rock Reservation,North Dakota
Source: *BioIn 1, 11, 19; NotNaAm; WhNaAH*

Rains, Albert McKinley
American. Politician
Dem. rep. from AL, 1945-65.
b. Mar 11, 1902 in Groveoak, Alabama
d. Mar 22, 1991 in Gadsden, Alabama
Source: *BiDrAC; BiDrUSC 89; BioIn 5, 17; CurBio 91N; NewYTBS 91; WhAmP; WhoGov 72*

Rains, Claude
American. Actor
Starred in *The Invisible Man,* 1933; *Casablanca,* 1942; *Notorious,* 1946.
b. Nov 9, 1889 in London, England
d. May 30, 1967 in Sandwich, New Hampshire
Source: *BiDFilm, 81, 94; BiE&WWA; BioIn 2, 7, 8, 9, 13, 14, 15, 17, 21; CmMov; CurBio 49; DcAmB S8; FacFETw; FilmEn; FilmgC; ForYSC; HalFC 80, 84, 88; IntDcF 1-3, 2-3; ItaFilm; LegTOT; MotPP; MovMk; NatCAB 62; NotNAT B; ObitT 1961; OlFamFa; OxCFilm; PenEncH; WhAm 4; WhoHol B; WhoHrs 80; WhScrn 74, 77, 83; WhThe; WorAl; WorAlBi; WorEFlm*

Rainwater, James
[Leo James Rainwater]
American. Physicist
Shared Nobel Prize in physics, 1975, for analyzing shape of atomic nucleus.
b. Dec 9, 1917 in Council, Idaho
d. May 31, 1986 in Yonkers, New York
Source: *AmMWSc 76P, 79, 82, 86; BiESc; BioIn 14, 15, 20; CamDcSc; IntWW 74, 75, 76, 77, 78, 79, 80, 81, 82, 83; McGMS 80; NobelP; NotTwCS; WhAm 9; Who 82, 83, 85, 88; WhoAm 74, 76, 78, 80, 82, 84; WhoAtom 77; WhoE 77, 79, 81, 83, 85; WhoNob, 90, 95; WhoWor 78, 80, 82, 84; WorAlBi*

Raisa, Rosa
[Rose Burstein]
Polish. Opera Singer
Dramatic soprano, noted for Tosca role; Chicago Civic Opera star.
b. May 30, 1893 in Bialystok, Poland
d. Sep 28, 1963 in Los Angeles, California
Source: *Baker 78, 84, 92; BiDAmM; BioIn 2, 5, 6, 9, 11, 12, 14; BriBkM 80; CmOp; IntDcOp; InWom, SUP; MetOEnc; MusSN; NewAmDM; NewEOp 71; NewGrDA 86; NewGrDM 80; NewGrDO; OxDcOp; PenDiMP; WhAm 4*

Raitt, Bonnie
American. Singer, Songwriter
Blues singer; winner of 4 Grammys, 1990, for *Nick of Time.*
b. Nov 8, 1949 in Burbank, California
Source: *ASCAP 80; Baker 92; BioIn 11, 12, 13, 16; BkPepl; ConMus 3; CurBio*

90; EncRk 88; EncRkSt; GrLiveH; HarEnR 86; IlEncRk; InWom SUP; LegTOT; NewGrDA 86; News 90, 90-2; NewYTBS 77; OnThGG; PenEncP; RkOn 78; RolSEnR 83; VarWW 85; WhoAm 78, 80, 82, 84, 86, 88; WhoAmW 81, 91; WhoEnt 92; WhoHol 92; WhoRocM 82

Raitt, John Emmet
American. Singer
Stage, TV vocalist, 1940s-60s; starred in Broadway's *Carousel,* 1945.
b. Jan 19, 1917 in Santa Ana, California
Source: *Baker 84; BiE&WWA; BioNews 74; CmpEPM; ConTFT 5; EncMT; FilmgC; HalFC 88; NotNAT; OxCPMus; VarWW 85; WhoAm 84; WhoHol A; WhoThe 81; WhoWest 74; WhoWor 84; WorAlBi*

Rajai, Mohammed Ali
Iranian. Political Leader
Former prime minister who served as pres., Jul 24-Aug 30, 1981.
b. 1933 in Quazin, Persia
d. Aug 30, 1981 in Tehran, Iran
Source: *NewYTBS 81*

Rajneesh, Bhagwan Shree
[Osho Rajneesh]
Indian. Religious Leader
Cult leader known for preaching blend of Eastern religion, pop psychology, free love; deported from US, 1985, for immigration violations.
b. Dec 11, 1931 in Kuthwara, India
d. Jan 19, 1990 in Pune, India
Source: *AnObit 1990; BioIn 14, 15, 16, 17; ConAu 93; DivFut; EncO&P 1S1, 2; EncWB; FacFETw; IntAu&W 77, 82; News 90, 90-2; RelLAm 91*

Rakosi, Matyas
Hungarian. Politician
General secretary Hungarian Socialist Workers Party, 1945-56.
b. Mar 14, 1892 in Ada
d. Feb 5, 1971 in Gorki, Union of Soviet Socialist Republics
Source: *BioIn 1, 2, 3, 4, 6, 8, 9, 10, 18; ColdWar 1, 2; ConAu 29R; CurBio 49, 71N; DcTwHis; EncCW; EncRev; FacFETw; NewYTBE 71; ObitOF 79*

Rakowski, Mieczyslaw Franciszek
Polish. Political Leader
Poland's prime minister, 1988-89; general secretary of the Polish United Worker's Party, 1989-90.
b. Dec 1, 1926 in Kowalewko, Poland
Source: *BioIn 12, 13, 16; CurBio 89; IntAu&W 89; IntWW 74, 75, 76, 77, 78, 79, 80, 81, 82, 83, 89, 91, 93; NewYTBS 88; WhoEmL 87; WhoSoCE 89; WhoSSW 88; WhoWor 78, 80, 82, 91*

Raleigh, Walter, Sir
English. Courtier, Navigator, Historian
Tried to colonize VA, introducing tobacco to England; favorite of Queen Elizabeth beheaded for treason.
b. 1552 in Devonshire, England
d. Oct 29, 1618 in London, England
Source: *AtlBL; BbD; Benet 87, 96; BiD&SB; BioIn 1, 2, 3, 4, 5, 6, 7, 8, 9, 10, 11, 12, 13, 15, 16, 17, 18, 19, 20, 21; BlmGEL; BritAu; CamGEL; CasWL; Chambr 1; ChhPo, S1; CroE&S; CrtT 1; DcBiPP; DcEnA A; DcEnL; DcEuL; DcLEL; Dis&D; Drake; EncAAH; EncCRAm; EncSoH; EvLB; Expl 93; HarEnUS; HisDBrE; HisDStE; LinLib L, S; LngCEL; McGEWB; MouLC 1; NewC; NewCol 75; OxCAmH; OxCEng 67; OxCShps; PenC ENG; REn; REnAL; RGFBP; WebBD 83; WhAm HS; WhDW; WhWE; WorAl*

Raleigh, Walter Alexander, Sir
English. Educator, Essayist
English literature professor at Oxford, 1904-22; wrote *The English Novel,* 1894.
b. Sep 5, 1861 in London, England
d. May 18, 1922 in Oxford, England
Source: *BioIn 2, 3, 14; CamGEL; CamGLE; CasWL; Chambr 3; ChhPo, S1, S2, S3; DcEnA, A; DcEnL; DcEuL; DcNaB 1922; EvLB; GrBr; LngCTC; NewC; NewCBEL; OxCEng 67, 85, 95; RComWL; REn; TwCA, SUP*

Ralf, Torsten
Swedish. Opera Singer
Tenor, noted for Wagner, Verdi repertories; NY Met. star, 1940s.
b. Jan 2, 1901 in Malmo, Sweden
d. Apr 27, 1954 in Stockholm, Sweden
Source: *Baker 78, 84; BioIn 1, 3, 10; CmOp; MetOEnc; NewEOp 71; NewGrDM 80; OxDcOp; PenDiMP*

Ralphs, Mick
[Mott the Hoople]
English. Musician
Guitarist, vocalist, with hard-rock group, 1969-73.
b. Mar 31, 1948 in Hereford, England
Source: *OnThGG; WhoRocM 82*

Ralston, Esther
"The American Venus"
American. Actor
Played heroine roles in over 150 films, 1918-40.
b. Sep 17, 1902 in Bar Harbor, Maine
d. Jan 14, 1994 in Ventura, California
Source: *BioIn 8, 18, 19; EncAFC; Film 2; FilmEn; FilmgC; ForYSC; HalFC 80, 84, 88; InWom, SUP; LegTOT; MotPP; MovMk; SilFlmP; SweetSg B; ThFT; TwYS; VarWW 85; What 2; WhoAmW 77; WhoHol 92, A; WomWMM*

Ralston, Vera
[Vera Helena Hruba]
American. Actor
Films include *Accused of Murder; The Man Who Died Twice.*
b. Jul 12, 1919 in Prague, Czechoslovakia
Source: *FilmEn; FilmgC; HalFC 88; InWom SUP; LegTOT; MotPP; MovMk; VarWW 85; WhoHol A*

Ram, Jagjivan
Indian. Politician
Served as minister of labor, agriculture, railways, defense, 1970-79; main force behind drive for independence.
b. Apr 5, 1908 in Chandwa, India
d. Jul 6, 1986 in New Delhi, India
Source: *AnObit 1986; BioIn 11, 12, 15; ConNews 86-4; CurBio 78, 86N; FarE&A 78, 79, 80, 81; IntWW 74, 75, 76, 77, 78, 79, 80, 81, 82, 83; IntYB 80, 81, 82; NewYTBS 77, 86; Who 74, 82, 83, 85; WhoWor 74*

Ramakrishna, Sri
Indian. Religious Leader
Considered sainted wise man by Hindus; followers founded Ramakrishna Mission, 1897.
b. Feb 18, 1834 in Kamapukur, India
d. Aug 16, 1886 in Calcutta, India
Source: *BiDAmCu; NewCol 75*

Raman, Chandrasekhara Venkata, Sir
Indian. Physicist
Won 1930 Nobel Prize for developing Raman Effect.
b. Nov 7, 1888 in Madras, India
d. Nov 21, 1970 in Bangalore, India
Source: *AsBiEn; BiESc; BioIn 14, 15, 16, 17, 20; CamDcSc; ConAu 113; CurBio 48, 71; DcScB; InSci; LarDcSc; REn; WhAm 6; WhDW; WhLit; WhoLA; WhoNob, 90, 95; WorAl*

Ramaphosa, Cyril
[Matamela Cyril Ramaphosa]
South African. Labor Union Official
General secretary, National Union of Mineworkers, South Africa, 1982-91; chm. African Nat. Congress, 1994—; led successful strike, 1984, costing the mineowners $225 million.
b. Nov 17, 1952 in Johannesburg, South Africa
Source: *BioIn 14, 15, 20, 21; ConBlB 3; CurBio 95; DcCPSAf; IntWW 91; News 88-2; NewYTBS 85; WhoWor 97*

Rama Rau, Santha
Indian. Author
First book, *Home to India,* 1945, seeks Indian nationalism; autobiography, *Gifts of Passage,* 1962.
b. Jan 24, 1923 in Madras, India
Source: *AmAu&B; BiE&WWA; BioIn 2, 5, 7, 10, 19, 20; ConAu X; CurBio 45, 59; DcLEL 1940; IntAu&W 89, 91, 93; IntWW 83, 91, 93; InWom, SUP; LiExTwC; LinLib L; ModWoWr; NewC; PenC ENG; TwCWr; Who 85, 92, 94; WhoAmW 64, 66, 68, 72; WhoWor 74; WorAu 1950*

Rambeau, Marjorie
American. Actor
Broadway, film star; Oscar nominee for *Promise Path,* 1940.
b. Jul 15, 1889 in San Francisco, California
d. Jul 7, 1970 in Palm Springs, California

Source: *BioIn 3, 9, 11, 21; EncAFC; Film 1, 2; FilmEn; FilmgC; ForYSC; HalFC 80, 84, 88; HolCA; InWom, SUP; LegTOT; MotPP; MovMk; NewYTBE 70; OlFamFa; OxCAmT 84; ThFT; TwYS; Vers B; WhoHol B; WhScrn 74, 77, 83; WhThe*

Rambert, Marie, Dame
[Cyvia Rambam; Myriam Rambam]
English. Dancer, Director
Key figure in development of ballet in Britain; founded Ballet Rambert, 1926.
b. Feb 20, 1888 in Warsaw, Poland
d. Jun 12, 1982 in London, England
Source: *AnObit 1982; BiDD; BioIn 3, 4, 5, 6, 9, 12; BlueB 76; CnOxB; ConAu 103, 107; ContDcW 89; CurBio 81, 82, 82N; DancEn 78; DcArts; DcNaB 1981; FacFETw; IntDcB; IntDcWB; IntWW 74, 75, 76, 77, 78, 79, 80, 81, 82; InWom, SUP; NewGrDM 80; NewOxM; NewYTBS 82; PolBiDi; WhDW; Who 74, 82; WhoThe 77; WhoWor 74, 76, 78, 82; WomFir; WorAlBi*

Rambo, Dack
[Norman J Rambo]
American. Actor
Played Jack Ewing on TV series "Dallas."
b. Nov 13, 1941 in Delano, California
d. Mar 21, 1994 in Delano, California
Source: *BioIn 13, 14, 19, 20; ConTFT 5, 13; LegTOT; VarWW 85; WhoHol A; WhoTelC*

Rameau, Jean-Philippe
French. Composer
Wrote *Treatise on Harmony,* 1722, which became cornerstone of modern music theory.
b. Sep 25, 1683 in Dijon, France
d. Sep 12, 1764 in Paris, France
Source: *Baker 78, 84, 92; BlkwCE; BriBkM 80; CmOp; CmpBCM; CnOxB; DcArts; DcBiPP; DcCom 77; DcCom&M 79; EncEnl; GrComp; IntDcOp; MetOEnc; MusMk; NewAmDM; NewEOp 71; NewGrDM 80; NewGrDO; NewOxM; OxCFr; OxCMus; OxDcOp; REn; WhDW*

Ramey, Samuel Edward
American. Opera Singer
Leading bass with NYC Opera, 1973—; noted for dramatic, buffo roles.
b. Mar 28, 1942 in Colby, Kansas
Source: *Baker 84, 92; BioIn 13, 14, 15, 16; CelR 90; CurBio 81; IntWWM 90; MetOEnc; NewAmDM; NewGrDA 86; NewGrDO; NewYTBS 77, 86; PenDiMP; WhoAm 82, 84, 86, 88, 90, 92, 94, 95, 96, 97; WhoAmM 83; WhoOp 76*

Ramgoolam, Seewoosagur, Sir
Mauritian. Political Leader
Founder, first prime minister of Mauritius.
b. Sep 18, 1900 in Belle River, Mauritius
d. Dec 15, 1985 in Port Louis, Mauritius
Source: *AfSS 78, 79, 80, 81, 82; AnObit 1985; BioIn 10, 12, 13, 14, 21; FacFETw; IntWW 74, 75, 76, 77, 78, 79, 80, 81, 82, 83; IntYB 78, 79, 80, 81, 82; Who 74, 82, 83, 85; WhoGov 72; WhoWor 74, 76, 78, 80; WorDWW*

Ramirez, Raul
Mexican. Tennis Player
Won doubles with Brian Gottfried, Wimbledon, 1976.
b. Jun 10, 1953 in Ensenada, Mexico
Source: *BuCMET; LegTOT; WhoAm 78, 80, 82; WhoIntT; WhoWest 92*

Ramo, Roberta Cooper
American. Lawyer
Attorney, 1967—; president, American Bar Association, 1995—.
b. Aug 8, 1942 in Denver, Colorado
Source: *BioIn 19; News 96, 96-1; WhoAm 95, 96, 97; WhoAmL 83, 85, 96; WhoAmW 95, 97; WhoEmL 87; WhoWest 89, 92, 94; WomFir*

Ramones, The
[Dee Dee Ramone; Joey Ramone; Johnny Ramone; Marky Ramone]
American. Music Group
New wave band, formed 1974; provided most of music for, starred in 1979 film *Rock 'n' Roll High School;* members unrelated.
Source: *BioIn 15, 20; ConMuA 80A; ConMus 9; EncPR&S 89; EncRk 88; EncRkSt; HarEnR 86; IlEncRk; NewGrDA 86; PenEncP; RkOn 85; RolSEnR 83; WhoRock 81; WhoRocM 82; WhsNW 85*

Ramon y Cajal, Santiago
Spanish. Neurologist
Shared 1906 Nobel Prize in medicine for research on the nervous system.
b. May 1, 1852 in Petilla de Aragon, Spain
d. Oct 18, 1934 in Madrid, Spain
Source: *AsBiEn; BiDPsy; BiESc; BiHiMed; BioIn 1, 2, 3, 6, 7, 8, 9, 12, 14, 15, 16, 17, 20, 21; CamDcSc; DcHiB; DcScB; LarDcSc; NamesHP; NobelP; NotTwCS; OxCMed 86; RAdv 14; WhDW; WhoNob, 90, 95; WorAl; WorAlBi; WorScD*

Ramos, Fidel V(aldez)
Philippine. Political Leader
Pres., Philippines, 1992—.
b. Mar 18, 1928 in Lingayen, Philippines
Source: *BioIn 14, 15; CurBio 94; FacFETw; IntWW 91; WhoWor 91*

Rampal, Jean-Pierre
French. Musician
Noted flutist; many French composers wrote works for him.
b. Jan 7, 1922 in Marseilles, France
Source: *Baker 78, 84; BioIn 14, 16; BriBkM 80; CelR 90; ConMus 6; CurBio 70; FacFETw; IntWW 91; IntWWM 80, 90; LegTOT; MusSN; NewAmDM; NewGrDM 80; News 89-2; PenDiMP; WhoAm 86, 88; WhoAmM 83; WhoEnt 92; WhoFr 79; WhoMus 72; WhoWor 74, 91; WorAlBi*

Rampling, Charlotte
[Mrs. Jean-Michel Jarre]
English. Actor
Best known for role in *Georgy Girl,* 1966; other films include *DOA,* 1988; *The Verdict,* 1982.
b. Feb 5, 1946 in Sturmer, England
Source: *BiDFilm 94; BioIn 13, 15, 16; ConTFT 1, 6; FilmgC; HalFC 88; IntMPA 75, 76, 77, 78, 79, 80, 81, 82, 84, 86, 88, 92, 94, 96; IntWW 89, 91, 93; VarWW 85; WhoHol 92, A*

Ramsay, Allan
Scottish. Poet
Wrote popular pastoral, *The Gentle Shepherd,* 1725.
b. Oct 15, 1686 in Leadhills, Scotland
d. Jan 7, 1758 in Edinburgh, Scotland
Source: *Alli; BbD; BiD&SB; BioIn 2, 3, 9; BlkwCE; BlmGEL; BritAu; CamGEL; CamGLE; CasWL; ChhPo, S1, S3; CmScLit; CnE&AP; DcArts; DcEnA; DcEnL; DcEuL; DcLEL; DcNaB; Dis&D; EvLB; GrWrEL P; NewC; NewCBEL; OxCEng 67, 85, 95; OxCMus; OxCThe 83; PenC ENG; REn; RfGEnL 91; WebAB 74; WebE&AL*

Ramsay, Allan
Scottish. Artist
Portraitist, court painter to George III, 1767.
b. 1713 in Edinburgh, Scotland
d. 1784
Source: *Alli; BioIn 2, 3, 4, 6, 7, 10, 11, 12, 14, 19; DcArts; DcBrECP; DcNaB; IntDcAA 90; McGDA; NewCBEL; NewCol 75; OxCArt; OxDcArt; REn*

Ramsay, Jack
[John T Ramsay]
American. Basketball Coach
NBA coach since 1968 with several teams, now with Indiana, 1986—; with Portland, 1977, won NBA championship.
b. Feb 21, 1925 in Philadelphia, Pennsylvania
Source: *BasBi; BiDAmSp BK; BioIn 13; OfNBA 87; WhoAm 84, 86, 88; WhoBbl 73; WhoMW 88; WhoSpor; WhoWest 84*

Ramsay, William, Sir
Scottish. Scientist
Best known for discovery of inert gases; won Nobel Prize, 1904.
b. Oct 2, 1852 in Glasgow, Scotland
d. Jul 23, 1916 in Hazelmere, England
Source: *AsBiEn; BiESc; BioIn 1, 2, 3, 4, 6, 9, 14, 15, 19, 20; CamDcSc; DcInv; DcNaB 1912; DcScB; Dis&D; GrBr; InSci; LarDcSc; LinLib L, S; McGEWB; NobelP; NotTwCS; RAdv 14; REn; WhDW; WhLit; WhoNob, 90, 95; WorAl; WorAlBi; WorScD*

Ramsbotham, Peter, Sir
English. Diplomat
Has held many diplomatic posts, including governor of Bermuda, 1977-80.
b. Oct 8, 1919 in London, England
Source: *BioIn 10, 11; IntWW 74, 75, 76, 77, 78, 79, 80, 81, 82, 83, 89, 91; Who 74, 82, 83, 85, 88, 90, 92*

Ramses II
Egyptian. Ruler
King, 1279-13 BC during 19th dynasty.
b. fl. 13th cent. BC

Ramsey, Anne
American. Actor
Had 37-year show business career, but best known for one of last roles—as mother in *Throw Momma From the Train,* 1987, for which she received Oscar nomination.
b. 1929?
d. Aug 11, 1988 in Los Angeles, California
Source: *NewYTBS 88*

Ramsey, Arthur Michael, Lord
English. Religious Leader
Archbishop of Canterbury, 1961-74; pres., World Council of Churches, 1961-68.
b. Nov 14, 1904 in Cambridge, England
d. Apr 23, 1988 in Oxford, England
Source: *BioIn 4, 5, 6, 7, 10; ConAu 77; CurBio 60, 88; DcEcMov; EncWB; FacFETw; IntAu&W 82; IntWW 74; LinLib L, S; NewCol 75; NewYTBS 88; WhAm 9; WhE&EA; Who 74; WhoWor 74, 76, 78; WrDr 76, 80, 82, 84, 86, 88*

Ramsey, Frank Vernon, Jr.
American. Basketball Player
Guard, Boston, 1954-64; won seven NBA championships; Hall of Fame, 1981.
b. Jul 31, 1931 in Corydon, Kentucky
Source: *BiDAmSp BK; BioIn 11; OfNBA 87*

Ramsey, Mike
[Michael Allen Ramsey]
American. Hockey Player
Defenseman, Buffalo, 1980-93; member US Olympic gold medal-winning team, 1980-93.
b. Dec 3, 1960 in Minneapolis, Minnesota
Source: *Ballpl 90; BiDAmSp Sup; HocEn; HocReg 87*

Ramsey, Norman
American. Scientist
Won Nobel Prize in physics, 1989, for work that led to development of the atomic clock.
b. Aug 27, 1915 in Washington, District of Columbia
Source: *AmMWSc 92; BioIn 3, 4, 5, 11, 16; ConAu P-1; IntWW 91; LarDcSc; Who 92; WhoAm 74, 76, 78, 80, 82, 84, 86, 88, 90, 92, 94; WhoE 91, 93; WhoFrS 84; WhoNob 90; WhoTech 89; WhoWor 89, 91, 93; WorAlBi; WrDr 92*

Ram Singh
Indian. Religious Leader, Political Activist
Leader of the Sikh Namdhari movement; attempted to oust the British from India.
b. 1816 in Bhaini, India
d. 1885 in Mergui, Burma
Source: *BioIn 15*

Rand, A(ddison) Barry
American. Business Executive
Executive VP, operations, Xerox Corp., 1992—.
b. Nov 5, 1944 in Washington, District of Columbia

Rand, Ayn
American. Author
Novels *The Fountainhead,* 1943; *Atlas Shrugged,* 1957, reflect "objectivist" philosophy.
b. Feb 2, 1905 in Saint Petersburg, Russia
d. Mar 6, 1982 in New York, New York
Source: *AmAu&B; AmNov; AmWomWr; AnObit 1982; ArtclWW 2; Au&Arts 10; Benet 87, 96; BenetAL 91; BioAmW; BioIn 2, 4, 5, 6, 7, 8, 10, 11, 12, 13, 14, 15, 16, 17, 18, 20, 21; BlmGWL; CamGLE; CamHAL; CasWL; CelR; ConAu 13R, 27NR, 105; ConLC 3, 30, 44, 79; ConNov 72, 76, 82; ConPopW; CurBio 82; DcAmC; DcArts; EncMcCE; EncSF, 93; EncUnb; EncWHA; FacFETw; ForWC 70; IntAu&W 76, 77; InWom SUP; JeAmHC; LegTOT; LibW; MajTwCW; NewEScF; NewYTBS 82; Novels; OxCAmL 65, 83, 95; OxCWoWr 95; PenC AM; PolProf E; REn; REnAL; RfGAmL 94; ScF&FL 1, 2, 92; ScFSB; TwCA SUP; TwCSFW 81, 86, 91; TwCYAW; TwoTYeD; WebAB 74, 79; WebE&AL; WhAm 8; WhoAm 74, 76, 78, 80, 82; WhoAmW 66, 68, 70, 72, 74, 75, 77, 81, 83; WhoTwCL; WorAl; WorAlBi; WorLitC; WrDr 76, 80, 82; WrPh*

Rand, Ellen Gertrude Emmet
American. Artist
Celebrity portrait painter, noted for craftmanship, coloring; after 1929 crash, sold paintings for up to $5,000 each.
b. Mar 4, 1875 in San Francisco, California
d. Dec 18, 1941 in New York, New York
Source: *DcWomA; InWom SUP; NatCAB 40; NotAW; WhAm 2*

Rand, James Henry
American. Business Executive
Formed company that became Remington-Rand, 1926.
b. Nov 18, 1886 in North Tonawanda, New York
d. Jun 3, 1968 in Freeport, Bahamas
Source: *BiDAmBL 83; BioIn 1, 2, 8, 10, 15; HisDcDP; NatCAB 54; ObitOF 79; WhAm 5*

Rand, Paul
American. Designer
Professor of graphic design, Yale, 1956-69; wrote *Thoughts on Design,* 1970.
b. Aug 15, 1914 in New York, New York
d. Nov 26, 1996 in Norwalk, Connecticut
Source: *AuBYP 2, 3; BioIn 1, 3, 5, 7, 8, 9, 10, 12, 14, 16, 19; BlueB 76; ConAu 21R, 154; ConDes 84, 90, 97; ConGrA 3; DcTwDes; IlsCB 1946, 1957; McGDA; NewYTBS 27; SmATA 6; ThrBJA; WhAmArt 85; WhoAm 74, 76, 78, 80, 82, 84, 94, 95, 96, 97; WhoAmA 73, 76, 78, 80, 82, 84, 86, 89, 91, 93; WhoE 91; WhoGrA 62, 82*

Rand, Sally
[Helen Beck]
American. Dancer
Exotic fan dance was sensation of 1933 Chicago World's Fair.
b. Jan 2, 1904 in Elkton, Missouri
d. Aug 31, 1979 in Glendora, California
Source: *BiDD; BioIn 7, 12; DcAmB S10; DcArts; EncVaud; FilmgC; GoodHs; HalFC 80, 84, 88; InWom, SUP; LegTOT; LibW; NewYTBS 79; OxCAmT 84; TwYS; WebAB 74, 79; What 1; WhoAmW 70; WhoHol A; WhScrn 83; WorAl*

Randall, Dudley
American. Poet
Works include "The Black Poets," 1971; "After the Killing," 1973.
b. Jan 14, 1914 in Washington, District of Columbia
Source: *AfrAmAl 6; BenetAL 91; BiDrLUS 70; BioIn 20; BlkAWP; BlkLC; BlkWr 1; BroadAu; ConAu 23NR, 25R; ConBlB 8; ConLC 1; ConPo 75, 80, 85, 91; DcLB 41; DcLEL 1940; DcTwCCu 5; DrAP 75; DrAPF 91; IntvTCA 2; IntWWP 82; LivgBAA; MichAu 80; SchCGBL; WhoBlA 85; WhoLibS 66; WhoMW 74; WrDr 80, 82, 84, 86, 88, 90, 92, 94, 96*

Randall, James Garfield
American. Historian, Author
Books on Pres. Lincoln, Civil War include *Lincoln and the South,* 1946.
b. Jun 24, 1881 in Indianapolis, Indiana
d. Feb 20, 1953 in Champaign, Illinois
Source: *AmAu&B; BioIn 1, 2, 3, 4, 8, 13; ConAu 118; DcAmB S5; EncSoH; IndAu 1816; NatCAB 39; REnAL; TwCA SUP; WhAm 3*

Randall, Samuel J
American. Government Official
Dem., Speaker of House, 1876-81; strengthened speaker's power by classifying rules of House of Representatives.
b. Oct 10, 1828 in Philadelphia, Pennsylvania

d. Apr 13, 1890 in Washington, District of Columbia
Source: *AmBi; ApCAB; BiDrAC; DcAmB; EncAB-H 1974; NatCAB 3; TwCBDA; WebAB 79; WhAm HS; WhAmP*

Randall, Tony
[Leonard Rosenberg]
American. Actor
Played Felix Unger in TV comedy "The Odd Couple," 1970-75; won Emmy, 1975.
b. Feb 26, 1924 in Tulsa, Oklahoma
Source: *BioIn 5, 6, 7, 9, 11, 13, 15; BkPepl; CelR 90; ConTFT 1, 7; CurBio 61; EncAFC; FilmgC; HalFC 88; IntMPA 86, 92; LesBEnT 92; MotPP; MovMk; NotNAT; VarWW 85; WhoAm 86, 90; WhoEnt 92A; WhoHol A; WhoTelC; WhoThe 81; WhoWor 74; WorAlBi; WorEFlm*

Randhawa, Mohinder Singh
Indian. Author
India's leading art historian; co-wrote *Indian Painting: The Scene, Themes, and Legends,* 1968.
b. Feb 2, 1909 in Zira, India
d. Mar 3, 1986
Source: *ConAu 28NR, 29R; DcLEL 1940; IntAu&W 77, 82, 86; WhoWor 74, 76; WrDr 76, 80, 82, 84*

Randi, James
[Randall James Hamilton Zwinge]
"The Amazing Randi"
Canadian. Magician
Conjurer who discredits parapsychology; wrote expose *The Magic of Uri Geller,* 1975.
b. Aug 7, 1928 in Toronto, Ontario, Canada
Source: *BioIn 12, 15; ConAu 117; CurBio 87; EncO&P 1S3, 2, 3; EncPaPR 91; LegTOT; News 90, 90-2; WhoAm 84, 86, 88, 90, 92, 94, 95, 96, 97; WhoE 85; WhoEnt 92; WhoUSWr 88; WhoWrEP 89, 92, 95; WrDr 90, 92, 94, 96*

Randisi, Robert Joseph
[Nick Carter; Tom Cutter; W B Longley; J R Roberts]
American. Author
Won Shamus award for mystery novel *The Sterling Collection,* 1983.
b. Aug 24, 1951 in New York, New York
Source: *BioIn 14; ConAu 116; TwCCr&M 85, 91; TwCWW 91; WrDr 86, 92, 94*

Randolph, Asa Philip
American. Labor Union Official
Organizer, pres. of Brotherhood of Sleeping Car Porters, 1925-68.
b. Apr 15, 1889 in Crescent City, Florida
d. May 16, 1979 in New York, New York
Source: *AfrAmAl 6; AfrAmOr; AmPeW; AmRef; AmSocL; BiDAmL; BiDAmLL; BiDMoPL; BioIn 1, 2, 3, 4, 5, 6, 7, 8, 9, 10, 11, 12, 13, 15, 16, 17, 18, 19, 20, 21; ConAu 85; ConBlB 3; CurBio 40, 51, 79; DcAmB S10; DcTwHis; Ebony 1; EncAB-H 1974, 1996; EncSoH; HeroCon; InB&W 80, 85; IntWW 74, 78; OxCAmH; SelBAAf; SelBAAu; WebAB 74, 79; WhAm 7; WhoAm 74, 76; WhoBlA 75; WhoLab 76*

Randolph, Boots
[Homer Louis Randolph, III]
American. Musician
Hit song "Yakety Sax," 1963.
b. Jun 3, 1927 in Paducah, Kentucky
Source: *BgBkCoM; BioIn 14; CounME 74, 74A; EncFCWM 83; EncRk 88; HarEnCM 87; IlEncCM; LegTOT; PenEncP; RkOn 74*

Randolph, Edmund Jennings
American. Statesman
First US attorney general, 1789-94.
b. Aug 10, 1753 in Williamsburg, Virginia
d. Sep 12, 1813 in Millwood, Virginia
Source: *Alli; AmBi; ApCAB; BiAUS; BiDrAC; BiDrUSE 71, 89; BiDSA; BioIn 3, 4, 6, 7, 8, 10, 11, 15, 16; CyAG; DcAmB; DcAmDH 80, 89; Drake; EncAB-H 1974; EncCRAm; McGEWB; REnAL; TwCBDA; WebAB 74, 79; WhAm HS; WhAmP; WhAmRev; WorAl*

Randolph, Georgiana Ann
[Craig Rice; Daphne Sanders; Michael Venning]
American. Author
Mystery novels include *The Corpse Steps Out,* 1940.
b. Jun 5, 1908 in Chicago, Illinois
d. Aug 28, 1957
Source: *BioIn 1, 4, 14; ConAu 116; CrtSuMy; DetWom; EncMys; FemiCLE; GrWomMW; InWom SUP; LegTOT; Novels; TwCCr&M 80, 85, 91; WhAm 3*

Randolph, Jennings
American. Politician
Dem. senator from WV, 1959-85.
b. Mar 8, 1902 in Salem, West Virginia
Source: *AlmAP 78, 80, 82, 84; BiDrAC; BiDrUSC 89; BioIn 6, 7, 8, 9, 10, 11, 12, 14; BlueB 76; CngDr 74, 77, 79, 81, 83; CurBio 62; IntWW 74, 75, 76, 77, 78, 79, 80, 81, 82, 83, 89; IntYB 78, 79, 80, 81, 82; NewYTBS 84; PolProf J, K, NF; PolsAm 84; WhoAm 74, 76, 78, 80, 82, 84; WhoAmP 73, 75, 77, 79, 81, 83, 85, 87, 89, 91, 93; WhoE 74, 75, 77; WhoGov 72, 75, 77; WhoSSW 78, 80, 82, 84; WhoWor 80, 82*

Randolph, John
[Randolph of Roanoke]
American. Statesman
Senator from VA, 1800-29; strong states' rights advocate; opposed Jefferson.
b. Jun 2, 1773 in Cawsons, Virginia
d. May 24, 1833 in Roanoke, Virginia
Source: *Alli; AmBi; AmOrN; AmPolLe; ApCAB; BenetAL 91; BiAUS; BiD&SB; BiDLA; BiDrAC; BiDrUSC 89; BioIn 2, 3, 4, 5, 6, 7, 8, 9, 11, 12, 15, 16, 18, 21; CelCen; CyAG; CyAL 1; DcAmB; DcAmC; DcNAA; Drake; EncAAH; EncAB-H 1974, 1996; EncSoH; HarEnUS; LinLib S; McGEWB; NatCAB 5; OxCAmH; PeoHis; PolPar; REn; REnAL; TwCBDA; WebAB 74, 79; WhAm HS; WhAmP; WorAl; WorAlBi*

Randolph, Mary
American. Author
Wrote early Southern cookbook *The Virginia Housewife,* 1824.
b. Aug 9, 1762 in Virginia
d. Jan 23, 1828 in Washington, District of Columbia
Source: *NotAW; PeoHis*

Randolph, Peyton
American. Continental Congressman, Lawyer
First pres., Continental Congress, 1774-75.
b. Sep 1721 in Williamsburg, Virginia
d. Oct 22, 1775 in Williamsburg, Virginia
Source: *AmBi; ApCAB; BiAUS; BiDrAC; BiDrUSC 89; BiDrUSE 71, 89; BiDSA; BlkwEAR; DcAmB; Drake; EncAR; EncCRAm; EncSoH; NatCAB 2; OxCAmH; TwCBDA; WhAm HS; WhAmRev; WorAl; WorAlBi*

Randolph, Willie
[William Larry Randolph, Jr]
American. Baseball Player
Second baseman, 1975—, mostly with Yankees; known for fielding; four-time AL All-Star.
b. Jul 6, 1954 in Holly Hill, South Carolina
Source: *Ballpl 90; BaseReg 86, 87; BioIn 12, 14, 21; LegTOT; NewYTBS 76, 77; WhoAm 88; WhoBlA 92*

Rangel, Charles Bernard
American. Politician
Dem. congressman from NY, 1971—.
b. Jun 11, 1930 in New York, New York
Source: *AlmAP 92; BiDrUSC 89; BioIn 9, 10, 13, 14, 16; BlkAmsC; CngDr 85, 87, 89; ConBlB 3; CurBio 84; EncWB; NegAl 89A; NewYTBE 70, 71; NewYTBS 74; PolsAm 84; WhoAm 74, 76, 78, 80, 82, 84, 86, 88, 90, 92, 94, 95, 96, 97; WhoAmP 85, 91; WhoBlA 85, 88, 92; WhoE 89, 91, 93, 95, 97; WhoGov 75, 77*

Rank, J(oseph) Arthur
"King Arthur"
English. Film Executive
Monopolized British film industry, 1930-40s; owned over half of the studios, 1,000 theaters.
b. Dec 23, 1888 in Hull, England
d. Mar 29, 1972 in Sutton Scotney, England
Source: *BioIn 1, 3; CurBio 45, 72; DcArts; DcFM; DcTwBBL; EncWM; FilmEn; FilmgC; OxCFilm; WhAm 5; WorEFlm*

Ranke, Leopold von
German. Historian
Noted for *History of the Popes*, 1834-39.
b. Dec 21, 1795 in Wiehe, Germany
d. May 23, 1886 in Berlin, Germany
Source: *BbD; Benet 87, 96; BiD&SB; BioIn 2, 4, 5, 7, 11, 12, 13, 14, 15; CasWL; CelCen; DcEuL; EuAu; LinLib L, S; LuthC 75; McGEWB; NewC; OxCEng 67, 85, 95; OxCGer 76, 86; REn; WhDW*

Rankin, Arthur
American. Actor
Leading man, 1921-35, in films *Little Miss Smiles; Wild Party*.
b. Aug 30, 1900 in New York, New York
d. Mar 23, 1947 in Hollywood, California
Source: *BioIn 1; Film 2; NotNAT B; TwYS; WhoHol B; WhScrn 74, 77, 83*

Rankin, J(ames) Lee
American. Lawyer
US solicitor general, 1956-61.
b. Jul 8, 1907
d. Jun 26, 1996 in California
Source: *BioIn 3, 4, 5, 6, 11; CurBio 96N; PolProf E, J; WhoAm 74, 76*

Rankin, Jeannette
American. Suffragist, Politician
First woman to serve in Congress, 1917-19; only member to oppose US entry into WW I, II.
b. Jul 11, 1880 in Missoula, Montana
d. May 18, 1973 in Carmel, California
Source: *AmPolLe; AmPolW 80; BiDMoPL; BiDrAC; BiDrUSC 89; BioAmW; BioIn 4, 7, 8, 9, 10, 11, 12; BioNews 75; ConAu 41R; EncAB-H 1974; FacFETw; GrLiveH; HeroCon; HisWorL; InWom; LibW; LinLib S; NewYTBE 72, 73; PeoHis; PolPar; RComAH; WebAB 74, 79; WhAm 5; WhAmP; What 2; WhoAmW 70, 72, 74; WomCon*

Rankin, Judy
[Judith Torluemke Rankin]
American. Golfer
Turned pro, 1962; first woman to win $100,000 in one yr., 1976; leading money winner, 1976, 1977.
b. Feb 18, 1945 in Saint Louis, Missouri
Source: *BiDAmSp OS; BioIn 11, 20; ConAu 107; EncWomS; GoodHs; InWom SUP; LegTOT; WhoAm 78, 80, 82, 84; WhoAmW 79, 81, 83, 85, 87, 89; WhoEmL 87; WhoGolf; WhoIntG; WhoSpor; WorAl*

Rankin, K(arl) L(ott)
American. Diplomat
Ambassador to Taiwan, 1953-58; to Yugoslavia, 1958-61.
b. Sep 4, 1898 in Manitowoc, Wisconsin
d. Jan 15, 1991 in Kennebunk, Maine
Source: *BioIn 3, 4, 5, 11, 17; ConAu P-1; WhAm 10; WhoAm 74, 76, 78, 80, 82, 84, 86, 88, 90; WhoWor 84, 87, 89*

Ransohoff, Martin
American. Producer
Films include *Cincinnati Kid*, 1965; *Catch 22*, 1970; *Class*, 1983.
b. 1927 in New Orleans, Louisiana
Source: *BioIn 7; FilmEn; FilmgC; HalFC 80, 84, 88; IntMPA 75, 76, 77, 78, 79, 80, 81, 82, 84, 86, 88, 92, 94, 96; LesBEnT, 92; NewYTET; VarWW 85; WhoAm 74, 76, 78, 80, 82, 84, 86, 88, 90, 92, 94, 95, 96, 97; WhoEnt 92*

Ransom, John Crowe
American. Poet
Founder, editor *Kenyan Review*, 1939-59; wrote verse volume *Chills and Fevers*, 1924.
b. Apr 30, 1888 in Pulaski, Tennessee
d. Jul 5, 1974 in Gambier, Ohio
Source: *AmAu&B; AmCulL; AmWr; Benet 87, 96; BenetAL 91; BioIn 1, 2, 4, 5, 6, 7, 8, 9, 10, 11, 12, 13, 14, 15, 16, 17, 19; CamGEL; CamGLE; CamHAL; CasWL; CelR; ChhPo, S2, S3; CnDAL; CnE&AP; CnMWL; ConAmA; ConAu 5R, 6NR, 34NR, 49; ConLC 2, 4, 5, 11, 24; ConLCrt 77, 82; ConPo 70, 75; CurBio 64, 74, 74N; CyWA 58; DcAmB S9; DcArts; DcLB 45, 63; DcLEL; EncSoH; EncWL 2, 3; EvLB; FacFETw; FifSWrA; Focus; GrWrEL P; IntWWP 77; LinLib L; LngCTC; MajTwCW; MakMC; McGEWB; ModAL, S1, S2; NewYTBS 74; ObitT 1971; OhA&B; OxCAmL 65, 83, 95; OxCEng 85, 95; OxCTwCP; PenC AM; RAdv 1, 14, 13-1; REn; REnAL; RfGAmL 87, 94; RGFAP; RGTwCWr; SixAP; SouWr; TwCA, SUP; TwCWr; WebAB 74, 79; WebE&AL; WhAm 6; WhoAm 74; WhoTwCL; WhoWor 74; WorAl; WorAlBi; WrPh*

Ransome, Arthur Mitchell
English. Author, Poet
Wrote *Swallows and Amazons*, 1930, based on childhood memories.
b. Jan 18, 1884 in Leeds, England
d. Jun 3, 1967, England
Source: *Alli SUP; AuBYP 2; CarSB; CasWL; ConAu 73; DcLEL; EvLB; JBA 34, 51; LngCTC; NewC; PenC ENG; REn; SmATA 22; TwCA; WhoChL; WhoLA*

Rao, P. V. Narasimha
Indian. Political Leader
India's 9th Prime Minister, 1991-96.
b. Jun 28, 1921 in Andhra, India
Source: *CurBio 92; News 93-2; Who 88; WhoWor 84, 87*

Rapacki, Adam
Polish. Government Official
Polish foreign minister, 1956-68; proposed Rapacki Paln to UN, 1957.
b. Dec 24, 1909 in Lvov, Poland
d. Oct 10, 1970 in Warsaw, Poland
Source: *BiDInt; BioIn 4, 5, 9; CurBio 58, 70; NewYTBE 70; ObitT 1961; WhAm 5; WhDW*

Raphael
[Raffaello Sanzio d'Urbino]
Italian. Artist, Architect
Master of the High Renaissance; responsible for many paintings inside Vatican: *The School of Athens*.
b. Mar 28, 1483 in Urbino, Italy
d. Apr 6, 1520 in Rome, Italy
Source: *Alli; AtlBL; Benet 87, 96; BioIn 1, 2, 3, 4, 5, 6, 7, 8, 9, 11, 12, 13, 14, 15, 16, 20, 21; ChhPo; DcArts; DcCathB; Dis&D; EncWT; IntDcAA 90; IntDcAr; LegTOT; LinLib L, S; LuthC 75; MacEA; McGDA; McGEWB; NewC; OxCArt; OxCEng 85, 95; OxDcArt; RAdv 14, 13-3; REn; WhDW; WhoArch; WorAl; WorAlBi*

Raphael
Spanish. Singer
Superstar performer of popular music in Spain since the 1960s; by 1990 received 250 gold records.
b. 1943 in Linares, Spain
Source: *BioIn 17; CurBio 91*

Raphael, Chaim
[Jocelyn Davey]
English. Economist, Author
Chief of information division of Her Majesty's Treasury, 1959-68; wrote crime novels under pseudonym.
b. Jul 14, 1908
d. Oct 10, 1994 in London, England
Source: *BioIn 6; ConAu 16NR, 85, 146; CurBio 95N; TwCCr&M 80, 85, 91; Who 82, 83, 85, 88, 90, 92, 94; WrDr 86, 88, 90, 92, 94, 96*

Raphael, Frederic Michael
English. Screenwriter
Won Oscar for *Darling*, 1965.
b. Aug 14, 1931 in Chicago, Illinois
Source: *Au&Wr 71; BioIn 13; ConAu 1NR; ConDr 82A, 88A; ConLC 14; ConNov 86, 91; ConTFT 2; DcLEL 1940; DcLP 87A; DrAPF 91; FilmgC; HalFC 84, 88; IntAu&W 77, 91; IntMPA 86, 92; IntWW 91; ModBrL S1; VarWW 85; Who 85, 92; WhoAm 86, 90; WorAu 1950; WrDr 86, 92*

Raphael, Sally Jessy
American. TV Personality
TV talk-show host, 1983—; red glasses are her trademark; won Emmys, 1989-90; has radio phone-in show, 1988-91.
b. Feb 25, 1943 in Easton, Pennsylvania
Source: *BioIn 15, 16; CelR 90; ConTFT 11; CurBio 90; LegTOT; News 92; WhoAm 95, 96, 97; WhoAmW 95, 97; WhoE 95; WhoEnt 92*

Raphaelson, Samson
American. Author, Screenwriter
Wrote play *The Jazz Singer*, 1925.
b. Mar 30, 1896 in New York, New York
d. Jul 16, 1983 in New York, New York
Source: *AmAu&B; BenetAL 91; BiE&WWA; BioIn 4, 13, 15; ConAu 65, 110; DcLB 44; EncAFC; FilmEn; FilmgC; HalFC 80, 84, 88; IntDcF 1-4,*

2-4; IntMPA 81, 82, 84; LegTOT; McGEWD 72; NewYTBS 83; NotNAT; OxCAmT 84; REnAL; TwCA SUP; VarWW 85; WhAm 8; WhoAm 74, 76, 78, 80, 82; WhoAmJ 80; WhThe; WorEFlm*

Raposo, Joseph
American. Composer, Puppeteer
Co-creator of TVs ''Sesame Street'' with Jim Henson; wrote song ''It's Not Easy Being Green''; nominated for Oscar for music for *The Great Muppet Caper.*
b. Feb 8, 1937 in Fall River, Massachusetts
d. Feb 5, 1989 in Bronxville, New York
Source: *BioIn 16; ConAu 127; NewYTBS 89; SmATA 61; WhAm 9; WhoAm 88*

Rapp, Danny
[Danny and the Juniors]
American. Singer
Had hit single ''At the Hop,'' 1957.
b. May 10, 1941 in Philadelphia, Pennsylvania
d. Apr 4, 1983 in Quartzside, Pennsylvania
Source: *WhoRocM 82*

Rapp, George
German. Religious Leader
Founded religious communistic societies in PA, IN; followers called Rappites.
b. Nov 1, 1757 in Iptingen, Germany
d. Aug 7, 1847 in Economy, Pennsylvania
Source: *AmBi; BenetAL 91; BiDAmCu; BioIn 7, 9, 15, 19; DcAmB; DcAmReB 1, 2; EncAAH; EncARH; McGEWB; NewGrDA 86; WhAm HS; WorAl; WorAlBi*

Rare Earth
[Gil Bridges; Edward Cuzman; Peter Hoorelbeke; Kenny James; Ray Monette; Mark Olson; John Persh; Rob Richards; Michael Urso]
American. Music Group
Detroit group, reportedly first white act signed by Motown; known for recording earlier Motown hits: ''Get Ready,'' 1970.
Source: *EncPR&S 89; EncRk 88; PenEncP; RkOn 78; RolSEnR 83; WhoRock 81; WhoRocM 82*

Rascals, The
[Eddie Brigati; Felix Cavaliere; Gene Cornish; Dino Danelli; Buzzy Feiten; Robert Popwell; Ann Sutton]
American. Music Group
Blue-eyed soul group formed 1965; number one hits ''Good Lovin','' 1966; ''Groovin','' 1967.
Source: *BiDAmM; ConMuA 80A; EncPR&S 89; EncRk 88; IlEncRk; NewAmDM; NewGrDA 86; PenEncP; RkOn 78; RolSEnR 83; WhoRock 81; WhoRocM 82*

Rascoe, Burton
American. Journalist, Editor, Critic
Books include *Titans of Literature,* 1932.
b. Oct 22, 1892 in Fulton, Kentucky
d. Mar 19, 1957 in New York, New York
Source: *AmAu&B; BenetAL 91; BiDAmNC; BioIn 1, 4, 9; LiHiK; NotNAT B; OxCAmL 65, 83; REnAL; TwCA, SUP; WhAm 3; WhE&EA; WhThe*

Rashad, Ahmad
[Bobby Moore]
American. Football Player, Sportscaster
Wide receiver, 1972-74, 1976-82, mostly with Minnesota; with NBC Sports, 1982—; husband of Phylicia.
b. Nov 19, 1949 in Portland, Oregon
Source: *BiDAmSp FB; BioIn 13, 14, 15, 16; CelR 90; LegTOT; WhoAfA 96; WhoAm 84, 86, 88, 90, 92, 94, 95, 96, 97; WhoBlA 77, 80, 85, 88, 90, 92, 94; WhoFtbl 74*

Rashad, Phylicia
[Phylicia Ayers-Allen; Mrs. Ahmad Rashad]
American. Actor
Played Claire Huxtable on ''The Cosby Show,'' 1984-92.
b. Jun 19, 1948 in Houston, Texas
Source: *AfrAmAl 6; BioIn 14, 15, 16; BlksAmF; CelR 90; ConNews 87-3; ConTFT 6; DrBlPA 90; IntMPA 92, 94, 96; LegTOT; WhoAfA 96; WhoAm 90; WhoBlA 92, 94; WhoEnt 92; WhoHol 92; WorAlBi*

Rashi
[Shelomoh Yitzhaki]
French. Scholar
Best known for commentaries on Old Testament, Talmud; influenced Christian thinking, Martin Luther.
b. 1040 in Troyes, France
d. Jul 13, 1105 in Troyes, France
Source: *BioIn 14, 17; CasWL; EuAu; EvEuW; JeHun; LuthC 75; McGEWB; RAdv 14, 13-4*

Rashidov, Sharaf Rashidovich
Russian. Editor
Edited *Red Uzbekistan, Lenin's Way,* 1940s.
b. Nov 6, 1917 in Dzhizak, Russia
d. Oct 31, 1983
Source: *ConAu 111; FarE&A 78, 79, 80, 81; IntWW 74, 75, 76, 77, 78, 79, 80, 81, 82, 83; SovUn; WhoSocC 78; WhoWor 74*

Raskin, A(braham) H(enry)
Canadian. Journalist
Reporter, columnist, editor for *NY Times,* 1934-77; regarded as dean of American labor reporters.
b. Apr 26, 1911 in Edmonton, Alberta, Canada
d. Dec 22, 1993 in New York, New York
Source: *ConAu 104, 143; CurBio 78, 94N; EncTwCJ; IntAu&W 89, 91, 93; WhoAm 74, 76, 78, 80, 82, 84, 86, 88, 90*

Raskin, Ellen
American. Children's Author, Illustrator
Won Newbery Medal for self-illustrated *Figgs and Phantoms,* 1975; *The Westing Game,* 1979.
b. Mar 13, 1928 in Milwaukee, Wisconsin
d. Aug 8, 1984 in New York, New York
Source: *ALA 80; BioIn 8, 9, 10, 12, 14, 15, 19; BkP; ChhPo, S1, S2; ChlBkCr; ChlLR 1, 12; ConAu 21R, 37NR, 113; DcLB 52; IlsBYP; IlsCB 1957; IntAu&W 76; MajAI; OxCChiL; SmATA 2, 38; ThrBJA; TwCChW 78, 83, 89; TwCYAW; WhAm 9; WhoAm 80, 82, 84, 86; WhoUSWr 88; WhoWrEP 89; WrDr 80, 82, 84*

Raskin, Judith
American. Opera Singer
Soprano; popular first on TV; NY Met., 1962-72; noted Mozart singer.
b. Jun 21, 1928 in New York, New York
d. Dec 21, 1984 in New York, New York
Source: *AnObit 1984; Baker 78, 84, 92; BioIn 6, 7, 8, 11, 12, 14; CurBio 64, 85, 85N; IntDcOp; IntWWM 77, 80; InWom, SUP; MetOEnc; MusSN; NewAmDM; NewGrDA 86; NewGrDO; NewYTBS 84; PenDiMP; WhAm 8; WhoAm 74, 76, 78, 80, 82, 84; WhoAmM 83; WhoAmW 66, 68, 70, 72, 74, 75; WhoWor 74*

Raskob, John J
American. Businessman
With Pierre du Pont organized E I du Pont de Nemours Co., 1902; as treasurer of GM, 1914, introduced modern accounting, auditing procedures to automotive industry.
b. Mar 19, 1879 in Lockport, New York
d. Oct 14, 1950 in Centreville, Maryland
Source: *DcAmB S4; NatCAB 38; WhAm 3*

Rasmussen, Knud Johan Victor
Danish. Explorer
First to traverse Northwest Passage by dog sled; sought to prove that Eskimos were related to American Indians.
b. Jun 7, 1879, Greenland
d. Dec 21, 1933
Source: *BioIn 5, 11, 14; ConAu 113; InSci; McGEWB; NewCol 75; OxCCan; OxCShps; PenC EUR; REn; SmATA 34; WebBD 83; WhWE*

Raspberries, The
[Jim Bonfanti; Wally Bryson; Eric Carmen; Michael McBride; Scot McCord; David Smalley]
American. Music Group
Formed 1970 in Cleveland; most hits written, sung by Eric Carmen.
Source: *BioIn 16; CelR 90; ConMuA 80A; EncRk 88; PenEncP; RkOn 78; RolSEnR 83; WhoRock 81; WhoRocM 82*

Raspberry, William
American. Journalist
Syndicated columnist for *Washington Post,* 1966—; often writes about minority affairs.
b. Oct 12, 1935 in Okolona, Mississippi
Source: *BioIn 15; BlkWr 1; ConAu 110, 122; ConBlB 2; DcTwCCu 5; EncTwCJ; WhoAm 86, 90; WhoBlA 88, 92; WhoE 86*

Rasputin, Grigori Efimovich
Russian. Religious Figure
Known for strong influence in court of Czar Nicholas II; assassinated.
b. Jan 23, 1871 in Tobolsk, Russia
d. Dec 31, 1916 in Saint Petersburg, Russia
Source: *Dis&D; LngCTC; LuthC 75; NewCol 75; REn; WebBD 83; WorAl*

Ratelle, Jean
[Joseph Gilbert Yvon Jean Ratelle]
Canadian. Hockey Player
Center, NY Rangers, 1960-75, Boston, 1975-81; scored 491 career goals; won Lady Byng Trophy twice.
b. Oct 3, 1940 in Lac Saint Jean, Quebec, Canada
Source: *HocEn; WhoAm 74, 76; WhoHcky 73*

Rathbone, Basil
English. Actor
Played Sherlock Holmes in series of 1930-40s films.
b. Jun 13, 1892 in Johannesburg, South Africa
d. Jul 21, 1967 in New York, New York
Source: *BiDFilm, 81, 94; BiE&WWA; BioIn 2, 3, 6, 8, 9, 10, 14, 15, 16, 17, 21; CmMov; CurBio 51, 67; DcAmB S8; FacFETw; FamA&A; Film 2; FilmEn; FilmgC; ForYSC; HalFC 80, 84, 88; IlWWBF A; IntDcF 1-3, 2-3; ItaFilm; LegTOT; MotPP; MovMk; NotNAT A, B; ObitT 1961; OlFamFa; OxCAmT 84; OxCFilm; PenEncH; RadStar; SaTiSS; ScF&FL 1; WhoHol B; WhoHrs 80; WhScrn 74, 77, 83; WhThe; WorAl; WorAlBi; WorEFlm*

Rathbone, Monroe Jackson
American. Businessman
Pres., chm. of board of Standard Oil Co., 1954-65; developed processes of major importance: cracking process, high octane aviation fuel, synthetic rubber.
b. Mar 1, 1900 in Parkersburg, West Virginia
d. Aug 2, 1976 in Baton Rouge, Louisiana
Source: *BioIn 3, 4, 5, 6, 7, 8, 10, 11, 13; CurBio 57; DcAmB S10; NatCAB 62; WhAm 4, 7; Who 74; WhoAm 74, 76; WhoWor 74*

Rathbun-Nealy, Melissa
American. Soldier
US female soldier captured by Iraqis during Persian Gulf War.
b. 1971 in Grand Rapids, Michigan

Rathenau, Walter
German. Industrialist
Mobilized German production, WW I; assassinated by anti-Semitics.
b. 1867 in Berlin, Germany
d. Jun 24, 1922 in Berlin, Germany
Source: *EncSoA; McGEWB; REn*

Rather, Dan(iel Irvin)
American. Broadcast Journalist
Anchor, "The CBS Evening News," 1981—; co-editor, "60 Minutes," 1975-81; host of "48 Hours," 1988—; winner of ten Emmys.
b. Oct 31, 1931 in Wharton, Texas
Source: *AuNews 1; BioIn 10, 11, 12, 13, 14, 15, 16; BioNews 74; BkPepl; CelR 90; ConAu 9NR, 53; ConTFT 5; CurBio 75; EncAJ; EncTwCJ; IntAu&W 89, 91, 93; IntMPA 86, 92, 94, 96; IntWW 83, 89, 91, 93; JrnUS; LegTOT; LesBEnT 92; PolProf NF; VarWW 85; WhoAm 76, 78, 80, 82, 84, 86, 88, 90, 92, 94, 95, 96, 97; WhoAmP 95; WhoE 85, 86, 89, 91; WorAlBi*

Ratoff, Gregory
American. Actor, Director
Directed *Intermezzo,* 1939; starred in *Seventh Heaven,* 1937; *All About Eve,* 1950.
b. Apr 20, 1893 in Saint Petersburg, Russia
d. Dec 14, 1960 in Solothurn, Switzerland
Source: *BiDFilm; CurBio 43, 61; FilmgC; MotPP; MovMk; NotNAT B; Vers A; WhAm 4; WhScrn 77; WhThe*

Ratsiraka, Didier
Political Leader
Pres. of Madagascar since 1976.
b. Nov 4, 1936 in Vatomandry, Madagascar
Source: *AfSS 78, 79, 80, 81, 82; BioIn 21; IntWW 74, 75, 76, 77, 78, 79, 80, 81, 82, 83, 89, 91, 93; IntYB 79, 80, 81, 82; WhoAfr; WhoWor 78, 80, 82, 84, 87, 89, 91, 93*

Rattigan, Terence Mervyn, Sir
English. Dramatist
Wrote *The Windslow Boy,* 1946; *Separate Tables,* 1956.
b. Jun 10, 1911 in Cornwall Gardens, England
d. Nov 30, 1977 in Hamilton, Bermuda
Source: *Au&Wr 71; BiE&WWA; BioIn 1, 2, 4, 5, 7, 10, 11, 12, 13; CasWL; CnMD; CnThe; ConAu 73, 85; ConBrDr; ConDr 73, 93; ConLC 7; CroCD; CurBio 56, 78; DcLEL; DcNaB 1971; EvLB; GayLL; GrBr; GrWrEL DR; IntDcT 2; IntWW 74, 75, 76, 77; LngCTC; McGEWD 72; ModBrL; NewC; NewCBEL; OxCEng 85, 95; OxCFilm; OxCThe 83; PenC ENG; REn; TwCWr; WebE&AL; WhE&EA; WhoTwCL; WorAl; WorAlBi; WorAu 1950; WrDr 76*

Rattle, Simon
English. Conductor
Controversial conductor of Birmingham Symphony Orchestra, 1980-91; music director of city of Birmingham Symphony Orchestra, 1991—.
b. Jan 19, 1955 in Liverpool, England
Source: *Baker 84; BioIn 13, 14, 15, 16; CurBio 88; DcArts; IntWW 82, 83, 89, 91, 93; IntWWM 90; NewAmDM; NewGrDM 80; News 89; NewYTBS 85, 92; OxDcOp; PenDiMP; Who 82, 83, 85, 88, 90, 92, 94; WhoAm 90, 92, 94, 95, 96, 97; WhoAmM 83; WhoEnt 92; WhoWest 92; WhoWor 82, 87, 89, 91, 95, 97*

Rattner, Abraham
American. Artist
Paintings known for intense, vivid colors depicting religious or moral themes.
b. Jul 8, 1895 in Poughkeepsie, New York
d. Feb 14, 1978 in New York, New York
Source: *BioIn 1, 4, 5, 6, 11; BriEAA; ConArt 77; CurBio 48, 78, 78N; DcAmArt; DcCAA 71, 77, 88, 94; McGDA; NewYTBS 78; ObitOF 79; PhDcTCA 77; PrintW 83, 85; WhAm 7; WhAmArt 85; WhoAm 74, 76, 78, 80; WhoAmA 73, 76, 78N, 80N, 82N, 84N, 86N, 89N, 91N, 93N; WhoWor 74; WorArt 1950*

Ratushinskaya, Irina
American. Poet
KGB political prisoner, 1983-86; wrote hundreds of poems in confinement; memoir of prison life, *Grey Is the Colour of Hope,* published in 1988.
b. Mar 4, 1954 in Odessa, Union of Soviet Socialist Republics
Source: *BiDSovU; BioIn 15, 16; ConAu 129; ConLC 54; ContDcW 89; CurBio 88; DcArts; EncCoWW; FacFETw; IntWW 89, 91; LiExTwC; ModWoWr; NewYTBS 87; RadHan; RAdv 14; WorAu 1980*

Ratzenberger, John Dezso
American. Actor
Played Clifford Claven in TV series "Cheers," 1982-93.
b. Apr 6, 1947 in Bridgeport, Connecticut
Source: *ConTFT 3; WhoAm 86, 88, 90, 92; WhoEnt 92; WorAlBi*

Ratzinger, Joseph Alois, Cardinal
German. Religious Leader
Heads Sacred Congregation for the Defense of Faith, a Vatican agency.
b. Apr 16, 1927 in Marktyl am Inn, Germany
Source: *BioIn 16; CurBio 86; IntWW 82, 83, 89, 91, 93; NewYTBS 85; WhoRel 92; WhoWor 82, 84, 87, 89, 91, 95, 96, 97*

Rau, Dhanvanthi Rama, Lady
[Dhanvanthi Handoo]
Indian. Feminist
Pres. of International Planned Parenthood Federation, 1963-71; mother of Santha Rama Rau.
b. May 10, 1893 in Hubli, India
d. Jul 19, 1987 in Bombay, India
Source: *BioIn 15; ContDcW 89; CurBio 54, 87, 87N; FacFETw; IntDcWB; IntWW 74, 75, 76, 77, 78, 79, 80, 81, 82, 83; NewYTBS 87*

Rauh, Joseph Louis, Jr.
American. Lawyer, Political Activist
Cofounder, Americans for Democratic Action, 1946; behind-the-scenes leader of NAACP.
b. Jan 3, 1911 in Cincinnati, Ohio
d. Sep 3, 1992 in Washington, District of Columbia
Source: *BioIn 5, 7, 9, 10, 11, 12, 14, 15; NewYTBS 85; WhoAm 88, 90; WhoAmL 85; WhoAmP 91*

Rausch, James Stevens
American. Religious Leader
Bishop of Phoenix, 1977-81.
b. Sep 4, 1928 in Albany, Minnesota
d. May 18, 1981 in Phoenix, Arizona
Source: *AmCath 80; NewYTBS 81; WhoAm 76, 78, 80; WhoRel 75, 77*

Rauschenberg, Robert
[Milton Rauschenberg]
American. Artist
Collages, called "combines," include *Gloria,* 1956; *Summer Rental,* 1960.
b. Oct 22, 1925 in Port Arthur, Texas
Source: *AmArt; AmCulL; AmDec 1960; Benet 87, 96; BiDD; BiDrAC; BioIn 4, 5, 6, 7, 8, 9, 10, 11, 12, 13, 14, 15, 17, 18, 19, 20; BlueB 76; BriEAA; CelR, 90; CenC; CmpGMD; CnOxB; ConArt 77, 83, 89, 96; ConDr 77E; ConPhot 88, 95; CurBio 65, 87; DcAmArt; DcArts; DcCAA 71, 77, 88, 94; DcCAr 81; DcTwCCu 1; EncAB-H 1974, 1996; FacFETw; ICPEnP A; IntDcAA 90; IntWW 74, 75, 76, 77, 78, 79, 80, 81, 82, 83, 89, 91, 93; LegTOT; MakMC; McGDA; McGEWB; ModArCr 1; News 91, 91-2; NewYTBS 81; OxCArt; OxCTwCA; OxDcArt; PhDcTCA 77; PrintW 83, 85; WebAB 74, 79; WhDW; WhoAm 74, 76, 78, 80, 82, 84, 86, 90, 92, 94, 95, 96, 97; WhoAmA 73, 76, 78, 80, 82, 84, 86, 89, 91, 93; WhoE 74; WhoWor 74, 76, 78, 84, 87, 89, 91, 93, 95; WorAlBi; WorArt 1950*

Rauschenbusch, Walter
American. Theologian
Socialist leader of Social Gospel movement, 1900s; wrote *Christianity and the Social Crisis,* 1907.
b. Oct 4, 1861 in Rochester, New York
d. Jul 25, 1918 in Rochester, New York
Source: *AmAu&B; AmDec 1910; AmRef; AmSocL; BiDAmLf; BioIn 2, 3, 4, 6, 7, 10, 12, 14, 15, 16, 19; DcAmB; DcAmReB 1, 2; DcNAA; EncAB-H 1974, 1996; EncARH; EncSoB; LuthC 75; McGEWB; NatCAB 19; OxCAmH; OxCAmL 65, 83, 95; PeoHis; RelLAm 91; REnAL; ThTwC 87; WebAB 74, 79; WhAm 1*

Raushenbush, Stephen
American. Military Leader
Helped develop battle plan to defeat German U-boats, WW II.
b. 1896 in New York, New York
d. Jul 4, 1991 in Sarasota, Florida
Source: *AmAu&B; AmMWSc 73S; BioIn 17; NewYTBS 91; WhAm 10*

Ravaillac, Francois
French. Assassin
Assassinated Henry IV of France May 14, 1610; executed for crime.
b. 1578 in Angouleme, France
d. May 27, 1610
Source: *BioIn 21; DcBiPP; Dis&D; OxCFr*

Ravel, Maurice Joseph
French. Composer
Best known for ballet *Bolero,* 1928, used as theme for movie *10,* 1981.
b. Mar 7, 1875 in Ciboure, France
d. Dec 28, 1937 in Paris, France
Source: *AtlBL; Benet 96; DcCM; NewCol 75; OxCFr; REn; WebBD 83; WorAl*

Raven, Peter H(amilton)
American. Botanist
Director, Missouri Botanical Garden, 1971—; spoke out about the causes and consequences of the degradation of the environment.
b. Jun 13, 1936 in Shanghai, China
Source: *AmMWSc 76P, 79, 82, 86, 89, 92, 95; BioIn 12, 13; CurBio 94; IntWW 89, 91, 93; WhoAm 76, 78, 80, 82, 86, 88, 90, 92, 94, 95, 96, 97; WhoFrS 84; WhoMW 80, 82, 84, 86, 90, 93; WhoScEn 96*

Rawl, Lawrence G
American. Business Executive
Chm., CEO, Exxon Corp., 1986-93.
b. May 4, 1928 in Lyndhurst, New Jersey
Source: *BioIn 15; CurBio 92; Dun&B 90; IntWW 91; St&PR 91; WhoAm 90; WhoFI 89; WhoWor 91*

Rawlings, Jerry John
Ghanaian. Political Leader
Led three military coups to overthrow govt., 1979-81; head of state, 1982—; cmdr. in chief of Armed Forces, 1982—.
b. Jun 22, 1947 in Accra, Gold Coast
Source: *AfSS 80, 81, 82; BioIn 13, 14, 15; CurBio 82; DcAfHiB 86; DcTwHis; EncRev; IntWW 83, 91; NewYTBS 82; WhoAfr; WhoWor 84, 87, 89, 91, 93, 95, 96, 97*

Rawlings, Marjorie Kinnan
American. Author
Won 1939 Pulitzer for *The Yearling;* filmed, 1946.
b. Aug 8, 1896 in Washington, District of Columbia
d. Dec 14, 1953 in Saint Augustine, Florida
Source: *AmAu&B; AmNov; AmWomWr; ArtclWW 2; Benet 87, 96; BenetAL 91; BioAmW; BioIn 14, 15, 16, 17, 19, 20; BlmGWL; ChlBkCr; CnDAL; ConAu 104, 137; CurBio 42, 54; CyWA 58; DcAmB S5; DcLB 9, 22, 102; DcLEL; EvLB; FacFETw; FifSWrA; GrWrEL N; InWom; LegTOT; LibW; LinLib L; LngCTC; MajAI; ModAL; ModWoWr; NotAW MOD; Novels; OxCAmL 65, 83, 95; OxCWoWr 95; PenC AM; PeoHis; REn; REnAL; RfGAmL 87, 94; SouWr; ThrBJA; TwCA, SUP; TwCChW 78, 83, 89; TwCLC 4; TwCWr; TwCYAW; WhAm 3; WorAl; WrChl; YABC 1*

Rawlins, John A
American. Army Officer
General Grant's advisor; army chief of staff, 1865; town in WY is named in his honor.
b. Feb 13, 1831 in Galena, Illinois
d. Sep 6, 1869 in Washington, District of Columbia
Source: *AmBi; ApCAB; BiAUS; BiDrUSE 71; DcAmB; DcBiPP; Drake; NatCAB 4; TwCBDA; WhAm HS*

Rawlinson, Herbert
English. Actor
Screen career, 1911-51; films include *Count of Monte Cristo; Swiss Family Robinson.*
b. Nov 15, 1883 in Brighton, England
d. Jul 12, 1953 in Woodland Hills, California
Source: *CanWW 70; Film 1; MotPP; MovMk; TwYS; WhoHol B; WhScrn 74, 77*

Rawls, Betsy
[Elizabeth Earle Rawls]
American. Golfer
Turned pro, 1951; won US Women's Open, four times, LPGA twice; leading money winner, 1952, 1959.
b. May 4, 1928 in Spartanburg, South Carolina
Source: *BiDAmSp OS; BioIn 15; EncWomS; InWom SUP; WhoGolf; WhoSpor*

Rawls, Lou(is Allen)
American. Singer
Began career as gospel singer; known for smooth, love ballads including "You'll Never Find," 1976, "Lady Love," 1978; has won numerous Grammys.
b. Dec 1, 1936 in Chicago, Illinois
Source: *AfrAmBi 1; Baker 84, 92; BiDAfM; BiDJaz; BioIn 13, 14, 15; BkPepl; CelR 90; CurBio 84; DrBlPA 90; EncPR&S 89; IlEncBM 82; InB&W 85; NegAl 89; NewAmDM; PenEncP;*

RkOn 78; VarWW 85; WhoAfA 96; WhoAm 80, 82, 84, 86, 88, 90, 92, 94; WhoBlA 80, 85, 88, 90, 92, 94; WhoEnt 92; WhoHol A; WhoRock 81; WhoWest 74; WorAl; WorAlBi

Ray, Aldo
[Aldo DaRe]
American. Actor
Played tough guy roles since 1951 in films *Green Berets; The Naked and the Dead.*
b. Sep 25, 1926 in Pen Argyl, Pennsylvania
d. Mar 27, 1991 in Martinez, California
Source: *AnObit 1991; BiDFilm, 81, 94; BioIn 2, 17, 18; ConTFT 1, 8, 9; FilmEn; FilmgC; ForYSC; GangFlm; HalFC 80, 84, 88; IntMPA 75, 76, 77, 78, 79, 80, 81, 82, 84, 86, 88; ItaFilm; LegTOT; MotPP; MovMk; NewYTBS 91; OxCFilm; VarWW 85; WhoHol A; WorAl; WorAlBi; WorEFlm*

Ray, Charles
American. Actor
Star of 118 silent, talking films, including *Nobody's Widow,* 1927.
b. Mar 15, 1891 in Jacksonville, Illinois
d. Nov 23, 1943 in Los Angeles, California
Source: *BioIn 11; CurBio 44; Film 1, 2; FilmEn; FilmgC; ForYSC; HalFC 80, 84, 88; MotPP; MovMk; NotNAT B; SilFlmP; TwYS, A; WhoHol B; WhScrn 74, 77, 83*

Ray, Charlotte E
American. Lawyer
First female African American lawyer in the US.
b. Jan 13, 1850 in New York, New York
d. Jan 4, 1911 in Woodside, New York
Source: *InB&W 85; InWom SUP; NotAW*

Ray, Dixy Lee
[Margaret Ray]
American. Politician, Zoologist
Dem. governor of WA, 1977-81; received UN Peace Medal, 1973; wrote *Trashing the Planet,* 1990.
b. Sep 3, 1914 in Tacoma, Washington
d. Jan 2, 1994 in Fox Island, Washington
Source: *AlmAP 78, 80; AmMWSc 73P, 76P; AmPolW 80; AmWomM; AmWomSc; BiDrGov 1789, 1978; BioIn 6, 9, 10, 11, 12; BioNews 74; BlueB 76; CelR; ConAu 134, 143; CurBio 73, 94N; EncWB; GoodHs; IntWW 74, 75, 76, 77, 78, 79, 80, 81, 82, 83, 89, 91, 93; IntYB 78, 79, 80, 81, 82; InWom, SUP; LegTOT; LibW; LinLib S; NewYTBE 73; NotTwCS; WhoAm 74, 76, 78, 80, 82; WhoAmP 75, 77, 79, 81, 83; WhoAmW 58, 61, 79, 81, 83; WhoGov 75, 77; WhoWest 78, 80, 82; WomPO 78; WorAl; WorAlBi; WrDr 94, 96*

Ray, Edward
English. Golfer
Touring pro, first half of 20th c., won British Open, 1912, US Open, 1920.
b. Mar 28, 1877 in Isle of Jersey, England
d. Aug 28, 1943 in London, England
Source: *WhoGolf*

Ray, Elizabeth
American. Secretary
Worked for Con. Wayne Hays; kept on payroll as mistress.
b. 1942
Source: *BioIn 10, 11*

Ray, James Earl
American. Assassin
Killed Martin Luther King, Jr., April 4, 1968; sentenced to 99 years in prison.
b. Mar 10, 1928 in Alton, Illinois
Source: *BioIn 8, 9, 10, 11, 12, 13, 15, 16, 17; CivRSt; LegTOT; PolProf J*

Ray, John
[John Wray]
English. Botanist
Known for his contributions to taxonomy.
b. Nov 29, 1627 in Black Notley, England
d. Jan 17, 1705 in Black Notley, England
Source: *Alli; BiESc; BioIn 2, 3, 4, 7, 11, 12, 14, 15; CamDcSc; CasWL; Chambr 2; DcEnL; DcLEL; DcNaB, C; DcScB; EvLB; InSci; LarDcSc; LinLib L; McGEWB; NewC; NewCBEL; OxCEng 67, 85, 95*

Ray, Johnnie
[John Alvin Ray]
"The Prince of Wails"
American. Singer
Emotionally charged 1950s singing idol; had number 1 hit single, "Cry," 1952.
b. Jan 10, 1927 in Dallas, Oregon
d. Feb 24, 1990 in Los Angeles, California
Source: *AnObit 1990; ASCAP 66, 80; Baker 92; BiDAmM; BioIn 16, 17, 21; EncRk 88; FilmgC; HalFC 80, 84, 88; LegTOT; NewAmDM; NewGrDA 86; NewYTBS 90; OxCPMus; PenEncP; RkOn 74; RolSEnR 83; VarWW 85; WhoHol A; WorAl; WorAlBi*

Ray, Man
American. Artist, Photographer
Co-founded Dadaism, 1917; developed rayograph photographical technique.
b. Aug 27, 1890 in Philadelphia, Pennsylvania
d. Nov 18, 1976 in Paris, France
Source: *Benet 87, 96; BioIn 5, 6, 7, 8, 9, 10, 11, 12, 13, 14, 15, 16, 17, 20; BriEAA; ConAu 29NR, 69, 77; CurBio 65, 77N; DcAmArt; DcFM; DcTwCCu 2; DcTwDes; EncFash; FacFETw; Film 2; FilmEn; FilmgC; HalFC 80, 84, 88; ICPEnP; IntDcAA 90; IntWW 74, 75, 76; MakMC; McGDA; McGEWB; MiSFD 9N; NewYTBE 70, 72; NewYTBS 76, 88; OxCFilm; PeoHis; PhDcTCA 77; REn; WebAB 74, 79; WhAmArt 85; WorAl; WorAlBi; WorArt 1950*

Ray, Nicholas
[Raymond N Kienzle]
American. Director
Films include *They Live By Night,* 1948; *Rebel Without a Cause,* 1955.
b. Aug 7, 1911 in La Crosse, Wisconsin
d. Jun 16, 1979 in New York, New York
Source: *Alli, 78, 79; ItaFilm; LegTOT; MiSFD 9N; MovMk; NewYTBE 72; OxCFilm; WhScrn 83; WorEFlm; WorFDir 2*

Ray, Robert D
American. Politician
Rep. governor of Iowa, 1969-83.
b. Sep 26, 1928 in Des Moines, Iowa
Source: *AlmAP 82; BioIn 15; CurBio 77; Dun&B 90; IntWW 91; WhoAm 82, 90; WhoAmP 87, 91; WhoAmW 72, 74, 75, 77, 81; WhoMW 74, 76, 78, 80, 82, 90*

Ray, Satyajit
Indian. Director
India's best-known filmmaker; works include trilogy about Bengali village life, *World of Apu,* 1960; won Oscar for lifetime achievement, 1992; 2 awards for *Agantuck* from Nat. Film Festival in New Delhi, 1992.
b. May 2, 1921 in Calcutta, India
d. Apr 23, 1992 in Calcutta, India
Source: *AnObit 1992; Benet 87, 96; BiDFilm, 81, 94; BioIn 5, 6, 7, 8, 9, 10, 12, 13, 14, 15, 16; ConAu 114, 137; ConLC 16, 76; ConTFT 11; CurBio 61, 92N; DcArts; DcFM; DrIndFM; FarE&A 78, 79, 80, 81; FilmEn; FilmgC; HalFC 80, 84, 88; IntDcF 1-2, 2-2; IntMPA 84, 86, 88, 92; IntWW 74, 75, 76, 78, 79, 80, 81, 82, 83, 89, 91; LegTOT; MakMC; McGEWB; MiSFD 9; MovMk; NewYTBE 73; NewYTBS 92; OxCFilm; VarWW 85; WhAm 10; Who 74, 82, 83, 85, 88, 90, 92; WhoWor 74, 76, 78, 82, 84, 87, 89, 91; WorEFlm; WorFDir 2*

Ray, Shorty
[Hugh Ray]
American. Football Executive
NFL supervisor of officials, technical advisor, 1938-56; Hall of Fame, 1966.
b. Sep 21, 1884 in Highland Park, Illinois
d. Sep 16, 1956
Source: *BioIn 1, 8, 17; WhoFtbl 74*

Rayburn, Gene
[Eugene Rubessa]
American. TV Personality
Best known as host of TV game shows including "Match Game PM," 1975, 1983-84.
b. Dec 22, 1917 in Christopher, Illinois
Source: *ConTFT 3; IntMPA 86, 92, 94, 96; LegTOT; LesBEnT, 92; VarWW 85; WhoAm 74, 76, 86, 88; WhoEnt 92; WorAl*

Rayburn, Sam(uel Taliaferro)
"Mr. Democrat"
American. Politician
Dem. Speaker of House for periods from 1940-61.
b. Jan 6, 1882 in Roane County, Tennessee
d. Nov 16, 1961 in Bonham, Texas
Source: *AmPolLe; BiDrUSC 89; BioIn 1, 2, 3, 4, 5, 6, 7, 8, 9, 10, 11, 12, 13, 14, 15, 16, 18, 19, 21; CurBio 40, 49, 62; DcAmB S7; EncAAH; EncAB-H 1974, 1996; EncSoH; FacFETw; LegTOT; McGEWB; NewCol 75; ObitT 1961; OxCAmH; WebAB 74, 79; WhAm 4; WhAmP; WorAl; WorAlBi*

Raye, Martha
[Margaret Teresa Yvonne Reed]
American. Comedian, Singer
Known for wide-mouthed zaniness; in films from 1936; won special Oscar, 1968.
b. Aug 27, 1916 in Butte, Montana
d. Oct 19, 1994 in Los Angeles, California
Source: *BiDAmM; BiE&WWA; BioIn 2, 3, 6, 9, 10, 11, 14, 15, 16, 18, 20, 21; BioNews 74; CelR; CmpEPM; ConTFT 4, 14; CurBio 63, 95N; EncAFC; EncMT; EncVaud; FilmEn; FilmgC; ForYSC; FunnyW; Funs; GoodHs; HalFC 80, 84, 88; IntMPA 77, 80, 84, 86, 88, 92, 94; InWom, SUP; JoeFr; LegTOT; LesBEnT 92; MotPP; MovMk; News 95, 95-1; NewYTBE 72; NewYTBS 85, 94; NewYTET; ThFT; VarWW 85; WhoAm 74, 76, 78, 80, 82, 84; WhoAmW 68, 70, 72, 74, 81, 83; WhoCom; WhoHol 92, A; WhoThe 72, 77, 81; WorAl; WorAlBi*

Rayleigh, John William Strutt, Baron
English. Physicist, Educator
Won 1904 Nobel Prize for co-discovering argon; pioneered in molecular acoustics.
b. Nov 12, 1842 in Essex, England
d. Jun 30, 1919 in Witham, England
Source: *AsBiEn; BiESc; BioIn 3, 4, 8, 12, 13, 14, 20; CamDcSc; DcInv; ICPEnP; InSci; LarDcSc; LinLib S; McGEWB; NamesHP; NewCol 75; NewGrDM 80; WorAl*

Raymond, Alex(ander Gillespie)
American. Cartoonist
Best known for characters: Flash Gordon, Jungle Jim.
b. Oct 2, 1909 in New Rochelle, New York
d. Sep 6, 1956 in Westport, Connecticut
Source: *BiDScF; BioIn 2, 4, 15; ConAu 112; DcAmB S6; EncACom; EncSF, 93; LegTOT; ScF&FL 1; WhAm 3; WhAmArt 85; WorECom*

Raymond, Gene
American. Actor
Married Jeanette MacDonald, 1937-65; leading man in B-pictures, 1940s-50s.
b. Aug 13, 1908 in New York, New York
Source: *BiDAmM; BiE&WWA; BioIn 10, 11; ConTFT 7; EncAFC; FilmEn; FilmgC; ForYSC; HalFC 80, 84, 88; HolP 30; IntMPA 75, 76, 77, 78, 79, 80, 81, 82, 84, 86, 88, 92, 94, 96; LegTOT; MotPP; MovMk; VarWW 85; What 5; WhoAm 74, 76, 78, 80, 82, 84, 86, 88, 90, 96; WhoEnt 92; WhoHol 92, A; WhoThe 72, 77, 81; WhoWest 84, 87, 89; WhoWor 78, 80, 82, 84, 87, 89; WorAl; WorAlBi*

Raymond, Henry Jarvis
American. Politician, Editor
Co-founder, editor, NY *Times,* 1851-69; a founder of Republican Party, 1856.
b. Jan 24, 1820 in Lima, New York
d. Jun 18, 1869 in New York, New York
Source: *Alli; AmAu; AmAu&B; AmBi; AmLegL; ApCAB; BbD; BenetAL 91; BiAUS; BiDAmJo; BiD&SB; BiDrAC; BiDrUSC 89; BioIn 2, 9, 10, 13, 15, 16, 17; CyAL 2; DcAmAu; DcAmB; DcNAA; Drake; HarEnUS; LegTOT; NatCAB 8; OxCAmH; OxCAmL 65, 83, 95; REnAL; TwCBDA; WebAB 74, 79; WhAm HS; WhAmP*

Raymond, James C
American. Cartoonist
Worked on "Blondie" for over 40 yrs.
b. Feb 25, 1917 in Riverside, Connecticut
d. Oct 14, 1981 in Boynton Beach, Florida
Source: *BioIn 12, 13; NewYTBS 81*

Rayner, Chuck
[Claude Earl Rayner]
Canadian. Hockey Player
Goalie, 1940-53, mostly with NY Rangers; won Hart Trophy, 1950; Hall of Fame, 1973.
b. Aug 11, 1920 in Sutherland, Saskatchewan, Canada
Source: *WhoHcky 73; WhoSpor*

Rayner, Claire Berenice
[Sheila Brandon]
English. Author
Former nurse who writes nonfiction books on medicine, sex.
b. Jan 22, 1931 in London, England
Source: *Au&Wr 71; BioIn 14; ConAu 13NR, 30NR; DcLP 87A; IntAu&W 91; InWom SUP; PenNWW A, B; TwCRGW; TwCRHW 90; Who 85, 92; WrDr 86, 92*

Rea, Gardner
American. Cartoonist
One of the original contributors to *New Yorker* mag., 1925; works characterized by minimal detail, wiggly lines.
b. Aug 12, 1892 in Ironton, Ohio
d. Dec 27, 1966 in Long Island, New York
Source: *AmAu&B; BioIn 1, 7, 8; ConAu 93; CurBio 46, 67; WhAm 4; WorECar*

Read, Albert Cushing
American. Naval Officer, Aviator
Rear admiral, 1941-46; commanded first Atlantic crossing in air, from Newfoundland to Portugal, via Azores, May 1919.
b. Mar 29, 1887 in Lyme, New Hampshire
d. Oct 10, 1967 in Miami, Florida
Source: *BiDWWGF; BioIn 8, 9; InSci; NatCAB 53; ObitOF 79; WebAMB; WhAm 4, 4A, 8*

Read, George
American. Continental Congressman, Lawyer
Signed Declaration of Independence, 1776; helped Delaware become first state to ratify Constitution.
b. Sep 18, 1733 in North East, Maryland
d. Sep 21, 1798 in New Castle, Delaware
Source: *Alli; AmBi; ApCAB; BiAUS; BiDrAC; BiDrACR; BiDrUSC 89; BioIn 7, 8, 9, 15, 16; DcAmB; Drake; EncAR; EncCRAm; EncSoH; HarEnUS; NatCAB 3; TwCBDA; WebAB 74, 79; WhAm HS; WhAmP; WhAmRev*

Read, Herbert, Sir
English. Poet, Critic
Interpreted modern British art from 1930; wrote *The Innocent Eye,* 1933.
b. Dec 4, 1893 in Kirbymoorside, England
d. Jun 12, 1968 in Malton, England
Source: *Benet 87; BioIn 12, 13; CamGLE; CasWL; CnE&AP; ConAu 25R, 85; ConLC 4; CurBio 62, 68; DcArts; DcLB 20, 149; DcLEL; DcTwDes; EncSF; EncWL 2, 3; EngPo; EvLB; LegTOT; LinLib L; LngCTC; McGDA; NewC; ObitT 1961; OxCTwCA; OxDcArt; PenC ENG; REn; RfGEnL 91; ScF&FL 1; ScFSB; ThTwC 87; TwCA; WhAm 5; WhDW; WhE&EA; WhLit; WhoLA*

Read, Mary
English. Pirate
Companion of Anne Bonny; member of the crew of pirate Capt. Rackam.
b. 1692, England
d. Dec 4, 1720, Jamaica
Source: *EncAmaz 91; GayLesB*

Read, Piers Paul
English. Author
Non-fiction works include *Alive: The Story of the Andes Survivors,* 1974.
b. Mar 7, 1941 in Beaconsfield, England
Source: *Au&Wr 71; BioIn 12, 13, 19; ConAu 21R, 38NR; ConDr 73, 77B; ConLC 4, 10, 25; ConNov 76, 82, 86, 91, 96; DcLB 14; DcLEL 1940; IntAu&W 76, 77, 82, 86, 89, 91, 93; IntWW 89, 91, 93; Novels; RGTwCWr; ScF&FL 92; SmATA 21; Who 74, 82, 83, 85, 88, 90, 92, 94; WhoAm 82, 84, 86, 88, 90, 92, 94, 95, 96, 97; WorAu 1970; WrDr 76, 80, 82, 84, 86, 88, 90, 92, 94, 96*

Read, Thomas Buchanan
American. Poet, Artist
Noted for verse *Sheridan's Ride,* 1865.
b. Mar 12, 1822 in Corner Ketch, Pennsylvania
d. May 11, 1872 in New York, New York
Source: *Alli; AmAu; AmAu&B; AmBi; ApCAB; ArtsNiC; BbD; BenetAL 91; BibAL; BiD&SB; BioIn 2, 13; Chambr 3; ChhPo, S1; CnDAL; CyAL 2; DcAmArt; DcAmAu; DcAmB; DcBiPP; DcLEL; DcNAA; DcVicP 2; Drake; EvLB; HarEnUS; IlBEAAW; LinLib L, S; NatCAB 6; NewYHSD; OhA&B; OxCAmL 65, 83, 95; REnAL; TwCBDA; WhAm HS*

Reade, Charles
English. Author, Dramatist
Wrote classic *The Cloister and the Hearth,* 1861.
b. Jun 8, 1814 in Ipsden, England
d. Apr 11, 1884 in London, England
Source: *Alli, SUP; AtlBL; BbD; Benet 87, 96; BiD&SB; BioIn 1, 2, 5, 6, 8, 10, 11, 12, 14, 16; BlmGEL; BritAu 19; CamGEL; CamGLE; CamGWoT; CasWL; CelCen; Chambr 3; CyWA 58; DcArts; DcBiA; DcBiPP; DcEnA; DcEnL; DcEuL; DcLB 21; DcLEL; DcNaB; Dis&D; EncWT; EvLB; GrWrEL N; HsB&A; IntDcT 2; LinLib L, S; MouLC 4; NewC; NewCBEL; NinCLC 2; NotNAT A, B; Novels; OxCAusL; OxCEng 67, 85, 95; OxCThe 67, 83; PenC ENG; RAdv 1, 14, 13-1; REn; RfGEnL 91; StaCVF; VicBrit; WebE&AL; WorAl; WorAlBi*

Ready, William Bernard
Canadian. Educator, Librarian, Author
Books on Tolkein include *Notes on Tolkein,* 1972.
b. Sep 16, 1914 in Cardiff, Wales
Source: *BiDrLUS 70; BioIn 2, 3, 4, 6, 7; BkC 6; CanWW 70; CathA 1952; ConAu 22NR; DrLC 69; IntAu&W 76, 77, 82; WhoAm 74, 76, 78, 80; WhoE 74; WhoLibI 82; WhoLibS 55; WrDr 76, 80, 82, 84, 86, 88*

Reagan, Maureen Elizabeth
[Mrs. Dennis Revell]
American. Politician
Daughter of Ronald Reagan, Jane Wyman; active in CA politics.
b. Jan 4, 1941 in Los Angeles, California
Source: *BioIn 12, 14, 15, 16; WhoAmW 91*

Reagan, Michael Edward
American. Businessman
Adopted son of Ronald Reagan, Jane Wyman; California-based radio show host.
b. Mar 18, 1946 in Los Angeles, California
Source: *BioIn 12, 13, 14, 15, 16*

Reagan, Nancy Davis
[Anne Frances Robbins]
American. First Lady
Appeared in high school play *First Lady,* 1939; last movie *Hellcats* with Ronald Reagan, 1957; active in anti-drug campaign.
b. Jul 6, 1921 in New York, New York
Source: *BioAmW; BioIn 13, 14, 15, 16; BioNews 74; BkPepl; CelR 90; ConAu 33NR, 110; CurBio 82; IntWW 91, 93; InWom SUP; NewYTBE 71; NewYTBS 80, 88; WhoAm 86; WhoAmW 87, 91; WhoE 89; WhoWest 74, 92; WhoWor 87, 91; WorAlBi; WrDr 92*

Reagan, Ronald Prescott
American.
Son of Ronald, Nancy Reagan; former ballet dancer for Joffrey Ballet Co., 1980-83; reporter for "Good Morning America," 1986-90; host of "The Ron Reagan Show," 1991-92.
b. May 20, 1958 in Los Angeles, California
Source: *BioIn 11, 12, 14, 15, 16; CurBio 92*

Reagan, Ronald (Wilson)
"Dutch"; "The Gipper"; "The Great Communicator"
American. US President
40th pres., Rep., 1981-89; applied "Reaganomics" to spur economy; known for conservative policies and appointments; oldest, first divorced president in office. Diagnosed with Alzheimer's disease, 1994.
b. Feb 6, 1911 in Tampico, Illinois
Source: *AmDec 1980; AmJust; AmOrTwC; AmPolLe; Ballpl 90; Benet 87; BenetAL 91; BestSel 90-1; BiDAmL; BiDAmLL; BiDFilm 94; BiDrGov 1789; BiDrUSE 89; BioIn 2, 3, 7, 8, 9, 10, 11, 12, 13, 14, 15, 16, 17, 18, 19, 20, 21; BlueB 76; CelR, 90; CmCal; CngDr 81, 83, 85, 87; ColdWar 1, 2; ConAu 47NR, 85; CurBio 49, 67, 82; DcAmC; DcTwHis; EncAB-H 1974, 1996; EncAFC; EncCW; EncMcCE; EncWB; FacFETw; FacPr 89, 93; FilmEn; FilmgC; GangFlm; HalFC 80, 84, 88; HealPre; HisEAAC; IntDcF 1-3, 2-3; IntMPA 82, 84, 86, 88, 92, 94, 96; IntWW 74, 75, 76, 77, 78, 79, 80, 81, 82, 83, 89, 91, 93; IntYB 78, 79, 80, 81, 82; LegTOT; LesBEnT, 92; LinLib S; MovMk; NatCAB 63N; NewYTBE 70; NewYTBS 74, 79, 80, 84, 87; OxCAmL 83; OxCSupC; PeoHis; PolProf J; RComAH; Who 82, 83, 85, 88, 90, 92, 94; WhoAm 74, 76, 78, 80, 82, 84, 86, 88, 90, 92, 94, 95, 96, 97; WhoAmP 73, 75, 77, 79, 81, 83, 85, 87, 89, 91, 93, 95; WhoE 81, 83, 85, 86, 89; WhoGov 72, 75, 77; WhoHol 92; WhoWest 74, 76, 89, 92, 94, 96; WhoWor 74, 76, 78, 80, 82, 84, 87, 89, 91, 93, 95, 96, 97; WorAl; WorAlBi; WorEFlm*

Reagon, Bernice Johnson
American. Musician, Museum Director
Founder of folk-music group, Sweet Honey in the Rock, 1973—; curator, National Museum of American History, Smithsonian Institution, 1988-93.
b. Oct 4, 1942 in Albany, Georgia
Source: *AmWomHi; BioIn 12, 14, 18, 20; ConAu 147; ConBlB 7; NotBlAW 1; RadHan; WhoAfA 96; WhoAm 92; WhoAmW 66; WhoBlA 92, 94*

Reagon, Toshi
American. Musician
Albums include *Demonstrations,* 1985; *The Rejected Stone,* 1994.
b. Jan 27, 1964
Source: *GayLesB*

Reard, Louis
French. Fashion Designer
Introduced two-piece bathing suit, the bikini, 1946.
b. 1897, France
d. Sep 16, 1984 in Lausanne, Switzerland
Source: *BioIn 14*

Reardon, John
American. Opera Singer, Actor
Baritone who had NY Met. debut, 1965; featured in TV, stage dramas.
b. Apr 8, 1930 in New York, New York
d. Apr 16, 1988 in Santa Fe, New Mexico
Source: *Baker 78, 84, 92; BiE&WWA; BioIn 8, 9, 10, 11, 15, 16; CurBio 74, 88, 88N; MetOEnc; MusSN; NewAmDM; NewGrDA 86; NewGrDM 80; NewGrDO; NewYTBE 72; NewYTBS 88; WhAm 9; WhoAm 74, 76, 78, 80, 82, 84, 86, 88; WhoAmM 83; WhoE 74; WhoOp 76; WhoWor 74, 82*

Reardon, Ken(neth Joseph)
Canadian. Hockey Player
Defenseman, Montreal, 1940-42, 1945-50; Hall of Fame, 1966.
b. Apr 1, 1921 in Winnipeg, Manitoba, Canada
Source: *BioIn 2; HocEn; WhoHcky 73*

Reasoner, Harry
American. Broadcast Journalist
Original co-editor, with Mike Wallace, of "60 Minutes," 1968-70, 1978-91.
b. Apr 17, 1923 in Dakota City, Iowa
d. Aug 6, 1991 in Norwalk, Connecticut
Source: *AmAu&B; AnObit 1991; AuNews 1; BioIn 7, 8, 10, 11, 12, 13, 17, 18; BioNews 75; CelR, 90; ConAu 111, 135; ConTFT 6, 10; CurBio 66, 91N; EncAJ; EncTwCJ; IntMPA 75, 76, 77, 78, 79, 80, 81, 82, 84, 86, 88; JrnUS; LegTOT; LesBEnT, 92; News 92, 92-1; NewYTBS 91; NewYTET; VarWW 85; WhAm 10; WhoAm 74, 76, 78, 80, 82, 84, 86, 88, 90; WhoE 74, 75, 91; WhoTelC; WorAl*

Rebbot, Olivier
French. Photojournalist
Freelance photographer who covered Nicaraguan civil war, Iranian revolution; died of gunshot wounds in El Salvadorean civil war.

b. 1949?, France
d. Feb 10, 1981 in Hialeah, Florida
Source: *BioIn 12; ConAu 103; ICPEnP A; NewYTBS 81*

Rebecca
Hebrew. Biblical Figure
Mother of twins, Jacob, Esau, after twenty years of childlessness; wife of Isaac.
b. fl. 1860BC
Source: *InWom SUP; NewCol 75; OxCEng 85*

Reber, Grote
American. Radio Performer
Built first radio telescope, 1937.
b. Dec 22, 1911 in Wheaton, Illinois
Source: *AsBiEn; BiESc; BioIn 8, 14, 16, 20; CamDcSc; LarDcSc; LegTOT; NotTwCS; WorAl; WorAlBi; WorInv*

Rebikov, Vladimir Ivanovich
Russian. Composer
Wrote short opera *The Christmas Tree;* fairy-tale opera *Yolka,* 1903.
b. May 31, 1866 in Krasnoyarsk, Russia
d. Dec 1, 1920 in Yalta, Union of Soviet Socialist Republics
Source: *Baker 84, 92; BiDSovU; BioIn 4; NewEOp 71; NewGrDO; OxCMus*

Rebozo, Bebe
[Charles Gregory Rebozo]
American. Real Estate Executive, Banker
Chm., Key Biscayne Bank, 1964-90; close friend of Richard Nixon.
b. Nov 17, 1912 in Tampa, Florida
Source: *BioIn 9, 10, 12; PolProf NF; WhoAm 74, 76, 78, 80, 82, 84, 86, 88, 90, 92, 94, 95, 96; WhoFI 74; WhoSSW 73; WorAl*

Rebuffat, Gaston Louis Simon
French. Mountaineer, Author
Known for ascents of Mt. Blanc; wrote *Men and the Matterhorn.*
b. May 7, 1921 in Marseilles, France
d. May 31, 1985 in Paris, France
Source: *ConAu 116; WhoFr 79*

Recamier, Julie, Madame
[Jeanne Francoise Juliette Adelaide Recamier]
French. Socialite
Queen of Parisian society, 1815-49; friend of Chateaubriand; portrait by Jacques Louis David in Louvre.
b. Dec 4, 1777 in Lyons, France
d. May 11, 1849 in Paris, France
Source: *LinLib L, S; NewCol 75; OxCFr; REn*

Rechy, John Francisco
American. Author
Novels concern underground homosexual life: *City of Night,* 1963.
b. Mar 10, 1934 in El Paso, Texas
Source: *AmAu&B; BioIn 13, 15, 16; CamGLE; CamHAL; ConAu 4AS, 5R, 6NR; ConLC 18; ConNov 86; DrAPF 91; IntvTCA 2; OxCAmL 83; PenC AM; WhoAm 86; WorAu 1975; WrDr 86*

Red Cloud, Chief
[Mahpiua Luta]
American. Native American Chief
Led Sioux, Cheyenne in resisting development of Bozeman Trail; signed Fort Laramie Treaty, 1868.
b. 1822 in Nebraska
d. 1909 in Pine Ridge, South Dakota
Source: *AmBi; BioIn 1, 3, 4, 7, 9, 10, 11, 15, 17, 20, 21; DcAmB; DcAmMiB; GenMudB; HarEnMi; LegTOT; McGEWB; NewCol 75; NotNaAm; OxCAmH; REnAW; WebAB 74, 79; WebAMB; WebBD 83; WhAm 4, HSA; WhNaAH*

Redding, Jay Saunders
American. Educator
First black professor on Cornell's arts/science faculty; helped found field of Afro-American studies.
b. Oct 13, 1906 in Washington, Delaware
d. Mar 2, 1988 in Ithaca, New York
Source: *Au&Wr 71; BioIn 1, 2, 3, 4, 8, 9, 10, 15, 16, 17, 18; ConAu 5NR; CurBio 69, 88; DrAS 74E, 82E; InB&W 80, 85; SelBAAf; SelBAAu; TwCA SUP; WhoAm 86; WhoBlA 85*

Redding, Otis
American. Singer, Songwriter
Hits include "Dock of the Bay," 1968.
b. Sep 9, 1941 in Dawson, Georgia
d. Dec 10, 1967 in Madison, Wisconsin
Source: *AfrAmAl 6; Baker 84, 92; BiDAfM; BiDAmM; BioIn 8, 10, 12, 15, 16; ConMus 5; DcArts; DcTwCCu 5; DrBlPA, 90; EncPR&S 89; EncRk 88; EncRkSt; FacFETw; IlEncBM 82; InB&W 80, 85; LegTOT; NegAl 89; NewAmDM; NewGrDA 86; OxCPMus; PenEncP; RkOn 74; RolSEnR 83; SoulM; WhAm 4A; WhoRock 81; WhoRocM 82; WhScrn 77, 83; WorAl; WorAlBi*

Reddy, Helen
"Queen of Housewife Rock"
Australian. Singer, Songwriter
Hit single, "I Am Woman," 1972, became feminist movement theme song; Grammy award winner, 1973.
b. Oct 25, 1941 in Melbourne, Australia
Source: *BioIn 13; BioNews 74; BkPepl; ConMus 9; ConTFT 5; CurBio 75; EncPR&S 89; EncRk 88; HalFC 88; IntMPA 86, 92; InWom SUP; LegTOT; NewYTBE 73; PenEncP; RkOn 78; WhoAm 74, 76, 78, 80, 82, 84, 86, 88, 90; WhoAmW 75, 81; WhoEnt 92; WhoHol 92, A; WhoRocM 82; WhoWest 82; WorAl; WorAlBi*

Reddy, N(eelam) Sanjeeva
Indian. Political Leader
Pres., India, 1977-82.
b. May 13, 1913 in Illure, India
d. Jun 1, 1996 in Bangalore, India
Source: *BioIn 16; CurBio 81; FarE&A 79; IntWW 83; IntYB 79; NewYTBS 79; WhoWor 84*

Redenbacher, Orville
American. Businessman, Manufacturer
Developed hybrid yellow popping corn, 1952; became best-selling popcorn in US under name Orville Redenbacher's Popcorn.
b. Jul 16, 1907 in Brazil, Indiana
d. Sep 19, 1995 in Coronado, California
Source: *BioIn 11, 12, 15, 21; Entr; LegTOT; News 96, 96-1*

Redfield, James
American. Author
Wrote *The Celestine Prophecy: An Adventure,* 1994.
b. 1950 in Birmingham, Alabama
Source: *News 95, 95-2*

Redford, Robert
[Charles Robert Redford, Jr.]
American. Actor, Director, Author
Box office draw since film *Barefoot in the Park,* 1967; won Oscar for directing *Ordinary People,* 1980.
b. Aug 18, 1937 in Santa Monica, California
Source: *Au&Arts 15; BiDFilm, 81, 94; BiE&WWA; BioIn 9, 11, 12, 13, 14, 16; BioNews 74; BkPepl; CelR, 90; ConAu 107; ConTFT 1, 3, 11; CurBio 71, 82; DcTwCCu 1; EncAFC; EnvEnDr; FacFETw; FilmgC; HalFC 88; IntDcF 1-3, 2-3; IntMPA 75, 76, 77, 78, 79, 81, 82, 84, 86, 88, 92, 94, 96; IntWW 75, 76, 77, 78, 79, 80, 81, 82, 83, 89, 91, 93; LegTOT; MiSFD 9; MotPP; MovMk; News 93-2; NewYTBS 74; OxCFilm; VarWW 85; Who 92; WhoAm 74, 76, 78, 80, 82, 84, 86, 88, 90, 92, 94, 95, 96, 97; WhoEnt 92; WhoHol 92, A; WhoWor 78, 91; WorAl; WorAlBi; WorEFlm*

Redgrave, Corin
English. Actor
Son of Sir Michael; brother of Vanessa, Lynn; films include *A Man for all Seasons,* 1966.
b. Jul 16, 1939 in London, England
Source: *BioIn 10, 13; CnThe; ConAu 154; ConTFT 5, 14; EncWT; FilmEn; FilmgC; HalFC 84, 88; IntMPA 88, 92, 94, 96; ItaFilm; VarWW 85; WhoHol 92, A; WhoThe 72, 77, 81*

Redgrave, Lynn
English. Actor
Starred in *Georgy Girl,* 1967; TV series "House Calls," 1979-81; TV spokeswoman for Weight Watchers.
b. Mar 8, 1943 in London, England
Source: *BioIn 7, 8, 9, 10, 11, 12, 16; BioNews 74; BlueB 76; CelR 90; ConTFT 1, 7, 15; CurBio 69; FacFETw; FilmgC; HalFC 84, 88; IntMPA 75, 76, 77, 78, 79, 81, 82, 84, 86, 88, 92, 94, 96; IntWW 91, 93; InWom, SUP; ItaFilm; LegTOT; MotPP; MovMk; NewYTBS 74; NotNAT; OxCFilm; VarWW 85; Who 82, 83, 85, 88, 90, 92,*

94; WhoAm 78, 80, 82, 84, 86, 88, 90, 92, 94, 95, 96, 97; WhoAmW 70, 72, 74, 75, 83, 89, 91, 93, 95, 97; WhoE 81; WhoEnt 92; WhoHol 92; WhoThe 72, 77, 81; WhoWest 78; WhoWor 74, 76, 78, 80, 82, 84, 87; WorAl; WorAlBi

Redgrave, Michael Scudamore, Sir
English. Actor
Starred in *The Quiet American,* 1958; *The Go-Between,* 1970.
b. Mar 20, 1908 in Bristol, England
d. Mar 21, 1985 in Denham, England
Source: *Au&Wr 71; CmMov; ConAu 143; CurBio 50; DcNaB 1981; FilmgC; IntAu&W 76, 77; IntDcT 3; MotPP; MovMk; NotNAT; OxCFilm; OxCThe 67, 83; PlP&P; VarWW 85; WhAm 8; Who 82; WhoE 74; WhoHol A; WhoThe 77; WhoWor 74, 76, 78, 84; WorAl; WorEFlm*

Redgrave, Vanessa
English. Actor
Won 1977 Oscar for *Julia;* starred in *Blow-up; Camelot; Playing for Time.*
b. Jan 30, 1937 in London, England
Source: *BiDFilm, 94; BioIn 7, 8, 9, 10, 11, 12, 14, 15, 16, 17, 18, 20; BkPepl; BlueB 76; CamGWoT; CelR, 90; CnThe; ConAu 148; ContDcW 89; ConTFT 1, 7, 15; CurBio 66; DcArts; EncEurC; EncWT; FacFETw; FilmgC; HalFC 84, 88; IntDcF 1-3, 2-3; IntDcT 3; IntDcWB; IntMPA 75, 76, 77, 78, 79, 81, 82, 84, 86, 88, 92, 94, 96; IntWW 74, 75, 76, 77, 78, 79, 80, 81, 82, 83, 89, 91, 93; InWom, SUP; ItaFilm; LegTOT; MotPP; MovMk; News 89-2; NewYTBS 86; OxCFilm; OxCThe 67, 83; VarWW 85; Who 74, 82, 83, 85, 88, 90, 92, 94; WhoAm 80, 82, 84, 86, 88, 90, 92, 94, 95, 96, 97; WhoAmW 70, 72, 74, 75, 83, 85, 87, 89, 91, 93, 95, 97; WhoEnt 92; WhoHol 92, A; WhoThe 72, 77, 81; WhoWor 74, 76, 78, 80, 82, 84, 87, 89, 91, 93, 95, 96, 97; WorAl; WorAlBi; WorEFlm*

Redhead, Hugh McCulloch
American. Advertising Executive
President of Campbell-Ewald Co., Detroit, 1968-75; died in plane crash.
b. Jul 18, 1920 in Saint Louis, Missouri
d. Sep 12, 1975 in Uniontown, Pennsylvania
Source: *BioIn 9, 10; NewYTBS 75; St&PR 75; WhAm 7; WhoAdv 72*

Red Hot Chili Peppers, The
American. Music Group
One of the trailblazing bands in the world of alternative rock; albums include *Mother's Milk,* 1989 and *Blood Sugar Sex Magik,* 1991.
Source: *BiDJaz A; BioIn 17, 20, 21; ConMus 7; EncRkSt; News 93-1*

Redi, Francesco
Italian. Author, Physician, Naturalist
Tested theory of spontaneous generation; wrote *Bacco in Toscana,* 1685.
b. Feb 18, 1626 in Arezzo, Italy
d. Mar 1, 1698 in Pisa, Italy
Source: *AsBiEn; BiESc; BioIn 3, 7, 15; CasWL; DcBiPP; DcCathB; DcEuL; DcItL 1, 2; DcScB; EuAu; EvEuW; InSci; LarDcSc; OxCEng 67, 85, 95; OxCMed 86; PenC EUR*

Red Jacket
American. Native American Chief
Seneca chief; urged Native American neutrality during the American Revolution.
b. 1756? in New York
d. Jan 20, 1830 in New York
Source: *BioIn 21; EncCRAm; NotNaAm; REnAW; WebAB 74, 79*

Redman, Ben Ray
[Jeremy Lord]
American. Critic, Editor
Noted reviewer in *Saturday Review of Literature,* 1926-61.
b. Feb 21, 1896 in New York, New York
d. Aug 1, 1961 in Hollywood, California
Source: *AmAu&B; AnMV 1926; Au&Wr 71; BenetAL 91; BioIn 6; ConAu 93; DcAmB S7; NotNAT B; REnAL; WhAm 4*

Redman, Don
American. Jazz Musician, Composer
Saxophonist; arranger; led own band, 1930s; director for Pearl Bailey.
b. Jul 29, 1900 in Piedmont, West Virginia
d. Nov 30, 1964 in New York, New York
Source: *AfrAmAl 6; AllMusG; ASCAP 66; Baker 84; BiDJaz; BioIn 16; CmpEPM; DcTwCCu 5; IlEncJ; NegAl 76, 83, 89; NewAmDM; NewGrDA 86; NewGrDJ 88; OxCPMus; PenEncP; WhoJazz 72*

Redman, Joshua
American. Musician
Saxophonist; released albums *Wish,* 1993; *Spirit of the Moment,* 1995.
b. 1969 in Berkeley, California
Source: *AllMusG; ConMus 12; DcTwCCu 5*

Redman, Joyce
Irish. Actor
Oscar nominee for *Tom Jones,* 1963; *Othello,* 1965.
b. 1918 in County Mayo, Ireland
Source: *BiE&WWA; BioIn 1; CnThe; ConTFT 5; FilmgC; HalFC 84, 88; NotNAT; PlP&P; VarWW 85; WhoHol 92, A; WhoThe 72, 77, 81*

Redon, Odilon
French. Artist
Noted for delicate floral studies, fantastic imagery.
b. Apr 22, 1840 in Bordeaux, France
d. Jul 6, 1916 in Paris, France
Source: *AtlBL; BioIn 2, 3, 4, 6, 7, 8, 9, 11, 12, 13, 15, 16, 20; ClaDrA; DcArts; DcTwCCu 2; IntDcAA 90; LegTOT; McGDA; McGEWB; OxCArt; OxCFr; OxDcArt; PhDcTCA 77; REn; WhDW*

Redpath, Jean
Scottish. Singer
Traditional folksinger; plans to record all the songs of Robert Burns; albums include *A Fine Song for Singing,* 1987.
b. Apr 28, 1937 in Edinburgh, Scotland
Source: *BioIn 13, 14; ConMus 1; CurBio 84; InWom SUP; PenEncP*

Redstone, Sumner (Murray)
American. Business Executive
Invented "multiplex" movie theaters, 1960s; owner of Viacom, Inc., entertainment giant, 1987—; holdings include cable's Showtime, MTV; purchased Paramount Communications, 1994.
b. May 27, 1923 in Boston, Massachusetts
Source: *BioIn 15, 16; ConNews 87-4; ConTFT 12; CurBio 96; Dun&B 86, 88, 90; IntMPA 88, 92, 94, 96; News 94, 94-1; WhoAm 74, 76, 78, 80, 82, 84, 86, 88, 90, 92, 94, 95, 96, 97; WhoAmJ 80; WhoAmL 78, 79, 83, 85, 87, 90, 92, 94, 96; WhoE 74, 75, 77, 79, 81, 83, 85, 86, 89, 91, 93, 95, 97; WhoEnt 92; WhoFI 74, 75, 77, 79, 81, 83, 85, 87, 89, 92, 94, 96; WhoWor 78, 80, 82, 84, 87, 89, 91, 93, 95, 96, 97*

Reed, Alan
[Teddy Bergman]
American. Actor
Cartoon voice of Fred Flintstone; played Falstaff Openshaw on radio show "Allen's Alley."
b. Aug 20, 1907 in New York, New York
d. Jun 14, 1977 in Los Angeles, California
Source: *ASCAP 66; NewYTBS 77; RadStar; Vers A; WhAm 7; WhoAm 74, 76; WhoHol A; WhScrn 83*

Reed, Austin Leonard
English. Retailer
Founded Austin Reed, Ltd., men's clothier, 1900.
b. 1873
d. May 5, 1954 in Gerrards Cross, England
Source: *DcNaB 1951; ObitT 1951*

Reed, Carol, Sir
English. Director
Won Oscar for *Oliver,* 1968; films include *Third Man; Fallen Idol.*
b. Dec 30, 1906 in London, England
d. Apr 25, 1976 in London, England
Source: *Benet 87, 96; BiDFilm, 81, 94; BioIn 1, 2, 3, 9, 10, 11, 12, 13, 15, 17, 20; BlueB 76; CmMov; CurBio 50, 76N; DcArts; DcFM; DcNaB 1971; EncEurC; FacFETw; FilmEn; FilmgC; HalFC 80, 84, 88; IlWWBF; IntDcF 1-2, 2-2; IntMPA 75, 76; IntWW 74, 75, 76; LegTOT; MiSFD 9N; MovMk; NewYTBE 70; NewYTBS 76; OxCFilm; WhAm 7;*

Who 74; WhoThe 77A; WhoWor 74; WhThe; WorAl; WorAlBi; WorEFlm; WorFDir 1

Reed, Dean
"The Frank Sinatra of Russia"
American. Singer
Sang "Tutti Frutti," "Blue Suede Shoes," in Russia.
b. 1939 in Denver, Colorado
d. Jun 17, 1986, German Democratic Republic
Source: *BioIn 9, 11; ConNews 86-3*

Reed, Donna
[Donna Belle Mullenger]
American. Actor
Won Oscar for *From Here To Eternity,* 1953, but gained greatest success on TVs "Donna Reed Show," 1958-66.
b. Jan 27, 1921 in Denison, Iowa
d. Jan 14, 1986 in Beverly Hills, California
Source: *AnObit 1986; BiDFilm, 81, 94; BioIn 1, 5, 6, 10, 14, 15, 17; ConNews 86-1; ConTFT 3; FilmEn; FilmgC; ForYSC; HalFC 80, 84, 88; IntDcF 1-3, 2-3; IntMPA 75, 76, 77, 78, 79, 80, 81, 82, 84, 86; InWom, SUP; LegTOT; MGM; MotPP; MovMk; NewYTBS 86; What 5; WhoAm 84; WhoHol A; WorAl; WorAlBi; WorEFlm*

Reed, Frank H
American. Hostage
Educator in Lebanon seized by Organization of Islamic Dawn Sep 9, 1986 and held captive 1,329 days; released Apr 30, 1990.
b. 1933 in Malden, Massachusetts

Reed, Henry Hope
American. Critic, Educator
Considered first to popularize Wordsworth in US; died in sinking of *Arctic.*
b. Jul 11, 1808 in Philadelphia, Pennsylvania
d. Sep 27, 1854
Source: *Alli; AmAu&B; ApCAB; ChhPo, S2; CyAL 2; DcAmAu; DcAmB; DcNAA; Drake; EvLB; NatCAB 2; TwCBDA; WhAm HS*

Reed, Ishmael Scott
American. Author
Satirist; books include *Chattanooga,* 1973; *Flight to Canada,* 1976.
b. Feb 22, 1938 in Chattanooga, Tennessee
Source: *AmAu&B; Benet 87; BioIn 14, 15, 16; BlkAWP; ConLC 11; CurBio 86; DrAP 75; DrAPF 91; InB&W 85; IntvTCA 2; LivgBAA; ModAL S1; PostFic; WhoAm 86; WhoWest 92*

Reed, Jack
American. Politician
Dem. senator, RI, 1997—.
b. Nov 12, 1949
Source: *AlmAP 96; CngDr 93, 95; WhoAmP 95*

Reed, Jerry
[Jerry Hubbard]
"The Alabama Wild Man"
American. Songwriter, Singer
Country music guitarist; wrote popular, offbeat song "When You're Hot, You're Hot," 1971.
b. Mar 20, 1937 in Atlanta, Georgia
Source: *Baker 84, 92; BgBkCoM; BioIn 12, 14; CounME 74, 74A; EncFCWM 83; EncRk 88; HarEnCM 87; IlEncCM; LegTOT; MiSFD 9; OnThGG; OxCPMus; PenEncP; RkOn 74; RolSEnR 83; VarWW 85; WhoAm 74, 76, 78, 80, 82, 84, 86, 88; WhoEnt 92; WhoHol 92; WhoRocM 82; WorAl; WorAlBi*

Reed, John Shedd
American. Railroad Executive
Chm., CEO of Santa Fe Industries, 1973-83.
b. Jun 9, 1917 in Chicago, Illinois
Source: *BlueB 76; IntWW 89, 91; St&PR 75, 84, 87; WhoAm 74, 76, 78, 80, 82, 84, 86, 88, 90, 92, 94, 95, 96, 97; WhoFI 74, 75, 77, 79, 81, 89; WhoMW 80, 82, 84, 90, 93, 96*

Reed, John Shepard
American. Financier
Chm., CEO, Citicorp, 1984—; world's largest private banking institution.
b. Feb 7, 1939 in Chicago, Illinois
Source: *BioIn 14, 15; CurBio 85; Dun&B 88; St&PR 87, 91, 93, 96, 97; WhoAm 86, 88, 90, 92, 94, 95, 96, 97; WhoE 86, 89, 91, 95, 97; WhoFI 87, 89, 92, 94, 96; WhoWor 87, 89, 91, 93, 95, 96, 97*

Reed, John Silas
American. Author, Journalist
Wrote *Ten Days That Shook the World,* 1919, considered finest eyewitness account of Russian Revolution; film *Reds* based on his life, 1981; only American buried in Red Square, Moscow.
b. Oct 22, 1887 in Portland, Oregon
d. Oct 19, 1920 in Moscow, Union of Soviet Socialist Republics
Source: *AmRef; AmSocL; BiDAmJo; ConAu 106; DcAmB; EncAB-H 1974, 1996; LiExTwC; McGEWB; NatCAB 19; WebAB 74; WhAm 1, 4A*

Reed, Lou
[Velvet Underground]
American. Singer, Songwriter
Had hit single "Walk on the Wild Side," 1973; albums include *Transformer,* 1972; *Street Hassle,* 1978; *New York,* 1988; designated Knight of France's Order of Arts and Letters, 1992.
b. Mar 2, 1944 in New York, New York
Source: *Baker 84; BioIn 16; ConLC 21; ConMuA 80A; CurBio 89; EncPR&S 89; EncRk 88; HarEnR 86; IlEncRk; IntWW 91; MugS; NewAmDM; PenEncP; RkOn 78, 84; RolSEnR 83; WhoAm 84, 90; WhoEnt 92; WhoRock 81; WhoRocM 82; WorAlBi*

Reed, Myrtle
[Katherine LaFarge Norton]
American. Author
Popular novelist; wrote best-selling *Lavender and Old Lace,* 1902.
b. Sep 27, 1874 in Chicago, Illinois
d. Aug 17, 1911 in Chicago, Illinois
Source: *AmAu&B; AmWomWr; BenetAL 91; ChhPo, S1, S3; DcAmAu; DcAmB; DcNAA; FemiCLE; InWom, SUP; LibW; NotAW; PenNWW A, B; REnAL; ScF&FL 1; TwCBDA*

Reed, Oliver
[Robert Oliver Reed]
English. Actor
Leading man, 1960—; films include *Oliver!,* 1968; *The Three Musketeers,* 1974.
b. Feb 13, 1938 in London, England
Source: *BioIn 11, 12; CelR; ConTFT 3; DcArts; EncEurC; FilmAG WE; FilmEn; FilmgC; ForYSC; HalFC 80, 84, 88; IlWWBF, A; IntDcF 1-3, 2-3; IntMPA 75, 76, 77, 78, 79, 80, 81, 82, 84, 86, 88, 92, 94, 96; IntWW 79, 80, 81, 82, 83, 89, 91, 93; ItaFilm; LegTOT; MovMk; OxCFilm; VarWW 85; Who 82, 83, 85, 88, 90, 92; WhoAm 76, 78, 80, 82, 84, 86, 88, 90, 92; WhoEnt 92; WhoHol 92, A; WhoHrs 80; WhoWor 84, 87, 89, 91, 93, 95, 96; WorAl; WorAlBi*

Reed, Peter Hugh
American. Critic, Author
Founded *American Music Lover* mag. (later) *American Record Guide,* 1935; edited until 1957.
b. Jun 14, 1892 in Washington, District of Columbia
d. Sep 25, 1969 in Wingdale, New York
Source: *Baker 78, 84; BioIn 8*

Reed, Ralph
[Ralph Eugene Reed, Jr.]
American. Political Activist
Executive director, Christian Coalition, 1989-97.
b. Jun 24, 1961 in Portsmouth, Virginia
Source: *CurBio 96; News 95, 95-1*

Reed, Rex
American. Critic, Journalist
Syndicated film critic noted for gossipy accounts of Hollywood greats.
b. Oct 2, 1939 in Fort Worth, Texas
Source: *AuNews 1; BioIn 8; BkPepl; CelR, 90; ConAu 27NR, 53; ConTFT 8; CurBio 72; EncTwCJ; HalFC 84, 88; NewYTBE 72; VarWW 85; WhoAm 84, 86, 88; WhoE 74; WhoEnt 92; WhoHol A; WhoUSWr 88; WhoWrEP 89; WrDr 86, 92*

Reed, Robert
[John Robert Rietz]
American. Actor
Played the father on TV series "The Brady Bunch," 1969-74.
b. Oct 19, 1932 in Chicago, Illinois
d. May 12, 1992 in Pasadena, California
Source: *AnObit 1992; BioIn 17, 18, 19; ConTFT 6, 11; ForYSC; IntMPA 92;*

LegTOT; News 92; VarWW 85; WhoHol 92, A; WorAl; WorAlBi

Reed, Stanley Forman
American. Supreme Court Justice
Appointed by FDR, 1938-57.
b. Dec 31, 1884 in Maysville, Kentucky
d. Apr 2, 1980 in Huntington, New York
Source: *AmBench 79; BioIn 1, 2, 4, 5, 11, 12, 15; CngDr 74, 77, 79; CurBio 42, 80; DcAmB S10; DrAS 74P; NewCol 75; NewYTBS 80; OxCSupC; SupCtJu; WebAB 74, 79; WebBD 83; WhAm 7; WhoAm 78, 80; WhoGov 72*

Reed, Susan
American. Singer
Recorded folk songs from around the world, 1950s; albums include *Folk Songs,* 1958.
b. 1927 in Columbia, South Carolina
Source: *BioIn 2; EncFCWM 69; InWom SUP; VarWW 85; WhoHol 92, A*

Reed, Thomas Brackett
American. Politician
Rep. congressman from Maine, 1877-99; speaker of the House of Representatives, 1889-91, 1895-99; introduced the Reed Rules, 1890, affecting congressional procedures.
b. Oct 18, 1839 in Portland, Maine
d. Dec 7, 1902 in Washington, District of Columbia
Source: *AmBi; AmPolLe; ApCAB; BiDrAC; BiDrUSC 89; BioIn 6, 7, 8, 9, 13, 14; CyAG; DcAmB; DcNAA; EncAB-H 1974, 1996; HarEnUS; HisWorL; LinLib S; McGEWB; NatCAB 2; OxCAmH; TwCBDA; WebAB 74, 79; WhAm 1; WhAmP*

Reed, Walter
American. Surgeon
Tracked mosquito to yellow fever virus; Washington, DC hospital named for him.
b. Sep 13, 1851 in Belroi, Virginia
d. Nov 22, 1902 in Washington, District of Columbia
Source: *AmBi; AmDec 1900; AsBiEn; BiESc; BiHiMed; BiInAmS; BioIn 1, 2, 3, 4, 5, 6, 7, 8, 9, 11, 13, 18, 20; CamDcSc; DcAmB; DcAmMeB, 84; DcAmMiB; DcScB; EncAB-H 1974, 1996; EncSoH; EncWM; FacFETw; GayN; HarEnMi; InSci; LarDcSc; LegTOT; LinLib S; McGEWB; MemAm; NatCAB 13, 33; NewCol 75; NotTwCS; OxCAmH; OxCMed 86; REn; WebAB 74, 79; WebBD 83; WhAm HS; WhDW; WorAl; WorAlBi; WorScD*

Reed, Willis, Jr.
American. Basketball Player
Center, NY Knicks, 1965-73; NBA MVP, 1970; Hall of Fame, 1981; wrote autobiography, *A View from the Rim,* 1971.
b. Jun 25, 1942 in Hico, Louisiana
Source: *AfrAmBi 2; BasBi; BiDAmSp BK; BioIn 9, 10, 11, 12, 13, 16; ConAu 104; CurBio 73; InB&W 80, 85; LegTOT; NegAl 89; NewYTBE 70; NewYTBS 74, 77, 82; OfNBA 87; WhoAfA 96; WhoAm 74, 78, 80, 84, 86, 88, 90, 92, 94, 95, 96, 97; WhoBbl 73; WhoBlA 75, 77, 80, 85, 88, 90, 92, 94; WhoE 89, 91, 95, 97; WhoSpor; WorAl; WorAlBi*

Reedy, George Edward
American. Journalist
Replaced Pierre Salinger as press secretary to LBJ, 1964-65; wrote *The Twilight of the Presidency,* 1970.
b. Aug 5, 1917 in East Chicago, Indiana
Source: *BioIn 5, 6, 7, 8, 10, 11; BlueB 76; EncTwCJ; IndAu 1967; IntAu&W 89, 91, 93; IntWW 74, 75, 76, 77, 78, 79, 80, 81, 82, 83, 89, 91, 93; WhoAm 74, 76, 78, 80, 82, 84, 86, 88, 90, 92, 94, 95, 96, 97; WhoAmP 73, 77; WhoMW 92; WhoUSWr 88; WhoWrEP 89, 92, 95; WrDr 92*

Reems, Harry
[Herbert Streicher]
American. Actor
Pornography star in films: *Deep Throat; Devil and Miss Jones.*
b. Aug 27, 1947 in New York, New York
Source: *BioIn 11, 15, 17; ConAu 61; WhoHol 92*

Rees, Ennis (Samuel, Jr.)
American. Children's Author
Books include *Tiny Tall Tales,* 1967; *The Little Green Alphabet Book,* 1968.
b. Mar 17, 1925 in Newport News, Virginia
Source: *AuBYP 2, 3; BioIn 8, 9, 15; ChhPo S1; ConAu 1R, 2NR; DrAP 75; DrAPF 80, 91; DrAS 74E, 78E, 82E; IntAu&W 76, 77, 82; IntWWP 77, 82; SmATA 3*

Rees, Roger
Welsh. Actor
Star of *Nicholas Nickleby* in London, on Broadway, TV; won Tony, 1982.
b. May 5, 1944 in Aberystwyth, Wales
Source: *BioIn 14, 15; ConTFT 1, 4; IntMPA 92, 94, 96; VarWW 85; WhoAm 94, 96, 97; WhoEnt 92; WhoHol 92; WhoThe 77, 81*

Reese, Della
[Delareese Patricia Early]
American. Singer, Actor
Gold records include "Don't You Know?," 1959; first woman to host TV variety show, "Della," 1969-70.
b. Jul 6, 1932 in Detroit, Michigan
Source: *Baker 84, 92; BiDAfM; BiDAmM; BiDJaz; BioIn 9, 10, 11; BioNews 74; CurBio 71; DrBlPA, 90; EncRk 88; InB&W 80, 85; IntMPA 94, 96; InWom, SUP; LegTOT; NotBlAW 2; OxCPMus; PenEncP; RkOn 74, 82; VarWW 85; WhoAm 74, 76, 78, 86, 88; WhoAmW 66, 68, 70, 72, 74, 75; WhoBlA 75, 77, 80, 88, 92; WhoEnt 92; WhoHol 92, A; WorAl; WorAlBi*

Reese, Don(ald Francis)
American. Football Player
Defensive lineman, 1974-81; jailed, 1977, for trafficking drugs; wrote *SI* article, 1982, exposing drug abuse in NFL.
b. Sep 4, 1951 in Mobile, Alabama
Source: *BioIn 13; FootReg 81; WhoBlA 80, 85, 90*

Reese, Harry B
American. Candy Manufacturer
Introduced popular chocolate-covered peanut butter cup, 1923.
b. 1879
d. 1956
Source: *Entr*

Reese, Lizette Woodworth
American. Poet
Wrote verse volume *Wild Cherry,* 1923; popular sonnet "Tears."
b. Jan 9, 1856 in Waverly, Maryland
d. Dec 17, 1935 in Baltimore, Maryland
Source: *Alli SUP; AmAu&B; AmWom; AmWomWr; AnCL; ArtclWW 2; BenetAL 91; BiDAmM; BiD&SB; BiDSA; BioIn 1, 4, 8, 11, 15; ChhPo, S2, S3; CnDAL; ConAmA; ConAmL; DcAmAu; DcAmB S1; DcLB 54; DcLEL; DcNAA; FemiCLE; InWom, SUP; LibW; LngCTC; NatCAB 1; NotAW; OxCAmL 65, 83, 95; OxCTwCP; REn; REnAL; SouWr; TwCA, SUP; WhAm 1, 2*

Reese, Mason
American. Actor
Best known for TV commercials since 1970; won three Clios.
b. Apr 11, 1966 in Los Angeles, California
Source: *BioIn 11, 13; BioNews 74; ConAu 97; NewYTBE 73*

Reese, Pee Wee
[Harold Henry Reese]
"The Little Colonel"
American. Baseball Player
Shortstop, Brooklyn/LA, 1940-42, 1946-58; part of keystone combination with Jackie Robinson; had 2,170 career hits; Hall of Fame, 1984.
b. Jul 23, 1919 in Elkton, Kentucky
Source: *Ballpl 90; BiDAmSp BB; BioIn 1, 2, 3, 4, 5, 6, 8, 14, 15, 17; CurBio 50; WhoProB 73; WhoSpor*

Reeve, Christopher
American. Actor
Best known for title role in *Superman* film series, 1978, 1980, 1983, 1987; paralyzed in horseriding accident, 1995; campaigns for spinal cord injury research.
b. Sep 25, 1952 in New York, New York
Source: *BioIn 11, 12, 13, 14, 15, 16; CelR 90; ConTFT 1, 3, 6; CurBio 82; HalFC 80, 84, 88; HolBB; IntMPA 80, 81, 82, 84, 88, 92, 94, 96; IntWW 89, 91, 93; LegTOT; VarWW 85; WhoAm 82, 84, 86, 88, 90, 92, 94, 95, 96, 97;*

WhoEnt 92; WhoHol 92; WhoHrs 80; WorAlBi

Reeves, Dan(iel Edward)
American. Football Player, Football Coach
Running back, Dallas, 1965-72; head coach, Denver, 1981-92; NY Giants, 1993-96; Atlanta Falcons, 1997—; NFL coach of the year award, 1993.
b. Jan 19, 1944 in Rome, Georgia
Source: *BiDAmSp FB; BioIn 16, 18; FootReg 87; WhoAm 84, 86, 88, 92, 94, 95, 96, 97; WhoAmA 91; WhoE 95, 97; WhoWest 84, 87, 89, 92*

Reeves, Dan(iel F)
American. Football Executive
Owner, Baltimore-LA Rams, 1941-71; pioneer in televising road games; Hall of Fame, 1967.
b. Jun 30, 1912 in New York, New York
d. Apr 15, 1971 in Los Angeles, California
Source: *CmCal; NewYTBE 71; WhAm 5; WhoFtbl 74*

Reeves, George
[George Basselo]
American. Actor
Typecast in TV series "The Adventures of Superman."
b. Jan 6, 1914 in Ashland, Kentucky
d. Jun 16, 1959 in Beverly Hills, California
Source: *BioIn 5, 17; FilmEn; FilmgC; ForYSC; HalFC 80, 84, 88; LegTOT; MotPP; NotNAT B; WhoHol B; WhoHrs 80; WhScrn 74, 77, 83*

Reeves, Jim
"Gentleman Jim"
American. Singer
Influential Country-Western performer, 1950s-60s; biggest hit: "He'll Have to Go," 1960; killed in plane crash.
b. Aug 20, 1924 in Galloway, Texas
d. Jul 31, 1964 in Tennessee
Source: *AmPS A; BioIn 14, 15; CounME 74, 74A; EncFCWM 69, 83; IlEncCM; LegTOT; NewGrDA 86; NotNAT B; OxCPMus; PenEncP; RkOn 74, 82; WhoHol B; WhScrn 74, 77, 83*

Reeves, Keanu
American. Actor
Films include *Bill and Ted's Excellent Adventure,* 1989; *My Own Private Idaho,* 1991.
b. Sep 4, 1964 in Beirut, Lebanon
Source: *BioIn 15, 16; ConTFT 9; CurBio 95; IntMPA 92, 94, 96; LegTOT; News 92, 92-1; WhoAm 94, 95, 96, 97; WhoAsA 94; WhoHol 92*

Reeves, Martha
[Martha and the Vandellas]
American. Singer
Lead singer, Martha and the Vandellas, 1962-72; hit single "Heat Wave," 1964.
b. Jul 18, 1941 in Detroit, Michigan
Source: *Baker 84, 92; BioIn 16; ConMus 4; EncRk 88; LegTOT; NewGrDA 86; PenEncP; WhoBlA 77, 85; WhoRocM 82*

Reeves, Rosser
American. Advertising Executive
Champion of hard-sell advertising; chm., Ted Bates & Co., retired, 1966; Copywriter's Hall of Fame, 1964.
b. Sep 10, 1910 in Danville, Virginia
d. Jan 24, 1984 in Chapel Hill, North Carolina
Source: *AdMenW; AnObit 1984; BioIn 5, 7, 8, 11, 12, 13, 20; BlueB 76; ConAu 89, 111; WhAm 8; WhoAm 74, 76, 78, 80, 82; WhoE 74; WhoFI 74; WhoWor 84, 87*

Reeves, Steve
American. Actor
Former "Mr. World," "Mr. Universe," who gained fame in Italian costume epics *Hercules,* 1957; *Goliath and the Barbarians,* 1959.
b. Jan 21, 1926 in Glasgow, Montana
Source: *Film 2; FilmEn; FilmgC; ForYSC; HalFC 80, 84, 88; IntMPA 75, 76, 77, 78, 79, 80, 81, 82, 84, 86, 88, 92, 94, 96; ItaFilm; LegTOT; MotPP; MovMk; VarWW 85; WhoHol 92, A; WhoHrs 80; WorEFlm*

Regan, Donald Thomas
American. Government Official
White House Chief of Staff under Reagan, 1985-87; secretary of Treasury, 1981-86.
b. Dec 21, 1918 in Cambridge, Massachusetts
Source: *BiDrUSE 89; BioIn 12, 13, 14, 15, 16; CngDr 83; ConAu 106, 127; CurBio 81; IntWW 74, 75, 76, 77, 78, 79, 80, 81, 82, 83, 89, 91, 93; NewYTBS 80, 85; St&PR 75; Who 82, 83, 85, 88, 90, 92, 94; WhoAm 74, 76, 78, 80, 82, 84, 86, 88, 90, 92, 94, 95, 96, 97; WhoAmP 85, 91; WhoE 74, 81, 83, 85, 86; WhoFI 74, 75, 77, 79, 81, 83, 85; WhoWor 82, 84, 87, 89, 91*

Regan, Phil
"Singing Policeman"
American. Singer
Theme song was "Happy Days Are Here Again," which he sang at Harry Truman's inauguration.
b. May 28, 1906 in New York, New York
d. Feb 11, 1996 in Santa Barbara, California
Source: *BioIn 21; CmpEPM; ForYSC; IntMPA 75, 76, 77, 78, 79, 80, 81, 82, 84, 86, 88; RadStar; WhoHol 92, A*

Reger, Max
[Johann Baptist Joseph Maximilian]
German. Composer
Noted for contrapuntal organ works; German Max Reger Society founded, 1920.
b. Mar 19, 1873 in Brand, Bavaria
d. May 11, 1916 in Leipzig, Germany
Source: *AtlBL; Baker 78, 84; BioIn 1, 2, 3, 4, 5, 8, 9, 12, 16; BriBkM 80; CompSN, SUP; DcCom 77; DcCom&M 79; LegTOT; LuthC 75; MusMk; NewAmDM; NewCol 75; NewGrDM 80; NewOxM; OxCMus; PenDiMP A; WebBD 83*

Reggio, Godfrey
American. Filmmaker
Made *Koyaanisqatsi,* 1983; *Anima Mundi,* 1991.
b. 1940 in New Orleans, Louisiana
Source: *CurBio 95; WhoAm 97*

Regine
[Regina Zylberberg]
"Queen of the Night"
French. Business Executive
Owns nightclubs bearing her name in NY, Paris.
b. Dec 26, 1929 in Etterbeck, Belgium
Source: *BioIn 10, 12, 15; CelR 90; CurBio 80; InWom SUP; NewYTBS 79; WhoFr 79*

Regnault, Henri Victor
French. Scientist
Director, Sevres Porcelain Co., 1854-70; researched specific heats, hydrocarbons.
b. Jul 20, 1810 in Aix-la-Chapelle, France
d. Jan 19, 1878 in Auteuil, France
Source: *AsBiEn; BioIn 5, 14; CamDcSc; DcBiPP; DcCathB; DcInv; DcScB; Dis&D; InSci; LarDcSc; NewCol 75*

Rehan, Ada
American. Actor
Leading lady of Daly's Theater in NY, 1879-99; best known for her rolee of Katherine in *Taming of the Shrew.*
b. Apr 22, 1860 in Limerick, Ireland
d. Jan 8, 1916 in New York, New York
Source: *AmBi; AmWom; ApCAB; BioIn 1, 6, 9, 10, 13, 16; CamGWoT; DcAmB; DcIrB 78, 88; EncWT; Ent; FamA&A; IntDcT 3; InWom; LinLib L; NatCAB 1; NotAW; NotNAT A, B; OxCAmL 65; OxCAmT 84; OxCThe 67, 83; PlP&P; TwCBDA; WebAB 74, 79; WhAm 1; WhoStg 1906, 1908; WhThe; WomWWA 14*

Rehnquist, William Hubbs
American. Supreme Court Justice
Conservative justice appointed by Nixon, 1971; named chief justice by Reagan, 1986—.
b. Oct 1, 1924 in Milwaukee, Wisconsin
Source: *AmPolLe; BiDFedJ A; BioIn 9, 10, 11, 12, 13, 14, 15, 16; CelR 90; CngDr 74, 77, 79, 81, 83, 85, 87, 89, 91, 93, 95; CurBio 72; DrAS 74P, 78P, 82P; EncWB; FacFETw; IntWW 83, 91; NatCAB 63N; NewYTBE 71; NewYTBS 86; OxCSupC; RComAH; SupCtJu; WebAB 74, 79; Who 85, 92; WhoAm 74, 76, 78, 80, 82, 84, 86, 88, 90, 92, 94, 95, 96, 97; WhoAmL 78, 79, 83, 85, 87, 90, 92, 94, 96; WhoAmP 73, 75, 77, 79, 81, 83, 85, 87, 89, 91, 93, 95; WhoE 77,*

79, 81, 83, 85, 86, 89, 91, 93, 95, 97; WhoGov 72, 75, 77; WhoSSW 73, 75, 76; WhoWor 78, 80, 82, 84, 87, 89, 91, 93, 95, 96, 97; WorAlBi

Reich, Robert B(ernard)
American. Government Official
Contributing Editor, *New Republic,* 1982-93; US Secretary of Labor, 1993-97.
b. Jun 24, 1946 in Scranton, Pennsylvania
Source: *BioIn 13; CurBio 93; IntWW 93; WhoAm 92, 94, 95, 96, 97; WhoE 93, 95, 97; WhoFI 94, 96; WhoWor 96, 97*

Reich, Steve
American. Composer
One of best known exponents of minimal music; often created overlapping rhythms; wrote "Desert Music," 1984.
b. Oct 3, 1936 in New York, New York
Source: *Baker 78, 84, 92; BiDAmM; BiDD; BioIn 12, 13, 14, 15; BriBkM 80; ConAmC 76, 82; ConAu 8NR, 61; ConCom 92; ConMus 8; ConTFT 13; CpmDNM 81; CurBio 86; DcArts; DcCM; DcTwCCu 1; EncWB; IntWW 89, 91, 93; IntWWM 80, 85, 90; NewAmDM; NewGrDA 86; NewGrDM 80; NewOxM; NewYTBS 82, 86; PenDiMP, A; PenEncP; PrintW 83, 85; WhoAm 74, 76, 78, 80, 82, 84, 86, 88, 90, 92, 94, 95, 96, 97; WhoAmM 83; WhoEnt 92; WorAlBi*

Reich, Wilhelm
American. Psychoanalyst
Headed Vienna Seminar for Psychoanalytic Therapy, 1924-30.
b. Mar 24, 1897, Austria
d. Nov 3, 1957 in Lewisburg, Pennsylvania
Source: *AmAu&B; BiDNeoM; BiDPsy; BioIn 1, 4, 7, 8, 9, 10, 11, 12, 13, 14, 15, 16, 20; DcAmMeB 84; EncO&P 1, 2, 3; EncPaPR 91; EncUnb; FacFETw; MakMC; NewAgE 90; NewYTBE 71; OxCPhil; PenC AM; RadHan; ThTwC 87; TwCA SUP; TwCLC 57; UFOEn; WhoTwCL*

Reichardt, Johann Friedrich
German. Composer, Conductor
Wrote first German Liederspiel, 1800; his Singspiels helped development of native opera.
b. Nov 25, 1752 in Konigsberg, Germany
d. Jun 27, 1814 in Giebichenstein, Germany
Source: *Baker 78, 84, 92; BioIn 1, 4; DcBiPP; MusMk; NewAmDM; NewEOp 71; NewGrDM 80; NewGrDO; NewOxM; OxCGer 76, 86; OxCMus; OxDcOp; WebBD 83*

Reichelderfer, Francis Wylton
American. Meteorologist
Headed US Weather Bureau, 1938-63.
b. Aug 6, 1895 in Harlan, Indiana
d. Jan 26, 1983 in Washington, District of Columbia
Source: *AmMWSc 82; IntWW 83; McGMS 80; WhoWor 80*

Reichmann, Paul
Canadian. Real Estate Executive
Owner of Olympia & York Developments, one of the richest, most powerful real estate developers in the world.
b. 1931 in Vienna, Austria
Source: *BioIn 11, 12, 13, 15, 16; CurBio 91; IntWW 91; NewYTBS 80; WhoAm 90; WhoFI 92*

Reichmann, Theodor
German. Opera Singer
Baritone with Vienna Opera, 1880s-90s; noted for William Tell role.
b. Mar 15, 1848 in Rostock, Germany
d. May 22, 1903 in Marbach, Switzerland
Source: *Baker 84; NewEOp 71*

Reichstein, Tadeus
Swiss. Chemist
First to synthesize Vitamin C, 1933; shared Nobel Prize, 1950.
b. Jul 20, 1897 in Wloclawek, Poland
d. Aug 1, 1996 in Basel, Switzerland
Source: *BiESc; BioIn 2, 3, 5, 15, 20; CurBio 51, 96N; InSci; IntWW 74, 75, 76, 77, 78, 79, 80, 81, 82, 83, 89, 91, 93; IntYB 78, 79, 80, 81, 82; LarDcSc; McGEWB; McGMS 80; NewCol 75; NewYTBS 27; NobelP; NotTwCS; Who 74, 82, 83, 85, 88, 90, 92, 94; WhoAm 88, 90, 92, 94, 95; WhoNob, 90, 95; WhoScEn 94, 96; WhoWor 74, 76, 78, 82, 84, 87, 89, 91, 93, 95, 96; WhoWorJ 72; WorAl; WorAlBi*

Reid, Beryl
English. Actor
Won 1967 Tony for *The Killing of Sister George.*
b. Jun 17, 1920 in Hereford, England
d. Oct 13, 1996 in London, England
Source: *BioIn 13, 14; ConTFT 6; FilmEn; FilmgC; HalFC 84, 88; IlWWBF; IntMPA 88, 92, 94, 96; VarWW 85; Who 82, 83, 85, 88, 90, 92, 94; WhoHol A; WhoThe 72, 77, 81*

Reid, Elliott
American. Actor
Supporting actor since 1940 in films *Gentlemen Prefer Blondes,* 1953; *Absent-Minded Professor,* 1961.
b. Jan 16, 1920 in New York, New York
Source: *BiE&WWA; BioIn 2; FilmEn; ForYSC; HalFC 80, 84, 88; MotPP; NotNAT; RadStar; Vers A; WhoHol 92, A*

Reid, Harry
American. Politician
Dem. senator, NV, 1987—.
b. Dec 2, 1939 in Searchlight, Nevada
Source: *AlmAP 84, 92, 96; BiDrUSC 89; BioIn 20; CngDr 83, 85, 87, 89, 91, 93, 95; IntWW 89, 91, 93; PolsAm 84; WhoAm 88, 90, 92, 94, 95, 96, 97; WhoAmP 83, 85, 87, 89, 91, 93, 95; WhoWest 84, 87, 89, 92, 94, 96; WhoWor 89, 91*

Reid, Helen Rogers
[Mrs. Ogden Mills Reid]
American. Newspaper Executive
Pres. of *NY Herald Tribune,* 1947-53; chm., 1953-55; zealous feminist, appealed to women readers.
b. Nov 23, 1882 in Appleton, Wisconsin
d. Jul 27, 1970 in New York, New York
Source: *AmAu&B; BiCAW; BiDAmBL 83; BioIn 1, 16; ConAu 115; CurBio 41, 52, 70; DcAmB S4; DcLB 29; EncAB-A 20; EncAJ; ForWC 70; InWom, SUP; JrnUS; NatCAB 33, 56; NewYTBE 70; NotAW MOD; OxCAmH; WebAB 74, 79; WhAm 2, 5, 7; WhJnl; WhoAmW 58, 68, 70, 72; WomComm; WomWWA 14*

Reid, Kate
[Daphne Kate Reid]
Canadian. Actor
Won critical acclaim, 1984, playing Linda Loman in revival of *Death of a Salesman* on Broadway.
b. Nov 4, 1930 in London, England
d. Mar 7, 1993 in Stratford, Ontario, Canada
Source: *AnObit 1993; BiE&WWA; BioIn 14, 18, 19; CamGWoT; CanWW 70, 79, 80, 81, 83, 89; ConTFT 1, 5; CreCan 2; CurBio 85, 93N; HalFC 80, 84, 88; IntMPA 88, 92; InWom SUP; NotNAT; OxCCanT; OxCThe 83; VarWW 85; WhAm 11; WhoAm 74, 76, 78, 80, 82, 84, 86, 88; WhoAmW 72, 74; WhoHol 92, A; WhoThe 72, 77, 81*

Reid, Ogden Mills
American. Newspaper Publisher
Editor, publisher of *NY Tribune,* 1913-24; bought *NY Herald* to form *NY Herald Tribune;* editor from 1924.
b. May 16, 1882 in New York, New York
d. Jan 3, 1947 in New York, New York
Source: *AmAu&B; BiDAmBL 83; BioIn 1; DcAmB S4; EncAB-A 20; EncAJ; NatCAB 33; OxCAmH; WebAB 74, 79; WhAm 2; WhJnl*

Reid, Thomas
Scottish. Philosopher
Founded Scottish, or common-sense, school of philosophy.
b. Apr 26, 1710 in Strachan, Scotland
d. Oct 7, 1796 in Glasgow, Scotland
Source: *Alli; BbD; BiD&SB; BiDPsy; BioIn 3, 13, 14; BlkwCE; BritAu; CamGEL; CamGLE; CasWL; CmScLit; CyEd; DcBiPP; DcEnA; DcEnL; DcEuL; DcLB 31A; DcNaB; EncEnl; EncEth; EvLB; LuthC 75; McGEWB; NamesHP; NewC; NewCBEL; OxCEng 67, 85, 95; OxCPhil; PenC ENG; RAdv 14, 13-4; WebE&AL*

Reid, Tim
American. Actor
Played Venus Flytrap in TV series "WKRP in Cincinnati," 1978-82;

played Frank Parrish in "Frank's Place."
b. Dec 19, 1944 in Norfolk, Virginia
Source: *AfrAmBi 2; BioIn 14, 15, 16; CelR 90; ConTFT 1, 7, 14; DrBlPA 90; IntMPA 94, 96; LegTOT; VarWW 85; WhoAfA 96; WhoBlA 90, 92, 94; WhoHol 92; WorAlBi*

Reid, Vernon
Musician, Songwriter
Guitarist; 1988 album *Vivid* with band Living Colour went platinum.
b. 1959, England
Source: *BioIn 13, 16; ConMus 2; WhoBlA 92*

Reid, Wallace Eugene
American. Actor
Silent screen star in over 100 films, 1910-22; died from morphine drug addiction.
b. Apr 15, 1891 in Saint Louis, Missouri
d. Jan 18, 1923 in Los Angeles, California
Source: *Film 1; FilmgC; MotPP; MovMk; St&PR 75; TwYS; WhoHol B; WhScrn 74, 77*

Reid, Whitelaw
American. Journalist, Diplomat
Editor, *New York Tribune*, from 1872; Ambassador to France, England; unsuccessful vice-presidential nominee, 1892.
b. Oct 27, 1837 in Xenia, Ohio
d. Dec 15, 1912 in London, England
Source: *Alli; AmAu; AmAu&B; AmBi; ApCAB, X; BbD; BenetAL 91; BiDAmJo; BiD&SB; BioIn 2, 5, 10, 14, 16; CivWDc; CyAL 2; DcAmAu; DcAmB; DcAmDH 80, 89; DcLB 23; DcNAA; Drake; EncAB-H 1974, 1996; EncAJ; GayN; HarEnUS; JrnUS; LegTOT; LinLib L, S; NatCAB 3, 22; OhA&B; OxCAmH; OxCAmL 65, 83, 95; PresAR; REnAL; TwCBDA; WebAB 74, 79; WhAm 1; WhCiWar; WhoWor 74*

Reid Dick, William, Sir
English. Sculptor
Did stone carvings of royalty, large bronzes.
b. Jan 13, 1878 in Glasgow, Scotland
d. Oct 1, 1961 in London, England
Source: *BioIn 14; DcNaB 1961; GrBr*

Reifel, Ben
American. Politician
First member of the Sioux Nation to serve in the US Congress, 1961-71.
b. Sep 19, 1906 in Rosebud Reservation, South Dakota
d. Jan 2, 1990 in Sioux Falls, South Dakota
Source: *BioIn 9, 16, 21; EncNAB; EncNoAI; NotNaAm; WhAm 10; WhoAm 74, 76; WhoGov 72, 75*

Reiffel, Leonard
American. Scientist, Journalist
Won Peabody Award for "The World Tomorrow," 1968; syndicated columnist, 1966-76; expert on physics, outer space.
b. Sep 30, 1927 in Chicago, Illinois
Source: *AmMWSc 76P, 79, 89, 92, 95; BlueB 76; ConAu 101; ScF&FL 92; St&PR 91, 93, 96, 97; WhoAm 74, 76, 78, 80, 82, 84, 86, 88, 90, 92, 94, 95, 96, 97; WhoFI 92; WhoFrS 84; WhoTech 82, 84, 89*

Reik, Theodor
American. Psychoanalyst, Author
Pupil of Freud; disagreed with him on theories of sex, love; wrote *The Psychology of Sex Relations*, 1945.
b. May 12, 1888 in Vienna, Austria
d. Dec 31, 1969 in New York, New York
Source: *AmAu&B; BioIn 1, 2, 4, 7, 8, 9, 10; ConAu 5NR, 5R, 25R; DcAmB S8; EncAB-A 16; RAdv 14, 13-5; REn; REnAL; TwCA SUP; WhAm 5; WhoWorJ 72*

Reilly, Charles Nelson
American. Comedian
Won Tony for *How to Succeed in Business without Really Trying*, 1961; TV includes game shows, situation comedies, varieties.
b. Jan 13, 1931 in New York, New York
Source: *BiE&WWA; BioIn 12, 17; ConTFT 3; IntMPA 82, 84, 86, 88, 92, 94, 96; LegTOT; NotNAT; PlP&P A; VarWW 85; WhoAm 74, 76, 78, 80, 82, 84, 86, 88, 92; WhoEnt 92; WhoHol 92, A; WhoThe 72, 77, 81; WorAl; WorAlBi*

Reilly, Sidney George
[Sigmund Rosenblum]
British. Spy
Began with British intelligence, 1896; disappeared into USSR in 1925, fate unknown.
b. 1874 in Odessa, Russia
d. 1925?
Source: *BiDSovU; BioIn 4, 8, 14, 15; SpyCS*

Reilly, William Kane
American. Government Official
Administrator of the Environmental Protection Agency under Pres. Bush, 1988-93.
b. Jan 26, 1940 in Decatur, Illinois
Source: *BioIn 16; CurBio 89; DcLP 87B; NatLAC; NewYTBS 92; WhoAm 82, 84, 86, 88, 90, 92, 94, 95, 96; WhoAmP 89, 91, 93, 95; WhoE 93; WhoWest 96*

Reiner, Carl
American. Actor, Author
Creative force behind TV's "The Dick Van Dyke Show," 1961-66; won several Emmys; appeared on Broadway, TV, film.
b. Mar 20, 1922 in New York, New York
Source: *BiE&WWA; BioIn 4, 5, 6, 8, 13, 15; CelR, 90; ConAu 112, 138; ConTFT 5; CurBio 61; EncAFC; FacFETw; FilmEn; FilmgC; HalFC 80, 84, 88; IlWWHD 1A; IntMPA 86, 92; JoeFr; LegTOT; LesBEnT, 92; MiSFD 9; MovMk; VarWW 85; WhoAm 74, 76, 78, 80, 82, 84, 86, 88, 90, 92, 94, 95, 96, 97; WhoCom; WhoEnt 92; WhoHol 92, A; WomWMM; WorAl; WorAlBi*

Reiner, Fritz
Hungarian. Conductor
Noted Wagner, Strauss interpreter; director of Metropolitan Opera, 1948-53; Chicago Symphony, 1953-62.
b. Dec 10, 1888 in Budapest, Austria-Hungary
d. Nov 15, 1963 in New York, New York
Source: *Baker 78, 84, 92; BiDAmM; BioIn 1, 2, 3, 4, 6, 7, 8, 11, 12, 13, 20; BriBkM 80; CmOp; CurBio 41, 53, 64; DcAmB S7; FacFETw; IntDcOp; LegTOT; LinLib S; MetOEnc; MusSN; NatCAB 60; NewAmDM; NewEOp 71; NewGrDA 86; NewGrDM 80; NewGrDO; NotNAT B; ObitT 1961; OxDcOp; PenDiMP; WhAm 4; WhScrn 77, 83; WorAl; WorAlBi*

Reiner, Rob(ert)
American. Actor, Director
Played Michael Stivic on "All in the Family," 1971-78; won two Emmys; directed films *Stand by Me*, 1986; *When Harry Met Sally*, 1989; *Sleepl ess in Seattle*, 1993; *The Princess Bride*, 1987.
b. Mar 6, 1947 in New York, New York
Source: *BioIn 9, 11, 12, 15, 16; CelR 90; ConTFT 5; CurBio 88; IntMPA 86, 92, 94, 96; IntWW 91; LesBEnT 92; News 91, 91-2; NewYTBS 87; VarWW 85; WhoAm 86, 90, 96, 97; WhoEnt 92; WhoHol A; WorAlBi*

Reinhardt, Ad(olph Frederick)
American. Artist
Precursor of minimal art; known for monochromatic, black works.
b. Dec 24, 1913 in Buffalo, New York
d. Aug 30, 1967 in New York, New York
Source: *BioIn 4, 5, 6, 7, 8, 11, 12, 13, 14, 17, 20; BriEAA; ConArt 77, 83, 89; ConAu 111; DcAmArt; DcAmB S8; DcCAA 71, 77, 88, 94; FacFETw; MakMC; McGDA; OxCTwCA; OxDcArt; PhDcTCA 77; WhAm 4; WorAlBi; WorArt 1950*

Reinhardt, Django (Jean Baptiste)
Belgian. Jazz Musician, Composer
Swing guitarist with gypsy heritage; first European to influence American jazz.
b. Jan 23, 1910 in Liverchies, Belgium
d. May 16, 1953 in Fontainebleau, France
Source: *AllMusG; Baker 84, 92; BioIn 1, 3, 6, 9, 10, 11, 12, 15, 16; CmpEPM; ConMus 7; DcArts; IlEncJ; LegTOT; NewAmDM; NewGrDJ 88, 94;*

NewGrDM 80; NewOxM; OnThGG; OxCPMus; PenEncP; WhAm 4A

Reinhardt, Max
[Maximilian Goldman]
American. Director, Producer
Expressionism in German films was directly influenced by his way of handling lights, sets, crowds.
b. Sep 9, 1873 in Baden, Austria
d. Oct 31, 1943 in New York, New York
Source: *BiDAmM; BioIn 2, 3, 4, 5, 7, 8, 9, 11, 12, 13, 14, 15, 17, 20; CamGWoT; CmOp; CnThe; CurBio 43; DcArts; DcFM; EncEurC; EncTR, 91; EncWB; EncWT; Ent; FacFETw; FilmEn; FilmgC; GrStDi; HalFC 80, 84, 88; IntDcOp; IntDcT 3; LegTOT; LinLib L, S; LngCTC; MakMC; MetOEnc; MiSFD 9N; NewGrDM 80; NewGrDO; NotNAT A, B; OxCAmT 84; OxCFilm; OxCGer 76, 86; OxCThe 67, 83; OxDcOp; PlP&P; REn; TheaDir; WhAm 2; WhDW; WhThe; WorEFlm*

Reinhart, Charles S
American. Artist
Revolutionized art of magazine, book illustration; most noted works in oil and watercolor: *September Morning,* 1879; *Fishermen of Villerville,* 1886.
b. May 16, 1844 in Pittsburgh, Pennsylvania
d. Aug 30, 1896 in New York, New York
Source: *AmBi; ApCAB; ArtsNiC; DcAmB; EarABI SUP; NatCAB 7; TwCBDA; WhAm HS*

Reinhold, Judge
[Edward Ernest Reinhold]
American. Actor
Films include *Ruthless People,* 1986; *Beverly Hills Cop,* 1984.
b. May 21, 1956? in Wilmington, Delaware
Source: *BioIn 14, 15; ConTFT 5; EncAFC; IntMPA 86, 92; LegTOT; WhoEnt 92; WorAlBi*

Reinking, Ann H
American. Actor, Dancer
Two-time Tony nominee whose plays include *Pippin,* 1972; films include *Annie,* 1982; won Tony for *Chicago,* 1997.
b. Nov 10, 1949 in Seattle, Washington
Source: *BiDD; BioIn 13, 15; ConTFT 4; HalFC 88; InWom SUP; NewYTBS 78, 81; VarWW 85; WhoAm 86, 90; WhoEnt 92; WhoThe 81*

Reisenberg, Nadia
Russian. Pianist
Specialized in radio performances, played all Mozart concertos.
b. Jul 14, 1904 in Vilna, Russia
d. Jun 10, 1983 in New York, New York
Source: *Baker 84, 92; InWom, SUP; NewAmDM; NewGrDA 86; NewYTBS 83*

Reiser, Paul
American. Actor, Comedian
Stand-up comic; starred in TV comedy "My Two Dads," 1987-90; star of "Mad About You," 1992—.
b. Mar 30, 1957 in New York, New York
Source: *BioIn 15; ConAu 153; ConTFT 5, 12; CurBio 96; IntMPA 92, 94, 96; News 95, 95-2; WhoAm 95, 96, 97*

Reiser, Pete
[Harold Patrick Reiser]
"Pistol Pete"
American. Baseball Player
Outfielder, 1940-42, 1946-52, mostly with Brooklyn; led NL in batting, 1941.
b. Mar 17, 1919 in Saint Louis, Missouri
d. Oct 25, 1981 in Palm Springs, California
Source: *Ballpl 90; BioIn 1, 6, 8, 10, 12, 19, 21; LegTOT; NewYTBE 72, 73; NewYTBS 76; WhoProB 73; WhoSpor*

Reisman, Simon
[Sol Simon Reisman]
Canadian. Government Official
Canada's chief negotiator at historic free-trade talks with US, 1985-87.
b. Jun 19, 1919 in Montreal, Quebec, Canada
Source: *BioIn 15, 16; CanWW 31, 70, 79, 80, 81, 83, 89; ConNews 87-4; WhoCanB 86; WhoCanF 86*

Reisner, George Andrew
American. Archaeologist, Educator
Noted Egyptologist; found Queen Hetephere's tomb at Giza.
b. Nov 5, 1867 in Indianapolis, Indiana
d. Jun 6, 1942 in Cairo, Egypt
Source: *ApCAB X; BioIn 2, 9; CurBio 42; DcAmB S3; IndAu 1816; InSci; LuthC 75; WhAm 2; WhE&EA; WhNAA*

Reiss, Albert
German. Opera Singer
Tenor, noted for Wagnerian roles; with NY Met., 1901-20.
b. Feb 22, 1870 in Berlin, Germany
d. Jun 20, 1940 in Nice, France
Source: *Baker 78, 84, 92; BioIn 14; MetOEnc; NewEOp 71; NewGrDM 80; NewGrDO*

Reiss, Stuart
American. Designer
Set decorator; won Oscars for *Diary of Anne Frank,* 1959; *Fantastic Voyage,* 1966.
b. Jul 15, 1921 in Chicago, Illinois
Source: *ConTFT 5; IntMPA 86, 92*

Reisz, Karel
British. Director
Films include *Morgan; Isadora; Saturday Night & Sunday Morning.*
b. Jul 21, 1926 in Ostrava, Czechoslovakia
Source: *BiDFilm, 81, 94; BioIn 12, 16; BlueB 76; ConTFT 5, 13; DcArts; EncEurC; FilmEn; FilmgC; HalFC 80, 84, 88; IlWWBF; IntDcF 1-2, 2-2; IntMPA 75, 76, 77, 78, 79, 80, 81, 82, 84, 86, 88, 92, 94, 96; IntWW 74, 75, 76, 77, 78, 79, 80, 81, 82, 83, 89, 91, 93; MiSFD 9; MovMk; OxCFilm; VarWW 85; Who 82, 83, 85, 88, 90, 92, 94; WhoWor 74, 76, 78, 82, 84, 95, 96; WorEFlm; WorFDir 2*

Reith, John Charles Walsham
[First Baron Reith]
"Father of BBC"
English. Government Official
First director of the BBC, 1920s.
b. Jul 20, 1889 in Stonehaven, Scotland
d. Jun 16, 1971 in Edinburgh, Scotland
Source: *CmScLit; ConAu 113; CurBio 40, 71, 71N; DcNaB 1971; DcTwBBL; DcTwHis; GrBr; InSci; LngCTC; ObitT 1971; WhDW*

Reitman, Ivan
Canadian. Director, Producer
Films include box office hits: *Stripes,* 1981; *Ghostbusters,* 1984.
b. Oct 26, 1946 in Komarno, Czechoslovakia
Source: *BioIn 11, 14, 15, 16; CanWW 31, 89; ConNews 86-3; ConTFT 7, 14; EncAFC; HalFC 84, 88; IntMPA 88, 92, 94, 96; LegTOT; MiSFD 9; NewYTBS 86; VarWW 85; WhoAm 84, 86, 88, 90, 92, 94, 95, 96, 97; WhoEnt 92; WhoWor 95, 96, 97*

Reitsch, Hanna
German. Aviator
Foremost of Germany's female pilots who served during WWII.
b. Mar 29, 1912 in Hirschberg, Germany
d. Aug 24, 1979 in Frankfurt am Main, Germany (West)
Source: *BioIn 2, 3, 5, 7, 12, 14, 15; ConAu 89; EncTR, 91; FacFETw; InWom, SUP; NewYTBS 79*

R.E.M.
[Bill Berry; Peter Buck; Mike Mills; Michael Stipe]
American. Music Group
Winner of three Grammy Awards, *Out of Time,* 1991.
Source: *BioIn 17, 18, 20, 21; EncRkSt; MiSFD 9; ObitT 1951; PenDiMP; WhoAm 94, 95, 96, 97*

Remarque, Erich Maria
[Erich Paul Remark]
American. Author
Wrote *All Quiet on the Western Front,* 1929; adapted to film, 1930.
b. Jun 22, 1898 in Osnabruck, Germany
d. Sep 25, 1970 in Locarno, Switzerland
Source: *AmAu&B; Benet 87, 96; BenetAL 91; BiDMoPL; BiGAW; BioIn 14, 15, 16, 17, 21; CasWL; ClDMEL 47, 80; ConAu 29R, 77; ConLC 21; CyWA 58; DcArts; DcLB 56; EncTR, 91; EncWL, 2, 3; EvEuW; FacFETw; FilmgC; HalFC 80, 84, 88; LegTOT; LiExTwC; LinLib L, S; LngCTC; MajTwCW; McGEWB; ModGL; NotNAT*

B; Novels; ObitT 1961; OxCEng 67, 85, 95; OxCGer 76, 86; PenC EUR; RAdv 14, 13-2; REn; REnAL; RfGWoL 95; TwCA, SUP; TwCWr; WhAm 5; WhoTwCL; WhScrn 77, 83; WorAl; WorAlBi

Rembrandt (Harmenszoon van Rijn)
Dutch. Artist
Master of light, shadow; notable works include *Nightwatch,* 1642; *Flight into Egypt,* 1627.
b. Jul 15, 1607 in Leiden, Netherlands
d. Oct 4, 1669, Netherlands
Source: *AtlBL; BioIn 10; NewC; NewEOp 71; REn; WhDW; WorAl*

Remenyi, Eduard
Hungarian. Musician, Composer
Violin soloist to Queen Victoria, 1854; had brilliant American tour, 1880s; said to be unexcelled for vigor, pathos.
b. Jul 17, 1830 in Heves, Hungary
d. May 15, 1898 in San Francisco, California
Source: *Baker 78, 84; BiDAmM; BioIn 2; NewGrDM 80; OxCMus*

Remick, Lee
[Mrs. William "Kip" Gowans]
American. Actor
Film and Broadway star; noted for role of mother in film *The Omen,* 1976; Oscar nominee for *Days of Wine and Roses,* 1963.
b. Dec 14, 1935 in Quincy, Massachusetts
d. Jul 2, 1991 in Los Angeles, California
Source: *AnObit 1991; BiDFilm, 81, 94; BioIn 5, 6, 7, 9, 10, 11, 13, 14, 16, 17, 18, 21; BkPepl; BlueB 76; CelR 90; ConTFT 7, 10; CurBio 66, 91N; DcArts; FilmEn; FilmgC; ForYSC; HalFC 80, 84, 88; IntDcF 1-3, 2-3; IntMPA 86, 88; IntWW 74, 75, 76, 77, 78, 79, 80, 81, 82, 83, 89, 91; InWom, SUP; LegTOT; LesBEnT 92; MotPP; MovMk; News 92; NewYTBS 91; NotNAT; OxCFilm; VarWW 85; WhAm 10; WhoAm 74, 76, 78, 86, 90; WhoAmW 79, 81, 83, 85, 87, 91; WhoHol A; WorAl; WorAlBi; WorEFlm*

Remington, Eliphalet
American. Manufacturer
Manufactured the Remington rifle, 1828, with father.
b. Oct 27, 1793 in Suffield, Connecticut
d. Apr 4, 1889 in Silver Springs, Florida
Source: *AmBi; AntBDN F; BiDAmBL 83; BioIn 18; DcAmB; NatCAB 9; TwCBDA; WebAB 74, 79; WhAm HS; WorAl; WorAlBi*

Remington, Frederic
American. Artist, Sculptor
Paintings, bronze sculptures depict the Old West.
b. Oct 4, 1861 in Canton, New York
d. Dec 26, 1909 in Ridgefield, Connecticut
Source: *AmAu; AmAu&B; AmBi; ApCAB X; ArtsAmW 1; AtlBL; Benet 87; BenetAL 91; BibAL; BioIn 1, 2, 3, 4, 5, 6, 7, 8, 9, 10, 11, 12, 13, 14, 15, 16, 17, 20; ClaDrA; CnDAL; ConAu 108; DcAmArt; DcAmAu; DcAmB; DcArts; DcLB 12; DcLEL; DcNAA; EncAAH; EncAB-H 1974, 1996; EncFWF; FifWWr; GayN; IlBEAAW; LegTOT; LinLib L, S; McGDA; McGEWB; MemAm; NatCAB 22; OxCAmH; OxCAmL 65, 83; OxDcArt; PeoHis; REn; REnAL; REnAW; SmATA 41; WebAB 74, 79; WhAm 1; WhCiWar; WhNaAH; WhoFtbl 74; WorAl; WorAlBi*

Rempp, Adolph
American. Restaurateur
Introduced papaya extract tenderizer; later became Adolph's Meat Tenderizer.
b. 1911
d. Apr 26, 1988 in Morro Bay, California
Source: *BioIn 15; Entr*

Remsen, Ira
American. Chemist, Educator, University Administrator
Discovered saccharin, Remsen's law; pres., John Hopkins U, 1901-13.
b. Feb 10, 1846 in New York, New York
d. Mar 5, 1927 in Carmel, California
Source: *Alli SUP; AmAu&B; AmBi; ApCAB; BiDAmEd; BiDAmS; BiDSA; BiESc; BioIn 1, 3, 6, 12; DcAmAu; DcAmB; DcNAA; DcScB; InSci; LegTOT; LinLib S; NatCAB 9, 37; OxCAmH; TwCBDA; WebAB 74, 79; WhAm 1; WhNAA; WorAl; WorAlBi*

Renaldo, Duncan
"The Cisco Kid"
American. Actor, Producer
Best known as star of Western series, playing the Cisco Kid.
b. Apr 23, 1904 in Camden, New Jersey
d. Sep 3, 1980 in Santa Barbara, California
Source: *BioIn 4, 78, 79, 80; LegTOT; MotPP; MovMk; WhAm 7; What 3; WhoAm 76; WhoHol A; WhoWest 74, 76; WhScrn 83*

Renan, (Joseph) Ernest
French. Historian
Wrote first biography to treat Jesus as historical figure: *Life of Jesus,* 1863.
b. Jan 27, 1823 in Treguier, France
d. Oct 2, 1892 in Paris, France
Source: *BbD; Benet 87, 96; BiD&SB; BioIn 1, 2, 3, 4, 5, 7, 8, 12, 13, 16, 18; CasWL; CelCen; ClDMEL 47; DcBiPP; DcEuL; Dis&D; EuAu; EvEuW; GuFrLit 1; LinLib L, S; LuthC 75; McGEWB; NewC; NewCBEL; NinCLC 26; OxCEng 67, 85, 95; OxCFr; OxCLiW 86; PenC EUR; RComWL; REn; WhDW*

Renard, Jules
French. Dramatist, Author
Wrote autobiography, *Poil de Carotte,* 1894, which was basis for his best-known play, 1900.
b. Feb 22, 1864 in Chalons-sur-Mayenne, France
d. May 22, 1910 in Paris, France
Source: *BioIn 1, 7; CasWL; ClDMEL 47, 80; CnMD; ConAu 117; Dis&D; EncWL; Ent; EuAu; EvEuW; GuFrLit 1; McGEWD 72, 84; ModWD; NotNAT B; OxCFr; PenC EUR; TwCLC 17*

Renaud, Madeleine
French. Actor
With France's national theatre company, Comedie Francaise, 1923-46; co-founded Renaud-Barrault Company, 1947.
b. Feb 21, 1903
d. Sep 23, 1994 in Neuilly, France
Source: *BioIn 3; ContDcW 89; CurBio 94N; DcTwCCu 2; EncEurC; EncWT; Ent; FilmAG WE; FilmEn; IntDcWB; IntWW 74, 75, 76, 77, 78, 79, 80, 81, 82; InWom; Who 74, 82, 83, 85, 88, 90, 92, 94*

Renaud, Maurice
French. Opera Singer
Dramatic baritone; noted for costuming, make-up; NYC star, 1906-12.
b. Jul 24, 1861 in Bordeaux, France
d. Oct 16, 1933 in Paris, France
Source: *Baker 78, 84; BioIn 14; CmOp; MetOEnc; MusSN; NewEOp 71; NewGrDM 80; OxDcOp*

Renault, Gilbert (Leon Etienne Theodore)
French. Soldier, Banker
Much-decorated WW II French Resistance leader.
b. Aug 6, 1904 in Vannes, France
d. Jul 30, 1984 in Guingamp, France
Source: *AnObit 1984; ConAu 113; FacFETw*

Renault, Louis
French. Educator, Diplomat
Shared 1907 Nobel Peace Prize for work at The Hague Peace Conferences, 1899, 1907.
b. May 21, 1843 in Autun, France
d. Feb 8, 1918 in Barbizon, France
Source: *BioIn 9, 11, 15; LinLib L; NobelP; OxCLaw; WhoNob, 90, 95*

Renault, Louis
French. Auto Manufacturer
Developed largest motor plant in France; arrested for aiding Nazis during occupation of France, 1944.
b. 1877? in Paris, France
d. Oct 24, 1944 in Paris, France
Source: *BioIn 4, 8, 16; CurBio 44; Entr; InSci; LegTOT; WorInv*

Renault, Mary
[Mary Challans]
English. Author
Wrote historical novels depicting life in ancient Greece, Rome: *The King Must Die,* 1958.
b. Sep 4, 1905 in London, England
d. Dec 13, 1983 in Cape Town, South Africa
Source: *AnObit 1983; ArtclWW 2; Au&Wr 71; AuBYP 2, 3; Benet 87, 96; BioIn 13, 14, 16, 19, 20; BlmGWL; BlueB 76; CamGEL; CamGLE; ConAu 81, 111; ConLC 3, 11, 17; ConNov 72, 76, 82; CurBio 59, 84N; CyWA 89; DcArts; DcLB Y83N; DcNaB 1981; EncBrWW; EncSoA; FacFETw; FemiCLE; GayLesB; GayLL; GrWomW; GrWrEL N; IntAu&W 76, 77; IntWW 74, 75, 76, 77, 78, 79, 80, 81, 82, 83; InWom SUP; LinLib L; LngCTC; ModBrL S1, S2; ModCmwL; ModWoWr; NewC; NewYTBS 83; Novels; OxCEng 85, 95; RAdv 1; REn; RfGEnL 91; RGTwCWr; SmATA 23, 36N; TwCRHW 90, 94; TwCWr; WhAm 8; Who 74, 83, 85N; WhoAmW 66, 68, 70, 72; WhoWor 74, 76, 78; WorAl; WorAlBi; WorAu 1950; WrDr 76, 80, 82, 84*

Rendell, Ruth
English. Author
Mystery writer, wrote *A Demon in My View,* 1976; *A Fatal Inversion,* 1987.
b. Feb 17, 1930 in London, England
Source: *ArtclWW 2; BioIn 12, 13, 14, 15, 16, 17, 18, 19, 20, 21; BlmGWL; ConAu 32NR, 109; ConLC 28, 48; ConNov 91; CrtSuMy; CurBio 94; DcArts; DcLB 87; EncBrWW; EncWB; FemiCLE; GrWomMW; IntAu&W 89, 91, 93; IntWW 89, 91, 93; InWom SUP; LegTOT; MajTwCW; Novels; RAdv 14; TwCCr&M 80, 85, 91; WorAlBi; WorAu 1980; WrDr 82, 84, 86, 88, 90, 92, 94, 96*

Renfro, Mel(vin Lacy)
American. Football Player
Ten-time all-pro defensive back, Dallas, 1964-77.
b. Dec 30, 1941 in Houston, Texas
Source: *BiDAmSp Sup; BioIn 10; WhoAfA 96; WhoBlA 77, 80, 85, 88, 90, 92, 94; WhoFtbl 74*

Reni, Guido
Italian. Artist
Painted mythological, religious scenes; noted for *Crucifixion of St. Peter.*
b. Nov 4, 1575 in Bologna, Italy
d. Aug 18, 1642 in Bologna, Italy
Source: *AtlBL; BioIn 4, 8, 9, 10, 12, 14, 15, 16, 19; ClaDrA; DcArts; IntDcAA 90; LegTOT; LinLib S; LuthC 75; McGDA; McGEWB; NewCol 75; OxCArt; OxCEng 85, 95; OxDcArt; REn; WebBD 83; WhDW*

Renick, Marion Lewis
American. Children's Author
Books on sports include *Sam Discovers Hockey,* 1975.
b. Mar 9, 1905 in Springfield, Ohio
Source: *AuBYP 2, 3; ConAu 1NR, 1R; MorJA; OhA&B; SmATA 1; WhoAmW 66, 68*

Rennie, Michael
English. Actor
Played Harry Lime in TV series "The Third Man," 1960.
b. Aug 29, 1909 in Bradford, England
d. Jun 10, 1971 in Harrogate, England
Source: *BiE&WWA; BioIn 5, 9, 10; DcAmB S9; FilmAG WE; FilmEn; FilmgC; ForYSC; HalFC 80, 84, 88; IlWWBF; ItaFilm; LegTOT; MotPP; MovMk; NewEScF; NewYTBE 71; NotNAT B; ObitT 1971; WhoHol B; WhoHrs 80; WhScrn 74, 77, 83; WorAl; WorAlBi*

Reno, Janet
American. Government Official
Attorney General, 1993—.
b. Jul 21, 1938 in Miami, Florida
Source: *BioIn 18, 19, 20, 21; CopCroC; CurBio 93; EncWHA; GrLiveH; IntWW 93; LegTOT; News 93-3; NewYTBS 93; Who 94; WhoAm 86, 88, 90, 92, 94, 95, 96, 97; WhoAmL 83, 85, 87, 94, 96; WhoAmW 95, 97; WhoSSW 84; WhoWor 95, 96, 97; WomLaw; WomStre*

Reno, Mike
Canadian. Singer
With Ann Wilson, had hit single "Almost Paradise," 1984.
b. Jan 8, 1955 in Vancouver, British Columbia, Canada
Source: *RkOn 85*

Renoir, (Pierre) Auguste
French. Artist
Impressionist painter; subjects: nudes, flowers, social scenes, represent optimistic view of life.
b. Feb 25, 1841 in Limoges, France
d. Dec 17, 1919 in Cagnes-sur-Mer, France
Source: *AtlBL; Benet 87, 96; BioIn 1, 2, 3, 4, 5, 6, 7, 8, 9, 10, 11, 12, 13, 14, 15, 16, 17, 18, 19, 21; ClaDrA; IntDcAA 90; LegTOT; LinLib S; McGEWB; NewCol 75; OxCArt; OxCFr; RAdv 14, 13-3; REn; WebBD 83; WhDW; WorAl*

Renoir, Jean
French. Director, Screenwriter
Best known for film *The Rules of the Game,* 1939; son of artist, Auguste Renoir.
b. Sep 15, 1894 in Paris, France
d. Feb 12, 1979 in Beverly Hills, California
Source: *Au&Wr 71, 78, 79; IntWW 74, 75, 76, 77, 78; ItaFilm; LegTOT; MakMC; MiSFD 9N; MovMk; NewYTBS 79; OxCFilm; OxDcArt; RAdv 14; REn; WhAm 7; WhDW; Who 74; WhoAm 74, 76, 78; WhoFr 79; WhoHol A; WhoWor 74; WhScrn 83; WorAl; WorAlBi; WorEFlm; WorFDir 1*

Rense, Paige
American. Editor
Editor-in-chief, *Architectural Digest, Bon Apetit* mags; wrote *Decorating for Celebrities.*
b. 1934? in Des Moines, Iowa
Source: *BioIn 16; EncTwCJ; InWom SUP; NewYTBS 81, 90; WhoAm 86, 90; WhoAmW 87, 91*

Rentner, Maurice
Manufacturer
First manufacturer of ready-made dresses to use designers to create original fashions, 1920s; introduced shirt-waist dress, soft tailored suit, short dinner dress.
b. Mar 3, 1889? in Warsaw, Poland
d. Jul 7, 1958 in New York, New York
Source: *BioIn 4, 5, 11; ConFash; EncFash; NatCAB 57*

Rentzel, Lance
American. Football Player
Wide receiver, 1965-74, mostly with Dallas; led NFL in TD's, 1969; suspended, 1973, for indecent conduct.
b. Oct 14, 1943 in Flushing, New York
Source: *BioIn 9, 10, 13; WhoFtbl 74*

Renvall, Johan Bengt Erik
American. Dancer
A leading performer, choreographer with American Ballet Theatre, 1978—, principle dancer, American Ballet Theatre, 1987—.
b. Sep 22, 1959 in Stockholm, Sweden
Source: *BioIn 13, 16; ConNews 87-4; WhoE 83; WhoEnt 92*

Renwick, James, Jr.
American. Architect
Designs include Smithsonian, Corcoran Galleries, Washington, DC.
b. Nov 1, 1818 in Bloomingdale, New York
d. Jun 23, 1895 in New York, New York
Source: *AmBi; ApCAB; BiDAmAr; BioIn 2, 11, 12; BriEAA; DcAmB; DcD&D; EncAAr 1, 2; IntDcAr; LegTOT; LinLib S; MacEA; McGDA; McGEWB; NatCAB 11; OxCAmH; TwCBDA; WebAB 74, 79; WhAm HS; WhoArch; WorAl; WorAlBi*

REO Speedwagon
[Kevin Cronin; Neal Doughty; Alan Gratzer; Bruce Hall; Gregg Philbin; Gary Richrath]
American. Music Group
Album *High Infidelity,* 1981, sold over six million copies; hit single "Can't Fight This Feeling," 1985.
Source: *BioIn 12; ConMuA 80A; EncPR&S 89; EncRk 88; EncRkSt; HarEnR 86; NewAmDM; PenEncP; RkOn 85; RolSEnR 83; WhoRock 81; WhoRocM 82*

Repin, Ilya Yefimovich
Russian. Artist
Leading Russian painter, 1800s; many portraits of Tolstoy have often been reproduced.
b. Aug 5, 1844 in Tschuguev, Russia
d. Oct 29, 1930 in Knokkala, Finland
Source: *BioIn 2; McGDA; NewCol 75; WebBD 83*

Replacements, The
American. Music Group
Rock and roll band formed in the 1980s; hit single "I'll Be You," 1989.
Source: *BioIn 15, 19, 20; ConMus 7; EncPR&S 89; EncRkSt; NewYTBS 95*

Repplier, Agnes
American. Essayist
Known for collections of scholarly essays: *Compromises,* 1904.
b. Apr 1, 1858 in Philadelphia, Pennsylvania
d. Dec 15, 1950 in Philadelphia, Pennsylvania
Source: *Alli SUP; AmAu&B; BiD&SB; BioIn 1, 2, 4, 9; CathA 1930; ChhPo, S1; CnDAL; ConAmA; ConAmL; DcAmAu; DcAmB S4; DcLEL; LngCTC; NotAW; OxCAmL 65, 83, 95; REn; REnAL; TwCA, SUP; TwCBDA; WhAm 3; WhE&EA; WhNAA; WomWWA 14*

Repton, Humphry
English. Landscape Architect
One of the foremost exponents of English landscape gardening; park at Cobham, Kent an example of his work; wrote *Sketches & Hints on Landscape Gardening,* 1795.
b. 1752 in Bury Saint Edmunds, England
d. Mar 24, 1818 in Romford, England
Source: *BioIn 1, 4, 7, 9, 10, 15; DcBrBI; DcD&D; DcNaB; IntDcAr; MacEA; McGDA; OxCArt; OxCDecA; OxDcArt; WhoArch*

Reshevsky, Samuel
American. Chess Player
Started as a child chess prodigy at age 8; won 7 US chess championships between 1936 and 1971; first full-time professional chess player, 1936-54.
b. Nov 26, 1911 in Ozorkow, Poland
d. Apr 4, 1992 in Suffern, New York
Source: *AnObit 1992; BioIn 1, 2, 3, 4, 5, 10, 12, 17, 18, 19; CurBio 55, 92N; GolEC; NewYTBS 81, 92; OxCChes 84; WhoAm 82, 84*

Resnais, Alain
French. Director
Films include *Hiroshima Mon Amour; Last Year at Marienbad.*
b. Jun 3, 1922 in Vannes, France
Source: *Benet 87, 96; BiDFilm, 81, 94; BioIn 5, 6, 7, 8, 10, 11, 12, 13, 15, 16; ConLC 16; ConTFT 5; CurBio 65; DcArts; DcFM; DcTwCCu 2; EncEurC; FacFETw; FilmEn; FilmgC; HalFC 80, 84, 88; IntDcF 1-2, 2-2; IntMPA 78, 79, 80, 81, 82, 84, 86, 88, 92, 94, 96; IntWW 74, 75, 76, 77, 78, 79, 80, 81, 82, 83, 89, 91, 93; ItaFilm; LegTOT; MakMC; MiSFD 9; MovMk; OxCFilm; REn; VarWW 85; Who 82, 83, 85, 88, 90, 92, 94; WhoFr 79; WhoWor 74, 76, 78, 82, 84, 87, 89, 91, 93, 95, 96; WomWMM; WorAl; WorAlBi; WorEFlm; WorFDir 2*

Resnik, Judy
[Judith Resnik]
"J R"
American. Astronaut
Second American woman in space; died in explosion of space shuttle *Challenger.*
b. Apr 5, 1949 in Akron, Ohio
d. Jan 28, 1986 in Cape Canaveral, Florida
Source: *AnObit 1986; FacFETw; NewYTBS 86*

Resnik, Muriel
American. Writer
Wrote the play *Any Wednesday,* 1964.
d. Mar 6, 1995 in New York, New York
Source: *AmWomD; BiE&WWA; BioIn 20; NewYTBS 95; NotNAT, A*

Resnik, Regina
American. Opera Singer
Soprano, changed to mezzo-soprano, 1950s; starred in NY Met. since 1946; taught opera seminars.
b. Aug 20, 1922 in New York, New York
Source: *Baker 78, 84, 92; BioIn 1, 2, 4, 6, 7, 8, 9, 11, 13, 14; CurBio 56; IntDcOp; IntWW 74, 75, 76, 77, 82; IntWWM 77, 80, 90; InWom, SUP; MetOEnc; MusSN; NewAmDM; NewEOp 71; NewGrDM 80; NewGrDO; OxDcOp; PenDiMP; WhoAm 86, 90; WhoEnt 92A; WhoMus 72; WhoWor 74; WhoWorJ 72*

Resor, Stanley Burnett
American. Advertising Executive
Pres., 1916-55, chm., 1955-61, J Walter Thompson advertising agency.
b. Apr 30, 1879 in Cincinnati, Ohio
d. Oct 29, 1962 in New York, New York
Source: *CurBio 49, 62; DcAmB S7; WhAm 4*

Resor, Stanley Rogers
American. Government Official
Civilian secretary of the Army, 1965-71.
b. Dec 5, 1917 in New York, New York
Source: *BioIn 7, 8, 11; CurBio 69; PolProf J; WhoAm 74, 76, 78, 84, 86, 88, 90, 92, 94, 95, 96, 97; WhoAmL 87, 90, 96; WhoE 95; WhoGov 72*

Respighi, Ottorino
Italian. Composer, Musician
Wrote opera *Belfagor,* 1923; tone poem *Pini di Roma,* 1924.
b. Jul 9, 1879 in Bologna, Italy
d. Apr 18, 1936 in Rome, Italy
Source: *Baker 78, 84, 92; BioIn 3, 4, 6, 8, 11, 12, 20; BriBkM 80; CmOp; CompSN, SUP; DancEn 78; DcArts; DcCathB; DcCom 77; DcCom&M 79; DcPup; FacFETw; LegTOT; McGEWB; MetOEnc; MusMk; NewAmDM; NewEOp 71; NewGrDM 80; NewGrDO; NewOxM; OxCMus; OxDcOp; PenDiMP A; REn; WhDW*

Reston, James (Barrett)
American. Journalist
Wrote *NY Times* column, "Washington," 1974-87; won Pulitzers for nat. reporting, 1945, 1957.
b. Nov 3, 1909 in Clydebank, Scotland
d. Dec 6, 1995 in Washington, District of Columbia
Source: *AmAu&B; AuNews 1, 2; BiDAmNC; BioIn 1, 2, 3, 4, 5, 6, 7, 8, 9, 10, 11, 12, 15, 17, 18, 21; BlueB 76; CelR; ConAu 31NR, 65, 150; CurBio 43, 80, 96N; EncTwCJ; EncWB; IntAu&W 76, 77, 89, 91; IntWW 74, 75, 76, 77, 78, 79, 80, 81, 82, 83, 89, 91, 93; JrnUS; LegTOT; LinLib S; NewYTBS 95; OhA&B; PolProf E; REnAL; St&PR 75, 84, 87; WebAB 74, 79; WhAm 11; WhoAm 74, 76, 78, 80, 82, 84, 90, 92, 94, 95, 96; WhoE 83, 85, 86, 89; WhoSSW 73; WhoWor 74, 78, 80, 82, 84, 87, 89, 91, 93, 95; WorAl; WorAlBi; WrDr 76, 80, 82, 84, 86, 88, 90, 92, 94, 96*

Rethberg, Elizabeth
[Elizabeth Sattler]
American. Opera Singer
Described as "world's most perfect singer;" with NY Met., 1922-42.
b. Sep 22, 1894 in Schwarzenburg, Germany
d. Jun 6, 1976 in Yorktown Heights, New York
Source: *NewEOp 71*

Retton, Mary Lou
[Mrs. Shannon Kelley]
American. Gymnast
First American woman to win individual medal in gymnastics, 1984 Olympics; *SI's* Sportswoman of 1984.
b. Jan 24, 1968 in Fairmont, West Virginia
Source: *BiDAmSp BK; BioIn 13, 14, 15, 16; ConNews 85-2; CurBio 86; EncWomS; LegTOT; NewYTBS 84, 85; WhoSpor; WomFir; WorAlBi*

Reuben, David Robert
American. Psychiatrist, Author
Wrote *Everything You Always Wanted to Know About Sex,* 1969.
b. Jul 29, 1933 in Chicago, Illinois
Source: *Au&Wr 71; AuNews 1; BioNews 74; WhoAm 76, 78, 80, 82, 84, 86; WhoWest 74; WorAl; WorAlBi; WrDr 76, 86, 92*

Reulbach, Ed(ward Marvin)
"Big Ed"
American. Baseball Player
Pitcher, 1905-17, mostly with Cubs; had 40 career shutouts, including two in one day, 1908.
b. Dec 4, 1882 in Detroit, Michigan

d. Jul 17, 1961 in Glens Falls, New York
Source: *Ballpl 90; BiDAmSp BB; BioIn 3, 6, 15; WhoProB 73*

Reuter, Ernst
German. Politician
Mayor of West Berlin from 1948 to 1953; foe of communism, supported German friendship with West.
b. Jul 29, 1889 in Apenrade, Germany
d. Sep 29, 1953 in Berlin, Germany (West)
Source: *BioIn 1, 2, 3, 16; CurBio 49, 53; ObitT 1951*

Reuter, Paul Julius Von
[Israel Beer Josaphat]
English. Journalist
Founded news service using telegraph lines, carrier pidgeons, 1849; now called Reuter's News Agency.
b. Jul 21, 1816 in Kassel, Germany
d. Feb 25, 1899 in Nice, France
Source: *BioIn 14; DcBiPP; REn; WhDW; WorAl*

Reuther, Roy
American. Labor Union Official
Brother of Walter; one of organizers of UAW.
b. 1909 in Wheeling, West Virginia
d. Jan 10, 1968 in Detroit, Michigan
Source: *BiDAmL; BiDAmLL; BioIn 8, 10; ObitOF 79*

Reuther, Walter Philip
American. Labor Union Official
Pres., UAW, 1946-70; instrumental in introducing unionization to auto companies.
b. Sep 1, 1907 in Wheeling, West Virginia
d. May 10, 1970 in Pellston, Michigan
Source: *AmAu&B; AmSocL; BiDAmL; BiDAmLL; BioIn 1, 2, 3, 4, 5, 6, 7, 8, 9, 10, 11, 12, 13, 14, 15, 16, 17, 19, 21; CurBio 41, 49, 70; DcAmB S8; DcPol; DcTwHis; EncAB-H 1974, 1996; EncABHB 5; LinLib S; McGEWB; MorMA; NewYTBE 70; OxCAmH; WebAB 74, 79; WhAm 5; WhDW; WorAl*

Revard, Carter
American. Poet
Poems collected in *Ponca War Dancers,* 1980.
b. 1931
Source: *BioIn 21; DcNAL; NatNAL; NotNaAm*

Revel, Jean Francois
French. Author, Philosopher
Columnist for *L'Express* mag., 1966-81; books include *Ideas of Our Times,* 1972.
b. Jan 19, 1924 in Marseilles, France
Source: *BioIn 10, 11; ConAu 127; CurBio 75; IntAu&W 89; IntWW 83, 91; NewYTBE 71; NewYTBS 77; WhoWor 74*

Revelle, Roger Randall
American. Oceanographer, Educator
Combined study of sea with geography, geology, geophysics, and meteorology; founding director of Center for Population Studies, Harvard U, 1964.
b. Mar 7, 1909 in Seattle, Washington
d. Jul 15, 1991 in San Diego, California
Source: *AmMWSc 92; BioIn 14; CurBio 91N; IntWW 91; NewYTBS 91; WhoAm 88*

Revels, Hiram Rhodes
American. Politician
First black man sworn into Senate office; Rep. from MS, 1870-71.
b. Sep 27, 1827 in Fayetteville, North Carolina
d. Jan 16, 1901 in Aberdeen, Mississippi
Source: *AfrAmAl 6; ApCAB; BiAUS; BiDrAC; BiDrUSC 89; BioIn 17; BlkAmsC; BlkCO; DcAmB; TwCBDA; WebAB 74; WhAm HS; WhAmP*

Reventlow, Lance
American. Auto Racer
Son of millionairess Barbara Hutton; developed *Scarab* racing car to compete with Europeans, late 1950s; died in plane crash.
b. Feb 24, 1936 in London, England
d. Jul 25, 1972 in Colorado
Source: *BioIn 5, 9, 13, 14; NewYTBE 72*

Revere, Anne
American. Actor
Best known for playing wise mothers in films, 1940s-50s; won supporting actress Oscar for role as Elizabeth Taylor's mother in *National Velvet,* 1945; career cut short for refusing to testify about alleged communism.
b. Jun 25, 1903 in New York, New York
d. Dec 18, 1990 in Locust Valley, New York
Source: *AnObit 1990; BiE&WWA; BioIn 7, 17; FilmEn; FilmgC; ForYSC; HalFC 80, 84, 88; HolCA; IntMPA 77, 88; InWom; LegTOT; NewYTBS 90; NotNAT; PlP&P; VarWW 85; WhAm 10; What 1; WhoAm 80; WhoHol A*

Revere, Paul
American. Patriot, Designer
Rode from Boston to Lexington, MA to warn of British attack, Apr 18, 1775; famous cry: "The British are coming!"; famed silversmith.
b. Jan 1, 1735 in Boston, Massachusetts
d. May 10, 1818 in Boston, Massachusetts
Source: *AmBi; AmRev; AntBDN Q; ApCAB; Benet 87, 96; BenetAL 91; BiDAmM; BioIn 1, 2, 3, 4, 5, 6, 7, 8, 9, 10, 11, 12, 14, 15, 16, 19, 20; BlkwEAR; BriEAA; DcAmArt; DcAmB; DcD&D; DcNiCA; Dis&D; Drake; EarABI; EncAB-H 1974, 1996; EncAI&E; EncAR; EncCRAm; EncNAB; HarEnMi; HarEnUS; LegTOT; LinLib S; McGDA; McGEWB; MorMA; NatCAB 1; NewCol 75; NewYHSD; OxCAmH; OxCAmL 65, 83, 95; OxCDecA; RComAH; REn; REnAL; TwCBDA; WebAB 74, 79; WebAMB; WebBD 83; WhAm HS; WhAmRev; WhDW; WorAl; WorAlBi; WorECar*

Revill, Clive Selsby
New Zealander. Actor
Character actor, 1959—; films include *The Empire Strikes Back,* 1980; *Zorro, the Gay Blade,* 1981.
b. Apr 18, 1930 in Wellington, New Zealand
Source: *BiE&WWA; EncMT; FilmEn; FilmgC; HalFC 88; IntMPA 92; VarWW 85; WhoHol A; WhoThe 81*

Revolta, Johnny
[John Revolta]
American. Golfer
Touring pro, 1930s-40s; won PGA, 1935; Hall of Fame, 1963.
b. Apr 5, 1911 in Saint Louis, Missouri
d. Mar 3, 1991 in Palm Springs, California
Source: *BiDAmSp Sup; BioIn 17; NewYTBS 91; WhoGolf*

Revson, Charles Haskell
American. Cosmetics Executive
Founded Revlon, Inc, 1932; pres., 1932-62; chm., 1962-75.
b. Oct 11, 1906 in Manchester, New Hampshire
d. Aug 24, 1975 in New York, New York
Source: *BioIn 4, 5, 10, 11, 13; BusPN; ConAmBL; DcAmB S9; NewYTBS 75; ObitT 1971; St&PR 75; WhAm 6; WhoAm 74; WhoFI 74, 75; WhoWor 74; WorAl*

Revson, Peter Jeffrey
American. Auto Racer
Nephew of Charles Revson; killed during practice for auto race.
b. Feb 27, 1939 in New York, New York
d. Mar 22, 1974 in Johannesburg, South Africa
Source: *BioIn 9, 10, 12; BioNews 74; ObitT 1971*

Rexroth, Kenneth
American. Poet
Beat generation writer, 1950s; interested in mystical forms of experience.
b. Dec 22, 1905 in South Bend, Indiana
d. Jun 6, 1982 in Montecito, California
Source: *AmAu&B; AnObit 1982; Benet 87, 96; BenetAL 91; BioIn 4, 7, 8, 9, 10, 12, 13, 15, 17, 19, 20; BlueB 76; CamGLE; CamHAL; CelR; ChhPo, S3; CmCal; CnE&AP; ConAu 5NR, 5R, 14NR, 34NR, 107; ConDr 73, 77, 82, 93; ConLC 1, 2, 6, 11, 22, 49; ConPo 70, 75, 80; CurBio 81, 82, 82N; CyWA 89; DcLB 16, 48, 165, Y82A; DcLEL 1940; DrAP 75; DrAPF 80; EncWL 2, 3; FacFETw; GrWrEL P; IndAu 1917; IntAu&W 76, 77; IntWW 74, 75, 76, 77, 78, 79, 80, 81, 82; IntWWP 77; LegTOT; LinLib L; LNinSix; MajTwCW; ModAL, S1, S2; NewCon; OxCAmL 65, 83, 95;*

OxCTwCP; PenC AM; RAdv 1, 14, 13-1; REn; REnAL; RfGAmL 87, 94; RGTwCWr; TwCA SUP; WebE&AL; WhAm 6, 8; WhoAm 74, 76, 78, 80, 82; WhoTwCL; WhoWest 74; WhoWor 74; WrDr 76, 80, 82

Rey, Alejandro
Argentine. Actor, Director
Played Carlos Ramirez in TV series "The Flying Nun," 1967-70.
b. Feb 8, 1930 in Buenos Aires, Argentina
d. May 21, 1987 in Los Angeles, California
Source: *BioIn 15; HalFC 88; NewYTBS 87; VarWW 85; WhAm 9; WhoAm 74, 76*

Rey, Alvino
[Alvin McGurney]
American. Bandleader, Musician
Pioneer in development of electric guitar; featured guitarist on King Family TV series, 1960s.
b. Jul 1, 1911 in Oakland, California
Source: *BiDAmM; BioIn 9, 12; CmpEPM; LegTOT; OnThGG; PenEncP; RadStar*

Rey, Fernando
[Fernando Casado Arambillet]
Spanish. Actor
Character actor; played criminal mastermind in *The French Connection*, 1971.
b. Sep 20, 1917 in La Coruna, Spain
d. Mar 9, 1994 in Madrid, Spain
Source: *BioIn 11, 12, 15, 19, 20; ConTFT 8, 13; CurBio 79, 94N; EncEurC; FilmAG WE; FilmEn; FilmgC; HalFC 88; IntDcF 1-3, 2-3; IntMPA 86, 88, 92, 94; IntWW 79, 91; MovMk; NewYTBS 87; VarWW 85*

Rey, Hans Augustus
American. Illustrator
Collaborated with wife Margret on *Curious George* series of children's books, 1941-66.
b. Sep 16, 1898 in Hamburg, Germany
d. Aug 26, 1977 in Boston, Massachusetts
Source: *ConAu 5R, 6NR, 73; SmATA 1, 26; WhoAmA 84N*

Rey, Margret (Elizabeth)
American. Children's Author
Collaborated with husband, Hans, on *Curious George* books, 1941-66.
b. May 16, 1906 in Hamburg, Germany
d. Dec 21, 1996 in Cambridge, Massachusetts
Source: *AuBYP 3; BioIn 13, 15, 16; ChlLR 5; ConAu 105; IntAu&W 91; SmATA 26; TwCChW 78, 83, 89, 95; WhoAm 95, 96, 97; WhoAmW 95, 97; WrDr 84, 86, 88, 90, 92, 94, 96*

Reyer, (Louis) Ernest (Etienne)
French. Composer
Wrote operas *Sigurd*, 1884; *Salammbo*, 1890.
b. Dec 1, 1823 in Marseilles, France
d. Jan 15, 1909 in Levandou, France
Source: *Baker 78; BioIn 7; CmOp; GrComp; MetOEnc; NewEOp 71; NewGrDM 80; OxCMus; OxDcOp*

Reyes, Alfonso
Mexican. Essayist
Regarded by many as one of Spanish America's greatest prose writers; best known for *Vision de Anahuac, 1519*, 1917; excelled in histories, criticisms.
b. May 17, 1889 in Monterrey, Mexico
d. Dec 27, 1959 in Mexico City, Mexico
Source: *AtlBL; Benet 87, 96; BenetAL 91; BioIn 1, 4, 5, 7, 8, 9, 10, 11, 12, 13, 15, 16, 18; CasWL; ConAu 131; CyWA 58; DcHiB; DcMexL; DcSpL; DcTwCCu 4; EncLatA; EncWL, 2, 3; FacFETw; HispWr; LatAmWr; LinLib L; McGEWB; ModLAL; OxCSpan; PenC AM; REn; SpAmA; TwCLC 33; TwCWr; WhAm 3; WhNAA; WorAu 1950*

Reymont, Wladyslaw Stanislaw
Polish. Author
Known for *The Peasants*, 1902-09, prose epic of village life; won Nobel Prize, 1924.
b. May 2, 1867 in Kobiele Wielkie, Poland
d. Dec 5, 1925 in Warsaw, Poland
Source: *Benet 87, 96; BioIn 1, 5, 9, 12; CasWL; ClDMEL 47, 80; ConAu 104; EncWL, 2, 3; EvEuW; ModSL 2; PenC EUR; RAdv 14; REn; TwCA, SUP; TwCLC 5; TwCWr; WhoNob, 90, 95; WhoTwCL; WorAl*

Reynaud, Paul
French. Politician
Led committee that formed 1958 Constitution; premier, 1940.
b. Oct 15, 1878 in Barcelonayye, France
d. Sep 21, 1966 in Neuilly, France
Source: *BiDFrPL; BiDInt; BioIn 1, 2, 3, 4, 7, 17; CurBio 40, 50, 66; DcPol; DcTwHis; EncTR 91; FacFETw; HisEWW; LinLib S; ObitT 1961; WhAm 4; WhWW-II; WorAl; WorAlBi*

Reynolds, Albert
Irish. Political Leader
Succeeded Charles Haughey as prime minister of Ireland, 1992-94.
b. Nov 3, 1932 in Rooskey, Ireland
Source: *BioIn 17, 20; CurBio 94; IntWW 91; Who 92; WhoWor 93, 95, 96, 97*

Reynolds, Allie
American. Baseball Player
Set AL record of two no-hit, no-run games in 1951.
b. Feb 10, 1919
d. Dec 27, 1994 in Oklahoma City, Oklahoma
Source: *CurBio 95N*

Reynolds, Burt
American. Actor
First *Cosmopolitan* centerfold; films include *Best Friends*, 1983; *Sharky's Machine*, 1984; *Stick*, 1985; TV Series "Evening Shade," 1990-94.
b. Feb 11, 1936 in Waycross, Georgia
Source: *BiDFilm 81, 94; BioIn 10, 11, 12, 13, 14, 15, 16; BkPepl; CelR, 90; ConTFT 1, 6, 13; CurBio 73; DcArts; EncAFC; FilmEn; FilmgC; ForYSC; HalFC 80, 84, 88; IntDcF 1-3, 2-3; IntMPA 75, 76, 77, 78, 79, 80, 81, 82, 84, 86, 88, 92, 94, 96; IntWW 89, 91, 93; ItaFilm; LegTOT; MiSFD 9; MotPP; MovMk; NewYTBE 72; NewYTBS 81; RkOn 85; VarWW 85; WhoAm 74, 76, 78, 80, 82, 84, 86, 88, 90, 92, 94, 95, 96, 97; WhoEnt 92; WhoHol A; WorAl; WorAlBi*

Reynolds, Debbie (Marie Frances)
American. Actor, Singer
Starred in *The Unsinkable Molly Brown*, 1964; *Singing in the Rain*, 1952.
b. Apr 1, 1932 in El Paso, Texas
Source: *BiDFilm, 81, 94; BioIn 3, 4, 5, 7, 8, 9, 10, 11, 12, 13, 16; BkPepl; CelR, 90; CmMov; CmpEPM; ConTFT 3; EncAFC; EncMT; FilmEn; FilmgC; ForYSC; GoodHs; HalFC 80, 84, 88; IntDcF 1-3, 2-3; IntMPA 75, 76, 77, 78, 79, 80, 81, 82, 84, 86, 88, 92, 94, 96; InWom, SUP; LegTOT; MGM; MotPP; MovMk; OxCFilm; OxCPMus; PlP&P A; RkOn 74; VarWW 85; WhoAm 74, 76, 78, 80, 82, 84, 86, 88, 90, 92, 94, 95, 96, 97; WhoAmW 64, 66, 68, 70, 72, 74, 95, 97; WhoHol 92, A; WhoWest 74; WhoWor 74; WorAl; WorAlBi; WorEFlm*

Reynolds, Frank
American. Broadcast Journalist
Chief anchorman, ABC World News Tonight, 1978-83.
b. Nov 29, 1923 in East Chicago, Indiana
d. Jul 20, 1983 in Washington, District of Columbia
Source: *AnObit 1983; BiDAmJo; BioIn 8, 12, 13, 14, 16; ConAu 109, 114; EncAJ; EncTwCJ; JrnUS; LesBEnT; NewYTBS 83; VarWW 85; WhAm 8; WhoAm 74, 76, 78, 80, 82; WhoWor 74*

Reynolds, Jack
[John Sumner Reynolds]
"Hacksaw"
American. Football Player
Two-time all-pro linebacker, 1970-84, mostly with LA Rams.
b. Nov 22, 1947 in Cincinnati, Ohio
Source: *BioIn 12, 14; FootReg 85; WhoAm 78, 80, 82, 84*

Reynolds, Joshua, Sir
English. Artist
Painted over 2000 portraits, historical scenes; first pres., Royal Academy, 1768; intimate of Johnson, Garrick.
b. Jul 16, 1723 in Plympton, England
d. Feb 23, 1792 in London, England
Source: *Alli; AtlBL; BbD; Benet 87, 96; BiD&SB; BioIn 1, 3, 4, 5, 6, 7, 8, 9, 10, 11, 12, 13, 14, 15, 16, 17, 18; BlkwCE; BlmGEL; CamGEL; CamGLE; CasWL; Chambr 2; ChhPo, S1, S2; ClaDrA;*

DcArts; DcBiPP; DcBrECP; DcEnL; DcEuL; DcLB 104; DcLEL; DcNaB; Dis&D; EncEnl; EvLB; IntDcAA 90; LegTOT; LinLib S; LitC 15; LngCEL; McGDA; McGEWB; NewC; NewCBEL; OxCArt; OxCEng 67, 85, 95; OxDcArt; PenC ENG; RAdv 14, 13-3; REn; WhDW; WorAl; WorAlBi

Reynolds, Marjorie
[Marjorie Goodspeed]
American. Actor
Played wife of William Bendix on TV's "Life of Riley," 1953-58.
b. Aug 12, 1921 in Buhl, Idaho
d. Feb 1, 1997 in Manhattan Beach, California
Source: *BiDD; BioIn 18; EncAFC; FilmEn; FilmgC; ForYSC; HalFC 80, 84, 88; IntMPA 75, 76, 77, 78, 79, 80, 81, 82, 84, 86, 88, 92, 94, 96; MotPP; MovMk; SweetSg C; WhoHol 92, A*

Reynolds, Quentin James
American. Journalist
Correspondent for *Collier's* mag., WW II; wrote *The Wounded Don't Cry,* 1941.
b. Apr 11, 1902 in New York, New York
d. Mar 17, 1965 in California
Source: *AmAu&B; AuBYP 2, 3; BiDAmJo; BioIn 16; ConAu 73; CurBio 41, 65; DcAmB S7; LngCTC; REnAL; St&PR 75; TwCA SUP; WhAm 4; WhScrn 77*

Reynolds, Richard S
American. Manufacturer
Created kitchen-wrap foil, 1947.
b. Aug 5, 1881 in Bristol, Tennessee
d. Jul 29, 1955 in Louisville, Kentucky
Source: *CurBio 55; Entr*

Reynolds, Ricky
American. Musician
Guitarist with heavy-metal, Dixie boogie group Black Oak Arkansas, 1971-77.
b. Oct 29, 1948 in Black Oak, Arkansas
Source: *OnThGG*

Reynolds, Robert Rice
American. Politician
Dem. senator from NC, 1933-45; known for conservative, isolationist views.
b. Jun 18, 1884 in Asheville, North Carolina
d. Feb 13, 1963 in Asheville, North Carolina
Source: *BiDrAC; BiDrUSC 89; BioIn 6, 8; CurBio 40, 63; DcAmB S7; EncAB-A 2; EncSoH; NatCAB 50; WhAm 4*

Reynolds, William
American. Actor
Played special agent Tom Colby on TV show "The FBI," 1967-73.
b. Dec 9, 1931 in Los Angeles, California
Source: *ForYSC; WhoHol 92, A; WhoHrs 80*

Reynolds, William Bradford
"Brad"
American. Government Official, Lawyer
US assistant attorney general for civil rights, 1981-87.
b. Jun 21, 1942 in Bridgeport, Connecticut
Source: *BioIn 12, 13, 14, 15, 16; CurBio 88; NewYTBS 81; WhoAm 82, 84, 86, 88, 90, 92, 94, 95, 96, 97; WhoAmL 78, 79, 83, 85, 87, 90, 96; WhoAmP 83, 85, 87, 89, 91, 93, 95; WhoE 89; WhoSSW 95, 97*

Rezanov, Nikolay Petrovich
Russian. Businessman, Diplomat
Co-founder of the Russian-American Co., a trading firm that influenced the development of Alaska.
b. Apr 8, 1764 in Saint Petersburg, Russia
d. Mar 13, 1807 in Krasnoyarsk, Russia
Source: *BioIn 2, 5; DcAmB; WhAm HS*

Reznicek, Emil von
Austrian. Composer
Wrote comic operas *Donna Diana,* 1894; *Til Eulenspiegel,* 1902.
b. May 4, 1860 in Vienna, Austria
d. Aug 2, 1945 in Berlin, Germany
Source: *Baker 84; MusMk; NewEOp 71; NewOxM; OxCMus; OxDcOp*

Reznor, Trent
[Nine Inch Nails]
American. Singer, Musician
Grammy, Best Metal Performance, "Wish," 1992.
b. May 17, 1965 in Mercer, Pennsylvania
Source: *ConMus 13*

Rheaume, Manon
Canadian. Hockey Player
First woman to play in a NHL game; tended goal for Tampa Bay Lightning in the first period of a pre-season game, 1992.
b. 1972, Canada

Rhee, Syngman
Korean. Statesman
First pres. of Korea, 1948-60; forced from office for political abuses.
b. Mar 26, 1875 in Hwanghai, Korea
d. Jul 19, 1965 in Honolulu, Hawaii
Source: *AsAmAlm; BioIn 1, 2, 3, 4, 5, 6, 7, 10, 12, 13, 15, 18, 20; ColdWar 1, 2; CurBio 47, 65; DicTyr; EncCW; EncWM; FacFETw; HisDcKW; HisWorL; LegTOT; LinLib L, S; McGEWB; NotAsAm; ObitOF 79; ObitT 1961; WhAm 4; WhDW; WorAl; WorAlBi*

Rhine, J(oseph) B(anks)
American. Psychologist
Wrote *New Frontiers of the Mind,* 1937; *The Reaches of the Mind,* 1947.
b. Sep 29, 1895 in Waterloo, Pennsylvania
d. Feb 20, 1980 in Hillsboro, North Carolina
Source: *AmAu&B; AmMWSc 73S, 78S; AsBiEn; BiDPara; BiDPsy; BioIn 1, 2, 12, 13; ConAu 4NR, 5R, 93; CurBio 49, 80, 80N; DcAmB S10; DivFut; EncO&P 1, 1S3, 2, 3; EncPaPR 91; InSci; IntEnSS 79; LiveLet; NewYTBS 80; WebAB 74, 79; Who 74; WhoAm 74, 76, 78; WhoWor 74; WorAl; WorAlBi*

Rhoades, Everett Ronald
American. Physician
First member of the Kiowa Tribe to receive a medical doctorate degree; assistant US Surgeon General, 1982-93.
b. 1931 in Lawton, Oklahoma
Source: *AmMWSc 73P, 76P, 79, 82, 86, 89, 92, 95; BioIn 21; NotNaAm; WhoSSW 73, 75*

Rhodes, Cecil John
English. Government Official
Prime minister, Cape Colony, South Africa, 1890-96; founded Rhodes scholarships.
b. Jul 5, 1853 in Bishop's Stortford, England
d. Mar 26, 1902 in Cape Town, South Africa
Source: *Benet 87, 96; BenetAL 91; BioIn 1, 2, 3, 4, 5, 6, 7, 8, 9, 10, 11, 13, 14, 15, 16, 17, 20, 21; DcAfHiB 86; DcNaB S2; DicTyr; Dis&D; EncSoA; LinLib S; LngCTC; McGEWB; NewC; OxCEng 85, 95; REn; VicBrit; WhDW*

Rhodes, Dusty
[James Lamar Rhodes]
American. Baseball Player
Outfielder, NY/San Francisco Giants, 1952-57, 1959; known for heroics in 1954 World Series.
b. May 13, 1927 in Mathews, Alabama
Source: *Ballpl 90; BioIn 3, 7, 10, 12, 14, 16; WhoProB 73*

Rhodes, Erik
[Ernest Rhoades Sharne]
American. Actor
Character actor, 1934-39; films include *The Gay Divorcee,* 1934; *Top Hat,* 1935.
b. Feb 10, 1906 in El Reno, Oklahoma
d. Feb 17, 1990 in Oklahoma City, Oklahoma
Source: *BiE&WWA; BioIn 16, 17; EncAFC; FilmEn; FilmgC; ForYSC; HalFC 80, 84, 88; HolCA; MovMk; NewYTBS 90; NotNAT; PlP&P; WhoHol A*

Rhodes, Hari
American. Actor, Author
Played in TV series "Daktari," 1966-68; "Bold Ones," 1969-71.
b. Apr 10, 1932 in Cincinnati, Ohio
Source: *BlkAWP; ConAu 17R; DrBlPA, 90; InB&W 80; LegTOT; WhoHol 92, A*

Rhodes, James Allen
American. Politician
Rep. governor of OH, 1963-70; 1975-83.

b. Sep 13, 1909 in Jackson, Ohio
Source: *BioIn 7, 8, 10, 11, 12, 15; BioNews 75; ConAu 105; CurBio 49, 76; IntWW 75, 76, 77, 78, 79, 80, 81, 82, 83; PolProf J, NF; WhoAm 76, 78, 80, 82; WhoAmP 73, 75, 77, 79, 81, 83, 85, 87, 89, 91, 93, 95; WhoGov 75, 77; WhoMW 80, 82; WhoWor 78, 82*

Rhodes, James Ford
American. Historian
Works on American history include 1917 Pulitzer winner *History of the Civil War.*
b. May 1, 1848 in Cleveland, Ohio
d. Jan 22, 1927 in Brookline, Massachusetts
Source: *AmAu&B; AmBi; AmLY; BenetAL 91; BiD&SB; BioIn 1, 6, 13, 15; Chambr 3; DcAmAu; DcAmB; DcAmC; DcLB 47; DcNAA; EncAB-H 1974; HarEnUS; InSci; LinLib L, S; McGEWB; NatCAB 7; OhA&B; OxCAmH; OxCAmL 65, 83, 95; REnAL; TwCA, SUP; TwCBDA; WebAB 74, 79; WhAm 1; WhNAA*

Rhodes, John Jacob
American. Politician
Rep. congressman from AZ, 1953-83; minority leader, 1973-81.
b. Sep 18, 1916 in Council Grove, Kansas
Source: *BiDrAC; BiDrUSC 89; BioIn 9, 10, 11, 12; BlueB 76; CngDr 87; ConAu 103; CurBio 76; IntWW 75, 76, 77, 78, 79, 80, 81, 82, 83, 89, 91, 93; NewYTBE 72, 73; NewYTBS 76, 80; PolProf J, K, NF; WhoAm 74, 76, 78, 80, 82, 84, 86, 88, 90, 92, 94, 95, 96, 97; WhoAmL 92; WhoAmP 87; WhoGov 72, 75, 77; WhoWest 74, 76, 78, 80, 82*

Rhodes, Zandra
English. Designer
Revolutionary dress designer; uses silks, chiffons, jerseys in unusual creations.
b. Sep 11, 1940 in Chatham, England
Source: *BioIn 15, 16, 21; ConDes 84, 90; ConFash; ConNews 86-2; DcArts; EncFash; IntWW 91, 93; InWom SUP; LegTOT; Who 92; WhoFash 88; WorFshn*

Rhone, Sylvia
American. Music Executive
CEO, EastWest Records America, 1991—.
b. Mar 11, 1952 in Philadelphia, Pennsylvania
Source: *ConBlB 2; ConMus 13; WhoAm 96, 97; WhoAmW 97; WhoBlA 92*

Rhys, Ernest Percival
English. Editor
Editor, Everyman's Library, an inexpensive series of classic literature that influenced the reading preferences of several generations.
b. Jul 17, 1859 in London, England
d. May 25, 1946 in London, England
Source: *BioIn 1, 4, 5; DcLEL; DcNaB 1941; EngPo; OxCEng 85; OxCLiW 86; TwCA, SUP; WhE&EA*

Rhys, Jean
[Ella Gwendolen Rees Williams]
English. Author
Wrote *After Leaving Mr. MacKenzie,* 1931; *Good Morning, Midnight,* 1939.
b. Aug 24, 1894 in Rosea, Dominica
d. May 14, 1979 in Exeter, England
Source: *ArtclWW 2; Benet 87; BenetAL 91; BioIn 9, 10, 11, 12; BlmGEL; BlueB 76; CamGEL; CamGLE; CaribW 1; CnMWL; ConAu 25R, 85; ConLC 2, 4, 6, 14, 19; ConNov 72, 76; ContDcW 89; CurBio 72, 79, 79N; CyWA 89; DcArts; EncWL; GrWomW; GrWrEL N; IntAu&W 76, 77; IntDcWB; InWom SUP; LegTOT; LngCTC; MajTwCW; ModBrL S1, S2; ModWoWr; NewCBEL; NewYTBS 78, 79; Novels; PenC ENG; RAdv 13-1; ShSCr 21; ShSWr; Who 74; WhoTwCL; WorAl; WorAlBi; WorAu 1950; WrDr 76, 80*

Riad, Mahmoud
Egyptian. Diplomat
Egyptian Minister of foreign affairs, 1964-72; secretary general, League of Arab States, 1972-79.
b. Jan 8, 1917, Egypt
d. Jan 25, 1992 in Cairo, Egypt
Source: *BioIn 9, 17, 18; ConAu 131, 136; CurBio 71, 92N; HisEAAC; IntWW 76, 77, 78, 79, 80, 81; MidE 78, 79, 80, 81, 82; WhoArab 81; WhoWor 78, 80, 82; WrDr 94, 96*

Ribalta, Francisco
Spanish. Artist
Influential painter; recognized as the earliest Spanish *tenebroso.*
b. 1565 in Castellon de la Plana, Spain
d. Jan 12, 1628 in Valencia, Spain
Source: *BioIn 17, 19; DcArts; IntDcAA 90; McGDA; OxCArt; OxDcArt*

Ribbentrop, Joachim von
German. Diplomat
German foreign affairs minister, 1938-45; hanged as war criminal.
b. Apr 30, 1893 in Wesel, Germany
d. Oct 16, 1946 in Nuremberg, Germany
Source: *Benet 87, 96; BiDExR; BioIn 1, 8, 11, 14, 16, 18, 21; CurBio 41, 46; DcPol; DcTwHis; Dis&D; EncTR, 91; FacFETw; HisEWW; LegTOT; LinLib S; LngCTC; REn; WhDW; WhWW-II; WorAl; WorAlBi*

Ribbs, Willy T
American. Auto Racer
First African-American to qualify for the Indianapolis 500, 1991.
b. Jan 3, 1956 in San Jose, California
Source: *BioIn 13, 15, 16; ConBlB 2; WhoBlA 90*

Ribeiro, Aquilino Gomez
Portuguese. Author
The most influential Portuguese fiction writer of the early 20th c.
b. Sep 13, 1885 in Beira Alta, Portugal
d. May 27, 1963 in Lisbon, Portugal
Source: *BioIn 1, 6; CasWL; EncWL 2; LiExTwC; ModSpP P; ObitOF 79*

Ribera, Jusepe (Jose) de
"Lo Spagnoletto"
Spanish. Artist
A leader of Neapolitan school, noted colorist; did *St. Jerome,* 1644.
b. Feb 17, 1590? in Jativa, Spain
d. Sep 2, 1652 in Naples, Italy
Source: *AtlBL; McGDA; McGEWB; NewCol 75; OxCArt; WebBD 83*

Ribicoff, Abraham Alexander
American. Politician
Liberal Dem. senator from CT, 1963-81; HEW secretary under JFK, 1961-62.
b. Apr 9, 1910 in New Britain, Connecticut
Source: *BiDrAC; BiDrGov 1789; BiDrUSC 89; BiDrUSE 71, 89; BioIn 2, 3, 4, 5, 6, 7, 8, 9, 10, 11, 12, 13; CngDr 74; ConAu 108; CurBio 55; IntWW 91; InWom SUP; PolProf K; Who 92; WhoAm 90; WhoAmL 79, 85; WhoAmP 91; WhoE 89; WhoFash, 88; WhoGov 77; WhoWor 84; WorAlBi*

Ricardo, David
English. Author, Economist
Advocate of free int'l trade; wrote *Principles of Political Economy and Taxation,* 1817.
b. Apr 19, 1772 in London, England
d. Sep 11, 1823 in Gatcomb Park, England
Source: *Alli; BbD; Benet 87, 96; BiD&SB; BiDLA; BioIn 2, 3, 4, 8, 10, 11, 12, 13, 14, 15, 16, 17, 20; BlkwCE; BritAu 19; CamGEL; CamGLE; CasWL; CelCen; Chambr 2; DcAmC; DcBiPP; DcEnA; DcEnL; DcEuL; DcLB 107, 158; DcLEL; DcNaB; EvLB; GrEconB; JeHun; LinLib L, S; McGEWB; NewC; NewCBEL; OxCEng 67, 85, 95; RAdv 14, 13-3; REn; WebE&AL; WhoEc 81, 86; WorAl; WorAlBi*

Ricca, Paul
[Felice Delucia]
"The Waiter"
Italian. Criminal
Ruthless boss of Chicago crime syndicate for four decades between 1931-72.
b. Nov 14, 1897 in Naples, Italy
d. Oct 11, 1972 in Chicago, Illinois
Source: *BioIn 9; DrInf; NewYTBE 72; ObitOF 79*

Riccardo, John Joseph
American. Auto Executive
Pres., Chrysler Corp., 1970-79.
b. Jul 2, 1924 in Little Falls, New York
Source: *BioIn 12; EncABHB 5; IntWW 76, 77, 78, 79, 80, 81, 82, 83; NewYTBS 75, 79; WhoAm 76, 78, 80; WhoFI 74, 77, 79, 81; WhoMW 78*

Ricci, Matteo
Italian. Missionary
Jesuit priest who introduced Christianity into Chinese cities; wrote Chinese classic *On the Nature of God.*
b. Oct 6, 1552 in Macerata, Papal States
d. May 11, 1610, China
Source: *BiESc; BioIn 3, 4, 7, 10, 14, 18, 19; DcBiPP; DcCathB; DcScB; InSci; LuthC 75; McGEWB; NewCol 75; WebBD 83; WhDW; WhWE*

Ricci, Nina
[Marie Nielli]
French. Designer
Opened fashion house, 1932; signature perfume *L'Air du Temps.*
b. 1883 in Turin, Italy
d. Nov 29, 1970 in Paris, France
Source: *BioIn 9; DcArts; DcTwDes; EncFash; FairDF FRA; LegTOT; NewYTBE 70; WhoFash, 88; WorFshn*

Ricci, Nino
Canadian. Author
Won Governor General's Award for Fiction in English for *Lives of the Saints,* 1990.
b. Aug 23, 1959 in Leamington, Ontario, Canada
Source: *ConAu 137; ConCaAu 1; ConLC 70; WhoCanL 92; WrDr 96*

Ricci, Ruggiero
American. Violinist
Child prodigy; repertoire included all of Paganini's works; celebrated "Golden Jubilee" of performing, 1978.
b. Jul 24, 1918 in San Francisco, California
Source: *Baker 78, 84, 92; BiDAmM; BioIn 11, 12, 14; BriBkM 80; IntWW 74, 75, 76, 77, 78, 79, 80, 81, 82, 83, 89, 91, 93; IntWWM 77, 90; MusSN; NewAmDM; NewGrDA 86; NewGrDM 80; PenDiMP; WhoAm 82, 84, 86, 88, 90, 92, 94, 95, 96, 97; WhoAmM 83; WhoE 74; WhoEnt 92; WhoMus 72; WhoWor 74, 91*

Ricci-Curbastro, Gregorio
Italian. Mathematician
A leader in the creation of absolute differential calculus.
b. Jan 12, 1853 in Lugo, Papal States
d. Aug 6, 1925 in Bologna, Italy
Source: *DcScB*

Riccio, Andrea
Italian. Sculptor
Known for his small bronze sculptures and statuettes.
b. 1470 in Padua, Italy
d. 1532 in Padua, Italy
Source: *BioIn 15; McGDA; OxCArt; PenDiDA 89*

Rice, Alice Caldwell Hegan
American. Children's Author
Wrote classic *Mrs. Wiggs of the Cabbage Patch,* 1901.
b. Jan 11, 1870 in Shelbyville, Kentucky
d. Feb 10, 1942 in Louisville, Kentucky
Source: *AmAu&B; AmLY; AmWomWr; BiDSA; CarSB; ChhPo; CnDAL; ConAmL; DcAmAu; DcAmB S3; DcBiA; DcNAA; EvLB; InWom, SUP; LibW; LinLib L, S; LngCTC; NatCAB 14; NotAW; OxCAmL 65; OxCChiL; REn; REnAL; SouWr; TwCA, SUP; TwCWr; WhAm 1; WhNAA; WomWWA 14*

Rice, Anne
[Howard Allen O'Brien]
American. Author
Wrote best-selling series, *The Vampire Chronicles; The Witching Hour,* 1990.
b. Oct 4, 1941 in New Orleans, Louisiana
Source: *AmWomWr SUP; Au&Arts 9; BenetAL 91; BestSel 89-2; BioIn 15, 16, 17, 18, 20, 21; BlmGWL; ConAu 12NR, 36NR, 53NR, 65; ConLC 41; ConNov 96; ConPopW; CurBio 91; DcTwCCu 1; DrAPF 91; FemiCLE; LegTOT; News 95, 95-1; NewYTBS 90; OxCAmL 95; PenEncH; RAdv 14; RGTwCWr; ScF&FL 92; TwCYAW; WhoAm 90, 92, 94, 95, 96, 97; WhoAmW 91, 93, 95, 97; WhoWrEP 92, 95; WorAu 1985; WrDr 80, 82, 84, 86, 88, 90, 92, 94, 96*

Rice, Cale Young
American. Poet, Author
Collections of plays include *From Dusk to Dusk,* 1898.
b. Dec 7, 1872 in Dixon, Kentucky
d. Jan 23, 1943 in Louisville, Kentucky
Source: *AmAu&B; AmLY; BenetAL 91; BiDSA; BioIn 2, 4; ChhPo, S1, S2, S3; DcAmAu; DcNAA; LiHiK; LngCTC; NatCAB 34; OxCAmL 83; REnAL; SouWr; TwCA, SUP; WhAm 2; WhLit; WhNAA*

Rice, Condoleezza
American. Political Scientist, Educator
Director, Soviet and East European affairs, National Security Council, 1989-91.
b. Nov 14, 1954
Source: *BioIn 17, 18, 19, 21; ConAu 154; ConBlB 3; NotBlAW 2; WhoAfA 96; WhoBlA 92, 94*

Rice, Craig
[Georgiana Ann Randolph]
American. Author
Wrote detective fiction with a comic touch: *Trial by Fury,* 1941.
b. Jun 5, 1908 in Chicago, Illinois
d. Aug 28, 1957 in Los Angeles, California
Source: *BioIn 1, 4, 14; ConAu 116; CrtSuMy; DetWom; EncMys; FemiCLE; GrWomMW; InWom SUP; LegTOT; Novels; TwCCr&M 80, 85, 91; WhAm 3*

Rice, Elmer
[Elmer Leopold Reizenstein]
American. Dramatist
Wrote Pulitzer-winner *Street Scene,* 1929; *We, The People,* 1933.
b. Sep 28, 1892 in New York, New York
d. May 8, 1967 in Southampton, England
Source: *AmAu&B; AmNov; ASCAP 66; Benet 87, 96; BenetAL 91; BiE&WWA; BioIn 1, 2, 4, 5, 6, 7, 8, 9, 11, 12, 13; CamGLE; CamGWoT; CamHAL; CasWL; CnDAL; CnMD; CnThe; ConAmA; ConAu 25R, P-2; ConLC 7, 49; CrtSuDr; CyWA 58, 89; DcAmB S8; DcArts; DcLB 4, 7; DcLEL; EncSF 93; EncWL, 2, 3; EncWT; Ent; EvLB; FacFETw; FilmgC; GrWrEL DR; HalFC 80, 84, 88; IntDcT 2; LegTOT; LinLib L; LngCTC; MajTwCW; McGEWD 72, 84; ModAL; ModWD; NotNAT A, B; Novels; ObitT 1961; OxCAmL 65, 83, 95; OxCAmT 84; OxCEng 67, 85, 95; OxCThe 67, 83; PenC AM; PlP&P; RAdv 14, 13-2; REn; REnAL; REnWD; RfGAmL 87, 94; RGTwCWr; ScF&FL 1, 2; ScFEYrs; TwCA, SUP; TwCWr; WebE&AL; WhE&EA; WhNAA; WhoTwCL; WhThe; WorAlBi*

Rice, Grantland
[Henry Grantland Rice]
American. Journalist, Poet
Coined term "the four horsemen" to describe U of Notre Dame football players; won 1943 Oscar for best one-reel film; wrote syndicated column "The Sportlight" from 1930.
b. Nov 1, 1880 in Murfreesboro, Tennessee
d. Jul 13, 1954 in New York, New York
Source: *AmAu&B; Ballpl 90; BenetAL 91; BiDAmJo; BiDAmSp OS; BiDSA; BioIn 1, 3, 4, 7, 16, 19, 21; ChhPo, S1, S3; ConAu 114; CurBio 41, 54; DcAmB S5; DcLB 29, 171; EncAB-A 26; EncAJ; JrnUS; LegTOT; LinLib L, S; NatCAB 41; RadStar; REnAL; WebAB 74, 79; WhAm 3; WhJnl; WhoGolf; WhScrn 77; WorAl; WorAlBi*

Rice, Gregory
American. Track Athlete
Distance runner undefeated for 65 major races in a row.
b. Jan 3, 1916 in Deer Lodge, Michigan
d. May 19, 1991 in Hackensack, New Jersey
Source: *CurBio 91N*

Rice, Jerry (Lee)
American. Football Player
Wide receiver, San Francisco, 1985—; holds NFL records for TD receptions in consecutive games and in season, set in 1987; NFL MVP, 1987, Super Bowl MVP, 1988.
b. Oct 13, 1962 in Starkville, Mississippi
Source: *AfrAmSG; BioIn 13, 15, 16; ConBlB 5; CurBio 90; FootReg 87; LegTOT; News 90; NewYTBS 87; WhoAfA 96; WhoAm 90, 92, 94, 95, 96, 97; WhoBlA 88, 90, 92, 94; WhoWest 89, 92, 94, 96; WorAlBi*

Rice, Jim
[James Edward Rice]
American. Baseball Player
Outfielder, Boston, 1974-89; led AL in home runs three times, RBIs twice; AL MVP, 1978.
b. Mar 8, 1953 in Anderson, South Carolina
Source: *Ballpl 90; BaseReg 86, 87; BiDAmSp BB; BioIn 11, 12, 13, 16; CurBio 79; InB&W 80, 85; LegTOT; WhoAfA 96; WhoAm 80, 82, 84, 86, 88; WhoBlA 77, 80, 85, 88, 90, 92, 94; WhoE 86, 89; WhoSpor; WorAl; WorAlBi*

Rice, Linda Johnson
American. Publishing Executive
President, Johnson Publishing Co., 1987—, publishers of *Ebony*.
b. Mar 22, 1958 in Chicago, Illinois
Source: *ConBlB 9; NotBlAW 2; WhoAfA 96; WhoAm 95, 96, 97; WhoAmW 97; WhoBlA 88, 90, 92, 94*

Rice, Norm(an Blann)
American. Politician
Mayor of Seattle, 1990—.
b. May 4, 1943 in Denver, Colorado
Source: *BioIn 20; ConBlB 8; WhoAfA 96; WhoBlA 80, 85, 88, 90, 92, 94*

Rice, Sam
[Edgar Charles Rice]
American. Baseball Player
Outfielder, 1915-34, mostly with Washington; had 2,987 career hits, .322 batting average; Hall of Fame, 1963.
b. Feb 20, 1892 in Morocco, Indiana
d. Oct 13, 1974 in Rossmoor, Maryland
Source: *BioIn 10; NewYTBS 74; WhoProB 73*

Rice, Thomas Dartmouth
"Jim Crow"
American. Actor
Known for song-and-dance act, "Jim Crow," that perpetuated the popular minstrel shows of 19th c.
b. May 20, 1808 in New York, New York
d. Sep 19, 1860 in New York, New York
Source: *AmAu&B; AmBi; ApCAB; BiDAmM; BioIn 3, 6, 11; DcAmB; Drake; EncAAH; Ent; FamA&A; NatCAB 11; NewAmDM; NewGrDA 86; NewGrDM 80; NotNAT B; OxCAmL 65; OxCPMus; OxCThe 67, 83; PlP&P; PseudAu; REnAL; WebAB 74, 79; WhAm HS*

Rice, Tim(othy Miles Bindon)
English. Librettist
Wrote lyrics for popular rock musical *Jesus Christ, Superstar,* 1971; won Tony, Grammy for *Evita,* 1980.
b. Nov 10, 1944 in Amersham, England
Source: *CamGWoT; ConAu 46NR, 103; ConDr 73, 77D; ConLC 21; ConTFT 2, 13; Ent; FacFETw; IntWW 91; IntWWM 90; LinLib L; NewYTBE 71; OxCPMus; OxCThe 83; VarWW 85; Who 82, 83, 85, 88, 90, 92, 94; WhoAm 74, 76, 78, 80, 82, 84, 86, 88, 94, 95, 96; WhoThe 77, 81; WhoWor 74, 76, 84, 87, 89, 91, 93, 95, 96, 97*

Rice-Davies, Mandy
English. Call Girl, Restaurateur, Actor
Involved in 1963 British political-sex scandal known as Profumo affair.
b. 1944
Source: *BioIn 9, 10, 15; InWom SUP; NewYTBS 76; What 3; WhoHol 92*

Rich, Adam
American. Actor
Played Nicholas Bradford on TV series "Eight Is Enough" 1977-81.
b. Oct 12, 1968 in New York, New York
Source: *BioIn 11, 15; LegTOT*

Rich, Adrienne (Cecile)
American. Poet
Works explore themes of sexuality, reelationships: *Diving into the Wreck: Poems 1971-72; An Atlas of the Difficult World: Poems, 1988-1991,* 1991; won The Lenore Marshall/ *Nation* Poetry Prize, 1992; won the Los Angeles Times Book Award, 1992.
b. May 16, 1929 in Baltimore, Maryland
Source: *AmCulL; AmWomWr, 92; AmWr S1; ArtclWW 2; Benet 87, 96; BenetAL 91; BioIn 9, 10, 11, 12, 13, 14, 15, 16; BlmGWL; CamGLE; CamHAL; ConAu 9R, 20NR, 53NR; ConLC 3, 6, 7, 11, 18, 36, 73, 76; ConPo 70, 75, 80, 85, 91, 96; ContDcW 89; CroCAP; CurBio 76; DcArts; DcLB 5, 67; DcLEL 1940; DrAP 75; DrAPF 91; EncWB; EncWHA; EncWL 3; FacFETw; FemiCLE; FemiWr; GayLesB; GayLL; GrWomW; GrWrEL P; HanAmWH; InB&W 85; IntDcWB; IntWW 89, 91, 93; IntWWP 77; JeAmWW; LegTOT; LinLib L; MagSAmL; MajTwCW; ModAL, S1, S2; ModAWP; ModAWWr; ModWoWr; NewYTBS 87; OxCAmL 83, 95; OxCTwCP; OxCWoWr 95; PenBWP; PenC AM; PeoHis; PoeCrit 5; RadHan; RAdv 1, 14, 13-1; RfGAmL 87, 94; RGFAP; RGTwCWr; WhoAm 76, 78, 80, 82, 84, 86, 88, 90, 92, 94, 95, 96, 97; WhoAmW 58, 81, 83, 95, 97; WhoE 85; WhoUSWr 88; WhoWest 87, 89, 92, 94; WhoWrEP 89, 92, 95; WomFir; WorAu 1950; WrDr 76, 80, 82, 84, 86, 88, 90, 92, 94, 96*

Rich, Buddy
[Bernard Rich]
American. Jazz Musician
All-time great drummer, with Tommy Dorsey, 1939-42; formed Buddy Rich band, 1960s.
b. Jun 30, 1917 in New York, New York
d. Apr 2, 1987 in Los Angeles, California
Source: *AllMusG; AnObit 1987; Baker 84, 92; BgBands 74; BiDAmM; BiDJaz; BioIn 7, 8, 9, 10, 11, 12, 15, 16, 17; CmpEPM; ConMus 13; ConNews 87-3; CurBio 73, 87, 87N; EncJzS; FacFETw; IlEncJ; LegTOT; NewAmDM; NewGrDA 86; NewGrDJ 88, 94; NewGrDM 80; NewYTBS 74, 87; OxCPMus; PenEncP; VarWW 85; WhAm 9; WhoAm 74, 76, 78, 80, 82, 84, 86; WhoJazz 72; WorAl; WorAlBi*

Rich, Charlie
[Charles Allan Rich]
"The Silver Fox"
American. Musician, Singer
Pop-country star whose hits include "Behind Closed Doors," 1973; won Grammy.
b. Dec 14, 1932 in Forrest City, Arkansas
d. Jul 25, 1995 in Hammond, Louisiana
Source: *ArtsEM; Baker 84, 92; BgBkCoM; BioIn 12, 14, 21; BioNews 74; BkPepl; ConMuA 80A; CounME 74, 74A; EncFCWM 83; EncPR&S 89; EncRk 88; HalFC 84; HarEnCM 87; IlEncRk; LegTOT; NewAmDM; NewGrDA 86; News 96, 96-1; OxCPMus; PenEncP; RkOn 74; RolSEnR 83; VarWW 85; WhAm 11; WhoAm 78, 80, 82, 84, 86, 88, 92, 94, 95; WhoEnt 92; WorAl; WorAlBi*

Rich, Claudius James
English. Businessman
While living in Baghdad his work was the foundation for Mesopotamian archaelogical studies.
b. Mar 28, 1787 in Dijon, France
d. Oct 5, 1820 in Shiraz, Persia
Source: *Alli; DcBiPP; DcNaB; NewCBEL*

Rich, Irene
[Irene Luther]
American. Actor
Radio star of "Dear John;" featured in films, 1918-50; radio sponsor for Welch's Grape Juice, 1930s.
b. Oct 13, 1897 in Buffalo, New York
d. Apr 23, 1988 in Santa Barbara, California
Source: *BioIn 7; Film 1; FilmgC; ForYSC; IntMPA 75, 76, 77, 78, 79, 80, 81, 82, 84, 86, 88; MotPP; MovMk; ThFT; TwYS; VarWW 85; WhoHol A; WorAl; WorAlBi*

Rich, John
American. Director, Producer
Won Emmys for "The Dick Van Dyke Show," 1963; "All in the Family," 1972.
b. Jul 6, 1925 in Rockaway Beach, New York
Source: *BlueB 76; ConTFT 4; FilmEn; FilmgC; HalFC 80, 84, 88; IntMPA 75, 76, 77, 78, 79, 80, 81, 82, 84, 86, 88, 92; LesBEnT 92; MiSFD 9; NewYTET; WhoAm 74, 76, 78, 80, 82, 84, 86, 88, 90, 92, 94, 95, 96, 97; WhoEnt 92; WhoWor 80, 82*

Rich, Lee
American. TV Executive
Pres., Lorimar Productions; co. produced TV shows "Dallas," "Knots Landing."
b. Dec 10, 1926 in Cleveland, Ohio
Source: *BioIn 14, 16; ConTFT 6; Dun&B 86; IntMPA 92, 94, 96; LesBEnT 92; NewYTET; WhoAm 90; WhoFI 87; WhoTelC*

Rich, Louise Dickinson
American. Author
Wrote bestseller *We Took to the Woods,* 1942, after making her home in the Maine wilderness.
b. Jun 14, 1903 in Huntington, Massachusetts
d. Apr 9, 1991 in Mattapoisett, Massachusetts
Source: *AmAu&B; AmWomWr; AmWomWr; AuBYP 2, 3; BenetAL 91; BioIn 16, 17; ConAu 73, 134; CurBio 91N; DcAmChF 1960; InWom; NewYTBS 91; REnAL; SmATA 54, 67; TwCA SUP; WhoAmW 58, 61, 64, 66, 68, 70, 72*

Richard, Cliff
[Harry Roger Webb]
British. Singer
Hit singles include "Devil Woman," 1976; "She's So Beautiful," 1985.
b. Oct 14, 1940 in Lucknow, India
Source: *Au&Wr 71; BioIn 6, 8, 10, 11, 12, 13, 16; BlueB 76; ConMuA 80A; ConMus 14; ConTFT 5; DcArts; EncEurC; EncPR&S 89; EncRk 88; EncRkSt; FilmAG WE; FilmEn; FilmgC; HalFC 80, 84, 88; HarEnR 86; IlEncRk; IlWWBF, A; IntMPA 75, 76, 77, 78, 79, 80, 81, 82, 84, 86, 88, 92, 94, 96; IntWW 76, 77, 78, 79, 80, 81, 82, 83, 89, 91, 93; LegTOT; NewGrDM 80; OxCPMus; PenEncP; RkOn 78; RolSEnR 83; VarWW 85; Who 82, 83, 85, 88, 90, 92, 94; WhoHol 92, A; WhoRock 81; WrDr 86, 88, 90, 92, 94, 96*

Richard, Duke of York
English. Statesman
Served under King Henry VI as lieutenant, protector, 1430s-50s; declared heir apparent, killed in battle.
b. 1411
d. 1460 in Wakefield, England
Source: *Alli; WebBD 83*

Richard, Gabriel
French. Clergy, Educator, Printer
Started first newspaper in MI, 1809; co-founded U of MI, 1817.
b. Oct 15, 1767 in Saintes, France
d. Sep 13, 1832 in Detroit, Michigan
Source: *ApCAB; BiAUS; BiDrAC; BiDrUSC 89; BioIn 1, 2, 5, 6, 7, 19; DcAmB; Drake; WhAm HS*

Richard, Henri
[Joseph Henri Richard]
"Pocket Rocket"
Canadian. Hockey Player
Center, Montreal, 1955-75; won 11 Stanley Cups, more than any NHL player; brother of Maurice; Hall of Fame, 1979.
b. Feb 29, 1936 in Montreal, Quebec, Canada
Source: *BioIn 4, 8, 10; HocEn; WhAmArt 85; WhoAm 74; WhoHcky 73*

Richard, J(ames) R(odney)
American. Baseball Player
Pitcher, Houston, 1971-80; tied record for most strikeouts in first ML start, 15, 1971; suffered stroke, 1980.
b. Mar 7, 1950 in Vienna, Louisiana
Source: *Ballpl 90; BiDAmSp Sup; BioIn 11, 12, 13; InB&W 80; NewYTBS 80, 81, 82; WhoAm 82; WhoBlA 77, 80, 85; WhoProB 73*

Richard, Maurice
[Joseph Henri Maurice Richard]
"Rocket"
Canadian. Hockey Player
Right wing, Montreal, 1942-60; first NHL player to score 50 goals in season (1944-45), 500 in career (544 total); Hall of Fame, 1961.
b. Aug 4, 1921 in Montreal, Quebec, Canada
Source: *BioIn 15, 20; CurBio 58; FacFETw; HocEn; LegTOT; WhoHcky 73; WorAl*

Richard, Zachary
American. Singer, Musician
Cajun singer and accordionist; debut album *Bayou des Mysteres,* 1976.
b. Sep 8, 1950 in Lafayette, Louisiana
Source: *BioIn 11; ConMus 9*

Richard I
"Richard the Lionhearted"
English. Ruler
Subject of many legends of chivalry; reigned, 1189-99.
b. Sep 8, 1157 in Oxford, England
d. Apr 6, 1199 in Chaluz, France
Source: *Alli; CasWL; McGEWB; NewC; NewCol 75; REn; WebBD 83; WorAl*

Richard II
English. Ruler
Son of Edward the Black Prince, grandson of Edward III; succeeded grandfather, 1377-99.
b. Jan 6, 1367 in Bordeaux, France
d. Feb 14, 1400 in Leicester, England
Source: *NewCol 75; WebBD 83*

Richard III
English. Ruler
Ruled, 1483-85; killed during battle of Bosworth Field by Earl of Richmond, who became Henry VII.
b. Oct 2, 1452 in Fotheringhay Castle, England
d. Aug 22, 1485 in Leicester, England
Source: *McGEWB; NewC; NewCol 75; REn; WebBD 83*

Richards, Ann
American. Politician
Dem. governor of TX, 1990-95.
b. Sep 1, 1933 in Lakeview, Texas
Source: *AlmAP 92; BioIn 13, 14; CurBio 91; GrLiveH; IntWW 91; LegTOT; News 91, 91-2; WhoAmP 91; WhoAmW 91; WhoSSW 91; WomPO 78; WomStre*

Richards, Bob
American. Track Athlete
Pole vaulter; won gold medals, 1952, 1956 Olympics.
b. Feb 20, 1926 in Champaign, Illinois
Source: *BioIn 2, 3, 4, 6, 7, 8, 10, 14; CmCal; CurBio 57; WhoSpor; WhoTr&F 73*

Richards, Dickinson Woodruff
American. Physician
Shared Nobel Prize with Andre Cournand, 1956, for discoveries concerning heart catheterization and the circulatory system.
b. Oct 30, 1895 in Orange, New Jersey
d. Feb 23, 1973 in Lakeville, Connecticut
Source: *BiESc; BioIn 4, 5, 6, 9, 10, 11; DcAmB S9; DcAmMeB 84; InSci; LarDcSc; McGMS 80; NotTwCS; OxCMed 86; WebAB 74, 79; WhAm 5; WhoNob, 90, 95*

Richards, Ellen Henrietta Swallow
American. Chemist
Sanitary chemist; leader in home economics movement; author *Cost of Cleanness,* 1908.
b. Dec 3, 1842 in Dunstable, Massachusetts
d. 1911 in Jamaica Plain, Massachusetts
Source: *Alli SUP; AmBi; AmWom; AmWomSc; ApCAB; BiDAmEd; BiDAmS; BiInAmS; BioIn 15, 16, 17, 18, 20, 21; DcAmB; HerW; InWom, SUP; LibW; NatCAB 7; NotAW; TwCBDA; WhAm 1*

Richards, Ivor Armstrong
English. Critic
Author of many literary criticism books; known as a "critic's critic."
b. Feb 26, 1893 in Sandbach, England
d. Sep 7, 1979 in Cambridge, England
Source: *AmAu&B; BioIn 1, 4, 9, 10, 12, 13; CasWL; Chambr 3; ChhPo S3; ConAu 89; ConPo 70, 75; DcLEL; DcNaB 1971; DrAP 75; EncWL; EvLB; GrBr; IntAu&W 76, 77; IntWW 74, 75, 76, 77, 78, 79; IntWWP 77; LngCTC; MakMC; McGEWB; ModBrL, S1; NewC; NewCBEL; NewYTBS 79; OxCAmL 65; OxCEng 67; PenC ENG; RAdv 1; REn; TwCA, SUP; TwCWr; WebAB 74, 79; WebE&AL; WhAm 7; Who 74; WhoAm 74, 76; WhoLA; WrDr 76*

Richards, Keith
[The Rolling Stones; Naker Phelge; Keith Richard]
English. Musician, Singer
Lead and rhythm guitarist, vocalist, Rolling Stones, 1962—;wrote "Satisfaction " with Mick Jagger bringing superstardom to the Rolling Stones.
b. Dec 18, 1943 in Dartford, England
Source: *Baker 84, 92; BioIn 11, 12, 13; ConAu 107; ConLC 17; ConMus 11; CurBio 89; IntWW 89, 91, 93; LegTOT; News 93-3; OnThGG; WhoAm 76, 78, 80, 82, 84, 86, 88, 90, 92, 94, 95, 96, 97; WhoEnt 92; WhoRocM 82; WhoWor 96; WorAlBi*

Richards, Laura Elizabeth Howe
[Mrs. Henry Richards]
American. Author
Daughter of Julia and Samuel Howe; wrote classic children's tale *Captain January,* 1910; movie starred Shirley Temple, 1936.
b. Feb 27, 1850 in Boston, Massachusetts
d. Jan 14, 1943 in Gardiner, Maine
Source: *AmAu&B; AmLY; AmWomPl; AmWomWr; BioIn 15, 19; DcAmB S3; LibW; NatCAB 15, 39; NotAW; REnAL; TwCBDA; WebAB 74, 79; WhAm 2; WomWWA 14*

Richards, Lloyd George
American. Director, Actor
First black director of Broadway play, *A Raisin in the Sun,* 1959; dean of drama school, Yale U., 1979-91.
b. 1922? in Toronto, Ontario, Canada
Source: *BioIn 14, 15; ConBlB 2; CurBio 87; DrBlPA 90; InB&W 85; NewYTBS 87; NotNAT; WhoAm 86, 88; WhoBlA 85, 92; WhoE 86; WhoEnt 92*

Richards, Michael
American. Actor
Plays Cosmo Kramer on "Seinfeld;" winner of two Emmys for that role.
b. Jul 21, 1948 in Culver City, California
Source: *WhoAdv 90; WhoSSW 88*

Richards, Paul Rapier
American. Baseball Player, Baseball Manager, Baseball Executive
Catcher, 1932-46; as general manager, turned White Sox, Orioles into pennant contenders.
b. Nov 21, 1908 in Waxahachie, Texas
d. May 4, 1986 in Waxahachie, Texas
Source: *BiDAmSp Sup; BioIn 2, 5, 6, 14, 15, 19; NewYTBS 84; WhAm 9; WhoProB 73; WhoSSW 73*

Richards, Rene
[Richard Raskind]
American. Tennis Player, Transsexual
Wrote autobiography *Second Serve,* 1983.
b. Aug 19, 1934
Source: *BioIn 11, 14*

Richards, Richard
American. Politician
Appointed GOP chm. by Ronald Reagan.
b. May 14, 1932 in Ogden, Utah
d. Dec 1988
Source: *BioIn 12, 13; NewYTBS 81; PolPar; WhoAmP 73, 75, 77, 79, 81, 83, 85, 87, 89, 91, 93, 95*

Richards, Stanley
American. Dramatist, Author
Wrote dozens of plays, many produced around the world: *Journey to Bahia,* 1964.
b. Apr 23, 1918 in New York, New York
d. Jul 26, 1980 in New York, New York
Source: *BioIn 12, 78, 79, 80, 81; OxCCan; WhoE 74*

Richards, Theodore William
American. Chemist
Won Nobel Prize, 1914; developed techniques for determining atomic weights of oxygen, silver.
b. Jan 31, 1868 in Germantown, Pennsylvania
d. Apr 2, 1928 in Cambridge, Pennsylvania
Source: *AmBi; AmDec 1910; ApCAB SUP; AsBiEn; BiESc; BioIn 3, 5, 6, 8, 9, 11, 19, 20; CamDcSc; DcAmB; DcScB; Dis&D; InSci; LarDcSc; McGEWB; NatCAB 12, 40; NotTwCS; WebAB 74, 79; WhAm 1; WhDW; WhLit; WhoNob, 90, 95; WorAl; WorScD*

Richards, William Trost
American. Artist
Painted landscapes, sea pictures; some work in NY Metropolitan Museum's permanent collection.
b. Nov 14, 1838 in Philadelphia, Pennsylvania
d. Nov 8, 1905 in Newport, Rhode Island
Source: *AmBi; ApCAB; DcAmB; EarABI; TwCBDA; WhAm 1*

Richardson, Benjamin
English. Manufacturer
Helped introduce modern glass-making techniques to England.
b. 1802 in Stourbridge, England
d. 1887
Source: *PenDiDA 89*

Richardson, Bill
[William Blaine Richardson]
American. Politician, Government Official
Dem. rep. from NM, 1983-97; amb. to UN, 1997—.
b. Nov 15, 1947 in Pasadena, California
Source: *AlmAP 84, 88, 92, 96; BiDrUSC 89; CngDr 83, 85, 87, 89, 91, 93, 95; CurBio 96; PolsAm 84; USBiR 74; WhoAm 84, 86, 88, 90, 92, 94, 95, 96, 97; WhoAmP 83, 85, 87, 89, 91, 93, 95; WhoE 95; WhoEmL 87; WhoHisp 91, 92, 94; WhoWest 84, 87, 89, 92, 94, 96*

Richardson, Bobby
[Robert Clinton Richardson]
American. Baseball Player, Baseball Coach
Second baseman, NY Yankees, 1955-66; led AL in hits, 209, 1962.
b. Aug 19, 1935 in Sumter, South Carolina
Source: *Ballpl 90; BioIn 5, 6, 7, 14, 15, 16, 21; CurBio 66; WhoProB 73*

Richardson, Dorothy Miller
English. Author
One of first to use "stream of consciousness" style; wrote 13-vol. novel, *Pilgrimage.*
b. May 17, 1873 in Abingdon, England
d. Jun 17, 1957 in Beckenham, England
Source: *AmAu&B; ArtclWW 2; BioIn 2, 4, 5, 6, 8, 10, 11, 13, 14, 16, 18, 20, 21; BlmGWL; CasWL; Chambr 3; ConAu 104; CyWA 58; DcLEL; DcNaB MP; EncWL, 3; EvLB; FacFETw; GrWrEL N; LngCTC; ModBrL, S1; NewC; NewCBEL; OxCEng 67, 85, 95; PenC ENG; RAdv 1; REn; RGTwCWr; TwCA, SUP; TwCWr; WebE&AL; WhoLA; WomNov*

Richardson, Elliot Lee
American. Government Official
Govt. posts include secretary of HEW, defense, commerce, under Nixon, Ford.
b. Jul 20, 1920 in Boston, Massachusetts
Source: *BiDrUSE 71, 89; BioIn 8, 9, 10, 11, 12, 14, 16; BioNews 74; BlueB 76; ConAu 111; CurBio 71; DcAmDH 89; IntWW 74, 75, 76, 77, 78, 79, 80, 81, 82, 83, 89, 91, 93; IntYB 78, 79, 80, 81, 82; NewYTBE 70, 72, 73; NewYTBS 75; PolProf NF; Who 82, 83, 85, 88, 90, 92, 94; WhoAm 74, 76, 78, 80, 82, 84, 86, 90, 92, 94, 95, 96, 97; WhoAmL 79, 87, 92, 94; WhoAmP 73, 75, 77, 79, 81, 83; WhoE 79, 81, 83, 85, 89; WhoGov 72, 75, 77; WhoSSW 73, 76, 95, 97; WhoWor 78, 80, 82; WorAl; WorAlBi*

Richardson, George Taylor
Canadian. Hockey Player
Amateur player, early 1900s; Hall of Fame, 1950; killed in action, WW I.
b. 1880? in Kingston, Ontario, Canada
d. Feb 9, 1916, France
Source: *WhoHcky 73*

Richardson, Henry Handel
[Ethel Florence Lindsey Richardson; Henrietta Richardson Robertson]
Australian. Author
Wrote trilogy of novels, *The Fortunes of Richard Mahony,* 1917-30.
b. Jan 3, 1870 in Melbourne, Australia
d. Mar 20, 1946 in Hastings, England
Source: *ArtclWW 2; Benet 87, 96; BioIn 1, 2, 3, 4, 5, 6, 8, 9, 10, 12, 16; BlmGEL; BlmGWL; CamGEL; CamGLE; CasWL; ContDcW 89; CurBio 46; CyWA 58; DcArts; DcLEL; DcNaB 1941; EncWL, 2, 3; EvLB; FemiCLE; GrWrEL N; IntDcWB; IntLitE; InWom SUP; LiExTwC; LngCTC; McGEWB;*

ModCmwL; ModWoWr; NewC; Novels; OxCAusL; OxCEng 67, 85, 95; PenC ENG; PenNWW B; RAdv 14, 13-1; REn; RfGEnL 91; RfGShF; RGTwCWr; TwCA, SUP; TwCLC 4; TwCRHW 94; TwCWr; WebE&AL; WhoTwCL

Richardson, Henry Hobson
American. Architect
Developed Romanesque revival in US; buildings in MA include Boston's Trinity Church, 1877.
b. Sep 29, 1838 in Saint James, Louisiana
d. Apr 27, 1886 in Brookline, Massachusetts
Source: *AmBi; AmCulL; ApCAB; AtlBL; BiDAmAr; BioIn 2, 3, 6, 7, 8, 9, 10, 11, 12, 13, 14, 15, 19; DcAmB; DcAmLiB; DcArts; DcD&D; EncAAr 1, 2; EncAB-H 1974, 1996; EncMA; HarEnUS; LinLib S; McGDA; McGEWB; NatCAB 6; OxCAmH; OxCAmL 65; OxCArt; PenDiDA 89; PeoHis; REn; TwCBDA; WebAB 74, 79; WhAm HS; WhDW; WhoArch; WorAl*

Richardson, Jack
American. Dramatist
Won Obie for *The Prodigal,* 1960.
b. Feb 18, 1935 in New York, New York
Source: *AmAu&B; BenetAL 91; BiE&WWA; BioIn 10, 12; CnMD; CnThe; ConAu 5R; ConDr 77, 82, 88; CroCD; DcLB 7; McGEWD 72, 84; ModWD; NotNAT; OxCAmL 83; PenC AM; PlP&P; REnWD; WorAu 1950; WrDr 80, 82, 84, 86, 88, 90, 92, 94, 96*

Richardson, John, Sir
Scottish. Naturalist, Explorer
Surveyed over 900 miles of Canadian Arctic Coast.
b. Nov 5, 1787 in Dumfries, Scotland
d. Jun 5, 1865 in Grasmere, England
Source: *Alli; ApCAB; BbtC; BioIn 11; CelCen; DcBiPP; DcCanB 9; DcNaB; Drake; InSci; MacDCB 78; OxCCan; WhWE*

Richardson, Lee
[Lee David Richard]
American. Actor
Played in TV soap operas "Search for Tomorrow," "Guiding Light."
b. Sep 11, 1926 in Chicago, Illinois
Source: *BiE&WWA; ConTFT 7, 15; NotNAT; WhoAm 82; WhoE 74, 75*

Richardson, Lewis Fry
Scottish. Physicist
The first to accurately predict the weather through mathematics.
b. Oct 11, 1881 in Newcastle-upon-Tyne, England
d. Sep 30, 1953 in Kilmun, Scotland
Source: *BiDMoPL; BiESc; BioIn 3, 12, 15, 20; DcNaB 1951; LarDcSc; NotTwCS; WhDW; WhE&EA*

Richardson, Micheal Ray
"Sugar Ray"
American. Basketball Player
Guard, 1978-85; led NBA in steals three times; banned from league play at least two yrs. for drug problems, 1986.
b. Apr 11, 1955 in Lubbock, Texas
Source: *BioIn 14, 15; NewYTBS 84; OfNBA 85*

Richardson, Miranda
English. Actor
Played an IRA terrorist in *The Crying Game.* 1992; also in *Enchanted April,*, 1992; *Damage,* 1992.
b. Mar 3, 1958 in Lancashire, England
Source: *BiDFilm 94; ConTFT 15; CurBio 94; IntMPA 92, 94, 96; LegTOT; Who 90, 92, 94; WhoAm 94, 95, 96, 97; WhoAmW 95, 97; WhoHol 92; WhoWor 95, 96, 97*

Richardson, Natasha
English. Actor
Appeared in *The Handmaid's Tale.*
b. May 11, 1963 in London, England
Source: *ConTFT 6, 13; IntMPA 92, 94, 96; LegTOT; NewYTBS 93; WhoHol 92*

Richardson, Nolan
American. Basketball Coach
Coach, Tulsa Univ., 1980-85; Univ. of Arkansas, 1985—.
b. Dec 27, 1941 in El Paso, Texas
Source: *ConBlB 9; WhoAfA 96; WhoBlA 88, 90, 92, 94*

Richardson, Owen Williams, Sir
English. Scientist
Known for thermionic effect named after him; won 1928 Nobel Prize in physics.
b. Apr 26, 1879 in Dewsbury, England
d. Feb 15, 1959 in Alton, England
Source: *AsBiEn; BiESc; DcNaB 1951; DcScB; LarDcSc; ObitT 1951; WhAm 3; WhoNob*

Richardson, Ralph David, Sir
"The Duke of Dark Corners"
English. Actor
One of most acclaimed figures in English-speaking theater; starred in over 200 plays, 100 films.
b. Dec 19, 1902 in Cheltenham, England
d. Oct 10, 1983 in London, England
Source: *AnObit 1983; BiDFilm; BiE&WWA; CurBio 50, 83N; FamA&A; FilmgC; IntMPA 82; IntWW 74, 75, 76, 77, 78, 79, 80, 81, 82, 83; MovMk; NewYTBS 83; OxCFilm; OxCThe 67, 83; VarWW 85; Who 74, 82, 83; WhoThe 77; WhoWor 74; WorAl*

Richardson, Samuel
English. Author
Wrote *Pamela or Virtue Rewarded,* 1740, often considered first modern English novel.
b. Jul 31, 1689 in Derbyshire, England
d. Jul 4, 1761 in London, England
Source: *Alli; AtlBL; BbD; Benet 87, 96; BiD&SB; BioIn 1, 2, 3, 5, 7, 8, 9, 10, 12, 13, 14, 15, 18, 21; BlkwCE; BlmGEL; BlmGWL; BritAu; BritWr 3; CamGEL; CamGLE; CasWL; CnDBLB 2; CrtT 2, 4; CyWA 58; DcArts; DcBiA; DcBiPP; DcEnA, A; DcEnL; DcEuL; DcLB 39, 154; DcLEL; DcNaB, C; EncEnl; EvLB; GrWrEL N; LegTOT; LinLib L, S; LitC 1; LngCEL; MagSWL; McGEWB; MouLC 2; NewC; NewCBEL; NewEOp 71; Novels; OxCChiL; OxCEng 67, 85, 95; OxCGer 76, 86; PenC ENG; RAdv 1, 14, 13-1; REn; RfGEnL 91; WebE&AL; WhDW; WorAl; WorAlBi; WorLitC*

Richardson, Scovel
American. Judge
Served on US Court of International Trade (formerly Customs Court) from 1957.
b. Feb 4, 1912 in Nashville, Tennessee
d. Mar 30, 1982 in New Rochelle, New York
Source: *AmBench 79; BiDFedJ; BioIn 8, 12, 13; BlueB 76; CngDr 74, 77, 79, 81; Ebony 1; InB&W 80; NegAl 76, 83, 89; NewYTBS 82; WhoAfA 96; WhoAm 74, 76, 78, 80, 82; WhoAmL 78, 79; WhoBlA 75, 77, 80, 85, 90, 92, 94; WhoE 79, 81; WhoGov 72, 75, 77*

Richardson, Sid
American. Oilman
One of richest men in America, late 1950s; independent oil producer from 1919; owned, operated several TX cattle ranches.
b. Apr 25, 1891 in Athens, Texas
d. Sep 29, 1959
Source: *BioIn 3, 4, 5; WhAm 3, 4*

Richardson, Susan
American. Actor
Played Susan Bradford on TV series "Eight Is Enough," 1977-81.
b. Mar 11, 1952 in Coatesville, Pennsylvania
Source: *BioIn 11*

Richardson, Tony
English. Producer, Director
Produced, directed films *A Taste of Honey,* 1962; *Tom Jones,* 1963, which won an Oscar.
b. Jun 5, 1928 in Shipley, England
d. Nov 15, 1991 in Los Angeles, California
Source: *AnObit 1991; BiDFilm, 81, 94; BiE&WWA; BioIn 6, 8, 9, 12, 16; BlueB 76; ConAu X; ConTFT 3, 11; CurBio 63, 92N; DcArts; DcFM; EncEurC; EncWT; Ent; FacFETw; FilmEn; FilmgC; HalFC 80, 84, 88; IlWWBF; IntDcF 1-2, 2-2; IntMPA 75, 76, 77, 78, 79, 80, 81, 82, 84, 86, 88, 92; IntWW 74, 75, 76, 77, 78, 79, 80, 81, 82, 83, 89, 91; LegTOT; MiSFD 9N; MovMk; NewC; NewYTBS 91; NotNAT; OxCFilm; OxCThe 83; VarWW 85; WhAm 10; Who 74, 82, 83, 85, 88, 90, 92; WhoEnt 92; WhoThe 72, 77, 81; WhoWor 84, 87, 89, 91; WomWMM; WorAl; WorAlBi; WorEFlm; WorFDir 2*

Richberg, Donald R(andall)
American. Lawyer, Author
Helped shape New Deal legislation; co-author of NRA.
b. Jul 10, 1881 in Knoxville, Tennessee
d. Nov 27, 1960 in Charlottesville, Virginia
Source: *AmAu&B; BiDAmBL 83; BioIn 2, 3, 5, 6, 7, 9; ChhPo S1; ConAu 113; CurBio 49, 61; DcAmB S6; DcAmC; EncAB-A 32; FacFETw; NatCAB 49; PeoHis; WhAm 4; WhNAA*

Richelieu, Armand Jean du Plessis, Cardinal
[Duc de Armand Jean du Plessis]
"Eminence Rouge"
French. Statesman
Chief minister to Louis XIII 1624-42; most powerful figure in French domestic, foreign policy of period.
b. Sep 9, 1585 in Paris, France
d. Dec 4, 1642 in Paris, France
Source: *Benet 96; BiD&SB; BioIn 19, 20; DicTyr; HarEnMi; NewC; NewCol 75; OxCEng 95; OxCFr; OxCThe 67; REn; WorAl*

Richelieu, Louis Francois Armand de
French. Soldier, Diplomat
Grandnephew of Cardinal Richelieu.
b. 1696
d. 1788
Source: *BioIn 7*

Richer, Jean
French. Astronomer
His measurements of the orbit of Mars contributed to the first accurate calculations of the size and orbits of the planets of the solar system.
b. 1630
d. 1696 in Paris, France
Source: *AsBiEn; BiESc; BioIn 5, 7; DcScB*

Richet, Charles Robert
French. Scientist
Won Nobel Prize, 1913; studied hypersensitivity of foreign bodies injected into the body, known as anaphylaxis.
b. Aug 26, 1850 in Paris, France
d. Dec 4, 1935 in Paris, France
Source: *AsBiEn; BiDPara; BiDPsy; BiESc; BioIn 2, 3, 9, 15, 20; DcScB; EncO&P 1; EncPaPR 91; InSci; LarDcSc; McGEWB; NamesHP; NotTwCS; OxCMed 86; WhoNob, 90, 95; WorScD*

Richie, Lionel (Brockman)
American. Singer
Former lead singer, Commodores; had nine number one songs in nine consecutive years; won five Grammys; won Oscar for best song, 1985.
b. Jun 20, 1949 in Tuskegee, Alabama
Source: *AfrAmAl 6; AfrAmBi 1; AmSong; Baker 92; BioIn 12, 13, 14, 15, 16; BkPepl; CelR 90; ConMus 2; CurBio 84; DrBlPA 90; EncPR&S 89; EncRk 88; EncRkSt; HarEnR 86; LegTOT; NegAl 89; NewAmDM; NewGrDA 86; PenEncP; RkOn 85; SoulM; VarWW 85; WhoAm 86, 90; WhoBlA 88, 90, 92; WhoEnt 92; WorAlBi*

Richler, Mordecai
Canadian. Author
Wrote *The Apprenticeship of Duddy Kravitz,* 1959; filmed, 1974; won Commonwealth Prize for *Solomon Gursky Was Here,* 1989.
b. Jan 27, 1931 in Montreal, Quebec, Canada
Source: *Au&Wr 71; AuNews 1; Benet 87, 96; BenetAL 91; BioIn 9, 10, 11, 12, 13, 14, 15, 16, 17, 18, 19, 20, 21; BioNews 75; BlueB 76; CamGLE; CanWr; CanWW 31, 70, 79, 80, 81, 83, 89; CasWL; ChlLR 17; ConAu 31NR, 65; ConCaAu 1; ConLC 3, 5, 9, 13, 18, 46, 70; ConNov 72, 76, 82, 86, 91; CreCan 1; CurBio 75; CyWA 89; DcArts; DcChlFi; DcLB 53; DcLEL 1940; EncAHmr; EncWL 2, 3; FacFETw; GrWrEL N; HalFC 84, 88; IntAu&W 76, 77, 86, 89, 91, 93; IntvTCA 2; IntWW 74, 75, 76, 77, 78, 79, 80, 81, 82, 83, 89, 91, 93; LegTOT; LiExTwC; MagSWL; MajAI; MajTwCW; ModCmwL; Novels; OxCCan; OxCCanL; OxCCan SUP; PenC ENG; RAdv 14, 13-1; REnAL; RfGEnL 91; RGTwCWr; SmATA 27, 44; TwCWr; WebE&AL; Who 74, 82, 83, 85, 88, 90, 92, 94; WhoAm 76, 78, 80, 82, 84, 86, 88, 90, 92, 94, 95, 96, 97; WhoCanL 85, 87, 92; WhoTwCL; WhoWor 74, 78, 80, 82, 84, 87, 89, 91, 93, 95, 96, 97; WhoWrEP 89, 92, 95; WorAl; WorAlBi; WorAu 1950; WrDr 76, 80, 82, 84, 86, 88, 90, 92, 94, 96*

Richman, Charles
American. Actor
Film star, 1915-42; films include *Life of Emile Zola,* 1937; *Dark Victory,* 1939.
b. Jan 12, 1870 in Chicago, Illinois
d. Dec 1, 1940 in New York, New York
Source: *CurBio 41; ForYSC; NotNAT B; Vers B; WhoHol B; WhoStg 1906, 1908; WhScrn 74, 77; WhThe*

Richman, Harry
American. Singer
Top nightclub entertainer, 1920s-30s; noted for cane, top hat.
b. Aug 10, 1895 in Cincinnati, Ohio
d. Nov 3, 1972 in Burbank, California
Source: *ASCAP 66, 80; BiE&WWA; BioIn 14; CmpEPM; EncMT; EncVaud; HalFC 80, 84, 88; InSci; NewYTBE 72; NotNAT A, B; OxCAmT 84; OxCPMus; What 1; WhoHol B; WhoWorJ 72; WhScrn 77, 83; WhThe; WorAl*

Richman, Milton
American. Journalist
Sports editor, UPI, 1972-85; baseball Hall of Fame, 1981.
b. Jan 29, 1922 in New York, New York
d. Jun 9, 1986 in New York, New York
Source: *Ballpl 90; ConAu 69, 119; WhoAm 84; WhoAmJ 80*

Richter, Burton
American. Scientist, Educator
Shared 1976 Nobel Prize in physics; co-discovered subatomic particle J/psi.
b. Mar 22, 1931 in New York, New York
Source: *AmMWSc 73P, 76P, 79, 82, 86, 89, 92, 95; BiESc; BioIn 11, 13, 15, 20; CamDcSc; CurBio 77; FacFETw; IntWW 77, 78, 79, 80, 81, 82, 83, 89, 91, 93; LarDcSc; LegTOT; McGMS 80; NewYTBS 76; NobelP; NotTwCS; Who 82, 83, 85, 88, 90, 92, 94; WhoAm 76, 78, 80, 82, 84, 86, 88, 90, 92, 94, 95, 96, 97; WhoFrS 84; WhoNob, 90, 95; WhoScEn 94, 96; WhoTech 84, 89, 95; WhoWest 78, 80, 82, 84, 87, 89, 92, 94, 96; WhoWor 78, 80, 82, 84, 87, 89, 91, 93, 95, 96, 97; WorAl; WorAlBi; WorScD*

Richter, Charles Francis
American. Inventor
Invented Richter Scale, 1935, to determine severity of earthquakes.
b. Apr 26, 1900 in Hamilton, Ohio
d. Sep 30, 1985 in Pasadena, California
Source: *AmMWSc 73P, 76P, 79; BiESc; BioIn 9, 10; CamDcSc; ConNews 85-4; CurBio 75, 85, 85N; LarDcSc; NewYTBE 71; NewYTBS 85; RAdv 14; WhAm 9; WhoAm 74, 76, 78, 80, 82, 84; WhoWest 74; WorAl*

Richter, Conrad Michael
American. Author
Won 1951 Pulitzer for *The Town.*
b. Nov 13, 1890 in Pine Grove, Pennsylvania
d. Oct 30, 1968 in Pottsville, Pennsylvania
Source: *AmAu&B; AmNov; CnDAL; ConAu 5R; CurBio 51, 68; CyWA 58; DcLEL; ModAL; OxCAmL 65; PenC AM; REn; REnAL; SmATA 3; TwCA; WhAm 5; WhE&EA*

Richter, Curt Paul
American. Scientist
Psychobiologist, Johns Hopkins Medical School, 1922-88; credited with discovery of biorhythms.
b. Feb 20, 1894 in Denver, Colorado
d. Dec 21, 1988 in Baltimore, Maryland
Source: *AmMWSc 73P, 76P, 79, 82, 86, 89, 92; BioIn 16, 17; BlueB 76; FacFETw; IntWW 74, 75, 76, 77, 78, 79, 80, 81, 82, 83; McGMS 80; WhAm 9; WhoAm 74, 76, 86, 88*

Richter, Hans
Hungarian. Conductor
Bayreuth conductor, 1876-1912; then regarded as finest interpreter of Wagner, German classics.
b. Apr 4, 1843 in Raab, Hungary
d. Dec 5, 1916 in Bayreuth, Germany
Source: *Baker 78, 84, 92; BioIn 4, 8, 11, 20; BriBkM 80; CmOp; IntDcOp; MetOEnc; MusMk; MusSN; NewAmDM;*

NewEOp 71; NewGrDM 80; NewGrDO; OxCMus; OxDcOp; PenDiMP; WebBD 83; WhDW

Richter, Hans
German. Filmmaker
Made first abstract film *Rhythm 21,* 1921; known for *Dada: Art and Anti-art,* 1964.
b. Apr 6, 1888 in Berlin, Germany
d. Feb 1, 1976 in Locarno, Switzerland
Source: *BioIn 6, 8, 9, 10, 11, 13, 15, 20; ConArt 77, 83; ConAu 30NR, 65, 73; DcFM; EncWB; FacFETw; FilmEn; FilmgC; HalFC 80, 84, 88; IntDcF 1-2, 2-2; MovMk; OxCFilm; OxCTwCA; PhDcTCA 77; WhoAmA 78N, 80N, 82N, 84N, 86N, 89N, 91N, 93N; WhoHol C; WhScrn 83; WorECar; WorEFlm; WorFDir 1*

Richter, Jean Paul F
German. Author
Works, which were popular in his lifetime, include novel, *Titan,* 1803.
b. Mar 21, 1763 in Wunsiedel, Bavaria
d. Nov 14, 1825 in Bayreuth, Germany
Source: *AtlBL; BiD&SB; DcBiA; NewCol 75; REn*

Richter, Karl
German. Musician, Conductor
Leader, developer, Munich Bach Choir, Orchestra, 1950s.
b. Oct 15, 1926 in Plauen, Germany
d. Feb 16, 1981 in Munich, Germany (West)
Source: *AnObit 1981; Baker 84, 92; BioIn 2, 8, 12; BriBkM 80; FacFETw; IntWW 74, 75, 76, 77, 78, 79, 80; IntWWM 77, 80; NewAmDM; NewGrDM 80; NewYTBS 81; PenDiMP; WhoWor 74, 78*

Richter, Sviatoslav Theofilovich
Russian. Pianist
Int'l concertist; hero of Socialist Labour, 1975; noted for impeccable style.
b. Mar 20, 1915 in Zhitomir, Russia
Source: *Baker 84; BioIn 16; CurBio 61; FacFETw; IntWW 91; IntWWM 90; MusMk; MusSN; NewAmDM; NewGrDM 80; PenDiMP; Who 92; WhoMus 72; WhoWor 74, 78, 80, 82, 84, 87, 89, 91, 93, 95; WorAlBi*

Richthofen, Ferdinand Paul Wilhelm
German. Geographer, Geologist
Pioneer in geomorphology; contributed much to evolution of geographical methodology.
b. May 5, 1833 in Carlsruhe, Prussia
d. Oct 6, 1905 in Berlin, Germany
Source: *BioIn 8; DcScB; Geog 7; WhWE*

Richthofen, Manfred von, Baron
"The Red Baron"
German. Aviator
WW I flying ace credited with shooting down 80 enemy aircraft; killed in action.
b. May 2, 1892 in Breslau, Germany
d. Apr 21, 1918, France
Source: *BioIn 18, 19, 21; HarEnMi; WorAl; WorAlBi*

Ricimer
Roman. Military Leader
Appointed several rulers to the throne of the Western Roman Empire, 456-472 AD.
d. Aug 18, 472
Source: *BioIn 9; DcBiPP; HarEnMi; McGEWB; OxDcByz*

Rickard, Tex
[George L Rickard]
"Man with the Midas Touch"
American. Boxing Promoter
Sponsored first million-dollar gate, Dempsey-Carpentier fight, 1921.
b. Jan 2, 1870 in Sherman, Texas
d. Jun 5, 1929 in Miami Beach, Florida
Source: *BioIn 12, 21; WhoBox 74; WhoSpor; WhScrn 83*

Rickenbacker, Eddie
[Edward Vernon Rickenbacker]
American. Aviator
Won Medal of Honor in WW I; head of Eastern Airlines, 1938-63.
b. Oct 8, 1890 in Columbus, Ohio
d. Jul 23, 1973 in Zurich, Switzerland
Source: *AmAu&B; ApCAB X; BiDAmBL 83; BiDAmSp OS; BioIn 1, 2, 3, 5, 6, 7, 8, 9, 10, 11, 12, 18; CelR; ConAu 41R, 101; CurBio 40, 52, 73, 73N; DcAmB S9; FacFETw; HarEnMi; InSci; LegTOT; MedHR 94; ObitT 1971; OhA&B; WebAB 74, 79; WebAMB; WhAm 5; WhDW; WhoSpor; WorAl*

Ricketts, Howard T
American. Scientist, Physician, Engineer
Early researcher in rickettsial diseases; developed use of laboratory animals for experimentation; died of spotted fever while trying to study it.
b. Feb 9, 1871 in Findlay, Ohio
d. May 3, 1910 in Mexico City, Mexico
Source: *DcAmB S1; DcScB*

Rickey, Branch
[Wesley Branch Rickey]
"The Mahatma"
American. Baseball Player, Baseball Manager, Baseball Executive
Catcher, appearing in 119 ML games; as vp, Brooklyn, 1942-50, broke ML color barrier by signing Jackie Robinson, 1946.
b. Dec 20, 1881 in Stockdale, Ohio
d. Dec 9, 1965 in Columbia, Missouri
Source: *Ballpl 90; BiDAmSp BB; BioIn 1, 2, 4, 6, 7, 10, 12, 13, 14, 15, 16, 17, 19, 21; CurBio 45, 66; DcAmB S7; EncAB-H 1974; EncWB; FacFETw; LegTOT; RComAH; WebAB 74; WhAm 4; WhoProB 73; WhoSpor; WorAl; WorAlBi*

Rickey, George Warren
American. Sculptor
Major figure in kinetic sculpture; works in Museum of Modern Art, NYC; edited *Contemporary Art, 1942-72,* 1973.
b. Jun 6, 1907 in South Bend, Indiana
Source: *AmArt; BioIn 7, 8, 16; BriEAA; ConArt 83, 89; ConAu 65; CurBio 80; DcCAA 88; FacFETw; WhAmArt 85; WhoAm 84, 90, 97; WhoAmA 84, 91*

Rickles, Don
American. Comedian
Well known for comedy style based on insults.
b. May 8, 1926 in New York, New York
Source: *BioIn 8, 10, 11, 12; BioNews 75; CelR, 90; ConTFT 2; EncAFC; FilmgC; ForYSC; HalFC 80, 84, 88; IntMPA 92, 94, 96; JoeFr; LegTOT; NewYTBS 80; VarWW 85; WhoAm 74, 76, 78, 80, 82, 84, 86, 90; WhoCom; WhoEnt 92; WhoHol 92, A; WhoHrs 80; WorAl; WorAlBi*

Rickover, Hyman George
"Father of the Atomic Submarine"
American. Naval Officer
Admiral who spent 63 yrs. in navy; oversaw navy's transition to nuclear equipment.
b. Jan 27, 1900 in Makov, Russia
d. Jul 8, 1986 in Arlington, Virginia
Source: *AmAu&B; AmMWSc 79, 82, 86; AsBiEn; BioIn 3, 4, 5, 6, 7, 8, 10, 11, 12, 13, 14, 15, 17, 18, 20; BlueB 76; ColdWar 2; ConAu 119; ConNews 86-4; CurBio 53, 86; DcAmMiB; EncAB-H 1996; EncWB; FacFETw; InSci; IntWW 74, 75, 76, 77, 78, 79, 80, 81, 82, 83; JeAmHC; LinLib S; McGMS 80; WebAB 74, 79; WebAMB; WhAm 9; WhDW; WhoAm 74, 76, 78, 80, 82, 84, 86; WhoAtom 77; WhoGov 72, 75, 77; WhoWor 74, 78, 80, 82, 84, 87; WhoWorJ 72; WorAl; WorDWW*

Rickword, Edgell
[John Edgell Rickword]
English. Poet, Editor
Founder, editor, "Left Review," 1934-38.
b. Oct 22, 1898 in Colchester, England
d. Mar 15, 1982, England
Source: *AnObit 1982; BioIn 10, 12, 13, 17, 20; CamGLE; ConAu 36NR, 101, 106; ConLCrt 82; ConPo 70, 75, 80; DcLB 20; GrWrEL P; IntAu&W 76; ModBrL; NewCBEL; OxCEng 85, 95; OxCTwCP; RfGEnL 91; RGFMBP; WorAu 1950; WrDr 76, 80, 82*

Rico, Don(ato)
American. Illustrator, Writer
Edited Marvel Comics: *Captain America; Daredevil,* 1939-57, 1977-85.
b. Sep 26, 1917 in Rochester, New York
d. Mar 27, 1985 in Los Angeles, California
Source: *BioIn 15; ConAu 28NR, 81, 115; ScF&FL 92; SmATA 43N*

Ricordi, Giovanni
Italian. Publisher
Founded family-run music publishing co. in Milan, 1808.
b. 1785
d. 1853
Source: *Baker 78, 92; BioIn 4, 12; MetOEnc; NewAmDM; NewEOp 71; NewGrDM 80; OxDcOp; WebBD 83*

Ridder, Bernard Herman
American. Newspaper Publisher
Last of three surviving sons in Ridder Publications family; chm. emeritus, 1973; merged with Knight Newspapers, 1974.
b. Mar 20, 1883 in New York, New York
d. May 5, 1975 in West Palm Beach, Florida
Source: *BioIn 7, 10; DcAmB S9; NewYTBS 75; ObitOF 79; St&PR 75; WhAm 6; WhLit*

Riddle, Nelson
American. Musician, Composer
Known for collaborations with Frank Sinatra, 1950s; won Oscar, 1974, for score of *The Great Gatsby.*
b. Jun 1, 1921 in Oradell, New Jersey
d. Oct 6, 1985 in Los Angeles, California
Source: *AnObit 1985; Baker 84, 92; BiDAmM; BiDJaz; BioIn 13, 14, 15; CmpEPM; ConAmC 76, 82; ConNews 85-4; ConTFT 5; FacFETw; FilmgC; HalFC 80, 84, 88; IntMPA 84, 86; LegTOT; NewAmDM; NewGrDA 86; NewGrDJ 88, 94; NewYTBS 85; OxCPMus; PenEncP; RkOn 74; VarWW 85; WhoAm 82; WorAlBi*

Riddleberger, James Williams
American. Diplomat
US ambassador to Yugoslavia, Greece, Austria, 1953-68.
b. Sep 21, 1904 in Washington, District of Columbia
d. Oct 17, 1982 in Woodstock, Virginia
Source: *BioIn 4, 5; CurBio 57, 83; WhoAmP 81, 83*

Ride, Sally K
[Mrs. Steven A. Hawley]
American. Astronaut
First US woman in space, aboard space shuttle *Challenger,* 1983.
b. May 26, 1951 in Los Angeles, California
Source: *BioIn 13, 14, 15, 16; CurBio 83; FacFETw; HerW 84; IntWW 91; InWom SUP; NewYTBS 83; WhoAm 90; WhoAmW 91; WhoSpc; WorAlBi*

Rider-Kelsey, Corinne
"Mme. Rider-Reed"
American. Singer
Soprano concert soloist, oratorio singer, early 1900s.
b. Feb 24, 1877 in Bergen, Norway
d. Jul 10, 1947 in Toledo, Ohio
Source: *Baker 78, 84, 92; BioIn 4; InWom; NewGrDA 86; NotAW; WomFir*

Ridge, John Rollin
American. Writer
Published *The Life and Adventures of Joaquin Murietta,* 1954.
b. Mar 19, 1827 in Georgia
d. Oct 5, 1867 in California
Source: *AmAu&B; BiNAW, B, SupB; BioIn 18, 21; ChhPo S1; ConAu 144; DcNAA; DcNAL; EncNoAI; NatNAL; NotNaAm; OxCAmL 65, 83, 95; REnAL; RfGAmL 94*

Ridge, Lola
American. Poet
Described NY in *The Ghetto and Other Poems,* 1918.
b. Dec 12, 1873 in Dublin, Ireland
d. May 19, 1941 in New York, New York
Source: *AmWomWr; BioIn 15; DcLB 54; FemiCLE; InWom SUP; NotAW*

Ridgeley, Andrew
English. Musician
Guitarist, drummer; hit single "Wake Me Up Before You Go-Go," 1984.
b. Jan 26, 1963 in Bushey, England
Source: *BioIn 14, 15; LegTOT*

Ridgeway, Rick
American. Adventurer
Wrote *The Last Step: The American Ascent of K2,* 1980.
b. Aug 12, 1949 in Long Beach, California
Source: *BioIn 15; ConAu 93*

Ridgway, Matthew Bunker
American. Army Officer
Commanded one of first airborne divisions formed by US Army; one of first to parachute in D-Day invasion of Normandy, Jun 1944; received Medal of Freedom, 1986.
b. Mar 3, 1895 in Fort Monroe, Virginia
d. Jul 26, 1993 in Fox Chapel, Pennsylvania
Source: *BiDWWGF; BioIn 1, 2, 3, 4, 6, 8, 9, 10, 11, 15; CmdGen 1991; ColdWar 2; DcAmMiB; DcTwHis; FacFETw; HarEnMi; IntWW 83, 91; LinLib S; McGEWB; PeoHis; PolProf E, J, T; WebAB 79; WebAMB; WhAm 11; Who 74, 82, 83, 85, 88, 90, 92; WhoAm 74, 76; WhoWor 74, 78, 80, 82, 84, 87; WhWW-II; WorAl; WorAlBi; WrDr 76, 80, 86, 90*

Riding, Laura
[Laura Riding Jackson]
American. Writer
Wrote verse, fiction, criticism, including novel *Trojan Ending,* 1937; often collaborated with Robert Graves.
b. Jan 16, 1901 in New York, New York
d. Sep 2, 1991 in Wabasso, Florida
Source: *AmAu&B; AmWomWr; AnObit 1991; ArtclWW 2; Benet 87; BenetAL 91; BioIn 13, 15, 16, 17, 18, 19; BlueB 76; CamGEL; CamGLE; CamHAL; ChhPo, S1; CnDAL; CnE&AP; ConAmA; ConAu 28NR, 65, 135, X; ConLC 3, 7, 70; ConPo 70, 75, 80, 85, 91; ContDcW 89; DcLB 48; DcLEL; DcLP 87B; EvLB; FemiCLE; GrWrEL P; IntAu&W 77; IntDcWB; IntWW 74, 75, 76, 77, 78, 79, 80, 81, 82, 83, 89, 91; IntWWP 77; InWom, SUP; LngCTC; ModWoWr; NewCBEL; NewYTBS 91; OxCAmL 65, 83, 95; OxCEng 85, 95; OxCTwCP; OxCWoWr 95; PenBWP; PenC AM; PenNWW A, B; RAdv 1, 14, 13-1; REnAL; RfGAmL 87, 94; RGFAP; SixAP; TwCA, SUP; WhE&EA; WhLit; WhNAA; Who 74, 82, 83, 85, 90; WhoAm 86, 90; WhoTwCL; WrDr 76, 80, 82, 84, 86, 88, 90, 92, 94N*

Riebeeck, Jan Anthonisz van
Dutch. Colonizer
By establishing Cape Town in 1652, he opened up South Africa to white colonists.
b. Apr 21, 1619 in Culemborg, Netherlands
d. Jan 18, 1677 in Batavia, Dutch East Indies
Source: *BioIn 8, 10*

Riefenstahl, Leni
[Helene Bertha Amalie Riefenstahl]
German. Director
Friend of Hitler, who filmed propaganda documentary, *Triumph of the Will,* 1934; imprisoned by French following WW II.
b. Aug 22, 1902 in Berlin, Germany
Source: *Benet 87; BiDFilm, 81, 94; BioIn 5, 8, 10, 11, 12, 14, 15, 18, 19, 20, 21; ConAu 108; ConLC 16; ConPhot 82, 88, 95; ContDcW 89; CurBio 75; DcArts; DcFM; EncEurC; EncTR, 91; EncWB; FacFETw; Film 2; FilmEn; FilmgC; HalFC 80, 84, 88; ICPEnP A; IntDcF 1-2, 2-2; IntDcWB; IntWW 83, 89, 91, 93; InWom SUP; LegTOT; MacBEP; MakMC; MiSFD 9; OxCFilm; ReelWom; VarWW 85; WhDW; WhoEnt 92; WhoHol 92, A; WhoWor 74, 76, 82, 84, 87, 89, 91, 93, 95; WomFir; WomWMM; WorAl; WorEFlm; WorFDir 1*

Riegger, Wallingford
American. Composer
Wrote orchestral works, ballet, film scores; composed "Symphony No. 3," 1948; developed electronic instruments.
b. Apr 29, 1885 in Albany, Georgia
d. Apr 2, 1961 in New York, New York
Source: *Baker 78, 84; BiDAmM; BioIn 1, 3, 4, 5, 6, 8, 13; BriBkM 80; CnOxB; CompSN; ConAmC 76, 82; DancEn 78; DcAmB S7; DcCM; MusMk; NewAmDM; NewGrDA 86; NewGrDM 80; NewOxM; OxCMus; WhAm 4*

Riegle, Donald Wayne, Jr.
American. Politician
Dem. senator from MI, 1977-95.
b. Feb 4, 1938 in Flint, Michigan
Source: *AlmAP 88, 92; BiDrAC; BiDrUSC 89; BioIn 8, 9, 10, 11, 15, 16; CngDr 87, 89; ConAu 61; CurBio 86; IntWW 91; PolsAm 84; WhoAm 74, 76,*

78, 80, 82, 84, 86, 88, 90, 92, 94, 95; WhoAmP 91; WhoGov 72, 75, 77; WhoMW 74, 76, 78, 80, 82, 84, 86, 88, 90, 92, 93; WhoWor 80, 82, 87, 89, 91, 96

Riel, Louis David, Jr.
Canadian. Revolutionary
Led Indian rebellions against govt. land threats, 1870, 1885; hanged for treason.
b. Oct 23, 1844 in Saint Boniface, Manitoba, Canada
d. Nov 16, 1885 in Regina, Saskatchewan, Canada
Source: *ApCAB; BioIn 1, 3, 4, 5, 7, 8, 9, 10, 11, 12; DcNAA; EncNAB; EncRev; MacDCB 78; NewCol 75; OxCCan; RelLAm 91; REnAW; WhAm HS; WhNaAH*

Riemann, Georg Friedrich
German. Mathematician
Developed non-Euclidean system of geometry; name applied to elliptic geometry.
b. Sep 17, 1826 in Breselanz, Germany
d. Jul 20, 1866 in Selasca, Italy
Source: *AsBiEn; DcScB; McGEWB; NewCol 75*

Riemenschneider, Tilman
German. Artist
Late Gothic German sculptor; leader of the Lower Franconia school.
b. 1460 in Heilgenstadt, Germany
d. Jul 7, 1531 in Wurzburg, Germany
Source: *AtlBL; BioIn 5, 6, 8, 12, 13, 14; DcArts; McGDA; McGEWB; OxCGer 76, 86; OxDcArt*

Rifkin, Jeremy
American. Author, Political Activist
Wrote *Algeny,* 1983; *Declaration of a Heretic,* 1985.
b. Jan 26, 1945 in Denver, Colorado
Source: *BioIn 10, 14, 15, 16; ConAu 50NR, 121, 129; CurBio 86; News 90, 90-3; WhoUSWr 88; WhoWrEP 89; WrDr 88, 90, 92, 94, 96*

Rifkind, Simon H(irsch)
American. Lawyer, Judge
Adviser on Jewish affairs to US army; helped set up Municipal Assistance Corp. to rescue New York City from bankruptcy, 1975.
b. Jun 5, 1901, Russia
d. Nov 14, 1995 in New York, New York
Source: *BiDFedJ; BioIn 1, 13; ConAu 150; CurBio 96N; WhAm 11; WhoAm 74, 76, 78, 80, 82, 84, 86, 88, 90, 92, 94, 95, 96; WhoAmL 78, 79, 83, 87, 94; WhoE 74, 95; WhoWor 96*

Rigaud, Hyacinthe
[Hyacinthe Francois Honore Rigau y Ros]
French. Artist
French Baroque painter who specialized in portraits.
b. Jul 28, 1659, France
d. Dec 29, 1743 in Paris, France
Source: *BioIn 1, 3, 6, 11; ClaDrA; DcArts; DcBiPP; McGDA; OxCFr; OxDcArt*

Rigby, Bob
American. Soccer Player
Goalie in NASL, 1973-79; had goals against average of under two per game.
b. Jul 3, 1951 in Ridley Park, Pennsylvania
Source: *AmEnS; WhoSpor*

Rigby, Cathy
[Mrs. Tom McCoy]
American. Gymnast
First American to win medal (silver) for int'l gymnastics, 1970; first non-russian in competition in USSR to win gold medal, 1970.
b. Dec 12, 1952 in Long Beach, California
Source: *AmDec 1970; BioIn 9, 10, 11, 12, 15, 17; BioNews 74; EncWomS; GoodHs; HerW, 84; InWom SUP; LegTOT; NewYTBE 72; WhoSpor; WomFir*

Rigby, Harry
American. Producer
Co-produced long-running Broadway hit musicals *Sugar Babies; Irene.*
b. Feb 21, 1925 in Pittsburgh, Pennsylvania
d. Jan 17, 1985 in New York, New York
Source: *BioIn 14; EncMT; NewYTBS 85; NotNAT; WhAm 8; WhoAm 84; WhoThe 81*

Rigg, Diana
English. Actor
Played Emma Peel on TV series "The Avengers," 1965-68.
b. Jul 20, 1938 in Doncaster, England
Source: *BioIn 7, 9, 10, 13, 16; CamGWoT; CelR, 90; ConTFT 3, 13; CurBio 74; DcArts; FilmEn; FilmgC; ForYSC; HalFC 80, 84, 88; IlWWBF; IntMPA 77, 80, 84, 86, 88, 92, 94, 96; IntWW 78, 80, 81, 82, 83, 89, 91; InWom SUP; LegTOT; MotPP; OxCThe 83; PlP&P; VarWW 85; Who 74, 82, 83, 85, 88, 90, 92, 94; WhoAm 76, 78, 80, 82, 86, 88, 90, 92, 95, 96, 97; WhoAmW 83; WhoEnt 92; WhoHol 92, A; WhoHrs 80; WhoThe 72, 77, 81; WhoWor 84, 87, 89, 91, 93, 95, 96, 97; WorAl; WorAlBi*

Riggins, John
American. Football Player
Running back, 1971-85; mostly with Washington; led NFL in TDs, twice; MVP, 1983 Super Bowl.
b. Aug 4, 1949 in Centralia, Kansas
Source: *BiDAmSp FB; BioIn 10, 13, 14, 15, 16; FootReg 85, 86; NewYTBS 83, 84, 91; WhoE 85; WhoFtbl 74; WhoSpor*

Riggs, Bobby
[Robert Larimore Riggs]
American. Tennis Player
Defeated by Billie Jean King in the "Match of the Century," 1973.
b. Feb 25, 1918 in Los Angeles, California
d. Oct 25, 1995 in Leucadia, California
Source: *BiDAmSp OS; BiDWomA; BioIn 1, 2, 8, 9, 10, 11, 12, 13, 14, 16; BuCMET; CmCal; ConArt 89; ContDcW 89; CurBio 49, 96N; EncFash; FacFETw; IntWW 91; InWom SUP; LegTOT; News 96, 96-2; NewYTBE 73; NewYTBS 95; OxDcArt; PrintW 85; TwCPaSc; Who 92; WhoAm 76, 78, 80, 82; WhoArt 84; WhoSpor; WhoWest 82; WhoWor 91; WorAl*

Riggs, Lynn
American. Dramatist
Noted for romantic comedy, *Green Grow the Lilacs,* 1931.
b. Aug 31, 1899 in Claremore, Oklahoma
d. Jun 30, 1954 in New York, New York
Source: *AmAu&B; BenetAL 91; BioIn 3, 4, 5, 6, 9, 11, 16, 17; CnDAL; CnMD; ConAmA; CrtSuDr; CyWA 58; McGEWD 72, 84; ModWD; NatCAB 45; NatNAL; NotNAT B; OxCAmL 65, 83, 95; OxCAmT 84; PlP&P; REn; REnAL; REnAW; TwCA, SUP; TwCLC 56; WhThe*

Riggs, Marlon
American. Filmmaker
Maker of documentaries from a black gay male sensibility; made *Tongues Untied,* 1989.
b. 1957 in Fort Worth, Texas
d. 1994
Source: *BioIn 19, 20; ConBlB 5; GayLesB*

Righetti, Dave
[David Allen Righetti]
American. Baseball Player
Relief pitcher, NY Yankees, 1979, 1981-90; San Francisco, 1991—; held ML record for saves in a season, 46, 1986, until broken by Bobby Thigpen, 1990; threw no-hitter, 1983.
b. Nov 28, 1958 in San Jose, California
Source: *Ballpl 90; BaseReg 86, 87; BioIn 11, 13, 14; NewYTBS 83*

Righteous Brothers, The
[Bobby Hatfield; Bill Medley]
American. Music Group
Duo formed 1962; personified "white soul" with harmony ballads; hit song "You've Lost That Lovin' Feelin'," 1964.
Source: *BiDAmM; ConMuA 80A; EncPR&S 74, 89; EncRk 88; EncRkSt; HarEnR 86; IlEncBM 82; IlEncRk; NewAmDM; PenEncP; RkOn 74; RolSEnR 83; SoulM; WhoRock 81; WhoRocM 82*

Righter, Carroll
American. Astrologer
Hollywood columnist on astrology from 1939.
b. Feb 2, 1900 in Salem, New Jersey
d. Apr 30, 1988 in Santa Monica, California
Source: *BioIn 3, 4, 5, 8, 9, 10, 15, 16; CelR; ConAu 93, 125; CurBio 72, 88, 88N*

Riis, Jacob August
American. Journalist
NYC police reporter, 1877-88; exposed slum conditions; wrote autobiography, *Making of an American,* 1901.
b. May 3, 1849 in Ribe, Denmark
d. May 26, 1914 in Barre, Massachusetts
Source: *AmAu&B; AmBi; AmRef; AmSocL; BbD; BiD&SB; BiDSocW; BioIn 1, 3, 6, 7, 8, 9, 10, 13; DcAmAu; DcAmB; DcAmImH; DcAmMeB 84; DcNAA; EncAB-H 1974, 1996; HarEnUS; MacBEP; McGEWB; NatCAB 13; OxCAmL 65, 83, 95; REn; REnAL; TwCBDA; WebAB 74, 79; WhAm 1; WhAmArt 85; WorAl*

Rijo, Jose Antonio Abreu
Dominican. Baseball Player
Pitcher since 1984, with Cincinnati, 1988—; MVP, 1990 World Series.
b. May 13, 1965 in San Cristobal, Dominican Republic
Source: *Ballpl 90; BaseEn 88; WhoBlA 92; WhoHisp 92*

Riklis, Meshulam
"Rik"
American. Business Executive
Chm., McCrory Corp., 1975-85, Rapid-Am Corp., 1957—; owns Faberge perfumes; married to Pia Zadora.
b. Dec 2, 1923 in Istanbul, Turkey
Source: *BioIn 7, 8, 9, 10, 11, 12, 16; CurBio 71; Dun&B 79, 86, 88, 90; IntWW 74, 75, 76, 77, 78, 79, 80, 81, 82, 83, 89, 91, 93; NewYTBE 72; Tst 93; WhoAm 74, 76, 78, 80, 82, 84, 86, 88, 92, 95, 96, 97; WhoE 74, 83, 85, 86, 89; WhoFI 74, 75, 77, 79, 81, 83, 85, 87, 89, 92*

Riles, Wilson Camanza
American. Educator
CA Superintendent of Public Instruction, 1971-82; won Spingarn, 1972.
b. Jun 27, 1917 in Alexandria, Louisiana
Source: *AfrAmBi 2; BioIn 14; CurBio 71; InB&W 80, 85; LEduc 74; NewYTBE 70; WhoAfA 96; WhoAm 78, 80, 82, 84, 86, 88, 90, 92, 94, 95, 96, 97; WhoAmP 73, 75, 77, 79, 81, 83, 85, 87, 89, 91, 93, 95; WhoBlA 75, 85, 88, 90, 92, 94; WhoWest 74, 76, 78, 80, 82, 84, 89, 92, 94, 96*

Riley, Bridget
English. Artist
Op-artist; early work is in black & white geometric shapes, lines; won many awards.
b. Apr 24, 1931 in London, England
Source: *BiDWomA; BioIn 8, 9, 10, 11, 12, 16; BlueB 76; ConArt 77, 83, 89; ConBrA 79; ContDcW 89; CurBio 81; DcCAr 81; IntDcWB; IntWW 74, 75, 76, 77, 78, 79, 80, 81, 82, 83, 89, 91, 93; McGDA; OxCTwCA; OxDcArt; PhDcTCA 77; PrintW 83, 85; TwCPaSc; Who 85; WhoArt 80, 82, 84, 96; WhoWor 74; WorArt 1950*

Riley, Charles Valentine
American. Scientist
Contributed greatly to the study of entomology.
b. Sep 18, 1843 in Chelsea, England
d. Sep 14, 1895 in Washington, District of Columbia
Source: *Alli SUP; AmBi; ApCAB; BiDAmS; BiInAmS; BioIn 9; DcAmAu; DcAmB; DcNAA; InSci; NatCAB 9; TwCBDA; WhAm HS*

Riley, James Whitcomb
"Hoosier Poet"
American. Poet
Wrote poems "Little Orphan Annie"; "The Raggedy Man."
b. Oct 7, 1849 in Greenfield, Indiana
d. Jul 22, 1916 in Indianapolis, Indiana
Source: *Alli SUP; AmAu; AmAu&B; AmBi; ApCAB X; ASCAP 66, 80; BbD; Benet 87, 96; BenetAL 91; BibAL; BiD&SB; BioIn 1, 2, 3, 4, 5, 6, 7, 8, 9, 10, 11, 12, 13, 14, 15, 19; BlkAWP; CamGEL; CamGLE; CamHAL; CarSB; CasWL; Chambr 3; ChhPo, S1, S2; ChlBkCr; ChrP; CnDAL; ConAu 118, 137; DcAmAu; DcAmB; DcArts; DcEnA A; DcLEL; DcNAA; EncAAH; EncAHmr; EvLB; GayN; GrWrEL P; IndAu 1816; JBA 34; LinLib L, S; LngCTC; MajAl; McGEWB; OxCAmL 65, 83, 95; OxCChiL; PenC AM; RAdv 1, 14, 13-1; REn; REnAL; RfGAmL 87, 94; SmATA 17; Str&VC; TwCLC 51; WebAB 74, 79; WhFla; WorAl; WorAlBi*

Riley, Jeannie C
[Jeannie C Stephenson]
American. Singer
1960s pop-country hits include "Harper Valley PTA."
b. Oct 19, 1945 in Anson, Texas
Source: *BioIn 14; ConAu 129; EncRk 88; HarEnCM 87; PenEncP; RkOn 74; WhoAm 82; WhoEnt 92; WhoSSW 73*

Riley, Pat(rick James)
American. Basketball Coach
Coach, LA Lakers, 1981-90, won four NBA championships; New York Knicks, 1991-95; Miami Heat, 1995—

b. Mar 20, 1945 in Rome, New York
Source: *BasBi; BiDAmSp BK; BioIn 13, 14, 15, 16; ConAu 147; CurBio 88; LegTOT; News 94, 94-3; NewYTBS 82, 90; OfNBA 87; WhoAm 84, 86, 88, 90, 92, 94, 95, 96, 97; WhoBbl 73; WhoE 93, 95, 97; WhoWest 84, 87, 89; WorAlBi*

Riley, Richard W(ilson)
American. Government Official
Secretary of Education, 1993—.
b. Jan 2, 1933 in Greenville, South Carolina
Source: *BiDrGov 1978, 1983; BioIn 15, 18, 19; CurBio 93; WhoAm 80, 82, 84, 86, 94, 95, 96, 97; WhoAmL 78, 79, 92; WhoAmP 73, 75, 77, 79, 81, 83, 85, 87, 89, 91, 93, 95; WhoE 95; WhoGov 75, 77; WhoSSW 75, 76, 80, 82, 86; WhoWor 82, 87, 96*

Rilke, Rainer Maria
German. Poet
Poems include *Life and Songs; Sonnets to Orpheus.*
b. Dec 4, 1876 in Prague, Bohemia
d. Dec 29, 1926 in Muzot, Switzerland
Source: *AtlBL; CasWL; ClDMEL 47; CnMWL; CyWA 58; EncWL; EvEuW; LngCTC; ModGL; OxCEng 67; PenC EUR; RComWL; REn; TwCA; TwCWr; WhAm 4A; WhoTwCL*

Rillieux, Norbert
American. Engineer
Made great impact on the sugar-refining industry with discovery of a vacuum pan evaporator, 1846.
b. 1806
d. 1894
Source: *AfrAmAl 6; BioIn 4, 6, 8, 9, 10, 11, 15, 17, 21; BlksScM; DcAmNB; InB&W 80, 85; NegAl 76, 83, 89; WorInv*

Rimbaud, (Jean Nicolas) Arthur
French. Poet
Wrote only from ages 16-19; great influence on Symbolist movement.
b. Oct 20, 1854 in Charlesville, France
d. Nov 10, 1891 in Marseilles, France
Source: *AtlBL; Benet 87, 96; BioIn 1, 2, 3, 4, 5, 6, 7, 8, 9, 10, 11, 12, 13, 14, 16, 17, 20; CasWL; ClDMEL 47, 80; CyWA 58; DcArts; DcEuL; Dis&D; EuAu; EuWr 7; EvEuW; GayLesB; GrFLW; GuFrLit 1; LegTOT; LinLib L, S; LngCTC; MagSWL; McGEWB; ModRL; NinCLC 4, 35; OxCEng 67, 85, 95; OxCFr; PenC EUR; PoeCrit 3; RAdv 14, 13-2; RComWL; REn; RfGWoL 95; RGFMEP; WhDW; WorAl; WorAlBi; WorLitC*

Rimmer, William
American. Sculptor
Figures include *The Dying Centaur; Alexander Hamilton.*
b. Feb 20, 1816 in Liverpool, England
d. Aug 20, 1879 in Boston, Massachusetts
Source: *Alli SUP; AmBi; AntBDN C; ApCAB; BenetAL 91; BioIn 1, 7, 9, 10, 11, 15; BriEAA; DcAmArt; DcAmAu; DcAmB; McGDA; McGEWB; NatCAB 4; NewYHSD; OxCAmH; OxCAmL 65, 83, 95; OxCArt; OxDcArt; REnAL; WebAB 74, 79; WhAmArt 85; WhAm HS*

Rimsky-Korsakov, Nikolai Andreevich
Russian. Composer
Known for brilliant instrumentation in symphonies; wrote 16 operas including *The Snow Maiden,* 1881.
b. Mar 18, 1844 in Tikhvin, Russia
d. Jun 21, 1908 in Saint Petersburg, Russia
Source: *AtlBL; McGEWB; NewCol 75; REn; WorAl*

Rinaldi, Kathy
American. Tennis Player
Wimbledon's youngest competitor in 74 yrs., 1981.
b. Mar 24, 1967 in Jensen Beach, Florida
Source: *BioIn 12, 13, 14; WhoIntT*

Rindt, Jochen
Austrian. Auto Racer
World Grand Prix champion, 1970; appeared in film *Grand Prix,* 1966.
b. Apr 18, 1942 in Mainz, Germany
d. Sep 5, 1970 in Monza, Italy
Source: *BioIn 9, 10, 12, 15, 16; WhScrn 83*

Rinehart, Frederick Roberts
American. Publisher
A founder, Farrar and Rinehart, 1929, with brother Stanley.
b. 1903 in Allegheny, Pennsylvania
d. Jun 15, 1981 in New York, New York
Source: *ConAu 104; NewYTBS 81*

Rinehart, Mary Roberts
American. Author, Dramatist
Wrote popular novels, mysteries including *The Circular Staircase,* 1908; *Tish,* 1916; mother of Frederick, Stanley.
b. Aug 12, 1876 in Pittsburgh, Pennsylvania
d. Sep 22, 1958 in New York, New York
Source: *AmAu&B; AmNov; AmWomD; AmWomPl; AmWomWr; ApCAB X; ArtclWW 2; Benet 87; BenetAL 91; BioAmW; BioIn 14, 16, 19, 20; ConAmL; ConAu 108; CorpD; CrtSuMy; DcAmB S6; DcBiA; DcLEL; DetWom; EncMys; EvLB; GrWomMW; GrWrEL N; HalFC 80, 84, 88; InWom, SUP; LegTOT; LinLib L, S; LngCTC; ModWD; NotAW MOD; NotNAT B; Novels; ObitT 1951; OxCAmL 65, 83, 95; OxCAmT 84; OxCWoWr 95; PenC AM; PenNWW A; REn; REnAL; RfGAmL 87, 94; ScF&FL 92; TwCA, SUP; TwCCr&M 80, 85, 91; TwCLC 52; TwCRGW; TwCRHW 90, 94; TwCWr; WebAB 74, 79; WhAm 3; WhLit; WhNAA; WhThe; WomFir; WomStre; WomWWA 14; WorAl; WorAlBi*

Rinehart, Stanley Marshall, Jr.
American. Publisher
A founder, Farrar and Rinehart, 1929, which became Holt, Rinehart & Winston, 1960.
b. Aug 18, 1897 in Pittsburgh, Pennsylvania
d. Apr 26, 1969 in South Miami, Florida
Source: *BioIn 3, 8; ConAu 29R; CurBio 54, 69; DcAmB S8; WhAm 5*

Rinehart, William H
American. Sculptor
Neo-classicist; finest works include *Clytie,* 1872.
b. Sep 13, 1825 in Union Bridge, Maryland
d. Oct 28, 1874 in Rome, Italy
Source: *AmBi; ApCAB; DcAmB; McGDA; NatCAB 2; OxCArt; TwCBDA; WhAm HS*

Ring, Blanche
American. Actor, Singer
Silent films include *Yankee Girl,* 1915; *It's the Old Army Game,* 1926.
b. Apr 24, 1872 in Boston, Massachusetts
d. Jan 13, 1961 in Santa Monica, California
Source: *BiDAmM; EncMT; Film 1, 2; InWom, SUP; WhAm 4; WhoHol B; WhoStg 1908; WhScrn 74, 77*

Ringer, Robert J
American. Author
Wrote *Looking Out for 1,* 1977.
b. 1938
Source: *BioIn 10; ConAu 81; NewYTBS 79; WrDr 92*

Ringgold, Faith
American. Artist, Writer
Multimedia artist known for her "story quilts;" wrote and illustrated award-winning children's book *Tar Beach,* 1992.
b. Oct 8, 1930 in New York, New York
Source: *AfrAmAl 6; Au&Arts 19; BiDWomA; BioIn 9, 11, 12, 13, 16; BlkAuII 92; ConAu 154; ConBlB 4; CurBio 96; EncWB; IntDcWB; InWom SUP; NegAl 89; NorAmWA; SmATA 71; TwCChW 95; WhoAfA 96; WhoAm 92, 94, 95, 96, 97; WhoAmA 84, 91, 93; WhoAmW 95, 97; WhoBlA 80, 85, 88, 90, 92, 94; WhoE 86; WhoWor 96, 97; WorArt 1980*

Ringling, Charles
[Ringling Brothers]
American. Circus Owner
With four brothers, started small circus, 1880s; merged with Forepaugh-Sells, Barnum & Bailey, 1907; established Sarasota as winter resort.
b. Dec 2, 1863 in McGregor, Iowa
d. Dec 3, 1926 in Sarasota, Florida
Source: *BiDAmBL 83; DcAmB; DcArts; LegTOT; WebAB 74, 79; WebBD 83; WhAm 4, HSA; WhFla*

Ringling Brothers
[Alfred C Ringling; Alfred T Ringling; Charles Ringling; John Ringling; Otto Ringling]
American. Circus Owners
Brothers who started small circus in Baraboo, WI, 1880s; merged with Forepaugh-Sells, Barnum & Bailey, 1907.
Source: *BioIn 8; OxCAmT 84; WhAmArt 85*

Ringo, Jim
[James Ringo]
American. Football Player
Center, Green Bay, 1953-63, Philadelphia, 1964-67; Hall of Fame, 1981.
b. Nov 21, 1932 in Orange, New Jersey
Source: *BiDAmSp FB; BioIn 17; LegTOT; WhoFtbl 74; WhoSSW 91*

Ringo, John(ny)
American. Outlaw
Idealized figure of "gentleman bandit"; member of Clanton gang, enemy of the Earps.
b. 1844?
d. Jul 14, 1882 in Tombstone, Arizona
Source: *BioIn 11, 15, 17; EncACr; REnAW*

Ringwald, Molly
American. Actor
Star of five feature films, including *The Breakfast Club,* 1985; *Pretty in Pink,* 1986.
b. Feb 18, 1968 in Roseville, California
Source: *BiDFilm 94; BioIn 13, 14, 15, 16; CelR 90; ConNews 85-4; ConTFT 6, 13; CurBio 87; HalFC 88; IntMPA 86, 88, 92, 94, 96; LegTOT; VarWW 85; WhoAm 92; WhoEnt 92; WhoHol 92; WorAlBi*

Rinkoff, Barbara Jean
American. Children's Author
First book, *A Map is a Picture,* 1965, used as elementary school text.
b. Jan 25, 1923 in New York, New York
d. Feb 18, 1975 in Mount Kisco, New York
Source: *AuBYP 2, 3; ConAu 57, P-2; IntAu&W 76; MorBMP; SmATA 4, 27N, 46; WhAm 6; WhoAmW 75*

Rinuccini, Ottavio
Italian. Poet, Librettist
Wrote text for Peri's *Dafne,* 1594; considered first true opera.
b. Jan 20, 1562 in Florence, Italy
d. Mar 28, 1621 in Florence, Italy
Source: *Baker 84, 92; BiD&SB; BioIn 13; CasWL; EvEuW; MetOEnc; NewEOp 71; NewGrDM 80; NewGrDO; OxDcOp; REn*

Riopelle, Jean-Paul
Canadian. Artist
Leading exponent of nonfigurative and "action" painting; awarded the Champion of the Order of Canada, 1969.
b. Oct 7, 1923 in Montreal, Quebec, Canada
Source: *BioIn 13, 16, 17; BlueB 76; CanWW 31, 70, 79, 80, 81, 83, 89; ConArt 77, 83, 89, 96; CreCan 1; CurBio 89; DcArts; FacFETw; IntWW*

74, 75, 76, 77, 78, 79, 80, 81, 82, 83, 89, 91, 93; McGDA; OxCTwCA; OxDcArt; PrintW 83, 85; WhoAm 74; WhoArt 80; WhoWor 74; WorArt 1950

Riordan, Richard J
American. Politician
Rep. Mayor of Los Angeles, 1993—.
b. 1930 in Flushing, New York
Source: *Dun&B 88*

Rios Montt, Jose Efrain
Guatemalan. Political Leader
Became pres. after bloodless coup, 1982; overthrown in another coup, 1983.
b. Jun 16, 1926? in Huehuetenango, Guatemala
Source: *BioIn 13, 15; CurBio 83; IntWW 83, 91; NewYTBS 82; WorDWW*

Riperton, Minnie
American. Singer
Had five-octave voice range; hits include "Lovin' You," 1974.
b. Nov 8, 1948 in Chicago, Illinois
d. Jul 12, 1979 in Los Angeles, California
Source: *BlkWAm; DrBlPA; IlEncBM 82; NewYTBS 79; PenEncP; RkOn 78; WhoBlA 77; WhoRock 81*

Ripken, Bill
[William Oliver Ripken]
American. Baseball Player
Second baseman, Baltimore, 1987-92; part of double play combination with brother, Cal.
b. Dec 16, 1964 in Havre de Grace, Maryland
Source: *Ballpl 90; BaseEn 88; BaseReg 87*

Ripken, Cal(vin Edwin, Jr.)
American. Baseball Player
Shortstop, Baltimore, 1978—; AL rookie of year, 1982, MVP, 1983 and 1991. Played in his 2131st consecutive game 9/06/95, breaking Lou Gehrig's long standing record.
b. Aug 24, 1960 in Havre de Grace, Maryland
Source: *Ballpl 90; BaseReg 86, 87; BioIn 13, 14, 15, 16; ConNews 86-2; CurBio 92; LegTOT; NewYTBS 84, 95; WhoAm 88; WhoE 89*

Ripken, Cal(vin Edwin, Sr.)
American. Baseball Manager
Minor league pitcher; manager, Baltimore, 1987-88; first to manage two sons in MLs.
b. Dec 17, 1935 in Aberdeen, Maryland
Source: *Ballpl 90; BaseEn 88; BaseReg 87; BioIn 13, 14, 15*

Ripley, Alexandra
American. Author
Chosen by Margaret Mitchell's estate, 1988, to write sequel to *Gone with the Wind—Scarlett,* 1991.
b. Jan 8, 1934 in Charleston, South Carolina
Source: *BioIn 16; ConAu 38NR, 119; CurBio 92; TwCRHW 90, 94; WhoAmW 93*

Ripley, Elmer Horton
"Rip"
American. Basketball Player, Basketball Coach
Played 20 yrs. in pro leagues, early 1900s; coached 24 yrs. at several colleges, with Harlem Globetrotters, Canadian Olympic team, 1928-60; Hall of Fame.
b. Jul 21, 1891 in Staten Island, New York
d. Apr 29, 1982 in New York, New York
Source: *BioIn 12, 13; FacFETw; NewYTBS 82; WhoBbl 73*

Ripley, George
American. Clergy, Social Reformer
Transcendentalist, founded the *Dial,* 1840.
b. Oct 3, 1802 in Greenfield, Massachusetts
d. Jul 4, 1880 in New York, New York
Source: *Alli; AmAu; AmAu&B; AmBi; AmRef; ApCAB; Benet 87, 96; BenetAL 91; BiDAmJo; BiD&SB; BiDTran; BioIn 3, 5, 6, 8, 9, 11, 15, 16, 19; CamGEL; CamGLE; CamHAL; CasWL; CelCen; Chambr 3; CnDAL; CyAL 2; CyEd; DcAmAu; DcAmB; DcAmReB 1, 2; DcEnL; DcLB 1, 64, 73; DcLEL; DcNAA; Drake; EncAB-H 1974; EncARH; HarEnUS; JrnUS; McGEWB; NatCAB 3; OxCAmH; OxCAmL 65, 83, 95; PenC AM; REn; REnAL; TwCBDA; WebAB 74, 79; WhAm HS; WorAl; WorAlBi*

Ripley, Robert Leroy
American. Cartoonist
First published *Believe It or Not* cartoons, 1918.
b. Dec 25, 1893 in Santa Rosa, California
d. May 27, 1949 in New York, New York
Source: *Alli; AmAu&B; BioIn 1, 2, 4, 5, 6, 9, 10, 11, 13, 14; CurBio 45, 49; DcAmB S4; JrnUS; NatCAB 41; OxCAmL 65; REnAL; WebAB 74, 79; WhAm 2; WhE&EA; WhoHol B; WhScrn 74, 77; WorAl; WorECar*

Ripley, William Zebina
American. Economist, Anthropologist
Expert on railroad transportation; drew plans that consolidated regional railways, 1920-23; wrote *Races of Europe,* 1899.
b. Oct 13, 1867 in Medford, Massachusetts
d. Aug 16, 1941 in New York, New York
Source: *ApCAB X; BioIn 3; DcAmAu; DcAmB S3; DcNAA; NatCAB 32; WhAm 1; WhoEc 86*

Rippy, Rodney Allen
American. Actor
1970s child commercial star for Jack-in-the Box hamburger chain.
b. Jul 29, 1968 in Long Beach, California
Source: *BioIn 10, 11; DrBlPA, 90; InB&W 80; LegTOT; WhoAfA 96; WhoBlA 92, 94; WhoHol A*

Risdon, Elizabeth
American. Actor
Played in over 60 films beginning in 1913; films include *Huckleberry Finn; Random Harvest.*
b. Apr 26, 1888 in London, England
d. Dec 20, 1956 in Santa Monica, California
Source: *Film 1; FilmgC; ForYSC; MotPP; MovMk; ThFT; Vers A; WhoHol B; WhScrn 74, 77*

Risling, David
American. Educator
Member of the board of the National Indian Education Association, 1970-77.
b. Apr 10, 1921 in Weitchpec, California
Source: *BioIn 21; NotNaAm*

Ritchard, Cyril
Australian. Actor, Director
Best known for portrayal of Captain Hook in Broadway's *Peter Pan,* won Tony, 1954.
b. Dec 1, 1897 in Sydney, Australia
d. Dec 18, 1977 in Chicago, Illinois
Source: *BiE&WWA; CamGWoT; CurBio 57, 78; EncMT; FilmgC; IlWWBF; NewC; NotNAT; OxCAmT 84; OxCPMus; Who 74; WhoAm 74; WhoHol A; WhoThe 72, 77; WhoWor 74; WhScrn 83; WorAl; WorAlBi*

Ritchey, George Willis
American. Astronomer
Designed reflector telescope at Washington's Naval Observatory, 1931.
b. Dec 31, 1864 in Tuppers Plains, Ohio
d. Nov 4, 1945 in Azusa, California
Source: *BiESc; BioIn 7; DcAmB S3; DcScB; InSci; WebBD 83; WhAm 4*

Ritchie, Jean
American. Singer, Author
Folk singer who popularized songs, tales of KY mountains, 1950s.
b. Dec 8, 1922 in Viper, Kentucky
Source: *ASCAP 66, 80; BgBkCoM; BiDAmM; BioIn 5, 8, 14, 16, 19; ConMus 4; CurBio 59; EncFCWM 69; InWom, SUP; LibW; NewAmDM; NewGrDA 86; PenEncP; WhoAmW 58, 61, 68*

Ritchie, Thomas
American. Journalist
Encouraged by Thomas Jefferson, he founded *Richmond Enquirer,* 1804; *Washington Union,* semi-official organ for President Polk, 1845; his

journalism was powerful influence on nat. politics.
b. Nov 5, 1778 in Tappahannock, Virginia
d. Dec 3, 1854 in Washington, District of Columbia
Source: *Alli; AmBi; ApCAB; BiAUS; BiDAmJo; BioIn 15, 16; DcAmB; DcLB 43; Drake; JrnUS; NatCAB 7; PolPar; WhAm HS*

Ritchie Family, The
[Cheryl Mason Jacks; Gwendolyn Oliver; Cassandra Ann Wooten]
American. Music Group
Made hit disco record ''Brazil,'' 1975; from old Cugat classic.
Source: *BioIn 3; EncFCWM 69; RkOn 74, 78; RolSEnR 83; WhoRocM 82*

Ritenour, Lee
''Captain Fingers''
American. Musician, Songwriter
Guitarist; 1981 album *Rit* put him in the pop music spotlight.
b. Jan 11, 1952 in Los Angeles, California
Source: *AllMusG; BioIn 12, 14, 15, 16; ConMus 7; LegTOT; NewAgMG; NewGrDJ 88; OnThGG; PenEncP; RkOn 85; WhoRocM 82*

Ritola, Ville
Finnish. Track Athlete
Long-distance runner; won five gold medals, 1924, 1928 Olympics.
b. Jan 18, 1896 in Peraseinajoki, Finland
d. Apr 24, 1982 in Helsinki, Finland
Source: *AnObit 1982; WhoTr&F 73*

Ritt, Martin
American. Director
Maverick director of *Norma Rae,* 1979, *Hud,* 1963, *The Long Hot Summer,* 1958; once blacklisted in Hollywood.
b. Mar 2, 1920 in New York, New York
d. Dec 8, 1990 in Santa Monica, California
Source: *BiDFilm, 81; BiE&WWA; BioIn 16; BioNews 74; ConTFT 6, 9; CurBio 79, 91N; DcFM; FacFETw; FilmEn; FilmgC; HalFC 84, 88; IlWWHD 1; IntDcF 1-2, 2-2; IntMPA 86; IntWW 74, 75, 76, 77, 78, 79, 80, 81, 82, 83, 89, 91N; ItaFilm; MovMk; NewYTBS 86, 90; NotNAT; OxCFilm; VarWW 85; WhoAm 74, 76, 78, 80, 82, 84, 86, 88, 90; WhoHol A; WhoWor 74; WorEFlm; WorFDir 2*

Rittenhouse, David
American. Astronomer, Mathematician
First director of US Mint, 1792; built observatory, collimating telescope, 1785; observed transit of Venus.
b. Apr 5, 1732 in Germantown, Pennsylvania
d. Jun 26, 1796 in Philadelphia, Pennsylvania
Source: *Alli; AmBi; AmRev; AntBDN D; ApCAB; BiAUS; BiDAmS; BiDrACR; BiInAmS; BioIn 1, 2, 7, 10, 12, 14, 15, 21; BlkwEAR; CyAL 1; DcAmB; DcBiPP; DcScB; Drake; EncAB-H 1974, 1996; EncCRAm; EncEnl; HarEnUS; InSci; McGEWB; NatCAB 1; NewCol 75; OxCAmH; OxCDecA; TwCBDA; WebAB 74, 79; WhAm HS; WhAmRev*

Ritter, John(athan Southworth)
American. Actor
Won Emmy for role in ''Three's Company,'' 1977-84; played Harry Hooperman in ''Hooperman,'' 1987-89; Hearts Afire 1992-95; son of Tex Ritter.
b. Sep 17, 1948 in Burbank, California
Source: *BioIn 11, 12; BkPepl; CelR 90; ConTFT 2, 10; CurBio 80; HalFC 84, 88; HolBB; IntMPA 84, 86, 88, 92, 94, 96; LegTOT; LesBEnT 92; VarWW 85; WhoAm 78, 80, 82, 84, 86, 88, 90, 92, 94, 96, 97; WhoEnt 92; WhoHol 92, A; WorAl; WorAlBi*

Ritter, Karl
German. Geographer
Founded scientific geography, correlating environment with development of man.
b. Aug 17, 1779, Germany
d. Sep 28, 1859 in Berlin, Germany
Source: *BioIn 5, 8; CyEd; DcBiPP; McGEWB; NewCol 75; RAdv 14; WhDW*

Ritter, Tex
[Woodward Maurice Ritter]
American. Singer, Actor
Singing cowboy in over 60 films; won Oscar, 1952, for *High Noon;* first country music Hall of Famer, 1964.
b. Jan 12, 1907 in Murval, Texas
d. Jan 2, 1974 in Nashville, Tennessee
Source: *BioIn 8; BioNews 74; CounME 74, 74A; EncFCWM 69; FilmgC; ForYSC; HalFC 80, 84, 88; NewYTBE 70; NewYTBS 74; WhoHol B; WhScrn 77; WorAl; WorAlBi*

Ritter, Thelma
American. Actor
Films include *All About Eve,* 1950; *Pillow Talk,* 1959; *Bird Man of Alcatraz,* 1961; six-time Oscar nominee.
b. Feb 14, 1905 in New York, New York
d. Feb 5, 1969 in New York, New York
Source: *BiDFilm, 81, 94; BiE&WWA; BioIn 2, 4, 5, 8, 10, 11; CurBio 57, 74, 74N; EncAFC; FilmEn; FilmgC; ForYSC; HalFC 80, 84, 88; IntDcF 1-3, 2-3; InWom, SUP; LegTOT; MotPP; MovMk; NotNAT B; OxCFilm; Vers A; WhAm 5; WhoAmW 68, 70; WhoHol B; WhScrn 74, 77, 83; WorAl; WorAlBi; WorEFlm*

Ritts, Herb
American. Photographer
Famous for celebrity portraits, including Madonna, Kim Basinger.
b. 1954
Source: *BioIn 15, 16; News 92, 92-2*

Ritz, Al
American. Comedian
Eldest member of comedy team; appeared in 21 films with brothers.
b. Aug 27, 1901 in Newark, New Jersey
d. Dec 22, 1965 in New Orleans, Louisiana
Source: *BioIn 10; EncVaud; Film 1; FilmEn; FilmgC; HalFC 80, 84, 88; LegTOT; MotPP; OxCFilm; WhoHol B; WhScrn 74, 77, 83*

Ritz, Cesar
Swiss. Hotel Executive, Restaurateur
Owner of fashionable hotels in Europe, US; name became synonymous with elegance, wealth.
b. Feb 23, 1848 in Niederwald, Switzerland
d. Nov 1, 1918 in Lucerne, Switzerland
Source: *BioIn 1, 9; WebBD 83*

Ritz, Harry
[Herschel Joachim]
American. Comedian
The youngest, last surviving brother of famous comedy team, the Ritz Brothers.
b. May 22, 1906 in Newark, New Jersey
d. Mar 29, 1986 in San Diego, California
Source: *BioIn 10, 14; FilmEn; FilmgC; HalFC 80, 84, 88; LegTOT; MotPP; OxCFilm; WhoHol B; WhScrn 74*

Ritz, Jimmy
[James Joachim]
American. Comedian
Member of comedy team with brothers; appeared in film *The Three Musketeers,* 1939.
b. Oct 5, 1905 in New York, New York
d. Nov 17, 1985 in Los Angeles, California
Source: *Funs; HalFC 84; NewYTBS 85; OxCFilm*

Ritz Brothers
[Al Ritz; Harry Ritz; Jimmy Ritz]
American. Comedy Team
Slapstick routines featured in 1930s-40s films; highlights include *The Three Musketeers,* 1939.
Source: *BiDD; EncAFC; Film 1; FilmEn; FilmgC; ForYSC; Funs; HalFC 80, 84, 88; JoeFr; MotPP; MovMk; NewYTBS 86; ObitOF 79; OxCFilm; QDrFCA 92; VarWW 85; WhoCom; WhoHol 92, A, B; WhScrn 74, 77*

Rivadavia, Bernardino
Argentine. Political Leader
First pres., Argentine republic, 1826-27; introduced many important cultural initiatives.
b. May 20, 1780 in Buenos Aires, Argentina
d. Sep 2, 1845 in Cadiz, Spain
Source: *ApCAB; BiDLAmC; BioIn 1, 2, 16; EncLatA; HisDcSE; McGEWB*

Rivera, Chita
[Concita del Rivero]
American. Singer
Created role of Anita in *West Side Story* on Broadway, 1957; won Tony for role of Anna in *The Rink*, 1984.
b. Jan 23, 1933 in Washington, District of Columbia
Source: *BiDD; BiE&WWA; BioIn 13, 14; CelR 90; CnOxB; ConTFT 1, 8; CurBio 84; DancEn 78; DcHiB; EncMT; HalFC 80, 84, 88; IntMPA 92, 94, 96; InWom SUP; LegTOT; NotHsAW 93; NotNAT; OxCPMus; VarWW 85; WhoAm 82, 84, 86, 88, 90, 92, 94, 95, 96, 97; WhoAmW 87, 91, 93, 95, 97; WhoHisp 91, 92, 94; WhoHol 92, A; WhoThe 72, 77, 81; WorAl; WorAlBi*

Rivera, Diego
Mexican. Artist
Painted murals depicting peasants, workers; revived fresco technique.
b. Dec 8, 1886 in Guanajuato, Mexico
d. Nov 25, 1957 in Mexico City, Mexico
Source: *ArtLatA; ArtsAmW 2; AtlBL; Benet 87; BioIn 1, 2, 3, 4, 5, 6, 7, 8, 9, 10, 11, 12, 14, 15, 16, 17, 18, 19, 20; CmCal; ConArt 77, 83; CurBio 48, 58; DcArts; DcHiB; DcTwCCu 4; EncAL; EncLatA; FacFETw; IntDcAA 90; LegTOT; LinLib S; McGDA; McGEWB; ModArCr 2; OxCAmL 65; OxCArt; OxDcArt; REn; WhAm 3; WorAl; WorAlBi; WorArt 1950*

Rivera, Geraldo
"Rock-and-Roll Newsman"
American. Journalist
Investigative reporter; TV shows include "20/20," 1978-85; "Geraldo," 1987—; won Emmys, 1980, 1981; wrote autobiography, *Exposing Myself*, 1991.
b. Jul 4, 1943 in New York, New York
Source: *AuBYP 3; BioIn 9, 10, 12, 13, 15, 16; BioNews 74; CelR, 90; ConAu 32NR, 108; ConTFT 6; CurBio 75; DcHiB; EncAJ; EncTwCJ; HispAmA; HispWr; IntMPA 78, 79, 80, 81, 82, 84, 86, 88, 92, 94, 96; LegTOT; LesBEnT, 92; News 89-1; NewYTBE 71; NewYTET; SmATA 28, 54; VarWW 85; WhoAm 78, 80, 82, 84, 86, 90, 92, 94, 95, 96, 97; WhoE 74; WhoEnt 92; WhoHisp 92; WhoTelC*

Rivers, Joan
[Joan Alexandra Molinsky]
American. Comedian, TV Personality
Known for daring wit; had own talk show "The Late Show," 1986-87; won Emmy for guest hosting "The Tonight Show," 1983; syndicated talk show "The Joan Rivers Show."
b. Jun 8, 1937 in New York, New York
Source: *BioIn 13, 14, 15, 16, 17, 18, 19, 20; BkPepl; CelR 90; ConAu X; ConTFT 1; CurBio 70, 87; EncAFC; FunnyW; HalFC 88; IntAu&W 91; IntMPA 92; InWom SUP; LesBEnT 92; VarWW 85; WhoAm 74, 76, 78, 80, 82, 84, 86, 88, 90, 94, 95, 96, 97; WhoAmW 89, 91, 95, 97; WhoEnt 92; WhoHol A; WhoUSWr 88; WhoWrEP 89, 92, 95; WorAl; WorAlBi; WrDr 92*

Rivers, Johnny
American. Singer
Songs include "Poor Side of Town," 1966.
b. Nov 7, 1942 in New York, New York
Source: *ConMuA 80A; EncPR&S 89; EncRk 88; EncRkSt; LegTOT; PenEncP; RkOn 78; RolSEnR 83; WhoAfA 96; WhoAm 74; WhoBlA 75, 77, 80, 85, 90, 92, 94; WhoRock 81; WhoRocM 82; WorAl; WorAlBi*

Rivers, L(ucius) Mendel
American. Government Official
Conservative Dem. congressman from SC, 1940-70; champion of American military might, urged escalation of Vietnam war.
b. Sep 28, 1905 in Berkeley County, South Carolina
d. Dec 28, 1970 in Birmingham, Alabama
Source: *BiDrAC; BiDrUSC 89; BioIn 5, 7, 8, 9, 11, 12; CurBio 71; DcAmB S8; NatCAB 56; NewYTBE 70; WhAm 5; WhAmP; WorAl*

Rivers, Larry
American. Artist
Pioneered in pop art movement: *Double Portrait of Birdie*, 1954.
b. Aug 17, 1923 in New York, New York
Source: *AmArt; Benet 87, 96; BioIn 3, 4, 5, 6, 7, 8, 9, 10, 11, 12, 13, 14; BlueB 76; BriEAA; CelR; ConArt 77, 83, 89, 96; ConAu 117, 124; CurBio 69; DcAmArt; DcCAA 71, 77, 88, 94; DcCAr 81; EncWB; IntDcAA 90; IntWW 83, 89, 91, 93; LegTOT; McGDA; MugS; OxCTwCA; OxDcArt; PhDcTCA 77; PrintW 83, 85; WhoAm 74, 76, 78, 80, 82, 84, 86, 94, 97; WhoAmA 73, 76, 78, 80, 82, 84, 91; WhoE 74, 85, 86; WhoWor 74; WorAl; WorAlBi; WorArt 1950*

Rivers, Thomas Milton
American. Physician, Scientist
Leading researcher in viral disease, 1930s-40s.
b. Sep 3, 1888 in Jonesboro, California
d. May 12, 1962 in New York, New York
Source: *AmDec 1920; BioIn 5, 6, 7; DcAmB S7; DcAmMeB 84; FacFETw; InSci; OxCMed 86; WhAm 4*

Rives, Amelie Louise
American. Author
Wrote novel *Shadows of Flames*, 1915; one of earliest realistic accounts of drug addiction.
b. Aug 23, 1863 in Richmond, Virginia
d. Jun 15, 1945 in Charlottesville, Virginia
Source: *ApCAB; CurBio 45; InWom SUP; NotAW; NotNAT B; ObitOF 79; OxCAmL 83; REnAL; TwCA SUP; TwCBDA; WomWWA 14*

Rivlin, Alice Mitchell
American. Economist
Head of economic studies, Brookings Institute, 1983-87; Member of staff, Brookings Institute, 1983—; director, CBO, 1975-83; director, OMB, 1994—.
b. Mar 4, 1931 in Philadelphia, Pennsylvania
Source: *AmEA 74; AmMWSc 73S, 78S; AmWomM; BioIn 12, 13, 14; ConAu 33R; CurBio 82; HanAmWH; InWom SUP; NewYTBS 75, 82; WhoAm 74, 76, 78, 80, 82, 84, 86, 88, 90, 92, 94, 95, 96, 97; WhoAmP 79; WhoAmW 66, 68, 70, 72, 74, 81, 83, 85, 87, 89, 91, 93, 95, 97; WhoEc 81, 86; WhoFI 87, 89, 92, 96; WhoGov 77; WhoWor 96*

Rixey, Eppa Jephtha
American. Baseball Player
Pitcher, 1912-33, mostly with Cincinnati; had 266 career wins, 39 shutouts; Hall of Fame, 1963.
b. May 3, 1891 in Culpeper, Virginia
d. Feb 28, 1963 in Cincinnati, Ohio
Source: *WhoProB 73*

Rizal, Jose
Philippine. Patriot
Exiled by Spanish govt. for novel *The Lost Eden*, 1886, which criticized Spanish regime, clergy; executed.
b. Jun 19, 1861 in Calamba, Philippines
d. Dec 30, 1896 in Manila, Philippines
Source: *Benet 87, 96; BioIn 15, 17, 18, 19; CasWL; DcMPSA; DcOrL 2; Dis&D; HisDcSE; McGEWB; NewCol 75; NinCLC 27; PenC CL; RAdv 14; REn*

Rizzo, Frank Lazzaro
"Cisco Kid"; "The Toughest Cop in America"
American. Politician
Police commissioner of Philadelphia, 1967-72; mayor of Philadelphia, 1972-80; running for third term at time of death.
b. Oct 23, 1920 in Philadelphia, Pennsylvania
d. Jul 16, 1991 in Philadelphia, Pennsylvania
Source: *BioIn 12, 13, 15, 16; CurBio 73, 91N; News 92; NewYTBE 71; NewYTBS 91; PolProf NF; WhoE 74; WhoGov 77*

Rizzuto, Phil(ip Francis)
"Scooter"
American. Baseball Player, Sportscaster
Shortstop, NY Yankees, 1941-42, 1946-56; known for fielding; AL MVP, 1950.
b. Sep 25, 1918 in New York, New York
Source: *Ballpl 90; BiDAmSp BB; BioIn 1, 2, 3, 4, 5, 7, 8, 14, 15, 16, 17, 18, 20, 21; CurBio 50; WhoAm 80, 82; WhoProB 73*

Roa (y Garcia), Raul
Cuban. Author, Diplomat, Lawyer
Foreign minister, 1959-76; known for aggressive diplomatic style and staunch defense of Castro's revolution.
b. Apr 18, 1907 in Havana, Cuba
d. Jul 6, 1982 in Havana, Cuba
Source: *AnObit 1982; BioIn 10, 12, 13; ConAu 107; CurBio 73, 82, 82N; DcTwCuL; NewCol 75; NewYTBS 82; WhoSocC 78*

Roach, Hal
American. Director, Producer
Developed comedy serials, "Laurel & Hardy"; "Our Gang"; later produced feature films only; won Oscars for *The Music Box,* 1932; *Bored of Education,* 1936.
b. Jan 14, 1892 in Elmira, New York
d. Nov 2, 1992 in Bel Air, California
Source: *AnObit 1992; BiDFilm 94; BioIn 9, 10, 11, 14, 15, 17, 18, 19; CmCal; CmMov; ConTFT 12; DcArts; DcFM; EncAFC; FilmEn; FilmgC; HalFC 80, 84, 88; IntDcF 1-4, 2-4; IntMPA 92; LegTOT; NewYTBS 84, 92; OxCFilm; TwYS B; WorEFlm*

Roach, John
American. Shipbuilder
Called father of modern shipbuilding in America; built Navy ships *Chicago, Boston, Atlanta;* made first compound engines in US.
b. Dec 25, 1813 in Mitchelstown, Ireland
d. Jan 10, 1887 in New York, New York
Source: *AmBi; BiDAmBL 83; BioIn 7, 12; DcAmB; NatCAB 3; TwCBDA; WhAm HS*

Roach, Max(well Lemuel)
American. Jazz Musician
Modern jazz pioneer who played drums for Dizzie Gillespie, Coleman Hawkins at first behop recording session, 1944.
b. Jan 10, 1924 in Elizabeth City, North Carolina
Source: *AllMusG; Baker 84, 92; BiDAfM; BiDJaz; BioIn 14, 15, 16; ConMus 12; CurBio 86; DcTwCCu 5; DrBlPA 90; EncJzS; InB&W 85; IntWW 89, 91, 93; LegTOT; NegAl 89; NewAmDM; NewGrDA 86; NewGrDJ 88; NewYTBS 85; OxCPMus; PenEncP; WhoAfA 96; WhoAm 74, 76, 78, 80, 82, 84, 86, 88, 90, 92, 94, 95, 96, 97; WhoBlA 85, 88, 90, 92, 94; WhoE 74; WhoEnt 92; WorAl; WorAlBi*

Roark, Garland
[George Garland]
American. Author
Adventure stories include *Wake of the Red Witch,* 1946; *Should the Wind be Fair,* 1960.
b. Jul 26, 1904 in Groesbeck, Texas
d. Feb 9, 1985 in Nacogdoches, Texas
Source: *AmAu&B; AmNov; BenetAL 91; BioIn 1, 2; ConAu 1NR, 1R, 115; REnAL; TwCWW 82, 91; WhoSSW 73, 75; WrDr 84*

Robards, Jason
American. Actor
Stage actor who became leading screen star in over 100 films, 1921-61.
b. Dec 31, 1892 in Hillsdale, Michigan
d. Apr 4, 1963 in Sherman Oaks, California
Source: *BioIn 5, 6, 10, 11, 14; EncAFC; FilmEn; FilmgC; MotPP; MovMk; TwYS; WhoHol B; WhScrn 74, 77, 83*

Robards, Jason, Jr.
American. Actor
Won Oscars for *All the President's Men,* 1976, *Julia,* 1977; won Tony for *The Disenchanted,* 1959; once wed to Lauren Bacall.
b. Jul 22, 1922 in Chicago, Illinois
Source: *BiDFilm 81, 94; BiE&WWA; BioIn 4, 5, 6, 7, 10, 11, 13, 14, 17, 19, 21; BkPepl; CamGWoT; CelR, 90; CnThe; ConTFT 1, 7, 15; CurBio 59; EncAFC; Ent; FilmEn; FilmgC; HalFC 88; IntDcF 1-3, 2-3; IntMPA 75, 76, 77, 78, 79, 80, 81, 82, 84, 86, 88, 92, 94, 96; IntWW 91; ItaFilm; LegTOT; MotPP; MovMk; NotNAT; OxCAmT 84; OxCThe 83; VarWW 85; WhoAm 86, 90; WhoEnt 92; WhoHol 92; WhoThe 72, 77, 81; WhoWor 74; WorAlBi*

Robarts, John Parmenter
Canadian. Politician
Progressive Conservative premier of Ontario, 1961-71.
b. Jan 11, 1917 in Banff, Alberta, Canada
d. Oct 18, 1982 in Toronto, Ontario, Canada
Source: *BioIn 6, 13; BlueB 76; CanWW 81; CurBio 63, 83; IntWW 74, 75, 76, 77, 78; IntYB 78, 79, 81; WhAm 8; WhoAm 74, 76, 78; WhoCan 82; WhoWor 74*

Robb, Charles Spittal
American. Politician, Lawyer
Dem. senator, VA, 1989—; governor, 1982-86; husband of Lynda Bird Johnson.
b. Jun 26, 1939 in Phoenix, Arizona
Source: *AlmAP 92; BiDrGov 1978; BioIn 8, 11, 12, 14, 16; CngDr 89; ConNews 87-2; CurBio 89; IntWW 82, 83, 89, 91, 93; NewYTBS 92; PolsAm 84; WhoAm 78, 80, 82, 84, 86, 88, 90, 92, 94, 95, 96, 97; WhoAmA 89, 91; WhoAmP 91; WhoSSW 78, 80, 82, 86, 88, 91, 93, 95; WhoWor 82, 84, 87, 89, 91*

Robbe-Grillet, Alain
French. Author, Filmmaker
Best known for writing *Last Year at Marienbad,* 1961.
b. Aug 18, 1922 in Brest, France
Source: *Au&Wr 71; AuSpks; Benet 87, 96; BioIn 7, 8, 9, 10, 11, 12, 13, 16, 17; CasWL; ClDMEL 80; CnMWL; ConAu 9R, 33NR; ConFLW 84; ConLC 1, 2, 4, 6, 8, 10, 14, 43; ConTFT 8; ConWorW 93; CrtSuMy; CurBio 74; CyWA 89; DcArts; DcFM; DcLB 83; DcTwCCu 2; EncWL, 2, 3; EuWr 13; EvEuW; FacFETw; FilmEn; FilmgC; GrFLW; GuFrLit 1; HalFC 80, 84, 88; IntAu&W 76, 77, 82, 89, 91, 93; IntDcF 1-4, 2-4; IntWW 74, 75, 76, 77, 78, 79, 80, 81, 82, 83, 89, 91, 93; ItaFilm; LegTOT; LinLib L; MajTwCW; MakMC; McGEWB; MiSFD 9; ModFrL; ModRL; Novels; OxCFilm; PenC EUR; RAdv 14, 13-2; REn; RfGWoL 95; ScF&FL 1, 2; TwCCr&M 80B, 85B, 91, 91B; TwCWr; VarWW 85; WhDW; Who 74, 82, 83, 85, 88, 90, 92, 94; WhoFr 79; WhoTwCL; WhoWor 74, 76, 78, 84, 87, 89, 91, 93, 95, 96, 97; WorAl; WorAlBi; WorAu 1950; WorEFlm*

Robbie, Joe
[Joseph Robbie, Jr]
American. Football Executive
Founder, president, Miami Dolphins, 1965-90.
b. Jul 7, 1916 in Sisseton, South Dakota
d. Jan 7, 1990 in Miami, Florida
Source: *BioIn 10, 11, 14, 16; BioNews 74; NatCAB 63N; NewYTBS 90; WhAm 10; WhoAm 74, 76, 78, 80, 82, 84, 86, 88; WhoAmL 79; WhoAmP 73, 75, 77, 79, 81, 83, 85, 87, 89; WhoFtbl 74; WhoMW 74, 76; WhoSSW 73, 75, 78, 80, 82, 84, 86, 88*

Robbins, Carrie Fishbein
American. Designer
Noted for costume scenic designs for stage: *Grease,* 1972; *Agnes of God,* 1983.
b. Feb 7, 1943 in Baltimore, Maryland
Source: *BioIn 16; CamGWoT; ConDes 90; ConTFT 5; NotNAT; NotWoAT; WhoAm 84; WhoAmW 85, 87, 89; WhoThe 77, 81*

Robbins, Frank
American. Cartoonist
Drew comic strip "Johnny Hazard," 1944-84; comic books include *Batman.*
b. Sep 9, 1917 in Boston, Massachusetts
Source: *BioIn 14, 15; ConAu 109; EncACom; IlsBYP; SmATA 42; WhAmArt 85; WhoAmA 73, 76, 78, 80N, 82N, 84N, 86N, 89N, 91N, 93N; WorECom*

Robbins, Fredrick Chapman
American. Scientist, Educator
Won Nobel Prize in medicine, 1954, for work on poliomyelitis virus.
b. Aug 25, 1916 in Auburn, Alabama
Source: *AmMWSc 82, 92; BiESc; BioIn 15; BlueB 76; FacFETw; IntWW 91; McGMS 80; NobelP; Who 83, 92; WhoAm 84, 90; WhoMW 92; WhoNob, 90; WhoWor 82, 91; WorAlBi*

Robbins, Harold
American. Author
Known for commercially rather than critically successful novels, including one of the most read in history: *The Carpetbaggers,* 1961.
b. May 21, 1916 in New York, New York
Source: *AmAu&B; AmNov; BenetAL 91; BioIn 16; BkPepl; CelR, 90; ConAu*

26NR, 54NR, 73; ConLC 5; CurBio 70; DcLP 87B; FacFETw; FilmgC; HalFC 80, 84, 88; IntAu&W 76, 77, 89, 93; IntvTCA 2; IntWW 74, 75, 76, 77, 78, 79, 80, 81, 82, 83, 89, 91, 93; LegTOT; MajTwCW; OxCAmL 95; RAdv 14; TwCWr; Who 85, 92, 94; WhoAm 78, 80, 82, 84, 86, 88, 90, 92, 94, 95, 96, 97; WhoUSWr 88; WhoWor 78, 80, 82, 84, 87, 89, 91; WhoWrEP 89, 92, 95; WorAl; WorAlBi; WrDr 86, 90

Robbins, Irvine
American. Businessman
With Burton Baskin, started Baskin-Robbins ice cream stores, 1947.
b. 1917
Source: *BioIn 9, 10; Entr; NewYTBS 76*

Robbins, Jerome
[Jerome Rabinowitz]
American. Choreographer
With NY City Ballet, 1949—; winner of Tony, Oscar for *West Side Story;* winner of Tony for *Jerome Robbins Broadway,* 1989.
b. Oct 11, 1918 in New York, New York
Source: *AmCulL; BiDD; BiE&WWA; BioIn 1, 2, 3, 4, 5, 6, 7, 8, 9, 10, 13, 14, 15, 16; BlueB 76; CamGWoT; CelR, 90; CmMov; CnOxB; CnThe; ConTFT 4, 11; CurBio 47, 69; DancEn 78; DcArts; DcTwCCu 1; EncMcCE; EncMT; EncWT; Ent; FacFETw; FilmEn; FilmgC; GrStDi; HalFC 80, 84, 88; IntDcB; IntWW 74, 75, 76, 77, 78, 79, 80, 81, 82, 83, 89, 91, 93; JeHun; LegTOT; MiSFD 9; NewGrDA 86; NewOxM; NewYTBS 74, 90; NotNAT; OxCAmT 84; OxCFilm; OxCPMus; PlP&P; RAdv 14; RComAH; TheaDir; WebAB 74, 79; WhDW; Who 74, 82, 83, 85, 88, 90, 92, 94; WhoAm 74, 76, 78, 80, 82, 84, 86, 88, 90, 92, 94, 95, 96, 97; WhoE 81, 83, 85, 86, 89, 91, 93, 95, 97; WhoEnt 92; WhoThe 72, 77, 81; WhoWor 74, 78, 80, 82, 84, 87, 89, 91, 93, 95, 96, 97; WhoWorJ 72; WorAl; WorAlBi; WorEFlm*

Robbins, Marty
[Martin David Robinson]
American. Singer
Country-western star won Grammy, 1959, for "El Paso."
b. Sep 26, 1925 in Glendale, Arizona
d. Dec 8, 1982 in Nashville, Tennessee
Source: *AmSong; AnObit 1982; Baker 84, 92; BgBkCoM; BiDAmM; BioIn 9, 10, 13, 14, 15, 16, 17; ConAu 108; ConMus 9; CounME 74, 74A; EncFCWM 69, 83; EncRk 88; HarEnCM 87; HarEnR 86; IlEncCM; LegTOT; NewAmDM; NewGrDA 86; NewYTBS 82; OxCPMus; PenEncP; PopAmC SUP; RkOn 74; WhAm 8; WhoAm 74, 76, 78, 80, 82; WhoRock 81; WorAl; WorAlBi*

Robbins, Tim(othy Francis)
American. Actor, Director
In films *Bull Durham,* 1988; *The Player,* 1992.
b. Oct 16, 1958 in West Covina, California
Source: *BiDFilm 94; BioIn 16; ConTFT 7, 15; CurBio 94; IntMPA 92, 94, 96; LegTOT; MiSFD 9; News 93-1; WhoAm 94, 95, 96, 97; WhoHol 92; WhoWor 95, 96, 97*

Robbins, Tom
[Thomas Eugene Robbins]
American. Author
Wrote *Another Roadside Attraction,* 1971; *Even Cowgirls Get the Blues,* 1976.
b. Jul 22, 1936 in Blowing Rock, North Carolina
Source: *BenetAL 91; BestSel 90-3; BioIn 11, 12, 13; ConAu 29NR, 81; ConLC 9, 32, 64; ConNov 86, 91, 96; ConPopW; CurBio 93; DcLB Y80B; IntWW 91, 93; LegTOT; MajTwCW; OxCAmL 83, 95; PostFic; ScF&FL 92; WhoAm 82, 84, 86, 88, 90, 92, 94, 95, 96, 97; WhoUSWr 88; WhoWrEP 89, 92, 95; WrDr 84, 86, 88, 90, 92, 94, 96*

Robelo, Alfonso
Nicaraguan. Revolutionary
Founder and leader, Nicaraguan Democratic Movement, 1978; original member of ruling junta, National Restruction, 1979; formed rebel (Contra) guerilla army, 1982.
b. 1940, Nicaragua
Source: *ConNews 88-1*

Robert, Hubert
French. Artist
One of first curators at Louvre; draftsman for Gardens of Versailles during Revol ution; escaped death when another by same name was sent to guillotine.
b. 1733 in Paris, France
d. 1808 in Paris, France
Source: *BioIn 11, 15, 18; BlkwCE; ClaDrA; DcBiPP; Dis&D; MacEA; McGDA; NewCol 75; OxCArt; OxDcArt; WebBD 83; WhDW*

Robert, Paul
French. Lexicographer, Author
Compiled *Le Robert,* established as standard dictionary for contemporary French usage, 1964.
b. Oct 9, 1910 in Orleansville, Algeria
d. Aug 11, 1980 in Mougins, France
Source: *AnObit 1980; BioIn 12; ConAu 101; WhoFr 79*

Robert, Rene Paul
Canadian. Hockey Player
Right wing, 1970-82, mostly with Buffalo on high-scoring French Connection Line with Gilbert Perreault, Rick Martin.
b. Dec 31, 1948 in Three Rivers, Quebec, Canada
Source: *BioIn 10; HocEn*

Robert Guiscard
Norwegian. Ruler
Fought to gain control of southern Italy, Rome, Sicily, Byzantine Empire.
b. 1015
d. 1085
Source: *DicTyr; NewCol 75; OxDcByz; WebBD 83*

Robert I
[Robert the Bruce]
Scottish. Ruler
Ruled, 1306-1329; battles with England led to Treaty of Northampton, 1328, recognizing his throne.
b. Mar 21, 1274 in Turnberry, Scotland
d. Jun 7, 1329 in Cardross, Scotland
Source: *BioIn 10, 16, 20; McGEWB; NewCol 75; WebBD 83*

Roberti, Ercole
Italian. Artist
One of greatest Ferrara painters; did portraits, altarpieces.
b. 1450? in Ferrara, Italy
d. 1496
Source: *McGDA; OxCArt*

Roberts, Barbara
American. Politician
Dem. governor, OR, 1991-94.
b. Dec 21, 1936 in Corvallis, Oregon
Source: *AlmAP 92; BiDrGov 1988; BioIn 20; IntWW 91, 93; LegTOT; WhoAm 86, 88, 90, 92, 94, 95; WhoAmP 83, 85, 87, 89, 91, 93, 95; WhoAmW 87, 89, 91, 93; WhoWest 87, 89, 92, 94, 96; WhoWomW 91*

Roberts, Charles George Douglas, Sir
Canadian. Author
Developed modern Canadian literature; wrote novels, verses of maritime provinces.
b. Jan 10, 1860 in Douglas, New Brunswick, Canada
d. Nov 26, 1943 in Toronto, Ontario, Canada
Source: *Alli SUP; ApCAB, SUP; BbD; BiD&SB; BioIn 1, 4, 5, 9, 10, 13; CanNov; CanWr; Chambr 3; ChhPo, S1, S2, S3; ConAmL; CreCan 2; CurBio 44; DcAmAu; DcArts; DcBiA; DcNAA; EvLB; GrWrEL P; JBA 34; LinLib L, S; LngCTC; MacDCB 78; NatCAB 11; OxCAmL 65, 83, 95; OxCCan; OxCEng 67; PenC ENG; REn; REnAL; TwCA, SUP; WebE&AL; WhAm 3; WhE&EA; WhLit*

Roberts, Cokie
[Mary Martha Corinne Morrison Claiborne Boggs]
American. Broadcast Journalist
Special correspondent for ABC, 1988—; reports on politics, Congress and public policy; co-host of "This Week," 1996—.
b. Dec 27, 1943 in New Orleans, Louisiana

Source: *BioIn 15; CurBio 94; LegTOT; LesBEnT 92; News 93; WhoAm 92; WomComm; WomStre*

Roberts, Dennis J(oseph)
American. Politician
Dem. governor of RI, 1951-59.
b. Apr 8, 1903
d. Jun 30, 1994 in Providence, Rhode Island
Source: *BiDrGov 1789; BioIn 3, 4; CurBio 94N*

Roberts, Doris
American. Actor
Won Emmy, 1983, for "St. Elsewhere"; nominated for "Remington Steele," 1985; plays include *Cheaters,* 1978.
b. Nov 4, 1930 in Saint Louis, Missouri
Source: *ConTFT 2, 4; EncAFC; NotNAT; VarWW 85; WhoAm 80, 82, 84, 86, 88, 90, 92, 94, 95, 96, 97; WhoAmW 95, 97; WhoEnt 92; WhoHol 92, A; WhoThe 77, 81; WhoWor 80, 82, 84, 87; WorAlBi*

Roberts, Edward Glenn
"Fireball"
American. Auto Racer
During 15-yr. career won 32 stock car races; killed in World 600-mile race.
b. 1927 in Tavares, Florida
d. Jul 24, 1964 in Charlotte, North Carolina
Source: *BioIn 6, 7, 10; WebAB 74*

Roberts, Elizabeth Madox
American. Author
Novels of KY, pioneer life include *The Great Meadow,* 1930.
b. 1886 in Perryville, Kentucky
d. Mar 13, 1941 in Orlando, Florida
Source: *AmAu&B; AnCL; ArtclWW 2; Benet 87, 96; BenetAL 91; BioIn 4, 5, 6, 7, 8; BkCL; ChhPo, S1, S3; CnDAL; ConAmA; ConAmL; ConAu 111; CurBio 41; CyWA 58; DcAmB S3; DcLEL; DcNAA; EncWL; InWom, SUP; LegTOT; LngCTC; ModAL; Novels; OxCAmL 65; PenC AM; REn; REnAL; SmATA 27, 33; Str&VC; TwCA, SUP; TwCChW 78, 83; WebAB 74, 79; WhAm 1; WhE&EA*

Roberts, Eric
American. Actor
Films include *Star 80,* 1983, *The Pope of Greenwich Village,* 1984; brother of Julia.
b. Apr 18, 1956 in Biloxi, Mississippi
Source: *BioIn 11; ConTFT 2, 7, 15; HalFC 84, 88; IntMPA 86, 88, 92, 94, 96; LegTOT; VarWW 85; WhoAm 90, 92, 94, 95, 96, 97; WhoEnt 92; WhoHol 92; WorAlBi*

Roberts, Frederick Sleigh
British. Army Officer
Commander-in-chief of India, 1885-93, of Ireland, 1895-99; captured major S. African cities while in command there, 1899-1900.
b. Sep 30, 1832 in Cawnpore, India
d. Nov 14, 1914 in Saint Omer, France
Source: *CelCen; DcAfHiB 86; DcInB; DcNaB 1912; Dis&D; HarEnMi; HisDBrE; LinLib S; McGEWB; NewCol 75; WebBD 83; WhoMilH 76*

Roberts, Gene
[Eugene Leslie Roberts, Jr]
"The Frog"
American. Newspaper Editor
Exec. editor, *Philadelphia Inquirer,* 1972-90; member, Pulitzer Prize Board, 1982—.
b. Jun 15, 1932 in Goldsboro, North Carolina
Source: *BioIn 13; ConAu 97; EncTwCJ; WhoAm 74, 76, 78, 80, 82, 84, 90, 96, 97; WhoAmP 91; WhoE 74, 75, 81, 91; WhoSSW 86*

Roberts, Gordon
Canadian. Hockey Player
Left wing for several amateur teams, 1910-20; Hall of Fame, 1971.
b. Sep 5, 1891
d. Sep 2, 1966
Source: *WhoHcky 73*

Roberts, Julia
[Julie Fiona Roberts]
American. Actor
Starred in films *Pretty Woman,* 1990, *Flatliners,* 1990; received Oscar nomination for *Steel Magnolias,* 1989.
b. Oct 28, 1967 in Smyrna, Georgia
Source: *BiDFilm 94; BioIn 16; ConTFT 9; CurBio 91; IntDcF 2-3; IntMPA 92, 94, 96; IntWW 91, 93; LegTOT; News 91, 91-3; WhoAm 92, 94; WhoAmW 93; WhoEnt 92; WhoHol 92*

Roberts, Kenneth Lewis
American. Author
Noted for historical novels including *Northwest Passage,* 1937; adapted to film, 1940; won special Pulitzer, 1957.
b. Dec 8, 1885 in Kennebunk, Maine
d. Jul 21, 1957 in Kennebunkport, Maine
Source: *AmAu&B; AmNov; CasWL; CnDAL; ConAmA; DcLEL; EvLB; LngCTC; ModAL; OxCAmL 65; OxCCan; PenC AM; REn; REnAL; TwCA; TwCWr; WhAm 3; WhLit*

Roberts, Marcus
American. Pianist
Jazz pianist; albums include *The Truth Is Spoken Here,* 1989 and *Deep in the Shed,* 1990.
b. Aug 7, 1963 in Jacksonville, Florida
Source: *AllMusG; BioIn 16; ConMus 6; CurBio 94*

Roberts, Oral
American. Evangelist
Founder, pres., Oral Roberts U, Tulsa, OK, 1963—.
b. Jan 24, 1918 in Ada, Oklahoma
Source: *AmDec 1960, 1970; BioIn 5, 6, 8, 9, 10, 11, 12, 13, 14, 15, 16; CelR; ConAu 41R; LegTOT; NewYTBE 73; PrimTiR; RelLAm 91; TwCSAPR; WebAB 74, 79; WhoAm 76, 80, 82, 92, 94, 95, 96, 97; WhoRel 75, 85, 92; WhoSSW 95, 97; WorAl; WorAlBi*

Roberts, Pat
American. Politician
Rep. senator, KS, 1997—.
b. Apr 20, 1936
Source: *AlmAP 82, 84, 88, 92, 96; CngDr 89, 91, 93, 95; LegTOT; PolsAm 84; WhoMW 86*

Roberts, Pernell
American. Actor
TV series roles in "Bonanza," 1959-65; "Trapper John, MD," 1979-86.
b. May 18, 1930 in Waycross, Georgia
Source: *BioIn 13; ConTFT 3; HalFC 80, 84, 88; IntMPA 86, 88, 92, 94, 96; LegTOT; VarWW 85; WhoAm 86, 90; WhoEnt 92; WhoHol A; WhoTelC; WorAlBi*

Roberts, Rachel
Welsh. Actor
Starred in *Saturday Night and Sunday Morning; This Sporting Life; O Lucky Man.*
b. Sep 20, 1927 in Llanelly, Wales
d. Nov 26, 1980 in Los Angeles, California
Source: *AnObit 1980; LegTOT; MotPP; NewYTBE 73; NewYTBS 80; OxCFilm; WhAm 7; Who 74; WhoAm 74, 78, 80; WhoHol A; WhoThe 72, 77, 81; WhoWor 74; WhScrn 83*

Roberts, Robin Evan
American. Baseball Player
Pitcher, 1948-66, mostly with Philadelphia; had 286 career wins; Hall of Fame, 1976.
b. Sep 30, 1926 in Philadelphia, Pennsylvania
Source: *Ballpl 90; BiDAmSp BB; BioIn 3, 4, 5, 6, 10, 11, 14, 15; CurBio 53; NewYTBS 74; WhoProB 73*

Roberts, Steven K
American. Cyclist
Designer of computerized bicycle-like vehicle BEHEMOTH (Big Electronic Human-Energized Machine.Only Too Heavy).
b. Dec 2, 1952 in San Diego, California
Source: *BioIn 14, 16; News 92, 92-1*

Roberts, Tony
[David Anthony Roberts]
American. Actor
Stage performances received two Tony nominations: *How Now, Dow Jones,* 1967; *Play It Again, Sam,* 1969; appeared in films, TV.
b. Oct 22, 1939 in New York, New York
Source: *ConTFT 2, 7, 15; EncAFC; FilmEn; HalFC 84, 88; IntMPA 88, 92, 94, 96; LegTOT; NotNAT; VarWW 85; WhoAm 78, 80, 82, 84, 86, 88, 90, 92, 94, 95, 96, 97; WhoEnt 92; WhoHol 92, A; WhoThe 77, 81; WorAlBi*

Roberts, Xavier
American. Businessman
Creator of Cabbage Patch Kids, soft sculpture collector dolls, 1978.
b. Oct 31, 1955 in Cleveland, Georgia
Source: *BioIn 12, 13, 14, 15; ConNews 85-3; NewYTBS 83*

Robertson, Alvin
American. Basketball Player
Guard, San Antonio, 1984-89; Milwaukee Bucks, 1990-93; Detroit Pistons 1993; Denver Nuggets, 1993—; set NBA record for steals in a season, led league, 1986, 1987; member US Olympic team, 1984.
b. Jul 22, 1962 in Barberton, Ohio
Source: *BasBi; BioIn 14, 15, 17; BlkOlyM; NewYTBS 84; OfNBA 87; WhoAm 90; WhoBlA 85, 92; WhoMW 92*

Robertson, Cliff
American. Actor
Won Oscar, 1969, for *Charley;* starred in *PT 109,* 1962.
b. Sep 9, 1925 in La Jolla, California
Source: *BiDFilm, 81, 94; BiE&WWA; BioIn 8, 11, 12, 13, 14; BkPepl; CelR, 90; CmMov; ConTFT 3; CurBio 69; FilmEn; FilmgC; ForYSC; GangFlm; HalFC 80, 84, 88; IntDcF 1-3, 2-3; IntMPA 77, 78, 79, 80, 81, 82, 84, 86, 88, 92, 94, 96; LegTOT; MiSFD 9; MotPP; MovMk; NewYTBE 72; VarWW 85; WhoAm 86, 88, 90, 92, 94, 95, 96, 97; WhoEnt 92; WhoHol 92, A; WhoHrs 80; WorAl; WorAlBi; WorEFlm*

Robertson, Dale
American. Actor
Appeared in TV series "Death Valley Days," 1968-72; "Tales of Wells Fargo," 1957-62.
b. Jul 14, 1923 in Oklahoma City, Oklahoma
Source: *ASCAP 66; BiE&WWA; BioIn 4, 8, 12, 18; ConAu 107; ConTFT 5; FilmEn; FilmgC; HalFC 80, 84, 88; IntMPA 75, 76, 77, 78, 80, 81, 82, 84, 86, 88, 92, 94, 96; ItaFilm; MotPP; VarWW 85; WhoEnt 92; WhoHol 92, A; WorAl; WorAlBi*

Robertson, Don
American. Songwriter
Country music hits include "I Really Don't Want to Know"; "Please Help Me I'm Falling."
b. Dec 5, 1922 in Beijing, China
Source: *ASCAP 66; BioIn 14, 15; EncFCWM 69, 83; PenEncP; RkOn 74; WhoEnt 92*

Robertson, James D, III
American. Business Executive
Chm., CEO, American Express Company, 1977—.
b. Nov 19, 1935 in Atlanta, Georgia
Source: *CelR 90*

Robertson, Oscar Palmer
"Big O"
American. Basketball Player
Nine-time all-star guard, 1960-74, with Cincinnati, Milwaukee; led NBA in assists six time; MVP, 1964; Hall of Fame, 1979.
b. Nov 24, 1938 in Charlotte, Tennessee
Source: *BiDAmSp BK; BioIn 16; BlkOlyM; CurBio 66; FacFETw; InB&W 80, 85; NegAl 89; OfNBA 87; WhoAfA 96; WhoAm 74, 90, 92, 94, 95, 96, 97; WhoBbl 73; WhoBlA 75, 88, 90, 92, 94; WhoFI 92, 94; WorAl; WorAlBi*

Robertson, Pat
[Marion Gordon Robertson]
American. Evangelist, TV Personality
Founder, pres., Christian Broadcasting Network, 1977—; host of "700 Club," 1968—; ran for pres., 1988.
b. Mar 22, 1930 in Lexington, Virginia
Source: *AmDec 1970; BioIn 10, 11, 12, 13, 16; CurBio 87; DcAmC; IntAu&W 86, 89; InWom; LegTOT; News 88-2; NewYTBS 87; PrimTiR; RelLAm 91; TwCSAPR; WhoAm 78, 80, 82, 84, 88, 90, 92, 94, 95, 96, 97; WhoRel 85, 92; WhoWrEP 89; WorAlBi*

Robertson, Robbie
[The Band; Jaime Robbie Robertson]
Canadian. Musician, Composer
Guitarist, vocalist with The Band, 1966-76; composed soundtrack for *The Color of Money,* 1986.
b. Jul 5, 1944 in Toronto, Ontario, Canada
Source: *BioIn 15, 16; ConMus 2; LegTOT; WhoAm 82; WhoRocM 82*

Robertson, William
Scottish. Author, Historian
Wrote *History of Scotland,* 1759; *History of America,* 1777.
b. Sep 19, 1721 in Borthwick, Scotland
d. Jun 11, 1793 in Edinburgh, Scotland
Source: *Alli; ApCAB; BbD; BenetAL 91; BiD&SB; BioIn 1, 3, 4, 5, 6, 17; BlkwCE; BritAu; CamGEL; CamGLE; CasWL; CmScLit; DcBiPP; DcEnA; DcEnL; DcEuL; DcLB 104; DcLEL; DcNaB; Drake; EncEnl; EvLB; NewC; NewCBEL; OxCAmL 65, 83, 95; OxCEng 67, 85, 95; PenC ENG; REn; WhDW*

Robertson, William Robert, Sir
English. Army Officer
Field Marshal, WW I, first man in British army to rise from private to highest rank.
b. Jan 29, 1860 in Welbourne, England
d. Feb 12, 1933 in London, England
Source: *BioIn 2, 6; DcNaB 1931; DcTwHis; HarEnMi; NewCol 75; WhLit; WhoMilH 76*

Robeson, Eslanda Cardoza Goode
American. Political Activist, Writer
Helped found the Council on African Affairs, 1941, with husband Paul and other influential African-Americans; author of *African Journey,* 1945.
b. 1896 in Washington, District of Columbia
d. Dec 13, 1965 in New York, New York
Source: *BioIn 14, 15; BlksScM; BlkWrNE; ConAu 141; CurBio 91N; HarlReB; InB&W 80, 85; InWom SUP; NegAl 89; NotAW MOD; NotBlAW 1; SelBAAf*

Robeson, Paul Leroy
American. Singer, Actor
Jerome Kern wrote "Ol' Man River" for him, which he sang in play, movie *Showboat,* 1928, 1936.
b. Apr 9, 1898 in Princeton, New Jersey
d. Jan 23, 1976 in Philadelphia, Pennsylvania
Source: *BiE&WWA; BioNews 74; ConMus 8; CurBio 41; EncMT; FilmgC; IntWW 74; MovMk; OxCAmL 65; OxCFilm; OxCThe 67; PlP&P; REn; WhAm 6; Who 74; WhoBlA 75; WorAl*

Robespierre, Maximilien Francois de
"The Incorruptible"
French. Revolutionary
Led French Revolution; major figure in Reign of Terror.
b. May 6, 1758 in Arras, France
d. Jul 28, 1794 in Paris, France
Source: *DcEuL; NewC; NewCol 75; OxCFr; REn; WebBD 83; WorAl*

Robey, George, Sir
English. Comedian, Actor
Films include *Birds of a Feather,* 1935; *The Pickwick Papers,* 1952.
b. Sep 20, 1869 in London, England
d. Nov 29, 1954 in Saltdean, England
Source: *BioIn 3, 4, 9; CamGWoT; CnThe; EncMT; EncWT; Ent; Film 1, 2; FilmgC; HalFC 80, 84, 88; IlWWBF, A; NewC; NotNAT A; ObitOF 79; ObitT 1951; OxCFilm; OxCPMus; OxCThe 67; QDrFCA 92; WhLit; WhoHol B; WhScrn 74, 77, 83; WhThe*

Robillard, Duke
American. Musician, Singer
Guitarist; formed bands Roomful of Blues and Black Cat in 1960s; Pleasure Kings, early 1980s; worked with Legendary Blues Band.
b. 1949 in Burrillville, Rhode Island
Source: *BioIn 13, 15; ConMus 2; WhoRocM 82*

Robin, Leo
American. Lyricist
Wrote lyrics for Bob Hope's theme song "Thanks for the Memory," which won 1938 Oscar.
b. Apr 6, 1895 in Pittsburgh, Pennsylvania
d. Dec 29, 1984 in Woodland Hills, California
Source: *AmSong; ASCAP 66; BiDAmM; BiE&WWA; BioIn 14, 15; CmpEPM;*

EncMT; IntMPA 84; VarWW 85; WhoAm 74, 76

Robin Hood
English. Legendary Figure, Hero
Legendary 12th c. hero who robbed from rich to give to poor.
Source: *DcAmSR; DcBiPP; REn*

Robins, Denise Naomi
[Ashley French; Harriet Gray; Julia Kane]
English. Author
Her 200 romance novels include *Dark Corridor.*
b. Feb 1, 1897 in London, England
d. May 1, 1985 in London, England
Source: *ConAu 116; PenNWW B; WhE&EA; WrDr 84*

Robins, Elizabeth
[C E Raimond]
American. Author, Actor
Played Ibsen roles in London, 1890s; novels include *My Little Sister,* 1913.
b. 1865 in Louisville, Kentucky
d. May 8, 1952 in Brighton, England
Source: *AmAu&B; BbD; BenetAL 91; BiDSA; Chambr 3; CnDAL; LngCTC; OhA&B; OxCAmL 65, 83, 95; OxCThe 67; REn; REnAL; TwCA, SUP; WhAm 5; WhThe; WomNov; WomWWA 14*

Robinson, Arthur H(oward)
American. Cartographer, Geographer
Creates maps using Robinson map projection, which creates maps without distorting the earth's spherical features; created map of worlf for Rand McNally, 1963.
b. Jan 5, 1915 in Montreal, Quebec, Canada
Source: *AmMWSc 73S; BioIn 18, 21; CurBio 96; WhoAm 74, 76, 78, 80, 82, 84, 86, 88, 90, 92, 94, 95, 96, 97*

Robinson, Bill
"Bojangles"
American. Actor, Dancer
Tap dancer known for stairway dance, appearances in Shirley Temple films.
b. May 25, 1878 in Richmond, Virginia
d. Nov 25, 1949 in New York, New York
Source: *AfrAmAl 6; AmCulL; BiDD; BioIn 1, 2, 3, 4, 5, 7, 9, 10, 16, 17, 18, 19, 20; BlksAmF; BlksB&W, C; BlksBF; CamGWoT; CmpEPM; CnOxB; ConBlB 11; CurBio 41, 50; DancEn 78; DcAmB S4; DcTwCCu 5; DrBlPA, 90; EncMT; EncVaud; Ent; FacFETw; FilmEn; FilmgC; ForYSC; HalFC 80, 84, 88; InB&W 80, 85; IntDcF 1-3, 2-3; LegTOT; MovMk; NegAl 76, 83, 89; NewAmDM; NewGrDA 86; NewGrDJ 88, 94; NotNAT B; OxCAmT 84; OxCPMus; WebAB 74, 79; WhAm 2; WhoHol B; WhScrn 74, 77, 83; WhThe; WorAl; WorAlBi*

Robinson, Boardman
American. Artist, Illustrator
Widely reprinted, influential political cartoonist, *NY Tribune,* 1910-14; illustrated books include *Moby Dick,* 1942.
b. Sep 6, 1876 in Somerset, Nova Scotia, Canada
d. Sep 5, 1952 in Stamford, Connecticut
Source: *AmAu&B; ArtsAmW 1; BioIn 1, 3, 12; BriEAA; ChhPo; CurBio 41, 52; DcAmArt; DcAmB S5; DcCAA 71, 77, 88; EncAJ; IlBEAAW; IlsCB 1744; McGDA; WhAm 3; WhAmArt 85; WhoAmA 84N, 89N, 91N, 93N; WorECar*

Robinson, Brooks Calbert, Jr.
American. Baseball Player
Third baseman, Baltimore, 1955-77, known for fielding; AL MVP, 1964; Hall of Fame, 1983.
b. May 18, 1937 in Little Rock, Arkansas
Source: *AmCath 80; Ballpl 90; BiDAmSp BB; BioIn 6, 7, 8, 9, 10, 11, 13, 14, 15, 16; ConAu 116; CurBio 73; FacFETw; WhoAm 74, 76, 78, 80, 82, 84, 86, 88, 90, 92, 94; WhoProB 73; WorAlBi*

Robinson, Claude Everett
American. Pollster
Pioneer, with Gallup, in public opinion research; founder, pres., Opinion Research Corp., 1938-60.
b. Mar 22, 1900 in Portland, Oregon
d. Aug 7, 1961 in New York, New York
Source: *BioIn 5, 6; DcAmB S7; NatCAB 46; WhAm 4*

Robinson, David (Maurice)
"The Admiral"
American. Basketball Player
Center with the San Antonio Spurs, 1989—; member U.S. Olympic Team, 1988, 1992.
b. Aug 6, 1965 in Key West, Florida
Source: *AfrAmSG; BiDAmSp Sup; BioIn 14, 15, 16; BlkOlyM; CurBio 93; LegTOT; News 90; NewYTBS 87; OfNBA 87; WhoAfA 96; WhoAm 92, 94, 95, 96, 97; WhoBlA 92, 94; WhoSSW 95, 97; WhoWor 95, 96, 97; WorAlBi*

Robinson, Earl Hawley
American. Composer, Singer
Wrote famous "Ballad for Americans," 1939, recorded by Paul Robeson, and Joe Hill.
b. Jul 2, 1910 in Seattle, Washington
d. Jul 20, 1991 in Seattle, Washington
Source: *Baker 84, 92; BiDAmM; BioIn 1, 8, 17, 18; ConAu 2NR, 43NR, 45, 135; CpmDNM 81; CurBio 45; EncAL; EncFCWM 69; IntWWM 77, 85, 90; NewAmDM; NewGrDA 86; NewGrDO; News 92, 92-1; NewYTBS 91; VarWW 85; WhAm 10; WhoAm 74, 76, 78, 80, 82, 84, 86, 88, 90; WhoWest 74, 76, 78*

Robinson, Eddie
[Edward Gay Robinson]
American. Football Coach
With Grambling State U., 1941—; became the winningest coach in college and pro football history, 1985.
b. Feb 13, 1919 in Jackson, Louisiana
Source: *AfrAmBi 2; AfrAmSG; Ballpl 90; BiDAmSp FB; BioIn 10, 13, 14, 15, 16; CurBio 88; InB&W 80, 85; NewYTBS 85; WhoAfA 96; WhoBlA 92, 94; WhoFtbl 74; WhoSpor*

Robinson, Edward
American. Geographer, Scholar
Considered father of biblical geography; wrote *Physical Geography of the Holy Land,* 1865.
b. Apr 10, 1794 in Southington, Connecticut
d. Jan 27, 1863 in New York, New York
Source: *Alli; AmAu; AmAu&B; AmBi; ApCAB; BioIn 2, 12; CyAL 1; DcAmAu; DcAmB; DcBiPP; DcEnL; DcNAA; Drake; HarEnUS; LuthC 75; NatCAB 2; TwCBDA; WhAm HS*

Robinson, Edward G
[Emanuel Goldenberg]
American. Actor
Played gangsters in *Little Caesar; Brother Orchid; Key Largo;* won special Oscar, 1972.
b. Dec 12, 1893 in Bucharest, Romania
d. Jan 26, 1973 in Beverly Hills, California
Source: *BiDFilm; BiE&WWA; CmMov; ConAu 45; CurBio 50, 73; FilmgC; ForYSC; MotPP; MovMk; NewYTBE 72, 73; OxCFilm; WhAm 5; WhoHol B; WhoWorJ 72; WhThe; WorAl; WorEFlm*

Robinson, Edwin Arlington
American. Poet
Pulitzer winners include *Collected Poems,* 1921; *Man Who Died Twice,* 1924; narrative poem, *Tristram,* 1927.
b. Dec 22, 1869 in Head Tide, Maine
d. Apr 6, 1935 in New York, New York
Source: *AmAu&B; AmBi; AmCulL; AmLY; AmWr; AnMV 1926; AtlBL; Benet 87, 96; BenetAL 91; BioIn 1, 2, 3, 4, 5, 6, 7, 8, 9, 10, 11, 12, 13, 14, 15, 17, 19; CamGEL; CamGLE; CamHAL; CasWL; Chambr 3; ChhPo, S1, S2, S3; CnDAL; CnE&AP; CnMWL; ConAmA; ConAmL; ConAu 133; CyWA 58; DcAmAu; DcAmB S1; DcArts; DcLB 54; DcLEL; DcNAA; EncWL, 2, 3; EvLB; FacFETw; GayN; GrWrEL P; LegTOT; LinLib L, S; LngCTC; MajTwCW; McGEWB; ModAL, S1; NatCAB 33; NewGrDA 86; OxCAmH; OxCAmL 65, 83, 95; OxCEng 67; OxCTwCP; PenC AM; PoeCrit 1; RAdv 1, 14, 13-1; RealN; REn; REnAL; RfGAmL 87, 94; RGFAP; RGTwCWr; SixAP; TwCA, SUP; TwCLC 5; TwCWr; WebAB 74, 79; WebE&AL; WhAm 1; WhDW; WhNAA; WhoTwCL*

Robinson, Forbes
English. Opera Singer
Bass; popular singer-actor; repertory of over 70 roles.
b. May 21, 1926 in Cheshire, England
Source: *Baker 84; BioIn 15; BlueB 76; CmOp; IntWW 74, 75, 76, 77, 78, 79, 80, 81, 82, 83; IntWWM 77, 80; NewGrDM 80; OxDcOp; PenDiMP; Who 74, 82, 83, 85, 88N; WhoMus 72; WhoOp 76; WhoWor 74, 76, 78*

Robinson, Francis Arthur
American. Manager
Assistant manager of Metropolitan Opera House, 1952-76.
b. Apr 28, 1910 in Henderson, Kentucky
d. May 14, 1980 in New York, New York
Source: *WhAm 7; WhoAm 78, 80; WhoE 74, 75, 77*

Robinson, Frank
American. Baseball Player, Baseball Manager
Outfielder, 1956-76; won AL triple crown, 1966; only player to be named MVP in both leagues; manager, Cleveland, 1975-77; San Francisco, 1981-84; Baltimore, 1988-91; Hall of Fame, 1982; baseball's first black manager.
b. Aug 31, 1935 in Beaumont, Texas
Source: *AfrAmAl 6; AfrAmBi 1; AfrAmSG; Ballpl 90; BiDAmSp BB; BioIn 6, 7, 8, 9, 10, 11, 12, 13, 16; BioNews 74; CelR; CmCal; ConBlB 9; CurBio 71; FacFETw; InB&W 80, 85; LegTOT; NegAl 89; News 90, 90-2; NewYTBS 74; WhoAfA 96; WhoAm 74, 76, 78, 80, 82, 84, 86, 88, 90, 92, 94, 95, 96, 97; WhoBlA 75, 77, 80, 85, 88, 90, 92, 94; WhoE 89, 91, 93, 95, 97; WhoProB 73; WhoSpor; WhoWest 84; WorAl; WorAlBi*

Robinson, Harriet Jane Hanson
American. Writer, Suffragist
Organized the Nat. Women Suffrage Assn. of MA, 1881.
b. Feb 8, 1825 in Boston, Massachusetts
d. Dec 22, 1911 in Malden, Massachusetts
Source: *Alli SUP; AmAu&B; AmRef; AmWom; AmWomWr; AmWomWr; ApCAB; ArtclWW 2; BenetAL 91; BioIn 12, 13, 15; DcAmAu; DcAmB; DcNAA; FemiCLE; InWom SUP; NatCAB 3; NotAW; OxCAmL 65, 83, 95; PeoHis; REnAL; TwCBDA; WhAm 1*

Robinson, Henry Morton
American. Author, Poet
Wrote best-selling novel *The Cardinal,* 1950.
b. Sep 7, 1898 in Boston, Massachusetts
d. Jan 13, 1961 in New York, New York
Source: *AmAu&B; AmNov; BenetAL 91; BioIn 1, 2, 3, 4, 5, 6; CathA 1952; ChhPo; ConAu 116; CurBio 50, 61; DcAmB S7; DcCathB; REnAL; TwCA SUP; WhAm 4; WhNAA*

Robinson, Jackie
[Jack Roosevelt Robinson]
American. Baseball Player
Infielder, Brooklyn, 1947-56; first black player in MLs; won NL batting title, NL MVP, 1949; Hall of Fame, 1962; won Spingarn, 1956.
b. Jan 31, 1919 in Cairo, Georgia
d. Oct 24, 1972 in Stamford, Connecticut
Source: *AfrAmAl 6; AfrAmSG; AmDec 1940; Ballpl 90; BiDAmSp BB; BioIn 12, 13, 14, 15, 16, 17, 18, 19, 20, 21; CmCal; ConBlB 6; ConHero 1; CurBio 47, 72, 72N; DcTwCCu 5; EncAACR; EncAB-H 1974, 1996; FacFETw; HeroCon; LegTOT; LinLib S; McGEWB; NatCAB 60; NegAl 76, 83, 89; NewYTBE 71, 72; PolProf T; RComAH; WebAB 74, 79; WhAm 5; WhoHol B; WhoProB 73; WhoSpor; WhScrn 77, 83; WorAl*

Robinson, James Harvey
American. Historian, Educator
Founder, NYC's New School for Social Research, 1919; wrote *Mind in the Making,* 1921.
b. Jun 29, 1863 in Bloomington, Illinois
d. Feb 16, 1936 in New York, New York
Source: *AmAu&B; AmBi; BenetAL 91; BiDAmEd; BioIn 1, 4, 12, 15, 17; DcAmAu; DcAmB S2; DcLB 47; DcNAA; LinLib L, S; McGEWB; NewCol 75; OxCAmH; OxCAmL 65; PeoHis; REnAL; TwCA, SUP; TwCBDA; WebAB 74, 79; WhAm 1; WhDW*

Robinson, Jay
American. Actor
Played in films, 1953-58, until drug conviction led to long career decline; came back in 1970s in *The Robe; Wild Party.*
b. Apr 14, 1930 in New York, New York
Source: *BiE&WWA; FilmgC; ForYSC; HalFC 80, 84, 88; NotNAT; VarWW 85; WhoAm 90; WhoHol 92, A*

Robinson, Joan Mary Gale Thomas
English. Children's Author
Self-illustrated books include *Teddy Robinson; Mary-Mary* series.
b. 1910 in Gerrards Cross, England
d. Aug 20, 1988
Source: *Au&Wr 71; AuBYP 3; BioIn 14; ConAu 5NR, 5R; OxCChiL; SmATA 7; TwCChW 89; WhoChL; WrDr 88*

Robinson, John Alexander
American. Football Coach
Head coach USC, 1976-82, won nat. championship, 1978; in NFL with LA Rams, 1983- 91.
b. Jul 25, 1935 in Chicago, Illinois
Source: *BiDAmSp Sup; FootReg 87; St&PR 91; WhoAm 78, 80, 82, 84, 86, 88, 90, 92; WhoWest 87, 89, 92, 94; WorAlBi*

Robinson, Larry
[Laurence Clark Robinson]
Canadian. Hockey Player
Defenseman, Montreal, 1972-89; LA Kings 1989-92; won Norris Trophy twice, five Stanley Cups.
b. Jun 2, 1951 in Winchester, Ontario, Canada
Source: *HocEn; HocReg 87; WorAlBi*

Robinson, Lennox
[Esme Stuart Lennox Robinson]
Irish. Author, Dramatist
Hired by Yeats as director of Abbey Theater, 1909-58; wrote *Ireland's Abbey Theater: A History,* 1899-1951.
b. Oct 4, 1886 in Douglas, Ireland
d. Oct 14, 1958 in Dublin, Ireland
Source: *BiDIrW; BioIn 4, 5, 7, 9, 13; CamGEL; CamGWoT; CasWL; ChhPo, S1; CnMD; CnThe; ConAu 120; CrtSuDr; DcIrB 78, 88; DcIrL, 96; DcIrW 1, 2; DcLB 10; DcLEL; DcNaB 1951; EncWL; EncWT; EvLB; FacFETw; IriPla; LngCTC; McGEWD 72, 84; ModBrL; ModIrL; ModWD; NewC; NewCBEL; NotNAT A, B; ObitT 1951; OxCEng 67, 85; OxCThe 67, 83; PlP&P; REnWD; RfGEnL 91; TwCA, SUP; WhAm 3; WhE&EA; WhLit; WhThe*

Robinson, M(aurice) R(ichard)
American. Editor, Publisher
Founded Scholastic Magazines Inc., 1920.
b. Dec 24, 1895 in Wilkinsburg, Pennsylvania
d. Feb 7, 1982 in Pelham, New York
Source: *BioIn 4, 5, 6, 9, 11, 12, 13; ChhPo S1; CurBio 56, 82, 82N; EncTwCJ; NewYTBS 82; St&PR 75; WhAm 8; WhoAm 74, 76, 78, 80, 82; WhoFI 81*

Robinson, Mary
Irish. Political Leader
First female pres. of Ireland, 1990—.
b. May 21, 1944 in Ballina, Ireland
Source: *BioIn 17, 18, 19, 20; CurBio 91; IntWW 91, 93; InWom SUP; News 93-1; Who 92, 94; WhoWomW 91; WhoWor 95, 96, 97; WomFir; WomLaw; WomStre*

Robinson, Max C
American. Broadcast Journalist
First black to anchor network TV news, 1978 on ABC; won several Emmys; died of AIDS.
b. May 1, 1939 in Richmond, Virginia
d. Dec 20, 1988 in Washington, District of Columbia
Source: *ConAu 110; ConBlB 3; InB&W 85; LesBEnT; VarWW 85; WhoAm 82; WhoBlA 75, 77, 80, 85*

Robinson, Randall
American. Lawyer
Executive director, TransAfrica, Inc., 1977-.
b. c. 1942 in Richmond, Virginia
Source: *ConBlB 7*

Robinson, Robert, Sir
English. Chemist
Won 1947 Nobel Prize for research in plant chemistry.
b. Sep 13, 1886 in Chesterfield, England
d. Feb 8, 1975 in Missenden, England
Source: *AsBiEn; Au&Wr 71; BiESc; BioIn 1, 2, 3, 4, 6, 9, 10, 11, 12, 14, 15, 17, 19, 20; CamDcSc; ConAu 113; DcNaB 1971; InSci; IntWW 74; LarDcSc; McGMS 80; NobelP; NotTwCS; ObitT 1971; WhAm 6; Who 74; WhoNob, 90, 95; WhoWor 74; WorScD*

Robinson, Smokey
[Smokey Robinson and the Miracles; William Robinson, Jr]
American. Singer, Songwriter
Hits include "Shop Around," 1961; "Tracks of My Tears," 1965; "Tears of a Clown," 1970; Rock and Roll Hall of Fame, 1986, Songwriters Hall of Fame, 1986; Grammy award winner, 1987.
b. Feb 19, 1940 in Detroit, Michigan
Source: *AfrAmAl 6; ASCAP 80; Baker 84, 92; BioIn 9, 12, 13, 15, 16; ConAu 116, X; ConBlB 3; ConLC 21; ConMuA 80A; ConMus 1; CurBio 80; DcArts; DrBlPA, 90; Ebony 1; EncPR&S 74, 89; EncRk 88; IlEncBM 82; IlEncRk; InB&W 85; LegTOT; NegAl 89; NewAmDM; NewGrDA 86; OxCPMus; PenEncP; PseudN 82; RkOn 78; VarWW 85; WhoAfA 96; WhoAm 78, 80, 82, 84, 86, 90; WhoBlA 75, 77, 80, 85, 88, 90, 92; WhoEnt 92; WhoHol 92; WhoRock 81; WhoRocM 82; WorAlBi*

Robinson, Sugar Ray
[Walker Smith]
American. Boxer
Welterweight champ, 1946-51; five-time middleweight champ, 1951-60; considered greatest fighter, pound for pound, who ever lived.
b. May 3, 1921 in Detroit, Michigan
d. Apr 12, 1989 in Culver City, California
Source: *AfrAmSG; AmDec 1950; AnObit 1989; BiDAmSp BK; BioIn 14, 15, 16; BoxReg; CelR; CurBio 51, 89, 89N; DrBlPA 90; FacFETw; ItaFilm; NegAl 89; News 89-3; NewYTBS 89; WebAB 74; WhoAm 74, 76, 78, 80; WhoBlA 75, 77, 80, 85, 88, 90N; WhoHol A; WorAl*

Robinson, Tom
[Tom Robinson Band]
English. Singer, Musician
Formed group to voice political views; songs include "War Babies," 1983.
b. Jul 1, 1948 in Cambridge, England
Source: *ConMuA 80A; EncRk 88; HarEnR 86; PenEncP; WhoRocM 82; WhsNW 85*

Robinson, W. Heath
English. Cartoonist, Illustrator
Popular cartoons featured fantastic machinery; illustrated children's classics.
b. May 31, 1872 in London, England
d. Sep 13, 1944 in London, England
Source: *CurBio 44; DcNaB 1941; McGDA; OxCChiL; SmATA 17; WorECar*

Robinson, Wilbert
"Uncle Robbie"
American. Baseball Player, Baseball Manager
Catcher, 1886-1902, mostly with Baltimore; manager, Brooklyn, 1914-31; Hall of Fame, 1945.
b. Jun 2, 1864 in Hudson, Massachusetts
d. Aug 8, 1934 in Atlanta, Georgia
Source: *BioIn 3, 5, 7, 8, 10, 14, 15, 19; LegTOT; WhoProB 73; WhoSpor*

Robison, Paula Judith
American. Musician
Noted flutist; made NYC debut, 1961; attempted to re-establish flute as solo concert instrument.
b. Jun 8, 1941 in Nashville, Tennessee
Source: *Baker 84, 92; BioIn 10, 11, 13; BioNews 74; CurBio 82; IntWWM 90; InWom SUP; NewGrDA 86; NewGrDM 80; NewYTBE 73; NewYTBS 77; WhoAm 80, 82, 84, 86, 88, 90, 92, 94, 95, 96, 97; WhoAmM 83; WhoAmW 83, 85, 87, 89, 95, 97; WhoEnt 92*

Robitaille, Luc
Canadian. Hockey Player
Left wing, LA, 1986-94; Pittsburgh, 1994—; NHL rookie of the year 1986-87; won Calder Trophy, 1987.
b. Feb 17, 1966 in Montreal, Quebec, Canada
Source: *BioIn 15; HocReg 86, 87; WhoAm 92, 94, 95, 96, 97; WhoWest 92, 94; WhoWor 95, 96*

Robitscher, Jonas Bondi, Jr.
American. Psychiatrist, Author
Crusader against abuses in forensic psychiatry: *The Power of Psychiatry,* 1980.
b. Oct 28, 1920 in New York, New York
d. Mar 25, 1981 in Atlanta, Georgia
Source: *AmMWSc 79, 82; AnObit 1981; ConAu 21R, 103; WhAm 7; WhoAm 80; WhoAmL 79*

Robson, Flora McKenzie, Dame
English. Actor
Actress since age five; played in over 100 plays, more than 60 films.
b. Mar 28, 1902 in South Shields, England
d. Jul 7, 1984 in Brighton, England
Source: *AnObit 1984; BiE&WWA; CurBio 51, 84; IntMPA 82; IntWW 74, 75, 76, 77, 78, 79, 80, 81, 82, 83; MotPP; MovMk; NewYTBS 84; NotNAT; OxCFilm; OxCThe 83; VarWW 85; Vers A; WhAm 8; Who 85N; WhoThe 81; WhoWor 74, 76, 78*

Robson, May
[Mary Jeanette Robison]
American. Actor
Oscar nominee for Apple Annie in *Lady for a Day,* 1933.
b. Apr 19, 1858 in Melbourne, Australia
d. Oct 20, 1942 in Beverly Hills, California
Source: *AmWomPl; BioIn 21; CurBio 42; DcAmB S3; EncAFC; Film 1; FilmEn; FilmgC; HalFC 80, 84, 88; HolCA; LegTOT; LibW; MotPP; MovMk; NotAW; OlFamFa; OxCFilm; PlP&P; ThFT; TwYS; Vers A; WhAm 2; WhNAA; WhoHol B; WhScrn 74, 77, 83*

Robustelli, Andy
[Andrew Robustelli]
American. Football Player
Seven-time all-pro end, LA Rams, 1951-55, NY Giants, 1956-64; Hall of Fame, 1971.
b. Dec 6, 1930 in Stamford, Connecticut
Source: *BiDAmSp FB; BioIn 11, 16; LegTOT; WhoFtbl 74*

Rocard, Michel Louis Leon
French. Politician
Moderate socialist prime minister of France, succeeding Jacques Chirac, 1988-91.
b. Aug 23, 1930 in Courbevoie, France
Source: *BiDFrPL; BioIn 13, 16; ColdWar 2; CurBio 88; EncWB; IntWW 82, 83, 89, 91; NewYTBS 88; Who 90, 92, 94; WhoWor 89, 91, 93, 95, 96, 97*

Rocca, Lodovico
Italian. Composer
Operas include *Il Dibuk,* 1939; *Monte Ivnor,* 1939.
b. Nov 29, 1895 in Turin, Italy
Source: *Baker 78, 84, 92; IntWWM 77, 80, 85; NewEOp 71; NewGrDM 80; NewGrDO; OxDcOp; WhoMus 72*

Rochambeau, Jean Baptiste Donatien de Vimeur, Comte
French. Army Officer
Led French force aiding Americans in Revolution; helped defeat Cornwallis at Yorktown, 1781.
b. Jul 1, 1725 in Vendome, France
d. May 10, 1807 in Loire-et-cher, France
Source: *AmBi; ApCAB; Benet 96; DcAmB; Drake; HarEnMi; McGEWB; NewCol 75; REn; TwCBDA; WebAB 74; WebBD 83; WhAm HS; WhAmRev*

Rochberg, George
American. Composer
Acclaimed for award-winning "Night Music," 1948; "Violin Concerto," 1975.
b. Jul 5, 1918 in Paterson, New Jersey
Source: *AmComp; ASCAP 66; Baker 78, 84, 92; BioIn 9, 10, 11, 13, 14, 16; BriBkM 80; CompSN SUP; ConAmC 82; ConCom 92; CpmDNM 72, 77, 78, 79, 81, 82; CurBio 85; DcCM; DcCom&M 79; DcTwCCu 1; EncWB; IntWWM 77, 80, 85, 90; NewAmDM; NewGrDA 86; NewGrDM 80; NewGrDO; OxCMus;*

PenDiMP A; WhoAm 74, 76, 78, 80, 82, 84, 86, 88, 90, 92, 94, 95, 96, 97; WhoAmM 83; WhoEnt 92; WhoWor 74

Roche, John P
American. Author, Educator
Political science works include *The History of Marxist-Leninist Organizational Theory,* 1985.
b. May 7, 1923 in New York, New York
Source: *AmAu&B; AmMWSc 73S; ConAu 69; DcLP 87B; DrAS 82H; IntWW 91; WhoAm 86, 90; WhoGov 72; WrDr 86, 88, 92*

Roche, Kevin
[Eammon Kevin Roche]
American. Architect
Won Pritzker Prize, 1982, architecture's most prestigious award, for outstanding work during career.
b. Jun 14, 1922 in Dublin, Ireland
Source: *BioIn 8, 9, 11, 12, 13, 15, 16; BriEAA; ConArch 80, 87; ConDes 97; ConNews 85-1; CurBio 70; EncAAr 2; IntDcAr; IntWW 75, 76, 77, 79, 81, 83, 91; MacEA; WhoAm 86, 88, 90, 92, 94, 95, 96, 97; WhoScEn 94, 96; WhoWor 91, 93, 95, 96, 97*

Rochefort, Henri
[Victor Henri Marquis de Rochefort-Lucay]
French. Journalist
Founded anti-imperalist journals, *La Lanterne,* 1868; *La Marseillaise,* 1869; exiled, 1889-95.
b. Jan 31, 1830 in Paris, France
d. Jun 30, 1913 in Aix-les-Bains, France
Source: *NewCol 75; OxCFr; WebBD 83*

Rochester, Nathaniel
American. Merchant, Banker
Founded Rochester, NY, 1824.
b. Feb 21, 1752 in Virginia
d. May 17, 1831 in Rochester, New York
Source: *ApCAB; BioIn 4; DcAmB; HarEnUS; NatCAB 9; TwCBDA; WebBD 83; WhAm HS; WhAmRev*

Rochot, Philippe
French. Hostage
French TV crew member in Lebanon seized by Revolutionary Justice Organization Mar 8, 1986 and released Jun 20, 1986.

Rock, Arthur
American. Business Executive
Chairman, Scientific Data Systems, 1962-69, which merged with Xerox, 1969; director, Xerox Corp., 1969-72.
b. Aug 19, 1926 in Rochester, New York
Source: *BioIn 8, 13; St&PR 75, 84, 87, 91, 93; WhoAm 74, 76, 78, 80, 82, 84, 86, 88, 90, 92, 94, 95, 96, 97; WhoFI 74, 85, 87, 89, 92, 94, 96; WhoWest 96*

Rock, Chris
American. Actor, Comedian
Films include *New Jack City,* 1988; *Boomerang,* 1992; featured performer on "Saturday Night Live," 1990-93.
b. 1967 in New York, New York
Source: *ConBlB 3; ConTFT 13; LegTOT*

Rock, John
American. Physician
Developed birth control pill, 1944; established first fertility clinic.
b. Mar 24, 1890 in Marlborough, Massachusetts
d. Dec 4, 1984 in Peterborough, New Hampshire
Source: *AnObit 1984; BioIn 7, 10, 11, 13; BlueB 76; CelR; ConAu 114; ConNews 85-1; CurBio 64, 85, 85N; IntWW 74, 75, 76, 77, 78, 79, 80, 81; NewYTBS 84; NotTwCS; WhAm 8; WhoAm 74, 76, 78*

Rockefeller, Abby Aldrich
American. Philanthropist, Art Patron
Wife of oil millionaire John D; known for primitive American art collection housed at Williamsburg.
b. Oct 26, 1874 in Providence, Rhode Island
d. Apr 15, 1948 in New York, New York
Source: *BioIn 19; DcAmB S4; GrLiveH; NotAW*

Rockefeller, David
American. Banker
CEO and chm., Chase Manhattan Bank, 1969-80; son of John, Jr.
b. Jun 12, 1915 in New York, New York
Source: *BiDAmBL 83; BioIn 1, 5, 6, 7, 8, 9, 10, 11, 12, 13, 14, 15, 18, 20, 21; BlueB 76; CelR, 90; CurBio 59; Dun&B 79; EncWB; FacFETw; IntWW 74, 76, 77, 78, 79, 80, 81, 82, 83, 89, 91, 93; IntYB 78, 79, 80, 81, 82; NewYTBE 70, 73; NewYTBS 95; PolProf J, K; St&PR 75, 91; Who 74, 82, 83, 85, 88, 90, 92, 94; WhoAm 74, 76, 78, 80, 82, 84, 86, 88, 90, 92, 94, 95, 96, 97; WhoAmA 73, 76, 78, 80, 82, 84, 86, 89, 91, 93; WhoE 74, 75, 77, 79, 81, 86, 89, 91, 93, 95, 97; WhoFI 74, 75, 77, 79, 81, 92; WhoWor 74, 76, 78, 80, 82, 84, 87, 89, 91; WorAl; WorAlBi*

Rockefeller, Happy
[Margaretta Large Rockefeller; Mrs. Nelson Rockefeller]
American.
Second wife, widow of former vp, NY governor.
b. Jun 9, 1926
Source: *BioNews 74; InWom SUP; NewYTBS 74; WhoAm 86, 90; WhoAmW 77*

Rockefeller, John D(avison)
American. Oilman
Founded Standard Oil of OH, 1870; U of Chicago, 1890; Rockefeller Foundation, 1913.
b. Jul 8, 1839 in Richford, New York
d. May 23, 1937 in Ormond Beach, Florida
Source: *AmBi; AmSocL; ApCAB SUP; Benet 87; BioIn 1, 2, 3, 4, 5, 6, 7, 8, 9, 10, 11, 12, 13; ChhPo S1; DcAmB S2; DcAmSR; DcNAA; Dis&D; EncAB-H 1974, 1996; HarEnUS; LinLib S; LuthC 75; McGEWB; NatCAB 11, 29; OhA&B; OxCAmH; OxCMed 86; REn; REnAL; TwCBDA; WebAB 74, 79; WhAm 1; WhFla; WorAl*

Rockefeller, John D(avison), Jr.
American. Philanthropist
Helped to restore colonial Williamsburg, VA, 1926-60.
b. Jan 29, 1874 in Cleveland, Ohio
d. May 11, 1960 in Tucson, Arizona
Source: *BiDInt; BioIn 2, 3, 4, 5, 6, 7, 10; CurBio 41, 60; DcAmB S6; FacFETw; LinLib S; McGEWB; NatCAB 44; NatLAC; OhA&B; WhAm 4; WorAl*

Rockefeller, John D(avison), III
American. Philanthropist
Head, Rockefeller Foundation, 1952-71.
b. Mar 21, 1906 in New York, New York
d. Jul 10, 1978 in Westchester County, New York
Source: *BiDInt; BiE&WWA; BioIn 3, 4, 5, 6, 7, 8, 9, 10, 11, 12, 13; BlueB 76; CelR; ConAu 77, 81; CurBio 53; DcAmB S10; IntWW 74, 75, 76, 77, 78; IntYB 78; St&PR 75; WhAm 7; Who 74; WhoAm 74, 76, 78; WhoAmA 73, 76, 78, 80N, 82N, 84N, 86N, 89N, 91N, 93N; WhoGov 72; WhoWor 74, 76, 78*

Rockefeller, John D(avison), IV
American. Politician
Dem. senator from WV, 1985—.
b. Jun 18, 1937 in New York, New York
Source: *AlmAP 92; BiDrGov 1789, 1978, 1983; BiDrUSC 89; BioIn 5, 7, 8, 9, 10, 11, 13, 14; CelR 90; CngDr 89; IntWW 89, 91, 93; NewYTBE 70; PolsAm 84; WhoAm 74, 76, 78, 80, 82, 84, 86, 88, 90, 92, 94, 95, 96, 97; WhoAmP 73, 75, 77, 79, 81, 83, 85, 87, 89, 91, 93, 95; WhoE 74, 75; WhoGov 72, 77; WhoScEn 94; WhoSSW 78, 80, 82, 84, 86, 88, 91, 93, 95, 97; WhoWor 82, 84, 87, 89, 91, 96; WorAl; WorAlBi*

Rockefeller, Laurance Spelman
American. Business Executive
Director, Rockefeller Center, 1936-78; vice chairman, Rockefeller Bros. Fund, 1980-82; director, Reader's Digest Assn., 1973—; active in conservation projects.
b. May 26, 1910 in New York, New York
Source: *BioIn 5, 6, 7, 8, 10, 11, 13; BusPN; CurBio 59; FacFETw; IntWW 74, 75, 76, 77, 78, 79, 80, 81, 82, 83, 89, 91, 93; NatLAC; NewYTBE 70; St&PR 84, 87; Who 74, 82, 83, 85, 88, 90, 92, 94; WhoAm 86, 90; WhoAmA 91; WhoE 74; WhoFI 74; WhoGov 72; WhoWor 84, 87, 91; WorAl; WorAlBi*

Rockefeller, Mary French
[Mrs. Laurance S. Rockefeller]
American. Philanthropist
Member, national board of YWCA, 1951-88.
b. May 1, 1910 in New York, New York
d. Apr 17, 1997 in New York, New York
Source: *BioIn 18; BlueB 76; IntYB 78, 79, 80, 81, 82; St&PR 75, 84, 87; WhoAm 74, 76, 78, 80, 82, 84, 86, 88, 90, 92, 97; WhoAmA 86, 89, 91, 93; WhoAmW 61, 64, 66, 68, 70, 72, 74, 75, 95; WhoE 74, 75, 77; WhoFI 74, 75, 77, 96; WhoGov 72, 75; WhoThSc 1996; WhoWor 78, 80, 82, 84, 87, 89, 91, 93, 95, 96, 97; WorAlBi*

Rockefeller, Nelson A(ldrich)
American. US Vice President
Moderate Rep. governor of NY, 1959-73; vp under Ford, 1974-76.
b. Jul 8, 1908 in Bar Harbor, Maine
d. Jan 26, 1979 in New York, New York
Source: *AmPolLe; BiDInt; BiDrUSC 89; BiDrUSE 89; BioIn 1, 2, 3, 4, 5, 6, 7, 8, 9, 10, 11, 12, 13; BioNews 74; BlueB 76; CurBio 41, 51; DcAmB S10; DcAmDH 80, 89; DcPol; EncAB-H 1974, 1996; EncCW; EncLatA; EncWB; FacFETw; IntWW 74, 75, 76, 77, 78; IntYB 78, 79; LinLib S; NewYTBE 70, 73; NewYTBS 74, 79; OxCAmH; PolProf E, J, K, T; VicePre; WebAB 74, 79; WhAm 7; Who 74; WhoAm 74, 76, 78; WhoAmA 73, 76, 78, 80N, 82N, 84N, 86N, 89N, 91N, 93N; WhoAmP 73, 75, 77; WhoE 74, 75, 77; WhoGov 72, 75, 77; WhoSSW 76; WhoWor 74, 76, 78; WorAl*

Rockefeller, Rodman C
American. Business Executive
Son of Nelson; chm., Ibec Inc., 1980-85, Pocantico Development, 1980—.
b. Apr 24, 1932 in New York, New York
Source: *Dun&B 79, 86; St&PR 75, 84, 87; WhoAm 76, 78, 86, 90; WhoFI 74*

Rockefeller, Sharon Percy
American.
Wife of John D, IV; daughter of Charles H Percy; twin sister, Valerie, murdered in bizarre unsolved mystery, 1960s.
b. Dec 10, 1944 in Oakland, California
Source: *BioIn 9; LesBEnT 92; WhoAm 84, 92, 95, 96, 97; WhoAmP 81, 83, 85, 87, 89, 91, 93, 95; WhoAmW 91, 93, 95*

Rockefeller, William
American. Industrialist
The head of export operations for standard oil; brother of John.
b. May 31, 1841 in Richford, New York
d. Jun 24, 1922 in Tarrytown, New York
Source: *AmBi; ApCAB SUP; BiDAmBL 83; BioIn 10; DcAmB; NatCAB 11; NewYTBS 74; WhAm 1; WhoAm 86; WhoWor 89*

Rockefeller, Winthrop
American. Politician
Governor of AR, 1967-71.
b. May 1, 1912 in New York, New York
d. Feb 22, 1973 in Palm Springs, California
Source: *BiDrGov 1789; BioIn 1, 4, 5, 6, 7, 8, 9, 10, 11, 12, 13, 16, 18; BioNews 74; CurBio 59, 73, 73N; DcAmB S9; FacFETw; NewYTBE 73; PolProf J, NF; WhAm 5, 6; WhoAm 74; WhoAmA 73, 89N, 91N, 93N; WhoFI 74; WhoSSW 73; WhoWor 74*

Rockin' Dopsie
[Alton Rubin]
American. Musician, Singer
Zydeco accordionist, known as the Crowned Prince of Zydeco, who recorded *Saturday Night Zydeco,* 1989 and *Louisiana Music,* 1991.
b. Feb 10, 1932 in Carencro, Louisiana
d. Aug 26, 1993 in Opelousas, Louisiana
Source: *BioIn 19; ConMus 10; GuBlues; PenEncP*

Rockne, Knute Kenneth
American. Football Coach
Head coach, Notre Dame, 1918-31; known for "Four Horsemen" backfield, 1924, "Win one for the Gipper" pep talk, 1920; died in plane crash.
b. Mar 4, 1888 in Voss, Norway
d. Mar 31, 1931 in Bazaar, Kansas
Source: *AmBi; BiDAmSp FB; BioIn 1, 2, 3, 4, 5, 6, 7, 8, 9, 10, 11, 12; DcAmB; DcCathB; IndAu 1917; McGEWB; NatCAB 25; OxCAmH; WebAB 74, 79; WhAm 1; WhoFtbl 74; WorAl*

Rockpile
[Billy Bremer; Dave Edmunds; Nick Lowe; Terry Williams]
British. Music Group
Pub-rock group, 1976-81; recorded one album *Seconds of Pleasure,* 1980.
Source: *BioIn 15; ConMuA 80A, 80B; RkOn 85; RolSEnR 83; WhoRock 81; WhoRocM 82; WhsNW 85*

Rockwell
[Kennedy Gordy]
American. Singer
Son of Berry Gordy, Jr; had hit single "Somebody's Watching Me," 1984, with Michael Jackson singing chorus.
b. Mar 15, 1964 in Detroit, Michigan
Source: *RkOn 85*

Rockwell, Doc
[George L Rockwell]
American. Cartoonist
Best known for "Doc Rockwell's Mustard Plaster."
b. 1889 in Providence, Rhode Island
d. Mar 3, 1978 in Brunswick, Maine
Source: *BioIn 9, 11; NewYTBS 78; ObitOF 79; WhScrn 83*

Rockwell, George Lincoln
American. Political Activist
Organized American Nazi Party, 1958; advocated extermination of all American Jews.
b. Mar 9, 1918 in Bloomington, Illinois
d. Aug 25, 1967 in Arlington, Virginia
Source: *BiDExR; BioIn 6, 7, 8, 11, 12, 20, 21; DcAmB S8; LegTOT; NewYTBS 78; PolProf J, K; WhDW*

Rockwell, Norman
American. Illustrator
Drew 317 nostalgic covers for *Saturday Evening Post,* 1916-63; received Presidential Freedom Medal, 1977.
b. Feb 3, 1894 in New York, New York
d. Nov 8, 1978 in Stockbridge, Massachusetts
Source: *AmCulL; Benet 87, 96; BenetAL 91; BioIn 1, 2, 3, 4, 5, 6, 7, 9, 10, 11, 12, 13, 14, 15, 16, 18, 19, 20; BlueB 76; CelR; ChhPo S2; ConAu 81, 89; CurBio 45, 79N; DcArts; EncAJ; IlrAm 1880, C; IlsBYP; IlsCB 1744; LegTOT; LinLib S; NewYTBE 71; NewYTBS 78; PrintW 83, 85; REn; REnAL; SmATA 23; WebAB 74, 79; WhAm 7; WhoAm 74, 76, 78; WhoAmA 73, 76, 78, 80N, 82N, 84N, 86N, 89N, 91N, 93N; WhoGrA 62; WhoWor 74; WorAl; WorAlBi*

Rockwell, Willard F
American. Manufacturer, Engineer
Founded Rockwell-Standard, Rockwell Manufacturing Co.
b. Mar 31, 1888 in Boston, Massachusetts
d. Oct 16, 1978 in Pittsburgh, Pennsylvania
Source: *Entr; ObitOF 79; St&PR 75; WhoFI 77*

Rodale, Jerome Irving
American. Author, Publisher
Pres., Rodale Press, 1932-71, publishers of ecology, health books.
b. Aug 16, 1898 in New York, New York
d. Jun 7, 1971 in New York, New York
Source: *AmAu&B; BioIn 7, 8, 9, 10, 12, 13, 17; EncTwCJ; NewYTBE 71; WhAm 5*

Roddenberry, Gene
[Eugene Wesley Roddenberry]
American. Writer, Producer
Creator of TV series "Star Trek," 1966-69; and "Star Trek: The Next Generation," 1987—; wrote screenplays for *Star Trek* films.
b. Aug 19, 1921 in El Paso, Texas
d. Oct 24, 1991 in Los Angeles, California
Source: *AnObit 1991; Au&Arts 5; BioIn 14, 15, 16, 17, 18, 19, 20; ConAu 37NR, 110, 135; ConLC 17, 70; ConSFA; ConTFT 3, 10; EncSF 93; FilmgC; HalFC 84; IntMPA 84, 86, 88, 92; LesBEnT; NewEScF; News 92, 92-2; NewYTBS 91; ScF&FL 1, 2, 92; SmATA 45, 69; TwoTYeD; VarWW 85; WhAm*

10; WhoAm 74, 76, 78, 80, 82, 84, 86, 88, 90; WhoSciF

Roddick, Anita Lucia Perella
English. Businesswoman, Social Reformer
Founder of the Body Shop; produces shampoos, lotions and creams from natural ingredients; uses business as a vehicle for social and environmental concerns.
b. Oct 23, 1942 in Littlehampton, England
Source: *BioIn 16; CurBio 92; News 89*

Rode, Jacques Pierre Joseph
French. Violinist
Played solo for Napoleon, 1800; wrote caprices, concertos.
b. Feb 16, 1774 in Bordeaux, France
d. Nov 25, 1830 in Bordeaux, France
Source: *Baker 84; OxCMus; WebBD 83*

Roderick, David Milton
American. Business Executive
Chairman, CEO, US Steel Corporation, 1979.
b. May 3, 1924 in Pittsburgh, Pennsylvania
Source: *BioIn 15; CurBio 87; Dun&B 88; EncABHB 9; IntWW 83, 89, 91; St&PR 91; WhAm 11; WhoAm 74, 76, 78, 80, 82, 84, 86, 88, 90; WhoE 77, 79, 81, 83, 85, 86, 89, 91; WhoFI 74, 77, 79, 81, 83, 85, 87, 89; WhoWor 82, 84, 91*

Rodford, Jim
[Argent; Kinks; James Rodford]
English. Musician
Bassist with Argent, 1969-76; Kinks, since 1978.
b. Jul 7, 1945 in Saint Albans, England

Rodgers, Bill
[William Henry Rodgers]
American. Track Athlete
Won Boston Marathon, 1975, 1978-79; NY Marathon, 1976-79.
b. Dec 23, 1947 in Hartford, Connecticut
Source: *BiDAmSp OS; BioIn 11, 12, 13, 16, 20; ConAu 101; CurBio 82; LegTOT; WhoAm 82, 84, 86, 88, 90, 92, 94, 95; WhoSpor; WorAl*

Rodgers, Bob
[Robert Leroy Rodgers]
"Buck"
American. Baseball Manager
Catcher, 1961-69; manager, Montreal, 1985-91; NL manager of yr., 1987.
b. Aug 16, 1938 in Delaware, Ohio
Source: *BaseReg 86, 87; BioIn 16; WhoAm 82, 86; WhoE 86*

Rodgers, Christopher Raymond Perry
American. Naval Officer
Rear-admiral; superintendent, Naval Academy, 1874-81; pres. of Int'l Conference which fixed prime (Greenwich) meridian time, universal day.
b. Nov 14, 1819 in New York, New York
d. Jan 8, 1892 in Washington, District of Columbia
Source: *AmBi; DcAmB; Drake; HarEnUS; NatCAB 4; NewCol 75; TwCBDA; WebAB 74; WebAMB; WhAm HS*

Rodgers, Guy William, Jr.
American. Basketball Player
Guard, 1958-70, with five NBA teams; led NBA in assists, 1963, 1967.
b. Sep 1, 1935 in Philadelphia, Pennsylvania
Source: *BiDAmSp BK; BioIn 5, 6, 7; OfNBA 87; WhoAfA 96; WhoBlA 92, 94*

Rodgers, Jimmie
[James Charles Rodgers]
"Brakeman"
American. Singer, Songwriter
Father of modern country music; had million-selling single "Blue Yodel"; country music Hall of Fame, 1961.
b. Sep 8, 1897 in Meridian, Mississippi
d. May 26, 1933 in New York, New York
Source: *ASCAP 66, 80; Baker 78, 84, 92; BgBkCoM; BioIn 2, 4, 10, 11, 12, 14, 15, 18, 21; BluesWW; CmpEPM; ConMus 3; CounME 74; DcArts; EncFCWM 69, 83; EncRk 88; HarEnCM 87; HarEnR 86; LegTOT; NewAmDM; NewGrDA 86; NewGrDM 80; OnThGG; PenEncP; RolSEnR 83; WhoRock 81; WorAl; WorAlBi*

Rodgers, Jimmy F
American. Singer
Hits include "Kisses Sweeter Than Wine," 1957; "Honeycomb," 1957.
b. Sep 18, 1933 in Camas, Washington
Source: *BioIn 14, 15; EncFCWM 69; EncRk 88; HarEnR 86*

Rodgers, John
American. Naval Officer
Commissioned lt. in newly organized US Navy, 1798; fought in War of 1812; pres., Board of Navy Commissions, 1815-37.
b. 1773 in Harford County, Maryland
d. Aug 10, 1838 in Philadelphia, Pennsylvania
Source: *AmBi; ApCAB; BioIn 8, 12; DcAmB; Drake; EncAB-A 26; GenMudB; OxCShps; TwCBDA; WebAB 74, 79; WebAMB; WebBD 83; WhAm HS*

Rodgers, Johnathan (Arlin)
American. TV Executive
President, CBS Television Stations Division, 1990—.
b. Jan 18, 1946 in San Antonio, Texas
Source: *AfrAmBi 1; ConBlB 6; DcTwCCu 5; WhoAm 92, 94, 95, 96; WhoEnt 92; WhoMW 92, 93, 96*

Rodgers, Johnny
American. Football Player
All-America running back, won Heisman Trophy, 1972; in NFL with San Diego, 1977-78.
b. Jul 5, 1951 in Omaha, Nebraska
Source: *BioIn 9, 10, 14; InB&W 80; WhoFtbl 74; WhoSpor*

Rodgers, Mary
[Mrs. Henry Guettel]
American. Composer
Scores include *Once Upon a Mattress,* 1959; daughter of Richard.
b. Jan 11, 1931 in New York, New York
Source: *ASCAP 66; AuBYP 2S; BiE&WWA; BioIn 11, 19; ChlBkCr; ChlLR 20; ConAmC 76, 82; ConAu 8NR, 49, 55NR; ConLC 12; DcAmChF 1960; EncMT; FifBJA; IntAu&W 77, 91, 93; InWom; MajAI; NewAmDM; NewCBMT; NotNAT; OxCPMus; OxDcOp; ScF&FL 1, 2, 92; SmATA 8; TwCChW 78, 83, 89, 95; VarWW 85; WhoAm 78, 80, 82, 84, 86, 88, 92; WhoAmW 61, 70, 72, 74, 75; WhoEnt 92; WhoThe 81; WrDr 80, 82, 84, 86, 88, 90, 92, 94, 96*

Rodgers, Nile
American. Musician
Guitarist who produces albums for other musicians, including Madonna.
b. Sep 19, 1952 in New York, New York
Source: *BioIn 11, 13, 14, 15, 16; ConMus 8; InB&W 85; LegTOT; NewGrDA 86; OnThGG; SoulM; WhoAm 94, 95*

Rodgers, Richard
[Rodgers and Hammerstein; Rodgers and Hart]
American. Composer
Won Pulitzers for *Oklahoma,* 1943; *South Pacific,* 1949; wrote music for 40 Broadway hits.
b. Jul 28, 1902 in New York, New York
d. Dec 30, 1979 in New York, New York
Source: *AmPS; AmSong; ASCAP 66, 80; Baker 78, 84; Benet 87; BenetAL 91; BiDD; BiE&WWA; BioIn 1, 2, 3, 4, 5, 6, 7, 8, 9, 10, 11, 12, 13, 14, 15, 16, 17, 19, 21; BlueB 76; CamGWoT; CelR; CmMov; CmpEPM; ConAmC 76, 82; ConAu 89; ConMus 9; CurBio 51, 80, 80N; DcTwCCu 1; EncAB-H 1974, 1996; EncMT; EncWT; FacFETw; FilmEn; FilmgC; IntMPA 77; IntWW 74, 75, 76, 77, 78, 79; IntWWM 77; LegTOT; LinLib L, S; McGEWD 72, 84; MnPM; MusMk; NatCAB 61; NewAmDM; NewCBMT; NewGrDA 86; NewGrDM 80; NewOxM; NewYTBS 79; NotNAT, A; OxCAmH; OxCAmL 65; OxCAmT 84; OxCFilm; OxCPMus; OxDcOp; PenDiMP A; PenEncP; PlP&P; PopAmC, SUP; RAdv 14; REn; REnAL; Sw&Ld C; WebAB 74, 79; WhAm 7; Who 74; WhoAm 74, 76, 78; WhoGov 72; WhoMus 72; WhoThe 72, 77, 81; WhoWor 74, 78; WhoWorJ 72, 78; WhScrn 83; WorAl; WorAlBi*

Rodham, Hugh
American.
Father of Hillary Rodham Clinton.
d. Apr 7, 1993 in Little Rock, Arkansas
Source: *BioIn 18*

Rodia, Simon
[Sam Rodia; Simon Rodilla]
American. Architect
Designed complex of towers, now a cultural monument, without any plans, training in Los Angeles, 1921-54.
b. 1879?, Italy
d. 1965 in Martinez, California
Source: *BioIn 2, 5, 7, 9, 10, 11, 16, 18; CmCal; FolkA 87; MacEA*

Rodin, Auguste
[Francois Auguste Rene Rodin]
French. Sculptor
Works include *The Thinker; The Kiss; The Burghers of Calais.*
b. Nov 12, 1840 in Paris, France
d. Nov 17, 1917 in Meudon, France
Source: *AntBDN C; AtlBL; Benet 87; BioIn 1, 2, 3, 4, 6, 7, 8, 9, 10, 11, 12, 13, 14, 15, 16, 17, 18, 19, 20, 21; DcArts; DcNiCA; DcTwCCu 2; Dis&D; IntDcAA 90; LegTOT; LinLib S; McGDA; McGEWB; NewC; NewCol 75; OxCArt; OxCFr; OxDcArt; PhDcTCA 77; RAdv 14, 13-3; REn; WebBD 83; WhAmArt 85A; WorAl; WorAlBi*

Rodin, Judith
American. Educator, University Administrator
President, University of Pennsylvania, 1994—.
b. c. Sep 9, 1944 in Philadelphia, Pennsylvania
Source: *AmMWSc 86, 89, 92, 95; BioIn 11; IntWW 89, 91, 93; WhoE 86*

Rodino, Peter Wallace, Jr.
American. Politician
Dem. con. from NJ, 1949-89; chm., House Judiciary Committee during Nixon's impeachment hearings, 1974.
b. Jun 7, 1909 in Newark, New Jersey
Source: *AlmAP 84, 88; AmCath 80; BiDrAC; BiDrUSC 89; BioIn 3, 10, 11, 12, 15; CngDr 74, 77, 79, 81, 83, 85, 87; CurBio 54; EncWB; IntWW 74, 75, 76, 77, 78, 79, 80, 81, 82, 83, 89, 91, 93; NewYTBS 74; PolsAm 84; WhoAm 74, 76, 78, 80, 82, 84, 86, 88, 90, 92, 94, 95; WhoAmP 73, 75, 77, 79, 81, 83, 85, 87, 89, 91, 93, 95; WhoE 74, 89, 91, 93; WhoGov 72, 75, 77; WhoWor 78; WorAl*

Rodman, Dennis (Keith)
"Worm"
American. Basketball Player
Forward, Detroit, 1986-92, San Antonio, 1993-95; Chicago, 1995—; defensive player of year, 1990-91.
b. May 13, 1961 in Trenton, New Jersey
Source: *ConBlB 12; CurBio 96; News 91, 96, 91-3; OfNBA 87; WhoAfA 96; WhoAm 92, 96, 97; WhoBlA 90, 92, 94; WhoSSW 95*

Rodman, Selden
American. Writer
Best known for narrative poem, "Lawrence: The Last Crusade," 1937; books include *Haiti: The Black Republic,* 1954.
b. Feb 19, 1909 in New York, New York
Source: *AmAu&B; AuBYP 2S; BenetAL 91; BioIn 4, 11; ChhPo, S1; ConAu 5NR, 5R, 25NR, 51NR; LinLib L; OxCAmL 65, 83, 95; OxCTwCP; REn; REnAL; SmATA 9; TwCA SUP; WhoAm 74, 76, 78; WhoAmA 73, 76, 78, 80, 82, 84, 86, 89, 91, 93; WhoWor 74*

Rodney, Caesar
American. Politician, Continental Congressman
Rode overnight through storm to ratify Declaration of Independence, 1776; governor of DE, 1778-81.
b. Oct 7, 1728 in Dover, Delaware
d. Jun 29, 1784 in Dover, Delaware
Source: *AmBi; ApCAB; BiAUS; BiDrAC; BiDrACR; BiDrUSC 89; BioIn 3, 6, 7, 8, 9; DcAmB; Drake; EncAR; EncCRAm; EncSoH; HarEnUS; HisWorL; NatCAB 5; TwCBDA; WhAm HS; WhAmP; WhAmRev; WorAl; WorAlBi*

Rodney, George Brydges, Baron
English. Naval Officer
His victories over French, Spanish, Dutch in Caribbean waters contributed to Britain's command of the seas, 1800s.
b. Feb 19, 1719 in Walton-on-Thames, England
d. May 24, 1792 in London, England
Source: *Alli; ApCAB; DcNaB; EncAR; McGEWB; NewCBEL; NewCol 75; OxCShps; REn; WebBD 83; WhDW*

Rodnina, Irina
[Rodnina and Zaitsev; Mrs. Aleksandr Zaitsev]
Russian. Skater
With Alexei Ulanov, won gold medal in pairs figure skating, 1972 Olympics; with Aleksandr Zaitsev, won gold medals, 1976, 1980 Olympics.
b. Sep 12, 1949, Union of Soviet Socialist Republics
Source: *BioIn 11, 12, 17; ContDcW 89; IntDcWB; InWom SUP; LegTOT*

Rodriguez, Andres
Paraguayan. Political Leader
Pres. of Paraguay 1989-93; responsible for overthrowing repressive dictatorship of Alfredo Stroessner.
b. Jun 19, 1923 in Borja, Paraguay
d. Apr 21, 1997 in New York, New York
Source: *CurBio 91; IntWW 91*

Rodriguez, Chi-Chi
[Juan Rodriguez]
Puerto Rican. Golfer
Turned pro, 1960; had eight career wins; known as crowd favorite; wrote *Chi-Chi's Secrets of Power Golf,* 1967.
b. Oct 23, 1934 in Rio Piedras, Puerto Rico
Source: *BioIn 13, 14, 15, 16; CurBio 69; NewYTBS 87; WhoGolf; WhoHisp 92; WhoIntG*

Rodriguez, Johnny
[John Raul Davis Rodriguez]
American. Singer
Country music star, who mixed Spanish, English lyrics in his hits, including "You'll Always Come Back to Hurting Me."
b. Dec 10, 1951 in Sabinal, Texas
Source: *BgBkCoM; BioIn 10, 12, 14; CounME 74, 74A; EncFCWM 83; HarEnCM 87; IlEncCM; LegTOT; WhoAm 82; WhoHisp 92; WhoHol 92*

Rodriguez, Robert
American. Filmmaker
Directed *El Mariachi,* 1993; *From Dusk Till Dawn,* 1995.
b. c. 1969 in San Antonio, Texas
Source: *CurBio 96; DcHiB*

Rodzinski, Artur
Yugoslav. Conductor
Controversial director NY Philharmonic, 1943-47, Chicago Symphony, 1947.
b. Jan 2, 1894 in Split, Yugoslavia
d. Nov 27, 1958 in Boston, Massachusetts
Source: *Baker 84; BiDAmM; BioIn 2, 4, 5, 7, 10, 11; BriBkM 80; CurBio 40, 59; NewEOp 71; NewGrDM 80; WhAm 3; WhoPolA*

Roe, Edward Payson
American. Clergy, Author
Wrote best-selling novels *Barriers Burned Away,* 1872; *Opening a Chestnut Burr,* 1874.
b. Mar 7, 1838 in New Windsor, New York
d. Jul 19, 1888 in Cornwall-on-Hudson, New York
Source: *Alli SUP; AmAu; AmAu&B; AmBi; ApCAB; BbD; BibAL; BiD&SB; BioIn 13; CarSB; Chambr 3; DcAmAu; DcAmB; DcLEL; DcNAA; MnBBF; NatCAB 7; OxCAmL 65; REnAL; TwCBDA; WhAm HS*

Roe, Tommy
American. Singer
Styled singing after Buddy Holly; had hit singles "Sheila," 1962; "Sweet Pea," 1966; "Dizzy," 1969.
b. May 9, 1942 in Atlanta, Georgia
Source: *EncPR&S 89; EncRk 88; LegTOT; PenEncP; RkOn 74; RolSEnR 83; WhoRock 81*

Roebling, John Augustus
American. Designer, Engineer
Pioneered design, construction of suspension bridges.
b. Jun 12, 1806 in Mulhouse, France
d. Jul 22, 1869 in New York, New York
Source: *AmBi; ApCAB; BiInAmS; BioIn 1, 2, 3, 4, 5, 7, 9, 10, 11, 13; DcAmAu;*

DcAmB; DcNAA; Drake; EncAB-H 1974, 1996; HarEnUS; InSci; LinLib S; MacEA; McGDA; McGEWB; NatCAB 4; OxCAmH; REn; TwCBDA; WebAB 74, 79; WhAm HS; WorAl

Roebling, Mary G(indhart)
American. Banker
First woman to head a major American bank; pres., Trenton NJ Trust Co., 1937-72.
b. Jul 29, 1906
d. Oct 25, 1994 in Trenton, New Jersey
Source: *AmWomM; CurBio 95N*

Roebling, Washington Augustus
American. Engineer
Succeeded father as chief engineer on Brooklyn Bridge, 1869-83.
b. May 26, 1837 in Saxonburg, Pennsylvania
d. Jul 21, 1926 in Trenton, New Jersey
Source: *AmBi; ApCAB; BioIn 2, 4, 5, 7, 9, 13, 15; DcAmAu; DcAmB; HarEnUS; InSci; MacEA; McGEWB; NatCAB 4, 26; REn; TwCBDA; WebAB 74, 79; WhAm 1*

Roebuck, Alvah Curtis
American. Merchant
Watchmaker who was partner with Richard W Sears, 1887; sold shares, 1897.
b. Jan 9, 1864 in Lafayette, Indiana
d. Jun 18, 1948 in Chicago, Illinois
Source: *BioIn 2, 7, 10; ObitOF 79*

Roeder, David
[The Hostages]
American. Hostage
One of 52 held by terrorists, Nov 1979-Jan 1981.
b. 1940?
Source: *BioIn 12; NewYTBS 81*

Roeg, Nicholas (Jack)
English. Filmmaker
Director of photography, *A Funny Thing Happened on the Way to the Forum,* 1964; *Fahrenheit 451,* 1966; directed *The Man Who Fell to Earth,* 1976.
b. Aug 15, 1928 in London, England
Source: *BiDFilm; BioIn 10, 13; CurBio 96; DcFM; IlWWBF; IntMPA 77, 80, 82, 84, 86, 88; ItaFilm; OxCFilm; WorAlBi; WorEFlm*

Roehm, Carolyne Jane Smith
American. Fashion Designer
Pres. of Carolyne Roehm, Inc., a fashion design house, 1984—.
b. May 7, 1951 in Jefferson City, Missouri
Source: *BioIn 15, 16; CurBio 92; EncFash; WhoAm 90; WhoAmW 91; WhoFash 88*

Roemer, Buddy
[Charles Elson Roemer, III]
American. Politician
Dem. governor of Louisiana, 1988-1991.
b. Oct 4, 1943 in Shreveport, Louisiana
Source: *AlmAP 82, 84, 88, 92; BiDrUSC 89; BioIn 15, 16; CngDr 81, 83, 85, 87; CurBio 90; IntWW 89, 91, 93; News 91; PolsAm 84; WhoAm 82, 84, 86, 88, 90; WhoAmP 83, 85, 87, 89, 91, 93, 95; WhoE 85; WhoSSW 82, 86, 88, 91; WhoWor 89, 91*

Roentgen, David
German. Furniture Designer
Cabinetmaker to Queen Marie Antoinette of France; often used wood inlays and bronze appliques.
b. Aug 11, 1743
d. Feb 12, 1807 in Wiesbaden, Germany
Source: *AntBDN G; BioIn 2, 5, 10, 11; DcD&D; McGDA; PenDiDA 89*

Roentgen, Wilhelm Konrad
German. Scientist
Revolutionized medicine with discovery of X-rays, 1895; won first Nobel Prize in physics, 1901.
b. Mar 27, 1845 in Lennep, Prussia
d. Feb 10, 1923 in Munich, Germany
Source: *AsBiEn; InSci; LinLib S; McGEWB; NewCol 75; REn; WhoNob; WorAl; WorAlBi*

Roeser, Donald
[Blue Oyster Cult]
American. Singer, Musician
Known for guitar solos; wrote hit single "Don't Fear the Reaper," 1976.
b. Nov 12, 1947 in Long Island, New York
Source: *ASCAP 80; OnThGG*

Roethke, Theodore (Huebner)
American. Poet
Among many award-winning works: *The Waking: Poems 1933-53,* 1954, won Pulitzer; *Words for the Wind,* 1958, won Bollingen.
b. May 25, 1908 in Saginaw, Michigan
d. Aug 1, 1963 in Bainbridge Isle, Washington
Source: *AmAu&B; AmCulL; AmWr; AnCL; AtlBL; Benet 87, 96; BenetAL 91; BioIn 3, 4, 6, 7, 8, 9, 10, 11, 12, 13, 14, 15, 16, 17, 18, 19; CamGEL; CamGLE; CamHAL; CasWL; ChhPo, S1, S2, S3; CnDAL; CnE&AP; ConAu 2BS, 81; ConLC 1, 3, 8, 11, 19, 46; ConPo 75, 80A, 85A; CroCAP; DcAmB S7; DcArts; DcLB 5; DcLEL 1940; DcTwCCu 1; EncWL, 2, 3; FacFETw; FifWWr; GrWrEL P; LegTOT; LinLib L; LngCTC; MagSAmL; MajTwCW; MakMC; McGEWB; MichAu 80; ModAL, S1, S2; NewCon; NewGrDA 86; ObitT 1961; OxCAmL 65, 83, 95; OxCEng 85, 95; OxCTwCP; PenC AM; PoeCrit 15; RAdv 1, 14, 13-1; REn; REnAL; RfGAmL 87, 94; RGFAP; RGTwCWr; TwCA SUP; TwCWr; WebAB 74, 79; WebE&AL; WhAm 4; WhDW; WhoPNW; WhoTwCL; WorAl; WorAlBi; WrPh*

Rogell, Albert S
American. Director, Producer
Made Hollywood's first coop. film, 1921; worked on over 2,000 films including *The Black Cat,* 1941.
b. Aug 21, 1901 in Oklahoma City, Oklahoma
d. Apr 7, 1988
Source: *EncAFC; FilmEn; FilmgC; HalFC 84, 88; IntMPA 86, 88; TwYS; VarWW 85*

Rogell, Billy
[William George Rogell]
American. Baseball Player
Shortstop, 1925, 1927-40, mostly with Detroit; known for fielding.
b. Nov 24, 1904 in Springfield, Illinois
Source: *Ballpl 90; BaseEn 88; BioIn 17, 20, 21; WhoProB 73*

Rogers, Adrian Pierce
American. Religious Leader
Pres., Southern Baptist Convention, largest Protestant denomination in US, 1979- 80, 1986-88.
b. Sep 12, 1931 in West Palm Beach, Florida
Source: *BioIn 12, 16; ConNews 87-4; NewYTBS 79; WhoAm 90; WhoRel 92*

Rogers, Bernard William
American. Military Leader
General who became supreme Allied commander in Europe, Jun 1979.
b. Jul 16, 1921 in Fairview, Kansas
Source: *BioIn 11, 14; CmdGen 1991; CurBio 84; IntWW 78, 79, 80, 81, 82, 83, 89, 91, 93; NewYTBE 70; NewYTBS 79; WebAB 74; WebAMB; Who 82, 83, 85, 88, 90, 92, 94; WhoAm 74, 76, 78, 80, 82, 84, 86, 88, 90, 92, 94, 95, 96, 97; WhoSSW 95; WhoWor 87, 89, 93, 95, 96; WorDWW*

Rogers, Bill
[William Charles Rogers]
American. Golfer
Turned pro, 1974; won British Open, 1981.
b. Sep 10, 1951 in Waco, Texas
Source: *BiNAW Sup; NewYTBS 81; WhoAm 82, 84, 86, 88; WhoIntG*

Rogers, Bruce
American. Designer
Best known for designing limited edition books; designed Centaur type.
b. May 14, 1870 in Lafayette, Indiana
d. May 18, 1957 in New Fairfield, Connecticut
Source: *BioIn 1, 2, 3, 4, 10, 12, 15, 16, 17; ChhPo, S2; ConAu 123; CurBio 46, 57; IndAu 1917; ObitT 1951; OxCAmL 65, 83, 95; OxCDecA; REnAL; WebAB 74, 79; WhAm 3; WhoAmA 80N, 82N, 84N, 86N, 89N, 91N, 93N*

Rogers, Buddy
[Charles Rogers]
American. Actor
Starred in *Wings,* 1927, first picture to win Oscar; husband of Mary Pickford.
b. Aug 13, 1904 in Olathe, Kansas
Source: *BioIn 1, 9, 16; EncAFC; FilmEn; FilmgC; ForYSC; HalFC 80, 84, 88; IntMPA 75, 76, 77, 78, 79, 80, 81, 82, 84, 86, 88, 92, 94, 96; LegTOT; MotPP; MovMk; RadStar; SilFlmP; TwYS; VarWW 85; What 3; WhoHol 92, A; WorAl; WorAlBi*

Rogers, Carl Ransom
American. Psychologist, Author
Iconoclast who pioneered development of encounter groups, "self-actualization"; wrote *On Becoming a Person,* 1961.
b. Jan 8, 1902 in Oak Park, Illinois
d. Feb 4, 1987 in La Jolla, California
Source: *AmMWSc 73S, 78S; BiDAmEd; BioIn 4, 6, 10, 11, 12, 13; ConAu 1NR, 1R; CurBio 62, 87; EncWB; LuthC 75; RAdv 14, 13-5; WhAm 9; WhoAm 74, 76, 78, 80, 82, 84, 86; WhoWest 74, 84*

Rogers, Darryl D
American. Football Coach
Collegiate coach, 1965-84; in NFL with Detroit, 1985-88.
b. May 28, 1935 in Los Angeles, California
Source: *FootReg 85, 87; WhoAm 86, 88; WhoMW 90*

Rogers, Don(ald Lavert)
American. Football Player
Safety; first round draft pick of Cleveland, 1984; died of cocaine overdose.
b. Sep 17, 1962 in Texarkana, Arkansas
d. Jun 27, 1986 in Sacramento, California
Source: *BioIn 15; FootReg 85, 86*

Rogers, Edith
American. Politician
Rep. congresswoman from MA, 1925-60; her legislation created Women's Army Corps, 1942.
b. Mar 19, 1881 in Saco, Maine
d. Sep 10, 1960 in Boston, Massachusetts
Source: *BioIn 1, 3, 4, 5, 6, 10, 12; CurBio 42, 60; DcAmB S6; NatCAB 44; WhAm 4*

Rogers, Fred McFeely
American. Educator, TV Personality
Producer, host, "Mister Rogers Neighborhood," 1965—; ordained Presbyterian minister.
b. Mar 20, 1928 in Latrobe, Pennsylvania
Source: *ASCAP 66; BioIn 13; ConAu 107; ConTFT 6; CurBio 71; IntMPA 86, 88; NewYTBS 75, 83; WhoAm 74, 76, 78, 80, 82, 84, 86, 88, 90, 92, 94, 95, 96, 97; WhoE 74, 93, 95, 97; WhoEnt 92; WhoTelC*

Rogers, George Washington, Jr.
American. Football Player
Running back, won Heisman Trophy, 1980; in NFL with New Orleans, 1981-84, Washington, 1985-87; led NFL in rushing, 1981.
b. Dec 8, 1958 in Duluth, Georgia
Source: *BiDAmSp FB; FootReg 87*

Rogers, Ginger
[Virginia Katherine McMath]
American. Dancer
Won Oscar, 1940, for *Kitty Foyle;* frequent dance partner of Fred Astaire.
b. Jul 16, 1911 in Independence, Missouri
d. Apr 25, 1995 in Rancho Mirage, California
Source: *Baker 92; BiDAmM; BiDD; BiDFilm, 81, 94; BiE&WWA; BioAmW; BioIn 1, 2, 6, 7, 8, 9, 10, 11, 12, 17, 18, 19, 20, 21; BlueB 76; CelR, 90; CmCal; CmMov; CmpEPM; CnOxB; ConTFT 3, 14; CurBio 67, 95N; DancEn 78; DcArts; EncAFC; EncMT; FacFETw; Film 2; FilmEn; FilmgC; ForYSC; GangFlm; GoodHs; GrLiveH; HalFC 80, 84, 88; IntDcF 1-3, 2-3; IntMPA 75, 76, 77, 78, 79, 80, 81, 82, 84, 86, 88, 92, 94, 96; IntWW 74, 75, 76, 77, 78, 79, 80, 81, 82, 83, 89, 91, 93; InWom, SUP; LegTOT; MotPP; MovMk; NewGrDA 86; News 95; NewYTBE 72; NewYTBS 95; OxCFilm; OxCPMus; OxCThe 83; RAdv 14; ThFT; VarWW 85; WhAm 11; WhoAm 74, 76, 78, 80, 82, 84, 86, 88, 90, 92, 94, 95; WhoAmW 58, 61, 64, 66, 68, 70, 72, 83, 85, 89, 91, 93; WhoEnt 92; WhoHol 92, A; WhoThe 77, 81; WhoWor 74; WorAl; WorAlBi; WorEFlm*

Rogers, Isaiah
American. Architect
Designed first modern hotel in America, Tremont House, Boston, 1828-29.
b. Aug 17, 1800 in Marshfield, Massachusetts
d. Apr 13, 1869
Source: *BiDAmAr; BriEAA; DcAmB; IntDcAr; MacEA; McGDA; WhAm HS*

Rogers, James Gamble
American. Architect
Designs include Northwestern U, Chicago.
b. Mar 3, 1867 in Bryant Station, Kentucky
d. Oct 1, 1947
Source: *BiDAmAr; BioIn 1, 13; DcAmB S4; MacEA; NewCol 75; WhAm 2*

Rogers, John
American. Religious Leader
Founded the Rogerenes, liberal religious sect advocating pacifism, separation of church and state.
b. Dec 12, 1648 in Milford, Connecticut
d. Oct 28, 1721 in New London, Connecticut
Source: *Alli; AmAu; AmWrBE; ApCAB; BenetAL 91; BioIn 16; DcAmB; DcNAA; OxCAmL 65, 83, 95; WebAB 74, 79; WhAm HS*

Rogers, John
American. Sculptor
Noted for popular statuette "Rogers groups" depicting Civil War, genre scenes, 1860s-80s.
b. Oct 30, 1829 in Salem, Massachusetts
d. Jul 26, 1904 in New Canaan, Connecticut
Source: *AmBi; ApCAB; BioIn 1, 2, 4, 7, 8, 9, 10, 11; BriEAA; DcAmArt; DcAmB; Dis&D; Drake; HarEnUS; McGDA; McGEWB; NatCAB 8; NewCol 75; NewYHSD; OxCAmH; OxCAmL 65; OxCArt; OxDcArt; PenDiDA 89; TwCBDA; WebAB 74, 79; WebBD 83; WhAm 1; WhAmArt 85*

Rogers, John W., Jr.
American. Business Executive
Founder and president, Ariel Capital Management, 1983—.
b. Mar 31, 1958 in Chicago, Illinois
Source: *ConBlB 5*

Rogers, Kenny
[Kenny Rogers and The First Edition; Kenneth Ray Rogers]
American. Singer
Pop-country hits include "Lady," 1980; "She Believed in Me," 1970.
b. Aug 21, 1938 in Houston, Texas
Source: *Baker 84, 92; BioIn 11, 12, 13, 16, 18, 19; BkPepl; CelR 90; ConAu 85; ConMus 1; ConTFT 8; CurBio 71; EncFCWM 83; EncRkSt; HarEnCM 87; IntMPA 88, 92, 94, 96; LegTOT; PenEncP; VarWW 85; WhoAm 86, 88, 90, 92, 94, 95, 96, 97; WhoEnt 92; WhoHol 92; WorAlBi*

Rogers, Lynn L(eroy)
American. Biologist
Involved in a field study of black bears in northeastern Minnesota, closely tracking more than one hundred bears; called one of the major pioneering studies of large mammals.
b. Apr 9, 1939 in Grand Rapids, Michigan
Source: *AmMWSc 79, 82, 86, 89, 92, 95; CurBio 94*

Rogers, Mary Cecilia
American. Victim
Murder was inspiration for Edgar Allan Poe's story *Mystery of Marie Roget.*
b. 1820
d. Jul 25, 1841 in Weehawken, New Jersey
Source: *ApCAB; BioIn 1, 2, 4, 8, 9; InWom, SUP*

Rogers, Mary Joseph(ine)
American. Religious Leader
Founded the Maryknoll Sisters, a religious missionary order.
b. Oct 27, 1882 in Boston, Massachusetts
d. Oct 9, 1955 in New York, New York
Source: *BioAmW; BioIn 4, 6, 12, 19; DcAmB S5; DcAmReB 2; DcWomA; InWom SUP; LibW; NotAW MOD; ObitOF 79; PeoHis; WhAmArt 85; WomFir*

Rogers, Randolph
American. Sculptor
Neo-classicist; did Columbus doors for US Capitol.
b. Jul 6, 1825 in Waterloo, New York
d. Jan 15, 1892 in Rome, Italy
Source: *AmBi; ApCAB; ArtsEM; ArtsNiC; BiAUS; BioIn 7, 9; BriEAA; DcAmArt; DcAmB; Drake; IlBEAAW; McGDA; NatCAB 8; NewYHSD; OxCAmH; TwCBDA; WhAmArt 85; WhAm HS*

Rogers, Robert
American. Pioneer, Soldier
Led famed Rogers Rangers during French and Indian Wars, 1750s; hero of Kenneth Roberts's *Northwest Passage*.
b. Nov 7, 1731 in Methuen, Massachusetts
d. May 18, 1795 in London, England
Source: *AmAu; AmAu&B; AmBi; AmRev; AmWrBE; Benet 87, 96; BenetAL 91; BiD&SB; BioIn 4, 5, 8, 9, 12, 16, 20; CamHAL; DcAmAu; DcAmB; DcAmMiB; DcCanB 4; DcLEL; DcNAA; EncAAH; EncCRAm; EncNAB; HarEnMi; MacDCB 78; McGEWB; NewCBEL; NewCol 75; OxCAmH; OxCAmL 65, 83, 95; OxCCan; REn; REnAL; WebAB 74, 79; WebAMB; WhAm HS; WhNaAH; WhoMilH 76; WhWE; WorAlBi*

Rogers, Rosemary
[Marina Mayson]
American. Author
Romantic, fantasy novels include *The Crowd Pleasers,* 1978; *Love Play,* 1981.
b. Dec 7, 1933 in Panadura, Ceylon
Source: *ArtclWW 2; BioIn 13, 14, 15; ConAu 3NR, 23NR, 49; IntAu&W 91; InWom SUP; NewYTBS 79; PenNWW A; TwCRHW 90; WhoAm 86, 90; WhoUSWr 88; WhoWrEP 89; WorAl; WrDr 86, 92*

Rogers, Roy
[Leonard Slye]
"King of the Cowboys"
American. Actor, Singer
With *Sons of the Pioneers,* 1932-38; in TV series "The Roy Rogers Show," 1951-64.
b. Nov 5, 1912 in Cincinnati, Ohio
Source: *BiDAmM; BioIn 1, 3, 4, 5, 8, 9, 10, 11, 12, 13, 14, 15, 16, 18, 20, 21; BkPepl; CelR 90; CmCal; CmMov; CmpEPM; ConAu 112; ConMus 9; CounME 74, 74A; CurBio 48, 83; DcArts; EncACom; EncFCWM 69, 83; FacFETw; FilmEn; FilmgC; ForYSC; HalFC 80, 84, 88; IntMPA 82, 92; MovMk; NewAmDM; OxCFilm; PenEncP; RadStar; SaTiSS; VarWW 85; WhoAm 74, 76, 78, 80, 82; WhoHol 92; WorAl; WorAlBi; WorEFlm*

Rogers, Samuel
English. Author
Known more for friendships with Byron, Wordsworth than for poetry.
b. Jul 30, 1763 in London, England
d. Dec 18, 1855 in London, England
Source: *Alli; BbD; Benet 87, 96; BiD&SB; BiDLA; BioIn 3, 4, 5, 12, 17; BlmGEL; BritAu 19; CamGEL; CamGLE; CasWL; CelCen; ChhPo, S1, S2, S3; CrtT 2; DcBiPP; DcEnA; DcEnL; DcEuL; DcLB 93; DcLEL; DcNaB; EvLB; GrWrEL P; MouLC 3; NewC; NewCBEL; OxCEng 67, 85, 95; PenC ENG; REn; RfGEnL 91; WebE&AL*

Rogers, Shorty
[Milton M Rogers]
American. Jazz Musician
Trumpeter, bandleader; noted as outstanding arranger for Woody Herman, 1940s.
b. Apr 14, 1924 in Lee, Massachusetts
Source: *AllMusG; Baker 84, 92; BiDJaz; BioIn 20; CmpEPM; IlEncJ; LegTOT; NewAmDM; NewGrDA 86; NewGrDJ 88, 94; NewGrDM 80; OxCPMus; PenEncP; WorAl; WorAlBi*

Rogers, Wayne
American. Actor
Played Trapper John in TV series "M*A*S*H," 1972-75.
b. Apr 7, 1933 in Birmingham, Alabama
Source: *BioIn 10, 11, 12, 21; BioNews 74; ConTFT 3; IntMPA 88, 92, 94, 96; LegTOT; VarWW 85; WhoAm 82, 84, 86, 88, 90, 92; WhoHol 92, A*

Rogers, Will, Jr.
American. Actor, Lecturer
Portrayed father in film *The Story of Will Rogers,* 1950.
b. Oct 12, 1912 in New York, New York
Source: *BioIn 1, 2; CurBio 53; Film 2; ForYSC; IntMPA 75, 76, 77, 78, 79, 80, 81, 82, 84, 86, 88, 92; VarWW 85; WhoHol 92, A*

Rogers, Will(iam Penn Adair)
American. Actor, Humorist, Lecturer
"Comedy roper" in Ziegfeld Follies from 1914; columnist, 1926-35; killed with Wiley Post in plane crash.
b. Sep 5, 1879 in Oologah, Oklahoma
d. Aug 15, 1935 in Point Barrow, Alaska
Source: *AmAu&B; AmBi; Benet 87, 96; BenetAL 91; BiDAmJo; BiDAmNC; BiDFilm, 81, 94; BiNAW, B; BioIn 1, 2, 3, 4, 5, 6, 7, 8, 9, 10, 11, 12, 13, 14, 15, 16, 17, 18, 19, 20, 21; CamGLE; CamGWoT; CamHAL; ChhPo S3; CmCal; CnDAL; ConAu 105, 144; DcAmB S1; DcLB 11; DcNAA; EncAAH; EncAB-H 1974, 1996; EncAFC; EncAHmr; EncMT; EncNAB; EncNoAI; EncVaud; Ent; EvLB; FacFETw; Film 1, 2; FilmEn; FilmgC; Funs; HalFC 80, 84, 88; IntDcF 1-3; JrnUS; LegTOT; LinLib L, S; LngCTC; MorMA; MotPP; MovMk; NatCAB 33; NatNAL; NotNaAm; NotNAT A, B; OxCAmH; OxCAmL 65, 83; OxCAmT 84; OxCFilm; OxCThe 67; PenC AM; PeoHis; PlP&P; QDrFCA 92; RadStar; RAdv 14; REn; REnAL; REnAW; SaTiSS; TwCA, SUP; TwCLC 8; TwYS; WebAB 74, 79; WhAm 1; WhJnl; WhoCom; WhoHol B; WhScrn 74, 77, 83; WhThe; WorAl; WorEFlm*

Rogers, William Pierce
American. Government Official
Secretary of State under Nixon, 1969-73.
b. Jun 23, 1913 in Norfolk, New York
Source: *AmPolLe; BiDrUSE 71, 89; BioIn 2, 3, 4, 5, 8, 9, 10, 11, 12, 14, 16; BlueB 76; DcAmDH 80, 89; DcPol; IntYB 78, 79, 80, 81, 82; NewYTBS 86; Who 74, 82, 83, 85, 88, 90, 92, 94; WhoAm 74, 76, 78, 80, 82, 84, 86, 88, 90, 94; WhoAmL 78, 79, 83, 85, 90, 94; WhoAmP 73, 75, 77, 79, 81, 83, 85; WhoGov 72; WhoSSW 73, 75, 76*

Roget, Peter Mark
English. Lexicographer, Physician
Compiled *Thesaurus of English Words and Phrases,* 1852; still standard reference work.
b. Jan 18, 1779 in London, England
d. Sep 12, 1869 in West Malvern, England
Source: *Alli; BiHiMed; BioIn 2, 3, 8, 9, 12, 17; DcBiPP; DcNaB; InSci; NewC; NewCol 75; OxCMed 86*

Rohatyn, Felix George
"Felix the Fixer"
American. Banker
Chaired emergency efforts to save NYC from bankruptcy, 1975.
b. May 29, 1928 in Vienna, Austria
Source: *BiDAmBL 83; BioIn 9, 10, 11, 12, 13, 14, 15, 16; CelR 90; ConAu 118; CurBio 78; Dun&B 90; IntWW 93; NewYTBE 72; NewYTBS 74, 75, 76, 81, 84; PolProf NF; St&PR 84, 91; WhoAm 74, 76, 78, 80, 82, 84, 86, 88, 90, 92, 94, 95, 96, 97; WhoFI 85, 87, 92, 94; WhoWor 96*

Rohde, Ruth Bryan Owen
American. Politician, Diplomat
Ambassador to Denmark, 1933; first American woman to hold major diplomatic post.
b. Oct 2, 1885 in Jacksonville, Illinois
d. Jul 26, 1958 in Copenhagen, Denmark
Source: *BioIn 16; DcAmB S5; DcAmDH 80, 89; EncWB; LibW; NotAW MOD; WhAm 3*

Rohm, Ernst
German. Soldier
Leader of Storm Troops (SS, SA), 1930-34; executed.
b. Nov 28, 1887 in Munich, Germany
d. Jul 2, 1934 in Munich, Germany
Source: *BiDExR; BioIn 2, 8, 14, 16, 18; DcPol; EncRev; EncTR 91; OxCGer 76, 86; REn; WorAl; WorAlBi*

Rohmer, Eric
[Jean-Marie Maurice Scherer]
French. Director
Films include *My Night at Maud's,* 1970; *Full Moon in Paris,* 1984.
b. Dec 1, 1920 in Nancy, France

Source: *Benet 87, 96; BiDFilm, 81, 94; BioIn 9, 11, 12, 13, 14; CelR; ConAu 110; ConLC 16; ConTFT 12; CurBio 77; DcArts; DcTwCCu 2; EncEurC; FacFETw; FilmEn; FilmgC; HalFC 80, 84, 88; IntDcF 1-2, 2-2; IntMPA 92, 94, 96; IntWW 74, 75, 76, 77, 78, 79, 80, 81, 82, 83, 89, 91, 93; LegTOT; MiSFD 9; MovMk; NewYTBE 71; OxCFilm; RAdv 14; VarWW 85; Who 92, 94; WhoAm 76, 78, 80, 82, 84, 86, 88, 90, 92, 94, 95; WhoEnt 92; WhoFr 79; WhoWor 78, 80, 82, 84, 87, 89, 91, 93, 95, 96, 97; WorAl; WorAlBi; WorEFlm; WorFDir 2*

Rohmer, Sax
[Arthur Sarsfield Ward]
English. Author
Best known for "Fu-Manchu" series, which includes more than 30 novels.
b. Feb 15, 1883 in London, England
d. Jun 1, 1959 in London, England
Source: *BioIn 1, 4, 5, 6, 9, 13; CorpD; CrtSuMy; DcLB 70; EncMys; EncSF, 93; EvLB; FacFETw; LngCTC; MnBBF; NewC; NewEScF; Novels; PenC ENG; PenEncH; RAdv 14; ScF&FL 1, 92; ScFEYrs; SpyFic; SupFW; TwCA, SUP; TwCCr&M 80, 85, 91; TwCLC 28; TwCWr; WhoHr&F; WhoLA; WhoSpyF; WorAl; WorAlBi*

Rohrer, Heinrich
Swiss. Physicist
Shared the Nobel Prize for Physics with Ruska for their invention of the scanning tunneling microscope, 1986.
b. Jun 6, 1933, Switzerland
Source: *AmMWSc 89, 92, 95; BioIn 14, 15; CamDcSc; IntWW 89, 91, 93; LarDcSc; NobelP; NotTwCS; Who 90, 92, 94; WhoAm 90, 92, 94, 95, 96, 97; WhoNob 90, 95; WhoScEn 94, 96; WhoScEu 91-4; WhoWor 89, 91, 93, 95, 96, 97; WorAlBi*

Roh Tae Woo
Korean. Political Leader
Pres., S Korea, 1988-93; election marked the country's peaceful shift toward democracy; sentenced to 22-1/2 years in prison for crimes committed with former president Chun Doo-hwan, 1996.
b. Dec 4, 1932 in Taegu, Korea
Source: *BioIn 14, 15; CurBio 88; FacFETw; IntWW 89, 91, 93; NewYTBS 87; WhoAsAP 91; WhoWor 91, 93*

Rojankovsky, Feodor Stepanovich
Russian. Artist
Won 1956 Caldecott for *Frog Went A-Courtin'*.
b. Dec 24, 1891 in Mitava, Russia
d. Oct 21, 1970 in Bronxville, New York
Source: *AuBYP 2; BkP; Cald 1938; ChhPo, S1; IlsBYP; IlsCB 1744, 1946, 1957; JBA 51; NewbC 1956; NewYTBE 70; WhAm 5; WhoChL*

Rojas, Fernando de
Spanish. Author
Wrote Spanish classic *La Celestina*, 1499, considered comparable to *Don Quixote*.
b. 1475 in Toledo, Spain
d. Apr 1541 in Talavera, Spain
Source: *BioIn 5, 7, 10; CasWL; CyWA 58; DcEuL; DcSpL; EuAu; GrFLW; McGEWD 84; NewC; OxCEng 85; OxCSpan; OxCThe 83; PenC EUR; RAdv 14, 13-2; REn; RfGWoL 95; WhDW*

Rojas Pinilla, Gustavo
Colombian. Political Leader
President of Colombia, 1953-57; came to power in coup, ousted in one.
b. Mar 12, 1900 in Tunja, Colombia
d. Jan 17, 1975 in Bogota, Colombia
Source: *BiDLAmC; BioIn 3, 4, 5, 10, 16; CurBio 56, 75N; DcCPSAm; EncLatA; IntWW 74; McGEWB; NewYTBE 70; NewYTBS 75; ObitT 1971; WhAm 6*

Rojas Zorrilla, Francisco de
Spanish. Dramatist
Wrote tragedy *Garcia del Castanar.*
b. 1607 in Toledo, Spain
d. 1648 in Madrid, Spain
Source: *Benet 87, 96; BioIn 7, 8; CamGWoT; CasWL; DcSpL; EuAu; EvEuW; McGEWD 72, 84; NewCBEL; NewCol 75; OxCSpan; OxCThe 67, 83; REn; WebBD 83*

Roker, Al
[Albert Lincoln Roker, Jr.]
American. TV Personality
Weatherman, "Today," show, 1995—.
b. c. 1954 in New York, New York
Source: *ConBlB 12*

Roker, Roxie
American. Actor
Played Helen Willis on "The Jeffersons," 1975-85.
b. Aug 28, 1929 in Miami, Florida
d. Dec 2, 1995 in Los Angeles, California
Source: *BioIn 10, 21; ConTFT 8, 15; DrBlPA, 90; InB&W 85; LegTOT; News 96, 96-2; NotNAT A; VarWW 85; WhoAfA 96; WhoAm 80, 82; WhoBlA 85, 92, 94; WhoHol 92*

Rokossovsky, Konstantin Konstantinovich
Russian. Army Officer
Soviet WW II general; commanded forces defending Moscow, crushing German resistance outside of Stalingrad.
b. Dec 21, 1896
d. Aug 3, 1968 in Moscow, Union of Soviet Socialist Republics
Source: *ColdWar 1; CurBio 44, 68; FacFETw; GenMudB; NewCol 75; ObitT 1961; SovUn; WebBD 83*

Roland (de La Platiere), Jeanne-Marie
French. Revolutionary
Salon became forum for Girondin faction; influenced husband's ministry under King Louis XVI; famous last word: "O Liberty, what crimes are committed in thy name!"
b. Mar 17, 1754 in Paris, France
d. Nov 8, 1793 in Paris, France
Source: *BioIn 5, 6, 7, 8, 15; BlkwCE; CmFrR; DcWomA; EncCoWW; InWom SUP; OxCFr*

Roland, Duane
[Molly Hatchet]
American. Musician
Guitarist with heavy metal band since 1975.
b. Dec 3, 1952 in Jeffersonville, Indiana
Source: *OnThGG; WhoRocM 82*

Roland, Gilbert
American. Actor
Latin lover in films including *Camille*, 1936.
b. Dec 11, 1905 in Juarez, Mexico
Source: *BioIn 8, 10, 11, 12, 14, 16, 19, 20; Film 2; FilmEn; FilmgC; ForYSC; GangFlm; HalFC 80, 84, 88; HispAmA; HolP 30; IntMPA 75, 76, 77, 78, 79, 80, 81, 82, 84, 86, 88, 92, 94; ItaFilm; LegTOT; MexAmB; MotPP; MovMk; NewYTBS 94; TwYS; VarWW 85; WhoAm 86; WhoHisp 91, 92, 94N; WhoHol 92, A; WorAl; WorAlBi; WorEFlm*

Roland, Ruth
American. Actor
Starred in 11 silent films, 1915-23.
b. Aug 26, 1897 in San Francisco, California
d. Sep 22, 1937 in Los Angeles, California
Source: *Film 1; FilmgC; MotPP; TwYS; WhoHol B; WhScrn 74, 77*

Roldos Aguilera, Jamie
Ecuadorean. Political Leader
Youngest pres. in Western Hemisphere, tried to lead country toward democracy.
b. Nov 5, 1940 in Guayaquil, Ecuador
d. May 24, 1981 in Guachanama, Ecuador
Source: *ConAu 108; NewYTBS 79, 81*

Rolfe, John
English. Colonial Figure
Introduced tobacco cultivation to VA, 1612; married Pocahontas, 1614.
b. 1585
d. 1622 in Bermuda Hundred, Virginia
Source: *AmBi; AmWrBE; ApCAB SUP; BenetAL 91; BioIn 1, 4, 6; DcAmB; DcNaB; EncAAH; EncAB-H 1974, 1996; EncCRAm; McGEWB; NewCol 75; OxCAmH; OxCAmL 65, 83, 95; REn; REnAL; WhAm HS; WhDW; WhNaAH*

Rolfe, Red
[Robert Abial Rolfe]
American. Baseball Player, Baseball Manager
Third baseman, NY Yankees, 1931, 1934-42; manager, Detroit, 1949-52; manager of year, 1950.
b. Oct 11, 1908 in Penacook, New Hampshire
d. Jul 8, 1969 in Gilford, New Hampshire
Source: *Ballpl 90; BiDAmSp Sup; BioIn 8, 9, 14; DcAmB S8; LegTOT; WhoProB 73*

Rolland, Romain
[Saint Just]
French. Author, Dramatist
Won Nobel Prize, 1915, for epic *Jean Christophe*, 1904-12.
b. Jan 29, 1866 in Clamecy, France
d. Dec 30, 1944 in Vezelay, France
Source: *Baker 78, 84, 92; Benet 87, 96; BiDMoPL; BioIn 1, 2, 3, 4, 5, 8, 9, 10, 11, 12, 13, 15, 16, 17; CamGWoT; CasWL; ClDMEL 47, 80; CnMD; CnMWL; ConAu 118; CurBio 43; CyWA 58; DcAmSR; DcArts; DcBiA; DcLB 65; DcTwCCu 2; EncTR; EncWL 2, 3; EncWT; Ent; EvEuW; FacFETw; GuFrLit 1; LegTOT; LinLib L, S; LngCTC; MakMC; McGEWB; McGEWD 72, 84; ModFrL; ModRL; ModWD; NewC; NewEOp 71; NewGrDM 80; NewGrDO; NobelP; NotNAT B; Novels; OxCEng 67; OxCFr; OxCMus; PenC EUR; RAdv 14, 13-2; RComWL; REn; RfGWoL 95; TwCA, SUP; TwCLC 23; TwCWr; WhDW; WhE&EA; WhoNob, 90, 95; WhoTwCL; WorAl; WorAlBi*

Rolle, Esther
American. Actor
Played Florida Evans in two TV series "Maude," 1972-74; "Good Times," 1974-78.
b. Nov 8, 1933? in Pompano Beach, Florida
Source: *BioNews 74; BlksAmF; ConTFT 3; InB&W 85; IntMPA 86, 92; InWom SUP; LegTOT; NewYTBS 74; NotNAT; VarWW 85; WhoAm 86, 90; WhoAmW 91; WhoBlA 85, 88, 92; WhoThe 81; WorAlBi*

Roller, Alfred
Austrian. Designer
Influential opera designer; did sets for Mahler in Vienna.
b. Feb 10, 1864 in Vienna, Austria
d. Jun 21, 1935 in Vienna, Austria
Source: *EncWT; IntDcOp; MetOEnc; NewEOp 71; NewGrDM 80; NewGrDO; OxDcOp*

Rollin, Betty
American. Author, Broadcast Journalist
Wrote *First, You Cry*, 1976, about her coping with breast cancer, became a TV movie starring Mary Tyler Moore; with NBC since 1971, one of the first female reporters to become a network journalist.
b. Jan 3, 1936 in New York, New York
Source: *ArtclWW 2; BioIn 11, 12, 13, 14, 15; ConAu 7NR, 13R, 22NR; CurBio 94; EncTwCJ; ForWC 70; InWom SUP; LegTOT; WhoAm 80, 82, 84, 86, 88, 90, 92, 94, 95, 96, 97; WhoAmW 95, 97; WhoTelC*

Rolling Stones, The
[Mick Jagger; Brian Jones; Keith Richard; Mick Taylor; Charlie Watts; Ron Wood; Bill Wyman]
English. Music Group
Group formed, 1962; first US single "Not Fade Away," 1964; inducted into the Rock and Roll Hall of Fame in 1989.
Source: *BiDAmM; BioIn 7, 8, 10, 14, 15, 16, 17, 18, 19, 20, 21; BioNews 75; CelR; ConAu X; ConMuA 80A, 80B; ConMus 3; DcArts; DcCAr 81; DcTwCCu 1; EncPR&S 74, 89; EncRk 88; EncRkSt; FacFETw; HarEnR 86; IlEncRk; MugS; NewAmDM; NewGrDM 80; NewYTBS 83; ObitOF 79; OxCPMus; PenEncP; RkOn 74, 78; RolSEnR 83; VarWW 85; WhAm 5; WhoAm 74, 88; WhoAmP 83, 85, 87, 89, 91; WhoHol 92; WhoRock 81; WhoRocM 82; WhoVenC 86*

Rollini, Adrian
American. Jazz Musician
Bass saxist, later specialized on vibraphone, from 1935; led combos, 1940s-50s.
b. Jun 28, 1904 in New York, New York
d. May 15, 1956 in Homestead, Florida
Source: *BiDAmM; BiDJaz; BioIn 4; CmpEPM; IlEncJ; NewGrDA 86; NewGrDJ 88, 94; OxCPMus; PenEncP; WhoJazz 72*

Rollins, Carl Purington
American. Printer
Typographer; promoted simplicity, good taste in book design.
b. Jan 7, 1880
d. Nov 20, 1960
Source: *BioIn 1, 5, 6; CurBio 48, 61; OxCAmL 65, 83, 95; WhAm 4; WhAmArt 85*

Rollins, Howard Ellsworth, Jr.
American. Actor
In feature films *Ragtime*, 1981; *A Soldier's Story*, 1984; in television series "In the Heat of the Night," 1988-93.
b. Oct 17, 1950 in Baltimore, Maryland
d. Dec 8, 1996 in New York, New York
Source: *BioIn 14, 15; ConNews 86-1; ConTFT 6; IntMPA 88; JohnWSW; VarWW 85; WhoAm 92, 94, 95, 96; WhoEnt 92*

Rollins, Kenny
[Fabulous Five]
American. Basketball Player
Center, U of KY; member, gold medal-winning US Olympic team, 1948; played three yrs. in pros.
b. Sep 14, 1923 in Charleston, Missouri
Source: *WhoBbl 73*

Rollins, Sonny
[Theodore Walter Rollins]
American. Jazz Musician
Outstanding tenor saxist during, 1950s-60s; wrote music, played soundtrack for film *Alfie*, 1965.
b. Sep 7, 1930 in New York, New York
Source: *AllMusG; BiDAfM; BiDJaz; BioIn 10, 11, 12, 13, 16; ConMus 7; CurBio 76; DcArts; DrBlPA, 90; IlEncBM 82; IlEncJ; InB&W 85; NewAmDM; NewGrDA 86; NewGrDJ 88, 94; NewGrDM 80; WhoAm 76, 78, 80, 82, 90, 92, 94, 95, 96, 97; WhoBlA 90, 92, 94; WhoE 74; WhoEnt 92; WorAlBi*

Rollins, Wayne Monte
American. Basketball Player
Center 1977-93, mostly with Atlanta Hawks; led NBA in blocked shots, 1983.
b. Jun 16, 1955 in Winter Haven, Florida
Source: *OfNBA 87; WhoBlA 92*

Rolls, Charles Stewart
English. Auto Manufacturer
With F Royce formed Rolls-Royce Ltd, 1906.
b. Aug 27, 1877 in Hendre, England
d. Jul 12, 1910
Source: *BioIn 3, 7, 8, 9, 15, 17; DcNaB S2; DcTwBBL; InSci; WhDW; WorAl*

Roloff, Lester
American. Clergy
Radio ministry sponsored homes for rebellious children.
b. 1914?
d. Nov 2, 1982 in Normangee, Texas
Source: *BioIn 13; PrimTiR*

Rolvaag, Karl Fritjof
American. Government Official
Ambassador to Iceland, 1967-69; Dem. governor of MN, 1963-67.
b. Jul 18, 1913 in Northfield, Minnesota
d. Dec 20, 1990 in Northfield, Minnesota
Source: *BiDrGov 1789; BioIn 6, 7, 17; CurBio 64, 91N; WhAm 10; WhoAm 74; WhoAmP 73, 75, 77*

Rolvaag, Ole Edvart
American. Author
Wrote *Giants in the Earth*, 1927, describing Norwegian immigrants.
b. Apr 22, 1876 in Helgeland, Norway
d. Nov 5, 1931 in Northfield, Minnesota
Source: *AmAu&B; AmBi; Benet 87, 96; BenetAL 91; BioIn 2, 5, 9, 10, 12, 14, 16; CasWL; ClDMEL 80; CnDAL; ConAmA; CyWA 58; DcAmB; DcLEL; DcNAA; EncAAH; EncFWF; EncWL; EvLB; FacFETw; LngCTC; McGEWB; ModAL; OxCAmL 65; PenC AM; RAdv 14, 13-2; REn; REnAL; REnAW; TwCA, SUP; TwCWr; WebAB 74, 79; WebE&AL; WhAm 1; WhNAA*

Romains, Jules
French. Author, Philosopher
Founded literary movement, Unanimisme, 1908; wrote 27-vol. *Men of Good Will,* 1932-46.
b. Aug 26, 1885 in Velay, France
d. Aug 14, 1972 in Paris, France
Source: *Au&Wr 71; Benet 87, 96; BioIn 1, 4, 5, 7, 9, 10, 12, 16, 17; CamGWoT; CasWL; ClDMEL 47, 80; CnMD; CnMWL; ConAu 34NR, 85; ConLC 7; DcArts; DcLB 65; DcTwCCu 2; Dis&D; EncO&P 1, 2, 3; EncPaPR 91; EncWL 2, 3; EncWT; Ent; EvEuW; FacFETw; GuFrLit 1; LegTOT; LinLib L, S; LngCTC; MajTwCW; MakMC; McGEWD 72, 84; ModFrL; ModRL; ModWD; NewYTBE 72; NotNAT B; Novels; ObitT 1971; OxCEng 67; OxCFr; OxCThe 67, 83; PenC EUR; RAdv 14, 13-2; REn; ScF&FL 1A, 92; TwCA, SUP; TwCWr; WhAm 5; WhDW; WhE&EA; WhoThe 77; WhoTwCL; WhThe*

Roman, Ruth
American. Actor
Played in TV's "Long Hot Summer," 1965-66; films include *Dallas,* 1943.
b. Dec 23, 1924 in Boston, Massachusetts
Source: *ConTFT 5; FilmEn; FilmgC; ForYSC; GangFlm; HalFC 80, 84, 88; IntMPA 84, 86, 88, 92, 94, 96; LegTOT; MotPP; MovMk; VarWW 85; WhoHol A; WorEFlm*

Romani, Felice
Italian. Librettist
Foremost of his time; wrote approximately 100 librettos.
b. Jan 31, 1788 in Genoa, Italy
d. Jan 28, 1865 in Moneglia, Italy
Source: *Baker 78, 84, 92; BioIn 9; BriBkM 80; CmOp; IntDcOp; MetOEnc; NewEOp 71; NewGrDM 80; NewGrDO; NotNAT B; OxCThe 67*

Roman Nose
American. Native American Leader
Played key roles in the battle against white advancement in the American West.
b. 1830?
d. 1868
Source: *BioIn 11, 12; EncNAB; NotNaAm; WhNaAH*

Romano, Joseph
Israeli. Olympic Athlete, Victim
One of 11 members of Israeli Olympic team kidnapped and killed by Arab terrorists during Summer Olympic Games.
b. 1940?, Libya
d. Sep 5, 1972 in Munich, Germany (West)
Source: *BioIn 9*

Romano, Umberto
American. Artist, Educator
Noted for portraits of Martin Luther King, Jr., John F Kennedy.
b. Feb 26, 1906 in Bracigliano, Italy
d. Sep 27, 1982 in New York, New York
Source: *BioIn 13; CurBio 54, 82; NewYTBS 82; WhAm 8; WhoAm 74, 76, 78, 80, 82; WhoAmA 73; WhoWor 74*

Romanoff, Mike
[Harry Gerguson]
American. Restaurateur
Posed as Russian prince; owned most famous restaurant in Hollywood.
b. 1890 in Vilnius, Lithuania
d. Sep 1, 1971 in Los Angeles, California
Source: *BioIn 1, 2, 3, 4, 5, 6, 7, 9, 10; FilmgC; HalFC 80, 84, 88; LegTOT; What 3; WhoHol B*

Romanov, Anastasia
Russian. Princess
Daughter of Czar Nicholas II; long thought to have escaped family's execution, but never proven.
b. Jun 5, 1901 in Saint Petersburg, Russia
d. Jul 16, 1918 in Ekaterinburg, Union of Soviet Socialist Republics
Source: *NewCol 75*

Romantics, The
["Coz" (George) Canler; Rich Cole; Jimmy Marinos; Wally Palmer; Mike Skill]
American. Music Group
Gold album *In Heat,* 1983; top ten single "Talking in Your Sleep."
Source: *RkOn 85; WhoRocM 82; WhsNW 85*

Rombauer, Irma von Starkloff
American. Author
Wrote *The Joy of Cooking,* first published 1931, the most popular American cookbook in mid-20th c.
b. Oct 30, 1877 in Saint Louis, Missouri
d. Oct 14, 1962 in Saint Louis, Missouri
Source: *BioIn 2, 3, 6; CurBio 53, 62; InWom SUP*

Romberg, Bernhard
German. Composer, Musician
Cellist; wrote opera *Alma,* 1824; chamber music, cello works.
b. Nov 11, 1767 in Dinklage, Germany
d. Aug 13, 1841 in Hamburg, Germany
Source: *Baker 78, 84; BriBkM 80; OxCMus*

Romberg, Sigmund
American. Composer
Wrote operettas *Maytime,* 1917; *Student Prince,* 1924; 2000 songs including "Stout Hearted Men."
b. Jul 29, 1887 in Nagykanizsa, Austria-Hungary
d. Nov 9, 1951 in New York, New York
Source: *AmPS; AmSong; ASCAP 66, 80; Baker 78, 84, 92; BestMus; BiDAmM; BioIn 1, 2, 3, 4, 5, 6, 10, 12, 14, 15, 16; BriBkM 80; CmpEPM; ConAmC 76, 82; CurBio 45, 51; DcAmB S5; EncMT; EncWT; FacFETw; FilmEn; FilmgC; HalFC 80, 84, 88; LegTOT; LinLib S; MusMk; NewAmDM; NewCBMT; NewGrDA 86; NewGrDM 80; NewGrDO; NewOxM; NotNAT A, B; OxCAmH; OxCAmT 84; OxCMus; OxCPMus; OxDcOp; PenEncP; PlP&P; PopAmC; Sw&Ld C; WebAB 74, 79; WhAm 3; WhThe; WorAl; WorAlBi*

Rome, Harold J(acob)
American. Songwriter
Wrote score for *Call Me Mister,* 1946; song "Fanny," 1954; Theatre Hall of Fame, 1991.
b. May 27, 1908 in Hartford, Connecticut
d. Oct 26, 1993 in New York, New York
Source: *AmSong; ASCAP 66; BiDAmM; BiE&WWA; BioIn 1, 5, 6, 9, 10, 12, 15; CmpEPM; CurBio 42, 94N; EncMT; NewCBMT; NewGrDA 86; NotNAT; OxCAmT 84; WhAm 11; WhoAm 74, 76, 78, 80, 82, 84, 86, 88, 90, 92, 94; WhoAmA 73; WhoEnt 92; WhoMus 72; WhoWor 74; WhoWorJ 72, 78; WorAl*

Romer, Alfred Sherwood
American. Paleontologist
Mapped evolutionary record of vertebrate adaptations to the environment.
b. Dec 28, 1894 in White Plains, New York
d. Nov 5, 1973 in Cambridge, Massachusetts
Source: *BiESc; BioIn 10, 13, 14, 20; DcAmB S9; DcScB S2; LarDcSc; McGMS 80; NatCAB 61; NotTwCS; ObitOF 79; WhAm 6; WhoAm 74*

Romer, Roy R
American. Politician
Dem. governor of Colorado, 1987—.
b. Oct 31, 1928 in Garden City, Kansas
Source: *AlmAP 88, 92; BioIn 15; IntWW 91; WhoAm 90; WhoAmP 87, 91; WhoWest 92; WhoWor 91*

Romero, Carlos Humberto
Salvadoran. Political Leader
President of El Salvador, 1977-79; ousted in coup.
b. 1924 in Chalatenango, El Salvador
Source: *BioIn 12; IntWW 80; IntYB 79, 80, 81, 82; WhoWor 78; WorDWW*

Romero, Cesar
American. Actor
Latin lover in films, 1933—; played The Joker in "Batman" TV series.
b. Feb 15, 1907 in New York, New York
d. Jan 1, 1994 in Santa Monica, California
Source: *BiDFilm, 81; BioIn 4, 8, 11, 14, 19, 20; ConTFT 1, 12; DcHiB; EncAFC; FilmEn; FilmgC; ForYSC; GangFlm; HalFC 80, 84, 88; HispAmA; HolP 30; IntMPA 75, 76, 77, 78, 79, 80, 81, 82, 84, 86, 88, 92, 94; ItaFilm; LegTOT; MotPP; MovMk; WhoHisp 91, 92, 94N; WhoHol 92, A; WhoHrs 80; WorAl; WorAlBi; WorEFlm*

Romero, George A
American. Filmmaker, Screenwriter
Wrote, directed cult classic *Night of the Living Dead,* 1968.
b. 1940? in New York, New York
Source: *BioIn 13, 14, 15; ConAu 116; ConTFT 6; IntDcF 1-2, 2-2; IntMPA 92; VarWW 85*

Romero Barcelo, Carlos Antonio
Puerto Rican. Politician
Governor of Puerto Rico, 1977-85.
b. Sep 4, 1952 in San Juan, Puerto Rico
Source: *CurBio 77; WhoAm 84; WhoAmP 85*

Romero y Galdamez, Oscar Arnulfo
Salvadoran. Religious Leader
Archbishop of San Salvador who advocated human rights; assassinated.
b. Aug 15, 1917 in Ciudad Barrios, El Salvador
d. Mar 24, 1980 in San Salvador, El Salvador
Source: *BioIn 12, 13; NewYTBS 80*

Romiti, Cesare
"Il Duro"
Italian. Auto Executive
CEO of Fiat, Europe's auto giant, since 1980.
b. Jun 24, 1923 in Rome, Italy
Source: *BioIn 15; IntWW 83, 89, 91, 93; WhoFI 96; WhoWor 84, 89, 95, 96, 97*

Romm, Mikhail
Russian. Director
Films include *Nine Days in One Year; Lenin.*
b. Jan 24, 1901 in Irkutsk, Russia
d. Nov 1, 1971 in Moscow, Union of Soviet Socialist Republics
Source: *BiDFilm, 81, 94; DcFM; FilmEn; FilmgC; HalFC 80, 84, 88; IntDcF 1-2; NewYTBE 71; OxCFilm; WorEFlm*

Rommel, Erwin Johannes Eugin
"Desert Fox"
German. Army Officer
Former Hitler bodyguard best known for commanding German forces in Africa, 1941-43.
b. Nov 15, 1891 in Heidenheim, Germany
d. Jul 18, 1944 in Herrligen, Germany
Source: *CurBio 42, 44; EncTR; McGEWB; NewCol 75; OxCGer 76; REn; WhoMilH 76; WhWW-II; WorAl*

Romney, George
English. Artist
Famed London portraitist; painted Emma Hart (Lady Hamilton) over 50 times.
b. Dec 15, 1734 in Lancashire, England
d. Nov 15, 1802 in Kendal, England
Source: *Alli; AtlBL; BioIn 1, 3, 4, 5, 6, 7, 9, 10, 13, 14, 15; BkIE; DcArts; DcBiPP; DcBrECP; DcNaB; Dis&D; EncEnl; IntDcAA 90; LegTOT; LinLib S; McGDA; McGEWB; NewC; NewCol 75; OxCArt; OxCEng 67, 85, 95; OxDcArt; WebBD 83; WhDW*

Romney, George (Wilcken)
American. Auto Executive, Politician
Rep. governor of MI, 1962-69; pres., chm., American Motors, 1954-62.
b. Jul 8, 1907 in Chihuahua, Mexico
d. Jul 26, 1995 in Bloomfield Hills, Michigan
Source: *BiDrGov 1789; BiDrUSE 71, 89; BioIn 4, 5, 6, 7, 8, 9, 10, 11, 21; BlueB 76; CelR; ConAu 106; CurBio 58, 95N; EncABHB 5; IntWW 74, 75, 76, 77, 78, 79, 80, 81, 82, 83; LinLib S; Ward 77G; WhoAm 74, 76, 78, 80, 82, 84, 86, 88, 92, 94; WhoAmP 73, 75, 77, 79, 81, 83, 85; WhoFI 74; WhoGov 72, 75; WhoMW 74, 76, 78; WhoWor 74, 76, 78*

Romney, Seymour Leonard
American. Physician, Educator
Co-chairperson of Physicians for Choice; expert on human reproduction, population control.
b. Jun 8, 1917 in New York, New York
Source: *AmMWSc 82, 92; WhoAm 74, 76, 78, 80, 82, 84, 86, 88, 90, 92, 94, 95, 96, 97; WhoE 74*

Romulo, Carlos Pena
Philippine. Statesman, Journalist
One of the founders of UN, 1945; first Asian to serve as pres. of UN General Assembly.
b. Apr 14, 1899 in Manila, Philippines
d. Dec 15, 1985 in Manila, Philippines
Source: *AmAu&B; BiDrAC; BiDrUSC 89; BioIn 1, 2, 3, 4, 5, 6, 8, 10, 14, 15; CathA 1930; ConAu 13R; CurBio 43, 57; DcTwHis; FarE&A 78, 79, 80, 81; IntAu&W 77, 82; IntWW 74, 76, 77, 78, 79, 80, 81, 82, 83; IntYB 81, 82; McGEWB; WhNAA; WhoUN 75; WhoWor 74*

Romulus
Roman. Legendary Figure
Twin brother of Remus whose father was god Mars; founder, 753 BC, first king of Rome, 753-716 BC.
Source: *CasWL; DcBiPP; DcCanB 1; DcCathB; NewCol 75*

Ronald, Landon, Sir
[L R Russell]
English. Conductor, Composer
London light opera conductor, from 1909; interpreted Elgar; brother of Henry Russell.
b. Jun 7, 1873 in London, England
d. Aug 14, 1938 in London, England
Source: *Baker 78, 84, 92; BioIn 2; DcNaB 1931; NewEOp 71; NewGrDM 80; NewOxM; OxCMus; PenDiMP; WhE&EA; WhThe*

Ronan, William John
American. Government Official, Educator
First chm. of NYC's Metropolitan Transit Authority, 1968-74.
b. Nov 8, 1912 in Buffalo, New York
Source: *AmMWSc 73S, 78S; BioIn 5, 7, 8; CurBio 69; Dun&B 86; NewYTBE 70; NewYTBS 74; St&PR 84, 91; WhoAm 74, 76, 78, 80, 82, 84, 86, 88, 90, 92, 94, 95, 96, 97; WhoFI 92, 94, 96; WhoSSW 93, 95, 97; WhoWor 80, 82, 84, 87, 89, 91, 93, 95, 96, 97*

Roney, William Chapoton, Jr.
American. Financier
Partner in William C Roney and Co., 1949-84.
b. Dec 19, 1924 in Detroit, Michigan
d. Apr 26, 1984 in Grosse Pointe, Michigan
Source: *AmCath 80; St&PR 75; WhoAm 74, 76, 78, 80, 82; WhoFI 75, 77; WhoSecI 86*

Ronne, Finn
American. Explorer, Geographer
Made nine Antarctic trips, from 1933; explored over 3600 miles by dog sled; wrote *Antarctic Command,* 1961.
b. Dec 20, 1899 in Horten, Norway
d. Jan 12, 1980 in Bethesda, Maryland
Source: *AmMWSc 73S, 76P; AnObit 1980; BioIn 1, 4, 8, 12; ConAu 1NR, 1R, 97; CurBio 48, 80, 80N; FacFETw; InSci; WhAm 7; WhoAm 74, 76, 78; WhoWor 74*

Ronning, Chester A
Canadian. Diplomat
Instrumental in arranging peace talks between US and N Vietnam, 1966.
b. Dec 13, 1894 in Fancheng, China
d. Dec 31, 1984 in Camrose, Alberta, Canada
Source: *BioIn 13; CanWW 70; ConAu 114; NewYTBS 85*

Ronsard, Pierre de
French. Poet
Leader of the Pleiade; helped establish French sonnet; wrote *Amours,* 1552-59.
b. Sep 11, 1524 in Vendomois, France
d. Dec 26, 1585 in Touraine, France
Source: *AtlBL; BbD; Benet 87, 96; BiD&SB; BioIn 1, 4, 5, 7, 9, 10, 13, 21; BlmGEL; CasWL; ChhPo S3; CyWA 58; DcArts; DcBiPP; DcCathB; DcEuL; DeafPAS; Dis&D; EncDeaf; EuAu; EuWr 2; EvEuW; GrFLW; GuFrLit 2; LegTOT; LitC 6; LngCEL; McGEWB; NewC; NewGrDM 80; OxCEng 67, 85, 95; OxCFr; OxCMus; PenC EUR; PoeCrit 11; RAdv 14, 13-2; RComWL; REn; RfGWoL 95; WhDW; WorAl; WorAlBi*

Ronstadt, Linda
American. Singer
Has six platinum albums; starred on Broadway in *The Pirates of Penzance,* 1981; with James Ingram, singer of Academy Award winning song "Somewhere Out There," 1988.
b. Jul 15, 1946 in Tucson, Arizona
Source: *Baker 84; BiDAmM; BioIn 9, 10, 11, 12, 13, 16; BkPepl; CelR 90; ConMuA 80A; ConMus 2; ConTFT 9;*

CurBio 78; DcHiB; EncFCWM 83; EncPR&S 74, 89; EncRk 88; EncRkSt; GoodHs; GrLiveH; HarEnCM 87; IlEncCM; IlEncRk; InWom SUP; LegTOT; MexAmB; NewAmDM; NewGrDA 86; NewYTBS 86; NotHsAW 93; OxCPMus; RkOn 78; RolSEnR 83; VarWW 85; WhoAm 86, 90; WhoAmW 91; WhoEnt 92; WhoHisp 92; WhoHol 92; WhoRock 81; WhoRocM 82; WorAl; WorAlBi

Roomful of Blues
American. Music Group
Founded in 1967 by Duke Robillard; known for bluesy big band sound; current lineup listed above.
Source: *ConMus 7; PenEncP; St&PR 96; WhoRocM 82*

Rooney, Andy
[Andrew Aitken Rooney]
American. Author, Producer
Feature commentator on "60 Minutes," 1978—; author of eight books.
b. Jan 14, 1919 in Albany, New York
Source: *BiDAmNC; BioIn 12, 13, 14, 15, 16; CelR 90; ConTFT 5; CurBio 82; EncAHmr; EncTwCJ; IntMPA 92; LegTOT; LesBEnT 92; MajTwCW; NewYTET; VarWW 85; WhoAm 74, 76, 78, 80, 82, 84, 86, 88, 90, 92, 94, 95, 96, 97; WhoCom; WhoE 91, 93; WhoTelC; WhoUSWr 88; WhoWrEP 89, 92, 95; WorAlBi; WrDr 92, 96*

Rooney, Art(hur Joseph)
American. Football Executive
Owner, Pittsburgh Steelers, 1933-88; Hall of Fame, 1964.
b. Jan 27, 1901 in Coulterville, Pennsylvania
d. Aug 25, 1988 in Pittsburgh, Pennsylvania
Source: *BiDAmSp FB; BioIn 16, 17; LegTOT; News 89-1; NewYTBS 75, 88; WhAm 9; WhoAm 74, 76, 78, 80, 82, 84, 86, 88; WhoE 74, 79, 81, 83, 85, 86; WhoFtbl 74; WorAl; WorAlBi*

Rooney, John (James)
American. Politician
Influential NYC Dem. congressman, 1944-74.
b. Nov 29, 1903 in New York, New York
d. Oct 26, 1975 in Washington, District of Columbia
Source: *BiDrAC; BiDrUSC 89; BioIn 5, 7, 8, 9, 10, 11, 12; CurBio 64, 76; WhAm 6; WhoAm 74; WhoAmP 73; WhoE 74; WhoGov 72, 75*

Rooney, Mickey
[Joe Yule, Jr.]
American. Actor
Played Andy Hardy in film series, 1937-46; on Broadway in *Sugar Babies.*
b. Sep 23, 1920 in New York, New York
Source: *ASCAP 66, 80; BiDD; BiDFilm, 94; BioIn 7, 9, 10, 12, 13, 14, 15; CelR, 90; CmMov; CmpEPM; CurBio 42, 65; DcArts; EncAFC; Film 2; FilmEn; FilmgC; GangFlm; HalFC 80, 84, 88; IntDcF 1-3, 2-3; IntMPA 86, 92, 94, 96; ItaFilm; LegTOT; MGM; MotPP; MovMk; NewYTBS 81; OxCFilm; QDrFCA 92; VarWW 85; WhoAm 74, 76, 78, 80, 86, 90, 92, 94, 95, 96, 97; WhoCom; WhoEnt 92; WhoHol 92; WhoHrs 80; WorAl; WorAlBi; WorEFlm*

Rooney, Pat
American. Actor
Vaudeville star in *Show Business,* 1924; silent films, 1915-33.
b. Jul 4, 1880 in New York, New York
d. Sep 9, 1962 in New York, New York
Source: *ASCAP 66, 80; BiDD; BioIn 6; CmpEPM; DancEn 78; DcAmB S7; EncVaud; Film 2; NotNAT B; OxCAmT 84; WhoHol B; WhScrn 74, 77, 83*

Roos, Frank John, Jr.
American. Author, Educator
Wrote *An Illustrated Handbook of Art History,* 1937.
b. Jan 10, 1903 in Chicago, Illinois
d. Feb 2, 1967
Source: *BioIn 8; OhA&B; WhAm 4*

Roosa, Robert V(incent)
American. Economist, Government Official
With Federal Reserve Bank of New York, 1941-61; undersecretary of the Treasury for monetary affairs, 1961-64; concerned with the management of the country's debt.
b. Jun 21, 1918
d. Dec 23, 1993 in Port Chester, New York
Source: *AmMWSc 73S; BioIn 5, 6, 9, 11, 12; BlueB 76; ConAu 143; CurBio 94N; WhAm 11; WhoAm 74, 76, 78, 80, 82, 84, 86, 88, 92*

Roosa, Stuart Allen
American. Astronaut
Member of *Apollo 14,* Mar 1971.
b. Aug 16, 1933 in Durango, Colorado
d. Dec 12, 1994
Source: *IntWW 74; NewYTBE 71; WhoAm 86; WhoSSW 73; WhoWor 74, 76, 78, 80, 82, 84; WorDWW*

Roose-Evans, James
English. Author, Director
Wrote series of children's books, *The Adventures of Odd and Elsewhere,* beginning in 1971; has written radio plays, documentaries.
b. Nov 11, 1927 in London, England
Source: *ConAu 29R, 35NR; OxCChiL; OxCLiW 86; SmATA 65; TheaDir; TwCChW 78, 83, 89, 95; WhoThe 72, 77, 81; WrDr 76, 80, 82, 84, 86, 88, 90, 92, 94, 96*

Roosevelt, Alice Lee
[Mrs. Theodore Roosevelt]
American.
First wife of Theodore Roosevelt; mother of Alice Longworth.
b. Jul 29, 1861 in Chestnut Hill, Massachusetts
d. Feb 14, 1884 in New York, New York
Source: *FacPr 89; GoodHs; NotAW*

Roosevelt, Anna C(urtenius)
American. Archaeologist, Anthropologist
Conducted archaeological digs in the Amazon region since 1983; great-granddaughter of US pres. Theodore Roosevelt.
b. May 24, 1946, China

Roosevelt, Anna Eleanor
[Mrs. James A Halsted]
American.
Only daughter of Franklin and Eleanor Roosevelt; author of children's books.
b. May 3, 1906 in Hyde Park, New York
d. Dec 1, 1975 in New York, New York
Source: *BioAmW; BioIn 11, 12; ConAu 61; WhoE 74*

Roosevelt, Edith Kermit Carow
[Mrs. Theodore Roosevelt]
American. First Lady
Second wife of Theodore Roosevelt; married 1886.
b. Aug 16, 1861 in Norwich, Connecticut
d. Sep 30, 1948 in Oyster Bay, New York
Source: *BioIn 16, 17; FacPr 89; ForWC 70; InWom, SUP; NatCAB 14; NotAW; TwCBDA; WhAm 2, 2C; WomWWA 14*

Roosevelt, Eleanor
[Anna Eleanor Roosevelt; Mrs. Franklin Delano Roosevelt]
"The First Lady of the World"
American. First Lady, Social Reformer
Married Franklin D Roosevelt, 1905; US representative to UN, 1945, 1947-52, 1961; often chosen in polls as world's "most influential woman."
b. Oct 11, 1884 in New York, New York
d. Nov 7, 1962 in New York, New York
Source: *AmAu&B; AmDec 1930; AmJust; AmOrTwC; AmPeW; AmPolLe; AuBYP 2, 3; Benet 87; BenetAL 91; BiDAmNC; BiDInt; BiDSocW; BioIn 1, 2, 3, 4, 5, 6, 7, 8, 9, 10, 11, 12, 13, 14, 15, 16, 17, 18, 19, 20, 21; ConAu 89; ConHero 1; ContDcW 89; CurBio 40, 49, 63; DcAmB S7; DcAmDH 80, 89; DcPol; DcTwHis; EncAACR; EncAB-H 1974, 1996; EncCW; EncMcCE; EncWHA; FacFETw; FacPr 89; FemiCLE; GayLesB; GrLiveH; HanAmWH; HeroCon; HerW, 84; HisWorL; IntDcWB; InWom, SUP; JrnUS; LegTOT; LibW; LinLib L, S; LngCTC; McGEWB; MemAm; NatCAB 57; NotAW MOD; ObitT 1961; OxCAmH; OxCAmL 65, 83; PolPar; PolProf E, K, T; PorAmW; RadStar; RAdv 13-3; RComAH; REn; REnAL; SmATA 50; WebAB 74, 79; WhAm 4; WhAmP; WhoAmW 58, 61; WhWW-II; WomComm; WomFir; WomPubS 1925; WomStre; WorAl; WorAlBi*

Roosevelt, Elliott
American., Military Leader, Author
Son of Franklin and Eleanor Roosevelt; as WW II Air Corps general played key role in D-Day Invasion of Normandy, 1944; mayor of Miami Beach, 1065-69; author of trilogy on family.
b. Sep 23, 1910 in New York, New York
d. Oct 27, 1990 in Scottsdale, Arizona
Source: *AmAu&B; AnObit 1990; AuNews 1; BiDWWGF; BioIn 1, 2, 7, 9, 10, 11, 17; ConAu 105, 132; CurBio 46, 91N; NewYTBS 90; WhAm 10; WhoAm 74, 76; WrDr 90*

Roosevelt, Franklin D(elano)
"FDR"
American. US President
Dem., 32nd pres; served longest term, 1933-45; created New Deal to combat Depression; increased influence of federal govt. through expanded bureaucracy; died in office.
b. Jan 30, 1882 in Hyde Park, New York
d. Apr 12, 1945 in Warm Springs, Georgia
Source: *AmAu&B; AmDec 1930; AmOrTwC; AmPolLe; ApCAB X; Benet 87, 96; BiDInt; BiDrAC; BiDrGov 1789; BiDrUSE 71, 89; BioIn 1, 2, 3, 4, 5, 6, 7, 8, 9, 10, 11, 12, 13; ColdWar 1, 2; ConAu 116; ConHero 2; CopCroC; CurBio 42, 45; DcAmB S3; DcNAA; DcTwHis; Dis&D; EncAAH; EncAB-A 5; EncAB-H 1974, 1996; EncCW; EncTR 91; EncUrb; EvLB; FacFETw; FacPr 89, 93; FilmgC; HalFC 80, 84, 88; HarEnMi; HealPre; HisEWW; HisWorL; LegTOT; LinLib L; LngCTC; McGEWB; MemAm; NatCAB 37; OxCAmH; OxCAmL 65, 83, 95; OxCSupC; PolPar; REn; REnAL; WebAB 74, 79; WhAm 2, 2C, 4A, HSA; WhAmP; WhDW; WhWW-II; WorAl; WorAlBi*

Roosevelt, Franklin Delano, Jr.
American. Politician
Fourth child of Franklin and Eleanor Roosevelt; Liberal Party congressman from NY, 1950-54.
b. Aug 17, 1914 in Campobello Island, New Brunswick, Canada
d. Aug 17, 1988 in Poughkeepsie, New York
Source: *BiDrAC; BiDrUSC 89; BioIn 1, 2, 3, 6, 7, 11; CurBio 50, 88; IntWW 74, 75, 76, 77, 78, 79, 80, 81; NewYTBS 88; PolProf J, K; WhAm 9; WhoAm 74, 76; WhoE 74, 75, 77; WhoGov 72*

Roosevelt, James
American., Politician
First son of Franklin and Eleanor Roosevelt; Democratic congressman from CA, 1955-66; author of several books on family; awarded Navy Cross and Silver Star during World War II.
b. Dec 23, 1907 in New York, New York
d. Aug 13, 1991 in Newport Beach, California
Source: *AnObit 1991; BiDrAC; BiDrUSC 89; BioIn 1, 2, 3, 7, 8, 11, 15, 17, 18; ConAu 12NR, 69, 135; CurBio 50, 91N; NewYTBS 91; PolProf T; WhAm 10; WhoAm 74, 76, 78, 80, 82, 84, 86, 88, 90; WhoAmP 73; WhoWor 80, 84*

Roosevelt, John Aspinal
American.
Youngest child of Franklin and Eleanor Roosevelt; supported Republican candidates in later years.
b. Mar 13, 1916 in Hyde Park, New York
d. Apr 27, 1981 in New York, New York
Source: *BioIn 1, 2, 3, 4, 12; PolProf T; St&PR 75; WhAm 7; WhoAm 80*

Roosevelt, Kermit
American.
Son of Theodore Roosevelt; traveled with father to Africa, S America; wrote *War in the Garden of Eden,* 1919; died in military service.
b. Oct 10, 1889 in Oyster Bay, New York
d. Jun 4, 1943 in Fort Richardson, Alaska
Source: *AmAu&B; BenetAL 91; BioIn 1; CurBio 43; DcAmB S3; DcNAA; InSci; LegTOT; NatCAB 33; REnAL; WhAm 2; WhNAA*

Roosevelt, Quentin
American.
Son of Theodore Roosevelt; shot down, killed in action, WW I.
b. Nov 19, 1897 in Washington, District of Columbia
d. Jul 14, 1918 in Cambrai, France
Source: *BioIn 1, 5; InSci*

Roosevelt, Sara Delano
American.
Mother of President Franklin D Roosevelt.
b. Sep 21, 1855 in Newburgh, New York
d. Sep 7, 1941 in Hyde Park, New York
Source: *BioAmW; CurBio 41; InWom*

Roosevelt, Theodore
American. US President
Rep., 26th pres., 1901-09; promoted activist foreign policy, conservation; first American to win Nobel Peace Prize, 1906, for mediating end to Russo-Japanese War.
b. Oct 27, 1858 in New York, New York
d. Jan 6, 1919 in Oyster Bay, New York
Source: *Alli SUP; AmAu&B; AmBi; AmDec 1900; AmLY; AmOrTwC; AmPolLe; AmRef; ApCAB, SUP; BbD; Benet 87, 96; BenetAL 91; BiD&SB; BiDInt; BiDrAC; BiDrGov 1789; BiDrUSC 89; BiDrUSE 71, 89; BiInAmS; BioIn 1, 2, 3, 4, 5, 6, 7, 8, 9, 10, 11, 12, 13, 14, 15, 16, 17, 18, 19, 20, 21; BritAS; Chambr 3; ChhPo, S1, S2, S3; ConAu 115; CopCroC; CyAG; DcAmAu; DcAmB; DcAmC; DcAmImH; DcAmMiB; DcAmSR; DcLB 47; DcNAA; Dis&D; EncAAH; EncAB-H 1974, 1996; EncEnv; EncFWF; EncSoH; EnvEnc; EvLB; Expl 93; FacFETw; FacPr 89, 93; FilmgC; GayN; HalFC 80, 84, 88; HarEnUS; HealPre; HisWorL; InSci; LegTOT; LinLib L, S; LngCTC; McGEWB; MemAm; NatCAB 9, 11, 14; NatLAC; NobelP; OxCAmH; OxCAmL 65, 83, 95; OxCMus; OxCShps; PenC AM; PolPar; PresAR; RAdv 14, 13-3; RComAH; REn; REnAL; REnAW; TwCBDA; VicePre; WebAB 74, 79; WebAMB; WhAm 1, 4A, HSA; WhAmP; WhDW; WhoNob, 90, 95; WorAl; WorAlBi*

Roosevelt, Theodore, Jr.
American., Military Leader
Eldest son of Theodore Roosevelt; only general to land with first wave of troops in D-Day Invasion of Normandy, June 6, 1944.
b. Sep 13, 1887 in Oyster Bay, New York
d. Jul 12, 1944 in Cherbourg, France
Source: *AmAu&B; BiDWWGF; BioIn 1, 5, 7; ChhPo; CurBio 44; DcAmB S3; DcNAA; LinLib L; MedHR, 94; NatCAB 48; WebAMB; WhAm 2*

Root, Elihu
American. Statesman
US Secretary of War, 1899-1904, State, 1905-09; won Nobel Peace Prize, 1912, for efforts toward international peace.
b. Feb 15, 1845 in Clinton, New York
d. Feb 7, 1937 in New York, New York
Source: *AmAu&B; AmBi; AmPeW; AmPolLe; ApCAB, SUP, X; BiDInt; BiDrAC; BiDrUSC 89; BiDrUSE 71, 89; BiInAmS; BioIn 1, 3, 4, 6, 7, 9, 10, 11, 14, 15, 16, 19; CyAG; DcAmB S2; DcAmDH 80, 89; DcAmMiB; DcAmSR; DcNAA; DcTwHis; EncAB-H 1974, 1996; FacFETw; HarEnMi; HarEnUS; HisWorL; LegTOT; LinLib L, S; McGEWB; NatCAB 7, 14, 26; NobelP; OxCAmH; OxCLaw; PolPar; REnAL; TwCBDA; WebAB 74, 79; WebAMB; WhAm 1; WhAmP; WhoMilH 76; WhoNob, 90, 95; WorAl; WorAlBi*

Root, Jack
American. Boxer
First champ of light-heavyweight division, 1903; Hall of Fame, 1961.
b. May 26, 1876, Austria
d. Jun 10, 1963 in Los Angeles, California
Source: *BiDAmSp BK; BioIn 6; WhoBox 74*

Root, John Wellborn
American. Architect
Member, Chicago school; developed steel frame office buildings, 1880s.
b. Jan 10, 1850 in Lumpkin, Georgia
d. Jan 15, 1891 in Chicago, Illinois
Source: *BiDAmAr; BioIn 3, 8, 10; DcAmB; EncAB-H 1974, 1996; EncMA; IntDcAr; MacEA; McGDA; NatCAB 8; NewCol 75; OxCAmH; OxCAmL 65, 83,*

95; WebAB 74, 79; WebBD 83; WhAm 4, HS; WhoArch; WorAl; WorAlBi

Root, Lynn
American. Dramatist
Wrote Broadway play with all-black cast: *Cabin In the Sky,* 1940; filmed, 1942.
b. Apr 11, 1905 in Morgan, Minnesota
Source: *BiE&WWA; NotNAT*

Root, Oren
American. Lawyer, Politician
Special assistant to Gov. Nelson Rockefeller (NY), 1959-64.
b. Jun 13, 1911
d. Jan 14, 1995 in Bedford, New York
Source: *AmCath 80; BioIn 2, 3, 6, 8, 20, 21; ConAu 85; CurBio 95N; WhAm 11; WhoAm 74, 76, 78, 80, 82, 84, 86, 88, 90, 92, 94, 95; WhoAmL 78, 79, 83; WhoFI 74*

Rootes, William Edward Rootes, Baron
English. Business Executive
Chairman, Chrysler UK, 1967-73; director, Lucas Industries, 1973—.
b. Jun 14, 1917 in Loose, England
d. 1992
Source: *IntWW 81, 91; Who 74, 92; WhoFI 77*

Roper, Daniel C(alhoun)
American. Lawyer, Politician
Head of Internal Revenue Service, 1917-20, first to enforce Prohibition; FDR's first secretary of Commerce, 1933-38.
b. Apr 1, 1867 in Marlboro, South Carolina
d. Apr 11, 1943 in Washington, District of Columbia
Source: *BiDrUSE 71; BioIn 8, 10; CurBio 43; DcAmB S3; EncAB-A 1; NatCAB 31; WhAm 2*

Roper, Elmo Burns, Jr.
American. Businessman
Public opinion analyst; rival of George Gallup; developed modern opinion polls.
b. Jul 31, 1900 in Hebron, Nebraska
d. Apr 30, 1971 in Norwalk, Connecticut
Source: *AmAu&B; CurBio 45, 71; DcAmB S9; EncAB-A 30; EncAI&E; NewYTBE 71*

Rorem, Ned
American. Composer
Won 1976 Pulitzer for Bicentennial commission: *Air Music;* published many diaries.
b. Oct 23, 1923 in Richmond, Indiana
Source: *AmAu&B; AmComp; ASCAP 66, 80; Baker 78, 84, 92; BiDAmM; BioIn 1, 4, 6, 7, 8, 9, 10, 11, 12, 13, 14, 15, 16, 19, 20; BlueB 76; BriBkM 80; CelR 90; CompSN, SUP; ConAmC 76, 82; ConAu 17R, 32NR; ConCom 92; CpmDNM 72, 73, 79, 80, 81, 82; CurBio 67; CyWA 89; DcCM; DcTwCCu 1; EncWB; GayLL; IndAu 1917; IntWWM 77, 80, 85, 90; LegTOT; LinLib L; MetOEnc; MusMk; NewAmDM; NewEOp 71; NewGrDA 86; NewGrDM 80; NewGrDO; NewOxM; NewYTBS 76; WhoAm 74, 76, 78, 80, 82, 84, 86, 88, 90, 92, 94, 95, 96, 97; WhoAmM 83; WhoE 74, 75, 77, 79, 81, 83, 85, 86, 89, 91; WhoMus 72; WhoUSWr 88; WhoWor 74, 76, 82, 87; WhoWrEP 89, 92, 95; WorAu 1975*

Rorke, Hayden
American. Actor
Best known as Dr. Alfred Bellows on TV's "I Dream of Jeannie," 1965-70; appeared in over 50 films, 70 plays.
b. Oct 23, 1910 in New York, New York
d. Aug 19, 1987 in Toluca Lake, California
Source: *ConTFT 5; EncAFC*

Rorschach, Hermann
Swiss. Psychiatrist
Developed Rorschach inkblot test, 1921, used in psychological analysis.
b. Nov 8, 1884 in Zurich, Switzerland
d. Apr 2, 1922 in Herisau, Switzerland
Source: *AsBiEn; BiDPsy; BioIn 5, 14; NamesHP; WorAl; WorAlBi*

Rosa, Carl
German. Impresario
Formed London's Carl Rosa Opera Co., 1870s; often producing operas in English.
b. Mar 21, 1842 in Hamburg, Germany
d. Apr 30, 1889 in Paris, France
Source: *Baker 78, 84, 92; MusMk; NewEOp 71; NewGrDM 80; OxDcOp; PenDiMP*

Rosa, Salvator
Italian. Artist, Poet
Member, Neapolitan school; painted battle scenes, marines, romantic landscapes.
b. Jun 20, 1615 in Naples, Italy
d. Mar 15, 1673 in Rome, Italy
Source: *AtlBL; Baker 84; BbD; BiD&SB; BioIn 1, 2, 5, 6, 7, 9, 10, 13, 19; ClaDrA; DcArts; DcBiPP; DcEuL; IntDcAA 90; McGDA; McGEWB; NewCol 75; NewGrDM 80; OxCArt; OxCEng 85, 95; OxCMus; OxDcArt*

Rosas, Juan Manuel de
Argentine. Political Leader, Military Leader
Dictator of Argentina, 1835-52; defeated at the Battle of Caseros, February 3, 1852.
b. Mar 30, 1793 in Buenos Aires, Argentina
d. Mar 14, 1877 in Southampton, England
Source: *Benet 87, 96; BiDLAmC; BioIn 2, 3, 6, 9, 12, 13, 16; DcHiB; EncLatA; HisDcSE; HisWorL; McGEWB; REn*

Rosay, Francoise
[Francoise Brandy de Naleche]
French. Actor
Star in over 100 films, 1913-74.
b. Apr 19, 1891 in Paris, France
d. Mar 28, 1974 in Paris, France
Source: *BiE&WWA; BioIn 5, 6, 10, 14; EncEurC; Film 2; FilmAG WE; FilmEn; FilmgC; ForYSC; HalFC 80, 84, 88; IlWWBF A; IntDcF 1-3, 2-3; InWom; ItaFilm; MotPP; MovMk; NewYTBS 74; ObitT 1971; OxCFilm; Who 74; WhoHol B; WhoThe 72; WhScrn 77, 83; WhThe; WorEFlm*

Rosbaud, Hans
Austrian. Conductor
Led Aix-en-Provence Festival, 1947-59; noted for performing modern works.
b. Jul 22, 1895 in Graz, Austria
d. Dec 30, 1962 in Lugano, Switzerland
Source: *Baker 78, 84, 92; BioIn 6, 14, 17; BriBkM 80; CmOp; IntDcOp; MetOEnc; NewAmDM; NewEOp 71; NewGrDM 80; NewGrDO; OxDcOp; PenDiMP; WhAm 4*

Rosberg, Keke
Swedish. Auto Racer
Formula One racer; world champion, 1982.
b. Dec 6, 1948 in Stockholm, Sweden
Source: *BioIn 14, 15; WhoWor 82*

Rosburg, Bob
[Robert Rosburg]
American. Golfer
Turned pro, 1953; won PGA, 1959.
b. Oct 21, 1926 in San Francisco, California
Source: *WhoGolf*

Rose, Axl
[Guns N' Roses; William Bailey]
American. Singer
Lead singer, rock group Guns n' Roses, 1986—; albums include *Appetite for Destruction,* 1987; *Use Your Illusion I, II,* 1991.
b. Feb 6, 1962 in Lafayette, Indiana
Source: *BioIn 16; News 92, 92-1; WhoEnt 92*

Rose, Billy
[William S Rosenburg]
American. Producer, Lyricist
Musicals included *Jumbo,* 1935; *Carmen Jones,* 1943; opened NYC's famed nightclub Diamond Horseshoe, 1938; wed to Fanny Brice.
b. Sep 6, 1899 in New York, New York
d. Feb 10, 1966 in Montego Bay, Jamaica
Source: *AmPS; ASCAP 66, 80; BiDAmNC; BiE&WWA; BioIn 1, 2, 3, 4, 5, 6, 7, 8, 15, 17; ChhPo S2; CmpEPM; ConAu 116; CurBio 40, 66; DcAmB S8; EncMT; EncVaud; FacFETw; HalFC 80, 84, 88; JeAmHC; LegTOT; NewGrDA 86; NotNAT A, B; OxCAmT 84; OxCPMus; PenEncP; Sw&Ld C; WhAm 4; WhThe; WorAl; WorAlBi*

Rose, Carl
[Earl Cros]
Cartoonist, Illustrator
Contributed cartoons to *New Yorker* mag. from 1925; illustrated many books for children, adults.
b. 1903 in New York, New York
d. Jun 21, 1971 in Rowayton, Connecticut
Source: *BioIn 14; ConAu 29R; SmATA 31; WorECar*

Rose, Charlie
[Charles Peete Rose, Jr.]
American. TV Personality
Host of "Nightwatch," 1984-90; "The Charlie Rose Show," 1991—.
b. Jan 5, 1942 in Henderson, North Carolina
Source: *ConTFT 12; CurBio 95; IntMPA 96*

Rose, David
English. Songwriter, Conductor
Music director for many TV shows; won 22 Grammys, four Emmys; wrote "Holiday for Strings," 1943; once wed to Judy Garland.
b. Jun 15, 1910 in London, England
d. Aug 23, 1990 in Burbank, California
Source: *AnObit 1990; ASCAP 66; BiDAmM; BioIn 1, 3, 6, 17; CmpEPM; FilmgC; HalFC 80, 84, 88; IntMPA 75, 76, 77, 78, 79, 80, 81, 82, 84, 86, 88; NewYTBS 90; OxCPMus; PenEncP; PopAmC; RadStar; RkOn 74; VarWW 85; WhAm 10; WhoAm 74, 76, 78, 80, 82, 84, 86, 88; WhoAmA 80, 82, 84, 86, 89, 91, 93; WhoWest 82, 84, 87; WhoWor 80, 84; WhoWorJ 72*

Rose, Fred
American. Singer
Popularized country music, 1940s-50s; often collaborated with Gene Autry.
b. Aug 24, 1897 in Evansville, Indiana
d. Dec 1, 1954 in Nashville, Tennessee
Source: *ASCAP 66, 80; BgBkCoM; BiDAmM; BioIn 3, 16; CmpEPM; EncFCWM 69; HarEnCM 87A; IlEncCM; NewAmDM; NewGrDA 86; OxCPMus; PenEncP*

Rose, George Walter
English. Actor
Won Tonys for *The Mystery of Edwin Drood,* 1986; *My Fair Lady,* 1976.
b. Feb 19, 1920 in Bicester, England
d. May 5, 1988 in Puerto Plata, Dominican Republic
Source: *BiE&WWA; ConTFT 4; CurBio 84, 88; FilmgC; MovMk; NotNAT; VarWW 85; WhoAm 94; WhoHol A; WhoThe 77*

Rose, Helen Bronberg
[Mrs. Harry Rose]
American. Fashion Designer
Won Oscars for designs in *The Bad and the Beautiful,* 1952; *I'll Cry Tomorrow,* 1955; designed wedding dress for Princess Grace, 1956.
b. 1904? in Chicago, Illinois
d. Nov 9, 1985 in Palm Springs, California
Source: *ConAu 117; WhoAm 76; WhoAmW 74; WorFshn*

Rose, Leonard
[Leonard Rozofsky]
American. Musician, Educator
Well-known cellist, teacher, who was first cellist with the NY Philharmonic, 1944-56.
b. Jul 27, 1918 in Washington, District of Columbia
d. Nov 16, 1984 in White Plains, New York
Source: *AnObit 1984; Baker 78, 84; BiDAmM; BioIn 2, 4, 7, 9, 11, 14; BriBkM 80; CurBio 77, 85N; IntWW 76, 77, 78, 79, 80, 81, 82, 83; IntWWM 77, 80; MusSN; NewAmDM; NewGrDA 86; NewGrDM 80; NewYTBE 71; NewYTBS 84; PenDiMP; WhAm 8; WhoAm 74, 76, 78, 80, 82, 84; WhoAmM 83; WhoMus 72; WhoWor 74, 78, 80*

Rose, Murray
[Iain Murray Rose]
Australian. Swimmer
Won three gold medals, 1956 Olympics.
b. Jan 6, 1939 in Nairn, Scotland
Source: *BioIn 5, 6, 7, 10*

Rose, Pete(r Edward)
"Charlie Hustle"
American. Baseball Player, Baseball Manager
Outfielder-infielder, 1963-86, mostly with Cincinnati; holds many ML hitting records, including most hits in career, 4,256, passing Ty Cobb, 1985; banished from baseball for gambling on games, 1989.
b. Apr 14, 1941 in Cincinnati, Ohio
Source: *Ballpl 90; BaseReg 86, 87; BiDAmSp BB; BioIn 14, 15, 16, 17, 18, 19, 20; LegTOT; News 91, 91-1; NewYTBE 73; NewYTBS 84, 85, 89; WhoAm 86, 88, 90, 92, 94, 95, 96, 97; WhoMW 88, 90; WhoProB 73; WorAl; WorAlBi*

Rose, Vincent
American. Bandleader, Songwriter
Led dance bands, 1920s-30s; wrote "Avalon," 1920; "Pretty Baby," 1931.
b. Jun 13, 1880 in Palermo, Sicily, Italy
d. May 20, 1944 in Rockville Centre, New York
Source: *ASCAP 66, 80; BiDAmM; CmpEPM; OxCPMus*

Rose, Wendy
[Bronwen Elizabeth Edwards; Chiron Khanshandel]
American. Poet, Writer
Poetry collections include *Hopi Roadrunner Dancing,* 1973; *The Halfbreed Chronicles and Other Poems,* 1985.
b. May 7, 1948 in Oakland, California
Source: *BioIn 11; ConAu 5NR, 51NR, 53, X; ConLC 85; DcNAL; DrAP 75; DrAPF 80; EncNAB; FemiCLE; InWom SUP; NatNAL; NotNaAm; PenNWW A, B; PoeCrit 13; RfGAmL 94; SmATA 12*

Roseanne
American. Comedian, Actor
Housewife-turned-comedian; star of TV comedy "Roseanne," 1988-97.
b. Nov 3, 1952 in Salt Lake City, Utah
Source: *BioIn 15; IntMPA 96; News 89-1; NewYTBS 91; WhoAm 96, 97; WhoAmW 95, 97; WhoEnt 92*

Rosebery, Archibald Philip Primrose, Earl
English. Political Leader, Author, Statesman
Liberal leader, 1894-5, appointed by Victoria after Gladstone retired; wrote biographies.
b. May 7, 1847 in London, England
d. May 21, 1929 in Epsom, England
Source: *BiD&SB; BioIn 3, 5, 6, 8, 9, 10, 21; Chambr 3; CmScLit; EvLB; LngCTC; NewCol 75; OxCEng 67*

Roseboro, Johnny
"Gabby"
American. Baseball Player
Catcher, 1957-70, mostly with Dodgers.
b. May 13, 1933 in Ashland, Ohio
Source: *Ballpl 90; ConAu 102; InB&W 85; WhoAm 74; WhoBlA 85; WhoProB 73*

Rosecrans, William Starke
American. Army Officer, Diplomat
Union general, led Army of the Cumberland; defeated at Chickamauga, 1863; minister to Mexico, 1860s.
b. Sep 6, 1819 in Delaware County, Ohio
d. Mar 11, 1898 in Redondo Beach, California
Source: *AmBi; ApCAB; BiAUS; BiDrAC; BiDrUSC 89; BioIn 1, 2, 6, 7, 16; CivWDc; CmCal; DcAmB; DcAmDH 80, 89; DcAmMiB; DcCathB; Drake; HarEnMi; HarEnUS; NatCAB 4; OxCAmH; TwCBDA; WebAB 74, 79; WebAMB; WhAm HS; WhCiWar; WorAl; WorAlBi*

Rose-Marie
[Rose-Marie Mazzatta]
American. Comedian
Played Sally Rogers on "The Dick Van Dyke Show," 1961-66.
b. Aug 15, 1925 in New York, New York
Source: *VarWW 85; WhoHol A; WorAl*

Rosen, Al(bert Leonard)
"Flip"
American. Baseball Player, Baseball Executive
Third baseman, Cleveland, 1947-56; led AL in home runs, RBIs twice; AL MVP, 1953 ; general manager, Houston, 1980-85, San Francisco, 1985-92.

b. Mar 1, 1925 in Spartanburg, South Carolina
Source: *BioIn 2, 3, 4, 5; CurBio 54; WhoAm 86, 88; WhoMus 72; WhoProB 73; WhoWest 87*

Rosen, Barry
[The Hostages]
American. Hostage
One of 52 held by terrorists, Nov 1979-Jan 1981.
b. 1944?
Source: *BioIn 13; ConAu 136; NewYTBS 81; WrDr 94, 96*

Rosen, Benjamin M(aurice)
American. Entrepreneur
Established, with brother Harold, Rosen Motors, 1993, which designed a new power train that runs on electricity.
b. Mar 11, 1933 in New Orleans, Louisiana
Source: *Dun&B 86, 88, 90; LElec; WhoAm 86, 88, 90, 92, 94, 95, 96, 97; WhoE 95; WhoFI 87, 89, 94, 96; WhoSSW 91, 93, 95, 97; WhoWor 95*

Rosen, Harold A.
American. Entrepreneur, Engineer
Established, with brother Maurice, Rosen Motors, 1993, which designed a new power train that runs on electricity.
b. Mar 20, 1926 in New Orleans, Louisiana
Source: *AmMWSc 79, 82, 86, 92, 95; LElec; WhoEng 80, 88; WhoScEn 96*

Rosen, Moishe Martin
American. Religious Leader
Founded Jews for Jesus, 1970.
b. Apr 12, 1932 in Kansas City, Missouri
Source: *ConAu 4NR; RelLAm 91; WhoRel 85, 92; WhoWest 78, 80, 82, 92*

Rosen, Nathaniel
American. Musician
First American cellist to win coveted Tchaikovsky award, Moscow, 1978.
b. Jun 9, 1948? in Altadena, California
Source: *Baker 84; BioIn 11; IntWWM 90; NewGrDA 86; WhoAm 86, 90; WhoE 91; WhoEmL 87; WhoEnt 92*

Rosen, Sidney
American. Children's Author
Biographies of scientists include *Harmonious World of Johann Kepler,* 1962.
b. Jun 5, 1916 in Boston, Massachusetts
Source: *AmMWSc 73P, 76P, 79, 82, 86, 89, 92, 95; BioIn 9; ConAu 9R; IntAu&W 76, 77, 82, 86, 89; LEduc 74; SmATA 1; WhoMW 90; WrDr 76, 80, 82, 84, 86, 88, 90, 92, 94, 96*

Rosenbach, Abraham Simon Wolf
"Dr. Rosenbach"
American. Bookseller, Author
Legendary rare-book dealer; helped build America's finest book collections; wrote three memoirs.
b. Jul 22, 1876 in Philadelphia, Pennsylvania
d. Jul 1, 1952 in Philadelphia, Pennsylvania
Source: *AmAu&B; BioIn 1, 2, 3, 4, 5, 7, 13, 18, 20; ChhPo, S1, S2; DcAmB S5; LngCTC; OxCAmL 65; REnAL; WebAB 74, 79; WhAm 3*

Rosenberg, Alfred
"Grand Inquisitor of the Third Reich"
German. Political Leader, Author
Nazi ideologist; molded Hitler's policies; hanged by war tribunal.
b. Jan 12, 1893 in Reval, Russia
d. Oct 16, 1946 in Nuremberg, Germany
Source: *BiDExR; BiDSovU; BioIn 1, 8, 9, 14, 16, 18, 21; CurBio 41, 46; DcPol; DcTwHis; Dis&D; EncRev; EncTR, 91; HisEWW; LngCTC; ObitOF 79; REn; WhWW-II*

Rosenberg, Anna Marie
American. Government Official
Named assistant secretary of Defense by Truman, 1950, highest position ever held by woman in nat. military establishment.
b. Jul 19, 1900 in Budapest, Austria-Hungary
d. May 9, 1983 in New York, New York
Source: *CurBio 43, 51; LibW; PolProf T; WhoAmW 70*

Rosenberg, Ethel Greenglass
American. Traitor
US communist convicted of giving secrets to USSR; first civilian executed for espionage.
b. Sep 28, 1915 in New York, New York
d. Jun 19, 1953 in Ossining, New York
Source: *ColdWar 2; ConAu 16NR; DcAmB S5; EncMcCE; HanAmWH; InWom, SUP; NotAW MOD; PolProf E, T; SpyCS; WebAB 79; WhoAmW 77; WomFir; WorAl*

Rosenberg, Evelyn Edelson
American. Artist
Sculptor, printmaker; innovative works produced by using plastic explosives.
b. 1942 in Washington, District of Columbia
Source: *BioIn 16; News 88-2*

Rosenberg, Hilding
Swedish. Composer, Conductor
Once led Stockholm Opera; wrote opera oratorio *Joseph and His Brothers,* 1948.
b. Jun 21, 1892 in Bosjokloster, Sweden
Source: *Baker 78, 84; CompSN, SUP; DcCM; IntWWM 80; NewAmDM; NewEOp 71; NewGrDM 80; OxDcOp*

Rosenberg, Issac
English. Poet
Wrote of experiences in WW I: *Youth,* 1918; killed in action.
b. Nov 25, 1890 in Bristol, England
d. Apr 19, 1918, France
Source: *BioIn 11; ConAu 107; DcLB 20; DcLEL; EncWL 2; NewYTBS 75; OxCEng 85; REn; TwCA SUP; TwCLC 12*

Rosenberg, Jakob
American. Art Historian
Museum curator, who was authority on Rembrandt, Baroque, Renaissance art.
b. Sep 5, 1893 in Berlin, Germany
d. Apr 7, 1980 in Cambridge, Massachusetts
Source: *AmAu&B; BioIn 10, 12, 13, 20; ConAu 97; NewYTBS 80; WhAm 7; WhAmArt 85; WhoAm 74, 76, 78; WhoAmA 73, 76, 78, 80, 82, 84N, 86N, 89N, 91N, 93N; WhoWorJ 72, 78*

Rosenberg, Julius
American. Traitor
With wife Ethel convicted of espionage; executed.
b. May 12, 1918 in New York, New York
d. Jun 19, 1953 in Ossining, New York
Source: *AmDec 1950; BioIn 2, 3, 4, 6, 7, 8, 9, 10, 11, 12, 13, 15, 17, 18, 19, 20, 21; ColdWar 1, 2; DcAmB S5; EncCW; EncMcCE; LegTOT; PolProf E, T; SpyCS; WebAB 74, 79; WorAl; WorAlBi*

Rosenberg, Steven A
American. Surgeon
Chief of surgery, National Cancer Institute, who has developed cancer treatment using interleukin-2, 1985.
b. Aug 2, 1940 in New York, New York
Source: *AmMWSc 92; BioIn 14; CurBio 91; News 89-1; NewYTBS 85; WhoAm 78, 90*

Rosenbloom, Carroll D
American. Football Executive, Businessman
Owner, Baltimore Colts, 1953-72; traded team for LA Rams, 1972; drowned while swimming.
b. Mar 5, 1907 in Baltimore, Maryland
d. Apr 2, 1979 in Miami, Florida
Source: *BioIn 11; NewYTBS 79; WhAm 7; WhoFtbl 74*

Rosenbloom, Georgia
[Georgia Frontiere-Rosenbloom]
"Madam Ram"
American. Football Executive
First woman owner of NFL team; inherited LA Rams on death of husband, 1979.
b. 1926 in Saint Louis, Missouri
Source: *NewYTBS 79; WhoAm 84, 86*

Rosenbloom, Maxie
"Slapsie Maxie"
American. Boxer, Actor, TV Personality
Colorful light-heavyweight champion, 1930-34; Hall of Fame, 1973.
b. Sep 6, 1904 in New York, New York
d. Mar 6, 1976 in South Pasadena, California

Source: *BiDAmSp BK; BoxReg; IntMPA 75; MotPP; MovMk; WhoBox 74; WhScrn 83*

Rosendahl, Bruce R
American. Physicist
Studies rifts in Africa to reveal earth's geological history.
b. 1947? in New York
Source: *BioIn 15, 16; ConNews 86-4*

Rosenfeld, Alvin Hirsch
American. Editor, Author
Most of his writings deal with Holocaust: *A Double Dying: Reflections on Holocaust Literature,* 1980.
b. Apr 28, 1938 in Philadelphia, Pennsylvania
Source: *ConAu 4NR, 24NR, 49; DrAS 74E, 78E, 82E*

Rosenfeld, Harry N(athan)
American. Government Official, Lawyer
Commissioner, US Displaced Persons Commission, 1948-52; credited with originating term "baby boom."
b. Aug 17, 1911
d. Jun 2, 1995 in Washington, District of Columbia
Source: *CurBio 95N*

Rosenfeld, Henry J
American. Fashion Designer
Opened dress manufacturing co., 1942; sold lower-priced fashions with expensive fabrics.
b. May 17, 1911 in New York, New York
d. Feb 5, 1986 in New York, New York
Source: *CurBio 48; WhoAm 74*

Rosenfeld, Paul
American. Critic
Covered music, art, literature; books include *Discoveries of a Music Critic,* 1936.
b. May 4, 1890 in New York, New York
d. Jul 21, 1946 in New York, New York
Source: *AmAu&B; Baker 78, 84; BenetAL 91; BioIn 1, 4, 5, 12, 13; CnDAL; CurBio 46; DcAmB S4; DcNAA; EncAJ; NewGrDA 86; NewGrDM 80; OxCAmL 65, 83, 95; REnAL; TwCA, SUP; WhAm 2; WhAmArt 85; WhJnl*

Rosenman, Dorothy
American. Political Activist
Housing expert and advocate; co-founder of Citizens Housing Council, 1934; National Committee on Housing chairperson, 1941-47.
b. Jan 17, 1900 in New York, New York
d. Jan 13, 1991 in New York, New York
Source: *BioIn 1, 17; CurBio 91N; NewYTBS 91; WhoAm 76, 78; WhoAmW 58*

Rosenquist, James Albert
American. Artist
Pop artist; known for controversial *F-1-11,* 1965 on canvas that was 11 ft. longer than original US bomber.
b. Nov 29, 1933 in Grand Forks, North Dakota
Source: *AmArt; BioIn 14, 15; ConArt 89; CurBio 70; DcCAA 71, 88; NewYTBS 86; OxDcArt; PrintW 85; WhoAm 74, 76, 78, 80, 82, 84, 86, 88, 90, 92, 94, 95, 96; WhoAmA 91; WhoE 74; WhoWor 74; WorAl; WorAlBi*

Rosenshontz
American. Entertainers
Family entertainment duo formed in 1974; children's records include *Rosenshontz Tickles You,* 1983.
Source: *ConMus 9*

Rosenstein, Nettie
American. Designer, Philanthropist
Noted for classic "little black dress;" won Coty, 1947.
b. Sep 26, 1893 in Vienna, Austria
d. Mar 13, 1980 in New York, New York
Source: *NewYTBS 80; WhAm 7; WhoAm 74, 76; WhoAmW 58, 61, 64, 66, 68, 70, 72, 74; WorFshn*

Rosenstock, Joseph
Polish. Conductor, Pianist
Led NYC Opera, 1948-55; Tokyo Philharmonic, 1930s-40s, 1960s.
b. Jan 27, 1895 in Krakow, Poland
d. Oct 17, 1985 in New York, New York
Source: *Baker 78, 84, 92; BiDAmM; BioIn 14, 15; CmOp; CurBio 54, 86, 86N; IntWWM 77, 80; MetOEnc; MusSN; NewEOp 71; NewGrDO; NewYTBS 85; WhAm 9; WhoMus 72; WhoWor 74; WhoWorJ 72, 78*

Rosenthal, Abraham Michael
Canadian. Editor, Author
Executive editor of *NY Times* since 1977.
b. May 2, 1922 in Sault Ste. Marie, Ontario, Canada
Source: *AmAu&B; BiDAmNC; BioIn 5, 6, 7, 10, 11, 12, 13; EncTwCJ; IntAu&W 86; IntWW 74, 75, 76, 77, 78, 79, 80, 81, 82, 83, 89, 91, 93; WhoAm 74, 76, 78, 80, 82, 84, 86, 88, 90, 92; WhoE 74, 83, 85, 86, 89, 91; WhoFI 74; WhoUSWr 88; WhoWor 78, 84, 87, 89, 91, 93, 95; WhoWrEP 89, 92, 95*

Rosenthal, Benjamin Stanley
American. Politician
Dem. congressman from NY, 1962-82; leader in saving NYC from bankruptcy, 1977.
b. Jun 8, 1923 in New York, New York
d. Jan 4, 1983 in Washington, District of Columbia
Source: *AlmAP 82; AnObit 1983; BiDrAC; BiDrUSC 89; BioIn 8, 13; CngDr 81; NewYTBS 83; WhAm 8; WhoAm 74, 76, 78, 80, 82; WhoAmJ 80; WhoAmP 73, 75, 77, 79, 81, 83; WhoE 74, 75, 77, 79, 81; WhoGov 72, 75, 77*

Rosenthal, Ida Cohen
American. Merchant
Seamstress; founded Maidenform Brassiere Co. with husband, 1923.
b. Jan 9, 1886 in Minsk, Russia
d. Mar 28, 1973 in New York, New York
Source: *BioIn 12, 15; NatCAB 57; NotAW MOD; WhAm 5*

Rosenthal, Jean E
[Eugenie Rosenthal]
American. Designer
Lighting designer for Broadway productions; lighting consultant for a Kennedy Airport terminal, NY.
b. Mar 16, 1912 in New York, New York
d. May 1, 1969 in New York, New York
Source: *NotAW MOD; ObitOF 79*

Rosenthal, Joe
[Joseph J Rosenthal]
American. Photojournalist
Won Pulitzer for picture of Marines raising US flag on Iwo Jima, during WW II.
b. Oct 9, 1911 in Washington, District of Columbia
Source: *BioIn 4; ConAu 69; CurBio 45; EncAJ; ICPEnP A; MacBEP*

Rosenthal, Moriz
"Little Giant of Piano"
Polish. Pianist
Pupil of Chopin, Liszt; made US debut, 1888; called "perfect pianist."
b. Dec 18, 1862 in Bemberg, Poland
d. Sep 3, 1946 in New York, New York
Source: *Baker 78, 84, 92; BiDAmM; BioIn 1, 2, 4, 7, 11, 16, 21; BriBkM 80; CurBio 46; MusSN; NewAmDM; NewCol 75; NewGrDA 86; NewGrDM 80; NotTwCP; OxCMus; PenDiMP*

Rosenwald, Julius
American. Businessman
Pres., chm., Sears, Roebuck, 1910-32; helped develop catalog business.
b. Aug 12, 1862 in Springfield, Illinois
d. Jan 6, 1932 in Chicago, Illinois
Source: *AmBi; AmSocL; BiDAmBL 83; BioIn 1, 2, 3, 4, 7, 8, 9, 10, 11, 12, 14, 15, 17, 18, 19; DcAmB; EncAACR; EncAAH; EncAB-H 1974, 1996; JeHun; LinLib S; McGEWB; NatCAB 26; PeoHis; WebAB 74, 79; WhAm 1*

Rosenzweig, Franz
German. Theologian
One of the most influential Jewish scholars in the early twentieth century; wrote *The Star of Redemption.*
b. Dec 25, 1886 in Kassel, Germany
d. Dec 10, 1929 in Frankfurt am Main, Germany
Source: *BioIn 1, 2, 3, 6, 7, 9, 15, 16, 17; LuthC 75; McGEWB; OxCPhil; RAdv 14, 13-4*

Rosewall, Ken(neth R)
Australian. Tennis Player
Youngest ever to win Australian nat. singles championship, 1953; won US Open, 1956, 1970.
b. Nov 2, 1934 in Sydney, Australia
Source: *BioIn 2, 9, 10, 11, 12, 14, 15, 16; BuCMET; CelR; CurBio 56; WhoWor 78; WorAl; WorAlBi*

Roskolenko, Harry
[Colin Ross]
American. Author
Writings draw on his extensive travel; autobiography *When I Was Last on Cherry Street,* 1965 tells of his early life in NYC.
b. Sep 21, 1907 in New York, New York
d. Jul 17, 1980 in New York, New York
Source: *BioIn 15; ConAu 13R, 17NR, 101; DrAPF 80; NewYTBS 80; OxCAusL; ScF&FL 1, 2, 92; WrDr 76, 80, 82, 84*

Rosovsky, Henry
American. Educator, Economist
Dean, Harvard U., 1973-84; wrote *Japanese Economic Growth,* 1973.
b. Sep 1, 1927 in Danzig, Germany
Source: *AmEA 74; AmMWSc 73S, 78S; ConAu 105; IntWW 83; St&PR 91, 96, 97; WhoAm 74, 76, 78, 80, 82, 84, 86, 88, 90, 92, 94, 95, 96, 97; WhoAmJ 80; WhoE 74, 75, 77; WhoEc 81, 86*

Ross, Alex(ander)
Scottish. Golfer
Touring pro, early 1900s; won US Open, 1907; brother of Donald.
b. 1881, Scotland
d. Jun 25, 1952 in Miami, Florida
Source: *WhoGolf*

Ross, Art(hur Howie)
Canadian. Hockey Player, Hockey Coach
Defenseman, Montreal Wanderers, 1917-18; coached 18 yrs., mostly with Boston, 1924-45; designed modern puck, nets; trophy given to NHL player with most points in season named for him; Hall of Fame, 1945.
b. Jan 13, 1886 in Naughton, Ontario, Canada
d. Aug 5, 1964 in Boston, Massachusetts
Source: *BioIn 7; HocEn; WhoHcky 73*

Ross, Barney
[Barnet David Rasofsky]
American. Boxer, Actor
World light- and welterweight champ, 1930s; film *Monkey on My Back* depicted life.
b. Dec 23, 1907 in New York, New York
d. Jan 18, 1967 in Chicago, Illinois
Source: *WhoBox 74; WhoHol B; WhScrn 74, 77, 83*

Ross, Betsy
[Elizabeth Griscom Ross]
American. Colonial Figure
Made first US flag at George Washington's request, 1775.
b. Jan 1, 1752 in Philadelphia, Pennsylvania
d. Jan 30, 1836 in Philadelphia, Pennsylvania
Source: *AmBi; AmRev; ApCAB SUP; BioIn 1, 2, 3, 4, 5, 6, 7, 8, 9, 10, 11, 13, 19, 21; BlkwEAR; DcAmB; EncCRAm; EncWHA; ForWC 70; HarEnUS; HerW, 84; LegTOT; LibW; LinLib S; NatCAB 12; NotAW; OxCAmH; REnAL; WebAB 74, 79; WhAm HS; WhAmRev; WorAl; WorAlBi*

Ross, Bobby
American. Football Coach
Head coach, San Diego Chargers, 1992-96; Detroit Lions, 1997—.
b. Dec 26, 1936 in Richmond, Virginia

Ross, David
American. Director, Producer
Won Obies for *Uncle Vanya,* 1956; *Hedda Gabler,* 1960.
b. Jul 7, 1891 in New York, New York
d. Nov 12, 1975 in New York, New York
Source: *ConAu 61, 65; RadStar; WhAm 6; WhoAm 74; WhoHol C; WhScrn 77, 83*

Ross, Diana
[The Supremes; Mrs. Arne Naess; Diane Ross]
American. Singer
Lead vocalist with The Supremes; group had 15 consecutive hits over 10-yr. period; went solo, 1969; appeared in films, stage; won special Tony for *The Wiz,* 1977.
b. Mar 26, 1944 in Detroit, Michigan
Source: *AfrAmAl 6; AfrAmBi 2; Baker 84, 92; BiDAfM; BioIn 7, 8, 9, 10, 11, 12, 13, 16; BkPepl; BlksAmF; CelR, 90; ConAu 146; ConBlB 8; ConMus 1; ContDcW 89; ConTFT 5; CurBio 73; DrBlPA, 90; Ebony 1; EncPR&S 89; EncRk 88; EncRkSt; EncWB; FacFETw; GoodHs; HalFC 80, 84, 88; HarEnR 86; HerW 84; IlEncBM 82; IlEncRk; InB&W 80, 85; IntDcWB; IntMPA 77, 80, 84, 86, 88, 92, 94, 96; IntWW 82, 83, 89, 91, 93; InWom SUP; LegTOT; MovMk; NegAl 89; NewAmDM; NewGrDA 86; NewYTBE 72; NotBlAW 1; OxCPMus; PenEncP; RkOn 78; RolSEnR 83; SoulM; VarWW 85; WhoAfA 96; WhoAm 74, 86, 88, 90, 92, 94, 95, 96, 97; WhoAmW 72, 87, 89, 91, 93, 95, 97; WhoBlA 85, 88, 90, 92, 94; WhoEnt 92; WhoHol 92, A; WhoRock 81; WhoRocM 82; WhoWor 89, 91, 93, 95, 96, 97; WorAl; WorAlBi*

Ross, Donald James
Scottish. Architect
Designed over 500 golf courses in US; Pinehurst No. 2 considered one of world's best courses; brother of Alex.
b. Nov 23, 1873 in Dornoch, Scotland
d. Apr 26, 1948 in Pinehurst, North Carolina
Source: *BioIn 1, 4; NatCAB 39; ObitOF 79; WhoGolf*

Ross, George
American. Continental Congressman, Lawyer
Signed Declaration of Independence for Pennsylvania; as Judge of Admiralty, his career was later marked by controversy.
b. Mar 10, 1730 in New Castle, Delaware
d. Jul 14, 1779 in Lancaster, Pennsylvania
Source: *AmBi; AmRev; ApCAB; BiAUS; BiDrAC; BiDrUSC 89; BioIn 7, 8, 9; DcAmB; Drake; EncAR; EncCRAm; HarEnUS; NatCAB 10; TwCBDA; WhAm HS; WhAmP; WhAmRev*

Ross, Harold Wallace
American. Editor
With financial backing from heir to Fleischman yeast fortune, founded *New Yorker* mag., 1925. Editor of *New Yorker* 1925-1951.
b. Nov 6, 1892 in Aspen, Colorado
d. Dec 6, 1951 in Boston, Massachusetts
Source: *AmAu&B; Benet 96; BiDAmJo; BioIn 1, 2, 3, 4, 5, 7, 8, 10, 14, 15, 16, 17, 18, 20, 21; CurBio 43, 52; DcAmB S5; LngCTC; REn; REnAL; WebAB 74, 79; WhAm 3; WhDW*

Ross, Herbert David
American. Director
Films include *The Turning Point,* 1977; *Footloose,* 1984.
b. May 13, 1927 in New York, New York
Source: *BiE&WWA; BioIn 16; CmMov; ConTFT 6; CurBio 80; EncAFC; FilmgC; HalFC 88; IntMPA 92; NotNAT; VarWW 85; WhAmArt 85; WhoAm 86, 92, 94, 95, 96, 97; WhoE 86; WhoEnt 92; WorEFlm*

Ross, Ishbel
American. Author
Wrote novels, biographies of famous women: *The President's Wife,* 1972.
b. 1897, Scotland
d. Sep 21, 1975 in New York, New York
Source: *AmAu&B; AmNov; AuSpks; BioIn 2, 10, 11, 16; ConAu 61, 93; ForWC 70; InWom, SUP*

Ross, James Clark, Sir
Scottish. Explorer
Located north magnetic pole, 1831.
b. Apr 15, 1800 in Balsarroch, Scotland
d. Sep 21, 1862 in Aylsbury, Scotland
Source: *Alli; ApCAB; BioIn 3, 6, 8, 9, 10, 11, 12, 13, 18, 21; BritAu 19; CamDcSc; CelCen; DcCanB 9; DcLEL; DcNaB; DcScB; Expl 93; InSci; LarDcSc; MacDCB 78; McGEWB; NewC; NewCBEL; NewCol 75; OxCCan;*

OxCEng 67, 85, 95; OxCShps; WhDW; WhWE

Ross, Joe E
American. Comedian
Films since 1960s include *The Love Bug,* 1969; *The Boatniks,* 1970.
b. Mar 15, 1905 in New York, New York
d. Aug 13, 1982 in Los Angeles, California
Source: *HalFC 84; WhoHol A*

Ross, John
American. Native American Chief
Led eastern Cherokees to Oklahoma, 1838-39; trip known as "trail of tears."
b. Oct 2, 1790 in Lookout Mountain, Tennessee
d. Aug 1, 1866 in Washington, District of Columbia
Source: *Alli; AmBi; ApCAB; BiNAW, B, SupB; BioIn 4, 5, 9, 11, 12, 13, 14, 17, 20; DcAmB; Drake; EncNAB; EncNoAI; EncWM; HarEnUS; HisWorL; McGEWB; NatCAB 11; NewCol 75; PeoHis; REnAW; WebAB 74, 79; WhAm HS; WhCiWar; WhNaAH*

Ross, Katharine
American. Actor
Starred in *The Graduate,* 1967; *Butch Cassidy and the Sundance Kid,* 1969; *The Stepford Wives,* 1975.
b. Jan 29, 1943 in Hollywood, California
Source: *BioIn 15; ConTFT 3; FilmgC; ForYSC; HalFC 84; IntMPA 77, 78, 79, 80, 81, 82, 84, 86, 88, 92, 94, 96; MotPP; MovMk; SweetSg D; VarWW 85; WhoAm 86, 88, 90, 92; WhoEnt 92; WhoHol 92, A; WorAl; WorAlBi*

Ross, Lanny
[Lancelot Patrick Ross]
American. Singer
Popular radio tenor, 1930s-50s; had own TV show, early 1950s.
b. Jan 19, 1906 in Seattle, Washington
d. Apr 26, 1988 in New York, New York
Source: *ASCAP 66, 80; BioIn 7, 12, 15, 16; CmpEPM; ForYSC; IntMPA 75, 76, 77, 78, 79, 80, 81, 82, 84, 86; NewYTBS 88; RadStar; SaTiSS; What 1; WhoHol A*

Ross, Marion
American. Actor
Best known for her role as Marion Cunningham on "Happy Days," 1974-83.
b. Oct 25, 1928? in Albert Lea, Minnesota
Source: *ConTFT 3; InWom SUP; LegTOT; VarWW 85; WhoAm 86, 90; WhoEnt 92; WhoHol 92; WhoTelC*

Ross, Nellie Taylor
American. Politician
First woman governor in US, Dem. of WY, 1925-27; first woman director of US Mint, 1933-53.
b. Nov 29, 1876 in Saint Joseph, Missouri
d. Dec 19, 1977 in Washington, District of Columbia
Source: *BiDrAC; CurBio 40, 78; GoodHs; LibW; NewYTBS 77; WebAB 79; WhAmP; WorAl*

Ross, Percy Nathan
American. Business Executive, Philanthropist, Journalist
Earned fortune, about $20 million, in plastic bag business; spends $1 million annually in charities, gives away money through newspaper column, "Thanks a Million," 1983—; hosts radio talk show *Thanks a Million,* 1990—.
b. Nov 22, 1916 in Laurium, Michigan
Source: *ConNews 86-2; NewYTBS 79; WhoAm 86, 88, 90, 92, 94, 95, 96, 97*

Ross, Ronald, Sir
English. Scientist, Physician
Discovered causes of malaria, 1897; won Nobel Prize for medicine, 1902.
b. May 13, 1857 in Almora, India
d. Sep 16, 1932 in London, England
Source: *AsBiEn; BiESc; BiHiMed; BioIn 1, 2, 3, 4, 6, 7, 9, 10, 14, 15, 18, 20; CamDcSc; ChhPo S3; DcInB; DcNaB 1931; DcScB; GrBr; InSci; LarDcSc; LinLib S; LngCTC; NobelP; NotTwCS; OxCMed 86; ScF&FL 1; WhoNob, 90, 95; WorAl; WorAlBi; WorScD*

Ross, Roy G
American. Religious Leader
Co-founder, National Council of Churches, 1950, serving as general secretary, 1952-63.
b. Jun 25, 1898 in Forrest, Illinois
d. Jan 8, 1978 in Pompano Beach, Florida
Source: *BioIn 2, 3, 6, 11; NewYTBS 78; ObitOF 79*

Ross, Steven J
American. Business Executive
Chm., Time Warner, Inc.
b. Sep 19, 1927 in New York, New York
d. Dec 20, 1992 in Los Angeles, California
Source: *BioIn 10, 12, 13, 14, 15, 16; Dun&B 90; IntMPA 92; IntWW 91; NewYTBS 89; St&PR 91; WhoAm 90; WhoE 91; WhoFI 92; WhoWor 84*

Rossant, James Stephane
American. Architect
Owner, James Rossant Architects, 1994—; professor of architecture, currently at Harvard, 1985—; has designed several cities.
b. Aug 17, 1928 in New York, New York
Source: *AmArch 70; WhoAm 82, 84, 86, 88, 90, 92, 94, 95, 96, 97*

Rosse, William Parsons, 3rd Earl of
Irish. Astronomer
Built 72-inch diameter mirror for use in the Victorian Age's biggest reflecting telescope.
b. Jun 17, 1800 in York, England
d. Oct 31, 1867 in Monkstown, Ireland
Source: *Alli; AsBiEn; BiESc; BioIn 8; CelCen; DcBiPP; DcScB; LarDcSc; WhDW*

Rossegger, Peter
Austrian. Author
His novels advocated social reform in rural Austria.
b. Jul 31, 1843 in Alpl, Austria
d. Jun 26, 1918 in Krieglach, Austria

Rossellini, Isabella
Italian. Actor, Model
Daughter of Ingrid Bergman and Roberto Rossellini; films include *Blue Velvet,* 1986.
b. Jun 18, 1952 in Rome, Italy
Source: *BioIn 11, 12, 13, 14, 15, 16; ConTFT 7, 15; CurBio 88; HalFC 88; IntMPA 88, 92, 94, 96; IntWW 91, 93; ItaFilm; LegTOT; WhoAm 90, 92, 94, 95, 96, 97; WhoAmW 95, 97; WhoHol 92, A; WhoWor 97*

Rossellini, Renzo
Italian. Composer
Wrote 130 movie scores including *Open City,* 1945; brother of Roberto.
b. Feb 2, 1908 in Rome, Italy
d. May 14, 1982 in Monte Carlo, Monaco
Source: *AnObit 1982; Baker 78, 84, 92; BioIn 12; DcFM; IntWW 74, 75, 76, 77, 78; IntWWM 77, 80; ItaFilm; NewEOp 71; NewGrDM 80; NewGrDO; OxDcOp; WhoHol A; WhoMus 72; WhoOp 76; WhoWor 74*

Rossellini, Roberto
Italian. Director
Directed *Open City,* 1946; *Stromboli,* 1950; husband of Ingrid Bergman.
b. May 8, 1906 in Rome, Italy
d. Jun 3, 1977 in Rome, Italy
Source: *Benet 87; IntWW 74, 75, 76, 77; ItaFilm; LegTOT; MakMC; MiSFD 9N; MovMk; NewYTBE 71; NewYTBS 74, 77; OxCFilm; REn; WhoWor 74; WorAl; WorAlBi; WorEFlm; WorFDir 1*

Rossen, Robert
American. Director, Producer
Won Oscar for *All the King's Men,* 1949; other films include *Body and Soul,* 1947; *Hustler,* 1961.
b. Mar 16, 1908 in New York, New York
d. Feb 18, 1966 in New York, New York
Source: *AmFD; BiDFilm, 81, 94; BioIn 2, 7, 8, 11, 12, 14, 15; CmMov; ConAu 113; CurBio 50, 66; DcAmB S8; DcFM; DcLB 26; FilmEn; FilmgC; GangFlm; HalFC 80, 84, 88; IlWWHD 1; IntDcF 1-2, 2-2; LegTOT; MiSFD 9N; MovMk;*

OxCFilm; WhAm 4; WorAl; WorAlBi; WorEFlm; WorFDir 1

Rossetti, Christina Georgina
English. Poet
Often modeled for brother, Dante; best verse appears in *Goblin Market,* 1862.
b. Dec 5, 1830 in London, England
d. Dec 29, 1894 in London, England
Source: *Alli, SUP; AnCL; ArtclWW 2; AtlBL; BbD; Benet 87, 96; BiD&SB; BioIn 1, 2, 3, 4, 5, 6, 7, 8, 9, 10, 11, 12, 13, 14, 15, 16, 18, 19, 20, 21; BlmGEL; BritAu 19; CamGEL; CarSB; CasWL; CelCen; Chambr 3; ChhPo, S1, S2, S3; CnE&AP; CrtT 3; CyWA 58; DcArts; DcBiPP; DcEnA, A; DcEnL; DcEuL; DcLB 163; DcLEL; DcNaB; EvLB; GrWrEL P; InWom, SUP; JBA 34; LinLib L, S; LngCEL; MajAI; McGEWB; MouLC 4; NewC; NewCBEL; NinCLC 2; OxCChiL; OxCEng 67, 85, 95; PenBWP; PenC ENG; RAdv 1; REn; Str&VC; VicBrit; WebE&AL; WomNov*

Rossetti, Dante Gabriel
English. Poet, Artist
Pre-Raphaelite paintings include *Dante's Dream,* 1871; wrote famed sonnet "The Blessed Damozel," 1850; son of Gabriele.
b. May 12, 1828 in London, England
d. Apr 9, 1882 in Birchington, England
Source: *Alli; AntBDN B; AtlBL; BbD; Benet 87, 96; BiD&SB; BioIn 1, 2, 3, 4, 5, 6, 7, 8, 9, 10, 11, 12, 13, 14, 15, 16, 17, 18, 19; BlmGEL; BritAu 19; BritWr 5; CamGEL; CamGLE; Chambr 3; ChhPo, S1, S2, S3; CnDBLB 4; CnE&AP; CrtT 3, 4; CyWA 58; DcArts; DcBiPP; DcBrBI; DcEnA; DcEnL; DcLB 35; DcLEL; DcNaB; DcNiCA; Dis&D; EncO&P 1, 2, 3; EvLB; GrWrEL P; IntDcAA 90; LegTOT; LinLib L, S; LngCEL; LuthC 75; McGDA; McGEWB; MouLC 4; NewC; NewCBEL; NinCLC 4; OxCArt; OxCEng 67, 85, 95; OxDcArt; PenC ENG; RAdv 1, 14, 13-1; RComWL; REn; RfGEnL 91; VicBrit; WebE&AL; WhDW; WorAl; WorAlBi; WorLitC*

Rossetti, Gabriele Pasquale Giuseppe
Italian. Poet, Scholar
Professor of Italian, London College, 1831-47; fathered three famed intellectuals.
b. Feb 28, 1783 in Vasto, Italy
d. Apr 24, 1854 in London, England
Source: *Alli; BiD&SB; BioIn 9; CasWL; DcEuL; EvEuW*

Rossetti, William Michael
English. Critic
Founder, Pre-Raphaelite Brotherhood; edited their organ *The Germ,* from 1850; brother of Christina, Dante.
b. Sep 25, 1829 in London, England
d. Feb 5, 1919 in London, England
Source: *Alli, SUP; Benet 87, 96; BiD&SB; BioIn 9, 10, 11, 15, 16, 19; BritAu 19; CamGEL; CamGLE; CelCen; Chambr 3; ChhPo, S1, S2, S3; DcEnA, A; DcEnL; DcEuL; DcLEL; DcNaB 1912; EvLB; NewC; NewCBEL; OxCEng 67, 85, 95; REn; WhLit*

Rossi, Gaetano
Italian. Librettist
Wrote over 120 librettos for noted composers.
b. 1780 in Verona, Italy
d. Jan 27, 1855 in Verona, Italy
Source: *NewEOp 71; NewGrDM 80*

Rossi, Peter Henry
American. Educator
Sociology professor, U of MA, 1974-92; author of several books on subject: *Why Families Move,* 1980.
b. Dec 27, 1921 in New York, New York
Source: *AmAu&B; AmMWSc 73S, 78S; ConAu 1R, 4NR, 19NR, 41NR; WhoAm 74, 76, 78, 80, 82, 84, 86, 88, 90, 92, 94, 95, 96, 97; WhoE 74*

Rossi-Lemeni, Nicola
Turkish. Opera Singer
Bass; with NY Met., 1950s; noted for roles of Mephistopheles, Emperor Jones.
b. Nov 6, 1920 in Constantinople, Turkey
d. Mar 12, 1991 in Bloomington, Indiana
Source: *Baker 78, 84, 92; BioIn 15; CmOp; IntDcOp; IntWWM 77, 80, 90; MetOEnc; NewAmDM; NewEOp 71; NewGrDM 80; NewGrDO; NewYTBS 91; OxDcOp; PenDiMP; WhoMus 72*

Rossini, Gioacchino Antonio
Italian. Composer
Best-known operas include *Barber of Seville,* 1816; *William Tell,* 1829.
b. Feb 29, 1792 in Pesaro, Italy
d. Nov 13, 1868 in Passy, France
Source: *AtlBL; NewCol 75; OxCFr; WebBD 83*

Rossner, Judith
American. Author
Wrote *Looking for Mr. Goodbar,* 1975; filmed, 1977.
b. Mar 31, 1935 in New York, New York
Source: *AmWomWr SUP; ArtclWW 2; AuNews 2; BenetAL 91; BestSel 90-3; BioIn 12; ConAu 17R, 18NR; ConLC 6, 9, 29; ConNov 86, 91, 96; DcLB 6; DrAF 76; DrAPF 80, 87, 91; IntAu&W 86, 91, 93; InWom SUP; LegTOT; MajTwCW; ModAL S2; Novels; WhoAm 76, 78, 80, 82, 84, 86, 88, 90, 92, 94, 95, 96; WhoAmW 79, 81, 83, 85, 87, 89, 95; WhoUSWr 88; WhoWrEP 89, 92, 95; WorAu 1975; WrDr 76, 80, 82, 84, 86, 88, 90, 92, 94, 96*

Rostand, Edmond Alexis
French. Dramatist
Wrote *Cyrano de Bergerac,* 1897.
b. Apr 1, 1868 in Marseilles, France
d. Dec 2, 1918 in Paris, France
Source: *AtlBL; BiD&SB; CasWL; ClDMEL 47; CnMD; CnThe; CyWA 58; EncWL; EvEuW; LngCTC; McGEWD 84; NewC; OxCEng 85; PenC EUR; REn; TwCA SUP; WorAl*

Rosten, Leo C(alvin)
[Leonard Q Ross]
American. Author
Best known for character Hyman Kaplan who is subject of several humorous works: *The Education of H*Y*M*A*N K*A*P*L*A*N,* 1937; adapted as musical play, 1968; wrote *The Joys of Yiddish,* 1968.
b. Apr 11, 1908 in Lodz, Poland
d. Feb 19, 1997 in New York, New York
Source: *AmAu&B; Benet 87; BenetAL 91; BioIn 13, 14, 15; ConAu 5R, 6NR; ConNov 86, 91; CurBio 42; DcLP 87A; EncAHmr; EncTwCJ; IntAu&W 91; LngCTC; OxCAmL 65; PenC AM; REn; REnAL; TwCA, SUP; Who 85, 92; WhoAm 86, 90; WhoEnt 92; WrDr 86, 92*

Rosten, Norman
American. Writer
Wrote play *Mister Johnson,* 1956.
b. Jan 1, 1914
d. Mar 7, 1995 in New York, New York
Source: *AmAu&B; ASCAP 80; BenetAL 91; BiE&WWA; BioIn 1, 3, 4, 20, 21; ChhPo; ConAu 21NR, 77, 147; CurBio 95N; DrAF 76; DrAP 75; DrAPF 80; IntAu&W 77; NotNAT; REn; REnAL; TwCA SUP*

Rostenkowski, Daniel David
American. Politician
Dem. congressman from IL, 1959—; chm. of Ways and Means Committee, 1981—.
b. Jan 2, 1928 in Chicago, Illinois
Source: *AlmAP 88; AmCath 80; BiDrAC; BiDrUSC 89; BioIn 11, 13, 14, 15; CngDr 87; CurBio 82; NewYTBS 85; PolsAm 84; WhoAm 74, 86, 88; WhoAmP 87, 89; WhoGov 72, 75, 77; WhoMW 90; WorAlBi*

Rostow, Eugene Victor
American. Lawyer, Economist
Headed Arms Control Disarmament Agency, 1981-83; ousted by Reagan over policy dispute.
b. Aug 25, 1913 in New York, New York
Source: *BioIn 5, 6, 11, 12, 13, 16; ConAu 5R; CurBio 61; DrAS 74P, 78P, 82P; IntWW 74, 75, 76, 77, 78, 79, 80, 81, 82, 83, 89, 91, 93; Who 74, 82, 83, 85, 88, 90, 92, 94; WhoAm 74, 76, 78, 80, 82, 84, 86, 88, 90, 92, 94, 95, 96, 97; WhoAmL 78, 79, 85; WhoE 95; WhoWor 74, 78; WrDr 86, 92*

Rostow, Walt Whitman
American. Economist
Author of many books on economic history; one of JFK's most influential

advisers, 1961; Lyndon B. Johnson's National Security advisor, 1966-69.
b. Oct 7, 1916 in New York, New York
Source: *AmAu&B; AmMWSc 73S, 78S; AmPolLe; BioIn 5, 6, 7, 8, 11, 14, 16, 17, 18; BlueB 76; ConAu 13R; CurBio 61; DcAmDH 80, 89; DrAS 74H, 78H, 82H; EncAB-H 1974; EncAI&E; EncWB; GrEconS; IntAu&W 77; IntWW 74, 75, 76, 77, 78, 79, 80, 81, 82, 83, 89, 91, 93; IntYB 78, 79, 80, 81, 82; NatCAB 63N; PolProf J, K; Who 74, 82, 83, 85, 88, 90, 92, 94; WhoAm 74, 76, 78, 80, 82, 84, 86, 88, 90, 92, 94, 95, 96, 97; WhoAmP 73, 75, 77, 79, 81, 83, 85, 87, 89, 91, 93, 95; WhoEc 86; WhoFI 89; WhoGov 72; WhoScEn 96; WhoWor 74; WrDr 76, 86, 92*

Rostropovich, Mstislav Leopoldovich
Russian. Musician, Educator, Conductor
Renowned cellist; director, Washington's National Symphony, 1977-94; won Lenin Prize, 1963.
b. Aug 12, 1927 in Baku, Union of Soviet Socialist Republics
Source: *Baker 84, 92; BiDSovU; BioIn 13, 14, 16; ColdWar 2; CurBio 66, 88; FacFETw; IntWW 74, 75, 76, 77, 78, 79, 80, 81, 82, 83, 89, 91, 93; IntWWM 77, 85, 90; NewAmDM; NewGrDA 86; NewGrDO; NewYTBS 75, 81, 85; PenDiMP; SovUn; VarWW 85; Who 92; WhoAm 86, 90, 92, 94, 95, 96, 97; WhoE 89, 91, 95, 97; WhoEnt 92; WhoWor 89, 91, 93, 95, 96, 97; WorAlBi*

Roswaenge, Helge
Danish. Opera Singer
Celebrated dramatic tenor; with Berlin State Opera, 1920s-40s; often compared to Caruso.
b. Aug 29, 1897 in Copenhagen, Denmark
d. Jul 19, 1972 in Munich, Germany
Source: *Baker 78, 84, 92; BioIn 7, 9, 10; CmOp; NewAmDM; NewEOp 71; NewGrDM 80; PenDiMP; WhScrn 77*

Roszak, Theodore
American. Sculptor
Designed 37-foot aluminum eagle for facade of US Embassy, London, 1960.
b. May 1, 1907 in Poznan, Poland
d. Sep 3, 1981 in New York, New York
Source: *AmAu&B; AnObit 1981; BioIn 1, 3, 4, 5; BriEAA; ConArt 77, 83, 89, 96; CurBio 66, 81, 81N; DcAmArt; DcCAA 71, 77, 88, 94; DcCAr 81; FacFETw; McGDA; NewYTBS 81; OxCTwCA; PhDcTCA 77; WhAm 8; WhoAm 74, 76, 78, 80; WhoAmA 73, 76, 78, 80, 82N, 84N, 86N, 89N, 91N, 93N; WhoArt 80, 82, 84; WhoWor 74, 76; WorArt 1950*

Roszak, Theodore
American. Historian, Author
Writings condemn technocratic culture: *The Making of a Counter Culture,* 1969.
b. 1933 in Chicago, Illinois
Source: *AmAu&B; BioIn 10, 12, 13, 20; ConAu 45NR, 77; CurBio 82; EncSF 93; EnvEnc; RadHan; RAdv 14; ScF&FL 92; WhoAm 74, 76, 78, 80; WorAu 1975*

Rote, Kyle
American. Football Player, Sportscaster
Six-time all-pro running back-end, NY Giants, 1951-61; author of books on football.
b. Oct 27, 1928 in San Antonio, Texas
Source: *ASCAP 66, 80; BioIn 2, 7, 10, 11; ConAu 21R; CurBio 65; NewYTBE 73; WhoFI 79; WhoFtbl 74; WhoSpor*

Rote, Kyle, Jr.
American. Soccer Player
Forward in NASL, mostly with Dallas, 1973-78; rookie of year, 1974; son of Kyle.
b. Dec 25, 1950 in Dallas, Texas
Source: *BiDAmSp OS; BioIn 10, 11, 12; BioNews 74; NewYTBE 73; NewYTBS 74; WhoSpor*

Roth, Ann
American. Designer
Costume designer for *Working Girl,* 1988; *The Birdcage,* 1996.
b. 1932? in Philadelphia, Pennsylvania

Roth, David Lee
[Van Halen]
American. Singer, Musician
Lead singer, Van Halen, 1974-84; had best-selling solo album *Crazy from the Heat.*
b. Oct 10, 1955 in Bloomington, Indiana
Source: *BioIn 14, 15; EncPR&S 89; LegTOT; WhoRocM 82; WorAlBi*

Roth, Henry
American. Author
Wrote novel recalling ghetto life: *Call It Sleep,* 1934; also *Shifting Landscape,* 1987.
b. Feb 8, 1906 in Tysmenica, Austria
d. Oct 13, 1995 in Albuquerque, New Mexico
Source: *AmAu&B; Benet 96; BenetAL 91; BioIn 7, 10, 12, 14, 15, 16, 17, 19, 20, 21; BlueB 76; CamGLE; CamHAL; CasWL; ConAu 38NR, 149, P-1; ConLC 2, 6, 11; ConNov 72, 76, 82, 86, 91, 96; CurBio 89, 96N; DcLB 28; EncWL, 2, 3; GrWrEL N; IntAu&W 76, 77; JeAmFiW; JeAmHC; LegTOT; MajTwCW; ModAL; NewYTBS 95; OxCAmL 95; PenC AM; RAdv 1, 14; RfGAmL 87, 94; RGTwCWr; WebE&AL; WhoAm 74, 76, 78, 80, 82, 84, 94, 95, 96; WhoTwCL; WhoWor 74; WorAlBi; WorAu 1950; WrDr 76, 80, 82, 84, 86, 88, 90, 92, 94, 96*

Roth, Lillian
American. Singer
Broadway performer at age eight; wrote autobiography *I'll Cry Tomorrow,* 1954, filmed 1955.
b. Dec 13, 1910 in Boston, Massachusetts
d. May 12, 1980 in New York, New York
Source: *BiE&WWA; BioIn 3, 4, 9, 12, 15; CmpEPM; ConAu 97; DcAmB S10; EncAFC; EncVaud; Film 1; FilmEn; FilmgC; ForYSC; HalFC 80, 84, 88; InWom SUP; LegTOT; MovMk; NewYTBS 80; NotNAT, A; PlP&P; ThFT; What 3; WhoHol A; WhoThe 77, 81; WhScrn 83; WorAl*

Roth, Mark Stephan
American. Bowler
Four-time PBA money leader; has won 33 pro titles; PBA Hall of Fame.
b. Apr 10, 1951 in New York, New York
Source: *BiDAmSp BK; BioIn 11; NewYTBS 79; WhoAm 80, 82*

Roth, Philip (Milton)
American. Author
Won National Book Award for *Goodbye Columbus,* 1959, adapted to movie; wrote controversial best seller, *Portnoy's Complaint,* 1969; *Patrimony: A True Story,* 1991; won 1994 Faulkner Award for Fiction for *Operation Shylock: A Confession,* 1993.
b. Mar 19, 1933 in Newark, New Jersey
Source: *AmAu&B; AmCulL; AmWr S3; Ballpl 90; Benet 87, 96; BenetAL 91; BestSel 90-3; BioIn 5, 7, 8, 9, 10, 11, 12, 13, 14, 15, 16; BlueB 76; BroV; CamGEL; CamGLE; CamHAL; CasWL; CelR, 90; ConAu 1NR, 1R, 22NR, 36NR, 55NR; ConLC 1, 2, 3, 4, 6, 9, 15, 22, 31, 47, 66, 86; ConNov 72, 76, 82, 86, 91, 96; ConPopW; CurBio 70, 91; CyWA 89; DcArts; DcLB 2, 28, 173, Y82A; DcLEL 1940; DcTwCCu 1; DrAF 76; DrAPF 80, 87, 91; EncSF, 93; EncWL, 2, 3; FacFETw; GrWrEL N; HalFC 84, 88; IntAu&W 76, 77, 82, 89, 91, 93; IntvTCA 2; IntWW 74, 75, 76, 77, 78, 79, 80, 81, 82, 83, 89, 91, 93; JeAmHC; LegTOT; LinLib L; MagSAmL; MajTwCW; ModAL, S1, S2; NewYTBE 71; Novels; OxCAmL 65, 83, 95; OxCEng 85, 95; PenC AM; RAdv 1, 14, 13-1; REn; REnAL; RfGAmL 87, 94; RfGShF; RGTwCWr; ScF&FL 1, 2; ScFSB; TwCWr; WebAB 74, 79; WebE&AL; Who 90, 92, 94; WhoAm 74, 76, 78, 80, 82, 84, 86, 88, 90, 92, 94, 95, 96, 97; WhoAmJ 80; WhoE 85, 86, 89, 91, 93, 95, 97; WhoTwCL; WhoUSWr 88; WhoWor 74, 76, 78, 80, 82, 84, 87, 89, 91, 93, 95, 96, 97; WhoWorJ 78; WhoWrEP 89, 92, 95; WorAl; WorAlBi; WorAu 1950; WorLitC; WrDr 76, 80, 82, 84, 86, 88, 90, 92, 94, 96*

Roth, William Victor, Jr.
American. Politician
Rep. senator from DE, 1971—; chairman senate Finance Committee.
b. Jul 22, 1921 in Great Falls, Montana
Source: *AlmAP 88, 92; BiDrAC; BiDrUSC 89; BioIn 13; CngDr 87, 89; CurBio 83; IntWW 91; PolsAm 84; WhoAm 86, 88; WhoAmP 73, 75, 77, 79,*

81, 83, 85, 87, 89, 91, 93, 95; WhoE 89; WhoWor 89

Rotha, Paul
[Paul Thompson]
English. Filmmaker, Author
Produced documentaries that often exposed social ills; wrote classic work on cinema *The Film Till Now,* 1930.
b. Jun 3, 1907 in London, England
d. Mar 7, 1984 in Wallingford, England
Source: *AnObit 1984; Au&Wr 71; BioIn 4, 10, 13, 14, 15; BlueB 76; ConAu 9R, 112; CurBio 84N; DcFM; DcNaB 1981; EncEurC; FilmEn; FilmgC; HalFC 80, 84; IlWWBF; IntAu&W 76, 77; IntDcF 2-2; IntMPA 75, 76, 77, 78, 79, 80, 81, 82, 84; IntWW 74, 75, 76, 77, 78, 79, 80, 81, 82, 83; OxCFilm; WhE&EA; Who 74, 82, 83; WhoWor 74, 76, 78; WorEFlm; WorFDir 1; WrDr 76, 80, 82, 84*

Rothenberg, Jerome
American. Poet
Avant-garde poet with interest in N American Indian poetry, Jewish mystics: *Poland/1931,* 1969.
b. Dec 11, 1931 in New York, New York
Source: *BioIn 10, 12; CamHAL; ConAu 1NR, 45; ConLC 6, 57; ConPo 70, 75, 80, 85, 91; CroCAP; DcLB 5; DcLEL 1940; DrAP 75; DrAPF 80, 87, 91; Focus; IntAu&W 77, 82, 86, 89, 91; OxCTwCP; PenC AM; RAdv 1; WhoAm 76, 78, 80, 82, 84, 86, 88, 90, 92, 94, 95, 96, 97; WhoUSWr 88; WorAu 1970; WrDr 76, 80, 82, 84, 86, 88, 90, 92, 94, 96*

Rothenberg, Susan
American. Artist
Painter who used horse as major motif, 1970s, human images, 1980s.
b. Jan 20, 1945 in Buffalo, New York
Source: *AmArt; BiDWomA; BioIn 12, 13, 14, 15, 16; ConArt 83, 89, 96; CurBio 85; DcCAA 88, 94; DcCAr 81; GrLiveH; IntWW 89, 91, 93; InWom SUP; News 95, 95-3; NewYTBS 84; NorAmWA; PrintW 83, 85; WhoAm 82, 84, 86, 88, 90, 92, 94, 95, 96; WhoAmA 80, 82, 84, 86, 89, 91, 93; WhoAmW 87, 89, 91, 93, 95; WhoE 86; WorArt 1980*

Rothenstein, William, Sir
English. Artist
Portraits, lithographs now in Tate, National Portrait Galleries.
b. Jan 29, 1872 in Bradford, England
d. Feb 14, 1945 in Oxford, England
Source: *BioIn 3, 4, 5, 6, 10, 11, 14, 16; ChhPo, S1, S3; ClaDrA; CurBio 45; DcArts; DcBrAr 1; DcBrBI; DcLEL; DcNaB 1941; DcVicP 2; GrBr; LngCTC; McGDA; ObitOF 79; OxCTwCA; OxDcArt; PhDcTCA 77; TwCA, SUP; TwCPaSc; WhLit*

Rothermere, Esmond Cecil Harmsworth, Viscount
English. Newspaper Publisher, Politician
Owner of Britain's largest newspaper chain, inherited from his father, Harold S Harmsworth.
b. May 29, 1898 in London, England
d. Jul 12, 1978 in London, England
Source: *BioIn 1, 11; ConAu 89; CurBio 48, 78; IntWW 76, 78; IntYB 78; Who 74; WhoWor 74*

Rothermere, Harold Sidney Harmsworth
English. Journalist
Owner, publisher of several newspaper chains in Britain including *London Daily Mail,* 1890s-1940.
b. Apr 26, 1868 in London, England
d. Nov 26, 1940 in Hamilton, Bermuda
Source: *BioIn 2, 12; NatCAB 31; NewCol 75; WebBD 83*

Rothier, Leon
French. Opera Singer
First basso; made NY Met. debut, 1910, as Mephistopheles.
b. Dec 26, 1874 in Reims, France
d. Dec 6, 1951 in New York, New York
Source: *Baker 78, 84, 92; BiDAmM; BioIn 1, 2, 4, 10, 11; MetOEnc; MusSN; NewEOp 71; NewGrDA 86; NewGrDO; WhAm 5*

Rothko, Mark
[Marcus Rothkovich]
American. Artist
Pioneer abstract expressionist; known for huge canvases containing simple rectangles of glowing, shifting color.
b. Sep 25, 1903 in Daugavpils, Russia
d. Feb 25, 1970 in New York, New York
Source: *AmCulL; AtlBL; Benet 87, 96; BioIn 3, 4, 5, 6, 7, 8, 9, 10, 11, 12, 13, 14, 16, 17, 19, 20; BriEAA; ConArt 77, 83, 89, 96; CurBio 61, 70; DcAmArt; DcAmB S8; DcArts; DcCAA 71, 77, 88, 94; DcTwCCu 1; EncAB-H 1974, 1996; FacFETw; IntDcAA 90; JeHun; LegTOT; MakMC; McGDA; McGEWB; ObitT 1961; OxCArt; OxCTwCA; OxDcArt; PhDcTCA 77; WebAB 74, 79; WhAm 5; WhAmArt 85; WhDW; WhoAmA 78N, 80N, 82N, 84N, 86N, 89N, 91N, 93N; WorAl; WorAlBi; WorArt 1950*

Rothmuller, Marko A
Yugoslav. Opera Singer
Baritone highly regarded for Wagner roles; with NY Met., early 1960s.
b. Dec 31, 1908 in Trnjani, Yugoslavia
d. Jan 20, 1993 in Bloomington, Indiana
Source: *Baker 84; IntWWM 90; PenDiMP; WhoAm 84; WhoEnt 92; WhoMW 84; WhoWorJ 72, 78*

Rothschild, Alain de, Baron
French. Banker
Senior member of French branch of famous banking family; spokesman, Leader of France's Jewish community.
b. Jan 7, 1910 in Paris, France
d. Oct 17, 1982 in New York, New York
Source: *AnObit 1982; BioIn 13; IntWW 83; NewYTBS 82; WhoFr 79*

Rothschild, Edmund Leopold de
English. Banker
Chm., N M Rothschild & Sons, 1970-75.
b. Jan 16, 1916 in London, England
Source: *BlueB 76; IntWW 74, 75, 76, 77, 78, 79, 80, 81, 82, 83, 89, 91, 93; Who 74, 82, 83, 85, 88, 90, 92, 94; WhoCan 73, 75, 77, 80, 82*

Rothschild, Guy Edouard Alphonse Paul de, Baron
French. Banker
With Banque Rothschild until govt. nationalization, 1981.
b. May 21, 1909 in Paris, France
Source: *BioIn 13, 14, 15; CurBio 73; IntWW 83, 89, 91, 93; NewYTBS 82; Who 85, 92*

Rothschild, Judith
American. Artist
Abstract painter; worked in oils and relief collage.
d. Mar 6, 1993 in New York, New York
Source: *AmArt; NewYTBS 93; WhoAmA 76, 78, 80, 82, 84, 86, 89, 91, 93*

Rothschild, Lionel Nathan Rothschild, Baron
English. Banker, Government Official
First Jewish member of Parliament, 1858-74; son of Nathan Mayer Rothschild.
b. Nov 22, 1808 in London, England
d. Jun 3, 1879 in London, England
Source: *NewCol 75; WorAl*

Rothschild, Mayer Amschel
German. Financier
Founded Rothschild family financial dynasty, Frankfurt, Germany.
b. Feb 23, 1743 in Frankfurt am Main, Germany
d. Sep 19, 1812
Source: *NewCol 75; WebBD 83; WhDW; WorAl*

Rothschild, Miriam Louisa
English. Scientist
World expert on fleas; author of six volume *Illustrated Catalogue of the Rothschild Collection of Fleas in the British Museum.*
b. Aug 5, 1908 in Ashton Wold, England
Source: *CurBio 92; IntDcWB; InWom SUP; Who 90, 92; WhoWor 91; WomFir*

Rothschild, Nathan Meyer
British. Banker
Opened British branch of family bank, 1805; son of Mayer Rothschild.
b. Sep 16, 1777 in Frankfurt, Germany
d. Jul 28, 1836
Source: *BioIn 15, 20, 21; DcBiPP; DcNaB; NewCol 75; WorAl*

Rothschild, Philippe de, Baron
French. Vintner
Known for producing some of world's finest wines; turned family vineyards in Bordeaux, France into popular tourist attraction.
b. Apr 13, 1902 in Paris, France
d. Jan 20, 1988 in Paris, France
Source: *AnObit 1988; BioIn 8, 9; News 88-2; NewYTBE 72; NewYTBS 88; WhoFr 79*

Rothstein, Arnold
American. Gambler
Accused of masterminding "Black Sox" baseball scandal, 1919; murdered in hotel room while playing cards.
b. Jan 24, 1882 in New York, New York
d. Nov 6, 1928 in New York, New York
Source: *BioIn 1, 3, 5, 6, 9; CopCroC; DrInf; NewCol 75*

Rothstein, Arthur
American. Photographer
With *Look* magazine, 1940-71; known for photos of American Dust Bowl during Great Depression.
b. Jul 17, 1915 in New York, New York
d. Nov 11, 1985 in New Rochelle, New York
Source: *AnObit 1985; BiDAmJo; BioIn 10, 13, 14, 15, 16; ConAu 6NR, 57, 117; ConPhot 82, 88, 95; EncAJ; EncTwCJ; ICPEnP; MacBEP; NewYTBS 85; WhAm 9; WhAmArt 85; WhoAm 82, 84; WhoAmA 80, 82, 84, 86N, 89N, 91N, 93N; WhoE 86; WhoWor 82*

Rothstein, Ron
American. Basketball Coach
Coach, Detroit, 1992.
b. Dec 27, 1942 in New York, New York
Source: *WhoAm 90*

Rothstein, Ruth
American. Business Executive
Director, Cook County Hospital, Chicago, chief, Cook County Bureau of Health Services.
b. Apr 5, 1923 in New York, New York

Rothwax, Harold
American. Judge
Judge, Criminal Court of the City of New York, 1970-86; New York Supreme Court, 1987—.
b. Aug 28, 1930 in New York, New York
Source: *BioIn 21; News 96, 96-3*

Rothwell, Walter Henry
English. Conductor
Organized, led LA Philharmonic, 1919-27.
b. Sep 22, 1872 in London, England
d. Mar 12, 1927 in Los Angeles, California
Source: *Baker 78, 84, 92; BiDAmM; BioIn 2; NewEOp 71; NewGrDA 86*

Rotimi, Ola
Nigerian. Dramatist
African playwright's work includes *Our Husband Has Gone Mad Again,* 1977; *Kurunmi,* 1989.
b. Apr 13, 1938 in Sapele, Nigeria
Source: *AfrA; BioIn 10, 14, 17, 19; BlkWr 1; CamGWoT; ConAu 124; ConBlB 1; ConDr 88, 93; CrtSuDr; EncWL 3; IntvTCA 2; McGEWD 84; OxCThe 83; WrDr 88, 90, 92, 94, 96*

Rouault, Georges
French. Artist
Expressionistic paintings include "The Old King."
b. May 27, 1871 in Paris, France
d. Feb 13, 1958 in Paris, France
Source: *AtlBL; Benet 87, 96; BioIn 1, 2, 3, 4, 5, 6, 7, 8, 9, 10, 11, 12, 14, 16, 17; ClaDrA; ConArt 77, 83; CurBio 45, 58; DancEn 78; DcArts; DcTwCCu 2; IntDcAA 90; LegTOT; LinLib S; MakMC; McGDA; McGEWB; NewCol 75; ObitT 1951; OxCArt; OxCTwCA; OxDcArt; PhDcTCA 77; REn; WebBD 83; WhAm 3; WhDW; WorArt 1950*

Roudebush, Richard L(owell)
American. Government Official
Administrator, VA, 1974-77.
b. Jan 18, 1918 in Noblesville, Indiana
d. Jan 28, 1995 in Sarasota, Florida
Source: *BiDrAC; BiDrUSC 89; BioIn 10, 11; CurBio 95N; NewYTBS 74; WhoAmP 85, 91*

Roueche, Berton
American. Author
Staff writer, *The New Yorker,* 1944-94, specializing in medical reporting; books include *The River World,* 1978.
b. Apr 16, 1911 in Kansas City, Missouri
d. Apr 28, 1994 in Amagansett, New York
Source: *AmAu&B; Au&Wr 71; BenetAL 91; BioIn 5, 13, 14, 15, 19, 20; ConAu 1NR, 1R, 48NR, 145; CurBio 59, 94N; DrAF 76; DrAPF 80, 87, 89; EncAJ; EncTwCJ; IntAu&W 76; REnAL; ScF&FL 1, 2; SmATA 28; WhAm 11; WhoAm 74, 76, 78, 80, 82, 84, 86, 88, 90, 92, 94; WhoUSWr 88; WhoWor 74, 76; WhoWrEP 89, 92; WorAu 1975; WrDr 90, 92, 94, 96*

Rouget de Lisle, Claude Joseph
French. Songwriter
Known for writing words, music to French national anthem "La Marseillaise," 1792.
b. May 10, 1760 in Lons-le-Saunier, France
d. Jun 20, 1836 in Choisy le Roi, France
Source: *BbD; BiD&SB; CasWL; DcEuL; EuAu; EvEuW; NewC; OxCEng 67; OxCFr; REn*

Rounds, David
American. Actor
Won 1980 Tony for *Mornings at Seven.*
b. Oct 9, 1930 in Bronxville, New York
d. Dec 9, 1983 in Lomontville, New York
Source: *BioIn 13; ConAu 111; NewYTBS 83; NotNAT; WhAm 8; WhoAm 82; WhoHol A, B*

Roundtree, Richard
American. Actor
Best-known film, *Shaft,* 1971; others include *City Heat,* 1984.
b. Sep 7, 1942 in New Rochelle, New York
Source: *AfrAmAl 6; BioIn 9, 11; BlksAmF; CelR; ConTFT 3; DcTwCCu 5; DrBlPA, 90; Ebony 1; FilmEn; FilmgC; InB&W 80, 85; IntMPA 77, 84, 86, 88, 92, 94, 96; MovMk; NewYTBE 72; VarWW 85; WhoAfA 96; WhoAm 76, 78, 80, 82, 84, 86, 88, 90, 92; WhoBlA 75, 77, 80, 85, 88, 90, 92, 94; WhoEnt 92; WhoHol A; WorAl*

Rounseville, Robert Field
American. Actor, Opera Singer
Films include *Tales of Hoffmann,* 1951; *Carousel,* 1955.
b. Mar 25, 1914 in Attleboro, Massachusetts
d. Aug 6, 1974 in New York, New York
Source: *BiE&WWA; BioIn 10; EncMT; NewYTBS 74; WhAm 6; WhoAm 74; WhoHol B; WhoThe 77*

Rountree, William M(anning)
American. Diplomat, Government Official
Asst. secretary of state for Near Eastern, South Asian, and African affairs, 1955-59; ambassador to Pakistan, 1959-62; Sudan, 1962-65; South Africa, 1965-70; Brazil, 1970-73.
b. Mar 28, 1917
d. Nov 3, 1995 in Gainesville, Florida
Source: *BioIn 5; BlueB 76; CurBio 96N; IntWW 74, 75, 76, 77; IntYB 78, 79, 80, 81, 82; USBiR 74; WhoAm 74, 76; WhoAmP 73, 75, 77, 79, 81, 83, 85, 87, 89, 91, 93, 95; WhoWor 74*

Rourke, Constance Mayfield
American. Author
Wrote *American Humor: A Study of the National Character,* 1931; *Audubon,* 1936.
b. Nov 14, 1885 in Cleveland, Ohio
d. Mar 23, 1941 in Grand Rapids, Michigan
Source: *AmAu&B; AnCL; CnDAL; ConAmA; CurBio 41; DcAmB S3; ModAL; MorJA; NotAW; OhA&B; OxCAmL 65; PenC AM; REn; REnAL; TwCA SUP; WhAm 1; YABC 1*

Rourke, Mickey
[Philip Andre Rourke, Jr.]
American. Actor
Films include *9 1/2 Weeks,* 1986; *Bar Fly,* 1987; known for playing difficult characters.
b. 1956 in Schenectady, New York
Source: *BioIn 13, 14, 15; ConTFT 5, 12; IntDcF 2-3; IntMPA 92, 94, 96; IntWW*

91; News 88; WhoAm 88, 94, 95, 96, 97; WhoEnt 92; WorAlBi

Rous, Francis Peyton
American. Scientist, Physician, Engineer
Shared Nobel Prize in medicine, 1966, for 1911 report on chicken viruses.
b. Oct 5, 1879 in Baltimore, Maryland
d. Feb 16, 1970 in New York, New York
Source: *AsBiEn; BiESc; BioIn 11, 12, 15, 20; CamDcSc; CurBio 67, 70; DcAmB S8; InSci; McGEWB; McGMS 80; NewYTBE 70; OxCMed 86; WebAB 74; WhAm 5; WhoNob, 90, 95; WorAl*

Rouse, James W(ilson)
American. Real Estate Executive, Urban Planner
Known for revitalization of inner cities; developed enclosed regional shopping mall; designed, built Columbia, MD, 1960s.
b. Apr 26, 1914 in Easton, Maryland
d. Apr 9, 1996 in Columbia, Maryland
Source: *BioIn 11, 12, 13, 14, 16; CurBio 82, 96N; WhoAm 74; WhoFI 75*

Roush, Edd J
[Eddie Roush]
American. Baseball Player
Outfielder, 1913-29, 1931, mostly with Cincinnati; led NL in batting twice; had .323 lifetime batting average; Hall of Fame, 1962.
b. May 8, 1893 in Oakland City, Indiana
d. Mar 21, 1988 in Bradenton, Florida
Source: *BiDAmSp BB; BioIn 6, 7; NewYTBS 88; WhoProB 73*

Rousseau, Henri
French. Artist
Primitive painter whose works possess dreamlike quality: *The Sleeping Gypsy,* 1897.
b. May 21, 1844 in Laval, France
d. Sep 2, 1910 in Paris, France
Source: *AtlBL; Benet 87; BioIn 1, 2, 3, 4, 5, 6, 7, 8, 9, 10, 11, 12; DcArts; DcTwCCu 2; IntDcAA 90; LegTOT; McGDA; McGEWB; NewCol 75; OxCArt; OxCFr; OxDcArt; PhDcTCA 77; REn; WebBD 83; WhDW; WorAl; WorAlBi*

Rousseau, Jean Jacques
French. Philosopher, Author
Influential political, educational reformer; wrote *Social Contract,* 1762; *Confessions,* published, 1781.
b. Jun 28, 1712 in Geneva, Switzerland
d. Jul 2, 1778 in Ermenonville, France
Source: *AtlBL; BbD; Benet 87, 96; BiD&SB; BioIn 1, 2, 3, 4, 5, 6, 7, 8, 9, 10, 11, 12, 13, 14; CasWL; ChhPo S1, S2; CmFrR; CyEd; CyWA 58; DcAmSR; DcBiA; DcBiPP; DcEnL; DcEuL; Dis&D; EncUnb; EuAu; EuWr 4; EvEuW; GolEC; LinLib L, S; LngCEL; LuthC 75; McGEWB; NamesHP; NewC; NewCBEL; NewEOp 71; OxCEng 67, 85; OxCFr; OxCGer 76; OxCLaw; OxCMus; PenC EUR; RAdv 1, 14, 13-3; RComWL; REn; WhNaAH; WorAl; WorAlBi*

Rousseau, (Pierre Etienne) Theodore
French. Artist
Landscapes include *Under the Birches;* led Barbizon School, painted dirctly from nature.
b. Apr 15, 1812 in Paris, France
d. Dec 22, 1867 in Barbizon, France
Source: *ArtsNiC; AtlBL; BioIn 4, 5, 7, 8, 9, 11; ClaDrA; DcBiPP; IntDcAA 90; LegTOT; LinLib S; McGDA; McGEWB; NewCol 75; NewYHSD; OxCFr; OxDcArt; ThHEIm*

Roussel, Albert
French. Composer
Wrote opera ballet *Padmavati,* 1918; often used Oriental scales, rhythms.
b. Apr 5, 1869 in Tourcoing, France
d. Aug 23, 1937 in Royan, France
Source: *Baker 78, 84; BioIn 3, 4, 6, 8, 12; BriBkM 80; CnOxB; CompSN; DcCM; DcCom&M 79; DcTwCC, A; DcTwCCu 2; FacFETw; LegTOT; McGEWB; MetOEnc; MusMk; NewAmDM; NewCol 75; NewGrDM 80; NewOxM; OxCFr; OxCMus; OxDcOp; PenDiMP A; WebBD 83*

Roux, Wilhelm
German. Scientist
Founded experimental embryology.
b. Jun 9, 1850 in Jena, Germany
d. Sep 15, 1924 in Halle, Germany
Source: *BioIn 12, 14; DcScB; InSci; LarDcSc; NewCol 75; WebBD 83*

Rovere, Richard Halworth
American. Author, Editor
Political columnist for *The New Yorker,* 1948-79; books include *Affairs of State: The Eisenhower Years,* 1956.
b. May 5, 1915 in Jersey City, New Jersey
d. Nov 23, 1979 in Poughkeepsie, New York
Source: *AmAu&B; BioIn 2, 4, 8, 11; ConAu 3NR, 49, 89; DcLEL 1940; OxCAmL 65; REnAL; WhoAm 74, 76, 78; WhoWor 74*

Rowan, Carl Thomas
American. Presidential Aide, Journalist
First black man to sit on National Security Council, 1964-65; has written syndicated newspaper column since 1965.
b. Aug 11, 1925 in Ravenscraft, Tennessee
Source: *AfrAmAl 6; AfrAmBi 2; AmAu&B; BiDAmNC; BioIn 2, 4, 5, 6, 7, 8, 9, 10, 11, 14, 16, 17, 18, 21; BlksCm; BlkWr 1, 2; ConAu 89; ConBlB 1; CurBio 58; EncTwCJ; EncWB; FacFETw; InB&W 80; JrnUS; LivgBAA; NegAl 89A; PolProf K; SchCGBL; SelBAAf; SelBAAu; Who 82, 83, 85, 88, 90, 92, 94; WhoAfA 96; WhoAm 74, 76, 78, 80, 82, 84, 86, 88, 90, 92, 94, 95, 96, 97; WhoAmP 73, 75, 77, 79, 81; WhoBlA 75, 77, 80, 85, 90, 92, 94; WhoSSW 73, 75; WhoUSWr 88; WhoWor 74; WhoWrEP 89, 92, 95*

Rowan, Dan
[Rowan and Martin]
American. Comedian
Co-star of TV comedy series "Laugh-In," 1968-73; straight man to Dick Martin for over 20 yrs; won two Emmys.
b. Jul 2, 1922 in Beggs, Oklahoma
d. Sep 22, 1987 in Englewood, Florida
Source: *AnObit 1987; BioIn 8, 10, 15; BioNews 74; ConAu 125; ConNews 88-1; CurBio 69, 87, 87N; FilmgC; ForYSC; HalFC 80, 84, 88; JoeFr; LegTOT; NewYTBS 87; VarWW 85; WhoAm 84; WhoHol A; WorAlBi*

Rowe, James Henry, Jr.
American. Government Official
Assistant to FDR who helped form, carry out New Deal.
b. Jun 1, 1909 in Butte, Montana
d. Jun 17, 1984 in Washington, District of Columbia
Source: *BioIn 11; NewYTBS 84; PolProf E; WhAm 8; WhoAm 74, 76, 78, 80, 82*

Rowe, Nicholas
English. Poet, Dramatist
Poet laureate from 1715; tragic plays include *Tamerlane,* 1702; noted as first modern editor of Shakespeare.
b. Jun 20, 1674 in Little Barford, England
d. Dec 6, 1718 in London, England
Source: *Alli; BbD; Benet 87, 96; BiD&SB; BioIn 3, 10, 12, 13; BlmGEL; BritAu; CamGEL; CamGLE; CamGWoT; CasWL; Chambr 2; ChhPo; CnThe; CrtSuDr; CrtT 2; DcArts; DcEnA; DcEnL; DcEuL; DcLB 84; DcLEL; DcNaB; DcPup; EncWT; Ent; EvLB; GrWrEL DR; IntDcT 2; LegTOT; LitC 8; McGEWD 72, 84; NewC; NewCBEL; NotNAT B; OxCEng 67, 85, 95; OxCThe 67, 83; PenC ENG; PoLE; REn; REnWD; RfGEnL 91; WebE&AL*

Rowe, Schoolboy
[Lynwood Thomas Rowe]
American. Baseball Player
Pitcher, 1933-43, 1946-49, mostly with Detroit; tied AL record for consecutive wins in season, 16, 1940.
b. Jan 11, 1912 in Waco, Texas
d. Jan 8, 1961 in El Dorado, Arkansas
Source: *BioIn 1, 3, 5, 6; DcAmB S7; WhoProB 73*

Rowen, Hobart
American. Journalist
With *Washington Post* since 1966; economics columnist since 1975.
b. Jul 31, 1918 in Burlington, Vermont
d. Apr 13, 1995 in Sherman Oaks, California
Source: *BiDAmNC; ConAu 9R, 148; EncTwCJ; JrnUS; WhoAm 74, 76, 78, 80, 82, 84, 86, 88, 90, 92, 94, 95; WhoE 89, 95; WhoFI 74, 94, 96; WhoSSW 73*

Rowland, Henry Augustus
American. Physicist
First physics professor, Johns Hopkins U, 1875-1901; invented concave diffraction for spectroscope.
b. Nov 27, 1848 in Honesdale, Pennsylvania
d. Apr 16, 1901 in Baltimore, Maryland
Source: *AmBi; ApCAB; AsBiEn; BiDAmS; BiESc; BiInAmS; BioIn 1, 2, 3, 4, 5, 6, 11, 12, 14; DcAmB; DcNAA; DcScB; EncAB-H 1974; InSci; LarDcSc; LinLib S; McGEWB; NatCAB 11; NewCol 75; OxCAmH; TwCBDA; WebAB 74, 79; WhAm 1*

Rowland, Pleasant
American. Business Executive
Founder and pres., Pleasant Company, creator of American Girl Collection and New Baby Collection of dolls and books.
b. Mar 8, 1946 in Chicago, Illinois
Source: *News 92; WhoMW 84*

Rowlands, Gena (Catherine)
[Mrs. John Cassavetes]
American. Actor
Oscar nominee, 1980, for *Gloria;* won 1987 Emmy for *The Betty Ford Story.*
b. Jun 19, 1936 in Cambria, Wisconsin
Source: *BiE&WWA; BioIn 4, 10, 12, 16; ConTFT 5; CurBio 75; FilmgC; ForYSC; IntMPA 76, 77, 78, 79, 80, 81, 82, 84, 86, 88, 92; InWom SUP; MotPP; NotNAT; VarWW 85; WhoAm 86, 88, 90, 92, 94, 95, 96, 97; WhoAmW 89, 91, 93; WhoEnt 92; WhoHol 92, A; WorAl*

Rowlandson, Thomas
English. Cartoonist
Best known for series of drawings, *Tours of Dr. Syntax,* 1812, 1820, 1821.
b. Jul 1756 in London, England
d. Apr 22, 1827 in London, England
Source: *Alli; AntBDN B; AtlBL; Benet 87, 96; BiDLA; BioIn 1, 2, 3; BkIE; CelCen; ChhPo, S2; ClaDrA; DcArts; DcBiPP; DcBrBI; DcBrWA; DcPup; Dis&D; IntDcAA 90; LegTOT; LinLib L, S; McGDA; NewC; NewCBEL; OxCArt; OxCEng 85, 95; OxCShps; OxDcArt; REn; WhDW; WorECom*

Rowley, James Joseph
American. Government Official
Director, Secret Service, 1961-73; reorganized and improved training procedures.
b. Oct 14, 1908 in New York, New York
d. Nov 1, 1992 in Leisure World, Maryland
Source: *BioIn 6, 10, 18, 19*

Rowling, Wallace Edward
New Zealander. Politician
Pres., Labour Party, 1970-73; prime minister, 1974-75; leader of Opposition, 1975-83.
b. Nov 27, 1927 in Motueka, New Zealand
Source: *BioIn 13; BlueB 76; FarE&A 78, 79, 80, 81; IntWW 74, 75, 76, 77, 78, 79, 80, 81, 82, 83, 89, 91, 93; WhAm 11; Who 74, 82, 83, 85, 92, 94; WhoAm 86, 88; WhoWor 76, 78, 80, 82, 84, 87*

Rowse, A(lfred) L(eslie)
English. Scholar, Biographer
Noted authority on Elizabethan England; wrote many books on subject: *The Sp irit of English History,* 1943.
b. Dec 4, 1903 in Saint Austell, England
Source: *Au&Wr 71; Benet 87, 96; BioIn 2, 4, 6, 7, 11, 12, 13, 14, 16; ChhPo, S1; ConAu 1NR, 1R, 8AS, 45NR; ConPo 70, 75, 85, 91, 96; CurBio 79; DcArts; EngPo; IntAu&W 76, 77, 82, 86, 89, 91; IntWW 74, 75, 76, 77, 78, 79, 80, 81, 82, 83, 89, 91, 93; IntWWP 77, 82; LngCEL; LngCTC; ModBrL; NewC; NewCBEL; OxCEng 85, 95; RAdv 13-3; TwCA SUP; WhE&EA; Who 74, 82, 83, 85, 88, 90, 92, 94; WhoWor 74, 76, 78, 84, 87, 89, 91, 93, 95, 96, 97; WrDr 76, 86, 92, 94, 96*

Roxana
Married Alexander the Great, 327 BC; murdered along with son, Alexander IV.
d. 311?BC
Source: *DcBiPP; EncAmaz 91; InWom; NewCol 75; OxCClL, 89; WebBD 83*

Roxon, Lillian
American. Journalist
Wrote *Rock Encyclopedia,* 1969.
b. 1933
d. Aug 9, 1973 in New York, New York
Source: *BioIn 8, 10; ConAu 111; NewYTBE 70, 73*

Roxy Music
[Brian Eno; Bryan Ferry; John Gustafson; Eddie Jobson; Andrew MacKay; Phil Manzanera; Paul Thompson]
English. Music Group
Hit singles include "The Same Old Scene," 1980; "Avalon," 1982.
Source: *Alli; AmEA 74; BioIn 11, 12, 14, 15, 16, 17, 18, 19, 20; ConMuA 80A; DcBiPP; EncPR&S 89; EncRk 88; EncRkSt; HarEnR 86; IlEncRk; IntvTCA 2; NewAgMG; OxCPMus; PenEncP; RkOn 85; RolSEnR 83; WhAm 2; WhoRock 81; WhoRocM 82*

Roy, Gabrielle
Canadian. Author
Wrote *The Tin Flute,* 1945; adapted to film, 1983.
b. Mar 22, 1909 in Saint Boniface, Manitoba, Canada
d. Jul 13, 1983 in Quebec, Quebec, Canada
Source: *AnObit 1983; Benet 87, 96; BenetAL 91; BioIn 3, 4, 9, 10, 12, 13, 14, 17; BlmGWL; CanWr; CasWL; CathA 1952; ConAu 5NR, 53, 110; ConCaAu 1; ConLC 10, 14; CreCan 2; DcLB 68; EncWL 2, 3; FemiCLE; GrFLW; InWom SUP; LinLib L; MagSWL; MajTwCW; ModCmwL; ModFrL; ModWoWr; Novels; OxCAmL 65; OxCCan; OxCCanL; OxCCan SUP; PenC ENG; REn; REnAL; RfGWoL 95; TwCA SUP; TwCWr; WhoAm 82*

Roy, Mike
[Michael Roy]
American. Chef
Wrote many cookbooks; hosted radio cooking show, "At Your Service," 1950-76.
b. Jul 18, 1912 in Hanaford, North Dakota
d. Jun 26, 1976 in Los Angeles, California
Source: *BioIn 10; ConAu 61, 65*

Roy, Patrick
Canadian. Hockey Player
Goalie, Montreal, 1984-95, Colorado, 1995—; member Stanley Cup Championship teams, 1986, 93, 96; won Vezina Trophy, 1989; Conn Smythe Trophy, 1986, 1993.
b. Oct 5, 1965 in Quebec, Quebec, Canada
Source: *BioIn 15, 19, 20, 21; News 94, 94-2; WhoAm 92, 94, 95, 96, 97; WhoSpor; WhoWor 95, 96; WorAlBi*

Roy, Ram Mohun
Indian. Social Reformer
Denounced the caste system; called for religious and educational reform in India.
b. May 22, 1772 in Radhanagar, India
d. Sep 27, 1833 in Bristol, England
Source: *BioIn 16; EncRev; McGEWB*

Roy, Ross
American. Advertising Executive
Founder, chm., Ross Roy, Inc., 1926-83.
b. Jul 22, 1898 in Kingston, Ontario, Canada
d. Aug 16, 1983 in Grosse Pointe Shores, Michigan
Source: *AnObit 1983; BioIn 7, 13; NewYTBS 83; St&PR 75, 84, 87; WhAm 8; WhoAdv 72; WhoAm 74, 76, 78, 80, 82; WhoFI 75, 77, 79*

Royal, Darrell K
American. Football Coach
Head coach, U of TX, 1957-77; won three national championships.
b. Jul 6, 1924 in Hollis, Oklahoma
Source: *BiDAmSp FB; BioIn 9, 10; WhoAm 84, 86, 88*

Royall, Anne Newport
American. Journalist, Traveler
Sometimes called first American newspaperwoman; published Washington gossip sheet, 1830.
b. Jun 11, 1769 in Baltimore, Maryland
d. Oct 1, 1854 in Washington, District of Columbia
Source: *Alli; AmAu; AmAu&B; AmBi; AmWomWr; ApCAB; BenetAL 91; BibAL; BiDAmJo; BiDSA; BioAmW; BioIn 15, 16, 17; DcAmAu; DcAmB; DcLEL; DcNAA; Drake; EncAB-H 1974, 1996; EncSoH; GoodHs; InWom, SUP;*

LibW; NotAW; OxCAmL 65, 83, 95; PenNWW A; REnAL; WebAB 74, 79; WhAm HS; WomComm; WomFir

Royce, Frederick Henry, Sir
English. Auto Manufacturer
Founded Royce Ltd., 1904; with C S Rolls formed Rolls-Royce Ltd., 1906.
b. Mar 27, 1863 in Peterborough, England
d. Apr 22, 1933
Source: *DcTwBBL; InSci; WebBD 83; WorAl*

Royce, Josiah
American. Author, Philosopher
Foremost American idealist, Harvard professor, 1892-1916; wrote *The Spirit of Modern Philosophy,* 1892.
b. Nov 20, 1855 in Grass Valley, California
d. Sep 14, 1916 in Cambridge, Massachusetts
Source: *Alli SUP; AmAu&B; AmBi; AmPeW; ApCAB; Benet 87, 96; BenetAL 91; BiD&SB; BiDInt; BiDPara; BiDPsy; BiInAmS; BioIn 1, 2, 3, 4, 5, 6, 8, 9, 10, 12, 13, 14, 15, 16, 17, 19; CmCal; DcAmAu; DcAmB; DcAmReB 1, 2; DcLEL; DcNAA; EncAB-H 1974, 1996; EncARH; EncEth; EncO&P 1, 2, 3; EncPaPR 91; EvLB; FacFETw; GayN; InSci; LegTOT; LinLib L, S; LuthC 75; McGEWB; NatCAB 11, 25; OxCAmL 65, 83, 95; OxCPhil; PenC AM; RAdv 14, 13-4; REn; REnAL; REnAW; TwCA, SUP; TwCBDA; WebAB 74, 79; WebE&AL; WhAm 1; WhDW; WorAl; WorAlBi; WrPh P*

Royer, William Blackburn, Jr.
[The Hostages]
American. Hostage
One of 52 held by terrorists, Nov 1979-Jan 1981.
b. Oct 21, 1931 in Pennsylvania
Source: *NewYTBS 81; USBiR 74*

Royko, Mike
American. Journalist
Reporter, columnist with Chicago newspapers, 1959-97; won Pulitzer for commentary, 1972.
b. Sep 19, 1932 in Chicago, Illinois
d. Apr 29, 1997 in Chicago, Illinois
Source: *BiDAmNC; BioIn 10, 11, 19, 20; CelR 90; ConAu 26NR, 89; ConPopW; CurBio 94; EncAHmr; EncAJ; EncTwCJ; JrnUS; LegTOT; LiJour; WhoAm 74, 76, 78, 80, 82, 84, 86, 88, 90, 92, 94, 95, 96, 97; WhoMW 74, 78, 80, 82, 84, 86, 88, 90, 92, 93; WhoUSWr 88; WhoWrEP 89, 92, 95; WorAl; WorAlBi; WrDr 80, 86, 92, 96*

Royle, Selena
American. Actor
Usually played mother in films: *Courage of Lassie,* 1946; *A Date with Judy,* 1948.
b. 1904 in New York, New York
d. Apr 23, 1983 in Guadalajara, Mexico
Source: *BioIn 13, 14; ConAu 109; EncAFC; FilmEn; ForYSC; HalFC 80, 84, 88; IntMPA 75, 76, 77, 78, 79, 80, 81, 82, 84, 86, 88; LegTOT; MGM; Vers B; WhoHol A; WhThe*

Royo, Aristides
Panamanian. Politician
Pres. of Panama, 1978-82; resigned.
b. Aug 14, 1940 in La Chorrera, Panama
Source: *BioIn 12; IntWW 79, 80, 81, 82, 83, 91; IntYB 80, 81, 82; WhoWor 82*

Royster, Vermont C(onnecticut)
American. Newspaper Editor
Reporter, columnist, *Wall Street Journal,* 1948-86; won Pulitzer, 1953, for editorial writing; editorial page editor, 1958-71; wrote weekly column, "Thinking Things Over."
b. Apr 30, 1914 in Raleigh, North Carolina
d. Jul 22, 1996 in Raleigh, North Carolina
Source: *AmAu&B; BiDAmJo; BiDAmNC; BioIn 3, 7, 8, 9, 13, 16; BlueB 76; CurBio 53, 96N; DcLB 127; DrAS 74E; EncTwCJ; IntAu&W 77, 89, 91, 93; IntWW 74, 75, 76, 77, 78, 79, 80, 81, 82, 83, 89, 91, 93; JrnUS; WhoAm 74, 86, 90, 92, 94, 95, 96, 97; WhoSSW 73, 82; WhoWor 78; WrDr 76, 86, 92*

Rozanov, Vasili Vasilyevich
Russian. Author
Published first detailed account of Dostoyevski: *Legend of the Grand Inquisitor,* 1890.
b. May 2, 1856 in Vetluga, Russia
d. Feb 5, 1919 in Moscow, Russia
Source: *CasWL; ClDMEL 47; DcRusL; EncWL; EuAu; EvEuW; ModSL 1; PenC EUR; REn*

Roze, Marie
[Marie Ponsen]
French. Opera Singer
Soprano; admired as Carmen, 1870s-80s.
b. Mar 2, 1846 in Paris, France
d. Jun 21, 1926 in Paris, France
Source: *Baker 84, 92; BioIn 3; NewEOp 71; PenDiMP*

Rozelle, Pete
[Alvin Ray Rozelle]
"Boy Commissioner"
American. Football Executive
Commissioner of NFL, 1960-89; merged NFL/AFL, 1966; Hall of Fame, 1985.
b. Mar 1, 1926 in South Gate, California
d. Dec 6, 1996 in Rancho Santa Fe, California
Source: *BiDAmSp FB; BioIn 6, 7, 8, 12, 13; CelR, 90; CurBio 64; LegTOT; NewYTBS 27; WhoAm 74, 76, 78, 80, 82, 84, 86, 88, 90, 92, 94, 95, 96, 97; WhoE 85, 86, 89; WhoFtbl 74; WorAl; WorAlBi*

Rozhdestvensky, Gennadi Nikolaevich
Russian. Conductor
Led BBC Symphony Orchestra, 1978-81; Moscow Chamber Orchestra, since 1974.
b. 1931 in Moscow, Union of Soviet Socialist Republics
Source: *Baker 84; IntWW 74, 75, 82, 91; IntWWM 90; NewAmDM; PenDiMP; Who 74, 82, 83, 85, 88, 90, 92; WhoEnt 92; WhoMus 72; WhoWor 74, 78, 80, 82, 84, 87, 89, 91, 93, 95*

Rozier, Mike
American. Football Player
Running back, won Heisman Trophy, 1983; in NFL with Houston, 1985-90; Atlanta, 1990-91.
b. Mar 1, 1961 in Camden, New Jersey
Source: *BiDAmSp FB; BioIn 14; FootReg 87; InB&W 85; WhoAfA 96; WhoBlA 92, 94; WhoSpor*

Rozsa, Miklos
American. Composer
Arranged film background music, 1930s-70s; scored *Ben Hur,* 1959.
b. Apr 18, 1907 in Budapest, Hungary
d. Jul 27, 1995 in Los Angeles, California
Source: *AmComp; Baker 78, 84, 92; BioIn 1, 10, 13, 16, 17, 18, 21; CmMov; CmpEPM; ConAmC 76, 82; ConTFT 8, 15; CpmDNM 76, 79, 80, 82; CurBio 92, 95N; DcCM; FilmEn; FilmgC; GangFlm; HalFC 80, 84, 88; IntDcF 1-4, 2-4; IntMPA 75, 76, 77, 78, 79, 80, 81, 82, 84, 86, 88, 92, 94; IntWW 91, 93; IntWWM 77, 80, 90; ItaFilm; LegTOT; NewAmDM; NewGrDA 86; NewGrDM 80; NewYTBS 95; OxCFilm; OxCMus; OxCPMus; PenDiMP A; WhoAm 92, 94; WhoAmM 83; WhoEnt 92; WhoHrs 80; WhoMus 72; WhoWor 74; WorEFlm*

Ruark, Robert Chester
American. Author
Best-selling works include *Horn of the Hunter,* 1953; wrote autobiography *Old Man and the Boy,* 1957.
b. Dec 29, 1915 in Wilmington, North Carolina
d. Jul 1, 1965 in London, England
Source: *AmAu&B; BioIn 1, 2, 3, 4, 5, 6, 7, 20; ConAu P-2; DcAmB S7; LngCTC; REn; REnAL; WhAm 4; WhScrn 77; WorAl*

Rubbia, Carlo
Italian. Physicist
Known for high-energy experiments with subatomic particles; shared Nobel Prize, 1984.
b. Mar 31, 1934 in Gorizia, Italy
Source: *AmMWSc 89, 92, 95; BioIn 14, 15; CurBio 85; IntWW 89, 91, 93; LarDcSc; NewYTBS 84; NobelP; NotTwCS; Who 88, 90, 92, 94; WhoAm 78, 86, 88, 90, 92, 94, 95; WhoNob, 90, 95; WhoScEn 94, 96; WhoScEu 91-4;*

WhoWor 84, 87, 89, 91, 93, 95, 96, 97; WorAlBi; WorScD

Rubell, Steve
American. Businessman
Co-founded Studio 54, New York's most fashionable disco dance club of the 1970s.
b. 1944?
d. Jul 25, 1989 in New York, New York
Source: *AnObit 1989; BioIn 11, 12, 14; NewYTBS 89*

Rubens, Alma
American. Actor
Silent film star, 1916-29; heroin addiction cut career short.
b. Feb 8, 1897 in San Francisco, California
d. Jan 23, 1931 in Los Angeles, California
Source: *BioIn 12; Film 1, 2; FilmEn; FilmgC; HalFC 80, 84, 88; LegTOT; MotPP; MovMk; NotNAT B; SilFlmP; TwYS; WhoHol B; WhScrn 74, 77, 83*

Rubens, Peter Paul, Sir
Flemish. Artist
Baroque style painter, known for brilliant coloring; sacred, historical subjects include *Rape of the Sabines.*
b. Jun 29, 1577 in Siegen, Prussia
d. May 30, 1640 in Antwerp, Belgium
Source: *AtlBL; Benet 87, 96; BioIn 1, 2, 3, 4, 5, 6, 7, 8, 9, 10, 11, 12, 13, 14, 15, 19, 20, 21; ChhPo; ClaDrA; DcArts; DcBiPP; DcCathB; Dis&D; IntDcAA 90; LegTOT; LinLib S; LuthC 75; McGDA; McGEWB; NewC; NewCol 75; OxCArt; OxCEng 85, 95; OxDcArt; RAdv 14, 13-3; REn; WhDW; WorAl*

Rubicam, Raymond
American. Advertising Executive
Co-founded one of largest advertising agencies in US, Young & Rubicam, 1923.
b. Jun 16, 1892 in New York, New York
d. May 8, 1978 in Scottsdale, Arizona
Source: *AdMenW; BioIn 1, 5, 6, 8, 10, 11, 13, 20; CurBio 43, 78N; DcAmB S10; NatCAB 62; St&PR 75; WhAm 7; WhoAm 74, 76, 78; WhoFI 74; WhoWest 74, 76, 78; WorAl; WorAlBi*

Rubik, Erno
Hungarian. Educator
Created Rubik's cube, 1974.
b. Jul 13, 1944 in Budapest, Hungary
Source: *BioIn 12, 15; CurBio 87; IntWW 83, 89, 91, 93; LegTOT; NewYTBS 86*

Rubin, Barbara Jo
American. Jockey
First female jockey to ride winning horse on US track, 1969.
b. Nov 21, 1949 in Highland, Illinois
Source: *BiDAmSp OS; BioIn 8; CurBio 69; EncWomS; InWom SUP; WhoSpor; WomFir*

Rubin, Benny
American. Comedian
Vaudeville comedian, tap dancer; worked with Jack Benny, Eddie Cantor, 1920s; helped launch careers of Milton Berle, George Burns.
b. Feb 2, 1899 in New York, New York
d. Jul 16, 1986 in Los Angeles, California
Source: *BioIn 15; ConAu 119; EncAFC; EncVaud; Film 2; FilmEn; ForYSC; QDrFCA 92; RadStar; TwYS; Vers A; WhoHol A*

Rubin, Gayle
American. Scholar
First person to receive a BA in women's studies from the University of Michigan, 1972; writes on many topics including feminist theory.
b. Jun 1949
Source: *GayLesB*

Rubin, Jerry
[The Chicago 7]
American. Author, Political Activist
Original "yippie" member; one of first defendants tried, convicted under anti-riot provision in 1968 Civil Rights Act.
b. Jul 14, 1938 in Cincinnati, Ohio
d. Nov 28, 1994 in Los Angeles, California
Source: *AmAu&B; BiDAmLf; BioIn 8, 10, 11, 12, 13, 16, 20, 21; ConAu 69; EncWB; FacFETw; HisWorL; LNinSix; MugS; News 95, 95-2; NewYTBS 76, 88, 94; PolProf J*

Rubin, Reuven
Israeli. Artist
Romantic impressionist, noted for landscapes of Holy Land; first minister to Romania from Israel, 1948-49.
b. Nov 13, 1893 in Galati, Romania
d. Oct 13, 1974 in Tel Aviv, Israel
Source: *BioIn 8, 10; ClaDrA; CurBio 43, 75, 75N; IntWW 74, 75; WhAm 6; WhoWor 74; WhoWorJ 72*

Rubin, Rick
[Frederick Jay Rubin]
American. Music Executive, Producer
Co-founder of Def Jam Records, 1984; founder pres., Def American Records, 1988—; producer of rock, punk, rap music.
b. Mar 10, 1963 in Lido Beach, New York
Source: *ConMus 9; WhoAm 94, 95, 96, 97; WhoEnt 92*

Rubin, Robert E.
American. Government Official
Chm., National Economic Council, 1993-95; Secretary of the Treasury, 1995—.
b. Aug 29, 1938 in New York, New York
Source: *CngDr 95; NewYTBS 94; St&PR 91, 93; WhoAm 84, 90, 97; WhoAmP 93, 95; WhoFI 92; WhoSecI 86; WhoWor 97*

Rubin, Theodore Isaac
American. Psychiatrist, Author
Columnist, *Ladies Home Journal,* 1968—; books include *Lisa and David,* 1961.
b. Apr 11, 1923 in New York, New York
Source: *AmAu&B; AmMWSc 73P; AuNews 1; BiDrAPA 77, 89; BioIn 7, 9, 10, 12; BioNews 74; ConAu 108, 110; CurBio 80; WhoAm 74, 76, 78, 80, 82, 84, 86, 88, 90, 92, 94, 95, 96, 97; WhoMedH; WhoWor 74, 76; WrDr 76, 92*

Rubin, Vitalii
Russian. Author, Educator
Advocate of human rights, free emigration while in Soviet concentration camp.
b. Sep 14, 1923 in Moscow, Union of Soviet Socialist Republics
d. Oct 18, 1981 in Beersheba, Israel
Source: *ConAu 69, 105; NewYTBS 81*

Rubin, William Stanley
American. Museum Director
Director, Department of Painting and Sculpture, Museum of Modern Art, NYC, 1967- 1988.
b. Aug 11, 1927 in New York, New York
Source: *BioIn 14, 15, 16; ConAu 77; CurBio 86; DrAS 82H; WhoAm 86, 88; WhoAmA 89; WhoE 89*

Rubini, Giovanni-Battista
Italian. Opera Singer
Celebrated European tenor, 1830s-40s; first to make extensive use of musical sob.
b. Apr 7, 1794 in Romano, Italy
d. Mar 2, 1854 in Romano, Italy
Source: *Baker 84; NewEOp 71*

Rubinstein, Anton Gregorovitch
Russian. Pianist
Virtuoso who rivaled Liszt; established prize for piano playing, composition, 1890.
b. Nov 28, 1829 in Kherson, Russia
d. Nov 20, 1894 in Peterhof, Russia
Source: *AtlBL; NewCol 75; OxCMus; WebBD 83*

Rubinstein, Arthur
American. Pianist
Ranked with Rachmaninoff, Horowitz among greatest pianists of 20th c; considered world's finest interpreter of Chopin.
b. Jan 28, 1887 in Lodz, Poland
d. Dec 20, 1982 in Geneva, Switzerland
Source: *AnObit 1982; Baker 78, 92; BiDAmM; BlueB 76; CelR; ConAu 108, 113; CurBio 66, 83; FacFETw; HalFC 84; IntWW 81; LinLib S; MusSN; NewGrDM 80; NewYTBS 76, 82; PenDiMP; WebAB 74, 79; Who 82, 83; WhoAm 82; WhoFr 79; WhoWor 78; WhoWorJ 78; WorAl; WorAlBi*

Rubinstein, Helena
American. Cosmetics Executive
Founder, pres. of Helena Rubinstein, Inc, 1902.
b. Dec 25, 1870 in Krakow, Poland
d. Apr 1, 1965 in New York, New York
Source: *AmWomM; BiDAmBL 83; BioAmW; BioIn 7, 8, 9, 10, 11, 12, 15, 16, 18; CurBio 43, 65; DcAmB S7; Entr; HerW, 84; InWom SUP; LegTOT; NatCAB 50; NotAW MOD; WhAm 4; WomFir; WorAl; WorAlBi*

Rubinstein, John Arthur
American. Actor
Won Tony for *Children of a Lesser God,* 1980; son of Arthur Rubinstein.
b. Dec 8, 1946 in Beverly Hills, California
Source: *ASCAP 80; BioIn 14, 15; HalFC 84; NewYTBS 80, 85; OxCAmT 84; VarWW 85; WhoAm 76, 78, 80, 82, 84, 86, 88, 90, 92; WhoEnt 92; WhoHol A; WhoRocM 82*

Rubirosa, Porfirio
Dominican. Diplomat
Playboy, sportsman, whose wives included Doris Duke, Barbara Hutton.
b. 1909
d. Jul 5, 1965 in Paris, France
Source: *BioIn 3, 4, 7, 10, 12; ObitOF 79*

Rubloff, Arthur
American. Real Estate Executive
Best known projects include Ft. Dearborn Project; North Loop Plan.
b. Jun 25, 1902 in Duluth, Minnesota
d. May 24, 1986 in Chicago, Illinois
Source: *BioIn 3, 12, 15; BlueB 76; St&PR 75; WhoAm 74, 82; WhoFI 74*

Ruby, Harry
American. Songwriter
Prolific Broadway composer; collaborated with Bert Kalmar on "Three Little Words," 1930; film based on their partnership, 1950.
b. Jan 27, 1895 in New York, New York
d. Feb 23, 1974 in Woodland Hills, California
Source: *AmPS; AmSong; ASCAP 66, 80; BiDAmM; BiE&WWA; BioIn 4, 5, 6, 10, 15, 16; CmpEPM; EncMT; HalFC 80, 84, 88; LegTOT; NewAmDM; NewCBMT; NewGrDA 86; NotNAT B; ObitOF 79; OxCAmT 84; OxCPMus; PopAmC, SUPN; WhAm 6; WhThe; WorAl; WorAlBi*

Ruby, Jack
[Jacob Rubenstein]
American. Murderer
Killed Lee Harvey Oswald on TV, 1963.
b. Mar 23, 1911 in Chicago, Illinois
d. Jan 3, 1967 in Dallas, Texas
Source: *AmDec 1960; BioIn 6, 7, 8, 9, 10, 11; FacFETw; LegTOT; ObitOF 79; PolProf J; WorAl; WorAlBi*

Ruchlis, Hy(man)
American. Children's Author
Science books include *Your Changing Earth,* 1963; *Wonder of Electricity,* 1965.
b. Apr 6, 1913 in New York, New York
d. Jun 30, 1992 in West Palm Beach, Florida
Source: *AuBYP 2, 3; BioIn 7, 9, 18; ConAu 1R, 2NR, 47NR, 139; DcLP 87A; SmATA 3, 72*

Ruckelshaus, William Doyle
American. Government Official
EPA administrator under Nixon, 1970-73; Reagan, 1983-85.
b. Jul 24, 1934 in Indianapolis, Indiana
Source: *BioIn 13, 14; CurBio 71; Dun&B 90; IntWW 74, 75, 76, 77, 78, 79, 83, 91; NewYTBE 72, 73; NewYTBS 83; St&PR 84, 87, 91; WhoAm 86, 90; WhoAmP 73, 91; WhoFI 85; WhoGov 72; WhoSSW 91*

Rucker, Darius
[Hootie and the Blowfish]
American. Musician, Singer, Songwriter
Won Grammy, Best New Artist, with Hootie and the Blowfish, 1995; debut album, *Cracked Rear View,* 1994.
b. May 13, 1966 in Charleston, South Carolina
Source: *BioIn 21*

Ruckert, Friedrich
German. Poet
Attempted to popularize Oriental poetic forms, ideas in Germany; works include "Songs on Children's Deaths," 1872.
b. May 16, 1788 in Schweinfurt, Germany
d. Jan 31, 1866 in Neuss, Germany
Source: *BbD; Benet 87, 96; BiD&SB; BioIn 7; CasWL; CelCen; DcEuL; Dis&D; EuAu; EvEuW; LinLib L; NewGrDM 80; OxCGer 76, 86; PenC EUR; REn*

Rudd, Hughes Day
American. Broadcast Journalist
Correspondent, ABC and CBS News; won Emmy, Peabody.
b. Sep 14, 1921 in Wichita, Kansas
d. Oct 13, 1992 in Toulouse, France
Source: *AmAu&B; BioIn 10; ConAu 73, 139; LesBEnT, 92; PeoHis; WhAm 10; WhoAm 74, 76, 78, 80, 82, 84, 86; WhoTelC*

Rudd, Mark
American. Revolutionary
Member of anti-war group, Students for Dem. Society, 1966; indicted as leader of Weatherman "Days of Rage" demonstration, Chicago, 1969.
b. Jun 2, 1947 in Irvington, New Jersey
Source: *BioIn 9, 10, 11, 20; LNinSix; MugS; PolProf J*

Rudd, Paul Ryan
American. Actor
TV shows include "Beacon Hill," 1975; "Beaulah Land," 1980; "Knots Landing," 1980.
b. May 5, 1940 in Boston, Massachusetts
Source: *ConTFT 5; CurBio 77; NewYTBS 76; WhoAm 78, 80, 82, 84, 86, 88, 90, 92, 94, 95; WhoEnt 92; WhoThe 81*

Rudd, Phil(lip)
Australian. Musician
Drummer, AC-DC, since 1974.
b. May 19, 1946 in Melbourne, Australia
Source: *WhoRocM 82*

Ruddy, Al(bert Stotland)
Canadian. Producer
Films include *The Godfather,* 1972; *Cannonball Run II,* 1984.
b. Mar 28, 1934 in Montreal, Quebec, Canada
Source: *BioIn 11; ConTFT 9; HalFC 84, 88; IntMPA 86, 92; VarWW 85; WhoAm 76, 78, 80*

Rudel, Julius
Austrian. Conductor
Led NYC Opera, 1957-79; Buffalo Philharmonic, 1979-85.
b. Mar 6, 1921 in Vienna, Austria
Source: *Baker 78, 84, 92; BiDAmM; BiE&WWA; BioIn 5, 6, 7, 8, 9, 10, 11, 13, 14; BlueB 76; BriBkM 80; CelR; CmOp; CurBio 65; IntDcOp; IntWWM 80, 90; MetOEnc; MusSN; NatCAB 63N; NewAmDM; NewEOp 71; NewGrDA 86; NewGrDM 80; NewGrDO; NewYTBE 71; OxDcOp; PenDiMP; WhoAm 74, 76, 78, 80, 82, 84, 86, 88, 90, 92, 94, 95, 96, 97; WhoE 74, 75, 77, 85, 95; WhoEnt 92; WhoGov 72, 75, 77; WhoOp 76; WhoWor 74, 76; WhoWorJ 72, 78*

Rudenko, Lyudmila
Russian. Chess Player
Won first world chess competition for women, 1950; first woman international grandmaster, 1977.
b. Jul 27, 1904 in Saint Petersburg, Russia
d. Mar 2, 1986 in Leningrad, Union of Soviet Socialist Republics
Source: *GolEC*

Rudensky, Morris
[Max Motel Friedman]
"Red"
American. Criminal
Safecracker with Al Capone, Bugsy Moran; spent 35 yrs. in prison; released, 1944, became law-abiding citizen.
b. 1908 in New York, New York
d. Apr 21, 1988 in Saint Paul, Minnesota
Source: *BioIn 9; DrInf*

Ruder, David Sturtevant
American. Government Official, Educator, Lawyer
Chm. of the Securities and Exchange Commission, 1987-89; served on the faculty of Northwestern U, IL, 1961-87.
b. May 25, 1929 in Wausau, Wisconsin
Source: *BioIn 15, 16; CurBio 88; DrAS 74P, 78P, 82P; WhoAm 74, 76, 78, 80, 82, 84, 86, 88, 90, 92, 94, 95, 96, 97; WhoAmL 78, 79, 83, 85, 87, 90, 96; WhoAmP 91; WhoFI 89*

Ruder, Melvin
American. Editor
Founder, editor, *Hungry Horse News*, 1946-78; won Pulitzer for local reporting, 1965.
b. Jan 19, 1915 in Manning, North Dakota
Source: *St&PR 75; WhoAm 86, 90; WhoWest 74*

Rudhyar, Dane
American. Author, Composer
His polytonal music was the first played in US, NY Met., 1917; prolific writer on astrology.
b. Mar 23, 1895 in Paris, France
d. Sep 13, 1985 in San Francisco, California
Source: *AmAu&B; AmComp; ArtsAmW 2; AstEnc; Baker 78, 84, 92; BiDAmM; BioIn 1, 14; ConAmC 76, 82; ConAu 21NR, 29R, 117; CpmDNM 81, 82; DcCM; EncO&P 1S1, 2, 2S1, 3; IntAu&W 76, 77; IntWWM 77, 80; NewAgE 90; NewGrDA 86; NewGrDM 80; OxCMus; ScF&FL 1, 2, 92; WhAm 10; WhoAm 74, 76, 78, 80, 82, 84; WhoAmM 83; WrDr 76, 80, 82, 84*

Rudi, Joe
[Joseph Oden Rudi]
American. Baseball Player
Outfielder, 1967-82, mostly with great Oakland teams of 1970s; led AL in hits, 1972.
b. Sep 7, 1946 in Modesto, California
Source: *Ballpl 90; BaseEn 88; BioIn 10, 11; WhoAm 78, 80, 82; WhoProB 73*

Rudkin, Margaret Fogarty
American. Business Executive
Founder, Pepperidge Farms baking firm, 1937.
b. Sep 14, 1897 in New York, New York
d. Jun 1, 1967 in New Haven, Connecticut
Source: *AmWomM; BioIn 17; ConAmBL; CurBio 67; DcAmB S8; EncWB; InWom, SUP; NotAW MOD; ObitOF 79; WhAm 4; WhoAmW 61, 64, 66, 68; WomFir*

Rudman, Warren Bruce
American. Politician
Rep. senator from NH, 1981-92; co-authored Gramm-Rudman deficit reduction law, 1985.
b. May 18, 1930 in Boston, Massachusetts
Source: *AlmAP 88, 92; BiDrUSC 89; BioIn 14, 16; CngDr 81, 83, 85, 87, 89; CurBio 89; IntWW 81, 82, 83, 89, 91, 93; NewYTBS 76, 90; PolsAm 84; WhoAm 82, 84, 86, 88, 90, 92, 94, 95, 96, 97; WhoAmP 73, 75, 87, 91; WhoE 89, 91, 93; WhoGov 75, 77; WhoSSW 91; WhoWor 82, 87, 89, 91*

Rudner, Rita
American. Comedian
Stand-up comedian; cohosted TV program "Funny People," 1988; co-author and actress in film *Peter's Friends* 1993.
b. 1956 in Miami, Florida
Source: *BioIn 16; ConTFT 12; IntMPA 96; LegTOT; News 93-2; WhoHol 92*

Rudnick, Paul
American. Dramatist
Wrote *I Hate Hamlet*, 1991; *Jeffrey*, 1993.
b. 1957 in Piscataway, New Jersey
Source: *ConAu 139; ConTFT 15; News 94, 94-3; WhoAm 95, 96, 97*

Rudolf, Max
German. Conductor
Led Cincinnati Symphony, 1958-70; Met. Opera Assn., 1973-75.
b. Jun 15, 1902 in Frankfurt am Main, Germany
d. Mar 1, 1995 in Philadelphia, Pennsylvania
Source: *Baker 78, 84, 92; BioIn 4, 6, 9, 13, 20; BlueB 76; BriBkM 80; IntWWM 77, 80, 90; LinLib S; MetOEnc; NewAmDM; NewEOp 71; NewGrDA 86; NewGrDM 80; NewGrDO; NewYTBS 88, 95; PenDiMP; WhoAm 74, 76, 78, 80, 82, 84, 86, 88, 90, 92, 94, 95, 96; WhoAmM 83; WhoE 95; WhoEnt 92; WhoOp 76; WhoSSW 76; WhoWor 74, 82, 84, 87, 89, 91, 93, 95*

Rudolf II
Ruler
Ruled Holy Roman Empire, 1576-1612; son of Maximilian II; granted Bohemians religious freedom, 1608.
b. Jul 18, 1552 in Vienna, Austria
d. Jan 20, 1612 in Prague, Czechoslovakia
Source: *BioIn 9; NewCol 75; WebBD 83*

Rudolf of Hapsburg
Austrian. Prince
Archduke, prince of Austria; only son of Emperor Franz Joseph.
b. Aug 21, 1858 in Laxenberg, Austria
d. Jan 30, 1889 in Vienna, Austria
Source: *BioIn 9; NewCol 75; WebBD 83*

Rudolph, Paul Marvin
American. Architect
Designs include Art & Architecture Bldg., Yale U.
b. Oct 23, 1918 in Elkton, Kentucky
Source: *AmArch 70; BioIn 4, 5, 6, 7, 9, 11, 13, 14, 15, 16; ConArch 80, 87, 94; CurBio 72; DcD&D; EncWB; IntDcAr; IntWW 74, 75, 76, 77, 78, 79, 80, 81, 82, 83, 89, 91, 93; MacEA; McGDA; WhoAm 74, 78, 80, 82, 84; WhoArch; WhoE 74, 89; WhoWor 74*

Rudolph, Wilma (Glodean)
American. Track Athlete
Sprinter; first American woman to win three gold medals, 1960 Olympics.
b. Jun 23, 1940 in Clarksville, Tennessee
d. Nov 12, 1994 in Nashville, Tennessee
Source: *AfrAmAl 6; AfrAmBi 2; AfrAmSG; BiDAmSp OS; BioIn 5, 6, 7, 8, 9, 10, 11, 12, 13, 16, 20, 21; BlkAmWO; BlkOlyM; BlkWAm; ConBlB 4; ConHero 2; ContDcW 89; CurBio 61, 95N; EncWomS; FacFETw; GoodHs; GrLiveH; HerW, 84; InB&W 85; IntDcWB; InWom, SUP; LegTOT; LibW; LinLib S; NegAl 76, 83, 89; News 95, 95-2; NewYTBS 94; NotBlAW 1; WhoAfA 96; WhoBlA 77, 80, 85, 90, 92, 94; WhoTr&F 73; WomFir; WorAl; WorAlBi*

Ruehl, Mercedes
American. Actor
Won Tony for *Lost in Yonkers*;; won Oscar for best supporting actress in *The Fisher King*, 1992.
Source: *BioIn 16, 18, 19; ConTFT 9; IntMPA 92, 94; News 92; WhoAm 92, 94, 95, 96, 97; WhoAmW 93, 95, 97; WhoE 93*

Ruffin, Clovis
American. Fashion Designer
Ready-to-wear designer, part of Kreisler Group; youngest designer to win Coty, 1973.
d. Apr 7, 1992 in New York, New York
Source: *BioIn 11, 17, 18; NewYTBS 92; WhoAm 80, 82; WhoFash; WorFshn*

Ruffin, David
American. Singer
Member of 1960s pop group The Temptations; hits included "Ain't Too Proud to Beg," and "My Girl;" died from a drug overdose.
b. Jan 18, 1941 in Meridian, Mississippi
d. Jun 1, 1991 in Philadelphia, Pennsylvania
Source: *AnObit 1991; BioIn 12; ConMus 6; DcArts; EncRk 88; InB&W 85; LegTOT; News 91; NewYTBS 91; PenEncP; RkOn 78; RolSEnR 83; SoulM; WhoBlA 92N; WhoRock 81; WhoRocM 82*

Ruffin, Edmund
American. Chemist
The leading figure in soil chemistry.
b. Jan 5, 1794 in Prince George County, Virginia
d. Jun 18, 1865 in Amelia County, Virginia
Source: *Alli; AmAu&B; AmBi; AmSocL; ApCAB; BiDAmJo; BiDAmS; BiDSA; BiInAmS; BioIn 1, 3, 4, 7, 12, 16, 17, 19; CivWDc; DcAmB; DcNAA; Drake; EncAAH; EncAB-H 1974, 1996; EncSoH; HarEnUS; McGEWB; NatCAB*

5; OxCAmH; PeoHis; WebAB 74, 79; WebAMB; WhAm HS; WhAmP; WhCiWar

Ruffin, Jimmy
American. Singer
Hits include "What Becomes of the Brokenhearted," 1966; "Hold on to My Love," 1980.
b. May 7, 1939 in Meridian, Mississippi
Source: *EncRk 88; EncRkSt; IlEncBM 82; PenEncP; RkOn 74, 78; SoulM*

Ruffing, Red
[Charles Herbert Ruffins]
American. Baseball Player
Pitcher, 1924-42, 1945-47, mostly with Yankees; had 273 career wins, 48 shutouts; Hall of Fame, 1967.
b. May 5, 1905 in Granville, Illinois
d. Feb 17, 1986 in Cleveland, Ohio
Source: *AnObit 1986; CurBio 41, 86; WhoProB 73*

Ruffo, Titta
[Ruffo Cafiero Titta]
Italian. Opera Singer
Famed baritone, noted for Verdi roles.
b. Jun 9, 1877 in Pisa, Italy
d. Jul 6, 1953 in Florence, Italy
Source: *Baker 78, 84, 92; BioIn 3, 7, 11, 14; BriBkM 80; CmOp; IntDcOp; MetOEnc; MusSN; NewAmDM; NewEOp 71; NewGrDA 86; NewGrDM 80; NewGrDO; OxDcOp; PenDiMP; WhScrn 74, 77, 83*

Ruggles, Carl
American. Composer, Artist
Controversial atonal musical works include *Sun-Treader,* 1931; had recent popularity.
b. Mar 11, 1876 in Marion, Massachusetts
d. Oct 24, 1971 in Bennington, Vermont
Source: *ASCAP 80; Baker 78, 84, 92; BiDAmM; BioIn 1, 3, 4, 7, 8, 9, 13, 17, 19, 20, 21; BriBkM 80; CompSN, SUP; ConAmC 76, 82; DcCM; FacFETw; MusMk; NewGrDA 86; NewGrDM 80; NewOxM; NewYTBE 71; OxCMus; WhAm 5; WhAmArt 85*

Ruggles, Charles
American. Actor
Character actor in films *Charley's Aunt,* 1915; *Ruggles of Red Gap,* 1916.
b. Feb 8, 1892 in Los Angeles, California
d. Dec 23, 1970 in Santa Monica, California
Source: *BiE&WWA; Film 1; MovMk; OxCFilm; WhAm 5; WhScrn 74, 77; WorEFlm*

Ruiz, Rosie
American. Track Athlete
Declared winner, then disqualified from Boston Marathon for cheating, 1981.
b. 1954?
Source: *BioIn 16; NewYTBS 81*

Rukeyser, Louis (Richard)
American. Broadcast Journalist, Author
Host, PBS series "Wall Street Week," 1970—; author *How To Make Money in Wall Street.*
b. Jan 30, 1933 in New York, New York
Source: *BioIn 11, 12, 13, 14, 15; ConAu 36NR, 65; CurBio 83; EncTwCJ; IntWW 89, 91, 93; JrnUS; LegTOT; WhoAm 82, 84, 86, 88, 90, 92, 94, 95, 96, 97; WhoE 89, 91, 93, 95, 97; WhoFI 87, 89, 92, 94, 96; WhoTelC; WhoWor 95, 96, 97; WorAlBi*

Rukeyser, Muriel
American. Poet
Comprehensive collection of poetry released in 1979: *The Collected Poems of Muriel Rukeyser;* wrote on social themes, feminism.
b. Dec 15, 1913 in New York, New York
d. Feb 12, 1980 in New York, New York
Source: *AmAu&B; AmWomWr; AnObit 1980; ArtclWW 2; AuBYP 2, 3; Benet 87, 96; BenetAL 91; BioIn 4, 7, 8, 10, 11, 12, 13, 14, 15, 17, 19, 20; BlmGWL; BlueB 76; CamGLE; CamHAL; CasWL; ChhPo, S1; CnDAL; ConAu 5R, 26NR, 93; ConLC 6, 10, 15, 27; ConPo 70, 75, 80; ContDcW 89; CurBio 43, 80N; DcAmB S10; DcLB 48; DcLEL; DrAP 75; DrAS 74E, 78E; EncWL 3; FemiCLE; FemiWr; ForWC 70; GayLesB; GrLiveH; GrWomW; GrWrEL P; HanAmWH; IntDcWB; IntWW 78, 79; IntWWP 82; InWom, SUP; JeAmWW; LegTOT; LibW; LinLib L; MajTwCW; ModAL, S1, S2; ModWoWr; NewYTBS 80; OxCAmL 65, 83, 95; OxCTwCP; OxCWoWr 95; PenBWP; PenC AM; PoeCrit 12; RAdv 1, 14; REn; REnAL; RfGAmL 87, 94; SixAP; SmATA 22N; TwCA, SUP; TwCWr; WebE&AL; WhAm 7; WhoAm 74, 76, 78, 80; WhoAmW 58, 61, 64, 66, 68, 70, 72, 74, 83; WhoWor 74, 76; WorAl; WorAlBi; WrDr 76, 80*

Rukeyser, William Simon
American. Editor
Managing editor, *Fortune,* 1980-86; commentator, "TV's Good Morning America," 1978-85.
b. Jun 8, 1939 in New York, New York
Source: *BlueB 76; ConAu 37NR, 69; IntAu&W 91; WhoAm 74, 76, 78, 80, 82, 84, 86, 88, 90, 92, 94, 95, 96, 97; WhoFI 87; WhoSSW 95, 97; WhoWor 74*

Rule, Jane
Canadian. Writer
Novels include *Desert of the Heart,* 1964; *Lesbian Images,* 1975.
b. Mar 28, 1931 in Plainfield, New Jersey
Source: *ArtclWW 2; BenetAL 91; BioIn 16, 19; BlmGWL; CamGLE; CaW; ConAu 12NR, 18AS, 25R, 30NR; ConLC 27; ConNov 86, 91; DcLB 60; FemiCLE; GayLesB; IntAu&W 77, 82, 86, 91, 93; OxCCan; OxCCanL; OxCCan SUP; OxCWoWr 95; RGTwCWr; ScF&FL 92; WhoAmW 74, 75; WhoCanL 85, 87, 92; WrDr 76, 80, 82, 84, 86, 88, 90, 92, 94, 96*

Rule, Janice
[Mrs. Ben Gazzara]
American. Actor
Former nightclub dancer, leading lady; became psychoanalyst, mid-1970s.
b. Aug 15, 1931 in Norwood, Ohio
Source: *BiDFilm, 81; BiE&WWA; BioIn 2, 6, 14; FilmEn; FilmgC; HalFC 80, 84, 88; IntMPA 75, 76, 77, 78, 79, 80, 81, 82, 84, 86, 88, 92, 94, 96; InWom, SUP; MotPP; NotNAT; WhoAm 76; WhoAmW 68A, 70, 72, 74; WhoHol 92, A; WhoThe 77, 81; WorAl*

Rulfo, Juan
Mexican. Author
Author of novel *Pedro Paramo,* 1955.
b. May 16, 1918 in Sayula, Mexico
d. Jan 7, 1986 in Mexico City, Mexico
Source: *AnObit 1986; Benet 87, 96; BenetAL 91; BioIn 7, 13, 14, 15, 16, 17, 18; CasWL; ConAu 26NR, 85, 118; ConFLW 84; ConLC 8, 80; DcCLAA; DcHiB; DcLB 113; DcMexL; DcTwCCu 4; EncLatA; EncWL 2, 3; HispLC; HispWr; LatAmWr; MajTwCW; ModLAL; NewYTBS 86; Novels; OxCSpan; PenC AM; PenEncH; RAdv 14, 13-2; TwCWr; WhoSSW 73; WorAu 1970*

Rumann, Sig(fried)
German. Actor
Character actor, 1929-66; made over 100 films: *A Night at the Opera.*
b. Oct 11, 1884 in Hamburg, Germany
d. Feb 14, 1967 in Julian, California
Source: *BioIn 21; EncAFC; FilmEn; HolCA; MovMk; OlFamFa; WhoHol B*

Ruml, Beardsley
American. Business Executive
Financial expert; chm., Federal Reserve Bank, NYC, 1941-47; devised 1943 tax bill adopted by Congress.
b. Nov 5, 1894 in Cedar Rapids, Iowa
d. Apr 18, 1960 in Danbury, Connecticut
Source: *BiDAmBL 83; BioIn 1, 2, 4, 5, 6; CurBio 43, 60; DcAmB S6; EncAB-H 1974, 1996; NatCAB 44; WhAm 3A*

Rumor, Mariano
Italian. Political Leader
Christian Democratic prime minister of Italy; led five coalition governments, 1968-75.
b. Jun 16, 1915 in Vicenza, Italy
d. Jan 22, 1990 in Vicenza, Italy
Source: *BioIn 8, 9, 16, 17; CurBio 69, 90, 90N; DcPol; FacFETw; IntWW 74, 75, 76, 77, 78, 79, 80, 81, 82, 83, 89; IntYB 78, 79, 80, 81, 82; NewYTBE 73; NewYTBS 90; WhoEIO 82; WhoWor 74*

Rumsfeld, Donald (Harold)
American. Government Official
Rep. congressman from IL, 1963-69; director, OEO, 1969-70; ambassador to

NATO, 1973-74; received Presidential Medal of Freedom, 1977.
b. Jul 9, 1932 in Chicago, Illinois
Source: *BiDrAC; BiDrUSC 89; BiDrUSE 89; BioIn 8, 9, 10, 11, 12, 13; BioNews 75; BlueB 76; CurBio 70; Dun&B 86; IntWW 74, 75, 91; NewYTBE 71; NewYTBS 74, 83; PolProf NF; WhoAm 74, 76, 78, 80, 82, 84, 86, 88, 90; WhoAmP 73, 75, 77, 79, 81, 83, 85, 89, 91, 93, 95; WhoFI 79, 81, 83, 85, 87, 92; WhoGov 72, 75, 77; WhoSSW 73; WhoWest 82; WhoWor 74, 78, 80, 82, 84, 91*

Runcie, Robert Alexander Kennedy
English. Religious Leader
Archbishop of Canterbury, 1980-91.
b. Oct 21, 1921 in Liverpool, England
Source: *BioIn 12, 13, 14, 15, 16; BlueB 76; ConAu 28NR, 108; CurBio 80; FacFETw; IntWW 80, 81, 82, 83; News 89; NewYTBS 79; Who 90; WhoAm 82, 84, 86, 88, 90; WhoRel 92; WhoWor 80, 82, 84, 87, 89, 91, 93, 95, 96, 97*

Rundgren, Todd
American. Musician, Singer
Music influenced by "British invasion"; songs include "Hello It's Me," 1973.
b. Jun 22, 1948 in Upper Darby, Pennsylvania
Source: *BioIn 15; ConMuA 80A, 80B; ConMus 11; EncPR&S 74, 89; EncRk 88; EncRkSt; HarEnR 86; IlEncRk; LegTOT; NewGrDA 86; OnThGG; PenEncP; RkOn 74, 78; RolSEnR 83; WhoAm 80, 82, 84, 86, 88, 90, 92, 94, 95, 96, 97; WhoEnt 92; WhoRock 81; WhoRocM 82; WorAlBi*

Run-DMC
American. Rap Group
First black rap group to enter music mainstream; albums include *Run-DMC,* 1984 and *Raising Hell,* 1986.
Source: *BioIn 16; CelR 90; ConMus 4; ConTFT 9; EncPR&S 89; IntMPA 92*

Rundstedt, Karl Rudolf Gerd von
German. Military Leader
WW II field marshal, 1940; commander-in-chief on Western front, 1942-45.
b. Dec 12, 1875 in Aschersleben, Germany
d. Feb 24, 1953 in Hannover, Germany (West)
Source: *BioIn 1, 3, 11, 14, 17; CurBio 41, 53; DcTwHis; FacFETw; GenMudB; HarEnMi; McGEWB; REn; WhoMilH 76*

Runeberg, Johan Ludwig
Finnish. Poet
Finland's greatest poet; composed national hymn; wrote in Swedish *Kung Fjalar,* 1844.
b. Feb 5, 1804 in Jakobstad, Finland
d. May 6, 1877 in Borga, Finland
Source: *BioIn 12; CasWL; CelCen; EuAu; LinLib L; NewCol 75; REn*

Runnels, Tom
American. Baseball Manager
Succeeded Buck Rodgers as manager of the Montreal Expos, 1991—.
b. Apr 17, 1955 in Greeley, Colorado
Source: *BioIn 14; NewYTBS 85*

Runyan, Paul Scott
"Little Poison"
American. Golfer
Turned pro, 1922; had over 50 PGA wins including PGA, 1934, 1938; Hall of Fame, 1959.
b. Jul 12, 1908 in Hot Springs, Arkansas
Source: *BiDAmSp OS; BioIn 15; WhoGolf*

Runyon, Damon
[Alfred Damon Runyon]
American. Journalist, Author
Used slang, metaphors in writings of romanticized underworld criminals; wrote *Guys and Dolls,* 1932.
b. Oct 4, 1884 in Manhattan, Kansas
d. Dec 10, 1946 in New York, New York
Source: *AmAu&B; Ballpl 90; Benet 87; BenetAL 91; BiDAmNC; CamGEL; CamGLE; CamHAL; CasWL; ChhPo; CnDAL; CnMWL; ConAu 107; CurBio 47; DcAmB S4; DcLEL; DcNAA; EncAJ; EncMys; EvLB; FacFETw; Film 2; FilmgC; GangFlm; HalFC 80, 84, 88; JrnUS; LegTOT; LinLib L; LngCTC; ModAL; ModWD; NotNAT A, B; Novels; OxCAmL 65, 83; OxCAmT 84; PenC AM; PlP&P; REn; REnAL; TwCA, SUP; TwCWr; WebAB 74, 79; WebE&AL; WhAm 2; WhDW; WhoHol B; WhScrn 77, 83; WorAl; WorAlBi*

RuPaul
[RuPaul Andre Charles]
American. Actor, Model, Singer
Transvestite performer; wrote autobiography, *Lettin' It All Hang Out,* 1995.
b. 1960 in New Orleans, Louisiana
Source: *DcTwCCu 5; GayLesB*

Rupp, Adolph Frederick
"Baron"
American. Basketball Coach
Coach, U of KY, 1931-72, compiling 874-190 record; Hall of Fame.
b. Sep 2, 1901 in Halstead, Kansas
d. Dec 10, 1977 in Lexington, Kentucky
Source: *BiDAmSp BK; DcAmB S10; NewYTBS 77; ObitOF 79; WhAm 7; WhoAm 74, 76, 78; WhoBbl 73; WhoSSW 73, 75; WorAl*

Ruppe, Loret Miller
American. Government Official
Director of Peace Corps, 1981-89; US Ambassador to Norway 1989-93.
b. Jan 3, 1936 in Milwaukee, Wisconsin
d. Aug 6, 1996 in Bethesda, Maryland
Source: *AmWomM; BioIn 15; ConNews 86-2; WhoAm 84, 92, 94, 95, 96, 97; WhoAmP 81, 83, 85, 87, 89, 91, 93, 95; WhoAmW 93, 95; WhoWor 93, 95*

Ruscha, Edward
American. Artist, Photographer
Pop artist whose classics include *The Los Angeles County Museum on Fire;* notorious for his 3-D word paintings.
b. Dec 16, 1937 in Omaha, Nebraska
Source: *AmArt; BioIn 9, 13, 15; ConArt 77, 83, 89; ConPhot 82, 88; CurBio 89; DcAmArt; DcCAA 71, 77, 88, 94; DcTwCCu 1; ICPEnP A; IntWW 91; OxCTwCA; PrintW 85; WhoAm 74, 76, 78, 80, 82, 84, 86, 88, 90, 92, 94, 95, 96, 97; WorArt 1980*

Rush
[Geddy Lee; Alex Liefson; Neil Peart; John Rutsey]
Canadian. Music Group
Formed 1971; use laser, visual projections; hit album *Power Windows,* 1985.
Source: *ConMuA 80A; ConMus 8; EncPR&S 89; EncRk 88; EncRkSt; HarEnR 86; NewYHSD; PenEncP; RkOn 85; RolSEnR 83; WhoRock 81; WhoRocM 82*

Rush, Barbara
American. Actor
TV shows include "Peyton Place," 1968-69; "Flamingo Road," 1981-82.
b. Jan 4, 1929 in Denver, Colorado
Source: *ConTFT 5; FilmgC; HalFC 84; IntMPA 86, 92; InWom SUP; MotPP; MovMk; VarWW 85; WhoAm 86; WhoEnt 92; WhoHol A; WorAlBi; WorEFlm*

Rush, Benjamin
American. Physician, Continental Congressman
Most famous American doctor of his time; signed Declaration of Independence, 177 6; surgeon general, Continental Army, 1777-78; hero of Philadelphia, 1793, durin g yellow fever epidemic.
b. Dec 24, 1745 in Philadelphia, Pennsylvania
d. Apr 19, 1813 in Philadelphia, Pennsylvania
Source: *Alli; AmAu; AmAu&B; AmBi; AmSocL; AmWrBE; ApCAB; BenetAL 91; BiAUS; BiDAmEd; BiDrAC; BiESc; BiHiMed; BioIn 1, 2, 3, 4, 5, 6, 7, 8, 9, 10, 13; BlkwEAR; CyAG; CyAL 1; CyEd; DcAmAu; DcAmB; DcAmMeB; DcAmSR; DcBiPP; DcLEL; DcNAA; Drake; EncAB-H 1974, 1996; HanAmWH; HarEnUS; HisWorL; InSci; McGEWB; NamesHP; OxCAmH; OxCMed 86; REn; REnAL; WebAB 74, 79; WhAmP; WorAl*

Rush, Billy
[Southside Johnny and the Asbury Jukes]
American. Musician
Guitarist with Southside Johnny and the Asbury Jukes since 1974.
b. Aug 26, 1952
Source: *WhoRocM 82*

Rush, (David) Kenneth
American. Diplomat, Government Official
Active in politics, law; ambassador to Germany, 1969-72; to France, 1974-77; advised Nixon, Ford on economic policy.
b. Jan 17, 1910 in Walla Walla, Washington
d. Dec 11, 1994 in Delray Beach, Florida
Source: *BioIn 4, 9, 10, 12, 16, 20, 21; BlueB 76; CngDr 74; CurBio 75, 95N; DcAmDH 80, 89; IntWW 74, 75, 76, 77, 78, 79, 80, 81, 82, 83, 89, 91, 93; IntYB 78, 79, 80, 81, 82; NewYTBE 71, 72; PolProf NF; WhoAm 74, 76, 78, 80, 82, 84, 86, 88, 90, 92, 94, 95; WhoAmP 73, 75, 77, 79, 81, 83, 85, 87, 89, 91, 93, 95; WhoE 74; WhoGov 72, 75, 77; WhoWor 74, 76, 78, 80, 82, 84, 87, 89, 93, 95*

Rush, Richard
American. Director, Producer
Oscar nominee for *The Stunt Man,* 1980.
b. 1931? in New York, New York
Source: *BioIn 12; ConTFT 6; FilmgC; HalFC 84, 88; IntMPA 86, 92; WhoAm 82*

Rush, Tom
American. Singer, Songwriter
Blues albums include *Late Night Radio,* 1985.
b. Feb 8, 1941 in Portsmouth, New Hampshire
Source: *BiDAmM; BioIn 14, 15; ConMuA 80A; EncFCWM 69, 83; EncRk 88; HarEnR 86; IlEncRk; PenEncP; RolSEnR 83; WhoRock 81*

Rush, William
American. Sculptor
Noted for wooden carvings, especially of George Washington; one of PA Academy of Fine Arts founders.
b. Jul 5, 1756 in Philadelphia, Pennsylvania
d. Jan 17, 1833 in Philadelphia, Pennsylvania
Source: *AmBi; ApCAB; BioIn 2, 9, 11; BriEAA; CabMA; DcAmArt; DcAmB; FolkA 87; McGDA; McGEWB; NatCAB 8; NewYHSD; OxCAmL 65; OxCArt; OxDcArt; TwCBDA; WebAB 74, 79; WhAm HS*

Rushdie, Salman Ahmed
British. Author
His novel *The Satanic Verses,* 1989, condemned by Muslims as blasphemous to Islam; sentenced to death by Ayatollah Khomeini, 1989; in hiding since sentence; wrote *The Moor's Last Sigh,* 1995.
b. Jun 19, 1947 in Bombay, India
Source: *Benet 87; BioIn 13, 14, 15, 16; CamGLE; ConAu 33NR, 108, 111; ConLC 23, 55; ConNov 86; CurBio 86; CyWA 89; IntAu&W 91; IntWW 83, 91; NewYTBS 89, 90, 91; OxCEng 85; PostFic; ScFSB; Who 85, 92; WhoRel 92; WhoWor 91; WorAlBi; WorAu 1975; WrDr 86, 92*

Rushen, Patrice Louise
American. Pianist, Singer
Child prodigy; studied music at age three; jazzy dance hits include ''Feels So Real,'' 1984.
b. Sep 30, 1954 in Los Angeles, California
Source: *BiDJaz; BioIn 11, 13; EncJzS; InB&W 85; InWom SUP; NewGrDJ 88; RkOn 85; WhoBlA 92*

Rusher, William Allen
American. Publisher
Publisher of conservative mag., *The National Review,* 1957-1989; columnist, frequent tv guest.
b. Jul 19, 1923 in Chicago, Illinois
Source: *BiDAmNC; BioIn 10, 16; BlueB 76; ConAu 28NR, 103; DcAmC; WhoAm 74, 76, 78, 80, 82, 84, 86, 88, 90, 92, 94, 95, 96, 97; WhoE 74, 77, 79, 81, 91, 93; WhoWest 96; WrDr 76, 80, 82, 84, 86, 88, 90, 92, 94, 96*

Rushing, Jimmy
''Mister Five by Five''
American. Jazz Musician
Major blues singer, toured with swing bands; with Count Basie, 1935-48, 1960s.
b. Aug 26, 1903 in Oklahoma City, Oklahoma
d. Jun 8, 1972 in New York, New York
Source: *AfrAmAl 6; AllMusG; Baker 84, 92; BiDJaz; BioIn 15, 17; CmpEPM; EncJzS; IlEncJ; LegTOT; NegAl 76, 83, 89; NewAmDM; NewGrDA 86; NewGrDJ 88, 94; NewGrDM 80; NewYTBE 72; RolSEnR 83; WhoJazz 72; WhScrn 77, 83; WorAl; WorAlBi*

Rushmore, Robert (William)
American. Author
Noted for book on history of vocal music, *The Singing Voice,* 1971; novels include *If My Love Leaves Me,* 1975.
b. Jul 7, 1926 in Tuxedo Park, New York
d. Sep 20, 1986 in Poughkeepsie, New York
Source: *BioIn 11; ConAu 25R, 120; DrAF 76; DrAPF 80; IntAu&W 77; SmATA 8, 49N*

Rusie, Amos Wilson
''Hoosier Thunderbolt''
American. Baseball Player
Pitcher, 1889-1901, mostly with NY Giants; holds several ML pitching records; had 243 career wins; Hall of Fame, 1977.
b. May 31, 1871 in Mooresville, Indiana
d. Dec 6, 1942 in Seattle, Washington
Source: *BiDAmSp BB; BioIn 3; WhoProB 73*

Rusk, (David) Dean
American. Government Official
Secretary of State, 1961-69; defended US involvement in Vietnam.
b. Feb 9, 1909 in Cherokee County, Georgia
d. Dec 20, 1994 in Athens, Georgia
Source: *AmPolLe; BiDrUSE 71, 89; BioIn 1, 2, 3, 5, 6, 7, 8, 9, 10, 11, 12, 13, 16, 17, 18, 20, 21; BlueB 76; CelR; ColdWar 1, 2; ConAu 141, 147; CurBio 49, 61, 95N; DcAmDH 80, 89; DcPol; DcTwHis; EncAB-H 1974, 1996; EncCW; EncWB; FacFETw; HisDcKW; HisEAAC; HisWorL; IntWW 74, 75, 76, 77, 78, 79, 80, 81, 82, 83, 89, 91, 93; IntYB 78, 79, 80, 81, 82; LegTOT; LinLib S; News 95, 95-2; NewYTBS 88, 94; PeoHis; PolProf E, J, K, T; WhDW; Who 74, 82, 83, 85, 88, 90, 92, 94; WhoAm 74, 76, 78, 80, 82, 84, 86, 88, 90, 92, 94, 95; WhoAmP 73, 75, 77, 79, 81; WhoGov 72, 75, 77; WhoWor 74, 76, 78; WorAl; WorAlBi*

Ruska, Ernst
German. Scientist
Invented electron microscope, 1933; shared 1986 Nobel Prize in physics.
b. Dec 25, 1906 in Heidelberg, Germany
d. May 27, 1988 in Berlin, Germany (West)
Source: *AnObit 1988; AsBiEn; BioIn 5, 15, 16, 17, 20; FacFETw; NobelP; NotTwCS; WhoNob 90, 95*

Ruskin, John
English. Critic, Author
Wrote on art, social problems: *Modern Painters,* 1843-60; juvenile classic: *King of the Golden River,* 1851; defended pre-Raphaelites.
b. Feb 8, 1819 in London, England
d. Jan 20, 1900 in Coniston, England
Source: *Alli, SUP; ArtsNiC; AtlBL; BbD; Benet 87, 96; BiD&SB; BiDTran; BioIn 1, 2, 3, 4, 5, 6, 7, 8, 9, 10, 11, 12, 13, 14, 15, 16, 17, 18, 21; BlmGEL; BriEAA; BritAu 19; BritWr 5; CamGEL; CamGLE; CarSB; CasWL; CelCen; Chambr 3; ChhPo, S1, S2, S3; ClaDrA; CnDBLB 4; ConAu 114, 129; CrtT 3, 4; CyEd; CyWA 58; DcAmSR; DcArts; DcBiPP; DcBrBI; DcBrWA; DcEnA, A; DcEnL; DcEuL; DcLB 55, 163; DcLEL; DcNaB S1; DcNiCA; DcPup; DcVicP, 2; Dis&D; EncO&P 1, 2, 3; EncPaPR 91; EncUrb; EvLB; FamSYP; GrWrEL N; IntDcAr; LegTOT; LinLib L, S; LngCEL; MacEA; MagSWL; McGDA; McGEWB; MouLC 4; NewC; NewCBEL; OxCArt; OxCChiL; OxCDecA; OxCEng 67, 85, 95; OxDcArt; PenC ENG; RAdv 14; RComWL; REn; RfGEnL 91; SmATA 24; StaCVF; TwCLC 20, 63; VicBrit; WebE&AL; WhDW; WhoChL; WorAl; WorAlBi; WrChl*

Russell, Andy
[Andres Rabago]
American. Singer
Romantic-style vocalist of 1940s; recorded ''Besame Mucho.''
d. Apr 16, 1992 in Phoenix, Arizona

Source: *BioIn 1, 10, 17, 18; CmpEPM; ForYSC; NewYTBS 92; WhoHol A*

Russell, Anna
English. Comedian
Wrote *The Power of Being a Positive Stinker;* popular satirist of opera stars; had many hit recordings.
b. Dec 27, 1911 in London, England
Source: *ASCAP 66, 80; BiE&WWA; BioIn 7, 14, 15; CurBio 54; JoeFr; NewAmDM; NewGrDA 86; NewYTBS 74; NotNAT; OxCThe 67; Who 74, 82, 83, 85, 88, 90, 92, 94; WhoAmW 58, 66, 68, 70, 72, 74; WhoHol A; WhoWor 74*

Russell, Annie
American. Actor
Early 1900s star, inspired Florida's Annie Russell Theater, 1932.
b. Jan 12, 1864 in Liverpool, England
d. Jan 16, 1936 in Winter Park, Florida
Source: *AmBi; BioIn 4; CamGWoT; DcAmB S2; FamA&A; InWom, SUP; LibW; NatCAB 13; NotAW; NotNAT B; OxCAmT 84; OxCThe 67; PlP&P; WhoStg 1906, 1908; WhThe*

Russell, Bertrand Arthur William
Welsh. Mathematician, Author
Wrote popular books on philosophy, *Principia Mathematica,* 1910-13; won Nobel Prize, 1950.
b. May 18, 1872 in Monmouthshire, Wales
d. Feb 2, 1970 in Merionethshire, Wales
Source: *AsBiEn; AtlBL; Benet 96; BiDMoPL; BiESc; BlmGEL; CamGEL; CasWL; Chambr 3; ConAu 44NR, P-1; CurBio 51, 70; DcLEL; DcNaB 1961; DcScB; DcTwHis; EncEth; EncSF 93; EvLB; GrBr; IlEncMy; InSci; IntEnSS 79; LarDcSc; LinLib S; LngCEL; LngCTC; LuthC 75; MakMC; McGEWB; ModBrL; NewC; NewCBEL; OxCEng 67, 85, 95; PenC ENG; RAdv 14; REn; TwCA, SUP; TwCSFW 81; TwCWr; WebE&AL; WhAm 5; WhDW; WhE&EA; WhLit; WhoLA; WhoNob, 90, 95; WorAl; WorScD*

Russell, Bill
[William Felton Russell]
American. Basketball Player, Basketball Coach
Five-time MVP center, Boston, 1956-69; first black coach in NBA, with Boston, 1966-69, Seattle, 1973-77; Hall of Fame, 1975.
b. Feb 12, 1934 in Monroe, Louisiana
Source: *AfrAmAl 6; AfrAmBi 1; AfrAmSG; AmDec 1950, 1960; BasBi; BiDAmSp BK; BioIn 4, 5, 6, 7, 8, 9, 10, 11, 12; BlkWrNE; CelR; CmCal; ConAu 108; ConBlB 8; ConHero 1; CurBio 75; FacFETw; InB&W 80, 85; LegTOT; NegAl 76, 83, 89; NewYTBE 73; NewYTBS 87; WebAB 74, 79; WhoAfA 96; WhoAm 74, 76, 80, 82, 84, 86, 88, 90, 92, 94, 95, 96, 97; WhoBbl 73; WhoBlA 75, 77, 80, 85, 88, 92, 94; WhoSpor; WhoWest 87, 89, 94, 96; WorAl; WorAlBi*

Russell, Blair
Canadian. Hockey Player
Forward for amateur Montreal Victorias, early 1900s; Hall of Fame, 1965.
b. Sep 17, 1880
d. Dec 7, 1961 in Montreal, Quebec, Canada
Source: *WhoHcky 73*

Russell, Charles Marion
American. Artist
Great painter of American West; museum in Great Falls, MT.
b. Mar 19, 1864 in Saint Louis, Missouri
d. Oct 24, 1926 in Great Falls, Montana
Source: *AmAu&B; ArtsAmW 1; BioIn 4, 5, 6, 7, 8, 9, 10, 11, 12, 14; BriEAA; DcAmArt; DcNAA; GayN; IlBEAAW; IlrAm 1880, B; McGEWB; NewCol 75; REnAW; TwCWW 82; WhAm 1; WhNaAH*

Russell, Charles Taze
American. Religious Leader
Founded Russellites, 1878, which became Jehovah's Witnesses, 1931.
b. Feb 16, 1852 in Pittsburgh, Pennsylvania
d. Oct 31, 1916 in Pampa, Texas
Source: *AmAu&B; AmBi; AmDec 1900; ApCAB X; BiDAmCu; BioIn 19; ChhPo S1; DcAmB; DcAmReB 1, 2; DcNAA; EncARH; LuthC 75; McGEWB; NatCAB 12; NewCol 75; RelLAm 91; WebAB 74, 79; WhAm 1; WorAl; WorAlBi*

Russell, Donald Joseph
American. Businessman
Pres., chm., Southern Pacific Co., 1964-72; introduced computer automation to co., 1960s.
b. Jan 3, 1900 in Denver, Colorado
d. Dec 13, 1985 in San Francisco, California
Source: *AmCath 80; BioIn 2, 6; BlueB 76; CurBio 86; IntWW 74, 75, 76, 77, 78, 79, 80, 81, 82, 83; IntYB 78, 79, 80, 81, 82; WhAm 9; WhoAm 74, 76; WhoWest 74, 76, 78*

Russell, Edward Frederick Langley, Baron of Liverpool
English. Judge, Author
Prosecuted war criminals after WW II; wrote *Scourge of the Swastika.*
b. Apr 10, 1895 in Liverpool, England
d. Apr 8, 1981 in Hastings, England
Source: *Au&Wr 71; BioIn 5, 12; ConAu 103; DcNaB 1981; IntAu&W 76, 77; NewYTBS 81; WhoWor 74; WrDr 80*

Russell, Ernie
[Ernest Russell]
Canadian. Hockey Player
Forward with amateur Montreal Wanderers, early 1900s; Hall of Fame, 1965.
b. Oct 21, 1883 in Montreal, Quebec, Canada
d. Feb 23, 1963 in Montreal, Quebec, Canada
Source: *WhoHcky 73*

Russell, Franklin Alexander
New Zealander. Author
Books about animals include *The Sea Has Wings,* 1973; *Lotor the Raccoon,* 1972.
b. Oct 9, 1926, New Zealand
Source: *AmAu&B; AuBYP 2, 3; ConAu 11NR, 17R; SmATA 11; WhoAm 80, 82; WrDr 86, 92*

Russell, Gail
"Hollywood's Haunted Heroine"
American. Actor
Films include *The Unlimited; The Unseen;* career ended by alcoholism, emotional problems.
b. Sep 23, 1924 in Chicago, Illinois
d. Aug 26, 1961 in Los Angeles, California
Source: *BioIn 10, 11, 15; FilmEn; FilmgC; ForYSC; HalFC 80, 84, 88; HolP 40; InWom SUP; MotPP; MovMk; NotNAT B; WhoHol B; WhScrn 74, 77, 83*

Russell, George William
[A.E.]
Irish. Poet, Dramatist, Editor
Literary revival figure; helped form Irish National Theater; wrote drama *Deirdre,* 1907.
b. Apr 10, 1867 in County Armagh, Ireland
d. Jul 17, 1935 in Bournemouth, England
Source: *AtlBL; Benet 96; BiDIrW; BioIn 1, 2, 3, 5, 6, 8, 9, 11, 13, 15, 16, 17, 18; CamGEL; CamGLE; CasWL; Chambr 3; ChhPo, S1, S2, S3; CnDBLB 5; ConAu 104; DcArts; DcIrB 78, 88; DcIrL 96; DcIrW 1; DcLEL; DcNaB 1931; EncWL 2, 3; EvLB; GrWrEL P; IlEncMy; LinLib L; LngCTC; McGEWD 72, 84; ModBrL; ModIrL; ModWD; NewC; NewCBEL; OxCEng 67, 85, 95; PlP&P; PoIre; REn; RfGEnL 91; ScF&FL 1; TwCA, SUP; WebE&AL; WhE&EA*

Russell, Harold
American. Actor
The first disabled actor to win an Oscar, 1946.
b. Jan 14, 1914 in North Sydney, Nova Scotia, Canada
Source: *BioIn 1, 2, 3, 5, 7, 8, 9, 12, 16; ConAu 129; FilmEn; FilmgC; HalFC 80, 84, 88; LegTOT; PenEncP; What 2; WhoAm 88; WhoFI 87; WhoHol 92, A*

Russell, Henry
English. Impresario, Teacher
Founder, manager, Boston Opera, 1909-14; noted for novel method of voice teaching.
b. Nov 14, 1871 in London, England
d. Oct 11, 1937 in London, England
Source: *Baker 78, 84, 92; NewEOp 71; NewGrDO*

Russell, Henry Norris
American. Astronomer
Postulated, confirmed correlation between star's brightness/type of

spectrum, called Hertzsprung-Russell diagram.
b. Oct 25, 1877 in Oyster Bay, New York
d. Feb 18, 1957 in Princeton, New Jersey
Source: *AmDec 1910; ApCAB X; AsBiEn; BiESc; BioIn 1, 3, 4, 5, 6, 11, 13, 14, 16, 19, 20; CamDcSc; DcAmB S6; DcScB; InSci; LarDcSc; LuthC 75; NatCAB 2, 62; NotTwCS; ObitOF 79; WebAB 74, 79; WhAm 3; WhDW; WhNAA; WorAlBi; WorScD*

Russell, Honey
[John Russell]
American. Basketball Player, Basketball Coach
High scoring defensive player with several pro teams; college coach for 20 yrs; first coach, Boston Celtics, 1947-48; Hall of Fame, 1964.
b. May 31, 1903 in New York, New York
d. Nov 15, 1973 in Livingston, New Jersey
Source: *BiDAmSp BK; BioIn 9, 10; NewYTBE 73; ObitOF 79; WhoBbl 73; WhoSpor*

Russell, Jane
American. Actor
Better known for buxom pinup poster accompaning 1943's *The Outlaw* than for film itself.
b. Jun 21, 1921 in Bemidji, Minnesota
Source: *BiDFilm, 81, 94; BioIn 2, 3, 5, 8, 9, 10, 11, 14, 15, 16, 18; CelR; CmMov; CmpEPM; ConTFT 9; DcArts; EncAFC; FilmEn; FilmgC; ForYSC; GangFlm; HalFC 80, 84, 88; IntDcF 1-3, 2-3; IntMPA 75, 76, 77, 78, 79, 80, 81, 82, 84, 86, 88, 92, 94, 96; InWom, SUP; LegTOT; MotPP; MovMk; NewYTBE 71; OxCFilm; SweetSg D; VarWW 85; WhoAm 74, 76, 78, 80, 82; WhoAmW 58, 66, 68, 70, 72, 74; WhoHol 92, A; WorAl; WorAlBi; WorEFlm*

Russell, John, Lord
English. Historian, Politician
Prime minister, 1846-52, 1865-66; wrote *Memoirs of Thomas Moore,* 1853-66.
b. Aug 18, 1792 in London, England
d. May 28, 1878 in Richmond, England
Source: *Alli, SUP; BbD; BioIn 21; BritAu 19; CyEd; DcBiPP; DcEnL; DcLEL; DcNaB; EvLB; HisDBrE; McGEWB; NewC; NewCBEL; OxCEng 67, 85, 95; VicBrit; WhCiWar; WhDW*

Russell, Ken
[Henry Kenneth Alfred Russell]
English. Director
BBC feature film director; films include *Altered States,* 1980.
b. Jul 3, 1927 in Southampton, England
Source: *BiDFilm, 81, 94; BioIn 9, 10, 11, 12, 14, 16, 18; BlueB 76; CelR, 90; ConAu 105; ConTFT 5, 13; CurBio 75; DcArts; EncEurC; FilmEn; FilmgC; HalFC 80, 84, 88; IlEncRk; IlWWBF, A; IntDcF 1-2, 2-2; IntMPA 75, 76, 77, 78, 79, 80, 81, 82, 84, 86, 88, 92, 94, 96; IntWW 74, 75, 76, 77, 78, 79, 80, 81, 82, 83, 89, 91, 93; IntWWM 90; LegTOT; MiSFD 9; NewGrDO; OxCFilm; Who 74, 82, 83, 85, 88, 90, 92, 94; WhoAm 74, 76, 78, 80, 82, 84, 86, 88, 90, 92, 94, 95, 96, 97; WhoEnt 92; WhoHol 92; WhoHrs 80; WhoWor 74, 95, 96; WorAl; WorAlBi; WorEFlm; WorFDir 2*

Russell, Kurt (Von Vogel)
American. Actor
Films include *Silkwood,* 1983; *Big Trouble in Little China,* 1986; son of actor Bing Russell.
b. Mar 17, 1951 in Springfield, Massachusetts
Source: *BioIn 12, 13; ConTFT 3, 11; FilmgC; HolBB; IntMPA 86, 88, 92, 94, 96; VarWW 85; WhoAm 86, 90, 92, 94, 95, 96, 97; WhoEnt 92; WhoHol 92, A; WorAlBi*

Russell, Leon
[Hank Wilson]
American. Singer
Country-rock star, 1960s-70s; honky-tonk pianist; did duo with Willie Nelson "One for the Road."
b. Apr 2, 1941 in Lawton, Oklahoma
Source: *Baker 84, 92; ConMuA 80A; EncFCWM 83; EncPR&S 74, 89; EncRk 88; EncRkSt; HarEnR 86; IlEncRk; LegTOT; NewGrDA 86; OnThGG; PenEncP; RkOn 78; RolSEnR 83; WhoAm 78, 80, 82; WhoRock 81; WhoRocM 82*

Russell, Lillian
[Helen Louise Leonard]
"The American Beauty"
American. Singer, Actor
In vaudeville, light opera, including Tony Pastor shows from 1880.
b. Dec 4, 1861 in Clinton, Iowa
d. Jun 6, 1922 in Pittsburgh, Pennsylvania
Source: *AmBi; AmWom; Baker 92; BiDAmM; BioAmW; BioIn 2, 3, 5, 6, 9, 12, 14, 15, 16, 17; CamGWoT; CmpEPM; DcAmB; DcAmImH; EncMT; FamA&A; HalFC 80, 84, 88; InWom, SUP; LegTOT; LibW; NatCAB 4; NewAmDM; NewGrDA 86; NewGrDO; NotAW; NotNAT A, B; NotWoAT; OxCAmL 65; OxCAmT 84; OxCPMus; OxCThe 67; PlP&P; REn; WebAB 74, 79; WhAm 1; WhoHol B; WhoStg 1906, 1908; WhScrn 74, 77; WhThe; WomWWA 14; WorAl; WorAlBi*

Russell, Mark
[Mark Ruslander]
American. Comedian
Political humorist who rose to popularity after the Watergate scandal.
b. Aug 23, 1932 in Buffalo, New York
Source: *BiDAmNC; BioIn 8, 11, 12, 19; ConAu 108, 113; ConMus 6; ConTFT 12; CurBio 81; Who 92; WhoAm 80, 82, 84, 86, 88, 90, 92, 94, 95, 96, 97; WhoCom; WhoEnt 92*

Russell, Morgan
American. Artist
Abstract painter; one of the founders of Synchromism.
b. 1886 in New York, New York
d. May 29, 1953 in Philadelphia, Pennsylvania
Source: *ArtsAmW 2; BioIn 3, 5, 17; BriEAA; DcAmArt; DcCAA 71, 77, 88; McGDA; ObitOF 79; OxCTwCA; OxDcArt; PhDcTCA 77; WhAmArt 85; WhoAmA 78N, 80N, 82N, 84N, 86N, 89N, 91N, 93N*

Russell, Nipsey
American. Comedian, Actor
Co-hosted "The Les Crane Show" on TV; first black regularly employed as MC on national TV.
b. Oct 13, 1924 in Atlanta, Georgia
Source: *ConTFT 6; DrBlPA, 90; InB&W 85; LegTOT; NegAl 89; VarWW 85; WhoAfA 96; WhoAm 82; WhoBlA 85, 92, 94; WhoHol 92; WorAl*

Russell, Pee Wee
[Charles Ellsworth Russell]
American. Jazz Musician
Clarinetist; popular soloist in Dixieland bands, small combos for over 40 yrs.
b. Mar 27, 1906 in Saint Louis, Missouri
d. Feb 15, 1969 in Alexandria, Virginia
Source: *AllMusG; ASCAP 66, 80; Baker 84, 92; BiDAmM; BiDJaz; BioIn 2, 4, 6, 8, 11, 12, 16; CmpEPM; CurBio 44, 69; DcAmB S8; EncJzS; IlEncJ; LegTOT; NewAmDM; NewGrDA 86; NewGrDJ 88, 94; NewGrDM 80; OxCPMus; PenEncP; WhoHol B; WhoJazz 72; WorAl; WorAlBi*

Russell, Richard Brevard, Jr.
American. Politician
Dem. senator from GA, 1933-71; leader of Senate's Southern Bloc; ran for pres., 1952.
b. Nov 2, 1897 in Winder, Georgia
d. Jan 21, 1971 in Washington, District of Columbia
Source: *BiDrAC; BiDrUSC 89; BioIn 1, 2, 3, 4, 5, 6, 7, 8, 9, 11, 12; CurBio 49, 71; DcAmB S9; EncAB-H 1974, 1996; NatCAB 56; NewYTBE 71; ObitT 1971; WhAm 5; WhAmP*

Russell, Rosalind
American. Actor
Films include *His Girl Friday; My Sister Eileen; Auntie Mame.*
b. Jun 4, 1911 in Waterbury, Connecticut
d. Nov 28, 1976 in Beverly Hills, California
Source: *BiDFilm, 94; BiE&WWA; BioIn 3, 4, 5, 6, 7, 9, 10, 11, 12, 14, 18; CelR; ConAu 111, 116; CurBio 43; EncMT; GoodHs; IntMPA 77; InWom; MotPP; MovMk; NatCAB 60; NewYTBE 71; NotNAT; OxCFilm; ThFT; WhAm 7; Who 74; WhoAm 74, 76, 78; WhoAmW 58, 61, 64, 66, 68, 70, 72, 74; WhoHol A; WhoThe 77; WomWMM; WorAl; WorAlBi; WorEFlm*

Russell, Solveig Paulson
American. Children's Author
Informational books include *Johnny Appleseed,* 1967; *The Mushmen,* 1968.
b. Mar 1904 in Salt Lake City, Utah
Source: *AuBYP 2, 3; BioIn 7, 9; ConAu 1R, 5NR; SmATA 3; WhoPNW*

Russell, Sydney Gordon, Sir
English. Author, Designer
Furniture designer whose books include *The Story of Furniture,* 1947.
b. May 20, 1892 in London, England
d. Oct 7, 1980 in Campden, England
Source: *Au&Wr 71; BioIn 2, 5, 6, 14, 15, 16; ConTFT 4; HalFC 88; IntMPA 92; IntWW 78, 80, 81; IntYB 78, 80, 81; Who 74; WhoArt 80; WhoWor 74*

Russell, Theresa
American. Actor
Films include *Bad Timing/A Sexual Obsession,* 1980; *Black Widow,* 1986; *Whore,* 1991.
b. 1957 in San Diego, California
Source: *BiDFilm 94; ConTFT 4, 10; HalFC 88; IntMPA 82, 84, 86, 88, 92, 94, 96; LegTOT; WhoHol 92*

Russo, Anthony J, Jr.
American. Engineer
Charged, with Daniel Ellsberg, of conspiracy in connection with Pentagon Papers, 1971; case dismissed, 1974.
b. 1937
Source: *BioIn 9, 10; St&PR 91*

Russo, Vito
American. Writer
Wrote book *The Celluloid Closet,* 1981, about Hollywood's anti-gay history.
b. 1946 in New York, New York
d. 1990
Source: *BioIn 17; ConAu 107; GayLesB; GayLL; IntAu&W 86*

Russwurm, John Brown
American. Journalist, Abolitionist
Co-founded first black newspaper: *Freedom's Journal,* 1827.
b. Oct 1, 1799 in Port Antonio, Jamaica
d. Jun 17, 1851 in Monrovia, Liberia
Source: *BiDAmJo; BioIn 7, 8, 9, 11; DcAmB; DcAmNB; McGEWB; WebAB 74, 79; WhAm HS*

Rustin, Bayard
"Mr. March"
American. Civil Rights Leader
Adviser to Rev. M L King, Jr; organized first Freedom Ride, "Journey of Reconciliation," 1947; march on Washington, 1963.
b. Mar 17, 1910 in West Chester, Pennsylvania
d. Aug 24, 1987 in New York, New York
Source: *AfrAmAl 6; AmPeW; AmSocL; AnObit 1987; BiDAmL; BiDAmLf; BioIn 7, 8, 9, 11, 12, 14, 15, 16, 19, 20, 21; BlkWr 1; CivR 74; CivRSt; ConAu 25NR, 53, 123; ConBlB 4; ConIsC 1; CurBio 67, 87, 87N; Ebony 1; EncAB-H 1974, 1996; EncAL; EncWB; FacFETw; GayLesB; InB&W 80, 85; LegTOT; LivgBAA; NegAl 76, 89; PolPar; PolProf E, J, K, NF, T; RadHan; SchCGBL; SelBAAf; WhoAm 74, 76, 78, 80, 82, 84, 86; WhoBlA 75, 77, 80, 85; WhoWor 74; WorAl; WorAlBi*

Rutan, Burt
American. Aircraft Designer
Designed history-making *Voyager* —first plane to circumnavigate world without refueling, Dec 1986; brother of Dick.
b. 1943 in Student, California
Source: *BioIn 14; ConNews 87-2; WhoAm 86; WhoFrS 84*

Rutan, Dick
[Richard Rutan]
American. Pilot
Former fighter pilot/stuntman; with Jeana Yeager, made longest flight without refueling, flying *Voyager* around the world, Dec 1986.
Source: *BioIn 12, 14, 15, 16, 18, 19, 20; ConHero 1*

Rutgers, Henry
American. Soldier, Philanthropist
Queen's College changed name to Rutgers University in his honor.
b. Oct 7, 1745 in New York, New York
d. Feb 17, 1830 in New York, New York
Source: *AmBi; ApCAB; DcAmB; Drake; NatCAB 3; TwCBDA; WhAm HS; WhAmRev*

Ruth
Hebrew. Biblical Figure
Central figure in the Book of Ruth; known for heroism, devotion.
b. fl. 1000BC
Source: *BioIn 11, 12; EncEarC; InWom SUP*

Ruth, Babe
[George Herman Ruth]
"The Bambino"; "The Sultan of Swat"
American. Baseball Player
Outfielder, 1914-35, mostly with Yankees; held over 50 records at retirement; instrumental in baseball becoming national pastime; original member, Hall of Fame, 1936.
b. Feb 6, 1895 in Baltimore, Maryland
d. Aug 16, 1948 in New York, New York
Source: *Ballpl 90; BiDAmSp BB; BioIn 1, 2, 3, 4, 5, 6, 7, 8, 9, 10, 11, 12, 13, 14, 15, 16, 17, 18, 19, 20, 21; BioNews 74; ConAu 116; CurBio 44, 48; DcAmB S4; DcCathB; EncAB-H 1974, 1996; FacFETw; Film 2; LegTOT; McGEWB; OxCAmH; RComAH; WebAB 74, 79; WhDW; WhoHol B; WhoProB 73; WhoSpor; WhScrn 74, 77, 83; WorAl; WorAlBi*

Rutherford, Ann
Canadian. Actor
Played Polly Benedict in Andy Hardy series, 1940s; films include *Secret Life of Walter Mitty,* 1947; retired, 1950.
b. Nov 2, 1917 in Toronto, Ontario, Canada
Source: *EncAFC; FilmEn; FilmgC; HalFC 80, 84, 88; IntMPA 86; LegTOT; MGM; MotPP; MovMk; SweetSg C; ThFT; WhoHol 92, A*

Rutherford, Ernest, Baron
[Baron Rutherford of Nelson]
British. Physicist
Founded modern atomic theory, pioneered work in radio-activity, 1904; first to split atom, 1920; Nobelist, 1908.
b. Aug 30, 1871 in Spring Grove, New Zealand
d. Oct 19, 1937 in Cambridge, England
Source: *AsBiEn; BiESc; BioIn 13, 14, 15, 17, 19, 20; CamDcSc; DcInv; DcNaB 1931; DcScB; FacFETw; GrBr; InSci; LarDcSc; MakMC; McGEWB; NobelP; NotTwCS; RAdv 14, 13-5; ThTwC 87; WhDW; WhE&EA; WhLit; WhoNob, 90, 95; WorAlBi; WorScD*

Rutherford, Joseph Franklin
"Judge Rutherford"
American. Religious Leader
Legal adviser for "Russellites," 1907; leader, 1917; founder, president Jehovah's Witnesses, 1925.
b. Nov 1869 in Versailles, Missouri
d. Jan 9, 1942 in San Diego, California
Source: *ApCAB X; BiDAmCu; BioIn 1, 19; CurBio 40, 42; DcAmB S3; DcAmReB 1, 2; DcNAA; LuthC 75; NewCol 75; RelLAm 91; WhNAA; WorAl; WorAlBi*

Rutherford, Margaret
[Dame Margot Rutherford]
English. Actor
Won 1963 Oscar for *The VIP's;* played Miss Marple in four Agatha Christie films.
b. May 11, 1892 in Balham, England
d. May 22, 1972 in Chalfont, England
Source: *BiE&WWA; BioIn 4, 5, 6, 7, 9, 10, 11, 13, 17; CnThe; ContDcW 89; CurBio 64, 72, 72N; DcArts; DcNaB 1971; EncEurC; EncWT; Ent; FilmAG WE; FilmEn; FilmgC; ForYSC; HalFC 80, 84, 88; IlWWBF, A; IntDcF 1-3, 2-3; IntDcWB; InWom, SUP; ItaFilm; LegTOT; MotPP; MovMk; NewYTBE 72; NotNAT A, B; ObitT 1971; OxCFilm; OxCThe 67, 83; QDrFCA 92; WhAm 5; WhoAmW 68, 70, 72, 74; WhoHol B; WhoThe 72; WhScrn 77, 83; WhThe; WomFir; WorAl; WorAlBi*

Rutherford, Michael
English. Singer, Musician
Guitarist, bassist, vocalist, original member of Genesis.
b. Oct 2, 1950, England
Source: *WhoRocM 82*

Rutherfurd, Lewis Morris
American. Physicist
Astrophysicist; the first to devise telescopes intended for celestial photography.
b. Nov 25, 1816 in Morrisania, New York
d. May 30, 1892 in Tranquility, New Jersey
Source: *AmBi; ApCAB; BiDAmS; BiInAmS; BioIn 7, 11, 14; DcAmB; DcScB; NatCAB 6; TwCBDA; WhAm HS*

Rutherfurd, Lucy Page Mercer
American. Secretary
Social secretary to Eleanor Roosevelt, who allegedly had affair with FDR; with him at his death.
b. 1891
d. 1948
Source: *BioIn 10*

Rutledge, Ann
American. Historical Figure
Little fact to support claim to being Lincoln's fiancee; they were friends.
b. 1816 in New Salem, Illinois
d. Aug 25, 1835 in New Salem, Illinois
Source: *BioIn 2, 3, 5; InWom; NewCol 75; NotAW; OxCAmH; REn; WhAm HS*

Rutledge, Edward
American. Continental Congressman
Youngest of signers of Declaration of Independence, 1776; governor of SC, 1798-1800; brother of John Rutledge.
b. Nov 23, 1749 in Charleston, South Carolina
d. Jan 23, 1800 in Charleston, South Carolina
Source: *AmBi; ApCAB; BiAUS; BiDrAC; BiDrGov 1789; BiDrUSC 89; BiDSA; BioIn 3, 7, 8, 9; BlkwEAR; DcAmB; Drake; EncAR; EncCRAm; EncSoH; HarEnUS; NatCAB 12; TwCBDA; WhAm HS; WhAmP; WhAmRev; WorAl; WorAlBi*

Rutledge, John
American. Politician, Judge
Active in SC politics from 1761; governor, 1779-82; chief justice SC Surpeme Court, 1791-95; helped ratify US Constitution, 1788.
b. Sep 1739 in Charleston, South Carolina
d. Jul 18, 1800 in Charleston, South Carolina
Source: *Alli; AmBi; AmPolLe; AmRev; ApCAB; BiAUS; BiDFedJ; BiDrAC; BiDrACR; BiDrUSC 89; BiDSA; BioIn 1, 2, 5, 7, 8, 9, 11, 15, 16; BlkwEAR; CyAG; DcAmB; Drake; EncAR; EncCRAm; EncSoH; HarEnUS; LinLib S; McGEWB; NatCAB 1; OxCAmH; OxCLaw; OxCSupC; SupCtJu; TwCBDA; WebAB 74, 79; WhAm HS; WhAmP; WhAmRev*

Ruttan, Susan
American. Actor
Plays Roxanne on TV series "L.A. Law," 1986—.
Source: *BioIn 15, 17, 19; ConTFT 7; WhoAm 92; WhoEnt 92; WorAlBi*

Ruttman, Troy
American. Auto Racer
Winner, 1952 Indianapolis 500, the youngest racer to do so.
b. Mar 11, 1930 in Mooreland, Oklahoma
d. May 19, 1997 in Lake Havasu City, Arizona

Ruysdael, Jacob van
[Jacob van Ruisdael]
Dutch. Artist
Landscape painter, etcher known for forest, shore, mountain scenes.
b. 1628 in Haarlem, Netherlands
d. Mar 14, 1682 in Amsterdam, Netherlands
Source: *AtlBL; BioIn 18, 19; DcArts; IntDcAA 90; LegTOT; McGEWB; OxCAmL 65; OxCArt; OxDcArt; REn; WebBD 83; WhDW; WorAl; WorAlBi*

Ruzici, Virginia
"The Gipsy"
Romanian. Tennis Player
Won French Open, 1978.
b. Jan 31, 1955 in Cimpia-Turzii, Romania
Source: *BuCMET; OfEnT; WhoIntT*

Ruzicka, Leopold Stephen
Swiss. Chemist
Won Nobel Prize, 1939, for work on polymethylenes and higher terpenes.
b. Sep 13, 1887 in Vukovar, Yugoslavia
d. Sep 26, 1976 in Zurich, Switzerland
Source: *BiESc; McGMS 80; ObitOF 79; WhAm 7; WhoNob, 90, 95*

Ryan, Claude
Canadian. Journalist
Publisher, *Le Devoir,* newspaper in Montreal, 1964-78; entered liberal politics, 1979-82.
b. Jan 26, 1925 in Montreal, Quebec, Canada
Source: *BioIn 11, 12; CanWW 31, 70, 79, 80, 81, 83, 89; ConAu 111; DcVicP; IntWW 83; NewYTBS 78; OxCCan SUP; WhoAm 80, 82, 84; WhoE 74, 75, 77, 79, 81, 83; WhoWor 74, 76, 78*

Ryan, Cornelius John
American. Journalist
Noted for lively accounts of WW II history; writings include *The Longest Day: June 6, 1944,* 1959, co-wrote screenplay for film, 1972.
b. Jun 5, 1920 in Dublin, Ireland
d. Nov 23, 1974 in New York, New York
Source: *BioIn 10, 11, 12; ConAu 38NR, 53, 69; ConLC 7; DcAmB S9; IntAu&W 76; NewYTBS 74, 79; WhAm 6; Who 74; WhoAm 74; WhoE 74; WhoWor 74; WorAl; WorAu 1970*

Ryan, Irene Noblette
American. Actor
Played Granny Clampett on TV series "Beverly Hillbillies," 1962-71.
b. Oct 17, 1903 in El Paso, Texas
d. Apr 26, 1973 in Santa Monica, California
Source: *FilmgC; MovMk; RadStar; WhoHol B; WhScrn 74, 77*

Ryan, Leo Joseph
American. Politician
Dem. congressman from CA murdered by member of Jim Jones' Peoples Temple.
b. May 5, 1925 in Lincoln, Nebraska
d. Nov 19, 1978 in Jonestown, Guyana
Source: *BiDrUSC 89; BioIn 11, 14; CngDr 74; NewYTBS 78; WhAm 7; WhoAm 74, 76, 78; WhoAmP 73, 75, 77; WhoGov 75, 77; WhoWest 76, 78*

Ryan, Meg
[Margaret Hyra]
American. Actor
Best known role, opposite Billy Crystal in *When Harry Met Sally,* 1989; in *Sleepless in Seattle,* 1993; in *French Kiss,* 1995.
b. Nov 19, 1961 in Fairfield, Connecticut
Source: *BioIn 13, 16; CelR 90; ConTFT 9; IntMPA 92, 94, 96; IntWW 91, 93; WhoAm 92, 94, 95, 96, 97; WhoAmW 95, 97; WhoHol 92*

Ryan, Nolan
[Lynn Nolan Ryan, Jr]
American. Baseball Player
Pitcher, 1966, 1968-93; holds many ML pitching records, including seven no-hitters, career strikeouts, strikeouts in one season; first player to make $1 million a year, 1979.
b. Jan 31, 1947 in Refugio, Texas
Source: *Ballpl 90; BaseReg 86, 87; BiDAmSp BB; BioIn 8, 9, 10, 11, 12, 13, 14, 15, 18; CmCal; CurBio 70; FacFETw; LegTOT; News 89; NewYTBE 70, 73; WhoAm 74, 76, 78, 80, 82, 84, 86, 88, 90, 92, 94, 95, 96, 97; WhoSpor; WhoSSW 86; WorAl; WorAlBi*

Ryan, Peggy
[Margaret O'Rene Ryan]
American. Actor
Played Jenny on TV show "Hawaii Five-O," 1969-76.
b. Aug 28, 1924 in Long Beach, California
Source: *BiDD; BioIn 10, 13, 17; EncAFC; FilmEn; FilmgC; ForYSC; HalFC 80, 84, 88; HolP 40; IntMPA 75, 76, 77, 78, 79, 80, 81, 82, 84, 86, 88; InWom SUP; LegTOT; MotPP; WhoHol 92, A; WorAl*

Ryan, Robert (Bushnell)
American. Actor
Leading man, 1940-73, whose films include *Crossfire,* 1947; *The Dirty Dozen,* 1967.
b. Nov 11, 1913 in Chicago, Illinois
d. Jul 11, 1973 in New York, New York

Source: *BiDFilm, 81; BiE&WWA; BioIn 5, 6, 10, 16, 20; CelR; CmMov; ForYSC; OxCFilm; WhAm 5; WhoE 74; WhoThe 72; WhThe; WorEFlm*

Ryan, Sylvester James
American. Judge
Presided over many famous cases while serving on nation's busiest Federal court, S. District of NY, 1960-76.
b. Sep 10, 1896 in New York, New York
d. Apr 10, 1981 in New York, New York
Source: *AmBench 79; NewYTBS 81; WhAm 7; WhoAm 74, 76; WhoAmL 79; WhoE 74; WhoGov 72*

Ryan, T(ubal) Claude
American. Aircraft Manufacturer
Founded company that built Lindbergh's "Spirit of St. Louis."
b. Jan 3, 1898 in Parsons, Kansas
d. Sep 11, 1982 in San Diego, California
Source: *BioIn 2, 9, 11, 12, 13; CmCal; CurBio 43, 82; NewYTBS 82; St&PR 75; WhAm 10; WhoAm 74, 76, 78*

Ryan, Thomas Fortune
American. Financier
Helped found American Tobacco.
b. Oct 17, 1851 in Lovingston, Virginia
d. Nov 23, 1928 in New York, New York
Source: *BiDAmBL 83; BioIn 1, 21; DcAmB; DcCathB; EncAB-H 1974; WebAB 74, 79; WhAm 1; WorAl*

Ryan, Tom Kreusch
American. Cartoonist
Draws syndicated cartoon, "Tumbleweeds," 1965—; published 20 paperback compilations, 1970-87.
b. Jun 6, 1926 in Anderson, Indiana
Source: *BioIn 11; WhoAm 80, 82, 84, 86, 88, 90, 92, 94, 95, 96, 97; WorECom*

Ryan, Tommy
American. Boxer
Middleweight champion, 1895-1907.
b. Mar 31, 1870 in Redwood, New York
d. Aug 3, 1948 in Van Nuys, California
Source: *BiDAmSp BK; BioIn 1; BoxReg; WhoBox 74; WhoSpor*

Rydell, Bobby
[Robert Ridarelli]
American. Musician
Singer, drummer; popular, 1959-65; hits include "Forget Him," 1963.
b. Apr 26, 1942 in Philadelphia, Pennsylvania
Source: *BiDAmM; BioIn 12; EncRk 88; EncRkSt; FilmgC; HalFC 80, 84, 88; LegTOT; PenEncP; RkOn 74, 84; RolSEnR 83; WhoHol 92, A; WhoRock 81; WorAl; WorAlBi*

Ryden, Ernest Edwin
American. Religious Leader
Wrote, translated over 40 hymns; helped form Lutheran Church in America, 1962.
b. Sep 12, 1886 in Kansas City, Missouri
d. Jan 1, 1981 in Providence, Rhode Island
Source: *BioIn 12; ConAu 102; NewYTBS 81; WhAm 7; WhNAA; WhoRel 75*

Ryder, Albert Pinkham
American. Artist
Legendary hermit-crank of American art; early landscapes may be tiniest ever exhibited as finished work: *The Golden Hour,* 1870s, measures 7 1/2 by 12 1/2.
b. Mar 19, 1847 in New Bedford, Massachusetts
d. Mar 28, 1917 in Elmhurst, New York
Source: *AmBi; AmCulL; ApCAB; AtlBL; Benet 87, 96; BioIn 1, 2, 3, 4, 5, 6, 7, 8, 9, 10, 12, 13, 16, 17, 19; BriEAA; DcAmArt; DcAmB; DcArts; DcSeaP; EncAB-H 1974, 1996; GayN; IlBEAAW; IntDcAA 90; LegTOT; McGDA; McGEWB; OxCAmH; OxCAmL 65; OxCArt; OxCShps; OxDcArt; REn; WebAB 74, 79; WhAm 1; WorAl; WorAlBi*

Ryder, Alfred
[Alfred Jacob Corn]
American. Actor, Director
On radio show "The Rise of the Goldbergs," 1930-33.
b. Jan 5, 1919 in New York, New York
Source: *BiE&WWA; MotPP; NotNAT; WhoHol 92, A; WhoThe 72, 77, 81*

Ryder, James Arthur
American. Business Executive
Founded leasing business, 1937; later became Ryder Systems Inc.
b. Jul 28, 1913 in Columbus, Ohio
d. Mar 25, 1997 in Coral Gables, Florida
Source: *BioIn 5, 9, 12; St&PR 75; WhoAm 74, 76, 78; WhoFI 74*

Ryder, Mitch
[Mitch Ryder and the Detroit Wheels; William S Levise, Jr.]
American. Singer
Lead vocalist in mid-60s blue-eyed soul band; had less-successful solo career.
b. Feb 26, 1945 in Detroit, Michigan
Source: *BioIn 13; ConMus 11; EncRk 88; LegTOT; NewGrDA 86; PenEncP; WhoRocM 82*

Ryder, Winona
[Winona Laura Horowitz]
American. Actor
Played May Welland in *The Age of Innocence,* 1993.
b. Oct 29, 1971 in Rochester, Minnesota
Source: *BiDFilm 94; BioIn 16, 18; ConTFT 8; CurBio 94; IntMPA 92, 94, 96; IntWW 93; LegTOT; News 91, 91-2; WhoAm 92, 94, 95, 96, 97; WhoAmW 95, 97; WhoHol 92*

Rykiel, Sonia
"Queen of Knits"
French. Fashion Designer
Designs include tight knits, clinging dresses and the inside-out look.
b. May 6, 1930 in Paris, France
Source: *BioIn 10, 12; ConDes 84, 90, 97; ConFash; CurBio 90; DcTwDes; EncFash; IntWW 91, 93; InWom SUP; WhoFash 88; WorFshn*

Rykov, Aleksey Ivanovich
Russian. Government Official
Right-wing Bolshevik leader; alliance with Stalin ended when Stalin adopted left-wing economic policies.
b. Feb 25, 1881 in Saratov, Russia
d. Mar 14, 1938 in Moscow, Union of Soviet Socialist Republics
Source: *BiDSovU; BioIn 10, 11, 16; FacFETw; SovUn*

Rylands, John
English. Merchant, Philanthropist
Textile tycoon; Manchester's noted Rylands Library founded as memorial.
b. 1801
d. 1888
Source: *BioIn 10; DcNaB*

Ryle, Gilbert
English. Philosopher, Editor
Opinions were influential in modern philosophy for over 25 yrs.
b. Aug 19, 1900, England
d. Oct 6, 1976 in Islip, England
Source: *Au&Wr 71; Benet 87, 96; BioIn 10, 11, 12, 14; BlueB 76; ConAu 69, 73; DcLEL 1940; DcNaB 1971; IntEnSS 79; IntWW 74, 75, 76; LngCTC; MakMC; McGEWB; NewCBEL; OxCEng 67, 85, 95; OxCPhil; RAdv 14, 13-4; ThTwC 87; WhAm 7; Who 74; WhoWor 74, 76; WorAu 1950; WrDr 76, 80*

Ryle, Martin, Sir
English. Astronomer
Researched radio astronomy; shared 1974 Nobel Prize in physics.
b. Sep 27, 1918 in Oxford, England
d. Oct 14, 1984 in Cambridge, England
Source: *AnObit 1984; BiESc; BioIn 3, 7, 10, 14, 15, 20; CamDcSc; ConAu 133; CurBio 73, 85, 85N; DcNaB 1981; IntWW 74, 75, 76, 77, 78, 79, 80, 81, 82, 83; LarDcSc; McGMS 80; NewYTBS 74, 84; NobelP; NotTwCS; Who 74, 82, 83, 85N; WhoNob, 90, 95; WhoWor 74, 76, 78, 80, 82, 84; WorScD*

Rypien, Mark
Canadian. Football Player
Quarterback, Washington Redskins, 1987-94; Cleveland Browns, 1994—; Superbowl MVP, 1992.
b. Oct 2, 1962 in Calgary, Alberta, Canada
Source: *News 92, 92-3*

Rysanek, Leonie
Austrian. Opera Singer
Soprano; NY Met. debut, 1959, replacing Callas; admired for Verdi, Strauss roles.
b. Nov 12, 1926 in Vienna, Austria
Source: *Baker 78, 84, 92; BioIn 13, 16; CmOp; CurBio 66; IntDcOp; IntWW 81, 82, 83, 89, 91, 93; IntWWM 90; InWom SUP; MetOEnc; MusSN; NewAmDM; NewEOp 71; NewGrDA 86; NewGrDM 80; NewGrDO; NewYTBS 83; OxDcOp; PenDiMP; WhoAm 80, 82, 84, 86, 88, 90, 92, 94, 95, 96, 97; WhoEnt 92; WhoMus 72; WhoWor 74, 89, 91*

Ryskind, Morrie
American. Journalist, Dramatist
Won Pulitzer for play *Of Thee I Sing,* 1932; wrote film *My Man Godfrey,* 1936; co-authored several Marx Brothers films.
b. Oct 20, 1895 in New York, New York
d. Aug 24, 1985 in Crystal City, Virginia
Source: *AmAu&B, 80; LegTOT; ModWD; NewCBMT; NewYTBS 85; NotNAT; OxCAmT 84; VarWW 85; WhAm 8; WhNAA; WhoAm 78, 80, 82, 84; WhoThe 77A; WhoWorJ 72, 78; WhThe*

Ryun, Jim
[James Ronald Ryun]
American. Track Athlete
Middle-distance runner; set world record in mile, 1967; won silver medal in 1,500 meters, 1968 Olympics.
b. Apr 29, 1947 in Wichita, Kansas
Source: *BiDAmSp OS; BioIn 7, 8, 9, 10, 11, 12; BioNews 74; CelR; CurBio 68; FacFETw; LegTOT; NewCol 75; NewYTBE 72; WhoAm 76, 78, 80, 82, 84; WhoSpor; WhoTr&F 73; WorAl; WorAlBi*

S

S(ymbionese) L(iberation) A(rmy)
[Angela Atwood; Donald David "Cinque Mtume" DeFreeze; Emily "Yolanda" Harris; William "Teko" Harris; Russell "Bo" Little; Nancy Ling Pery; Joseph "Osceola" Romero; Kathy Soliah; Steven Soliah; Patricia "Mizmoon" Soltysik; William "Cujo" Wolfe]
American. Revolutionaries
Kidnapped Patricia Hearst, February 1974.
Source: *GoodHs; NewYTBS 74*

Saarinen, Aline Bernstein
American. Critic, Author
With *NY Times,* 1947-59; wrote *The Proud Possessors,* 1958; wife of Eero.
b. Mar 25, 1914 in New York, New York
d. Jul 13, 1972 in New York, New York
Source: *AmAu&B; CurBio 56, 72; ForWC 70; NewYTBE 72; WhAm 5; WhoAmW 66, 68, 70, 72; WhoGov 72*

Saarinen, Eero
American. Architect
Often collaborated with father, Eliel; designed St. Louis' Jefferson Memorial Arch, 1947; husband of Aline.
b. Aug 20, 1910 in Kyrkslatt, Finland
d. Sep 1, 1961 in Ann Arbor, Michigan
Source: *AmCulL; AmDec 1940, 1950; AtlBL; Benet 87; BioIn 2, 3, 4, 5, 6, 7, 8, 9, 10, 11, 12, 13, 14, 16, 19; BriEAA; ConArch 80, 87, 94; ConAu 113; ConDes 84; CurBio 49, 61; DcAmB S7; DcArts; DcD&D; DcNiCA; DcTwDes; EncAAr 1, 2; EncMA; FacFETw; IntDcAr; LegTOT; LinLib S; MacEA; McGDA; McGEWB; ModArCr 2; ObitT 1961; OxCAmH; OxCArt; PenDiDA 89; PlP&P; REn; WebAB 74, 79; WhAm 4; WhoAmA 78N, 80N, 82N, 84N, 86N, 89N, 91N, 93N; WhoArch; WorAl; WorAlBi*

Saarinen, Eliel
Flemish. Architect
Influenced modern architecture by rejecting edecticism with simple lines.
b. Aug 28, 1873 in Rantasalmi, Finland
d. Jul 1, 1950 in Bloomfield Hills, Michigan
Source: *BioIn 1, 2, 3, 8, 10, 12, 13, 14, 16, 19, 21; BriEAA; ConArch 80, 87; CurBio 42, 50; DcArts; DcD&D; DcTwDes; EncAAr 1, 2; EncMA; FacFETw; IntDcAr; LegTOT; LinLib L, S; MacEA; McGDA; McGEWB; OxCAmH; OxCArt; PenDiDA 89; WebAB 74, 79; WhAm 3; WhAmArt 85; WhoArch*

Saatchi, Charles
English. Advertising Executive
Co-founder, director, Saatchi & Saatchi Co., an advertising agency, 1970-94.
b. Jun 9, 1943, England
Source: *BioIn 12, 13, 14, 15, 16; ConNews 87-3; DcTwBBL; IntWW 91, 93; NewYTBS 80; Who 82, 83, 85, 88, 90, 92, 94; WhoAdv 90; WhoAm 88, 90, 92; WhoFI 89, 92, 96; WhoWor 89, 91, 93, 95, 96, 97*

Saatchi, Maurice
English. Advertising Executive
Cofounder (with brother Charles) of Saatchi & Saatchi, an advertising agency, 1970, chairman, 1985-94; cofounded New Saatchi Agency (with brother), 1995.
b. Jun 21, 1946 in Baghdad, Iraq
Source: *BioIn 12, 13, 14, 15, 16; CurBio 89; DcTwBBL; IntWW 91, 93; News 95; NewYTBS 80; Who 88, 90, 92, 94; WhoAdv 90; WhoAm 88, 90, 92, 94, 95, 96; WhoFI 89, 92, 94, 96; WhoWor 89, 91, 93, 95, 96, 97*

Saavdedra, Lamas Carlos
Argentine. Educator, Lawyer
Won Nobel Peace Prize, 1936, for espousal of antiwar pact submitted to League of Nations.
b. Nov 1, 1878 in Buenos Aires, Argentina
d. May 5, 1959 in Buenos Aires, Argentina
Source: *WhoNob*

Sabatier, Paul
French. Chemist
Won Nobel Prize, 1912; studied organic processes, molecular structure.
b. Nov 5, 1854 in Carcassonne, France
d. Aug 14, 1941 in Toulouse, France
Source: *AsBiEn; BiESc; BioIn 3, 6, 11, 14, 15, 19, 20; CurBio 41; DcScB; InSci; LarDcSc; McGEWB; NobelP; NotTwCS; WhoNob, 90, 95; WorAl; WorAlBi*

Sabatini, Gabriela
Argentine. Tennis Player
As amateur, youngest player ever to win a round at US Open, 1984; won US Open, 1990; retired, 1996.
b. May 16, 1970 in Buenos Aires, Argentina
Source: *BioIn 14, 15, 16; BuCMET; ConNews 85-4; CurBio 92; DcHiB; IntWW 89, 91, 93; LegTOT; NewYTBS 92; WhoAm 92, 94, 95, 96, 97; WhoAmW 93, 95, 97; WhoWor 93, 95, 96*

Sabatini, Rafael
Italian. Author, Dramatist
Wrote historical novels: *Scaramouche,* 1921; *Captain Blood,* 1922.
b. Apr 29, 1875 in Jesi, Italy
d. Feb 13, 1950 in Aldenbogen, Switzerland
Source: *BioIn 2, 4, 11, 14; DcBiA; DcLEL; DcNaB MP; EvLB; FilmgC; HalFC 80, 84, 88; LegTOT; LngCTC; NewC; NotNAT B; REn; TwCA, SUP; TwCLC 47; TwCRGW; TwCRHW 90, 94; TwCWr; WhAm 2; WhE&EA; WhLit; WhoSpyF; WhThe*

Sabato, Ernesto
Argentine. Author
Works examine human condition, survival of moral values; won Miguel de Cervantes Prize, 1985.
b. Jun 24, 1911 in Rojas, Argentina
Source: *Benet 87, 96; BenetAL 91; BioIn 14, 16; CasWL; ConAu 32NR, 97; ConLC 10, 23; CurBio 85; CyWA 89; DcArts; DcCLAA; DcHiB; DcLB 145; DcTwCCu 3; EncLatA; EncWL, 2, 3;*

HispLC; HispWr; IntAu&W 76, 77, 82, 86; IntvLAW; IntWW 74, 75, 76, 77, 78, 79, 80, 81, 82, 83, 89, 91, 93; LatAmWr; LegTOT; MajTwCW; McGEWB; ModLAL; OxCSpan; PenC AM; RAdv 14, 13-2; SpAmA; WhoWor 74, 78, 80, 82, 87, 89, 91, 93, 95, 96; WorAu 1975

Saberhagen, Bret William
American. Baseball Player
Pitcher, KC, 1984—; NY Mets 1991-94; Denver, 1995—; fifth youngest in ML history to win 20 games, 1985, youngest to win Cy Young Award, 1985; won Cy Young Award, 1989.
b. Apr 13, 1964 in Chicago Heights, Illinois
Source: *Ballpl 90; BaseReg 86, 87; BioIn 14, 15; ConNews 86-1; NewYTBS 85, 86, 91; WhoAm 90, 96, 97; WhoMW 90; WorAlBi*

Sabich, Spider
[Vladimir Sabich]
American. Skier
Two-time world champion skier accidentally killed by Claudine Longet.
b. 1943
d. Mar 21, 1976 in Aspen, Colorado
Source: *BioIn 10, 11*

Sabin, Albert Bruce
American. Biologist
Developed oral polio vaccine, 1954; superior in some ways to Salk vaccine.
b. Aug 26, 1906 in Bialystok, Russia
d. Mar 3, 1993 in Washington, District of Columbia
Source: *AmMWSc 76P, 79, 82, 86, 89, 92; AsBiEn; BiESc; BioIn 4, 5, 6, 7, 8, 10, 11, 12, 13; CurBio 58; EncWB; FacFETw; InSci; IntWW 83, 91; LarDcSc; McGMS 80; WebAB 74, 79; Who 74, 85, 92; WhoAm 80, 82, 84, 86, 88, 90, 92; WhoTech 89; WhoWor 89, 93; WorAl; WorAlBi; WorScD*

Sabin, Florence Rena
American. Scientist
Known for her study of the lymphatic system and bloodcells.
b. Nov 9, 1871 in Central City, Colorado
d. Oct 3, 1953 in Denver, Colorado
Source: *AmWomSc; BiDAmEd; BiHiMed; BioAmW; BioIn 1, 2, 3, 4, 5, 8, 9, 10, 11, 12, 15, 16, 17, 19, 20; CamDcSc; ContDcW 89; CurBio 45, 53; DcAmB S5; DcAmMeB 84; DcScB; GoodHs; HerW 84; InSci; IntDcWB; InWom, SUP; LibW; LinLib S; NatCAB 40; NotAW MOD; NotTwCS; NotWoLS; ObitOF 79; OxCMed 86; PeoHis; WhAm 3; WomFir; WomSc; WomWWA 14; WorScD*

Sablon, Jean Georges
French. Singer, Composer
Has appeared in musicals, variety shows, and nightclubs worldwide; dubbed the "French Bing Crosby."
b. Mar 25, 1906 in Nogent-sur-Marne, France
d. Feb 24, 1994 in Cannes-la-Bocca, France
Source: *BiE&WWA; BioIn 1; OxCPMus*

Sabo, Chris(topher Andrew)
American. Baseball Player
Third baseman, Cincinnati Reds, 1988-94; Baltimore Orioles, 1994-95; Chicago White Sox, 1995—; NL rookie of year, 1988.
b. Jan 19, 1962 in Detroit, Michigan
Source: *Ballpl 90; BaseReg 88; BioIn 16*

Sabu
[Sabu Dastagir]
Indian. Actor
Best known for title role in *Elephant Boy,* 1937.
b. Mar 15, 1924, Mysore
d. Dec 2, 1963 in Chatsworth, California
Source: *BioIn 6, 10, 15, 16; CmMov; DcArts; EncEurC; FilmEn; FilmgC; HalFC 80, 84, 88; HolP 40; IlWWBF; ItaFilm; LegTOT; MotPP; MovMk; NotNAT B; ObitT 1961; OxCFilm; WhoHol B; WhoHrs 80; WhScrn 74, 77, 83; WorEFlm*

Sacagawea
[Mrs. Toussaint Charbonneau]
American. Native American Guide
Shoshone Indian who served as interpreter, guide on Lewis and Clark Expedition, 1804.
b. 1787?
d. Dec 2, 1812? in Fort Lisa, Nebraska
Source: *DcAmB; LinLib S; OxCAmL 65, 83, 95; REnAW; WebAB 74, 79; WhAm HS; WorAl; WorAlBi*

Sacchini, Antonio
Italian. Composer
Operas include *Oedipe a Colone,* 1786; had short-lived fame.
b. Jun 14, 1730 in Florence, Italy
d. Oct 6, 1786 in Paris, France
Source: *Baker 78, 84, 92; BioIn 4; IntDcOp; MusMk; NewEOp 71; NewGrDM 80; NewOxM; OxCMus; OxDcOp*

Sacco, Nicola
[Sacco and Vanzetti]
Italian. Political Activist
Tried, executed for murder during robbery; case became most notorious of century due to widespread charges of mistrial.
b. Apr 22, 1891 in Apulia, Italy
d. Aug 23, 1927 in Boston, Massachusetts
Source: *AmBi; BiDAmL; BioIn 1, 2, 3, 4, 5, 6, 7, 8, 9, 10, 11, 12, 13, 14, 15, 16, 17; CopCroC; DcAmB; DcAmImH; LegTOT; McGEWB; NewCol 75; WebAB 74, 79; WhAm 4; WhDW; WorAl; WorAlBi*

Sacher, Paul
Swiss. Conductor
Founded Basel's Kammer Orchestra, 1926, introducing contemporary composers.
b. Apr 28, 1906 in Basel, Switzerland
Source: *Baker 78, 84, 92; BioIn 3, 4, 15; DcArts; IntWW 74, 75, 76, 77, 78, 79, 80, 81, 82, 83, 89, 91, 93; IntWWM 77, 80, 85, 90; NewAmDM; NewGrDM 80; PenDiMP; WhoMus 72; WhoWor 74, 76, 78*

Sacher-Masoch, Leopold von
Austrian. Author
Word "masochism" derived from abnormality often depicted in his novels.
b. Jan 27, 1836? in Lemberg, Austria
d. Mar 9, 1895 in Lindheim, Germany
Source: *BbD; Benet 87, 96; BiD&SB; DcArts; Dis&D; EuAu; EvEuW; NinCLC 31; OxCGer 76; OxCMed 86; REn*

Sachs, Hans
German. Composer, Poet
Famed poet of the Meistersinger; wrote over 6000 works; main figure in Wagner's opera.
b. Nov 5, 1494 in Nuremberg, Germany
d. Jan 19, 1576 in Nuremberg, Germany
Source: *Baker 78, 84, 92; BbD; Benet 87, 96; BiD&SB; BioIn 5, 7, 11; CasWL; CmMedTh; CnThe; CyWA 58; DcArts; DcBiPP; DcEuL; DcPup; EncWT; Ent; EuAu; EvEuW; LinLib L; LuthC 75; McGEWB; McGEWD 72, 84; NewAmDM; NewC; NewCBEL; NewEOp 71; NewGrDM 80; NewOxM; NotNAT B; OxCEng 67, 95; OxCGer 76, 86; OxCMus; OxCThe 67, 83; OxDcOp; PenC EUR; RAdv 14, 13-2; REn; REnWD; RfGWoL 95*

Sachs, Jeffrey D(avid)
American. Economist
Freelance economic adviser to foreign governments since 1985.
b. 1954 in Michigan
Source: *CurBio 93; WhoEc 86*

Sachs, Nelly (Leonie)
German. Poet
Won Nobel Prize in literature, 1966, for poetry, dramas.
b. Dec 10, 1891 in Berlin, Germany
d. May 12, 1970 in Stockholm, Sweden
Source: *Benet 87, 96; BioIn 7, 8, 9, 10, 11, 20; BlmGWL; CasWL; ClDMEL 80; ConAu 25R, P-2; ConLC 14, 98; ContDcW 89; CurBio 67, 70; EncCoWW; EncWL, 2, 3; FacFETw; GrWomW; IntDcWB; InWom; LadLa 86; LegTOT; LiExTwC; LinLib L, S; McGEWB; ModGL; ModWoWr; NewYTBE 70; NobelP; OxCGer 76, 86; PenBWP; PenC EUR; RAdv 14; RfGWoL 95; TwCWr; WhAm 5; WhoNob; WomFir; WomWrGe; WorAl; WorAlBi; WorAu 1950*

Sachs, Samuel, II
American. Museum Director
Director, Detroit Institute of Arts, 1985—; co-author *Fakes and Forgeries.*
b. Nov 30, 1935 in New York, New York
Source: *WhoAm 76, 78, 80, 84, 86, 88, 90, 92, 94, 95, 96, 97; WhoAmA 73, 76, 78, 80, 82, 84, 86, 89, 91, 93; WhoMW 74, 76, 78, 86, 90, 92, 93, 96*

Sachse, Leopold
German. Director
Stage director of Wagnerian operas, NY Met., 1935-43; Stage director of NY City Opera, 1945-51.
b. Jan 5, 1880 in Berlin, Germany
d. Apr 4, 1961 in Englewood Cliffs, New Jersey
Source: *Baker 78, 84, 92; BioIn 5; NewEOp 71*

Sack, Erna
"European Nightingale"
German. Opera Singer
Coloratura soprano, formerly contralto; American performances, 1930s, 1954.
b. 1903, Germany
d. Mar 2, 1972
Source: *Baker 84; NewYTBE 72; WhoHol A; WhScrn 77, 83*

Sackheim, Maxwell Byron
American. Advertising Executive
Co-founded Book of the Month Club, 1926.
b. Sep 25, 1890 in Kovna, Russia
d. Dec 2, 1982 in Largo, Florida
Source: *BioIn 2, 8, 10; ConAu 108; WhAm 9*

Sackler, Howard Oliver
American. Dramatist
Won Pulitzer, 1969, for *The Great White Hope.*
b. Dec 19, 1929 in New York, New York
d. Oct 14, 1982 in Ibiza, Spain
Source: *AnObit 1982; ChhPo S2; ConAu 61, 108; ConDr 73, 82; ConLC 14; McGEWD 84; NewYTBS 82; NotNAT; OxCAmL 83; OxCThe 83; PlP&P; WhAm 8; WhoAm 82; WrDr 76, 80*

Sacks, Oliver Wolf
American. Physician, Neurologist
Staff neurologist, Beth Abraham Hospital, New York, 1966—; author of *Awakenings,* 1973.
b. Jul 9, 1933 in London, England

Sackville-West, Edward Charles
English. Author, Critic
Witty novels include *Piano Quintet,* 1925; *The Sun in Capricorn,* 1934; son of Victoria Mary.
b. Nov 13, 1901 in London, England
d. Jul 4, 1965 in Clogheen, Ireland
Source: *BioIn 3, 4; CathA 1952; ChhPo S2; DcLEL; DcNaB 1961; EvLB; LngCTC; ModBrL; NewC; NewCBEL; PenC ENG; REn; TwCA, SUP; TwCWr; WhE&EA*

Sackville-West, Vita
[Mrs. Harold Nicholson; Victoria Mary Sackville-West]
English. Poet, Author
Wrote *The Edwardians,* 1930, *Pepita,* 1937; mother of Nigel and Benjamin.
b. Mar 9, 1892 in Sevenoaks, England
d. Jun 2, 1962 in Cranbrook, England
Source: *ArtclWW 2; BioIn 3, 4, 5, 6, 7, 8, 10, 11, 12, 13; BlmGWL; Chambr 3; ChhPo, S1, S2, S3; ConAu 93, 104; ContDcW 89; DcArts; DcLEL; DcNaB 1961; EncBrWW; EncWL; EvLB; FacFETw; FemiCLE; GayLesB; GrBr; IntDcWB; InWom SUP; LngCTC; ModBrL; ModWoWr; NewC; NewCBEL; OxCEng 85, 95; PenC ENG; PenNWW B; RAdv 1, 14; REn; TwCA, SUP; TwCWr; WhoLA; WomFir*

Sadat, Anwar el
Egyptian. Political Leader
Pres., 1970-81; awarded 1978 Nobel Peace Prize with Menachem Begin, for reaching Camp David peace agreement; slain in 1981.
b. Dec 25, 1918 in Mit Abul-Kum, Egypt
d. Oct 6, 1981 in Cairo, Egypt
Source: *BioIn 11; BioNews 75; BkPepl; ConAu 101, 104; CurBio 71, 81; IntYB 79; NewCol 75; NewYTBE 70, 72; WhoNob; WhoWor 78*

Sadat, Jehan Raouf
Egyptian., Educator
Widow of Anwar Sadat; lecturer in Arabic literature at Cairo U; outspoken advocate of women's rights; wrote autobiography *A Woman of Egypt,* 1987.
b. Aug 1934? in Cairo, Egypt
Source: *BioIn 10, 11, 14, 15; CurBio 86; InWom SUP; NewYTBS 78, 87*

Saddler, Donald
American. Choreographer
Won Tonys for *Wonderful Town,* 1953; *No, No, Nanette,* 1971.
b. Jan 24, 1920 in Van Nuys, California
Source: *BiDD; BiE&WWA; BioIn 6, 9; CnOxB; ConTFT 2; DancEn 78; EncMT; NotNAT; VarWW 85; WhoAm 92; WhoEnt 92; WhoThe 77, 81*

Sade
[Helen Folasade Adu]
Nigerian. Singer
Debut album *Diamond Life,* 1984, sold over six million copies; second albu m *Promise,* 1985, was platinum.
b. Jan 16, 1959 in Ibadan, Nigeria
Source: *Baker 92; BioIn 14, 15, 16; CelR 90; ConMus 2; CurBio 86; DrBlPA 90; EncPR&S 89; EncRk 88; LegTOT; News 93-2; PenEncP; SoulM; WhoAm 94, 95, 96, 97*

Sade, Marquis (Donatien Alphonse Francoise) de
French. Author
Works first considered pornographic; believed sexual, criminal acts to be normal; term sadism derived from name.
b. Jun 2, 1740 in Paris, France
d. Dec 2, 1814 in Charenton, France
Source: *AtlBL; CasWL; EuAu; EvEuW; McGEWB; NewC; OxCEng 67; OxCFr; PenC EUR; REn*

Sadik, Nafis
Pakistani. Physician
Executive director, United Nations Population Fund, 1987—; urges equality between men and women in order for population programs to be successful.
b. Aug 18, 1929 in Jaunpur, India
Source: *CurBio 96; IntWW 89, 91, 93; WhoWor 95, 96, 97*

Sadler, Barry
American. Singer
Wrote and sang popular Vietnam-era song, "The Ballad of the Green Berets," 1966.
b. 1941 in Leadville, Colorado
d. Nov 5, 1989 in Murfreesboro, Kentucky
Source: *BioIn 7, 9, 15, 16; FacFETw; NewYTBS 89; RkOn 74, 78; RolSEnR 83; WhoRock 81*

Saerchinger, Cesar Victor Charles
American. Author, Editor, Conductor
Editor, *Who's Who in Music and Musical Gazetteer,* 1918; conductor, CBS radio series, "The Story Behind the Headlines," 1938-48.
b. Oct 23, 1889 in Aachen, Germany
d. Oct 10, 1971
Source: *AmAu&B; Baker 84; BioIn 9; ConAu 33R; CurBio 40; NewYTBE 71; WhAm 5*

Safdie, Moshe
Israeli. Architect
Created master design in urban housing, Habitat 67, for Montreal's Expo 67, 1967.
b. Jul 14, 1938 in Haifa, Palestine
Source: *BioIn 8, 9, 10, 11, 16; BlueB 76; CanWW 31, 70, 79, 80, 81, 83, 89; ConArch 80, 87, 94; ConAu 69; CurBio 68; IntAu&W 91, 93; IntDcAr; IntWW 74, 75, 76, 77, 78, 79, 80, 81, 82, 83, 89, 91, 93; WhoAm 74, 76, 78, 80, 82, 84, 86, 88, 90, 92, 94, 95, 96; WhoE 74; WhoWor 74, 76, 78, 84, 87, 89, 91, 93, 95; WrDr 80, 82, 84, 86, 88, 90, 92, 94, 96*

Safer, Morley
Canadian. Broadcast Journalist
Vietnam correspondent, 1964-71; correspondent, "60 Minutes," 1970—
b. Nov 8, 1931 in Toronto, Ontario, Canada

Source: *BioIn 11, 12, 13, 16; BlueB 76; CelR 90; ConAu 93; ConCaAu 1; ConTFT 12; CurBio 80; DcAmDH 80, 89; EncAJ; EncTwCJ; IntMPA 84, 86, 88, 92, 94, 96; JrnUS; LegTOT; LesBEnT 92; WhoAm 74, 76, 78, 80, 82, 84, 86, 88, 90, 92, 94, 95, 96, 97; WhoE 91, 93; WhoTelC; WorAl; WrDr 92, 94, 96*

Safire, William L
American. Author, Journalist
Washington columnist, *NY Times,* 1973—; won Pulitzer, 1978.
b. Dec 17, 1929 in New York, New York
Source: *BioIn 8, 9, 10, 11, 12, 13, 15, 16; ConAu 17R, 31NR; ConLC 10; CurBio 73; DcAmC; EncTwCJ; IntAu&W 91; IntWW 91; PolProf NF; WhoAm 86, 90; WhoAmP 91; WhoE 91; WhoGov 72; WhoSSW 73; WhoUSWr 88; WhoWor 91; WorAlBi; WrDr 92*

Sagal, Katey
American. Actor
Plays Peg Bundy in TV series "Married with Children," 1987—.
b. 1956
Source: *BioIn 15, 16; ConTFT 5; LegTOT*

Sagan, Carl (Edward)
American. Astronomer, Biologist
Has popularized science through book and TV series *Cosmos.*
b. Nov 9, 1934 in New York, New York
d. Dec 20, 1996 in Seattle, Washington
Source: *AmMWSc 73P, 76P, 79, 82, 86, 89, 92, 95; AsBiEn; Au&Arts 2; BiESc; BioIn 6, 8, 10, 11, 12, 13, 14, 15, 16, 17, 20, 21; BlueB 76; ConAu 11NR, 25R, 36NR; ConHero 1; ConIsC 2; ConLC 30; ConPopW; CurBio 70; EncSF, 93; FacFETw; IntAu&W 76, 89; IntWW 76, 77, 78, 79, 80, 81, 82, 83, 89, 91, 93; LarDcSc; LegTOT; MajTwCW; NewEScF; NewYTBS 27, 79, 85; NotTwCS; RAdv 14, 13-5; ScF&FL 92; SmATA 58; UFOEn; WhoAm 74, 76, 78, 80, 82, 84, 86, 88, 90, 92, 94, 95, 96, 97; WhoE 74, 75, 77, 79, 81, 83, 85, 86, 89, 91, 93; WhoFrS 84; WhoScEn 94, 96; WhoTelC; WhoUSWr 88; WhoWor 78, 80, 82, 84, 87, 89, 91, 93, 95; WhoWrEP 89, 92, 95; WorAl; WorAlBi; WorAu 1975; WorScD; WrDr 76, 80, 82, 84, 86, 88, 90, 92, 94, 96*

Sagan, Francoise
[Francoise Quoirez]
French. Author
Wrote award-winning *Bonjour Tristesse,* 1945, filmed, 1958.
b. Jun 21, 1935 in Cajarc, France
Source: *Benet 87, 96; BioIn 3, 4, 5, 7, 8, 10, 11, 12, 13, 14, 16, 17; BlmGWL; CasWL; ClDMEL 80; ConAu 6NR, 39NR, 49; ConLC 3, 6, 9, 17, 36; ContDcW 89; ConWorW 93; CurBio 60; DcArts; DcLB 83; DcTwCCu 2; EncCoWW; EncWL, 2, 3; EvEuW; FacFETw; FilmEn; FilmgC; FrenWW; GuFrLit 1; HalFC 80, 84, 88; IntAu&W 76, 77, 89; IntDcWB; IntWW 74, 75, 76, 77, 78, 79, 80, 81, 82, 83, 89, 91, 93; InWom, SUP; ItaFilm; LegTOT; LinLib L; LngCTC; MajTwCW; McGEWD 84; ModFrL; ModRL; ModWoWr; Novels; PenC EUR; PenNWW A, B; REn; TwCWr; WhDW; Who 74, 82, 83, 85, 88, 90, 92, 94; WhoAmW 66, 68, 70, 72; WhoFr 79; WhoTwCL; WhoWor 74, 82, 84, 87, 89, 91, 93, 95, 96; WorAl; WorAlBi; WorAu 1950*

Sagansky, Jeff
American. TV Executive
Pres., entertainment programming, CBS, 1990-94; executive vp, Sony US, 1994—.
b. 1952 in Wellesley, Massachusetts
Source: *IntMPA 92; LesBEnT 92; News 93-2; WhoEnt 92*

Sage, Margaret Olivia
[Mrs. Russell Sage]
American. Philanthropist
Gave $10 million to found Russell Sage Foundation, 1907, for improvement in living conditions in US.
b. Sep 8, 1828 in Syracuse, New York
d. Nov 4, 1918 in New York, New York
Source: *AmBi; DcAmB; NotAW; WebAB 74; WhAm 1; WomWWA 14; WorAl; WorAlBi*

Sage, Russell
American. Financier
Associated with Jay Gould in railroading, stock market operations, 1850s-80s; amassed fortune.
b. Aug 4, 1816 in Oneida County, New York
d. Nov 4, 1906 in New York, New York
Source: *AmBi; ApCAB; BiAUS; BiDAmBL 83; BiDrAC; BiDrUSC 89; BioIn 7, 21; DcAmB; HarEnUS; LinLib S; NatCAB 10; TwCBDA; WebAB 74, 79; WhAm 1; WorAl; WorAlBi*

Sager, Carole Bayer
[Mrs. Robert Daly]
American. Singer, Songwriter
Won 1986 Grammy for "That's What Friends Are For."
b. Mar 8, 1947 in New York, New York
Source: *BioIn 11, 14, 15; CelR 90; ConAu 146; ConTFT 13; PenEncP; RkOn 85; RolSEnR 83; WhoAm 80, 82, 84, 86, 88, 90, 92, 94, 95, 96, 97; WhoAmW 95; WhoRocM 82*

Sager, Ruth
American. Geneticist
Discovered that genetic material was also contained apart from the chromosomes in the nucleus of the cell.
b. Feb 7, 1918
d. Mar 29, 1997 in Brookline, Massachusetts
Source: *AmMWSc 73P, 76P, 79, 82, 86, 89, 92, 95; AmWomSc; BioIn 7, 8, 16, 20; InWom, SUP; LibW; NotTwCS; WhoAm 82, 84, 90, 92, 94, 95, 96; WhoAmW 68A, 79, 81, 83, 85, 89, 91, 93, 95; WhoFrS 84; WhoScEn 94, 96*

Saget, Bob
[Robert Saget]
American. Actor, Comedian
Played Danny Tanner on TV comedy "Full House," 1987-94; hosted TV show "America's Funniest Home Videos," 1990-97.
b. May 17, 1956 in Philadelphia, Pennsylvania
Source: *BioIn 16; ConTFT 7; IntMPA 96; LegTOT; WhoEnt 92; WhoHol 92*

Sahl, Mort (Lyon)
American. Comedian
Offbeat nightclub, TV political satirist; known for ironic views of passing scene; wrote autobiography, *Heartland,* 1976.
b. May 11, 1927 in Montreal, Quebec, Canada
Source: *BioIn 4, 5, 6, 7, 9, 10, 11, 13, 16; BioNews 74; CmCal; ConAu 113; ConTFT 7; CurBio 60; Ent; FacFETw; FilmgC; HalFC 84; IntWW 89, 91; JoeFr; LegTOT; WhoAm 86, 90; WhoCom; WhoEnt 92; WhoHol 92, A; WorAl; WorAlBi*

Said, Edward W
American. Political Activist, Educator
Prominent American spokesperson for Palistinian Causes; wrote *Orientalism,* 1978.
b. Nov 1, 1935 in Jerusalem, Palestine
Source: *BioIn 15, 16; CamGLE; ConAu 21R; CurBio 89; CyWA 89; DcLB 67; IntWW 91; LiExTwC; NewYTBS 80; WhoAm 90; WhoUSWr 88; WhoWrEP 89; WorAu 1975; WrDr 92*

Said bin Taimur
Ruler
Impoverished citizens of his oil-rich country during reign as Sultan of Muscat and Oman, 1932-70; deposed by son, Quabus bin Said.
b. Aug 13, 1910 in London, England
d. Oct 19, 1972 in London, England
Source: *BioIn 4, 9, 10, 11, 17; CurBio 57, 78, 78N*

Saidenberg, Daniel
American. Musician, Conductor
Cellist; created Saidenberg Little Symphony, 1940; led IL Symphony, 1930s.
b. Nov 12, 1906 in Winnipeg, Manitoba, Canada
d. May 18, 1997 in New York, New York
Source: *BioIn 2, 9; IntWWM 77, 80, 85; WhoAm 74, 76, 78, 80, 82, 84, 86, 88, 90; WhoAmA 73, 76, 78, 80, 82, 84, 86, 89, 91, 93; WhoEnt 92; WhoMus 72*

Said ibn Sultan
Arab. Ruler
Sayyid of Muscat, Oman, and Zanzibar, 1806-56; established Zanzibar as a commerce capital.
b. 1791, Oman
d. Oct 19, 1856, At Sea

Sain, Johnny
[John Franklin Sain]
American. Baseball Player, Baseball Coach
Pitcher, 1942, 1946-55; had 139 career wins; controversial pitching coach for 13 yrs.
b. Sep 15, 1918 in Havana, Arkansas
Source: *Ballpl 90; BioIn 1, 2, 3, 4, 6, 7, 8, 9, 10, 14, 15; WhoProB 73*

Saint, Assotto
American. Writer
Poetry collections include *Stations,* 1989; also performed theatrical works.
b. Oct 2, 1957, Haiti
d. 1994
Source: *GayLesB*

Saint, Eva Marie
American. Actor
Won Oscar, 1955, for *On the Waterfront,* her first film; other films include *North by Northwest,* 1959; *Grand Prix,* 1966.
b. Jul 4, 1924 in Newark, New Jersey
Source: *BiDFilm 94; BiE&WWA; BioIn 2, 3, 4, 10; BioNews 74; ConTFT 3, 5; CurBio 55; FilmEn; FilmgC; ForYSC; GangFlm; HalFC 80, 84, 88; IntDcF 1-3, 2-3; IntMPA 77, 78, 79, 80, 81, 82, 84, 86, 88, 92, 94, 96; InWom, SUP; LegTOT; MotPP; MovMk; WhoAm 74, 76, 78, 80, 82, 84, 86, 88, 90, 92, 94, 95, 96, 97; WhoAmW 58, 61, 64, 66, 68, 70, 95, 97; WhoEnt 92; WhoHol 92, A; WorAl; WorAlBi; WorEFlm*

Saint Clair, Arthur
American. Military Leader
First governor of Northwest Territory, 1787-1802; removed from office by Jeffers on in 1802 for criticizing act which made Ohio a state.
b. Mar 23, 1736 in Thurso, Scotland
d. Aug 31, 1818 in Ligonier, Pennsylvania
Source: *Alli; AmBi; ApCAB; BiAUS; BiDrAC; BiDrUSE 71; DcAmB; Drake; NewCol 75; OhA&B; OxCAmH; REnAL; TwCBDA; WebAB 74; WebAMB; WhAm HS; WorAl*

St. Clair, Bob
American. Football Player
Tackle, San Francisco, 1953-63; Hall of Fame, 1990.
b. Feb 18, 1931 in San Francisco, California
Source: *BioIn 17; WhoSpor*

Saint Clair, James Draper
American. Lawyer
Chief Watergate counsel to Richard Nixon, Jan-Aug 1974; argued against impeachment before House Judiciary Committee, Feb 1974.
b. Apr 14, 1920 in Akron, Ohio
Source: *BioIn 10; NewYTBS 74; PolProf NF; WhoAm 86, 90; WhoAmL 85, 92*

Saint Cyr, Lillian
[Marie VanShaak]
American. Entertainer
Burlesque queen who made as much as $7,500 per week at height of career.
b. Jun 3, 1917 in Minneapolis, Minnesota
Source: *BioIn 10; InWom SUP; WhoHol A*

Saint Denis, Ruth
American. Dancer, Choreographer
Early modern dance exponent; noted for eclectic style from Oriental movements.
b. Jan 20, 1877 in Newark, New Jersey
d. Jun 21, 1968 in Los Angeles, California
Source: *BiDD; CurBio 49, 68; IntDcWB; McGEWB; NotAW MOD; WebAB 79; WhAm 5; WhoHol B; WhScrn 83*

Sainte-Beuve, Charles Augustin
French. Critic
First professional literary critic; wrote *Port-Royal,* 1840-59.
b. Dec 23, 1804 in Boulogne-sur-Mer, France
d. Oct 13, 1869 in Paris, France
Source: *AtlBL; BbD; Benet 87, 96; BiD&SB; BioIn 1, 2, 3, 4, 5, 6, 7, 9, 10; CasWL; CelCen; CyWA 58; DcArts; DcBiPP; DcEnL; DcEuL; Dis&D; EuAu; EvEuW; LinLib L, S; McGEWB; NewC; NewCBEL; NinCLC 5; OxCEng 67, 85; OxCFr; OxCThe 67; PenC EUR; RComWL; REn*

Sainte-Clair Deville, Henri Etienne
French. Chemist
Invented first cost-effective process for making aluminum.
b. Mar 11, 1818 in Saint Thomas, Danish West Indies
d. Jul 1, 1881 in Boulogne, France
Source: *BioIn 3, 6*

Sainte-Marie, Buffy
[Beverly Sainte-Marie]
American. Singer, Composer
Won Oscar for best song from *An Officer and a Gentleman,* 1982; has composed over 300 songs.
b. Feb 20, 1941 in Craven, Saskatchewan, Canada
Source: *ASCAP 80; BiDAmM; BioIn 14, 21; CivR 74; ConAu 107; ConLC 17; CurBio 69; EncFCWM 69, 83; EncRk 88; GoodHs; HarEnCM 87; IlEncCM; IlEncRk; InWom SUP; LegTOT; NewAmDM; NewGrDA 86; PenEncP; RkOn 74, 78; RolSEnR 83; WhoAm 74, 76, 78, 80, 82; WhoAmW 70, 72, 74, 75, 83; WhoRock 81; WhoRocM 82; WhoWor 74; WorAl; WorAlBi*

Saint-Exupery, Antoine (Jean Baptiste Marie Roger) de
French. Author, Aviator
Wrote fable *The Little Prince,* 1943;autobiography *Wind, Sand, and Stars,* 1939; opened transatlantic airmail routes to S America, Africa.
b. Jun 29, 1900 in Lyons, France
d. Jul 31, 1944, France
Source: *AtlBL; CasWL; ConAu 108; CurBio 40, 45; MajAI; ModRL; OxCFr; PenC EUR; REn; TwCA, SUP; TwCWr; WhoTwCL*

Saint Gaudens, Augustus
American. Sculptor
Leading sculptor of late 19th c. known for equestrian statue of General Sherman in Central Park, NYC.
b. Mar 1, 1848 in Dublin, Ireland
d. Aug 3, 1907 in Cornish, New Hampshire
Source: *AmAu&B; AmBi; ApCAB; AtlBL; DcAmB; EncAB-H 1974; OxCAmL 65; REn; REnAL; TwCBDA; WebAB 74; WhAm 1*

Saint Georges, Jules
French. Author, Librettist
Wrote, alone or in collaboration, over 80 opera books for noted French composers.
b. Nov 7, 1801 in Paris, France
d. Dec 23, 1875 in Paris, France
Source: *NewEOp 71*

Saint Jacques, Raymond
[Charles Arthur Johnson]
American. Actor
Films include *Cotton Comes to Harlem,* 1970; *Glory,* 1990.
b. Mar 1, 1930 in Hartford, Connecticut
d. Aug 27, 1990 in Los Angeles, California
Source: *BioIn 15; BlksAmF; ConTFT 9; DrBlPA 90; FacFETw; FilmEn; FilmgC; HalFC 88; IntMPA 86, 88; MovMk; NewYTBE 73; NewYTBS 90; VarWW 85; WhoAm 86, 90; WhoBlA 75, 92N; WhoHol A*

St. James, Lyn
[Evelyn Cornwall]
American. Auto Racer
First woman to be named rookie of the year at the Indianapolis 500, 1992.
b. Mar 13, 1947 in Cleveland, Ohio
Source: *BioIn 12, 16; News 93-2; WhoAdv 90; WhoAm 94, 95, 96, 97; WhoAmW 91, 93, 95, 97; WhoFI 89*

Saint James, Susan
[Susan Miller]
American. Actor
Appeared in TV series "The Name of the Game"; "McMillan and Wife"; "Kate and Allie."
b. Aug 14, 1946 in Long Beach, California
Source: *BioIn 13, 14, 15; CelR 90; ConTFT 2, 8; FilmEn; FilmgC; ForYSC; HalFC 80, 84, 88; HolBB; IntMPA 77, 78, 79, 80, 81, 82, 84, 86, 88, 92, 94,*

96; InWom SUP; LegTOT; WhoAm 74, 76, 80, 82, 84, 86, 88, 90, 92; WhoAmW 72, 74, 75; WhoEnt 92; WhoHol 92, A; WorAl; WorAlBi

Saint John, Betta
[Betty Streidler]
American. Actor
Ingenue in original Broadway cast of *South Pacific,* 1949; films include *The Law vs. Billy the Kid,* 1954.
b. Nov 26, 1929 in Hawthorne, California
Source: *FilmEn; FilmgC; HalFC 84, 88; IntMPA 86, 88; WhoHol A*

Saint John, Howard
American. Actor
Films include *L'il Abner,* 1959; *Don't Drink the Water,* 1969.
b. Oct 9, 1905 in Chicago, Illinois
d. Mar 13, 1974 in New York, New York
Source: *BiE&WWA; FilmgC; MovMk; WhoHol B; WhScrn 77*

Saint John, Jill
[Jill Oppenheim; Mrs. Robert Wagner]
American. Actor
Began acting at age 6; has appeared on radio, TV, film; appeared in film *Tony Rome,* 1967.
b. Aug 9, 1940 in Los Angeles, California
Source: *BioIn 13, 16; ConTFT 3; EncAFC; FilmgC; HalFC 84, 88; IntMPA 92; InWom SUP; MotPP; MovMk; WhoAm 86, 90; WhoEnt 92; WorAlBi*

Saint John, Robert
American. Journalist, Author
War correspondent with AP, WW II; books on Middle-Eastern affairs include *The Tongue of the Prophets,* 1952.
b. Mar 9, 1902 in Chicago, Illinois
Source: *AmAu&B; ConAu 1R, 5NR; CurBio 42; IntAu&W 91; WhoAm 84; WhoWor 74; WrDr 86, 92*

Saint Johns, Adela Rogers
American. Author, Journalist
Noted for inside stories of Hollywood film community; wrote *The Tramp,* short story based on Hollywood experiences.
b. May 20, 1894 in Los Angeles, California
d. Aug 10, 1988 in Arroyo Grande, California
Source: *AmWomWr; AuNews 1; CelR; ConAu 108; CurBio 76, 88; DcLB 29; EncAJ; EncTwCJ; ForWC 70; GoodHs; InWom SUP; LibW; WhoAm 74, 76, 78; WhoAmW 64, 66, 68, 70, 72, 74, 75; WorAl; WrDr 76, 80, 82, 84*

St. Laurent, Andre
"Ace"
Canadian. Hockey Player
Center, 1973-85; involved in controversial free agent compensation case with Dale McCourt, Rogie Vachon, 1979.
b. Feb 16, 1953 in Rouyn Noranda, Quebec, Canada
Source: *HocEn; HocReg 85*

Saint Laurent, Louis Stephen
Canadian. Political Leader
Prime Minister, Liberal Party, 1948-57.
b. Feb 1, 1882 in Compton, Quebec, Canada
d. Jul 24, 1973 in Quebec, Quebec, Canada
Source: *CanWW 70; CurBio 48, 73; NewYTBE 73; OxCCan; WhAm 5; WhoWor 74*

Saint Laurent, Yves Mathieu
French. Fashion Designer
Responsible for "chic beatnik" and "little boy look" of 1960s.
b. Aug 1, 1936 in Oran, Algeria
Source: *BioIn 13, 16; BkPepl; CelR 90; ConDes 90; CurBio 64; DcTwDes; EncFash; Entr; FacFETw; IntWW 91; NewYTBS 76, 83; Who 92; WhoFash 88; WhoWor 84, 91; WorAlBi; WorFshn*

Saint-Saens, (Charles) Camille
French. Musician, Composer
Best known for opera *Samson et Delila,* 1877, several symphonies.
b. Oct 9, 1835 in Paris, France
d. Dec 16, 1921 in Algiers, Algeria
Source: *AtlBL; Baker 78, 84, 92; Benet 87, 96; BioIn 1, 2, 3, 4, 5, 6, 7, 8, 9, 12, 13, 16, 20; BriBkM 80; CelCen; CmOp; CmpBCM; DancEn 78; DcArts; DcCom 77; DcCom&M 79; DcPup; DcTwCCu 2; EncPaPR 91; GrComp; IntDcOp; LegTOT; LinLib S; LuthC 75; McGEWB; MetOEnc; MusMk; NewAmDM; NewEOp 71; NewGrDM 80; NewGrDO; NewOxM; NotNAT B; OxCFr; OxCMus; OxDcOp; PenDiMP A; REn; WhDW; WorAl; WorAlBi*

Saintsbury, George Edward Bateman
English. Author, Educator, Critic
Critical writings include *Elizabethan Literature,* 1906; *A Scrapbook,* 1922-24.
b. Oct 10, 1845 in Southampton, England
d. Jan 28, 1933 in Bath, England
Source: *Alli SUP; AtlBL; BbD; BiD&SB; BioIn 1, 2, 5, 8, 11, 13; BlmGEL; Chambr 3; ChhPo, S2, S3; DcEnA, A; DcLEL; DcNaB 1931; EvLB; LngCEL; LngCTC; ModBrL; NewC; NewCBEL; OxCEng 67, 85, 95; PenC ENG; RAdv 1; TwCA, SUP; WhLit*

Saint-Simon, Claude-Henri de Rouvroy
French. Philosopher
Saint-Simonianism was system of social thought combining religious dogma with socialism.
b. Oct 17, 1760 in Paris, France
d. May 19, 1825 in Paris, France
Source: *ApCAB; BbD; BiD&SB; CasWL; DcEuL; EuAu; EvEuW; OxCEng 67, 95; OxCFr; OxCPhil; REn*

Saint-Subber, Arnold
American. Producer
Productions include *The Little Foxes,* 1967; *Gigi,* 1973.
b. Feb 18, 1918 in Washington, District of Columbia
Source: *BiE&WWA; BlueB 76; CamGWoT; CelR; NotNAT; WhoAm 78; WhoThe 72, 77, 81*

Saito, Yoshishige
Japanese. Artist
Rose to prominence with his surrealistic series of Japanese demons, 1956; later works moved to non-expressive mode.
b. May 4, 1904 in Tokyo, Japan
Source: *ConArt 77, 83, 89, 96; OxCTwCA; PhDcTCA 77; WhoWor 74; WhWW-II*

Sajak, Pat
American. TV Personality
Host of game show "Wheel of Fortune," 1981—, most successful show ever syndicated.
b. Oct 26, 1947 in Chicago, Illinois
Source: *CelR 90; ConNews 85-4; CurBio 89; IntMPA 92; LegTOT; WhoAm 90, 92, 94, 95, 96, 97; WhoEnt 92; WorAlBi*

Sakall, S. Z
[Eugene Gero Szakall]
"Cuddles"
Hungarian. Actor
Films include *Casablanca,* 1942; *Tea for Two,* 1950.
b. Feb 2, 1883 in Budapest, Austria-Hungary
d. Feb 12, 1955 in Los Angeles, California
Source: *FilmgC; MotPP; MovMk; Vers A; WhoHol B; WhScrn 74, 77*

Sakamoto, Ryuichi
Japanese. Composer, Musician
Composer and innovator in electronic keyboard work; released first solo album, *Thousand Knives,* in 1978; formed the Yellow Magic Orchestra, 1978; wrote film score for *The Last Emperor,* 1988, for which he won an Oscar, a Grammy, a Golden Globe, and the New York, Los Angeles, and British Film Critics Association awards for Best Original Score.
b. 1952, Japan

Sakharov, Andrei Dmitrievich
Russian. Physicist
National hero for building hydrogen bomb; led dissident movement in Soviet Union; won Nobel Peace Prize, 1975; exiled to Gorky, 1980-87.
b. May 21, 1921 in Moscow, Union of Soviet Socialist Republics
d. Dec 14, 1989 in Moscow, Union of Soviet Socialist Republics
Source: *BiDSovU; BioIn 8, 9, 10, 11, 12, 13, 14, 15, 16, 17, 18, 19, 20; ColdWar 1; ConAu 105, 128, 130; CurBio 71, 90, 90N; EncWB; FacFETw; IntWW 89; News 90-2; NewYTBE 73; NewYTBS 75, 80, 86, 89; NobelP; Who 90; WhoNob, 90; WhoWor 89; WorAlBi*

Saki
[Hector Hugh Munro]
Author
Satirist, short-story writer; works include *Chronicles of Clovis,* 1911; killed in WW I.
b. Dec 18, 1870 in Akyab, Burma
d. Nov 13, 1916 in Beaumont-Hamel, France
Source: *Alli SUP; AtlBL; Benet 87, 96; BioIn 1, 5, 9, 10, 12, 14, 15, 17, 18; CamGEL; CamGLE; CasWL; ChhPo; CnMWL; ConAu 104; CrtSuMy; CyWA 58; DcArts; DcLEL; DcNaB 1912; EncSF, 93; EvLB; FacFETw; GrBr; GrWrEL N; LegTOT; LngCTC; ModBrL; NewC; NewCBEL; NewEScF; Novels; OxCEng 67, 85, 95; PenC ENG; PenEncH; RAdv 1, 13-1; REn; RfGEnL 91; RfGShF; RGTwCWr; ScFEYrs; ShSCr 12; ShSWr; SupFW; TwCA, SUP; TwCLC 3; TwCWr; WhDW; WhoTwCL; WorAlBi; WorLitC*

Sakic, Joe
Canadian. Hockey Player
Center, Quebec, 1988-95; Colorado, 1995—; won Conn Smythe Trophy, 1996.
b. Jul 7, 1969 in Burnaby, British Columbia, Canada

Sakiestewa, Ramona
American. Artist
Hopi weaver; creates designs based on historic textiles.
b. 1949 in Albuquerque, New Mexico
Source: *BioIn 21; NotNaAm*

Saks, Gene
American. Director
Won Tony for musical, *I Love My Wife,* 1977.
b. Nov 8, 1921 in New York, New York
Source: *BiE&WWA; BioIn 11; CamGWoT; ConTFT 2, 9; EncAFC; FilmEn; FilmgC; HalFC 80, 84, 88; IntMPA 75, 76, 77, 78, 79, 80, 81, 82, 84, 86, 88, 92, 94, 96; IntWW 91; ItaFilm; LegTOT; MiSFD 9; NotNAT; TheaDir; WhoAm 74, 86, 90; WhoHol 92, A; WhoThe 72, 77, 81; WorAlBi*

Sala, George Augustus
English. Journalist
London *Daily Telegraph* correspondent, covering American Civil War; wrote travel books, novels.
b. Nov 24, 1828 in London, England
d. Dec 8, 1895 in Brighton, England
Source: *BbD; BenetAL 91; DcEnL; EvLB; NinCLC 46; OxCAusL; OxCEng 85, 95; REnAL; ScFEYrs; StaCVF*

Saladin Yusuf ibn Ayyub
[Salah al-Din]
Moslem. Ruler
Sultan of Egypt, Syria, 1174; united Muslim territories; considered great Muslim hero.
b. 1138, Mesopotamia
d. 1193
Source: *NewC; NewCol 75; WebBD 83*

Salam, Abdus
Pakistani. Physicist
Shared 1979 Nobel Prize in physics with Sheldon Glashow and Steven Weinberg.
b. Jan 29, 1926 in Jhang, Pakistan
d. Nov 21, 1996 in Oxford, England
Source: *AmMWSc 86, 89, 92, 95; BiESc; BioIn 12, 13, 14, 15, 16, 19, 20; BlueB 76; CamDcSc; CurBio 88; FacFETw; FarE&A 78, 79, 80, 81; IntWW 74, 75, 76, 77, 78, 79, 80, 81, 82, 83, 89, 91, 93; IntWWE; LarDcSc; NewYTBS 27; NobelP; NotTwCS; RAdv 14; Who 74, 82, 83, 85, 88, 90, 92, 94; WhoAm 88, 90, 92, 94, 95; WhoAtom 77; WhoNob, 90, 95; WhoScEn 94, 96; WhoScEu 91-3; WhoUN 75; WhoWor 74, 76, 78, 80, 82, 84, 87, 89, 91, 93, 95, 96, 97; WorAlBi; WorScD*

Salam, Saeb
Lebanese. Political Leader
Prime minister, 1952-53, 1960-61, 1970-73.
b. 1905 in Beirut, Lebanon
Source: *BioIn 4; DcMidEa; IntWW 74, 75, 76, 77, 78, 79, 80, 81, 82, 83, 89, 91, 93; MidE 78, 79, 80, 81, 82; WhoWor 74*

Salant, Richard S
American. Broadcasting Executive
President of CBS, 1961-79.
b. Apr 14, 1914 in New York, New York
d. Feb 16, 1993 in Southport, Connecticut
Source: *BioIn 16; CurBio 61; EncTwCJ; IntMPA 86, 92; LesBEnT; WhoAm 86; WorAlBi*

Salazar, Alberto
American. Track Athlete
Won NY City Marathon, 1980, 1981; Boston Marathan, 1982.
b. Aug 7, 1958 in Havana, Cuba
Source: *BioIn 12, 13, 14, 16; CurBio 83; NewYTBS 81; WhoAm 84, 86, 88, 92, 94, 95, 96, 97; WhoHisp 91, 92, 94*

Salazar, Antonio de Oliveira
Portuguese. Statesman
Premier, dictator of Portugal, 1932-68.
b. Apr 28, 1889, Portugal
d. Jul 27, 1970 in Lisbon, Portugal
Source: *BioIn 17, 21; ConAu 113; CurBio 41, 52, 70; DcTwHis; DicTyr; EncTR 91; FacFETw; McGEWB; NewYTBE 70; PolLCWE; WhDW; WorAlBi*

Sale, Charles Partlow
"Chic"
American. Actor
Films include *It's a Great Life,* 1936; *You Only Live Once,* 1937.
b. 1885 in Huron, South Dakota
d. Nov 7, 1936 in Los Angeles, California
Source: *BioIn 3; DcNAA; WhAm 1; WhScrn 74, 77*

Sale, Richard Bernard
American. Author, Director, Screenwriter
Published more than 400 short stories; screenplays include *Mr. Belvidere Goes to College,* 1949; directed *The Girl Next Door,* 1953.
b. Dec 17, 1911 in New York, New York
d. Mar 4, 1993 in Los Angeles, California
Source: *BioIn 14; ConAu 9R; EncAFC; HalFC 88; IntAu&W 91; IntMPA 92; TwCCr&M 91; WrDr 92*

Salem, Mamdouh
Egyptian. Political Leader
Prime minister under Sadat, 1975-78; interior minister, 1971-75.
b. 1918 in Alexandria, Egypt
d. Feb 24, 1988 in London, England
Source: *BioIn 15; IntWW 74, 75, 83; NewYTBS 88*

Salem, Peter
American. Patriot
Killed a British commander at the Battle of Bunker Hill, 1775.
b. 1750
d. 1816
Source: *BioIn 7, 8, 9, 10; DcAmNB; InB&W 80, 85*

Salerno-Sonnenberg, Nadja
Italian. Violinist
Concert star, 1981—; youngest to win the Naumburg competition, 1981.
b. Jan 10, 1961 in Rome, Italy
Source: *Baker 92; BioIn 15, 16; ConMus 3; CurBio 87; LegTOT; News 88; NewYTBS 87; WhoAm 96, 97; WhoAmM 83; WhoAmW 93, 95, 97; WhoEnt 92*

Sales, Soupy
[Milton Hines; Milton Supman]
American. TV Personality
Starred in "Soupy Sales Show," 1953-66; known for pie-throwing act.
b. Jan 8, 1930 in Wake Forest, North Carolina

Source: *ASCAP 66, 80; BioIn 14, 16; CurBio 67; EncAFC; FilmgC; HalFC 88; LesBEnT 92; MotPP; WhoHol A; WorAlBi*

Salgado, Sebastiao
Brazilian. Photojournalist
Creator of photographic shows and books, including *Other Americas,* 1984.
b. 1944 in Aimores, Brazil
Source: *ICPEnP A; News 94, 94-2; NewYTBS 91*

Salhany, Lucie
[Lucille S Salhany]
American. Business Executive
Chm. Fox television, 1993-94; first woman to head a broadcast network; United ParamountNetwork, 1994—.
b. May 25, 1946 in Cleveland, Ohio
Source: *ConTFT 12; WomFir*

Salieri, Antonio
Italian. Conductor, Composer
Thirty five operas include *Tarare,* 1787; his envy of Mozart depicted in 1985 Oscar-winning film, *Amadeus.*
b. Aug 18, 1750 in Legnano, Italy
d. May 7, 1825 in Vienna, Austria
Source: *Baker 78, 84, 92; BioIn 4, 5, 6, 9, 12, 14, 18; BriBkM 80; CmOp; DcArts; DcBiPP; IntDcOp; MetOEnc; MusMk; NewAmDM; NewEOp 71; NewGrDM 80; NewGrDO; NewOxM; NewYTBS 81; OxCMus; OxDcOp; PenDiMP A*

Salinas, Luis Omar
American. Poet
Poetry frequently uses surrealistic images and metaphors; published collection *Crazy Gypsy,* 1970.
b. Jun 27, 1937 in Robstown, Texas
Source: *BioIn 13, 16; ChiLit; ChiSch; ConAu 131; ConLC 90; DcHiB; DcLB 82; HispLC; HispWr; IntWWP 77; MexAmB; WhoHisp 91, 92, 94*

Salinas (y Serrano), Pedro
Spanish. Poet
Verse volumes include *Presagios,* 1923; *La Voza Ti Debida,* 1934.
b. Nov 27, 1891 in Madrid, Spain
d. Dec 4, 1951 in Boston, Massachusetts
Source: *Benet 87; BioIn 1, 2, 3, 4, 8, 10; CasWL; ClDMEL 47, 80; CnMWL; ConAu 117; DcLB 134; DcSpL; EncWL 2, 3; EvEuW; LiExTwC; ModRL; ModSpP S; OxCSpan; PenC EUR; RAdv 14, 13-2; REn; TwCA SUP; TwCLC 17; TwCWr; WebBD 83; WhAm 3*

Salinas de Gortari, Carlos
Mexican. Political Leader
Succeeded Miguel de la Madrid as pres. of Mexico, 1988-94.
b. Apr 3, 1948 in Mexico City, Mexico
Source: *BioIn 15, 16; DcCPCAm; DcHiB; IntWW 89, 91, 93; News 92; NewYTBS 87, 88, 89; WhoAm 94, 95, 96; WhoSSW 91, 93, 95; WhoWor 91, 95, 96, 97*

Salinger, J(erome) D(avid)
American. Author
Best known for poignant human comedy, *Catcher in the Rye,* 1951, popular with teens at the time.
b. Jan 1, 1919 in New York, New York
Source: *AmAu&B; AmWr; Au&Arts 2; Au&Wr 71; Benet 87, 96; BenetAL 91; BioIn 2, 4, 5, 6, 7, 8, 9, 10, 11, 12, 13, 14, 15, 16, 17, 19; CamGEL; CamGLE; CamHAL; CasWL; CelR 90; ChlLR 18; CnMWL; ConAu 5R, 39NR; ConLC 12, 56; ConNov 86, 91, 96; ConPopW; CyWA 89; DcArts; DcLB 102; DcLEL 1940; DrAPF 87, 91; EncAB-H 1974, 1996; FacFETw; IntAu&W 89, 91, 93; IntvTCA 2; IntWW 91, 93; MajAI; MajTwCW; MakMC; ModAL S1; NewCon; OxCAmL 83, 95; OxCChiL; OxCEng 85, 95; PenC AM; RAdv 14, 13-1; REn; REnAL; RfGAmL 87, 94; RfGShF; RGTwCWr; ShSCr 2; SmATA 67; TwCYAW; WebAB 74, 79; WhDW; Who 74, 82, 83, 85, 88, 90, 92, 94; WhoAm 74, 76, 78, 80, 82, 84, 92, 94, 95, 96, 97; WhoUSWr 88; WhoWor 74, 84, 95, 96, 97; WhoWrEP 89, 92, 95; WorAlBi; WrDr 86, 90, 94, 96*

Salinger, Pierre Emil George
American. Journalist, Politician
Press secretary to JFK; chief foreign correspondent for ABC News, 1979-87; senior editor, ABC News for Europe, 1988-90; senior editor, ABC News, 1988-93.
b. Jun 14, 1925 in San Francisco, California
Source: *BiDrAC; BiDrUSC 89; BioIn 14, 15; ConAu 14NR, 17R; CurBio 61, 87; EncTwCJ; IntAu&W 89; IntWW 91; LesBEnT 92; PolProf J, K; Who 92; WhoAm 86, 90, 97; WhoTelC; WhoUSWr 88; WhoWrEP 89; WorAlBi; WrDr 86, 92*

Salisbury, Harrison Evans
American. Journalist
Staff writer with *NY Times,* 1949-73; won Pulitzer, 1955; best-sellers include *Black Nights, White Snow,* 1978.
b. Nov 14, 1908 in Minneapolis, Minnesota
d. Jul 5, 1993 in Providence, Rhode Island
Source: *AmAu&B; Au&Wr 71; BenetAL 91; BiDAmJo; BioIn 3, 4, 5, 6, 7, 10, 11, 12, 13, 14, 15, 16, 17, 19, 21; CelR 90; ConAu 1R, 3NR, 15AS, 30NR; ConLC 81; CurBio 55, 82; EncTwCJ; EncWB; IntAu&W 76, 77, 82, 89, 91, 93; IntWW 74, 75, 76, 77, 78, 79, 80, 81, 82, 83, 89, 91, 93; MajTwCW; MinnWr; PolProf E, J; REnAL; WhAm 11; Who 74, 82, 83, 85, 88, 90, 92; WhoAm 74, 76, 78, 80, 82, 84, 86, 88, 90, 92; WhoE 74; WhoWor 74, 78; WorAl; WorAlBi; WorAu 1950; WrDr 76, 86, 92*

Salisbury, Robert Arthur Talbot, 3rd Marquess
English. Statesman
Prime minister, 1885-1902, during England's greatest power.
b. Feb 3, 1830 in Hatfield, England
d. Aug 22, 1903 in Hatfield, England
Source: *CelCen; DcInB; McGEWB; WhDW*

Salk, Jonas E(dward)
American. Scientist, Physician
Developed anti-polio vaccine, one of the greatest triumphs in medical history, 1953.
b. Oct 28, 1914 in New York, New York
d. Jun 23, 1995 in La Jolla, California
Source: *AmMWSc 76P, 79, 82, 86, 89, 92, 95; AsBiEn; BiDrAPH 79; BiESc; BioIn 3, 4, 5, 6, 7, 8, 9, 10, 11, 12, 13, 14, 15, 16; BioNews 75; BlueB 76; CelR 90; ConAu 49; ConHero 1; CurBio 54, 95N; FacFETw; InSci; IntMed 80; IntWW 74, 75, 76, 77, 78, 79, 80, 81, 82, 83, 89, 91, 93; IntYB 78, 79, 80, 81, 82; JeAmHC; LarDcSc; LngCTC; McGEWB; McGMS 80; NewYTBS 90; OxCAmH; RComAH; WebAB 74, 79; WhAm 11; WhDW; Who 74, 82, 83, 85, 88, 90, 92, 94; WhoAm 74, 76, 78, 80, 82, 84, 86, 88, 90, 92, 94, 95; WhoAmJ 80; WhoFrS 84; WhoScEn 94; WhoWest 76, 78, 80, 82, 84, 87, 89, 92, 94; WhoWor 74, 78, 80, 82, 84, 87, 89, 91, 93, 95; WhoWorJ 72, 78; WorAl; WorAlBi*

Salk, Lee
American. Psychologist, Author
Family columnist with *McCall's;* wrote books on pediatric psychology; *Familyhood: Nurturing the Values That Matter,* 1992.
b. Dec 27, 1926 in New York, New York
d. May 4, 1992 in New York, New York
Source: *AnObit 1992; AuNews 1; BioIn 10, 11, 12, 15, 17, 18, 19; ConAu 104, 137; CurBio 79, 92N; NewYTBS 92; WhAm 10; WhoAm 80, 82, 84, 86, 88, 90; WhoWor 82*

Salmi, Albert
American. Actor
TV western actor; films include *Caddy Shack,* 1980.
b. Mar 11, 1928 in New York, New York
d. Apr 22, 1990 in Spokane, Washington
Source: *BiE&WWA; BioIn 16, 17; ConTFT 5; FilmEn; FilmgC; ForYSC; HalFC 80, 84, 88; IntMPA 77, 80, 84, 86, 88; NewYTBS 90; NotNAT; VarWW 85; WhoHol A*

Salome
Hebrew. Biblical Figure
Princess; granddaughter of Herod the Great; asked for head of John the Baptist in payment for dancing.
b. 14
d. 62
Source: *Dis&D; NewCol 75; WebBD 83*

Salomon, Alice
American. Educator
Founded first German school of social work.
b. Apr 19, 1872 in Berlin, Germany
d. Aug 30, 1948 in New York, New York
Source: *BioIn 1, 2; InWom SUP; ObitOF 79; WhE&EA; WhoLA*

Salomon, Haym
American. Patriot
Aided finances of American Revolution; made large loans to new govt., to patriots.
b. 1740 in Leszno, Poland
d. Jan 6, 1785 in Philadelphia, Pennsylvania
Source: *AmBi; AmRev; ApCAB; BiDAmBL 83; BioIn 1, 2, 3, 4, 5, 6, 7, 8, 9, 10, 11, 14, 15, 17; DcAmB; DcAmSR; EncAI&E; HarEnUS; JeHun; NatCAB 11; OxCAmH; PolBiDi; WebAB 74, 79; WhAm HS; WhAmP; WhAmRev*

Salt
[Salt 'n Pepa; Cheryl James]
American. Rapper
Grammy. Best Rap Performance by a Group or Duo, "None of Your Business," 1994.
b. Mar 8, 1964 in New York, New York

Salt, Jennifer
American. Actor
Leading lady, 1960s-70s: *Midnight Cowboy,* 1969; *Play It Again Sam,* 1972.
b. Sep 4, 1944 in Los Angeles, California
Source: *ConTFT 7; FilmEn; HalFC 84, 88; WhoHol 92, A*

Salt, Waldo
American. Screenwriter
Won Oscars, 1969, 1978 for screenplays: *Midnight Cowboy; Coming Home.*
b. Oct 18, 1914 in Chicago, Illinois
d. Mar 9, 1987 in Los Angeles, California
Source: *AnObit 1987; BioIn 15; ConAu 111, 121; ConTFT 6; DcLB 44; FilmEn; FilmgC; HalFC 80, 84, 88; IntDcF 1-4, 2-4; IntMPA 75, 76, 77, 78, 79, 80, 81, 82, 84, 86; VarWW 85; WhAm 9; WhoAm 84, 86*

Salten, Felix
[Siegmund Salzmann]
Hungarian. Children's Author
Wrote *Bambi,* 1926, translated, 1928, as *Bambi: A Life in the Woods.*
b. Sep 6, 1869 in Budapest, Hungary
d. Oct 8, 1945 in Zurich, Switzerland
Source: *AuBYP 2; BioIn 1, 4, 5, 8, 13, 19, 20; ChlBkCr; ClDMEL 47; ConAu 108, 137; CyWA 58; LegTOT; LinLib L; LngCTC; MajAI; OxCChiL; OxCGer 76, 86; ScF&FL 1; SmATA 25; TwCA, SUP; WhAm 2; WhE&EA; WhoChL; WrChl*

Salter, Andrew
American. Psychologist
Developed techniques for autohypnosis; wrote *What Is Hypnosis?,* 1944.
b. May 9, 1914
d. Oct 7, 1996 in New York, New York
Source: *InSci*

Salt n Pepa
[Spinderella; Sandy "Pepa" Denton; Cheryl "Salt" James]
American. Rap Group
Popular female rap group; singles "Push It," 1987, "Let's Talk about Sex," 1992.
Source: *BioIn 20, 21; ConMus 6*

Saltonstall, Leverett
American. Politician
Rep. governor of MA, 1939-44; senator, 1945-66.
b. Sep 1, 1892 in Chestnut Hill, Massachusetts
d. Jun 17, 1979 in Dover, Massachusetts
Source: *BiDrAC; BiDrGov 1789; BiDrUSC 89; BioIn 1, 3, 4, 7, 11, 12; BlueB 76; CurBio 44, 56, 79, 79N; DcAmB S10; NewYTBS 79; PolProf E, J, K, T; WhAm 7; WhAmP; WhoAm 74, 76, 78; WhoAmL 78, 79; WhoAmP 73, 75, 77, 79*

Saltzman, Charles E(skridge)
American. Business Executive, Government Official
Assistant secretary of state for occupied areas, 1947-49; partner, Goldman, Sachs & Co., 1956-73.
b. Sep 19, 1903
d. Jun 16, 1994 in New York, New York
Source: *BiDWWGF; BioIn 1, 3; CurBio 94N; IntWW 74, 75, 76, 77, 78, 79, 80, 81, 82, 83, 89, 91, 93; WhAm 11; Who 74, 82, 83, 85, 88, 90, 92, 94; WhoAm 74, 76, 78, 80, 82, 84, 86, 88, 90, 92; WhoFI 74, 75, 77, 79*

Sam and Dave
[Sam Moore; Dave Prater]
American. Music Group
Black singing duo known for pop, soul hits including "Soul Man," 1967.
Source: *BioIn 16; ConMuA 80A; ConMus 8; EncPR&S 89; EncRk 88; HarEnR 86; InB&W 80; NewYTBS 88; PenEncP; RkOn 78; RolSEnR 83; WhoHol 92; WhoRock 81; WhoRocM 82*

Samaranch, Juan Antonio
[Juan Antonio Samaranch Torello]
Spanish. Olympic Official
Pres., International Olympic Committee, 1979—.
b. Jul 17, 1920 in Barcelona, Spain
Source: *BioIn 14, 15, 16; ConNews 86-2; CurBio 94; IntWW 91; Who 82, 83, 85, 88, 90, 92, 94; WhoWor 84, 87, 89, 91, 93, 95, 96, 97*

Samaras, Lucas
American. Artist
Experimental artist, noted for his "assemblages," three dimensional still lifes: *The Room,* 1964.
b. Sep 14, 1936 in Kastoria, Greece
Source: *AmArt; BioIn 8, 9, 10, 14, 17; BriEAA; ConArt 77, 83, 89, 96; ConPhot 82, 88, 95; CurBio 72; DcAmArt; DcCAA 71, 77, 88, 94; DcCAr 81; ICPEnP A; MacBEP; OxCTwCA; OxDcArt; PhDcTCA 77; PrintW 83, 85; WhoAm 82, 84, 86, 88; WhoAmA 73, 76, 78, 80, 82, 84, 86, 89, 91, 93; WhoArt 80; WorArt 1980*

Samaroff, Olga
American. Pianist
Ranked among best pianists, early 1900s; wed to Leopold Stokowski, 1911-23.
b. Aug 8, 1882 in San Antonio, Texas
d. May 17, 1948 in New York, New York
Source: *Baker 78, 84, 92; BiDAmEd; BioIn 15, 16, 20; BriBkM 80; CurBio 46, 48; DcAmB S4; FacFETw; InWom; LibW; MusSN; NewAmDM; NewGrDA 86; NewGrDM 80; NotAW; PeoHis; WhAm 2; WomFir*

Sammarco, Mario
Italian. Opera Singer
Baritone with European, American operas, from 1900; noted for *Tosca, Rigoletto* roles.
b. Dec 13, 1868 in Palermo, Sicily, Italy
d. Jan 24, 1930 in Milan, Italy
Source: *Baker 78, 84; BioIn 10; CmOp; MetOEnc; NewEOp 71; NewGrDM 80; OxDcOp*

Sammartino, Peter
American. Educator
Founder, pres. Fairleigh Dickinson University, 1942-1967.
b. Aug 15, 1904 in New York, New York
d. Mar 29, 1992 in Rutherford, New Jersey
Source: *BiDAmEd; BioIn 3, 5, 14, 17, 18; ConAu 7NR, 57, 137; CurBio 92N; WhAm 10; WhoAm 74, 76, 78, 80, 82, 84, 86, 88, 90, 92; WhoGov 75; WhoWor 74*

Samms, Emma
[Emma Samuelson]
English. Actor
Succeeded Pamela Sue Martin in role of Fallon Carrington Colby in TV series "Dynasty," "The Colbys."
b. Aug 28, 1960 in London, England
Source: *BioIn 13, 14, 15; ConTFT 4; IntMPA 94, 96; LegTOT; WhoEnt 92; WhoHol 92; WorAlBi*

Samoset
American. Native American Chief
Chief of the Abenaki; first chief to negotiate land transfer between native Americans and English settlers, 1625.
b. 1590?
d. 1653?

Source: *ApCAB; EncNAB; HarEnUS; NotNaAm; WebAB 74; WhNaAH*

Samper Pizano, Ernesto
Colombian. Political Leader
Pres., Colombia, 1994—.
b. Aug 3, 1950 in Bogota, Colombia
Source: *WhoWor 95, 96, 97*

Sample, Bill
American. Police Officer
Founder, pres., Sunshine Foundation, 1977; grants wishes to terminally ill children.
b. Dec 2, 1935 in Philadelphia, Pennsylvania
Source: *BioIn 12, 15; ConNews 86-2*

Sample, Paul Starrett
American. Artist
Paintings of genre subjects in a simplified manner include *Janitor's Holiday*.
b. Sep 14, 1896 in Louisville, Kentucky
d. Feb 26, 1974 in Norwich, Vermont
Source: *ArtsAmW 1; BioIn 1, 5, 6; IlBEAAW; McGDA; WhAm 6; WhAmArt 85; WhoAm 74; WhoAmA 73, 76, 78*

Samples, Junior
[Alvin Samples]
American. Comedian
Bib-overalled, 300 lb. star of TV's "Hee-Haw," 1969-83.
b. Apr 10, 1927? in Cumming, Georgia
d. Nov 13, 1983 in Cumming, Georgia
Source: *BioIn 13; HarEnCM 87; NewYTBS 83*

Sampras, Pete(r)
American. Tennis Player
First American since 1984, youngest man ever to win US Open, 1990; ranked number one for 82 consecutive weeks until April 10, 1995; won at Wimbledon, 1993, 1994, 1995, 1997.
b. Aug 12, 1971 in Washington, District of Columbia
Source: *BioIn 16; BuCMET; CurBio 94; LegTOT; News 94, 94-1; NewYTBS 91; WhoAm 92, 94, 95, 96, 97; WhoSpor; WhoWor 95, 96, 97*

Sampson, Charles
American. Rodeo Performer
First black world rodeo champion, 1982.
b. 1957?
Source: *BioIn 13; ConBlB 13*

Sampson, Deborah
[Robert Shirtliff]
American. Soldier
Spent three years in Continental Army disguised as a man.
b. Dec 17, 1760 in Massachusetts
d. 1827
Source: *AmBi; AmRev; ApCAB; BioAmW; BioIn 18, 20, 21; ContDcW 89; DcNAA; Drake; EncAmaz 91; EncAR; EncCRAm; EncWHA; GoodHs; HanAmWH; HarEnUS; HerW, 84; IntDcWB; InWom, SUP; LibW; NatCAB 8; NotAW; NotBlAW 1; OxCAmL 65, 83, 95; WebAMB; WhAmRev; WomFir*

Sampson, Edith Spurlock
American. Judge
First African-American woman to serve as circuit court judge, 1925 and as United Nations alternate delegate, 1950.
b. Oct 13, 1901 in Pittsburgh, Pennsylvania
d. Oct 8, 1979 in Chicago, Illinois
Source: *Ebony 1; InB&W 80, 85; InWom, SUP; NegAl 89A; NotBlAW 1; WhAm 7; WhoAm 74, 76; WhoAmW 66, 68, 70, 72, 74; WhoMW 74, 76*

Sampson, Ralph Lee
"The Stick"
American. Basketball Player
Seven-foot, four-inch center, played 1983-92, mostly with Houston; NBA rookie of yr., 1984; with Akeem Olajuwon, formed team's famed "Twin Towers" combination.
b. Jul 7, 1960 in Harrisonburg, Virginia
Source: *BiDAmSp BK; BioIn 16; NewYTBS 82, 83, 86; OfNBA 87; WhoBlA 85, 88, 92*

Sampson, Will, Jr.
American. Actor
Acting debut as Chief Bromden in *One Flew Over the Cuckoo's Nest;* 1975.
b. 1943 in Okmulgee, Oklahoma
d. Jun 2, 1987 in Houston, Texas

Sampson, William T
American. Military Leader
Commanded North Atlantic squadron, Spanish-American War.
b. Feb 9, 1840 in Palmyra, New York
d. May 6, 1902 in Washington, District of Columbia
Source: *AmBi; ApCAB, SUP; NatCAB 9; OxCAmH; TwCBDA; WebAMB; WhAm 1*

Samrin, Heng
Cambodian. Political Leader
Became pres. of Cambodia following Vietnam's invasion; held office 1979-93.
b. May 25, 1934 in Prey Veng Province
Source: *BioIn 11, 18; ColdWar 1, 2; EncWB; IntWW 91; WhoWor 91*

Samson
Biblical Figure
Known for tremendous strength used against Philistines; secret betrayed by Delilah.
Source: *Benet 96; BiB N; BioIn 1, 2, 4, 6, 7, 8, 9, 10, 12, 17; DcBiPP; DcCathB; DcNaB; Dis&D; NewCol 75; WhoRocM 82*

Samsonov, Aleksandr Vasilievich
Russian. Military Leader
General; defeated by Germans at Battle of Tannenberg; suicide victim.
b. 1859
d. Aug 29, 1914 in Tannenberg, Prussia
Source: *HarEnMi; NewCol 75; WhoMilH 76*

Samstag, Nicholas
American. Advertising Executive, Author
Pres., Nicholas Samstag, Inc., 1933-39; wrote *The Uses of Ineptitude,* 1962.
b. Dec 25, 1903 in New York, New York
d. Mar 26, 1968
Source: *AuBYP 2, 3; BioIn 8; ConAu 5R, 25R*

Sam the Sham and the Pharaohs
[Butch Gibson; David Martin; Jerry Patterson; Domingo Samudio; Ray Stinnet]
American. Music Group
1960s rock-and-roll band best known for first hit, "Wooly Bully," 1965.
Source: *Alli, SUP; BioIn 1, 15, 21; ChhPo S2; DcVicP 2; Drake; DrAPF 89, 91, 93, 97; Dun&B 86, 88; EncPR&S 74, 89; EncRk 88; InB&W 80; MorBAP; NewYHSD; NewYTBS 95; PenDiMP; PenEncP; RkOn 78, 84; RolSEnR 83; St&PR 96, 97; WhoLibS 55; WhoRock 81; WhoRocM 82*

Samuel
Hebrew. Biblical Figure
Judge, great prophet who was influential in establishing Israeli monarchy.
b. fl. 11th cent. BC
Source: *DcCathB; EncEarC; EncPaPR 91; NewC; NewCol 75; WebBD 83; Who 92*

Samuel, Maurice
American. Journalist, Author
Writings on Jewish subjects include: *The Gentlemen and the Jew,* 1950.
b. Feb 8, 1895 in Macin, Romania
d. May 4, 1972 in New York, New York
Source: *AmAu&B; AmNov; BenetAL 91; BioIn 2, 4, 6, 9, 11; ConAu 33R, 102; JeAmFiW; REnAL; ScF&FL 1; TwCA SUP; WhAm 5; WhoWorJ 72*

Samuels, Ernest
American. Educator, Author
Won Pulitzer for three-vol. biography on Henry Adams, 1965.
b. May 19, 1903 in Chicago, Illinois
d. Feb 12, 1996 in Evanston, Illinois
Source: *AmAu&B; DcLB 111; DrAS 74E, 78E, 82E; IntAu&W 82; OxCAmL 65, 83; WhAm 11; WhoAm 74, 76, 78, 80, 82, 84, 86, 88, 90, 92, 94, 95, 96; WhoAmJ 80; WhoWorJ 72, 78; WorAu 1950; WrDr 76, 80, 82, 84, 86, 92, 94, 96*

Samuelson, Joan
[Joan Benoit]
American. Track Athlete
Won Boston Marathon, 1983, posting fastest time ever for woman runner: 2:22.42.

b. Mar 16, 1957 in Cape Elizabeth, Maine
Source: *ConNews 86-3; CurBio 96; LegTOT; NewYTBS 83, 84; WhoSpor; WomFir*

Samuelson, Paul Anthony
American. Economist
Won Nobel Prize, 1970; best known for writing textbook: *Economics: An Introductory Analysis,* 1948.
b. May 15, 1915 in Gary, Indiana
Source: *AmAu&B; AmMWSc 73S, 78S; BioIn 5, 7, 9, 11, 12, 14, 15, 17, 19; BlueB 76; ConAu 5R; CurBio 65; EncAB-H 1974, 1996; GrEconS; IndAu 1917; IntAu&W 91, 93; IntWW 74, 75, 76, 77, 78, 79, 80, 81, 82, 83, 89, 91, 93; JeAmHC; McGEWB; NewYTBE 70, 71; NewYTBS 86; NobelP; PolProf K, NF; RAdv 14; ThTwC 87; WebAB 74, 79; Who 92; WhoAm 74, 76, 78, 80, 82, 84, 86, 88, 90, 92, 94, 95, 96, 97; WhoE 74, 77, 79, 81, 83, 85, 86, 89, 91, 93, 95, 97; WhoEc 81, 86; WhoFI 79, 81, 83, 85, 89, 92, 94, 96; WhoNob, 90, 95; WhoScEn 96; WhoWor 74, 78, 80, 82, 84, 87, 89, 91, 93, 95, 96, 97; WorAl; WorAlBi; WrDr 76, 80, 82, 84, 86, 88, 90, 92, 94, 96*

Samuelsson, Bengt Ingemar
Swedish. Scientist
Shared 1982 Nobel Prize in medicine for researching prostaglandins and their role in lowering blood pressure.
b. May 21, 1934 in Halmstad, Sweden
Source: *AmMWSc 95; BiESc; BioIn 13, 14, 15; IntMed 80; LarDcSc; NewYTBS 82; NobelP; Who 85, 88, 90, 92, 94; WhoAm 88, 90, 92, 94, 95; WhoMedH; WhoNob, 90, 95; WhoScEn 94, 96; WhoWor 78, 80, 82, 84, 87, 89, 91, 93, 95, 96, 97; WorAlBi*

Sananikone, Phoui
Laotian. Political Leader
Prime minister of Laos, 1950-51, 1959-60; formed govt. in exile, 1978.
b. Sep 6, 1903, Laos
d. Dec 4, 1983 in Paris, France
Source: *BiDD; BioIn 8, 9, 10; CurBio 59, 84, 84N; FarE&A 78, 79, 80, 81; IntWW 74, 75, 76, 77, 78, 79, 80, 81, 82, 83; WhoWor 74*

Sanapia
American. Physician
Last known Comanche eagle doctor.
b. 1895 in Fort Sill, Oklahoma
d. 1984 in Oklahoma
Source: *BioIn 21; EncNAR; NotNaAm; RelLAm 91*

Sanborn, David
American. Musician
Saxophonist; won Grammy for best rhythm and blues instrumental performance for *Voyeur,* 1981 and best pop instrumental for *Close Up,* 1989.
b. Jul 30, 1945 in Tampa, Florida
Source: *AllMusG; BioIn 13, 16; ConMus 1; CurBio 92; EncJzS; LegTOT; NewGrDJ 88; PenEncP; SoulM; WhoAm 94, 95, 96, 97*

Sanborn, Pitts
American. Critic, Author
Music editor, NYC papers, from 1905; wrote *Metropolitan Book of the Opera,* 1937.
b. Oct 19, 1878 in Port Huron, Michigan
d. Mar 7, 1941 in New York, New York
Source: *Baker 84; BiDAmM; CurBio 41; TwCA*

Sanchez, Salvador
"Chava"
Mexican. Boxer
WBC featherweight champ, 1980-82.
b. Feb 5, 1959 in Santiago de Tianquistenco, Mexico
d. Aug 12, 1982 in Queretaro, Mexico
Source: *AnObit 1982; BoxReg; NewYTBS 82*

Sanchez-Vicario, Arantxa
Spanish. Tennis Player
Won French Open, 1989.
b. Dec 18, 1971 in Barcelona, Spain
Source: *IntWW 93*

Sand, George
[Amandine Lucile Dupin Dudevant]
French. Author
Novels include *Lelia,* 1833; noted for her unconventionality, liaison with Chopin.
b. Sep 1, 1804 in Paris, France
d. Jun 8, 1876 in Nohant, France
Source: *AtlBL; BbD; Benet 87, 96; BiD&SB; BioIn 1, 2, 3, 4, 5, 6, 7, 8, 9, 10, 11, 12, 14, 15, 16, 17, 18, 19, 20; BlmGEL; BlmGWL; CasWL; CelCen; ContDcW 89; CyWA 58; DcAmSR; DcArts; DcBiA; DcEnL; DcEuL; DcLB 119; DcPup; DcWomA; EuAu; EuWr 6; EvEuW; FemiCLE; FemiWr; FrenWW; GoodHs; GrFLW; GrWomW; GuFrLit 1; HerW 84; IntDcWB; InWom SUP; LegTOT; LinLib L, S; McGEWB; NewCBEL; NinCLC 2, 42, 57; NotNAT B; Novels; OxCEng 67, 85, 95; OxCFr; PenC EUR; PenNWW B; RAdv 14; RComWL; REn; RfGWoL 95; ScF&FL 1; WhDW; WorAl; WorAlBi; WorLitC*

Sand, Paul
[Pablo Sanchez]
American. Actor
TV series include "St. Elsewhere," 1982-84; films: *The Main Event,* 1979.
b. Mar 5, 1941 in Los Angeles, California
Source: *ConTFT 4; HalFC 88; NewYTBE 71; NotNAT; VarWW 85; WhoHol 92, A; WhoThe 81*

Sanda, Dominique
[Dominique Varaigne]
French. Actor
Top int'l star, 1970s; films include *The Garden of Finzi-Continis,* 1971.
b. 1948 in Paris, France
Source: *BioIn 10, 17; FilmAG WE; FilmEn; FilmgC; HalFC 80, 84, 88; IntDcF 1-3, 2-3; ItaFilm; LegTOT; MovMk; WhoHol 92, A*

Sandberg, Ryne (Dee)
American. Baseball Player
Infielder, Philadelphia, 1981; Chicago Cubs, 1982-94; 1996—; known for fielding; NL MVP, 1984.
b. Sep 18, 1959 in Spokane, Washington
Source: *Ballpl 90; BaseReg 86, 87; BioIn 14, 15, 16; CurBio 94; LegTOT; WhoAm 86, 88, 90, 92, 94; WhoMW 88, 90, 92, 93; WorAlBi*

Sandburg, Carl (August)
American. Poet, Author
Won three Pulitzers in Poetry, 1918, 1940, 1951.
b. Jan 6, 1878 in Galesburg, Illinois
d. Jul 22, 1967 in Flat Rock, North Carolina
Source: *AmAu&B; AmCulL; AmDec 1910, 1930; AmWr; AnCL; ApCAB X; ASCAP 66, 80; AtlBL; AuBYP 2, 3; Benet 87, 96; BenetAL 91; BiDAmJo; BiDAmM; BiDAmNC; BioIn 1, 2, 3, 4, 5, 6, 7, 8, 9, 10, 11, 12, 13, 14, 15, 16, 17, 18, 19, 20; CamGEL; CamGLE; CamHAL; CasWL; Chambr 3; ChhPo, S1, S2, S3; ChlBkCr; CnDAL; CnE&AP; CnMWL; ConAmA; ConAmL; ConAu 5R, 25R, 35NR; ConLC 1, 4, 10, 15, 35; CurBio 40, 63; CyWA 58; DcAmB S8; DcArts; DcLB 17, 54; DcLEL; EncAAH; EncAB-H 1974, 1996; EncAJ; EncAL; EncFCWM 69; EncWL, 2, 3; EvLB; FacFETw; GrWrEL P; LegTOT; LinLib L, S; LngCTC; MagSAmL; MajAI; MajTwCW; MakMC; McGEWB; ModAL, S1, S2; MorMA; NewGrDA 86; ObitT 1961; OxCAmH; OxCAmL 65, 83, 95; OxCEng 67, 85, 95; OxCTwCP; PenC AM; PeoHis; PoeCrit 2; RAdv 1, 14, 13-1, 13-3; RealN; REn; REnAL; RfGAmL 87, 94; RGFAP; RGTwCWr; SixAP; SmATA 8; Str&VC; TwCA, SUP; TwCWr; WebAB 74, 79; WebE&AL; WhAm 4; WhDW; WhE&EA; WhoTwCL; WisWr; WorAl; WorAlBi; WorLitC; WrChl*

Sandburg, Helga
American. Children's Author
Young adults novels include *Gingerbread,* 1964; daughter of Carl.
b. Nov 24, 1918 in Elmhurst, Illinois
Source: *AuBYP 2, 3; BioIn 8, 9, 11, 16; BlueB 76; ConAu 1R, 5NR; ConPo 70; ForWC 70; IntAu&W 82, 86, 91; IntWWP 77, 82; MichAu 80; SmATA 3, 10AS; ThrBJA; WhoAm 74, 76, 78, 80, 82, 84, 86, 88, 90, 92, 94, 95, 96, 97; WhoAmW 77; WhoUSWr 88; WhoWrEP 89, 92, 95; WrDr 80, 82, 84, 86, 88, 90, 92, 94, 96*

Sande, Earl
American. Jockey
Winner of KY Derby, 1923, 1925, 1930; member of racing Hall of Fame.
b. 1898 in Groton, South Dakota
d. Aug 18, 1968 in Jacksonville, Florida

Source: *BioIn 3, 5, 6, 8, 10, 12; DcAmB S8; DcBiPP; LegTOT; WhScrn 83*

Sander, Jil
[Heidemarie Jiline Sander]
German. Fashion Designer
Established Jil Sander collection, 1973.
b. Nov 27, 1943 in Wesselburen, Germany
Source: *ConDes 97; ConFash; News 95, 95-2*

Sanderlin, George William
American. Children's Author
Historical books include *Benjamin Franklin: As Others Saw Him,* 1971.
b. Feb 5, 1915 in Baltimore, Maryland
Source: *BioIn 9; ConAu 13R; DrAS 74E, 78E, 82E; IntAu&W 89; SmATA 4; WhoUSWr 88; WhoWrEP 89; WrDr 86, 92*

Sanders, Barry
American. Football Player
Runningback, Detroit Lions 1989—; won Heisman Trophy as junior at Oklahoma State, 1988.
b. Jul 16, 1968 in Wichita, Kansas
Source: *AfrAmSG; ConBlB 1; CurBio 93; News 92, 92-1; WhoAfA 96; WhoAm 92, 94, 95, 96, 97; WhoBlA 92, 94; WhoMW 93, 96*

Sanders, Bernard
American. Politician
In 1990, became the first independent, Socialist candidate elected to the US House of Representatives since 1920.
b. Sep 8, 1941 in New York, New York
Source: *AlmAP 92, 96; BioIn 16; CngDr 91, 93, 95; CurBio 91; EncAL; WhoAm 92, 94, 95, 96, 97; WhoAmP 85, 87, 89, 91, 93, 95; WhoE 83, 85, 86, 91, 93, 95, 97; WhoEmL 87*

Sanders, Colonel
[Harland David Sanders]
American. Restaurateur
Established Kentucky Fried Chicken franchise, using a secret recipe, at age 66.
b. Sep 9, 1890 in Henryville, Indiana
d. Dec 16, 1980 in Louisville, Kentucky
Source: *AnObit 1980; BioIn 17; BusPN; ConAu 102; CurBio 73, 81; DcAmB S10; NewYTBS 80; WhoAm 74; WhoSSW 73*

Sanders, Deion (Luwynn)
"Neion Deion"; "Prime Time"
American. Football Player, Baseball Player
Cornerback and punt returner, Atlanta, 1989-94, San Francisco, 1994-95, Dallas, 1995—; outfielder, NY Yankees, 1988-90; Atlanta Braves, 1991-94; Cincinnati Reds, 1994—.
b. Aug 9, 1967 in Fort Myers, Florida
Source: *AfrAmSG; BioIn 16; ConBlB 4; CurBio 95; News 92; WhoAfA 96; WhoAm 92, 94, 95, 96, 97; WhoBlA 92, 94; WhoSSW 95, 97*

Sanders, Dori(nda)
American. Writer
Author of *Clover,* 1990; *Her Own Place,* 1993.
b. c. 1935 in York, South Carolina
Source: *ConBlB 8; WhoAfA 96; WhoBlA 92, 94*

Sanders, Ed
[Black Hobart; James Edward Sanders]
American. Satirist
Anarchist, social critic; wrote best-selling non-fiction book *The Family: The Story of Charles Manson's Dune Buggy Attack Battalion,* 1971; organizer, lead singer, cult folk-rock group The Fugs, 1965-70.
b. Aug 17, 1939 in Kansas City, Missouri
Source: *AmAu&B; BioIn 10, 13, 17; ConAu 13NR, 13R; ConLC 53; ConPo 70, 75, 80, 85, 91; DcLB 16; DrAF 76; DrAP 75; DrAPF 80, 89; IntAu&W 91, 93; IntWWP 77; MugS; PenC AM; WrDr 76, 80, 82, 84, 86, 88, 90, 92*

Sanders, George
American. Actor
Won Oscar, 1950, for *All About Eve;* married to Zsa Zsa and Magda Gabor.
b. Jul 3, 1906 in Saint Petersburg, Russia
d. Apr 25, 1972 in Castelldefels, Spain
Source: *BiDFilm, 81, 94; BioIn 2, 4, 5, 6, 8, 9, 10, 12, 18; CurBio 43, 72, 72N; DcAmB S9; DcArts; Film 2; FilmEn; FilmgC; ForYSC; HalFC 80, 84, 88; IlWWBF, A; IntDcF 1-3, 2-3; ItaFilm; LegTOT; MotPP; MovMk; NewYTBE 72; NotNAT A; ObitT 1971; OxCFilm; WhAm 5; WhoHol B; WhoHrs 80; WhScrn 77, 83; WorAl; WorAlBi; WorEFlm*

Sanders, Joseph
[Joseph Richard Sanders, Jr.]
American. Designer
Designed exhibits *Moving Back Barriers: The Legacy of Carter G. Woodson,* Library of Congress, 1994; *Black Male: Representations of Masculinity in Contemprary Art,* 1994-95, Whitney Museum.
b. Oct 11, 1954 in Atchison, Kansas
Source: *ConBlB 11*

Sanders, Lawrence
American. Author
Best-selling novels include *The Anderson Tapes,* 1970, filmed 1971; *T he First Deadly Sin,* 1973; *The Devil in the White House,* 1988.
b. 1920 in New York, New York
Source: *AuSpks; BestSel 89-4; BioIn 12, 14, 16, 17; ConAu 33NR, 81; ConLC 41; ConPopW; CrtSuMy; CurBio 89; EncSF, 93; IntAu&W 76, 77, 91, 93; LegTOT; MajTwCW; Novels; RAdv 14; ScF&FL 92; ScFSB; TwCCr&M 80, 85, 91; WhoAm 80, 82, 84, 86, 88, 90, 92, 94, 95, 96, 97; WhoUSWr 88; WhoWrEP 89, 92, 95; WorAl; WorAlBi; WrDr 82, 84, 86, 88, 90, 92, 94, 96*

Sanders, Marlene
American. Broadcast Journalist
Correspondent, producer of CBS News documentaries since 1978.
b. Jan 10, 1931 in Cleveland, Ohio
Source: *BioIn 10, 11, 12, 14, 16; ConAu 65; CurBio 81; EncTwCJ; ForWC 70; GoodHs; InWom SUP; LesBEnT, 92; Who 92; WhoAm 80, 82, 84, 86, 88, 90, 92, 94, 95, 96, 97; WhoAmW 79, 81, 83, 85, 87, 89, 91, 93, 95, 97; WhoE 95; WhoEnt 92; WhoTelC; WomFir; WomWMM*

Sanders, Marty
[Jay and the Americans]
American. Musician, Songwriter
Guitarist, songwriter with clean-cut vocal quintet of 1960s.
b. Feb 28, 1941
Source: *WhoRocM 82*

Sanders, Richard Kinard
American. Actor
Played Les Nessman on TV series "WKRP in Cincinnati," 1978-82.
b. Aug 23, 1940 in Harrisburg, Pennsylvania
Source: *WhoAm 80, 82, 84, 86, 88, 90, 92, 94, 95, 96, 97; WhoEnt 92*

Sanders, Summer
American. Swimmer
Won two gold medals in swimming events, 1992.
b. 1972
Source: *BioIn 21; WhoAm 97; WhoAmW 93, 95, 97; WhoWor 95, 96*

Sanderson, Derek Michael
"Turk"
Canadian. Hockey Player
Colorful center, 1965-78, mostly with Boston; won Calder Trophy, 1966; wrote autobiography, *I've Got to Be Me,* 1970.
b. Jun 16, 1946 in Niagara Falls, Ontario, Canada
Source: *BioIn 9, 10, 11, 13; CurBio 75; HocEn; NewYTBE 70, 72, 73; NewYTBS 74, 83; WhoAm 76, 78; WhoHcky 73*

Sanderson, Ivan Terence
[Terence Roberts]
American. Zoologist, Author
Importer of rare animals, 1950s; popular nature books include *Animal Treasure,* 1937.
b. Jan 30, 1911 in Edinburgh, Scotland
d. Feb 19, 1973
Source: *AmAu&B; AmMWSc 73P; AuBYP 2, 3; EncSF, 93; EncSUPP; IlsCB 1744, 1946; LinLib L; NatCAB 57; NewYTBE 73; REnAL; ScF&FL 1, 2; SmATA 6; TwCA, SUP; UFOEn*

Sanderson, Julia
[The Singing Sweethearts; Julia Sackett]
American. Singer, Actor
Often starred with husband, Frank Crumit, on stage, radio, 1900-40s;

started Battle of Sexes Game Show, 1939-43.
b. Aug 22, 1887 in Springfield, Massachusetts
d. Jan 27, 1975 in Springfield, Massachusetts
Source: *BiE&WWA; BioIn 3, 10; CmpEPM; EncMT; Film 1; InWom; NotNAT B; OxCAmT 84; OxCPMus; RadStar; SaTiSS; WhAm 6; WhoStg 1908; WhScrn 77; WhThe*

Sanderson, Sybil
American. Opera Singer
Dramatic soprano; more successful in Paris than NY or London, 1880s-90s.
b. Dec 7, 1865 in Sacramento, California
d. May 15, 1903 in Paris, France
Source: *AmWom; Baker 84; CmOp; IntDcOp; InWom; NewEOp 71*

Sandler, Adam
American. Actor, Comedian
Appeared on "Saturday Night Live."
b. Sep 9, 1966 in New York, New York
Source: *LegTOT*

Sandler and Young
[Tony Sandler; Ralph Young]
American. Music Group
Popular singing duo, 1960s-70s, combining suave European Tony Sandler and comedic American Ralph Young.
Source: *CmpEPM*

Sando, Joe
American. Historian
Wrote works that chronicle the life, culture, and history of the Pueblo people; books include *The Pueblo Indians,* 1976.
b. Aug 1, 1923 in Jemez Pueblo, New Mexico
Source: *NotNaAm*

Sandow, Eugene
[Karl Frederick Mueller]
"The Mighty Monarch of Muscle"
German. Entertainer
Physical cultist; performed in London's music halls, 1800s.
b. Apr 10, 1867 in Konigsberg, Germany
d. Oct 14, 1925 in London, England
Source: *BiDD; BioIn 7, 12; EncVaud; Ent; Film 1; OxCAmT 84; WhScrn 77, 83*

Sandoz, Mari
American. Author
Wrote *Old Jules,* 1935; books on Indians include *These Were the Sioux,* 1961.
b. May 11, 1900 in Sheridan County, Nebraska
d. Mar 10, 1966 in New York, New York
Source: *AmAu&B; AuBYP 2; CnDAL; ConAu 1R; OxCAmL 65; REn; REnAL; SmATA 5; ThrBJA; TwCA, SUP; WhAm 4; WhNAA*

Sandrich, Jay H
American. Director
Has directed TV sitcoms, including "Mary Tyler Moore Show," 1970-77; "Soap," 1977-79.
b. Feb 24, 1932 in Los Angeles, California
Source: *BioIn 15; ConTFT 4; IntMPA 88; LesBEnT; NewYTET; WhoAm 86, 88; WhoTelC*

Sands, Bobby
[Robert Gerard Sands]
Irish. Hunger Striker, Revolutionary
IRA member, elected to Parliament while in prison; first of 10 hunger strikers to die demanding political prisoner rather than criminal status.
b. Mar 9, 1954 in Belfast, Northern Ireland
d. May 5, 1981 in Belfast, Northern Ireland
Source: *AnObit 1981; BioIn 12; DcIrB 88; DcIrL 96; NewYTBS 81*

Sands, Diana Patricia
American. Actor
Best known for stage role in *A Raisin in the Sun,* 1960; won Obie, 1964.
b. Aug 22, 1934 in New York, New York
d. Sep 21, 1973 in New York, New York
Source: *BiE&WWA; DcAmB S9; HalFC 84; InWom SUP; MotPP; NewYTBE 73; WhAm 6; WhoAmW 72, 74; WhoBlA 75; WhoHol B; WhScrn 83; WomWMM*

Sands, Dorothy
American. Actor, Director
One of top performers in Grand Street Follies, 1920s.
b. Mar 5, 1893 in Cambridge, Massachusetts
d. Sep 11, 1980 in Croton-on-Hudson, New York
Source: *BiE&WWA; BioIn 12; ConAu 102; NotNAT; PlP&P; WhoAmW 58, 61; WhoThe 72, 77, 81; WhScrn 83*

Sands, Tommy
[Thomas Adrian Sands]
American. Singer
Had hit song "Teenage Crush," 1957; film, TV star, 1950s-60s; first husband of Nancy Sinatra.
b. Aug 27, 1937 in Chicago, Illinois
Source: *ASCAP 66; BiDAmM; BioIn 4, 12; FilmEn; FilmgC; ForYSC; HalFC 80, 84, 88; IntMPA 75, 76, 77, 78, 79, 80, 81, 82, 84, 86, 88, 92, 94, 96; LegTOT; MotPP; PenEncP; RkOn 74; WhoHol A*

Sandwich, John Montagu
[4th Earl of Sandwich]
English. Politician
First Lord of Admiralty, 1771-82; selfishness led to ruin of British navy; much-hated man in 18th c. England; supposed inventor of sandwich.
b. Nov 3, 1718 in Wiltshire, England
d. Apr 30, 1792 in London, England
Source: *AmRev; BioIn 1, 2, 6, 17, 19; EncAR; WhAmRev*

Sandy, Gary
American. Actor
Played Andy Travis on TV series "WKRP in Cincinnati," 1978-82.
b. Dec 25, 1946? in Dayton, Ohio
Source: *BioIn 11, 12; ConTFT 6; WhoAm 82*

Sandys, Edwin, Sir
English. Statesman
One of founders of VA; joint mgr. of colony, 1617.
b. Dec 9, 1561, England
d. Oct 1629
Source: *Alli; ApCAB; BioIn 1, 3, 6, 12; DcBiPP; DcEnL; DcNaB; HarEnUS; McGEWB; NewCBEL; NewCol 75; OxCAmH; WebBD 83*

Saneyev, Viktor
Russian. Track Athlete
Triple jumper; won gold medals, 1968, 1972 Olympics.
b. Oct 3, 1945, Union of Soviet Socialist Republics
Source: *BioIn 17; IntWW 81, 82, 83, 89, 91; LesBEnT; WhoTr&F 73*

Sanford, Isabel Gwendolyn
American. Actor
Best known for role of Louise Jefferson on TV series "The Jeffersons," 1974-85.
b. Aug 29, 1933? in New York, New York
Source: *BioIn 10, 13; ConTFT 2; IntMPA 88; WhoAm 86, 90; WhoAmW 91; WhoBlA 85, 88; WhoEnt 92; WhoTelC*

Sanford, Terry
American. Educator, Politician
Governor of NC, 1961-65; pres. of Duke U., 1969-85; senator from NC, 1987-1993.
b. Aug 20, 1917 in Laurinburg, North Carolina
Source: *AlmAP 88, 92; BiDrGov 1789; BiDrUSC 89; BioIn 6, 7, 8, 9, 10, 12, 14, 15; BlueB 76; CngDr 87, 89, 91; ConAu 17R; CurBio 61; IntWW 74, 75, 76, 77, 78, 79, 80, 81, 82, 83, 89, 91, 93; LEduc 74; NewYTBS 86; PolPar; PolProf J, K, NF; WhoAm 74, 76, 78, 80, 82, 84, 86, 88, 90, 92, 94, 95, 96, 97; WhoAmL 90, 92, 94, 96; WhoAmP 73, 75, 77, 79, 81, 83, 85, 87, 89, 91, 93, 95; WhoSSW 84, 86, 88, 91, 95, 97; WhoUSWr 88; WhoWor 78, 84, 87, 89, 91; WhoWrEP 89, 92, 95*

Sang, Samantha
Australian. Singer
Soft rock singer; had hit single "Emotion," 1977, written by Barry and Robin Gibb.
b. Aug 5, 1953 in Melbourne, Australia
Source: *LegTOT; RkOn 78, 84; WhoRock 81*

Sanger, Frederick
English. Biologist
Won two Nobel Prizes in chemistry: in 1958 for studies on insulin, in 1980 for research on nucleic acids.
b. Aug 13, 1918 in Rendcomb, England
Source: *AmMWSc 89, 92, 95; AsBiEn; BiESc; BioIn 5, 6, 8, 12, 14, 15, 16, 19, 20, 21; BlueB 76; CamDcSc; CurBio 81; FacFETw; IntWW 74, 75, 76, 77, 78, 79, 80, 81, 82, 83, 89, 91, 93; LarDcSc; McGEWB; McGMS 80; NewYTBS 80; NobelP; NotTwCS; Who 74, 82, 83, 85, 88, 90, 92, 94; WhoAm 88, 90, 92, 94, 95; WhoNob, 90, 95; WhoScEn 94, 96; WhoWor 74, 76, 78, 82, 84, 87, 89, 91, 93, 95, 96, 97; WorAlBi; WorScD*

Sanger, Margaret
[Margaret Higgins]
American. Nurse, Social Reformer
Founded National Birth Control League, 1914; wrote *Women, Morality, and Birth Control,* 1931.
b. Sep 14, 1883 in Corning, New York
d. Sep 6, 1966 in Tucson, Arizona
Source: *AmAu&B; BenetAL 91; BioIn 2, 3, 4, 7, 8, 9, 10, 11; ConAu 89; ContDcW 89; CurBio 44, 66; DcAmSR; EncAB-H 1974; FacFETw; HerW, 84; IntDcWB; LinLib L, S; LngCTC; LuthC 75; MemAm; ObitT 1961; OxCAmL 65, 83; OxCMed 86; TwoTYeD; WebAB 74; WhAm 4; WomFir; WorAlBi*

Sangster, Margaret Elizabeth
[Margaret Elizabeth Murson]
American. Social Reformer
Founded American Birth Control League, 1917; opened first clinic, 1921.
b. Feb 22, 1838 in New Rochelle, New York
d. Jun 4, 1912 in Glen Ridge, New Jersey
Source: *Alli SUP; AmAu; AmAu&B; AmBi; AmWom; ApCAB; BbD; BiD&SB; ChhPo S3; DcAmB; NotAW; REnAL; TwCBDA; WhAm 1; WomNov*

Sanguillen, Manny
[Manuel Dejesus Sanguillen]
Panamanian. Baseball Player
Catcher, 1967, 1969-80, mostly with Pittsburgh; had .296 lifetime batting average.
b. Mar 21, 1944 in Colon, Panama
Source: *Ballpl 90; BioIn 9, 10; InB&W 80; LegTOT; WhoBlA 77, 80, 85; WhoProB 73*

Sankara
Indian. Philosopher, Theologian
Founder of Advaita Vedanta School of thought, upon which modern Indian philosophy is based.
b. 700? in Kaladi, India
d. 750? in Kedarnath, India
Source: *CasWL; McGEWB*

San Martin, Jose de
Argentine. Revolutionary, Statesman
Fought in revolutions to liberate Argentina, Chile, Peru from Spain, 1812-22.
b. Feb 25, 1778 in Yapeyu, Argentina
d. Aug 17, 1850 in Boulogne-sur-Mer, France
Source: *ApCAB; Benet 87, 96; BenetAL 91; BiDLAmC; BioIn 1, 2, 3, 4, 5, 7, 8, 9, 10, 11, 12, 15, 16, 17, 19, 20; Drake; EncLatA; EncRev; GenMudB; HarEnMi; HisDcSE; HisWorL; LegTOT; McGEWB; NewCol 75; REn; WhDW; WhoMilH 76; WorAl; WorAlBi*

Sann, Paul
American. Journalist
Executive editor, *NY Post,* 1949-77; nonfiction books include *The Lawless Decade,* 1957.
b. Mar 7, 1914 in New York, New York
Source: *AmAu&B; Au&Wr 71; BioIn 10; ConAu 5NR, 13R, 120; IntAu&W 86; ScF&FL 92; WhAm 9; WhoAm 74, 76, 78, 80, 82, 84, 86; WhoE 74; WrDr 80, 82, 84, 86*

Sansom, Odette Marie Celine
[Odette Marie Celine Churchill; Odette Marie Celine Hallowes]
British. Spy
British spy in France, 1942-43; captured, sent to concentration camp; freed, 1945.
b. Apr 28, 1912 in Amiens, France
Source: *BioIn 2, 3, 4, 7; EncE 75; IntWW 74, 75, 76, 77, 78, 79, 80, 81, 82, 83, 89, 91, 93; InWom SUP; SpyCS; Who 74, 82, 83, 85, 88, 90, 92, 94; WhoWor 74, 76, 78; WhWW-II*

Sansom, William
English. Author
Best known for sketches of London life: *The Stories of William Sansom,* 1963.
b. Jan 18, 1912 in London, England
d. Apr 20, 1976 in London, England
Source: *Au&Wr 71; Benet 87, 96; BioIn 2, 4, 7, 10, 17, 20; BlmGEL; BlueB 76; CamGLE; CnMWL; ConAu 5R, 42NR, 65; ConLC 2, 6; ConNov 72, 76; CyWA 89; DcLB 139; DcLEL 1940; EncWL 2, 3; GrWrEL N; IntAu&W 76, 77; LngCTC; MajTwCW; ModBrL, S1; NewC; NewCBEL; Novels; OxCEng 85, 95; PenC ENG; RAdv 1; REn; RfGEnL 91; RfGShF; RGTwCWr; ScF&FL 1, 2; ShSCr 21; TwCA SUP; TwCWr; WhAm 7; Who 74; WhoHr&F; WhoWor 74; WrDr 76*

Sansovino, Andrea
[Andrea Andrea]
Italian. Artist
Renaissance sculptures include *Baptism of Christ.*
b. 1460 in Monte Sansavino, Italy
d. 1529
Source: *BioIn 9, 15, 18; LuthC 75; McGDA; NewCol 75; OxCArt; WhDW*

Sansovino, Jacopo
[Jacopo Tatti]
Italian. Artist
Renaissance sculptures include *St. John the Baptist.*
b. 1486 in Florence, Italy
d. Nov 27, 1570 in Venice, Italy
Source: *BioIn 1, 2, 5, 10, 12, 14, 15, 17, 18; DcArts; DcCathB; IntDcAA 90; IntDcAr; MacEA; McGEWB; NewCol 75; OxCArt; OxDcArt; WhoArch*

Santa Anna, Antonio Lopez de
"Perpetual Dictator"
Mexican. Political Leader
Pres. of Mexico intermittently, 1833-55; captured the Alamo in TX revolution, 1836.
b. 1794 in Jalapa, Mexico
d. Jun 20, 1876 in Mexico City, Mexico
Source: *ApCAB; BiDLAmC; BioIn 15, 16, 17, 18; DcHiB; DicTyr; EncLatA; HarEnMi; HisWorL; OxCAmH; REn; REnAL; WhAm HS; WhoMilH 76; WorAl; WorAlBi*

Santana
[Jose Areas; David Brown; Michael Carabello; Ndugu Chancler; Tom Coster; Armando Pereza; Gregg Rolie; Carlos Santana; Michael Shrieve; Greg Waler]
American. Music Group
Music is a mix of latin, jazz, rock; hits include "Evil Ways," 1970; "Hold On," 1982.
Source: *Alli; AmMWSc 89; AntBDN D; ApCAB; BiNAW Sup, SupB; BioIn 14; ConAu 129, X; ConMuA 80A; DcBrECP; DcBrWA; DcNaB; DrRegL 75; Dun&B 90; EncASM; EncPR&S 89; EncRk 88; EncRkSt; HarEnR 86; IlEncRk; InB&W 80; MacEA; NewAgMG; NewYHSD; OxCPMus; PenEncP; RkOn 74, 78; RolSEnR 83; SmATA X; Who 94N; WhoAmW 66, 68; WhoRock 81; WhoRocM 82; WhoScEu 91-1*

Santana, Carlos
[Devadip Carlos Santana]
Mexican. Musician
Guitarist, founder of rock band Santana, 1966; Grammy award, 1989.
b. Jul 20, 1947 in Autlan, Mexico
Source: *Baker 84, 92; BioIn 11, 12, 13, 16, 17, 20; BkPepl; ConMus 1; DcHiB; EncPR&S 89; LegTOT; NewAmDM; NewGrDA 86; NewGrDJ 88; OnThGG; RkWW 82; WhoAm 80, 82, 84, 86, 88, 90, 92, 94, 95, 96, 97; WhoEnt 92; WhoHisp 91, 92, 94; WhoRocM 82*

Santander, Francisco de Paula
Colombian. Revolutionary, Politician
Aided Bolivar in revolt against Spain; pres. of New Granada, 1832-36.
b. 1792
d. 1840
Source: *ApCAB; BioIn 16; DcHiB; Drake*

Santayana, George
American. Philosopher, Author, Educator
Wrote philosophic *Realms of Being,* 1927-40; novel *Last Puritan,* 1935; memoirs *Persons and Places,* 1944-53.
b. Dec 16, 1863 in Madrid, Spain
d. Sep 26, 1952 in Rome, Italy
Source: *AmAu&B; AmDec 1910; AmWr; AtlBL; Benet 87, 96; BenetAL 91; BiD&SB; BioIn 1, 2, 3, 4, 5, 6, 7, 8, 9, 11, 12, 13, 14, 15, 16, 18, 20; CamGEL; CamGLE; CamHAL; CasWL; Chambr 3; ChhPo, S1, S2; CnDAL; ConAmA; ConAmL; ConAu 115; CurBio 44, 52; CyWA 58; DcAmAu; DcAmB S5; DcAmC; DcHiB; DcLB 54, 71, DS13; DcLEL; EncAB-H 1974, 1996; EncEth; EncUnb; EncWL, 2, 3; EvLB; FacFETw; GayLesB; GayN; GrWrEL N; LegTOT; LiExTwC; LinLib L, S; LngCTC; MakMC; McGEWB; ModAL, S1; MorMA; Novels; ObitT 1951; OxCAmH; OxCAmL 65, 83, 95; OxCArt; OxCEng 67, 85, 95; OxCPhil; OxCTwCP; OxDcArt; PenC AM; RAdv 14, 13-4; REn; REnAL; RfGAmL 87; ThTwC 87; TwCA, SUP; TwCBDA; TwCLC 40; TwCWr; TwoTYeD; WebAB 74, 79; WebE&AL; WhAm 3; WhE&EA; WhLit; WhoLA; WhoTwCL; WorAl; WorAlBi; WrPh P*

Santee, Wes
American. Track Athlete
Known as America's greatest miler, 1950s.
b. Mar 25, 1932 in Ashland, Kansas
Source: *BioIn 3, 4, 10, 21; WhoTr&F 73*

Santiago, Benito
American. Baseball Player
Catcher, San Diego, 1982-92; Florida, 1992-94; Cincinnati, 1995—; had 34-game hitting streak, 1987; NL rookie of year, 1987; highest pay ever for catcher, $3.3 million, 1992.
b. Sep 3, 1965 in Ponce, Puerto Rico
Source: *Ballpl 90; BaseEn 88; BaseReg 87, 88; BioIn 15; LegTOT; WhoHisp 91, 92, 94*

Santillana, Inigo Lopez de Mendoza
Spanish. Poet
First to write sonnets in Spanish.
b. Aug 19, 1398 in Carrion, Spain
d. Mar 25, 1458 in Guadalajara, Spain
Source: *BbD; Benet 96; BiD&SB; CasWL; DcEuL; DcSpL; EuAu; EvEuW; PenC EUR; REn*

Santmyer, Helen Hooven
American. Author
Wrote in obscurity for 60 yrs. before republication of fourth book *".And Ladies of the Club,"* 1984, became best-seller.
b. Nov 25, 1895 in Xenia, Ohio
d. Feb 21, 1986 in Xenia, Ohio
Source: *AmAu&B; AnObit 1986; BenetAL 91; BioIn 14, 15, 17, 21; ConAu 1R, 15NR, 33NR, 118; ConLC 33; CurBio 85, 86, 86N; DcLB Y84B; DrAPF 80; FacFETw; InWom SUP; MajTwCW; NewYTBS 84; OhA&B; TwCRHW 90, 94; WhoAmW 75; WorAu 1985; WrDr 76, 80, 82, 84*

Santo, Ron(ald Edward)
American. Baseball Player
Third baseman, 1960-74, mostly with Cubs; known for fielding; had lifetime .277 average.
b. Feb 25, 1940 in Seattle, Washington
Source: *Ballpl 90; BaseEn 88; BiDAmSp BB; BioIn 7, 8, 9, 10, 15, 18, 19, 21; WhoAm 74; WhoProB 73*

Santorum, Rick
American. Politician
Rep. senator from PA, 1995—.
b. May 10, 1958
Source: *AlmAP 92, 96; BioIn 20, 21; CngDr 93; WhoAm 92, 94, 95, 96, 97; WhoE 93, 95, 97*

Santos, Jose Eduardo dos
Angolan. Political Leader
Pres., Angola, 1979—.
b. Aug 28, 1942 in Luanda, Angola
Source: *BioIn 13, 15, 16, 17, 18, 19, 20, 21; ColdWar 1, 2; CurBio 94; DcAfHiB 86S; DcCPSAf; EncWB; FacFETw; IntWW 91; WhoWor 91*

Santos-Dumont, Alberto
Brazilian. Balloonist
First to combine gasoline motor with propeller on a balloon, 1898; designed, flew box-kite type machine, 1906.
b. 1873 in Minas Gerais, Brazil
d. 1932, Brazil
Source: *BiDMoPL; BioIn 2, 3, 4, 6, 7, 8, 11, 12, 14, 19; EncLatA; InSci; LinLib S; McGEWB; REn; WhDW*

Saperstein, Abe
[Abraham Saperstein]
"Little Caesar"
American. Basketball Executive
Formed Harlem Globetrotters, 1927; clowning gradually became team trademark; Hall of Fame, 1970.
b. Jul 4, 1903 in London, England
d. Mar 15, 1966 in Chicago, Illinois
Source: *BioIn 1, 7, 21; LegTOT; ObitOF 79; WhoBbl 73; WhoSpor*

Sapir, Edward
American. Anthropologist, Author
Studied ethnology and linguistics of some Native Americans.
b. Jan 26, 1884 in Louenburg, Germany
d. Feb 4, 1939 in New Haven, Connecticut
Source: *BenetAL 91; BiDPsy; BioIn 1, 2, 4, 7, 12, 14, 16, 17; DcAmB S2; DcLB 92; DcNAA; IntDcAn; MakMC; McGEWB; NamesHP; NatCAB 33; OxCAmH; OxCCan; RAdv 14, 13-3; REnAL; REnAW; ThTwC 87; WebAB 74, 79; WhAm 1; WhDW*

Sapir, Pinchas
Israeli. Government Official
Minister of commerce, finance, and other cabinet positions, 1955-74.
b. 1909 in Suwalki, Poland
d. Aug 12, 1975 in Beersheba, Israel
Source: *WhoWor 74; WhoWorJ 72*

Sapp, Carolyn
American. Beauty Contest Winner
Miss America, 1992.

Sapphire
[Ramona Lofton]
American. Writer
Wrote book of poetry, *American Dreams,* 1994; novel, *Push,* 1996.
b. c. 1951
Source: *News 96*

Sappho
"The Tenth Muse"
Greek. Poet
Lyric poet often compared to Homer; poems celebrate love of women.
b. 612BC, Greece
Source: *AtlBL; BbD; Benet 87, 96; BiD&SB; BioIn 13, 14; CasWL; ClMLC 3; ContDcW 89; CyWA 58; EncAmaz 91; EncCoWW; FemiCLE; GayLesB; GrFLW; GrWomW; IntDcWB; InWom SUP; NewC; NewGrDM 80; OxCChiL; OxCEng 85; PenC CL; RAdv 13-2; RComWL; REn; RfGWoL 95*

Saragat, Giuseppe
Italian. Political Leader
One of founders of post-war Italian Republic; first socialist pres. of Italy, 1964-71.
b. Sep 19, 1898 in Turin, Italy
d. Jun 11, 1988 in Rome, Italy
Source: *AnObit 1988; BioIn 1, 4, 7, 16; CurBio 56, 65, 88, 88N; DcPol; FacFETw; IntWW 74, 75, 76, 77, 78, 79, 80, 81, 82, 83; IntYB 78, 79, 80; NewYTBS 88; WhAm 11; WhDW; Who 74, 82, 83, 85, 88; WhoGov 72; WhoWor 74, 91*

Sarah
Hebrew. Biblical Figure
Mother of Isaac, wife of Abraham; life was a continuous test of faith.
b. fl. 1900BC
Source: *BioIn 1; FolkA 87; InWom SUP*

Sarandon, Chris
American. Actor
Starred in *Dog Day Afternoon,* 1975; *Protocol,* 1984.
b. Jul 24, 1942 in Beckley, West Virginia
Source: *BioIn 15; ConTFT 4, 15; HalFC 80, 84, 88; IntMPA 84, 86, 88, 92, 94, 96; LegTOT; NewYTBS 76; WhoEnt 92; WhoHol 92, A; WhoThe 81*

Sarandon, Susan
[Susan Abigail Tomalin]
American. Actor
Films include *The Rocky Horror Picture Show,* 1975; *Atlantic City,* 1981; *Bull Durham,* 1988; and *Thelma and Louise,* 1991.
b. Oct 4, 1946 in New York, New York
Source: *BiDFilm 94; BioIn 13, 14, 15, 16; CelR 90; ConNews 86-2; ConTFT 3, 10; CurBio 89; FilmEn; HalFC 80, 84, 88; HolBB; IntDcF 1-3, 2-3; IntMPA 80, 84, 86, 88, 92, 94, 96; InWom SUP; ItaFilm; LegTOT; News 95, 95-3; NewYTBS 83; WhoAm 86, 90; WhoAmW 91; WhoEnt 92; WhoHol 92; WorAlBi*

Sarasate, Pablo de
[Martin Meliton S y Navascuez]
Spanish. Violinist, Composer
Celebrated virtuoso; had enormously successful worldwide tours, many noted works written for him.
b. Mar 10, 1844 in Pamplona, Spain
d. Sep 20, 1908 in Biarritz, France
Source: *Baker 78, 84, 92; BioIn 1, 2, 4, 7, 8, 14; BriBkM 80; DcCom&M 79; GrComp; MusMk; NewAmDM; NewGrDM 80; NewOxM; OxCMus; PenDiMP*

Sarasin, Jean Francois
French. Author
Wrote witty, satirical verse, popular with Parisian society, 1640s.
b. 1614
d. Dec 5, 1654
Source: *OxCFr*

Sarazen, Gene
[Gene Saraceni; Eugene Sarazen]
American. Golfer
Turned pro, 1920; has seven major tournament wins including 1935 Masters; one of four players to win all major titles; invented the sand wedge, 1930s.
b. Feb 27, 1901 in Harrison, New York
Source: *BiDAmSp OS; BioIn 2, 6, 9, 10, 13; LegTOT; NewYTBE 72, 73; NewYTBS 82; WebAB 74, 79; WhoGolf; WorAl*

Sarbanes, Paul S(pyros)
American. Politician
Dem. senator from MD, 1977—.
b. Feb 3, 1933 in Salisbury, Maryland
Source: *AlmAP 80, 92; BiDrUSC 89; BioIn 10, 11; CngDr 83, 89; IntWW 77, 78, 79, 80, 81, 82, 83, 89, 91, 93; PolsAm 84; WhoAm 74, 76, 78, 80, 82, 84, 86, 88, 90, 92, 94, 95, 96, 97; WhoAmP 73, 77, 79, 81, 83, 85, 87, 89, 91, 93, 95; WhoE 74, 75, 77, 79, 81, 83, 85, 86, 89, 91, 93, 95, 97; WhoGov 72, 75, 77; WhoWor 80, 82, 84, 87, 89, 91*

Sarcey, Francisque
French. Journalist, Critic
Wrote influential eight-volume work on the theater, late 1800s.
b. Oct 8, 1827 in Dourban, France
d. May 15, 1899 in Paris, France
Source: *BbD; BiD&SB; BioIn 1; CamGWoT; ClDMEL 47; DcEuL; Dis&D; EncWT; NotNAT A, B; OxCFr; OxCThe 67*

Sardi, Vincent, Sr.
American. Restaurateur
Opened Sardi's restaurant in Manhattan's theatre district, 1921.
b. Dec 23, 1885 in Canelli, Italy
d. Nov 19, 1969 in New York, New York
Source: *BioIn 3, 4, 8, 9; CurBio 57, 70*

Sardi, Vincent, Jr.
American. Restaurateur
Owner, Sardi's restaurant, NY.
b. Jul 23, 1915 in New York, New York
Source: *BiE&WWA; BioIn 4, 12; CelR; WhoAm 76, 78, 80, 82, 84, 86*

Sardou, Victorien
French. Dramatist
Wrote over 70 popular plays including historical melodramas starring Sarah Bernhardt.
b. Sep 7, 1831 in Paris, France
d. Nov 8, 1908 in Paris, France
Source: *AtlBL; BbD; Benet 87, 96; BiD&SB; BioIn 1, 5, 7, 11; CamGWoT; CasWL; CelCen; ClDMEL 47; CnThe; DcArts; DcBiPP A; DcEuL; Dis&D; EncO&P 1, 2, 3; EncWT; Ent; EuAu; EvEuW; GuFrLit 1; IntDcT 2; LinLib L, S; LngCTC; McGEWD 72, 84; MetOEnc; ModWD; NewC; NewCBEL; NewEOp 71; NewGrDM 80; NewGrDO; NotNAT A, B; OxCAmT 84; OxCFr; OxCThe 67, 83; OxDcOp; PenC EUR; PlP&P; REn; REnWD; WhDW; WhLit; WhoStg 1908*

Sarduy, Severo
Cuban. Author
Author of novel *Cobra,* 1972.
b. Feb 25, 1937 in Camaguey, Cuba
d. Aug 1993
Source: *Benet 96; BenetAL 91; BioIn 18, 20; CaribW 4; ConAu 89, 142; ConLC 6, 81, 97; ConWorW 93; CubExWr; DcCLAA; DcLB 113; DcTwCCu 4; DcTwCuL; EncWL 2, 3; HispWr; IntvLAW; LiExTwC; ModLAL; OxCSpan; RAdv 14; SpAmA*

Sarett, Lew R
American. Poet
Books of verse focus on Native American: *Slow Smoke,* 1925.
b. May 16, 1888 in Chicago, Illinois
d. Aug 17, 1954 in Gainesville, Florida
Source: *AmAu&B; AnMV 1926; ChhPo, S1, S2; CnDAL; ConAmA; ConAmL; OxCAmL 65; REn; REnAL; TwCA, SUP; WhAm 3; WhNAA*

Sarg, Tony
[Anthony Frederick Sarg]
American. Puppeteer, Children's Author
Created his famed marionettes, 1915; wrote, illustrated *Tony Sarg's Wonder Zoo,* 1927.
b. Apr 24, 1882, Guatemala
d. Mar 7, 1942 in Nantucket, Massachusetts
Source: *AmAu&B; ConICB; CurBio 42; DcAmB S3; IlrAm 1880, C; JBA 34, 51; OxCChiL; REnAL; WhAm 2; WorECar*

Sargeant, Winthrop
American. Critic, Author
Music critic for *New Yorker* mag., 1949-72.
b. Dec 10, 1903 in San Francisco, California
d. Aug 15, 1986 in Salisbury, Connecticut
Source: *AnObit 1986; Baker 78, 84, 92; BioIn 9, 15; BlueB 76; ConAu 29R, 120; IntAu&W 77, 86; NewGrDA 86; NewYTBS 86; WhAm 9; WhoAm 74, 76, 78, 80, 82, 84, 86; WhoWor 74; WrDr 76, 80, 82, 84, 86*

Sargent, Alvin
American. Screenwriter
Wrote Oscar-winning screenplays for *Julia,* 1977; *Ordinary People,* 1980.
b. Apr 12, 1927 in Philadelphia, Pennsylvania
Source: *ConAu 48NR, 111, 121; ConDr 88A; ConTFT 12; HalFC 88; IntMPA 92, 94, 96*

Sargent, Ben
American. Cartoonist, Author
Won 1982 Pulitzer for editorial cartooning.
b. Nov 26, 1948 in Amarillo, Texas
Source: *BioIn 15, 16; ConAu 113, 114, 115, 116, 117, 118; ConGrA 2; WhoAm 84, 86, 88, 90, 92, 94, 95; WorECar*

Sargent, Dick
American. Actor
Replaced Dick York as Darrin on TV series ''Bewitched,'' 1969-72.
b. Apr 19, 1933 in Carmel, California
d. Jul 8, 1994 in Los Angeles, California
Source: *BioIn 17, 20; FilmgC; HalFC 88; IntMPA 80, 81, 82, 84, 86, 88, 92; LegTOT; Who 92; WhoAm 74, 82; WhoHol 92, A*

Sargent, George
English. Golfer
Touring pro, early 1900s; won US Open, 1909; first to use movies for golf instruction, 1930.
b. 1880 in Dorking, England
d. Jun 18, 1962 in Atlanta, Georgia
Source: *WhoGolf*

Sargent, Herb
Writer
Won Emmys for ''Lily,'' 1974; ''Saturday Night Live,'' 1976, 1977.
Source: *ConTFT 15; VarWW 85*

Sargent, John Singer
American. Artist
Portrait painter who had many famous subjects; *Madame X* is in Metropolitan Museum of Art, NYC.
b. Jan 12, 1856 in Florence, Italy
d. Apr 15, 1925 in London, England
Source: *AmBi; AmCulL; ApCAB, X; ArtsAmW 3; AtlBL; Benet 87, 96; BioIn 1, 2, 3, 4, 6, 7, 9, 10, 11, 12, 13, 14, 15, 16, 19, 20; BriEAA; ChhPo, S1; ClaDrA; DcAmArt; DcAmB; DcArts; DcBrAr 1; DcBrBI; DcBrWA; DcNaB 1922; DcVicP, 2; EncAB-H 1974, 1996; FacFETw; GayN; HarEnUS; IntDcAA 90; LegTOT; LinLib S; LngCTC; McGDA; McGEWB; MorMA; NatCAB 11; OxCAmH; OxCAmL 65; OxCArt; OxDcArt; PeoHis; PhDcTCA 77; RComAH; REn; REnAL; ThHElm; TwCBDA; TwCPaSc; WebAB 74, 79; WhAm 1; WhDW; WorAl; WorAlBi*

Sargent, Malcolm, Sir
"Ambassador of Music"
English. Conductor
Led British orchestras, 1920s-60s; made frequent int'l tours; commemorative stamp issued in his honor, 1980.
b. Apr 29, 1895 in Stamford, England
d. Oct 3, 1967 in London, England
Source: *Baker 78, 84; BioIn 1, 2, 3, 4, 5, 7, 8, 11; BriBkM 80; CurBio 45, 68; DcNaB 1961; FacFETw; MusSN; NewAmDM; NewEOp 71; NewGrDM 80; ObitT 1961; OxCMus; OxDcOp; PenDiMP; WhScrn 77, 83*

Sarkis, Elias
Lebanese. Political Leader
Pres. of Lebanon, 1976-82; also gained fame as head of Central Bank.
b. Jul 20, 1924 in Shibaniyah, Lebanon
d. Jun 27, 1985 in Paris, France
Source: *AnObit 1985; BioIn 11, 12, 14, 15; ConNews 85-3; CurBio 79, 85, 85N; DcMidEa; FacFETw; IntWW 78, 79, 80, 81, 82, 83; MidE 78, 79, 80, 81, 82; NewYTBS 76, 85; WhoWor 78, 80, 82, 84*

Sarney, Jose
[Jose Ribamar Ferreira da Costa]
Brazilian. Political Leader
Brazil's first civilian pres. since 1964; assumed power, 1985.
b. Apr 30, 1930 in Sao Bento, Brazil
Source: *BioIn 14, 15; CurBio 86; DcCPSAm; IntWW 89, 91, 93; NewYTBS 85; WhoWor 87*

Sarnoff, David
American. Business Executive
Chairman, RCA; one of first to see that TV would replace radio in popularity.
b. Feb 27, 1891 in Minsk, Russia
d. Dec 12, 1971 in New York, New York
Source: *AmDec 1920, 1950; BiDAmBL 83; BioIn 1, 2, 3, 4, 5, 6, 7, 8, 9, 10, 11, 12, 14, 15, 17, 19, 20; ConAu 113; CurBio 40, 51, 72, 72N; DcAmB S9; EncAB-A 25; EncAB-H 1974, 1996; EncAJ; EncTwCJ; EncWB; FacFETw; InSci; JeAmHC; JeHun; LinLib L, S; McGEWB; NatCAB 56; NewYTBE 70, 71; ObitT 1971; PolProf E; SaTiSS; WebAB 74, 79; WhAm 5; WhoWorJ 72; WorAl; WorAlBi*

Sarnoff, Robert W(illiam)
American. Business Executive
Chm., RCA, 1970-75.
b. Jul 2, 1918 in New York, New York
d. Feb 22, 1997 in New York, New York
Source: *BioIn 2, 4, 8, 10, 11; BusPN; CurBio 56; EncTwCJ; IntMPA 88; St&PR 84; Who 74; WhoAm 74; WorAl*

Saro-Wiwa, Ken
Nigerian. Writer
Author of *Sozaboy: A Novel in Rotten English.*
b. Oct 10, 1941 in Bori, Nigeria
d. Nov 10, 1995 in Port Harcourt, Nigeria
Source: *BlkWr 2; DcLB 157; HeroCon; News 96, 96-2*

Saroyan, William
American. Author, Dramatist
Won Pulitzer Prize, 1940, for *The Time of Your Life.*
b. Aug 31, 1908 in Fresno, California
d. May 18, 1981 in Fresno, California
Source: *AmAu&B; AmNov; AnObit 1981; Au&Wr 71; Benet 87, 96; BenetAL 91; BiE&WWA; BioIn 1, 2, 3, 4, 5, 6, 7, 8, 9, 10, 11, 12, 13, 14, 15, 17, 20; BlueB 76; CamGLE; CamGWoT; CamHAL; CasWL; CelR; CmCal; CnDAL; CnMD; CnMWL; CnThe; ConAmA; ConAmD; ConAu 5R, 30NR, 103; ConDr 73, 77, 93; ConLC 1, 8, 10, 11, 29, 56; ConNov 72, 76; CrtSuDr; CurBio 40, 72, 81, 81N; CyWA 58, 89; DcArts; DcLB 7, 9, 86, Y81A; DcLEL; DrAF 76; DrAPF 80; EncWL, 2, 3; EncWT; Ent; EvLB; FacFETw; FilmEn; FilmgC; GrWrEL DR, N; HalFC 80, 84, 88; IntAu&W 76, 77; IntDcT 2; IntWW 74, 75, 77, 78, 79, 80, 81, 81N; LegTOT; LinLib L, S; LngCTC; MagSAmL; MajTwCW; McGEWB; McGEWD 72, 84; ModAL, S1; ModWD; NewCBEL; NewYTBS 75, 79, 81; NotNAT, A; Novels; OxCAmL 65, 83, 95; OxCAmT 84; OxCThe 67, 83; PenC AM; PlP&P; RAdv 1, 14, 13-2; REn; REnAL; REnWD; RfGAmL 87, 94; RfGShF; ShSCr 21; SmATA 23, 24N; TwCA, SUP; TwCWr; WebAB 74, 79; WebE&AL; WhAm 7; WhE&EA; Who 74; WhoAm 74, 76, 78, 80; WhoThe 72, 77, 81; WhoTwCL; WhoWor 74; WorAl; WorAlBi; WorLitC; WrDr 76, 80, 82*

Sarraute, Nathalie
French. Author
Wrote novels *Tropismes,* 1939; *Le planetarium,* 1959.
b. Jul 18, 1900 in Ivanovo-Voznessensk, Russia
Source: *Benet 96; BioIn 6, 7, 8, 9, 10, 11, 12, 13; CasWL; ConAu 9R, 23NR; ConFLW 84; ConLC 1, 2, 8, 10, 31, 80; ConWorW 93; CyWA 89; DcLB 83; DcTwCCu 2; EncCoWW; EncWB; EncWL 2, 3; EuWr 12; FacFETw; FrenWW; GrWomW; GuFrLit 1; IntAu&W 82, 86, 89, 91; IntDcT 2; IntWW 80, 81, 82, 83, 89, 91, 93; InWom, SUP; LiExTwC; LinLib L; MajTwCW; ModFrL; RfGWoL 95; Who 82, 83, 85, 88, 90, 92, 94; WhoFr 79; WhoWor 84, 87, 89, 91, 93, 95, 96, 97*

Sarrazin, Michael
[Jacques Michel Andre Sarrazin]
Canadian. Actor
Starred in *The Reincarnation of Peter Proud,* 1975.
b. May 22, 1940 in Quebec, Quebec, Canada
Source: *ConTFT 5, 12; FilmEn; FilmgC; HalFC 80, 84, 88; IntMPA 77, 78, 79, 80, 81, 82, 84, 86, 88, 92, 94, 96; ItaFilm; LegTOT; NewYTBE 70; WhoEnt 92; WhoHol 92, A; WorAl*

Sarria, Jose
American. Entertainer
Pioneer in gay political theater; active in AIDS fundraising.
Source: *GayLesB*

Sarris, Andrew George
American. Author
Books on film include *Politics and Cinema,* 1978.
b. Oct 31, 1928 in New York, New York
Source: *AmAu&B; BioIn 13; OxCFilm; WhoAm 76, 78, 80, 82, 84, 86, 88, 90, 92, 94, 95, 96, 97; WhoE 74, 75, 93; WhoEnt 92; WhoUSWr 88; WhoWor 78; WhoWrEP 89, 92, 95*

Sartain, John
American. Engraver
Pioneer mezzotint engraver; introduced pictorial illustration to American periodicals.
b. Oct 24, 1808 in London, England
d. Oct 25, 1897 in Philadelphia, Pennsylvania
Source: *Alli; AmAu&B; AmBi; ApCAB; ArtsNiC; BioIn 8; DcAmArt; DcAmAu; DcAmB; DcNAA; Drake; HarEnUS; McGDA; NatCAB 6; NewYHSD; TwCBDA; WhAmArt 85; WhAm HS*

Sarti, Giuseppe
Italian. Composer, Conductor
Held musical posts in Denmark, Russia; his 70 operas now forgotten.
b. Dec 1, 1729 in Faenza, Italy
d. Jul 28, 1802 in Berlin, Germany
Source: *Baker 78, 84, 92; BioIn 4; BriBkM 80; DcBiPP; MusMk; NewEOp 71; NewGrDM 80; NewGrDO; NewOxM; OxCMus; OxDcOp*

Sarto, Andrea del
[Andrea Domenico d'Agnolodi Francisco]
"Andrew the Faultless"
Italian. Artist
Noted for superbly colored religious frescoes, easel painting: *Madonna of the Harpies,* 1517.
b. Jul 16, 1486 in Florence, Italy
d. Sep 29, 1531 in Florence, Italy
Source: *AtlBL; Benet 87, 96; BioIn 1, 2, 5, 7, 9; Dis&D; LegTOT; McGDA; REn*

Sarton, May
[Eleanor Marie Sarton]
American. Author, Poet
Writings include verse vol. *A Durable Fire,* 1972; novel *As We Are Now,* 1973.
b. May 3, 1912 in Wondelgem, Belgium
d. Jul 16, 1995 in York, Maine
Source: *AmAu&B; AmWomWr; ArtclWW 2; Benet 87, 96; BenetAL 91; BioAmW; BioIn 4, 5, 8, 10, 11, 12, 13, 14, 15, 16, 17, 18, 19, 20, 21; BlmGWL; BlueB 76; CamGLE; CamHAL; ConAu 1NR, 1R, 34NR; ConLC 4, 14, 49, 91; ConNov 72, 76, 82, 86, 91; ConPo 70, 75, 80, 85, 91; CurBio 82, 95N; CyWA 89; DcLB 48, Y81B; DrAF 76; DrAP 75; DrAPF 80, 87, 91; DrAS 74E, 78E, 82E; EncWL 2; FemiCLE; GayLesB; GrWomW; IntAu&W 76, 77, 86, 91, 93; IntvTCA 2; IntWWP 77; InWom SUP; LegTOT; MajTwCW; ModAL, S1, S2; ModWoWr; NewYTBS 83; Novels; OxCAmL 65, 83; OxCWoWr 95; PenC AM; RAdv 1; REnAL; ScF&FL 1; SmATA 36; TwCA SUP; WhoAm 74, 76, 78, 80, 82, 90, 92; WhoAmW 58, 64, 66, 68, 70, 72, 81, 83, 85, 87, 89, 91, 93, 95; WhoWor 74; WrDr 76, 80, 82, 84, 86, 88, 90, 92, 94, 96*

Sartre, Jean-Paul
French. Author, Dramatist
Major exponent of 20th-c. existentialism; wrote *Being and Nothingness,* 1943; refused Nobel Prize in literature, 1964.
b. Jun 21, 1905 in Paris, France
d. Apr 15, 1980 in Paris, France
Source: *AnObit 1980; Au&Wr 71; Benet 87, 96; BiDFrPL; BiDNeoM; BiDPsy; BiE&WWA; BlmGEL; CamGWoT; CasWL; CelR; ClDMEL 47, 80; CnMD; CnMWL; CnThe; ConAu 9R, 21NR, 97; ConLC 1, 4, 7, 9, 13, 18, 24, 52; CroCD; CurBio 71, 80N; CyWA 58, 89; DcArts; DcLB 72; DcTwCCu 2; DramC 3; EncUnb; EncWL, 2, 3; EncWT; Ent; EuWr 12; EvEuW; FacFETw; FilmEn; FilmgC; GrFLW; GuFrLit 1; HalFC 80, 84, 88; IntAu&W 76, 77; IntWW 74, 75, 76, 77, 78, 79; ItaFilm; LegTOT; LinLib L, S; LngCTC; LuthC 75; MagSWL; MajMD 2; MajTwCW; MakMC; McGEWB; McGEWD 72, 84; ModFrL; ModRL; ModWD; NewYTBS 80; NobelP; NotNAT, A; Novels; OxCEng 67, 85, 95; OxCFr; OxCPhil; OxCThe 67; PenC EUR; PlP&P; RadHan; RAdv 14, 13-2, 13-4; RComWL; REn; REnWD; ScF&FL 1, 2, 92; ThTwC 87; TwCA SUP; TwCWr; TwoTYeD; WhAm 7; WhDW; Who 74; WhoFr 79; WhoNob; WhoThe 72, 77, 81; WhoTwCL; WhoWor 74, 78; WhScrn 83; WorAl; WorAlBi; WorLitC; WrPh, P*

Sasakawa, Ryoichi
Japanese. Industrialist, Philanthropist
Wealthy businessman amassed power through generous gifts to charitable organizarions; the UN has received more than $50 million from his foundation.
Source: *BioIn 13, 15, 21; NewYTBS 74, 95*

Sasser, James R(alph)
American. Politician
Dem. senator from TN, 1977-94; US ambassador to China, 1996—.
b. Sep 30, 1936 in Memphis, Tennessee
Source: *AlmAP 82, 92; BiDrUSC 89; CngDr 77, 79, 81, 83, 85, 87, 89; CurBio 93; IntWW 81, 82, 83, 89, 91, 93; NewYTBS 90; WhoAm 78, 80, 82, 84, 86, 88, 90, 92, 94, 95, 97; WhoAmL 78; WhoAmP 77, 79, 81, 83, 85, 87, 89, 91, 93, 95; WhoGov 77; WhoSSW 78, 80, 82, 86, 88, 91; WhoWor 80, 82, 84, 87, 89, 91*

Sassetta
[Stefano di Giovanni]
Italian. Artist
Noted painter of international Gothic style; drew panels on life of St. Francis, 1437-44.
b. 1395? in Siena, Italy
d. 1450 in Siena, Italy
Source: *AtlBL; OxCArt*

Sassoon, Siegfried
English. Poet, Soldier, Author
Prize-winning *Memoirs of a Fox-Hunting Man,* 1928, best known of semi-atobiographical trilogy.
b. Sep 8, 1886 in Brenchley, England
d. Sep 1, 1967 in Purton, England
Source: *AtlBL; Benet 87, 96; BioIn 12, 14, 15, 16, 17, 18, 21; BlmGEL; BritAS; CamGEL; CamGLE; CasWL; Chambr 3; CnE&AP; CnMWL; ConAu 25R, 36NR, 104; ConLC 36; CyWA 58; DcArts; DcLB 20; EncWL 2, 3; EngPo; FacFETw; GrWrEL P; LinLib L; LngCEL; LngCTC; MajTwCW; ModBrL S1, S2; NewC; ObitT 1961; PenC ENG; PoeCrit 12; RAdv 14, 13-1; REn; RfGEnL 91; TwCA SUP; WhAm 4; WhDW; WhE&EA; WhoTwCL; WorAlBi*

Sassoon, Vidal
English. Hairstylist
Founder, chm., Vidal Sassoon, Inc; wrote *A Year of Beauty and Health,* 1976.
b. Jan 17, 1928 in London, England
Source: *AmDec 1960; BioIn 7, 8, 10, 12, 13; BioNews 74; BkPepl; CelR, 90; ConAu 15NR, 65; Dun&B 86, 88; EncFash; IntWW 89, 91, 93; LegTOT; WhoAm 76, 78, 80, 82, 84, 86, 88, 90, 92, 96; WhoAmJ 80; WhoFI 96; WhoWest 82, 84, 87, 89, 92, 94, 96; WhoWor 97; WorAl; WorFshn*

Sasway, Benjamin H
American. Political Activist
First person indicted for violation of Selective Service Act since draft revival, 1980.
b. 1961? in Vista, California
Source: *BioIn 13; NewYTBS 82*

Satanta
American. Native American Chief
Principal war chief of the Kiowa; served prison sentences.
b. 1820 in Oklahoma
d. Sep 11, 1878 in Huntsville, Texas
Source: *BioIn 21; NotNaAm; PeoHis*

Satcher, David
American. Physician
Director, Centers for Disease Control and Prevention, 1994—.
b. Mar 2, 1941 in Anniston, Alabama
Source: *AmMWSc 89, 92, 95; BiDrAPH 79; BioIn 19, 20; BlksScM; ConBlB 7; NotTwCS; St&PR 84, 87, 91, 93, 96; WhoAfA 96; WhoAm 92, 95, 96, 97; WhoBlA 77, 80, 85, 88, 90, 92, 94; WhoMedH; WhoScEn 96; WhoSSW 84, 86; WhoWor 96*

Sather, Glen Cameron
"Slats"
Canadian. Hockey Player, Hockey Coach, Hockey Executive
Left wing, 1966-77; coach, GM, pres., Edmonton, 1977-89; won five Stanley Cups.
b. Sep 2, 1943 in High River, Alberta, Canada
Source: *BioIn 14; HocEn; NewYTBE 71; NewYTBS 85; WhoAm 84, 86, 90, 92, 94, 95, 96, 97; WhoHcky 73; WhoWest 87, 89, 92, 94, 96*

Satherly, Arthur Edward
"Uncle Art"
American. Music Executive
Record industry pioneer; helped launch careers of Gene Autry, Tex Ritter, Roy Rogers.
b. Oct 19, 1889 in Bristol, England
d. Feb 10, 1986 in Fountain Valley, California
Source: *WhAm 9; WhoAm 76*

Satie, Erik
French. Composer
Avant-garde works include *Socrate,* 1918; influenced Debussy, Ravel, and Les Six group; wrote chiefly for piano.
b. May 17, 1866 in Honfleur, France
d. Jul 1, 1925 in Paris, France
Source: *AtlBL; Baker 78, 84; Benet 87; BiDD; BioIn 1, 2, 3, 4, 5, 6, 7, 8, 9, 10, 11, 12, 16, 17, 18, 20, 21; BriBkM 80; CmpBCM; CnOxB; CompSN, SUP; DancEn 78; DcCM; DcCom 77; DcCom&M 79; DcTwCC, A; DcTwCCu 2; FacFETw; IntDcB; LegTOT; MakMC; McGEWB; MusMk; NewAmDM; NewCol 75; NewEOp 71; NewGrDM 80; NewOxM; OxCFilm; OxCMus; OxDcOp; PenDiMP A; RAdv 14; REn; WhDW;*

WhScrn 77, 83; WorAl; WorAlBi; WorEFlm

Sato, Eisaku
Japanese. Political Leader
Premier, 1964-72; developed Japan into major economic, industrial nation; shared 1974 Nobel Peace Prize for helping stabilize Pacific area.
b. Mar 27, 1901 in Tabuse, Japan
d. Jun 3, 1975 in Tokyo, Japan
Source: *BioIn 6, 7, 8, 9, 10, 11, 15; CurBio 65, 75, 75N; DcPol; FacFETw; IntWW 74, 75; LegTOT; McGEWB; NewYTBS 74, 75; NobelP; ObitT 1971; WhAm 6; WhoGov 72; WhoNob, 90, 95; WhoWor 74; WorAlBi*

Satriani, Joe
American. Musician
Lead guitarist for Mick Jagger's world tour, 1988; Hit album *Surfing with the Alien.*
b. 1957 in Carle Place, New York
Source: *BioIn 16; ConMus 4; News 89-3*

Saubel, Katherine Siva
American. Historian
Helped found the Malki Museum, the first non-profit tribal museum on a Native American reservation in California; named Elder of the Year by the California State Indian Museum, 1987.
b. 1920
Source: *BioIn 21; NotNaAm; WhoAmW 97*

Saud (Ibn Abdul Aziz al Saud)
Saudi. Ruler
Ruled Saudi Arabia, 1953-64; deposed by brother, Faisal.
b. Jan 15, 1902, Kuwait
d. Feb 23, 1969 in Athens, Greece
Source: *BioIn 1, 3, 4, 5, 6, 7, 8, 9; CurBio 54, 69; NewCol 75*

Saudek, Robert
American. TV Executive
Known for producing cultural programming, including "Omnibus"; past president, NY's Museum of Broadcasting.
b. Apr 11, 1911 in Pittsburgh, Pennsylvania
d. Mar 13, 1997 in Baltimore, Maryland
Source: *BlueB 76; LesBEnT 92; St&PR 75; WhoEnt 92; WhoWor 74, 76*

Sauer, George (Henry)
American. Football Coach
Head coach, Univ. of New Hampshire, 1937-41; Univ. of Kansas, 1946-47, winner of two Bix Six titles.
b. Dec 11, 1910
d. Feb 5, 1994 in Waco, Texas
Source: *BiDAmSp Sup; BioIn 1; CurBio 94N*

Saunders, Allen
American. Cartoonist
Did comic strips Mary Worth, Steve Roper.
b. Mar 24, 1899 in Lebanon, Indiana
d. Jan 28, 1985 in Maumee, Ohio
Source: *BioIn 14; ConAu 69, 118; EncACom; NewYTBS 86; WhoAm 82; WorECom*

Saunders, Charles E, Sir
Canadian. Scientist
Developed early-maturing spring wheat grown in Western Canada: Marquis wheat, 1920s.
b. Feb 2, 1867 in London, Ontario, Canada
d. Jul 25, 1937 in Toronto, Ontario, Canada
Source: *Alli; McGEWB*

Saunders, Lori
American. Actor
Played Bobbi Jo on TV series "Petticoat Junction," 1965-70.
b. Oct 4, 1941 in Kansas City, Missouri
Source: *WhoHol 92, A*

Saunders, Stuart T(homas)
American. Businessman
Headed PA Railroad, 1964; Penn Central Railroad, 1968-70.
b. Jul 16, 1909 in McDowell, Wyoming
d. Feb 7, 1987 in Richmond, Virginia
Source: *BioIn 4, 6, 7, 8, 9, 11, 12, 15; CurBio 66, 87, 87N; EncAB-A 35; EncABHB 1; IntWW 74, 75, 76, 77, 78, 79, 80, 81; NewYTBS 87; PolProf J, NF; WhAm 9; WhoAm 74; WhoE 74*

Saunders, William Laurence
American. Engineer, Inventor
Patented stone-cutting machines and drills.
b. Nov 1, 1856 in Columbus, Georgia
d. Jun 25, 1931 in Tenerife, Canary Islands, Spain
Source: *DcAmB; NatCAB 14, 26; WhAm 1; WhNAA*

Saura (Atares), Carlos
Spanish. Director, Screenwriter
Leading figure in Spanish cinema; films include *Cria,* 1976; *Carmen,* 1983.
b. Jan 4, 1932 in Huesca, Spain
Source: *BiDFilm 94; BioIn 11, 13, 16; ConAu 114, 131; ConLC 20; CurBio 78; EncEurC; FilmEn; HispWr; IntDcF 1-2, 2-2; IntMPA 92, 94, 96; IntWW 89, 91, 93; MiSFD 9; NewYTBE 71; WorEFlm; WorFDir 2*

Saussure, Nicolas Thoedore de
Swiss. Chemist
Experiments in biochemistry of plants supplied groundwork for later development of phytochemistry.
b. Oct 14, 1767 in Geneva, Switzerland
d. Apr 18, 1845 in Geneva, Switzerland
Source: *BioIn 6; DcScB*

Sauter, Eddie
[Edward Ernest Sauter]
American. Jazz Musician, Songwriter
Trumpeter; arranged for Benny Goodman, Red Norvo, 1930s-40s; co-led Sauter-Finegan band, 1950s.
b. Dec 2, 1914 in New York, New York
d. Apr 21, 1981 in Nyack, New York
Source: *AnObit 1981; ASCAP 66, 80; BiDAmM; BioIn 12, 16; CmpEPM; ConAmC 76A, 82; IlEncJ; NewAmDM; NewGrDA 86; NewGrDJ 88, 94; NewYTBS 81; OxCPMus; PenEncP; WhAm 7; WhoJazz 72*

Sauve, Jeanne Mathilde Benoit
[Mrs. Maurice Sauve]
Canadian. Political Leader
First woman, 23rd governor-general (queen's representative) of Canada, 1984-90.
b. Apr 26, 1922 in Prud'Homme, Saskatchewan, Canada
d. Jan 26, 1993 in Montreal, Quebec, Canada
Source: *AmCath 80; BioIn 13, 14, 15; CanWW 83, 89; ContDcW 89; CurBio 84; IntDcWB; IntWW 89; InWom SUP; NewYTBS 83, 85; Who 92; WhoAm 86, 90; WhoAmW 91; WhoE 91; WhoWor 91*

Sauveur, Albert
American. Scientist
A pioneer in the field of physical metallurgy.
b. Jun 21, 1863 in Louvain, Belgium
d. Jan 26, 1939 in Boston, Massachusetts
Source: *BioIn 4, 12; DcAmB S2; DcNAA; DcScB; InSci; NatCAB 29; WhAm 1; WhNAA*

Savage, Augusta Christine
American. Sculptor
First black member National Assn. of Women Painters and Sculptors, 1934; noted for portrait sculpture.
b. Feb 29, 1892 in Green Cove Springs, Florida
d. Mar 26, 1962 in New York, New York
Source: *BiDWomA; BioIn 12, 20; DcWomA; InWom SUP; NotAW MOD*

Savage, Edward
American. Artist
Noted for portraits of George, Martha Washington.
b. Nov 26, 1761 in Princeton, Massachusetts
d. Jul 6, 1817 in Princeton, Massachusetts
Source: *AmBi; ApCAB; BioIn 1, 3, 5, 7, 10; BriEAA; DcAmArt; DcAmB; Drake; McGDA; NewYHSD; WhAm HS*

Savage, Fred
American. Actor
Played Kevin Arnold on "The Wonder Years," 1988-93.
b. Jul 9, 1976 in Chicago, Illinois
Source: *BioIn 16; ConTFT 8, 15; IntMPA 92, 94, 96; LegTOT; News 90, 90-1; WhoHol 92*

Savage, Henry Wilson
American. Impresario
Founded Boston Light Opera Co., 1895, presenting opera in English at moderate prices; also produced *Merry Widow,* 1907.
b. Mar 21, 1859 in Alton, New Hampshire
d. Nov 29, 1927 in Boston, Massachusetts
Source: *Baker 78, 84; BiDAmM; DcAmB; EncMT; NewEOp 71; NewGrDA 86; NotNAT B; WhAm 1; WhThe*

Savage, John
American. Journalist
Editorial writer for *States* (Washington, DC), 1857-61.
b. Dec 13, 1828 in Dublin, Ireland
d. Sep 9, 1888 in Laurelside, Pennsylvania
Source: *Alli; AmAu; AmAu&B; ApCAB; BbD; BiD&SB; ChhPo S1; CyAL 2; DcAmAu; DcAmB; DcIrL 96; DcNAA; DcNaB; Drake; HarEnUS; NatCAB 11; PoIre; TwCBDA; WhAm HS*

Savage, John
[John Youngs]
American. Actor
Films include *Salvador,* 1986; *The Onion Field,* 1979.
b. Aug 25, 1950? in Old Bethpage, New York
Source: *ConTFT 5; St&PR 87; VarWW 85; WhoEnt 92*

Savage, Richard
English. Poet
Reputation gained from biography by Samuel Johnson, friendship with Alexander Pope.
b. 1697
d. Aug 1, 1743 in Bristol, England
Source: *Alli; BbD; Benet 87, 96; BioIn 2, 3, 5, 9; BlmGEL; BritAu; CasWL; Chambr 2; ChhPo, S1; DcBiPP; DcEnA; DcEnL; DcEuL; DcLB 95; EvLB; GrWrEL P; NewC; NewCBEL; OxCEng 67, 85, 95; PenC ENG; REn; RfGEnL 91; WebE&AL*

Savage, Rick
[Def Leppard]
"Sav"
English. Musician
Bassist with heavy metal group formed 1977.
b. Dec 2, 1960 in Sheffield, England

Savalas, Telly
[Aristoteles Savalas]
American. Actor
Played Kojak on TV police drama of same name, 1973-78; first shaved head for role of Pontius Pilate in *The Greatest Story Ever Told,* 1965.
b. Jan 21, 1923 in Garden City, New York
d. Jan 22, 1994 in Universal City, California
Source: *BioNews 74; BkPepl; ConTFT 2, 7, 12; CurBio 76; FilmgC; HalFC 88; IntMPA 92; IntWW 76, 77, 78, 79, 80, 81, 82, 89; MotPP; MovMk; NewYTBE 73; VarWW 85; WhoAm 86, 92; WhoEnt 92; WhoHol A; WorAlBi*

Savant, Marilyn vos
American. Journalist
IQ of 228 is highest ever recorded; column, "Ask Marilyn," appears in *Parade* magazine.
b. Aug 11, 1946 in Saint Louis, Missouri
Source: *BioIn 15, 16; News 88-2*

Savard, Denis Joseph
Canadian. Hockey Player
Center, Chicago, 1980-90; Montreal, 1990-93; Tampa Bay, 1993—.
b. Feb 4, 1961 in Pointe Gatineau, Quebec, Canada
Source: *HocEn; HocReg 87; WhoAm 96, 97; WhoMW 90*

Savard, Serge A
"The Senator"
Canadian. Hockey Player
Defenseman, 1966-83, mostly with Montreal; won Conn Smythe Trophy, 1969, Masterton Trophy, 1979; Hall of Fame, 1986.
b. Jan 22, 1946 in Montreal, Quebec, Canada
Source: *BioIn 12; HocEn; WhoAm 84, 86, 90; WhoE 91; WhoHcky 73*

Savelli, Luca
Roman. Politician
Led middle class revolt against Pope Gregory IX, 1234.
d. 1266

Savery, Thomas
English. Inventor
Constructed the first steam engine.
b. 1650 in Shilstone, England
d. 1715 in London, England
Source: *AsBiEn; BiESc; BioIn 14; DcInv; DcNaB; InSci; NewCBEL; WorInv*

Savimbi, Jonas Malheiro
Angolan. Political Leader
Founded National Union for the Total Independence of Angola, 1966.
b. Aug 3, 1934 in Munhango, Angola
Source: *BioIn 14, 15, 16; ColdWar 1; ConBlB 2; ConNews 86-2; CurBio 86; DcCPSAf; DcTwHis; EncRev; EncWB; FacFETw; IntWW 91; WhoAfr*

Savitch, Jessica Beth
American. Broadcast Journalist
With NBC News, 1977-83; wrote autobiography, *Anchorwoman,* 1982.
b. Feb 2, 1948 in Kennett Square, Pennsylvania
d. Oct 23, 1983 in New Hope, Pennsylvania
Source: *BioIn 11; ConAu 108; CurBio 83, 84; LesBEnT; NewYTBS 83; WhAm 8; WhoAm 82*

Savitskaya, Svetlana Y
Russian. Cosmonaut
First woman to walk in space, Jul 25, 1984.
b. 1947?
Source: *BiDSovU; BioIn 13, 14, 15; FacFETw; InWom SUP*

Savitt, Jan
Russian. Bandleader
Led popular dance band, 1930s-40s.
b. Sep 4, 1913 in Saint Petersburg, Russia
d. Oct 4, 1948 in Sacramento, California
Source: *ASCAP 66, 80; CmpEPM; PenEncP*

Savo, Jimmy
American. Actor, Comedian
Broadway performer who starred in several 1930s films.
b. 1896 in New York, New York
d. Sep 6, 1960 in Teni, Italy
Source: *BiDAmM; EncAFC; EncMT; JoeFr; NotNAT A, B; PlP&P; WhoCom; WhoHol B; WhScrn 74, 77; WhThe*

Savonarola, Girolamo
Italian. Religious Leader
Preached against corruptions in secular life; burned at stake for heresy, 1498.
b. Sep 21, 1452 in Ferrara, Italy
d. May 23, 1498 in Florence, Italy
Source: *BbD; Benet 87; BiD&SB; BioIn 15, 16, 17, 20; BlmGEL; CasWL; DcCathB; DcItL 1, 2; Dis&D; EncRev; EuAu; EvEuW; HisWorL; LegTOT; LinLib S; LuthC 75; McGEWB; NewC; OxCEng 85, 95; PenC EUR; REn; WhDW; WorAl; WorAlBi*

Savoy Brown
[Miller Anderson; Eric Dillon; James Leverton; Kim Simmonds; Stan Webb]
English. Music Group
Heavy rock group formed 1966; albums include *Rock & Roll Warriors,* 1981.
Source: *ConMuA 80A; HarEnR 86; IlEncRk; OnThGG; PenEncP; RkOn 85A; RolSEnR 83; WhoRock 81; WhoRocM 82*

Sawchuk, Terry
[Terrance Gordon Sawchuk]
Canadian. Hockey Player
Goalie, 1949-70, mostly with Detroit; holds NHL record for career shutouts, 103; died of injuries received in fight with teammate; Hall of Fame, 1971.
b. Dec 28, 1929 in Winnipeg, Manitoba, Canada
d. May 31, 1970 in Mineola, New York
Source: *BioIn 10, 11; FacFETw; HocEn; LegTOT; NewYTBE 70; WhoHcky 73; WhoSpor*

Sawyer, Amos
Liberian. Political Leader
Pres. interim government of Liberia, 1990.
b. Jun 15, 1945 in Greenville, Liberia
Source: *BioIn 16, 17, 21; ConBlB 2; WhoAfr*

Sawyer, Charles
American. Government Official
Ambassador to Belgium, 1944-45; secretary of Commerce, 1948-53.
b. Feb 10, 1887 in Cincinnati, Ohio
d. Apr 7, 1979 in Palm Beach, Florida
Source: *BiDrUSE 71, 89; BioIn 1, 2, 3, 10, 11, 12; ConAu 85, P-2; CurBio 79, 79N; NewYTBS 79; PolProf T; St&PR 75; WhAm 7; Who 74; WhoAm 74, 76; WhoAmP 73, 75, 77, 79*

Sawyer, Diane (K.)
American. Broadcast Journalist
Former staff assistant to Nixon; first female correspondent on TV's "60 Minutes," 1984-89; host of "Prime Time Live," 1989—; co-anchor, "Day One," 1995—; co-anchor, "Turning Point."
b. Dec 22, 1945 in Glasgow, Kentucky
Source: *BioIn 12, 13, 16; CelR 90; ConAu 109, 115; ConTFT 10; CurBio 85; EncTwCJ; IntMPA 86, 88, 92, 94, 96; InWom SUP; JrnUS; LegTOT; LesBEnT 92; News 94; NewYTBS 81; WhoAm 86, 88, 90, 92, 94, 95, 96, 97; WhoAmW 87, 89, 91, 93, 95, 97; WhoE 91; WomStre; WorAlBi*

Sawyer, Eugene, Jr.
American. Politician
Alderman, elected acting mayor of Chicago replacing Harold Washington, 1987.
b. Sep 4, 1934 in Greensboro, Alabama
Source: *NewYTBS 87; WhoAm 88; WhoAmP 73, 75, 77, 79, 81, 83, 85, 87, 89, 91, 93, 95*

Sawyer, Forrest
American. Broadcast Journalist
Covered Persian Gulf War for ABC; correspondent, Nightline, ABC, 1992—; anchor, World News Sunday, ABC; ABC News "Day One".
Source: *LesBEnT 92; WhoAm 88, 90, 92, 94, 95, 96, 97; WhoE 95*

Sawyer, John E(dward)
American. Educator
Pres., Andrew W. Mellon Foundation, 1975-87; pres., Williams College, 1961-73.
b. May 5, 1917
d. Feb 7, 1995 in Woods Hole, Massachusetts
Source: *AmMWSc 73S, 78S; BioIn 5, 6, 7, 9; CurBio 95N; EncAI&E; LEduc 74; WhAm 11; WhoAm 74, 76, 78, 80, 82, 84, 86, 88, 90, 92, 94, 95; WhoWor 76*

Sawyer, Ruth
American. Children's Author
Won Newbery Medal for autobiography *Roller Skates,* 1936.
b. Aug 5, 1880 in Boston, Massachusetts
d. Jun 3, 1970 in Hancock, Maine
Source: *AmAu&B; AmLY; AmWomPl; AmWomWr; AnCL; AuBYP 2, 3; BioAmW; BioIn 2, 4, 6, 7, 8, 9, 11, 12, 14, 19; BkCL; CarSB; ChhPo; ChlBkCr; ChlLR 36; ConAu 37NR, 73; DcLB 22; HerW; InWom SUP; JBA 51; MajAI; NewbMB 1922; NotAW MOD; OxCChiL; SmATA 17; TwCA, SUP; TwCChW 78, 83, 89, 95; WhAm 5; WhE&EA; WhNAA; WhoAmW 58, 70, 72; WomNov; WrChl*

Sax, Adolphe (Antoine-Joseph)
Belgian. Inventor
Developed the saxophone, 1842, and other instruments used by military bands.
b. Nov 6, 1814 in Dinant, Belgium
d. Feb 4, 1894 in Paris, France
Source: *Baker 78, 84, 92; BioIn 1, 2, 3, 5; BriBkM 80; MusMk; NewAmDM; NewGrDM 80; NewGrDO; NewOxM; WebBD 83; WhDW*

Sax, Charles Joseph
Belgian. Manufacturer
Made brass instruments at factory established in Brussels, 1815.
b. Feb 1, 1791 in Dinant, Belgium
d. Apr 26, 1865 in Paris, France
Source: *Baker 84; WebBD 83*

Saxbe, William Bart
American. Diplomat
Rep. senator from OH, 1969-74; attorney general, 1973-74; ambassador to India, 1974-76.
b. Jun 25, 1916 in Mechanicsburg, Ohio
Source: *BiDrAC; BiDrUSC 89; CngDr 74; CurBio 74; IntWW 83, 89; NewYTBE 73; PolProf NF; WhoAm 76, 78, 80, 82, 84, 86, 88, 90, 92, 94, 95, 96, 97; WhoAmP 85, 91; WhoGov 72*

Saxe, Maurice
French. Military Leader
One of greatest generals of his time for victories at Fontenoy, 1745, Racoux, 1746.
b. Oct 28, 1696 in Saxony, France
d. Nov 30, 1750 in Chambord, France
Source: *BioIn 2, 4, 6, 7, 16; NewCol 75; OxCFr; OxCGer 76*

Saxon, Charles David
American. Cartoonist
Best known for humorous, satiric commentary on suburban upper class liftstyle in cartoons appearing on covers of *New Yorker* magazine since 1956.
b. Nov 13, 1920 in New York, New York
d. Dec 6, 1988 in Stamford, Connecticut
Source: *AmAu&B; ConAu 118, 127; WhAm 9; WhoAm 74, 76, 78; WhoAmA 73, 76, 78, 80, 82, 84, 86, 89, 91N, 93N; WhoE 74; WhoGrA 82*

Saxon, John
[Carmen Orrico]
American. Actor
Starred in TV series "The Bold Ones," 1969-72; film *The Cardinal,* 1963.
b. Aug 5, 1935 in New York, New York
Source: *BioIn 5; FilmEn; FilmgC; ForYSC; GangFlm; HalFC 80, 84, 88; IntMPA 75, 76, 77, 78, 79, 80, 81, 82, 84, 86, 88; ItaFilm; LegTOT; MotPP; MovMk; WhoHol A; WhoHrs 80; WorAl*

Sayao, Bidu
"The Brazilian Nightingale"
Brazilian. Opera Singer
Soprano prima donna with NY Met., 1937-52; noted for Manon role, jewel collection.
b. May 11, 1902 in Rio de Janeiro, Brazil
Source: *Baker 78, 84, 92; BioIn 11, 13, 14, 15; BriBkM 80; CmOp; CurBio 42; IntDcOp; MetOEnc; MusSN; NewAmDM; NewEOp 71; NewGrDA 86; NewGrDM 80; OxDcOp; PenDiMP*

Sayer, Leo
[Gerald Sayer]
English. Singer
Pop-rock hits include "Have You Ever Been In Love," 1982.
b. May 21, 1948 in Shoreham, England
Source: *BioIn 11; BkPepl; ConMuA 80A; EncRk 88; EncRkSt; HarEnR 86; IlEncRk; LegTOT; OxCPMus; PenEncP; RkOn 74, 78; RolSEnR 83; WhoRock 81*

Sayers, Dorothy Leigh
English. Author
Dectective stories feature sleuth, Lord Peter Wimsey; first woman ever to receive degree from Oxford in medieval linguistics.
b. Jun 13, 1893 in Oxford, England
d. Dec 17, 1957 in Witham, England
Source: *ArtclWW 2; BioIn 2, 4, 8, 10, 11, 12, 13; CasWL; Chambr 3; CnMD; ConAu 104, 119; CorpD; DcLEL; DcNaB 1951; EncMys; EncWL; EngPo; EvLB; GrBr; GrWrEL N; InWom; LinLib S; LngCTC; ModBrL, S1; ModWD; NewC; NewCBEL; NotNAT B; OxCEng 67; PenC ENG; PenNWW A; REn; TwCA, SUP; TwCWr; WhAm 3; WhLit; WhThe*

Sayers, Gale Eugene
American. Football Player
Four-time all pro running back, Chicago, 1965-71; led NFL in rushing, 1966, 1969; wrote *I Am Third,* 1970; Hall of Fame, 1977.
b. May 30, 1940 in Wichita, Kansas
Source: *BiDAmSp FB; ConAu 73; InB&W 85; NewYTBE 70, 72; WhoAm 86, 88; WhoBlA 88; WhoFtbl 74*

Sayles, John
American. Filmmaker
Films include *Eight Men Out,* 1988; *Passion Fish,* 1992; *Lone Star,* 1996.
b. Sep 28, 1950 in Schenectady, New York
Source: *BiDFilm 94; BioIn 13, 14, 15, 16, 17, 19, 21; CelR 90; ConLC 7, 10, 14; ConTFT 1, 6, 13; CurBio 84; EncSF 93; HalFC 88; IntDcF 1-4, 2-2; IntMPA 84, 86, 88, 92, 94, 96; LegTOT; LesBEnT; MiSFD 9; NewYTBS 83; Novels; WhoHol 92; WorAlBi; WorFDir 2; WrDr 88, 90, 92, 94, 96*

Sayles Belton, Sharon
American. Politician
Mayor of Minneapolis, 1994—.
b. c. 1952 in Saint Paul, Minnesota
Source: *ConBlB 9*

Scaasi, Arnold
American. Fashion Designer
Made-to-order designer of First Lady Barbara Bush.
b. May 8, 1930 in Montreal, Quebec, Canada
Source: *BioIn 5, 11, 12, 13, 16; CelR 90; WhoAm 84*

Scaasi, Arnold
American. Fashion Designer
One of the last true custom designers in US; famous for his fur, feather-trimmed evening clothes.
b. May 8, 1931 in Montreal, Quebec, Canada
Source: *BioIn 13, 16; CelR 90; ConFash; FairDF US; WhoFash 88; WorFshn*

Scaggs, Boz
[William Royce Scaggs]
American. Musician, Singer
Won Grammy for "Lowdown," 1976; other hits include "Miss Sun," 1980.
b. Jun 8, 1944 in Dallas, Texas
Source: *ASCAP 80; BioIn 16, 20; ConMuA 80A; ConMus 12; EncPR&S 89; EncRk 88; EncRkSt; IlEncBM 82; IlEncRk; LegTOT; NewAmDM; NewGrDA 86; OnThGG; PenEncP; RkOn 74, 78; RolSEnR 83; SoulM; WhoAm 78, 80, 82, 84, 86, 88, 90, 92, 94; WhoEnt 92; WhoRock 81; WorAlBi*

Scala, Gia
[Giovanna Sgoglio]
American. Actor
Leading lady, 1950s-60s: *The Guns of Navarone,* 1961; died of accidental drug, alcohol overdose.
b. Mar 3, 1934 in Liverpool, England
d. Apr 30, 1972 in Hollywood Hills, California
Source: *FilmEn; FilmgC; HalFC 80, 84, 88; LegTOT; MotPP; MovMk; NewYTBE 72; WhoHol B; WhScrn 77, 83*

Scalchi, Sofia
Italian. Opera Singer
Noted mezzo-soprano; sang at NY Met.'s opening season, 1883; famed for high register.
b. Nov 29, 1850 in Turin, Italy
d. Aug 22, 1922 in Rome, Italy
Source: *Baker 78, 84, 92; BioIn 1; InWom; MetOEnc; NewEOp 71; NewGrDM 80; NewGrDO*

Scali, John (Alfred)
American. Journalist, Diplomat
Senior correspondent, ABC News; US ambassador to UN, 1973-75.
b. Apr 27, 1918 in Canton, Ohio
d. Oct 9, 1995 in Washington, District of Columbia
Source: *BioIn 9, 10, 11, 12; CelR; ConAu 65; CurBio 73, 96N; EncTwCJ; IntAu&W 89, 91, 93; IntWW 74, 75, 76, 77, 78, 79, 80, 81, 82, 83, 89; LesBEnT 92; NewYTBE 71, 72; USBiR 74; WhAm 11; WhoAm 74, 76, 80, 82, 84, 86, 88, 90, 94, 95, 96; WhoAmP 73; WhoE 95; WhoGov 75; WhoSSW 73; WhoUN 75; WhoWor 74, 76, 78*

Scalia, Antonin
American. Supreme Court Justice
Appointed to court by Ronald Reagan, 1986.
b. Mar 11, 1936 in Trenton, New Jersey
Source: *AmPolLe; BioIn 14, 15, 17, 18; CngDr 83, 85, 87, 89, 91, 93, 95; CurBio 86; EncWB; FacFETw; IntWW 89, 91, 93; LegTOT; News 88-2; NewYTBS 86; OxCSupC; SupCtJu; Who 90, 92, 94; WhoAm 74, 76, 78, 80, 82, 84, 86, 88, 90, 92, 94, 95, 96, 97; WhoAmL 78, 79, 83, 87, 90, 92, 94, 96; WhoAmP 87, 89, 91, 93, 95; WhoE 85, 86, 89, 91, 93; WhoGov 75, 77; WhoWor 89, 91, 93, 96; WorAlBi*

Scaliger, Joseph Justus
French. Scholar
Founded Julian period of scientific chronology.
b. Aug 4, 1540 in Agen, France
d. Jan 21, 1609 in Leyden, France
Source: *AsBiEn; BbD; BiD&SB; CyEd; DcBiPP; DcEuL; EvEuW; InSci; LinLib L, S; LuthC 75; NewC; OxCEng 67, 85, 95; OxCFr; PenC EUR; WorAl; WorAlBi*

Scamozzi, Vincenzo
Italian. Architect
Influential designer of cathedrals, theaters, palaces; architectural theories helped usher in English Neoclassic era.
b. 1552 in Vicenza, Italy
d. 1616, Italy
Source: *CamGWoT; DcBiPP; MacEA; McGDA; NotNAT B; OxCArt; OxCThe 67, 83; PlP&P; WhoArch*

Scanlon, Hugh Parr
English. Labor Union Official
Pres., Amalgamated Union of Engineering Workers, 1968-78.
b. Oct 26, 1913, Australia
Source: *BioIn 8, 9; IntWW 74, 75, 76, 77, 78, 93; Who 74*

Scarbury, Joey
American. Singer
Hit single "Believe It or Not," 1981, theme from TV show "Greatest American Hero."
b. Jun 7, 1955 in Ontario, California
Source: *RkOn 85*

Scargill, Arthur
English. Labor Union Official
Pres., Nat. Union of Mineworkers, 1981—; led Britain's longest, most violent post WW II strike, 1984-85.
b. Jan 11, 938 in Barnsley, England
Source: *BioIn 14, 15; CurBio 85; EncWB; FacFETw; IntWW 91; Who 92*

Scarlatti, Alessandro
Italian. Composer
Established Italian opera overture; wrote 200 masses, 115 operas, including *Il Tigrane,* 1715; father of Domenico.
b. May 2, 1660 in Palermo, Sicily, Italy
d. Nov 24, 1725 in Naples, Italy
Source: *AtlBL; Baker 78, 84; Benet 87; BioIn 3, 4, 5, 7, 10, 12, 14; BriBkM 80; CmOp; CmpBCM; DcCom 77; DcCom&M 79; GrComp; IntDcOp; LegTOT; MetOEnc; MusMk; NewAmDM; NewCBEL; NewEOp 71; NewGrDM 80; NewOxM; OxCMus; OxDcOp; PenDiMP A; REn; WorAl; WorAlBi*

Scarlatti, Domenico Girolamo
Italian. Composer
Founded modern keyboard technique; first to use arpeggios in performances; wrote over 500 harpsichord sonatas.
b. Oct 26, 1685 in Naples, Italy
d. Jul 23, 1757 in Naples, Italy
Source: *AtlBL*

Scarne, John
American. Magician, Business Executive
Authority on games of chance; wrote *Scarne on Dice.*
b. Mar 4, 1903 in Steubenville, Ohio
d. Jul 7, 1985 in Englewood, New Jersey
Source: *BioIn 14; ConAu 116; WhoAm 76, 78, 80, 82, 84, 86, 88, 90, 92, 94, 95, 96, 97*

Scarpelli, Glenn
American. Actor
Played Alex in TV series "One Day at a Time," 1980-83.
b. Jul 6, 1968 in Staten Island, New York
Source: *VarWW 85*

Scarry, Richard (McClure)
American. Children's Author, Illustrator
Prolific writer of "best ever" picture books; won Edgar mystery award, 1976.
b. Jun 5, 1919 in Boston, Massachusetts
d. Apr 30, 1994 in Gstaad, Switzerland

Source: *AuBYP 2, 3; BioIn 9, 10, 12, 14, 16, 19, 20; ChlBkCr; ChlLR 3, 41; ConAu 17R, 18NR, 39NR, 145; ConLC 86; DcLB 61; FamAIYP; IlsCB 1957; IntAu&W 77, 82, 86, 91, 93; MajAI; NewYTBS 94; OxCChiL; PiP; SmATA 2, 35, 75, 90; ThrBJA; TwCChW 78, 83, 89, 95; WhAm 11; WhoAm 78, 80, 82, 84, 86, 88, 90, 92, 94; WrDr 76, 80, 82, 84, 86, 88, 90, 92, 94, 96*

Scavullo, Francesco
American. Photographer
Freelance photographer known for pictures of models, celebrities appearing in popular magazines.
b. Jan 16, 1929 in Staten Island, New York
Source: *BioIn 13, 14, 15, 17; CelR 90; ConAu 43NR, 102; CurBio 85; EncFash; ICPEnP A; LegTOT; MacBEP; WhoAdv 90; WhoAm 78, 80, 82, 84, 86, 88, 90, 92, 94, 95, 96, 97*

Schaap, Dick
[Richard J Schaap]
American. Journalist
Sportscaster with ABC News, 1980—.
b. Sep 27, 1934 in New York, New York
Source: *AmAu&B; BioIn 15; ConAu 5NR, 9R; LiJour; WhoE 74*

Schacht, Al(exander)
"Clown Prince of Baseball"
American. Baseball Player
Pitcher, Washington, 1919-21, with 14 ML wins; better known for entertaining fans before game.
b. Nov 11, 1892 in New York, New York
d. Jul 14, 1984 in Waterbury, Connecticut
Source: *Ballpl 90; BioIn 14; NewYTBS 84; WhoProB 73*

Schacht, Hjalmar Horace Greeley
German. Financier
Germany's "financial wizard"; saved country from inflation by issuing the Rentenmark, 1923; made Minister of Economics by Hitler; acquitted at Nuremberg trails.
b. Jan 22, 1877 in Tingleff, Germany
d. Jun 4, 1970 in Munich, Germany (West)
Source: *BiDExR; ConAu 113; CurBio 44, 70; McGEWB; REn; WhWW-II*

Schadow, Gottfried
[Johann Gottfried Schadow]
German. Sculptor
Member of Neo-classic school; best known for monuments of Fredrick the Great, Blucher, Luther.
b. May 20, 1764 in Berlin, Germany
d. Jan 27, 1850 in Berlin, Germany
Source: *BioIn 2, 6, 11, 12; CelCen; DcBiPP; LuthC 75; McGDA; NewCol 75; OxCArt; OxDcArt; WorECar*

Schaefer, Germany
[Herman A Schaefer]
American. Baseball Player
Infielder, early 1900s; known for antics while stealing bases.
b. Feb 4, 1878 in Chicago, Illinois
d. May 16, 1919 in Saranac Lake, New York
Source: *BioIn 2, 3, 5; WhoProB 73*

Schaefer, Jack Warner
American. Author
Wrote dozens of Western novels including *Shane,* 1949, adapted to film, 1953, translated into 35 languages.
b. Nov 19, 1907 in Cleveland, Ohio
d. Jan 24, 1991 in Santa Fe, New Mexico
Source: *AmAu&B; Au&Wr 71; AuBYP 2, 3; BioIn 5, 8, 9, 11, 14; ConAu 15NR, 17R, 133, P-1; DcAmChF 1960; EncFWF; FifWWr; IntMPA 82, 86; NewYTBS 91; OhA&B; REnAW; SmATA 3, 66; ThrBJA; TwCChW 89; TwCWW 82, 91; WhoAm 74, 76, 78, 80, 82, 84, 86, 88, 90; WhoWest 74*

Schaefer, Rudolph Jay
American. Brewer
Chm., F & M Schaefer Brewing Co., 1950-69.
b. Jul 9, 1900 in Larchmont, New York
d. Sep 2, 1982 in New York, New York
Source: *NewYTBS 82; St&PR 75; WhoAm 74*

Schaefer, Thomas E
[The Hostages]
American. Hostage
One of 52 held by terrorists, Nov 1979-Jan 1981.
b. 1931?
Source: *NewYTBS 81*

Schaefer, Vincent Joseph
American. Meteorologist
Performed experiments to investigate the nature of precipitation.
b. Jul 4, 1906 in Schenectady, New York
d. Jul 25, 1993 in Schenectady, New York
Source: *AmMWSc 73P, 76P, 79; AsBiEn; BiESc; BioIn 1, 2, 5; ConAu 120; CurBio 48; InSci; LarDcSc; McGMS 80; WhoAm 74, 76, 78, 80, 82, 84; WhoTech 89*

Schaefer, William Donald
American. Politician
Dem. governor of MD, 1987—; mayor of Baltimore, 1971-87.
b. Nov 2, 1921 in Baltimore, Maryland
Source: *AlmAP 88, 92; BiDrGov 1983, 1988; BioIn 12, 13, 16; CelR 90; ConNews 88-1; CurBio 88; IntWW 89, 91, 93; WhoAm 78, 80, 82, 84, 86, 88, 90, 92, 94, 95; WhoAmP 73, 75, 77, 79, 81, 83, 85, 87, 89, 91, 93, 95; WhoE 74, 75, 77, 79, 81, 83, 85, 86, 89, 91, 93, 95; WhoGov 75, 77; WhoWor 89, 91, 93, 95*

Schafer, Natalie
American. Actor
Veteran stage comedienne since 1944; played Lovey on TV series "Gilligan's Island," 1964-67.
b. Nov 5, 1902 in Rumson, New Jersey
d. Apr 10, 1991 in Beverly Hills, California
Source: *FilmEn; HalFC 88; IntMPA 88; NewYTBS 91; VarWW 85*

Schaff, Philip
American. Theologian
Noted church scholar; founder, first president, American Society of Church History, 1888.
b. Jan 1, 1819 in Chur, Switzerland
d. Oct 20, 1893 in New York, New York
Source: *Alli, SUP; AmAu; AmAu&B; AmBi; ApCAB; BbD; BiD&SB; BioIn 1, 15, 17, 19; CyAL 2; DcAmAu; DcAmB; DcAmReB 1, 2; DcLB DS13; DcNAA; Drake; EncARH; HarEnUS; LuthC 75; McGEWB; NatCAB 3; NewCol 75; OxCAmH; PeoHis; RelLAm 91; REnAL; TwCBDA; WebAB 74, 79; WhAm HS*

Schaffner, Franklin James
American. Director
Won best director Oscar, 1970, for *Patton.*
b. May 3, 1920 in Tokyo, Japan
d. Jul 2, 1989 in Santa Monica, California
Source: *BioIn 16; ConTFT 7; FacFETw; HalFC 88; IntMPA 88; IntWW 79, 80, 81, 82, 83, 89; LesBEnT 92; NewYTBS 89; PeoHis*

Schalk, Franz
Austrian. Conductor
Led Vienna State Opera, from 1918.
b. May 27, 1863 in Vienna, Austria
d. Sep 2, 1931 in Edlach, Austria
Source: *Baker 78, 84, 92; CmOp; IntDcOp; MetOEnc; NewEOp 71; NewGrDM 80; NewGrDO; OxDcOp; PenDiMP*

Schalk, Ray(mond William)
"Cracker"
American. Baseball Player
Catcher, 1912-29, mostly with Cubs; known for fielding; Hall of Fame, 1955.
b. Aug 12, 1892 in Harvel, Illinois
d. May 19, 1970 in Chicago, Illinois
Source: *Ballpl 90; BiDAmSp BB; BioIn 7, 8, 14, 15; DcAmB S8; LegTOT; WhoProB 73*

Schally, Andrew Victor
American. Biochemist
Discovered pituitary hormone TRH, 1969, human ovulation hormone LHRH, 1971; shared Nobel Prize, 1977.
b. Nov 30, 1926 in Wilno, Poland
Source: *AmMWSc 76P; WhoMedH; WhoNob, 90, 95; WhoScEn 94, 96; WhoSSW 78, 80, 82, 84, 86, 88, 91, 93, 95, 97; WhoTech 89; WhoWor 78, 80,*

82, 84, 87, 89, 91, 93, 95, 96, 97; WorAlBi; WorScD

Schaltzberg, Jerry Ned
American. Director
Films include *Panic in Needle Park,* 1972; *Honeysuckle Rose,* 1980.
b. Jun 26, 1927 in New York, New York
Source: *ConTFT 4; HalFC 84; WhoAm 86*

Schama, Simon
English. Historian, Educator
Wrote *Citizens: A Chronicle of the French Revolution,* 1989, noted for its unusual colorful narrative and stylistic qualities.
b. Feb 13, 1945 in London, England
Source: *BestSel 89-4; ConAu 105; CurBio 91; IntAu&W 91, 93; IntWW 91; WhoAm 84, 94, 95, 96, 97; WhoWor 93, 95; WrDr 90, 92*

Schanberg, Sydney Hillel
American. Journalist
Columnist, associate editor, *NY Times,* 1959-85; columnist, associate editor, *Newsday,* 1986—' won Pulitzer, 1975.
b. Jan 17, 1934 in Clinton, Massachusetts
Source: *BiDAmNC; BioIn 14, 15; ConAu 69; CurBio 90; IntAu&W 91; IntWW 89, 91, 93; WhoAm 76, 78, 80, 82, 84, 86, 88, 90, 92, 94, 95, 96, 97; WhoAmJ 80; WhoE 77, 79, 81, 83, 85, 86, 89, 91, 95*

Schank, Roger C(arl)
American. Scientist
Creative computer scientist founded Cognitive Science Society; Yale professor and chairman of department of Computer Science, from 1980; founded Institute for the Learning Sciences, 1989.
b. Mar 12, 1946 in New York, New York
Source: *BioIn 13, 14, 15, 16; ConAu 132; News 89-2; WhoAm 84, 86, 88, 90, 92, 94, 95, 96, 97; WhoE 86; WhoFrS 84; WhoTech 89*

Schapiro, Meyer
[Meir Schapiro]
American. Historian, Educator
Art historian; faculty member of art history dept. at Columbia U, 1928-1973; professor emeritus, 1973-96.
b. Sep 23, 1904 in Siauliai, Lithuania
d. Mar 3, 1996 in New York, New York
Source: *AmAu&B; BioIn 7, 10, 11, 12, 14, 15, 17, 20, 21; ConAu 97, 151; CurBio 84, 96N; DrAS 74H, 78H; EncAL; FacFETw; IntAu&W 91; NewYTBS 27, 75; ThTwC 87; WhAm 11; Who 74, 82, 83, 85, 88, 90, 92, 94; WhoAm 74, 76, 78, 82, 84, 86, 88, 90, 92, 94, 95, 96; WhoAmA 73, 76, 78, 80, 82, 84, 86, 89, 91, 93; WhoWorJ 72, 78; WorAu 1975; WrDr 86, 88, 90, 92, 94, 96*

Schary, Dore
American. Producer, Screenwriter
Early in career wrote several film scripts including *Boys Town,* 1938; later switched to producing.
b. Aug 31, 1905 in Newark, New Jersey
d. Jul 7, 1980 in New York, New York
Source: *AmAu&B; AnObit 1980; BenetAL 91; BiDFilm, 81, 94; BiE&WWA; BioIn 1, 2, 3, 4, 5, 6, 9, 10, 12, 17, 20; BlueB 76; ConAu 1NR, 1R, 101; ConDr 73, 77, 93; CurBio 48, 80, 80N; DcAmB S10; DcFM; EncMcCE; FacFETw; FilmEn; FilmgC; HalFC 80, 84, 88; IntDcF 1-4, 2-4; IntMPA 75, 76, 77, 78, 79, 80, 81, 82; LegTOT; LinLib L, S; MGM A; MiSFD 9N; ModWD; NatPD 77; NewYTBS 80; NotNAT; OxCFilm; REnAL; WhAm 7; WhoAm 74, 76, 78, 80; WhoAmJ 80; WhoE 74, 75, 77, 79, 81; WhoThe 72, 77, 81; WhoWor 74, 76, 78, 80; WhoWorJ 72, 78; WorAl; WorAlBi; WorAu 1950; WorEFlm; WrDr 76, 80*

Schaudinn, Fritz Richard
German. Zoologist
Discovered syphilis organism, Spirochaeta pallida, 1905.
b. Sep 19, 1871 in Roseningken, Prussia
d. Jun 22, 1906 in Hamburg, Germany (West)
Source: *AsBiEn; BiESc; BiHiMed; BioIn 9; CamDcSc; DcScB; InSci; LarDcSc; NewCol 75; OxCMed 86; WebBD 83; WhDW*

Schauffler, Robert Haven
American. Poet, Essayist
Writings include *The Unknown Brahms,* 1933; *The Days We Celebrate,* 1940.
b. Apr 8, 1879 in Brunn, Austria
d. Nov 24, 1964
Source: *AmAu&B; Baker 78, 84; BenetAL 91; BioIn 4, 7; ChhPo, S1, S2, S3; OhA&B; REn; REnAL; TwCA, SUP; WhAm 4; WhE&EA; WhNAA*

Schaufuss, Peter
Danish. Dancer
Principal dancer, NYC Ballet, 1974-77; Nat. Ballet of Canada, 1977-83; English Nat. Ballet, 1984-90.
b. Apr 26, 1949 in Copenhagen, Denmark
Source: *BiDD; BioIn 12, 13, 16; CnOxB; CurBio 82; FacFETw; IntDcB; IntWW 91; NewYTBS 75; Who 92; WhoAm 78, 80, 82, 90; WhoEnt 92; WhoWor 91*

Schawlow, Arthur Leonard
American. Physicist, Educator
With Nicolaas Bloembergen, shared 1981 Nobel Prize in physics for studies of laser spectroscopy.
b. May 5, 1921 in Mount Vernon, New York
Source: *AmMWSc 76P, 79, 82, 86, 89, 92, 95; BioIn 8, 11, 12, 13, 14, 15, 18, 20; BlueB 76; CamDcSc; IntWW 74, 75, 76, 77, 78, 79, 80, 81, 82, 83, 89, 91, 93; LarDcSc; NobelP; Who 83, 85, 88, 90, 92, 94; WhoAm 74, 76, 78, 80, 82, 84, 86, 88, 90, 92, 94, 95, 96, 97; WhoAtom 77; WhoEng 80, 88; WhoFrS 84; WhoNob, 90, 95; WhoScEn 94, 96; WhoTech 89; WhoWest 74, 76, 78, 80, 82, 84, 87, 89, 92, 94, 96; WhoWor 74, 76, 78, 82, 84, 87, 89, 91, 93, 95, 96, 97; WorAlBi*

Schayes, Dolph
[Adolph Schayes]
American. Basketball Player, Basketball Coach
Forward, 1949-64, mostly with Syracuse; led NBA in rebounding, 1951; coached five seasons; coach of year, 1966; Hall of Fame, 1972.
b. May 19, 1928 in New York, New York
Source: *BasBi; BiDAmSp BK; BioIn 4, 5, 6, 8, 9, 10, 14; LegTOT; OfNBA 87; PeoHis; WhoAm 74; WhoBbl 73; WhoE 74; WhoSpor*

Scheel, Walter
German. Diplomat
Pres., Federal Republic of Germany, 1974-79.
b. Jul 8, 1919 in Solingen, Germany
Source: *BioIn 8, 9, 10; CurBio 71; IntWW 74, 75, 76, 77, 78, 79, 80, 81, 82, 83, 89, 91, 93; IntYB 78, 79, 80, 81, 82; NewYTBS 74; Who 74, 82, 83, 85, 88, 90, 92, 94; WhoFI 96; WhoWor 74, 76, 78, 84, 87, 89, 91, 93, 95*

Scheele, Karl Wilhelm
Swedish. Chemist
Discovered oxygen, 1772, chlorine, 1774; prior to Priestly's publications.
b. Dec 9, 1742 in Stralsund, Swedish Pomerania
d. May 26, 1786 in Koping, Sweden
Source: *AsBiEn; BiESc; BioIn 1, 3, 5, 6, 7, 9, 10, 12; InSci; LinLib L, S; McGEWB; WhDW; WorAl; WorAlBi*

Scheer, Robert
American. Journalist
Anti-war activist, 1960s; wrote *How the United States Got Involved in Vietna m,* 1965; reporter, *LA Times,* 1976-1993.
b. Apr 14, 1936 in New York, New York
Source: *AmAu&B; BioIn 8, 11, 13; ConAu 106; PolProf J*

Scheff, Fritzi
"Little Devil of the Opera"
Austrian. Opera Singer
Soprano who sang over 30 roles; most noted for Broadway light opera, 1906-30s.
b. Aug 30, 1879 in Vienna, Austria
d. Apr 8, 1954 in New York, New York
Source: *Baker 78, 84, 92; BioIn 3; CmOp; CmpEPM; EncMT; EncVaud; Film 1; InWom, SUP; MetOEnc; NewEOp 71; NewGrDA 86; NewGrDM 80; NewGrDO; NotNAT B; OxCAmT 84; OxCPMus; WhoHol B; WhoStg 1906, 1908; WhScrn 74, 77, 83; WhThe*

Scheffer, Victor B(lanchard)
American. Conservationist, Zoologist
US government biologist, 1937-69; accepted idea that wildlife is a "resource" to be managed.
b. Nov 27, 1906 in Manhattan, Kansas
Source: *BioIn 10; CurBio 94; IntAu&W 93; WhoAm 74, 76; WrDr 94, 96*

Scheidemann, Philipp
German. Political Leader
Proclaimed start of Weimar Republic, 1918; first chancellor, 1919.
b. Jun 26, 1865 in Kassel, Germany
d. Nov 29, 1939 in Copenhagen, Denmark
Source: *EncTR 91; FacFETw; NewCol 75; REn*

Scheider, Roy Richard
American. Actor
Starred in *Jaws I, II,* 1975, 1978; Oscar nominee: *All That Jazz,* 1979.
b. Nov 10, 1935 in Orange, New Jersey
Source: *BioIn 13; CelR 90; ConTFT 5; FilmgC; HalFC 84; IntMPA 86; NewYTBS 80; WhoAm 76, 78, 80, 82, 84, 86, 88, 90, 94; WhoEnt 92; WhoHol A; WorAl*

Schell, Johnathan Edward
American. Journalist
Staff writer,*New Yorker,* 1968-87; author of many books and articles on the Vietnam war.
b. Aug 21, 1943 in New York, New York
Source: *BioIn 12, 13; ConLC 35; CurBio 92; IntAu&W 91; WhoAm 88; WhoWrEP 89; WrDr 92*

Schell, Maria Margarethe
Austrian. Actor
Short American career debuted with *The Brothers Karamazov,* 1958; returned to European screen.
b. Jan 5, 1926 in Vienna, Austria
Source: *BioIn 14; ConTFT 6; CurBio 61; FilmEn; HalFC 84, 88; IntMPA 86, 92; InWom SUP; WorAlBi*

Schell, Maximilian
Austrian. Actor
Won Oscar, 1961, for *Judgment at Nuremberg;* brother of Maria Schell.
b. Dec 8, 1930 in Vienna, Austria
Source: *BiDFilm 94; BiE&WWA; BioIn 6, 7, 11, 14, 17; CelR; ConAu 116; ConTFT 5; CurBio 62; FilmAG WE; FilmEn; FilmgC; ForYSC; HalFC 80, 84, 88; IntDcF 1-3, 2-3; IntMPA 75, 76, 77, 78, 79, 80, 81, 82, 84, 86, 88, 92, 94, 96; IntWW 74, 75, 76, 77, 78, 79, 80, 81, 82, 83, 89, 91, 93; ItaFilm; LegTOT; MiSFD 9; MotPP; MovMk; WhoAm 74, 76, 78, 80, 82, 84, 86, 88, 90, 92, 94, 95, 96, 97; WhoEnt 92; WhoHol 92, A; WhoWor 74, 78, 82, 84, 87, 89, 91, 93, 95, 96; WorAl; WorAlBi; WorEFlm*

Schell, Orville H, Jr.
American. Businessman
Chairman of NYC Ballet, 1975-87.
b. Jul 11, 1908 in New Rochelle, New York
d. Jun 17, 1987 in Danbury, Connecticut
Source: *NewYTBS 87; WhoAm 86*

Schell, Orville H(ickock), 3rd.
American. Journalist, Author
Books on China include *Modern China: The Story of a Revolution,* 1972.
b. May 20, 1940 in New York, New York
Source: *AuBYP 2S, 3; BioIn 11; ConAu 25R; IntAu&W 91; SmATA 10; WrDr 86, 92*

Schelling, Ernest Henry
"Uncle Ernest"
American. Pianist, Composer, Conductor
Led children's concerts, 1920s-30s; wrote fantasy *A Victory Ball,* 1923.
b. Jul 26, 1876 in Belvidere, New Jersey
d. Dec 8, 1939 in New York, New York
Source: *AmBi; ASCAP 66; Baker 84; BiDAmM; CurBio 40; DcAmB S2; OxCMus; WhAm 1*

Schelling, Friedrich Wilhelm Joseph von
German. Philosopher
Spokesman of Romantic thought, ideals; father of existential tendencies in modern art.
b. Jan 27, 1775 in Wurttemberg, Germany
d. Aug 20, 1854 in Bad Ragaz, Switzerland
Source: *BbD; Benet 87, 96; BiD&SB; BiDPsy; BiDTran; BioIn 7, 11, 17; BlkwCE; CasWL; CelCen; CyEd; DcBiPP; DcEuL; DcLB 90; Dis&D; EncEth; EuAu; EvEuW; InSci; LinLib L, S; LuthC 75; McGEWB; NamesHP; NewC; OxCEng 67, 85, 95; OxCGer 76, 86; OxCPhil; PenC EUR; RAdv 13-4; REn*

Schembechler, Bo
[Glenn Edward Schembechler]
American. Football Coach, Baseball Executive
Assistant coach, Ohio State under Woody Hayes, 1958-62; head coach, U of M, 1969-89; president, Detroit Tigers, 1990—.
b. Apr 1, 1929 in Barberton, Ohio
Source: *BiDAmSp FB; BioIn 10, 11, 12, 16; ConAu 139; News 90, 90-3; NewYTBS 76; WhoAm 84, 86, 88, 90, 92, 94; WhoFtbl 74; WhoMW 92; WhoSpor*

Schenck, Joseph M
American. Film Executive, Producer
Chm., 20th Century-Fox, 1935-41; produced all of Buster Keaton's Silent films.
b. Dec 25, 1878 in Rybinsk, Russia
d. Oct 22, 1961 in Beverly Hills, California
Source: *FilmEn; FilmgC; OxCFilm; WhAm 4*

Schenck, Nicholas Michael
American. Film Executive
Pres., Loew's, Inc., 1927-55.
b. Nov 14, 1881 in Rybinsk, Russia
d. Mar 3, 1969 in Miami Beach, Florida
Source: *BioIn 8; DcAmB S8; DcFM; FilmEn; FilmgC; OxCFilm; WhAm 5; WorEFlm*

Schenck, Robert Cumming
American. Politician
Whig-Rep. congressman from OH, 1843-51, 1863-71; minister to Brazil, 1851-53, to England, 1871-76.
b. Oct 4, 1809 in Franklin, Ohio
d. Mar 23, 1890 in Washington, District of Columbia
Source: *Alli SUP; AmBi; ApCAB; BiAUS; BiDrAC; BiDrUSC 89; BioIn 7, 10, 12, 16; DcAmB; DcAmDH 80, 89; Drake; HarEnUS; NatCAB 3; OhA&B; TwCBDA; WhAm HS; WhAmP; WhCiWar*

Schenk, Ard
Dutch. Skater
Won three speed skating gold medals, 1972 Olympics.
b. Sep 19, 1944 in Anna Paulowna, Netherlands
Source: *BioIn 10*

Schenkel, Chris(topher Eugene)
American. Sportscaster
Broadcaster for more than 50 yrs. including 30 yrs. on ABC's Pro Bowling.
b. Aug 21, 1924 in Bippus, Indiana
Source: *BioIn 6, 9, 10; BioNews 74; LesBEnT, 92; WhoAm 86*

Schenkkan, Robert
American. Dramatist
Winner of Pulitzer Prize for drama, *The Kentucky Cycle,* 1992.
b. Mar 19, 1953 in Chapel Hill, North Carolina
Source: *ConAu 132; ConTFT 4*

Scherchen, Hermann
German. Conductor
Led European orchestras, from 1911; conducted premieres of many ultramodern works.
b. Jun 21, 1891 in Berlin, Germany
d. Jun 12, 1966 in Florence, Italy
Source: *Baker 78, 84, 92; BioIn 4, 5, 7, 11; BriBkM 80; CmOp; DcArts; FacFETw; MusSN; NewAmDM; NewEOp 71; NewGrDM 80; NewGrDO; OxDcOp; PenDiMP; WhAm 5*

Scherer, Ray(mond Lewis)
American. Broadcast Journalist, Business Executive
Former NBC News correspondent, now vp, RCA, 1975—.
b. Jun 7, 1919 in Fort Wayne, Indiana

Source: *ConAu 104; Dun&B 88; LElec; LesBEnT 92; St&PR 84, 87; WhoAm 74, 76, 78, 80, 82, 84, 86; WhoWor 74*

Scherman, Harry
American. Publisher, Author
Co-founded Book of the Month Club, 1926.
b. Feb 1, 1887 in Montreal, Quebec, Canada
d. Nov 12, 1969 in New York, New York
Source: *AmAu&B; BioIn 1, 6, 7, 8, 9, 12; CurBio 43, 63, 70; DcAmB S8; EncTwCJ; NatCAB 58; WhAm 5; WhE&EA; WhoWorJ 72*

Scherman, Thomas Kielty
American. Conductor
Founded NYC's Little Orchestra Society, 1947-75; son of Harry.
b. Feb 12, 1917 in New York, New York
d. May 14, 1979 in New York, New York
Source: *Baker 84; BioIn 10; ConAu 106; CurBio 54, 79; NewYTBS 79; WhoWor 74*

Scherr, Max
American. Lawyer, Publisher
Founded the radical *Berkeley Barb,* 1965; editor until 1973.
b. 1916?
d. Oct 31, 1981 in Berkeley, California
Source: *AnObit 1982; BioIn 8, 12; ConAu 105*

Scheuer, Philip K(latz)
American. Critic, Editor
Film, drama critic, LA *Times,* 1927-67.
b. Mar 24, 1902 in Newark, New Jersey
d. Feb 18, 1985 in Hollywood, California
Source: *BiE&WWA; ConAu 115; IntMPA 75*

Schiaparelli
[Elsa Schiaparelli]
Italian. Fashion Designer
Known for exaggerated shoulders, nipped waistline, bizarre hats; introduced "shocking pink," 1939.
b. Sep 10, 1890 in Rome, Italy
d. Nov 14, 1973 in Paris, France
Source: *BioIn 1, 2, 3, 5, 9, 10; ConAu 113; ConFash; ContDcW 89; CurBio 40, 51, 74, 74N; EncFash; FairDF FRA; InWom SUP; LegTOT; LinLib S; NewYTBE 73; WhAm 6; Who 74; WhoFash 88; WhoWor 74; WomFir; WorAlBi; WorFshn*

Schiaparelli, Giovanni
Italian. Explorer, Scientist
Director, Milan Observatory, 1862-1900; discovered asteroid Hesperia, 1861.
b. Mar 14, 1835 in Savigliano, Italy
d. Jul 4, 1910 in Milan, Italy
Source: *AsBiEn; NewCol 75*

Schick, Bela
American. Scientist, Physician
Developed Schick test for diphtheria, 1913; wrote *Child Care Today,* 1932.
b. Jul 16, 1877 in Bolgar, Austria-Hungary
d. Dec 6, 1967 in New York, New York
Source: *BioIn 3, 4, 6, 8, 9; CurBio 44, 68; DcAmMeB 84; EncAB-A 40; InSci; JeAmHC; NatCAB 53; ObitT 1961; WebAB 74, 79; WhAm 4*

Schick, Jacob
American. Inventor
Introduced electric razor, 1931.
b. Sep 16, 1877 in Des Moines, Iowa
d. Jul 3, 1937 in New York, New York
Source: *BioIn 11; Entr; NatCAB 30; WorAl; WorAlBi*

Schickel, Richard
American. Critic, Author
Time magazine movie critic, 1973—.
b. Feb 10, 1933 in Milwaukee, Wisconsin
Source: *AuNews 1; BioIn 10; ConAu 1NR, 1R, 34NR; ConTFT 10; IntAu&W 91, 93; IntWW 89, 91, 93; WhoAm 74, 76, 78, 80, 82, 84, 86, 88, 92, 94, 95, 96, 97; WhoE 74; WhoEnt 92; WhoUSWr 88; WhoWrEP 89, 92, 95; WorAu 1980; WrDr 76, 80, 82, 84, 86, 88, 90, 92*

Schickele, Peter
American. Composer, Musician
Created mythical, zany composer, PDQ Bach, who lampoons music classics; wrote score, lyrics for *Oh, Calcutta.*
b. Jul 17, 1935 in Ames, Iowa
Source: *ASCAP 66, 80; Baker 78, 84, 92; BioIn 8, 11, 12, 14; ConAmC 76, 76A, 82; ConAu 85; ConMus 5; CpmDNM 78, 79, 81, 82; CurBio 79; IntWWM 90; NewAmDM; NewGrDA 86; NewGrDM 80; NewGrDO; PenEncP; WhoAm 76, 78, 80, 82, 84, 86, 88, 90, 92, 94, 95, 96, 97; WhoAmM 83; WhoEnt 92; WhoWor 74*

Schieffer, Bob
American. Broadcast Journalist
Anchor, correspondent, CBS News, since 1969.
b. Feb 25, 1937 in Austin, Texas
Source: *BioIn 15; ConAu 69; EncTwCJ; IntWW 91; JrnUS; LesBEnT, 92; WhoAm 86, 90; WhoTelC*

Schiele, Egon
Austrian. Artist
Expressionist painter; concentrated on the erotic portrayal of the human figure.
b. Jun 12, 1890 in Tulln, Austria
d. Oct 31, 1918 in Vienna, Austria
Source: *Benet 87, 96; BioIn 4, 5, 7, 9, 10, 11, 12, 14, 17; DcArts; EncWB; FacFETw; IntDcAA 90; McGDA; ModArCr 4; OxCTwCA; OxDcArt; PhDcTCA 77*

Schiff, Dorothy
American. Publisher, Journalist
First woman publisher in US; bought controlling interest in *New York Post,* 1939; responsible for turning it into a tabloid with scandal, glamour, columnists; sold to Rupert Murdoch, 1976.
b. Mar 11, 1903 in New York, New York
d. Aug 30, 1989 in New York, New York
Source: *AmAu&B; AnObit 1989; BiDAmBL 83; BiDAmNC; BioAmW; BioIn 4, 5, 7, 8, 10, 11, 16, 19; CelR; ConAu 114, 121, 129; CurBio 45, 65, 89, 89N; DcLB 127; EncAJ; EncTwCJ; ForWC 70; GoodHs; IntWW 74, 75, 76, 77, 78, 79, 80; InWom, SUP; LegTOT; LibW; NewYTBS 76, 89; WhoAm 74, 76; WhoAmW 58, 61, 64, 66, 68, 70, 72, 74, 75, 77; WhoE 74, 75, 77; WhoWor 74; WhoWorJ 72, 78; WorAl*

Schiff, Jacob Henry
American. Philanthropist
His banking syndicates played major role in railroad, industrial mergers, 1890s; created Semitic Museum at Harvard.
b. Jan 10, 1847 in Frankfurt am Main, Germany
d. Sep 25, 1920
Source: *AmBi; BiDAmBL 83; BioIn 5, 8, 9, 11, 12, 14, 15, 17, 19, 21; DcAmB; DcNAA; EncAB-H 1974, 1996; EncABHB 6; HarEnUS; McGEWB; NatCAB 13; WhAm 1*

Schiffer, Claudia
German. Model
Model noted for her physical similarity to Brigitte Bardot.
b. Aug 24, 1971 in Dusseldorf, Germany
Source: *BioIn 16; IntWW 93*

Schifrin, Lalo Claudio
Argentine. Composer
Wrote for films, TV; four Grammys include score for TV's "Mission Impossible."
b. Jun 21, 1932 in Buenos Aires, Argentina
Source: *Baker 84; BiDAmM; BioIn 8, 9; ConTFT 5; HalFC 88; IntMPA 84, 92; NewAmDM; NewGrDA 86; NewGrDJ 88; NewGrDM 80; OxCPMus; PenEncP; RkOn 82; WhoAm 82, 88; WhoEnt 92; WorEFlm*

Schifter, Peter Mark
American. Conductor
Has been guest director of operas in Washington, DC; Seattle; Philadelphia; and other US cities.
b. 1950 in Westfield, New Jersey
d. Sep 10, 1993 in New York, New York
Source: *BioIn 12; WhoAmM 83*

Schikaneder, Emanuel
[Johann Jakob Schikaneder]
Austrian. Producer, Actor, Librettist
Collaborated with Mozart on *Die Zauberflote,* 1791.
b. Sep 1, 1748 in Straubing, Austria
d. Sep 21, 1812 in Vienna, Austria
Source: *BioIn 9; NewEOp 71; OxCMus*

Schildkraut, Joseph
American. Actor
Won Oscar, 1937, for *The Life of Emile Zola;* son of Rudolph.
b. Mar 22, 1896 in Vienna, Austria
d. Jan 21, 1964 in New York, New York
Source: *BiE&WWA; BioIn 10; CurBio 56, 64; DcAmB S7; EncAB-A 35; FamA&A; FilmgC; ForYSC; MotPP; MovMk; NotNAT A; TwYS; WhAm 4; WhoHol B; WhScrn 74, 77, 83; WhThe; WorAl; WorAlBi*

Schildkraut, Rudolph
American. Actor
Silent films include *Turkish Delight; The King of Kings,* 1927.
b. 1865 in Constantinople, Turkey
d. Jul 30, 1930 in Los Angeles, California
Source: *Film 1; FilmEn; NotNAT B; TwYS; WhoHol B; WhScrn 74, 77, 83*

Schiller, Friedrich von
[Johann Christoph Friedrich von Schiller]
German. Author, Dramatist
Leading German playwright; wrote historical drama *Wilhelm Tell,* 1804.
b. Nov 10, 1759 in Marbach, Germany
d. May 9, 1805 in Weimar, Germany
Source: *AtlBL; Baker 78, 84; BbD; Benet 87; BiD&SB; BioIn 1, 2, 3, 4, 5, 6, 7, 9, 10, 11, 13; BlkwCE; CasWL; CelCen; ChhPo, S1, S2; CnThe; CyWA 58; DcArts; DcBiPP; DcEnL; DcEuL; EncWT; Ent; EuAu; EuWr 5; EvEuW; GrFLW; LegTOT; LinLib L, S; LuthC 75; McGEWB; McGEWD 72, 84; MetOEnc; NewC; NewCBEL; NewEOp 71; NewGrDM 80; NotNAT A, B; OxCEng 67, 85, 95; OxCFr; OxCGer 76; OxCPhil; OxCThe 67, 83; OxDcOp; PenC EUR; RAdv 14, 13-2; RComWL; REn; REnWD; WorAlBi; WrPh*

Schiller, Karl (August Fritz)
German. Government Official
Directed reconstruction of Hamburg after the Second World War.
b. Apr 24, 1911
d. Dec 26, 1994 in Hamburg, Germany
Source: *BioIn 8, 9, 10, 20, 21; CurBio 71, 95N; IntWW 74, 75, 76, 77, 78, 79, 80, 81, 82, 83, 89, 91, 93; IntYB 78, 79, 80, 81, 82; Who 74, 82, 83, 85, 88, 90, 92, 94; WhoWor 74, 78, 80, 82*

Schilling, Peter
German. Singer
First single, ''Major Tom (Coming Home),'' was int'l hit, 1983.
b. Jan 28, 1956 in Stuttgart, Germany (West)
Source: *RkOn 85*

Schillinger, Joseph
American. Composer, Musician
Composers Gershwin, Levant and others used his musical system.
b. Sep 1, 1895 in Kharkov, Russia
d. Mar 23, 1943 in New York, New York
Source: *Baker 78, 84; BiDAmM; BioIn 1, 2, 11; ConAmC 76, 82; CurBio 43; DcAmB S3; DcCM; EncAB-A 11; NewAmDM; NewGrDA 86; NewGrDM 80; OxCMus*

Schillings, Max von
German. Conductor, Composer
Wrote opera, *Mona Lisa,* 1915.
b. Apr 19, 1868 in Duren, Germany
d. Jul 23, 1933 in Berlin, Germany
Source: *Baker 78, 84, 92; MetOEnc; NewEOp 71; NewGrDM 80; NewGrDO; OxCGer 76, 86; OxCMus; OxDcOp; PenDiMP A*

Schilt, Jan
American. Astronomer
Invented Schilt photometer, which measures distance of stars from Earth.
b. Feb 23, 1894 in Gouda, Netherlands
d. Jan 9, 1982 in Englewood, New Jersey
Source: *AnObit 1982; BioIn 12, 13; NewYTBS 82; WhAm 8*

Schindler, Alexander Moshe
American. Religious Leader
Leader in nat. Jewish, Zionist organizations since early 1960s; pres., Union of American Hebrew Congregations, 1973—.
b. Oct 4, 1925 in Munich, Germany
Source: *BioIn 15; CurBio 87; IntWW 89, 91, 93; NewYTBE 73; WhoAm 76, 78, 80, 82, 84, 86, 88, 90, 92, 94, 95, 96, 97; WhoE 74, 75, 77, 86, 89, 91, 95, 97; WhoRel 75, 77, 85, 92; WhoWor 78, 80, 82; WhoWorJ 72, 78*

Schine, G(erard) David
American. Businessman
Music, hotel exec., who produced *The French Connection,* 1971; directed special govt. investigations, 1952-53.
b. Sep 11, 1927 in Gloversville, New York
d. Jun 19, 1996 in Burbank, California
Source: *BioIn 3, 8, 10, 11; EncMcCE; PolProf E; St&PR 84, 91; WhAm 11; WhoAm 74, 76, 78, 80, 82, 84, 86, 88, 90, 92, 94, 95, 96; WhoWor 74*

Schioetz, Aksel
''The Voice of Denmark''
Danish. Singer, Educator
Broadcast daily patriotic songs defying Nazi occupation during WW II.
b. Sep 1, 1906 in Roskilde, Denmark
d. Apr 19, 1975 in Copenhagen, Denmark
Source: *ConAu 111; CurBio 49, 75; MusSN*

Schipa, Tito
Italian. Opera Singer
Tenor with NY Met., 1932-35, 1940; noted for Rossini, Bellini roles.
b. Jan 2, 1889 in Lecce, Italy
d. Dec 16, 1965 in New York, New York
Source: *Baker 78, 84; BioIn 1, 4, 6, 7, 11, 12, 16, 18, 21; LegTOT; MusSN; NewEOp 71; WhAm 4; WhoHol B; WhScrn 74, 77, 83*

Schippers, Thomas
American. Conductor
Youngest ever to lead NY Met., 1955; conducted record number of Met. premieres; led Cincinnati Orchestra, 1970-77.
b. Mar 9, 1930 in Kalamazoo, Michigan
d. Dec 16, 1977 in New York, New York
Source: *Baker 78, 84, 92; BiDAmM; BioIn 3, 4, 5, 6, 7, 8, 9, 10, 11, 21; BlueB 76; BriBkM 80; CelR; CmOp; CurBio 70, 78, 78N; DcAmB S10; IntDcOp; IntWW 74, 75, 76, 77; IntWWM 77, 80; MetOEnc; MusSN; NewAmDM; NewEOp 71; NewGrDA 86; NewGrDM 80; NewGrDO; NewYTBS 77; OxDcOp; PenDiMP; WhAm 7; WhoAm 74, 76, 78; WhoMus 72; WhoMW 74, 76; WhoOp 76; WhoWor 74; WorAl; WorAlBi*

Schirmer, Gustave
German. Publisher, Musician
Founded Schirmer music publishing co., 1866; published Wagner's works.
b. Sep 19, 1829 in Konigsee, Germany
d. Aug 6, 1893 in Eisenach, Germany
Source: *DcAmB; WebAB 74; WhAm HS*

Schirra, Wally
[Walter Marty Schirra, Jr]
American. Astronaut, Businessman
Pilot, Gemini 6, 1965; commander, Apollo 7, 1968.
b. Mar 12, 1923 in Hackensack, New Jersey
Source: *AmMWSc 73P; BioIn 6, 7, 8, 9, 10, 13, 16; CurBio 66; FacFETw; IntWW 74, 75, 76, 77; LegTOT; WebAMB; WhoAm 74, 76, 78, 80, 82, 84, 86, 88, 90, 92, 94, 95, 96, 97; WhoFI 96; WhoScEn 94, 96; WhoSpc; WhoTech 89; WhoWest 96; WhoWor 74, 78, 80, 82, 84, 87, 89, 91, 93, 95, 96, 97; WorAl; WorAlBi*

Schisgal, Murray Joseph
American. Dramatist
Avant-garde playwright with comic-sad heroes: *Luv,* 1963, ran on Broadway for 900 performances; sreenplays include *Tootsie,* 1982.
b. Nov 25, 1926 in New York, New York
Source: *BiE&WWA; BioIn 15; CnMD SUP; ConDr 82, 88; ConLC 6; ConTFT 5; CroCD; CurBio 68; DrAPF 87, 91; EncAHmr; IntAu&W 86; McGEWD 72; ModAL; ModWD; NotNAT; WhoAm 86,*

90, 97; WhoEnt 92; WorAu 1950; WrDr 86, 92

Schlafly, Phyllis Stewart
American. Anti-Feminist, Author, Politician
Outspoken ultra-conservative opponent of ERA; wrote many books championing conservatism, warning against communism: *A Choice, Not an Echo,* 1964.
b. Aug 15, 1924 in Saint Louis, Missouri
Source: *AmSocL; AuNews 1; BiDAmNC; BioIn 13, 14, 15; BioNews 74; ConAu 26NR; CurBio 78; DcAmC; EncWB; IntAu&W 89, 91, 93; InWom SUP; NewYTBS 80; PolProf NF; WhoAm 76, 78, 80, 82, 84, 86, 88, 90, 92, 94, 95, 96, 97; WhoAmP 73, 89, 91, 93, 95; WhoAmW 58, 61, 79, 81, 83, 85, 87, 89, 91, 93, 95, 97; WhoEnt 92; WhoMW 84, 86, 88, 90, 92; WhoUSWr 88; WhoWrEP 89, 92, 95*

Schlamme, Martha
Austrian. Singer, Actor
Known for singing folk songs in 12 languages; made Broadway debut, 1968, in *Fiddler on the Roof.*
b. 1930 in Vienna, Austria
d. Oct 6, 1985 in Jamestown, New York
Source: *BioIn 6, 7; CurBio 64, 86; InWom; WhoAm 74*

Schlegel, Friedrich von
[Karl Wilhelm Friedrich von Schlegel]
German. Critic
Wrote history of literature; studies of ancient Indian language; wrote novel *Lucinde,* 1799.
b. Mar 10, 1772 in Hannover, Germany
d. Jan 12, 1829 in Dresden, Germany
Source: *AtlBL; BbD; BiD&SB; BiDTran; BioIn 5, 7, 14, 16, 17; BlkwCE; CasWL; DcArts; DcBiPP; DcCathB; DcEuL; EuAu; EuWr 5; LinLib L; LuthC 75; McGDA; McGEWB; NewC; NewCBEL; OxCEng 67, 85, 95; OxCGer 76, 86; PenC EUR; REn; REnWD; RfGWoL 95; WorAl; WorAlBi*

Schleicher, Kurt von
German. Political Leader
Chancellor of Germany, 1932-33; succeeded by Hitler.
b. Apr 7, 1882 in Brandenburg, Germany
d. Jun 30, 1934 in Berlin, Germany
Source: *BioIn 5, 14; DcTwHis; EncTR, 91; NewCol 75; REn; WebBD 83*

Schleiden, Matthias Jakob
German. Botanist
Study of plant structure established that plants are made up of cells; theorized importance of nucleus in mitosis.
b. Apr 5, 1804 in Hamburg, Germany
d. Jun 23, 1881 in Frankfurt am Main, Germany
Source: *AsBiEn; BiESc; BioIn 4, 12, 14; DcScB; LarDcSc; WorAlBi*

Schleiermacher, Friedrich Ernst Daniel
German. Theologian, Philosopher
One of the founders of modern Protestant theology.
b. Nov 21, 1768 in Breslau, Germany
d. Feb 12, 1834 in Berlin, Germany
Source: *Benet 87; BioIn 2, 7, 8, 9, 11, 12; CelCen; DcBiPP; EncUnb; LinLib L, S; McGEWB*

Schlein, Miriam
[Miriam Weiss]
American. Children's Author
Writer since 1952: *Giraffe: The Silent Giant,* 1976; *The Boy Who Became Pharaoh,* 1979.
b. Jun 6, 1926 in New York, New York
Source: *AuBYP 2, 3; BioIn 5, 6, 7, 9; ChlLR 41; ConAu 1R, 2NR, 52NR; CurBio 59; IntAu&W 91; InWom; MorJA; PenNWW A; SmATA 2, 87; TwCChW 89; WhoAmW 58, 61, 91; WrDr 92*

Schlesinger, Arthur M(eier), Jr.
American. Historian, Author
Special asst. to presidents Kennedy, Johnson, 1961-64; wrote *A Thousand Days,* 1965; *Robert Kennedy and His Times,* 1978.
b. Oct 15, 1917 in Columbus, Ohio
Source: *AuNews 1; Benet 87, 96; BenetAL 91; BioIn 1, 2, 3, 4, 5, 6, 7, 8, 10, 11, 12, 13, 14, 15; ColdWar 2; ConAu 1NR, 1R, 28NR; ConLC 84; CurBio 46, 79; EncAB-H 1996; EncAI&E; EncWB; IntAu&W 91; IntWW 89; MajTwCW; NewYTBS 79; OhA&B; OxCAmL 65; PenC AM; PolProf E, J, K, T; RAdv 14, 13-3; REn; REnAL; SmATA 61; WebAB 79; Who 92; WhoAm 86, 90, 97; WhoE 97; WhoUSWr 88; WhoWor 91, 97; WhoWrEP 89; WorAlBi; WrDr 92*

Schlesinger, Frank
American. Astronomer, Educator
Developed method for determining stellar distances by photography.
b. May 11, 1871 in New York, New York
d. Jul 10, 1943 in Old Lyme, Connecticut
Source: *BioIn 1, 20; CurBio 43; DcAmB S3; DcScB; InSci; NatCAB 14, 32; WhAm 2; WhNAA*

Schlesinger, James Rodney
American. Government Official
Secretary of Defense, 1973-75; Energy, 1977-79.
b. Feb 15, 1929 in New York, New York
Source: *AmMWSc 73S; BioIn 9, 10, 11, 12, 14; CngDr 74; ColdWar 2; CurBio 73; EncAI&E; EncWB; IntWW 74, 75, 76, 77, 78, 79, 80, 81, 82, 83, 89, 91, 93; IntYB 78, 79, 80, 81, 82; NewYTBE 71, 72; NewYTBS 74, 76; Ward 77D; WhoAm 74, 76, 78, 80, 82, 84, 86, 88, 90, 92, 94, 95, 96, 97; WhoAmP 73, 75, 77, 79, 81, 83, 85, 87, 89, 91, 93, 95; WhoE 77, 79, 81, 83; WhoFI 79; WhoGov 72, 75, 77; WhoSSW 73, 75, 76; WhoWor 74, 78, 80, 82, 84, 87, 89, 91, 93, 95, 96, 97; WorAlBi*

Schlesinger, John Richard
English. Director
Won Oscar, 1969, for *Midnight Cowboy.*
b. Feb 16, 1926 in London, England
Source: *BiDFilm; BioIn 16; CurBio 70; DcFM; FilmgC; HalFC 88; IntDcF 2-2; IntMPA 92; IntWW 74, 75, 76, 77, 78, 79, 80, 81, 82, 83, 89, 91, 93; MovMk; NewGrDO; OxCFilm; Who 74, 82, 83, 85, 88, 90, 92, 94; WhoAm 78, 80, 82, 84, 86, 88, 90, 92, 94, 95, 96, 97; WhoEnt 92; WhoThe 81; WhoWor 74, 76, 78, 82, 84, 87, 89, 91, 93, 95, 96, 97; WorEFlm*

Schlessinger, David
American. Businessman
Founded Encore Books, discount bookstore chain, 1973.
b. Mar 3, 1955 in Philadelphia, Pennsylvania
Source: *ConNews 85-1*

Schlessinger, Laura
American. Author, Physiologist, Radio Performer
Host of "The Dr. Laura Schlessinger Show," 1990—; author of *Courage, and Conscience,* 1996.
b. c. 1947 in New York, New York
Source: *ConAu 152; News 96, 96-3*

Schley, Winfield Scott
American. Naval Officer
Led battle of Santiago, Spanish-American War, 1898; controversy arose about credit of battle between him and W T Sampson.
b. Oct 9, 1839 in Frederick County, Maryland
d. Oct 2, 1909 in New York, New York
Source: *Alli SUP; AmBi; ApCAB, SUP, X; BiDSA; BioIn 1, 13; DcAmAu; DcAmB; DcAmMiB; DcNAA; HarEnMi; HarEnUS; LinLib L, S; NatCAB 4, 9; OxCShps; TwCBDA; WebAMB; WhAm 1*

Schlicter, Art(hur E)
American. Football Player
Quarterback, Baltimore/Indianapolis, 1982, 1984-85; suspended for gambling, 1983.
b. Apr 25, 1960 in Washington Court House, Ohio
Source: *BioIn 15, 16; FootReg 85*

Schlieffen, Alfred, Graf von
German. Military Leader
WW I field marshal; developed "swinging door" plan to crush French resistance.
b. Feb 28, 1833 in Berlin, Germany
d. Jan 4, 1913 in Berlin, Germany
Source: *NewCol 75; WebBD 83; WhoMilH 76; WorAl; WorAlBi*

Schliemann, Heinrich
German. Archaeologist
Excavated cities for remains of Homeric age; known for discovery of ancient Troy.
b. Jan 6, 1822 in Neubuckow, Germany
d. Dec 26, 1890 in Naples, Italy
Source: *Alli SUP; AmBi; BbD; Benet 87, 96; BiD&SB; BioIn 1, 2, 4, 5, 6, 7, 8, 9, 10, 11, 12, 13, 14, 16, 17, 19, 20, 21; CelCen; CmCal; DcScB; InSci; LegTOT; McGDA; McGEWB; NewC; OxCClL, 89; OxCGer 76, 86; REn; WhAm HS; WhDW; WorAl; WorAlBi*

Schlink, Frederick John
American. Consultant
Headed Consumers' Research until 1983; wrote *Eat, Drink and Be Wary*, 1935.
b. Oct 26, 1891
d. Jan 15, 1995 in Phillpsburg, New Jersey
Source: *AmAu&B; BioIn 8; ConAu 65, 147; CurBio 95N; InSci; WhE&EA; WhNAA; WhoAm 74, 76, 78, 80*

Schlondorff, Volker
German. Director, Screenwriter
Directed, wrote screen adaptation of *The Tin Drum*, 1980; won best foreign film Oscar.
b. Mar 31, 1939 in Wiesbaden, Germany
Source: *BiDFilm, 81, 94; BioIn 12, 13, 14, 16; CurBio 83; EncEurC; FilmEn; HalFC 84, 88; IntDcF 1-2, 2-2; IntMPA 81, 82, 84, 86, 88, 92, 94, 96; IntWW 89, 91, 93; MiSFD 9; OxCFilm; WhoWor 84, 87, 89, 91, 93, 95, 96; WorFDir 2*

Schlumberger, Jean
French. Jeweler
Had own salon at Tiffany's, 1956-87; set well-known 128-carat Tiffany diamond; prominent jewelry designer.
b. Jun 24, 1907 in Muhlhausen, Germany
d. Aug 29, 1987 in Paris, France
Source: *AnObit 1987; CelR; EncFash; FacFETw; NewYTBS 87; St&PR 75; WhoFash 88; WorFshn*

Schlusnus, Heinrich
German. Opera Singer
Baritone with Berlin Opera, 1917-45; noted as Lieder singer, had several US tours.
b. Aug 6, 1888 in Braubach, Germany
d. Jun 19, 1952 in Frankfurt, Germany (West)
Source: *Baker 78, 84, 92; BioIn 2; CmOp; IntDcOp; MetOEnc; NewEOp 71; NewGrDM 80; NewGrDO; OxDcOp; PenDiMP*

Schmedes, Erik
Danish. Opera Singer
One of leading heroic tenors of his day; with Vienna Opera, 1898-1924.
b. Aug 6, 1866 in Gjentofte, Denmark
d. Mar 23, 1931 in Vienna, Austria
Source: *Baker 84; CmOp; NewEOp 71; NewGrDM 80; NewGrDO; OxDcOp; PenDiMP*

Schmeling, Max(imilian)
"The Black Uhlan"
German. Boxer
World heavyweight champ, 1930-32; KO'd Joe Louis, 1936; Hall of Fame, 1970.
b. Sep 28, 1905 in Brandenburg, Germany
Source: *BioIn 1, 2, 5, 7, 8, 9, 10, 11, 14, 16, 19; BoxReg; EncTR, 91; FacFETw; LegTOT; What 1; WhoBox 74; WhoHol 92, A; WorAl*

Schmemann, Alexander
Russian. Clergy, Theologian
Eastern Orthodox leader; promoted religious freedom in Soviet Union.
b. 1921 in Estonia, Union of Soviet Socialist Republics
d. Dec 13, 1983 in Crestwood, New York
Source: *AnObit 1983; BioIn 13, 19; ConAu 111, 117; DcEcMov; EncARH; NewYTBS 83; RelLAm 91*

Schmid, Eduard
[Kasimir Edschmid]
German. Author
Wrote first German expressionist novellas.
b. Oct 5, 1890 in Darmstadt, Germany
d. Aug 31, 1966 in Vulpera, Switzerland
Source: *BioIn 1, 2, 7, 16; CasWL; ClDMEL 47, 80; ConAu 113; DcLB 56; EncWL; ModGL; OxCGer 76, 86; PenC EUR*

Schmidt, Alfred
German. Hostage
Engineer in Lebanon seized by Strugglers for Freedom January 21, 1987 and released September 7, 1987.
Source: *AmEA 74; WhoWor 80*

Schmidt, Benno Charles, Jr.
American. University Administrator, Lawyer
Pres., Yale U, 1986-92; pres., CEO Edison Project, national private school system, 1992—.
b. Mar 20, 1942 in Washington, District of Columbia
Source: *CurBio 86; IntWW 91; NewYTBS 85; Who 90, 92, 94; WhoAm 86, 88, 90, 92, 94, 95, 96; WhoAmL 87, 90; WhoE 86, 89, 91; WhoSSW 95, 97; WhoWor 89, 91, 93, 95; WorAlBi; WrDr 92, 94, 96*

Schmidt, Helmut Heinrich Waldemar
German. Political Leader
Chancellor, W Germany, 1974-82; author of several books on political affairs.
b. Dec 23, 1918 in Hamburg, Germany
Source: *BioIn 16; ColdWar 2; CurBio 74; FacFETw; IntWW 76, 77, 91; IntYB 79; NewYTBS 74, 76, 77; Who 85, 92; WhoWor 84; WorAlBi*

Schmidt, Joe
[Joseph Paul Schmidt]
American. Football Player, Football Coach
Ten-time all-pro middle linebacker, Detroit, 1953-65; head coach, Detroit, 1967-72; Hall of Fame, 1973.
b. Jan 18, 1932 in Pittsburgh, Pennsylvania
Source: *BiDAmSp FB; BioIn 5, 6, 8, 17; LegTOT; WhoFtbl 74*

Schmidt, Mike
[Michael Jack Schmidt]
American. Baseball Player
Infielder, Philadelphia, 1972-89; led NL in home runs eight times, RBIs four ti mes; NL MVP, 1980-81, 86.
b. Sep 27, 1949 in Dayton, Ohio
Source: *Ballpl 90; BaseEn 88; BaseReg 87, 88; BiDAmSp BB; BioIn 10, 11, 12, 13, 14, 15, 16, 17, 18, 20; ConAu 126; FacFETw; LegTOT; News 88-3; NewYTBS 74, 89; WhoAm 80, 82, 84, 86, 88, 90, 92, 94, 95, 96, 97; WhoE 86, 89, 95; WhoSpor; WorAl; WorAlBi*

Schmidt, Milt(on Conrad)
Canadian. Hockey Player, Hockey Coach, Hockey Executive
Center, Boston, 1936-55; won Art Ross Trophy, 1940, Hart Trophy, 1951; coach, Boston, 1955-66, GM, 1967-73; Hall of Fame, 1961.
b. Mar 5, 1918 in Kitchener, Ontario, Canada
Source: *BioIn 9, 10; HocEn; WhoAm 76; WhoE 74, 75; WhoHcky 73*

Schmidt, Tim(othy B)
[Poco; The Eagles]
American. Singer, Musician
Joined The Eagles, 1977, replacing Randy Meisner.
b. Oct 30, 1947 in Oakland, California
Source: *RkOn 85*

Schmidt-Isserstedt, Hans
German. Conductor
Led int'l orchestras, 1935-60s; had US debut, 1963.
b. May 5, 1900 in Berlin, Germany
d. May 28, 1973 in Hamburg, Germany (West)
Source: *Baker 78, 84, 92; BioIn 9, 10; BriBkM 80; CmOp; NewAmDM; NewEOp 71; NewGrDM 80; NewGrDO; NewYTBE 73; OxDcOp; PenDiMP; WhAm 6; WhoMus 72*

Schmidt-Rottluf, Karl
German. Artist
Helped form German Expressionist group, Die Brucke, 1905; drew vividly colored landscapes, nudes.
b. Dec 1, 1884 in Rottluff, Germany
d. Aug 9, 1976 in Wiesbaden, Germany (West)
Source: *ConArt 83; McGDA; OxCArt; OxCGer 76; WhoWor 74*

Schmiechen, Richard Kurt
American. Producer
Won Academy Award for documentary *The Times of Harvey Milk,* 1984.
b. Jul 10, 1947 in Saint Louis, Missouri
d. Apr 7, 1993 in California

Schmitt, Bernadotte Everly
American. Author, Educator
Modern history authority; won Pulitzer, 1931, for *The Coming of War,* 1914.
b. May 19, 1886 in Strasburg, Virginia
d. Mar 22, 1969 in Alexandria, Virginia
Source: *AmAu&B; BioIn 4, 5, 8, 10; ConAu 1R, 103; CurBio 42, 69; NatCAB 55; ObitOF 79; OhA&B; OxCAmL 65; TwCA, SUP; WhE&EA; WhNAA*

Schmitt, Gladys
American. Author, Editor
Wrote historical, biographical, biblical works with love as recurring theme.
b. May 31, 1909 in Pittsburgh, Pennsylvania
d. Oct 3, 1972 in Pittsburgh, Pennsylvania
Source: *AmAu&B; AmNov; AmWomWr; Au&Wr 71; BenetAL 91; BioIn 1, 2, 3, 4, 9, 12; ConAu 1R, 2NR, 37R; CurBio 43, 72, 72N; OxCAmL 65, 83, 95; REnAL; TwCA SUP; WhAm 5; WhoAmW 58, 64, 66, 68, 70, 72, 74*

Schmitt, Harrison Hagan
American. Politician, Astronaut
Conservative Rep. senator from NM, 1977-83; piloted lunar module, Apollo 17, 1972.
b. Jul 3, 1935 in Santa Rita, New Mexico
Source: *AmMWSc 95; BiDrUSC 89; BioIn 10, 11, 12, 13, 14; CngDr 77, 79; CurBio 74; FacFETw; IntWW 83, 91; NewYTBE 72; NewYTBS 79; WhoAm 78, 80, 82, 84, 86, 88, 90, 92, 94, 95, 96, 97; WhoAmP 77, 79, 81, 83, 85, 87, 89, 91, 93, 95; WhoEng 88; WhoGov 72, 75, 77; WhoScEn 94, 96; WhoSSW 73, 75, 76; WhoWest 78, 80, 82; WhoWor 80, 82; WorAlBi*

Schmoke, Kurt L(idell)
American. Politician
Mayor of Baltimore, 1987—.
b. Dec 1, 1949 in Baltimore, Maryland
Source: *BioIn 15, 16; ConBlB 1; CurBio 95; InB&W 85; NegAl 89A; WhoAm 90; WhoAmP 89; WhoBlA 92; WhoE 91*

Schnabel, Artur
American. Pianist
Had US debut, 1921; interpreter of Beethoven, Bach.
b. Apr 17, 1882 in Lipnik, Austria
d. Aug 15, 1951 in Axenstein, Switzerland
Source: *Baker 78, 84, 92; BioIn 1, 2, 3, 4, 6, 7, 9, 10, 11, 12, 16, 21; BriBkM 80; CurBio 42, 51; DcAmB S5; DcArts; FacFETw; LegTOT; MusMk; MusSN; NewAmDM; NewGrDA 86; NewGrDM 80; NotTwCP; ObitT 1951; OxCMus; PenDiMP; REn; WhAm 3*

Schnabel, Julian
American. Artist
Neo-expressionist whose paintings are encrusted with crockery, plaster; had one-man show, NYC, 1981.
b. Oct 26, 1951 in New York, New York
Source: *AmArt; BioIn 12, 13, 14, 15; ConArt 83, 89, 96; CurBio 83; DcCAA 88, 94; DcCAr 81; IntWW 91, 93; LegTOT; News 97-1; NewYTBS 84; PrintW 85; WhoAm 84, 86, 88, 90, 92, 94, 95, 96; WhoAmA 86, 89, 91, 93; WhoE 85, 86; WhoWor 97; WorArt 1980*

Schnabel, Karl Ulrich
Austrian. Musician
Performed duo-piano concerts with wife, Helen Fogel, 1939-74; son of Artur.
b. Aug 6, 1909 in Berlin, Germany
Source: *Baker 78, 84, 92; IntWWM 77, 80, 85, 90; NewGrDM 80; PenDiMP; WhoAm 74, 76, 78, 80, 82, 84, 86, 88, 90, 92, 94, 95; WhoEnt 92; WhoMus 72; WorAl; WorAlBi*

Schneerson, Menachem Mendel
American. Religious Leader
Spiritual leader of orthodox Lubavitch Sect, most powerful branch of Hasidism.
b. Apr 18, 1902 in Nikolayev, Russia
d. Jun 12, 1994 in New York, New York
Source: *BioIn 4, 13; CurBio 83, 94N; EncARH; News 92, 94; OrJudAm; RelLAm 91; WhoAmJ 80; WhoRel 85; WhoWorJ 78*

Schneider, Alan
[Abram Leopoldovich]
American. Director
Won Tony, 1962, for *Who's Afraid of Virginia Woolf.*
b. Dec 12, 1917 in Kharkov, Union of Soviet Socialist Republics
d. May 3, 1984 in London, England
Source: *AnObit 1984; BiE&WWA; BioIn 8, 9, 13; BlueB 76; CamGWoT; CelR; ConTFT 1; CurBio 69, 84, 84N; EncWT; FacFETw; GrStDi; LesBEnT; NewYTBS 84; NewYTET; NotNAT; OxCAmT 84; TheaDir; WhAm 8, 11; WhoAm 82; WhoThe 72, 77, 81; WhoWor 84, 87, 89, 91*

Schneider, Alexander
American. Musician
First to present all of Bach's unaccompanied violin works in concert; often accompanied Casals.
b. Oct 21, 1908 in Vilna, Russia
d. Feb 4, 1993 in New York, New York
Source: *Baker 78, 84; BiDAmM; BioIn 2, 8, 9, 10, 11, 14, 15, 18, 19; BriBkM 80; CurBio 76, 93N; IntWWM 90; NewAmDM; NewGrDA 86; NewGrDM 80; NewYTBS 93; PenDiMP; WhAm 11; WhoAm 74, 76, 78, 80, 82, 84, 86, 88, 90, 92; WhoWor 74*

Schneider, Bert
American. Producer
Won Oscar, 1974, for documentary *Hearts and Minds.*
b. 1933?
Source: *HalFC 88; NewYTBS 75; WhoAm 76; WhoAmA 76*

Schneider, Herman
American. Children's Author
Writes science books for juveniles with wife Nina: *Let's Find Out about the Weather,* 1956.
b. May 31, 1905 in Kreschov, Poland
Source: *Au&Wr 71; AuBYP 2, 3; BioIn 6, 7, 10; ConAu 16NR, 29R; IntAu&W 76, 77, 82; MorJA; SmATA 7*

Schneider, John
American. Actor, Singer
Played Bo Duke on TV series "The Dukes of Hazard."
b. Apr 8, 1954 in Mount Kisco, New York
Source: *BgBkCoM; BioIn 12; ConTFT 5; HarEnCM 87; IntMPA 92, 94, 96; LegTOT; VarWW 85; WhoHol 92*

Schneider, Maria
French. Actor
Starred with Marlon Brando in controversial film *Last Tango in Paris,* 1972.
b. Mar 27, 1952 in Paris, France
Source: *BioIn 9, 10, 17; FilmEn; HalFC 80, 84, 88; ItaFilm; LegTOT; MovMk; NewYTBE 73; WhoHol 92, A*

Schneider, Nina
[Mrs. Herman Schneider]
American. Children's Author
Writes juvenile books with husband; first adult novel *The Woman Who Lived in a Prologue,* 1980.
b. Jan 29, 1913 in Antwerp, Belgium
Source: *Au&Wr 71; AuBYP 2, 3; BioIn 6, 7, 9; ConAu 15NR, 29R; DrAPF 80, 87, 91; MorJA; SmATA 2; WhoAmW 61, 64*

Schneider, Romy
[Rosemarie Albach-Retty]
Austrian. Actor
Starred in *The Cardinal,* 1963.
b. Sep 23, 1938 in Vienna, Austria
d. May 29, 1982 in Paris, France
Source: *AnObit 1982; BiDFilm, 81, 94; BioIn 4, 6, 7, 11, 12, 13, 17; ConTFT 2; CurBio 65, 82, 82N; DcArts; EncEurC; FilmAG WE; FilmEn; FilmgC; ForYSC; HalFC 80, 84, 88; IntDcF 1-3, 2-3; IntMPA 75, 76, 77, 78, 79, 80, 81, 82; InWom, SUP; ItaFilm; LegTOT; MotPP; MovMk; NewYTBS 82; OxCFilm; WhoAm 74; WhoAmW 70, 72; WhoHol A; WhoWor 74; WorAl; WorEFlm*

Schneirla, Theodore Christian
American. Animal Expert
Animal psychologist; studied the behavior patterns of army ants.
b. Jul 23, 1902 in Bay City, Michigan
d. Aug 20, 1968 in New York, New York
Source: *BiDPsy; BioIn 4, 8; CurBio 55, 68; InSci; ObitOF 79; WhAm 5*

Schnellenberger, Howard Leslie
American. Football Coach
Head coach, U of Miami, 1979-83; won nat. championship, 1983.
b. Mar 13, 1934 in Saint Meinrad, Indiana
Source: *BioIn 13, 14; NewYTBS 85; WhoAm 88; WhoSSW 84, 86, 88*

Schnering, Otto
American. Candy Manufacturer
Made Baby Ruth candy bar, 1910s, named for Pres. Cleveland's daughter.
b. Oct 9, 1891 in Chicago, Illinois
d. Jan 19, 1953 in Cary, Illinois
Source: *BioIn 2, 3, 4; Entr; NatCAB 41; WhAm 3; WorAl*

Schnittke, Alfred
Russian. Composer
Original experimental composer; works defy categorization.
b. Nov 24, 1934 in Engels, Union of Soviet Socialist Republics
Source: *Baker 78, 84; BioIn 18, 19; ConCom 92; CurBio 92; IntWW 89, 91, 93; IntWWM 90; PenDiMP A; Who 92, 94*

Schnitzler, Arthur
Austrian. Author, Dramatist
Plays are psychological observations, mostly with erotic themes: *La Ronde,* 1900.
b. May 15, 1862 in Vienna, Austria
d. Oct 21, 1931 in Vienna, Austria
Source: *AtlBL; Benet 87, 96; BioIn 1, 4, 6, 9, 10, 11, 13, 18; CamGWoT; CasWL; ClDMEL 47, 80; CnMD; CnThe; ConAu 104; CyWA 89; DcArts; DcLB 81, 118; Dis&D; EncWL 2, 3; EncWT; Ent; EuWr 8; EvEuW; FacFETw; FilmgC; GrFLW; HalFC 80, 84, 88; IntDcT 2; LinLib L, S; LngCTC; MajMD 1; McGEWB; McGEWD 72, 84; ModGL; ModWD; NewCBEL; NotNAT A, B; Novels; OxCGer 76, 86; OxCThe 67, 83; PenC EUR; RAdv 14, 13-2; REn; REnWD; RfGShF; RfGWoL 95; ShSCr 15; TwCA, SUP; TwCLC 4; WhDW; WhE&EA; WhoLA; WorAl; WorAlBi*

Schnorr, Ludwig von Carolsfeld
German. Opera Singer
Leading tenor with Dresden Opera, 1860s; created role of Tristan in Wagner's opera, 1865.
b. Jul 2, 1836 in Munich, Germany
d. Jul 21, 1865 in Dresden, Germany
Source: *Baker 84; NewEOp 71; NewGrDM 80*

Schocken, Theodore
American. Publisher
Pres., Schocken Books, Inc., 1965-76.
b. Oct 8, 1914 in Zwickau, Germany
d. Mar 20, 1975 in White Plains, New York
Source: *BioIn 10, 12; ConAu 104; DcAmB S9; NatCAB 59; NewYTBS 75; WhAm 6; WhoAm 74; WhoWor 74, 76; WhoWorJ 72*

Schoech, Othmar
Swiss. Composer, Conductor
Choral, orchestral leader, 1915-40s; song cycles include *Elegie,* 1923.
b. Sep 1, 1886 in Brunnen, Switzerland
d. Mar 8, 1957 in Zurich, Switzerland
Source: *Baker 84; BriBkM 80; NewEOp 71; NewGrDM 80; OxCMus*

Schoellkopf, Caroline Rose Hunt
American. Businesswoman
Heiress to Hunt oil fortune; richest woman in US, 1987.
b. 1923? in Texas
Source: *BioIn 12, 15; InWom SUP*

Schoenbach, Sol Israel
American. Musician
Prize-winning bassoonist; with Philadelphia Orchestra, 1937-57.
b. Mar 15, 1915 in New York, New York
Source: *NewGrDA 86; WhoAm 74, 76, 78, 80, 82, 84, 86, 88, 90; WhoAmJ 80; WhoAmM 83; WhoEnt 92*

Schoenberg, Arnold
American. Composer
Invented 12-tone musical system, 1921; wrote opera *Moses und Aron,* 1951, song cycle *Pierrot Lunaire,* 1912.
b. Sep 13, 1874 in Vienna, Austria
d. Jul 13, 1951 in Brentwood, California
Source: *ASCAP 66, 80; AtlBL; Baker 78, 84; Benet 87, 96; BioIn 14, 15, 16, 17, 19, 20; BriBkM 80; CmCal; CmOp; CnOxB; CompSN, SUP; ConAmC 76, 82; ConAu 109; CurBio 42, 51; DcAmB S5; DcCM; DcCom 77; DcCom&M 79; DcTwCC, A; EncAB-H 1974, 1996; FacFETw; IntDcOp; JeHun; LegTOT; McGEWB; MetOEnc; MusMk; NewAmDM; NewEOp 71; NewGrDA 86; NewGrDM 80; NewOxM; OxCAmH; OxCEng 85, 95; OxCGer 76; OxCMus; OxDcOp; PenDiMP A; RAdv 14, 13-3; REn; ThTwC 87; WebAB 74; WhAm 3; WhDW; WorAl; WorAlBi*

Schoenbrun, David
American. Journalist
War correspondent for CBS News, 1945-63; ABC News, 1963-79; author of seven best-selling books: *Soldiers of the Night,* 1980.
b. Mar 15, 1915 in New York, New York
d. May 23, 1988 in New York, New York
Source: *AmAu&B; BioIn 5, 6; ConAu 3NR, 49, 125; CurBio 60, 88, 88N; EncAJ; EncTwCJ; IntAu&W 91; LesBEnT; WhoAm 84; WhoWor 74; WrDr 80, 82, 84, 86, 88, 90*

Schoendienst, Red
[Albert Fred Schoendienst]
American. Baseball Player, Baseball Manager
Second baseman, 1945-63, mostly with St. Louis; known for fielding; had .289 lifetime batting average; managed St. Louis to two pennants, one World Series win, 1960s.
b. Feb 2, 1923 in Germantown, Illinois
Source: *Ballpl 90; BiDAmSp BB; BioIn 15, 19; CurBio 64; WhoAm 74, 76, 78, 90, 92, 94, 95, 96, 97; WhoProB 73; WhoSpor*

Schoenfeld, Gerald
American. Theater Owner
Chm., Shubert Organization, 1972—; owns 50 percent of Broadway's theaters.
b. 1924 in New York, New York
Source: *BioIn 15; ConNews 86-2; ConTFT 6; OxCAmT 84*

Schoen-Rene, Anna
American. Teacher
Singing teacher at Juilliard School of Music whose students included Paul Robeson.
b. Jan 12, 1864 in Koblenz, Germany
d. Nov 13, 1942 in New York, New York
Source: *Baker 92; CurBio 43; NewEOp 71*

Schofield, John McAllister
American. Military Leader
Civil War general; commander of US Army, 1888-95, succeeding Sheridan.
b. Sep 29, 1831 in Gerry, New York
d. Mar 4, 1906 in Saint Augustine, Florida
Source: *AmBi; ApCAB; BiAUS; BiDrUSE 71, 89; BiInAmS; BioIn 1, 7, 9, 10; CivWDc; CmdGen 1991; DcAmAu; DcAmB; DcAmMiB; DcNAA; Drake; HarEnMi; HarEnUS; MedHR 94; NatCAB 4; TwCBDA; WebAB 74, 79; WebAMB; WhAm 1; WhCiWar*

Scholder, Fritz
American. Artist
Member of the Luiseno tribe; known for his paintings and lithographs; won New Mexico's Governor's Award in Visual Arts, 1983.
b. Oct 6, 1937 in Breckenridge, Minnesota
Source: *AmArt; BioIn 9, 10, 14, 15, 17, 21; CurBio 85; DcCAA 88, 94; EncNAB; IlBEAAW; NotNaAm; PrintW 83, 85; WhoAm 76, 78, 80, 82, 84, 86, 88, 90, 92, 94, 95, 96, 97; WhoAmA 73, 76, 78, 80, 82, 84, 86, 89, 91, 93; WhoWest 74, 76, 78, 84; WhoWor 78, 80, 82, 84, 87, 93; WorArt 1980*

Scholem, Gershom Gerhard
Israeli. Educator, Author
Wrote, taught Jewish mysticism known as Kabbalah.
b. Dec 5, 1897 in Berlin, Germany
d. Feb 20, 1982 in Jerusalem, Israel
Source: *AnObit 1982; BioIn 14, 15, 16, 17, 20; ConAu 39NR, 45, 106; IntWW 81, 82; McGEWB; MidE 80; WhoWor 82; WhoWorJ 78; WorAu 1970*

Scholes, Percy Alfred
English. Musicologist
Presented music appreciation in informative, interesting manner: *Oxford Companion to Music,* 1938.
b. Jul 1877 in Leeds, England
d. Aug 2, 1958 in Vevey, Switzerland
Source: *Baker 84; LngCTC; OxCMus; TwCA SUP; WhoLA*

Scholl, William M
"Doctor Scholl"
American. Physician
Founder, pres., Scholl Manufacturing Co., 1908-68.
b. Jun 22, 1882 in LaPorte, Indiana
d. Mar 30, 1968 in Chicago, Illinois
Source: *IndAu 1917; WhAm 5*

Schollander, Don(ald Arthur)
American. Swimmer
Won two gold medals, 1964 Olympics.
b. Apr 30, 1946 in Charlotte, North Carolina
Source: *BiDAmSp BK; BioIn 7, 8, 9, 10; CmCal; CurBio 65*

Scholz, Jackson Volney
American. Track Athlete, Children's Author
Finished second in 1924 Olympic race which was adapted into 1981 film *Chariots of Fire;* wrote boys' sports books.
b. Mar 15, 1897 in Buchanan, Michigan
d. Oct 26, 1986 in Delray Beach, Florida
Source: *AuBYP 2, 3; BiDAmSp OS; BioIn 6, 8, 13; ConAu 5R, 120; MorJA; NewYTBS 86*

Scholz, Tom
American. Singer, Musician
Founded hard-rock group Boston, 1975; hits include "Amanda," 1986; has also invented, made electronic equipment for musicians.
b. Mar 10, 1947 in Toledo, Ohio
Source: *BioIn 15, 16; BkPepl; ConNews 87-2; LegTOT; OnThGG; RkOn 84; RolSEnR 83; WhoRocM 82*

Schomburg, Arthur Alfonso
[Arturo Alfonso Schomburg]
American. Historian
Private collection of African American books, prints, and artifacts became the basis for the 135th St. branch of the NY Public Library's Division of Negro Literature, History, and Prints; curator, 1932-38.
b. Jan 24, 1874 in San Juan, Puerto Rico
d. Jun 10, 1938 in New York, New York
Source: *BioIn 1, 16, 19; ConBlB 9; DcAmLiB; DcAmNB; DcTwCCu 5; WhoColR*

Schonbein, Christian Friedrich
German. Chemist
Discovered ozone gas, 1840.
b. Oct 18, 1799 in Metzingen, Germany
d. Aug 29, 1868 in Sauersberg, Germany
Source: *AsBiEn; BiESc; BioIn 2; DcBiPP; DcScB; InSci; LarDcSc; NewCol 75*

Schonberg, Harold C
American. Critic
With *NY Times,* 1960-80; won Pulitzer for distinguished criticism, 1971.
b. Nov 29, 1915 in New York, New York
Source: *AmAu&B; AuBYP 3; Baker 84; BioIn 15, 16; ConAu 112; IntAu&W 91; IntWW 83, 91; IntWWM 90; NewGrDA 86; WhoAm 86, 90; WhoEnt 92; WrDr 92*

Schonfield, Hugh J
English. Author, Educator
Authority on Judaism; wrote controversial *The Passover Plot,* 1965.
b. May 17, 1901 in London, England
d. Jan 24, 1988 in London, England
Source: *Au&Wr 71; ConAu 9R, 124*

Schongauer, Martin
German. Artist, Engraver
First painter to practice engraving; historical, religious subjects include *Madonna of the Rose Bower,* 1473.
b. 1450 in Colmar, Germany
d. Feb 2, 1491 in Breisach, Germany
Source: *AtlBL; NewCol 75; WebBD 83*

Schoolcraft, Henry Rowe
American. Explorer, Naturalist
Native American culture expert; wrote *The Myth of Hiawatha,* 1856, which inspired Longfellow's poem.
b. Mar 28, 1793 in Albany County, New York
d. Dec 10, 1864 in Washington, District of Columbia
Source: *Alli; AmAu; AmAu&B; AmBi; ApCAB; BbD; Benet 87, 96; BenetAL 91; BiAUS; BiDAmS; BiD&SB; BiInAmS; BioIn 1, 3, 4, 8, 9, 13, 16; CelCen; CyAL 1; DcAmAu; DcAmB; DcBiPP; DcNAA; DcScB; Drake; EncAAH; EncAB-H 1974, 1996; HarEnUS; IlBEAAW; InSci; IntDcAn; LegTOT; LinLib L; McGEWB; MichAu 80; NatCAB 5; NewYHSD; OxCAmH; OxCAmL 65, 83, 95; OxCCan; REn; REnAL; REnAW; TwCBDA; WebAB 74, 79; WhAm HS; WhNaAH; WhWE*

Schoonmaker, Frank Musselman
American. Author
Leading figure in US during Prohibition; wrote *The Complete Book of Wine,* 1934.
b. Aug 20, 1905 in Spearfish, South Dakota
d. Jan 11, 1976 in New York, New York
Source: *AmAu&B; BioIn 10; ConAu 61; NewYTBS 76; ObitOF 79*

Schoonmaker, Thelma
American. Filmmaker
Film editor of *Taxi Driver,* 1976; *The Age of Innocence,* 1993.
b. 1940 in Algiers, Algeria

Schopenhauer, Arthur
German. Philosopher, Author
Exponent of philosophical pessimism; major work: *The World as Will and Idea,* 1819.
b. Jan 22, 1788 in Danzig, Germany
d. Sep 20, 1860 in Frankfurt am Main, Germany
Source: *AtlBL; Baker 78, 84, 92; BbD; Benet 87, 96; BiD&SB; BiDPsy; BioIn 1, 2, 3, 4, 5, 7, 8, 9, 10, 12, 13, 14, 16, 17, 20; CasWL; CelCen; CyEd; CyWA 58; DcBiPP; DcEuL; DcLB 90; Dis&D; EncEth; EncUnb; EuAu; EuWr 5; EvEuW; IlEncMy; LegTOT; LinLib L, S; LngCEL; LuthC 75; McGEWB; NamesHP; NewC; NewCBEL; NewGrDM 80; NinCLC 51; OxCEng 67, 85, 95; OxCGer 76, 86; OxCPhil; PenC EUR; RAdv 14, 13-4; RComWL; REn; TwoTYeD; WhDW; WorAl; WorAlBi; WrPh P*

Schopf, J(ames) William
American. Geologist, Educator, Chemist
Discovered oldest amino acids in 1967.
b. Sep 27, 1941 in Urbana, Illinois
Source: *AmMWSc 73P, 76P, 79, 82, 86, 89, 92, 95; BioIn 11; CurBio 95; WhoAm 78, 80, 82, 84, 86, 88, 96; WhoScEn 96; WhoWest 74, 76; WhoWor 97*

Schorer, Mark
American. Author, Educator
Wrote encyclopedic biography, *Sinclair Lewis: An American Life,* 1961.
b. May 17, 1908 in Sauk City, Wisconsin
d. Aug 11, 1977 in Oakland, California
Source: *AmAu&B; Au&Wr 71; Benet 87; BenetAL 91; BioIn 4, 11, 17; BlueB 76; CnDAL; ConAu 5R, 7NR, 73; ConLC 9; ConLCrt 77, 82; ConNov 72, 76; DcAmB S10; DcLB 103; DrAF 76; DrAS 74E; IntAu&W 76, 77; IntWW 74, 75, 76, 77; LinLib L; Novels; OxCAmL 65, 83, 95; PenC AM; REn; REnAL; ScF&FL 1, 2; TwCA, SUP; WhoAm 74, 76; WhoWor 74; WrDr 76*

Schorr, Daniel Louis
American. Broadcast Journalist
Controversial CBS News correspondent, 1943-76; won three Emmys for Watergate coverage; suspended for disclosing confidential govt. information to *Village Voice* newspaper, 1976.
b. Aug 31, 1916 in New York, New York
Source: *BiDAmNC; BioIn 13, 14, 15; ConAu 65; CurBio 59, 78; EncTwCJ; IntMPA 86, 92; JrnUS; LesBEnT, 92; NewYTBS 76; PolProf NF; WhoAm 74, 76, 78, 80, 82, 84, 86, 88, 90, 92, 94, 95, 96, 97; WhoAmJ 80; WhoE 95; WhoTelC; WhoWor 74; WorAl*

Schorr, Friedrich
Hungarian. Opera Singer
Baritone with NY Met., 1924-43; noted Wagnerian singer.

b. Sep 2, 1888 in Nagyvarad, Austria-Hungary
d. Aug 14, 1953 in Farmington, Connecticut
Source: *Baker 78, 84, 92; BiDAmM; BioIn 1, 2, 3, 4, 10, 11, 14; CmOp; CurBio 42, 54; IntDcOp; LegTOT; MetOEnc; MusSN; NatCAB 41; NewAmDM; NewEOp 71; NewGrDA 86; NewGrDM 80; NewGrDO; OxDcOp; PenDiMP*

Schott, Marge
[Margaret Schott]
American. Business Executive
Socialite; owner, Cincinnati Reds, 1985—; suspended from NL for one year following derogatory racial and ethnic remarks, 1992; suspended again in 1996 through the 1998 season.
b. Aug 18, 1928 in Cincinnati, Ohio
Source: *BioIn 14, 15, 16; ConNews 85-4; NewYTBS 85; WhoAm 88, 90, 92, 94, 95, 96, 97; WhoAmW 89, 91, 93, 95; WhoMW 88, 90, 92, 93, 96*

Schottland, Charles I(rwin)
American. Government Official
Commissioner, US Social Security Administration, 1954-59.
b. Oct 29, 1906
d. Jun 27, 1995 in Tucson, Arizona
Source: *BioIn 4, 5, 21; BlueB 76; ConAu 13R, 149; CurBio 95N; WhoAm 74, 76, 78, 80, 82, 84, 86, 88, 90, 92, 94, 95, 96; WhoAmJ 80; WhoWorJ 72, 78*

Schrader, Paul Joseph
American. Director, Writer
Directed, wrote films *American Gigolo*, 1980; *Blue Collar*, 1978; *Hardcore*, 1979.
b. Jul 22, 1946 in Grand Rapids, Michigan
Source: *BioIn 10, 11, 13, 14, 15, 16; ConAu 37R, 41NR; ConDr 82A, 88A; ConLC 26; ConTFT 4; CurBio 81; DcLB 44; HalFC 88; IntDcF 2-2; IntMPA 92; IntWW 91, 93; WhoAm 82, 88, 90, 92, 94, 95, 96, 97; WhoEnt 92; WhoWor 95; WorFDir 2*

Schram, Emil
American. Businessman
Pres. of NY Stock Exchange, 1941-51; pres. of United Service Organizations, 1953-57.
b. Nov 23, 1893 in Peru, Indiana
d. Sep 18, 1987 in Peru, Indiana
Source: *BioIn 1, 2, 3, 15; CurBio 41, 53, 87, 87N; NewYTBS 87; WhAm 9; Who 74, 82, 83, 85, 88; WhoAm 74*

Schramm, Tex(as Edward)
American. Football Executive
Dallas Cowboys, GM, 1960-1989; pres., 1966-1989; pres., World League of American Football, 1989-91.
b. Jun 2, 1920 in Los Angeles, California
Source: *BioIn 13, 16; WhoAm 86, 90; WhoFtbl 74; WhoSSW 73, 75, 86, 91*

Schranz, Karl
Austrian. Skier
World Cup Alpine champion, 1969, 1970.
b. Nov 18, 1938 in Saint Anton, Austria
Source: *BioIn 8, 9; CurBio 71; WhoWor 74*

Schreiber, Avery
[Burns and Schreiber]
American. Actor, Comedian
Starred with Jack Burns in "Burns and Schreiber Comedy Hour," 1973.
b. Apr 9, 1935 in Chicago, Illinois
Source: *ConTFT 7; EncAFC; LegTOT; WhoAm 74; WhoEnt 92; WhoHol 92, A*

Schreiber, Hermann Otto Ludwig
[Lujo Bassermann]
Austrian. Historian, Author
Books include *Vanished Cities*, 1957; *The Oldest Profession*, 1967.
b. May 4, 1920 in Wiener Neustadt, Austria
Source: *Au&Wr 71; ConAu 36NR; DcLP 87A; IntAu&W 86, 91; WrDr 76, 86, 88*

Schreker, Franz
German. Composer
Operas include *Der Ferne Klang*, 1912; *Christophorous*, cancelled by Nazis, 1933, first performed, 1978.
b. Mar 23, 1878, Monaco
d. Mar 21, 1934 in Berlin, Germany
Source: *Baker 78, 84, 92; BioIn 1, 3, 7, 8, 9, 12, 17, 18, 19; CmOp; CompSN, SUP; DcCom 77; IntDcOp; MetOEnc; NewAmDM; NewEOp 71; NewGrDM 80; NewGrDO; OxCMus; OxDcOp*

Schreyer, Edward Richard
Canadian. Political Leader
Premier of Manitoba, 1969-77; governor-general, 1979-84, succeeded by Jeanne Sauve.
b. Dec 21, 1935 in Beausejour, Manitoba, Canada
Source: *AmCath 80; BioIn 11, 12, 13; BlueB 76; CanWW 31, 80, 81, 83, 89; CurBio 81; IntWW 74, 75, 76, 77, 78, 79, 80, 81, 82, 83, 89, 91, 93; IntYB 80, 81, 82; Who 82, 83, 85, 88, 90, 92, 94; WhoAm 74, 76, 78, 80, 82, 84; WhoCan 73, 75, 77, 80, 82, 84; WhoE 81, 83, 85; WhoMW 76, 78; WhoWor 74, 76, 78, 80, 82, 87*

Schrieffer, John Robert
American. Physicist, Educator
Shared 1972 Nobel Prize in physics for developing BCS (researchers' initials) theory of superconductivity.
b. May 31, 1931 in Oak Park, Illinois
Source: *AmMWSc 76P, 79, 82, 86, 89, 92, 95; BioIn 9, 10, 15, 20; BlueB 76; CamDcSc; IntWW 74, 75, 76, 77, 78, 79, 80, 81, 82, 83, 89, 91, 93; LarDcSc; McGMS 80; NobelP; WebAB 74, 79; Who 74, 82, 83, 85, 88, 90, 92, 94; WhoAm 74, 78, 80, 82, 84, 86, 88, 90, 92, 94, 95, 96, 97; WhoAtom 77; WhoE 74, 75, 77, 79, 81, 85; WhoFrS 84; WhoNob, 90, 95; WhoScEn 94, 96; WhoSSW 93, 95, 97; WhoTech 89; WhoWest 82, 87, 89, 92; WhoWor 74, 80, 82, 84, 87, 89, 91, 93, 95, 96, 97; WorAl; WorAlBi; WorScD*

Schriner, Sweeney
[David Schriner]
Canadian. Hockey Player
Left wing, NY Americans, 1934-39, Toronto, 1939-46; won Calder Trophy, 1935, Art Ross Trophy, 1936, 1937; Hall of Fame, 1962.
b. Nov 30, 1911 in Calgary, Alberta, Canada
Source: *BioIn 17; HocEn; WhoHcky 73; WhoSpor*

Schroder, Gerhard
[Gerhard Schroeder]
German. Politician
Christian Democratic Union leader; foreign affairs minister, 1961-66, defense minister, 1966-69.
b. Sep 11, 1910 in Saarbrucken, Germany
d. Dec 31, 1989 in Sylt Island, Germany (West)
Source: *BioIn 5, 6, 7, 16, 17; CurBio 62, 90, 90N; IntWW 74, 75, 76, 77, 78, 79, 80, 81, 82, 83, 89; IntYB 78, 79, 80, 81, 82; NewYTBS 90; WhoWor 74, 76, 78*

Schroder, Ricky
American. Actor
Appeared in remake of *The Champ*, 1979; won Golden Globe award.
b. Apr 13, 1970 in Staten Island, New York
Source: *BioIn 11, 12, 13, 14, 16; ConTFT 2, 3; HalFC 84, 88; IntMPA 84, 86, 88, 92; LegTOT; VarWW 85; WhoEnt 92*

Schroder-Devrient, Wilhelmine
"The Queen of Tears"
German. Opera Singer
Famed soprano with Dresden Opera, 1822-47; first great singing actress.
b. Dec 6, 1804 in Hamburg, Germany
d. Jan 26, 1860 in Coburg, Germany
Source: *Baker 78, 84, 92; BioIn 7, 14, 15, 19; BriBkM 80; CmOp; IntDcOp; InWom, SUP; MetOEnc; NewAmDM; NewEOp 71; NewGrDM 80; NewGrDO; OxDcOp*

Schroeder, Barbet
American. Director
Directed *Reversal of Fortune*, 1990; *Kiss of Death*, 1995.
b. Apr 26, 1941 in Tehran, Iran
Source: *BiDFilm 94; ConAu 143; ConTFT 9; FilmEn; HalFC 84, 88; IntMPA 88, 92, 94, 96; IntWW 91, 93; LegTOT; MiSFD 9; News 96, 96-1; WrDr 96*

Schroeder, Jay Brian
American. Football Player
Minor league baseball player, 1980-83; quarterback, Washington, 1985-88; LA Raiders, 1989-93; Cincinnati, 1993—.

b. Jun 28, 1961 in Milwaukee, Wisconsin
Source: *BioIn 14, 16; FootReg 86, 87*

Schroeder, Patricia Scott
[Mrs. James White Schroeder]
American. Politician
Liberal Dem. congresswoman from CO, 1973-95.
b. Jul 30, 1940 in Portland, Oregon
Source: *AlmAP 88; WhoWest 74, 76, 78, 80, 82, 84, 87, 89, 92, 94, 96; WomPO 76*

Schroeder, William J
American. Transplant Patient
Second human to receive artificial heart, Nov 1984; survived longest, 620 days.
b. Feb 14, 1932 in Jasper, Indiana
d. Aug 6, 1986 in Louisville, Kentucky
Source: *ConNews 86-4; NewYTBS 86*

Schroedinger, Erwin
Austrian. Physicist
Shared 1933 Nobel Prize for quantum mechanics concept; discovered new productive forms of atomic theory.
b. Aug 12, 1887 in Vienna, Austria
d. Jan 4, 1961 in Alpbach, Austria
Source: *AsBiEn; BiESc; ConAu 113; DcScB; MakMC; McGEWB; WhAm 4; WhDW; WhoNob; WorAl*

Schuba, Beatrix
Austrian. Skater
Two-time world champion figure skater, 1971-72; won gold medal, 1972 Olympics.

Schubert, Franz Peter
Austrian. Composer
Created the German lieder; symphonies include B Minor (*The Unfinished,* 1822) and C Major; wrote "Ave Maria."
b. Jan 31, 1797 in Vienna, Austria
d. Nov 19, 1828 in Vienna, Austria
Source: *AtlBL; Baker 92; BioIn 1, 2, 3, 4, 5, 6, 7, 8, 9, 10, 11, 12, 13; CelCen; DcArts; DcBiPP; DcCathB; Dis&D; LinLib S; McGEWB; NewC; NewEOp 71; NewGrDO; NotNAT B; OxCEng 85, 95; OxCGer 76; OxCMus; REn; WhDW; WorAl*

Schuch, Ernst von
Austrian. Conductor
Led Dresden Court Opera for 40 yrs; debuted 50 new operas, including *Der Rosenkavalier.*
b. Nov 23, 1846 in Graz, Austria
d. May 10, 1914 in Dresden, Germany
Source: *Baker 78, 84, 92; CmOp; IntDcOp; MetOEnc; NewEOp 71; NewGrDM 80; OxDcOp; PenDiMP*

Schul, Bob
American. Track Athlete
Middle-distance runner; first American to win gold medal in 5,000-meters, 1964 Olympics.
b. Sep 28, 1937 in West Milton, Ohio
Source: *WhoTr&F 73*

Schulberg, Budd Wilson
American. Author, Journalist
Wrote *What Makes Sammy Run?* 1941; prize-winning film scenario, *On the Waterfront,* 1954.
b. Mar 27, 1914 in New York, New York
Source: *Benet 87; BenetAL 91; BioIn 14, 15, 16; ConAu 19NR; ConDr 73, 88A; ConLC 48; ConNov 76, 91; ConTFT 6; CurBio 41, 51; DcFM; DrAPF 87, 91; FilmgC; HalFC 88; IntMPA 77, 96; IntvTCA 2; IntWW 74, 91; LngCTC; ModAL; NewYTBE 72; NotNAT; OxCAmL 65; OxCFilm; PenC AM; REnAL; WhoAm 86, 90; WhoUSWr 88; WhoWrEP 89; WorAlBi; WrDr 92*

Schulberg, Stuart
American. Producer
Exec. producer of news documentaries for NBC; producer, "Today Show," 1968-76.
b. Nov 17, 1922 in Los Angeles, California
d. Jun 28, 1979 in New York, New York
Source: *BioIn 11, 12; ConAu 89; NewYTBS 79; NewYTET*

Schuler, Mike
[Michael Harold Schuler]
American. Basketball Coach
Coach, Portland, 1986-89; Clippers, 1990-92; NBA coach of year, 1987.
b. Sep 22, 1940 in Portsmouth, Ohio
Source: *OfNBA 87; WhoAm 88, 90, 92; WhoWest 87, 89, 92*

Schuller, Gunther
American. Composer, Conductor
Noted horn player, 1940s-50s; popularized "cool jazz" style; instrumental in ragtime revival; wrote operas, third-stream music.
b. Nov 22, 1925 in New York, New York
Source: *AllMusG; AmComp; Baker 78, 84; BiDAmM; BiDJaz; BioIn 6, 7, 8, 9, 10, 12, 14, 15; BlueB 76; BriBkM 80; CompSN, SUP; ConAmC 76, 82; ConAu 28NR, 69; ConCom 92; CpmDNM 77, 78, 80, 81, 82; CurBio 64; DcCM; DcTwCCu 1; EncJzS; IntAu&W 91, 93; IntWW 74, 75, 76, 77, 78, 79, 80, 81, 82, 83, 89, 91, 93; IntWWM 77, 80, 90; LEduc 74; McGEWB; MetOEnc; MusMk; NewAmDM; NewEOp 71; NewGrDA 86; NewGrDJ 88; NewGrDM 80; NewOxM; OxCMus; OxCPMus; PenDiMP, A; PenEncP; WebAB 74, 79; WhoAm 74, 76, 78, 80, 82, 84, 86; WhoAmM 83; WhoE 74, 77, 83; WhoWest 87; WhoWor 74; WrDr 76, 80, 82, 84, 86, 88, 90, 92, 94, 96*

Schuller, Robert Harold
American. Evangelist, Author
Popular televangelist emphasizes optimistic thinking: *The Be Happy Attitudes,* 1985.
b. Sep 16, 1926 in Alton, Iowa
Source: *BioIn 11, 12, 13, 14, 15, 16; ConAu 9R, 14NR, 46NR; CurBio 79; IntAu&W 77, 86, 91; RelLAm 91; WhoAm 76, 78, 80, 82, 84, 86, 88, 90, 95, 96, 97; WhoAmA 80; WhoRel 75, 77, 85, 92; WhoWest 80, 87, 89, 92, 94; WorAlBi; WrDr 76, 86, 92*

Schulman, Sarah (Miriam)
American. Writer
Wrote novel *After Delores,* 1988, winner of the American Library Association Gay/Lesbian Book Award.
b. Jul 28, 1958 in New York, New York
Source: *BioIn 19, 20; ConAu 118; GayLesB; GayLL*

Schultes, Richard Evans
American. Educator, Scientist
Did botanical research in the Amazon region, collecting 24,000 plant specimens.
b. Jan 12, 1915 in Boston, Massachusetts
Source: *AmMWSc 73P, 76P, 79, 82, 86, 89, 92, 95; BioIn 12; ConAu 25NR, 50NR, 108; CurBio 95; EnvEnDr; IntWW 89, 91, 93; NotTwCS; WhoAm 74, 76, 78, 80, 82, 84, 86, 90, 92, 94, 95, 96, 97; WhoE 95; WhoFrS 84; WhoRel 75, 77; WhoScEn 94, 96*

Schultz, Dave
[David William Schultz]
"The Hammer"
Canadian. Hockey Player
Left wing, 1971-80, mostly with Philadelphia; holds NHL record for most penalties in season, 472 (1974-75); second to Tiger Williams in career penalties (2,294).
b. Oct 14, 1949 in Waldheim, Saskatchewan, Canada
Source: *BioIn 12, 13; HocEn; NewYTBS 74, 75*

Schultz, Dutch
[Arthur Flegenheimer]
"The Dutchman"
American. Criminal
Major NYC bootlegger, racketeer of Prohibition era; known for ruthlessness; ordered rival "Legs" Diamond killed, 1931.
b. Aug 6, 1902 in New York, New York
d. Oct 24, 1935 in Newark, New Jersey
Source: *BioIn 1, 2, 6; CopCroC; DcAmB S1; DrInf; FacFETw; LegTOT; WebAB 74, 79; WorAl; WorAlBi*

Schultz, Harry D
American. Financier
Among books on stocks, investments: *Schultz's Bear Market Strategy,* 1981.
b. Sep 11, 1923
Source: *BioIn 13; ConAu 14NR, 21R*

Schultz, Howard M.
American. Business Executive
Chairman and CEO, Starbucks Coffee Co., 1987—.
b. 1953 in New York, New York

Schultz, Michael A.
American. Director
Directed *Cooley High,* 1975; *The Last Dragon,* 1985.
b. Nov 10, 1938 in Milwaukee, Wisconsin
Source: *ConBlB 6; ConTFT 10; FilmEn; WhoAfA 96; WhoBlA 94; WhoThe 72, 77, 81*

Schultz, Richard D(ale)
American. Olympic Official
Executive director, United States Olympic Committee, 1995—.
b. Sep 5, 1929 in Grinnell, Iowa
Source: *CurBio 96; WhoAm 76, 78, 80, 82, 84, 86, 88, 90, 92, 94, 95, 96, 97; WhoFI 96; WhoMW 93, 96*

Schultz, Theodore William
American. Educator
Won Nobel Prize in economics, 1979.
b. Apr 30, 1902 in Arlington, South Dakota
Source: *AmAu&B; AmMWSc 73S, 78S; BioIn 4, 12, 15; ConAu 85; GrEconS; IntAu&W 91; IntWW 91; LEduc 74; NewYTBS 79; Who 92; WhoAm 74, 76, 80, 82, 84, 86, 88, 90, 92, 94, 95, 96, 97; WhoEc 86; WhoFI 83, 85, 89, 92, 94; WhoMW 80, 82, 84, 86, 88, 90, 92, 93, 96; WhoNob, 90, 95; WhoScEn 96; WhoWor 74, 80, 82, 84, 87, 89, 91, 93, 95, 96, 97; WorAlBi; WrDr 90*

Schultze, Carl Emil
"Bunny"
American. Cartoonist
Drew "Foxy Grandpa" comic series, 1900-27.
b. May 25, 1866 in Lexington, Kentucky
d. Jan 18, 1939 in New York, New York
Source: *AmAu&B; ChhPo; DcNAA; WhAm 1; WhAmArt 85; WorECom*

Schultze, Charles Louis
American. Economist
Chaired Jimmy Carter's Council of Economic Advisers, 1977-81.
b. Dec 12, 1924 in Alexandria, Virginia
Source: *AmEA 74; AmMWSc 92; BioIn 7, 8, 9, 11; ConAu 114; CurBio 70; IntWW 74, 75, 76, 77, 78, 79, 80, 81, 82, 83, 89, 91, 93; IntYB 78, 79, 80, 81, 82; NewYTBS 76, 77; PolProf J; WhoAm 74, 76, 78, 80, 84, 86, 88, 90, 92, 94, 95, 96, 97; WhoAmP 77, 79, 81; WhoE 77, 79, 81; WhoGov 77; WhoMedH; WorAlBi*

Schulz, Charles Monroe
American. Cartoonist
Created "Peanuts" comic strip, 1950; won Emmy, 1966.
b. Nov 26, 1922 in Minneapolis, Minnesota
Source: *AmAu&B; AuBYP 2, 3; BiDrAPA 89; BioIn 14, 15; BkPepl; CelR 90; ConAu 6NR, 9R; ConLC 12; CurBio 60; EncACom; EncTwCJ; IntAu&W 91; IntWW 91; LesBEnT 92; MinnWr; SmATA 10; ThrBJA; WebAB 79; WhoAm 86, 90, 97; WhoAmA 84, 91; WhoEnt 92; WhoWor 84, 89, 97; WorAlBi; WrDr 86, 88, 92*

Schumacher, E(rnst) F(riedrich)
English. Economist, Writer
Wrote *Small Is Beautiful,* 1973; *A Guide for the Perplexed,* 1977; works fused economic philosophy and Christian and Buddhist theology.
b. Aug 16, 1911 in Bonn, Germany
d. Sep 4, 1977 in Romont, Switzerland
Source: *BioIn 14; ConAu 34NR, 73, 81; ConLC 80; DcNaB 1971; EnvEnc*

Schumacher, Joel
American. Writer
Films include *St. Elmo's Fire,* 1985.
b. 1942 in New York, New York
Source: *HalFC 88; IntMPA 88; MiSFD 9; VarWW 85*

Schumacher, Kurt
German. Politician
Leader, West German Social Democratic Party, 1945-52.
b. Oct 13, 1895 in Kulm, Germany
d. Aug 21, 1952 in Bonn, Germany
Source: *BioIn 1, 2, 3, 7, 18; ColdWar 1, 2; CurBio 52; DcTwHis; EncGRNM; EncTR 91; EncWB; ObitT 1951*

Schuman, Patricia Glass
American. Publishing Executive
Pres., Neal-Schuman Publishers, 1976—; pres., American Library Assn., 1990—
b. Mar 15, 1943 in New York, New York
Source: *ConAu 14NR, 33R; News 93-2; WhoAmM 83; WhoAmW 91, 93, 95, 97; WhoE 97; WhoLibI 82*

Schuman, Robert
French. Statesman, Economist
Founder, European Coal and Steel Community.
b. Jun 29, 1886, Luxembourg
d. Sep 4, 1963 in Metz, France
Source: *BiDInt; BioIn 1, 2, 3, 5, 6, 9, 17, 19; CurBio 48, 63; DcTwHis; EncCW; HisEWW; McGEWB; ObitT 1961; WhAm 4; WhDW; WorAl; WorAlBi*

Schuman, William Howard
American. Composer
First to receive Pulitzer in music, 1943.
b. Aug 4, 1910 in New York, New York
d. Feb 15, 1992 in New York, New York
Source: *Baker 84; BiDAmM; BiE&WWA; BioIn 13, 14, 16; ConCom 92; CurBio 42, 62; DancEn 78; DcCM; EncAB-H 1974; FacFETw; IntWW 74, 91; MusMk; NewAmDM; NewGrDA 86; NewOxM; NewYTBS 85; OxCMus; PenDiMP A; REnAL; WebAB 74; WhoAm 86, 90; WhoMus 72; WhoWor 74, 91*

Schumann, Clara Josephine Wieck
German. Pianist
Brilliant performer; wife of Robert Shumann, friend of Brahms.
b. Sep 13, 1819 in Leipzig, Germany
d. May 20, 1896 in Frankfurt am Main, Germany
Source: *Baker 84; HerW; InWom, SUP*

Schumann, Elisabeth
American. Opera Singer
Soprano with Vienna State Opera, 1919-38; noted for Wagner, R Strauss roles.
b. Jun 13, 1885 in Merseburg, Germany
d. Apr 23, 1952 in New York, New York
Source: *Baker 78, 84; BiDAmM; BioIn 4, 6, 10, 11, 12, 14, 15, 16, 18, 20; BriBkM 80; CmOp; FacFETw; IntDcOp; MetOEnc; MusSN; NewEOp 71; NewGrDM 80; ObitT 1951*

Schumann, Maurice
French. Politician
Foreign affairs minister, 1969-73.
b. Apr 10, 1911 in Paris, France
Source: *BiDFrPL; BioIn 2, 7, 8, 9, 17; CurBio 70; HisEWW; IntAu&W 76, 77, 82, 89; IntWW 74, 75, 76, 77, 78, 79, 80, 81, 82, 83, 89, 91, 93; IntYB 78, 79, 80, 81, 82; WhE&EA; Who 74, 82, 83, 85, 88, 90, 92, 94; WhoFr 79; WhoWor 74, 78, 82, 84, 87, 89, 91, 93, 95, 96, 97*

Schumann, Robert Alexander
German. Composer
Led Romantic movement; career as pianist ended due to hand injury.
b. Jun 8, 1810 in Zwickau, Germany
d. Jul 29, 1856 in Endenick, Germany
Source: *AtlBL; Baker 84, 92; BbD; BiD&SB; BioIn 1, 2, 3, 4, 5, 6, 7, 8, 9, 10, 11, 12, 13; CelCen; DcArts; EncPaPR 91; IntDcOp; LuthC 75; McGEWB; NewGrDO; OxCGer 76; OxCMus; REn*

Schumann, Walter
American. Composer, Conductor
Won Emmy for theme to TV's "Dragnet," 1955.
b. Oct 8, 1913 in New York, New York
d. Aug 21, 1958 in Minneapolis, Minnesota
Source: *ASCAP 66, 80; Baker 78, 84, 92; BioIn 5; ConAmC 76, 82; NotNAT B*

Schumann-Heink, Ernestine Rossler
American. Opera Singer
Brilliant contralto; famed for Wagnerian roles, German Lieder; noted radio performer.
b. Jun 15, 1861 in Lieben, Bohemia
d. Nov 16, 1936 in Hollywood, California
Source: *AmBi; BiDAmM; DcAmB S2; InWom SUP; NotAW; REn; WebAB 74; WhAm 1; WhScrn 77; WomWWA 14*

Schumer, Charles E(llis)
American. Politician
Dem. congressman from NY, 1981—.
b. Nov 23, 1950 in New York, New York
Source: *BiDrUSC 89; BioIn 13; CngDr 81, 83, 85, 87; CurBio 95; NewYTBS 91; WhoAm 82, 84, 86, 88, 90, 92, 94, 95, 96, 97; WhoE 83, 85, 86, 89, 91, 93, 95, 97; WhoGov 77*

Schumpeter, Joseph Alois
American. Economist
Wrote *Theory of Economic Development,* 1911.
b. Feb 8, 1883 in Trest, Moravia
d. Jan 8, 1950 in Taconic, Connecticut
Source: *AmSocL; BioIn 2, 8, 10, 11, 12, 13, 14, 15, 16, 17, 18, 19, 20, 21; DcAmB S4; EncAB-H 1974, 1996; McGEWB; NewCol 75; OxCAmH; RAdv 14; REnAL; WebAB 74, 79; WhAm 2; WhoEc 81, 86*

Schurman, Jacob Gould
Canadian. Philosopher, Diplomat
Ambassador to China, 1921-25; Germany, 1925-30.
b. May 22, 1854 in Prince Edward Island, Canada
d. Aug 13, 1942
Source: *Alli SUP; AmAu&B; ApCAB; BbD; BiD&SB; BiDInt; BioIn 4, 5, 16; Chambr 3; CurBio 42; DcAmAu; DcAmB S3; DcAmDH 80, 89; DcNAA; HarEnUS; LinLib L; NatCAB 4, 40; TwCBDA; WebAB 74, 79; WhAm 2*

Schurz, Carl
American. Politician
Reformist Rep. senator from MO, 1870-76; urged civil service revision.
b. Mar 2, 1829 in Cologne, Germany
d. May 14, 1906 in New York, New York
Source: *Alli, SUP; AmAu; AmAu&B; AmBi; AmPolLe; AmRef; AmRef&R; ApCAB; BbD; BenetAL 91; BiAUS; BiDAmJo; BiDrAC; BiDrUSC 89; BiDrUSE 71, 89; BiDSA; BioIn 1, 2, 3, 5, 6, 7, 8, 9, 10, 12, 15, 16, 17, 20, 21; CivWDc; CyAG; DcAmAu; DcAmB; DcAmDH 80, 89; DcAmImH; DcAmSR; DcLB 23; DcNAA; Drake; EncAAH; EncAB-H 1974, 1996; EncPaPR 91; EncSoH; HarEnUS; JrnUS; LinLib L, S; McGEWB; NatCAB 3; NatLAC; OxCAmH; OxCAmL 65, 83, 95; PolPar; REnAL; REnAW; TwCBDA; WebAB 74, 79; WhAm 1; WhAmP; WhCiWar; WhNaAH; WisWr; WorAl; WorAlBi*

Schuschnigg, Kurt von
Austrian. Political Leader
Chancellor of Austria, 1934-38; taught in US for 20 yrs.
b. Dec 14, 1897 in Riva, Italy
d. Nov 18, 1977 in Innsbruck, Austria
Source: *BioIn 11, 14; CathA 1952; DcPol; DcTwHis; EncTR; FacFETw; HisEWW; IntWW 74, 75, 76, 77; McGEWB; REn; WhDW; Who 74; WhoWor 74*

Schuster, Max Lincoln
American. Publisher
Founded Simon and Schuster, with Richard Simon, 1924.
b. Mar 2, 1897 in Kalusz, Austria
d. Dec 20, 1970 in New York, New York
Source: *AmAu&B; BioIn 9; ConAu 29R; CurBio 41, 71; DcAmB S8; REnAL; WhAm 10; WhoWorJ 72, 78*

Schutz, Heinrich
German. Composer
Regarded as finest German composer before Bach; wrote first German opera, *Daphne,* 1627; composed over 500 sacred works.
b. Oct 8, 1585 in Kostritz, Germany
d. Nov 6, 1672 in Dresden, Germany
Source: *AtlBL; Baker 78, 84, 92; Benet 87; BioIn 1, 4, 5, 7, 8, 12, 13, 15, 16, 17, 20; BriBkM 80; DcArts; DcCom 77; DcCom&M 79; GrComp; LegTOT; LuthC 75; McGEWB; MetOEnc; MusMk; MusSN; NewAmDM; NewEOp 71; NewGrDM 80; NewGrDO; NewOxM; OxCGer 76, 86; OxCMus; OxDcOp; PenDiMP A; REn; WhDW*

Schutzendorf, Gustav
German. Opera Singer
Best known of four brothers, all operatic baritones; with NY Met., 1922-35; wed to soprano Grete Stuckgold.
b. 1883 in Cologne, Germany
d. Apr 27, 1937 in Berlin, Germany
Source: *Baker 78, 84, 92; MetOEnc; NewEOp 71; NewGrDA 86; NewGrDM 80; OxDcOp*

Schuur, Diane
American. Singer
Two-time Grammy winner, best female jazz performance for *Timeless,* 1986 and *Diane Schuur and the Count Basie Orchestra,* 1987.
b. Dec 10, 1953
Source: *AllMusG; BioIn 16; ConMus 6; WhoAmW 91; WhoEnt 92*

Schuyler, James Marcus
American. Poet
Won Pulitzer Prize for Poetry, 1981.
b. Nov 9, 1923 in Chicago, Illinois
d. Apr 12, 1991 in New York, New York
Source: *AmAu&B; Benet 87; BenetAL 91; BlueB 76; ConAu 101, 134; ConLC 5, 70; ConPo 70, 75, 91; CroCAP; DcLEL 1940; DrAP 75; DrAPF 80, 91; IntAu&W 86, 91, 93; IntWWP 77, 82; NewYTBS 91; WhoAm 82, 84, 86, 88, 90; WhoUSWr 88; WhoWrEP 89, 92, 95; WorAu 1975; WrDr 76, 90*

Schuyler, Philip John
American. Statesman
Member of Continental Congress, 1778-81; one of NY's first two senators, 1780s-90s.
b. Nov 20, 1733 in Albany, New York
d. Nov 18, 1804 in Albany, New York
Source: *AmBi; ApCAB; BiAUS; BiDrAC; BiDrUSC 89; BioIn 6, 7, 8, 10, 16, 18; BlkwEAR; DcAmB; Drake; EncAR; EncCRAm; GenMudB; HarEnMi; McGEWB; NatCAB 1; OxCAmH; TwCBDA; WebAB 74, 79; WebAMB; WebBD 83; WhAm HS; WhNaAH*

Schwab, Charles
American. Business Executive
Founder and president Charles Schwab & Co., 1971—, largest discount brokerage in US.
b. 1937 in Sacramento, California
Source: *BioIn 12, 13, 15; Dun&B 90; News 89-3; NewYTBS 85; WhoAm 90; WhoFI 92; WhoWest 92*

Schwab, Charles Michael
American. Industrialist
First pres. of US Steel, 1901-03; became pres. of Bethlehem Steel, 1904, making it huge independent steel maker.
b. Feb 18, 1862 in Williamsburg, Pennsylvania
d. Sep 18, 1939 in New York, New York
Source: *AmBi; AmDec 1900; ApCAB X; BiDAmBL 83; BioIn 2, 3, 4, 7, 9, 10, 12; DcAmB S2; EncAB-H 1974, 1996; LinLib S; McGEWB; NatCAB 14; OxCAmH; WebAB 74, 79; WhAm 1; WorAl*

Schwann, Theodor
German. Physiologist
Regarded as father of cytology; co-founded cell theory; coined term metabolism.
b. Dec 7, 1810 in Neuss, Prussia
d. Jan 11, 1882 in Liege, Belgium
Source: *AsBiEn; BiESc; BioIn 4, 8, 9, 12, 14; CamDcSc; DcCathB; DcScB; InSci; LarDcSc; McGEWB; NewCol 75; WhDW; WorAl; WorAlBi*

Schwartz, Arthur
American. Songwriter
With Howard Dietz, wrote over 500 songs, including "Dancing in the Dark," "That's Entertainment."
b. Nov 25, 1900 in New York, New York
d. Sep 3, 1984 in Kintnersville, Pennsylvania
Source: *AmPS, 80; LegTOT; NewAmDM; NewCBMT; NewGrDA 86; NewGrDM 80; NewGrDO; NotNAT; OxCAmT 84; OxCPMus; PenEncP; PlP&P; PopAmC, SUP; Sw&Ld C; WhAm 8; WhoAm 76; WhoThe 77, 81; WorAl; WorAlBi*

Schwartz, David
American. Businessman
Founder and head of Rent-A-Wreck, an agency renting low cost, late model used vehicles, 1970—.
b. 1936
Source: *News 88-3; WhoAm 84*

Schwartz, Delmore (David)
American. Author, Editor, Critic
Edited *Partisan Review* mag., 1943-55.
b. Dec 8, 1913 in New York, New York
d. Jul 11, 1966 in New York, New York
Source: *AmAu&B; AmCulL; AmWr S2; AtlBL; Benet 87, 96; BenetAL 91; BioIn 4, 5, 7, 8, 10, 11, 12, 13, 14, 15, 17, 18, 19; CamGLE; CamHAL; CasWL; CnDAL; CnE&AP; CnMWL; ConAu 17R, 25R, 35NR, P-2; ConLC 2, 4, 10, 45, 87; ConLCrt 77, 82; ConPo 75, 80A; CurBio 60, 66; CyWA 89; DcAmB S8; DcArts; DcLB 28, 48; EncWL, 2, 3; FacFETw; GrWrEL P; JeAmFiW; LegTOT; LinLib L; MajTwCW; ModAL, S1, S2; OxCAmL 65, 83, 95; OxCTwCP; PenC AM; PoeCrit 8; RAdv 1, 14, 13-1; REn; REnAL; RfGAmL 87, 94; RGFAP; RGTwCWr; SixAP; TwCA, SUP; TwCWr; WebE&AL; WhAm 4; WhoTwCL; WorAl; WorAlBi*

Schwartz, Felice N(ierenberg)
American. Social Reformer
Founder, pres., CEO, Catalyst, 1962-1993.
b. Jan 16, 1925 in New York, New York
d. Feb 8, 1996 in New York, New York
Source: *AmWomM; CurBio 93; InWom SUP; WhoAmW 58, 61, 64, 66, 70, 85, 91; WhoE 77*

Schwartz, Jean
American. Songwriter
Prolific Broadway composer, 1900-1930s; wrote "Rock-a-Bye Your Baby to a Dixie Melody," 1918; "Chinatown My Chinatown," 1910.
b. Nov 4, 1878 in Budapest, Austria-Hungary
d. Nov 30, 1956 in Sherman Oaks, California
Source: *AmPS; AmSong; ASCAP 66, 80; BiDAmM; BioIn 4, 5, 6, 15, 16; CmpEPM; EncMT; NewCBMT; NewGrDA 86; NotNAT B; OxCAmT 84; OxCPMus; PopAmC; Sw&Ld C; WhThe*

Schwartz, Maurice
American. Actor, Director, Producer
Films include *Bird of Paradise,* 1951; *Slaves of Babylon,* 1953.
b. Jun 18, 1890 in Sedikov, Russia
d. May 10, 1960 in Tel Aviv, Israel
Source: *BioIn 4, 5, 10, 20; CamGWoT; CurBio 56, 60; FilmEn; NotNAT B; OxCAmT 84; OxCThe 67; TheaDir; WhAm 4; WhoHol B; WhScrn 74, 77; WhThe*

Schwartz, Melvin
American. Physicist
Shared Nobel Prize in physics, 1988, for co-discovering neutrinos, subatomic particles.
b. Nov 2, 1932 in New York, New York
Source: *AmMWSc 73P, 76P, 79, 82, 86, 89, 92, 95; BioIn 16, 18, 20; LarDcSc; LElec; NobelP 91; NotTwCS; Who 90, 92, 94; WhoAm 74, 76, 78, 80, 82, 84, 86, 88, 90, 92, 94, 95, 96, 97; WhoE 95, 97; WhoFrS 84; WhoNob 90, 95; WhoScEn 94, 96; WhoWor 91, 93, 95, 96, 97; WhoWorJ 72, 78; WorAlBi*

Schwartz, Stephen L(awrence)
American. Dramatist, Composer
Wrote music, lyrics for *Godspell,* 1971; *Butterflies Are Free,* 1969.
b. Mar 6, 1948 in Roslyn, New York
Source: *ConAu 85; ConTFT 5; EncMT; NotNAT; OxCPMus; SmATA 19; WhoAm 78, 80, 82, 84, 86, 88, 92, 94, 95, 96, 97; WhoEnt 92; WhoThe 81*

Schwary, Ronald L
American. Producer
Films include *A Soldier's Story,* 1984; won Oscar for *Ordinary People,* 1980.
b. May 23, 1944 in Oregon
Source: *VarWW 85; WhoAm 90; WhoEnt 92*

Schwarz, Gerard
American. Composer, Musician
Trumpet virtuoso who is one of most sought-after conductors in US.
b. Aug 19, 1947 in Weehawken, New Jersey
Source: *Baker 84; BioIn 14, 15, 16; BriBkM 80; CurBio 86; IntWW 89, 91, 93; IntWWM 90; NewAmDM; NewGrDA 86; NewGrDM 80; NewYTBS 75, 86; PenDiMP; WhoAm 82, 96, 97; WhoAmM 83; WhoWest 96*

Schwarz-Bart, Andre
French. Author
His *Last of the Just* was a significant post WWII Novel.
b. 1928 in Metz, France
Source: *Benet 87, 96; BioIn 5, 10; ConAu 89; ConLC 2, 4, 24; CyWA 89; IntAu&W 76, 77; REn; TwCWr; Who 74, 82, 83, 85, 88, 90, 92, 94; WhoWor 74; WorAu 1950*

Schwarzenegger, Arnold Alois
Austrian. Actor
Five times Mr. Universe, six times Mr. Olympia; films include *Twins,* 1988; *Total Recall,* 1990.
b. Jul 30, 1947 in Graz, Austria
Source: *BioIn 10, 13, 14, 15, 16; CelR 90; ConAu 21NR, 81; ConTFT 4; CurBio 79, 91; HalFC 88; IntMPA 92; IntWW 91, 93; News 91-1; NewYTBS 76, 82; WhoAm 84, 86, 88, 90, 92, 94, 95, 96, 97; WhoEnt 92; WorAlBi*

Schwarzhaupt, Elisabeth
German. Politician
First woman cabinet member in West Germany, health minister, 1961-66.
b. Jan 7, 1901 in Frankfurt am Main, Germany
d. Oct 29, 1986 in Frankfurt, Germany (West)
Source: *BioIn 7, 8, 15; CurBio 67, 87, 87N; IntWW 74; InWom SUP; NewYTBS 86*

Schwarzkopf, Elisabeth
German. Opera Singer
Soprano who performed in US, 1950s-70s; renowned Mozart singer.
b. Dec 9, 1915 in Jarotschin, Poland
Source: *Baker 78, 84, 92; BioIn 3, 4, 5, 6, 7, 8, 10, 11, 12, 13, 14, 15; BriBkM 80; CmOp; ContDcW 89; CurBio 55; DcArts; FacFETw; IntDcOp; IntDcWB; IntWW 74, 75, 76, 77, 78, 79, 80, 81, 82, 83, 89, 91, 93; IntWWM 90; InWom; LegTOT; MetOEnc; MusMk; MusSN; NewAmDM; NewEOp 71; NewGrDM 80; OxDcOp; PenDiMP; Who 74, 82, 83, 85, 88, 90, 92, 94; WhoHol 92; WhoMus 72; WhoWor 80, 82, 93; WorAl; WorAlBi*

Schwarzkopf, H. Norman
American. Military Leader
Retired army general; responsible for military plan Operation Desert Shield/Storm, January 16, 1991-February 28, 1991.
b. Aug 22, 1934 in Trenton, New Jersey
Source: *CurBio 91; FacFETw; IntWW 91; NewYTBS 91; WhoAm 90*

Schwarzschild, Martin
American. Astronomer
Wrote *Structure and Evolution of the Stars,* 1958; had a part in creating Stratosphere-based astronomy.
b. May 21, 1912, Germany
d. Apr 10, 1997 in Langhorne, Pennsylvania
Source: *AmMWSc 73P, 76P, 79, 82, 86, 89, 92, 95; BioIn 5, 7, 8, 14; BlueB 76; IntWW 74, 75, 76, 77, 78, 79, 80, 81, 82, 83, 89, 91, 93; McGMS 80; WhoAm 74, 76, 78, 80, 82, 84, 86, 88, 90, 92, 94, 95, 96, 97; WhoE 95; WhoFrS 84; WhoScEn 94, 96; WhoWor 74*

Schwatka, Frederik
American. Explorer, Naturalist
Explored AK's Yukon River, 1883-84; wrote *Nimrod of the North,* 1885.
b. Sep 29, 1849 in Galena, Illinois
d. Nov 2, 1892 in Portland, Oregon
Source: *AmBi; ApCAB; DcAmB; NatCAB 1; TwCBDA; WhAm HS*

Schweickart, Russell L
American. Astronaut
Lunar module pilot on *Apollo 9,* 1969.
b. Oct 25, 1935 in Neptune, New Jersey
Source: *IntWW 74; WhoAm 86; WhoGov 72; WhoSSW 73; WhoWor 91*

Schweiker, Richard Schultz
American. Government Official
Rep. senator from PA, 1969-81; secretary of HHS, 1981-83.
b. Jun 1, 1926 in Norristown, Pennsylvania
Source: *BiDrAC; BiDrUSC 89; BiDrUSE 89; BioIn 8, 9, 10, 11, 12, 13, 14; BioNews 74; CngDr 74, 77, 79; CurBio 77; IntWW 74, 75, 76, 77, 78, 79, 80, 81, 82, 83, 89, 91, 93; NatCAB 63N; NewYTBS 76, 80; PolProf NF; WhoAm 74, 76, 78, 80, 82, 84, 86, 88, 90, 92, 94, 95, 96, 97; WhoAmP 73, 75, 77, 79,*

81, 83, 85, 87, 89, 91, 93; WhoE 74, 75, 77, 79, 81; WhoGov 72, 75, 77; WhoIns 86, 88, 90, 92, 93, 94; WhoWor 78, 80, 82; WorAl; WorAlBi

Schweitzer, Albert
French. Missionary, Physician
Founded Lambarene Hospital, French Equatorial Africa, 1913; won 1952 Nobel Peace Prize; known for humanitarianism, ''reverence of life'' philosohy.
b. Jan 14, 1875 in Kaysersberg, Germany
d. Sep 4, 1965 in Lambarene, Gabon
Source: *Baker 78, 84, 92; Benet 87, 96; BiDMoPL; BioIn 1, 2, 3, 4, 5, 6, 7, 8, 9, 10, 11, 12, 13, 14, 15, 16, 17, 18, 19, 20, 21; BriBkM 80; ConAu 93; ConHero 2; CurBio 48, 65; DcAfHiB 86; DcTwHis; EncEth; EnvEnc; FacFETw; HeroCon; InSci; LegTOT; LinLib L, S; LngCTC; LuthC 75; McGEWB; MusMk; MusSN; NewAmDM; NewCol 75; NewGrDM 80; NewYTBS 75; NobelP; ObitT 1961; OxCGer 76, 86; OxCMed 86; OxCMus; PenDiMP; REn; ThTwC 87; TwCA SUP; TwCWr; WebBD 83; WhAm 4; WhDW; WhE&EA; WhoNob, 90, 95; WorAl; WorAlBi*

Schweitzer, Pierre-Paul
French. Banker
Director of French treasury, 1953-60; chairman, International Monetary Fund, 1963-73; nephew of Albert Schweitzer.
b. May 29, 1912
d. Jan 2, 1994 in Paris, France
Source: *BioIn 19, 20; CurBio 94N; IntWW 74, 75, 76, 77, 78, 79, 80, 81, 82, 83, 89, 91, 93; IntYB 78, 79, 80, 81, 82; WhAm 11; Who 74, 82, 83, 85, 88, 90, 92, 94; WhoAm 74, 76, 78, 80, 82, 84, 86, 88, 90, 92; WhoFI 74, 75, 77, 79, 81, 83; WhoFr 79; WhoGov 72; WhoSSW 73; WhoWor 74, 76, 78, 80, 82, 84, 87, 89*

Schweppe, Jacob
Swiss. Inventor
Pioneered method of carbonating still water into soda water, 1792.
b. 1740
d. 1821
Source: *Entr*

Schwimmer, David
American. Actor
Plays Ross Geller on TV's ''Friends,'' 1994—.
b. Nov 12, 1966 in New York, New York
Source: *ConTFT 15; News 96, 96-2*

Schwinden, Ted
American. Politician
Dem. governor of Montana, 1981-89.
b. Aug 31, 1925 in Wolf Point, Montana
Source: *AlmAP 82, 84, 88; BiDrGov 1978, 1983, 1988; BioIn 20; IntWW 81, 82, 83, 89, 91, 93; IntYB 82; PolsAm 84; WhoAm 78, 80, 82, 84, 86, 88; WhoAmP 77, 79, 81, 83, 85, 87, 89, 91, 93, 95; WhoWest 80, 82, 84, 87, 89, 92, 94, 96; WhoWor 82, 87, 89, 91*

Schwinger, Julian (Seymour)
American. Physicist, Educator
Shared 1965 Nobel Prize in physics for developing theory of quantum electrodynamics.
b. Feb 12, 1918 in New York, New York
d. Jul 16, 1994 in Los Angeles, California
Source: *AmMWSc 73P, 76P, 79, 82, 86, 89, 92; AsBiEn; BiESc; BioIn 1, 4, 7, 8, 12, 14, 15, 20, 21; BlueB 76; CamDcSc; CurBio 67, 94N; IntWW 74, 75, 76, 77, 78, 79, 80, 81, 82, 83, 89, 91, 93; LarDcSc; LegTOT; McGMS 80; NobelP; NotTwCS; RAdv 14; ThTwC 87; WebAB 79; WhAm 11; Who 74, 82, 83, 85, 88, 90, 92, 94; WhoAm 74, 76, 78, 80, 82, 84, 86, 88, 90, 92, 94; WhoE 74; WhoFrS 84; WhoNob, 90, 95; WhoScEn 94; WhoWest 78, 80, 82, 84, 87, 89, 92, 94; WhoWor 74, 80, 82, 84, 87, 89, 91, 93; WorAl; WorAlBi; WorScD; WrDr 86, 88, 90, 92, 94, 96*

Schwinn, Edward R, Jr.
American. Business Executive
Pres., chief exec., Schwinn Bicycle Co., 1979—.
b. 1949?
Source: *BioIn 15; ConNews 85-4; Dun&B 90; WhoMW 82, 86*

Schwinn, Ignaz
American. Manufacturer
Bicycle pioneer, whose design has been successful from outset of co., 1895.
b. 1860
d. 1948
Source: *Entr*

Schwob, Marcel
French. Journalist, Author
Wrote *The Book of Monelle,* 1929; *Children's Crusade,* 1898.
b. Aug 23, 1867 in Chaville, France
d. Feb 26, 1905 in Paris, France
Source: *BioIn 1, 7, 13, 15, 19; ClDMEL 47, 80; ConAu 117; DcLB 123; EuAu; GuFrLit 1; OxCFr; PenC EUR; PenEncH; TwCLC 20*

Scipio Africanus, Publius Cornelius
[Scipio the Elder]
Roman. Army Officer
Most famous Roman general before Julius Caesar, known for victory over Hannibal at Zama.
b. 234BC
d. 183BC in Liternum, Campania
Source: *DcBiPP; REn*

Scobee, Dick
[Francis Richard Scobee]
American. Astronaut
Spacecraft commander who died in explosion of space shuttle *Challenger.*
b. May 19, 1939 in Auburn, Virginia
d. Jan 28, 1986 in Cape Canaveral, Florida
Source: *BioIn 16; NewYTBS 86*

Scobie, Ronald Mackenzie
British. Army Officer
Commander of British Land Forces in Adriatic, WW II; commander-in-chief of Allied forces in Greece.
b. Jun 8, 1893
d. 1969
Source: *CurBio 45; WhWW-II*

Scofield, John
American. Musician
Jazz guitarist; albums include *Decoy,* 1984 with Miles Davis.
b. Dec 26, 1951 in Dayton, Ohio
Source: *AllMusG; BioIn 12, 13, 16; ConMus 7; FacFETw; NewGrDJ 88, 94; OnThGG; PenEncP; WhoAm 94, 95, 96, 97*

Scofield, Paul
[David Paul Scofield]
English. Actor
Won Oscar, 1966, for *A Man for All Seasons.*
b. Jan 21, 1922 in Hurstpierpoint, England
Source: *BiE&WWA; BioIn 2, 3, 4, 6, 7, 8, 9, 10, 11, 14, 15, 16; BlueB 76; CamGWoT; CnThe; ConTFT 4, 13; CurBio 62; DcArts; EncMT; EncWT; Ent; FilmEn; FilmgC; ForYSC; HalFC 80, 84, 88; IlWWBF; IntMPA 82, 84, 86, 88, 92, 94, 96; IntWW 74, 75, 76, 77, 78, 79, 80, 81, 82, 83, 89, 91, 93; ItaFilm; LegTOT; MotPP; MovMk; NotNAT, A; OxCAmT 84; OxCFilm; OxCThe 67, 83; PlP&P; Who 74, 82, 83, 85, 88, 90, 92; WhoAm 94, 95, 96, 97; WhoHol 92, A; WhoThe 72, 77, 81; WhoWor 74, 76, 78, 84, 87, 89, 91, 93, 95, 96, 97; WorAl; WorAlBi*

Scopas
Greek. Sculptor
First to depict violent emotions on marble faces; known for architectural works, statues.
b. fl. 6th cent. BC in Paros, Greece
Source: *DcBiPP; NewCol 75; OxCArt; OxCClL, 89; OxDcArt; WebBD 83*

Scopes, John Thomas
American. Teacher
Tried for teaching theory of evolution against state law, ''monkey trial'' of 1925.
b. Aug 3, 1900 in Paducah, Kentucky
d. Oct 21, 1970 in Shreveport, Louisiana
Source: *DcAmB S8; LegTOT; NewYTBE 70; WorAl*

Score, Herb(ert Jude)
American. Baseball Player, Sportscaster
Pitcher, 1955-62, mostly with Cleveland; AL rookie of year, 1955; never fully recovered when hit in eye by line drive, 1957.
b. Jun 7, 1933 in Rosedale, New York

Source: *Ballpl 90; BiDAmSp Sup; BioIn 3, 4, 5, 6, 8, 11; WhoProB 73*

Scorel, Jan van
Dutch. Artist
Portraitist, religious painter; most of great altarpieces have perished.
b. 1495
d. 1562
Source: *BioIn 4, 11; McGDA; NewCol 75; OxCArt; OxDcArt*

Scoresby, William
English. Explorer
Pioneered in study of the Arctic; charted Greenland's coasts, 1820s.
b. Oct 5, 1789 in Whitby, England
d. Mar 22, 1857 in Torquay, England
Source: *Alli; ApCAB; BioIn 4, 18; BritAu 19; CelCen; DcBiPP; DcNaB, C; EncO&P 3; Geog 4; LarDcSc; NewCol 75; OxCShps; WhWE*

Scorpions
[Francis Buchholz; Matthias Jabs; Klaus Meine; Herman Rarebell; Rudolph Schenker]
German. Music Group
Formed in 1971; first American tour, 1979-80.
Source: *ConMus 12; EncRk 88; EncRkSt; IlEncRk; PenEncP; RkOn 85; WhoRocM 82*

Scorsese, Martin
American. Director, Screenwriter
Known for films *The Color of Money,* 1986; *Taxi Driver,* 1976.
b. Nov 17, 1942 in New York, New York
Source: *AmCulL; AmDec 1980; BenetAL 91; BiDFilm 81, 94; BioIn 10, 11, 12, 13, 14, 15, 16; CelR 90; ConAu 46NR, 110, 114; ConLC 20, 89; ConTFT 1, 5, 12; CurBio 79; DcArts; DcTwCCu 1; FacFETw; FilmEn; GangFlm; HalFC 84, 88; IlWWHD 1; IntDcF 1-2, 2-2; IntMPA 86, 88, 92, 94, 96; IntWW 82, 83, 89, 91, 93; LegTOT; MiSFD 9; MovMk; News 89-1; NewYTBE 73; NewYTBS 76, 85; Who 92, 94; WhoAm 74, 76, 78, 80, 82, 84, 86, 88, 90, 92, 94, 95, 96, 97; WhoEnt 92; WhoHol 92, A; WhoWor 84, 87, 91, 93, 95, 96, 97; WorAl; WorAlBi; WorFDir 2*

Scott, Adrian
[The Hollywood Ten]
American. Producer, Screenwriter
Blacklisted as Communist by film industry; sentenced to one yr. in prison.
b. Feb 6, 1912 in Arlington, New Jersey
d. 1973
Source: *FilmEn; FilmgC; GangFlm; HalFC 80, 84, 88; IntMPA 75, 76, 77, 78, 79, 80, 81, 82*

Scott, Arleigh Winston, Sir
West Indian. Political Leader
Governor-general of Barbados, 1967-76.
b. Mar 27, 1900, Barbados
d. Aug 9, 1976 in Georgetown, Barbados
Source: *IntWW 74; Who 74; WhoGov 72; WhoWor 74, 76*

Scott, Austin
American. Educator
Pres. of Rutgers U, 1891-1906.
b. Aug 10, 1848 in Maumee, Ohio
d. Aug 16, 1922 in Granville Centre, Massachusetts
Source: *DcAmB; NatCAB 3; TwCBDA; WhAm 1*

Scott, Austin Wakeman
American. Author, Educator
Authority on trust law; wrote classic *Scott on Trusts,* 1939.
b. Aug 31, 1884 in New Brunswick, New Jersey
d. Apr 9, 1981 in Boston, Massachusetts
Source: *ConAu 103; NewYTBS 74, 81; OxCLaw; WhAm 7*

Scott, Barbara Ann
Canadian. Skater
Two-time world champion figure skater; won gold medal, 1948 Olympics.
b. May 9, 1928 in Ottawa, Ontario, Canada
Source: *BioIn 1, 2, 3, 8, 10, 11, 16; CanWW 70; CurBio 48; InWom, SUP; WhoSpor*

Scott, Charles Prestwich
English. Editor
Editor, *Manchester Guardian,* 1872-1929, the forerunner of *The Guardian.*
b. Oct 26, 1846 in Bath, England
d. Jan 1, 1932 in Manchester, England
Source: *BioIn 1, 2, 5, 9, 14, 17; DcNaB 1931; GrBr; NewCBEL; WhDW*

Scott, Charles Wesly
[The Hostages]
American. Hostage
One of 52 held by terrorists, Nov 1979-Jan 1981.
b. 1933?
Source: *NewYTBS 81; WhoSSW 91*

Scott, Clarence
American. Businessman
Partner with brother, Edward, in million-dollar paper products business, begun 1879.
b. 1848 in Saratoga County, New York
d. 1912
Source: *Entr*

Scott, Cyril (Meir)
English. Composer, Author
Wrote opera *The Alchemist;* occult books include *The Initiate.*
b. Sep 27, 1879 in Oxton, England
d. 1970
Source: *Baker 78, 84, 92; BioIn 1, 3, 4, 8; BriBkM 80; CompSN, SUP; ConAu 111; DcNaB 1961; EncO&P 1S2, 1S3, 2, 3; MusMk; NewGrDM 80; NewGrDO; NewOxM; ObitT 1971; OxCMus; WhAm 6; WhE&EA; WhLit*

Scott, David Randolph
American. Astronaut
On flights of Gemini 8, 1966; Apollo 9, 1969; Apollo 15, 1971.
b. Jun 6, 1932 in San Antonio, Texas
Source: *BioIn 9, 10; CurBio 71; IntWW 74; NewYTBE 71; WhoAm 86, 88; WhoSSW 73; WhoWor 80*

Scott, Dred
American. Slave
Sued for his freedom, 1846; lost in Supreme Court, 1857; "Dred Scott Case" because landmark decision upholding slavery.
b. 1795 in Southampton County, Virginia
d. Sep 17, 1858 in Saint Louis, Missouri
Source: *AfrAmAl 6; AmBi; BenetAL 91; BioIn 1, 2, 6, 9, 10, 11, 12, 20; DcAmB; DcAmNB; EncAB-H 1974, 1996; InB&W 80, 85; LegTOT; McGEWB; WhAm HS; WorAl*

Scott, Duncan Campbell
Canadian. Poet
Wrote extensively on N American Indian: *Collected Poems,* 1926.
b. Aug 2, 1862 in Ottawa, Ontario, Canada
d. Dec 19, 1947 in Ottawa, Ontario, Canada
Source: *Benet 87, 96; BenetAL 91; BiD&SB; BioIn 1, 4, 5, 10, 11, 17; CamGEL; CamGLE; CanNov; CanWr; CasWL; Chambr 3; ChhPo, S1, S2, S3; ConAu 104, 153; ConCaAu 1; CreCan 2; DcLB 92; DcLEL; DcNAA; EvLB; GrWrEL P; LinLib L, S; LngCTC; MacDCB 78; OxCCan; OxCCanL; PenC ENG; RAdv 14, 13-1; REn; REnAL; RfGEnL 91; TwCA, SUP; TwCLC 6; WebE&AL; WhE&EA; WhLit; WhNaAH*

Scott, Edward Irvin
American. Businessman
Partner with brother Clarence, in million-dollar paper products business, begun 1879.
b. 1846 in Saratoga County, New York
d. 1931
Source: *Entr*

Scott, Evelyn
[Elsie Dunn; Ernest Soiza]
American. Author
Novels include *Migrations,* 1927; *The Wave,* 1929.
b. Jan 17, 1893 in Clarksville, Tennessee
d. Aug 3, 1963
Source: *AmAu&B; AmWomPl; AmWomWr; ArtclWW 2; BenetAL 91; BioAmW; BioIn 4, 9, 10, 12, 13, 14, 15, 16, 17; CnDAL; ConAmA; ConAmL; ConAu 104, 112; ConLC 43; DcLB 9, 48; DcLEL; FemiCLE; OxCAmL 65, 83, 95; OxCWoWr 95; PenNWW A; REnAL; SouWr; TwCA, SUP; TwCRHW 90, 94; WhE&EA; WhNAA*

Scott, George C(ampbell)
American. Actor
First performer to refuse Oscar, 1970, for *Patton.*

b. Oct 18, 1927 in Wise, Virginia
Source: *BiDFilm; BiE&WWA; BioIn 6, 8, 9, 10, 11, 13, 14, 15; BkPepl; CamGWoT; CelR 90; ConTFT 7; DcArts; HalFC 84, 88; IntDcT 3; IntMPA 86, 92; IntWW 74, 75, 76, 77, 83, 91, 93; NewYTBS 82; NotNAT; OxCFilm; WhoAm 74, 76, 78, 80, 82, 84, 86, 88, 90, 92, 94, 95, 96, 97; WhoEnt 92; WhoThe 81; WhoWor 74, 78; WorAlBi*

Scott, George Charles, Jr.
"Boomer"
American. Baseball Player
First baseman, 1966-79, mostly with Boston; led AL in home runs, RBIs, 1975.
b. Mar 23, 1944 in Greenville, Mississippi
Source: *BaseEn 88; InB&W 85; WhoBlA 80*

Scott, George Gilbert, Sir
English. Architect
Led Gothic revival; restored Westminster Abbey; designed Albert Memorial, 1863-72.
b. Jul 13, 1811 in Gawcott, England
d. Mar 27, 1878 in London, England
Source: *Alli, SUP; ArtsNiC; BioIn 3, 5, 10, 11, 13, 14, 16; CelCen; DcBiPP; DcD&D; DcNaB; IntDcAr; MacEA; McGDA; NewCol 75; OxCArt; VicBrit; WhDW; WhoArch*

Scott, Gloria Dean Randle
American. University Administrator
Pres., Bennett College, 1987—; first African-American pres. of the Girl Scouts 1975-78.
b. Apr 14, 1938 in Houston, Texas
Source: *AfrAmBi 1; BlkWAm; InB&W 85; InWom SUP; NotBlAW 1; WhoAfA 96; WhoAm 94, 95; WhoAmW 91; WhoBlA 85, 88, 90, 92, 94; WhoWor 96*

Scott, Gordon
[Gordon M Werschkul]
American. Actor
Was the 11th Tarzan in films, 1955-60.
b. Aug 3, 1927 in Portland, Oregon
Source: *FilmEn; FilmgC; ForYSC; HalFC 80, 84, 88; IntMPA 75, 76, 77, 78, 79, 80, 81, 82, 84, 86, 88, 92, 94, 96; ItaFilm; LegTOT; WhoHol 92, A; WhoHrs 80*

Scott, Hazel Dorothy
[Mrs. Adam Clayton Powell, Jr.]
American. Jazz Musician
Pianist, singer, popular in 1940s; sang "FDR Jones;" had own TV show.
b. Jun 11, 1920 in Port of Spain, Trinidad and Tobago
d. Oct 2, 1981 in New York, New York
Source: *AmPS B; AnObit 1981; ASCAP 66; BiDAfM; BiDAmM; BioIn 6, 8, 10; CmpEPM; CurBio 43, 81; DrBlPA; InB&W 80; InWom; WhoAmW 58; WhoHol A*

Scott, Hugh (Doggett), Jr.
American. Politician
Rep. minority leader, 1969-77; senator from PA, 1959-77.
b. Nov 11, 1900 in Fredericksburg, Virginia
d. Jul 21, 1994 in Falls Church, Virginia
Source: *BiDrAC; BiDrUSC 89; BioIn 1, 5, 6, 7, 8, 9, 10, 11, 12, 17, 20; BlueB 76; CelR; CurBio 94N; InB&W 85; IntWW 74, 75, 76, 77, 78, 79, 80, 81, 82, 83; NewYTBS 94; WhAm 11; WhoAm 74, 76, 78, 80, 82, 84, 86, 88, 90, 92, 94; WhoAmP 73, 75, 77, 79, 81, 83, 85, 87, 89, 91, 93; WhoWor 74; WorAl; WorAlBi*

Scott, Ken
[George Kenneth Scott]
American. Designer
First American to set up fashion house in Italy; known for scarves, colorful swimwear, 1950s-60s.
b. Nov 6, 1918 in Fort Wayne, Indiana
d. Feb 26, 1991 in Eze, France
Source: *BioIn 7, 8, 17; EncFash; NewYTBS 91; WorFshn*

Scott, Lizabeth
[Emma Matzo]
American. Actor
Played tough, shiftless blondes in 1940s-50s films: *Bad for Each Other,* 1953.
b. Sep 29, 1922 in Scranton, Pennsylvania
Source: *FilmEn; FilmgC; HalFC 80, 84, 88; IntMPA 77, 82, 96; InWom SUP; LegTOT; MotPP; MovMk; What 3; WhoAm 80; WhoHol 92, A; WorEFlm*

Scott, Martha Ellen
American. Actor
Broadway, film character actress nominated for Oscar for *Our Town,* 1940.
b. Sep 22, 1914 in Jamesport, Missouri
Source: *FilmgC; HalFC 88; HolP 40; InWom SUP; MovMk; NotNAT; WhoAm 74, 76, 82; WhoHol A; WhoThe 81; WorAlBi*

Scott, Mike
[Michael Warren Scott]
American. Baseball Player
Pitcher, 1980-92; threw no-hitter, 1986; won NL Cy Young Award, 1986.
b. Apr 26, 1955 in Santa Monica, California
Source: *Ballpl 90; BaseReg 86, 87; BioIn 15; NewYTBS 86; WhoAm 88, 90; WhoSpor; WorAlBi*

Scott, Norman
American. Opera Singer
Bass with NY Met., 1951-68.
b. Nov 30, 1928 in New York, New York
d. Sep 22, 1968 in New York, New York
Source: *BiDAmM; WhAm 5*

Scott, Paul Mark
English. Author
Wrote novels *The Raj Quartet,* 1976, adapted for TV, 1982.
b. Mar 25, 1920 in London, England
d. Mar 1, 1978 in London, England
Source: *Au&Wr 71; BioIn 10, 11, 12, 13; ConNov 72, 76, 82A; DcArts; DcLEL 1940; DcNaB 1971; GrBr; ObitOF 79; OxCEng 85, 95; TwCRHW 94; WorAu 1950; WrDr 76*

Scott, Peter Markham, Sir
English. Author, Naturalist
Founded World Wildlife Fund, designed panda logo, 1961; advocated existence of Loch Ness Monster; son of Robert.
b. Sep 14, 1909, England
d. Aug 29, 1989 in Bristol, England
Source: *Au&Wr 71; BioIn 7, 8, 12, 14, 16; BlueB 76; CurBio 89N; DcBrAr 1; DcNaB 1986; FacFETw; LngCTC; NewYTBS 89; OxCCan; WhE&EA; Who 74, 82, 83, 85, 88, 90N; WhoArt 80, 82, 84; WhoOcn 78; WhoWor 74, 89*

Scott, Pippa
[Phillippa Scott]
American. Actor
Appeared in films *Auntie Mame,* 1958; *Cold Turkey,* 1970.
b. Nov 10, 1935 in Los Angeles, California
Source: *BiE&WWA; FilmgC; ForYSC; HalFC 80, 84, 88; MotPP; WhoHol A*

Scott, Randolph
American. Actor
Made name as a Western hero who was fast on the draw but short on words: *Ride the High Country,* 1962.
b. Jan 23, 1898 in Orange County, Virginia
d. Mar 2, 1987 in Los Angeles, California
Source: *BiDFilm; BioIn 15, 16, 21; CmMov; ConNews 87-2; FilmgC; HalFC 88; IntMPA 82; LegTOT; MotPP; MovMk; NewYTBS 87; OxCFilm; WhoHol A; WorAlBi; WorEFlm*

Scott, Raymond
[Harry Warnow]
American. Songwriter, Bandleader
Led quintet, 1940s; with TV's "Your Hit Parade," 1950s; wrote "In an 18th Century Drawing Room."
b. Sep 10, 1909 in New York, New York
d. Feb 8, 1994 in North Hills, California
Source: *ASCAP 66, 80; BgBands 74; BiDAmM; BioIn 3, 6, 9, 12, 19, 20; CmpEPM; CurBio 41, 94N; MnPM; NewGrDJ 88; OxCPMus; PenEncP; PopAmC; RadStar; WhoHol 92; WhoJazz 72*

Scott, Ridley
English. Director
Films include *Alien,* 1979; *Blade Runner,* 1982; *Thelma and Louise* 1991.
b. 1939 in South Shields, England

Source: *BiDFilm 94; BioIn 13, 14, 15; ConTFT 5, 9; CurBio 91; DcArts; EncEurC; EncSF 93; HalFC 84, 88; IntDcF 2-2; IntMPA 92; IntWW 91; LegTOT; MiSFD 9; VarWW 85; WhoAm 92, 94, 95, 96, 97; WhoEnt 92*

Scott, Robert Falcon
English. Explorer
Led expedition to S Pole, 1912, only to find Roald Amundsen had already been there.
b. Jun 6, 1868 in London, England
d. Mar 27, 1912, South Pole
Source: *AnCL; AsBiEn; BioIn 1, 2, 3, 4, 5, 6, 7, 8, 9, 10, 11, 12, 13, 14, 15, 17, 18, 19, 20; DcNaB 1912; Expl 93; InSci; LinLib L, S; McGEWB; NewC; OxCEng 67, 85, 95; OxCShps; RAdv 14, 13-3; REn; WhDW; WhWE; WorAl*

Scott, Steve
American. Track Athlete
Second fastest miler in history.
b. 1956?
Source: *BiDAmSp OS; BioIn 12, 13, 16; NewYTBS 82*

Scott, Thomas Alexander
American. Railroad Executive
Head of Union rail transportation, Civil War; pres. of Pennsylvania Railroad, 1874-80.
b. Dec 28, 1823 in Fort Loudon, Pennsylvania
d. May 21, 1881 in Darby, Pennsylvania
Source: *AmBi; ApCAB; BiDAmBL 83; DcAmB; EncAB-H 1974, 1996; NatCAB 13; OxCAmH; REnAW; TwCBDA; WhAm HS; WhCiWar*

Scott, Tony
American. Musician
Top jazz clarinetist, 1950s-60s; adapted folk songs to jazz.
b. Jun 17, 1921 in Morristown, New Jersey
Source: *AllMusG; BiDAmM; BiDJaz; BioIn 5; CmpEPM; EncJzS; NewGrDA 86; NewGrDJ 88, 94; PenEncP; WhoAm 74; WhoE 74*

Scott, Walter
"Death Valley Scotty"
American. Adventurer
Built $2 million Moorish castle in Death Valley; tourist attraction today.
b. 1872
d. Jan 5, 1954 in Stovepipe Wells, California
Source: *BioIn 3, 7, 9, 10; CmCal; DcAmB S5; WebAB 74*

Scott, Walter, Sir
Scottish. Poet, Author, Historian
Father of historical novel; writings include *Ivanhoe*, 1820.
b. Aug 15, 1771 in Edinburgh, Scotland
d. Sep 21, 1832 in Abbotsford, Scotland
Source: *Alli; AnCL; AtlBL; BbD; Benet 87, 96; BiD&SB; BiDLA, SUP; BioIn 1, 2, 3, 4, 5, 6, 7, 8, 9, 10, 11, 12, 13, 14, 15, 17, 18, 19, 20, 21; BlmGEL; BritAu 19; BritWr 4; CamGEL; CamGLE; CarSB; CasWL; CelCen; Chambr 3; ChhPo, S1, S2, S3; CmScLit; CnDBLB 3; CnE&AP; CrtT 2, 4; CyWA 58; DcArts; DcBiA; DcBiPP; DcEnA, A; DcEnL; DcEuL; DcLB 93, 107, 116, 144, 159; DcLEL; DcNaB; DcPup; Dis&D; EncPaPR 91; EvLB; FamAYP; GrWrEL N, P; HalFC 80, 84, 88; HsB&A; LegTOT; LinLib L, S; LngCEL; MagSWL; McGEWB; MetOEnc; MnBBF; MouLC 3; NewC; NewCBEL; NewEOp 71; NewGrDM 80; NewGrDO; NinCLC 15; Novels; OxCChiL; OxCEng 67, 85, 95; OxCMus; OxCThe 83; OxDcOp; PenC ENG; PenEncH; PoChrch; PoeCrit 13; RAdv 1, 14, 13-1; RComWL; REn; RfGEnL 91; RfGShF; ScF&FL 92; Str&VC; SupFW; WebE&AL; WhDW; WhoChL; WhoHr&F; WorAl; WorAlBi; WorLitC; YABC 2*

Scott, Willard Herman, Jr.
American. TV Personality
Weatherman, "Today" show, 1980-95.
b. Mar 7, 1934 in Alexandria, Virginia
Source: *BioIn 12, 13; ConAu 109; NewYTBS 87; WhoAm 82, 84, 86, 88, 90, 92, 94, 95, 96, 97; WhoE 95; WhoTelC*

Scott, Winfield
"Old Fuss and Feathers"
American. Army Officer
Led US in Mexican War, 1846-48; Whig candidate for pres., 1852.
b. Jun 13, 1786 in Petersburg, Virginia
d. May 29, 1866 in West Point, New York
Source: *Alli; AmAu&B; AmBi; AmPolLe; ApCAB; BenetAL 91; BiAUS; BiDSA; BioIn 1, 2, 3, 4, 6, 7, 8, 9, 10, 12, 20; CelCen; CivWDc; CmdGen 1991; CyAG; DcAmAu; DcAmB; DcAmMiB; DcNAA; Drake; EncAB-H 1974, 1996; EncSoH; GenMudB; HarEnMi; HarEnUS; HisWorL; LegTOT; LinLib S; McGEWB; NatCAB 3; OxCAmH; PolPar; PresAR; REnAL; REnAW; TwCBDA; WebAB 74, 79; WebAMB; WhAm HS; WhCiWar; WhFla; WhNaAH; WhoMilH 76; WorAl; WorAlBi*

Scott, Zachary
American. Actor
Films include *Bandido*, 1956; *It's Only Money*, 1962.
b. Feb 24, 1914 in Austin, Texas
d. Oct 3, 1965 in Austin, Texas
Source: *BiE&WWA; BioIn 7, 10; FilmEn; FilmgC; ForYSC; HalFC 80, 84, 88; HolP 40; MotPP; MovMk; NotNAT B; WhoHol B; WhScrn 74, 77, 83; WorAl*

Scotti, Antonio
Italian. Opera Singer
Famed dramatic baritone, NY Met., 1900-33.
b. Jan 25, 1866 in Naples, Italy
d. Feb 26, 1936 in Naples, Italy
Source: *Baker 78, 84, 92; BiDAmM; BioIn 1, 3, 6, 11, 14; CmOp; IntDcOp; LegTOT; MetOEnc; MusSN; NewAmDM; NewEOp 71; NewGrDA 86; NewGrDM 80; NewGrDO; OxDcOp; PenDiMP; WhAm 1*

Scotto, Renata
Italian. Opera Singer
Soprano who made NY Met. debut, 1965.
b. Feb 24, 1934 in Savona, Italy
Source: *Baker 78, 84; BioIn 14; CelR 90; CmOp; IntDcOp; IntWW 74, 75, 76, 77, 78, 79, 80, 81, 82, 83, 91; IntWWM 90; InWom SUP; MetOEnc; MusSN; NewAmDM; NewEOp 71; NewGrDM 80; NewGrDO; NewYTBE 72; PenDiMP; WhoAm 86; WhoAmW 68, 70, 72, 74; WhoE 74; WhoMus 72; WhoWor 74, 78; WorAl; WorAlBi*

Scottsboro Boys
[Olen Montgomery; Clarence Norris; Haywood Patterson; Ozie Powell; Willie Roberson; Charlie Weems; Eugene Williams; Andy Wright; Roy Wright]
American. Criminals
Young defendants charged with rape; case dragged on for 20 years even though one of rape charges was recanted.
Source: *InB&W 80; NewCol 75*

Scourby, Alexander
American. Actor
Best known for resonant bass voice; most memorable screen role in *Giant*, 1956.
b. Nov 13, 1913 in New York, New York
d. Feb 22, 1985 in Boston, Massachusetts
Source: *BiE&WWA; BioIn 7, 8, 14; CurBio 65, 85, 85N; FilmEn; FilmgC; ForYSC; GangFlm; HalFC 80, 84, 88; ItaFilm; LegTOT; MotPP; MovMk; NewYTBS 85; NotNAT; RadStar; WhoE 74; WhoHol A; WhoThe 72, 77, 81; WorAl; WorAlBi*

Scowcroft, Brent
American. Presidential Aide
Head of National Security Council, 1975-77; 1989-93; member of Tower commission investigating Iran-Contra scandal, 1986-87.
b. Mar 19, 1925 in Ogden, Utah
Source: *AmMWSc 73S; WhoWor 80; WorDWW*

Scranton, George Whitfield
American. Manufacturer
Founded Scranton, PA, 1840.
b. May 11, 1811 in Madison, Connecticut
d. Mar 24, 1861 in Scranton, Pennsylvania
Source: *AmBi; BiDrAC; BiDrUSC 89; DcAmB; EncABHB 3; NatCAB 9; WhAm HS; WhAmP; WorAl*

Scranton, William Warren
American. Politician
Rep. governor of PA, 1963-66.
b. Jul 19, 1917 in Madison, Connecticut
Source: *BiDrAC; BiDrGov 1789; BiDrUSC 89; BioIn 6, 7, 10, 11, 12, 17; BioNews 74; CurBio 64; IntWW 83, 89, 91, 93; IntYB 78, 79, 80, 81, 82; NewYTBE 70; NewYTBS 76; PolProf J, K, NF; St&PR 75; WhoAm 74, 76, 78, 80, 82, 84; WhoAmP 73, 75, 77, 79, 81, 83, 85, 87, 89, 91, 93, 95; WhoE 86; WhoFI 89; WhoGov 72, 75, 77; WhoWor 74, 78, 80, 82; WorAl; WorAlBi*

Scriabin, Alexander Nicholaevich
[Alexsandr Scryabin]
Russian. Composer, Musician
Best known for composition *Prometheus.*
b. Jan 6, 1872 in Moscow, Russia
d. Apr 27, 1915 in Moscow, Russia
Source: *AtlBL; BioIn 1, 3, 4, 6, 7, 8, 9, 10, 12; DcCM; REn*

Scribe, (Augustin) Eugene
French. Dramatist
Wrote an estimated three to four hundred works; wrote *Encore une nuit de la Garde Nationale,* 1815.
b. 1791 in Paris, France
d. 1861 in Paris, France
Source: *AtlBL; Baker 78, 84, 92; BbD; Benet 87, 96; BiD&SB; BioIn 7, 10, 11, 14; BriBkM 80; CasWL; CelCen; CmOp; CnOxB; CnThe; DcArts; DcBiPP; DcEuL; Dis&D; DramC 5; EncWT; Ent; EuAu; EvEuW; GuFrLit 1; IntDcOp; IntDcT 2; LinLib L, S; McGEWD 72, 84; MetOEnc; NewCBEL; NewGrDM 80; NewGrDO; NinCLC 16; NotNAT A, B; OxCAmT 84; OxCFr; OxCThe 67, 83; OxDcOp; PenC EUR; REn; REnWD; RfGWoL 95*

Scribner, Charles
American. Publisher
Founded Baker and Scribner Publishers, 1846; changed to Charles Scribner's Sons, 1878.
b. Feb 21, 1821 in New York, New York
d. Aug 26, 1871 in Lucerne, Switzerland
Source: *AmAu&B; AmBi; ApCAB; BioIn 1; DcAmB; LegTOT; NatCAB 6; TwCBDA; WhAm HS; WhDW; WorAl; WorAlBi*

Scribner, Charles, Jr.
American. Publisher
Chairman, Scribner Book Cos., 1978-86; president, Charles Scribner's Sons, 1952 -77, chairman, 1977-78; was Ernest Hemingway's personal editor.
b. Jul 13, 1921 in Quogue, New York
d. Nov 11, 1995 in New York, New York
Source: *AmAu&B; BioIn 11, 14, 17, 19, 21; BlueB 76; CelR; ConAu 69, 150; IntAu&W 82; IntWW 74, 75, 76, 77, 78, 79, 80, 81, 82, 83, 89, 91, 93; LinLib L; PeoHis; SmATA 13, 87; St&PR 75, 84, 87; WhAm 11; WhoAm 74, 76, 78, 80, 82, 84, 86, 88, 90, 92, 94; WhoFI 74; WhoWor 74*

Scribner, Fred C(lark), Jr.
American. Government Official, Lawyer
Member, Republican National Committee, 1948-56; undersecretary of the Treasury, 1957-60; helped arrange Nixon-Kennedy debate, 1960.
b. Feb 14, 1908
d. Jan 5, 1994 in Portland, Maine
Source: *BioIn 4, 5; CurBio 94N; St&PR 75, 84, 87, 91, 93; WhAm 11; WhoAm 74, 76, 78, 80, 82, 84, 86, 88, 90, 92, 94; WhoAmL 78, 79, 83, 87; WhoAmP 73, 75, 77, 79, 81, 83, 85, 87, 89, 91, 93; WhoFI 92, 94*

Scripps, Edward Wyllis
American. Newspaper Publisher
Formed Scripps-McRae League of Newspapers which evolved into Scripps-Howard Newspapers; developed United Press International.
b. Jun 18, 1854 in Rushville, Illinois
d. Mar 12, 1926 in Monrovia, Liberia
Source: *AmAu&B; AmBi; BioIn 2, 3, 5, 7, 9, 10, 13, 14, 15, 16, 17, 20; DcAmB; EncAB-H 1974, 1996; McGEWB; NatCAB 28; OxCAmH; REnAL; WebAB 74, 79; WhAm 1*

Scripps, Robert Paine
American. Journalist
Editorial director of Scripps-Howard newspaper chain from 1917.
b. Oct 27, 1895 in San Diego, California
d. Mar 2, 1938
Source: *AmAu&B; AmBi; BioIn 4, 13; DcAmB S2; LinLib L, S; NatCAB 62; WhAm 1, 1C*

Scruggs, Earl Eugene
[Flatt and Scruggs]
American. Musician, Songwriter
Won Grammy, 1969, for "Foggy Mountain Breakdown."
b. Jan 6, 1924 in Flint Hill, North Carolina
Source: *Baker 84, 92; BiDAmM; BioIn 14, 15; ConMus 3; EncFCWM 69; EncRk 88; HarEnR 86; NewAmDM; NewGrDA 86; OxCPMus; WhoAm 76, 78, 80, 82, 84, 86, 88, 90, 92, 94, 95, 96, 97; WhoAmP 73; WhoEnt 92; WhoGov 72; WhoWor 74, 78*

Scruggs, Jan
American. Veterans' Leader
Vietnam veteran; created concept of Vietnam Veterans Memorial, 1982, with wall of names of deceased soldiers.
Source: *BioIn 16; ConHero 1*

Scudery, Madeleine de
French. Author
Wrote huge novels, which epitomized sentimental romances of her day: *Almahide, or the Slave as Queen,* 1660-63.
b. Nov 15, 1607 in Le Havre, France
d. Jun 2, 1701 in Paris, France
Source: *BbD; Benet 87, 96; BiD&SB; BioIn 5, 7, 9, 11, 17; BlmGWL; CasWL; ContDcW 89; CyWA 58; DcEuL; EncCoWW; EvEuW; FemiCLE; FrenWW; IntDcWB; InWom, SUP; LegTOT; LitC 2; NewC; NewCBEL; OxCEng 67, 85, 95; OxCFr; PenC EUR; PenNWW A; REn; WhDW*

Sculley, John
American. Business Executive
As president and CEO of Pepsi-Cola Co., 1977-83 used his marketing skills to create "the Pepsi generation;" Apple Computer, Inc., president and CEO, 1983-, chairman 1986-.
b. Apr 6, 1939 in New York, New York
Source: *BioIn 11, 13; ConAu 127; CurBio 88; Dun&B 79, 88, 90; IntWW 89, 91, 93; News 89; St&PR 84, 87, 91, 93, 96, 97; WhoAm 82, 84, 86, 88, 90, 92, 94, 95, 96; WhoFI 81, 87, 92, 94, 96; WhoTech 95; WhoWest 87, 89, 92, 94; WorAlBi*

Scully, Vince(nt Edward)
American. Sportscaster
With NBC Sports since 1982, covering among other things, baseball game of the week.
b. Nov 29, 1927 in New York, New York
Source: *BiDAmSp OS; BioIn 4, 6, 13; WhoAm 78, 80, 82, 84, 86, 88, 90, 92, 94, 95, 96, 97; WhoTelC; WhoWest 96*

Seaborg, Glenn Theodore
American. Chemist
Shared Nobel Prize, 1951, for identification of elements 94-102; chm., Atomic Energy Commission, 1961-71.
b. Apr 19, 1912 in Ishpeming, Michigan
Source: *AmMWSc 76P, 79, 82, 86, 89, 92, 95; AsBiEn; BiESc; BioIn 1, 2, 3, 4, 5, 6, 7, 9, 10, 11, 12, 14, 15, 19, 20, 21; BlueB 76; CamDcSc; ConAu 2NR, 49; CurBio 48, 61; EncWB; FacFETw; Future; InSci; IntAu&W 77, 93; IntWW 91; LinLib L, S; McGMS 80; NobelP; OxCAmH; RAdv 14; St&PR 87, 91; WebAB 74, 79; WhE&EA; Who 74, 82, 83, 85, 88, 90, 92, 94; WhoAm 74, 76, 78, 80, 82, 84, 86, 88, 90, 92, 94, 95, 96, 97; WhoAmP 73; WhoFrS 84; WhoNob, 90, 95; WhoScEn 94, 96; WhoWest 78, 80, 82, 84, 87, 89, 92, 94, 96; WhoWor 74, 76, 78, 80, 82, 84, 87, 89, 91, 93, 95, 96, 97; WorAl; WorAlBi; WrDr 94, 96*

Seabury, Samuel
[A Westchester Farmer]
American. Theologian, Pamphleteer, Religious Leader
Loyalist during Revolution who was first American-born Episcopalian bishop.
b. Nov 30, 1729 in Groton, Connecticut
d. Feb 25, 1796 in New London, Connecticut
Source: *Alli; AmAu&B; AmBi; AmWrBE; ApCAB; BenetAL 91; BioIn 3, 5, 6, 9,*

10, 11, 13, 14, 19; BlkwEAR; CnDAL; CyAL 1; DcAmAu; DcAmB; DcAmReB 1, 2; DcLB 31; DcLEL; DcNAA; Drake; EncAB-H 1974, 1996; EncARH; EncCRAm; HarEnUS; LuthC 75; McGEWB; NatCAB 3; OxCAmH; OxCAmL 65, 83, 95; REnAL; TwCBDA; WebAB 74, 79; WhAm HS

Seaga, Edward Phillip George
Jamaican. Political Leader
Prime minister of Jamaica, 1981-89.
b. May 28, 1930 in Boston, Massachusetts
Source: *BiDLAmC; BioIn 12, 13, 14, 16; CurBio 81; IntWW 91; NewYTBS 80; Who 92; WhoWor 87, 91*

Seagal, Steven
American. Actor
Martial arts expert; movies include: *Above the Law,* 1988; *Under Siege,* 1992.
b. Apr 10, 1951 in Lansing, Michigan
Source: *IntMPA 92, 94; WhoAm 94, 95, 96, 97*

Seagram, Joseph Edward Frowde
Canadian. Distiller
President of Joseph E Seagram & Sons from 1937.
b. Aug 11, 1903 in Waterloo, Ontario, Canada
d. Nov 28, 1979 in Waterloo, Ontario, Canada
Source: *CanWW 70, 79; IntYB 78, 79, 80; St&PR 75; WhAm 7; WhoAm 74; WhoCan 73, 75, 77, 80; WhoE 74; WhoFI 74; WhoMW 74; WhoWor 74*

Seagrave, Gordon Stifler
American. Surgeon, Author
Founded hospitals in Burma, practiced there for 40 yrs.
b. 1897 in Rangoon, Burma
d. Mar 28, 1965 in Namkham, Burma
Source: *BioIn 1, 2, 3, 4, 5, 6, 7, 8; CurBio 43, 65; DcAmB S7; InSci; OhA&B; WebAMB; WhAm 4*

Seagren, Bob
[Robert Lloyd Seagren]
American. Track Athlete
Pole vaulter; first American to vault 18 feet, 1972; won gold medal, 1968 Olympics, silver medal, 1972 Olympics.
b. Oct 17, 1946 in Pomona, California
Source: *BiDAmSp OS; BioIn 7, 8, 10; CmCal; CurBio 74; WhoSpor; WhoTr&F 73*

Seajay, Carol
American. Publisher
Co-founder of the feminist bookstore Old Wives Tales, 1976, San Francisco; publisher and editor, *Feminist Bookstore News,* 1976—.
Source: *BioIn 19; GayLesB*

Seal
[Sealhenry Olumide Samuel]
English. Singer, Songwriter
Debut album, *Seal,* 1991; won three Grammy Awards, 1996.
b. Feb 19, 1963 in Paddington, England
Source: *ConMus 14*

Seal, Elizabeth
Italian. Actor
Won Tony for *Irma La Douce,* 1961.
b. Aug 28, 1933 in Genoa, Italy
Source: *BiE&WWA; ConTFT 5; EncMT; HalFC 84, 88; NotNAT; VarWW 85; WhoHol 92; WhoThe 72, 77, 81*

Seale, Bobby G
American. Political Activist, Author
Co-founder, chairman, Black Panthers, 1966.
b. Oct 20, 1936 in Dallas, Texas
Source: *BiDAmLf; BioIn 14, 15; BlkWr 1; BlkWrNE; ConBlB 3; Dun&B 90; LivgBAA; MugS; NewYTBE 70; PolProf J, NF; WhoBlA 85, 88*

Seals, Dan Wayland
American. Singer, Songwriter
Member of pop duo England Dan and John Ford Coley, 1969-80; solo career, 1983—; hits include "Bop," 1988.
b. Feb 8, 1948 in McCarney, Texas
Source: *BioIn 14; ConMus 9; HarEnCM 87; WhoAm 94, 95, 96, 97*

Seals, Jim
[Seals and Crofts; James Seals]
American. Singer, Songwriter
Guitarist, vocalist with Seals and Crofts; had hit album *Diamond Girl,* 1973.
b. Oct 17, 1942 in Sindey, Texas
Source: *BkPepl; EncPR&S 89; WhoAm 82*

Seals and Crofts
[Dash Crofts; Jim Seals]
American. Music Group
Hit rock duo, popular during 1970s; songs show social concern.
Source: *BkPepl; ConMus 3; EncPR&S 74, 89; EncRk 88; HarEnR 86; IlEncRk; PenEncP; RkOn 74; WhoAm 78, 80, 82; WhoRocM 82*

Seaman, Owen, Sir
English. Editor
Editor of *Punch,* 1906-32.
b. Sep 18, 1861 in London, England
d. Feb 2, 1936 in London, England
Source: *Alli SUP; BioIn 2, 11, 14; Chambr 3; ChhPo, S1, S2, S3; DcNaB 1931; EvLB; GrBr; LngCTC; NewC; NewCBEL; NotNAT B; TwCA, SUP; WhE&EA; WhLit; WhThe*

Searchers, The
[Billy Adamson; Frank Allen; Bob Jackson; John McNally; Mike Pender]
English. Music Group
Second to The Beatles in popularity, 1960s; hits include "Love Potion No. 9," 1964.
Source: *BiDAmM; BioIn 12; DrAPF 80, 83, 85, 87; EncRk 88; EncRkSt; HarEnR 86; OxCPMus; PenEncP; ProFbHF; RkOn 78, 84; RolSEnR 83; WhoRock 81; WhoRocM 82*

Searle, Ronald William Fordham
English. Artist
Children's writer, film illustrator; created cartoon series, "St. Trinian's," 1941-53.
b. Mar 3, 1920 in Cambridge, England
Source: *Au&Wr 71; BioIn 14, 15; ConAu 9R, 25NR; FacFETw; IlsBYP; IlsCB 1946; IntWW 74, 91; NewC; OxCChiL; OxCTwCA; SmATA 24, 42; TwCPaSc; Who 92; WhoAm 86, 88; WhoArt 84; WhoGrA 62; WhoWor 74, 89; WrDr 76, 92*

Sears, Eleonora Randolph
"Mother of Squash"
American. Athlete
Socialite, all-around sportswoman who made breakthrough into all-male sports; first woman squash champion, 1928.
b. Sep 28, 1881 in Boston, Massachusetts
d. Mar 26, 1968 in Palm Beach, Florida
Source: *BiDAmSp OS; BioIn 12, 17, 21; InWom SUP; NotAW MOD*

Sears, Heather
English. Actor
b. Sep 28, 1935 in London, England
Source: *FilmEn, 78, 79, 80, 81, 82, 84, 86; MotPP; WhoHol 92, A; WhoThe 72, 77, 81*

Sears, Isaac
"King Sears"
American. Patriot
Led anti-British demonstrations in New York City before the American Revolution.
b. Jul 1, 1730 in West Brewster, Massachusetts
d. Oct 28, 1786 in Guangzhou, China
Source: *BioIn 12, 16; BlkwEAR; DcAmB; EncAR; EncCRAm; NatCAB 1; WebAB 74, 79; WhAm HS; WhAmRev*

Sears, John Patrick
American. Lawyer
Deputy counsel to Nixon, 1969-70; managed Reagan's presidential campaign, 1975-76, 1979-80.
b. Jul 3, 1940 in Syracuse, New York
Source: *BioIn 8, 10, 11, 12; NewYTBS 76; WhoAm 74, 76, 78, 80, 82, 84, 86, 88, 90, 92, 94, 95, 96, 97; WhoAmL 78, 79; WhoAmP 79, 81, 83, 85, 87, 89, 91, 93, 95; WhoSSW 73*

Sears, Richard Dudley
American. Tennis Player
First US nat. amateur tennis champ, 1881.
b. Oct 26, 1861 in Boston, Massachusetts
d. Apr 8, 1943 in Boston, Massachusetts
Source: *BiDAmSp OS; DcAmB S3*

Sears, Richard Warren
American. Merchant
Issued first mail order catalog, 1887; Sears, Roebuck opened, 1893.
b. Dec 7, 1863 in Stewartville, Minnesota
d. Sep 28, 1914 in Waukesha, Wisconsin
Source: *AmBi; ApCAB X; BiDAmBL 83; BioIn 2, 6, 7, 10, 20; DcAmB; EncAAH; WebAB 74, 79; WhAm 1; WhDW*

Sears, Robert Richardson
American. Psychologist, Educator
Psychology professor at several universities, specializing in child development; wrote *Patterns of Child Rearing,* 1957.
b. Aug 31, 1908 in Palo Alto, California
d. May 22, 1989 in Menlo Park, California
Source: *AmAu&B; AmMWSc 73S, 78S; BioIn 2, 3, 10, 12, 16, 17; ConAu 17R; CurBio 52, 89; InSci; NewYTBS 89; WhAm 10; WhoAm 74, 76, 78, 80, 82, 84, 86, 88*

Sears-Collins, Leah J.
American. Judge
First black woman to serve on the State Supreme Court of Georgia, 1992—.
b. Jun 13, 1955 in Heidelberg, Germany (West)
Source: *AfrAmBi 1; ConBlB 5; NotBlAW 2; WhoAmL 94, 96; WhoAmW 93, 95; WhoBlA 90; WhoSSW 93, 95*

Seaton, George
American. Screenwriter
Won Oscars for *Miracle on 34th Street,* 1947; *The Country Girl,* 1954.
b. Apr 17, 1911 in South Bend, Indiana
d. Jul 28, 1979 in Beverly Hills, California
Source: *BiDFilm, 81, 94; BioIn 9, 11, 12, 15; ConAu 89, 105; DcFM; DcLB 44; EncAFC; FilmEn; FilmgC; HalFC 80, 84, 88; IlWWHD 1A; IndAu 1967; IntDcF 1-2; IntMPA 75, 76, 77, 78, 79; LegTOT; MiSFD 9N; MovMk; WhAm 7; WhoAm 74, 76, 78; WhoWor 74; WhScrn 83; WorEFlm*

Seattle
American. Native American Chief
Chief of the Suquamish tribe; signed Port Elliott Treaty with the US government ceding native lands, 1855.
b. 1788?
d. Jun 7, 1866 in Washington
Source: *NotNaAm; WhNaAH*

Seaver, Tom
[George Thomas Seaver]
"Tom Terrific"
American. Baseball Player
Pitcher, 1967-86, mostly with Mets; 17th in ML history to win 300 games, 1985; won NL Cy Young Award three times.
b. Nov 17, 1944 in Fresno, California
Source: *Ballpl 90; BaseReg 86, 87; BiDAmSp BB; BioIn 7, 8, 9, 10, 11, 12, 13, 14, 15, 16; BkPepl; CelR; CmCal; CurBio 70; LegTOT; NewYTBE 70; NewYTBS 74, 77, 85; WhoAm 74, 76, 78, 80, 82, 84, 86, 88, 92, 94, 95, 96, 97; WhoE 95; WhoProB 73; WhoSpor*

Sebastian, John
[Lovin' Spoonful]
American. Singer
Co-founder, rock-folk group, Lovin' Spoonful, 1965.
b. Mar 17, 1944 in New York, New York
Source: *Baker 84, 92; BioIn 13, 14; ConMuA 80A, 80B; EncRk 88; IlEncRk; LegTOT; NewGrDA 86; RkOn 78, 82; RolSEnR 83; WhoAm 74; WhoHol 92; WhoRock 81; WhoRocM 82; WorAlBi*

Sebastiani, Samuele
American. Vintner
Established prosperous trade selling bulk wine to bottlers in US, 1825.
b. 1874
d. 1944
Source: *Entr*

Sebelius, Keith George
American. Politician
Rep. congressman from KS, 1969-81.
b. Sep 10, 1916 in Alamena, Kansas
d. Sep 5, 1982 in Norton, Kansas
Source: *BiDrAC; WhoMW 74, 76, 78, 80, 82*

Seberg, Jean
American. Actor
Discovered by Otto Preminger; films include *Saint Joan,* 1957; *Lilith,* 1964.
b. Nov 13, 1938 in Marshalltown, Iowa
d. Aug 31, 1979 in Paris, France
Source: *BiDFilm, 78, 79; InWom SUP; ItaFilm; LegTOT; MotPP; MovMk; NewYTBS 80; OxCFilm; WhoAmW 74; WhoFr 79; WhoHol A; WhoWor 74; WhScrn 83; WorEFlm*

Sebrell, W(illiam) H(enry), Jr.
American. Nutritionist
Medical director, Weight Watchers International, 1971-79; director, Weight Watchers Foundation, 1971-92.
b. Sep 11, 1901 in Portsmouth, Virginia
d. Sep 29, 1992 in Pompano Beach, Florida
Source: *AmMWSc 73P, 76P, 79; BiDrAPH 79; BioIn 2, 3, 18, 19; CurBio 92N; InSci; WhAm 10; WhoAm 74, 76, 78, 80, 82, 84, 86, 88, 90, 92; WhoWor 74*

Sebring, Jay
American. Hairstylist, Actor
Murdered, with Sharon Tate, by Charles Manson family.
b. Oct 10, 1933 in Alabama
d. Jul 8, 1969 in Los Angeles, California
Source: *BioIn 6; WhScrn 77, 83*

Secchi, Pietro Angelo
Italian. Astronomer
Jesuit priest known for work in spectroscopy; classified stars by their spectra, made solar-eclipse photo, 1860.
b. 1818 in Reggio Nell'Emilia, Italy
d. Feb 26, 1878 in Rome, Italy
Source: *AsBiEn; BiESc; DcAmB; DcCathB; DcScB; NewCol 75*

Secombe, Harry
Welsh. Actor, Comedian, Singer
With Spike Mulligan, Peter Sellers, originated, performed in BBC radio series, "The Goon Show," 1951-56.
b. Sep 8, 1921 in Swansea, Wales
Source: *BioIn 10, 13; BlueB 76; ConAu 57; EncMT; FilmgC; HalFC 80, 84, 88; IlWWBF; IntMPA 75, 76, 77, 78, 79, 80, 81, 82, 84, 86, 88, 92, 94, 96; Who 74, 82, 83, 85, 88, 90, 92; WhoHol 92, A; WhoMus 72; WhoThe 72, 77, 81; WrDr 76, 80, 82*

Secord, Laura Ingersoll
Canadian. Historical Figure
During War of 1812, warned British of surprise American attack at Beaver Dams, 1813.
b. 1775 in Massachusetts
d. Oct 17, 1868 in Chippewa, Ontario, Canada
Source: *BioIn 10; ColCR; MacDCB 78; NewCol 75; OxCCan; WomFir*

Secunda, Arthur
[Holland Arthur Secunda]
American. Artist
Abstract paintings reflect California environment through use of vibrant colors.
b. Nov 12, 1927 in Jersey City, New Jersey
Source: *PrintW 83, 85; WhoAm 76, 78, 80, 82, 84, 86, 88, 90, 92, 94, 95, 96; WhoAmA 73, 76, 78, 80, 82, 84, 86, 89, 91*

Secunda, Sholom
Russian. Conductor
Wrote over 40 operettas for NYC Yiddish Theater; noted for "Bei Mir Bist Du Schon," 1933.
b. Aug 23, 1894 in Alexandria, Russia
d. Jun 13, 1974 in New York, New York
Source: *ASCAP 66, 80; Baker 84, 92; BioIn 2, 10, 12, 13; ConAmC 76, 82; ConAu 49; NatCAB 58; NewYTBS 74; WhAm 6; WhoAm 74; WhoMus 72; WhoWorJ 72*

Sedaka, Neil
American. Singer, Songwriter
Wrote songs "Breaking Up is Hard to Do," 1960; "Love Will Keep Us Together," 1975.
b. Mar 13, 1939 in New York, New York
Source: *AmSong; BioIn 6, 10, 11, 12, 13, 14, 15, 16; BkPepl; ConAu 103; ConMuA 80A; ConMus 4; CurBio 78; EncPR&S 74, 89; EncRk 88; EncRkSt; HarEnR 86; IlEncRk; LegTOT; NewAmDM; NewGrDA 86; OxCPMus; PenEncP; RkOn 74, 78; RolSEnR 83; WhoAm 78, 80, 82, 84, 86, 88, 90, 92, 94, 95, 96, 97; WhoEnt 92; WhoHol 92; WhoRock 81; WhoRocM 82; WorAl; WorAlBi*

Seddon, Rhea
American. Astronaut
One of five women chosen for astronaut program, Jul, 1978.
b. 1947?
Source: *BioIn 11, 12; WhoSpc*

Sedelmaier, Joe
[John Josef Sedelmaier]
American. Director, Filmmaker
Advertising director who created "Where's the Beef" commercial for Wendy's, 1984.
b. May 31, 1933 in Orrville, Ohio
Source: *BioIn 13, 14, 15; ConNews 85-3; WhoAdv 90; WhoAm 80, 82, 84, 86, 88, 90, 92, 94, 95, 96, 97; WhoEnt 92; WhoWor 80, 82, 84, 87*

Sedgman, Frank
[Francis Arthur Sedgman]
Australian. Tennis Player
First Australian to win US Nat. singles title, 1951, 1952; Wimbledon, 1952.
b. Oct 29, 1927 in Mont Albert, Australia
Source: *BioIn 2, 3, 12; BuCMET; CurBio 51; Who 74, 82, 83, 85, 88, 90, 92, 94*

Sedgwick, Adam
English. Zoologist
Discovered an important zoological link between Annelida and Arthropoda.
b. Sep 28, 1854 in Norwich, England
d. Feb 27, 1913 in London, England
Source: *DcNaB 1912*

Sedgwick, Anne Douglas
American. Author
Wrote novels *Tante,* 1911; *Little French Girl,* 1924.
b. Mar 28, 1873 in Englewood, New Jersey
d. Jul 19, 1935
Source: *AmAu&B; AmBi; AmWomWr; BenetAL 91; BioIn 1; Chambr 3; CnDAL; ConAmA; ConAmL; DcAmB S1; DcLEL; DcNAA; EvLB; FemiCLE; InWom, SUP; LibW; LngCTC; NotAW; OhA&B; OxCAmL 65, 83, 95; REnAL; ScF&FL 1; TwCA, SUP; WhAm 1; WhE&EA; WhLit; WomWWA 14*

Sedgwick, Catherine Maria
"Marie Edgeworth of America"
American. Author
Best-known historical novel: *Hope Leslie,* 1827.
b. Dec 28, 1789 in Stockbridge, Massachusetts
d. Jul 31, 1867 in West Roxbury, Massachusetts
Source: *Alli; AmWom; ApCAB; ArtclWW 2; BenetAL 91; CarSB; ChhPo; DcAmB; DcEnL; DcLB 1; DcLEL; DcNAA; HarEnUS; NewCBEL; NotAW; OxCAmL 83; REnAL*

Sedgwick, John
American. Army Officer
Commanded Union troops at Antietam, Chancellorsville, etc; killed in Wilderness campaign.
b. Sep 13, 1813 in Cornwall Hollow, Connecticut
d. May 9, 1864 in Spotsylvania, Virginia
Source: *Alli; AmBi; ApCAB; BioIn 1, 7, 12; CivWDc; DcAmB; Drake; GenMudB; HarEnUS; NatCAB 4; NewCol 75; TwCBDA; WebAMB; WhAm HS; WhCiWar*

Sedney, Jules
Surinamese. Political Leader
Prime minister, Suriname, 1970-73; chm., Nat. Planning Council, 1980—.
b. Sep 28, 1922 in Paramaribo, Suriname
Source: *IntWW 74, 75, 76, 77, 78, 79, 80, 81, 82, 83, 89, 91, 93*

Sedran, Barney
[Heavenly Twins]
American. Basketball Player
Guard with several pro teams, 1912-26; Hall of Fame.
b. Jan 28, 1891 in New York, New York
d. Jan 14, 1969 in New York, New York
Source: *BioIn 9; ObitOF 79; WhoBbl 73; WhoSpor*

Seebeck, Thomas Johann
German. Physicist
Research in flow of electric current with a variety of conductors led to discovery of Seebeck effect.
b. Apr 9, 1770 in Tallinn, Estonia
d. Dec 10, 1831 in Berlin, Prussia
Source: *AsBiEn; BiESc; BioIn 12; CamDcSc; DcBiPP; DcInv; DcScB; InSci; LarDcSc*

Seeckt, Hans von
German. Military Leader
As general and leader of the Reichswehr, strengthened German army by stressing efficiency and a Russo-German alliance.
b. Apr 22, 1866 in Schleswig, Prussia
d. Dec 27, 1936 in Berlin, Germany
Source: *BioIn 1, 2, 3, 5, 14; DcTwHis; EncTR, 91; FacFETw; HarEnMi; WhoMilH 76*

Seed, Jenny
South African. Author
Children's historical novels include *The Bushman's Dream,* 1974.
b. May 18, 1930 in Cape Town, South Africa
Source: *BioIn 11, 21; ConAu 21R, X; IntAu&W 86; SmATA 8; TwCChW 78, 83, 89, 95; WhoWor 95, 96, 97; WrDr 76, 82, 84, 86, 88, 90, 92, 94, 96*

Seefried, Irmgard Maria Theresia
German. Opera Singer
Soprano with Vienna State Opera, 1940s; made NY Met. debut, 1953.
b. Oct 9, 1919 in Kongetvied, Germany
d. Nov 24, 1988 in Vienna, Austria
Source: *Baker 84; BriBkM 80; CurBio 56; IntWW 74; MusSN; NewGrDM 80; Who 74; WhoMus 72; WhoWor 74*

Seeger, Alan
American. Poet
Wrote "I Have a Rendevous with Death," 1916; killed in WW I.
b. Jun 22, 1888 in New York, New York
d. Jul 4, 1916 in Belloy en Senterre, France
Source: *AmAu&B; AmBi; Benet 87, 96; BenetAL 91; BibAL; BioIn 6, 7, 10, 12, 13, 15; CamGEL; CamGLE; CamHAL; Chambr 3; ChhPo, S3; CnDAL; DcAmB; DcAmC; DcLB 45; DcLEL; DcNAA; EvLB; FacFETw; LinLib L, S; LngCTC; NatCAB 20; OxCAmL 65, 83, 95; OxCTwCP; REn; REnAL; TwCA; TwCWr; WebAMB; WhAm 4*

Seeger, Pete(r)
[The Weavers]
American. Singer, Songwriter
Folksinger, guitarist, social activist; founded The Weavers, 1948; wrote modern folksong "If I Had a Hammer," 1958, popularized by Peter, Paul, and Mary, 1962.
b. May 3, 1919 in New York, New York
Source: *AmSocL; Baker 78, 84, 92; BgBkCoM; BioIn 6, 7, 8, 10, 11, 12, 13, 16; BioNews 74; BlueB 76; CelR, 90; CmpEPM; ConAu 33NR, 69; ConHero 2; ConMuA 80A; ConMus 4; CurBio 63; DcArts; EncAAH; EncAL; EncFCWM 69, 83; EncMcCE; EncRk 88; EncWB; FacFETw; HarEnR 86; HeroCon; IlEncRk; LegTOT; LNinSix; MusMk; NewAmDM; NewGrDA 86; NewGrDM 80; OxCPMus; PenEncP; PolPar; RadHan; RolSEnR 83; SmATA 13; WebAB 74, 79; WhoAm 74, 76, 78, 80, 82, 84, 86, 88, 90, 92, 94, 95, 96, 97; WhoEnt 92; WhoHol 92, A; WhoRock 81; WhoRocM 82; WhoWor 74; WorAl; WorAlBi*

Seeley, Blossom
[Mrs. Benny Fields]
American. Actor
Vaudville performer with husband; their life filmed as *Somebody Loves Me.*
b. Jul 16, 1892 in San Pablo, California
d. Apr 17, 1974 in New York, New York

Source: *BiE&WWA; HalFC 80, 84, 88; LegTOT; NewYTBS 74; NotNAT B; OxCAmT 84; WhoHol B; WhScrn 77*

Seferiades, Giorgos Styljanou
Greek. Author, Diplomat
Won 1963 Nobel Prize in literature; best known for unique style of poetry.
b. Feb 22, 1900 in Izmir, Turkey
d. Sep 20, 1971 in Athens, Greece
Source: *ConAu 5NR, 5R; CurBio 64; WhoNob*

Seferis, George
Greek. Poet
Widely translated pioneer of symbolism in Greek literature; won Nobel Prize for Literature, 1963.
b. Mar 13, 1900 in Smyrna, Ottoman Empire
d. Sep 20, 1971 in Athens, Greece
Source: *Benet 87, 96; BioIn 1, 13, 15, 17; ClDMEL 80; CnMWL; ConAu 5NR, 5R, 33R, 36NR, X; ConLC 5, 11; DcArts; EncWL 2, 3; EuWr 12; FacFETw; GrFLW; IntvTCA 2; LegTOT; LinLib L; MajTwCW; MakMC; McGEWB; NobelP; ObitOF 79; ObitT 1971; OxCEng 85, 95; PenC EUR; RAdv 14, 13-2; RComWL; RfGWoL 95; RGFMEP; WhoNob; WhoTwCL; WorAu 1950*

Sefton, William
[Heavenly Twins]
American. Track Athlete
With Earle Meadows, formed Heavenly Twins pole vaulting team; set world record, 1937.
b. Jan 21, 1915 in Los Angeles, California
Source: *WhoTr&F 73*

Segal, Erich Wolf
American. Author, Dramatist
Wrote *Love Story,* 1970; translated into 23 languages, filmed, 1970; *Oliver's Story,* 1977, filmed, 1978.
b. Jun 16, 1937 in New York, New York
Source: *AmAu&B; BioIn 8, 9, 10, 11, 12, 14, 15; BkPepl; ConAu 20NR, 36NR; ConLC 3, 10; CurBio 71; DcLB Y86B; DrAS 82F; HalFC 84, 88; MajTwCW; NewYTBE 71; Who 85, 92; WhoAm 86, 88; WhoE 74; WhoHol A; WhoUSWr 88; WhoWor 84; WhoWorJ 72; WhoWrEP 89; WrDr 86, 92*

Segal, George
American. Sculptor
Known for life-size sculpture done in plaster.
b. Nov 26, 1924 in New York, New York
Source: *AmArt; AmCulL; Benet 87; BioIn 6, 7, 8, 9, 10, 11, 12, 13, 14, 16, 19; BriEAA; CelR; ConArt 77, 83, 89, 96; CurBio 72; DcAmArt; DcCAA 71, 77, 88, 94; DcCAr 81; EncWB; FacFETw; McGDA; OxCTwCA; OxDcArt; PhDcTCA 77; PrintW 83, 85; WebAB 74, 79; WhoAm 74, 76, 78, 80, 82, 84, 86, 88, 90, 92, 94, 95, 96, 97; WhoAmA 73, 76, 78, 80, 82, 84, 86, 89, 91, 93; WhoWor 74; WorAlBi; WorArt 1950*

Segal, George
American. Actor
Starred in *A Touch of Class,* 1973; *Carbon Copy,* 1981.
b. Feb 13, 1934 in New York, New York
Source: *BiDFilm, 81; BioIn 7, 9, 10, 11, 12, 14; BkPepl; ConTFT 3; EncAFC; FilmEn; FilmgC; GangFlm; HalFC 80, 84, 88; IntMPA 75, 76, 77, 78, 79, 80, 81, 82, 84, 86, 88, 92, 94, 96; IntWW 77, 78, 79, 80, 81, 82, 83, 89, 91, 93; ItaFilm; LegTOT; MotPP; MovMk; VarWW 85; WhoAm 86, 88, 90, 92, 94, 95, 96, 97; WhoCom; WhoEnt 92; WhoHol 92, A; WorAl; WorAlBi*

Segal, Henry
American. Journalist
Editor, publisher of *American Israelite,* 1930-85, oldest English-Jewish newspaper in US.
b. 1901
d. Jul 18, 1985 in Cincinnati, Ohio
Source: *ConAu 116*

Segal, Lore Groszmann
American. Author
Children's fiction include *Lucinella,* 1976; *Tell Me a Trudy,* 1977.
b. Mar 8, 1928 in Vienna, Austria
Source: *AmAu&B; ConAu 5NR, 13R; DrAF 76; DrAPF 87, 91; IntAu&W 91; InWom SUP; LiExTwC; SmATA 4, 11AS, 66; WhoAm 86, 90; WhoAmW 87; WhoMW 84; WhoUSWr 88; WrDr 76, 86, 92*

Segal, Vivienne
American. Actor
Broadway star of operettas, musicals: *Desert Song,* 1926; *Pal Joey,* 1940.
b. Apr 19, 1897 in Philadelphia, Pennsylvania
d. Dec 29, 1992 in Los Angeles, California
Source: *BiDAmM; BiE&WWA; BioIn 6, 9, 16, 18; CmpEPM; EncMT; Film 2; FilmEn; ForYSC; HalFC 80, 84, 88; InWom SUP; MotPP; NotNAT; NotWoAT; OxCAmT 84; OxCPMus; ThFT; What 3; WhoHol 92, A; WhoThe 77A; WhThe*

Segantini, Giovanni
Artist
Portrayed allegorical scenes, peasants, alpine landscapes: *At The Watering Place.*
b. Jan 15, 1858 in Arco, Italy
d. Sep 28, 1899 in Samaden, Switzerland
Source: *BioIn 1, 13; ClaDrA; Dis&D; IntDcAA 90; McGDA; NewCol 75; OxCArt; OxDcArt; WebBD 83*

Segar, Elzie Crisler
American. Cartoonist
Created comic strip "Popeye," 1929.
b. Dec 8, 1894 in Chester, Illinois
d. Oct 13, 1938 in Santa Monica, California
Source: *BioIn 17; DcNAA; WebAB 74, 79; WorECom*

Seger, Bob
[The Silver Bullet Band; Robert Clark Seger]
American. Singer, Musician
Triple platinum albums *Stranger in Town,* 1978; *Against the Wind,* 1980.
b. May 6, 1945 in Ann Arbor, Michigan
Source: *ASCAP 80; BioIn 11, 12, 13, 14, 16; ConLC 35; ConMuA 80A; ConMus 15; ConNews 87-1; EncPR&S 89; EncRk 88; EncRkSt; HarEnR 86; IlEncRk; LegTOT; NewAmDM; NewGrDA 86; PenEncP; RkOn 74, 78; RolSEnR 83; WhoAm 86, 88, 90, 92, 94, 95; WhoEnt 92; WhoRock 81*

Segni, Antonio
Italian. Political Leader
Premier of Italy, 1955-57, 1959-60; pres., 1962-64; founder of Christian Dem. Party.
b. Feb 2, 1891 in Sardinia, Italy
d. Dec 1, 1972 in Rome, Italy
Source: *BioIn 4, 5, 6, 9, 10; CurBio 55, 73, 73N; LinLib S; NewYTBE 72; ObitT 1971; WhAm 5*

Segovia, Andres
Spanish. Musician
Brought classical guitar into mainstream of musical world during 71-yr. career.
b. Feb 18, 1894 in Linares, Spain
d. Jun 2, 1987 in Madrid, Spain
Source: *BioIn 1, 2, 3, 4, 5, 6, 7, 10, 11; CelR; ConAu 111; ConNews 87-3; CurBio 48, 64, 87; IntWW 74, 75, 76, 77, 78, 79, 80, 81, 82, 83; IntWWM 77; NewYTBS 86; WhAm 9; Who 74, 82, 83, 85; WhoAm 76, 78, 80, 82, 84, 86; WhoAmM 83; WhoMus 72; WhoWor 74, 78, 87; WorAl; WorAlBi*

Segrave, Henry O'Neal de Hane, Sir
English. Auto Racer, Boat Racer
Set several land and water speed records, 1920s.
b. Sep 22, 1896 in Baltimore, Maryland
d. Jun 13, 1930 in Lake Windermere, England
Source: *BioIn 6, 7, 8; DcNaB MP*

Segre, Emilio Gino
American. Physicist
Shared Nobel Prize for physics, 1959.
b. Feb 1, 1905 in Tivoli, Italy
d. Apr 22, 1989 in Lafayette, California
Source: *AmMWSc 73P, 76P, 79, 82, 86, 89, 92; AsBiEn; BiESc; BioIn 14, 15, 16; BlueB 76; CamDcSc; CmCal; ConAu 13NR, 128; CurBio 60, 89, 89N; InSci; IntAu&W 91; IntWW 83, 89N; McGMS 80; NewYTBS 89; NobelP; WebAB 74, 79; WebBD 83; Who 85, 90N; WhoAm 86, 88; WhoAmJ 80; WhoNob, 90, 95; WhoTech 89; WhoWest 87; WhoWor 87, 89; WorAlBi; WorScD; WrDr 86, 90*

Segretti, Donald H
American. Lawyer
His "dirty trick" activities were the first uncovered by Woodward & Bernstein, 1972; convicted of political espionage.
b. Sep 17, 1941 in San Marino, California
Source: *BioIn 9, 10, 11; NewYTBE 73; PolProf NF*

Segura, Pancho
[Francisco Segura]
Ecuadorean. Tennis Player
First S. American to win nat. professional singles championship, 1950, 1951.
b. Jun 20, 1921, Ecuador
Source: *BioIn 2, 3, 5, 10; BuCMET; CurBio 51; NewYTBE 71*

Seiberling, Frank Augustus
American. Businessman
Founder, pres., Goodyear Tire & Rubber Co., 1898-1921.
b. Oct 6, 1859 in Western Star, Ohio
d. Aug 11, 1955 in Akron, Ohio
Source: *ApCAB X; BiDAmBL 83; BioIn 7; DcAmB S5; WhAm 3*

Seibert, Earl Walter
Canadian. Hockey Player
Defenseman, 1931-46, with three NHL teams; Hall of Fame, 1963; son of Oliver, also in Hall of Fame.
b. Dec 7, 1911 in Kitchener, Ontario, Canada
d. May 20, 1990 in Agawam, Massachusetts
Source: *BioIn 16; HocEn; WhoHcky 73*

Seibert, Florence B(arbara)
American. Biochemist, Inventor
Developed first test for tuberculosis infection, internationally adopted 1952.
b. Oct 6, 1897 in Easton, Pennsylvania
d. Aug 23, 1991 in Saint Petersburg, Florida
Source: *AmMWSc 73P, 76P, 79, 89, 92; AmWomSc; BioIn 1, 2, 4, 6, 15; CurBio 91N; WhAm 10; WhoAm 74, 76; WhoAmW 58, 61, 64, 66, 68, 70, 72, 74*

Seibert, Michael
[Blumberg and Seibert]
American. Skater
With Judy Blumberg, won bronze medal in ice dancing, 1983 world championships.
b. 1959? in Washington, Pennsylvania
Source: *BioIn 12, 13, 14; NewYTBS 83, 84*

Seibert, Oliver L
Canadian. Hockey Player
Played for amateur teams, early 1900s; Hall of Fame, 1961; father of Earl, also in Hall of Fame.
b. Mar 18, 1881 in Berlin, Ontario, Canada
d. May 15, 1944
Source: *WhoHcky 73*

Seidelman, Susan
American. Director, Producer
Directed film *Desperately Seeking Susan,* 1984.
b. Dec 11, 1952 in Philadelphia, Pennsylvania
Source: *BioIn 14, 15, 16; ConTFT 3, 12; CurBio 90; GrLiveH; HalFC 88; IntMPA 92, 94, 96; IntWW 91, 93; LegTOT; MiSFD 9; ReelWom; WhoAm 90, 92, 94, 95, 96, 97; WhoAmW 91, 93, 95, 97; WhoEnt 92; WomFir*

Seidl, Anton
Hungarian. Conductor
Led NY Philharmonic, from 1891; noted Wagnerian.
b. May 7, 1850 in Budapest, Hungary
d. Mar 28, 1898 in New York, New York
Source: *ApCAB SUP, X; Baker 78, 84, 92; BiDAmM; BioIn 19; BriBkM 80; CmOp; DcAmB; HarEnUS; IntDcOp; MetOEnc; NatCAB 8; NewAmDM; NewEOp 71; NewGrDA 86; NewGrDM 80; NewGrDO; OxCMus; OxDcOp; PenDiMP; TwCBDA; WhAm HS*

Seifert, Elizabeth
American. Author
Wrote novels with a medical setting: *Young Dr. Galahad,* won Redbook Prize, 1938.
b. Jun 19, 1898 in Washington, Missouri
d. Jun 17, 1983 in Moberly, Missouri
Source: *AmWomWr; CurBio 51, 83N; IntAu&W 82X; InWom; WhoAmW 83; WrDr 84*

Seifert, Jaroslav
Czech. Poet
Won Nobel Prize for literature, 1984.
b. Sep 23, 1901 in Prague, Bohemia
d. Jan 10, 1986 in Prague, Czechoslovakia
Source: *AnObit 1986; Benet 87, 96; BioIn 14, 15, 17; CasWL; ClDMEL 80; ConAu 127; ConLC 34, 44, 93; DcArts; EncWL 2, 3; EvEuW; FacFETw; IntWW 74, 75, 76, 77, 78, 79, 80, 81, 82, 83; IntWWP 77; LegTOT; MajTwCW; ModSL 2; NewYTBS 86; NobelP; PenC EUR; RAdv 14, 13-2; WhoNob, 90, 95; WhoSocC 78; WhoWor 74; WorAu 1975*

Seiler, James, W
American. Broadcasting Executive
Founded American Research Bureau (later Arbitron), 1949; conducted first broadcast audience survey system.
b. 1917
d. Jan 2, 1983 in Silver Spring, Maryland
Source: *NewYTBS 82*

Seinfeld, Jerry
American. Comedian, Actor
Star of TV series "Seinfeld."
b. Apr 29, 1955 in New York, New York
Source: *BioIn 16; CurBio 92; News 92; WhoAm 92, 94, 95, 96; WhoEnt 92*

Seiss, Joseph Augustus
American. Clergy
Founded General Council of Evangelical Lutheran Church in N America; wrote many books on religion.
b. Mar 18, 1823 in Frederick County, Maryland
d. Jun 20, 1904 in Philadelphia, Pennsylvania
Source: *Alli, SUP; AmAu&B; ApCAB; BiDSA; ChhPo; DcAmAu; DcAmB; DcNAA; Drake; LuthC 75; NatCAB 7; RelLAm 91; TwCBDA; WhAm 1*

Sejanus, Lucius Aelius
Roman.
Head administrator of Roman Empire under Tiberius.
d. Oct 18, 31
Source: *BioIn 6, 8, 9; OxCClL, 89*

Selby, David
American. Actor
Starred in TV soap opera "Dark Shadows," 1966-71; played Richard Channing on TV drama "Falcon Crest," 1982-90.
b. Feb 5, 1941 in Morgantown, West Virginia
Source: *ConTFT 5; IntMPA 84, 86, 88, 92, 94, 96; WhoHol 92, A*

Selby, Hubert, Jr.
American. Author
Wrote *Last Exit to Brooklyn,* 1964, subject of obscenity trial in England, banned in Italy.
b. Jul 23, 1928 in New York, New York
Source: *AmAu&B; Benet 87, 96; BenetAL 91; BioIn 7, 8, 13, 17, 18; BlueB 76; CamGLE; CamHAL; CasWL; ConAu 13R, 33NR; ConLC 1, 2, 4, 8; ConNov 72, 76, 82, 86, 91, 96; DcArts; DcLB 2; DcLEL 1940; DrAF 76; DrAPF 87; IntAu&W 76, 77, 89; LegTOT; ModAL S1; Novels; OxCAmL 83, 95; RGTwCWr; ShSCr 20; WebE&AL; WhoAm 80, 82, 84, 86, 88, 90, 92, 94, 95, 96, 97; WhoEnt 92; WorAu 1970; WrDr 76, 80, 82, 84, 86, 88, 90, 92, 94, 96*

Selden, George Baldwin
American. Inventor
Developed gasoline engine, 1879; patented, 1895.
b. Sep 14, 1846 in Clarkon, New York
d. Jan 17, 1922 in Rochester, New York
Source: *BioIn 9; DcAmB; InSci; LinLib S; NatCAB 20; WebAB 74, 79; WhAm 4*

Selden, John
English. Judge, Orientalist
Noted for collection of remarks over 20-yr. period: *Table Talk,* 1689.
b. Dec 10, 1584 in Salvington, England
d. Nov 30, 1654 in London, England
Source: *Alli; Benet 87, 96; BiD&SB; BioIn 2, 3, 4, 9, 14, 15, 16; BritAu; CamGEL; CamGLE; CasWL; Chambr 1; CyEd; DcBiPP; DcEnA; DcEnL; DcEuL; DcLEL; DcNaB; EvLB; HisDStE; NewC; NewCBEL; OxCEng 67, 85, 95;*

OxCLaw; OxCShps; PenC ENG; REn; WebE&AL; WhDW

Seldes, George (Henry)
American. Journalist
Foreign correspondent, *Chicago Tribune,* 1919-28; advocate for freedom of the press; wrote *Even the Gods Cannot Change History,* 1976; *Witness to a Century,* 1987.
b. Nov 16, 1890 in Alliance, New Jersey
d. Jul 2, 1995 in Windsor, Vermont
Source: *AmAu&B; Au&Wr 71; BenetAL 91; BiDAmJo; BioIn 3, 4, 10, 14, 15, 16, 17, 21; ConAu 2NR, 5R, 149; CurBio 41, 95N; DcAmSR; EncAJ; IntAu&W 77, 86, 91, 93; NewYTBS 95; OxCAmL 65, 83; REnAL; TwCA, SUP; WhE&EA; WhJnl; WhNAA; WhoAm 74, 76, 78, 80, 82, 84, 86, 88, 90, 92, 94, 95; WrDr 76, 80, 82, 84, 86, 88, 90, 92, 94, 96*

Seldes, Gilbert Vivian
American. Critic, Author, Editor
CBS program director, 1937-45; wrote *The Seven Lively Arts,* 1924; novel *The Wings of the Eagle,* 1929; brother of George.
b. Jan 3, 1893 in Alliance, New Jersey
d. Sep 29, 1970 in New York, New York
Source: *AmAu&B; Au&Wr 71; BiDAmNC; BiE&WWA; BioIn 21; CnDAL; ConAu 5R; NewYTBE 70; OxCAmL 83; OxCFilm; PenC AM; REnAL; TwCA SUP; WebAB 79; WhAm 5*

Seldes, Marian
American. Actor
Won 1967 Tony for *A Delicate Balance.*
b. Aug 23, 1928 in New York, New York
Source: *BiE&WWA; BioIn 16; BlueB 76; CamGWoT; ConAu 19NR, 85; ConTFT 2, 15; ForYSC; NotNAT; NotWoAT; WhoAm 84, 86, 90; WhoE 74; WhoEnt 92; WhoHol 92, A; WhoThe 72, 77, 81*

Seldom Scene, The
[Mike Auldridge; T Michael Coleman; John Duffey; Ben Eldridge; Tom Gray; Phil Rosenthal; John Starling]
American. Music Group
Bluegrass band; name chosen because of infrequent concert appearnces; albums include *Scenic Roots,* 1990.
Source: *BgBkCoM; BioIn 14; ConMus 4; DcBrBI; DcVicP 2; EncFCWM 69; HarEnCM 87; MedHR; NewGrDA 86; NewYTBS 27; OnThGG; WhoRock 81; WhoRocM 82*

Selena
[Selena Quintanilla Perez]
American. Singer
Grammy Award singer of Tejano songs.
b. Apr 16, 1971 in Lake Jackson, Texas
d. Mar 31, 1995 in Corpus Christi, Texas
Source: *BioIn 20, 21; ConMus 16; DcHiB; News 95*

Seles, Monica
Yugoslav. Tennis Player
Won Grand Slam, 1990; ranked number 1 female tennis player by the Women's International Tennis Association, 1991. Stabbed during tennis match, 1994. Made comeback, 1995.
b. Dec 2, 1973 in Novi Sad, Yugoslavia
Source: *BioIn 15; BuCMET; CurBio 92; IntWW 91, 93; LegTOT; News 91-3; NewYTBS 90; WhoAm 92, 94, 95, 96, 97; WhoAmW 95, 97; WhoSpor; WhoWor 93, 95, 96, 97*

Selfridge, Harry Gordon
English. Businessman
Opened Selfridge and Co., Ltd., 1909.
b. Jan 11, 1858 in Ripon, Wisconsin
d. May 8, 1947 in London, England
Source: *BioIn 1, 2, 4, 5, 12, 14; DcNaB, 1941; DcTwBBL; GrBr; WebAB 74; WhAm 2; WhE&EA*

Selfridge, Thomas Etholen
American. Soldier
First fatality of powered airplane travel; Selfridge AFB, MI named for him.
b. Feb 8, 1882 in San Francisco, California
d. Sep 17, 1908 in Fort Meyer, Virginia
Source: *BioIn 6; InSci*

Selig, Bud
[Allan H. Selig]
American. Sports Executive
President and CEO, Milwaukee Brewers baseball team, 1970—; interim commissioner of Major League Baseball, 1991—.
b. Jul 30, 1934 in Milwaukee, Wisconsin
Source: *News 95, 95-2; WhoAm 74, 76, 78, 80, 82, 84, 86, 88, 90, 92, 94, 95, 96, 97; WhoMW 78, 80, 82, 84, 86, 88, 92, 93, 96*

Selim I
"Yavuz (The Grim)"
Ruler
Sultan, 1512-20; extended Ottomon Empire to include Syria, the Hejaz, and Egypt.
b. 1470 in Amasya, Ottoman Empire
d. Sep 22, 1520 in Corlu, Ottoman Empire

Selke, Frank J, Sr.
Canadian. Hockey Executive
With Conn Smythe, helped build Toronto Maple Leafs; became GM, Montreal, 1946-64, winning six Stanley Cups; NHL trophy given to best defensive forward named for him, 1978; Hall of Fame, 1976.
b. May 7, 1893 in Kitchener, Ontario, Canada
Source: *WhoHcky 73*

Selkirk, Alexander
Scottish. Adventurer
Lived alone on island, 1703-09; Daniel Defoe based *Robinson Crusoe* on account of his life.
b. 1676 in Largo, Scotland
d. 1721
Source: *Alli; ApCAB; Benet 87, 96; BioIn 1, 4, 5, 8, 9, 12, 13; BlmGEL; DcBiPP; DcEuL; DcNaB; Drake; LngCEL; NewC; NewCBEL; OxCEng 85, 95; OxCShps; REn; WhWE*

Sellars, Peter
American. Director
Director, American National Theater, J F Kennedy Center for Performing Arts.
b. 1958? in Pittsburgh, Pennsylvania
Source: *BioIn 13, 14, 15; CamGWoT; CurBio 86; IntWW 91; IntWWM 90; MetOEnc; NewGrDA 86; WhoAm 86; WhoEnt 92*

Sellecca, Connie
American. Actor
Played Christine Francis on TV series "Hotel," 1983-88.
b. May 25, 1955 in New York, New York
Source: *BioIn 11, 12, 15, 16; ConTFT 6, 13; IntMPA 92, 94, 96; LegTOT; VarWW 85; WhoAm 92; WorAlBi*

Selleck, Tom
[Thomas William Selleck]
"Clark Gable of the 80s"
American. Actor
Played Thomas Magnum on TV series "Magnum PI," 1980-88; won Emmy, 1984; star of film *Three Men and a Baby,* 1987.
b. Jan 29, 1945 in Detroit, Michigan
Source: *BioIn 12, 13, 14, 15, 16; CelR 90; ConTFT 1, 3, 12; CurBio 83; HalFC 88; IntMPA 86, 88, 92, 94, 96; IntWW 89, 91, 93; LegTOT; VarWW 85; WhoAm 86, 88, 90, 92, 94, 95, 96, 97; WhoEnt 92; WhoHol 92, A; WhoTelC; WorAlBi*

Sellers, Peter
[Richard Henry Peter Sellers]
English. Actor
Played Inspector Jacques Clouseau in *The Pink Panther* films, 1963-76.
b. Sep 8, 1925 in Portsmouth, England
d. Jul 24, 1980 in London, England
Source: *AnObit 1980, 78, 79, 80; ItaFilm; JoeFr; LegTOT; MotPP; MovMk; OxCFilm; QDrFCA 92; WhAm 7; Who 74; WhoCom; WhoHol A; WhoWor 74, 78; WhScrn 83; WorAl; WorAlBi; WorEFlm*

Sellinger, Frank
[Francis John Sellinger]
American. Brewer
Chief exec., Joseph Schlitz Brewing, 1980-82.
b. Jul 8, 1914 in Philadelphia, Pennsylvania
Source: *Dun&B 90; St&PR 84; WhoAm 80, 82, 84; WhoFI 81; WhoMW 80, 82*

Sellinger, Joseph A
American. University Administrator
Pres., Loyola of Baltimore, 1964-1993; transformed small commuter's college into one of the nation's leading Jesuit universities.
d. Apr 19, 1993 in Baltimore, Maryland

Selmon, Lee Roy
American. Football Player
Five-time all-pro defensive end, Tampa Bay, 1976-85.
b. Oct 20, 1954 in Eufaula, Oklahoma
Source: *BiDAmSp FB; BioIn 13; FootReg 85, 86; WhoAm 82, 84; WhoBlA 80, 85, 88, 90; WhoSpor*

Selvon, Samuel Dickson
[Sam Selvon]
Trinidadian. Author
Novels focus on Caribbean life: *Moses Ascending*, 1975; *I Hear Thunder*, 1963.
b. May 20, 1923 in San Fernando, Trinidad and Tobago
Source: *Benet 87; BenetAL 91; BioIn 13, 14; CamGLE; CasWL; ConAu 117, 128, X; ConNov 86, 91; DcLB 125; FifCWr; IntvWPC; LiExTwC; LngCTC; MajTwCW; RAdv 13-2; RfGEnL 91; SchCGBL; WebE&AL; Who 85, 92; WorAu 1950; WrDr 86, 92*

Selye, Hans
[Hugo Bruno Selye]
Canadian. Scientist
Authority on stress who linked it to disease, death; wrote *Stress without Distress*, 1974.
b. Jan 26, 1907 in Vienna, Austria
d. Oct 16, 1982 in Montreal, Quebec, Canada
Source: *AmMWSc 73P, 76P, 79, 82; AnObit 1982; BiDPsy; BioIn 2, 3, 4, 5, 6, 10, 11, 12, 13, 15; BlueB 76; CanWW 70, 79, 80, 81; ConAu 2NR, 5R, 108; CurBio 51, 81, 83, 83N; FacFETw; InSci; IntAu&W 76, 77; IntMed 80; IntWW 74, 75, 76, 77, 78, 79, 80, 81, 82; NewYTBS 82; WhAm 8; WhoAm 74, 76, 78, 80, 82; WhoWor 74, 78; WrDr 76, 80, 82*

Selzer, Richard (Alan)
American. Author
Wrote *Letters to a Young Doctor*, 1982; *Raising the Dead*, 1993; winner of the 1982 Pushcart Prize for fiction.
b. Jun 24, 1928 in Troy, New York
Source: *BioIn 15, 16; ConAu 14NR, 65; ConLC 74; CurBio 93; IntAu&W 86; WhoAm 84, 86, 88, 90; WorAu 1985*

Selznick, David O(liver)
American. Producer
Won Oscar, 1939, for producing *Gone With the Wind*.
b. May 10, 1902 in Pittsburgh, Pennsylvania
d. Jun 22, 1965 in Hollywood, California
Source: *BiDFilm; BioIn 7, 8, 9, 10, 11, 12, 13; CurBio 41, 65; DcArts; DcFM; FilmgC; NatCAB 54; OxCFilm; WebAB 74, 79; WhAm 4; WorEFlm*

Selznick, Irene Mayer
American. Producer
Known for threatrical productions on London, NYC stages, 1940s-60s; former wife of David O Selznick.
b. Apr 2, 1907 in New York, New York
d. Oct 10, 1990 in New York, New York
Source: *BiE&WWA; BioIn 13, 16, 17; ConAu 132; NewYTBS 90; NotNAT; NotWoAT; WhAm 10; WhoAm 84, 86, 88, 90*

Sembello, Michael
American. Singer, Musician
Guitarist for Stevie Wonder, 1973-79; had hit single "Maniac" from film *Flashdance*, 1983.
b. Apr 17, 1956? in Philadelphia, Pennsylvania
Source: *RkOn 85*

Sembene, Ousmane
Senegalese. Filmmaker
Made *La Noire de . . .*, (*Black Girl*) 1965; *Camp de Thiaroye*, (*The Camp at Thiaroye*) 1987; several of his films have been banned in African nations.
b. Jan 1, 1923 in Ziguinchor, Senegal
Source: *AfrA; AfSS 78, 79, 80, 81, 82; BiDFilm 94; BioIn 9, 11, 13, 14, 15, 16, 17, 18, 19, 20, 21; CasWL; ConBlB 13; CurBio 94; CyWA 89; DcAfHiB 86; DrBlPA, 90; EncWL, 2, 3; InB&W 80; IntAu&W 76; IntDcF 1-2, 2-2; MiSFD 9; ModBlW; ModFrL; PenC CL; RAdv 13-2; WorAu 1970; WorFDir 2*

Sembrich, Marcella
[Marcelline Kochanska]
Polish. Opera Singer
Soprano, great favorite of NY Met., 1898-1909; noted for Violetta role.
b. Feb 18, 1858 in Wisniewczyk, Poland
d. Jan 11, 1935 in New York, New York
Source: *Baker 78, 84, 92; BiDAmM; BioIn 1, 2, 3, 5, 7, 8, 10, 11, 13, 14; BriBkM 80; CmOp; DcAmB S1; EncAB-A 5; IntDcOp; InWom SUP; LibW; MetOEnc; MusSN; NatCAB 25; NewAmDM; NewEOp 71; NewGrDA 86; NewGrDM 80; NewGrDO; NotAW; OxDcOp; PenDiMP; WhAm 1*

Semenenko, Serge
American. Financier, Business Executive
Consultant to ailing companies who led group that bought Warner Brothers; with First National Bank of Boston, 1926-67.
b. Aug 23, 1903 in Odessa, Russia
d. Apr 24, 1980 in New York, New York
Source: *BioIn 6, 8, 12; IntYB 78; NewYTBS 80; St&PR 75; WhAm 7; WhoAm 74*

Semenov, Nikolai Nikolaevich
Russian. Chemist
First Soviet in homeland to win Nobel Prize, 1956, for research into mechanics of chemical reaction.
b. Apr 16, 1896 in Saratov, Russia
d. Sep 28, 1986 in Moscow, Russia
Source: *BiESc; BioIn 14, 15; McGEWB; McGMS 80; NobelP; WhDW; Who 82, 83, 85, 88N; WhoAtom 77; WhoNob, 90, 95; WhoSocC 78; WhoWor 74, 78, 80, 82; WorAl; WorAlBi*

Semmelweis, Ignaz Philipp
Hungarian. Physician
Discovered how pueperal fever is transmitted; helped greatly to reduce the death rate.
b. Jul 1, 1818 in Buda, Hungary
d. Aug 13, 1865 in Vienna, Austria
Source: *BiESc; BioIn 1, 2, 3, 4, 5, 6, 7, 9, 10, 12, 16; DcCathB; DcScB; LarDcSc; McGEWB; OxCMed 86; WorAlBi; WorScD*

Semple, Lorenzo, Jr.
Screenwriter
Films include *Never Say Never Again*, 1983; TV movies include *Rearview Mirror*, 1986.
Source: *BioIn 13; ConAu 125, 129; ConDr 88A; ConTFT 5; FilmgC; HalFC 80, 84, 88; IntDcF 1-4; IntMPA 84, 86, 88, 92, 94, 96; VarWW 85*

Semyonova, Marina
Russian. Dancer
Russia's first prima ballerina; best known for role of Nikya in *La Bayadere*.
b. Jun 12, 1908 in Saint Petersburg, Russia
Source: *BiDD; BioIn 14, 15, 17; NewYTBS 87*

Senanayake, Don Stephen
Ceylonese. Political Leader
First prime minister of Ceylon, 1947-52; regarded as father of country.
b. Oct 20, 1884 in Botale, Ceylon
d. Mar 22, 1952 in Colombo, Ceylon
Source: *BioIn 2, 3, 5, 11; CurBio 50, 52; DcNaB 1951; DcTwHis; NewCol 75; WhAm 3*

Senanayake, Dudley Shelton
Ceylonese. Statesman
Prime minister, 1952-53, 1960, 1965-70; son of Don Stephen.
b. Jun 19, 1911 in Colombo, Ceylon
d. Apr 12, 1973 in Colombo, Sri Lanka
Source: *BioIn 3, 5, 7, 9, 10; CurBio 52, 73N; NewCol 75; NewYTBE 73; WhAm 5; WhoGov 72*

Sendak, Maurice Bernard
American. Author, Illustrator
Won Caldecott for *Where the Wild Things Are*, 1963; first American to win H C Anderson's illustrator's award, 1970.
b. Jun 10, 1928 in New York, New York

Source: *AuBYP 3; BenetAL 91; BioIn 13, 16; CamGLE; ChlLR 17; ConAu 5R; CurBio 68, 89; DcLB 61; FacFETw; IlrAm 1880; IlsBYP; IlsCB 1946, 1957; IntAu&W 91; IntWW 91; MajTwCW; MetOEnc; MorJA; NewYTBE 70, 73; OxCChiL; PiP; SmATA 1; Str&VC; Who 92; WhoAm 86, 90, 97; WhoAmA 91; WhoEnt 92; WhoUSWr 88; WhoWor 97; WhoWrEP 89; WorAlBi; WrDr 86, 92*

Sender, Ramon Jose
Spanish. Author
Numerous strong novels include *Counterattack in Spain,* 1937; award-winning *Mr. Witt among the Rebels,* 1935.
b. Feb 3, 1902 in Alcolea de Cinca, Spain
d. Jan 15, 1982 in San Diego, California
Source: *AmAu&B; AnObit 1982; Benet 87, 96; BioIn 12, 13; CasWL; ClDMEL 47, 80; ConAu 5R; DcSpL; EncWL; EvEuW; IntAu&W 77; IntWW 80; ModRL; REn; TwCA, SUP; TwCWr; WhAm 8; Who 74, 82; WhoAm 74, 76*

Seneca, Lucius Annaeus, the Younger
Roman. Philosopher, Statesman, Dramatist
Famed stoic; wrote eight tragedies; committed suicide at Nero's command.
b. 4BC in Cordoba, Spain
d. 65AD in Rome, Italy
Source: *AtlBL; BbD; BiD&SB; BioIn 1, 2, 5, 7, 8, 10, 11, 12, 14, 17; CasWL; ClMLC 6; CnThe; CyEd; CyWA 58; DcArts; DcEnL; DcEuL; DcScB; Dis&D; DramC 5; EncEth; EncWT; InSci; IntDcT 2; LinLib L, S; LngCEL; LuthC 75; McGEWB; McGEWD 72; NewC; NotNAT B; OxCClL, 89; OxCEng 67, 85, 95; OxCSpan; OxCThe 67, 83; PenC CL; RComWL; REn; REnWD*

Senefelder, Aloys
German. Inventor
Invented lithography, 1796.
b. Nov 6, 1771 in Prague, Bohemia
d. Feb 26, 1834 in Munich, Germany
Source: *DcAmB; DcBiPP; DcCathB; LinLib L, S; NewCol 75; OxCArt; OxDcArt; WebBD 83*

Senesh, Hannah
Hungarian. Social Reformer
Anti-Nazi activist; shot by Nazi firing squad.
b. 1921 in Budapest, Hungary
d. Nov 7, 1944
Source: *BioIn 2, 4, 5, 7, 9, 10, 11, 13, 14, 15, 16, 17, 18, 19; ConAu 119; ContDcW 89; EncAmaz 91; HerW, 84; IntDcWB; InWom, SUP; WhWW-II*

Senesino
[Francesco Bernardi]
Italian. Opera Singer
Male mezzo-soprano; extremely popular in London, 1720s-30s; took name from hometown.
b. 1680 in Siena, Italy
d. 1750 in Siena, Italy
Source: *Baker 84, 92; CmOp; MetOEnc; NewAmDM; NewEOp 71; NewGrDM 80; OxDcOp; PenDiMP*

Senghor, Leopold Sedar
Senegalese. Political Leader, Poet
Pres. of Senegal, 1960-80; first book of verse: *Chants d'Ombre,* 1945.
b. Oct 9, 1906 in Joal, Senegal
Source: *AfrA; AfSS 78, 79, 80, 81, 82; Benet 87, 96; BiDFrPL; BioIn 5, 6, 7, 8, 9, 10, 11, 12, 13, 14, 17, 18, 20, 21; BlkLC; BlkWr 1, 2; CasWL; ClDMEL 80; ConAu 47NR, 116, 117, 118, 119, 120, 121, 122, 123, 124, 125; ConBlB 12; ConFLW 84; ConLC 54; ConWorW 93; CurBio 62, 94; DcAfHiB 86; DcArts; DcTwCCu 2; DcTwHis; EncWL 2, 3; FacFETw; GuFrLit 1; HisWorL; InB&W 80, 85; IntAu&W 77, 89, 91; IntWW 74, 75, 76, 77, 78, 79, 80, 81, 82, 83, 89, 91, 93; IntWWP 77, 82; IntYB 78, 79, 80, 81, 82; LegTOT; LiExTwC; LinLib L; MajTwCW; McGEWB; ModBlW; ModFrL; PenC CL; RAdv 14, 13-2; RGAfL; SchCGBL; SelBAAf; TwCWr; WhoGov 72; WhoTwCL; WhoWor 74, 76, 78, 80, 82, 95; WorAl; WorAlBi; WorAu 1950*

Sengstacke, John H(erman Henry)
American. Newspaper Publisher
President, editor of influential black newspaper *Chicago Defender* and affiliates since 1940; founded Negro Newspaper Publishers' Assn., 1940.
b. Nov 25, 1912 in Savannah, Georgia
d. May 28, 1997 in Chicago, Illinois
Source: *AfrAmAl 6; BioIn 2, 8; BlkWr 1; ConAu 101; CurBio 49; DcLB 127; EncTwCJ; InB&W 80, 85; NegAl 83, 89; SelBAAf; SelBAAu; St&PR 84, 87, 91; WhoAm 74, 76, 78, 80, 82, 84, 86, 88, 90, 92, 94, 95, 96, 97; WhoBlA 88, 92; WhoFI 75, 77, 92, 96; WhoMW 82, 88, 90, 92, 93, 96; WhoWor 95, 96, 97*

Senna, Ayrton
Brazilian. Auto Racer
Formula One World Champion, 1988, 1990, and 1991.
b. Mar 21, 1960 in Sao Paulo, Brazil
d. May 1, 1994 in Imola, Italy
Source: *BioIn 15, 16; IntWW 91, 93; News 91, 94; Who 94*

Sennacherib
Assyrian. Ruler
During reign destroyed Babylon, 689 BC, restored Nineveh; killed by son.
b. 705BC
d. 681BC
Source: *NewC; NewCol 75; WebBD 83; WhDW*

Sennett, Mack
[Michael Sinnott]
''King of Comedy''
American. Director, Producer
Created Keystone Kops; directed Charlie Chaplin, Harold Lloyd.
b. Jan 17, 1884 in Richmond, Quebec, Canada
d. Nov 5, 1960 in Woodland Hills, California
Source: *Benet 87, 96; BenetAL 91; BioIn 2; BioNews 75; CmCal; CmMov; DcFM; Film 1; FilmEn; FilmgC; McGEWB; MotPP; ObitT 1951; OxCFilm; REn; REnAL; TwYS, B; WebAB 74, 79; WhAm 4, HSA; WhScrn 83; WorAlBi; WorEFlm*

Seper, Franjo
Yugoslav. Religious Leader
Cardinal, Prefect, Sacred Congregation Doctrine of Faith, 1968-81.
b. Oct 2, 1905 in Osijek, Yugoslavia
d. Dec 31, 1981 in Rome, Italy
Source: *AnObit 1981; BioIn 8, 11, 12; IntWW 74, 75, 76, 77, 78, 79, 80, 81; NewYTBS 81; WhoSocC 78; WhoWor 74, 76, 78, 80, 82*

Sequoyah
[Sequoia; Sequoya; Sikwayi; Sogwal; George Gist; George Guess]
American. Linguist, Scholar
Created Cherokee syllabary; taught thousands to read, write; sequoia tree named for him.
b. 1770? in Taskigi, Tennessee
d. 1843 in Tamaulipas, Mexico
Source: *AmBi; ApCAB; BenetAL 91; BioIn 1, 2, 3, 4, 5, 7, 8, 9, 10, 17, 19, 21; DcAmB; DcAmSR; Drake; EncAAH; EncNoAI; HarEnUS; McGEWB; NatCAB 5; NewCol 75; NotNaAm; OxCAmH; OxCAmL 65, 83, 95; PeoHis; REnAW; WebAB 74, 79; WebBD 83; WhAm HS; WhDW; WhNaAH; WorAl; WorAlBi*

Serafin, Tullio
Italian. Conductor
Led Milan's La Scala, Rome Opera Co., 1909-50s; helped launch Maria Callas.
b. Dec 8, 1878 in Rottanova, Italy
d. Feb 2, 1968 in Rome, Italy
Source: *Baker 84, 92; BioIn 3, 4, 5, 6, 8, 11; BriBkM 80; CmOp; IntDcOp; MetOEnc; MusSN; NewAmDM; NewEOp 71; NewGrDA 86; NewGrDM 80; NewGrDO; ObitT 1961; OxDcOp; PenDiMP; WhAm 4A*

Seraphine, Danny
[Daniel Peter Seraphine]
American. Musician
Drummer with group since 1967; had number one hit ''Hard to Say I'm Sorry,'' 1982.
b. Aug 28, 1948 in Chicago, Illinois
Source: *ASCAP 80; WhoAm 86, 90*

Serban, Andrei George
Romanian. Director
Associate director, Yale Repertory Theatre, 1977-78; directed opera *Elektra,* 1991.
b. Jun 21, 1943 in Bucharest, Romania
Source: *BioIn 11, 12, 13; CamGWoT; ConTFT 8; CurBio 78; IntWWM 90; MetOEnc; OxCThe 83; WhoAm 78, 80, 82; WhoThe 81*

Seredy, Kate
Hungarian. Children's Author, Illustrator
Won 1938 Newbery Medal for *The White Stag.*
b. Nov 10, 1899 in Budapest, Austria-Hungary
d. Mar 7, 1975 in Middletown, New York
Source: *AnCL; Au&ICB; AuBYP 2; BioIn 13, 14, 19; BkCL; ChhPo; ChlBkCr; ChlLR 10; ConAu 5R, 57; CurBio 40, 75, 75N; DcLB 22; IlsCB 1744, 1946; JBA 51; LinLib L; MajAI; NewbMB 1922; OxCChiL; SmATA 1, 24, 24N; Str&VC; TwCChW 78, 83, 89, 95*

Sereno, Paul C.
American. Paleontologist
Unearthed the most complete Herrerasaurus skeleton, 1988.
b. Oct 11, 1957 in Aurora, Illinois

Serkin, Peter A(dolf)
American. Pianist
Noted for chamber music, contemporary compositions, fresh interpretations of classic, romantic music; son of Rudolph.
b. Jul 24, 1947 in New York, New York
Source: *Baker 84, 92; BioIn 14, 15, 16; CurBio 86; IntWW 89, 91, 93; IntWWM 90; NewAmDM; NewGrDA 86; NewYTBE 73; NewYTBS 80; NotTwCP; PenDiMP; WhoAm 84, 86, 90; WhoAmM 83; WhoE 74; WhoEnt 92; WhoMus 72; WhoWor 74*

Serkin, Rudolph
[Rudolf Serkin]
American. Pianist
Made US debut, 1933; specialized in Viennese classics.
b. Mar 28, 1903 in Eger, Bohemia
d. May 8, 1991 in Guilford, Vermont
Source: *AnObit 1991; Baker 78, 84, 92; BiDAmM; BioIn 2, 3, 4, 5, 6, 9, 11, 15, 16, 17, 18, 21; BlueB 76; BriBkM 80; CelR; CurBio 89, 90, 91N; DcArts; DcTwCCu 1; FacFETw; IntWW 74, 75, 76, 77, 78, 79, 80, 81, 82, 83, 89, 91, 91N; IntWWM 77, 80, 90; LegTOT; MusMk; MusSN; NewAmDM; NewGrDA 86; NewGrDM 80; News 92, 92-1; NewYTBS 91; NotTwCP; PenDiMP; REn; WhAm 10; Who 74, 82, 83, 85, 88, 90, 92N; WhoAm 74, 76, 78, 80, 82, 84, 86, 88, 90; WhoAmM 83; WhoE 74; WhoGov 72, 75; WhoMus 72; WhoWor 74, 78, 80, 82, 84, 87, 89, 91; WorAl; WorAlBi*

Serling, Rod
American. Author, Producer
Created, hosted TV series "Twilight Zone," 1959-65; "Night Gallery," 1970-73.
b. Dec 25, 1924 in Syracuse, New York
d. Jun 28, 1975 in Rochester, New York
Source: *AmAu&B; Au&Arts 14; AuNews 1; BenetAL 91; BioIn 4, 5, 6, 7, 10, 14, 16, 19; CelR; ConAu 57, 65; ConDr 73; ConLC 30; ConTFT 14; CurBio 59, 75N; DcLB 26; DcTwCCu 1; EncO&P 1S2, 2, 3; EncSF, 93; FilmEn; FilmgC; HalFC 80, 84, 88; IntMPA 75, 76; LegTOT; LinLib L; NewEScF; NewYTBS 75; NewYTET; REnAL; ScF&FL 1, 92; ScFSB; TwCSFW 81, 86, 91; WhAm 6; WhoAm 74; WhoHrs 80; WhoSciF; WhoWor 74; WhScrn 77, 83; WorAl; WorAlBi; WorEFlm*

Serpico, Frank
[Francisco Vincent Serpico]
American. Police Officer
Subject of film *Serpico,* 1973, which starred Al Pacino.
b. Apr 14, 1936 in New York, New York
Source: *BioIn 9, 13; CopCroC; NewYTBE 71*

Serra, Richard Anthony
American. Artist
Most innovative of minimalist sculptors.
b. Nov 2, 1939 in San Francisco, California
Source: *AmArt; BioIn 16; BriEAA; ConArt 83, 89; CurBio 85; IntWW 91; NewYTBS 89; OxCTwCA; PrintW 85; WhoAm 84, 86, 90; WhoAmA 84, 91*

Serraillier, Ian Lucien
English. Children's Author
Works depicting old English legends include *The Silver Sword,* 1960.
b. Sep 24, 1912 in London, England
d. Nov 28, 1994
Source: *Au&Wr 71; BioIn 15; ChlLR 2; ConAu 1NR, 1R; EngPo; IntAu&W 91; OxCChiL; SmATA 1, 3, 3AS; ThrBJA; TwCChW 83; WrDr 86, 92*

Serrano, Andres
American. Artist
Associated with debates on federal funding for artists and freedom of artistic expression due to work "Piss Christ," a photograph of a crucifix in urine.
b. Aug 15, 1950 in New York, New York
Source: *BioIn 17, 18; ConPhot 95; WhoAm 97; WhoAmA 89, 91, 93*

Serrault, Michel
French. Actor
Played the transvestite Zara in *La Cage aux Folles,* 1978.
b. 1928?
Source: *BioIn 12; ItaFilm; WhoFr 79*

Sert, Jose Luis
American. Architect
Dean, Harvard Graduate School of Design, 1953-69.
b. Jul 1, 1902 in Barcelona, Spain
d. Mar 15, 1983 in Barcelona, Spain
Source: *AmAu&B; AnObit 1983; BioIn 10; BlueB 76; CurBio 74, 83, 83N; EncMA; IntWW 74, 75, 76, 77, 78, 79, 80, 81, 82; McGDA; NewYTBS 83; WhAm 8; WhoAm 74, 76, 78, 82; WhoWor 74*

Serusier, Paul
[Louis Paul Henri Serusier]
French. Artist
Postimpressionist painter.
b. 1863? in Paris, France
d. Oct 6, 1927 in Morlaix, France
Source: *BioIn 4; ClaDrA; OxCTwCA; OxDcArt; PhDcTCA 77*

Servan-Schreiber, Jean-Jacques
French. Politician, Journalist
President, the Radical Party since 1977; founded news-magazine, *L'Express,* 1953-69.
b. Feb 13, 1924 in Paris, France
Source: *BiDFrPL; BioIn 13, 14; ConAu 102; EncWB; IntAu&W 76, 77, 86, 89; IntWW 74, 75, 76, 77, 78, 79, 80, 81, 82, 83, 89, 91, 93; LinLib L; Who 74, 82, 83, 85, 85E, 88, 90, 92, 94; WhoAm 94, 95, 96, 97; WhoFr 79; WhoWor 74, 76, 78, 80, 82, 84, 87, 89, 91, 93, 95, 96, 97*

Servetus, Michael
Spanish. Physician, Theologian
Published *De Trinitatis Erroribus,* 1531, opposing doctrine of Trinity.
b. Sep 29, 1511 in Villanueva de Sixena, Spain
d. Oct 27, 1553 in Geneva, Switzerland
Source: *AsBiEn; BbD; BiD&SB; BiESc; BioIn 1, 2, 3, 4, 5, 7, 9, 12, 17; DcScB; Dis&D; InSci; LarDcSc; LuthC 75; McGEWB; NewC; OxCEng 67, 85, 95; OxCMed 86*

Service, John Stewart
American. Diplomat
Foreign service officer fired from State dept. over doubts of his loyalty, 1951; Supreme Court ruled his rights were violated.
b. Aug 3, 1909 in Chengdu, China
Source: *BioIn 2, 3, 7, 9, 11; ConAu 113; EncCW; PolProf E, T*

Service, Robert William
"Canadian Kipling"
Canadian. Author, Poet
Wrote of northern frontier life: *Spell of the Yukon,* 1907; *Bar Room Ballads,* 1940.
b. Jan 16, 1874 in Preston, England
d. Sep 11, 1958 in Lancieux, France
Source: *BioIn 2, 3, 4, 5, 11, 12; CanNov; CanWr; CasWL; Chambr 3; ChhPo, S1, S2, S3; CnDAL; CnE&AP; CreCan 1; DcAmB S6; DcArts; DcLEL; DcNaB 1951; EvLB; FacFETw; GrWrEL P; LinLib S; LngCTC; MacDCB 78; NewC; OxCAmL 65; OxCCan; OxCEng 85, 95; PenC ENG; REn; REnAL; TwCA, SUP; TwCWr; WebE&AL; WhAm 3; WhNAA; WhoLA; WorAl*

Sesshu, Toyo
Japanese. Artist
Zen priest, master of ink paintings; noted for landscape scrolls: *Four Seasons Landscape,* ca. 1470-90.
b. 1420
d. 1506

Source: *McGDA; McGEWB; NewCol 75; REn; WebBD 83*

Sessions, Jeff
American. Politician
Rep. senator, AL, 1997—.
b. Dec 24, 1946

Sessions, Roger Huntington
American. Composer
Most popular work was first major composition *The Black Masters,* 1923.
b. Dec 28, 1896 in New York, New York
d. Mar 16, 1985 in Princeton, New Jersey
Source: *AmAu&B; AmComp; BiDAmM; BioIn 1, 3, 4, 5, 6, 7, 8, 10, 11, 12, 13; ConAmC 76, 82; ConAu 93; CurBio 75, 85; DcCM; IntWW 74, 75, 76, 77, 78, 79, 80, 81, 82, 83; IntWWM 77; McGEWB; OxCAmL 65; REnAL; WebAB 74, 79; WhoAm 74, 76, 78, 80, 82, 84; WhoAmM 83; WhoE 85; WhoMus 72; WhoWor 74; WorAl*

Sessions, William Steele
American. Government Official
Director of FBI, 1987-93.
b. May 27, 1930 in Fort Smith, Arkansas
Source: *AmBench 79; BioIn 15, 16; CurBio 88; IntWW 91; NewYTBS 87; WhoAm 78, 86, 88, 90, 92, 94, 95, 96, 97; WhoAmL 79, 83, 85, 87, 90, 92, 94, 96; WhoAmP 91; WhoGov 72, 75, 77; WhoSSW 82, 84, 86*

Seth, Vikram
Indian. Author
Published verse novel *The Golden Gate,* 1986; novel *A Suitable Boy,* 1993.
b. Jun 20, 1952 in Calcutta, India
Source: *AsAmAlm; BioIn 15, 18, 19, 20, 21; CamGLE; ConAu 50NR, 121, 127; ConLC 43, 90; ConNov 96; ConPo 91, 96; DcLB 120; IntWW 93; NotAsAm; OxCTwCP; RGTwCWr; WhoAm 94, 95, 96; WhoUSWr 88; WhoWrEP 89, 92, 95; WorAu 1985; WrDr 88, 90, 92, 94, 96*

Seton, Anya Chase
American. Author
Historical romances include *Dragonwyck,* 1944; daughter of Ernest Thompson.
b. 1916 in New York, New York
d. Nov 8, 1990 in Old Greenwich, Connecticut
Source: *AmAu&B; AmNov; Au&Wr 71; Benet 87; BenetAL 91; BioIn 14; ConAu 17R; CurBio 53; EncFWF; IntAu&W 89; InWom SUP; LngCTC; NewYTBS 90; OxCAmL 65; PenC AM; REn; REnAL; SmATA 3; TwCA SUP; TwCRHW 90; Who 85; WhoAm 86; WrDr 86*

Seton, Elizabeth Ann Bayley, Saint
[Mother Seton]
American. Religious Leader
Laid foundation of US parochial school system; founded Sisters of Charity, 1809; first American canonized, 1975.
b. Aug 28, 1774 in New York, New York
d. Jan 4, 1821 in Emmitsburg, Maryland
Source: *AmAu&B; AmBi; AmSocL; ApCAB; ArtclWW 2; BiDAmEd; BioNews 75; BlmGWL; DcAmAu; DcAmB; DcAmReB 1, 2; DcCathB; EncARH; EncSoH; GoodHs; InWom, SUP; LibW; McGEWB; NatCAB 2; NotAW; TwCBDA; WebAB 74, 79; WhAm HS; WomFir*

Seton, Ernest Thompson
American. Naturalist, Author
Noted animal fiction writer; instrumental in founding the Boy Scouts of America, 1910.
b. Aug 14, 1860 in South Shields, England
d. Oct 23, 1946 in Santa Fe, New Mexico
Source: *AmAu&B; AmLY; ApCAB X; ArtsAmW 1; Benet 87, 96; BenetAL 91; BioIn 1, 2, 3, 4, 5, 8, 10, 11, 12, 14, 15, 17; CamGEL; CamGLE; CanWr; ChhPo, S1; ChlBkCr; ConAmL; ConAu 109; CreCan 2; DcAmB S4; DcArts; DcBrAr 1; DcBrBI; DcLB 92, DS13; DcNAA; DcVicP 2; EncSoH; EncWB; EvLB; GayN; HarEnUS; IlBEAAW; IlsCB 1744; InSci; JBA 34; LinLib L, S; LngCTC; MacDCB 78; NatCAB 36; NatLAC; NewCBEL; OxCAmL 65, 83; OxCCan; OxCCanL; OxCChiL; REn; REnAL; SmATA 18; TwCA, SUP; TwCChW 78, 83, 89; TwCLC 31; TwCWr; WhAm 2; WhAmArt 85; WhE&EA; WhLit; WhNAA; WhNaAH; WhoChL*

Seton-Watson, Hugh
[George Hugh Nicholas Seton-Watson]
English. Government Official
Authority on E European affairs; wrote *The Russian Empire,* 1967.
b. Feb 15, 1916 in London, England
d. Dec 19, 1984 in Washington, District of Columbia
Source: *AnObit 1984; Au&Wr 71; Benet 87; BioIn 10, 14; ConAu 114, 117; DcNaB 1981; NewYTBS 84; Who 74, 82, 83, 85; WorAu 1950*

Seurat, Georges Pierre
French. Artist
Devised pointillist style of painting, tiny dots of color.
b. Dec 2, 1859 in Paris, France
d. Mar 29, 1891 in Paris, France
Source: *AtlBL; BioIn 1, 2, 4, 5, 6, 7, 8, 9, 11, 12, 13, 14, 15, 16, 17, 18, 21; ClaDrA; McGEWB; REn*

Seurat, Michel
French. Hostage
French researcher in Lebanon seized by Islamic Jihad May 22, 1985; reported dead March 5, 1986.

Seuss, Doctor
[Theodore Seuss Geisel]
American. Author, Illustrator
Wrote *How The Grinch Stole Christmas,* 1957; *The Cat in the Hat,* 1957; *Green Eggs and Ham,* 1960.
b. Mar 2, 1904 in Springfield, Massachusetts
d. Sep 24, 1991 in La Jolla, California
Source: *AmAu&B; ASCAP 66, 80; AuBYP 3; Benet 87; BenetAL 91; BioIn 13, 14, 15, 16; CamGLE; CelR 90; ChlLR 1, 9; ConAu 13R, 32NR, 135, X; ConGrA 3; ConLC 70; FacFETw; FamAIYP; IlsCB 1957; MajTwCW; News 92; NewYTBS 86; OxCChiL; REn; REnAL; SmATA 1, 67; TwCA, SUP; WebAB 74; WhoAm 86, 88; WhoWest 74; WhoWor 74; WrDr 86, 92*

Sevareid, Eric
[Arnold Eric Severeid]
American. Broadcast Journalist
Joined CBS as member of original news team assembled, 1939.
b. Nov 26, 1912 in Velva, North Dakota
d. Jul 9, 1992 in Washington, District of Columbia
Source: *AmAu&B; AuNews 1; BiDAmJo; BioIn 4, 5, 7, 8, 10, 11, 12, 16, 18, 19, 21; CelR; ConAu 69; ConTFT 12; CurBio 42, 66; DcAmDH 89; EncAJ; EncTwCJ; FacFETw; IntMPA 75, 76, 77, 78, 79, 80, 81, 82, 84, 86, 88, 92; IntWW 74, 75, 76, 77, 78, 79, 80, 83, 91; LegTOT; LesBEnT, 92; LinLib L, S; News 93-1; NewYTBS 79, 92; NewYTET; PeoHis; RadStar; SaTiSS; WhoAm 86, 90; WhoHol 92; WhoTelC; WhoWor 74; WorAl; WorAlBi*

Severini, Gino
Italian. Artist
Futurist, cubist whose paintings include *Dynamic Hieroglyph of the Bal Tabarin.*
b. Apr 7, 1883 in Cortona, Italy
d. Feb 29, 1966 in Paris, France
Source: *BioIn 4, 6, 7, 10, 11, 13, 14, 17, 21; ClaDrA; ConArt 77, 83; DcArts; FacFETw; IntDcAA 90; McGDA; McGEWB; NewCol 75; OxCArt; OxCTwCA; OxDcArt; PhDcTCA 77*

Severinsen, Doc
[Carl H Severinsen]
American. Musician, Bandleader
Joined "Tonight Show" orchestra, 1962; music director 1967-92.
b. Jul 7, 1927 in Arlington, Oregon
Source: *AllMusG; ASCAP 66, 80; Baker 84, 92; BiDAmM; BiDJaz; BioIn 8, 9, 10, 11, 12, 14, 16; CmpEPM; ConMus 1; ConTFT 12; EncJzS; EncJzS; NewAmDM; NewGrDA 86; NewGrDJ 88, 94; PenEncP; WhoAm 78, 80, 82, 84, 86, 88, 90, 92, 94, 95, 96, 97; WhoAmM 83; WhoE 74; WhoEnt 92; WhoTelC; WhoWest 94, 96; WhoWor 95; WorAl; WorAlBi*

Severn, William Irving
American. Author
Writes books of American history, magic for children: *Magic with Coins and Bills,* 1977; *Democracy's Messengers,* 1975.
b. May 11, 1914 in New York, New York
Source: *AuBYP 3; ConAu 1NR, 1R, 16NR, 36NR; SmATA 1, 41*

Sevier, John
American. Politician
First governor of TN, 1796-1801, 1803-09.
b. Sep 23, 1745 in New Market, Virginia
d. Sep 24, 1815 in Fort Decatur, Alabama
Source: *AmAu&B; AmBi; AmRev; ApCAB; BiAUS; BiDrAC; BiDrGov 1789; BiDrUSC 89; BioIn 1, 3, 4, 5, 6, 10, 16; DcAmB; Drake; EncAAH; EncAR; EncCRAm; EncSoH; HarEnUS; McGEWB; NatCAB 3; OxCAmH; REn; REnAW; TwCBDA; WebAB 74, 79; WebAMB; WhAm HS; WhAmP; WhAmRev; WhNaAH*

Sevigne, Marie de Rabutin-Chantal, Marquise de
French. Diarist
Prolific correspondent whose 1700 letters to her daughter reflected the social history of the reign of Louis XIV.
b. Feb 5, 1626 in Paris, France
d. Apr 17, 1696 in Grignan, France
Source: *Benet 87; BioIn 1, 4, 13, 14, 19; BlmGWL; CasWL; DcArts; EncCoWW; EuAu; FemiCLE; FrenWW; GuFrLit 2; IntDcWB; InWom SUP; LitC 11; OxCEng 85, 95; OxCFr; RAdv 13-2; REn; WorAlBi*

Seville, David
[Ross S Bagdasarian]
American. Singer
Wrote "The Chipmunk Song," 1958; led to animated TV series "The Alvin Show," 1960.
b. Jan 27, 1919 in Fresno, California
d. Jan 16, 1972 in Beverly Hills, California
Source: *ASCAP 80; BiDAmM; EncPR&S 74; LegTOT; PenEncP; RkOn 74; WhoHol B; WhoRock 81; WhScrn 77; WorAl*

Sevitzky, Fabien
Russian. Conductor
Led Indianapolis Symphony, 1937-55.
b. Sep 29, 1891 in Volotchok, Russia
d. Feb 2, 1967 in Athens, Greece
Source: *ASCAP 66; Baker 78, 84, 92; CurBio 46, 67; NewGrDA 86; WhAm 4; WhoMus 72*

Sewall, Samuel
American. Judge
Sentenced 19 people to death at Salem witchcraft trials, 1692; publicly confessed his error, 1697.
b. Mar 28, 1652 in Bishopstoke, England
d. Jan 1, 1730 in Boston, Massachusetts
Source: *Alli; AmAu; AmAu&B; AmBi; AmWrBE; ApCAB; BbD; Benet 87, 96; BenetAL 91; BiD&SB; BioIn 1, 2, 3, 4, 7, 8, 10, 14, 15; CamGEL; CamGLE; CamHAL; CasWL; CnDAL; DcAmAu; DcAmB; DcAmSR; DcLB 24; DcLEL; DcNaB; Drake; EncAB-H 1974, 1996; HarEnUS; LegTOT; McGEWB; NatCAB 5; OxCAmH; OxCAmL 65, 83, 95; OxCMus; PenC AM; REn; REnAL; REnAW; RfGAmL 87, 94; TwCBDA; WebAB 74, 79; WebE&AL; WhAm HS; WorAl; WorAlBi*

Seward, Anna
"The Swan of Lichfield"
English. Poet
Wrote poetic novel *Louisa,* 1782; provided James Boswell gossip about Samuel Johnson.
b. Dec 12, 1747 in Eyam, England
d. Mar 25, 1809 in Lichfield, England
Source: *Alli; ArtclWW 2; BiD&SB; BlmGEL; BritAu; CamGEL; CamGLE; CasWL; Chambr 2; ChhPo, S1; DcBiPP; DcBrAmW; DcEnL; DcEuL; DcLEL; DcNaB, C; EvLB; InWom, SUP; NewC; NewCol 75; OxCEng 67, 85, 95; PenC ENG; REn*

Seward, William Henry
American. Government Official
Secretary of State, appointed by Lincoln, 1861-69; his purchase of Alaska from Russia, 1867, was called "Seward's Folly."
b. May 16, 1801 in Florida, New York
d. Oct 10, 1872 in Auburn, New York
Source: *Alli; AmAu&B; AmBi; AmPolLe; ApCAB; BbD; BenetAL 91; BiAUS; BiD&SB; BiDrAC; BiDrGov 1789; BiDrUSC 89; BiDrUSE 71, 89; BioIn 1, 3, 4, 5, 6, 7, 8, 9, 10, 11, 12, 14, 16, 17, 18, 19, 21; CelCen; CivWDc; CopCroC; CyAG; CyAL 2; DcAmAu; DcAmB; DcAmDH 80, 89; DcAmSR; DcBiPP; DcNAA; Drake; EncAAH; EncAB-H 1974, 1996; HarEnUS; HisWorL; LegTOT; LinLib L, S; McGEWB; MorMA; NatCAB 2; OxCAmH; REn; REnAL; TwCBDA; WebAB 74, 79; WhAm HS; WhAmP; WhCiWar; WorAl*

Sewell, Anna
English. Author
Wrote *Black Beauty,* 1877.
b. Mar 30, 1820 in Yarmouth, England
d. Apr 25, 1878 in Norwich, England
Source: *ArtclWW 2; BioIn 1, 2, 4, 8, 9, 13, 16, 19; BlmGEL; BlmGWL; BritAu 19; CamGEL; CamGLE; CarSB; CasWL; ChlBkCr; ChlLR 17; DcArts; DcLB 163; DcLEL; DcNaB; EncBrWW; EvLB; FemiCLE; InWom; JBA 34; LegTOT; MajAI; NewC; NewCBEL; OxCChiL; OxCEng 67, 85, 95; REn; SmATA 24; StaCVF; TwCChW 78A, 83A, 89A, 95A; VicBrit; WhoChL; WrChl*

Sewell, Joe
[Joseph Wheeler Sewell]
American. Baseball Player
Infielder, 1920-33, mostly with Cleveland; hold ML record for fewest strikeouts, with one every 64 at-bats; Hall of Fame, 1977.
b. Oct 9, 1898 in Titus, Alabama
d. Mar 6, 1990 in Mobile, Alabama
Source: *Ballpl 90; BiDAmSp BB; BioIn 11, 14, 15, 16, 17; FacFETw; LegTOT; NewYTBS 90*

Sex Pistols, The
[Paul Cook; Steve Jones; Johnny Rotten; Sid Vicious]
English. Music Group
Hit songs include "God Save the Queen," 1977; was banned from radio in England.
Source: *BioIn 11, 15, 17, 18; ConMuA 80A; ConMus 5; DcArts; DrAPF 85, 87, 89, 91, 93, 97; EncPR&S 89; EncRk 88; EncRkSt; HarEnR 86; IlEncRk; NewAmDM; NewYTBS 79; OxCPMus; PenEncP; RolSEnR 83; St&PR 96, 97; WhoHol 92; WhoRock 81; WhoRocM 82; WhsNW 85*

Sexton, Anne Harvey
American. Poet
Wrote "confessional" verse; won Pulitzer for *Live or Die,* 1967; committed suicide.
b. Nov 9, 1928 in Newton, Massachusetts
d. Oct 4, 1974 in Weston, Massachusetts
Source: *AmAu&B; CasWL; ChhPo S1; ConAu 1R, 3NR, 53; ConLC 2, 4, 6, 15; ConPo 70, 75; CroCAP; ForWC 70; GrWrEL P; MakMC; ModAL, S1; NewYTBS 74; PenBWP; PenC AM; RAdv 1; SmATA 10; WebE&AL; WhAm 6; WhoAm 74; WhoAmW 68, 70, 72, 74, 75; WhoE 74; WhoTwCL; WorAu 1950*

Sexton, Leo
American. Track Athlete
Shot putter; won gold medal, 1932 Olympics.
b. Aug 27, 1909 in Danvers, Massachusetts
d. Sep 6, 1968 in Perry, Oklahoma
Source: *BioIn 8; ObitOF 79; WhoTr&F 73*

Seymour, Anne Eckert
American. Actor
Performed in memorable radio series, "Bulldog Drummond," "Inner Sanctum," and "The Romance of Helen Trent," 1932-61.
b. Sep 11, 1909 in New York, New York
d. Dec 8, 1988 in Los Angeles, California
Source: *BiE&WWA; FilmgC; InWom SUP; MotPP; MovMk; NotNAT; WhoAm 82; WhoHol A*

Seymour, Charles
American. Educator, Historian
President of Yale U, 1937-50; wrote *Diplomatic Background of the War,* 1916.
b. Jan 1, 1884 in New Haven, Connecticut
d. Aug 11, 1963 in New Haven, Connecticut
Source: *AmAu&B; CurBio 41, 63; REnAL; WhAm 4; WhNAA*

Seymour, Dan
American. Advertising Executive
Pres., chairman, J Walter Thompson Co., 1964-74.
b. Jun 28, 1914 in New York, New York
d. Jul 27, 1982 in New York, New York
Source: *BioIn 6, 7, 8, 13; NewYTBS 82; SaTiSS; St&PR 75; WhAm 8; WhoAdv 72; WhoAm 74, 76; WhoE 75; WhoFI 74, 75*

Seymour, Dan
American. Actor
Character actor; appeared in films *Casablanca,* 1942; *Key Largo,* 1948.
b. Feb 22, 1915 in Chicago, Illinois
d. May 25, 1993 in Santa Monica, California
Source: *BioIn 4, 19; EncAFC; FilmEn; FilmgC; ForYSC; HalFC 80, 84, 88; IntMPA 75, 76, 77, 78, 79, 80, 81, 82, 84, 86, 88, 92; MotPP; MovMk; RadStar; Vers A; WhoHol A*

Seymour, Horatio
American. Politician
Dem. presidential candidate, 1868; lost to Grant.
b. May 31, 1810 in Onondaga County, New York
d. Feb 12, 1886 in Utica, New York
Source: *AmBi; AmPolLe; ApCAB; BiDrGov 1789; BioIn 5, 7, 8, 9; CivWDc; CyAG; DcAmB; DcNAA; Drake; HarEnUS; McGEWB; NatCAB 3; NewCol 75; PolPar; PresAR; TwCBDA; WebAB 74, 79; WhAm HS; WhCiWar*

Seymour, Jane
English. Consort
Married Henry VIII, 1536; mother of Edward VI; died 12 days after son's birth.
b. 1509
d. Oct 24, 1537
Source: *Benet 87, 96; BioIn 18; DcNaB; Dis&D; InWom SUP; NewCol 75; REn; WebBD 83*

Seymour, Jane
[Joyce Penelope Wilhelmina Frankenberg]
English. Actor
Starred in TV mini-series, ''East of Eden,'' 1980; star of ''Dr. Quinn, Medicine Woman,'' 1993—.
b. Feb 15, 1951 in Hillingdon, England
Source: *BioIn 12, 16; CelR 90; ConTFT 1, 6, 13; HalFC 84, 88; HolBB; IntMPA 84, 86, 88, 92, 94, 96; LegTOT; News 94; NewYTBS 80; WhoAm 80, 82, 84, 86, 88, 90, 92, 94, 95, 96, 97; WhoAmW 91, 93, 95, 97; WhoEnt 92; WhoHol 92; WorAlBi*

Seymour, Lynn
Canadian. Dancer
Popular dramatic ballerina with Royal Ballet, 1957-77; director, prima ballerina, Bayerische Staatsoper, Munich, 1978-79.
b. Mar 8, 1939 in Wainwright, Alberta, Canada
Source: *BiDD; BioIn 6, 11, 12, 13; CanWW 70, 79, 80, 81, 83, 89; CnOxB; CreCan 2; CurBio 79; DancEn 78; DcArts; IntDcB; IntWW 77, 78, 79, 80, 81, 82, 83, 89, 91, 93; InWom SUP; Who 74, 82, 83, 85, 88, 90, 92, 94; WhoAm 80, 82; WhoWor 74, 82, 87, 89, 91, 93, 95*

Seyss-Inquart, Artur von
Austrian. Politician
German High Commissioner of The Netherlands, 1940-46; condemned, hanged by Int'l Military Tribunal for ''ruthless terrorism.''
b. Jul 2, 1892 in Stannern, Bohemia
d. Oct 16, 1946 in Nuremberg, Germany
Source: *BioIn 1, 14, 16, 18; CurBio 41, 46; Dis&D; REn; WhDW; WhWW-II*

Sforza, Carlo
Italian. Author, Educator, Statesman
Foreign minister, 1920-22, 1947-51; writings display knowledge of int'l politics.
b. Sep 25, 1872 in Lucca, Italy
d. Sep 4, 1952 in Rome, Italy
Source: *BiDInt; BioIn 1, 2, 3; ClDMEL 47; CurBio 42, 52; LinLib L, S; ObitOF 79; ObitT 1951; WhE&EA*

Sforza, Ludovico
[Duke of Milan]
''Il Moro''
Italian. Nobleman
Ruled, 1481-99; defeated by Louis XII of France, 1499; imprisoned, 1500.
b. Jul 27, 1451 in Vigevano, Italy
d. May 27, 1508 in Loches, France
Source: *NewCol 75; WebBD 83*

Shabazz, Attallah
American. Actor, Director
Daughter of Malcolm X; formed theater troupe, Nucleus, with Yolanda King, daughter of Martin Luther King, Jr.
b. Nov 16, 1958 in Mount Vernon, New York
Source: *BioIn 11, 12, 13, 16, 20; ConBlB 6; InB&W 80, 85; NotBlAW 1*

Shabazz, Betty
American. Civil Rights Activist
Wife of Malcolm X.
b. May 28, 1936 in Detroit, Michigan
d. Jun 23, 1997 in New York, New York
Source: *ConBlB 7; Ebony 1; InB&W 80; NegAl 76; NotBlAW 2; WhoAfA 96; WhoBlA 75, 77, 94*

Shackelford, Ted
American. Actor
Played Gary Ewing on TV series ''Knots Landing,'' 1980-93.
b. Jun 23, 1946 in Oklahoma City, Oklahoma
Source: *BioIn 13; ConTFT 8; LegTOT; VarWW 85; WhoAm 82, 84, 86, 88, 90, 92; WhoEnt 92; WhoHol 92; WorAlBi*

Shackleton, Ernest Henry, Sir
Irish. Explorer
Wrote *The Heart of the Antarctic,* 1909, which described expeditions.
b. Feb 15, 1874 in Kilkee, Ireland
d. Jan 5, 1922 in South Georgia, Antarctica
Source: *BioIn 2, 3, 4, 5, 6, 7, 8, 10, 11, 12, 14, 17, 18, 20; ConAu 118; DcIrB 78, 88; DcNaB 1922; FacFETw; GrBr; InSci; LinLib L, S; LngCTC; McGEWB; OxCShps; REn; WhDW; WhWE; WorAl*

Shadrach
[Meshach and Abednego]
Hebrew. Biblical Figure
In Bible, one of three miraculously saved from burning in a furnace.
Source: *BioIn 2, 4; NewCol 75*

Shadwell, Thomas
English. Dramatist, Poet
Wrote *Medal of John Bayes,* 1682; succeeded Dryden as poet laureate, 1688-92.
b. 1642 in Bromhill, England
d. Nov 20, 1692 in London, England
Source: *Alli; AtlBL; BbD; Benet 87, 96; BiD&SB; BioIn 3, 8, 12; BlmGEL; BritAu; CamGEL; CamGLE; CamGWoT; CasWL; Chambr 1; CrtT 2; DcArts; DcEnA; DcEnL; DcEuL; DcLEL; DcNaB; EncWT; Ent; EvLB; GrWrEL DR; LngCEL; McGEWD 72; MouLC 1; NewC; NewCBEL; NewGrDM 80; NotNAT B; OxCEng 67, 85, 95; OxCIri; OxCThe 67, 83; PenC ENG; PoLE; REn; REnWD; WebE&AL; WhDW*

Shaffer, Anthony
English. Author
Won 1971 Tony for *Sleuth.*
b. May 15, 1926 in Liverpool, England
Source: *BioIn 10, 13, 14; ConAu 110, 116; ConDr 73, 77, 82, 88; ConLC 19; ConTFT 6; DcLB 13; DcLEL 1940; DcLP 87A; EncWT; HalFC 84, 88; IntvTCA 2; LegTOT; NewCBEL; NotNAT; ScF&FL 92; TwCCr&M 85, 91; WhoThe 72, 77, 81; WrDr 76, 80, 82, 84, 86, 88, 90, 92*

Shaffer, Paul
Canadian. Musician, Composer
Best known as keyboardist, bandleader on TV show ''Late Night with David Letterman,'' 1982-93, and ''Late Show With David Letterman,'' 1993—.
b. Nov 28, 1949 in Thunder Bay, Ontario, Canada
Source: *BioIn 14, 15, 16; CanWW 31; ConMus 13; ConNews 87-1; ConTFT 7,*

15; LegTOT; WhoAm 92, 94, 95, 96, 97; WhoEnt 92; WorAlBi

Shaffer, Peter Levin
English. Dramatist
Wrote plays *Five Finger Exercise,* 1958; Tony-winner *Equus,* 1975; *Amadeus,* 1981.
b. May 15, 1926 in Liverpool, England
Source: *Benet 87; BioIn 13, 14, 15; BritWr S1; CamGLE; ConAu 25NR; ConDr 88; ConLC 18, 37; ConTFT 4; CurBio 67, 88; DcLP 87A; FacFETw; HalFC 84; IntAu&W 89; IntvTCA 2; IntWW 91; McGEWD 84; ModBrL S2; NewC; OxCAmT 84; OxCEng 85; PenC ENG; RAdv 13-2; REnWD; TwCCr&M 85; TwCWr; Who 92; WhoAm 90; WhoThe 81; WhoWor 87, 91; WrDr 86, 88*

Shafran, Daniel
Russian. Musician
Remarkable cellist, concertist; won first prize in Moscow competition, 1937.
b. Feb 13, 1923 in Leningrad, Union of Soviet Socialist Republics
Source: *Baker 78, 84; BiDSovU; BioIn 5; PenDiMP*

Shafter, William Rufus
American. Military Leader
Led volunteer expeditionary force which invaded Cuba, Spanish-American War, 1898.
b. Oct 16, 1835 in Kalamazoo County, Michigan
d. Nov 12, 1906 in Bakersfield, California
Source: *AmBi; ApCAB SUP; BioIn 1, 8, 16; CivWDc; DcAmB; DcAmMiB; HarEnMi; HarEnUS; MedHR 94; NatCAB 9; TwCBDA; WebAB 74, 79; WebAMB; WhAm 1*

Shaftesbury, Anthony Ashley Cooper, Earl
English. Philosopher, Statesman
Collected writings appeared in *Characteristics of Men, Manners, Opinions, Times,* 1711.
b. Feb 26, 1671 in London, England
d. Feb 15, 1713 in Naples, Italy
Source: *BbD; BioIn 19; BritAu; CasWL; DcEnA; DcEnL; DcEuL; DcLEL; EncEnl; EvLB; IlEncMy; NewC; OxCEng 67, 95; PenC ENG; RAdv 14; WebE&AL*

Shagan, Steve
[Stephen H Shagan]
American. Screenwriter
Oscar nominee for best screenplay: *Save the Tiger,* 1973; *Voyage of the Damned,* 1976.
b. Oct 25, 1927 in New York, New York
Source: *BioIn 12, 13; ConAu 6NR, 53; ConTFT 5; HalFC 84, 88; IntMPA 86, 92, 94, 96; NewYTBS 79; ScF&FL 92; VarWW 85; WhoAm 76, 78, 80, 82, 84, 86, 88, 90, 92, 94, 95, 96, 97; WhoWor 82; WrDr 82, 84, 86, 88, 90, 92, 94, 96*

Shagari, Alhaji Shehu Usman Aliyu
Nigerian. Political Leader
Overthrown in bloodless coup, Dec 31, 1983, by military leader Mohammed Buhari.
b. Apr 1925 in Shagari, Nigeria
Source: *AfSS 78, 79; BioIn 13, 14; CurBio 80; DcAfHiB 86; InB&W 85; IntWW 75, 76, 77, 91; NewYTBS 79; Who 92, 94; WhoWor 74, 76*

Shah, Indries
Indian. Religious Leader
Author of books on the "secret wisdom;" wrote *The Sufis,* 1964.
b. Jun 16, 1924
d. Nov 23, 1996 in London, England
Source: *BioIn 11*

Shaham, Gil
American. Violinist
Considered the finest violinist in his generation; stood in for Itzhak Perlman at the London Symphony Orchestra at age 17, 1989.
b. 1971

Shah Jahan
Indian. Ruler
Mughal emperor, 1628-58; directed building of the Taj Mahal.
b. Jan 5, 1592 in Lahore, India
d. Jan 22, 1666 in Agra, India

Shahn, Ben(jamin)
American. Artist
Noted for posters; used social, political themes in paintings: *Handball.*
b. Sep 12, 1898 in Kaunas, Lithuania
d. Mar 14, 1969 in New York, New York
Source: *AtlBL; Benet 87, 96; BioIn 1, 2, 3, 4, 5, 6, 7, 8, 9, 10, 12, 13, 14, 17, 21; BriEAA; ChhPo S1; ConArt 77, 83, 89, 96; ConAu 89, 121; ConPhot 82, 88; CurBio 54, 69; DcAmArt; DcAmB S8; DcArts; DcCAA 71, 77, 88, 94; EncAB-H 1974, 1996; FacFETw; ICPEnP A; IlsCB 1957; IntDcAA 90; LegTOT; MacBEP; McGDA; McGEWB; ModArCr 3; ObitT 1961; OxCAmL 65, 83, 95; OxCArt; OxCTwCA; OxDcArt; PhDcTCA 77; PrintW 83, 85; REn; SmATA 21N; WebAB 74, 79; WhAm 5; WhAmArt 85; WhoAmA 78N, 80N, 82N, 84N, 86N, 89N, 91N, 93N; WhoGrA 62; WorAl; WorAlBi; WorArt 1950*

Shaka
African. Military Leader
Founder, chief of Zulu Empire, 1816; ruthless, highly trained army crushed neighboring tribes into submission or extermination; slain after his insanity led to murder of over 7,000 Zulus.
b. 1787
d. Sep 22, 1828
Source: *BioIn 4, 6, 7, 8, 9, 10, 12, 14, 19, 20; DcAfHiB 86; DicTyr; GenMudB; HarEnMi; McGEWB*

Shakespeare, William
[Bard of Avon]
English. Dramatist, Poet
Considered greatest dramatist ever; wrote 154 sonnets, 37 plays.
b. Apr 23, 1564 in Stratford-upon-Avon, England
d. Apr 23, 1616 in Stratford-upon-Avon, England
Source: *Alli; AnCL; AtlBL; BbD; Benet 87, 96; BiD&SB; BiDRP&D; BioIn 1, 2, 3, 4, 5, 6, 7, 8, 9, 10, 11, 12, 13, 14, 15, 16, 17, 18, 19, 20, 21; BlmGEL; BritAu; BritWr 1; CamGEL; CamGLE; CamGWoT; CarSB; CasWL; Chambr 1, 2, 3; ChhPo, S1, S2, S3; CnDBLB 1; CnE&AP; CnThe; CroE&S; CrtSuDr; CrtT 1, 4; CyWA 58; DcArts; DcBiPP; DcEnA, A; DcEnL; DcEuL; DcLB 62, 172; DcLEL; DcNaB; DcPup; Dis&D; EncPaPR 91; EncWT; Ent; EvLB; FamAYP; FilmgC; GrWrEL DR, P; HalFC 80, 84, 88; HisDStE; IntDcT 2; LegTOT; LinLib L; LngCEL; LuthC 75; MagSWL; McGEWB; McGEWD 72, 84; MetOEnc; MouLC 1; NewC; NewCBEL; NewEOp 71; NewGrDM 80; NewGrDO; NotNAT A, B; OxCAmT 84; OxCEng 67, 85, 95; OxCFilm; OxCFr; OxCGer 76; OxCThe 67, 83; OxDcOp; PenC ENG; PlP&P, A; RComWL; REn; REnWD; RfGEnL 91; TwoTYeD; WebE&AL; WhDW; WhoHrs 80; WorAl; WorAlBi; WorLitC*

Shakur, Assata
[JoAnne Deborah Byron]
American. Civil Rights Activist
Member of the Black Liberation Army, 1970s; charged with several crimes; living in political asylum in Cuba.
b. Jul 16, 1947 in New York, New York
Source: *BioIn 20; ConBlB 6*

Shakur, Tupac
American. Rapper
Debut album *2Pacalypse Now,* 1992; died of gunshot wounds.
b. Jun 16, 1971 in New York, New York
d. Sep 13, 1996 in Las Vegas, Nevada
Source: *News 97-1; WhoAfA 96*

Shalala, Donna Edna
American. Political Scientist, University Administrator, Government Official
Secretary, Department of Health and Human Services, 1993—; chancellor of University of Wisconsin, Madison, 1988-93; first woman in history to head a Big Ten university.
b. Feb 14, 1941 in Cleveland, Ohio
Source: *AmWomM; BioIn 12, 13, 15, 16; CurBio 91; IntWW 91, 93; InWom SUP; News 92; NewYTBS 79, 87, 88; WhoAm 82, 84, 86, 88, 90, 92, 94, 95, 96, 97; WhoAmW 85, 87, 89, 91, 93, 95, 97; WhoE 83, 85, 86, 95; WhoMedH; WhoMW 90, 92, 93, 96; WhoWor 89, 91, 93, 95, 96, 97*

Shalamar
[Delisa Davis; Micki Free; Howard Hewett]
American. Music Group
Dance/pop group formed 1978; hits include "A Night to Remember," 1982.
Source: *BioIn 17; EncRk 88; EncRkSt; HarEnR 86; InB&W 85A; RkOn 85; RolSEnR 83; SoulM*

Shalamov, Varlam Tikhonovich
Russian. Poet, Author
Wrote about 17 yrs. in Gulag in *Kolyma Tales,* 1980.
b. Jun 18, 1907 in Vologda, Russia
d. Jan 17, 1982 in Moscow, Union of Soviet Socialist Republics
Source: *AnObit 1982; Benet 96; ConAu 105; ConLC 18; NewYTBS 82*

Shales, Tom
[Thomas William Shales]
American. Journalist
Syndicated columnist, *Washington Post,* 1971—; wrote *American Film Heritage,* 1972; wone Pulitzer Prize, 1988.
b. Nov 3, 1948 in Elgin, Illinois
Source: *BioIn 12, 15; ConAu 110, 112, X; ConTFT 15; LesBEnT 92; WhoAm 82, 84, 86, 88, 90, 92, 94; WhoE 91, 93; WhoEnt 92*

Shalikashvili, John (Malchase David)
American. Military Leader
Drafted into U.S. Army, 1958; Chairman, Joint Chiefs of Staff, 1993-97.
b. Jun 27, 1936 in Warsaw, Poland
Source: *BioIn 18, 19, 20, 21; CurBio 95; IntWW 93; News 94, 94-2; NewYTBS 93; Who 94*

Shalit, Gene
American. Critic, Journalist
With NBC since 1969; regular commentator, "Today" show, 1973— .
b. 1932 in New York, New York
Source: *BioIn 10; BkPepl; CelR 90; IntMPA 77, 78, 79, 80, 81, 82, 84, 86, 88, 92, 94, 96; LegTOT; LesBEnT 92; NewYTET; WhoAm 84, 86; WhoTelC*

Shambaugh, Jessie Field
"Mother of 4-H"
American. Educator
Started nat. farm organization, 4-H, clubs, 1910.
b. Jun 26, 1881 in Shenandoah, Iowa
d. Jan 15, 1971 in Clarinda, Iowa
Source: *InWom SUP; NotAW MOD; PeoHis; WomFir*

Shamir, Yitzhak
[Yitzhak Yerzernitsky]
Israeli. Political Leader
Prime minister of Israel, 1983-84; 1986-92.
b. Nov 3, 1914 in Kuzinoy, Poland
Source: *BioIn 13, 14, 15, 16; CurBio 83, 96; EncWB; FacFETw; IntWW 91; MidE 82; NewYTBS 80, 83, 88; PolLCME; WhoWor 87, 91*

Sha Na Na
[Lenny Baker; John "Bowser" Bauman; Johnny Contrado; "Dennis" Frederick Greene; "Jocko" John; Dan McBride; "Chico" Dave Ryan; Tony Santini; Simon Scott; Donald York]
American. Music Group
Formed in 1969; albums include *Remember Then,* 1978.
Source: *EncPR&S 74, 89; EncRk 88; HarEnR 86; IlEncRk; NewYTBS 77, 82; NotNAT; PenEncP; RkOn 74, 78; RolSEnR 83; WhoHol 92, A; WhoRock 81; WhoRocM 82*

Shandling, Garry
American. Comedian
Star of cable TV sitcom "It's Garry Shandling's Show," 1986-90; star of "The Larry Sanders Show," 1992—.
b. Nov 29, 1949 in Chicago, Illinois
Source: *BioIn 15, 16; ConTFT 9; CurBio 89; IntMPA 94, 96; LegTOT; News 95, 95-1; WhoAm 94, 95, 96, 97; WhoCom*

Shange, Ntozake
[Paulette Linda Williams]
American. Dramatist, Poet
Wrote play *For Colored Girls Who Have Considered Suicide/When the Rainbow is Enuf,* 1977, won Obie.
b. Oct 18, 1948 in Trenton, New Jersey
Source: *AfrAmAl 6; AfrAmW; AmWomD; AmWomWr SUP; ArtclWW 2; Au&Arts 9; BenetAL 91; BioIn 11, 12, 13, 14, 15, 16; BlkLC; BlkWAm; BlkWr 1, 2; BlmGWL; CamGWoT; ConAmD; ConAu 3BS, 27NR, 48NR, 85; ConBlAP 88; ConBlB 8; ConDr 82, 88, 93; ConLC 8, 25, 38, 74; ConPo 91, 96; ConTFT 5; ConWomD; CrtSuDr; CurBio 78, 79; CyWA 89; DcLB 38; DcTwCCu 5; DramC 3; DrAPF 80, 91; DrBlPA, 90; FemiCLE; FemiWr; GrWomW; InB&W 80, 85; IntDcT 2; InWom SUP; MagSAmL; MajTwCW; ModWoWr; MorBAP; NatPD 81; NegAl 83, 89; NewYTBS 76; NotBlAW 1; NotWoAT; OxCAmL 95; OxCWoWr 95; SchCGBL; SelBAAf; SelBAAu; TwCYAW; WhoAfA 96; WhoAm 80, 82, 84, 86, 88, 90, 92, 94, 95, 96, 97; WhoAmW 83, 95; WhoBlA 80, 85, 88, 90, 92, 94; WhoThe 81; WhoUSWr 88; WhoWrEP 89, 92, 95; WorAu 1975; WrDr 86, 92, 94, 96*

Shankar, Ravi
Indian. Musician, Composer
Plays the sitar; composed film score for *Ghandi,* 1982.
b. Apr 7, 1920 in Benares, India
Source: *AsAmAlm; ASCAP 80; AuBYP 3; Baker 78, 84, 92; BioIn 6, 7, 8, 9, 11, 13, 14; BriBkM 80; CelR; ConMus 9; ConTFT 12; CurBio 68; DcArts; EncRk 88; FacFETw; FarE&A 78, 79, 80, 81; IntDcF 1-4, 2-4; IntWW 74, 75, 76, 77, 78, 79, 80, 81, 82, 83, 89, 91, 93; IntWWM 77, 80, 90; LegTOT; MusMk; NewAgMG; NewAmDM; NewGrDA 86; NewGrDM 80; PenDiMP; PenEncP; Who 90, 92; WhoHol 92, A; WhoMus 72; WhoWor 74, 84, 87, 89, 91, 93, 95, 96; WorAl; WorEFlm*

Shankar, Uday
Indian. Dancer
Popularized Indian dance in West; created two ballets on Hindu themes.
b. 1901, India
d. Sep 26, 1977 in Calcutta, India
Source: *DcFM; IntWW 74; NewYTBS 77, 85; ObitOF 79*

Shanker, Albert
American. Teacher, Labor Union Official
Pres., NYC United Federation of Teachers, 1964-86.
b. Sep 14, 1928 in New York, New York
d. Feb 22, 1997 in New York, New York
Source: *AmDec 1980; BiDAmL; BiDAmLL; BioIn 8, 9, 10, 11, 12, 13, 14, 15; BlueB 76; CurBio 69; LEduc 74; NewYTBS 75; PolProf J, NF; WhoAm 76, 78, 80, 82, 84, 86, 88, 90, 92, 94, 95, 96, 97; WhoAmP 77, 79, 81, 83, 85, 87, 89, 91, 93, 95; WhoE 74, 75, 77, 79, 81, 91, 95; WhoLab 76; WhoWorJ 72, 78; WorAlBi*

Shanks, Michael
[Thomas William Shanks]
English. Economist, Government Official
Chm., National Consumer Council, 1977-84.
b. Apr 12, 1927 in London, England
d. Jan 13, 1984 in Sheffield, England
Source: *ConAu 8NR, 111; IntWW 74, 75, 76, 77, 78, 79, 80, 81, 82, 83; WhoWor 84*

Shanley, John Patrick
American. Dramatist
Wrote *Danny and the Deep Blue Sea: An Apache Dance,* 1984; wrote screenplay for film *Moonstruck,* 1987.
b. Oct 13, 1950 in New York, New York
Source: *ConAmD; ConAu 128, 133; ConDr 93; ConLC 75; ConTFT 9; IntMPA 92, 94, 96; LegTOT; MiSFD 9; WhoAm 95, 96, 97; WrDr 94, 96*

Shanley, Kathryn W.
American. Scholar
Served on many boards and committees including the American Indian Programm Steering Committee at Cornell Univ.
b. Dec 1, 1947 in Wolf Point, Montana
Source: *NotNaAm*

Shannon, Del
[Charles Westover]
American. Singer, Songwriter
Early rock singer; wrote, recorded no. 1 hit "Runaway," 1961; popularity waned with Beatles-led British Invasion.

b. Dec 30, 1939 in Coopersville, Michigan
d. Feb 8, 1990 in Santa Clarita, California
Source: *AmPS A; AnObit 1990; BioIn 12, 16, 17; EncPR&S 89; EncRk 88; FacFETw; HarEnR 86; LegTOT; NewGrDA 86; NewYTBS 90; PenEncP; RkOn 74, 82; RolSEnR 83; WhoRock 81; WorAlBi*

Shannon, Fred Albert
American. Historian, Educator
Won 1929 Pulitzer for *Organization and Administration of the Union Army,* 1861-65.
b. Feb 12, 1893 in Sedalia, Missouri
d. Feb 14, 1963 in Urbana, Illinois
Source: *AmAu&B; BioIn 4, 6; ConAu 111; DcAmB S7; EncAAH; OxCAmL 65; TwCA, SUP; WhAm 4; WhE&EA; WhNAA*

Shannon, James A(ugustine)
American. Physician
Director, National Institutes of Health, 1955-68; perfected usable form of quinacrine to combat malaira.
b. Aug 9, 1904
d. May 20, 1994 in Baltimore, Maryland
Source: *AmMWSc 76P, 79, 82, 86, 89, 92, 95; BioIn 7; BlueB 76; CurBio 94N; IntWW 74, 75, 76, 77, 78, 79, 80, 81, 82, 83, 89, 91, 93; WhoWor 74*

Shannon, William Vincent
American. Diplomat, Author
US ambassador to Ireland, 1977-81; wrote *Heir Apparent: Robert Kennedy and the Struggle for Power,* 1967.
b. Aug 24, 1927 in Worcester, Massachusetts
d. Sep 27, 1988 in Boston, Massachusetts
Source: *AmAu&B; AmCath 80; BiDAmNC; BioIn 11, 12, 13; ConAu 6NR, 9R; CurBio 79, 88; IntAu&W 76, 77, 89; IntWW 78, 79, 80, 81, 82, 83; IntYB 78, 79, 80, 81, 82; WhAm 9; WhoAm 74, 76, 78, 80, 82, 84, 86, 88; WhoAmP 85; WhoWor 78, 80, 82, 84*

Shante
[Lolita Gooden]
"Roxanne Shante"
American. Rapper
Controversial rap artist who recorded debut single "Roxanne'e Revenge," 1985 and "Have a Nice Day," 1987; released first album *Bad Sister,* 1990 and later *The Bitch is Back,* 1992.
b. 1970 in Long Island, New York
Source: *ConMus 10*

Shapira, Amitzur
Israeli. Olympic Athlete, Victim
One of 11 members of Israeli Olympic team kidnapped, killed by Arab terrorists during Summer Olympic Games.
b. 1932?
d. Sep 5, 1972 in Munich, Germany (West)
Source: *BioIn 9*

Shapiro, Arnold
American. Producer
Won Oscar for documentary *Scared Straight,* 1978.
b. Feb 1, 1941 in Los Angeles, California
Source: *LesBEnT 92; VarWW 85*

Shapiro, Harold Tafler
American. University Administrator, Educator
Pres., U of Michigan, 1979-87, Princeton, 1987—.
b. Jun 8, 1935 in Montreal, Quebec, Canada
Source: *BioIn 15; CanWW 31, 89; IntWW 91, 93; NewYTBS 87; WhoAm 80, 82, 84, 86, 88, 90, 92, 94, 95, 96, 97; WhoE 91, 93, 95, 97; WhoMW 80, 82, 84, 86; WhoWor 80, 87, 89, 91, 93, 95, 96, 97*

Shapiro, Jane
American. Author
Wrote *After Moondog,* 1992.
Source: *ConLC 76*

Shapiro, Karl Jay
American. Poet, Critic
Poems of WW II, *V-Letters & Other Poems,* won Pulitzer Prize, 1945.
b. Nov 10, 1913 in Baltimore, Maryland
Source: *AmAu&B; AmWr S2; AnCL; Benet 87; CamGLE; CamHAL; CanWW 89; CasWL; CnDAL; CnE&AP; ConAu 1NR, 6AS, 132; ConLC 4, 15, 53; ConPo 85; DcLB 48; DrAPF 87; IntAu&W 89; IntvTCA 2; IntWW 91; ModAL S1, S2; OxCAmL 83; PenC AM; RAdv 13-1; RfGAmL 87; TwCA SUP; WebAB 79; Who 92; WhoAm 86, 90; WhoE 91; WhoWor 91; WrDr 86, 88*

Shapiro, Stanley
American. Screenwriter, Producer
Co-wrote screenplay for Oscar-winning film *Pillow Talk,* 1959.
b. Jul 16, 1925 in New York, New York
d. Jul 21, 1990 in Los Angeles, California
Source: *BioIn 6, 17; CmMov; ConAu 132; EncAFC; FilmEn; FilmgC; HalFC 80, 84, 88; ScF&FL 92; VarWW 85; WrDr 88, 90, 92, 94, 96*

Shaplen, Robert Modell
American. Journalist
Staff writer, *New Yorker* magazine, 1952-88; wrote *Bitter Victory,* 1986.
b. Mar 22, 1917 in Philadelphia, Pennsylvania
d. May 15, 1988 in New York, New York
Source: *AmAu&B; ConAu 9R; IntAu&W 77, 82; WhAm 9; WhoAm 74, 76, 78, 80, 82, 84, 86; WhoUSWr 88; WhoWor 74; WhoWrEP 89; WrDr 76, 80, 82, 84, 86, 88*

Shapley, Harlow T
American. Astronomer
Director of Harvard Observatory, 1921-52; known for studies of the Milky Way; wrote *Galaxies,* 1943; *Readings in the World of Science,* 1943.
b. Nov 2, 1885 in Nashville, Missouri
d. Oct 20, 1972 in Boulder, Colorado
Source: *AmAu&B; CurBio 41, 52, 72; DcScB; EncAB-H 1974; McGEWB; OxCAmH; REnAL; TwCA, SUP; WebAB 74; WhAm 5*

Shapp, Milton J(errold)
American. Politician
Dem. governor of PA, 1971-79.
b. Jun 25, 1912 in Cleveland, Ohio
d. Nov 24, 1994 in Wynnewood, Pennsylvania
Source: *BiDrGov 1789, 1978; BioIn 7, 9, 10, 11, 12, 17, 20, 21; BioNews 74; CurBio 73, 95N; IntWW 77, 78, 79, 80, 81, 82, 83; PolProf NF; WhoAm 74; WhoAmP 85, 91; WhoE 74; WhoGov 72*

Sharaff, Irene
American. Designer
Won four Oscars for costume designs including *West Side Story,* 1961; Tony for *The King and I,* 1952.
b. 1910 in Boston, Massachusetts
d. Aug 16, 1993 in New York, New York
Source: *AnObit 1993; BiE&WWA; BioIn 16, 19; CamGWoT; CnOxB; ConDes 84, 90, 97; DancEn 78; EncFash; FilmgC; HalFC 80, 84, 88; IntDcF 1-4, 2-4; IntMPA 84, 86, 88, 92; IntWW 83; NotNAT; NotWoAT; OxCAmT 84; VarWW 85; WhoAm 84; WhoThe 77, 81*

Sharer, Donald A
[The Hostages]
American. Hostage
One of 52 held by terrorists, Nov 1979-Jan 1981.
b. 1941?
Source: *NewYTBS 81*

Sharett, Moshe
[Moshe Shertok]
Israeli. Government Official
Zionist leader; foreign minister, 1948-56; premier, 1953-55.
b. Oct 3, 1894 in Kherson, Russia
d. Jul 7, 1965 in Jerusalem, Israel
Source: *BioIn 1, 2, 3, 4, 7, 8, 13; CurBio 48, 65; DcMidEa; HisEAAC; ObitT 1961; WhAm 4*

Sharietmadari, Ayatollah Seyed
Iranian. Religious Leader
Islamic scholar who opposed Shah of Iran, led nation's conservative forces with Khomeini in exile.
b. 1902
Source: *BioIn 11*

Sharif, Nawaz
Pakistani. Political Leader
Prime minister of Pakistan, 1990-93, 1997—.

b. Dec 23, 1948 in Lahore, Pakistan
Source: *BioIn 19, 20*

Sharif, Omar
[Michael Shalhoub]
Egyptian. Actor
Starred in *Dr. Zhivago,* 1965, *Funny Girl,* 1968; bridge expert—daily bridge lessons published in syndicated newspapers.
b. Apr 10, 1932 in Alexandria, Egypt
Source: *BiDFilm, 81, 94; BioIn 8, 9, 10, 11, 13, 14, 16, 21; BkPepl; CelR; CmMov; ConTFT 5; CurBio 70; DcArts; FilmEn; FilmgC; HalFC 80, 84, 88; IntDcF 1-3, 2-3; IntMPA 77, 78, 79, 80, 81, 82, 84, 86, 88, 92, 94, 96; IntWW 74, 75, 76, 77, 78, 79, 80, 81, 82, 83, 89, 91; ItaFilm; LegTOT; MidE 78, 79, 80, 81, 82; MotPP; MovMk; OxCFilm; WhoAm 80, 82, 84, 86, 88, 90, 92, 94, 95, 96, 97; WhoEnt 92; WhoFr 79; WhoHol 92, A; WhoWor 74, 82, 84, 87, 89, 91; WorAl; WorAlBi; WorEFlm*

Sharkey, Jack
[Joseph Paul Zukauskas]
"Big Skee"
American. Boxer
Popular, cocky world heavyweight champ, 1932-33.
b. Oct 6, 1902 in Binghamton, New York
Source: *BiDAmSp BK; BioIn 2, 5, 9, 10, 13, 20; BoxReg; NewYTBS 83, 94; What 3; WhoBox 74*

Sharkey, Ray
American. Actor
Began acting on TV playing tough guys who were emotionally vulnerable; best known for his role of Sonny Steelgrave on "Wiseguy."
b. Nov 14, 1952 in New York, New York
d. Jun 11, 1993 in New York, New York
Source: *BioIn 12, 16; ConTFT 5; HalFC 84, 88; IntMPA 84, 86, 88, 92; LegTOT; News 94; WhAm 11; WhoHol 92*

Sharman, Bill
[William Walton Sharman]
American. Basketball Player, Basketball Coach
Guard, 1950-61, mostly with Boston; led NBA in free throw percentage seven yrs; coached seven yrs. in NBA, mostly with LA; coach of year, 1972; Hall of Fame, 1974.
b. May 25, 1926 in Abilene, Texas
Source: *Ballpl 90; BasBi; BiDAmSp BK; CmCal; NewYTBE 72; OfNBA 87; WhoAm 80, 82, 90; WhoBbl 73; WhoSpor; WhoWest 80, 92*

Sharmat, Marjorie Weinman
American. Children's Author
Prolific writer of books for juveniles: *Rex,* 1967, *Mooch the Messy,* 1976.
b. Nov 12, 1928 in Portland, Maine
Source: *AuBYP 2S, 3; BioIn 14, 19; ChlBkCr; ConAu 12NR, 25R, 39NR; FifBJA; FifWWr; IntAu&W 76, 77, 82, 86, 91, 93; MajAI; SmATA 4, 33, 74; TwCChW 78, 83, 89, 95; WrDr 76, 80, 82, 84, 86, 88, 90, 92, 94, 96*

Sharon, Ariel
"Arik"
Israeli. Government Official
Defense minister forced to resign because of role in Beirut massacre, 1982.
b. 1928 in Kafr Malal, Palestine
Source: *BioIn 9, 10, 11, 12, 13, 14, 15, 16; ColdWar 1, 2; CurBio 81; DcMidEa; EncWB; FacFETw; HarEnMi; HisEAAC; IntWW 75, 76, 77, 78, 79, 80, 81, 82, 83, 89, 91, 93; MidE 78, 79, 80, 81, 82; NewYTBS 81, 82, 90; WhoWor 82, 84, 87, 89, 91, 93, 97; WhoWorJ 78*

Sharon, Lois & Bram
[Sharon Hampson; Lois Lilienstein; Bram Morrison]
Music Group
Popular children's singing group formed in 1978.
Source: *ConMus 6*

Sharp, Granville
English. Philanthropist
Founded English Society for Abolition of Slaves, 1787.
b. Nov 10, 1735 in Durham, England
d. Jul 6, 1813 in Fulham, England
Source: *BioIn 2, 6, 8, 9, 10; DcAfL; DcBiPP; DcNaB; HisDBrE; NewCBEL; NewCol 75; WebBD 83*

Sharp, Margery
British. Author
b. 1905
Source: *Au&Wr 71; AuBYP 2, 3; BioIn 1, 2, 4, 8, 9, 13, 16, 17, 19; ChlBkCr; ChILR 27; ConAu 18NR, 21R, 134; ConNov 72, 76, 82, 86; DcLB 161; DcLEL; EncBrWW; EvLB; IntAu&W 76, 77, 89; IntWW 83, 91N; LngCTC; MajAI; NewC; OxCChiL; RAdv 1; REn; ScF&FL 1, 2, 92; SmATA 1, 29, 67; ThrBJA; TwCA, SUP; TwCChW 78, 83, 89, 95; WhLit; Who 85, 90, 92N; WhoWor 84, 91; WrDr 76, 80, 82, 84, 86, 88, 90*

Sharp, William
[Fiona MacLeod]
Scottish. Poet, Author
Wrote literary biographies, novels under own name; mystical verse prose under feminine pseudonym.
b. Sep 12, 1855 in Paisley, Scotland
d. Dec 12, 1905 in Castello de Manlace, Sicil, Italy
Source: *Alli SUP; AnCL; BbD; BiD&SB; BioIn 12, 16, 21; BritAu 19; CamGLE; CasWL; Chambr 3; ChhPo, S1, S2, S3; CmScLit; DcBiA; DcEnA, A; DcLB 156; DcLEL; DcNaB S2; EvLB; GrWrEL N; LngCTC; MnBBF; NewC; NewCBEL; OxCEng 67, 85, 95; OxCIri; PenC ENG; RfGEnL 91; ScF&FL 1; StaCVF; SupFW; TwCLC 39; VicBrit*

Sharp, Zerna A
American. Teacher
Originated *Dick and Jane* reader series for schools.
b. Aug 12, 1889 in Hillisburg, Indiana
d. Jun 17, 1981 in Frankfort, Indiana
Source: *AnObit 1981; BioIn 12, 13; ConAu 104; NewYTBS 81; SmATA 27N*

Sharpe, Sterling
American. Football Player
With Green Bay Packers, 1988-95; NFL receiving leader, 1989, 1992, 1993.
b. Apr 6, 1965 in Chicago, Illinois
Source: *BioIn 20; News 94, 94-3; WhoAm 95, 96, 97; WhoSpor*

Sharpton, Al(fred), Jr.
American. Political Activist, Clergy
NY ordained minister involved in racial crimes to promote justice; Tawana Brawley case, 1987.
b. Oct 3, 1954 in New York, New York
Source: *AfrAmAl 6; BioIn 16; CurBio 95; LegTOT; News 91, 91-2; NewYTBS 91*

Shastri, Lal Badahur
Indian. Statesman
Prime minister of India, 1964-66.
b. Oct 2, 1904 in Mughalsarai, India
d. Jan 11, 1966 in Tashkent, Union of Soviet Socialist Republics
Source: *BioIn 9; CurBio 64, 66; WhAm 2*

Shatner, William
American. Actor
Best known as James T Kirk on TV series "Star Trek," 1966-69, films based on series, 1979-89.
b. Mar 22, 1931 in Montreal, Quebec, Canada
Source: *BiE&WWA; BioIn 10, 12, 13, 14, 15, 16, 17, 19, 20, 21; BioNews 74; CanWW 31, 83, 89; CelR 90; ConAu 146; ConCaAu 1; ConTFT 1, 3; CurBio 87; EncSF 93; FilmEn; FilmgC; ForYSC; HalFC 80, 84, 88; IntMPA 84, 86, 88, 92, 94, 96; IntWW 91, 93; ItaFilm; LegTOT; LesBEnT 92; MiSFD 9; MotPP; MovMk; NotNAT; OxCCanT; ScF&FL 92; VarWW 85; WhoAm 74, 78, 80, 82, 84, 86, 88, 90, 92, 94, 95, 96, 97; WhoEnt 92; WhoHol 92, A; WhoHrs 80; WhoTelC; WhoThe 77, 81; WorAl; WorAlBi*

Shattuck, Roger Whitney
American. Author, Educator
Wrote award-winner, *Marcel Proust,* 1974.
b. Aug 20, 1923 in New York, New York
Source: *AmAu&B; Au&Wr 71; ConAu 5R; DrAP 75; DrAPF 87, 91; DrAS 82F; IntvTCA 2; SmATA 64; WhoAm 86, 90, 97; WhoUSWr 88; WhoWrEP 89; WorAu 1950; WrDr 86, 92*

Shaughnessy, Clark Daniel
American. Football Coach
Head coach at several colleges and in NFL, 1915-49; introduced modern T-formation at Rose Bowl, 1941.
b. Mar 6, 1892 in Saint Cloud, Minnesota
d. May 15, 1970 in Santa Monica, California
Source: *BiDAmSp FB; BioIn 4, 6, 8; DcAmB S8; NewYTBE 70; WhAm 5; WhoFtbl 74*

Shaughnessy, Mickey
[Joseph C Shaughnessy]
American. Actor, Comedian
Often cast in tough guy roles; films include *From Here to Eternity,* 1953; *Pocketful of Miracles,* 1961.
b. 1920 in New York, New York
d. Jul 23, 1985 in Cape May Court House, New Jersey
Source: *BioIn 14; EncAFC; FilmEn; FilmgC; ForYSC; HalFC 80, 84, 88; MovMk; NewYTBS 85; WhoHol A*

Shaver, Dorothy
American. Business Executive
Pres., Lord and Taylor specialty store from 1945; promoted American designers.
b. Jul 29, 1897 in Center Point, Arkansas
d. Jun 28, 1959 in Hudson, New York
Source: *AmWomM; BioIn 1, 2, 3, 4, 5, 7, 9, 11, 12, 17; ConAmBL; CurBio 46, 59; EncAB-A 28; InWom, SUP; NatCAB 56; NotAW MOD; WhAm 3; WhoAmW 58; WorFshn*

Shaver, Helen
Canadian. Actor
Films include *The Amityville Horror,* 1979.
b. Feb 24, 1951 in Saint Thomas, Ontario, Canada
Source: *BioIn 15; ConTFT 7, 14; IntMPA 92, 94, 96; VarWW 85; WhoHol 92*

Shavers, Ernie
American. Boxer
Heavyweight champion; 24 straight KOs, 1970s.
b. Aug 31, 1945 in Garland, Alabama
Source: *BioIn 11, 12, 13; NewYTBS 79; WhoBox 74*

Shaw, Albert
American. Editor
Founded current events mag., *Review of Reviews,* 1912-37.
b. Jul 23, 1857 in Shandon, Ohio
d. Jun 25, 1947 in New York, New York
Source: *Alli SUP; AmAu&B; ApCAB; BbD; BiDAmJo; BiD&SB; BioIn 1, 2, 10, 16, 17; DcAmAu; DcAmB S4; DcAmSR; DcLB 91; DcNAA; HarEnUS; LinLib L; NatCAB 9, 34; OhA&B; OxCAmL 65; REnAL; TwCBDA; WhAm 2; WhNAA*

Shaw, Artie
[Arthur Arshowsky]
American. Musician
Clarinetist, prominent swing bandleader, 1930s-40s; had biggest hit with Cole Po rter's "Begin the Beguine," 1938.
b. May 23, 1910 in New York, New York
Source: *AllMusG; ASCAP 66, 80; Baker 78, 84, 92; BiDAmM; BiDJaz; BioIn 1, 2, 3, 6, 7, 8, 9, 12, 13, 14, 15, 16, 17, 20; CelR, 90; CmpEPM; ConAu 144; ConMus 8; CurBio 41; DcArts; DcLP 87B; FacFETw; HalFC 84, 88; IlEncJ; LegTOT; NewAmDM; NewGrDA 86; NewGrDJ 88, 94; NewGrDM 80; NewYTBE 73; NewYTBS 85; OxCPMus; PenEncP; PeoHis; RadStar; What 2; WhoAm 74, 76, 78, 80, 82, 84, 86, 88, 90, 92, 94, 95, 96, 97; WhoE 74; WhoEnt 92; WhoHol 92, A; WhoJazz 72; WhoWor 74, 76; WorAl; WorAlBi; WrDr 96*

Shaw, Bernard
American. Broadcast Journalist
CNN's principal Washington anchor 1980—; one of three CNN correspondents in Baghdad during the Gulf War, 1991.
b. May 22, 1940 in Chicago, Illinois
Source: *AfrAmAl 6; BioIn 11, 12, 16; BlkWr 1; ConAu 109, 119; ConBlB 2; CurBio 95; DcTwCCu 5; NegAl 76; WhoAfA 96; WhoAm 90, 92, 94, 95, 96, 97; WhoBlA 90, 92, 94; WhoE 93*

Shaw, George Bernard
English. Dramatist, Critic
Greatest British dramatist since Shakespeare; wrote *Pygmalion,* 1913; won Nobel Prize, 1925.
b. Jul 26, 1856 in Dublin, Ireland
d. Nov 2, 1950 in Ayot Saint Lawrence, England
Source: *Alli SUP; AtlBL; Baker 78, 84, 92; Benet 87, 96; BiD&SB; BiDBrF 2; BiDIrW; BioIn 1, 2, 3, 4, 5, 6, 7, 8, 9, 10, 11, 12, 13, 14, 15, 16, 17, 18, 19, 20; BlmGEL; BritPl; BritWr 6; CamGEL; CamGLE; CamGWoT; CasWL; Chambr 3; ChhPo, S2, S3; CnMD; CnMWL; CnThe; ConAu 104, 128; CrtSuDr; CyWA 89; DcAmSR; DcArts; DcBiA; DcEnA A; DcIrB 78, 88; DcIrW 1, 2; DcLEL; DcNaB 1941; DcPup; DcTwHis; Dis&D; EncSF, 93; EncUnb; EncWL, 2, 3; EncWT; Ent; EvLB; FacFETw; Film 2; GrBr; GrStDi; GrWrEL DR; HalFC 84, 88; IlWWBF A; IntDcT 2; IriPla; LegTOT; LinLib L, S; LngCEL; LuthC 75; MagSWL; MajTwCW; MakMC; McGEWB; McGEWD 72, 84; ModBrL, S1; ModIrL; NewC; NewCBEL; NobelP; NotNAT A, B; Novels; OxCAmT 84; OxCEng 67, 85; OxCIri; OxCMus; OxCThe 67, 83; PenC ENG; PlP&P; RAdv 14, 13-2; RComWL; REn; RGTwCWr; ScF&FL 1; ScFEYrs; ScFSB; StaCVF; ThTwC 87; TwCA, SUP; TwCLC 3; TwCWr; TwoTYeD; VicBrit; WebE&AL; WhAm 3; WhDW; WhE&EA; WhLit; WhoNob, 90, 95; WhoStg 1906, 1908; WhoTwCL; WhScrn 77, 83; WorAl; WorAlBi; WrPh*

Shaw, Irwin
American. Author, Dramatist
Wrote *Rich Man, Poor Man,* 1970.
b. Feb 27, 1913 in New York, New York
d. May 16, 1984 in Davos, Switzerland
Source: *AmAu&B; AmNov; AnObit 1984; Au&Wr 71; AuNews 1; Benet 87; BenetAL 91; BiE&WWA; BioIn 1, 2, 4, 5, 6, 7, 8, 10, 12, 13, 14, 15, 16, 17, 20; BlueB 76; CelR; CnMD; CnThe; ConAu 13R, 21NR, 112; ConDr 73, 77, 82; ConLC 7, 23, 34; ConNov 72, 76, 82; ConPopW; CurBio 84N; CyWA 89; DcLB 6, 102, Y84N; DcTwCCu 1; DrAF 76; EncWL; EncWT; Ent; FacFETw; FilmEn; IntAu&W 76, 77, 82; IntWW 74, 75, 76, 77, 78, 79, 80, 81, 82, 83; ItaFilm; JeAmFiW; LinLib L; LngCTC; MajTwCW; McGEWD 72, 84; ModAL; ModWD; NewCon; NewYTBS 83, 84; NotNAT; Novels; OxCAmL 65, 83, 95; OxCAmT 84; PenC AM; RAdv 1; REn; REnAL; ShSWr; TwCA, SUP; TwCWr; WhAm 9; Who 74, 82, 83; WhoAm 74, 76, 78, 80, 82, 84, 86, 88; WhoThe 72, 77, 81; WhoTwCL; WhoWor 74, 78, 80, 82; WorAl; WorAlBi; WorEFlm; WrDr 76, 80, 82, 84*

Shaw, Mary
American. Actor
One of first actresses to introduce American audiences to Ibsen, Shaw.
b. Jan 25, 1854 in Boston, Massachusetts
d. May 18, 1929 in New York, New York
Source: *AmWomPl; BioIn 16; DcAmB; NotAW; NotNAT B; PeoHis; PlP&P; WhAm 1; WhoStg 1906, 1908; WhThe; WomWWA 14*

Shaw, Richard Norman
English. Architect
Led revolution in domestic architecture; designed economical, smaller houses; important work, New Scotland Yard, 1888-90.
b. Jul 5, 1831 in Edinburgh, Scotland
d. Jul 11, 1912 in Hampstead, England
Source: *AntBDN G; BioIn 11, 13, 15, 16; DcBrAr 1; DcD&D; DcNaB 1912; DcNiCA; EncMA; IntDcAr; McGDA; McGEWB; NewCol 75; OxCArt; VicBrit; WhDW; WhoArch*

Shaw, Robert
English. Actor, Dramatist, Author
Starred in *Jaws,* 1975; *The Deep,* 1977.
b. Aug 9, 1927 in Westhoughton, England
d. Aug 28, 1978 in Tourmakeady, Ireland
Source: *AuNews 1; BiDFilm 81, 94; BiDrAPA 77; BiE&WWA; BioIn 6, 7, 8, 9, 10, 11, 13, 14, 20, 21; BlueB 76; CelR; ConAu 1R, 4NR, 81; ConDr 73, 77; ConLC 5; ConNov 72, 76; CroCD; CurBio 78N; DcLB 13, 14; DcLEL 1940; EncWT; FilmAG WE; FilmEn; FilmgC; ForYSC; HalFC 80, 84, 88; IlWWBF; IntAu&W 76, 77; IntDcF 1-3, 2-3; ItaFilm; LegTOT; McGEWD 72; MovMk; NotNAT; PlP&P, A; WhAm 7;*

Who 74; WhoAm 76, 78; WhoHol A; WhoThe 72, 77; WhoWor 74; WorAl; WorAlBi; WorAu 1950; WrDr 76

Shaw, Robert Gould
American. Military Leader
White commander of a black regiment, the 54th Massachusetts; his career and story of 54th featured in film *Glory,* 1989.
b. Oct 10, 1837 in Boston, Massachusetts
d. Jul 18, 1863 in Charleston, South Carolina
Source: *AmBi; ApCAB; BioIn 4, 5, 7, 10, 12, 14, 15, 16, 17; Drake; EncAB-H 1974, 1996; GenMudB; NatCAB 8; NewCol 75; TwCBDA; WebAMB; WebBD 83; WhAm HS; WhCiWar*

Shaw, Robert Lawson
American. Conductor
Founder, director, Robert Shaw Chorale, 1948-65; leader of Atlanta Symphony, 1967-88; won many Grammys.
b. Apr 30, 1916 in Red Bluff, California
Source: *Baker 84, 92; BiDAmM; BioIn 1, 2, 4, 7, 8, 9, 11, 12; IntWWM 85; MusSN; NewGrDA 86; NewYTBS 80; WebAB 74, 79; WhoAm 82, 84, 86, 88, 90, 92, 94, 95, 96, 97; WhoAmM 83; WhoEnt 92; WhoFI 87; WhoSSW 88, 95; WhoWor 95*

Shaw, Wilbur
American. Auto Racer
Introduced crash helmet to US racing, 1932; won Indy 500, 1937 in car made by him; won again, 1939, 1940.
b. Oct 31, 1902 in Shelbyville, Indiana
d. Oct 30, 1954 in Fort Wayne, Indiana
Source: *BioIn 3, 5, 7, 10, 11, 12; DcAmB S5; IndAu 1917; WhoSpor*

Shawn, Dick
[Richard Schulefand]
American. Actor, Comedian
Appeared in films *It's a Mad Mad Mad Mad World,* 1963; *The Producers,* 1968.
b. Dec 1, 1929 in Buffalo, New York
d. Apr 17, 1987 in La Jolla, California
Source: *ConNews 87-3; ConTFT 5; EncAFC; FilmEn; FilmgC; ForYSC; HalFC 80; IntMPA 77, 80, 84, 86; MotPP; MovMk; VarWW 85; WhoHol A; WhoThe 77; WorAl; WorAlBi*

Shawn, Ted
[Edwin Meyers Shawn]
American. Dancer
With wife Ruth St. Denis, organized Denishawn Dancers, 1915; established, directed Jacob's Pillow Dance Festival, 1932-49.
b. Oct 21, 1891 in Kansas City, Missouri
d. Jan 9, 1972 in Orlando, Florida
Source: *AmAu&B; BiDD; BioIn 1, 2, 3, 4, 5, 6, 7, 8, 9, 10, 11, 12, 13, 17, 19, 21; CnOxB; ConAu 33R, X; CurBio 49, 72, 72N; DancEn 78; DcAmB S9; LegTOT; LinLib L; NewGrDM 80; NewYTBE 72; RAdv 14, 13-3; REnAL; WebAB 74, 79; WhScrn 77*

Shawn, Wallace
American. Actor, Dramatist
Known for collaboration, starring role in film *My Dinner with Andre,* 1981; son of *New Yorker* editor William Shawn.
b. Nov 12, 1943 in New York, New York
Source: *BioIn 13, 14, 15; ConAmD; ConAu 112; ConDr 77, 82, 88, 93; ConLC 41; ConTFT 1, 6, 14; CrtSuDr; CurBio 86; IntAu&W 86; IntMPA 92, 94, 96; LegTOT; NatPD 77, 81; WhoAm 88, 90, 92, 94, 95, 96, 97; WhoHol 92; WrDr 80, 82, 84, 86, 88, 90, 92, 94, 96*

Shawn, William
American. Editor
Editor, *New Yorker* mag., 1952-87; second editor in mag.'s history; responsible for publishing excerpts of *Catcher in the Rye, Silent Spring,* and *Hiroshima.*
b. Aug 31, 1907 in Chicago, Illinois
d. Dec 8, 1992 in New York, New York
Source: *AmAu&B; AnObit 1992; BioIn 2, 9, 10, 12, 13, 14, 15; BlueB 76; CelR; ConAu 108, 140; ConLC 76; DcLB 137; EncTwCJ; IntWW 74, 75, 76, 77, 78, 79, 80, 81, 82, 83, 89, 91; LegTOT; LiJour; News 93-3; NewYTBS 92; WhAm 10; WhoAm 74, 76, 82, 84, 86, 88, 90, 92; WhoE 75, 85, 86; WhoWor 74; WorAlBi*

Shays, Daniel
American. Soldier
Associated with 1786-87 rebellion, Springfield, MA.
b. 1747? in Hopkinton, Massachusetts
d. Sep 29, 1825 in Sparta, New York
Source: *AmBi; AmRef; AmSocL; ApCAB; BioIn 1, 4, 7, 15, 19, 20; DcAmB; DcAmMiB; Drake; EncAAH; EncAB-H 1974, 1996; EncAR; HarEnUS; McGEWB; NatCAB 2; REn; TwCBDA; WebAB 74, 79; WebAMB; WhAm HS; WhAmRev; WhDW; WorAl; WorAlBi*

Shazar, Zalman
Israeli. Political Leader
Third pres. of Israel, 1963-73; leader of Zionist movement.
b. Nov 24, 1889 in Mir, Russia
d. Oct 5, 1974 in Jerusalem, Israel
Source: *ConAu 53, 101; CurBio 64, 74, 74N; IntWW 74; NewYTBS 74; WhAm 6; WhoGov 72; WhoWor 74*

Shcharansky, Anatoly Borisovich
Russian. Scientist
Jewish dissenter who served nine yrs. in Soviet prisons, 1977-86.
b. Jan 20, 1948 in Ukraine, Union of Soviet Socialist Republics
Source: *BioIn 14, 15, 16; ConNews 86-2; CurBio 87; EncWB; FacFETw; IntWW 91; NewYTBS 78, 86; WorAlBi*

Shchedrin, Rodion Konstantinovich
Russian. Composer
Extremely popular works include Bizet's *Carmen* written as a ballet for ballerina wife, Maya Plisetskaya.
b. Dec 16, 1932 in Moscow, Union of Soviet Socialist Republics
Source: *Baker 84, 92; BiDSovU; BioIn 9; CnOxB; CurBio 91N; DcCM; Dun&B 90; IntWW 80, 81, 82, 83, 89, 91, 93; NewGrDM 80; NewGrDO; NewYTBS 91; SovUn; WhoAm 90; WhoAmL 90; WhoE 91; WhoFI 89; WhoRus; WhoWor 82, 84, 87, 89, 91, 93, 95*

Shcherbo, Vitaly
Belarussian. Gymnast
Win six gold medals in the 1992 Olympics, more than any other gymnast in history.
b. Jan 13, 1972 in Kherson, Union of Soviet Socialist Republics
Source: *CurBio 96*

Shea, John
[Victor Shea, III]
American. Actor
Films include *Missing,* 1982; *Windy City,* 1984.
b. Apr 14, 1949? in North Conway, New Hampshire
Source: *BioIn 12; ConTFT 5, 13; IntMPA 92, 94, 96; NewYTBS 79*

Shea, John A
American. Skater
Won two speed skating gold medals, 1932 Olympics.
Source: *DrRegL 75*

Shea, Lisa
American. Author
Wrote novel *Hula,* 1994.
b. Feb 13, 1953 in Washington, District of Columbia
Source: *ConAu 147; ConLC 86*

Shea, William Alfred
American. Lawyer
Credited with return of NL baseball to NYC, 1962; NY Mets' home stadium named for him.
b. Jun 21, 1907 in New York, New York
d. Oct 2, 1991 in New York, New York
Source: *BioIn 7, 17, 18, 19; CurBio 65; WhAm 10; WhoAm 86, 88, 90; WhoAmL 87, 90; WhoE 86, 89, 91; WhoFI 89; WhoMW 74; WhoRel 75*

Shean, Al
[Alfred Schoenberg]
American. Actor
Films include *52nd Street,* 1937; *People Are Funny,* 1946.
b. May 12, 1868 in Dornum, Germany
d. Aug 12, 1949 in New York, New York
Source: *BioIn 2; EncMT; Ent; Film 2; FilmgC; ForYSC; HalFC 80, 84, 88; JoeFr; NotNAT B; WhoHol B; WhScrn 74, 77, 83; WhThe*

Shear, Murray Jacob
"Father of Chemotherapy"
American. Biochemist
Pioneer in development of chemotherapy treatment while at National Cancer Institute, 1939-69.
b. Nov 7, 1899 in New York, New York
d. Sep 27, 1983 in Bethesda, Maryland
Source: *NewYTBS 83; WhoAm 74; WhoWorJ 72*

Shearer, Douglas
American. Engineer
Pioneer in film sound recording; won 12 Oscars, 1951-63.
b. 1899
d. Jan 5, 1971 in Culver City, California
Source: *BioIn 9; FilmEn; FilmgC; HalFC 80, 84, 88; IntDcF 1-4, 2-4*

Shearer, Moira
Scottish. Dancer, Actor
Ballerina with Sadler's Wells, 1942-52; best known for leading film, *The Red Shoes,* 1948.
b. Jan 17, 1926 in Dunfermline, Scotland
Source: *BiDD; BioIn 1, 2, 3, 4, 5, 6, 8, 12, 15, 18, 20; CnOxB; CurBio 50; DancEn 78; FilmEn; FilmgC; ForYSC; HalFC 80, 84, 88; IntDcB; InWom, SUP; LegTOT; MotPP; NewYTBS 88; Who 74, 82, 83, 85, 88, 90, 92, 94; WhoAmW 66, 68, 70, 72, 74, 75; WhoHol 92, A; WhoThe 77A; WhoWor 74; WhThe; WorAl; WorAlBi*

Shearer, Norma
"First Lady of the Screen"
American. Actor
Won 1930 Oscar for *The Divorcee;* married to Irving Thalberg, 1927.
b. Aug 10, 1900 in Montreal, Quebec, Canada
d. Jun 12, 1983 in Woodland Hills, California
Source: *AnObit 1983; BioIn 14, 16, 17; CanWW 70; CmMov; Film 2; FilmEn; FilmgC; HalFC 80, 84, 88; IntDcF 1-3, 2-3; InWom, SUP; LegTOT; MGM; MotPP; MovMk; NewYTBS 83; OxCFilm; ThFT; TwYS; WhoHol A; WorEFlm*

Sheares, Benjamin Henry
Singaporean. Political Leader
Pres., 1971-81; former gynecologist.
b. Aug 12, 1907, Singapore
d. May 12, 1981, Singapore
Source: *BioIn 10, 12, 13; FarE&A 78, 79, 80; IntWW 74, 75, 76, 77, 78, 79, 80, 81; IntYB 78, 79, 80, 81; NewYTBS 81; WhoWor 74, 76, 78, 80*

Shearing, George Albert
American. Musician
Popular blind pianist known for block chords; wrote jazz classic "Lullaby of Birdland."
b. Aug 13, 1919 in London, England
Source: *Baker 78, 84, 92; BiDAmM; BiDJaz; BioIn 4, 5, 11, 12, 13, 16; CelR 90; CmpEPM; CurBio 58; EncJzS; MusMk; NewAmDM; NewGrDA 86; NewGrDJ 88, 94; OxCPMus; PenEncP; WhoAm 86, 90, 92, 94, 95, 96, 97; WhoEnt 92; WhoHol A; WorAlBi*

Sheba
Ethiopian. Ruler
Biblical queen who made visit to Solomon to improve relations with Israel.
b. fl. 950BC, Ethiopia
Source: *WomWR*

Sheean, (James) Vincent
American. Journalist, Author
Covered world events from WW I to Korean War.
b. Dec 5, 1899 in Christian County, Illinois
d. Mar 15, 1975 in Arolo, Italy
Source: *AmAu&B; AmNov; AuBYP 2S, 3; BenetAL 91; BioIn 1, 2, 3, 4, 5, 10, 14, 16, 20; CnDAL; ConAmA; ConAu 61; CurBio 41, 75, 75N; DcAmB S9; EncAJ; IntAu&W 76, 77; LiJour; LinLib L, S; NewYTBS 74; OxCAmL 65, 83, 95; REn; REnAL; ScF&FL 1, 2; TwCA, SUP; WhAm 6; Who 74; WhoAm 74*

Sheed, Frank
[Francis Joseph Sheed]
Australian. Author, Publisher
Cofounded Roman Catholic publishing house in London, Sheed & Ward, 1926; wrote *Society and Sanity,* 1953.
b. Mar 20, 1897 in Sydney, Australia
d. Nov 20, 1981 in Jersey City, New Jersey
Source: *Au&Wr 71; BioIn 1, 9, 10, 12, 13, 14, 19; CathA 1930; ConAu 105, 129; CurBio 81, 82, 82N; FacFETw; WhoAm 74*

Sheed, Wilfrid John Joseph
American. Author
Satirical novels, *A Middle-class Education,* 1960; *The Hack,* 1963; son of Frank.
b. Dec 27, 1930 in London, England
Source: *BenetAL 91; BiDConC; ConAu 30NR; ConLC 2, 4, 10; ConNov 86, 91; CurBio 81; DcLB 6; DrAPF 91; FacFETw; IntAu&W 91; IntWW 91; LiExTwC; MajTwCW; OxCAmL 83; WhoAm 84, 86, 90; WorAu 1950; WrDr 92*

Sheedy, Ally
[Alexandra Elizabeth Sheedy]
American. Actor
Films include *The Breakfast Club; St. Elmos Fire,* 1985; member of Hollywood's "brat pack.".
b. Jun 13, 1962 in New York, New York
Source: *BioIn 12, 13, 14, 15; ConAu 85; ConTFT 2, 6, 8, 13; HalFC 88; IntMPA 86, 88, 92, 94, 96; InWom SUP; LegTOT; News 89-1; NewYTBS 86; SmATA 19, X; VarWW 85; WhoAm 92, 94, 95, 96, 97; WhoAmW 91, 93; WhoEnt 92; WhoHol 92; WorAlBi*

Sheehan, Daniel P
American. Lawyer
Founder and chief counsel of the Christic Institute, 1980-; legal team member involved in "Pentagon Papers" litigation.
b. 1945 in Warrensburg, New York
Source: *News 89-1*

Sheehan, Joseph Green
American. Psychologist, Educator, Author
Authority on speech problems.
b. May 27, 1918 in Battle Creek, Michigan
d. Nov 14, 1983 in Santa Monica, California
Source: *AmMWSc 73S, 78S; ConAu 111; WhAm 8; WhoAm 74, 76, 78, 80, 82*

Sheehan, Neil
American. Journalist, Author
Bureau chief for UPI during the Vietnam War; book *A Bright Shining Lie,* won Pulitzer Prize for nonfiction, 1988.
b. Oct 27, 1936 in Holyoke, Massachusetts
Source: *BestSel 89-2; BioIn 11, 16; ConAu 29R, 40NR; CurBio 89; EncTwCJ; IntAu&W 91; IntWW 93; LiJour; NewYTBE 71; NewYTBS 90; OxCAmL 95; WhoAm 74, 76, 78, 80, 82, 84, 86, 88, 90, 92, 94, 95, 96, 97; WhoE 93, 95, 97; WhoUSWr 88; WhoWrEP 89, 92, 95; WrDr 90, 92, 94, 96*

Sheehy, Gail Henion
American. Journalist, Author
Wrote *Passages: Predictable Crises of Adult Life,* 1976; *The Silent Passage: Menopause,* 1992.
b. Nov 27, 1937 in Mamaroneck, New York
Source: *BioIn 14, 15, 16; ConAu 1NR, 33NR, 49; CurBio 93; ForWC 70; InWom SUP; MajTwCW; WhoAm 78, 80, 82, 84, 86, 88, 90, 92, 94, 95, 96; WhoAmW 81, 93, 95; WhoUSWr 88; WhoWrEP 89, 92, 95; WorAl; WrDr 86, 92*

Sheekman, Arthur
American. Screenwriter
Collaborated on Marx Brothers' films; helped found Screen Writers Guild, 1930s.
b. Feb 5, 1901 in Chicago, Illinois
d. Jan 12, 1978 in Santa Monica, California
Source: *BioIn 11, 78*

Sheeler, Charles
American. Artist, Photographer
Abstractionist whose paintings include *Upper Deck;* depicted factories, machines.
b. Jul 16, 1883 in Philadelphia, Pennsylvania
d. May 7, 1965 in Dobbs Ferry, New York
Source: *AmCulL; ArtsAmW 2; Benet 87; BioIn 1, 2, 3, 4, 5, 6, 7, 8, 10, 11, 13, 14, 15, 16, 19, 20; BriEAA; ConPhot 82,*

88; CurBio 50, 65; DcAmArt; DcArts; DcCAA 71, 77, 88, 94; DcTwDes; EncAB-H 1974, 1996; FacFETw; GrAmP; ICPEnP; LinLib S; MacBEP; McGDA; McGEWB; WebAB 74, 79; WhAm 4; WhAmArt 85; WhoAmA 78N, 80N, 82N, 84N, 86N, 89N, 91N, 93N; WorAlBi

Sheen, Charlie
[Carlos Irwin Estevez]
American. Actor
Son of Martin Sheen; brother of Emilio Estevez; in films *Ferris Bueller's Day Off, Platoon,* 1986, *Major League,* 1988.
b. Sep 3, 1965 in Los Angeles, California
Source: *BioIn 15, 16; CelR 90; ConTFT 4, 10; DcHiB; HalFC 88; IntMPA 92, 94, 96; IntWW 91, 93; LegTOT; WhoAm 94, 95, 96, 97; WhoHisp 92, 94; WhoHol 92; WorAlBi*

Sheen, Fulton John, Bishop
American. Religious Leader, Author
Well-known spokesman for Catholic perspective, 1930s-70s; reached millions through radio, TV series, books: *Peace of Soul,* 1949.
b. May 8, 1895 in El Paso, Illinois
d. Dec 10, 1979 in New York, New York
Source: *AmAu&B; AmCath 80; BioIn 1, 2, 3, 4, 5, 7, 8, 9, 11, 12; CathA 1930; ConAu 5NR, 5R, 89; CurBio 41, 51; DcAmB S10; DcAmReB 2; IntAu&W 77; IntWW 74, 75, 76, 77, 78, 79; LinLib S; RelLAm 91; REnAL; TwCA SUP; WebAB 74, 79; WebBD 83; WhAm 7; Who 74; WhoAm 74, 76, 78; WhoE 74, 75; WhoHol A; WhoRel 77; WhoWor 74, 78; WorAl; WorAlBi; WrDr 76*

Sheen, Martin
[Ramon Estevez]
American. Actor
Films include *Apocalypse Now,* 1979; *Gandhi,* 1982; father of Charlie, Emilio Estevez.
b. Aug 3, 1940 in Dayton, Ohio
Source: *BiDFilm 94; BioIn 11, 12, 13, 14, 16, 17, 18, 20; CelR 90; ConTFT 2, 6, 13; CurBio 77; DcHiB; FilmEn; HalFC 80, 84, 88; HispAmA; IntDcF 1-3, 2-3; IntMPA 75, 76, 77, 78, 79, 80, 81, 82, 84, 86, 88, 92, 94, 96; IntWW 89, 91, 93; LegTOT; MiSFD 9; MovMk; NotNAT; VarWW 85; WhoAm 78, 80, 82, 84, 86, 88, 90, 92, 94, 95, 96, 97; WhoEnt 92; WhoHisp 91, 92, 94; WhoHol 92, A; WhoThe 72, 77, 81; WorAl; WorAlBi*

Shehu, Mehmet
"The Butcher"
Albanian. Politician
Prime Minister, 1954-81.
b. Jan 10, 1913 in Tirana, Albania
d. Dec 17, 1981 in Tirana, Albania
Source: *AnObit 1981; BioIn 4, 5, 12, 13; CurBio 58, 82N; FacFETw; IntWW 74, 75, 76, 77, 78, 79, 80, 81; NewYTBS 81; WhoSocC 78; WhoWor 78, 80*

Sheil, Bernard James, Archbishop
American. Religious Leader
Auxiliary bishop of Chicago, 1928-69; founder, director, Catholic Youth Organization, 1930-54.
b. Feb 18, 1888 in Chicago, Illinois
d. Sep 13, 1969 in Tucson, Arizona
Source: *BioIn 1, 2, 3, 4, 5, 7, 8; CurBio 68, 69; WhAm 5*

Sheila E
[Sheila Escovedo]
American. Singer, Musician
Has worked with Prince; had solo single "The Glamorous Life," 1984.
b. Dec 12, 1959 in San Francisco, California
Source: *BioIn 15; ConMus 3; DrBlPA 90; RkOn 85*

Sheinwold, Alfred
American. Bridge Player, Author
Has syndicated columns on bridge, backgammon; author, *Five Weeks to Winning Bridge,* 1959.
b. Jan 26, 1912 in London, England
d. Mar 8, 1997 in Sherman Oaks, California
Source: *ConAu 61; EncAI&E; WhoAm 86, 88*

Shelby, Carroll (Hall)
American. Auto Racer, Business Executive
Founder of Shelby-American, Inc., the company that created the tube-frame Cobra in 1962.
b. Jan 11, 1923 in Leesburg, Texas
Source: *BioIn 13, 14, 15, 16, 17, 19, 21; ConAu 17R; CurBio 93*

Shelby, Richard C.
American. Politician
Rep. senator, AL, 1987—.
b. May 6, 1934 in Birmingham, Alabama
Source: *AlmAP 80, 82, 84, 88, 92, 96; BiDrUSC 89; CngDr 79, 81, 83, 85, 87, 89, 91, 93, 95; IntWW 91; PolsAm 84; WhoAm 90; WhoAmP 91; WhoSSW 91; WhoWor 91*

Sheldon, Alice Hastings Bradley
[Raccoona Sheldon; James Tiptree, Jr.]
American. Author
Science fiction novelist; works include *Starry Rift,* 1986, *Brightness Falls from the Air,* 1985.
b. Aug 24, 1915 in Chicago, Illinois
d. May 19, 1987 in McLean, Virginia
Source: *ConAu 34NR, 108, 122; ConLC 48, 50; DcLB 8; EncSF, 93; MajTwCW; NewEScF; Novels; PenNWW B; RGTwCSF; ScF&FL 1, 92; ScFWr; WrDr 86*

Sheldon, Sidney
American. Author
Wrote *The Other Side of Midnight,* 1973; *Rage of Angels,* 1980; several screenplays, TV series, plays.
b. Feb 11, 1917 in Chicago, Illinois
Source: *ASCAP 66, 80; AuNews 1; BestSel 89-1; BiE&WWA; BioIn 10, 12, 16, 17, 20; BioNews 74; CelR 90; ConAu 29R, 33NR; ConPopW; ConTFT 8; CurBio 80; FilmEn; FilmgC; HalFC 80, 84, 88; IntAu&W 91, 93; IntMPA 82, 84, 86, 88, 92, 94, 96; IntWW 91, 93; LegTOT; MajTwCW; MiSFD 9; Novels; RAdv 14; ScF&FL 92; WhoAm 78, 80, 82, 84, 86, 88, 90, 92, 94, 95, 96, 97; WhoEnt 92; WhoUSWr 88; WhoWrEP 89, 92, 95; WorAl; WorAlBi; WrDr 80, 82, 84, 86, 88, 90, 92, 94, 96*

Sheldon, William Herbert
American. Physician, Psychologist
Correlated human somatypes with physique, personality.
b. Nov 19, 1898 in Warwick, Rhode Island
d. Sep 16, 1977 in Cambridge, Massachusetts
Source: *BiDPsy; BioIn 11; ConAu 116; DcAmB S10; WhAm 7; WhoAm 74, 76, 78*

Shelepin, Aleksandr (Nikolaevich)
Russian. Government Official
First secretary, Young Communist League, 1952-58; served in Politburo, 1964-75.
b. Aug 18, 1918
d. Oct 24, 1994
Source: *BiDSovU; BioIn 7, 8, 9, 10; CurBio 71, 95N; SovUn; WhoSocC 78*

Shell, Art
American. Football Player, Football Coach
Offensive tackle, Oakland, 1968-83; head coach LA Raiders, 1989-94; first black head coach in NFL history; Hall of Fame 1989.
b. Nov 26, 1946 in Charleston, South Carolina
Source: *AfrAmSG; BioIn 16, 20, 21; ConBlB 1; NewYTBS 89; WhoAfA 96; WhoAm 90; WhoBlA 92, 94; WhoWest 92*

Shelley, Carole Augusta
English. Actor
Won Tony, 1979, for *The Elephant Man;* Obie, 1982, for *Twelve Dreams.*
b. Aug 16, 1939 in London, England
Source: *ConTFT 4; NewYTBE 73; NotNAT; VarWW 85; WhoAm 80, 82, 84, 86, 88, 90, 92, 94, 95, 96, 97; WhoAmW 81, 83, 87, 89, 91, 93, 95, 97; WhoEnt 92; WhoThe 81*

Shelley, Mary Wollstonecraft
[Mrs. Percy Bysshe Shelley]
English. Author
Wrote *Frankenstein,* 1818.
b. Aug 30, 1797 in London, England
d. Feb 1, 1851 in Bournemouth, England

Source: *Alli; ArtclWW 2; AtlBL; BbD; Benet 87, 96; BiD&SB; BioIn 1, 2, 3, 4, 5, 7, 8, 9, 10, 11, 12, 13, 15, 16, 17, 18, 19, 20; BlmGEL; BlmGWL; BritAu 19; CasWL; Chambr 3; CnDBLB 3; CrtT 4; CyWA 58; DcArts; DcBiA; DcBiPP; DcLB 110, 116, 159; DcNaB; EncBrWW; EncSF, 93; FilmgC; GrWomW; HalFC 80, 84, 88; HerW; InWom; NewC; NewEScF; OxCEng 85, 95; PenC ENG; PenEncH; RAdv 1, 14, 13-1; REn; ScF&FL 1, 92; SmATA 29; WhDW; WhoHrs 80; WorAl; WorAlBi*

Shelley, Percy Bysshe
English. Poet
Romantic lyricist known for *Prometheus Unbound,* 1820.
b. Aug 4, 1792 in Field Place, England
d. Jul 8, 1822 in Viareggio, Italy
Source: *Alli; AtlBL; BbD; Benet 87, 96; BiD&SB; BioIn 1, 2, 3, 4, 5, 6, 7, 8, 9, 10, 11, 12, 13, 14, 15, 16, 17, 18, 19, 20; BlmGEL; BritAu 19; BritWr 4; CamGEL; CamGLE; CasWL; CelCen; Chambr 3; ChhPo, S1, S2, S3; CnDBLB 3; CnE&AP; CnThe; CrtSuDr; CrtT 2, 4; CyWA 58; DcArts; DcBiPP; DcEnA; DcEnL; DcEuL; DcLB 96, 110, 158; DcLEL; DcNaB, C; DcPup; Dis&D; EncPaPR 91; EncUnb; EncWT; EvLB; GrWrEL P; IlEncMy; LegTOT; LinLib L, S; LngCEL; MagSWL; McGEWB; McGEWD 72, 84; MouLC 2; NewC; NewCBEL; NinCLC 18; NotNAT B; OxCEng 67, 85, 95; OxCThe 67, 83; PenC ENG; PenEncH; PoeCrit 14; RadHan; RAdv 1, 14, 13-1; RComWL; REn; REnWD; RfGEnL 91; RGFBP; ScF&FL 1; TwoTYeD; WebE&AL; WhDW; WorAl; WorAlBi; WorLitC; WrPh*

Shepard, Alan Bartlett, Jr.
American. Astronaut
First American to travel in space, 1961.
b. Nov 18, 1923 in East Derry, New Hampshire
Source: *BioIn 5, 6, 7, 8, 9, 10, 12, 13, 16; ConHero 1; CurBio 61; FacFETw; InSci; IntWW 74, 91; WebAMB; WhoAm 74, 76, 78, 80, 82, 84, 86, 88, 90, 92, 94, 95, 96, 97; WhoFI 96; WhoScEn 94, 96; WhoSpc; WhoSSW 73, 75, 76; WhoWor 74, 78, 80, 82, 84, 87, 89, 91, 93, 95, 96, 97; WorAl; WorAlBi*

Shepard, Ernest Howard
English. Artist, Illustrator
Gained fame as illustrator of Milne's *Pooh* books.
b. Dec 10, 1879 in London, England
d. Mar 24, 1976 in Midhurst, England
Source: *Au&Wr 71; BioIn 1, 4, 5, 6, 8, 9, 10, 11, 12, 13; ChhPo, S1, S2; ConAu 9R, 23NR, 65; ConICB; DcBrAr 1, 2; DcBrBI; DcLB 160; DcNaB 1971; DcVicP 2; GrBr; IlsBYP; IlsCB 1744, 1946, 1957; MajAI; MorJA; NewYTBS 76; REn; SmATA 3, 24N, 33; Who 74; WhoChL*

Shepard, Odell
American. Author
Co-founder, Thoreau Society of America; won Pulitzer for *Pedlar's Progress, the Life of Bronson Alcott,* 1938.
b. Jul 22, 1884 in Rock Falls, Illinois
d. Jul 19, 1967 in New London, Connecticut
Source: *AmAu&B; BenetAL 91; BioIn 1, 4, 8; ChhPo, S1; ConAu 3NR, 5R, 25R; OxCAmL 65, 83, 95; OxCCan; REnAL; TwCA, SUP; WhAm 4*

Shepard, Sam
[Samuel Shepard Rogers, III]
American. Dramatist, Actor
Won Pulitzer for *Buried Child,* 1979; won several Obies; wrote film *The Right Stuff,* 1983; appeared in some films.
b. Nov 5, 1943 in Fort Sheridan, Illinois
Source: *AmCulL; AmWr S3; Au&Arts 1; Benet 87, 96; BenetAL 91; BiDFilm 94; BioIn 10, 11, 12, 13, 14, 15, 16, 17, 18, 19, 20; CamGLE; CamGWoT; CamHAL; CelR 90; ConAmD; ConAu 3BS, 22NR, 69; ConDr 73, 77, 82, 88, 93; ConLC 4, 6, 17, 34, 41, 44; CroCD; CrtSuDr; CurBio 79; CyWA 89; DcArts; DcLB 7; DcLEL 1940; DcTwCCu 1; DramC 5; EncWL 2, 3; EncWT; Ent; FacFETw; GrWrEL DR; HalFC 84, 88; IntAu&W 91, 93; IntDcF 2-4; IntDcT 2; IntMPA 84, 86, 88, 92, 94, 96; IntWW 89, 91, 93; LegTOT; LiExTwC; MagSAmL; MajTwCW; McGEWD 84; MiSFD 9; ModAL S1, S2; NatPD 77, 81; News 96; NewYTBS 80; NotNAT; OxCAmL 83, 95; OxCAmT 84; OxCThe 83; RAdv 14, 13-2; RfGAmL 87, 94; WhoAm 84, 86, 88, 90, 92, 94, 95, 96, 97; WhoEnt 92; WhoHol 92; WhoThe 77, 81; WorAlBi; WorAu 1970; WrDr 76, 80, 82, 84, 86, 88, 90, 92, 94, 96*

Shepherd, Cybill Lynne
American. Actor, Model
Played Maddie Hayes on TV series ''Moonlighting,'' 1985-89; plays Cybill Sheridan on ''Cybill,'' 1995—.
b. Feb 18, 1950 in Memphis, Tennessee
Source: *BioIn 16; ConTFT 7; CurBio 87; HalFC 88; IntMPA 82, 92; InWom SUP; MovMk; WhoAm 86, 90; WhoEnt 92; WhoHol A; WomWMM; WorAlBi*

Shepherd, Jean Parker
American. Actor, Author
Writings include *The America of George Ade,* 1961; *The Ferrari in the Bedroom,* 1973.
b. Jul 26, 1929 in Chicago, Illinois
Source: *AuNews 2; ConAu 77; WhoAm 74, 76*

Sheppard, Eugenia Benbow
American. Fashion Editor, Journalist
Wrote fashion column *Inside Fashion.*
b. 1910 in Columbus, Ohio
d. Nov 11, 1984 in New York, New York
Source: *AnObit 1984; BioIn 5, 6, 9; InWom, SUP; WhoAmW 61; WhoE 85A; WorFshn*

Sheppard, Jack
[John Sheppard]
English. Criminal
Thief, known for many escapes from prison; hanged; career is theme of several books, plays.
b. 1702 in Stepney, England
d. Nov 16, 1724 in London, England
Source: *BioIn 3, 4, 7, 8, 14; CamGEL; DcNaB; DrInf; NewC; NewCol 75; OxCEng 85, 95; OxCLaw*

Sheppard, Sam(uel)
''Doctor Sam''
American. Physician
Accused of murdering wife, 1954.
b. Nov 5, 1923 in Fort Sheridan, Illinois
d. Apr 6, 1970 in Columbus, Ohio
Source: *BioIn 7, 8*

Sheppard, T. G
[Bill Browser]
American. Singer, Musician
Country singer, guitarist who sang ''Make My Day,'' with Clint Eastwood, 1984.
b. Jul 20, 1944 in Jackson, Tennessee
Source: *BioIn 13, 14; HarEnCM 87; PenEncP; RkOn 85*

Shera, Jesse Hauk
American. Librarian, Educator
Leading authority on classification, documentation, history of US libraries.
b. Dec 8, 1903 in Oxford, Ohio
d. Mar 8, 1982 in Cleveland, Ohio
Source: *AmAu&B; BiDAmEd; BioIn 2, 3, 6, 7, 8, 9, 12, 13, 15, 16, 17; BlueB 76; ConAu 2NR, 5R, 106; CurBio 64, 82; LEduc 74; WhAm 8; WhoAm 74, 76, 78, 80, 82; WhoCon 73; WhoLibI 82*

Sheraton, Thomas
English. Designer, Furniture Designer
Advanced neoclassic designs; elegant style was delicate, simple, with emphasis on straight, vertical lines.
b. 1751 in Stockton, England
d. Oct 22, 1806 in London, England
Source: *Alli; AntBDN G; BioIn 2, 3, 4, 7, 16; BlmGEL; DcArts; DcD&D; DcNaB; LinLib L, S; LngCEL; McGDA; McGEWB; NewC; OxCDecA; OxCEng 67; PenDiDA 89; WorAl; WorAlBi*

Sheridan, Ann
[Clara Lou Sheridan]
''Oomph Girl''
American. Actor
Pin-up favorite, 1940s; films include *The Man Who Came to Dinner,* 1942.
b. Feb 21, 1915 in Denton, Texas
d. Jan 21, 1967 in Hollywood, California
Source: *BiDFilm, 81, 94; BioIn 1, 7, 8, 9, 14, 18; EncAFC; Film 2; FilmEn; FilmgC; GangFlm; HalFC 80, 84, 88; IntDcF 1-3, 2-3; InWom, SUP; LegTOT; MotPP; MovMk; SweetSg D; ThFT;*

WhAm 4; WhoHol B; WhScrn 74, 77, 83; WorAl; WorAlBi; WorEFlm

Sheridan, Clare Consuelo
English. Author, Artist
Sculpted bronze busts of many heads of state; wrote memoirs *To the Fair Winds,* 1957.
b. Sep 9, 1885 in London, England
d. May 31, 1970 in Sussex, England
Source: *BioIn 3, 4, 8, 11, 14; CathA 1952; DcBrAr 1; DcNaB 1961; DcWomA; FemiCLE; GrBr; IntDcWB; WhLit*

Sheridan, Nicollette
American. Actor
Played Paige Mathison on TV series "Knot's Landing," 1988-93.
b. Nov 21, 1963 in Sussex, England
Source: *BioIn 14, 15; CelR 90; ConTFT 10; IntMPA 94, 96; LegTOT*

Sheridan, Philip Henry
American. Military Leader
Civil War Union general credited with forcing Lee's surrender by blocking retreat from Appomattox, 1865.
b. Mar 6, 1831 in Albany, New York
d. Aug 5, 1888 in Nonquitt, Massachusetts
Source: *Alli SUP; AmAu&B; AmBi; ApCAB; BbD; BenetAL 91; BiD&SB; BioIn 1, 3, 4, 5, 6, 7, 8, 9, 11, 12, 14, 15, 16, 17, 18, 19, 20; CelCen; CivWDc; CmdGen 1991; DcAmAu; DcAmB; DcAmMiB; DcCathB; DcIrB 78, 88; DcNAA; Drake; EncAAH; EncAB-H 1974, 1996; HarEnMi; HarEnUS; HisWorL; LinLib S; McGEWB; NatCAB 4; OhA&B; OxCAmH; REn; REnAL; REnAW; TwCBDA; WebAB 74, 79; WebAMB; WhAm HS; WhCiWar; WhNaAH; WhoMilH 76; WorAl*

Sheridan, Richard Brinsley
Irish. Dramatist, Politician
Noted for three great comedies: *The Rivals,* 1775; *School for Scandal,* 1777; farce *The Critic,* 1779.
b. Oct 30, 1751 in Dublin, Ireland
d. Jul 7, 1816 in London, England
Source: *Alli; AtlBL; BbD; Benet 87, 96; BiD&SB; BiDIrW; BiDLA; BioIn 12; BlkwCE; BlmGEL; BritAu; BritWr 3; CamGEL; CamGLE; CamGWoT; CasWL; Chambr 2; ChhPo; CnDBLB 2; CnThe; CrtSuDr; CrtT 2; CyWA 58; DcArts; DcEnA; DcEnL; DcEuL; DcInB; DcIrB 78, 88; DcIrL 96; DcIrW 1; DcLB 89; DcLEL; DcNaB; DramC 1; EncEnl; EncWT; Ent; EvLB; GrWrEL DR; LinLib L, S; McGEWB; McGEWD 72, 84; MouLC 2; NewC; NewCBEL; NewEOp 71; NewGrDO; NinCLC 5; NotNAT A, B; OxCAmT 84; OxCEng 67, 85, 95; OxCIri; OxCThe 67, 83; OxDcOp; PenC ENG; PlP&P; PoIre; RAdv 14, 13-2; REn; REnWD; RfGEnL 91; WebE&AL; WhDW; WorAlBi; WorLitC*

Sherman, Allan
American. Comedian
Known for satiric song, "Hello Muddah, Hello Faddah," 1963.
b. Nov 30, 1924 in Chicago, Illinois
d. Nov 20, 1973 in Los Angeles, California
Source: *ASCAP 66, 80; AuBYP 2, 3; BioIn 6, 7, 8, 9, 10, 19; ChhPo S1; ConAu 45, 101; CurBio 66, 74, 74N; DcAmB S9; JoeFr; LegTOT; RkOn 74; WhAm 6; WhoCom; WhoRock 81; WorAl*

Sherman, Bobby
American. Singer, Actor
1960s teen hero; first single, "Little Woman," 1969, went gold; starred in TV's "Here Come the Brides," 1968-70.
b. Jul 22, 1945 in Santa Monica, California
Source: *EncPR&S 74; PenEncP; RkOn 78, 84*

Sherman, Cindy
American. Artist
Performance art depicts feminist view of women's role in society.
b. Jan 19, 1954 in Glen Ridge, New Jersey
Source: *AmArt; BioIn 12, 13, 14, 15, 16; ConPhot 95; CurBio 90; ICPEnP A; IntWW 91, 93; News 92, 92-3; NorAmWA; WhoAm 88, 90, 92, 94, 95, 96, 97; WhoAmA 86, 89, 91, 93; WhoAmW 85; WhoE 85, 86, 89; WorArt 1980*

Sherman, Frank Dempster
[Felix Carmen]
American. Poet, Educator, Architect
Wrote volumes of witty, light verse: *Lyrics of Joy,* 1904.
b. May 6, 1860 in Peekskill, New York
d. Sep 19, 1916
Source: *Alli SUP; AmAu; AmAu&B; BbD; BenetAL 91; BibAL; BiD&SB; BioIn 13; ChhPo, S1, S3; ChrP; CnDAL; DcAmAu; DcAmB; DcNAA; NatCAB 7; OxCAmL 65, 83, 95; REn; REnAL; ScF&FL 1; TwCBDA; WhAm 1, 4*

Sherman, George
American. Director
Director of low budget-westerns; first film *Wild Horse Rodeo,* 1937.
d. Mar 15, 1991 in Los Angeles, California
Source: *DcLP 87B; HalFC 88; IntMPA 75, 76, 78, 79, 81, 82, 84, 86; NewYTBS 91*

Sherman, Harry R
American. Producer
TV productions include "Eleanor and Franklin," 1976; "The Gathering," 1978; won three Emmys.
b. Sep 21, 1927 in Los Angeles, California
Source: *VarWW 85*

Sherman, James Schoolcraft
American. US Vice President
VP under William Howard Taft, 1909-12.
b. Oct 24, 1855 in Utica, New York
d. Oct 30, 1912 in Utica, New York
Source: *AmBi; AmPolLe; ApCAB X; BiDrAC; BiDrUSC 89; BiDrUSE 71, 89; BioIn 1, 4, 7, 8, 9, 10, 14; DcAmB; HarEnUS; NatCAB 14; VicePre; WebAB 74, 79; WhAm 1; WhAmP*

Sherman, Lowell
American. Actor, Director
Films include *Morning Glory,* 1933; *Born to Be Bad,* 1934.
b. Oct 11, 1885 in San Francisco, California
d. Dec 28, 1934 in Hollywood, California
Source: *BiDFilm, 81, 94; EncAFC; Film 1, 2; FilmEn; FilmgC; ForYSC; HalFC 80, 84, 88; MotPP; NotNAT B; SilFlmP; TwYS, A; WhoHol B; WhScrn 74, 77, 83; WhThe; WorEFlm*

Sherman, Richard Morton
American. Composer, Lyricist
Won Oscars for score of *Mary Poppins* and song "Chim, Chim, Cheree," 1964.
b. Jun 12, 1928 in New York, New York
Source: *ConAu 107; IntMPA 92; OxCPMus; WhoAm 74, 76, 78, 80, 82, 84, 86, 88*

Sherman, Roger
American. Continental Congressman
Influential member, first and second Continental Congress; signed Declaration of Independence, 1776; strict Puritan.
b. Apr 19, 1721 in Newton, Massachusetts
d. Jul 23, 1793 in New Haven, Connecticut
Source: *AmBi; AmPolLe; ApCAB; BiAUS; BiDrAC; BiDrUSC 89; BioIn 3, 4, 7, 8, 9, 12, 13, 15, 16; BlkwEAR; CyAG; DcAmB; Drake; EncAB-H 1974, 1996; EncCRAm; HarEnUS; HisWorL; McGEWB; NatCAB 2; OxCAmH; TwCBDA; WebAB 74, 79; WhAm HS; WhAmP; WhAmRev; WorAl; WorAlBi*

Sherman, Vincent
[Abram Orovitz]
American. Director
TV shows include "The Waltons," 1972-81; "Baretta," 1975-78.
b. Jul 16, 1906 in Vienna, Georgia
Source: *BioIn 11, 12, 14, 21; FilmEn; FilmgC; ForYSC; GangFlm; HalFC 80, 84, 88; IlWWHD 1; IntMPA 75, 76, 77, 78, 79, 80, 81, 82, 84, 86, 88, 92, 94, 96; ItaFilm; MiSFD 9; VarWW 85; WhoHol 92, A; WomWMM; WorEFlm*

Sherman, William Tecumseh
American. Military Leader
Civil War Union general famous for march through Atlanta to the sea, 1864; said "War is Hell," 1880.

b. Feb 8, 1820 in Lancaster, Ohio
d. Feb 14, 1891 in New York, New York
Source: *Alli, SUP; AmAu&B; AmBi; ApCAB; BbD; Benet 87, 96; BiAUS; BiD&SB; BiDrUSE 71, 89; BioIn 1, 2, 3, 4, 5, 6, 7, 8, 9, 10, 11, 12, 13; CelCen; CivWDc; CmCal; CmdGen 1991; DcAmAu; DcAmB; DcAmMiB; DcBiPP; DcNAA; Drake; EncAB-H 1974, 1996; EncABHB 6; GenMudB; HarEnMi; HarEnUS; HisWorL; LegTOT; LinLib S; McGEWB; MemAm; NatCAB 4; OhA&B; OxCAmH; OxCAmL 95; RComAH; REn; REnAL; REnAW; TwCBDA; WebAB 74, 79; WebAMB; WhAm HS; WhCiWar; WhDW; WhNaAH; WhoMilH 76; WorAl; WorAlBi*

Sherriff, Robert Cedric
English. Author, Dramatist
Wrote *Journey's End,* 1929; translated, performed in every European language.
b. Jun 6, 1896 in Hampton-Wick, England
d. Nov 13, 1975 in Kingston-upon-Thames, England
Source: *Au&Wr 71; BiE&WWA; BioIn 2, 4, 5, 8, 10, 13, 14; Chambr 3; CnMD; CnThe; ConAu 61; ConDr 73; CroCD; CyWA 58; DcLEL; DcNaB 1971; EncWT; Ent; EvLB; GrBr; IntAu&W 76; IntWW 74, 75; LngCTC; McGEWD 72; ModBrL; ModWD; NewC; NewCBEL; NewYTBS 75; NotNAT A, B; OxCEng 67, 85; OxCThe 67; PenC ENG; REn; TwCA, SUP; TwCWr; WhE&EA; Who 74; WhoThe 72; WhoWor 74; WhThe*

Sherrill, Henry Knox
American. Theologian
Bishop of the Episcopal Church, 1946-58; pres., National Council of Churches, 1950-52.
b. Nov 6, 1890 in New York, New York
d. May 12, 1980 in Boxford, Massachusetts
Source: *AnObit 1980; BiDInt; BioIn 1, 2, 5, 6, 12; BlueB 76; ConAu 97; CurBio 47, 80N; IntWW 74, 75, 76, 77, 78, 79, 80; RelLAm 91; WhAm 7; Who 74; WhoAm 74, 76; WhoWor 74*

Sherrill, Robert Glenn
American. Author
Wrote controversial books on political issues, including, *The Last Kennedy: Edward M Kennedy,* 1976.
b. Dec 24, 1925 in Frogtown, Georgia
Source: *ConAu 15NR; WhoSSW 73, 75, 76, 82*

Sherrington, Charles Scott, Sir
English. Physician, Educator
Shared Nobel Prize in medicine, 1932, with Edgar Adrian.
b. Nov 27, 1857 in London, England
d. Mar 4, 1952 in Eastbourne, England
Source: *AsBiEn; BiDPsy; BiESc; BiHiMed; BioIn 2, 3, 4, 5, 6, 7, 9, 12, 14, 15, 20; CamDcSc; DcLEL; DcNaB 1951; DcScB; EvLB; GrBr; LarDcSc; McGEWB; NamesHP; NewCBEL; NotTwCS; ObitOF 79; ObitT 1951; OxCMed 86; WhoNob, 90, 95; WorAl; WorScD*

Sherrod, Robert (Lee)
American. Journalist, Editor
With the *New York Herald Tribune, Time, Saturday Evening Post;* wrote *History of the Marine Corps Aviation in World War II,* 1952.
b. Feb 8, 1909
d. Feb 13, 1994 in Washington, District of Columbia
Source: *AmAu&B; BioIn 3, 6, 17, 19, 20; ConAu 77; CurBio 94N; EncTwCJ; IntAu&W 76, 77, 89; IntWW 74, 75, 76, 77, 78, 79, 80, 81, 82, 83, 89, 91, 93; WhoAm 74, 76, 78, 80, 82, 84, 86, 88, 90, 92, 94; WhoE 79, 89; WhoSSW 73, 75, 76; WhoWor 78*

Sherwin, Henry Alden
American. Manufacturer
Developed formula for first premixed paint; joined Edward Williams to form paint co., 1873.
b. Sep 27, 1842 in Baltimore, Vermont
d. Jun 26, 1916 in Willoughby, Ohio
Source: *Entr; NatCAB 21; WhAm 1*

Sherwood, Frances
American. Author
Wrote *Vindication,* 1993, a fictional biography of the writer Mary Wollstonecraft.
b. Jun 4, 1940 in Washington, District of Columbia
Source: *BioIn 19; ConAu 146; ConLC 81*

Sherwood, Mary Martha
English. Children's Author
Wrote children's classic *History of the Fairchild Family,* 1818-47.
b. May 6, 1775 in Stamford, England
d. Sep 22, 1851 in Worcester, England
Source: *Alli; ArtclWW 2; BiD&SB; BioIn 1, 8, 10; BritAu 19; CamGLE; CarSB; CasWL; Chambr 3; DcBiPP; DcBrAmW; DcEnL; DcEuL; DcInB; DcLB 163; DcNaB; EvLB; FemiCLE; InWom; NewC; NewCBEL; OxCChiL; OxCEng 67, 85, 95; PenNWW A; ScF&FL 1; WhoChL*

Sherwood, Robert Emmet
American. Dramatist, Author
Won Pulitzer for *Idiot's Delight,* 1936; *Abe Lincoln in Illinois,* 1938.
b. Apr 4, 1896 in New Rochelle, New York
d. Nov 14, 1955 in New York, New York
Source: *AmAu&B; CasWL; CnDAL; CnMD; DcLEL; OxCAmL 65; PenC AM; TwCA, SUP; WebAB 74*

Shevardnadze, Eduard Amvrosiyevich
Russian. Diplomat
Replaced Gromyko as minister of foreign affairs, 1985-90; resigned amid controversy.
b. Jan 25, 1928 in Mamati, Union of Soviet Socialist Republics
Source: *BiDSovU; BioIn 16; ColdWar 1, 2; CurBio 86; FacFETw; IntWW 81, 82, 83, 89, 91, 93; Who 88, 90, 92, 94; WhoSocC 78; WhoWor 87, 89, 91, 93, 95, 96, 97; WorAlBi*

Shevchenko, Arkady Nikolayevich
Russian. Diplomat
Adviser to Andrei Gromyko, UN official, who defected to US, 1978; wrote *Breaking with Moscow,* 1985.
b. Oct 11, 1930 in Gorlovka, Union of Soviet Socialist Republics
Source: *BiDSovU; BioIn 11, 12; ConAu 129; CurBio 85; IntWW 76, 91; NewYTBS 78; WhoUN 75*

Shevchenko, Taras
Ukrainian. Poet
Allegorical poems include "Neofity," 1857; "Maruja," 1859.
b. Mar 9, 1814 in Morintsy, Russia
d. Mar 10, 1861 in Saint Petersburg, Russia
Source: *BbD; BiD&SB; BlkwERR; CasWL; DcArts; DcRusL; EuAu; HanRL; NinCLC 54; PenC EUR; RAdv 13-2*

Shields, Alexander
American. Fashion Designer
Menswear designer; introduced caftan for male beachwear, lounging, 1971.
Source: *Alli; WhoAm 82; WorFshn*

Shields, Brooke
[Mrs. Andre Agassi; Christa Brooke Camille Shields]
American. Model, Actor
Appeared on over 30 magazine covers, 1981; films include *The Blue Lagoon,* 1980, *Endless Love,* 1981.
b. May 31, 1965 in New York, New York
Source: *BioIn 11, 12, 13, 14, 15; BkPepl; CelR 90; ConTFT 3, 9; CurBio 82; FilmEn; HalFC 80, 84, 88; IntMPA 79, 80, 81, 82, 84, 86, 88, 92, 94, 96; InWom SUP; LegTOT; News 96, 96-3; WhoAm 88, 90; WhoEnt 92; WhoHol 92; WorAl; WorAlBi*

Shields, James
American. Politician
Governor, Oregon Territory, 1849; senator from IL, 1849-55, from MN, 1858-59.
b. May 10, 1810 in Altimore, Ireland
d. Jun 1, 1879 in Oregon
Source: *AmBi; ApCAB; BiAUS; BiDrAC; DcAmB; Drake; HarEnUS; NatCAB 8; TwCBDA; WhAm HS; WhAmP; WhCiWar*

Shields, Larry
American. Jazz Musician
Pioneered hot-style clarinet; star of Chicago's Original Dixieland Band, 1916.
b. May 17, 1893 in New Orleans, Louisiana
d. Nov 22, 1953 in Hollywood, California
Source: *BiDAmM; BiDJaz; CmpEPM; NewGrDJ 88, 94; NewOrJ; WhoJazz 72*

Shields and Yarnell
[Robert Shields; Lorene Yarnell]
American. Entertainers
Mime duo; won first place Ted Mack amateur contest; on numerous TV specials.
Source: *DcEnL; DcNaB; VarWW 85; WhoAm 82, 84, 86, 88; WhoScEu 91-1*

Shilts, Randy (Martin)
American. Author, Journalist
Wrote *The Mayor of Castro Street: The Life and Times of Harvey Milk,* 1982; *And the Band Played On: Politics, People, and the AIDS Epidemic,* 1987.
b. Aug 8, 1951 in Davenport, Iowa
d. Feb 17, 1994 in Guerneville, California
Source: *Au&Arts 19; BioIn 12; ConAu 45NR, 127, 144; ConLC 85, 86; CurBio 93, 94N; GayLesB; GayLL; LegTOT; News 94, 94-3; WhAm 11; WhoAm 94*

Shimkin, Leon
American. Publisher
Helped build Simon & Schuster into leading book publisher, eventually becoming owner; responsible for publishing Carnegie's *How to Win Friends and Influence People,* 1937.
b. Apr 7, 1907 in New York, New York
d. May 25, 1988 in New Rochelle, New York
Source: *AmAu&B; BioIn 2, 3, 7, 16; CurBio 54, 88; NewYTBS 88; St&PR 84, 87; WhAm 9; WhoAm 74, 76, 78, 80, 82, 84; WhoFI 79, 81; WhoWorJ 72, 78*

Shimomura, Tsutomu
Japanese. Computer Scientist
Directed pursuit of noted computer hacker Kevin Mitnick, 1994-95.
b. 1965, Japan
Source: *News 96, 96-1*

Shinburn, Mark
[Baron Shindell]
American. Criminal
Fenced stolen goods through Fredericka Mandelbaum, eventually retired to Monaco under alias.
b. 1842
d. 1916
Source: *BioIn 8*

Shinn, Everett
American. Artist
One of "the eight" versatile creator of mag., children's book illustrations; pastel scenes of Paris, NYC.
b. Nov 7, 1876 in Woodstown, New Jersey
d. May 1, 1953 in New York, New York
Source: *BioIn 1, 3, 4, 5, 6, 10, 12, 14, 19, 20; BriEAA; ChhPo, S2; CurBio 51, 53; DcAmArt; DcAmB S5; DcCAA 71, 77, 88, 94; IlrAm 1880, A; IlsBYP; IlsCB 1744, 1946; McGDA; NatCAB 44; OxCTwCA; OxDcArt; PhDcTCA 77; SmATA 21; WhAm 3; WhAmArt 85; WhoAmA 78N, 80N, 82N, 84N, 86N, 89N, 91N, 93N*

Shippen, Katherine Binney
American. Children's Author
Historical children's books include *Passage to America,* 1950.
b. Apr 1, 1892 in Hoboken, New Jersey
d. Feb 20, 1980 in Suffern, New York
Source: *AnCL; AuBYP 2, 3; BioIn 2, 3, 6, 7, 9, 12, 13, 14; ConAu 5R, 93; CurBio 54; IntAu&W 76; InWom; MorJA; SmATA 1, 23N; Str&VC*

Shippen, Margaret
"Peggy"
American. Spy
Loyalist, second wife of Benedict Arnold; collaborated in treasonable correspondence, fled to England.
b. 1760 in Philadelphia, Pennsylvania
d. 1804
Source: *AmBi; BioIn 2, 3, 8, 9, 10, 11; InB&W 80; InWom*

Shiras, George, Jr.
American. Supreme Court Justice
Served as associate justice, 1892-1903.
b. Jan 26, 1832 in Pittsburgh, Pennsylvania
d. Sep 2, 1924 in Pittsburgh, Pennsylvania
Source: *ApCAB SUP; BiDFedJ; BioIn 2, 3, 5, 15; DcAmB; HarEnUS; NatCAB 2; OxCSupC; SupCtJu; TwCBDA; WebAB 74, 79; WhAm 1*

Shire, David (Lee)
American. Composer
Won best song Oscar for *Norma Rae,* 1979; Grammy for *Saturday Night Fever,* 1978.
b. Jul 3, 1937 in Buffalo, New York
Source: *AmSong; ASCAP 66; BioIn 15; ConTFT 5; HalFC 80, 84, 88; IntMPA 80, 84, 86, 88, 92, 94, 96; VarWW 85; WhoAm 80, 82, 84, 86, 88, 90, 92, 94, 95, 96, 97; WhoEnt 92; WhoWest 87, 89*

Shire, Talia Rose Coppola
[Mrs. Jack Schwartzman]
American. Actor
Played Adrian in *Rocky* films; sister of director Francis Ford Coppola.
b. Apr 25, 1946 in Jamaica, New York
Source: *BioIn 13; ConTFT 4; HalFC 88; InB&W 85; IntMPA 92; InWom SUP; NewYTBS 76, 82; WhoAm 86, 90; WhoEnt 92; WhoHol A; WorAlBi*

Shirelles, The
[Doris Kenner Jackson; Beverly Lee; Addie "Micki" Harris McFadden; Shirley Alston Owens]
American. Music Group
Their 1961 hit, "Dedicated to the One I Love," was the first million-selling singl e by an all-girl group.
Source: *AmPS A; BiDAmM; ConMus 11; EncPR&S 89; EncRk 88; EncRkSt; IlEncBM 82; InB&W 80, 85A; NewGrDA 86; PenEncP; RkOn 74; RolSEnR 83; SoulM; WhoRock 81; WhoRocM 82*

Shirer, William L(awrence)
American. Author, Journalist
Blacklisted during McCarthy era for supporting Hollywood Ten; wrote best-sellers *Berlin Diary,* 1941, *The Rise and Fall of the Third Reich,* 1960.
b. Feb 23, 1904 in Chicago, Illinois
d. Dec 28, 1993 in Boston, Massachusetts
Source: *AmAu&B; Au&Wr 71; AuBYP 2, 3; Benet 87, 96; BenetAL 91; BiDAmJo; BioIn 1, 2, 3, 4, 6, 7, 8, 11, 12, 13, 14, 15, 16; BlueB 76; ConAu 7NR, 9R, 55NR, 143; ConLC 81; CurBio 41, 62, 94N; DcLB 4; EncAJ; EncTR; EncTwCJ; EncWB; FacFETw; IntAu&W 76, 77, 82, 86, 89, 91, 93; IntWW 74, 75, 76, 77, 78, 79, 80, 81, 82, 83, 89, 91, 93; JrnUS; LinLib L; MajTwCW; NewYTBS 82, 86, 90; OxCAmL 65, 83; REn; REnAL; SmATA 45, 78; TwCA SUP; WebAB 74, 79; WhAm 11; WhE&EA; Who 74, 82, 83, 85, 88, 90, 92, 94; WhoAm 74, 76, 78, 80, 82, 84, 86, 88, 90, 92, 94; WhoUSWr 88; WhoWor 74, 78; WhoWrEP 89, 92; WorAl; WorAlBi; WrDr 76, 80, 82, 84, 86, 88, 90, 92, 94, 96*

Shirley, Anne
[Dawn O'Day; Dawn Evelyeen Paris]
American. Actor
Child star under name Dawn O'Day, 1922-34; received Oscar nomination for *Stella Dallas,* 1937.
b. Apr 17, 1918 in New York, New York
d. Apr 4, 1993 in Los Angeles, California
Source: *AnObit 1993; BioIn 10, 15, 19; EncAFC; Film 2; FilmEn; FilmgC; ForYSC; GangFlm; HalFC 80, 84, 88; InWom SUP; LegTOT; MotPP; MovMk; ThFT; TwYS; WhoHol 92, A*

Shirley, George Irving
American. Opera Singer
Tenor; won Met. Opera audition, 1961.
b. Apr 18, 1934 in Indianapolis, Indiana
Source: *Baker 84; BioNews 75; DrBlPA 90; InB&W 85; IntWW 83, 91; MetOEnc; MusSN; NegAl 89; NewAmDM; NewGrDA 86; NewYTBE 72; WhoAm 86, 88; WhoAmM 83; WhoEnt 92*

Shirley, James
English. Dramatist
Wrote 40 plays, including tragedy *The Traitor,* 1631; comedy of manners, *Lady of Pleasure,* 1635.
b. Sep 18, 1596 in London, England
d. Oct 29, 1666 in London, England
Source: *Alli; AtlBL; Benet 87, 96; BiDRP&D; BioIn 1, 3, 4, 5, 8, 11, 12, 13, 16, 19; BlmGEL; BritAu; CamGEL; CamGLE; CamGWoT; CasWL; Chambr 1; ChhPo; CnE&AP; CnThe; CroE&S; CrtSuDr; CrtT 1; CyWA 58; DcCathB; DcEnA; DcEnL; DcEuL; DcLB 58; DcLEL; DcNaB, C; EncWT; Ent; EvLB; GrWrEL DR; IntDcT 2; LngCEL; McGEWD 72, 84; MouLC 1; NewC; NewCBEL; NewGrDM 80; NewGrDO; NewOxM; NotNAT A, B; OxCEng 67, 85, 95; OxCIri; OxCMus; OxCThe 67, 83; PenC ENG; PlP&P; REn; REnWD; RfGEnL 91; WebE&AL*

Shirley, Ralph
[Rollo Ireton]
English. Publisher, Editor
Founded, edited *The Occult Review,* 1905-26.
b. Dec 30, 1865 in Oxford, England
d. Dec 29, 1946 in Oxford, England
Source: *ConAu 117; EncO&P 1, 2, 3; WhE&EA; WhLit*

Shirley, William
American. Colonial Figure
Governor of MA, 1740s-50s; headed British forces in America after Braddock's death.
b. Dec 2, 1694 in Preston, England
d. Mar 24, 1771 in Roxbury, Massachusetts
Source: *Alli; AmBi; AmWrBE; BenetAL 91; BiDrACR; BioIn 4, 6, 9, 14; DcAmB; DcAmMiB; DcNaB; Drake; EncAR; NatCAB 7; OxCAmH; REnAL; WebAB 74, 79; WhAm HS*

Shirley-Quirk, John Stanton
American. Opera Singer
Bass-baritone who sang multiple roles in *Death in Venice,* 1973; made NY Met. debut, 1974.
b. Aug 28, 1931 in Liverpool, England
Source: *Baker 84, 92; IntDcOp; IntWW 91; IntWWM 77, 90; MetOEnc; NewAmDM; NewGrDM 80; PenDiMP; Who 74, 82, 83, 85, 88, 90, 92, 94; WhoWor 74, 76, 78*

Shirley-Smith, Hubert
English. Engineer
Expert designer, builder of int'l steel bridges.
b. Oct 13, 1901 in Hendon, England
d. Feb 10, 1981
Source: *ConAu 113; Who 74*

Shively, Charles
American. Educator
Professor of American Studies, University of Massachusetts; active in Boston's Gay Liberation Front, 1970—.
b. Dec 8, 1937 in Stonelick Township, Ohio
Source: *DrAS 82H; GayLesB; WhoAmL 85*

Shklovsky, Iosif Samvilovitch
Russian. Astronomer, Educator
Researched extraterrestrial life; wrote *Intelligent Life in the Universe,* 1966.
b. Jul 1, 1916 in Glukhov, Russia
d. Mar 3, 1985 in Moscow, Union of Soviet Socialist Republics
Source: *ConAu 115; IntWW 83*

Shocked, Michelle
American. Singer, Songwriter
Known for social commentary folk music; *The Texas Campfire Tapes; Short, Sharp, Shocked; Captain Swing; Arkansas Traveller,* 1992.
b. 1963
Source: *BioIn 16; ConMus 4; News 89; PenEncP; WhoAmW 97*

Shockley, William B(radford)
American. Scientist
Co-winner of 1956 Nobel Prize for inventing transistor, which revolutionized electronics; also known for theories on racial differences.
b. Feb 13, 1910 in London, England
d. Aug 12, 1989 in Palo Alto, California
Source: *AmMWSc 82, 92; AsBiEn; BiESc; BioIn 9, 10, 12; BlueB 76; CamDcSc; CmCal; ConAu 113, 129; CurBio 89N; EncAB-H 1974, 1996; FacFETw; HisDcDP; LarDcSc; LElec; LinLib S; McGMS 80; NewYTBS 89; NobelP; PolProf NF; PorSil; WebAB 74, 79; WhAm 10; WhDW; Who 90N; WhoAm 74, 76, 78, 82, 84, 88; WhoFrS 84; WhoNob, 90, 95; WhoWest 87, 89; WhoWor 74, 76, 78, 80, 82, 84, 87, 89; WorAl; WorAlBi*

Shoemaker, Vaughn Richard
American. Cartoonist
Political cartoons found in *Chicago Daily News* won Pulitzers, 1938, 1947.
b. Aug 11, 1902 in Chicago, Illinois
d. Aug 18, 1991 in Carol Stream, Illinois
Source: *AmAu&B; EncTwCJ; NewYTBS 91; WhAmArt 85; WhoAm 86; WhoAmA 73, 91; WhoWor 74, 89*

Shoemaker, Willie
[William Lee Shoemaker]
"The Shoe"
American. Jockey
Won over 8,500 races, including four Kentucky Derbys.
b. Aug 19, 1931 in Fabens, Texas
Source: *BiDAmSp OS; BioIn 2, 3, 5, 6, 7, 8, 9, 10, 11, 12, 14, 15, 16, 17, 19; CelR; CmCal; ConAu 115; CurBio 66; FacFETw; IntWW 89, 91, 93; LegTOT; NewYTBE 70, 73; WebAB 74, 79; WhoAm 76, 78, 80, 82, 84, 86; WorAl; WorAlBi*

Sholes, Christopher Latham
American. Journalist, Printer
Invented typewriter, 1868.
b. Feb 14, 1819 in Mooresburg, Pennsylvania
d. Feb 17, 1890 in Milwaukee, Wisconsin
Source: *AmBi; ApCAB; BioIn 3, 5, 7, 8, 11, 12, 13, 15, 21; DcAmB; InSci; JrnUS; LinLib S; NatCAB 3; OxCAmH; WebAB 74, 79; WhAm HS; WorInv*

Sholokhov, Mikhail Aleksandrovich
Russian. Author
Novel *And Quiet Flows the Don,* depicted civil war as experienced by Cossack villagers; won Nobel Prize in literature, 1965.
b. May 24, 1905 in Kruzhilin, Russia
d. Feb 21, 1984 in Veshenskaya, Union of Soviet Socialist Republics
Source: *Benet 96; BioIn 1, 4, 5, 6, 7, 9, 10, 11, 12; CasWL; ClDMEL 47; CnMWL; ConAu 101; CurBio 42, 60, 84; CyWA 58; DcRusL; EncWL; EvEuW; IntAu&W 76, 77; IntWW 74, 77, 78, 79, 80, 81, 82, 83; LngCTC; MakMC; McGEWB; ModSL 1; PenC EUR; REn; TwCA, SUP; TwCWr; Who 74, 82, 83; WhoNob; WhoSocC 78; WhoTwCL; WhoWor 82; WorAl*

Shor, Toots
[Bernard Shor]
American. Restaurateur
Best known for NYC "watering spots" frequented by celebrities for over 35 yrs.
b. May 6, 1905 in Philadelphia, Pennsylvania
d. Jan 24, 1977 in New York, New York
Source: *BusPN; LegTOT; WhAm 7; WhoAm 74, 76*

Shore, Dinah
[Frances Rose Shore]
"Fannie"
American. Singer, Actor
Began singing, 1938; won ten Emmys for various TV shows; "Dinah Shore Chevy Show," 1956-63, where she sang the closing jingle, "See the U.S.A. in Your Chevrolet."
b. Mar 1, 1917 in Winchester, Tennessee
d. Feb 24, 1994 in Beverly Hills, California
Source: *Baker 84, 92; BioAmW; BioIn 1, 3, 4, 5, 6, 7, 9, 10, 11, 12, 16, 19, 20, 21; BioNews 74; BkPepl; CelR, 90; CmpEPM; ConTFT 3, 13; CurBio 42, 66, 94N; EncWomS; FilmEn; FilmgC; ForYSC; GoodHs; HalFC 80, 84, 88; IntMPA 84, 86, 88, 92, 94; InWom, SUP; LegTOT; LesBEnT, 92; MotPP; NewAmDM; NewGrDA 86; News 94, 94-3; NewYTBE 72; NewYTBS 81, 85, 94; OxCPMus; PenEncP; RadStar; RkOn 74; SaTiSS; WhoAm 86, 90; WhoEnt 92; WhoHol 92, A; WorAlBi*

Shore, Eddie
[Edward William Shore]
Canadian. Hockey Player
Defenseman, 1926-40, mostly with Boston; known for rough play; only defenseman to win Hart Trophy four times; Hall of Fame, 1945.
b. Nov 25, 1902 in Fort Qu'Appelle, Saskatchewan, Canada
d. Mar 16, 1985 in Springfield, Massachusetts
Source: *BioIn 2, 3, 5, 6, 8, 9, 10, 14; HocEn; LegTOT; NewYTBS 85; WhoHcky 73; WhoSpor; WorAl; WorAlBi*

Shorr, Kehat
Israeli. Olympic Athlete, Victim
One of 11 members of Israeli Olympic team kidnapped, killed by Arab terrorists during Summer Olympic games.
b. 1919?, Romania
d. Sep 5, 1972 in Munich, Germany (West)

Shorrock, Glenn
[The Little River Band]
Australian. Singer
Formed Little River Band, 1975; began solo career, 1982, with album *Villain of the Peace.*
b. Jun 30, 1944 in Sydney, Australia
Source: *RkOn 85; Who 92*

Short, Bobby
[Robert Waltrip Short]
American. Pianist
Quintessential supper-club singer; celebrated 25th season at Cafe Carlyle, 1992.
b. Sep 15, 1926 in Danville, Illinois
Source: *Baker 84, 92; BiDAfM; BiDJaz; CelR, 90; ConAu 107; CurBio 72; DrBlPA 90; EncJzS; EncJzS; InB&W 85; NewGrDA 86; OxCPMus; PenEncP; WhoAm 82, 88; WhoBlA 75, 92; WhoEnt 92; WhoHol 92; WorAlBi*

Short, James
Scottish. Astronomer, Manufacturer
Optician; invented the first accurate reflecting-telescope mirrors.
b. Jun 10, 1710 in Edinburgh, Scotland
d. Jun 14, 1768 in London, England
Source: *Alli; DcBiPP; DcNaB; DcScB*

Short, Martin
Canadian. Actor, Comedian
Regular cast member, "Saturday Night Live," 1984-85; created characters Ed Grimley, Nathan Thurm.
b. Mar 26, 1950 in Hamilton, Ontario, Canada
Source: *BioIn 14, 15; ConNews 86-1; ConTFT 5, 12; CurBio 92; IntMPA 92, 94, 96; LegTOT; WhoAm 90; WhoEnt 92; WhoHol 92*

Short, Walter Campbell
American. Army Officer
Commanded armed forces at Pearl Harbor, Feb-Dec 1941; retired 1942; found directly responsible for failure of defenses.
b. Mar 30, 1880 in Fillmore, Illinois
d. Sep 3, 1949 in Dallas, Texas
Source: *BiDWWGF; BioIn 1, 2, 4; CurBio 46, 49; DcAmB S4; DcAmMiB; HarEnMi; NatCAB 40; ObitOF 79; WebAMB; WhAm 2*

Shorter, Frank C
American. Track Athlete
Long-distance runner; won gold medal in marathon, 1972 Olympics, silver medal, 1976 Olympics.
b. Oct 31, 1947 in Munich, Germany (West)
Source: *BiDAmSp OS; BioIn 9, 13, 14; ConAu 132; NewYTBE 72, 73; NewYTBS 76; WhoAm 80, 82, 84, 86, 88; WhoTr&F 73; WorAlBi*

Shorter, Wayne
American. Composer, Musician
Saxophonist; co-leader of Weather Report 1970-85; formed own band 1985; leading figure in post-modern jazz.
b. Aug 25, 1933 in Newark, New Jersey
Source: *AllMusG; BiDAfM; BiDJaz; BioIn 13, 16; ConMus 5; CurBio 96; DcTwCCu 5; EncJzS; InB&W 80, 85; IntWW 89, 91, 93; LegTOT; NewAmDM; NewGrDA 86; NewGrDJ 88, 94; PenEncP; WhoAm 78, 80, 82, 84, 86, 88, 92, 94, 95, 96, 97; WhoEnt 92; WhoRocM 82*

Shorthouse, Joseph Henry
English. Author, Manufacturer
Wrote historical, religious novel *John Inglesant,* 1881.
b. Sep 9, 1834 in Birmingham, England
d. Mar 4, 1903 in London, England
Source: *BbD; BioIn 5, 9, 12, 13; BritAu 19; CamGEL; CamGLE; CasWL; CelCen; Chambr 3; ConAu 121; CyWA 58; DcBiA; DcEnA, A; DcEuL; DcLB 18; DcLEL; DcNaB S2; EvLB; GrWrEL N; NewC; NewCBEL; OxCEng 67, 85, 95; PenC ENG; REn; RfGEnL 91; WebE&AL*

Shortz, Will(iam Frederic)
American. Editor, Puzzle Maker
Editor in chief, *Games* magazine, 1989-93; puzzle editor, *NY Times,* 1993—.
b. Aug 26, 1952 in Crawfordsville, Indiana
Source: *CurBio 96; IndAu 1967; WhoAm 94, 95, 96, 97*

Shostakovich, Dmitri Dmitryevich
Russian. Composer
Best-known symphony, *Fifth,* celebrated 20th anniversary of Russian Revolution, 1937.
b. Sep 25, 1906 in Saint Petersburg, Russia
d. Aug 9, 1975 in Moscow, Union of Soviet Socialist Republics
Source: *Baker 78; CurBio 41, 75; DcCM; DcFM; NewEOp 71; NewYTBE 73; NewYTBS 75; OxCFilm; OxCMus; WhAm 6; WorEFlm*

Shostakovich, Maxim
Russian. Conductor
Son of Dmitri; led USSR State Orchestra, 1960s; noted for interpreting his father's works; defected to US, 1981.
b. May 10, 1938 in Leningrad, Union of Soviet Socialist Republics
d. Aug 9, 1975 in Moscow, Russia
Source: *Baker 78, 84, 92; BiDSovU; BioIn 7, 8; IntWW 91; IntWWM 90; NewAmDM; NewGrDM 80; PenDiMP; WhoAm 90; WhoSSW 91; WhoWor 82, 84, 87, 91*

Shotwell, James Thomson
American. Historian, Diplomat
Edited over 200 historical vols.: *Economic and Social History of the World War,* 1919-29.
b. Aug 6, 1874 in Strathroy, Ontario, Canada
d. Jul 15, 1965 in New York, New York
Source: *AmAu&B; AmPeW; BiDInt; BioIn 4, 5, 6, 7, 10; CurBio 44, 65; DcAmB S7; MacDCB 78; TwCA, SUP; WebBD 83; WhAm 4; WhE&EA; WhLit; WhNAA*

Show, Grant
American. Actor
Appears on TV's "Melrose Place."
b. Feb 27, 1962 in Detroit, Michigan
Source: *ConTFT 15*

Shrady, Henry M
American. Sculptor
Executed equestrian statues of George Washington, R E Lee, General Grant, 1901-02.
b. Oct 24, 1871 in New York, New York
d. Apr 12, 1922 in Elmsford, New York
Source: *AmBi; DcAmB; NatCAB 13; TwCBDA; WhAm 1; WhAmArt 85*

Shrapnel, Henry
English. Army Officer
Invented shrapnel shells, c. 1804.
b. Jun 3, 1761 in Bradford-on-Avon, England
d. Mar 13, 1842 in Southampton, England
Source: *DcBiPP; DcNaB; HarEnMi; WebBD 83*

Shreve, Henry Miller
American. Pilot
Steamboat captain; assisted in the development of the lower Mississippi River system.
b. Oct 21, 1785 in Burlington County, New Jersey
d. Mar 6, 1851 in Saint Louis, Missouri
Source: *AmBi; ApCAB; BioIn 1, 3, 18; DcAmB; Drake; McGEWB; NatCAB 2; REnAW; TwCBDA; WebAB 74, 79; WhAm HS; WorAl; WorAlBi*

Shreve, Susan Richards
American. Author
Won Edgar for juvenile mystery: *Lucy Forever and Miss Rosetree,* 1987.
b. May 2, 1939 in Toledo, Ohio
Source: *AuBYP 3; BioIn 13, 15, 16; ConAu 5AS, 5NR, 38NR, 49; ConLC 23; DcAmChF 1985; DrAPF 80, 91; IntWW 91, 93; MajAI; ScF&FL 92; SixBJA; SmATA 41, 46; WhoAm 88, 90, 92, 94, 95, 96, 97; WhoAmW 87, 89, 91, 93, 95, 97; WhoUSWr 88; WrDr 76, 80, 82, 84, 86, 92*

Shrimpton, Jean Rosemary
"Shrimp"
English. Model
Popular model at same time as Twiggy, 1960s.
b. Nov 6, 1942 in High Wycombe, England
Source: *BioIn 7, 8, 13; InWom SUP; WhoHol A*

Shriner, Herb
American. TV Personality
Pioneer TV humorist, emcee; known for his Hoosier stories, 1950s.
b. May 29, 1918 in Toledo, Ohio
d. Apr 23, 1970 in Delray Beach, Florida
Source: *ASCAP 66; BiE&WWA; BioIn 1, 2, 3, 4, 8; JoeFr; LegTOT; LesBEnT; NewYTBE 70; NewYTET; NotNAT B; RadStar; WhAm 5; WhoHol B; WhScrn 74, 77, 83; WorAl; WorAlBi*

Shriver, Eunice Mary Kennedy
[Mrs. Robert Sargent Shriver]
American. Social Reformer
Sister of John F Kennedy; vp, Joseph P Kennedy Foundation, 1956—; founder of International Special Olympics.
b. Jul 10, 1920 in Brookline, Massachusetts
Source: *BioIn 13, 15; CelR 90; CurBio 96; InWom SUP; WhoAm 86, 90; WhoAmW 77, 91*

Shriver, Maria (Owings)
[Mrs. Arnold Schwarzenegger]
American. Broadcast Journalist
Daughter of Sargent Shriver, Eunice Kennedy; co-anchor, CBS Morning News, 1985-86; "First Person with Maria Shriver," 1991—.
b. Nov 6, 1955 in Chicago, Illinois
Source: *BioIn 11, 16; ConNews 86-2; ConTFT 12; CurBio 91; LegTOT; LesBEnT 92; WhoAm 86, 88, 95, 96, 97; WhoAmW 95, 97; WhoEnt 92; WomStre*

Shriver, Pam(ela Howard)
American. Tennis Player
Professional tennis player, 1979—; winner of 21 singles titles and 92 doubles titles; gold medal in 1988 Olympic games in doubles.
b. Jul 4, 1962 in Baltimore, Maryland
Source: *BiDAmSp OS; BioIn 11, 12, 13, 14, 15; BuCMET; EncWomS; LegTOT; NewYTBS 82, 85; WhoAm 84, 86, 88, 90, 92, 94, 95, 96, 97; WhoAmW 93, 95, 97; WhoE 95; WhoIntT; WhoWor 96, 97*

Shriver, (Robert) Sargent
American. Lawyer, Government Official
Brother-in-law of John F Kennedy; first director of Peace Corps, 1961-66.
b. Nov 9, 1915 in Westminster, Maryland
Source: *AmCath 80; BioIn 5, 6, 7, 8, 9, 10, 11, 12, 14, 16; BlueB 76; CelR; DcAmDH 80, 89; FacFETw; IntWW 74, 75, 76, 77, 78, 79, 80, 81, 82, 83, 89, 91, 93; IntYB 78, 79, 80, 81, 82; LinLib S; NewYTBE 72; PresAR; Who 74, 82, 83, 85, 88, 90, 92, 94; WhoAm 74, 76, 78, 80, 82, 84, 86, 88, 92, 94, 95, 96, 97; WhoAmP 73, 75, 77, 79, 81, 83, 85, 87, 89, 91, 93, 95; WhoE 95; WhoWor 74, 78, 80, 82*

Shrontz, Frank Anderson
American. Business Executive
President of Boeing, world's largest aircraft maker, since 1985.
b. Dec 14, 1931 in Boise, Idaho
Source: *BioIn 11, 15; Dun&B 90; IntWW 89, 91, 93; St&PR 84, 87, 91, 93, 96; WhoAm 76, 78, 80, 82, 84, 86, 88, 90, 92, 94, 95, 96, 97; WhoAmP 75, 77, 79; WhoFI 87, 89, 92, 94, 96; WhoGov 75, 77; WhoWest 80, 82, 87, 89, 92, 94, 96; WhoWor 91, 93, 95, 96, 97*

Shubert, Jacob J
American. Manager, Producer
One of three brothers who built powerful Broadway theatrical empire; principal backer of Flo Ziegfeld.
b. Aug 15, 1880 in Shirvanta, Russia
d. Dec 26, 1963 in New York, New York
Source: *EncAB-H 1974; NotNAT A; OxCThe 67; PlP&P; WhAm 4*

Shubert, Lee
American. Theater Owner, Producer
With brothers, major owner of legitimate theater empire, 1920-53; produced countless Broadway hits.
b. Mar 15, 1875 in Shirvanta, Russia
d. Dec 25, 1953 in New York, New York
Source: *BioIn 3, 8, 17, 18, 19; CamGWoT; CnThe; DcAmB S5; EncWT; LegTOT; NotNAT A, B; OxCThe 67; PlP&P; WebAB 74, 79; WhAm 3; WhoStg 1908; WhThe; WorAl; WorAlBi*

Shue, Andrew
American. Actor
Appears on TV's "Melrose Place."
b. Feb 20, 1967 in South Orange, New Jersey
Source: *LegTOT*

Shue, Elizabeth
American. Actor
Starred in *Leaving Las Vegas,* 1995.
b. Jun 10, 1963 in Wilmington, Delaware

Shue, Gene
[Eugene William Shue]
American. Basketball Player, Basketball Coach
Guard, 1954-64; NBA coach 1966-89; with several teams, now with Washington, 1980—; coach of yr., 1969, 1982.
b. Dec 18, 1931 in Baltimore, Maryland
Source: *BasBi; BiDAmSp BK; OfNBA 87; WhoAm 84, 88, 92; WhoBbl 73; WhoE 85; WhoWest 89*

Shukairy, Ahmed
Palestinian. Political Leader
Founder, first head of PLO, 1964-67.
b. 1908 in Acre, Palestine
d. Feb 26, 1980 in Amman, Jordan
Source: *AnObit 1980; HisEAAC; NewYTBS 80*

Shukovsky, Joel
American. Writer
Co-created television comedy *Murphy Brown.*

Shukshin, Vasilii Makarovich
Russian. Actor, Author, Director
Short story writer identified with "New Slavophiles."
b. 1929, Union of Soviet Socialist Republics
d. Oct 2, 1974 in Moscow, Union of Soviet Socialist Republics
Source: *BiDSovU; BioIn 10, 11, 12, 16; ObitOF 79; ObitT 1971*

Shula, Don(ald Francis)
American. Football Coach, Football Executive
Co-owner, head coach, Miami, 1970-95; won Super Bowl, 1972, 1973, 1974, 1984, and 1985.
b. Jan 4, 1930 in Grand River, Ohio
Source: *BiDAmSp FB; BioIn 9, 10, 11, 12, 13, 14, 15; BioNews 74; CelR, 90; ConAu 106; CurBio 74; FootReg 87; LegTOT; News 92, 92-2; NewYTBE 73; NewYTBS 85; WhoAm 86, 88; WhoSSW 86, 91; WorAl; WorAlBi*

Shull, George Harrison
American. Botanist
Research on corn hybrids increased yields per acre 25-50%.
b. Apr 15, 1874 in Clark County, Ohio
d. Sep 28, 1954 in Princeton, New Jersey
Source: *BioIn 1, 3, 4, 6, 12, 14; DcAmB S5; EncAAH; InSci; IntWW 83; WhAm 3; WhNAA; WhoAm 84*

Shulman, Irving
American. Author, Educator
Novels include *The Amboy Dukes,* 1947; biographies: *Harlow: An Intimate Biography,* 1964; adapted to film, 1965.
b. May 21, 1913 in New York, New York
d. Mar 23, 1995 in Sherman Oaks, California

Source: *AmAu&B; AmNov; Au&Wr 71; BioIn 2, 4, 11, 20, 21; ConAu 1R, 6NR, 148; CurBio 56, 95N; SmATA 13; WhoAm 74, 76, 78, 80, 82, 84, 88, 90, 92; WhoE 74; WhoUSWr 88; WhoWorJ 72, 78; WhoWrEP 89, 92, 95; WrDr 76, 80, 82, 84, 86, 88, 90, 92, 94, 96*

Shulman, Max
American. Author, Dramatist
Humorous works include *Barefoot Boy with Cheek,* 1943; adapted to musical comedy, 1947; cowrote play *The Tender Trap,* 1954; creator, writer, TV series "The Many Loves of Dobie Gillis," 1959-63.
b. Mar 14, 1919 in Saint Paul, Minnesota
d. Aug 28, 1988 in Los Angeles, California
Source: *AmAu&B; AmNov; BiE&WWA; BioIn 2, 5, 6, 7, 13, 16; ConAu 89, 126; CurBio 59, 88, 88N; DcLB 11; DrAPF 80; IntMPA 75, 76, 77, 78, 79, 80, 81, 82, 84, 86, 88; LegTOT; NewYTBS 88; NotNAT; SmATA 59; St&PR 75; WhAm 9; WhoAm 74, 76, 78, 80, 82, 84, 86, 88; WhoE 74; WhoUSWr 88; WorAl*

Shulman, Morton
Canadian. Author, Physician
Wrote books on finance as a hobby: *How to Invest Your Money & Profit from Inflation,* 1979.
b. Apr 2, 1925 in Toronto, Ontario, Canada
Source: *AmMWSc 73P, 92; AuNews 1; BioIn 8, 10, 11, 12; CanWW 31, 83, 89; ConAu 14NR, 21R; ConCaAu 1; WhoMW 74*

Shultz, George Pratt
American. Government Official
Succeeded Alexander Haig as Reagan's secretary of state, 1982-88.
b. Dec 13, 1920 in New York, New York
Source: *AmMWSc 73S; AmPolLe; BiDrUSE 71, 89; BioIn 8, 9, 10, 11, 12, 13, 14, 15, 16, 18, 19; CngDr 74, 83, 85, 87; ColdWar 2; ConAu 104; CurBio 69, 88; DcAmDH 89; EncWB; IntAu&W 89; IntWW 74, 75, 76, 77, 78, 79, 80, 81, 82, 83, 89, 91, 93; NewYTBE 70, 72, 73; NewYTBS 80, 82; PolProf NF; St&PR 84; Who 74, 82, 83, 85, 88, 90, 92, 94; WhoAm 74, 76, 78, 80, 82, 84, 86, 88, 90, 92, 94, 95, 96, 97; WhoAmP 73, 75, 77, 79, 85, 87, 89, 91, 93, 95; WhoE 83, 85, 86, 89; WhoFI 79, 92, 94; WhoGov 72; WhoSSW 73, 75, 76; WhoWest 92, 94, 96; WhoWor 74, 82, 84, 87, 89, 91, 93, 95, 96, 97; WorAlBi; WrDr 86, 92*

Shumlin, Herman Elliott
American. Producer, Director
Directed plays *Grand Hotel; The Deputy.*
b. Dec 6, 1898 in Atwood, Colorado
d. Jun 14, 1979 in New York, New York
Source: *BiE&WWA; BioIn 11; CurBio 41, 79; DcAmB S10; FilmgC; NewYTBS 79; NotNAT; WhAm 7; WhoAm 74, 76, 78; WhoThe 77; WorEFlm*

Shushkevich, Stanislav
Russian. Government Official
One of President Boris Yeltsin's key partners during the establishment of the Russian commonwealth.

Shuster, Frank
[Wayne and Shuster]
Canadian. Comedian
Had documentary-style TV show with partner Johnny Wayne, "Wayne and Schuster Take an Affectionate Look at.," 1966.
b. Sep 5, 1916 in Toronto, Ontario, Canada
Source: *BioIn 5, 11; CreCan 2*

Shuster, Joe
American. Cartoonist
Best known for "Superman" cartoons.
b. Jul 10, 1914 in Toronto, Ontario, Canada
d. Jul 30, 1992 in Los Angeles, California
Source: *BiDScF; BioIn 19; ConLC 21; EncACom; JeHun; LegTOT; WorECom*

Shuster, Rosie
American. Writer
Multiple Emmy winner for NBC's "Saturday Night Live," 1970s.
b. Jun 19, 1950 in Toronto, Ontario, Canada
Source: *BioIn 12; ConTFT 4*

Shute, Denny
[Herman Densmore Shute]
American. Golfer
Turned pro, 1928; won British Open, 1933; last to win PGA two straight yrs., 1936, 1937; Hall of Fame, 1957.
b. Oct 25, 1904 in Cleveland, Ohio
d. May 13, 1974 in Akron, Ohio
Source: *LegTOT; NewYTBS 74; ObitOF 79; WhoGolf; WhoSpor*

Shute, Nevil
[Nevil Shute Norway]
English. Author, Aeronautical Engineer
Best known for novel of nuclear holocaust, *On the Beach,* 1963.
b. Jan 17, 1899 in Ealing, Australia
d. Jan 12, 1960 in Melbourne, Australia
Source: *Benet 87, 96; BioIn 3, 4, 5, 7, 11, 14, 17; CamGLE; ConAu 93, 102; ConLC 30; CurBio 42, 60; DcArts; DcLEL; DcNaB 1951; EncSF, 93; EvLB; FilmgC; GrBr; HalFC 80, 84, 88; InSci; LegTOT; LngCTC; ModBrL; NewC; NewCBEL; NewEScF; Novels; ObitT 1951; OxCAusL; PenC ENG; RAdv 14, 13-1; REn; ScF&FL 1, 92; ScFSB; TwCA, SUP; TwCCr&M 80; TwCRHW 90, 94; TwCSFW 81, 86, 91; TwCWr; WhAm 3, 4; WhE&EA; WhoTwCL; WorAl*

Shutt, Steve
[Stephen John Shutt]
Canadian. Hockey Player
Left wing, 1972-85, mostly with Montreal; set NHL record for most goals in season by left wing, 60 (1976-77).
b. Jul 1, 1952 in Toronto, Ontario, Canada
Source: *BioIn 11, 16; HocEn; HocReg 85; WhoAm 78, 80, 82, 84*

Shutta, Ethel
American. Actor
Sang in Ziegfeld Follies with Eddie Cantor in *Whoopee.*
b. Dec 1, 1896 in New York, New York
d. Feb 5, 1976
Source: *BiDAmM; BioIn 9, 10; InWom SUP; NewYTBE 70, 71; WhoHol C; WhoThe 72; WhThe*

Shuttlesworth, Dorothy Edwards
American. Children's Author
Noted for natural history books.
b. 1907 in New York, New York
Source: *AuBYP 2, 3; BioIn 7, 9; ConAu 1R, 4NR; FifBJA; ForWC 70; SmATA 3*

Shuttlesworth, Fred Lee
American. Clergy, Civil Rights Leader
Aid to Martin Luther King, Jr; founder, pres., AL Christian Movement for Human Rights, 1956-69.
b. Mar 18, 1922 in Mugler, Alabama
Source: *BioIn 7, 11; InB&W 85; NegAl 89; PolProf E, J, K; WhoBlA 85, 92*

Shyer, Charles
American. Screenwriter
Films include *Smokey and the Bandit,* 1977; *Private Benjamin,* 1980.
b. Oct 11, 1941 in Los Angeles, California
Source: *BioIn 14; ConTFT 8; MiSFD 9; VarWW 85*

Siad Barre, Mohamed
Somali. Political Leader
Pres., Somalia, 1969-91.
b. 1912? in Lugh, Somalia
d. Jan 2, 1995 in Lagos, Nigeria
Source: *BioIn 11, 13; ColdWar 1; IntWW 91; WhoWor 91*

Sibelius, Jean
Finnish. Composer
Romantic composer who drew themes from nature, folklore; known for seven symphonies, 1899-1924.
b. Dec 8, 1865 in Tavastehus, Finland
d. Sep 20, 1957 in Jarvenpaa, Finland
Source: *AtlBL; Baker 78, 84, 92; Benet 87, 96; BioIn 1, 2, 3, 4, 5, 6, 7, 8, 9, 10, 11, 12, 13, 14, 15, 16, 17, 19, 20; BriBkM 80; CnOxB; CompSN, SUP; DcCM; DcCom 77; DcCom&M 79; DcTwCC, A; FacFETw; LegTOT; MakMC; MusMk; NewAmDM; NewGrDM 80; NewOxM; NotNAT B; ObitT 1951; OxCEng 85, 95; OxCMus; OxDcOp; PenDiMP A; RAdv 14; REn; WhAm 3; WhDW; WorAl; WorAlBi*

Siberry, Jane
Canadian. Singer, Songwriter
Albums include *No Borders Here,* 1984 and *Bound by the Beauty,* 1989.
b. 1950? in Toronto, Ontario, Canada
Source: *BioIn 16; ConMus 6*

Sibley, Hiram
American. Businessman
Pres., Western Union Telegraph Co., 1856-69; built first transcontinental line, 1861; established Sibley College at Cornell U.
b. Feb 6, 1807 in North Adams, Massachusetts
d. Jul 12, 1888 in Rochester, New York
Source: *AmBi; ApCAB; BiDAmBL 83; BioIn 4, 9, 15; DcAmB; NatCAB 4; TwCBDA; WebAB 74, 79; WebBD 83; WhAm HS*

Sickles, Daniel Edgar
American. Government Official, Soldier
Acquitted for shooting Philip Key, son of Francis Scott; first time plea of temporary insanity used, 1859; credited with obtaining Central Park for NYC.
b. Oct 20, 1825 in New York, New York
d. May 3, 1914 in New York, New York
Source: *AmBi; ApCAB; BiAUS; BiDrAC; BioIn 3, 4, 6, 7, 8, 11, 12, 13; CivWDc; CopCroC; DcAmB; Drake; NatCAB 12; TwCBDA; WebAB 74, 79; WebAMB; WhAm 1; WhAmP*

Sickmann, Rodney Virgil
[The Hostages]
"Rocky"
American. Hostage
One of 52 held by terrorists, Nov 1979-Jan 1981.
b. 1958?
Source: *BioIn 12; NewYTBS 81*

Sidaris, Andy
American. Producer, Director
Won Emmys for "1968 Summer Olympics," 1969; "XII Winter Olympics," 1976.
b. Feb 20, 1932 in Chicago, Illinois
Source: *IntMPA 75, 76, 77, 78, 79, 80, 81, 82, 84, 86, 88, 92, 94, 96; VarWW 85*

Sidarouss, Stephanos, Cardinal
Egyptian. Religious Leader
Patriarch of Coptic Catholic Church, 1958-85; became cardinal, 1965.
b. Feb 22, 1904 in Cairo, Egypt
d. Aug 23, 1987 in Cairo, Egypt
Source: *BioIn 11, 15; IntWW 78; WhAm 11; WhoWor 76, 78, 80, 82, 84, 87*

Siddal, Elizabeth Eleanor
[Mrs. Dante Gabriel Rossetti]
"Lizzie"
English. Model, Artist
Body exhumed after death to recover manuscript Rossetti had buried with her.
b. 1834 in Sheffield, England
d. Feb 10, 1862
Source: *BioIn 9, 10, 11, 13; DcVicP, 2; DcWomA; OxCArt; WomArt*

Siddons, Sarah Kemble
English. Actor
Best known for tragic roles, especially Lady MacBeth, 1785-1812.
b. Jul 5, 1755 in Brecon, Wales
d. Jun 8, 1831 in London, England
Source: *CnThe; DcEuL; Ent; HerW, 84; InWom, SUP; NewC; NewCol 75; NotNAT A, B; OxCThe 67; PlP&P; REn*

Sidey, Hugh Swanson
American. Author, Journalist
Has written column, "The Presidency," for Time mag. since 1966.
b. Sep 3, 1927 in Greenfield, Iowa
Source: *BioIn 11, 15; ConAu 111, 124; EncTwCJ; WhoAm 74, 76, 78, 80, 82, 84, 86, 88, 90, 92, 94, 95, 96, 97; WhoWor 74*

Sidgwick, Henry
English. Educator, Author
Best-known work: *Methods of Ethics,* 1874.
b. May 31, 1838 in Yorkshire, England
d. Aug 28, 1900 in Cambridge, England
Source: *Alli SUP; BbD; BiD&SB; BiDBrF 1; BiDPara; BioIn 8, 9, 10, 16; BritAu 19; CamGEL; CamGLE; CasWL; CelCen; Chambr 3; ConAu 120; DcEnA, A; DcEuL; DcLEL; DcNaB S1; EncEth; EncO&P 1, 2, 3; EncPaPR 91; EvLB; GrEconB; LuthC 75; McGEWB; NewC; NewCBEL; OxCEng 67, 85, 95; OxCPhil; PenC ENG; RAdv 14; WhoEc 81, 86*

Sidney, Algernon
English. Politician, Author
First to write "God helps those who help themselves" in English in *Discourses Government,* 1698; charged with treason, executed for part in Ryehouse Plot.
b. 1622 in Penshurst, England
d. Dec 7, 1683 in London, England
Source: *Alli; BiD&SB; BioIn 13, 14, 17, 21; DcBiPP; DcEnA, A; DcEnL; DcNaB; EvLB; NewC; NewCol 75; OxCEng 67, 85, 95; REn; WebBD 83*

Sidney, George
American. Director, Producer
Won Oscars for shorts *Quicker'n A Wink,* 1940; *Of Pups and Puzzles,* 1941.
b. Oct 4, 1916 in New York, New York
Source: *BiDFilm; BioIn 15, 20; CmMov; DcFM; EncAFC; FilmEn; FilmgC; IlWWHD 1; IntDcF 1-2; IntMPA 75, 76, 77, 78, 79, 80, 81, 82, 84, 86, 88, 92, 94, 96; MiSFD 9; MovMk; WhoAm 74, 76, 78, 80, 82, 84; WhoEnt 92; WorEFlm; WorFDir 1*

Sidney, Philip, Sir
English. Poet, Statesman, Soldier, Courtier
Model of English chivalry; wrote pastoral *Arcadia,* 1590.
b. Nov 30, 1554 in Kent, England
d. Oct 17, 1586 in Arnhem, Netherlands
Source: *Alli; AtlBL; BbD; Benet 87, 96; BiD&SB; BiDRP&D; BioIn 1, 2, 3, 4, 5, 7, 8, 9, 10, 11, 12, 13, 14, 15, 16, 17, 18, 20, 21; BlmGEL; BritAu; BritWr 1; CamGEL; CamGLE; CamGWoT; CasWL; Chambr 1; ChhPo, S2, S3; CnDBLB 1; CnE&AP; CroE&S; CrtT 1, 4; CyWA 58; DcArts; DcBiPP; DcEnA; DcEnL; DcEuL; DcLB 167; DcLEL; DcNaB; EvLB; GrWrEL N, P; LinLib L, S; LitC 19; LngCEL; LuthC 75; MagSWL; McGEWB; MouLC 1; NewC; NewCBEL; OxCEng 67, 85, 95; PenC ENG; RAdv 1, 14, 13-1; REn; RfGEnL 91; RGFBP; WebE&AL; WhDW; WorAl; WorAlBi; WrPh*

Sidney, Sylvia
[Sophia Kosow]
American. Actor
Oscar nominee, 1973, for *Summer Wishes, Winter Dreams.*
b. Aug 8, 1910 in New York, New York
Source: *BiDFilm, 81, 94; BiE&WWA; BioIn 9, 12, 21; CelR; ConTFT 9; CurBio 81; Film 2; FilmEn; FilmgC; ForYSC; GangFlm; HalFC 80, 84, 88; IntDcF 1-3, 2-3; IntMPA 75, 76, 77, 78, 79, 80, 81, 82, 84, 86, 88, 92, 94, 96; InWom, SUP; LegTOT; MotPP; MovMk; NotNAT; OxCFilm; ThFT; What 3; WhoAm 76, 78, 80, 82, 84, 86, 88, 90, 92, 94, 95, 96, 97; WhoEnt 92; WhoHol 92, A; WhoThe 72, 77, 81; WomWMM; WorAl; WorAlBi; WorEFlm*

Siebert, Babe
[Albert Charles Siebert]
Canadian. Hockey Player
Left wing, 1925-39, with four NHL teams; won Hart Trophy, 1937; Hall of Fame, 1964; died from drowning at height of career.
b. Jan 14, 1904 in Plattsville, Ontario, Canada
d. Aug 25, 1939 in Saint Joseph, Ontario, Canada
Source: *HocEn; WhoHcky 73; WhoSpor*

Siebert, Muriel
"Rebel of Wall Street"
American. Business Executive
First female member of NY Stock Exchange, 1967; one of first to open discount brokerage.
b. 1932? in Cleveland, Ohio
Source: *BioIn 16; ConNews 87-2; EncABHB 7; InWom SUP; WhoAm 90; WhoAmW 91; WhoFI 89; WomFir*

Siegbahn, Kai Manne Boerje
Swedish. Physicist, Educator
Won 1981 Nobel Prize in physics for developing ESCA for chemical analysis; son of 1924 prize winner Manne.

b. Apr 20, 1918 in Lund, Sweden
Source: *AmMWSc 92; BioIn 13, 15; NobelP; Who 92; WhoAm 90; WhoNob, 90, 95; WhoWor 87, 91; WorAlBi*

Siegbahn, Karl Manne Georg
Swedish. Scientist
Won 1924 Nobel Prize in physics for discoveries in field of X-ray spectroscopy.
b. Dec 3, 1886 in Orebro, Sweden
d. Sep 26, 1978 in Stockholm, Sweden
Source: *AsBiEn; BiESc; DcScB S2; InSci; IntWW 74, 75, 76, 77, 78, 79N; LarDcSc; McGMS 80; ObitOF 79; WhAm 9; WhE&EA; Who 74; WhoNob, 90, 95; WhoWor 76; WorAl*

Siegel, Bernie S(hepard)
American. Surgeon
Promoter of self-healing; wrote *How to Live Between Office Visits,* 1993.
b. Oct 14, 1932 in New York, New York
Source: *ConAu 49NR; CurBio 93*

Siegel, Bugsy
[Benjamin Siegel]
American. Criminal
Helped organize Murder, Inc; began syndicate-controlled gambling in Las Vegas.
b. Feb 28, 1906 in New York, New York
d. Jun 20, 1947 in Beverly Hills, California
Source: *AmDec 1940; BioIn 1, 2, 8, 11, 18; DrInf; LegTOT*

Siegel, Don
American. Director
Won two Academy Awards for short films *Star in the Night,* and *Hitler Lives;* movies directed include *Dirty Harry,* 1971 and *Escape from Alcatraz,* 1979.
b. Oct 16, 1912 in Chicago, Illinois
d. Apr 20, 1991 in Nipomo, California
Source: *AnObit 1991; BiDFilm 94; BioIn 12, 15, 17, 18, 19; ConTFT 6, 10; FilmEn; FilmgC; GangFlm; HalFC 80, 84, 88; IlWWHD 1; IntDcF 1-2, 2-2; IntMPA 75, 76, 77, 78, 79, 80, 81, 82, 84, 86, 88; LegTOT; MiSFD 9N; MovMk; NewYTBE 71, 72; NewYTBS 91; OxCFilm; PenEncH; WhAm 10; WhoAm 74, 76, 78, 80, 82, 84, 86, 88, 90; WhoHrs 80*

Siegel, Jerry
American. Cartoonist
Created comic book's most lucrative character, Superman, 1933; mistakenly sold rights for only $130 in 1938.
b. Oct 17, 1914 in Cleveland, Ohio
d. Jan 28, 1996 in Los Angeles, California
Source: *BioIn 10, 21; ConAu X; EncACom; EncSF, 93; JeHun; LegTOT; WorECom*

Siegel, Larry
American. Writer
Won Emmys for "The Carol Burnett Show," 1971, 1973, 1978.
b. Oct 29, 1925 in New York, New York
Source: *VarWW 85*

Siegel, Morris J
American. Businessman
Chm., pres., Celestial Seasonings, biggest producer of herbal teas, 1971-84; sold to Kraft for $36 million.
b. Nov 21, 1949 in Salida, Colorado
Source: *BioIn 13; NewYTBS 83; WhoAm 80, 82, 84, 86, 88*

Siegel, Owen R
American. Manufacturer
Founded trophy-making co., RS Owens & Co., 1938; makes Oscars, Emmys, Clios, MTV Awards.
b. 1919 in Chicago, Illinois
Source: *BioIn 16; St&PR 84, 87*

Siegfried and Roy
[Siegfried Fischbacher; Roy Uwehudwigltorn]
American. Entertainers
Partners in illusion; have given over 10,000 performances in Las Vegas.
Source: *BioIn 17, 18, 19, 21*

Siegmeister, Elie
American. Composer, Conductor
Stage, orchestral works on native American themes include *Ozark Set,* 1943; founded, led American Ballad singers, 1939-44; wrote on music.
b. Jan 15, 1909 in New York, New York
d. Mar 10, 1991 in Manhasset, New York
Source: *AmAu&B; AmComp; ASCAP 66, 80; Au&Wr 71; AuBYP 2, 3; Baker 78, 84, 92; BiDAmM; BiE&WWA; BioIn 1, 2, 7, 8, 9, 11, 14, 16, 17; BlueB 76; BriBkM 80; CompSN, SUP; ConAmC 76, 82; ConAu 1NR, 1R, 46NR, 133; CpmDNM 73, 79, 80; DcCM; EncAL; IntWWM 77, 80, 85, 90; LegTOT; MusMk; NewAmDM; NewGrDA 86; NewGrDM 80; NewGrDO; NewOxM; NewYTBS 91; NotNAT; OxCMus; WhAm 10; WhoAm 74, 76, 78, 80, 82, 84, 86, 88, 90; WhoAmJ 80; WhoAmM 83; WhoE 83, 85; WhoMus 72; WhoWorJ 72; WrDr 76, 80, 82, 84*

Siemens, (Ernst) Werner von
German. Inventor, Industrialist
Developed electroplating process, 1841.
b. Dec 13, 1816 in Lenthe, Germany
d. Dec 6, 1892 in Berlin, Germany
Source: *BioIn 7, 12, 20; CamDcSc; DcScB; InSci; LarDcSc; NewCol 75; WhDW; WorAl; WorAlBi; WorInv*

Siemens, William, Sir
English. Inventor, Physicist, Engineer
Developed open-hearth steelmaking process, 1861; laid first cable between US and England, 1875.
b. Apr 4, 1823 in Lenthe, Germany
d. Nov 18, 1883 in London, England
Source: *AsBiEn; BioIn 16; DcNaB; NewCol 75; WebBD 83; WorAl; WorAlBi*

Sienkiewicz, Henryk Adam Aleksander Pius
Polish. Author
Best known for historical novel *Quo Vadis,* 1895; won Nobel Prize for literature, 1905.
b. May 5, 1846 in Okrzejska, Poland
d. Nov 15, 1916 in Vevey, Switzerland
Source: *AtlBL; BbD; BiD&SB; CasWL; ClDMEL 47; CyWA 58; DcBiA; DcEuL; EncWL; EuAu; EvEuW; LngCTC; ModSL 2; PenC EUR; REn; WhoNob, 95*

Siepi, Cesare
Italian. Opera Singer
Bass with NY Met., 1950-74; noted for Don Giovanni, Verdi roles.
b. Feb 10, 1923 in Milan, Italy
Source: *Baker 78, 84, 92; BiE&WWA; BioIn 4, 5, 6, 7, 11; BriBkM 80; CelR; CmOp; CurBio 55; FacFETw; IntDcOp; IntWWM 77, 80, 90; MetOEnc; MusSN; NewAmDM; NewEOp 71; NewGrDM 80; NewGrDO; NewYTBE 71; PenDiMP; WhoAm 74, 76, 78, 80, 82, 84, 86, 88, 90, 92, 94, 95, 96, 97; WhoEnt 92; WhoHol 92, A; WhoMus 72; WhoOp 76; WhoWor 74*

Sierra (Garcia), Ruben Angel
Puerto Rican. Baseball Player
Outfielder, Texas, 1982-92; Oakland, 1992-95; NY Yankees, 1995—; led AL in rbis, 1989.
b. Oct 6, 1965 in Rio Piedras, Puerto Rico
Source: *Ballpl 90; BaseEn 88; BaseReg 88; WhoAfA 96; WhoAm 90, 92, 94, 95; WhoBlA 92, 94; WhoHisp 91, 92, 94; WhoWest 92, 94; WorAlBi*

Sieyes, Emmanuel Joseph
French. Political Activist, Pamphleteer
Writings encouraged bourgeoisie during French Revolution; participated in political coup that brought Napoleon to power.
b. May 3, 1748 in Frejus, France
d. Jun 20, 1836 in Paris, France
Source: *BiDMoER 1; BioIn 16; CelCen; CmFrR; DcBiPP; EncEnl; EncRev; McGEWB; OxCFr; WhDW; WorAl; WorAlBi*

Sifford, Charlie
[Charles Luther Sifford]
American. Golfer
First African-American to join Professional Golfers' Assn. (PGA) tour, 1960.
b. Jun 2, 1922 in Charlotte, North Carolina
Source: *AfrAmSG; BioIn 8, 19, 21; ConBlB 4; InB&W 85; NegAl 89; WhoAfA 96; WhoBlA 92, 94*

Sigismund
Ruler
Ruled Holy Roman Empire, 1433-37; German king, 1410-37; king of Hungary, 1387-1437; son of Charles IV.
b. Feb 15, 1368 in Nuremberg, Germany
d. Dec 19, 1437 in Znojmo, Bohemia
Source: *BioIn 8; DcBiPP; DcCathB; Dis&D; LuthC 75; McGEWB; NewCol 75; WebBD 83*

Signac, Paul
French. Artist
Leading spokesman for the neo-impressionist movement; painted European coastal scenes.
b. Nov 11, 1863 in Paris, France
d. Aug 15, 1935 in Paris, France
Source: *AtlBL; BioIn 2, 3, 4, 5, 6, 8, 13, 14, 16; ClaDrA; DcArts; DcTwCCu 2; McGDA; OxCArt; OxDcArt; PhDcTCA 77; REn; ThHEIm; WhDW*

Signorelli, Luca
Italian. Artist
Member of Umbrian school; best-known frescoe: *Heaven and Hell,* 1499-1504.
b. 1441 in Cortona, Italy
d. Oct 16, 1523 in Cortona, Italy
Source: *AtlBL; BioIn 1, 5, 9, 16; DcCathB; IntDcAA 90; LuthC 75; McGDA; OxCArt; OxDcArt; REn*

Signoret, Simone Henrietta Charlotte
[Simone Kaminker; Mrs. Yves Montand]
German. Actor
Won Oscar for *Room at the Top,* 1958.
b. Mar 25, 1921 in Wiesbaden, Germany
d. Sep 30, 1985 in Normandy, France
Source: *AnObit 1991; BiDAmM; BiDFilm, 81, 94; BioIn 5, 9, 11, 13; CelR, 90; ConMus 12; ConTFT 6, 10; CurBio 60, 85, 88, 92N; DcArts; DcTwCCu 2; EncEurC; FacFETw; FilmAG WE; FilmEn; FilmgC; ForYSC; HalFC 80, 84, 88; IntDcF 1-3, 2-3; IntMPA 77, 80, 82, 84, 86, 88, 92; IntWW 74, 75, 76, 77, 78, 79, 80, 81, 82, 83, 89, 91; ItaFilm; LegTOT; MotPP; MovMk; News 92, 92-2; NewYTBS 91; OxCFilm; OxCPMus; WhAm 10; Who 82; WhoAm 74, 82; WhoFr 79; WhoHol 92, A; WhoWor 74, 76, 78, 84, 87, 89, 91; WorAl; WorAlBi; WorEFlm*

Signorile, Michelangelo
American. Journalist
Known for denouncing closeted gays who he felt most harmed the gay community; wrote *Outing Yourself,* 1995.
b. 1960
Source: *GayLesB*

Sigourney, Lydia Howard
"The Mrs. Hemans of America"
American. Poet
Wrote over 60 volumes of sentimental, sad verse: *Poems, Religious and Elegiac,* 1841.
b. Sep 1, 1791 in Norwich, Connecticut
d. Jun 10, 1865 in Hartford, Connecticut
Source: *AmBi; AmWom; ApCAB; BioIn 3, 4, 7, 9, 11, 12, 13, 15, 19; CelCen; DcAmB; DcLB 1; Drake; FemiCLE; NatCAB 1; NotAW; TwCBDA; WebAB 74; WhAm HS*

Sihanouk, Norodom
[Samdech Preah Norodom Sihanouk (Varman)]
Cambodian. Ruler
Ruled Cambodia, 1941-55, 1960-70, 1975-76, 1993—; gained independence from French rule, 1953.
b. Oct 31, 1922 in Pnom Penh, Cambodia
Source: *ColdWar 2; ConAu 106, 129; CurBio 54, 93; DcMPSA; DcTwHis; FacFETw; FarE&A 78, 79, 80, 81; IntWW 74, 75, 76, 77, 78, 79, 80, 81, 82, 83, 89, 91, 93; McGEWB; NewYTBS 79, 93; WhoAsAP 91; WhoWor 74, 82, 84, 87, 89, 91, 93, 95, 96; WorAlBi*

Sikelianos, Angelos
Greek. Poet
Significant 20th c. Greek lyrical poet.
b. Mar 28, 1884 in Leucas Island, Greece
d. Jun 19, 1951 in Athens, Greece
Source: *BioIn 1, 2, 10, 13; CasWL; ClDMEL 80; EncWL 2, 3; GrFLW; PenC EUR; RAdv 14; TwCLC 39; WorAu 1950*

Sikking, James B
American. Actor
Played Lt. Howard Hunter on TV series "Hill Street Blues," 1981-87.
b. Mar 5, 1934 in Los Angeles, California
Source: *ConTFT 6; IntMPA 92; VarWW 85; WhoTelC*

Sikorsky, Igor Ivanovich
American. Aeronautical Engineer
Developed first successful helicopter, 1939.
b. May 25, 1889 in Kiev, Russia
d. Oct 26, 1972 in Easton, Connecticut
Source: *AmAu&B; AmMWSc 73P; CurBio 40, 56, 72; DcAmB S9; FacFETw; McGMS 80; NewYTBE 72; WebAB 74; WhAm 5; WhDW; WorAl*

Silas, Paul Theron
American. Basketball Player, Basketball Coach
Forward, 1964-80, with six NBA teams; won three NBA championships; coach, San Diego, 1980-83.
b. Jul 12, 1943 in Prescott, Arizona
Source: *BiDAmSp BK; OfNBA 81, 87; WhoAfA 96; WhoBbl 73; WhoBlA 85, 92, 94*

Silber, John Robert
American. University Administrator
Pres. of Boston University, 1971-96; chancellor, Boston U, 1996—.
b. Aug 15, 1926 in San Antonio, Texas
Source: *BioIn 9, 10, 11, 12, 13, 16; DrAS 82P; IntWW 91; News 90-1; NewYTBS 89; WhoAm 90, 97; WhoE 91, 97; WhoWor 84; WrDr 92*

Siles Zuazo, Hernan
Bolivian. Political Leader
Leader of revolution, 1952; pres., 1956-60, 1982-85.
b. Mar 19, 1914 in La Paz, Bolivia
d. Aug 6, 1996 in Montevideo, Uruguay
Source: *BioIn 5, 6, 13, 16; CurBio 58, 85, 96N; DcCPSAm; EncLatA; IntWW 74, 75, 76, 77, 78, 79, 80, 81, 82, 83, 89, 91, 93; NewYTBS 82; WhoWor 74, 84, 87, 89, 91*

Silhouette, Etienne de
French. Social Reformer
Controller of finance, 1759, scorned by nobility for savings reforms; name used for anything plain or cheap; "silhouette" applied to profile outlines, the poor man's miniature.
b. Jul 5, 1709
d. 1767
Source: *AntBDN O; Benet 87, 96; DcBiPP; REn; WebBD 83; WorAl; WorAlBi*

Silk, Dave
[David Silk]
American. Hockey Player
Center in NHL, 1980-86; member US Olympic gold medal-winning team, 1980.
b. Jan 1, 1958 in Boston, Massachusetts
Source: *BioIn 13; HocEn; HocReg 86; NewYTBS 82*

Silk, George
American. Photographer, Journalist
Staff photographer, *Life* magazine, 1943-72; best known for sports, war pictures.
b. Nov 17, 1916 in Levin, New Zealand
Source: *BioIn 4; ConPhot 82, 88; EncTwCJ; ICPEnP A; MacBEP; WhoAm 74, 76, 78, 80, 82, 84, 86, 88, 90, 92, 94, 95, 96, 97*

Silkin, Jon
English. Poet
Books of verse include *The Lapidary Poems,* 1979.
b. Dec 2, 1930 in London, England
Source: *Au&Wr 71; BioIn 7, 10, 12, 14, 16; CamGLE; ChhPo, S3; CnE&AP; ConAu 5AS, 5R; ConLC 2, 6, 43; ConPo 70, 75, 80, 85, 91, 96; DcLB 27, 29; DcLEL 1940; EngPo; IntAu&W 77, 86, 89, 91, 93; IntvTCA 2; IntWW 76, 77, 78, 79, 80, 81, 82, 83, 89, 91, 93; IntWWP 77; LinLib L; ModBrL, S1, S2; NewC; OxCEng 85, 95; OxCTwCP; RGFMBP; RGTwCWr; Who 74, 82, 83, 85, 88, 90, 92, 94; WhoWor 82, 84, 87, 89, 91, 93, 95, 96, 97; WorAu 1950; WrDr 76, 80, 82, 84, 86, 88, 90, 92, 94, 96*

Silko, Leslie Marmon
American. Author
Writes novels with Native American themes; wrote *Ceremony,* 1977; *The Almanac of the Dead,* 1992.
b. Mar 5, 1948 in Albuquerque, New Mexico
Source: *AmWomWr, 92; Au&Arts 14; Benet 96; BenetAL 91; BioIn 12, 13; BlmGWL; CamGLE; CamHAL; ConAu 45NR, 115, 122; ConLC 23, 74; ConNov 86, 91, 96; ConPo 91, 96; ConPopW; CyWA 89; DcLB 143; DcNAL; DrAPF 80; EncNAB; GrWomW; InWom SUP; MagSAmL; ModWoWr; NatNAL; NotNaAm; OxCAmL 95; OxCWoWr 95; RAdv 14; RfGAmL 94; RfGShF; TwCWW 82, 91; WorAu 1985; WrDr 94, 96*

Silkwood, Karen
American. Nuclear Technician
Exposed to radiation on job; active to improve safety; played by Meryl Streep in movie *Silkwood,* 1983.
b. Feb 19, 1946
d. Nov 13, 1974 in Oklahoma City, Oklahoma
Source: *BioIn 10, 11, 14, 16; ConHero 1; FacFETw; LegTOT; NewYTBS 79*

Sill, Edward Rowland
American. Poet, Educator
Best known for *The Hermitage and Other Poems,* 1868.
b. Apr 29, 1841 in Windsor, Connecticut
d. Feb 27, 1887 in Cleveland, Ohio
Source: *Alli, SUP; AmAu; AmAu&B; AmBi; ApCAB; BenetAL 91; BibAL; BiDAmEd; BiDAmM; BiD&SB; BioIn 4, 13; Chambr 3; ChhPo, S1, S2; CmCal; CnDAL; CyEd; DcAmAu; DcAmB; DcLEL; DcNAA; LinLib L; NatCAB 7; OhA&B; OxCAmL 65, 83, 95; REn; REnAL; TwCBDA; WhAm HS*

Sillanpaa, Frans E
Finnish. Author
Wrote novel *The Maid Silja,* 1931; won 1939 Nobel Prize in literature.
b. Sep 16, 1888 in Hameenkyro, Finland
d. Jun 3, 1964 in Helsinki, Finland
Source: *CasWL; ConAu 93; CurBio 40, 64; EncWL; EvEuW; Novels; PenC EUR; REn; TwCA SUP; TwCWr; WhAm 4; WhoNob; WorAl*

Silliman, Benjamin
American. Educator, Chemist, Geologist
Yale U professor; founded *American Journal of Science,* 1818.
b. Aug 8, 1779 in Trumbull, Connecticut
d. Nov 24, 1864 in New Haven, Connecticut
Source: *Alli; AmAu; AmBi; ApCAB; AsBiEn; BbD; BbtC; BenetAL 91; BiDAmEd; BiDAmS; BiESc; BiInAmS; BioIn 1, 2, 5, 7, 8, 9, 17; CyAL 1; CyEd; DcAmAu; DcAmB; DcAmMeB, 84; DcBiPP; DcNAA; DcScB; Drake; EncAB-H 1974, 1996; HarEnUS; InSci; McGEWB; NatCAB 2; OxCAmH; OxCCan; PeoHis; REnAL; TwCBDA; WebAB 74, 79; WhAm HS*

Silliphant, Stirling Dale
American. Screenwriter, Producer
Won Oscar, Edgar for writing *In the Heat of the Night,* 1968.
b. Jan 16, 1918 in Detroit, Michigan
d. Apr 26, 1996 in Bangkok, Thailand
Source: *BioIn 14; CmMov; ConAu 14NR, 42NR, 73, 152; ConTFT 3; DcLB 26; HalFC 84, 88; IntMPA 86, 92; LesBEnT, 92; WhAm 11; WhoAm 76, 78, 80, 82, 84, 86, 88, 90, 92, 94, 95, 96; WhoEnt 92*

Sillitoe, Alan
English. Author
Novels, short stories adapted to film: *Saturday Night and Sunday Morning,* 1958.
b. Mar 4, 1928 in Nottingham, England
Source: *Au&Wr 71; AuNews 1; Benet 87, 96; BioIn 6, 8, 9, 10, 13, 15, 16; BlmGEL; BlueB 76; CamGLE; CnDBLB 8; ConAu 2AS, 8NR, 9R, 26NR, 55NR; ConLC 1, 3, 6, 10, 19, 57; ConNov 72, 76, 82, 86, 91, 96; ConPo 70, 75, 80, 85, 91; CyWA 89; DcArts; DcLB 14, 139; DcLEL 1940; EncSF, 93; EncWL, 2, 3; FacFETw; GrWrEL N; HalFC 80, 84, 88; IntAu&W 76, 77, 91, 93; IntvTCA 2; IntWW 74, 75, 76, 77, 78, 79, 80, 81, 82, 83, 89, 91, 93; IntWWP 77; LegTOT; LngCEL; LngCTC; MajTwCW; ModBrL, S1, S2; NewC; Novels; OxCEng 85, 95; PenC ENG; RAdv 1, 14, 13-1; REn; RfGEnL 91; RfGShF; RGTwCWr; ScF&FL 1, 2; ScFSB; SmATA 61; TwCSFW 81; TwCWr; WebE&AL; Who 74, 82, 83, 85, 88, 90, 92, 94; WhoTwCL; WhoWor 74, 76, 78, 80, 82, 84, 87, 89, 91, 93, 95, 96, 97; WorAl; WorAlBi; WorAu 1950; WrDr 76, 80, 82, 84, 86, 88, 90, 92, 94, 96*

Sillman, Leonard
American. Producer, Actor, Author
Wrote film *New Faces,* 1954; produced *An Angel Comes to Brooklyn,* 1945.
b. May 9, 1908 in Detroit, Michigan
d. Jan 23, 1982 in New York, New York
Source: *BiE&WWA; BioIn 5, 10, 12; ConAu 105; EncMT; NewYTBS 82; NotNAT, A; WhoThe 72, 77, 81*

Sills, Beverly
[Mrs. Peter B Greenough; Belle Silverman]
"Bubbles"
American. Opera Singer
Coloratura soprano, made operatic debut, 1947; director, NYC Opera, 1979-88; won two Emmys, Medal of Freedom, 1980.
b. May 25, 1929 in New York, New York
Source: *Baker 78, 84, 92; BiDAmM; BioIn 8, 9, 10, 11, 12, 13, 14, 15; BlueB 76; BriBkM 80; CelR, 90; CmOp; ConAu 89; ConMus 5; ContDcW 89; CurBio 69, 82; DcArts; DcTwCCu 1; EncWB; FacFETw; GoodHs; GrLiveH; HerW 84; IntDcOp; IntDcWB; IntWW 74, 75, 76, 77, 78, 79, 80, 81, 82, 83, 89, 91, 93; IntWWM 77, 80, 90; InWom SUP; LegTOT; LibW; MetOEnc; MusMk; MusSN; NewAmDM; NewEOp 71; NewGrDA 86; NewGrDM 80; NewGrDO; NewYTBE 71; NewYTBS 75, 76, 79, 87, 88; OxDcOp; PenDiMP; RAdv 14; Who 74, 82, 83, 85, 88, 90, 92, 94; WhoAm 74, 76, 78, 80, 82, 84, 86, 88, 90, 92, 94, 95, 96; WhoAmJ 80; WhoAmM 83; WhoAmW 75, 77, 79, 81, 83, 85, 87, 89, 91, 93, 95, 97; WhoE 74, 75, 77, 79, 81, 85, 86, 89, 91; WhoEnt 92; WhoGov 72, 75, 77; WhoOp 76; WhoWor 74, 76, 78, 80, 82, 84, 87, 89, 91, 93, 95, 96; WhoWorJ 78; WomFir; WorAl; WorAlBi*

Sills, Milton
American. Actor
Leading man in over 75 films, 1914-30.
b. Jan 10, 1882 in Chicago, Illinois
d. Sep 15, 1930 in Santa Barbara, California
Source: *BioIn 9, 17; DcAmB; DcNAA; Film 1, 2; FilmEn; FilmgC; ForYSC; HalFC 80, 84, 88; MovMk; NotNAT B; SilFlmP; TwYS; WhAm 1; WhoHol B; WhScrn 74, 77, 83*

Silone, Ignazio
[Secondo Tranquilli]
Italian. Author
Founding member, Italian Communist Party, 1921; wrote *Bread and Wine,* 1936.
b. May 1, 1900 in Pescina, Italy
d. Aug 22, 1978 in Geneva, Switzerland
Source: *Benet 87, 96; BiDMoPL; BioIn 1, 2, 3, 4, 5, 6, 7, 8, 10, 11, 12, 14, 15, 17; CasWL; ClDMEL 47, 80; CnMD; CnMWL; ConAu 34NR, 81, P-2; ConLC 4; CyWA 58; DcArts; DcItL 1, 2; EncWL, 2, 3; EuWr 12; EvEuW; FacFETw; GrFLW; IntAu&W 76; IntWW 74, 75, 76, 77, 78; LegTOT; LiExTwC; LinLib L, S; LngCTC; MajTwCW; MakMC; McGEWB; ModRL; NewYTBS 78; Novels; OxCEng 85, 95; PenC EUR; RAdv 14, 13-2; REn; RfGWoL 95; TwCA, SUP; TwCWr; Who 74; WhoTwCL; WhoWor 74*

Silver, Abba Hillel
American. Religious Leader
Zionist leader, early advocate of the state of Israel.
b. Jan 28, 1893 in Sirvintos, Lithuania
d. Nov 28, 1963 in Cleveland, Ohio
Source: *AmAu&B; BioIn 3, 6, 7, 8, 10, 16, 19; ConAu 1R; CurBio 41, 63, 64; DcAmB S7; DcAmReB 2; EncAB-A 37; JeAmHC; McGEWB; NatCAB 50; OhA&B; OxCAmH; RelLAm 91; WhAm 4*

Silver, Franelle
Canadian. Writer
Won Emmy for "The Carol Burnett Show," 1978.

b. Sep 12, 1952 in Toronto, Ontario, Canada
Source: *VarWW 85; WhoEnt 92*

Silver, Horace Ward Martin Tavares
American. Jazz Musician
Outstanding pianist, accompanist; noted for "funky" style popular in late 1950s.
b. Sep 28, 1928 in Norwalk, Connecticut
Source: *ASCAP 66; Baker 84, 92; BiDAfM; BiDAmM; BiDJaz; BioIn 13, 16; CmpEPM; EncJzS; IlEncJ; InB&W 80, 85; NewAmDM; NewGrDA 86; NewGrDJ 88, 94; NewGrDM 80; OxCPMus; PenEncP; WhoAm 74, 76, 78, 80, 82, 84, 86, 88, 90, 92, 94, 95, 96, 97; WhoBlA 75, 77, 80, 85, 88, 90, 92; WhoE 74; WorAl; WorAlBi*

Silver, Ron
American. Actor
Won best actor Tony for *Speed-the-Plow,* 1988; films include *Silkwood,* 1983.
b. Jul 2, 1946 in New York, New York
Source: *BioIn 15, 16, 17, 19; CelR 90; ConTFT 1, 4, 11; IntMPA 86, 88, 92, 94, 96; LegTOT; WhoAm 90, 92, 94, 95, 96, 97; WhoEnt 92; WhoHol 92*

Silvera, Frank
American. Actor
Character actor, 1952-70; appeared in TV series "High Chaparral," 1967-70.
b. Jul 24, 1914 in Kingston, Jamaica
d. Jun 11, 1970 in Pasadena, California
Source: *BiE&WWA; BioIn 6, 8; BlkAWP; BlksAmF; DrBlPA, 90; EarBlAP; FilmEn; FilmgC; ForYSC; HalFC 80, 84, 88; MovMk; NewYTBE 70; NotNAT B; WhAm 5; WhoHol B; WhScrn 74, 77, 83*

Silverberg, Robert
American. Author
Science fiction books include *Lord Valentine's Castle,* 1980.
b. Jan 15, 1935 in New York, New York
Source: *AmAu&B; AuBYP 2, 3; BenetAL 91; BioIn 12, 13, 15; ConAu 1NR, 1R, 3AS, 20NR, 36NR; ConLC 7; ConNov 96; ConPopW; DcLB 8; DcLP 87A; EncSF 93; IntAu&W 82, 91, 93; IntvTCA 2; LegTOT; MajAI; MajTwCW; NewEScF; RGTwCSF; ScF&FL 1, 2, 92; ScFWr; SmATA 13, 91; ThrBJA; TwCSFW 81, 86, 91; WhoAm 86, 90, 92, 94, 95, 96, 97; WhoUSWr 88; WhoWest 92, 94; WhoWrEP 89; WorAl; WorAlBi; WrDr 84, 86, 88, 90, 92, 94, 96*

Silverheels, Jay
[Harold J. Smith]
American. Actor
Played Tonto in *Lone Ranger* movies and TV series, 1948-61.
b. May 26, 1919 in Six Nations Indian Reserva Ontario, Canada
d. Mar 5, 1980 in Woodland Hills, California
Source: *AnObit 1980; DcAmB S10; FilmEn; FilmgC; HalFC 84, 88; LegTOT; WhoHol A*

Silverman, Fred
American. TV Executive
Only man to run all three TV networks' entertainment divisions; CBS, 1963-75; ABC, 1975-78; NBC, 1978-81.
b. Sep 13, 1937 in New York, New York
Source: *BioIn 10, 11, 12, 13, 16; ConTFT 7; CurBio 78; EncTwCJ; IntMPA 76, 77, 78, 79, 80, 81, 82, 84, 86, 88, 92, 94, 96; IntWW 83, 89, 91, 93; LegTOT; LesBEnT, 92; NewYTBS 78, 89; NewYTET; WhoAm 78, 80, 82, 84, 94, 95, 96, 97; WhoE 79, 81; WhoEnt 92; WhoFI 79, 81; WhoTelC; WhoWor 82*

Silverman, Sime
American. Publisher
Founder, editor of show business newspaper, *Variety,* 1905-33.
b. May 18, 1873 in Cortland, New York
d. Sep 22, 1933 in Los Angeles, California
Source: *AmAu&B; DcAmB; EncAJ; EncVaud; LegTOT; NatCAB 24; NotNAT A; OxCAmT 84; WebAB 74, 79; WhAm 4, HSA*

Silvers, Phil
[Philip Silversmith]
American. Comedian
Won three Emmys for playing Sergeant Bilko in TV series "The Phil Silvers" Show, 1955-59; films include *A Funny Thing Happened on the Way to the Forum,* 1966.
b. May 11, 1911 in New York, New York
d. Nov 1, 1985 in Los Angeles, California
Source: *AnObit 1985; ASCAP 66; BiE&WWA; CmMov; CmpEPM; ConNews 85-4; CurBio 57, 86; EncMT; Ent; FilmgC; ForYSC; Funs; IntMPA 81; LegTOT; MotPP; MovMk; NewYTBE 70; NotNAT, A; OxCAmT 84; QDrFCA 92; WhoAm 82; WhoHol A; WhoThe 77, 81*

Silverstein, Alvin
[Dr. A]
American. Children's Author
Scientific, juvenile books include *Human Anatomy & Physiology,* 1980.
b. Dec 30, 1933 in New York, New York
Source: *AuBYP 2S, 3; BioIn 11; ChlLR 25; ConAu 2NR, 49; ConLC 17; FifBJA; IntAu&W 76, 77, 82; MajAI; SmATA 8, 69; WhoE 91, 93*

Silverstein, Elliot
American. Director
Films include *Cat Ballou,* 1965; *A Man Called Horse,* 1970.
b. Aug 3, 1927 in Boston, Massachusetts
Source: *BioIn 7; FilmEn; HalFC 84, 88; IntMPA 86, 88, 92, 94, 96; MiSFD 9; WorEFlm*

Silverstein, Shel(by)
American. Cartoonist, Author
Self-illustrated best-sellers include *Where the Sidewalk Ends,* 1974; *A Light in the Attic,* 1981.
b. 1932 in Chicago, Illinois
Source: *BioIn 10, 11, 12, 13, 15, 16; ChlBkCr; ChlLR 5; ConAu 47NR, 107; EncFCWM 83; FifBJA; HarEnCM 87; IntAu&W 91, 93; LegTOT; MajAI; NewYTBS 81; PenEncP; RAdv 14; SmATA 27, 33; TwCChW 83, 89, 95; WhoAm 74, 76, 78, 80, 82, 84, 86, 88, 90, 92, 94, 95, 96, 97; WhoUSWr 88; WhoWrEP 89, 92, 95; WrDr 86, 88, 90, 92, 94, 96*

Silverstone, Alicia
American. Actor
Filed for emancipation from her parents at 15 so she could work in films as an adult; appeared in several MTV videos.
b. 1976 in San Francisco, California

Silvia
Swedish. Consort
Commoner who married King Carl Gustaf of Sweden, 1976.
b. Dec 23, 1943 in Heidelberg, Germany
Source: *BioIn 10, 11; NewYTBS 81; WhoWor 82, 87, 89, 91, 93, 95*

Sim, Alastair
English. Producer, Director
Films include *The Lavender Hill Mob,* 1951; starred in *A Christmas Carol,* 1951.
b. Oct 9, 1900 in Edinburgh, Scotland
d. Aug 19, 1976 in London, England
Source: *BioIn 11, 13, 16; CmMov; EncEurC; FilmAG WE; FilmEn; FilmgC; ForYSC; HalFC 80, 84, 88; IlWWBF; IntDcF 1-3, 2-3; IntMPA 75, 76; MotPP; MovMk; NewYTBS 76; OxCThe 83; QDrFCA 92; WhAm 7; Who 74; WhoHol A; WhoThe 72, 77; WhoWor 74; WhScrn 83*

Simak, Clifford Donald
American. Author
Wrote highly acclaimed science fiction, fantasy novels; won three Hugos; first in Fandom Hall of Fame, 1973; Grand Master, 1979.
b. Aug 3, 1904 in Millville, Wisconsin
d. Apr 25, 1988 in Minneapolis, Minnesota
Source: *BioIn 6, 7, 10, 12; ConAu 1NR, 1R; ConLC 1; DcLB 8; DcLEL 1940; IntAu&W 77; TwCSFW 86; WhoAm 84; WorAu 1950; WrDr 86*

Simcoe, John Graves
English. Government Official
First lt. governor of Upper Canada, 1792-74; established capital at York (now Toronto), 1793.

b. Feb 25, 1752 in Cotterstock, England
d. Oct 26, 1806 in Exeter, England
Source: *AmBi; AmRev; ApCAB; BioIn 8, 13; DcCanB 5; DcNaB; Drake; EncAR; HarEnMi; HarEnUS; MacDCB 78; NewC; NewCBEL; OxCCan; WebBD 83; WhAmRev*

Simenon, Georges
[Georges Sim]
Belgian. Author
Wrote over 500 books; created Chief Inspector Maigret, the Parisian detective featured in over 80 mysteries.
b. Feb 13, 1903 in Liege, Belgium
d. Sep 4, 1989 in Lausanne, Switzerland
Source: *AnObit 1989; Au&Wr 71; Benet 87, 96; BioIn 2, 3, 4, 5, 7, 8, 9, 10, 12, 13, 14, 15, 16, 17, 18, 19, 20; CasWL; ClDMEL 80; CnMWL; ConAu 35NR, 85, 129; ConFLW 84; ConLC 1, 2, 3, 8, 18, 47; CorpD; CrtSuMy; CurBio 70, 89N; CyWA 89; DcArts; DcLB 72, Y89N; DcTwCCu 2; EncEurC; EncMys; EncWL, 2, 3; EuWr 12; EvEuW; FacFETw; FilmgC; GuFrLit 1; HalFC 80, 84, 88; IntAu&W 76, 77, 82, 86, 89, 91; IntWW 74, 75, 76, 77, 78, 79, 80, 81, 82, 83, 89; LegTOT; LinLib L; LngCTC; MajTwCW; McGEWB; ModFrL; ModRL; NewYTBS 84, 89; Novels; OxCEng 67, 85, 95; OxCFr; PenC EUR; RAdv 13-2; REn; REnAL; TwCA, SUP; TwCCr&M 80B, 85B, 91, 91B; TwCWr; WhAm 10; WhDW; WhE&EA; Who 74, 82, 83, 85, 88, 90N; WhoFr 79; WhoTwCL; WhoWor 78, 82, 84, 87, 89; WorAlBi*

Simeon
[Symeon]
"The New Theologian"
Byzantine. Biblical Figure
Monk who preached mysticism; forced to resign, 1009; wrote hymns, sermons.
b. 949?
d. 1022?
Source: *Alli; NewCol 75; WebBD 83*

Simeone, Harry
American. Composer
Arranger for Fred Waring; co-wrote "The Little Drummer Boy," 1958.
b. May 9, 1911 in Newark, New Jersey
Source: *ASCAP 66, 80; ConAmC 76, 82; RkOn 82*

Simeon Stylites, Saint
[Simeon the Elder]
Syrian. Religious Leader
First most famed stylite "Pillar Dweller;" spent 35 yrs. on top of 50-ft. high pillar.
b. 390?
d. 459?
Source: *BioIn 1, 2, 3, 4, 5, 6, 7, 8, 11, 12; DcBiPP; DcCathB; LuthC 75; NewCol 75; WebBD 83*

Simic, Charles
American. Poet
Wrote award-winning verse, *Return to a Place Lit by a Glass of Milk,* 1975.
b. May 9, 1938 in Belgrade, Yugoslavia
Source: *Benet 87, 96; BenetAL 91; BioIn 9, 10, 13, 14, 15, 17, 18, 21; ConAu 4AS, 12NR, 29R, 33NR, 52NR; ConLC 6, 9, 22, 49, 68; ConPo 75, 80, 85, 91, 96; DcLB 105; DrAP 75; DrAPF 80, 91; Focus; IntvTCA 2; IntWW 91, 93; LegTOT; OxCAmL 95; OxCTwCP; RAdv 14, 13-1; WhoAm 78, 80, 82, 84, 86, 88, 90, 92, 94, 95, 96, 97; WhoE 91, 93, 95, 97; WhoUSWr 88; WhoWrEP 89, 92, 95; WorAu 1970; WrDr 76, 80, 82, 84, 86, 88, 90, 92, 94, 96*

Simionato, Guilietta
Italian. Opera Singer
La Scala's leading contralto, 1939-59; with NY Met., 1959-65.
b. May 12, 1916 in Forli, Italy
Source: *Baker 84; BioIn 11, 13, 14; CurBio 60; IntWWM 90; InWom SUP; MetOEnc; MusSN; NewAmDM; NewEOp 71; NewGrDM 80; PenDiMP; WhoEnt 92*

Simionescu, Mariana
Romanian. Tennis Player
Former wife of Bjorn Borg.
b. Nov 21, 1956 in Tirgu Neamt, Romania
Source: *BioIn 12, 13; WhoIntT*

Simmel, Georg
German. Sociologist, Philosopher
Principal translated works include *The Sociology of Georg Simmel,* 1950.
b. Mar 1, 1858 in Berlin, Germany
d. Sep 26, 1918 in Strassburg, Germany
Source: *BioIn 4, 5, 7, 11, 12, 14; DcSoc; MakMC; McGEWB; NewCol 75; RAdv 14, 13-3; ThTwC 87; TwCA SUP; TwCLC 64*

Simmer, Charlie
[Charles Robert Simmer]
"Chaz"
Canadian. Hockey Player
Left wing, LA, 1977-84, Boston, 1984-87; first left wing in NHL history to score 100 pts. in two consecutive seasons (1979-81).
b. Mar 20, 1954 in Terrace Bay, Ontario, Canada
Source: *HocEn; HocReg 87*

Simmons, Adele Smith
American. Philanthropist, Educator
Pres. of John D. and Catherine T. MacArthur Foundation, 1989—, the US's fourth largest private foundation.
b. Jun 21, 1941 in Lake Forest, Illinois
Source: *BioIn 11, 17; CurBio 91; IntWW 89, 91, 93; News 88; WhoAm 80, 82, 86, 88, 90, 92, 94, 95, 96, 97; WhoAmW 87, 89, 91, 93, 95, 97; WhoE 79, 81, 83, 86, 89; WhoEmL 87*

Simmons, Al(oysius Harry)
"Bucketfoot Al"
American. Baseball Player
Outfielder, 1924-41, 1943-44, mostly with Philadelphia; led AL in RBIs once, in batting twice; had .334 lifetime batting average; Hall of Fame, 1953.
b. May 22, 1903 in Milwaukee, Wisconsin
d. May 26, 1956 in Milwaukee, Wisconsin
Source: *BioIn 2, 3, 4, 5, 6, 7, 9, 10; DcAmB S6; WhoPolA; WhoProB 73; WhoSpor*

Simmons, Althea T. L
American. Lawyer, Civil Rights Leader
Worked her way through the ranks of the NAACP to become director of Washington office and chief lobbyist.
b. Apr 17, 1924 in Shreveport, Louisiana
d. Sep 13, 1990 in Washington, District of Columbia
Source: *BioIn 15; InB&W 80, 85; NewYTBS 87, 90; NotBlAW 1; WhoBlA 77, 80, 85, 88, 92N*

Simmons, Calvin
"Maestro Kid"
American. Conductor
Led Oakland Symphony from 1979.
b. Apr 27, 1950 in San Francisco, California
d. Aug 21, 1982 in Connery Pond, New York
Source: *AnObit 1982; Baker 84; BiDAfM; BioIn 11, 12, 13, 21; BlkCond; BlkOpe; DrBlPA 90; InB&W 80; IntWWM 77, 80; NewAmDM; NewGrDA 86; NewYTBS 82; PenDiMP; WhoBlA 77, 80; WhoWest 80, 82*

Simmons, Franklin
American. Sculptor
Marble, bronze portraits, monuments include General Grant in the capitol rotunda, 1900.
b. Jan 11, 1839 in Webster, Maine
d. Dec 8, 1913 in Rome, Italy
Source: *AmBi; ApCAB; BioIn 14; BriEAA; DcAmB; HarEnUS; NatCAB 11; NewYHSD; TwCBDA; WhAm 1; WhAmArt 85*

Simmons, Gene
[Kiss; Gene Klein]
American. Singer, Musician
Co-founded Kiss, 1972; dressed as fire-breathing, blood-spewing ghoul; invented Axe bass guitar, 1980.
b. Aug 25, 1949 in Haifa, Israel
Source: *BioIn 11, 12; ConTFT 8; LegTOT; RkOn 85; WhoAm 82, 84, 86, 88, 90, 92, 94, 95, 96, 97; WhoEnt 92; WhoHol 92; WhoRocM 82*

Simmons, Jean
English. Actor
Appeared in British, US films including *Big Country,* 1958; TV movies include "Thornbirds," 1983.
b. Jan 31, 1929 in London, England

Source: *BiDFilm, 81, 94; BioIn 1, 2, 3, 4, 5, 7, 10, 11, 16; BioNews 74; CelR, 90; CmMov; ConTFT 3, 4; CurBio 52; DcArts; EncEurC; FilmAG WE; FilmEn; FilmgC; ForYSC; HalFC 80, 84, 88; IlWWBF; IntDcF 1-3, 2-3; IntMPA 75, 76, 77, 78, 79, 80, 81, 82, 84, 86, 88, 92, 94, 96; IntWW 82, 83, 89, 91, 93; InWom, SUP; LegTOT; MotPP; MovMk; OxCFilm; Who 74, 82, 83, 85, 88, 90, 92, 94; WhoAm 74, 76, 78, 80, 82, 84, 86, 88, 90, 92, 94, 95, 96, 97; WhoAmW 58, 68, 70, 72, 74, 83, 85, 87, 89, 91, 93, 95, 97; WhoEnt 92; WhoHol 92, A; WorAl; WorAlBi; WorEFlm*

Simmons, Pat(rick)
[The Doobie Brothers]
American. Singer, Songwriter
Wrote Doobie hit "Black Water," 1974; began solo career, 1982.
b. Jan 23, 1950 in Aberdeen, Washington
Source: *OnThGG; RkOn 85*

Simmons, Richard
"The Clown Prince of Fitness"; "The Pied Piper of Pounds"
American. TV Personality, Author
Creator of diet program "Deal-a-Meal" and exercise video series "Sweatin' to the Oldies;" author of *Never Say Diet,* 1980.
b. Jul 12, 1948 in New Orleans, Louisiana
Source: *BioIn 12, 13; CelR 90; CurBio 82; LegTOT; NewYTBS 81; WhoTelC; WorAlBi*

Simmons, Russell
American. Music Executive
Co-owner and founder Def Jam Records; head of Rush Artist Management, 1985; produces rap artists Run-DMC and Public Enemy.
b. Oct 4, 1957 in New York, New York
Source: *BioIn 15, 16; ConBlB 1; ConMus 7; Dun&B 88; NewYTBS 87; WhoAm 94, 95, 96, 97*

Simmons, Ruth J(ean)
American. Educator
President of Smith College, 1995—.
b. Jul 3, 1945 in Grapeland, Texas
Source: *CurBio 96*

Simmons, Zalmon G
American. Manufacturer
Invented inventor's patent for bedspring as payment of debt, started bedding products firm.
b. Sep 10, 1828 in Euphrates, New York
d. Feb 11, 1910 in Kenosha, Wisconsin
Source: *Entr; NatCAB 15*

Simms, Ginny
[Virginia E Simms]
American. Singer, Radio Performer
Popular vocalist, Kay Kyser's band, 1930s-40s; own radio, TV show, early 1950s.
b. May 25, 1916 in San Antonio, Texas
d. Apr 4, 1994 in Palm Springs, California
Source: *CmpEPM; FilmgC; HalFC 80, 84, 88; LegTOT; MotPP; RadStar; WhoHol 92*

Simms, Hilda
American. Actor
Made Broadway debut in first play in US with all-black cast, *Anna Lucasta,* 1944.
b. Apr 15, 1920 in Minneapolis, Minnesota
d. Feb 6, 1994 in Buffalo, New York
Source: *BiE&WWA; BioIn 18, 19, 20; CurBio 44, 94N; DrBlPA, 90; InB&W 85; InWom; NegAl 76, 83, 89; NotBlAW 1; NotNAT; WhoHol 92, A; WhoThe 72, 77, 81*

Simms, Phil(ip)
American. Football Player
Quarterback, NY Giants, 1979-93; MVP, Super Bowl, 1987; giants retire number, 1 995.
b. Nov 3, 1955 in Lebanon, Kentucky
Source: *BioIn 12, 14, 15, 16, 17, 18, 20, 21; CelR 90; CurBio 94; FootReg 87; NewYTBS 79, 81; WhoAm 90; WorAlBi*

Simms, William Gilmore
American. Author
Works include romantic novel *Master Faber,* 1833; popular SC histories.
b. Apr 17, 1806 in Charleston, South Carolina
d. Jun 11, 1870 in Charleston, South Carolina
Source: *Alli; AmAu; AmAu&B; AmBi; ApCAB; BbD; Benet 87, 96; BenetAL 91; BibAL; BiD&SB; BiDSA; BioIn 1, 2, 3, 4, 5, 6, 8, 10, 11, 12, 13, 14, 15, 16, 18; CamGEL; CamGLE; CamHAL; CasWL; Chambr 3; ChhPo, S1, S2, S3; CnDAL; CyAL 2; CyWA 58; DcAmAu; DcAmB; DcBiA; DcEnL; DcLB 3, 30, 59, 73; DcLEL; DcNAA; Drake; EncFWF; EncSoH; EvLB; FifSWrB; GrWrEL N; HarEnUS; HsB&A, SUP; InB&W 80; LinLib L, S; McGEWB; NatCAB 6; NinCLC 3; Novels; OxCAmH; OxCAmL 65, 83, 95; OxCEng 67; PenC AM; PenEncH; RAdv 14; REn; REnAL; RfGAmL 87, 94; SouWr; TwCBDA; WebAB 74, 79; WebE&AL; WhAm 3, HS; WhNaAH*

Simon, Carly
American. Singer, Songwriter
Hits include "You're So Vain," 1972; "Jesse," 1980; "Coming Around Again," 1987; Grammy award winner, 1971.
b. Jun 25, 1945 in New York, New York
Source: *AmSong; ASCAP 80; BiDAmM; BioIn 9, 10, 11, 12, 13, 16; BkPepl; CelR 90; ConAu 105; ConLC 26; ConMuA 80A; ConMus 4; CurBio 76; EncRk 88; EncRkSt; FacFETw; GoodHs; HarEnR 86; HerW, 84; IlEncRk; InWom SUP; LegTOT; NewAmDM; NewGrDA 86; NewYTBS 74; PenEncP; RkOn 78; RolSEnR 83; WhoAm 86, 88, 90, 92, 94, 95, 96, 97; WhoAmW 89, 91, 93, 95, 97; WhoEnt 92; WhoRock 81; WhoRocM 82; WorAl; WorAlBi*

Simon, Claude Eugene Henri
French. Author
Won Nobel Prize, 1985, for pioneering work in new novel style of 1950s.
b. Oct 10, 1913 in Tananarive, Madagascar
Source: *Benet 87; BioIn 14, 15; CasWL; ConAu 33NR, 89; ConFLW 84; ConLC 4, 39; ConWorW 93; CurBio 92; CyWA 89; DcLB 83; EncWL; EuWr 13; FacFETw; GuFrLit 1; IntAu&W 91; IntWW 74, 91; MajTwCW; ModRL; NewYTBS 85; PenC EUR; RAdv 13-2; REn; TwCWr; Who 92; WhoNob, 90, 95; WhoTwCL; WhoWor 74, 91, 93, 95, 96, 97; WorAlBi*

Simon, Herbert Alexander
American. Psychologist, Economist
Awarded 1978 Nobel Prize in economics; developed a theory of business decision-making.
b. Jun 15, 1916 in Milwaukee, Wisconsin
Source: *AmMWSc 73S, 78S, 92; BioIn 11, 12, 14, 15, 16, 17, 20, 21; BlueB 76; ConAu 9NR, 13R; EncWB; GrEconS; HisDcDP; IntWW 91; NobelP; ThTwC 87; Who 83, 92; WhoAm 74, 76, 78, 80, 82, 84, 86, 90, 92, 94, 95, 96, 97; WhoE 79, 81, 83, 85, 86, 91, 93, 95, 97; WhoEc 86; WhoEng 88; WhoFI 83, 85, 92, 94, 96; WhoMW 92; WhoNob, 90, 95; WhoScEn 96; WhoTech 89; WhoWor 74, 80, 82, 84, 87, 91, 93, 95, 96, 97; WrDr 86, 92*

Simon, Joe
American. Singer
Rhythm and blues, soul singer; hit single "The Chokin' Kind," 1966.
b. Sep 2, 1943 in Simmesport, Louisiana
Source: *DrBlPA, 90; EncRk 88; GuBlues; IlEncBM 82; RkOn 78; SoulM; WhoRock 81*

Simon, John, Sir
English. Physician
His strong advocacy led to development of public health system standards and eventually to passage of Sanitary Act, 1866; Public Health Act, 1875.
b. Oct 10, 1816 in London, England
d. Jul 23, 1904 in London, England
Source: *Alli, SUP; BiHiMed; BioIn 1, 2, 7, 9; DcBiPP; DcNaB, S2; InSci; LarDcSc; OxCMed 86; WhDW*

Simon, John Ivan
American. Critic
Cultural critic for noted periodicals, from 1960; books on theater include *Movies into Film,* 1971.
b. May 12, 1925 in Subotica, Yugoslavia
Source: *BiE&WWA; ConAmTC; NotNAT; WhoAm 76, 78, 80, 82, 84, 90, 92, 94, 95, 96, 97; WhoEnt 92; WhoThe 77; WorAu 1950*

Simon, Neil
[Marvin Neil Simon]
American. Dramatist
Most of his outstanding plays have been adapted to film including *The Goodbye Girl,* 1977; has won 4 Tonys; Pulitzer Prize winner in drama for *Lost in Yonkers,* 1991; wrote autobiography, *Rewrites* 1996.
b. Jul 4, 1927 in New York, New York
Source: *AmAu&B; AmCulL; AuNews 1; Benet 87; BenetAL 91; BiE&WWA; BioIn 6, 7, 8, 9, 10, 11, 12, 13, 16; BlueB 76; CamGLE; CamGWoT; CamHAL; CelR, 90; CnThe; ConAu 21R, 26NR; ConDr 73, 77, 82, 88; ConLC 6, 11, 31, 39, 70; ConTFT 1, 6, 13; CroCD; CrtSuDr; CurBio 68, 89; CyWA 89; DcLB 7; DcLEL 1940; DcTwCCu 1; EncAFC; EncMT; EncWT; Ent; FacFETw; FilmEn; FilmgC; HalFC 80, 84, 88; IntAu&W 89, 91, 93; IntMPA 77, 80, 86, 88, 92, 94, 96; IntWW 74, 75, 76, 77, 78, 79, 80, 81, 82, 83, 89, 91, 93; ItaFilm; JeAmHC; LegTOT; LesBEnT 92; LinLib L; MagSAmL; MajTwCW; McGEWD 72, 84; ModAL; ModWD; NatPD 81; NewCBMT; NewYTBS 85, 91; NewYTET; NotNAT; OxCAmT 84; OxCPMus; OxCThe 83; PlP&P, A; RAdv 14; WebAB 74, 79; Who 74, 82, 83, 85, 88, 90, 92, 94; WhoAm 74, 76, 78, 80, 82, 84, 86, 88, 90, 92, 94, 95, 96, 97; WhoAmJ 80; WhoE 91, 93, 95, 97; WhoEnt 92; WhoThe 72, 77, 81; WhoWor 74, 78, 93, 95, 96, 97; WorAl; WorAlBi; WorAu 1950; WrDr 76, 82, 84, 86, 88, 90, 92, 94, 96*

Simon, Norma Feldstein
American. Children's Author
Children are sources for writings: *All Kinds of Families,* 1976.
b. Dec 24, 1927 in New York, New York
Source: *AuBYP 2, 3; ConAu 5R, 6NR, 21NR; SmATA 3, 68*

Simon, Norton Winfred
American. Business Executive
Founded Norton Simon Inc., which included Hunt-Wesson Foods, Canada Dry Corp; art collection valued at $50 million.
b. Feb 5, 1907 in Portland, Oregon
d. Jun 2, 1993 in Los Angeles, California
Source: *AnObit 1993; BioIn 12, 15; ConAmBL; CurBio 68, 93N; NewYTBE 70; NewYTBS 74; WhAm 11; WhoAm 78, 80, 82, 84, 86, 88; WhoAmA 84, 91; WhoWest 84, 87, 89*

Simon, Paul
[Simon and Garfunkel]
American. Songwriter, Singer
Has successful solo career; won 1987 Grammy for South African album *Graceland;* Emmy award winner, 1977; Rock and Roll Hall of Fame, 1990.
b. Oct 13, 1941 in Newark, New Jersey
Source: *AmSong; Baker 84, 92; BioIn 12, 13, 14, 15; BkPepl; CelR, 90; ConAu 116; ConLC 17; ConMus 1, 16; DcTwCCu 1; EncFCWM 83; EncPR&S 89; EncRk 88; EncRkSt; HalFC 88; HarEnR 86; IlEncRk; IntMPA 92, 94, 96; NewAmDM; News 92, 92-2; NewYTBE 72; OnThGG; OxCPMus; PenEncP; VarWW 85; WhoAm 86, 88, 90, 92, 94, 95, 96, 97; WhoEnt 92; WhoRock 81; WhoRocM 82; WhoWor 74; WorAl; WorAlBi*

Simon, Paul M(artin)
American. Politician
Dem. senator, IL, 1985-97; 1988 presidential candidate.
b. Nov 29, 1928 in Eugene, Oregon
Source: *AlmAP 92; BiDrUSC 89; BioIn 13, 14, 15, 16; CngDr 87, 89; ConAu 81; CurBio 88; EncWB; IntAu&W 89; IntWW 91; PolsAm 84; WhoAm 86, 90; WhoAmP 85, 91; WhoGov 77; WhoMW 92; WhoUSWr 88; WhoWor 87, 91; WhoWrEP 89*

Simon, Richard Leo
American. Publisher
With Max Schuster, founded Simon & Schuster Publishers, 1924.
b. Mar 6, 1899 in New York, New York
d. Jul 29, 1960 in Stamford, Connecticut
Source: *AmAu&B; BioIn 5, 6; CurBio 41, 60; DcAmB S6; NatCAB 44; ObitOF 79; WhAm 4; WorAl; WorAlBi*

Simon, Saint
Biblical Figure
One of Twelve Disciples; preached in Egypt; feast day Oct 28.
Source: *BioIn 2, 3, 4, 5, 6, 8, 9, 10, 11; McGDA; NewCol 75*

Simon, Simone
French. Actor
Movie idol in France, 1930s; US films include *Seventh Heaven,* 1937; *The Cat People,* 1942.
b. Apr 23, 1913 in Marseilles, France
Source: *BiDFilm; FilmgC; HalFC 84; HolP 30; IntMPA 76, 77; MotPP; MovMk; OxCFilm; ThFT; WorEFlm*

Simon, William E(dward)
American. Government Official
Secretary of Treasury, 1974-77.
b. Nov 27, 1927 in Paterson, New Jersey
Source: *BiDrUSE 89; BioIn 9, 10, 11, 12, 13, 14, 15, 16, 17, 19; BlueB 76; ConAmBL; ConAu 81; CurBio 74; DcAmC; IntWW 74, 75, 76, 77, 78, 79, 80, 81, 82, 83, 89, 91, 93; LinLib S; NewYTBE 73; NewYTBS 87; PolProf NF; Who 82, 85, 88, 90, 92, 94; WhoAm 74, 76, 78, 80, 82, 84, 86, 88, 90, 92, 95, 96, 97; WhoAmP 75, 77, 79, 81, 83, 85, 87, 89, 91, 93, 95; WhoE 77; WhoFI 83; WhoGov 75, 77; WhoSSW 76; WhoWor 76, 78; WorAl; WorAlBi*

Simon and Garfunkel
[Arthur Garfunkel; Paul Simon]
American. Music Group
Sixth grade classmates who formed folk-rock duo; number one hits "Mrs. Robinson," 1967; "Bridge Over Troubled Waters," 1970.
Source: *BioIn 17, 18, 19, 20; BlueB 76; ConMuA 80A; EncFCWM 69; EncPR&S 74, 89; EncRk 88; FacFETw; HarEnR 86; IntMPA 75, 76, 77, 78, 79, 80, 81; IntWW 89, 91; NewAmDM; NewGrDA 86; NewYTBE 72; NewYTBS 82, 87; PenEncP; RkOn 74, 78; RolSEnR 83; WhoAm 74, 80, 82, 84, 86; WhoRock 81; WhoRocM 82; WhoWor 74*

Simone, Nina
[Eunice Wayman]
American. Singer
Jazz/soul singer, noted for club, festival performances; albums include *Fodder On My Wings,* 1984.
b. Feb 21, 1933 in Tryon, North Carolina
Source: *AllMusG; ASCAP 66, 80; Baker 84, 92; BiDAfM; BiDAmM; BiDJaz; BioIn 6, 8, 9, 10, 12; BioNews 74; BlkWAm; ContDcW 89; CurBio 68; DcTwCCu 5; DrBlPA, 90; EncJzS; EncJzS; EncRk 88; HarEnR 86; IlEncBM 82; IlEncRk; InB&W 80, 85; IntWW 89, 91, 93; InWom SUP; LegTOT; NegAl 89; NewGrDA 86; NotBlAW 1; OxCPMus; PenEncP; RolSEnR 83; SoulM; WhoAm 74, 76, 78, 80, 82; WhoAmW 70, 72, 74, 81; WhoBlA 75, 77, 80, 85, 92; WhoHol 92; WhoRock 81; WorAl; WorAlBi*

Simoneau, Leopold
Canadian. Opera Singer
Tenor; active during 1940s-70s; noted for Mozart roles.
b. May 3, 1918 in Quebec, Quebec, Canada
Source: *Baker 78, 84, 92; CanWW 31, 70, 79, 80, 81, 83, 89; CreCan 1; IntDcOp; IntWWM 90; MetOEnc; NewAmDM; NewGrDM 80; OxDcOp; PenDiMP; WhoWor 74*

Simonetta
Italian. Author, Fashion Designer
Rome's leading designer, 1950s; established first "haute boutique," 1965.
b. Apr 10, 1922 in Rome, Italy
Source: *BioIn 4; ConFash; EncFash; IntWW 74, 91; InWom; LegTOT; WorFshn*

Simons, Elwyn L(aVerne)
American. Scientist
Formulated a theory that all higher primates arose in Africa about forty million years ago in the form of squirrel-like tree-living animals.
b. Jul 14, 1930 in Lawrence, Kansas
Source: *AmMWSc 76P, 79, 82, 86, 89, 92; ConAu 22NR, 105; CurBio 94; IntAu&W 86; IntWW 89, 91, 93; WhoAm 74, 78, 80, 82, 84, 86, 88, 90, 92, 94, 95; WhoScEn 94, 96; WhoSSW 95, 97*

Simons, Howard
American. Newspaper Editor
Managing editor, *Washington Post,* 1971-84; wrote *Simm's List Book,* 1977.
b. Jun 3, 1928 in Albany, New York
d. Jun 13, 1989 in Jacksonville Beach, Florida
Source: *BioIn 14; ConAu 65, 128; EncTwCJ; IntAu&W 89; NewYTBS 89; WhoAm 86, 88; WhoSSW 82*

Simple Minds
[Charlie Burchill; Mel Gaynor; John Giblin; Jim Kerr; Mick Mac Neil]
Scottish. Music Group
Punk-dance style hits include "Alive and Kicking," 1985.
Source: *EncPR&S 89; EncRk 88; EncRkSt; HarEnR 86; PenEncP; WhoRocM 82; WhsNW 85*

Simpson, Adele (Smithline)
American. Fashion Designer
Among highest paid designers in world, 1940s-50s; first to go "on tour" with her collections.
b. Dec 8, 1903 in New York, New York
d. Aug 23, 1995 in Greenwich, Connecticut
Source: *AmDec 1940; BioIn 9, 10, 11, 21; CelR; ConDes 90; CurBio 70, 95N; FairDF US; InWom, SUP; LegTOT; WhoAm 86, 90; WhoAmW 58, 64, 66, 68, 70, 72, 74, 91; WhoFash, 88; WorFshn*

Simpson, Alan Kooi
American. Politician
Rep. senator from WY, 1979-97; co-authored landmark Simpson-Mazzoli immigration law, 1986.
b. Sep 2, 1931 in Cody, Wyoming
Source: *AlmAP 82, 92; BiDrUSC 89; BioIn 13; CngDr 87, 89; CurBio 90; IntWW 89, 91, 93; NewYTBS 90; PolsAm 84; WhoAm 80, 82, 86, 88, 90, 92, 94, 95, 96, 97; WhoAmP 85, 91; WhoGov 75, 77; WhoWest 82, 89, 92, 94, 96; WhoWor 80, 82, 84, 89, 91*

Simpson, Carole
[Carole Simpson Marshall]
American. Broadcast Journalist
Anchor, ABC's "World News Staurday," 1988-93; anchor, ABC's "World News Sunday," 1993—.
b. Dec 7, 1940 in Chicago, Illinois
Source: *AfrAmAl 6; AfrAmBi 2; BioIn 18, 20; BlkWAm; ConBlB 6; DcTwCCu 5; Ebony 1; InB&W 80; InWom SUP; NotBlAW 1; WhoAfA 96; WhoAm 92, 94, 95; WhoBlA 75, 77, 80, 85, 88, 90, 92, 94*

Simpson, Cedric Keith
English. Physician, Author
Noted forensic scientist; wrote *Forty Years of Murder* 1979.
b. Jul 20, 1907 in Brighton, England
d. Jul 21, 1985
Source: *Au&Wr 71; BioIn 12; ConAu 111, 117; CopCroC; IntWW 83; Who 74, 82, 83, 85*

Simpson, Donald C
American. Producer
Films include *Flash Dance,* 1983; *Beverly Hills Cop,* 1984; *Top Gun,* 1986.
b. Oct 29, 1945 in Seattle, Washington
d. Jan 19, 1996 in Los Angeles, California
Source: *ConTFT 5; IntMPA 86; VarWW 85*

Simpson, James Young, Sir
Scottish. Physician
One of founders of modern gynecology, 1840; first to use anesthesia in childbirth.
b. Jun 7, 1811 in Bathgate, Scotland
d. May 6, 1870 in London, England
Source: *Alli, SUP; AsBiEn; BiESc; BiHiMed; BioIn 1, 2, 3, 4, 6, 8, 9, 10, 14; CelCen; ChhPo S1, S2; DcBiPP; DcNaB; InSci; LarDcSc; LinLib S; OxCMed 86; WorAl; WorAlBi*

Simpson, Jim
American. Broadcaster
Play-by-play football commentator on TV, 1962-79.
b. Dec 20, 1927 in Washington, District of Columbia
Source: *BioIn 9, 21; LesBEnT, 92; NewYTET; WhoTelC*

Simpson, Lorna
American. Artist
Known for conceptual photography.
b. Aug 13, 1960 in New York, New York
Source: *AfrAmAl 6; BioIn 21; ConBlB 4; DcTwCCu 5; IlBBlP; WhoAmW 91*

Simpson, Louis
[Louis Aston Marantz Simpson]
American. Author, Poet
Won 1964 Pulitzer for verse volume *At the End of the Open Road.*
b. Mar 27, 1923 in Kingston, Jamaica
Source: *Benet 87; BenetAL 91; BioIn 7, 8, 9, 10, 12, 13, 14, 15, 17, 20; BlueB 76; CamGEL; CamGLE; CamHAL; CaribW 1; ChhPo, S1, S3; CnE&AP; ConAu 1NR, 1R, 4AS; ConLC 4, 7, 9, 32; ConPo 70, 75, 80, 85, 91, 96; CroCAP; DcAfL; DcLB 5; DrAF 76; DrAP 75; DrAPF 80, 91; FacFETw; GrWrEL P; IntAu&W 86, 89, 91, 93; IntWW 79, 80, 81, 82, 83, 89, 91, 93; IntWWP 77, 82; LegTOT; LinLib L; MajTwCW; ModAL, S1; OxCAmL 65, 83, 95; OxCTwCP; PenC AM; RAdv 1, 14, 13-1; REn; REnAL; RfGAmL 87, 94; WebE&AL; WhoAm 74, 76, 78, 80, 82, 84, 86, 88, 90, 92, 94, 95, 96; WhoE 74; WhoTwCL; WhoUSWr 88; WhoWor 74; WhoWrEP 89, 92, 95; WorAl; WorAlBi; WorAu 1950; WrDr 76, 80, 82, 84, 86, 88, 90, 92, 94, 96*

Simpson, Mona Elizabeth
American. Author
Author's work includes *Anywhere but Here,* 1986; *The Lost Father,* 1992.
b. Jun 14, 1957 in Green Bay, Wisconsin
Source: *BioIn 15, 16; ConAu 122, 135; ConLC 44; CurBio 93; DrAPF 91; WrDr 92*

Simpson, Nicole Brown
[Mrs. O. J. Simpson]
American. Victim
Former wife of football star O. J. Simpson and famous murder victim.
b. May 19, 1959, Germany
d. Jun 13, 1994 in Los Angeles, California

Simpson, O(renthal) J(ames)
"Juice"
American. Football Player, Actor
Halfback, Buffalo, 1969-77, San Francisco, 1978-79; set many NFL rushing records including first to gain 2,000 yds. in season, 1973; Hall of Fame, 1985; acquitted of the murder of his former wife, Nicole Brown Simpson, and her friend, Ronald Goldman, 1995; found liable for those deaths in a civil trial, 1997.
b. Jul 9, 1947 in San Francisco, California
Source: *AfrAmBi 2; BiDAmSp FB; BioIn 8, 9, 10, 11, 12, 13, 14, 15, 16; BkPepl; CelR 90; ConAu 50NR; ConTFT 7; CurBio 69; DrBlPA 90; HalFC 88; InB&W 85; IntMPA 86, 92; LesBEnT, 92; NegAl 89; NewYTBE 70, 73; NewYTBS 75, 76; WhoAm 74, 86, 90; WhoBlA 77, 80, 85, 88, 90, 92; WhoFtbl 74; WhoHol A; WorAlBi*

Simpson, Scott
American. Golfer
Turned pro, 1977; won US Open, 1987.
b. Sep 17, 1955 in San Diego, California
Source: *BioIn 15, 16; ODwPR 91; WhoIntG*

Simpson, Valerie
[Ashford and Simpson; Mrs. Nickolas Ashford]
American. Singer
With husband, contributed original material to soundtrack of *The Wiz;* recorded two solo albums.
b. Aug 26, 1948 in New York, New York
Source: *BioIn 14, 15, 16; BioNews 74; BlkWAm; InB&W 85; NewGrDA 86; NewYTBS 85; WhoBlA 85, 88, 92; WhoRocM 82*

Simpson, Wallis (Bessie Wallis Warfield)
[Duchess of Windsor]
American.
Two-time divorcee for whom Edward VIII abdicated his throne to marry, 1936.
b. Jun 19, 1896 in Blue Ridge Summit, Pennsylvania
d. Apr 24, 1986 in Paris, France
Source: *AnObit 1986; BioIn 15; CelR; ConNews 86-3; CurBio 86N; FacFETw; NewYTBS 86; WebAB 74; Who 82R, 83R, 85R; WhoAm 80, 82; WhoWor 76, 78, 80, 82*

Simpson, William Hood
American. Army Officer
Commanded 9th Army in German invasion, WW II; four-star general, 1954.
b. May 19, 1888 in Weatherford, Texas
d. Aug 15, 1980 in San Antonio, Texas
Source: *AnObit 1980; BiDWWGF; BioIn 1, 3, 12; CurBio 45, 80; FacFETw; HarEnMi; NewYTBS 80; WebAB 74; WebAMB*

Sims, Billy Ray
American. Football Player
Halfback, won Heisman Trophy, 1978; in NFL with Detroit, 1980-86; career shortened by injuries.
b. Sep 18, 1955 in Saint Louis, Missouri
Source: *BiDAmSp FB; BioIn 11, 12, 14; FootReg 85, 86; InB&W 85; NewYTBS 78, 80; WhoBlA 85, 92*

Sims, James Marion
American. Scientist, Physician, Engineer
Originator of operative gynecology; established Woman's Hospital of NY, 1857.
b. Jan 25, 1813 in Lancaster County, Kentucky
d. Nov 13, 1883 in New York, New York
Source: *Alli, SUP; AmBi; ApCAB; BiDSA; BiHiMed; BioIn 1, 2, 3, 4, 5, 6, 7, 8, 9; DcAmAu; DcAmB; DcAmMeB; DcNAA; HarEnUS; InSci; NatCAB 2; OxCAmH; OxCMed 86; TwCBDA; WebAB 74, 79; WhAm HS*

Sims, Naomi
American. Model, Business Executive
Haute couture model, 1967-73; founder and chm., Naomi Sims Beauty Products; author of several beauty books for black women.
b. Mar 30, 1948 in Oxford, Mississippi
Source: *BioIn 8, 9, 10, 12, 15; ConAu 26NR, 69; InB&W 85; InWom SUP; NegAl 89; NotBlAW 1; SelBAAf; WhoBlA 92*

Sims, William Sowden
American. Military Leader
Wrote navigation textbook, 1880; adopted convoy system, WW I; co-wrote *The Victory at Sea*, won Pulitzer, 1920.
b. Oct 15, 1858 in Port Hope, Ontario, Canada
d. Sep 25, 1936 in Boston, Massachusetts
Source: *AmBi; ApCAB X; BioIn 4, 6, 7, 8, 9; DcAmB S2; DcAmMiB; DcNAA; EncAB-H 1974, 1996; EncAI&E; HarEnMi; LinLib S; McGEWB; NatCAB 27; OxCAmL 65; OxCShps; WebAB 74, 79; WebAMB; WhAm 1; WorAl*

Sims, Zoot
[John Haley Sims]
American. Jazz Musician
Saxophonist with Big Bands, 1940s; won Grammy, 1977.
b. Oct 29, 1925 in Inglewood, California
d. Mar 23, 1985 in New York, New York
Source: *AllMusG; AnObit 1985; ASCAP 80; Baker 84; CmpEPM; EncJzS; FacFETw; IlEncJ; IntWWM 77; LegTOT; NewAmDM; NewGrDA 86; NewGrDJ 88, 94; NewYTBS 85; OxCPMus; PenEncP; WhAm 8; WhoAm 74, 76, 78, 80, 82, 84*

Sin, Jaime L(achica)
Philippine. Clergy
Archbishop of Manila, 1974—; elevated to Cardinal, 1976.
b. Aug 31, 1928 in New Washington, Philippines
Source: *BioIn 11, 12; CurBio 95; FarE&A 78, 79, 80, 81; IntWW 77, 78, 79, 80, 81, 82, 83; WhoRel 92; WhoWor 80, 82, 84, 87, 89, 91, 95, 96, 97*

Sinatra, Barbara Marx Spencer
[Mrs. Frank Sinatra]
American.
Fourth, current wife of Frank Sinatra.
b. May 16, 1926 in Glendale, California
Source: *BioIn 10*

Sinatra, Christina
American.
Youngest daughter of Frank Sinatra.
b. Jun 20, 1948
Source: *BioIn 10*

Sinatra, Frank
[Francis Albert Sinatra]
"Ol' Blue Eyes"
American. Singer, Actor
Regarded as biggest entertainment attraction in 20th c; won Oscar, 1953, for *From Here to Eternity*.
b. Dec 12, 1915 in Hoboken, New Jersey
Source: *AllMusG; AmCulL; AmDec 1940; ASCAP 66, 80; Baker 78, 84, 92; BiDAmM; BiDFilm, 81, 94; BiDJaz; BioIn 12, 13, 14, 15, 16, 17, 18, 19, 20, 21; BkPepl; CelR 90; CmCal; CmMov; CmpEPM; ConMus 1; ConTFT 9; CurBio 43, 60; DcArts; DcTwCCu 1; EncAB-H 1974; EncAFC; EncJzS; EncPR&S 89; EncWB; FacFETw; FilmEn; FilmgC; ForYSC; GangFlm; HalFC 80, 84, 88; HarEnR 86; IntDcF 1-3, 2-3; IntMPA 75, 76, 77, 78, 79, 80, 81, 82, 84, 86, 88, 92, 94, 96; IntWW 74, 75, 76, 77, 78, 79, 80, 81, 82, 83, 89, 91, 93; LegTOT; LesBEnT 92; MGM; MiSFD 9; MovMk; MusMk; NewAmDM; NewGrDA 86; NewGrDJ 88, 94; NewGrDM 80; NewYTBS 90; OxCFilm; OxCPMus; PenEncP; RadStar; RAdv 14; RComAH; RkOn 74; RolSEnR 83; WebAB 74; Who 82, 83, 85, 88, 90, 92, 94; WhoAm 74, 76, 78, 80, 82, 84, 86, 88, 90, 92, 94, 95, 96, 97; WhoEnt 92; WhoHol 92; WhoMus 72; WhoRock 81; WhoWor 78, 80, 82, 84, 87, 89, 91, 93, 95, 96, 97; WorAl; WorAlBi; WorEFlm*

Sinatra, Frank, Jr.
American. Singer
Son of Frank; nightclub performer, cameo roles in TV, films.
b. Jan 10, 1944 in Jersey City, New Jersey
Source: *BioIn 6, 12; LegTOT; PenEncP; VarWW 85; WhoHol 92, A*

Sinatra, Nancy
American. Singer
Recorded "Something Stupid," with father, 1969.
b. Jun 8, 1940 in Jersey City, New Jersey
Source: *BioIn 7, 8, 9, 10, 14; CelR; ConTFT 11; FilmgC; ForYSC; HalFC 80, 84, 88; InWom SUP; LegTOT; PenEncP; RkOn 78; RolSEnR 83; WhoAm 74; WhoHol 92, A; WhoRocM 82*

Sinbad
[David Adkins]
American. Comedian, Actor
TV series "A Different World," 1988-91; "The Sinbad Show," 1993-94.
b. Nov 10, 1956 in Benton Harbor, Michigan
Source: *AfrAmAl 6; BioIn 15; ConBlB 1; ConTFT 10; DcLP 87B; DcTwCCu 5; DrBlPA 90; IntMPA 96; WhoBlA 92; WhoEnt 92*

Sinclair, Gordon
Canadian. Journalist, Radio Performer
Canadian editor who defended US in best-selling recorded editorial, "The Americans," 1973.
b. Jun 3, 1900 in Toronto, Ontario, Canada
d. May 17, 1984 in Toronto, Ontario, Canada
Source: *AuNews 1; BioIn 8, 10, 11, 13, 14; BioNews 74; CanWW 70, 79, 80, 81, 83; ConAu 102, 112; RkOn 78*

Sinclair, Harry Ford
American. Oilman
One of the key participants in the Teapot Dome scandal, 1922; founder of Sinclair Oil Corp.
b. Jul 6, 1876 in Wheeling, West Virginia
d. Nov 10, 1956 in Pasadena, California
Source: *BiDAmBL 83; BioIn 1, 4; DcAmB S6; WebAB 74, 79; WhAm 3; WorAl; WorAlBi*

Sinclair, Iain
Welsh. Author
Wrote *Downriver; or, The Vessels of Wrath*, 1991; won the James Tait Black Memorial Book Prize, 1992.
b. Jun 11, 1943 in Cardiff, Wales
Source: *ConAu 132; ConLC 76; ConPo 91, 96; ScF&FL 92; WrDr 92, 94, 96*

Sinclair, Jo
[Ruth Seid]
American. Author
Novelist, short story writer: *The Changelings,* 1955.
b. Jul 1, 1913 in New York, New York
d. Apr 4, 1995 in Jenkintown, Pennsylvania
Source: *AmAu&B; AmNov, X; AmWomWr; Au&Wr 71; BioAmW; BioIn 1, 2, 4, 14, 18, 20, 21; BlmGWL; ConAu 5R, 148, X; ConNov 72, 76, 82, 86; CurBio 46, 95N; DcLB 28; DcLP 87B; IntAu&W 76, 77; InWom, SUP; JeAmWW; Novels; OhA&B; PenNWW B; TwCA SUP; WhoAm 74, 76, 78, 80, 82, 84, 86, 88, 90, 92, 94, 95, 96; WhoAmW 58, 61, 64, 66, 68, 70, 72, 74; WhoUSWr 88; WhoWorJ 72, 78; WhoWrEP 89, 92, 95; WrDr 76, 80, 82, 84, 86, 88*

Sinclair, Madge
[Madge Walters]
American. Actor
Three-time Emmy nominee for role on TV's "Trapper John, MD," 1980-86.
b. Apr 28, 1938 in Kingston, Jamaica
d. Dec 20, 1995 in Los Angeles, California
Source: *BioIn 14, 21; BlksAmF; ConTFT 4, 15; DrBlPA 90; InB&W 85; IntMPA 92, 94, 96; WhoAfA 96; WhoEnt 92; WhoHol 92, A*

Sinclair, Upton Beall
[Clarke Fitch; Frederick Garrison; Arthur Stirling]
American. Author
Wrote *The Jungle,* 1906; 1943 Pulitzer winner *Dragon's Teeth.*
b. Sep 20, 1878 in Baltimore, Maryland
d. Nov 25, 1968 in Bound Brook, New Jersey
Source: *AmRef; AmSocL; BiDAmJo; CasWL; ConLC 15; CurBio 62; DcAmB S8; EncAB-H 1996; ModAL; OxCAmL 65; OxCEng 67; OxCFilm; PenC AM; RAdv 1; REn; REnAL; SmATA 9; TwCA, SUP; WebE&AL; WorEFlm*

Sinden, Donald (Alfred)
English. Actor
British films include *The Cruel Sea,* 1953; *That Lucky Touch,* 1975.
b. Oct 9, 1923 in Plymouth, England
Source: *BioIn 13, 19; CamGWoT; CnThe; ConAu 132; ConTFT 7; DcArts; Ent; FilmAG WE; FilmEn; FilmgC; HalFC 80, 84, 88; IlWWBF; IntAu&W 89, 93; IntMPA 75, 76, 77, 78, 79, 80, 81, 82, 84, 86, 88, 92, 94, 96; IntWW 83, 89, 91, 93; OxCThe 83; VarWW 85; Who 74, 82, 83, 85, 88, 90, 92, 94; WhoEnt 92; WhoHol 92, A; WhoThe 72, 77, 81; WhoWor 96; WrDr 94, 96*

Sinding, Christian
Norwegian. Composer
Wrote piano work, "Rustle of Spring;" operas, four symphonies.
b. Jan 11, 1856 in Kongsberg, Norway
d. Dec 3, 1941 in Oslo, Norway
Source: *Baker 78, 84; BioIn 3, 8; CompSN; CurBio 42; LinLib S; MusMk; NewAmDM; NewGrDM 80; NewOxM; OxCMus*

Singer, Burns James Hyman
American. Author
Best known for documentary novel, *Living Silver,* 1958.
b. Apr 29, 1928 in New York, New York
d. Sep 8, 1964 in Plymouth, England
Source: *ConAu 89, 102; ConPo 75; WorAu 1950*

Singer, Isaac Bashevis
[Isaac Warshofsky]
American. Author
Foremost living writer of Yiddish literature; won Nobel Prize, 1978; awarded American Academy and Institute of Arts and Letters gold medal, 1989.
b. Jul 14, 1904 in Radzymin, Poland
d. Jul 24, 1991 in Miami, Florida
Source: *AmAu&B; AmWr; AnCL; AnObit 1991; Au&Wr 71; AuBYP 2, 3; AuNews 1, 2; AuSpks; Benet 87, 96; BenetAL 91; BioIn 6, 7, 8, 9, 10, 11, 12, 13, 14, 15, 16, 17, 18, 19, 20, 21; BlueB 76; CasWL; CelR; ChlBkCr; ChlLR 1; ConAu 1NR, 1R, 39NR, 134; ConLC 1, 3, 6, 9, 11, 15, 23, 38, 69, 70; ConNov 72, 76, 82, 86; CurBio 69, 91N; CyWA 89; DcArts; DcLB 6, 28, 52, Y91N; DcLP 87A; DcTwCCu 1; DrAF 76; EncAB-H 1996; EncWL 2, 3; FacFETw; GrWrEL N; IntAu&W 76, 77, 89, 91; IntvTCA 2; IntWW 74, 75, 76, 77, 78, 79, 80, 81, 82, 83, 89, 91; JeAmHC; LegTOT; LiExTwC; LinLib L, S; MagSWL; MajAI; MajTwCW; McGEWB; ModAL S1, S2; MorBMP; NewCon; News 92, 92-1; NewYTBS 78, 91; NobelP; Novels; OxCAmL 83, 95; OxCChiL; OxCEng 85, 95; PenC AM; PenEncH; PeoHis; PolBiDi; RAdv 14, 13-2; RfGAmL 87, 94; RfGShF; RGTwCWr; ScF&FL 1, 2, 92; ShSCr 3; ShSWr; SmATA 3, 27, 68; ThrBJA; TwCChW 78, 83, 89, 95; TwCWr; WebAB 74, 79; WebE&AL; WhAm 10; Who 82, 83, 85, 88, 90, 92N; WhoAm 74, 76, 78, 80, 82, 84, 86, 88, 90; WhoAmJ 80; WhoE 74, 79, 81, 83, 85, 86, 89, 91; WhoNob, 90, 95; WhoTwCL; WhoUSWr 88; WhoWor 74, 78, 80, 82, 84, 87, 89, 91; WhoWrEP 89; WorAl; WorAlBi; WorAu 1950; WorLitC; WrDr 76, 80, 82, 84, 86, 88, 90, 92, 94N; WrPh*

Singer, Isaac Merrit
American. Inventor
Manufactured first domestic sewing machine, 1851.
b. Oct 27, 1811 in Rensselaer, New York
d. Jul 23, 1875 in Torquay, England
Source: *AmBi; ApCAB; BioIn 5, 6, 7, 9, 11, 12; DcAmB; LegTOT; TwCBDA; WebAB 74, 79; WhAm HS; WhDW*

Singer, Jane Sherrod
American. Author
Juvenile books include *Ernest Hemingway, Man of Courage,* 1963.
b. May 26, 1917 in Wichita Falls, Texas
Source: *BioIn 15; ConAu 17NR, 25R, 115; ForWC 70; SmATA 4, 42N; WhoAmW 61, 64, 66, 68, 70, 74, 75, 77; WhoWest 74, 76, 78*

Singer, Peter
Austrian. Philosopher, Educator
Champion of animal rights; founder of the animal liberation movement; wrote *Animal Liberation: A New Ethic for Our Treatment of Animals,* 1975.
b. Jul 6, 1946 in Melbourne, Australia
Source: *ConAu 8NR, 57; CurBio 91; EnvEnc; IntWW 91; WrDr 84, 86, 88, 90, 92, 94, 96*

Singh, Giani Zail
Indian. Political Leader
Pres., India, 1982-87.
b. May 15, 1916 in Sandhwan, India
d. Dec 25, 1994 in Chandigarh, India
Source: *BioIn 13, 14, 15; CurBio 87, 95N; IntWW 83, 89, 91, 93; Who 88, 90, 92, 94; WhoWor 87*

Singh, (Sardar) Swaran
Indian. Government Official
Held various Indian cabinet positions, 1952-75.
b. Aug 19, 1907
d. Oct 30, 1994 in New Delhi, India
Source: *BioIn 7, 9, 20; CurBio 71, 95N; FarE&A 78, 79, 80, 81; IntWW 74, 75, 76, 77, 78, 79, 80, 81, 82, 83, 89, 91, 93; IntYB 78, 79, 80, 81, 82; Who 74, 82, 83, 85, 88, 90, 92, 94; WhoWor 74, 76, 78, 80*

Singh, V(ishwanath) P(ratap)
Indian. Political Leader
Prime Minister of India, 1989-1990; resigned after losing a parliamentary vote of confidence.
b. Jun 25, 1931 in Daiya, India
Source: *BioIn 15, 16; CurBio 90; IntWW 89, 91, 93; NewYTBS 89, 90; Who 92, 94; WhoAsAP 91; WhoWor 91*

Singher, Martial
French. Opera Singer
Baritone with NY Met., 1943-60; noted for French operas.
b. Aug 14, 1904 in Oloron Saint Marie, France
d. Mar 10, 1990 in Santa Barbara, California
Source: *Baker 78, 84; BioIn 1, 4, 5, 11, 15, 16; ConAu 131; CurBio 47, 90, 90N; IntWWM 90; MetOEnc; MusSN; NewAmDM; NewEOp 71; NewGrDA 86; NewGrDM 80; NewYTBS 90; PenDiMP; WhAm 10; WhoAm 74, 76, 78, 80, 82, 84, 86, 88; WhoAmM 83; WhoMus 72; WhoWest 74, 76, 78; WhoWor 74*

Singletary, Mike
[Michael Singletary]
American. Football Player
Four-time all-pro linebacker, Chicago, 1981-92; played major role in Super Bowl winning season, 1985-86.
b. Oct 9, 1958 in Houston, Texas
Source: *AfrAmSG; BiDAmSp FB; BioIn 14, 18, 19, 21; ConBlB 4; CurBio 93; FootReg 87; WhoAfA 96; WhoAm 86, 88, 90, 92, 94, 95, 96, 97; WhoBlA 85, 88, 90, 92, 94; WhoMW 88, 90; WhoSpor; WorAlBi*

Singleton, John (Daniel)
American. Filmmaker
Writer and director of *Boyz N the Hood,* 1991; *Poetic Justice,* 1993; *Higher Learning,* 1995.
b. Jan 6, 1968 in Los Angeles, California
Source: *AfrAmAl 6; BlkWr 2; ConAu 138; ConBlB 2; ConTFT 12; IntMPA 94, 96; LegTOT; News 94, 94-3; NewYTBS 91; SchCGBL; WhoAm 95, 96, 97*

Singleton, Penny
[Dorothy McNulty]
American. Actor
Starred as "Blondie" in film series, 1938-50.
b. Sep 15, 1908 in Philadelphia, Pennsylvania
d. 1952
Source: *BioIn 10, 11; BioNews 74; BusPN; EncAFC; FilmEn; FilmgC; HalFC 80, 84, 88; HolP 30; IntMPA 77, 84, 86, 88, 92, 94, 96; InWom SUP; LegTOT; MotPP; MovMk; QDrFCA 92; RadStar; ThFT; WhoHol 92, A*

Singleton, Zutty
[Arthur James Singleton]
American. Musician
Drummer with leading jazz groups for over 50 yrs.
b. May 14, 1898 in Bunkie, Louisiana
d. Jul 14, 1975 in New York, New York
Source: *Baker 84, 92; BiDAfM; BiDAmM; BiDJaz; BioIn 7, 10, 16; CmpEPM; EncJzS; InB&W 80, 85; LegTOT; NewAmDM; NewGrDA 86; NewGrDJ 88, 94; NewGrDM 80; NewYTBS 75; OxCPMus; WhoHol C; WhoJazz 72; WhScrn 77, 83; WorAl; WorAlBi*

Singmaster, Elsie
American. Author
Her novels describe Pennsylvania Dutch country she lived in.
b. Aug 29, 1897 in Schuylkill, Pennsylvania
d. Sep 30, 1958 in Gettysburg, Pennsylvania
Source: *AmAu&B; ConAu 110; ObitOF 79; WhAm 3*

Sinise, Gary
American. Actor
Appeared in *Forrest Gump,* 1994; *Apollo 13,* 1995; founded the Steppenwolf Theatre Company, Chicago, 1974.
b. Mar 17, 1955 in Chicago, Illinois
Source: *IntMPA 96; News 96, 96-1; WhoAm 96, 97*

Sinkwich, Frank
"Fireball Frankie"
American. Football Player
All-America halfback, won Heisman Trophy, 1942; in NFL with Detroit, 1943-44; NFL MVP, 1944.
b. Oct 10, 1920 in McKees Rocks, Pennsylvania
d. Oct 22, 1990 in Athens, Georgia
Source: *BioIn 3, 8, 14, 17; NewYTBS 90; WhoFtbl 74; WhoSpor*

Sinner, George Albert
American. Politician
Dem. governor of ND, 1985-93.
b. May 29, 1928 in Fargo, North Dakota
Source: *AlmAP 88, 92; IntWW 89, 91, 93; St&PR 91; WhoAm 86, 88, 90, 92, 94, 95, 96, 97; WhoAmP 73, 85, 87, 91; WhoMW 88, 90, 92, 93, 96; WhoWor 87, 89, 91, 93, 95*

Sinopoli, Giuseppe
Italian. Conductor, Composer
Music director, London Philharmonia Orchestra, 1983-87; musical director, 1987—; known for his intense and individual interpretation of music.
b. Nov 2, 1946 in Venice, Italy
Source: *Baker 84, 92; BioIn 14, 15; ConNews 88-1; CurBio 91; IntDcOp; IntWW 89, 91, 93; IntWWM 90; MetOEnc; NewAmDM; NewGrDM 80; NewGrDO; PenDiMP; Who 94*

Sinyavsky, Andrei D(onatovich)
[Abram Terts]
Russian. Author, Critic
Tried, convicted for slander to the Soviet State for literary work, *The Makepeace Experiment,* 1966; exiled to Paris, 1973.
b. Oct 8, 1925 in Moscow, Union of Soviet Socialist Republics
d. Feb 25, 1997 in Paris, France
Source: *Benet 87; BioIn 13, 15, 16, 21; ConAu 85; ConLC 8; CurBio 75; CyWA 89; DcRusLS; EncWL 2; FacFETw; HanRL; IntWW 91; LiExTwC; LinLib L; PenC EUR; RAdv 13-2; RfGShF; TwCWr; WhDW; WhoWor 91; WorAu 1950*

Siodmark, Curt
German. Producer, Director, Author
Science fiction books, films include *Donovan's Brain,* 1943.
b. Aug 10, 1902 in Dresden, Germany
Source: *ConAu 111, 113; ConDr 88A; DcLB 44; HalFC 88; IntMPA 92; NewEScF; ScFSB; TwCSFW 86, 91; WhoEnt 92; WhoSciF; WrDr 90*

Siouxie and the Banshees
English. Music Group
Punk rock band founded in 1976; the 1991 album *Superstition,* is their most cohesive work to date.
Source: *ConMus 8; EncRk 88; IlEncRk; PenEncP; WhoRocM 82; WhsNW 85*

Siple, Paul Allman
American. Explorer, Geographer
Originated wind-chill index.
b. Dec 18, 1908 in Montpelier, Ohio
d. Nov 25, 1968 in Arlington, Virginia
Source: *AmAu&B; BioIn 4, 5, 6, 8; CurBio 57, 69; InSci; OhA&B; WhAm 5*

Siqueiros, David A
Mexican. Artist
Last of Mexican Renaissance giants; did boldly colored murals promoting proletarian revolution.
b. Dec 29, 1896 in Chihuahua, Mexico
d. Jan 6, 1974 in Cuernavaca, Mexico
Source: *CurBio 59, 74; NewCol 75; NewYTBS 74; WhAm 6; WhoAmA 73*

Sirhan, Sirhan Bishara
Jordanian. Assassin
Shot Robert Kennedy, Jun 5, 1968; serving life sentence in San Quentin Prison.
b. Mar 19, 1944? in Jerusalem, Palestine
Source: *BioIn 8, 9, 10, 11, 12, 13, 15; PolProf J; WorAlBi*

Sirica, John Joseph
American. Judge
Presided over Watergate trial, 1973-75.
b. Mar 19, 1904 in Waterbury, Connecticut
d. Aug 14, 1992 in Washington, District of Columbia
Source: *BioIn 12, 13, 15; CngDr 85, 87, 89; ConAu 110; CurBio 74; EncWB; FacFETw; IntWW 77, 78, 79, 80, 81, 82, 83, 89, 91; News 93-2; NewYTBE 73; NewYTBS 92; WhoAm 86, 90; WhoAmL 83, 85; WhoSSW 73; WhoWor 84; WorAlBi*

Sirk, Douglas
[Dietlef Sierck]
Danish. Director
Films include *Magnificent Obsession,* 1954; *Imitation of Life,* 1959.
b. Apr 26, 1900 in Skagen, Denmark
d. Jan 14, 1987 in Lugano, Switzerland
Source: *AnObit 1987; BiDFilm, 81, 94; BioIn 10, 11, 12, 15, 16; CmMov; DcArts; DcFM; FacFETw; FilmEn; FilmgC; HalFC 80, 84, 88; IlWWHD 1; IntDcF 1-2, 2-2; IntMPA 75, 76, 77, 78, 79, 80, 81, 82, 84, 86; ItaFilm; LegTOT; MakMC; MiSFD 9N; NewYTBS 87; OxCFilm; RAdv 14; WorEFlm; WorFDir 1*

Sironi, Mario
Italian. Artist
Founding member of the Novecento group: *House and Trees,* 1948.
b. May 12, 1885 in Tempio Pausania, Sardinia, Italy
d. Aug 13, 1961 in Milan, Italy
Source: *BioIn 4, 6, 17; ConArt 77, 83; McGDA; ObitOF 79; OxCTwCA; PhDcTCA 77*

Sisco, Joseph John
American. Government Official
Asst. secretary of State, Near East and S Asian affairs, 1969-74; pres., American U, 1976-80.
b. Oct 31, 1919 in Chicago, Illinois
Source: *BioIn 10, 12; BlueB 76; CurBio 72; HisEAAC; IntWW 74, 75, 76, 77, 78, 79, 80, 81, 82, 83, 89, 91, 93; PolProf NF; USBiR 74; WhoAm 74, 76, 78, 80, 82, 84, 86, 88, 90, 92, 94, 95, 96, 97; WhoAmP 73, 75, 77, 79; WhoGov 72, 75; WhoSSW 73; WhoWor 78*

Siskel, Gene
[Eugene Karl Siskel]
American. Critic
Co-host of TV shows ''Sneak Previews,'' 1978-82; ''Siskel and Ebert,'', 1982—.
b. Jan 26, 1946 in Chicago, Illinois
Source: *BioIn 13, 14, 15, 16; CelR 90; ConAu 113, X; ConTFT 10; DcTwCCu 1; EncTwCJ; LegTOT; WhoAm 84, 86, 88, 90, 92, 94, 95, 96, 97; WhoEmL 87; WhoEnt 92; WhoMW 88, 90, 92, 93*

Siskind, Aaron
American. Photographer
Abstract photographer best known for expressing moods/feelings through photography.
b. 1903 in New York, New York
Source: *AmArt; AnObit 1991; BioIn 10, 12, 13; BriEAA; ConPhot 82, 88, 95; DcAmArt; DcArts; DcCAr 81; ICPEnP; MacBEP; NewYTBS 91; WhAm 10; WhAmArt 85; WhoAm 84, 88, 90*

Sisler, George Harold
''Gorgeous George''
American. Baseball Player
First baseman, 1915-22, 1924-30, mostly with St. Louis; holds ML record for hits in one season, 257, 1920; won AL batting title twice; Hall of Fame, 1939.
b. Mar 24, 1893 in Manchester, Ohio
d. Mar 26, 1973 in Richmond Heights, Missouri
Source: *BiDAmSp BB; BioIn 2, 3, 4, 5, 6, 7, 8, 9, 10; DcAmB S9; WhoProB 73*

Sisley, Alfred
French. Artist
Impressionist painter; *The Flood at Port Marly; Snow at Louveciennes,* both at Louvre.
b. Oct 30, 1839 in Paris, France
d. Jan 29, 1899 in Moret, France
Source: *AtlBL; Benet 87, 96; BioIn 2, 3, 4, 5, 6, 7, 9, 11, 12, 16, 18; ClaDrA; DcArts; DcNaB MP; IntDcAA 90; LegTOT; OxCArt; OxDcArt; REn; ThHElm; WhDW; WorAl; WorAlBi*

Sissle, Noble
American. Bandleader, Lyricist
Led Sizzling Syncopators, 1930s-60s; often collaborated with Eubie Blake; wrote ''I'm Just Wild About Harry.''
b. Jul 10, 1889 in Indianapolis, Indiana
d. Dec 17, 1975 in Tampa, Florida
Source: *AfrAmAl 6; AllMusG; ASCAP 66, 80; BgBands 74; BiDAfM; BiDAmM; BiDJaz; BioIn 8, 9, 10, 11, 15; BlkAmP; BlkAWP; BlksB&W, C; BlksBF; CamGWoT; CmpEPM; ConAu 112; DrBlPA, 90; EncAACR; EncMT; EncVaud; MorBAP; NegAl 76, 83, 89; NewAmDM; NewGrDA 86; NewGrDJ 88; OxCPMus; WhoJazz 72; WhScrn 77, 83*

Sissman, L(ouis) E(dward)
American. Poet, Essayist
Writings include ''Dying: An Introduction,'' 1968; ''Pursuit of Honor,'' 1971.
b. Jan 1, 1928 in Detroit, Michigan
d. Mar 10, 1976 in Boston, Massachusetts
Source: *BioIn 8, 10, 11, 12, 13; ConAu 13NR, 21R, 65; ConLC 9, 18; ConPo 75; DcLB 5; DcLEL 1940; DrAP 75; NatCAB 61; NewYTBS 76; OxCTwCP; WhAm 7; WhoAdv 72; WhoAm 74, 76; WhoE 74; WorAu 1950, 1975; WrDr 76*

Sisson, Charles Hubert
English. Poet
Satirical, politically critical works include ''Anchises,'' 1976; ''Exactions,'' 1980.
b. Apr 22, 1914 in Bristol, England
Source: *Au&Wr 71; BioIn 12, 14, 15; CamGLE; ConAu 1R, 3AS, 3NR; ConLC 8; ConPo 70, 75, 91; DcLB 27; EngPo; FacFETw; IntAu&W 77, 82, 86, 89, 91, 93; IntWW 77, 78, 79, 80, 81, 82, 83, 89, 91, 93; IntWWP 77, 82; MakMC; ModBrL S2; OxCEng 85; Who 74, 82, 83, 85, 88, 90, 92, 94; WhoTwCL; WhoWor 89; WrDr 76, 86, 92*

Sister Sledge
[Debbie Sledge; Joni Sledge; Kathy Sledge; Kim Sledge]
American. Music Group
Sister quartet known for hit ''We Are Family,'' 1979, which became theme for world champ Pittsburgh Pirates, 1979.
Source: *DrBlPA 90; EncRk 88; InB&W 80, 85A; Law&B 92; RkOn 85; SoulM*

Sister Souljah
[Lisa Williamson]
American. Rapper
Released album, *360 Degrees of Power,* 1992; autobiography, *No Disrespect,* 1995.
b. 1964 in New York, New York
Source: *ConBlB 11*

Sitter, Willem de
Dutch. Mathematician
His theoretical models regarding the nature of the universe were based on Einstein's theory of relativity.
b. May 6, 1872 in Sneek, Netherlands
d. Nov 20, 1934 in Leiden, Netherlands
Source: *AsBiEn; CamDcSc; DcScB; InSci; WorScD*

Sitting Bull
American. Native American Chief
Organized Native American forces at Battle of Little Bighorn, 1876.
b. 1831 in Grand River, South Dakota
d. Dec 15, 1890 in Grand River, South Dakota
Source: *AmBi; ApCAB; BenetAL 91; BioIn 15, 16, 17, 19, 20; DcAmB; EncAB-H 1974; EncNoAI; FilmgC; GayN; HalFC 80, 84, 88; HarEnMi; LegTOT; NatNAL; NotNaAm; RelLAm 91; REnAW; WebAB 74, 79; WebAMB; WhAm HS; WhDW; WhNaAH; WorAl; WorAlBi*

Sittler, Darryl Glen
Canadian. Hockey Player
Center, 1970-85, mostly with Toronto; set NHL record for most pts. in game, 10 (1976); Hall of Fame, 1989.
b. Sep 18, 1950 in Kitchener, Ontario, Canada
Source: *HocEn; HocReg 85; NewYTBS 76; WhoAm 78, 80, 82, 84; WhoHcky 73*

Sitwell, Edith, Dame
English. Poet
Wrote poetry volume *Street Songs,* 1943; biographical study *English Eccentrics,* 1933.
b. Sep 7, 1887 in Scarborough, England
d. Dec 9, 1964 in London, England
Source: *AnCL; ArtclWW 2; AtlBL; Benet 87, 96; BioIn 1, 2, 3, 4, 5, 6, 7, 8, 9, 10, 11, 12, 13, 14, 16, 17, 18, 20, 21; BlmGEL; BlmGWL; BritWr 7; CamGEL; CamGLE; CasWL; Chambr 3; ChhPo, S1, S2, S3; ClDMEL 47; CnDBLB 7; CnMWL; ConAu 9R, 35NR; ConLC 2, 9, 67; DcArts; DcLB 20; DcLEL; EncBrWW; EncWL, 2, 3; EngPo; EvLB; FacFETw; FemiCLE; GrWomW; GrWrEL P; InWom, SUP; LegTOT; LinLib L; LngCEL; LngCTC; MajTwCW; MakMC; McGEWB; ModBrL, S1, S2; ModWoWr; NewC; NewCBEL; ObitT 1961; OxCEng 67; OxCMus; PenBWP; PenC ENG; PoeCrit 3; RAdv 1, 14, 13-1; REn; RfGEnL 91; RGFMBP; TwCA, SUP; TwCWr; WebE&AL; WhAm 4; WhDW; WhoTwCL; WorAl; WorAlBi*

Sitwell, Osbert, Sir
English. Author
Wrote novel *Before the Bombardment,* 1926; five-volume memoirs of his eccentric family, 1944-50.
b. Dec 6, 1892 in London, England
d. May 4, 1969 in Montagnana, Italy
Source: *Benet 87; BioIn 1, 2, 3, 4, 5, 6, 7, 8, 9, 10, 11, 12, 13, 14, 17; BlmGEL; CamGEL; CamGLE; CasWL; Chambr 3; ConAu 25R, P-2; CurBio 65, 69; DcArts; DcLB 100; DcLEL; DcNaB 1961; EncSF, 93; EncWL; EvLB; FacFETw; GrWrEL P; LinLib L, S; LngCEL; LngCTC; ModBrL, S1; NewC; NewCBEL; Novels; ObitT 1961; OxCEng 67, 85; PenC ENG; RAdv 1, 13-1; REn; RfGEnL 91; ScF&FL 1, 2, 92; TwCA, SUP; TwCWr; WhAm 5; WhDW; WhE&EA; WhLit; WhoTwCL*

Sitwell, Sacheverell, Sir
English. Author, Critic
Known for art, music critiques: *German Baroque Art,* 1927; *Sacred and Profane Love,* 1940.
b. Nov 15, 1897 in Scarborough, England
d. Oct 1, 1988 in London, England
Source: *AnObit 1988; Au&Wr 71; Benet 87, 96; BioIn 2, 3, 4, 6, 8, 9, 10, 11, 12, 15, 16, 19; BlmGEL; BlueB 76; CamGEL; CamGLE; Chambr 3; ChhPo, S2; CnE&AP; ConAu 21R, 126; ConPo 70, 75, 80, 85; DcArts; DcLEL; DcNaB 1986; EncWL; EvLB; FacFETw; GrWrEL P; IntAu&W 76, 77, 82, 89, 91; IntWW 74, 75, 76, 77, 78, 79, 80, 81, 82, 83; IntWWP 77; LinLib L; LngCEL; LngCTC; ModBrL, S1; NewC; NewCBEL; NewYTBS 88; OxCEng 67, 85, 95; OxCTwCP; PenC ENG; REn; RfGEnL 91; RGTwCWr; TwCA, SUP; TwCWr; WhDW; WhE&EA; Who 74, 82, 83, 85, 88; WhoTwCL; WhoWor 74, 76, 78; WrDr 76, 80, 82, 84, 86, 88*

Six, Robert Forman
American. Business Executive
Flamboyant founder of Continental Airlines; introduced discount fares to industry, 1962.
b. Jun 25, 1907 in Stockton, California
d. Oct 6, 1986 in Beverly Hills, California
Source: *BioIn 4, 5, 6, 7, 8, 9, 10, 11; BlueB 76; CurBio 70, 86; IntWW 74, 75, 76, 77, 78, 79, 80, 81, 82, 83; IntYB 78, 79, 80, 81, 82; NewYTBS 86; St&PR 75, 84; WhAm 9; WhoAm 74, 76, 78, 80, 82, 84; WhoE 81, 83; WhoFI 74, 75, 77, 79, 81; WhoWest 74, 76, 78, 82; WhoWor 74*

Sjoberg, Alf
Swedish. Director
Head director of Sweden's Royal Dramatic Theater, 1930-40.
b. Jun 21, 1903 in Stockholm, Sweden
d. Apr 17, 1980 in Stockholm, Sweden
Source: *AnObit 1980; BiDFilm, 81, 94; BioIn 12, 15, 20; CamGWoT; DcFM; EncEurC; EncWT; FilmEn; FilmgC; HalFC 80, 84, 88; IntDcF 1-2, 2-2; IntDcT 3; IntWW 74, 75, 76, 77, 78; MiSFD 9N; OxCFilm; OxCThe 83; TheaDir; WhoWor 74, 76, 78; WhScrn 83; WorFDir 1*

Sjostrom, Victor
Swedish. Director
Pioneer of Swedish film industry.
b. Sep 20, 1879 in Silbodal, Sweden
d. Jan 3, 1960 in Stockholm, Sweden
Source: *BiDFilm, 81, 94; BioIn 15, 16; DcFM; EncEurC; Film 1; FilmEn; FilmgC; HalFC 80; IntDcF 1-2, 2-2; MiSFD 9N; MovMk; ObitT 1951; OxCFilm; WhoHol B; WorEFlm; WorFDir 1*

Sjowall, Maj
Swedish. Author, Poet
With husband, Per Wahloo, wrote detective novel series featuring Martin Beck as protagonist, 1965-75.
b. Sep 25, 1935 in Malmo, Sweden
Source: *Benet 87; BioIn 9, 10; ConAu 65; ConLC 7; CrtSuMy; EncMys; LegTOT; NewYTBE 71; Novels; TwCCr&M 85, 85B; WorAl; WorAlBi; WorAu 1970*

Skaggs, M(arion) B
American. Merchant
Founder, head, Safeway Stores, Inc., 1926-34; had 3,527 stores, 1931.
b. 1888
d. May 8, 1976 in Oakland, California
Source: *BioIn 10; NewYTBS 76; ObitOF 79*

Skaggs, Ricky
American. Musician, Singer
Won 1982 CMA awards for best male vocalist and newcomer of year.
b. Jul 18, 1954 in Cordell, Kentucky
Source: *Baker 92; BgBkCoM; BioIn 13, 14, 15, 16; ConMus 5; EncRk 88; HarEnCM 87; HarEnR 86; LegTOT; NewAmDM; NewGrDA 86; OnThGG; PenEncP; PrimTiR; WhoAm 90, 97; WhoEnt 92; WhoNeCM*

Skelly, Hal
American. Actor
Starred in seven films, 1929-33, including *The Dance of Life,* 1929.
b. 1891 in Allegheny, Pennsylvania
d. Jun 16, 1934 in West Cornwall, Connecticut
Source: *CmpEPM; Film 2; ForYSC; HalFC 80, 84, 88; OxCAmT 84; WhoHol B; WhScrn 74, 77, 83; WhThe*

Skelton, John
English. Poet
Poet laureate; tutor to Henry VIII; irregular rhyme-scheme called "skeltonic meter."
b. 1460?
d. Jun 21, 1529 in Westminster, England
Source: *Alli; AtlBL; Benet 87, 96; BiD&SB; BioIn 1, 2, 3, 5, 7, 8, 9, 11, 12, 13, 17, 20; BlmGEL; BritAu; BritWr 1; CamGEL; CamGLE; CamGWoT; CasWL; Chambr 1; ChhPo, S1, S3; CmMedTh; CnE&AP; CroE&S; CrtT 1, 4; DcArts; DcCathB; DcEnL; DcEuL; DcLEL; DcNaB; Dis&D; EvLB; GrWrEL P; LngCEL; McGEWB; McGEWD 72, 84; MouLC 1; NewC; NewCBEL; OxCEng 67, 85, 95; OxCThe 67, 83; PenC ENG; PoLE; RAdv 1, 14, 13-1; REn; RfGEnL 91; WebE&AL*

Skelton, Red
[Richard Skelton]
American. Comedian, Actor
Master of pantomime and slapstick comedy; hosted comedy-variety TV show, 1951-71.
b. Jul 18, 1913 in Vincennes, Indiana
Source: *ASCAP 66, 80; AuBYP 2S, 3; BioIn 2, 3, 4, 5, 6, 7, 10, 11, 12, 16; CelR; CmMov; ConAu 104; ConTFT 8; CurBio 47; EncAFC; FilmEn; FilmgC; Funs; HalFC 84, 88; IndAu 1967; IntMPA 84, 86, 88, 92, 94, 96; JoeFr; LegTOT; LesBEnT, 92; MGM; MotPP; MovMk; NewYTBS 77; RadStar; SaTiSS; ScF&FL 1; WhoAm 76, 78, 80, 82, 88, 90, 92, 94, 95, 96, 97; WhoCom; WhoEnt 92; WhoHol A; WorAl; WorAlBi*

Skelton, Robin
English. Poet
Major books of poetry include *The Hunting Dark,* 1971; *Timelight,* 1978.
b. Oct 12, 1925 in Easington, England
Source: *Au&Wr 71; AuNews 2; BioIn 10, 11, 14, 15, 16; CanWW 31, 70, 79, 80, 81, 83, 89; CaW; ChhPo S1; CnE&AP; ConAu 5AS, 5R, 28NR; ConCaAu 1; ConLC 13; ConPo 70, 75, 80, 85, 91, 96; DcLB 27, 53; DcLEL 1940; DrAP 75; DrAPF 80, 91; DrAS 74E, 78E, 82E; EngPo; IntAu&W 76, 77, 82, 89, 91, 93; IntWWP 77, 82; OxCCanL; OxCCan SUP; OxCTwCP; ScF&FL 92; Who 74, 82, 83, 85, 88, 90, 92, 94; WhoAmA 78, 80, 82; WhoCanL 85, 87, 92; WhoWest 74, 76; WorAu 1950; WrDr 76, 80, 82, 84, 86, 88, 90, 92, 94, 96*

Skerritt, Tom
[Thomas Roy Skerritt]
American. Actor
Films include *The Dead Zone,* 1983; *Alien,* 1979.
b. Aug 25, 1933 in Detroit, Michigan
Source: *BioIn 21; ConTFT 6, 13; HalFC 84, 88; IntMPA 88, 92, 94, 96; ItaFilm; LegTOT; VarWW 85; WhoAm 80, 82, 84, 94, 95, 96, 97; WhoHol 92, A; WorAlBi*

Skidmore, Louis
American. Architect
Partner in architectural firm that constructed town of Oak Ridge, TN.
b. Apr 8, 1897 in Lawrenceburg, Indiana
d. Sep 27, 1962 in Winter Haven, Florida
Source: *AmCulL; BioIn 2, 4, 6, 8, 13; ConArch 80, 87, 94; CurBio 51, 62; DcAmB S7; DcD&D; DcTwDes; EncAAr 1; EncMA; InSci; LegTOT; MacEA; McGDA; NatCAB 50; WhAm 4, 5; WorAl; WorAlBi*

Skinner, B(urrhus) F(rederic)
American. Psychologist, Author
Leading exponent of Behaviorism; father of programmed instruction and "Skinner" box.
b. Mar 20, 1904 in Susquehanna, Pennsylvania
d. Aug 18, 1990 in Cambridge, Massachusetts
Source: *AmAu&B; AmMWSc 73S, 78S; AmSocL; Au&Wr 71; Benet 87, 96; BenetAL 91; BiDAmEd; BioIn 1, 6, 7, 8, 9, 10, 11, 12, 13, 14, 17, 18, 19; ConAu 9R, 18NR, 42NR, 132; CurBio 64, 79, 90, 90N; EncAB-H 1974, 1996; EncSF; FacFETw; IntWW 74, 75, 76, 77, 78, 79,*

80, 81, 82, 83, 89, 91N; MajTwCW; MakMC; McGEWB; McGMS 80; News 91-1; NewYTBS 90; RAdv 14, 13-3; ScFSB; ThTwC 87; WebAB 74, 79; WhAm 10; Who 82, 83, 85, 88, 90; WhoAm 74, 76, 78, 80, 82, 84, 86, 88, 90; WhoWor 74, 84; WorAlBi; WorAu 1970; WrDr 76, 80, 90

Skinner, Cornelia Otis
American. Actor, Author
Daughter of Otis Skinner; appeared with him in *Blood and Sand,* 1921.
b. May 30, 1901 in Chicago, Illinois
d. Jul 9, 1979 in New York, New York
Source: *AmAu&B; AmWomD; AmWomPl; AmWomWr; ArtclWW 2; Au&Wr 71; Benet 87, 96; BenetAL 91; BiE&WWA; BioIn 2, 3, 4, 5, 7, 9, 12, 13, 16; CamGWoT; CelR; ChhPo; ConAu 17R, 89; CurBio 42, 64, 79N; DcAmB S10; DcLEL; EncWT; EvLB; FemiCLE; FilmgC; ForYSC; HalFC 80, 84, 88; IntWW 74; InWom, SUP; LegTOT; LinLib L; LngCTC; NewYTBS 79; NotNAT, A; NotWoAT; OxCAmL 65, 83, 95; OxCAmT 84; PenC AM; REn; REnAL; SmATA 2; TwCA SUP; TwCWr; Who 74; WhoAm 74; WhoHol A; WhoThe 72, 77; WhScrn 83; WorAl; WorAlBi; WrDr 76*

Skinner, Halcyon
American. Inventor
Made power looms for weaving carpets, 1856.
b. Mar 6, 1824 in Mantua, Ohio
d. Nov 28, 1900 in Mantua, Ohio
Source: *DcAmB; NatCAB 5; WhAm HS*

Skinner, Otis
American. Actor
One of American theater's greatest character actors; known for role in *Kismet,* 1911-14.
b. Jun 28, 1858 in Cambridge, Massachusetts
d. Jan 4, 1942 in New York, New York
Source: *AmAu&B; BenetAL 91; BioIn 1, 2, 3, 4, 5, 9, 10, 13; CamGWoT; CurBio 42; DcAmB S3; DcNAA; EncWT; FamA&A; Film 1, 2; FilmgC; HalFC 80, 84, 88; IntDcT 3; LinLib L, S; NatCAB 11, 32; NotNAT A, B; OxCAmL 65; OxCAmT 84; OxCThe 67, 83; PlP&P; REn; REnAL; TwYS; WebAB 74, 79; WhAm 1; WhoHol B; WhScrn 74, 77; WhThe; WorAl; WorAlBi*

Skinner, Samuel K(nox)
American. Government Official
US Secretary of Transportation 1988-92; White House chief of staff, 1991-92.
b. Jun 10, 1938 in Chicago, Illinois
Source: *BiDrUSE 89; BioIn 16; CngDr 89, 91; CurBio 89; News 92; NewYTBS 91; Who 94; WhoAm 82, 90, 92, 94, 95, 96, 97; WhoAmL 78, 79, 83, 85, 87; WhoAmP 91, 93, 95; WhoE 91, 93; WhoFI 92; WhoMW 96; WhoWor 91, 93*

Skipworth, Alison
American. Actor
Played dowagers, duchesses, 1930s; films include *If I Had A Million,* 1932.
b. Jul 25, 1870? in London, England
d. Jul 5, 1952 in New York, New York
Source: *FilmgC; MovMk; ThFT; Vers B; WhoHol B; WhoStg 1908; WhScrn 74, 83*

Skolnick, Mark H(enry)
American. Geneticist
Isolated two genes which cause breast cancer, BRCA1 in 1994 and BRCA2 in 1996.
b. Jan 28, 1946 in Temple, Texas
Source: *AmMWSc 79, 82, 86, 89, 92, 95; WhoAm 97*

Skolsky, Sidney
American. Journalist
Hollywood gossip columnist since 1933, coined term "sneak preview."
b. May 5, 1905 in New York, New York
d. May 3, 1983 in Hollywood, California
Source: *BioIn 2, 78, 79, 80, 81, 82; NewYTBS 83; WhAm 8; WhoAm 74, 76, 78, 80, 82; WhoWorJ 72, 78*

Skouras, Spyros Panagiotes
American. Producer
Pres., 20th Century Fox, 1942-62; launched cinemascope.
b. Mar 28, 1893 in Skourokhori, Greece
d. Aug 16, 1971 in Mamaroneck, New York
Source: *BioIn 5, 6, 8, 9; CurBio 43, 71; DcAmB S9; DcFM; FilmgC; NewYTBE 71; OxCFilm; WebAB 74, 79; WhAm 5; WorEFlm*

Skowron, Bill
[William Joseph Skowron]
"Moose"
American. Baseball Player
First baseman, NY Yankees, 1954-62; had lifetime .282 batting average.
b. Dec 18, 1930 in Chicago, Illinois
Source: *Ballpl 90; BaseEn 88; BiDAmSp Sup; BioIn 6, 14, 15*

Skrowaczewski, Stanislaw
American. Composer, Conductor
Wrote symphony at age eight; led MN Orchestra, 1960-79; Manchester, England's Halle Orchestra, 1984-91; musical advisor, St. Paul Chamber Orchestra, 1986-87.
b. Oct 3, 1923 in Lwow, Poland
Source: *ASCAP 80; Baker 78, 84, 92; BioIn 5, 7, 8, 9, 11; BlueB 76; BriBkM 80; CelR; ConAmC 82; CurBio 64; IntWW 74, 75, 76, 77, 78, 79, 80, 81, 82, 83, 89, 91, 93; IntWWM 77, 80, 85, 90; MusSN; NewAmDM; NewGrDA 86; NewGrDM 80; PenDiMP; WhoAm 74, 76, 78, 80, 82, 84, 86, 88, 90, 92, 94, 95, 96, 97; WhoAmM 83; WhoEnt 92; WhoMus 72; WhoMW 74, 76, 78, 80, 82, 90; WhoOp 76; WhoPoA 96; WhoSocC 78; WhoSoCE 89; WhoWor 74, 76, 78, 80, 82, 84, 87, 89, 91, 93, 95, 96, 97*

Skulnik, Menasha
Polish. Actor
Stage comedian, 1920-50, in Yiddish theater.
b. May 15, 1898? in Warsaw, Poland
d. Jun 4, 1970 in New York, New York
Source: *BiE&WWA; NewYTBE 70; WhAm 5; WhScrn 77*

Skurzynski, Gloria
American. Author
Juvenile books include *The Magic Pumpkin,* 1971; *What Happened in Hamelin,* 1979.
b. Jul 6, 1930 in Duquesne, Pennsylvania
Source: *ConAu 13NR, 30NR, 33R; DcAmChF 1960, 1985; FifBJA; SmATA 8, 9AS*

Slade, Bernard
[Bernard Slade Newbound]
Canadian. Dramatist
Stage plays include *Same Time Next Year,* 1975; *Fatal Attraction,* 1984; also wrote screenplays, TV scripts.
b. May 2, 1930 in Saint Catharines, Ontario, Canada
Source: *BioIn 15; CanWW 31, 89; CaP; ConAu 9AS, 49NR, 81; ConCaAu 1; ConDr 88, 93; ConLC 11, 46; ConTFT 1; CrtSuDr; DcLB 53; IntAu&W 91, 93; LesBEnT, 92; McGEWD 84; NatPD 81; NewYTBS 75; OxCAmT 84; OxCCanT; WhoAm 84, 86, 88, 90, 92, 94, 95, 96, 97; WhoEnt 92; WhoWor 84; WrDr 88, 90, 92, 94, 96*

Slade, Jack
[Joseph A Slade]
American. Murderer
Ruthless gunman of the American West; known for his senseless cruelty; lynched by vigilantes.
b. 1824 in Carlyle, Illinois
d. Mar 10, 1864 in Virginia City, Montana
Source: *DrInf*

Slash
[Guns N' Roses; Saul Hudson]
English. Musician
Debut album *Live? ! Like a Suicide,* 1986.
b. 1965 in Stoke-on-Trent, England
Source: *LegTOT; OnThGG; WhoAm 94, 95, 96, 97*

Slater, Christian
[Christian Hawkins]
American. Actor
Appeared in *The Legend of Billie Jean,* 1985; *Interview with the Vampire,* 1994.
b. Aug 18, 1969 in New York, New York
Source: *ConTFT 9; IntMPA 92, 94, 96; LegTOT; News 94, 94-1; WhoAm 94, 95, 96, 97; WhoHol 92*

Slater, Rodney E.
American. Government Official
Secretary of Transportation, 1997—.

b. Feb 23, 1955
Source: *AfrAmBi 2; WhoAfA 96; WhoAm 95, 96, 97; WhoBlA 88, 90, 92, 94; WhoFI 96*

Slatkin, Leonard
American. Conductor
Most promising American-born conductor since Leonard Bernstein; music director, St. Louis Symphony since 1979.
b. Sep 1, 1944 in Los Angeles, California
Source: *ASCAP 80; Baker 78, 84; BioIn 14, 15, 16; CelR 90; CurBio 86; IntWW 91, 93; IntWWM 80, 90; LegTOT; NewAmDM; NewGrDA 86; NewYTBS 84; PenDiMP; WhoAm 84, 90; WhoEnt 92; WhoMW 82, 92*

Slaughter, Enos Bradsher
"Country"
American. Baseball Player
Outfielder, 1938-42, 1946-59, mostly with St. Louis; led NL in RBIs, 1946; had lifetime .300 batting average.
b. Apr 27, 1916 in Roxboro, North Carolina
Source: *Ballpl 90; BiDAmSp BB; BioIn 1, 2, 3, 4, 5, 7, 8, 10, 11, 15, 16; WhoProB 73*

Slaughter, Frank Gill
[C V Terry]
American. Author, Surgeon
Best known for medical novels: *That None Should Die,* 1941.
b. Feb 25, 1908 in Washington, District of Columbia
Source: *AmAu&B; AmNov; Au&Wr 71; AuNews 2; BenetAL 91; BioIn 1, 2, 3, 4, 5, 7, 10, 11, 14; ConAu 5NR, 5R; ConLC 29; CurBio 42; DcLP 87A; InSci; IntAu&W 76, 77, 82, 86, 89, 91, 93; LngCTC; PenC AM; REnAL; TwCA SUP; TwCRGW; TwCRHW 90; Who 74, 82, 83, 85, 88, 90, 92, 94; WhoAm 86, 88, 90, 92, 94, 95, 96, 97; WrDr 76, 86, 92*

Slavenska, Mia
[Mia Corak]
Yugoslav. Dancer
Ballerina best known for role of "Blanche" in *Streetcar Named Desire,* 1952.
b. Feb 20, 1914 in Slavonski-Brod, Yugoslavia
Source: *BiDD; CnOxB; CurBio 54; IntDcB; WhoAm 82*

Slavin, Mark
Israeli. Olympic Athlete, Victim
One of 11 members of Israeli Olympic team kidnapped and killed by Arab terrorists during Summer Olympic Games.
b. 1954?, Union of Soviet Socialist Republics
d. Sep 5, 1972 in Munich, Germany (West)
Source: *BioIn 9*

Slavitt, David R
[Henry Sutton]
American. Author
Wrote *Vital Signs,* 1975.
b. Mar 23, 1935 in White Plains, New York
Source: *BioIn 15, 16; ConAu 3AS; ConLC 5, 14; ConNov 76; ConPo 85, 91; DcLP 87A; DrAP 75; DrAPF 91; IntAu&W 91; IntWW 91; ScF&FL 1, 2, 92; WhoWrEP 89; WrDr 86, 92, 94*

Slayton, Donald Kent
"Deke"
American. Astronaut
Flew on Apollo mission that docked with Russian Soyuz spaceship, 1975.
b. Mar 1, 1924 in Sparta, Wisconsin
d. Jun 13, 1993 in League City, Texas
Source: *AmMWSc 73P; AnObit 1993; BioIn 6, 9, 10, 11, 13, 16, 17, 19, 20; CurBio 76; FacFETw; IntWW 83; NewYTBE 73; WebAMB; WhAm 11; WhoAm 74, 76, 78, 80, 82, 84, 86, 88, 90, 92; WhoFI 87; WhoGov 72, 75, 77; WhoSpc; WhoSSW 73, 75, 76, 78, 93; WhoWor 74, 78, 80, 82, 84*

Sledge, Debbie
[Sister Sledge]
American. Singer
Part of pop-rock group with three sisters, 1970s-80s; best known hit: "We Are Family," 1979.
b. Jul 9, 1954 in Philadelphia, Pennsylvania
Source: *InB&W 85; InWom SUP*

Sledge, Joni
[Sister Sledge]
American. Singer
Late 1970s-early 1980s hits with three sisters include "We Are Family," 1979.
b. Sep 13, 1956 in Philadelphia, Pennsylvania
Source: *InB&W 85; InWom SUP*

Sledge, Kathy
[Sister Sledge]
American. Singer
Biggest hit with three sisters: "We Are Family," 1979.
b. Jan 6, 1959 in Philadelphia, Pennsylvania
Source: *InB&W 85; InWom SUP*

Sledge, Kim
[Sister Sledge]
American. Singer
Sang pop-rock tunes with three sisters, late 1970s-early 1980s.
b. Aug 21, 1957 in Philadelphia, Pennsylvania
Source: *InB&W 85; InWom SUP*

Sleet, Moneta, Jr.
American. Photojournalist
Staff photographer, *Ebony* and *Jet,* 1955—.
b. Feb 14, 1926 in Owensboro, Kentucky
d. Sep 30, 1996 in New York, New York
Source: *AfrAmAl 6; BioIn 19; ConBlB 5; NegAl 89; WhoE 74*

Slenczynska, Ruth
American. Pianist
Acclaimed protege; stopped performing at early age; wrote memoirs *Forbidden Childhood,* 1957, recounts problems.
b. Jan 15, 1925 in Sacramento, California
Source: *Baker 78, 84, 92; BiDAmM; BioIn 4, 5, 10; CmCal; IntWWM 77, 80; InWom; NewGrDA 86; WhoAm 76, 78; WhoAmW 58, 64, 66, 68, 70, 72, 74, 75, 77; WhoMus 72*

Slesar, Henry
American. Writer
Head writer for "The Edge of Night," 1968-83; "Capitol," 1984-87; won Emmy, 1974.
b. Jun 12, 1927 in New York, New York
Source: *BioIn 14; ConAu 1NR, 1R; DcLP 87A; EncSF, 93; IntAu&W 91, 93; LegTOT; NewEScF; ScFSB; TwCCr&M 80, 85, 91; TwCSFW 81, 86; VarWW 85; WrDr 76, 80, 82, 84, 86, 88, 90, 92, 94, 96*

Slezak, Erika
American. Actor
Won Emmys, 1984, 1986, for role of Victoria Lord Buchanan in soap opera "One Life to Live."
b. Aug 5, 1946 in Los Angeles, California
Source: *ConTFT 4; LegTOT; VarWW 85; WhoAm 90; WhoEnt 92*

Slezak, Leo
Czech. Opera Singer
Tenor, noted for Lohengrin role; wrote popular *What Time's the Next Swan*; father of Walter.
b. Aug 18, 1875? in Schonberg, Moravia
d. Jun 1, 1946 in Egern, Germany
Source: *Baker 84; BriBkM 80; CmOp; MusSN; WhAm 2; WhoHol B; WhScrn 74, 77, 83*

Slezak, Walter
American. Actor
Won 1955 Tony for *Fanny,* best known film role in *Lifeboat,* 1944.
b. May 3, 1902 in Vienna, Austria
d. Apr 21, 1983 in Flower Hill, New York
Source: *AnObit 1983; BiDAmM; BiE&WWA; BioIn 3, 4, 5, 6, 13, 14; CelR; CmMov; ConAu 109; CurBio 55, 83, 83N; EncAFC; EncMT; Film 2; FilmEn; FilmgC; ForYSC; HalFC 80, 84, 88; IntMPA 75, 76, 77, 78, 79, 80, 81, 82; ItaFilm; MotPP; MovMk; NewYTBS 83; NotNAT, A; OxCAmT 84; OxDcOp; Vers A; WhAm 8; WhoAm 76; WhoHol A; WhoThe 72, 77, 81; WhoWor 74; WorAl*

Slick, Grace Wing
[Jefferson Airplane; Mrs. Skip Johnson; Grace Barnett Wing]
American. Singer
Lead vocalist, Jefferson Starship, 1966-78; rock hits include "White Rabbit," 1967; pursued solo career.
b. Oct 20, 1939 in Chicago, Illinois
Source: *Baker 84; BioIn 9, 10, 11; BkPepl; CurBio 82; IntDcWB; InWom SUP; RkOn 85; WhoAm 74, 76, 78, 80, 82, 84, 86, 88, 90, 92, 94, 95, 96, 97; WhoAmW 70, 72, 74, 79, 81, 83, 85; WhoEnt 92; WhoRocM 82; WorAlBi*

Slim, William Joseph
English. Military Leader
Led Allied campaign to liberate Burma from Japanese, WW II.
b. Aug 6, 1891 in Bristol, England
d. Dec 14, 1970 in London, England
Source: *BioIn 1, 2, 3, 15, 17; ConAu 107; CurBio 45, 71; DcNaB 1961; DcTwHis; FacFETw; GenMudB; GrBr; HarEnMi; HisEWW; WhAm 5; WhoMilH 76; WhWW-II; WorAl; WorAlBi*

Slipher, Vesto Melvin
American. Astronomer
First to provide evidence suggesting the expanding universe theory.
b. Nov 11, 1875 in Mulberry, Indiana
d. Nov 8, 1969 in Flagstaff, Arizona
Source: *AmDec 1910; AsBiEn; BiESc; BioIn 8, 9, 12, 14, 20; CamDcSc; DcAmB S8; DcScB; InSci; LarDcSc; WebAB 74, 79; WhAm 5; WorScD*

Sliwa, Curtis
"The Rock"
American. Social Reformer
Founder, pres., Guardian Angels, 1979, civilian patrol group launched to help combat crime in NYC.
b. Mar 26, 1954 in New York, New York
Source: *BioIn 12, 13, 14, 15, 16; ConAu 111; CurBio 83; NewYTBS 88*

Sloan, Alfred Pritchard, Jr.
American. Industrialist
Founded Sloan-Kettering Institute for Cancer Research, 1945.
b. May 23, 1875 in New Haven, Connecticut
d. Feb 17, 1966 in New York, New York
Source: *ApCAB X; BiDAmBL 83; BioIn 2, 3, 4, 5, 6, 7, 9, 10; CurBio 40, 66; DcAmB S8; EncAB-H 1996; EncABHB 5; FacFETw; McGEWB; WhAm 4; WorAl*

Sloan, Hugh W
American. Presidential Aide
Treasurer of Nixon's re-election campaign, 1971.
b. Nov 1, 1940 in Princeton, New Jersey
Source: *BioIn 10; CanWW 89; NewYTBE 73; PolProf NF; WhoAm 86, 90; WhoCanB 86*

Sloan, John F
American. Artist
Member "The Eight" or "Ashcan" school; drew somber genre scenes of NY working people : *McSorley's Bar,* 1912.
b. Aug 2, 1871 in Lock Haven, Pennsylvania
d. Sep 8, 1951 in Hanover, New Hampshire
Source: *AtlBL; DcAmB S5; DcCAA 71; EncAB-H 1974; OxCAmL 65; REn; REnAL; WebAB 74; WhAm 3*

Sloan, Michael
American. Writer
Wrote for TV detective shows "Columbo," 1971-77; "Harry-O," 1974-76; "Switch," 1975-78.
b. Oct 14, 1946 in New York, New York
Source: *ConAu 130; ConTFT 5; ScF&FL 92; VarWW 85; WhoEnt 92; WrDr 94*

Sloan, Samuel
"Architect of Philadelphia"
American. Architect
Edited *The Architectural Review and American Builder's Journal,* 1868-70, first US periodical devoted to architecture; internationally recognized expert on designs for hospitals for the insane.
b. 1815 in Chester County, Pennsylvania
d. Jul 19, 1884 in Raleigh, North Carolina
Source: *Alli; ApCAB, X; BiDAmAr; BioIn 5, 14; BriEAA; DcAmAu; DcNAA; Drake; IntDcAr; MacEA; NewYHSD*

Sloane, Dennis
American. Scientist
Wrote *Birth Defects and Drugs in Pregnancy,* 1977, most comprehensive report on subject.
b. Jan 9, 1930 in Pretoria, South Africa
d. May 10, 1982 in Lexington, Massachusetts
Source: *BiDrACP 79; ConAu 106; NewYTBS 82; WhoAm 80*

Sloane, Eric
[Everard Jean Hinrichs]
American. Artist
Known for portraying nostalgic aspects of life in pre-industrial America.
b. Feb 27, 1910 in New York, New York
d. Mar 6, 1985 in New York, New York
Source: *AmArt; AmAu&B; AnObit 1985; ConAu 108, 115; CurBio 72, 85N; IlBEAAW; IlsCB 1957; NewYTBS 85; SmATA 42N, 52; WhAm 8; WhAmArt 85; WhoAm 74, 76, 78; WhoAmA 73, 76, 78, 80, 82, 86N, 89N, 91N, 93N*

Sloane, Everett
American. Actor
Films include *The Patsy,* 1964; *Brushfire,* 1962.
b. Oct 1, 1909 in New York, New York
d. Aug 6, 1965 in Brentwood, California
Source: *BiDFilm, 81, 94; BioIn 4, 7; CurBio 57, 65; FilmEn; FilmgC; HalFC 80, 84, 88; HolCA; IntDcF 1-3, 2-3; LegTOT; MotPP; MovMk; NotNAT B; RadStar; SaTiSS; Vers A; WhoHol B; WhScrn 74, 77, 83*

Sloane, Hans, Sir
English. Physician, Philanthropist
His collection of manuscripts, books, specimens became the nucleus of British Museum, 1759; physician to George II.
b. Apr 16, 1660 in Killyleagh, Ireland
d. Jan 11, 1753 in London, England
Source: *Alli; ApCAB; BiDIrW; BiHiMed; BioIn 2, 3, 5, 9, 10, 14, 17; BlkwCE; DcBiPP; DcIrB 78, 88; DcIrW 2; DcLEL; DcNaB; DcScB; HisDBrE; InSci; NewC; NewCBEL; OxCEng 67, 85, 95; OxCMed 86; REn; WhDW*

Sloane, John
Business Executive
Chm., W&J Sloane, 1933-55; manufactured reproductions of antique furniture.
b. Apr 20, 1883 in New York, New York
d. Aug 3, 1971 in Bennington, Vermont
Source: *BioIn 9, 11; EncAB-A 30; NatCAB 56; NewYTBE 71; WhAm 7*

Slobodkin, Louis
American. Sculptor, Author, Illustrator
Won Caldecott Medal for illustrating James Thurber's *Many Moons,* 1943; did sculptures for govt. buildings, wrote *Sculpture: Principles and Practice,* 1949.
b. Feb 19, 1903 in Albany, New York
d. May 8, 1975 in Miami Beach, Florida
Source: *AmAu&B; AuBYP 2, 3; BenetAL 91; BioIn 1, 2, 4, 5, 7, 8, 9, 10, 13, 14, 19; BkCL; BkP; Cald 1938; ChhPo; ChlBkCr; ConAu 13R, 57; CurBio 57, 75N; IlsBYP; IlsCB 1744, 1946, 1957; JBA 51; MajAI; NewYTBS 75; OxCChiL; REnAL; ScF&FL 1, 2; SmATA 1, 26; TwCChW 78, 83, 89, 95; WhAm 6; WhAmArt 85; WhoAm 74; WhoAmA 73, 76N, 78N, 80N, 82N, 84N, 86N, 89N, 91N, 93N; WhoWorJ 72, 78*

Slobodkina, Esphyr
American. Children's Author, Illustrator
Self-illustrated books include *Long Island Ducklings,* 1961.
b. Sep 22, 1909 in Siberia, Russia
Source: *AuBYP 2, 3; ChhPo; ConAu 1NR, 1R; ForWC 70; SmATA 1, 8AS; ThrBJA; TwCChW 83, 89; WhoAmA 91; WrDr 86, 92*

Slocum, Joshua
American. Author, Adventurer
Built ship *Spray;* sailed around the world alone, 1895-98.
b. Feb 20, 1844 in Wilmont Township, Nova Scotia, Canada
d. 1910?
Source: *AmAu&B; BenetAL 91; BioIn 2, 3, 4, 5, 9, 11, 12, 18, 21; DcAmAu; DcAmB; DcCanB 13; DcNAA; LngCTC; NewYTBS 75; OxCAmL 65, 83, 95;*

OxCShps; PeoHis; RAdv 14, 13-3; REnAL; WhAm 4, HSA; WhDW

Slonimsky, Nicolas
American. Musicologist
Wrote *Music Since 1900,* 1971; revised prestigious *Baker's Biographical Dictionary,* 1958.
b. Apr 27, 1894 in Saint Petersburg, Russia
d. Dec 25, 1995 in Los Angeles, California
Source: *AmAu&B; ASCAP 66, 80; Baker 78, 84, 92; BiDAmM; BiDSovU; BioIn 1, 2, 3, 4, 5, 15, 16, 17, 21; ConAmC 76, 82; ConAu 17R, 150; CurBio 55, 91, 96N; DcCM; IntAu&W 82; IntWW 89, 91, 93; IntWWM 85, 90; NewGrDA 86; NewGrDM 80; NewYTBS 95; OxCMus; PenDiMP; WhAm 11; WhoAm 74, 76, 78, 80, 82, 84, 86, 88, 90, 92, 94, 95, 96; WhoAmM 83; WhoEnt 92; WhoMus 72; WhoWest 96; WhoWorJ 72; WrDr 76, 80, 82, 84*

Slotnick, Barry Ivan
American. Lawyer
Regarded as America's most successful criminal defense attorney; clients have included Bernhard Goetz, reputed mobsters.
b. Jun 18, 1939
Source: *BioIn 14, 16; ConNews 87-4; WhoAm 88, 90, 92; WhoAmL 90, 94; WhoE 74, 75, 91; WhoFI 75*

Slotnick, Daniel Leonid
American. Scientist
Directed scientific team that developed advance computer, Illiac IV.
b. Nov 12, 1931 in New York, New York
d. Oct 25, 1985 in Baltimore, Maryland
Source: *AmMWSc 76P, 79, 82, 86, 89, 92; ConAu 117; WhAm 9; WhoAm 82, 84*

Slotta, Karl Heinrich
American. Biochemist
Discovered female hormone progesterone, 1935; helped develop birth control pill.
b. May 12, 1895 in Breslau, Germany
d. Jul 17, 1987 in Coral Gables, Florida
Source: *AmMWSc 76P, 79, 82, 86*

Slovik, Eddie
[Edward Donald Slovik]
American. Soldier
Only American executed during WW II for desertion.
b. 1920 in Detroit, Michigan
d. Jan 31, 1945 in Sainte Marie Mines, France
Source: *BioIn 3, 9, 10, 12, 15; BioNews 74; NewYTBS 87*

Slovo, Joe
South African. Political Leader, Lawyer
Founding member of South African Communist Party, 1953; general secretary, 1987.
b. 1926, Lithuania
d. Jan 6, 1995 in Johannesburg, South Africa
Source: *BioIn 12; DcCPSAf; EncRev; IntWW 91, 93; News 89-2; NewYTBS 95; RadHan; WhAm 11; WhoAfr; WhoWor 95*

Sluter, Claus
Dutch. Sculptor
Master of early Burgundian school, noted for works at Dijon.
b. 1350?
d. 1406? in Dijon, France
Source: *McGEWB; OxCArt; WebBD 83*

Sly and the Family Stone
[Gregg Errico; Lawence Graham, Jr; Jerry Martini; Cynthia Robinson; Fred Stone; Rose Stone; Sly Stone]
American. Music Group
Dance-rock hits include "Family Affair," 1971.
Source: *AmPS B; BiDAmM; BioIn 15, 16; EncPR&S 74, 89; EncRk 88; HarEnR 86; IlEncBM 82; IlEncRk; InB&W 80, 85A; NewAmDM; NewGrDA 86; PenEncP; RkOn 74; SoulM; WhoHol 92; WhoRocM 82*

Smale, John Gray
American. Business Executive
Chm., Procter & Gamble, 1986-90; director, General Motors Corp., 1992-95; chm. of the board and chm. executive committee, GM, 1996—.
b. Aug 1, 1927 in Listowel, Ontario, Canada
Source: *BioIn 12, 15, 16, 18; ConNews 87-3; Dun&B 90; IntWW 91; St&PR 75, 84, 87, 91, 93, 96, 97; WhoAm 76, 78, 80, 82, 84, 86, 88, 90, 94, 95, 96, 97; WhoFI 75, 77, 79, 81, 85, 87, 89, 92, 94, 96; WhoMW 74, 76, 78, 80, 82, 88, 90; WhoWor 82, 84, 87, 89, 91, 95, 96, 97*

Small, Albion W(oodbury)
American. Sociologist
First U.S. professor of sociology; made sociology a respected academic discipline in America; wrote *An Introduction to the Study of Society,* 1894.
b. May 11, 1854 in Buckfield, Maine
d. Mar 24, 1926 in Chicago, Illinois
Source: *Alli SUP; AmAu&B; AmBi; AmLY; BiDAmEd; BioIn 3, 5, 10, 11; DcAmB; DcNAA; DcSoc; EncARH; McGEWB; NatCAB 8, 25; TwCBDA; WhAm 1*

Smallens, Alexander
Russian. Conductor
Director, Radio City Music Hall, 1947-50; original conductor, *Porgy and Bess,* 1935.
b. Jan 1, 1889 in Saint Petersburg, Russia
d. Nov 24, 1972 in Tucson, Arizona
Source: *Baker 78, 84, 92; BiDAmM; BioIn 1, 2, 4, 8, 9, 10, 11; CurBio 47, 73, 73N; DancEn 78; MusSN; NewAmDM; NewEOp 71; NewGrDA 86; NewGrDM 80; NewYTBE 72; OxDcOp; PenDiMP; WhAm 5*

Smalley, David Bruce
[The Raspberries]
American. Musician
Bassist, guitarist with power pop group, 1970-73.
b. Jul 10, 1949 in Oil City, Pennsylvania

Small Faces, The
[Kenny Jones; Ian MacLagan; Steve Marriott; Rick Wills]
English. Music Group
Styled after rock group The Who; hits include "Tin Soldier," 1967.
Source: *BioIn 21; EncRk 88; EncRkSt; HarEnR 86; IlEncRk; OxCPMus; PenEncP; RkOn 78, 84; RolSEnR 83; WhoRock 81; WhoRocM 82*

Smalls, Charlie
American. Composer, Lyricist
Won Tonys for music, lyrics of *The Wiz,* 1975.
b. Oct 25, 1943 in New York, New York
d. Aug 27, 1987 in Bruges, Belgium
Source: *BioIn 12, 15; DrBlPA 90; WhAm 9; WhoAm 78, 80, 82, 84, 86; WhoBlA 85*

Smallwood, Joey
[Joseph Roberts Smallwood]
Canadian. Political Leader
Led Newfoundland and Labrador into Canadian Confederation; province's first premier, 1949-79.
b. Dec 24, 1900 in Gambo, Newfoundland, Canada
d. Dec 17, 1991 in Saint John's, Newfoundland, Canada
Source: *AnObit 1991; BioIn 2, 3, 5, 9, 10, 11, 15; BlueB 76; CanWW 83, 89; ConAu 105; CurBio 53; IntWW 83; OxCCan; WhAm 10; WhoCan 73, 75, 77, 80; WhoE 74, 75*

Smart, Christopher
English. Poet, Author
Noted for poem, "A Song to David," 1763.
b. Apr 22, 1722 in Shipbourne, England
d. May 21, 1771 in Kings Bench, England
Source: *Alli; AtlBL; Benet 87, 96; BiD&SB; BioIn 1, 2, 3, 4, 5, 6, 7, 8, 10, 12, 13, 14, 15, 17, 18; BlkwCE; BlmGEL; BritAu; CamGEL; CamGLE; CasWL; Chambr 2; ChhPo, S1, S3; CnE&AP; CrtT 2; DcArts; DcBiPP; DcEnA; DcEnL; DcLB 109; DcLEL; DcNaB, C; Dis&D; EvLB; LitC 3; LngCEL; MouLC 2; NewC; OxCChiL; OxCEng 67, 85, 95; OxCLiW 86; PenC ENG; PoeCrit 13; RAdv 1, 14, 13-1; REn; RfGEnL 91; WebE&AL*

Smart, Jack Scott
American. Actor
Films include *Some Like It Hot,* 1939; *The Fat Man,* 1951.
b. 1903

d. Jan 15, 1960 in Springfield, Illinois
Source: *WhoHol B; WhScrn 74, 77*

Smathers, George Armistead
American. Government Official
Dem. senator from FL, 1951-69.
b. Nov 14, 1913 in Atlantic City, New Jersey
Source: *BiDrAC; BiDrUSC 89; BioIn 2, 3, 5, 6, 7, 9, 11; CurBio 54; IntWW 74; PolProf E, J, K; WhoAm 74; WhoAmP 73, 75, 77, 79, 81, 83, 85, 87, 89, 91, 93, 95*

Smeal, Eleanor Marie Cutri
American. Feminist
Pres. of NOW, 1977-82, 1985-87.
b. Jul 30, 1939 in Ashtabula, Ohio
Source: *BioIn 11, 12, 13; CurBio 80; EncWB; InWom SUP; NewYTBS 77; WhoAm 84, 86, 90; WhoAmP 91; WhoAmW 87, 91*

Smedley, Agnes
American. Author, Journalist
Wrote eye-witness reports on China for magazines, newspapers, 1920s-40s; books include *Chinese Destinies,* 1933.
b. 1894? in Missouri
d. May 6, 1950 in Oxford, England
Source: *AmAu&B; BioAmW; BioIn 2, 4, 10; CurBio 44, 50; DcAmB S4; EncAJ; InWom; LibW; NotAW; TwCA, SUP; WhAm 3*

Smet, Pierre Jean de
Belgian. Missionary
Jesuit priest; mediated land talks between the US government and native American tribes.
b. Jan 30, 1801 in Dendermonde, Belgium
d. May 23, 1873 in Saint Louis, Missouri
Source: *AmAu&B; BenetAL 91; BioIn 1, 3, 4, 5, 6, 7, 9, 12, 15; DcNAA; EncNAB; MacDCB 78; NatCAB 2; OxCAmL 95; OxCCan; REnAL; WhAm HS*

Smetana, Bedrich
Czech. Musician, Conductor, Composer
Best known for opera *The Bartered Bride,* 1866.
b. Mar 2, 1824 in Litomischl, Bohemia
d. May 12, 1884 in Prague, Czechoslovakia
Source: *AtlBL; Baker 78, 84, 92; Benet 87; BioIn 1, 2, 3, 4, 5, 6, 7, 8, 9, 11, 12, 14, 20, 21; BriBkM 80; CmOp; CmpBCM; DcArts; DcCom 77; DcCom&M 79; DcPup; Dis&D; EncDeaf; GrComp; IntDcOp; LegTOT; McGEWB; MetOEnc; MusMk; NewAmDM; NewEOp 71; NewGrDM 80; NewGrDO; NewOxM; OxCEng 85, 95; OxCMus; OxDcOp; PenDiMP A; RAdv 14; REn; WhDW; WorAl; WorAlBi*

Smiley, Jane (Graves)
American. Author
Winner of Pulitzer Prize for *A Thousand Acres,* 1992.
b. Sep 26, 1949 in Los Angeles, California
Source: *BioIn 15, 16, 17, 18, 20, 21; ConAu 30NR, 50NR, 104; ConLC 53, 76; ConNov 96; ConPopW; CurBio 90; GrWomW; News 95; OxCWoWr 95; RAdv 14; WhoAm 90, 92, 94, 95, 96, 97; WhoAmW 93, 95, 97; WhoMW 96; WorAu 1985; WrDr 92, 94, 96*

Smirnoff, Yakov
[Yakov Pokhis]
American. Comedian
Known for TV beer commercial; comedy about native land.
b. Jan 24, 1951 in Odessa, Union of Soviet Socialist Republics
Source: *BioIn 13, 15, 16; ConNews 87-2; LegTOT; WhoCom; WhoEnt 92; WorAlBi*

Smith, A(rthur) J(ames) M(arshall)
Canadian. Poet, Critic
Leading figure in modern Canadian poetry: *Poems New and Collected,* 1967.
b. Nov 8, 1902 in Montreal, Quebec, Canada
d. Nov 21, 1980 in East Lansing, Michigan
Source: *AnObit 1980; Benet 87, 96; BioIn 1, 4, 5, 12, 13; CanWr; CasWL; ConAu 1R, 4NR, 102; ConCaAu 1; ConLC 15; ConPo 70, 75, 80; CreCan 2; DcLB 88; DcLEL, 1940; DrAP 75; DrAS 74E, 78E; IntWWP 77; LngCTC; ModCmwL; OxCCan; OxCCanL; OxCCan SUP; OxCTwCP; PenC ENG; REnAL; TwCA SUP; WebE&AL; WhAm 7; WhoAm 76, 78, 80; WrDr 76, 80, 82*

Smith, Adam
Scottish. Economist
Laid foundation for classical economics with *An Inquiry into the Nature and Causes of the Wealth of Nations,* 1776.
b. Jun 5, 1723 in Kirkcaldy, Scotland
d. Jul 17, 1790 in Edinburgh, Scotland
Source: *Alli; BbD; Benet 87, 96; BiD&SB; BiDPsy; BioIn 1, 2, 3, 4, 5, 6, 7, 8, 10, 11, 12, 13, 14, 15, 16, 17, 18, 19, 20, 21; BlkwCE; BlkwEAR; BlmGEL; BritAu; CamGEL; CamGLE; CasWL; CmScLit; CyEd; CyWA 58; DcAmC; DcBiPP; DcEnA; DcEnL; DcEuL; DcLB 104; DcLEL; DcNaB; Dis&D; EncEnl; EncEnv; EncEth; EvLB; GrEconB; HisDBrE; LinLib L, S; LngCEL; LuthC 75; McGEWB; NamesHP; NewC; OxCEng 67, 85, 95; OxCLaw; OxCPhil; PenC ENG; RAdv 14, 13-3; REn; WebE&AL; WhDW; WhoEc 81, 86; WorAl; WorAlBi*

Smith, Alex
Scottish. Golfer
Touring pro, early 1900s; won US Open, 1906, 1910; charter member, Hall of Fame, 1940.
b. 1872 in Carnoustie, Scotland
d. Apr 20, 1930 in Baltimore, Maryland
Source: *BiDAmSp OS; WhoGolf; WhoSpor*

Smith, Alexander
Scottish. Poet, Essayist
Labelled spasmodic poet; known for essays in *Dreamthorp,* 1863.
b. Dec 31, 1830? in Kilmarnock, Scotland
d. Jan 5, 1867 in Wardie, Scotland
Source: *Alli; BbD; BiD&SB; BioIn 2, 14, 15; BritAu 19; CamGEL; CamGLE; CasWL; Chambr 3; ChhPo, S1, S2, S3; CmScLit; DcBiPP; DcEnA; DcEnL; DcEuL; DcLB 32; DcLEL; EvLB; NewC; OxCEng 67, 85, 95; PenC ENG; REn; StaCVF; WebE&AL*

Smith, Alexis
[Mrs. Craig Stevens]
American. Actor
Won 1971 Tony award for *Follies.*
b. Jun 8, 1921 in Penticton, British Columbia, Canada
d. Jun 9, 1993 in Los Angeles, California
Source: *AnObit 1993; BioIn 19, 20, 21; CelR; ConTFT 3, 12; FilmEn; FilmgC; ForYSC; HalFC 80, 84, 88; IntMPA 75, 76, 77, 78, 79, 80, 81, 82, 84, 86, 88, 92, 94; InWom SUP; LegTOT; MotPP; MovMk; NewYTBE 71; PlP&P, A; WhAm 11; WhoAm 74, 76, 78, 80, 82, 84, 86, 88, 90, 92; WhoAmW 81, 83; WhoHol 92, A; WhoThe 77, 81; WorAl; WorAlBi; WorEFlm*

Smith, Alfred
Canadian. Hockey Player
Amateur player with several teams, early 1900s; Hall of Fame, 1962.
b. Jun 3, 1873 in Ottawa, Ontario, Canada
d. Aug 21, 1953 in Ottawa, Ontario, Canada
Source: *WhoHcky 73*

Smith, Alfred Emanuel
American. Political Leader
Four-term Dem. governor of NY; first Catholic to run for pres., 1928.
b. Dec 30, 1873 in New York, New York
d. Oct 4, 1944 in New York, New York
Source: *AmAu&B; AmOrTwC; AmPolLe; ApCAB X; BioIn 1, 2, 3, 4, 5, 6, 7, 8, 9, 10, 11, 13, 14, 16; CurBio 44; DcAmB S3; DcCathB; DcNAA; DcTwHis; EncAAH; EncAB-H 1974, 1996; LinLib S; MorMA; NatCAB 32; OxCAmH; OxCAmL 65; REn; REnAL; WebAB 74, 79; WhAm 2; WhAmP*

Smith, Allison
American. Actor
Played Jennie Lowell on TV series "Kate & Allie," 1984-88.
b. Dec 9, 1969 in Bergen County, New Jersey
Source: *BioIn 14, 15; InWom SUP; WorAlBi*

Smith, Amanda W
American. Manufacturer
Baked pies; sold by son, commercialized into business bearing her name.
b. 1860
d. 1947
Source: *Entr*

Smith, Anna Deavere
American. Actor, Dramatist
Staged one-woman performance *Twilight: Los Angeles 1992,* 1993; won 1993 OBIE Award for Best New American Play.
b. Sep 18, 1950 in Baltimore, Maryland
Source: *ConAu 133; ConBlB 6; ConLC 86; ConTFT 2, 14; CurBio 94; WhoAm 94, 95, 96, 97; WhoAmW 93, 95, 97; WrDr 94, 96*

Smith, Austin E(dward)
American. Physician
Wrote *The Drugs You Use,* 1948.
b. Nov 25, 1912
d. Oct 9, 1993 in Fort Myers, Florida
Source: *AmMWSc 73P; BioIn 2; CurBio 94N; InSci*

Smith, Barbara
American. Writer
Editor of *Home Girls: A Black Feminist Anthology,* 1983.
b. Nov 16, 1946 in Cleveland, Ohio
Source: *AfrAmAl 6; BlkWr 2; BlkWrNE; ConAu 142; FemiWr; GayLesB; GayLL; SchCGBL; WhoAfA 96; WhoBlA 88, 90, 92, 94; WrDr 96*

Smith, Barbara
American. Restaurateur
Proprietor of B. Smith's, a restaurant in New York and Washington; wrote cookbook *B. Smith's Entertaining and Cooking for Friends,* 1995.
b. Aug 24, 1949 in Pittsburgh, Pennsylvania
Source: *ConBlB 11*

Smith, Bessie
American. Singer, Songwriter
Blues singer, 1920s; discovered by Ma Rainey; first recording "Gulf Coast Blues," 1923.
b. Apr 15, 1894? in Chattanooga, Tennessee
d. Sep 26, 1937 in Clarksdale, Mississippi
Source: *AfrAmAl 6; AllMusG; AmCulL; AmDec 1920; Baker 78, 84, 92; BiDAfM; BioAmW; BioIn 4, 5, 7, 8, 9, 10, 11, 12, 19, 20, 21; BlkWAm; BluesWW; ConBlB 3; ConMus 3; DcAmB S2; DcAmNB; DcArts; DcTwCCu 5; DrBlPA, 90; GayLesB; GoodHs; GrLiveH; GuBlues; HerW; IlEncJ; InB&W 80; InWom SUP; LegTOT; NegAl 76, 83, 89; NewAmDM; NewGrDA 86; NewGrDJ 88, 94; NewGrDM 80; NotAW; NotBlAW 1; OxCPMus; PenEncP; WebAB 74; WhAm 4, HSA; WhoJazz 72; WhScrn 77, 83; WorAl; WorAlBi*

Smith, Betty
[Betty Wehner]
American. Author
Wrote best-seller *A Tree Grows in Brooklyn,* 1943; filmed, 1945; on Broadway, 1951.
b. Dec 15, 1904 in New York, New York
d. Jan 17, 1972 in Shelton, Connecticut
Source: *AmAu&B; AmNov; BenetAL 91; BioIn 1, 2, 3, 4, 5, 9, 10; CnDAL; ConAu 5R; CurBio 43, 72, 72N; CyWA 58; HalFC 84, 88; LegTOT; LinLib L; LngCTC; NotWoAT; Novels; OxCAmL 65, 83; PenC AM; REn; REnAL; TwCA SUP; WhAm 5; WhE&EA; WhoAmW 58, 61*

Smith, Billy
[William John Smith]
Canadian. Hockey Player
Goalie, NY Islanders, 1972-90; first goalie to score goal in NHL (1979); won Vezina Trophy, 1982, Jennings Trophy, 1983.
b. Dec 12, 1950 in Perth, Ontario, Canada
Source: *BioIn 13; HocEn; HocReg 87; NewYTBS 83*

Smith, Bob
"Buffalo Bob"
American. Entertainer
Creator, star of children's TV show "Howdy Doody," 1947-60.
b. Nov 27, 1917 in Buffalo, New York
Source: *BioIn 15, 16; LegTOT; WhoAm 78; WorAl; WorAlBi*

Smith, Bruce (Bernard)
American. Football Player
Player with Buffalo Bills, 1985—.
b. Jun 18, 1963 in Norfolk, Virginia
Source: *CurBio 95; WhoAfA 96; WhoAm 92, 94, 95, 96, 97; WhoBlA 92, 94; WhoWor 95, 96*

Smith, Bruce P
"Boo"
American. Football Player
All-America halfback, won Heisman Trophy, 1941; in NFL with Green Bay, 1945-48, LA Rams, 1948.
b. Feb 8, 1920 in Faribault, Minnesota
d. Aug 28, 1967
Source: *BiDAmSp FB; BioIn 8, 11, 14; WhoFtbl 74*

Smith, Bubba
[Charles Aaron Smith]
American. Football Player
Two-time all-pro defensive end-tackle, 1967-76, mostly with Baltimore; made popular beer commercials.
b. Feb 28, 1945 in Orange, Texas
Source: *BiDAmSp FB; BioIn 9, 10, 11, 14, 15; ConTFT 7; LegTOT; WhoBlA 85, 88; WhoFtbl 74; WhoHol 92; WhoSpor*

Smith, C. Aubrey
English. Actor
Noted character actor in over 80 films, 1920s-40s.
b. Jul 21, 1863 in London, England
d. Dec 20, 1948 in Beverly Hills, California
Source: *Film 1; FilmgC; MotPP; MovMk; PlP&P; Vers A; WhoHol B; WhoStg 1908; WhScrn 74, 77*

Smith, Carleton Sprague
American. Musicologist
Expert on the Brazilian and Hispanic cultures; chief of the music division, New York Public Library, 1931-59.
b. Aug 8, 1905
d. Sep 19, 1994 in Washington, Connecticut
Source: *Baker 78, 84, 92; BioIn 5, 17, 20; CurBio 94N; IntWWM 80; NewGrDA 86; NewGrDM 80*

Smith, Cathy Evelyn
Canadian. Singer
Convicted, sentenced to three yrs. in prison, for injecting fatal drug dose to John Belushi, 1986; paroled, 1988.
b. 1947?
Source: *BioIn 13*

Smith, Chard Powers
American. Author, Lecturer
Writings include verse *Along the Wind,* 1925; novel *Ladies Day,* 1941.
b. Nov 1, 1894 in Watertown, New York
d. Oct 31, 1977
Source: *AmAu&B; AmNov; AnMV 1926; Au&Wr 71; BenetAL 91; BioIn 2, 4, 11; ChhPo S1; ConAu 5R, 73; OxCAmL 65, 83, 95; REnAL; TwCA, SUP; WhAm 7; WhE&EA; WhoAm 74, 76; WrDr 76*

Smith, Christopher Columbus
American. Manufacturer
Superior designs of his boats started venture of speedboat-building, marketing his Chris-Craft boats worldwide.
b. May 20, 1861 in Saint Clair, Michigan
d. Sep 9, 1939 in Mount Clemens, Michigan
Source: *BioIn 7; Entr; NatCAB 47*

Smith, Clarence
"Pinetop"
American. Jazz Musician
Pianist, vocalist; wrote "Pine Top's Boogie Woogie," 1928; accidentally murdered.
b. Jun 11, 1904 in Troy, Alabama
d. Mar 14, 1929 in Chicago, Illinois
Source: *Baker 84, 92; BiDAfM; BiDAmM; BiDJaz; BluesWW; GuBlues; InB&W 80, 85; WhoJazz 72*

Smith, Claydes
[Kool and the Gang]
American. Musician
Lead guitarist with Kool and the Gang.
b. Sep 6, 1948 in Jersey City, New Jersey

Source: *OnThGG*

Smith, Courtney Craig
American. Educator
Pres. of Swarthmore College, 1953-69; proponent of academic freedom; died of he art attack during campus demonstration.
b. Dec 20, 1916 in Winterset, Iowa
d. Jan 16, 1969 in Swarthmore, Pennsylvania
Source: *CurBio 59, 69; DcAmB S8; WhAm 5*

Smith, Cyrus Rowlett
American. Airline Executive
President, American Airlines, 1934-68.
b. Sep 9, 1899 in Minerva, Texas
d. Apr 4, 1990 in Annapolis, Maryland
Source: *BiDAmBL 83; BiDrUSE 71, 89; BiDWWGF; BioIn 5, 8, 10, 16; CurBio 45, 90; FacFETw; InSci; IntWW 83; NewYTBE 73; NewYTBS 90; WhAm 10; WhoAm 74, 76, 78, 80, 82, 84, 86; WhoFI 74*

Smith, David
American. Sculptor
Welded metal sculptures include *Zig*.
b. Mar 9, 1906 in Decatur, Indiana
d. May 23, 1965 in Albany, New York
Source: *AtlBL; Benet 87, 96; BioIn 1, 2, 3, 4, 5, 6, 7, 8, 9, 10, 11, 12, 13, 14, 15, 19, 20; BriEAA; CenC; ConArt 77, 83, 89; ConAu 113; DcAmArt; DcArts; DcCAA 71, 77, 88, 94; DcTwCCu 1; EncAB-H 1974, 1996; IntDcAA 90; McGDA; McGEWB; OxCArt; OxCTwCA; OxDcArt; PhDcTCA 77; WebAB 74, 79; WhAm 4; WhAmArt 85; WhDW; WhoAmA 78N, 80N, 82N, 84N, 86N, 89N, 91N, 93N; WorAlBi; WorArt 1950*

Smith, Dean Edwards
American. Basketball Coach
Coach, U of NC, 1961—; won NCAA championship, 1982; Hall of Fame, 1982.
b. Feb 28, 1931 in Emporia, Kansas
Source: *BiDAmSp BK; CurBio 94; WhoAm 78, 80, 82, 84, 86, 88, 90, 92, 94, 95, 96, 97; WhoSSW 86, 88, 91, 93, 95, 97*

Smith, Dennis
American. Author
Wrote *Report from Engine Co. 82*, 1972, about his experiences as a firefighter.
b. Sep 9, 1940 in New York, New York
Source: *BioIn 15; ConAu 10NR, 61; NewYTBE 72; WhoAm 82, 90; WhoE 79; WrDr 80, 82, 84, 86*

Smith, Dodie
[C L Anthony; Dorothy Gladys Smith]
English. Dramatist, Author
Wrote *The Hundred and One Dalmations*, 1956; filmed by Walt Disney, 1960.
b. May 3, 1896 in Whitefield, England
d. Nov 24, 1990
Source: *AnObit 1990; Au&Wr 71; BiE&WWA; BioIn 4, 9, 10, 11, 12, 13, 15, 17, 19, 21; BlmGWL; Chambr 3; ConAu 37NR, 133; ConBrDr; ConDr 77, 82, 88, 93; ConWomD; DcLB 10; DcLEL; DcLP 87A; FemiCLE; IntAu&W 89, 91; IntWW 77, 78, 79, 80, 81, 82, 83, 89; InWom SUP; LegTOT; LngCTC; MajAI; McGEWD 72, 84; NewC; NotNAT; OxCChiL; PenNWW A, B; PlP&P; REn; RGTwCWr; ScF&FL 1, 92; SmATA 4, 65, 82; TwCChW 83, 89, 95; Who 82, 83, 85, 88, 90; WhoThe 77, 81; WorAu 1950; WrDr 76, 86*

Smith, Donald Alexander
"Strathcona"
Canadian. Financier, Politician
A leader in syndicate that built Canadian Pacific Railway, 1880-85; pres., Bank of Montreal, 1887-1905.
b. Aug 6, 1820 in Morayshire, Scotland
d. Jan 21, 1914 in London, England
Source: *ApCAB; DcNaB 1912; McGEWB; OxCCan*

Smith, Edmund Kirby
[Edmund Kirby-Smith]
American. Military Leader
Last Confederate general to surrender in Civil War, May 1865; pres., U of Nashville, 1870-75.
b. May 16, 1824 in Saint Augustine, Florida
d. Mar 8, 1893 in Sewanee, Tennessee
Source: *AmBi; ApCAB; BiDAmEd; BiDConf; BioIn 1, 3, 5, 9, 17, 18; CivWDc; DcAmB; DcAmMiB; Drake; EncSoH; HarEnMi; HarEnUS; NatCAB 8; NewCol 75; TwCBDA; WebAMB; WhAm HS; WhCiWar; WhoMilH 76; WorAl; WorAlBi*

Smith, Ellison DuRant
"Cotton Ed"
American. Politician
Dem. senator from SC, 1909-44; critic of "New Deal."
b. Aug 1, 1864 in Lynchburg, South Carolina
d. Nov 17, 1944 in Lynchburg, South Carolina
Source: *ApCAB X; BiDrUSC 89; BioIn 1; CurBio 45; DcAmB S3; EncSoH; FacFETw; WhAm 2*

Smith, Emmitt
[Emmitt James Smith, III]
American. Football Player
Running back for the Dallas Cowboys, 1990—; led NFL in rushing, 1991-93, 1995.
b. May 15, 1969 in Pensacola, Florida
Source: *AfrAmSG; ConBlB 7; CurBio 94; News 94, 94-1; WhoSpor*

Smith, Ethel
[Ethel Goldsmith]
American. Organist
Film, radio performer, 1940s; helped popularize organ music.
b. Nov 22, 1910 in Pittsburgh, Pennsylvania
d. May 17, 1996 in Palm Beach, Florida
Source: *ASCAP 66, 80; BioIn 9; CmpEPM; InWom SUP; PenEncP; What 3; WhoHol A*

Smith, Frances Scott Fitzgerald Lanahan
"Scottie"
American., Writer
Only child of F Scott, Zelda Fitzgerald; wrote for *Washington Post; New Yorker*.
b. 1922?
d. Jun 18, 1986 in Montgomery, Georgia

Smith, Francis Marion
American. Financier
Prospector; co-discovered Nevada borax deposits, 1872; monopolized borax market, using "Twenty-Mule Team" trademark.
b. Feb 2, 1846 in Richmond, Wisconsin
d. Aug 27, 1931 in Oakland, California
Source: *BiDAmBL 83; BioIn 12; DcAmB; NatCAB 28; WebAB 74, 79; WhAm 1*

Smith, Frederick Wallace
American. Business Executive
Founded Federal Express, 1972; first corp. in history worth $1 billion in first decade of existence.
b. Aug 11, 1944 in Marks, Mississippi
Source: *ConAmBL; ConNews 85-4; St&PR 84, 87; WhoAm 82, 84, 86, 88, 90, 92, 94, 95, 96, 97; WhoFI 83, 85, 87, 89, 92, 94, 96; WhoSSW 86, 88, 91, 93, 97; WhoWor 95, 96, 97*

Smith, Geoff
English. Track Athlete
Won Boston Marathon, 1984, 1985.
b. 1954? in Liverpool, England
Source: *BioIn 13; NewYTBS 84*

Smith, Gerald Lyman Kenneth
American. Editor, Lecturer
Founded anti-Communist, anti-black, anti-Semitic group: Christian Nationalist Crusade.
b. Feb 27, 1898 in Pardeeville, Wisconsin
d. Apr 15, 1976 in Glendale, California
Source: *AmSocL; BiDExR; BioIn 1, 7, 8, 10, 11; ConAu 65; CurBio 43, 76; DcAmReB 2; RelLAm 91*

Smith, Gerard C(oad)
American. Government Official
Head of US Arms Control and Disarmament Agency, 1969-73; led American delegation to SALT.
b. May 4, 1914
d. Jul 4, 1994 in Easton, Maryland
Source: *BioIn 8, 9, 12; CurBio 94N; IntWW 74, 75, 76, 77, 78, 79, 80, 81, 82, 83, 89, 91, 93; PolProf NF; WhoAm 74, 76, 78; WhoAmP 73, 75, 77, 79, 81, 83, 85, 87, 89, 91, 93, 95; WhoGov 72*

Smith, Gerrit
American. Philanthropist
Aided temperance, abolition, women suffrage; helped John Brown.
b. Mar 6, 1797 in Utica, New York
d. Dec 28, 1874 in New York, New York
Source: *Alli; AmBi; AmPeW; AmRef; AmSocL; ApCAB; BbD; BiAUS; BiD&SB; BiDMoPL; BiDrAC; BiDrUSC 89; BioIn 2, 8, 9, 12, 15, 19; DcAmAu; DcAmB; DcAmSR; DcAmTB; DcNAA; Drake; HarEnUS; McGEWB; NatCAB 2; PolPar; TwCBDA; WebAB 74, 79; WhAm HS; WhCiWar*

Smith, Goldwin
English. Author
Wrote extensively on Canadian politics, urging separation from Britain, union with US: *Canada and the Canadian Question,* 1891.
b. Aug 13, 1823 in Reading, England
d. Jun 7, 1910 in Toronto, Ontario, Canada
Source: *Alli, SUP; ApCAB; BbD; BiD&SB; BioIn 1, 2, 4, 12, 14, 17; BritAu 19; CamGEL; CamGLE; CanWr; CelCen; Chambr 3; CyEd; DcBiPP; DcCanB 13; DcEnA, A; DcEnL; DcEuL; DcLB 99; DcLEL; DcNAA; DcNaB S2; Drake; EvLB; HarEnUS; HisDBrE; LinLib L, S; LngCTC; MacDCB 78; NewC; OxCCan; OxCCanL; OxCEng 67, 85, 95; REn; REnAL; WhAm 1; WhLit*

Smith, Gordon H.
American. Politician
Rep. senator, OR, 1997—.
b. May 25, 1952

Smith, H(arry) Allen
American. Author
Thirty-six books of humor include *Low Man on a Totem Pole,* 1941.
b. Dec 19, 1907? in McLeansboro, Illinois
d. Feb 24, 1976 in San Francisco, California
Source: *AmAu&B; AuNews 2; BiDrAC; BioIn 1, 3, 4, 6, 8, 10, 11, 12, 13, 15; CelR; ChhPo; ConAu 5NR, 5R, 65; CurBio 42; DcAmB S10; EncSF, 93; LngCTC; REn; REnAL; ScF&FL 2; TwCA SUP; WhAm 6; WhE&EA; WhoAm 74; WrDr 76*

Smith, Hamilton Othanel
American. Biologist, Physician
Won 1978 Nobel Prize in medicine for research on enzymes, molecular genetics.
b. Aug 23, 1931 in New York, New York
Source: *AmMWSc 76P, 79, 82, 86, 89, 92, 95; BiESc; BioIn 11, 12, 14, 15, 20; CamDcSc; LarDcSc; McGMS 80; Who 82, 83, 85, 88, 90, 92, 94; WhoAm 80, 82, 84, 86, 88, 90, 92, 94, 95, 96, 97; WhoE 79, 81, 83, 85, 86, 89, 91, 93, 95, 97; WhoFrS 84; WhoMedH; WhoNob, 90, 95; WhoScEn 94, 96; WhoWor 80, 82, 84, 87, 89, 91, 93, 95, 96, 97*

Smith, Harold
American. Boxing Promoter
Chm., Muhammad Ali Professional Sports, Inc; sought by FBI for embezzlement, 1981.
b. 1944?
Source: *NewYTBS 81*

Smith, Hazel Brannon
American. Journalist
Won Pulitzer Prize, 1964; fought against racism; owned the Durant MS *News,* and Lexington MS *Advertiser.*
b. 1914?
d. May 14, 1994 in Cleveland, Tennessee
Source: *BiDAmNC; BioIn 19, 20; CurBio 73, 94N; DcLB 127; GoodHs; InWom SUP; JrnUS; WomFir*

Smith, Hedrick Laurence
American. Journalist
Chief Washington correspondent for *NY Times,* 1979-85; won Pulitzers for cowriting *The Pentagon Papers,* 1972, for int'l reporting, 1974; wrote *The Power Game: How Washington Works,* 1988.
b. Jul 9, 1933 in Kilmacolm, Scotland
Source: *ConAu 11NR, 65; CurBio 91; EncTwCJ; WhoAm 86, 90, 97; WorAlBi; WrDr 86, 92*

Smith, Holland McTeire
"Howlin' Mad"
American. Military Leader
Led Marine invasion of Iwo Jima, 1945; regarded as father of modern amphibious warfare; only third Marine in history to reach full general.
b. Apr 20, 1882 in Seale, Alabama
d. Jan 12, 1967 in San Diego, California
Source: *CurBio 45, 67; WhAm 4*

Smith, Hooley
[Reginald Joseph Smith]
Canadian. Hockey Player
Defenseman, 1924-41, with four NHL teams, Hall of Fame, 1972.
b. Jan 7, 1905 in Toronto, Ontario, Canada
d. Aug 24, 1963 in Montreal, Quebec, Canada
Source: *HocEn; WhoHcky 73*

Smith, Horace
[Smith and Wesson]
American. Manufacturer, Inventor
Produced the first revolvers, 1857.
b. Oct 28, 1808 in Cheshire, Massachusetts
d. Jan 15, 1893
Source: *AntBDN F; BioIn 18; DcAmB; NatCAB 10; WhAm HS; WorInv*

Smith, Horton
"The Joplin Ghost"
American. Golfer
Turned pro, 1926; won 29 PGA tournaments, including first Masters, 1934; pres. of PGA, 1952-54.
b. May 22, 1908 in Springfield, Missouri
d. Oct 15, 1963 in Detroit, Michigan
Source: *BiDAmSp OS; BioIn 6; DcAmB S7; LegTOT; ObitOF 79; WhoGolf; WhoSpor*

Smith, Howard K(ingsbury)
American. Broadcast Journalist
Correspondent, CBS News, 1941-61; reporter, commentator, ABC News, 1961-79.
b. May 12, 1914 in Ferriday, Louisiana
Source: *AmAu&B; BiDAmJo; BioIn 11, 16; BlueB 76; ConAu 45; CurBio 43, 76; EncTwCJ; IntAu&W 77, 82, 93; IntMPA 86, 92; IntWW 74, 75, 76, 77, 78, 83; JrnUS; LesBEnT; WhoAm 74, 76, 78, 80, 82; WhoSSW 73, 75, 76; WhoTelC; WhoWor 74, 78; WorAlBi; WrDr 76, 86, 90*

Smith, Howard Worth
American. Politician
Congressman, 1931-36; wrote Smith Act, 1940, making illegal to be a Communist.
b. Feb 2, 1883 in Broad Run, Virginia
d. Oct 3, 1976 in Alexandria, Virginia
Source: *BiDrAC; BiDrUSC 89; BioIn 3, 5, 6, 7, 11; DcAmB S10; NewYTBS 76; WhAm 7; WhAmP; WhoAm 74, 76; WhoAmP 73, 75, 77, 79*

Smith, Iain Crichton
Scottish. Poet
Writes in English and Gaelic: *From Bourgeois Land,* 1969.
b. Jan 1, 1928 in Isle of Lewis, Scotland
Source: *BioIn 15; CamGLE; CasWL; ChhPo S2; CmScLit; ConAu 21R; ConLC 64; ConNov 72, 76, 82, 86, 91, 96; ConPo 70, 75, 80, 85, 91, 96; DcLB 40, 139; DcLEL 1940; EngPo; IntAu&W 76, 77, 86, 89, 91, 93; IntWWP 77; OxCTwCP; PenC ENG; RfGShF; RGTwCWr; WhoTwCL; WhoWor 95, 96, 97; WorAu 1970; WrDr 84, 86, 88, 90, 92, 94, 96*

Smith, Ian Douglas
Rhodesian. Political Leader
Last prime minister of Rhodesia, 1964-79; declared country's independence, 1965.
b. Apr 8, 1919 in Seluwke, Rhodesia
Source: *BioIn 13, 21; ColdWar 1; CurBio 66; DcAfHiB 86; IntWW 83, 89; McGEWB; NewYTBS 76, 78; Who 85, 92*

Smith, Jack
[John Francis Smith, Jr.]
American. Auto Executive
President and CEO, General Motors, 1992-95; chairman, 1996—.
b. Apr 6, 1938 in Worcester, Massachusetts
Source: *IntWW 89, 91, 93; News 94, 94-3; WhoAm 86, 88, 90, 92, 94, 95, 96, 97; WhoFI 89, 92, 94, 96; WhoMW 93, 96; WhoWor 95, 96, 97*

Smith, Jaclyn
American. Actor
Starred in "Charlie's Angels," 1976-80; TV movie *Rage of Angels,* 1983; was married to actor Dennis Cole.
b. Oct 26, 1947 in Houston, Texas
Source: *BioIn 11, 12, 13, 16; BkPepl; CelR 90; ConTFT 2, 7, 14; HolBB; IntMPA 84, 86, 88, 92, 94, 96; InWom SUP; LegTOT; WhoAm 86, 88, 90, 92, 94; WhoEnt 92; WhoHol 92; WhoTelC; WorAlBi*

Smith, James
American. Continental Congressman, Lawyer
Inconspicious Pennsylvania delegate; signed Declaration of Independence.
b. 1713, Northern Ireland
d. Jul 11, 1806 in York, Pennsylvania
Source: *AmBi; ApCAB; BiAUS; BiDrAC; BiDrUSC 89; DcAmB; Drake; NatCAB 2; REnAL; WhAm HS; WhAmP; WhAmRev*

Smith, Jedediah Strong
American. Fur Trader, Explorer
Advocate of western expansion; explorations helped open up the West.
b. Jan 6, 1799? in Bainbridge, New York
d. May 27, 1831
Source: *AmAu&B; AmBi; CmCal; DcAmB; EncAAH; EncWM; McGEWB; OxCAmH; OxCAmL 65; REnAW; WebAB 74, 79; WhAm HS; WhNaAH; WhWE; WorAl; WorAlBi*

Smith, Jeff
American. TV Personality, Chef, Author
Host of TV show "The Frugal Gourmet," 1973—, and author of 6 best-selling cookbooks.
b. Jan 22, 1939 in Seattle, Washington
Source: *BioIn 15; CurBio 91; News 91; NewYTBS 88; WrDr 92, 94, 96*

Smith, Jerome
[K C and the Sunshine Band]
American. Musician
Guitarist with the Sunshine Band since 1973.
b. Jun 18, 1953 in Miami, Florida
Source: *OnThGG*

Smith, Jerry
American. Football Player
All-pro tight end, Washington, 1965-78; first athlete to admit he had AIDS.
b. Jul 19, 1943 in Oakland, California
d. Oct 15, 1986 in Silver Spring, Maryland
Source: *ConNews 87-1*

Smith, Jessie Wilcox
American. Illustrator
Known for children's classics: *Little Women, Heidi.*
b. Sep 1863 in Philadelphia, Pennsylvania
d. May 3, 1935 in Philadelphia, Pennsylvania
Source: *AuBYP 2, 3; BioIn 2, 8, 11, 12, 13; DcWomA; IlrAm A; InWom SUP; JBA 34, 51; NatCAB 26; NotAW; OxCChiL; SmATA 21; WhAm 1*

Smith, Joe
[Smith and Dale; Joseph Seltzer]
American. Comedian
Part of vaudeville team, Smith and Dale, for 73 yrs.
b. Feb 17, 1884 in New York, New York
d. Feb 22, 1981 in Englewood, New Jersey
Source: *AnObit 1981; BioIn 8, 9, 10, 12; EncVaud; FacFETw; NewYTBS 81; QDrFCA 92; WhoHol A; WhScrn 83*

Smith, Joe
American. Jazz Musician
Trumpeter with Fletcher Henderson, McKinney's Cotton Pickers, 1920s.
b. Jun 28, 1902 in Ripley, Ohio
d. Dec 2, 1937 in New York, New York
Source: *Baker 84, 92; BiDAfM; BiDAmM; BiDJaz; CmpEPM; IlEncJ; InB&W 80, 85; LegTOT; NewGrDA 86; NewGrDJ 88, 94; PenEncP; WhoJazz 72; WorAl; WorAlBi*

Smith, John
English. Colonizer
Founder, leader of Jamestown, VA colony, 1607-09; explored, advocated colonization of New England.
b. Jan 1580? in Willoughby, England
d. Jun 21, 1631 in London, England
Source: *Alli; AmAu; AmAu&B; AmBi; AmWrBE; ApCAB; Benet 87, 96; BenetAL 91; BiD&SB; BioIn 1, 2, 3, 4, 5, 6, 7, 8, 9, 10, 11, 12, 13, 14, 15, 16, 17, 18, 19, 20; CamGEL; CasWL; CnDAL; CyAL 1; DcAmAu; DcAmB; DcLB 24, 30; DcLEL; DcNaB; EncCRAm; EvLB; Expl 93; FifSWrB; HisWorL; LinLib L, S; LitC 9; LuthC 75; McGEWB; NewC; OxCAmH; OxCAmL 65, 83, 95; OxCEng 67, 85, 95; PenC AM; PeoHis; RComAH; REn; REnAL; WebAB 74, 79; WebAMB; WebE&AL; WhAm HS; WhDW; WhNaAH; WhWE; WorAl; WorAlBi*

Smith, Joseph
American. Religious Leader
Founded Mormons, 1830; murdered by non-believers.
b. Dec 23, 1805 in Sharon, Vermont
d. Jun 27, 1844 in Carthage, Illinois
Source: *Alli; AmAu&B; AmBi; AmRef&R; AmSocL; ApCAB; Benet 87, 96; BenetAL 91; BiDAmCu; BioIn 1, 3, 4, 5, 6, 8, 9, 10, 11, 12, 13, 14, 15, 16, 17, 18, 19, 20, 21; CelCen; CyAG; DcAmB; DcAmReB 1, 2; DcBiPP; DcNAA; Dis&D; Drake; EncAAH; EncAB-H 1974, 1996; EncARH; HarEnUS; HisWorL; LegTOT; LinLib L, S; LuthC 75; McGEWB; MemAm; NatCAB 7, 16; NinCLC 53; OhA&B; OxCAmH; OxCAmL 65, 83, 95; PeoHis; RAdv 14; RComAH; REn; REnAL; REnAW; TwCBDA; WebAB 74, 79; WhAm HS; WhDW; WorAl; WorAlBi*

Smith, Joseph Fielding
American. Religious Leader
10th pres., Mormon Church, pres., Council of Apostles.
b. Jul 19, 1876 in Salt Lake City, Utah
d. Jul 2, 1972 in Salt Lake City, Utah
Source: *AmAu&B; BioIn 2, 5, 8, 9, 10, 18; ConAu 37R; DcAmB S9; RelLAm 91; WhAm 5*

Smith, Joshua (Isaac)
American. Business Executive
President and CEO, MAXIMA Corp., 1978—.
b. Apr 8, 1941 in Garrard County, Kentucky
Source: *AfrAmBi 1; ConBlB 10; WhoAfA 96; WhoBlA 85, 88, 90, 92, 94*

Smith, Juane Quick-to-See
American. Artist
Merged traditional Native American abstract art with contemporary styles; had several solo exhibitions of her work.
b. 1940 in Saint Ignatius, Montana
Source: *NotNaAm*

Smith, Kate
[Kathryn Elizabeth Smith]
American. Singer
Recorded over 2,000 songs, had 19 number one hits, best known for rendition of "God Bless America."
b. May 1, 1907 in Greenville, Virginia
d. Jun 17, 1986 in Raleigh, North Carolina
Source: *AnObit 1986; Baker 92; BioNews 74; ConAu 119; ConNews 86-3; CurBio 40, 65, 86; IntMPA 82; OxCPMus; PenEncP; RadStar; SaTiSS; ThFT; WebAB 74; WhAm 9; WhoAm 80, 82, 84*

Smith, Keely
American. Singer
Pop vocalist with husband, Louis Prima, 1950s-60s.
b. Mar 9, 1932 in Norfolk, Virginia
Source: *ASCAP 66; BiDAmM; BiDJaz; BioIn 13; CmpEPM; ForYSC; InWom, SUP; LegTOT; NewGrDJ 88; PenEncP; WhoAm 74; WhoHol 92, A; WorAl; WorAlBi*

Smith, Kenneth Danforth
American. Museum Director, Author
Director of Baseball Hall of Fame, Cooperstown, NY, 1963-79; baseball writer for *NY Mirror,* 1931-63.
b. Jan 8, 1902 in Danbury, Connecticut
d. Mar 1, 1991 in Tilantire Bridge, New York
Source: *ConAu 1NR; WhoAm 74, 76, 78*

Smith, Kent
American. Actor
Films include *Games,* 1967; *Taking Tiger Mountain,* 1983.
b. Mar 19, 1907 in New York, New York
d. Apr 23, 1985 in Los Angeles, California
Source: *AnObit 1985; BiE&WWA; BioIn 10, 14, 15; FilmEn; FilmgC; ForYSC; HalFC 80, 84, 88; HolP 40; IntMPA 77, 80, 82; MovMk; NewYTBS 85; NotNAT; VarWW 85; WhoHol A; WhoHrs 80; WhoThe 72, 77, 81*

Smith, Lee
American. Author
Fiction explores life in Appalachia; wrote *The Last Day the Dogbushes Bloomed,* 1968; *Black Mountain Breakdown,* 1981.
b. Mar 17, 1937 in New York, New York
Source: *ConAu 73, 114, 119; ConLC 25, 73*

Smith, Lee (Arthur)
American. Baseball Player
Relief pitcher, Chicago Cubs, 1980-87, Boston, 1988-90; St. Louis, 1990—; led NL in saves, 1983.
b. Dec 4, 1957 in Jamestown, Louisiana
Source: *Ballpl 90; BaseReg 87, 88; BiDAmSp Sup; WhoAfA 96; WhoAm 92, 94, 95, 96, 97; WhoBlA 85, 88, 90, 92, 94; WhoE 95, 97; WhoWest 96*

Smith, Lillian
American. Author
Wrote popular novel *Strange Fruit,* 1944; banned in Boston.
b. Dec 12, 1897 in Jasper, Florida
d. Sep 28, 1966 in Atlanta, Georgia
Source: *AmAu&B; AmNov; AmWomWr; ArtclWW 2; Benet 87, 96; BenetAL 91; BioAmW; BlmGWL; CnDAL; ConAu 25R, P-2; DcAmSR; EncSoH; FacFETw; FemiCLE; FemiWr; LinLib L; LngCTC; NotAW MOD; ODwPR 79; OxCAmL 65, 83; REn; REnAL; TwCA SUP; WhAm 4; WhE&EA; WhoAmW 58, 64, 66*

Smith, Liz
[Mary Elizabeth Smith]
American. Journalist
Gossip column runs in *NY Daily News,* over 60 syndicated papers.
b. Feb 2, 1923 in Fort Worth, Texas
Source: *BiDAmNC; BioIn 15, 16; CelR 90; ConAu 65; ConTFT 9; CurBio 87; ForWC 70; HalFC 88; InWom SUP; JrnUS; LegTOT; WhoAm 86, 90, 96, 97; WhoAmW 85, 87, 95, 97; WhoWrEP 89; WorAlBi*

Smith, Loring
American. Actor
Films include *The Clown,* 1953; *Hurry Sundown,* 1967.
b. Nov 18, 1895 in Stratford, Connecticut
d. Jul 8, 1981
Source: *BiE&WWA; NotNAT; WhoHol A; WhoThe 72, 77A; WhScrn 83; WhThe*

Smith, Lowell Herbert
American. Aviator
Commanded first around the world flight, using two planes in 57 hops from Seattle, Apr-Sep 1924.
b. Oct 8, 1892 in Santa Barbara, California
d. Nov 4, 1945 in Tucson, Arizona
Source: *BioIn 3; NatCAB 37; ObitOF 79; WhAm 2*

Smith, Madeline Hamilton
Scottish. Murderer
Allegedly poisoned lover, who had blackmailed her with letters she'd written him, 1857.
b. 1835
d. Apr 12, 1928
Source: *BioIn 2, 5, 10, 11*

Smith, Maggie Natalie
English. Actor
Won Oscars for *The Prime of Miss Jean Brodie,* 1969; *California Suite,* 1978.
b. Dec 28, 1934 in Ilford, England
Source: *BiDFilm; BioIn 15, 16; ContDcW 89; ConTFT 4; CurBio 70; EncMT; FacFETw; FilmgC; HalFC 88; IntMPA 92; IntWW 74, 75, 76, 77, 78, 79, 80, 81, 82, 83, 89, 91, 93; InWom SUP; MotPP; MovMk; NewYTBE 70; NewYTBS 82, 90; OxCThe 83; PlP&P; Who 92; WhoAm 86, 90; WhoEnt 92; WhoThe 81; WhoWor 87, 91; WorAlBi*

Smith, Margaret
American. Educator, Author
Rehabilitation specialist for visually handicapped; wrote *If Blindness Strikes, Don't Strike Out,* 1984.
b. Feb 27, 1939 in Detroit, Michigan

Smith, Margaret (Madeline) Chase
American. Politician
Rep. senator from ME, 1948-72; served longer than any other woman.
b. Dec 14, 1897 in Skowhegan, Maine
d. May 29, 1995 in Skowhegan, Maine
Source: *AmPolLe; AmWomM; BiDrAC; BiDrUSC 89; BioAmW; BioIn 15, 16; ConAu 73, 148; ContDcW 89; CurBio 45, 62, 95N; EncWB; HerW 84; IntWW 83, 91; InWom SUP; NewYTBE 70, 72; NewYTBS 75; PolProf E, J, K, NF, T; WhoAm 74; WhoAmP 73, 91; WhoAmW 87; WorAlBi*

Smith, Martin Cruz
[Nick Carter; Jake Logan; Martin Quinn; Simon Quinn]
American. Author
Prolific writer of popular fiction, spy novels, westerns; wrote best-seller *Gorky Park,* 1981.
b. Nov 3, 1942 in Reading, Pennsylvania
Source: *BenetAL 91; BestSel 89-4; BioIn 12, 14, 16; ConAu 6NR, 23NR, 43NR, 85; ConLC 25; ConPopW; CrtSuMy; CurBio 90; IntAu&W 91, 93; IntWW 91, 93; NatNAL; NewYTBS 81; RfGAmL 94; ScF&FL 1, 2, 92; TwCCr&M 85, 91; WhoAm 92, 94, 95, 96, 97; WorAlBi; WorAu 1975; WrDr 86, 88, 90, 92, 94, 96*

Smith, Mary Carter
American. Folklorist
Storyteller who helped preserve African American history and culture through various media.
b. Feb 10, 1919 in Birmingham, Alabama
Source: *BioIn 21; CurBio 96; WhoAfA 96; WhoBlA 92, 94*

Smith, Mayo
[Edward Mayo Smith]
American. Baseball Manager
Appeared in 73 ML games as player; managed nine yrs. with three teams; won World Series with Detroit, 1968.
b. Jan 17, 1915 in New London, Missouri
d. Nov 24, 1977 in Boynton Beach, Florida
Source: *Ballpl 90; BaseEn 88; BioIn 11; NewYTBS 77; ObitOF 79*

Smith, Merriman
"Smitty"
American. Journalist
Chief Washington correspondent for UPI, 1941-70; won Pulitzer, 1964, for coverage of John F Kennedy assassination.
b. Feb 10, 1913 in Savannah, Georgia
d. Apr 13, 1970 in Alexandria, Virginia
Source: *AmAu&B; BiDAmJo; BioIn 8, 9, 11, 16, 19; ConAu 1R, 2NR, 29R; EncTwCJ; LegTOT; NatCAB 56; WhAm 5; WorAl; WorAlBi*

Smith, Michael John
American. Astronaut
Spacecraft pilot who died in explosion of space shuttle *Challenger.*
b. Apr 30, 1945 in Beaufort, North Carolina
d. Jan 28, 1986 in Cape Canaveral, Florida
Source: *NewYTBS 86*

Smith, Michael W
American. Singer
Album, *Somewhere Somehow* has Christian themes.

Smith, Oliver
American. Producer, Designer
Winner of eight Tonys for designs including *The Sound of Music,* 1960.
b. Feb 13, 1918 in Waupun, Wisconsin
d. Jan 23, 1994 in New York, New York
Source: *BiDD; BiE&WWA; BioIn 1, 2, 4, 6, 7, 9, 13, 15, 19, 20; CamGWoT; CelR; CnOxB; ConDes 84, 90; CurBio 61, 94N; DancEn 78; EncWT; Ent; IntDcB; IntWW 83, 89, 91, 93; MetOEnc; NewYTBS 94; NotNAT; OxCAmT 84; PlP&P; WhAm 11;*

WhoAm 74, 76, 78, 80, 82, 84, 86, 88, 90, 92, 94; WhoE 74, 79, 81, 93; WhoEnt 92; WhoGov 72, 75, 77; WhoOp 76; WhoThe 72, 77, 81; WhoWor 74, 76

Smith, Owen Guinn
American. Track Athlete
Pole vaulter; won gold medal, 1948 Olympics; set record that stood 25 yrs.
b. May 20, 1920 in McKinney, Texas
Source: *WhoTr&F 73*

Smith, Ozzie
[Osborne Earl Smith]
"Wizard of Oz"
American. Baseball Player
Shortstop with San Diego, 1977-82; St. Louis, 1982—; holds ML record for most assists by shortstop, 1980; seven-time NL All-Star; 2,000 career hit, 1992; NL record, 13 straight Gold Glove Awards.
b. Dec 26, 1954 in Mobile, Alabama
Source: *AfrAmSG; Ballpl 90; BaseReg 86, 87; BiDAmSp Sup; BioIn 11, 13, 16; LegTOT; WhoAfA 96; WhoAm 88, 90, 92, 94, 95, 96, 97; WhoBlA 85, 88, 90, 92, 94; WhoMW 90, 92, 93, 96; WhoSpor; WorAlBi*

Smith, (Charles) Page
American. Historian
Writer of historical narratives including the 8 volume *People's History of the United States,* 1976-86.
b. Sep 6, 1917 in Baltimore, Maryland
d. Aug 28, 1995 in Santa Cruz, California
Source: *AmAu&B; BioIn 14; ConAu 1R, 2NR, 149; CurBio 90, 95N; DrAS 74H, 78H, 82H; IntAu&W 91, 93; WhoAm 74; WrDr 80, 82, 84, 86, 88, 90, 92, 94, 96*

Smith, Patti
American. Singer, Poet
Hit single "Because the Night," written with Bruce Springsteen, 1978.
b. Dec 30, 1946 in Chicago, Illinois
Source: *BioIn 16; ConAu 93; ConLC 12; ConMuA 80A; CurBio 89; DcArts; DrAPF 89; EncPR&S 89; EncRk 88; EncRkSt; HarEnR 86; IlEncRk; InWom SUP; LegTOT; NewGrDA 86; NewWmR; PenEncP; RkOn 85; RolSEnR 83; WhoEnt 92; WhoRock 81; WhoRocM 82; WorAl; WorAlBi*

Smith, Paul Joseph
American. Composer
Won Oscar, 1940, for work on Walt Disney classic *Pinocchio.*
b. Oct 30, 1906 in Calumet, Michigan
d. Jan 25, 1985 in Glendale, California
Source: *ASCAP 80; BioIn 14*

Smith, Perry Edward
American. Murderer
Subject of Truman Capote's book, *In Cold Blood;* killed family of four with partner Richard Hickock, 1959; hanged after many appeals.
b. Oct 27, 1928? in Lansing, Kansas
d. Apr 14, 1965
Source: *BioIn 7; MurCaTw*

Smith, Pete
[Peter Schmidt]
American. Producer
Produced, narrated shorts for MGM, 1936-55; over 20 nominated for Oscars.
b. Sep 4, 1892 in New York, New York
d. Jan 12, 1979 in Los Angeles, California
Source: *BioIn 9, 78, 79; What 4; WhScrn 83*

Smith, Red
[Walter Wellesley Smith]
American. Journalist
Sportswriter whose column appeared in over 500 newspapers; won Pulitzer.
b. Sep 25, 1905 in Green Bay, Wisconsin
d. Jan 15, 1982 in Stamford, Connecticut
Source: *AnObit 1982; BenetAL 91; BiDAmJo; BiDAmSp OS; BioIn 1, 2, 3, 4, 5, 6, 10, 11, 12, 13, 15, 16, 17; CelR; ConAu 77; CurBio 59, 82, 82N; DcLB 29, 171; EncTwCJ; FacFETw; JrnUS; LegTOT; NewYTBS 82, 86; REnAL; WebAB 74, 79; WhAm 8; WhoAm 76, 78, 80, 82; WorAl; WorAu 1975*

Smith, Rex
American. Actor, Singer
Had hit single "You Take My Breath Away," 1981; starred in Broadway, film versions of *Pirates of Penzance,* 1980.
b. Sep 19, 1956? in Jacksonville, Florida
Source: *BioIn 12; ConTFT 7; LegTOT; RkOn 85; WhoHol 92; WhoSSW 91*

Smith, Robert C
American. Politician
Rep. senator, NH, 1990—.
b. Mar 30, 1941 in Trenton, New Jersey
Source: *AlmAP 88; BiDrUSC 89; CngDr 89; WhoAm 88; WhoAmP 87; WhoE 89*

Smith, Robert H
American. Social Reformer
Co-founder with William Griffith Wilson (Bill W) of Alcoholics Anonymous (AA).
b. Aug 8, 1879 in Saint Johnsbury, Vermont
d. Nov 16, 1950 in Akron, Ohio
Source: *WorAlBi*

Smith, Robert Lee
American. Inventor, TV Personality
Founder, Equal Relationships Institute, 1981—; host, TV series "You and Your Big Ideas," 1959-64.
b. Sep 18, 1928 in Saint Louis, Missouri
Source: *ConAu 111*

Smith, Robert Weston
"Wolfman Jack"
American. Radio Personality
Rock 'n' Roll jockey icon famous for his gravelly voice and wolf-man howls.
d. Jul 1, 1995 in Belvidere, North Carolina
Source: *BioIn 10, 21; BioNews 74*

Smith, Robyn Caroline
[Mrs. Fred Astaire]
American. Jockey
First woman jockey to win major race.
b. Aug 14, 1944 in San Francisco, California
Source: *BioIn 9, 10, 11, 12; CurBio 76; HerW 84; InWom SUP; NewYTBE 71; NewYTBS 78; WhoAm 78, 80, 82*

Smith, Roger
American. Actor
Films include *The First Time,* 1969; husband, manager of Ann-Margret.
b. Dec 18, 1932 in South Gate, California
Source: *BioIn 16; FilmgC; ForYSC; HalFC 80, 84, 88; IntMPA 75, 76, 77, 78, 79, 80, 81, 82, 84, 86, 88, 92, 94, 96; ItaFilm; LegTOT; MotPP; MovMk; WhoAm 82; WhoHol 92, A; WorAl*

Smith, Roger Bonham
American. Auto Executive
Chm., GM, 1981-90.
b. Jul 12, 1925 in Columbus, Ohio
Source: *AutoN 79; BioIn 12, 13, 16; ConAmBL; CurBio 84; Dun&B 79, 90; EncABHB 5; IntWW 91; NewYTBS 85; St&PR 84, 87, 91, 93; Ward 77; Who 82, 83, 85, 88, 90, 92, 94; WhoAm 74, 76, 78, 80, 82, 84, 86, 88, 90, 92, 94, 95, 96; WhoE 85, 86, 89; WhoFI 74, 81, 83, 85, 87, 89, 92; WhoMW 84, 86, 88, 90, 92; WhoWor 84, 87, 89, 91*

Smith, Ronnie
[K C and the Sunshine Band]
American. Musician
Trumpeter with Sunshine Band since 1973.
b. 1952 in Hialeah, Florida

Smith, Samantha
American. Student, Actor
Wrote letter to Soviet leader Andropov, 1982, visited USSR as his guest, 1983; died in plane crash.
b. Jun 29, 1972 in Manchester, Maine
d. Aug 25, 1985 in Auburn, Maine
Source: *ConAu 117; ConNews 85-3; SmATA 45N*

Smith, Sammi
American. Singer
Won best female country vocalist Grammy, 1972, for "Help Me Make It Through the Night."
b. Aug 5, 1943 in Orange, California
Source: *BgBkCoM; BioIn 14; CounME 74, 74A; EncFCWM 83; HarEnCM 87; IlEncCM; PenEncP; RkOn 74, 78*

Smith, Samuel Francis
American. Poet, Clergy
Wrote patriotic hymn, "America," 1831.
b. Oct 21, 1808 in Boston, Massachusetts
d. Nov 16, 1895 in Boston, Massachusetts
Source: *Alli, SUP; AmAu; AmAu&B; AmBi; ApCAB; BiDAmM; BiD&SB; BioIn 1, 4, 13, 16; ChhPo, S1; CyAL 2; DcAmAu; DcAmB; DcLEL; DcNAA; Drake; EvLB; HarEnUS; LinLib L; LuthC 75; NatCAB 6; OxCAmL 65, 83, 95; PoChrch; REn; TwCBDA; WebAB 74, 79; WebE&AL; WhAm HS*

Smith, Seba
[Major Jack Downing]
American. Journalist
Wrote America's first political satires on Jacksonian democracy in newspapers, magazines.
b. Sep 17, 1792 in Buckfield, Maine
d. Jul 28, 1868 in Patchogue, New York
Source: *Alli; AmAu; AmAu&B; AmBi; ApCAB; BbD; Benet 87; BenetAL 91; BiD&SB; BioIn 11, 12, 13, 15; ChhPo, S1; CnDAL; CyAL 2; DcAmAu; DcAmB; DcEnL; DcLB 1, 11; DcLEL; DcNAA; Drake; EncAHmr; EncAJ; NatCAB 8; OxCAmL 65, 83, 95; REn; REnAL; RfGAmL 87, 94; TwCBDA; WebAB 74, 79; WhAm HS*

Smith, (Robert) Sidney
American. Cartoonist
Started Andy Gump comic strip, 1917; considered first to introduce continuity to strips by continuing stories day after day.
b. Feb 13, 1877 in Bloomington, Illinois
d. Oct 20, 1935 in Harvard, Illinois
Source: *AmAu&B; DcAmB S1; DcNAA; EncACom; WhAm 1, 4; WhAmArt 85; WhAm HSA; WorECom*

Smith, Sophia
American. Philanthropist
Founded Smith College; opened, 1875.
b. Aug 27, 1796 in Hatfield, Massachusetts
d. Jun 12, 1870 in Hadley, Massachusetts
Source: *AmAu&B; ApCAB; BioAmW; BioIn 2, 10; ContDcW 89; DcAmB; IntDcWB; InWom; LibW; MorMA; NatCAB 7; NotAW; OxCAmH; TwCBDA; WhAm HS; WomFir*

Smith, Stan(ley Roger)
American. Tennis Player
Winner of over 25 US singles, doubles titles.
b. Dec 14, 1946 in Pasadena, California
Source: *BiDAmSp OS; BioIn 10, 12; BuCMET; CelR; ConAu 85; LegTOT; NewYTBE 70; WhoAm 76, 78, 80, 82, 84, 86, 88, 90, 92, 94, 95, 96, 97; WhoIntT*

Smith, Stevie
[Florence Margaret Smith]
English. Poet
Poems include "A Good Time Was Had by All," 1937; "Novel on Yellow Paper," 1936.
b. Sep 20, 1903 in Hull, England
d. Mar 7, 1971 in Ashburton, England
Source: *Au&Wr 71; CasWL; ConAu P-2; ConLC 25; ConPo 75; DcLEL; LngCTC; ModBrL S1; OxCEng 85; WorAu 1950*

Smith, Sydney
English. Clergy, Essayist
Co-founded *Edinburgh Review,* 1802; wrote *Letters of Peter Plymley,* 1807, defending Catholic emancipation.
b. Jun 6, 1771 in Woodford, England
d. Feb 22, 1845 in London, England
Source: *Alli; AtlBL; BbD; BenetAL 91; BiD&SB; BioIn 1, 3, 4, 5, 6, 7, 8, 9, 10, 11, 12, 13, 17; BritAu 19; CamGEL; CamGLE; CasWL; CelCen; DcAmC; DcBiPP; DcEnA; DcEnL; DcEuL; DcLB 107; DcLEL; DcNaB; EvLB; LinLib L, S; NewC; OxCAmL 65, 83, 95; OxCEng 67, 85, 95; PenC ENG; WebE&AL; WhDW*

Smith, Theobald
American. Pathologist
Infectious disease specialist; did important research on animals, especially hogs, cattle.
b. Jul 31, 1859 in Albany, New York
d. Dec 10, 1934 in Princeton, New Jersey
Source: *AmBi; BiDSocW; BiESc; BiHiMed; BioIn 1, 2, 3, 5, 7, 9, 13; CamDcSc; DcAmB S1; DcAmMeB 84; DcNAA; DcScB; EncAB-H 1974; InSci; LarDcSc; NatCAB 35; OxCMed 86; WebAB 74, 79; WhAm 1*

Smith, Thorne
American. Author
Humorous works include *Topper,* 1926; became famous film series, TV show.
b. 1892? in Annapolis, Maryland
d. Jun 21, 1934 in Sarasota, Florida
Source: *AmAu&B; Benet 87; BenetAL 91; CnDAL; DcLEL; DcNAA; EncAHmr; FilmgC; HalFC 80, 84, 88; LegTOT; LngCTC; OxCAmL 65, 83, 95; REn; REnAL; TwCA*

Smith, Tommie
American. Track Athlete
Sprinter; won gold medal in 200 meters, 1968 Olympics; on winner's stand with John Carlos, protested treatment of blacks in US by raising clenched fists; expelled from games.
b. Jun 5, 1944 in Clarksville, Texas
Source: *AfrAmSG; BiDAmSp OS; BioIn 7, 11; BlkOlyM; CmCal; InB&W 80; WhoAfA 96; WhoBlA 77, 80, 85, 88, 90, 92, 94; WhoTr&F 73*

Smith, Tommy
[Thomas J Smith]
Canadian. Hockey Player
Left wing, Quebec, 1919-20; Hall of Fame, 1973.
b. Sep 27, 1885 in Ottawa, Ontario, Canada
d. Aug 1, 1966
Source: *HocEn*

Smith, Tony
[Anthony Peter Smith]
American. Sculptor
Created huge minimalist sculptures: *Cigarette,* 1961; *Throwback,* 1978.
b. 1912 in Orange, New Jersey
d. Dec 26, 1980 in New York, New York
Source: *AnObit 1980; BioIn 7, 8, 9, 12, 13; BriEAA; ConArt 77, 83, 89, 96; ConAu 105; DcAmArt; DcCAA 77, 88, 94; DcCAr 81; McGDA; NewYTBS 80; OxCTwCA; OxDcArt; PhDcTCA 77; WhAm 7; WhoAm 74, 76, 78; WhoAmA 73, 76, 78, 80, 82, 84, 86, 89, 91N, 93N; WorArt 1950*

Smith, Walter Bedell
"Beetle"
American. Army Officer
CIA director, 1950-53; ambassador to USSR, 1946-49.
b. Oct 5, 1895 in Indianapolis, Indiana
d. Aug 9, 1961 in Washington, District of Columbia
Source: *BiDWWGF; BioIn 1, 2, 3, 6, 11, 16, 17, 18; ColdWar 1, 2; CurBio 44, 53, 61; DcAmB S7; DcAmDH 80, 89; DcAmMiB; DcCathB; EncCW; HarEnMi; HisDcKW; HisEWW; IndAu 1917; PolProf E, T; REnAL; WebAB 74, 79; WebAMB; WhAm 4*

Smith, Will
[DJ Jazzy Jeff & The Fresh Prince]
"The Fresh Prince"
American. Actor, Rapper
Appeared on TV's "The Fresh Prince of Bel Air," 1990-96; in *Independence Day,* 1996.
b. Sep 25, 1968 in Philadelphia, Pennsylvania
Source: *ConBlB 8; CurBio 96; IntMPA 96; LegTOT; WhoAfA 96*

Smith, Willi Donnell
American. Fashion Designer
Began Willi Wear, Ltd, 1976; won 1983 Coty award for women's fashion.
b. Feb 29, 1948 in Philadelphia, Pennsylvania
d. Apr 17, 1987 in New York, New York
Source: *ConNews 87-3; InB&W 85; WhAm 9; WhoAm 80, 82, 84, 86; WhoBlA 85; WhoE 85, 86; WhoFash; WorFshn*

Smith, William
English. Geologist
Founder of stratigraphical geology; wrote *Geological Map of England,* 1815;

first recipient of geology's Wollaston Medal, 1831.
b. Mar 23, 1769 in Churchill, England
d. Aug 28, 1839 in Northampton, England
Source: *Alli; ApCAB; AsBiEn; BbtC; BiESc; BioIn 2, 3, 7, 8, 12, 14; BritAu 19; CamDcSc; DcBiPP; DcCanB 7; DcEnL; DcNAA; DcNaB; DcScB; InSci; LarDcSc; MacDCB 78; NewCol 75; OxCCan; WhDW*

Smith, William
[William Henry Joseph Berthol Bonaparte Smith]
"Willie the Lion"
American. Jazz Musician, Songwriter
One of great "stride" pianists, active from 1920s; subject of two short films, 1900s.
b. Nov 23, 1897 in Goshen, New York
d. Apr 18, 1973 in New York, New York
Source: *ASCAP 66; Baker 84; CmpEPM; EncJzS; WhoJazz 72*

Smith, William French
American. Government Official
US attorney general under Ronald Reagan, 1981-84.
b. Aug 26, 1917 in Wilton, New Hampshire
d. Oct 29, 1990 in Los Angeles, California
Source: *AnObit 1990; BiDrUSE 89; BioIn 12, 13; CngDr 81, 83; CurBio 82, 91N; FacFETw; IntWW 81, 82, 83, 89, 91N; IntYB 82; LEduc 74; NewYTBS 80, 90; WhAm 10; Who 82, 83, 85, 88, 90, 92N; WhoAm 80, 82, 84, 86, 88; WhoAmL 78, 79, 83, 87; WhoAmP 73, 75, 77, 79, 81, 83, 85, 87, 89; WhoBlA 90; WhoE 81, 83, 85; WhoGov 75, 77; WhoWest 74, 76, 78, 80; WhoWor 80, 82, 84, 87, 89*

Smith, William Jay
American. Children's Author, Poet
Wrote *The Tin Can and Other Poems,* 1966; honored for poetry, translations.
b. Apr 22, 1918 in Winnfield, Louisiana
Source: *AuBYP 2S, 3; BenetAL 91; BioIn 6, 8, 9, 10, 11, 12, 17, 19; BkCL; ChhPo, S1, S2, S3; ConAu 5R, 44NR; ConLC 6; ConPo 70, 75, 80, 85, 91, 96; CurBio 74; DcLB 5; DcLEL 1940; DrAP 75; DrAPF 91; DrAS 74E, 78E; FifBJA; IntAu&W 77; IntWWP 77; MajAI; OxCAmL 83, 95; OxCTwCP; PenC AM; SmATA 2, 22AS, 68; TwCChW 78, 83, 89, 95; WhoAm 74, 76, 78, 80, 82, 84, 86, 88, 90, 92, 94, 95, 96, 97; WhoUSWr 88; WhoWrEP 89, 92, 95; WorAu 1950; WrDr 76, 80, 82, 84, 86, 88, 90, 92, 94, 96*

Smith Brothers
[Andrew Smith; William Smith]
English. Manufacturers
First to market cough drops in prepacked boxes, 1872.
Source: *Alli, SUP; AntBDN N; ArtsEM; BbtC; BiAUS; BiD&SB; BiDBrA; BiDLA, SUP; BiDrAC; BiDRP&D; BiDrUSC 89; BioIn 3, 9, 17, 18; BlmGEL; CabMA; CasWL; Chambr 1, 3; DcBiPP; DcCanB 5; DcNaB; DcNiCA; DcVicP, 2; Drake; Entr; FolkA 87; IlDcG; IntMPA 82, 84, 86; LElec; MacDCB 78; MedHR; NegAl 83, 89; NewGrDM 80; NewYHSD; NewYTBE 70; NewYTBS 93; OxCCanL; OxCShps; OxCThe 67, 83; PeoHis; PoIre; ScF&FL 92; WhAm HS; WhE&EA; WhoAmM 83; WhoHol 92, A; WhoReal 83; WhoRocM 82; WhoScEu 91-1*

Smitherman, Geneva
American. Educator, Author
Linguist who specializes in black language; author, *Black Language and Culture,* 1975.
b. Dec 10, 1940 in Brownsville, Tennessee
Source: *BlkAWP; BlkWrNE; ConAu 130; DrAS 74E, 78F, 82F; InB&W 80, 85; LEduc 74; WhoBlA 75, 77, 80, 85, 92; WrDr 94, 96*

Smithers, Jan
American. Actor
Played Bailey on TV series "WKRP in Cincinnati," 1978-82.
b. Jul 3, 1949 in North Hollywood, California
Source: *BioIn 15; ConTFT 7; LegTOT; VarWW 85; WhoHol 92, A*

Smiths, The
English. Music Group
Rock band formed in 1982 in Manchester, England; dissoved in 1987.
Source: *BioIn 17; ConMus 3; DcArts; EncRk 88; EncRkSt; PenEncP*

Smithson, Harriet Constance
Irish. Actor
Played Shakespearean roles to delighted Parisian audiences, 1827-28.
b. Mar 18, 1800 in Ennis, Ireland
d. Mar 3, 1854
Source: *BioIn 5, 10, 11, 13; CamGWoT; CnThe; DcIrB 78, 88; DcNaB; InWom; OxCThe 67, 83*

Smithson, James (Louis Macie)
American. Scientist
Left estate money for founding of Smithsonian Institution, 1826.
b. 1765 in Paris, France
d. Jun 27, 1829 in Genoa, Italy
Source: *Alli; ApCAB; BiESc; BiInAmS; BioIn 1, 6, 7, 10, 13; DcNaB; DcScB; Drake; EncAAH; InSci; LarDcSc; TwCBDA; WhAm HS; WorAl; WorAlBi*

Smits, Jimmy
American. Actor
Starred in TV drama "LA Law," 1986-91; currently on "NYPD Blue," 1994—; won supporting actor Emmy, 1990.
b. Jul 9, 1955 in New York, New York
Source: *BioIn 15; ConTFT 6, 15; DcHiB; HolBB; IntMPA 92, 94, 96; LegTOT; WhoAm 95, 96, 97; WhoEnt 92; WhoHisp 91, 92, 94; WhoHol 92; WorAlBi*

Smohalla
American. Religious Leader
Responsible for revitalizing the Washani religion of the Pacific Northwest.
b. 1815? in Washington
d. 1895
Source: *AmBi; BioIn 11, 21; DcAmB; EncNAR; EncNoAI; NotNaAm; RelLAm 91; WebAB 74, 79; WhAm 4, HSA; WhNaAH*

Smokey Robinson and the Miracles
[Pete Moore; Claudette Rogers Robinson; William "Smokey" Robinson; Bobby Rogers; Ronnie White]
American. Music Group
All-Detroit group, formed 1957; hit singles "I Second That Emotion," 1965; "The Tears of a Clown," 1970.
Source: *InB&W 85A; NewYTBS 95; RolSEnR 83; WhoAmP 81; WhoRocM 82*

Smollett, Tobias George
"Smelfungus"
Scottish. Author, Physician, Translator
Novels include *Roderick Random,* 1748; *Humphrey Clinker,* 1770.
b. Mar 1721 in Dalquhurn, Scotland
d. Sep 17, 1771 in Monte Nero, Italy
Source: *Alli; AtlBL; BbD; Benet 96; BiD&SB; BiHiMed; BioIn 1, 2, 3, 5, 7, 8, 9, 10, 11, 12, 14, 15, 17, 18; BlkwCE; BlmGEL; BritAu; CamGEL; CasWL; Chambr 2; ChhPo; CrtT 2; CyWA 58; DcArts; DcBiA; DcBiPP; DcEnA; DcEnL; DcEuL; DcLEL; Dis&D; EncEnl; EvLB; LinLib S; LngCEL; McGEWB; MouLC 2; NewC; NotNAT B; OxCEng 67, 85, 95; OxCMed 86; OxCShps; PenC ENG; RAdv 1, 14, 13-1; REn; WebE&AL; WorAl*

Smoltz, John
American. Baseball Player
Pitcher, Atlanta Braves, 1988—; All Star, 1989, 1992-93; Cy Young award winner, 1996.
b. May 15, 1967 in Warren, Michigan
Source: *Ballpl 90*

Smoot, George
[George Fitzgerald Smoot, III]
American. Physicist
Studied microwave radiation, the residual heat, of the big bang, resulting in a better understanding of the early days of the universe.
b. Feb 20, 1945 in Yukon, Florida
Source: *AmMWSc 76P, 79, 82, 86, 89, 92, 95; CurBio 94; WhoAm 92, 94, 95, 96, 97; WhoScEn 94, 96*

Smothers, Dick
[The Smothers Brothers; Richard Smothers]
American. Comedian, Singer
Starred with brother Tommy in 1960s TV series, in Broadway play *I Love My Wife,* 1978-79.
b. Nov 20, 1938 in New York, New York
Source: *BiDAmM; BioIn 7, 16; ConTFT 3; CurBio 68; HalFC 84; IntMPA 92; NewYTBS 76; WhoAm 86, 90; WhoHol A; WorAl; WorAlBi*

Smothers, Tommy
[The Smothers Brothers; Thomas Bolyn Smothers, III]
American. Comedian, Singer
b. Feb 2, 1937 in New York, New York
Source: *BioIn 16; ConTFT 3; CurBio 68; EncAFC; HalFC 88; IntMPA 92; LegTOT; WhoAm 74, 90; WhoEnt 92; WhoHol A; WorAlBi*

Smucker, Jerome
American. Manufacturer
In 1915 apple butter was main product in his preserves co; jellies, jams added later.
b. 1858
d. 1948
Source: *Entr*

Smuin, Michael
American. Choreographer
Won Tony for musical revival *Anything Goes,* 1988.
b. Oct 13, 1938 in Missoula, Montana
Source: *BiDD; BioIn 10, 11, 13, 16; CnOxB; ConTFT 9; CurBio 84; WhoAm 80, 82, 84, 92, 94, 95, 96, 97; WhoEnt 92A; WhoWest 82*

Smuts, Jan Christian
South African. Soldier, Statesman
Commander of British forces in Africa during WW I; prime minister of S Africa, 1919-24, 1939-48.
b. May 24, 1870 in Cape Town, South Africa
d. Sep 11, 1950 in Irene, South Africa
Source: *Benet 87, 96; BioIn 2, 3, 4, 5, 6, 7, 8, 9, 10, 11, 12; Chambr 3; CurBio 41, 50; DcNaB 1941; DcTwHis; EncSoA; GrBr; LngCTC; McGEWB; NamesHP; OxCEng 67; REn; WhAm 3*

Smyslov, Vasili Vasil'evich
Russian. Chess Player
Held world chess championships, 1957-58.
b. Mar 23, 1921 in Moscow, Union of Soviet Socialist Republics
Source: *BiDSovU; BioIn 8, 15; CurBio 67; OxCChes 84*

Smyth, Ethel, Dame
English. Composer
Composed *Mass in D Major,* 1893; memoir *Impressions That Remained, As Time Went On,* 1936.
b. 1858
d. May 1944
Source: *ArtclWW 2; Baker 78, 84; CmOp; ContDcW 89; DcCom&M 79; FemiCLE; GayLesB; IntDcOp; IntDcWB; LngCTC; MetOEnc; MusMk; NewAmDM; NewEOp 71; NewGrDM 80; NewOxM; OxDcOp; PenDiMP A; RadHan*

Smythe, Conn
[Constantine Falkland Kerry Smythe]
Canadian. Hockey Executive
One of original organizers of NY Rangers; first owner, Toronto Maple Leafs, 1926-61; built Maple Leaf Gardens, 1931; Conn Smythe Trophy, NHL Smythe Division named for him; Hall of Fame, 1958.
b. Feb 1, 1895 in Toronto, Ontario, Canada
d. Nov 18, 1980 in Toronto, Ontario, Canada
Source: *BioIn 1, 2, 10, 12; CanWW 70; ColCR; NewYTBS 80; St&PR 75; WhoHcky 73*

Smythe, Reginald
English. Cartoonist
Created "Andy Capp," daily comic strip for London's *Daily Mirror,* 1956—.
b. Oct 7, 1917 in Hartlepool, England
Source: *AuNews 1; Who 92; WhoAm 86*

Snake, Reuben, Jr.
American. Native American Leader, Religious Leader
Chairman of the American Indian Movement, 1972-75; chairman of the Winnebago Tribe, 1975-ca. 1987.
b. 1937 in Winnebago, Nebraska
d. 1993 in Nebraska
Source: *BioIn 21; EncNAB; NotNaAm*

Snead, Sam(uel Jackson)
"Slammin' Sammy"
American. Golfer
Turned pro, 1934; has over 100 career wins, including PGA three times; wrote several books on golf: *Golf Begins at Forty,* 1978.
b. May 27, 1912 in Hot Springs, Virginia
Source: *BiDAmSp OS; BioIn 1, 2, 3, 5, 6, 9, 10, 11, 12, 13; CelR; ConAu 114; CurBio 49; FacFETw; IntWW 81, 82, 83, 89, 91, 93; LegTOT; NewYTBE 72; NewYTBS 74, 75, 81, 82; WebAB 74, 79; WhoAm 76, 78, 80, 82, 84, 86, 88, 90, 92, 94, 95, 96, 97; WhoGolf; WorAl; WorAlBi*

Sneider, Vernon John
American. Author
Wrote *Teahouse of the August Moon,* 1951; became play, film.
b. Oct 6, 1916 in Monroe, Michigan
d. May 1, 1981 in Monroe, Michigan
Source: *BioIn 4; ConAu 5R, 13NR, 103; CurBio 56, 81; IntAu&W 77; NewYTBS 81*

Snell, George D(avis)
American. Scientist
Research on immune system greatly enhanced organ transplants; shared Nobel Prize, 1980.
b. Dec 19, 1903 in Bradford, Massachusetts
d. Jun 6, 1996 in Bar Harbor, Maine
Source: *AmMWSc 73P, 76P, 79, 82, 86, 89, 92, 95; BiESc; BioIn 12, 14, 15, 20; BlueB 76; ConAu 106, 152; CurBio 86, 96N; IntWW 74, 75, 76, 77, 78, 79, 80, 81, 82, 83, 89, 91, 93; LarDcSc; McGMS 80; NewYTBS 80; NobelP; NotTwCS; WhAm 11; Who 82, 83, 85, 88, 90, 92, 94; WhoAm 74, 76, 78, 80, 82, 84, 86, 88, 90, 92, 94, 95, 96; WhoE 81, 83, 85, 86, 89, 91, 93, 95; WhoFrS 84; WhoNob, 90, 95; WhoScEn 94, 96; WhoWor 78, 82, 84, 87, 89, 91, 93, 95, 96; WorAlBi*

Snell, Peter George
New Zealander. Track Athlete
Set five middle-distance records, 1962, including the mile.
b. Dec 17, 1938 in Opunake, New Zealand
Source: *CurBio 62; WhoTr&F 73*

Snelling, Richard
American. Politician
Rep. governor of VT, 1977-85; 1990-91.
b. Feb 18, 1927 in Allentown, Pennsylvania
d. Mar 13, 1991
Source: *PolsAm 84; WhoAm 88; WhoAmP 87; WhoE 85; WhoWor 84*

Snepp, Frank Warren, III
American. Government Official, Author
With CIA, 1968-76; in Saigon during S Vietnam's fall, 1975; wrote *Decent Interval,* 1977.
b. May 3, 1943? in Kinston, North Carolina
Source: *BioIn 11, 13; ConAu 105*

Sneva, Tom
[Thomas Edsol Sneva]
American. Auto Racer
Won Indianapolis 500, 1983.
b. Jun 1, 1948 in Spokane, Washington
Source: *BiDAmSp OS; WhoAm 78, 80, 82, 84, 86, 88, 92, 94; WhoWest 94*

Snider, Dee
[Twisted Sister; Daniel Dee Snider]
American. Singer, Composer
Lead singer, Twisted Sister, 1976—; composes most of group's original songs.
b. Mar 15, 1955 in Massapequa, New York
Source: *BioIn 15; ConNews 86-1; RkOn 85*

Snider, Duke
[Edwin Donald Snider]
"The Silver Fox"
American. Baseball Player
Outfielder, 1947-64, mostly with Brooklyn/LA; led NL in home runs, RBIs once; Hall of Fame, 1980.
b. Sep 19, 1926 in Los Angeles, California
Source: *Ballpl 90; BiDAmSp BB; BioIn 3, 4, 5, 6, 7, 8, 9, 10, 14, 15, 16; CmCal; CurBio 56; FacFETw; LegTOT; WhoProB 73; WhoSpor*

Snider, Paul
Canadian. Murderer
Husband of Dorothy Stratten; killed wife, himself in lover's quarrel.
b. 1951?
d. Aug 14, 1980 in Los Angeles, California

Snipes, Wesley
American. Actor
Films include *Jungle Fever,* 1991; *White Men Can't Jump,* 1992.
b. Jul 31, 1962 in Orlando, Florida
Source: *AfrAmAl 6; ConBlB 3; CurBio 93; DcTwCCu 5; IntMPA 92, 94, 96; LegTOT; News 93-1; WhoAfA 96; WhoBlA 92, 94; WhoHol 92*

Snively, William Daniel, Jr.
American. Physician, Author
Books on medicine include *Sea Within,* 1960.
b. Feb 9, 1911 in Rock Island, Illinois
Source: *AmMWSc 73P, 76P, 79; BiDrACP 79; BioIn 8; IndAu 1967; WhoAm 74, 76, 78, 80, 82, 84, 86, 88, 90, 92; WhoWor 74, 82*

Snodgrass, W(illiam) D(eWitt)
[S S Gardens]
American. Poet
Won Pulitzer for *Heart's Needle,* 1959.
b. Jan 5, 1926 in Wilkinsburg, Pennsylvania
Source: *BenetAL 91; BioIn 5, 6, 10, 11, 12, 16; BlueB 76; CamGLE; CamHAL; CasWL; ChhPo, S1; ClDMEL 47; ConAu 1R, 36NR; ConLC 18; ConPo 85, 91, 96; CroCAP; CurBio 60; DcLEL 1940; DcLP 87A; IntAu&W 77, 82, 91; IntWW 74, 75, 76, 77, 78, 79, 80, 81, 82, 83, 89, 91, 93; IntWWP 77, 82; MajTwCW; MichAu 80; ModAL S1, S2; OxCAmL 83, 95; PenC AM; RAdv 14, 13-1; REn; REnAL; RfGAmL 87, 94; WebE&AL; WhoAm 74, 76, 78, 80, 82, 90; WhoTwCL; WhoUSWr 88; WhoWrEP 89; WorAl; WorAlBi; WorAu 1950; WrDr 86, 90, 94, 96*

Snodgress, Carrie
American. Actor
1970 Oscar nominee for *Diary of a Mad Housewife.*
b. Oct 27, 1946 in Chicago, Illinois
Source: *CelR; ConTFT 5; FilmEn; HalFC 80, 84, 88; IntMPA 82, 92; InWom SUP; LegTOT; MovMk; NewYTBE 70; WhoHol A; WorAl*

Snoop Doggy Dogg
[Calvin Broadus]
American. Rapper
Debut album *Doggystyle,* 1993.
b. 1971? in Long Beach, California
Source: *EncRkSt*

Snorri, Sturluson
Icelandic. Historian
Best known for saga *Heimskringla,* which tells history of Norway to 1177.
b. 1178
d. 1241
Source: *NewCol 75*

Snow, C(harles) P(ercy), Sir
English. Scientist, Author
His series of 11 novels, *Strangers and Brothers,* depicts stresses of contemporary British life.
b. Oct 15, 1905 in Leicester, England
d. Jul 1, 1980 in London, England
Source: *Au&Wr 71; AuSpks; Benet 96; BioIn 3, 4, 5, 12, 13, 14, 15, 17, 18; CasWL; ConAu 5R, 101; ConLC 1, 4, 6, 9, 13; ConNov 72, 76; CurBio 54, 61, 80; DcArts; DcLEL; DcNaB 1971; DcScB S2; EncMys; EncSF 93; EncWL 3; EvLB; GrBr; GrWrEL N; InSci; IntAu&W 76, 77; LinLib L, S; LngCEL; LngCTC; McGEWB; ModBrL, S1; NewC; NewCBEL; Novels; OxCEng 67, 95; PenC ENG; RAdv 1, 13-1, 13-5; REn; RGTwCWr; ScF&FL 1, 2; TwCA SUP; TwCWr; WebE&AL; WhE&EA; WhoTwCL; WorAl; WrDr 76, 80*

Snow, Carmel White
American. Fashion Editor
Edited *Harper's Bazaar,* 1932-57; promoted Parisian designers.
b. Aug 21, 1887? in Dublin, Ireland
d. May 7, 1961 in New York, New York
Source: *DcAmB S7; WhAm 4; WorFshn*

Snow, Clyde Collins
American. Scientist
Created the field of forensic anthropology.
b. Jan 7, 1928 in Fort Worth, Texas
Source: *AmMWSc 73P, 76P, 79, 82, 86, 89, 92, 95; FifIDA; WhoScEn 94; WhoSSW 95*

Snow, Don
Kenyan. Singer, Musician
Keyboardist, vocalist with Squeeze, 1982.
b. Jan 13, 1957, British East Africa
Source: *WhoRocM 82*

Snow, Dorothea Johnston
American. Children's Author
Wrote *Sequoyah: Young Cherokee Guide,* 1960; *Tomahawk Claim,* 1968.
b. Apr 7, 1909 in McMinnville, Tennessee
Source: *ConAu 1R, 3NR, 27NR; SmATA 9*

Snow, Edgar Parks
American. Journalist
Wrote of communism in China: *Red Star Over China,* 1937; *The Other Side of the River,* 1962.
b. Jul 19, 1905 in Kansas City, Missouri
d. Feb 15, 1972 in Eysins, Switzerland
Source: *AmAu&B; Au&Wr 71; BenetAL 91; ConAu 33R, 38NR, 81; CurBio 41, 72; JrnUS; REn; REnAL; TwCA, SUP; WhAm 5*

Snow, Hank
[Clarence Eugene Snow]
"The Singing Ranger"
American. Singer
Country music star, popular, 1950s; wrote hit "I'm Movin' On."
b. May 9, 1914 in Liverpool, Nova Scotia, Canada
Source: *Baker 84, 92; BgBkCoM; BiDAmM; BioIn 10, 12, 14, 15, 20; CanWW 31, 83, 89; CmpEPM; CounME 74, 74A; EncFCWM 69, 83; EncRk 88; HarEnCM 87; IlEncCM; LegTOT; NewAmDM; NewGrDA 86; OnThGG; OxCPMus; PenEncP; WhoAm 76, 78, 80, 82, 84; WorAl; WorAlBi*

Snow, Phoebe Laub
American. Singer
Albums include *Never Letting Go,* 1977; *Rock Away,* 1980.
b. Jul 17, 1952 in New York, New York
Source: *BiDJaz; BioIn 10, 13, 16; ConMus 4; EncJzS; EncPR&S 89; EncRk 88; IlEncRk; InWom SUP; NewYTBS 76; PenEncP; WhoAm 86; WhoRocM 82*

Snowe, Olympia J(ean)
American. Politician
Rep. congresswoman from ME, 1979-95; Senator, 1995—.
b. Feb 21, 1947 in Augusta, Maine
Source: *BiDrUSC 89; BioIn 12, 13; CurBio 95; WhoAmP 75, 77, 79, 81, 83, 85, 87, 89, 91, 93, 95; WhoE 79, 81, 83, 85, 86; WhoWomW 91*

Snyder, Gary Sherman
American. Poet
Won Pulitzer, 1975, for *Turtle Island.*
b. May 8, 1930 in San Francisco, California
Source: *AmAu&B; CasWL; ConAu 17R; ConLC 5; ConPo 85; CroCAP; CurBio 78; DrAP 75; ModAL S1; OxCAmL 83; OxCEng 85; PenC AM; REn; REnAL; WhoAm 86, 90; WhoUSWr 88; WhoWrEP 89; WorAu 1950; WrDr 86*

Snyder, Jimmy the Greek
[James Snyder; Demetrius George Synodinos]
American. Journalist, Sportscaster
Former pro gambler; analyst for CBS Sports, fired, 1988, for controversial racial statements.
b. Sep 9, 1919 in Steubenville, Ohio
d. Apr 21, 1996 in Las Vegas, Nevada
Source: *BioIn 9, 10, 11, 12; NewYTBS 88; WhoAm 76, 80, 82, 86; WhoTelC*

Snyder, John Wesley
American. Banker, Government Official
Influential Truman adviser who was secretary of Treasury, 1946-53; helped design reconstruction programs after WW II.
b. Jun 21, 1895 in Jonesboro, Arkansas
d. Oct 9, 1985 in Seabrook Is., South Carolina
Source: *BiDrUSE 71, 89; BioIn 3, 9, 10, 11; BlueB 76; CurBio 45, 86; IntWW 74, 75, 76, 77, 78, 79, 80, 81, 82, 83; IntYB 78, 79, 80, 81; St&PR 75; WhAm 9; Who 74, 82, 83, 85; WhoAm 74, 76, 78, 80, 82, 84; WhoAmP 73, 75, 77, 79*

Snyder, Mitch
American. Political Activist
Active with Community for Creative Non-Violence since 1973, on behalf of homeless people; apparent suicide victim.
b. Aug 14, 1943 in New York, New York
d. Jul 5, 1990 in Washington, District of Columbia
Source: *AnObit 1990; BioIn 16; ConHero 1; HeroCon; News 91, 91-1; NewYTBS 90; WhAm 10; WhoAm 88*

Snyder, Richard Elliot
American. Publisher
Chairman of Simon & Schuster, 1975-94; chairman and CEO, Golden Books Family Entertainment, Inc., 1996—.
b. Apr 6, 1933 in New York, New York
Source: *BioIn 12; St&PR 84, 87, 91; WhoAm 76, 78, 80, 82, 84, 86, 88, 90, 92, 94; WhoE 74, 75, 77, 89, 91; WhoFI 79, 81, 87, 92, 94; WorAlBi*

Snyder, Solomon H(albert)
American. Scientist
Identified, with Candace Pert, opiate receptors in the brain, 1973.
b. Dec 26, 1938 in Washington, District of Columbia
Source: *AmMWSc 73P, 76P, 79, 82, 86, 89, 92, 95; BiDrAPA 77, 89; BiESc; BioIn 11, 13, 17; CamDcSc; ConAu 14NR, 37R; CurBio 96; LarDcSc; WhoAm 74, 76, 78, 80, 82, 84, 86, 88, 90, 92, 94, 95, 96, 97; WhoE 74; WhoMedH; WhoScEn 94, 96*

Snyder, Tom
American. Broadcast Journalist, TV Personality
Best known as host of NBC latenight interview show "Tomorrow," 1973-81; host of "Late Late Show with Tom Snyder," 1994—.
b. May 12, 1936 in Milwaukee, Wisconsin
Source: *BioIn 10, 11, 12, 13; BkPepl; ConAu 109, 121; CurBio 80; EncAJ; EncTwCJ; IntMPA 77, 78, 79, 80, 81, 82, 84, 86, 88, 92, 94, 96; LegTOT; LesBEnT 92; NewYTET; VarWW 85; WhoAm 78, 80, 82; WhoTelC*

Soames, Christopher
[Baron of Fletching; Arthur Christopher John Soames]
English. Government Official
Governor of S Rhodesia, 1979-80; presided over its transition into independent Zimbabwe; son-in-law of Winston Churchill.
b. Oct 12, 1920 in Penn, England
d. Sep 16, 1987 in London, England
Source: *BioIn 5, 10, 12, 15; BlueB 76; CurBio 81, 87, 87N; IntWW 74, 75, 76, 77, 79; IntYB 78; NewYTBS 79, 87; OxCLaw; Who 74, 85; WhoWor 74, 76, 78*

Soane, John, Sir
English. Architect, Art Collector
Best-known works include Bank of England, 1788; Dulwich College Picture Gallery, 1811.
b. Sep 10, 1753 in Whitchurch, England
d. Jan 20, 1837 in London, England
Source: *AtlBL; BiDBrA; BioIn 1, 2, 3, 4, 6, 9, 11, 13, 14, 15, 16, 17; DcArts; DcBiPP; DcD&D; DcNaB; EncMA; IntDcAr; MacEA; McGDA; McGEWB; NewCol 75; OxCArt; OxCEng 85, 95; WebBD 83; WhDW; WhoArch*

Soares, Mario Alberto Nobre Lopes
Portuguese. Political Leader
First civilian president of Portugal in 60 yrs., 1986-96.
b. Dec 7, 1924 in Lisbon, Portugal
Source: *CurBio 75; IntWW 76, 77, 78, 79, 80, 81, 82, 83, 89, 91, 93; NewYTBS 76, 86; Who 92, 94; WhoWor 78, 80, 82, 84, 87, 89, 91, 93, 95, 96, 97; WorAlBi*

Sobchak, Anatoly Aleksandrovich
Russian. Politician
Mayor, St. Petersburg, Russia, 1991—.
b. 1937 in Chita, Union of Soviet Socialist Republics
Source: *CurBio 92; IntWW 91*

Sobell, Morton
American. Spy
Found guilty with Julius, Ethel Rosenberg of conspiracy to sell nuclear secrets, 1951.
b. Apr 11, 1917 in New York, New York
Source: *BioIn 2, 3, 4, 5, 6, 7, 8, 11; ConAu 53; EncCW; PolProf E, T; WrDr 76, 80, 82, 84*

Sobhuza II
"The Lion of Swaziland"
Swazi. Ruler
World's longest reigning monarch, 1921-82; estimated to have had nearly 100 wives, 500 children.
b. Jul 22, 1899 in Mbabane, Swaziland
d. Aug 21, 1982 in Mbabane, Swaziland
Source: *AfSS 79; AnObit 1982; CurBio 82; IntWW 78; NewCol 75; NewYTBS 82; WhoGov 72; WhoWor 78*

Sobieski, Carol
American. Writer
TV shows include "Peyton Place," 1964-69; films include *The Toy, Annie,* 19 82.
b. Mar 16, 1939 in Chicago, Illinois
Source: *BioIn 17; ConAu 124, 129, 132; ConTFT 1, 9; NewYTBS 90; VarWW 85*

Sobieski, John, III
Polish. Ruler
King of Poland, 1674-96; later years unsuccessful because of poor political conditions.
b. Aug 17, 1624 in Lvov, Poland
d. Jun 17, 1696 in Wilanow, Poland
Source: *McGEWB; WebBD 83*

Sobol, Louis
American. Journalist, Author
Manhattan columnist for *NY Journal-American,* King Features Syndicate.
b. Aug 10, 1896 in New Haven, Connecticut
d. Jan 19, 1948
Source: *AmAu&B; BioIn 1, 8, 14; ConAu 118, P-2; IntMPA 75, 76, 77, 78, 79, 80, 81, 82, 84, 86; WhAm 2, 9; WhE&EA*

Sobrero, Ascanio
Italian. Chemist
Discovered nitroglycerine, 1847.
b. Oct 12, 1812 in Casale, Italy
d. May 26, 1888 in Turin, Italy
Source: *AsBiEn; BiESc; InSci; LarDcSc*

Soby, James Thrall
American. Critic, Author
Contended that modern art could only be appreciated through knowledge of art of the past.
b. Dec 14, 1906 in Hartford, Connecticut
d. Jan 29, 1979 in Norwalk, Connecticut
Source: *AmAu&B; BioIn 3, 4, 5, 6, 11; ConAu 103; REnAL; TwCA SUP; WhAm 7; WhoAm 74, 76, 78; WhoAmA 73, 76, 78, 80, 80N, 82N, 84N, 86N, 89N, 91N, 93N*

Socinus, Faustus
Theologian
His teachings led to the development of Unitarianism.
b. Dec 5, 1539 in Siena, Italy
d. Mar 3, 1604 in Luclawice, Poland
Source: *BioIn 12*

Sockman, Ralph W
American. Religious Leader
Popular NYC pastor, 1916-61; broadcast weekly sermons for 35 yrs.
b. Oct 1, 1889 in Mount Vernon, Ohio
d. Aug 29, 1970 in New York, New York
Source: *AmAu&B; ConAu 5R, 89; CurBio 70; NatCAB 55; OhA&B; WhAm 5; WhNAA*

Socrates
Greek. Philosopher
Viewed philosophy as necessary pursuit of all intelligent men; teacher of Plato.
b. 470?BC in Athens, Greece
d. 399?BC in Athens, Greece
Source: *AsBiEn; AtlBL; BbD; Benet 96; BiD&SB; BiDPsy; BioIn 1, 2, 3, 4, 5, 6, 7, 8, 9, 10, 11, 12, 13; BlmGEL; CasWL; CyWA 58; EncEth; LegTOT; LngCEL; LuthC 75; NamesHP; NewC; OxCEng 67; OxCPhil; PenC CL; PlP&P; RComWL; REn; WhDW; WorAl; WorAlBi; WrPh P*

Soddy, Frederick
English. Chemist
Won Nobel Prize, 1921, for work on the origin of isotopes.
b. Sep 2, 1877 in Eastbourne, England
d. Sep 22, 1956 in Brighton, England
Source: *AsBiEn; BiESc; BioIn 3, 4, 5, 6, 12, 14, 15, 19, 20; CamDcSc; DcNaB 1951; DcScB; GrBr; InSci; LarDcSc; LinLib L, S; LngCTC; McGEWB; NobelP; NotTwCS; ObitT 1951; WhAm 3; WhDW; WhE&EA; WhoNob, 90, 95; WorAl; WorAlBi; WorScD*

Soderbergh, Steven
American. Filmmaker
Wrote, edited, directed *Sex, Lies, and Videotape,* winner of several awards, 1989 Cannes Film Festival.
b. 1963 in Georgia
Source: *BiDFilm 94; BioIn 16; CelR 90; ConTFT 11; IntMPA 96; IntWW 91, 93; LegTOT; MiSFD 9; NewYTBS 91; WhoAm 90; WhoEnt 92*

Soderblom, Nathan
Swedish. Theologian
Won Nobel Peace Prize, 1930, "for promotion of int'l understanding."
b. Jan 15, 1866 in Trono, Sweden
d. Jul 12, 1931 in Uppsala, Sweden
Source: *BiDInt; BioIn 1, 2, 6, 7, 8, 9, 11, 12, 15, 16; DcEcMov; FacFETw; LuthC 75; McGEWB; NobelP; WhE&EA; WhoLA; WhoNob, 90, 95*

Soderman, Danuta
"Queen of Christian Broadcasting"
American. TV Personality
Co-host of Christian Broadcasting Company's "700 Club," 1985—.
Source: *BioIn 14; PrimTiR*

Sodero, Cesare
Italian. Conductor
Metropolitan Opera conductor who directed grand opera, symphony performances on radio.
b. Aug 2, 1886 in Naples, Italy
d. Dec 16, 1947 in New York, New York
Source: *ASCAP 66, 80; Baker 78, 84, 92; BiDAmM; BioIn 1, 3; ConAmC 76A, 82; CurBio 43, 48; MetOEnc; NatCAB 38; NewEOp 71; RadStar*

Soderstrom, Elisabeth Anna
Swedish. Opera Singer
Soprano, who is also versatile actress known for more than 50 operatic roles in ten languages.
b. May 7, 1927 in Stockholm, Sweden
Source: *CurBio 85; IntWW 74, 75, 76, 77, 78, 79, 80, 81, 82, 83, 89, 91, 93; IntWWM 77, 85; InWom SUP; NewAmDM; PenDiMP; WhoAmM 83; WhoMus 72; WhoOp 76*

Soeharto
Indonesian. Political Leader
Pres., Indonesia, 1967—.
b. Jun 8, 1921 in Java, Indonesia
Source: *BioIn 14, 15, 17, 18, 19; CurBio 92; IntYB 78, 79, 80, 81, 82; Who 90, 92, 94; WhoAsAP 91; WhoWor 78, 80, 82, 84, 87, 89, 91, 93, 95, 96, 97*

Soft Cell
[Marc Almond; Dave Ball]
English. Music Group
Formed 1979; hit single "Tainted Love," 1982, was on charts for 43 straight weeks.
Source: *EncRk 88; EncRkSt; HarEnR 86; RkOn 85; WhsNW 85*

Soft Machine
[Roy Babbington; Elton Dean; Hugh Hopper; Phil Howard; John Marshall; Mike Ratledge]
English. Music Group
Jazz sounding group; albums include *The Land of Cockayne,* 1981.
Source: *Alli, SUP; BiDJaz A; BioIn 9, 16, 17; CabMA; ConMuA 80A; DcVicP, 2; Dun&B 86, 88; EncRk 88; HarEnR 86; IlEncRk; MnBBF; NewCBEL; NewGrDJ 88, 94; NewYTBS 80; OxCChiL; PenEncP; PeoHis; PoIre; RolSEnR 83; Who 92, 94; WhoAm 90, 92, 94; WhoAmP 93, 95; WhoArt 80, 82, 84, 96; WhoE 97; WhoRock 81; WhoRocM 82; WhoSSW 88, 91, 93*

Soglow, Otto
American. Cartoonist
Created "Little King" comic strip, 1934.
b. Dec 23, 1900 in New York, New York
d. Apr 3, 1975 in New York, New York
Source: *AmAu&B; BenetAL 91; BioIn 3, 10, 14; ChhPo, S3; ConAu 57, 93; CurBio 40, 75N; EncTwCJ; NatCAB 63; NewYTBS 75; REnAL; SmATA 30N; WhAm 6; WhAmArt 85; WhoAm 74; WhoAmA 73, 76N, 78N, 80N, 82N, 84N, 86N, 89N, 91N, 93N; WorECom*

Sohappy, David, Sr.
American. Political Activist
Leading figure in battle for Northwest Coast Indian fishing rights.
b. Apr 25, 1925 in Yakima Indian Reservation,Washington
d. May 7, 1991 in Hood River, Washington
Source: *BioIn 21; EncNAB; NotNaAm*

Sokolsky, George E
American. Journalist, Author
Conservative columnist for Hearst Syndicate, 1944-62.
b. Sep 5, 1893 in Utica, New York
d. Dec 13, 1962 in Otis, Massachusetts
Source: *AmAu&B; ConAu 89; CurBio 41, 63; WhAm 4*

Solal, Martial
French. Pianist
Jazz pianist; has composed music for more than 30 films, among them *Breathless.*
b. Aug 23, 1927 in Algiers, Algeria
Source: *AllMusG; BiDJaz; BioIn 6; ConMus 4; EncJzS; NewGrDJ 88, 94; NewGrDM 80; PenEncP; WhoFr 79; WhoWor 74*

Solari, Andrea
Italian. Artist
A painter strongly influenced by Leonrdo da Vinci; student of the Milanese school.
d. 1524
Source: *OxDcArt*

Solarz, Stephen Joshua
American. Politician
Liberal Dem. congressman from NY, 1975-93
b. Sep 12, 1940 in New York, New York
Source: *AlmAP 88, 92; BiDrUSC 89; BioIn 12; CngDr 87; CurBio 86; NewYTBS 91; WhoAm 78, 80, 82, 84, 86, 88, 90, 92, 94, 95, 96; WhoAmJ 80; WhoAmP 87; WhoE 77, 79, 81, 85, 86, 89, 91, 93; WhoGov 75, 77*

Soleri, Paolo
American. Architect
Designed the planned community of Arcosanti, AZ, 1970; combines needs of architecture, ecology for 5,000 people.
b. Jun 21, 1919 in Turin, Italy
Source: *BioIn 8, 9, 10, 11, 12, 13, 14, 16; BriEAA; CelR; ConArch 80, 87, 94; ConAu 106; CurBio 72; IntDcAr; IntWW 82, 83, 89, 91, 93; MacEA; WhoAm 76, 82, 84, 86, 88, 90, 92, 94, 95, 96, 97; WhoAmA 73, 76, 78, 80, 82, 84, 86, 89, 91, 93; WhoWest 92, 94; WhoWor 84, 87, 89, 91, 93, 95; WrDr 82, 84, 86, 88, 90, 92, 94, 96*

Solomon
Hebrew. Ruler, Author
Ruled Israel; renowned for wisdom, wealth; during reign nation rose to its greatest; wrote *The Song of Solomon.*
b. 973?BC
d. 933?BC
Source: *DcOrL 3; Dis&D; NewC; WebBD 83; WhDW*

Solomon
[Solomon Cutner]
English. Pianist
Child prodigy; concert repertoire focused on Mozart, Brahms, Shubert; retired, 1956.
b. Aug 9, 1902 in London, England
d. Feb 22, 1988 in London, England
Source: *AnObit 1988; Baker 78, 84, 92; BioIn 1, 2, 9, 21; BriBkM 80; DcNaB 1986; FacFETw; IntWWM 77, 80; NewAmDM; NewGrDM 80; NewYTBS 88; NotTwCP; PenDiMP; Who 74, 82, 83, 85, 88*

Solomon, Hannah Greenebaum
American. Social Reformer
Founded National Council of Jewish Women, 1890.
b. Jan 14, 1858 in Chicago, Illinois
d. Dec 7, 1942 in Chicago, Illinois
Source: *HanAmWH; InWom SUP; LibW; NatCAB 36; NotAW; WomFir; WomWWA 14*

Solomon, Harold Charles
"Solly"
American. Tennis Player
Winner of Baltimore Grand Prix Tennis Tournament, 1979; German Championship, 1980.
b. Sep 17, 1952 in Washington, District of Columbia
Source: *OfEnT; WhoAm 78, 80, 82, 84; WhoIntT*

Solomon, Izler
American. Conductor
Led Indianapolis Symphony, 1956-75.
b. Jan 11, 1910 in Saint Paul, Minnesota
Source: *Baker 78, 84, 92; BiDAmM; BioIn 1, 2, 4, 11, 15; BlueB 76; MusSN; NewGrDA 86; NewYTBS 87; WhoAm 74, 76, 78, 80; WhoMus 72; WhoMW 74, 76, 78, 80; WhoWorJ 72, 78*

Solomon, Neil
American. Physician, Journalist
Writes syndicated medical column, L.A. Times, 1974-.
b. Feb 27, 1932 in Pittsburgh, Pennsylvania
Source: *AmMWSc 73P, 76P, 79, 82, 86, 89, 92, 95; ConAu 27NR; IntMed 80; WhoAm 76, 78, 80, 82, 84, 86, 88; WhoAmJ 80; WhoE 74, 75; WhoGov 77; WhoMedH*

Solomon, Samuel Joseph
American. Airline Executive
Associated with various US airlines; chm., Aviation Historical Foundation.
b. Jul 11, 1899 in Washington, District of Columbia
d. Dec 8, 1977 in Bethesda, Maryland
Source: *BioIn 10, 12; IntYB 78; NatCAB 60; St&PR 75; WhAm 7; WhoAm 74, 76, 78*

Solotaroff, Theodore
American. Author
Editor of *American Review* mag., 1972-77.
b. Oct 9, 1928 in Elizabeth, New Jersey
Source: *BioIn 13; ConAu 8NR, 9R; DrAF 76; DrAPF 80, 91; WhoAm 90; WhoWorJ 72; WhoWrEP 89*

Soloviev, Sergei Mikhailovich
Russian. Historian
Wrote *History of Russia,* 1851-79, describing story of Russian people, govt.
b. May 5, 1820 in Moscow, Russia
d. Oct 4, 1879
Source: *CasWL; NewCol 75; WebBD 83*

Solow, Robert Merton
American. Economist, Educator
MIT economics professor, 1958-95; W. Edwards Deming professor, NYU, 1996—; won Nobel Prize in economics, 1987, for theories of economic growth of national income.
b. Aug 23, 1924 in New York, New York
Source: *BioIn 15, 16; IntWW 91; NewYTBS 87; Who 90, 92; WhoAm 86, 90, 97; WhoE 91, 97; WhoFI 83, 92; WhoNob, 90, 95; WhoWor 91, 97; WhoWorJ 78; WorAlBi*

Solti, Georg, Sir
English. Musician, Conductor
Winner of 22 Grammys, 1962-83; music director of Chicago Symphony 22 years; artistic director of Salzburg Easter Festival, 1992.
b. Oct 21, 1912 in Budapest, Hungary
Source: *Baker 78, 84, 92; BioIn 4, 5, 6, 8, 9, 10, 11, 12, 13, 14, 15, 18, 21; BioNews 74; BlueB 76; BriBkM 80; CelR; CmOp; ConMus 13; CurBio 64; DcArts; FacFETw; IntDcOp; IntWW 74, 75, 76, 77, 78, 79, 80, 81, 82, 83, 89, 91, 93; IntWWM 77, 80, 85, 90; MetOEnc; MusMk; MusSN; NewAmDM; NewEOp 71; NewGrDA 86; NewGrDM 80; NewGrDO; NewYTBE 71, 72; OxDcOp; PenDiMP; VarWW 85; Who 74, 82, 83, 85, 88, 92, 94; WhoAm 74, 76, 78, 80, 82, 84, 86, 88, 90, 92, 94, 95, 96, 97; WhoAmM 83; WhoEnt 92; WhoFr 79; WhoMus 72; WhoMW 74, 76, 78, 80, 82, 84, 86, 88, 90, 92, 93, 96; WhoOp 76; WhoWor 74, 76, 78, 80, 82, 84, 87, 89, 91, 93, 95; WorAl; WorAlBi*

Soltysik, Patricia Michelle
[S(ymbionese) L(iberation) A(rmy)]
"Mizmoon"; "Zoya"
American. Revolutionary
Member of terrorist group that kidnapped Patricia Hearst, 1974.
b. May 17, 1950
d. May 24, 1974 in Los Angeles, California
Source: *BioIn 10; GoodHs*

Solzhenitsyn, Aleksandr (Isayevich)
Russian. Author
Exiled to Siberia, 1953; won Nobel Prize for literature, 1970; wrote *Gulag Archipelago,* 1973.
b. Dec 11, 1918 in Kislovodsk, Union of Soviet Socialist Republics
Source: *AuNews 1; Benet 87, 96; BenetAL 91; BiDSovU; BioIn 14, 15, 16, 17, 18, 19, 20, 21; BioNews 74; CasWL; CelR 90; ColdWar 1, 2; ConAu 69; ConHero 1; ConLC 1, 2, 4, 7, 9, 10, 18, 26, 34, 78; CurBio 69, 88; CyWA 89; DcRusLS; EncWL; EuWr 13; FacFETw; HalFC 88; IntAu&W 89, 91, 93; IntWW 74, 75, 76, 77, 78, 79, 80, 81, 82, 83, 89, 91, 93; IntYB 78, 79, 80, 81, 82; LiExTwC; MagSWL; MajTwCW; MakMC; ModSL 1; NewYTBE 72; NewYTBS 74; NobelP; PenC EUR; RadHan; RAdv 14, 13-2; RComWL; REn; TwCWr; WhDW; Who 92; WhoAm 86, 90, 94, 95, 96, 97; WhoE 91, 95; WhoNob 90; WhoTwCL; WhoWor 91, 95, 96, 97; WhoWrEP 89; WorAlBi; WorAu 1950; WorLitC*

Some, Malidoma Patrice
Upper Voltan. Writer
Writer and speaker whose goal is to spread his knowledge of the spiritual life of his people to the whole world.
b. 1956 in Dano, Upper Volta
Source: *BioIn 20, 21; ConAu 145; ConBlB 10*

Somers, Brett
American. Actor
Ex-wife of Jack Klugman.
b. Jul 11, 1927
Source: *LegTOT; WhoHol 92, A*

Somers, Suzanne
[Mrs. Alan Hamel; Suzanne Mahoney]
American. Actor
Star of TV's "Three's Company," 1977-81; also star of TV's "Step by Step," 1991 —.
b. Oct 16, 1946 in San Bruno, California
Source: *BioIn 11, 16; BkPepl; ConAu 139; ConTFT 3, 11; HalFC 84, 88; IntAu&W 91; IntMPA 81, 82, 84, 86, 88, 92, 94, 96; InWom SUP; LegTOT; TwCRHW 90; WhoAm 82; WhoAmW 97; WhoEnt 92; WhoHol 92; WhoTelC; WorAl; WorAlBi; WrDr 92*

Somes, Michael (George)
English. Dancer
Leading male dancer with Royal Ballet, 1951-61; asst. director, 1963-70.
b. Sep 28, 1917 in Horsley, England
d. Nov 18, 1994 in London, England
Source: *BiDD; BioIn 3, 4, 5, 11, 20, 21; BlueB 76; CnOxB; CurBio 55, 95N; DancEn 78; IntDcB; NewYTBS 94; Who 74, 82, 83, 85, 88, 90, 92, 94; WhoHol 92, A; WhoThe 77A; WhoWor 74; WhThe; WorAl*

Sommer, Elke
[Elke Schletze]
American. Actor
Sexy blonde in films since 1959, including *A Shot in the Dark,* 1964; *The Prisoner of Zenda,* 1979.
b. Nov 5, 1941 in Berlin, Germany
Source: *BioIn 7, 10, 16; ConTFT 3; FilmgC; ForYSC; HalFC 88; IntMPA 75, 76, 77, 78, 79, 80, 81, 82, 84, 86, 88; IntWW 91; InWom SUP; MotPP; MovMk; WhoAm 76, 78, 80, 82, 84, 86, 88, 90, 92; WhoAmW 74; WhoEnt 92; WhoHol A; WorAl; WorAlBi*

Sommer, Frederick
American. Photographer, Artist
Known for 1940s "assemblage" pictures: *Coyotes,* 1945; works have also included landscapes, geometric forms.
b. Sep 7, 1905 in Angri, Italy
Source: *BioIn 17; BriEAA; ConPhot 82, 88, 95; DcCAr 81; ICPEnP; MacBEP; WhAmArt 85; WhoAm 82; WhoAmA 78, 80, 82, 84, 86, 89, 91, 93*

Sommers, Ben
American. Manufacturer
Pres., Capezio, makers of dance, theatrical shoes, 1940-85.
b. Dec 1, 1906 in New York, New York
d. Apr 30, 1985 in New York, New York
Source: *BiE&WWA; BioIn 14; NewYTBS 84; WhoAmJ 80; WhoE 74, 75, 77, 79, 81, 83, 85, 86*

Somogi, Judith
American. Conductor
Music director, conductor, Utica (NY) Symphony, 1977-88; first female to conduct an opera in US.
b. May 13, 1937 in New York, New York
d. Mar 23, 1988 in Long Island, New York
Source: *Baker 84, 92; BioIn 12; IntWWM 80; NewAmDM; NewGrDA 86; NewYTBS 80; WhoAm 84; WhoAmM 83*

Somoza, Anastasio
Nicaraguan. Political Leader
President, 1937-47, 1951-56; assassinated.
b. Feb 1, 1896 in San Marcos, Nicaragua
d. Sep 29, 1956 in Managua, Nicaragua
Source: *BioIn 1, 2, 3, 4, 7, 11, 12, 16, 17, 19; ColdWar 1; CurBio 42, 56; LegTOT; McGEWB; WhAm 3; WorAl*

Somoza Debayle, Anastasio
Nicaraguan. Political Leader
Pres. of Nicaragua, 1967-72; 1974-79.
b. Dec 5, 1925 in Leon, Nicaragua
d. Sep 17, 1980 in Asuncion, Nicaragua
Source: *BiDLAmC; BioIn 8, 10, 11, 12; ColdWar 2; CurBio 78; DcCPCAm; DicTyr; EncLatA; EncWB; FacFETw; HisWorL; IntWW 74, 75, 76, 77, 78, 79, 80; IntYB 78, 79, 80; LegTOT; NewYTBS 79, 80; WhoGov 72; WhoWor 74, 76, 78; WorAl; WorAlBi; WorDWW*

Sondergaard, Gale (Edith Holm)
[Mrs. Herbert Biberman]
American. Actor
Known for playing villainous women; won first supporting actress Oscar for *Anthony Adverse,* 1937; blacklisted with husband, late 1940s-50s.
b. Feb 15, 1899 in Litchfield, Minnesota
d. Aug 14, 1985 in Woodland Hills, California
Source: *AnObit 1985; BiE&WWA; BioIn 10, 11; BioNews 74; EncMcCE; FilmEn; FilmgC; HalFC 80, 84, 88; HolCA; IntMPA 82; InWom SUP; LegTOT; MotPP; MovMk; NotNAT; OlFamFa; ThFT; Vers A; WhoAm 82; WhoHol A; WhoHrs 80; WhoThe 77; WomFir*

Sondheim, Stephen (Joshua)
American. Composer, Lyricist
One of America's most acclaimed lyricists; wrote lyrics for *West Side Story,* 1957; *Gypsy,* 1959.
b. Mar 22, 1930 in New York, New York
Source: *AmCulL; AmDec 1970; AmPS; AmSong; ASCAP 66, 80; Au&Arts 11; Baker 78, 84, 92; Benet 87; BenetAL 91; BestMus; BiDAmM; BiE&WWA; BioIn 9, 10, 12, 13, 16; BkPepl; BlueB 76; BriBkM 80; CamGWoT; CamHAL; CelR, 90; ConAmC 76, 82; ConAu 47NR, 103; ConCom 92; ConLC 30, 39; ConMus 8; ConTFT 1, 11; CurBio 73; DcArts; DcTwCCu 1; EncMT; EncWB; EncWT; Ent; FacFETw; GayLesB; HalFC 80, 84, 88; IntMPA 88, 92, 94, 96; IntWW 76, 77, 78, 79, 80, 81, 82, 83, 89, 91, 93; IntWWM 77, 90; JeHun; LegTOT; NatPD 77; NewAmDM; NewCBMT; NewGrDA 86; NewGrDM 80; NewGrDO; NewOxM; News 94; NewYTBS 84; NotNAT, A; OxCAmL 95; OxCAmT 84; OxCPMus; OxCThe 83; OxDcOp; PenEncP; PlP&P, A; PopAmC SUP; RAdv 14; Who 82, 83, 85, 88, 90, 92, 94; WhoAm 74, 76, 78, 80, 82, 84, 86, 88, 90, 92, 94, 95, 96, 97; WhoE 75, 77, 91, 93, 95; WhoEnt 92; WhoThe 72, 77, 81; WhoWor 78, 80, 82, 84, 87, 89, 91, 93, 95; WorAl; WorAlBi; WrDr 82, 84, 86, 88, 90, 92, 94, 96*

Sonneck, Oscar George Theodore
American. Musicologist, Librarian
First chief, Music Division, Library of Congress, 1902-17; edited *Musical Quarterly,* 1915-28; wrote on American music.
b. Oct 6, 1873 in Jersey City, New Jersey
d. Oct 30, 1928 in New York, New York
Source: *AmAu&B; Baker 78, 84; BiDAmM; BiGAW; BioIn 1, 3, 17; ConAmC 76, 82; DcAmB; DcAmLiB; DcNAA; EncAAH; NatCAB 25; NewGrDM 80; OxCAmH; OxCMus; REnAL; WhAm 1*

Sonnenfeldt, Helmut
American. Government Official
Senior member of Nixon's National Security Council, 1969-74.
b. Sep 13, 1926 in Berlin, Germany
Source: *BioIn 10, 12; EncCW; IntWW 75, 76, 77, 78, 79, 80, 81, 82, 83, 89, 91, 93; NewYTBE 73; PolProf NF; USBiR 74; WhoAm 74, 76, 78, 80, 82, 84, 86, 88, 90, 92, 94, 95, 96, 97; WhoAmJ 80; WhoAmP 81, 83, 85, 87, 89, 91, 93, 95; WhoE 91; WhoGov 72, 75, 77*

Sonnier, Jo-El
American. Musician, Singer
Cajun music artist; recorded *Cajun Life,* 1984 for which he rececived a Grammy Award nomination; also released *Hello Happiness Again,* 1992, *Cajun Valentine,* and *The Scene in Cajun Music.*
b. 1946 in Rayne, Louisiana
Source: *ASCAP 80; ConMus 10*

Sonny and Cher
[Cher; Sonny Bono]
American. Music Group
1960s pop hits include "I Got You Babe."
Source: *BioIn 9, 16, 17, 18, 20, 21; BioNews 74; EncPR&S 89; EncRk 88; HarEnR 86; IntMPA 75, 76, 77, 78, 79, 80, 81, 82; IntWW 89, 91, 93; LesBEnT, 92; NewGrDA 86; NewYTBS 84, 88, 95; PenEncP; RkOn 74; RolSEnR 83; WhoAmP 89, 91, 93; WhoHol A; WhoRocM 82*

Sons of the Pioneers
[Pat Brady; Roy Lanham; Rob Nolan; Lloyd Perryman; Rusty Richards; Roy Rogers; Tim Spencer; Dale Warren]
American. Music Group
One of first highly successful, durable Western singing groups, 1930s; hits include "Cool Water," 1948.
Source: *AmPS B; ASCAP 66, 80; BgBkCoM; BiDAmM; BioIn 7, 15; BioNews 74; CmpEPM; ConMuA 80B; CounME 74, 74A; CurBio 48; EncFCWM 69, 83; HarEnCM 87; IlEncCM; MotPP; NewAmDM; NewGrDA 86; NewYTBE 72; ObitOF 79; OnThGG; OxCPMus; PenEncP; WhoHol 92, A; WhScrn 77, 83*

Sontag, Henriette
German. Opera Singer
Celebrated European soprano, 1820s-40s; noted for Rossini roles.
b. Jan 3, 1806 in Koblenz, Germany
d. Jun 17, 1854 in Mexico City, Mexico
Source: *ApCAB; Baker 78, 84, 92; BioIn 7, 14, 15, 19; BriBkM 80; CmOp; ContDcW 89; IntDcOp; IntDcWB; InWom; MetOEnc; NewAmDM; NewEOp 71; NewGrDM 80; OxDcOp; PenDiMP*

Sontag, Susan
American. Author, Critic
One of most influential contemporary American critics, utilizing new sensibility to evaluate art; wrote novels *The Benefactor,* 1963; *Death Kit,* 1967.
b. Jan 16, 1933 in New York, New York

Source: *AmAu&B; AmWomWr; AmWr S3; ArtclWW 2; Benet 87, 96; BenetAL 91; BioIn 6, 7, 8, 9, 10, 11, 12, 13, 14, 15, 16, 17, 18, 19, 20, 21; BlueB 76; CamGLE; CamHAL; CelR; ConAu 17R, 25NR, 51NR; ConLC 1, 2, 10, 13, 31; ConNov 72, 76, 82, 86, 91, 96; ConPopW; ContDcW 89; CurBio 69, 92; CyWA 89; DcArts; DcLB 2, 67; DcLEL 1940; DrAF 76; DrAPF 80, 91; EncWB; EncWHA; EncWL 2, 3; FacFETw; FemiCLE; GayLesB; GrLiveH; HanAmWH; IntAu&W 76, 77; IntDcWB; IntWW 89, 91, 93; InWom SUP; JeAmFiW; JeAmWW; LegTOT; LibW; LiExTwC; LiJour; LinLib L; MajTwCW; ModAL, S2; ModAWWr; ModWoWr; NewYTBS 78, 80; NotWoAT; Novels; OxCAmL 83, 95; OxCFilm; OxCWoWr 95; PenC AM; PolProf J; RAdv 1, 14, 13-1; RfGAmL 94; ThTwC 87; TwCRHW 94; Who 85, 88, 90, 92, 94; WhoAm 86, 90, 96, 97; WhoAmW 87, 91, 97; WhoTwCL; WomWMM; WorAl; WorAlBi; WorAu 1950; WrDr 76, 80, 82, 84, 86, 88, 90, 92, 94, 96*

Sonzogno, Edoardo
Italian. Publisher
Sole proprietor of newspaper, *Il Secolo,* 1861-1909; printed French, Italian operas, 1874-1909.
b. Apr 21, 1836 in Milan, Italy
d. Mar 14, 1920 in Milan, Italy
Source: *Baker 78, 84, 92; MetOEnc; NewAmDM; NewEOp 71; NewGrDM 80; OxDcOp*

Soo, Jack
[Goro Suzuki]
American. Actor
Played Yemana on TV series "Barney Miller," 1975-79.
b. Oct 28, 1915 in Oakland, California
d. Jan 11, 1979 in Los Angeles, California
Source: *BioIn 11; MotPP; NewYTBS 79; WhoHol A; WhScrn 83*

Soong, T. V
[Sung Tsu-Wen]
Chinese. Statesman
Leading financier of Chinese Nationalist regime; brother of Madam Chiang-Kai-Shek; founded Bank of China, 1936.
b. Dec 4, 1894 in Shanghai, China
d. Apr 24, 1971 in San Francisco, California
Source: *CurBio 41, 71, 71N; NewYTBE 71; WhAm 5*

Sophocles
Greek. Poet, Dramatist
Wrote *Antigone, Oepidus Rex,* c. 429 BC.
b. 496?BC in Colonus, Greece
d. 406?BC in Athens, Greece
Source: *AncWr; AtlBL; BbD; Benet 87, 96; BiD&SB; BioIn 1, 2, 3, 5, 8, 10, 12; CamGWoT; CasWL; ChhPo S2; ClMLC 2; CnThe; CyWA 58; DcArts; DcEnL; Dis&D; DramC 1; EncWT; Ent; GrFLW; Grk&L; IntDcT 2; LegTOT; LuthC 75; MagSWL; McGEWB; McGEWD 72, 84; MetOEnc; NewC; NewEOp 71; NewGrDM 80; NewGrDO; NotNAT A, B; OxCClL, 89; OxCEng 67, 85, 95; OxCThe 67, 83; OxDcByz; PenC CL; PlP&P; RAdv 14, 13-2; RComWL; REn; REnWD; RfGWoL 95; WhDW; WorAl; WorAlBi*

Sopwith, Thomas O. M, Sir
English. Aeronautical Engineer, Aviator
Founded Sopwith Aviation, 1912; designed Sopwith Pup, Sopwith Camel, planes used extensively by British in WW I.
b. Jan 18, 1888
d. Jan 27, 1989 in Winchester, England
Source: *AnObit 1989; BioIn 16; FacFETw; IntWW 83, 89N; NewYTBS 89; Who 85, 88, 90N; WhoAm 88; WhoWor 74*

Sor, Fernando
[Fernando Sors]
Spanish. Composer, Musician
Guitar virtuoso, popular in London, Paris, 1820s; wrote guitar music.
b. Feb 13, 1778 in Barcelona, Spain
d. Jul 8, 1839 in Paris, France
Source: *Baker 78, 84; BioIn 11; DcHiB; NewGrDM 80; NewOxM; OxCMus; PenDiMP*

Sordello
[Sordel]
Italian. Troubador, Poet
Composer of about forty poems on love, chivalry, and mortality.
b. c. 1189 in Goito, Italy
d. c. 1269
Source: *ClMLC 15; DcBiPP*

Sorel, Edward
[Edward Schwartz]
American. Artist
One of the founders of the Push Pin Studios, 1953; drawings appear in many American magazines including *The New Yorker* and *Esquire.*
b. Mar 26, 1929 in New York, New York
Source: *BioIn 8, 12, 15, 16, 17, 19, 20; ConAu 9R, 33NR; ConGrA 1; CurBio 94; EncSF, 93; IlrAm 1880; IlsBYP; IlsCB 1957; SmATA 37, 65; WhoAm 74, 76, 78, 80, 82, 84, 86, 88, 90, 92, 94, 95, 96, 97; WhoAmA 76, 78, 80, 82, 84, 86, 89, 91, 93; WhoE 74; WhoGrA 82; WhoWor 74, 76; WorECar*

Soren, David
[Howard David Soren]
American. Archaeologist
Discovered lost Roman city of Kourion (destroyed by earthquake in 364), 1984.
b. Oct 7, 1946 in Philadelphia, Pennsylvania
Source: *AmMWSc 95; ConNews 86-3; DrAS 78H, 82H; WhoAm 90, 92, 94, 95, 96, 97; WhoEmL 87; WhoScEn 94, 96; WhoWest 89, 92, 94, 96*

Soren, Tabitha
American. Broadcast Journalist
MTV news correspondent.
b. Aug 19, 1967 in San Antonio, Texas
Source: *LegTOT*

Sorensen, Ted
[Theodore Chaikin Sorensen]
American. Government Official
Assistant, special counsel to JKF, 1953-63; wrote *The Kennedy Legacy,* 1969.
b. May 8, 1928 in Lincoln, Nebraska
Source: *AmAu&B; ConAu 2NR, 45; CurBio 61; IntWW 83, 91; PolProf K; WhoAm 84, 86, 90, 97; WhoAmL 92; WhoAmP 85, 91; WrDr 86, 92*

Sorensen, Virginia
[Mrs. Alec Waugh]
American. Children's Author
Won 1957 Newbery for *Miracles on Maple Hill.*
b. Feb 17, 1912 in Provo, Utah
d. Dec 24, 1991
Source: *AmAu&B; AmNov; ArtclWW 2; Au&Wr 71; AuBYP 2, 3; BenetAL 91; BioIn 2, 4, 6, 7, 9, 10; ConAu 13R, 22NR, 139; CurBio 50; DcAmChF 1960; EncFWF; InWom; MajAI; MorBMP; MorJA; NewbC 1956; OxCAmL 83, 95; OxCChiL; SmATA 2, 15AS, 72; TwCA SUP; TwCChW 78, 83, 89, 95; TwCWW 82, 91; WhAm 10; WhoAm 74, 76, 78, 80, 82, 84, 86, 88, 90; WhoAmW 58, 72, 74; WhoWor 74; WrDr 76, 80, 82, 84, 86, 88, 90, 92, 94N*

Sorge, Richard
German. Journalist, Spy
Soviet spy who organized spy ring in Japan, 1935-44; caught and executed, 1944.
b. 1895 in Baku, Russia
d. 1944 in Tokyo, Japan
Source: *BiDSovU; BioIn 2, 3, 4, 7, 8, 11, 14, 17; EncTR, 91; HisEWW; SpyCS; WhDW; WhWW-II*

Soria, Dario
American. Business Executive
Pres., Cetra-Soria Records, 1950-53, EMI, 1953-57; produced Met. Opera Historic Broadcasting Recording Series, 1975-80.
b. May 21, 1912 in Rome, Italy
d. Mar 28, 1980 in New York, New York
Source: *BioIn 10, 11, 12; MetOEnc; NewYTBS 80; WhAm 7; WhoAm 74, 76, 78, 80*

Sorin, Edward Frederick
American. Clergy, Educator
Roman Catholic priest; founder, first pres., U of Notre Dame, 1844-65.
b. Feb 6, 1814 in Ahuille, France
d. Oct 31, 1893 in South Bend, Indiana
Source: *AmAu&B; ApCAB; BiDAmEd; DcAmB; TwCBDA; WebAB 74, 79; WhAm HS*

Soros, George
[Dzjchdzhe Shorash]
American. Financier
First American to earn $1 billion in one year; started the Quantum Fund, 1969.
b. Aug 12, 1930 in Budapest, Hungary
Source: *BioIn 12; WhoAm 94, 95, 96, 97; WhoFI 92, 94*

Sorvino, Mira
American. Actor
Won Oscar, Best Supporting Actress, *Mighty Aphrodite,* 1994.
b. 1969 in Tenafly, New Jersey

Sorvino, Paul
American. Actor
Starred in *That Championship Season,* on Broadway, 1972, film, 1982.
b. 1939 in New York, New York
Source: *BioIn 13, 14; ConTFT 4; EncAFC; FilmEn; HalFC 80, 84, 88; IntMPA 80, 84, 86, 88, 92, 94, 96; LegTOT; NewYTBE 72; NewYTBS 82; PlP&P A; VarWW 85; WhoAm 86, 90, 95, 96, 97; WhoEnt 92; WhoHol 92, A; WhoThe 77, 81; WorAl; WorAlBi*

Sosa, Mercedes
Argentine. Singer
Songs reflect the pain of exile, fear of political violence and struggle for justice.
b. 1935 in Tucuman, Argentina
Source: *BioIn 16; ConMus 3; DcHiB; NewYTBS 88*

Sosnik, Harry
American. Conductor
Led band, 1930s-40s; wrote TV scores, songs.
b. Jul 13, 1906 in Chicago, Illinois
Source: *ASCAP 66, 80; CmpEPM; St&PR 75; WhoAm 74, 76, 78, 80, 82, 84, 86, 88; WhoEnt 92*

Soss, Wilma Porter
American. Business Executive
Founder, pres., Federation of Women Shareholders in American Business, 1947-86.
b. Mar 13, 1900 in San Francisco, California
d. Oct 10, 1986 in New York, New York
Source: *BioIn 15; CurBio 65, 87; NewYTBS 86; WhoAmW 87*

Sostratus
Greek. Architect
Built lighthouse for Ptolemy Philadelphus at Alexandria; model for similar structures of period.
b. fl. 3rd cent. BC
Source: *BioIn 14; DcBiPP; WebBD 83*

Sotheby, John
English. Auctioneer
Founded Covent Gardens Auction Rooms, 1744.
d. 1807
Source: *WebBD 83*

Sotheby, Samuel Leigh
English. Auctioneer
Entered family business, 1817; expert in Cataloguing; wrote on early printing.
b. Aug 31, 1805
d. Jun 19, 1861 in Buckfastleigh Abbey, England
Source: *Alli; BioIn 12; DcBiPP; DcNaB; WebBD 83*

Sothern, Ann
[Harriet Lake]
American. Actor
Lighthearted heroine of *Maisie* film series, 1939-47; starred on TV in comedies "Private Secretary," 1954-57; "The Ann Sothern Show," 1958-61.
b. Jan 22, 1909 in Valley City, North Dakota
Source: *ASCAP 66; BioIn 16; CmpEPM; ConTFT 8; CurBio 56; EncAFC; EncMT; Film 2; FilmEn; FilmgC; GangFlm; HalFC 80, 84, 88; IntDcF 1-3; IntMPA 86, 92, 94, 96; InWom SUP; LegTOT; MGM; MotPP; MovMk; OxCFilm; RadStar; SaTiSS; ThFT; WhoAm 80, 82; WhoCom; WhoHol A; WhoThe 77A; WhThe; WorAlBi; WorEFlm*

Sothern, Edward Askew
English. Entertainer
Noted for role in *Our American Cousin,* from 1858; appeared night of Lincoln assassination.
b. Apr 1, 1826 in Liverpool, England
d. Jan 20, 1881 in London, England
Source: *Alli; AmBi; DcAmB; DcNaB; EncWT; FamA&A; NatCAB 5; NewC; NotNAT A; OxCAmH; OxCAmL 65; OxCThe 67, 83; REnAL; TwCBDA; WhAm HS*

Sothern, Edward Hugh
American. Entertainer
Founded Shakespearian Repertory Co. with wife, Julia Marlowe, 1900-16; son of Edward Askew.
b. Dec 6, 1859 in New Orleans, Louisiana
d. Oct 28, 1933 in New York, New York
Source: *AmAu&B; AmBi; ApCAB X; BioIn 1, 2, 3, 4, 5, 13; ChhPo; DcAmB; DcNAA; FamA&A; LinLib S; NatCAB 5; NotNAT A, B; OxCAmH; OxCAmL 65; OxCThe 67, 83; REn; REnAL; TwCBDA; WebAB 74, 79; WhAm 1; WhoStg 1906, 1908; WhScrn 74, 77; WhThe*

Soto, Gary
American. Writer
Published poetry collections *The Elements of San Joaquin,* 1977; *Black Hair,* 1985; children's book *Pacific Crossing,* 1992; memoir *Living up the Street,* 1985.
b. Apr 12, 1952 in Fresno, California
Source: *Au&Arts 10; ChiLit; ChiSch; ChlBkCr; ChlLR 38; ConAu 50NR, 119, 125; ConLC 32, 80; ConPo 85, 91, 96; ConSSWr; DcHiB; DcLB 82; DrAPF 80; HispAmA; HispLC; HispWr; MexAmB; OnHuMoP; OxCAmL 95; OxCTwCP; RfGAmL 94; SmATA 80; TwCYAW; WhoAm 92; WhoHisp 91, 92, 94; WhoWest 87; WorAu 1975; WrDr 86, 88, 90, 92, 94, 96*

Soto, Mario Melvin
Dominican. Baseball Player
Pitcher, Cincinnati, 1977—; led NL in complete games, 1983, 1984; three-time NL All-Star.
b. Jul 12, 1956 in Bani, Dominican Republic
Source: *Ballpl 90; BaseReg 86, 87; BioIn 13; NewYTBS 84, 86*

Soul, David
American. Actor
Starred in TV shows "Here Come the Brides," "Starsky and Hutch."
b. Aug 28, 1946 in Chicago, Illinois
Source: *BioIn 13; ConTFT 3; HalFC 84; IntMPA 88; WhoAm 80, 82; WhoHol A*

Soule, Olan
American. Actor
Films include *The Apple Dumpling Gang,* 1975; *St. Ives,* 1976.
b. Feb 28, 1909 in La Harpe, Illinois
d. Feb 1, 1994 in Corona, California
Source: *ConTFT 9, 13; EncAFC; RadStar; VarWW 85; WhoHol 92, A*

Soundgarden
American. Music Group
Heavy metal rock band; albums include *Louder Than Love,* 1989.
Source: *BioIn 20; ConMus 6; EncRkSt*

Soupault, Philippe
French. Author
Wrote poem "The Magnetic Fields," 1919, with Andre Breton, considered the work that gave birth to the surrealist movement.
b. Aug 2, 1897 in Chaville, France
d. Mar 11, 1990 in Paris, France
Source: *AnObit 1990; Benet 87, 96; BioIn 1, 9, 10, 16, 17; CasWL; ClDMEL 47, 80; ConAu 116, 131, 147; ConLC 68; DcTwCCu 2; EncWL, 2, 3; FacFETw; GuFrLit 1; IntAu&W 77, 89, 91; IntWW 74, 75, 76, 77, 78, 79, 80, 81, 82, 83, 89; IntWWP 77; ModFrL; ModRL; ModWD; NewYTBS 90; OxCFr; REn; WhoFr 79; WhoWor 74; WorAu 1950*

Souphanouvong, Prince
Laotian. Political Leader
President of Laos, 1975-86.
b. 1912 in Luang Prabang, Lao People's Democratic Republic
d. Jan 9, 1995, Lao People's Democratic Republic
Source: *IntWW 83, 91; NewYTBE 70, 73; NewYTBS 74; WhoWor 84, 87, 91*

Sour, Robert B(andler)
American. Lyricist
Hit songs include "Body and Soul," 1930.
b. Oct 31, 1905 in New York, New York
d. Mar 6, 1985 in New York, New York
Source: *BiDAmM; BioIn 14; ConAu 115; WhAm 8; WhoAm 74, 76, 78, 80*

Sousa, John Philip
American. Composer, Conductor
Wrote 140 marches, including "Stars and Stripes Forever," 1897.
b. Nov 6, 1854 in Washington, District of Columbia
d. Mar 6, 1932 in Reading, Pennsylvania
Source: *AmAu&B; AmBi; AmCulL; ApCAB SUP, X; ASCAP 66, 80; AtlBL; Baker 78, 84, 92; Benet 87, 96; BenetAL 91; BiDAmM; BioIn 1, 2, 3, 4, 5, 6, 7, 8, 9, 10, 13, 14, 15, 18, 19, 20; BriBkM 80; CmpEPM; ConMus 10; DcAmAu; DcAmB; DcArts; DcNAA; EncAB-H 1974, 1996; EncMT; GayN; HalFC 80, 84, 88; LegTOT; LinLib L, S; McGEWB; MemAm; MusMk; NatCAB 9, 33; NewAmDM; NewGrDA 86; NewGrDM 80; NewOxM; NotNAT B; OxCAmH; OxCAmL 65; OxCAmT 84; OxCMus; OxCPMus; OxDcOp; PenEncP; PopAmC; REn; REnAL; TwCBDA; WebAB 74, 79; WebAMB; WhAm 1; WhDW; WhoStg 1906, 1908; WhThe; WorAl; WorAlBi*

Soustelle, Jacques
French. Government Official, Anthropologist
Governor-general of Algeria, 1955-56; minister of information, 1958; has written extensively of anthropological expeditions to Mexico.
b. Feb 3, 1912 in Montpellier, France
d. Aug 7, 1990 in Neuilly-sur-Seine, France
Source: *AnObit 1990; BiDFrPL; BioIn 4, 5, 7, 9, 17; ConAu 132; CurBio 58, 90, 90N; DcPol; FacFETw; IntDcAn; IntWW 74, 75, 76, 77, 78, 79, 80, 81, 82, 83, 89, 91N; NewYTBS 90; Who 74, 82, 83, 85, 88, 90; WhoFr 79*

Soutar, William
Scottish. Poet
Prominent figure in the Scottish Renaissance movement; in later years wrote "Whigmaleeries."
b. Apr 28, 1898 in Perth, Scotland
d. Oct 15, 1943 in Perth, Scotland
Source: *BioIn 3, 12; CamGEL; CamGLE; CasWL; ChhPo, S1, S2, S3; CmScLit; DcLEL; EncWL; EngPo; EvLB; NewCBEL; OxCEng 85, 95; OxCTwCP; PenC ENG; RGTwCWr; TwCWr; WhE&EA; WhLit*

Souter, David Hackett
American. Supreme Court Justice
Conservative justice appointed to Supreme Court by George Bush, 1990, replacing retiring William Brennan.
b. Sep 17, 1939 in Melrose, Massachusetts
Source: *CngDr 91, 93, 95; CurBio 91; FacFETw; IntWW 91, 93; News 91-3; SupCtJu; Who 94; WhoAm 78, 80, 82, 84, 86, 88, 90, 92, 94, 95, 96, 97; WhoAmL 78, 85, 87, 90, 92, 94, 96; WhoAmP 91; WhoE 79, 81, 83, 85, 86, 89, 91, 93, 95, 97; WhoWor 96*

South, Joe
American. Musician, Singer, Songwriter
Won two Grammys, 1969, for "Games People Play."
b. Feb 28, 1942 in Atlanta, Georgia
Source: *BioIn 8; EncPR&S 89; HarEnR 86; IlEncRk; PenEncP; RkOn 74; RolSEnR 83; WhoRock 81*

Southall, Ivan Francis
Australian. Author
Novels for young adults deal with how children cope with various disasters: *Hills End*, 1962; *To the Wild Sky*, 1967.
b. Jun 8, 1921 in Canterbury, Australia
Source: *Au&Wr 71; AuBYP 2, 3; ChlLR 2; ConAu 7NR, 9R; IntAu&W 91; IntWW 91; SenS; SmATA 3, 68; ThrBJA; TwCChW 89; WhoAm 97; WhoWor 87, 91; WrDr 86, 92*

Southampton, Henry Wriothesley, Earl
English. Statesman
Active in London co. of VA, colonization of America, early 1600s; only benefactor acknowledged by Shakespeare.
b. Oct 6, 1573
d. Nov 10, 1624, Netherlands
Source: *ApCAB; Benet 87, 96; BioIn 7, 8, 11, 14; BlmGEL; DcArts; DcBiPP; LngCEL; NewC; NewCBEL; REn*

Souther, J(ohn) D(avid)
[The Souther-Hillman-Furay Band]
American. Singer, Songwriter
Guitarist, vocalist with country-rock band, 1973-75.
b. Nov 2, 1945 in Detroit, Michigan
Source: *ConMuA 80A; RkOn 85; WhoRock 81*

Souther-Hillman-Furay Band, The
[Richie Furay; James Gordon; Paul Harris; Chris Hillman; Al Perkins; J(ohn) D(avid) Souther]
American. Music Group
Country-rock band formed 1973; first album was gold; disbanded, 1975, with members going on to solo careers.
Source: *Alli, SUP; BiDLA; BiDSA; ChhPo S1, S3; ConMuA 80A; DcNaB; EngPo; IlEncRk; OnThGG; RkOn 78, 85; RolSEnR 83; WhoAmA 73, 76, 78; WhoHol 92; WhoNeCM A; WhoRock 81; WhoRocM 82*

Southern, Terry
American. Writer
Writes satirical novels, screenplays; known for satire on pornography, *Candy*, 1958, later published as *Lollipop*, 1962; films include *Easy Rider*, 1969.
b. May 1, 1924 in Alvarado, Texas
d. Oct 29, 1995 in New York, New York
Source: *AmAu&B; Au&Wr 71; BioIn 6, 7, 8, 10; BlueB 76; CasWL; ConAu 1NR, 1R, 55NR, 150; ConDr 73, 77A; ConLC 7; ConNov 72, 76, 82, 86, 91, 96; ConTFT 15; DcLB 2; DrAF 76; DrAPF 91; HalFC 88; IntAu&W 76, 77, 91, 93; Novels; PenC AM; RGTwCWr; WhoAm 76, 78, 80, 82; WhoTwCL; WorAu 1950; WrDr 76, 80, 82, 84, 86, 88, 90, 92, 94, 96*

Southey, Robert
English. Poet, Author
One of "Lake Poets;" poet laureate, 1813-43.
b. Aug 12, 1774 in Bristol, England
d. Mar 21, 1843 in Keswick, England
Source: *Alli; AtlBL; BbD; Benet 87, 96; BiD&SB; BiDLA; BioIn 1, 2, 3, 5, 6, 7, 8, 9, 10, 11, 12, 13, 16, 17, 20; BlmGEL; BritAu 19; BritWr 4; CamGEL; CamGLE; CasWL; CelCen; Chambr 3; ChhPo, S1, S2, S3; CnE&AP; CrtT 2, 4; CyWA 58; DcArts; DcBiPP; DcEnA, A; DcEnL; DcEuL; DcLB 93, 107, 142; DcLEL; DcNaB; Dis&D; EvLB; GrWrEL P; LegTOT; LinLib L, S; LngCEL; MouLC 3; NewC; NewCBEL; NinCLC 8; OxCChiL; OxCEng 67, 85, 95; PenC ENG; PoLE; RAdv 14; REn; RfGEnL 91; SmATA 54; WebE&AL; WhDW; WhoChL*

Southside Johnny and the Asbury Jukes
[Gene Bacia; Steve Becker; Al Berger; Ricky Gazda; Kevin Kavanaugh; "Southside" Johnny Lyon; Eddie Manion; Carlo Novi; Tony Palligrosi; Kenny Pentifallo; Richie Rosenberg; Billy Rush]
American. Music Group
Rhythm and blues influenced rock band formed 1974; albums featured Bruce Springsteen songs.
Source: *ConMuA 80A; EncPR&S 89; EncRk 88; HarEnR 86; IlEncRk; PenEncP; RkOn 78, 85; RolSEnR 83; WhoRock 81; WhoRocM 82*

Southworth, Emma Dorothy Eliza Nevitte
American. Author
Wrote novels of Southern life: *The Hidden Hand*, 1859.
b. Dec 26, 1819 in Washington, District of Columbia
d. Jun 30, 1899 in Georgetown, Virginia
Source: *AmAu; AmBi; AmWom; AmWomWr; ApCAB; ArtclWW 2; BioIn 17; DcAmB; InWom, SUP; LibW; NatCAB 1; NewCol 75; NinCLC 26; NotAW; PenNWW A; REn; REnAL; SouWr; TwCBDA; WebAB 74, 79; WhAm 1*

Soutine, Chaim
French. Artist
Expressionist, used heavy impasto; often painted distorted portraits, slaughterhouse scenes.
b. 1894 in Smilovich, Russia
d. Aug 9, 1943 in Paris, France
Source: *AtlBL; BioIn 1, 2, 4, 6, 8, 10, 11, 12, 13, 14, 16, 18, 21; ConArt 83; DcTwCCu 2; MakMC; McGDA; McGEWB; NewCol 75; OxCArt; OxCTwCA; OxDcArt*

Souvanna, Phouma
Laotian. Prince, Political Leader
Neutralist prime minister of Laos, 1951-75.
b. Oct 7, 1901 in Luang Prabang, Laos
d. Jan 10, 1984 in Vientiane, Laos
Source: *AnObit 1984; BioIn 5, 6, 7, 8, 9, 10; CurBio 62, 84; IntWW 74; NewYTBS 84; WhoGov 77; WhoWor 74*

Souzay, Gerard
[Gerard Marcel Tisserand]
French. Opera Singer
Baritone, noted for Lieder, French art songs; popular concertist, 1960s-80s.
b. Dec 8, 1920? in Angers, France
Source: *Baker 78, 84; BioIn 11; CurBio 66; IntWW 74, 75, 76, 77, 78, 79, 80, 81, 82, 83, 89, 91, 93; IntWWM 77, 80; MusMk; MusSN; NewGrDM 80; Who 92; WhoFr 79; WhoMus 72; WhoOp 76; WhoWor 74*

Sovern, Michael I(ra)
American. University Administrator
Pres., Columbia U, 1980-93.
b. Dec 1, 1931 in New York, New York
Source: *BioIn 8, 10, 12; BlueB 76; CurBio 81; DrAS 74P, 78P, 82P; IntWW 89, 91, 93; NewYTBS 80; WhoAm 74, 76, 78, 80, 82, 84, 86, 88, 90, 92, 94, 95, 96, 97; WhoAmL 78, 79, 87, 90, 92, 94; WhoE 74, 83, 85, 86, 89, 91, 93; WhoWor 84, 87, 89, 91, 93, 95, 96, 97*

Sowell, Thomas
American. Economist, Author
Controversial conservative economist, believes affirmative action and minimum wages laws are detrimental to black Americans; books include *Ethnic America,* 1981; *Preferential Policies,* 1990.
b. Jun 30, 1930 in Gastonia, North Carolina
Source: *AmEA 74; AmMWSc 73S, 78S; BiDAmNC; BioIn 12, 13, 14, 15, 17; BlkWr 1, 2; BlkWrNE A; ConAu 26NR, 41R; ConBlB 2; ConIsC 2; CurBio 81; DcAmC; InB&W 85; NegAl 89; SchCGBL; SelBAAf; WhoAfA 96; WhoAm 76, 82, 84, 86, 88, 90, 92, 94, 95, 96, 97; WhoBlA 75, 77, 80, 85, 90, 92, 94; WhoEc 81; WrDr 92, 94, 96*

Sowerby, Leo
American. Organist, Composer
Wrote Pulitzer-winning poem, "Canticle of the Sun," 1944.
b. May 1, 1895 in Grand Rapids, Michigan
d. Jul 7, 1968 in Port Clinton, Ohio
Source: *AmComp; ASCAP 66, 80; Baker 78, 84, 92; BiDAmM; BioIn 1, 3, 4, 8; BriBkM 80; CompSN; ConAmC 76, 82; DcCM; DcCom&M 79; MusMk; NewAmDM; NewGrDA 86; NewGrDM 80; OxCAmL 65; OxCMus; REnAL; WhAm 5*

Soyer, David
American. Musician
Cellist; won five Grammys for Guarnieri Quarter recordings, 1965-74.
b. Feb 24, 1923 in Philadelphia, Pennsylvania
Source: *BioIn 9, 11; IntWWM 77, 80; NewYTBE 71; PenDiMP; WhoAm 76, 78, 80, 82, 84, 86, 88, 90, 92, 94, 95, 96, 97; WhoAmM 83; WhoEnt 92*

Soyer, Isaac
American. Artist
With brothers, Moses, Raphael, leading exponent of realism; paintings of Depression Era working class: *Employment Agency,* 1941.
b. Apr 20, 1907 in Tambov, Russia
d. Jul 8, 1981 in New York, New York
Source: *BioIn 17; BriEAA; CurBio 41, 81, 81N; McGDA; WhAm 8; WhAmArt 85; WhoAm 74, 76, 78; WhoE 74; WorArt 1950*

Soyer, Moses
American. Artist
Twin brother of Raphael; social realism genre painter; major works include *Girl at Sewing Machine,* 1940.
b. Dec 25, 1899 in Tambov, Russia
d. Sep 2, 1974 in New York, New York
Source: *BioIn 6, 7, 8, 10, 12, 14, 17; BriEAA; CelR; CurBio 41, 74, 74N; DcAmArt; DcAmB S9; DcCAA 71, 77, 88, 94; McGDA; NatCAB 58; NewYTBS 74; OxCTwCA; OxDcArt; WhAm 6; WhAmArt 85; WhoAm 74; WhoAmA 73, 76N, 78N, 80N, 82N, 84N, 86N, 89N, 91N, 93N; WorArt 1950*

Soyer, Raphael
American. Artist
Social realist; known for paintings showing men, women during the Depression.
b. Dec 25, 1899 in Tambov, Russia
d. Nov 4, 1987 in New York, New York
Source: *AmArt; AnObit 1987; BiDSovU; BioIn 1, 2, 3, 6, 8, 9, 10, 11, 12, 13, 14, 15, 16, 17; BriEAA; CelR; ConAu 81, 124; CurBio 41, 88, 88N; DcAmArt; DcCAA 71, 77, 88, 94; GrAmP; McGDA; NewYTBE 72; NewYTBS 87; OxDcArt; PhDcTCA 77; PrintW 83, 85; WhAm 9; WhAmArt 85; WhoAm 74, 76, 78, 80, 82, 84, 86; WhoAmA 73, 76, 78, 80, 82, 84, 86; WhoWorJ 72; WorArt 1950*

Soyinka, Wole
[Akinwande Oluwole Soyinka]
Nigerian. Author
Works deal with life in Nigeria; first African, first black to win Nobel Prize for literature, 1986.
b. Jul 13, 1934 in Abeokuta, Nigeria
Source: *AfSS 78, 79, 80, 81, 82; Benet 87, 96; BioIn 8, 10, 12, 13; BlkLC; BlkWr 1, 2; BlmGEL; CamGEL; CamGLE; CamGWoT; CasWL; CnThe; ConAu 13R, 27NR, 39NR; ConBlB 4; ConDr 73, 77, 82, 88, 93; ConLC 3, 5, 14, 36, 44; ConNov 96; ConPo 70, 75, 80, 85, 91, 96; ConTFT 6; CrtSuDr; CurBio 74; CyWA 89; DcArts; DcLB 125; DramC 2; DrBlPA, 90; EncWL 2, 3; EncWT; Ent; FacFETw; GrWrEL DR; InB&W 80, 85; IntAu&W 76, 77; IntDcT 2; IntLitE; IntWW 74, 75, 76, 77, 78, 79, 80, 81, 82, 83, 89, 91, 93; IntWWP 77; LegTOT; LiExTwC; LngCTC; MajTwCW; MakMC; McGEWD 84; ModBlW; ModCmwL; ModWD; NewYTBS 87; NobelP; Novels; OxCEng 85, 95; OxCThe 83; OxCTwCP; PenC CL, ENG; RadHan; RAdv 14, 13-2; REnWD; RfGEnL 91; RGAfL; SchCGBL; WebE&AL; Who 90, 92, 94; WhoNob 90, 95; WhoWor 74, 82, 84, 87, 89, 91, 93, 95, 96, 97; WorAlBi; WorAu 1950; WorLitC; WrDr 76, 80, 82, 84, 86, 88, 90, 92, 94, 96*

Spaak, Paul-Henri
Belgian. Lawyer, Politician
Three-time premier of Belgium; among creators of NATO, secretary-general, 1957-61.
b. Jan 25, 1899 in Schaerbeeck, Belgium
d. Jul 31, 1972 in Brussels, Belgium
Source: *BiDInt; BioIn 21; ConAu 37R; CurBio 45, 58, 72, 72N; DcTwHis; EncCW; FacFETw; HisEWW; McGEWB; NewYTBE 72; ObitT 1971; PolLCWE; WhAm 5*

Spaatz, Carl Andrew
American. Army Officer
In charge of strategic bombing against Germany, Japan, WW II.
b. Jun 28, 1891 in Boyertown, Pennsylvania
d. Jul 14, 1974 in Washington, District of Columbia
Source: *BioIn 10, 11, 12; ConAu 49; CurBio 42, 74; DcAmB S9; DcAmMiB; NatCAB 58; NewYTBS 74; WebAB 74; WhAm 6; Who 74*

Spacek, Sissy
[Mrs. Jack Fiske; Mary Elizabeth Spacek]
American. Actor
Won Oscar, 1980, for *Coal Miner's Daughter.*
b. Dec 25, 1949 in Quitman, Texas
Source: *BioIn 12, 13, 16; BkPepl; CelR 90; ConAu 77; CurBio 78; DcArts; FilmEn; HalFC 88; HolBB; IntDcF 1-3, 2-3; IntMPA 82, 88, 92, 94, 96; IntWW 83, 89, 91; LegTOT; NewYTBS 86; WhoAm 86, 88, 90, 92, 94, 95, 96, 97;*

WhoAmW 81, 83, 85, 87, 89, 91, 93, 95, 97; WhoHol 92, A; WorAlBi

Spacey, Kevin
American. Actor
Won Tony award, best featured actor (Drama), *Lost in Yonkers,* 1991; Oscar, best supporting actor, *The Usual Suspects,* 1995.
b. Jul 26, 1959 in South Orange, New Jersey
Source: *ConTFT 9; IntMPA 92, 94, 96; LegTOT; News 96; WhoAm 92, 94, 95, 96, 97; WhoEnt 92; WhoHol 92*

Spader, James
American. Actor
Films include *sex, lies, and videotape,* 1989; *White Palace,* 1990.
b. Feb 7, 1960 in Boston, Massachusetts
Source: *BioIn 15, 16; CelR 90; ConTFT 9; IntMPA 92, 94, 96; LegTOT; News 91, 91-2; WhoAm 92, 94, 95, 96, 97; WhoEnt 92; WhoHol 92; WhoWor 95, 96, 97*

Spaeth, Sigmund Gottfried
"The Tune Detective"
American. Musicologist
Wrote syndicated column, books on music; helped popularize classical music.
b. Apr 10, 1885 in Philadelphia, Pennsylvania
d. Nov 12, 1965 in New York, New York
Source: *AmAu&B; ASCAP 66; Baker 84; BiDAmM; ChhPo S1; CmpEPM; ConAu 5R; CurBio 42, 66; REnAL; TwCA, SUP; WhAm 4; WhNAA*

Spahn, Warren Edward
American. Baseball Player
Pitcher, Boston/Milwaukee Braves, 1942, 1946-65; had 363 career wins, 63 shutouts; Hall of Fame, 1973.
b. Apr 23, 1921 in Buffalo, New York
Source: *Ballpl 90; BiDAmSp BB; BioIn 4, 5, 6, 7, 8, 9, 10; CurBio 62; FacFETw; WebAB 74, 79; WhoAm 74; WhoProB 73; WorAlBi*

Spalding, Albert
American. Violinist
Int'l concertist, 1910-40s; wrote violin pieces; son of Albert Goodwill.
b. Aug 15, 1888 in Chicago, Illinois
d. May 26, 1953 in New York, New York
Source: *ASCAP 66, 80; Baker 78, 84, 92; BiDAmM; BioIn 1, 2, 3, 4, 5, 9, 10, 11, 14, 16; BriBkM 80; ConAmC 76, 82; CurBio 44, 53; DcAmB S5; LinLib S; MusSN; NatCAB 42; NewAmDM; NewGrDA 86; RadStar; WebAB 74, 79; WhAm 3*

Spalding, Albert Goodwill
American. Baseball Player, Businessman
Pitcher, Chicago, 1876-78; won 47 games, 1876; Hall of Fame, 1939; founded sporting goods firm, 1876.
b. Sep 2, 1850 in Byron, Illinois
d. Sep 9, 1915 in Point Loma, California
Source: *BiDAmBL 83; BiDAmSp BB; BioIn 2, 3, 7, 11; DcAmB; DcNAA; Entr; NatCAB 3; OxCAmH; WebAB 74, 79; WhAm 1; WhoProB 73*

Spallanzani, Lazzaro
Italian. Explorer, Scientist
Disproved theory of spontaneous generation.
b. Jan 12, 1729 in Scandiano, Italy
d. Feb 11, 1799 in Pavia, Italy
Source: *AsBiEn; BiESc; BiHiMed; BioIn 6, 9, 12, 14, 15; CamDcSc; DcCathB; DcScB; Dis&D; EncEnl; InSci; McGEWB; NewCol 75; OxCMed 86; WhDW; WorAl; WorAlBi; WorScD*

Spandau Ballet
[Tony Hadley; John Keeble; Gary Kemp; Martin Kemp; Steve Norman]
English. Music Group
Formed 1979; known for flamboyant, then classic dress; hit single "True," 1983.
Source: *Alli; BioIn 17; ConAu X; DrAPF 83, 85, 87, 89, 91, 93, 97; EncPR&S 89; EncRk 88; EncRkSt; HarEnR 86; PenEncP; RkOn 85; SmATA X; WhsNW 85*

Spanel, Abram N
American. Businessman, Inventor, Philanthropist
Founded International Latex (now Playtex) Corp., 1932; held over 2,000 patents.
b. May 15, 1901 in Odessa, Russia
d. Mar 30, 1985 in Princeton, New Jersey
Source: *BioIn 14; NewYTBS 85; WhoAm 82; WhoFI 74*

Spanier, Muggsy
[Francis Joseph Spanier]
American. Jazz Musician
Noted Dixieland cornetist; with Ted Lewis, 1929-36; led own band, early 1940s; used plunger mute.
b. Nov 9, 1906 in Chicago, Illinois
d. Feb 12, 1967 in Sausalito, California
Source: *AllMusG; Baker 84, 92; BiDJaz; BioIn 7, 8; CmpEPM; EncJzS; IlEncJ; LegTOT; MusMk; NewAmDM; NewGrDA 86; NewGrDJ 88, 94; NewGrDM 80; ObitT 1961; OxCPMus; PenEncP; WhAm 4; WhoHol B; WhoJazz 72; WhScrn 74, 77; WorAl; WorAlBi*

Spann, Otis
American. Pianist
Blues music pianist and boogie-woogie piano master; played with Muddy Waters band, 1953-1969; released *Otis Spann Is the Blues,* 1960, which includes song "This Is the Blues," and *Cryin' Time,* 1969; inducted into Blues Hall of Fame, 1980.
b. Mar 21, 1939 in Jackson, Mississippi
d. Apr 24, 1970 in Chicago, Illinois

Spano, Joe
American. Actor
Played Henry Goldblum on TV series "Hill Street Blues," 1981-87.
b. Jul 7, 1946 in San Francisco, California
Source: *ConTFT 5; VarWW 85; WhoAm 90; WhoEnt 92; WhoHol 92; WhoWest 89*

Spargo, John
American. Museum Director
Founder, director, curator, Bennington Historical Museum, 1927-54.
b. Jan 31, 1876 in Stithians, England
d. Aug 17, 1966 in Bennington, Vermont
Source: *AmAu&B; AmLY; BiDAmLf; BioIn 1, 7, 9; ConAu 89; DcAmB S8; DcAmImH; DcAmSR; EncAB-A 6, 39; EncAL; LinLib L; NatCAB 52; OxCAmH; REnAL; WhAm 4; WhLit; WhNAA*

Spark, Muriel Sarah
Scottish. Author
Satirist; best-known novel, *The Prime of Miss Jean Brodie,* 1961, was adapted to film, stage.
b. Feb 1, 1918 in Edinburgh, Scotland
Source: *BioIn 13, 16; CmScLit; CnDBLB 7; ConAu 12NR, 36NR; ConLC 18; ConNov 86, 91; ConPo 91; CyWA 89; DcLB 15; EncBrWW; FacFETw; FemiCLE; HalFC 88; IntAu&W 91; IntWW 83, 91; InWom SUP; LiExTwC; MajTwCW; ModBrL S1; NewC; PenC ENG; RAdv 1; REn; RfGEnL 91; TwCWr; WebE&AL; Who 85, 92; WhoAm 86, 90; WhoWor 84, 91; WorAlBi; WorAu 1950; WrDr 86, 92*

Sparkman, John Jackson
American. Government Official
Dem. senator from AL, 1947-79; Adlai Stevenson's vice presidential running mate, 1952.
b. Dec 20, 1899 in Morgan County, Alabama
d. Nov 16, 1985 in Huntsville, Alabama
Source: *BiDrAC; BiDrUSC 89; BioIn 2, 3, 5, 7, 9, 10, 11; CurBio 50, 86; EncSoH; IntWW 83; IntYB 78, 79, 80; WhAm 9; Who 74; WhoAm 74; WhoAmP 73; WhoGov 72, 75, 77; WhoSSW 73*

Sparks, Jared
American. Editor, Historian
Pres. of Harvard, 1849-53; edited *North American Review,* 1820s; wrote about US history.
b. May 10, 1789 in Willington, Connecticut
d. Mar 14, 1866
Source: *Alli; AmAu; AmAu&B; AmBi; ApCAB; Benet 87, 96; BenetAL 91; BiDAmEd; BiD&SB; BioIn 3, 6, 9, 11, 14; CelCen; CyAL 1; DcAmAu; DcAmB; DcAmBC; DcBiPP; DcLB 1, 30; DcNAA; Drake; EncAB-H 1974, 1996; HarEnUS; LinLib L, S; LuthC 75; McGEWB; NatCAB 5; OxCAmH; OxCAmL 65, 83, 95; REn; REnAL; TwCBDA; WebAB 74, 79; WhAm HS*

Sparks, Ned
[Edward A Sparkman]
American. Actor
Character actor, 1922-47; films include *Magic Town,* 1947.
b. 1883 in Guelph, Ontario, Canada
d. Apr 2, 1957 in Apple Valley, California
Source: *BioIn 4; EncAFC; Film 1, 2; FilmEn; FilmgC; HalFC 80, 84, 88; LegTOT; MotPP; MovMk; TwYS; Vers A; WhoHol B; WhScrn 74, 77, 83*

Spartacus
Thracian. Slave
Led slave revolt, Servile War, 73-71 BC; finally beaten after winning several battles against the Romans.
d. 71BC
Source: *Benet 87, 96; BioIn 1, 3, 5, 6, 7, 8, 9, 20; DcAmSR; EncRev; GenMudB; HarEnMi; LegTOT; LinLib S; McGEWB; OxCClL, 89; REn; WebBD 83; WhDW; WorAl; WorAlBi*

Spassky, Boris Vasilyevich
Russian. Chess Player, Journalist
World chess champion, 1969-72; lost title to Bobby Fischer, 1972.
b. Jan 30, 1937 in Leningrad, Union of Soviet Socialist Republics
Source: *BiDSovU; BioIn 15, 17, 18; CurBio 72; FacFETw; IntAu&W 89; IntWW 74, 91; OxCChes 84; WhoWor 76, 78*

Spaulding, Charles Clinton
American. Insurance Executive
President, North Carolina Mutual Life Insurance Co., 1923-52, building it into the largest all-black business enterprise in the world in 1952.
b. Aug 1, 1874 in Clarkton, North Carolina
d. Aug 1, 1952 in Durham, North Carolina
Source: *BiDAmBL 83; BioIn 1, 2, 3, 5, 6, 8, 9, 12, 20; ConBlB 9; DcAmB S5; DcAmNB; EncSoH; InB&W 80, 85; NatCAB 42; WhoColR*

Speaker, Tris(tram E)
''Spoke''; ''The Grey Eagle''
American. Baseball Player
Outfielder, 1907-28, mostly with Boston, Cleveland; holds ML record for doubles in career, 793; Hall of Fame, 1937.
b. Apr 4, 1888 in Hubbard City, Texas
d. Dec 8, 1958 in Lake Whitney, Texas
Source: *Ballpl 90; BiDAmSp BB; BioIn 2, 3, 4, 5, 6, 7, 8, 9, 10, 13, 14, 15, 17; FacFETw; LegTOT; WhoProB 73; WhScrn 83; WorAlBi*

Speakes, Larry Melvin
American. Government Official
Deputy press secretary under Reagan, 1981-87.
b. Sep 13, 1939 in Cleveland, Mississippi
Source: *BioIn 15, 16; IntWW 91; WhoAm 84, 90, 97; WhoAmP 91; WhoFI 92; WhoGov 75*

Speaks, Oley
American. Songwriter
Hits include ''On the Road to Mandalay,'' 1907; ''Sylvia,'' 1914.
b. Jun 28, 1874 in Canal Winchester, Ohio
d. Aug 27, 1948 in New York, New York
Source: *ASCAP 66, 80; Baker 78, 84, 92; BiDAmM; CmpEPM; ConAmC 76, 82; DcAmB S4; InWom SUP; NewAmDM; NewGrDA 86; NotNAT B; OxCMus; OxCPMus; PopAmC; WhAm 2*

Speare, Elizabeth George
American. Children's Author
Won Newbery Medals for *The Witch of Blackbird Pond,* 1959; *The Bronze Bow,* 1962.
b. Nov 21, 1908 in Melrose, Massachusetts
d. Nov 15, 1994 in Tucson, Arizona
Source: *AmAu&B; AmWomWr; Au&Wr 71; AuBYP 2, 3; BioIn 14, 17, 19, 20, 21; ChlBkCr; ChlLR 8; ConAu 1R, 147; CurBio 59, 95N; DcAmChF 1960; ForWC 70; IntAu&W 77, 82; InWom; MajAI; MorBMP; MorJA; NewbC 1956; OxCChiL; SmATA 5, 62, 83; TwCChW 78, 83, 89; TwCYAW; WhAm 11; WhoAm 74, 76, 78, 80, 82, 84, 86, 88, 90, 92, 94; WhoAmW 64, 66, 68, 70, 72, 74, 93; WrDr 76, 80, 82, 84, 86, 88, 90, 92, 94, 96*

Speck, Frank Gouldsmith
American. Anthropologist
Cultural anthropologist; pioneered studies in ethnoscience and ethnomusicology; known for work on Algonquin Indians.
b. Nov 8, 1881 in New York, New York
d. Feb 6, 1950 in Philadelphia, Pennsylvania
Source: *AmAu&B; BenetAL 91; BioIn 2, 13, 14; DcAmB S4; OxCCan; REnAL; WhAm 2A; WhLit*

Speck, Richard Franklin
American. Murderer
Killed eight student nurses in Chicago, July 13-14, 1966.
b. Dec 6, 1941 in Kirkwood, Illinois
d. Dec 5, 1991 in Joliet, Illinois
Source: *BioIn 7, 15; MurCaTw; NewYTBS 91*

Specter, Arlen
American. Politician
Rep. senator from PA, 1981—.
b. Feb 12, 1930 in Wichita, Kansas
Source: *AlmAP 82, 84, 88, 92, 96; BiDrUSC 89; BioIn 7, 12, 16; CngDr 81, 83, 85, 87, 89, 91, 93, 95; CurBio 88; IntWW 81, 82, 83, 89, 91, 93; IntYB 82; LegTOT; PolsAm 84; WhoAm 84, 86, 88, 90, 92, 94, 95, 96, 97; WhoAmP 73, 75, 77, 79, 81, 83, 85, 87, 89, 91, 93, 95; WhoAmW 70; WhoE 74, 75, 83, 85, 86, 89, 91, 93, 95, 97; WhoWor 82, 87, 89, 91*

Spector, Phil(lip Harvey)
American. Producer
Devised ''wall of sound'' technique of sound arrangement, 1962; highlights lead vocals; inducted into Rock-'n'-Roll Hall of Fame, 1989.
b. Dec 26, 1940 in New York, New York
Source: *BioIn 9, 12, 16; ConMus 4; CurBio 89; DcArts; EncPR&S 89; EncRk 88; IlEncBM 82; IlEncRk; LegTOT; MusMk; NewGrDA 86; News 89-1; OxCPMus; PenEncP; RkWW 82; RolSEnR 83; SoulM; WhoAm 78, 80, 82, 84, 86, 88, 90, 92, 94, 95, 96, 97; WhoEnt 92; WhoHol 92; WhoRock 81; WhoRocM 82; WhoWest 92, 94; WorAl; WorAlBi*

Spectorsky, Auguste Compte
American. Journalist
Associate publisher, *Playboy* mag., 1956-72; best known for witty book, *The Exurbanites,* 1955.
b. Aug 13, 1910 in Paris, France
d. Jan 17, 1972 in Saint Croix, Virgin Islands of the United States
Source: *AmAu&B; ConAu P-2; CurBio 60, 72; NewYTBE 72; REnAL; WhAm 5*

Spedding, Frank Harold
American. Chemist
Pioneered advances in cheaper production of rare-earth metals; was instrumental in developing methods of extracting pure uranium for use in nuclear chain reaction experiments.
b. Oct 22, 1902 in Hamilton, Ontario, Canada
d. Dec 15, 1984 in Ames, Iowa
Source: *AmMWSc 76P, 79, 82; AnObit 1984; AsBiEn; BiESc; BioIn 1, 3, 8, 14, 15; BlueB 76; IntWW 74, 75, 76, 77, 78, 79, 80, 81, 82, 83; LarDcSc; McGMS 80; NotTwCS; WhAm 8; WhoAm 74, 76; WhoTech 84; WhoWor 74*

Speer, Albert
German. Architect
Germany's official architect under Hitler; helped plan war economy with Goering.
b. Mar 19, 1905 in Mannheim, Germany
d. Sep 1, 1981 in London, England
Source: *AnObit 1981; BiDExR; BioIn 1, 2, 3, 8, 9, 10, 11, 12, 13, 14, 15, 16, 18, 21; ConArch 80; ConAu 40NR, 65, 104; CurBio 76, 81, 81N; DcArts; DcTwHis; EncTR, 91; FacFETw; HisEWW; HisWorL; LegTOT; MacEA; NewCol 75; NewYTBS 81; WhWW-II*

Speicher, Eugene Edward
American. Artist
Portraitist; best example of realistic painting, *Lilya,* 1930.
b. Apr 5, 1883 in Buffalo, New York
d. May 11, 1962 in Woodstock, New York

Source: *BioIn 1, 2, 4, 6; BriEAA; CurBio 47, 62; DcCAA 71; McGDA; OxCAmH; WhAm 4*

Speidel, Hans
German. Military Leader
Part of abortive plot to assassinate Hitler, 1944; commanded Allied land forces in central Europe for NATO, 1957-63.
b. Oct 28, 1897 in Metzingen, Germany
d. Nov 28, 1984 in Bad Honnef, Germany (West)
Source: *BioIn 2, 3, 4, 11, 14, 17; ConAu 114, 133; CurBio 85, 85N; EncTR, 91; HarEnMi; IntWW 74, 75, 76, 77, 78, 79, 80, 81, 82, 83; IntYB 78, 79, 80, 81, 82; NewYTBS 84; Who 74, 82, 83, 85; WhWW-II*

Speight, Johnny
English. Writer
Created BBC series "Till Death Do Us Part," 1966-75; adapted in US as "All in the Family," 1971.
b. Jun 2, 1921? in London, England
Source: *BioIn 10; ConAu 117; ConDr 73, 77, 82C; DcLEL 1940; IntAu&W 77, 91; Who 92; WrDr 76, 80, 82, 84, 86, 88, 90, 92, 94, 96*

Speke, John Hanning
English. Explorer
Discovered Lake Victoria, 1858, confirmed as source of the Nile, 1862.
b. May 4, 1827 in Jordans, England
d. Sep 18, 1864 in Bath, England
Source: *Alli; BbD; BiD&SB; BioIn 4, 5, 6, 8, 9, 18, 20, 21; BritAu 19; CamGEL; CamGLE; CelCen; DcAfHiB 86; DcBiPP; DcLB 166; DcLEL; DcNaB; EvLB; Expl 93; HisDBrE; LinLib L, S; McGEWB; NewC; NewCBEL; OxCEng 67, 85, 95; WhWE*

Spelling, Aaron
American. Producer
Most successful TV producer; shows include "Charlie's Angels," "Dynasty," "Hotel," "Beverly Hills 90210."
b. Apr 22, 1923 in Dallas, Texas
Source: *BioIn 16; CelR 90; ConTFT 3, 12; CurBio 86; IntMPA 92; LesBEnT, 92; NewYTBS 91; St&PR 91; WhoAm 86, 90, 92, 94, 95, 96, 97; WhoEnt 92; WhoHol A; WhoTelC; WorAlBi*

Spelling, Tori
[Victoria Spelling]
American. Actor
Plays Donna Martin on TV series "Beverly Hills 90210;" daughter of Aaron Spelling.
b. May 16, 1973 in Los Angeles, California
Source: *LegTOT*

Spellman, Francis Joseph
American. Religious Leader
Appointed Archbishop of NY, 1939, cardinal, 1946 by Pope Pius XII.
b. May 4, 1889 in Whitman, Massachusetts
d. Dec 2, 1967 in New York, New York
Source: *AmAu&B; BioIn 1, 2, 3, 4, 5, 6, 7, 8, 9, 11, 12; CathA 1930; ChhPo; ColdWar 2; ConAu 113; CurBio 40, 47, 68; DcAmB S8; DcAmReB 1, 2; EncAB-H 1974, 1996; EncARH; LinLib S; McGEWB; WebAB 74, 79; WhAm 4; WhNAA; WorAl; WorAlBi*

Spemann, Hans
German. Educator, Biologist
Won Nobel Prize in medicine, 1935, for work on embryonic development.
b. Jun 27, 1869 in Stuttgart, Germany
d. Sep 12, 1941 in Freiburg, Germany
Source: *AsBiEn; BiESc; BioIn 3, 6, 12, 14, 15, 20; DcScB; InSci; LarDcSc; McGEWB; NobelP; NotTwCS; WhoNob, 90, 95; WorAl; WorAlBi*

Spence, Basil Urwin, Sir
English. Architect
Designed new Coventry Cathedral, 1951.
b. Aug 13, 1907 in Bombay, India
d. Nov 18, 1976 in Eye, England
Source: *Au&Wr 71; BioIn 3, 5, 9, 11, 14, 21; ConArch 87, 94; ConDes 84, 97; DcBrAr 1; DcNaB 1971; GrBr; IntWW 74, 75, 76; WebBD 83; Who 74; WhoWor 74*

Spence, Lewis
[James Lewis Thomas Chalmers Spence]
Scottish. Editor, Poet, Folklorist
Wrote on occult, Mexican mythology: *The Occult Sciences in Atlantis,* 1943.
b. Nov 25, 1874 in Dundee, Scotland
d. Mar 3, 1955 in Edinburgh, Scotland
Source: *BioIn 3, 4; ChhPo, S1, S3; CmScLit; ConAu 115; EncO&P 1, 2, 3; EvLB; ObitT 1951; OxCTwCP; PenC ENG; ScF&FL 1; TwCA SUP; WhLit; WhoLA*

Spencer, Herbert
English. Philosopher
Applied Darwin's doctrine of evolution to philosophy, ethics; wrote *Principles of Sociology,* 1876-96.
b. Apr 27, 1820 in Derby, England
d. Dec 8, 1903 in Brighton, England
Source: *Alli, SUP; AsBiEn; BbD; Benet 87, 96; BiD&SB; BiDPsy; BiESc; BioIn 1, 3, 4, 5, 6, 7, 8, 9, 10, 11, 13, 14, 15, 16, 19, 21; BlmGEL; BritAu 19; CamGEL; CamGLE; CasWL; CelCen; Chambr 3; CyEd; DcAmC; DcAmSR; DcBiPP; DcEnA, A; DcEnL; DcLB 57; DcLEL; DcNaB S2; DcScB; DcSoc; Dis&D; EncEth; EncUnb; EncUrb; EvLB; InSci; IntDcAn; LarDcSc; LinLib L, S; LngCEL; LuthC 75; McGEWB; NamesHP; NewC; NewCBEL; OxCEng 67, 85, 95; OxCLaw; OxCPhil; PenC ENG; RAdv 14, 13-3, 13-4; REn; VicBrit; WebE&AL; WhAm HS; WhDW; WorAl; WorAlBi; WrPh P*

Spencer, Percy Le Baron
American. Inventor
Invented the microwave oven, 1946.
b. Jul 9, 1894 in Howland, Maine
d. Sep 7, 1970 in Newton, Massachusetts
Source: *NewYTBE 70; WhAm 5*

Spencer, Stanley, Sir
English. Artist
Drew surrealistic religious paintings including *Resurrection* series, 1945-50.
b. Jun 30, 1891 in Cookham-on-Thames, England
d. Dec 14, 1959 in Taplow, England
Source: *BioIn 1, 2, 3, 4, 5, 6, 7, 9, 11, 12, 14, 17; ConArt 77, 83; DcArts; DcBrAr 1; DcNaB 1951; FacFETw; GrBr; IntDcAA 90; McGDA; NewCol 75; ObitT 1951; OxCArt; OxCTwCA; OxDcArt; PhDcTCA 77; TwCPaSc; WhDW; WorArt 1950*

Spencer, William
American. Author
Historical writings include *Historical Dictionary of Morocco,* 1980.
b. Jun 1, 1922 in Erie, Pennsylvania
Source: *AuBYP 2, 3; BioIn 11; ConAu 8NR, 17R, 23NR; DrAS 74H, 78H; Dun&B 90; IntAu&W 76, 77, 82, 86, 89, 91, 93; IntMed 80; SmATA 9; WhoFla; WrDr 76, 80, 82, 84, 86, 88, 90, 92, 94, 96*

Spencer Davis Group, The
[Spencer Davis; Muff Winwood; Stevie Winwood; Pete York]
English. Music Group
Hits include "Gimme Some Lovin'," 1967.
Source: *ConMuA 80A, 80B; EncPR&S 89; EncRk 88; IlEncRk; RkOn 78; RolSEnR 83; WhoHol 92; WhoRock 81; WhoRocM 82; WhScrn 83*

Spender, Stephen (Harold)
English. Author, Poet
Wrote autobiography *World Within World,* 1951; *Collected Poems,* 1954.
b. Feb 28, 1909 in London, England
d. Jul 16, 1995 in London, England
Source: *Au&Wr 71; AuBYP 2S, 3; Benet 87, 96; BioIn 1, 2, 3, 4, 5, 8, 9, 10, 11, 12, 13, 14, 15, 16, 17, 18, 19, 20, 21; BlmGEL; BlueB 76; BritWr S2; CamGEL; CamGLE; CasWL; Chambr 3; ChhPo, S2, S3; CnDBLB 7; CnE&AP; CnMD; CnMWL; ConAu 9R, 31NR, 54NR, 149; ConLC 1, 2, 5, 10, 41, 91; ConLCrt 77, 82; ConPo 70, 75, 80, 85, 91, 96; CurBio 40, 77, 95N; CyWA 58, 89; DcArts; DcLB 20; DcLEL; EncWB; EncWL, 2, 3; EngPo; EvLB; FacFETw; GayLL; GrWrEL P; IntAu&W 76, 77, 91, 93; IntWW 74, 75, 76, 77, 78, 79, 80, 81, 82, 83, 89, 91, 93; IntWWP 77; LegTOT; LinLib L, S; LngCEL; LngCTC; MajTwCW; MakMC; ModBrL, S1, S2; ModWD; NewC; NewCBEL; NewYTBS 95; OxCEng 67, 85, 95; OxCTwCP; PenC ENG; RAdv 1, 14, 13-1; REn; RfGEnL 91; RGTwCWr; TwCA, SUP; TwCWr; WebE&AL; WhDW; WhE&EA; Who 74, 82, 83, 85, 88, 90, 92, 94; WhoAm 76; WhoTwCL; WhoWor 74, 78, 80, 82, 91; WorAl; WorAlBi;*

WrDr 76, 80, 82, 84, 86, 88, 90, 92, 94, 96

Spengler, Oswald
German. Philosopher
Best known for *Decline of the West,* 1918-22.
b. May 29, 1880 in Blankenburg, Germany
d. May 8, 1936 in Munich, Germany
Source: *Benet 87, 96; BiDExR; BioIn 2, 4, 7, 9, 10, 12, 13, 14; CasWL; ConAu 118; EncGRNM; EncRev; EncTR, 91; EvEuW; FacFETw; LegTOT; LinLib L, S; LngCTC; LuthC 75; MakMC; McGEWB; OxCGer 76, 86; RAdv 14, 13-3; REn; ThTwC 87; TwCA, SUP; TwCLC 25; TwCWr; WhDW; WorAl; WorAlBi; WrPh P*

Spenkelink, John Arthur
American. Murderer
First person involuntarily executed in US since 1967.
b. 1949 in Buena Park, California
d. May 25, 1979 in Starke, Florida
Source: *BioIn 11, 12*

Spenser, Edmund
English. Poet
Developed Spenserian stanza used in allegorical epic *The Faerie Queen,* 1596.
b. 1552? in London, England
d. Jan 13, 1599 in London, England
Source: *Alli; AtlBL; BbD; Benet 87, 96; BiD&SB; BiDRP&D; BioIn 1, 2, 3, 4, 5, 6, 7, 8, 9, 10, 11, 12, 14, 15, 18, 19, 20, 21; BlmGEL; BritAu; CamGEL; CamGLE; CasWL; Chambr 1; ChhPo, S1, S2; CnDBLB 1; CnE&AP; CroE&S; CrtT 1, 4; CyEd; CyWA 58; DcArts; DcEnA; DcEnL; DcEuL; DcIrL 96; DcLB 167; DcLEL; DcNaB; EvLB; GrWrEL P; LegTOT; LinLib L, S; LitC 5; LngCEL; LuthC 75; MagSWL; McGEWB; MouLC 1; NewC; NewCBEL; OxCEng 67, 85, 95; OxCIri; PenC ENG; PoeCrit 8; PoLE; RAdv 1, 14, 13-1; RComWL; REn; RfGEnL 91; RGFBP; WebE&AL; WhDW; WorAl; WorAlBi; WorLitC; WrPh*

Speransky, Mikhail
Russian. Political Leader
Chief adviser to Czar Alexander, 1808-12, under Nicholas I was responsible for systemized Russian laws, 1833.
b. 1772
d. 1839
Source: *NewCol 75*

Sperling, Godfrey, Jr.
American. Journalist
Chief of Washington Bureau, *Christian Science Monitor,* 1973-83; senior Washington columnist, 1984—.
b. Sep 25, 1915 in Long Beach, California
Source: *BiDAmNC; BioIn 9; WhoAm 74, 76, 78, 80, 82, 84, 86, 88, 90, 92, 94, 95, 96, 97; WhoSSW 73*

Sperry, Armstrong W
American. Author, Illustrator, Children's Author
Most of writings based on his travel adventures throughout the world.
b. Nov 7, 1897 in New Haven, Connecticut
d. Apr 28, 1976 in Hanover, New Hampshire
Source: *AnCL; CurBio 41; IlsCB 1744, 1946; JBA 34, 51; NewbMB 1922; SmATA 1, 27; Str&VC*

Sperry, Elmer Ambrose
American. Inventor
Invented gyrocompass and numerous electrical devices.
b. Oct 12, 1860 in Cortland, New York
d. Jun 10, 1930 in New York, New York
Source: *AmBi; ApCAB X; AsBiEn; BiDAmBL 83; BiESc; BioIn 3, 4, 5, 6, 9, 12, 13, 19, 20, 21; DcAmB; DcScB; EncAB-H 1974, 1996; InSci; LinLib S; NatCAB 15, 23; NewCol 75; OxCAmH; OxCShps; WebAB 74, 79; WhAm 1; WhDW; WorAl*

Sperry, Roger W(olcott)
American. Biologist
Won Nobel Prize, 1981, for contributions to understanding human brain.
b. Aug 20, 1913 in Hartford, Connecticut
d. Apr 17, 1994 in Pasadena, California
Source: *AmMWSc 73S, 78S, 82, 86, 89, 92; BiESc; BioIn 12, 13, 14, 15, 19, 20, 21; BlueB 76; CamDcSc; CurBio 86, 94N; IntWW 74, 75, 76, 77, 78, 79, 80, 81, 82, 83, 89, 91, 93; LarDcSc; McGMS 80; NewYTBS 81; WhAm 11; Who 83, 85, 88, 90, 92, 94; WhoAm 74, 76, 78, 80, 82, 84, 86, 88, 90, 92, 94; WhoFrS 84; WhoNob, 90, 95; WhoScEn 94; WhoUSWr 88; WhoWest 82, 84, 87, 89, 92, 94; WhoWor 74, 84, 87, 89, 91, 93; WhoWrEP 89, 92; WorAlBi*

Sperti, George Speri
American. Scientist, Inventor
Holder of over 100 patents including Preparation H and Aspercreme.
b. Jan 17, 1900 in Covington, Kentucky
d. Apr 29, 1991 in Cincinnati, Ohio
Source: *AmCath 80; AmMWSc 73P, 76P, 79, 82, 86, 89; BioIn 2, 14, 17; CurBio 91N; InSci; IntWW 74, 75, 76, 77, 78, 79, 80, 81, 82, 83, 89, 91; InWom SUP; News 89-2; WhAm 10; WhoAm 74, 76, 78, 80, 86, 88; WhoEnt 92; WorInv*

Spethmann, Dieter
German. Business Executive
Chairman of German steelmaker Thyssen since 1973.
b. 1926? in Essen, Germany
Source: *BioIn 15; IntWW 77*

Spewack, Bella Cohen
[Mrs. Samuel Spewack]
American. Dramatist, Journalist
With husband, wrote Broadway hits *Boy Meets Girl,* 1935, *Kiss Me Kate,* 1949.
b. Mar 25, 1899 in Bucharest, Romania
d. Apr 27, 1990 in New York, New York
Source: *AmAu&B; AmWomD; AmWomPl; Au&Wr 71; BenetAL 91; BiDAmM; BiE&WWA; BioIn 4, 7, 9, 16; CnMD; ConAu 33R; ConDr 73, 82D; DcAmB S9; EncAFC; EncMT; FilmEn; IntMPA 88; InWom, SUP; McGEWD 72, 84; ModWD; NewCBMT; NewYTBS 76, 90; NotNAT, B; NotWoAT; OxCAmT 84; REn; REnAL; TwCA, SUP; WhAm 5, 10; WhJnl; WhoAm 74, 76; WhoThe 77; WhThe; WomWMM*

Spewack, Samuel
Russian. Dramatist
With wife Bella, wrote Broadway hits *Boy Meets Girl,* 1935, *Kiss Me Kate,* 1949.
b. Sep 16, 1899 in Bachmut, Russia
d. Oct 14, 1971 in New York, New York
Source: *AmAu&B; Au&Wr 71; BenetAL 91; BiDAmM; BiE&WWA; BioIn 4, 7, 9, 16; CnMD; ConAu 33R; DcAmB S9; EncAFC; FilmEn; McGEWD 72, 84; ModWD; NewCBMT; NewYTBE 71; NotNAT B; OxCAmT 84; REn; REnAL; TwCA, SUP; WhAm 5; WhJnl; WhThe*

Spheeris, Penelope
American. Filmmaker
Founded music video production company, Rock n' Reel, 1974. Films *The Decline of Western Civilization I-II,* 1980-88 depict punk and heavy-metal movements.
b. 1945
Source: *ConTFT 11; IntMPA 88, 92, 94, 96; LegTOT; MiSFD 9; News 89-2; WhoAm 92, 94, 95, 96, 97; WhoAmW 95; WhoEnt 92*

Spicer, Jack
American. Poet
Wrote first book of poetry, *After Lorca,* 1957, in which he "communicates" with the Spanish poet Federico Garcia Lorca.
b. 1925 in Hollywood, California
d. 1965
Source: *AmAu&B; BenetAL 91; BioIn 12, 13; ConAu 85; ConLC 8, 18, 72; ConPo 80A, 85A; DcLB 5, 16; GayLL; OxCAmL 83, 95; OxCTwCP; PenC AM*

Spiegel, Sam
[S P Eagle]
American. Producer
Won Oscars for *On the Waterfront,* 1954; *The Bridge on the River Kwai,* 1957; *Lawrence of Arabia,* 1962.
b. Nov 11, 1904 in Jaroslau, Austria
d. Dec 31, 1985, St. Martin
Source: *BiDFilm, 81, 94; FilmgC; IntMPA 82; OxCFilm; WhoAm 78, 80, 82, 84; WhoAmA 73, 76, 78, 80, 82, 84; WhoAmJ 80; WhoWorJ 72, 78; WorEFlm*

Spiegelman, Art
[Joe Cutrate; Al Flooglebuckle; Skeeter Grant]
American. Cartoonist, Writer
Published *Maus: A Survivor's Tale I: My Father Bleeds History,* 1986 and *Maus: A Survivor's Tale II: And Here My Troubles Began,* 1991; both about the experiences of a Jew in Nazi-occupied Poland; won Pulitzer Prize, 1992, for these books.
b. Feb 15, 1948 in Stockholm, Sweden
Source: *Au&Arts 10; BioIn 10; ConAu 41NR, 55NR, 125; ConGrA 3; ConLC 76; CurBio 94; EncACom; MugS; TwCYAW; WhoAm 92, 94, 95, 96, 97; WhoE 95, 97*

Spielberg, David
American. Actor
Noted for TV, stage, film work; won Obie for *Sleep,* 1971.
b. Mar 6, 1939 in Mercedes, Texas
Source: *BioIn 11; ConTFT 1, 5; HalFC 84, 88; VarWW 85; WhoEnt 92; WhoHol 92*

Spielberg, Steven
American. Director, Producer
Films include *Jaws,* 1975; *ET,* 1982; *Schindler's List,* 1993; *Jurassic Park.*
b. Dec 18, 1947 in Cincinnati, Ohio
Source: *AmDec 1980; Au&Arts 8; BenetAL 91; BiDFilm 81, 94; BioIn 10, 13, 14, 15, 16, 17, 18, 19, 20, 21; CelR 90; ConAu 32NR, 77; ConHero 1; ConLC 20; ConTFT 1, 10; CurBio 78, 96; DcArts; DcTwCCu 1; EncSF 93; FacFETw; FilmEn; FilmgC; HalFC 88; IlWWHD 1; IntDcF 1-2, 2-2; IntMPA 75, 76, 77, 78, 79, 80, 81, 82, 84, 86, 88, 92, 94, 96; IntWW 83, 89, 91, 93; JeHun; LegTOT; LesBEnT 92; MiSFD 9; NewEScF; News 93; NewYTBS 82; ScF&FL 92; ScFSB; SmATA 32; Who 88, 90, 92, 94; WhoAm 80, 82, 84, 86, 88, 90, 92, 94, 95, 96, 97; WhoEnt 92; WorAlBi; WorFDir 2*

Spielhagen, Friedrich von
German. Writer
Popular social novelist; wrote *Problematische Naturen,* 1861.
b. Feb 24, 1829 in Magdeburg, Prussia
d. Feb 25, 1911 in Berlin, Germany
Source: *Benet 87; OxCGer 86*

Spier, Peter Edward
American. Artist, Author
Self-illustrated children's books include *Gobble, Growl, Grunt,* 1971.
b. Jun 6, 1927 in Amsterdam, Netherlands
Source: *AuBYP 2S, 2SA, 3; BioIn 16; BkP; ConAu 5R, 41NR; IlsBYP; IlsCB 1946, 1957; MajAI; SmATA 4; ThrBJA; WhoAm 74, 76, 78, 80, 82, 84, 86, 88, 90, 94, 95, 96, 97; WhoAmA 76, 78, 80, 82, 84, 86, 89, 91, 93*

Spigelgass, Leonard
American. Dramatist
Oscar nominee for best original story: *Mystery Street,* 1950.
b. Nov 26, 1908 in New York, New York
d. Feb 14, 1985 in Los Angeles, California
Source: *BiE&WWA; BioIn 14; ConAu 103, 115; IntMPA 77, 80, 82; NotNAT; WhoAm 74, 76; WhoThe 72, 77*

Spillane, Mickey
[Frank Morrison Spillane]
American. Author
Known for Mike Hammer detective stories.
b. Mar 9, 1918 in New York, New York
Source: *AmAu&B; Benet 87, 96; BenetAL 91; BioIn 2, 3, 4, 5, 6, 9, 11, 12, 14, 15, 17, 21; CelR, 90; ConAu 25R, 28NR, X; ConLC 3, 13; CorpD; CrtSuMy; CurBio 81; DcArts; DcTwCCu 1; EncMys; FacFETw; FilmgC; HalFC 80, 84, 88; IntAu&W 91; LegTOT; LinLib L; LngCTC; MajTwCW; Novels; OxCAmL 65, 83, 95; PenC AM; RAdv 14; REn; SmATA 66; SpyFic; TwCCr&M 80, 85, 91; TwCWr; WebAB 74, 79; WhoAm 76, 78, 80, 82, 84, 86, 88, 90, 92, 94, 95, 96, 97; WhoHol 92, A; WhoWrEP 89; WorAl; WorAlBi; WrDr 76, 80, 82, 84, 86, 88, 90, 92, 94, 96*

Spilsbury, Bernard Henry, Sir
English. Pathologist
Homicide expert; subject of *Scalpel of Scotland Yard,* 1952; committed suicide.
b. 1877 in Leamington, England
d. Dec 17, 1947 in London, England
Source: *BioIn 1, 2, 5, 7, 10, 14; CopCroC; DcNaB 1941; GrBr; InSci; LngCTC; ObitOF 79*

Spinal Tap
American. Music Group
Fictitious British heavy metal band made famous in the film *This Is Spinal Tap,* 1984; first appeared on television's "The TV Show," 1978.
Source: *BioIn 15, 18, 20; ConMus 8; ConTFT 3; EncRkSt; WhoAm 80, 82, 84, 86, 88, 90, 92, 94; WhoEnt 92*

Spingarn, Arthur Barnett
American. Lawyer, Civil Rights Leader
Pres., NAACP, 1940-65; honorary pres., 1966-71.
b. Mar 28, 1878 in New York, New York
d. Dec 1, 1971 in New York, New York
Source: *BioIn 7, 9, 16; CurBio 65, 72; DcAmBC; DcAmB S9; EncAACR; NewYTBE 71; WhAm 5*

Spingarn, Joel Elias
American. Author, Educator
Founded NAACP, 1913, pres., 1930-31; originated Spingarn Medal, 1914.
b. May 17, 1875 in New York, New York
d. Jul 26, 1939 in New York, New York
Source: *AmAu&B; AmBi; AmLY; AmRef; AmSocL; AnMV 1926; BioIn 3, 4, 9, 11, 15, 17, 19; ChhPo; CnDAL; DcAmAu; DcAmB S2; DcLEL; DcNAA; EncAB-H 1974, 1996; LinLib L; NatCAB 17; OxCAmL 65; REn; REnAL; TwCA; WebAB 74, 79; WhAm 1; WhNAA; WorAl*

Spinks, Leon
American. Boxer
Won gold medal, 1976 Olympics; won world heavyweight title from Muhammad Ali, 1977.
b. Jul 11, 1953 in Saint Louis, Missouri
Source: *BiDAmSp BK; BioIn 11, 12, 16; BlkOlyM; LegTOT; NewYTBS 89*

Spinks, Michael
American. Boxer
Defeated Larry Holmes to become WBC heavyweight champ, 1985.
b. Jul 29, 1956 in Saint Louis, Missouri
Source: *BiDAmSp Sup; BioIn 12, 13, 16; BlkOlyM; BoxReg; InB&W 80; LegTOT; WhoAfA 96; WhoAm 86, 88, 90, 92, 94, 95, 96, 97; WhoBlA 88, 90, 92, 94*

Spinola, Antonio (Sebastiao Ribeiro) de
American. Military Leader, Political Leader
Pres., Portugal, 1974.
b. Apr 11, 1910
d. Aug 13, 1996 in Lisbon, Portugal
Source: *CurBio 96N; IntWW 74, 75, 76, 77, 78, 79, 80, 81, 82, 83, 89, 91, 93*

Spinoza, Baruch (Benedictus de)
Dutch. Philosopher
Exponent of rational pantheism; wrote *Ethics Demonstrated with Geometrical Order,* 1674.
b. Nov 24, 1632 in Amsterdam, Netherlands
d. Feb 20, 1677 in The Hague, Netherlands
Source: *BbD; Benet 87, 96; BiD&SB; BlkwCE; CasWL; DcEuL; Dis&D; EncUnb; EvEuW; IlEncMy; LegTOT; LinLib L, S; McGEWB; NewC; OxCEng 67; OxCLaw; OxCPhil; PenC EUR; RAdv 14, 13-4; RComWL; REn; TwoTYeD; WorAl; WorAlBi; WrPh P*

Spitalny, Phil
American. Bandleader
Conducted female orchestra, 1935-55.
b. Nov 7, 1890 in Odessa, Russia
d. Oct 11, 1970 in Miami, Florida
Source: *ASCAP 66, 80; BiDAmM; BioIn 9; CmpEPM; NewAmDM; NewGrDA 86; RadStar; SaTiSS; WhoHol B; WhScrn 74, 77, 83; WorAl*

Spitta, Philipp
[Julius August Philipp Spitta]
German. Author, Educator
Leading figure in late-19th c. musicology; wrote first comprehensive biography of Bach, 1873.
b. Dec 27, 1841 in Wechold, Germany

d. Apr 13, 1894 in Berlin, Germany
Source: *Baker 78, 84; BriBkM 80; LuthC 75; NewGrDM 80; NewOxM; OxCMus*

Spitteler, Karl Friedrich Georg
[Felix Tandem]
Swiss. Poet
Best-known epic poem: *Olympischer Fruhling,* 1900-10; Nobelist, 1919.
b. Apr 24, 1845 in Liestal, Switzerland
d. Dec 28, 1924 in Lucerne, Switzerland
Source: *BioIn 15, 19; ConAu 109; Dis&D; EvEuW; LinLib L; WhoNob*

Spitz, Mark Andrew
American. Swimmer
First athlete to win seven gold medals in single Olympic games, 1972; Sports Hall of Fame, 1991.
b. Feb 10, 1950 in Modesto, California
Source: *BiDAmSp BK; BioIn 16; BioNews 74; CurBio 72; FacFETw; NewYTBE 72, 73; WhoAm 74, 76; WorAlBi*

Spitzer, Andre
Israeli. Olympic Athlete, Victim
One of 11 members of Israeli Olympic team kidnapped and killed by Arab terrorists during Summer Olympic Games.
b. 1945?, Romania
d. Sep 5, 1972 in Munich, Germany (West)
Source: *BioIn 9*

Spitzer, Lyman, Jr.
American. Astronomer
Called the father of satellite astronomy.
b. Jun 26, 1914
d. Mar 31, 1997 in Princeton, New Jersey
Source: *AmMWSc 73P, 76P, 79, 82, 86, 89, 92, 95; AsBiEn; BiESc; BioIn 5, 10, 14, 20; BlueB 76; ConAu 116; InSci; IntAu&W 77, 86, 89, 91, 93; IntWW 74, 75, 76, 77, 78, 79, 80, 81, 82, 83, 89, 91, 93; LarDcSc; McGMS 80; NotTwCS; Who 74, 82, 83, 85, 88, 90, 92, 94; WhoAm 74, 76, 78, 80, 82, 84, 86, 88, 90, 92, 94, 95, 96, 97; WhoE 74, 75, 77; WhoFrS 84; WhoScEn 96; WhoTech 82, 84, 89, 95; WhoWor 74, 76, 78; WorAl; WorAlBi; WrDr 76, 80, 82, 84, 86, 88, 90, 92, 94, 96*

Spitzweg, Carl
German. Artist
Best known early Victorian painter in Germany.
b. Feb 5, 1808 in Munich, Germany
d. Sep 23, 1885 in Munich, Germany
Source: *BioIn 10, 11, 14, 20; ClaDrA; McGDA; OxCArt; OxCGer 76, 86; WorECar*

Spivak, Charlie
American. Bandleader, Musician
Played lead trumpet with his popular band, 1940s-50s; disbanded with demise of big bands.
b. Feb 17, 1906 in New Haven, Connecticut
d. Mar 1, 1982 in Greenville, South Carolina
Source: *CmpEPM; NewYTBS 82; OxCPMus; PenEncP; WhoJazz 72*

Spivak, Lawrence E(dmund)
American. TV Personality, Producer
Co-founder, producer, panel member, *Meet the Press,* on radio, TV, 1945-1975.
b. Jun 11, 1900 in New York, New York
d. Mar 9, 1994 in Washington, District of Columbia
Source: *BioIn 4, 6, 9; CurBio 56, 94N; IntMPA 82, 92; WhAm 11; WhoAm 76, 78, 80, 82, 84, 86, 88, 90, 92; WhoAmJ 80; WhoEnt 92; WhoSSW 73; WhoWorJ 72; WorAlBi*

Spivakov, Valdimir (Teodorovich)
Russian. Violinist
Founded the Moscow Virtuosi, a 26-member chamber orchestra, 1979.
b. Sep 12, 1944 in Ufa, Union of Soviet Socialist Republics
Source: *CurBio 96*

Spivakovsky, Tossy
Russian. Musician
Concert master of Berlin Philharmonic pre Nazism; violin soloist, 1941—.
b. Feb 4, 1907 in Odessa, Russia
Source: *Baker 78, 84, 92; BioIn 1, 2, 3, 4, 9; IntWW 74, 75, 76, 77, 78, 79, 80, 81, 82, 83, 89, 91, 93; IntWWM 85, 90; NewGrDA 86; PenDiMP; WhoAmM 83; WhoWor 74; WhoWorJ 72*

Spock, Benjamin McLane
American. Physician, Author
Wrote *Common Sense Book of Baby Care,* 1946; sold over 40 million copies.
b. May 2, 1903 in New Haven, Connecticut
Source: *AmAu&B; AmPeW; Au&Wr 71; AuNews 1; BioIn 13, 16; BioNews 74; CelR 90; ConAu 35NR; ConHero 1; CurBio 56, 69; EncAB-H 1974, 1996; FacFETw; IntWW 91; MajTwCW; NewYTBE 72; PolProf NF; RComAH; REnAL; WebAB 79; Who 90, 92; WhoAm 86, 90, 97; WhoAmP 91; WhoMedH; WhoWor 91, 97; WrDr 86, 92*

Spode, Josiah
English. Artist
Potter; developed fine English porcelain called Spode ware, 1799.
b. Jul 16, 1754
d. 1827
Source: *DcArts; LegTOT; NewCol 75; PenDiDA 89; WebBD 83; WhDW*

Spofford, Charles M(erville)
American. Lawyer
Pres. Metropolitan Opera Assn., 1946-50; initiator of Lincoln Center for the Performing Arts.
b. Nov 17, 1902 in Saint Louis, Missouri
d. Mar 23, 1991 in Hampton, New York
Source: *BiDWWGF; BiE&WWA; BioIn 2, 9, 17; CurBio 91N; NewYTBS 91; Who 74, 82, 83, 85, 88, 90, 92N; WhoAmL 79; WhoE 74*

Spohr, Louis Ludwig
German. Violinist, Composer, Conductor
Traveling violin virtuoso, opera conductor; known for chamber works.
b. Apr 5, 1784 in Brunswick, Germany
d. Oct 22, 1859 in Cassel, Germany
Source: *OxCMus*

Spokane Garry
American. Native American Chief
Chief of the Spokane; tribe signed treaty with US government ceding land, 1887.
b. 1811? in Washington
d. Jan 12, 1892? in Washington
Source: *BioIn 21; EncNAB; NotNaAm; WhNaAH*

Spong, John
American. Religious Leader
Controversial Episcopal bishop approves of women and homosexual clergy, and monogamous homosexual relationships affirmed by the church.
b. Jun 16, 1931 in Charlotte, North Carolina
Source: *BioIn 15; IntWW 91; News 91, 91-3; WhoAm 90; WhoE 91; WhoRel 92*

Spontini, Gasparo
Italian. Composer, Conductor
Wrote opera *La Vestale,* 1807; developed modern orchestral conducting.
b. Nov 14, 1774 in Majolati, Italy
d. Jan 24, 1851 in Majolati, Italy
Source: *Baker 84; BioIn 1, 4, 7, 8, 12; BriBkM 80; CmOp; DcCom 77; DcCom&M 79; GrComp; MusMk; NewEOp 71; NewOxM; OxCMus*

Spooner, Bill
[The Tubes]
American. Musician
Guitarist with The Tubes since late 1960s.
b. Apr 16, 1949 in Phoenix, Arizona

Spooner, John Coit
American. Politician
US Senator; wrote Spooner Act (1902), giving Pres. Theodore Roosevelt authority to build the Panama Canal.
b. Jan 6, 1843 in Lawrenceburg, Indiana
d. Jun 11, 1919 in New York, New York
Source: *AmBi; ApCAB, X; BiDrAC; BiDrUSC 89; BioIn 5; DcAmB; EncAAH; EncAB-H 1974; HarEnUS; IndAu 1967; NatCAB 1, 14; TwCBDA; WebAB 74, 79; WhAm 1; WhAmP*

Spooner, William Archibald
English. Educator
"Spoonerisms" are unconscious consonant transpositions.

b. Jul 22, 1844 in London, England
d. 1930
Source: *Benet 87, 96; BioIn 8, 11, 14; DcNaB 1922; GrBr; LngCTC; REn*

Spotswood, Alexander
English. Colonial Figure
Lt. governor, Colony of Virginia, 1710-22; improved tobacco production, Indian relationships.
b. 1676 in Tangiers, Morocco
d. Jun 7, 1740 in Annapolis, Maryland
Source: *AmBi; AmWrBE; ApCAB; BenetAL 91; BiDrACR; BiDSA; BioIn 8, 15; DcAmB; DcNaB, C; Drake; EncAB-H 1974, 1996; EncCRAm; McGEWB; NatCAB 13; NewCol 75; OxCAmH; OxCAmL 65, 83, 95; REnAL; TwCBDA; WhAm HS; WhWE*

Spotted Tail
[Sinte Gleska]
American. Native American Chief
Chief of the Sioux; proponent of nonviolent resolution with the white population; assassinated by fellow tribesman, Crow Dog.
b. 1823?
d. Aug 5, 1881
Source: *BioIn 5, 11; EncNAB; EncNoAI; NotNaAm*

Spottswood, Stephen Gill
American. Religious Leader
African Methodist Episcopal Zion bishop, who was chm., NAACP, 1961-74.
b. Jul 18, 1897 in Boston, Massachusetts
d. Dec 1, 1974 in Washington, District of Columbia
Source: *AfrAmAl 6; BioIn 6, 10, 12; CurBio 62, 75, 75N; DcAmB S9; Ebony 1; EncWM; InB&W 80; NegAl 76, 83, 89; NewYTBS 74; WhAm 6; WhoAm 74; WhoBlA 75, 77, 80, 85; WhoSSW 73; WhoWor 74*

Sprague, Frank Julian
American. Engineer
Constructed first major electric trolley system in US in Richmond, VA, 1887.
b. Jul 25, 1857 in Milford, Connecticut
d. Oct 25, 1934 in New York, New York
Source: *AmBi; ApCAB X; BioIn 1, 3, 7, 10; DcAmB S1; EncAB-H 1974, 1996; InSci; McGEWB; NatCAB 3, 24; WebAB 74, 79; WhAm 1*

Sprague, R(obert) C(hapman)
American. Businessman
Founder of Sprague Electric Co., pioneer in electronic components of radio and TV receivers.
b. Aug 3, 1900 in New York, New York
d. Sep 27, 1991 in Williamstown, Massachusetts
Source: *AmMWSc 92; BioIn 2, 5, 17; CurBio 91N; Dun&B 88; IntYB 78, 79, 80, 81, 82; LElec; NewYTBS 91; St&PR 91; WhAm 10; WhoAm 74, 76, 78, 80, 86, 88, 90; WhoE 75, 77; WhoFI 74, 75, 77, 85*

Spreckels, Claus
"Sugar King"
German. Manufacturer
Owner of largest sugar refinery on the West Coast, 1883.
b. Jul 9, 1828 in Lamstedt, Germany
d. Jan 10, 1908 in San Francisco, California
Source: *BiDAmBL 83; BioIn 7; CmCal; DcAmB; WebAB 74, 79; WhAm 1*

Springer, Axel Caesar
German. Publisher
Created Europe's largest newspaper empire, including *Die Welt, Bild Zeitung.*
b. May 2, 1912 in Hamburg, Germany
d. Sep 22, 1985 in Berlin, Germany (West)
Source: *ConAu 117; CurBio 68, 85; IntWW 74; WhoWor 74*

Springer, Ya'acov
Israeli. Olympic Athlete, Victim
One of 11 members of Israeli Olympic team kidnapped and killed by Arab terrorists during Summer Olympic Games.
b. 1920?
d. Sep 5, 1972 in Munich, Germany (West)
Source: *BioIn 9*

Springfield, Dusty
[Mary Isobel Catherine O'Brien]
English. Singer
Popular vocalist, 1963-69; hits include "Wishin' and Hopin,'" 1964.
b. Apr 16, 1939 in Hampstead, England
Source: *BiDAmM; BioIn 21; ConMuA 80A; EncPR&S 74; EncRk 88; EncRkSt; HarEnR 86; IlEncRk; InWom SUP; LegTOT; OxCPMus; PenEncP; RkOn 74, 78; RolSEnR 83; WhoRock 81; WhoRocM 82; WorAl; WorAlBi*

Springfield, Rick
[Richard Springfield]
Australian. Actor, Musician, Singer
Former star of soap opera "General Hospital" who had Grammy-winning hit "Jessie's Girl," 1981.
b. Aug 23, 1949 in Sydney, Australia
Source: *BioIn 12, 13; ConMus 9; EncPR&S 89; EncRk 88; EncRkSt; IntMPA 88, 92, 94, 96; LegTOT; PenEncP; RkOn 78; RolSEnR 83; WhoHol 92; WhoTelC; WorAlBi*

Springsteen, Bruce
"The Boss"
American. Singer, Songwriter
Album *Born in the USA,* most popular rock album of all time, 1985.
b. Sep 23, 1949 in Freehold, New Jersey
Source: *AmDec 1980; AmSong; ASCAP 80; Baker 84, 92; BioIn 10, 11, 12, 13, 16; CelR 90; ConAu 111; ConLC 17; ConMuA 80A; ConMus 6; CurBio 78, 92; DcArts; DcTwCCu 1; EncPR&S 89; EncRk 88; EncRkSt; FacFETw; HarEnR 86; IlEncRk; IntWW 82, 83, 89, 91, 93; LegTOT; NewAmDM; NewGrDA 86; NewYTBS 85; OnThGG; OxCPMus; PenEncP; RkOn 74, 78; RolSEnR 83; WhoAm 80, 82, 84, 86, 88, 90, 92, 94, 95, 96, 97; WhoEnt 92; WhoRock 81; WhoRocM 82; WhoWor 97; WorAl; WorAlBi*

Sprinkel, Beryl Wayne
American. Economist
Undersecretary of Treasury for monetary affairs, Reagan administration, 1981-85.
b. Nov 20, 1923 in Richmond, Missouri
Source: *CurBio 87; IntWW 91; NewYTBS 85; WhoAm 86, 90, 97; WhoAmP 89; WhoFI 92; WrDr 92*

Sproul, Robert Gordon
American. Educator
Pres. of U of CA, 1930-58.
b. May 22, 1891 in San Francisco, California
d. Sep 10, 1975 in Berkeley, California
Source: *BiDAmEd; BioIn 1, 6, 7, 10, 11; CmCal; CurBio 45, 75, 75N; DcAmB S9; EncAB-A 6; LinLib S; WhAm 6; Who 74; WhoAm 74*

Spruance, Raymond Ames
American. Naval Officer, Statesman
Naval commander, US forces in Japanese defeat at Midway, 1942.
b. Jul 3, 1886 in Baltimore, Maryland
d. Dec 13, 1969 in Pebble Beach, California
Source: *BiDWWGF; BioIn 16; CurBio 44, 70; DcAmB S8; DcAmMiB; FacFETw; HarEnMi; NatCAB 55; OxCAmH; OxCShps; WebAB 74, 79; WebAMB; WhAm 5; WorAl*

Spry, Constance
English. Artist, Author
Internationally noted flower arranger; wrote *Flower Decoration,* 1935.
b. Dec 5, 1886 in Derby, England
d. Jan 3, 1960 in Windsor, England
Source: *BioIn 5, 10, 14, 18; ContDcW 89; CurBio 60; DcNaB 1951; GrBr; IntDcWB; InWom, SUP; ObitT 1951; WomFir*

Spurrier, Steve(n Orr)
American. Football Player
All-America quarterback, won Heisman Trophy, 1966; in NFL, mostly with San Francisco, 1967-76.
b. Apr 20, 1945 in Miami Beach, Florida
Source: *BiDAmSp FB; BioIn 7, 8, 21; WhoFtbl 74; WhoSpor*

Spuzich, Sandra Ann
American. Golfer
Turned pro, 1962; won US Women's Open, 1966.
b. Apr 3, 1937 in Indianapolis, Indiana
Source: *BioIn 7; WhoGolf*

Spy
[Leslie Ward]
English. Cartoonist
Contributed to *Vanity Fair* for 36 yrs; recollections in *Forty Years of Spy,* 1915.
b. Nov 21, 1851 in London, England
d. May 15, 1922 in London, England
Source: *BioIn 8, 11, 12, 14, 16; ClaDrA; DcBrAr 1; DcNaB 1922; DcVicP, 2; GrBr; LinLib LP; LngCTC; PseudAu; VicBrit; WorECar*

Spychalski, Marian
Polish. Architect, Politician
Organized Polish Worker's Party, 1942; mayor of Warsaw, 1944-45; marshal of Poland, 1963-80.
b. Dec 6, 1906 in Lodz, Poland
d. Jun 7, 1980 in Warsaw, Poland
Source: *AnObit 1980; BioIn 8; IntWW 74, 75, 76, 77, 78, 79, 80; IntYB 78, 79, 80; WhoSocC 78*

Spyri, Johanna Heuser
Swiss. Author
Best known for ever-popular *Heidi,* 1880; adapted to films, TV shows.
b. Jun 12, 1827 in Hirzel, Switzerland
d. Jul 7, 1901 in Zurich, Switzerland
Source: *AnCL; AuBYP 2; CarSB; JBA 34, 51; OxCChiL; OxCGer 76; SmATA 19; WhoChL*

Spyropoulos, Jannis
Greek. Artist
Painting style ranged from naturalistic to abstract to non-objective abstract; later paintings concentrate on surface, texture.
b. Mar 12, 1912 in Pylos, Greece
Source: *BioIn 5, 6; IntWW 74, 75, 76, 77, 78, 79, 80, 81, 82, 83, 89, 91, 93; OxCTwCA; WhoWor 74, 78*

Squanto
American. Native American Guide
Member of Wampanoag tribe; taught Pilgrims wilderness survival.
b. 1585?
d. 1622 in Chatham Harbor, Massachusetts
Source: *AmBi; DcAmB; WebAB 74; WhAm HS*

Squeeze
[John Bentley; Paul Carrack; Chris Difford; Julian Holland; Harry Kakoulli; Gilson Lavis; Don Snow; Glenn Tilbrook]
English. Music Group
Formed 1974 in London; had hit album *East Side Story,* 1981.
Source: *Alli; BiDLA; BioIn 1; ConMus 5; DcInB; DcNaB; EncPR&S 89; EncRk 88; EncRkSt; HarEnR 86; IlEncRk; PenEncP; RkOn 85; RolSEnR 83; WhoRocM 82; WhsNW 85*

Squibb, Edward Robinson
American. Manufacturer
Founded E R Squibb pharmaceutical firm, 1858.
b. Jul 4, 1819 in Wilmington, Delaware
d. Oct 25, 1900 in New York, New York
Source: *Alli SUP; BiDAmS; BiInAmS; BioIn 1, 4, 5, 6, 7; DcAmB; DcAmMeB 84; DcNAA; InSci; NatCAB 19; WebAB 74, 79; WhAm HS*

Squier, Billy
American. Singer, Musician
Guitarist whose singles include "Everybody Wants You," 1982; "Eye On You," 1984.
b. May 12, 1950 in Wellesley, Massachusetts
Source: *LegTOT; PenEncP; RkOn 85; RolSEnR 83; WhoRocM 82*

Squire, Chris
English. Singer, Musician
Self-taught bassist who formed Yes, 1968; had solo album *Fish Out of the Water,* 1975.
b. Mar 4, 1948 in London, England
Source: *WhoRocM 82*

Squires, James Radcliffe
American. Poet
Poetry was influenced by Greek mythology; wrote *Cornar,* 1940.
b. May 23, 1917 in Salt Lake City, Utah
d. Feb 14, 1993
Source: *ConLC 51, 81; WhoAm 74, 76, 78, 80, 82, 84, 86, 88, 90, 92; WhoMW 74, 76; WhoUSWr 88*

Stabile, Mariano
Italian. Opera Singer
Baritone; sang Falstaff more than 1,000 times; retired, 1960.
b. May 12, 1888 in Palermo, Sicily, Italy
d. Jan 11, 1968 in Milan, Italy
Source: *Baker 78, 84, 92; BioIn 3, 8; CmOp; IntDcOp; MetOEnc; NewEOp 71; NewGrDM 80; NewGrDO; PenDiMP*

Stabler, Ken(neth Michael)
"Snake"
American. Football Player
Quarterback, 1970-84, mostly with Oakland; known for passing; led NFL in passing, 1973.
b. Dec 25, 1945 in Foley, Alabama
Source: *BioIn 16; CurBio 79; WhoAm 80, 82; WhoFtbl 74; WorAl; WorAlBi*

Stace, W(alter) T(erence)
Philosopher, Author
Combined naturalism and religion in his theories; wrote prolifically in the field; *Mysticism and Philophy,* 1960.
b. Nov 17, 1886 in London, England
d. Aug 2, 1967 in Laguna Beach, California
Source: *AmAu&B; BioIn 3, 5, 6, 8, 10, 11; ConAu 1R, 2NR; NatCAB 55; WhAm 5, 7; WhLit*

Stacey, Thomas Charles Gerard
English. Author
Travel books include *A Malayan Journey,* 1953; editor, *Chamber's Encyclopedia Yearbook,* 1969-72.
b. Jan 11, 1930 in Bletchingley, England
Source: *Au&Wr 71; ConAu 9R, 21NR, 47NR; DcLEL 1940; IntAu&W 91; WhoWor 76, 95, 96, 97; WrDr 86, 92*

Stack, Robert Langford
American. Actor
Starred in TV series "The Untouchables," 1959-63.
b. Jan 13, 1919 in Los Angeles, California
Source: *BiDFilm; FilmgC; HalFC 84; MotPP; MovMk; WhoAm 74, 76, 78, 80, 82, 84, 86, 88, 90, 92, 94, 95, 96, 97; WhoEnt 92; WorAl*

Stacton, David Derek
American. Author
Biographical-historical novels include *Kaliyuga; or, A Quarrel with the Gods,* 1965.
b. Apr 25, 1925 in Minden, Nevada
d. Jan 20, 1968 in Fredensborg, Sweden
Source: *AmAu&B; ConAu 5R, 6NR; ObitOF 79; OxCAmL 83; WorAu 1950*

Stacy, Hollis
American. Golfer
Turned pro, 1974; won US Women's Open, 1977, 1978, 1984.
b. Mar 16, 1954 in Savannah, Georgia
Source: *BiDAmSp Sup; BioIn 9, 11; InWom SUP; WhoAm 86, 88; WhoGolf; WhoIntG; WhoSpor*

Stacy, James
[Maurice W Elias]
American. Actor
Lost arm, leg in motorcycle accident; starred in TV movie *Just a Little Inconvenience,* 1977; once married to Connie Stevens.
b. Dec 23, 1936 in Los Angeles, California
Source: *BioIn 18; ConTFT 6; VarWW 85; WhoHol 92, A*

Stader, Maria
Swiss. Opera Singer
Lyric soprano; performances limited to recordings, stage concerts.
b. Nov 5, 1951 in Budapest, Hungary
Source: *Baker 84; CurBio 58; WhoMus 72; WhoWor 74*

Stadler, Craig Robert
"The Walrus"
American. Golfer
Turned pro, 1975; won Masters, 1982; leading money winner on tour, 1982.
b. Jun 2, 1953 in San Diego, California
Source: *NewYTBS 82; WhoAm 84, 86, 88, 90, 92, 94, 95, 96, 97; WhoIntG; WhoWest 94, 96*

Stael, Nicolas de
French. Artist
Painted mainly in watercolor; known for *Footballers* series, 1952; suicide victim.
b. Jan 5, 1914 in Saint Petersburg, Russia
d. Mar 22, 1955 in Antibes, France
Source: *AtlBL; BioIn 3, 4, 5, 6, 7, 11, 12, 16, 17; McGDA; McGEWB; OxCTwCA; OxDcArt; WhDW*

Stael-Holstein, Anne Louise Germaine Necker, Baroness de
French. Author, Socialite
Influenced French Romanticism; *Delphine,* 1802, *Corinne,* 1807, considered first modern, feminist, romantic novels; critic of Napoleon, consequently exiled from Paris many times.
b. Apr 22, 1766 in Paris, France
d. Jul 14, 1817 in Paris, France
Source: *Benet 87; BioIn 14, 15; CasWL; CmFrR; FemiCLE; GuFrLit 1; IntDcWB; InWom SUP; McGEWB; OxCEng 85; OxCFr; OxCGer 86; REn; WorAlBi*

Stafford, Jean
American. Author
Collection of short stories, *Collected Stories,* won Pulitzer, 1970.
b. Jul 1, 1915 in Covina, California
d. Mar 26, 1979 in White Plains, New York
Source: *AmAu&B; AmNov; AmWomWr, 92; ArtclWW 2; Benet 87, 96; BenetAL 91; BioAmW; BioIn 2, 3, 4, 7, 11, 12, 13, 14, 15, 16, 17, 18, 19, 20; BlmGWL; BlueB 76; CamGLE; CamHAL; CnDAL; ConAu 1R, 3NR, 85; ConLC 4, 7, 19, 68; ConNov 72, 76; CurBio 79N; CyWA 89; DcAmB S10; DcLB 173; DcLEL 1940; DrAF 76; EncWL; FacFETw; FemiCLE; GrWomW; GrWrEL N; IntAu&W 76, 77; InWom, SUP; LegTOT; LinLib L; MajTwCW; ModAL; ModWoWr; Novels; OxCAmL 65, 83, 95; OxCWoWr 95; PenC AM; RAdv 1; REn; REnAL; RfGAmL 87, 94; RfGShF; ShSWr; SmATA 22N; TwCA SUP; TwCWW 82, 91; WhAm 7; WhoAm 74, 76, 78; WhoAmW 58, 64, 66, 68, 70, 72, 74; WhoE 74; WhoTwCL; WhoWor 74; WorAl; WorAlBi; WrDr 76, 80*

Stafford, Jim
[James Wayne Stafford]
American. Singer, Songwriter
Novelty songwriter; had hit singles "Spiders and Snakes," 1974; "My Girl Bill," 1974.
b. Jan 16, 1944 in Eloise, Florida
Source: *BioIn 10, 14; EncFCWM 83; LegTOT; RkOn 74, 78*

Stafford, Jo
American. Singer
Popular performer, 1940s-50s; sang with Tommy Dorsey through mid-1944.
b. Nov 12, 1918 in Coalinga, California
Source: *BiDAmM; CmpEPM; InWom, SUP; LegTOT; RadStar; WhoAm 74, 90; WhoHol 92; WorAl; WorAlBi*

Stafford, Robert Theodore
American. Politician
Republican senator from VT, 1971-89.
b. Aug 8, 1913 in Rutland, Vermont
Source: *AlmAP 82; BiDrAC; BiDrUSC 89; BioIn 5, 9, 10, 12, 13, 16; CngDr 74, 77, 79, 81, 83, 85, 87; CurBio 60; NewYTBE 71; WhoAm 74, 76, 78, 80, 82, 84, 86, 88, 90, 92, 94, 95, 96, 97; WhoAmL 96; WhoAmP 85, 91; WhoE 74, 75, 77, 79, 81, 83, 85, 86, 89; WhoWor 80, 82, 87, 89*

Stafford, Thomas P(atten)
American. Astronaut, Businessman
Flew on Gemini VI, IX, and Apollo X flights.
b. Sep 17, 1930 in Weatherford, Oklahoma
Source: *AmMWSc 73P; BioIn 7, 8, 9, 10, 11; CurBio 77; IntWW 74; Law&B 89A; NewYTBS 75; WhoAm 74, 76, 78, 80, 82, 84, 86, 88, 90, 92, 94, 95, 96, 97; WhoScEn 94, 96; WhoSSW 73, 75, 95, 97; WhoWor 74, 78, 80, 82, 84, 87; WorAl; WorAlBi*

Stafford, William Edgar
American. Poet
Poems dealt with conflicts between natural, artificial worlds; won Nat. Book Award, 1962, for *Traveling through the Dark.*
b. Jan 17, 1914 in Hutchinson, Kansas
d. Aug 28, 1993 in Lake Oswego, Oregon
Source: *BenetAL 91; BioIn 15, 18, 19, 20; ConAu 5NR, 5R, 142; ConLC 4; ConPo 91; CroCAP; ModAL S1; OxCAmL 65; PenC AM; RAdv 1; WhoAm 84, 86, 90; WhoPNW; WhoUSWr 88; WhoWrEP 89; WorAu 1950; WrDr 92, 96*

Stagg, Amos Alonzo
American. Football Coach
Collegiate coach for 57 yrs., 1890-1946; introduced huddle and many innovative plays used today, including end around, double reverse.
b. Aug 16, 1862 in West Orange, New Jersey
d. Mar 17, 1965 in Stockton, California
Source: *BasBi; BiDAmSp FB; BioIn 1, 2, 3, 4, 5, 6, 7, 8, 9, 10, 12, 20, 21; CurBio 44, 65; DcAmB S7; FacFETw; LegTOT; NatCAB 11, 18; NewYTBS 81; OxCAmH; WebAB 74, 79; WhAm 4; WhNAA; WhoBbl 73; WhoFtbl 74; WhoSpor; WhScrn 83; WorAl; WorAlBi*

Staggers, Harley O(rrin)
American. Politician
Dem. WV Congressman, 1949-81.
b. Aug 3, 1907 in Keyser, Washington
d. Aug 20, 1991 in Cumberland, Maryland
Source: *AlmAP 78, 80, 88; BiDrAC; BiDrUSC 89; BioIn 9, 11, 12; CngDr 74, 77, 79; CurBio 71; NewYTBS 91; PolProf J, NF; PolsAm 84; WhAm 10; WhoAm 74, 76, 78, 80, 84, 86, 88; WhoAmP 73, 75, 77, 79, 81, 83, 85, 87, 89, 91; WhoE 74, 75, 77, 86; WhoGov 72, 75, 77; WhoSSW 78, 80, 82, 86, 88*

Stahl, Ben(jamin Albert)
American. Artist, Illustrator
Best known for illustrations in the *Saturday Evening Post,* 1933-63; won many awards.
b. Sep 7, 1910 in Chicago, Illinois
d. Oct 19, 1987 in Sarasota, Florida
Source: *BioIn 1, 2, 7, 8, 10, 11, 12, 15, 16; ConAu 29R, 123; IlrAm 1880, E; IlsBYP; IlsCB 1957; NewYTBS 87; ScF&FL 1, 2, 92; SmATA 5, 54N; WhAm 9; WhAmArt 85; WhoAm 74, 76, 78, 80, 82, 84, 86; WhoAmA 73, 76, 78, 80, 82, 84, 86; WhoSSW 73, 75, 76; WhoWor 80, 82*

Stahl, Franklin William
American. Geneticist
Together with Mathew Meselsohn, 1958, demonstrated how DNA replicates itself.
b. Oct 8, 1929 in Boston, Massachusetts
Source: *AmMWSc 76P, 79, 82, 86, 89, 92, 95; BioIn 14, 20; LarDcSc*

Stahl, Lesley (Rene)
American. Broadcast Journalist
Longtime correspondent, CBS News; moderator, "Face the Nation," 1983-91; co-editor and correspondent "60 Minutes," 1991—; coined expression "The Peggy Principle."
b. Dec 16, 1941 in Lynn, Massachusetts
Source: *AuNews 2; BioIn 11, 14, 21; CelR 90; ConAu 107; ConTFT 12; CurBio 96; EncTwCJ; InWom SUP; LegTOT; LesBEnT 92; News 97-1; WhoAm 86, 90; WhoAmW 91; WhoE 91; WomStre; WorAlBi*

Stahlberg, Kaarlo Juho
Finnish. Political Leader
Principle author of Finland's Constitution; independent Finland's first president, 1919-25.
b. Jan 28, 1865 in Suomusselmi, Finland
d. Sep 22, 1952 in Helsinki, Finland
Source: *BioIn 3, 8; OxCLaw*

Stakman, Elvin Charles
American. Agriculturist
Plant pathologist who pioneered techniques to identify and fight food crop diseases.
b. May 17, 1885 in Algoma, Wisconsin
d. Jan 22, 1979 in Saint Paul, Minnesota
Source: *AmMWSc 76P; BioIn 1, 2, 3, 7, 8, 11, 12, 14; BlueB 76; CurBio 49, 79N; InSci; IntWW 74, 75, 76, 77, 78, 79; NewYTBS 79; WhAm 7*

Stalin, Joseph
[Iosif Visarionovich Djugashvili]
Russian. Political Leader
Successor of Lenin who was dictator, 1929-53; attempted to establish socialism by force, terror.
b. Dec 21, 1879 in Gori, Russia
d. Mar 5, 1953 in Moscow, Union of Soviet Socialist Republics
Source: *Benet 87, 96; BioIn 13, 14, 15, 16, 17, 18, 19, 20, 21; ColdWar 1, 2; CurBio 42, 53; DcRusL; EncMcCE; EncTR 91; GrLGrT; HisDcKW; HisWorL; LegTOT; LinLib L; MakMC; McGEWB; ObitT 1951; OxCEng 85; RAdv 14, 13-3; REn; WhAm 3, 4; WhDW; WhoEc 81; WorAl; WorAlBi*

Stalin, Svetlana Alliluyeva
[Svetlana Peters]
Russian. Author
Daughter of Joseph Stalin who defected to West, 1967; wrote memoirs *Twenty Letters to a Friend,* 1967.
b. Feb 28, 1926 in Moscow, Union of Soviet Socialist Republics
Source: *BioIn 15; CurBio 68; NewYTBE 73; WhoAm 74, 82, 84*

Staller, Ilona
"Cicciolina"
Italian. Actor, Politician
Actress in pornographic films; member of Italian Parliament 1987—.
b. 1951 in Budapest, Hungary
Source: *News 88-3*

Stallings, George Augustus, Jr.
American. Religious Leader
Priest, founder of an independent African-American Roman Catholic church in Washington, DC, 1989—.
b. Mar 17, 1948 in New Bern, North Carolina
Source: *AfrAmAl 6; BioIn 16; News 90-1; RelLAm 91; WhoAfA 96; WhoBlA 85, 92, 94*

Stallings, Laurence
American. Dramatist, Screenwriter
Co-wrote play *What Price Glory?,* 1924.
b. Nov 25, 1894 in Macon, Georgia
d. Feb 28, 1968
Source: *AmAu&B; BenetAL 91; BiE&WWA; BioIn 3, 4, 8, 10, 12, 15; CnDAL; ConAmA; ConAmL; ConAu 89; DcLB 7, 44; FilmEn; FilmgC; HalFC 80, 84, 88; LegTOT; McGEWD 72, 84; ModWD; NatCAB 55; NotNAT B; Novels; OxCAmL 65, 83, 95; PenC AM; PlP&P; REn; REnAL; SouWr; TwCA, SUP; WhAm 4A; WhThe; WorAl; WorAlBi*

Stallone, Sylvester (Enzio)
American. Actor, Director
Best known for *Rocky* film series, 1976-90; *Rambo* films, 1984, 1985, 1988.
b. Jul 6, 1946 in New York, New York
Source: *BiDFilm 94; BioIn 11, 12, 13, 15, 16; BkPepl; CelR 90; ConAu 77; ConTFT 1, 8; CurBio 77, 94; DcTwCCu 1; FilmEn; HalFC 80, 84, 88; HolBB; IntDcF 1-3, 2-3; IntMPA 78, 79, 80, 81, 82, 84, 86, 88, 92, 94, 96; IntWW 89, 91, 93; LegTOT; MiSFD 9; News 94, 94-2; VarWW 85; WhoAm 78, 80, 82, 84, 86, 88, 90, 92, 94, 95, 96, 97; WhoEnt 92; WhoHol 92; WhoWor 97; WorAl; WorAlBi*

Stallworth, John(ny Lee)
American. Football Player
Three-time all-pro wide receiver, Pittsburgh, 1974-87; led NFL in receiving, 1979; won four Super Bowls.
b. Jul 15, 1952 in Tuscaloosa, Alabama
Source: *BiDAmSp FB; BioIn 16; FootReg 87; WhoBlA 80, 85, 92*

Stambuliski, Aleksandr
[Alexandr Stamboliski]
Bulgarian. Political Leader
Leader of Peasant's Party; premier, 1920-23, until assassinated.
b. Mar 1, 1879 in Slavovitsa, Bulgaria
d. Jun 12, 1923 in Slavovitsa, Bulgaria
Source: *NewCol 75; WebBD 83*

Stammler, Rudolf
German. Judge
Renowned legal philosopher of the 20th century; wrote *Lehre von dem richtigen Rechte,* 1902.
b. Feb 19, 1856 in Alsfeld, Germany
d. Apr 25, 1938 in Wernigerode, Germany

Stamos, John
American. Actor
Played Jesse on TV series "Full House," 1987-95.
b. Aug 19, 1963 in Los Angeles, California
Source: *BioIn 13, 14, 16; ConTFT 4, 13; IntMPA 94, 96; LegTOT; WhoAm 95, 96, 97; WhoHol 92*

Stamos, Theodoros
American. Painter
Abstract expressionist; painted in thin washes of pigment.
b. Dec 31, 1922
d. Feb 2, 1997 in Yianina, Greece
Source: *BioIn 4, 5, 6, 11; BriEAA; ConArt 83, 89, 96; DcAmArt; DcCAA 71, 77, 88, 94; DcCAr 81; McGDA; OxCTwCA; PhDcTCA 77; PrintW 83, 85; WhAmArt 85; WhoAm 82, 84, 86, 88, 90, 92, 94, 95, 96; WhoAmA 73, 76, 78, 80, 82, 84, 86, 89, 91; WhoWor 74; WorArt 1950*

Stamp, Terence
English. Actor
Films include *Superman II,* 1980; *Monster Island,* 1981.
b. Jul 22, 1940 in London, England
Source: *BioIn 14, 16, 20, 21; FilmEn; FilmgC; HalFC 80, 84, 88; IlWWBF; IntMPA 75, 76, 82, 92; IntWW 82, 91; ItaFilm; MotPP; MovMk; OxCFilm; WhoHol A; WorAl; WorEFlm; WrDr 92*

Stampfli, Jakob
Swiss. Political Leader
Pres. Swiss Confederation, 1856, 1859, 1862; helped fashion Swiss federal bank and shaped its policies.
b. Feb 23, 1820 in Janzenhaus, Switzerland
d. May 15, 1879 in Bern, Switzerland
Source: *IntWWM 90*

Stander, Lionel (Jay)
American. Actor
Played Max on TV series "Hart to Hart," 1979-84.
b. Jan 11, 1909 in New York, New York
d. Nov 30, 1994
Source: *BiE&WWA; ConTFT 5; EncAFC; FilmgC; HalFC 84, 88; IntMPA 92; MotPP; MovMk; NewYTBE 71; NotNAT; Vers A; WhoAm 84; WhoHol A*

Standing, Guy, Sir
Actor
Prominent on British, American stage; appeared in Hollywood films, 1930s: *Death Takes a Holiday,* 1934.
b. Sep 1, 1873 in London, England
d. Feb 24, 1937 in Los Angeles, California
Source: *FilmEn; FilmgC; ForYSC; HalFC 80, 84, 88; HolCA; MotPP; NotNAT B; WhoHol B; WhoStg 1906, 1908; WhScrn 74, 77, 83; WhThe*

Standing Bear
American. Native American Leader
Leader of the Ponca tribe; led a band of his tribesmen to resettle their former lands in Nebraska, 1879.
b. 1829?
d. Sep 1908
Source: *BioIn 4, 9, 11; NotNaAm; WhNaAH*

Standish, Miles
American. Colonial Figure
Military leader, Plymouth Colony, 1620-25.
b. 1584 in Lancashire, England
d. Oct 3, 1656 in Duxbury, Massachusetts
Source: *AmBi; Benet 87, 96; BenetAL 91; DcAmMiB; Drake; EncCRAm; HarEnUS; LegTOT; LinLib L, S; NatCAB 5; OxCAmH; OxCAmL 83; REn; REnAL; WebAB 74, 79; WebAMB; WhNaAH; WorAl; WorAlBi*

Stanfield, Andy
[Andrew Stanfield]
American. Track Athlete
Sprinter; gold medalist in 200-meter, 400-meter relays, 1952 Olympics.
b. Dec 29, 1927 in Washington, District of Columbia
Source: *BlkOlyM; WhoSpor; WhoTr&F 73*

Stanford, Charles Villiers, Sir
Irish. Composer, Conductor
b. Sep 30, 1852 in Fublin, Ireland

d. Mar 29, 1924 in London, England
Source: *Baker 78, 84, 92; BioIn 4, 5, 6, 11, 14, 16; BriBkM 80; CelCen; CmOp; DcArts; DcCom&M 79; DcIrB 78, 88; DcNaB 1922; GrBr; LuthC 75; MusMk; NewAmDM; NewEOp 71; NewGrDM 80; NewGrDO; NewOxM; OxCEng 85, 95; OxCMus; OxDcOp; PenDiMP A; VicBrit*

Stanford, Leland
[Amasa Leland Stanford]
American. Railroad Executive, Politician
Pres., Central Pacific, Southern Pacific railroads, 1860s-90s; governor of CA, 1861-63; founded Stanford U, 1885, in memory of son.
b. Mar 9, 1824 in Watervliet, New York
d. Jun 21, 1893 in Palo Alto, California
Source: *AmBi; AmSocL; ApCAB; BiAUS; BiDAmBL 83; BiDrAC; BiDrGov 1789; BiDrUSC 89; BioIn 2, 3, 6, 7, 8, 9, 10, 11, 12, 13, 15, 17, 19; CmCal; DcAmB; Drake; EncAB-H 1974, 1996; EncABHB 2; GayN; HarEnUS; LegTOT; LinLib S; McGEWB; MemAm; NatCAB 2; OxCAmH; REnAW; TwCBDA; WebAB 74, 79; WhAm HS; WhAmP; WhCiWar*

Stanford, Sally
[Marcia Busby; Sally Gump]
American. Politician
Ran San Francisco's most celebrated brothel, 1930s-40s; mayor of Sausalito, CA, 1976-78.
b. May 5, 1903 in Baker City, Oregon
d. Feb 2, 1982 in Greenbrae, California
Source: *AnObit 1982; BioIn 2, 10, 11, 12, 14; ConAu 105; InWom SUP; NewYTBS 82; WomPO 76*

Stanford-Tuck, Robert Roland
English. Military Leader
WW II flying ace; decorated for fighting in Battle of Britain.
b. Jul 1, 1916
d. May 5, 1987 in London, England
Source: *Who 74, 82, 83, 85*

Stang, Arnold
American. Comedian, Actor
Performer on radio beginning 1935; known for film performance in *The Man With the Golden Arm,* 1955.
b. Sep 28, 1925 in Chelsea, Massachusetts
Source: *ASCAP 66; BiE&WWA; ConTFT 2; EncAFC; FilmEn; ForYSC; IntMPA 86, 92; LegTOT; Vers A; WhoEnt 92; WhoHol 92, A*

Stangl, Franz Paul
Austrian. Government Official
Commanded Nazi concentration camps in Poland, 1942-43, where 400,000 Jews were killed under his supervision.
b. Mar 26, 1908? in Altmunster, Austria
d. Jun 28, 1971 in Dusseldorf, Germany (West)
Source: *BioIn 7, 8, 9, 10; NewYTBE 71; WhWW-II*

Stanislavsky, Konstantin Sergeyevich
[Konstantin Sergeyevich Alexeyev]
Russian. Actor, Director
Co-founder, Moscow Art Theatre; developed theory of actor identifying with role, called Stanislavsky System.
b. Jan 17, 1863 in Moscow, Russia
d. Aug 7, 1938 in Moscow, Union of Soviet Socialist Republics
Source: *DcRusL; EncWT; LngCTC; NewGrDM 80; NewGrDO; OxCFilm; OxCThe 67; REn*

Stankiewicz, Richard Peter
American. Artist
Pioneer in junk art; created sculptures from scrap metal *The Bride.*
b. Oct 18, 1922 in Philadelphia, Pennsylvania
d. Mar 27, 1983 in Worthington, Massachusetts
Source: *BioIn 4, 5, 6, 7, 8; BlueB 76; ConArt 77; CurBio 83; DcAmArt; McGDA; WhoAm 74, 76, 78, 80, 82; WhoAmA 73, 76, 78, 80, 82; WhoE 74, 83*

Stanky, Eddie
[Edward Raymond Stanky]
"Muggsy"; "The Brat"
American. Baseball Player, Baseball Manager
Infielder, 1943-53, known for brash play, fielding; managed for eight yrs.
b. Sep 3, 1916 in Philadelphia, Pennsylvania
Source: *Ballpl 90; BaseEn 88; BiDAmSp Sup; BioIn 1, 2, 3, 5, 7, 11, 12; CurBio 51; LegTOT; WhoProB 73*

Stanley, Allan Herbert
Canadian. Hockey Player
Defenseman, 1948-69, with five NHL teams; won four Stanley Cups with Toronto; Hall of Fame, 1981.
b. Mar 1, 1926 in Timmins, Ontario, Canada
Source: *HocEn; WhoHcky 73*

Stanley, Barney
[Russell Stanley]
Canadian. Hockey Player
Right wing in pro hockey 15 yrs, through 1920s; Hall of Fame, 1962.
b. Jun 1, 1893 in Paisley, Ontario, Canada
d. May 16, 1971
Source: *WhoHcky 73*

Stanley, Francis Edgar
American. Inventor, Auto Manufacturer
With twin brother, Freelan, built steam-powered "Stanley Steamer," 1887; founded Stanley Motor Co., 1902; killed in auto accident.
b. Jun 1, 1849 in Kingfield, Maine
d. Jul 31, 1918 in Wenham, Massachusetts
Source: *BioIn 5, 7, 21; DcAmB; NatCAB 18; WebAB 74, 79; WhAm 4, HSA; WorAl; WorInv*

Stanley, Frederick Arthur, Earl of Derby
[Lord Stanley of Preston]
English. Political Leader, Hockey Pioneer
Governor-general of Canada, 1888-93; donated Stanley Cup, presented to amateur hockey teams, 1893-1912, to pros ever since.
b. Jan 15, 1841 in London, England
d. Jun 14, 1908 in Kent, England
Source: *ApCAB; CelCen; DcCanB 13; DcNaB S2; WhoHcky 73*

Stanley, Freelan O
American. Inventor, Auto Manufacturer
Built steam-powered "Stanley Steamer," 1897, with twin brother, Francis; one of their cars set world speed record, 1906.
b. Jun 1, 1849 in Kingfield, Maine
d. Oct 2, 1940 in Boston, Massachusetts
Source: *BioIn 5, 7; CurBio 40; EncABHB 4; InSci; WebAB 74, 79; WhAm 1; WorAlBi*

Stanley, Henry Morton, Sir
[Stanley and Livingstone]
English. Explorer, Journalist
Best known for finding David Livingstone in Africa, 1871; fought on both sides in US Civil War.
b. Jan 31, 1841 in Denbigh, Wales
d. May 10, 1904 in London, England
Source: *ABCMeAm; Alli SUP; AmAu&B; AmBi; BbD; Benet 87, 96; BiD&SB; BioIn 1, 2, 3, 4, 5, 6, 7, 8, 9, 10, 11, 12; BritAu 19; CamGEL; CamGLE; CarSB; Chambr 3; DcAfHiB 86; DcAmAu; DcAmB; DcBrBI; DcEnA, A; DcNaB S2; EncPaPR 91; EvLB; Expl 93; HisDBrE; LegTOT; LinLib L, S; McGEWB; NatCAB 4; NewCBEL; OxCAmH; OxCAmL 65, 83, 95; OxCEng 67, 85, 95; OxCLiW 86; RAdv 14, 13-3; REn; REnAL; VicBrit; WebAB 74, 79; WhAm 1; WhCiWar; WhDW; WhWE; WorAl*

Stanley, Kim
[Patricia Kimberly Reid]
American. Actor
Method actress; nominated for Oscar, 1964, for *Seance on a Wet Afternoon,* 1964.
b. Feb 11, 1925 in Tularosa, New Mexico
Source: *BiE&WWA; BioIn 1, 3, 4, 5, 6, 7, 12, 14, 16; CnThe; CurBio 55; FilmEn; FilmgC; ForYSC; IntMPA 86, 88, 92, 94, 96; InWom, SUP; MotPP; MovMk; NewYTBS 79; NotNAT; NotWoAT; OxCAmT 84; WhoAm 74; WhoAmW 58, 66, 68, 70, 72, 74, 75, 91; WhoHol 92, A; WhoThe 72, 77; WorAl; WorAlBi*

Stanley, Mickey
[Mitchell Jack Stanley]
American. Baseball Player
Outfielder, Detroit, 1964-78, known for fielding; played errorless ball, 1968, 1970; played shortstop, 1968 World Series.

b. Jul 20, 1942 in Grand Rapids, Michigan
Source: *Ballpl 90; BaseEn 88; WhoProB 73*

Stanley, Paul
[Kiss; Paul Eisen]
American. Singer, Musician
Guitarist who co-founded Kiss, 1972.
b. Jan 20, 1949 in New York, New York
Source: *WhoRocM 82*

Stanley, Ralph Edmond
American. Singer, Songwriter
One of the patriarchs of bluegrass; co-founder of Stanley Brothers and the Clinch Mountain Boys, 1946-66; now Ralph Stanley and the Clinch Mountain Boys.
b. Feb 25, 1927 in Stratton, Virginia
Source: *BiDAmM; BioIn 15; ConMus 5; IlEncCM; NewAmDM; WhoAm 90; WhoEnt 92*

Stanley, Wendell Meredith
American. Chemist
Won Nobel Prize, 1946, for work on viruses; isolated influenza virus, prepared vaccine against it.
b. Aug 16, 1904 in Ridgeville, Indiana
d. Apr 15, 1971 in Salamanca, Spain
Source: *AmMWSc 82; AsBiEn; BiESc; BioIn 1, 3, 5, 6, 7, 8, 9, 10, 11, 15, 19, 20; CamDcSc; DcAmB S9; DcAmMeB 84; DcScB S2; IndAu 1917; InSci; LarDcSc; McGEWB; McGMS 80; NatCAB 57; NotTwCS; WebAB 74, 79; WhAm 5; WhDW; WhoNob, 90, 95; WorAl; WorScD*

Stans, Maurice Hubert
American. Government Official
Secretary of Commerce, 1969-72, under Richard Nixon; involved in Vesco scandal.
b. Mar 22, 1908 in Shakopee, Minnesota
Source: *BiDFilm; BiDrUSE 71, 89; BioIn 4, 5, 6, 8, 9, 10, 12; ConAu 113; CurBio 58; IntWW 74, 75, 76, 77, 78, 79, 80, 81, 82, 83, 91, 93; NewYTBE 70, 71, 73; WhoAm 74, 76, 78, 80, 82, 84, 86, 88, 90, 92, 94, 95, 96, 97; WhoAmP 91; WhoSSW 73; WorAl; WorAlBi*

Stansfield, Lisa
English. Singer
Pop/soul vocalist; formed group Blue Zone, 1986; first solo album *Affection,* 1989.
b. Apr 11, 1966 in Rochdale, England
Source: *ConMus 9; EncRkSt; LegTOT*

Stanton, Edwin McMasters
American. Statesman
Secretary of War, 1862-68; dismissal caused impeachment charges against Johnson, 1868.
b. Dec 19, 1814 in Steubenville, Ohio
d. Dec 24, 1869 in Washington, District of Columbia
Source: *Alli; AmBi; AmPolLe; ApCAB; BiAUS; BiDrUSE 71, 89; BioIn 3, 5, 6, 7, 9, 10, 12, 15, 17; CivWDc; CyAG; DcAmB; DcAmMiB; Drake; EncAB-H 1974, 1996; HarEnUS; LinLib S; McGEWB; NatCAB 2; OxCAmH; TwCBDA; WebAB 74, 79; WhAm HS; WhCiWar; WorAl*

Stanton, Elizabeth Cady
[Mrs. Henry Brewster Stanton]
American. Feminist, Social Reformer
Co-founded women's rights movement with Lucretia Mott; first pres., National Woman Suffrage Assn., 1869-90.
b. Nov 12, 1815 in Johnstown, New York
d. Oct 26, 1902 in New York, New York
Source: *Alli SUP; AmAu; AmAu&B; AmBi; AmJust; AmOrN; AmRef; AmRef&R; AmSocL; AmWom; AmWomWr, 92; ApCAB; ArtclWW 2; BbD; Benet 87, 96; BenetAL 91; BiCAW; BiDAmJo; BiD&SB; BioAmW; BioIn 14, 15, 16, 17, 18, 19, 20, 21; BlmGWL; CamHAL; ContDcW 89; DcAmAu; DcAmB; DcAmReB 1, 2; DcAmSR; DcLB 79; DcNAA; EncAB-H 1974, 1996; EncARH; EncNAB; EncRev; EncWHA; FemiWr; GayN; GoodHs; GrLiveH; HanAmWH; HarEnUS; HerW, 84; HisWorL; IntDcWB; InWom, SUP; LegTOT; LibW; LinLib L, S; McGEWB; NatCAB 3; NotAW; OxCAmH; OxCAmL 65, 83, 95; OxCWoWr 95; PolPar; PorAmW; RadHan; RComAH; REn; REnAL; TwCBDA; TwoTYeD; WebAB 74, 79; WhAm 1; WhAmP; WomFir; WorAl; WorAlBi*

Stanton, Frank Lebby
"Riley of the South"
American. Poet, Journalist
Wrote one of American journalism's first columns, "Just From GA" in *Atlanta Constitution,* beginning 1889; published poems *Up from GA,* 1902.
b. Feb 22, 1857 in Charleston, South Carolina
d. Jan 7, 1927 in Atlanta, Georgia
Source: *AmAu&B; ASCAP 66, 80; BbD; BiDAmNC; BiDSA; ChhPo, S1, S2; DcAmAu; DcAmB; DcNAA; LinLib L, S; NatCAB 11; OxCAmL 65, 83, 95; REn; REnAL; WhAm 1*

Stanton, Frank Nicholas
American. TV Executive
Pres. of CBS, 1946-71; TV Academy Hall of Fame, 1986.
b. Mar 20, 1908 in Muskegon, Michigan
Source: *BiDAmJo; BiE&WWA; BioIn 15, 16; CurBio 45, 65; EncTwCJ; IntWW 83, 89; NewYTBE 71; WhoAm 86, 90; WhoTelC*

Stanton, Henry Brewster
American. Social Reformer
Active in anti-slavery activities, beginning 1834; married Elizabeth Cady, 1840.
b. Jun 27, 1805 in Griswold, Connecticut
d. Jan 7, 1887 in New York, New York
Source: *Alli, SUP; AmBi; ApCAB, X; BiD&SB; DcAmAu; DcAmB; DcNAA; HarEnUS; NatCAB 2; TwCBDA; WhAm HS*

Stanwyck, Barbara
[Ruby Stevens]
American. Actor
Starred in over 80 films; received Oscar nominations for *Stella Dallas,* 1937, *The Lady Eve,* 1941, *Double Indemnity,* 1944, *Sorry, Wrong Number,* 1948; won Emmys for "The Big Valley" and "The Thorn Birds."
b. Jul 16, 1907 in New York, New York
d. Jan 20, 1990 in Santa Monica, California
Source: *AnObit 1990; BiDFilm, 81, 94; BiE&WWA; BioAmW; BioIn 1, 2, 3, 6, 9, 10, 11, 12, 13, 16; CelR, 90; CmMov; ConTFT 3, 8; CurBio 47, 90, 90N; DcArts; EncAFC; FacFETw; Film 2; FilmEn; FilmgC; ForYSC; GoodHs; HalFC 80, 84, 88; IntDcF 1-3, 2-3; IntMPA 77, 80, 84, 86, 88; IntWW 79, 80, 81, 82, 83, 89; InWom, SUP; LegTOT; MotPP; MovMk; NewYTBS 81, 90; OxCFilm; SweetSg D; ThFT; WhAm 10; WhoAm 74, 76, 78, 80, 82, 84, 86, 88; WhoAmW 58, 61, 64, 66, 68, 70, 72, 87, 89; WhoHol A; WhoThe 77A; WhoWor 74, 89; WhThe; WorAl; WorAlBi; WorEFlm*

Stapledon, Olaf
[William Olaf Stapledon]
English. Educator, Author
Science fiction novels include *Death into Life,* 1946.
b. May 10, 1886 in Wallasey, England
d. Sep 6, 1950 in Cheshire, England
Source: *Benet 87; BioIn 2, 4, 7, 12, 13, 14, 17, 20, 21; ConAu 111; DcLB 15; EncSF; EvLB; LngCTC; NewCBEL; NewEScF; Novels; REn; RGSF; RGTwCSF; ScF&FL 1, 2, 92; ScFEYrs; ScFSB; ScFWr; TwCA, SUP; TwCLC 22; TwCSFW 81, 86, 91; TwCWr; WhE&EA; WhLit; WhoSciF*

Staples, Brent
American. Journalist
Editorial writer, *New York Times,* 1983—; wrote *Parallel Time: Growing Up Black and White,* 1994.
b. 1951 in Chester, Pennsylvania
Source: *ConAu 153; ConBlB 8*

Staple Singers, The
[Cleotha Staple; Mavis Staple; Pervis Staple; Roebuck "Pop" Staple; Yvonne Staple]
American. Music Group
Family group formed, 1954; soul hits include "Let's Do It Again," 1975.
Source: *BiDAfM; BiDAmM; DcTwCCu 5; EncRk 88; EncRkSt; HarEnR 86; IlEncRk; InB&W 85A; NewGrDA 86; PenEncP; RkOn 78, 84; SoulM; WhoRock 81*

Stapleton, Jean
[Jeanne Murray; Mrs. William Putch]
American. Actor
Played Edith Bunker on TV series "All in the Family," 1971-79.
b. Jan 19, 1923 in New York, New York
Source: *BiE&WWA; BioIn 9, 10; BioNews 74; BkPepl; CelR; ConTFT 1, 7; CurBio 72; EncAFC; FilmEn; ForYSC; HalFC 80, 84, 88; IntMPA 77, 78, 79, 80, 81, 82, 84, 86, 88, 92; InWom SUP; LegTOT; NewYTBE 71, 72; NewYTBS 86; NotNAT; WhoAm 74, 86, 88, 90; WhoAmW 74, 75, 77, 87, 89; WhoCom; WhoHol 92, A; WhoTelC; WhoThe 77; WhoWest 74; WorAl; WorAlBi*

Stapleton, Maureen
[Louis Maureen Stapleton]
American. Actor
Won Tony for *The Gingerbread Lady,* 1970; won Oscar for *Reds,* 1982.
b. Jun 21, 1925 in Troy, New York
Source: *BiE&WWA; BioIn 2, 3, 5, 6, 7, 9, 10, 12, 13, 14, 16, 18, 21; BioNews 74; CamGWoT; CelR, 90; CnThe; ConTFT 4, 11; CurBio 59; EncAFC; Ent; FamA&A; FilmEn; FilmgC; ForYSC; HalFC 80, 84, 88; IntMPA 75, 76, 77, 78, 79, 80, 81, 82, 84, 86, 88, 92, 94, 96; InWom, SUP; ItaFilm; LegTOT; MotPP; MovMk; NewYTBE 71; NewYTBS 81; NotNAT; NotWoAT; OxCAmT 84; OxCThe 83; WhoAm 74, 76, 78, 80, 82, 84, 86, 88, 90, 92, 94, 95, 96, 97; WhoAmW 66, 68, 70, 72, 74, 75, 77, 81, 83, 85, 87, 89, 91, 93, 95, 97; WhoEnt 92; WhoHol 92, A; WhoThe 72, 77, 81; WhoWor 74, 76; WorAl; WorAlBi*

Stapleton, Ruth Carter
American.
Baptist evangelist, spiritual healer; sister of Jimmy Carter.
b. Aug 7, 1929 in Archery, Georgia
d. Sep 26, 1983 in Fayetteville, North Carolina
Source: *AnObit 1983; BioIn 10; ConAu 81, 110; InWom SUP; NewYTBS 83*

Starch, Daniel
American. Advertising Executive, Psychologist
Marketing research expert; wrote *Principles of Advertising,* 1923.
b. Mar 8, 1883 in La Crosse, Wisconsin
d. Feb 8, 1979
Source: *AdMenW; AmAu&B; AmMWSc 73S, 78S; BioIn 4, 6, 10, 11, 12, 20; ConAu 37R, 133; CurBio 63; NewYTBS 79; REnAL; WhAm 7; WhNAA; WhoAm 74, 76, 78*

Stargell, Willie
[Wilver Dornel Stargell]
"Pops"
American. Baseball Player
Outfielder, Pittsburgh, 1962-82; led NL in home runs twice, in RBIs once; Hall of Fame, 1988; coach, Ptiisgurgh, 1982-85; coach, Atlanta Braves, 1985-88.
b. Mar 4, 1941 in Earlsboro, Oklahoma
Source: *AfrAmSG; BiDAmSp BB; BioIn 9, 10, 11, 12, 13, 21; ConAu 118, 146; CurBio 80; InB&W 80; LegTOT; WhoAfA 96; WhoAm 80, 82, 92, 94, 95, 96, 97; WhoBlA 77, 80, 85, 88, 90, 92, 94; WhoE 95; WhoProB 73; WhoSpor; WhoWor 96; WorAl; WorAlBi*

Stark, Harold Raynsford
American. Naval Officer
Chief of US naval operations, 1939-41; relieved of command after Pearl Harbor attack.
b. Nov 12, 1880 in Wilkes-Barre, Pennsylvania
d. Aug 20, 1972 in Washington, District of Columbia
Source: *BiDWWGF; BioIn 1, 10; CurBio 72, 72N; DcAmB S9; DcAmMiB; LinLib S; NewYTBE 72; ObitOF 79; OxCShps; WebAMB; WhAm 5; WhWW-II*

Stark, Johannes
German. Scientist
Discovered Doppler effect in canal rays; won 1919 Nobel Prize in physics.
b. Apr 15, 1874 in Schickenhof, Germany
d. Jun 21, 1957 in Traunstein, Germany (West)
Source: *AsBiEn; BiESc; BioIn 3, 4, 14, 15, 20; CamDcSc; DcScB; EncTR, 91; InSci; LarDcSc; NobelP; NotTwCS; WhoNob, 90, 95*

Stark, John
American. Army Officer
Revolutionary War officer; won battle of Bennington, VT, 1777.
b. Aug 28, 1728 in Londonderry, New Hampshire
d. May 8, 1822 in Manchester, New Hampshire
Source: *Alli; AmBi; AmRev; ApCAB; BioIn 2, 3, 7, 9, 10, 16; DcAmB; Drake; EncAR; EncCRAm; GenMudB; HarEnUS; LinLib S; NatCAB 1; OxCAmH; TwCBDA; WebAB 74, 79; WebAMB; WhAm HS; WhAmRev; WhoMilH 76; WorAl; WorAlBi*

Stark, Koo
[Kathleen Stark]
American. Actor
Involved in publicized romanace with Britain's Prince Andrew, 1982.
b. 1957? in New York, New York
Source: *BioIn 13*

Stark, Ray
American. Filmmaker
Films produced include *Funny Girl,* 1968; *The Way We Were,* 1973; *Biloxi Blues,* 1987.
b. Oct 13, 1917?
Source: *CelR 90; ConTFT 6; HalFC 88; IntMPA 86; NewYTBS 80; WhoAm 84; WhoEnt 92; WhoWest 92*

Starker, Janos
Hungarian. Musician
Cello virtuoso; int'l reputation as first cellist with many symphonies.
b. Jul 5, 1924 in Budapest, Hungary
Source: *Baker 78, 84, 92; BioIn 4, 6, 9, 10, 11, 12, 13, 15; BlueB 76; BriBkM 80; CurBio 63; FacFETw; IntWW 74, 75, 76, 77, 78, 79, 80, 81, 82, 83, 89, 91, 93; IntWWM 77, 80, 90; MusSN; NewAmDM; NewGrDA 86; NewGrDM 80; NewYTBE 72; NewYTBS 82; PenDiMP; Who 74, 82, 83, 85, 88, 90, 92, 94; WhoAm 74, 76, 78, 80, 82, 84, 86, 88, 90; WhoAmM 83; WhoEnt 92; WhoMus 72*

Starkie, Walter Fitzwilliam
Irish. Author, Educator
Taught Romance languages, Trinity College, 1926-47; best known for stories of his life among the gypsies: *In Sara's Tents,* 1953.
b. Aug 9, 1894 in Killiney, Ireland
d. Nov 2, 1976 in Madrid, Spain
Source: *Au&Wr 71; BiDIrW; BioIn 1, 4, 6, 7, 11, 17; BlueB 76; CarSB; CathA 1930; ConAu 69, 77; CurBio 64, 77; DcIrB 88; DcIrW 2; IntAu&W 77; IntWW 74, 75, 76; LngCTC; NewC; NewCBEL; NewGrDM 80; NewYTBS 76; TwCA, SUP; WhAm 7; WhE&EA; Who 74; WhoAm 74, 76; WhoMus 72*

Starkweather, Charles
American. Murderer
Killed 11 people, 1958; executed, 1959.
b. Nov 24, 1938 in Lincoln, Nebraska
d. Jun 24, 1959 in Lincoln, Nebraska
Source: *BioIn 10*

Starling, Ernest Henry
English. Physiologist
Collaborated with William Bayliss on digestive, kidney function studies; discovered secretin, 1912; wrote *Principles of Human Physiology,* 1912.
b. Apr 17, 1866 in London, England
d. May 2, 1927 in Kingston, Jamaica
Source: *AsBiEn; BiESc; BiHiMed; BioIn 2, 4, 8, 9, 14, 20; CamDcSc; DcNaB 1922; DcScB; InSci; LarDcSc; NewCol 75; OxCMed 86; WhLit; WorAl; WorAlBi; WorScD*

Starr, Bart
[Bryan B Starr]
American. Football Player
Quarterback, Green Bay, 1956-71; set several NFL passing records; led league in passing three times; MVP, Super Bowl, 1967, 1968; Hall of Fame, 1977.
b. Jan 9, 1934 in Montgomery, Alabama
Source: *BioIn 7, 8, 9, 10, 11, 12, 13, 15, 17, 20; BioNews 75; CurBio 68; LegTOT; NewYTBS 81; WhoAm 82, 84, 86, 88, 92, 94, 95, 96; WhoFtbl 74; WhoSpor; WorAl; WorAlBi*

Starr, Belle
[Myra Belle Shirley]
American. Pioneer, Outlaw
Cattle rustler; harbored Jesse James, 1881.
b. Feb 5, 1848? in Carthage, Missouri
d. Feb 3, 1889 in Briartown, Oklahoma
Source: *AmAu&B; BioIn 3, 5, 6, 7, 8, 9, 10, 11, 13, 14, 15, 16, 17; ContDcW 89; DrInf; EncAmaz 91; GoodHs; HalFC 80, 84, 88; IntDcWB; LegTOT; LibW; NotAW; REnAW; WhAm HS; WorAl; WorAlBi*

Starr, Kay
[Kathryn Stark]
American. Singer
Popular vocalist, 1940s-50s; combined blues, country, swing; hit single: "Wheel of Fortune," 1952.
b. Jul 21, 1924 in Doughtery, Oklahoma
Source: *BiDAmM; BioIn 2; CmpEPM; NewGrDJ 88; PenEncP; RkOn 74*

Starr, Ringo
[The Beatles; Richard Starkey]
English. Singer, Musician
Drummer with The Beatles; started solo career, 1970; starred in film *Caveman,* 1981; inducted into Rock and Roll Hall of Fame with The Beatles, 1988.
b. Jul 7, 1940 in Liverpool, England
Source: *Baker 78, 84, 92; BioIn 6, 7, 8, 9, 10, 11, 12, 13, 16; BkPepl; BlueB 76; CelR, 90; ConMuA 80A; ConMus 10; ConTFT 7; CurBio 65; EncPR&S 89; EncRk 88; EncRkSt; FilmEn; ForYSC; HarEnR 86; IlEncRk; IntMPA 92, 94, 96; IntWW 74, 75, 76, 77, 78, 79, 80, 81, 82, 83, 89, 91, 93; ItaFilm; LegTOT; MiSFD 9; MotPP; NewAmDM; NewGrDM 80; OxCPMus; PenEncP; RkOn 78; RolSEnR 83; WhoAm 78, 80, 82, 84, 86, 88, 90, 92, 94, 95, 96, 97; WhoEnt 92; WhoHol 92, A; WhoRock 81; WhoRocM 82; WhoWor 74, 78, 80, 82, 84, 87, 89, 91, 93, 95, 96, 97; WorAl; WorAlBi*

Starrett, Vincent
[Charles Vincent Emerson Starrett]
American. Author, Critic
Books include *Bookman's Holiday,* 1942; *Private Life of Sherlock Holmes,* 1933.
b. Oct 26, 1886 in Toronto, Ontario, Canada
d. Jan 4, 1974 in Chicago, Illinois
Source: *AmAu&B; AuBYP 2, 3; BenetAL 91; BioIn 4, 7, 8, 10, 14; ChhPo, S2; ConAu 31NR, 45, 73; CrtSuMy; DcLEL; EncMys; NewYTBS 74; REn; REnAL; ScF&FL 1, 92; TwCA, SUP; TwCCr&M 80, 85, 91; WhAm 6; WhLit; WhNAA*

Starship
[Don Baldwin; Craig Chaquico; Pete Sears; Grace Slick; Mickey Thomas]
American. Music Group
Made up of members of Jefferson Starship; hit album *Knee Deep in the Hoopla,* 1985.
Source: *ConMus 5; EncPR&S 89; EncRk 88; FacFETw; NewAmDM; PenEncP; WhoAmP 75; WhoRocM 82*

Starzl, Thomas Earl
American. Surgeon
Pioneer in organ transplantation; performed first human-liver transplant, 1963.
b. Mar 11, 1926 in Le Mars, Iowa
Source: *BioIn 11, 12; CurBio 93; WhoAm 74, 76, 80, 82, 84, 88, 90, 92, 94, 95, 96, 97; WhoWest 74, 76, 78, 80*

Stassen, Harold Edward
American. Lawyer, Politician
Rep. Governor of MN, 1938-45; youngest governor in US history; best known for many attempts at presidential nomination.
b. Apr 13, 1907 in West Saint Paul, Minnesota
Source: *AmAu&B; BiDrGov 1789; BioIn 1, 2, 3, 4, 5, 6, 8, 10, 11; BlueB 76; CurBio 40, 48; FacFETw; IntWW 83; IntYB 78, 79, 80, 81, 82; LinLib S; PolProf E, T; WebAB 74, 79; Who 74, 82, 83, 85, 88, 90, 92, 94; WhoAm 74, 76, 78, 80, 82; WhoAmL 83, 85; WhoAmP 73; WhoWor 78, 80, 82; WorAl; WorAlBi*

Stastny, Anton
Czech. Hockey Player
Left wing, Quebec, 1980—; defected with brothers Peter and Marian.
b. Aug 5, 1959 in Bratislava, Czechoslovakia
Source: *BioIn 12, 13; HocEn; HocReg 87; NewYTBS 81; WhoFI 92*

Stastny, Marian
Czech. Hockey Player
Right wing, Quebec, 1981-85, Toronto, 1985-87; defected with brothers Anton and Peter.
b. Jan 8, 1953 in Bratislava, Czechoslovakia
Source: *BioIn 13; HocEn; HocReg 86; NewYTBS 81*

Stastny, Peter
Czech. Hockey Player
Center, Quebec, 1980-1990, NJ, 1990—; one of four players in NHL history to break in with three consecutive 100-pt. seasons; won Calder Trophy, 1981, first non-North American player honored.
b. Sep 18, 1956 in Bratislava, Czechoslovakia
Source: *BioIn 12, 13; HocEn; HocReg 87; NewYTBS 81*

Statler, Ellsworth Milton
American. Hotel Executive
Started Statler chain of hotels, Buffalo, NY, 1904.
b. Oct 26, 1863 in Somerset County, Pennsylvania
d. Apr 16, 1928 in New York, New York
Source: *BioIn 2, 3, 7, 8, 10; ConMus 8; DcAmB; WebAB 74, 79; WhAm 1*

Statler Brothers
[Phillip Balsley; Lew C DeWitt; Don S Reid; Harold W Reid]
American. Music Group
Durable country harmony group; hit singles since early 1960s.
Source: *BgBkCoM; BiDAmM; ConMus 8; CounME 74, 74A; EncFCWM 69, 83; HarEnCM 87; IlEncCM; NewAmDM; NewGrDA 86; PenEncP; RkOn 74, 78; WhoAmP 75, 77, 79, 81, 83, 85, 87; WhoHol 92; WhoRock 81*

Status Quo
English. Music Group
Pop hits include *Dear John,* 1982; *The Wanderer,* 1984.
Source: *AfrAmPr; Alli, SUP; BbtC; BiAUS; BiDBrA; BiDLA; BiDrAC; BiDrUSC 89; BioIn 11, 19; CabMA; Chambr 2, 3; ChhPo, S1; ConMuA 80A; CyAL 1; DcBiPP; DcBrBI; DcBrWA; DcLP 87A; DcNaB, C; EncRk 88; EncRkSt; FolkA 87; IlEncRk; InB&W 80; Law&B 89A, 89B, 92; NewC; NewCBEL; NewYHSD; OxCPMus; PenEncP; PeoHis; PoIre; RkOn 78; RolSEnR 83; St&PR 96, 97; WhAm HS; WhoAfA 96; WhoAmP 85; WhoHol 92; WhoRock 81; WhoRocM 82; WhScrn 77, 83*

Staub, Rusty
[Daniel Joseph Staub]
American. Baseball Player
Outfielder, 1963-85; led NL in pinch hits, 1983, 1984; had .279 lifetime batting average.
b. Apr 1, 1944 in New Orleans, Louisiana
Source: *Ballpl 90; BaseReg 86; BiDAmSp BB; BioIn 8, 9, 11, 12, 14, 15, 16; LegTOT; NewYTBE 72, 73; NewYTBS 85; WhoAm 74, 76, 78; WhoProB 73*

Staubach, Roger Thomas
American. Football Player
Quarterback, won Heisman Trophy, 1963; in NFL with Dallas, 1969-79; MVP, Super Bowl, 1972; Hall of Fame, 1985.
b. Feb 5, 1942 in Cincinnati, Ohio
Source: *BiDAmSp FB; BioIn 6, 9, 10, 11, 12, 15, 16; ConAu 104; CurBio 72; NewYTBE 71, 72; NewYTBS 84, 89; WhoAm 74, 76, 78, 80, 82, 84, 86, 88, 90, 92, 94, 95, 96; WhoFtbl 74; WorAlBi*

Staudinger, Hermann
German. Chemist, Author
Won 1953 Nobel Prize for work in synthetics.
b. Mar 23, 1881 in Worms, Germany
d. Sep 9, 1965 in Freiburg, Germany (West)
Source: *AsBiEn; BiESc; BioIn 2, 3, 6, 7, 8, 14, 15, 19, 20; CamDcSc; ConAu 113; CurBio 65; DcScB; InSci; LarDcSc;*

McGMS 80; NobelP; NotTwCS; WhAm 4; WhoNob, 90, 95

Stauffenberg, Claus (Schenk Graf) Von
[Klaus Graf Schenk von Stauffenberg]
German. Army Officer
Part of conspiracy against Hitler; failed in assassination attempt, Jul 1944; shot to death by firing squad.
b. Nov 15, 1907 in Upper Franconia, Germany
d. Jul 20, 1944 in Rastenburg, Germany
Source: *BioIn 2, 8, 10; EncTR; HisWorL; OxCGer 76; WhWW-II*

Staunton, Howard
English. Chess Player
Organizer of first world chess tournament, 1851; wrote several books on subject.
b. 1810 in Westmoreland, England
d. Jun 22, 1874 in London, England
Source: *Alli; BioIn 10, 11, 12, 14, 15; CelCen; DcBiPP; DcNaB; GolEC; NewCBEL; OxCChes 84*

Staupers, Mabel K.
American. Civil Rights Activist
Executive secretary, National Association of Colored Graduate Nurses, 1934-49; president, 1940-50; helped pursuade the American Nurses' Association to remove all barriers to black membership.
b. Feb 27, 1890, Barbados
d. Nov 29, 1989 in Washington, District of Columbia
Source: *ConBlB 7*

Stautner, Ernie
[Ernest Stautner]
American. Football Player
Nine-time all-pro defensive tackle, Pittsburgh, 1950-63; Hall of Fame, 1969.
b. Apr 2, 1925 in Calm, Bavaria
Source: *BiDAmSp FB; BioIn 10, 17; LegTOT; WhoFtbl 74; WhoSpor*

Stavisky, Serge Alexandre
French. Criminal
Swindler; sold worthless bonds to French working people.
b. Nov 10, 1886 in Slobodka, Russia
d. Jan 8, 1934 in Chamonix-Mont-Blanc, France
Source: *BioIn 2, 4, 5, 10, 11, 14, 17; REn*

Stavropoulos, George Peter
American. Fashion Designer
Best known for chiffon evening wear for women; influenced by classical Greek scu lpture; dressed such celebrities as Elizabeth Taylor, Maria Callas.
b. Jan 22, 1920 in Tripolis, Greece
d. Dec 10, 1990 in New York, New York
Source: *BioIn 14, 16; ConFash; CurBio 85, 91N; EncFash; FairDF US; NewYTBS 90; WhoAm 82; WorFshn*

Stead, Christina (Ellen)
Australian. Author
Feminist novelist; best-known novel *The Man Who Loved Children,* 1940.
b. Jul 17, 1902 in Sydney, Australia
d. Mar 31, 1983 in Sydney, Australia
Source: *AnObit 1983; ArtclWW 2; Au&Wr 71; AuLitCr; AuWomWr; Benet 87, 96; BioIn 1, 4, 8, 9, 10, 11, 13, 14, 15, 16, 17, 18, 19, 20, 21; BlmGEL; BlmGWL; CamGLE; CasWL; ConAu 13R, 33NR, 40NR, 109; ConLC 2, 5, 8, 32, 80; ConNov 72, 76, 82; ContDcW 89; CyWA 89; DcArts; DcLEL; EncBrWW; EncWL 2, 3; EvLB; FacFETw; FarE&A 78, 79, 80, 81; FemiCLE; FemiWr; GrWomW; GrWrEL N; IntAu&W 76, 77; IntDcWB; IntLitE; IntWW 77, 78, 79, 80, 81, 82, 83N; InWom, SUP; LegTOT; LngCTC; MajTwCW; ModCmwL; ModWoWr; NewCBEL; NewYTBS 83; Novels; OxCAusL; OxCEng 85, 95; RAdv 1, 14, 13-1; RfGEnL 91; RfGShF; RGTwCWr; ScF&FL 1, 2, 92; TwCA, SUP; TwCWr; WhAm 8; WhE&EA; Who 74, 82, 83; WhoTwCL; WhoWor 74, 76; WorAl; WrDr 76, 80, 82, 84*

Steber, Eleanor
American. Opera Singer
Soprano; NY Met., 1940-66; noted for Mozart, Verdi, Puccini roles.
b. Jul 17, 1916 in Wheeling, West Virginia
d. Oct 3, 1990 in Langhorne, Pennsylvania
Source: *Baker 78, 84; BiDAmM; BioIn 1, 2, 3, 4, 5, 9, 10, 11, 12, 13; BriBkM 80; CmOp; CurBio 43, 91N; FacFETw; IntDcOp; IntWWM 90; InWom, SUP; MetOEnc; MusSN; NewAmDM; NewEOp 71; NewGrDA 86; NewGrDM 80; NewGrDO; NewYTBE 73; NewYTBS 90; PenDiMP; WhoAm 74, 76, 78, 80, 82, 84, 86, 90; WhoAmM 83; WhoAmW 58, 83, 87; WhoMus 72; WhoWor 74*

Stedman, Edmund Clarence
American. Author, Journalist
Edited *Victorian Poets,* 1875; 11-volume *Library of American Literature,* 1888-90.
b. Oct 8, 1833 in Hartford, Connecticut
d. Jan 18, 1908 in New York, New York
Source: *Alli, SUP; AmAu; AmAu&B; AmBi; ApCAB, X; Benet 87; BenetAL 91; BibAL; BiD&SB; BioIn 3, 5, 13, 15, 16; Chambr 3; ChhPo, S1, S2, S3; CivWDc; CnDAL; CyAL 2; DcAmAu; DcAmB; DcEnA A; DcEnL; DcLB 64; DcLEL; DcNAA; Drake; EvLB; GayN; HarEnUS; JrnUS; LinLib L; NatCAB 3; OxCAmL 65, 83, 95; OxCCan; REn; REnAL; TwCBDA; WhAm 1; WhCiWar; WhLit*

Steegmuller, Francis
American. Author
Best known for biographies; *Cocteau: A Biography* won Nat. Book Award, 1971.
b. Jul 3, 1906 in New Haven, Connecticut
Source: *AmAu&B; Au&Wr 71; Benet 87, 96; BenetAL 91; BioIn 2, 4, 12, 17, 20; ChhPo; ConAu 2NR, 49; ConNov 72, 76; DcLB 111; DcLP 87A; DrAPF 80, 91; IntAu&W 76, 77, 82, 86, 89, 91; NewYTBS 80; OxCAmL 83, 95; REnAL; TwCA SUP; WhAm 11; WhE&EA; Who 74, 82, 83, 85, 88, 90, 92, 94; WhoAm 74, 76, 78, 80, 82, 84, 86, 88, 90, 92, 94; WrDr 76, 80, 82, 84, 86, 88, 90, 92, 94, 96*

Steel, Anthony
English. Actor
Films include *The Monster Club,* 1981.
b. May 21, 1920 in London, England
Source: *FilmEn; FilmgC; ForYSC; HalFC 80, 84, 88; IlWWBF; IntMPA 75, 76, 77, 78, 79, 80, 81, 82, 84, 86, 88, 92; ItaFilm; WhoHol A*

Steel, Danielle Fernande
[Danielle Schuelein-Steel]
American. Author
Author of romantic bestsellers *The Promise,* 1979; *Full Circle,* 1984; *Fine Things,* 1987; *Jewels,* 1991.
b. Aug 14, 1947 in New York, New York
Source: *BioIn 16; CelR 90; ConAu 19NR, 36NR, 81; CurBio 89; SmATA 66; TwCRHW 90; WhoAm 86, 88, 90, 92, 94, 95, 96; WhoAmW 81, 83, 85, 89, 91, 93, 95; WhoUSWr 88; WhoWor 95; WhoWrEP 89, 92, 95; WorAlBi; WrDr 92*

Steel, Dawn
American. Producer, Film Executive
Films include *Fatal Attraction,* 1987; pres. of Columbia Pictures, 1987-90.
b. Aug 19, 1946 in New York, New York
Source: *BioIn 16; ConAu 151; ConTFT 5; IntMPA 86, 92, 94, 96; IntWW 89, 91, 93; News 90, 90-1; ReelWom; WhoAm 86, 88, 90; WhoAmW 89, 91; WhoEnt 92; WhoWest 89, 92; WomFir*

Steel, Flora Annie Webster
English. Author
Wrote on India: *On the Face of the Waters,* 1896.
b. Apr 2, 1847 in Harrow, England
d. Apr 12, 1929
Source: *BioIn 16, 21; ConAu 116; InWom, SUP; LngCTC; TwCA*

Steele, Bob
[Robert North Bradbury, Jr.]
American. Actor
Cowboy star in over 150 films, 1927-71; appeared in TV comedy "F-Troop." 1965-67.
b. Jan 23, 1906? in Pendleton, Oregon
d. Dec 21, 1988 in Burbank, California
Source: *BioIn 8, 16; Film 2; FilmEn; FilmgC; TwYS; Vers A; WhoHol A*

Steele, Richard, Sir
[Isaac Bickerstaff]
British. Author, Editor
Founded periodical papers *Tatler,* 1709, *Spectator,* 1711, *Guardian,* 1713; wrote comedy *The Conscious Lover,* 1712.
b. Mar 1672 in Dublin, Ireland
d. Sep 1, 1729 in Carmarthen, Wales
Source: *Alli; AtlBL; BbD; Benet 87, 96; BiD&SB; BiDIrW; BioIn 1, 2, 3, 4, 5, 6, 8, 9, 11, 12, 15, 17, 18, 21; BlkwCE; BlmGEL; BritAu; BritWr 3; CamGEL; CamGLE; CamGWoT; CasWL; Chambr 2; ChhPo; CnDBLB 2; CnThe; CrtSuDr; CrtT 2, 4; CyWA 58; DcArts; DcEnA; DcEnL; DcEuL; DcIrB 78, 88; DcIrL 96; DcIrW 1, 2; DcLB 84, 101; DcLEL; DcNaB; Dis&D; EncEnl; EncWT; Ent; EvLB; GrWrEL DR, N; IntDcT 2; LegTOT; LiJour; LinLib L, S; LitC 18; LngCEL; LuthC 75; McGEWB; McGEWD 72, 84; MouLC 2; NewC; NewCBEL; NotNAT A, B; OxCEng 67, 85, 95; OxCIri; OxCThe 67, 83; PenC ENG; PlP&P; PoIre; RAdv 1, 14, 13-1; REn; REnWD; RfGEnL 91; WebE&AL; WhDW; WorAl; WorAlBi*

Steele, Shelby
American. Author, Educator
Writing focuses on racial issues, specifically the notion that white society is inherently racist and all blacks are victimized by racism; book *The Content of Our Character,* nominated for National Book Award, 1991.
b. Jan 1, 1946 in Chicago, Illinois
Source: *AfrAmAl 6; AmDec 1980; ConBlB 13; CurBio 93; News 91, 91-2; NewYTBS 90; WhoAfA 96; WhoAm 94, 95, 96, 97; WhoBlA 92, 94; WrDr 92, 94, 96*

Steele, Tommy
English. Actor
Films include *The Happiest Millionaire,* 1967; *Finian's Rainbow,* 1968.
b. Dec 17, 1936 in London, England
Source: *BioIn 4, 5, 7, 8, 11, 13; BlueB 76; ConAu 129; ConTFT 3; EncMT; EncRk 88; EncRkSt; FilmAG WE; FilmEn; FilmgC; ForYSC; HalFC 80, 84, 88; IlWWBF, A; IntMPA 75, 76, 77, 78, 79, 80, 82, 84, 86, 88, 92, 94, 96; IntWW 79, 80, 81, 82, 83, 89, 91, 93; IntWWM 90; MotPP; OxCFilm; OxCPMus; PenEncP; RolSEnR 83; Who 74, 82, 83, 85, 88, 90, 92, 94; WhoHol 92, A; WhoRocM 82; WhoThe 72, 77, 81; WhoWor 76*

Steele, Willie
American. Track Athlete
Long jumper; won gold medal, 1948 Olympics.
b. Jul 14, 1923 in Seeley, California
Source: *WhoTr&F 73*

Steeleye Span
[Kemp; Martin Carthy; Bob Johnson; John Kirkpatrick; Peter Knight; Maddy Prior]
British. Music Group
Pioneered electronic folk music; albums include *Sails of Silver,* 1980.
Source: *Alli, SUP; AuBYP 2, 3; BiDLA; BioIn 8, 17, 18; ConMuA 80A; EncPR&S 89; EncRk 88; HarEnR 86; IlEncRk; NewYTBS 91; PenEncP; PoIre; RolSEnR 83; WhoAm 84, 86; WhoAmP 83; WhoRock 81; WhoRocM 82; WhoWest 87, 89*

Steelman, John Roy
American. Government Official
Held several govt. posts beginning 1934; first to serve as asst. to US pres., under Truman, 1946-52.
b. Jun 23, 1900 in Thornton, Arkansas
Source: *BioIn 1, 2, 3, 10, 11; CurBio 41, 52; PolProf T*

Steely Dan
[Jeff Baxter; Walter Becker; Denny Dias; Donald Fagen; James Hodder; David Palmer]
American. Music Group
Formed, 1972; lively, bluesy jazz hits include FM, 1978; "Deacon Blues," 1978.
Source: *Alli; BioIn 12; ChhPo, S1; ConMuA 80A; ConMus 5; DcNaB; DrAPF 85, 87, 89, 91, 93, 97; Dun&B 88, 90; EncPR&S 89; EncRk 88; EncRkSt; HarEnR 86; IlEncRk; NewAmDM; NewGrDA 86; OnThGG; OxCCan; PenEncP; RkOn 74, 78; RolSEnR 83; WhoAm 80, 82, 84, 86, 94, 95, 96, 97; WhoEnt 92; WhoHol 92; WhoRock 81; WhoRocM 82*

Steen, Alann
American. Hostage
Journalism professor in Lebanon seized by Islamic Jihad January 24, 1987 and held captive 1,774 days; released December 3, 1991.
Source: *BioIn 19*

Steen, Jan
Dutch. Artist
Prolific painter of genre scenes depicting taverns, middle-class life.
b. 1626 in Leiden, Netherlands
d. Feb 3, 1679 in Leiden, Netherlands
Source: *AtlBL; ClaDrA; DcArts; Dis&D; IntDcAA 90; LegTOT; McGDA; OxCArt; WhDW*

Steen, Roger
[The Tubes]
American. Musician
Guitarist with The Tubes since late 1960s.
b. Nov 13, 1949 in Pipestone, Minnesota

Steenburgen, Mary
[Mrs. Ted Danson]
American. Actor
Won Oscar, 1981, for *Melvin and Howard;* star of TV's "Ink," 1996-97.
b. 1953 in Little Rock, Arkansas
Source: *BioIn 12, 13, 16; CelR 90; ConTFT 7, 14; HalFC 88; IntMPA 86, 88, 92, 94, 96; JohnWSW; LegTOT; WhoAm 86, 88, 90, 92, 94, 95, 96, 97; WhoAmW 87, 89, 91, 93, 95, 97; WhoEnt 92; WhoHol 92; WorAlBi*

Stefanik, Milan Rastislav
Czech. Astronomer, Military Leader
Army general who was one of Czechoslovakia's founders in 1918.
b. Jul 21, 1880 in Kosariska, Austria-Hungary
d. Apr 4, 1919 in Wenor, Czechoslovakia

Stefansson, Vihjalmur
Canadian. Explorer
Led Canadian Arctic Expedition, 1913-18; discovered new lands in Arctic archipelago.
b. Nov 3, 1879 in Arnes, Manitoba, Canada
d. Aug 26, 1962 in Hanover, New Hampshire
Source: *CurBio 62; WebAB 74; WebBD 83; WorAl*

Steffani, Agostino
Italian. Composer
Noted operas include *SoloMe,* 1685.
b. Jul 25, 1654 in Castelfranco, Italy
d. Feb 12, 1728 in Frankfurt am Main, Germany
Source: *Baker 84, 92; BioIn 4; BriBkM 80; DcCathB; LuthC 75; MusMk; NewAmDM; NewEOp 71; NewGrDM 80; NewGrDO; NewOxM; OxCMus; OxDcOp*

Steffens, Lincoln
[Joseph Lincoln Steffens]
American. Journalist, Social Reformer
Muckraking editor who exposed government, business corruption.
b. Apr 6, 1866 in San Francisco, California
d. Aug 9, 1936 in Carmel, California
Source: *AmAu&B; AmBi; AmDec 1900; AmJust; AmRef; AmSocL; Benet 87; BenetAL 91; BiDAmJo; BiDAmLf; BioIn 1, 2, 3, 4, 5, 6, 8, 9, 10, 11, 12, 13, 15, 16, 19; CmCal; ConAu 117; CyWA 89; DcAmAu; DcAmB S2; DcAmSR; DcLEL; DcNAA; EncAB-H 1974, 1996; EncAJ; FacFETw; GayN; JrnUS; LegTOT; LiJour; LinLib L, S; LngCTC; McGEWB; MemAm; ModAL; NatCAB 14; OxCAmH; OxCAmL 65, 83; PenC AM; PeoHis; REn; REnAL; REnAW; TwCA, SUP; TwCLC 20; WebAB 74, 79; WebE&AL; WhAm 1; WorAl; WorAlBi*

Steger, Will
American. Pilot, Explorer
First person to fly solo around the world; explored both the North & South Poles.
b. 1945 in Minneapolis, Minnesota
Source: *BioIn 16; News 90*

Stegner, Wallace (Earle)
American. Author
Writings deal with American West; won Pulitzer, 1972, for *Angle of Repose*.
b. Feb 18, 1909 in Lake Mills, Iowa
d. Apr 13, 1993 in Santa Fe, New Mexico
Source: *AmAu&B; AmCulL; AmNov; AnObit 1993; Au&Wr 71; AuNews 1; Benet 87, 96; BenetAL 91; BestSel 90-3; BioIn 2, 3, 4, 9, 10, 11, 12, 13, 14, 15, 16, 17, 18, 19, 20, 21; BlueB 76; CmCal; CnDAL; ConAu 1NR, 1R, 9AS, 21NR, 46NR, 141; ConLC 9, 49, 81; ConNov 72, 76, 82, 86, 91; CurBio 77, 93N; CyWA 89; DcLB 9, Y93N; DrAF 76; DrAPF 80, 91; DrAS 74E, 78E, 82E; EncFWF; FifWWr; IntAu&W 76, 77, 91, 93; LegTOT; LinLib L; MajTwCW; ModAL; NewYTBS 93; Novels; OxCAmL 65, 83, 95; OxCCan; PenC AM; RAdv 1, 14; REn; REnAL; REnAW; RfGAmL 94; TwCA, SUP; TwCWW 82, 91; WhAm 11; WhE&EA; WhNAA; WhoAm 74, 76, 78, 80, 82, 84, 86, 88, 90, 92; WhoUSWr 88; WhoWest 74, 76; WhoWrEP 89, 92; WorAlBi; WrDr 76, 80, 82, 84, 86, 88, 90, 92, 94N*

Steichen, Edward Jean
American. Photographer, Artist
Brother-in-law of Carl Sandburg; pictures ranged from impressionistic to straight documentary.
b. Mar 27, 1879, Luxembourg
d. Mar 25, 1973 in West Redding, Connecticut
Source: *BiDAmJo; BriEAA; ConPhot 82; CurBio 73; DcAmArt; DcAmB S9; DcTwDes; EncAB-H 1974, 1996; MacBEP; McGEWB; NatCAB 60; NewYTBE 73; ObitOF 79; OxCAmL 65; REn; REnAL; WebAB 74, 79; WhAm 5; WorFshn*

Steig, William
American. Cartoonist, Illustrator, Children's Author
Drawings featured in *The New Yorker;* won 1970, 1977 Caldecotts; wrote *The Amazing Bone*, 1977.
b. Nov 14, 1907 in New York, New York
Source: *AmAu&B; AuBYP 2, 3; BenetAL 91; BioIn 8, 9, 10, 12, 13, 14, 15, 16, 17, 18, 19, 20; ChlBkCr; ChlLR 15; ConAu 21NR, 77; CurBio 44; DcAmChF 1960; DcLB 61; EncTwCJ; IlsBYP; IlsCB 1967; MajAI; NewYTBE 72; OxCChiL; REnAL; SmATA 18, 70; ThrBJA; TwCChW 78, 83, 89, 95; WhoAm 74, 76, 78, 80, 82, 84, 86, 88, 90, 92, 94, 95, 96, 97; WhoAmA 73, 76, 78, 80, 82, 84, 86, 89; WhoE 74; WhoGrA 82; WhoWor 74; WorECar; WrDr 80, 82, 84, 86, 88, 90, 92, 94, 96*

Steiger, Rod
American. Actor
Won Oscar, 1967, for *In the Heat of the Night*.
b. Apr 14, 1925 in Westhampton, New York
Source: *BiDFilm, 81, 94; BiE&WWA; BioIn 4, 5, 6, 7, 8, 10, 11, 12, 13, 14, 21; BkPepl; BlueB 76; CelR, 90; CmMov; ConTFT 3, 10; CurBio 65; FilmEn; FilmgC; ForYSC; GangFlm; HalFC 80, 84, 88; IntDcF 1-3, 2-3; IntMPA 75, 76, 77, 78, 79, 80, 81, 82, 84, 86, 88, 92, 94, 96; IntWW 74, 75, 76, 77, 78, 79, 80, 81, 82, 83, 89, 91, 93; ItaFilm; LegTOT; MotPP; MovMk; OxCFilm; WhoAm 74, 76, 78, 80, 82, 84, 86, 88, 90, 92, 94, 95, 96, 97; WhoEnt 92; WhoHol 92, A; WhoHrs 80; WhoWor 74, 78; WorAl; WorAlBi; WorEFlm*

Stein, Aaron Marc
[George Bagby; Hampton Stone]
American. Author
Mystery story writer; won Grand Master Edgar Award, 1979.
b. Nov 15, 1906 in New York, New York
d. Aug 29, 1985 in New York, New York
Source: *BioIn 14; ConAu 6NR, 9R, 117; EncMys; IntAu&W 77, 82; Novels; TwCCr&M 80, 85, 91; WhAm 9; WhoAm 82, 84; WrDr 82, 84, 86*

Stein, Clarence S
American. Architect, Urban Planner
Style emphasizes walls and minimal ornamentation; planned town of Greenbelt, MD.
b. Jun 19, 1882 in Rochester, New York
d. Feb 7, 1975 in New York, New York
Source: *AmArch 70; BlueB 76; EncUrb; IntWW 74, 75; WhAm 7; WhoAm 74, 76*

Stein, Gertrude
American. Author
Center of American expatriates in 1920s Paris; named members the "Lost Generation."
b. Feb 3, 1874 in Allegheny, Pennsylvania
d. Jul 27, 1946 in Neuilly, France
Source: *AmAu&B; AmCulL; AmWomD; AmWomPl; AmWomWr, 92; AmWr; ArtclWW 2; AtlBL; Benet 87, 96; BenetAL 91; BioAmW; BioIn 1, 2, 3, 4, 5, 6, 7, 8, 9, 10, 11, 12, 13, 14, 15, 17, 18, 19, 20, 21; BlmGWL; CamGEL; CamGLE; CamHAL; CasWL; Chambr 3; ChhPo S1; CmCal; CnDAL; CnE&AP; CnMD; CnMWL; ConAmA; ConAmL; ConAu 104, 132; ContDcW 89; CyWA 89; DcAmB S4; DcArts; DcLB 4, 54, 86; DcLEL; DcNAA; EncAB-A 6; EncAB-H 1974, 1996; EncWHA; EncWL 2, 3; EncWT; EvLB; FacFETw; FemiCLE; GayLesB; GayLL; GoodHs; GrLiveH; GrWomW; GrWrEL N; HanAmWH; HerW, 84; IntDcWB; InWom, SUP; JeAmWW; JeHun; LegTOT; LibW; LiExTwC; LinLib L, S; LngCTC; MajTwCW; MakMC; McGEWB; MetOEnc; ModAL, S1, S2; ModAWWr; ModWD; ModWoWr; MorMA; NatCAB 38; NewEOp 71; NewGrDA 86; NewGrDO; NotAW; NotNAT A, B; NotWoAT; Novels; OxCAmH; OxCAmL 65, 83, 95; OxCAmT 84; OxCChiL; OxCEng 67, 85, 95; OxCTwCP; OxCWoWr 95; PenBWP; PenC AM; PeoHis; RAdv 1, 14, 13-1; RComAH; RComWL; REn; REnAL; RfGAmL 87, 94; RfGShF; RGTwCWr; SixAP; Tw; TwCA, SUP; TwCLC 1, 6, 28, 48; TwCWr; WebAB 74, 79; WebE&AL; WhAm 2; WhAmArt 85; WhDW; WhLit; WhNAA; WhoTwCL; WomFir; WomNov; WorAl; WorAlBi; WorLitC*

Stein, Herbert
American. Economist
Free-market advocate; member, Pres. Nixon's Council of Economic Advisers, 1969-74, chm., 1971-74; member, Pres. Reagan's Economic Policy Advisory Board, 1981.
b. Aug 27, 1916 in Detroit, Michigan
Source: *AmAu&B; AmEA 74; AmMWSc 73S; BioIn 8, 9, 10, 12, 16, 17, 19, 20; BlueB 76; ConAu 106; CurBio 73; IntWW 74, 75, 76, 77, 78, 79, 80, 81, 82, 83, 89, 91, 93; NewYTBE 71; PolProf NF; St&PR 91; WhoAm 74, 76, 78, 80, 82, 84, 86, 88, 90, 92, 94, 95, 96, 97; WhoEc 81, 86; WhoFI 83, 92; WhoGov 72, 75; WrDr 86, 88, 90, 92, 94, 96*

Stein, Horst
German. Conductor
Led Hamburg State Opera, 1972-77, Hamburg Philharmonic, 1973-76.
b. May 28, 1928 in Elberfeld, Germany
Source: *Baker 78, 84; IntWWM 90; NewEOp 71; NewGrDM 80; NewGrDO; OxDcOp; PenDiMP; WhoMus 72; WhoWor 74*

Stein, James R
American. Writer
Won Emmys for "Lily," 1974; "The Carol Burnett Show," 1978.
b. Jan 9, 1950 in Chicago, Illinois
Source: *St&PR 87; VarWW 85; WhoEnt 92*

Stein, Joseph
American. Dramatist, Librettist
Won Tony for play *Fiddler on the Roof*, 1965; wrote film version, 1972.
b. May 30, 1912 in New York, New York
Source: *BiE&WWA; BioIn 15; CanWW 89; ConAu 13R, 31NR; ConDr 77D, 82D; ConTFT 4; EncMT; IntMPA 77; LegTOT; NatPD 77; NewCBMT; NotNAT; OxCAmT 84; VarWW 85; WhoAm 80, 82, 84, 86, 90; WhoEnt 92; WhoThe 72, 77, 81; WhoUSWr 88; WhoWrEP 89, 92*

Stein, Jules Caesar
American. Record Company Executive
Founder, pres., Music Corporation of America, 1924-46; chm., 1946-73; today MCA, Inc. is considered a major entertainment agency.

b. Apr 26, 1896 in South Bend, Indiana
d. Apr 29, 1981 in Los Angeles, California
Source: *BioIn 7, 8, 10, 13; CurBio 81; IntMPA 79; NewYTBS 74; WhAm 7; WhoAm 80; WhoFI 74; WhoWest 76*

Stein, Mark
[Vanilla Fudge]
American. Singer, Musician
Keyboardist, vocalist with group formed 1966.
b. Mar 11, 1947 in Bayonne, New Jersey

Stein, William Howard
American. Chemist
Shared 1972 Nobel Prize in chemistry with Stanford Moore.
b. Jun 25, 1911 in New York, New York
d. Feb 2, 1980 in New York, New York
Source: *AmMWSc 76P, 79; BiESc; BioIn 9, 10, 12; DcScB S2; LarDcSc; NotTwCS; WebAB 74, 79; WhAm 7; Who 74; WhoAm 74, 76, 78, 80; WhoAmJ 80; WhoE 77, 79; WhoNob, 90, 95; WhoWor 74; WorAl*

Steinbach, Terry Lee
American. Baseball Player
Catcher, Oakland, 1986—; MVP, 1988 All-Star Game.
b. Mar 2, 1962 in New Ulm, Minnesota
Source: *Ballpl 90; BaseEn 88; BaseReg 87, 88; WhoAm 97*

Steinbeck, John (Ernst)
American. Author
Won 1962 Nobel Prize; wrote *Of Mice and Men,* 1937; *The Grapes of Wrath,* 1939; *East of Eden,* 1952.
b. Feb 27, 1902 in Salinas, California
d. Dec 20, 1968 in New York, New York
Source: *AgeMat; AmAu&B; AmCulL; AmNov; AmWr; Au&Arts 12; AuBYP 2S, 3; Benet 87, 96; BenetAL 91; BiDAmJo; BiE&WWA; BioIn 1, 2, 3, 4, 5, 6, 7, 8, 9, 10, 11, 12, 13, 14, 15, 16, 17, 19, 20, 21; CamGEL; CamGLE; CamGWoT; CamHAL; CasWL; CmCal; CnDAL; CnMD; CnMWL; CnThe; ConAmA; ConAu 1NR, 1R, 25R, 35NR; ConLC 1, 5, 9, 13, 21, 34, 45, 59, 75; CurBio 40, 63; CyWA 58, 89; DcAmB S8; DcAmC; DcAmSR; DcArts; DcLB 7, 9, DS2; DcLEL; DcTwCCu 1; EncAAH; EncAB-H 1974, 1996; EncFWF; EncWL, 2, 3; EncWT; EvLB; FacFETw; FifWWr; FilmEn; FilmgC; GrWrEL N; HalFC 80, 84, 88; LegTOT; LinLib L, S; LngCTC; MagSAmL; MajTwCW; MakMC; McGEWB; McGEWD 72, 84; ModAL, S2; ModWD; MorMA; NatCAB 61; NobelP; NotNAT B; Novels; ObitT 1961; OxCAmH; OxCAmL 65, 83, 95; OxCAmT 84; OxCEng 67, 85, 95; OxCFilm; OxCThe 67, 83; PenC AM; RAdv 1, 14, 13-1; RComAH; RComWL; REn; REnAL; REnAW; RfGAmL 87, 94; RfGShF; RGTwCWr; ScF&FL 1, 2, 92; ShSCr 11; ShSWr; SmATA 9; TwCA, SUP; TwCRHW 90, 94; TwCWr; TwCWW 82, 91; TwCYAW; WebAB 74, 79; WebE&AL; WhAm 5; WhDW; WhoNob, 90, 95; WhoTwCL; WhThe; WorAl; WorAlBi; WorLitC*

Steinberg, David
Canadian. Actor, Comedian
Off-beat comic; hosted David Frost, Dick Cavett shows on TV; directed film *Paternity,* 1981.
b. Aug 9, 1942 in Winnipeg, Manitoba, Canada
Source: *BioIn 9, 10, 12; CanWW 31, 81, 83, 89; ConTFT 7, 15; IntMPA 88, 92, 94, 96; MiSFD 9; WhoAm 74, 76, 78, 80, 82, 84, 86, 88, 90, 92, 94, 96, 97; WhoCom; WhoEnt 92; WhoHol A; WorAl*

Steinberg, Saul
American. Artist, Cartoonist
Known for cartoons, cover-art for *New Yorker;* works combine many styles including cubism, pointalism.
b. Jun 15, 1914 in Romanic-Sarat, Romania
Source: *AmArt; AmAu&B; Benet 87; BenetAL 91; BioIn 1, 2, 3, 4, 5, 7, 8, 9, 11, 12, 13, 17; CelR; ConArt 77, 83, 89, 96; ConAu 89; CurBio 57; DcAmArt; DcArts; DcCAA 71, 77, 88, 94; EncAI&E; IntWW 74, 75, 76, 77, 78, 79, 80, 81, 82, 83, 89, 91, 93; LegTOT; LinLib L; McGDA; OxCAmL 65, 83, 95; OxCTwCA; PhDcTCA 77; REn; SmATA 67; WebAB 74, 79; WhAmArt 85; WhoAm 74, 76, 78, 80, 82, 84, 86, 88, 90, 92, 94, 95, 96; WhoAmA 78, 80, 82, 84, 89, 91, 93; WhoGrA 62; WhoWor 74; WorArt 1950; WorECar*

Steinberg, William
[Hans Wilhelm Steinberg]
American. Conductor
Director, Pittsburgh Symphony, 1952-76; Boston Symphony, 1968-72.
b. Aug 1, 1899 in Cologne, Germany
d. May 16, 1978 in New York, New York
Source: *Baker 78, 84, 92; BiDAmM; BioIn 4, 5, 6, 7, 8, 10, 11, 12; BlueB 76; BriBkM 80; CelR; CmOp; CurBio 40, 58, 78N; FacFETw; IntWW 74, 75, 76, 77, 78; IntWWM 77; LinLib S; MetOEnc; MusSN; NatCAB 60; NewAmDM; NewEOp 71; NewGrDA 86; NewGrDM 80; PenDiMP; WhAm 7; Who 74; WhoAm 74, 76, 78; WhoE 74, 75, 77; WhoWor 74*

Steinberger, Jack
American. Physicist
Shared Nobel Prize in physics, 1988, for codiscovering subatomic particles called neutrinos, with two other Americans.
b. May 25, 1921 in Bad Kissinger, Germany
Source: *AmMWSc 76P, 79, 82, 86, 89, 92, 95; CamDcSc; IntWW 74, 75, 76, 77, 78, 79, 80, 81, 82, 83, 89, 91, 93; LarDcSc; LegTOT; NobelP 91; NotTwCS; Who 90, 92, 94; WhoAm 74, 76, 78, 88, 90, 92, 94, 95; WhoNob 90, 95; WhoScEn 94, 96; WhoWor 78, 91, 93, 95, 96, 97; WorAlBi*

Steinbrenner, George Michael, III
American. Baseball Executive
Shipbuilding executive; controversial principal owner of NY Yankees, 1973-90; ordered by commissioner to give up managing partnership of Yankees for alleged association with gamblers.
b. Jul 4, 1930 in Rocky River, Ohio
Source: *BioIn 10, 11, 12, 16; BioNews 74; BusPN; CurBio 79; Dun&B 90; NewYTBE 73; St&PR 87, 91; WhoAm 76, 78, 80, 82, 84, 86, 88, 90, 92, 94, 95, 96, 97; WhoE 79, 81, 83, 85, 86, 89, 91, 93, 95, 97; WhoFI 74, 75; WhoSSW 86, 88*

Steinem, Gloria
American. Feminist, Journalist
Well-known activist for women's rights; co-founded *Ms.* mag., 1971; founded groups Coalition of Labor Union Women, Women USA; inducted into Nationa l Women's Hall of Fame, 1993.
b. Mar 25, 1934 in Toledo, Ohio
Source: *AmAu&B; AmDec 1970; AmSocL; AmWomWr SUP; BenetAL 91; BioIn 7, 8, 9, 10, 11, 12, 13, 16, 18; BioNews 74; BkPepl; BlmGWL; CelR 90; ConAu 28NR, 51NR, 53; ConHero 1; ConLC 63; ContDcW 89; CurBio 72, 88; DcTwCCu 1; EncAB-H 1996; EncTwCJ; EncWB; EncWHA; FacFETw; FemiCLE; FemiWr; ForWC 70; GoodHs; GrLiveH; HanAmWH; IntAu&W 89, 91, 93; IntDcWB; IntWW 89, 91, 93; InWom SUP; LegTOT; LiJour; MajTwCW; News 96; OxCAmL 95; OxCWoWr 95; PolPar; PolProf NF; RadHan; RComAH; WhoAm 76, 78, 80, 82, 84, 86, 88, 90, 92, 94, 95, 96, 97; WhoAmW 74, 75, 77, 79, 81, 83, 85, 87, 89, 91, 93, 95, 97; WomFir; WorAl; WorAlBi*

Steiner, Max
Austrian. Composer, Conductor
Wrote music for *Gone With the Wind,* 1939; Oscar-winning scores for *The Informer,* 1935; *Now, Voyager,* 1942.
b. May 10, 1888 in Vienna, Austria
d. Dec 28, 1971 in Hollywood, California
Source: *ASCAP 66, 80; Baker 78, 84; BioIn 1, 6, 9, 10; CmMov; CmpEPM; ConAmC 76, 82; CurBio 43, 72, 72N; DcFM; FacFETw; FilmEn; FilmgC; GangFlm; HalFC 80, 84, 88; IntDcF 1-4, 2-4; ItaFilm; LegTOT; NewAmDM; NewGrDA 86; NewGrDM 80; NotNAT B; OxCFilm; OxCPMus; PopAmC; WhAm 5; WhoHrs 80; WorAl; WorAlBi; WorEFlm*

Steiner, Rudolf
Austrian. Philosopher
Studied spirituality as independent of senses—''anthroposophy;'' founded Anthroposophical Society, 1912.
b. Feb 27, 1861 in Kraljevic, Austria
d. Mar 30, 1925 in Durnach, Switzerland

Source: *BiDAmCu; BioIn 2, 4, 5, 9, 10, 11, 12, 13, 14, 15, 17, 21; ConAu 107; EncO&P 1, 2, 3; EncPaPR 91; LngCTC; LuthC 75; MacEA; MakMC; NewAgE 90; OxCGer 76, 86; RAdv 14; RelLAm 91; ThTwC 87; TwCLC 13*

Steinitz, Wilhelm
German. Chess Player
Editor of *International Chess Magazine,* 1885-1891; won first official world championship, 1866.
b. May 17, 1836 in Prague, Bohemia
d. Aug 12, 1900 in New York, New York
Source: *BioIn 14, 15, 17, 18; GolEC; NewCol 75; OxCChes 84*

Steinman, David Barnard
American. Engineer, Designer
Known for designing world's great bridges, including George Washington Bridge, NY, 1938; Mackinac Bridge, MI, 1957.
b. Jun 11, 1886 in New York, New York
d. Aug 22, 1960 in New York, New York
Source: *AmAu&B; BioIn 2, 4, 5, 8, 20; DcAmB S6; InSci; McGMS 80; WebAB 74, 79; WhAm 4; WhE&EA; WhNAA*

Steinmetz, Charles Proteus
American. Engineer
His more than 100 inventions turned electricity into useful household tool.
b. Apr 9, 1865 in Breslau, Prussia
d. Oct 26, 1923 in Schenectady, New York
Source: *AmBi; AmDec 1900; AsBiEn; BioIn 2, 3, 4, 5, 6, 7, 8, 9, 11, 13, 18, 20, 21; DcAmAu; DcAmB; DcNAA; DcScB; EncAB-H 1974, 1996; GayN; InSci; LarDcSc; LinLib S; McGEWB; MemAm; NatCAB 13, 23; OxCAmH; WebAB 74, 79; WhAm 1; WorAl; WorInv*

Steinway, Henry Engelhard
[Henry Engelhard Steinweg]
German. Manufacturer
Founded Steinway and Sons piano manufacturers in NY, 1853.
b. Feb 15, 1797 in Wolfshagen, Germany
d. Nov 30, 1896 in New York, New York
Source: *AmBi; ApCAB; BiDAmBL 83; BioIn 21; DcAmB; NatCAB 2; REn; WebAB 74; WhAm HS; WorAl*

Stella, Frank Philip
American. Artist
Leader of "Minimal Art" movement; paintings emphasize shape and color.
b. May 12, 1936 in Malden, Massachusetts
Source: *AmCulL; BioIn 12, 13; BriEAA; ConArt 83; CurBio 71, 88; DcCAA 71; EncAB-H 1974, 1996; IntWW 83; MakMC; McGEWB; OxCTwCA; WebAB 74, 79; WhoAm 86, 90, 92, 94, 95, 96; WhoAmA 84*

Stella, Joseph
American. Artist
Realist-turned-semiabstractionist painter: *Battle of Lights, Coney Island,* 1913; *Brooklyn Bridge,* 1919.
b. Jun 13, 1880 in Munra Lucano, Italy
d. Nov 5, 1946 in New York, New York
Source: *BioIn 1, 2, 4, 5, 6, 9, 11; ConArt 83; CurBio 46; DcAmB S4; DcCAA 71; McGDA; McGEWB; NatCAB 36; OxCTwCA; REnAL; WhAm 2; WhAmArt 85*

Stempel, Robert
American. Auto Executive
Succeeded Roger Smith as chm. of GM, 1990-92; first engineer in GM history to hold position.
b. 1933 in New Jersey
Source: *AmMWSc 92; BioIn 11, 13, 15, 16; Dun&B 90; IntWW 91; News 91, 91-3; St&PR 84; WhoAm 90; WhoFI 92; WhoMW 92; WhoWor 91*

Stemrick, Greg(ory Earl, Sr.)
American. Football Player
Defensive back, 1975-83, mostly with Houston; suspended by NFL for drug involvement, 1983.
b. Oct 25, 1951 in Cincinnati, Ohio
Source: *FootReg 85*

Stendhal
[Marie Henri Beyle]
French. Author, Critic
Wrote *The Red and the Black,* 1831; *The Charterhouse of Parma,* 1839.
b. Jan 23, 1783 in Grenoble, France
d. Mar 23, 1842 in Paris, France
Source: *AtlBL; Baker 78, 84, 92; Benet 87, 96; BiD&SB; BioIn 1, 2, 3, 4, 5, 6, 7, 8, 9, 10, 11, 12, 13, 14, 15, 19, 20, 21; CasWL; CelCen; CyWA 58; DcArts; DcBiA; DcBiPP; DcEuL; DcLB 119; DcPup; Dis&D; EuAu; EuWr 5; EvEuW; GrFLW; GuFrLit 1; LegTOT; LinLib L, S; MagSWL; McGEWB; NewC; NewCBEL; NewGrDM 80; NewGrDO; NinCLC 23; Novels; OxCEng 67, 95; OxCFr; OxDcOp; PenC EUR; PseudAu; RAdv 14, 13-2; RComWL; REn; RfGWoL 95; WhDW; WorLitC*

Stenerud, Jan
American. Football Player
Placekicker, 1967-85, mostly with Kansas City; set NFL record for most 100-pt. seasons in career, seven.
b. Nov 26, 1943 in Fetsund, Norway
Source: *BioIn 9, 10, 13, 14; FootReg 85, 86; NewYTBE 71; NewYTBS 83*

Stengel, Casey
[Charles Dillon Stengel]
"The Old Professor"
American. Baseball Player, Baseball Manager
Outfielder, 1912-25; managed for 25 yrs., including NY Yankees, 1949-60, where he won 10 pennants, seven World Series.
b. Jul 30, 1890 in Kansas City, Missouri
d. Sep 29, 1975 in Glendale, California
Source: *BiDAmSp BB; CurBio 49, 75; DcAmB S9; NewYTBS 74, 75; WebAB 74; WhAm 6; WhoAm 74; WhoE 74; WhoSpor; WhScrn 77, 83; WorAl; WorAlBi*

Stenmark, Ingemar
Swedish. Skier
World Cup Alpine champion, 1976-78; won gold medals in men's slalom, giant slalom, 1980 Olympics.
b. Mar 18, 1956 in Josesjo, Sweden
Source: *BioIn 11, 12, 13, 15; CurBio 82; FacFETw; NewYTBS 82, 88; WorAl; WorAlBi*

Stennis, John C(ornelius)
American. Politician
Dem. senator from MS, 1947-89.
b. Aug 3, 1901 in Kemper County, Mississippi
d. Apr 23, 1995 in Jackson, Mississippi
Source: *BiDrAC; BiDrUSC 89; BioIn 1, 3, 5, 6, 8, 9, 10, 11, 12; BlueB 76; CngDr 74, 77, 79, 81, 83, 85, 87; CurBio 53, 95N; IntWW 74, 75, 76, 77, 78, 79, 80, 82, 83, 89, 91, 93; IntYB 78, 79, 80, 81, 82; NewYTBS 85; PolProf E, J, K, NF, T; WhAm 11; WhoAm 74, 76, 78, 80, 82, 84, 86, 88, 90, 92, 94, 95; WhoAmL 79; WhoAmP 73, 75, 77, 79, 81, 83, 85, 87, 89, 91, 93; WhoGov 72, 75, 77; WhoSSW 73, 75, 76, 78, 80, 82, 86, 88; WhoWor 78, 80, 82, 84, 87, 89; WorAl; WorAlBi*

Stephanie, Princess
[Stephanie Marie Elisabeth Grimaldi]
Monacan. Princess
Daughter of Princess Grace, Prince Rainier; career attempts include swimsuit designer, model and singer.
b. Feb 1, 1965 in Monaco-Ville, Monaco
Source: *BioIn 7, 12, 13, 16; CurBio 86; EncCoWW; LegTOT*

Stephanopoulos, George (Robert)
American. Government Official
Senior advisor to pres. Bill Clinton, 1993-96.
b. Feb 10, 1961 in Fall River, Massachusetts
Source: *BioIn 13; CurBio 95; LegTOT; News 94, 94-3; NewYTBS 92, 93; WhoAm 95, 96, 97; WhoAmP 93, 95*

Stephen, Leslie, Sir
English. Author, Critic
First editor, *Dictionary of National Biography,* 1882-91; wrote biographies: *Thomas Hobbs,* 1904; father of Virginia Woolf.
b. Nov 28, 1832 in London, England
d. Feb 22, 1904 in London, England
Source: *Alli, SUP; AtlBL; BbD; Benet 87, 96; BiD&SB; BioIn 1, 2, 3, 4, 5, 6, 7, 8, 9, 10, 11, 12, 13, 14, 16, 21; BlmGEL; BritAu 19; BritWr 5; CamGEL; CamGLE; CasWL; CelCen; Chambr 3; ChhPo S1; ConAu 123; DcArts; DcEnA, A; DcEnL; DcEuL; DcLB 57, 144; DcLEL; DcNaB S2; EvLB; LinLib L, S; LngCEL; LngCTC;*

McGEWB; MouLC 4; NewC; NewCBEL; OxCEng 67, 85, 95; PenC ENG; REn; TwCLC 23; VicBrit; WebE&AL; WorAl; WorAlBi

Stephens, Alexander Hamilton
American. Politician
Elected vp of US Confederate States, 1862-65; imprisoned May-Oct 1865; served in US Congress following Civil War.
b. Feb 11, 1812 in Crawfordsville, Georgia
d. Mar 4, 1883 in Atlanta, Georgia
Source: *Alli, SUP; AmAu&B; AmBi; ApCAB; BbD; BenetAL 91; BiAUS; BiD&SB; BiDConf; BiDrAC; BiDrGov 1789; BiDrUSC 89; BiDSA; BioIn 1, 3, 4, 5, 6, 7, 9, 15, 16, 21; CivWDc; CyAG; DcAmAu; DcAmB; DcBiPP; DcNAA; Drake; EncAAH; EncAB-H 1974, 1996; EncSoH; HarEnUS; LinLib L, S; McGEWB; NatCAB 3; OxCAmH; REnAL; TwCBDA; WebAB 74, 79; WhAm HS; WhAmP; WhCiWar; WorAl*

Stephens, Alice Barber
American. Artist
Noted magazine, book illustrator, 1875-1904.
b. Jul 1, 1858 in Salem, New Jersey
d. Jul 13, 1932 in Rose Valley, Pennsylvania
Source: *BioIn 15, 17; ChhPo; ConICB; DcAmB; IlrAm 1880, A; InWom, SUP; LibW; NatCAB 13, 23; NorAmWA; NotAW; SmATA 66; TwCBDA; WhAm 1; WhAmArt 85; WomArt; WomWWA 14*

Stephens, Ann Sophia
American. Author, Editor
Wrote first dime novel *Malaeska; or the Indian Wife of the White Hunter,* 1860.
b. May 30, 1810 in Seymour, Connecticut
d. Aug 20, 1886 in Newport, Rhode Island
Source: *BlmGWL; DcLB 73; FemiCLE; LibW; NotAW; OxCAmL 83, 95*

Stephens, Helen
American. Track Athlete
Sprinter; won two gold medals, 1936 Olympics.
b. Feb 3, 1918 in Fulton, Missouri
d. Jan 17, 1994 in Saint Louis, Missouri
Source: *BiDAmSp OS; BioIn 3, 17, 19; WhoSpor; WhoTr&F 73*

Stephens, James
English. Author, Poet
Noted for prose fantasy *Crock of Gold,* 1912.
b. 1882 in Dublin, Ireland
d. Dec 26, 1950 in London, England
Source: *AnCL; AuBYP 2S, 3; Benet 87, 96; BiDIrW; BioIn 1, 2, 3, 4, 5, 6, 7, 10, 11, 12, 13, 14, 21; CamGEL; CamGLE; CarSB; CasWL; Chambr 3; ChhPo, S1, S2, S3; CnE&AP; ConAu 104; CyWA 58; DcIrW 1; DcLB 19, 162; DcLEL; EncWL; EvLB; FacFETw; GrWrEL P; LinLib L; LngCTC; McGEWB; ModBrL, S1; NewC; NewCBEL; OxCEng 67, 85, 95; PenC ENG; PoIre; RAdv 1; REn; ScF&FL 1, 92; Str&VC; SupFW; TwCA, SUP; TwCLC 4; TwCWr; WhAm 3; WhDW*

Stephens, John Lloyd
American. Traveler, Author, Diplomat
Supervised construction of railway across Isthmus of Panama; wrote of travels: *Incidents of Travel in Yucatan,* 1843.
b. Nov 28, 1805 in Shrewsbury, New Jersey
d. Oct 12, 1852 in New York, New York
Source: *Alli; AmAu&B; AmBi; ApCAB; BbD; BenetAL 91; BiAUS; BiD&SB; BioIn 1, 3, 6, 7, 8, 10; CyAL 2; DcAmAu; DcAmB; DcAmDH 80, 89; DcNAA; Drake; EncLatA; HarEnUS; InSci; IntDcAn; NatCAB 5; OxCAmH; OxCAmL 65, 83, 95; REn; REnAL; TwCBDA; WhAm HS; WhDW*

Stephens, Robert, Sir
English. Actor
Films include *Cleopatra,* 1963; *The Shout,* 1978.
b. Jul 14, 1931 in Bristol, England
d. Nov 12, 1995 in London, England
Source: *BioIn 9, 21; BlueB 76; CamGWoT; CnThe; ConTFT 6, 13, 15; FilmAG WE; FilmEn; FilmgC; HalFC 80, 84, 88; IlWWBF; IntMPA 92, 94, 96; IntWW 74, 75, 76, 77, 78, 79, 80, 81, 82, 83, 89, 91, 93; ItaFilm; NewYTBS 95; VarWW 85; WhAm 11; Who 74, 82, 83, 85, 88, 90, 92, 94; WhoHol 92, A; WhoThe 72, 77, 81; WhoWor 74, 84, 87, 91, 93, 95, 96*

Stephenson, George
English. Engineer, Inventor
Patented steam blast locomotive; developed railway system.
b. Jun 9, 1781 in Wylam, England
d. Aug 12, 1848 in Chesterfield, England
Source: *AsBiEn; BiESc; BioIn 1, 2, 3, 4, 5, 6, 7, 8, 9, 10, 11, 12, 13, 14, 16, 17, 20; CelCen; DcBiPP; DcInv; DcNaB; InSci; LinLib S; MacEA; McGDA; McGEWB; NewCol 75; WebBD 83; WhDW; WorAl; WorAlBi; WorInv*

Stephenson, Henry
British. Actor
Character actor in over 100 films, 1917-49.
b. Apr 16, 1871, West Indies
d. Apr 24, 1956 in San Francisco, California
Source: *CmMov; EncAFC; Film 1, 2; FilmEn; FilmgC; HalFC 80, 84, 88; HolCA; MotPP; MovMk; NotNAT B; Vers A; WhoHol B; WhScrn 74, 77, 83*

Stephenson, Jan Lynn
American. Golfer
Turned pro, 1974; won US Women's Open, 1983; rookie of the year, 1974.
b. Dec 22, 1951 in Sydney, Australia
Source: *NewYTBS 76, 81, 82, 83; WhoAm 78, 84, 86, 88, 90, 92, 94, 95, 96, 97; WhoAmW 79, 89, 91, 93; WhoGolf; WhoIntG*

Stephenson, Skip
[Charles Frederick Stephenson]
American. TV Personality, Comedian
Co-host of TV series "Real People."
b. Apr 18, 1948? in Omaha, Nebraska
Source: *BioIn 12*

Stephenson, William
Spy
WW II spymaster; launched Anglo-American espionage program that helped defeat Nazis; subject of bestseller *A Man Called Intrepid.*
b. Jan 11, 1896 in Winnipeg, Manitoba, Canada
d. Jan 31, 1989 in Hamilton, Bermuda
Source: *AnObit 1989; BioIn 16; FacFETw; NewYTBS 89; Who 85, 88, 90N*

Stepinac, Alojzije
Yugoslav. Religious Leader
Roman Catholic archbishop of Zagreb, 1937-53; cardinal, 1953-60; imprisoned by Communists, 1946-51.
b. May 8, 1898 in Krasic, Croatia
d. Feb 10, 1960 in Krasic, Yugoslavia
Source: *BioIn 1, 2, 3, 5, 6, 12, 15; CurBio 53, 60; DcCathB; EncWB; LuthC 75*

Steppenwolf
[George Biondo; Robert Cochran; Wayne Cook; Jerry Edmonton; John Kay]
American. Music Group
Songs include "Born to Be Wild," 1968.
Source: *Alli; BiDAmM; ConMuA 80A; DcEnL; DcNaB; DrAPF 80, 83, 85, 87, 89, 91, 93, 97; EncPR&S 74, 89; EncRk 88; EncRkSt; FolkA 87; HarEnR 86; IlEncRk; InSci; MedHR; NewAmDM; NewGrDA 86; PenEncP; PoLE; RkOn 78; RolSEnR 83; WhDW; WhoRock 81; WhoRocM 82; WorInv*

Steptoe, Patrick Christopher
English. Physician
Gynecologist; with Robert Edwards, pioneered in vitro fertilization; responsible for first test-tube baby, Louise Brown, born, 1978.
b. Jun 9, 1913 in Oxford, England
d. Mar 21, 1988 in Canterbury, England
Source: *BioIn 11, 12; CurBio 79, 88; DcNaB 1986; FacFETw; LarDcSc; NewYTBS 78, 88; Who 82, 83, 85, 88; WhoWor 82, 84*

Sterban, Richard
[The Oak Ridge Boys]
American. Singer
Bass vocalist with country-pop group.
b. Apr 24, 1943 in Camden, New Jersey
Source: *WhoAm 90*

Sterling, Bruce
American. Author
One of the founders of the cyberpunk movement; author of *The Hacker Countdown: Law and Disorder on the Electronic Frontier,* 1992.
b. Apr 14, 1954 in Brownsville, Texas
Source: *ConAu 44NR, 119; ConLC 72; EncSF 93; IntAu&W 89, 91, 93; NewEScF; News 95; ScF&FL 92; TwCSFW 86, 91; WrDr 88, 90, 92, 94, 96*

Sterling, Claire
Author
Author of *Time of the Assassins* and *The Terror Network.*
d. Jun 17, 1995 in Arezzo, Italy
Source: *BioIn 14, 21; InWom SUP; NewYTBS 81, 95*

Sterling, Ford
[George Ford Stitch]
American. Actor
With Max Sennett's Keystone serials, 1912-21.
b. Nov 3, 1880 in La Crosse, Wisconsin
d. Oct 13, 1939 in Los Angeles, California
Source: *Film 1; FilmEn; FilmgC; MovMk; QDrFCA 92; SilFlmP; TwYS; WhoHol B; WhScrn 74, 77, 83*

Sterling, George
American. Poet
Leader of bohemian art colony, Carmel, CA, 1908-15.
b. Dec 1, 1869 in Sag Harbor, New York
d. Nov 18, 1926 in San Francisco, California
Source: *AmAu&B; AnMV 1926; BenetAL 91; BibAL; BioIn 1, 2, 8, 12, 13, 15, 16; CasWL; ChhPo, S1, S2, S3; CmCal; ConAmL; ConAu 117; DcAmB; DcLB 54; DcLEL; DcNAA; OxCAmL 65, 83, 95; PenEncH; REn; REnAL; TwCA, SUP; TwCLC 20; WhAm 1; WhLit*

Sterling, Jan
[Jan Sterling Andriance; Mrs. Paul Douglas]
American. Actor
Made Broadway debut, 1938; nominated for Oscar for *The High and the Mighty,* 1954.
b. Apr 3, 1923 in New York, New York
Source: *BiE&WWA; BioIn 2; ConTFT 7; FilmEn; FilmgC; GangFlm; HalFC 80, 84, 88; IntMPA 75, 76, 77, 78, 79, 80, 81, 82, 84, 86, 88, 92, 94, 96; InWom, SUP; LegTOT; MotPP; MovMk; NotNAT; WhoHol A; WhoThe 77, 81; WorAl; WorAlBi*

Sterling, John Ewart Wallace
American. University Administrator
Pres., Stanford U, for two decades; received honorary knighthood from Elizabeth II, 1976.
b. Aug 6, 1906 in Linwood, Ontario, Canada
d. Jul 1, 1985 in Woodside, California
Source: *BiDAmEd; BioIn 1, 2, 3, 14; CanWW 70, 79, 80, 81, 83; DrAS 74H, 78H, 82H; LEduc 74; WhAm 8, 11; WhoAm 74, 76, 78, 80, 82, 84; WhoWest 84*

Sterling, Robert
[William Sterling Hart]
American. Actor
Played George Kerby in TV's "Topper," 1953-56; appeared in some films.
b. Nov 13, 1917 in New Castle, Pennsylvania
Source: *BiE&WWA; BioIn 3; FilmEn; FilmgC; ForYSC; HalFC 80, 84, 88; IntMPA 75, 76, 77, 78, 79, 80, 81, 82, 84, 86, 88, 92, 94, 96; LegTOT; MGM; MotPP; VarWW 85; WhoHol 92, A*

Stern, Arthur Cecil
American. Environmentalist
Pioneering expert in field of air pollution; co-author, *Fundamentals of Air Pollution,* 1984.
b. Mar 14, 1909 in Petersburg, Virginia
d. Apr 17, 1992 in Chapel Hill, North Carolina
Source: *BioIn 4, 8, 17, 18; InSci; WhAm 10; WhoAm 74, 76, 78, 80, 86, 88, 90; WhoCon 73; WhoEng 88; WhoTech 89*

Stern, Bert
American. Photographer
Commercial photographer who ascribed to motto "less is more;" known for Smirnoff ads of martini glass in front of pyramids, 1955, portfolio of Marilyn Monroe silkscreen prints, 1967.
b. Oct 3, 1929 in New York, New York
Source: *ConPhot 82, 88, 95; ICPEnP A; WhoAdv 90; WhoAm 74, 76*

Stern, Bill
[William Stern]
American. Sportscaster
Sports announcer with NBC radio, TV, 1930s-50s; known for flamboyant anecdotes.
b. Jul 1, 1907 in Rochester, New York
d. Nov 19, 1971 in Rye, New York
Source: *BiDAmSp OS; BioIn 1, 5, 9; ConAu 89; CurBio 41, 72, 72N; DcAmB S9; EncAJ; IntMPA 75, 76, 77, 78, 79; NewYTBE 71; RadStar; SaTiSS; WhAm 5; WhoHol B; WhScrn 74, 77, 83*

Stern, Carl Leonard
American. Broadcast Journalist
NBC News legal affairs correspondent, 1967-93; director Office of Public Affairs, justice dept., 1993—.
b. Aug 7, 1937 in New York, New York
Source: *ConAu 97; EncTwCJ; WhoAm 80, 82, 84, 86, 88, 90, 92, 94, 95, 96, 97; WhoAmL 79, 83, 85, 94, 96; WhoE 95*

Stern, David Joel
American. Basketball Executive
Succeeded Larry O'Brien as commissioner of NBA, 1984—.
b. Sep 22, 1942 in New York, New York
Source: *BiDAmSp BK; WhoAm 86, 88, 90, 92, 94, 95, 96, 97; WhoE 86, 89, 91*

Stern, Howard (Allan)
American. Radio Performer
Nationally syndicated, New York based radio host known for obnoxious behavior; movie *Private Parts,* 1997.
b. Jan 12, 1954 in New York, New York
Source: *BioIn 16; ConAu 146; ConTFT 12; CurBio 96; LegTOT; News 88-2, 93-3; WhoAm 94, 95, 96, 97; WhoE 95*

Stern, Isaac
American. Violinist
Made debut age 11; int'l concertist; made soundtrack for *Fiddler on the Roof,* 1971; French Legion of Honor, 1979.
b. Jul 21, 1920 in Kreminiecz, Union of Soviet Socialist Republics
Source: *AmMWSc 92; Baker 78, 84, 92; BiDAmM; BioIn 1, 2, 3, 4, 5, 7, 8, 9, 11, 12, 16; BlueB 76; BriBkM 80; CelR, 90; CmCal; ConMus 7; ConTFT 15; CurBio 49, 89; DcTwCCu 1; FacFETw; IntWW 74, 75, 76, 77, 78, 79, 80, 81, 82, 83, 89, 91, 93; IntWWM 77, 80, 90; LegTOT; MusMk; MusSN; NewAmDM; NewGrDA 86; NewGrDM 80; NewYTBE 70; PenDiMP; WebAB 74, 79; Who 74, 82, 83, 85, 88, 90, 92, 94; WhoAm 74, 76, 78, 80, 82, 84, 86, 88, 90, 92, 94, 95, 96, 97; WhoAmJ 80; WhoAmM 83; WhoE 74, 97; WhoEnt 92; WhoGov 72, 75, 77; WhoHol 92, A; WhoMus 72; WhoWor 74, 76, 78, 80, 82, 84, 87, 89, 91, 93, 95, 96, 97; WhoWorJ 72, 78; WorAl; WorAlBi*

Stern, James
Irish. Author
Short story writer usually set in Ireland or Africa: *Something Wrong,* 1938.
b. Dec 26, 1904 in County Meath, Ireland
d. Nov 22, 1993 in Tisbury, England
Source: *BioIn 10, 19; ConAu 21R; ConNov 72, 76, 82, 86; IntAu&W 76, 77, 82, 86; WhoWor 76; WorAu 1950; WrDr 76, 80, 82, 84, 86, 88, 90, 92*

Stern, Leonard B
Writer, Producer
Won Emmys for scripts of "The Bilko Show," 1956; "Get Smart," 1967.
b. Dec 23, 1923 in New York, New York
Source: *BioIn 15, 16; ConAmBL; CurBio 91; LesBEnT 92; NewYTET; VarWW 85; WhoAm 88*

Stern, Leonard Norman
American. Business Executive
CEO, Hartz Group, Inc. (pet supplies), 1959—; owner of *The Village Voice.*

b. Mar 28, 1938 in New York, New York
Source: *BioIn 10, 11, 12; BusPN; Dun&B 90; WhoAm 74, 76, 78, 80, 82, 84, 86, 88, 90, 92, 95, 96, 97; WhoFI 92*

Stern, Max
American. Business Executive
Founded, Hartz Mountain Corp., 1932.
b. 1898 in Fulda, Germany
d. May 20, 1982 in New York, New York
Source: *BioIn 5, 10, 11, 12, 13, 15; NewYTBS 82; WhAm 8*

Stern, Otto
American. Physicist, Educator
Won Nobel Prize in physics, 1943, for development of molecular beams, discovery of magnetic moment of the proton.
b. Feb 17, 1888 in Soran, Germany
d. Aug 17, 1969 in Berkeley, California
Source: *AsBiEn; BiESc; BioIn 3, 5, 8, 9, 10, 13, 14, 15, 20; CamDcSc; DcAmB S8; DcScB; InSci; LarDcSc; LegTOT; LinLib S; McGEWB; McGMS 80; NobelP; NotTwCS; ObitOF 79; WebAB 74, 79; WebBD 83; WhAm 9; WhoNob, 90, 95; WorAl; WorAlBi*

Stern, Philip Van Doren
American. Author
Novelist, historian, widely acclaimed for Civil War era books.
b. Sep 10, 1900 in Wyalusing, Pennsylvania
d. Jul 31, 1984 in Sarasota, Florida
Source: *AmAu&B; AmNov; BenetAL 91; ConAu 5R, 6NR; NewYTBS 84; REnAL; ScF&FL 92; SmATA 13; WhE&EA; WhNAA; WhoAm 82, 84*

Stern, Richard Gustave
American. Author
Relatively obscure novelist since 1960; admired by other writers: *Packages,* 1980.
b. Feb 25, 1928 in New York, New York
Source: *AmAu&B; Au&Wr 71; BenetAL 91; BioIn 16; ConAu 1NR, 1R, 52NR; ConLC 4; ConNov 72, 76, 86, 91; CurBio 94; CyWA 89; DrAF 76; DrAPF 80; IntAu&W 91; PenC AM; WhoAdv 90; WhoAm 74, 76, 78, 80, 82, 84, 86, 88, 90, 92, 94, 95, 96, 97; WhoUSWr 88; WhoWrEP 89, 92, 95; WorAu 1950; WrDr 76, 86, 92*

Stern, Sandor
Canadian. Writer, Director
Wrote screenplays *Fast Break; The Amityville Horror.*
b. Jul 13, 1936 in Timmins, Ontario, Canada
Source: *ConTFT 15; MiSFD 9; VarWW 85; WhoEnt 92*

Stern, Stewart
American. Screenwriter
Films include *Rebel Without a Cause,* 1955; Oscar-winning *Rachel, Rachel,* 1966.
b. Mar 22, 1922 in New York, New York
Source: *BioIn 10, 14, 17; ConAu 113; ConDr 77, 77A; DcLB 26; FilmEn; IntMPA 75, 76, 77, 78, 79, 80, 81, 82, 84, 86, 88, 92, 94, 96; WorEFlm*

Sterne, Laurence
[Mister Yorick]
English. Author, Theologian
Wrote *Tristram Shandy,* 1760-67; *Sentimental Journey,* 1768.
b. Nov 24, 1713 in Clonmel, Ireland
d. Mar 18, 1768 in London, England
Source: *Alli; AtlBL; BbD; Benet 87, 96; BiD&SB; BiDIrW; BioIn 1, 2, 3, 4, 5, 6, 7, 8, 9, 10, 12, 13, 14, 15, 18, 20; BlkwCE; BlmGEL; BritAu; BritWr 3; CamGEL; CamGLE; CasWL; Chambr 2; ChhPo S3; CnDBLB 2; CrtT 2, 4; CyWA 58; DcArts; DcBiA; DcBiPP; DcEnA; DcEnL; DcEuL; DcIrB 78, 88; DcIrL 96; DcIrW 1; DcLB 39; DcLEL; DcNaB; Dis&D; EncEnl; EvLB; GrWrEL N; LegTOT; LinLib L, S; LitC 2; LngCEL; MagSWL; McGEWB; MouLC 2; NewC; NewCBEL; Novels; OxCEng 67, 85, 95; OxCGer 76, 86; OxCIri; PenC ENG; PoIre; RAdv 1, 14, 13-1; RComWL; REn; RfGEnL 91; WebE&AL; WhDW; WorAl; WorAlBi; WorLitC*

Sterne, Maurice
American. Artist
Modern classicist, painted 20 murals for Dept. of Justice Bldg; works done on Bali made island famous.
b. Jul 13, 1878 in Libau, Russia
d. Jul 23, 1957 in New York, New York
Source: *BioIn 1, 2, 4, 5, 7, 10; BriEAA; CurBio 43, 57; DcAmArt; DcAmB S6; DcCAA 71, 77, 88; IlBEAAW; McGDA; PhDcTCA 77; WhAm 3; WhAmArt 85; WhoAmA 80N, 82N, 84N, 86N, 89N, 91N, 93N*

Sterrett, Cliff
American. Cartoonist
Creator of "Polly and her Pals" comic strip, 1912-58.
b. Dec 12, 1883 in Fergus Falls, Minnesota
d. Dec 28, 1964 in Ogunquit, Maine
Source: *BioIn 7; WhAm 7; WhAmArt 85; WhoAmA 89N, 91N, 93N; WorECom*

Stetson, John Batterson
American. Manufacturer
Formed John B Stetson Co., 1885; made wide-brimmed, high-crowned cowboy hats.
b. May 5, 1830 in Orange, New Jersey
d. Feb 18, 1906 in De Land, Florida
Source: *AmBi; BioIn 2, 6, 13, 18; DcAmB; Entr; NatCAB 11; NewCol 75; TwCBDA; WebAB 74, 79; WhAm 1; WhFla*

Stettinius, Edward R, Jr.
American. Government Official
Lend-lease administrator, 1941-43; secretary of State, 1944-45; first US delegate to UN, 1945.
b. Oct 22, 1900 in Chicago, Illinois
d. Oct 31, 1949 in Greenwich, Connecticut
Source: *CurBio 40, 49; DcAmB S4; EncAB-H 1974; McGEWB; NatCAB 38; PolProf T; WhAm 1, 2*

Steuben, Friedrich Wilhelm Ludolf Gerhard Augustin, Baron
American. Soldier
American Revolutionary War general; trained Continental Army; Washington's advisor.
b. Sep 17, 1730 in Magdeburg, Prussia
d. Nov 28, 1794 in Remsen, New York
Source: *DcNAA; McGEWB; NewCol 75; OxCAmH; REnAL; WebAMB*

Stevens, Albert William
American. Soldier, Balloonist
First photographer to capture Earth's curving shape on camera in 1930; took first photos of Earth during a solar eclipse.
b. Mar 13, 1886 in Belfast, Maryland
d. Mar 26, 1949 in Redwood City, California
Source: *BioIn 1, 2, 3; DcVicP 2; InSci; NatCAB 37; ObitOF 79; WhAm 7*

Stevens, Andrew
American. Actor
Films include *The Fury,* 1978; played Casey Denault on TV series "Dallas," 1987-88; son of Stella.
b. Jun 10, 1955? in Memphis, Tennessee
Source: *BioIn 11; ConTFT 3; HalFC 80, 84, 88; IntMPA 82, 92, 94, 96; LegTOT; MiSFD 9; VarWW 85; WhoAm 80, 82, 84, 86, 88, 90, 92, 94, 95, 96; WhoEnt 92; WhoHol 92; WhoWor 80, 82*

Stevens, Cat
[Stephen Demetri Georgiou; Yosef Islam]
English. Singer, Songwriter
Rock-folk singer; had hits "Moon Shadow," 1971, "Morning Has Broken," 1972; quit music business, became Muslim, 1981.
b. Jul 21, 1948 in London, England
Source: *BiDAmM; BioIn 10, 12, 16; BioNews 74; ConMuA 80A; ConMus 3; EncPR&S 89; EncRk 88; HarEnR 86; IlEncRk; NewAmDM; NewYTBE 71; PenEncP; RkOn 78, 84; WhoAm 80, 82; WhoRock 81; WhoRocM 82; WorAl; WorAlBi*

Stevens, Connie
[Concetta Ingolia]
American. Actor, Singer
Starred in TV series "Hawaiian Eye," 1959-63; "Wendy and Me," 1964-65, with George Burns.
b. Aug 8, 1938 in New York, New York

Source: *BiDAmM; BioIn 6, 13, 16, 18; ConTFT 3; EncAFC; FilmEn; FilmgC; ForYSC; HalFC 80, 84, 88; IntMPA 75, 76, 77, 78, 79, 80, 81, 82, 84, 86, 88, 92, 94, 96; InWom, SUP; LegTOT; MotPP; RkOn 74; WhoAm 86, 88, 90, 92, 94, 97; WhoEnt 92; WhoHol 92, A; WhoRock 81; WorAl; WorAlBi*

Stevens, Edmund William
American. Journalist
Pulitzer Prize for distinguished reporting on international affairs; "This Is Russia—Uncensored," 1950.
b. Jul 22, 1910 in Denver, Colorado
d. May 24, 1992 in Peredelkino, Russia
Source: *AmAu&B; BioIn 2; ConAu 109, 137; CurBio 92N; EncTwCJ; WhAm 10; WhoAm 74, 76, 78, 80, 82, 84, 86, 88, 90; WhoWor 82, 91*

Stevens, Emily A
American. Actor
Known for alluring woman roles: *The Unchastened Woman,* 1915; died of drug overdose; cousin of Minnie Fiske.
b. Feb 27, 1882 in New York, New York
d. Jan 2, 1928 in New York, New York
Source: *DcAmB; Film 1; WhoHol B; WhScrn 74, 77, 83*

Stevens, George, Jr.
American. Producer
Won Emmys for "Salute to James Cagney," 1975; "The Kennedy Center Honors: A Celebration of the Performing Arts," 1984.
b. Apr 3, 1932 in Los Angeles, California
Source: *BioIn 7, 11; BlueB 76; CelR; ConAu 118, 125; ConTFT 4; CurBio 65; FilmEn; HalFC 84, 88; IntMPA 75, 76, 77, 78, 79, 80, 81, 82, 84, 86, 88, 92, 94, 96; LesBEnT 92; MiSFD 9; VarWW 85; WhoAm 74, 76, 78, 80, 82, 84, 86, 88, 90, 92, 94, 95, 96, 97; WhoAmP 93, 95; WhoEnt 92*

Stevens, George (Cooper)
American. Director
Won Oscars for *A Place in the Sun,* 1951; *Giant,* 1956.
b. Dec 18, 1904 in Oakland, California
d. Mar 8, 1975 in Lancaster, California
Source: *AmAu&B; BiDFilm, 81, 94; BioIn 10, 12, 14, 15, 19; CelR; CmMov; ConAu 116; CurBio 52, 75N; DcAmB S9; DcArts; DcFM; EncAFC; FacFETw; Film 1; FilmEn; FilmgC; HalFC 80, 84, 88; IlWWHD 1; IntDcF 1-2, 2-2; IntMPA 75; IntWW 74; LegTOT; MiSFD 9N; MovMk; NewYTBS 75; OxCFilm; WhAm 6; Who 74; WhoAm 74; WhoWor 74; WhScrn 77, 83; WorAl; WorAlBi; WorEFlm; WorFDir 1*

Stevens, Inger
[Inger Stensland]
American. Actor
Starred in "The Farmer's Daughter," 1963-66.
b. Oct 18, 1934 in Stockholm, Sweden
d. Apr 30, 1970 in Hollywood, California
Source: *BiE&WWA; BioIn 6, 8, 16, 17; FilmEn; FilmgC; ForYSC; InWom; LegTOT; MotPP; MovMk; NewYTBE 70; NotNAT B; WhAm 5; WhScrn 74, 77*

Stevens, Jeremy
Writer
Won Emmy for "The Electric Company," 1973; wrote for "What's Happening;" "Barbara Mandrell Show."
Source: *Alli; VarWW 85*

Stevens, John
American. Inventor, Shipbuilder
Built first oceangoing steamboat, 1808; first American steam locomotive, 1825; established first US patent laws, 1790.
b. 1749 in New York, New York
d. Mar 6, 1838 in Hoboken, New Jersey
Source: *AmBi; ApCAB X; BiDAmBL 83; BiInAmS; BioIn 1, 2, 3, 6, 9, 11, 14; BlkwEAR; DcAmB; Drake; HarEnUS; InSci; LinLib S; McGEWB; NatCAB 11; OxCAmH; REn; WebAB 74, 79; WhAm HS; WhAmRev; WhDW; WorInv*

Stevens, John Frank
American. Engineer
Civil engineer; aided in building of Great Northern Railway, 1890, Panama Canal, 1904-14.
b. Apr 25, 1853 in West Gardiner, Maine
d. Jun 2, 1943 in Southern Pines, North Carolina
Source: *BioIn 8, 9; DcAmB S3; NatCAB 32; WhAm 4*

Stevens, John Paul
American. Supreme Court Justice
Appointed 101st justice to Supreme Court, 1975—.
b. Apr 20, 1920 in Chicago, Illinois
Source: *AmBench 79; BiDFedJ A; BioIn 9, 10, 11, 12, 13; CelR 90; CngDr 77, 79, 81, 83, 85, 87, 89, 91, 93, 95; CurBio 76; DrAS 78P, 82P; EncWB; FacFETw; IntWW 76, 77, 78, 79, 80, 81, 82, 83, 89, 91, 93; LegTOT; LesBEnT; LinLib S; NatCAB 63N; NewYTBS 75; OxCSupC; PolProf NF; SupCtJu; WebAB 79; Who 82, 83, 85, 88, 90, 92, 94; WhoAm 74, 76, 78, 80, 82, 84, 86, 88, 90, 92, 94, 95, 96, 97; WhoAmL 78, 79, 83, 85, 87, 90, 92, 94, 96; WhoAmP 85, 87, 89, 91, 93, 95; WhoE 79, 81, 83, 85, 86, 89, 91, 93; WhoGov 75, 77; WhoMW 74; WhoWor 78, 80, 82, 84, 95, 96; WorAl; WorAlBi*

Stevens, K. T
[Gloria Wood]
American. Actor
Films include *Bob, Carol, Ted, and Alice,* 1969; daughter of Sam Wood.
b. Jul 20, 1919 in Hollywood, California
Source: *ConTFT 2; FilmgC; HalFC 84, 88; IntMPA 86, 92; WhoHol A; WhoThe 77A*

Stevens, Leslie
American. Screenwriter
Co-wrote science fiction film *Buck Rogers in the 25th Century,* 1979.
b. Feb 13, 1924 in Washington, District of Columbia
Source: *BiE&WWA; FilmEn; FilmgC; HalFC 80, 84, 88; IntMPA 75, 76, 77, 78, 79, 80, 81, 82, 84, 86, 88, 92, 94, 96; LesBEnT 92; MiSFD 9; NewYTET; NotNAT; VarWW 85; WorEFlm*

Stevens, Mark
American. Actor
Films include *Destination Tokyo,* 1944; *Gun Fever,* 1958.
b. Dec 13, 1922 in Cleveland, Ohio
Source: *BioIn 3; FilmEn; IntMPA 84, 86, 88, 92, 94, 96; MotPP; VarWW 85*

Stevens, Morton
American. Composer, Conductor
Won Emmys for themes to "You're Dead," 1970; "Hawaii 5-0," 1974.
b. Jan 30, 1929 in Newark, New Jersey
Source: *ASCAP 66, 80; BioIn 17; NewYTBS 91; VarWW 85*

Stevens, Nettie Maria
American. Biologist, Geneticist
Among the first to discover that chromosomes determine sex.
b. Jul 7, 1861 in Cavendish, Vermont
d. May 4, 1912 in Baltimore, Maryland
Source: *AmWomSc; BiInAmS; BioIn 11, 12, 15, 19, 20; CamDcSc; DcNAA; DcScB S2; IntDcWB; InWom SUP; LarDcSc; LibW; NotAW; NotTwCS; NotWoLS; WomFir; WomSc; WorScD*

Stevens, Onslow
[Onslow Ford Stevenson]
American. Actor
Appeared in films *This Side of Heaven,* 1934; *The Couch,* 1962.
b. Mar 29, 1906 in Los Angeles, California
d. Jan 5, 1977 in Van Nuys, California
Source: *BiE&WWA; BioIn 11; FilmgC; MovMk; NewYTBS 77; NotNAT; Vers A; WhoHol A; WhoThe 72; WhThe*

Stevens, Ray
[Harold Ray Ragsdale]
American. Musician, Singer
Pianist, country-western singer, 1970s.
b. Jan 24, 1939 in Clarksdale, Georgia
Source: *BgBkCoM; BioIn 14; ConMus 7; EncFCWM 83; EncPR&S 74; EncRk 88; HarEnCM 87; IlEncCM; IlEncRk; LegTOT; RkOn 82; WhoAm 76, 78, 80, 82; WhoRock 81*

Stevens, Rise
American. Opera Singer
Attractive mezzo-soprano; NY Met., 1938-61; films include *Going My Way,* 1944.
b. Jun 11, 1913 in New York, New York
Source: *Baker 78, 84, 92; BiDAmM; BioIn 1, 2, 3, 4, 5, 6, 7, 10, 11, 13, 15, 16, 18; BriBkM 80; CmOp; CmpEPM;*

CurBio 41; FacFETw; FilmgC; ForYSC; HalFC 80, 84, 88; IntDcOp; IntWWM 90; InWom, SUP; LinLib S; MetOEnc; MusSN; NewAmDM; NewEOp 71; NewGrDA 86; NewGrDM 80; NewGrDO; OxDcOp; PenDiMP; RadStar; What 4; WhoAm 82; WhoAmW 85; WhoHol 92, A; WorAl; WorAlBi

Stevens, Robert Livingston
American. Inventor, Shipbuilder
Built over 20 ferries, steamboats; invented inverted T-rail for railroads, 1830; son of John.
b. Oct 18, 1787 in Hoboken, New Jersey
d. Apr 20, 1856 in Hoboken, New Jersey
Source: *AmBi; ApCAB; BiDAmBL 83; BiInAmS; BioIn 11, 14; DcAmB; Drake; HarEnUS; InSci; NatCAB 11; OxCAmH; TwCBDA; WebAB 74, 79; WhAm HS; WorInv*

Stevens, Robert Ten Broeck
American. Business Executive, Government Official
Pres., JP Stevens, 1929-45; secretary of Army, 1953-55, during close of Korean War testified at Army-McCarthy hearings.
b. Jul 31, 1899 in Fanwood, New Jersey
d. Jan 30, 1983 in Edison, New Jersey
Source: *ConAmBL; CurBio 53, 83; EncMcCE; IntWW 80, 81; NewYTBS 83; PolProf E; WhoAm 78; WhoWor 74*

Stevens, Roger L(acey)
American. Producer
Won Tonys for Broadway productions of *A Man For All Seasons,* 1962; *Death of a Salesman,* 1984; chm. of board, Kennedy Center, Washington, DC, 1961-88.
b. Mar 12, 1910 in Detroit, Michigan
Source: *BioIn 3, 4, 5, 7, 11, 13; BlueB 76; CamGWoT; CurBio 55; NewYTBE 71; NotNAT; VarWW 85; WhoAm 86, 90, 92, 94, 95, 96, 97; WhoE 93; WhoEnt 92; WhoThe 81*

Stevens, S(tanley) S(mith)
American. Psychologist, Educator
Noted psychophysicist; founded Harvard's Psychoacoustic Laboratory, 1940s.
b. Nov 4, 1906 in Ogden, Utah
d. Jan 18, 1973 in Vail, Colorado
Source: *AmMWSc 73P; BioIn 1, 9, 10, 11, 14; ConAu 116; DcScB S2; GuPsyc; McGMS 80; ThTwC 87*

Stevens, Shadoe
American. TV Personality
Replaced Casey Kasem as host of "American Top 40."
Source: *BioIn 16; CelR 90*

Stevens, Shane
American. Author
Novels deal with life in Harlem: *Go Down Dead,* 1967.
b. Oct 8, 1941 in New York, New York
Source: *ConAu 21R, 43NR; DrAF 76; DrAPF 80, 87; IntAu&W 76*

Stevens, Siaka Probyn
Sierra Leonean. Political Leader
First president, prime minister, of Sierra Leone, 1971-85.
b. Aug 24, 1905 in Moyamba, Sierra Leone
d. May 29, 1988 in Freetown, Sierra Leone
Source: *AfSS 78, 79, 80, 81, 82; BioIn 8, 15, 16, 18, 21; DcAfHiB 86; IntWW 74, 75, 76, 77, 78, 79, 80, 81, 82, 83; IntYB 79, 80, 81, 82; Who 85; WhoGov 72; WhoWor 74, 76, 78, 80, 82, 84*

Stevens, Stella
[Estelle Egglestone]
American. Actor
Best known for role of Appassionata von Climax in film *Lil' Abner,* 1959.
b. Oct 1, 1938 in Hot Coffee, Mississippi
Source: *BiDFilm, 81; BioIn 16, 21; ConTFT 7; FilmgC; HalFC 84, 88; IntMPA 77, 78, 79, 80, 81, 82, 84, 86, 88, 92; InWom SUP; MiSFD 9; MotPP; NewYTBE 73; WhoAm 74; WhoHol A; WorAlBi*

Stevens, Ted
[Theodore Fulton Stevens]
American. Politician
Rep. senator from AK, 1968—.
b. Nov 18, 1923 in Indianapolis, Indiana
Source: *AlmAP 78; WhoWest 76, 78, 80, 82, 84, 87, 89, 92, 94, 96; WhoWor 80, 82, 84, 87, 89, 91; WorAl; WorAlBi*

Stevens, Thaddeus
American. Abolitionist, Politician
Organized Rep. party in VT; fathered the 14th admendment; active during Reconstruction period.
b. Apr 4, 1792 in Danville, Vermont
d. Aug 11, 1868 in Washington, District of Columbia
Source: *AmBi; AmPolLe; AmRef; ApCAB; BiAUS; BiDrAC; BiDrUSC 89; BioIn 1, 3, 4, 5, 7, 8, 9, 12, 13, 14, 15, 16, 20; CivWDc; CyAG; CyEd; DcAmB; DcAmSR; Drake; EncAACR; EncAAH; EncAB-H 1974, 1996; HarEnUS; HisWorL; LegTOT; LinLib S; McGEWB; NatCAB 4, 7; OxCAmH; PeoHis; PolPar; RComAH; REn; REnAL; TwCBDA; WebAB 74, 79; WhAm HS; WhAmP; WhCiWar*

Stevens, Wallace
American. Poet, Author
Won 1955 Pulitzer for *Collected Poems;* noted for verse theme: reality mixed with imagination.
b. Oct 2, 1879 in Reading, Pennsylvania
d. Aug 2, 1955 in Hartford, Connecticut
Source: *AgeMat; AmAu&B; AmCulL; AmWr; AtlBL; Benet 87, 96; BenetAL 91; BioIn 1, 2, 3, 4, 5, 6, 7, 8, 9, 10, 11, 12, 13, 14, 15, 16, 17, 19; CamGLE; CamHAL; CasWL; ChhPo S2; CnDAL; CnE&AP; CnMWL; ConAmA; ConAu 104, 124; CyWA 58; DcAmB S5; DcArts; DcLB 54; DcLEL; DcTwCCu 1; EncAB-H 1974, 1996; EncWL 2, 3; FacFETw; GrWrEL P; LegTOT; LinLib L, S; LngCTC; MagSAmL; MajTwCW; MakMC; McGEWB; ModAL, S1, S2; MorMA; NewGrDA 86; OxCAmL 65, 83, 95; OxCEng 95; OxCTwCP; PenC AM; PoeCrit 6; RAdv 1, 14, 13-1; RComAH; REn; REnAL; RfGAmL 87, 94; RGFAP; RGTwCWr; SixAP; TwCA, SUP; TwCLC 3, 12, 45; TwCWr; WebAB 74, 79; WebE&AL; WhAm 3; WhDW; WhoTwCL; WorAl; WorAlBi; WorLitC; WrPh*

Stevenson, Adlai Ewing
American. US Vice President
Served under Grover Cleveland, 1893-97.
b. Oct 23, 1835 in Christian County, Kentucky
d. Jun 14, 1914 in Chicago, Illinois
Source: *AmBi; AmPolLe; ApCAB SUP; BiDrAC; BiDrUSC 89; BiDrUSE 71, 89; BiDSA; BioIn 1, 4, 7, 8, 9, 10, 17; DcAmB; DcNAA; EncAAH; HarEnUS; NatCAB 2; TwCBDA; VicePre; WebAB 74, 79; WhAm 1; WhAmP; WorAl*

Stevenson, Adlai Ewing, II
American. Diplomat, Politician
UN ambassador, 1961-65; lost to Eisenhower in presidential races, 1952, 1956.
b. Feb 5, 1900 in Los Angeles, California
d. Jul 14, 1965 in London, England
Source: *AmAu&B; AmDec 1950; AmOrTwC; AmPolLe; BiDInt; BioIn 1, 2, 3, 4, 5, 6, 7, 8, 9, 10, 11, 12, 13; ColdWar 2; ConAu P-1; CurBio 49, 61, 65; DcAmB S7; DcAmDH 80, 89; DcPol; DcTwHis; EncAAH; EncAB-A 36; EncAB-H 1974, 1996; FacFETw; LinLib S; McGEWB; NatCAB 53; OxCAmH; OxCAmL 65; PresAR; REn; REnAL; WebAB 74, 79; WhAm 4; WhAmP; WhDW; WhScrn 77; WorAl*

Stevenson, Adlai Ewing, III
American. Politician, Lawyer
Dem. senator from IL, 1970-81.
b. Oct 10, 1930 in Chicago, Illinois
Source: *BiDrAC; BiDrUSC 89; BioIn 3, 7, 8, 9, 10, 11, 13; CurBio 74; IntWW 83, 91; LElec; WhoAm 74, 76, 78, 80, 82, 84, 86, 88, 90, 92, 94, 95, 96, 97; WhoAmL 85, 90, 92, 94, 96; WhoAmP 73, 75, 77, 79, 81, 83, 85, 87, 89, 91, 93, 95; WhoGov 72, 75, 77; WhoMW 74, 76, 78, 80, 82; WhoWor 80, 82, 84; WorAl; WorAlBi*

Stevenson, Bryan (Allen)
American. Lawyer
Founder and director, Equal Justice Initiative of Alabama, 1995—; works to fight inequities in the justice system.
b. Nov 14, 1959 in Milton, Delaware
Source: *BioIn 21; CurBio 96; WhoAm 96, 97; WhoAmL 92, 94*

Stevenson, Coke Robert
American. Politician
Prominent in TX politics, 1920s-40s; governor of TX, 1943-47.
b. Mar 20, 1888 in Mason County, Texas
d. Jun 28, 1975 in San Angelo, Texas
Source: *BioIn 1, 10, 11; WhAm 6*

Stevenson, Janet
American. Author
Many of her writings deal with women in unexpected roles: *Woman Aboard,* 1969.
b. Feb 4, 1913 in Chicago, Illinois
Source: *AuBYP 2S, 3; BioIn 11; ConAu 13R, 29NR; ForWC 70; SmATA 8; WhoAmW 61, 66, 68, 70*

Stevenson, McLean
American. Actor
Played Henry Blake on "M*A*S*H," 1972-75.
b. Nov 14, 1929 in Bloomington, Illinois
d. Feb 15, 1996 in Tarzana, California
Source: *BioIn 10, 12, 17, 21; BioNews 74; ConTFT 6; CurBio 80, 96N; LegTOT; News 96, 96-3; WhoAm 80; WhoCom; WhoHol 92, A; WhoTelC*

Stevenson, Parker
American. Actor
Starred in TV series "Hardy Boys Mysteries," 1978-79.
b. Jun 4, 1951? in Philadelphia, Pennsylvania
Source: *BioIn 12, 13; IntMPA 86, 92*

Stevenson, Robert
American. Director
Films include Disney classics *Mary Poppins,* 1964; *The Love Bug,* 1968.
b. Mar 31, 1905 in London, England
d. Apr 30, 1986 in Santa Barbara, California
Source: *AnObit 1986; BioIn 14, 15; ConAu 120; FilmEn; FilmgC; HalFC 80, 84, 88; IlWWBF; IlWWHD 1; IntAu&W 77; IntDcF 2-2; IntMPA 75, 76, 77, 78, 79, 80, 81, 82, 84, 86; MiSFD 9N; MovMk; NewYTBS 86; WhAm 9; Who 74, 82, 83, 85; WhoAm 78, 80, 82; WhoHrs 80; WhoWest 80; WorEFlm; WorFDir 1*

Stevenson, Robert Louis (Balfour)
Scottish. Author, Poet, Essayist
Wrote *Treasure Island; A Child's Garden of Verses; Dr. Jekyll and Mr. Hyde.*
b. Nov 13, 1850 in Edinburgh, Scotland
d. Dec 3, 1894 in Vailima, Samoa
Source: *Alli SUP; AnCL; ApCAB SUP; AtlBL; AuBYP 2, 3; BbD; Benet 87, 96; BenetAL 91; BiD&SB; BioIn 1, 2, 3, 4, 5, 6, 7, 8, 9, 10, 11, 12, 13, 14, 15, 16, 17, 18, 19, 20, 21; BlmGEL; BritAu 19; BritWr 5; CamGEL; CamGLE; CarSB; CasWL; CelCen; Chambr 3; ChhPo, S1, S2, S3; ChlBkCr; ChlLR 10, 11; ChrP; CmCal; CmScLit; CnDBLB 5; CrtSuMy; CrtT 3; CyWA 58; DcArts; DcBiA; DcBrBI; DcEnA, A; DcEuL; DcLB 18, 57, 141, 156, 174, DS13; DcLEL; DcNaB, C; DcPup; Dis&D; EncMys; EncPaPR 91; EncSF, 93; EvLB; FamAYP; FilmgC; GrWrEL N; HalFC 80, 84, 88; JBA 34; LegTOT; LinLib L, S; LngCEL; MagSWL; MajAI; McGEWB; MnBBF; MouLC 4; NewC; NewCBEL; NewEScF; NinCLC 5, 14; Novels; OxCAmL 65, 83, 95; OxCAusL; OxCChiL; OxCEng 67, 85, 95; OxCMus; PenC ENG; PenEncH; PeoHis; RAdv 1, 14, 13-1; REn; REnAL; RfGEnL 91; RfGShF; ScF&FL 1, 92; ScFSB; ShSCr 11; ShSWr; StaCVF; Str&VC; SupFW; TwCChW 78A, 83A, 89A, 95A; TwCYAW; VicBrit; WebE&AL; WhDW; WhoChL; WhoHr&F; WhoHrs 80; WorAl; WorAlBi; WorLitC; WrChl; YABC 2*

Stevenson, Teofilo
Cuban. Boxer
Amateur heavyweight boxer; second man to win three successive Olympic boxing gold medals, 1972-1980.
b. Mar 23, 1952 in Delicias, Cuba
Source: *BioIn 15; BlkOlyM; InB&W 80; NewYTBS 82*

Stevin, Simon
[Simon Stevinus]
Dutch. Mathematician, Engineer
Introduced decimal fractions into common use; developed hydrostatics; wrote *La Thiende,* 1585.
b. 1548 in Bruges, Belgium
d. 1620 in The Hague, Netherlands
Source: *AsBiEn; BiESc; BioIn 1, 8, 14, 15, 16; CamDcSc; CasWL; DcBiPP; DcCathB; DcInv; DcScB; InSci; LarDcSc; NewCol 75; WhDW; WorAl; WorAlBi; WorInv; WorScD*

Steward, Emanuel
American. Boxing Trainer
Trainer of Thomas Hearns, Milton McCrory.
b. Jul 7, 1944 in Bluefield, West Virginia
Source: *BioIn 12; BoxReg; WhoAfA 96; WhoBlA 85, 88, 90, 92, 94*

Steward, Julian Haynes
American. Anthropologist
Founded cultural ecology theory.
b. Jan 31, 1902 in Washington, District of Columbia
d. Feb 6, 1972 in Urbana, Illinois
Source: *BioIn 9, 10; ConAu 33R; FacFETw; IntEnSS 79; WhAm 5*

Stewart, Al
Scottish. Singer
Hit singles include "Year of the Cat," 1977; "Time Passages," 1978.
b. Sep 5, 1945 in Glasgow, Scotland
Source: *ASCAP 80; BioIn 11; ConMuA 80A; EncRkSt; HarEnR 86; IlEncRk; LegTOT; PenEncP; RkOn 74, 78; RolSEnR 83; WhoAm 80, 82; WhoRock 81*

Stewart, Alexander Peter
American. Military Leader
General active during Civil War in western, Atlanta campaigns; commanded Army of Tennessee.
b. Oct 2, 1821 in Rogersville, Tennessee
d. Aug 30, 1908 in Biloxi, Mississippi
Source: *AmBi; ApCAB; BiDConf; BioIn 1, 3, 5, 17; CivWDc; DcAmB; NatCAB 4; TwCBDA; WebAMB; WhAm 1; WhCiWar*

Stewart, Alexander Turney
American. Merchant, Philanthropist
Started NYC dry-goods store, 1823; developed into world's largest retail store, 1862; founded Garden City, 1869.
b. Oct 12, 1803 in Lisburn, Northern Ireland
d. Apr 10, 1876 in New York, New York
Source: *AmBi; ApCAB; BiAUS; BiDAmBL 83; BioIn 1, 4, 6, 7, 10, 15, 18; DcAmB; Dis&D; Drake; EncAB-H 1974; HarEnUS; McGEWB; NatCAB 7; OxCAmH; TwCBDA; WebAB 74, 79; WhAm HS*

Stewart, Anita
American. Actor
Starred for Vitagraph, 1911-17; with Louis B. Mayer, 1918-28; retired with advent of talkies.
b. Feb 17, 1896 in New York, New York
d. May 4, 1961 in Beverly Hills, California
Source: *Film 1; FilmgC; TwYS; WhoHol B; WhScrn 74, 77*

Stewart, Black Jack
[John Sherratt Stewart]
Canadian. Hockey Player
Defenseman, 1938-52, mostly with Detroit; Hall of Fame, 1964.
b. May 6, 1917 in Pilot Mound, Manitoba, Canada
Source: *HocEn; WhoHcky 73*

Stewart, Dave
[David Keith Stewart]
American. Baseball Player
Pitcher since 1981, with Oakland, 1986-92; Toronto, 1993—; has won at least 20 games, 1987-90; MVP, 1989 World Series; with Fernando Valenzuela, pitched no-hitter on same day, 1990; first pitchers to accomplish since 1898.
b. Feb 19, 1957 in Oakland, California
Source: *Ballpl 90; BaseEn 88; BaseReg 88; BioIn 16; News 91, 91-1; NewYTBS 89; WhoAfA 96; WhoBlA 85, 88, 90, 92, 94; WhoWest 92; WorAlBi*

Stewart, David
[The Eurythmics]
English. Musician
Guitarist with Eurythmics; singles include "Would I Lie to You?" 1985.
b. Sep 19, 1952 in Sunderland, England

Stewart, Donald Ogden
American. Author, Actor
Hollywood scenarist, humorist; wrote *Parody Outline of History,* 1921.
Hollywood scenarist, humorist; wrote *Parody Outline of History,* 1921.
b. Nov 30, 1894 in Columbus, Ohio
d. Aug 2, 1980 in London, England
Source: *AmAu&B; AnObit 1980; BenetAL 91; BiE&WWA; BioIn 4, 10, 12, 13, 14, 15, 17; CarSB; ConAu 43NR, 81, 101; Conv 1; CurBio 41, 80N; DcAmB S10; DcLB 4, 11, 26; DcLEL; EncAFC; FilmEn; FilmgC; HalFC 80, 84, 88; IntDcF 1-4, 2-4; LegTOT; NotNAT; OhA&B; OxCAmL 65, 83, 95; PenC AM; REnAL; TwCA, SUP; WhAm 7, 10; WhJnl; WhNAA; WhoAm 74; WhoThe 77A; WhScrn 83; WhThe; WorEFlm*

Stewart, Ellen
American. Producer
Opened boutique, La Mama, NYC, 1962; produced, directed plays by int'l, avant-garde playwrights.
b. Oct 7, 1931 in New Orleans, Louisiana
Source: *BioIn 10, 13; CelR; ConTFT 5; CurBio 73; NotNAT; PlP&P; WhoThe 77, 81; WhThe*

Stewart, George Rippey
American. Author, Educator
Versatile writer, known for novels *Storm,* 1941; *Earth Abides,* 1951.
b. May 31, 1895 in Sewickley, Pennsylvania
d. Aug 22, 1980 in San Francisco, California
Source: *AmAu&B; AmNov; Au&Wr 71; BioIn 1, 2, 4, 9, 12, 13; CnDAL; ConAu 1R, 3NR, 101; CurBio 42, 80; EncSF; FifWWr; IntAu&W 77; OxCAmL 65; REnAL; ScF&FL 1, 2; SmATA 3, 23N; TwCA SUP; TwCSFW 81; WhAm 7; WhE&EA; WhNAA; WhoAm 74; WrDr 76, 80, 82*

Stewart, J(ohn) I(nnes) M(ackintosh)
[Michael Innes]
Scottish. Author
Wrote detective stories concerning sleuth Inspector Appleby: *The Spider Strikes,* 1939.
b. Sep 30, 1906 in Edinburgh, Scotland
d. Nov 12, 1994
Source: *Au&Wr 71; Benet 96; BioIn 14, 15, 16, 17, 20; ConAu 47NR, 85, 147; ConLC 7, 14, 32, 86; ConNov 72, 76; CrtSuMy; DcLEL; EncMys; EvLB; LegTOT; LngCTC; NewC; NewCBEL; Novels; OxCAusL; OxCEng 95; PenC ENG; REn; RGTwCWr; TwCA, SUP; TwCCr&M 80, 85, 91; TwCWr; Who 74, 82, 83, 85, 88, 90, 92, 94; WhoSpyF; WorAl; WorAlBi; WrDr 76, 94, 96*

Stewart, Jackie
[John Young Stewart]
Scottish. Auto Racer
World Grand Prix champ, 1969, 1971, 1973; auto racing commentator, ABC.
b. Jun 11, 1939 in Dunbartonshire, Scotland
Source: *BioIn 8, 9, 10, 11, 12, 16; FacFETw; IntWW 76, 77, 78, 79, 80, 81, 82, 83, 89, 91, 93; LegTOT; Who 74, 82, 83, 85, 88, 90, 92, 94; WorAl; WorAlBi*

Stewart, James (Maitland)
[Jimmy Stewart]
American. Actor
Hollywood great; best known for *Mr. Smith Goes to Washington,* 1939, *It's a Wonderful Life,* 1946.
b. May 20, 1908 in Indiana, Pennsylvania
d. Jul 2, 1997 in Beverly Hills, California
Source: *AmCulL; BiDFilm, 81, 94; BiE&WWA; BioIn 1, 2, 3, 4, 5, 6, 7, 8, 9, 10, 11, 12, 13; BkPepl; BlueB 76; CelR, 90; CmCal; CmMov; ConTFT 4; DcArts; EncAFC; FacFETw; FilmEn; FilmgC; ForYSC; GangFlm; HalFC 80, 84, 88; IntDcF 1-3, 2-3; IntMPA 77, 84, 86, 88, 92, 94, 96; IntWW 74, 75, 76, 77, 78, 79, 80, 81, 82, 83, 89, 91, 93; LegTOT; MGM; MotPP; MovMk; NewYTBS 90; OxCFilm; PlP&P; VarWW 85; Who 74, 82, 83, 85, 88, 90, 92, 94; WhoAm 74, 76, 78, 80, 82, 84, 86, 88, 90, 92, 94, 95, 96, 97; WhoEnt 92; WhoHol 92, A; WhoHrs 80; WhoThe 77, 81; WhoWor 74, 78, 84, 89, 91, 93, 95, 96, 97; WorAl; WorAlBi; WorEFlm*

Stewart, John
American. Singer, Songwriter
Best known for writing song "Daydream Believer," 1967, which was number one hit for The Monkees, 1967; member of Kingston Trio, 1961-67.
b. Sep 5, 1939 in San Diego, California
Source: *BioIn 14; ConMuA 80A; EncFCWM 83; HarEnCM 87; HarEnR 86; IlEncCM; IlEncRk; IntWWM 80; PenEncP; RkOn 85; RolSEnR 83; WhoAdv 90; WhoAm 74, 76; WhoEnt 92; WhoRock 81*

Stewart, Jon
[Jon Stuart Liebowitz]
American. TV Personality, Actor, Comedian
Host of "The Jon Stewart Show."
b. 1963 in Lawrence, New Jersey

Stewart, Luisa Harris
American. Basketball Player
Led Delta State to three national championships in the 1970s; one of first two women inducted into Basketball Hall of Fame, 1992.
b. Feb 10, 1955 in Minter City, Mississippi

Stewart, Martha
American. Author
Author of gourmet food and lifestyle books; was lifestyle contributor to NBC's "Today;" created own line of paints.
b. 1941? in Nutley, New Jersey
Source: *AmDec 1980; BioIn 12, 16; CurBio 93; GrLiveH; News 92-1*

Stewart, Mary (Florence Elinor)
English. Author
Wrote trilogy about Merlin, King Arthur: *The Last Enchantment,* 1979.
b. Sep 17, 1916 in Sunderland, England
Source: *ArtclWW 2; Au&Wr 71; Benet 87, 96; BioIn 5, 8, 9, 10, 11, 12, 14, 16; BlmGWL; ChlBkCr; ConAu 1NR, 1R; ConLC 7, 35; ConPopW; CrtSuMy; DcLEL 1940; EncBrWW; EncMys; FemiCLE; IntAu&W 76, 77, 82, 89, 91, 93; InWom SUP; LngCEL; LngCTC; NewYTBS 79; Novels; OxCChiL; ScF&FL 1, 2, 92; SJGFanW; SmATA 12; TwCCr&M 80, 85, 91; TwCRGW; TwCRHW 90, 94; TwCWr; TwCYAW; Who 74, 82, 83, 85, 88, 90, 92, 94; WhoAm 74, 76, 78, 80, 82, 84, 86, 88, 90, 92, 94, 95, 96, 97; WhoAmW 70, 72, 74, 75, 77; WhoUSWr 88; WhoWor 74, 76; WhoWrEP 89, 92, 95; WorAlBi; WorAu 1950; WrDr 76, 80, 82, 84, 86, 88, 90, 92, 94, 96*

Stewart, Michael
[Michael Rubin]
American. Dramatist
Won Tonys for *Bye, Bye Birdie,* 1961; *Hello Dolly!* 1964.
b. Aug 1, 1929 in New York, New York
d. Sep 20, 1987 in New York, New York
Source: *BiE&WWA; BioIn 12, 15; ConTFT 1, 5; EncMT; NewCBMT; NotNAT; OxCAmT 84; VarWW 85; WhAm 9; WhoAm 82, 84, 86; WhoThe 77, 81*

Stewart, Nels(on Robert)
"Old Poison"
Canadian. Hockey Player
Center, 1925-40, mostly with Montreal Maroons; won Hart Trophy, 1926, 1930, Art Ross Trophy, 1926; first to score 300 goals; Hall of Fame, 1962.
b. Dec 29, 1902 in Montreal, Quebec, Canada
d. Aug 21, 1957 in Toronto, Ontario, Canada
Source: *BioIn 2, 4; HocEn; ObitOF 79; WhoHcky 73*

Stewart, Patrick
English. Actor
Played Captain Jean-Luc Picard on "Star Trek: The Next Generation," 1987-94; won and was nominated for several Lawrence Olivier Awards.
b. Jul 13, 1940 in Mirfield, England
Source: *BioIn 18, 19, 20, 21; ConTFT 7, 14; CurBio 94; IntMPA 94, 96; News 96, 96-1; WhoAm 94, 95, 96, 97; WhoHol 92, A; WhoThe 72, 77, 81*

Stewart, Paul
American. Actor
Made acting debut in Orson Welles' *Citizen Kane,* 1941; typically cast in gangster roles.
b. Mar 13, 1908 in New York, New York
d. Feb 17, 1986 in Los Angeles, California
Source: *AnObit 1986; BioIn 14; FilmEn; FilmgC; ForYSC; GangFlm; HalFC 80, 84, 88; HolCA; IntMPA 84, 86; MovMk; RadStar; Vers A; WhoAm 74, 76, 78, 80, 82, 84; WhoHol A*

Stewart, Potter
American. Supreme Court Justice
Conservative Eisenhower Rep; justice, 1958-81; youngest to resign.
b. Jan 13, 1915 in Jackson, Michigan
d. Dec 7, 1985 in Hanover, New Hampshire
Source: *AmBench 79; AnObit 1985; BiDFedJ; BioIn 5, 6, 7, 8, 9, 10, 11, 12, 13, 14, 15, 17; BlueB 76; CelR; CngDr 74, 77, 79, 81, 83, 85, 87; ConNews 86-1; CurBio 59, 86, 86N; DrAS 74P, 78P, 82P; EncWB; FacFETw; IntWW 74, 75, 76, 77, 78, 79, 80, 81, 82, 83; IntYB 78, 79, 80, 81, 82; LegTOT; LinLib S; NewYTBS 85; OxCSupC; PolProf E, J, K, NF; SupCtJu; WebAB 74, 79; Who 74, 82, 83, 85; WhoAm 74, 76, 78, 80, 82, 84; WhoAmL 78, 79, 83, 85; WhoAmP 73, 75, 77, 79, 81, 83, 85; WhoE 79, 81, 83, 85; WhoGov 72, 75, 77; WhoSSW 73, 75, 76; WhoWor 74, 78, 80, 82, 84; WorAl; WorAlBi*

Stewart, Rod(erick David)
English. Singer
Singer with Jeff Beck Group, 1968-69; Faces, 1969-75; solo performer, 1975—.
b. Jan 10, 1945 in North London, England
Source: *ASCAP 80; BioIn 9, 10, 11, 12, 13, 16; BkPepl; CelR 90; ConMuA 80A; ConMus 2; CurBio 79; EncPR&S 74, 89; EncRk 88; EncRkSt; HarEnR 86; IlEncRk; IntWW 89, 91, 93; LegTOT; NewAmDM; OxCPMus; PenEncP; RkOn 74, 78; RolSEnR 83; WhoAm 78, 80, 82, 84, 86, 88, 90, 92, 94, 95, 96, 97; WhoEnt 92A; WhoMW 90; WhoRock 81; WhoRocM 82; WhoWor 95, 96, 97; WorAl; WorAlBi*

Stewart, Slam
[Leroy Stewart]
American. Jazz Musician, Composer
Innovative bassist with Art Tatum, Benny Goodman; recorded "Flat Foot Floogie" with Slim Gaillard, 1938.
b. Sep 21, 1914 in Englewood, New Jersey
d. Dec 10, 1987 in Binghamton, New York
Source: *AllMusG; AnObit 1987; BiDAmM; BiDJaz; BioIn 15, 16; CmpEPM; DrBlPA 90; EncJzS; InB&W 80, 85; NewGrDA 86; NewGrDJ 88, 94; NewYTBS 87; PenEncP; WhoAm 82, 84, 86; WhoJazz 72*

Stewart, Thomas
[Thomas James Stewart, Jr.]
American. Opera Singer
Baritone with various operas including the NY Met, 1960—; Wagnerian soloist.
b. Aug 19, 1928 in San Saba, Texas
Source: *Baker 78, 84; BiDAmM; BioIn 11, 13; CmOp; CurBio 74; IntWW 78, 79, 80, 81, 82, 83, 89, 91, 93; IntWWM 80; MetOEnc; MusSN; NewAmDM; NewEOp 71; NewGrDA 86; NewGrDM 80; OxDcOp; WhoAm 78, 80, 82, 84, 86, 88, 90, 92, 94, 95, 96, 97; WhoAmM 83; WhoEnt 92; WhoOp 76; WhoWor 78, 80, 82, 84*

Stewart, Wynn
American. Singer, Songwriter
Formed country-western band, The Tourists, 1960s; hit single "Something Pretty," 1968.
b. Jun 7, 1934 in Morrisville, Missouri
d. Jul 17, 1985 in Hendersonville, Tennessee
Source: *BgBkCoM; BiDAmM; BioIn 14; ConAu 116, 154; CounME 74, 74A; EncFCWM 69, 83; HarEnCM 87; IlEncCM; PenEncP*

Stibitz, George R.
American. Inventor, Mathematician
Inventor of first electric calculator.
d. Jan 13, 1995 in Hanover, New Hampshire
Source: *NewYTBS 95*

Stich, Michael
Tennis Player
Won Grand Slam, 1991.
Source: *BioIn 17; NewYTBS 91*

Stich-Randall, Teresa
American. Opera Singer
Soprano; NY Met debut, 1961; sang Aida at age 15.
b. Dec 24, 1927 in West Hartford, Connecticut
Source: *Baker 84, 92; CmOp; IntDcOp; IntWWM 80, 90; MetOEnc; NewAmDM; NewEOp 71; NewGrDA 86; NewGrDM 80; NewGrDO; OxDcOp; PenDiMP; WhoAm 74; WhoMus 72*

Stickley, Gustav
[Gustav Stoeckel]
American. Journalist, Furniture Designer
Editor, publisher, *The Craftsman Magazine,* 1901; founded furniture works hops; created Mission style furniture.
b. Mar 9, 1858 in Osceola, Wisconsin
d. Apr 21, 1942 in New York, New York
Source: *AmCulL; AmRef; BioIn 3, 7, 11, 13, 15, 16, 19, 20; NatCAB 14; WhAm 4*

Stickney, Dorothy
American. Actor
Co-starred in Broadway's *Life With Father* with husband Howard Lindsay, 1939-43.
b. Jun 21, 1900 in Dickinson, North Dakota
Source: *BiE&WWA; CurBio 42; ForYSC; InWom, SUP; MotPP; NotNAT; WhoHol 92, A; WhoThe 72, 77, 81*

Stieb, Dave
[David Andrew Stieb]
American. Baseball Player
Pitcher, Toronto, 1979-92; led AL in ERA, 1985; five-time AL All-Star; pitched no-hitter, 1990.
b. Jul 22, 1957 in Santa Ana, California
Source: *Ballpl 90; BaseReg 86, 87; BiDAmSp Sup; BioIn 13; WhoAm 84, 86, 88, 90, 92; WhoE 89*

Stiedry, Fritz
Austrian. Conductor
Principal Wagner conductor, NY Met., 1946-58.
b. Oct 11, 1883 in Vienna, Austria
d. Aug 9, 1968 in Zurich, Switzerland
Source: *Baker 78, 84, 92; BiDAmM; BiDSovU; BioIn 2, 4, 8, 11; CmOp; MetOEnc; MusSN; NewEOp 71; NewGrDA 86; NewGrDM 80; NewGrDO; PenDiMP*

Stiegel, Henry William
American. Manufacturer
Iron, glass maker; founder Flint Glass Co., 1772; glassware now collector's items.
b. May 13, 1729 in Cologne, Germany
d. Jan 10, 1785 in Charming Forge, Pennsylvania
Source: *AmBi; AntBDN H; BioIn 1, 3, 8, 17; BriEAA; DcAmB; EncCRAm; IlDcG; McGEWB; NewCol 75; OxCAmH; OxCDecA; PenDiDA 89; WebAB 74, 79; WhAm HS*

Stieglitz, Alfred
"Father of Modern Photography"
American. Photographer, Editor
Work characterized by technical innovations taking pictures at night or in rain; influenced by artists Matisse, Picasso.
b. Jan 1, 1864 in Hoboken, New Jersey
d. Jul 13, 1946 in New York, New York
Source: *AmAu&B; AmCulL; AtlBL; Benet 87, 96; BiDAmJo; BioIn 1, 2, 4, 5, 6, 7, 8, 9, 10, 11, 12, 13, 14, 15, 16, 17, 18, 19, 20, 21; BriEAA; ConPhot 82, 88; CurBio 46; DcAmArt; DcAmB S4; DcArts; DcTwDes; EncAB-H 1974, 1996; EncAJ; FacFETw; GayN; ICPEnP; JeAmHC; LegTOT; MacBEP; McGDA; McGEWB; ObitOF 79; OxCAmH; OxCAmL 65; OxCTwCA; OxDcArt; REn; REnAL; WebAB 74, 79; WhAm 2; WhAmArt 85; WhNAA; WorAl; WorAlBi*

Stiers, David Ogden
American. Actor
Played Major Winchester on "M*A*S*H," 1977-83.
b. Oct 31, 1942 in Peoria, Illinois
Source: *BioIn 11, 12, 13; ConTFT 6; HalFC 88; IntMPA 92, 94, 96; LegTOT;*

VarWW 85; WhoAm 80, 82, 84, 86, 88, 90, 92, 94, 95, 96, 97; WhoEnt 92; WhoHol 92; WhoWest 82

Stiffel, Theodopholous
American. Businessman
Started TA Stiffel Co., 1932, artfully fashioned, high-priced lamps.
b. 1899 in Memphis, Tennessee
d. 1971
Source: *Entr*

Stigler, George Joseph
American. Economist
Intellectual anchor of Chicago school of economics movement; won Nobel Prize in economics, 1982; wrote *The Economist as Preacher,* 1982.
b. Jun 17, 1911 in Renton, Washington
d. Dec 1, 1991 in Chicago, Illinois
Source: *AmAu&B; AmMWSc 73S, 78S; BioIn 13, 14, 15, 16, 17, 18, 19, 20; BlueB 76; ConAu 41R; CurBio 83; GrEconS; IntWW 74, 75, 76, 77, 78, 79, 80, 81, 82, 83, 89, 91; NewYTBS 82; NobelP; RAdv 14; WhAm 10; Who 85, 88, 90, 92; WhoAm 74, 76, 78, 80, 82, 84, 86, 88, 90; WhoEc 81, 86; WhoFI 83, 85, 89, 92; WhoMW 84, 86, 88, 90; WhoNob, 90, 95; WhoWor 82, 84, 87, 89, 91; WorAlBi; WrDr 76, 84, 92*

Stignani, Ebe
Italian. Opera Singer
Mezzo-soprano; with Milan's La Scala, 1926-56; known for Italian roles.
b. Jul 10, 1907 in Naples, Italy
d. Oct 5, 1974 in Imola, Italy
Source: *Baker 84; BioIn 1, 2, 3, 4, 9, 10, 11, 14, 17; BriBkM 80; CurBio 49, 91N; InWom; MusSN; NewEOp 71; NewGrDM 80; WhAm 6*

Stigwood, Robert Colin
Australian. Producer
Won Tony for *Evita,* 1980.
b. Apr 16, 1934 in Adelaide, Australia
Source: *ConAu 102; ConTFT 5; CurBio 79; HalFC 84, 88; IntMPA 86, 92; IntWW 83, 89, 91, 93; VarWW 85; WhoAm 86, 88, 90, 92, 94, 95, 96, 97; WhoE 93; WhoEnt 92; WhoWor 84, 87*

Still, Andrew Taylor
American. Physician
Founder of osteopathy; believed all disease derived from dislocation of vertebrae.
b. Aug 6, 1828 in Jonesville, Virginia
d. Dec 12, 1917 in Kirksville, Missouri
Source: *AmBi; BioIn 2, 4, 9; DcAmB; DcAmMeB 84; DcNAA; LinLib L, S; NatCAB 14, 26; NewAgE 90; NewCol 75; WebAB 74, 79; WhAm 1*

Still, Clyfford
American. Artist
Pioneer in use of mural sized canvas.
b. Oct 30, 1904 in Grandin, North Dakota
d. Jun 23, 1980 in Baltimore, Maryland
Source: *AnObit 1980; BioIn 1, 3, 5, 6, 8, 9, 10, 12, 14, 15, 19, 20, 21; BriEAA; CelR; ConArt 77, 83, 89, 96; CurBio 71, 80N; DcAmArt; DcAmB S10; DcArts; DcCAA 71, 77, 88, 94; DcCAr 81; EncWB; McGDA; NewCol 75; NewYTBS 80; OxCTwCA; OxDcArt; PhDcTCA 77; REn; WhAm 4, 7, 8; WhAmArt 85; WhoAm 74, 76, 78, 80; WhoAmA 73, 76, 78, 80, 82N, 84N, 86N, 89N, 91N, 93N; WhoE 74; WhoWor 74; WorArt 1950*

Still, William Grant
''''Dean of Afro-American Composers''''
American. Composer, Conductor
First black to lead major US orchestra, LA Philharmonic, 1936; wrote ''Afro-American Symphony,'' 1931.
b. May 11, 1895 in Woodville, Mississippi
d. Dec 3, 1978 in Los Angeles, California
Source: *AfrAmAl 6; AmComp; ASCAP 66, 80; Baker 78, 84, 92; BiDAfM; BiDAmM; BioIn 1, 2, 3, 4, 6, 8, 9, 10, 11, 12, 13; BlkOpe; BriBkM 80; CmCal; CompSN, SUP; ConAmC 76, 82; CurBio 41, 79, 79N; DcAfAmP; DcAmB S10; DcCM; DcTwCCu 5; DrBlPA, 90; Ebony 1; EncAACR; FacFETw; InB&W 80, 85; McGEWB; MetOEnc; NegAl 76, 83, 89; NewAmDM; NewCol 75; NewEOp 71; NewGrDA 86; NewGrDM 80; NewGrDO; NewOxM; NewYTBS 78; ObitOF 79; OxCMus; OxDcOp; REnAL; SelBAAu; WebAB 74, 79; WhoAm 74, 76; WhoBlA 75, 77; WhoMus 72*

Stiller, Ben
American. Actor, Director
Appeared in *Empire of the Sun,* and *Reality Bites.*
b. 1966 in New York, New York
Source: *ConTFT 12; IntMPA 96*

Stiller, Jerry
[Stiller and Meara]
American. Comedian, Actor
Formed successful comedy team with wife Anne Meara; in film *Those Lips, Those Eyes;* plays Frank Costanza on ''Seinfeld,'' 1993—.
b. Jun 8, 1926? in New York, New York
Source: *BioNews 75; CelR 90; LegTOT; VarWW 85; WhoAm 86, 88; WhoHol A*

Stiller, Mauritz
Swedish. Director
Pioneer of Swedish cinema; discovered Greta Garbo.
b. Jul 17, 1883 in Helsinki, Finland
d. Nov 8, 1928 in Stockholm, Sweden
Source: *BiDFilm, 81, 94; BioIn 9, 10, 12, 15; DcFM; EncEurC; FilmEn; FilmgC; HalFC 80, 84, 88; IntDcF 1-2, 2-2; MiSFD 9N; MovMk; OxCFilm; TwYS, A; WhScrn 77, 83; WorEFlm; WorFDir 1*

Stillman, Irwin Maxwell
American. Physician
Wrote *The Doctor's Quick Weight-Loss Diet,* 1966.
b. Sep 11, 1895 in New York, New York
d. Aug 27, 1975 in Bal Harbour, Florida
Source: *BioIn 10, 12; BioNews 74; ConAu 49, 61; NatCAB 59; NewYTBS 75*

Stillman, James
American. Banker
Pres. of NY's National City Bank (now Citibank) made it one of the more powerful institutions in US.
b. Jun 9, 1850 in Brownsville, Texas
d. Mar 15, 1918 in New York, New York
Source: *BiDAmBL 83; BioIn 3, 10, 21; DcAmB; EncABHB 6; NatCAB 15; WhAm 1*

Stills, Stephen
[Buffalo Springfield; Crosby, Stills, Nash, and Young]
American. Musician, Singer, Songwriter
Vocalist, guitarist, Buffalo Springfield band, 1966-68; Crosby, Stills, Nash, 1968-69, 1977, 1982; Crosby, Stills, Nash, & Young, 1969-71; solo career, 1971—; solo hits include ''Love the One You're With,'' 1971.
b. Jan 3, 1945 in Dallas, Texas
Source: *ASCAP 80; BioIn 13; ConMuA 80A; ConMus 5; EncPR&S 74, 89; EncRk 88; HarEnR 86; IlEncRk; LegTOT; OnThGG; PenEncP; WhoAm 94, 95, 96, 97; WhoRocM 82; WorAl; WorAlBi*

Stilwell, Joseph Warren
''Vinegar Joe''
American. Army Officer
Commander of the 6th Army; chief-of-staff to Chiang Kai-Shek; disagreement over role of Chinese forces led to his loss of command by FDR, 1944.
b. Mar 19, 1883 in Palatka, Florida
d. Oct 12, 1946 in San Francisco, California
Source: *BiDWWGF; BioIn 1, 5, 9, 10, 11, 13, 17, 18; CurBio 42, 46; DcAmB S4; DcAmMiB; DcTwHis; EncAB-H 1974, 1996; HarEnMi; McGEWB; NatCAB 33; REnAL; WebAB 74, 79; WebAMB; WhAm 2; WhoMilH 76; WhWW-II; WorAl*

Stilwell, Richard Dale
American. Opera Singer
Lyric baritone who joined NYC Opera, 1970; known for role of Pelleas in *Pelleas et Melisande.*
b. May 6, 1942 in Saint Louis, Missouri
Source: *Baker 92; BioIn 10, 11; ColdWar 2; CurBio 86; IntWW 89, 91, 93; NewAmDM; PenDiMP; WhoAm 74, 76, 78, 80, 82, 84, 86, 88, 90, 92, 94, 95, 96, 97; WhoOp 76*

Stimson, Henry Lewis
[Harry Stimson]
American. Government Official
Secretary of War, 1940-45; led expansion, operation of US Army, WW II; advised use of atomic bomb on Japan.
b. Sep 21, 1867 in New York, New York
d. Oct 20, 1950 in Huntington, New York
Source: *AmPolLe; BiDInt; BiDrUSE 71, 89; BioIn 1, 2, 3, 4, 5, 6, 7, 8, 9, 10, 11, 13, 15, 16, 17, 18; ColdWar 2; CurBio 40, 50; DcAmB S4; DcAmDH 80, 89; DcAmMiB; DcPol; DcTwHis; EncAB-H 1974; EncTR 91; FacFETw; HarEnUS; HisEWW; HisWorL; LinLib S; McGEWB; NatCAB 37; OxCAmH; REnAL; WebAB 74, 79; WhAm 3; WorAl*

Stine, R. L.
American. Author
Teen horror fiction writer known for *Goosebumps* series.
b. Oct 8, 1943 in Columbus, Ohio
Source: *BioIn 20, 21; ChILR 37; ConAu 22NR; OnHuMoP; WhoWrEP 89*

Sting
[The Police; Gordon Matthew Sumner]
English. Musician, Singer, Songwriter
Self-taught musician, force behind success of *The Police,* 1976-83; solo performer, 1985—.
b. Oct 2, 1951 in Newcastle-upon-Tyne, England
Source: *Baker 92; BioIn 16; CelR 90; ConMus 2; ConTFT 2, 7; CurBio 85; DcArts; EncPR&S 89; EncRkSt; EnvEnDr; HalFC 88; IntMPA 88, 92, 94, 96; IntWW 89, 91, 93; ItaFilm; LegTOT; NewAmDM; News 91; NewYTBS 84; WhoAm 84, 86, 88, 90, 92, 94, 95, 96, 97; WhoEnt 92; WhoHol 92; WhoRocM 82; WhoWor 93, 95, 96, 97; WorAlBi*

Stingley, Darryl
American. Football Player
Wide receiver, New England, 1973-78; paralyzed by Jack Tatum tackle during preseason game, 1978.
b. Sep 18, 1951 in Chicago, Illinois
Source: *BioIn 11, 12, 13, 18; BlkWrNE A; InB&W 85; NewYTBS 78, 82; WhoBlA 80, 85, 88*

Stipe, Michael
[R.E.M; John Michael Stipe]
American. Singer, Songwriter
Grammy, Best Pop Vocal—Group, "Losing My Religion," 1991.
b. Jan 4, 1960 in Decatur, Georgia
Source: *LegTOT; WhoAm 94, 95, 96, 97*

Stirling, Lord
[William Alexander]
American. Military Leader
Continental army general; defended the NYC area in various battles, Mar 1776-Jan 1780.
b. 1726 in New York, New York
d. Sep 15, 1783 in New York, New York
Source: *AmBi; AmRev; ApCAB; BiInAmS; BioIn 8, 12, 15; DcAmB; DcNaB; Drake; EncAR; EncCRAm; HarEnMi; HarEnUS; NatCAB 1; TwCBDA; WebAB 74; WebAMB; WhAm HS; WhAmP; WhAmRev*

Stirling, James
Scottish. Architect
Major designs include Queen's College-Oxford, 1967-71; Fogg Museum, Harvard U., 1979.
b. Apr 22, 1926 in Glasgow, Scotland
d. Jun 25, 1992 in London, England
Source: *AnObit 1992; ConArch 80; DcArts; DcD&D; EncWB; IntDcAr; IntWW 75, 76, 77, 78, 79, 80, 81, 82, 83, 89, 91; MacEA; NewYTBS 92; WhAm 10; Who 92; WhoArch; WhoArt 96; WhoWor 78, 82, 84, 87, 89, 91*

Stirner, Max
German. Philosopher
Writings lent ideological inspiration to anarchists; wrote *Der Einzige und Sein Eigentum,* 1845.
b. Oct 25, 1806 in Bayreuth, Bavaria
d. Jun 26, 1856 in Berlin, Germany
Source: *BioIn 9, 10, 11, 19; DcLB 129; Dis&D; McGEWB; OxCGer 76, 86; OxCPhil; REn*

Stitt, Sonny
[Edward Stitt]
American. Jazz Musician
Saxophonist with Dizzy Gillespie, 1940s; led own combo, 1950s-60s.
b. Feb 2, 1924 in Boston, Massachusetts
d. Jul 22, 1982 in Washington, District of Columbia
Source: *AllMusG; AnObit 1982; Baker 84, 92; BiDAfM; BiDAmM; BiDJaz; BioIn 13, 16; CmpEPM; DrBlPA, 90; EncJzS; IlEncJ; InB&W 80, 85; LegTOT; NewAmDM; NewGrDA 86; NewGrDJ 88, 94; NewYTBS 82; PenEncP; WhoAm 82; WorAl; WorAlBi*

Stock, Frederick A
American. Conductor
Led Chicago Symphony for 48 yrs.
b. Nov 11, 1872 in Dulich, Germany
d. Oct 20, 1942 in Chicago, Illinois
Source: *Baker 78, 84; BiDAmM; BriBkM 80; CurBio 42; DcAmB S3; MusSN; NewGrDM 80; OxCMus; WhAm 2*

Stockdale, James
American. Army Officer
Vietnam War POW; Ross Perot's vice-presidential candidate, 1992.
b. Dec 23, 1923 in Abington, Illinois
Source: *BioIn 11, 12, 13, 18, 20, 21; WhoAm 90*

Stocker, Wally
[The Babys]
English. Singer, Musician
Guitarist, vocalist with power pop group, 1976-81.
b. Mar 17, 1954 in London, England

Stockhausen, Karlheinz
German. Composer
Avant-garde works emphasize time-space music, electronic devices, audience participation; *Sirius* dedicated to space pioneers, 1976.
b. Aug 28, 1928 in Modrath, Germany
Source: *Baker 78, 84, 92; BioIn 6, 7, 8, 9, 10, 12, 13, 14, 15, 20, 21; BriBkM 80; CnOxB; CompSN, SUP; ConCom 92; CurBio 71; DcArts; DcCM; DcCom 77; DcCom&M 79; FacFETw; IntDcOp; IntWW 74, 75, 76, 77, 78, 79, 80, 81, 82, 83, 89, 91, 93; IntWWM 77, 80, 90; MakMC; McGEWB; MetOEnc; MusMk; NewAmDM; NewGrDM 80; NewGrDO; NewOxM; NewYTBE 71; OxCMus; OxDcOp; PenDiMP A; RAdv 14; WhDW; Who 74, 82, 83, 85, 88, 90, 92, 94; WhoMus 72; WhoWor 74, 78, 82, 84, 87, 89, 91, 93, 95, 96, 97*

Stockman, David Allen
American. Government Official
Directed OMB, 1981-85; wrote *Triumph of Politics,* 1986.
b. Nov 10, 1946 in Fort Hood, Texas
Source: *AlmAP 80; CngDr 78; CurBio 81; IntWW 81, 82, 83, 89, 91, 93; IntYB 82; NewYTBS 80, 85; WhoAm 78, 80, 82, 84, 86, 92, 94, 95, 96, 97; WhoAmP 85, 91, 95; WhoFI 83, 85, 89, 92, 94; WhoGov 77; WhoMW 78, 80*

Stockton, Dave
[David Knapp Stockton]
American. Golfer
Turned pro, 1964; won PGA, 1970, 1976.
b. Nov 2, 1941 in San Bernardino, California
Source: *BioIn 19, 21; NewYTBE 71; NewYTBS 74; WhoAm 78, 80, 82, 84, 86, 88, 90, 92, 94, 95, 96, 97; WhoGolf; WhoIntG; WhoWest 94, 96*

Stockton, Dick
American. Tennis Player
US Open mixed champion, 1975; World mixed champion, 1975-77; WCT World champion, 1977.
b. Feb 18, 1951 in New York, New York
Source: *BioIn 10, 11; WhoIntT*

Stockton, Frank
[Francis Richard Stockton]
American. Author
Known for puzzling short story *The Lady or the Tiger,* 1884.
b. Apr 5, 1834 in Philadelphia, Pennsylvania
d. Apr 20, 1902 in Washington, District of Columbia
Source: *Alli SUP; AmBi; ApCAB, X; BiD&SB; BioIn 14, 15, 19; Chambr 3; CnDAL; ConAu 108, 137; DcAmAu; DcAmB; DcBiA; DcEnA A; DcNAA; EncMys; FamSYP; JBA 34; LinLib L; LngCTC; MajAI; NatCAB 1; NewYHSD; OxCAmL 65; OxCEng 67; RAdv 1; REn;*

REnAL; ScFEYrs; SmATA 44; TwCBDA; WebAB 74, 79; WhAm 1; WhAmArt 85

Stockton, John (Houston)
American. Basketball Player
With Utah Jazz, 1984—; member, US Olympic Basketball Team, 1992.
b. Mar 26, 1962 in Spokane, Washington
Source: *BasBi; CurBio 95; LegTOT; WhoAm 92, 94, 95, 96, 97; WorAlBi*

Stockton, Richard
American. Continental Congressman, Lawyer
Signed Declaration of Independence, 1776; promoted Princeton College; grandfather of Robert Field.
b. Oct 1, 1730 in Princeton, New Jersey
d. Feb 28, 1781 in Princeton, New Jersey
Source: *AmBi; AmPolLe; ApCAB; BiAUS; BiDrAC; BiDrUSC 89; BioIn 1, 3, 4, 7, 8, 9, 10, 11, 18; DcAmB; Drake; EncAR; EncCRAm; HarEnUS; NatCAB 12; TwCBDA; WhAm HS; WhAmP; WhAmRev*

Stockton, Robert Field
American. Naval Officer
Captured Santa Barbara, Los Angeles in Mexican War; declared CA a territory of US; Stockton, CA named for him.
b. Aug 20, 1795 in Princeton, New Jersey
d. Oct 7, 1866 in Princeton, New Jersey
Source: *AmBi; ApCAB; BiAUS; BiDrAC; BiDrUSC 89; BioIn 1, 2, 4, 16; CmCal; DcAmB; DcAmDH 80, 89; DcAmMiB; Drake; HarEnMi; HarEnUS; McGEWB; NatCAB 4; OxCAmH; REnAW; TwCBDA; WebAB 74, 79; WebAMB; WhAm HS; WhAmP*

Stockwell, Dean
American. Actor
Child star of 1940s; films include *Blue Velvet,* 1986, *Married to the Mob,* 1988; stars as TVs first holographic character in "Quantum Leap," 1988-93.
b. Mar 5, 1936 in Hollywood, California
Source: *BiDFilm 94; BioIn 1, 2, 9, 16; ConTFT 5, 12; CurBio 91; FilmEn; FilmgC; ForYSC; HalFC 84, 88; IntMPA 77, 84, 86, 92; LegTOT; MGM; MotPP; MovMk; VarWW 85; WhoAm 90, 92, 94, 95, 96, 97; WhoEnt 92A; WhoHol 92, A; WhoWor 95, 96, 97; WorAl*

Stockwell, Guy
American. Actor
Films include *Please Don't Eat the Daisies,* 1960; *Airport 1975,* 1974.
b. Nov 16, 1938 in North Hollywood, California
Source: *FilmgC; ForYSC; HalFC 88; WhoHol A*

Stoddard, Alexandra
American. Interior Decorator
Wrote *Style for Living,* 1974; host of "Homes Across America" on the Home and Garden cable network, 1994—.
b. Nov 6, 1941 in Weston, Massachusetts
Source: *CurBio 96; WhoWor 91*

Stoddard, Brandon
American. Broadcasting Executive
Pres. of ABC's Entertainment, 1985-89; pres. ABC Productions, 1989—.
b. Mar 31, 1937 in Bridgeport, Connecticut
Source: *BioIn 11, 12, 13, 14, 15, 16; CurBio 89; IntMPA 92, 94, 96; LesBEnT 92; WhoAm 80, 82, 84, 86, 88, 90, 92, 94, 95, 96, 97; WhoEnt 92; WhoFI 85*

Stoddard, Richard Henry
"Nestor of American Literature"
American. Poet
Literary editor, *NY Mail and Express,* 1880-1903.
b. Jul 12, 1825 in Hingham, Massachusetts
d. May 12, 1903
Source: *Alli, SUP; AmAu; AmAu&B; AmBi; ApCAB; BbD; BenetAL 91; BibAL 8; BiD&SB; BioIn 4, 9, 12, 16; Chambr 3; ChhPo, S1; CnDAL; ConAu 114; CyAL 2; DcAmAu; DcAmB; DcEnA A; DcEnL; DcLB 3, 64, DS13; DcLEL; DcNAA; Drake; EvLB; HarEnUS; LinLib L; NatCAB 3; OxCAmL 65, 83, 95; REn; REnAL; TwCBDA; WhAm 1*

Stoessel, Albert
American. Conductor, Composer, Violinist
Associated with NY Oratorio Society, Juilliard School; wrote *Technic of the Baton,* 1920.
b. Oct 11, 1894 in Saint Louis, Missouri
d. May 12, 1943 in New York, New York
Source: *ASCAP 66, 80; Baker 78, 84; ConAmC 76, 82; CurBio 43; DcAmB S3; NewAmDM; NewGrDA 86; NewGrDM 80; OxCMus; WhAm 2*

Stoffels, Hendrijke
Dutch. Mistress, Model
Housekeeper, mistress of Rembrandt, 1645-63.
b. 1622
d. 1663
Source: *BioIn 9*

Stofflet, Ty(rone Earl)
American. Softball Player
Known as fastest softball pitcher in the world, at speeds exceeding 100 mph.
b. Jul 29, 1941 in Coplay, Pennsylvania
Source: *BioIn 12, 16; ConNews 87-1; NewYTBS 85*

Stokely, Alfred Jehu
American. Business Executive
With Stokely-Van Camp, Inc. since 1938; chm., CEO, 1978-81.
b. Mar 26, 1916 in Newport, Tennessee
Source: *BioIn 9; St&PR 75, 84, 87, 91; WhoAm 74, 76, 78, 80, 82; WhoFI 74, 75, 77, 79, 81; WhoWor 74*

Stokely, Anna
American. Business Executive
With sons established canning business, 1898; has become major nat. food packer.
b. 1852
d. 1916
Source: *Entr*

Stokely, James
American. Businessman
With mother, brother, established food packing business, 1898.
b. 1875
d. 1922
Source: *Entr*

Stokely, John
American. Businessman
With brother, mother established cannery which grew in six years to major industry.
b. 1876
d. 1919
Source: *Entr*

Stoker, Bram
Irish. Author
Published best-selling horror story *Dracula,* 1897.
b. Nov 8, 1847 in Dublin, Ireland
d. Apr 20, 1912 in London, England
Source: *Alli SUP; Benet 87, 96; BioIn 5, 6, 8, 10, 11, 12, 13, 14, 15, 16, 17, 18, 20, 21; CamGLE; CnDBLB 5; ConAu 150; CyWA 58; DcArts; DcIrL, 96; DcLB 36, 70; DcLEL; EncMys; EncO&P 1, 2, 3; EncSF; EvLB; FilmgC; GrWrEL N; HalFC 80, 84, 88; LegTOT; LngCTC; NewEScF; NotNAT B; Novels; OxCEng 85, 95; OxCIri; PenC ENG; PenEncH; RAdv 14; REn; RfGEnL 91; ScF&FL 1, 92; StaCVF; SupFW; TwCA, SUP; TwCCr&M 80; TwCLC 8; VicBrit; WhDW; WhLit; WhoChL; WhoHr&F; WhoHrs 80; WorAl; WorAlBi; WorLitC*

Stokes, Carl B(urton)
American. Politician
Mayor, Cleveland, 1967-71; one of the first big city black mayors in America.
b. Jun 21, 1927 in Cleveland, Ohio
d. Apr 4, 1996 in Cleveland, Ohio
Source: *BioIn 7, 8, 9, 10, 11, 12; BlueB 76; ConAu 69, 152; CurBio 68, 96N; Ebony 1; InB&W 80, 85; PolProf J, NF; WhAm 11; WhoAfA 96; WhoAm 74, 76, 78, 80, 82, 84, 86, 88, 90, 92, 94, 95, 96; WhoAmP 73, 75, 77, 79, 81, 83, 85, 87, 89, 91, 93, 95; WhoBlA 75, 77, 80, 85, 88, 90, 92, 94; WhoWor 74*

Stokes, Donald Gresham Stokes, Baron
English. Auto Executive
Pres. British Leyland, 1975-79; Dutton-Forshaw Motor Group Ltd., 1980-90.
b. Mar 22, 1914 in London, England
Source: *BioIn 10; BlueB 76; IntWW 74, 75, 76, 77, 78, 79, 80, 81; IntYB 80, 81; Who 74; WhoAm 84, 86, 90; WhoWor 74*

Stokes, Doris
English. Psychic, Author
Internationally known psychic medium; wrote *Voices in My Ear: The Autobiography of a Medium,* 1980.
b. 1919 in Grantham, England
Source: *BioIn 16; ConAu 115, 122; EncO&P 1S3, 2, 3*

Stokes, George Gabriel, Sir
English. Physicist, Mathematician
Developed law of viscosity, which has to do with a solid globe's motion in fluid; created theorem of vector analysis called Stokes's theorem.
b. Aug 13, 1819 in Skreen, Ireland
d. Feb 1, 1903 in Cambridge, England
Source: *Alli, SUP; AsBiEn; BiESc; BioIn 8, 12, 14, 16, 17; BritAu 19; CamDcSc; CelCen; DcBiPP; DcInv; DcIrB 78, 88; DcNaB S2; DcScB; InSci; LarDcSc*

Stokes, Louis
American. Politician
Dem. congressman representing Ohio, 1969—.
b. Feb 23, 1925 in Cleveland, Ohio
Source: *AfrAmAl 6; AfrAmBi 1; AlmAP 78, 80, 82, 84, 88, 92, 96; BiDrAC; BiDrUSC 89; BioIn 9, 12, 13, 14, 16; BlkAmsC; BlueB 76; CivR 74; CngDr 74, 77, 79, 81, 83, 85, 87, 89, 91, 93, 95; ConBlB 3; Ebony 1; PolsAm 84; WhoAfA 96; WhoAm 74, 76, 78, 80, 82, 84, 86, 88, 90, 92, 94, 95, 96, 97; WhoAmL 78, 79; WhoAmP 73, 75, 77, 79, 81, 83, 85, 87, 89, 91, 93, 95; WhoBlA 75, 77, 80, 85, 88, 90, 92, 94; WhoGov 72, 75, 77; WhoMW 74, 76, 78, 80, 82, 84, 86, 88, 90, 92, 93, 96; WhoWor 74*

Stokes, William
Irish. Physician
Most renowned modern doctor in Europe; leader in Dublin School of anatomical diagnosis.
b. Oct 1, 1804 in Dublin, Ireland
d. Jan 10, 1878 in Howth, Ireland
Source: *Alli, SUP; BiHiMed; BioIn 5, 9, 14; CelCen; DcBiPP; DcIrB 78, 88; DcNaB; InSci; OxCMed 86; WhDW*

Stokowski, Leopold (Anton Stanislaw Boleslawawicz)
American. Conductor, Musician
Led Philadelphia Orchestra, 1914-36; formed American Symphony Orchestra, 1962; film *Fantasia,* 1940, helped popularize the classics.
b. Apr 18, 1882 in London, England
d. Sep 13, 1977 in Nether Wallop, England
Source: *ASCAP 66; Baker 78, 84; BiDAmM; BioIn 15, 16, 17, 19, 21; BioNews 74; BlueB 76; BriBkM 80; CelR; ChhPo S2; ConAmC 76, 82; CurBio 41, 53, 77, 77N; DcArts; FacFETw; FilmEn; FilmgC; HalFC 80, 84, 88; IntWW 76, 77; IntWWM 77; LegTOT; MetOEnc; MusMk; MusSN; NewAmDM; NewEOp 71; NewGrDA 86; NewGrDM 80; NewYTBE 70; NewYTBS 77; OxCAmH; PenDiMP; PolBiDi; RadStar; REn; WebAB 74, 79; WhAm 7; Who 74; WhoAm 74, 78; WhoE 74; WhoHol A; WhoMus 72; WhoWor 74; WhScrn 83; WorAl; WorAlBi*

Stoll, George E
American. Composer
Film scores include *For Me and My Gal,* 1942; won Oscar for *Anchors Aweigh,* 1945.
b. May 7, 1905 in Minneapolis, Minnesota
d. Jan 18, 1985 in Monterey, California
Source: *CmpEPM; FilmEn; FilmgC; VarWW 85*

Stoltz, Rosine
[Victorine Noel]
French. Opera Singer
Paris Opera mezzo-soprano, 1830s-40s; noted for adventuresome life.
b. Feb 13, 1815 in Paris, France
d. Jul 28, 1903 in Paris, France
Source: *Baker 78, 84, 92; BioIn 3, 11; InWom; MetOEnc; NewEOp 71; NewGrDM 80; NewGrDO; OxDcOp; PenDiMP*

Stoltzman, Richard Leslie
American. Musician
Clarinet virtuoso, known for combining traditional, contemporary material from classical, jazz sources.
b. Jul 12, 1942 in Omaha, Nebraska
Source: *Baker 92; CurBio 86; IntWWM 77, 80, 90; WhoAm 80, 82, 84, 86, 88, 90, 92, 94, 95, 96, 97; WhoAmM 83; WhoEnt 92*

Stolypin, Piotr Arkadevich
Russian. Political Leader
Premier, minister of Interior for Czar Nicholas II, 1906-11.
b. Apr 14, 1862 in Baden, Russia
d. Sep 14, 1911 in Kiev, Russia
Source: *BioIn 10; McGEWB; NewCol 75*

Stolz, Robert
German. Composer
Wrote 2,000 songs, 50 operettas, music for films; won Oscars, 1941, 1944.
b. Aug 25, 1886 in Graz, Austria
d. Jun 27, 1975 in Berlin, Germany (West)
Source: *BiE&WWA; CurBio 43, 75, 75N; WhoMus 72; WhoWor 74; WhThe*

Stolz, Teresa
[Teresina Stolzova]
Bohemian. Opera Singer
Soprano; first Italian Aida, 1872; often sang Verdi roles.
b. Jun 2, 1834 in Elbe Kosteletz, Bohemia
d. Aug 23, 1902 in Milan, Italy
Source: *Baker 78, 84, 92; BioIn 15; CmOp; IntDcOp; InWom; MetOEnc; NewEOp 71; NewGrDM 80; NewGrDO; OxDcOp; PenDiMP*

Stommel, Henry Melson
American. Oceanographer, Meteorologist
Ocean current research led to development of means for determining absolute velocity of mean ocean currents from observations of the density alone.
b. Sep 27, 1920 in Wilmington, Delaware
Source: *AmMWSc 73P, 76P, 79, 82, 86, 89, 92; BioIn 14; IntWW 74; McGMS 80; WhAm 10; WhoAm 90; WhoFrS 84; WhoWor 74*

Stompanato, Johnny
American. Criminal
Killed by Lana Turner's daughter after argument; death judged justifiable homicide.
b. 1926
d. Apr 4, 1958 in Hollywood, California
Source: *EncACr*

Stone, Chuck
[Charles Sumner Stone]
American. Journalist
Special asst. to US congressman, Adam Clayton Powell, 1965-67; syndicated columnist, *Philadelphia Daily News,* 1973-91.
b. Jul 21, 1924 in Saint Louis, Missouri
Source: *BiDAmNC; BioIn 12; BlkAWP; BlkWr 2; BlkWrNE; ConAu 77; ConBlB 9; DcTwCCu 5; InB&W 80, 85; LivgBAA; WhoAfA 96; WhoBlA 90, 92, 94; WhoE 74*

Stone, Dick
[Richard Bernard Stone]
American. Politician
Senator from FL, 1975-81; ambassador to Central America, 1980-84.
b. Sep 22, 1928 in New York, New York
Source: *BiDrUSC 89; CngDr 77, 79; NewYTBS 80, 83; Who 74; WhoAm 78, 80; WhoAmJ 80; WhoAmP 73, 75, 77, 79, 81, 83, 85, 87, 89, 91, 93, 95; WhoGov 72, 75, 77; WhoSSW 78, 80; WhoWor 80, 82*

Stone, Dorothy
American. Actor, Dancer
Daughter of Fred Stone; dance partner with husband, Charles Collins, in *The Gay Divorcee,* 1933, 1941; *The Red Mill,* 1945.
b. Jun 3, 1905 in New York, New York
d. Sep 24, 1974 in Montecito, California
Source: *BiDD; BiE&WWA; NotNAT B; WhoHol B; WhoMus 72; WhScrn 77, 83; WhThe*

Stone, Doug
[Doug Brooks]
American. Singer, Songwriter
Country music singer; released debut album *Doug Stone,* 1990, which became platinum record; also recorded *I Thought It Was You,* 1992 and *From the Heart,* 1992.
b. Jun 19, 1956 in Atlanta, Georgia
Source: *BgBkCoM; ConMus 10; LegTOT*

Stone, Edward C, Jr.
American. Physicist, Educator
Project Scientist for Voyager Project, 1972—; Director, Jet Propulsion Laboratory, 1991—.
b. Jan 23, 1936 in Knoxville, Iowa
Source: *AmMWSc 73P, 92; BioIn 11, 12, 16; CurBio 90; WhoAm 90; WhoTech 89; WhoWest 92*

Stone, Edward Durell
American. Architect
Designed JFK Center, Washington, DC; New York Cultural Center; US Embassy in New Delhi.
b. Mar 9, 1902 in Fayetteville, Arkansas
d. Aug 6, 1978 in New York, New York
Source: *AmArch 70; BiE&WWA; BioIn 4, 5, 6, 7, 9, 11, 14; BlueB 76; BriEAA; CelR; ConArch 80, 87, 94; DcAmB S10; DcTwDes; EncAAr 1, 2; EncAB-A 33; EncMA; FacFETw; IntDcAr; IntWW 74, 75, 76, 77, 78; MacEA; NewYTBS 78; WebAB 74, 79; WhAm 7; WhoAm 74, 76, 78; WhoAmA 80N, 82N, 84N, 86N, 89N, 91N, 93N; WhoFI 74; WhoWor 74; WorAl; WorAlBi*

Stone, Ezra (Chaim)
American. Director, Producer
Best known as Henry Aldrich on radio show "The Aldrich Family;" director of numerous movies, plays, TV shows.
b. Dec 2, 1917 in New Bedford, Massachusetts
d. Mar 3, 1994 in Perth Amboy, New Jersey
Source: *AmAu&B; BiE&WWA; BioIn 19, 21; BlueB 76; ConTFT 1, 13; IntMPA 82, 92, 94; LesBEnT 92; NotNAT; WhAm 11; WhoAm 74, 76, 78, 80, 82, 84, 86, 88, 90, 92, 94; WhoE 89; WhoEnt 92; WhoHol 92, A*

Stone, Fred Andrew
American. Actor
Scarecrow in original Broadway version of *The Wizard of Oz,* 1903.
b. Aug 19, 1873 in Valmont, Colorado
d. Mar 6, 1959 in North Hollywood, California
Source: *BioIn 3, 5; EncMT; Film 1, 2; FilmEn; NotNAT A, B; PlP&P; TwYS; Vers A; WhAm 3; WhoHol B; WhScrn 74, 77; WhThe*

Stone, George Robert
American. Baseball Player
Outfielder, 1903, 1905-10, mostly with St. Louis; led AL in batting, 1906; had .301 lifetime batting average.
b. Sep 7, 1877 in Lost Nation, Iowa
d. Jan 3, 1945 in Clinton, Iowa
Source: *BioIn 4; WhoProB 73*

Stone, Grace Zaring
American. Author
Wrote *The Heaven and Earth of Dona Elena,* 1929.
b. Jan 9, 1891 in New York, New York
d. Sep 29, 1991 in Stonington, Connecticut
Source: *AnObit 1991; BioIn 17, 18; ConAu 135, P-2; ConLC 70*

Stone, Harlan Fiske
American. Supreme Court Justice
Associate justice, 1925-41; chief justice, 1941-46.
b. Oct 11, 1872 in Chesterfield, New Hampshire
d. Apr 22, 1946 in Washington, District of Columbia
Source: *AmDec 1920; AmJust; AmPolLe; ApCAB X; BiDFedJ; BiDrUSE 71, 89; BioIn 1, 2, 3, 4, 5, 7, 8, 9, 10, 11, 15; CopCroC; CurBio 41, 46; DcAmB S4; EncAB-H 1974, 1996; FacFETw; LegTOT; McGEWB; NatCAB 34; OxCAmH; OxCLaw; OxCSupC; PolProf T; RComAH; SupCtJu; WebAB 74, 79; WhAm 2; WorAl; WorAlBi*

Stone, Harold J
American. Actor
Starred in TV series "The Goldbergs," 1952; "My World and Welcome to It," 1969-72; "Bridget Loves Bernie," 1972-73.
b. 1911
Source: *FilmgC; HalFC 88; WhoHol A*

Stone, I(sidor) F(einstein)
"Godfather of New Left Journalism"
American. Journalist, Author, Pamphleteer
Edited newsletter *I F Stone's Bi-Weekly,* 1953-71; wrote *Underground to Palestine,* 1946; *The Trial of Socrates,* 1988.
b. Dec 24, 1907 in Philadelphia, Pennsylvania
d. Jun 18, 1989 in Boston, Massachusetts
Source: *ABCMeAm; AmPeW; AmSocL; BiDAmJo; BioIn 8, 9, 10, 11, 12, 13, 14, 15, 16, 17, 18, 19, 20; CelR; ConAu 40NR, 61; CurBio 72; EncAB-H 1996; EncAJ; EncTwCJ; EncWB; JrnUS; NewYTBS 78; PolProf E, J, K; WebAB 74, 79; WhE&EA; WhoAm 74, 76, 78, 80, 82, 84, 86, 88; WhoWor 74; WorAl; WorAu 1970; WrDr 80*

Stone, Irving
American. Author
Noted for biographical novels: *Lust for Life; The Agony and the Ecstasy; The Origin.*
b. Jul 14, 1903 in San Francisco, California
d. Aug 26, 1989 in Los Angeles, California
Source: *AmAu&B; AmNov; AnObit 1989; Au&Wr 71; AuNews 1; Benet 87, 96; BenetAL 91; BioIn 2, 4, 5, 6, 7, 8, 9, 10, 12, 14, 15, 16, 17; BlueB 76; CelR; CmCal; ConAu 1NR, 1R, 3AS, 23NR, 129; ConLC 7; ConNov 72, 76, 82, 86; ConPopW; CurBio 67, 89, 89N; CyWA 89; DrAS 74E, 78E, 82E; FacFETw; HalFC 84, 88; IntAu&W 76, 77, 89, 91; IntWW 74, 75, 76, 77, 78, 79, 80, 81, 82, 83, 89; LegTOT; LinLib L; LngCTC; MajTwCW; News 90, 90-2; NewYTBS 80, 89; Novels; OxCAmL 83, 95; PenC AM; RAdv 14; REn; REnAL; SmATA 3, 64; TwCA, SUP; TwCRHW 90, 94; TwCWr; WhAm 10; WhE&EA; WhNAA; WhoAm 74, 76, 78, 80, 82, 84, 86, 88; WhoAmJ 80; WhoWor 74, 78; WhoWorJ 72, 78; WorAl; WorAlBi; WrDr 76, 80, 82, 84, 86, 88, 90*

Stone, John Richard Nicholas, Sir
English. Economist, Educator
Won 1984 Nobel Prize in economics.
b. Aug 30, 1913 in London, England
Source: *IntWW 89; NewYTBS 84; Who 74, 85, 92; WhoEc 81, 86; WhoNob, 90, 95*

Stone, Lewis
American. Actor
Was Judge Hardy in Andy Hardy film series.
b. Nov 15, 1879 in Worcester, Massachusetts
d. Sep 11, 1953 in Los Angeles, California
Source: *BioIn 3, 7, 17, 21; EncAFC; Film 1, 2; FilmEn; FilmgC; ForYSC; HalFC 80, 84, 88; HolCA; IntDcF 1-3; LegTOT; MGM; MotPP; MovMk; NotNAT B; OlFamFa; TwYS; Vers B; WhAm 3; WhoHol B; WhoHrs 80; WhScrn 74, 77; WorAl*

Stone, Louis
American. Businessman, Publisher
Founder, *Louis Stone Monthly Investment Letter,* 1953-85.
b. 1910 in New York, New York
d. Mar 16, 1985 in New York, New York
Source: *ConAu 115*

Stone, Lucy
American. Feminist, Suffragist, Editor
Founded *Woman's Journal,* 1870; voice of Woman's Suffrage Assn. for 50 yrs.
b. Aug 13, 1818 in West Brookfield, Massachusetts
d. Oct 18, 1893 in Dorchester, Massachusetts
Source: *AmAu&B; AmBi; AmOrN; AmRef; AmSocL; AmWom; ApCAB; Benet 87, 96; BenetAL 91; BiDAmJo; BiD&SB; BioAmW; BioIn 3, 4, 6, 8, 9, 10, 11, 12, 13, 14, 15, 16, 18, 19, 21; ContDcW 89; DcAmB; DcAmSR; DcLB 79; Drake; EncWHA; FemiCLE; GoodHs; GrLiveH; HanAmWH; HarEnUS; HerW, 84; HisWorL; IntDcWB; InWom, SUP; LegTOT; LibW; McGEWB; NatCAB 2, 29; NotAW; OxCAmH; OxCAmL 65, 83, 95; PolPar; REn; TwCBDA; WebAB 74, 79; WhAm HS; WhAmP; WhCiWar; WomFir; WorAl; WorAlBi*

Stone, Marvin Lawrence
American. Journalist
Editor-in-chief, *US News & World Report,* mag., 1976-85.
b. Feb 26, 1924 in Burlington, Vermont
Source: *ConAu 69; WhoAm 74, 76, 78, 80, 82, 84, 86, 88, 90, 92, 94, 95, 96,*

97; WhoE 85, 86, 89; WhoSSW 76, 95, 97; WhoWorJ 72

Stone, Melville Elijah
American. Newspaper Publisher
Founded Chicago's first penny newspaper, *Daily News,* 1875; general manager, AP in IL and later in NY, 1893-1921.
b. Aug 22, 1848 in Hudson, Illinois
d. Feb 15, 1929 in New York, New York
Source: *AmAu&B; AmBi; ApCAB, X; BiDAmJo; BioIn 7, 9; ChhPo S1; DcAmB; DcNAA; EncAB-H 1974, 1996; JrnUS; LinLib L, S; NatCAB 1, 21; REnAL; WebAB 74, 79; WhAm 1*

Stone, Michael Patrick William
American. Government Official
Secretary of the Army, 1989-1993; presided over Army's response to the Iraqi invasion of Kuwait in 1990.
d. May 18, 1995 in San Francisco, California

Stone, Milburn
American. Actor
Played Doc Adams on "Gunsmoke," 1955-75; won Emmy, 1968.
b. Jul 5, 1904 in Burton, Kansas
d. Jun 12, 1980 in La Jolla, California
Source: *AnObit 1980; BioIn 4, 5, 12; EncAFC; FilmEn; FilmgC; ForYSC; HalFC 80, 84, 88; HolCA; LegTOT; MotPP; WhoHol A; WhoHrs 80; WhScrn 83*

Stone, Oliver
American. Screenwriter, Director
Won best picture, best director Oscars for *Platoon,* 1986; best director Oscar for *Born on the Fourth of July,*. 1990; also made *JFK,* 1991.
b. Sep 15, 1946 in New York, New York
Source: *Au&Arts 15; BiDFilm 94; BioIn 12, 16; CelR 90; ConAu 110; ConLC 73; ConTFT 1, 6, 13; CurBio 87; DcTwCCu 1; GangFlm; HalFC 88; IntDcF 2-2; IntMPA 86, 88, 92, 94, 96; IntWW 89, 91, 93; LegTOT; MiSFD 9; News 90; NewYTBS 81, 84; WhoAm 82, 84, 86, 88, 90, 92, 94; WhoEnt 92; WhoHol 92; WhoWor 80; WorAlBi*

Stone, Paula
American. Producer
Starred with family as *The Stepping Stones* in vaudeville.
b. Jan 20, 1916 in New York, New York
Source: *BiE&WWA; BioIn 3; ForYSC; NotNAT; WhoHol A; WhoThe 77A; WhThe*

Stone, Peter H
American. Screenwriter
Won Oscar for *Father Goose,* 1964; won Tonys for *1776,* 1969; *Woman of the Year,* 1980; *Titanic,* 1997.
b. Feb 27, 1930 in Los Angeles, California
Source: *ConAu 7NR; ConDr 82D; ConTFT 6; HalFC 84, 88; IntAu&W 91; IntMPA 86; NotNAT; SmATA 65; VarWW 85; WhoAm 86, 90; WhoE 89; WhoEnt 92*

Stone, Robert Anthony
American. Author
Wrote *A Hall of Mirrors,* 1967; *Children of Light,* 1986.
b. Aug 21, 1937 in New York, New York
Source: *AmAu&B; BioIn 13; ConAu 85; ConLC 23; ConNov 86; CurBio 86; OxCAmL 83; WhoAm 86, 90, 97; WhoUSWr 88; WhoWrEP 89*

Stone, Sharon
American. Actor
Films include *Basic Instinct,* 1992; *Casino,* 1995.
b. Mar 10, 1958 in Meadville, Pennsylvania
Source: *ConTFT 7, 14; CurBio 96; IntMPA 94, 96; LegTOT; News 93; WhoAm 94, 95, 96, 97; WhoAmW 93, 95, 97*

Stone, Sidney
American. TV Personality
Commercial announcer for Milton Berle's TV series, 1948-51; coined phrase, "Tell ya what I'm gonna do!"
b. 1903?
d. Feb 12, 1986 in New York, New York
Source: *LesBEnT*

Stone, Sly
[Sly and the Family Stone; Sylvester Stewart]
American. Singer, Musician
Led rock/blues group, 1970s; hits include "If You Want Me to Stay," 1973.
b. Mar 15, 1944 in Dallas, Texas
Source: *BiDAmM; BioIn 10, 12, 16; ConMus 8; DrBlPA, 90; InB&W 80, 85; NewAmDM; NewGrDA 86; WhoBlA 80; WhoRocM 82; WorAl; WorAlBi*

Stone, Thomas
American. Lawyer, Continental Congressman
Signed Declaration of Independence, 1776; moderate patriot; rarely spoke in Congress.
b. 1743 in Charles County, Maryland
d. Oct 5, 1787 in Alexandria, Virginia
Source: *AmBi; ApCAB; BiAUS; BiDrAC; BiDrUSC 89; BioIn 7, 8, 9; DcAmB; Drake; EncAR; EncCRAm; HarEnUS; NatCAB 8; TwCBDA; WhAm HS; WhAmP; WhAmRev*

Stone, W. Clement
American. Businessman, Philanthropist
Founder, CEO, chm. of board, worldwide Combined Insurance Co. of America, 1939-81; exponent of Positive Mental Attitude; editor, publisher, *Success: The Magazine of Achievers.*
b. May 4, 1902 in Chicago, Illinois
Source: *Au&Wr 71; CurBio 72; Dun&B 90; St&PR 91; WhoAm 86, 90; WhoAmP 85, 89; WhoIns 92; WhoMW 90*

Stoneham, Horace
American. Baseball Executive
Principal owner, pres., NY/San Francisco Giants, 1936-76; known for moving team to San Francisco following 1957 season.
b. Jul 10, 1903 in Jersey City, New Jersey
d. Jan 7, 1990 in Scottsdale, Arizona
Source: *AnObit 1990; BiDAmSp BB; BioIn 7, 15, 16; FacFETw; NewYTBS 90*

Stoneman, George
American. Military Leader, Politician
Union general; commanded troops that brought on Battle of Williamsburg, 1862; part of Atlanta campaign, 1864; Dem. governor of CA, 1883-87.
b. Aug 8, 1822 in Busti, New York
d. Sep 5, 1894 in Buffalo, New York
Source: *AmBi; ApCAB; BiDrGov 1789; BioIn 1, 7, 11; CivWDc; CmCal; DcAmB; Drake; HarEnUS; NatCAB 4; TwCBDA; WebAMB; WhAm HS; WhCiWar*

Stones, Dwight
American. Track Athlete
High jumper; won bronze medal, 1972, 1976 Olympics; set world record 10 times.
b. Dec 6, 1953 in Los Angeles, California
Source: *BioIn 10, 11, 12, 14, 21; NewYTBS 75, 79, 84; WhoTr&F 73; WorAl; WorAlBi*

Stonesifer, Patty
American. Computer Executive
Vice president, consumer division, Microsoft Corp, 1994-96.
b. 1956 in Indiana
Source: *News 97-1*

Stoney, George Johnstone
English. Physicist
Coined the word "electron."
b. Feb 15, 1826 in Oakley Park, Ireland
d. Jul 5, 1911 in London, England
Source: *AsBiEn; BiESc; BioIn 14; CamDcSc; DcNaB S2; DcScB; InSci; LarDcSc*

Stoodard, George Dinsmore
American. University Administrator
President, U of IL, 1946-53; wrote *The Meaning of Intelligence,* 1943.
b. Oct 8, 1897 in Carbondale, Pennsylvania
d. Dec 28, 1981 in New York, New York
Source: *AmAu&B; AmMWSc 73S; BiDAmEd; ConAu 106; CurBio 46, 82; WhoAm 80, 82; WhoWor 80*

Stookey, Paul
[Peter, Paul, and Mary; Noel Paul Stockey]
American. Singer, Songwriter
Member, folk-singing group, Peter, Paul and Mary, 1961-1971; 1978—; wrote, recorded The "Wedding Song (There Is Love,)" 1971.
b. Dec 30, 1937 in Baltimore, Maryland
Source: *ASCAP 66; BioIn 12, 14, 21; EncFCWM 69; LegTOT; WhoAm 84, 86, 90; WhoEnt 92; WorAlBi*

Stoopnagle, Lemuel Q, Colonel
[Stoopnagle and Budd; F Chase Taylor]
American. Actor
Part of radio team, 1930-37, famous for nonsense words, silly inventions.
b. Oct 4, 1897 in Buffalo, New York
d. May 29, 1950 in Boston, Massachusetts
Source: *CurBio 47, 50; JoeFr; WhScrn 77*

Stopes, Marie Charlotte Carmichael
English. Scientist
Cofounded first birth control clinic in Britain, 1921; candid books on marriage were forerunners of today's books on sex: *Married Love,* 1918.
b. Oct 15, 1880 in Edinburgh, Scotland
d. Oct 2, 1958 in Dorking, England
Source: *BiDBrF 1; BioIn 14, 16, 17, 20; ChhPo S2; ConAu 115; DcNaB 1951; GrBr; HumSex; InWom SUP; LngCTC; NewCol 75; OxCEng 85, 95; OxCMed 86; WebBD 83; WhoLA; WomFir; WomNov*

Stoppard, Tom
[Tomas Straussler]
English. Author
Award-winning dramatist: *Rosencrantz and Guildenstern Are Dead,* 1967; *The Real Thing,* 1984; *Arcadia,* 1995.
b. Jul 3, 1937 in Zlin, Czechoslovakia
Source: *Au&Wr 71; Benet 87, 96; BioIn 8, 9, 10, 11, 12, 13; BlmGEL; BlueB 76; BritWr S1; CamGEL; CamGLE; CamGWoT; CelR 90; CnDBLB 8; CnThe; ConAu 39NR, 81; ConBrDr; ConDr 73, 77, 82, 88, 93; ConLC 1, 3, 4, 5, 8, 15, 29, 34, 63, 91; ConTFT 1, 4, 12; CroCD; CrtSuDr; CurBio 74; CyWA 89; DcArts; DcLB 13, Y85A; DcLEL 1940; DramC 6; EncWB; EncWL, 2, 3; EncWT; Ent; FacFETw; GrWrEL DR; HalFC 88; IntAu&W 76, 89, 91, 93; IntDcT 2; IntMPA 92, 94, 96; IntWW 74, 75, 76, 77, 78, 79, 80, 81, 82, 83, 89, 91, 93; LegTOT; MagSWL; MajMD 1; MajTwCW; MakMC; McGEWD 72, 84; MiSFD 9; ModBrL S1, S2; ModWD; News 95; NewYTBE 72; NewYTBS 74, 84; NotNAT; OxCAmT 84; OxCEng 85, 95; OxCThe 83; PlP&P A; RAdv 14, 13-2; RfGEnL 91; RGTwCWr; WebE&AL; Who 74, 82, 83, 85, 88, 90, 92, 94; WhoAm 80, 82, 84, 86, 88, 90, 92, 94, 95, 96, 97; WhoEnt 92; WhoThe 72, 77, 81; WhoTwCL; WhoWor 82, 84, 87, 89, 91, 93, 95, 96, 97; WorAl; WorAlBi; WorAu 1970; WorLitC; WrDr 76, 80, 82, 84, 86, 88, 90, 92, 94, 96*

Storch, Larry
American. Actor, Comedian
Starred on TV series "F Troop," 1965-67.
b. Jan 8, 1923 in New York, New York
Source: *BiE&WWA; BioIn 3; ConTFT 6; ForYSC; HalFC 80, 84, 88; IntMPA 96; LegTOT; MotPP; NotNAT; WhoCom; WhoHol 92, A*

Storey, David Malcolm
English. Author, Dramatist
Wrote *This Sporting Life,* 1960, filmed, 1963.
b. Jul 13, 1933 in Wakefield, England
Source: *CnThe; ConAu 81; ConDr 73, 77; ConNov 76; CurBio 73; DcLEL 1940; EncWT; IntAu&W 91; IntMPA 81; IntWW 91; McGEWD 84; ModBrL S1; NotNAT; OxCEng 85; TwCWr; Who 92; WhoThe 81; WhoWor 91*

Storm, Gale
[Josephine Cottle]
American. Actor
Starred in "My Little Margie," 1952-55; "The Gale Storm Show," 1956-62.
b. Apr 5, 1922 in Bloomington, Texas
Source: *BiDAmM; BioIn 3, 4, 10, 12, 18; FilmEn; FilmgC; ForYSC; HalFC 80, 84, 88; HolP 40; IntMPA 75, 76, 77, 78, 79, 80, 81, 82, 84, 86, 88, 92, 94, 96; InWom, SUP; LegTOT; MotPP; MovMk; PenEncP; RadStar; RkOn 74; SweetSg D; WhoAmW 58; WhoHol 92, A; WhoRock 81; WorAl; WorAlBi*

Stormer, Fredrik (Carl Mulertz)
Norwegian. Physicist, Mathematician
Created mathematical theory of auroral phenomena.
b. Sep 3, 1874 in Skien, Norway
d. Aug 13, 1957 in Oslo, Norway
Source: *BioIn 2, 4, 5, 20; DcScB; InSci; NotTwCS*

Storr, (Charles) Anthony
English. Psychiatrist
Wrote *Human Aggression,* 1968; *The Art of Psychotherapy,* 1979.
b. May 18, 1920 in Bentley, England
Source: *ConAu 17NR, 41NR, 97; CurBio 94; IntAu&W 89, 91, 93; IntWW 91, 93; Who 74, 82, 83, 85, 88, 90, 92, 94; WhoWor 95, 96, 97; WorAu 1985; WrDr 86, 88, 90, 92, 94, 96*

Story, Joseph
American. Supreme Court Justice
Associate justice, 1811-45; pioneer in organizing, directing teaching at Harvard Law School; wrote *Equity Jurisprudence,* 1836.
b. Sep 18, 1779 in Marblehead, Massachusetts
d. Sep 10, 1845 in Cambridge, Massachusetts
Source: *Alli; AmAu; AmAu&B; AmBi; AmJust; AmPolLe; ApCAB; BenetAL 91; BiAUS; BiDAmEd; BiD&SB; BiDFedJ; BiDrAC; BiDrUSC 89; BioIn 1, 2, 3, 5, 6, 8, 9, 11, 14, 15; CyAG; CyAL 2; DcAmAu; DcAmB; DcAmC; DcBiPP; DcEnL; DcNAA; Drake; EncAB-H 1974, 1996; HarEnUS; LinLib L, S; McGEWB; NatCAB 2; OxCAmH; OxCAmL 65, 83, 95; OxCLaw; OxCSupC; REnAL; SupCtJu; TwCBDA; WebAB 74, 79; WhAm HS; WhAmP; WorAl; WorAlBi*

Story, Liz
American. Pianist, Composer
First solo album *Solid Colors* released in 1983.
b. Oct 28, 1956 in San Diego, California
Source: *Baker 92; BioIn 16; ConMus 2; NewAgMG*

Story, William Wetmore
American. Sculptor, Author, Lawyer
Best known as neoclassic sculptor; wrote books on Italy: *Vallombrosa,* 1881.
b. Feb 12, 1819 in Salem, Massachusetts
d. Oct 7, 1895 in Vallombrosa, Italy
Source: *Alli, SUP; AmAu; AmAu&B; AmBi; ApCAB; BbD; BenetAL 91; BibAL 8; BiD&SB; BiDTran; BioIn 4, 5, 7, 8, 9, 10, 11; BriEAA; CasWL; Chambr 3; ChhPo, S1; CyAL 2; DcAmArt; DcAmAu; DcAmB; DcBiPP; DcEnL; DcLB 1; DcLEL; DcNAA; Drake; EvLB; HarEnUS; McGDA; NatCAB 5; NewYHSD; OxCAmH; OxCAmL 65, 83, 95; REnAL; TwCBDA; WhAmArt 85; WhAm HS*

Stoss, Veit
German. Sculptor
Master wood carver, active in Krakow, Nuremberg.
b. 1445 in Nuremberg, Germany
d. 1533 in Nuremberg, Germany
Source: *McGEWB; NewCol 75*

Stottlemyre, Mel(vin Leon)
American. Baseball Player
Pitcher, NY Yankees, 1964-74; had three 20-game winning seasons, 164 career wins.
b. Nov 13, 1941 in Hazelton, Missouri
Source: *Ballpl 90; BaseEn 88; BiDAmSp Sup; BioIn 14, 18; WhoAm 74; WhoProB 73*

Stotz, Charles Morse
American. Architect, Author
Pioneer in architectural restoration; wrote on PA architecture.
b. Aug 1, 1898 in Pittsburgh, Pennsylvania
d. Mar 5, 1985 in Fort Myers, Florida
Source: *AmArch 70; ConAu 115; WhoAm 74, 76*

Stouffer, Vernon B
American. Businessman, Restaurateur
Operated chain of restaurants, formed corp., 1929; introduced frozen dishes, 1954.
b. Aug 22, 1901 in Cleveland, Ohio
d. Jul 26, 1974 in Lakewood, Ohio

Source: *Entr; ObitOF 79; WhAm 6; WhoAm 74*

Stout, Juanita Kidd
American. Judge
First African-American woman elected judge in the US; Municipal Court of Philadelphia, 1959.
b. Mar 7, 1919 in Wewoka, Oklahoma
Source: *AmBench 79; BioIn 6, 7, 16; BlkWAm; Ebony 1; InWom; NegAl 89; NotBlAW 1; WhoAfA 96; WhoAm 76, 78, 96, 97; WhoAmL 79, 83; WhoAmP 91; WhoAmW 61, 64, 66, 68, 72, 74, 75, 85, 87, 89, 91, 93, 95, 97; WhoBlA 75, 77, 80, 85, 88, 90, 92, 94; WhoE 74, 75, 91; WomPO 78*

Stout, Rex Todhunter
American. Author
Founded Vanguard Press, 1926; created detective Nero Wolfe, 1934.
b. Dec 1, 1886 in Noblesville, Indiana
d. Oct 27, 1975 in Danbury, Connecticut
Source: *AmAu&B; AuNews 2; CasWL; ConAu 61; ConLC 3; ConNov 76; CorpD; CurBio 46; EncMys; EvLB; IndAu 1917; LngCTC; PenC AM; REn; TwCA SUP; WhAm 6; WhoAm 74, 76*

Stout, William Bushnell
American. Engineer, Inventor
Built first commercial monoplane, 1919; gasoline driven passenger rail car, 1933.
b. Mar 16, 1880 in Quincy, Illinois
d. Mar 20, 1956
Source: *BioIn 2, 3, 4, 9, 19; CurBio 57; FacFETw; InSci; WhAm 3*

Stoutenburg, Adrien Pearl
[Lace Kendall]
American. Children's Author
Books include *Fee, Fi, Fo, Fum: Friendly & Funny Giants,* 1969; *A Cat Is,* 1971.
b. Dec 1, 1916 in Dafur, Minnesota
Source: *AmAu&B; Au&Wr 71; AuBYP 2, 3; ConAu 5R; ConPo 75; DrAP 75; MinnWr; PenNWW A, B; SmATA 3; ThrBJA; WhoAm 82; WhoWest 74; WrDr 86*

Stove, Betty
Dutch. Tennis Player
One of best doubles players; currently coaches Hana Mandlikova.
b. Jun 24, 1945 in Rotterdam, Netherlands
Source: *BuCMET; InWom SUP; OfEnT; WhoIntT*

Stover, Russell
American. Candy Manufacturer
Perfected Eskimo Pie, 1921; pres., Russell Stover Candies, 1925-43.
b. May 6, 1888 in Alton, Kansas
d. May 11, 1954 in Miami Beach, Florida
Source: *BioIn 3, 4, 6; Entr; NatCAB 43*

Stow, (Julian) Randolph
Australian. Author
Novels on Australia include *Tourmaline,* 1963.
b. Nov 28, 1935 in Geraldton, Australia
Source: *AuLitCr; Benet 87, 96; BioIn 6, 9, 10, 17; BlueB 76; CamGLE; CasWL; ConAu 13R, 33NR; ConLC 23, 48; ConNov 72, 76, 82, 86, 91, 96; ConPo 70, 75, 80, 85; CyWA 89; DcChlFi; DcLEL 1940; EncSF 93; GrWrEL N; IntAu&W 76, 77, 82, 89, 91, 93; IntLitE; IntWWP 77; LiExTwC; MajTwCW; ModCmwL; NewC; OxCAusL; OxCTwCP; PenC ENG; RAdv 14, 13-1; RfGEnL 91; RGTwCWr; ScF&FL 1, 2, 92; ScFSB; TwCWr; WebE&AL; Who 74, 82, 83, 85, 90, 92, 94; WorAu 1950; WrDr 76, 80, 82, 84, 86, 88, 90, 92, 94, 96*

Stowe, Harriet (Elizabeth) Beecher
American. Author
Wrote *Uncle Tom's Cabin,* 1852.
b. Jun 14, 1811 in Litchfield, Connecticut
d. Jul 1, 1896 in Hartford, Connecticut
Source: *Alli, SUP; AmAu; AmAu&B; AmBi; AmRef; AmSocL; AmWomWr; AtlBL; BbD; BiD&SB; CarSB; CasWL; Chambr 3; CyWA 58; DcAmB; DcAmReB 1, 2; EncAAH; EncAB-H 1974, 1996; HarEnUS; InWom, SUP; LibW; LinLib S; MajAI; McGEWB; NatCAB 1; NotAW; OxCAmL 95; OxCEng 85, 95; PenC AM; RAdv 1; REn; RfGAmL 94; TwCBDA; WebAB 74, 79; WhAm HS; WhAmP*

Stowe, Leland
American. Journalist
Foreign correspondent, *NY Herald Tribune,* 1926-39; won Pulitzer, 1930; war correspondent, *Chicago Daily News,* 1939-43.
b. Nov 10, 1899 in Southbury, Connecticut
d. Jan 16, 1994 in Ann Arbor, Michigan
Source: *AmAu&B; BiDAmJo; BioIn 1, 3, 4, 16, 17, 19, 20; BlueB 76; ConAu 53NR, 77, 143; CurBio 40, 94N; DcLB 29; EncAJ; EncTwCJ; IntAu&W 77, 89, 91; IntWW 74, 75, 76, 77, 78, 79, 80, 81, 82, 83, 89, 91, 93; JrnUS; LinLib L; NewYTBS 94; REnAL; SmATA 60, 78; TwCA SUP; WhoAm 74, 76, 78, 80, 82, 84, 86, 88, 90, 92, 94, 95, 96, 97; WhoWor 74*

Stowe, Madeleine
American. Actor
Appeared in *The Last of the Mohicans.*
b. Aug 18, 1958 in Los Angeles, California
Source: *ConTFT 12; IntMPA 94, 96; LegTOT; WhoAm 95, 96, 97; WhoAmW 95, 97; WhoHisp 94; WhoHol 92*

Strabo
Greek. Geographer, Historian
Wrote *Historical Sketches; Geographical Sketches* describing earth as a globe.
b. 63?BC in Amasia, Pontus
d. 22AD
Source: *AsBiEn; BbD; BiD&SB; BiESc; BioIn 18, 20; CasWL; DcScB; Grk&L; InSci; OxCEng 67, 85, 95; OxDcByz; PenC CL; REn; WhWE; WorAl; WorAlBi*

Stracciari, Riccardo
Italian. Opera Singer
Baritone who sang *Figaro* over 90 times.
b. Jun 26, 1875 in Casalecchio, Italy
d. Oct 10, 1955 in Rome, Italy
Source: *Baker 84, 92; BioIn 4, 10, 12; CmOp; IntDcOp; MetOEnc; NewEOp 71; NewGrDM 80; NewGrDO; OxDcOp*

Strachey, (Giles) Lytton
English. Biographer, Historian
Revolutionized art of biography with humanized criticism; most famous work: *Queen Victoria,* 1921.
b. Mar 1, 1880 in London, England
d. Jan 21, 1932 in Hungerford, England
Source: *AtlBL; Benet 87, 96; BiDMoPL; BioIn 1, 2, 3, 4, 5, 8, 9, 10, 12, 13, 14, 15, 19, 20, 21; BlmGEL; BritWr S2; CamGEL; CamGLE; CasWL; Chambr 3; CnMWL; ConAu 110; CyWA 58; DcArts; DcLB 149, DS10; DcLEL; DcNaB 1931; EncWL, 2, 3; EvLB; FacFETw; GayLesB; GrBr; LegTOT; LinLib L, S; LngCEL; LngCTC; MakMC; ModBrL; NewC; NewCBEL; OxCEng 67, 85, 95; PenC ENG; RAdv 13-3; REn; TwCA, SUP; TwCLC 12; TwCWr; WebE&AL; WhDW; WhE&EA; WhLit; WhoLA; WhoTwCL; WorAl; WorAlBi*

Stradella, Alessandro
Italian. Composer
Adventuresome life subject of 19th-c. operas, books; wrote opera *Il Corispeo.*
b. Oct 1, 1642 in Naples, Italy
d. Feb 28, 1682 in Genoa, Italy
Source: *Baker 84; BioIn 3, 4; CmOp; MusMk; NewEOp 71; OxCMus*

Stradivari, Antonio
[Antonius Stradivarius]
Italian. Violin Maker
Workmanship perfected violin; earliest known, 1666.
b. 1644 in Cremona, Italy
d. Dec 17, 1737 in Cremona, Italy
Source: *Baker 78, 84, 92; BioIn 1, 2, 3, 6, 10, 15; BriBkM 80; DcArts; DcCathB; Dis&D; LegTOT; LinLib S; MusMk; NewAmDM; NewCol 75; NewGrDM 80; NewOxM; OxCMus; WebBD 83*

Straight, Beatrice Whitney
American. Actor
Won Tony, 1953, for performance in *The Crucible;* Oscar, 1976, for *Network.*
b. Aug 2, 1918 in Long Island, New York
Source: *BiE&WWA; ConTFT 7; ForWC 70; HalFC 88; IntMPA 92; InWom SUP; NotNAT; VarWW 85; WhoAm 78, 80, 82, 84, 86, 88, 90, 92, 94, 95, 96; WhoAmW 85; WhoE 89, 91, 93, 95; WhoEnt 92;*

WhoHol A; WhoThe 81; WhoWor 91; WorAlBi

Strait, George
American. Singer
Country singer; CMA entertainer of year, 1989, 1990; album *Does Fort Worth Ever Cross Your Mind* was CMA album of year, 1985.
b. May 10, 1952 in Pearsall, Texas
Source: *BgBkCoM; CelR 90; ConMus 5; HarEnCM 87; LegTOT; PenEncP; WhoAm 88, 90, 92, 94, 95, 96, 97; WhoEnt 92; WhoNeCM*

Strakosch, Maurice
Czech. Impresario
Presented first season of Italian Opera, NYC, 1850s.
b. Jan 15, 1825 in Butschowitz, Moravia
d. Oct 9, 1887 in Paris, France
Source: *ApCAB; Baker 78, 84, 92; MetOEnc; NewEOp 71; NewGrDA 86; NewGrDO; WhAm HS*

Strand, Mark
American. Poet
Publications include *Reasons for Moving,* 1968; won Edgar Award for *The Story of Our Lives,* 1974; published collection of poems *The Continuous Life,* 1990.
b. Apr 11, 1934 in Summerside, Prince Edward Island, Canada
Source: *AmAu&B; Benet 87, 96; BenetAL 91; BioIn 9, 10, 11, 12, 13, 15, 17, 20; ChhPo S2; ConAu 21R, 40NR; ConLC 6, 8, 18, 41, 71; ConPo 70, 75, 80, 85, 91, 96; CroCAP; DcLB 5; DcLEL 1940; DrAP 75; DrAPF 80, 91; DrAS 82E; EncWL 3; Focus; IntAu&W 86; IntWWP 77; LegTOT; LinLib L; ModAL S2; ODwPR 91; OxCAmL 83, 95; OxCTwCP; RAdv 1, 14, 13-1; SmATA 41; WhoAm 76, 78, 80, 82, 84, 86, 88, 90, 92, 94, 95, 96, 97; WhoE 74; WhoUSWr 88; WhoWest 94; WhoWrEP 89, 92, 95; WorAu 1970; WrDr 76, 80, 82, 84, 86, 88, 90, 92, 94, 96*

Strand, Paul
American. Photographer, Filmmaker
First to use ''candid camera'' trick; produced film documentaries.
b. Oct 16, 1890 in New York, New York
d. Mar 31, 1976 in Yvelines, France
Source: *Benet 87, 96; BioIn 6, 7, 8, 9, 10, 11, 12, 13, 16, 17, 18, 20; BriEAA; ConAu 65; ConPhot 82, 88; CurBio 65, 76N; DcAmArt; DcAmB S10; DcArts; DcFM; DcTwDes; EncAJ; FacFETw; FilmEn; ICPEnP; LegTOT; MacBEP; NewYTBS 76; OxCFilm; WebAB 74, 79; WhAm 7; WhAmArt 85; WhoAm 74, 76; WhoWor 74; WorEFlm*

Strange, Curtis
American. Golfer
Turned pro, 1976; leading money winner on tour, 1985; won US Open, 1988, 1989.
b. Jan 30, 1955 in Norfolk, Virginia
Source: *BioIn 16; IntWW 91; LegTOT; News 88; NewYTBS 90; WhoAm 90; WhoE 86; WhoEmL 87; WhoFI 87; WhoIntG; WhoWor 89; WorAlBi*

Strasberg, Lee
[Israel Strassberg]
American. Actor, Acting Teacher
Directed Actor's Studio, 1950-82; taught Stanislavsky acting method, also known as ''method acting.''
b. Nov 17, 1901 in Budzanow, Austria
d. Feb 17, 1982 in New York, New York
Source: *AnObit 1982; BiDFilm 94; BiE&WWA; BioIn 5, 6, 10, 11, 12, 13, 14, 20; BlueB 76; CamGWoT; CelR; CnThe; ConAu 13R, 29NR, 106; CurBio 60, 82, 82N; EncWB; EncWT; Ent; FacFETw; FilmEn; FilmgC; HalFC 80, 84; IntDcT 3; IntMPA 81, 82; IntWW 74, 75, 76, 77, 78, 79, 80, 81; LegTOT; NewYTBS 75, 82; NotNAT; OxCAmT 84; OxCThe 83; PlP&P; TheaDir; WhAm 8; WhoAm 74, 76, 78, 80; WhoE 77, 79, 81; WhoHol A; WhoThe 72, 77, 81; WhoWor 74; WorAl; WorAlBi*

Strasberg, Susan Elizabeth
American. Actor, Author
Created lead role on stage in *Diary of Anne Frank,* 1955.
b. May 22, 1938 in New York, New York
Source: *BiE&WWA; ConAu 120; CurBio 58; FilmgC; HalFC 88; IntMPA 92; InWom, SUP; MotPP; MovMk; NewYTBS 80; NotNAT; WhoAm 86, 90; WhoEnt 92; WhoHol A; WorAlBi*

Strasburger, Eduard Adolf
German. Biologist
Plant cytologist who explained nuclear division in plants.
b. Feb 1, 1844 in Warsaw, Poland
d. May 18, 1912 in Bonn, Germany
Source: *AsBiEn; BiESc; BioIn 2; CamDcSc; DcScB; LarDcSc*

Strasfogel, Ignace
Polish. Conductor
Associate conductor, Metropolitan Opera Assn., 1951-1974.
b. Jul 17, 1909 in Warsaw, Poland
d. Feb 6, 1994 in New York, New York
Source: *BioIn 10, 19; BlueB 76; WhAm 11; WhoAm 74, 76, 78, 80, 82, 84, 86, 88, 90, 92, 94; WhoEnt 92; WhoMus 72; WhoOp 76; WhoWor 74, 76; WhoWorJ 72, 78*

Strassman, Marcia
American. Actor
Played Julie Kotter in TV series ''Welcome Back, Kotter,'' 1975-79.
b. Apr 28, 1948 in New York, New York
Source: *BioIn 11, 13; ConTFT 7; LegTOT; VarWW 85; WhoHol 92*

Strassmann, Fritz
German. Chemist
Opened field of atomic energy when he found neutron-induced nuclear fissure in uranium.
b. Feb 22, 1902 in Boppard, Germany
d. Apr 22, 1980 in Mainz, Germany
Source: *BiESc; BioIn 12, 20; McGMS 80; NotTwCS; WhoWor 74, 76, 78*

Stratas, Teresa
[Anastasia Strataki]
Canadian. Opera Singer
Soprano; NY Met., since late 1950s; won three Grammys, one Tony.
b. May 26, 1939 in Toronto, Ontario, Canada
Source: *Baker 84; BioIn 16; CanWW 89; CreCan 2; FacFETw; IntWW 91; IntWWM 90; NewAmDM; NewYTBS 90; PenDiMP; WhoAm 74, 76, 78, 80, 86, 90; WhoAmW 66, 68, 70, 72, 74, 75; WhoHol 92; WhoMus 72; WhoWor 84, 91*

Stratemeyer, Edward L
American. Children's Author
Syndicate produced *The Rover Boys, Hardy Boys, Bobbsey Twins, Nancy Drew,* etc.
b. Oct 4, 1862 in Elizabeth, New Jersey
d. May 10, 1930 in Newark, New Jersey
Source: *AmAu&B; BiD&SB; CarSB; ConAu P-2; DcAmAu; EncMys; HsB&A; OxCAmL 65; REn; REnAL; SmATA 1; TwCBDA; WebAB 74; WhAm 1*

Stratemeyer, George E, General
American. Army Officer
US Air Force general, commanding general China-Burma-India, WW II; Far East Air Forces, 1949-52.
b. Nov 24, 1890 in Cincinnati, Ohio
d. Aug 9, 1969 in Winter Park, Florida
Source: *CurBio 51, 69; WhAm 5*

Stratten, Dorothy
[Dorothy Hoogstratten; Mrs. Paul Snider]
Canadian. Actor, Model
Former Playboy centerfold shot to death by estranged husband; life story subject of film *Star 80,* 1983.
b. Feb 28, 1960 in Vancouver, British Columbia, Canada
d. Aug 14, 1980 in Los Angeles, California
Source: *BioIn 12, 16, 17*

Stratton, Julius A(dams)
American. Scientist
President, MIT, 1959-66; expert on radar for US Secretary of War during World War II.
b. May 18, 1901
d. Jun 22, 1994 in Boston, Massachusetts
Source: *AmMWSc 76P, 79, 82, 86, 89, 92; BioIn 1, 4, 5, 6, 7, 20, 21; BlueB 76; CurBio 94N; LElec; WhAm 11; Who 74, 82, 83, 85, 88, 90, 92, 94; WhoAm 74, 76, 78, 80, 84, 86, 88, 90, 92, 94; WhoE 83, 85, 86, 89; WhoWor 74*

Stratton, Monty Franklin Pierce
"Gander"
American. Baseball Player
Pitcher, White Sox, 1934-38; lost leg in hunting accident, 1938; life story filmed, 1949, starring Jimmy Stewart.
b. May 21, 1912 in Celeste, Texas
d. Sep 29, 1982 in Greenville, Texas
Source: *NewYTBS 82; WhoProB 73*

Stratton, Samuel S(tuddiford)
American. Politician
Fifteen term US representative from NY.
b. Sep 27, 1916 in Yonkers, New York
d. Sep 13, 1990 in Gaithersburg, Maryland
Source: *AlmAP 78, 80, 82, 84, 88; BiDrAC; BiDrUSC 89; BioIn 7; CngDr 74, 77, 79, 81, 83, 85, 87; CurBio 91N; NewYTBS 90; PolsAm 84; WhAm 10; WhoAm 74, 76, 78, 80, 82, 84, 86, 88, 90; WhoAmP 73, 75, 77, 79, 81, 83, 85, 87, 89; WhoE 74, 75, 77, 79, 81, 83, 85, 86, 89; WhoGov 72, 75, 77*

Straub, Peter
American. Author
Horror novelist's titles include *Ghost Story,* 1979 and *The Talisman,* 1984, co-written with Stephen King and the fastest-selling book in publishing history.
b. Mar 2, 1943 in Milwaukee, Wisconsin
Source: *BestSel 89-1; BioIn 12, 13, 14, 15, 16; ConAu 28NR, 85; ConLC 28; CurBio 89; DcLB Y84B; IntAu&W 91; IntvTCA 2; LegTOT; MajTwCW; PenEncH; RAdv 14; ScF&FL 92; ScFSB; WhoAm 90; WhoEnt 92; WhoWrEP 89; WrDr 80, 82, 84, 86, 88, 90, 92*

Straus, Isidor
American. Merchant, Philanthropist
Purchased R H Macy & Co., 1896; developed Abraham & Straus, 1892; lost in Titanic disaster.
b. Feb 6, 1845 in Otterberg, Germany
d. Apr 15, 1912 in At Sea
Source: *AmBi; ApCAB X; BiDAmBL 83; BiDrAC; BiDrUSC 89; BioIn 4, 5; DcAmB; JeAmHC; McGEWB; NatCAB 10; OxCAmH; WebAB 74, 79; WhAm 1; WorAl; WorAlBi*

Straus, Jack Isidor
American. Merchant
Pres., chief exec., Macy's, beginning 1940, who oversaw company's expansion to 93 stores in 14 states.
b. Jan 13, 1900 in New York, New York
d. Sep 19, 1985 in New York, New York
Source: *BiDAmBL 83; BioIn 2, 3, 6, 7, 8, 9, 14; BlueB 76; CurBio 52, 85N; IntWW 74; IntYB 78, 79, 80, 81, 82; NewYTBS 85; St&PR 75, 84; WhAm 9; WhoAm 74, 76, 80, 82, 84; WhoFI 74; WhoWorJ 72, 78; WorAl; WorAlBi*

Straus, Nathan
American. Merchant, Philanthropist
With brother Isidor became owner of R H Macy & Co., 1896; leader in campaign for pasteurized milk in NY, 1892.
b. Jan 31, 1848 in Otterberg, Bavaria
d. Jan 11, 1931 in New York, New York
Source: *AmBi; ApCAB X; BiDAmBL 83; BioIn 1, 2, 4, 8, 9, 14, 17; DcAmB; DcAmMeB 84; DcNAA; JeAmHC; LinLib S; NatCAB 10, 22; OxCAmH; WebAB 74, 79; WhAm 1; WorAl; WorAlBi*

Straus, Oscar Solomon
American. Lawyer, Diplomat
First ambassador to Turkey; secretary of Commerce, Labor under Theodore Roosevelt, 1906-09; wrote *The Hague Tribunal,* 1904.
b. Dec 23, 1850 in Otterberg, Germany
d. May 3, 1926 in New York, New York
Source: *Alli SUP; AmAu&B; AmBi; AmPeW; ApCAB, SUP; BiDAmBL 83; BiD&SB; BiDInt; BiDrUSE 71, 89; BiDSA; BioIn 1, 2, 4, 5, 8, 9, 10, 14, 16; CyAG; DcAmAu; DcAmB; DcNAA; HarEnUS; JeAmHC; NatCAB 10, 14, 40; REnAL; TwCBDA; WebAB 74, 79; WhAm 1*

Straus, Oskar
Austrian. Composer
Wrote 50 operettas including *Chocolate Soldier,* 1909; filmed, 1941.
b. Apr 6, 1870 in Vienna, Austria
d. Jan 11, 1954 in Bad Ischl, Austria
Source: *Baker 78; BioIn 3, 4; CmpEPM; CurBio 44, 54; NotNAT B; ObitOF 79; OxCMus; REn; WhAm 3; WhThe*

Straus, Roger W(illiams), Jr.
American. Publisher
Founder, pres., Farrar, Straus & Co., 1945.
b. Jan 3, 1917 in New York, New York
Source: *AmMWSc 73P; BiDAmBL 83; BioIn 12, 16; CelR 90; CurBio 80; IntWW 91; NewYTBS 80; WhE&EA; WhoAm 86, 90; WorAlBi*

Strauss, David Friedrich
German. Theologian
Described Gospels as "historical myth;" his *Leben Jesu,* 1835, was turning point in study of historical Jesus.
b. Jan 27, 1808 in Stuttgart, Germany
d. Feb 28, 1874 in Ludwigsburg, Germany
Source: *Benet 87, 96; BiD&SB; BiDTran; BioIn 7, 10, 13, 14, 20; CelCen; DcBiPP; DcEuL; DcLB 133; EncUnb; LuthC 75; McGEWB; NewCBEL; NewCol 75; OxCEng 85, 95; OxCGer 76, 86; REn*

Strauss, Franz Josef
German. Politician
West German Defense Minister, 1956-62; Finance Minister, 1966-69; pres. of Bavaria, 1978-80.
b. Sep 6, 1915 in Munich, Germany
d. Oct 3, 1988 in Munich, Germany
Source: *AnObit 1988; BioIn 4, 5, 6, 7, 8, 9, 10, 11, 12, 13, 15, 16, 18, 21; ColdWar 1, 2; CurBio 57, 87, 88, 88N; DcTwHis; EncCW; EncWB; FacFETw; IntWW 74, 75, 76, 77, 78, 79, 80, 81, 82, 83; IntYB 78, 79, 80, 81, 82; NewYTBS 88; WhAm 11; Who 74, 82, 83, 85, 88; WhoWor 74, 84, 87, 89*

Strauss, Johann, Sr.
"The Father of the Waltz"
Austrian. Composer, Conductor
Published 152 waltzes; led orchestra at Viennese dance halls.
b. Mar 14, 1804 in Vienna, Austria
d. Sep 25, 1849 in Vienna, Austria
Source: *Baker 78, 84; BioIn 1, 4, 5, 7, 9, 11, 12, 16, 20; BriBkM 80; DcCom 77; LegTOT; NewAmDM; NewCol 75; NewGrDM 80; NotNAT B; OxCMus; OxCPMus; OxDcOp; WebBD 83*

Strauss, Johann, Jr.
"The Waltz King"
Austrian. Composer, Conductor, Violinist
Wrote 16 operettas, 400 waltzes, including *The Blue Danube,* 1864.
b. Oct 25, 1825 in Vienna, Austria
d. Jun 3, 1899 in Vienna, Austria
Source: *AtlBL; Baker 78, 84; Benet 87, 96; BiDD; BioIn 1, 2, 3, 4, 5, 6, 7, 9, 10, 11, 12, 16, 20; BriBkM 80; CelCen; CmOp; CmpBCM; CnOxB; DancEn 78; DcCom 77; DcCom&M 79; GrComp; LinLib S; McGEWB; MetOEnc; MusMk; NewAmDM; NewEOp 71; NewGrDM 80; NotNAT B; OxCAmT 84; OxCGer 76, 86; OxCMus; OxCPMus; OxDcOp; PenDiMP A; REn; WhDW; WorAl; WorAlBi*

Strauss, Joseph Baermann
American. Engineer
Best known as chief engineer for Golden Gate Bridge, 1937.
b. Jan 9, 1870 in Cincinnati, Ohio
d. May 16, 1938 in Los Angeles, California
Source: *AmBi; BioIn 2, 4, 7, 15; DcAmB S2; InSci; LinLib S; NatCAB 27; OhA&B; WhAm 1*

Strauss, Levi
American. Manufacturer
Settled in San Francisco, 1850, to make denim pants for miners.
b. 1829?
d. 1902
Source: *BioIn 4, 11, 14, 16, 17, 18, 20; EncAB-H 1996; Entr; JeHun; LegTOT; WebAB 74, 79; WorAl; WorAlBi*

Strauss, Lewis Lichtenstein
American. Author, Government Official
Chm., Atomic Energy Commission, 1953-58; helped shape US thermonuclear policy; wrote *Men & Decisions,* 1962.
b. Jan 31, 1896 in Charleston, West Virginia
d. Jan 21, 1974 in Brandy Station, Virginia

Source: *BiDrUSE 71, 89; BioIn 1, 3, 4, 5, 6, 10, 11; BioNews 74; ConAu 45; CurBio 47, 74; LinLib S; PolProf E, T; WhAm 6; Who 74; WhoWor 74*

Strauss, Peter
American. Actor
Won Emmy, 1979, for *The Jericho Mile;* starred in *Rich Man, Poor Man,* 1976.
b. Feb 20, 1947 in Croton-on-Hudson, New York
Source: *ConTFT 5; IntMPA 77, 78, 79, 80, 81, 82, 84, 86, 88, 92, 94, 96; ItaFilm; WhoAm 78, 80, 82, 84, 86, 88, 90, 92, 94, 95, 96, 97; WhoEnt 92; WhoHol 92, A; WorAl; WorAlBi*

Strauss, Richard Georg
German. Conductor, Composer
Wrote operas *Salome,* 1905; *Rosenkavalier,* 1911; one of last German romantics.
b. Jun 11, 1864 in Munich, Germany
d. Sep 8, 1949 in Garmisch, Germany (West)
Source: *AtlBL; Baker 84; CurBio 44, 49; DcCM; NewYTBS 91; OxCGer 76; REn; WhAm 2; WhoAm 90; WhoAmL 90; WhoAmP 91*

Strauss, Robert
American. Actor
In films, 1942-61; appeared in *Stalag 17,* 1953; *The Seven Year Itch,* 1955.
b. Nov 8, 1913 in New York, New York
d. Feb 20, 1974 in New York, New York
Source: *BiE&WWA; BioIn 10; BioNews 75; EncAFC; FilmEn; FilmgC; ForYSC; HalFC 80, 84, 88; HolCA; IntMPA 75; MovMk; NewYTBS 75; NotNAT B; Vers A; WhoHol C; WhScrn 77, 83*

Strauss, Robert Schwarz
American. Presidential Aide, Lawyer
Chm., Dem. Nat. Committee, 1972-77; worked to reelect Carter, 1979-81; US Ambassador to Russia, 1991-93.
b. Oct 19, 1918 in Lockhart, Texas
Source: *BioIn 10, 11, 12; CurBio 74, 92; EncWB; IntWW 89, 91, 93; NewYTBS 76, 80, 91; PolProf NF; WhoAm 78, 80, 82, 84, 86, 88, 90, 92, 94, 95, 96; WhoAmL 87, 90; WhoAmP 85; WhoGov 77; WhoSSW 95; WhoWor 93, 95; WorAl*

Strauss, Theodore
Writer
TV shows include "Born of Fire;" won Emmy for "They've Killed President Lincoln," 1971.
Source: *VarWW 85*

Stravinsky, Igor Fedorovich
American. Composer
Noted for ballets *The Firebird,* 1910, *Rite of Spring,* 1913; greatly influenced modern music.
b. Jun 17, 1882 in Oranienbaum, Russia
d. Apr 6, 1971 in New York, New York
Source: *AmAu&B; AmCulL; AnCL; ASCAP 66; Baker 84; BiDAmM; ConAu 29R, 107; CurBio 40, 53, 71; DcCM; EncAB-H 1974; FacFETw; MakMC; McGEWB; MusSN; NewGrDM 80; REn; WebAB 74, 79; WhAm 5, 7*

Stravinsky, Vera de Bossett
Russian. Artist
Second wife of Igor Stravinsky, married, 1940.
b. Dec 25, 1888 in Saint Petersburg, Russia
d. Sep 17, 1982 in New York, New York
Source: *AnObit 1982; NewYTBE 71; NewYTBS 82*

Straw, Syd
American. Singer, Songwriter
Performed backup singer for musician Pat Benatar in late 1970s; released debut album, *Surprise,* 1989; later recorded *War and Peace,* 1996 and contributed song "People of Earth" to *Party of Five* television soundtrack, 1996.
b. c. 1958 in Vermont

Strawberry, Darryl Eugene
American. Baseball Player
Outfielder, NY Mets, 1983-90; LA Dodgers, 1991-94; SF Giants, 1994-95; NY Yankees, 1995—; NL rookie of year, 1983; led NL in home runs, 1988.
b. Mar 12, 1962 in Los Angeles, California
Source: *Ballpl 90; BaseReg 86, 87; BioIn 16; CurBio 84; NewYTBS 82, 83, 84; WhoAm 90; WhoBlA 92; WhoWest 92; WorAlBi*

Strawbs
[Rod Coombes; Dave Cousins; Chas Cronk; Dave Lambert]
British. Music Group
Music mixes folk/bluegrass; songs include "Part of the Union," 1973.
Source: *ConMuA 80A; EncRk 88; HarEnR 86; IlEncRk; ObitOF 79; PenEncP; RolSEnR 83; WhoRock 81; WhoRocM 82*

Strawser, Neil Edward
American. Broadcast Journalist
CBS News correspondent since 1952.
b. Aug 16, 1927 in Rittman, Ohio
Source: *WhoAm 76, 78, 80, 82, 84, 86*

Stray Cats
[Jim "Slim Jim Phantom" McDonnell; Lee Rocker; Brian Setzer]
American. Music Group
Rock group formed, 1979; albums include *Built for Speed,* 1982.
Source: *BioIn 15; ConMus 11; EncRk 88; EncRkSt; HarEnR 86; IlEncRk; PenEncP; RkOn 85; RolSEnR 83; WhsNW 85*

Strayhorn, Billy
[William Strayhorn]
American. Jazz Musician
Pianist, arranger, Duke Ellington's band, 1938-67; wrote "Take the A' Train," 1941.
b. Nov 29, 1915 in Dayton, Ohio
d. May 31, 1967 in New York, New York
Source: *AfrAmAl 6; AllMusG; ASCAP 66, 80; Baker 78, 84, 92; BiDAfM; BiDAmM; BiDJaz; BioIn 7, 8; CmpEPM; ConAmC 76, 82; ConMus 13; DrBlPA, 90; EncJzS; EncJzS; IlEncJ; LegTOT; NewAmDM; NewGrDA 86; NewGrDJ 88, 94; NewGrDM 80; OxCPMus; PenEncP; WhoJazz 72*

Streep, Meryl
[Mary Louise Streep]
American. Actor
Won Oscar for *Sophie's Choice,* 1983; Emmy, 1978, for *Holocaust.*
b. Jun 22, 1949 in Summit, New Jersey
Source: *AmDec 1980; BiDFilm 94; BioIn 11, 12, 13, 16; CamGWoT; CelR 90; ContDcW 89; ConTFT 8; CurBio 80; DcArts; DcTwCCu 1; GrLiveH; HalFC 84, 88; HolBB; IntDcF 1-3, 2-3; IntMPA 82, 84, 86, 88, 92, 94, 96; IntWW 83, 89, 91, 93; InWom SUP; LegTOT; News 90, 90-2; NewYTBS 76, 79, 91; Who 90, 92; WhoAm 86, 90, 92, 94, 95, 96, 97; WhoAmW 87, 89, 91, 93, 95, 97; WhoEnt 92; WhoHol 92; WhoThe 81; WhoWor 89, 91, 93, 95, 96, 97; WorAlBi*

Street, George Edmund
English. Architect
A champion of Gothic revival; designed over 250 buildings including London's Royal Courts of Justice, 1874-81.
b. Jun 20, 1824 in Woodford, England
d. Dec 18, 1881 in London, England
Source: *Alli, SUP; ArtsNiC; BioIn 5, 14, 16; CelCen; DcArts; DcBiPP; DcD&D; DcNaB; IntDcAr; MacEA; McGDA; NewCBEL; NewCol 75; OxCArt; VicBrit; WhoArch*

Streeter, Edward
American. Author
Wrote *Father of the Bride,* 1949; *Chairman of the Bored,* 1961.
b. Aug 1, 1891 in New York, New York
d. Mar 31, 1976 in New York, New York
Source: *AmAu&B; Au&Wr 71; BioIn 1, 5, 7, 10, 13, 15; ConAu 1R, 2NR, 65; DcLB 11; EncAHmr; OxCAmL 65, 83, 95; REnAL; WhAm 7; WhNAA; WhoAm 74, 76; WorAu 1950*

Streeter, Ruth
American. Military Leader
Commanded Marine Corps. Women's Reserve during WWII.
b. Oct 2, 1895 in Brookline, Massachusetts
d. Sep 30, 1990 in Morristown, New Jersey
Source: *BioIn 1; CurBio 91N; InWom SUP; NewYTBS 90; WebAMB*

Strehler, Giorgio
Italian. Director
Responsible for bringing Italian theatre to international attention via his Piccolo Teatro di Milano, 1949—; an advocate of theatre as a force in contemporary society.
b. Aug 14, 1921 in Trieste, Italy
Source: *BioIn 11, 15, 17, 20; CamGWoT; CmOp; CurBio 91; DcItL 2; EncWT; Ent; GrStDi; IntDcOp; IntDcT 3; IntWW 93; MetOEnc; NewGrDM 80; NewGrDO; OxCThe 83; OxDcOp; TheaDir; WhoOp 76; WhoWor 97*

Streibert, Theodore Cuyler
American. Government Official
First director, US Information Agency, 1953-57.
b. Aug 29, 1899 in Albany, New York
d. Jan 18, 1987 in Syosset, New York
Source: *BioIn 3, 4, 11; CurBio 55, 87; PolProf E; WhAm 9; WhoAm 74, 76, 78; WhoWor 74*

Streich, Rita
German. Opera Singer
Soprano; Vienna debut, 1953; noted for Mozart, Strauss roles.
b. Dec 18, 1920 in Barnaul, Union of Soviet Socialist Republics
Source: *Baker 84, 92; BioIn 4, 14; CmOp; IntDcOp; IntWW 74; MetOEnc; NewAmDM; NewGrDM 80; NewGrDO; OxDcOp; PenDiMP; WhoMus 72; WhoOp 76; WhoWor 74*

Streicher, Julius
German. Journalist, Politician
Edited anti-Semitic *The Stormer,* 1923-45; executed after Nuremberg trial.
b. Feb 12, 1885 in Fleinhausen, Germany
d. Oct 16, 1946 in Nuremberg, Germany
Source: *BiDExR; BioIn 1, 12, 14, 16, 18; CurBio 46; DcTwHis; Dis&D; EncTR, 91; HisEWW; REn; WhDW; WhWW-II*

Streisand, Barbra (Joan)
[Barbra Streisand]
American. Singer, Actor, Director
Won Oscar, 1968, for *Funny Girl;* albums include *The Lodgers,* 1985; received special Grammy Legend Award for lifetime achievement, 1992; directed and starred in *The Mirror Has Two Faces,* 1996; Emmy award winner, 1964 for TV special, "My Name is Barbra."
b. Apr 24, 1942 in New York, New York
Source: *AmDec 1960; ASCAP 80; Baker 84, 92; BiDAmM; BiDFilm, 81, 94; BiE&WWA; BioAmW; BioIn 6, 7, 8, 9, 10, 11, 12, 13, 16; BkPepl; BlueB 76; CelR, 90; CmMov; ConAu 144; ConMuA 80A; ConMus 2; ContDcW 89; ConTFT 1, 7; CurBio 64, 92; DcArts; DcTwCCu 1; EncAFC; EncMT; EncPR&S 89; FacFETw; FilmEn; FilmgC; ForWC 70; ForYSC; GoodHs; GrLiveH; HalFC 80, 84, 88; IntDcF 1-3, 2-3; IntDcWB; IntMPA 75, 76, 77, 78, 79, 80, 81, 82, 84, 86, 88, 92, 94, 96; IntWW 74, 75, 76, 77, 78, 79, 80, 81, 82, 83, 89, 91, 93; InWom, SUP; LegTOT; LibW; MiSFD 9; MotPP; MovMk; NewAmDM; NewGrDA 86; News 92, 92-2; NotNAT, A; OxCFilm; OxCPMus; PenEncP; PlP&P; ReelWom; RkOn 78; WebAB 74, 79; Who 94; WhoAm 74, 76, 78, 80, 82, 84, 86, 88, 90, 92, 94, 95, 96, 97; WhoAmJ 80; WhoAmW 66, 68, 70, 72, 74, 75, 79, 81, 83, 85, 87, 89, 91, 93, 95, 97; WhoE 74; WhoEnt 92; WhoHol 92, A; WhoRock 81; WhoThe 72, 77, 81; WhoWor 74, 78, 89; WomFir; WomWMM; WorAl; WorAlBi*

Streithorst, Tom
American. Broadcast Journalist
Covered Middle East, Latin America for NBC News from early 1960s.
b. 1932
d. Feb 19, 1981 in Palo Alto, California
Source: *ConAu 103; WhAm 7*

Strenger, Hermann Josef
German. Business Executive
Chairman of Bayer, prominent German chemical firm, since 1984.
b. Sep 26, 1928? in Cologne, Germany
Source: *BioIn 15; IntWW 82, 83, 89, 91; WhoFI 96; WhoWor 95, 96, 97*

Strepponi, Giuseppina
Italian. Opera Singer
Famed soprano, late 1830s; wife of Verdi.
b. Sep 18, 1815 in Lodi, Italy
d. Nov 15, 1897 in Busseto, Italy
Source: *Baker 78, 84, 92; CmOp; IntDcOp; InWom; MetOEnc; NewAmDM; NewEOp 71; NewGrDM 80; NewGrDO; OxDcOp; PenDiMP*

Stresemann, Gustav
German. Statesman
Chancellor, then foreign minister, who helped negotiate Locarno Pact, 1925; shared 1926 Nobel Peace Prize with Aristide Briand.
b. May 10, 1878 in Berlin, Germany
d. Oct 3, 1929 in Berlin, Germany
Source: *BiDInt; BioIn 3, 4, 6, 9, 10, 11, 15, 16; DcTwHis; Dis&D; EncTR, 91; HisWorL; McGEWB; NewCol 75; NobelP; OxCGer 76, 86; REn; WhDW; WorAl; WorAlBi*

Stribling, Thomas Sigismund
American. Author
Trilogy depicting life in the South includes 1933 Pulitzer-winning novel, *The Store.*
b. Mar 4, 1881 in Clinton, Tennessee
d. Jul 8, 1965 in Florence, Alabama
Source: *AmAu&B; BioIn 7, 8, 10, 12, 13, 14, 15; CasWL; CnDAL; ConAmA; DcAmB S7; DcLEL; EncAAH; EncMys; EncSoH; EncWL; LngCTC; OxCAmL 65; PenC AM; REn; TwCA; WhAm 4; WhE&EA; WhNAA*

Stribling, Young
[William Lawrence Stribling]
"Georgia Peach"
American. Boxer
Had 126 KOs out of 286 fights; defeated by Schmeling for heavyweight crown, 1931.
b. Dec 26, 1904 in Bainbridge, Georgia
d. Oct 2, 1933 in Macon, Georgia
Source: *BioIn 8; BoxReg; WhoBox 74*

Strindberg, August
[Johan August Strindberg]
Swedish. Dramatist, Author
Developed realism, symbolism in work: *Miss Julie; The Ghost Sonata.*
b. Jan 22, 1849 in Stockholm, Sweden
d. May 14, 1912 in Stockholm, Sweden
Source: *AtlBL; Benet 87; BiD&SB; BioIn 1, 2, 3, 4, 5, 6, 7, 8, 9, 10, 11, 12, 13, 14, 15, 16, 17, 18, 19; BlmGEL; CamGWoT; CasWL; ClDMEL 47, 80; CnMD; CnThe; ConAu 104, 135; CyWA 58; DcArts; DcEuL; DcScanL; Dis&D; EncWL, 2, 3; EncWT; Ent; EuAu; EuWr 7; EvEuW; FacFETw; GrFLW; IntDcT 2; LegTOT; LinLib L, S; LngCEL; LngCTC; MagSWL; MajMD 2; McGEWB; McGEWD 72, 84; ModWD; NewC; NewCBEL; NewEOp 71; NewYTBS 74; NotNAT A, B; OxCAmT 84; OxCEng 67, 85; OxCGer 76, 86; OxCThe 67, 83; PenC EUR; PhDcTCA 77; PlP&P A; RAdv 14, 13-2; RComWL; REn; REnWD; RfGWoL 95; TwCA, SUP; TwCLC 1, 8, 21, 47; WhDW; WhLit; WhoTwCL; WorAl; WorAlBi; WorLitC; WrPh*

Stringfield, Sherry
American. Actor
Played Dr. Susan Lewis on TV's "ER," 1994-96.
b. Jun 24, 1967 in Colorado Springs, Colorado

Stritch, Elaine
American. Actor, Singer
Film, stage performer; appeared in film *September,* 1987.
b. Feb 2, 1928 in Detroit, Michigan
Source: *BiE&WWA; BioIn 16; CelR, 90; ConTFT 7; CurBio 88; EncMT; FilmgC; HalFC 88; IntMPA 92; IntWW 91; InWom SUP; MotPP; NewYTBE 70; NotNAT; OxCAmT 84; WhoAm 76, 90; WhoEnt 92; WhoHol A; WhoThe 77; WorAlBi*

Strode, Hudson
American. Author, Educator, Lecturer
Biographies include *Jefferson Davis; Confederate President,* 1959.
b. Oct 31, 1893 in Cairo, Illinois
d. Sep 22, 1976 in Tuscaloosa, Alabama
Source: *AmAu&B; BioIn 2, 4, 10; ConAu 13R, 69; REnAL; TwCA, SUP; WhNAA; WhoAm 74*

Strode, Woody
[Woodrow Wilson Woolwine Strode]
American. Actor
In films since 1941: *The Cotton Club,* 1984.
b. Jul 25, 1914 in Los Angeles, California
d. Dec 31, 1994 in Glendora, California
Source: *BioIn 13, 20, 21; BlksAmF; CelR; CmMov; DrBlPA, 90; FilmEn; FilmgC; HalFC 84, 88; IntMPA 88, 92, 94; ItaFilm; NewYTBE 71; WhoHol 92, A*

Stroessner, Alfredo
Paraguayan. Political Leader
President of Paraguay, longest ruling political leader in Latin America, 1954-89; ousted in military coup.
b. Nov 3, 1912 in Encarnacion, Paraguay
Source: *BiDLAmC; BioIn 5, 8, 9, 11, 12, 13, 16; CurBio 58, 81; DcCPSAm; DcHiB; DcPol; DcTwHis; DicTyr; EncLatA; FacFETw; IntWW 74, 75, 76, 77, 78, 79, 80, 81, 82, 83, 89, 91, 93; McGEWB; WhoWor 82, 87, 89, 91; WorDWW*

Stroh, Bernard
American. Brewer
Established brewery, 1850; introduced Bohemian-style beer.
b. 1822
d. 1882
Source: *BusPN; Entr*

Stroh, Peter W
American. Brewer
Chairman and CEO Stroh Brewery, 1982—.
b. Dec 18, 1927 in Detroit, Michigan
Source: *BioIn 15; ConNews 85-2; WhoAm 88; WhoFI 87; WhoMW 92*

Stromberg, Hunt
American. Producer
Produced Nelson Eddy-Jeanette MacDonald films, *The Thin Man* series for MGM, 1930s.
b. Jul 12, 1894 in Louisville, Kentucky
d. Aug 23, 1968 in Los Angeles, California
Source: *FilmEn; FilmgC; HalFC 80, 84, 88; IntDcF 1-4, 2-4; WhAm 5*

Stromgren, Bengt Georg Daniel
Danish. Physicist, Astronomer
Pioneered studies of gas clouds in space.
b. Jan 21, 1908 in Goteborg, Sweden
d. Jul 4, 1987 in Copenhagen, Denmark
Source: *BiESc; BioIn 2, 14, 15, 16; FacFETw; IntWW 74, 75, 76, 77, 78, 79, 80; McGMS 80; NewYTBS 87; WhAm 9; WhoAm 74, 76; WhoWor 74, 78*

Strong, Anna Louise
American. Journalist
Advocated communism in her newsletter, *Letter from China.*
b. Nov 24, 1885 in Friend, Nebraska
d. Mar 29, 1970 in Beijing, China
Source: *AmAu&B; AmWomWr; BioIn 1, 2, 3, 4, 8, 9, 11, 13, 14, 15, 19; ConAu 29R; CurBio 49, 70; DcAmB S8; EncAJ; FemiCLE; InWom, SUP; JrnUS; LibW; NewYTBE 70; NotAW MOD; ObitT 1961; OhA&B; TwCA, SUP; WhAm 5; WhNAA; WomWWA 14*

Strong, Austin
American. Author
Wrote play *Seventh Heaven,* 1920, which was filmed, 1937.
b. Jan 18, 1881 in San Francisco, California
d. Sep 17, 1952 in Nantucket, Massachusetts
Source: *AmAu&B; BenetAL 91; BioIn 1, 3; LngCTC; ModWD; NotNAT B; OxCAmL 65, 83; REnAL; WhAm 3; WhLit; WhNAA; WhThe*

Strong, James Matthew
Irish. Politician
Member, N Ireland Parliament, killed with father, by IRA terrorists.
b. Jun 21, 1932
d. Jan 21, 1981 in Armagh, Northern Ireland
Source: *AnObit 1981; BioIn 12*

Strong, Ken(neth E)
American. Football Player
Halfback-kicker, 1929-39, 1944, 1947, mostly with NY Giants; led NFL in field goals, 1944; Hall of Fame, 1967.
b. Aug 6, 1906 in West Haven, Connecticut
d. Oct 5, 1979 in New York, New York
Source: *Ballpl 90; BioIn 12, 17; LegTOT; NewYTBS 79; WhoFtbl 74; WhoSpor*

Strong, Maurice Frederick
Canadian. Environmentalist
Known for his environmetal activism; secretary-general, UN Conference on Environment and Development, 1990-92 (better known as the Earth Summit).
b. Apr 29, 1929 in Oak Lake, Manitoba, Canada
Source: *BioIn 9, 10, 11, 13, 15, 16; BlueB 76; CanWW 83, 89; CurBio 73; IntWW 91; News 93-1; NewYTBE 71; Who 92; WhoAm 74, 76, 78, 80, 82, 84, 86, 94, 95; WhoCanB 86; WhoCanF 86; WhoFI 81, 83, 94; WhoScEn 96; WhoUN 75, 92; WhoWest 84*

Strong, Philip Duffield
American. Author
Wrote *State Fair,* 1932; made into film several times.
b. Jan 27, 1899 in Keosauqua, Iowa
d. Apr 26, 1957 in Washington, Connecticut
Source: *AmAu&B; AuBYP 2S; ConAmA*

Stronge, Norman, Sir
[Charles Norman Lockhart Stronge]
Irish. Politician
Speaker of House of Commons, N Ireland, 1945-69; killed in terrorist attack on his home.
b. Jul 23, 1894 in Bryansford, Northern Ireland
d. Jan 21, 1981 in Armagh, Northern Ireland
Source: *AnObit 1981; BioIn 12; IntWW 74, 75, 76, 77, 78, 79, 80; Who 74; WhoWor 74, 76, 78*

Stroud, Robert Franklin
"Birdman of Alcatraz"
American. Ornithologist, Criminal
60 yrs. in prison for murder portrayed in film starring Burt Lancaster, *Birdman of Alcatraz,* 1961.
b. 1890 in Seattle, Washington
d. Nov 21, 1963 in Springfield, Missouri
Source: *BioIn 4, 6; WebAB 74*

Strougal, Lubomir
Czech. Political Leader
Prime minister of Czechoslovakia, 1970-88.
b. Oct 19, 1924 in Veseli nad Luznici, Czechoslovakia
Source: *BioIn 8, 9; IntWW 74, 75, 76, 77, 78, 79, 80, 81, 82, 83, 89, 91, 93; IntYB 81, 82; WhoGov 72; WhoSocC 78; WhoSoCE 89; WhoWor 74, 76, 78, 80, 82, 84, 87, 89, 91*

Stroup, Thomas Bradley
American. Educator, Author
Wrote *Religious Rite and Ceremony in Milton's Poetry,* 1968.
b. Dec 21, 1903 in Fletcher, North Carolina
Source: *DrAS 74E, 78E, 82E*

Strouse, Charles
American. Composer
Won Tonys for *Bye Bye Birdie,* 1959; *Applause,* 1970; *Annie,* 1977.
b. Jun 7, 1928 in New York, New York
Source: *AmPS; AmSong; ASCAP 66, 80; Baker 84; BiDAmM; BiE&WWA; BioIn 9, 10, 12; CelR 90; ConAmC 82; ConTFT 1, 11; EncMT; NewAmDM; NewCBMT; NewGrDA 86; NewGrDM 80; NotNAT; OxCAmT 84; OxCPMus; PopAmC SUP; WhoAm 74, 76, 78, 80, 82, 84, 86, 88, 90; WhoThe 72, 77, 81; WorAl; WorAlBi*

Strouse, Norman H(ulbert)
American. Advertising Executive
Became pres. of J Walter Thompson in 1955.
b. Nov 4, 1906 in Olympia, Washington
d. Jan 19, 1993 in Saint Helena, California
Source: *BioIn 5, 6, 7, 8; ChhPo S1; CurBio 60, 93N; St&PR 75*

Strout, Richard Lee
American. Journalist
Known for political analyses in *Christian Science Monitor* and weekly column "TRB From Washington" in *New Republic.*
b. Mar 14, 1898 in Cohoes, New York
d. Aug 19, 1990 in Washington, District of Columbia
Source: *AmAu&B; BiDAmJo; BiDAmNC; BioIn 8, 10, 11, 12, 13, 16, 17; ConAu 69, 132; CurBio 80, 90, 90N; NewYTBS 90; WhAm 10; WhoAm 74, 76, 78, 80, 82, 84, 86*

Strudwick, Shepperd
American. Actor
Career began in 1928; over 200 roles in plays, movies, TV.
b. Sep 22, 1907 in Hillsboro, North Carolina
d. Jan 15, 1983 in New York, New York
Source: *BiE&WWA; BioIn 13; FilmEn; FilmgC; ForYSC; HalFC 80; IntMPA 75, 76, 77, 78, 79, 80, 81, 82, 84; LegTOT; MovMk; NewYTBS 83; NotNAT; WhAm 8; WhoAm 74, 76, 82; WhoHol A; WhoThe 72, 77, 81*

Struss, Karl
American. Filmmaker
Won first Oscar given for cinematography, 1927.
b. Nov 30, 1886 in New York, New York
d. Dec 16, 1981 in Santa Monica, California
Source: *AnObit 1981; BioIn 12, 19; CmMov; FilmEn; FilmgC; ICPEnP; IntDcF 1-4, 2-4; MacBEP; NewYTBS 81; WhoHrs 80; WorEFlm*

Struther, Jan
[Joyce Maxtone Graham]
English. Author
Best known for *Mrs. Miniver,* 1940.
b. Jun 6, 1901 in London, England
d. Jul 20, 1953 in New York, New York
Source: *BioIn 1, 3, 4, 16; ChhPo, S1, S2; CurBio 41, 53; EncAB-A 24; EncBrWW; EngPo; FemiCLE; InWom; LngCTC; NewC; REn; TwCA, SUP; WhAm 3*

Struthers, Sally Anne
American. Actor
Played Gloria on "All in the Family," 1971-78; won two Emmys.
b. Jul 28, 1948 in Portland, Oregon
Source: *BkPepl; ConTFT 2, 7; CurBio 74; HalFC 84, 88; IntMPA 92; InWom SUP; NewYTBE 72; WhoAm 78, 80, 82, 84, 86, 88, 90; WhoHol A; WhoTelC; WorAl; WorAlBi*

Strutt, Joseph
English. Author
Wrote *Manners, Customs, Habits of People of England,* 1774-76.
b. Oct 27, 1749 in Chelmsford, England
d. Oct 16, 1802 in London, England
Source: *Alli; BioIn 3, 11; BkIE; BritAu; CamGLE; DcBiPP; DcBrECP; DcBrWA; DcEnL; DcLEL; DcNaB; DcPup; NewC; NewCBEL; OxCEng 67, 85, 95; REn*

Struve, Otto
American. Astronomer, Educator
Director, Yerkes and McDonald Observatories, 1932-47.
b. Aug 12, 1897 in Kharkov, Russia
d. Apr 6, 1963 in Berkeley, California
Source: *AsBiEn; BiDSovU; BiESc; BioIn 2, 3, 4, 5, 6, 7; DcAmB S7; DcScB; InSci; LarDcSc; McGMS 80; WebAB 74, 79; WebBD 83; WhAm 4*

Stryper
American. Music Group
Christian rock band that tosses miniature Bibles into the audience during concerts.
Source: *Alli; BiDrAPA 89; BioIn 16, 17; ConMus 2; WhoHisp 91, 92, 94*

Stuart, Bruce
Canadian. Hockey Player
Amateur player for several teams, early 1900s; Hall of Fame, 1961.
b. 1882 in Ottawa, Ontario, Canada
d. Oct 28, 1961 in Ottawa, Ontario, Canada
Source: *WhoHcky 73*

Stuart, Charles Edward Louis Philip
"Bonnie Prince Charlie"
English.
Grandson of James II who unsuccessfully tried to seize Hanoverian throne, 1745.
b. Dec 31, 1720 in Rome, Italy
d. Jan 31, 1788 in Rome, Italy
Source: *Alli; McGEWB; NewC; REn; WhoMilH 76*

Stuart, Gilbert Charles
American. Artist
Noted for three portraits of George Washington, 1795-96.
b. Dec 3, 1755 in North Kingstown, Rhode Island
d. Jul 9, 1828 in Boston, Massachusetts
Source: *AmBi; AmCulL; ApCAB; AtlBL; BriEAA; DcAmB; DcArts; DcBiPP; Drake; EncAB-H 1974; HarEnUS; IlBEAAW; McGEWB; NatCAB 5; NewYHSD; OxCAmL 65; REn; REnAL; TwCBDA; WebAB 74, 79; WhAm HS; WorAl*

Stuart, Hod
[Horace Hodgson Stuart]
Canadian. Hockey Player
Defenseman, 1898-1907, with several amateur teams; Hall of Fame, 1945; drowned.
b. 1880 in Ottawa, Ontario, Canada
d. Jun 23, 1907 in Belleville, Ontario, Canada
Source: *WhoHcky 73*

Stuart, James
English. Architect, Artist
Published *The Antiquities of Athens,* 1762, which had first illustrations of Greek architecture; work spurred the classic revival period.
b. 1713
d. 1788
Source: *Alli; BiDBrA; BlkwCE; DcArts; DcBiPP; DcBrECP; DcNaB; IntDcAr; MacEA; McGDA; NewCBEL; NewCol 75; OxCArt; PenDiDA 89; WhoArch*

Stuart, Jeb
[James Ewell Brown Stuart]
American. Army Officer
Commanded all Confederate cavalry, 1862-64.
b. Feb 6, 1833 in Patrick County, Virginia
d. May 12, 1864 in Richmond, Virginia
Source: *AmBi; ApCAB; BiDConf; BioIn 1, 3, 4, 5, 6, 7, 8, 9, 12, 15, 18, 19, 20, 21; CivWDc; DcAmB; DcAmMiB; EncAB-H 1974, 1996; EncSoH; GenMudB; HarEnMi; HarEnUS; HisWorL; McGEWB; NatCAB 4; OxCAmH; TwCBDA; WebAB 74, 79; WebAMB; WhAm HS; WhCiWar; WhoMilH 76*

Stuart, Jesse Hilton
American. Author, Poet
Prolific regional writer named poet laureate of KY, 1954; best-known work: *Man with a Bull-Tongue Plow,* 1934.
b. Aug 8, 1907 in W-Hollow, Kentucky
d. Feb 17, 1984 in Ironton, Ohio
Source: *AmAu&B; AmNov; Au&Wr 71; AuBYP 3; ConAu 5R; ConLC 14; ConNov 72, 76; CurBio 84; CyWA 58; OxCAmL 65; RAdv 1; REn; SixAP; SmATA 2; TwCA SUP; TwCWr; WhAm 8; WhoAm 82*

Stuart, Kenneth James
American. Illustrator, Art Director
Art editor *Saturday Evening Post,* 1943-62; art director, Reader's Digest Assn., 1962-77.
b. Sep 21, 1905 in Milwaukee, Wisconsin
d. Feb 27, 1993 in Norwalk, Connecticut
Source: *BioIn 18; WhAmArt 85; WhoAm 74, 76, 78, 80, 82, 84, 86, 88, 90, 92, 94, 95, 96; WhoAmA 91, 93; WhoE 85, 86, 89; WhoWor 80*

Stuart, Lyle
American. Publisher
Pres. of Lyle Stuart, Inc., 1954-89; wrote *The Secret Life of Walter Winchell,* 1953.
b. Aug 11, 1922 in New York, New York
Source: *BioIn 6, 8, 9, 11; CelR; ConAu 81; DcAmSR; IntWW 91, 93; WhoAm 78, 80, 82, 84, 86, 88, 90, 92, 94, 95, 96, 97*

Stuart, Marty
[John Marty Stuart]
American. Singer, Songwriter, Musician
Country and bluegrass singer, guitarist and mandolinist; debut album, *Ridge Runner,* 1982; won 1993 Grammy for "The Whiskey Ain't Workin'"
b. Sep 30, 1958 in Philadelphia, Mississippi
Source: *BgBkCoM; ConMus 9; LegTOT; WhoAm 94, 95, 96, 97; WhoNeCM*

Stuart, Mel
American. Director
Won Emmys for "The Roots of Madness," 1967; "Making of the President," 1970.
b. Sep 2, 1928 in New York, New York
Source: *FilmgC; HalFC 88; LesBEnT 92; MiSFD 9; NewYTET; VarWW 85; WhoAm 80, 82*

Stuart, Ruth McEnery
American. Author
Wrote Southern life tales in dialect: *In Simpkinsville,* 1897.
b. May 21, 1849 in Marksville, Louisiana
d. May 6, 1917 in White Plains, New York
Source: *NotAW; REn*

Stubbs, George
English. Artist
Animal painter, noted for drawings of horses.
b. Aug 24, 1724 in Liverpool, England
d. Jul 10, 1806 in London, England
Source: *Alli; AtlBL; Benet 87; BioIn 1, 2, 3, 4, 5, 6, 7, 9, 10, 11, 13, 14, 15; BlkwCE; BritAS; DcArts; DcBiPP; DcBrECP; DcBrWA; DcNaB; EncEnl; IntDcAA 90; LegTOT; McGDA; NewCol 75; OxCArt; OxDcArt; WhDW; WorAl; WorAlBi*

Stubbs, Levi
[The Four Tops]
American. Singer
Original member of group.
b. Jun 6, 1936 in Detroit, Michigan
Source: *BioIn 15; WhoBlA 92; WhoRocM 82*

Stuckey, Williamson Sylvester
American. Businessman
Opened first candy shop, 1938; became nat. restaurant chain, with stores off US highways, after WW II.
b. 1909
d. Jan 7, 1977 in Eastman, Georgia
Source: *BioIn 8, 11; NewYTBS 77*

Studds, Gerry E(astman)
American. Politician
Dem. congressman from MA, 1973-83, 1983-96; censured by House, Jul 1983, for homosexual affair with page.
b. May 12, 1937 in Mineola, New York
Source: *AlmAP 92; BiDrUSC 89; CngDr 87, 89; GayLesB; LesBEnT; WhoAm 74, 76, 78, 80, 82, 84, 86, 88, 90, 92, 94, 95, 96, 97; WhoAmP 73, 75, 77, 79, 81, 83, 85, 87, 89, 91, 93, 95; WhoE 77, 79, 81, 83, 85, 86, 89, 91, 93, 95, 97; WhoGov 75, 77*

Studebaker, Clement
American. Manufacturer
Formed wagon co., 1852; experimented with autos, 1897; major product, 1902.
b. Mar 12, 1831 in Pinetown, Pennsylvania
d. Nov 27, 1901 in South Bend, Indiana
Source: *BiDAmBL 83; DcAmB; EncWM; NatCAB 11; WebAB 74, 79; WhAm 1; WorAl; WorAlBi*

Studebaker, John Mohler
American. Auto Manufacturer
Joined brother's firm, 1858, pres. from 1901.
b. Oct 10, 1833 in Gettysburg, Pennsylvania
d. Mar 16, 1917
Source: *BioIn 1; NatCAB 11; WhAm 1*

Studer, Cheryl
American. Opera Singer
Internationally known versatile soprano.
b. Oct 24, 1955 in Midland, Michigan
Source: *Baker 92; CurBio 92; IntWWM 90; NewGrDO; NewYTBS 91; OxDcOp; WhoAm 92; WhoEnt 92*

Studi, Wes
[Wesley Studie]
American. Actor
Appeared in films *Dances With Wolves, The Last of the Mohicans,* and *Geronimo.*
b. c. 1944 in Nofire Hollow, Oklahoma
Source: *News 94, 94-3*

Stuhldreher, Harry A
[Four Horsemen of Notre Dame]
American. Football Player
All-America quarterback under Knute Rockne at Notre Dame, 1922-24.
b. Oct 14, 1901 in Massillon, Ohio
d. Jan 22, 1965 in Pittsburgh, Pennsylvania
Source: *DcAmB S7; OhA&B; WhoFtbl 74; WhScrn 83*

Stulberg, Louis
American. Labor Union Official
Pres. of International Ladies Garment Workers Union, 1966-75.
b. Apr 14, 1901, Poland
d. Dec 14, 1977 in New York, New York
Source: *BiDAmL; BiDAmLL; BioIn 5, 11; NewYTBS 77; WhAm 7; WhoAm 74, 76; WhoLab 76; WhoWorJ 72, 78*

Stumpf, Richard J
American. Engineer
Co-inventor, Sensurround; won two Oscars for sound engineering, 1974, 1981.
b. Oct 15, 1926 in Glendale, California
Source: *VarWW 85*

Sturgeon, Theodore Hamilton
[Edward Hamilton Waldo]
American. Author
Books include *My People Is the Enemy,* 1964.
b. Feb 26, 1918 in Staten Island, New York
d. May 8, 1985 in Eugene, Oregon
Source: *AmAu&B; BioIn 7, 10, 12; ConAu 81; LinLib L; PenC AM; REnAL; WhoAm 74, 76, 78, 80, 82, 84; WorAl; WorAu 1950*

Sturgeon, William
English. Physicist
Developed the electromagnet.
b. May 22, 1783 in Whittington, England
d. Dec 4, 1850 in Prestwich, England
Source: *Alli; AsBiEn; BiESc; BioIn 2, 3, 14; CamDcSc; CelCen; DcBiPP; DcInv; DcNaB; DcScB; InSci; LarDcSc; WhDW*

Sturges, Preston
[Edmond P Biden]
American. Director, Screenwriter
Wrote, directed Oscar-winning *The Great McGinty,* 1940.
b. Aug 29, 1898 in Chicago, Illinois
d. Aug 6, 1959 in New York, New York
Source: *AmFD; BenetAL 91; BiDFilm, 81, 94; BioIn 1, 4, 5, 7, 8, 9, 10, 12, 13; CmMov; ConAu 114, 149; CurBio 41, 59; DcAmB S6; DcArts; DcFM; DcLB 26; EncAFC; FacFETw; FilmEn; FilmgC; HalFC 80, 84, 88; IlWWHD 1; IntDcF 1-2, 2-2; LegTOT; MiSFD 9N; ModWD; MovMk; NatCAB 61; ObitT 1951; OxCFilm; REnAL; TwCLC 48; WhAm 3; WhThe; WorEFlm; WorFDir 1*

Sturm, Charles Francois
[Jacques Charles Francois Sturm]
French. Mathematician
Sturm's theorem, concerning the theory of equations, was named in honor of his work.
b. Sep 29, 1803 in Geneva, Switzerland
d. Dec 18, 1855 in Paris, France
Source: *DcBiPP; DcScB; InSci; LarDcSc*

Sturtevant, Alfred Henry
American. Geneticist
Responsible for mapping specific genes of chromosomes in fruit flies.
b. Nov 21, 1891 in Jacksonville, Illinois
d. Apr 5, 1970 in Pasadena, California
Source: *AmDec 1910; BiESc; BioIn 6, 8, 9, 20; CamDcSc; DcScB; LarDcSc; McGMS 80; WhAm 5; WorScD*

Sturtzel, Howard Allison
[Paul Annixter]
American. Children's Author
Wrote nature novels with wife: *Windigo,* 1963.
b. Jun 25, 1894 in Minneapolis, Minnesota
Source: *BioIn 6, 9; ConAu 1R, 6NR; DcLP 87A; SmATA 1*

Sturtzel, Jane Levington
American. Children's Author
With husband, wrote nature novels: *The Year of the She-Grizzly,* 1978.
b. Jun 22, 1903 in Detroit, Michigan
Source: *AuBYP 3; BioIn 9; ConAu 1R, 6NR; DcLP 87A; PenNWW A; SmATA 1*

Stuyvesant, Peter
[Petrus Stuyvesant]
Dutch. Colonial Figure
One-legged governor of New Amsterdam, now NY, 1647-64.
b. 1610 in Scherpenzeel, Netherlands
d. Feb 1672 in New York, New York
Source: *AmBi; DcAmB; EncAB-H 1974; EncCRAm; HisWorL; LegTOT; McGEWB; RComAH; REn; REnAL; WebAB 74, 79; WhAm HS; WhNaAH; WorAl*

Stydahar, Joe
[Joseph Leo Stydahar]
"Jumbo Joe"
American. Football Player
Four-time all-pro defensive tackle, Chicago, 1936-42, 1945-46; Hall of Fame, 1967.
b. Mar 17, 1912 in Kaylor, Pennsylvania
d. Mar 23, 1977 in Beckley, West Virginia
Source: *BioIn 6, 8, 11, 17; LegTOT; NewYTBS 77; WhoFtbl 74*

Styles, Re
[The Tubes]
American. Singer
Dancer, singer with The Tubes since late 1960s.
b. Mar 3, 1950

Styne, Jule
[Julius Kerwin Stein]
American. Songwriter
Won best song Oscar for "Three Coins in the Fountain," 1954; other songs included in films "I'll Walk Alone," 1945; "Funny Girl," 1968.
b. Dec 31, 1905 in London, England
d. Sep 20, 1994 in New York, New York
Source: *AmPS; AmSong; ASCAP 66, 80; Baker 78, 84, 92; BestMus; BiDAmM; BiE&WWA; BioIn 1, 5, 6, 9, 10, 11, 12, 13, 14, 15, 16, 20, 21; CelR, 90; CmpEPM; ConAmC 76, 82; ConTFT 4, 13; CurBio 83, 94N; EncMT; FacFETw; FilmEn; FilmgC; HalFC 80, 84, 88; IntMPA 77, 80, 92, 94; IntWW 89, 91, 93; LegTOT; NewAmDM; NewCBMT; NewGrDA 86; NewGrDM 80; NewGrDO; News 95, 95-1; NewYTBS 87, 94; NotNAT; OxCAmT 84; OxCPMus; PopAmC, SUP; Sw&Ld C; WhAm 11; WhoAm 74, 76, 78, 80, 82, 84, 86, 88, 90, 92, 94; WhoThe 72, 77, 81; WhoWor 74; WorAl; WorAlBi*

Styron, William Clark, Jr.
American. Author
Won Pulitzer for *The Confessions of Nat Turner,* 1968; wrote novel *Sophie's Choice,* 1979, filmed, 1982.
b. Jun 11, 1925 in Newport News, Virginia
Source: *Benet 87; BenetAL 91; BioIn 15, 16; BroV; CamGLE; CamHAL; CasWL; CelR 90; ConAu 5NR, 5R, 33NR; ConLC 15, 60; ConNov 86, 91; CurBio 86; CyWA 89; DrAPF 91; EncWB; FacFETw; FifSWrA; IntAu&W 91; IntvTCA 2; IntWW 91; MajTwCW; ModAL S1, S2; OxCAmL 65; PenC AM; PeoHis; RAdv 1, 13-1; REn; REnAL; RfGAmL 87; TwCRHW 90; TwCWr; WhoAm 86, 90; WhoE 91; WhoUSWr 88; WhoWor 87, 91; WhoWrEP 89; WorAlBi; WrDr 86, 92; WrPh*

Styx
[John Curulewski; Dennis DeYoung; Chuck Panozzo; John Panozzo; Tommy Shaw; James Young]
American. Music Group
Hard pop group formed 1963, popular among young teens; hit single "Babe," 1979.
Source: *Alli; AntBDN Q; ASCAP 80; ConMuA 80A; DcCanB 1; DcNaB; EncPR&S 89; EncRk 88; EncRkSt; Film 1; InB&W 80; NewGrDA 86; NewYTBS 27; OxCCan; PenEncP; RkOn 78, 85, 85A; RolSEnR 83; WhoHol 92; WhoRock 81; WhoRocM 82*

Suarez, Xavier Louis
Cuban. Politician, Lawyer
Mayor, Miami, FL, 1985-93; first Cuban-American mayor in Miami.
b. May 21, 1949 in Las Villas, Cuba
Source: *ConNews 86-2; NewYTBS 85; WhoAm 86, 88, 90, 92, 94, 95, 96, 97; WhoAmL 94, 96; WhoAmP 87, 89, 91, 93, 95; WhoHisp 92; WhoSSW 88, 91, 93, 95*

Suarez Gonzales, Adolfo
Spanish. Political Leader
Prime minister, 1976-81.
b. Sep 25, 1932 in Cebreros, Spain
Source: *CurBio 77; WhoWor 84, 91; WorAl; WorAlBi*

Subic, Joseph, Jr.
[The Hostages]
American. Hostage
One of 52 held by terrorists, Nov 1979-Jan 1981.
b. 1957?
Source: *NewYTBS 81*

Sublette, William L
American. Explorer, Naturalist
Established firm to transport people across Rocky Mts., 1823-30.
b. 1799 in Lincoln County, Kentucky
d. Jul 23, 1845 in Pittsburgh, Pennsylvania
Source: *DcAmB; WhAm HS*

Suchocka, Hanna
Polish. Politician
Prime minister, Poland, 1992-93.
b. Apr 3, 1946 in Pleszew, Poland
Source: *CurBio 94; IntWW 93; NewYTBS 93; WhoWor 93, 95*

Suckow, Ruth
American. Author
Books describe small-town Iowa: *The Folks,* 1934.
b. Aug 6, 1892 in Hawarden, Iowa
d. Jan 23, 1960 in Claremont, California
Source: *AmAu&B; AmNov; AmWomPl; AmWomWr; ArtclWW 2; BenetAL 91; BioAmW; BioIn 2, 4, 5, 7, 8, 12, 17; ChhPo; CnDAL; ConAmA; ConAmL; ConAu 113; DcLB 9, 102; DcLEL; EncFWF; FemiCLE; FifWWr; GrWrEL N; InWom, SUP; LngCTC; ModWoWr; NotAW MOD; OxCAmL 65, 83, 95; PeoHis; REn; REnAL; RfGAmL 87, 94; ShSCr 18; TwCA, SUP; TwCWW 91; WhoAmW 58*

Sucre, Antonio J. de
Venezuelan. Revolutionary
Pres. of Bolivia, 1825-28.
b. 1795 in Cumana, Venezuela
d. Jun 4, 1830 in Pasto, Colombia
Source: *ApCAB; Drake; REn*

Sudarkasa, Niara
[Gloria Albertha Marshall]
American. University Administrator
First woman pres. of historically black Lincoln U, PA 1987—.
b. Aug 14, 1938 in Fort Lauderdale, Florida
Source: *BioIn 16; BlkWAm; ConBlB 4; NotBlAW 1; WhoAfA 96; WhoAm 88, 90, 94; WhoAmW 91, 93, 97; WhoBlA 85, 88, 90, 92, 94; WhoWor 96*

Sudermann, Hermann
German. Dramatist
Works concerned ideas of honor, reputation: *Honor,* 1893; *St. John's Fire,* 1900.
b. Sep 30, 1857 in Matziken, Prussia
d. Nov 21, 1928 in Berlin, Germany
Source: *BbD; Benet 87, 96; BiD&SB; BioIn 1, 5, 18; CamGWoT; CasWL; ClDMEL 47, 80; CnMD; ConAu 107; CyWA 58; DcLB 118; Dis&D; EncWT; Ent; EvEuW; IntDcT 2; LinLib L, S; LngCTC; McGEWB; McGEWD 72, 84; ModWD; NewC; NewCBEL; NotNAT B; OxCEng 67; OxCGer 76, 86; OxCThe 67, 83; PenC EUR; REn; TwCA, SUP; TwCLC 15; WhDW*

Sue, Eugene Joseph Marie
French. Author, Physician
Wrote romances *The Wandering Jew,* 1845; *Mysteries of Paris,* 1842.
b. Jan 20, 1804 in Paris, France
d. Aug 3, 1857 in Annecy, France
Source: *BbD; BiD&SB; CasWL; CyWA 58; DcBiA; DcEuL; EncMys; EuAu; EvEuW; NewC; OxCEng 67; OxCFr; OxCThe 67; PenC EUR; REn*

Suenens, Leon Joseph, Cardinal
American. Religious Leader
Primate, Belgium, 1961-79.

b. Jul 6, 1904
d. May 6, 1996 in Brussels, Belgium
Source: *BioIn 6, 7, 8, 9, 10, 11, 12, 13, 20; ConAu 61, 152; CurBio 96N; WhoWor 74, 76, 78, 80, 82*

Suesse, Dana Nadine
"Girl Gershwin"
American. Composer, Musician
Child prodigy pianist; composed orchestral pieces as well as pop tunes: "You Oughta Be in Pictures," 1934.
b. Dec 3, 1911 in Shreveport, Louisiana
d. Oct 16, 1987 in New York, New York
Source: *Baker 84; CmpEPM; ConAmC 82; CurBio 40, 88; InWom, SUP*

Suetonius
Roman. Biographer
Wrote lives of Roman literary figures, biographies of first 11 emperors.
b. 69?
d. 140?
Source: *AncWr; AtlBL; BiD&SB; CasWL; DcArts; NewC; OxCEng 67; RAdv 14, 13-2, 13-3; REn; RfGWoL 95; WorAl; WorAlBi*

Suggs, Louise
American. Golfer
Turned pro, 1948; has 50 LPGA wins including US Women's Open, 1949, 1952; Hall of Fame, 1961.
b. Sep 7, 1923 in Lithia Springs, Georgia
Source: *BiDAmSp OS; BioIn 1, 6; CurBio 62; EncWomS; InWom, SUP; LegTOT; WhoGolf; WhoSpor*

Sugiura, Kanematsu
American. Scientist
Pioneer in development of chemotherapy for cancer treatment, 1912.
b. Jun 5, 1892 in Tsushima-Shi, Japan
d. Oct 21, 1979 in White Plains, New York
Source: *AmMWSc 79; DcAmB S10; NewYTBS 79*

Suharto, General
Indonesian. Political Leader
President since 1968.
b. Jun 8, 1921 in Kemusa, Dutch East Indies
Source: *BioIn 10, 14; CurBio 67; FacFETw; FarE&A 79; IntWW 80, 81, 82, 83, 91; IntYB 78; NewYTBS 91; Who 92; WhoWor 87, 91; WorAlBi*

Suhl, Yuri
American. Author
Wrote on Holocaust for children, adults: *On the Other Side of the Gate,* 1975.
b. Jul 30, 1908 in Podhajce, Poland
d. Nov 8, 1986 in New York, New York
Source: *AuBYP 2S, 3; BioIn 11, 15, 16, 19; ChlLR 2; ConAu 2NR, 45, 121; IntAu&W 76; SmATA 1AS, 8, 50N; WhoWorJ 72, 78*

Sui, Anna
American. Fashion Designer
Launched own fashion line, c. 1980.
b. c. 1955 in Dearborn Heights, Michigan
Source: *AsAmAlm; ConFash; CurBio 93; News 95, 95-1; NotAsAm; WhoAm 94, 95, 96; WhoAmW 95, 97; WhoAsA 94; WhoWor 97*

Sui, Yang Chien
Chinese. Political Leader
First of Sui emperors; reunited China, killed, succeeded by son.
b. 541
d. 604
Source: *McGEWB; NewCol 75*

Suits, C(hauncey) G(uy)
American. Physicist, Inventor
Developed method of measuring temperature of arcs, determined practical applications like radio circuits, beacons, and submarine signals.
b. Mar 12, 1905 in Oshkosh, Wisconsin
d. Aug 14, 1991 in Pilot Knob, New York
Source: *AmMWSc 73P, 76P, 79, 82, 86, 89, 92; BioIn 1, 2, 4, 7, 17, 20; BlueB 76; CurBio 91N; InSci; IntWW 74, 75, 76, 77, 78, 79, 80, 81, 82, 83, 89, 91; McGMS 80; NewYTBS 91; WhAm 10; WhoAm 74, 76, 78, 86, 88, 90; WhoEng 88; WhoWor 74*

Suk, Josef
Bohemian. Violinist, Composer
Wrote symphony *Asrael,* 1907; son-in-law of Dvorak.
b. Jan 4, 1874 in Krecovic, Bohemia
d. May 29, 1935 in Beneschau, Czechoslovakia
Source: *Baker 78, 84, 92; BioIn 3, 4, 8, 14; DcCom&M 79; NewAmDM; NewCol 75; NewGrDM 80; NewOxM; OxCMus*

Sukarno, Achmed
Indonesian. Political Leader
First pres. of Indonesia, 1945-67, headed authoritarian government with strong ties to Communist China.
b. Jun 1, 1901 in Surabaya, Dutch East Indies
d. Jun 21, 1970 in Jakarta, Indonesia
Source: *ConAu 113; CurBio 47, 70; DcPol; McGEWB; NewYTBE 70; WhAm 5; WhWW-II*

Sukenik, Eliazer Lipa
Israeli. Archaeologist
Expert on Biblical manuscripts.
b. 1889
d. Feb 28, 1953 in Jerusalem, Israel
Source: *BioIn 3; ObitOF 79*

Sukhomlinov, Vladimir Aleksandrovich
Russian. Military Leader
General most responsible for prematurely involving Russia in World War I.
b. Aug 16, 1848, Russia
d. Feb 2, 1926 in Berlin, Germany
Source: *BiDSovU; BioIn 17*

Sukman, Harry
American. Composer, Conductor, Pianist
Won Oscar for score of *Song Without End,* 1960.
b. Dec 2, 1912 in Chicago, Illinois
d. Dec 2, 1984
Source: *ASCAP 66, 80; BioIn 14; VarWW 85*

Suleiman I
[Suleiman the Magnificent]
Turkish. Ruler
Ottoman sultan, 1520-66; empire reached height of power under him.
b. Apr 27, 1496 in Trebizona, Turkey
d. Sep 5, 1566 in Szigetvar, Hungary
Source: *McGEWB; NewCol 75; REn; WebBD 83; WhDW; WhoMilH 76*

Sulla, Lucius C
Roman. Army Officer, Political Leader
Used army to seize control of state, 82 BC; revived Roman office of dictator; his was notorious for cruelty.
b. 138BC
d. 78BC in Campania, Campania
Source: *LinLib S; McGEWB; NewCol 75; REn*

Sullavan, Margaret
American. Actor
First wife of Henry Fonda; won Drama Critics award for *The Voice of the Turtle,* 1943.
b. May 16, 1896 in Norfolk, Virginia
d. Jan 1, 1960 in New Haven, Connecticut
Source: *BiDFilm; BioAmW; CmMov; CurBio 44, 60; FilmgC; MotPP; MovMk; OxCFilm; OxCThe 67; ThFT; WhAm 3; WhScrn 77*

Sullivan, A(loysius) M(ichael)
American. Editor
Edited *Dun's Review,* 1954-61.
b. Aug 9, 1896 in Harrison, New Jersey
d. Jun 10, 1980 in Montclair, New Jersey
Source: *AmCath 80; AnCL; BioIn 1, 3, 12; BkC 3; CathA 1930; ChhPo, S1, S2; ConAu 97, P-2; CurBio 53, 80; Po&Wr 77; REnAL; WhAm 7; WhE&EA*

Sullivan, Andrew
American. Editor, Writer
Editor, *New Republic,* 1991—.
b. c. 1964, England
Source: *News 96, 96-1*

Sullivan, Anne
[Mrs. John A. Macy]
American. Teacher
Perkins Institute teacher of Helen Keller, 1887; companion until death, 1936.
b. Apr 14, 1866 in Feeding Hills, Massachusetts
d. Oct 20, 1936 in Forest Hills, New York

Source: *AmBi; BioIn 14, 18, 20, 21; InWom, SUP; LegTOT; NotAW; WebAB 74*

Sullivan, Arthur Seymour, Sir
[Gilbert and Sullivan]
English. Composer, Author
With W S Gilbert produced 14 comic operas; wrote "Onward Christian Soldiers," 1871.
b. May 14, 1842 in London, England
d. Nov 22, 1900 in London, England
Source: *Alli; AtlBL; AuBYP 2S; Baker 78, 84; BioIn 1, 2, 3, 4, 5, 6, 7, 8, 9, 10, 11, 12, 13; BriBkM 80; CelCen; CmOp; DcCom 77; DcCom&M 79; DcNaB S1; Dis&D; FilmgC; GrComp; LinLib L, S; McGEWB; MusMk; NewC; NewGrDM 80; NotNAT A, B; OxCMus; REn; REnWD*

Sullivan, Barry
[Patrick Barry]
American. Actor
Leading man in films since 1940s: *Another Time, Another Place,* 1958; *Harlow,* 1965.
b. Aug 12, 1912 in New York, New York
d. Jun 6, 1994 in Sherman Oaks, California
Source: *BiE&WWA; BioIn 4, 18, 19, 20; FilmEn; FilmgC; ForYSC; GangFlm; HalFC 80, 84, 88; IntMPA 75, 76, 78, 79, 80, 81, 82, 84, 86, 88, 92, 94; ItaFilm; LegTOT; MotPP; MovMk; NotNAT; VarWW 85; WhoAm 82, 84; WhoHol 92, A; WorAl*

Sullivan, C(harles) Gardner
American. Screenwriter, Filmmaker
Wrote scenarios of early Western films.
b. Sep 18, 1886? in Stillwater, Minnesota
d. Sep 5, 1965 in Hollywood, California
Source: *ConAu 113; DcLB 26; OxCFilm*

Sullivan, Daniel P
American. Government Official
FBI agent who helped track down John Dillinger and Barker-Karpis gang.
b. 1912 in Washington, District of Columbia
d. Jul 4, 1982 in Miami, Florida
Source: *NewYTBS 82*

Sullivan, Danny
American. Auto Racer
Won Indianapolis 500, 1985.
b. Mar 9, 1950 in Louisville, Kentucky
Source: *BioIn 15; CelR 90; NewYTBS 85; WhoAm 94, 95, 96, 97*

Sullivan, Ed(ward Vincent)
American. TV Personality
"Toast of the Town" variety show evolved into "The Ed Sullivan Show," 1948-71.
b. Sep 28, 1902 in New York, New York
d. Oct 13, 1974 in New York, New York
Source: *AmDec 1950; BiDAmJo; BiDAmNC; BiDD; BioIn 2, 3, 4, 5, 6, 7, 8, 10, 12, 16, 17, 19; CelR; ConAu 89; CurBio 52, 74, 74N; EncAJ; EncTwCJ; FacFETw; IntMPA 75; IntWW 74; LegTOT; LinLib L, S; NewYTBS 74; NewYTET; PlP&P; SaTiSS; WebAB 74, 79; WhAm 6; WhoAm 74; WhoHol B; WhoWor 74; WhScrn 77, 83; WorAl; WorAlBi*

Sullivan, Francis Loftus
English. Actor
Character actor, often in villainous roles: *Oliver Twist,* 1948; *The Prodigal,* 1955.
b. Jan 6, 1903 in London, England
d. Nov 19, 1956 in New York, New York
Source: *BioIn 3, 4; FilmAG WE; FilmEn; FilmgC; ForYSC; HalFC 80; IlWWBF; MotPP; NotNAT B; PlP&P; Vers A; WhAm 3; WhoHol B; WhScrn 74, 77, 83; WhThe*

Sullivan, Frank
American. Journalist
Best known for cliche phrases; wrote Christmas poems for *The New Yorker,* 1932-74.
b. Sep 22, 1892 in Saratoga, New York
d. Feb 19, 1976 in Saratoga, New York
Source: *AmAu&B; Benet 87, 96; BenetAL 91; BiDAmNC; BioIn 3, 4, 7, 9, 10, 13, 14, 15; ChhPo S1; ConAu 65, P-2; JrnUS; LegTOT; LngCTC; NewYTBS 76; OxCAmL 83, 95; REn; REnAL; TwCA, SUP; WhAm 6; WhoAm 74, 76*

Sullivan, Haywood Cooper
American. Baseball Executive
Catcher, Boston Red Sox, 1952, 1955-60; Kansas City, 1961-63; appeared in 312 ML games in seven yrs., mostly as catcher; co-owner Boston Red Sox, 1985-94.
b. Dec 15, 1930 in Donaldsonville, Georgia
Source: *BaseEn 88; WhoAm 84, 86, 88, 90, 92, 94, 95; WhoE 83, 85, 86, 91, 95*

Sullivan, John
American. Politician
President (before title of governor) of NH, 1786, 1787, 1789; member of first, second Continental Congresses, 1774, 1775.
b. Feb 17, 1740 in Somersworth, New Hampshire
d. Jan 23, 1795 in Durham, North Carolina
Source: *Alli; AmBi; AmRev; ApCAB; BenetAL 91; BiAUS; BiDFedJ; BiDrAC; BiDrACR; BiDrUSC 89; BioIn 4, 6, 7, 8, 10, 11; BlkwEAR; DcAmB; DcAmMiB; Drake; EncAR; EncCRAm; HarEnMi; HarEnUS; NatCAB 1; NewCBEL; OxCAmH; REnAL; TwCBDA; WebAB 74, 79; WebAMB; WhAm HS; WhAmP; WhAmRev; WhNaAH; WhoMilH 76*

Sullivan, John L(awrence)
"Boston Strong Boy"
American. Boxer
Last bare-knuckle heavyweight champ, 1882-92; Hall of Fame, 1954.
b. Oct 15, 1858 in Boston, Massachusetts
d. Feb 2, 1918 in Abingdon, Massachusetts
Source: *AmBi; BiDAmSp BK; BioIn 1, 2, 3, 4, 5, 6, 9, 10, 11, 12; DcAmB; DcAmTB; DcNAA; McGEWB; OxCAmH; REnAL; WebAB 74, 79; WhAm 4, HS, HSA; WhoBox 74*

Sullivan, Kathleen
American. Broadcast Journalist
Anchors "ABC World News This Morning."
b. May 17, 1954? in Pasadena, California
Source: *BioIn 15, 16; CelR 90; InWom SUP; LegTOT; WhoAm 90; WhoRel 92*

Sullivan, Kathryn D
American. Astronaut
First woman to walk in space, with shuttle *Challenger,* Oct 1984.
b. 1951? in New Jersey
Source: *BioIn 11; NewYTBS 84; WhoAmW 91; WhoSpc*

Sullivan, Leon H
American. Civil Rights Leader, Clergy
Pioneer of protest economic boycotts for stores failing to employ blacks; created job-training agency Opportunities Industrialization Centers of America, Inc.
b. Oct 16, 1922 in Charleston, West Virginia
Source: *BioIn 8, 9, 10, 11, 12, 13; ConBlB 3; CurBio 69; NegAl 89; WhoAm 90; WhoBlA 92; WhoRel 92*

Sullivan, Louis Henri
American. Architect
Pioneer in modern functional architecture who abandoned Victorian Gothic ornamentation for simple, uncluttered lines.
b. Sep 3, 1856 in Boston, Massachusetts
d. Apr 14, 1924 in Chicago, Illinois
Source: *AmAu&B; AmBi; AtlBL; BiDAmAr; BriEAA; DcAmB; DcNAA; EncAAr 1, 2; EncAB-H 1974, 1996; McGDA; McGEWB; MemAm; OxCAmH; OxCAmL 65; REn; REnAL; WebAB 74, 79; WhAm 1; WhDW; WhoArch*

Sullivan, Louis W(ade)
American. Government Official
US Secretary of Health and Human Services 1989-93.
b. Nov 3, 1933 in Atlanta, Georgia
Source: *AfrAmAl 6; AfrAmBi 1; AmMWSc 73P, 76P, 79, 82, 86, 89, 92, 95; BiDrUSE 89; BioIn 16; BlksScM; CngDr 89, 91; CurBio 89; DiAASTC; InB&W 85; IntWW 89, 91, 93; WhoAfA 96; WhoAm 78, 82, 84, 86, 88, 90, 92, 94, 95, 96, 97; WhoAmP 89, 91, 93, 95; WhoBlA 80, 85, 88, 90, 92, 94; WhoE 91, 93; WhoFrS 84; WhoMedH;*

WhoScEn 94; WhoSSW 95, 97; WhoWor 91, 93, 95

Sullivan, Mark
American. Author
Wrote six-vol. history, *Our Times: The United States, 1900-1925,* 1926-36.
b. Sep 10, 1874 in Avondale, Pennsylvania
d. Aug 13, 1952 in Avondale, Pennsylvania
Source: *AmAu&B; Benet 87; BenetAL 91; BiDAmNC; BioIn 3, 4, 5, 9, 14; CathA 1952; DcAmB S5; DcAmSR; EncAJ; MorMA; NatCAB 42; OxCAmH; OxCAmL 65, 83, 95; REn; REnAL; TwCA, SUP; WhAm 3; WhLit; WhNAA*

Sullivan, Maxine
American. Singer, Musician
Famous for 1937 rendition of "Loch Lomond."
b. May 13, 1911 in Pittsburgh, Pennsylvania
d. Apr 7, 1987 in New York, New York
Source: *AllMusG; AnObit 1987; BiDAfM; BiDAmM; BiDJaz; BioIn 10, 14, 15, 17; BlkWAm; CmpEPM; DrBlPA, 90; EncJzS; IlEncJ; InB&W 80, 85; InWom SUP; NegAl 83, 89; NewAmDM; NewGrDA 86; NewGrDJ 88, 94; NewYTBS 87; NotBlAW 2; OxCPMus; PenEncP; WhoJazz 72*

Sullivan, Mike
[Michael J Sullivan]
American. Politician
Dem. governor of Wyoming, 1987-93.
b. Sep 23, 1939 in Omaha, Nebraska
Source: *AlmAP 88, 92; BiDrGov 1983, 1988; BioIn 16; IntWW 89, 91, 93; WhoAm 88, 90; WhoAmP 87, 89, 91, 93, 95; WhoWest 87, 89, 92; WhoWor 89, 91*

Sullivan, Pat(rick J)
American. Football Player
All-America quarterback, won Heisman Trophy, 1971; in NFL with Atlanta, 1972-75.
b. Jan 18, 1950 in Birmingham, Michigan
Source: *BiDAmSp FB; BioIn 14; NewYTBE 71; WhoFtbl 74*

Sullivan, Susan
American. Actor
Played Maggie Gioberti Channing on TV series "Falcon Crest," 1981-89.
b. Nov 18, 1944 in New York, New York
Source: *BioIn 15; ConTFT 2; LegTOT; VarWW 85*

Sullivan, Tom
American. Singer, Actor, Composer
Blind performer who wrote *If You Could See What I Hear,* 1976; made into movie, 1982.
b. Mar 27, 1947 in Boston, Massachusetts
Source: *BioIn 10, 11, 12, 17; ConTFT 2; VarWW 85; WhoEnt 92*

Sullivan, Walter
[Walter Seager Sullivan, Jr.]
American. Journalist
Science editor of *NY Times* 1964-87; wrote *We Are Not Alone,* 1964.
b. Jan 12, 1918 in New York, New York
d. Mar 19, 1996 in Riverside, Connecticut
Source: *AmAu&B; AmMWSc 92; ConAu 2NR, 151; CurBio 80; EncTwCJ; IntAu&W 91; IntWW 83, 91; JrnUS; NewYTBS 27; WhAm 11; WhoAm 82, 90; WhoWrEP 89; WrDr 80, 82, 84, 86, 88, 90, 92*

Sullivan, William Hallisey, Jr.
American. Football Executive
Owner, president, New England Patriots, 1975-88; president, AFL, 1963-69.
b. Sep 13, 1915 in Lowell, Massachusetts
Source: *NewYTBS 86; WhoAm 74, 76, 78, 80, 82, 84, 86, 88, 90, 92, 94, 95, 96, 97; WhoE 74, 79, 81, 83, 85, 86, 93; WhoFtbl 74*

Sullivan, William Healy
American. Diplomat
US ambassador to Iran, 1977-79, to Philippines, 1973-77.
b. Oct 12, 1922 in Cranston, Rhode Island
Source: *BioIn 9, 11, 12, 14; CurBio 79; IntWW 74, 75, 76, 77, 78, 79, 80, 81, 82, 83, 89; MidE 78, 79, 80, 81, 82; NewYTBS 79; PolProf J, K; USBiR 74; WhoAm 76, 78; WhoAmP 77, 79; WhoGov 72, 75, 77; WhoWor 74, 76, 78*

Sully, Maximilien de Bethune, Duc
French. Statesman
Wrote *Royal Economics,* 1638.
b. 1560, France
d. 1641, France
Source: *BiD&SB; OxCFr; REn*

Sully, Thomas
American. Artist
Painted over 2,000 portraits, 500 historical scenes.
b. Jun 8, 1783 in Horncastle, England
d. Nov 5, 1872 in Philadelphia, Pennsylvania
Source: *Alli SUP; AmBi; ApCAB; ArtsNiC; Benet 87, 96; BioIn 1, 2, 4, 7, 9, 10, 11, 12, 13, 14; BriEAA; ChhPo; DcAmArt; DcAmAu; DcAmB; Drake; EncAB-H 1974, 1996; HarEnUS; LegTOT; LinLib S; McGDA; NatCAB 5; NewYHSD; OxCAmH; OxCAmL 65; OxCArt; OxDcArt; REn; TwCBDA; WebAB 74, 79; WhAm HS; WorAl; WorAlBi*

Sully Prudhomme
[Rene-Francois-Armand Prudhomme]
French. Poet
Won first Nobel Prize for literature, 1901.
b. Mar 16, 1839 in Paris, France
d. Sep 7, 1907 in Paris, France
Source: *AtlBL; Benet 87, 96; BiD&SB; CasWL; ClDMEL 47, 80; EuAu; LinLib L, S; OxCFr; PenC EUR; REn; TwCLC 31; WorAl; WorAlBi*

Sulzberger, Arthur Hays
American. Journalist
Board chm. of *NY Times* from 1957, publisher from 1935.
b. Sep 12, 1891 in New York, New York
d. Dec 11, 1968 in New York, New York
Source: *AmAu&B; BioIn 1, 2, 3, 7, 8, 12, 16, 19; ConAu 89; CurBio 43, 69; DcAmB S8; DcLB 127; EncAJ; JrnUS; LinLib L, S; ObitT 1961; REnAL; WebAB 74, 79; WhAm 5*

Sulzberger, Arthur O(chs)
"Punch"
American. Newspaper Executive
Pres., publisher of *NY Times* 1963-92; CEO *NY Times,* 1963—.
b. Feb 5, 1926 in New York, New York
Source: *BioIn 7, 8, 10, 11, 13, 15, 16, 17, 18, 19; BlueB 76; CelR, 90; CurBio 66; DcLB 127; Dun&B 79, 88, 90; EncAJ; EncWB; IntWW 74, 75, 76, 77, 78, 79, 80, 81, 82, 83, 89, 91, 93; NewYTBS 87; PolProf K; St&PR 93, 96, 97; Who 74, 82, 83, 85, 88, 90, 92, 94; WhoAm 74, 76, 78, 80, 82, 84, 86, 88, 90, 92, 94, 95, 96, 97; WhoE 74, 75, 77, 79, 81, 83, 85, 86, 89, 91, 93, 95, 97; WhoFI 74, 75, 77, 79, 81, 83, 85, 87, 89, 92, 94, 96; WhoWor 74, 78, 87; WorAlBi*

Sulzberger, Arthur O(chs), Jr.
American. Newspaper Executive
Publisher, *The New York Times,* 1992—.
b. Sep 22, 1951 in Mount Kisco, New York
Source: *NewYTBS 87; WhoAm 92, 94, 95, 96, 97; WhoE 89, 91, 93, 95, 97; WhoWor 96*

Sulzberger, C(yrus) L(eo)
American. Author
Books include *Such a Peace: The Roots and Ashes of Yalta,* 1982.
b. Oct 27, 1912 in New York, New York
d. Sep 20, 1993 in Paris, France
Source: *Au&Wr 71; BiDAmNC; BioIn 3, 4, 7, 8, 9, 10, 11, 19; ConAu 23NR, 53; CurBio 44; IntAu&W 76; IntWW 74, 75, 76, 77, 78, 79, 80, 81, 82, 83, 89, 91, 93; REnAL; WhAm 11; WhoAm 74, 76, 78, 80, 82, 84, 86, 90, 92, 94; WhoWor 74, 89; WrDr 92*

Sulzer, Salomon
"Father of Modern Synagogue Music"
Austrian. Composer
Most renowned cantor of 19th century.
b. Mar 30, 1804 in Hohenems, Austria

d. Jan 17, 1890 in Vienna, Austria
Source: *Baker 78, 84, 92; BioIn 2; NewGrDM 80*

Sumac, Yma
Peruvian. Singer
Flamboyant concertist, billed as Inca princess; voice ranged five octaves.
b. Sep 10, 1928 in Ichocan, Peru
Source: *Baker 84; CurBio 55; ForYSC; HalFC 80, 84, 88; PenEncP; WhoAmW 58, 61, 68, 72, 74; WhoHol A; WhoMus 72*

Summer, Donna
[LaDonna Andrea Gaines]
American. Singer
Disco hits include "Hot Stuff," 1979; "Last Dance," 1978; "Dinner With Gershwin," 1987; Grammy award winner, 1984.
b. Dec 31, 1948 in Boston, Massachusetts
Source: *ASCAP 80; BiDAfM; BioIn 11, 12, 13; BkPepl; CelR 90; ConMuA 80A; ConMus 12; CurBio 79; DrBlPA 90; EncPR&S 89; EncRk 88; EncRkSt; HerW; IlEncBM 82; IntWW 89, 91, 93; InWom SUP; LegTOT; NewGrDA 86; OxCPMus; PenEncP; RkOn 74; RolSEnR 83; SoulM; WhoAm 80, 82, 84, 86, 88, 90, 92; WhoAmW 87, 89, 91; WhoBlA 85; WhoEnt 92; WhoHol 92; WhoRock 81; WorAlBi*

Summerall, Pat
[George Summerall]
"Gary Cooper of Sportscasters"
American. Sportscaster
Announcer for CBS Sports, 1962-94; covered 11 Super Bowls; Sportscaster of Year, 1977; announcer for Fox Sports, 1994—.
b. 1931? in Lake City, Florida
Source: *LegTOT; LesBEnT; WhoAm 86, 92, 94, 95, 96, 97; WhoFtbl 74; WhoWest 96*

Summerfield, Arthur Ellsworth
American. Government Official
Postmaster General under Eisenhower, 1953-61.
b. Mar 17, 1899 in Pinconning, Michigan
d. Apr 26, 1972 in West Palm Beach, Florida
Source: *BiDrUSE 71, 89; BioIn 2, 3, 4, 5, 9, 10, 11, 17; CurBio 52, 72; DcAmB S9; IntYB 78; LinLib S; NewYTBE 72; PolProf E; WhAm 5; Who 74*

Summers, Andy
[The Police; Andrew James Somers; Andrew James Summers]
English. Musician, Songwriter
Guitarist with The Police; scored movie *Down and Out in Beverly Hills,* 1986; now solo.
b. Dec 31, 1942 in Poulton-Fylde, England
Source: *BioIn 12, 13, 16; ConMus 3; LegTOT; OnThGG; WhoAm 94, 95, 96, 97; WhoRocM 82*

Summers, Anne Fairhurst
Editor, Writer
Editor-in-chief of Ms. magazine, 1987-89; author of *Damned Whores and God's Police,* 1975.
b. Mar 12, 1945 in Deniliquin, Australia
Source: *AmWomWr; BioIn 16; News 90-2; OxCAusL; WhoAm 94; WhoAmW 91, 93; WhoE 91, 93, 95*

Summersby, Kay
[Kathleen McCarthy-Morrogh]
English. Secretary
Wartime companion romantically linked to Eisenhower.
b. 1908 in County Cork, Ireland
d. Jan 20, 1975 in Southampton, England
Source: *BioIn 1, 7, 10, 11, 17; BioNews 74*

Summerskill, Edith Clara, Baroness
English. Physician
Member, House of Commons, 1938-61; chm., Labour Party, 1954-55.
b. Apr 19, 1901 in London, England
d. Feb 4, 1980 in London, England
Source: *BiDBrF 2; BioIn 7, 8, 12; CurBio 43, 63, 80N; DcNaB 1971; InSci; IntWW 77; InWom, SUP; NewYTBS 80; WhoWor 74; WomFir*

Summerville, Slim
[George J Summerville]
American. Comedian
One of original Keystone Cops, known for "hick" roles; films include *All Quiet on the Western Front,* 1930.
b. Jul 10, 1896 in Albuquerque, New Mexico
d. Jan 6, 1946 in Laguna Beach, California
Source: *CurBio 46; Film 1; FilmgC; HalFC 84; MotPP; MovMk; NotNAT B; TwYS; WhScrn 77, 83*

Sumner, Charles
American. Politician, Orator
Senator from MA, 1851-74; abolitionist; injured by Southern colleague for ardent attacks against slavery, 1856.
b. Jan 6, 1811 in Boston, Massachusetts
d. Mar 11, 1874 in Washington, District of Columbia
Source: *Alli, SUP; AmAu; AmAu&B; AmBi; AmOrN; AmPeW; AmPolLe; AmRef; ApCAB; BbD; Benet 87, 96; BenetAL 91; BiAUS; BiD&SB; BiDMoPL; BiDrAC; BiDrUSC 89; BiDTran; BioIn 2, 3, 4, 5, 6, 7, 8, 9, 11, 12, 13, 15, 16, 17, 20, 21; CelCen; CivWDc; CyAG; CyAL 2; DcAmAu; DcAmB; DcAmDH 80, 89; DcAmSR; DcBiPP; Dis&D; Drake; EncAACR; EncAAH; EncAB-H 1974, 1996; HarEnUS; LegTOT; LinLib L, S; McGEWB; NatCAB 3; OxCAmH; OxCAmL 65, 83, 95; PolPar; RComAH; REn; REnAL; TwCBDA; WebAB 74, 79; WhAm HS; WhAmP; WhCiWar; WorAl; WorAlBi*

Sumner, Edwin V
American. Army Officer
Commander, Department of the West, 1858-61.
b. Jan 30, 1797 in Boston, Massachusetts
d. Mar 21, 1863 in Syracuse, New York
Source: *AmBi; ApCAB; DcAmB; Drake; TwCBDA; WebAMB; WhAm HS*

Sumner, James Batcheller
American. Chemist
Shared Nobel Prize, 1946, for crystallization of enzymes.
b. Nov 19, 1887 in Canton, Massachusetts
d. Aug 19, 1955 in Buffalo, New York
Source: *AsBiEn; BiESc; BioIn 1, 3, 4, 6, 15, 19, 20; DcAmB S5; DcScB; InSci; LarDcSc; McGMS 80; NatCAB 46; WebAB 74, 79; WhAm 3; WhoNob, 90, 95; WorAl; WorScD*

Sumner, Jessie
American. Politician
Rep. congresswoman from IL, 1939-47; opposed to Pres. Roosevelt's New Deal programs.
b. 1899?
d. Aug 10, 1994 in Watseka, Illinois

Sumner, William Graham
American. Educator, Economist, Sociologist
Laissez-faire economist whose best-known work was *Folkways,* 1907.
b. Oct 30, 1840 in Paterson, New Jersey
d. Apr 12, 1910 in Englewood, New Jersey
Source: *Alli SUP; AmAu; AmAu&B; AmBi; AmSocL; ApCAB; BenetAL 91; BiDAmEd; BiD&SB; BioIn 1, 2, 3, 10, 11, 14, 19; DcAmAu; DcAmB; DcAmC; DcAmSR; DcSoc; EncAB-H 1974, 1996; EncABHB 6; GayN; HarEnUS; LinLib L, S; McGEWB; MorMA; NatCAB 11, 25; OxCAmH; OxCAmL 65, 83, 95; REn; REnAL; WebAB 74, 79; WhAm 1; WorAl*

Sumners, Rosalyn
American. Skater
World champion figure skater, 1983.
b. Apr 20, 1964 in Palo Alto, California
Source: *BioIn 13*

Sumter, Thomas
American. Army Officer
Brigadier general in Revolution; Dem. senator from SC, 1802-10; Fort Sumter, SC named for him.
b. Aug 14, 1734 in Hanover County, Virginia
d. Jun 1, 1832 in Stateburg, Virginia
Source: *AmBi; AmRev; ApCAB; BiAUS; BiDrAC; BiDrUSC 89; BioIn 5, 16; BlkwEAR; DcAmB; Drake; EncAR; EncCRAm; EncSoH; HarEnMi; HarEnUS; NatCAB 1; TwCBDA; WebAB 74, 79; WebAMB; WhAm HS; WhAmP; WhAmRev; WhoMilH 76*

Sunay, Cevdet
Turkish. Political Leader
Pres. of Turkey, 1966-73.
b. Feb 10, 1900 in Trabzon, Turkey
d. May 22, 1982 in Istanbul, Turkey
Source: *AnObit 1982; BioIn 7, 8, 11, 12, 13; CurBio 69, 82N; DcPol; IntWW 75, 76, 77, 78, 79, 80, 81, 82; IntYB 78, 79, 81; MidE 78, 79, 80, 81; WhoGov 72; WhoWor 74, 78*

Sundance Kid, The
[Harry Longabaugh]
American. Outlaw
Celebrated bankrobber, trainrobber, 1901-09; portrayed by Robert Redford in popular 1969 film.
d. 1909?
Source: *BioIn 10, 13; LegTOT; PeoHis; REnAW*

Sunday, Billy
[William Ashley Sunday]
"Parson"; "The Evangelist"
American. Baseball Player, Evangelist
Outfielder, 1883-90, known for fielding, base stealing; as popular evangelist, fought against Sunday baseball.
b. Nov 18, 1862 in Ames, Iowa
d. Nov 6, 1935 in Chicago, Illinois
Source: *AmBi; AmSocL; Ballpl 90; BioIn 15, 17, 18, 19; ConAu 120; DcAmB S1; DcAmReB 1, 2; DcAmTB; DcNAA; EncAAH; EncARH; GayN; HisWorL; LngCTC; LuthC 75; McGEWB; PrimTiR; RelLAm 91; TwCSAPR; WebAB 74, 79; WhAm 1; WhoProB 73; WorAl*

Sundburg, Jim
[James Howard Sundburg]
American. Baseball Player
Catcher, 1974-89, mostly with Texas; led AL catchers in fielding seven times; awarded golden glove, 1980.
b. May 18, 1951 in Galesburg, Illinois
Source: *BaseReg 86, 87*

Sunderland, Thomas E(lbert)
American. Businessman, Lawyer
Antitrust law and international negotiations expert; progressive pres. of United Fruit Co.
b. Apr 28, 1907 in Ann Arbor, Michigan
d. Mar 1, 1991 in Scottsdale, Arizona
Source: *BioIn 5, 6, 17; BlueB 76; CurBio 91N; IntWW 74, 75, 76, 77, 78, 79, 80, 81, 82, 83, 89, 91; NewYTBS 91; WhAm 10; WhoAm 74, 76, 78, 80, 82, 84, 86, 88, 90; WhoAmL 78, 79, 83, 85, 87, 90; WhoWor 74, 76, 78, 80*

Sundlun, Bruce George
American. Politician
Dem. governor, RI, 1990—.
b. Jan 19, 1920 in Providence, Rhode Island
Source: *AlmAP 92; BioIn 11, 12; Dun&B 88; IntWW 91, 93; St&PR 75, 84, 87, 91; WhoAm 74, 76, 78, 80, 82, 84, 86, 88, 90, 92; WhoAmP 91; WhoE 79, 81, 93; WhoWor 76, 82*

Sung Chiao-jen
Chinese. Political Activist
Founded Kuomintang Nationalist Party; assassinated while boarding a train; death helped start second revolution of 1913.
b. Apr 5, 1882 in Taoyuan, China
d. Mar 22, 1913 in Shanghai, China
Source: *BioIn 9*

Sun Ra
[Herman "Sonny" Blount]
American. Bandleader, Composer, Musician
Leader of the Sun Ra Arkestra; influenced modern jazz for more than four decades.
b. May 22, 1914 in Birmingham, Alabama
d. May 30, 1993 in Birmingham, Alabama
Source: *AllMusG; AnObit 1993; Baker 92; BioIn 11, 12, 13, 16; ConMus 5; DcTwCCu 5; DrBlPA 90; EncJzS; FacFETw; InB&W 85; NewAmDM; NewGrDA 86; NewGrDJ 88, 94; News 94, 94-1; OxCPMus; PenEncP; WhoAm 90*

Sunshine, Linda
American. Author
Author *Plain Jane Works Out,* 1983, spoof of *Jane Fonda's Workout Book.*
b. 1948?
Source: *ConAu 154*

Sununu, John Henry
American. Presidential Aide, Politician
Chief of staff under George Bush, 1989-91; Rep. governor of NH, 1983-89.
b. Jul 2, 1939 in Havana, Cuba
Source: *AlmAP 88; AmMWSc 73P, 79, 82, 86, 89, 92, 95; BioIn 13; WhoAm 86; WhoAmP 85, 87; WhoE 83, 85, 86; WhoGov 75, 77; WhoWor 87*

Sun Yat-Sen
[Sun Wen]
"Father of Modern China"
Chinese. Political Leader
Led revolution that overthrew Manchu dynasty, 1911; principal founder of Chinese Nationalist Party, 1912; pres., South China Republic, 1921.
b. Nov 12, 1866, Macao
d. Mar 12, 1925 in Beijing, China
Source: *Benet 96; BioIn 18, 20; EncRev; HisWorL; LegTOT; McGEWB; NewCol 75; OxCEng 67; RadHan; REn; WhDW; WorAl; WorAlBi*

Sun Yat-Sen, Chingling Soong, Madame
[Ching-ling Sung Sun]
Chinese. Political Leader
Widow of Sun Yat-sen; deputy chairman of People's Republic of China; ardent communist.
b. Jan 27, 1893 in Shanghai, China
d. May 29, 1981 in Beijing, China
Source: *BioIn 1, 4, 5, 9, 10; CurBio 44, 81; NewYTBS 81*

Supertramp
[Bob C Benberg; Richard Davies; John Anthony Helliwell; Rodger Hodgson; Dougie Thompson]
English. Music Group
Albums include *.Famous Last Words,* 1982.
Source: *Alli; ConMuA 80A; DcNaB, C; DrRegL 75; EncRk 88; EncRkSt; EngPo; HarEnR 86; IlEncRk; NewCBEL; PenEncP; RkOn 85; RolSEnR 83; WhoAmP 75, 77, 79, 81, 83; WhoRock 81; WhoRocM 82*

Supervia, Conchita
Spanish. Opera Singer
Mezzo-soprano; London debut, 1930; noted for Rossini roles, controversial Carmen.
b. Dec 8, 1899 in Barcelona, Spain
d. Mar 30, 1936 in London, England
Source: *Baker 84; BioIn 3, 5, 7, 10; InWom; NewEOp 71*

Suppe, Franz von
Austrian. Composer
Influenced development of German and Austrian light opera; prolific until middle of 20th century.
b. Apr 18, 1819 in Spalato, Austria
d. May 21, 1895 in Vienna, Austria
Source: *Baker 84; BioIn 4, 7, 12; MetOEnc; NewAmDM; NewOxM; OxCPMus*

Supremes, The
[Florence Ballard; Cindy Birdsong; Diana Ross; Jean Terrell; Mary Wilson]
American. Music Group
Detroit trio, formed 1962; hits include "Baby Love," 1964; Hall of Fame, 1988.
Source: *Alli, SUP; BioIn 9, 14, 15, 16, 17, 18, 19, 20; BlkWAm; ConAu X; DcLP 87B; DcWomA; EncPR&S 74; EncRk 88; EncRkSt; EngPo; HarEnR 86; IlEncBM 82; InB&W 80, 85, 85A; IntMPA 75, 76, 78, 79, 81, 82; InWom, SUP; NegAl 76, 83, 89; NewGrDA 86; NewYTBE 72; NewYTBS 76; ObitOF 79; PenEncP; PenNWW A; ScF&FL 92; SmATA X; SoulM; TwCRHW 90, 94; WhoAm 74, 76, 78, 80, 82, 84, 86; WhoAmW 70, 72, 74, 75, 77, 79, 81, 83, 85, 87; WhoBlA 75, 77, 80; WhoHol 92; WhoRocM 82; WhoWest 74, 76; WhoWor 84, 87; WomPO 78; WrDr 84, 86, 88, 90, 92, 96*

Surratt, John Harrison
American. Criminal
Friend of John Wilkes Booth, tried as conspirator in assassination of A Lincoln.
b. 1844 in Prince George's County, Maryland
d. Apr 21, 1916
Source: *BioIn 7, 17; DcNAA; HarEnUS; WhAm HS; WhCiWar*

Surratt, Mary Eugenia Jenkins
American. Criminal
Boardinghouse operator; hanged as conspirator in Lincoln's assassination.
b. May 1820 in Waterloo, Maryland
d. Jul 7, 1865 in Washington, District of Columbia
Source: *BioIn 1, 3; LibW; NatCAB 4; NotAW; WebAB 74, 79*

Surtees, John
British. Auto Racer
Motorcycle, car racing champ, 1950s-60s.
b. Feb 11, 1934
Source: *BioIn 7, 8, 10, 11, 12; EncMot; IntWW 81, 82, 83, 89, 91, 93; Who 74, 82, 83, 85, 88, 90, 92, 94*

Surtees, Robert Smith
English. Author
Humorous character, sporting grocer John Jorrocks appeared in *Jorrocks's Jaunts and Jollities,* 1838.
b. May 17, 1805 in Newcastle-upon-Tyne, England
d. Mar 16, 1864 in Brighton, England
Source: *AtlBL; BioIn 14; BlmGEL; BritAS; BritAu 19; Chambr 3; CyWA 58; DcEuL; DcLEL; DcNaB, C; EvLB; LngCEL; NewC; NinCLC 14; OxCEng 67, 85, 95; PenC ENG; REn; StaCVF; WebE&AL*

Survivor
[Dave Bickler; Marc Droubay; Stephan Ellis; Dennis Keith Johnson; Jim Peternik; R Gary Smith; Frankie Sullivan]
American. Music Group
Had number one hit "Eye of the Tiger," theme song from *Rocky III,* 1982.
Source: *BioIn 13; EncRkSt; PenEncP; RkOn 85; WhoRocM 82*

Susann, Jacqueline
American. Author, Actor
Wrote sex-filled novels *Valley of the Dolls,* 1966; *Once Is Not Enough,* 1973.
b. Aug 20, 1921 in Philadelphia, Pennsylvania
d. Sep 21, 1974 in New York, New York
Source: *AmAu&B; ArtclWW 2; AuNews 1; AuSpks; BioAmW; BioIn 10, 11, 13, 15, 17, 21; BlmGWL; ConAu 53, 65; ConLC 3; CurBio 72, 74, 74N; DcAmB S9; ForWC 70; HalFC 80, 84, 88; InWom SUP; LegTOT; LibW; MajTwCW; NewYTBE 73; NewYTBS 74; WhAm 6; WhoAm 74; WhoHol B; WhScrn 77, 83; WorAl*

Su Shih
[Su Tung-p'o]
Chinese. Poet
Considered to be the greatest poet of the Sung dynasty.
b. 1036 in Mei-shan, China
d. 1101
Source: *BioIn 18; ClMLC 15*

Suslov, Mikhail Andreevich
Russian. Politician
Worked under Stalin, Khrushchev, Brezhnev; senior member of Politburo, 1952-82.
b. Nov 21, 1902 in Shakhovskol, Russia
d. Jan 26, 1982 in Moscow, Union of Soviet Socialist Republics
Source: *AnObit 1982; BiDSovU; BioIn 4, 5, 6, 7, 8, 9, 12, 13, 16, 18; ColdWar 1; CurBio 57, 82; IntWW 74, 78; IntYB 78, 79; NewYTBS 82; SovUn; WhoSocC 78; WhoWor 74*

Suso, Heinrich
[Heinrich Seuse]
"Sweet Suso"
German. Mystic
Popular Dominican preacher; thought to have written first German prose autobiography, early 1360s.
b. Mar 21, 1295? in Uberlingen, Germany
d. Jan 25, 1366 in Ulm, Germany
Source: *CasWL; DcBiPP; DcEuL; EvEuW; LuthC 75; NewCol 75; OxCGer 76*

Susskind, David Howard
American. Producer
Well-known TV talk show host; producer of films, plays, TV shows; won Emmys, 1970s.
b. Dec 19, 1920 in Brookline, Massachusetts
d. Feb 22, 1987 in New York, New York
Source: *BiE&WWA; BioIn 11; BkPepl; ConNews 87-2; ConTFT 5; CurBio 60, 87; FilmgC; IntMPA 82; IntWW 74, 75, 76, 77, 78, 79, 80, 81, 82, 83; NotNAT; WhAm 9; WhoAm 74, 76, 78, 80, 82, 84, 86; WhoE 74; WhoWor 74, 78; WorAl*

Susskind, Walter
British. Conductor
Led St. Louis Symphony, 1968-75.
b. May 1, 1913 in Prague, Bohemia
d. Mar 25, 1980 in Berkeley, California
Source: *AnObit 1980; Baker 78, 84; BioIn 2, 10, 12; BlueB 76; CanWW 70; CreCan 2; IntWW 74, 75, 76, 77, 78, 79; IntWWM 77; MusMk; NewAmDM; NewGrDA 86; NewGrDM 80; PenDiMP; WhAm 7; Who 74; WhoAm 74, 76, 78, 80; WhoMus 72; WhoMW 74, 80; WhoWor 74, 76, 78, 80*

Sutcliffe, Rick
[Richard Lee Sutcliffe]
American. Baseball Player
Pitcher, LA Dodgers, 1976-81; Cleveland Indians, 1982-84; Chicago Cubs, 1984—; won NL rookie of year, 1979, Cy Young Award, 1984.
b. Jun 21, 1956 in Independence, Missouri
Source: *Ballpl 90; BaseReg 86, 87; WhoMW 90; WhoSpor*

Suter, Gary
American. Hockey Player
Defenseman, Calgary, 1985—; won Calder Trophy, 1986.
b. Jun 24, 1964 in Madison, Wisconsin
Source: *BioIn 21; HocReg 87*

Sutermeister, Heinrich
Swiss. Composer
Works include *Madam Bovary,* 1967; radio, TV operas.
b. Aug 12, 1910 in Feuerthalen, Switzerland
Source: *Baker 78, 84, 92; BioIn 8; CmOp; CompSN, SUP; CpmDNM 80; DcCM; IntWW 74, 75, 76, 77, 78, 79, 80, 81, 82, 83, 89, 91, 93; IntWWM 77, 80, 85, 90; NewEOp 71; NewGrDM 80; NewGrDO; OxDcOp; PenDiMP A; WhoMus 72*

Sutherland, Donald
Canadian. Actor
Played Hawkeye in film version of *M*A*S*H,* 1970; other films include *Ordinary People,* 1980.
b. Jul 17, 1934 in Saint John, New Brunswick, Canada
Source: *BiDFilm, 94; BioIn 13, 14, 16, 17; BkPepl; CanWW 81, 83, 89; CelR, 90; ConTFT 6, 13; CurBio 81; DcArts; FilmEn; FilmgC; IntDcF 1-3, 2-3; IntMPA 82, 84, 86, 88; LegTOT; MovMk; NewYTBE 70; OxCCanT; VarWW 85; WhoAm 76, 78, 80, 82, 84, 86; WhoHol 92, A; WomWMM; WorAl; WorAlBi*

Sutherland, Earl Wilbur, Jr.
American. Scientist, Physician, Engineer
Won Nobel Prize in medicine, 1971, for his career research on hormones.
b. Nov 19, 1915 in Burlingame, Kansas
d. Mar 9, 1974 in Miami, Florida
Source: *AmMWSc 73P; BioIn 14, 15, 20; ConAu 49; DcAmB S9; DcAmMeB 84; LarDcSc; McGMS 80; NewYTBE 71; NewYTBS 74; OxCMed 86; WebAB 74, 79; WhAm 6; Who 74; WhoAm 74; WhoNob, 90, 95; WhoSSW 73, 75; WhoWor 74; WorAl*

Sutherland, Graham Vivian
English. Artist
Commissioned to paint a portrait of Winston Churchill, 1954; so disliked, Churchill's family destroyed it.
b. Aug 24, 1903 in London, England
d. Feb 17, 1980 in Hampstead, England
Source: *AnObit 1980; CurBio 55, 80; DcBrAr 1; IntWW 74, 75, 76, 77, 78, 79; Who 74; WhoWor 74*

Sutherland, Joan, Dame
Australian. Opera Singer
Leading coloratura soprano, 1960s-70s; won Grammy for best classical vocalist, 1981.
b. Nov 7, 1929 in Sydney, Australia
Source: *Baker 84; CelR; CurBio 60; IntWW 83; InWom; NewEOp 71; NewYTBE 70; NewYTBS 82; Who 85; WhoAm 86; WhoAmM 83*

Sutherland, Keifer
Canadian. Actor
Films include *Stand By Me,* 1986, *Bright Lights, Big City,* 1988, *Flatliners,* 1990; son of Donald.
b. Dec 21, 1966 in London, England
Source: *BioIn 13; CelR 90; ConTFT 5*

Sutherland, Thomas M
American. Hostage
Dean, American University of Beirut seized by Islamic Jihad June 19, 1985 and held captive for 2,353 days; released November 18, 1991.
Source: *BioIn 10*

Sutter, Bruce
[Howard Bruce Sutter]
American. Baseball Player
Relief pitcher, 1976-89; set NL records for saves in season, in career; won NL Cy Young Award, 1979.
b. Jan 8, 1953 in Lancaster, Pennsylvania
Source: *Ballpl 90; BaseReg 86, 87; BioIn 12, 13; WhoAm 82, 84, 86, 88; WhoSpor; WhoSSW 86, 88*

Sutter, John Augustus
[Johann August Suter]
American. Pioneer
Discovery of gold on his land started 1848 CA gold rush.
b. Feb 15, 1803 in Kandern, Germany
d. Jun 18, 1880 in Washington, District of Columbia
Source: *AmAu&B; AmBi; ApCAB; BenetAL 91; BioIn 1, 2, 3, 4, 6, 7, 8, 9, 12, 20; CmCal; DcAmB; EncAAH; HarEnUS; McGEWB; NatCAB 4; OxCAmH; OxCAmL 65, 83, 95; PeoHis; REnAW; WebAB 74, 79; WhAm HS; WhNaAH; WorAl; WorAlBi*

Suttner, Bertha Felicie Sophie Kinsky von
Austrian. Editor, Writer
First woman to win Nobel Peace Prize, 1905; wrote *Lay Down Your Arms,* 1889.
b. Jun 9, 1843 in Prague, Czechoslovakia
d. Jun 21, 1914 in Vienna, Austria
Source: *CasWL; EuAu; EvEuW; HerW; LuthC 75; OxCGer 76; ScF&FL 1; WhLit; WhoNob*

Sutton, Carol
American. Editor
First woman to head news operation of major US daily newspaper, 1974.
b. Jun 29, 1933 in Saint Louis, Missouri
d. Feb 19, 1985 in Louisville, Kentucky
Source: *BioIn 10, 14; ConAu 115; InWom SUP; WhoAmW 75, 77; WomFir*

Sutton, Don(ald Howard)
American. Baseball Player
Pitcher, 1966-88; tied NL record for most one-hit games in career, five; 19th ML pitcher to win 300 games, 1986.
b. Apr 2, 1945 in Clio, Alabama
Source: *Ballpl 90; BaseReg 86, 87; BiDAmSp BB; BioIn 11, 12, 13; LegTOT; WhoAm 78, 80, 82, 84, 86, 88, 92; WhoWest 87; WorAl; WorAlBi*

Sutton, Hal Evan
American. Golfer
Touring pro, 1980s; won PGA, 1983; leading money winner on tour, 1983.
b. Apr 28, 1958 in Shreveport, Louisiana
Source: *WhoAm 84, 86, 88*

Sutton, Horace (Ashley)
American. Author
Travel books include *Travelers: The American Tourist from Stagecoach to Space Shuttle,* 1980; editor-in-chief of Citicorp Publishing Co. 1984-87.
b. May 17, 1919 in New York, New York
d. Oct 26, 1991 in New York, New York
Source: *BioIn 3, 5, 17; CelR; ConAu 10NR, 13R, 135; WhAm 10; WhoAm 74, 76, 78, 80, 82, 84, 86, 88, 90; WhoWor 74*

Sutton, John
English. Actor
In films since 1937, usually playing hero's rival: *Of Human Bondage,* 1964.
b. Oct 22, 1908 in Rawalpindi, India
d. 1963
Source: *FilmEn; FilmgC; ForYSC; HalFC 80, 84, 88; IntMPA 75, 76, 78, 79, 80, 81, 82; MotPP; MovMk; WhoHol A, B; WhScrn 74, 77, 83*

Sutton, Margaret Beebe
Children's Author
Best known for Judy Bolton series.
b. Jan 22, 1903
Source: *AuBYP 2, 3; ConAu 1R; ForWC 70; SmATA 1*

Sutton, Walter Stanborough
American. Geneticist
Proved that chromosones contain the building blocks of inheritance.
b. 1877 in Utica, New York
d. Nov 10, 1916 in Kansas City, Kansas
Source: *BiInAmS; BioIn 20; DcScB; NotTwCS; WorScD*

Sutton, Willie
[William Francis Sutton, Jr]
"The Actor"
American. Criminal
Stole $2 million in 35 years of bank robbing; disguises earned him nickname.
b. Jun 30, 1901 in New York, New York
d. Nov 2, 1980 in Spring Hill, Florida
Source: *BioIn 2, 3, 8, 9, 10, 11, 12; DcAmB S10; DrInf; FacFETw; LegTOT*

Suu Kyi, Aung San
Burmese. Political Activist
Political dissident, under house arrest in Rangoon, 1989-95; won Nobel Peace Prize, 1991.
b. 1945? in Rangoon, Burma
Source: *BioIn 16; ConHero 2; News 92, 96, 92-2, 96-2*

Suvorov, Aleksandr V
Russian. Military Leader
Commanded Austro-Russian forces against French in French Revolutionary Wars, 1798-99; never beaten in battle.
b. Nov 25, 1729 in Moscow, Russia
d. May 17, 1800 in Saint Petersburg, Russia
Source: *McGEWB; NewCol 75*

Suzman, Helen
South African. Politician
Member of South African Parliament, 1953-89; noted for her battle against apartheid.
b. Jul 11, 1917 in Germiston, South Africa
Source: *BioIn 7, 8, 9, 10, 11, 15, 16; ConAu 145; ContDcW 89; CurBio 68; DcCPSAf; EncSoA; EncWB; IntDcWB; IntWW 91, 93; News 89-3; NewYTBE 70; RadHan; Who 74, 82, 83, 85, 88, 90, 92, 94; WomFir; WomLaw*

Suzman, Janet
South African. Actor
Active in British theater since 1962; Oscar nominee for *Nicholas and Alexandra,* 1971.
b. Feb 9, 1939 in Johannesburg, South Africa
Source: *BioIn 10, 11, 12; CamGWoT; CnThe; ConTFT 1, 4; CurBio 76; Ent; FilmAG WE; FilmgC; HalFC 80, 84, 88; IntDcT 3; IntMPA 84, 86, 88, 92, 94, 96; IntWW 76, 78, 79, 80, 81, 82, 83, 89, 91, 93; InWom SUP; ItaFilm; OxCThe 83; Who 82, 83, 85, 88, 90, 92, 94; WhoEnt 92; WhoHol 92, A; WhoThe 72, 77, 81; WhoWor 74*

Suzuki, Daisetz Teitaro
Japanese. Author, Educator, Philosopher
Introduced Zen Buddhism to Western world.
b. Oct 18, 1870 in Kanazawa, Japan
d. Jul 12, 1966 in Tokyo, Japan
Source: *BiDAmCu; BioIn 4, 5, 15, 17, 19; ConAu 111, 121; CurBio 58, 66; DcAmReB 1, 2; EncARH; EncWB; IlEncMy; MajTwCW; NewCol 75; RelLAm 91; WhE&EA*

Suzuki, David T(akayoshi)
Canadian. Broadcast Journalist, Environmentalist
Host of CBC's "The Nature of Things with David Suzuki," 1979—.
b. Mar 24, 1936 in Vancouver, British Columbia, Canada
Source: *AmMWSc 73P, 76P, 79, 82, 86, 89, 92, 95; CurBio 95; WhoAm 78, 86, 88*

Suzuki, Pat
[Chiyoko Suzuki]
American. Singer, Actor
Starred in *Flower Drum Song,* 1958.
b. Sep 23, 1931 in Cressy, California
Source: *CurBio 60; InWom; WhoAm 74; WhoAmW 66, 68, 70, 72; WhoHol 92, A; WhoWor 74*

Suzuki, Zenko
Japanese. Political Leader
Prime minister, 1980-82.
b. Jan 11, 1911? in Yamada, Japan
Source: *BioIn 12, 13; CurBio 81; FarE&A 78, 79, 80, 81; IntWW 77, 78, 79, 80, 81, 82, 83, 89, 91, 93; NewYTBS 80, 81; WhoWor 80, 82, 84, 87, 89, 91, 93*

Suzy
American. Journalist
Gossip column syndicated to more than 100 newspapers.
b. Jun 10, in El Paso, Texas
Source: *BioIn 6, 7, 10, 15, 16; CelR, 90; FairDF FRA; InWom, SUP; PenNWW B; WhoAm 78, 80, 82, 84, 86*

Svanholm, Set
Swedish. Opera Singer, Director
Tenor, formerly baritone, noted for Wagner roles; NY Met., 1946-56; director, Swedish Royal Opera, 1956-63.
b. Sep 2, 1904 in Vasteras, Sweden
d. Oct 4, 1964 in Saltsjoe-Duvnaes, Sweden
Source: *Baker 78, 84; BioIn 3, 4, 7, 11, 16; CmOp; CurBio 56, 64; IntDcOp; MetOEnc; MusSN; NewEOp 71; NewGrDM 80; ObitT 1961; OxDcOp; PenDiMP; WhAm 4*

Svedberg, Theodor H. E
Swedish. Chemist
Won 1926 Nobel Prize for developing the ultracentrifuge; work later used for studying polymers.
b. Aug 30, 1884 in Flerang, Sweden
d. Feb 25, 1971 in Orebro, Sweden
Source: *AsBiEn; BiESc; DcScB; NewYTBE 71; WhAm 5; WhoNob; WorAl*

Sverdrup, H(arald) U(lrik)
Norwegian. Meteorologist, Oceanographer
His research explained equatorial countercurrents; assisted in the creation of methods to predict surf and breakers.
b. Nov 15, 1888 in Sogndal, Norway
d. Aug 21, 1957 in Oslo, Norway
Source: *BioIn 2, 4; DcScB; LarDcSc; McGMS 80; ObitOF 79; WhAm 3*

Sverdrup, Otto
Norwegian. Explorer
Famous for expedition to N Pole, 1898-1902, aboard the *Fram.*
b. Jan 1, 1855 in Helgeland, Norway
d. Nov 26, 1930 in Oslo, Norway
Source: *MacDCB 78; NewCol 75; OxCCan*

Svetlanov, Evgeni Fyodorovich
Russian. Composer, Conductor
Led State Orchestra of USSR, 1965-79.
b. Sep 6, 1928 in Moscow, Union of Soviet Socialist Republics
Source: *Baker 84; IntWW 74, 75, 83; WhoWor 74*

Svetlova, Marina
American. Dancer, Choreographer
Prima ballerina with Met. Opera, 1943-50.
b. May 3, 1922 in Paris, France
Source: *BiDD; BioIn 5; CnOxB; DancEn 78; IntWWM 77; WhoAm 74, 76, 78, 80, 82, 84, 86, 88, 90, 92, 94, 95, 96, 97; WhoAmW 61, 64, 66, 68, 70, 72, 74, 77, 79, 81, 83, 85, 87, 89, 91, 93, 95, 97; WhoEnt 92; WhoWor 74, 76*

Svoboda, Ludvik
Czech. Political Leader
Pres. of Czechoslovakia, 1968-75.
b. Nov 25, 1895 in Horznatin, Moravia
d. Sep 20, 1979 in Prague, Czechoslovakia
Source: *BioIn 8, 12; EncCW; FacFETw; IntWW 74, 75, 76, 77, 78, 79; IntYB 78, 79; NewYTBS 79; WhoGov 72; WhoSocC 78; WhoWor 74; WorDWW*

Swados, Elizabeth A
[Liz Swados]
American. Author, Composer, Director
Composer, director for *Nightclub Cantata,* 1977.
b. Feb 5, 1951 in Buffalo, New York
Source: *ConAu 97; ConLC 12; ConTFT 1; CurBio 79; NewYTBS 77, 78; WhoAm 86; WhoThe 81*

Swados, Harvey
American. Author
Works concerned disillusionment of American life: *Standing Fast,* 1970.
b. Oct 28, 1920 in Buffalo, New York
d. Dec 11, 1972 in Holyoke, Massachusetts
Source: *AmAu&B; AuBYP 2S, 3; BenetAL 91; BioIn 5, 6, 9, 10; ConAu 5R, 6NR, 37R; ConLC 5; ConNov 72; DcLB 2; DcLEL 1940; EncAL; IntAu&W 76; JeAmFiW; LiJour; LinLib L; ModAL; NewYTBE 72; Novels; OxCAmL 65, 83, 95; PenC AM; REnAL; WhAm 5; WorAu 1950*

Swaggart, Jimmy Lee
American. Evangelist
TV preacher who claims to have 200 million followers; strong right-wing views; involved in sex scandal, banned from pulpit, 1988.
b. Mar 15, 1935 in Ferriday, Louisiana
Source: *BioIn 13; ConNews 87-3; CurBio 87; RelLAm 91; WhoAm 95, 96, 97; WhoRel 92*

Swaminathan, M(onkombu) S(ambisivan)
Indian. Geneticist
Leader in ''Green Revolution'' introducing high-yield rice, wheat crops; promoted improved farming tehcniques.
b. Aug 7, 1925 in Kumbakonam, India
Source: *IntWW 91; Who 74; WhoWor 91*

Swan, Joseph Wilson, Sir
English. Physicist, Chemist
Inventor of dry photographic plate; created electric light bulb that became prototype for Edison's later invention.
b. Oct 31, 1828 in Sunderland, England
d. May 27, 1914 in Warlingham, England
Source: *AsBiEn; BiESc; BioIn 1, 8, 12, 20; DcNaB 1912; ICPEnP; InSci; LarDcSc; MacBEP; WhDW; WorAl; WorAlBi*

Swanberg, William Andrew
American. Author
Pulitzer-winning biographer whose books include *Citizen Hearst,* 1961; *Luce and His Empire,* 1972.
b. Nov 23, 1907 in Saint Paul, Minnesota
d. Sep 17, 1992 in Southbury, Connecticut
Source: *Au&Wr 71; BioIn 10; ConAu 5R, 8NR; ConLC 76; DcLEL 1940; MinnWr; WhAm 10; WhoAm 74, 76, 78, 80, 82, 84, 86, 88, 90, 92; WorAu 1950; WrDr 76, 80, 86*

Swann, Donald (Ibrahim)
Welsh. Composer, Lyricist, Entertainer
Starred with Michael Flanders in two-man show *At the Drop of a Hat,* 1950s.
b. Sep 30, 1923 in Llanelly, Wales
d. Mar 23, 1994 in London, England
Source: *Au&Wr 71; BiE&WWA; BioIn 5, 7, 8, 9, 19, 20; BlueB 76; ConAu 16NR, 21R, 41NR, 144; CurBio 70, 94N; IntAu&W 77, 82; IntWW 74, 75, 76, 77, 78, 79, 80, 81, 82, 83, 89, 91, 93; IntWWM 77, 80, 85, 90; JoeFr; NewYTBS 94; NotNAT; OxCPMus; OxCThe 67; WhAm 11; Who 74, 82, 83, 85, 88, 90, 92, 94; WhoMus 72; WhoThe 72, 77, 81; WhoWor 74, 76, 78, 89; WrDr 76, 80, 82, 84, 86, 88, 90, 92, 94, 96*

Swann, Lynn Curtis
American. Football Player
Wide receiver, Pittsburgh, 1974-82; led NFL in receiving TDs, 1975.
b. Mar 7, 1952 in Alcoa, Tennessee
Source: *BiDAmSp FB; BioIn 11; NewYTBS 77, 78, 79; WhoAfA 96; WhoAm 78, 80, 82, 84, 86, 88, 90, 92, 94, 95, 96, 97; WhoBlA 77, 80, 85, 90, 92, 94; WhoFtbl 74*

Swann, Michael Meredith, Sir
English. Educator
Chancellor of U of York since 1980.
b. Mar 1, 1920 in Shortlands, England

Source: *BioIn 3, 9; BlueB 76; DcNaB 1986; IntWW 74, 76, 77, 78, 79, 80; WhAm 10; Who 74; WhoWor 74, 76, 78, 82, 84, 87*

Swanson, Carl A
American. Businessman
Food processing firm in 1920s was nucleus of first frozen dinner production, 1953.
b. May 1, 1876 in Karlskrona, Sweden
d. Oct 9, 1949 in Chicago, Illinois
Source: *Entr; NatCAB 40*

Swanson, Gloria May Josephine
[Josephine Swenson]
American. Actor
Starred in *Sunset Boulevard,* 1950.
b. Mar 27, 1897 in Chicago, Illinois
d. Apr 4, 1983 in New York, New York
Source: *AnObit 1983; BiDFilm; BiE&WWA; CurBio 83; Film 1; FilmgC; IntMPA 82; MovMk; NewYTBS 83; OxCFilm; ThFT; WhAm 8; Who 82; WhoAm 82; WhoHol A; WhoThe 81*

Swart, Charles Robberts
South African. Political Leader
First South African state president, 1961-67; last governor general, 1960-61.
b. Dec 5, 1894, Orange Free State
d. Jul 16, 1982 in Bloemfontein, South Africa
Source: *AfSS 78, 79, 80, 81, 82; AnObit 1982; BioIn 5, 13; CurBio 60; EncSoA; IntWW 74, 75, 76, 77, 78, 79, 80, 81, 82, 83; IntYB 78, 79, 80, 81; NewYTBS 82; WhAm 8; WhE&EA; Who 74, 82; WhoWor 74*

Swarthout, Gladys
American. Opera Singer
NY Met. mezzo-soprano, 1929-45; renowned as Carmen; made five films.
b. Dec 25, 1904 in Deepwater, Missouri
d. Jul 6, 1969 in La Ragnaia, Italy
Source: *Baker 84; BiDAmM; BioIn 1, 3, 4, 8, 9, 11, 14; CmOp; CurBio 44, 69; FilmEn; FilmgC; ForYSC; HalFC 80, 84, 88; InWom, SUP; LegTOT; LinLib S; MusSN; NewEOp 71; NewGrDM 80; ObitT 1961; RadStar; ThFT; WhAm 5; What 2; WhoAmW 58, 61, 64, 66, 68, 70; WhoHol B; WhoMus 72; WhScrn 74, 77, 83*

Swarthout, Glendon (Fred)
American. Author
Books include *Where the Boys Are,* 1960; *Skeletons,* 1979.
b. Apr 8, 1918 in Pinckney, Michigan
d. Sep 23, 1992 in Scottsdale, Arizona
Source: *AnObit 1992; AuBYP 2, 3; BenetAL 91; BioIn 4, 11, 13; ConAu 1NR, 1R, 47NR, 139; ConLC 35, 76; ConNov 72, 76, 82, 86, 91; DcAmChF 1960; DcLEL 1940; DrAPF 80; EncFWF; FourBJA; IntAu&W 76, 77, 86, 91, 93; MagSAmL; MichAu 80; Novels; SmATA 26; TwCWW 82, 91; TwCYAW; WhAm 10; WhoAm 80, 82, 86, 88, 90; WhoUSWr 88; WhoWest 74, 76, 78; WhoWrEP 89, 92, 95; WrDr 76, 80, 82, 84, 86, 88, 90, 92, 94N*

Swayne, Noah Haynes
American. Supreme Court Justice
Appointed by Abraham Lincoln; served, 1862-81.
b. Dec 7, 1804 in Frederick County, Virginia
d. Jun 8, 1884 in New York, New York
Source: *ApCAB; BiAUS; BiDFedJ; BioIn 2, 5, 15; DcAmB; Drake; HarEnUS; NatCAB 4; OxCSupC; SupCtJu; TwCBDA; WebAB 74, 79; WhAm HS; WhCiWar*

Swayze, John Cameron, Sr.
American. Journalist
Did commercials for Timex watches; radio, TV news commentator, NBC, 1947-56.
b. Apr 4, 1906 in Wichita, Kansas
d. Aug 15, 1995 in Sarasota, Florida
Source: *BioIn 3, 13, 21; ConAu 102, 149; EncAJ; EncTwCJ; IntMPA 75, 76, 78, 79, 80, 81, 82, 84, 86, 88, 92, 94; LegTOT; LesBEnT; News 96, 96-1; NewYTET; SaTiSS; WhAm 11; WhoAm 74, 76, 78, 80, 82, 84, 86, 88, 90, 92, 94, 95; WhoE 74; WhoEnt 92; WhoWor 78, 82, 84, 87, 89; WorAl; WorAlBi*

Swayze, Patrick
American. Actor
In films *Dirty Dancing,* 1987, *Ghost,* 1990.
b. Aug 18, 1952 in Houston, Texas
Source: *ConTFT 4; CurBio 91; HolBB; IntMPA 94, 96; LegTOT; VarWW 85; WhoHol 92*

Swearingen, John Eldred
American. Business Executive
Chm., CEO of Continental Illinois Corp., 1984-87; CEO of Standard Oil of Indiana, 1960-83.
b. Sep 7, 1918 in Columbia, South Carolina
Source: *AmMWSc 73P, 79, 82, 86, 89, 92, 95; BioIn 6, 11, 12, 13; CurBio 79; IntWW 74, 75, 76, 77, 78, 79, 80, 81, 82, 83, 89, 91, 93; NewYTBS 84; WhoAm 74, 76, 78, 80, 82, 84, 86, 88, 90, 92; WhoFI 74, 75, 77, 79, 81, 83, 87, 89; WhoMW 74, 76, 78, 80, 82, 86, 88, 92; WhoWor 74, 76, 78, 80, 82, 84, 87, 89*

Swedenborg, Emanuel
Swedish. Scientist, Mystic
Religious works rejected traditional doctrines of original sin, eternal damnation.
b. Jan 29, 1688 in Stockholm, Sweden
d. Mar 29, 1772
Source: *BbD; Benet 87, 96; BenetAL 91; BiD&SB; BiDPsy; BiHiMed; BioIn 1, 3, 4, 5, 6, 7, 8, 9, 10, 14, 15, 16, 18, 19, 20; BlmGEL; CasWL; CyWA 58; DcEuL; DcScanL; DcScB; Dis&D; EncEnl; EncO&P 1, 2, 3; EncPaPR 91; EncSF, 93; EuAu; EvEuW; IlEncMy; LarDcSc; LinLib L, S; LngCEL; LuthC 75; McGEWB; NamesHP; NewC; NewCBEL; OxCEng 67, 85, 95; RAdv 14; RComWL; REn; WorAl; WorAlBi; WrPh P*

Sweelinck, Jan Pieterszoon
Dutch. Composer, Organist
Famed organ teacher; wrote choral, church music.
b. 1562 in Amsterdam, Netherlands
d. Oct 16, 1621 in Amsterdam, Netherlands
Source: *AtlBL; Baker 78, 84, 92; BioIn 1, 4, 7, 12; DcCathB; LuthC 75; McGEWB; MusSN; NewAmDM; NewGrDM 80; NewOxM; OxCMus; WhDW*

Sweeney, John J(oseph)
American. Labor Union Official
President, AFL-CIO, 1995—.
b. May 5, 1934 in New York, New York
Source: *CurBio 96; NewYTBS 76*

Sweet, Blanche
[Sarah Blanche Sweet]
American. Actor
Starred in first feature length film made in US: *Judith of Bethulia,* 1913.
b. Jun 18, 1896 in Chicago, Illinois
d. Sep 6, 1986 in New York, New York
Source: *AnObit 1986; BiE&WWA; BioIn 9, 10, 11, 15, 18; Film 1, 2; FilmgC; ForYSC; IntDcF 1-3, 2-3; MotPP; MovMk; NewYTBS 86; NotNAT; OxCFilm; SweetSg A; TwYS; WhoHol A*

Sweet, John Howard
Canadian. Publisher
Publisher of *US News and World Report,* 1951-78; board chm., 1973-83.
b. Mar 21, 1907 in Emerson, Manitoba, Canada
d. Aug 14, 1988 in Bethesda, Maryland
Source: *BioIn 16; BlueB 76; CanWW 70, 79, 80, 81, 83; EncTwCJ; IntYB 78, 79; WhAm 9; WhoAm 74, 76, 78, 80, 82, 84, 86, 88; WhoE 77, 79, 81, 83, 85, 86; WhoFI 74; WhoSSW 73; WhoWor 74*

Sweet, Matthew
American. Singer, Songwriter, Musician
Rock and roll singer/guitarist; began solo career 1986; albums include *Girlfriend,* 1991.
b. Oct 6, 1964 in Lincoln, Nebraska
Source: *ConMus 9*

Sweet, Rachel
American. Singer
Hit album *Fool Around;* single "Baby."
b. 1966 in Akron, Ohio
Source: *BioIn 12; NewWmR*

Sweet Honey in the Rock
[Ysaye Maria Barnwell; Nitanju Bolade; Evelyn Harris; Aisha Kahlil; Bernice Johnson Reagon]
American. Music Group
Politically active gospel singers; album *B'lieve I'll Rin On. See, What the Ends Gonna Be,* 1978.

Source: *BlkWAm; ConMus 1; InB&W 85A; PenEncP; PeoHis; WomPO 76, 78*

Swenson, Inga
American. Actor
Played Gretchen Kraus on TV series "Benson," 1979-85.
b. Dec 29, 1932 in Omaha, Nebraska
Source: *BiE&WWA; EncMT; FilmgC; HalFC 80, 84, 88; InWom SUP; LegTOT; NotNAT; WhoAm 74; WhoHol A; WhoTelC; WhoThe 77, 81*

Swenson, May
American. Poet
Wrote *New and Selected Things Taking Place,* 1978.
b. May 28, 1919 in Logan, Utah
Source: *AmAu&B; AnCL; AnObit 1989; ArtclWW 2; AuBYP 2S, 3; Benet 87, 96; BenetAL 91; BioIn 8, 9, 10, 12, 14, 15, 16, 17, 19, 20; ChhPo S1, S2; ConAu 5R, 36NR, 130; ConLC 4, 14, 61; ConPo 70, 75, 80, 85; CroCAP; DcLEL 1940; DrAP 75; FemiCLE; Focus; IntWWP 77, 82; InWom SUP; MajTwCW; ModAL S2; ModWoWr; OxCTwCP; OxCWoWr 95; PoeCrit 14; RAdv 1, 14; SmATA 15; WhoAm 74, 76, 78, 80, 82, 84, 86, 88; WhoAmW 81, 85, 87, 89; WhoUSWr 88; WhoWor 74; WhoWrEP 89; WorAu 1950; WrDr 76, 80, 82, 84, 86, 88, 90*

Swenson, Rick
American. Athlete
Five-time winner of the Alaskan Iditarod Trail sled dog race.

Swerling, Jo
American. Screenwriter, Dramatist
Co-author of play *Guys and Dolls,* 1951; won Tony.
b. May 18, 1897 in Bardichov, Russia
Source: *BiE&WWA; BioIn 15; DcLB 44; FilmEn; FilmgC; HalFC 84; IntDcF 1-4, 2-4; IntMPA 75, 76, 78, 79, 80, 81, 82, 84, 86, 88, 92, 94, 96; NotNAT; VarWW 85; WorEFlm*

Swift, Elizabeth Ann
[The Hostages]
American. Hostage
One of 52 held by terrorists, Nov 1979-Jan 1981.
b. Dec 3, 1940 in Washington, District of Columbia
Source: *BioIn 12; NewYTBS 81; USBiR 74; WhoGov 72*

Swift, Graham (Colin)
English. Author
Wrote novels *The Sweet-Shop Owner,* 1980; *Ever After,* 1992.
b. Aug 16, 1949 in London, England
Source: *BioIn 14, 17; CamGLE; ConAu 46NR, 117, 122; ConLC 41, 88; ConNov 86, 91, 96; CyWA 89; IntAu&W 91, 93; IntWW 91, 93; RGTwCWr; Who 94; WorAu 1980; WrDr 86, 88, 90, 92, 94, 96*

Swift, Gustavus Franklin
American. Manufacturer
Developed refrigerated railroad cars.
b. Jun 24, 1839 in Sandwich, Massachusetts
d. Mar 29, 1903 in Chicago, Illinois
Source: *AmBi; ApCAB X; BiDAmBL 83; BioIn 3, 6, 7, 15; DcAmB; EncAAH; EncAB-H 1974, 1996; NatCAB 14; OxCAmH; WebAB 74, 79; WhAm 1; WorAl*

Swift, Jonathan
[Isaac Bickerstaff]
English. Satirist, Author, Clergy
Wrote *Gulliver's Travels,* 1726.
b. Nov 30, 1667 in Dublin, Ireland
d. Oct 19, 1745 in Dublin, Ireland
Source: *Alli; AtlBL; BbD; Benet 87, 96; BiD&SB; BiDIrW; BioIn 1, 2, 3, 4, 5, 6, 7, 8, 9, 10, 11, 12, 13, 14, 15, 16, 17, 18, 20, 21; BlkwCE; BlmGEL; BritAu; BritWr 3; CamGEL; CamGLE; CarSB; CasWL; Chambr 2; ChhPo, S1, S3; CnDBLB 2; CnE&AP; CrtT 2, 4; CyWA 58; DcArts; DcBiA; DcBiPP; DcEnA, A; DcEnL; DcEuL; DcIrB 78, 88; DcIrL, 96; DcIrW 1, 2; DcLB 95, 101; DcLEL; DcNaB; DcPup; Dis&D; EncEnl; EncSF, 93; EvLB; GrWrEL N, P; HalFC 80, 84, 88; HsB&A; LegTOT; LinLib L, S; LitC 1; LngCEL; LuthC 75; MagSWL; McGEWB; MouLC 2; NewC; NewCBEL; NewEScF; Novels; OxCEng 67, 85, 95; OxCIri; OxCMus; PenC ENG; PoeCrit 9; PoIre; RadHan; RAdv 1, 14; RComWL; REn; RfGEnL 91; RGFBP; ScF&FL 1; ScFEYrs; ScFSB; SmATA 19; WebE&AL; WhDW; WhoChL; WorAl; WorAlBi; WorLitC; WrChl; WrPh*

Swift, Kay
American. Musician, Songwriter
Pianist-arranger; songs include "Forever and a Day."
b. Apr 19, 1897 in New York, New York
d. Jan 28, 1993 in Southington, Connecticut
Source: *AnObit 1993; ASCAP 66; BioIn 18, 19; CmpEPM; ConAmC 76; EncMT; InWom SUP; NewGrDA 86; NewYTBS 93*

Swigert, Ernest Goodnough
American. Manufacturer
Founder, pres., Hyster Co., 1929-71, manufacturer of lift trucks, cranes.
b. Aug 4, 1892 in Portland, Oregon
d. Nov 30, 1986 in Portland, Oregon
Source: *BioIn 4, 15; CurBio 57, 87; WhAm 9*

Swigert, Jack
[John Leonard Swigert, Jr]
American. Astronaut, Politician
Commanded *Apollo 13;* elected to Congress from CO, 1982; died before sworn in.
b. Aug 30, 1931 in Denver, Colorado
d. Dec 27, 1982 in Washington, District of Columbia
Source: *AmMWSc 73P, 79; AnObit 1982; BioIn 21; IntWW 74, 75, 76, 77; NewYTBS 82; WhAm 8; WhoAm 76, 78, 80, 82; WhoAmP 75, 77, 79; WhoGov 72, 75; WhoSSW 73, 75, 76; WhoWest 82, 84; WhoWor 78; WorDWW*

Swimmer, Ross
American. Native American Chief, Government Official, Business Executive
Principal chief of the Cherokee, 1975-85; head of the Bureau of Indian Affairs, 1985-89; president, Cherokee Nation Industries, Inc., 1992—.
b. Oct 26, 1943 in Oklahoma City, Oklahoma
Source: *NotNaAm*

Swinburne, Algernon Charles
English. Poet, Dramatist, Critic
Wrote *Atalanta in Calydon,* 1865; *Poems and Ballads,* 1866.
b. Apr 5, 1837 in London, England
d. Apr 10, 1909 in London, England
Source: *AtlBL; BbD; Benet 87, 96; BiD&SB; BioIn 1, 2, 3, 5, 6, 7, 8, 9, 10, 11, 12, 13, 14, 16, 17, 18, 19, 20; BlmGEL; BritAu 19; BritWr 5; CamGEL; CamGLE; CarSB; CasWL; CelCen; Chambr 3; ChhPo, S1, S2, S3; CnDBLB 4; CnE&AP; ConAu 105, 140; CrtSuDr; CrtT 3, 4; CyWA 58; DcArts; DcBiPP; DcEnA, A; DcEnL; DcEuL; DcLEL; DcNaB S2; Dis&D; EncUnb; EvLB; GrWrEL P; LinLib S; LngCEL; MagSWL; McGEWB; MouLC 4; NewC; NewCBEL; NotNAT B; OxCEng 67, 85, 95; PenC ENG; RAdv 1; RComWL; REn; RfGEnL 91; RGFBP; TwoTYeD; VicBrit; WebE&AL; WhDW; WhLit; WorAl; WorAlBi*

Swinburne, Laurence
American. Children's Author
Books include *RFK: The Last Knight,* 1969; *Detli,* 1970.
b. Jul 2, 1924 in New York, New York
Source: *BioIn 11; ConAu 15NR, 61; SmATA 9*

Swing, Raymond Gram
American. Broadcast Journalist
Best known for radio commentaries in 1930s; liberal views attacked by House Committee on Un-American Activities.
b. Mar 25, 1887 in Cortland, New York
d. Dec 22, 1968 in Washington, District of Columbia
Source: *AmAu&B; BiDAmJo; ConAmC 76, 82; ConAu 89; CurBio 40, 69; DcAmDH 80, 89; EncAJ; LegTOT; LngCTC; OhA&B; OxCAmH; RadStar; TwCA SUP; WhAm 5; WorAl*

Swinnerton, Frank Arthur
[Simon Pure]
English. Author, Critic
Wrote popular tale *Nocturne,* 1917; critique *Georgian Literary Scene,* 1935.
b. Aug 12, 1884 in Wood Green, England

d. Nov 6, 1982 in Cranleigh, England
Source: *AnObit 1982; BioIn 5, 6, 11, 13; Chambr 3; ChhPo S3; ConAu 108; ConNov 72, 76; CyWA 58; DcLEL; DcNaB 1981; EvLB; IntWW 74, 75, 76, 77, 78, 79, 80, 81, 82; LngCTC; ModBrL; NewC; NewCBEL; NewYTBS 76, 82; PenC ENG; RAdv 1; REn; TwCA, SUP; TwCWr; WhAm 8; WhE&EA; Who 74, 82, 83; WhoLA; WhoWor 74, 76, 78, 80; WrDr 76, 80*

Swinnerton, James Guilford
American. Cartoonist
Created early comic strips "Little Jimmy," "The Canyon Kiddies."
b. Nov 13, 1875 in Eureka, California
d. Sep 5, 1974 in Palm Springs, California
Source: *ArtsAmW 1; BioIn 6, 9, 10; ConAu 93; IlBEAAW; NewYTBS 74; WhAm 6; WhoAmA 84N; WorECom*

Swinton, Ernest Dunlop, Sir
English. Army Officer
Instrumental in development of tank, WW I.
b. Oct 21, 1868 in Bangalore, Mysore
d. Jan 15, 1951 in Oxford, England
Source: *BioIn 2, 3, 9; DcNaB 1951; InSci; WhDW; WhLit*

Swit, Loretta
[Mrs. Dennis Holahan]
American. Actor
Played Margaret Houlihan in TV series "M*A*S*H," 1972-83; won Emmy award for best supporting actress in a comedy series 1979-81.
b. Nov 4, 1939 in Passaic, New Jersey
Source: *BioNews 74; HalFC 84; IntMPA 86, 94, 96; WhoAm 84, 86, 95, 96, 97; WhoAmW 85, 87, 95; WhoHol A*

Switzer, Barry
American. Football Coach
Head coach, U of Oklahoma, 1973-89; won three national championships; head coach, Dallas Cowboys, 1994—; won Super Bowl, 1996.
b. Oct 5, 1937 in Crossett, Arkansas
Source: *BiDAmSp FB; BioIn 13; ConAu 143; NewYTBS 86; WhoAm 80, 82, 84, 86, 88, 95, 96, 97; WhoFtbl 74; WhoSpor; WhoSSW 78, 80, 82, 84, 95; WrDr 96*

Switzer, Carl
[Our Gang]
"Alfalfa"
American. Actor
In *Our Gang* film series, 1935-42; specialty was off-key singing; shot in brawl.
b. Aug 7, 1927 in Paris, Illinois
d. Jan 21, 1959 in Sepulveda, California
Source: *BioIn 5, 9; FilmEn; FilmgC; MotPP; NotNAT B; WhoHol B; WhScrn 74, 77, 83*

Switzer, Katherine Virginia
American. Track Athlete
First woman to officially run in Boston Marathon, 1967.
b. Jan 5, 1947 in Amberg, Germany
Source: *BioIn 12; NewYTBS 76, 82; WhoAmW 77, 85, 87*

Swoopes, Sheryl
American. Basketball Player
Member of gold-medal winning US Women's Olympic Basketball Team, 1996.
b. Mar 25, 1971 in Brownfield, Texas
Source: *ConBlB 12; CurBio 96*

Swope, Gerard
American. Industrialist
Pres., General Electric, 1922-39, 1942-44.
b. Dec 1, 1872 in Saint Louis, Missouri
d. Nov 20, 1957 in New York, New York
Source: *BiDAmBL 83; BioIn 1, 4, 5, 6, 11; CurBio 41, 58; DcAmB S6; EncAB-A 2; EncWB; InSci; NatCAB 45; ObitOF 79; OxCAmH; WebAB 74, 79; WhAm 3*

Swope, Herbert Bayard
American. Journalist, Editor
Won Pulitzer for WW I coverage; executive editor of *NY World,* 1920-29.
b. Jan 5, 1882 in Saint Louis, Missouri
d. Jun 20, 1958 in Sands Point, New York
Source: *BiDAmJo; BioIn 1, 4, 5, 6, 7, 13, 14, 16; CurBio 44, 58; DcAmB S6; EncAJ; JrnUS; NatCAB 45; REn; REnAL; WebAB 74, 79; WhAm 3; WorAl; WorAlBi*

Syberberg, Hans Jurgen
German. Director, Screenwriter
Films include seven-hr. *Our Hitler: A Film from Germany,* 1977.
b. 1935 in Pomerania, Prussia
Source: *BioIn 10, 11, 12, 13, 14, 16, 17, 19; ConAu 93; CurBio 83; EncEurC; WorFDir 2*

Sydenham, Thomas
"The English Hippocrates"
English. Scientist, Engineer, Physician
Introduced use of quinine; invented liquid laudanum.
b. Sep 10, 1624
d. Dec 29, 1689 in London, England
Source: *Alli; BiESc; BiHiMed; BioIn 5, 7, 9, 17; CamDcSc; DcBiPP; DcNaB; DcScB; InSci; LarDcSc; McGEWB; NewCBEL; OxCMed 86; WhDW; WorScD*

Sykes, George
"Tardy George"
American. Military Leader
Commanded Union's Fifth Corps at Gettysburg, 1863.
b. Oct 9, 1822 in Dover, Delaware
d. Feb 8, 1880 in Brownsville, Texas
Source: *AmBi; ApCAB; BioIn 7; CivWDc; DcAmB; HarEnUS; NatCAB 4; TwCBDA; WhAm HS; WhCiWar*

Sykes, Mark, Sir
English. Statesman
Expert on Mideast policy who helped promote Balfour Declaration, 1917.
b. Mar 16, 1879 in London, England
d. Feb 16, 1919 in Paris, France
Source: *BioIn 2, 10; DcNaB 1912; HisDBrE*

Sylbert, Paul
Designer, Director
Won Oscar, 1978, for *Heaven Can Wait.*
b. 1928
Source: *BioIn 13; ConTFT 9; VarWW 85; WhoAm 96, 97*

Sylbert, Richard
American. Art Director
Films include *Breathless; The Cotton Club;* won Oscar for *Who's Afraid of Virginia Woolf,* 1966.
b. Apr 16, 1928 in New York, New York
Source: *BioIn 12, 13; ConDes 90, 97; ConTFT 9; FilmgC; HalFC 84, 88; IntDcF 1-4, 2-4; VarWW 85; WhoAm 96, 97*

Sylvers, The
[Charmaine Sylver; Edmund Sylver; Foster Sylver; James Sylver; Joseph Sylver; Leon Sylver; Olympia-Ann Sylver]
American. Music Group
Family group of singers, began recording, 1972; soul hits include "Boogie Fever," 1976; "Hot Line," 1977.
Source: *BioIn 11; InB&W 80; RkOn 84*

Sylvester, James Joseph
English. Mathematician
Co-founder of algebraic invariants theory with Arthur Cayley.
b. Sep 3, 1814 in London, England
d. Mar 15, 1897 in London, England
Source: *Alli SUP; AmBi; ApCAB; BiDAmS; BiESc; BiInAmS; BioIn 15; CamDcSc; DcAmB; DcBiPP; DcNaB; DcScB; InSci; LarDcSc; OxCAmH; PeoHis; WhAm HS; WhDW*

Symington, J. Fife, III
American. Politician
Rep. governor, AR, 1991—; indicted on 23 counts of attempted extortion and wire and bankruptcy fraud in 1996.
b. Aug 12, 1945 in New York, New York
Source: *AlmAP 92; WhoWest 92*

Symington, Stuart
[William Stuart Symington]
American. Politician
Democratic senator from MO, 1952-77; known champion of the military; first US Air Force secretary, 1947-50.

b. Jun 26, 1901 in Amherst, Massachusetts
d. Dec 14, 1988 in New Canaan, Connecticut
Source: *AnObit 1988; BiDrAC; BiDrUSC 89; BioIn 1, 2, 3, 4, 5, 6, 9, 10, 11, 12, 16; BlueB 76; CelR; CngDr 74; CurBio 45, 56, 89, 89N; EncCW; EncMcCE; FacFETw; InSci; IntWW 74, 75, 76, 77, 78, 79, 80, 81; IntYB 78, 79; LinLib S; NewYTBS 88, 89; PolPar; PolProf E, J, K, NF, T; WhAm 9; Who 74, 82, 83, 85, 88; WhoAm 74, 76, 84, 86, 88; WhoAmP 73, 75, 77, 79, 89; WhoGov 72, 75, 77; WhoMW 74, 76; WhoWor 74; WorAl; WorAlBi*

Symms, Steven Douglas
American. Politician
Rep. senator from ID, 1980—.
b. Apr 23, 1938 in Nampa, Idaho
Source: *AlmAP 88; BiDrUSC 89; CngDr 87; IntWW 81, 82, 83, 89, 91, 93; WhoAm 74, 76, 78, 80, 82, 84, 86, 88, 90; WhoAmP 87; WhoWest 74, 76, 78, 80, 82, 84, 87, 89; WhoWor 82, 87, 91*

Symonds, John Addington
English. Historian, Poet, Translator
Noted for seven-volume *History of Italian Renaissance,* 1875-86; translation of Cellini autobiography, 1888.
b. Oct 5, 1840 in Bristol, England
d. Apr 19, 1893 in Rome, Italy
Source: *Alli, SUP; AtlBL; BbD; Benet 87, 96; BiD&SB; BioIn 7, 8, 9, 10, 14, 16, 20, 21; BritAu 19; CamGEL; CamGLE; CasWL; CelCen; ChhPo, S1, S2, S3; DcEnA; DcEuL; DcLB 144; DcLEL; Dis&D; EvLB; GayLesB; LinLib L, S; MouLC 4; NewC; NewCBEL; NinCLC 34; OxCEng 67, 85, 95; PenC ENG; REn; VicBrit*

Symons, Arthur William
Welsh. Critic, Poet
Wrote verse volume *Silhouettes,* 1892; critique *Symbolist Movement in Literature,* 1899.
b. Feb 28, 1865 in Milford Haven, Wales
d. Jan 22, 1945 in Wittersham, England
Source: *Alli SUP; AtlBL; BiD&SB; CasWL; Chambr 3; CnE&AP; DcNaB 1941; EvLB; LngCTC; ModBrL; NewC; OxCEng 67, 85, 95; OxCTwCP; PenC ENG; REn; TwCA, SUP; TwCWr; WebE&AL*

Symons, George James
English. Meteorologist
Worked to make meteorology more accurate and standardized in its measurements.
b. Aug 6, 1838 in London, England
d. Mar 10, 1900 in London, England
Source: *BioIn 4; DcNaB S1; InSci; LarDcSc*

Symons, Julian (Gustave)
English. Author
Mystery writer; won 1961 Edgar for *Progress of a Crime.*
b. May 30, 1912 in London, England
d. Nov 19, 1994
Source: *Benet 87, 96; BioIn 4, 9, 13, 14, 15, 17, 19, 20, 21; BlueB 76; ConAu 3AS, 3NR, 33NR, 49, 147; ConLC 2, 14, 32, 86; ConNov 82, 86, 91; ConPo 80, 85, 91; CrtSuMy; DcLB 87, 155, Y92; DcLEL 1940; EncMys; EngPo; IntAu&W 76, 77, 89, 91, 93; IntWW 91, 93; LngCTC; MajTwCW; ModBrL; NewCBEL; NewYTBS 94; Novels; OxCTwCP; RGTwCWr; ScF&FL 92; TwCA SUP; TwCCr&M 80, 85, 91; WhAm 11; WhE&EA; Who 74, 82, 83, 85, 88, 90, 92, 94; WhoAm 82, 84, 86, 88, 90, 92, 94, 95; WhoSpyF; WorAl; WorAlBi; WrDr 76, 80, 82, 84, 86, 88, 90, 92, 94, 96*

Syms, Sylvia
American. Singer
Popular Cabaret singer.
b. Dec 2, 1917 in New York, New York
d. May 10, 1992 in New York, New York
Source: *BioIn 17, 18; NewYTBS 92*

Syms, Sylvia
English. Actor
Leading lady in films: *The World of Suzie Wong,* 1960; *The Victim,* 1961.
b. Dec 3, 1934 in London, England
Source: *BioIn 19; ConTFT 3, 13; FilmAG WE; FilmEn; FilmgC; HalFC 80, 84, 88; IlWWBF; IntMPA 75, 76, 78, 79, 80, 81, 82, 84, 88, 92, 94, 96; ItaFilm; MotPP; WhoHol 92, A*

Synge, John Millington
Irish. Author, Dramatist
Wrote about peasants of W Ireland; *The Playboy of the Western World,* 1907.
b. Apr 16, 1871 in Dublin, Ireland
d. Mar 24, 1909 in Dublin, Ireland
Source: *AtlBL; Benet 87, 96; BiDIrW; BioIn 1, 3, 4, 5, 6, 7, 8, 9, 10, 11, 12, 13, 14, 17, 18; BlmGEL; CamGEL; CamGWoT; CasWL; Chambr 3; ChhPo S1; CnDBLB 5; CnMD; CnMWL; CnThe; CrtSuDr; CyWA 58; DcEuL; DcIrB 78, 88; DcIrL; DcIrW 1; DcLEL; DcNaB S2; Dis&D; DramC 2; EncWL, 2, 3; EncWT; Ent; EvLB; FacFETw; IriPla; LinLib L, S; LngCEL; LngCTC; MagSWL; McGEWD 72, 84; ModBrL, S1, S2; ModIrL; ModWD; NewC; NewEOp 71; NewGrDO; NotNAT B; OxCEng 67, 85; OxCThe 67, 83; PenC ENG; PlP&P; PoIre; RAdv 14; RComWL; REn; REnWD; TwCA; TwCLC 37; TwCWr; WebE&AL; WhDW; WhoTwCL; WorAl; WorAlBi*

Synge, Richard Laurence Millington
English. Chemist
Shared Nobel Prize, 1952, for invention of partition chromatography.
b. Oct 28, 1914 in Liverpool, England
Source: *AsBiEn; BiESc; BioIn 3, 6; BlueB 76; IntWW 74, 75, 76, 77, 78, 79, 80, 81, 82, 83, 89, 91, 93; LarDcSc; McGMS 80; Who 74, 82, 83, 85, 88, 90, 92, 94; WhoNob, 90, 95; WhoScEn 94, 96; WhoWor 74, 76, 78, 82, 84, 87, 89, 91, 93, 95, 96, 97; WorAl*

Szabo, Violette Bushell
English. Spy
Special Operations Executive agent, WW II; captured while on mission, executed in concentration camp; life was subject of film *Carve Her Name With Pride,* 1958.
b. 1918
d. Jan 26, 1945, Germany
Source: *BioIn 7, 8; WhWW-II*

Szabolcsi, Bence
Hungarian. Musicologist, Educator
Authority on Hungarian composer, Bela Bartok.
b. Aug 2, 1899 in Budapest, Austria-Hungary
d. Jan 21, 1973 in Budapest, Hungary
Source: *Baker 78, 84, 92; ConAu 116; NewGrDM 80; WhoMus 72; WhoWor 74; WhoWorJ 72, 78*

Szasz, Thomas Stephen
American. Psychiatrist, Educator
Books on mental illness include *Insanity: The Idea and Its Consequences,* 1986.
b. Apr 15, 1920 in Budapest, Hungary
Source: *AmAu&B; AmMWSc 73S, 76P, 79, 82, 86, 89, 92, 95; BiDrAPA 77; BioIn 9, 10, 12, 13, 15; ConAu 9NR, 17R; CurBio 75; IntAu&W 77, 82, 86, 89, 91, 93; IntWW 76, 77, 78, 79, 80, 81, 82, 83, 89, 91, 93; MakMC; NewYTBE 71; WhoAm 74, 76, 78, 80, 82, 84, 86, 88, 90, 92, 94, 95, 96, 97; WhoE 91, 95; WhoMedH; WhoScEn 94, 96; WhoWor 74; WorAu 1975; WrDr 76, 80, 82, 84, 86, 88, 90, 92, 94, 96*

Szell, George
American. Conductor
Led Cleveland Symphony, from 1946, molding it into one of nation's finest.
b. Jun 7, 1897 in Budapest, Austria-Hungary
d. Jul 30, 1970 in Cleveland, Ohio
Source: *Baker 78, 84, 92; BiDAmM; BioIn 1, 2, 3, 4, 6, 7, 8, 9, 11, 13, 18; BriBkM 80; CurBio 45, 70; DcAmB S8; FacFETw; IntDcOp; LegTOT; LinLib S; MetOEnc; MusSN; NatCAB 61; NewAmDM; NewGrDA 86; NewGrDM 80; NewGrDO; NewYTBE 70; ObitT 1961; OxCAmH; OxDcOp; PenDiMP; WebAB 74, 79; WorAl; WorAlBi*

Szenkar, Eugen
Brazilian. Conductor
Directed Dusseldorf Symphony, 1950s; Brazilian Symphony, 1940s.
b. Apr 9, 1891 in Budapest, Austria-Hungary
d. Mar 28, 1977 in Duesseldorf, Germany
Source: *Baker 78, 84, 92; NewEOp 71*

Szent-Gyorgyi, Albert (von Nagyrapolt)
American. Biochemist
Won Nobel Prize, 1937, for discovery of Vitamin C; first Hungarian to win Nobel.
b. Sep 16, 1893 in Budapest, Austria-Hungary
d. Oct 22, 1986 in Woods Hole, Massachusetts
Source: *AmMWSc 73P, 76P, 79, 82, 86; AsBiEn; BioIn 2, 3, 4, 10, 11, 14, 15, 16, 20; BlueB 76; ConAu 120; ConNews 87-2; CurBio 55, 87, 87N; FacFETw; IntWW 74, 75, 76, 77, 78, 79, 80, 81, 82, 83; LarDcSc; LinLib S; McGEWB; McGMS 80; NewYTBS 86; NobelP; NotTwCS; WebAB 74, 79; WhAm 9; Who 74, 82, 83, 85; WhoAm 74, 76, 78, 80, 84, 86; WhoE 77, 79, 81, 83, 85, 86; WhoNob, 90, 95; WhoWor 74, 76, 78, 82, 84, 87; WorAl; WorAlBi; WorScD*

Szeryng, Henryk
Mexican. Violinist
Int'l concertist since 1933; recorded nearly 250 works, mostly in Romantic style.
b. Sep 22, 1921? in Zelazowa Wola, Poland
d. Mar 3, 1988 in Kassel, Germany (West)
Source: *Baker 84; BioIn 6, 8; CurBio 68, 86; IntWW 74, 75, 76, 77; MusSN; NewGrDM 80; NewYTBS 83; Who 74; WhoAm 86; WhoAmM 83; WhoFr 79; WhoSSW 73, 75; WhoWor 74*

Szewinska, Irena Kirszenstein
Polish. Track Athlete
Sprinter; won gold medal in 200 meters, 1968 Olympics.
b. May 24, 1946 in Leningrad, Union of Soviet Socialist Republics
Source: *WhoTr&F 73*

Szigeti, Joseph
American. Violinist
Great concert performer; pioneered in performing Bartok, contemporary composers.
b. Sep 2, 1892 in Budapest, Hungary
d. Feb 20, 1973 in Lucerne, Switzerland
Source: *Baker 78, 84, 92; BioIn 1, 2, 3, 4, 5, 7, 9, 10, 11, 12, 13, 14, 18; BriBkM 80; ConAu P-1; CurBio 40, 58, 73, 73N; FacFETw; MusMk; MusSN; NewAmDM; NewGrDM 80; NewYTBE 73; ObitT 1971; PenDiMP; WhAm 5; WhoMus 72; WhScrn 83*

Szilard, Leo
American. Scientist
With Enrico Fermi, achieved first nuclear chain reaction, 1942.
b. Feb 11, 1898 in Budapest, Austria-Hungary
d. May 30, 1964 in La Jolla, California
Source: *AmPeW; AsBiEn; BiDMoPL; BiESc; BioIn 1, 5, 6, 7, 8, 9, 10, 11, 12, 13; CamDcSc; ConAu 113; CurBio 47, 64; DcAmB S7; DcScB; EncSF, 93; EncWB; FacFETw; InSci; JeHun; LarDcSc; McGEWB; McGMS 80; NotTwCS; ObitT 1961; OxCAmH; PeoHis; PolProf T; ScF&FL 1; ScFSB; TwCSFW 81, 86, 91; WebAB 74, 79; WhAm 4; WhoSciF; WorAl; WorAlBi; WorInv*

Szmuness, Wolf
Polish. Scientist
Epidemiologist, best known for hepatitis-B vaccine.
b. Mar 12, 1919 in Warsaw, Poland
d. Jun 6, 1982 in Flushing, New York
Source: *AnObit 1982; BioIn 12, 13; NewYTBS 82*

Szoka, Edmund Casimir, Cardinal
American. Religious Leader
Archbishop of Detroit, 1981-90; chief financial officer at the Vatican, 1990—
b. Sep 14, 1927 in Grand Rapids, Michigan
Source: *AmCath 80; BioIn 13; IntWW 89, 91, 93; RelLAm 91; WhoAm 76, 78, 80, 82, 84, 86, 88, 90, 95, 96, 97; WhoMW 82, 84, 88, 90; WhoRel 85, 92; WhoWor 91, 95, 96*

Szold, Henrietta
American. Social Reformer
Founder, pres., Hadassah, US women's Zionist group, 1912-26; practiced nursing in Holy Land.
b. Dec 21, 1860 in Baltimore, Maryland
d. Feb 13, 1945 in Jerusalem, Palestine
Source: *BioAmW; BioIn 1, 2, 3, 4, 5, 6, 7, 8, 9, 10, 11, 12, 13, 14, 15, 16, 17, 19, 21; ContDcW 89; CurBio 40, 45; DcAmB S3; DcAmImH; DcAmReB 1, 2; EncARH; EncWHA; FacFETw; GoodHs; GrLiveH; HerW; IntDcWB; InWom, SUP; JeAmHC; JeHun; LibW; McGEWB; NotAW; RelLAm 91; WhAm 2; WomFir; WomWWA 14; WorAl; WorAlBi*

Szyk, Arthur
Polish. Artist
Miniaturist, manuscript illuminator; noted for fine book illustration.
b. Jun 3, 1894 in Lodz, Poland
d. Sep 13, 1951 in New Canaan, Connecticut
Source: *BioIn 1, 2, 3, 5, 16; ChhPo; CurBio 46, 51; DcAmB S5; IlsBYP; IlsCB 1946; PolBiDi; WhAm 3; WhAmArt 85; WhoAmA 84, 89N, 91N, 93N; WorECar*

Szymanowski, Karol Maciej
Russian. Composer
Works include opera *Krol Roger,* 1926.
b. Oct 6, 1882 in Timoshovka, Russia
d. Mar 29, 1937 in Lausanne, Switzerland
Source: *Baker 84; DcCM*

T

T, Mr.
[Lawrence Tero; Lawrence Tureaud]
American. Actor
Former celebrity bodyguard; star of TV's "A-Team."
b. May 21, 1952 in Chicago, Illinois
Source: *BioIn 13; BlksAmF; ConTFT 5; InB&W 85; VarWW 85; WhoAfA 96; WhoBlA 85, 88, 90, 92, 94; WhoHol 92; WorAlBi*

T. Rex
[Marc Bolan; Steven Currie; Mickey Finn; Jack Green; Bill Legend; Steven Peregrine Took]
English. Music Group
Rock group formed 1967; up and down career eventually landed hit song "Bang A Gong (Get it On)," 1972.
Source: *BiDrAPA 89; BioIn 13; ConMus 11; EncPR&S 89; EncRk 88; EncRkSt; ForYSC; IntMPA 94; LinLib LP; RkOn 78; RolSEnR 83; WhoHol 92; WhoRock 81; WhoRocM 82*

Tabb, John Banister
American. Poet
Wrote religious verse *The Rosary in Rhyme,* 1904.
b. Mar 22, 1845 in Amelia County, Virginia
d. Nov 19, 1909
Source: *AmAu; AmAu&B; AmBi; BenetAL 91; BibAL 8; BiD&SB; BiDSA; Chambr 3; ChhPo, S1; CnDAL; DcAmAu; DcAmB; DcLEL; DcNAA; EvLB; LinLib L; NatCAB 13; OxCAmL 65, 83; REnAL; SouWr; TwCBDA; WhAm 1*

Tabbert, William
American. Actor, Singer
Broadway shows include *South Pacific; Seven Lively Arts; Fanny.*
b. Oct 5, 1921 in Chicago, Illinois
d. Oct 20, 1974 in Dallas, Texas
Source: *BiE&WWA; BioIn 10; CmpEPM; EncMT; NewYTBS 74; NotNAT B; ObitOF 79; WhThe*

Tabei, Junko
Japanese. Mountaineer
First woman to climb to summit of Mt. Everest, 1975.
b. 1940 in Tokyo, Japan
Source: *GoodHs; InWom SUP; WorAl; WorAlBi*

Taber, Gladys Bagg
American. Journalist, Author
Wrote popular "Stillmeadow" books; columnist, *Ladies Home Journal,* 1938-49.
b. Apr 12, 1899 in Colorado Springs, Colorado
d. Mar 11, 1980 in Hyannis, Massachusetts
Source: *AmAu&B; AmNov; Au&Wr 71; BioIn 15; ConAu 4NR, 5R, 97; CurBio 52, 80; ForWC 70; WhoAm 74*

Tabor, Elizabeth Bonduel McCourt Doe
[Mrs. Horace Tabor]
"Baby Doe"; "Silver Queen"
American. Pioneer
Douglas Moore's opera, *The Ballad of Baby Doe,* 1955, based on marriage to Horace Tabor.
b. 1854 in Oshkosh, Wisconsin
d. Mar 7, 1935 in Leadville, Colorado
Source: *NewCol 75*

Tabor, Horace Austin Warner
"Hod"; "Silver Dollar"
American. Government Official
Wealth gained from silver mine; first mayor of Leadville, CO, 1878; went broke when US adopted gold standard.
b. Nov 26, 1830 in Holland, Vermont
d. Apr 10, 1899 in Denver, Colorado
Source: *AmBi; ApCAB; BiDAmBL 83; BiDrAC; BiDrUSC 89; BioIn 4, 10; DcAmB; McGEWB; NatCAB 11; REnAW; TwCBDA; WhAm HS; WhAmP*

Tabori, Kristoffer
American. Actor
Son of actress Viveca Lindfors; starred in TV series "Chicago Story," 1982.
b. Aug 4, 1952 in Los Angeles, California
Source: *NotNAT; WhoHol 92, A*

Tabouis, Genevieve
French. Journalist
Noted European political analyst; foreign news editor of *L'Oeuvre,* 1932-40.
b. Feb 23, 1892
d. Sep 22, 1985 in Paris, France
Source: *ConAu 117; CurBio 40, 85; WhE&EA; Who 82, 83, 85; WhoFr 79*

Tacitus, Cornelius
[Gaius Tacitus; Publius Tacitus]
Roman. Historian, Orator
Writings on Roman history include *Annals, Dialogue on Oratory.*
b. 55
d. 117
Source: *Alli; AtlBL; BbD; Benet 87, 96; BiD&SB; BioIn 1, 4, 5, 7, 8, 9, 10, 11, 12; BlmGEL; CasWL; CyWA 58; DcEnL; LngCEL; LuthC 75; NewC; OxCEng 67, 85, 95; OxCGer 76; PenC CL; RComWL; REn; WhDW*

Taddei, Giuseppe
Italian. Opera Singer
Dramatic baritone, noted for Verdi, buffo roles.
b. Jun 26, 1916 in Genoa, Italy
Source: *Baker 84, 92; BioIn 14, 16; CmOp; IntWWM 90; MetOEnc; NewAmDM; NewEOp 71; NewGrDM 80; NewGrDO; OxDcOp; PenDiMP; WhoMus 72; WhoOp 76*

Taeuber, Conrad
American. Sociologist
Together with wife Irene Barnes-Taeuber, contributed to founding of demography as a field.
b. Jun 15, 1906 in Hosmer, South Dakota
Source: *ConAu 28NR, 45; IntEnSS 79; IntYB 78, 79, 80, 81, 82; RAdv 14; WhoAm 74, 76, 78, 80, 82, 84, 86, 88, 90, 92, 94, 95, 96, 97; WhoE 77; WhoSSW 73, 75, 76; WhoTech 89*

Taeuber-Arp, Sophie
Swiss. Artist
Sculptor; active in Dada movement; wed to Jean Arp; best work done, 1935-38.
b. Jan 19, 1889 in Davos, Switzerland
d. Jan 13, 1943 in Zurich, Switzerland
Source: *ConArt 77, 83; DcWomA; EncWB; InWom SUP; McGDA; OxCTwCA; OxDcArt; PhDcTCA 77; WomArt*

Taft, Charles Phelps
American. Lawyer, Religious Leader
One of the founders, World Council of Churches; son of Pres. William Howard Taft.
b. Sep 20, 1897
d. Jun 24, 1983 in Cincinnati, Ohio
Source: *AmAu&B; Au&Wr 71; BioIn 1, 3, 7, 9, 13; BlueB 76; ConAu 105; CurBio 45, 83; IntWW 74, 75, 76, 77, 78, 79, 80, 81, 82, 83; NewYTBS 83; OhA&B; REnAL; WhAm 8; Who 74, 82, 83; WhoAm 74, 76, 78, 80, 82; WhoAmP 83*

Taft, Helen Herron
[Mrs. William Howard Taft]
American. First Lady
Persuaded mayor of Tokyo to donate 3,000 cherry trees to nation's capital.
b. Jun 2, 1861 in Cincinnati, Ohio
d. May 22, 1943 in Washington, District of Columbia
Source: *BioIn 16, 17, 19; DcNAA; FacPr 89; GoodHs; InWom, SUP; NatCAB 14; NotAW; OhA&B; WomWWA 14*

Taft, Henry Waters, II
American. Business Executive
Former pres. Outward Bound, U.S.A; pres. and treasurer Brystal-Myers Co., 1962-73; grand nephew of pres. William Howard Taft.
b. Jul 5, 1926 in New York, New York
d. Mar 18, 1991 in Camden, Maine
Source: *BioIn 17; NewYTBS 91; WhoAm 74, 76, 78, 80, 82, 84, 86; WhoE 74; WhoFI 74*

Taft, Lorado
American. Sculptor
Best-known works include *Solitude of the Soul,* Chicago; Ferguson Fountain of the Great Lakes, Chicago.
b. Apr 29, 1860 in Elmwood, Illinois
d. Oct 30, 1936 in Chicago, Illinois
Source: *AmBi; AmLY; ApCAB SUP; BioIn 1, 4, 8, 11; DcAmAu; DcAmB S2; DcNAA; EncAB-A 2; GayN; HarEnUS; LinLib L, S; McGDA; OxCAmH; OxCAmL 65; REnAL; TwCBDA; WebAB 74; WhAm 1, 4A; WhNAA*

Taft, Robert A(lphonso)
"Mr. Republican"
American. Politician
Rep. senator from OH, 1939-53; son of William Howard; sponsored Taft-Hartley Labor Relations Act, 1947.
b. Sep 8, 1889 in Cincinnati, Ohio
d. Jul 31, 1953 in New York, New York
Source: *AmDec 1950; AmPolLe; BiDrAC; BiDrUSC 89; BioIn 1, 2, 3, 4, 5, 6, 7, 8, 9, 10, 11, 13; ColdWar 2; CurBio 40, 48, 53; DcAmB S5; EncAAH; EncAB-H 1974, 1996; EncWB; FacFETw; LinLib S; NatCAB 47; OhA&B; PolProf E, T; REn; REnAL; WebAB 74, 79; WhAm 3; WhAmP; WhoAmW 58; WorAl*

Taft, Robert A(lphonso), Jr.
American. Politician
Rep. senator from OH, 1971-76; grandson of Pres. Taft; son of Sen. Taft.
b. Feb 26, 1917 in Cincinnati, Ohio
d. Dec 6, 1993 in Cincinnati, Ohio
Source: *BiDrAC; BioIn 3, 4, 5, 6, 7, 8, 9, 10, 11, 12; CngDr 74; CurBio 67; IntWW 83; NewYTBE 70; PolProf NF; WhoAm 86*

Taft, William (Howard)
American. US President
Rep., 27th pres., 1909-13; created labor dept., 1911; Supreme Court justice, 1921-30.
b. Sep 15, 1857 in Cincinnati, Ohio
d. Mar 8, 1930 in Washington, District of Columbia
Source: *AmBi; AmDec 1900; AmJust; AmLY; AmPeW; AmPolLe; ApCAB SUP, X; Ballpl 90; Benet 87, 96; BenetAL 91; BiDFedJ; BiDInt; BiDrAC; BiDrUSE 71, 89; BioIn 1, 2, 3, 4, 5, 6, 7, 8, 9, 10, 11, 12, 13; CyAG; DcAmB; DcAmC; DcAmSR; DcNAA; Dis&D; EncAAH; EncAB-H 1974, 1996; EncSoH; FacFETw; FacPr 89, 93; HarEnUS; HealPre; HisWorL; LegTOT; LinLib L, S; McGEWB; NatCAB 14, 23; OhA&B; OxCAmH; OxCAmL 65, 83; OxCLaw; OxCSupC; PolPar; RComAH; REn; REnAL; SupCtJu; TwCBDA; WebAB 74, 79; WhAm 1; WhAmP; WhDW; WorAl; WorAlBi*

Taggard, Genevieve
American. Poet, Editor
Founder, editor of *Measure,* 1920-26; wrote *Slow Music,* 1946.
b. Nov 28, 1894 in Waitsburg, Washington
d. Nov 8, 1948 in New York, New York
Source: *AmAu&B; BenetAL 91; BioIn 1, 4, 15; ChhPo, S1, S2, S3; CmCal; CnDAL; ConAmA; DcAmB S4; DcNAA; FemiCLE; InWom, SUP; LibW; ModWoWr; NewCol 75; NotAW; OxCAmL 65, 83, 95; OxCTwCP; REn; REnAL; SixAP; TwCA, SUP; WhAm 2; WhE&EA*

Tagliabue, Carlo
Italian. Opera Singer
Internationally known baritone; noted for Verdi, Wagner roles.
b. Jan 13, 1898 in Como, Italy
d. Apr 5, 1978 in Monza, Italy
Source: *Baker 84, 92; BioIn 11; CmOp; MetOEnc; NewAmDM; NewEOp 71; NewGrDM 80; NewGrDO; WhScrn 83*

Tagliabue, Paul John
American. Football Executive, Lawyer
Commissioner of NFL, 1989—.
b. Nov 24, 1940 in Jersey City, New Jersey
Source: *BioIn 16; CurBio 92; News 90-2; NewYTBS 89; WhoAm 90, 92, 94, 95, 96, 97; WhoAmL 90, 92; WhoE 91, 93*

Tagliavini, Ferrucio
Italian. Opera Singer
Leading Italian lyric tenor during WW II; with NY Met., 1946-54.
b. Aug 14, 1913 in Reggio Emilia, Italy
d. Jan 28, 1995 in Reggio Emilia, Italy
Source: *Baker 84; CurBio 47; ItaFilm; MusSN; NewYTBS 95*

Taglioni, Maria
Italian. Dancer
Member of dancing family; known for ballet *La Sylphide.*
b. Apr 23, 1804 in Stockholm, Sweden
d. Apr 24, 1884 in Marseilles, France
Source: *CelCen; DancEn 78; InWom; NewC; NewCol 75; OxCFr; WebBD 83; WhDW*

Tagore, Rabindranath, Sir
[Ravindranath Thakur]
Indian. Poet
Won Nobel Prize for literature, 1913; known for mysticism, religious feeling.
b. May 6, 1861 in Calcutta, India
d. Aug 7, 1941 in Calcutta, India
Source: *Benet 87, 96; BiDMoPL; BioIn 1, 2, 4, 5, 6, 7, 8, 9, 10, 11, 12, 13, 14, 15, 16, 17, 20, 21; CamGEL; CasWL; Chambr 3; ChhPo, S1, S2; CnMD; CnThe; ConAu 120; CurBio 41; DcAmSR; DcArts; DcLEL; DcNaB 1941; DcOrL 2; DcTwHis; EncWL 2, 3; EncWT; Ent; EvLB; FacFETw; GrWrEL P; HisWorL; IlEncMy; IntDcT 2; LegTOT; LinLib L, S; LngCTC; MajTwCW; MakMC; McGEWB; McGEWD 84; ModCmwL; ModWD; NewC; NewGrDM 80; NobelP; NotNAT B; Novels; OxCEng 67, 85, 95; OxCPhil; OxCThe 67, 83; PenC CL, ENG; PoeCrit 8; RAdv 14; REn; REnWD; RfGEnL 91; RfGShF; RfGWoL 95; TwCA, SUP; TwCLC 53; TwCWr; WebE&AL; WhDW; WhLit; WhoNob, 90, 95; WhoTwCL; WorAl; WorAlBi*

Taha Hussein
Egyptian. Educator, Author
Outstanding Islamic scholar, author of over 40 books; blinded in childhood; wrote *An Egyptian Childhood,* 1932; *The Tree of Misfortune,* 1944.
b. Nov 14, 1889 in Maghagha, Egypt
d. Oct 28, 1973 in Cairo, Egypt
Source: *ConAu 45; CurBio 53, 73; NewYTBE 73; WhAm 6; WhoWor 74*

Tahse, Martin
American. Producer
Exec. producer of ABC's "Afternoon Specials;" won Emmys, 1980, 1981.
b. Apr 24, 1930 in Cincinnati, Ohio

Source: *BiE&WWA; VarWW 85; WhoAm 74, 76, 78; WhoWor 74*

Tailleferre, Germaine
[Les Six]
French. Composer
Only woman composer in group of post-WW I composers.
b. Apr 19, 1892 in Pau-Saint Maur, France
d. Nov 7, 1983 in Paris, France
Source: *AnObit 1983; Baker 78, 84; BioIn 3, 4, 13, 15, 17, 19; BriBkM 80; ContDcW 89; IntDcWB; IntWWM 80; InWom; NewAmDM; NewGrDM 80; NewOxM; NewYTBS 82, 83; OxCMus; PenDiMP A; WhoFr 79; WomFir*

Taine, Hippolyte Adolphe
French. Philosopher
Attempted scientific study of human nature, history; wrote *History of English Literature,* 1864.
b. Apr 21, 1828 in Vouziers, France
d. Mar 9, 1893 in Paris, France
Source: *AtlBL; BbD; BiD&SB; BiDPsy; BioIn 1, 2, 3, 5, 7, 9, 10; CasWL; CelCen; ClDMEL 47; CyWA 58; DcArts; DcBiPP; DcEnL; DcEuL; Dis&D; EuAu; EvEuW; LinLib L, S; McGEWB; NamesHP; NewC; NewCBEL; NinCLC 15; OxCEng 67; OxCFr; PenC EUR; REn; WhDW; WorAl; WorAlBi*

Tairov, Aleksandr Yakovlevich
Russian. Producer, Director
Founded Moscow's Kamerny (Chamber) Theatre 1914; producer-director 1914-49; known for avant garde staging style.
b. Jun 24, 1885 in Romny, Russia
d. Sep 25, 1950 in Moscow, Union of Soviet Socialist Republics
Source: *BiDSovU; BioIn 3, 14; CamGWoT; FacFETw; NotNAT B; OxCThe 83; SovUn*

Taishoff, Sol Joseph
American. Editor, Publisher
Co-founded *Broadcasting* magazine.
b. Oct 8, 1904 in Minsk, Russia
d. Aug 15, 1982 in Washington, District of Columbia
Source: *BiDAmJo; BioIn 12, 13, 16; ConAu 73; EncTwCJ; NewYTBS 82; NewYTET; St&PR 75; WhAm 8; WhoAm 74, 76, 78, 80, 82; WhoFI 74, 75, 77, 79, 81; WhoSSW 73; WhoWor 74, 76, 78, 80; WhoWorJ 72*

Tait, Arthur Fitzwilliam
English. Artist
Self-taught painter for Currier & Ives; specialized in animal subjects: *The Life of a Hunter.*
b. Aug 5, 1819 in Liverpool, England
d. Apr 28, 1905 in Yonkers, New York
Source: *ApCAB; BioIn 3, 7, 9, 10, 14, 15; BriEAA; DcAmArt; DcAmB; EarABI; IlBEAAW; NewYHSD; TwCBDA; WhAm 1; WhAmArt 85*

Tait, Peter Guthrie
Scottish. Physicist, Mathematician
Co-developer of quaternions, a form of advanced algebra.
b. Apr 28, 1831 in Dalkeith, Scotland
d. Jul 4, 1901 in Edinburgh, Scotland
Source: *Alli, SUP; BioIn 4; BritAu 19; CelCen; DcNaB, S2; DcScB; InSci; LarDcSc*

Tai-Tsung
Chinese. Ruler
Second emperor of Sung Dynasty, 960-1249; consolidated power, developed civil-service examination system.
b. 939, China
d. 997, China

Taj Mahal
American. Singer, Songwriter, Composer
Blues performer; composed scores for films *Sounder, Sounder II,* and *Brothers.*
b. May 17, 1942 in New York, New York
Source: *BiDJaz A; ConMus 6; EncFCWM 83; InB&W 80, 85; NewGrDA 86; OnThGG*

Tajo, Italo
b. Apr 25, 1915 in Pinerolo, Italy
d. Mar 29, 1993 in Cincinnati, Ohio
Source: *Baker 84, 92; BioIn 1, 3, 4, 11, 13, 14, 18; CmOp; IntDcOp; IntWWM 77, 80, 90; MetOEnc; NewAmDM; NewEOp 71; NewGrDA 86; NewGrDM 80; NewGrDO; NewYTBS 93; OxDcOp; PenDiMP; WhAm 11; WhoAm 78, 80, 82, 84, 86, 88; WhoAmM 83; WhoEnt 92; WhoOp 76*

Takada, Kenzo
Japanese. Fashion Designer
Ready-to-wear designs sold around the world; specializes in clothing, shoes, accessories.
b. Feb 28, 1940, Japan
Source: *WhoFash; WorFshn*

Takahama Kyoshi
Japanese. Poet
Contributed much to modern Japanese haiku; wrote *Susumu beki haiku no michi,* 1918.
b. Feb 22, 1874 in Matsuyama, Japan
d. Apr 8, 1959 in Kamakura, Japan

Takamine, Jokichi
Japanese. Biochemist
First person to isolate a pure hormone (adrenalin or epinephrine) in its natural state.
b. Nov 3, 1854 in Takaoka, Japan
d. Jul 22, 1922 in New York, New York
Source: *AsAmAlm; AsBiEn; BiDAmS; BiESc; BioIn 3, 4, 11, 20; CamDcSc; DcAmB; DcAmMeB 84; NatCAB 40; NotAsAm; WhAm 1*

Take 6
[Alvin "Vinnie" Chea; Cedric Dent; Mark Kibble; Claude V. McKnight, III; David Thomas; Mervyn Warren]
American. Music Group
Gospel/jazz group; Grammy Awards: best jazz vocal group for "Spread Love," 1989 and best soul gospel album *Take 6,* 1989.
Source: *Alli; BioIn 16, 17; ConMus 6; DcTwCCu 5; DrRegL 75; NewCBEL; WhoAmP 85; WhoHol 92, A; WhoRocM 82*

Takehara Han
Japanese. Dancer
Became Japan's best known Jiutamai dancer of the 20th c.
b. Feb 4, 1903 in Tokushima, Japan

Takei, George
American. Actor
Played Sulu on TV's "Star Trek," 1966-69, also in film series.
b. Apr 20, 1937 in Los Angeles, California
Source: *ConTFT 5, 14; EncSF 93; IntMPA 86, 92, 94, 96; VarWW 85*

Takei, Kei
Japanese. Choreographer, Dancer
Founder of the Moving Earth dance company, 1969; choreography blurs traditional distinction between dance and drama.
b. Dec 30, 1946 in Tokyo, Japan
Source: *BiDD; News 90, 90-2; WhoEnt 92*

Takemitsu, Toru
Japanese. Composer
Co-founded an experimental laboratory in Tokyo, 1951, to examine oriental music and avant-garde western techniques.
b. Oct 8, 1930 in Tokyo, Japan
d. Feb 20, 1996 in Tokyo, Japan
Source: *Baker 78, 84, 92; BioIn 8, 11, 17, 21; BriBkM 80; CompSN SUP; ConCom 92; ConMus 6; DcCM; IntDcF 1-4, 2-4; IntWWM 77, 80, 90; JapFilm; NewAmDM; NewGrDM 80; NewOxM; NewYTBS 27; PenDiMP A; WhoWor 78, 80, 82*

Takeshita, Noboru
Japanese. Political Leader
Succeeded Yasuhiro Nakasone as prime minister, 1987.
b. Feb 26, 1924 in Shimane, Japan
Source: *CurBio 88; FacFETw; FarE&A 80, 81; IntWW 80, 81, 82, 83, 89, 91, 93; NewYTBS 87; WhoAsAP 91; WhoWor 87, 89, 91, 93*

Takhtadzhian, Armen Leonovich
Russian. Botanist
Expert on plant classification; author of *Flowering Plants: Classification and Phylogeny,* 1993.
b. May 28, 1910 in Shusha, Russia
Source: *WhoSocC 78*

Taktakishvili, Otar Vasilevich
Russian. Composer
Music shows Caucasus influence; has written piano concertos, symphonic poems.
b. Jul 27, 1924 in Tiflis, Union of Soviet Socialist Republics
Source: *Baker 84; BioIn 9*

Tal, Mikhail Nekhemyevich
Russian. Chess Player
International Grandmaster, 1957, world champion, 1960-61.
b. 1936 in Riga, Union of Soviet Socialist Republics
d. Jun 28, 1992 in Moscow, Union of Soviet Socialist Republics
Source: *BioIn 11; GolEC; OxCChes 84*

Talbot, John Michael
American. Musician, Singer
Member of country-rock band Mason Proffit, 1969-1973; became a Franciscan monk, late 1970s; developed a classical, contemplative musical style.
b. May 8, 1954 in Oklahoma City, Oklahoma
Source: *BioIn 14, 15; ConMus 6; NewAgMG*

Talbot, Lyle
[Lyle Henderson]
American. Actor
Character actor in over 100 films since 1932; in TV series "The Bob Cummings Show," 1955-59.
b. Feb 8, 1902 in Pittsburgh, Pennsylvania
d. Mar 3, 1996 in San Francisco, California
Source: *BiE&WWA; ConTFT 7; EncAFC; FilmEn; FilmgC; HalFC 84; HolCA; IntMPA 94, 96; MovMk; NotNAT; Vers B; WhDW; WhoAm 74; WhoHol A*

Talbot, Nita
American. Comedian
Appeared in film *The Day of the Locust,* 1975.
b. Aug 8, 1930 in New York, New York
Source: *ConTFT 8; EncAFC; FilmgC; ForWC 70; ForYSC; HalFC 80, 84, 88; InWom SUP; WhoHol 92, A; WorAl*

Talbot, William Henry Fox
"Father of Photography"
English. Photographer, Inventor
Developed several photographic processes, including method for taking instant pictures, 1851.
b. Feb 11, 1800 in Lacock Abbey, England
d. Sep 17, 1877 in Lacock Abbey, England
Source: *Alli; AsBiEn; BioIn 2, 4, 7, 8, 9, 10, 11, 12, 13, 16, 18, 19, 20; CamDcSc; CelCen; DcBiPP, A; DcBrWA; DcInv; DcScB; EncAJ; ICPEnP; InSci; LarDcSc; MacBEP; NewCol 75; OxCDecA; VicBrit; WhDW; WorInv*

Talese, Gay
American. Author, Journalist
Wrote *Honor Thy Father,* 1971; *Thy Neighbor's Wife,* 1980.
b. Feb 7, 1932 in Ocean City, New Jersey
Source: *BioIn 9, 10, 12; ConAu 9NR; ConLC 37; CurBio 72; EncAJ; EncTwCJ; IntAu&W 86; LegTOT; LiJour; LinLib L; MajTwCW; NewYTBS 80; WhoAm 74, 76, 78, 80, 82, 84, 86, 88, 90, 92, 94, 95, 96, 97; WhoE 74; WhoUSWr 88; WhoWor 74, 76, 93; WhoWrEP 89, 92, 95; WorAu 1975; WrDr 86, 88, 90, 92, 94, 96*

Talking Heads, The
[David Byrne; Chris Frantz; Jerry Harrison; Martina Weymouth]
American. Music Group
New wave group begun, 1977; combine traditional rock styles with Afro-American music; had hit single "Burning Down the House," 1983.
Source: *BioIn 14, 15, 16, 17, 20; ConMuA 80A; ConMus 1; DcArts; EncPR&S 89; EncRk 88; EncRkSt; HarEnR 86; NewAmDM; NewYTBS 85, 86; OxCPMus; PenEncP; RkOn 85; RolSEnR 83; WhoRock 81; WhoRocM 82; WhsNW 85*

Tallchief, Maria
American. Dancer
Prima ballerina who appeared in film *Million Dollar Mermaid,* 1952.
b. Jan 24, 1925 in Fairfax, Oklahoma
Source: *BiDD; BioAmW; BioIn 2, 3, 4, 5, 6, 7, 9, 10, 12, 13; BlueB 76; CnOxB; CurBio 51; DancEn 78; FacFETw; GoodHs; GrLiveH; HanAmWH; HerW; IntDcB; InWom, SUP; LegTOT; LibW; LinLib S; NotNaAm; WebAB 74, 79; WhoAm 74, 76, 78, 80, 82, 84, 86, 88, 90, 92, 94, 95, 96, 97; WhoAmW 58, 61, 64, 66, 68, 70, 72, 74, 81, 83, 85, 87, 89, 91, 93, 95; WhoEnt 92; WhoHol 92, A; WhoMus 72; WhoMW 80, 82, 84, 86, 88, 92; WhoThe 77A; WhoWor 74, 76, 78, 80, 82, 84; WhThe*

Tallchief, Marjorie
American. Dancer
Ballerina; first American to achieve position of premiere danseuse etoile with Paris Opera.
b. Oct 19, 1927 in Fairfax, Oklahoma
Source: *BiDD; BioIn 3, 4, 5, 9, 10, 11, 13; CnOxB; DancEn 78; IntWW 74, 75, 76, 77, 78, 79, 80, 81, 82, 83, 89, 91, 93; InWom, SUP; WhoHol 92*

Tallent, Garry Wayne
[E Street Band]
American. Musician
Bassist who joined Bruce Springsteen's band, 1971.
b. Oct 27, 1949 in Detroit, Michigan
Source: *WhoRocM 82*

Talley, Gary
[The Box Tops]
American. Musician
Bass guitarist with Memphis-based group, 1966-70.
b. Aug 17, 1947
Source: *WhoRocM 82*

Talleyrand-Perigord, Charles Maurice de
French. Statesman
Minister of Foreign Affairs, 1797-99; opposed Louisiana Purchase, 1803.
b. Feb 13, 1754 in Paris, France
d. May 17, 1838 in Paris, France
Source: *BbD; Benet 87, 96; BiD&SB; BioIn 12, 19, 20, 21; CelCen; CmFrR; DcBiPP; Dis&D; HarEnUS; LinLib L, S; LuthC 75; OxCFr; REn; WhAm HS; WhDW; WorAl; WorAlBi*

Tallis, Thomas
[Thomas Tallys]
"Father of English Cathedral Music"
English. Organist, Composer
Among first to set English words to music for Anglican liturgy; organist of the chapel royal.
b. 1515? in Greenwich, England
d. Nov 23, 1585 in Greenwich, England
Source: *Alli; AtlBL; Baker 84; DcBiPP; DcCathB; DcNaB; LuthC 75; NewCol 75; OxCMus; WhDW*

Tallmadge, Thomas Eddy
American. Architect
Designed numerous churches; wrote *Architecture in America,* 1927.
b. Apr 24, 1876 in Washington, District of Columbia
d. Jan 1, 1940
Source: *BiDAmAr; DcNAA; MacEA; WhAm 1; WhAmArt 85; WhNAA*

TallMountain, Mary
American. Poet
Published poetry collections *There Is No Word for Goodbye,* 1981; *A Quick Brush of Wings,* 1991.
b. 1918 in Nulato, Alaska
d. Sep 2, 1994
Source: *BioIn 21; ConAu 146; ConLC 86; NatNAL; NotNaAm*

Talma, Francois Joseph
French. Actor
Greatest tragic actor of his time; introduced realistic scenery, costuming.
b. Jan 15, 1763 in Paris, France
d. Oct 19, 1826 in Paris, France
Source: *BbD; BioIn 2, 3, 4, 5, 7; CamGWoT; CelCen; CnThe; DcBiPP; Dis&D; EncWT; NewCol 75; NotNAT A, B; OxCFr; OxCThe 67; WebBD 83*

Talmadge, Constance
American. Comedian
Silent film star, 1914-29; retired when talking pictures began.
b. Apr 19, 1900 in New York, New York

d. Nov 23, 1973 in Los Angeles, California
Source: *BioAmW; BioIn 7, 10, 15; DcAmB S9; EncAFC; Film 1, 2; FilmEn; FilmgC; InWom, SUP; MotPP; MovMk; NewYTBE 73; ObitT 1971; OxCFilm; TwYS; WhAm 6; What 1; WhoAmW 72; WhoHol B; WhScrn 77; WorEFlm*

Talmadge, Eugene
American. Politician
Dem. governor of GA, 1933-37, 1940-43.
b. Sep 23, 1884 in Forsyth, Georgia
d. Dec 21, 1946 in Atlanta, Georgia
Source: *AmOrTwC; BioIn 1, 3, 4, 9, 10; CurBio 41, 47; DcAmB S4; EncAB-A 1; EncSoH; NatCAB 38; PolPar; WhAm 2*

Talmadge, Herman Eugene
American. Politician
Dem. governor of GA, 1948-55; US senator, 1957-81; son of Eugene.
b. Aug 9, 1913 in Telfair County, Georgia
Source: *AlmAP 80; BiDrAC; BiDrUSC 89; BioIn 1, 2, 3, 4, 5, 8, 9, 10, 11, 12; BlueB 76; CngDr 74, 77, 79; CurBio 47; EncAAH; IntWW 74, 75, 76, 77, 78, 79, 80, 81, 82, 83; NewYTBS 79; WhoAm 74, 76, 78, 80, 82, 84; WhoAmP 73, 75, 77, 79; WhoWor 78, 80; WorAl*

Talmadge, Norma
American. Actor
Played suffering heroine in films, 1910-30.
b. May 26, 1897 in Jersey City, New Jersey
d. Dec 24, 1957 in Las Vegas, Nevada
Source: *BiDFilm, 81, 94; BioAmW; BioIn 4, 5, 6, 7, 9, 12, 18; DcAmB S6; EncAFC; Film 1; FilmEn; FilmgC; ForYSC; HalFC 84; IntDcF 1-3, 2-3; InWom; MotPP; MovMk; NatCAB 48; NotNAT B; OxCFilm; ThFT; TwYS; WhAm 3; WhScrn 83; WorAl; WorEFlm*

Talmadge, Thomas de Witt
American. Clergy, Author
Chaplain for Union Army during Civil War; sermons printed weekly in various papers for 30 yrs; wrote *The Earth Girdled,* 1895.
b. Jan 7, 1832 in Bound Brook, New Jersey
d. Apr 12, 1902 in Washington, District of Columbia
Source: *AmAu&B; NewCol 75; WhAm 1*

Talman, William
American. Actor
Played D.A. Burger on TV show "Perry Mason," 1957-66.
b. Feb 4, 1915 in Detroit, Michigan
d. Aug 30, 1968 in Encino, California
Source: *FilmgC; ForYSC; HalFC 80, 84, 88; MotPP; WhoHol B; WhScrn 77, 83*

Talvela, Martti Olavi
Finnish. Opera Singer
Bass, noted for portrayal of bass roles by Wagner and Mussorgsky.
b. Feb 4, 1935 in Hiitola, Finland
d. Jul 22, 1989 in Juva, Finland
Source: *Baker 84; CurBio 83, 89; IntWW 74, 75, 76, 77, 78, 79, 80, 81, 82, 89; MusSN; NewYTBS 74; WhoAm 84, 86, 88; WhoOp 76; WhoWor 84, 87, 89*

Tamagno, Francesco
Italian. Opera Singer
Probably greatest tenor di forza of all time; created role of Othello, 1887.
b. Dec 28, 1850 in Turin, Italy
d. Aug 31, 1905 in Varese, Italy
Source: *Baker 78, 84, 92; BriBkM 80; CmOp; IntDcOp; MetOEnc; NewAmDM; NewEOp 71; NewGrDM 80; NewGrDO; OxDcOp; PenDiMP*

Tamayo, Rufino
Mexican. Artist
Fused ancient Mexican with modern French art; painted nationalistic murals in Mexico City, 1950s.
b. Aug 26, 1899 in Oaxaca, Mexico
d. Jun 24, 1991 in Mexico City, Mexico
Source: *AnObit 1991; ArtLatA; BioIn 1, 2, 3, 4, 5, 6, 8, 9, 10, 11, 12, 13, 14, 15, 17, 18; ConArt 83, 89, 96; CurBio 53; DcArts; DcHiB; DcTwCCu 4; EncLatA; IntDcAA 90; McGDA; NewCol 75; News 92, 92-1; NewYTBS 91; OxCArt; OxCTwCA; OxDcArt; PhDcTCA 77; PrintW 83, 85; REn; WhoAm 74, 76, 78, 80, 82; WhoAmA 73, 76, 78, 80, 82, 84, 86, 89, 91, 93N; WhoSSW 73, 75; WhoWor 74; WorArt 1950*

Tamayo y Baus, Manuel
Spanish. Dramatist
Internationally known for play, *Un drama nuevo,* 1867.
b. Sep 15, 1829 in Madrid, Spain
d. Jun 20, 1898 in Madrid, Spain
Source: *BioIn 1, 3, 7, 10; CamGWoT; CasWL; ClDMEL 47; DcEuL; DcSpL; EuAu; EvEuW; LinLib L; McGEWD 72, 84; NinCLC 1; NotNAT B; OxCSpan; OxCThe 67, 83; PenC EUR*

Tamberlik, Enrico
Italian. Singer
Internationally renowned tenor of the 19th c. known for powerful, resonant high notes.
b. Mar 16, 1820 in Rome, Italy
d. Mar 13, 1889 in Paris, France
Source: *Baker 78, 84, 92; BioIn 4, 7, 14; BriBkM 80; CmOp; DcBiPP; MetOEnc; NewAmDM; NewGrDM 80; NewGrDO; OxDcOp; PenDiMP*

Tamblyn, Russ
American. Actor
Oscar nominee for *Peyton Place,* 1957; dancing star of *Seven Brides for Seven Brothers,* 1954; *West Side Story,* 1961.
b. Dec 30, 1935 in Los Angeles, California
Source: *BiDD; CmMov; ConTFT 9; FilmgC; ForYSC; HalFC 84; IntMPA 84, 88, 92, 94, 96; MotPP; MovMk; WhoHol A*

Tambo, Oliver
South African. Political Activist
Pres. of South Africa's outlawed African National Congress, 1949—; formally ap pointed pres., 1977-89.
b. Oct 27, 1917 in Transkei, South Africa
d. Apr 24, 1993 in Johannesburg, South Africa
Source: *AfSS 78, 79, 80, 81, 82; BioIn 13; CurBio 87, 93N; EncRev; FacFETw; IntWW 74, 75, 76, 77, 78, 79, 80, 81, 82, 83, 89, 91; LegTOT; News 91, 91-3; RadHan; WhoWor 74*

Tamburini, Antonio
Italian. Opera Singer
Celebrated baritone, idol of London, Paris, 1830s-40s; created many roles.
b. Mar 28, 1800 in Faenza, Italy
d. Nov 9, 1876 in Nice, France
Source: *Baker 78, 84, 92; BioIn 7, 14; BriBkM 80; CelCen; CmOp; DcBiPP; MetOEnc; NewAmDM; NewEOp 71; NewGrDM 80; NewGrDO; OxDcOp; PenDiMP*

Tamerlane
[Timur]
"The Prince of Destruction"
Mongolian. Conqueror
Descendant of Genghis Khan; invaded Russia, Asia Minor.
b. 1336 in Kesh, Persia
d. 1405
Source: *Benet 87, 96; BioIn 1, 2, 3, 4, 5, 6, 7, 8, 10, 11, 12, 15, 17, 20; DcBiPP; DicTyr; GenMudB; HarEnMi; HisWorL; LegTOT; LinLib S; McGEWB; NewCol 75; OxCChes 84; OxDcByz; WebBD 83; WhDW*

Tamiris, Helen
American. Choreographer, Dancer
Choreographed Broadway musical *Annie Get Your Gun,* 1948.
b. Apr 24, 1902? in New York, New York
d. Aug 25, 1966 in New York, New York
Source: *BiDD; InWom SUP; NotAW MOD; NotNAT B; NotWoAT; WhAm 4*

Tamiroff, Akim
American. Actor
Character actor who played villain roles, 1933-70; Oscar nominee for *For Whom the Bell Tolls.*
b. Oct 29, 1901 in Baku, Russia
d. Sep 17, 1972 in Palm Springs, California
Source: *BiDFilm; BiE&WWA; FilmgC; MotPP; MovMk; NewYTBE 72; NotNAT B; OxCFilm; Vers A; WhAm 5; WhoHol B; WhScrn 77; WorEFlm*

Tamm, Igor Evgenevich
Russian. Physicist, Educator
Shared Nobel Prize in physics, 1958, with I M Frank.
b. Jul 8, 1895 in Vladivostok, Russia
d. Apr 12, 1971 in Moscow, Union of Soviet Socialist Republics
Source: *AmMWSc 82; BiDSovU; BiESc; McGMS 80; ObitOF 79; ObitT 1971; WhoNob, 90, 95; WhoSocC 78; WorAl*

Tammann, Gustav Heinrich Johann Apollon
Russian. Chemist
One of the founders of metallurgy; pioneered research of metals and alloys and their internal structure and physical properties.
b. Jun 9, 1861 in Jamburg, Russia
d. Dec 17, 1938 in Gottingen, Germany
Source: *BioIn 2; DcScB*

Tan, Amy
American. Author
Wrote *The Joy Luck Club,* 1989, *The Kitchen God's Wife,* 1991, and *The Hundred Secret Senses,* 1995.
b. Feb 19, 1952 in Oakland, California
Source: *AmWomWr 92, SUP; AsAmAlm; Au&Arts 9; BestSel 89-3; BlmGWL; ConAu 136; ConLC 59; CurBio 92; DcLB 173; GrLiveH; IntAu&W 91; LegTOT; ModWoWr; NotAsAm; OxCAmL 95; OxCWoWr 95; SmATA 75; TwCYAW; WorAu 1985; WrDr 94, 96*

Tanaka, Kakuei
Japanese. Political Leader
Prime minister, 1972-74; convicted of bribery, 1983.
b. May 4, 1918 in Kariwa, Japan
d. Dec 16, 1993 in Tokyo, Japan
Source: *AnObit 1993; BioIn 12, 13; CurBio 72, 94N; EncWB; FacFETw; FarE&A 78, 79, 80, 81; IntWW 74, 75, 76, 77, 78, 79, 80, 81, 82, 83, 91, 93; IntYB 78, 79; NewCol 75; NewYTBE 72; NewYTBS 76, 93; WhoWor 74; WorAl; WorAlBi*

Tanana, Frank Daryl
American. Baseball Player
Pitcher, 1973—; seventh in ML history to record 2,000 strikeouts.
b. Jul 3, 1953 in Detroit, Michigan
Source: *BaseReg 86, 87; BiDAmSp Sup; BioIn 11*

Tandy, James Napper
Irish. Revolutionary
Founder, Society of United Irishmen, 1791; hero of ballad "The Wearing of the Green."
b. 1740 in Dublin, Ireland
d. Apr 24, 1803 in Bordeaux, France
Source: *DcIrB 78; DcNaB; NewCol 75*

Tandy, Jessica
[Mrs. Hume Cronyn]
American. Actor
Three-time Tony winner; performances include *A Streetcar Named Desire,* 1948; oldest to win Oscar, 1990, for *Driving Miss Daisy.*
b. Jun 7, 1909 in London, England
d. Sep 11, 1994 in Easton, Connecticut
Source: *BiDFilm 94; BiE&WWA; BioIn 1, 2, 4, 5, 7, 10, 11, 12, 13; CamGWoT; CelR, 90; CnThe; ConTFT 1, 7, 13; CurBio 56, 84, 94N; FacFETw; FilmEn; FilmgC; ForYSC; GrLiveH; HalFC 80, 84, 88; IntDcT 3; IntMPA 75, 76, 78, 79, 80, 81, 82, 84, 88, 92, 94; IntWW 91, 93; InWom, SUP; LegTOT; MotPP; MovMk; News 90, 95, 95-1; NewYTBS 74, 81, 82; NotNAT; NotWoAT; OxCAmL 83; OxCAmT 84; OxCThe 83; PlP&P; WhAm 11; Who 74, 82, 83, 85, 88, 90, 92, 94; WhoAm 74, 76, 78, 80, 82, 84, 86, 88, 90, 92, 94; WhoAmW 58, 61, 64, 66, 68, 70, 72, 74, 79, 81, 83, 85, 87, 89, 91, 93; WhoE 91, 93; WhoEnt 92; WhoHol 92, A; WhoThe 72, 77, 81; WhoWor 74, 76; WorAl; WorAlBi*

Tanen, Ned Stone
Producer
Films include *The Breakfast Club,* 1985; *St. Elmo's Fire,* 1985.
b. 1931 in Los Angeles, California
Source: *BioIn 13, 14, 16; Dun&B 79; VarWW 85; WhoAm 80, 82, 84, 86, 88, 90, 95, 96, 97; WhoWest 89*

Taney, Roger Brooke
American. Supreme Court Justice
Appointed, 1836; ruled against Scott in Dred Scott case, 1857, arguing that blacks needed to remain slaves as long as they were in US.
b. Mar 17, 1777 in Calvert County, Maryland
d. Oct 12, 1864 in Washington, District of Columbia
Source: *Alli; AmBi; AmJust; AmPolLe; ApCAB; BiAUS; BiDFedJ; BiDrUSE 71, 89; BiDSA; BioIn 2, 3, 4, 5, 6, 7, 8, 9, 10, 11, 12, 14, 15, 18, 19, 20; ChhPo; CyAG; DcAmB; DcCathB; Drake; EncAB-H 1974, 1996; EncSoH; HarEnUS; LinLib L, S; McGEWB; MorMA; NatCAB 1; OxCAmH; OxCLaw; OxCSupC; REn; REnAL; SupCtJu; TwCBDA; WebAB 74, 79; WhAm HS; WhCiWar; WhDW; WorAl*

Taneyev, Sergey Ivanovich
Russian. Composer, Pianist
Chief composer of counterpoint in 19th c. Russia; composed operatic trilogy *Oresteia,* 1895.
b. Nov 25, 1856 in Vladimir, Russia
d. Jun 19, 1915 in Moscow, Russia
Source: *Baker 84; BioIn 1; BriBkM 80; MetOEnc; NewAmDM; NewGrDM 80; NewGrDO; NewOxM*

Tange, Kenzo
American. Architect, Educator
Combines modern designs with Japanese traditions for urban buildings, cultural centers, sports facilities, and govt. headquarters.
b. Sep 4, 1913 in Osaka, Japan
Source: *BioIn 5, 6, 7, 9, 11, 12, 13; ConArch 80, 87, 94; CurBio 87; DcArts; DcD&D; EncMA; EncWB; FarE&A 78, 79, 80, 81; IntDcAr; IntWW 74, 75, 76, 77, 78, 79, 80, 81, 82, 83, 89, 91, 93; MacEA; MakMC; McGDA; McGEWB; NewCol 75; WhoAm 74, 76, 82; WhoArch; WhoScEn 96; WhoWor 74, 76, 78, 89, 91*

Tanguay, Eva
"I Don't Care Girl"
Canadian. Actor
Vaudeville, musical, comedy darling; starred in *Sambo Girl.*
b. Aug 1, 1878 in Marbleton, Quebec, Canada
d. Jan 11, 1947 in Los Angeles, California
Source: *AmPS B; BiDD; BioIn 1, 5, 16, 17; CmpEPM; DcAmB S4; EncVaud; Ent; Film 1; InWom, SUP; LibW; NewAmDM; NewGrDA 86; NotAW; NotNAT B; NotWoAT; OxCAmT 84; OxCPMus; WhoCom; WhoHol B; WhoStg 1908; WhScrn 77, 83; WhThe*

Tanguy, Yves
American. Artist
Surrealist painter whose permanent collections are in museums throughout US, Paris.
b. Jan 5, 1900 in Paris, France
d. Jan 15, 1955 in Woodbury, Connecticut
Source: *BioIn 1, 3, 4, 14; BriEAA; ConArt 77, 83; DcArts; DcCAA 71, 77, 88, 94; DcTwCCu 2; FacFETw; IntDcAA 90; LegTOT; McGDA; McGEWB; NewCol 75; OxCArt; OxCTwCA; OxDcArt; PhDcTCA 77; REn; WhAm 3; WhoAmA 78N, 80N, 82N, 86N, 89N, 91N, 93N; WorArt 1950*

Tanizaki Jun'ichiro
Japanese. Author
Works alternately marked by both eroticism and an adherence to traditional standards of beauty.
b. Jul 24, 1886 in Tokyo, Japan
d. Jul 30, 1965 in Yugawara, Japan
Source: *Benet 87; BioIn 7, 10, 12, 13; CasWL; ConAu 25R, 93; ConLC 8, 14, 28; EncWL 2; GrFLW; McGEWB; ObitOF 79*

Tannen, Deborah Frances
American. Linguist, Author
Author of *You Just Don't Understand: Women and Men in Conversation,* 1990.
b. Jun 7, 1945 in New York, New York
Source: *CurBio 94; WhoAm 94, 95, 96, 97; WhoAmW 95, 97*

Tannenbaum, Frank
American. Educator, Historian
Expert on Mexico, Latin America; wrote *Peace By Revolution,* 1933.
b. Mar 1893, Austria
d. Jun 1, 1969 in New York, New York

Source: *AmAu&B; BioIn 2, 8, 16; ConAu 9R; IntEnSS 79; NewCol 75; RAdv 14; WhNAA*

Tanner, Alain
Swiss. Filmmaker
Films include *Charles Dead or Alive,* and *The Women from Rose Hill.*
b. Dec 6, 1929 in Geneva, Switzerland
Source: *BiDFilm 94; BioIn 13, 16; ConTFT 8; CurBio 90; EncEurC; FilmEn; HalFC 88; IntDcF 1-2, 2-2; IntWW 91; MiSFD 9; WhoWor 89, 95; WorFDir 2*

Tanner, Henry Ossawa
American. Artist
Most renowned of all black artists; member National Academy of Art and Design.
b. Jun 21, 1859 in Pittsburgh, Pennsylvania
d. May 25, 1937 in Etaples, France
Source: *AfrAmAl 6; AfroAA; AmBi; ApCAB X; BioIn 1, 3, 4, 6, 7, 8, 9, 11, 17, 19, 21; BriEAA; ConBlB 1; DcAmArt; DcAmB S2; DcAmNB; EncAB-H 1974, 1996; GayN; InB&W 80, 85; McGDA; McGEWB; ModArCr 4; NatCAB 3; NegAl 76, 83, 89; WebAB 74, 79; WhAm 1; WhoAmA 80N, 82N, 86N, 89N, 91N, 93N; WhoColR*

Tanner, Marion
American. Philanthropist, Socialite
Real life model for Auntie Mame, immortalized in novel by nephew Patrick Dennis.
b. Mar 6, 1891 in Buffalo, New York
d. Oct 30, 1985 in New York, New York
Source: *BioIn 14; NewYTBS 85*

Tanner, Roscoe
[Leonard Roscoe Tanner, III]
"Cannonball Kid"
American. Tennis Player
Serve timed at 155 mph; lost to Borg in five-set Wimbledon final, 1979.
b. Oct 15, 1951 in Lookout Mountain, Tennessee
Source: *BioIn 10, 12, 14; LegTOT; NewYTBS 84; WhoAm 80, 82; WhoIntT*

Tanner, Valno Alfred
Finnish. Statesman
Headed Social Democratic Party, 1950s-60s; opposed Soviet expansion.
b. Mar 12, 1881 in Helsinki, Finland
d. Apr 19, 1966 in Helsinki, Finland
Source: *BioIn 1, 4, 5, 7, 8; CurBio 60, 66; ObitOF 79*

Tanny, Vic
[Victor A Iannidinardo]
American. Businessman
Owner, first chain of stylish gyms, health clubs, 1939.
b. 1912
d. Jun 11, 1985 in Tampa, Florida
Source: *BioIn 5; ConNews 85-3; NewYTBS 85*

Tao-chi
Chinese. Artist
One of first Individualist painters well known in China, the West; landscapes have often been forged.
b. 1630 in Wuzhou, China
d. 1717?
Source: *BioIn 3; McGDA; OxCArt*

Taoka Kazuo
"Kuma"
Japanese. Criminal
Leader of Yamaguchi-gumi criminal organization which dealt in exortion, gambling, labor racketeering, loansharking, prostitution, show business, smuggling.
b. Mar 28, 1912 in Sanshomura, Japan
d. Jul 30, 1981 in Amagasaki, Japan
Source: *BioIn 11*

Tapahonso, Luci
American. Poet
Poetry collections include *One More Shiprock Night,* 1981; *Saanii Dahataal, The Women Are Singing,* 1993.
b. 1953 in Shiprock, New Mexico
Source: *BioIn 14, 21; ConAu 145; NatNAL; NotNaAm*

Tappan, Eva March
American. Children's Author, Educator
Wrote educational books: *American Hero Stories,* 1906.
b. Dec 26, 1854 in Blackstone, Massachusetts
d. Jan 29, 1930 in Worcester, Massachusetts
Source: *AmAu&B; AmLY; BiDAmEd; BiD&SB; BioIn 15; CarSB; ChhPo, S1; DcAmAu; DcAmB; DcNAA; InWom SUP; JBA 34; NatCAB 22; NotAW; REnAL; TwCA; TwCBDA; WhAm 1; WhNAA; WomNov; WomWWA 14*

Tappan, William J
American. Manufacturer
Founded stove co., 1881, which later diversified into microwave ovens.
b. 1860
d. 1937
Source: *Entr*

Tarantino, Quentin
American. Director, Writer, Actor
Oscar, Best Original Screenplay, *Pulp Fiction,* 1994.
b. Mar 27, 1963 in Knoxville, Tennessee
Source: *ConTFT 13; CurBio 95; IntMPA 96; LegTOT; News 95, 95-1; NewYTBS 92; WhoAm 95, 96, 97; WhoWor 96, 97*

Tarasova, Alla Konstantinovna
Russian. Actor
Award winning actress with the Moscow Art Theatre; played Anna in *Anna Karenina,* 1937.
b. Jan 25, 1898 in Kiev, Russia
d. Apr 5, 1973 in Moscow, Union of Soviet Socialist Republics
Source: *BiDSovU; EncWT; SovUn; WhoWor 74; WhScrn 77; WhThe*

Tarbell, Ida Minerva
American. Author, Editor
Leader of "muckracking" movement in journalism; wrote *Life of Abraham Lincoln,* 1900.
b. Nov 5, 1857 in Erie County, Pennsylvania
d. Jan 6, 1944 in Bethel, Connecticut
Source: *AmAu&B; AmRef; AmSocL; AmWomHi; AmWomWr; ApCAB X; ArtclWW 2; BiDAmJo; BiD&SB; BioIn 1, 2, 3, 4, 5, 6, 8, 9, 10, 11, 13; CnDAL; CurBio 44; DcAmAu; DcAmB S3; DcLEL; DcNAA; EncAB-H 1974, 1996; EncTwCJ; GoodHs; HarEnUS; HerW; InWom, SUP; LibW; LinLib S; McGEWB; NatCAB 14; NotAW; OxCAmH; OxCAmL 65, 83; REn; REnAL; TwCA, SUP; WebAB 74, 79; WhAm 2; WhLit; WhNAA; WomComm; WomNov; WomWWA 14; WorAl*

Tarde, Gabriel
[Jean Gabriel de Tarde]
French. Sociologist, Criminologist
Introduced theory of social interaction placing emphasis on individuals instead of group.
b. Mar 12, 1843 in Sarlat, France
d. May 13, 1904 in Paris, France
Source: *BiDPsy; BioIn 1, 6; ClDMEL 47; CopCroC; DcSoc; EncSF 93; NamesHP; OxCFr; OxCLaw; REn; ScF&FL 1; ScFEYrs*

Targ, William
American. Publisher
Senior editor, Putnam's Sons, 1974—; writes on book collecting.
b. Mar 4, 1907 in Chicago, Illinois
Source: *AmAu&B; BioIn 10; ChhPo, S3; ConAu 61; St&PR 75; WhoAm 74, 76, 78, 80, 82, 84, 86, 88, 90, 92, 95; WhoWor 82, 84, 87, 89; WhoWorJ 72, 78*

Tarkanian, Jerry
American. Basketball Coach
Coach, UNLV, 1973-1992; Fresno State, 1995—.
b. Aug 8, 1930 in Euclid, Ohio
Source: *BiDAmSp BK; BioIn 9, 11, 13, 14, 15, 16, 17, 18, 19, 21; LegTOT; News 90; NewYTBS 83; WhoAm 86, 88, 92, 94; WhoBbl 73; WhoSpor; WhoSSW 95*

Tarkenton, Fran(cis Asbury)
American. Football Player, TV Personality
Scrambling quarterback, 1961-79; mostly with Minnesota; Hall of Fame, 1986; co-host TV series, "That's Incredible," 1980-84.
b. Feb 3, 1940 in Richmond, Virginia
Source: *BiDAmSp FB; BioIn 6, 7, 8, 9, 10, 11, 12, 13, 15, 17, 21; CelR; ConAu 103; CurBio 69; FacFETw; LegTOT; NewYTBE 70, 71, 72; WhoAm 74, 76,*

78, 80, 82, 84, 86, 88, 92, 94, 95, 96; WhoFtbl 74; WorAl; WorAlBi

Tarkington, Booth
[Newton Booth Tarkington]
American. Author, Dramatist
Won Pulitzers for *The Magnificent Ambersons,* 1919; *Alice Adams,* 1922.
b. Jul 29, 1869 in Indianapolis, Indiana
d. May 16, 1946 in Indianapolis, Indiana
Source: *AmAu&B; AmCulL; ApCAB X; AtlBL; BbD; Benet 87; BenetAL 91; BiD&SB; BioIn 1, 2, 3, 4, 5, 6, 8, 10, 11, 12, 13, 14, 16, 17, 19; CamGLE; CamGWoT; CamHAL; CarSB; CasWL; Chambr 3; ChhPo S2; ChlBkCr; CnDAL; ConAmA; ConAmL; ConAu 110; CurBio 46; CyWA 58; DcAmAu; DcAmB S4; DcAmC; DcArts; DcBiA; DcLB 102; DcLEL; DcNAA; EncAAH; EncAB-A 15; EvLB; FacFETw; FilmgC; GayN; GrWrEL N; HalFC 80, 84, 88; IndAu 1816; JBA 34; LegTOT; LinLib L, S; LngCTC; McGEWB; McGEWD 72, 84; MnBBF; ModAL; ModWD; MorMA; NatCAB 4, 42; NotNAT B; Novels; OxCAmL 65, 83; OxCAmT 84; OxCEng 67, 85; OxCThe 67, 83; PenC AM; PlP&P; REn; REnAL; RfGAmL 87; SmATA 17; TwCA, SUP; TwCBDA; TwCChW 89; TwCWr; WebAB 74, 79; WebE&AL; WhAm 2; WhAmArt 85; WhE&EA; WhLit; WhNAA; WhoChL; WorAl; WorAlBi*

Tarkovsky, Andrei (Arsenyich)
Russian. Director
Made films *My Name is Ivan,* 1963; *Andrei Rublev,* 1966.
b. Apr 4, 1932 in Sarvrashye, Union of Soviet Socialist Republics
d. Dec 29, 1986 in Paris, France
Source: *AnObit 1986; BiDFilm, 81, 94; ConAu 127; ConLC 75; DcArts; EncSF 93; FilmEn; HalFC 80, 84, 88; IntDcF 1-2, 2-2; MiSFD 9N; NewYTBS 86; OxCFilm; WorFDir 2*

Tarleton, Banastre, Sir
English. Army Officer
Led British Troops in American Revolution; with Cornwallis at surrender; noted for cruelty.
b. Aug 21, 1754 in Liverpool, England
d. Jan 25, 1833 in Shropshire, England
Source: *Alli; AmBi; AmRev; ApCAB; BiDLA; BiDSA; BioIn 4, 7, 10; BlkwEAR; DcNaB; Drake; EncAR; EncCRAm; GenMudB; HarEnMi; HarEnUS; McGEWB; NewCBEL; WhAmRev*

Tarlton, Richard
English. Comedian
Queen Elizabeth I's favorite clown; probably model for Yorick in Shakespeare's *Hamlet.*
d. Sep 3, 1588 in London, England
Source: *Alli; BiDRP&D; BioIn 2, 3; BlmGEL; CamGLE; CamGWoT; LngCEL; NewC; NewCBEL; OxCEng 85, 95; OxCMus; REn*

Tarnower, Herman
American. Physician, Author
Wrote *The Complete Scarsdale Medical Diet,* 1979; murdered by longtime companion, Jean Harris.
b. Mar 18, 1910 in New York, New York
d. Mar 10, 1980 in Purchase, New York
Source: *BiDrACP 79; BioIn 12, 13; ConAu 89, 97; LegTOT; NewYTBS 80*

Tarsis, Valery Yakovlevich
Swiss. Author
Dissident deprived of Soviet citizenship during lecture of Britain, 1966.
b. Sep 23, 1906 in Kiev, Russia
d. Mar 3, 1983 in Bern, Switzerland
Source: *ConAu 109; DcRusLS; HanRL; NewYTBS 83; TwCWr; WhoAm 78; WorAu 1950*

Tarski, Alfred
American. Mathematician
Major contributor to algebra, mathematical logic, measure theory, metamathematics, set theory; wrote number of books including *Ordinal Algebras,* 1956.
b. Jan 14, 1902 in Warsaw, Poland
d. Oct 26, 1983 in Berkeley, California
Source: *AmAu&B; AmMWSc 73P; AnObit 1983; BiESc; BioIn 15; BlueB 76; ConAu 111; DcScB S2; IntWW 74, 75, 76, 77, 78, 79, 80, 81, 82, 83; LarDcSc; McGEWB; OxCPhil; ThTwC 87; WhAm 8; WhoAm 74, 76; WhoWor 74, 76, 78*

Tartikoff, Brandon
American. TV Executive
Pres., NBC Entertainment, 1980-90, credited with successes "The Cosby Show," "Cheers;" Chairman, NBC Entertainment, 1989-91; Chairman, Paramount Pictures, 1991-92; Chairman, New World Entertainment, Ltd., 1994—.
b. Jan 13, 1949 in Long Island, New York
Source: *ConNews 85-2; ConTFT 5, 10; CurBio 87; IntMPA 84, 86, 88, 92, 94, 96; LegTOT; LesBEnT; WhoAm 86, 88, 90, 92, 94, 95, 96, 97; WhoEnt 92; WhoFI 94, 96; WhoTelC; WhoWest 89, 92, 94*

Tartini, Giuseppe
Italian. Composer, Violinist
Wrote 50 violin sonatas; developed "Tartini harmonic" for finer intonation.
b. Apr 8, 1692 in Istria, Italy
d. Feb 26, 1770 in Padua, Italy
Source: *Baker 78, 84, 92; BioIn 1, 2, 3, 4, 6, 7, 8, 12, 14; BriBkM 80; CmpBCM; DcArts; DcBiPP; DcCathB; DcCom 77; GrComp; McGEWB; MusMk; NewAmDM; NewCol 75; NewGrDM 80; NewOxM; OxCMus; REn; WebBD 83; WhDW*

Tartt, Donna (Louise)
American. Author
Wrote *The Secret History,* 1992.
b. 1964? in Greenwood, Mississippi
Source: *ConAu 142; ConLC 76; LegTOT*

Tashman, Lilyan
American. Actor
Elegant leading lady of silents and early talkies, 1921-34, in *No, No Nanette.*
b. Oct 23, 1899 in New York, New York
d. Mar 21, 1934 in New York, New York
Source: *BioIn 10; EncAFC; Film 2; FilmEn; FilmgC; HalFC 80, 84, 88; InWom SUP; LegTOT; MovMk; NotNAT B; SilFlmP; ThFT; TwYS; WhoHol B; WhScrn 74, 77; WhThe; WorAl*

Tasman, Abel Janszoon
Dutch. Explorer
Discovered Tasmania and New Zealand, 1642.
b. 1603
d. 1659
Source: *BioIn 5, 11, 12, 18, 19, 20; Expl 93; LegTOT; McGEWB; NewC; NewCol 75; OxCAusL; OxCShps; REn; WebBD 83; WhDW; WhWE*

Tassell, Gustave
American. Designer
With the death of Norman Norell, 1972, carried on the designer's classic, luxurious line.
b. Feb 4, 1926 in Philadelphia, Pennsylvania
Source: *ConFash; EncFash; FairDF US; WhoAm 74, 76, 78; WhoFash 88; WorFshn*

Tasso, Torquato
Italian. Author
Best-known epic *Jerusalem Delivered,* 1575; re-wrote because of criticism, 1587.
b. Mar 11, 1544 in Sorrento, Italy
d. Apr 25, 1595 in Rome, Italy
Source: *AtlBL; BbD; Benet 87, 96; BiD&SB; BioIn 1, 2, 5, 7, 8, 13, 14, 20; BlmGEL; CamGWoT; CasWL; CnThe; CroE&S; CyWA 58; DcArts; DcBiPP; DcCathB; DcEuL; DcItL 1, 2; Dis&D; EncWT; Ent; EuAu; EuWr 2; EvEuW; GrFLW; IntDcT 2; LinLib L, S; LitC 5; LngCEL; McGEWB; McGEWD 72, 84; NewC; NewCBEL; NewEOp 71; NewGrDM 80; NewGrDO; NotNAT B; OxCEng 67, 85, 95; OxCThe 67, 83; OxDcOp; PenC EUR; PlP&P; RAdv 14; RComWL; REn; REnWD; RfGWoL 95; WhDW; WorAl; WorAlBi*

Tata, J(ehangir) R(atanji) D(adbhoy)
Indian. Industrialist
Grandson of Jamshedji Nusserwanji Tata; became chairman of Tata Sons, 1938.
b. Jul 29, 1904
d. Nov 29, 1993, Switzerland
Source: *BioIn 5, 8; CurBio 94N; IntYB 78, 79, 80, 81, 82*

Tata, Jamshedji Nusserwanji
Indian. Industrialist, Philanthropist
Major architect of India's industrial development; gave generously to fund several research institutions.
b. Mar 3, 1839 in Navsari, India
d. May 19, 1904 in Nauheim, Germany
Source: *BioIn 1, 6, 7; DcNaB S2*

Tate, Allen (John Orley)
American. Poet, Critic
Poems include *The Golden Mean and Other Poems,* 1923; novels include *The Fathers,* 1938.
b. Nov 19, 1899 in Winchester, Kentucky
d. Feb 9, 1979 in Nashville, Tennessee
Source: *AmAu&B; AmWr; Au&Wr 71; Benet 87; BenetAL 91; BiDConC; BioIn 3, 4, 5, 7, 8, 9, 10, 11, 12, 13, 14, 15, 16, 17, 18, 19, 21; BlueB 76; CamGEL; CamGLE; CamHAL; CasWL; CathA 1952; ChhPo, S2, S3; CnDAL; CnE&AP; ConAmA; ConAu 5R, 32NR, 85; ConLC 2, 4, 6, 9, 11, 14, 24; ConLCrt 77, 82; ConNov 72, 76; ConPo 70, 75; CurBio 79N; DrAF 76; DrAP 75; DrAS 74E, 78E, 82E; EncWL 2, 3; FacFETw; FifSWrA; GrWrEL P; IntAu&W 76, 77; IntWW 74, 75, 76, 77, 78; IntWWP 77; LegTOT; LiHiK; LinLib L; LngCTC; MajTwCW; McGEWB; ModAL, S1, S2; NewYTBS 79; OxCAmL 65, 83; OxCEng 85; OxCTwCP; PenC AM; PeoHis; RAdv 1, 14; REn; REnAL; RfGAmL 87; RGFAP; SixAP; SouWr; TwCA, SUP; TwCWr; WebAB 74, 79; WebE&AL; WhAm 7; WhE&EA; WhoAm 74, 76, 78; WhoSSW 73, 75, 76; WhoTwCL; WhoWor 74, 76, 78; WorAl; WorAlBi; WrDr 76, 80*

Tate, Henry, Sir
English. Art Collector, Manufacturer
Sugar magnate; founded Britain's renowned Tate Gallery, 1897.
b. 1819
d. 1899
Source: *BioIn 6, 8; DcNaB S1; REn*

Tate, James
American. Poet
Winner of Pulitzer Prize for poetry, *Selected Poems,* 1992.
b. Dec 8, 1943 in Kansas City, Missouri
Source: *BenetAL 91; BioIn 9, 12; ConAu 21R, 29NR; ConLC 25; ConPo 80, 85, 91; DcLB 169; OxCAmL 83; OxCTwCP; RAdv 14; WhoAm 74, 76, 78, 82, 84; WhoUSWr 88; WhoWrEP 89, 92, 95; WorAu 1970; WrDr 80, 82, 84, 86, 88, 90, 92*

Tate, Nahum
English. Poet
Poet laureate, 1692-1715, best known for "Panacea, a poem on Tea," 1700.
b. Sep 12, 1652 in Dublin, Ireland
d. Aug 12, 1715 in London, England
Source: *Alli; AnCL; Benet 87, 96; BiDIrW; BioIn 3, 9, 12; BlmGEL; BritAu; CamGLE; CamGWoT; CasWL; Chambr 2; ChhPo; DcArts; DcBiPP; DcEnA; DcEnL; DcEuL; DcIrB 78, 88; DcIrL, 96; DcIrW 1; DcLEL; DcNaB; EvLB; GrWrEL DR; IntDcT 2; LuthC 75; NewC; NewCBEL; NewGrDM 80; NewGrDO; NotNAT B; OxCEng 67, 85, 95; OxCIri; OxCMus; OxCThe 67, 83; PenC ENG; PlP&P; PoChrch; PoIre; PoLE; REn; RfGEnL 91*

Tate, Sharon
[Mrs. Roman Polanski]
American. Actor
Murdered by Charles Manson family.
b. Jan 24, 1943 in Dallas, Texas
d. Aug 9, 1969 in Bel Air, California
Source: *BioIn 7, 8, 11, 13; FilmgC; ForYSC; HalFC 80, 84, 88; ItaFilm; LegTOT; MotPP; WhoHol B; WhoHrs 80; WhScrn 74, 77, 83*

Tati, Jacques
[Jacques Tatischeff]
French. Comedian, Director
Won Oscar, 1958, for *Mon Oncle;* inspired by Charlie Chaplin and Buster Keaton.
b. Oct 9, 1908 in Le Pecq, France
d. Nov 5, 1982 in Paris, France
Source: *AnObit 1982; BiDFilm, 81, 94; BioIn 3, 5, 6, 9, 11, 12; ConAu 108; CurBio 61, 83N; DcArts; DcFM; DcTwCCu 2; EncEurC; Ent; FacFETw; FilmAG WE; FilmEn; FilmgC; HalFC 80, 84, 88; IntDcF 1-2, 2-2; IntWW 74, 75, 76, 77, 78, 79, 80, 81, 82, 83N; ItaFilm; JoeFr; LegTOT; MiSFD 9N; MotPP; MovMk; NewYTBS 82; OxCFilm; QDrFCA 92; Who 74, 82, 83, 83N; WhoCom; WhoHol A; WhoWor 74, 82; WorEFlm; WorFDir 2*

Tatlin, Vladimir Yevgrapovich
Ukrainian. Artist, Sculptor
Led Constructivism movement in Moscow; known for monument to the Third International, 1920.
b. Dec 28, 1885 in Kharkov, Ukraine
d. May 31, 1953 in Moscow, Union of Soviet Socialist Republics
Source: *BioIn 13, 14, 15, 16; ConArt 83; DcTwDes; FacFETw; IntDcAA 90; OxCArt; OxDcArt; PenDiDA 89; WhoArch*

Tatum, Art(hur)
American. Jazz Musician
All-time great jazz pianist, noted for original technique, improvisation; led trio, 1943-55; recorded "Sweet Lorraine."
b. Oct 13, 1910 in Toledo, Ohio
d. Nov 4, 1956 in Los Angeles, California
Source: *AmCulL; Baker 84, 92; BiDAfM; BiDAmM; BiDJaz; BioIn 4, 5, 10, 11, 12, 13, 14, 15, 16, 17, 19, 20; CmpEPM; DcAmB S6; DcArts; DrBlPA, 90; EncJzS; IlEncJ; InB&W 80; LegTOT; NegAl 76, 83, 89; NewAmDM; NewGrDM 80; WebAB 74, 79; WhAm 4; WhoJazz 72; WhScrn 77, 83; WorAl; WorAlBi*

Tatum, Donn B
American. Business Executive
Chm., Walt Disney Co., 1971-80; major figure in the development of Walt Disney World and Tokyo Disneyland.
b. Jan 9, 1913 in Los Angeles, California
d. May 31, 1993 in Pacific Palisades, California
Source: *BioIn 9; IntMPA 92; WhoAm 90; WhoEnt 92; WhoFI 89*

Tatum, Edward Lawrie
American. Biochemist, Geneticist, Educator, Author
Won 1958 Nobel Prize for work in genetics.
b. Dec 14, 1909 in Boulder, Colorado
d. Nov 5, 1975 in New York, New York
Source: *AsBiEn; BiESc; BioIn 3, 4, 5, 6, 7, 10, 11, 12, 13, 14, 15, 20; BlueB 76; ConAu 113; CurBio 59; DcAmB S9; DcAmMeB 84; LarDcSc; McGMS 80; NotTwCS; OxCMed 86; WebAB 74, 79; WhAm 6; WhoAm 74, 76; WhoNob, 90, 95; WorAl; WorScD*

Tatum, Jack
[John David Tatum]
"The Assassin"
American. Football Player
Three-time all-pro defensive back, 1971-80, mostly with Oakland; known for aggressiveness; wrote *They Call Me Assassin,* 1979.
b. Nov 18, 1948 in Cherryville, North Carolina
Source: *BiDAmSp FB; BioIn 10, 12; ConAu 104; NewYTBS 80; WhoAm 78, 80; WhoBlA 77, 80, 85, 90; WhoFtbl 74*

Taube, Henry
American. Educator
Won Nobel Prize in chemistry, 1983.
b. Nov 30, 1915 in Neudorf, Saskatchewan, Canada
Source: *AmMWSc 73P, 76P, 79, 82, 86, 89, 92, 95; BiESc; BioIn 3, 5, 7, 8, 9, 13; BlueB 76; IntWW 74, 75, 76, 77, 78, 79, 80, 81, 82, 83, 89, 91, 93; LarDcSc; McGMS 80; NobelP; NotTwCS; Who 85, 88, 90, 92, 94; WhoAm 74, 76, 78, 80, 82, 84, 86, 88, 90, 92, 94, 95, 96, 97; WhoFrS 84; WhoNob, 90, 95; WhoScEn 94, 96; WhoWest 87, 89, 92, 94, 96; WhoWor 74, 84, 87, 89, 91, 93, 95, 96, 97; WorAlBi*

Tauber, Richard
British. Opera Singer, Actor
Tenor, noted for Mozart, Lehar operetta roles; films include *Blossom Time,* 1932.
b. May 16, 1892 in Linz, Austria
d. Jan 8, 1948 in London, England
Source: *Baker 78, 84; BioIn 1, 2, 3, 4, 5, 7, 9, 11, 12, 14, 17, 18; BriBkM 80; CmOp; EncMT; FacFETw; FilmgC; ForYSC; HalFC 80, 84, 88; IlWWBF, A; MusMk; MusSN; NewCol 75; NewEOp 71; NewOxM; OxCFilm; OxCPMus; OxDcOp; WhAm 2; WhoHol B; WhScrn 74, 77, 83*

Taubes, Frederic
American. Artist
Exhibits at one-man shows, museums throughout US, Europe, Palestine; books on art include *The Technique of Oil Painting,* 1941.
b. Apr 15, 1900 in Lvov, Poland
d. Jun 21, 1981 in Nyack, New York
Source: *BioIn 1, 2, 3, 10; ConAu 9NR, 17R, 104; CurBio 43; DcCAA 71, 77, 88, 94; McGDA; WhAmArt 85; WhoAmA 73, 76, 78, 80, 82N, 86N, 89N, 91N, 93N*

Taubman, A(dolph) Alfred
American. Businessman
Founder and chm. Taubman Co., 1950—, a major developer of successful shopping malls nationwide.
b. Jan 31, 1925 in Pontiac, Michigan
Source: *BioIn 13, 14, 15; CurBio 93; Dun&B 90; IntWW 91; NewYTBS 83; WhoAm 90; WhoE 89; WhoFI 92; WhoMW 92*

Taubman, (Hyman) Howard
American. Journalist, Author, Critic
Drama critic, *NY Times,* 1960-72.
b. Jul 4, 1907 in New York, New York
d. Jan 8, 1996 in Sarasota, Florida
Source: *AmAu&B; Baker 78, 84, 92; BiDAmM; BiE&WWA; BioIn 5, 20, 21; BlueB 76; CurBio 59, 96N; IntAu&W 76, 77; IntWW 74, 75, 76, 77, 78, 79, 80, 81, 82, 83, 89, 91, 93; NewGrDA 86; NewGrDM 80; NewYTBS 27; NotNAT; WhoAm 74, 76; WhoThe 72, 77A; WhThe*

Taupin, Bernie
English. Lyricist
Wrote lyrics for Elton John's gold records; inducted into Songwriters Hall of Fame, 1992.
b. May 22, 1950 in Sleaford, England
Source: *BioIn 11, 12; EncPR&S 74; EncRk 88; IlEncRk; LegTOT; WhoRocM 82*

Taurog, Norman
American. Director
Won Oscar for *Skippy,* 1931.
b. Feb 23, 1899 in Chicago, Illinois
d. Apr 7, 1981 in Rancho Mirage, California
Source: *AnObit 1981; BioIn 12, 15; CmMov; DcFM; EncAFC; Film 1; FilmEn; FilmgC; HalFC 80, 84, 88; IlWWHD 1; IntDcF 1-2; IntMPA 75, 76, 78, 79, 80, 81; LegTOT; MiSFD 9N; MovMk; NewYTBS 81; TwYS, A; WhAm 7; WhoAm 74, 76, 78, 80; WhScrn 83; WorEFlm; WorFDir 1*

Tausig, Karl
Polish. Pianist, Composer
Internationally renowned concert pianist known for excellent dexterity and tone; student of Liszt.
b. Nov 4, 1841 in Warsaw, Poland
d. Jul 17, 1871 in Leipzig, Germany
Source: *Baker 84; BioIn 2, 7, 16; NewAmDM; OxCMus; PenDiMP*

Taussig, Frank William
American. Economist
Major contributor to trade theory; wrote text *Princples of Economics,* 1911.
b. Dec 28, 1859 in Saint Louis, Missouri
d. Nov 11, 1940 in Saint Louis, Missouri
Source: *Alli SUP; AmAu&B; AmLY; BiDAmEd; BioIn 2, 3, 4, 14; CurBio 40; DcAmAu; DcAmB S2; DcNAA; HarEnUS; NatCAB 8, 30; ObitOF 79; OxCAmH; REnAL; WhAm 1; WhNAA; WhoEc 81, 86*

Taussig, Helen Brooke
American. Physician
Developed surgical procedure for treating "blue babies;" warned US of Thalidomide peril.
b. May 24, 1898 in Cambridge, Massachusetts
d. May 20, 1986 in Kennett Square, Pennsylvania
Source: *AmMWSc 76P, 79, 82; AmWomSc; BiDrACP 79; BioIn 1, 2, 3, 5, 7, 8, 9, 11, 13, 14, 15, 16, 18, 20; ContDcW 89; CurBio 46, 86; GoodHs; InSci; IntDcWB; InWom, SUP; LarDcSc; LibW; McGMS 80; NewYTBS 86; NotTwCS; NotWoLS; WhAm 9; WhoAm 74, 76, 78; WhoAmW 58, 61, 64, 66, 68, 70, 72, 74, 79, 83, 85; WhoWor 74; WomFir; WorScD*

Tavernier, Bertrand
French. Director
Films center around basic human experiences: *'Round Midnight,* 1986; *Let Joy Reign Supreme,* 1975.
b. Apr 25, 1941 in Lyons, France
Source: *BiDFilm 94; BioIn 13; ConAu 123; ConTFT 7; CurBio 88; EncEurC; FilmEn; HalFC 80, 84, 88; IntDcF 1-2, 2-2; IntMPA 79, 80, 81, 82, 84, 86, 88, 92, 94, 96; LegTOT; MiSFD 9; NewYTBS 85; WhoFr 86; WhoWor 87; WorFDir 2*

Tawley, Howard
Canadian. Politician
New Democratic Party premier of Manitoba, 1981—.
b. Nov 21, 1934 in Brampton, Ontario, Canada

Tawney, Richard Henry
English. Historian, Author
Best known for his comparative study *Religion and the Rise of Capitalism,* 1926.
b. Nov 30, 1880 in Calcutta, India
d. Jan 16, 1962 in London, England
Source: *BioIn 2, 4, 5, 6, 10, 12, 14; CasWL; ConAu 93; DcLEL; DcNaB 1961; DcSoc; DcTwHis; GrBr; LngCTC; MakMC; McGEWB; NewC; NewCBEL; OxCEng 85; PenC AM, ENG; REn; TwCA, SUP; WhE&EA; WhLit; WhoEc 81, 86*

Tax, Sol
American. Anthropologist
Studies of native American tribes led to pioneering use of transactional analysis.
b. Oct 30, 1907 in Chicago, Illinois
d. Jan 4, 1995 in Chicago, Illinois
Source: *AmAu&B; AmMWSc 73S, 76P; BioIn 17, 20, 21; BlueB 76; ConAu 5R; EncNAB; FifIDA; IntDcAn; IntEnSS 79; IntWW 74, 75, 76, 77, 78, 79, 80, 81, 82, 83, 89, 91, 93; WhoAm 74, 76, 78, 80, 82, 84, 88, 90; WhoGov 72, 75; WhoWor 74; WhoWorJ 72, 78*

Tayback, Vic
[Victor Tabback]
American. Actor
Played Mel on TV series "Alice," 1976-85.
b. Jan 6, 1929 in New York, New York
d. May 25, 1990 in Glendale, California
Source: *BioIn 11, 16, 17; HalFC 88; LegTOT; WhoAm 80, 82, 84; WhoHol A; WhoTelC*

Taylor, A(lan) J(ohn) P(ercivale)
English. Author, Historian
Britain's most popular historian; wrote at least 30 books; his 60-year career convinced him that events are often shaped by accident.
b. Mar 25, 1906 in Birkdale, England
d. Sep 7, 1990 in Barnet, England
Source: *Au&Wr 71; Benet 87, 96; BioIn 4, 7, 10, 11, 13, 15, 17, 18, 19, 20; BlueB 76; ConAu 5R; CurBio 83, 90; DcNaB 1986; EncTR; IntAu&W 76, 77, 91; IntWW 74, 75, 76, 77, 78, 79, 80, 81, 82, 83, 89; LngCTC; MajTwCW; NewC; NewCBEL; NewYTBS 90; OxCCan SUP; OxCEng 85, 95; RAdv 14; REn; WhAm 10; WhDW; WhE&EA; Who 74, 82, 83, 85, 88, 90; WhoWor 74, 76, 78, 84, 87, 89; WorAu 1950; WrDr 76, 80, 82, 84, 86, 90*

Taylor, Ann
English. Children's Author, Poet
With sister Jane, wrote *Original Poems for Infant Minds,* 1804.
b. Jun 30, 1782 in London, England
d. Dec 20, 1866
Source: *Alli; BioIn 8, 14, 15, 16; BlmGEL; BlmGWL; BritAu 19; CarSB; ChhPo, S1, S2, S3; ChrP; DcBiPP; DcEnL; DcEuL; DcLB 163; DcNaB; EncBrWW; EvLB; InWom, SUP; NewC; NewCBEL; OxCChiL; OxCEng 67; PenNWW A; SmATA 35, 41; Str&VC; WhoChL*

Taylor, Arthur Robert
American. TV Executive
President, CBS, Inc., 1972-76.
b. Jul 6, 1935 in Elizabeth, New Jersey
Source: *BioIn 9, 10, 11; BlueB 76; IntWW 74, 75, 76, 77, 78, 79, 80, 81, 82, 83, 89, 91, 93; NewYTBE 72; Who 83, 85, 88, 90, 92, 94; WhoAm 74, 76, 78, 80, 82, 84, 86, 88, 90, 92, 94, 95, 96, 97; WhoE 89; WhoFI 74, 77, 79, 81, 83; WhoWor 87, 89*

Taylor, Bayard
[James Bayard Taylor]
American. Traveler, Author
Wrote *Travels in Arabia,* 1872; *Egypt and Iceland,* 1874.
b. Jan 11, 1825 in Kennett Square, Pennsylvania
d. Dec 19, 1878 in Berlin, Germany
Source: *Alli, SUP; AmAu; AmAu&B; AmBi; ApCAB; ArtsAmW 1; BbD; Benet 87; BenetAL 91; BibAL 8; BiD&SB; BiGAW; BioIn 1, 2, 3, 9, 10, 15, 16; CamGEL; CamGLE; CamHAL; CasWL; CelCen; Chambr 3; ChhPo, S1, S3; CmCal; CnDAL; CyAL 2; DcAmAu; DcAmB; DcAmDH 80, 89; DcBiA; DcBiPP; DcEnA A; DcEnL; DcLB 3; DcLEL; DcNAA; Drake; EncAHmr; EvLB; FolkA 87; GrWrEL P; HarEnUS; IlBEAAW; JrnUS; LinLib L, S; NatCAB 3; NewYHSD; OxCAmH; OxCAmL 65, 83; OxCEng 67; PenC AM; PeoHis; REn; REnAL; REnAW; RfGAmL 87, 94; TwCBDA; WebAB 74, 79; WhAm HS*

Taylor, Billy
[William Edward Taylor]
American. Jazz Musician
Noted jazz pianist, since 1937; had weekly TV show, 1960s; member, Jazz Hall of Fame, 1979.
b. Jul 24, 1921 in Greenville, North Carolina
Source: *AfrAmAl 6; AllMusG; ASCAP 80; Baker 84, 92; BiDJaz; BioIn 13, 14, 16, 17; BlkCond; CmpEPM; ConMus 13; DcTwCCu 5; DrBlPA, 90; Ebony 1; EncJzS; FacFETw; InB&W 80, 85; IntWWM 77; LegTOT; NewAmDM; NewGrDA 86; NewGrDJ 88, 94; NewYTBE 71; OxCPMus; PenEncP; WhoAfA 96; WhoAm 74, 76, 78, 80, 82, 84, 86, 88, 96, 97; WhoBlA 77, 80, 85, 90, 92, 94; WhoJazz 72; WorAl; WorAlBi*

Taylor, Cecil Percival
American. Musician
Jazz pianist, who combines classical, contemporary music; innovator in harmony rhythm.
b. Mar 15, 1933 in Long Island, New York
Source: *Baker 92; BiDAfM; BiDJaz; ConMus 9; CurBio 86; EncJzS; InB&W 80, 85; WhoAm 80, 82, 84, 86, 88, 90, 92, 94, 95, 96, 97*

Taylor, Charles Alonzo
"The Master of Melodrama"
American. Producer, Dramatist
Suspense plays include *The Child Wife,* 1901.
b. Jan 20, 1864 in Greenfield, Massachusetts
d. Mar 20, 1942 in Glendale, California
Source: *CurBio 42; DcAmB S3*

Taylor, Charles McArthur
Liberian. Military Leader
Self-proclaimed president of Liberia.
b. 1948?, Liberia
Source: *BioIn 16; CurBio 92*

Taylor, Charley
American. Football Player
Halfback, receiver, 1965-77, mostly with Washington; Hall of Fame, 1984.
b. Sep 28, 1942 in Dallas, Texas
Source: *BioIn 9; LegTOT; WhoBlA 85*

Taylor, Cyclone
[Fred Taylor]
Canadian. Hockey Player
Forward-defenseman, 1906-21; Hall of Fame, 1945.
b. Jun 23, 1883 in Tara, Ontario, Canada
d. Jun 10, 1979
Source: *BioIn 8, 11; WhoHcky 73*

Taylor, Dave
[David Andrew Taylor]
Canadian. Hockey Player
Right wing, LA, 1977—; with Marcel Dionne, Charlie Simmer, formed high-scoring Royal Line, early 1980s.
b. Dec 4, 1955 in Levack, Ontario, Canada
Source: *HocEn; HocReg 87*

Taylor, (Joseph) Deems
American. Composer, Critic
Editor, *Musical America,* 1927-29; commentator, narrator on radio, 1933-66.
b. Dec 22, 1885 in New York, New York
d. Jul 3, 1966 in New York, New York
Source: *AmAu&B; AmComp; ApCAB X; ASCAP 66, 80; Baker 78, 84, 92; BiDAmM; BioIn 1, 3, 4, 5, 6, 7, 8, 11; ChhPo, S2; CompSN; ConAmC 76, 82; ConAu 89; CurBio 40, 66; DcAmB S8; DcCM; DcCom&M 79; FilmgC; LegTOT; LinLib L, S; MetOEnc; NewAmDM; NewCol 75; NewEOp 71; NewGrDA 86; NewGrDM 80; NewGrDO; NotNAT B; OxCAmH; OxCAmL 65; OxCAmT 84; OxCMus; OxDcOp; RadStar; REnAL; TwCA, SUP; WebAB 74, 79; WhAm 4; WhJnl; WhScrn 77, 83; WhThe*

Taylor, Edward
American. Poet
Only two of his works were published in his lifetime, re-discovered, 1939: "God's Determinations Touching His Elect," 1685.
b. 1642 in Coventry, England
d. Jun 24, 1729 in Westfield, Massachusetts
Source: *Alli; AmAu&B; AmBi; AmWr; AmWrBE; ApCAB; AtlBL; Benet 87, 96; BenetAL 91; BioIn 5, 6, 7, 9, 10, 12, 14, 17; CasWL; ChhPo, S1; CnDAL; CnE&AP; CrtT 3; CyWA 58; DcAmB S1; DcLEL; GrWrEL P; LinLib L; LitC 11; McGEWB; OxCAmL 65; OxCEng 67; PenC AM; RAdv 1, 14; REn; REnAL; RfGAmL 87, 94; RGFAP; WebE&AL; WhAm HS*

Taylor, Elizabeth Rosemond
English. Actor
Won Oscars for *Butterfield 8,* 1960; *Who's Afraid of Virginia Woolf?* 1966.
b. Feb 27, 1932 in London, England
Source: *BiDFilm; BioIn 1, 2, 3, 4, 5, 6, 7, 8, 9, 10, 11; BkPepl; CmCal; FilmgC; IntDcWB; MovMk; OxCFilm; Who 94; WhoAm 86, 95, 96, 97; WhoAmW 87, 95, 97; WhoWor 87, 95, 96, 97; WorAl; WorEFlm*

Taylor, Estelle
[Estelle Boylan]
American. Actor
Married Jack Dempsey, 1925-31; films include *The Ten Commandments,* 1956.
b. May 20, 1899 in Wilmington, Delaware
d. Apr 15, 1958 in Hollywood, California
Source: *BioIn 4; Film 2; FilmEn; FilmgC; ForYSC; HalFC 80, 84, 88; InWom, SUP; LegTOT; MotPP; NotNAT B; SilFlmP; ThFT; TwYS; WhoHol B; WhScrn 74, 77, 83; WorAl*

Taylor, Frederick Winslow
American. Engineer, Inventor
Conducted first time-and-motion studies to improve efficiency, 1881.
b. Mar 20, 1856 in Germantown, Pennsylvania
d. Mar 21, 1915 in Philadelphia, Pennsylvania
Source: *AmBi; AmDec 1900; AsBiEn; BiDAmBL 83; BiDAmSp OS; BiInAmS; BioIn 2, 4, 5, 7, 8, 9, 10, 11, 12, 13, 17, 20, 21; DcAmB; DcNAA; DcScB; EncAB-H 1974, 1996; EncABHB 4; MemAm; NatCAB 14, 23; NewCol 75; NotTwCS; OxCAmH; PeoHis; WebAB 74, 79; WhAm 1; WorAl*

Taylor, George
American. Colonial Figure, Continental Congressman
Ironmaster; served less than a year in Congress; signed Declaration of Independence, 1776.
b. 1716, Northern Ireland
d. Feb 22, 1781 in Easton, Pennsylvania
Source: *AmBi; ApCAB; BiAUS; BiDrAC; BiDrUSC 89; BioIn 7, 8, 9; DcAmB; DcIrB 78, 88; Drake; EncAR; EncCRAm; HarEnUS; NatCAB 5; NewCol 75; TwCBDA; WhAm HS; WhAmP; WhAmRev*

Taylor, Graham
American. Clergy, Sociologist
Founder, warden, Chicago Commons Social Settlement, 1894-1938.
b. May 2, 1851 in Schenectady, New York
d. Sep 26, 1938
Source: *AmLY; BiDSocW; BioIn 3, 4, 7; DcAmB S2; DcNAA; NatCAB 29; OxCAmH; OxCAmL 65, 83, 95; WhAm 1; WorAl; WorAlBi*

Taylor, Henry Junior
American. Journalist, Diplomat
Non-fiction works include *Men and Power,* 1946.
b. Sep 2, 1902 in Chicago, Illinois

d. Feb 26, 1984 in New York, New York
Source: *AmAu&B; BiDAmNC; BioIn 1; ConAu 112, P-2; IntWW 74; St&PR 75; WhAm 8; WhoAm 74, 76, 78, 80, 82*

Taylor, J(ohn) H(enry)
[Great Triumvirate]
English. Golfer
With James Braid, Harry Vardon, dominated game, late 19th, early 20th c; won British Open five times.
b. Mar 19, 1871 in North Devon, England
d. Feb 10, 1963 in Devonshire, England
Source: *BioIn 6, 13, 14; DcNaB 1941, 1961; GrBr; ObitT 1961; WhoGolf*

Taylor, J. T
[Kool and the Gang; James Taylor]
American. Singer
Vocalist with Kool and the Gang since 1978.
b. Aug 16, 1953 in South Carolina

Taylor, James Vernon
"Sweet Baby James"
American. Singer, Songwriter
Has nine gold albums, four platinum albums, three gold singles for his folk-rock songs.
b. Mar 12, 1948 in Boston, Massachusetts
Source: *Baker 92; BkPepl; HarEnR 86; RkOn 74; WhoAm 74, 76, 78, 80, 82, 84, 86, 88, 90, 92, 94, 95, 96, 97; WhoEnt 92; WhoWest 74*

Taylor, Jane
English. Poet
Wrote *Twinkle, Twinkle Little Star;* sister of Ann.
b. Sep 26, 1783 in Holborn, England
d. Apr 12, 1824 in Ongar, England
Source: *Alli; ArtclWW 2; BioIn 2, 6, 8, 13, 15, 16; BlmGEL; BlmGWL; CarSB; ChhPo, S1, S3; ChrP; DcBiPP; DcEnL; DcEuL; DcNaB; EncBrWW; EvLB; FemiCLE; InWom, SUP; NewCBEL; OxCChiL; OxCEng 67, 85, 95; PenNWW A; PoChrch; SmATA 35, 36, 41; Str&VC; WhoChL*

Taylor, Jeremy
Irish. Religious Leader
Anglican minister; wrote *Holy Living, Holy Dying,* 1650-51.
b. Aug 1613 in Cambridge, England
d. Aug 13, 1667 in Lisburn, Northern Ireland
Source: *Alli; BbD; Benet 87, 96; BiD&SB; BioIn 1, 2, 3, 5, 8, 9, 10, 12, 21; BlmGEL; BritAu; CamGEL; CamGLE; CasWL; Chambr 1; ChhPo, S1; CrtT 1; CyEd; DcBiPP; DcEnA; DcEnL; DcEuL; DcLB 151; DcLEL; DcNaB, C; EvLB; IlEncMy; LinLib L, S; LngCEL; LuthC 75; MouLC 1; NewC; NewCBEL; OxCEng 67, 85, 95; PenC ENG; REn; WebE&AL*

Taylor, Jim
[James Taylor]
American. Football Player
Fullback, 1958-67, mostly with Green Bay; had greatest success paired with Paul Hornung in backfield; Hall of Fame, 1976.
b. Sep 20, 1935 in Baton Rouge, Louisiana
Source: *BioIn 6, 7, 8, 15, 17; LegTOT; WhoFtbl 74; WhoSpor*

Taylor, John Russell
English. Critic
Film critic, London *Times,* 1962-73; books include *Hollywood 1940s,* 1985.
b. Jun 19, 1935 in Dover, England
Source: *Au&Wr 71; ConAu 5R, 37NR; ConTFT 5; DcLEL 1940; IntAu&W 77, 89, 91, 93; IntMPA 92, 94, 96; IntWW 77, 78, 79, 80, 81, 82, 83, 89, 91, 93; Who 74, 82, 85, 88, 90, 92, 94; WhoArt 96; WhoThe 72, 77, 81; WhoWest 76, 78; WhoWor 84, 87, 89, 91, 93, 95, 96, 97; WrDr 76, 80, 82, 84, 86, 88, 90, 92, 94, 96*

Taylor, June
[June Taylor Dancers]
American. Choreographer, Dancer
Best known for TV work; signature routine done for "Jackie Gleason Show," 1952-59, 1962-70 was the overhead shot of a circular formation.
b. 1918 in Chicago, Illinois
Source: *BiDD; BiE&WWA; CnOxB; NotNAT*

Taylor, Kenneth Douglas
Canadian. Diplomat
Ambassador to Iran, 1977-80; helped six Americans escape from Iran during hostage crisis, 1980.
b. Oct 5, 1934 in Calgary, Alberta, Canada
Source: *CanWW 31, 81, 83, 89; WhoAm 82, 84, 86, 88*

Taylor, Kent
[Louis Weiss]
American. Actor
Hero in B-pictures: *Tangier, Tombstone;* began film career, 1931; played Blackie in TV series "Boston Blackie," 1951-53.
b. May 11, 1907 in Nashua, Iowa
d. Apr 13, 1987 in Los Angeles, California
Source: *BioIn 15, 17; FilmEn; FilmgC; ForYSC; HalFC 80, 84, 88; IntMPA 75, 76, 78, 79, 80, 81, 82, 84, 86; MovMk; VarWW 85; WhoHol A; WhoHrs 80; WorAl*

Taylor, KoKo
[Cora Walton]
American. Singer, Songwriter
Blues singer; recorded million-selling single "Wang Dang Doodle," 1964; won Grammy Award for best blues recording for *Blues Explosion,* 1984; recipient of annual W.C. Handy Award, 1983-1992.
b. 1935 in Memphis, Tennessee
Source: *BioIn 19; BlkWAm; BluesWW; ConMus 10; DcTwCCu 5; PenEncP; RolSEnR 83*

Taylor, Kristin Clark
American. Business Executive
Director of White House media relations, 1989-90; vice-president of external affairs, Student Loan Marketing Association, 1994—.
b. Mar 26, 1959 in Detroit, Michigan
Source: *ConBlB 8; WhoAm 90, 94, 95, 96, 97; WhoAmW 91, 93; WhoEmL 93*

Taylor, Laurette
[Laurette Cooney]
American. Actor
Star of plays *Peg o' My Heart,* 1912; *Glass Menagerie,* 1945.
b. Apr 1, 1887? in New York, New York
d. Dec 7, 1946 in New York, New York
Source: *CurBio 45, 47; DcAmB S4; FamA&A; FilmgC; NotAW; ObitOF 79; OxCAmL 65; OxCThe 67, 83; PlP&P; TwYS; WhAm 2; WhoHol B; WhScrn 74, 77*

Taylor, Lawrence Julius
American. Football Player
Linebacker, NY Giants, 1981—; MVP, 1987.
b. Feb 4, 1959 in Williamsburg, Virginia
Source: *BioIn 13; ConNews 87-3; FootReg 87; WhoAfA 96; WhoBlA 85, 90, 92, 94*

Taylor, Livingston
American. Singer
Brother of James Taylor; hit single "I Will Be in Love with You," 1978.
b. Nov 21, 1950 in Boston, Massachusetts
Source: *RkOn 85; RolSEnR 83*

Taylor, Lucy Beaman Hobbs
American. Dentist, Social Reformer
First woman to receive degree in dentistry, 1866.
b. Mar 14, 1833 in Franklin County, New York
d. Oct 3, 1910 in Lawrence, Kansas
Source: *GoodHs; InWom SUP; LibW; NotAW*

Taylor, Margaret Smith
[Mrs. Zachary Taylor]
American. First Lady
Devoted wife without social ambition; daughter acted as White House hostess.
b. Sep 21, 1788 in Calvert County, Maryland
d. Aug 18, 1852 in Pascagoula, Kentucky
Source: *AmWom; ApCAB; BioIn 16, 17; FacPr 89; GoodHs; NatCAB 4; NotAW; TwCBDA*

Taylor, Maxwell Davenport
American. Military Leader
Chm., US Joint Chiefs of Staff, 1962-64; played a major role in determining American military, diplomatic strategy from WW II to Vietnam War.
b. Aug 26, 1901 in Keytesville, Missouri
d. Apr 19, 1987 in Washington, District of Columbia
Source: *BiDWWGF; BioIn 1, 3, 4, 5, 6, 7, 8, 9, 11, 12; BlueB 76; CmdGen 1991; ColdWar 2; ConNews 87-3; CurBio 46, 61, 87; DcAmDH 80, 89; DcAmMiB; FacFETw; HarEnMi; IntWW 74, 75, 76, 77, 78, 79, 80, 81, 82, 83; WebAMB; WhAm 9; Who 74, 82, 83, 85; WhoAm 74, 76, 78, 80, 82, 84; WhoWor 74, 78; WorAl*

Taylor, Meshach
American. Actor
Played Anthony on TV series *Designing Women,* 1986-93; plays Shel on TV series *Dave's World,* 1993—.
b. Apr 11, in Boston, Massachusetts
Source: *BioIn 16, 18, 19; ConTFT 8; IntMPA 92, 94, 96; WhoAfA 96; WhoAm 92, 94, 95, 96, 97; WhoBlA 92, 94; WhoEnt 92*

Taylor, Mick
[The Rolling Stones]
English. Musician
Guitarist; replaced Brian Jones, 1969-74.
b. Jan 17, 1948 in Hertfordshire, England
Source: *BioIn 8, 11; LegTOT; OnThGG; WhoRocM 82*

Taylor, Paul
American. Choreographer
Award-winning productions include *Musette,* 1983; formed own co., NYC, 1952—.
b. Jul 29, 1930 in Allegheny, New York
Source: *BiDD; BioIn 5, 6, 7, 8, 10, 11, 12, 13, 14, 15, 17, 18, 19, 21; BlueB 76; CelR 90; CmpGMD; CnOxB; ConTFT 12; CurBio 64; DancEn 78; DcArts; DcTwCCu 1; FacFETw; IntDcB; LegTOT; News 92, 92-3; NewYTBS 81, 87; RAdv 14; WhoAm 74, 76, 78, 80, 82, 84, 86, 88, 92, 94, 95, 96, 97; WhoE 74; WhoWor 74, 76, 78, 80, 82, 84, 87, 89, 91, 93, 95; WorAlBi*

Taylor, Peter (Hillsman)
American. Author
Master storyteller; won PEN/Faulkner best fiction award, 1985.
b. Jan 8, 1917 in Trenton, New Jersey
d. Nov 2, 1994 in Charlottesville, Virginia
Source: *AmAu&B; Benet 96; BenetAL 91; BioIn 3, 4, 8, 9, 13, 14, 15, 17, 20, 21; BlueB 76; CamGLE; CamHAL; ConAu 9NR, 50NR, 147; ConLC 1, 4, 18, 37, 44, 50, 71; ConNov 82, 86, 91; CurBio 84, 87, 95N; CyWA 89; DcLB Y94N; DcLEL 1940; FifSWrA; LegTOT; MajTwCW; ModAL, S2; NewYTBS 94; Novels; OhA&B; OxCAmL 83, 95; PenC AM; REnAL; RfGShF; RGTwCWr; ShSCr 10; ShSWr; SouWr; TwCA SUP; WhoAm 74, 76, 78, 80, 84; WhoUSWr 88; WhoWrEP 89, 92, 95; WorAlBi; WrDr 82*

Taylor, Phoebe Atwood
[Alice Tilton]
American. Author
Crime novels include *The Cape Cod Mystery,* 1931; *Punch with Care,* 1946.
b. May 18, 1910 in Boston, Massachusetts
d. Jan 9, 1976 in Boston, Massachusetts
Source: *ConAu 61; EncMys; TwCA, SUP; TwCCr&M 80*

Taylor, Regina
American. Actor
Won Golden Globe, 1993, for best actress, "I'll Fly Away," 1991-93.
b. c. 1959 in Dallas, Texas
Source: *ConBlB 9*

Taylor, Richard Edward
Canadian. Physicist
Shared Nobel Prize in physics, 1990, for breakthrough discoveries about the structure of matter; first to observe traces of quarks, subatomic particles forming the basis of 99% of earth's matter.
b. Nov 2, 1929 in Medicine Hat, Alberta, Canada
Source: *AmMWSc 79, 82, 86, 89, 92, 95; BioIn 17, 18, 20; IntWW 91, 93; LarDcSc; Who 92, 94; WhoAm 86, 88, 90, 92, 94, 95, 96, 97; WhoScEn 94, 96; WhoWest 74, 76, 87, 89, 92, 94, 96; WhoWor 95, 96, 97*

Taylor, Robert
[Arlington Spangler Brugh]
"The Man with the Perfect Profile"
American. Actor
Romantic star with MGM for 25 years.
b. Aug 5, 1911 in Filley, Nebraska
d. Jun 8, 1969 in Santa Monica, California
Source: *BiDFilm, 81, 94; BioIn 2, 3, 5, 6, 8, 9, 10, 14, 17; CmMov; CurBio 52, 69; DcAmB S8; EncMcCE; FacFETw; FilmEn; FilmgC; ForYSC; GangFlm; HalFC 80, 84, 88; IntDcF 1-3, 2-3; LegTOT; MGM; MotPP; MovMk; OxCFilm; WhoHol B; WhScrn 74, 77, 83; WorAl; WorAlBi; WorEFlm*

Taylor, Rod(ney)
Australian. Actor
Best known as resourceful hero in Hitchcock's *The Birds,* 1963.
b. Jan 11, 1930 in Sydney, Australia
Source: *CelR; ConTFT 6; FilmgC; HalFC 84; IntMPA 92, 94, 96; MotPP; MovMk; WhoAm 74, 76, 78, 80, 82, 84, 86, 88, 90, 92; WhoEnt 92A; WhoHol A; WorAl*

Taylor, Ronnie
English. Filmmaker
Won Oscar for cinematography of *Gandhi,* 1982.
Source: *HalFC 84, 88; VarWW 85; WhoRocM 82*

Taylor, Samuel (Albert)
American. Dramatist
Plays include *Sabrina Fair,* 1953; *No Strings,* 1962.
b. Jun 13, 1912 in Chicago, Illinois
Source: *AmAu&B; BiE&WWA; ConAu 25R; ConDr 73, 77D; McGEWD 72, 84; NotNAT; OxCAmT 84; WhoAm 74, 76, 78, 80, 82, 84, 86, 88, 90, 92, 94, 95, 96, 97; WhoEnt 92; WhoThe 72, 77, 81; WhoWor 80; WrDr 76, 80, 82, 84, 86, 88, 90, 92, 94, 96*

Taylor, Susan L.
American. Editor, Journalist
Editor of black women's magazine, *Essence,* 1980—.
b. Jan 23, 1946 in New York, New York
Source: *BioIn 18, 20, 21; ConBlB 10; InB&W 85; NotBlAW 1; WhoAfA 96; WhoAm 84; WhoBlA 94*

Taylor, Susie Baker King
American.
Author of *Reminiscences of My Life in Camp,* 1902 about her life as a slave and Civil War nurse.
b. Aug 5, 1848 in Isle of Wight, Georgia
d. Oct 12, 1912 in Boston, Massachusetts
Source: *BlksScM; BlkWAm; BlkWrNE; FemiCLE; HerW 84; InB&W 85; InWom SUP; NotBlAW 1*

Taylor, Sydney Brenner
American. Children's Author
Wrote *All-of-a-Kind Family* series.
b. Oct 31, 1904? in New York, New York
d. Feb 12, 1978 in New York, New York
Source: *AuBYP 2; BkCL; ConAu 4NR, 5R, 77; MorBMP; MorJA; SmATA 1; WrDr 76*

Taylor, Walter
American. Vintner
Established winery, 1880, in NY's Finger Lake district.
b. 1858
d. 1934
Source: *Entr*

Taylor, William Desmond
[William Cunningham Dean Tanner]
American. Director
Pres., Screen Actors Guild; homicide victim whose death was a scandal when affairs with popular leading ladies discovered.
b. Apr 26, 1877 in Carlow, Ireland
d. Feb 2, 1922 in Hollywood, California
Source: *BioIn 15, 16, 17; EncAFC; FilmEn; LegTOT; MiSFD 9N; TwYS, A; WhoHol B; WhScrn 74, 77, 83*

Taylor, Zachary
"Old Rough and Ready"
American. US President
12th pres., 1849-50; hero of US-Mexican War, 1846-48.
b. Nov 24, 1784 in Orange County, Virginia
d. Jul 9, 1850 in Washington, District of Columbia
Source: *AmAu&B; AmBi; AmPolLe; ApCAB; BenetAL 91; BiAUS; BiDrAC; BiDrUSE 71, 89; BiDSA; BioIn 1, 2, 3, 4, 5, 6, 7, 8, 9, 10, 11, 12, 13, 14, 15, 16, 17, 18, 19, 20; CelCen; CyAG; DcAmB; DcAmMiB; DcBiPP; DcNaB; Drake; EncAAH; EncAB-H 1974, 1996; EncSoH; FacPr 89, 93; GenMudB; HarEnMi; HarEnUS; HealPre; HisWorL; LegTOT; LinLib L, S; McGEWB; NatCAB 4; OxCAmH; OxCAmL 65, 83; PolPar; RComAH; REnAL; REnAW; TwCBDA; WebAB 74, 79; WebAMB; WhAm HS; WhAmP; WhDW; WhFla; WhNaAH; WhoMilH 76; WorAl; WorAlBi*

Tchaikovsky, Peter Ilyich
[Petr Ilich Chaikovshy]
Russian. Composer
Known for classical ballet scores *Swan Lake,* 1877; *Nutcracker Suite,* 1892; *Sleeping Beauty,* 1889.
b. May 7, 1840 in Votiwsk, Russia
d. Nov 6, 1893 in Saint Petersburg, Russia
Source: *AtlBL; Baker 84; CmOp; GayLesB; LegTOT; McGEWB; MetOEnc; MusMk; NewC; NewEOp 71; OxCEng 67, 85; REn; WorAl; WorAlBi*

Tchelitchew, Pavel
American. Artist, Designer
Stage designer; abstract painter, portraitist, noted for multiple imagery.
b. Sep 21, 1898, Russia
d. Jul 31, 1957 in Rome, Italy
Source: *BioIn 11, 21; BriEAA; CamGWoT; ChhPo; ConArt 77, 83; CurBio 43, 57; DcAmB S6; DcCAA 71, 77, 88, 94; IntDcB; McGDA; NewCol 75; OxCTwCA; OxDcArt; PhDcTCA 77*

Tcherepnin, Alexander Nikolayevich
American. Pianist, Composer
Experimented with nine-note scale, rhythmic polyphony; wrote opera, *Farmer and the Nymph,* 1952.
b. Jan 20, 1899 in Saint Petersburg, Russia
d. Sep 29, 1977 in Paris, France
Source: *Baker 84; DcCM; IntWW 74; WebBD 83; WhAm 7; WhoAm 74; WhoMus 72; WhoWor 74*

Tcherepnin, Nicholas
[Nicolai Tcherepnin]
Russian. Composer, Conductor
Wrote ballets, symphonies; led Diaghilef Ballet, 1909-14; father of Alexander.
b. May 14, 1873 in Saint Petersburg, Russia
d. Jun 26, 1945 in Paris, France
Source: *Baker 84; BiDD; CnOxB; NewEOp 71; NewOxM; OxCMus; WebBD 83*

Tcherkassky, Marianna Alexsavena
American. Dancer
Principal dancer, American Ballet Theatre since 1976, known for purity of style.
b. Oct 28, 1952 in Glen Cove, New York
Source: *CurBio 85; WhoAm 78, 80, 82, 84, 86, 88, 92, 94, 95, 96, 97; WhoAmW 83, 85, 89, 91, 93, 95; WhoWor 95, 96, 97*

Tchernichowski, Saul Gutmanovich
Israeli. Poet
Poems, sonnets reflect fervent Jewish nationalism.
b. Aug 20, 1875 in Crimea, Ukraine
d. Oct 14, 1943 in Jerusalem, Palestine
Source: *CasWL; ConAu 116; PenC CL; WorAu 1950*

Teacher, Brian
American. Tennis Player
Won Australian Open, 1980.
b. Dec 23, 1954 in San Diego, California
Source: *WhoIntT*

Teagarden, Charles
"Little T"
American. Jazz Musician
Trumpeter with Big Bands, late 1920s-63; brother of Jack.
b. Jul 19, 1913 in Vernon, Texas
d. Dec 10, 1984 in Las Vegas, Nevada
Source: *AnObit 1984; BiDAmM; BiDJaz; CmpEPM; EncJzS; IlEncJ*

Teagarden, Jack
[Weldon John Teagarden]
"Big T"
American. Jazz Musician, Bandleader
Great jazz trombonist, vocalist; led own band, 1939-46; in film *Birth of the Blues,* 1941.
b. Aug 20, 1905 in Vernon, Texas
d. Jan 15, 1964 in New Orleans, Louisiana
Source: *AllMusG; Baker 92; BgBands 74; BioIn 4, 5, 6, 7, 9, 12, 13, 20; CmpEPM; ConMus 10; FacFETw; IlEncJ; LegTOT; NewAmDM; NewGrDA 86; NewGrDJ 88, 94; NewGrDM 80; OxCAmH; OxCPMus; PenEncP; WhAm 4; WhoHol B; WhoJazz 72; WhScrn 74, 77; WorAlBi*

Teague, Olin E
American. Politician
Dem. senator from TX, 1946-79; identified with veterans affairs.
b. Apr 6, 1910 in Woodward, Oklahoma
d. Jan 23, 1981 in Bethesda, Maryland
Source: *AlmAP 78; AnObit 1981, 1984; BiDrAC; CurBio 52, 81, 81N; NewYTBS 81; WhAm 7*

Teague, Walter Dorwin
"Dean of Industrial Design"
American. Designer
Known for industrial designs for Kodak, Ford Motor Co., US Steel.
b. Dec 18, 1883 in Decatur, Indiana
d. Dec 5, 1960 in Flemington, New Jersey
Source: *AmAu&B; BioIn 5, 6, 8; ChhPo S1; ConDes 84; CurBio 42, 61; DcArts; DcD&D; DcTwDes; EncAB-A 32; FacFETw; IndAu 1917; McGDA; NatCAB 50; ObitOF 79; PenDiDA 89; WhAm 4; WhAmArt 85*

Teale, Edwin Way
American. Naturalist, Author
Wrote over 25 books; won Pulitzer for *Wandering Through Winter,* 1966.
b. Jun 2, 1899 in Joliet, Illinois
d. Oct 18, 1980 in Norwich, Connecticut
Source: *AmAu&B; AnObit 1980; Au&Wr 71; AuBYP 2, 3; BenetAL 91; BioIn 1, 2, 3, 4, 5, 6, 7, 8, 9, 10, 12, 13, 15; ConAu 1R, 2NR, 102; CurBio 61, 81, 81N; InSci; LinLib L, S; NewYTBS 80; OxCAmL 83, 95; REnAL; SmATA 7, 25N; Str&VC; ThrBJA; TwCA SUP; WhAm 7; WhNAA; WhoAm 74, 76, 78, 80; WhoWor 74; WrDr 76, 80, 82, 84*

Tears for Fears
[Roland Orzabal; Curt Smith]
English. Music Group
Bath, England duo; had number one hit "Everybody Wants to Rule the World," 1985.
Source: *ConMus 6; EncRk 88; EncRkSt; HarEnR 86; PenEncP; RkOn 85*

Teasdale, Sara
American. Author, Poet
Writings include *Rivers to the Sea,* 1915; *Stars Tonight,* 1930.
b. Aug 8, 1884 in Saint Louis, Missouri
d. Jan 28, 1933 in New York, New York
Source: *AmAu&B; AmBi; AmWomPl; AnCL; AnMV 1926; ApCAB X; ArtclWW 2; Benet 87, 96; BenetAL 91; BiDAmM; BiDSA; BioAmW; BioIn 4, 5, 8, 11, 12, 14, 15, 16; BkCL; BlmGWL; CasWL; ChhPo, S1, S2, S3; CnDAL; ConAmA; ConAmL; ConAu 104; DcAmB; DcLEL; DcNAA; EvLB; FacFETw; FemiCLE; GayLL; GrLiveH; GrWrEL P; InWom, SUP; LegTOT; LibW; LinLib L; LngCTC; ModWoWr; NatCAB 39; NotAW; OxCAmL 65, 83, 95; OxCTwCP; OxCWoWr 95; PeoHis; RAdv 1; REn; REnAL; RfGAmL 87, 94; SixAP; SmATA 32; Str&VC; TwCA, SUP; TwCWr; WebAB 74, 79; WhAm 1, 7; WhNAA; WomWWA 14; WorAl; WorAlBi*

Tebaldi, Renata
Italian. Opera Singer
Outstanding postwar soprano; noted for Verdi, Puccini roles.
b. Feb 1, 1922 in Pesaro, Italy
Source: *Baker 78, 84, 92; BioIn 2, 3, 4, 5, 6, 7, 9, 10, 11, 14, 15, 18, 21; BriBkM 80; CmOp; CurBio 55; DcArts;*

FacFETw; IntDcOp; IntWW 74, 75, 76, 77, 78, 79, 80, 81, 82, 83, 89, 91, 93; IntWWM 77, 80; InWom, SUP; LegTOT; MetOEnc; MusMk; MusSN; NewAmDM; NewEOp 71; NewGrDA 86; NewGrDM 80; NewGrDO; NewYTBE 73; OxDcOp; PenDiMP; Who 74, 82, 83, 85, 88, 90, 92, 94; WhoAm 74, 76, 78, 80, 82, 86, 88, 90, 92, 94, 95, 96, 97; WhoAmM 83; WhoAmW 66, 68, 70, 72, 74, 75, 83; WhoHol 92, A; WhoMus 72; WhoOp 76; WhoWor 74; WorAl; WorAlBi

Tebbel, John William
American. Author, Educator
Writings include *Your Body: How to Keep It Healthy,* 1950; *A Voice in the Streets,* 1954.
b. Nov 16, 1912 in Boyne City, Michigan
Source: *BioIn 3; ConAu 85; CurBio 53; DrAS 74E, 78E, 82E; WhoAm 86*

Tebbetts, Birdie
[George Robert Tebbetts]
American. Baseball Player, Baseball Manager
Catcher, 1936-42, 1946-52, mostly with Detroit; managed for 11 yrs.
b. Nov 10, 1912 in Burlington, Vermont
Source: *Ballpl 90; BioIn 16, 21; WhoProB 73*

Tebbit, Norman Beresford
English. Political Leader
Conservative member of Parliament, 1970-92; chm., Conservative Party, 1985-87.
b. Mar 29, 1931 in London, England
Source: *CurBio 87; IntWW 82, 83, 89, 91, 93; IntYB 78, 79, 80, 81, 82; NewYTBS 86; WhoWor 87, 89*

Tebelak, John Michael
American. Dramatist, Director
Wrote, directed rock musical *Godspell.*
b. 1949
d. Apr 2, 1985 in New York, New York
Source: *ConAu 115*

Technotronic
[MC Eric; Thomas (Jo Bogaert) DeQuincey; Manuela Barbara (Ya Kid K) Kamosi]
American. Music Group
Studio house band with rap and vocals; debut album *Pump Up the Jam: The Album,* 1989 went gold.
Source: *ConMus 5; OxCMus*

Tecumseh
American. Native American Chief
Shawnee Indian chief, tried to unite tribes to resist westward expansion of whites.
b. Mar 1768 in Oldtown, Ohio
d. Oct 5, 1813 in Thamesville, Ontario, Canada
Source: *AmBi; ApCAB; Benet 87, 96; BenetAL 91; BioIn 1, 2, 4, 5, 6, 7, 8, 9, 10, 11, 12, 14, 15, 16, 17, 18, 19, 20; DcAmB; DcAmMiB; DcCanB 5; EncAAH; EncAB-H 1974, 1996; EncNAB; EncNoAI; GenMudB; HarEnMi; HarEnUS; HisWorL; MacDCB 78; McGEWB; MorMA; NatCAB 11; NatNAL; NotNaAm; OxCAmH; OxCAmL 65, 83, 95; OxCCan; RComAH; REn; REnAL; REnAW; WebAB 74, 79; WebAMB; WhAm HS; WhNaAH; WhoMilH 76; WorAl; WorAlBi*

Tedder, Arthur William Tedder, Baron
English. Military Leader, Author, University Administrator
Marshall of Royal Air Force; responsible for Allied Air Forces in Mediterranean, 1943.
b. Jul 11, 1890 in Stirling, Scotland
d. Jun 3, 1967 in Surrey, England
Source: *BioIn 1, 3, 7, 8, 11, 14; CurBio 43, 67; HisEWW; ObitOF 79; ObitT 1961; WhAm 4; WhWW-II; WorAl*

Teena Marie
[Mary Christine Brockert]
""Lady T""
American. Singer
Often works with Rick James; hits include "I Need Your Lovin';" "It Must be Magic."
b. 1957 in Santa Monica, California
Source: *EncPR&S 89; IlEncBM 82; RkOn 85*

Teicher, Louis
[Ferrante and Teicher]
American. Pianist, Composer
Part of Ferrante and Teicher piano team, 1947—.
b. Aug 24, 1924 in Wilkes-Barre, Pennsylvania
Source: *ASCAP 66, 80; BioIn 6, 7; LegTOT; WhoAm 74, 76, 78, 80, 82, 84, 86, 88; WhoAmJ 80*

Teichmann, Howard Miles
American. Dramatist, Biographer
Best-known play: *The Solid Gold Cadillac,* 1953; biographies include those of Henry Fonda, Alexander Woollcott.
b. Jan 22, 1916 in Chicago, Illinois
d. Jul 7, 1987 in New York, New York
Source: *BiE&WWA; ConAu 69; ConTFT 1; McGEWD 72; NatPD 77; NewYTBS 87; NotNAT; WhAm 9; WhoAm 80, 82, 84, 86; WhoE 79, 83, 85, 86*

Teilhard de Chardin, Pierre
French. Clergy, Philosopher, Paleontologist
Attempted to reconcile evolution with Catholic doctrine; helped discover Peking Man, 1929; wrote *Phenomenon of Man,* published 1955.
b. May 1, 1881 in Auvergne, France
d. Apr 10, 1955 in New York, New York
Source: *Benet 87, 96; BioIn 3, 4, 5, 6, 7, 8, 9, 10, 11, 12, 13; CasWL; ClDMEL 80; ConAu 105; DcCathB; DcScB; DcTwCCu 2; EncHuEv; EncUnb; FacFETw; Geog 7; GuFrLit 1; InSci; LarDcSc; LegTOT; LinLib L, S; LngCTC; LuthC 75; MakMC; McGEWB; NewCol 75; OxCEng 85, 95; RAdv 14; ThTwC 87; WhAm 4, HSA; WorAl; WorAlBi; WorAu 1950; WrPh P*

Teisserenc de Bort, Leon-Philippe
French. Meteorologist
Discoverer of the stratosphere.
b. Nov 5, 1855 in Paris, France
d. Jan 2, 1913 in Cannes, France

Tekakwitha, Kateri, Saint
[Catherine Tegakovita]
"Lily of the Mohawks"
American. Religious Figure
First Native American to be canonized by the Roman Catholic Church.
b. 1656 in Ossernenon, New York
d. Apr 17, 1680 in Caughnawaga, Quebec, Canada
Source: *BioAmW; BioIn 2, 3, 4, 5, 6, 7, 11, 18, 19, 21; DcAmReB 1; DcCanB 1; EncARH; EncNAR; EncNoAI; InWom, SUP; LibW; MacDCB 78; NotAW; NotNaAm; WebAB 74, 79; WhNaAH*

Te Kanawa, Kiri, Dame
New Zealander. Opera Singer
Soprano; performed at wedding of Prince Charles, Lady Diana Spencer, 1981.
b. Mar 6, 1944 in Gisborne, New Zealand
Source: *Baker 84, 92; BriBkM 80; CelR 90; CmOp; ConMus 2; ContDcW 89; CurBio 78; DcArts; EncWB; FarE&A 81; IntWW 81, 82, 83, 89, 91, 93; IntWWM 90; ItaFilm; MetOEnc; NewAmDM; NewGrDM 80; NewGrDO; NewYTBS 82; OxDcOp; PenDiMP; Who 82, 83, 85, 88, 90, 92; WhoAm 86, 88, 90, 92, 94, 95, 96, 97; WhoAmW 87; WhoWor 84, 87, 89, 91, 93, 95, 96, 97; WorAlBi*

Tekere, Edgar Zivanai
Zimbabwean. Government Official
Secretary general who was arrested for murder during guerrilla attacks in Zimbabwe, 1980.
b. Apr 1, 1937, Rhodesia
Source: *BioIn 12; NewYTBS 80*

Tekulve, Kent(on Charles)
American. Baseball Player
Relief pitcher, 1975-89; pitched in more games as reliever than anyone in ML history, 1,050.
b. Mar 5, 1947 in Cincinnati, Ohio
Source: *Ballpl 90; BaseReg 86, 87; BiDAmSp Sup; BioIn 12, 13; LegTOT; NewYTBS 79; WhoAm 82, 84*

Telemann, Georg Philipp
German. Composer
Wrote over 600 overtures, 50 operas, including *Sokrates,* 1721.
b. Mar 14, 1681 in Magdeburg, Germany
d. Jun 25, 1767 in Hamburg, Germany
Source: *AtlBL; Baker 78, 84, 92; BioIn 1, 4, 7, 10, 12, 20; BriBkM 80; CmOp;*

CmpBCM; DcArts; DcCom 77; DcCom&M 79; EncEnl; GrComp; IntDcOp; LuthC 75; McGEWB; MetOEnc; MusMk; NewAmDM; NewCol 75; NewGrDM 80; NewGrDO; NewOxM; OxCMus; OxDcOp; WorAl; WorAlBi

Telkes, Maria (de)
American. Chemist
Pioneer in application of solar energy to water distillation and home heating, 1970s.
b. Dec 12, 1900, Austria-Hungary
d. Dec 2, 1995 in Budapest, Hungary
Source: *AmMWSc 73P, 76P, 79, 82, 86, 89, 92, 95; BioIn 2, 4, 15, 20; CurBio 96N; ForWC 70; InSci; NotTwCS; WhoAm 74, 76, 78, 80, 82; WhoAmW 58, 64, 66, 68, 70, 72, 79, 81; WhoFrS 84; WhoWor 74, 78*

Tell, William
[Wilhelm Tell]
Swiss. Legendary Figure
In legend, shot an apple from son's head with arrow.
b. 1282
Source: *NewCol 75; OxCGer 76*

Teller, Edward
"Father of the Hydrogen Bomb"
American. Physicist, Educator, Author
Worked on the Manhattan Project developing atomic bomb, 1940s.
b. Jan 15, 1908 in Budapest, Austria-Hungary
Source: *AmAu&B; AmDec 1940; AmMWSc 73P, 73S, 76P, 79, 82, 86, 89, 92, 95; AsBiEn; BiESc; BioIn 3, 4, 5, 6, 8, 11, 12, 13, 14, 15, 16, 17, 18, 20; BlueB 76; CamDcSc; CelR; CmCal; ColdWar 1, 2; ConAu 33NR, P-1; CurBio 54, 83; EncAB-H 1974, 1996; EncWB; FacFETw; InSci; IntWW 74, 75, 76, 77, 78, 79, 80, 81, 82, 83, 89, 91, 93; IntWWE; IntYB 78, 79; LarDcSc; LegTOT; LinLib L, S; MajTwCW; McGMS 80; NotTwCS; OxCAmH; PolProf E, K, T; RAdv 14; WebAB 74, 79; WhDW; Who 74, 82, 83, 85, 88, 90, 92, 94; WhoAm 74, 76, 78, 80, 82, 84, 86, 88, 90, 92, 94, 95, 96, 97; WhoFrS 84; WhoScEn 94, 96; WhoTech 82, 84, 89, 95; WhoWest 82, 84; WhoWor 74, 78, 80, 82, 84; WhoWorJ 72, 78; WorAl; WorAlBi; WorInv*

Telva, Marion
American. Opera Singer
Contralto, NY Met., 1920-33.
b. Sep 26, 1897 in Saint Louis, Missouri
d. Oct 23, 1962 in Norwalk, Connecticut
Source: *Baker 84; BiDAmM; BioIn 6; InWom, SUP; MetOEnc; NewEOp 71; WhAm 4*

Temin, Howard Martin
American. Scientist, Educator
Shared 1975 Nobel Prize in medicine for work with tumor viruses, cells.
b. Dec 10, 1934 in Philadelphia, Pennsylvania
Source: *AmMWSc 73P, 76P, 79, 82, 86, 89, 92; BiESc; BioIn 10, 14, 15, 19, 20, 21; FacFETw; LarDcSc; WhAm 11; WhoAm 74, 76, 78, 80, 82, 84, 86, 88, 90, 92, 94; WhoFrS 84; WhoMW 78, 80, 82, 84, 86, 88, 90, 92, 93; WhoNob, 90, 95; WhoScEn 94; WhoWor 78, 80, 82, 84, 87, 89, 91, 93; WorAl; WorScD*

Tempest, Marie
English. Actor
Appeared in stage comedies, 1899-1942, including *Marriage of Kitty.*
b. Jul 15, 1864 in London, England
d. Oct 15, 1942 in London, England
Source: *BioIn 3, 5, 10, 14; CnThe; ContDcW 89; CurBio 42; DcNaB 1941; EncMT; EncWT; Ent; FamA&A; Film 1; FilmgC; GrBr; HalFC 80, 84, 88; IntDcWB; LegTOT; OxCAmT 84; OxCPMus; OxCThe 67, 83; PlP&P; REn; WhAm 2; WhoHol B; WhoStg 1906, 1908; WhScrn 77, 83; WhThe; WorAl*

Templeton, Alec
American. Pianist
Famed blind entertainer, noted for piano parodies, novelty vocals, 1930s-40s; own radio show, 1940.
b. Jul 4, 1910 in Cardiff, Wales
d. Mar 28, 1963 in Greenwich, Connecticut
Source: *ASCAP 66, 80; Baker 84; BiDAmM; BioIn 1, 5, 6, 11; CmpEPM; ConAmC 76; CurBio 40, 63; NewGrDA 86; NotNAT B; RadStar; WhAm 4; WhoHol B*

Templeton, Fay
American. Actor
Appearances on stage, vaudeville included *Fiddle-Dee-Dee.*
b. Dec 25, 1865 in Little Rock, Arkansas
d. Oct 3, 1939 in San Francisco, California
Source: *BioIn 3; CamGWoT; CmpEPM; EncMT; InWom, SUP; LibW; NewGrDA 86; NotAW; NotNAT B; OxCAmH; OxCAmT 84; OxCPMus; WhAm 1; WhoHol B; WhoStg 1906, 1908; WhScrn 74, 77; WhThe*

Templeton, Garry Lewis
"Jump Steady"; "Tempy"
American. Baseball Player
Shortstop, Padres, 1976—; led NL in hits, 1979.
b. Mar 24, 1956 in Lockney, Texas
Source: *BaseReg 86, 87; BiDAmSp Sup; InB&W 80; WhoAfA 96; WhoBlA 88, 90, 92, 94*

Temptations, The
[Dennis Edwards; Melvin Franklin; Eddie Kendricks; David Ruffin; Otis Williams; Paul Williams]
American. Music Group
Group formed in 1964; hits include "My Girl;" "Just My Imagination."
Source: *AmBench 79; BiDAmM; BioIn 12, 17, 18; ConMuA 80A; ConMus 3; DcTwCCu 5; EncPR&S 74, 89; EncRk 88; EncRkSt; HarEnR 86; IlEncRk; InB&W 80, 85, 85A; IntMPA 75, 76, 77, 78, 79, 80, 81, 82, 84, 86, 88, 92; NewAmDM; NewGrDA 86; NewYTBS 92, 95; OxCPMus; PenEncP; RkOn 84; SoulM; WhAmArt 85; WhoHol 92, A; WhoRock 81; WhoRocM 82; WorAl; WorAlBi*

Tenace, Gene
[Fury Gene Tenace]
American. Baseball Player
Catcher-first baseman, 1969-83, mostly with Oakland; holds ML record for hitting home run in first two at-bats, 1972 World Series; fifth ML player to hit four home runs in World Series, 1972.
b. Oct 10, 1946 in Russellton, Pennsylvania
Source: *Ballpl 90; BaseEn 88; BioIn 9, 10, 11; NewYTBE 73; WhoProB 73*

Ten Boom, Corrie
Dutch. Author
Wrote of experiences in concentration camp: *The Hiding Place,* 1971; movie starred Julie Harris, 1975.
b. Apr 15, 1892 in Amsterdam, Netherlands
d. Apr 15, 1983 in Placentia, California
Source: *BioIn 10, 11, 12, 13; ConAu 109, 111; ConHero 2; FacFETw; HeroCon; RelLAm 91; WomFir*

Ten CC
[Paul Burgess; Lol Creme; Kevin Godley; Graham Gouldman; Eric Stewart]
English. Music Group
Formed in 1972; albums include *Windows in the Jungle,* 1983.
Source: *BioIn 11; ConMuA 80A; EncRk 88; HarEnR 86; IlEncRk; MiSFD 9; OxCPMus; PenEncP; RkOn 78; RolSEnR 83; WhoRock 81; WhoRocM 82*

Tenggren, Gustaf Adolf
American. Illustrator
Books include *Canterbury Tales,* 1961; *King Arthur and the Knights of the Round Table,* 1962.
b. Nov 3, 1896, Sweden
d. Apr 6, 1970 in West Southport, Maine
Source: *BioIn 8; IlsBYP; IlsCB 1744, 1946; MorJA; SmATA 18; WhAm 6; WhAmArt 85*

Teniers, David, the Younger
Flemish. Artist
Paintings express tone, atmosphere: *The Dance in Front of the Castle,* 1645.
b. Dec 14, 1610 in Antwerp, Belgium
d. Apr 25, 1690 in Brussels, Belgium
Source: *AtlBL; BioIn 2, 11, 12; ClaDrA; DcBiPP; DcCathB; IntDcAA 90; McGDA; OxCArt; OxCEng 85, 95; OxDcArt*

Tennant, Veronica
Canadian. Dancer
Principal dancer with National Ballet Canada, 1965-89.
b. Jan 15, 1946 in London, England
Source: *BiDD; BioIn 14, 16; CanWW 79, 80, 81, 83; CnOxB; CreCan 1; SmATA 36; WhoAm 84*

Tennenbaum, Silvia
American. Author, Lecturer
Wrote *Rachel, the Rabbi's Wife,* 1978; articles, book reviews for *Midstream; Newsday* mags.
b. Mar 10, 1928, Germany
Source: *ConAu 21NR, 77*

Tenniel, John, Sir
English. Illustrator, Artist
Best known for illustrations in *Alice's Adventures in Wonderland.*
b. Feb 28, 1820 in London, England
d. Feb 25, 1914 in London, England
Source: *Alli; AntBDN B; ArtsNiC; Benet 87, 96; BioIn 1, 2, 3, 8, 9, 11, 12, 13, 16, 17, 19; CamGLE; CelCen; ChhPo, S1, S2; ChlBkCr; ChlLR 18; ClaDrA; ConAu 111; DcArts; DcBiPP; DcBrBI; DcBrWA; DcNaB 1912; DcPup; DcVicP, 2; IlsBYP; JBA 34, 51; LegTOT; LinLib L; LngCTC; MajAI; McGDA; NewC; NewCBEL; OxCArt; OxCChiL; OxCEng 85, 95; OxDcArt; REn; SmATA 27, 74; StaCVF; Str&VC; VicBrit; WhDW; WhLit; WhoChL; WorECar*

Tennille, Toni
[The Captain and Tennille; Mrs. Daryl Dragon]
American. Singer
Had 1975 hit "Love Will Keep Us Together," written by Neil Sedaka.
b. May 8, 1943 in Montgomery, Alabama
Source: *BioIn 11, 12, 13, 21; BkPepl; LegTOT; WhoAmW 81, 83; WorAl; WorAlBi*

Tennstedt, Klaus
German. Conductor
Musical director, conductor of London Philharmonic Orchestra, 1983-87; conducto r laureate, 1987—.
b. Jun 6, 1926 in Merseburg, Germany
Source: *Baker 78, 84, 92; BioIn 11, 12, 13; CurBio 83; DcArts; IntWW 82, 83, 89, 91, 93; IntWWM 90; MetOEnc; NewAmDM; NewGrDA 86; NewGrDM 80; NewGrDO; NewYTBS 77; PenDiMP; Who 85, 88, 90, 92, 94; WhoAm 80, 82, 84, 86, 88, 90, 92, 94, 95, 96, 97; WhoEnt 92; WhoWor 84, 87, 89, 91, 93, 95*

Tennyson, Alfred, Lord
English. Poet
Poet laureate, 1850-92; wrote *Idylls of the King,* 1885; "Charge of the Light Brigade," 1854.
b. Aug 6, 1809 in Somersby, England
d. Oct 6, 1892 in Haslemere, England
Source: *Alli, SUP; AnCL; AtlBL; AuBYP 2, 3; BbD; Benet 87, 96; BiD&SB; BioIn 12, 13, 16, 17, 18, 19, 20; BlmGEL; BritAu 19; BritWr 4; CamGEL; CamGWoT; CasWL; CelCen; Chambr 3; ChhPo, S1, S2, S3; CnDBLB 4; CnE&AP; CnThe; CrtSuDr; CrtT 3, 4; CyWA 58; DcArts; DcBiPP; DcEnA, A; DcEnL; DcEuL; DcLEL; DcNaB; DcPup; Dis&D; EncPaPR 91; EvLB; GrWrEL P; IlEncMy; LegTOT; LngCEL; LuthC 75; MagSWL; McGEWB; McGEWD 72, 84; MouLC 4; NewC; NewCBEL; NewEOp 71; NinCLC 30; NotNAT B; OxCEng 67, 85, 95; OxCMus; OxCThe 67, 83; PenC ENG; PenEncH; PoLE; RAdv 1, 14; RComWL; REn; REnWD; RfGEnL 91; Str&VC; VicBrit; WebE&AL; WhDW; WorAl; WorAlBi; WorLitC*

10,000 Maniacs
[Jerry Augustyniak; Robert Buck; Dennis Drew; Steve Gustafson; Natalie Merchant]
American. Music Group
Rock group; hit singles include *Like the Weather,* 1987 and *Trouble Me,* 1989.
Source: *Alli; BioIn 15, 16, 21; ConMus 3; EncRkSt; OnThGG*

Ten Years After
[Chick Churchill; Alvin Lee; Rick Lee; Leo Lyons]
British. Music Group
Major blues band, 1967-75; albums include *Goin' Home,* 1975.
Source: *BioIn 11; ConMuA 80A; EncPR&S 89; EncRk 88; EncRkSt; HarEnR 86; IlEncRk; PenEncP; RolSEnR 83; WhoRock 81; WhoRocM 82*

Tenzing Norgay
[Namgyal Wangdi]
Mountaineer
With Sir Edmund Hillary, first to reach summit of Mt. Everest, 1953.
b. May 15, 1914 in Solo Khumbu, Nepal
d. May 9, 1986 in Darjeeling, India
Source: *BioIn 3, 4, 5, 7, 8, 9, 10, 11, 14, 15, 16, 17, 19; CurBio 54; FarE&A 78, 79, 80, 81; IntWW 76, 77, 78, 79, 81, 82, 83; NewYTBS 86; Who 82, 83, 85*

Ter-Arutunian, Rouben
Russian. Designer
Best known for innovative stage designs for ballet, Broadway including *Redhead,* 1959; works in both realism, abstractionism.
b. Jul 24, 1920 in Tiflis, Union of Soviet Socialist Republics
d. Oct 17, 1992 in New York, New York
Source: *AnObit 1992; BiDD; BiE&WWA; BioIn 6, 7, 8, 19; CamGWoT; CnOxB; ConDes 84, 90, 97; ConTFT 7; CurBio 63, 93N; DancEn 78; EncWT; NewEOp 71; NewYTBS 92; NotNAT; WhoAm 74, 76, 78, 80, 82; WhoE 74; WhoOp 76; WhoThe 72, 77, 81; WhoWor 74*

Ter Borch, Gerard
Dutch. Artist
Noted for small portraits, genre painting, including *Guitar Lesson.*
b. 1617 in Zwolle, Netherlands
d. Dec 8, 1681 in Deventer, Netherlands
Source: *McGDA; McGEWB; NewCol 75; OxCArt*

Terbrugghen, Hendrick
Dutch. Artist
Genre works, influenced by Caravaggio, include *The Flute Player,* 1621.
b. 1588
d. 1629
Source: *BioIn 5, 19; DcArts; IntDcAA 90; McGDA; NewCol 75; OxCArt; OxDcArt; WhDW*

Terence
[Publius Terentius Afer]
Roman. Dramatist, Poet
Comedies modeled on Greek originals; more subtle, refined than Plautus's.
b. 185?BC
d. 159BC
Source: *AtlBL; BbD; Benet 87, 96; BiD&SB; CasWL; ClMLC 14; CnThe; CyWA 58; DcEnL; LngCEL; LuthC 75; McGEWD 84; NewC; OxCEng 67; OxCThe 67; PenC CL; PlP&P; RComWL; REn; REnWD*

Teresa, Mother
[Agnes Gonxha Bojaxhiu]
"Saint of the Gutters"
Albanian. Missionary
Catholic nun widely respected for int'l humanitarian efforts for poor; founded Missionaries of Charity, 1950, Superior General, 1950-97; awarded Nobel Peace Prize, 1979.
b. Aug 27, 1910 in Skopje, Yugoslavia
Source: *BioIn 16, 17, 18, 19, 20; CurBio 73; FacFETw; FarE&A 81; IntDcWB; IntWW 89, 91, 93; InWom SUP; News 93-1; NewYTBS 79; Who 92, 94; WhoNob, 90; WhoRel 92; WhoWor 87, 91, 93, 95, 96, 97; WorAlBi*

Tereshkova-Nikolaeva, Valentina
Russian. Cosmonaut
First woman in space; orbited earth 48 times, 1963.
b. Mar 6, 1937 in Maslennikovo, Union of Soviet Socialist Republics
Source: *IntWW 74; WhoWor 74*

TerHorst, Jerald Franklin
American. Journalist
White House press secretary under Ford, who resigned after 30 days because of Ford's pardon of Richard Nixon, 1974.
b. Jul 11, 1922 in Grand Rapids, Michigan
Source: *AuNews 1; BiDAmNC; BioIn 10, 12; BioNews 74; ConAu 107; CurBio 75; EncTwCJ; NewYTBS 74; PolProf NF; WhoAm 74, 76, 78, 80, 82, 84, 86, 88, 90, 92, 94, 95, 96, 97; WhoSSW 95*

Terhune, Albert Payson
American. Journalist, Author
Popular canine stories include *Lad, a Dog,* 1928.
b. Dec 21, 1872 in Newark, New Jersey
d. Feb 18, 1942 in Pompton Lakes, New Jersey
Source: *AmAu&B; AmLY; AuBYP 2, 3; BenetAL 91; BiD&SB; BioIn 2, 5, 7, 8, 9, 11, 12, 19; ChhPo; ChlBkCr; CnDAL; ConAu 111, 136; CurBio 42; DcAmAu; DcAmB S3; DcLB 9; DcNAA; EvLB; JBA 34; LinLib L; MajAI; NatCAB 34; OxCAmL 65, 83, 95; OxCChiL; REnAL; SmATA 15; TwCA, SUP; TwCBDA; TwCChW 89, 95; WebAB 74, 79; WhAm 2; WhLit; WhNAA; WorAl; WorAlBi*

Terhune, Mary Virginia
American. Author
Wrote romantic novels, household quotes; mother of Albert Payson.
b. Dec 31, 1831 in Dennisville, Virginia
d. Jun 3, 1922 in New York, New York
Source: *Alli SUP; AmAu; AmAu&B; AmBi; AmWom; ApCAB; BbD; BiD&SB; BiDSA; CarSB; Drake; NotAW; OxCAmL 83; REnAL; TwCBDA; WhAm 1*

Terkel, Studs (Louis)
American. Author, Journalist
Books based on tape-recorded interviews include Pulitzer winner *The Good War,* 1985.
b. May 16, 1912 in New York, New York
Source: *AmAu&B; AuNews 1; BenetAL 91; BioIn 7, 10, 11, 12, 13, 14, 16, 17, 18, 19, 21; CelR 90; ConAu 57; ConLC 38; CurBio 74; EncAJ; FacFETw; IntAu&W 89; IntWW 83, 89, 91, 93; LegTOT; LiJour; LinLib L; OxCAmL 83, 95; WhoAm 74, 76, 78, 80, 82, 84, 86, 88, 90, 92, 94, 95, 96, 97; WhoHol 92; WhoMW 74, 76, 80, 82, 84, 86, 88, 92, 93, 96; WhoUSWr 88; WhoWor 95, 96, 97; WhoWrEP 89, 92, 95; WorAl; WorAlBi; WrDr 76, 86, 94, 96*

Terman, Lewis Madison
American. Psychologist
Publisher of the Stanford-Binet intelligence test.
b. Jan 15, 1877 in Johnson County, Indiana
d. Dec 21, 1956 in Palo Alto, California
Source: *AmDec 1910; BiDAmEd; BiDPsy; BioIn 4, 5, 9, 10, 12, 14, 16, 18; DcAmB S6; DcAmImH; EncWB; IndAu 1917; InSci; NamesHP; ObitOF 79; OxCAmH; REnAL; WebAB 74, 79; WhAm 3; WhE&EA; WhNAA*

Ternina, Milka
Croatian. Opera Singer
Outstanding Wagnerian soprano; sang first NY, London *Tosca,* 1901.
b. Dec 19, 1863 in Belgisc
d. May 18, 1941 in Zagreb, Yugoslavia
Source: *Baker 78, 84, 92; BioIn 1, 11; CmOp; InWom; MetOEnc; MusSN; NewEOp 71; NewGrDM 80; NewGrDO; OxDcOp; PenDiMP*

Terra, Daniel J(ames)
American. Art Collector, Diplomat
Founded Terra Museum of American Art, Chicago, 1980; ambassador at large for cultural affairs, 1981-89.
b. Jun 9, 1911 in Philadelphia, Pennsylvania
d. Jun 28, 1996 in Washington, District of Columbia
Source: *BioIn 12, 13; CurBio 87, 96N; St&PR 87; WhAm 11; WhoAm 76, 78, 80, 82, 84, 86, 90, 92, 94, 95, 96; WhoAmA 84; WhoAmP 81, 83, 85, 87, 89, 91, 93, 95; WhoFI 74, 75, 77, 79, 81, 83, 85; WhoMW 74, 76, 78, 80, 82, 86; WhoWor 76, 78, 82, 84*

Terrell, Mary Church
American. Social Reformer
Worked to improve women's rights, equality for black people; first pres., Nat. Association of Colored Women, 1896-1904.
b. Sep 23, 1863 in Memphis, Tennessee
d. Jul 24, 1954 in Annapolis, Maryland
Source: *BiDSocW; BioIn 17, 18, 19, 20, 21; BlkWrNE; ConBlB 9; CurBio 42, 54; DcAmB S5; DcAmNB; EncAACR; EncSoH; HanAmWH; InWom; LegTOT; NegAl 76, 83, 89; NotBlAW 1; PeoHis; SelBAAf; WhAm 3; WomEdUS; WomFir; WorAl; WorAlBi*

Terrell, Tammi
American. Singer
Best known for duets with Marvin Gaye: "Your Precious Love," 1967; "Ain't Nothing Like the Real Thing," 1968.
b. Apr 29, 1945 in Philadelphia, Pennsylvania
d. Mar 16, 1970 in Philadelphia, Pennsylvania
Source: *RolSEnR 83*

Terris, Norma
American. Actor
Played Magnolia Hawks in *Showboat,* 1927, 1932.
b. Nov 13, 1904 in Columbus, Kansas
d. Nov 15, 1989 in Lyme, Connecticut
Source: *AnObit 1989; EncMT; Film 2; WhoHol A; WhoThe 77A; WhThe*

Terris, Susan
American. Children's Author
Writings include *The Upstairs Witch and the Downstairs Witch,* 1970; *Ammanda, the Panda, and the Redhead,* 1975.
b. May 6, 1937 in Saint Louis, Missouri
Source: *AuBYP 2S; BioIn 9; ConAu 12NR, 29R; FifBJA; IntAu&W 76, 77, 82, 89, 91, 93; SmATA 3, 77; WhoAmW 75; WhoWrEP 89, 92, 95; WrDr 76, 80, 82, 84, 86, 88, 90, 92, 94, 96*

Terry, Alfred Howe
American. Military Leader, Lawyer
Major-general who led campaign against Sioux involving Custer massacre at Little Big Horn, 1876.
b. Nov 10, 1827 in Hartford, Connecticut
d. Dec 16, 1890 in New Haven, Connecticut
Source: *AmBi; ApCAB; BioIn 7, 17; CivWDc; DcAmB; DcAmMiB; Drake; HarEnUS; NatCAB 4; NewCol 75; REnAW; TwCBDA; WebAB 74, 79; WebAMB; WebBD 83; WhAm HS; WhCiWar; WhNaAH*

Terry, Bill
[William Harold Terry]
"Memphis Bill"
American. Baseball Player, Baseball Manager
First baseman, NY Giants, 1923-36; last player to bat .400 in NL, 1930; Hall of Fame, 1954.
b. Oct 30, 1898 in Atlanta, Georgia
d. Jan 9, 1989 in Jacksonville, Florida
Source: *AnObit 1989; BiDAmSp BB; BioIn 2, 4, 5, 7, 8, 9, 14, 15, 16, 20; NewYTBS 89; WhoProB 73; WhoSpor*

Terry, Ellen Alicia, Dame
English. Actor
Acting partner with Henry Irving, 1878-1902; carried on famed correspondence with George Bernard Shaw.
b. Feb 27, 1848 in Coventry, England
d. Jul 21, 1928 in Kent, England
Source: *FamA&A; Film 1; HerW; IntDcWB; LngCTC; NewC; OxCThe 67; PlP&P; REn; WhAm 1; WhDW; WhoStg 1906, 1908; WhScrn 77; WorAl*

Terry, Luther Leonidas
American. Physician
Surgeon general, whose study revealed smoking hazardous to health, 1964.
b. Sep 15, 1911 in Red Level, Alabama
d. Mar 29, 1985 in Philadelphia, Pennsylvania
Source: *AmMWSc 73P, 76P, 79, 82; BiDrACP 79; BioIn 5, 6, 11; ConAu P-2; CurBio 61; FacFETw; InSci; IntWW 74, 75, 76, 77, 78, 79, 80, 81, 82, 83; SmATA 11; St&PR 84; WhAm 8; WhoAm 74, 76, 78, 80, 82, 84; WhoE 85; WhoWor 82*

Terry, Megan
[Megan Duffy]
American. Dramatist
Plays include Obie winner, *The Tommy Allen Show,* 1970.
b. Jul 22, 1932 in Seattle, Washington
Source: *AmWomD; AmWomWr; ArtclWW 2; BenetAL 91; BioIn 10, 12, 15, 16; CamGWoT; ConAmD; ConAu 3BS, 43NR, 77; ConDr 73, 77, 82, 88, 93; ConLC 19; ConTFT 5; ConWomD; CroCD; CrtSuDr; DrAP 75; DrAPF 80; EncWT; FemiCLE; GrLiveH; IntAu&W 89, 91, 93; IntDcT 2; InWom SUP; McGEWD 84; ModWoWr; NatPD 81; NotNAT; NotWoAT; OxCThe 83;*

OxCWoWr 95; PlP&P; RAdv 14; WhoAm 76, 78, 80, 82, 84, 86, 88, 90, 92, 94, 95, 96, 97; WhoAmW 95, 97; WhoEnt 92; WhoThe 77, 81; WhoWor 80; WorAu 1970; WrDr 76, 80, 82, 84, 86, 88, 90, 92, 94, 96

Terry, Paul H
American. Cartoonist, Producer
Best known for animation of Mighty Mouse.
b. Feb 19, 1887 in San Mateo, California
d. Oct 25, 1971 in New York, New York
Source: *BioIn 9; DcFM; FilmgC; WorECom*

Terry, Randall A.
American. Social Reformer
Controversial leader of anti-abortion group Operation Rescue, 1984—.
b. Apr 25, 1959 in Rochester, New York
Source: *BioIn 16; CurBio 94; News 91; St&PR 87*

Terry, Sonny
American. Singer, Musician
Harmonica player and blues singer; partner to guitarist Brownie McGhee.
b. Oct 24, 1911 in Greensboro, Georgia
d. Mar 11, 1986 in Mineola, New York
Source: *AnObit 1986; Baker 92; BiDAfM; BiDAmM; BiDJaz; BluesWW; CmpEPM; DrBlPA, 90; EncFCWM 69; EncJzS; EncRk 88; GuBlues; IlEncJ; InB&W 80; NewAmDM; NewGrDA 86; NewYTBS 86; OxCPMus; PenEncP; WhAm 9; WhoRock 81*

Terry, Walte
American. Critic
Dance critic, 193
b. May 14, 1913
York
d. Oct 4, 1982 in
Source: *AmAu&B;*
2, 3; BioIn 8, 13; C
21R, 107; DancEn 7
NewYTBS 82; SmATA
WhoAm 74, 76, 78, 8

Terry-Thomas
[Thomas Terry Hoar-Ste
English. Actor, Comedia
Character actor known fo
smile; films include *I'm*
Jack, 1960, *Those Magn*
Their Flying Machines,
b. Jul 14, 1911 in London,
d. Jan 8, 1990 in Godalming
Source: *AnObit 1990; BioIn*
11, 13, 16, 17; ConTFT 10;
90, 90N; DcArts; DcNaB 198
EncEurC; FacFETw; FilmEn; FilmgC; ForYSC; HalFC 80, 84, 88; IlWWBF; IntDcF 2-3; IntMPA 75, 76, 78, 79, 80, 81, 82; IntWW 82, 83, 89; ItaFilm; LegTOT; MotPP; MovMk; NewYTBS 90; QDrFCA 92; Who 74, 82, 83, 85, 88, 90; WhoCom; WhoHol A; WhoHrs 80; WhoWor 74, 76; WorAl; WorAlBi

Tertullian, Quintus Septimus Florens
Roman. Writer
Known as one of fathers of church; writings attack official attitude toward Christianity.
b. 160?
d. 230?
Source: *BbD; BiD&SB; BioIn 1, 2, 3, 5, 6, 7, 9; CasWL; DcCathB; Grk&L; LinLib L, S; McGEWB; NewC; OxCEng 67; PenC CL; WhDW*

Teschemacher, Frank
American. Jazz Musician
Hot clarinetist, active, 1920s-30s.
b. Mar 14, 1906 in Kansas City, Missouri
d. Feb 29, 1932 in Chicago, Illinois
Source: *AllMusG; BiDAmM; BiDJaz; BioIn 16; CmpEPM; IlEncJ; NewAmDM; NewGrDA 86; NewGrDJ 88, 94; NewGrDM 80; OxCPMus; PenEncP; WhAm 4, HSA; WhoJazz 72*

Teschner, Richard
Austrian. Puppeteer
Improved on existing Javanese rod puppets; helped popularize ro puppets in Europe and the US.
b. Mar 22, 1879 in Carlsbad, Bohemia
d. Jul 4, 1948 in Vienna, Austria
Source: *BioIn 2; DcPup; Ent*

Tesh, John
American. TV

Utice,

d. Jul 1, 1996 in Sydney, Nova Scotia, Canada
Source: *BioIn 14, 17, 21; ConAu 105, 152; ConDr 82; ConLC 40; ConTFT 5; CrtSuDr; CurBio 91, 96N; HalFC 84; IntMPA 86, 92, 94, 96; NewYTBS 27, 80, 82; VarWW 85; WhAm 11; WhoAm 82, 84, 86, 88, 90, 92, 94, 95, 96; WhoEnt 92; WorAu 1985; WrDr 84, 86, 88, 90, 92, 94, 96*

Tesla, Nikola
American. Engineer, Inventor
Pioneer in electric power, marketed first electric appliance, three blade fan, 1889.
b. Jul 10, 1856 in Smiljan, Austria-Hungary
d. Jan 7, 1943 in New York, New York
Source: *ApCAB SUP; AsBiEn; BiESc; BioIn 12, 13, 14, 15, 16, 18, 20, 21; CamDcSc; ChhPo S3; CurBio 43; DcAmB S3; DcNAA; DcScB; EncO&P 2S1, 3; GayN; InSci; LarDcSc; LegTOT; McGEWB; NewCol 75; NotTwCS; ObitOF 79; OxCAmH; WebAB 74, 79; WhAm 2; WhDW; WorAl; WorAlBi; WorInv*

Testaverde, Vinny
"Miami Nice"
American. Football Player
Quarterback, won Heisman Trophy, 1986; signed with Tampa Bay as America's richest draft pick, 1987.
b. Nov 13, 1963 in New York, New York
Source: *ConNews 87-2; LegTOT; WhoSpor*

Tetrazzini, Luisa
Italian. Opera Singer
Soprano who debuted in NYC, 1908: 33 operas include *Rigoletto*
b. Jun 29, 187

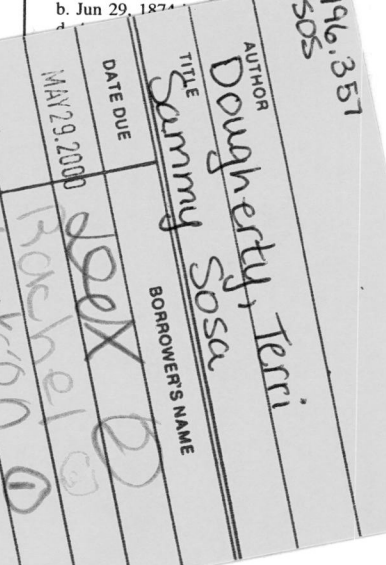

d. Apr 13, 1868 in Magdela, Ethiopia
Source: *DcAfHiB 86; McGEWB*

Tex, Joe
[Joseph Arrington, Jr.]
American. Singer
Had 1964 hit "Hold On to What You've Got."
b. Aug 8, 1933 in Rogers, Texas
d. Aug 13, 1982 in Navasota, Texas
Source: *BioIn 13; EncPR&S 89; EncRk 88; GuBlues; InB&W 80; LegTOT; NewGrDA 86; OxCPMus; PenEncP;*

RkOn 78; RolSEnR 83; SoulM; WhoBlA 77; WhoRock 81

Tex and Jinx
[Jinx Falkenburg; Tex McCrary]
American. Radio Performers
Husband and wife team; produced own radio, TV shows, 1940s-50s.
Source: *BioIn 1, 2, 3, 12, 17; CurBio 53*

Texas Tornadoes, The
[Freddie (Baldemar Huerta) Fender; Flaco (Leonardo Jiminez) Jiminez; Augie Meyers; Doug Sahm]
American. Music Group
Country/rock group; solo performers before joining together in 1989; Grammy award for best Mexican-American performance, 1991.
Source: *ConMus 8; WhoRocM 82*

Tey, Josephine
[Elizabeth Mackintosh]
Scottish. Author
Mystery novels include *Brat Farrar,* 1949; *To Love and Be Wise,* 1950.
b. 1897 in Inverness, Scotland
d. Feb 13, 1952
Source: *CamGLE; Chambr 3; DcLEL; EncMys; EvLB; InWom SUP; LegTOT; LngCTC; NewC; PenC ENG; REn; TwCA SUP; TwCCr&M 80, 85, 91; TwCLC 14; TwCWr*

Teyte, Maggie, Dame
[Margaret Tate]
English. Opera Singer
Lead singer in opera, 1907-19; London stage musicals include *A Little Dutch Girl,* 1920.
b. Apr 17, 1888 in Wolverhampton, England
d. May 27, 1976 in London, England
Source: *Baker 78, 84, 92; BioIn 10, 11, 12, 14; BriBkM 80; CmOp; ConAu 65; ContDcW 89; CurBio 45, 76, 76N; DcArts; EncMT; FacFETw; IntDcOp; IntDcWB; InWom SUP; MetOEnc; MusSN; NewAmDM; NewEOp 71; NewGrDA 86; NewGrDM 80; NewGrDO; NewYTBS 76; OxDcOp; PenDiMP; Who 74*

Thackeray, William Makepeace
[Jeames; Mister Brown; George Savage Fitzboodle; Michael Angelo Titmarsh; Theophile Wagstaff; Charles James Yellowplush]
British. Author
Wrote satirical novel *Vanity Fair,* 1848.
b. Jul 18, 1811 in Calcutta, India
d. Dec 24, 1863 in London, England
Source: *Alli; AtlBL; BbD; Benet 87, 96; BiD&SB; BioIn 1, 2, 3, 4, 5, 6, 7, 8, 9, 10, 11, 12, 13, 14, 15, 16, 18, 21; BlmGEL; BritAu 19; BritWr 5; CamGEL; CamGLE; CarSB; CasWL; CelCen; Chambr 3; ChhPo, S1, S2, S3; CnDBLB 4; CrtT 3, 4; CyWA 58; DcArts; DcBiA; DcBiPP; DcBrBI; DcBrWA; DcEnA, A; DcEnL; DcEuL; DcInB; DcIrL 96; DcLB 159, 163; DcLEL; DcPup; Dis&D; EncO&P 3; EvLB; FamSYP; GrWrEL N; HsB&A; LegTOT; LinLib L, S; LngCEL; MagSWL; McGEWB; MouLC 3; NewC; NewCBEL; NinCLC 5, 14, 22, 43; Novels; OxCAmL 65, 83, 95; OxCEng 67, 85, 95; OxCIri; PenC ENG; PseudAu; RAdv 1, 14; RComWL; REn; RfGEnL 91; ScF&FL 1A, 92; SmATA 23; StaCVF; VicBrit; WebE&AL; WhDW; WhoChL; WorAl; WorAlBi; WorLitC*

Thalberg, Irving Grant
"The Boy Wonder"
American. Producer
Head of MGM production under Louis Mayer, 1923-36.
b. May 30, 1899 in New York, New York
d. Sep 14, 1936 in Santa Monica, California
Source: *AmCulL; BiDFilm; BioIn 16, 17, 19; CmCal; ConAu 41R; DcAmB S2; DcArts; DcFM; FilmgC; NatCAB 27; OxCFilm; WebAB 74, 79; WhAm 4, HSA; WorAl; WorEFlm*

Thales
Greek. Philosopher
First to search for rational explanation of natural phenomenon replacing superstition with science.
b. 600BC in Miletus, Asia Minor
d. 540BC
Source: *AsBiEn; BiD&SB; BiESc; CasWL; DcInv; Grk&L; NewC; PenC CL; REn; WorAl*

Thalheimer, Richard
American. Businessman
Founder and pres. The Sharper Image, 1977—.
b. 1948 in Little Rock, Arkansas
Source: *BioIn 13; ConNews 85-2; News 88; St&PR 91*

Thalmann, Ernst
German. Political Leader
Communist leader responsible for creating Kommunistische Partei Deutschlands into second most powerful Communist Party; executed at Buchenwald concentration camp.
b. Apr 16, 1886 in Hamburg, Germany
d. Aug 18, 1944 in Buchenwald, Germany
Source: *EncGRNM; EncTR 91*

Thang, Ton Duc
Vietnamese. Government Official
Pres., Vietnam, 1969-80.
b. Aug 20, 1888 in Long Xuyen Province, Vietnam
d. Mar 30, 1980 in Hanoi, Vietnam
Source: *AnObit 1980; BioIn 8, 9; IntWW 74; WhoWor 74, 76, 78*

Thani, Shiekh Khalifa Ben Hamad al
Qatari. Ruler
Amir of Qatar, 1972—; expanded economic, social reform; stopped most of royal family's extravagance, privileges.
b. 1932 in Rayyan, Qatar
Source: *WhoWor 74*

Thant, U
Burmese. Statesman
Secretary-general, UN, 1962-72; focused on problems of Third World.
b. Jan 22, 1909 in Pantanaw, Burma
d. Nov 25, 1974 in New York, New York
Source: *BioIn 12, 18; ColdWar 1; ConAu 108; CurBio 62, 75N; EncCW; IntWW 74; LegTOT; LinLib S; McGEWB; NewYTBS 74; ObitT 1971; OxCLaw; WhAm 6; WhDW; Who 74; WhoAm 74; WhoWor 74; WorAl; WorAlBi*

Thao, Tran Duc
Vietnamese. Philosopher
Existentialist thinker with ties to Sartre.
b. 1917 in Hanoi, Vietnam
d. Apr 24, 1993 in Paris, France

Tharaud, Jean
French. Author
With brother Jerome, wrote many magazine articles and books; *Notre cher Peguy,* 1926.
b. May 9, 1877 in Saint-Junien, France
d. Apr 9, 1952 in Paris, France
Source: *BioIn 1, 2, 3, 4; ObitOF 79; ObitT 1951*

Tharaud, Jerome
French. Author
With brother Jean, wrote many magazine articles and books; *Dingley,* 1902.
b. May 18, 1874 in Saint-Junien, France
d. Jan 28, 1953 in Varengeville-sur-Mer, France
Source: *BioIn 1, 3, 4; ObitOF 79; ObitT 1951; TwCA*

Tharoor, Shashi
Indian. Author
Author of *The Great Indian Novel,* 1991, a retelling of India's history.
b. 1956 in London, England
Source: *BioIn 19, 20, 21; ConAu 141; ConLC 70; ConNov 96; IntAu&W 91; NotAsAm; WorAu 1985; WrDr 96*

Tharp, Louise Hall
American. Author
Biographies include *The Peabody Sisters of Salem,* 1950; *Mrs. Jack,* 1965.
b. Jun 19, 1898 in Oneonta, New York
Source: *AmAu&B; Au&Wr 71; AuBYP 2, 3; ChhPo; ConAu 1R, 33NR; CurBio 55; ForWC 70; MorJA; RAdv 1; SmATA 3; WhoAm 74; WorAu 1950*

Tharp, Twyla
American. Choreographer, Dancer
Choreographer, Paul Taylor Dance Co., 1963-65; founder Twyla Tharp Dance Founda tion, 1965-87; artistic associate

and resident choreographer American Ballet Th eatre, 1987-91.
b. Jul 1, 1941 in Portland, Indiana
Source: *BiDD; BioIn 10; CelR 90; ConTFT 12; CurBio 75; DcArts; DcTwCCu 1; FacFETw; GoodHs; GrLiveH; IntDcB; IntWW 89, 91, 93; InWom SUP; LegTOT; LibW; NewGrDA 86; News 92; NewYTBS 76; NotWoAT; RAdv 14; WhoAm 78, 80, 82, 84, 86, 88, 92, 94, 95, 96, 97; WhoAmW 79, 81, 83, 85, 87, 89, 91, 93, 95, 97; WhoE 79, 81, 83, 85, 86, 89, 91, 93, 95, 97; WhoEnt 92; WomFir; WorAl; WorAlBi*

Thatcher, Margaret (Hilda Roberts)
"Iron Lady"
English. Political Leader
Britian's first female prime minister, 1979-91.
b. Oct 13, 1925 in Grantham, England
Source: *ColdWar 1, 2; ConHero 1; ContDcW 89; CurBio 75, 89; DcAmC; EncCW; EncWB; HisDBrE; HisWorL; IntDcWB; IntWW 74; InWom SUP; LegTOT; NewYTBS 75, 79, 83, 95; PolLCWE; Who 82, 83, 85, 88, 90, 92; WhoAmW 74; WhoWor 87; WomStre; WomWR; WorAlBi*

Thaw, Harry Kendall
American. Murderer
Killed architect Stanford White in Madison Square Garden, 1906; ruled insane.
b. Feb 1, 1871 in Pittsburgh, Pennsylvania
d. Feb 22, 1947 in Miami Beach, Florida
Source: *BioIn 1, 5, 6, 8, 9, 11; DcAmB S4; EncACr; WorAl*

Thaxter, Celia
American. Poet
Verse volumes include *Driftwood,* 1879.
b. Jun 29, 1835 in Portsmouth, New Hampshire
d. Aug 26, 1894 in Appledore, New Hampshire
Source: *BenetAL 91; BioIn 1, 2, 6, 13; ChrP; FemiCLE; NotAW; OxCAmL 83; REn*

Thaxter, Phyllis
American. Actor
Mother of Skye Aubrey; films include *Sea of Grass,* 1947.
b. Nov 20, 1920 in Portland, Maine
Source: *BiE&WWA; FilmgC; HalFC 84; MGM; MovMk; NotNAT; WhoHol A; WhoThe 77, 81*

Thayer, Abbott Handerson
American. Artist
Painted landscapes, portraits, 1879-91; turned later to figure paintings.
b. Aug 12, 1849 in Boston, Massachusetts
d. May 29, 1921 in Monadnock, New Hampshire
Source: *AmBi; ApCAB; BioIn 2, 4, 9, 11, 13; BriEAA; DcAmB; McGDA; PeoHis; WhAm 1*

Thayer, Ernest L
American. Author
Wrote *Casey at the Bat,* 1888.
b. Aug 14, 1863 in Lawrence, Massachusetts
d. Aug 21, 1940 in Santa Barbara, California
Source: *AuBYP 2; BioIn 6; EvLB*

Thayer, Mary Van Rensselaer
[Molly Thayer]
American. Journalist, Author
Wrote two biographies of Jacqueline Kennedy.
b. 1903? in Southampton, New York
d. Dec 12, 1983 in Washington, District of Columbia
Source: *ConAu 111*

Thayer, Sylvanus, General
"Father of the Military Academy"
American. Educator, Military Leader
Superintendent, West Point, 1817-33; instituted reforms, established efficient organization.
b. Jun 9, 1785 in Braintree, Massachusetts
d. Sep 7, 1872 in Braintree, Massachusetts
Source: *Alli; AmBi; ApCAB; BiDAmEd; BioIn 4, 5, 8, 11, 13; CivWDc; CyEd; DcAmAu; DcAmB; DcAmMiB; DcNAA; Drake; HarEnUS; McGEWB; NatCAB 7; OxCAmH; TwCBDA; WebAB 74, 79; WebAMB; WhAm HS; WhCiWar*

Thayer, Tiffany Ellsworth
American. Screenwriter, Actor
Appeared in films, 1920-25; wrote *Devil on Horseback,* 1936; *Chicago Deadline,* 1949.
b. Mar 1, 1902 in Freeport, Illinois
d. Aug 23, 1959 in Nantucket, Massachusetts
Source: *AmAu&B; TwCA, SUP; WhAm 3; WhE&EA*

Thebom, Blanche
American. Opera Singer
Mezzo-soprano; starred with NY Met., 1940-67.
b. Sep 19, 1919 in Monessen, Pennsylvania
Source: *Baker 84; BiDAmM; BioIn 2, 3, 4, 5, 10; BioNews 74; CurBio 48; IntWWM 77, 80; InWom, SUP; NewEOp 71; WhoAm 74, 76; WhoAmW 58, 64, 66, 68, 70, 72, 74, 75; WhoWor 74*

Thedosius I
Roman. Ruler
Ruled Holy Roman Empire before division of East, West, 379-395; proclaimed son, Honorius, emperor of the West, 395.
b. Jan 11, 346? in Cauca, Spain
d. Jan 17, 395 in Milan, Spain
Source: *BioIn 1, 6, 9; LinLib S; McGEWB; NewCol 75; WebBD 83*

Theiler, Max
American. Scientist, Physician, Engineer
Research on yellow fever led to developing vaccine; won Nobel Prize in medicine, 1951.
b. Jan 30, 1899 in Pretoria, South Africa
d. Aug 11, 1972 in New Haven, Connecticut
Source: *AsBiEn; BiESc; BioIn 2, 3, 4, 5, 6, 9, 10, 14, 15, 20; CamDcSc; CurBio 52, 72, 72N; DcAmMeB 84; EncSoA; InSci; LarDcSc; McGEWB; McGMS 80; NewYTBE 72; NobelP; NotTwCS; OxCMed 86; WhAm 5; WhoNob, 90, 95*

Theismann, Joe
[Joseph Robert Theismann]
American. Football Player, Sportscaster
Two-time all-pro quarterback, 1971-85, mostly with Washington; suffered career-en ding broken leg during game; anallyst, CBS NFL broadcasts, 1987-88; analyst, ESPN NFL broadcasts, 1988—.
b. Sep 9, 1949 in New Brunswick, New Jersey
Source: *BiDAmSp FB; BioIn 12, 13; FootReg 86; NewYTBS 82, 84; WhoAm 80, 82, 84, 86, 88, 94, 95, 96, 97; WhoE 85; WhoFtbl 74; WhoSSW 95; WhoWor 80*

Themistocles
Greek. Military Leader
Athenian commander who developed naval strength; led victory against Persians at Salamis, 480 BC.
b. 524?BC
d. 460?BC
Source: *BioIn 20, 21; DcBiPP; GenMudB; LegTOT; McGEWB; NewCol 75; OxCClL 89; REn; WhDW; WorAl; WorAlBi*

Theocritus
Greek. Poet
Originator of pastoral poetry; sensitivity to nature imitated by later poets.
b. 310BC in Syracuse, Sicily, Italy
d. 250BC
Source: *BbD; BiD&SB; CasWL; ChhPo; CyWA 58; DcArts; DcBiPP; DcEnL; Grk&L; LegTOT; McGEWB; NewC; OxCEng 67; PenC CL; RAdv 14; RComWL; REn; WhDW; WorAlBi*

Theodora
Roman. Consort
Married Justinian I, 523; became joint ruler of Byzantine empire, 527.
b. 508
d. 548
Source: *Benet 87, 96; DcBiPP; Dis&D; InWom, SUP; NewCol 75; PlP&P; REn; WebBD 83; WomFir*

Theodoracopulos, Taki
Greek. Journalist
Columnist for the English magazine *Spectator.*
b. Aug 11, 1937 in Athens, Greece
Source: *BioIn 12; CelR 90; ConAu 129*

Theodorakis, Mikis
Greek. Composer
Revitalized modern Greek music; wrote score for *Zorba the Greek,* 1964.
b. Jul 29, 1925 in Chios, Greece
Source: *Baker 78, 84, 92; BioIn 8, 9, 10, 12, 16, 18; CurBio 73; EncEurC; FilmEn; IntDcF 1-4, 2-4; IntMPA 88, 92, 94, 96; IntWW 74, 75, 76, 77, 78, 79, 80, 81, 82, 83, 89, 91, 93; IntWWM 80; ItaFilm; MusMk; NewGrDM 80; OxCFilm; OxCPMus; WhoFr 79; WhoWor 74, 78, 80, 82, 84, 87, 89, 91, 93, 95; WorEFlm*

Theodorescu, Ion N
Romanian. Poet, Translator
Romania's poet laureate; wrote verse volume *Cuvinte Potrivite,* 1927.
b. May 20, 1880 in Bucharest, Romania
d. Jul 14, 1967 in Bucharest, Romania
Source: *ClDMEL 80; ConAu 116; WorAu 1970*

Theorell, (Axel) Hugh Teodor
Swedish. Biochemist
Won 1955 Nobel Prize for medicine; pioneered enzyme research.
b. Jul 6, 1903 in Linkoping, Sweden
d. Aug 15, 1982 in Stockholm, Sweden
Source: *AnObit 1982; AsBiEn; CurBio 56, 82N; IntWW 81; NewYTBS 82; Who 83N; WhoNob; WhoWor 78*

Theresa, Saint
Spanish. Religious Figure, Author
Noted for mystic visions; reformed Carmelite order.
b. Mar 28, 1515 in Avila, Spain
d. Oct 4, 1582 in Alva, Spain
Source: *DcBiPP; DcEuL; InWom; LinLib L; McGEWB; NewC; NewCol 75; OxCEng 67, 85, 95; REn*

Therese of Lisieux, Saint
"The Little Flower"
French. Religious Figure
Carmelite nun called the "greatest saint of modern times"; patron of aviators, foreign ministers.
b. Jan 2, 1873 in Alencon, France
d. Sep 30, 1897 in Lisieux, France
Source: *DcCathB; Dis&D; LuthC 75; NewCol 75*

Theriault, Yves
Canadian. Author
Prolific writer for radio and TV; books include *Agaguk,* 1958; *N'Tsuk.*
b. Nov 28, 1916 in Quebec, Quebec, Canada
d. Oct 20, 1983 in Montreal, Quebec, Canada
Source: *BenetAL 91; BioIn 10; CanWr; CanWW 70, 79, 80, 81, 83; CasWL; ConAu 102; ConLC 79; CreCan 1; DcLB 88; OxCCan; OxCCanT; REnAL*

Theroux, Paul Edward
American. Author
Wrote prize-winning novel *Picture Palace,* 1978; best-selling travel yarn *Kingdom By the Sea,* 1983.
b. Apr 10, 1941 in Medford, Massachusetts
Source: *Au&Wr 71; ConLC 28; ConNov 86; ConPo 70; NewYTBS 76, 78; OxCAmL 83; SmATA 44; WhoAm 86; WrDr 86*

Thespis
Greek. Actor, Dramatist, Poet
Invented tragedy in Greek tradition; originated actor's role; actors called thespians in his honor.
b. fl. 6th cent. BC in Attica, Greece
Source: *Benet 87, 96; BlmGEL; CamGWoT; CasWL; DcArts; DcBiPP; EncWT; Ent; Grk&L; LegTOT; LinLib L, S; NewC; NewCol 75; NotNAT B; OxCClL, 89; OxCThe 67, 83; PenC CL; REn; WorAl; WorAlBi*

They Might Be Giants
American. Music Group
Pop-rock duo; wildly inventive videos caught the attention of MTV viewers.
Source: *AntBDN G; BioIn 16; ConMus 7; DcBrWA; DcVicP 2*

Thibault, Conrad
American. Singer
Baritone; active in radio, 1930s.
b. Nov 13, 1908 in Northbridge, Massachusetts
d. Aug 1, 1987 in New York, New York
Source: *BiDAmM; CmpEPM; WhoAm 74, 76, 78, 80, 82, 84, 86*

Thicke, Alan
Canadian. Actor
Star of TV series "Growing Pains," 1985-92.
b. Mar 1, 1947 in Kirkland Lake, Ontario, Canada
Source: *ConTFT 6; CurBio 87; IntMPA 96; LegTOT; WhoHol 92; WorAlBi*

Thiebaud, (Morton) Wayne
American. Artist
Realist painter best known for use of light, structure.
b. Nov 15, 1920 in Mesa, Arizona
Source: *AmArt; BioIn 10, 11, 12, 15, 17, 19, 20, 21; CmCal; ConArt 77, 83, 89, 96; ConAu 45; CurBio 87; DcAmArt; DcCAA 71, 77, 88, 94; DcCAr 81; IntWW 89, 91, 93; News 91, 91-1; OxCTwCA; PhDcTCA 77; PrintW 83, 85; WhoAm 74, 76, 78, 80, 82, 84, 86, 88, 92, 96; WhoAmA 73, 76, 78, 80, 82, 84, 86, 89, 91, 93; WhoWor 74, 76; WorArt 1950*

Thierry, Augustin
[Jacques-Nicolas-Augustin Thierry]
French. Historian
Best known for Romantic interpretations of Middle Ages.
b. 1795 in Blois, France
d. 1856
Source: *BioIn 11; DcEuL; Dis&D; OxCFr; WebBD 83*

Thiers, Adolphe
[Louis-Adolphe Thiers]
French. Statesman
Held public office, 1832-73; premier, 1836, 1840; first pres. of Third Republic, 1871-73, resigned.
b. Apr 15, 1797 in Marseilles, France
d. Sep 3, 1877 in Saint-Germain-en-Laye, France
Source: *BiDFrPL; BioIn 8, 9, 10, 11, 17; OxCFr; WebBD 83*

Thigpen, Bobby
[Robert Thomas Thigpen]
American. Baseball Player
Relief pitcher, Chicago White Sox, 1986—; set ML record for saves in a season, 57, 1990, breaking Dave Righetti's mark.
b. Jul 17, 1963 in Tallahassee, Florida
Source: *Ballpl 90; LegTOT; WhoAm 92, 94*

Thill, Georges
French. Opera Singer
Leading tenor, Paris Opera, 1925 to end of WW II.
b. Dec 14, 1897 in Paris, France
d. Oct 17, 1984 in Draguignan, France
Source: *AnObit 1984; Baker 84, 92; BioIn 4, 10, 14; CmOp; IntDcOp; MetOEnc; NewEOp 71; NewGrDM 80; NewGrDO; NewYTBS 84; OxDcOp; PenDiMP*

Thin Lizzy
[Eric Bell; Brian Downey; Scott Gorham; Phil Lynott; Garry Moore; Brian Robertson; Midge Ure; Darren Wharton; Snowy White]
Irish. Music Group
Hard-nosed rock band, known for successful album *Jailbreak,* 1976.
Source: *ConMuA 80A; ConMus 13; CurBio 48, 54; EncPR&S 89; EncRk 88; EncRkSt; HarEnR 86; IlEncRk; LesBEnT, 92; OnThGG; PenEncP; RkOn 78; RolSEnR 83; WhoRock 81; WhoRocM 82*

Thinnes, Roy
American. Actor
On TV in "Long, Hot Summer," 1965-66; "Invaders," 1966-68; "Falcon Crest," 1983.
b. Apr 6, 1936 in Chicago, Illinois
Source: *ConTFT 6; FilmgC; IntMPA 84; WhoAm 82, 84; WhoHol A*

Third World
[Bunny "Rugs" Clarke; Michael "Ibo" Cooper; Stephen "Cat" Coore; Richard Daley; Orvin "Carrot" Jarrett; Willie Stewart]
Jamaican. Music Group
Reggae band formed 1973; hits include "Sense of Purpose," 1985.

Source: *BioNews 74; ConMus 13; EncPR&S 89; InB&W 85A; RkOn 85*

Thirty-Eight Special
[Don Barnes; Steve Brookins; Jeff Carlisi; Jack Grondin; Larry Junstron; Donnie Van Zandt]
American. Music Group
Formed 1979; albums include *Tour de Force,* 1984.
Source: *EncPR&S 89; HarEnR 86; PenEncP; RkOn 85; RolSEnR 83; WhoRock 81; WhoRocM 82*

Thoma, Hans
German. Artist
Influenced by Courbet; early landscapes depict native Black Forest.
b. Oct 2, 1839 in Bernau, Germany
d. Nov 7, 1924 in Karlsruhe, Germany
Source: *ClaDrA; Dis&D; LuthC 75; McGDA; NewCol 75; OxCArt; OxDcArt; WebBD 83*

Thomas, Saint
[Teoma]
"Doubting Thomas"
Biblical Figure
One of 12 Apostles; his life is outlined in John's Gospel; remembered for doubting the Resurrection.
d. 53
Source: *Alli; Benet 87, 96; BiB N; BioIn 1, 2, 3, 4, 5, 6, 7, 8, 9, 10, 11, 14, 15; ChhPo; DcBrECP; DcCathB; DcNaB; DcVicP 2; DcWomA; InWom SUP; McGDA; NewC; REn; WebBD 83*

Thomas, (Charles Louis) Ambroise
French. Composer
Wrote operas *Mignon,* 1866; *Hamlet,* 1868.
b. Aug 5, 1811 in Metz, France
d. Feb 12, 1896 in Paris, France
Source: *Baker 78, 84, 92; BioIn 3, 4, 7, 12; BriBkM 80; CelCen; CmOp; CmpBCM; DcCathB; DcCom 77; DcCom&M 79; Dis&D; GrComp; IntDcOp; LinLib S; MetOEnc; MusMk; NewAmDM; NewCol 75; NewEOp 71; NewGrDM 80; NewGrDO; NewOxM; NotNAT B; OxCEng 85, 95; OxCMus; OxDcOp; PenDiMP A*

Thomas, B(illy) J(oe)
American. Singer
Hits include "Raindrops Keep Fallin' On My Head," 1970; "Somebody Done Somebody Wrong Song," 1974.
b. Aug 7, 1942 in Houston, Texas
Source: *EncFCWM 83; EncPR&S 74; WhoAm 84, 86, 88, 90, 92, 94; WhoEnt 92*

Thomas, Betty
[Betty Thomas Nienhauser]
American. Actor
Played Lucy Bates on TV series "Hill Street Blues," 1981-87.
b. Jul 27, 1948 in Saint Louis, Missouri
Source: *BioIn 13; ConTFT 7, 15; IntMPA 92, 94, 96; VarWW 85; WhoTelC*

Thomas, Bill
American. Designer
Won Oscar for costume designs in *Spartacus,* 1960.
b. Oct 13, 1921 in Chicago, Illinois
Source: *IntMPA 75, 76, 77, 78, 79, 80, 81, 82, 84, 86, 88; VarWW 85*

Thomas, Billy
[Our Gang]
"Buckwheat"
American. Actor
Played Buckwheat in "Our Gang" comedies, 1934-44.
b. Mar 12, 1931 in Los Angeles, California
d. Oct 10, 1980 in Los Angeles, California
Source: *NewYTBS 80; WhScrn 83*

Thomas, Brandon
English. Actor, Dramatist
Wrote *Charley's Aunt,* 1892.
b. Dec 25, 1856 in Liverpool, England
d. Jun 19, 1914 in London, England
Source: *BioIn 4, 5; CamGWoT; LngCTC; McGEWD 72, 84; ModWD; NotNAT A, B; OxCThe 83; WhLit; WhThe*

Thomas, Caitlin Macnamara
[Mrs. Dylan Thomas]
Welsh. Author
Married Dylan Thomas, 1937; wrote of life together in *Leftover Life to Kill,* 1957.
b. Dec 8, 1913 in London, England
Source: *BioIn 4*

Thomas, Charles Allen
American. Business Executive
Pres., Monsanto Chemical Co., 1951-60; chairman, 1960-65.
b. Feb 15, 1900 in Scott County, Kentucky
d. Mar 30, 1982 in Albany, Georgia
Source: *AmMWSc 73P, 76P, 79, 82; AnObit 1982; BioIn 1, 2, 3, 4, 5, 12, 13; CurBio 50, 82N; FacFETw; InSci; IntWW 74; IntYB 78, 79, 80, 81, 82; NewYTBS 82; St&PR 75; WhAm 8; WhoAm 74, 76, 78, 80, 82; WhoWor 74, 76, 78, 80*

Thomas, Clarence
American. Supreme Court Justice
Member of US Supreme Court, 1991—; controversy surrounding nomination involved accusations of sexual harassment by former EEOC colleague Anita Hill.
b. Jun 23, 1948 in Savannah, Georgia
Source: *AfrAmAl 6; AfrAmBi 1; BioIn 13, 14, 15, 18; CngDr 91, 93, 95; ConBlB 2; CurBio 92; InB&W 85; LegTOT; News 92, 92-2; NewYTBS 91; OxCSupC; SupCtJu; WhoAfA 96; WhoAm 82, 84, 86, 88, 92, 94, 95, 96, 97; WhoAmL 92, 94, 96; WhoAmP 89, 91, 93, 95; WhoBlA 85, 88, 90, 92, 94; WhoE 93; WhoEmL 89; WhoFI 87, 89, 92, 94; WhoWor 96*

Thomas, Craig
American. Politician
Rep. senator from WY, 1995—.
b. Feb 17, 1933
Source: *AlmAP 92, 96; BioIn 20, 21; CngDr 91, 93, 95; WhoAm 90, 92, 94, 95, 96, 97; WhoAmP 91, 93, 95; WhoWest 92, 94, 96*

Thomas, Craig D
[David Grant]
Welsh. Author
Best-selling novel *Firefox,* 1977, adapted to successful film, 1982.
b. Nov 24, 1942 in Cardiff, Wales
Source: *ConAu 108, 112; Novels; WrDr 86, 94*

Thomas, D(onald) M(ichael)
English. Author
Wrote best-seller *The White House,* 1981.
b. Jan 27, 1935 in Carnkie, England
Source: *BioIn 12; ConAu 45NR, 61; ConNov 96; ConPo 70, 75, 96; DcLEL 1940; EncSF 93; IntAu&W 77, 82, 89, 91, 93; IntWW 89, 91, 93; OxCEng 95; OxCTwCP; RGTwCWr; Who 85, 88, 90, 92, 94; WhoWor 87; WrDr 76, 80, 94, 96*

Thomas, Danny
[Amos Jacobs]
American. Actor, Comedian, Producer
Starred in "Make Room for Daddy," 1953-64, later called "Danny Thomas Show"; father of Marlo.
b. Jan 6, 1914 in Deerfield, Michigan
d. Feb 6, 1991 in Los Angeles, California
Source: *BiDAmM; BioIn 3, 4, 5, 6, 8, 9, 10, 11, 13, 14, 15; BioNews 74; CelR, 90; CmpEPM; ConTFT 3; CurBio 59, 91N; EncAFC; FilmEn; FilmgC; ForYSC; HalFC 80, 84, 88; IntMPA 75, 76, 77, 80, 84, 86, 88; JoeFr; LegTOT; MotPP; News 91, 91-3; NewYTET; WhAm 10; WhoAm 74, 76, 78, 80, 82, 84, 86, 88, 90; WhoHol A; WorAl; WorAlBi*

Thomas, Dave
[Rex David Thomas]
American. Business Executive, Restaurateur
Founder of Wendy's International, 1969; known for his folksy TV commercials.
b. Jul 2, 1932 in Atlantic City, New Jersey
Source: *ConNews 86-2; CurBio 95; LegTOT; News 93-2; St&PR 87; WhoAm 84, 86; WhoFI 83*

Thomas, Dave
[McKenzie Brothers; Doug McKenzie]
Canadian. Comedian, Screenwriter
As Doug McKenzie, had hit album with Rick Moranis *Great White North,* 1981.
b. May 20, 1949 in Saint Catharines, Ontario, Canada
Source: *BioIn 12, 13; ConAu 115, 152; ConTFT 6, 13; IntMPA 96; News 93-2*

Thomas, Debi
American. Skater
First black figure skater to win world championship, 1986; won bronze medal, 1988 Olympics.
b. Mar 25, 1967 in Poughkeepsie, New York
Source: *AfrAmBi 1; BlkOlyM; CelR 90; ConNews 87-2; EncWomS; LegTOT; NewYTBS 85; NotBlAW 2; WhoAfA 96; WhoAm 94, 95, 96, 97; WhoAmW 89, 91; WhoBlA 88, 90, 92, 94; WhoSpor*

Thomas, Dennis
[Kool and the Gang]
"Dee Tee"
American. Musician
Plays flute, saxophone with Kool and the Gang.
b. Feb 9, 1951 in Jersey City, New Jersey

Thomas, Dylan Marlais
Welsh. Author
Wrote *A Child's Christmas in Wales; Under Milk Wood,* 1954.
b. Oct 27, 1914 in Swansea, Wales
d. Nov 9, 1953 in New York, New York
Source: *AtlBL; BlmGEL; CasWL; ConPo 75; DcArts; DcLEL; DcNaB 1951; EncWL; EvLB; GrBr; LinLib S; LngCEL; LngCTC; MakMC; McGEWB; McGEWD 72; ModBrL, S1; ModWD; NewC; OxCEng 67, 85, 95; PenC ENG; RfGShF; TwCA; TwCWr; WhAm 4, HSA; WhE&EA*

Thomas, E. Donall
American. Physician
Won Nobel Prize in medicine, 1990, for work in transplanting human organs and bone marrow.
b. Mar 15, 1920 in Mart, Texas
Source: *AmMWSc 92; Who 92; WhoAm 90; WhoNob 90; WhoWest 92*

Thomas, Edith Matilda
American. Poet, Editor
Wrote *The Inverted Torch,* 1890.
b. Aug 12, 1854 in Chatham, Ohio
d. Sep 13, 1925 in New York, New York
Source: *Alli SUP; AmAu; AmAu&B; AmBi; AmWom; AmWomPl; ApCAB, X; BbD; BenetAL 91; BiD&SB; BlmGWL; ChhPo, S1, S2, S3; DcAmAu; DcAmB; DcNAA; InWom, SUP; LibW; NatCAB 9; NotAW; OhA&B; OxCAmL 65, 83, 95; REn; REnAL; TwCBDA; WhAm 1; WomWWA 14*

Thomas, Edward
English. Poet, Author
Writings focus on nature, melancholy; wrote travel books, biographies before meeting Robert Frost and switching to poetry.
b. Mar 3, 1878 in London, England
d. Apr 9, 1917 in Arras, France
Source: *AnCL; AtlBL; Benet 87; BioIn 3, 4, 5, 6, 8, 9, 10, 11, 12, 13, 14, 15, 16, 17, 21; CamGEL; CamGLE; ChhPo, S1, S2, S3; CnE&AP; CnMWL; ConAu 106; DcLB 19, 98, 156; DcLEL; EncWL 2, 3; FacFETw; GrWrEL P; LngCTC; ModBrL, S1, S2; NewC; NewCBEL; OxCEng 67, 85; OxCLiW 86; OxCTwCP; PenC ENG; RAdv 14; REn; RfGEnL 91; RGFMBP; TwCA, SUP; TwCLC 10; TwCWr; WebE&AL; WhDW; WhoTwCL*

Thomas, Elizabeth Marshall
American. Writer
Wrote books based on her study of animal behavior, *The Hidden Life of Dogs,* 1993; *The Tribe of the Tiger,* 1994.
b. Sep 13, 1931 in Boston, Massachusetts
Source: *Au&Wr 71; BioIn 15, 19, 21; ConAu 17R; CurBio 96; IntAu&W 82, 93; ScF&FL 92*

Thomas, Elmer
American. Politician
Dem. senator from OK, 1927-51.
b. Sep 8, 1876 in Greencastle, Indiana
d. Sep 19, 1965
Source: *BioIn 1, 2, 7, 11; CurBio 49, 65; DcAmB S7; WhAm 4*

Thomas, Frank
[Frank Edward Thomas, Jr.]
"The Big Hurt"
American. Baseball Player
With the Chicago White Sox, 1990—; AL MVP, 1994.
b. May 27, 1968 in Columbus, Georgia
Source: *AfrAmSG; ConBlB 12; CurBio 94; News 94, 94-3; WhoAfA 96; WhoAm 92, 94, 95, 96, 97; WhoBlA 94; WhoMW 93, 96*

Thomas, Franklin Augustine
American. Lawyer
Pres. of Ford Foundation, 1979-96.
b. May 27, 1934 in New York, New York
Source: *BioIn 11, 12, 13; CurBio 81; Ebony 1; InB&W 80, 85; NewYTBS 79; Who 83, 85, 88, 90, 92, 94; WhoAm 76, 78, 80, 82, 84, 86, 88, 90, 92, 94, 95, 96, 97; WhoBlA 88; WhoE 95, 97; WhoFrS 84*

Thomas, George Henry
"The Rock of Chickamauga"
American. Military Leader
Distinguished Civil War general; accepted surrender of Atlanta, 1864.
b. Jul 31, 1816 in Southampton County, Virginia
d. Mar 28, 1870 in San Francisco, California
Source: *AmBi; ApCAB; BioIn 1, 3, 6, 7, 8, 9, 10, 13, 15, 17; CivWDc; DcAmB; DcAmMiB; DcBiPP; Drake; EncAB-H 1974, 1996; EncSoH; HarEnMi; HarEnUS; LinLib S; McGEWB; NatCAB 4; OxCAmH; PeoHis; TwCBDA; WebAB 74, 79; WebAMB; WhAm HS; WhCiWar; WhoMilH 76; WorAl*

Thomas, Gerald
English. Producer, Director
Noted for *Carry On* comedy film series, 1957-70s.
b. Dec 20, 1920 in Hull, England
Source: *BioIn 19; ConTFT 5; FilmEn; FilmgC; HalFC 80, 84, 88; IlWWBF; IntMPA 75, 76, 77, 78, 79, 80, 81, 82, 84, 86, 88, 92, 94; MiSFD 9*

Thomas, Gwyn
Welsh. Author
Wrote *Where Did I Put My Pity?; The Love Man; The Keep.*
b. Jul 6, 1913 in Porth, Wales
d. Apr 13, 1981 in Cardiff, Wales
Source: *AnObit 1981; ArtclWW 2; Au&Wr 71; BioIn 8, 10, 11, 12, 13, 19; CasWL; ConAu 9NR, 65, 103; ConDr 73, 77, 93; ConNov 76; CroCD; DcLB 15; DcLEL 1940; DcNaB 1981; EncWT; IntAu&W 76, 77; LngCTC; OxCLiW 86; TwCWr; Who 74; WhoThe 72, 77, 81; WorAu 1950; WrDr 76, 80, 82*

Thomas, Helen A.
[Mrs. Douglas B. Cornell]
American. Journalist
UPI White House bureau chief, 1974—.
b. Aug 4, 1920 in Winchester, Kentucky
Source: *BioIn 12; BioNews 75; ConAu 101; CurBio 93; WhoAm 74, 76, 78, 80, 82, 84, 86, 88, 90, 92, 94, 95, 96, 97; WhoAmW 66, 68, 70, 72, 74, 81, 85, 89, 91, 93, 95, 97; WhoE 95; WhoWor 74; WomFir*

Thomas, Henry
American. Actor
Played Elliott, ET's "friend," in film *ET,* 1981.
b. Sep 8, 1972 in San Antonio, Texas
Source: *BioIn 13; ConTFT 6; LegTOT; VarWW 85*

Thomas, Isaiah
American. Publisher
Founded American Antiquarian Society, 1812.
b. Jan 30, 1750 in Boston, Massachusetts
d. Apr 4, 1831 in Worcester, Massachusetts
Source: *Alli; AmAu; AmAu&B; AmBi; ApCAB; BiD&SB; BioIn 15, 16, 17; CyAL 1; DcAmB; DcLB 43, 73; Drake; EarABI; JrnUS; OxCAmL 65; OxCChiL; REnAL; TwCBDA; WebAB 74; WhAm HS*

Thomas, Isiah
[Isiah Lord Thomas, III]
"Pocket Magic"
American. Basketball Player, Basketball Executive
Guard, Detroit, 1981-94; holds NBA record for most assists in season, 1985; MVP, All-Star Game, 1984, 1986; MVP, championship series, 1990; vice president, Toronto Raptors, 1994—.
b. Apr 30, 1961 in Chicago, Illinois
Source: *AfrAmBi 1; AfrAmSG; BasBi; BiDAmSp BK; BioIn 12; CelR 90; ConBlB 7; CurBio 89; News 89-2; NewYTBS 81; OfNBA 87; WhoAfA 96; WhoAm 86, 88, 90, 92, 94, 95, 96, 97; WhoBlA 88, 90, 92, 94; WhoE 97; WhoMW 88, 90, 92, 93, 96*

Thomas, Jess
American. Opera Singer
Tenor, noted for Wagner roles; NY Met. debut, 1963.
b. Apr 8, 1927 in Hot Springs, South Dakota
d. Oct 11, 1993 in San Francisco, California
Source: *AnObit 1993; Baker 84; BiDAmM; BioIn 6, 7, 9, 11, 13, 16, 19, 20; CmOp; CurBio 64, 94N; IntWWM 77, 80, 90; MetOEnc; MusSN; NewEOp 71; NewGrDA 86; NewGrDM 80; NewYTBE 71; NewYTBS 93; OxDcOp; PenDiMP; WhAm 11; WhoAm 74, 76, 78, 80, 82, 84, 86, 88, 90, 92, 94; WhoAmM 83; WhoE 74; WhoEnt 92; WhoOp 76; WhoWor 74, 78, 82, 87, 89*

Thomas, John Charles
American. Opera Singer
Baritone; radio, film star; popular concert performer, 1940s-50s; NY Met., 1933-45.
b. Sep 6, 1891 in Meyersdale, Pennsylvania
d. Dec 13, 1960 in Apple Valley, California
Source: *Baker 78, 84, 92; BioIn 1, 2, 4, 5; CurBio 43, 61; DcAmB S6; MetOEnc; MusSN; NewEOp 71; NewGrDA 86; NewGrDO; OxCAmT 84; PenDiMP; RadStar; WhAm 4; WhoHol B; WhScrn 74, 77*

Thomas, Jonathan Taylor
[Jonathan Weiss]
American. Actor
Plays Randy Taylor on TV's "Home Improvement," 1991—.
b. Sep 8, 1981 in Bethlehem, Pennsylvania

Thomas, Joyce Carol
American. Author
Wrote 1982 award-winning young adult novel *Marked By Fire.*
b. May 25, 1938 in Ponca City, Oklahoma
Source: *Au&Arts 12; BioIn 13; BlkAuII, 92; BlkWr 1, 2; ChlLR 19; ConAu 48NR, 113, 116; ConBlAP 88; ConLC 35; DcLB 33; DrAPF 80; FemiCLE; MajAI; MajTwCW; MorBAP; OnHuMoP; OxCWoWr 95; ScF&FL 92; SchCGBL; SmATA 7AS, 40, 78; TwCYAW; WhoAfA 96; WhoAm 88, 97; WhoAmW 87, 89; WhoBlA 75, 77, 80, 85, 88, 90, 92, 94; WhoUSWr 88; WhoWor 96, 97; WhoWrEP 89, 92, 95*

Thomas, Kurt
American. Gymnast
First US male to win gold medal in world gymnastic competition, 1978.
b. Mar 29, 1956 in Terre Haute, Indiana
Source: *BiDAmSp BK; BioIn 11, 12; ConAu 114, 154; LegTOT; WhoHol 92; WhoSpor; WorAl*

Thomas, Lewis
American. Physician, Author
Wrote *The Lives of a Cell: Notes of a Biology Watcher,* 1974; *The Medusa and the Snail,* 1979.
b. Nov 25, 1913 in Flushing, New York
d. Dec 3, 1993 in New York, New York
Source: *AmDec 1970; AmMWSc 73P, 76P, 79, 82, 86, 89, 92; AnObit 1993; Benet 96; BioIn 10, 12, 13, 14, 16, 17, 19, 20, 21; ConAu 38NR, 85, 143; ConLC 35; CurBio 75, 94N; CyWA 89; DcNaB; IntMed 80; IntWW 77, 78, 79, 80, 81, 82, 83, 89, 91, 93; LEduc 74; MajTwCW; NewYTBS 79, 93; RAdv 14, 13-1, 13-5; WhAm 11; WhoAm 74, 76, 78, 80, 82, 84, 86, 88, 90, 92, 94; WhoE 74; WhoFrS 84; WhoWor 78, 80, 82, 84, 87, 89, 91; WorAlBi; WorAu 1975; WrDr 82, 84, 86, 88, 90, 92, 94, 96*

Thomas, Lowell Jackson
American. Author, Radio Performer
Wrote *With Lawrence in Arabia,* 1924; hosted "High-Adventure," 1957-59.
b. Apr 6, 1892 in Woodington, Ohio
d. Aug 29, 1981 in Pawling, New York
Source: *AmAu&B; AmSocL; Au&Wr 71; AuBYP 2, 3; AuNews 1, 2; BiDAmJo; ConAu 3NR, 45, 104; CurBio 40, 81; IntMPA 79; JBA 34; NewYTBS 78; OhA&B; OxCCan; REnAL; TwCA, SUP; WebAB 74, 79; WhE&EA; WhNAA; Who 74; WhoAm 80; WhoHol A; WorAl; WrDr 80*

Thomas, Lowell Jackson, Jr.
American. Author, Producer
Writings include *The Silent War in Tibet,* 1959; *Famous First Flights That Changed History,* 1968.
b. Oct 6, 1923 in London, England
Source: *AmAu&B; AuBYP 2, 3; ConAu 85; IntMPA 82; SmATA 15; WhoAm 84, 86; WhoAmP 85; WhoHol A; WhoWest 74*

Thomas, Marlo
[Mrs. Phil Donahue; Margaret Thomas]
American. Actor
Starred in "That Girl," 1966-71; won Emmys for "Free to Be. You and Me," 1977; "Nobody's Child," 1986.
b. Nov 21, 1938 in Detroit, Michigan
Source: *BioIn 8, 9, 10, 11; BkPepl; CelR, 90; ConTFT 10; HalFC 84; IntMPA 77, 78, 79, 80, 81, 82, 84, 86, 88, 92, 94, 96; LegTOT; NewYTBE 73; VarWW 85; WhoAm 86; WhoAmW 85; WhoHol 92, A*

Thomas, Martha Carey
American. Educator, Feminist
Pres., Bryn Mawr College, 1894-1922.
b. Jan 2, 1857 in Baltimore, Maryland
d. Dec 2, 1935 in Philadelphia, Pennsylvania
Source: *AmAu&B; AmBi; AmRef; AmWomM; BiDAmEd; BioIn 1, 10, 11, 12, 14, 15, 19, 20; ContDcW 89; DcAmAu; DcAmB S1; DcNAA; EncAB-H 1996; FemiWr; GayLesB; GoodHs; GrLiveH; IntDcWB; InWom, SUP; LibW; McGEWB; NotAW; TwCBDA; WebAB 74, 79; WomEdUS; WomFir; WomWWA 14; WorAl; WorAlBi*

Thomas, Norman Mattoon
"Conscience of America"
American. Author, Political Leader
Writings include *The Conscientious Objector in America,* 1923; *What's the Matter with New York?,* 1932.
b. Nov 20, 1884 in Marion, Ohio
d. Dec 19, 1968 in Huntington, New York
Source: *Benet 96; ConAu 101; CurBio 44, 62, 69; EncAB-H 1974, 1996; OhA&B; OxCAmL 65; PenC AM; REn; REnAL; WebAB 74; WhAm 5*

Thomas, Philip Michael
American. Actor
Played Ricardo Tubbs on TV series "Miami Vice," 1984-89.
b. May 26, 1949 in Los Angeles, California
Source: *BlksAmF; ConTFT 6; IntMPA 88, 92, 94, 96; LegTOT; WhoAfA 96; WhoBlA 85, 88, 90, 92, 94; WhoHol 92, A*

Thomas, Pinklon
American. Boxer
WBC heavyweight champion, 1984; lost title to Trevor Berbick, 1986.
b. 1957? in Pontiac, Michigan
Source: *BioIn 12; NewYTBS 82, 85*

Thomas, Piri
American. Author
Wrote autobiographies *Down These Mean Streets,* 1967; *Seven Long Times,* 1974.
b. Sep 30, 1928 in New York, New York
Source: *AmAu&B; BiDHisL; BioIn 7, 8, 9, 10, 13, 16, 17, 20; CaribW 4; ConAu 73; ConLC 17; DcHiB; DrAF 76; DrAP 75; DrAPF 80; HispAmA; HispWr; IntAu&W 77; MorBAP; WhoE 74; WhoHisp 92, 94; WrDr 76*

Thomas, Richard Earl
American. Actor
Played John Boy in "The Waltons," 1972-77; published two books of poetry.

b. Jun 13, 1951 in New York, New York
Source: *ConAu 107; CurBio 75; FilmgC; HalFC 84; IntMPA 86; WhoAm 84, 86*

Thomas, Robert B
American. Publisher
Founded, edited *Old Farmer's Almanac,* 1792-1844.
b. Apr 24, 1766 in Grafton, Massachusetts
d. May 19, 1846 in West Bolyston, Massachusetts
Source: *Alli; AmAu&B; AmBi; CasWL; DcAmAu; DcAmB; REnAL; WhAm HS*

Thomas, Ronald Stuart
Welsh. Poet
Poems express bleak view of man: *The Stones of the Field,* 1946.
b. Mar 29, 1913 in Cardiff, Wales
Source: *BioIn 6, 10, 12, 14, 15, 17, 18; CasWL; ChhPo, S1, S2; CnE&AP; ConAu 89; ConLC 6, 13; ConPo 70, 75; DcLEL 1940; IntAu&W 89, 91, 93; IntWW 79, 80, 81, 82, 83, 89, 91, 93; LngCTC; ModBrL, S1; NewC; NewCBEL; NewYTBS 83; OxCLiW 86; PenC ENG; TwCWr; WebE&AL; Who 85, 88, 90, 92, 94; WhoTwCL; WorAu 1950; WrDr 76*

Thomas, Ross (Elmore)
''Oliver Bleeck''
American. Writer
Author of political thrillers such as *Chinaman's Chance,* 1978.
b. Feb 19, 1926 in Oklahoma City, Oklahoma
d. Dec 18, 1995 in Santa Monica, California
Source: *Au&Wr 71; BioIn 14, 15, 21; ConAu 22NR, 33R, 150; ConLC 39; CrtSuMy; EncMys; Novels; SpyFic; TwCCr&M 80, 85, 91; WhAm 11; WhoAm 74, 76, 78, 80, 82, 84, 86, 88, 90, 92, 94, 95, 96; WhoSSW 73; WrDr 76, 80, 82, 84, 86, 88, 90, 92, 94, 96*

Thomas, Samuel Bath
American. Manufacturer, Businessman
Introduced English muffins to US, 1880.
b. 1855
d. 1919
Source: *Entr*

Thomas, Seth
American. Manufacturer
Founded Seth Thomas Clock Co., 1853.
b. Aug 19, 1785 in Wolcott, Connecticut
d. Jan 29, 1859 in Plymouth, Connecticut
Source: *AmBi; ApCAB X; BiDAmBL 83; BioIn 2, 6; DcAmB; DcNiCA; Entr; LegTOT; NatCAB 3; WebAB 74, 79; WhAm HS*

Thomas, Sidney Gilchrist
English. Inventor, Scientist
Discovered method to allow phosphoric ores to be used, Bessemer converter, 1875.
b. Apr 16, 1850 in London, England
d. Feb 1, 1885 in Paris, France
Source: *BiESc; BioIn 2, 7; DcNaB; DcScB; InSci; LarDcSc; OxCLiW 86; WorInv*

Thomas, Theodore
German. Conductor
Director, Cincinnati College of Music, 1878-98; violinist with symphonies.
b. Oct 11, 1835 in Essen, Germany
d. Jan 4, 1905 in Chicago, Illinois
Source: *AmBi; ApCAB; Baker 78, 84; BioIn 1, 2, 3, 7, 8, 9; BriBkM 80; DcAmB; DcNAA; HarEnUS; LinLib S; McGEWB; MetOEnc; NatCAB 2; NewAmDM; NewEOp 71; NewGrDA 86; NewGrDM 80; OxCAmH; OxCAmL 65; OxCMus; PenDiMP; REn; TwCBDA; WebAB 74, 79; WhAm 1; WhDW*

Thomas, Thurman Lee
American. Football Player
NFL running back, Buffalo Bills, 1988— ; AP MVP, 1991.
b. May 16, 1966 in Houston, Texas
Source: *News 93-1; WhoBlA 92*

Thomas, Tony
Writer
Co-created *Blossom, Nurses,* and *Herman's Head.*
Source: *BioIn 16; ConTFT 13; SelBAAf; WhoHol A*

Thomas, Vivien
American. Scientist
With no formal medical training, helped develop intricate surgical techniques; surgical research technician, Vanderbilt Univ. Medical School, 1930-41; research assoc., Johns Hopkins Univ. School of Medicine, 1941-70.
b. 1910 in Nashville, Tennessee
d. 1985
Source: *ConBlB 9*

Thomas, W(illiam) I(saac)
American. Sociologist, Educator
Sociology professor; author of *Sex and Society,* 1907.
b. Aug 13, 1863 in Russell County, Virginia
d. Dec 5, 1947 in Berkeley, California
Source: *BioIn 1, 6, 10, 11, 14; DcAmB S4; DcNAA; DcSoc; McGEWB; NatCAB 44; RAdv 14, 13-3; ThTwC 87; WhAm 2*

Thomas a Kempis
[Thomas Hamerken]
German. Theologian, Author
Wrote influential *The Imitation of Christ,* c. 1427.
b. 1380? in Kempen, Germany
d. Jul 25, 1471 in Agnietenberg, Netherlands
Source: *AtlBL; Benet 87, 96; BiD&SB; BioIn 1, 2, 5, 6, 7, 20; CasWL; CyWA 58; DcCathB; DcEnL; DcEuL; DcSpL; EuAu; LitC 11; McGEWB; NewC; OxCEng 67, 85, 95; OxCGer 76; PenC EUR; PseudAu; RComWL; REn; WhDW; WorAl*

Thomas Aquinas, Saint
[Tommaso d'Aquino]
''Angelic Doctor''; ''Doctor of the School''
Italian. Theologian, Philosopher
Synthesis of theology, philosophy known as Thomism; wrote *Summa Theologica.*
b. 1225 in Roccasecca, Italy
d. Mar 7, 1274 in Fossannova, Italy
Source: *BbD; BiD&SB; BioIn 1, 2, 3, 4, 5, 6, 7, 8, 9, 10, 11, 12, 13, 14, 15, 17, 18, 20; CasWL; CyWA 58; DcCathB; DcEuL; EncEth; EuAu; EvEuW; IlEncMy; McGDA; NewC; OxCEng 67; OxCFr; PenC EUR; RAdv 13-4; RComWL; REn; WebBD 83*

Thomason, Harry
American. Writer
Co-created television comedies *Designing Women* and *Evening Shade.*
Source: *BioIn 12, 17, 18; WhoAm 92*

Thomason, John William, Jr.
American. Military Leader
WW I colonel; wrote, illustrated from military experiences: *Fix Bayonets,* 1926.
b. Feb 28, 1893 in Huntsville, Texas
d. Mar 12, 1944 in San Diego, California
Source: *AmAu&B; ArtsAmW 1; BioIn 1, 4, 6, 8, 13; CurBio 44; DcNAA; EncFWF; IlBEAAW; NatCAB 33; REnAL; TexWr; TwCA, SUP; TwCWW 82; WhAm 2; WhAmArt 85*

Thomaz, Americo
[Americo Deus Rodrigues Tomas]
Portuguese. Political Leader
Elected pres., 1958; twice again, under suspicious circumstances, until ousted in 1974.
b. Nov 19, 1894 in Lisbon, Portugal
d. Sep 18, 1987 in Cascais, Portugal
Source: *CurBio 58, 87; DcPol; FacFETw; IntWW 74; WhoWor 74*

Thomopoulos, Anthony Denis
American. TV Executive
Pres., ABC Broadcast Group, 1983-85; pres., ABC, 1978-83; chm. and CEO, United Artists Pictures, 1986—.
b. Feb 7, 1938 in Mount Vernon, New York
Source: *BioIn 11; IntMPA 86; LesBEnT; VarWW 85; WhoAm 86; WhoFI 83; WhoTelC*

Thompson, Bradbury James
American. Designer
On faculty of Yale School of Art and Architecture, 1956—; designed Time-Life *Library of Art* series, 1965; designer of over 100 US postage stamps, 1958-92.
b. Mar 25, 1911 in Topeka, Kansas
d. Nov 1, 1995
Source: *WhoAm 84, 86; WhoAmA 84; WhoGrA 62; WhoWor 87*

Thompson, Daley
[Francis Daley Thompson]
English. Track Athlete
Second person to win two gold medals in decathlon, 1980, 1984 Olympics.
b. Jul 30, 1958 in London, England
Source: *BioIn 11, 12, 13; CurBio 86; FacFETw; IntWW 89, 91; NewYTBS 79, 84*

Thompson, David
English. Explorer, Geographer
First white man to explore Columbia River from source to mouth, 1811; maps helped outline US-Canadian boundary, 1816-26.
b. Apr 30, 1770 in London, England
d. Feb 10, 1857 in Montreal, Quebec, Canada
Source: *AmBi; ApCAB; BbtC; BenetAL 91; BioIn 1, 4, 5, 7, 8, 9, 12, 14, 17, 18, 20; DcAmB; DcCanB 8; DcLB 99; DcLEL; Expl 93; HarEnUS; IntDcAn; MacDCB 78; McGEWB; NewCBEL; OxCAmH; OxCAmL 65; OxCCan; REnAL; REnAW; WebAB 74, 79; WhAm HS; WhDW; WhNaAH; WhWE; WorAl; WorAlBi*

Thompson, David O'Neil
American. Basketball Player
Guard, Denver, 1976-82, Seattle, 1982-84; MVP, NBA All-Star game, 1979.
b. Jul 13, 1954 in Shelby, North Carolina
Source: *BiDAmSp BK; NewYTBS 82; WhoAm 84; WhoBbl 73; WhoBlA 85*

Thompson, Dorothy
American. Journalist
Columnist for *NY Herald Tribune Syndicate,* 1936-41; writer, *Ladies Home Journal,* mag, 1937-61.
b. Jul 9, 1894 in Lancaster, New York
d. Jan 31, 1961 in Lisbon, Portugal
Source: *AmAu&B; AmSocL; AmWomWr; Benet 87, 96; BenetAL 91; BioAmW; BioIn 1, 2, 4, 5, 6, 7, 8, 9, 10, 11; ConAu 89; ContDcW 89; CurBio 40, 61; EncAB-H 1974, 1996; EncAJ; EncTR; EncTwCJ; EncWB; EvLB; FacFETw; GoodHs; IntDcWB; InWom; LegTOT; LibW; LinLib L, S; ObitT 1961; OxCAmH; OxCAmL 65, 83, 95; RadStar; REn; REnAL; TwCA, SUP; WebAB 74, 79; WhAm 4; WhE&EA; WhoAmW 58, 61; WomFir; WomPO 76; WomStre; WorAl; WorAlBi*

Thompson, Edward Herbert
American. Archaeologist, Explorer, Author
Studied Mayan sites in Mexico; wrote *People of the Serpent,* 1932.
b. Sep 28, 1856 in Worcester, Massachusetts
d. May 11, 1935 in Plainfield, New Jersey
Source: *BioIn 4, 6, 8; DcAmB S1*

Thompson, Emma
English. Actor
Appeared in *Henry V,* 1989; won Oscar, Best Actress, *Howard's End,* 1993; Oscar, Best Adapted Screenplay, *Sense and Sensibility,* 1995.
b. Apr 15, 1959 in London, England
Source: *BiDFilm 94; BiNAW Sup, SupB; ConAu 154; ConTFT 11; CurBio 95; DcArts; IntMPA 92, 94, 96; IntWW 91, 93; LegTOT; News 93-2; Who 94; WhoAm 94, 95, 96, 97; WhoAmW 97; WhoWor 95, 96, 97*

Thompson, Ernest
[Richard Ernest Thompson]
American. Author
Wrote play *On Golden Pond,* 1978; won 1982 Oscar for screen adaptation.
b. Nov 6, 1950 in Bellows Falls, Vermont
Source: *ConAu 115; MiSFD 9; VarWW 85*

Thompson, Francis Joseph
English. Poet, Essayist
First volume *Poems,* 1893, contained best known poem "The Hound of Heaven."
b. Dec 18, 1859 in Preston, England
d. Nov 13, 1907 in London, England
Source: *AtlBL; BiD&SB; CasWL; CnE&AP; ConAu 104; CrtT 3; DcEuL; DcLEL; EncWL; EvLB; LngCTC; MouLC 4; NewC; OxCEng 67; PenC ENG; RAdv 1; REn; WebE&AL*

Thompson, Frank, Jr.
American. Politician
Dem. congressman from NJ, 1955-69, 1971-81.
b. Jul 26, 1918 in Trenton, New Jersey
d. Jul 22, 1989 in Baltimore, Maryland
Source: *AlmAP 78, 80; BiDrAC; BiDrUSC 89; BioIn 5, 8, 10, 11, 12, 16; CngDr 74, 77, 79; CurBio 59, 89N; NewYTBS 76, 80, 89; PolProf E, J, K; WhoAm 74, 76, 78, 80; WhoAmP 73, 75, 77, 79, 81, 83; WhoE 74, 75, 77, 79; WhoGov 72, 75, 77*

Thompson, Fred
American. Politician
Rep. senator from TN, 1994—.
b. Aug 19, 1942
Source: *AlmAP 96; CngDr 95; WhoAm 97; WhoSSW 97*

Thompson, George Selden
[George Selden]
American. Children's Author
Best known for *The Cricket in Times Square,* which won Newbery Medal, 1961, and was adapted to film, 1973.
b. May 14, 1929 in Hartford, Connecticut
d. Dec 5, 1989 in New York, New York
Source: *AuBYP 2, 3; BioIn 8, 9, 10, 14, 15, 16, 17, 19; ChlBkCr; ChlLR 8; ConAu 5R, 21NR, 37NR, 130; DcAmChF 1960; DcLB 52; FourBJA; IntAu&W 91; MajAI; OxCChiL; ScF&FL 1, 2, 92; SJGFanW; SmATA 4, 63, 73, X; TwCChW 78, 83, 89, 95; WrDr 80, 82, 84, 86, 88, 90*

Thompson, Hank
American. Singer, Musician, Bandleader
Led country music-swing band, Brazos Valley Boys, 1950s-70s; had 100 hit-chart records by 1966.
b. Sep 3, 1925 in Waco, Texas
Source: *ASCAP 66; Ballpl 90; BgBkCoM; BioIn 14, 15, 20; CounME 74, 74A; EncFCWM 69, 83; HarEnCM 87; IlEncCM; NewAmDM; NewGrDA 86; PenEncP*

Thompson, Hunter S(tockton)
[Sebastian Owl]
American. Journalist, Editor
Wrote *Hell's Angels: A Strange and Terrible Saga,* 1966; nat. affairs editor, *Rolling Stone* mag, 1969-74.
b. Jul 18, 1939 in Louisville, Kentucky
Source: *AmSocL; BioIn 12, 13; ConAu 17R, 46NR; ConLC 17, 40; ConPopW; CurBio 81; IntAu&W 76, 77, 82; News 92; NewYTBS 79; WhoAm 76, 78, 80, 82, 84, 86, 88, 90, 92; WhoE 74; WhoUSWr 88; WhoWest 89; WhoWrEP 89, 92, 95; WrDr 94, 96*

Thompson, J(ames) Walter
American. Advertising Executive
Founded one of major advertising firms, 1878; specialized in mag. marketing.
b. Oct 28, 1847 in Pittsfield, Massachusetts
d. Oct 16, 1928 in New York, New York
Source: *AdMenW; ApCAB X; BiDAmBL 83; BioIn 6, 7, 20; NatCAB 15, 21; WebAB 74, 79; WebBD 83*

Thompson, James Robert
American. Politician
Republican governor of IL, 1977-90, succeeded by Jim Edgar.
b. May 8, 1936 in Chicago, Illinois
Source: *AlmAP 88; AmMWSc 95; BiDrGov 1789; BioIn 10, 11; CurBio 79; IntYB 79, 80, 81, 82; WhoAm 78, 80, 82, 84, 86, 88, 90, 92, 94, 95, 96, 97; WhoAmL 79, 96; WhoGov 75, 77; WhoMW 78, 80, 82, 84, 86, 88, 90, 92; WhoScEn 94; WhoWor 82, 87, 89, 91; WorAl*

Thompson, John
American. Basketball Coach
Coach at Georgetown University, 1972— ; coached US Olympic men's basketball team, 1988.
b. Sep 2, 1941 in Washington, District of Columbia
Source: *AfrAmSG; BasBi; BiDAmSp BK; BioIn 12; CelR 90; CurBio 89; News 88-3; WhoAm 84, 86, 88, 90, 92, 94, 95, 96, 97; WhoBbl 73; WhoE 89; WhoSpor; WorAlBi*

Thompson, John S(parrow) D(avid), Sir
Canadian. Judge, Politician
Conservative prime minister, 1892-94; died while visiting Queen Victoria.
b. Nov 10, 1844 in Halifax, Nova Scotia, Canada

d. Dec 2, 1894 in Windsor Castle, England
Source: *ApCAB; BioIn 1, 4, 7, 8; DcCathB; DcNaB; MacDCB 78; OxCCan; PeoHis*

Thompson, John Taliaferro
American. Inventor
US military officer; invented firearms, machinery, airplane devices; ''Tommy Gun'' named for him, 1920.
b. Dec 31, 1860 in Newport, Kentucky
d. Jun 21, 1940
Source: *ApCAB X; CurBio 40; NatCAB 16, 29; WebAMB; WhAm 1*

Thompson, Karen
American. Social Reformer
Was involved in a case for guardianship of her companion, Sharon Kowalski, which Kowalski's parents opposed; was granted guardianship, 1991.
Source: *BioIn 15, 17; GayLesB*

Thompson, Kay
American. Singer
Noted for singing career with Williams Brothers, 1947-53; invented popular character in book, *Eloise,* 1955.
b. Nov 9, 1913 in Saint Louis, Missouri
Source: *AmAu&B; ASCAP 66, 80; CmpEPM; ConAu 85; CurBio 59; FourBJA; InWom; MotPP; SmATA 16; WhoAm 74; WhoHol A*

Thompson, Llewellyn E, Jr.
American. Diplomat
US ambassador to the Soviet Union, 1957-62; 1967-69.
b. Aug 24, 1904 in Las Animas, Colorado
d. Feb 6, 1972 in Washington, District of Columbia
Source: *BioIn 4, 5, 6, 7, 8, 9, 11, 16; ColdWar 2; DcAmDH 89; NewYTBE 72; PolProf J*

Thompson, Marshall
[James Marshall Thompson]
American. Actor
Played in TV show ''Daktari,'' 1966-69.
b. Nov 27, 1926 in Peoria, Illinois
d. May 25, 1992 in Royal Oak, Michigan
Source: *FilmgC; ForYSC; HalFC 84; IntMPA 84, 86, 88, 92; MGM; MotPP; MovMk; WhoHol A; WhoHrs 80*

Thompson, Mary
American. Centenarian
One of the oldest Americans, dying at age 120; daughter of slaves.
b. Mar 27, 1876?
d. Aug 3, 1996 in Orlando, Florida
Source: *NewYTBS 27*

Thompson, Mickey
American. Auto Racer
First American to exceed 400 mph on land, 1960, but not officially recognized for record because of car's mechanical problems; shot to death with wife.
b. 1928
d. Mar 23, 1988 in Bradbury, California
Source: *BioIn 6, 8, 9, 11, 12, 13; FacFETw*

Thompson, Moose
[Wilbur Thompson]
American. Track Athlete
Shot putter; won gold medal, 1948 Olympics.
b. Apr 6, 1921 in Frankfort, South Dakota
Source: *WhoTr&F 73*

Thompson, Oscar
American. Critic, Author
Editor, *Musical America,* 1936-43.
b. Aug 10, 1887 in Crawfordsville, Indiana
d. Jul 2, 1945 in New York, New York
Source: *AmAu&B; Baker 78, 84, 92; BiDAmM; CurBio 45; DcAmB S3; DcNAA; IndAu 1917; NewGrDA 86; NewGrDM 80; OxCAmH; WhAm 2; WhNAA*

Thompson, Paul W(illiams)
American. Publishing Executive
With *Reader's Digest,* 1957-71, retiring as vp.
b. Dec 19, 1906
d. Feb 9, 1996 in Daytona Beach, Florida
Source: *BiDWWGF; BioIn 21; CurBio 96N; InSci; WhoAm 74, 76, 78*

Thompson, Randall
American. Composer, Teacher
Wrote *Second Symphony,* 1932; choral piece, *Festival of Freedom,* 1942.
b. Apr 12, 1899 in New York, New York
d. Jul 9, 1984 in Boston, Massachusetts
Source: *AmComp; AmMWSc 73P; AnObit 1984; ASCAP 66, 80; Baker 78, 84, 92; BiDAmM; BioIn 1, 4, 8, 14, 17; BriBkM 80; CompSN, SUP; ConAmC 76, 82; ConAu 113; CpmDNM 82; IntWWM 77, 80; LegTOT; MusMk; NewAmDM; NewGrDA 86; NewGrDM 80; NewGrDO; NewYTBS 84; OxCMus; WhAm 8; WhoAm 74, 76, 78, 80, 82, 84; WhoE 75; WhoWor 74*

Thompson, Richard
English. Singer, Musician
Founding member of Fairport Convention 1967-1972; albums include *Shoot Out the Lights,* 1982 and *Amnesia,* 1988.
b. Apr 3, 1949 in London, England
Source: *BioIn 13; ConMus 7; DcArts; EncRk 88; EncRkSt; OnThGG; PenEncP; RolSEnR 83*

Thompson, Ruth Plumly
'''Royal Historian of Oz''''
American. Historian, Author
Wrote 19 ''Oz'' books after Baum's death, including *The Enchanted Island of Oz,* 1976.
b. Jul 27, 1891 in Philadelphia, Pennsylvania
d. Apr 6, 1976
Source: *ConAu 113, 134; DcLB 22; SmATA 66*

Thompson, Sada Carolyn
American. Actor
Played Kate Lawrence in ''Family,'' 1976-79; won Tony for *Twigs,* 1971.
b. Sep 27, 1929 in Des Moines, Iowa
Source: *BiE&WWA; BioNews 75; ConTFT 4; CurBio 73; HalFC 84; InWom SUP; NewYTBE 71; NotNAT; PlP&P A; WhoAm 74, 76, 78, 80, 82, 84, 86, 88, 92; WhoAmW 81, 83; WhoEnt 92; WhoHol A; WhoThe 81; WorAl*

Thompson, Sam(uel Luther)
American. Baseball Player
Outfielder, 1885-98, 1906; led NL in batting, 1887; had lifetime .331 batting average; Hall of Fame, 1974.
b. Mar 5, 1860 in Danville, Indiana
d. Nov 7, 1922 in Detroit, Michigan
Source: *Ballpl 90; BioIn 14, 15; WhoProB 73*

Thompson, Thomas
American. Journalist
At age 23 became youngest city editor with a major daily newspaper, *Houston Press,* 1957; wrote nonfiction best-sellers.
b. Oct 3, 1933 in Fort Worth, Texas
d. Oct 29, 1982 in Los Angeles, California
Source: *BioIn 13; ConAu 14NR, 65, 108; LiJour; NewYTBS 82; WrDr 80*

Thompson, Tiny
[Cecil Thompson]
Canadian. Hockey Player
Goalie, 1928-40, mostly with Boston; won Vezina Trophy four times; Hall of Fame, 1959.
b. May 31, 1905 in Sandon, British Columbia, Canada
d. Feb 9, 1981 in Calgary, Alberta, Canada
Source: *HocEn; WhoHcky 73; WhoSpor*

Thompson, Tommy George
American. Politician
Rep. governor of Wisconsin, 1987—.
b. Nov 19, 1941 in Elroy, Wisconsin
Source: *AlmAP 88; CurBio 95; IntWW 89, 91, 93; WhoAm 88, 90, 92, 94, 95, 96, 97; WhoAmL 79; WhoAmP 73, 75, 77, 79, 81, 83, 85, 87, 89, 91, 93, 95; WhoMW 74, 76, 78, 80, 88, 90, 92, 93, 96; WhoWor 89, 91*

Thompson, Vivian Laubach
American. Children's Author
Best known for book on the experience of moving: *Sad Day, Glad Day,* 1962.
b. Jan 7, 1911 in Jersey City, New Jersey
Source: *AuBYP 2, 3; BioIn 8, 9; ConAu 1NR, 1R; ForWC 70; SmATA 3; WrDr 76, 86*

Thompson, William Tappan
American. Humorist, Writer
Founder and editor of *Savannah Morning News,* 1850-82; wrote *Major Jones's Courtship,* 1843.
b. Aug 31, 1812 in Ravenna, Ohio
d. Mar 24, 1882 in Savannah, Georgia
Source: *AmAu; AmAu&B; AmBi; ApCAB; BenetAL 91; BibAL 8; BiDSA; BioIn 3, 8, 12, 13, 15; CnDAL; DcAmAu; DcAmB; DcLB 3, 11; DcLEL; DcNAA; EncAHmr; FifSWrB; NatCAB 9; OhA&B; OxCAmL 65, 83, 95; PeoHis; REnAL; SouWr; TwCBDA; WhAm HS*

Thompson Twins
[Tom Bailey; Alannan Currie; Joe Leway]
English. Music Group
Chesterfield, England group; hit singles include "Hold Me Now," 1984; "King for Just One Day," 1986.
Source: *EncPR&S 89; EncRk 88; EncRkSt; HarEnR 86; PenEncP; RkOn 85; WhsNW 85*

Thomson, Bobby
[Robert Brown Thomson]
"Nick the Greek"
American. Baseball Player
Outfielder, 1946-60; best known for home run that won pennant for NY Giants—"the shot heard round the world"—1951.
b. Oct 25, 1923 in Glasgow, Scotland
Source: *Ballpl 90; BiDAmSp Sup; BioIn 3, 4, 10, 11, 15, 16, 17; LegTOT; WhoProB 73*

Thomson, Charles Wyville, Sir
Scottish. Naturalist
Pioneered in deep-sea study; wrote oceanographic classic *Depths of the Sea,* 1873.
b. Mar 5, 1830 in Bonsyde, Scotland
d. Mar 10, 1882 in Bonsyde, Scotland
Source: *Alli SUP; AsBiEn; BiESc; BioIn 2, 6; BritAu 19; CamDcSc; CelCen; DcBiPP; DcNaB; DcScB; InSci; NewCol 75; WhDW; WhWE*

Thomson, Earl
Canadian. Track Athlete
Hurdler; won gold medal in 110-meter hurdles, 1920 Olympics.
b. Feb 15, 1895 in Prince Albert, Saskatchewan, Canada
d. Apr 19, 1971 in Annapolis, Maryland
Source: *BioIn 10; WhoTr&F 73*

Thomson, Elihu
American. Inventor, Scientist
Invented electric welding; obtained over 700 patents.
b. Mar 29, 1853 in Manchester, England
d. Mar 13, 1937 in Swampscott, Massachusetts
Source: *AmBi; ApCAB; BiESc; BioIn 3, 4, 5, 11, 17, 21; DcAmB S2; DcScB; HarEnUS; InSci; LarDcSc; LinLib S; NatCAB 10, 27; OxCAmH; TwCBDA; WebAB 74, 79; WhAm 1; WhDW; WorInv*

Thomson, George Paget, Sir
English. Physicist
Shared Nobel Prize in physics, 1937, with Clinton J Davisson.
b. May 3, 1892 in Cambridge, England
d. Sep 10, 1975 in Cambridge, England
Source: *AsBiEn; BiESc; BioIn 1, 2, 3, 5, 10, 11, 14, 15, 20; BlueB 76; CamDcSc; ConAu 4NR, 5R, 61; CurBio 47, 75, 75N; DcNaB 1971; DcScB S2; InSci; IntWW 74, 75; LarDcSc; LngCTC; McGEWB; McGMS 80; NotTwCS; ObitOF 79; WhAm 6; WhE&EA; Who 74; WhoLA; WhoNob, 90, 95; WhoWor 74, 76; WorAl*

Thomson, Gordon
Canadian. Actor
Played Adam Carrington on TV drama "Dynasty," 1982-89.
b. Mar 2, 1951 in Ottawa, Ontario, Canada
Source: *BioIn 13; ConTFT 8*

Thomson, James
Scottish. Poet
Best known collection *The Seasons,* 1730, emphasized blank verse, nature as a theme within itself.
b. Sep 11, 1700 in Ednam, Scotland
d. Aug 27, 1748 in Richmond, England
Source: *Alli; AtlBL; BbD; Benet 87, 96; BiD&SB; BioIn 1, 2, 3, 4, 5, 6, 7, 9, 10, 12, 16, 17; BlkwCE; BlmGEL; BritAu; CamGEL; CamGLE; CasWL; ChhPo, S1, S3; CmScLit; CnE&AP; CrtT 2, 4; DcArts; DcBiPP; DcEnA; DcEnL; DcEuL; DcLB 95; DcLEL; DcNaB; EvLB; GrWrEL P; LinLib L; LitC 16, 29; LngCEL; McGEWB; MouLC 2; NewC; NewCBEL; NotNAT B; OxCEng 67, 85, 95; OxCMus; OxCThe 67; PenC ENG; RAdv 1, 14, 13-1; REn; RfGEnL 91; RGFBP; WebE&AL; WhDW*

Thomson, James
[B V; Bysshe Vanolis]
Scottish. Poet, Essayist
Best known for "The City of Dreadful Night," 1874, which expressed his despair of current political affairs.
b. Nov 23, 1834, Scotland
d. Jun 3, 1882 in London, England
Source: *Alli SUP; AtlBL; BbD; Benet 87, 96; BiD&SB; BioIn 2, 9, 11, 14; BlmGEL; BritAu 19; CamGEL; CamGLE; CasWL; CelCen; ChhPo, S1, S2; CmScLit; CnE&AP; DcArts; DcEnA; DcEuL; DcLB 35; DcLEL; DcNaB; EvLB; GrWrEL P; LngCEL; MouLC 4; NewC; NewCBEL; NinCLC 18; OxCEng 67, 85, 95; PenC ENG; REn; RfGEnL 91; WebE&AL*

Thomson, Joseph John, Sir
English. Scientist
Won 1906 Nobel Prize in physics for experiments in conduction of electricity through gases.
b. Dec 18, 1856 in Manchester, England
d. Aug 30, 1940 in Cambridge, England
Source: *AsBiEn; BiESc; BioIn 1, 2, 3, 4, 5, 7, 9, 11, 12, 13, 14, 15, 17, 20; CamDcSc; CurBio 40; DcInv; DcNaB 1931; DcScB; FacFETw; GrBr; InSci; LinLib L, S; McGEWB; RAdv 14; WhDW; WhE&EA; WhoLA; WhoNob, 90, 95; WorAl; WorScD*

Thomson, Ken(neth Roy)
[Lord Thompson of Fleet]
Canadian. Business Executive
Owner Thomson Newspapers, Toronto, 1953—; chairman, International Thomson Organization, Ltd; son of Roy.
b. Sep 1, 1923 in Toronto, Ontario, Canada
Source: *St&PR 84, 87, 91, 93, 96, 97; WhoAm 74, 76, 78, 80, 82, 84, 86, 88; WhoE 85, 89; WhoFI 83, 85, 87; WhoWor 74, 87*

Thomson, Peter William
Australian. Golfer
International golfer, 1950-65; won British Open five times.
b. Aug 23, 1929 in Melbourne, Australia
Source: *BioIn 8, 9, 13; FarE&A 81; IntWW 83, 89, 91, 93; WhoGolf*

Thomson, Roy Herbert
[Lord Thompson of Fleet]
English. Newspaper Publisher, Business Executive
Founded media empire, Thomson Organization Ltd; today has publishing, travel, oil.
b. Jun 5, 1894 in Toronto, Ontario, Canada
d. Aug 4, 1976 in London, England
Source: *BioIn 3, 5, 6, 7, 8, 10, 11, 17, 20; CanWW 70; ConAu 69; CurBio 60, 76; DcNaB 1971; DcTwBBL; FacFETw; IntWW 74; WhAm 7; Who 74; WorAl*

Thomson, Tom
Canadian. Artist
Short painting career ended when found mysteriously drowned; his Canadian landscapes directly influenced the Group of Seven.
b. Aug 4, 1877 in Claremont, Ontario, Canada
d. Jul 8, 1917 in Canoe Lake, Ontario, Canada
Source: *ArtsAmW 3; BioIn 1, 2, 4, 8, 9, 10, 11, 13, 18; CreCan 1; IlBEAAW; McGDA; McGEWB; OxCArt; OxDcArt; PhDcTCA 77*

Thomson, Vernon Wallace
American. Politician
Rep. congressman from WI, 1960-75; member of Federal Election Commission, 1975-79.
b. Nov 5, 1905 in Richland Center, Wisconsin
d. Apr 2, 1988 in Washington, District of Columbia
Source: *BiDrAC; BiDrGov 1789; BiDrUSC 89; BioIn 4, 5, 15, 16; CngDr 74; CurBio 58, 88; WhAm 9; WhoAm 74, 76, 78, 80; WhoAmP 73, 75, 77, 79, 81, 83, 85, 87; WhoGov 72, 75; WhoMW 74, 76*

Thomson, Virgil Garnett
American. Composer, Musician, Critic
Wrote 100 musical portraits; opera *Four Saints in Three Acts,* 1934; won Oscar for score of *Louisiana Story,* 1948.
b. Nov 25, 1896 in Kansas City, Missouri
d. Sep 30, 1989 in New York, New York
Source: *AmComp; ASCAP 66; Baker 84; Benet 96; BiDAmM; BiE&WWA; CurBio 40, 66; DcCM; EncAAH; EncAB-H 1974, 1996; IntWW 83; McGEWB; NewYTBE 71; NotNAT; REn; REnAL; TwCA; WebAB 74, 79; WhoAm 86; WhoAmM 83; WhoMus 72*

Thon, William
American. Artist
Leans toward cubism; paintings are of architectural subjects.
b. Aug 8, 1906 in New York, New York
Source: *BioIn 1, 3, 4, 6, 7; McGDA; WhAmArt 85; WhoAm 74, 76, 78, 80, 82, 84, 86, 88, 90, 92, 94, 95, 96, 97; WhoAmA 73, 76, 78, 80, 82, 84, 86, 89, 91, 93*

Thorarensen, Jakob
Icelandic. Poet
Wrote poetry that championed the worker; *Snaljos,* 1914.
b. May 18, 1886 in Hunavatnssysla, Iceland
d. 1972, Iceland
Source: *BioIn 2; WhE&EA*

Thorborg, Kerstin
Swedish. Opera Singer
Sometimes considered greatest Wagnerian Mezzo-soprano of all time; NY Met., 1936-50.
b. May 19, 1896 in Hedemora, Sweden
d. Apr 12, 1970 in Falun, Sweden
Source: *Baker 78, 84, 92; BioIn 6, 8, 9, 11; CurBio 40, 70; IntDcOp; MetOEnc; MusSN; NewEOp 71; NewGrDA 86; NewGrDM 80; NewGrDO; NewYTBE 70; OxDcOp; PenDiMP*

Thoreau, Henry David
American. Author
Wrote essay *Civil Disobedience,* 1849; novel *Walden,* 1854.
b. Jul 12, 1817 in Concord, Massachusetts
d. May 6, 1862 in Concord, Massachusetts
Source: *Alli; AmAu; AmAu&B; AmBi; AmCulL; AmRef; AmSocL; AmWr; AnCL; ApCAB; AtlBL; BbD; BbtC; Benet 87, 96; BenetAL 91; BibAL 8; BiD&SB; BiDMoPL; BiDTran; BioIn 1, 2, 3, 4, 5, 6, 7, 8, 9, 10, 11, 12, 13, 14, 15, 16, 17, 18, 19, 20, 21; CamGEL; CamGLE; CamHAL; CasWL; CelCen; Chambr 3; ChhPo; CnDAL; CnE&AP; ColARen; CrtT 3, 4; CyAL 2; CyWA 58; DcAmAu; DcAmB; DcArts; DcEnA; DcLB 1; DcLEL; DcNAA; Dis&D; Drake; EncAAH; EncAB-H 1974, 1996; EncARH; EncEnv; EncEth; EnvEnc; EvLB; GrWrEL N; HarEnUS; IlEncMy; InSci; LegTOT; LinLib L, S; MagSAmL; McGEWB; MemAm; MouLC 3; NatCAB 2; NewGrDA 86; NinCLC 7, 21; OxCAmH; OxCAmL 65, 83, 95; OxCCan; OxCEng 67, 85, 95; OxCPhil; PenC AM; PeoHis; RadHan; RAdv 1, 14, 13-1; RComAH; RComWL; REn; REnAL; REnAW; RfGAmL 87, 94; RGFAP; TwCBDA; TwoTYeD; WebAB 74, 79; WebE&AL; WhAm HS; WorAl; WorAlBi; WorLitC; WrPh*

Thorek, Max
American. Surgeon
Founded International College of Surgeons, 1935; developed successful gall bladder surgery technique.
b. Mar 10, 1880, Austria-Hungary
d. Jan 25, 1960 in Chicago, Illinois
Source: *BioIn 2, 5, 7; CurBio 51, 60; DcAmB, S6; NatCAB 48; WhAm 3; WhAmArt 85*

Thorez, Maurice
French. Politician
Leader of French Communist party, secretary general, 1930-64, first pres., 1964.
b. Apr 28, 1900 in Noyelles Godault, France
d. Jul 11, 1964
Source: *BiDFrPL; BioIn 1, 2, 3, 4, 6, 7, 9, 17; ConAu 113; CurBio 46, 64; DcPol; DcTwCCu 2; DcTwHis; EncWB; ObitOF 79; ObitT 1961; WhAm 4*

Thorn, Gaston
Luxembourg. Politician
Pres., European Commission, exec. section of European Economic Community, 1981-84; prime minister of Luxembourg, 1974-79.
b. Sep 3, 1928, Luxembourg
Source: *EncWB; IntWW 74, 75, 76, 77, 78, 79, 80, 81, 82, 83, 89, 91, 93; IntYB 82; NewYTBS 75; Who 82, 83, 85; WhoEIO 82; WhoWor 74, 76, 78*

Thornburgh, Dick
[Richard Lewis Thornburgh]
American. Politician
Rep. governor of PA, 1979-87; succeeded Edwin Meese as US attorney general, 1988-91.
b. Jul 16, 1932 in Pittsburgh, Pennsylvania
Source: *AlmAP 88; BiDrGov 1978, 1983; BiDrUSE 89; BioIn 11; IntWW 89, 91, 93; NewYTBS 75, 78, 90; Who 92, 94; WhoAm 76, 78, 80, 82, 86, 88, 90, 92, 94, 95, 96, 97; WhoAmL 78, 79, 83, 90, 92, 94, 96; WhoAmP 79, 85; WhoE 74, 75, 77, 79, 81, 83, 85, 86, 89, 91, 93; WhoGov 72, 75, 77; WhoWor 82, 87, 89, 91*

Thorndike, Edward L(ee)
American. Psychologist
Animal behavior studies created groundwork for connectionism theory.
b. Aug 31, 1874 in Williamsburg, Massachusetts
d. Aug 9, 1949 in Montrose, New York
Source: *AmAu&B; AmDec 1900; AmLY; AmSocL; ApCAB X; BiDAmEd; BiDPsy; BioIn 2, 3, 4, 8, 12, 14, 15; ConAu 121; CurBio 49; DcAmAu; DcAmB S4; DcAmImH; DcNAA; EncAB-H 1974, 1996; InSci; LinLib L, S; LuthC 75; McGEWB; NamesHP; NatCAB 15, 51; ObitOF 79; OxCAmH; RAdv 14; REnAL; WebAB 74, 79; WhAm 2; WhE&EA; WhNAA*

Thorndike, Lynn
American. Historian
Wrote eight-vol. *History of Magic and Experimental Science,* 1923-58.
b. Jul 24, 1882 in Lynn, Massachusetts
d. Dec 28, 1965 in New York, New York
Source: *AmAu&B; BioIn 4, 5, 7, 8; ConAu 111; DcAmB S7; NatCAB 51; OhA&B; REnAL; TwCA SUP; WhAm 4; WhE&EA; WhNAA*

Thorndike, Sybil, Dame
[Agnes Sybil Thorndike]
English. Actor
Best known for her lead role in *Saint Joan,* 1923.
b. Oct 24, 1882 in Gainsborough, England
d. Jun 9, 1976 in Chelsea, England
Source: *BiE&WWA; BioIn 2, 3, 4, 9, 10, 11, 14; BlueB 76; CamGWoT; CnThe; ContDcW 89; CurBio 53, 76N; DcArts; DcNaB 1971; EncWT; Ent; Film 2; FilmEn; FilmgC; GrBr; HalFC 80, 84, 88; IlWWBF, A; IntDcWB; IntWW 74, 75, 76; InWom, SUP; LegTOT; MotPP; MovMk; NewC; NewYTBS 76; NotNAT A, B; OxCThe 67, 83; PlP&P; REn; WhAm 7; WhDW; Who 74; WhoAmW 74; WhoHol A; WhoThe 72, 77, 81N; WhoWor 74; WhScrn 83; WorAl; WorAlBi*

Thorne, Jim
American. Author, Adventurer
First non-Mexican to make successful dive off Acapulco cliff, 1965.
b. 1922 in Milwaukee, Wisconsin
Source: *ConAu 1NR, 1R*

Thornell, Jack Randolph
American. Photographer
With AP, 1964—; won Pulitzer, 1967.

b. Aug 29, 1939 in Vicksburg, Mississippi
Source: *WhoAm 74, 76, 78, 80, 82, 84, 86, 88, 90, 92, 94, 95, 96, 97; WhoSSW 73*

Thorneycroft, (George Edward) Peter
English. Politician
Member of Parliament, 1948-66; chairman, Conservative Party, 1975-81.
b. Jul 26, 1909
d. Jun 4, 1994 in London, England
Source: *BioIn 3, 4, 20; CurBio 94N; IntWW 93; WhAm 11; WhoWor 74, 76, 78, 84, 87, 89, 91, 93*

Thornhill, Claude
American. Songwriter, Bandleader
Led major dance band, 1940s; noted for novelty arrangements.
b. Aug 10, 1908 in Terre Haute, Indiana
d. Jul 1, 1965 in Caldwell, New Jersey
Source: *ASCAP 66, 80; Baker 84; BiDAmM; BioIn 7, 9, 12; CmpEPM; WhoHol B; WhoJazz 72; WhScrn 74, 77, 83*

Thornton, Charles Bates
''''Tex''''
American. Businessman
Helped establish Litton Industries, served as chm., CEO, 1953-81; headed ''Whiz Kids'' team at Ford Motor Co., 1946-48.
b. Jul 22, 1913 in Haskell, Texas
d. Nov 24, 1981 in Holmby Hills, California
Source: *AnObit 1981; BiDAmBL 83; BioIn 6, 8, 9, 12, 13; CelR; CurBio 70, 82; Dun&B 79; IntWW 74, 75, 76, 77, 78, 79, 80, 81; LElec; NewYTBS 81; WhAm 8; WhoAm 74, 76, 78, 80, 84; WhoFI 74, 75, 79, 81; WhoWest 74, 76, 78, 80, 82; WhoWor 74*

Thornton, Matthew
American. Continental Congressman, Physician
Congressman from NH; signed Declaration of Independence, 1776.
b. 1714?, Ireland
d. Jun 24, 1803 in Newburyport, Massachusetts
Source: *Alli; AmBi; ApCAB; BiAUS; BiDrAC; BiDrACR; BiDrUSC 89; BioIn 7, 8, 9; DcAmB; DcAmMeB, 84; DcIrB 78, 88; Drake; EncAR; EncCRAm; HarEnUS; NatCAB 11; TwCBDA; WhAm HS; WhAmP; WhAmRev*

Thornton, Willie Mae
''''Big Mama''''
American. Singer
Known for renditions of ''Have Mercy Baby''; ''Hound Dog''; ''Ball and Chain.''
b. Dec 11, 1926 in Montgomery, Alabama
d. Jul 25, 1984 in Los Angeles, California
Source: *AnObit 1984; BiDAfM; BioIn 19; BluesWW; ConAu 113; EncRk 88; GuBlues; HanAmWH; InB&W 80, 85; NewYTBS 84; NotBlAW 2; PenEncP; RkOn 74*

Thorp, Willard Long
American. Economist
Helped draft the Marshall Plan for the economic recovery of Europe after WW II.
b. May 24, 1899 in Oswego, New York
d. May 10, 1992 in Pelham, Massachusetts
Source: *AmMWSc 73S; BioIn 1, 2, 11, 16, 17, 18, 19; BlueB 76; ConAu 1R, 28NR, 130, 137; IntWW 74, 75, 76, 77, 78, 79, 80, 81, 82, 83, 89, 91; NewYTBS 90; WhAm 10; WhoAm 74, 76, 78; WhoE 91; WhoWor 74; WrDr 76*

Thorpe, Grace F.
American. Political Activist
Daughter of Olympian Jim Thorpe; made efforts to reinstate her father's medals and to establish a museum in his honor; former lobbyist for the National Congress of American Indians.
b. 1921
Source: *BioIn 21; NotNaAm*

Thorpe, Jeremy
[John Jeremy Thorpe]
English. Political Leader
Liberal MP, 1959-79; held balance of power in govt., mid-1970s.
b. Apr 29, 1929 in London, England
Source: *BioIn 7, 8, 10, 11, 12, 17; BlueB 76; CurBio 74; DcPol; FacFETw; IntWW 74, 75, 76, 77, 78, 79, 80, 81, 82, 83, 89, 91; IntYB 78, 79, 80, 81, 82; NewYTBS 74, 78; Who 74, 82, 83, 85, 88, 90, 92; WhoWor 74, 76, 78, 80, 82*

Thorpe, Jim
[James Francis Thorpe]
American. Track Athlete
Called ''greatest athlete ever''; only person ever to win gold medals in decathalon, pentathlon, 1912 Olympics; played pro baseball, football; first pres. of NFL, 1920-21; Burt Lancaster starred in film of life, 1951.
b. May 28, 1888 in Shawnee, Oklahoma
d. Mar 28, 1953 in Los Angeles, California
Source: *AmDec 1910; BiDAmSp FB; BiNAW SupB; BioIn 2, 3, 4, 5, 6, 7, 8, 9, 10, 11, 12, 13, 14, 15, 16, 17, 18, 19, 20, 21; ConHero 2; CurBio 50, 53; DcAmB S5; EncAB-H 1974, 1996; EncNAB; EncWB; FacFETw; HalFC 80, 84, 88; LegTOT; OxCAmH; RComAH; WebAB 74, 79; WhAm 4, HSA; WhoFtbl 74; WhoHol B; WhoProB 73; WhoSpor; WhoTr&F 73; WhScrn 74, 77; WorAl*

Thorpe, Thomas Bangs
American. Humorist
Created tall-tale ''The Big Bear of Arkansas.''
b. Mar 1, 1815 in Westfield, Massachusetts
d. Sep 20, 1878 in New York, New York
Source: *Alli; AmAu; AmAu&B; ApCAB; BibAL 8; BiDSA; BioIn 4, 6, 8, 12, 13, 15; CnDAL; CyAL 2; DcAmAu; DcAmB; DcEnL; DcLB 3, 11; DcLEL; DcNAA; Drake; EncAAH; EncAHmr; FifSWrB; GrWrEL N; HarEnUS; NatCAB 6; NewYHSD; OxCAmL 65, 83; PeoHis; RAdv 14; REnAL; REnAW; RfGAmL 87, 94; SouWr; TwCBDA; WebAB 74, 79; WebE&AL; WhAm HS*

Thorvaldsen, Albert Bertel
[Bertel Thorwaldsen]
Danish. Sculptor
Statues of various figures include Venus, Psyche, Jason.
b. 1770 in Copenhagen, Denmark
d. 1844
Source: *DcArts; DcNiCA; NewCol 75; OxCArt; WebBD 83*

Thou, Jacques Auguste de
French. Historian, Statesman
Wrote *Historia sui Temporis,* 1604-08.
b. Oct 8, 1553
d. May 7, 1617
Source: *DcBiPP; DcCathB; DcEuL; NewCBEL; NewCol 75; OxCFr; REn; WebBD 83*

Threadgill, Henry
American. Jazz Musician, Composer
Jazz saxophinist and composer; albums include *Easily Slip into Another World,* 1987.
b. Feb 14, 1944 in Chicago, Illinois
Source: *AllMusG; BiDJaz; BioIn 15; ConMus 9; NewGrDJ 88; PenEncP*

Three Dog Night
[Michael Allsup; James Greenspoon; Daniel Hutton; Skip Konte; Charles Negron; Joseph Schermine; Floyd Sneed; Cory Wells]
Australian. Music Group
Rock band formed, 1968; hits include ''Joy to the World,'' 1971.
Source: *BiDAmM; ConMuA 80A; ConMus 5; EncPR&S 74, 89; EncRk 88; EncRkSt; HarEnR 86; IlEncRk; NewAmDM; PenEncP; RkOn 78, 84; RolSEnR 83; WhoRock 81; WhoRocM 82*

Three Stooges, The
[Joe Besser; Joe DeRita; Larry Fine; Curly Howard; Moe Howard; Shemp Howard]
American. Comedy Team
Performed in vaudeville, 1923; made 200 short films, 1934-58.
Source: *BioIn 10, 11; EncAFC; FacFETw; FilmEn; ForYSC; Funs; GrMovC; HalFC 84, 88; IntDcF 1-3, 2-3; IntMPA 94N; JoeFr; MotPP; NewYTBS 75, 88; ObitOF 79; What 4; WhoCom; WhoHol 92, B; WhoHrs 80*

Threlkeld, Richard D
American. Broadcast Journalist
Correspondent CBS News, 1966-82; chief correspondent ABC News, 1982-89.
b. Nov 30, 1937 in Cedar Rapids, Iowa
Source: *ConAu 65; WhoAm 84, 86; WhoAmP 87, 89, 91, 93, 95; WhoTelC*

Throckmorton, Cleon
American. Designer
Pioneer in stage, set design; began career while working on Eugene O'Neill's plays, 1920s.
b. Oct 8, 1897 in Atlantic City, New Jersey
d. Oct 23, 1965
Source: *BiE&WWA; BioIn 7; CamGWoT; CurBio 43, 65; LegTOT; NotNAT B; OxCAmT 84; PlP&P; WhAm 4; WhAmArt 85; WhThe*

Throneberry, Marv(in Eugene)
"Marvelous Marv"
American. Baseball Player
First baseman, 1955, 1958-63; best known for time with NY Mets, where he became symbol of team's inept play in early yrs.
b. Sep 12, 1933 in Collierville, Tennessee
Source: *Ballpl 90; BaseEn 88; BioIn 20; LegTOT; WhoProB 73*

Thucydides
Greek. Historian
Wrote *History of the Peloponnesian War,* called first modern history.
b. c. 460BC in Athens, Greece
d. c. 399BC in Athens, Greece
Source: *AncWr; AtlBL; BbD; Benet 87, 96; BiD&SB; CasWL; ClMLC 17; CyWA 58; DcBiPP; DcEnL; Dis&D; GrFLW; Grk&L; McGEWB; NewC; OxCClL, 89; OxCEng 67, 85, 95; OxDcByz; PenC CL; RAdv 14; RComWL; REn; RfGWoL 95; WhDW*

Thuilier, Raymond
French. Chef
Known for his classic French cuisine with distinct sauces and multiple courses.
b. Jan 11, 1897 in Chambery, France
d. Jun 20, 1993 in Carita, France
Source: *AnObit 1993; BioIn 19; WhoFr 79*

Thulin, Ingrid
Swedish. Actor
Films include *Wild Strawberries; The Damned; Cries and Whispers.*
b. Jan 27, 1929 in Solleftea, Sweden
Source: *BiDFilm, 81, 94; BioIn 6, 11, 17; CelR; ConTFT 9; EncEurC; EncWT; FilmEn; FilmgC; ForYSC; HalFC 80, 84, 88; IntDcF 1-3, 2-3; IntMPA 75, 76, 77, 78, 79, 80, 81, 82, 84, 86, 88, 92, 94, 96; IntWW 74, 75, 76, 77, 78, 79, 80, 81, 82, 83, 89, 91, 93; InWom SUP; ItaFilm; LegTOT; MotPP; MovMk; OxCFilm; WhoEnt 92; WhoHol 92, A; WhoWor 74, 76, 78, 84, 87, 89, 91, 95, 96, 97; WomWMM; WorAl; WorAlBi; WorEFlm*

Thum, Marcella
American. Children's Author
Won Edgar for first book, *Mystery at Crane's Landing,* 1964; other books include *Margarite,* 1987.
Source: *AuBYP 2S, 3; BioIn 9, 13; ConAu 6NR, 9R, 21NR, 49NR; DcAmChF 1960; IntAu&W 77, 86, 89, 91, 93; SmATA 3, 28; TwCRHW 90, 94; WrDr 76, 80, 82, 84, 86, 88, 90, 92*

Thurber, Charles
American. Inventor
Patented, 1843, hand printing machine that preceded typewriter.
b. Jan 2, 1803 in East Brookfield, Massachusetts
d. Nov 7, 1886 in Nashua, New Hampshire
Source: *BioIn 12; DcAmB; WhAm HS*

Thurber, James Grover
American. Author
Major contributor to *New Yorker* mag., 1927-52; known for whimsical writings, cartoons; best-known short story: "The Secret Life of Walter Mitty"; book: *The Thurber Carnival,* 1945.
b. Dec 8, 1894 in Columbus, Ohio
d. Nov 2, 1961 in New York, New York
Source: *AmAu&B; AnCL; AtlBL; AuBYP 2; Benet 96; BiDAmNC; BkCL; CasWL; CnDAL; CnMWL; ConAmA; ConAu 73; ConLC 5, 11; CurBio 40, 62; EncAB-H 1996; OxCAmL 65; PenC AM; RGTwCWr; SJGFanW; TwCA*

Thurman, Howard
American. Educator
Baptist minister since 1925; taught theology, dean of chapel, Howard U., 1932-44; first full-time black professor, Boston U., School of Theology, 1953-65.
b. Nov 18, 1900 in Daytona Beach, Florida
d. Apr 10, 1981 in San Francisco, California
Source: *AnObit 1981; BioIn 19; BlkAWP; BlkWr 1; BlueB 76; CmCal; ConAu 25NR, 97, 103; ConBlB 3; CurBio 55, 81, 81N; DcAmReB 2; Ebony 1; LinLib L, S; LivgBAA; NegAl 83, 89; NewYTBS 81; RelLAm 91; SchCGBL; SelBAAf; SelBAAu; WhAm 7; WhoAm 74, 76, 78; WhoBlA 75, 77; WhoRel 77*

Thurman, Uma
American. Actor
Appeared in *Dangerous Liaisons,* 1988; *Henry and June,* 1990; *Pulp Fiction,* 1994.
b. Apr 29, 1970 in Boston, Massachusetts
Source: *ConTFT 10; CurBio 96; IntMPA 92, 94, 96; LegTOT; News 94, 94-2; WhoHol 92*

Thurmond, Nate
[Nathaniel Thurmond]
American. Basketball Player
Center, 1963-77, mostly with San Francisco-Golden State; known for rebounding; Hall of Fame, 1984.
b. Jul 25, 1941 in Akron, Ohio
Source: *BasBi; BiDAmSp BK; InB&W 80; NewYTBS 76; OfNBA 87; WhoAfA 96; WhoAm 78; WhoBbl 73; WhoBlA 75, 77, 80, 85, 88, 90, 92, 94; WhoSpor*

Thurmond, Strom
[James Strom Thurmond]
American. Politician
Dem., then Rep. senator from SC, 1955—; led segregationists, 1940s-50s; conducted longest Senate filibuster, 24 hrs., 1957.
b. Dec 5, 1902 in Edgefield, South Carolina
Source: *AlmAP 82, 84, 88, 92, 96; AmPolLe; BiDrAC; BiDrGov 1789; BiDrUSC 89; BioIn 1, 4, 5, 6, 7, 8, 9, 10, 11, 13, 18, 20, 21; BlueB 76; CelR, 90; CivRSt; CngDr 74, 77, 79, 81, 83, 85, 87, 89, 91, 93, 95; ConAu 89; CurBio 92; EncAAH; EncSoH; EncWB; IntWW 74, 75, 76, 77, 78, 79, 80, 81, 82, 83, 89, 91, 93; IntYB 78, 79, 80, 81, 82; LegTOT; PolPar; PolProf E, J, K, NF; PolsAm 84; WebAB 74, 79; WhoAm 74, 76, 78, 80, 82, 84, 86, 88, 90, 92, 94, 95, 96, 97; WhoAmP 73, 75, 77, 79, 81, 83, 85, 87, 89, 91, 93, 95; WhoGov 72, 75, 77; WhoSSW 73, 75, 76, 78, 80, 82, 84, 86, 88, 91, 93, 95, 97; WhoWor 74, 78, 80, 82, 84, 87, 89, 91; WorAl; WorAlBi*

Thurow, Lester C
American. Economist, Educator
Most influential economist of his generation; wrote *Zero-Sum Society,* 1980.
b. May 7, 1938 in Livingston, Montana
Source: *AmEA 74; BioIn 9, 10, 12, 15; ConAu 81; CurBio 90; WhoAm 88; WhoEc 86; WhoFI 85; WrDr 92*

Thurston, Howard
American. Magician
Practiced magic since childhood; toured US, 1907-08.
b. Jul 20, 1869 in Columbus, Ohio
d. Apr 13, 1936 in Miami, Florida
Source: *BioIn 4, 5, 7, 16; ChhPo; DcAmB S2; DcNAA; MagIlD; NatCAB 10; OhA&B; OxCAmT 84; WhAm 1; WhJnl*

Thyssen, Fritz
German. Industrialist
Early Nazi supporter; broke with party, fled to Switzerland, WW II.
b. Nov 9, 1873
d. Feb 8, 1951, Argentina
Source: *BioIn 1, 2, 3, 14; CurBio 40, 51; EncTR, 91; WorAl; WorAlBi*

Thyssen-Bornemisza de Kaszan, Hans Heinrich, Baron
Netherlands. Art Collector
Art collection considered finest in the world, second only to the Queen of England.
b. Apr 13, 1921 in The Hague, Netherlands
Source: *BioIn 12; CurBio 89; IntWW 91; Who 92*

Tiant, Luis Clemente
Cuban. Baseball Player
Pitcher, 1964-82, mostly with Boston; led AL in ERA twice.
b. Nov 23, 1940 in Havana, Cuba
Source: *BioIn 9, 10, 11; InB&W 80, 85; WhoAm 78, 80, 82; WhoBlA 77, 80; WhoProB 73; WorAl*

Tibbets, Paul Warfield
American. Pilot
Piloted the *Enola Gay,* plane that dropped atomic bomb on Hiroshima, Aug 6, 1945.
b. 1915
Source: *BioIn 10, 11, 12; St&PR 84, 87; WhWW-II*

Tibbett, Lawrence Mervil
American. Opera Singer, Actor
Popular leading baritone, NY Met., 1923-50; starred in film *New Moon* with Grace Moore, 1931.
b. Nov 16, 1896 in Bakersfield, California
d. Jul 15, 1960 in New York, New York
Source: *Baker 84; CurBio 45, 60; DcAmB S6; FilmgC; LinLib S; WhAm 4; WhoHol B; WhScrn 74, 77*

Tiberius Julius Caesar Augustus
[Tiberius Claudius Nero]
Roman. Ruler
Second Roman Emperor, AD 14-37.
b. Nov 16, 42BC in Rome, Italy
d. Mar 16, 37AD in Campania, Italy
Source: *GenMudB; McGEWB; NewCol 75; REn*

Tiburzi, Bonnie
American. Pilot
First woman hired by a major airline, American Airlines 727 fleet, 1973.
b. 1948?
Source: *BioIn 9, 12, 17; ConAu 136; SmATA 65; WomFir; WrDr 94*

Tichatschek, Joseph
German. Opera Singer
Principal tenor, Dresden Opera, 1837-70; admired by Wagner.
b. Jul 11, 1807 in Weckseldorf, Germany
d. Jan 18, 1886 in Dresden, Germany
Source: *Baker 84, 92; BioIn 14, 16; NewEOp 71; OxDcOp*

Tickner, Charlie
[Charles Tickner]
American. Skater
Four-time US champion figure skater, 1977-80; world champion, 1978.
b. Nov 13, 1953 in Oakland, California
Source: *BiDAmSp BK; BioIn 11, 12; LegTOT; WhoSpor; WorAl*

Ticknor, George
American. Historian
Wrote *History of Spanish Literature,* 1849; founded Boston Public Library, 1852.
b. Aug 1, 1791 in Boston, Massachusetts
d. Jan 26, 1871 in Boston, Massachusetts
Source: *Alli, SUP; AmAu; AmAu&B; AmBi; ApCAB; BbD; Benet 87; BenetAL 91; BiDAmEd; BiD&SB; BiDTran; BioIn 1, 2, 3, 5, 7, 11, 12, 16, 20; CasWL; Chambr 3; ChhPo S1; CyAL 1; DcAmAu; DcAmB; DcAmBC; DcAmLiB; DcBiPP; DcEnL; DcLB 1, 59, 140; DcNAA; DcSpL; Drake; EvLB; HarEnUS; LegTOT; NatCAB 6; NewYHSD; OxCAmH; OxCAmL 65, 83, 95; OxCEng 67; OxCSpan; PeoHis; REn; REnAL; TwCBDA; WebAB 74, 79; WhAm HS*

Tidyman, Ernest
American. Author, Screenwriter
Wrote novel, screenplay *Shaft,* won best screenplay Oscar for *The French Connection,* 1971.
b. Jan 1, 1928 in Cleveland, Ohio
d. Jul 14, 1984 in London, England
Source: *AnObit 1984; BioIn 8, 9, 12; ConAu 29NR, 73, 113; EncSF, 93; GangFlm; HalFC 84, 88; ScF&FL 92; TwCCr&M 80, 85, 91; WhAm 8; WhoAm 76, 78, 80, 82; WrDr 82, 84*

Tiede, Tom Robert
American. Journalist
Expert on war; correspondent for Newspaper Enterprise Assn., 1964-92.
b. Feb 24, 1937 in Huron, South Dakota
Source: *AmAu&B; BiDAmNC; WhoAm 74, 76, 78, 80, 82, 84, 86, 88, 90, 92, 96, 97; WhoE 74; WhoSSW 95; WhoWor 91, 93, 95, 96, 97*

Tiegs, Cheryl
American. Actor, Model
Highest paid model of 1970s; wrote *The Way to Natural Beauty,* 1980.
b. Sep 25, 1947 in Alhambra, California
Source: *BioIn 11, 12, 13; BkPepl; CelR 90; CurBio 82; InWom SUP; LegTOT; NewYTBS 78; WhoAm 84, 86; WhoAmW 85, 87*

Tiepolo, Giambattista
[Giovanni Battista Tiepol]
Italian. Artist
Works include frescoes, portraits, palace facades.
b. Mar 5, 1696 in Venice, Italy
d. Mar 27, 1770 in Madrid, Spain
Source: *AtlBL; McGEWB; OxCArt; REn; WebBD 83*

Tiepolo, Giovanni Domenico
Italian. Artist
Paintings include decorations of royal palace at Wurzburg.
b. 1727
d. 1804
Source: *BioIn 1, 3, 5, 9, 13; ClaDrA; McGDA; WebBD 83*

Tieri, Frank
"Funzi"; "Funzola"; "The Old Man"
Italian. Criminal
First man ever convicted of heading an organized-crime family, 1980; died before serving 10 yr. sentence.
b. 1904 in Castel Gandolfo, Italy
d. Mar 29, 1981 in New York, New York
Source: *BioIn 11, 12; NewYTBS 81*

Tierney, Gene
American. Actor
Played title role in *Laura,* 1944; wrote *Self-Portrait,* 1979.
b. Nov 11, 1920 in New York, New York
d. Nov 6, 1991 in Houston, Texas
Source: *AnObit 1991; BiDFilm, 81, 94; BioIn 5, 8, 9, 10, 11, 17, 18; CmMov; ConAu 116; ConTFT 11; FilmEn; FilmgC; ForYSC; GangFlm; HalFC 80, 84, 88; IntDcF 1-3, 2-3; IntMPA 75, 76, 77, 78, 79, 80, 81, 82, 84, 86, 88, 92; InWom, SUP; LegTOT; MotPP; MovMk; NewYTBS 91; WhAm 10; What 5; WhoHol 92, A; WorAl; WorAlBi; WorEFlm*

Tietjen, Heinz
German. Conductor, Producer
Director, Bayreuth Festival, 1931-44; noted Wagnerian producer.
b. Jun 24, 1881 in Tangiers, Morocco
d. Nov 1, 1967 in Bayreuth, Germany (West)
Source: *Baker 84, 92; CmOp; NewEOp 71; NewGrDO; OxDcOp*

Tietjens, Eunice
American. Poet, Author
Wrote poems *Profiles on China,* 1917; novel *Jake,* 1921.
b. Jul 29, 1884 in Chicago, Illinois
d. Sep 6, 1944 in Chicago, Illinois
Source: *AmAu&B; BenetAL 91; BioAmW; BioIn 4; ChhPo, S1, S2, S3; ConAmL; CurBio 44; DcLB 54; DcLEL; DcNAA; FemiCLE; InWom, SUP; JBA 34; NotAW; OxCAmL 65, 83, 95; OxCTwCP; REn; REnAL; TwCA, SUP; WhAm 2; WhNAA*

Tiffany
[Tiffany Renee Darwish]
American. Singer
Million-selling album, 1987; included "Could've Been," "I Think We're Alone Now."
b. Oct 2, 1971 in Norwalk, California
Source: *EncRkSt; LegTOT*

Tiffany, Charles Lewis
American. Jeweler
Founded exclusive jewelry store, Tiffany & Co., 1837; manufactured silverware, jewelry, art pieces.
b. Feb 15, 1812 in Killingly, Connecticut
d. Feb 18, 1902 in Irvington-on-Hudson, New York
Source: *AmBi; BioIn 7, 13, 15; DcAmB; Entr; LinLib S; NatCAB 2; TwCBDA; WebAB 74, 79; WhAm 1, 2; WorAl*

Tiffany, Louis Comfort
American. Artist, Designer
VP, director, Tiffany and Co. who discovered formula for making decorative glass, "Tiffany Favrile glass"; known for Tiffany lamps.
b. Feb 18, 1848 in New York, New York
d. Jan 17, 1933 in New York, New York
Source: *AmBi; AmCulL; AmDec 1900; AntBDN A; ApCAB; ArtsAmW 3; Benet 87, 96; BioIn 1, 2, 3, 4, 5, 6, 7, 8, 9, 10, 11, 12, 13, 15, 16, 17, 18, 19; BriEAA; CenC; DcAmB; DcArts; DcD&D; DcNiCA; DcTwDes; EncAB-H 1974, 1996; GayN; IlDcG; LinLib S; McGDA; McGEWB; NatCAB 7, 36; OxCDecA; OxDcArt; PenDiDA 89; PeoHis; PhDcTCA 77; REn; TwCBDA; WebAB 74, 79; WebBD 83; WhAm 1; WorAl; WorAlBi*

Tiffeau, Jacques Emile
French. Fashion Designer
Winner of two Coty Awards who designed coats, sportswear for Originala since 1976.
b. Oct 11, 1927 in Chenevelles, France
Source: *WhAm 9; WhoAm 74, 76, 78, 80, 82; WorFshn*

Tiffin, Pamela Kimberley
American. Model, Actor
Films include *The Pleasure Seekers,* 1964; *Harper,* 1966.
b. Oct 13, 1942 in Oklahoma City, Oklahoma
Source: *FilmgC; ForWC 70; HalFC 84; IntMPA 86; MotPP; WhoAm 74, 76, 78; WhoAmW 74; WhoHol A*

Tikaram, Tanita
American. Singer, Songwriter
Folk-rock performer; debut album *Ancient Heart,* 1988.
b. 1970, Germany (West)
Source: *BioIn 16; ConMus 9*

Tikhomirov, Vasily Dmitrievich
Russian. Dancer
Premier danseur Bolshoi Ballet 1893; Bolshoi teacher and director; helped maintain Bolshoi's classic techniques.
b. Mar 30, 1876 in Moscow, Russia
d. Jun 20, 1956 in Moscow, Union of Soviet Socialist Republics
Source: *BiDSovU; BioIn 4, 14; FacFETw*

Tilberis, Elizabeth
American. Editor
Editor-in-chief, *Harper's Bazaar,* 1992—
b. Sep 7, 1947 in Bath, England
Source: *News 94, 94-3; Who 92*

Tilbrook, Glenn
English. Singer, Musician
Guitarist, vocalist; collaborated with Chris Difford on over 600 songs.
b. Aug 31, 1957 in London, England
Source: *LegTOT; OnThGG; WhoRocM 82*

Tilden, Bill
[William Tatem, Jr. Tilden]
"Big Bill"
American. Tennis Player
US tennis champion, 1920-25, 1929; only man to win US championship six consecutive yrs.
b. Feb 10, 1893 in Philadelphia, Pennsylvania
d. Jun 5, 1953 in Hollywood, California
Source: *BioIn 17, 21; BuCMET; DcAmB S5; FacFETw; LegTOT; NotNAT B; RComAH; WebAB 74; WhAm 4; WhoHol B; WhoSpor; WhScrn 74, 77, 83*

Tilden, Samuel Jones
American. Politician, Lawyer
Dem. governor, NY, 1875-76; ran for pres. against Rutherford B Hayes.
b. Feb 9, 1814 in New Lebanon, New York
d. Aug 4, 1886 in Yonkers, New York
Source: *Alli SUP; AmAu&B; AmBi; AmPolLe; ApCAB; BiAUS; BiDrGov 1789; BioIn 2, 5, 7, 8, 9, 10; CelCen; CyAG; DcAmAu; DcAmB; DcNAA; Drake; EncAAH; EncAB-H 1974, 1996; HarEnUS; LinLib S; McGEWB; NatCAB 3; OxCAmH; REn; REnAL; TwCBDA; WebAB 74, 79; WhAm HS; WhAmP; WhCiWar; WorAl*

Till, Emmett (Louis)
American. Victim
Lynched for allegedly whistling at a white woman; event was a catalyst for protests asking Congress for an anti-lynching bill.
b. Jul 25, 1941 in Chicago, Illinois
d. Aug 28, 1955 in Tallahatchie County, Mississippi
Source: *BioIn 10, 11; ConBlB 7; EncAACR; InB&W 80*

Tiller, Rogers
[Terence Rogers Tiller]
English. Poet, Writer
Major poetry works include *The Inward Animal,* 1943; *Unarm, Eros* 1947.
b. Sep 19, 1916 in Truro, England
Source: *ConAu 101; ConPo 70, 75, 85; DcLEL 1940; IntWWP 77; ModBrL; TwCWr; WrDr 76, 86*

Tilley, Samuel Leonard, Sir
Canadian. Politician
Created the National Policy trade protection program.
b. May 8, 1818 in Gagetown, New Brunswick, Canada
d. Jun 25, 1896 in Saint John, New Brunswick, Canada
Source: *ApCAB; DcCanB 12; DcNaB; Drake; MacDCB 78; McGEWB; OxCCan*

Tillich, Paul Johannes
American. Theologian
Wrote *The Shaking of the Foundation,* 1948; *Theology of Culture,* 1959.
b. Aug 20, 1886 in Starzeddal, Germany
d. Oct 22, 1965 in Chicago, Illinois
Source: *AmAu&B; Benet 96; BioIn 3, 4, 5, 6, 7, 8, 9, 10, 11, 12; BioNews 74; ConAu 5R; CurBio 54, 65; DcAmReB 1, 2; EncAB-A 37; EncAB-H 1974, 1996; EncARH; LngCTC; McGEWB; OxCAmL 65; OxCGer 76; RAdv 14, 13-4; REn; REnAL; TwCA SUP; WebAB 74, 79; WhAm 4*

Tillis, Mel(vin)
American. Singer, Songwriter
Has written over 450 songs; CMA entertainer of year, 1976.
b. Aug 8, 1932 in Pahokee, Florida
Source: *Baker 84, 92; BgBkCoM; BiDAmM; BioIn 12, 13; BkPepl; ConMus 7; CounME 74, 74A; EncFCWM 69, 83; HarEnCM 87; IlEncCM; LegTOT; PenEncP; WhoAm 78, 80, 82, 84, 86, 88, 92, 94, 95, 96, 97; WhoEnt 92*

Tillis, Pam
American. Singer, Songwriter
Album *Put Yourself in My Place,* 1991 includes hits *Don't Tell Me What to Do* and *I've Already Fallen.*
b. Jul 24, 1957 in Plant City, Florida
Source: *BgBkCoM; BioIn 13; ConMus 8; LegTOT; WhoAm 94, 95, 96, 97*

Tillstrom, Burr
American. Puppeteer
Creator, puppeteer, "Kukla, Fran, & Ollie" puppet show, on TV, 1947-57.
b. Oct 13, 1917 in Chicago, Illinois
d. Dec 6, 1985 in Palm Springs, California
Source: *ASCAP 66, 80; BioIn 2, 3, 10, 14, 15; CelR; ConNews 86-1; CurBio 51, 86, 86N; FacFETw; IntMPA 75, 76, 77, 78, 79, 80, 81, 82, 84, 86; LegTOT; PupTheA, SUP; WebAB 74, 79; WhAm 9; WhoAm 74, 76, 78, 80, 82, 84; WorAl; WorAlBi*

Tilson Thomas, Michael
American. Conductor
Principal guest conductor, LA Philharmonic, 1981-85; principal conductor of the London Symphony Orchestra 1988-95; conductor, San Francisco Symphony, 1995—; winner of two Grammy awards.

b. Dec 21, 1944 in Hollywood, California
Source: *Baker 84; BiDAmM; BioIn 21; CurBio 71, 96; IntWW 91, 93; IntWWM 77, 80; MusSN; NewGrDM 80; NewYTBE 71; Who 90, 92, 94; WhoAm 86, 95, 96, 97; WhoAmM 83; WhoMus 72; WhoWest 96; WhoWor 84, 96, 97*

Tilton, Charlene
American. Actor
Played Lucy Ewing Cooper on TV drama "Dallas", 1978-85, 1988—.
b. Dec 1, 1958? in San Diego, California
Source: *BioIn 12, 20; ConTFT 8; InWom SUP; LegTOT; WhoHol 92; WhoTelC*

Timbuk 3
American. Music Group
Pop/rock duo; made *Cutting Edge,* MTV showcase, 1985.
Source: *ConMus 3*

Timerman, Jacobo
Argentine. Author, Journalist
Wrote *Prisoner Without a Name, Cell Without a Number,* 1981, detailing events during capture in Argentina, 1977-79.
b. Jan 6, 1923 in Bar, Union of Soviet Socialist Republics
Source: *BioIn 11, 12, 13, 14, 17; ConAu 32NR, 109, 120; CurBio 81; DcHiB; EncWB; HeroCon; HispWr; LegTOT; NewYTBS 79; WhoWor 89*

Timken, Henry
American. Inventor, Manufacturer
Patented Timken spring, 1877.
b. Aug 16, 1831 in Bremen, Germany
d. Mar 16, 1909 in San Diego, California
Source: *BioIn 21; DcAmB; WhAm 4, HSA*

Timmerman, George Bell, Jr.
American. Politician
Governor, SC, 1955-59; made efforts to oppose racial desegregation.
b. Aug 12, 1912
d. Nov 29, 1994 in Columbia, South Carolina
Source: *AmBench 79; BiDrGov 1789; BioIn 4, 5, 11, 20, 21; CurBio 95N; PolProf E; WhAm 11; WhoAm 74, 76, 78, 80, 82, 84, 86, 88, 90, 92; WhoAmL 78, 79, 83, 90; WhoGov 75, 77; WhoWor 82, 84, 87, 89, 93*

Timmermans, Felix
Flemish. Author
Prolific novelist and short story writer; wrote *Pallieter,* 1916.
b. Jul 5, 1886 in Lier, Belgium
d. Jan 24, 1947 in Lier, Belgium
Source: *Benet 87, 96; BioIn 1, 3; CasWL; CathA 1952; ClDMEL 47, 80; DcCathB; EncWL, 2, 3; EvEuW; ScF&FL 1; TwCWr*

Timoshenko, Semen Konstantinovich
Russian. Army Officer
WW II hero helped defeat German troops on Soviet western front.
b. Feb 19, 1895 in Urmanka, Russia
d. Mar 31, 1970 in Moscow, Union of Soviet Socialist Republics
Source: *BiDSovU; BioIn 1, 4, 6, 8, 9; CurBio 70; HarEnMi; LinLib S; ObitOF 79; ObitT 1961; SovUn; WhoMilH 76; WorAl*

Timrod, Henry
"Laureate of the Confederacy"
American. Poet
Wrote war verse inspirational to Southern cause.
b. Dec 8, 1828 in Charleston, South Carolina
d. Oct 6, 1867 in Columbia, South Carolina
Source: *Alli; AmAu; AmAu&B; AmBi; Benet 87, 96; BenetAL 91; BibAL 8; BiD&SB; BiDSA; BioIn 1, 2, 3, 7, 8, 9, 12; CamGEL; CamGLE; CamHAL; CasWL; Chambr 3; ChhPo, S1, S2; CnDAL; CyAL 1; DcAmAu; DcAmB; DcLB 3; DcLEL; DcNAA; EvLB; FifSWrB; GrWrEL P; LinLib L, S; NinCLC 25; OxCAmL 65, 83, 95; PenC AM; RAdv 14, 13-1; REn; REnAL; RfGAmL 87, 94; SouWr; TwCBDA; WebAB 74, 79; WhAm HS; WhCiWar*

Tinbergen, Jan
Dutch. Economist
Shared 1969 Nobel Prize for work in econometrics, math economics.
b. Apr 12, 1903 in The Hague, Netherlands
d. Jun 9, 1994
Source: *AmEA 74; BioIn 8, 9, 13, 14, 15, 17, 20, 21; ConAu 2NR, 5R, 145; Future; GrEconS; IntEnSS 79; IntWW 74, 75, 76, 77, 78, 79, 80, 81, 82, 83, 89, 91, 93; IntYB 78, 79, 80, 81, 82; McGEWB; NobelP; ThTwC 87; WhAm 11; Who 74, 82, 83, 85, 88, 90, 92, 94; WhoAm 74, 76, 90, 92, 94; WhoEc 81, 86; WhoFI 92, 94; WhoNob, 90, 95; WhoUN 75; WhoWor 74, 76, 78, 80, 82, 84, 87, 89, 91, 93*

Tinbergen, Nikolaas
Dutch. Scientist
Shared 1973 Nobel Prize for animal behavior studies; noted for researching gulls; one of the founders of ethology.
b. Apr 15, 1907 in The Hague, Netherlands
d. Dec 21, 1988 in London, England
Source: *AmMWSc 89, 92; AnObit 1988; Au&Wr 71; BiESc; BioIn 10, 11, 12; BlueB 76; CamDcSc; CurBio 75, 89; DcNaB 1986; FacFETw; IntAu&W 77; IntDcAn; IntEnSS 79; IntWW 74, 75, 76, 77, 78, 79, 80, 81, 82, 83; LarDcSc; MakMC; McGMS 80; NewYTBS 88; NotTwCS; RAdv 14, 13-3, 13-5; WhAm 9; Who 74, 82, 83, 85, 88; WhoAm 74, 76, 88; WhoNob, 90, 95; WhoWor 74, 76, 78, 80, 82, 84, 87, 89; WorAl; WorAlBi; WrDr 88*

Tindemans, Leo(nard)
Belgian. Political Leader
Active in politics since 1960s; prime minister of Belgium, 1974-78; minister of Foreign Relations, 1981-89.
b. Apr 16, 1922 in Zwijndrecht, Belgium
Source: *BioIn 11, 21; CurBio 78; IntWW 74, 75, 76, 77, 78, 79, 80, 81, 82, 83, 89, 91, 93; IntYB 78, 79, 80, 81, 82; PolLCWE; Who 82, 83, 85, 88, 90, 92, 94; WhoWor 76, 78, 84, 87, 89, 91*

Ting, Samuel Chao Chung
American. Scientist
Shared 1976 Nobel Prize in physics; co-discovered subatomic particle J/psi.
b. Jan 27, 1936 in Ann Arbor, Michigan
Source: *AmMWSc 86; BiESc; BioIn 11, 12; CamDcSc; IntWW 77, 78, 79, 80, 81, 82, 83, 89, 91, 93; LarDcSc; McGMS 80; NewYTBS 76; Who 82, 83, 85, 88, 90, 92, 94; WhoAm 76, 78, 80, 82, 84, 86, 88, 90, 92, 94, 95, 96, 97; WhoE 77, 79, 81, 83, 85, 86, 89, 91, 93, 95, 97; WhoNob, 90, 95; WhoScEn 94, 96; WhoWor 78, 80, 82, 84, 87, 89, 91, 93, 95, 96, 97; WorAl; WorScD*

Tinguely, Jean
Swiss. Sculptor
Began using motion in sculpture, 1940s; advanced to complex machine art: *Homage to NY,* 1960.
b. May 22, 1925 in Fribourg, Switzerland
d. Aug 30, 1991 in Bern, Switzerland
Source: *AnObit 1991; BioIn 5, 6, 7, 8, 10, 11, 13, 17, 18; ConArt 77, 83, 89, 96; CurBio 66, 91N; DcCAr 81; DcTwCCu 2; EncWB; McGDA; ModArCr 4; NewCol 75; NewYTBS 91; OxCTwCA; OxDcArt; PhDcTCA 77; WhoAm 74; WhoWor 74; WorArt 1950*

Tinker, Grant Almerin
American. TV Executive, Producer
Pres., MTM Enterprises, 1970-81; chm, CEO, NBC, 1981-86; former husband of Mary Tyler Moore.
b. Jan 11, 1926 in Stamford, Connecticut
Source: *ConTFT 5; CurBio 82; IntMPA 86; LesBEnT; NewYTBS 86; NewYTET; St&PR 84, 87; WhoAm 86; WhoE 83; WhoFI 83; WhoTelC*

Tinker, Joe
[Joseph Bert Tinker]
American. Baseball Player
Shortstop, 1902-16, mostly with Cubs; part of double play combination of Tinker to Evers to Chance; Hall of Fame, 1946.
b. Jul 27, 1880 in Muscotah, Kansas
d. Jul 27, 1948 in Orlando, Florida
Source: *Ballpl 90; BiDAmSp BB; BioIn 1, 3, 7, 10, 14, 15; LegTOT; WhoProB 73*

Tinney, Cal(vin Lawrence)
American. Radio Performer
Homespun philosopher with Texas accent; known for radio show, early 1940s.

b. Feb 2, 1908 in Pontotoc County, Oklahoma
Source: *CurBio 43; JoeFr; RadStar*

Tintoretto
[Jacopo Robusti]
Italian. Artist
Paintings known for unusual body movement, light, spacing.
b. Sep 29, 1518 in Venice, Italy
d. May 31, 1594 in Venice, Italy
Source: *AtlBL; Benet 87, 96; BioIn 1; DcArts; DcCathB; Dis&D; IntDcAA 90; LegTOT; LinLib S; LuthC 75; McGDA; McGEWB; NewC; NewCol 75; OxDcArt; REn; WebBD 83; WorAl; WorAlBi*

Tiny Tim
[Herbert Buckingham Khaury]
American. Entertainer
Falsetto singer, best known for song "Tiptoe through the Tulips."
b. Apr 12, 1922 in New York, New York
d. Nov 30, 1996 in Minneapolis, Minnesota
Source: *BioIn 8, 9, 10, 11, 14, 21; BioNews 75; LegTOT; WhoAm 74; WhoHol A*

Tiomkin, Dimitri
American. Composer, Pianist
Wrote music for over 100 films; four Oscar-winning scores include *High Noon*, 1952.
b. May 10, 1899 in Saint Petersburg, Russia
d. Nov 11, 1979 in London, England
Source: *AmPS; Baker 84; BiDAmM; BioIn 1, 3, 5, 6, 8, 9, 12, 15; BlueB 76; CmMov; CmpEPM; ConAu 93; DcArts; DcFM; FacFETw; FilmEn; FilmgC; IntDcF 1-4, 2-4; IntMPA 77; IntWW 74, 75, 76, 77, 78, 79; IntWWM 77; MusMk; OxCFilm; PopAmC, SUP; WebAB 74, 79; WhAm 7; WhoAm 74, 76, 78; WhoHrs 80; WhoWor 74, 78; WorEFlm*

Tippett, Michael Kemp, Sir
English. Composer
Works include oratorio *A Child of Our Time*, 1941; opera *The Knot Garden*, 1970.
b. Jan 2, 1905 in London, England
Source: *Baker 84, 92; BioIn 1, 4, 6, 7, 8, 10, 11, 12, 13; BioNews 74; ConAu 109; CurBio 74; DcArts; DcCM; IntWW 74, 75, 76, 77, 78, 79, 80, 81, 82, 83, 89, 91, 93; IntWWM 77; McGEWB; MusSN; NewGrDO; NewOxM; OxCEng 85; OxCMus; WhDW; Who 94; WhoMus 72; WhoWor 74, 76, 78, 82, 84, 87, 89, 91, 93, 95, 96, 97*

Tippu Tib
[Muhammed Bin Hamid]
Arab. Businessman
Trader; monopolized elephant hunting, built roads and plantations in the upper Congo area.
b. 1837
d. Jun 14, 1905, Zanzibar

Tirpitz, Alfred von
German. Naval Officer
Cruiser squadron commander, East Asia, 1896-97; secretary of State in Imperial Navy, 1897-1916.
b. Mar 19, 1849 in Kustrin, Prussia
d. Mar 6, 1930 in Ebenhausen, Germany
Source: *BioIn 6, 7, 17; DcTwHis; FacFETw; HarEnMi; LinLib S; NewCol 75; OxCGer 76, 86; OxCShps; REn; WebBD 83; WhDW; WorAl; WorAlBi*

Tisch, Laurence Alan
American. Business Executive
Known for rescuing failing companies like CBS, 1986.
b. Mar 15, 1923 in New York, New York
Source: *BioIn 5, 8, 10, 12, 13; ConAmBL; ConTFT 5; CurBio 87; IntWW 89, 91, 93; News 88-2; WhoAm 74, 76, 78, 80, 82, 84, 86, 88, 90, 92, 94, 95, 96, 97; WhoE 74, 83, 85, 86, 89, 91, 93, 95, 97; WhoEnt 92; WhoFI 74, 75, 77, 79, 81, 83, 85, 87, 89, 92, 94, 96; WhoWor 87, 89, 91, 93, 95, 96*

Tisdale, Wayman Lawrence
American. Basketball Player
Forward, Indiana, 1985; member, US Olympic team, 1984.
b. Jun 9, 1964 in Tulsa, Oklahoma
Source: *BiDAmSp BK; NewYTBS 84; OfNBA 87; WhoAfA 96; WhoBlA 92, 94*

Tiselius, Arne Wilhelm Kaurin
Swedish. Chemist
Won Nobel Prize, 1948, for research on serum protein.
b. Aug 10, 1902 in Stockholm, Sweden
d. Oct 29, 1971 in Stockholm, Sweden
Source: *AsBiEn; BiESc; BioIn 14, 15, 19, 20; CamDcSc; DcScB; InSci; LarDcSc; McGEWB; McGMS 80; ObitOF 79; WhAm 5; WhoNob, 90, 95; WorScD*

Tissot, James Joseph Jacques
French. Artist
Painter known for portrayal of people in late Victorian society.
b. Oct 15, 1836 in Nantes, France
d. Aug 8, 1902 in Buillon Abbey, France
Source: *BioIn 8, 9, 10, 11, 12, 14, 15, 16; ClaDrA; DcVicP 2; EncO&P 2, 3; McGDA; OxCArt; OxDcArt; ThHEIm*

Tisza, Kalman
Hungarian. Politician
Prime minister, 1875-90; wide-ranging reforms strengthened, modernized Hungary.
b. Dec 16, 1830 in Geszt, Hungary
d. Mar 23, 1902 in Budapest, Austria-Hungary
Source: *WhDW*

Titian
[Tiziano Vecellio]
Italian. Artist
Works include *Assumption of the Virgin*, 1518; *La Bella*, 1537; master colorist.
b. 1477 in Pieve di Cadore, Italy
d. Aug 27, 1576 in Venice, Italy
Source: *AtlBL; Benet 87, 96; BioIn 1, 2, 3, 4, 5, 6, 7, 8, 9, 10, 11, 12, 13; ClaDrA; DcBiPP; DcCathB; Dis&D; LinLib S; LuthC 75; McGDA; McGEWB; NewC; NewCol 75; OxCArt; REn; WebBD 83*

Tito
[Josip Broz Tito]
Yugoslav. Political Leader
Established Yugoslavia as communist state after WW II; pres., 1953-80.
b. May 25, 1892 in Kumrovec, Yugoslavia
d. May 4, 1980 in Ljubljana, Yugoslavia
Source: *AnObit 1980; BiDMarx; BioIn 1, 2, 3, 4, 5, 6, 7, 8, 9, 10, 11, 12, 13, 14, 15, 16, 17, 18, 19, 20, 21; ColdWar 1, 2; ConAu 97; CurBio 43, 55, 80N; DcAmSR; DcPol; DicTyr; EncCW; EncRev; FacFETw; GenMudB; GrLGrT; HisEWW; IntWW 74, 75, 76, 77, 78, 79; IntYB 78, 79, 80; LegTOT; LinLib S; McGEWB; NewCol 75; NewYTBS 80; WhDW; Who 74; WhoGov 72; WhoMilH 76; WhoWor 74, 76, 78; WhWW-II; WorAl; WorAlBi*

Titov, Gherman Stepanovich
Russian. Cosmonaut
Pilot of first space flight of more than 24 hrs., 1961.
b. Sep 11, 1935 in Verkhneye, Union of Soviet Socialist Republics
Source: *BioIn 6, 7, 15, 17; CurBio 62; IntWW 83; WhoWor 74*

Tittle, Y(elberton) A(braham)
American. Football Player
Three-time all-pro quarterback, 1948-64, enjoying greatest success with NY Giants; led NFL in passing, 1963; Hall of Fame, 1971.
b. Oct 24, 1926 in Marshall, Texas
Source: *BiDAmSp FB; BioIn 4, 6, 7, 8, 9, 10, 11, 15, 17; CurBio 64; NewYTBE 70; WhoFtbl 74*

Titus
Roman. Ruler
Ruled, AD 79-81; empire was peaceful during reign; aided Pompeii after volcano, Rome after fires.
b. Dec 30, 40 in Rome, Italy
d. Sep 13, 81 in Rome, Italy
Source: *BioIn 2, 4, 5, 10, 14, 17; REn; WhDW*

Tizard, Henry Thomas, Sir
English. Scientist
Developed Watson-Watts radio beam aircraft detector—radar.
b. Aug 23, 1885 in Gillingham, England
d. Oct 9, 1959 in Oxford, England
Source: *BiESc; BioIn 1, 2, 3, 5, 6, 7, 8, 14, 20; CurBio 59; DcNaB 1951; GrBr; HisEWW; InSci; LarDcSc; WhWW-II*

Tjader, Cal(len Radcliffe, Jr.)
American. Jazz Musician
Vibist; with Brubeck octet, 1949-51, George Shearing, 1950s; won 1981 Grammy.
b. Jul 16, 1925 in Saint Louis, Missouri
d. May 5, 1982, Philippines
Source: *AllMusG; BioIn 12, 13, 16; CmpEPM; EncJzS; FacFETw; LegTOT; NewAmDM; NewGrDA 86; NewGrDJ 88; NewYTBS 82; PenEncP; WhoAm 74*

TLC
[Lisa "Left Eye" Lopes; Rozonda "Chilli" Thomas; Tionne "T-Boz" Watkins]
American. Music Group
Released albums *Ooooooohhh. . .On the TLC Tip,* 1992; *Crazysexycool,* 1994.
Source: *ConMus 15; EncRkSt; News 96, 96-1*

Tobey, Mark
American. Artist
Painter known for calligraphy in white on a dark background; influenced by Chinese calligraphers.
b. Dec 11, 1890 in Centerville, Wisconsin
d. Apr 24, 1976 in Basel, Switzerland
Source: *ArtsAmW 3; BioIn 1, 2, 3, 4, 5, 6, 7, 9, 10, 11, 13, 14, 18; BriEAA; CelR; ConArt 77, 83, 89, 96; ConAu 65; CurBio 57, 76N; DcAmArt; DcAmB S10; DcCAA 71, 77, 88, 94; EncWB; IntDcAA 90; IntWW 74, 75, 76; McGDA; ObitOF 79; OxCArt; OxCTwCA; OxDcArt; PeoHis; PhDcTCA 77; PrintW 83, 85; REn; WebAB 74, 79; WhAm 7; WhAmArt 85; WhDW; WhoAm 74, 76; WhoAmA 73, 76, 78N, 80N, 82N, 84N, 86N, 89N, 91N, 93N; WhoWor 74; WorArt 1950*

Tobias, Andrew Previn
American. Writer
Columnist, *Playboy* mag., 1983-87; *Time,* 1989—; contributor *Worth Magazine*; noted for books on money management.
b. Apr 20, 1947 in New York, New York
Source: *BioIn 9; ConAu 14NR, 37R; WhoAm 84, 86, 88, 90, 92, 94, 95, 96, 97; WhoUSWr 88; WhoWrEP 89, 92, 95; WrDr 86*

Tobias, Channing Heggie
American. Social Reformer
Minister active in NAACP, 1940s-50s.
b. Feb 1, 1882 in Augusta, Georgia
d. Nov 5, 1961 in New York, New York
Source: *BioIn 2, 3, 4, 6, 12; CurBio 45, 62; DcAmB S7; DcAmNB; InB&W 80; WhAm 4*

Tobias, George
American. Actor
Character actor as the hero's sidekick, 1939-70; films include *Ninotchka; Silk Stockings.*
b. Jul 14, 1901 in New York, New York
d. Feb 27, 1980 in Hollywood, California
Source: *BiE&WWA; BioIn 12; EncAFC; FilmEn; FilmgC; ForYSC; HalFC 80, 84, 88; HolCA; IntMPA 78, 79, 80; LegTOT; MotPP; MovMk; NewYTBS 80; NotNAT; Vers A; WhoHol A; WhoThe 81N; WhScrn 83; WorAl*

Tobin, Daniel Joseph
American. Labor Union Official
Pres., Teamsters, 1907-52.
b. Apr 1875 in County Clare, Ireland
d. Nov 14, 1955
Source: *BiDAmL; BiDAmLL; BioIn 1, 3, 4, 5, 11; DcAmB S5; DcCathB; NatCAB 42; WhAm 3; WorAl*

Tobin, James
American. Economist
Follower of John Maynard Keynes who believed in government intervention in economics; won Nobel Prize, 1981.
b. Mar 5, 1918 in Champaign, Illinois
Source: *AmEA 74; AmMWSc 73S, 78S; BioIn 4, 5, 7, 9, 11, 12, 13, 14, 15; BlueB 76; ConAu 5NR, 53; CurBio 84; GrEconS; IntAu&W 77; IntWW 74, 75, 76, 77, 78, 79, 80, 81, 82, 83, 89, 91, 93; NewYTBS 81, 85; NobelP; PolProf K; Who 83, 85, 88, 90, 92, 94; WhoAm 74, 76, 78, 80, 82, 84, 86, 88, 90, 92, 94, 95, 96, 97; WhoE 85, 86, 89, 91, 93, 95, 97; WhoEc 81, 86; WhoFI 87, 89, 92, 94, 96; WhoNob, 90, 95; WhoScEn 96; WhoWor 82, 84, 87, 89, 91, 93, 95, 96, 97; WorAlBi; WrDr 76, 80, 82, 84, 86, 88, 90, 92, 94, 96*

Tobin, Richard L(ardner)
American. Journalist
With *NY Herald Tribune,* 1932-56; wrote *Invasion Journal,* 1944.
b. Aug 9, 1910
d. Sep 10, 1995 in Southbury, Connecticut
Source: *AmAu&B; BioIn 1, 5; ConAu 1NR, 1R, 149; CurBio 95N; St&PR 75; WhoAm 74, 76, 78; WhoMW 86, 88*

Toch, Ernst
American. Composer, Musician
Seven symphonies include 1956 Pulitzer-winning *Third Symphony;* wrote piano pieces, film scores.
b. Dec 7, 1887 in Vienna, Austria
d. Oct 1, 1964 in Los Angeles, California
Source: *AmComp; ASCAP 66, 80; Baker 78, 84, 92; BioIn 1, 2, 3, 7, 8, 12; BriBkM 80; CompSN, SUP; ConAmC 76, 82; DcCM; HalFC 84, 88; IntWWM 77, 80; LegTOT; NewAmDM; NewEOp 71; NewGrDA 86; NewGrDM 80; NewGrDO; NewOxM; OxCAmH; OxCMus; PenDiMP A; WhAm 4*

Tocqueville, Alexis, Comte de
French. Author
Noted for classic, two-volume: *Democracy in America,* 1835.
b. Jul 29, 1805 in Vernevil, France
d. Apr 16, 1859 in Cannes, France
Source: *AmBi; ApCAB; AtlBL; BbD; BiD&SB; CasWL; CnDAL; CyAG; DcEuL; Drake; EuAu; GuFrLit 1; NewC; NewCBEL; NewCol 75; OxCAmH; OxCAmL 65, 83, 95; OxCEng 67; OxCFr; PenC AM; REn; REnAL; WhDW*

Todd, Alexander (Robertus), Sir
English. Chemist
Won Nobel Prize for work in biochemistry, 1957.
b. Oct 2, 1907 in Glasgow, Scotland
d. Jan 10, 1997 in Cambridge, England
Source: *AmMWSc 95; AsBiEn; BiESc; ConAu 146; CurBio 58; InSci; IntWW 93; LarDcSc; LinLib S; NobelP; NotTwCS; WhoAm 76, 90, 92, 94, 95; WhoNob, 90, 95; WhoScEn 94; WhoWor 74, 76, 78, 80, 82, 87, 89, 91, 93, 95, 96, 97; WorScD*

Todd, Ann
English. Actor
Films include *The Paradine Case,* 1947; *The Seventh Veil,* 1946.
b. Jan 24, 1909 in Hartford, England
d. May 6, 1993 in London, England
Source: *BiE&WWA; BioIn 1, 12, 18, 19; ConAu 129; EncEurC; FilmAG WE; FilmEn; FilmgC; HalFC 80, 84, 88; IlWWBF; IntMPA 86, 88, 92; ItaFilm; LegTOT; MotPP; MovMk; OxCFilm; Who 85; WhoHol 92, A; WhoThe 81*

Todd, Mabel Loomis
American. Author
First editor of poems, letters of Emily Dickinson, 1890-95.
b. Nov 10, 1856 in Cambridge, Massachusetts
d. Oct 14, 1932 in Hog Island, Maine
Source: *AmAu&B; AmWomWr; BenetAL 91; BiD&SB; BioIn 14, 15, 17; ChhPo; CnDAL; DcAmAu; DcAmB; DcNAA; InWom, SUP; LibW; NatCAB 28, 41; NotAW; OxCAmL 65, 83, 95; REnAL; TwCA, SUP; WhNAA*

Todd, Mike
[Avron Hirsch Goldbogen; Michael Todd]
American. Producer
Produced 1956 Oscar-winning *Around the World in 80 Days;* wed to Elizabeth Taylor; killed in plane crash.
b. Jun 22, 1909 in Minneapolis, Minnesota
d. Mar 22, 1958 in Grants, New Mexico
Source: *CurBio 55, 58; DcAmB S6; DcFM; EncMT; FilmgC; LegTOT; NatCAB 62; ObitOF 79; OxCFilm; WhAm 3; WorAl; WorAlBi*

Todd, Richard
[Richard Andrew Palethorpe-Todd]
Irish. Actor
Oscar nominee for *The Hasty Heart,* 1949.
b. Jun 11, 1919 in Dublin, Ireland
Source: *BioIn 4, 11, 13, 19; CmMov; ConTFT 3; CurBio 55; FilmAG WE; FilmEn; FilmgC; ForYSC; HalFC 80, 84, 88; IlWWBF; IntMPA 75, 76, 77, 78, 79, 80, 81, 82, 84, 86, 88, 92, 94, 96;*

ItaFilm; LegTOT; MotPP; MovMk; NewYTBS 78, 84; Who 74, 82, 83, 85, 88, 90, 92, 94; WhoAm 74, 76; WhoHol 92, A; WhoThe 77, 81; WhoWor 74; WorAl

Todd, Richard
American. Football Player
Quarterback, 1976-85, mostly with NY Jets; set NFL record for completed passes in game: 42, 1980.
b. Nov 19, 1953 in Birmingham, Alabama
Source: *BioIn 11, 12, 13; CurBio 82; FootReg 86, 87; NewYTBS 84; WhoAm 84*

Todd, Sweeney
"Demon Barber of Fleet Street"
English. Murderer
Life was subject of Broadway musical *Sweeney Todd;* supposedly slashed hi s victims' throats, used bodies in meat pies.

Todd, Thelma
American. Actor
Made over 60 films, 1926-36, last released post-humously.
b. Jul 29, 1905 in Lawrence, Massachusetts
d. Dec 18, 1935 in Santa Monica, California
Source: *BiDD; BioIn 11; EncAFC; Film 2; FilmEn; FilmgC; ForYSC; Funs; HalFC 80, 84, 88; InWom SUP; JoeFr; LegTOT; MotPP; MovMk; NotNAT B; QDrFCA 92; ThFT; TwYS; WhoCom; WhoHol B; WhoHrs 80; WhScrn 74, 77, 83; WorAl*

Todman, Bill
[William Seldon Todman]
American. Producer
With Mark Goodson, created TV game shows "What's My Line"; "Match Game."
b. Jul 31, 1916 in New York, New York
d. Jul 29, 1979 in New York, New York
Source: *ConAu 89; IntMPA 77; LegTOT; NatCAB 62; NewYTBS 79; WhAm 7, 8; WhoAm 82; WhoTelC*

Toffenetti, Dario Louis
Italian. Restaurateur
Owner, operator, Toffenetti restuarants, Hotel, 1950s-62.
b. Jan 20, 1889 in Valdi Sole, Austria
d. Jan 16, 1962 in New York, New York
Source: *BioIn 1, 6, 9; NatCAB 53; ObitOF 79; WhAm 4*

Toffler, Alvin
American. Author
Wrote *Future Shock,* 1970; *The Third Wave,* 1980.
b. Oct 4, 1928 in New York, New York
Source: *AmAu&B; BioIn 10, 12, 13; ConAu 13R, 15NR, 46NR; ConIsC 1; ConPopW; CurBio 75; DcLEL 1940; EncSF, 93; Future; IntAu&W 89, 91, 93; LegTOT; MajTwCW; NewYTBS 80; WhoAm 74, 76, 78, 80, 82, 84, 86, 88, 92, 94, 95, 96; WhoE 75; WhoUSWr 88; WhoWrEP 89, 92, 95; WrDr 76, 80, 82, 84, 86, 88, 90, 92, 94, 96*

Togliatti, Palmiro
[Ercole Ercoli]
Italian. Political Leader
A founder, head of Italian Communist Party, 1921-44; exiled under Mussolini for 18 yrs.
b. Mar 26, 1893 in Genoa, Italy
d. Aug 21, 1964 in Yalta, Union of Soviet Socialist Republics
Source: *BioIn 1, 2, 3, 4, 7, 9, 21; ConAu 113, 133; CurBio 47, 64; DcTwHis; EncCW; EncRev; EncWB; ObitT 1961; PolLCWE; WhAm 4; WhDW; WorAl; WorAlBi*

Togo, Heihachiro
Japanese. Naval Officer
Considered Japan's greatest naval hero; led Japanese fleet in Russo-Japanese War, 1904-05.
b. Dec 22, 1848 in Kagoshima, Japan
d. May 30, 1934 in Tokyo, Japan
Source: *BioIn 5, 8; GenMudB; HarEnMi; NewCol 75; WebBD 83; WorAlBi*

Tojo, Hideki
[Eiki Tojo]
Japanese. Army Officer, Political Leader
Prime minister, 1941; directed Japanese military operations, WW II; hanged for war crimes.
b. Dec 30, 1884 in Tokyo, Japan
d. Dec 23, 1948 in Tokyo, Japan
Source: *BioIn 1, 2, 3, 7, 8, 9, 10, 12, 13, 15, 18, 20; CurBio 41, 49; DcPol; FacFETw; HarEnMi; HisEWW; LegTOT; LinLib S; McGEWB; NewCol 75; REn; WhoMilH 76; WhWW-II; WorAl*

Tokatyan, Armand
Bulgarian. Opera Singer
Tenor; with NY Met., 1922-46.
b. Feb 12, 1899 in Plovdiv, Bulgaria
d. Jun 12, 1960 in Pasadena, California
Source: *Baker 84; NewEOp 71*

Toklas, Alice B(abette)
American. Secretary
Close companion of Gertrude Stein from 1907; her famed *Autobiography,* was actually written by Stein, 1933.
b. Apr 30, 1877 in San Francisco, California
d. Mar 7, 1967 in Paris, France
Source: *AmAu&B; AmWomWr; BioIn 1, 6, 8, 9, 10, 11, 12, 13; CmCal; CnDAL; ConAu 25R, 81; DcAmB S8; GayLesB; GayLL; InWom SUP; LngCTC; NotAW MOD; ObitOF 79; OxCAmL 65, 95; REn*

Tokutomi Soho, pseud.
Japanese. Publisher
Exerted influence in Japan through the publication of Japan's first general periodical and the respected newspaper, *Kokumn Shimbum.*
b. Mar 13, 1863 in Tsumori, Japan
d. Nov 3, 1957 in Atami, Japan
Source: *BioIn 12*

Tokyo Rose
[Iva Toguri d'Aquino]
American. Traitor
WW II propaganda commentator for Radio Tokyo; imprisoned, then received presidential pardon, 1977.
b. Jul 4, 1916 in Los Angeles, California
Source: *FacFETw; GoodHs; LegTOT; NewYTBS 76; What 3; WhWW-II; WorAl; WorAlBi*

Toland, Gregg
American. Filmmaker
Photography talents in chiaroscuro and deep-focus photography are showcased in movies such as *Citizen Kane,* 1941.
b. May 29, 1904 in Charleston, Illinois
d. Sep 28, 1948 in Hollywood, California
Source: *BiDFilm 94; BioIn 1, 13; CurBio 48; DcArts; DcFM; FilmEn; FilmgC; GangFlm; HalFC 80, 84, 88; IntDcF 1-4, 2-4; ObitOF 79; OxCFilm; WorEFlm*

Toland, John Willard
American. Journalist, Author, Historian
Historical works include 1970 Pulitzer winner *The Rising Sun.*
b. Jun 29, 1912 in La Crosse, Wisconsin
Source: *AmAu&B; Au&Wr 71; ConAu 1R, 6NR; SmATA 38; WhoAm 86, 97; WhoWor 87, 97; WorAu 1950; WrDr 86*

Tolbert, William Richard, Jr.
Liberian. Political Leader
Pres. of Liberia, 1971-80.
b. May 13, 1913 in Bensonville, Liberia
d. Apr 12, 1980 in Monrovia, Liberia
Source: *AfSS 78, 79; BioIn 9, 10, 12; CurBio 74, 80; DcAfHiB 86S; InB&W 80, 85; IntWW 74, 75, 76, 77, 78, 79; NewYTBE 72; WhoAm 74, 76; WhoGov 72; WhoWor 74, 76, 78*

Toledano, Ralph de
American. Journalist, Author
Syndicated columnist, King Features, 1960-71; publications include *RFK: The Man Who Would Be President,* 1967; *J Edgar Hoover: The Man & His Times,* 1973.
b. Aug 17, 1916 in Tangiers, Morocco
Source: *AmAu&B; AuNews 1; BiDAmNC; ConAu 9R, 31NR; CurBio 62; DcAmC; IntAu&W 76, 86; LinLib L; WhoAm 74, 76, 78, 80, 82, 84, 86, 88, 90, 92, 94, 95, 96, 97; WhoUSWr 88; WhoWrEP 89, 92, 95; WrDr 76, 80, 82, 84, 86, 88, 90, 92, 94, 96*

Toledo, Fernando Alvarez de
[Duke of Alva]
Spanish. Army Officer
Through use of cautious tactics rose to chief of Spanish Army, 1541;

governor-general of Netherlands, 1567-73.
b. Jul 10, 1515 in Oropesa, Spain
d. Apr 21, 1582 in Thomar, Spain
Source: *ApCAB*

Toler, Sidney
American. Actor
Replaced Warner Oland in Charlie Chan film series, 1938-47.
b. Apr 28, 1874 in Warrensburg, Missouri
d. Feb 12, 1947 in Beverly Hills, California
Source: *BioIn 1; DcNAA; EncAFC; Film 2; FilmEn; FilmgC; ForYSC; GangFlm; HalFC 80, 84, 88; HolCA; LegTOT; MotPP; MovMk; NotNAT B; ObitOF 79; WhoHol B; WhoHrs 80; WhScrn 74, 77, 83; WhThe; WorAl*

Tolkien, J(ohn) R(onald) R(euel)
English. Author
Wrote *The Hobbit,* 1938; *The Lord of the Rings,* 1954-56.
b. Jan 3, 1892 in Bloemfontein, South Africa
d. Sep 2, 1973 in Bournemouth, England
Source: *AnCL; Au&Arts 10; Au&Wr 71; AuBYP 2; AuNews 1; Benet 96; BioIn 4, 6, 7, 8, 9, 10, 11, 12, 13, 14, 16, 17, 18, 19, 20; CasWL; CelR; ChhPo, S1, S2, S3; CnMWL; ConAu 45, 117; ConLC 1, 2, 3; ConNov 72, 76; ConPopW; DcArts; DcLEL; DcNaB 1971; EncSF 93; EncWL, 3; GrBr; LngCTC; MajAI; MakMC; ModBrL, S1; MorJA; NewC; NewCBEL; OxCEng 67, 95; PenC ENG; RAdv 1; REn; RGTwCWr; SJGFanW; SmATA 2; TwCChW 78, 95; TwCWr; TwCYAW; WebE&AL; WhAm 6; WhDW; WhoChL; WhoTwCL; WhoWor 74; WorAu 1950*

Toller, Ernst
German. Poet, Dramatist
Pacifist who organized Students' League for Peace during WW I.
b. Dec 1, 1893 in Samotschin, Germany
d. May 22, 1939 in New York, New York
Source: *Benet 87, 96; BiDMoPL; BiGAW; BioIn 1, 4, 7, 9, 17, 19; CamGWoT; CasWL; ClDMEL 47, 80; CnMD; CnMWL; CnThe; ConAu 107; DcLB 124; EncGRNM; EncTR, 91; EncWL, 2, 3; EncWT; Ent; EvEuW; FacFETw; IntDcT 2; LiExTwC; LinLib L; LngCTC; McGEWB; McGEWD 72, 84; ModGL; ModWD; NotNAT B; OxCEng 67, 85, 95; OxCGer 76, 86; OxCThe 67, 83; PenC EUR; PlP&P; RAdv 14, 13-2; REn; REnWD; RfGWoL 95; TwCA, SUP; TwCLC 10; WhAm 4, HSA; WhDW; WhE&EA; WhoTwCL; WhThe*

Tolliver, William (Mack)
American. Artist
Created many paintings of the deep South including *High Cotton,* 1985; *Ceremony in Red,* 1986.
b. Dec 1951 in Vicksburg, Mississippi
Source: *ConBlB 9; WhoSSW 88, 91*

Tolman, Edward Chace
American. Psychologist
Behaviorist; advanced theory of behaviorial unit as purposive and not merely conditioned reflex.
b. Apr 14, 1886 in West Newton, Massachusetts
d. Nov 19, 1959 in Berkeley, California
Source: *BiDPsy; BioIn 5, 6, 14, 15; DcAmB, S6; McGEWB; NamesHP; ThTwC 87; WhAm 4*

Tolman, Richard C(hace)
American. Chemist, Physicist
Experiments led to discovery of electron as charged particle in electrical flow in metals; determined mass of electron.
b. Mar 4, 1881 in West Newton, Massachusetts
d. Sep 5, 1948 in Pasadena, California
Source: *BioIn 1, 2, 3; DcAmB S4; DcNAA; DcScB; InSci; WhAm 2; WhNAA*

Tolson, Clyde Anderson
American. Government Official
Joined FBI, 1928; named associate director, 1947.
b. May 22, 1900 in Laredo, Missouri
d. Apr 14, 1975 in Washington, District of Columbia
Source: *BioIn 3, 9, 10, 11; WhAm 6; WhoAm 74; WhoGov 72; WhoSSW 73*

Tolstoy, Alexey Nikolaevich
Russian. Author
Historical novel, *Peter the Great,* 1929-34, called a masterpiece of Soviet literature.
b. Jan 10, 1883 in Nikolaevski-Samarskom, Russia
d. Feb 22, 1945 in Moscow, Union of Soviet Socialist Republics
Source: *ConAu 107; EncWL 2, 3; McGEWD 84; RAdv 13-2; WhDW*

Tolstoy, Leo Nikolayevich
Russian. Author
Wrote *War and Peace,* 1865-69; *Anna Karenina,* 1875-77.
b. Sep 9, 1828 in Yasnaya Polyana, Russia
d. Nov 20, 1910 in Astapovo, Russia
Source: *AtlBL; ClDMEL 47; CnMD; CyWA 58; DcEuL; EncWT; EuAu; FilmgC; LngCTC; McGEWD 72; ModWD; NewGrDM 80; NotNAT B; OxCChes 84; OxCChiL; OxCEng 67; OxCThe 67; PlP&P; RComWL; REn; REnWD; WorAl*

Tomasi di Lampedusa, Guiseppe
Italian. Author
Novelist; wrote of decline of Sicilian upper class in 1860s: *The Leopard,* published posthumously, 1960.
b. Dec 23, 1896 in Palermo, Sicily, Italy
d. Jul 26, 1957 in Rome, Italy
Source: *CasWL; ConAu 111; EvEuW; OxCEng 67*

Tomasson, Helgi
Icelandic. Dancer, Choreographer
"Premier danseur" with NY City Ballet, 1970-85; artistic director, San Francisco ballet, 1985—.
b. Oct 8, 1942 in Reykjavik, Iceland
Source: *BiDD; BioIn 7, 8, 11, 12, 13; CnOxB; CurBio 82; IntDcB; WhoAm 78, 80, 82, 84, 86, 88, 90, 92, 94, 95, 96, 97; WhoE 79, 81, 83; WhoEnt 92; WhoWest 87, 89, 92, 94; WhoWor 95*

Tomba, Alberto
"Tomba la Bomba"
Italian. Skier
Won gold medals in slalom, giant slalom, 1988, 1992 Olympics.
b. Dec 19, 1966 in San Lazzaro di Savenna, Italy
Source: *CurBio 93; LegTOT; News 92, 92-3; WhoWor 95, 96*

Tombalbaye, Nagarta Francois
Chadian. Political Leader
Pres. of Chad since 1960; killed in military coup.
b. Jun 15, 1918 in Badaya, Chad
d. Apr 13, 1975 in Fort Lamy, Chad
Source: *WhAm 6; WhoWor 74*

Tombaugh, Clyde W(illiam)
American. Astronomer
Discovered planet, Pluto, 1930.
b. Feb 4, 1906 in Streator, Illinois
d. Jan 17, 1997 in Las Cruces, New Mexico
Source: *AmMWSc 86; AsBiEn; BiESc; BioIn 4, 6, 10, 12; CamDcSc; FacFETw; InSci; IntWW 74, 75, 76, 77, 78, 79, 80, 81, 82, 83, 89, 91, 93; LarDcSc; WhDW; WhoAm 74, 76, 88, 90, 92, 94, 95, 96, 97; WhoScEn 94, 96; WhoWest 74, 76, 78; WhoWor 74*

Tomei, Marisa
American. Actor
Oscar, Best Supporting Actress, *My Cousin Vinny,* 1993.
b. Dec 4, 1964 in New York, New York
Source: *ConTFT 12; IntMPA 94, 96; LegTOT; News 95, 95-2; WhoAm 94, 95, 96, 97; WhoAmW 95, 97*

Tomes, Margot
American. Illustrator
Award winning artist/illustrator of more than 40 books.
b. Aug 10, 1917 in Yonkers, New York
d. Jun 25, 1991 in New York, New York
Source: *BioIn 8, 13, 14, 16, 17, 18, 19; ChlBkCr; FifBJA; NewYTBS 91; SmATA 27, 36; WhoAmA 91*

Tomlin, Bradley Walker
American. Artist
Abstract painter; body of work consists mainly of poetic Cubist still lifes.
b. Aug 19, 1899 in Syracuse, New York
d. May 11, 1953 in New York, New York
Source: *BioIn 3, 4, 10, 14; BriEAA; ConArt 77, 83; DcAmArt; DcAmB S5;*

DcCAA 71, 77, 88, 94; EncAB-A 7; McGDA; OxCTwCA; OxDcArt; PhDcTCA 77; WhAm 3; WhAmArt 85; WhoAmA 78N, 80N, 82N, 84N, 86N, 89N, 91N, 93N; WorArt 1950

Tomlin, Lily
[Mary Jane Tomlin; Mary Jane Tomlinson]
American. Comedian
Starred in *Nine to Five,* 1980; won Tony for *The Search for Signs of Intelligent Life in the Universe,* 1986.
b. Sep 1, 1939 in Detroit, Michigan
Source: *ASCAP 80; BioIn 9, 10, 11, 12; BkPepl; CelR; ConLC 17; ConTFT 2, 6, 13; CurBio 73; EncAFC; GoodHs; GrLiveH; HalFC 80, 84, 88; IntMPA 84, 86, 88, 92, 94, 96; JoeFr; LegTOT; NewYTBE 73; NewYTBS 76, 85; QDrFCA 92; WhoAm 74, 76, 78, 80, 82, 84, 86, 88, 90, 92, 94, 95, 96; WhoAmW 79, 81, 83, 85, 89, 91, 93, 95, 97; WhoCom; WhoEnt 92; WhoHol 92, A; WorAl; WorAlBi*

Tomlin, Pinky
American. Songwriter
Co-wrote popular hit, "The Object of My Affection," 1934; used in film *Times Square Lady,* 1935.
b. Sep 9, 1908 in Eros, Arkansas
d. Dec 15, 1987 in Los Angeles, California
Source: *ASCAP 66, 80; BioIn 12, 15; CmpEPM; WhoHol A*

Tomlinson, Henry Major
English. Author
Noted for travel tale *The Sea and the Jungle,* 1912; novel *All Our Yesterdays,* 1930.
b. Jun 21, 1873 in London, England
d. Feb 5, 1958 in London, England
Source: *BioIn 1, 2, 3, 4, 5, 6, 9, 13, 14, 17; CyWA 58; DcLB 36; DcLEL; DcNaB 1951; EvLB; InSci; LngCTC; ModBrL; NewC; NewCBEL; OxCEng 67; OxCShps; PenC ENG; REn; REnAL; TwCA, SUP; TwCWr; WhDW*

Tomlinson, Jill
English. Children's Author
Animal tales include *Penguin's Progress,* 1975.
b. Dec 27, 1931 in Twickenham, England
d. 1976, England
Source: *Au&Wr 71; BioIn 9, 13; ConAu P-2; IntAu&W 76; SmATA 3, 24, 24N; WrDr 76, 80, 82, 84, 86*

Tomonaga Shinichiro
Japanese. Physicist
Shared 1965 Nobel Prize; researched quantum electrodynamics.
b. Mar 31, 1906 in Tokyo, Japan
d. Jul 8, 1979 in Tokyo, Japan
Source: *WhoNob*

Tom Petty and the Heartbreakers
[Ron Blair; Mike Campbell; Stan Lynch; Tom Petty; Benmont Tench]
American. Music Group
Rock group formed by Tom Petty, 1975; album *Damn the Torpedoes,* 1979, sold over 2.5 million copies.
Source: *BioIn 11, 12, 17, 20, 21; EncPR&S 89; EncRk 88; HarEnR 86; IlEncRk; PenEncP; RkOn 85; RolSEnR 83; WhoHol 92; WhoRocM 82*

Tompkins, Daniel D
American. US Vice President
Vp under James Monroe, 1817-25.
b. Jun 21, 1774 in Scarsdale, New York
d. Jun 11, 1825 in Staten Island, New York
Source: *BiAUS; BiDrGov 1789; HarEnUS; NatCAB 6; WebAB 79*

Tompkins, Sally Louisa
American. Philanthropist
Operated Civil War hospital in own home; commissioned captain in Confederate calvary, only woman to be so honored.
b. Nov 9, 1833 in Mathews County, Virginia
d. Jul 25, 1916 in Richmond, Virginia
Source: *BiDConf; BioIn 5, 16, 21; DcAmB; EncSoH; InWom SUP; LibW; NotAW; WebAB 74, 79; WebAMB; WhCiWar; WomFir*

Tompkins, Susie
American. Fashion Designer, Business Executive
Founder, owner of Esprit Clothing, noted for mail order catalogue, trendy, colorful outfits.
b. 1943
Source: *ConNews 87-2*

Toms, Carl
English. Designer
Won Tony for stage designs in *Sherlock Holmes,* 1975; first head of design, associate director with National Theater, 1970—.
b. May 29, 1927, England
Source: *ConDes 84, 90, 97; ConTFT 6, 13; IntWWM 77, 80; NotNAT; VarWW 85; Who 82, 83, 85, 88, 90, 92, 94; WhoOp 76; WhoThe 72, 77, 81*

Tomseth, Victor Lloyd
[The Hostages]
American. Hostage
One of 52 held by terrorists, Nov 1979-Jan 1981.
b. Apr 14, 1941 in Springfield, Oregon
Source: *BioIn 12; NewYTBS 81; USBiR 74*

Tom Thumb, General
[Charles Sherwood Stratton]
American. Circus Performer
Midget, whose height never exceeded 33 inches; hired by PT Barnum, 1842.
b. Jan 4, 1838 in Bridgeport, Connecticut
d. Jul 15, 1883 in Middleboro, Massachusetts
Source: *AmBi; ApCAB; BioIn 1, 2, 3, 4, 5, 6, 8, 11, 12; DcAmB; Drake; NatCAB 10; NewCol 75; NotNAT A; OxCAmH; WhAm HS*

Tone, Franchot
[Stanislas Pascal Franchot Tone]
American. Actor
Typecast in playboy roles at MGM, 1930s; Oscar nominee for *Mutiny on the Bounty,* 1935.
b. Feb 27, 1905 in Niagara Falls, New York
d. Sep 18, 1968 in New York, New York
Source: *BiDFilm 94; BiE&WWA; BioIn 8, 9, 14; CmMov; CurBio 68; DcAmB S8; EncAFC; FilmEn; FilmgC; ForYSC; HalFC 80, 84, 88; ItaFilm; LegTOT; MGM; MotPP; MovMk; NotNAT B; ObitOF 79; OxCAmT 84; OxCFilm; PlP&P; WhAm 5; WhoHol A; WhScrn 74, 77, 83; WorAl; WorAlBi; WorEFlm*

Tone, Theobald Wolfe
Irish. Revolutionary
One of the founders of United Irishmen, 1791.
b. 1763
d. 1798
Source: *Alli; BiDIrW; BioIn 13, 16, 17, 18; CasWL; Chambr 2; CmFrR; DcBiPP; DcIrB 78, 88; DcIrW 2; DcNaB; NewCol 75; OxCIri; PoIre; REn; WebBD 83; WhDW*

Tonegawa, Susumu
Japanese. Scientist
Won Nobel Prize in medicine, 1987, for discovering how body makes antibodies to fight disease.
b. Sep 5, 1939 in Nagoya, Japan
Source: *AmMWSc 86, 89, 92, 95; BioIn 15, 18, 20; IntWW 89, 91, 93; LarDcSc; NobelP 91; NotTwCS; Who 90, 92, 94; WhoAm 84, 86, 88, 90, 92, 94, 95, 96, 97; WhoAsA 94; WhoE 91, 95, 97; WhoMedH; WhoNob 90, 95; WhoScEn 94, 96; WhoWor 89, 91, 93, 95, 96, 97; WorAlBi*

Tone-Loc
[Anthony Terrell Smith]
American. Rapper
Rap singer; had multi-platinum hit single "Wild Thing," 1988; won several Grammys, 1990.
b. Mar 3, 1966 in Los Angeles, California

Tonge, Israel
English. Revolutionary
With Titus Oakes, invented Popish Plot, 1678, plan to assassinate Charles II, replace with brother James.
b. 1621
d. 1680
Source: *BioIn 2; DcNaB*

Toole, John Kennedy
American. Author
Wrote posthumously published best-seller *The Confederacy of Dunces,* 1980, which won Pulitzer.
b. 1937 in New Orleans, Louisiana
d. Mar 26, 1969 in Biloxi, Mississippi
Source: *BenetAL 91; BiDConC; BioIn 12, 13, 15, 17, 19; CamGLE; CamHAL; ConAu 104; ConLC 19, 64; CyWA 89; DcLB Y81B; EncAHmr; OxCAmL 83, 95; RGTwCWr; WorAlBi; WorAu 1975*

Toombs, Robert Augustus
American. Statesman
Dem. con. from GA, 1845-53; left to become secretary of State of Confederacy.
b. Jul 2, 1810 in Wilkes County, Georgia
d. Dec 15, 1885 in Washington, Georgia
Source: *AmBi; ApCAB; BiAUS; BiDConf; BiDrAC; BioIn 5, 7, 16; CivWDc; CyAG; DcAmB; DcAmDH 80, 89; Drake; EncSoH; McGEWB; NatCAB 4; NewCol 75; TwCBDA; WebAB 74, 79; WebBD 83; WhAm HS; WhAmP; WhCiWar*

Toomer, Jean
[Nathan Pinchback Toomer]
American. Author, Poet
A Harlem Renaissance writer; wrote *Cane,* 1923.
b. Dec 26, 1894 in Washington, District of Columbia
d. Mar 30, 1967 in Doylestown, Pennsylvania
Source: *AfrAmAl 6; AfrAmW; AmAu&B; AmWr S3; BioIn 2, 8, 9, 10, 12, 14, 15, 17, 19, 20; BlkAmP; BlkAmW 1; BlkAWP; BlkLC; BlkWr 1; BlkWrNE; BroadAu; CamGLE; CamHAL; ConAu 85; ConBlB 6; ConLC 1, 4, 13, 22; CyWA 89; DcAmNB; DcLB 45, 51; DcTwCCu 5; EarBlAP; EncAACR; EncSoH; EncWL 2, 3; FifSWrA; GrWrEL N; InWom SUP; LegTOT; LinLib L; MajTwCW; ModAL S1; ModBlW; MorBAP; NegAl 76, 83, 89; OxCAmL 65, 83, 95; OxCTwCP; PenC AM; PoeCrit 7; RAdv 14; REnAL; RfGAmL 87, 94; RfGShF; SchCGBL; SelBAAf; SelBAAu; ShSCr 1; SouBlCW; SouWr; Tw; WebE&AL; WorAu 1950*

Toomer, Ronald V
American. Designer, Business Executive
Designed more than 80 roller coasters worldwide.
b. 1930 in Pasadena, California
Source: *BioIn 16; News 90-1*

Toomey, Bill
[William Toomey]
American. Track Athlete
Won gold medal in decathlon, 1968 Olympics.
b. Jan 10, 1939 in Philadelphia, Pennsylvania
Source: *CmCal; WhoSpor; WhoTr&F 73*

Toomey, Mary Rand
[Mrs. Bill Toomey]
American. Track Athlete
As member of British team, won gold medal in long jump, silver in pentathlon, bronze in 400 meter relay, 1960 Olympics.
b. Feb 10, 1940
Source: *WhoTr&F 73*

Toomey, Regis
American. Actor
Character actor in over 150 films, 1929—, TV shows ''Burke's Law,'' 1963-65.
b. Aug 13, 1898 in Pittsburgh, Pennsylvania
d. Oct 12, 1991 in Woodland Hills, California
Source: *AnObit 1991; BioIn 17, 18; Film 2; FilmgC; HalFC 84; IntMPA 82, 84, 86, 92; MotPP; MovMk; NewYTBS 91; Vers A; WhoHol A; WorAl*

Toon, Malcolm
American. Diplomat
Has served as US ambassador to Czechoslovakia, Yugoslavia, Israel, USSR.
b. Jul 4, 1916 in Troy, New York
Source: *BioIn 8, 11, 16; BlueB 76; CurBio 78; DcAmDH 80, 89; IntWW 74, 75, 76, 77, 78, 79, 80, 81, 82, 83, 89, 91, 93; IntYB 78, 79, 80, 81, 82; USBiR 74; WhoAm 74, 76, 78, 80, 82, 84, 86, 88, 90, 92, 94, 95, 96, 97; WhoAmP 73, 75, 77, 79, 81, 83, 85, 87, 89, 91, 93, 95; WhoGov 72, 75, 77; WhoWor 74, 76, 78, 82*

Toots and the Maytals
[Raleigh Gordon; Frederick ''Toots'' Hibbert; Nathaniel ''Jerry'' Mat]
Jamaican. Music Group
Reggae band, 1962-83; hit albums include *Reggae Greats,* 1985.
Source: *ConMuA 80A; HarEnR 86; IlEncRk; RolSEnR 83*

Toplady, Augustus Montague
English. Clergy
Wrote ''Rock of Ages,'' 1776.
b. Nov 4, 1740 in Farnham, England
d. Aug 11, 1778 in London, England
Source: *Alli; BbD; BiD&SB; BioIn 3; BritAu; CasWL; Chambr 2; ChhPo; DcBiPP; DcEnL; DcLEL; DcNaB; EncWM; EvLB; LuthC 75; NewC; NewCBEL; OxCEng 67, 85, 95; OxCMus; PoChrch*

Topol, Chaim
Israeli. Actor
Oscar nominee for Tevye in *Fiddler on the Roof,* 1971.
b. Sep 9, 1935 in Tel Aviv, Palestine
Source: *BioIn 8, 9, 13; FilmgC; IntWW 77, 78, 79, 80, 81, 82, 83, 89, 91, 93; NewYTBE 71; OxCThe 83; WhoHol A; WhoWor 82, 84, 87, 89, 91, 93, 95, 96, 97; WhoWorJ 78*

Topolski, Feliks
English. Artist
Official war artist, 1940-45; mural in Buckingham Palace: *The Coronation of Elizabeth II.*
b. Aug 14, 1907 in Warsaw, Poland
d. Aug 24, 1989 in London, England
Source: *AnObit 1989; BioIn 1, 4, 5, 7, 11, 14, 16; BlueB 76; ConAu 112; DcBrAr 1; DcNaB 1986; IlsBYP; IlsCB 1946; IntWW 74, 75, 76, 77, 78, 79, 80, 81, 82, 83, 89; NewYTBS 89; OxCArt; OxCTwCA; OxDcArt; PhDcTCA 77; PolBiDi; TwCPaSc; WhAm 10; Who 74, 82, 83, 85, 88; WhoArt 80, 82, 84; WhoGrA 62, 82; WhoSoCE 89; WhoWor 74, 82; WorArt 1950*

Topping, Dan(iel Reid)
American. Baseball Executive
Owner, NY Yankees, 1945-66.
b. Jun 11, 1912 in Greenwich, Connecticut
d. May 18, 1974 in Miami, Florida
Source: *BiDAmSp BB; BioIn 10, 15; NewYTBS 74; WhAm 6*

Torborg, Jeff(rey Allen)
American. Baseball Manager
ML catcher, 1964-73; manager, Cleveland, 1977-79, Chicago White Sox, 1989—; AL manager of year, 1990.
b. Nov 26, 1941 in Westfield, New Jersey
Source: *Ballpl 90; BaseEn 88; WhoAm 74, 76, 78, 90, 92; WhoMW 90*

Toren, Marta
Swedish. Actor
Films include *Casbah, Sword in the Sand.*
b. May 21, 1926 in Stockholm, Sweden
d. Feb 19, 1957 in Stockholm, Sweden
Source: *BioIn 1, 4; FilmEn; FilmgC; HalFC 80, 84, 88; ItaFilm; MotPP; NotNAT B; ObitOF 79; WhoHol B; WhScrn 74, 77, 83*

Tork, Peter
[The Monkees]
American. Singer, Musician
Bass guitarist, vocalist with The Monkees on popular TV series, 1966-68.
b. Feb 13, 1944 in Washington, District of Columbia
Source: *LegTOT*

Torme, Mel(vin Howard)
''The Velvet Fog''
American. Singer, Songwriter
Versatile film, TV entertainer from 1940s; wrote ''The Christmas Song''; won 1983 Grammy.
b. Sep 13, 1925 in Chicago, Illinois
Source: *AllMusG; ASCAP 66, 80; Baker 84, 92; BiDAmM; BiDJaz; BioIn 6, 11, 12, 13, 15, 16, 17, 20; CelR, 90; CmpEPM; ConAu 118, 143; ConMus 4; CurBio 83; EncJzS; FilmgC; ForYSC; IlEncJ; IntMPA 84, 86, 88, 92, 94, 96; LegTOT; NewAmDM; NewGrDA 86;*

NewGrDJ 88, 94; OxCPMus; PenEncP; RadStar; RkOn 74; WhoAm 74, 76, 78, 80, 82, 84, 86, 88, 90; WhoHol 92, A; WorAl; WorAlBi; WrDr 96

Torn, Rip
[Elmore Torn, Jr.]
American. Actor
Films from 1956 include *Sweet Bird of Youth; Heartland;* married Geraldine Page, 1961.
b. Feb 6, 1931 in Temple, Texas
Source: *BiE&WWA; BioIn 8, 9, 11, 12, 20, 21; ConTFT 4; CurBio 77; FilmEn; FilmgC; ForYSC; HalFC 80, 84, 88; IntDcF 1-3; IntMPA 75, 76, 77, 78, 79, 80, 81, 82, 84, 86, 88, 92, 94, 96; LegTOT; MiSFD 9; MovMk; NotNAT; WhoAm 78, 80, 82, 84, 86, 88, 90, 92, 94, 95, 96, 97; WhoEnt 92; WhoHol 92, A; WhoThe 72, 77, 81; WorAl; WorAlBi*

Torquemada, Tomas de
Spanish. Religious Figure
Monk, Inquisitor-General, who organized the Spanish Inquisition, 1483; in charge of removing Jews, Muslims from Spain.
b. 1420, Spain
d. 1498
Source: *BioIn 2, 4, 7, 20; BlmGEL; DcBiPP; DcCathB; DicTyr; LngCEL; LuthC 75; NewC; OxCEng 85, 95; OxCSpan; WhDW; WorAl; WorAlBi*

Torrance, Jack
"Baby Elephant"; "Baby Jack"
American. Track Athlete
Shot putter; held world record, 1934-59.
b. Jun 20, 1913 in Weathersby, Mississippi
d. Nov 10, 1969 in Baton Rouge, Louisiana
Source: *BioIn 8; WhoTr&F 73*

Torre, Joe
[Joseph Paul Torre]
American. Baseball Player, Baseball Manager
Catcher-infielder, 1960-77; led NL in batting, RBIs, won MVP, 1971; manager, NY Mets, 1977-82; Atlanta Braves, 1982-84; California Angels, 1984-90; St. Louis Cardinals, 1990-95; NY Yankees, 1996—.
b. Jul 18, 1940 in New York, New York
Source: *Ballpl 90; BiDAmSp BB; BioIn 7, 8, 9, 11, 15; CurBio 72; LegTOT; News 97-1; NewYTBE 71; NewYTBS 74, 77; WhoAm 74, 76, 78, 80, 82, 84, 92, 94, 95; WhoE 79, 81, 97; WhoMW 92, 93; WhoProB 73; WorAl; WorAlBi*

Torrence, Dean
[Jan and Dean]
American. Singer
Formed singing duo with junior high school friend, Jan Berry, 1958; has designed album covers.
b. Mar 10, 1941 in Los Angeles, California

Torrence, Ernest
American. Actor, Opera Singer
Films, 1921-33, include *Covered Wagon; King of Kings.*
b. Jun 16, 1878 in Edinburgh, Scotland
d. May 15, 1933 in New York, New York
Source: *BioIn 17; Film 2; FilmEn; FilmgC; ForYSC; HalFC 80, 84, 88; HolCA; MotPP; MovMk; NotNAT B; SilFlmP; TwYS; WhoHol B; WhScrn 74, 77, 83; WhThe*

Torrence, Gwen(dolyn Lenna)
American. Track Athlete
Won two gold medals, 200-meter and 4x100-meter relay, 1992 Olympics; won gold in 4x100-meter relay, 1996 Olympics.
b. Jun 12, 1965 in Atlanta, Georgia
Source: *CurBio 96; EncWomS; WhoAmW 97; WhoWor 97*

Torrence, Jackie
American. Folklorist
Began telling stories to three and four-year olds; became known as "The Story Lady."
b. Feb 12, 1944 in Chicago, Illinois
Source: *BioIn 18, 20; NotBlAW 1; WhoBlA 92*

Torrence, Ridgely
[Frederic Ridgely Torrence]
American. Poet, Dramatist
His *Plays for a Negro Theater,* 1917, sparked interest in blacks as a source of literary material; won many awards for poetry, admired by A E Houseman, other poets.
b. Feb 27, 1875 in Xenia, Ohio
d. Dec 25, 1950 in New York, New York
Source: *AmAu&B; BenetAL 91; BioIn 2, 3, 4, 8, 9, 15; CnDAL; ConAmL; DcAmAu; EvLB; ModAL; OhA&B; OxCAmL 65, 83; OxCTwCP; REnAL; TwCA, SUP; WhAm 3; WhNAA*

Torre-Nilsson, Leopoldo
Argentine. Director
Art cinema director; *The House of the Angel,* 1957, brought world attention to him, Argentinian films.
b. May 5, 1924 in Buenos Aires, Argentina
d. Sep 8, 1978 in Buenos Aires, Argentina
Source: *DcFM; FilmEn; FilmgC; HalFC 84; IntWW 74, 79N; OxCFilm; WorEFlm*

Torresola, Griselio
Puerto Rican. Attempted Assassin
Tried to shoot way into Blair House to kill Harry Truman; killed in attempt.
d. Nov 1, 1950 in Washington, District of Columbia
Source: *BioIn 8, 9, 10*

Torrey, Bill
[William Arthur Torrey]
Canadian. Hockey Executive
NY Islanders, 1972-93; Florida Panthers 1993—; built team that won four consecutive Stanley Cups, 1979-83.
b. Jun 23, 1934 in Montreal, Quebec, Canada
Source: *BioIn 12, 13; NewYTBS 80, 81; WhoAm 74, 76, 78, 80, 82, 84, 86, 88, 92, 95; WhoE 79, 81, 85, 86, 89, 91*

Torricelli, Evangelista
Italian. Scientist
Developed barometer, invented its earliest form, 1643; also improved telescope.
b. Oct 15, 1608 in Piancaldoli, Italy
d. Oct 25, 1647 in Florence, Italy
Source: *AsBiEn; BiESc; BioIn 5, 9, 12, 14; CamDcSc; DcBiPP; DcCathB; DcInv; DcScB; Dis&D; InSci; LarDcSc; LinLib S; McGEWB; NewC; NewCol 75; WebBD 83; WhDW; WorAl; WorAlBi; WorInv; WorScD*

Torricelli, Robert G.
American. Politician
Dem. senator, NJ, 1997—.
b. Aug 26, 1951
Source: *AlmAP 84, 88, 92, 96; BioIn 21; CngDr 83, 85, 87, 89, 91, 93, 95; PolsAm 84; WhoAm 84, 86, 88, 90, 92, 94, 95, 96, 97; WhoAmP 75, 77, 79, 81, 83, 85, 87, 89, 91, 93, 95; WhoE 83, 85, 86, 89, 91, 93, 95, 97*

Torrijos Herrera, Omar
Panamanian. Political Leader
Engineered 1968 coup, instituted reforms as Chief of Government, 1972-78; main architect of Panama Canal treaties with US, 1979; against opposition granted asylum to Shah of Iran, 1979; killed in plane crash.
b. Feb 13, 1929 in Santiago de Veraguas, Panama
d. Jul 31, 1981, Panama
Source: *BiDLAmC; BioIn 9, 10, 11, 12, 14, 16, 17; BioNews 74; CurBio 73, 81, 81N; DcCPCAm; IntWW 74, 75, 76, 77, 78, 79, 80, 81; IntYB 78, 79, 80, 81; NewYTBE 73; NewYTBS 77, 81; WhoWor 78, 80; WorAl*

Torrio, Johnny
[John Torrio]
American. Criminal
Prohibition-era crime boss involved in Chicago brothel chain, bootlegging and casinos; cohort of Al Capone; served various prison sentences, but retired wealthy.
b. Feb 1882 in Orsara, Italy
d. Apr 16, 1957 in New York, New York
Source: *BioIn 9, 16; CopCroC*

Torroja (y Miret), Eduardo
Spanish. Architect, Engineer
Pioneered concrete-shell structure design; founded Technical Institute of Construction and Cement, 1951-61.

b. Aug 27, 1899 in Madrid, Spain
d. Jun 15, 1961 in Madrid, Spain
Source: *ConArch 80, 87; DcD&D; EncMA; McGDA; WhoArch*

Tors, Ivan
Hungarian. Producer, Director
Produced TV shows ''Sea Hunt,'' 1957-61; ''Flipper,'' 1964-68.
b. Jun 12, 1916 in Budapest, Austria-Hungary
d. Jun 4, 1983 in Mato Grosso, Brazil
Source: *BioIn 7, 8, 12, 13; CelR; ConAu 103, 110; CurBio 69, 83N; FilmEn; FilmgC; HalFC 80, 84, 88; IntMPA 75, 76, 77, 78, 79, 80, 81, 82; LesBEnT; NewYTBS 83; NewYTET; WhAm 8; WhoAm 74, 76, 78, 80, 82; WhoHol A; WhoHrs 80*

Tortelier, Paul
French. Musician, Composer
Noted cellist; wrote cello concertos.
b. Mar 21, 1914
d. Dec 18, 1990 in Villarceaux, France
Source: *AnObit 1990; Baker 78, 84, 92; BioIn 11, 14, 16, 17; IntWW 74, 75, 76, 77, 78, 79, 80, 81, 82, 83, 89; IntWWM 77, 80, 90; MusMk; NewAmDM; NewGrDM 80; NewYTBS 90; PenDiMP; WhAm 10; Who 74, 82, 83, 85, 88, 90; WhoMus 72; WhoWor 74, 76, 78, 89*

Torvill, Jayne
[Torvill and Dean]
English. Skater
With Christopher Dean, won gold medal in ice dancing, 1984 Olympics.
b. 1958? in Nottingham, England
Source: *BioIn 13*

Toscanini, Arturo
Italian. Conductor
Considered finest maestro of his time; director, La Scala, from 1898; NBC Symphony, 1937-54; directed from memory.
b. Mar 25, 1867 in Parma, Italy
d. Jan 16, 1957 in New York, New York
Source: *AmCulL; Baker 78, 84, 92; BiDAmM; BioIn 1, 2, 3, 4, 5, 6, 7, 8, 10, 11, 12, 13, 14, 15, 16, 17, 19, 20; BriBkM 80; CmOp; ConMus 14; CurBio 42, 54, 57; DcAmB S6; DcArts; DcCathB; FacFETw; IntDcOp; LegTOT; LinLib S; McGEWB; MetOEnc; MusMk; MusSN; NewAmDM; NewEOp 71; NewGrDA 86; NewGrDM 80; NewGrDO; ObitT 1951; OxCAmH; OxCMus; OxDcOp; PenDiMP; RadStar; REn; WebAB 74, 79; WhAm 3; WhDW; WhScrn 77, 83; WorAl; WorAlBi*

Tosh, Peter
[Bob Marley and the Wailers; Winston Hubert MacIntosh MacIntosh]
Jamaican. Singer
Original Wailer; one of the founding fathers of Jamaica's vibrant music of revolution—reggae.
b. Oct 9, 1944 in Westmoreland, Jamaica
d. Sep 11, 1987 in Kingston, Jamaica
Source: *AnObit 1987; BioIn 12, 15, 16; ConBlB 9; ConMuA 80A; ConMus 3; DcTwCCu 5; DrBlPA 90; EncPR&S 89; EncRk 88; HarEnR 86; InB&W 80, 85; LegTOT; News 88-2; NewYTBS 87; OnThGG; RkOn 85; RolSEnR 83; WhoRock 81*

Tosti, Francesco Paolo
Italian. Composer
Singing teacher to Britain's royal family; wrote ''Goodbye Forever and Forever.''
b. Apr 7, 1846 in Ortona, Italy
d. Dec 6, 1916 in Rome, Italy
Source: *Baker 78, 84; BioIn 7, 12; GrComp; NewGrDM 80; OxCMus; WebBD 83*

Totenberg, Nina
American. Journalist
Legal affairs correspondent National Public Radio, 1975—; interviewed Anita Hill about her claim of sexual harassment against then-nominee to the Supreme Court Clarence Thomas, 1991; reporter, ''Inside Washington,'' 1992—; reporter ''Nightline'', 1993—
b. Jan 14, 1944 in New York, New York
Source: *CurBio 96; News 92, 92-2; WhoAm 94, 95, 96, 97; WhoAmW 97; WhoE 93, 95; WomStre*

Totheroh, Dan
American. Dramatist
Plays include *Wild Birds,* 1922.
b. Jul 22, 1894 in Oakland, California
d. 1976
Source: *AmAu&B; CnDAL; CnMD; ConAmA; ModWD; OxCAmL 65; PenC AM; REnAL; WhoThe 77A; WhThe*

Toto
[Bobby Kimball; Steve Lukather; David Paich; Jeff Porcaro; Mike Porcaro; Steve Porcaro]
American. Music Group
Formed late 1970s; hits include ''Rosanna,'' 1982; ''Africa,'' 1983.
Source: *ConMuA 80A; EncAFC; EncPR&S 89; EncRk 88; EncRkSt; Film 1; FilmAG WE; HarEnR 86; ItaFilm; MotPP; NewGrDA 86; ObitOF 79; PenEncP; RkOn 85; RolSEnR 83; WhoHol 92; WhoRock 81; WhoRocM 82*

Totter, Audrey
American. Actor
Played in TV show ''Medical Center,'' 1972-76; appeared on stage, film.
b. Dec 20, 1918 in Joliet, Illinois
Source: *BioIn 16, 18; FilmEn; FilmgC; ForYSC; GangFlm; HalFC 80, 84, 88; IntMPA 84, 86, 94, 96; LegTOT; MGM; MotPP; MovMk; WhoHol 92, A*

Tough, Dave
American. Jazz Musician
A top drummer, 1940s; with Spivak, Goodman, Woody Herman, others.
b. Apr 26, 1908 in Oak Park, Illinois
d. Dec 6, 1948 in Newark, New Jersey
Source: *BiDAmM; BiDJaz; CmpEPM; IlEncJ; WhoJazz 72*

Touhy, Roger
''The Terrible''
American. Criminal
Chicago crime boss involved in bootlegging, gambling; imprisoned 1934-59 for a kidnapping, later found to be a hoax; killed by gunmen shortly after release.
b. 1898 in Chicago, Illinois
d. Dec 17, 1959 in Chicago, Illinois
Source: *BioIn 5; DrInf*

Toulouse-Lautrec (Monfa), (Henri Marie Raymond de)
French. Artist
Postimpressionist painter known for physical deformity; drawings of Paris cabarets.
b. Nov 24, 1864 in Albi, France
d. Sep 9, 1901 in Malrome, France
Source: *AntBDN A; AtlBL; Dis&D; NewCol 75; OxCFr; REn; WorAl*

Toumanova, Tamara
Russian. Dancer
Prima ballerina from age 12; starred in film *Days of Glory,* 1944.
b. Mar 2, 1919 in Siberia, Russia
d. May 29, 1996 in Santa Monica, California
Source: *BiDD; BioIn 21; CnOxB; ContDcW 89; DancEn 78; FilmgC; HalFC 84; IntDcB; IntDcWB; NewYTBS 27; WhoHol A; WhoThe 77A*

Toure, Ahmed Sekou
Guinean. Political Leader
Leader of Guinea since its independence, 1958-84; black Africa's longest surviving head of state.
b. Jan 9, 1922 in Faranah, Guinea
d. Mar 26, 1984 in Cleveland, Ohio
Source: *AfSS 78, 79, 80, 81, 82; AnObit 1984; BiDMarx; BioIn 14, 18, 20, 21; CurBio 59; DcAfHiB 86; DcTwHis; InB&W 80, 85; IntWW 74, 75, 76, 77, 78, 79, 80, 83; IntYB 79, 80, 81, 82; NewCol 75; NewYTBS 84; WhoGov 72; WhoWor 78, 80, 82*

Toure, Ali Farka
Malian. Singer, Musician
Malian guitarist who played with American blues legend John Lee Hooker in France in the 1970s; collaborated with Ry Cooder to produce *Talking Timbuktu,* 1994, which received *Down Beat* Critics Poll's ''Beyond Album of the Year'' Award; also released *The Source* in 1992.
b. 1942 in Niafenke, Mali

Tourel, Jennie
American. Opera Singer
Mezzo-soprano, noted for Carmen; NY Met., 1944-57.

b. Jun 18, 1910 in Montreal, Quebec, Canada
d. Nov 23, 1973 in New York, New York
Source: *Baker 84; BiDAmM; BioIn 1, 2, 3, 4, 6, 9, 10, 11; BioNews 74; CmOp; CurBio 47, 74, 74N; InWom, SUP; NewEOp 71; NewYTBE 73; WhAm 6; WhoAmW 58, 61, 64; WhoHol B; WhoWor 74; WhoWorJ 72; WhScrn 77, 83*

Tournefort, Joseph Pitton de
"The Father of Botany"
French. Scientist
Founded system of classifying plants, discarded, mid-18th c.
b. Jun 3, 1656 in Aix-en-Provence, France
d. Nov 28, 1708 in Paris, France
Source: *BioIn 4; DcBiPP; DcCathB; DcScB; InSci; LarDcSc*

Tourneur, Cyril
English. Dramatist
The Revenger's Tragedy, 1607; *The Atheist's Tragedy,* 1611, are considered most important of his dramas.
b. 1575
d. Feb 28, 1626 in Kinsdale, Ireland
Source: *Alli; AtlBL; Benet 87, 96; BiD&SB; BiDRP&D; BioIn 1, 3, 5, 7, 12, 16; BlmGEL; BritAu; BritWr 2; CamGEL; CamGLE; CamGWoT; CasWL; Chambr 1; CnE&AP; CnThe; CroE&S; CrtSuDr; CrtT 1, 4; CyWA 58; DcArts; DcEnL; DcLEL; DcNaB; EncWT; Ent; EvLB; GrWrEL DR; IntDcT 2; LngCEL; McGEWD 72, 84; MouLC 1; NewC; NewCBEL; NotNAT B; OxCEng 67, 85, 95; OxCThe 67, 83; PenC ENG; RAdv 14, 13-2; REn; REnWD; RfGEnL 91; WebE&AL*

Tournier, Michel
French. Author
Novel *Le Roides Aulnes,* 1970, awarded Prix Goncourt, France's highest literary award.
b. Dec 19, 1924 in Paris, France
Source: *Benet 96; BioIn 10, 13, 16; ConAu 3NR, 36NR, 49; ConFLW 84; ConLC 6, 23, 36, 95; CurBio 90; CyWA 89; DcLB 83; DcTwCCu 2; EncWL 2, 3; GuFrLit 1; IntAu&W 76, 77, 82, 91; IntWW 74, 75, 76, 77, 78, 79, 80, 81, 82, 83, 89, 91, 93; MajTwCW; ModFrL; PostFic; RAdv 14, 13-2; SmATA 23; TwCChW 83B; WhoFr 79; WhoWor 84, 87, 89, 91, 93, 95, 96, 97; WorAu 1975*

Toussaint l'Ouverture, Pierre Dominique
Haitian. Slave, Political Leader
Self-educated slave who played dominant role in Negro Rebellion, 1791, bringing law, order to Haiti by 1801.
b. May 20, 1743 in Cape Francois, Haiti
d. Apr 7, 1803 in Fort-de-Joux, France
Source: *Drake; LinLib S; NewCol 75; REn; WhAm HS*

Tovey, Donald Francis, Sir
English. Musicologist, Composer, Author
Wrote opera *The Bride of Dionysus,* 1935.
b. Jul 17, 1875 in Eton, England
d. Jul 10, 1940 in Edinburgh, Scotland
Source: *Baker 78, 84; BioIn 2, 3, 4, 6, 9, 10, 12, 21; BriBkM 80; CurBio 40; DcNaB, 1931; EvLB; LngCTC; MusMk; NewCBEL; NewGrDM 80; REn; TwCA SUP; WhDW*

Tower, Joan Peabody
American. Composer
Works include *Percussion Quartet,* 1963; *Hexachords for Flute,* 1972.
b. Sep 6, 1938 in New Rochelle, New York
Source: *Baker 84, 92; BioIn 13; ConAmC 82; WhoAm 88, 90, 92, 94, 95; WhoAmW 74, 75, 77, 85, 87, 89, 91, 93; WhoEnt 92*

Tower, John Goodwin
American. Politician
Conservative Rep. senator from TX, 1961-85; nomination to be Bush's secretary of defense rejected by Senate, 1989.
b. Sep 29, 1925 in Houston, Texas
d. Apr 5, 1991 in Brunswick, Georgia
Source: *BiDrAC; BiDrUSC 89; BioIn 5, 6, 8, 9, 10, 11, 12, 13; BlueB 76; CngDr 74, 77, 79, 81, 83; ConAu 106; CurBio 68; IntWW 83, 89; IntYB 82; NewYTBS 80, 83; WhAm 10; WhoAm 74, 76, 78, 80, 82, 84, 86, 88, 90; WhoAmP 73, 75, 77, 79, 81, 83, 85, 87, 89; WhoGov 72, 75, 77; WhoSSW 73, 75, 76, 78, 80, 82; WhoWor 78, 80, 82; WorAl; WorAlBi*

Towers, John Henry
American. Naval Officer
One of the first officers of Navy in aviation service; Asst. director, Naval Aviation, WW I.
b. Jan 30, 1885 in Rome, Georgia
d. Apr 1, 1955 in Washington, District of Columbia
Source: *BiDWWGF; BioIn 1, 3, 4, 16, 17; DcAmB S5; NatCAB 41; ObitT 1951; WebAMB; WebBD 83; WhAm 3*

Towle, Katherine Amelia
American. Military Leader, Educator
First director of Women's Marines; in regular Marine Corps, 1948-53.
b. Apr 30, 1898 in Towle, California
d. Mar 1, 1986 in Pacific Grove, California
Source: *BioIn 1, 2; CurBio 86; InWom, SUP; LibW; WebAMB; WhAm 9; WhoAmW 58, 61, 64, 66*

Towne, Charles Hanson
American. Poet, Editor
Wrote *Pretty Girls Get There,* 1940; *Gentlemen Behave,* 1941.
b. Feb 2, 1877 in Louisville, Kentucky
d. Feb 28, 1949 in New York, New York
Source: *AmAu&B; ASCAP 66, 80; BenetAL 91; BioIn 1, 4, 5; ChhPo, S1, S2; DcAmB S4; DcNAA; NotNAT B; OxCCan; REnAL; TwCA, SUP; WhAm 2; WhScrn 83*

Towne, Robert (Burton)
[P. H. Vazak; Edward Wain]
American. Writer, Filmmaker
Won Oscar for *Chinatown,* 1974.
b. 1936 in San Pedro, California
Source: *BioIn 10, 12, 13, 15, 16, 17, 21; ConAu 108; ConDr 82A; ConLC 87; ConTFT 8; CurBio 89; DcLB 44; HalFC 84, 88; IntMPA 84, 86, 92, 94, 96; LegTOT; MiSFD 9; VarWW 85; WhoAm 84, 86, 94, 95, 96, 97*

Townes, Charles Hard
American. Physicist
Shared Nobel Prize, 1964, for work in quantum electronics; one of builders of first successful maser, 1954.
b. Jul 28, 1915 in Greenville, South Carolina
Source: *AmMWSc 76P, 79, 82, 86, 89, 92, 95; AsBiEn; BiESc; BioIn 6, 7, 8, 9, 11, 12; BlueB 76; CamDcSc; FacFETw; IntWW 74, 75, 76, 77, 78, 79, 80, 81, 82, 83, 89, 91, 93; LarDcSc; LElec; McGMS 80; WebAB 74, 79; Who 74, 82, 83, 85, 88, 90, 92, 94; WhoAm 74, 76, 78, 80, 82, 84, 86, 88, 90, 92, 94, 95, 96, 97; WhoFrS 84; WhoNob, 90, 95; WhoScEn 94, 96; WhoWest 74, 76, 78, 80, 82, 84, 87, 89, 92, 94, 96; WhoWor 74, 80, 82, 84, 87, 89, 91, 93, 95, 96, 97*

Towns, Forrest
American. Track Athlete
Hurdler; won gold medal, 110 meter hurdles, 1936 Olympics; first to run hurdles under 14 seconds.
b. Feb 6, 1914 in Fitzgerald, Georgia
d. Apr 9, 1991 in Athens, Georgia
Source: *WhoTr&F 73*

Townsend, Francis Everett
American. Social Reformer, Physician
Pres., Townsend National Weekly, Inc., United Publishing Co., pres., Townsend Foundation.
b. Jan 13, 1867 in Livingston City, Illinois
d. Sep 1, 1960 in Los Angeles, California
Source: *AmDec 1930; AmRef; AmSocL; BioIn 1, 5, 7, 13, 15, 19; DcAmB S6; DcTwHis; FacFETw; OxCAmH; WebAB 74, 79; WhAm 4; WorAl*

Townsend, George Alfred
"Gath"
American. Author
Wrote *Campaigns of a Non-Combatant,* 1865; *The Entailed Hat,* 1884.
b. Jan 30, 1841 in Georgetown, Delaware
d. Apr 15, 1914 in New York, New York
Source: *Alli, SUP; AmAu; AmAu&B; AmBi; ApCAB; BbD; BenetAL 91; BiD&SB; BioIn 1, 3; ChhPo S1; CivWDc; DcAmAu; DcAmB; DcNAA; HarEnUS; JrnUS; NatCAB 1; OxCAmL*

65, 83, 95; REnAL; TwCBDA; WhAm 1; WhCiWar

Townsend, John Sealy Edward, Sir
Irish. Physicist
Pioneer in electrical conduction of gases; first person to measure the unit electrical charge (e).
b. Jun 7, 1868 in Galway, Ireland
d. Feb 16, 1957 in Oxford, England
Source: *BiESc; BioIn 1, 4, 8, 14; DcNaB 1951; DcScB; InSci; LarDcSc; WhLit*

Townsend, Lynn Alfred
American. Auto Executive
Pres., Chrysler Corp., 1961-66; board chm., 1967-75.
b. May 12, 1919 in Flint, Michigan
Source: *BioIn 6, 7, 8, 10, 11; BlueB 76; BusPN; CurBio 66; EncABHB 5; IntWW 81; IntYB 78, 79, 80, 81, 82; PolProf J; St&PR 75; WhoAm 74, 76, 78, 80; WhoFI 74, 75; WhoMW 74, 76; WhoWor 74*

Townsend, Peter Wooldridge
English. Author
Books on history, travel include *Earth, My Friend,* 1959; *Duel of Eagles,* 1961.
b. Nov 22, 1914 in Rangoon, Myanmar
d. Jun 19, 1995 in Paris, France
Source: *Au&Wr 71; Who 85; WrDr 86*

Townsend, Robert
American. Filmmaker, Actor
Co-wrote, directed, produced, and appeared in *Hollywood Shuffle,* 1987, and *The Five Heartbeats,* 1991.
b. Feb 6, 1957 in Chicago, Illinois
Source: *BioIn 14, 15, 16; ConBlB 4; ConTFT 3, 13; CurBio 94; DrBlPA 90; IntMPA 88, 92, 94, 96; LegTOT; MiSFD 9; WhoAfA 96; WhoAm 94, 95, 96, 97; WhoBlA 92, 94; WhoEnt 92*

Townsend, Willard Saxby
American. Labor Union Official
Pres., United Transport Service Employees of America, 1940-57.
b. Dec 4, 1895 in Cincinnati, Ohio
d. Feb 3, 1957 in Chicago, Illinois
Source: *BiDAmL; BiDAmLL; BioIn 1, 4; CurBio 48; DcAmB S6; InB&W 80, 85; WhAm 3; WorAl*

Townsend, William Cameron
American. Missionary
Founded Wycliffe Bible Translators, Inc., 1935, nonprofit group that translated New Testament into over 130 languages.
b. 1896
d. Apr 23, 1982 in Lancaster, South Carolina
Source: *BioIn 10, 12, 13, 15, 19; ConAu 106; DcAmReB 2*

Townsend, William H(enry)
American. Lawyer, Author
Expert on Pres. Lincoln; held one of largest collections of Lincoln memorabilia in US; wrote *Lincoln the Litigant.*
b. May 31, 1890 in Glensboro, Kentucky
d. Jul 25, 1964 in Lexington, Kentucky
Source: *AmAu&B; BioIn 6, 7, 8; ConAu 111; EncAB-A 6; EncAB-H 1974; NatCAB 51; WhAm 4*

Townshend, Peter Dennis Blandford
[The Who]
English. Musician
Called one of rock music's most intelligent, inventive songwriters; wrote opera *Tommy.*
b. May 19, 1945 in London, England
Source: *ConAu 107; CurBio 83; HarEnR 86; IntWW 89, 91, 93; IntWWM 90; WhoAm 80*

Toye, Clive Roy
English. Soccer Executive
Chm. of the now defunct NASL; president, Toronto Blizzard, 1979—; has written books about soccer for children.
b. Nov 23, 1932 in Plymouth, England
Source: *SmATA 30; WhoAm 84, 86; WhoE 77, 79, 81, 83, 85, 86*

Toye, Francis
English. Author, Journalist
Music critic for London newspapers; wrote *Guiseppi Verdi: His Life and Work,* 1931.
b. Jan 27, 1883 in Winchester, England
d. Oct 31, 1964 in Florence, Italy
Source: *Baker 78, 84; BioIn 1, 4, 7; NewGrDM 80; OxCMus*

Toynbee, Arnold Joseph
English. Historian
Writings include *Nationality and War,* 1915; *Hellenism,* 1959; *Mankind and Mother Earth,* 1976.
b. Apr 14, 1889 in London, England
d. Oct 22, 1975 in York, England
Source: *Au&Wr 71; AuNews 2; BioIn 1, 2, 3, 4, 5, 6, 7, 8, 10, 11, 12, 13, 14, 15, 16, 20; CasWL; ConAu 5R, 61; CurBio 47; CyWA 58; DcLEL; DcNaB 1971; EvLB; GrBr; IntWW 74, 75; LinLib S; LngCTC; MakMC; McGEWB; NewC; NewCBEL; OxCEng 67, 85, 95; REn; TwCA, SUP; TwCWr; WebE&AL; WhAm 6; WhDW; WhE&EA; WhLit; Who 74; WhoAm 74; WhoLA; WhoWor 74*

Toynbee, Philip
[Theodore Philip Toynbee]
English. Author, Critic, Journalist
Wrote *Tea with Mrs. Goodman,* 1947; *The Garden to the Sea,* 1953.
b. Jun 25, 1916 in Oxford, England
d. Jun 15, 1981 in Saint Briavels, England
Source: *AnObit 1981; Au&Wr 71; BioIn 4, 12; BlueB 76; ConAu 1R, 4NR, 104; ConNov 72, 76; ConPo 70, 75, 80; DcLEL; DcNaB 1981; EvLB; IntAu&W 76, 77; IntWWP 77; LngCTC; ModBrL; NewCBEL; Novels; PenC ENG; REn; TwCA SUP; TwCWr; WhE&EA; Who 74; WhoTwCL; WrDr 76, 80, 82*

Toyoda, Eiji
Japanese. Auto Executive
With Toyota Motor Co. since 1937; chm., 1982—.
b. Sep 12, 1913 in Kinjo, Japan
Source: *ConNews 85-2; FarE&A 78, 79, 80, 81; IntWW 74, 75, 76, 77, 78, 79, 80, 81; WhoAm 74, 76, 78, 80, 82, 84, 86, 88, 92, 94, 95, 96; WhoWor 74, 78, 80, 82, 84, 87, 89, 91, 93, 95, 97*

Toyoda, Shoichiro
"The Crown Prince"
Japanese. Auto Executive
President, Toyota Motor Corporation, 1982-92; chm., 1992—.
b. Feb 27, 1925, Japan
Source: *IntWW 93; WhoFI 96; WhoWor 74, 76, 89, 91, 93, 95, 96, 97*

Tozzer, Alfred Marston
American. Anthropologist, Archaeologist
Expert on Mayan Indians attempted to decipher their hieroglyphics; wrote many scholarly works on the subject.
b. Jul 4, 1877 in Lynn, Massachusetts
d. Oct 5, 1954 in Cambridge, Massachusetts
Source: *BioIn 3, 4; InSci; IntDcAn; WhAm 3; WhLit; WhNAA*

Tozzi, Giorgio
American. Opera Singer, Actor
Bass-baritone; NY Met. debut, 1955; starred in Broadway's *Most Happy Fella,* 1979-80.
b. Jan 8, 1923 in Chicago, Illinois
Source: *Baker 78, 84, 92; BioIn 4, 5, 6, 8, 11; CelR; CmOp; CurBio 61; IntDcOp; IntWWM 90; MetOEnc; MusSN; NewAmDM; NewEOp 71; NewGrDA 86; NewGrDM 80; NewGrDO; PenDiMP; WhoAm 74, 76, 78, 80, 82, 84, 86, 88; WhoAmM 83; WhoMus 72; WhoOp 76; WhoWor 74*

Trabert, Tony
[Marion Anthony Trabert]
American. Tennis Player
Won US Open championship singles title, 1953, 1955; doubles, 1954; Wimbledon championship, 1955.
b. Sep 16, 1930 in Cincinnati, Ohio
Source: *BiDAmSp OS; BioIn 3, 4, 10, 12; BuCMET; CurBio 54; LegTOT; WhoHol A; WhoSpor; WhoTelC*

Tracy, Arthur
"The Street Singer"
American. Singer
Appeared with accordion on radio shows, films, 1930s-50s: film *The Big Broadcast,* 1932.
b. Jun 25, 1903 in Philadelphia, Pennsylvania

Source: *BioIn 7, 10; EncVaud; FilmgC; ForYSC; HalFC 80, 84, 88; SaTiSS; WhoHol 92, A*

Tracy, Edward A
American. Hostage
Writer in Lebanon seized by Revolutionary Justice Organization Oct 21, 1986 and held captive 1,755 days; released Aug 11, 1991.

Tracy, Lee
American. Actor
Oscar nominee for *The Best Man,* 1964.
b. Apr 4, 1898 in Atlanta, Georgia
d. Oct 18, 1968 in Santa Monica, California
Source: *BiE&WWA; BioIn 5, 8, 11, 18, 21; CamGWoT; EncAFC; Film 2; FilmEn; FilmgC; ForYSC; HalFC 80, 84, 88; HolP 30; LegTOT; MotPP; MovMk; NotNAT B; OlFamFa; OxCAmT 84; WhAm 5; WhoHol B; WhScrn 74, 77, 83; WhThe; WorAl; WorAlBi*

Tracy, Spencer Bonaventure
American. Actor
Leading man considered one of world's greatest actors; won Oscars for *Captains Courageous,* 1937; *Boy's Town,* 1938; co-starred with Katharine Hepburn in nine films.
b. Apr 5, 1900 in Milwaukee, Wisconsin
d. Jun 10, 1967 in Beverly Hills, California
Source: *BiDFilm; BiE&WWA; CmMov; CurBio 43, 67; DcAmB S8; EncWB; FilmEn; FilmgC; MotPP; MovMk; OxCFilm; PlP&P; WebAB 79; WhAm 4; WhScrn 83; WorEFlm*

Traetta, Tommaso
Italian. Composer
Operas include *Il Farnace,* 1751; works now neglected.
b. Mar 30, 1727 in Bitonto, Italy
d. Apr 6, 1779 in Venice, Italy
Source: *Baker 78, 84, 92; BlkwCE; DcBiPP; MusMk; NewAmDM; NewEOp 71; NewGrDM 80; NewOxM; OxCMus; OxDcOp*

Traffic
[Jim Capaldi; Dave Mason; Stevie Winwood; Chris Wood]
English. Music Group
Rock band formed 1967; known for hit albums: *Traffic,* 1968.
Source: *ConMuA 80A; EncPR&S 74, 89; EncRk 88; EncRkSt; HarEnR 86; IlEncRk; OxCPMus; PenEncP; RkOn 78; RolSEnR 83; WhoRock 81; WhoRocM 82*

Trafficante, Santo, Jr.
American. Criminal
Mafia don; testified before Congress that he was part of a 1960 assassination plot against Fidel Castro.
b. Nov 14, 1915? in Tampa, Florida
d. Mar 17, 1987 in Houston, Texas
Source: *BioIn 11*

Trafton, George
American. Football Player
Center, Chicago, 1920-33; Hall of Fame, 1964.
b. Dec 6, 1896 in Chicago, Illinois
d. Sep 5, 1971
Source: *BiDAmSp FB; BioIn 8, 17; LegTOT; WhoFtbl 74; WhoSpor*

Trafzer, Clifford Earl
American. Historian
Writings include *The Kit Carson Campaign,* 1982; *Yakima, Palouse, Cayuse, Umatilla, Walla Walla, and Wanapum Indians: An Historical Bibliography,* 1992.
b. Mar 1, 1949 in Mansfield, Ohio
Source: *ConAu 26NR, 109; DrAS 78H, 82H; NotNaAm*

Traglia, Luigi, Cardinal
Italian. Religious Leader
Dean of Roman Catholic Sacred College of Cardinals, 1974-77.
b. Apr 3, 1896 in Albano Laziale, Italy
d. Nov 22, 1977 in Rome, Italy
Source: *BioIn 5, 11; IntWW 74; WhoWor 74*

Traikov, Georgi
Bulgarian. Politician
Chief of state, 1964-72; first deputy prime minister, 1949-64.
b. 1898, Bulgaria
d. Jan 14, 1975
Source: *IntWW 74; NewCol 75; WhoGov 72; WhoSocC 78; WhoWor 74*

Train, Arthur Cheney
American. Lawyer, Author
Wrote *Mr. Tutt* stories.
b. Sep 6, 1875 in Boston, Massachusetts
d. Dec 22, 1945 in New York, New York
Source: *DcAmB S3; REnAL; TwCA; WhAm 2*

Train, Russell Errol
American. Government Official
EPA administrator, 1973-77; pres., World Wildlife Fund, 1978-85.
b. Jun 4, 1920 in Washington, District of Columbia
Source: *BioIn 8, 9, 10, 12; BlueB 76; CurBio 70; IntWW 74, 75, 76, 77, 78, 79, 80, 81, 82, 83, 89, 91, 93; NatLAC; NewYTBE 70; NewYTBS 84; PolProf NF; WhoAm 74, 76, 78, 82, 84, 86, 88, 92, 94, 95, 96, 97; WhoAmP 73, 75, 77, 79; WhoGov 72, 75, 77; WhoSSW 73; WhoWor 84, 93*

Trajan
[Marcus Ulpius Trajanus]
Roman. Ruler
Ruled, 98-117; known for building bridges, roads, Trajan's Forum, Trajan's Column.
b. Sep 18, 53? in Italica, Spain
d. Aug 8, 117 in Selinus, Cilicia
Source: *BioIn 5, 7, 8, 9, 14, 17, 20; DicTyr; EncEarC; GrLGrT; HarEnMi; HisWorL; LegTOT; LinLib S; McGEWB; NewC; NewCol 75; OxCClL 89; REn; WebBD 83; WhDW; WorAl; WorAlBi*

Trammell, Alan Stuart
American. Baseball Player
Shortstop, Detroit, 1977-96; MVP, 1984 World Series.
b. Feb 21, 1958 in Garden Grove, California
Source: *BaseReg 86, 87; BiDAmSp Sup; WhoAm 86, 88, 92; WhoMW 88, 90*

Trampler, Walter
American. Musician
Viola virtuoso; known for performances with Budapest String Quartet.
b. Aug 25, 1915 in Munich, Germany
Source: *Baker 78, 84, 92; BioIn 9, 11; BriBkM 80; CurBio 71; IntWWM 77, 80; MusSN; NewAmDM; NewGrDA 86; NewGrDM 80; NewYTBS 77; PenDiMP; WhoAm 74, 76; WhoAmM 83; WhoE 74, 75; WhoMus 72; WhoWor 74*

Traore, Moussa
Malian. Political Leader
President, Republic of Mali, 1968-91; ousted, Mar 26, 1991.
b. Sep 25, 1936 in Kayes, Mali
Source: *AfSS 78, 79, 80, 81, 82; BioIn 21; DcAfHiB 86S; EncRev; IntWW 74, 75, 76, 77, 78, 79, 80, 81, 82, 83, 89, 91, 93; WhoGov 72; WhoWor 74, 76, 78, 80, 82, 84, 87, 89, 91*

Traphagen, Ethel Leigh
American. Fashion Designer
Founded first school of fashion design in US, 1923.
b. Oct 10, 1882 in New York, New York
d. Apr 29, 1963 in New York, New York
Source: *CurBio 48, 63; NatCAB 54*

Trapp, Maria Augusta von
American. Singer, Author
Fled Nazi-occupied Austria, formed Trapp Family Singers, 1930s; life story was inspiration for play *The Sound of Music,* 1959.
b. Jan 26, 1905 in Vienna, Austria
d. Mar 28, 1987 in Morrisville, Vermont
Source: *AmAu&B; BioIn 12, 13; ConAu 81; ConNews 87-3; CurBio 68, 87; InWom SUP; NewYTBS 87; SmATA 16; WhoAm 74, 76, 78, 80, 82, 84, 86; WhoE 74; WorAl*

Trask, Diana
Australian. Singer, Actor
Folk singer with Grand Ole Opry, 1960s-70s.
b. Jun 23, 1940
Source: *BioIn 5, 14; CounME 74, 74A; EncFCWM 83; HarEnCM 87; IlEncCM*

Traub, Marvin Stuart
American. Business Executive
Chm., Bloomingdales dept. store chain, 1978-92.

b. Apr 14, 1925 in New York, New York
Source: *ConNews 87-3; St&PR 87; WhoAm 76, 78, 80, 82, 84, 86, 88, 90, 95; WhoFI 89, 92*

Traube, Shepard
American. Producer, Director
Founder, Society of Stage Directors and Choreographers; directed *Angel Street*, 1940s.
b. Feb 27, 1907 in Malden, Massachusetts
d. Jul 23, 1983 in New York, New York
Source: *BiE&WWA; BioIn 13; ConAu 111; NotNAT; WhAm 8; WhoAm 78, 80, 82; WhoThe 72, 77, 81*

Traubel, Helen
American. Opera Singer
Leading NY Met. Wagnerian soprano, 1939-53; forced to resign due to nightclub appearances.
b. Jun 20, 1899 in Saint Louis, Missouri
d. Jul 28, 1972 in Santa Monica, California
Source: *Baker 78, 84; BiDAmM; BioIn 12, 15, 19, 20; BriBkM 80; CmOp; CurBio 40, 52, 72; DcAmB S9; FilmgC; HalFC 80, 84, 88; IntDcOp; InWom; LinLib S; MetOEnc; MusSN; NewAmDM; NewEOp 71; NewGrDA 86; NewGrDM 80; NewYTBE 72; OxDcOp; PenDiMP; WhAm 5; WhScrn 77; WorAl; WorAlBi*

Trauner, Alexander
French. Art Director
Set designer; won Oscar for *The Apartment*, 1960.
b. Aug 3, 1906 in Budapest, Hungary
Source: *FilmEn; FilmgC; HalFC 80, 84, 88; OxCFilm; VarWW 85; WorEFlm*

Travanti, Daniel J(ohn)
American. Actor
Won two Emmys for role of Frank Furillo on TV series "Hill Street Blues," 1981-87.
b. Mar 7, 1940 in Kenosha, Wisconsin
Source: *VarWW 85; WhoAm 86, 95, 96, 97; WhoTelC*

Traven, B
[Berick Traven Torsvan]
Mexican. Author
Wrote *Treasure of the Sierra Madre*, 1935; filmed, 1948.
b. Feb 23, 1882? in Schwiebus, Germany
d. Mar 27, 1969 in Mexico City, Mexico
Source: *AmAu&B; CasWL; CnMWL; ConAu P-2; ConLC 11; EncWL; HalFC 80; OxCAmL 83; OxCEng 85; OxCGer 76; PenC AM, EUR; REnAL; TwCA SUP; WebE&AL; WhAm 5*

Travers, Ben
English. Dramatist
Known for series of farces, 1920s-30s: *Rookery Nook*, 1926.
b. Nov 12, 1886 in London, England
d. Dec 18, 1980 in London, England
Source: *AnObit 1980; Au&Wr 71; BiE&WWA; BioIn 4, 10, 11, 12, 13, 14; BlmGEL; CamGLE; CamGWoT; ConAu 102, 133; ConDr 73, 77, 93; CroCD; DcLB 10; EncWT; Ent; FilmgC; GrWrEL DR; HalFC 80, 84, 88; IntAu&W 76, 77; LngCTC; McGEWD 72, 84; NewCBEL; NewYTBS 80; NotNAT, A; OxCEng 85, 95; OxCThe 83; RfGEnL 91; WhDW; WhE&EA; Who 74; WhoThe 72, 77, 81; WrDr 76, 80, 82*

Travers, Bill
English. Actor, Producer, Director
Films include *Born Free*, 1966; *Ring of Bright Water*, 1969.
b. Jan 3, 1922 in Newcastle-upon-Tyne, England
Source: *BioIn 19, 20; FilmEn; FilmgC; HalFC 80, 84, 88; IlWWBF; IntMPA 77, 80, 88, 92, 94; MovMk; VarWW 85; WhoHol 92, A*

Travers, Jerry
[Jerome Dunstan Travers]
American. Golfer
One of five amateurs to win US Open, 1915; charter member, Hall of Fame, 1940.
b. May 19, 1887 in New York, New York
d. Mar 29, 1951 in East Hartford, Connecticut
Source: *BiDAmSp OS; BioIn 2; DcAmB S5; ObitOF 79; WhoGolf; WhoSpor*

Travers, Mary
[Peter, Paul, and Mary]
American. Singer
Member of folk music trio, popular in 1960s; hits include number-one single "Leavin' on a Jet Plane," 1969.
b. Nov 7, 1937 in Louisville, Kentucky
Source: *ASCAP 66; BioIn 12, 14, 21; EncFCWM 69; WhoAm 74; WhoRock 81; WhoRocM 82; WhoWor 74*

Travers, P(amela) L(yndon)
Australian. Author
Wrote *Mary Poppins*, 1934; filmed by Walt Disney, 1964.
b. Aug 9, 1906 in Queensland, Australia
d. Apr 23, 1996 in London, England
Source: *AnCL; ArtclWW 2; AuBYP 2; AuWomWr; Benet 96; BioIn 1, 2, 3, 4, 6, 7, 8, 9, 10, 11, 13; ChlLR 2; ConAu 33R; CurBio 96; JBA 51; LngCTC; MorBMP; NewC; NewCBEL; RAdv 14; REn; ScF&FL 1; SmATA 4; TwCA, SUP; TwCChW 78, 83, 95; WhoChL; WrDr 86, 94, 96*

Travis, Dempsey Jerome
American. Real Estate Executive, Mortgage Banker
Founded, heads many businesses including Travis Realty Co., 1949—; wrote *Autobiography of Black Politics*, 1987.
b. Feb 25, 1920 in Chicago, Illinois
Source: *BioIn 9, 10, 13; ConAu 15NR, 85; InB&W 85; WhoAm 74, 76, 78, 80, 82, 84, 86, 88, 90, 92, 94, 95, 96, 97; WhoBlA 85, 88; WhoFI 74, 75, 77, 79, 81, 85; WhoMW 74, 76, 78, 80, 82, 84; WhoWor 74, 76*

Travis, Merle Robert
American. Musician, Singer
Country Music Hall of Fame, 1977; compositions include "16 Tons," "Old Mountain Dew"; created "Travis-style" guitar playing.
b. Nov 29, 1917 in Rosewood, Kentucky
d. Oct 20, 1983 in Park Hill, Oklahoma
Source: *Baker 84; BiDAmM; CounME 74, 74A; EncFCWM 83; IlEncCM; NewYTBS 83; VarWW 85; WhAm 8; WhoAm 76, 80, 82*

Travis, Randy
[Randy Traywick]
American. Singer
Country singer; had number one single "Forever and Ever, Amen," 1987; Grammy award winner, 1987; has won numerous other awards.
b. May 4, 1959 in Monroe, North Carolina
Source: *Baker 92; CelR 90; ConMus 9; CurBio 89; EncRkSt; LegTOT; News 88; PenEncP; WhoAm 88; WhoHol 92; WorAlBi*

Travis, William Barret
American. Military Leader
Hero of Texas Revolution; commanded The Alamo, where all were slain by Santa Anna.
b. Aug 9, 1809 in Red Banks, South Carolina
d. Mar 6, 1836 in San Antonio, Texas
Source: *AmBi; BioIn 1, 3, 4, 5, 6, 7, 8, 10, 11, 16; DcAmB; Drake; EncAAH; EncSoH; HarEnMi; McGEWB; WebAB 74, 79; WebAMB; WhAm HS; WorAlBi*

Travolta, John
American. Actor
Starred in TV's "Welcome Back Kotter," 1975-79; films: *Saturday Night Fever*, 1977; *Grease*, 1978; *Look Who's Talking*, 1989; *Pulp Fiction*, 1994; *Get Shorty*, 1995.
b. Feb 18, 1954 in Englewood, New Jersey
Source: *BiDD; BiDFilm 81, 94; BioIn 11, 12, 13; BkPepl; CelR 90; ConTFT 2, 13; CurBio 78, 96; FilmEn; HalFC 80, 84, 88; HarEnR 86; HolBB; IntDcF 1-3, 2-3; IntMPA 84, 86, 88, 92, 94, 96; IntWW 81, 82, 83, 89, 91, 93; LegTOT; News 95, 95-2; NewYTBS 83; RkOn 78; WhoAm 78, 80, 82, 84, 86, 88, 90, 92, 94, 95, 96, 97; WhoEnt 92; WhoHol 92; WhoRock 81; WorAl; WorAlBi*

Traynor, John
[Jay and the Americans; Jay Traynor]
American. Singer
Lead singer, original "Jay" of Jay and the Americans, 1961-62.
Source: *BiDAmM; ConMuA 80A; EncPR&S 89; EncRk 88; NewAmDM; PenEncP; RkOn 74; RolSEnR 83; WhoRock 81; WhoRocM 82*

Traynor, Pie
[Harold Joseph Traynor]
American. Baseball Player
Infielder, Pittsburgh, 1920-37; had 100 or more RBIs seven times, .320 lifetime batting average; Hall of Fame, 1948.
b. Nov 11, 1899 in Framingham, Massachusetts
d. Mar 16, 1972 in Pittsburgh, Pennsylvania
Source: *Ballpl 90; BiDAmSp BB; BioIn 2, 3, 4, 6, 7, 8, 9, 10, 13, 14, 15; DcAmB S9; FacFETw; LegTOT; NewYTBE 72; ObitOF 79; WhoProB 73; WhoSpor*

Treacher, Arthur
[Arthur Veary]
American. Actor
Played butler in films, 1930s-40s; sidekick on Merv Griffin's TV show.
b. Jul 2, 1894 in Brighton, England
d. Dec 14, 1975 in Manhasset, New York
Source: *BiE&WWA; BioIn 8, 10; CelR; EncAFC; Film 2; FilmEn; FilmgC; ForYSC; HalFC 80, 84, 88; HolCA; IntMPA 75; LegTOT; MotPP; MovMk; NewYTBS 75; NotNAT B; Vers B; WhoHol C; WhScrn 77, 83; WorAl; WorAlBi*

Treas, Terri
American. Actor
Films include *All That Jazz,* 1979; *The Best Little Whorehouse in Texas,* 1982.
b. Jul 19, 1959 in Kansas City, Kansas
Source: *VarWW 85*

Treat, Lawrence
[Lawrence Arthur Goldstone]
American. Author
Mystery novels include *Venus Unarmed,* 1961; *Murder in the Mind,* 1967.
b. Dec 21, 1903 in New York, New York
Source: *BioIn 12, 16; ConAu 49; CrtSuMy; IntAu&W 89, 91, 93; SmATA 59; TwCCr&M 80, 85, 91; WhoAm 82, 84, 86, 88, 90, 92, 94, 95, 96, 97; WhoUSWr 88; WhoWrEP 89, 92, 95; WrDr 82, 84, 86, 88, 90, 92, 94, 96*

Trebek, Alex
Canadian. TV Personality
Host of syndicated TV game show "Jeopardy!," 1984—.
b. Jul 22, 1940 in Sudbury, Ontario, Canada
Source: *LegTOT; VarWW 85; WhoAm 90, 92, 94, 95, 96, 97; WhoEnt 92; WhoTelC; WhoWest 96*

Tree, Herbert Beerbohm
English. Actor, Manager
Began acting, 1878; managed the Haymarket Theatre, 1887-97; produced 18 Shakespeare plays.
b. Dec 17, 1853 in Kensington, England
d. Jul 2, 1917 in London, England
Source: *BioIn 2, 3, 4, 5, 6, 9, 10, 12; BlmGEL; CamGWoT; CnThe; DcNaB 1912; FamA&A; Film 1; NewC; NotNAT A, B; OxCAmT 84; OxCThe 67; PlP&P; VicBrit; WhAm 1; WhDW; WhLit; WhoHol B; WhScrn 77; WhThe; WorAl*

Tree, Marietta Endicott Peabody
American. Government Official
US rep. to Human Rights Committee, UN, 1961-64; served on staff of UN Secretariat until 1967.
b. Apr 12, 1917 in Lawrence, Massachusetts
d. Aug 15, 1991 in New York, New York
Source: *CurBio 61; WhoAm 86; WhoAmW 79*

Treece, Henry
English. Author, Poet, Dramatist
Versatile writer whose novels include *Red Queen, White Queen,* 1958; *Oedipus,* 1964.
b. Dec 22, 1911 in Staffordshire, England
d. Jun 10, 1966 in Barton-on-Humber, England
Source: *AuBYP 2, 3; BioIn 19; CamGLE; ChlBkCr; ConAu 1R, 6NR, 25R; DcLB 160; DcLEL; EvLB; LngCEL; LngCTC; ModBrL; MorJA; NewC; NewCBEL; OxCChiL; PenC ENG; REn; ScF&FL 1, 2; SmATA 2; TwCA SUP; TwCChW 78, 83, 89; TwCRHW 90, 94; TwCWr; TwCYAW; WhoChL*

Trefflich, Henry Herbert Frederick
"Monkey King of America"
American. Animal Dealer
Sold over 1.5 million monkeys, many of which were used for research and lab experiments; supplied Cheetah for *Tarzan* films.
b. Jan 9, 1908 in Hamburg, Germany
d. Jul 7, 1978 in Bound Brook, New Jersey
Source: *BioIn 3, 11; ConAu 77, P-2; CurBio 53, 78; WhAm 7; WhoAm 74, 76, 80*

Tregaskis, Richard William
American. Author
Wrote best-selling *Guadalcanal Diary,* 1943.
b. Nov 28, 1916 in Elizabeth, New Jersey
d. Aug 15, 1973 in Honolulu, Hawaii
Source: *AmAu&B; Au&Wr 71; AuBYP 2, 3; BioIn 7, 9, 10, 12, 13; ConAu 1R, 2NR, 45; CurBio 73; NatCAB 59; NewYTBE 73; SmATA 3, 26; WebAMB; WhAm 6; WhoAm 74*

Treitel, Jonathan
English. Writer
Author of *The Red Cabbage Cafe,* 1991, a novel of post-Revolution Russia.
b. 1959, England
Source: *ConLC 70*

Treitschke, Heinrich Gotthard von
German. Historian
Member of Prussian school of history, 19th-c. Germany; supported idea of united Germany under Prussian leadership.
b. Sep 15, 1834 in Dresden, Germany
d. Apr 28, 1896 in Berlin, Germany
Source: *BiD&SB; BioIn 1, 4, 7, 9; CasWL; DcEuL; EuAu; McGEWB; OxCGer 76; REn*

Trelawny, Edward John
English. Adventurer
Wrote *Recollections of the Last Days of Shelley and Byron,* 1858.
b. Nov 13, 1792 in London, England
d. Aug 13, 1881 in Sompting, England
Source: *Alli; Benet 87, 96; BiD&SB; BioIn 17, 18, 21; BritAu 19; CasWL; CelCen; DcAmAu; DcEnA; DcLB 110, 116, 144; DcLEL; DcNaB; EvLB; NewC; NewCBEL; OxCEng 67, 85, 95; PenC ENG; REn*

Tremayne, Les
American. Actor
Long-time radio actor in "The First Nighter," 1933-43; "The Thin Man," 1945-50; had character roles in US films from 1951: *The Fortune Cookie,* 1966.
b. Apr 16, 1913 in London, England
Source: *FilmgC; ForYSC; HalFC 84, 88; IntMPA 75, 76, 77, 78, 79, 80, 81, 82, 84, 86, 88, 92, 94, 96; RadStar; SaTiSS; WhoAm 74, 76, 78, 80, 82; WhoHol 92, A; WhoWor 80, 82*

Tremblay, Michel
Canadian. Dramatist
Plays include *Les Belles-Soeurs,* 1968.
b. Jun 25, 1942 in Montreal, Quebec, Canada
Source: *Benet 96; BioIn 11, 15, 16, 17; CamGWoT; CanWW 31; CaP; ClDMEL 80; ConAu 116, 128; ConCaAu 1; ConLC 29; ConWorW 93; DcLB 60; EncWL 3; GayLL; IntDcT 2; IntWW 91, 93; MajTwCW; McGEWD 84; OxCCanL; OxCCan SUP; OxCCanT; OxCThe 83; WhoCanL 85, 87, 92; WhoWor 95; WorAu 1970*

Trenary, Jill
American. Skater
Three-time US figure skating champion; world champion, 1990.
b. 1969 in Minneapolis, Minnesota

Trench, Richard Chenevix
Irish. Poet, Scholar
Noted philologist who popularized study of language: *Study of Words.*
b. Sep 5, 1807 in Dublin, Ireland
d. Mar 28, 1886 in London, England
Source: *Alli, SUP; BbD; Benet 87, 96; BiD&SB; BiDIrW; BioIn 5, 12, 19; BritAu 19; CamGEL; CamGLE; CelCen; Chambr 3; ChhPo, S1, S2; DcBiPP; DcEnL; DcEuL; DcIrB 78, 88; DcIrL 96; DcLEL; DcNaB, C; EvLB; LuthC*

75; NewC; NewCBEL; OxCEng 67, 85, 95; OxCIri; PoIre; REn

Trenchard, Hugh Montague, First Viscount
"Father of the RAF"
English. Military Leader
Marshall of Royal Air Force from 1927.
b. Feb 3, 1873 in Taunton, England
d. Feb 10, 1956 in London, England
Source: *CopCroC; DcNaB 1951; DcTwHis; GrBr; HarEnMi; HisEWW; WhAm 3; WhE&EA; WhoMilH 76; WorAl; WorAlBi*

Trendelenburg, Friedrich Adolf
German. Educator, Philosopher
Professor; wrote a number of scholarly books supporting the philosophy of Plato and Aristotle, against that of Kant and Hegel.
b. Nov 30, 1802 in Eutin, Germany
d. Jan 24, 1872 in Berlin, Germany
Source: *BiD&SB; CelCen; CyEd; OxCLaw*

Trendle, George Washington
American. Producer
Creator of "The Lone Ranger," "The Green Hornet," "Sergeant Preston of the Yukon" radio series, 1930s-40s.
b. Jul 4, 1884 in Norwalk, Ohio
d. May 11, 1972 in Grosse Pointe, Michigan
Source: *BioIn 9; EncMys; NewYTBE 72; WhAm 5*

Trenet, Charles
French. Singer, Songwriter
Writer of pop classic *Beyond the Sea.*
b. May 18, 1913 in Perpignan, France
Source: *BioIn 1, 6, 15, 16; CurBio 89; DcTwCCu 2; NewYTBS 87; OxCPMus; PenEncP; WhoFr 79; WhoHol 92*

Treptow, Martin A
American. Soldier
Ronald Reagan made reference to him in Inaugural speech, 1981.
b. 1894 in Bloomer, Wisconsin
d. Jul 28, 1918 in Chateau Thierry, France
Source: *BioIn 12*

Tretiak, Vladislav
Russian. Hockey Player
Goalie, Soviet national team, 1970s; wrote *The Hockey I Love,* translated, 1977; Hall of Fame, 1989.
b. Apr 25, 1952, Union of Soviet Socialist Republics
Source: *BioIn 10, 11, 13*

Treurnicht, Andries Petrus
South African. Politician
Leader of South African Conservative Party; advocate of separate national areas based on race.
b. Feb 19, 1921 in Piketberg, South Africa
Source: *AfSS 78, 79, 80, 81, 82; BioIn 12; DcCPSAf; IntWW 74, 75, 76, 77, 78, 79, 80, 81, 82, 83, 89, 91; IntYB 81, 82; News 92; NewYTBS 82; WhAm 11; WhoWor 89, 91, 93*

Trevelyan, George Macaulay
English. Historian, Author
Known for dramatic histories of England, including *England under Queen Anne,* 1930-34.
b. Feb 16, 1876 in Stratford-upon-Avon, England
d. Jul 21, 1962 in Cambridge, England
Source: *ArizL; BioIn 1, 2, 3, 4, 5, 6, 7, 10, 11, 13, 14, 18, 19; BlueB 76; CamGEL; CasWL; Chambr 3; ChhPo S2; ConAu 89; DcLEL; DcNaB 1961; EvLB; GrBr; LinLib L; LngCTC; McGEWB; ModBrL; NewC; NewCBEL; OxCEng 67; PenC ENG; RAdv 14, 13-3; REn; TwCA, SUP; WebE&AL; WhAm 4; WhE&EA; WhLit; WhoLA; WorAl; WorAlBi*

Trevino, Elizabeth Borton de
American. Children's Author
Won Newbery Medal for *I, Juan de Pareja,* 1966.
b. Sep 2, 1904 in Bakersfield, California
Source: *AuBYP 2; BioIn 14, 19; ConAu 9NR, 17R; DcAmChF 1960; NewbC 1966; ScF&FL 1, 2; SmATA 1, 5AS, 29; ThrBJA; WhoAm 74, 76, 78, 80, 82; WhoAmW 70, 72, 74; WhoSSW 73, 75, 76*

Trevino, Lee Buck
American. Golfer
Turned pro, 1960; first to win US, British, Canadian opens in same yr., 1971; struck by lightning on golf course, 1975, which changed his swing; wrote autobiography *They Call Me Super Mex,* 1983.
b. Dec 1, 1939 in Dallas, Texas
Source: *BiDAmSp OS; ConAu 113; CurBio 71; FacFETw; IntWW 81, 82, 83, 89, 91, 93; WebAB 74, 79; WhoAm 74, 76, 78, 80, 82, 84, 86, 88, 90, 92, 94, 95, 96, 97; WhoGolf; WhoIntG; WhoSSW 73, 75, 76, 78, 80, 82; WhoWor 74*

Trevithick, Richard
English. Inventor
Built first passenger steam train, 1801.
b. Apr 13, 1771 in Illogan, England
d. Apr 22, 1833 in Dartford, England
Source: *AsBiEn; BioIn 1, 2, 3, 4, 5, 6, 7, 9, 12, 14; DcBiPP; DcInv; DcNaB; InSci; NewCol 75; OxCLiW 86; WebBD 83; WhDW; WorAl; WorAlBi; WorInv*

Trevor, Claire
American. Actor
Won Oscar for *Key Largo,* 1948.
b. Mar 8, 1909 in New York, New York
Source: *BiDFilm, 81, 94; BioIn 9, 18; CmMov; ConTFT 9; FilmEn; FilmgC; ForYSC; GangFlm; HalFC 80, 84, 88; IntDcF 2-3; IntMPA 84, 86, 88; InWom SUP; LegTOT; MotPP; MovMk; OxCFilm; ThFT; VarWW 85; WhoAm 74; WhoHol 92, A; WhoThe 77A; WhThe; WomWMM; WorAl; WorAlBi; WorEFlm*

Trevor, William
[William Trevor Cox]
Irish. Author, Dramatist
Works deal with domestic, private relationships in English, Irish counties, towns; wrote *The Children of Dynmouth,* 1976; *Two Lives: Reading Turgenev; My House in Umbria,* 1991.
b. May 24, 1928 in Mitchelstown, Ireland
Source: *Benet 87, 96; BiDIrW; BioIn 10, 13, 14, 17, 18, 19, 20; BlueB 76; CamGLE; ConAu 4NR, 9NR, 9R, 37NR, 55NR, X; ConBrDr; ConDr 73, 77, 82, 88, 93; ConLC 7, 9, 14, 25, 71; ConNov 72, 76, 82, 86, 91, 96; CurBio 84; CyWA 89; DcIrL, 96; DcIrW 1; DcLB 14, 139; DcLEL 1940; EncWB; EncWL 3; FacFETw; IntAu&W 76, 77, 82, 86, 89, 91, 93; IntWW 81, 82, 83, 89, 91, 93; MajTwCW; ModBrL S1, S2; ModIrL; NewC; Novels; OxCEng 85, 95; OxCIri; RfGEnL 91; RfGShF; ScF&FL 92; ShSCr 21; ShSWr; TwCWr; Who 74, 82, 83, 85, 88, 90, 92, 94; WhoWor 74, 76, 84, 87, 89, 91, 93, 95; WorAu 1950; WrDr 76, 80, 82, 84, 86, 88, 90, 92, 94, 96*

Trevor-Roper, Hugh Redwald
[Baron Dacre of Glanton]
English. Historian
Books covering period from Roman Empire to Nazi Germany include *The Crisis of the Seventeenth Century,* 1967; *The Last Days of Hitler,* 1947.
b. Jan 15, 1914 in Glanton, England
Source: *ConAu 101; CurBio 83; IntWW 83; LngCTC; REn; TwCA SUP; Who 85; WhoWor 97; WrDr 86*

Treybig, James G
American. Computer Executive
Pres. and CEO Tandem Computers, 1974—.
b. 1940 in Clarendon, Texas
Source: *BioIn 13, 15; Dun&B 90; News 88-3; WhoFI 89; WhoWest 92*

Tribble, Isreal, Jr.
[Israel Tribble, Jr.]
American. Educator
President and CEO, Florida Education Fund, 1985—.
b. Sep 4, 1940 in Philadelphia, Pennsylvania
Source: *BioIn 20; ConBlB 8; WhoAfA 96; WhoBlA 77, 92, 94*

Tribe, Laurence Henry
American. Lawyer, Educator
Authority on Constitutional law; clients include Sun Myung Moon, Hare Krishnas.
b. Oct 10, 1941 in Shanghai, China
Source: *CurBio 88; DrAS 74P, 78P, 82P; IntWW 89, 91, 93; WhoAm 82, 84, 86, 88, 90, 92, 94, 95, 96; WhoAmL 83,*

85, 90, 92, 94; WhoE 91, 93, 95; WhoEmL 87

Tribe Called Quest, A
American. Rap Group
Have won accolades for their use of complex musical structures and the fresh collage of sonic information they have produced.
Source: *BioIn 8; ConMus 8; McGEWB; NewYTBE 73*

Trible, Paul Seward, Jr.
American. Politician
Rep. senator from VA, 1983-89.
b. Dec 29, 1946 in Baltimore, Maryland
Source: *AlmAP 88; BiDrUSC 89; BioIn 13; CngDr 77, 79, 81, 87; IntWW 83, 89, 91, 93; WhoAm 78, 80, 82, 84, 86, 88, 90, 96, 97; WhoAmP 77, 79, 81, 83, 85, 87, 89, 91, 93, 95; WhoEmL 87; WhoFI 96; WhoGov 77; WhoSSW 78, 80, 82, 84, 86, 88; WhoWor 84, 87, 89*

Tricky
[Adrian Thaws]
English. Producer, Composer, Singer, Songwriter
Invented the genre known as "trip-hop;" member of group Massive Attack, 1990-1995; released solo debut album, *Maxinquaye,* 1995 and later *Tricky Presents Grass Roots,* 1996; also recorded *Nearly God,* 1996.
b. c. 1967 in Bristol, England

Trifa, Valerian
American. Religious Leader
Orthodox archbishop ordered out of U.S. for hiding pro-Nazi activities while a student leader in pre-WW II Romania.
b. Jun 28, 1914 in Campeni, Romania
d. Jan 28, 1987 in Cascais, Portugal
Source: *AnObit 1987; BlueB 76; NewYTBS 87; RelLAm 91; WhoAm 82, 84; WhoRel 85*

Trifonov, Yuri Valentinovich
Russian. Author
Major contributor to 20th-c. Russian literature; tales of Stalinist era include *The House on the Embankment,* 1983.
b. Aug 28, 1925 in Moscow, Union of Soviet Socialist Republics
d. Mar 21, 1981 in Moscow, Union of Soviet Socialist Republics
Source: *AnObit 1981; ClDMEL 80; ConAu 103; EncWL 2; FacFETw; IntWW 80; WhoSocC 78; WorAu 1975*

Trigere, Pauline
American. Fashion Designer
Leading designer of ladies' ready-to wear clothes; known for cutting, designing directly from bolts of cloth; won Coty Award, 1949, 1951, 1959.
b. Nov 4, 1912 in Paris, France
Source: *AmDec 1940; BioIn 2, 5, 10, 11; BioNews 74; CelR, 90; ConDes 84, 90, 97; ConFash; CurBio 60; EncFash; FairDF US; GoodHs; InWom, SUP; LegTOT; LibW; WhoAm 74, 76, 78, 80, 82, 84, 86, 88, 92, 94, 95, 96, 97; WhoAmW 58, 61, 64, 66, 68, 70, 72, 74, 81, 83, 91, 93, 95, 97; WhoFash 88; WorFshn*

Trihey, Harry
[Henry Judah Trihey]
Canadian. Hockey Player
Center, Montreal Shamrocks, 1897-1901; Hall of Fame, 1950.
b. Dec 25, 1877 in Montreal, Quebec, Canada
d. Dec 9, 1942 in Montreal, Quebec, Canada
Source: *WhoHcky 73*

Trillin, Calvin Marshall
American. Author
Books include *Uncivil Liberties,* 1982; *If You Can't Say Something Nice,* 1987; *American Stories,* 1991.
b. Dec 5, 1935 in Kansas City, Missouri
Source: *AuNews 1; ConAu 85; OxCAmL 83; WhoAm 86, 97*

Trilling, Diana (Rubin)
American. Author, Critic
Wife of Lionel; wrote *Mrs. Harris: The Death of the Scarsdale Diet Doctor,* 1981.
b. Jul 21, 1905 in New York, New York
d. Oct 23, 1996 in New York, New York
Source: *AmWomM; AmWomWr; ArtclWW 2; Au&Wr 71; BenetAL 91; BioIn 3, 11, 12, 13; ConAu 5R, 10NR, 46NR, 154; CurBio 79; ForWC 70; IntAu&W 86, 89; InWom SUP; MajTwCW; NewYTBS 27; OxCAmL 83, 95; REnAL; WhoAm 80, 82, 84, 86, 88, 90, 92, 94, 95, 96, 97; WhoWorJ 72, 78; WorAu 1975; WrDr 86, 88, 90, 92, 94, 96*

Trilling, Lionel
American. Author, Critic
Volumes of essays include *The Opposing Self,* 1955; *The Middle of the Journey,* 1947.
b. Jul 4, 1905 in New York, New York
d. Nov 5, 1975 in New York, New York
Source: *AmAu&B; AmNov; AmWr S3; Benet 87, 96; BenetAL 91; BioIn 1, 2, 3, 4, 10, 11, 12, 13, 14, 15, 16, 17, 19, 20; BlueB 76; CamGLE; CamHAL; CasWL; CelR; CnDAL; ConAu 9R, 10NR, 61; ConLC 9, 11, 24; ConLCrt 77, 82; ConNov 72, 76; CyWA 89; DcAmB S9; DcAmC; DcArts; DcLB 28, 63; DcLEL; DrAS 74E; EncWL, 2, 3; FacFETw; GrWrEL N; IntAu&W 76; IntWW 74, 75; JeAmFiW; JeAmHC; LegTOT; LinLib L; LngCTC; MajTwCW; MakMC; ModAL, S2; NewYTBE 71; NewYTBS 75, 76; Novels; ObitT 1971; OxCAmL 65, 83, 95; OxCEng 85, 95; PenC AM; PeoHis; RAdv 1, 14, 13-1; REn; REnAL; RfGAmL 87, 94; RGTwCWr; ThTwC 87; TwCA SUP; TwCWr; WebAB 74, 79; WhAm 6, 7; Who 74; WhoAm 74, 76; WhoE 74, 75; WhoTwCL; WhoWor 74; WhoWorJ 72, 78; WorAl; WorAlBi*

Trintignant, Jean-Louis Xavier
French. Actor
Films include *And God Created Woman,* 1957; *A Man and a Woman,* 1966.
b. Dec 11, 1930 in Polenc, France
Source: *BiDFilm; BioNews 74; CurBio 88; FilmgC; IntMPA 84; IntWW 83; MotPP; MovMk; OxCFilm; VarWW 85; WhoHol A; WhoWor 74; WorAl; WorEFlm*

Tripp, Paul
American. Children's Author, Actor, Producer
Created, produced TV shows for children; wrote script, lyrics for film *The Christmas That Almost Wasn't,* 1966; also starred in film.
b. Feb 20, 1916 in New York, New York
Source: *ASCAP 66, 80; ConAu 21R; ConTFT 2; SmATA 8; WhoAm 84, 86, 88, 90, 92; WhoE 74, 75, 77, 81, 83, 85, 86, 89; WhoEnt 92; WhoHol A*

Trippe, Juan Terry
American. Airline Executive
Founded Pan Am, 1928; had first transatlantic passenger service, 1939.
b. Jun 27, 1899 in Sea Bright, New Jersey
d. Apr 3, 1981 in New York, New York
Source: *BiDAmBL 83; BioIn 1, 2, 3, 4, 7, 8, 12, 13, 15, 16; CurBio 42, 55, 81; FacFETw; InSci; OxCAmH; St&PR 75; WhAm 7; Who 74; WhoE 74; WhoFI 74, 75, 77; WorAl*

Trippi, Charlie
[Charles L Trippi]
"Scintillating Sicilian"; "Triple-Threat Trippi"
American. Football Player
Running back, Chicago Cards, 1947-55; Hall of Fame, 1968.
b. Dec 14, 1922 in Pittston, Pennsylvania
Source: *BioIn 1, 8; LegTOT; WhoFtbl 74*

Tripplehorn, Jean
American. Actor
Appeared in *Basic Instinct.*
b. 1963 in Tulsa, Oklahoma

Tristano, Leonard Joseph
"Lennie"
American. Jazz Musician
Blind avant-garde pianist, active, late 1940s; noted for jazz improvisations.
b. Mar 19, 1919 in Chicago, Illinois
d. Nov 18, 1978 in Jamaica, New York
Source: *Baker 84; BiDAmM; BioIn 5, 8, 11, 12, 15, 16; CmpEPM; DcAmB S10; EncJzS; NewGrDM 80; WhoE 74*

Tritt, Travis
American. Singer, Songwriter, Musician
Country music singer; debut album *Country Club,* 1990 went gold; Grammy, vocal collaboration with Mary Stuart, for "The Whisky Ain't Workin,'" 1992.
b. Feb 9, 1963 in Marietta, Georgia

Source: *BgBkCoM; ConMus 7; LegTOT; WhoAm 94, 95, 96, 97*

Triumph
[Rick Emmet; Mike Levine; Gil Moore]
Canadian. Music Group
Albums include *Best Of*, 1985.
Source: *BioIn 19; EncPR&S 89; HarEnR 86; RkOn 85; WhoRocM 82*

Trnka, Jiri
Czech. Filmmaker, Illustrator
Award-winning puppet film producer: *The Animals and the Brigands*, 1946; *Favorite Tales from Grimm and Andersen*, 1959.
b. Feb 24, 1912 in Pilsen, Bohemia
d. Dec 30, 1969 in Prague, Czechoslovakia
Source: *BioIn 14, 15, 19; ConAu 111; DcFM; EncEurC; FilmEn; HalFC 84; IlsCB 1957; IntDcF 1-2, 2-4; MajAI; OxCFilm; SmATA 32, 43; ThrBJA; WhoGrA 62; WorECar; WorEFlm*

Troell, Jan
Swedish. Director
Films include *The Emigrants*, 1971; *The New Land*, 1973; *Flight of the Eagle*, 1978; often edits, photographs works.
b. Jul 23, 1931 in Limhamn, Sweden
Source: *ConTFT 8; EncEurC; FilmEn; HalFC 80, 84, 88; IntDcF 1-2; IntMPA 75, 76, 77, 78, 79, 80, 81, 82, 84, 86, 88, 92, 94, 96; MiSFD 9; MovMk; WorEFlm; WorFDir 2*

Troggs, The
[Ronnie Bond; Chris Britton; Tony Murray; Reg Presley]
British. Music Group
Cabaret, club performers since 1966; albums include *Love is All Around*, 1967.
Source: *BioIn 12; ConMuA 80A; EncRk 88; EncRkSt; HarEnR 86; RkOn 78, 84; RolSEnR 83; WhoRock 81; WhoRocM 82*

Trohan, Walter
American. Journalist
With *Chicago Tribune*, 1929-71, as Washington correspondent, executive director; wrote *Political Animals*, 1975.
b. Jul 4, 1903 in Mount Carmel, Pennsylvania
Source: *BioIn 1, 10; ConAu 81; EncTwCJ; WhoAm 74, 76, 78, 80, 82, 84, 86, 88, 90, 92, 94, 95; WhoWor 80, 82, 84, 87, 89, 91, 93, 95*

Trollope, Anthony
English. Author
Wrote 50 novels including *Barsetshire Chronicles*, 1850s-60s.
b. Apr 24, 1815 in London, England
d. Dec 6, 1882 in London, England
Source: *Alli, SUP; AtlBL; BbD; Benet 87, 96; BenetAL 91; BiD&SB; BioIn 1, 2, 3, 4, 5, 6, 7, 8, 9, 10, 11, 12, 13, 14, 15, 16, 17, 18, 19; BlmGEL; BritAS; BritAu 19; BritWr 5; CamGEL; CamGLE; CasWL; CelCen; Chambr 3; ChhPo S2; CnDBLB 4; CrtT 3, 4; CyWA 58; DcArts; DcBiA; DcBiPP; DcEnA; DcEnL; DcEuL; DcIrL 96; DcLB 21, 57, 159; DcLEL; DcNaB; Dis&D; EncSF, 93; EvLB; GrWrEL N; HsB&A; LegTOT; LinLib L, S; LngCEL; MagSWL; McGEWB; MouLC 4; NewC; NewCBEL; NinCLC 6, 33; Novels; OxCAusL; OxCEng 67, 85, 95; PenC ENG; RAdv 1, 14, 13-1; REn; REnAL; RfGEnL 91; RfGShF; ScF&FL 1; ScFEYrs; ScFSB; SmATA 22; StaCVF; VicBrit; WebE&AL; WhDW; WorAl; WorAlBi; WorLitC; WrPh*

Trollope, Frances
English. Author
Wrote controversial, much resented *Domestic Manners of the Americans*, 1832; mother of Anthony.
b. Mar 10, 1780 in Bristol, England
d. Oct 6, 1863 in Florence, Italy
Source: *Alli; ArtclWW 2; BbD; Benet 87, 96; BenetAL 91; BiD&SB; BioIn 1, 2, 3, 4, 5, 6, 8, 9, 10, 11, 12, 13; BlmGEL; BritAu 19; CamGEL; CamGLE; CasWL; Chambr 3; ContDcW 89; DcAmImH; DcEnA; DcEnL; DcLEL; DcNaB; EvLB; FemiCLE; LegTOT; NewC; NewCBEL; NinCLC 30; OhA&B; OxCAmH; OxCAmL 65, 83, 95; OxCEng 67, 85, 95; PenC ENG; REn; REnAL*

Tromp, Solco Walle
Dutch. Geologist, Author
Wrote *Neo-Materialism; Physical Physics.*
b. Mar 9, 1909 in Batavia, Dutch East Indies
d. Mar 17, 1983, Netherlands
Source: *BiDPara; ConAu 116; EncO&P 2*

Trotman, Alexander J.
American. Auto Executive
Chairman and CEO of Ford Motor Co., 1993—.
b. Jul 22, 1933 in Middlesex, England
Source: *AutoN 79; Dun&B 86, 88, 90; WhoAm 90, 96, 97; WhoFI 87, 94, 96; WhoMW 96; WhoWor 96, 97*

Trotsky, Leon
[Lev Davidovitch Bronstein]
Russian. Political Leader, Author
Organized 1917 revolution; banished, 1929, after power struggle with Stalin.
b. Nov 8, 1879 in Elisavetgrad, Russia
d. Aug 21, 1940 in Mexico City, Mexico
Source: *Benet 87, 96; BiDMarx; BiDSovU; BioIn 1, 2, 3, 4, 5, 6, 7, 8, 9, 10, 11, 12, 13, 14, 15, 16, 17, 18, 19, 20, 21; CasWL; ColdWar 1, 2; ConAu 118; CurBio 40; DcAmC; DcAmSR; DcRusL; DcTwHis; EncRev; Film 1; HarEnMi; HisEWW; HisWorL; JeHun; LegTOT; LinLib L, S; LngCTC; MakMC; McGEWB; OxCPhil; RadHan; RAdv 14, 13-3; REn; ThTwC 87; TwCLC 22; WhoHol B; WhScrn 77, 83; WorAl; WorAlBi*

Trotta, Margarethe Von
German. Filmmaker
Work focuses on concerns and relationships of women; films include *Rosa Luxemburg*, 1986; *Love and Fear*, 1988.
b. Feb 21, 1942 in Berlin, Germany
Source: *BioIn 14, 16; ConAu 126; ContDcW 89; CurBio 88; EncEurC; HalFC 84; IntDcF 2-2; ReelWom; WorFDir 2*

Trotta, Maurice S
American. Educator, Author
Labor arbitrator, wrote books on industrial labor relations.
b. Aug 15, 1907 in New York, New York
d. Jul 11, 1976 in Newton, New Jersey
Source: *AmMWSc 73S; ConAu 111; WhoLab 76*

Trotter, John Scott
American. Musician, Songwriter
Pianist, arranger for Bing Crosby radio shows, 1930s-40s; won Oscar for scoring *Pennies From Heaven*, 1961.
b. Jun 14, 1908 in Charlotte, North Carolina
d. Oct 29, 1975 in Los Angeles, California
Source: *ASCAP 66, 80; BioIn 4, 10; CmpEPM; NewYTBS 75; ObitOF 79; RadStar; WhoHol C; WhScrn 77, 83*

Trotter, Monroe
[William Monroe Trotter]
American. Civil Rights Activist, Editor
Co-founder and editor, *The Guardian*, a Boston newspaper, 1901-34.
b. Apr 7, 1872 in Chillicothe, Ohio
d. Apr 7, 1934 in Boston, Massachusetts
Source: *AfrAmAl 6; AmDec 1900; BiDAmJo; BioIn 1, 5, 8, 9, 16, 21; BlkWrNE; ConBlB 9; DcAmNB; DcTwCCu 5; EncAB-H 1974, 1996; EncAJ; EncWB; InB&W 80, 85; NegAl 76, 83, 89; SelBAAf; SelBAAu; WhoColR*

Trottier, Bryan John
"Trots"
American. Hockey Player
Center, NY Islanders, 1975-90; Pittsburgh, 1990-93; won Art Ross, Hart trophies, 1979; 15th player in NHL history to score 500 goals (1990).
b. Jul 17, 1956 in Val Marie, Saskatchewan, Canada
Source: *CurBio 85; HocEn; HocReg 87; NewYTBS 75, 78; WhoAm 80, 82, 84, 86, 88, 90, 92, 94, 95, 96, 97; WhoE 95*

Troup, Bobby
[Robert William Troup]
American. Actor, Songwriter, Singer
Former bandleader who played Dr. Joe Early in TV series "Emergency," 1972-77; wrote "Daddy," 1941; "Route 66," 1946.
b. Oct 18, 1918 in Harrisburg, Pennsylvania

Source: *AllMusG; ASCAP 66, 80; BioIn 10; CmpEPM; ForYSC; PenEncP; WhoEnt 92; WhoHol 92, A*

Trout, Dizzy
[Paul Howard Trout]
American. Baseball Player
Pitcher, 1939-52, 1957, mostly with Detroit; led AL in wins, 1943.
b. Jun 29, 1915 in Sandcut, Indiana
d. Feb 28, 1972 in Chicago, Illinois
Source: *Ballpl 90; BiDAmSp Sup; BioIn 2, 3, 9; NewYTBE 72; ObitOF 79*

Trout, Robert
"''Iron Man of Radio''"
American. Broadcast Journalist
Coined term "fireside chats" for FDR's radio broadcasts, which he announced; known for ad-libbing, stamina.
b. Oct 15, 1908 in Wake County, North Carolina
Source: *BiDAmJo; BioIn 1, 7; CelR; CurBio 65; EncAJ; EncTwCJ; LesBEnT; NewYTET; RadStar; SaTiSS; WhoAm 74, 76*

Trowbridge, John Townsend
American. Journalist, Author
Best known for juvenile antislavery novels, *Cudjo's Cave,* 1864; *Jack Hazard Series,* 1871-74; narrative poem, "Darius Green and His Flying Machine," 1903.
b. Sep 18, 1827 in Ogdensburg, New York
d. Feb 12, 1916 in Arlington, Massachusetts
Source: *Alli, SUP; AmAu; AmAu&B; AmBi; ApCAB; BbD; BenetAL 91; BibAL 8; BiD&SB; BioIn 1, 2, 5; CarSB; ChhPo, S1; CyAL 2; CyWA 58; DcAmAu; DcAmB; DcBiA; DcEnL; DcLEL; DcNAA; Drake; HarEnUS; LinLib L, S; NatCAB 3; OxCAmL 65; REnAL; TwCBDA; WhAm 1*

Trower, Robin
[Procol Harum]
English. Musician
Albums include *Beyond the Mist,* 1985.
b. Mar 9, 1945 in London, England
Source: *ConMuA 80A; EncPR&S 74, 89; EncRk 88; HarEnR 86; IlEncRk; LegTOT; PenEncP; RolSEnR 83; WhoRock 81; WhoRocM 82*

Troy, Hannah
American. Fashion Designer
Creator of the petite size for women; introduced Italian styles to the US.
b. Feb 10, 1905 in New York, New York
d. Jun 22, 1993 in Miami Beach, Florida
Source: *WhoAmW 58, 61, 64, 66*

Troyanos, Tatiana
American. Opera Singer
Mezzo-soprano; starred in *Ariodante,* opening of Kennedy Center, 1971.
b. Sep 12, 1938 in New York, New York
d. Aug 21, 1993 in New York, New York
Source: *AnObit 1993; Baker 84, 92; BioIn 12, 13, 19, 20; CelR 90; CmOp; CurBio 79, 93N; IntDcOp; IntWWM 90; InWom SUP; LegTOT; MetOEnc; NewAmDM; NewGrDA 86; NewGrDM 80; NewGrDO; NewYTBS 76, 93; OxDcOp; PenDiMP; WhAm 11; WhoAm 78, 80, 82, 84, 86, 88, 92, 94; WhoAmM 83; WhoAmW 81, 83, 85; WhoMus 72; WhoOp 76*

Troyat, Henri
[Lev Tarassoff]
French. Author
Well-known French author, wrote a series of biographical novels on Russian literary figures.
b. Nov 1, 1911 in Moscow, Russia
Source: *Benet 87, 96; BiDSovU; BioIn 17, 18; CasWL; ClDMEL 80; ConAu 2NR, 33NR, 45; ConLC 23; CurBio 92; DcTwCCu 2; EncWL; GuFrLit 1; IntAu&W 76, 77, 82, 89; IntWW 74, 75, 76, 77, 78, 79, 80, 81, 82, 83, 89, 91, 93; LinLib L; MajTwCW; PenC EUR; REn; TwCWr; Who 74, 82, 83, 85, 88, 90, 92, 94; WhoAm 74, 76, 78, 80, 82; WhoFr 79; WhoWor 74, 76, 78, 87; WorAu 1950*

Troyon, Constant
French. Artist
Member, Barbizon School; noted for landscapes and animal scenes, particularly cows.
b. Aug 18, 1810 in Sevres, France
d. Feb 21, 1865 in Paris, France
Source: *ArtsNiC; BioIn 1, 4, 5, 8; ClaDrA; McGDA; McGEWD 72; NewCol 75; OxDcArt*

Trudeau, Arthur G(ilbert)
American. Military Leader
Chief Army Research & Development Command, 1958-62; won Silver Star for gallantry at Porkchop Hill.
b. Jul 5, 1902 in Middlebury, Vermont
d. Jun 5, 1991 in Chevy Chase, Maryland
Source: *BiDWWGF; BioIn 3, 4, 5, 11, 17; CurBio 91N; EncAI&E; InSci; NewYTBS 91; PolProf K; WhAm 10; WhoAm 74, 76*

Trudeau, Edward Livingston
American. Physician
First to establish sanitarium, laboratories for pulmonary tuberculosis study in US, 1884, at Saranac Lake, NY.
b. Oct 5, 1848 in New York, New York
d. Nov 15, 1915
Source: *AmAu&B; AmBi; BiInAmS; BioIn 1, 2, 3, 4, 5, 8, 9; DcAmB; DcAmMeB, 84; DcNAA; NatCAB 13; OxCMed 86; WhAm 1*

Trudeau, Garry
[Garretson Beckman Trudeau]
American. Cartoonist
Created comic strip "Doonesbury"; won Pulitzer, 1975.
b. 1948 in New York, New York
Source: *AmDec 1970; Au&Arts 10; AuNews 2; CelR 90; ConAu 81; ConLC 12; ConTFT 7; CurBio 75; EncACom; EncAJ; EncTwCJ; FacFETw; LegTOT; News 91, 91-2; WhoAm 84, 86, 95, 96, 97; WhoAmA 84; WhoE 95; WorAlBi; WorECom; WrDr 86, 88, 90, 92*

Trudeau, Margaret Joan Sinclair
Canadian. Author, Socialite
Ex-wife of Pierre Trudeau; wrote *Beyond Reason,* 1979.
b. Sep 10, 1948 in Vancouver, British Columbia, Canada
Source: *BioNews 74; BkPepl; ConAu 93; InWom SUP*

Trudeau, Pierre Elliott
Canadian. Political Leader
Colorful Liberal prime minister, 1969-79, 1980-84.
b. Oct 18, 1919 in Montreal, Quebec, Canada
Source: *BioIn 8, 9, 10, 11, 12, 13; BlueB 76; CanWW 31, 70, 79, 80, 81, 83, 89; ConAu 3NR, 45; CurBio 68; DcTwHis; EncWB; FacFETw; IntWW 74, 75, 76, 77, 78, 79, 80, 81, 82, 83, 89, 91, 93; IntYB 78, 79, 80, 81, 82; LinLib L, S; NewYTBS 80, 84; OxCCan SUP; Who 74, 82, 83, 85, 88, 90, 92, 94; WhoAm 74, 76, 78, 80, 82, 84, 86, 88, 90, 92, 94, 95, 96, 97; WhoAmL 94; WhoCan 73, 75, 77, 80, 82; WhoE 74, 75, 77, 79, 81, 83, 85, 86, 89, 91, 93; WhoWor 74, 76, 78, 80, 82, 84, 87, 89, 91, 93, 95, 96, 97; WorAl; WorAlBi*

Trudell, John
American. Actor, Musician, Political Activist
Joined group that occupied Alcatraz Island, 1969; took part in the Trail of Broken Treaties, 1972.
b. 1947 in Niobrara, Nebraska
Source: *BioIn 21; EncNAB; NotNaAm*

Trueblood, D(avid) Elton
American. Theologian
Philosophy professor; wrote *The Essence of Spiritual Religion,* 1936.
b. Dec 12, 1900
d. Dec 20, 1994 in Lansdale, Pennsylvania
Source: *AmAu&B; BioIn 2, 3, 6, 7, 10, 12; ConAu 41R; CurBio 95N; DrAS 74P, 78P, 82P; IndAu 1967; WhE&EA; WhoAm 74, 76, 78, 82, 84, 86, 88, 90, 92, 94; WhoRel 77*

Truex, Ernest
American. Actor
Films include *It's a Wonderful World,* 1939; *Fluffy,* 1965.
b. Sep 19, 1890? in Kansas City, Missouri
d. Jun 27, 1973 in Fallbrook, California
Source: *BiE&WWA; BioIn 9, 10; CurBio 41, 73, 73N; EncAFC; EncMT; Film 1, 2; FilmEn; FilmgC; HalFC 80, 84, 88; MotPP; MovMk; NatCAB 62; ObitOF*

79; TwYS; Vers A; WhoHol B; WhScrn 77; WhThe; WorAl

Truffaut, Francois
French. Director
New Wave director who was admired for depictions of children, obsessed men, and women driven by strong passions; won Oscar, 1973.
b. Feb 6, 1932 in Paris, France
d. Oct 21, 1984 in Neuilly-sur-Seine, France
Source: *AnObit 1984; Benet 87, 96; BiDFilm, 81, 94; BioIn 6, 7, 8, 9, 10, 11, 12, 13, 14, 15, 16, 17, 18, 20; CelR; ConAu 34NR, 81, 113; ConLC 20; ConTFT 2; CurBio 69, 85N; DcArts; DcFM; DcTwCCu 2; EncEurC; FacFETw; FilmEn; FilmgC; HalFC 80, 84, 88; IntDcF 1-2, 2-2; IntMPA 75, 76, 77, 78, 79, 80, 81, 82, 84; IntWW 74, 75, 76, 77, 78, 79, 80, 81, 82, 83; ItaFilm; LegTOT; MakMC; McGEWB; MiSFD 9N; MovMk; NewYTBS 84; OxCFilm; RAdv 14, 13-3; WhAm 8, 11; Who 74, 82, 83; WhoAm 74, 76, 78, 80, 82, 84; WhoFr 79; WhoHol A; WhoHrs 80; WhoWor 74, 76, 78, 80, 82, 84, 95, 96; WorAl; WorAlBi; WorEFlm; WorFDir 2*

Truitt, Anne
American. Artist, Sculptor
Produced paintings and sculptures over the last five decades; helped create American abstract art.
b. Mar 16, 1921 in Baltimore, Maryland
Source: *BiDWomA; BioIn 13, 15, 19, 20, 21; BriEAA; ConAmWS; ConArt 77, 83, 89, 96; DcCAA 77, 88, 94; InWom SUP; News 93-1; NorAmWA; WhoAm 90; WhoAmA 73, 76, 78, 80, 82, 84, 86, 89, 91; WrDr 88, 90, 92, 94, 96*

Trujillo (Molina), Rafael Leonidas
Dominican. Politician
Dictator of Dominican Republic, 1931-61; assassinated.
b. Oct 24, 1891 in San Cristobal, Dominican Republic
d. May 30, 1961 in Ciudad Trujillo, Dominican Republic
Source: *BiDLAmC; BioIn 1, 2, 3, 4, 5, 6, 7, 8, 9, 10, 12, 16, 17, 18; ColdWar 1, 2; CurBio 41, 61; DcHiB; DicTyr; EncLatA; McGEWB; ObitT 1961; WhAm 4; WorAl*

Truly, Richard H
American. Astronaut, Government Official
Commander, Columbia Flight 2, NASA, 1981; commander, Columbia Flight 2, Challen ger Flight 3, 1983; dir, Space Shuttle program, 1986-89; administrator, NSASA, 1989-92.
b. Nov 12, 1937 in Fayette, Mississippi
Source: *WhoSSW 73; WhoWor 74; WorDWW*

Truman, Bess
[Mrs. Harry S Truman; Elizabeth Virginia Wallace]
"The Boss"
American. First Lady
Publicity shy, gracious, unassuming White House hostess, married 1919.
b. Feb 13, 1885 in Independence, Missouri
d. Oct 18, 1982 in Kansas City, Missouri
Source: *AnObit 1982; BioIn 1, 2, 3, 5, 6, 7, 8, 9, 10, 11, 12, 13; CurBio 47, 83; LegTOT; NewYTBE 72; NewYTBS 82; WhoAm 74, 76, 78, 80; WhoAmW 72, 74*

Truman, Harry S
"Give 'em Hell, Harry"
American. US President
Dem., 33rd pres., 1945-53; made decision to drop atomic bomb on Japan, 1945.
b. May 8, 1884 in Lamar, Missouri
d. Dec 26, 1972 in Kansas City, Missouri
Source: *Au&Wr 71; BiDrAC; BiDrUSE 71; ColdWar 2; ConAu 106; CurBio 42, 45, 73; DcAmSR; EncAB-H 1974; HisEWW; ObitT 1971; OxCAmH; OxCAmL 65; REn; WhAm 5; WhDW; WhoGov 72; WorAl*

Truman, Margaret
[Mrs. Clifton Daniel, Jr; Mary Margaret Truman]
American. Author
Daughter of Harry Truman; wrote *Letters from Father*, 1981.
b. Feb 17, 1924 in Independence, Missouri
Source: *BestSel 90-1; BiDAmM; BioIn 1, 2, 3, 4, 5, 6, 7, 8, 9, 10, 12, 15, 17, 21; BioNews 74; CelR, 90; ConAu 29NR, 105; CurBio 50, 87; GrWomMW; InWom, SUP; MajTwCW; NewYTBS 80; WhoAm 74, 76, 78, 80, 82, 84, 86, 88, 90, 92, 94, 95, 96, 97; WhoAmW 91, 93, 95, 97; WrDr 86, 88, 90, 92, 94, 96*

Trumbauer, Frank(ie)
American. Songwriter, Bandleader
C-melody saxist; with Paul Whiteman, 1927-36; recorded classics with Beiderbecke.
b. May 30, 1901 in Carbondale, Illinois
d. Jun 11, 1956 in Kansas City, Missouri
Source: *ASCAP 66, 80; BgBands 74; BiDAmM; BiDJaz; BioIn 4, 7, 20; CmpEPM; NewAmDM; NewGrDA 86; NewGrDJ 88, 94; OxCPMus; PenEncP; WhAm 4; WhoJazz 72*

Trumbauer, Horace
American. Architect
Built French Renaissance-style mansions, mostly in NYC, Philadelphia
b. Dec 28, 1869 in Philadelphia, Pennsylvania
d. Sep 18, 1938 in Philadelphia, Pennsylvania
Source: *BiDAmAr; BioIn 4; BriEAA; DcAmB S2; MacEA; NatCAB 28; WhAm 4, HSA*

Trumbo, Dalton
[The Hollywood Ten]
American. Screenwriter, Author
Wrote novel *Johnny Got His Gun*, 1939; screenplays *Thirty Seconds Over Tokyo*, 1945; *Exodus*, 1960.
b. Dec 9, 1905 in Montrose, Colorado
d. Sep 10, 1976 in Los Angeles, California
Source: *AmAu&B; AuSpks; Benet 87, 96; BenetAL 91; BioIn 2, 4, 5, 9, 11, 14, 16, 17, 19; CmCal; ConAu 10NR, 21R, 69; ConDr 73, 77A; ConLC 19; ConNov 72, 76; CurBio 41, 76N; DcFM; DcLB 26; EncMcCE; FilmEn; FilmgC; HalFC 80, 84, 88; IntAu&W 76, 77; IntDcF 1-4, 2-4; IntMPA 75, 76; ItaFilm; LegTOT; LiExTwC; Novels; ObitOF 79; OxCAmL 95; OxCFilm; PolProf T; REnAL; RGTwCWr; ScF&FL 1, 2; TwCA, SUP; TwCYAW; WhAm 7; WhE&EA; WhoAm 74, 76, 78; WhoWor 76; WorEFlm; WrDr 76*

Trumbull, John
American. Poet, Judge
Most popular of Hartford Wits; wrote mock epic *M'Fingal*, 1782, satirizing stupidity of British.
b. Apr 24, 1750 in Watertown, Connecticut
d. May 11, 1831 in Detroit, Michigan
Source: *Alli; AmAu; AmAu&B; AmBi; AmWrBE; ApCAB; Benet 87, 96; BenetAL 91; BiAUS; BibAL 8; BiD&SB; BioIn 2, 3, 9, 10, 12, 14, 15; CamGEL; CamGLE; CamHAL; CasWL; ChhPo, S1; CnDAL; CyAL 1; DcAmAu; DcAmB; DcEnL; DcLB 31; DcLEL; DcNAA; Drake; EncAHmr; EncCRAm; EvLB; GrWrEL P; HarEnUS; NatCAB 7; NinCLC 30; OxCAmL 65, 83, 95; PenC AM; REn; REnAL; RfGAmL 87, 94; TwCBDA; WebAB 74, 79; WebE&AL; WhAm HS; WhAmRev*

Trumbull, John
American. Artist
Did historical scenes, portraits of eminent Americans.
b. Jun 6, 1756 in Lebanon, Connecticut
d. Nov 10, 1843 in New York, New York
Source: *Alli; AmAu&B; AmBi; AmRev; AntBDN J; ApCAB; BiAUS; BioIn 1, 2, 3, 4, 5, 6, 7, 8, 9, 10, 11, 13, 14, 15; BriEAA; DcAmArt; DcAmB; DcArts; DcBiPP; DcBrECP; DcNAA; Drake; EncAB-H 1974, 1996; EncAR; EncCRAm; HarEnUS; IntDcAA 90; LegTOT; LinLib S; McGDA; McGEWB; MorMA; NatCAB 3; NewYHSD; OxCAmH; OxCAmL 65; OxDcArt; TwCBDA; WebAB 74, 79; WhAm HS; WhAmRev; WorAl; WorAlBi*

Trumbull, Jonathan
"Brother Jonathan"
American. Politician, Judge
Governor of CT, 1769-84; friend, counselor to George Washington.
b. Oct 12, 1710 in Lebanon, Connecticut
d. Aug 17, 1785 in Lebanon, Connecticut

Source: *Alli; AmBi; AmRev; ApCAB; BiAUS; BiDAmBL 83; BiDrACR; BioIn 1, 3, 4, 6, 8, 10; CyAL 1; DcAmB; DcAmSR; Drake; EncAR; EncCRAm; HarEnUS; NatCAB 10; OxCAmH; OxCAmL 65, 83, 95; REn; TwCBDA; WebAB 74, 79; WhAm HS; WhDW; WorAl; WorAlBi*

Trumka, Richard Louis
American. Labor Union Official, Lawyer
National pres., UMW, 1981-82; sec. treasurer, AFL-CIO, 1995—.
b. Jul 24, 1949 in Waynesburg, Pennsylvania
Source: *CurBio 86; IntWW 89, 91, 93; NewYTBS 82; WhoAm 84, 86, 88, 92, 95, 96, 97; WhoE 89; WhoFI 87, 89, 92, 96*

Trump, Donald John
American. Business Executive
Pres., billion-dollar Trump Organization, one of Manhattan's most grandiose builders.
b. 1946 in New York, New York
Source: *ConAmBL; CurBio 84; IntWW 89, 91, 93; NewYTBS 84; WhoAm 84, 86, 88, 90, 92, 94, 95, 96, 97; WhoE 91, 93, 95, 97; WhoFI 87, 89, 92, 94, 96; WhoSSW 88, 91*

Trump, Ivana Winkelmayr
American. Businesswoman
Former wife of NY billionaire Donald Trump; wrote tell-all *For Love Alone,* 1992.
b. Feb 20, 1949 in Zlin, Czech Republic
Source: *BioIn 14, 15, 16; CelR 90*

Truth, Sojourner
[Isabella VanWagener]
American. Abolitionist, Feminist
Freed slave who advocated emancipation, women's rights; noted orator.
b. 1797 in Ulster County, New York
d. Nov 26, 1883 in Battle Creek, Michigan
Source: *AfrAmAl 6; AfrAmOr; AmBi; AmOrN; AmRef; AmSocL; AmWomWr 92; BenetAL 91; BioAmW; BioIn 1, 3, 4, 5, 6, 7, 8, 9, 10, 11, 13; BlksScM; BlmGWL; ContDcW 89; DcAmNB; DcAmReB 1, 2; EncAB-H 1974, 1996; EncARH; EncWHA; FemiCLE; FemiWr; GoodHs; GrLiveH; HerW, 84; HisWorL; InB&W 80, 85; IntDcWB; InWom, SUP; LegTOT; LibW; McGEWB; NegAl 76, 83, 89; NewCol 75; NotAW; NotBlAW 1; OxCAmL 95; RadHan; RComAH; WebAB 74, 79; WhAmP; WomPubS 1800; WorAl; WorAlBi*

Tryon, Thomas
American. Author, Actor
Writes supernatural fiction: *The Other,* 1971; *Harvest Home,* 1973 ; *By the Rivers of Babylon,* 1992.
b. Jan 14, 1926 in Hartford, Connecticut
d. Sep 4, 1991 in Los Angeles, California
Source: *AnObit 1991; AuNews 1; AuSpks; BioIn 10, 11; BioNews 75; BkPepl; CelR; ConAu 29R, 32NR, 135; ConLC 3, 11; ConPopW; ConTFT 5, 10; Conv 1; CurBio 77, 91N; IntAu&W 76, 77, 91, 93; IntMPA 82; LegTOT; MajTwCW; NewYTBS 91; Novels; PenEncH; ScF&FL 1, 2, 92; WhAm 10; WhoAm 74, 76, 78, 80, 82, 84, 86, 88, 90; WorAl; WrDr 76, 80, 82, 84, 86, 88*

Ts'ai, Lun
Chinese. Inventor
Made paper from bamboo pulp, circa 105.
b. 50? in Guiyang, China
d. 118?
Source: *AsBiEn; WebBD 83*

Tsang, Daniel C.
American. Librarian
Co-founded Alliance Working for Asian Rights and Empowerment (AWARE), 1993; research topics include the lesbian/gay Asian press.
b. Oct 27, 1949, Hong Kong
Source: *GayLesB*

Tsankov, Aleksandur
Bulgarian. Political Leader
Became prime minister of Bulgaria after a 1923 military coup; served until 1926, a period of civil unrest.
b. 1879 in Oriakhova, Bulgaria
d. Jul 17, 1959 in Belgrano, Argentina
Source: *BiDExR; ObitOF 79*

Tsatsos, Constantinos
Greek. Political Leader
First elected pres. of the republic of Greece, 1975-80.
b. Jul 1, 1899 in Athens, Greece
d. Oct 8, 1987 in Athens, Greece
Source: *IntWW 83; WhoWor 87*

Tschirky, Oscar
"Oscar of the Waldorf"
American. Hotel Executive
Maitre d'hotel, Waldorf-Astoria, NYC, 1931-43; executive, 1943-50; originated Waldorf salad.
b. Sep 28, 1866 in Locle, Switzerland
d. Nov 6, 1950 in New Paltz, New York
Source: *BioIn 1, 2; CurBio 47, 50; LegTOT; WhAm 3; WorAl; WorAlBi*

Tsedenbal, Yumzahgin
Mongolian. Politician
Chm. of Presidium of People's Great Hural (head of state), 1974-84.
b. Sep 17, 1916
d. Apr 20, in Moscow, Russia
Source: *BioIn 9; IntWW 83; WhoWor 84*

Tsegaye, Gabre-Medhin
Ethiopian. Poet, Dramatist
Plays deal with Ethiopian life and history; author of more than 20 plays; most famous English verse play, *Oda Oak Oracle,* 1965.
b. Aug 17, 1935 in Ambo, Ethiopia
Source: *AfrA; BioIn 10; CamGWoT; ConAu X; ConDr 82, 88*

Tshabalala, Headman
South African. Singer
Member of Ladysmith Black Mambazo.
d. Dec 10, 1991 in Pinetown, South Africa
Source: *BioIn 17; NewYTBS 91*

Tshombe, Moise
Congolese. Political Leader
Prominent in secession of Katanga Province from Congo, 1960; president of Katanga, 1960-63; premier of Congo, 1963-65.
b. Nov 10, 1919 in Musumba, Congo
d. Jun 29, 1969 in Algiers, Algeria
Source: *BioIn 5, 6, 18, 21; ColdWar 1; CurBio 61, 69; DcPol; FacFETw; LinLib S; McGEWB; NewCol 75; ObitOF 79; ObitT 1961; WhDW; WorAl*

Tsiolkovsky, Konstantin Eduardovich
Russian. Scientist
Formulated mathematical fundamentals of modern astronautics; advocated space travel via rocket propulsion, 1883; presented plans for multistage rocket, 1929.
b. Sep 17, 1857 in Izhevskoye, Union of Soviet Socialist Republics
d. Sep 19, 1935 in Kaluga, Union of Soviet Socialist Republics
Source: *AsBiEn; BiESc; BioIn 10; ConAu 119; DcScB; DeafPAS; EncSF 93; LarDcSc; McGEWB; NewCol 75; ScFEYrs; TwCSFW 86A; WorAl*

Tsiranana, Philibert
African. Political Leader
Pres. of Madagascar, 1959-72; first of the republic; declared independence in 1960.
b. Oct 18, 1912 in Anahidrano, Madagascar
d. Apr 16, 1978 in Tananarive, Madagascar
Source: *BioIn 21; IntWW 74, 75, 76, 77; NewCol 75; NewYTBS 78; ObitOF 79; WhoGov 72; WhoWor 74*

Tsongas, Paul E(fthemios)
American. Politician, Lawyer
Dem. senator from MA, 1979-85; presidential candidate, 1992.
b. Feb 14, 1941 in Lowell, Massachusetts
d. Jan 18, 1997 in Boston, Massachusetts
Source: *AlmAP 78, 80, 82, 84; BiDrUSC 89; BioIn 10, 11, 12, 13; CngDr 79; ConAu 108; CurBio 81; IntWW 81, 82, 83, 89, 91, 93; NewYTBS 85, 92; PolsAm 84; WhoAm 78, 80, 82, 84, 86, 88, 90, 92, 94, 95, 96, 97; WhoAmP 75, 77, 79, 81, 83, 85, 87, 89, 91, 93, 95; WhoE 79, 81, 83, 85; WhoWor 80, 82*

Tsui, Kitty
American. Writer
Books include *The Words of a Woman Who Breathes Fire,* 1983; *Breathless,* 1995.
b. 1952, Hong Kong
Source: *BioIn 19; DrAPF 80; GayLesB*

Tsvetayeva, Marina Ivanovna
Russian. Poet
Modernist poet influenced by Pasternak, folk music; suicide victim.
b. Sep 26, 1892? in Moscow, Russia
d. Aug 31, 1941 in Yelabuga, Union of Soviet Socialist Republics
Source: *BioIn 14; CasWL; ClDMEL 47, 80; DcRusL; DcRusLS; EvEuW; IntDcWB; ModSL 1; PenBWP; PenC EUR; WorAu 1950*

Tu, Fu
Chinese. Poet
Verse shows hatred of war, love of nature.
b. 712 in Gongxian, China
d. 777 in Tanzhou, China
Source: *Benet 87; BioIn 2, 3, 4, 8, 9, 14; CasWL; DcOrL 1; GrFLW; IndCTCL; LinLib L; McGEWB; PenC CL; REn; WhDW; WorAl*

Tubb, Ernest
"The Texas Trubadour"
American. Singer, Musician, Songwriter
Country music legend who wrote over 150 songs including hit "Walking the Floor over You," 1941.
b. Feb 9, 1914 in Crisp, Texas
d. Sep 6, 1984 in Nashville, Tennessee
Source: *AnObit 1984; Baker 84; BgBkCoM; BioIn 14, 15; CmpEPM; ConAu 114; ConMus 4; CounME 74, 74A; CurBio 83, 84N; EncFCWM 69, 83; HarEnCM 87; IlEncCM; LegTOT; NewAmDM; NewGrDA 86; NewGrDM 80; NewYTBS 84; OxCPMus; PenEncP; RadStar; WhoAm 80*

Tubes, The
[Rich Anderson; Michael Cotten; Prairie Prince; Bill Spooner; Roger Steen; Re Styles; Fee Waybill; Vince Welnick]
American. Music Group
Begun late 1960s, combining rock, theater, satire; appeared in film *Xanadu,* 1980.
Source: *ConMuA 80A; EncRk 88; EncRkSt; HarEnR 86; IlEncRk; RkOn 85; RolSEnR 83; WhDW; WhoRock 81; WhoRocM 82; WorAl*

Tubman, Harriet Ross
"Moses of Her People"
American. Abolitionist
Leader of Underground Railroad; helped over 300 slaves escape.
b. 1826 in Dorchester, Maryland
d. Mar 10, 1913 in Auburn, New York
Source: *AmBi; ApCAB; BioAmW; DcAmB; EncAB-H 1974; GoodHs; HerW; InB&W 80; InWom; NewCol 75; NotAW; NotBlAW 1; REnAL; WebAB 74; WhAm HSA; WhAmP; WorAl*

Tubman, William Vacanarat Shadrach
Liberian. Political Leader
President of Liberia, 1944-71.
b. Nov 29, 1895 in Harper, Liberia
d. Jul 23, 1971 in London, England
Source: *BioIn 1, 3, 4, 5, 6, 7, 8, 9, 10, 11, 18, 20, 21; CurBio 55, 71; DcAfHiB 86; DcTwHis; EncWM; InB&W 80, 85; McGEWB; NewCol 75; WhAm 5; WhoGov 72*

Tuchman, Barbara Wertheim
American. Author, Historian
Wrote about people at war or at brink of war; won Pulitzers for *The Guns of August,* 1962, *Stillwell and the American Experience in China, 1911-45,* 1971.
b. Jan 30, 1912 in New York, New York
d. Feb 6, 1989 in Greenwich, Connecticut
Source: *AmAu&B; AmWomWr; Au&Wr 71; Benet 87; BenetAL 91; BioIn 13, 16; BlueB 76; ConAu 1R, 3NR, 24NR, 127; CurBio 63, 89, 89N; EncWB; IntAu&W 91; IntWW 83, 89N; InWom, SUP; LibW; MajTwCW; NewYTBS 78, 89; OxCAmL 65; RAdv 13-3; WhAm 9; WhoAm 74, 76, 78, 80, 82, 84, 86, 88; WhoAmJ 80; WhoAmW 58, 61, 64, 66, 68, 70, 72, 74, 75, 77, 81, 83, 85, 87, 89; WhoE 74; WhoUSWr 88; WhoWor 74, 78, 80, 82, 87, 89; WomFir; WorAu 1950; WrDr 76, 86, 88*

Tuck, Lily
American. Author
Wrote *Interviewing Matisse, or, The Women Who Died Standing Up,* 1991.
b. 1938, France
Source: *ConAu 139; ConLC 70; WrDr 96*

Tucker, Forrest Meredith
American. Actor
Crusty character actor best known as Sgt. O'Rourke on TV series "F Troop," 1965-67.
b. Feb 12, 1919 in Plainfield, Indiana
d. Oct 25, 1986 in Woodland Hills, California
Source: *BiE&WWA; BioNews 74; ConNews 87-1; ConTFT 3, 4; FilmgC; IntMPA 82; MotPP; MovMk; WhAm 9; WhoAm 74, 76, 80, 82, 84, 86; WhoHol A*

Tucker, Lorenzo
"The Black Valentino"
American. Actor
One of the first major black screen actors; starred in many all-black movies, 1920s-40s.
b. Jun 27, 1907 in Philadelphia, Pennsylvania
d. Aug 19, 1986 in Los Angeles, California
Source: *BioIn 15, 16; BlksAmF; BlksB&W, C; DrBlPA, 90; InB&W 80; WhoBlA 80, 85*

Tucker, Mary Bradham
American. Model
The first Pepsi girl, seen on calendars, early 1900s.
b. 1903
d. May 26, 1984 in Edenton, North Carolina
Source: *BioIn 13*

Tucker, Orrin
American. Bandleader
Led dance bands, 1930s-40s; recorded "Oh, Johnny, Oh" with Bonnie Baker, 1939.
b. Feb 17, 1911 in Saint Louis, Missouri
Source: *ASCAP 66, 80; BgBands 74; BiDAmM; CmpEPM; PenEncP; SaTiSS; WhoHol 92*

Tucker, Preston Thomas
American. Auto Manufacturer
Developed rear engine car, 1940s.
b. Sep 21, 1903 in Capac, Michigan
d. Jan 7, 1956 in Ypsilanti, Michigan
Source: *BioIn 2, 4, 5, 9, 10, 11, 13; BusPN; EncABHB 5; FacFETw; ObitOF 79; WhAm 3*

Tucker, Richard
[Reuben Tickel]
American. Opera Singer, Actor
Considered best operatic tenor, 1940s-50s.
b. Aug 28, 1913 in New York, New York
d. Jan 8, 1975 in Kalamazoo, Michigan
Source: *Baker 78, 84, 92; BioIn 2, 3, 4, 5, 6, 7, 8, 9, 10, 11, 13, 21; CelR; CurBio 56, 75, 75N; DcAmB S9; FacFETw; IntDcOp; IntWW 74; MetOEnc; MusSN; NewAmDM; NewEOp 71; NewGrDA 86; NewGrDM 80; NewGrDO; NewYTBE 73; OxDcOp; PenDiMP; WhAm 6; WhoAm 74; WhoWor 74; WhScrn 77*

Tucker, Sophie
[Sophia Kalish]
American. Singer
Vaudeville performer billed as "last of the red-hot Mamas."
b. Jan 13, 1884, Russia
d. Feb 9, 1966 in New York, New York
Source: *AmAu&B; Baker 92; BiDAmM; BiE&WWA; BioAmW; BioIn 2, 3, 7, 11, 12, 13, 16; CamGWoT; CmpEPM; ConMus 12; ContDcW 89; CurBio 45, 66; EncMT; Film 2; FilmgC; ForYSC; FunnyW; GoodHs; GrLiveH; HalFC 80, 84, 88; IntDcWB; InWom; JoeFr; LegTOT; LibW; NewGrDA 86; NotAW MOD; NotNAT A; ObitT 1961; OxCAmH; OxCAmT 84; OxCPMus; PenEncP; ThFT; WebAB 74, 79; WhAm 4; WhoAmW 61, 64; WhoCom; WhoHol B; WhScrn 74, 77, 83; WhThe; WorAl; WorAlBi*

Tucker, Sterling
American. Civil Rights Leader
Executive director, Washington, DC Urban League, 1956-78; books include *Black Reflections on White Power,* 1969; *For Blacks Only,* 1970.
b. Dec 21, 1923 in Akron, Ohio
Source: *CivR 74; InB&W 80; LivgBAA; SelBAAf; WhoAm 78, 80, 82, 84, 86, 88; WhoAmP 73, 75, 77, 79; WhoGov 72, 75*

Tucker, Tanya (Denise)
American. Singer
First hit at age 14; millionaire by 16; hit song "Delta Dawn," 1973.
b. Oct 10, 1958 in Seminole, Texas
Source: *BgBkCoM; BioIn 10, 11, 12, 14, 16, 20; BioNews 75; CelR 90; ConMus 3; CounME 74, 74A; EncFCWM 83; EncRk 88; HarEnCM 87; IlEncCM; LegTOT; RkOn 78, 85; RolSEnR 83; WhoAm 80, 82, 84, 86, 88, 90, 92, 94, 95, 96, 97; WhoAmW 81, 83, 85, 95, 97; WhoEnt 92; WhoHol 92, A; WhoNeCM; WhoRock 81; WhoWest 82; WorAlBi*

Tucker, Tommy
"Little Tommy Tucker"
American. Bandleader
Led hotel-style dance bands, 1930s-50s; best known song was "I Don't Want to Set the World on Fire."
b. May 18, 1908 in Souris, North Dakota
d. Jul 10, 1989 in Sarasota, Florida
Source: *ASCAP 66, 80; BgBands 74; BiDAmM; CmpEPM; LegTOT; WhoAm 74; WhoMus 72; WhoRocM 82*

Tuckwell, Barry Emmanuel
Australian. Musician
Virtuoso horn player; edited horn literature.
b. Mar 5, 1931 in Melbourne, Australia
Source: *Baker 84, 92; BioIn 16; CurBio 79; IntWW 81, 82, 83, 89, 91, 93; NewAmDM; NewGrDM 80; NewYTBS 78; PenDiMP; TwCBrS; Who 82, 83, 85, 88, 90, 92, 94; WhoAm 80, 82, 84, 86, 88, 90, 92, 94, 95, 96, 97; WhoAmM 83; WhoMus 72; WhoWor 76, 82, 84*

Tudjman, Franjo
Croatian. Political Leader
Pres., of Croatia, 1990—.
b. May 14, 1922 in Veliko-Tgroviste, Croatia
Source: *IntWW 93; News 96, 96-2; WhoSoCE 89; WhoWor 95, 96, 97*

Tudor, Antony
[William Cook]
English. Choreographer
Best known for revolutionary use of psychological themes in ballet.
b. Apr 4, 1908? in London, England
d. Apr 20, 1987 in New York, New York
Source: *AnObit 1987; BiDD; BiE&WWA; BioIn 11, 13; CnOxB; ConNews 87-4; CurBio 45, 87; DcTwCCu 1; IntDcB; LegTOT; NewGrDA 86; NewOxM; NewYTBS 87; WhAm 9; WhoAm 74, 76, 80, 82, 84, 86; WorAl*

Tudor, John Thomas
American. Baseball Player
Pitcher, 1979-91; led NL in shutouts, 1985.
b. Feb 2, 1954 in Schenectady, New York
Source: *Ballpl 90; BaseReg 86, 87; BioIn 14*

Tuffin, Sally
English. Fashion Designer
Fashions designed for youth; firm of Foale & Tuffin, Ltd. was major fashion influence during the Youth Rebellion, 1965.
Source: *EncFash; WorFshn*

Tufts, Sonny
[Bowen Charles Tufts, III]
American. Actor
Began film career, 1943; appeared in *No Escape*, 1953.
b. Jul 16, 1911 in Boston, Massachusetts
d. Jun 5, 1970 in Santa Monica, California
Source: *BioIn 8, 10; EncAFC; FilmEn; FilmgC; HalFC 80, 84, 88; HolP 40; LegTOT; MotPP; MovMk; NewYTBE 70; ObitOF 79; What 2; WhoHol B; WhoHrs 80; WhScrn 74, 77*

Tugwell, Rexford Guy
American. Author, Political Scientist
Adviser to FDR during Depression; appointed gov. of Puerto Rico, 1941.
b. Jul 10, 1891 in Sinclairville, New York
d. Jul 21, 1979 in Santa Barbara, California
Source: *AmAu&B; AmMWSc 73S; AmPolLe; BioIn 1, 6, 7, 8, 10, 11, 12; BlueB 76; ConAu 85, 89; CurBio 41, 79; DcAmB S10; EncAAH; EncAB-H 1974, 1996; EncWB; IntAu&W 76; IntWW 74, 75, 76, 77, 78, 79; NewYTBE 70; NewYTBS 79; OxCAmH; PolProf T; REnAL; WebAB 74, 79; WhAm 7; WhoAm 74, 76, 78; WhoEc 86; WhoWest 74, 76, 78; WhoWor 74, 78; WrDr 76, 80*

Tukhachevski, Mikhail Nikolayevich
Russian. Military Leader
Commanded Russian offensive in Russo-Polish War, 1919-20; led modernization of Red Army, 1935; charged with treason by Stalin, executed.
b. Feb 16, 1893 in Slednevo, Russia
d. Jun 11, 1937 in Moscow, Russia
Source: *NewCol 75; WebBD 83; WhoMilH 76*

Tulane, Paul
American. Merchant, Philanthropist
New Orleans clothier; donated fortune to U of Louisiana; name changed to Tulane U, 1884.
b. May 10, 1801 in Princeton, New Jersey
d. Mar 27, 1887 in Princeton, New Jersey
Source: *AmBi; ApCAB; BioIn 3; DcAmB; HarEnUS; NatCAB 9; TwCBDA; WhAm HS*

Tully, Alice
American. Singer, Philanthropist
Former operatic soprano; donated Alice Tully Hall, chamber music recital hall in Lincoln Center for Performing Arts, NYC.
b. Oct 11, 1902 in Corning, New York
d. Dec 10, 1993 in New York, New York
Source: *AnObit 1993; Baker 84, 92; BioIn 13, 14, 15, 16, 17, 19, 20, 21; CelR 90; CurBio 84, 94N; InWom, SUP; NewAmDM; NewGrDA 86; NewYTBS 77, 82, 93*

Tully, Grace George
American. Secretary
Personal secretary to FDR, 1928-45; wrote memoirs, *F.D.R.: My Boss*, 1949.
b. Aug 9, 1900 in Bayonne, New Jersey
d. Jun 15, 1984 in Washington, District of Columbia
Source: *BioIn 2, 12, 14; ConAu 113; NewYTBS 80, 84; WhoGov 72*

Tully, Tom
American. Actor
Oscar nominee for *The Caine Mutiny*, 1954.
b. Aug 21, 1902 in Durango, California
d. Apr 27, 1982 in Newport Beach, California
Source: *FilmgC; ForYSC; IntMPA 82; MotPP; MovMk; Vers A; WhoHol A*

Tune, Tommy
[Thomas James Tune]
American. Director, Choreographer
Won Tonys for *A Day in Hollywood/A Night in the Ukraine*, 1980; *Nine*, 1982; only person to win 9 Tonys in 4 different categories.
b. Feb 28, 1939 in Wichita Falls, Texas
Source: *BiDD; BioIn 13, 14; CelR 90; CnOxB; ConTFT 1, 7, 14; CurBio 83; GrStDi; IntMPA 86, 88, 92, 94, 96; IntWW 89, 91, 93; LegTOT; News 94, 94-2; NewYTBS 80; OxCAmT 84; TheaDir; WhoAm 80, 82, 84, 86, 88, 90, 92, 94, 95, 96, 97; WhoE 91, 93; WhoEnt 92; WhoHol 92, A; WhoThe 81; WorAl; WorAlBi*

Tung Chee-hwa
Chinese. Political Leader
Chief Executive, Hong Kong, 1997—.
b. May 29, 1937 in Shanghai, China

Tunis, Edwin Burdett
American. Children's Author
Self-illustrated works include *Frontier Living*, 1961.
b. Dec 8, 1897 in New York
d. Aug 7, 1973
Source: *AuBYP 2; ConAu 5R, 45; IlsCB 1946, 1957; MorJA; SmATA 1; WhoAmA 73*

Tunnard, Christopher
American. Architect
Urban planning authority; known for idea of "linear" or "super" city on Atlantic sea board; won National Book Award, 1963, for *Man-Made America: Chaos or Control*.

b. Jul 7, 1910 in Victoria, British Columbia, Canada
d. Feb 14, 1979 in New Haven, Connecticut
Source: *AmAu&B; BioIn 5, 11, 12; ConAu 5R, 6NR, 85; CurBio 59, 79N; NewYTBS 79; WhAm 7; WhoAm 74, 76, 78; WhoWor 74*

Tunnell, Em(len)
American. Football Player, Football Coach
Defensive back, 1948-61, mostly with NY Giants; first black full-time coach in NFL as assistant coach with Giants, 1963-73; first black man in Hall of Fame, 1967.
b. Mar 29, 1925 in Bryn Mawr, Pennsylvania
d. Jul 22, 1975 in Pleasantville, New York
Source: *AfrAmSG; BiDAmSp FB; BioIn 6, 10, 17, 21; InB&W 80; LegTOT; NewYTBS 75; ObitOF 79; WhoFtbl 74; WhoSpor*

Tunney, Gene
[James Joseph Tunney]
American. Boxer, Businessman
Beat Jack Dempsey in famous "long count fight," 1922, to become heavyweight champ; retired unbeaten.
b. May 25, 1898 in New York, New York
d. Nov 7, 1978 in Greenwich, Connecticut
Source: *AmAu&B; BiDAmSp BK; BioIn 1, 2, 3, 4, 5, 6, 7, 8, 9, 10, 11, 12, 14, 17, 21; CelR; ConAu 111; CurBio 40, 79N; FacFETw; Film 2; IntWW 74; LegTOT; NewYTBS 78; OxCAmH; REnAL; WebAB 74, 79; WhoAm 74; WhoBox 74; WhScrn 83; WorAl; WorAlBi*

Tunney, John Varick
American. Politician
Dem. senator from CA, 1971-77; son of boxer Gene.
b. Jun 26, 1934 in New York, New York
Source: *BiDrAC; BiDrUSC 89; BioIn 7, 8, 9, 10, 11; BlueB 76; CngDr 74; ConAu 61; CurBio 71; IntWW 83, 91; NewYTBE 71; WhoAm 74, 76, 78, 80, 82, 84, 86, 88, 92, 94, 95, 96, 97; WhoAmP 73, 75, 77, 79, 81, 83, 85, 87, 89, 91, 93, 95; WhoGov 75, 77; WhoWest 74, 76*

Tupac Amaru
[Jose Gabriel Condorcanqui]
Peruvian. Nobleman
Inca, who lead Indian rebellion in Americas, 1780, resulting in minor reforms in Peru.
b. 1742 in Tinta, Peru
d. 1781
Source: *ApCAB; EncLatA; HisDcSE; McGEWB; NewCol 75*

Tupper, Earl Silas
American. Inventor
Former DuPont chemist who founded Tupperware Home Parties, Inc., 1945.
b. Jul 28, 1907 in Berlin, New Hampshire
d. Oct 3, 1983 in San Jose, California
Source: *Entr; NewYTBS 83*

Tura, Cosme
[Cosimo Tura]
Italian. Artist
Founder, master of Ferrarese school of painting; works include allegorical frescoes, Pieta, 1472.
b. 1430 in Ferrara, Italy
d. 1495 in Ferrara, Italy
Source: *AtlBL; DcCathB; IntDcAA 90; McGEWB; NewCol 75; OxCArt; OxDcArt; WebBD 83*

Turbay Ayala, Julio Cesar
Colombian. Political Leader
Pres., 1978-82; permanent representative UN, 1967; ambassador to US, 1974-76.
b. Jun 18, 1916 in Bogota, Colombia
Source: *BioIn 11, 12; CurBio 79; DcCPSAm; IntWW 74, 79, 80, 81, 82, 83, 89, 91, 93; IntYB 79, 80, 81, 82; NewYTBS 78; WhoWor 74, 80, 82*

Turcotte, Ron
Canadian. Jockey
Leading jockey, 1960s-70s; rode Secretariat to Triple Crown, 1973.
b. Jul 22, 1941 in Drummond, New Brunswick, Canada
Source: *BioIn 10, 11, 12, 13, 16; CurBio 74*

Tureck, Rosalyn
American. Pianist
Specialized in Bach; founded Int'l Bach Society, 1966.
b. Dec 14, 1914 in Chicago, Illinois
Source: *Baker 78, 84, 92; BioIn 1, 2, 4, 5, 8, 11, 12, 14, 21; BlueB 76; BriBkM 80; CurBio 59; IntAu&W 82, 89; IntWW 74, 75, 76, 77, 78, 80, 81, 82, 83, 89, 91, 93; IntWWM 77, 80, 90; InWom; MusSN; NewAmDM; NewGrDA 86; NewGrDM 80; NotTwCP; PenDiMP; Who 74, 82, 83, 85, 88, 90, 92, 94; WhoAm 74, 76, 78, 80, 82, 84, 86, 88, 90, 92, 94, 95, 96, 97; WhoAmW 66, 68, 70, 74, 79, 81, 83, 85, 87, 89, 91, 93, 95, 97; WhoEnt 92; WhoMus 72; WhoWor 74; WhoWorJ 72, 78; WomCom; WrDr 76, 80, 82, 84, 86, 88, 90, 92, 94, 96*

Turenne, Henri de La Tour Auvergne, Viscount
French. Military Leader
Fought in Thirty Years War; emphasized mobility, surprise in military operations.
b. Sep 11, 1611 in Sedan, France
d. Jul 27, 1675 in Sasbach, Germany
Source: *LinLib S; NewCol 75; OxCFr; REn; WhDW; WorAl*

Turgenev, Ivan Sergeevich
Russian. Author
First major 19th-c. Russian novelist known abroad; wrote his masterpiece, *Fathers and Sons,* 1862; a popular comedy, *A Month in the Country,* 1850.
b. Nov 9, 1818 in Orel, Russia
d. Sep 3, 1883 in Bougival, France
Source: *AtlBL; BbD; BiD&SB; BioIn 12, 13, 14, 15, 16, 20; BlmGEL; CamGWoT; CasWL; ClDMEL 47; CnThe; CyWA 58; DcBiA; DcEuL; DcRusL; EuAu; HanRL; LinLib L; McGEWB; McGEWD 84; OxCEng 85, 95; OxCThe 83; PenC EUR; RComWL; RfGShF; RfGWoL 95*

Turing, Alan (Mathison)
English. Mathematician
Was instrumental in the design of an automatic computing engine while with England's National Physical Laboratory, 1946-48.
b. Jun 23, 1912 in London, England
d. Jun 1954
Source: *BiESc; BioIn 3, 4, 5, 8, 11, 12, 13, 14, 15, 17, 18, 20, 21; CamDcSc; DcNaB 1951; DcScB; EncWB; FacFETw; GayLesB; GrBr; HisDcDP; InSci; LarDcSc; LegTOT; MakMC; NotTwCS; OxCPhil; PorSil; RAdv 14*

Turischeva, Ludmila
[Mrs. Valeri Borzov]
Russian. Gymnast
Won gold medals, 1968, 1972, 1976 Olympics.
b. Oct 7, 1952 in Grozny, Union of Soviet Socialist Republics
Source: *BiDSovU; BioIn 11; ContDcW 89; InWom SUP; WorAl*

Turkle, Brinton Cassaday
American. Children's Author
Self-illustrated juvenile books include *The Adventures of Obadiah,* 1972; *Rachel & Obadiah,* 1978.
b. Aug 15, 1915 in Alliance, Ohio
Source: *BioIn 8, 9, 10, 12, 14, 20; BkP; ChhPo S2; FamAIYP; IlsBYP; IlsCB 1957; SmATA 2; ThrBJA; TwCChW 89; WrDr 86, 92*

Turkus, Burton B
"Mr. Arsenic"
American. Lawyer
Cracked organized crime syndicate, Murder, Inc., 1940s.
b. 1902? in New York, New York
d. Nov 22, 1982 in New York, New York
Source: *AnObit 1982; BioIn 2, 13; ConAu 108; NewYTBS 82; WhoAmL 79; WhoLab 76*

Turlington, Christy
American. Model
Her face was used on mannequins at the Metropolitan Museum of Art's costume galleries.
b. Jan 2, 1969 in Walnut Creek, California

Source: *WhoAm 95, 96, 97; WhoAmW 95; WhoWor 97*

Turnbull, Agnes Sligh
American. Author
Wrote of rural PA in 14 novels including *Rolling Years,* 1936.
b. Oct 14, 1888 in New Alexandria, Pennsylvania
d. Jan 31, 1982 in Livingston, New Jersey
Source: *AmAu&B; AmNov; AmWomWr; AnObit 1982; Au&Wr 71; AuBYP 2, 3; BenetAL 91; ConAu 1R, 2NR, 105; InWom, SUP; NewYTBS 82; REnAL; TwCA, SUP; WhE&EA; WhNAA; WhoAm 74, 76, 78, 80, 82; WhoAmW 58, 61, 64, 66, 68, 70, 72, 74*

Turnbull, Collin M(acmillan)
English. Anthropologist
Best known for studies on Pygmy groups: *The Forest People,* 1961; *The Mountain People,* 1971.
b. Nov 25, 1924 in Harrow, England
d. Jul 28, 1994 in Kilmarnock, Virginia
Source: *AmMWSc 73S; BioIn 11, 14; ConAu 3NR; CurBio 80; WhoAm 86, 88; WorAu 1970; WrDr 92*

Turnbull, Wendy
"Rabbit"
Australian. Tennis Player
Won mixed doubles with John Lloyd: 1982 French Open, 1983 Wimbledon.
b. Nov 26, 1952 in Brisbane, Australia
Source: *BioIn 14, 16; NewYTBS 84; WhoIntT*

Turner, Donald F(rank)
American. Lawyer
Specialist in antitrust law; wrote *Antitrust Policy,* 1959; *Antitrust Law,* 1980.
b. Mar 19, 1921
d. Jul 19, 1994 in Derwood, Maryland
Source: *BioIn 7, 8, 11, 20; BlueB 76; CurBio 94N; DrAS 74P, 78P; PolProf J; WhAm 11; WhoAm 74, 76, 78, 80, 82, 84, 86, 88, 90, 92, 94, 95; WhoAmL 83, 85, 90, 92; WhoE 74*

Turner, Eva, Dame
English. Opera Singer
Dramatic soprano; 35-year career earned her the unofficial title of England's greatest soprano; won renown in title role in Puccini's "Turandot."
b. Mar 10, 1892 in Oldham, England
d. Jun 16, 1990 in London, England
Source: *AnObit 1990; Baker 92; BioIn 2, 3, 5, 14, 15, 17, 21; CmOp; DcArts; DcNaB 1986; FacFETw; IntDcOp; IntWWM 90; InWom; MetOEnc; NewEOp 71; NewGrDM 80; NewGrDO; NewYTBS 90; OxDcOp; PenDiMP; Who 83, 85, 88, 90; WhoMus 72*

Turner, Frederick Jackson
American. Historian
Originated frontier theory emphasizing significance of receding frontier in American social, economic development.
b. Nov 14, 1861 in Portage, Wisconsin
d. Mar 14, 1932 in Pasadena, California
Source: *AmAu&B; AmBi; AmSocL; Benet 87, 96; BenetAL 91; BioIn 1, 3, 5, 7, 8, 9, 10, 11, 12, 13, 14, 15, 19, 20; CamGEL; CamGLE; CamHAL; CasWL; ConAu 113; DcAmB; DcLB 17; DcNAA; EncAAH; EncAB-H 1974, 1996; EvLB; FacFETw; GayN; HarEnUS; MakMC; McGEWB; MemAm; NatCAB 13; OxCAmH; OxCAmL 65, 83, 95; PenC AM; PeoHis; RAdv 14, 13-3; RComAH; REn; REnAL; REnAW; ThTwC 87; TwCA, SUP; WebAB 74; WebE&AL; WhAm 1; WisWr*

Turner, Henry McNeal
American. Religious Leader
Commissioned chaplain by Lincoln, first black commissioned, 1863; forced out, 1865.
b. Feb 1, 1834 in Abbeville, South Carolina
d. May 8, 1915 in Windsor, Ontario, Canada
Source: *AfrAmAl 6; BiDSA; BioIn 6, 8, 9, 10, 11, 17, 18, 19; DcAmAu; DcAmB; DcAmNB; DcAmReB 1, 2; EncAACR; EncAB-H 1974, 1996; EncSoH; EncWM; McGEWB; RelLAm 91; TwCBDA; WhAm 1; WhoColR; WorAlBi*

Turner, Ike
[Ike and Tina Turner]
American. Singer, Songwriter
Wrote, sang hit songs "A Fool in Love (Tell Me What's Wrong)," 1960; "Goodbye, So Long," 1971.
b. Nov 5, 1931 in Clarksdale, Mississippi
Source: *Baker 84, 92; BiDAfM; BioIn 15; DcTwCCu 1; DrBlPA 90; EncPR&S 89; EncRk 88; LegTOT; NewAmDM; OnThGG; OxCPMus; PenEncP; SoulM; WhoHol 92, A; WhoRock 81; WorAlBi*

Turner, Janine
[Janine Gauntt]
American. Actor
Plays Maggie O'Connell on the Emmy winning TV show, "Northern Exposure."
b. Dec 1962 in Lincoln, Nebraska
Source: *IntMPA 94, 96; LegTOT; News 93-2*

Turner, Jesse
American. Hostage
Computer science instructor in Lebanon seized by Islamic Jihad January 24, 1987 and held captive 1,731 days; released October 21, 1991.
Source: *BioIn 13, 17*

Turner, Joe
""Big Joe""
American. Jazz Musician
Blues vocalist; rock pioneer; recorded classic "Shake, Rattle, and Roll," 1954.
b. May 18, 1911 in Kansas City, Missouri
d. Nov 24, 1985 in Hollywood, California
Source: *BiDJaz; BioIn 11, 12, 14, 15, 16, 17; DrBlPA 90; EncPR&S 74, 89; EncRk 88; NewGrDA 86; NewGrDJ 88, 94; RkOn 74, 78; RolSEnR 83; WhoJazz 72; WhoRocM 82*

Turner, John Napier
Canadian. Political Leader
Liberal Party leader who succeeded Pierre Trudeau as prime minister, 1984; defeated by Conservative Brian Mulroney, Sep 1984.
b. Jun 7, 1929 in Richmond, England
Source: *AmCath 80; BlueB 76; CurBio 84; FacFETw; IntWW 74, 75, 76, 77, 78, 79, 80, 81, 82, 83, 89, 91, 93; NewYTBS 84; Who 82, 83, 85, 88, 90, 92, 94; WhoAm 74, 76, 78, 80, 82, 84, 88, 94, 95, 96, 97; WhoCan 73, 75, 77, 80, 82, 84; WhoE 74, 75, 77, 85; WhoWor 74, 76, 78, 84, 89, 93, 95, 96, 97*

Turner, Joseph Mallord William
English. Artist
Foremost English Romantic painter; noted for impressionistic oils, watercolors of seascapes.
b. Apr 23, 1775 in London, England
d. Dec 19, 1851 in London, England
Source: *Alli; ArtsNiC; AtlBL; Benet 87, 96; BioIn 1, 2, 3, 4, 5, 6, 7, 8, 9, 10, 11, 12, 13, 14, 15, 16; CelCen; ChhPo, S1, S3; ClaDrA; DcArts; DcBiPP; DcBrBI; DcBrECP; DcBrWA; DcNaB; DcSeaP; DcVicP, 2; EncEnv; LinLib S; McGDA; McGEWB; NewC; NewCBEL; OxCArt; OxCShps; OxDcArt; RAdv 14, 13-3; REn; VicBrit; WhDW*

Turner, Kathleen
[Mary Kathleen Turner]
American. Actor
Star of feature films *Romancing the Stone,* 1984; *Jewel of the Nile,* 1985.
b. Jun 19, 1954 in Springfield, Missouri
Source: *BiDFilm 94; BioIn 14, 15, 16; CelR 90; ConNews 85-3; ConTFT 5, 12; CurBio 86; EncAFC; HalFC 88; HolBB; IntDcF 1-3, 2-3; IntMPA 86, 88, 92, 94, 96; IntWW 89, 91, 93; ItaFilm; LegTOT; NewYTBS 86; VarWW 85; WhoAm 86, 88, 90, 92, 94, 95, 96, 97; WhoAmW 89, 91, 93, 95, 97; WhoEnt 92; WhoHol 92*

Turner, Lana
[Julia Jean Mildred Frances Turner]
"The Sweater Girl"
American. Actor
Allegedly discovered while drinking a soda at Top Hat Malt Shop; films include *Imitation of Life,* 1959.
b. Feb 8, 1920 in Wallace, Idaho
d. Jun 29, 1995 in Los Angeles, California
Source: *BiDFilm, 94; BioAmW; BioIn 1, 2, 4, 6, 8, 9, 10, 11, 12, 13, 14, 15, 16, 18, 21; BlueB 76; CelR, 90; CmMov; CurBio 43, 95N; DcArts; FilmEn; FilmgC; ForYSC; GoodHs; HalFC 80, 84, 88; IntDcF 1-3, 2-3; IntMPA 84, 86, 88, 92; InWom, SUP; LegTOT; MGM;*

MotPP; MovMk; NewYTBE 71; NewYTBS 95; OxCFilm; ThFT; VarWW 85; WhoAm 74, 76, 78, 80, 82, 84, 86, 88, 92, 94; WhoEnt 92; WhoHol A; WorAl; WorAlBi; WorEFlm

Turner, Morrie
American. Cartoonist, Author
Broke cartoon strip color barrier with syndicated comic *Wee Pals,* 1970s; books include *All God's Chillun Got Soul,* 1980.
b. Dec 11, 1923 in Oakland, California
Source: *BioIn 15; ConAu 15NR, 29R, X; Ebony 1; EncACom; WhoAm 80; WorECom*

Turner, Nat
American. Slave
Led only effective slave rebellion in US history, 1831.
b. Oct 2, 1800 in Southampton County, Virginia
d. Nov 11, 1831 in Jerusalem, Virginia
Source: *AfrAmAl 6; AmBi; ApCAB; BenetAL 91; BioIn 1, 3, 4, 6, 7, 8, 9, 10, 11, 16, 17, 18, 19, 20, 21; DcAmB; DcAmNB; DcAmSR; EncAAH; EncAB-H 1974, 1996; EncARH; EncSoH; HarEnUS; HisWorL; LegTOT; LinLib S; NatCAB 13; NegAl 76, 83, 89; NewCol 75; OxCAmL 83; WebAB 74, 79; WhAm HS; WhCiWar; WorAl; WorAlBi*

Turner, Roscoe Wilson
American. Aviator
Stunt flier, air racer; held cross-country speed records, nat. air races, 1933-38; awarded Distinguished Flying Cross, 1952.
b. Sep 29, 1895 in Corinth, Mississippi
d. Jun 23, 1970 in Indianapolis, Indiana
Source: *NewYTBE 70; WhAm 5; WhoSSW 82; WhScrn 83*

Turner, Stansfield
American. Government Official
Retired Naval admiral; directed CIA, 1977-81.
b. Dec 1, 1923 in Chicago, Illinois
Source: *BioIn 11, 12, 13, 14; ConAu 118, 124; CurBio 78; EncAI&E; IntAu&W 89; IntWW 77, 78, 79, 80, 81, 82, 83, 89, 91, 93; IntYB 78, 79, 80, 81, 82; NewYTBS 77; WhoAm 74, 76, 78, 80, 82, 84, 86, 88, 90, 92, 94, 95, 96, 97; WhoAmP 77, 79, 81, 83, 85, 87, 89, 91, 93, 95; WhoE 79, 81; WhoFI 89, 92; WhoGov 72, 77; WhoSSW 88; WorAl; WorAlBi*

Turner, Ted
[Robert Edward Turner, III]
"The Mouth of the South"
American. Impresario, Businessman
Winner of America's Cup, 1977; owner of Atlanta Braves, Hawks; developed first all-news cable network, Cable News Network (CNN).
b. Nov 19, 1938 in Cincinnati, Ohio
Source: *AmDec 1970; Ballpl 90; BiDAmSp OS; BioIn 13, 14, 15, 16, 17, 18, 19, 20, 21; CelR 90; ConAmBL; ConAu 120, X; ConTFT 5; CurBio 79; DcTwCCu 1; EncAB-H 1996; EncTwCJ; EncWB; FacFETw; IntMPA 86, 88, 92, 94, 96; IntWW 91, 93; LegTOT; LesBEnT, 92; News 89-1; NewYTBE 72; St&PR 93, 96, 97; WhoAm 80, 82, 84, 86, 88, 90, 92, 94, 95, 96, 97; WhoEnt 92; WhoFI 83, 85, 87, 89, 94, 96; WhoSpor; WhoSSW 86, 88, 91, 95, 97; WhoWor 96, 97; WorAl; WorAlBi*

Turner, Thomas Wyatt
American. Civil Rights Leader, Educator
Charter member, NAACP; founded Federation of Colored Catholics, 1915; active in black voter registration, 1920s.
b. Apr 16, 1877 in Hughesville, Maryland
d. Apr 21, 1978 in Washington, District of Columbia
Source: *BioIn 13, 19, 21; BlksScM; FacFETw; InB&W 80; NatCAB 61; NewYTBS 78; ObitOF 79; WhoColR*

Turner, Tina
[Ike and Tina Turner; Anna Mae Bullock]
American. Singer
Won Grammys for "Proud Mary," 1972; "What's Love Got to Do With It?," 1984.
b. Nov 26, 1939 in Nutbush, Tennessee
Source: *AfrAmAl 6; Baker 84, 92; BiDAfM; BioIn 8, 9, 13, 14, 15, 16; BlkWAm; CelR 90; ConAu 147; ConMus 1; CurBio 84; DcTwCCu 5; DrBlPA, 90; EncPR&S 89; EncRk 88; EncRkSt; GrLiveH; HarEnR 86; InB&W 80, 85; IntMPA 88, 92, 94, 96; IntWW 91; InWom SUP; NegAl 89; NewAmDM; NewGrDA 86; NotBlAW 1; OxCPMus; PenEncP; RkOn 85; SoulM; WhoAm 84, 86, 88, 90, 92, 94, 95, 96, 97; WhoAmW 89, 91; WhoBlA 92; WhoEnt 92; WhoHol 92, A; WhoRock 81; WhoRocM 82; WorAl; WorAlBi*

Turnesa, Jim
[James Turnesa]
American. Golfer
Turned pro, 1931; won PGA, 1952.
b. Dec 9, 1914 in Elmsford, New York
d. Aug 27, 1971 in Elmsford, New York
Source: *BioIn 9; NewYTBE 71; ObitOF 79; WhoGolf*

Turow, Scott
American. Author
Lawyer-turned-best-selling author; wrote *The Burden of Proof,* 1990; *Presumed Innocent* filmed, 1990, starring Harrison Ford.
b. Apr 12, 1949 in Chicago, Illinois
Source: *BestSel 90-3; BioIn 11, 15, 16; ConAu 40NR, 73; ConPopW; CurBio 91; LegTOT; TwCCr&M 91; WhoAm 88, 90; WhoMW 92; WorAu 1985; WrDr 92*

Turpin, Ben
American. Comedian
Known for crossed eyes, somersaults; appeared in film *Swing High,* 1930s.
b. Sep 17, 1869 in New Orleans, Louisiana
d. Jul 1, 1940 in Santa Barbara, California
Source: *BioIn 2, 4, 11, 17; CurBio 40; DcAmB S2; Film 1; FilmgC; Funs; LegTOT; MotPP; MovMk; SilFlmP; TwYS; WhAm 4, HSA; WhScrn 74, 77, 83; WorAl; WorAlBi; WorEFlm*

Turpin, Dick
[Richard Turpin]
English. Criminal
Horse thief hanged at York; subject of W H Ainsworth's novel, *Rockwood,* 1834.
b. 1706 in Essex, England
d. Apr 10, 1739 in York, England
Source: *Benet 87, 96; BioIn 1, 4, 6, 8, 10; BlmGEL; CamGEL; DcArts; DcNaB; DrInf; FilmgC; HalFC 84, 88; LngCEL; NewC; NewCol 75; REn; WhDW*

Turtle Island String Quartet
[Darol Anger; David Balakrishnan; Jeremy Cohen; Mark Summer]
American. Music Group
Acoustic string quartet; albums include *Skylife,* 1990.
Source: *ConMus 9; DrAS 82H; NewAgMG*

Turtles, The
[Howard Kaylan; Don Murray; Al Nichol; Jim Pons; Chuck Portz; John Seiter; Jim Tucker]
American. Music Group
Underrated cult band during Beatles era; hits include "Happy Together," 1967.
Source: *BiDAmM; ConMuA 80A; CurBio 59; EncPR&S 89; EncRk 88; EncRkSt; HarEnR 86; IlEncRk; InB&W 80; PenEncP; RkOn 78, 84; RolSEnR 83; WhoHol 92; WhoRock 81; WhoRocM 82*

Turturro, John
American. Actor
Films include *Do the Right Thing,* 1989; *Quiz Show,* 1994; *Unstrung Heroes,* 1995.
b. Feb 28, 1957 in New York, New York
Source: *BiDFilm 94; BioIn 14, 15, 17, 18, 19, 20; ConTFT 9; CurBio 96; IntMPA 92, 94, 96; IntWW 93; LegTOT; MiSFD 9; WhoAm 92, 94, 95, 96, 97; WhoEnt 92; WhoHol 92; WhoWor 95, 96, 97*

Tushingham, Rita
English. Actor
Had award-winning performance in *A Taste of Honey,* 1961.
b. Mar 14, 1942 in Liverpool, England
Source: *BioIn 7, 11; BlueB 76; ConTFT 7; CurBio 65; FilmEn; FilmgC; HalFC 84, 88; IlWWBF; IntMPA 75, 76, 77, 78, 79, 80, 81, 82, 84, 86, 92, 94, 96; InWom, SUP; MotPP; MovMk; OxCFilm; Who 74, 82, 83, 85, 88, 90, 92, 94; WhoAmW 70, 72, 74; WhoHol A; WhoThe 72, 77, 81; WhoWor 74, 76; WorAl; WorAlBi; WorEFlm*

Tussaud, Marie Gresholtz, Madame
Swiss. Wax Modeler
Created Madame Tussaud museum of waxwork figures in London.
b. Dec 7, 1760 in Bern, Switzerland
d. Apr 15, 1850 in London, England
Source: *InWom; NewCol 75; WebBD 83*

Tutankhamen
[Tut-Ankh—Amen]
"King Tut"
Egyptian. Ruler
Boy ruler of 18th Dynasty; tomb, with magnificent contents, found 1922, in Valley of Kings.
b. 1358BC
d. 1340BC
Source: *DcBiPP; NewCol 75; WebBD 83*

Tuthill, Harry J
American. Cartoonist
Created wryly cynical syndicated comic strip, "The Bungle Family," 1925-45.
b. 1886 in Chicago, Illinois
d. Jan 25, 1957 in Saint Louis, Missouri
Source: *WorECom*

Tuttle, Lurene
American. Actor
TV shows include "Life With Father," 1953-55; Julia, 1968-71.
b. Aug 20, 1906 in Pleasant Lake, Indiana
d. May 28, 1986 in Encino, California
Source: *ForWC 70; LegTOT; Vers A; WhoHol A*

Tuttle, Merlin Devere
American. Animal Expert
World-renowned authority on bats.
b. Aug 26, 1941 in Honolulu, Hawaii
Source: *AmMWSc 76P, 79, 82, 86, 89, 92, 95; BioIn 15, 16; CurBio 92*

Tutu, Desmond (Mpilo)
South African. Religious Leader
First black Anglican bishop of Johannesburg, S Africa; won Nobel Peace Prize, 1984.
b. Oct 7, 1931 in Klerksdrop, South Africa
Source: *AfSS 81, 82; BioIn 12, 13, 14, 15, 16; BlkLC; BlkWr 1; ConAu 125; ConBlB 6; ConHero 1; ConLC 80; CurBio 85; DcCPSAf; DcEcMov; DcTwHis; EncWB; FacFETw; HeroCon; IntWW 81, 82, 83, 89, 91, 93; LegTOT; NewYTBS 84; NobelP; RadHan; SchCGBL; Who 82, 83, 88, 92; WhoAfr; WhoNob, 90, 95; WhoRel 92; WhoWor 87, 89, 91, 93, 95, 96, 97*

Tutuola, Amos
Nigerian. Author
Novels with Yoruba folklore as background include *The Feather Woman of the Jungle*, 1962; *The Wild Herbalist of the Remote Town*, 1980.
b. Jun 20, 1920 in Abeokuta, Nigeria
d. Jun 8, 1997 in Ibadan, Nigeria
Source: *AfrA; AfSS 78, 79, 80, 81, 82; Au&Wr 71; Benet 87, 96; BioIn 3, 6, 7, 10, 13, 14; BlkLC; BlkWr 1, 2; CamGEL; CamGLE; CasWL; CnMWL; ConAu 9R, 27NR; ConLC 5, 14, 29; ConNov 72, 76, 82, 86, 91, 96; CyWA 89; DcAfHiB 86; DcLB 125; DcLEL 1940; GrWrEL N; IntAu&W 76, 77, 82; IntvTCA 2; IntWW 74, 75, 76, 77, 78, 79, 80, 81, 82, 83, 89, 91, 93; LegTOT; LinLib L; LngCTC; MajTwCW; McGEWB; ModBlW; ModCmwL; Novels; PenC CL, ENG; RAdv 14, 13-2; RfGEnL 91; RGAfL; RGTwCWr; ScF&FL 1, 2; SchCGBL; SelBAAf; TwCWr; WebE&AL; WhDW; WhoHr&F; WhoWor 84, 87, 89, 91, 93, 95, 96; WorAu 1950; WrDr 76, 80, 82, 84, 86, 88, 90, 92, 94, 96*

Tuve, Merle Antony
American. Physicist
Scientific discoveries led to development of radar and nuclear energy.
b. Jun 27, 1901 in Canton, South Dakota
d. May 20, 1982 in Bethesda, Maryland
Source: *AmMWSc 76P, 79, 82; BiESc; BioIn 5, 6, 12, 13; BlueB 76; CamDcSc; ConAu 106; DcScB S2; IntWW 74, 75, 76, 77, 78, 79, 80, 81, 82, 83N; McGMS 80; WhAm 8; WhoAm 74, 76, 78, 80; WhoGov 72; WhoWor 74*

Twachtman, John Henry
American. Artist
Impressionist landscape painter; known for scenes of Yellowstone, Niagara: "Snowbound," 1902.
b. Aug 4, 1853 in Cincinnati, Ohio
d. Aug 8, 1902 in Gloucester, Massachusetts
Source: *AmBi; ApCAB; ArtsAmW 3; BioIn 1, 12, 19, 20; BriEAA; DcAmArt; DcAmB; IlBEAAW; McGDA; McGEWB; NatCAB 13; NewCol 75; OxCAmH; WebBD 83; WhAmArt 85*

Twain, Mark
[Samuel Langhorne Clemens]
"The People's Author"
American. Author, Journalist
Wrote *Tom Sawyer*, 1876; *Huckleberry Finn*, 1885.
b. Nov 30, 1835 in Florida, Missouri
d. Apr 21, 1910 in Redding, Connecticut
Source: *Alli, SUP; AmAu; AmAu&B; AmBi; AmCulL; AmOrN; AmRef; AmWr; AnCL; ApCAB; ArizL; AtlBL; AuBYP 2, 3; BbD; Benet 87, 96; BenetAL 91; BiDAmJo; BiD&SB; BiDPara; BiDSA; BioIn 1, 2, 3, 4, 5, 6, 7, 8, 9, 10, 11, 12, 13, 14, 15, 16, 17, 18, 19, 20, 21; CamGEL; CamGLE; CamHAL; CarSB; CasWL; CelCen; Chambr 3; ChhPo, S1; ChlBkCr; CnDAL; ConAu 104, 135; CrtSuMy; CrtT 3, 4; CyAL 2; CyWA 58, 89; DcAmAu; DcAmB; DcAmC; DcArts; DcBiPP; DcEnA, A; DcEnL; DcLB 11, 12, 23, 64, 74; DcLEL; DcNAA; Dis&D; Drake; EncAAH; EncAB-H 1974, 1996; EncAHmr; EncFWF; EncMys; EncO&P 1, 2, 3; EncPaPR 91; EncSF, 93; EncSoH; EncUnb; EncWL; EvLB; FamAYP; FifSWrB; FilmgC; GayN; GrWrEL N; HalFC 80, 84, 88; HarEnUS; JBA 34; JrnUS; LegTOT; LiJour; LinLib L, S; LngCTC; MagSAmL; MajAI; McGEWB; MemAm; ModAL, S1; NatCAB 6; NewEScF; NewGrDA 86; NotNAT B; Novels; OnHuMoP; OxCAmH; OxCAmL 65, 83, 95; OxCAusL; OxCChiL; OxCEng 67, 85, 95; PenC AM; RAdv 1, 14, 13-1; RComAH; RComWL; RealN; REn; REnAL; REnAW; RfGAmL 87, 94; RfGShF; ScF&FL 1, 92; ScFEYrs; ScFSB; ShSCr 6; ShSWr; SJGFanW; SouWr; SupFW; TwCA; TwCBDA; TwCChW 78A, 83A, 89A, 95A; TwCLC 6, 12, 19, 36, 48; TwCSFW 81, 86, 91; TwCYAW; TwoTYeD; WebAB 74, 79; WebE&AL; WhAm 1; WhCiWar; WhDW; WhLit; WhoChL; WhoTwCL; WorAl; WorAlBi; WorLitC; WrChl; YABC 2*

Twain, Shania
[Eileen Twain]
Canadian. Singer, Songwriter
Won Grammy, Best Country Album, *The Woman in Me*, 1995.
b. 1965 in Windsor, Ontario, Canada
Source: *CanWW 31; ConMus 17; News 96, 96-3*

Tway, Bob
[Robert Tway]
American. Golfer
Touring pro, 1980s; won PGA, 1986.
b. May 4, 1958 in Oklahoma City, Oklahoma
Source: *BioIn 15; NewYTBS 87*

Tweed, Boss
[William Marcy Tweed]
American. Politician
Tammany Hall boss; stole millions from city treasury; exposed by Nast cartoons, 1870.
b. Apr 3, 1823 in New York, New York
d. Apr 12, 1878 in New York, New York
Source: *AmBi; AmPolLe; ApCAB; Benet 87, 96; BiAUS; BiDrAC; BiDrUSC 89; BioIn 5, 6, 7, 10, 11, 16, 17, 21; CabMA; CyAG; DcAmB; EncAB-H 1974, 1996; HarEnUS; LegTOT; McGEWB; NatCAB 3; OxCAmH; REn; WebAB 74, 79; WhAm HS; WhAmP; WorAl; WorAlBi*

Tweedale, Violet Chambers
British. Author
Wrote over 30 works dealing with occult: *Ghosts I Have Seen*, 1919.
b. 1862
d. Dec 10, 1936
Source: *ConAu 116; EncO&P 1*

Twelvetrees, Helen
[Helen Jurgens]
American. Actor
1930s films include *Millie, Bedtime Story*.
b. Dec 25, 1908 in New York, New York
d. Feb 14, 1958 in Pennsylvania
Source: *BioIn 4, 5, 11; Film 2; FilmgC; ForYSC; HalFC 80, 84, 88; HolP 30;*

MotPP; MovMk; NotNAT B; ObitOF 79; ThFT; WhoHol B; WhoHrs 80; WhScrn 74, 77, 83

Twiggy
[Leslie Hornby]
English. Model
Ultra-thin model, 1966-76; sang and danced in critically acclaimed musical *My One and Only,* with Tommy Tune, 1983.
b. Sep 19, 1949 in London, England
Source: *AmDec 1960; CelR, 90; ConAu 103; ConTFT 3; CurBio 68; EncFash; FilmgC; GoodHs; HalFC 84, 88; IntMPA 75, 76, 77, 78, 79, 80, 81, 82, 84, 86, 88, 92, 94, 96; IntWW 91; InWom, SUP; LegTOT; NewYTBS 83; Who 85, 88, 90, 92, 94; WhoAm 84, 86, 92, 94; WhoEnt 92; WhoHol 92, A; WorAl*

Twining, Nathan F(arragut)
American. Air Force Officer
Became general, 1950; chm., Joint Chiefs of Staff, 1957-60; instrumental in formulating Indochina policy.
b. Oct 11, 1897 in Monroe, Wisconsin
d. Mar 29, 1982 in Lackland Air Force Base, Texas
Source: *AnObit 1982; BiDWWGF; BioIn 1, 2, 3, 4, 5, 11, 12, 13; BlueB 76; CurBio 53, 82; HarEnMi; IntWW 74, 75, 76, 77, 78, 79, 80, 81, 82N; NewYTBS 82; PolProf E; WebAMB; WhAm 8; Who 74, 83N; WhoAm 74, 76, 78; WhoWor 74; WhWW-II; WorAl; WorAlBi*

Twining, Thomas
English. Merchant
Known for specialty teas; popularized tea in England by opening first tea house, 1717.
b. 1675
d. 1741
Source: *Entr*

Twisted Sister
[Jay Jay French; Mark "the Animal" Mendoza; Eddie "Fingers" Ojeda; A J Pero; Dee Snider]
American. Music Group
Heavy metal group formed 1976, known for wild attire, hard rock sound; first single "We're Not Gonna Take It," 1984.
Source: *BioIn 15; EncPR&S 89; PenEncP; RkOn 85*

Twitchell, Paul
Cultist, Author
Founder, cult sect Eck, 1968.
b. 1908?
d. 1971
Source: *ConAu 111, 132; EncO&P 1S3, 2, 3; ScF&FL 1A, 2, 92*

Twitty, Conway
[Harold Lloyd Jenkins]
"The High Priest of Country Music"
American. Singer, Songwriter
Began as rock-n-roll singer, later turned to country music: "Lonely Boy Blue," 1960.
b. Sep 1, 1933 in Friars Point, Mississippi
d. Jun 5, 1993 in Springfield, Missouri
Source: *Baker 84, 92; BgBkCoM; BioIn 14, 15, 16, 18, 19, 20, 21; BioNews 75; CelR 90; ConMus 6; CounME 74, 74A; EncFCWM 83; EncRk 88; ForYSC; HarEnCM 87; HarEnR 86; IlEncCM; LegTOT; NewAmDM; NewGrDA 86; News 94, 94-1; OxCPMus; PenEncP; RolSEnR 83; WhoAm 78, 80, 82, 84, 86, 88; WhoEnt 92; WhoHol 92, A; WhoRock 81; WhoRocM 82; WorAl; WorAlBi*

Twombly, Cy
[Edward Parker Twombly, Jr.]
American. Artist
Paintings, drawings reflect his love for antiquity: *Discoveries on Commodus,* 1963; elected to the American Academy and Institute of Arts and Letters, 1987.
b. Apr 25, 1929 in Lexington, Virginia
Source: *AmArt; BioIn 8, 11, 12, 14, 15, 16, 17, 20, 21; ConArt 77, 83, 89, 96; CurBio 88; DcAmArt; DcCAA 71, 77, 88; IntWW 91, 93; OxCTwCA; OxDcArt; PhDcTCA 77; PrintW 85; WhoAm 82, 84, 86, 88, 94, 96; WhoAmA 84, 91; WorArt 1980*

Tworkov, Jack
American. Artist
Leader of NY school of Abstract Expressionism.
b. Aug 15, 1900 in Biala, Poland
d. Sep 4, 1982 in Provincetown, Massachusetts
Source: *AnObit 1982; BioIn 3, 5, 6, 7, 10, 13, 14, 16; BriEAA; ConArt 77, 83, 89, 96; ConAu 107; CurBio 82, 82N; DcAmArt; DcCAA 71, 77, 88, 94; DcCAr 81; NewYTBS 82; OxCTwCA; OxDcArt; PhDcTCA 77; PrintW 83, 85; SmATA 31N, 47; WhAm 8; WhAmArt 85; WhoAm 74, 76, 78, 80, 82; WhoAmA 73, 76, 78, 80, 82, 84N, 86N, 89N, 91N, 93N; WhoAmJ 80; WhoWor 74; WhoWorJ 72, 78; WorArt 1950*

Twyman, Jack
[John Kennedy Twyman]
American. Basketball Player
Forward, 1955-66, mostly with Cincinnati; led NBA in field goal percentage, 1958; Hall of Fame, 1982.
b. May 11, 1934 in Pittsburgh, Pennsylvania
Source: *BasBi; BiDAmSp BK; BioIn 6; Dun&B 86, 88, 90; OfNBA 87; WhoAm 86, 90, 94, 95, 96, 97; WhoBbl 73; WhoFI 87, 89, 94, 96; WhoMW 88, 90; WhoSpor*

Tydings, Millard Evelyn
American. Politician
Dem. senator from MD, 1927-51; headed McCarthy investigation which cleared State Dept., 1950.
b. Apr 6, 1890 in Havre de Grace, Maryland
d. Feb 9, 1961 in Havre de Grace, Maryland
Source: *BiDrAC; BiDrUSC 89; BioIn 2, 5, 6, 11; CurBio 45, 61; DcAmB S7; EncAB-A 32; EncSoH; NewCol 75; WhAm 4; WhAmP; WorAl*

Tyler, Anne
American. Author
Called chronicler of modern American family: *Morgan's Passing,* 1980; *Dinner at the Homesick Restaurant,* 1982; won Pulitzer Prize for fiction for *Breathing Lessons,* 1989.
b. Oct 25, 1941 in Minneapolis, Minnesota
Source: *AmWomWr; ArtclWW 2; Au&Arts 18; Benet 96; BenetAL 91; BestSel 89-1; BioIn 10, 11, 12, 13, 14, 15, 16, 17, 18, 19, 20, 21; BlmGWL; ConAu 9R, 11NR, 33NR, 53NR; ConLC 7, 11, 18, 28, 44, 59; ConNov 72, 76, 82, 86, 91, 96; ConPopW; CurBio 81; CyWA 89; DcLB 6, 143, Y82A; DcLEL 1940; DcTwCCu 1; DrAF 76; DrAPF 80, 83, 87, 91; EncWL 3; FemiCLE; FifSWrA; GrWomW; IntAu&W 76, 77, 91, 93; IntvTCA 2; IntWW 91, 93; InWom SUP; LegTOT; MagSAmL; MajTwCW; ModAL S2; ModAWWr; ModWoWr; News 95; NewYTBS 77; OxCAmL 83, 95; OxCWoWr 95; RAdv 14; RfGAmL 94; RGTwCWr; SmATA 7, 90; TwCYAW; Who 94; WhoAm 76, 78, 80, 82, 84, 86, 88, 90, 92, 94, 95, 96, 97; WhoAmW 68, 70, 72, 74, 75, 79, 81, 83, 85, 87, 89, 91, 93, 95, 97; WhoE 74, 75, 77, 95, 97; WhoEmL 87; WhoUSWr 88; WhoWor 95, 96, 97; WhoWrEP 89, 92, 95; WorAlBi; WorAu 1970; WrDr 76, 80, 82, 84, 86, 88, 90, 92, 94, 96*

Tyler, Bonnie
[Gaynor Hopkins]
Welsh. Singer
Raspy-voiced singer who had number one hit "Total Eclipse of the Heart," 1983.
b. Jun 8, 1953 in Swansea, Wales
Source: *BioIn 13, 14; EncFCWM 83; EncRkSt; LegTOT; PenEncP; RkOn 85; WhoRock 81; WhoRocM 82*

Tyler, John
American. US President
Took office after Harrison's death, 1841-45, making him first vice president to take such action.
b. Mar 29, 1790 in Charles City, Virginia
d. Jan 18, 1862 in Richmond, Virginia
Source: *Alli; AmAu&B; AmBi; AmPolLe; ApCAB; BenetAL 91; BiAUS; BiDConf; BiDrAC; BiDrGov 1789; BiDrUSC 89; BiDrUSE 71, 89; BioIn 1, 2, 3, 4, 5, 6, 7, 8, 9, 10, 11, 12, 13, 14, 15, 16, 17, 18, 19, 20; CelCen; CyAG; DcAmB;*

DcBiPP; Drake; EncAAH; EncAB-H 1974, 1996; EncSoH; FacPr 89, 93; HarEnUS; HealPre; LegTOT; LinLib L, S; McGEWB; NatCAB 6; OxCAmH; OxCAmL 65, 83; OxCSupC; PolPar; PresAR; RComAH; REn; REnAL; TwCBDA; VicePre; WebAB 74, 79; WhAm HS; WhAmP; WhCiWar; WhDW; WorAl; WorAlBi

Tyler, Julia Gardiner
[Mrs. John Tyler]
American. First Lady
Became Tyler's second wife in secret ceremony, 1844.
b. May 4, 1820 in Gardiner's Island, New York
d. Jul 10, 1889 in Richmond, Virginia
Source: *AmWom; ApCAB; BioIn 16, 17; FacPr 89; GoodHs; InWom, SUP; NatCAB 6; NotAW*

Tyler, Letitia Christian
[Mrs. John Tyler]
American. First Lady
First president's wife to die in White House.
b. Nov 12, 1790 in New Kent County, Virginia
d. Sep 10, 1842 in Washington, District of Columbia
Source: *Alli; AmAu&B; AmBi; AmPolLe; ApCAB; BenetAL 91; BiAUS; BiDConf; BiDrAC; BiDrGov 1789; BiDrUSC 89; BiDrUSE 71, 89; BioIn 1, 2, 3, 4, 5, 6, 7, 8, 9, 10, 11, 12, 13, 14, 15, 16, 17, 18, 19, 20; CelCen; CyAG; DcAmB; DcBiPP; Drake; EncAAH; EncAB-H 1974, 1996; EncSoH; FacPr 89, 93; GoodHs; HarEnUS; HealPre; InWom, SUP; LegTOT; LinLib L, S; McGEWB; NatCAB 6; NotAW; OxCAmH; OxCAmL 65, 83; OxCSupC; PolPar; PresAR; RComAH; REn; REnAL; TwCBDA; VicePre; WebAB 74, 79; WhAm HS; WhAmP; WhCiWar; WhDW; WorAl; WorAlBi*

Tyler, Liv
American. Actor
Appeared in *Silent Fall,* 1994.
b. Jul 1, 1977 in New York, New York
Source: *LegTOT*

Tyler, Parker
American. Poet, Critic
Wrote *The Young and Evil,* 1933; *Chaplin,* 1948; *Classics of the Foreign Film,* 1962.
b. Mar 6, 1907 in New Orleans, Louisiana
d. Jul 24, 1974 in New York, New York
Source: *AmAu&B; BenetAL 91; BioIn 4, 10, 14; ChhPo; ConAu 5NR, 5R, 49; GayLL; OxCFilm; REnAL; TwCA SUP*

Tyler, Richard
Australian. Fashion Designer
Started Richard Tyler collection with wife Lisa Trafficante, late 1980s, opened Los Angeles showroom, Tyler Trafficante, 1988.
b. Sep 22, 1950 in Sunshine, Australia
Source: *WhoAm 97; WhoWor 97*

Tyler, Steven
[Aerosmith; Steven Tallarico]
American. Musician, Singer
Vocalist with heavy-metal band since 1970; hit album *Toys in the Attic,* 1975, went platinum.
b. Mar 26, 1948 in Yonkers, New York
Source: *BkPepl; CurBio 96; LegTOT; WhoAm 95, 96, 97; WhoRocM 82*

Tyler, Wat
English. Revolutionary
Lead Peasant's Revolt, 1381, against Richard II; was killed after demands were met; Richard II revoked agreement.
d. 1381 in Smithfield, England
Source: *BioIn 7; BlmGEL; DcAmSR; DcBiPP; DcNaB; EncRev; LinLib S; LngCEL; NewCol 75; OxCEng 85, 95; WhDW*

Tylor, Edward Bennett, Sir
English. Anthropologist
Founder of modern anthropology; developed theory of animism in *Primitive Culture,* 1871.
b. Oct 2, 1832 in London, England
d. Jan 2, 1917 in Wellington, England
Source: *DcBiPP; DcEnA; NamesHP; WhDW*

Tynan, Kenneth Peacock
English. Critic, Author
Reviewer for *London Observer,* 1954-58, 1960-63; wrote musical *Oh! Calcutta,* 1969.
b. Apr 2, 1927 in Birmingham, England
d. Jul 26, 1980 in Santa Monica, California
Source: *Benet 87, 96; BiE&WWA; BlueB 76; ConAu 13R, 101; CroCD; CurBio 63, 80; DcArts; DcLEL 1940; DcNaB 1971; IntAu&W 76, 77; IntWW 74, 77, 78, 79, 80; LngCTC; ModBrL; NewC; NotNAT; OxCEng 85, 95; OxCThe 83; PenC ENG; Who 74; WhoThe 77; WhoWor 74, 78, 80; WorAu 1950; WrDr 76*

Tyndale, William
[William Hutchins; William Tindale]
English. Translator
Translated New Testament into English, 1525; basis for King James version.
b. 1484? in Gloucester, England
d. Oct 6, 1536 in Antwerp, Belgium
Source: *Alli; BritAu; CasWL; Chambr 1; CroE&S; DcBiPP; DcEnA; DcEnL; DcEuL; DcLEL; EvLB; LngCEL; NewC; NewCol 75; OxCEng 67; PenC ENG; REn; WebBD 83; WebE&AL*

Tyndall, John
English. Physicist, Author
Helped popularize science; his experiments showed why the sky is the color blue; wrote *On Radiation,* 1865.
b. Aug 2, 1820 in Leighlin Bridge, Ireland
d. Dec 4, 1893 in Hindhead, England
Source: *Alli, SUP; AsBiEn; Baker 78, 84; BbD; BiD&SB; BiDIrW; BiDTran; BiESc; BiHiMed; BioIn 1, 2, 6, 8, 9, 10, 12, 14; BritAu 19; CamDcSc; CamGLE; CelCen; Chambr 3; CyEd; DcBiPP; DcEnA; DcEnL; DcIrB 78, 88; DcIrW 2; DcNaB; DcScB; EvLB; InSci; LarDcSc; LinLib L, S; LuthC 75; McGEWB; NewCBEL; OxCEng 67, 85, 95; WorAl; WorAlBi; WorScD*

Tyne, George
American. Actor, Director
Directed TV shows: "Sanford and Son," 1972-77; "The Ghost and Mrs. Muir," 1968-70.
b. Aug 6, 1917 in Philadelphia, Pennsylvania
Source: *VarWW 85; WhoAm 80, 82; WhoHol 92*

Tyner, McCoy Alfred
American. Pianist, Composer
Jazz recording artist; member of John Coltrane Quartet 1960-65.
b. Dec 11, 1938 in Philadelphia, Pennsylvania
Source: *Baker 84; BiDJaz; BioIn 12, 13, 16; ConMus 7; NewAmDM; NewGrDA 86; NewGrDJ 88; PenEncP; WhoBlA 92*

Typhoid Mary
[Mary Mallon]
American. Cook
Immune to typhoid fever, but carried virus during NY epidemics, 1904, 1914.
b. 1870
d. Nov 11, 1938 in New York, New York
Source: *BioIn 5; GoodHs; InWom SUP; LegTOT; LibW; WebAB 74, 79; WorAl; WorAlBi*

Tyrrell, James, Sir
English. Courtier
Sir Thomas More claimed he was responsible for murders of Edward V, brother Richard.
d. May 6, 1502 in London, England
Source: *BioIn 3, 11; DcNaB; NewC*

Tyrrell, Joseph Burr
Canadian. Geologist
Pioneered in Canadian metal mining, mineral findings; discovered Kirkland Lake gold deposits, 1900s.
b. Nov 1, 1858 in Weston, Ontario, Canada
d. Aug 26, 1957 in Toronto, Ontario, Canada
Source: *BioIn 1, 2, 4, 5, 11, 12; DcScB; InSci; LarDcSc; MacDCB 78; OxCCan; RAdv 14; WhLit; WhNAA*

Tyrrell, Susan
American. Actor
Oscar nominee for *Fat City,* 1972.
b. 1946 in San Francisco, California

Source: *ConTFT 6; FilmEn; HalFC 80, 84, 88; IntMPA 75, 76, 77, 78, 79, 80, 81, 82, 84, 86, 88, 92, 94, 96; ItaFilm; NewYTBE 72; WhoHol 92, A*

Tyson, Cicely
[Mrs. Miles Davis]
American. Actor
Won Emmy, 1973, for "The Autobiography of Miss Jane Pitman"; star of film, *Sounder*, 1972.
b. Dec 19, 1939 in New York, New York
Source: *BioIn 9, 10, 11, 12, 13, 14, 15, 16; BlksAmF; BlkWAm; CelR 90; CurBio 75; DrBlPA, 90; GoodHs; GrLiveH; HalFC 84, 88; InB&W 85; IntMPA 86, 92; InWom SUP; MovMk; NegAl 89; NewYTBE 72; NotBlAW 1; NotNAT; NotWoAT; WhoAm 86, 90; WhoAmW 85, 87, 91; WhoBlA 85, 92; WhoEnt 92; WhoHol A; WhoThe 81; WorAlBi*

Tyson, Don
American. Business Executive
President, Tyson Foods, 1956-67, chairman and CEO, 1967-95.
b. Apr 21, 1930 in Olathe, Kansas
Source: *Dun&B 86, 88, 90; News 95, 95-3; St&PR 75, 84, 87, 91, 93; WhoFI 74*

Tyson, Ian
[Ian and Sylvia]
Canadian. Singer, Songwriter
Former rodeo performer; played blues, folk material; formed duo, 1959.
b. Sep 25, 1933 in Victoria, British Columbia, Canada
Source: *BiDAmM; BioIn 8, 10, 14, 16, 20, 21; DcCAr 81; TwCPaSc; WhoRocM 82*

Tyson, Laura D'Andrea
American. Economist, Government Official
Chm., President's Council of Economic Advisors, 1993-95; chair, National Economics Council, 1995—.
b. Jun 28, 1947 in Bayonne, New Jersey
Source: *AmEA 74; AmMWSc 78S; BioIn 18, 19, 20, 21; CurBio 96; News 94, 94-1; NewYTBS 93; WhoAm 95, 96, 97; WhoAmW 95, 97; WhoE 95; WhoFI 96; WhoScEn 96; WhoWor 96, 97*

Tyson, Mike
American. Boxer
Youngest heavyweight champion ever, defeating defending WBC champ, Trevor Berbick, Nov 1986; lost championship to "Buster" Douglas, Feb 1990; sentenced to 6-year prison term for the rape of Desiree Washington, 1992.
b. Jun 1, 1966 in New York, New York
Source: *AfrAmSG; AmDec 1980; BioIn 16; CelR 90; ConNews 86-4; CurBio 88; IntWW 91; LegTOT; NegAl 89; NewYTBS 86, 91; WhoAfA 96; WhoAm 90; WhoBlA 92, 94; WhoSpor; WhoWor 89; WorAlBi*

Tyson, Sylvia Fricker
[Ian and Sylvia; Mrs. Ian Tyson]
Canadian. Singer, Songwriter
With husband formed folksinging country duo; hits include "You Were on My Mind," 1964.
b. Sep 19, 1940 in Chatham, Ontario, Canada
Source: *ASCAP 80; WhoRocM 82*

Tyus, Wyomia
American. Track Athlete
Sprinter; first woman to win gold medal in 100 meters twice, 1964, 1968 Olympics.
b. Aug 29, 1945 in Griffin, Georgia
Source: *AfrAmBi 1; BiDAmSp OS; BioIn 10, 11, 15, 16, 17, 19, 21; BlkAmWO; BlkOlyM; InB&W 80, 85; InWom SUP; NotBlAW 2; WhoAfA 96; WhoBlA 77, 80, 85, 88, 90, 92, 94; WhoSpor; WhoTr&F 73; WorAl; WorAlBi*

Tyzack, Margaret Maud
English. Actor
Noted for work on London stage; plays include *Mornings at Seven*, 1984; a lso on TV, films.
b. Sep 9, 1931
Source: *FilmgC; HalFC 84, 88; Who 82, 83, 85, 88, 90, 92, 94; WhoHol A; WhoThe 72, 81*

Tzara, Tristan
Romanian. Author, Poet
Leader of Dada movement in French literature; edited *Dada* magazine, 1916-20.
b. Apr 4, 1896 in Moinesti, Romania
d. Dec 24, 1963 in Paris, France
Source: *Benet 87, 96; BiDMoPL; BioIn 4, 6, 8, 9, 10, 11, 12, 17; CasWL; ClDMEL 80; ConAu 153; ConLC 47; DcTwCCu 2; EncWL 2, 3; EvEuW; FacFETw; LiExTwC; MakMC; ModFrL; ModWD; OxCFr; PenC EUR; REn; TwCWr; WhE&EA; WhoTwCL; WorAlBi; WorAu 1950*

Tz'u Hsi
Chinese. Ruler
Empress Dowager 1861-1908, who resisted foreign encroachment, modernization; last great Manchu leader.
b. Nov 29, 1835 in Beijing, China
d. Nov 14, 1908 in Beijing, China
Source: *McGEWB; NewCol 75; WhDW*

U

U2
[Adam Clayton; David Howell "The Edge" Evans; Paul "Bono Vox" Hewson; Larry Mullen, Jr.]
Irish. Music Group
Rock band; albums include *War,* 1983; Grammy winner *The Joshua Tree,*2 1987.
Source: *CelR 90; ConMus 2, 12; DcArts; EncPR&S 89; EncRk 88; EncRkSt; HarEnR 86; NewAmDM; OxCPMus; PenEncP; RkOn 85; RolSEnR 83; WhsNW 85*

UB 40
[James Brown; Ali Campbell; Robin Campbell; Earl Falconer; Norman Hassan; Brian Travers; Michael Virture; Terence "Astro" Wilson]
English. Music Group
Reggae group formed 1978; named for number of British unemployment benefits card.
Source: *Alli, SUP; BbtC; BiDLA; BioIn 15, 16, 17, 18, 20; BlkAmP; BlkAmWO; BlkAWP; CabMA; ChhPo; ConAu 151; ConMuA 80A; ConMus 4; DcBrBI; DcNAA; DrAPF 80, 83, 85, 87, 89, 91, 93, 97; DrRegL 75; Dun&B 88, 90; EncPR&S 89; EncRk 88; FolkA 87; HarEnR 86; InB&W 80; Law&B 84; LesBEnT 92; MedHR; NewYTBS 84, 92; PenEncP; RkOn 85; SmATA 85; Who 83S; WhoAfA 96; WhoAmA 80, 82, 84, 86, 89, 91, 93; WhoAmP 85; WhoBlA 80, 85; WhoRocM 82; WhoScEu 91-1; WhsNW 85*

Ubell, Earl
American. Broadcast Journalist
Health editor *Parade* mag., 1983—; director TV news, NBC News, 1972-76.
b. Jun 21, 1926 in New York, New York
Source: *BioIn 5, 9; ConAu 37R; SmATA 4; St&PR 96, 97; WhoAm 74, 76, 78, 80, 82, 84, 86, 88, 90, 92, 94, 95, 96, 97; WhoUSWr 88; WhoWrEP 89, 92, 95*

Uccello, Paolo
[Paolo di Dono]
Italian. Artist
Developed foreshortening, linear perspective: *Rout of San Romano,* 1450s.
b. 1396 in Florence, Italy
d. Dec 10, 1475 in Florence, Italy
Source: *AtlBL; BioIn 14, 19; DcBiPP; DcCathB; REn; WhDW*

Uchida, Mitsuko
Japanese. Pianist
Japanese Suntory Music Award for outstanding contribution to interntional music in Japan, 1987.
b. Dec 20, 1948 in Tokyo, Japan
Source: *Baker 92; BioIn 16; CurBio 91; IntWW 89, 91, 93; IntWWM 90; News 89-3; NewYTBS 88; NotTwCP; PenDiMP*

Udall, Mo(rris King)
American. Politician
Sought Dem. presidential nomination, 1976; keynote speaker, Dem. Nat. Convention, 1980; congressman from AZ, 1970s.
b. Jun 15, 1922 in Saint Johns, Arizona
Source: *AlmAP 88, 92; BiDrAC; BiDrUSC 89; BioIn 8, 9, 10, 11, 12, 13, 16; BioNews 74; BlueB 76; CngDr 85, 87, 89; ConAu 45; CurBio 69; IntWW 91; NewYTBS 80; PolsAm 84; REnAW; WhoAm 74, 76, 78, 80, 82, 84, 86, 88, 90, 92, 94, 95, 96; WhoAmL 79; WhoAmP 73, 75, 77, 79, 81, 83, 85, 87, 89, 91, 93, 95; WhoE 95; WhoGov 72, 75, 77; WhoWest 74, 76, 78, 80, 82, 84, 87, 89, 92, 94; WorAl; WorAlBi*

Udall, Nicholas
English. Dramatist
Wrote *Ralph Roister Doister,* first complete English comedy, c. 1553.
b. 1505 in Hampshire, England
d. Dec 1556 in London, England
Source: *Alli; BbD; BiD&SB; BiDRP&D; BioIn 3, 4, 5, 7, 11, 12, 16; BlmGEL; BritAu; CamGEL; CamGLE; CamGWoT; CasWL; CmMedTh; CnThe; CroE&S; CrtSuDr; CyWA 58; DcArts; DcEnA; DcEnL; DcEuL; DcLEL; DcNaB; EncWT; Ent; EvLB; GrWrEL DR; LngCEL; McGEWD 72, 84; NewC; NewCBEL; NotNAT B; OxCEng 67, 85; OxCThe 67, 83; PenC ENG; REn; WebE&AL*

Udall, Stewart Lee
American. Government Official
Secretary of Interior, 1961-69; brother of Morris.
b. Jan 31, 1920 in Saint Johns, Arizona
Source: *AmAu&B; BiDrAC; BiDrUSC 89; BiDrUSE 71, 89; BioIn 5, 6, 7, 8, 9, 10, 11, 12; ConAu 69; CurBio 61; EncAAH; IntWW 74, 75, 76, 77, 78, 79, 80, 81, 82, 83, 89, 91, 93; LinLib L, S; NewYTBS 93; REnAW; WhoAm 74, 76, 78, 80, 82, 84, 86, 88; WhoWor 78; WorAl; WorAlBi*

Udet, Ernst
German. Aviator
Stunt flier who shot down 62 planes during WW I; killed while experimenting with "new weapon."
b. Apr 26, 1896 in Frankfurt am Main, Germany
d. Nov 17, 1941
Source: *BioIn 5, 8, 11, 12, 14, 16; EncTR, 91; HisEWW; InSci; ObitOF 79; WhoMilH 76; WhWW-II*

Udry, Janice May
American. Children's Author
Writings include *Danny's Pig,* 1960; *The Sunflower Garden,* 1969.
b. Jun 14, 1928 in Jacksonville, Illinois
Source: *AuBYP 2, 3; BkP; ConAu 5R; SmATA 4; ThrBJA; WrDr 92*

Ueberroth, Peter Victor
American. Businessman, Baseball Executive
Pres., LA Olympic Organizing Committee, 1979-84; succeeded Bowie Kuhn as baseball commissioner, 1984-89, succeeded by A Bartlett Giamatti.
b. Sep 2, 1937 in Evansville, Illinois
Source: *Ballpl 90; BiDAmSp OS; BioIn 13, 14, 15, 16; CurBio 85; EncWB;*

IntWW 91; NewYTBS 84; St&PR 75; WhoAm 86, 88, 92; WorAlBi

Uecker, Bob
[Robert George Uecker]
American. Baseball Player, Actor
Catcher, 1962-67, known for beer commercials, starring role in TV series "Mr. Belvedere," 1984-90.
b. Jan 26, 1935 in Milwaukee, Wisconsin
Source: *Ballpl 90; BioIn 13; LegTOT; WhoAm 86, 88, 90, 92, 94, 95, 96, 97; WhoEnt 92; WhoHol 92; WhoProB 73; WorAlBi*

Ufer, Walter
American. Artist
Painter known for his Indian portraits and southwestern landscapes.
b. Jul 22, 1876 in Louisville, Kentucky
d. Aug 2, 1936 in Santa Fe, New Mexico
Source: *ArtsAmW 1; BioIn 1, 9, 11, 14; IlBEAAW; WhAm 1; WhAmArt 85*

UFO
[Neil Carter; Paul Chapman; Phil Mogg; Andy Parker; Michael Schenker; Pete Way]
British. Music Group
Formed 1971; hard-rock band whose hits include *The Wild, the Willing, and the Innocent,* 1982.
Source: *ConMuA 80A; EncRk 88; HarEnR 86; IlEncRk; PenEncP; RolSEnR 83; WhAmArt 85; WhoRock 81; WhoRocM 82*

Uggams, Leslie (Marian Crayne)
American. Singer, Actor
Won Tony for *Hallelujah Baby,* 1968; played Kizzy in TV epic, "Roots," 1977.
b. May 25, 1943 in New York, New York
Source: *AfrAmAl 6; BiDAfM; BiDAmM; BioIn 6, 7, 8, 11, 14; BlksAmF; CelR, 90; ConTFT 6; CurBio 67; DcTwCCu 5; DrBlPA, 90; EncMT; FilmgC; HalFC 84, 88; InB&W 85; IntMPA 75, 76, 77, 78, 79, 80, 81, 82, 84, 86, 88, 92, 94, 96; InWom, SUP; LegTOT; NegAl 76, 83, 89; NewAmDM; NewYTBS 86; NotBlAW 2; NotNAT; WhoAfA 96; WhoAm 74, 76, 78, 80, 82, 84, 86, 88, 90, 92, 94, 95; WhoAmW 68, 70, 74, 75, 81, 83, 95, 97; WhoBlA 75, 77, 80, 85, 88, 90, 92, 94; WhoEnt 92; WhoHol 92, A; WorAl; WorAlBi*

Uhde, Hermann
German. Opera Singer
Noted bass-baritone, noted for Wagnerian roles; died on stage.
b. Jul 20, 1914 in Bremen, Germany
d. Oct 10, 1965 in Copenhagen, Denmark
Source: *Baker 84, 92; BioIn 7; CmOp; MetOEnc; NewEOp 71; NewGrDM 80; NewGrDO; OxDcOp; PenDiMP; WhAm 4*

Uhlman, Wes(ley Carl)
American. Politician, Lawyer
Mayor of Seattle, 1970-78.
b. Mar 13, 1935 in Cashmere, Washington
Source: *WhoAm 84; WhoAmP 73, 75, 77, 79, 81, 83, 85, 87, 89, 91, 93, 95; WhoGov 77; WhoWest 74, 80*

Uhnak, Dorothy
American. Author
Crime novels include *The Ledger,* 1970.
b. 1933 in New York, New York
Source: *AmWomWr; ArtclWW 2; AuNews 1; BioIn 13, 14; ConAu 29NR, 81; EncMys; FemiCLE; GrWomMW; IntAu&W 91, 93; InWom SUP; NewYTBE 71; NewYTBS 81; Novels; ThrtnMM; TwCCr&M 80, 85, 91; WrDr 76, 82, 84, 86, 88, 90, 92, 94, 96*

Uhry, Alfred
American. Dramatist
Won 1988 Pulitzer for first play, *Driving Miss Daisy.*
b. 1937?
Source: *BioIn 16; ConAu 127, 133; ConLC 55; OxCAmL 95; WhoAm 90; WhoEnt 92; WhoWor 91; WrDr 92*

Ukrainka, Lesia
[Larisa Kvitka-Kosach]
Russian. Poet
Wrote collection of poems *On the Wings of Song,* 1892; play *Cassandra,* 1908.
b. 1871 in Ukraine, Russia
d. 1913
Source: *NewCol 75*

Ulanova, Galina
Russian. Dancer
Retired from Russian ballet to teach; appeared on film, 1950s.
b. Jan 10, 1910 in Saint Petersburg, Russia
Source: *BiDD; BiDSovU; BioIn 3, 4, 5, 6, 10, 14, 17; CnOxB; ContDcW 89; CurBio 58; DancEn 78; DcArts; FacFETw; IntDcB; IntDcWB; IntWW 83, 91; InWom SUP; NewGrDM 80; RAdv 14; WhDW; Who 85, 92; WhoAmW 66, 68, 70, 72; WhoHol A; WhoWor 74; WorAlBi*

Ulbricht, Walter
German. Political Leader
Member, People's Chamber, 1949-73; chm., Council of State of German Democratic Republic, 1960-73.
b. Jun 30, 1893 in Leipzig, Germany
d. Aug 1, 1973 in Berlin, German Democratic Republic
Source: *BioIn 6, 7, 8, 9, 10, 14, 18, 20; ColdWar 1, 2; ConAu 113; CurBio 52, 73, 73N; DcTwHis; DicTyr; EncCW; EncGRNM; EncRev; EncTR 91; FacFETw; HisEWW; HisWorL; McGEWB; NewYTBE 73; ObitT 1971; OxCGer 76, 86; WhAm 5; WhDW; WhoGov 72; WorAl; WorAlBi*

Ulibarri, Sabine (Reyes)
American. Writer
Published collection of poetry *Al cielo se sube a pie,* 1961; also published several collections of short stories.
b. Sep 21, 1919 in Santa Fe, New Mexico
Source: *ChiLit; ConAu 105; ConLC 83; DrAS 74F, 78F, 82F; HispAmA*

Ullman, Al(bert Conrad)
American. Politician
Dem. congressman from OR, 1956-81.
b. Mar 9, 1914 in Great Falls, Montana
d. Oct 11, 1986 in Bethesda, Maryland
Source: *AlmAP 78, 80; BiDrAC; BiDrUSC 89; BioIn 10, 15; BioNews 75; BlueB 76; CngDr 74, 77, 79; CurBio 75, 87, 87N; IntWW 78, 79, 80, 81, 82, 83; NewYTBS 74; WhAm 9; WhoAm 74, 76, 78, 80, 82, 84, 86; WhoAmP 73, 75, 77, 79, 81, 83, 85; WhoGov 72, 75, 77; WhoWest 74; WorAl*

Ullman, James Ramsey
American. Author
Wrote books about mountaineering: *Kingdom of Everest,* 1947.
b. Nov 24, 1907 in New York, New York
d. Jun 20, 1971 in Boston, Massachusetts
Source: *AmAu&B; Au&Wr 71; AuBYP 2, 3; BenetAL 91; BioIn 1, 2, 4, 7, 9, 10, 11, 14; ConAu 1R, 3NR, 29R; CurBio 45, 71; FourBJA; LngCTC; NatCAB 56; NewYTBE 71; REn; REnAL; ScF&FL 1, 2; SmATA 7; TwCA SUP; WhAm 5; WhNAA*

Ullman, Norm(an Victor Alexander)
Canadian. Hockey Player
Center, 1955-77, mostly with Detroit, Toronto; scored 490 goals in NHL; Hall of Fame, 1982.
b. Dec 26, 1935 in Provost, Alberta, Canada
Source: *HocEn; WhoAm 74, 76; WhoHcky 73*

Ullman, Tracey
English. Actor
First American hit "They Don't Know," 1984; star of TV show "The Tracey Ullman Show," 1986-90; films include *I Love You to Death,* 1990.
b. Dec 30, 1959 in Slough, England
Source: *BioIn 14, 15, 16; CelR 90; ConTFT 4, 9; CurBio 88; EncRk 88; IntMPA 92, 94, 96; IntWW 93; LegTOT; NewYTBS 89; PenEncP; RkOn 85; WhoAm 90, 92, 94, 95, 96, 97; WhoAmW 91, 93, 95, 97; WhoCom; WhoEnt 92; WhoHol 92; WhoWor 91*

Ullmann, Liv (Johanne)
[Mrs. Donald Saunders]
Norwegian. Actor
Star of Ingmar Bergman films; goodwill ambassador, UNICEF, 1980—.
b. Dec 16, 1938 in Tokyo, Japan
Source: *BiDFilm; BioIn 13, 14, 16; BioNews 74; CelR 90; ConAu 102;*

ContDcW 89; ConTFT 3; CurBio 73; EncEurC; HalFC 84, 88; IntDcWB; IntMPA 84, 86, 92; IntWW 76, 77, 78, 79, 80, 81, 82, 83, 89, 91, 93; InWom SUP; LegTOT; MovMk; NewYTBE 72; NewYTBS 82; Who 82, 83, 85, 88, 90, 92, 94; WhoAm 84, 86, 88, 90, 92, 94, 95, 96, 97; WhoEnt 92; WhoHol 92, A; WhoWor 87, 89, 91, 93, 95, 96; WorAlBi

Ullstein, Hermann
German. Publisher
Partner, Ullstein Publisher, which was taken over by Nazis.
b. 1875
d. Nov 23, 1943 in New York, New York
Source: *ConAu 116; CurBio 44; ObitOF 79*

Ulmer, James
"Blood"
American. Musician
Sound based on blues, hard rock, avant-garde jazz; albums include *Free Lancing,* 1982.
b. Feb 2, 1942 in Saint Matthews, South Carolina
Source: *BiDJaL; BiDJaz; BioIn 12, 15; InB&W 85; NewAmDM; NewGrDA 86; NewGrDJ 88, 94; PenEncP; RolSEnR 83*

Ulreich, Nura Woodson
American. Illustrator
Wrote, illustrated children's book *The Kitten Who Listened,* 1950.
b. Dec 1899 in Kansas City, Missouri
d. 1950
Source: *IlsBYP; IlsCB 1744, 1946; InWom; PenNWW A*

Ulric, Lenore
American. Actor
Played in *Tiger Rose; Camille; Intrigue.*
b. Jul 21, 1894 in New Ulm, Minnesota
d. Dec 30, 1970 in Orangeburg, New York
Source: *BiE&WWA; FamA&A; Film 1; FilmgC; InWom; MotPP; MovMk; NewYTBE 70; ObitOF 79; ThFT; TwYS; WhScrn 74, 77*

Ulrichs, Karl Heinrich
German. Writer
Played an early role in the fight for gay rights in Germany; came out with his own scientific theories defenging his sexuality, 1862.
b. Aug 28, 1825, Germany
d. Jul 14, 1895
Source: *BioIn 20; GayLesB; HumSex*

Ulvaeus, Bjorn
Swedish. Singer, Musician
With group since 1973; hits include "Dancing Queen," 1977; "Take a Chance on Me," 1978.
b. Apr 25, 1945 in Stockholm, Sweden
Source: *RolSEnR 83*

Umberto II
[Umberto Nicola Giovanni Maria of Savoy]
Italian. Ruler
Italy's last king; reigned May 9-Jun 2, 1946; monarchy abolished by Mussolini.
b. Sep 15, 1904 in Racconigi, Italy
d. Mar 18, 1983 in Geneva, Switzerland
Source: *CurBio 43, 83N; NewYTBS 83*

Umeki, Miyoshi
Japanese. Singer, Actor
Films include *Flower Drum Song,* 1961; won Oscar for *Sayonara,* 1957.
b. Apr 3, 1929 in Holdaido, Japan
Source: *BioIn 5, 6, 9; FilmEn; FilmgC; ForYSC; HalFC 80, 84, 88; InWom SUP; LegTOT; MotPP; MovMk; VarWW 85; WhoHol 92, A; WorAl*

Unamuno (y Jugo), Miguel de
Spanish. Philosopher, Author
Major work *The Tragic Sense of Life in Men and Nations,* 1913.
b. Sep 29, 1864 in Bilbao, Spain
d. Dec 31, 1936 in Salamanca, Spain
Source: *AtlBL; Benet 87, 96; BioIn 1, 2, 3, 4, 5, 6, 7, 8, 9, 10, 12, 14, 16, 17; CasWL; ClDMEL 47, 80; CnMD; CnMWL; ConAu 104, 131; CyWA 89; DcAmC; DcArts; DcHiB; DcLB 108; DcSpL; Dis&D; EncUnb; EncWL 2, 3; EncWT; EuWr 8; EvEuW; GrFLW; HispLC; HispWr; IlEncMy; LiExTwC; LinLib L; LngCTC; LuthC 75; MajTwCW; MakMC; McGEWB; McGEWD 72, 84; ModRL; ModSpP S; ModWD; NewCBEL; Novels; OxCEng 67, 95; OxCSpan; OxCThe 67; PenC EUR; RAdv 14, 13-2; REn; RfGShF; RfGWoL 95; ShSCr 11; TwCA, SUP; TwCLC 2, 9; TwCWr; WhDW; WhoTwCL; WorAl; WorAlBi; WrPh*

Underhill, Evelyn
English. Author
Through her lectures and works furthered the development and acceptance of mystical theology.
b. Dec 6, 1875 in Wolverhampton, England
d. Jun 15, 1941 in London, England
Source: *ArtclWW 2; BioIn 1, 2, 5, 10, 11, 12, 16, 17, 19; Chambr 3; ContDcW 89; DcLEL; DcNaB 1941; DivFut; EncBrWW; EvLB; FemiCLE; IntDcWB; InWom; LngCTC; LuthC 75; NewC; NewCBEL; OxCCanL; OxCEng 85, 95; REn; ScF&FL 1; TwCA, SUP; TwCWr; WhE&EA; WhLit; WomNov*

Underwood, Blair
American. Actor
Appeared on TV's "L.A. Law," 1987-94; won NAACP Image Award, 1994.
b. Aug 25, 1964 in Tacoma, Washington
Source: *AfrAmBi 2; ConBlB 7; DrBlPA 90; IntMPA 94, 96; LegTOT; WhoAfA 96; WhoBlA 92, 94; WhoHol 92*

Underwood, John Thomas
American. Manufacturer
Introduced Underwood typewriter, 1897.
b. Apr 12, 1857 in London, England
d. Jul 2, 1937 in Wianno, Massachusetts
Source: *BiDAmBL 83; BioIn 4; DcAmB S2; NatCAB 29; WhAm 4, HSA*

Underwood, Oscar Wilder
American. Government Official
Dem. senator from AL, 1914-27.
b. May 6, 1862 in Louisville, Kentucky
d. Jan 25, 1929 in Fairfax County, Virginia
Source: *AmBi; AmPolLe; ApCAB SUP, X; BiDrAC; BiDrUSC 89; BioIn 4, 8, 12, 15; DcAmB; DcNAA; EncAAH; EncAB-H 1974; EncSoH; FacFETw; NatCAB 12, 21; TwCBDA; WebAB 74, 79; WhAm 1; WhAmP*

Undset, Sigrid
Norwegian. Author
Won Nobel Prize in literature, 1928; wrote three-vol. historical novel, *Kristin Lavransatter,* 1922.
b. May 20, 1882 in Kalundborg, Denmark
d. Jun 10, 1949 in Lillehammer, Norway
Source: *AtlBL; AuBYP 2, 3; Benet 87, 96; BioIn 1, 2, 3, 4, 5, 7, 8, 9, 10, 11, 12, 14, 15, 17, 20; BlmGWL; CasWL; CathA 1930; ClDMEL 47, 80; ConAu 104, 129; ContDcW 89; CurBio 40, 49; CyWA 58; DcArts; DcCathB; DcScanL; EncCoWW; EncWL 2, 3; EuWr 9; EvEuW; FacFETw; FemiWr; GoodHs; GrFLW; GrWomW; InWom, SUP; LadLa 86; LegTOT; LiExTwC; LinLib L, S; LngCTC; MajTwCW; McGEWB; ModWoWr; NobelP; Novels; OxCEng 67; PenC EUR; RAdv 14, 13-2; REn; RfGWoL 95; TwCA, SUP; TwCLC 3; TwCWr; WhAm 2; WhoNob, 90, 95; WomFir; WorAl; WorAlBi; WorLitC*

Ungaretti, Giuseppe
Italian. Poet
Themes of personal sorrow, grief are based on self: *Il Dolore,* 1946.
b. Feb 10, 1887 in Alexandria, Egypt
d. Jun 1, 1970 in Milan, Italy
Source: *CasWL; ClDMEL 47; CnMWL; ConAu P-2; ConLC 7, 15; EncWL; EvEuW; ModRL; NewYTBE 70; PenC EUR; REn; TwCWr; WhoTwCL; WorAu 1950*

Ungaro, Emanuel Matteotti
French. Fashion Designer
Avant-garde designs are noted for print patterns, flowers, abstracts.
b. Feb 13, 1933 in Aix-en-Provence, France
Source: *BioIn 9, 14, 15, 16; ConDes 90; CurBio 80; DcTwDes; EncFash; IntWW 91, 93; WhoAm 96; WhoFash 88; WhoWor 91, 93, 95, 96; WorFshn*

Unger, Caroline
Austrian. Opera Singer
Contralto known for turning Beethoven around to see audience applause after

first performance of ninth symphony, 1824.
b. Oct 28, 1803 in Vienna, Austria
d. Mar 23, 1877 in Florence, Italy
Source: *Baker 78, 84, 92; CmOp; InWom; MetOEnc; NewEOp 71; NewGrDM 80; OxDcOp*

Unger, Garry Douglas
"Iron Man"
Canadian. Hockey Player
Center, 1967-83; held NHL record for consecutive games played (914, from 1968-79) until broken by Doug Jarvis, 1986.
b. Dec 7, 1947 in Edmonton, Alberta, Canada
Source: *HocEn; WhoAm 74, 76, 78, 80, 82, 84; WhoHcky 73*

Unger, Irwin
American. Educator, Historian
Won Pulitzer for history, 1965; writings include *The Vulnerable Years: The United States, 1896-1917.*
b. May 2, 1927 in New York, New York
Source: *ConAu 7NR, 9R; DrAS 74H, 78H, 82H; EncAAH; OxCAmL 65; WhoAm 74, 76, 78, 80, 82, 84, 86, 88, 90, 92, 94, 95, 96, 97*

Ungerer, Tomi
[Jean Thomas Ungerer]
French. Children's Author, Illustrator
Writings include *Moon Man,* 1967; *The Joy of Frogs,* 1985.
b. Nov 28, 1931 in Strasbourg, France
Source: *AmAu&B; Au&Wr 71; AuBYP 2, 3; BioIn 5, 7, 8, 9, 10, 11, 12, 13, 14, 16, 19; BkP; ChhPo; ChlBkCr; ChlLR 3; ConAu 41R, X; FamAIYP; IlsCB 1957; IntAu&W 77; LinLib L; OxCChiL; SmATA 5; ThrBJA; TwCChW 78, 83, 89, 95; Who 90, 92, 94; WhoAm 86, 88; WhoGrA 62, 82; WhoUSWr 88; WhoWrEP 89*

Unitas, Johnny
[John Constantine Unitas]
American. Football Player
Quarterback, 1956-73, mostly with Baltimore; holds many NFL passing records, including most 300-yd. passing games, 27; MVP, three times; Hall of Fame, 1979.
b. May 7, 1933 in Pittsburgh, Pennsylvania
Source: *BiDAmSp FB; BioIn 13, 16, 17, 20; BioNews 74; CurBio 62; FacFETw; LegTOT; NewYTBE 71; NewYTBS 74; WebAB 79; WhoAm 74, 76, 78, 80, 82, 84, 86, 88, 90, 92; WhoFtbl 74; WhoSpor; WorAlBi*

Unkelbach, Kurt
American. Children's Author
Books on cats, dogs include *Uncle Charlie's Poodle,* 1975; wrote *Straw Hat,* 1937, which was produced on Broadway.
b. Nov 21, 1913 in New Britain, Connecticut
Source: *ApCAB SUP; AuBYP 2S, 3; BioIn 9; ConAu 8NR, 21R; SmATA 4; WhoE 74*

Unruh, Howard B
American. Murderer
Killed 13 people in 12 minutes in Camden, NJ, Jun 9, 1949.
b. 1921? in Camden, New Jersey
Source: *BioIn 2; DrInf*

Unruh, Jesse Marvin
American. Politician
Influential CA assemblyman who aided John, Robert Kennedy presidential campaigns.
b. Sep 30, 1922 in Newton, Kansas
d. Aug 4, 1987 in Marina del Rey, California
Source: *BioIn 5, 6, 7, 8, 9, 11; CurBio 69, 87; PolProf J, K; WhAm 9; WhoAm 74, 76, 78, 80, 82, 84, 86; WhoGov 75; WhoWest 74, 84, 87*

Unseld, Wes(tley Sissel)
American. Basketball Player
Center, 1968-81, mostly with Washington; led NBA in rebounding, 1975; NBA MVP, 1969; Hall of Fame, 1988.
b. Mar 14, 1946 in Louisville, Kentucky
Source: *BasBi; BiDAmSp BK; BioIn 16; InB&W 85; LegTOT; OfNBA 87; WhoAfA 96; WhoAm 90, 92, 94, 95, 96, 97; WhoBbl 73; WhoBlA 77, 80, 85, 88, 90, 92, 94; WhoE 89, 91, 95, 97; WorAl; WorAlBi*

Unser, Al, Sr.
American. Auto Racer
One of three drivers to win Indianapolis 500 four times.
b. May 29, 1939 in Albuquerque, New Mexico
Source: *BiDAmSp OS; BioIn 9, 11, 12, 13, 14, 21; CelR; LegTOT; WhoAm 74, 76, 78, 80, 82, 84, 86, 88, 92, 94, 95, 96, 97; WhoWest 94, 96; WorAl; WorAlBi*

Unser, Al, Jr.
"Little Al"
American. Auto Racer
Raced with father for first time, 1983 Indianapolis 500; won Indianapolis 500 by .043 second, closest finish in race's history.
b. Apr 19, 1962
Source: *BioIn 13, 14, 15, 16; LegTOT; NewYTBS 83, 85*

Unser, Bobby
[Robert William Unser]
American. Auto Racer
Won Indianapolis 500, 1968, 1975, 1981.
b. Feb 20, 1934 in Albuquerque, New Mexico
Source: *BiDAmSp OS; BioIn 9, 10, 11, 12, 13; ConAu 97; LegTOT; NewYTBS 74; WhoAm 74, 76, 78, 80, 82, 84, 86, 88, 90, 92, 94, 95, 96, 97; WhoSpor; WhoWest 94; WorAl; WorAlBi*

Unsworth, Barry (Foster)
English. Author
Won Booker Prize for Fiction for *Sacred Hunger,* 1992.
b. Aug 10, 1930 in Wingate, England
Source: *BioIn 21; ConAu 25R, 30NR; ConLC 76; IntWW 93; WrDr 76, 80, 82, 84, 86, 88, 90, 92*

Unsworth, Geoffrey
English. Filmmaker
Cameraman, who won Oscar for cinematography, 1972, for *Cabaret.*
b. 1914 in London, England
d. 1978
Source: *EncEurC; FilmEn; FilmgC; HalFC 80, 84, 88; IntDcF 1-4, 2-4; ItaFilm; WorEFlm*

Untermeyer, Jean Starr
American. Author
Wrote *Growing Pains,* 1918; translated Hermann Broch's *The Death of Virgil,* 1945.
b. Mar 13, 1886 in Zanesville, Ohio
d. Jul 27, 1970 in New York, New York
Source: *AmAu&B; AmWomWr; AnMV 1926; Au&Wr 71; BenetAL 91; ChhPo, S2, S3; CnDAL; ConAmL; ConAu 29R; ForWC 70; InWom, SUP; NewYTBE 70; OhA&B; OxCAmL 65, 83, 95; REnAL; TwCA SUP; WhAm 5, 7; WhNAA; WhoAmW 58, 61, 64, 66, 68, 70, 72; WhoWorJ 72, 78*

Untermeyer, Louis
American. Author, Editor
Best known for anthologies used by colleges.
b. Oct 1, 1885 in New York, New York
d. Dec 18, 1977 in Newtown, Connecticut
Source: *AmAu&B; AmLY; AnCL; AnMV 1926; ApCAB X; Au&Wr 71; AuBYP 2, 3; Benet 87, 96; BenetAL 91; BioIn 1, 4, 5, 6, 7, 8, 9, 11, 13, 14, 15; BlueB 76; CelR; Chambr 3; ChhPo, S1, S2, S3; CnDAL; ConAmA; ConAmL; ConAu 5R, 31NR, 73; ConPo 70, 75; CurBio 67, 78N; DcAmB S10; DcLEL; EvLB; FacFETw; IntAu&W 76, 77; IntWW 74, 75, 76, 77; IntWWP 77, 82; LegTOT; LinLib L, S; LngCTC; NewYTBS 77; OxCAmL 65, 83, 95; OxCTwCP; REn; REnAL; ScF&FL 1, 2; SmATA 2, 26N, 37; TwCA, SUP; TwCWr; WhAm 7; WhNAA; Who 74; WhoAm 74, 76; WhoWorJ 72; WorAl; WorAlBi; WrDr 76*

Unwin, Stanley, Sir
English. Publisher, Author
Founder, George Allen & Unwin Ltd., book publishers, 1914.
b. Dec 19, 1884 in London, England
d. Oct 13, 1968 in London, England
Source: *BioIn 1, 2, 5, 8, 14, 18; ConAu 5R; CurBio 49, 68; DcNaB 1961; GrBr; LinLib L; LngCTC; ObitT 1961; WhAm 5; WhE&EA; WhLit*

Upchurch, John Jorden
American. Labor Union Official
Founded Ancient Order of United Workmen, 1868; forerunner of fraternal societies.
b. Mar 26, 1820 in Franklin County, North Carolina
d. Jan 18, 1887 in Steelville, Missouri
Source: *ApCAB; DcAmB; DcNAA; HarEnUS; WhAm HS*

Updike, Daniel Berkeley
American. Printer, Publisher
Known for improving typography in US; founded The Merrymount Press, Boston, 1893.
b. Feb 24, 1860 in Providence, Rhode Island
d. Dec 28, 1941 in Boston, Massachusetts
Source: *BenetAL 91; BioIn 1, 4, 10, 12; CurBio 42; DcAmBC; DcAmB S3; DcNAA; LinLib L; OxCAmL 65, 83, 95; OxCDecA; REnAL; WhAm 2; WhAmArt 85*

Updike, John (Hoyer)
American. Author
Won Pulitzer, 1981, for *Rabbit Is Rich;* National Book Critics Circle Award, Pultizer Prize, for *Rabbit at Rest,* 1990.
b. Mar 18, 1932 in Shillington, Pennsylvania
Source: *AmAu&B; AmCulL; AmWr; AnCL; Au&Wr 71; AuBYP 2, 3; Benet 87, 96; BenetAL 91; BioIn 5, 6, 7, 8, 9, 10, 11, 12, 13, 14, 15, 16; BlueB 76; BroV; CamGEL; CamGLE; CamHAL; CasWL; CelR, 90; ChhPo; ConAu 1BS, 1NR, 1R, 4NR, 33NR, 51NR; ConLC 1, 2, 3, 5, 7, 9, 13, 15, 23, 34, 43, 45, 70; ConNov 72, 76, 82, 86, 91, 96; ConPo 70, 75, 80, 85, 91, 96; ConPopW; CurBio 84; CyWA 89; DcArts; DcLB 2, 5, 143, DS3, Y80A, Y82A; DcLEL 1940; DcTwCCu 1; DrAF 76; DrAPF 80, 91; EncAB-H 1974, 1996; EncSF 93; EncWL, 2, 3; FacFETw; FolkA 87; GrWrEL N; IntAu&W 76, 77, 89, 91, 93; IntvTCA 2; IntWW 74, 75, 76, 77, 78, 79, 80, 81, 82, 83, 89, 91, 93; IntWWP 77; LegTOT; LinLib L, S; MagSAmL; MajTwCW; MakMC; ModAL, S1, S2; NewYTBS 89; Novels; OxCAmL 65, 83, 95; OxCEng 85, 95; PenC AM; RAdv 1, 14, 13-1; REn; REnAL; RfGAmL 87, 94; RfGShF; RGTwCWr; ScF&FL 1, 2, 92; ShSCr 13; ShSWr; TwCWr; WebAB 74, 79; WebE&AL; Who 74, 82, 83, 85, 88, 90, 92, 94; WhoAm 74, 76, 78, 80, 82, 84, 86, 88, 90, 92, 94, 95, 96, 97; WhoE 85, 86, 91, 93, 95, 97; WhoTwCL; WhoUSWr 88; WhoWor 74, 78, 80, 82, 84, 87, 91, 93, 95, 96, 97; WhoWrEP 89, 92, 95; WorAl; WorAlBi; WorAu 1950; WorLitC; WrDr 76, 80, 82, 84, 86, 88, 90, 92, 94, 96; WrPh*

Upjohn, Lawrence Northcote
American. Manufacturer
Pres., Upjohn Pharmaceuticals, 1930-44.
b. 1873
d. Jun 2, 1967 in Kalamazoo, Michigan
Source: *BioIn 7, 9; EncAB-A 39; NatCAB 53; ObitOF 79*

Upjohn, Richard
American. Architect
Designs include Trinity Church, NYC.
b. Jan 22, 1802 in Shaftesbury, England
d. Aug 17, 1878 in Garrison, New York
Source: *Alli; AmBi; AmCulL; ApCAB; BiDAmAr; BioIn 1, 8, 9, 15, 19; BriEAA; DcAmB; DcD&D; EncAAr 1, 2; HarEnUS; IntDcAr; LegTOT; MacEA; McGDA; McGEWB; NatCAB 2; NewYHSD; OxCAmH; OxCAmL 65; TwCBDA; WebAB 74, 79; WhAm HS; WhFla; WhoArch; WorAl; WorAlBi*

Uppman, Theodor
American. Opera Singer
Baritone, created title role in Britten's *Billy Budd,* 1951.
b. Jan 12, 1920 in San Jose, California
Source: *Baker 84, 92; BioIn 4, 6, 9, 13; CmOp; IntWWM 77, 80, 90; MetOEnc; NewAmDM; NewEOp 71; NewGrDA 86; NewGrDM 80; NewGrDO; PenDiMP; WhoAm 74, 76, 78, 80, 82, 84, 86, 88, 90, 92, 94, 95, 96, 97; WhoAmM 83; WhoEnt 92; WhoOp 76; WhoWor 74*

Upshaw, Dawn
American. Singer
Lyric soprano has performed with most outstanding orchestras and chamber groups in the US and Europe.
b. Jul 17, 1960 in Nashville, Tennessee
Source: *Baker 92; BioIn 16; ConMus 9; CurBio 90; NewGrDO; News 91, 91-2; WhoAm 92, 94, 95, 96, 97; WhoAmW 93*

Upshaw, Gene
[Eugene Upshaw]
American. Football Player, Football Executive
Guard, Los Angeles Raiders, 1967-82; exec. director, NFL Players Assn., 1980—; Hall of Fame, 1987.
b. Aug 15, 1945 in Robstown, Texas
Source: *AfrAmBi 2; AfrAmSG; BiDAmSp FB; BioIn 12, 13, 14, 15; ConNews 88-1; InB&W 80; LegTOT; WhoAfA 96; WhoAm 86, 88, 90, 94, 95, 96, 97; WhoBlA 77, 80, 85, 88, 90, 92, 94; WhoFtbl 74; WhoSpor; WhoWor 96; WorAlBi*

Upshaw, William David
American. Author, Politician
Dem. congressman from GA, 1919-27.
b. Oct 15, 1866 in Newnan, Georgia
d. Nov 21, 1952
Source: *BiDrAC; BiDrUSC 89; BiDSA; BioIn 3, 4; DcAmB S5; DcAmTB; NatCAB 41; WhAm 3; WhAmP*

Upson, Ralph Hazlett
American. Aeronautical Engineer
Chief engineer, aeronautical dept., Goodyear Tire & Rubber Co., 1914-20; produced many US balloons, airships, WW I.
b. Jun 21, 1888 in New York, New York
d. Aug 13, 1968
Source: *BioIn 8, 10; NatCAB 54; WhAm 5*

Upton, Florence Kate
English. Illustrator
Created "Golliwogg" series for children, popular, 1890s-1910.
b. Feb 22, 1873 in Flushing, New York
d. Oct 17, 1922 in London, England
Source: *BioIn 8, 14, 18, 20; DcBrAr 2; DcWomA*

Upton, Francis Robbins
American. Mathematician, Physicist
As asst. to Edison, helped with various inventions that led to the modern use of electricity.
b. 1852 in Peabody, Massachusetts
d. Mar 10, 1921 in Orange, New Jersey

Urban, Joseph Maria
Austrian. Designer, Architect
Designed the Tsar's Bridge, Leningrad, USSR; best known for interior, set designs of theaters, opera houses.
b. May 26, 1872 in Vienna, Austria
d. Jul 10, 1933 in New York, New York
Source: *AmBi; DcAmB; MacEA; OxCAmH; OxCThe 67; WebAB 74, 79; WhAm 1*

Urban II, Pope
[Odo of Lagery]
French. Religious Leader
French pope, 1088-99; launched First Crusade, 1095.
b. 1035? in Chatillon-sur-Marne, France
d. Oct 29, 1099
Source: *DcCathB; McGEWB; NewCol 75; WebBD 83; WorAl*

Ure, Mary
Scottish. Actor
Married John Osborne, Robert Shaw; films include *Sons and Lovers,* 1960.
b. Feb 18, 1933 in Glasgow, Scotland
d. Apr 3, 1975 in London, England
Source: *BiE&WWA; BioIn 9, 10; EncWT; FilmAG WE; FilmEn; FilmgC; ForYSC; HalFC 80, 84, 88; IntMPA 75; LegTOT; MotPP; MovMk; NewYTBE 72; NewYTBS 75; NotNAT B; ObitOF 79; ObitT 1971; OxCThe 83; PlP&P; WhAm 6; Who 74; WhoAmW 68, 70, 72, 74; WhoHol C; WhoWor 74; WhScrn 77, 83; WhThe*

U'Ren, William Simon
American. Statesman
Best known for bringing about direct election of senators, the direct presidential primary.
b. Jan 10, 1859 in Lancaster, Wisconsin
d. Mar 8, 1949 in Portland, Oregon
Source: *AmRef; BioIn 1, 8, 15; DcAmB S4; WebAB 74, 79; WhAm 4*

Urey, Harold Clayton
American. Chemist
Work with separation of isotopes aided in making first atomic bomb; won Nobel Prize, 1934.
b. Apr 29, 1893 in Walkerton, Indiana
d. Jan 6, 1981 in La Jolla, California
Source: *AmAu&B; AmMWSc 76P, 79; AnObit 1981; AsBiEn; BiESc; BioIn 1, 3, 5, 6, 9, 10, 11, 12, 13, 14, 15, 19, 20; CamDcSc; ConAu 102; CurBio 41, 60, 81; DcScB S2; EncAB-H 1974; IndAu 1917; InSci; IntWW 74, 75, 76, 77, 78, 79, 80, 81; LarDcSc; LinLib S; McGEWB; McGMS 80; NewYTBS 81; OxCAmH; WebAB 74, 79; WhAm 7; WhDW; Who 74, 82; WhoAm 74, 76, 78, 80; WhoAtom 77; WhoNob, 90, 95; WhoWest 78, 80, 82; WhoWor 74; WorAl; WorScD*

Uriah Heep
[Mick Box; David Byron; Ken Hensley; Al Napier; Paul Newton]
English. Music Group
Rock group whose albums include *Demons And Wizards,* 1972; not liked by critics.
Source: *ConMuA 80A; EncPR&S 74, 89; EncRk 88; HarEnR 86; IlEncRk; PenEncP; RkOn 78; RolSEnR 83; WhoRock 81; WhoRocM 82*

Urich, Robert
American. Actor
Actor has appeared on numerous TV series, including "S.W.A.T.," 1975-76 and "Spenser for Hire," 1985-88.
b. Dec 19, 1947 in Toronto, Ohio
Source: *BioIn 15, 16; ConNews 88-1; ConTFT 3; HalFC 88; IntMPA 86, 88, 92; LesBEnT 92; VarWW 85; WhoAm 86, 90, 94, 95, 96, 97; WhoEnt 92; WorAlBi*

Uris, Harold David
American. Philanthropist
With brother, Percy, financed many of NYC's skyscrapers.
b. May 26, 1905 in New York, New York
d. Mar 28, 1982 in Palm Beach, Florida
Source: *NewYTBS 82; St&PR 75; WhoAm 74, 76*

Uris, Leon Marcus
American. Author
Wrote *Exodus,* 1958; *Trinity,* 1976.
b. Aug 3, 1924 in Baltimore, Maryland
Source: *AmAu&B; Au&Wr 71; AuNews 1, 2; ConAu 1NR, 1R; ConLC 7, 32; ConNov 86; CurBio 59; IntWW 83; REn; REnAL; WebAB 79; WhoAm 86; WrDr 86*

Urquhart, Brian Edward
English. Diplomat
Served as chief aide to UN secretaries-general, 1945-85; wrote biography *Hammarskjold,* 1972.
b. Feb 28, 1919 in Bridport, England
Source: *BioIn 13, 14, 15, 16; BlueB 76; ConAu 26NR, 105; CurBio 86; IntWW 83, 91; NewYTBS 82; Who 74, 82, 83, 85, 92, 94; WhoE 83, 85, 86, 89; WhoUN 75; WhoWor 80, 82, 84, 89; WrDr 76, 80, 82, 84, 86, 88, 90, 92, 94, 96*

Urquhart, Jane
Canadian. Author
Novels set in the Victorian Era include *The Whirlpool,* 1986.
b. Jun 21, 1949 in Geraldton, Ontario, Canada
Source: *BlmGWL; CanWW 31, 89; ConAu 32NR, 113; ConCaAu 1; ConLC 90; IntAu&W 93; ScF&FL 92; WhoCanL 85, 87, 92*

Urrutia Lleo, Manuel
Cuban. Judge, Political Leader
Pres. of Cuba, 1959; dismissed by Castro six months later.
b. Dec 8, 1901 in Yaguajay, Cuba
d. Jul 5, 1981 in New York, New York
Source: *AnObit 1981; BioIn 5, 12; ConAu 104; CurBio 59, 81, 81N; NewYTBS 81*

Ursuleac, Viorica
Romanian. Opera Singer
Considered the ideal soprano by R Strauss; noted also for Mozart, Wagner roles.
b. Mar 26, 1899 in Czernowitz, Romania
Source: *Baker 78, 84; BioIn 14, 15; CmOp; InWom; MetOEnc; NewEOp 71; PenDiMP*

Urtain, Jose Manuel Ibar
Spanish. Boxer
European heavyweight champ, 1970.
b. May 14, 1943, Spain
Source: *BioIn 8; WhoBox 74*

Uspenskii, Petr Dem'yanovich
[P D Uspensky]
Russian. Author
Writings include *Tertium Organum,* 1920; *A New Model of the Universe,* 1931.
b. 1878 in Moscow, Russia
d. 1947 in Virginia Water, England
Source: *BioIn 1; LngCTC; TwCA SUP*

Ussachevsky, Vladimir Alexis
Composer
Works using electronic sound include *The Creation,* 1961; a founder, Princeton Electronic Music Center, 1959.
b. Nov 3, 1911 in Hailar, China
d. Jan 4, 1990 in New York, New York
Source: *AmComp; Baker 84; BioIn 15, 16; ConAmC 82; DcCM; NewAmDM; NewGrDA 86; NewYTBS 90; WhoAm 86, 88; WhoAmM 83*

Ussher, James
Irish. Religious Leader
Archbishop of Armagh, 1625; upheld doctrine of divine right of kings.
b. Jan 4, 1581 in Dublin, Ireland
d. Mar 21, 1656 in Reigate, England
Source: *Alli; BbD; Benet 87, 96; BiD&SB; BiDIrW; BioIn 1, 3, 5, 8, 12; BritAu; CamGLE; Chambr 1; DcBiPP; DcEnA; DcEnL; DcIrB 78, 88; DcIrW 2; DcNaB; EvLB; LinLib L, S; LuthC 75; NewC; NewCBEL; OxCEng 67, 85, 95; OxCIri; REn*

Ustinov, Dmitri Fedorovich
Russian. Government Official
Politburo member, minister of defense, 1976-84.
b. Oct 30, 1908 in Samara, Russia
d. Dec 20, 1984 in Moscow, Union of Soviet Socialist Republics
Source: *ColdWar 1; IntWW 74, 75, 76, 81, 82, 83; IntYB 81, 82; NewYTBS 76, 84; WhoWor 74, 80, 82*

Ustinov, Peter Alexander
English. Actor
All-around entertainer in films, stage, TV; Oscar nominee for *Quo Vadis,* 1951.
b. Apr 16, 1921 in London, England
Source: *Benet 87; BiE&WWA; BioIn 13, 14, 15, 16; CelR 90; ConAu 13R, 25NR, 51NR; ConDr 82, 88; ConTFT 8; FacFETw; HalFC 88; IntAu&W 91; IntMPA 92; IntvTCA 2; IntWW 91; MovMk; NewYTBS 84; NotNAT; OxCFilm; OxCThe 67; PlP&P; TwCWr; Who 85, 92; WhoAm 86, 90, 97; WhoEnt 92; WhoHol A; WhoThe 81; WhoWor 87, 91, 97; WorAlBi; WorEFlm; WrDr 86, 92*

Ut, Huynh Cong
Vietnamese. Photojournalist
Won 1973 Pulitzer for photograph of children running, crying from their napalmed village near Saigon.
b. Mar 29, 1951 in Saigon, Vietnam
Source: *AsAmAlm; MacBEP; NotAsAm; WhoAm 74, 76*

Utamaro, Kitagawa
Japanese. Artist
Best known Japanese master of color print; paintings center around beautiful women's occupations, amusements.
b. 1753
d. 1806
Source: *BioIn 2; DcArts; McGDA; McGEWB; NewCol 75; OxCArt*

Utley, Freda
American. Journalist, Author
Wrote *Will the Middle East Go West?,* 1957.
b. Jan 23, 1898 in London, England
d. Jan 21, 1978 in Washington, District of Columbia
Source: *AmAu&B; BioIn 1, 2, 5, 8, 11; BlueB 76; ConAu 77, 81; CurBio 58, 78, 78N; DcAmB S10; EncAJ; EncMcCE; FacFETw; InWom, SUP; NewYTBS 78; WhAm 7; WhoAm 74, 76; WhoAmW 58, 64, 66, 68, 70, 72; WhoSSW 73*

Utley, (Clifton) Garrick
American. Journalist
Foreign correspondent for NBC, 1963-64; British correspondent, 1973-79.
b. Nov 19, 1939 in Chicago, Illinois
Source: *ConAu 69; IntAu&W 89; LegTOT; LesBEnT 92; Who 82, 83, 85, 88, 90, 92, 94; WhoAm 76, 78, 80, 82, 84, 86, 88, 90, 92, 94; WhoE 91; WhoSSW 73, 75*

Utley, Mike
American. Football Player
Offensive lineman for Detroit Lions until a paralyzing spinal column injury occurred during a game, 1991.
b. Dec 20, 1965 in Seattle, Washington

Utrillo, Maurice
French. Artist
Style based on modified form of Cubism; known for Parisian street scenes, houses.
b. Dec 25, 1883 in Paris, France
d. Nov 5, 1955 in Dax, France
Source: *AtlBL; Benet 87, 96; BioIn 1, 2, 3, 4, 5, 7, 8, 9, 10, 12, 13, 16, 17; ClaDrA; CurBio 53, 56; DcArts; DcTwCCu 2; LegTOT; McGDA; ObitT 1951; OxCArt; OxCFr; OxCTwCA; OxDcArt; PhDcTCA 77; REn; WhDW*

Uttley, Alice Jane Taylor
[Alison Uttley]
English. Children's Author
Books based on farm life, animals include *Little Grey Rabbit's Christmas,* 1939.
b. Dec 17, 1884 in Derbyshire, England
d. May 7, 1976 in High Wycombe, England
Source: *Au&Wr 71; AuBYP 2, 3; BioIn 3, 8, 10, 12, 14, 16; BlmGWL; CamGLE; ChhPo; ConAu 7NR, 53, 65, X; DcLB 160; DcLEL; FemiCLE; LngCTC; OxCChiL; OxCEng 85, 95; PenNWW B; ScF&FL 1; SmATA 3, 26, X; TwCChW 78, 83, 89, 95; WhoChL; WrDr 76*

Utzon, Jorn
Danish. Architect
Best known for designing Opera House, Sydney, Australia, 1956; built, 1960-73.
b. Apr 9, 1918 in Copenhagen, Denmark
Source: *BioIn 7, 10, 11, 12, 14; ConArch 80, 87, 94; DcD&D; DcTwDes; EncMA; IntDcAr; IntWW 74, 75, 76, 77, 78, 79, 80, 81, 82, 83, 89, 91, 93; MacEA; WhDW; WhoArch; WhoScEn 96*

V

Vaaler, Johan
Norwegian. Inventor, Educator
Patented the paper clip, 1899.

Vaccaro, Brenda
American. Actor
Husky-voiced entertainer on TV, film, stage; nominated for three Tonys, won Emmy for "The Shape of Things," 1974.
b. Nov 18, 1939 in New York, New York
Source: *BiE&WWA; BioIn 8; CelR; ConTFT 2, 7, 15; EncAFC; FilmEn; FilmgC; HalFC 80, 84, 88; IntMPA 76, 77, 78, 79, 80, 81, 82, 84, 86, 88, 92, 94, 96; InWom SUP; LegTOT; NotNAT; WhoAm 74, 76, 78, 80, 82, 84, 86, 88, 90, 92, 94; WhoAmW 74, 83; WhoEnt 92; WhoHol 92, A; WhoThe 72, 77, 81; WorAl*

Vachon, Rogie
[Rogatien Rosaire Vachon]
Canadian. Hockey Player
Goalie, 1966-82, with four NHL teams; won Vezina Trophy, 1968; involved in controversial free agent compensation case with Dale McCourt, 1978-79.
b. Sep 8, 1945 in Palmarolle, Quebec, Canada
Source: *BioIn 11; HocEn; WhoAm 78, 80, 82, 90, 92, 94, 95, 96, 97; WhoHcky 73; WhoWest 87, 89, 92, 94, 96*

Vadim, Roger
[Roger Vadim Piemiannikov]
French. Director
Wrote book about former wives: *Bardot, Deneuve, Fonda,* 1983.
b. Jan 26, 1928 in Paris, France
Source: *BiDFilm, 81, 94; BioIn 4, 5, 10, 11, 13, 14, 15, 16; ConAu 143; ConTFT 5; CurBio 84; DcFM; DcTwCCu 2; EncEurC; FilmEn; FilmgC; HalFC 84, 88; IntDcF 1-2, 2-2; IntMPA 84, 86, 88, 92, 94, 96; IntWW 74, 75, 76, 77, 78, 79, 80, 81, 82, 83, 89, 91; ItaFilm; MiSFD 9; MovMk; NewYTBE 70; OxCFilm; WhoEnt 92; WhoFr 79; WhoHol 92, A; WhoWor 74, 84, 87, 91; WorAl; WorEFlm; WorFDir 2*

Vagelos, P. Roy
[Pindaros Vagelos]
American. Businessman
Enjoys highest credibility in pharmaceutical industry as president and CEO of Merck & Co., 1985-.
b. Aug 10, 1929 in Westfield, New Jersey
Source: *AmMWSc 92; BioIn 7, 14, 15; Dun&B 90; IntWW 91; News 89; St&PR 91; WhoAm 90; WhoE 91; WhoFI 92*

Vai, Steve
American. Musician, Songwriter
Guitarist; performed and recorded with Frank Zappa, David Lee Roth and Whitesnake.
b. 1961 in New York, New York
Source: *ConMus 5*

Vaid, Urvashi
American. Writer
Public Information Director and Executive Director for the National Gay and Lesbian Task Force, 1986-92; wrote book *Virtual Equality,* 1995.
b. 1958, India
Source: *BioIn 20; GayLesB; NotAsAm*

Vail, Alfred Lewis
American. Manufacturer, Inventor
Manufactured telegraph, 1838; received test message between Washington, DC and Baltimore, "What hath God wrought!" 1844.
b. Sep 25, 1807 in Morristown, New Jersey
d. Jan 18, 1859 in Morristown, New Jersey
Source: *AmBi; ApCAB; DcAmB; NatCAB 4; TwCBDA; WebAB 74, 79; WhAm HS*

Vail, Theodore Newton
American. Businessman
Pres., American Telegraph & Telephone Co., 1907-20.
b. Jul 16, 1845 in Carroll County, Ohio
d. Apr 16, 1920 in Baltimore, Maryland
Source: *AmBi; ApCAB X; BiDAmBL 83; BioIn 6, 7, 10; DcAmB; DcNAA; EncAB-H 1974, 1996; HarEnUS; InSci; NatCAB 28; OhA&B; OxCAmH; WebAB 74, 79; WhAm 1; WorAl*

Vaive, Rick Claude
Canadian. Hockey Player
Right wing, 1978-93, mostly with Toronto, currently with Chicago; had three 50-goal seasons.
b. May 14, 1959 in Ottawa, Ontario, Canada
Source: *HocEn; HocReg 87*

Valachi, Joe
[Joseph M. Valachi]
American. Criminal
Hit man, turned informer to Justice Dept., 1963.
b. Sep 22, 1904 in New York, New York
d. Apr 3, 1971 in El Paso, Texas
Source: *BioIn 8, 9; NewYTBE 71; ObitOF 79*

Valadon, Suzanne
French. Artist
Mother of Utrillo; influenced in painting by Gauguin, Degas; figures usually from working class.
b. Sep 23, 1869 in Bessines, France
d. Apr 7, 1938 in Paris, France
Source: *IntDcWB; McGDA; OxCArt; OxCTwCA*

Valdengo, Giuseppe
Italian. Opera Singer
Baritone with NY Met., 1947-60.
b. May 24, 1920 in Turin, Italy
Source: *Baker 84; BioIn 13; IntWWM 90; MetOEnc; PenDiMP; WhoWor 74*

Valdes-Leal, Juan de
Spanish. Artist
Paintings include *The Two Cadavers;* series on life of St. Jerome.
b. 1622
d. 1690
Source: *NewCol 75; WebBD 83*

Valdez, Luis (Miguel)
American. Director, Writer
Founder, El Teatro Campesino, 1965—, most influential Chicano theater in US; won Obie, 1969; Emmy, 1973.
b. Jun 26, 1940 in Delano, California
Source: *BenetAL 91; BioIn 12, 14, 15, 16; CamGWoT; ChiLit; ChiSch; ConAmD; ConAu 32NR, 101; ConDr 82, 88, 93; ConLC 84; ConTFT 5; CrtSuDr; CyWA 89; DcHiB; DcLB 122; HispAmA; HispLC; HispWr; MiSFD 9; TheaDir; VarWW 85; WhoHisp 92; WhoThe 81; WhoWest 89; WrDr 84, 86, 88, 90, 92, 94, 96*

Vale, Jerry
[Gerano Louis Vitaliamo]
American. Singer
Hit singles include "Innamorata," 1956; "Dommage, Dommage," 1966.
b. Jul 8, 1932 in New York, New York
Source: *AmPS A, B; PenEncP; RkOn 74, 82*

Valens, Ritchie
[Richard Valenzuela]
American. Singer
Had number one single "La Bamba," 1958; life story filmed, 1987.
b. May 13, 1941 in Pacoima, California
d. Feb 3, 1959 in Clear Lake, Iowa
Source: *BioIn 15, 20; DcHiB; EncPR&S 74; EncRk 88; EncRkSt; HarEnR 86; LegTOT; PenEncP; RkOn 74; RolSEnR 83; WhoRock 81*

Valente, Benita
American. Opera Singer
Lyric soprano with NY Met. since 1973.
Source: *Baker 84; BioIn 12, 13, 14, 15, 16, 19; CurBio 88; IntWWM 85, 90; MetOEnc; NewAmDM; NewGrDA 86; NewYTBE 73; NewYTBS 75, 85; WhoAm 78, 80, 82, 84, 86, 88, 90; WhoAmM 83; WhoAmW 97; WhoOp 76*

Valenti, Jack Joseph
American. Film Executive, Government Official
Assistant to LBJ, 1963-66; pres., Motion Picture Assn., 1966—.
b. Sep 5, 1921 in Houston, Texas
Source: *BioIn 6, 7, 8, 10, 11, 13, 16; BlueB 76; BusPN; CelR 90; ConAu 73; CurBio 68; FilmgC; HalFC 84, 88; IntMPA 86, 92; IntWW 83, 91; LesBEnT, 92; NewYTBS 82, 91; WhoAm 74, 76, 78, 80, 82, 84, 86, 88, 90, 92, 94, 95, 96, 97; WhoE 85, 86; WhoEnt 92; WhoGov 72, 75; WhoSSW 73; WhoTelC; WhoWor 74, 78, 80, 82, 84, 87; WorAl*

Valentina
[Nicholaena Sanina Schlee]
American. Fashion Designer
Known for soft, flowing, bias-cut clothing, 1930s-40s.
b. May 1, 1904 in Kiev, Russia
d. Sep 14, 1989 in New York, New York
Source: *AmDec 1930; BioIn 1, 2, 3, 6, 16, 21; ConFash; CurBio 89N; EncFash; FairDF US; InWom, SUP; WorFshn*

Valentine, Dean
American. Broadcasting Executive
One of the most powerful executives in television comedy; pres., Disney Television.

Valentine, Karen
American. Actor
TV shows include "Room 222," 1969-74; "Karen," 1975.
b. May 25, 1947 in Santa Rosa, California
Source: *BioIn 10, 13; ConTFT 3; HalFC 84, 88; IntMPA 84, 86, 88, 92, 94, 96; LegTOT; WhoAmW 87; WhoEmL 87; WhoHol 92*

Valentine, Scott
American. Actor
Played Nick in TV series "Family Ties," 1985-87.
b. Jun 3, 1958 in Saratoga Springs, New York
Source: *BioIn 15; ConTFT 5; WhoHol 92*

Valentino
[Valentino Garavani]
Italian. Fashion Designer
Opened ready-to-wear boutique in Milan, 1969; designs known for elegance, simple lines, styles.
b. May 11, 1932 in Milan, Italy
Source: *BioIn 7, 10, 12, 14, 16; CelR, 90; ConDes 84, 90, 97; ConFash; CurBio 73; DcArts; EncFash; IntWW 91, 93; LegTOT; WhoAm 76, 78, 96, 97; WhoFash, 88; WhoWor 82, 84, 87, 89, 91, 93, 95, 96, 97; WorFshn*

Valentino, Rudolph
[Rodolfo d'Antonguella]
American. Actor
Starred in *The Sheik,* 1921; *Blood and Sand,* 1922.
b. May 6, 1895 in Castellaneta, Italy
d. Aug 23, 1926 in New York, New York
Source: *AmBi; AmCulL; BiDD; BiDFilm, 81, 94; BioIn 1, 2, 3, 5, 6, 7, 8, 9, 10, 11, 12, 14, 15, 16, 17, 18, 19, 20; CmCal; CmMov; DcArts; DcNAA; FacFETw; Film 1, 2; FilmEn; FilmgC; HalFC 80, 84, 88; IntDcF 1-3, 2-3; LegTOT; MotPP; MovMk; NotNAT B; OxCFilm; SilFlmP; TwYS; WebAB 74, 79; WhAm 1; WhDW; WhoHol B; WhScrn 74, 77, 83; WomWMM; WorAl; WorAlBi; WorEFlm*

Valenzuela, Fernando
[Fernando Anguamea]
"El Toro"
Mexican. Baseball Player
Pitcher, LA Dodgers, 1980-91; CA Angels, 1991-92; won NL rookie of year, Cy Young Award, 1981; first Mexican to win 20 games in NL, 1986; with Dave Stewart, pitched no-hitter on same day, 1990, first with same-day no-hitters since 1898.
b. Nov 1, 1960 in Navajoa, Mexico
Source: *Ballpl 90; BaseReg 85, 86, 87; BioIn 12, 13, 14, 15, 16; CurBio 82; HispAmA; LegTOT; NewYTBS 81, 86; WhoAm 84, 86, 88, 90, 92; WhoHisp 91, 92, 94; WhoSpor; WhoWest 87, 89; WorAlBi*

Valeriani, Richard Gerard
American. Broadcast Journalist
With NBC News since, 1961; Pentagon correspondent since, 1982.
b. Aug 29, 1932 in Camden, New Jersey
Source: *ConAu 12NR, 65; EncTwCJ; WhoAm 74, 76, 78, 80, 82, 84, 86, 88, 90, 92, 94, 95, 96, 97; WhoE 95; WhoSSW 73; WhoTelC*

Valerio, James Robert
American. Artist
Realist painter; won many awards.
b. Dec 2, 1938 in Chicago, Illinois
Source: *BioIn 13; DcCAA 88; PrintW 85; WhoAm 84, 86, 88; WhoAmA 78, 80, 82, 84, 86, 89, 91, 93; WhoE 83, 85, 86*

Valery, Paul Ambroise
French. Poet, Critic
Wrote *The Graveyard by the Sea.*
b. Oct 30, 1871 in Sete, France
d. Jul 20, 1945 in Paris, France
Source: *AtlBL; CasWL; ChhPo S2; ClDMEL 47, 80; CnMD; CnMWL; CurBio 45; Dis&D; EncWL; EvEuW; LngCTC; McGEWB; ModRL; NewC; OxCEng 67; OxCFr; PenC EUR; REn; TwCA, SUP; TwCWr; WhAm 4; WhDW; WhoLA; WhoTwCL*

Vallee, Rudy
[Hubert Prior Vallee]
"The Vagabond Lover"
American. Actor, Singer
Saxophonist, vaudeville performer; known for using megaphone, theme song "My Time Is Your Time."
b. Jul 28, 1901 in Island Pond, Vermont
d. Jul 3, 1986 in Hollywood, California
Source: *AmCulL; AmPS; AnObit 1986; ASCAP 66, 80; Baker 92; BgBands 74; BiE&WWA; BioIn 1, 2, 6, 9, 10, 11, 12, 15, 16, 19; CmpEPM; ConAu 2NR, 119, X; CurBio 63, 86, 86N; DcArts; EncAFC; EncMT; EncVaud; FacFETw; Film 2; FilmEn; FilmgC; ForYSC; HalFC 80, 84, 88; IntMPA 75, 76, 77, 78, 79, 80, 81, 82, 84, 86; LegTOT; MotPP; MovMk; NewAmDM; NewGrDA 86; NewGrDM 80; NewYTBS 86; OxCPMus; PenEncP; RadStar; WebAB 74, 79; WhoHol A; WorAl; WorAlBi*

Valleria, Alwina
[Alwina Schoening]
American. Opera Singer
Soprano, noted for Wagnerian roles; with NY Met., 1883.
b. Oct 12, 1848 in Baltimore, Maryland
d. Feb 17, 1925 in Nice, France

Source: *Baker 78, 84, 92; BiDAmM; BioIn 13; InWom SUP; MetOEnc; NewEOp 71; NewGrDA 86; NewGrDM 80; NewGrDO*

Valletti, Cesare
Italian. Opera Singer
Tenor with NY Met., 1952-62; admired for Mozart, Rossini roles.
b. Dec 18, 1922 in Rome, Italy
Source: *Baker 84, 92; IntDcOp; IntWWM 90; MetOEnc; NewEOp 71; NewGrDM 80; NewGrDO; WhoMus 72*

Valli, Alida
[Alida Maria Altenburger]
Italian. Actor
Films include *Third Man; Paradise Case.*
b. May 31, 1921 in Pola, Italy
Source: *BiDFilm, 81, 94; BioIn 11; EncEurC; FilmAG WE; FilmEn; FilmgC; ForYSC; HalFC 80, 84, 88; IntDcF 1-3, 2-3; IntMPA 75, 76, 77, 78, 79, 80, 81, 82, 84, 86, 88, 92, 94, 96; InWom SUP; ItaFilm; LegTOT; MotPP; MovMk; OxCFilm; WhoHol 92, A; WorEFlm*

Valli, Frankie
[The Four Seasons; Francis Castelluccio]
American. Singer
Hits include "Sherry"; "Big Girls Don't Cry"; "My Eyes Adored You."
b. May 3, 1937 in Newark, New Jersey
Source: *BioIn 15; BkPepl; ConMus 10; IlEncRk; LegTOT; NewAmDM; NewGrDA 86; RkOn 74, 78; WhoAm 78, 80, 82, 84, 86, 88, 92, 94; WhoEnt 92; WorAl; WorAlBi*

Vallone, Raf(faele)
Italian. Actor
Leading man in Italian films; films include *Obsession,* 1976; *The Godfather: Part III,* 1991.
b. Feb 17, 1918 in Tropea, Italy
Source: *ConTFT 1; FilmgC; HalFC 84, 88; IntMPA 84, 86, 92; MovMk; WhoHol A; WorEFlm*

Valtman, Edmund Siegfried
American. Cartoonist
Won 1962 Pulitzer for political, anti-Castro cartoon.
b. May 31, 1914 in Tallinn, Russia
Source: *WhoAm 74, 76; WhoAmA 84, 91; WhoE 91; WorECar*

Valvano, Jim
[James Thomas Valvano]
American. Basketball Coach, Sportscaster
Coach, NC State U, 1980-1990; won NCAA championship, 1983; college basketball analyst.
b. Mar 10, 1946 in New York, New York
d. Apr 28, 1993 in Durham, North Carolina
Source: *BioIn 13, 15, 16; NewYTBS 80, 83, 89; WhAm 11; WhoAm 84, 86, 88, 90, 92; WhoEmL 87; WhoSSW 86*

Van Allen, James Alfred
American. Physicist
Specialist in earth's radiation belts; won many awards.
b. Sep 7, 1914 in Mount Pleasant, Iowa
Source: *AmMWSc 73P, 76P, 79, 82, 86, 89, 92, 95; AsBiEn; BiESc; BioIn 5, 6, 8, 11, 12, 14, 16, 17, 20; BlueB 76; CurBio 59; FacFETw; IntWW 74, 75, 76, 77, 78, 79, 80, 81, 82, 83, 89, 91, 93; LarDcSc; LegTOT; McGMS 80; OxCAmH; WebAB 74, 79; Who 74, 82, 83, 85, 88, 90, 92, 94; WhoAm 74, 76, 78, 80, 82, 84, 86, 88, 90, 92, 94, 95, 96; WhoFrS 84; WhoScEn 94, 96; WhoWor 74; WorAl*

VanAllsburg, Chris
American. Children's Author, Illustrator
Won Caldecotts for *Jumanji,* 1981; *The Polar Express,* 1985.
b. Jun 18, 1949 in Grand Rapids, Michigan
Source: *AuBYP 3; BioIn 14, 15, 16; ChlLR 5, 13; ConAu 113, 117; CurBio 96; DcLB 61; FifBJA; NewYTBS 89; TwCChW 89; WhoAm 86, 90*

VanAlstyne, Egbert Anson
American. Songwriter, Musician
Wrote over 700 songs, including "In the Shade of the Old Apple Tree."
b. Mar 5, 1882 in Chicago, Illinois
d. Jul 9, 1951 in Chicago, Illinois
Source: *AmPS; ASCAP 66, 80; BiDAmM; BioIn 2, 3, 4, 6, 10; CmpEPM; NotNAT; REnAL*

Van Andel, Jay
American. Business Executive
Co-founder, chairman of Amway Corp., 1970—.
b. Jun 3, 1924 in Grand Rapids, Michigan
Source: *BioIn 9, 10, 11, 12, 13, 17; ConAmBL; Dun&B 86, 88, 90; St&PR 75, 84, 87, 91; WhoAm 74, 76, 78, 80, 82, 84, 86, 88, 90, 92, 94, 95, 96, 97; WhoFI 74, 75, 85, 87, 89, 92, 94, 96; WhoMW 76, 78, 84, 86, 90, 92, 93; WhoWor 74*

Van Ark, Joan
American. Actor
Played Val Ewing on TV series "Knots Landing," 1979-93.
b. Jun 16, 1946 in New York, New York
Source: *BioIn 6, 12, 15, 16; CelR 90; ConTFT 7; IntMPA 92; WhoAm 86, 90; WhoAmW 87, 91; WhoEnt 92; WhoHol A; WorAlBi*

Vanbiesbrouck, John
American. Hockey Player
Goalie, NY Rangers, 1983-93; FL Panthers, 1993—; won Vezina Trophy, 1986.
b. Sep 4, 1963 in Detroit, Michigan
Source: *BioIn 14, 21; HocReg 87; NewYTBS 85; WhoAm 92, 94, 95, 96, 97; WhoSSW 95, 97*

Van Brocklin, Norm (an Mack)
"The Dutchman"
American. Football Player, Football Coach
Quarterback, 1949-60, mostly with LA Rams; holds NFL record for yds. passing, 554, in single game, 1951; MVP, 1960; Hall of Fame, 1971.
b. Mar 15, 1926 in Parade, South Dakota
d. May 2, 1983 in Monroe, Georgia
Source: *AnObit 1983; CmCal; ConAu 109; LegTOT; NewYTBS 83; WhoAm 74; WhoFtbl 74; WorAl; WorAlBi*

Vanbrugh, John, Sir
English. Dramatist, Architect
Designed Castle Howard, Yorkshire; Blenheim Palace, Woodstock; plays include *The Provoked Wife,* 1697.
b. Jan 24, 1664 in London, England
d. Mar 16, 1726 in London, England
Source: *Alli; AtlBL; BbD; Benet 87, 96; BiD&SB; BiDBrA; BioIn 1, 2, 3, 5, 6, 7, 8, 10, 12, 13, 14, 16, 17, 18; BlkwCE; BlmGEL; BritAu; BritWr 2; CamGEL; CamGLE; CamGWoT; CasWL; Chambr 2; ChhPo S1; CnThe; CrtSuDr; CrtT 2; CyWA 58; DcArts; DcD&D; DcEnA; DcEnL; DcEuL; DcLB 80; DcLEL; DcNaB; EncWT; Ent; EvLB; GrWrEL DR; IntDcAr; IntDcT 2; LitC 21; LngCEL; MacEA; McGDA; McGEWB; McGEWD 72, 84; MouLC 2; NewC; NewCBEL; NewCol 75; NewGrDO; NotNAT A, B; OxCArt; OxCEng 67, 85, 95; OxCThe 67, 83; PenC ENG; PlP&P; RAdv 14, 13-2; REn; REnWD; RfGEnL 91; WebE&AL; WhDW; WhoArch*

Van Buren, Abigail
[Pauline Esther Friedman; Mrs. Morton Phillips]
"Dear Abby"; "Popo"
American. Journalist
Wrote *Dear Abby on Marriage,* 1962; twin sister of Ann Landers.
b. Jul 4, 1918 in Sioux City, Iowa
Source: *AmAu&B; BioAmW; BioIn 14, 15, 16; CelR, 90; ConAu 1R, X; CurBio 60; DcLP 87B; EncAJ; EncTwCJ; ForWC 70; InWom, SUP; JrnUS; LegTOT; LibW; PenNWW B; WebAB 74, 79; WhoAm 74, 76, 78, 80, 82, 84, 86, 88, 90, 92, 94, 95, 96, 97; WhoAmJ 80; WhoAmW 66, 68, 70, 72, 74, 75, 77, 79, 81, 83, 85, 95, 97; WorAl; WorAlBi*

Van Buren, Hannah Hoes
[Mrs. Martin Van Buren]
American.
Died 18 yrs. before husband became pres.
b. Mar 8, 1783 in Kinderhook, New York
d. Feb 5, 1819 in Albany, New York
Source: *ApCAB; BioIn 16, 17; FacPr 89; GoodHs; InWom, SUP; NotAW*

Van Buren, Martin
American. US President
Eighth pres., Dem., 1837-41; opposed annexation of Texas, established independent treasury system.

b. Dec 5, 1782 in Kinderhook, New York
d. Jul 24, 1862 in Kinderhook, New York
Source: *Alli; AmAu&B; AmBi; AmPolLe; ApCAB; BbD; Benet 87, 96; BenetAL 91; BiAUS; BiD&SB; BiDrAC; BiDrGov 1789; BiDrUSC 89; BiDrUSE 71, 89; BioIn 1, 2, 3, 4, 5, 6, 7, 8, 9, 10, 11, 12, 13, 14, 15, 16, 17, 18, 19, 20; CelCen; CyAG; DcAmAu; DcAmB; DcAmDH 80, 89; DcAmSR; DcNAA; Drake; EncAAH; EncAB-H 1974, 1996; FacPr 89, 93; HealPre; LegTOT; LinLib L, S; McGEWB; NatCAB 6; OxCAmH; OxCAmL 65, 83; PolPar; PresAR; RComAH; REn; REnAL; TwCBDA; VicePre; WebAB 74, 79; WhAm HS; WhAmP; WhCiWar; WhDW; WorAl; WorAlBi*

Van Buren, Steve W
American. Football Player
Four-time all-pro halfback, Philadelphia, 1944-51; led NFL in rushing four times; Hall of Fame, 1965.
b. Dec 28, 1920 in La Ceiba, Honduras
Source: *BiDAmSp FB; BioIn 1, 2, 6, 7, 8, 9, 10; WhoFtbl 74*

Van Camp, Gilbert C
American. Business Executive
Pres., Van Camp Packing Co, 1882-98.
b. Dec 25, 1817 in Brookline, Indiana
d. Apr 4, 1900 in Indianapolis, Indiana
Source: *NatCAB 28*

Vance, Cyrus Roberts
American. Lawyer, Government Official
Secretary of State, 1977-80.
b. Mar 27, 1917 in Clarksburg, West Virginia
Source: *AmPolLe; BiDrUSE 89; BioIn 6, 8, 10, 11, 12, 13, 14, 16; BlueB 76; CngDr 77, 79; ColdWar 2; ConAu 121; CurBio 62; DcAmDH 80, 89; EncWB; IntWW 74, 75, 76, 77, 78, 79, 80, 81, 82, 83, 89, 91, 93; IntYB 78, 79, 80, 81, 82; NewYTBS 76; Who 88, 92, 94; WhoAm 74, 76, 78, 80, 82, 84, 86, 88, 90, 92, 94, 95, 96, 97; WhoAmL 78, 79, 87, 90, 92; WhoAmP 73, 75, 77, 79, 81, 83, 85, 87, 89, 91, 93, 95; WhoE 74, 77, 79, 81, 83, 85, 86, 89, 91, 93, 95, 97; WhoFI 89; WhoGov 72, 77; WhoWor 78, 80, 82, 84; WorAlBi*

Vance, Dazzy
[Clarence Arthur Vance]
American. Baseball Player
Pitcher, 1915, 1918, 1922-35, mostly with Brooklyn; led NL in strikeouts seven straight yrs; Hall of Fame, 1955.
b. Mar 4, 1891 in Orient, Iowa
d. Feb 16, 1961 in Homosassa Springs, Florida
Source: *Ballpl 90; BioIn 5, 6, 7, 8, 14, 15; LegTOT; WhoProB 73; WhoSpor*

Vance, Kenny
[Jay and the Americans]
American. Singer
Part of clean-cut vocal quintet of 1960s; solo debut, 1975.
b. Dec 9, 1943
Source: *WhoRocM 82*

Vance, Louis Joseph
American. Author
Wrote *The Lone Wolf,* 1914; *The Trembling Flame,* 1931.
b. Sep 19, 1879 in Washington, District of Columbia
d. Dec 16, 1933 in New York, New York
Source: *AmAu&B; AmBi; BioIn 14; ConAu 112; DcAmB S1; DcNAA; EncMys; LngCTC; ScF&FL 1; TwCA; TwCCr&M 80, 85, 91; WhAm 1; WhLit; WhNAA*

Vance, Vivian
American. Actor
Best known as Ethel Mertz in "I Love Lucy," 1951-59; also starred in "The Lucy Show," 1962-65.
b. Jul 26, 1912 in Cherryvale, Kansas
d. Aug 17, 1979 in Belvedere, California
Source: *BioIn 4, 7, 8, 10, 11, 12; DcAmB S10; FilmgC; ForYSC; IntMPA 77; InWom, SUP; MotPP; WhoAm 74; WhoCom; WhoHol A; WorAl*

Van Cleef, Lee
American. Actor
Western/action films include *High Noon,* 1952; *The Good, the Bad, and the Ugly,* 1967.
b. Jan 9, 1925 in Somerville, New Jersey
d. Dec 16, 1989 in Oxnard, California
Source: *AnObit 1989; BioIn 16, 17; CmMov; ConTFT 8; FilmEn; FilmgC; ForYSC; GangFlm; HalFC 80, 84, 88; IntDcF 1-3, 2-3; IntMPA 75, 76, 77, 78, 79, 80, 81, 82, 84, 86, 88; ItaFilm; LegTOT; MotPP; MovMk; NewYTBS 89; OxCFilm; WhAm 10; WhoAm 78, 80, 82, 84, 86, 88; WhoHol A; WhoHrs 80; WorAl; WorAlBi*

Van Cortlandt, Oloff Stevenszen
Dutch. Politician
Deputy mayor of NYC, 1667; Van Cortlandt Park, NYC, named after him.
b. 1600 in Wijk, Netherlands
d. Apr 5, 1684 in New York, New York
Source: *ApCAB; BiDAmBL 83; DcAmB; WhAm HS*

Van Cortlandt, Stephanus
American. Politician
Merchant who was first American-born mayor of NYC, 1677.
b. May 7, 1643 in New York, New York
d. Nov 25, 1700 in New York, New York
Source: *AmBi; ApCAB; BiDAmBL 83; DcAmB; EncCRAm; NatCAB 5; TwCBDA; WebAB 74, 79; WhAm HS*

Vancouver, George
English. Explorer
Wrote *A Voyage of Discovery to the North Pacific Ocean and Round the World,* 1798.
b. Jun 22, 1757 in King's Lynn, England
d. May 10, 1798 in Petersham, England
Source: *Alli; ApCAB; BbD; BbtC; BenetAL 91; BiD&SB; BioIn 3, 4, 5, 9, 11, 12, 18, 20; BritAu; DcCanB 4; DcNaB, C; Drake; Expl 93; MacDCB 78; NewC; OxCAmL 65; OxCCan; OxCEng 67; REn; WhAm HS; WhWE; WorAl; WorAlBi*

Van Damme, Jean-Claude
[Jean-Claude Van Varenberg]
"Muscles from Brussels"
Belgian. Bodybuilder, Actor
Martial-arts films include *Bloodsport; Universal Soldier,* 1992.
b. Oct 18, 1960 in Brussels, Belgium
Source: *IntMPA 92, 94; WhoHol 92*

Vandegrift, Alexander Archer
American. Army Officer
Entered Marines, 1909; became general, 1945; received Medal of Honor.
b. Mar 13, 1887 in Charlottesville, Virginia
d. May 8, 1973 in Bethesda, Maryland
Source: *BiDWWGF; BioIn 1, 2, 6, 7, 9, 10; CurBio 43, 73, 73N; DcAmB S9; DcAmMiB; HarEnMi; MedHR, 94; WebAB 74, 79; WebAMB; WhAm 6; WorAl*

Vandenberg, Arthur Hendrick
American. Politician
Rep. senator from MI, 1928-51.
b. Mar 22, 1884 in Grand Rapids, Michigan
d. Apr 18, 1951 in Grand Rapids, Michigan
Source: *AmAu&B; AmPeW; AmPolLe; ApCAB X; BiDInt; BiDrAC; BiDrUSC 89; BioIn 1, 2, 3, 5, 6, 9, 10, 11; ColdWar 2; ConAu 120; CurBio 51; DcAmB S5; DcAmDH 80, 89; DcTwHis; EncAB-H 1974, 1996; FacFETw; LinLib L, S; OxCAmH; WebAB 74, 79; WhAm 3; WhAmP; WhLit; WhWW-II; WorAl*

Vandenberg, Arthur Hendrick, Jr.
American. Government Official, Presidential Aide
Exec. asst. to General Dwight D Eisenhower, 1952; director, Govt. Affairs Foundation, Inc., 1953-68.
b. Jun 30, 1907 in Grand Rapids, Michigan
d. Jan 18, 1968 in Grand Rapids, Michigan
Source: *BioIn 3, 10, 11; WhAm 4A*

Vandenberg, Hoyt Sanford
American. Army Officer
Chief of Staff, US Air Force, 1948-53; head of air mission to Russia, 1943-44.
b. Jan 24, 1899 in Milwaukee, Wisconsin

d. Apr 2, 1954 in Washington, District of Columbia
Source: *BiDWWGF; BioIn 1, 2, 3, 4, 11, 12, 16; CurBio 45, 54; DcAmB S5; DcAmMiB; EncAI&E; WebAMB; WhAm 3*

Van Depoele, Charles Joseph
American. Inventor, Scientist
Held over 250 patents, including the electric railway, 1883.
b. Apr 27, 1846 in Lichtervelde, Belgium
d. Mar 18, 1892 in Lynn, Massachusetts
Source: *BiInAmS; DcAmB; NatCAB 13; TwCBDA; WebAB 74, 79; WhAm HS*

Vanderbilt, Alfred G
English. Horse Racing Official
Chm. of New York Racing Association, 1971-75.
b. Sep 22, 1912 in London, England
Source: *BioIn 1; NewYTBS 75; WhoAm 76*

Vanderbilt, Amy
American. Journalist, Author
Etiquette expert who wrote syndicated newspaper column, regularly revised *Complete Book of Etiquette,* 1952.
b. Jul 22, 1908 in Staten Island, New York
d. Dec 27, 1974 in New York, New York
Source: *AmAu&B; AmWomWr; Au&Wr 71; BiDAmNC; BioIn 3, 5, 6, 7, 9, 10; CelR; ConAu 1R, 3NR, 53; CurBio 54, 75, 75N; DcAmB S9; EncAJ; EncTwCJ; InWom, SUP; LegTOT; LinLib L; NewYTBS 74; ObitOF 79; WhAm 6; WhoAm 74; WhoAmW 58, 61, 64, 66, 68, 70; WhoE 74; WorAl; WorAlBi*

Vanderbilt, Cornelius
American. Financier
Fortune made in shipping business, stock market, estimated at $100 million; Vanderbilt U., Nashville, named after him.
b. May 27, 1794 in Staten Island, New York
d. Jan 4, 1877 in New York, New York
Source: *AmBi; ApCAB; BiDAmBL 83; BioIn 1, 3, 5, 6, 7, 9, 11, 13, 14, 15, 16, 17, 21; CelCen; DcAmB; DcAmDH 80, 89; Drake; EncAB-H 1974, 1996; EncABHB 2; HarEnUS; LegTOT; LinLib S; McGEWB; MemAm; NatCAB 6; OxCAmH; RComAH; REn; REnAL; TwCBDA; WebAB 74, 79; WhAm HS; WhCiWar; WhDW; WorAl; WorAlBi*

Vanderbilt, Cornelius
American. Financier, Philanthropist
Eldest son of William H, grandson of Cornelius Vanderbilt.
b. Nov 27, 1843 in Staten Island, New York
d. Sep 12, 1899 in New York, New York
Source: *AmBi; ApCAB, SUP; BiDAmBL 83; BioIn 2, 3, 7, 12, 16; DcAmB; EncABHB 2; HarEnUS; NatCAB 6, 34; TwCBDA; WebAB 74, 79; WhAm 1*

Vanderbilt, Cornelius, Jr.
American. Journalist, Filmmaker
Founder, pres., Vanderbilt Newspapers, Inc., 1923; wrote *Park Avenue,* 1930; *Farewell to Fifth Avenue,* 1935.
b. Apr 30, 1898 in New York, New York
d. Jul 7, 1974 in Miami Beach, Florida
Source: *AmAu&B; Au&Wr 71; AuNews 1; BioIn 5, 10, 16; BlueB 76; ConAu 49, P-1; DcAmB S9; LinLib L; WhAm 6; WhNAA; Who 74; WhoAm 74*

Vanderbilt, Gloria Morgan
[Gloria Cooper]
American. Designer
Best known for Gloria Vanderbilt jeans that influenced "designer jeans" craze, 1980s; appeared on stage, film; writes poetry, designs fabrics.
b. Feb 20, 1924 in New York, New York
Source: *BiDAmBL 83; BiE&WWA; BioAmW; BioIn 4, 5, 8, 9, 10, 11, 12, 13, 14, 15, 16; BioNews 74; CelR 90; ConAu 22NR, 89; CurBio 72; Entr; ForWC 70; InWom SUP; NewYTBS 79, 85, 87; NotNAT; WhoAm 76, 78, 80, 82, 84, 86, 88; WhoAmW 83, 85, 87, 89, 91, 93, 95; WomFir*

Vanderbilt, Harold Stirling
American. Businessman
Invented card game contract bridge, 1925.
b. Jul 6, 1884 in Oakdale, New York
d. Jul 4, 1970 in Newport, Rhode Island
Source: *BioIn 7, 8, 9, 21; NewYTBE 70; ObitOF 79; OxCShps; WebAB 74, 79; WhAm 5, 7*

Vanderbilt, William Henry
American. Financier, Railroad Executive
Succeeded father Cornelius as pres., NY Central Railroad, 1877.
b. May 8, 1821 in New Brunswick, New Jersey
d. Dec 8, 1885 in New York, New York
Source: *AmBi; ApCAB; BiDAmBL 83; BiDrGov 1789; BioIn 3, 5, 7; DcAmB; EncAB-H 1974, 1996; HarEnUS; NatCAB 6, 30; NewYTBS 81; TwCBDA; WebAB 74, 79; WhAm HS; WorAl*

Vanderbilt, William Henry
American. Politician, Philanthropist
Rep. governor of RI, 1939-40; founded non-profit South Forty Corp to help rehabilitate prisoners.
b. Nov 24, 1902 in New York, New York
d. Apr 14, 1981 in South Williamston, Massachusetts
Source: *NewYTBS 81; St&PR 75; WhoAm 74*

Vanderbilt, William Kissam
American. Businessman
Pres., P.& L.E. Railroad; director NY Central Railroad; founder, pres., The New Theater.
b. Dec 12, 1849 in New York, New York
d. Jul 22, 1920 in Paris, France
Source: *ApCAB SUP; BiDAmBL 83; BioIn 16; CurBio 44; DcAmB; NatCAB 6, 30; WebAB 74, 79; WhAm 1; WorAl*

Vandercook, John Womack
American. Author, Broadcast Journalist
Writings include *Tom-Tom,* 1926; *Murder in New Guinea,* 1959.
b. Apr 22, 1902 in London, England
d. Jan 6, 1963 in Delhi, New York
Source: *AmAu&B; BioIn 1, 6; CurBio 42, 63; EncMys; NotNAT B; REnAL; WhAm 4; WhE&EA; WhNAA*

Van der Klugt, Cor
Dutch. Business Executive
President of Philips, Dutch electronics firm, since 1986.
b. 1924?, Netherlands

Vanderlyn, John
American. Artist
First nude exhibited in US caused scandal, 1815; portraits of famous people include Andrew Jackson, James Monroe.
b. Oct 15, 1775 in Kingston, New York
d. Sep 23, 1852 in Kingston, New York
Source: *AmBi; ApCAB; BiAUS; DcAmB; Drake; OxCAmL 65; TwCBDA; WebAB 74; WhAm HS*

Vander Meer, Johnny
[John Samuel Vander Meer]
"Double No-Hit"; "The Dutch Master"
American. Baseball Player
Pitcher, 1937-51; only pitcher to throw consecutive no-hitters, 1938.
b. Nov 2, 1914 in Prospect Park, New Jersey
Source: *Ballpl 90; BiDAmSp Sup; BioIn 2, 6, 9, 11; FacFETw; LegTOT; WhoProB 73; WorAl*

Van der Meer, Simon
Dutch. Physicist
Shared Nobel Prize in physics with Carlo Rubbia, 1984; studied subatomic particles, links to basic forces of nature.
b. Nov 24, 1925 in The Hague, Netherlands
Source: *AmMWSc 89, 92, 95; BioIn 13, 14, 15; IntWW 89, 91, 93; LarDcSc; LegTOT; NobelP; NotTwCS; Who 88, 90, 92, 94; WhoNob, 90, 95; WhoScEn 94, 96; WhoWor 87, 89, 91, 93, 95, 96, 97; WorAlBi*

Van Der Post, Laurens (Jan), Sir
South African. Author
Wrote *In a Province,* 1934; *The Heart of the Hunter,* 1961.
b. Dec 13, 1906 in Philioppis, South Africa
d. Dec 15, 1996 in London, England
Source: *Au&Wr 71; Benet 87, 96; BioIn 4, 8, 9, 10, 13, 15, 16; BlueB 76; CamGEL; CamGLE; CasWL; ConAu 5R, 35NR; ConLC 5; ConNov 72, 76, 82, 86, 91, 96; DcArts; DcLEL; EncSoA;*

GrWrEL N; IntAu&W 76, 77, 82, 89, 91, 93; IntWW 74, 75, 76, 77, 78, 79, 80, 81, 82, 83, 89, 91, 93; LiExTwC; LinLib L; LngCTC; ModCmwL; NewYTBS 27; Novels; OxCEng 85, 95; PenC ENG; RAdv 14, 13-3; REn; RfGEnL 91; RGTwCWr; TwCWr; Who 74, 82, 83, 85, 85N, 88, 90, 92, 94; WhoAm 74, 76, 78; WhoWor 74, 76, 78; WorAu 1950; WrDr 76, 80, 82, 84, 86, 88, 90, 92, 94, 96

Vandervelde, Emile
Belgian. Statesman
Belgian minister of justice, 1919, foreign affairs, 1925; first pres., International Socialist Bureau.
b. Jan 25, 1866 in Ixelles, Belgium
d. Dec 27, 1938 in Brussels, Belgium
Source: *BiDInt; NewCol 75; WebBD 83*

Vander Zalm, William
[Wilhelmus Nicholass Theodoros Maria Vander Zalm]
Canadian. Political Leader
Social Credit premier of British Columbia, 1986-91.
b. May 29, 1934 in Noordwykerhout, Netherlands
Source: *BioIn 15, 16; CanWW 83, 89; ConNews 87-3; IntWW 91; Who 92; WhoAm 90; WhoWest 92*

VanDerZee, James
American. Photographer
Known for photographs of Harlem, begun in 1915.
b. Jun 29, 1886 in Lenox, Massachusetts
d. May 15, 1983 in Washington, District of Columbia
Source: *BioIn 9, 10, 12; ConAu 104, 109; ConPhot 82; InB&W 80; NegAl 83; NewYTBE 71; NewYTBS 83; PeoHis; WhAm 7; WhAmArt 85; WhoAm 74, 76, 78*

Van Devanter, Willis
American. Supreme Court Justice
Served on US Supreme Court, 1910-37.
b. Apr 17, 1859 in Marion, Indiana
d. Feb 8, 1941 in Washington, District of Columbia
Source: *BiDFedJ; BioIn 1, 2, 5, 8, 11, 15; CurBio 41; DcAmB S3; NatCAB 12; OxCSupC; REnAW; SupCtJu; WebAB 74, 79; WhAm 1*

Van Devere, Trish
[Patricia Dressel; Mrs. George C Scott]
American. Actor
Co-starred with husband in several films: *Where's Poppa?*, 1970, *Day of the Dolphin*, 1973.
b. Mar 9, 1945 in Englewood Cliffs, New Jersey
Source: *BioIn 9, 11; ConTFT 3; FilmEn; HalFC 88; IntMPA 84, 86, 88, 92, 94, 96; InWom SUP; WhoAm 88*

Vandeweghe, Kiki
[Ernest Maurice Vandeweghe]
American. Basketball Player
Forward, Denver, 1980-84, Portland, 1984-89; NY Knicks, 1989-92; LA Clippers, 1992-93; led NBA in three-point field goal percentage, 1987.
b. Aug 1, 1958 in Wiesbaden, Germany (West)
Source: *BasBi; BioIn 15; OfNBA 87*

Van Dine, S. S
[Willard Huntington Wright]
American. Author, Critic
Wrote popular Philo Vance detective stories including *Canary Murder Case*, 1927.
b. Oct 15, 1888 in Charlottesville, Virginia
d. Apr 11, 1939 in New York, New York
Source: *AmAu&B; BenetAL 91; BioIn 4, 6, 14, 18; CnDAL; ConAu 115; DcAmB S2; DcNAA; EncMys; EvLB; FilmgC; LngCTC; OxCAmL 65, 83, 95; PenC AM; REnAL; TwCA, SUP; TwCWr; WhAm 1; WhLit; WhNAA*

Van Doren, Carl Clinton
American. Critic, Biographer
Won Pulitzer for biography of *Benjamin Franklin*, 1938; brother of Mark.
b. Sep 10, 1885 in Hope, Illinois
d. Jul 18, 1950 in Torrington, Connecticut
Source: *CnDAL; ConAmA; ConAmL; ConAu 111; DcAmB S4; DcLEL; EvLB; LngCTC; NatCAB 39; OxCAmL 83; REn; REnAL; TwCA; TwCWr; WebAB 79; WhAm 3*

Van Doren, Charles Lincoln
American. Editor
VP, *Encyclopedia Britannica*, 1973-82.
b. Feb 12, 1926 in New York, New York
Source: *BioIn 4, 5, 6, 10, 11, 20; ConAu 4NR, 5R; DrAS 74E, 78E, 82E; IntAu&W 89; PolProf E; WhoAm 84, 86, 90; WhoFI 83; WhoUSWr 88; WhoWrEP 89*

Van Doren, Dorothy Graffe
American. Author
Writings include *Strangers*, 1926; *The Country Wife*, 1950; *Men, Women and Cats*, 1962.
b. May 2, 1896 in San Francisco, California
d. Feb 21, 1993 in Sharon, Connecticut
Source: *AmAu&B; AmNov; BioIn 18; ConAu 1R, 141; ForWC 70; InWom; REnAL; WhAm 10; WhE&EA; WhLit; WhoAm 74, 76, 78; WhoAmW 58, 61, 64, 66, 68, 70, 72, 74*

Van Doren, Mamie
[Joan Lucille Olander]
American. Actor
Films include *Untamed Youth; Ain't Misbehavin'*.
b. Feb 6, 1933 in Rowena, South Dakota
Source: *BioIn 3, 14, 15; FilmgC; ForYSC; HalFC 80, 84, 88; IntMPA 75, 76, 77, 78, 79, 80, 81, 82, 84, 86, 88, 92, 94, 96; InWom, SUP; ItaFilm; LegTOT; MotPP; MovMk; WhoHol A; WhoHrs 80; WorAl; WorAlBi*

Van Doren, Mark
American. Poet, Critic, Author
Won Pulitzer for poetry, 1939; writings include *That Shining Place*, 1969.
b. Jun 13, 1894 in Hope, Illinois
d. Dec 10, 1972 in Torrington, Connecticut
Source: *AmAu&B; Au&Wr 71; Benet 87, 96; BenetAL 91; BiDAmEd; BiE&WWA; BioIn 1, 3, 4, 5, 7, 8, 9, 10, 12, 15, 17; CasWL; ChhPo, S1, S2, S3; CnDAL; CnE&AP; ConAmA; ConAu 1R, 3NR, 37R; ConLC 6, 10; ConNov 72; ConPo 70; CurBio 40, 73, 73N; DcArts; DcLB 45; DcLEL; EvLB; GrWrEL P; LinLib L; LngCTC; MajTwCW; ModAL, S1; NewYTBE 72; Novels; OxCAmL 65, 83; OxCTwCP; PenC AM; RAdv 1; REn; REnAL; RfGAmL 87; ScF&FL 1, 2; SixAP; TwCA, SUP; TwCWr; WebAB 74, 79; WhAm 5; WhNAA; WorAl; WorAlBi*

Vandross, Luther
American. Singer, Musician
With *Power of Love*, 1991, has created 8 consecutive platinum records.
b. Apr 20, 1951 in New York, New York
Source: *AfrAmAl 6; BioIn 12, 13, 14, 15, 16; ConBlB 13; ConMus 2; CurBio 91; DrBlPA 90; EncPR&S 89; EncRk 88; EncRkSt; InB&W 85; IntWW 91; LegTOT; NewYTBS 91; PenEncP; RkOn 85; SoulM; WhoEnt 92*

Van Druten, John William
English. Dramatist
Plays include *I Remember Mama*, 1944, from Kathryn Forbes' book; *Anatomy of Murder*, 1957, from Robert Traver's book.
b. Jun 1, 1901 in London, England
d. Dec 19, 1957 in Indio, California
Source: *CurBio 44, 58; McGEWD 72; ModAL; ModBrL; ModWD; NewC; OxCAmL 65; OxCThe 67; PenC AM; PlP&P; REn; REnAL; TwCA, SUP; TwCWr; WhAm 3*

Van Dusen, Henry Pitney
American. Clergy, Educator
Helped found World Council of Churches, 1948.
b. Dec 11, 1897 in Philadelphia, Pennsylvania
d. Feb 13, 1975 in Belle Meade, New Jersey
Source: *AmAu&B; BiDAmEd; BioIn 2, 3, 6, 7, 10, 11, 18, 19; ConAu 1R, 3NR, 57; CurBio 50, 75; DcAmReB 1, 2; DrAS 74P; RelLAm 91; WhAm 6; WhNAA; WhoAm 74*

Van Duyn, Mona
American. Poet
US poet laureate, 1992-93; won Pulitzer Prize for poetry, *Near Changes*, 1991.
b. May 9, 1921 in Waterloo, Iowa
Source: *AmAu&B; AmWomWr SUP; ArtclWW 2; Benet 96; BenetAL 91; BioIn 12, 16; ConAu 7NR, 9R; ConLC 3, 7, 63; ConPo 70, 75, 80, 85, 91; DcLB 5; DrAP 75; DrAPF 80, 91; EncWHA; FemiCLE; GrWomW; IntWW 93; InWom SUP; News 93-2; OxCAmL 95; OxCTwCP; OxCWoWr 95; RAdv 14; WhoAm 90; WhoAmW 91; WhoWrEP 89; WorAu 1970; WrDr 76, 80, 82, 84, 86, 88, 90, 92, 94, 96*

Van Dyck, Anthony, Sir
Flemish. Artist
Court painter to Charles I of England; set style for English portraiture which lasted a century.
b. Mar 22, 1599 in Antwerp, Belgium
d. Dec 9, 1641 in London, England
Source: *AtlBL; Benet 96; BioIn 14; IntDcAA 90; LegTOT; McGDA; McGEWB; NewC; NewCol 75; OxCArt; OxCEng 95; REn; WebBD 83; WorAlBi*

Van Dyke, Dick
American. Actor, Comedian
Won three Emmys for TV series "The Dick Van Dyke Show," 1961-66.
b. Dec 13, 1925 in West Plains, Missouri
Source: *BioIn 6, 7, 9, 10, 11, 16, 18; CelR, 90; ConAu 112; ConTFT 3, 13; CurBio 63; EncAFC; FilmEn; FilmgC; ForYSC; Funs; HalFC 80, 84, 88; IntMPA 75, 76, 77, 78, 79, 80, 81, 82, 84, 86, 88, 92, 94, 96; JoeFr; LegTOT; LesBEnT 92; MotPP; MovMk; OxCPMus; QDrFCA 92; WhoAm 74, 76, 78, 80, 82, 84, 86, 88, 90, 92, 94, 95, 96, 97; WhoCom; WhoEnt 92; WhoHol 92, A; WhoTelC; WhoWest 74; WhoWor 74, 76; WorAl; WorAlBi; WorEFlm*

Vandyke, Henry Jackson, Jr.
American. Clergy, Poet, Educator
Wrote *The White Bees, and Other Poems*, 1909; *Chosen Poems*, 1927.
b. Nov 10, 1852 in Germantown, Pennsylvania
d. Apr 10, 1933 in Princeton, New Jersey
Source: *Alli SUP; AmAu&B; AmBi; ApCAB; BbD; BiD&SB; Chambr 3; ChhPo, S1, S2; ConAmL; DcAmAu; DcAmB; DcNAA; EvLB; JBA 34; LngCTC; REnAL; Str&VC; TwCA, SUP; WhAm 1; WhNAA*

Van Dyke, Jerry
American. Actor
Brother of Dick Van Dyke; starred in TV series "My Mother the Car," 1965-66.
b. Jul 27, 1931 in Danville, Illinois
Source: *BioIn 16; ConTFT 12; ForYSC; IntMPA 96; MotPP; VarWW 85; WhoCom; WhoEnt 92; WhoHol 92, A; WorAl*

Van Dyke, W(oodbridge) S(trong)
"One Shot Woody"; "Woody"
American. Director, Producer
Nickname earned from reputation as casual director; resulted in spontaneous performances from actors.
b. Mar 21, 1887 in San Diego, California
d. Feb 5, 1943 in Brentwood, California
Source: *BiDFilm; CmMov; DcFM; Film 1; FilmgC; MovMk; ObitOF 79; OxCFilm; TwYS; WhScrn 77; WorEFlm*

Van Dyken, Amy
American. Swimmer
First American woman to win four gold medals in any event during a single Olympic Game, 1996.
b. Feb 1, 1973 in Engelwood, Colorado
Source: *EncWomS; News 97-1; WhoAmW 97; WhoWor 97*

Vane, John Robert, Sir
English. Scientist
Shared Nobel Prize in medicine, 1982, for discoveries relating to prostaglandins.
b. Mar 29, 1927 in Tardebigg, England
Source: *AmMWSc 89, 92, 95; BiESc; BioIn 13, 14, 15; BlueB 76; CurBio 86; IntMed 80; IntWW 83, 89, 91, 93; LarDcSc; NewYTBS 82; NobelP; Who 74, 82, 83, 85, 88, 92, 94; WhoAm 88, 90, 92, 94, 95; WhoMedH; WhoNob, 90, 95; WhoScEn 94, 96; WhoWor 78, 80, 82, 84, 87, 89, 91, 93, 95, 96, 97; WorAlBi*

Van Eyck, Hubert
Flemish. Artist
Co-founder, with brother Jan, of Flemish School; only extant piece, Lamb altarpiece, Ghent.
b. 1370
d. 1426
Source: *AtlBL; LegTOT; LinLib S; McGDA; McGEWB; NewC; REn*

Van Eyck, Jan
Flemish. Artist
Noted for descriptive realism, intensive color; perfected, but did not discover oil technique.
b. 1371 in Maeseyck, Netherlands
d. 1440
Source: *ClaDrA; McGDA; McGEWB; NewC; REn*

Van Fleet, James Alward
American. Army Officer
Served in Mexican Border campaign, 1916-17; deputy chief of staff European Command, Germany, 1947-48.
b. Mar 19, 1892 in Coytesville, New Jersey
d. Sep 23, 1992 in Polk City, Florida
Source: *BiDWWGF; BioIn 1, 2, 3, 4, 9, 18, 19; CurBio 48; DcAmMiB; HarEnMi; WebAMB; WhoAm 74, 76, 78, 80, 82, 84; WhoWor 74, 76*

Van Fleet, Jo
[Mrs. William Bales]
American. Actor
Won Oscar for her first film *East of Eden*, 1955; Tony for *Trip to Bountiful*, 1954.
b. Dec 30, 1919 in Oakland, California
d. Jun 10, 1996 in New York, New York
Source: *BiE&WWA; ConTFT 5; FilmEn; FilmgC; ForYSC; HalFC 80, 84, 88; HolCA; IntMPA 86, 92, 94, 96; InWom SUP; ItaFilm; LegTOT; MotPP; MovMk; NotNAT; VarWW 85; Vers A; WhoAm 82; WhoEnt 92; WhoHol 92, A; WhoThe 81; WorAl*

Vangelis
[Evangelos Papathanassiou]
Greek. Composer
Won Oscar for score of *Chariots of Fire*, 1982.
b. Mar 29, 1943 in Volos, Greece
Source: *BioIn 13; EncEurC; EncRk 88; EncRkSt; HalFC 88; HarEnR 86; IlEncRk; IntMPA 92, 94, 96; IntWW 91; ItaFilm; LegTOT; NewAgMG; RkOn 85; RolSEnR 83; WhoRocM 82*

Van Gogh, Vincent Willem
Dutch. Artist
Works in brilliant colors, swirling brush strokes became popular 50 years after death, include *Sunflowers*.
b. Mar 30, 1853 in Groot Zundert, Netherlands
d. Jul 29, 1890 in Auvers, France
Source: *AtlBL; McGDA; NewCol 75; OxCFr; REn*

Van Halen
[Michael Anthony; Sammy Hagar; David Lee Roth; Alex Van Halen; Eddie (Edward) Van Halen]
American. Music Group
California-based, heavy metal rock band; first number-one hit was "Jump," 1984.
Source: *BioIn 14, 15, 16, 17, 21; BlkOlyM; CelR 90; ConMuA 80A; ConMus 8; EncPR&S 89; EncRk 88; EncRkSt; HarEnR 86; PenEncP; RkOn 85; RolSEnR 83; WhoRock 81; WhoRocM 82*

Van Halen, Alex
[Van Halen]
American. Musician
Drummer, brother of Eddie Van Halen; inducted into Hollywood Rock Walk, 1991.
b. May 8, 1955 in Nijmegen, Netherlands
Source: *EncPR&S 89; LegTOT*

Van Halen, Eddie
[Van Halen; Edward Van Halen]
Dutch. Musician, Singer
One of world's top guitarists with band Van Halen since 1974.
b. Jan 26, 1957 in Nijmegen, Netherlands
Source: *BioIn 12, 14, 15; ConNews 85-2; EncPR&S 89; LegTOT; OnThGG;*

WhoAm 86, 88, 90, 92, 94, 95, 96, 97; WhoEnt 92; WhoRocM 82; WorAlBi

Van Hamel, Martine
Canadian. Dancer
Principal dancer, American Ballet Theatre, 1973—; won dance awards.
b. Nov 16, 1945 in Brussels, Belgium
Source: *BiDD; BioIn 8, 10, 11, 12, 13, 14; CreCan 2; CurBio 79; IntDcB; InWom SUP; WhoAm 78, 80, 82, 84, 86, 88; WhoAmW 83, 85, 89, 91; WhoE 85, 86, 89*

Van Heusen, Jimmy
[Edward Chester Babcock; James Van Heusen]
American. Songwriter
''Architect of melody,'' known for collaborations with Sammy Kahn; with Kahn, won Oscars for ''All the Way,'' 1957, ''High Hopes,'' 1959, ''Call Me Irresponsible,'' 1963.
b. Jan 26, 1913 in Syracuse, New York
d. Feb 7, 1990 in Rancho Mirage, California
Source: *AmSong; AnObit 1990; ASCAP 66, 80; Baker 92; BestMus; BiE&WWA; BioIn 4, 9, 14, 15, 16, 17; CelR; CmpEPM; ConTFT 11; CurBio 70, 86, 90, 90N; FacFETw; FilmgC; HalFC 84, 88; IntMPA 86, 88; LegTOT; NewAmDM; NewGrDA 86; NewGrDM 80; NewYTBS 90; NotNAT; OxCPMus; PopAmC, SUP; WhAm 10; WhoThe 81; WorAl; WorAlBi*

Van Heusen, John
American. Designer
Designed first semisoft shirt collar, 1919.
b. Apr 14, 1869 in Albany, New York
d. Dec 18, 1931 in Scarsdale, New York
Source: *Entr; NatCAB 24*

Van Horne, Harriet
American. Critic, Journalist
Syndicated columnist since 1967; writings focus on quality of radio, TV.
b. May 17, 1920 in Syracuse, New York
Source: *BiDAmNC; BioIn 3, 5, 11; CelR; ConAu 113; CurBio 54; EncTwCJ; InWom, SUP; WhoAm 80, 84; WhoAmW 58, 61, 64, 66, 68, 72, 74, 83*

Van Horne, William Cornelius, Sir
American. Railroad Executive
Pres., C.,M.&St.P. Railroad, 1888-99.
b. Feb 3, 1843 in Will County, Illinois
d. Sep 11, 1915 in Montreal, Quebec, Canada
Source: *ApCAB; BiDAmBL 83; DcAmB; DcNaB 1912; HarEnUS; OxCCan; WhAm 1*

Vanik, Charles Albert
American. Politician
Dem. congressman from OH, 1954-79.
b. Apr 7, 1913 in Cleveland, Ohio
Source: *AlmAP 80; BiDrAC; BiDrUSC 89; BioIn 11, 12; CngDr 79; PolProf J, NF; WhoAm 80; WhoAmP 85, 91; WhoGov 77*

Vanilla Fudge
[Carmine Appice; Tim Bogert; Vincent Martell; Mark Stein]
American. Music Group
One of first heavy-rock bands, formed 1966; known for psychedelic light shows.
Source: *BiDAmM; ConMuA 80A; EncPR&S 74; EncRk 88; EncRkSt; IlEncRk; PenEncP; RkOn 78; RolSEnR 83; WhoRock 81; WhoRocM 82*

Vanilla Ice
American. Rapper
White solo rap star; received American Music Award, 1991.
b. Oct 31, 1967 in Miami, Florida
Source: *ConMus 6; News 91, 91-3*

Van Itallie, Jean-Claude
American. Dramatist
Won Obie for *The Serpent,* 1969; other plays include *The Traveler,* 1986.
b. May 23, 1936 in Brussels, Belgium
Source: *BioIn 15; CamGWoT; ConAmD; ConAu 1NR, 2AS, 45, 48NR; ConDr 73, 77, 82, 88, 93; ConLC 3; ConTFT 3; CroCD; DcLB 7; Ent; IntAu&W 82; IntDcT 2; IntWWP 77, 82; McGEWD 72, 84; ModWD; NatPD 77; NotNAT; OxCThe 83; PlP&P; RAdv 13-2; WhoAm 74, 76, 78, 84, 86, 88, 90, 92, 94, 95, 96, 97; WhoEnt 92; WhoThe 72, 77, 81; WhoUSWr 88; WhoWor 74, 76; WhoWrEP 89, 92, 95; WorAu 1970; WrDr 76, 80, 82, 84, 86, 88, 90, 92, 94, 96*

Vanity
[Denise Mathews]
American. Singer, Actor
Recorded album *Nasty Girl* with Vanity 6; solo *Wild Animal,* 1985; in film *The Last Dragon,* 1985.
b. Jan 3, 1961 in Niagara Falls, New York
Source: *BioIn 14, 15, 16; DrBlPA 90; IntAu&W 86*

VanKamp, Merete
[Merete Kamp]
Danish. Actor
Played Daisy in TV movie ''Princess Daisy,'' 1983.
b. Nov 17, 1961 in Kolding, Denmark
Source: *BioIn 13; ConTFT 4*

Van Lew, Elizabeth
American. Spy
VA unionist; federal agent during Civil War.
b. Oct 17, 1818 in Richmond, Virginia
d. Sep 25, 1900 in Richmond, Virginia
Source: *BioIn 3, 6, 9, 11, 19; GoodHs; HerW, 84; InWom; NotAW; WebAMB*

Van Leyden, Lucas
[Lucas Hugensz]
Dutch. Artist
Noted for copperplate engravings; considered founder of Dutch genre painting.
b. 1494 in Leiden, Netherlands
d. 1533 in Leiden, Netherlands
Source: *AtlBL; McGDA; NewCol 75; OxCArt*

Van Loon, Hendrik Willem
American. Historian, Author
Wrote six best-sellers including *The Story of Mankind,* 1921.
b. Jan 14, 1882 in Rotterdam, Netherlands
d. Mar 10, 1944 in New York, New York
Source: *AmAu&B; AnCL; AuBYP 2, 3; Benet 87; BenetAL 91; BioIn 1, 2, 3, 4, 7, 8, 9, 12, 14; ChhPo S2; ChlBkCr; ConAmA; ConAmL; ConAu 117; CurBio 44; DcAmB S3; DcLEL; DcNAA; JBA 34; LinLib L, S; LngCTC; NatCAB 33; NewbMB 1922; OxCAmL 65, 83, 95; REn; REnAL; ScF&FL 1; SmATA 18; TwCA, SUP; WhAm 2; WhAmArt 85; WhNAA; WrChl*

Vannelli, Gino
Canadian. Singer, Songwriter
One of first pop artists to perform without guitars or bass ''Wheels of Life,'' 1979; ''Living Inside Myself.''
b. Jun 16, 1952 in Montreal, Quebec, Canada
Source: *ASCAP 80; BioIn 11, 12; LegTOT; RkOn 85*

Van Niel, Cornelius B(ernardus)
American. Biologist, Educator
Microbiologist who was first to explain photosynthesis.
b. Nov 4, 1897 in Haarlem, Netherlands
d. Mar 10, 1985 in Carmel, California
Source: *AmMWSc 82; ConAu 115; FacFETw; McGMS 80; WhAm 8; WhoAm 76*

Van Nostrand, David
American. Publisher
Publishing co. was largest US outlet for scientific, military, technical works.
b. Dec 5, 1811 in New York, New York
d. Jun 14, 1886
Source: *AmAu&B; ApCAB; DcAmB*

Vanocur, Sander
American. Broadcast Journalist
With ABC News since 1977; chief diplomatic correspondent since 1981.
b. Jan 8, 1928 in Cleveland, Ohio
Source: *BiDAmNC; BioIn 6, 9; ConAu 109, 120; ConTFT 12; CurBio 63; EncTwCJ; IntMPA 84, 86, 92, 94, 96; LegTOT; LesBEnT, 92; WhoAm 74, 76, 78, 80, 82, 84, 86; WhoHol A; WhoSSW 73*

Van Paassen, Pierre
[Pieter Antonie Laurusse Van Paassen]
Canadian. Journalist, Author, Clergy
Religious writings include *Days of Our Years,* 1939; *To Number Our Days,* 1964.
b. Feb 7, 1895 in Goreum, Netherlands
d. Jan 8, 1968 in New York, New York
Source: *AmAu&B; BenetAL 91; BioIn 1, 4, 7, 8, 11; CurBio 42, 68; EncAJ; REnAL; TwCA, SUP; WhAm 4A*

Van Patten, Dick Vincent
American. Actor
Appeared in "I Remember Mama," 1949-57; played Tom Bradford on "Eight Is Enough," 1977-81.
b. Dec 9, 1928 in Kew Gardens, New York
Source: *BiE&WWA; BioIn 12; EncAFC; HalFC 84, 88; IntMPA 86, 92; NotNAT; WhoAm 78, 80, 82, 84, 86, 88, 92, 94, 95, 96, 97; WhoEnt 92; WhoHol A; WhoThe 77; WorAl; WorAlBi*

Van Patten, Joyce
American. Actor
Began career as child actress in radio, stage; TV shows include "Danny Kaye Show."
b. Mar 9, 1934 in New York, New York
Source: *BiE&WWA; ConTFT 4; EncAFC; FilmEn; FilmgC; HalFC 80, 84, 88; IntMPA 88, 92; LegTOT; NotNAT; WhoEnt 92; WhoHol 92, A; WhoThe 72, 77, 81*

Van Patten, Vince(nt)
American. Actor, Tennis Player
Supporting actor, 1970s; films include *Wild Horses;* son of Dick Van Patten.
b. Oct 17, 1957 in New York, New York
Source: *BioIn 14, 21; ItaFilm; NewYTBS 84; WhoHol 92, A; WhoIntT*

Van Peebles, Mario
American. Actor
Films included *The Cotton Club,* 1984; *Heartbreak Ridge,* 1987; *New Jack City,* 1991.
b. Jan 15, 1957 in Mexico City, Mexico
Source: *BioIn 15, 16; ConBlB 2; ConTFT 6, 13; CurBio 93; DcTwCCu 5; DrBlPA 90; InB&W 85; IntMPA 92, 94, 96; LegTOT; NewYTBS 91; WhoBlA 92; WhoHol 92*

Van Peebles, Melvin
American. Actor, Dramatist, Composer
Wrote, directed play *Ain't Supposed to Die a Natural Death,* 1971.
b. Aug 21, 1932 in Chicago, Illinois
Source: *ASCAP 80; BiDAfM; BioIn 8, 9, 10, 12, 13, 15, 16, 17, 19, 20, 21; BlkAmP; BlkAWP; BlksAmF; BlkWr 1, 2; CelR; ConAu 27NR, 85; ConBlAP 88; ConBlB 7; ConDr 77D, 82D, 88D; ConLC 2, 20; ConTFT 7; DcTwCCu 5; DrBlPA, 90; Ebony 1; EncAFC; FilmEn; FilmgC; HalFC 80, 84, 88; InB&W 80, 85; IntDcF 1-2; IntMPA 77, 80, 86, 92, 94, 96; LegTOT; LinLib L; LivgBAA; MiSFD 9; MorBAP; NegAl 76; NewYTBE 72; NotNAT; PlP&P A; SchCGBL; SelBAAf; SelBAAu; WhoAfA 96; WhoBlA 75, 77, 80, 85, 88, 90, 92, 94; WhoHol 92, A; WhoThe 77, 81*

Van Rensselaer, Stephen
American. Army Officer, Politician
Congressman from NY, 1822-29; first pres., NY Board of Agriculture, 1820.
b. Nov 1, 1764 in New York, New York
d. Jan 26, 1839 in Albany, New York
Source: *AmBi; ApCAB; BiAUS; BiDrAC; BiDrUSC 89; BiInAmS; BioIn 19; CyEd; DcAmB; DcAmMiB; Drake; EncAAH; EncAR; HarEnMi; NatCAB 2; OxCAmH; WebAB 74, 79; WebAMB; WhAm HS; WhAmP*

Van Rooy, Anton
Dutch. Opera Singer
Bass-baritone; Wagnerian star, banned from Bayreuth, 1903.
b. Jan 1, 1870 in Rotterdam, Netherlands
d. Nov 28, 1932 in Munich, Germany
Source: *Baker 78, 84; MetOEnc; NewEOp 71; NewGrDA 86; NewGrDM 80; PenDiMP*

Van Sant, Gus
American. Filmmaker
Films directed include *Drugstore Cowboy,* 1989; *My Own Private Idaho.*
b. 1952 in Louisville, Kentucky
Source: *Au&Arts 17; ConAu 152; CurBio 92; IntMPA 94, 96; LegTOT; News 92, 92-2; NewYTBS 91; WhoAm 95, 96, 97*

Van Shelton, Ricky
American. Singer, Songwriter
Country singer; debut album *Wild-Eyed Dream,* 1987 went gold.
b. Jan 12, 1952 in Grit, Virginia
Source: *BioIn 16; ConMus 5; WhoAm 90, 92, 94, 95; WhoEnt 92*

Van Slyke, Andy
[Andrew James Van Slyke]
American. Baseball Player
Centerfielder, St. Louis Cardinals 1979-87; currently with the Philadelphia Phillies.
b. Dec 21, 1960 in Utica, New York
Source: *Ballpl 90; BioIn 16, 21; News 92; WhoAm 92, 94, 95, 96, 97; WhoE 95; WhoSpor; WhoWor 96*

Van Slyke, Helen Lenore Vogt
American. Author
Wrote best-sellers *A Necessary Woman,* 1979; *No Love Lost,* 1979.
b. Jul 9, 1919 in Washington, District of Columbia
d. Jul 3, 1979 in New York, New York
Source: *ConAu 89; InWom SUP; WhoAdv 72; WrDr 76*

Van't Hoff, Jacobus Henricus
Dutch. Chemist
First to win Nobel Prize, 1901; researched stereochemistry.
b. Aug 30, 1852 in Rotterdam, Netherlands
d. Mar 1, 1911 in Berlin, Germany
Source: *AsBiEn; BiESc; BioIn 14, 15, 19; DcScB; Dis&D; InSci; LarDcSc; McGEWB; WhoNob, 90, 95; WorAl; WorScD*

Van Vechten, Carl
American. Author, Critic
Wrote *Parties,* 1930; *Pavlova,* 1947.
b. Jun 17, 1880 in Cedar Rapids, Iowa
d. Dec 21, 1964 in New York, New York
Source: *AmAu&B; AmWr S2; Baker 78, 84, 92; Benet 87, 96; BenetAL 91; BiDAmM; BioIn 2, 3, 4, 5, 6, 7, 8, 12, 15, 16, 20; CnDAL; ConAmA; ConAmL; ConAu 89; ConLC 33; ConPhot 82, 88; CyWA 58; DancEn 78; DcAmB S7; DcLB 4, 9, 51A; DcLEL; GayLesB; GrWrEL N; ICPEnP A; LegTOT; LngCTC; MacBEP; NewGrDA 86; NotNAT B; OxCAmL 65, 83, 95; PenC AM; REn; REnAL; RfGAmL 87, 94; RGTwCWr; TwCA, SUP; WebE&AL; WhAm 4*

Van Vleck, John Hasbrouck
American. Physicist
Shared Nobel Prize in physics, 1977, with Anderson, Mott; studied electronic structures.
b. Mar 13, 1899 in Middletown, Connecticut
d. Nov 28, 1980 in Cambridge, Massachusetts
Source: *AnObit 1980; BioIn 12, 13, 14, 15, 19, 20; CamDcSc; ConAu 102; DcAmB S10; DcScB S2; IntWW 74; LarDcSc; NewYTBS 80; WhAm 7; Who 74; WhoAm 74; WhoNob, 90, 95; WhoWor 74; WorScD*

Van Vooren, Monique
American. Actor, Author
Appeared in movie *Damn Yankees,* 1958; wrote novel *Night Sanctuary,* 1981.
b. Mar 17, 1933 in Brussels, Belgium
Source: *BiE&WWA; ConAu 107; ForYSC; InWom; MotPP; WhoAm 74, 76; WhoAmW 70, 72; WhoHol 92, A; WhoHrs 80*

Van Wachem, Lodewijk Christiaan
Dutch. Business Executive
President of Royal Dutch Petroleum Co. since 1982.
b. Jul 31, 1931 in Pangkalan Brandan, Dutch East Indies
Source: *BioIn 15; Dun&B 90; IntWW 78, 79, 80, 81, 82, 83, 89, 91, 93; St&PR 91; Who 82, 83, 85, 88, 90, 92, 94; WhoAm 88, 90, 92, 94, 95, 96, 97; WhoFI 89, 92, 94, 96; WhoSSW 88, 91, 93; WhoWor 89, 93, 95, 96, 97*

Van Westerborg, Edward
American. Publisher
Founded *Facts on File,* 1941; headed publications until 1975.
b. 1900?, Netherlands
d. May 7, 1988 in Walnut Creek, California

Van Zandt, Marie
American. Opera Singer
Coloratura soprano; Paris Opera-Comique, 1880s.
b. Oct 8, 1861 in New York, New York
d. Dec 31, 1919 in Cannes, France
Source: *AmWom; ApCAB; Baker 78, 84; InWom; NewEOp 71; NewGrDM 80; PenDiMP*

Van Zant, Ronnie
[Lynyrd Skynard; Ronald Van Zant]
American. Musician, Singer
Founding member of one of best rock bands in history, 1973-77; group ended when he and others were killed in plane crash.
b. Jan 15, 1949 in Jacksonville, Florida
d. Oct 20, 1977 in Gillsburg, Mississippi
Source: *BioIn 11; LegTOT; WhoRocM 82*

Vanzetti, Bartolomeo
[Sacco and Vanzetti]
Italian. Political Activist
Tried, executed for murder during robbery; case became most notorious of century due to widespread charges of mistrial.
b. Jun 11, 1888 in Villafalletto, Italy
d. Aug 23, 1927 in Boston, Massachusetts
Source: *AmBi; BiDAmL; BioIn 2, 3, 4, 5, 6, 7, 8, 9, 10, 11, 12, 13, 14, 15, 16, 17, 20; CopCroC; DcAmB; DcAmSR; LegTOT; REn; WebAB 74, 79; WhAm 4; WhDW; WorAl; WorAlBi*

Varda, Agnes
French. Screenwriter, Director
Directed *Elsa,* 1966; *Lions Love,* 1969.
b. May 30, 1928 in Brussels, Belgium
Source: *BiDFilm, 81, 94; BioIn 7, 9, 12, 13, 15, 16; ConAu 116, 122; ConLC 16; ContDcW 89; ConTFT 8; CurBio 70; DcFM; DcTwCCu 2; EncEurC; FilmEn; FilmgC; HalFC 80, 84, 88; IntAu&W 76, 77, 82; IntDcF 1-2, 2-2; IntDcWB; IntMPA 79, 80, 81, 82, 84, 86, 88; IntWW 74, 75, 76, 77, 78, 79, 80, 81, 82, 83, 89, 91, 93; InWom SUP; ItaFilm; MiSFD 9; OxCFilm; ReelWom; WhoAmW 70, 72; WhoFr 79; WhoHol A; WhoWor 74, 76, 78, 84, 91; WomWMM; WorEFlm; WorFDir 2*

Vardon, Harry
"Great Triumvirate"
English. Golfer
With James Braid, JH Taylor, dominated game, late 19th, early 20th c; only player to win British Open six times.
b. May 9, 1870 in Isle of Jersey, England
d. Mar 20, 1937 in London, England
Source: *BioIn 9, 13; WhoGolf*

Vare, Glenna Collett
American. Golfer
Dominated women's golf, 1922-35; won 49 amateur titles; Vare Trophy, given to women golfers, named for her; charter member, Hall of Fame.
b. Jun 20, 1903 in New Haven, Connecticut
d. Feb 3, 1989 in Gulfstream, Florida
Source: *BiDAmSp OS; BioIn 11, 16, 17; FacFETw; GoodHs; InWom SUP; NewYTBS 89; WhoGolf; WorAl; WorAlBi*

Varese, Edgar
American. Composer, Author
Founded, directed International Composers Guild, 1921-27; developed electronic music, 1917.
b. Dec 22, 1883 in Paris, France
d. Nov 6, 1965 in New York, New York
Source: *AtlBL; Baker 78, 84; BriBkM 80; DcAmB S7; DcCM; DcTwCC; FacFETw; NewGrDM 80; OxCMus; WebAB 74; WhAm 4*

Varesi, Felice
French. Opera Singer
Baritone, noted for Verdi roles.
b. 1813 in Calais, France
d. Mar 13, 1889 in Milan, Italy
Source: *Baker 84, 92; CmOp; MetOEnc; NewEOp 71; NewGrDM 80; NewGrDO; OxDcOp*

Vargas, Alberto
[Joaquin Alberto Vargas y Chavez]
American. Artist
Created pinups for *Esquire; Playboy* magazines.
b. Feb 9, 1895 in Arequipa, Peru
d. Dec 30, 1983 in Los Angeles, California
Source: *BioIn 11; NewYTBS 83*

Vargas, Getulio Dornelles
Brazilian. Lawyer, Political Leader
Pres. of Brazil, 1930-45.
b. Apr 19, 1883 in Sao Borja, Brazil
d. Aug 24, 1954 in Rio de Janeiro, Brazil
Source: *BiDLAmC; CurBio 40, 51, 54; DcPol; McGEWB; WhAm 3; WhDW; WhWW-II*

Vargas Llosa, Mario
Peruvian. Author
Work includes *The Real Life of Alejandro Mayta,* 1986.
b. Mar 28, 1936 in Arequipa, Peru
Source: *Benet 87; BenetAL 91; BioIn 7, 10, 11, 12, 14, 15, 16, 17, 18, 19, 20, 21; CasWL; ConAu 18NR, 32NR, 73; ConFLW 84; ConLC 3, 6, 9, 10, 15, 31, 42, 85; CurBio 76; CyWA 89; DcArts; DcCLAA; DcCPSAm; DcHiB; DcLB 145; DcTwCCu 3; EncLatA; EncWL, 2, 3; FacFETw; HispLC; HispWr; IntAu&W 89; IntvLAW; IntWW 74, 75, 76, 77, 78, 79, 80, 81, 82, 83, 89, 91, 93; LatAmWr; LegTOT; LiExTwC; MagSWL; MajTwCW; ModLAL; NewYTBS 89, 90; Novels; OxCSpan; PenC AM; PostFic; RAdv 14, 13-2; SpAmA; TwCWr; WhoAm 86, 88; WhoTwCL; WhoWor 74, 78, 80, 82, 84, 87, 91, 93, 95; WorAu 1970*

Varipapa, Andy
American. Bowler
Won national bowling championships in 1940s.
b. 1894
d. Aug 25, 1984 in Huntington, New York
Source: *BioIn 1, 10; NewYTBS 84; WhoSpor*

Varley, F(rederick) H(orseman)
[Group of Seven]
Canadian. Artist
Landscape, portrait painter; original member of group influential in Canadian painting, 1920s; famous for *Stormy Weather, Georgian Bay,* 1920.
b. Jan 2, 1881 in Sheffield, England
d. Sep 8, 1969 in Toronto, Ontario, Canada
Source: *BioIn 11; CreCan 1; IlBEAAW; McGDA; WhoAmA 78N*

Varmus, Harold E(lliot)
American. Government Official, Scientist
With J. Michael Bishop won the 1989 Nobel Prize for Physiology or medicine for their work on the origins of cancer; director, National Institutes of Health, 1993—.
b. Dec 18, 1939 in Oceanside, New York
Source: *AmMWSc 82, 86, 89, 92, 95; CurBio 96; IntWW 91; LarDcSc; Who 92; WhoAm 90; WhoNob 90; WhoWest 92; WhoWor 91; WorAlBi*

Varnay, Astrid
Swedish. Opera Singer
Dramatic soprano; made NY Met., debut, 1941, substituting for Lotte Lehmann without rehearsal.
b. Apr 25, 1918 in Stockholm, Sweden
Source: *Baker 78, 84; BiDAmM; BioIn 2, 3, 4, 6, 10, 11; BriBkM 80; CmOp; CurBio 51; IntWWM 80, 90; InWom, SUP; MetOEnc; MusSN; NewAmDM; NewEOp 71; NewGrDA 86; NewGrDM 80; NewYTBS 74; OxDcOp; PenDiMP; WhoMus 72*

Varnedoe, (John) Kirk (Train)
American. Art Historian
Director of the Dept. of Painting and Sculpture at the Museum of Modern Art, 1989—.
b. Jan 18, 1946 in Savannah, Georgia
Source: *BioIn 15, 16, 17; CurBio 91; NewYTBS 90; WhoAm 90, 92, 94, 95, 96, 97; WhoAmA 76, 78, 80, 82, 84, 86, 89, 91, 93; WhoE 95*

Varney, Jim
American. Actor
Plays TV commercial character Ernest P Worrell; star of film *Ernest Goes to Camp,* 1987.
b. Jun 15, 1949 in Lexington, Kentucky
Source: *ConNews 85-4; ConTFT 11; IntMPA 92, 94, 96; WhoHol 92*

Varsi, Diane
American. Actor
Won Oscar for her first film *Peyton Place,* 1957.
b. Feb 23, 1938 in San Francisco, California
d. Nov 19, 1992 in Los Angeles, California
Source: *AnObit 1992; BioIn 18, 19; FilmgC; ForYSC; HalFC 80, 84, 88; IntMPA 84, 86, 88, 92; InWom SUP; LegTOT; MotPP; MovMk; NewYTBE 72; WhoAm 74; WhoHol 92, A; WorAl*

Varviso, Silvio
Swiss. Conductor
Director, Stockholm Royal Opera, 1965-72; Paris Opera, since 1981.
b. Feb 26, 1924 in Zurich, Switzerland
Source: *Baker 78, 84, 92; IntWWM 90; MetOEnc; NewAmDM; NewEOp 71; NewGrDM 80; NewGrDO; PenDiMP; WhoOp 76; WhoWor 74*

Vasarely, Victor
French. Artist
Considered originator of post-war Op Art; geometric works include *Orion MC,* 1963.
b. Apr 9, 1908 in Pecs, Austria-Hungary
d. Mar 15, 1997 in Paris, France
Source: *BioIn 8, 9, 10; ClaDrA; ConArt 77, 83, 89; CurBio 71; DcArts; DcCAr 81; DcTwCCu 2; EncWB; IntDcAA 90; IntWW 74, 75, 76, 77, 78, 79, 80, 81, 82, 83, 89, 91, 93; McGDA; OxCTwCA; OxDcArt; PhDcTCA 77; PrintW 83, 85; WhoAm 74, 76, 78, 80, 82, 84, 86, 88, 95; WhoArt 80, 82, 84; WhoFI 85; WhoFr 79; WhoWor 82, 84, 87, 89; WorArt 1950*

Vasari, Giorgio
Italian. Architect, Artist, Author
Published *Lives of Most Eminent Painters and Sculptors,* 1550, first work of art history.
b. Jul 30, 1511 in Arezzo, Italy
d. Jun 27, 1574 in Florence, Italy
Source: *AtlBL; Benet 87, 96; BiD&SB; BioIn 14, 18, 21; CamGWoT; CasWL; ClaDrA; DcArts; DcCathB; DcEuL; DcItL 1, 2; EncWT; EuAu; IntDcAA 90; IntDcAr; LegTOT; LinLib L, S; MacEA; McGDA; McGEWB; NewC; NewCBEL; OxCArt; OxCEng 67, 85, 95; OxDcArt; PenC EUR; REn; WhDW; WhoArch; WorAl; WorAlBi*

Vashti
Persian. Ruler
Dethroned, maybe beheaded, for refusing to flaunt her beauty for group of princes at her husband's, the king's, request.
b. fl. 519BC
Source: *BioIn 9; EncAmaz 91; NewCol 75*

Vasily III
Russian. Ruler
Grand prince of Moscow 1505-1533; consolidated several independent principalities into Muscovite state; father of Ivan the Terrible.
b. 1479
d. Dec 3, 1533 in Moscow, Russia

Vassallo, Jesse
American. Swimmer
World's best individual medley swimmer, 1978-82.
b. 1961
Source: *BioIn 11, 13; NewYTBS 84*

Vassar, Matthew
English. Brewer, Merchant
Founded Vassar College, 1865.
b. Apr 29, 1792 in East Tuddingham, England
d. Jun 23, 1868 in Poughkeepsie, New York
Source: *AmBi; ApCAB; BioIn 10, 15; CyAL 2; DcAmB; HarEnUS; LinLib L, S; NatCAB 5; NewCol 75; OxCAmH; TwCBDA; WebAB 74, 79; WebBD 83; WhAm HS*

Vassilenko, Sergei
Russian. Composer
Wrote operas *Christopher Columbus,* 1933; *Buran,* 1939; works inspired by Russian folk songs, the East.
b. Mar 30, 1872 in Moscow, Russia
d. Mar 11, 1956 in Moscow, Union of Soviet Socialist Republics
Source: *Baker 78, 84; NewEOp 71*

Vaughan, Arky
[Joseph Floyd Vaughan]
American. Baseball Player
Shortstop, 1932-43, 1947-48, mostly with Pittsburgh; led NL in batting, 1935; had lifetime .318 batting average.
b. Mar 9, 1912 in Clifty, Arkansas
d. Aug 30, 1952 in Eagleville, California
Source: *Ballpl 90; BiDAmSp BB; BioIn 14, 15; LegTOT; WhoProB 73; WhoSpor*

Vaughan, Bill
[William Edward Vaughan]
American. Journalist, Author
Wrote nationally syndicated column "Starbeams."
b. Oct 8, 1915 in Saint Louis, Missouri
d. Feb 26, 1977 in Kansas City, Kansas
Source: *BiDAmNC; BioIn 6, 11; ConAu 5R, 69; WhAm 7; WhoAm 74, 76; WhoMW 74, 76*

Vaughan, Harry Hawkins
American. Army Officer
Military aide to Harry S Truman during vice presidential, presidential years, 1944-53.
b. Nov 26, 1893 in Glasgow, Missouri
d. May 20, 1981 in Fort Belvoir, Virginia
Source: *BioIn 1, 2, 8, 11, 12; CurBio 49, 81; PolProf T*

Vaughan, Henry
Welsh. Poet
Best known for *The Retreat; The World.*
b. Apr 17, 1622 in Llansantfraed, Wales
d. Apr 23, 1695 in Newton, England
Source: *Alli; AtlBL; BbD; Benet 87, 96; BiD&SB; BiDRP&D; BioIn 1, 2, 3, 5, 6, 7, 10, 12, 19, 21; BlmGEL; BritAu; BritWr 2; CamGEL; CasWL; ChhPo, S2; CnE&AP; CroE&S; CrtT 1; DcArts; DcEnA; DcEnL; DcEuL; DcLEL; DcNaB; EvLB; GrWrEL P; IlEncMy; LinLib L; LngCEL; MouLC 1; NewC; NewCBEL; OxCEng 67; PenC ENG; RAdv 1, 14, 13-1; REn; WebE&AL*

Vaughan, Sarah Lois
American. Singer
Jazz vocalist, pianist; career took off after winning contest at Apollo Theater, NYC, 1940s.
b. Mar 27, 1924 in Newark, New Jersey
d. Apr 3, 1990 in Hidden Hills, California
Source: *Baker 84; BiDJaz; BioIn 13, 14, 15, 16; BioNews 74; CelR 90; CmpEPM; ConMus 2; ContDcW 89; CurBio 57, 80, 90, 90N; DrBlPA 90; EncJzS; FacFETw; IntWW 83, 89; InWom SUP; NegAl 89; NewAmDM; NewGrDA 86; NewGrDJ 88; News 90; NewYTBS 90; NotBlAW 1; OxCPMus; PenEncP; WhoAm 86, 88; WhoAmW 85, 87; WhoBlA 85, 90, 92N; WhoWor 84, 89; WorAlBi*

Vaughan, Stevie Ray
American. Musician
Guitarist; Grammy for "In Step," 1990; died in helicopter crash.
b. Oct 3, 1954 in Dallas, Texas
d. Aug 27, 1990 in East Troy, Wisconsin
Source: *AnObit 1990; BioIn 13, 16; EncPR&S 89; EncRkSt; FacFETw; News 91-1; NewYTBS 90; OnThGG; PenEncP*

Vaughan Williams, Ralph
English. Composer
Works include chorals, songs, symphonies including "London," 1914; "Pastoral," 1922.
b. Oct 12, 1872 in Ampney, England
d. Aug 26, 1958 in London, England
Source: *AtlBL; Baker 78, 84, 92; Benet 87, 96; BioIn 1, 2, 3, 4, 5, 6, 7, 8, 9, 10, 11, 12, 14, 15, 16, 20; BriBkM 80; CmOp; CompSN, SUP; ConAu 115; CurBio 53, 58; DcArts; DcCM; DcCom 77; DcCom&M 79; DcNaB 1951; DcTwCC, A; FacFETw; GrBr; IntDcOp; LegTOT; LinLib S; MakMC; McGEWB; MetOEnc; MusMk; NewAmDM; NewEOp 71; NewGrDM 80; NewGrDO;*

NewOxM; ObitT 1951; OxCEng 85, 95; OxCFilm; OxCMus; OxDcOp; PenDiMP A; RAdv 14; REn; WhAm 3; WhDW; WhE&EA

Vaughn, Robert
American. Actor
Played Napoleon Solo in TV series "The Man from UNCLE," 1964-67.
b. Nov 22, 1932 in New York, New York
Source: *BioIn 7, 8, 10, 11, 17; BioNews 74; BlueB 76; ConAu 61; ConTFT 3, 5; CurBio 67; FilmEn; FilmgC; ForYSC; HalFC 80, 84, 88; IntMPA 75, 76, 77, 78, 79, 80, 81, 82, 84, 86, 88, 92, 94, 96; ItaFilm; LegTOT; MotPP; MovMk; WhoAm 74, 76, 78, 80, 82, 84, 86, 88, 90, 92, 94, 95, 96, 97; WhoHol 92, A; WhoHrs 80; WhoTelC; WorAlBi; WorEFlm*

Vaux, Calvert
American. Architect
Park landscapes include Central Park, NYC; South Park, Chicago.
b. Dec 20, 1824 in London, England
d. Nov 19, 1895 in New York, New York
Source: *Alli; AmBi; ApCAB; BiDAmAr; BioIn 2, 3, 9, 13; DcAmAu; DcAmB; DcNAA; HarEnUS; IntDcAr; MacEA; NatCAB 9; OxCAmH; TwCBDA; WhAm HS; WhoArch*

Veblen, Thorstein Bunde
American. Economist
Divided society into economic classes; wrote *The Theory of the Leisure Class,* 1899.
b. Jul 30, 1857 in Valders, Wisconsin
d. Aug 3, 1929 in Palo Alto, California
Source: *AmAu&B; AmBi; DcAmB; DcAmSR; DcLEL; EncAB-H 1974, 1996; EvLB; LinLib S; LngCTC; ModAL; OxCAmH; OxCAmL 65, 83; PenC AM; REn; REnAL; WhoTwCL; WorAl*

Vedder, Eddie
[Pearl Jam; Eddie Mueller]
American. Singer, Songwriter
Debut album *Ten,* 1991.
b. Dec 23, 1964 in Chicago, Illinois

Vedder, Elihu
American. Artist
Painted five decorative panels, mosaic Minerva in the Congressional Library in Washington, DC.
b. Feb 26, 1836 in New York, New York
d. Jan 29, 1923 in Rome, Italy
Source: *AmAu&B; AmBi; AmLY; ApCAB, X; ArtsNiC; BenetAL 91; BioIn 5, 7, 9, 12, 15; BriEAA; ChhPo S1; DcAmArt; DcAmB; DcNAA; Drake; EarABI, SUP; HarEnUS; IlrAm 1880; LinLib S; McGDA; NatCAB 6; NewYHSD; OxCAmL 65, 83, 95; PeoHis; REnAL; TwCBDA; WhAm 1; WhAmArt 85*

Vee, Bobby
[Robert Velline]
American. Singer
Teen idol singer similar to Frankie Avalon, Fabian; songs include "Take Good Care of My Baby," 1961.
b. Apr 30, 1943 in Fargo, North Dakota
Source: *AmPS A; BiDAmM; BioIn 12; EncPR&S 89; EncRk 88; EncRkSt; HarEnR 86; LegTOT; PenEncP; RkOn 74, 82; RolSEnR 83; WhoHol 92, A; WhoRock 81*

Veeck, Bill
[William Louis Veeck]
"P T Barnum of Baseball"
American. Baseball Executive
Owner of three ML baseball teams; introduced gimmicks such as exploding scoreboards, ethnic nights to game.
b. Feb 9, 1914 in Chicago, Illinois
d. Jan 2, 1986 in Chicago, Illinois
Source: *AnObit 1986; Ballpl 90; BiDAmSp BB; BioIn 11, 13; BioNews 74; ConAu 118; ConNews 86-1; CurBio 48, 86, 86N; FacFETw; LegTOT; NewYTBS 82, 86; WebAB 74, 79; WhAm 9; WhoAm 76, 78, 80, 82, 84; WhoMW 78, 80; WhoProB 73*

Vega, Suzanne
American. Singer, Songwriter
Blends jazz, rock and roll, and minimalism; had hit single "Luka," 1987.
b. Jul 11, 1959 in Santa Monica, California
Source: *BioIn 14, 15; ConMus 3; ConNews 88-1; CurBio 94; EncRkSt; LegTOT; NewGrDA 86; PenEncP; WhoAm 94; WhoAmW 95*

Veidt, Conrad
British. Actor
Played in German films, 1917-34, including *Diary of a Lost Girl.*
b. Jan 22, 1893 in Berlin, Germany
d. Apr 3, 1943 in Hollywood, California
Source: *BiDFilm, 81, 94; BioIn 9, 15, 20; CurBio 43; DcArts; EncEurC; Film 1, 2; FilmAG WE; FilmEn; FilmgC; ForYSC; HalFC 80, 84, 88; IlWWBF; IntDcF 1-3, 2-3; ItaFilm; LegTOT; MotPP; MovMk; NotNAT B; OxCFilm; PenEncH; TwYS; WhoHol B; WhoHrs 80; WhScrn 74, 77, 83; WorAl; WorEFlm*

Veil, Simone Annie Jacob
French. Political Leader
Pres., European Parliament, 1979-82; chm., legal affairs committee, 1982, 1984-89.
b. Jul 13, 1927 in Nice, France
Source: *BiDFrPL; BioIn 16; ContDcW 89; CurBio 80; IntWW 83, 91; IntYB 82; InWom SUP; NewYTBS 74; Who 83, 92; WhoWor 87, 91*

Velarde, Pablita
American. Artist
Her art chronicles the lives of the Pueblo people; she revived traditional forms of making art; won the Palmes Academiques from the French government, 1954.
b. Sep 19, 1918 in Santa Clara, New Mexico
Source: *BioIn 7, 9, 10, 11, 19, 20, 21; HerW, 84; InWom SUP; NotNaAm; WhoAmA 73, 76, 78, 80, 82*

Velasco Alvarado, Juan
Peruvian. Political Leader
Pres. of Peru after 1958 coup; ousted in 1975 coup.
b. Jun 16, 1910 in Piura, Peru
d. Dec 24, 1977 in Lima, Peru
Source: *BiDLAmC; BioIn 8, 9, 10, 11, 13; CurBio 70, 78, 78N; DcCPSAm; EncLatA; EncWB; IntWW 74, 75, 76, 77, 78; NewCol 75; NewYTBS 77; WhoGov 72; WhoWor 74, 76; WorDWW*

Velasco Ibarra, Jose Maria
Ecuadorean. Political Leader
Served as pres. of Ecuador five times between 1934-72; ousted by military off and on.
b. Mar 19, 1893 in Quito, Ecuador
d. Mar 30, 1979 in Quito, Ecuador
Source: *BiDLAmC; BioIn 1, 5, 6, 8, 9, 11, 12, 16, 21; CurBio 52, 79, 79N; DcCPSAm; DcHiB; DicTyr; EncLatA; FacFETw; IntWW 74, 75, 76, 77, 78; McGEWB; NewCol 75; NewYTBS 79; WhoGov 72; WhoWor 74*

Velazquez, Diego Rodriguez de Silva
Spanish. Artist
Greatest Spanish Baroque painter; superb colorist, noted for portraits, genre scenes.
b. Jun 6, 1599 in Seville, Spain
d. Aug 6, 1660 in Madrid, Spain
Source: *AtlBL; McGDA; McGEWB; NewC; NewCol 75; OxCArt; RAdv 14; REn*

Velde, Willem van de
Dutch. Artist
Known for paintings of naval battles; member of family of famous 17th century painters, draftsmen.
b. 1633 in Leiden, Netherlands
d. 1707 in London, England
Source: *McGDA; NewCol 75; WebBD 83; WhDW*

Velez, Clemente Soto
Puerto Rican. Social Reformer, Poet
Campaigned to prevent Puerto Rico from becoming the 51st state.
d. Apr 16, 1993 in San Juan, Puerto Rico
Source: *BiDHisL; BioIn 16*

Velez, Eddie
[Edwin Velez]
American. Actor
Best known for episodic TV; films include *Extremities,* 1986.
b. Jun 4, 1958 in New York, New York
Source: *ConTFT 5; WhoHol 92*

Velez, Lupe
[Maria Guadalupe Velez de Villalobos]
Mexican. Actor
Starred in *Mexican Spitfire* film series, 1940s; married Johnny Weissmuller, 1933-38.
b. Jul 18, 1910 in San Luis Potosi, Mexico
d. Dec 14, 1944 in Beverly Hills, California
Source: *BioIn 7, 10; CurBio 45; FilmEn; FilmgC; InWom; MotPP; MovMk; NotNAT B; ThFT; TwYS; WhoHol B; WhScrn 74, 77*

Velluti, Giovanni Battista
Italian. Opera Singer
Male soprano, considered last great castrato; shocked, fascinated Londoners, 1820s.
b. Jan 28, 1780 in Monterone, Italy
d. Jan 22, 1861 in Sambruson, Italy
Source: *CmOp; NewEOp 71; NewGrDO; OxCMus; OxDcOp*

Velvet Underground, The
[John Cale; Sterling Morrison; Lou Reed; Marueen Tucker]
American. Music Group
Formed, 1965; never sold many records but influenced David Bowie, the Cars, the Sex Pistols, and others.
Source: *BiDAmM; BioIn 12, 14, 15, 16, 17, 21; ConAu X; ConMuA 80A; ConMus 7; DcArts; EncPR&S 74, 89; EncRk 88; EncRkSt; HarEnR 86; IlEncRk; NewAmDM; NewGrDA 86; NewYTBS 95; OxCPMus; PenEncP; RolSEnR 83; WhoRock 81; WhoRocM 82*

Vendler, Helen Hennessy
American. Educator, Critic
Harvard English professor; poetry criticism appears in *New Yorker; New Yorker Review of Books.*
b. Apr 30, 1933 in Boston, Massachusetts
Source: *AmWomWr; BioIn 14, 15; ConAu 25NR, 41R; CurBio 86; DrAS 82E; IntAu&W 77, 91; MajTwCW; WhoAm 86, 90, 97; WhoAmW 85, 87, 91, 97; WhoUSWr 88; WhoWrEP 89; WorAu 1975; WrDr 86, 92*

Venizelos, Eleutherios Kyriakos
Greek. Statesman
Premier of Greece, 1910; leader of opposition to Tsaldares govt., 1933-35; condemned to death but received amnesty from King George II.
b. Aug 23, 1864 in Mournies, Crete
d. Mar 18, 1936 in Paris, France
Source: *McGEWB; WebBD 83; WhDW*

Venkataraman, Ramaswamy
Indian. Political Leader
President of India, 1987-92.
b. Dec 4, 1910 in Rajamadam, India
Source: *BioIn 15, 16, 19, 21; IntWW 83, 89, 91, 93; NewYTBS 87; Who 83, 85, 88, 90, 92, 94; WhoAsAP 91; WhoWor 82, 84, 87, 91, 93, 95*

Venter, J. Craig
American. Scientist
With the Institute for Genomic Research, Gaithersburg, MD, 1992—.
b. Oct 14, 1946 in Salt Lake City, Utah
Source: *AmMWSc 82, 86, 89, 92, 95; CurBio 95; WhoFrS 84*

Ventura, Charlie
American. Jazz Musician
Noted tenor saxist; with Gene Krupa, 1940s.
b. Dec 2, 1916 in Philadelphia, Pennsylvania
d. Jan 17, 1992 in Pleasantville, New Jersey
Source: *AllMusG; AnObit 1992; BgBands 74; BiDJaz; BioIn 17, 19; CmpEPM; EncJzS; EncJzS; NewAmDM; NewGrDJ 88, 94; PenEncP; WhoJazz 72*

Ventures, The
[Bob Bogle; Johnny Durrill; Nokie Edwards; Howie Johnston; Jerry McGee; Mel Taylor; Don Wilson]
American. Music Group
Instrumental rock group, formed 1960; hits include "Walk, Don't Run," 1960; "Hawaii Five-O," 1969.
Source: *AmPS A; CurBio 44; DrRegL 75; EncPR&S 74, 89; EncRk 88; EncRkSt; HarEnR 86; NewAmDM; NewGrDA 86; NewYTBS 27, 82, 88; ObitOF 79; PenEncP; RkOn 74; RolSEnR 83; WhoHol 92, A; WhoRock 81; WhoRocM 82*

Venturi, Ken(neth)
American. Sportscaster, Golfer
Won US Open, 1964; golf commentator for CBS since 1968.
b. May 15, 1931 in San Francisco, California
Source: *BioIn 4, 5, 7, 9, 10, 11; CmCal; CurBio 66; WhoGolf; WhoTelC*

Venturi, Robert
American. Architect
Winner, Pritzker Architecture Prize, 1991; best-known works are the Salisbury Wing of the British National Gallery and the Seattle Art Museum.
b. Jun 25, 1925 in Philadelphia, Pennsylvania
Source: *AmArch 70; AmCulL; AmDec 1960, 1970; BioIn 9, 10, 11, 12, 13; BlueB 76; BriEAA; CelR; ConArch 80; ConAu 61; CurBio 75; DcArts; DcTwCCu 1; DcTwDes; EncAAr 2; EncAB-H 1996; EncWB; IntDcAr; IntWW 76, 77, 78, 79, 80, 81, 82, 83, 89, 91, 93; MacEA; NatCAB 63N; News 94; PenDiDA 89; Who 88, 90, 92, 94; WhoAm 74, 76, 78, 80, 82, 84, 86, 88, 90, 92, 94, 95, 96, 97; WhoAmA 78, 80, 82, 84, 86, 89, 91, 93; WhoE 74, 77, 85A, 86, 89, 93, 95, 97; WhoWor 74; WrDr 76, 80, 82, 84, 86, 88, 90, 92, 94, 96*

Venuta, Benay
[Venuta Rose Crooke]
American. Actor, Singer
Played on stage since 1928 in *Anything Goes; Annie Get Your Gun.*
b. Jan 27, 1911 in San Francisco, California
Source: *BiE&WWA; BioIn 21; CmpEPM; NewYTBS 95; NotNAT; WhoHol A; WhoThe 72, 77, 81*

Vera
[Vera Neumann]
American. Designer
Founded Vera Co., 1945.
b. Jul 24, 1910 in Stamford, Connecticut
d. Jun 15, 1993 in North Tarrytown, New York
Source: *DcLP 87B; FairDF US; WorFshn*

Vera, Billy
[Billy Vera & the Beaters]
American. Singer
Had number one single "At This Moment," 1986.
b. May 28, 1945 in Riverside, California
Source: *BioIn 15*

Vera-Ellen
[Vera-Ellen Rohe]
American. Dancer, Actor
Films include *White Christmas,* 1954; *Web of Violence,* 1959.
b. Feb 16, 1926 in Cincinnati, Ohio
d. Aug 30, 1981 in Los Angeles, California
Source: *AnObit 1981; BioIn 5, 11, 12, 13; CmMov; CmpEPM; CurBio 59, 81, 81N; FilmEn; FilmgC; HalFC 80; InWom, SUP; MotPP; MovMk; WhoHol A; WhScrn 83; WorEFlm*

Verdi, Giuseppe Fortunino Francesco
Italian. Composer
Composed 27 operas, including *Rigoletto; La Traviata; Aida.*
b. Oct 10, 1813 in Le Roncole, Italy
d. Jan 27, 1901 in Milan, Italy
Source: *AtlBL; NewC; NewCol 75; REn; WebBD 83*

Verdi-Fletcher, Mary (Regina)
American. Dancer
President and founder, Cleveland Ballet Dancing Wheels, the first dance company in the US that included people in wheelchairs, 1980—.
b. Jun 4, 1955 in Bratenahl, Ohio

Verdon, Gwen
[Gwyneth Evelyn Verdon]
American. Dancer, Actor
Won Tonys for *Can Can,* 1953; *Damn Yankees,* 1956; *New Girl in Town,* 1958; *Red Head,* 1959.
b. Jan 13, 1925 in Culver City, California
Source: *BiDD; BiE&WWA; BioIn 3, 4, 5, 6, 8, 12, 16, 18; CamGWoT; CelR, 90; ConTFT 3; CurBio 60; DancEn 78; EncAFC; EncMT; FilmEn; GrLiveH; HalFC 80, 84, 88; IntMPA 88, 92, 94, 96; InWom, SUP; LegTOT; MotPP; NewAmDM; NewGrDA 86; NewYTBS 81; NotNAT; NotWoAT; OxCAmT 84; OxCPMus; WhoAm 74, 76, 78, 80, 82, 86, 88, 90, 92, 94, 95, 96, 97; WhoAmW 83, 85; WhoEnt 92; WhoHol 92, A; WhoThe 77, 81; WorAl; WorAlBi*

Verdugo, Elena
American. Actor
Played Millie Bronson in "Meet Millie," 1952-56; Nurse Consuelo Lopez in "Marcus Welby, MD," 1969-76.
b. Apr 20, 1926 in Hollywood, California
Source: *FilmEn; FilmgC; ForYSC; HalFC 80, 84, 88; LegTOT; MovMk; WhoHol A*

Verdy, Violette
[Nelly Guillerm]
French. Dancer, Director
Toured US, Europe, 1957-58; artistic director Boston Ballet, 1980-84; teaches NYC Ballet, 1984—.
b. Dec 1, 1933 in Pont-L'Abbe, France
Source: *BioIn 11, 12, 13, 14; CnOxB; CurBio 80; DancEn 78; IntDcB; InWom SUP; WhoAm 74, 76, 78, 80, 82, 84, 86, 88; WhoAmW 70, 72, 74, 75, 83, 85; WhoE 83, 85; WhoFr 79; WhoWor 74*

Vereen, Ben(jamin Augustus)
American. Entertainer
Won Tony for *Pippin',* 1972; played Chicken George in TV miniseries "Roots ," 1977.
b. Oct 10, 1946 in Miami, Florida
Source: *Baker 84, 92; BiDAfM; BiDD; BioIn 9, 10, 11, 12, 16; CelR, 90; ConBlB 4; ConTFT 2, 8; CurBio 78; DcBiPP; DcTwCCu 5; DrBlPA, 90; EncMT; HalFC 80, 84, 88; InB&W 80, 85; IntMPA 84, 86, 88, 92, 94, 96; LegTOT; NegAl 89; NewYTBE 72; NotNAT; WhoAm 76, 78, 80, 82, 84, 86, 88, 90, 92, 94, 95, 96, 97; WhoBlA 92; WhoEnt 92; WhoHol 92, A; WhoThe 77, 81; WorAl; WorAlBi*

Vereshchagin, Vasily Vasilyevich
Russian. Artist
Best known subjects are of the military, Turkish, Oriental life including *Blessing the Dead.*
b. Oct 26, 1842 in Cherepovets, Russia
d. 1904 in Lushun, China
Source: *BioIn 9; NewCol 75; WebBD 83*

Verga, Giovanni
Italian. Author
Novels, short stories of Sicilian life include *Mastro Don Gesnaldo,* 1889; *Cavalleria Rusticana,* 1880.
b. Aug 31, 1840 in Catania, Sicily, Italy
d. Jan 27, 1922 in Catania, Sicily, Italy
Source: *AtlBL; BbD; Benet 87, 96; BiD&SB; BioIn 1, 3, 4, 5, 6, 8, 9, 11, 12, 14; CamGWoT; CasWL; ClDMEL 47, 80; CnThe; ConAu 104, 123; CyWA 58; DcBiA; DcEuL; DcItL 1, 2; EncWL 2, 3; EncWT; EuWr 7; EvEuW; GrFLW; LinLib L; LngCTC; McGEWD 72, 84; ModRL; ModWD; NewGrDO; Novels; OxCEng 67, 85, 95; OxCThe 67, 83; PenC EUR; RAdv 14, 13-2; RComWL; REn; REnWD; RfGShF; RfGWoL 95; ShSCr 21; TwCA SUP; TwCLC 3; WhDW; WhoTwCL; WhThe; WorAl; WorAlBi*

Vergil
[Virgil; Publius Vergilius Maro]
Roman. Poet
Unfinished epic poem *Aeneid* was about the founding of Rome.
b. Oct 15, 70BC in Mantua, Gaul
d. Sep 21, 19BC in Brundisium, Italy
Source: *AncWr; AtlBL; BbD; Benet 87, 96; BiDLA; BioIn 1, 2, 4, 5, 6, 7, 9, 10, 12, 13; BlmGEL; CasWL; ClMLC 9; DcArts; DcBiA; DcEnL; DcEuL; Dis&D; GrFLW; Grk&L; LegTOT; LinLib L; LngCEL; MagSWL; McGEWB; MetOEnc; NewC; NewCBEL; NewEOp 71; NewGrDM 80; NewGrDO; OxCClL, 89; OxCEng 67, 85, 95; OxDcByz; PenC CL; PoeCrit 12; RAdv 14, 13-2; RComWL; REn; RfGWoL 95; WhDW; WorAl; WorAlBi*

Verissimo, Erico Lopes
Brazilian. Author
Novels set in Brazil, full of character, broad in scope include *Crossroads,* 1935.
b. Dec 17, 1905 in Rio Grande do Sul, Brazil
d. Nov 28, 1975 in Porto Alegre, Brazil
Source: *CasWL; EncWL; IntAu&W 76, 77; IntWW 74, 75; PenC AM; REn; TwCWr; WhoWor 74; WorAu 1950*

Verity, C(alvin) William, Jr.
American. Government Official
Succeeded Malcolm Baldridge as secretary of Commerce, 1987-89.
b. Jan 26, 1917 in Middletown, Ohio
Source: *BiDrUSE 89; BioIn 7, 10, 12, 15, 16; BlueB 76; CurBio 88; Dun&B 79; IntWW 74, 75, 76, 77, 78, 79, 80, 81, 82, 83, 89, 91, 93; NewYTBS 87; St&PR 75, 84, 87; WhoAm 74, 76, 78, 80, 82, 84, 88; WhoE 89; WhoFI 74, 75, 77, 81, 89; WhoMW 82; WhoWor 74, 89*

Verlaine, Paul (Marie)
French. Poet
Lyrics are known for musical tone, gracefulness: *Sagesse,* 1881.
b. Mar 30, 1844 in Metz, France
d. Jan 8, 1896 in Paris, France
Source: *AtlBL; BbD; Benet 87, 96; BiD&SB; BioIn 20; CasWL; ClDMEL 47, 80; CyWA 58; DcArts; DcEuL; Dis&D; EuAu; EuWr 7; EvEuW; GayLesB; GrFLW; GuFrLit 1; LegTOT; LinLib L, S; MagSWL; ModRL; NewC; NewCBEL; NewGrDM 80; NinCLC 2, 51; OxCEng 67, 85, 95; OxCFr; OxCMus; PenC EUR; PoeCrit 2; RAdv 14, 13-2; RComWL; REn; RGFMEP; WhDW; WorAl; WorAlBi*

Vermeer, Jan
[Jan van Delft; Jan van der Meer]
Dutch. Artist
Painted Dutch interiors, genre subjects; interested in light, color: *The Lacemaker.*
b. Oct 30, 1632 in Delft, Netherlands
d. Dec 15, 1675 in Delft, Netherlands
Source: *AtlBL; Benet 87, 96; BioIn 14, 15, 16, 17, 19; DcArts; IntDcAA 90; LegTOT; McGDA; McGEWB; NewC; NewCol 75; OxCArt; OxDcArt; REn; WebBD 83; WhDW; WorAl; WorAlBi*

Vermeij, Geerat J(acobus)
American. Biologist
Blind scientist who studies mollusks; demonstrated the importance of predation as a force in evolution.
b. Sep 28, 1946 in Groningen, Netherlands
Source: *AmMWSc 76P, 79, 82, 86, 89, 92, 95; BioIn 9, 11; CurBio 95; WhoScEn 96*

Vermeil, Dick
[Richard Albert Vermeil]
American. Football Coach, Sportscaster
Coach, Philadelphia Eagles, 1976-82; analyst for CBS Sports and ABC Sports, 1983-97; coach, St. Louis Rams, 1997—.
b. Oct 30, 1936 in Calistoga, California
Source: *BioIn 12, 13; NewYTBS 81; WhoAm 82; WhoTelC*

Verne, Jules
"The Founder of Science Fiction"
French. Author
Wrote *Twenty Thousand Leagues Under the Sea,* 1870; *Around the World in Eighty Days,* 1873; both adapted to film, 1954, 1956.
b. Feb 8, 1828 in Nantes, France
d. Mar 24, 1905 in Amiens, France
Source: *AtlBL; Au&Arts 16; AuBYP 2; BbD; Benet 87, 96; BiD&SB; BioIn 1, 2, 3, 4, 5, 6, 7, 8, 9, 10, 11, 12, 13, 14, 17, 18, 19, 21; CarSB; CasWL; CelCen; ChlBkCr; ClDMEL 80; ConAu 110, 131; CyWA 58; DcArts; DcBiA; DcBiPP; DcCathB; DcEnL; DcEuL; DcLB 123; DcPup; Dis&D; DivFut; EncSF; EuAu; EvEuW; FilmgC; GuFrLit 1; HalFC 80, 84, 88; JBA 34, 51; LegTOT; LinLib L, S; LngCEL; LngCTC; MagSWL; McGEWB; MnBBF; NewC; NewCBEL; NewEScF; Novels; OxCChiL; OxCEng 67, 85, 95; OxCFr; OxCShps; PenC EUR; REn; RGSF; ScF&FL 1, 92; ScFEYrs; ScFSB; ScFWr; SmATA 21;*

TwCLC 6, 52; TwCSFW 81A, 86A, 91A; WhDW; WhoChL; WhoHrs 80; WhoSciF; WorAl; WorAlBi; WrChl

Vernier, Pierre
French. Mathematician
Developed vernier scale for measuring linear or angular magnitudes.
b. Aug 19, 1580 in Ornans, France
d. Sep 14, 1637 in Ornans, France
Source: *BiESc; DcBiPP; DcCathB; DcScB; InSci; WebBD 83*

Vernon, Edward, Sir
"Old Grog"
English. Naval Officer
First to issue rum mixed with water, later called grog, 1740.
b. 1684
d. 1757
Source: *Alli; ApCAB; BioIn 3; DcBiPP; DcNaB; Drake; EncAR; HarEnUS; HisDBrE; NewCol 75; OxCShps; WebBD 83*

Vernon, Jackie
American. Comedian
Known for off-beat, satirical humor; played nightclubs, TV, films; trademark saying, "You had to be there."
b. 1928 in New York, New York
d. Nov 10, 1987 in Los Angeles, California
Source: *WhoCom; WhoHol A*

Vernon, John
[Adolphus Vernon Agopsowicz]
Canadian. Actor
Films include *Dirty Harry; Topaz; National Lampoon's Animal House.*
b. Feb 24, 1932 in Regina, Saskatchewan, Canada
Source: *ColCR; ConTFT 7, 15; DrAPF 91; FilmEn; FilmgC; HalFC 88; IntMPA 84, 92, 94, 96; ItaFilm; WhoHol 92, A*

Vernon, Lillian
American. Business Executive
Started a mail order business from her home, 1951; issued first catalog, 1956; company became the Lillian Vernon Corporation, 1965.
b. 1927 in Leipzig, Germany
Source: *CurBio 96; WhoAm 92, 94, 95, 96, 97; WhoAmW 93, 95; WhoE 97; WhoFI 94*

Vernon, Mickey
[James Barton Vernon]
American. Baseball Player
First baseman, 1939-43, 1946-60, mostly with Washington; won AL batting title, 1946, 1953; set several AL fielding records.
b. Apr 22, 1918 in Marcus Hook, Pennsylvania
Source: *Ballpl 90; BaseEn 88; BiDAmSp BB; BioIn 3, 4, 11, 15, 18; WhoProB 73*

Vernon, Mike
[Michael Vernon]
Canadian. Hockey Player
Goaltender, Calgary, 1982-94; Detroit, 1994—; won Conn Smythe Trophy, 1997.
b. Feb 24, 1963 in Calgary, Alberta, Canada

Veronese, Paolo
[Paolo Caliari]
"Painter of Pageants"
Italian. Artist
Noted for decorative, many-figured frescoes, altarpieces: *Marriage of Cana.*
b. 1528 in Verona, Italy
d. Apr 9, 1588 in Venice, Italy
Source: *AtlBL; Benet 87, 96; BioIn 1, 2, 4, 5, 6, 9, 15, 16; ClaDrA; DcArts; DcCathB; IntDcAA 90; LegTOT; McGDA; McGEWB; OxDcArt; REn; WhDW; WorAl; WorAlBi*

Veronis, John James
American. Publisher
Co-founder, *Psychology Today* mag; pres., Communications/Research/ Machines, Inc., 1967-71; founder, pres., *Book Digest* mag., NYC, 1973-79.
b. Mar 6, 1928 in New Brunswick, New Jersey
Source: *EncTwCJ; WhoAm 76, 78, 86, 88; WhoE 74, 75, 77; WhoFI 74, 75*

Verrazano, Giovanni da
Italian. Navigator, Explorer
Discovered mouth of Hudson River, 1524.
b. 1485? in Val di Greve, Italy
d. Nov 1528 in Puerto del Pico, Spain
Source: *AmBi; ApCAB; Benet 87, 96; BenetAL 91; BioIn 1, 2, 8, 9, 11, 15, 16, 18, 19, 20; CnDAL; EncCRAm; McGEWB; OxCCan; REn; REnAL; WhAm HS; WhDW; WhNaAH; WhWE; WorAl; WorAlBi*

Verrett, Shirley Carter
American. Opera Singer
Mezzo-soprano; made NY Met. debut, 1968; 1955 Marion Anderson winner.
b. May 31, 1933 in New Orleans, Louisiana
Source: *Baker 84; BioIn 13, 16; BioNews 75; CelR 90; DrBlPA 90; InB&W 85; IntWW 83, 91; IntWWM 90; InWom SUP; MetOEnc; MusSN; NegAl 89; NewAmDM; NewGrDA 86; NewYTBS 74; PenDiMP; WhoAm 86, 90; WhoAmM 83; WhoAmW 85, 87; WhoBlA 85, 92; WhoEnt 92; WhoWor 84, 91*

Verrill, Alpheus Hyatt
American. Explorer, Author, Inventor
Developed autochrome natural color photo process; wrote over 100 books.
b. Jul 23, 1871 in New Haven, Connecticut
d. Nov 14, 1954 in Chiefland, Florida
Source: *AmAu&B; BioIn 3; DcAmB S5; ObitOF 79; REnAL; WhAm 3; WhNAA*

Verrocchio, Andrea del
[Andrea di Michele di Francesco Cioni]
Italian. Artist
Sculptures include bronze of David; paintings include *Baptism of Christ.*
b. 1435 in Florence, Italy
d. Oct 7, 1488 in Venice, Italy
Source: *AtlBL; BioIn 1, 5, 8, 11, 15, 18; DcArts; DcCathB; IntDcAA 90; LegTOT; McGDA; McGEWB; NewCol 75; OxCArt; OxDcArt; REn; WebBD 83*

Versace, Gianni
Italian. Fashion Designer
Known for bondage inspired designs and his use of metal-mesh materials.
b. Dec 2, 1946 in Reggio di Calabria, Italy
d. Jul 15, 1997 in Miami Beach, Florida
Source: *BioIn 15, 16, 17, 18, 19, 20, 21; ConDes 84, 90, 97; ConFash; ConNews 88-1; CurBio 93; DcArts; EncFash; IntWW 89, 91, 93; LegTOT; WhoAm 84, 86, 88, 92, 94, 95, 96, 97; WhoFash 88; WhoWor 84, 87, 89, 91, 93, 95, 97*

Versalles, Zoilo Casanova
"Zorro"
Cuban. Baseball Player
Shortstop, Washington Senators 1959-60, Minnesota Twins 1961-67, Los Angeles Dodgers 1968, Cleveland Indians 1969, Washington Senators 1969, Atlanta Braves 1971. American League MVP, 1965.
b. Dec 18, 1939 in Vedado, Cuba
d. Jun 9, 1995 in Bloomington, Minnesota
Source: *Ballpl 90; BaseEn 88; BioIn 7, 8, 11*

Vertes, Marcel
Hungarian. Artist
Designed scenery, costumes for ballets: *Bluebeard; Helen of Troy;* exhibits in museums around the world.
b. Aug 10, 1895 in Ujpest, Austria-Hungary
d. Oct 31, 1961 in Paris, France
Source: *BioIn 1, 2, 3, 4, 5, 6; ClaDrA; CurBio 61, 62; DancEn 78; EncFash; McGDA; NotNAT B; WhAm 4; WhAmArt 85; WhoAmA 80N, 82N, 84N, 86N, 89N, 91N, 93N; WhoArt 80, 82, 84; WhoGrA 62*

Veruschka
[Countess Vera VonLehndorff]
German. Model, Actor
Films include *Blow Up,* 1966.
b. 1943
Source: *BioIn 10, 11, 14, 15; InWom SUP; WhoHol A*

Verwoerd, Hendrik F
South African. Political Leader
Prime minister, 1958-66; assassinated.
b. Sep 8, 1901 in Amsterdam, Netherlands
d. Sep 6, 1966 in Cape Town, South Africa
Source: *BioIn 5, 6, 7, 8; CurBio 59, 67; WhAm 4*

Very, Jones
American. Author
Wrote religious verse, 1837; wrote sonnets, 1839; published book *Essays and Poems*, 1839.
b. Aug 28, 1813 in Salem, Massachusetts
d. May 8, 1880 in Salem, Massachusetts
Source: *Alli, SUP; AmAu; AmAu&B; AmBi; ApCAB; AtlBL; Benet 87, 96; BenetAL 91; BibAL 8; BiDAmM; BiD&SB; BiDTran; BioIn 6, 8, 11, 12; CamGEL; CamGLE; CamHAL; CasWL; Chambr 3; ChhPo, S1; CnDAL; CyAL 2; DcAmAu; DcAmB; DcLB 1; DcLEL; DcNAA; Drake; EvLB; GrWrEL P; MouLC 3; NatCAB 6; NinCLC 9; OxCAmL 65, 83, 95; PenC AM; RAdv 14, 13-1; REn; REnAL; RfGAmL 87, 94; WebAB 74, 79; WebE&AL; WhAm HS*

Vesalius, Andreas
Belgian. Scientist
Anatomist who was the first to dissect the human body.
b. Dec 31, 1514 in Brussels, Belgium
d. Oct 15, 1564 in Zante, Greece
Source: *AsBiEn; BiD&SB; BiDPsy; BiESc; BiHiMed; BioIn 1, 2, 3, 4, 5, 6, 7, 8, 9, 11, 12, 13, 14, 15, 16, 18, 19, 20; CamDcSc; DcBiPP; DcCathB; DcScB; InSci; LarDcSc; LinLib L, S; McGEWB; OxCMed 86; RAdv 14; REn; WorAl; WorAlBi; WorScD*

Vesco, Robert Lee
American. Financier
Indicted for using illegal funds to gain control of US companies, 1970s; contributed large sum to re-elect Nixon used to finance Watergate break-in, 1972; fled to Costa Rica to avoid charges.
b. Dec 4, 1935 in Detroit, Michigan
Source: *BioIn 10, 11, 12, 13; BioNews 74; BusPN; PolProf NF; WhoE 74*

Vespasian
[Titus Flavius Sabinus Vespasianus]
Roman. Ruler
During reign, suppressed revolt of Batavians; began erection of Colosseum, AD 69-79.
b. Nov 17, 8 in Reate, Italy
d. Jun 24, 79 in Reate, Italy
Source: *PenC CL; REn*

Vespucci, Amerigo
[Americus Vespucius]
Italian. Navigator
America was named for him; discovered mouth of Rio de la Plata.
b. Mar 9, 1451 in Florence, Italy
d. Feb 22, 1512 in Seville, Spain
Source: *BbD; Benet 87, 96; BiD&SB; BioIn 1, 3, 4, 5, 7, 8, 9, 12, 14, 16, 17, 18, 19, 20; DcBiPP; DcCathB; Dis&D; Drake; Expl 93; HisDcSE; LinLib S; NatCAB 3; NewC; OxCAmH; OxCAmL 65; OxCShps; RAdv 14, 13-3; REn; REnAL; TwCBDA; WebAB 74; WhAm HS; WhWE*

Vessels, Billy
"Curly"
American. Football Player
Halfback, won Heisman Trophy, 1952; had brief NFL career with Baltimore, 1956.
b. Mar 22, 1931 in Cleveland, Ohio
Source: *BiDAmSp FB; BioIn 14; WhoFtbl 74*

Vessey, John William, Jr.
American. Military Leader
First man to rise through ranks from private to four-star general to chairman of Joint Chiefs of Staff, 1979-85; succeeded by William Crowe.
b. Jun 29, 1922 in Minneapolis, Minnesota
Source: *BioIn 13, 14, 15; IntWW 83, 91; NewYTBS 82, 84; WhoAm 82, 84, 86, 88, 90, 97; WhoMW 90, 92; WhoWor 87*

Vestris, Lucia Elizabeth, Madame
English. Opera Singer, Actor
Star of London stage, 1820-54; noted for "breeches parts, burlesques."
b. Jan 3, 1797 in London, England
d. Aug 8, 1856 in London, England
Source: *BioIn 8, 10; CelCen; DcBiPP; IntDcT 3; InWom; NewGrDM 80; NewGrDO; OxCThe 67; OxDcOp; PenDiMP*

Vezina, Georges
"The Chicoutimi Cucumber"
Hockey Player
Goalie, Montreal, 1917-25, considered best of his time; died of TB; Hall of Fame, 1945; Vezina Trophy, awarded to goalies, named in his honor.
b. Jan 1887 in Chicoutimi, Quebec, Canada
d. Mar 26, 1925
Source: *BioIn 2; HocEn; WhoHcky 73; WhoSpor*

Viardot-Garcia, Pauline
French. Opera Singer, Composer
Mezzo-soprano, noted for range, technique; friend of Turgenev.
b. Jul 18, 1821 in Paris, France
d. May 18, 1910 in Paris, France
Source: *Baker 78, 84; BioIn 1, 4, 5, 7, 8, 10, 11; CmOp; InWom; NewAmDM; NewCol 75; NewEOp 71; PenDiMP*

Vicious, Sid
[The Sex Pistols; John Simon Ritchie]
English. Singer
Bass player, vocalist with punk rock group, 1977-78; arrested for murder, 1978; died of drug overdose.
b. May 10, 1957 in London, England
d. Feb 2, 1979 in New York, New York
Source: *BioIn 11; LegTOT; NewYTBS 79; WhoRocM 82*

Vickers, Edward
English. Manufacturer
Co-founded Vickers' Sons & Co., 1867, for steel manufacturing.
b. 1804
d. 1897
Source: *WebBD 83*

Vickers, Jon
Canadian. Opera Singer
Among finest postwar heroic tenors; made recordings, operatic films; had NY Met. debut, 1960.
b. Oct 29, 1926 in Prince Albert, Saskatchewan, Canada
Source: *Baker 78, 84; BioIn 5, 6, 7, 8, 10, 11, 15, 16, 17, 19, 21; BlueB 76; BriBkM 80; CanWW 31, 70, 79, 80, 81, 83, 89; CmOp; CreCan 1; CurBio 61; FacFETw; IntDcOp; IntWW 74, 75, 76, 77, 78, 79, 80, 81, 82, 83, 89, 91, 93; IntWWM 77, 80, 90; LegTOT; MetOEnc; MusSN; NewAmDM; NewEOp 71; NewGrDM 80; OxDcOp; PenDiMP; Who 74, 82, 83, 85, 88, 90, 92, 94; WhoAm 74, 76, 78, 80, 82, 84, 86, 88; WhoAmM 83; WhoOp 76; WhoWor 74; WorAl; WorAlBi*

Vickers, Martha
[Martha MacVicar]
American. Actor
Married Mickey Rooney, 1949-51; films include *The Big Sleep*, 1946.
b. May 28, 1925 in Ann Arbor, Michigan
d. Nov 2, 1971 in Van Nuys, California
Source: *BioIn 10; FilmEn; FilmgC; ForYSC; HalFC 80, 84, 88; HolP 40; LegTOT; ObitOF 79; WhoHol B; WhScrn 74, 77, 83*

Vickrey, Robert (Remsen)
American. Artist
Paintings are of detailed, eerie tempera: *The Labyrinth*, 1951.
b. Aug 20, 1926 in New York, New York
Source: *AmArt; BioIn 3, 4, 7, 12; DcCAA 88; McGDA; PrintW 85; WhoAm 74, 76, 78, 80, 82, 84, 86, 88, 90, 92, 94, 95, 96; WhoAmA 73, 76, 78, 80, 82, 84, 86, 89, 91, 93; WhoWor 84, 87, 89*

Vickrey, William
American. Economist
Won Nobel Prize in economics, 1996.
b. Jun 21, 1914, Canada
d. Oct 11, 1996 in New York
Source: *AmEA 74; ConAu 41R; WhoEc 81, 86*

Vico, Giovanni Battista
Italian. Philosopher
Writings dealt with laws of evolution in society.
b. Jun 23, 1668 in Naples, Italy
d. Jan 23, 1744 in Naples, Italy
Source: *BioIn 3, 7, 8, 10, 13, 14, 15, 17, 19, 20; CyEd; DcBiPP; DcEuL; EuAu; EuWr 3; LngCTC; LuthC 75; NewCol 75; OxCLaw; REn*

Victor, Paul-Emile
French. Explorer
Founded French Polar Expeditions, 1947; explored polar regions from 1934 to 1987.
b. Jun 28, 1907 in Geneva, Switzerland
d. Mar 8, 1995 in Bora Bora, French Polynesia
Source: *BioIn 20; IntWW 74, 75, 76, 77, 78, 79, 80, 81, 82, 83, 89, 91, 93; NewYTBS 95; WhoFr 79; WhoWor 78*

Victor, Sally Josephs
American. Designer
Opened hat shop, 1934-68; won Coty, 1956.
b. Feb 23, 1905 in Scranton, Pennsylvania
d. May 14, 1977 in New York, New York
Source: *BioIn 12; CurBio 54, 77N; FairDF US; InWom; NatCAB 59; NewYTBS 77; WorFshn*

Victor Emmanuel II
Italian. Ruler
First king of Italy, 1861-78, who freed Italy from Austrian domination.
b. Mar 14, 1820 in Turin, Italy
d. Jan 9, 1878 in Rome, Italy
Source: *CelCen; Dis&D; LinLib S; NewCol 75*

Victor Emmanuel III
Italian. Ruler
King of Italy, 1900-46; relinquished power to son, 1944; abdicated, 1946.
b. Nov 11, 1869 in Naples, Italy
d. Dec 28, 1947 in Alexandria, Egypt
Source: *NewCol 75; WebBD 83*

Victoria, Queen
[Alexandrina Victoria]
English. Ruler
Had longest reign in British history, 1837-1901; featured growing industrialization, middle class prosperity.
b. May 24, 1819 in London, England
d. Jan 22, 1901 in Isle of Wight, England
Source: *Alli, SUP; BbD; Benet 87, 96; BiD&SB; BioIn 1, 2, 3, 4, 5, 6, 7, 8, 9, 10, 11, 12, 13, 14, 15, 16, 17, 18, 19, 20, 21; BlmGWL; ChhPo; ContDcW 89; DcBiPP; DcBrWA; DcEnL; DcLB 55; DcLEL; DcNaB; DcWomA; Dis&D; EncBrWW; EncFash; EncO&P 3; EncPaPR 91; EvLB; FemiCLE; GoodHs; HalFC 84, 88; HerW, 84; HisDBrE; HisWorL; IntDcWB; InWom, SUP; LegTOT; LinLib L, S; LngCEL; McGEWB; NewC; OxCEng 67, 85, 95; REn; VicBrit; WhCiWar; WhDW; WomFir; WomWR; WorAl; WorAlBi*

Victoria Ingrid Alice Desiree
Swedish. Princess
First child of King Carl Gustaf XVI of Sweden; will succeed father to throne.
b. Jul 4, 1977 in Stockholm, Sweden

Victorio
American. Native American Leader
Led small bands of Native Americans in resistance to US and Mexican troops.
b. 1820?
d. Oct 15, 1880
Source: *NotNaAm*

Vidal, Gore
[Eugene Luther Gore Vidal, Jr.]
American. Author, Dramatist
Wrote *Lincoln: A Novel,* 1984; *Empire,* 1987; won National Book Award for *United States: Essays, 1952-92,* 1993.
b. Oct 3, 1925 in West Point, New York
Source: *AmAu&B; AmCulL; AmNov; AuNews 1; AuSpks; Benet 87, 96; BenetAL 91; BestSel 90-2; BiE&WWA; BioIn 2, 3, 4, 5, 6, 7, 8, 9, 10, 11, 12, 13, 14, 15, 16, 17, 18, 19, 20, 21; BioNews 74; BkPepl; BlueB 76; CamGEL; CamGLE; CamHAL; CasWL; CelR, 90; CnMD; ConAmD; ConAu 5R, 13NR, 45NR; ConDr 73, 77, 82, 88, 93; ConGAN; ConLC 2, 4, 6, 8, 10, 22, 33, 72; ConNov 72, 76, 82, 86, 91, 96; ConPopW; ConTFT 3; CroCD; CurBio 83; CyWA 89; DcArts; DcLB 6, 152; DcLEL 1940; DcLP 87A; DrAF 76; DrAPF 80, 87, 91; EncMys; EncSF, 93; EncWL, 2, 3; EncWT; FacFETw; FilmEn; GayLesB; GrWrEL N; IntAu&W 76, 77, 89, 91, 93; IntvTCA 2; IntWW 74, 75, 76, 77, 78, 79, 80, 81, 82, 83, 89, 91, 93; ItaFilm; LegTOT; LiExTwC; LiJour; LinLib L; LngCTC; LNinSix; MagSAmL; MajTwCW; MakMC; McGEWD 72, 84; ModAL S2; ModWD; NatPD 81; NewEScF; News 96, 96-2; NotNAT, A; Novels; OxCAmL 65, 83, 95; OxCAmT 84; PenC AM; RAdv 1, 14, 13-1; REn; REnAL; RfGAmL 87; ScF&FL 1, 2, 92; ScFSB; TwCA SUP; TwCCr&M 91; TwCRHW 90, 94; TwCSFW 81, 86; TwCWr; WebAB 74, 79; WebE&AL; Who 74, 82, 83, 85, 88, 90, 92, 94; WhoAm 74, 76, 78, 80, 82, 84, 86, 88, 90, 92, 94, 95, 96, 97; WhoSpyF; WhoThe 72, 77, 81; WhoTwCL; WhoUSWr 88; WhoWor 74, 84; WhoWrEP 89, 92, 95; WorAl; WorAlBi; WorEFlm; WrDr 76, 80, 82, 84, 86, 88, 90, 92, 94, 96*

Videla, Jorge Rafael
Argentine. Political Leader
Pres. of Argentina, 1976-81; led coup that ousted Pres. Peron.
b. Aug 2, 1925 in Mercedes, Argentina
Source: *BiDLAmC; BioIn 10, 11, 12, 16; CurBio 78; DcCPSAm; EncWB; IntWW 76, 77, 78, 79, 80, 81, 82, 83, 89, 91, 93; IntYB 78, 79, 80, 81, 82; NewYTBS 75; WhoWor 78, 80*

Vidor, Florence
[Florence Cobb]
American. Actor
Successful on silent films; career ended with talkies.
b. Jul 23, 1895 in Houston, Texas
d. Nov 3, 1977 in Pacific Palisades, California
Source: *BioIn 9, 11; DcAmB S10; EncAFC; Film 1, 2; FilmEn; FilmgC; HalFC 80, 84, 88; MotPP; MovMk; NewYTBS 77; ObitOF 79; SilFlmP; TwYS; WhoHol A; WhScrn 83*

Vidor, King Wallis
American. Director
Directed *Hallelujah,* 1929; first Hollywood movie with all black cast.
b. Feb 8, 1894 in Galveston, Texas
d. Nov 1, 1982 in Paso Robles, California
Source: *AnObit 1982; BiDFilm; BioIn 3, 4, 8, 9, 10, 11, 12, 13; BkPepl; CmMov; CurBio 57, 83; Film 1; FilmgC; IntMPA 82; IntWW 83N; MovMk; NewYTBE 72; NewYTBS 82; OxCFilm; TwYS; Who 82; WhoAm 82*

Vieira Da Silva, Maria Helena
French. Artist
Abstract painter, inspired by the seasons, landscapes, urban streets, games and the horror of WW II.
b. Jun 13, 1908 in Lisbon, Portugal
d. Mar 6, 1992 in Paris, France
Source: *BiDWomA; BioIn 17, 18; ConArt 89; CurBio 92N; WhoArt 84*

Viereck, George Sylvester
American. Author, Editor
Edited *American Editor,* 1914-27; imprisoned during WW II for pro-German propaganda.
b. Dec 31, 1884 in Munich, Germany
d. Mar 18, 1962 in Holyoke, Massachusetts
Source: *AmAu&B; AmLY; BenetAL 91; BioIn 4, 6, 9, 11, 15; CasWL; ChhPo; ConAu 116; CurBio 40, 62; DcAmB S7; DcLB 54; EncAJ; LinLib L; OxCAmL 65, 83, 95; REnAL; ScF&FL 1, 92; SJGFanW; TwCA SUP; WhAm 4; WhJnl; WhLit; WhNAA*

Viereck, Peter Robert Edwin
American. Poet, Educator
Won 1949 Pulitzer for verse vol., *Terror and Decorum.*
b. Aug 5, 1916 in New York, New York
Source: *AmAu&B; BenetAL 91; CnDAL; CnE&AP; ConAu 1NR, 1R; ConPo 85, 91; CurBio 43; DrAPF 87, 91; DrAS 82E; IntAu&W 91; IntvTCA 2; IntWW 83, 91; ModAL; OxCAmL 65; PenC AM; REn; REnAL; TwCWr; WhoAm 86, 90; WhoUSWr 88; WhoWrEP 89; WrDr 86, 92*

Viertel, Peter
American. Author
Writings include *The Canyon,* 1940; *White Hunter, Black Heart,* 1953.
b. Nov 16, 1920 in Dresden, Germany
Source: *AmAu&B; AmNov; BioIn 2, 7, 12; ConAu 13R, 52NR; DcLEL 1940*

Vieuxtemps, Henri Francois Joseph
Belgian. Musician, Composer
Violinist who was professor, Brussels Conservatory of Music, 1871-81.
b. Feb 20, 1820 in Verviers, Belgium
d. Jun 6, 1881 in Mustapha, Algeria
Source: *NewCol 75; OxCMus*

Vig, Butch
American. Producer, Musician
Formed band Spooner with Duke Erikson, 1979; founded Smart Studios with Steve Marker, late 1970s; formed band Fire Town with Steve Marker and released debut album, *The Good Life*, in 1989; produced Nirvana's album *Nevermind*, 1991; formed group Garbage and released self-titled debut album, 1995.
b. 1956 in Viroqua, Wisconsin
Source: *ConMus 17*

Vigee-Lebrun, Marie-Louise-Elisabeth
French. Artist
Best known for her portraits, including over 25 of Marie-Antoinette.
b. Apr 16, 1755 in Paris, France
d. Mar 30, 1842 in Paris, France
Source: *NewCol 75; WebBD 83*

Vigeland, Gustav
[Adolf Gustav Vigeland]
Norwegian. Sculptor
His famous work, Fountain Square (located in Oslo's Frogner Park), consists of sculptures of all the periods in the human life cycle.
b. Apr 11, 1869 in Mandal, Norway
d. Mar 12, 1943 in Oslo, Norway
Source: *BioIn 1, 2, 5, 9; DcArts; McGDA; OxCArt; OxCTwCA; OxDcArt; PhDcTCA 77*

Vignola, Giacomo da
[Giacomo Barocchio; Giacomo Barozzi]
Italian. Architect
Succeeded Michelangelo as chief architect of St. Peter's, 1564; wrote on architectural theory.
b. Oct 1, 1507 in Vignola, Italy
d. Jul 7, 1573 in Rome, Italy
Source: *AtlBL; LuthC 75; McGEWB; NewCol 75; WebBD 83; WhDW*

Vigny, Alfred Victor, Comte de
French. Author, Poet, Dramatist
Early exponent of French romanticism; wrote historical novel *Cliq-Mars*, 1826; verse *Les Destinees*, 1864.
b. Mar 27, 1797 in Loches, France
d. Sep 17, 1863 in Paris, France
Source: *AtlBL; BbD; BiD&SB; BioIn 1, 2, 3, 4, 5, 6, 7, 8, 9, 11; CasWL; CnThe; CyWA 58; DcBiA; DcEuL; Dis&D; EuAu; EvEuW; McGEWB; McGEWD 72; NewC; OxCEng 67; OxCFr; PenC EUR; RComWL; REn; REnWD; WorAl; WorAlBi*

Vigo, Jean
French. Director
Experimental films banned as "anti-French" because they attacked the establishment.
b. Apr 26, 1905 in Paris, France
d. Oct 5, 1934 in Paris, France
Source: *BiDFilm, 81, 94; BioIn 9, 12, 15; DcArts; DcFM; DcTwCCu 2; EncEurC; FilmEn; FilmgC; HalFC 80, 84, 88; IntDcF 1-2, 2-2; MiSFD 9N; MovMk; OxCFilm; WorEFlm; WorFDir 1*

Vigoda, Abe
American. Actor
Played Detective Fish on "Barney Miller," 1975-77.
b. Feb 24, 1921 in New York, New York
Source: *BioIn 10, 16; ConTFT 3; EncAFC; HalFC 84, 88; IntMPA 96; LegTOT; WhoAm 78, 80, 82, 84, 86, 88, 92, 94; WhoCom; WhoEnt 92A; WhoHol A; WorAlBi*

Viguerie, Richard A(rt)
"Godfather of the New Right"
American. Publisher
Founder of the *Conservative Digest*, 1975.
b. Sep 23, 1933 in Golden Acres, Texas
Source: *BioIn 12, 13, 15; CurBio 83; DcAmC; IntWW 89, 91, 93; St&PR 84; WhoAdv 90; WhoAm 80, 82, 86, 88*

Vila, Bob
[Robert Joseph Vila]
American. TV Personality
Host of PBS's "This Old House," 1979-89, "Home Again With Bob Vila," 1990—.
b. Jun 20, 1946 in Miami, Florida
Source: *DcHiB; LegTOT; WhoAm 88, 90, 92, 94, 95, 96, 97; WhoEnt 92; WhoHisp 91, 92, 94*

Vila, George Raymond
American. Business Executive
Best known for contributions to rubber industry; chm., US Rubber Co., 1965-75, now called Uniroyal.
b. Mar 12, 1909 in Philadelphia, Pennsylvania
d. Jul 8, 1987 in New York, New York
Source: *BioIn 6, 7; BlueB 76; CurBio 63, 87; IntWW 74, 75, 76, 77, 78, 79, 80, 81; IntYB 78, 79, 80, 81, 82; NewYTBS 87; WhoAm 74, 76, 78, 80, 82, 84, 86, 88; WhoFI 74, 75; WhoWor 74*

Vilas, Guillermo
"Young Bull of the Pampas"
Argentine. Tennis Player
Won US Open, 1977; Italian, 1980.
b. Aug 17, 1952 in Mar del Plata, Argentina
Source: *BioIn 10, 11, 12, 13, 14, 16; BuCMET; CurBio 78; LegTOT; NewYTBS 77, 84; WhoIntT; WhoWor 78; WorAl*

Villa, Luz Corral de
[Mrs. Francisco "Pancho" Villa]
"Dona Lucha"
Mexican.
Known for her successful efforts to gain official recognition of her husband's revolutionary contributions to Mexico.
b. 1892 in Chihuahua, Mexico
d. Jul 6, 1981 in Chihuahua, Mexico
Source: *AnObit 1981; NewYTBS 81*

Villa, Pancho
[Doroteo Arango; Francisco Villa]
Mexican. Revolutionary
Notorious as bandit before fighting in revolution; viewed jointly as criminal, hero.
b. Jun 5, 1878 in Rio Grande, Mexico
d. Jul 20, 1923 in Parral, Mexico
Source: *BioIn 14, 15, 16, 17, 19, 20; DcHiB; EncRev; FacFETw; HisWorL; LegTOT; McGEWB; NewC; OxCAmH; REn; WhAm 4, HSA; WhDW; WorAl; WorAlBi*

Villa, Pancho
[Francisco Guilledo Villa]
Philippine. Boxer
World flyweight champ, 1923; Hall of Fame, 1961.
b. Aug 1, 1901 in Iloilo, Philippines
d. Jul 14, 1925 in Oakland, California
Source: *BoxReg; WhoBox 74*

Village People, The
[Alex Briley; David Hodo; Glenn M Hughes; Randy Jones; Jeff Olson; Felipe Rose; Ray Simpson; Victor Willis]
American. Music Group
Formed late 1970s; known for outrageous macho stage costumes; hit single "YMCA," 1979.
Source: *BioIn 10, 11; ConMuA 80A; ConMus 7; EncRk 88; EncRkSt; InB&W 85A; MorBAP; NewYTBS 76, 77; RkOn 85; RolSEnR 83; TwCPaSc; WhoAm 92, 94; WhoHol 92; WhoRock 81*

Villa-Lobos, Heitor
Brazilian. Composer
Wrote over 1,400 works including *Bachianas Brasileiras*, 1930-44, featuring national folk music.
b. Mar 5, 1887 in Rio de Janeiro, Brazil
d. Nov 17, 1959 in Rio de Janeiro, Brazil
Source: *AtlBL; Baker 78, 84, 92; BriBkM 80; CompSN, SUP; CurBio 45, 60; DcArts; DcBrazL; DcCM; DcCom 77; DcCom&M 79; EncLatA; FacFETw; HalFC 88; IntDcOp; LatAmCC; LegTOT; McGEWB; MusMk; NewAmDM; NewGrDM 80; NewGrDO; NewOxM; ObitT 1951; OxCMus; OxDcOp; PenDiMP A; REn; WhAm 3; WhDW; WorAl; WorAlBi*

Villanueva, Carlos Raul
Venezuelan. Architect
Responsible for the development of modern Venezuelan architecture.
b. May 30, 1900 in Croydon, England

d. Aug 16, 1975 in Caracas, Venezuela
Source: *BioIn 11; ConArch 80, 87, 94; DcD&D; DcHiB; DcTwCCu 3; EncLatA; EncMA; IntDcAr; IntWW 74, 75, 76; MacEA; McGDA; OxCArt; WhoArch; WhoWor 74*

Villard, Helen Francis Garrison
American. Social Reformer
Worked to further the women's movement, advancement of black people.
b. Dec 16, 1844 in Boston, Massachusetts
d. Jul 5, 1928 in Dobbs Ferry, New York
Source: *DcAmB; DcNAA*

Villard, Henry
[Ferdinand H G Hilgard]
American. Journalist, Businessman
Helped found Edison General Electric Co., 1890s; most important railroad promoter in US, 1879-83.
b. Apr 10, 1835 in Speyer, Bavaria
d. Nov 12, 1900 in Dobbs Ferry, New York
Source: *AmAu&B; AmBi; ApCAB; BenetAL 91; BiDAmBL 83; BiDAmJo; BioIn 1, 3, 11, 16, 17; CivWDc; DcAmB; DcLB 23; DcNAA; EncAB-H 1974, 1996; EncABHB 2; EncAJ; HarEnUS; JrnUS; NatCAB 3; OhA&B; OxCAmH; OxCAmL 65, 83, 95; REnAL; REnAW; TwCBDA; WebAB 74, 79; WhAm HS; WhCiWar; WorAl; WorAlBi*

Villard, Oswald (Garrison)
American. Journalist
Involved in founding NAACP; capital correspondent for *Evening Post,* Wash ington, DC, 1915.
b. Mar 13, 1872 in Wiesbaden, Germany
d. Oct 1, 1949 in New York, New York
Source: *AmAu&B; AmDec 1910; AmPeW; AmRef; AmSocL; BenetAL 91; BiDAmJo; BioIn 2, 4, 5, 6, 7, 10, 14, 15, 16, 17, 19; ConAu 113; CurBio 40, 49; DcAmB S4; DcAmSR; DcLB 25, 91; DcNAA; EncAACR; EncAB-H 1974, 1996; EncAJ; JrnUS; LegTOT; McGEWB; OxCAmH; OxCAmL 65, 83, 95; REn; REnAL; TwCA, SUP; WebAB 74, 79; WhAm 2; WhNAA; WorAl; WorAlBi*

Villechaize, Herve Jean Pierre
French. Actor
Played Tattoo on TV series "Fantasy Island," 1978-83.
b. Apr 23, 1943 in Paris, France
d. Sep 4, 1993 in Los Angeles, California
Source: *BioIn 13; ConTFT 5; HalFC 84, 88; IntMPA 84, 86, 92; News 94; WhAm 11; WhoAm 80, 82, 84, 86, 88; WhoEnt 92; WhoHol A; WhoTelC; WhoWest 82*

Villella, Edward Joseph
American. Dancer, Choreographer
Member, NY City Ballet, 1957—; soloist, 1958-60; principle soloist, 1960-83; artistic director, OK Ballet, 1983-86; founding artistic director, Miami City Ballet, 1985—.
b. Oct 1, 1936 in New York, New York
Source: *BiDD; BioIn 13; BioNews 74; CelR 90; CurBio 65; FacFETw; IntWW 83, 91; NewYTBS 80; St&PR 87; WhoAm 74, 76, 78, 80, 82, 84, 86, 88, 90, 92, 94, 95, 96, 97; WhoE 85, 86; WhoEnt 92; WhoGov 72, 75; WhoHol A; WhoSSW 86, 91, 93, 95, 97; WhoWor 74, 78, 80, 82, 84, 87, 89, 91, 93, 95, 96, 97; WorAlBi*

Villeneuve, Gilles
"Air Canada"
Canadian. Auto Racer
Won six Grand Prix races.
b. Jan 18, 1950 in Berthierville, Quebec, Canada
d. May 8, 1982 in Zolder, Belgium
Source: *AnObit 1982; WhoWor 82*

Villeneuve, Jacques
Canadian. Auto Racer
Won Indianapolis 500, 1995.
b. Apr 9, 1971 in Saint-Jean-sur-Richelieu, Quebec, Canada
Source: *News 97-1*

Villers, George
English. Nobleman, Dramatist
Prominent writer of the restoration; satirized Dryden in play *The Rehearsal,* 1671.
b. Jan 30, 1628 in London, England
d. Apr 16, 1687 in Yorkshire, England
Source: *AtlBL; DcEnL; DcLEL; EvLB; McGEWB; NewCol 75; OxCEng 67; OxCThe 67; REn*

Villiers, Alan John
Australian., Author
Writings include *Whaling in the Frozen South,* 1925; *The Bounty Ships of France,* 1972.
b. Sep 23, 1903 in Melbourne, Australia
d. Mar 3, 1982 in Oxford, England
Source: *AuBYP 3; BioIn 1, 4, 7, 10, 11, 13; BlueB 76; ConAu 1NR; IntAu&W 76, 77; IntWW 74, 75, 76, 77, 78, 79, 80, 81, 82N; OxCAusL; OxCShps; SmATA 10; WhE&EA; Who 74, 82, 83N; WhoAm 74; WhoWor 74, 76, 78; WrDr 82*

Villon, Francois
[Francois Des Loges; Francois de Montcorbier]
French. Poet
Wrote *Grand Testament,* 1461; became Rogue-hero of 19th c.
b. 1431? in Paris, France
d. 1463 in Paris, France
Source: *AtlBL; BbD; Benet 87, 96; BiD&SB; BioIn 1, 2, 4, 5, 6, 7, 8, 9, 13, 17; CasWL; ChhPo, S2, S3; CyWA 58; DcArts; DcBiPP; DcEuL; Dis&D; EuAu; EuWr 2; EvEuW; HalFC 84, 88; LegTOT; LinLib L; McGEWB; MediFra; NewC; NewCol 75; NewEOp 71; OxCEng 67, 85, 95; OxCFr; PenC EUR; PoeCrit 13; RAdv 14, 13-2; RComWL; REn; WorAl; WorAlBi*

Vinay, Ramon
Chilean. Opera Singer
Tenor, baritone with NY Met., 1946-61; famed for role, recording of *Otello.*
b. Aug 31, 1912 in Chillan, Chile
Source: *Baker 84, 92; BioIn 7, 21; IntDcOp; IntWWM 90; MetOEnc; NewEOp 71; NewGrDM 80; NewGrDO; NewYTBS 27; OxDcOp; PenDiMP*

Vincennes, Francois Marie Bissot
[Sieur DeVincennes]
Canadian. Explorer
Established fort on Wabash River, 1731.
b. 1700 in Montreal, Quebec, Canada
d. Mar 25, 1736
Source: *AmBi; DcAmB*

Vincent, Fay
[Francis Thomas Vincent, Jr.]
American. Baseball Executive
Succeeded A. Bartlett Giamatti as baseball commissioner, 1989-92.
b. May 29, 1938 in Waterbury, Connecticut
Source: *Ballpl 90; BioIn 15, 16; CurBio 91; Dun&B 88; IntMPA 88; IntWW 93; News 90, 90-2; NewYTBS 90; WhoAm 80, 82, 84, 86, 90, 92, 94; WhoE 83, 85, 86, 91, 93; WhoFI 87; WhoSSW 88; WhoWor 84*

Vincent, Gene
[Vincent Eugene Craddock]
American. Singer
Known for wild habits on/off stage; recorded "Pistol Packin' Mama," 1960.
b. Feb 11, 1935 in Norfolk, Virginia
d. Oct 12, 1971 in Hollywood, California
Source: *BiDAmM, 83*

Vincent, Jan-Michael
American. Actor
Films include *Buster and Billie; White Line Fever.*
b. Jul 15, 1944 in Ventura, California
Source: *BioIn 13; ConTFT 5; FilmEn; HalFC 80, 84, 88; IntMPA 80, 84, 86, 88, 92; LegTOT; WhoEnt 92; WhoHol A; WorAl; WorAlBi*

Vincent, Marjorie Judith
American. Beauty Contest Winner
Miss America, 1991; first black woman to be crowned by reigning black queen.
b. Nov 21, 1964 in Chicago, Illinois
Source: *ConBlB 2; WhoAfA 96; WhoBlA 92, 94*

Vincent de Paul, Saint
French. Religious Leader
Founded charities, Vincentians, Sisters of Charity, circa 1625; helped revive French Catholicism.
b. Apr 24, 1581 in Pouy, France
d. Sep 27, 1660 in Paris, France
Source: *DcCathB; LinLib S; McGEWB; NewCol 75; OxCFr*

Vines, Ellsworth
[Henry Ellsworth Vines, Jr.]
American. Tennis Player, Author
Youngest player to win US amateur championship, 1931; writings include *How to Play Tennis,* 1938.
b. Sep 28, 1911 in Pasadena, California
Source: *BiDAmSp OS; BioIn 1, 6, 7, 12, 14, 17, 19; BuCMET; CmCal; ConAu 109; NewYTBS 94; WhoGolf; WhoSpor*

Vinson, Carl
American. Politician
Dem. congressman from GA, 1914-65.
b. Nov 18, 1883 in Milledgeville, Georgia
d. Jun 1, 1981 in Milledgeville, Georgia
Source: *AnObit 1981; BiDrAC; BiDrUSC 89; BioIn 1, 2, 4, 5, 6, 7, 11, 12; CurBio 42, 81, 81N; EncCW; FacFETw; NewYTBS 81; PolProf E, J, K, T; WhAm 7; WhAmP*

Vinson, Cleanhead
[Eddie Vinson]
American. Jazz Musician, Singer
Saxophonist, vocalist; sang with Cootie Williams, 1940s; own band, 1960s.
b. Dec 18, 1917 in Houston, Texas
d. Jul 2, 1988 in Los Angeles, California
Source: *AllMusG; AnObit 1988; Baker 92; BiDAfM; BiDJaz; BioIn 13; BluesWW; CmpEPM; EncJzS; GuBlues; InB&W 80, 85; NewGrDJ 88, 94; NewYTBS 88; PenEncP; WhoJazz 72*

Vinson, Frederick Moore
American. Supreme Court Justice
Served on US Supreme Court, 1946-53; advocate of civil rights, liberal construction of the Constitution.
b. Jan 22, 1890 in Louisa, Kentucky
d. Sep 8, 1953 in Washington, District of Columbia
Source: *AmPolLe; BiDrAC; BiDrUSC 89; BiDrUSE 71, 89; BioIn 1, 2, 3, 4, 5, 10, 11, 15; EncSoH; LinLib S; OxCSupC; SupCtJu; WebAB 74, 79; WhAmP; WorAl*

Vinson, Helen
American. Actor
Supporting roles in films during 1930s-40s include *The Thin Man Goes Home,* 1945.
b. Sep 17, 1907 in Beaumont, Texas
Source: *BioIn 21; FilmEn; FilmgC; ForYSC; GangFlm; HalFC 80, 84, 88; HolCA; InWom SUP; MovMk; OlFamFa; ThFT; WhoHol 92, A; WhoThe 77; WhThe*

Vinton, Bobby
[Stanley Robert Vinton]
"The Polish Prince"
American. Singer
Hits include "Blue Velvet"; had sold over 25 million records by 1974.
b. Apr 16, 1935 in Canonsburg, Pennsylvania
Source: *ASCAP 66; BiDAmM; BioNews 74; ConAu 120; CurBio 77; EncPR&S 89; EncRk 88; EncRkSt; LegTOT; PenEncP; WhoAm 86; WhoEnt 92; WhoHol 92, A; WhoRock 81; WhoRocM 82; WorAl; WorAlBi*

Vinton, Will
American., Filmmaker
Uses claymation to create TV commercial characters.
b. Nov 17, 1938 in McMinnville, Oregon
Source: *BioIn 12, 13, 15; WhoAdv 90; WhoEnt 92*

Viola, Frank John, Jr.
American. Baseball Player
Pitcher, Minnesota Twins, 1982-89; NY Mets, 1989-91; Boston Red Sox, 1992-94; Toronto Blue Jays, 1994—.
b. Apr 19, 1960 in East Meadow, New York
Source: *Ballpl 90; BaseEn 88; BaseReg 87, 88; BioIn 14, 15, 16; NewYTBS 87; WhoAm 90, 92, 94, 95, 96, 97; WhoE 95; WorAlBi*

Viollet le Duc, Eugene Emmanuel
French. Architect
Supporter of Gothic revival in France; noted for restorations of churches, town halls.
b. Jan 27, 1814 in Paris, France
d. Sep 17, 1879 in Lausanne, Switzerland
Source: *McGEWB; NewCol 75*

Vionnet, Madeleine
French. Fashion Designer
Invented revolutionary bias cut for Women's Fashion, 1930s.
b. Jun 22, 1877 in Chilleurs-aux-Bois, France
d. Mar 2, 1975 in Paris, France
Source: *BioIn 5, 10; ConDes 90; ContDcW 89; DcTwDes; EncFash; IntDcWB; InWom SUP; NewYTBS 75; WhoFash 88; WomFir; WorFshn*

Viorst, Judith (Stahl)
American. Author, Poet
Writings include *The Village Square,* 1965; *People and Other Aggravations,* 1971.
b. Feb 2, 1931 in Newark, New Jersey
Source: *ArtclWW 2; AuBYP 3; BenetAL 91; BestSel 90-1; BioIn 15, 16; ChlBkCr; ConAu 2NR, 26NR, 49; ConPopW; DcLB 52; IntAu&W 86; InWom SUP; LegTOT; MajAI; SmATA 7, 70; TwCChW 83, 89, 95; WhoAm 82, 84, 86, 88, 90, 92, 94, 95, 96, 97; WhoAmW 95, 97; WhoSSW 73; WhoUSWr 88; WhoWrEP 89, 92, 95; WrDr 88, 92, 94, 96*

Viotti, Giovanni Battista
"The Father of the Modern Technique"
Italian. Musician, Composer
Foremost violinist of his time; played for royalty, directed the Paris Opera.
b. May 23, 1753 in Vercelli, Italy
d. Mar 3, 1824 in London, England
Source: *Baker 84; BioIn 1, 2, 3, 4, 7, 8, 14; CelCen; DcBiPP; DcCathB; OxCMus; WebBD 83*

Virchow, Rudolf
German. Pathologist, Political Leader
Founded cellular pathology.
b. Oct 31, 1821 in Schivelbein, Prussia
d. Sep 5, 1905 in Berlin, Germany
Source: *AsBiEn; BbD; BiD&SB; BiDMoPL; BiHiMed; CelCen; InSci; LarDcSc; OxCGer 76, 86; WebBD 83*

Viren, Lasse
Finnish. Track Athlete
Distance runner; won two gold medals, 1972 Olympics; won gold medals, 1972, 1976 Olympics for the 5,000- and 10,000- metre races.
b. Jul 22, 1949
Source: *BioIn 12; IntWW 81, 82, 83, 89, 91, 93; WhoTr&F 73*

Virtanen, Artturi Llmari
Finnish. Chemist
Won Nobel Prize, 1945, for work on preservation of fodder crops.
b. Jan 15, 1895 in Helsinki, Finland
d. Nov 11, 1973 in Helsinki, Finland
Source: *BiESc; McGMS 80; WhoNob*

Viscardi, Henry, Jr.
American. Businessman
Founder, trustee of Abilities Inc., NY, since 1942; pres., chm., Human Resources Center, since 1955.
b. May 10, 1912 in New York, New York
Source: *BioIn 2, 3, 7, 9, 15; ConAu 5NR, 5R; CurBio 54, 66; NewYTBE 72; WhoAm 74, 76, 78, 80; WhoE 74*

Visconti, Luchino
Italian. Director
Films' recurrent theme was moral disintegration of a family including *The Damned,* 1961.
b. Nov 2, 1906 in Milan, Italy
d. Mar 17, 1976 in Rome, Italy
Source: *Baker 84; Benet 87, 96; BiDFilm, 81, 94; BioIn 5, 6, 7, 8, 9, 10, 11, 12, 13, 14, 15, 18, 20; CamGWoT; CelR; CmOp; CnThe; ConAu 39NR, 65, 81; ConLC 16; CurBio 65, 76N; DcArts; DcBiPP; DcFM; EncEurC; EncWT; Ent; FacFETw; FilmEn; FilmgC; HalFC 80, 84, 88; IntDcF 1-2, 2-2; IntDcOp; IntDcT 3; IntMPA 75, 76; IntWW 74, 75; ItaFilm; LegTOT; MakMC; MetOEnc; MiSFD 9N; MovMk; NewEOp 71; NewGrDM 80; NewYTBS 76; OxCFilm; OxCThe 67, 83; OxDcOp; RAdv 14, 13-3; TheaDir; WhAm 6; Who 74; WhoOp 76; WhoWor 74; WhScrn 83; WorAl; WorAlBi; WorEFlm; WorFDir 1*

Vishnevskaya, Galina (Pavlovna)
Russian. Opera Singer
First Russian diva to sing with Metropolitan Opera, 1961, in title role of *Aida.*

b. Oct 25, 1926 in Leningrad, Union of Soviet Socialist Republics
Source: *Baker 78, 84, 92; BiDSovU; BioIn 14, 15, 21; BriBkM 80; CmOp; CurBio 66; FacFETw; IntDcOp; IntWW 74, 75, 76, 77, 78, 79, 80, 81, 82, 83, 89, 91, 93; IntWWM 77, 80, 85, 90; InWom, SUP; MetOEnc; MusSN; NewAmDM; NewEOp 71; NewGrDM 80; NewGrDO; OxDcOp; PenDiMP; SovUn; Who 74, 82, 83, 85, 88, 90, 92, 94; WhoAm 80, 82, 84, 86, 88, 90, 92, 94, 95, 96, 97; WhoAmM 83; WhoOp 76*

Vishnevsky, Alexandr Alekandrovich
Russian. Surgeon
Director, Institute of Surgery, 1948-75; noted for working with local anesthesia and open-heart surgery, late 1960s.
b. May 24, 1906 in Kazan, Russia
d. Nov 19, 1975, Union of Soviet Socialist Republics
Source: *IntWW 74; NewYTBS 75; WhoWor 74*

Vishniac, Roman
American. Photographer
Best known for photographs documenting doomed Jews in Nazi Germany.
b. Aug 19, 1897 in Saint Petersburg, Russia
d. Jan 22, 1990 in New York, New York
Source: *AnObit 1990; BioIn 4, 5, 7, 8, 10, 13, 16; ConPhot 82, 88, 95; CurBio 67, 90, 90N; FacFETw; ICPEnP; InSci; MacBEP; NewYTBS 90; WhAm 10; WhoAm 86, 88*

Visscher, William Lightfoot
American. Poet
Wrote over 1,000 poems which were published in newspapers.
b. Nov 25, 1842 in Owingsville, Kentucky
d. Feb 10, 1924 in Chicago, Illinois
Source: *AmAu&B; AmLY; DcAmB; DcNAA; JrnUS; WhAm 1*

Visser T. Hooft, Willem Adolf
Dutch. Religious Leader
Founding general-secretary, World Council of Churches, 1948-66.
b. Sep 20, 1900 in Haarlem, Netherlands
d. Jul 4, 1985 in Geneva, Switzerland
Source: *ConAu 116; CurBio 49, 85*

Vitale, Dick
[Richard Vitale]
American. Basketball Coach, Sportscaster
Coach, Detroit Pistons, 1978-79; flamboyant basketball commentator for ABC, ESPN.
b. Jun 9, 1939 in Garfield, New Jersey
Source: *BioIn 15, 16; News 88, 94; NewYTBS 79*

Vitale, Milly
Italian. Actor
Films since 1950s include *The Juggler,* 1953; *War and Peace,* 1956.
b. Jul 16, 1938 in Rome, Italy
Source: *FilmgC; ForYSC; HalFC 84, 88; IntMPA 75, 76, 77, 78, 79, 80, 81, 82, 84, 86, 88; WhoHol A*

Vitellius, Aulus
Roman. Ruler
Roman emperor, 69, after death of Otho; defeated, killed by Primus.
b. 15
d. 69
Source: *BioIn 14, 20; DcBiPP; NewCol 75; OxCClL; REn; WebBD 83*

Vitruvius
[Marcus Vitruvius Pollio]
Roman. Architect
Wrote only source of classical Greek, Roman architecture *De Architectura,* c.27-23 BC.
b. 70BC
d. 16BC
Source: *AsBiEn; AtlBL; PlP&P; REn*

Vitti, Monica
[Maria Louisa Ceciarelli]
Italian. Actor
Appeared mostly on stage in classical roles; first leading role in film: *L'Avventura.*
b. Nov 3, 1931 in Rome, Italy
Source: *BiDFilm; BioIn 11, 17; ContDcW 89; EncEurC; FilmAG WE; FilmEn; FilmgC; HalFC 84, 88; IntDcF 1-3, 2-3; IntDcWB; IntMPA 86, 92; IntWW 79, 80, 81, 82, 83, 89, 91, 93; InWom SUP; ItaFilm; MotPP; MovMk; OxCFilm; WhoHol 92, A; WorEFlm*

Vivaldi, Antonio Lucio
"The Red Priest"
Italian. Musician, Composer
Violinist, famous for over 100 concertos including *The Four Seasons.*
b. Mar 4, 1675 in Venice, Italy
d. Jul 27, 1741 in Vienna, Austria
Source: *AtlBL; NewCol 75; REn; WebBD 83*

Vizenor, Gerald
American. Author
Poetry collections include *Seventeen Chirps,* 1964; short stories collected in *Wordarrows,* 1978.
b. Oct 22, 1934 in Minneapolis, Minnesota
Source: *BenetAL 91; CamGLE; CamHAL; ConAu 22AS; DcNAL; EncNAB; IntWWP 77; NatNAL; NotNaAm; OxCAmL 95; TwCWW 91; WrDr 92*

Vlaminck, Maurice de
French. Artist
Painted in broad strokes, straight from paint tube to canvas; began with Fauvism ended with sinister realism.
b. Apr 4, 1876 in Paris, France
d. Oct 11, 1958 in Paris, France
Source: *AtlBL; Benet 87, 96; BioIn 1, 3, 4, 5, 6, 7, 8, 17; ClaDrA; ConArt 83; DcArts; DcTwCCu 2; IntDcAA 90; LegTOT; McGDA; McGEWB; NewCol 75; ObitT 1951; OxCArt; OxCTwCA; OxDcArt; PhDcTCA 77; REn*

Vlasic, Joseph
American. Business Executive
Created Vlasic Pickle Co., 1959; successful ad campaign made Vlasic synonymous with pickles.
b. 1904?, Yugoslavia
d. Jul 10, 1986 in Phoenix, Arizona
Source: *BioIn 15; Entr*

Vlieger, Simon Jacobsz de
Dutch. Artist
Best known for *Rescue,* 1630; *Seascape with a Boat.*
b. 1600 in Rotterdam, Netherlands
d. 1653 in Weesp, Netherlands
Source: *BioIn 5, 19; McGDA; OxCArt; OxCShps*

Voelker, John Donaldson
[Robert Traver]
American. Judge, Author
Wrote *Anatomy of a Murder,* 1957; made into film, 1959.
b. Jun 29, 1903 in Ishpeming, Michigan
d. Mar 18, 1991 in Ishpeming, Michigan
Source: *AmAu&B; BioIn 4, 5, 10, 17, 18; BlueB 76; ConAu 1R, 134, X; ConNov 72, 76; DcLP 87A; IntAu&W 76, 77; MichAu 80; NewYTBS 91; WhAm 10; WhoAm 74, 76, 78; WhoAmA 91; WorAu 1950; WrDr 76, 80, 82, 84, 86, 88, 90, 92, 94N*

Voelker, Paul Frederick
American. Educator, Author
Pres., Battle Creek College, 1925-33; wrote *Function of Ideals in Social Education,* 1921.
b. Sep 30, 1875 in Evart, Michigan
Source: *WhAm 5; WhNAA*

Vogel, Hans-Jochen
German. Politician
Leader, Social Dem. party, 1982-91; minister of justice, 1974-81.
b. Feb 3, 1926 in Gottingen, Germany
Source: *BioIn 10, 13, 14; CurBio 84; EncWB; IntWW 83, 89, 91, 93; IntYB 79, 80, 81, 82; Who 85, 88, 90, 92, 94; WhoWor 84, 87, 89, 91, 93, 95; WrDr 92*

Vogel, Paula (Anne)
American. Dramatist
Wrote play *The Baltimore Waltz,* 1989; won Obie Award, 1992.
b. Nov 16, 1951 in Washington, District of Columbia
Source: *ConAmD; ConAu 108; ConDr 93; ConLC 76; ConWomD; WhoEnt 92*

Vogelstein, Bert
American. Biologist
Cancer researcher who studies the genetics of cancer; helped to identify the genes called "tumor-supressors."
b. Jun 2, 1949
Source: *CurBio 96*

Vogl, Heinrich
German. Opera Singer
Leading Wagnerian tenor at Bayreuth, 1876-97.
b. Jan 15, 1845 in Aue, Germany
d. Apr 21, 1900 in Munich, Germany
Source: *Baker 78, 84, 92; CmOp; MetOEnc; NewEOp 71; NewGrDM 80; NewGrDO; OxDcOp; PenDiMP*

Vogues, The
[Charles Blasko; William Burkette; Hugh Geyer; Don Miller]
American. Music Group
Formed, 1960; hits include "Turn Around Look At Me," 1968.
Source: *DrRegL 75; EncPR&S 74; RkOn 78; WhoRock 81; WhoRocM 82*

Voight, Jon
American. Actor
Won Oscar, 1979, for *Coming Home.*
b. Dec 29, 1938 in Yonkers, New York
Source: *BiDFilm 94; BioIn 8, 10, 11, 12, 13, 14, 15; BioNews 74; BkPepl; CelR, 90; ConTFT 2, 7; CurBio 74; DcArts; FilmEn; FilmgC; ForYSC; HalFC 80, 84, 88; IntDcF 2-3; IntMPA 75, 76, 77, 78, 79, 80, 81, 82, 84, 86, 88, 92, 94, 96; IntWW 79, 80, 81, 82, 83, 89, 91, 93; ItaFilm; LegTOT; MovMk; NewYTBS 79; OxCFilm; WhoAm 74, 76, 78, 80, 82, 84, 86, 88, 90, 92, 94, 95, 96, 97; WhoEnt 92; WhoHol 92, A; WhoThe 77, 81; WhoWor 95, 96, 97; WorAl; WorAlBi*

Voinovich, George V(ictor)
American. Politician
Mayor of Cleveland, 1979-90; Rep. governor, OH, 1991—.
b. Jul 15, 1936 in Cleveland, Ohio
Source: *AlmAP 92; St&PR 75; WhoAm 84, 86, 88; WhoAmP 73, 85, 91; WhoMW 82, 92*

Voit, Willard Darby
American. Business Executive
Chm. of W J Voit Rubber Corp., 1960-70.
b. Nov 8, 1910 in Seattle, Washington
d. Feb 1980 in Newport Beach, California
Source: *St&PR 75; WhoAm 74, 76, 78*

Volcker, Paul Adolph
American. Government Official, Banker
Chm., Federal Reserve Board, 1979-87; known for reducing double-digit inflation.
b. Sep 5, 1927 in Cape May, New Jersey
Source: *AmPolLe; BioIn 6, 9, 10, 12, 13, 14, 15, 16; ConAu 114, 129; CurBio 73; EncABHB 7; EncWB; IntWW 83, 91; NewYTBS 75, 79, 88; PolProf NF; Who 85, 92; WhoAm 86, 88; WhoAmP 85, 91; WhoE 86; WhoFI 85, 92; WhoWor 82, 84, 87, 91; WorAlBi*

Volkov, Leon
American. Journalist
Defected to US from USSR, 1945; Soviet affairs specialist with *Newsweek* mag. for 20 yrs.
b. Jan 22, 1920
d. Jan 22, 1974 in Bethesda, Maryland
Source: *ConAu 45; NewYTBS 74*

Volkov, Vladislav Nikolayevich
Russian. Cosmonaut
Flight engineer, *Soyuz 7,* 1969; died in space due to faulty depressurization.
b. Nov 23, 1935 in Moscow, Union of Soviet Socialist Republics
d. Jun 30, 1971
Source: *NewYTBE 71; WhAm 5*

Vollbracht, Michaele J
American. Fashion Designer, Artist
Asst. to Geoffrey Beene, 1968-70; partner, chm., Michaele Vollbracht, NYC; won Coty, 1980.
b. Nov 17, 1947 in Quincy, Illinois
Source: *BioIn 11; WhoAm 82, 84*

Vollenweider, Andreas
Swiss. Musician
Cult harpist who combines jazz, classical styles; has million-selling albums *Behind the Gardens,* 1981; *Caverna Magica,* 1982.
b. 1953 in Zurich, Switzerland
Source: *Baker 92; BioIn 14, 15; ConNews 85-2; CurBio 87; LegTOT; NewAgMG*

Vollmann, William T.
American. Author
Often compared to Wolfe and Pynchon; wrote *An Afghanistan Picture Show,* 1992.
b. 1959 in Santa Monica, California
Source: *ConAu 134; ConLC 89; ConPopW; EncSF 93; WrDr 94, 96*

Vollmer, Lula
American. Dramatist
Plays include *The Shame Woman,* 1923; *Sentinels,* 1931.
b. 1898 in Keyser, North Carolina
d. May 2, 1955
Source: *AmAu&B; AmWomD; AmWomPl; BioIn 1, 3, 4, 16; CnMD; InWom SUP; ModWD; NotNAT B; OxCAmL 65; TwCA, SUP; WhAm 3; WhNAA; WhThe*

Volner, Jill Wine
American. Lawyer
Asst. special prosecutor during Watergate trial, 1973-75.
b. May 5, 1943 in Chicago, Illinois
Source: *BioNews 74; GoodHs; InWom SUP; NewYTBE 73; WhoAm 74, 76, 78, 80; WhoAmL 78, 79; WhoAmP 77, 79, 81, 83; WhoAmW 77, 79, 81, 83; WhoGov 75*

Volney, (Constantin) Francois Chasseboeuf, Comte de
French. Author
Best known for essay on the philosophy of history: *Les Ruines, ou Meditation sur les Revolutions des Empires,* 1791.
b. Feb 3, 1757 in Craon, France
d. Apr 25, 1820 in Paris, France
Source: *ApCAB; BbD; BbtC; BiD&SB; DcEuL; EncEnl; EuAu; OxCFr*

Volpe, John A(nthony)
American. Diplomat
US secretary of transportation, 1969-73; ambassador to Italy, 1973-77; Rep. governor of MA, 1960s.
b. Dec 8, 1908 in Wakefield, Massachusetts
d. Nov 11, 1994 in Nahunt, Massachusetts
Source: *AmCath 80; BiDrAC; BiDrGov 1789; BiDrUSE 71, 89; BioIn 6, 8, 10, 11, 12, 15; BlueB 76; CurBio 62, 95N; IntWW 74, 75, 76, 77, 78, 79, 80, 81, 82, 83, 89; PolProf K, NF; USBiR 74; WhoAm 74, 76; WhoAmP 73, 75, 77, 79; WhoEng 88; WhoFI 74; WhoGov 72, 75, 77; WhoSSW 73; WhoWor 74, 76*

Volpi, Alfredo
Brazilian. Artist
Abstract paintings marked by intricate geometric forms in bright colors.
b. 1895 in Lucca, Italy
d. May 30, 1988 in Sao Paulo, Brazil
Source: *McGDA; OxCTwCA*

Volstead, Andrew J
American. Politician
Ten-term congressman who personified Prohibition with passage of Volstead Act, 1919.
b. Oct 31, 1860 in Kenyon, Minnesota
d. Jan 20, 1947 in Granite Falls, Minnesota
Source: *BiDrAC; DcAmB S4; LinLib S; ObitOF 79; WhAm 2; WhAmP; WorAl*

Volta, Alessandro Giuseppe Antonio Anastasio
Italian. Physicist
The volt, a unit of electrical measurement, is named for him.
b. Feb 18, 1745 in Como, Italy
d. May 7, 1827 in Como, Italy
Source: *AsBiEn; DcScB; EncEnl; NewCol 75; WebBD 83*

Voltaire (Francois Marie Arouet de)
French. Author, Philosopher
Wrote *Candide,* 1759.
b. Nov 21, 1694 in Paris, France
d. May 30, 1778 in Paris, France
Source: *AsBiEn; AtlBL; BbD; Benet 87; BiD&SB; BiDPsy; BioIn 14, 15, 17, 18, 20; BlkwCE; BlmGEL; CamGWoT; CasWL; CnThe; CrtSuMy; CyWA 58; DcArts; DcBiA; DcEnL; DcEuL; DcPup;*

Dis&D; EncEth; EncSF, 93; EncWT; Ent; EuAu; EuWr 4; EvEuW; GrFLW; GuFrLit 2; IntDcT 2; LegTOT; LitC 14; LngCEL; LuthC 75; MagSWL; McGEWB; McGEWD 72, 84; MetOEnc; NamesHP; NewC; NewEOp 71; NewEScF; NewGrDO; Novels; OxCCan; OxCEng 67, 85, 95; OxCFr; OxCGer 76; OxCMus; OxCThe 67, 83; OxDcOp; PenC EUR; RAdv 14, 13-2; RComWL; REn; REnWD; RfGWoL 95; ScF&FL 1, 92; ScFEYrs; ScFSB; ShSCr 12; WorAlBi; WorLitC; WrPh P

Von Bekesy, Georg
American. Scientist
Won 1961 Nobel Prize in medicine for research on hearing.
b. Jun 3, 1899 in Budapest, Austria-Hungary
d. Jun 13, 1972 in Honolulu, Hawaii
Source: *BiESc; BioIn 6, 9, 10, 11, 14, 15, 20; CurBio 62, 72; DcAmMeB 84; WhAm 5; WhoNob, 90, 95*

VonBraun, Wernher
American. Scientist
Led development of V-2 missiles for Germany during WW II; directed rocket research in US.
b. Mar 23, 1912 in Wirsitz, Germany
d. Jun 1977 in Alexandria, Virginia
Source: *AmAu&B; AmMWSc 73P, 76P; AuBYP 2; BlueB 76; CelR; ConAu 5R, 9NR, 69; CurBio 52; InSci; IntWW 74; McGEWB; NewYTBE 70; WebAB 74, 79; WhAm 7; Who 74; WhoAm 74, 76; WhoSSW 73; WhoWor 74; WrDr 76*

Von Bulow, Claus
[Claus Borberg]
British. Businessman
Convicted, 1982, of injecting wife with insulin, resulting in irreversible coma.
b. Aug 11, 1926 in Copenhagen, Denmark
Source: *AmDec 1980; BioIn 12, 13, 14, 15, 16; FacFETw; LegTOT*

Von Bulow, Sunny
[Martha Sharp Crawford Von Bulow; Mrs. Claus Von Bulow]
American. Socialite, Victim
Husband convicted, 1982, of trying to murder her with insulin injection.
b. Sep 1, 1932 in Manassas, Virginia
Source: *BioIn 12, 13, 14, 15, 16; LegTOT*

VonDaeniken, Erich
Swiss. Author
Wrote *Chariots of the Gods?* 1968; *Unsolved Mysteries of the Past,* 1969.
b. Apr 14, 1935 in Zofingen, Switzerland
Source: *AuNews 1; BioNews 75; ConAu 17NR*

VonDoderer, Heimito
Austrian. Author
Best known for novel *Die Strudelhofstiege,* 1951.
b. Sep 5, 1896
d. Dec 23, 1966 in Vienna, Austria
Source: *CasWL; ConAu 25R; EncWL; EvEuW; LinLib L; ModGL; OxCGer 76; PenC EUR; REn; TwCWr; WhoTwCL; WorAu 1950*

Von Eckardt, Wolf
German. Critic, Author
Design critic, *Time* mag., 1981-85; writings include *Back to the Drawing Board! Planning Livable Cities,* 1979.
b. Mar 6, 1918 in Berlin, Germany
d. Aug 27, 1995 in Jaffrey, New Hampshire
Source: *ConAu 5R, 149; IntAu&W 89, 91, 93; WhoAm 74, 76, 78, 80, 82, 84, 86, 88, 90, 92, 94, 95, 96*

Von Euler, Ulf
Swedish. Biochemist
Co-winner of 1970 Nobel Prize for work on nerve hormones.
b. Feb 7, 1905 in Stockholm, Sweden
d. Mar 1983 in Stockholm, Sweden
Source: *AmMWSc 82; AnObit 1983; BiESc; IntWW 83; Who 83; WhoAm 82; WhoNob; WhoWor 82*

VonFurstenberg, Betsy
[Elizabeth Caroline Maria Agatha Felicitas Therese Furstenberg-Hedringen]
German. Actor
Stage performances include *Wonderful Town,* 1959, 1967.
b. Aug 16, 1932 in Westphalia, Germany
Source: *BiE&WWA; ConTFT 5; InWom SUP; MotPP; NotNAT; WhoAm 86, 90; WhoEnt 92; WhoHol A; WhoThe 81; WorAl*

VonHoffman, Nicholas
American. Journalist
Writings include *Mississippi Notebook,* 1964; *Two, Three, Many More,* 1969.
b. Oct 16, 1929 in New York, New York
Source: *AmAu&B; CelR 90; ConAu 34NR, 81; EncTwCJ; WhoAm 86, 90; WhoE 91; WhoSSW 73; WrDr 92*

Von Karman, Theodore
American. Aeronautical Engineer
Helped found, chm. of advisory group for aeronautical research, development for NATO, 1951-63.
b. May 11, 1881 in Budapest, Austria-Hungary
d. May 7, 1963 in Aachen, Germany (West)
Source: *BioIn 1, 2, 3, 4, 5, 6, 7, 8, 10, 12, 13, 14, 18, 20; LinLib L, S; McGMS 80; NotTwCS; OxCAmH; PeoHis; WebAB 74; WhAm 4*

Von Klitzing, Klaus
German. Physicist
Won 1985 Nobel Prize in physics for discovering the quantized Hall effect of electrical conductivity.
b. Jun 28, 1943 in Schroda, Germany
Source: *AmMWSc 89, 92, 95; BioIn 13, 14, 15, 20; IntWW 89, 91, 93; LarDcSc; NewYTBS 85; NobelP; NotTwCS; Who 88, 90, 92, 94; WhoNob, 90; WhoScEu 91-3; WhoWor 87*

von Lipsey, Roderick K.
American. Pilot, Government Official
Aide-de-camp to Chairman of Joint Chiefs of Staff Colin Powell, 1991-93; US Marine Corps pilot, 1980-91.
b. Jan 13, 1959 in Philadelphia, Pennsylvania
Source: *ConBlB 11*

Vonnegut, Kurt, Jr.
American. Author, Journalist
Wrote *Slaughterhouse Five,* 1969; *Breakfast of Champions,* 1973; *Hocus Pocus,* 1990, his 13th novel.
b. Nov 11, 1922 in Indianapolis, Indiana
Source: *AmAu&B; AmCulL; AmDec 1960; AmWr S2; Au&Arts 6; Au&Wr 71; AuNews 1; AuSpks; Benet 87, 96; BenetAL 91; BestSel 90-4; BioIn 2, 8, 9, 10, 11, 12, 13, 14, 15, 16, 17, 19, 21; BlueB 76; BroV; CamGEL; CamGLE; CamHAL; CasWL; CelR; ConAu 1NR, 1R, 25NR, 49NR; ConDr 77, 82, 93; ConLC 1, 2, 3, 4, 5, 8, 12, 22, 40, 60; ConNov 72, 76, 82, 86, 91, 96; ConPopW; ConSFA; ConTFT 6; CurBio 70, 91; CyWA 89; DcArts; DcLB 2, 8, 152, DS3, Y80A; DcLEL 1940; DcTwCCu 1; DrAF 76; DrAPF 80, 91; DrmM 1; EncAB-H 1974, 1996; EncSF, 93; EncWL 2, 3; FacFETw; GrWrEL N; IndAu 1917; IntAu&W 76, 77, 89, 91, 93; IntvTCA 2; IntWW 74, 75, 76, 77, 78, 79, 80, 81, 82, 83, 89, 91, 93; LegTOT; LinLib L, S; MagSAmL; MajTwCW; MakMC; ModAL S1, S2; MugS; NatPD 77, 81; NewEScF; Novels; OxCAmL 83, 95; OxCEng 85, 95; PenC AM; PostFic; RAdv 1, 14, 13-1; RfGAmL 87, 94; RGTwCSF; RGTwCWr; ScF&FL 1, 2, 92; ScFSB; ScFWr; ShSCr 8; SpyFic; TwCSFW 81, 86, 91; TwCYAW; TwoTYeD; WebAB 74, 79; WebE&AL; Who 83, 85, 88, 90, 92, 94; WhoAm 74, 76, 78, 80, 82, 84, 86, 88, 90, 92, 94, 95, 96, 97; WhoE 91, 93, 95, 97; WhoEnt 92; WhoHol 92; WhoHrs 80; WhoSciF; WhoSpyF; WhoTwCL; WhoUSWr 88; WhoWor 74, 76, 78, 80, 82, 84, 87, 89, 91, 93, 95, 96, 97; WhoWrEP 89, 92, 95; WorAl; WorAlBi; WorAu 1950; WorLitC; WrDr 76, 80, 82, 84, 86, 88, 90, 92, 94, 96*

Vonnegut, Mark
American. Author
Wrote *The Eden Express,* 1975; son of Kurt.
b. May 11, 1947 in Chicago, Illinois
Source: *AuNews 2; BioIn 11, 12; ConAu 65*

Von Neumann, John
American. Mathematician
Helped develop atomic, hydrogen bombs.
b. Dec 3, 1903 in Budapest, Austria-Hungary
d. Feb 8, 1957 in Washington, District of Columbia

Source: *AmDec 1930; BiDPsy; BiESc; BioIn 3, 4, 5, 6, 7, 8, 11, 12, 13, 14, 15, 16, 17, 18, 19, 20, 21; ConAu 117; CurBio 55, 57; DcAmB S6; EncAB-H 1974, 1996; FacFETw; HisDcDP; InSci; JeHun; LarDcSc; MakMC; McGEWB; McGMS 80; NatCAB 46; NotTwCS; OxCAmH; PorSil; RAdv 14, 13-3; RComAH; ThTwC 87; WebAB 74; WhAm 3*

Vonnoh, Robert William
American. Artist
Paintings exhibited at Metropolitan Museum, NYC, include *President Wilson's Family, La Mere Adele.*
b. Sep 17, 1858 in Hartford, Connecticut
d. Dec 28, 1933 in Lyme, Connecticut
Source: *AmBi; ApCAB, X; BioIn 15, 19; BriEAA; DcAmArt; DcAmB; NatCAB 7; TwCBDA; WhAm 1; WhAmArt 85*

von Praunheim, Rosa
[Holger Mischwitki]
German. Filmmaker
Films include *Army of Lovers,* 1979; *Dolly, Lotte and Maria,* 1988.
b. 1942 in Riga, Latvia
Source: *GayLesB; MiSFD 9*

VonSchmidt, Harold
American. Illustrator
Known for drawings of Western subjects in mags., private sales.
b. May 19, 1893 in Alameda, California
d. Jun 3, 1982 in Westport, Connecticut
Source: *ArtsAmW 1; BioIn 1, 2, 7, 9, 10, 12, 13; IlBEAAW; IlrAm 1880; NewYTBS 82; WhAm 8; WhAmArt 85*

VonStade, Frederica
[Mrs. Peter Elkus]
"Flicka"
American. Opera Singer
Mezzo-soprano; had NY Met. debut in 1970; noted for Wagner, Rossini roles.
b. Jun 1, 1945 in Somerville, New Jersey
Source: *BioIn 16; CelR 90; FacFETw; IntWW 91; IntWWM 90; InWom SUP; NewAmDM; NewGrDA 86; NewYTBS 83; PenDiMP; WhoAm 86, 88, 90; WhoAmW 83, 89*

VonSternberg, Josef
Austrian. Director
Films include *The Blue Angel,* 1931, which starred Marlene Dietrich, whom he discovered.
b. May 29, 1894 in Vienna, Austria
d. Dec 22, 1969 in Hollywood, California
Source: *BiDFilm; DcFM; FilmEn; FilmgC; MovMk; ObitOF 79; OxCFilm; TwYS; WhScrn 74, 77; WorEFlm*

VonStroheim, Erich
[Erich Oswald Stroheim]
German. Actor, Director
As actor, called "the man you love to hate"; directed many silent films including *Greed,* 1928.
b. Sep 22, 1885 in Vienna, Austria
d. May 12, 1957 in Paris, France
Source: *BiDFilm; DcFM; Film 1; FilmgC; MotPP; MovMk; ObitOF 79; OxCFilm; REn; TwYS; WebAB 74, 79; WhAm 3; WhoHol A; WhScrn 74, 83; WorAl; WorEFlm*

VonSydow, Max Carl Adolf
Swedish. Actor
Sensitive, versatile, powerful screen actor: *Hannah and Her Sisters,* 1985, *Pelle the Conqueror,* 1988.
b. Apr 10, 1929 in Lund, Sweden
Source: *BiDFilm; BioIn 16; CelR 90; ConTFT 5; CurBio 67; FilmgC; HalFC 84, 88; IntMPA 84, 86, 92; IntWW 74; MotPP; MovMk; OxCFilm; WhoAm 76, 78, 80, 82, 84, 86, 90; WhoEnt 92; WhoHol A; WhoWor 74, 76, 78, 91; WorAl; WorAlBi; WorEFlm*

Von Tilzer, Albert
[Albert Gumm]
American. Composer
Best known for song "Take Me Out to the Ball Game."
b. Mar 29, 1878 in Indianapolis, Indiana
d. Oct 1, 1956 in Los Angeles, California
Source: *AmPS; AmSong; ASCAP 66, 80; BiDAmM; BioIn 4, 6, 14, 15, 16; CmpEPM; NewGrDA 86; NotNAT B; OxCPMus; PopAmC; Sw&Ld C*

VonTilzer, Harry
[Harry Gumm]
American. Publisher, Songwriter
Published two thousand songs including "Wait Till the Sun Shines, Nellie"; "In the Sweet Bye-and-Bye."
b. Jul 8, 1872 in Detroit, Michigan
d. Jan 10, 1946 in New York, New York
Source: *ASCAP 66; CurBio 46; DcAmB S4; REnAL*

Von Wangenheim, Chris
German. Photographer
Fashion photographer whose admirable love of women produced "daring, provocative, brilliantly inventive photos."
b. Feb 21, 1942 in Breslau, Germany
d. Mar 9, 1981, St. Martin
Source: *ConAu 103; MacBEP; NewYTBS 81*

Von Zell, Harry
American. Actor
Known for mellow voice; featured on "George Burns and Gracie Allen Show," 1956-58; appeared in 30 movies.
b. Jul 11, 1906 in Indianapolis, Indiana
d. Nov 21, 1981 in Woodland Hills, California
Source: *BioIn 12, 13; CurBio 44, 82, 82N; ForYSC; LegTOT; RadStar; SaTiSS; WhoHol A; WhScrn 83; WorAl*

Voorhees, Donald
American. Conductor
Directed popular weekly radio concerts, Bell Telephone Hour, 1940s.
b. Jul 26, 1903 in Allentown, Pennsylvania
d. Jan 10, 1989 in Cape May Court House, New Jersey
Source: *Baker 92; BioIn 2, 4, 16; CurBio 50, 89, 89N; FacFETw; NewYTBS 89; RadStar; WhAm 9; WhoAm 74*

Voroshilov, Kliment Efremovich
Russian. Soldier, Politician
In command on the Leningrad front at outbreak of war with Germany, 1941; succeeded Stalin as chm. of Presidium, 1953-57.
b. Feb 4, 1881 in Verkhneye, Russia
d. Dec 2, 1969 in Moscow, Union of Soviet Socialist Republics
Source: *BiDSovU; BioIn 13, 16, 18; ColdWar 1, 2; CurBio 40, 70; FacFETw; WebBD 83; WhoMilH 76*

Vorster, Balthazar Johannes
[John Vorster]
South African. Lawyer, Politician
Prime minister, 1966-78; Pres., 1978-79; introduced "banning" (internal exile).
b. Dec 13, 1915 in Jamestown, South Africa
d. Sep 10, 1983 in Cape Town, South Africa
Source: *AfSS 78, 79, 80, 81, 82; AnObit 1983; BioIn 7, 8, 9, 10, 11, 12, 13, 21; CurBio 67, 83N; DcAfHiB 86S; DcPol; DcTwHis; EncSoA; HisWorL; IntWW 74, 75, 76, 77, 78, 79, 80, 81, 82, 83; IntYB 78, 79, 80, 81, 82; McGEWB; NewYTBS 76, 83; WhAm 8; WhDW; Who 74, 82, 83; WhoGov 72; WhoWor 74, 76, 78; WorAl; WorAlBi*

Vos, Cornelis de
Flemish. Artist
Best known for straightforward portraits including one of his family, 1621.
b. 1584
d. 1651
Source: *NewCol 75; OxCArt; OxDcArt*

Vos, Martin de
Flemish. Artist
Student of Frans Floris; after Floris' death he became leading Italianate artist in Antwerp.
b. 1532
d. Dec 4, 1603
Source: *McGDA; NewCol 75; OxCArt*

Voskovec, George
Czech. Actor, Director, Dramatist
On Broadway *Cabaret,* 1969; in film *Twelve Angry Men,* 1957.
b. Jun 19, 1905 in Sazova, Czechoslovakia
d. Jul 1, 1981 in Pearblossom, California
Source: *AnObit 1981; BiE&WWA; BioIn 6, 11, 12; ConAu 104; FilmgC; ForYSC; HalFC 80, 84, 88; MotPP; NewYTBS*

81; NotNAT; OxCThe 67; WhoHol A; WhoThe 72, 77, 81; WhScrn 83

Votipka, Thelma
American. Opera Singer
Debut in *Marriage of Figaro,* 1927; soprano with Metropolitan Opera, 1935-63.
b. Dec 20, 1898 in Cleveland, Ohio
d. Oct 24, 1972
Source: *InWom; NewYTBE 72; WhAm 5*

Vouet, Simon
French. Artist
Best-known paintings: *The Presentation,* 1641; *Allegory of Peace,* 1648.
b. Jan 9, 1590 in Paris, France
d. Jun 30, 1649 in Paris, France
Source: *BioIn 6, 11, 13, 19; ClaDrA; DcBiPP; IntDcAA 90; McGDA; NewCol 75; OxCArt; OxDcArt*

Vought, Chance Milton
American. Aeronautical Engineer
Taught to fly by the Wright brothers, 1910; designed planes Vought VE-7, 1919; Vought UO-1, 1922-25.
b. Feb 26, 1890 in New York, New York
d. Jul 25, 1930 in Long Island, New York
Source: *DcAmB; WebAB 74, 79; WhAm 4, HSA*

Vo Van Kiet
Vietnamese. Political Leader
Prime minister, Vietnam, 1991—.
b. 1922 in Cuu Long, Vietnam
Source: *DcMPSA; FarE&A 78, 79, 80, 81; IntWW 78, 79, 80, 81, 82, 83, 89, 91, 93; WhoWor 93, 95, 96, 97*

Vranitzky, Franz
Austrian. Government Official
Federal Chancellor of Austria 1986-97.
b. Oct 4, 1937 in Vienna, Austria
Source: *BioIn 16; CurBio 89; IntWW 89, 91, 93; PolLCWE; WhoWor 82, 87, 89, 91, 93, 95, 96, 97*

Vrba, Elisabeth S.
South African. Paleontologist
Was the first person to hypothesize that climate played a major role in the extinction of species and evolution.
b. 1942

Vreeland, Diana (Dalziel)
American. Fashion Editor
Fashion editor, *Harper's Bazaar,* 1937-62, editor-in-chief, *Vogue,* 1962-71; created spectacular fashion exhibits at Metropolitan Museum of Art 1971-89.
b. 1903 in Paris, France
d. Aug 22, 1989 in New York, New York
Source: *AnObit 1989; BioIn 6, 7, 11, 12, 13, 14, 16; BlueB 76; CelR; ConAu 111, 129; ContDcW 89; CurBio 78, 89, 89N; EncTwCJ; FacFETw; ForWC 70; GrLiveH; IntDcWB; InWom, SUP; LegTOT; LibW; News 90, 90-1; NewYTBS 84, 89; WhoAm 86, 88; WhoAmW 89; WhoFash, 88; WorAlBi; WorFshn*

Vronsky, Vitya
[Vronsky and Babin; Victoria Vronsky]
American. Pianist
Performed two-piano concerts with husband, Victor, since 1937.
b. Aug 22, 1909 in Evpatoria, Russia
Source: *Baker 78, 84, 92; BioIn 3, 4, 6, 11; InWom; NewGrDA 86; NewGrDM 80; PenDiMP; WhoAm 74; WhoAmM 83; WhoAmW 58, 64*

Vuckovich, Pete(r Dennis)
American. Baseball Player
Pitcher, 1975-83; led AL in wins, 1981; won AL Cy Young Award, 1982.
b. Oct 27, 1952 in Johnstown, Pennsylvania
Source: *Ballpl 90; BaseEn 88; BioIn 13; LegTOT; NewYTBS 83*

Vuillard, (Jean) Edouard
French. Artist
Painted commonplace subjects, domestic interiors: *Woman Sweeping,* 1892.
b. Nov 11, 1868 in Cuiseaux, France
d. Jun 21, 1940 in La Baule, France
Source: *AtlBL; BioIn 3, 4, 6, 8, 9, 11, 15, 16; ClaDrA; DcTwCCu 2; IntDcAA 90; LegTOT; McGDA; McGEWB; OxCArt; OxCTwCA; OxDcArt; PhDcTCA 77; WhDW; WorAl; WorAlBi*

Vynnychenko, Volodymyr
Ukrainian. Author
Known for realistic, unexpected conflicts; writings include *Nova Zapovid,* 1950.
b. Jul 27, 1880 in Kherson, Russia
d. Mar 6, 1951 in Paris, France
Source: *BlkwERR; ClDMEL 80; EncRev; EncWL 2, 3; LiExTwC; ModSL 2; PenC EUR*

Vyshinsky, Andrei Yanuarievich
Russian. Judge, Diplomat
Foreign minister, Soviet Union, 1949-53.
b. Dec 10, 1883 in Odessa, Union of Soviet Socialist Republics
d. Nov 22, 1954 in New York, New York
Source: *BiDSovU; CurBio 55; EncWB; FacFETw; WhAm 3*

Vysotsky, Vladimir Semyonovich
Russian. Actor, Singer, Songwriter
Best known as ballad singer whose songs were mildly critical of Soviet officials.
b. Jan 25, 1938 in Moscow, Union of Soviet Socialist Republics
d. Jul 25, 1980 in Moscow, Union of Soviet Socialist Republics
Source: *AnObit 1980; CamGWoT; DcRusLS; HanRL; NewYTBE 70; NewYTBS 80*

Vyvyan, Jennifer Brigit
English. Opera Singer
London's Covent Garden soprano, 1950s-60s; noted for Handel, Britten roles.
b. Mar 13, 1925 in Broadstairs, England
d. Apr 5, 1974 in London, England
Source: *Baker 84; Who 74; WhoMus 72*

W

Waals, Johannes Diderik van der
Dutch. Scientist
Won 1910 Nobel Prize in physics; known for theory of binary solutions, thermodynamic theory of capillarity.
b. Nov 23, 1837 in Leiden, Netherlands
d. Mar 9, 1923 in Amsterdam, Netherlands
Source: *AsBiEn; BiESc; BioIn 20; CamDcSc; DcScB; WhDW; WhoNob; WorScD*

Wachner, Linda
American. Business Executive
Owner and pres. Warnaco, Inc., an apparel conglomerate, 1986-; chm., CEO, authentic fitness Corp., 1991—.
b. Feb 3, 1946 in New York, New York
Source: *AmWomM; BioIn 15; ConAmBL; Dun&B 90; News 88-3; WhoAm 90; WhoAmW 91; WhoE 91; WhoFI 92; WhoWest 92*

Wachter, Ed(ward)
American. Basketball Player
Center, 1896-1924; first pro player to be sold to another team, 1902; Hall of Fame.
b. Jun 30, 1883 in Troy, New York
d. Mar 12, 1966 in Troy, New York
Source: *BioIn 9; WhoBbl 73*

Waddell, Rube
[George Edward Waddell]
American. Baseball Player
Pitcher, 1897, 1899-1901; led AL in strikeouts once, NL six consecutive yrs; Hall of Fame, 1946.
b. Oct 13, 1876 in Bradford, Pennsylvania
d. Apr 1, 1914 in San Antonio, Texas
Source: *Ballpl 90; BiDAmSp BB; BioIn 2, 3, 4, 5, 6, 7, 8, 9, 10, 14, 15, 16; LegTOT; WhoProB 73; WhoSpor*

Waddell, Tom
[Thomas Flubacher; Thomas Waddell]
American. Physician, Olympic Athlete
Olympic decathlon athlete, 1968; founded Gay Games, 1982.
b. 1937 in Paterson, New Jersey
d. Jul 11, 1987 in San Francisco, California
Source: *BioIn 15, 20; GayLesB; News 88-2; NewYTBS 87*

Waddles, Charleszetta, Mother
American.
Founder, Mother Waddles Perpetual Help Mission, Detroit, 1956—; provides help for the needy.
b. Oct 7, 1912 in Saint Louis, Missouri
Source: *BioIn 8, 9; ConBlB 10; Ebony 1; InB&W 85; NegAl 76, 89; NotBlAW 1; WhoBlA 88, 92*

Wade, Benjamin Franklin
American. Politician
Senator from OH, 1851-69; opposed Lincoln's reconstruction policy; awaited Johnson's impeachment, as head of senate, he would succeed him.
b. Oct 27, 1800 in Springfield, Massachusetts
d. Mar 2, 1878 in Jefferson, Ohio
Source: *AmBi; AmPolLe; ApCAB; BiAUS; BiDrAC; BiDrUSC 89; BioIn 1, 3, 6, 7; CivWDc; DcAmB; Drake; EncAB-H 1974, 1996; HarEnUS; McGEWB; NatCAB 2; OxCAmH; TwCBDA; WebAB 74, 79; WhAm HS; WhAmP; WhCiWar*

Wade, Virginia
''Ginny Fizz''; ''Our Ginny''
English. Tennis Player
Women's singles champion, Wimbledon, 1977.
b. Jul 10, 1945 in Bournemouth, England
Source: *BioIn 10, 11, 12, 13, 14; BuCMET; ConAu 132; CurBio 76; IntWW 81, 82, 83, 91; InWom SUP; LegTOT; NewYTBS 83; Who 88, 90, 92; WhoIntT; WhoWor 78, 80, 82, 84, 87, 89, 91, 93, 95, 96; WorAl*

Wadkins, Lanny
American. Golfer
Turned pro, 1971; won PGA, 1977.
b. Dec 5, 1949 in Richmond, Virginia
Source: *BioIn 9, 11, 13; LegTOT; WhoAm 74, 76, 92, 94, 95, 96, 97; WhoGolf; WhoIntG; WhoWor 95, 96*

Wadsworth, James Jeremiah
[Jerry Wadsworth]
American. Government Official
Helped negotiate partial ban on nuclear weapons as head of US delegation to UN, 1960.
b. Jun 12, 1905 in Groveland, New York
d. Mar 13, 1984 in Rochester, New York
Source: *BioIn 3, 4, 5, 8, 11, 12, 13, 14; BlueB 76; ConAu 112, P-2; CurBio 56, 84; IntWW 74, 75, 76; NewYTBS 84; WhoAm 74*

Wadsworth, James Samuel
American. Military Leader
Brigadier general of volunteers from 1861; played key role in Union victory at Gettysburg, 1863.
b. Oct 30, 1807 in Geneseco, New York
d. May 8, 1864 in Fredericksburg, Virginia
Source: *AmBi; ApCAB; BioIn 7; CivWDc; DcAmB; Drake; HarEnUS; NatCAB 5; TwCBDA; WhCiWar*

Waggoner, Lyle
American. Actor
TV shows include ''Wonder Woman,'' 1977-79; ''Carol Burnett Show,'' 1967-74.
b. Apr 13, 1935 in Kansas City, Kansas
Source: *ConTFT 7; IntMPA 75, 76, 77, 78, 79, 80, 81, 82, 84, 86, 88, 92, 94, 96; LegTOT; WhoAm 82; WhoHol 92; WorAl*

Wagnalls, Adam Willis
American. Publisher
With Isaac Funk founded publishing house, Funk & Wagnalls, 1890.
b. Sep 24, 1843 in Lithopolis, Ohio
d. Sep 3, 1924 in Northport, New York
Source: *AmAu&B; NatCAB 23; WhAm 1*

Wagner, Barbara
Canadian. Skater
Figure skater; with partner Bob Paul, won gold medal, pairs skating, 1960 Olympics.
b. May 5, 1938 in Toronto, Ontario, Canada
Source: *BioIn 10*

Wagner, Cosima Liszt
[Mrs. Richard Wagner]
Hungarian.
Daughter of Franz Liszt; married Wagner, 1870; created Bayreuth Festival.
b. Dec 25, 1837 in Bellagio, Austria
d. Apr 1, 1930 in Bayreuth, Germany
Source: *Baker 84; IntDcWB; NewCol 75; NewEOp 71; WebBD 83*

Wagner, Honus
[John Peter Wagner]
"The Flying Dutchman"
American. Baseball Player
Infielder, 1897-1917, mostly with Pittsburgh; led NL in batting eight times; had lifetime .329 batting average; one of five original Hall of Fame inductees, 1936.
b. Feb 24, 1874 in Mansfield, Pennsylvania
d. Dec 6, 1955 in Carnegie, Pennsylvania
Source: *AmDec 1900; Ballpl 90; BiDAmSp BB; BioIn 1, 2, 3, 4, 5, 6, 7, 8, 9, 10, 13, 14, 15, 17, 20, 21; DcAmB S5; FacFETw; LegTOT; WebAB 74, 79; WhoProB 73; WhoSpor; WorAl; WorAlBi*

Wagner, Jack Peter
American. Actor, Singer
Plays Frisco Jones on daytime drama "General Hospital"; hit single "All I Need," 1984.
b. Oct 3, 1959 in Washington, Missouri

Wagner, Jane
American. Writer, Director
Won three Emmys for Lily Tomlin specials; wrote film *The Incredible Shrinking Woman,* 1980.
b. Feb 2, 1935 in Morristown, Tennessee
Source: *AuBYP 2S, 3; BioIn 14; ConAu 42NR, 109; ConTFT 6; IntMPA 88, 92, 94, 96; InWom SUP; LegTOT; LesBEnT; MiSFD 9; SmATA 33; VarWW 85*

Wagner, Lindsay J
American. Actor
Emmy-winning star of TV series "Bionic Woman," 1976-78; TV films include *This Child Is Mine,* 1985.
b. Jun 22, 1949 in Los Angeles, California
Source: *BioIn 13, 15; CelR 90; ConTFT 3; HalFC 84, 88; IntMPA 92; InWom SUP; LesBEnT 92; NewAgE 90; WhoAm 86, 90; WhoEnt 92; WhoHol A; WorAlBi*

Wagner, Richard
[Wilhelm Richard Wagner]
German. Composer, Librettist, Poet
Opera themes derived from medieval legends; wrote *Lohengrin, Tristan, Die Meistersinger;* founded Bayreuth Festival, 1876.
b. May 22, 1813 in Leipzig, Germany
d. Feb 13, 1883 in Venice, Italy
Source: *AtlBL; Baker 78, 84; BbD; Benet 87, 96; BiD&SB; BioIn 1, 2, 3, 4, 5, 6, 7, 8, 9, 10, 11, 12, 13, 14, 15, 16, 17, 18, 19, 20; BriBkM 80; CamGWoT; CasWL; CelCen; ClDMEL 47, 80; CmOp; CmpBCM; CnOxB; DancEn 78; DcArts; DcBiPP; DcCom 77; DcCom&M 79; DcEuL; DcLB 129; Dis&D; EncRev; EncTR, 91; EuAu; EuWr 6; EvEuW; GrComp; IntDcOp; LegTOT; LinLib L; LuthC 75; McGEWB; MetOEnc; MusMk; NewAmDM; NewC; NewCBEL; NewCol 75; NewEOp 71; NewGrDM 80; NewOxM; NinCLC 9; NotNAT B; OxCEng 67, 85, 95; OxCFr; OxCGer 76, 86; OxCMus; OxCThe 67; OxDcOp; PenC EUR; PenDiMP A; RAdv 14, 13-3; REn; REnWD; WebBD 83; WhDW; WorAl; WorAlBi*

Wagner, Robert F(erdinand)
American. Politician
Dem. senator from NY, 1926-49; helped draft several New Deal measures.
b. Jun 8, 1877 in Hesse-Nasseau, Germany
d. May 4, 1953 in New York, New York
Source: *AmPolLe; BiDrAC; BiDrUSC 89; BioIn 1, 2, 3, 7, 8, 11; CurBio 41, 53; DcAmB S5; DcAmSR; DcCathB; EncAB-H 1974, 1996; LinLib S; McGEWB; NatCAB 48; NewYTBE 72; PolProf T; WebAB 74, 79; WhAm 3; WhAmP; WorAl*

Wagner, Robert Ferdinand, Jr.
American. Lawyer, Politician
NYC's 102nd mayor, 1954-65; U.S. ambassador to Spain, 1968; envoy to the Vatican, 1978-81.
b. Apr 20, 1910 in New York, New York
d. Feb 12, 1991
Source: *BiE&WWA; BioIn 3, 4, 5, 6, 7, 8, 9, 10, 11, 17, 18; CurBio 54; EncWB; IntWW 74; LinLib S; NewCol 75; NewYTBS 91; PolProf E; WhoAm 86, 90; WhoAmL 79, 90; WhoAmP 85; WhoE 89; WorAl; WorAlBi*

Wagner, Robert John, Jr.
"R J"
American. Actor
Star of TV series, 1960s-80s: "It Takes a Thief;" "Switch;" "Hart to Hart;" in films since 1951: *Prince Valiant,* 1954; widower of Natalie Wood.
b. Feb 10, 1930 in Detroit, Michigan
Source: *BioIn 4, 5, 9, 10, 11; BkPepl; FilmgC; MovMk; WhoAm 86; WhoHol A; WhoTelC; WorAl; WorEFlm*

Wagner, Robin
American. Designer
Won Tony for set design of *On the 20th Century,* 1978; other plays include *42nd Street, Dream Girls.*
b. Aug 31, 1933 in San Francisco, California
Source: *BiE&WWA; BioIn 21; CamGWoT; ConDes 84, 90; ConTFT 3, 11; MetOEnc; NotNAT; VarWW 85; WhoAm 88, 90; WhoEnt 92; WhoThe 72, 77, 81*

Wagner, Roger Frances
American. Musician
Founded chorale group which toured extensively in US, Canada, Latin America, 1946-65.
b. Jan 16, 1914 in Le Puy, France
d. Sep 17, 1992, France
Source: *ASCAP 66; Baker 84; WhoAm 86; WhoWest 87, 92*

Wagner, Siegfried (Helferich)
German. Composer, Conductor
Son of Richard Wagner; conducted father's works at Bayreuth Festival.
b. Jan 6, 1869 in Stiebschen, Switzerland
d. Aug 4, 1930 in Bayreuth, Germany
Source: *Baker 78, 84; BioIn 8, 10, 19; MetOEnc; NewCol 75; NewEOp 71; NewGrDM 80; OxCMus; OxDcOp; PenDiMP*

Wagner, Wieland Adolf Gottfried
German. Director, Producer
Scenic director of Bayreuth Festival from 1951; grandson of Richard Wagner, son of Siegfried.
b. Jan 5, 1917 in Bayreuth, Germany
d. Oct 16, 1966 in Munich, Germany (West)
Source: *Baker 84; BioIn 7, 8, 9, 13; ConDes 84; EncWT; IntDcOp; ObitT 1961; WhAm 4*

Wagner, Wolfgang
German. Producer
Director of Bayreuth Festival since 1966; grandson of Richard Wagner, son of Siegfried.
b. Aug 30, 1919 in Bayreuth, Germany
Source: *Baker 84; BioIn 11; IntAu&W 82; IntDcOp; IntWW 83, 89, 91, 93; IntWWM 90; MetOEnc; NewEOp 71; NewGrDM 80; OxDcOp; WhoEnt 92; WhoMus 72; WhoOp 76; WhoWor 74, 76, 78, 84*

Wagner-Jaurregg, Julius, von
Austrian. Scientist
Won 1927 Nobel Prize in medicine for discovery of therapeutic value of malaria inoculation in treatment of syphilitic paralysis.
b. Mar 7, 1857 in Wels, Austria
d. Sep 27, 1940 in Vienna, Austria
Source: *BiESc; CurBio 40; DcScB; WhoNob*

Wagner-Regeny, Rudolf
Romanian. Composer
Operas include *Johanna Balk,* 1941; director of the State Conservatory in East Berlin, 1950.
b. Aug 28, 1903 in Regen, Romania
d. Sep 18, 1969 in Berlin, German Democratic Republic
Source: *Baker 78, 84, 92; BioIn 8; CmOp; DcCM; NewEOp 71; NewGrDM 80; NewGrDO; NewOxM; OxCMus; OxDcOp*

Wagoner, Porter
American. Singer
With Grand Ole Opry, 1957—; won three CMA awards with Dolly Parton.
b. Aug 12, 1927 in West Plains, Missouri
Source: *Baker 84, 92; BioIn 14; EncFCWM 83; HarEnCM 87; LegTOT; NewAmDM; NewGrDA 86; PenEncP; WhoAm 74, 76, 78, 80, 82, 84, 86, 88, 90, 92, 94, 95, 96, 97; WhoEnt 92; WhoHol 92; WorAl; WorAlBi*

Wahl, Ken
American. Actor
Played undercover cop Vinnie Terranova on TV series, "Wiseguy," 1987-90.
b. Feb 14, 1957 in Chicago, Illinois
Source: *BioIn 12; CelR 90; ConTFT 7; HalFC 88; IntMPA 84, 86, 88, 92; WhoHol 92*

Wahlberg, Donnie
American. Singer
Lead vocals of the group.
b. Aug 17, 1969 in Massachusetts
Source: *BioIn 17*

Wahloo, Per
Swedish. Journalist, Author
With wife, Maj Sjowall, wrote police procedure mysteries.
b. Aug 5, 1926 in Gothenburg, Sweden
d. Jun 22, 1975 in Malmo, Sweden
Source: *BioIn 9, 10; ConAu 57, 61; ConLC 7; DetWom; EncMys; EncSF, 93; InWom SUP; LegTOT; LinLib L; NewYTBE 71; ScF&FL 92; ScFSB; TwCCr&M 80B, 85B, 91B; WorAl; WorAlBi*

Waihee, John David, III
American. Politician
Dem. governor of Hawaii, 1986—.
b. May 19, 1946 in Honokaa, Hawaii
Source: *AlmAP 88, 92; IntWW 89, 91, 93; PolsAm 84; WhoAm 84, 86, 88, 90, 92, 94, 95; WhoAmP 85, 87, 91; WhoAsA 94; WhoWest 84, 87, 89, 92, 94; WhoWor 89, 91, 93, 95*

Wain, Bea
American. Singer
Famous for renditions of "My Reverie," "Deep Purple," 1938; popular in 1930s-40s.
b. Apr 30, 1917 in New York, New York
Source: *CmpEPM; IntMPA 79; InWom SUP; RadStar*

Wain, John Barrington
English. Author, Critic
Wrote novel, *Hurry on Down,* 1953; critical appraisal, *Living World of Shakespeare,* 1964.
b. Mar 14, 1925 in Stoke-on-Trent, England
d. May 24, 1994 in Oxford, England
Source: *Au&Wr 71; Benet 87; BioIn 13; CamGLE; CasWL; CnDBLB 8; ConAu 4AS, 5R, 23NR, 145; ConLC 11, 15, 46; ConNov 86, 91; ConPo 85, 91; CyWA 89; EncWL; EngPo; IntAu&W 91; IntWW 83, 91; LngCTC; MajTwCW; ModBrL, S2; OxCEng 85, 95; PenC ENG; REn; Who 92; WhoTwCL; WhoWor 91; WorAu 1950; WrDr 86, 92, 96*

Wainwright, James
American. Actor
TV shows include "Jigsaw," 1972-73; "Daniel Boone," 1968.
b. Mar 5, 1938 in Danville, Illinois
Source: *HalFC 84, 88; WhoAm 78, 80, 82; WhoFI 87; WhoHol 92, A*

Wainwright, Jonathan Mayhew
American. Army Officer
Led US forces at Bataan, Corregidor, WW II; awarded Congressional Medal of Honor.
b. Aug 23, 1883 in Walla Walla, Washington
d. Sep 2, 1953 in San Antonio, Texas
Source: *BiDWWGF; BioIn 1, 3, 6, 7, 9, 10, 12, 17; CurBio 42, 53; DcAmB S5; HarEnMi; McGEWB; MedHR 94; NatCAB 44; WebAMB; WhAm 3; WhWW-II; WorAl*

Wainwright, Loudon, III
American. Musician, Singer
Acoustic guitarist; albums include *Fame and Wealth,* 1983.
b. Sep 5, 1947 in Chapel Hill, North Carolina
Source: *ASCAP 80; BioIn 9, 10, 11, 14, 15, 16; ConMuA 80A; EncRk 88; HarEnR 86; IlEncRk; NewYTBS 74, 88; PenEncP; RkOn 82; RolSEnR 83; WhoRocM 82*

Waissman, Kenneth
American. Producer
Won Tony for *Torch Song Trilogy,* 1983.
b. Jan 24, 1940 in Baltimore, Maryland
Source: *ConTFT 5; NewYTBS 74; NotNAT; VarWW 85; WhoThe 81*

Waite, John
[The Babys]
English. Singer, Songwriter
Had hit single, "Missing You," 1984.
b. Jul 4, 1955 in Lancaster, England
Source: *LegTOT; RkOn 85; WhoRocM 82*

Waite, Morrison Remick
American. Supreme Court Justice
Appointed by U S Grant; served on bench, 1874-88.
b. Nov 29, 1816 in Lyme, Connecticut
d. Mar 23, 1888 in Washington, District of Columbia
Source: *AmBi; AmJust; AmPolLe; ApCAB; BiAUS; BiDFedJ; BioIn 2, 3, 5, 6, 9, 11, 15; DcAmB; EncAB-H 1974, 1996; HarEnUS; McGEWB; NatCAB 1, 26; OxCAmH; OxCLaw; OxCSupC; SupCtJu; TwCBDA; WebAB 74, 79; WhAm HS*

Waite, Ralph
American. Actor
Played John Walton in TV series "The Waltons," 1972-80.
b. Jun 22, 1928 in White Plains, New York
Source: *BioIn 13; ConTFT 1, 8; HalFC 80, 84, 88; IntMPA 86, 92; LegTOT; MiSFD 9; WhoAm 86, 90; WhoEnt 92; WhoHol 92, A; WorAlBi*

Waite, Ric
Filmmaker
Cinematographer who won Emmy for *Captains and Kings,* 1977; theatrical films include *Brewster's Millions,* 1985.
Source: *IntMPA 86, 88, 92, 94; VarWW 85; WhoEnt 92*

Waite, Terry
[Terence Hardy Watte]
"Anglican Henry Kissinger"
English. Clergy, Diplomat
Special Anglican Church envoy to Mideast who helped negotiate release of hostages in Lebanon, 1986-87; kidnapped, held hostage himself, 1987-1991.
b. May 31, 1939 in Styal, England
Source: *BioIn 14, 15; ConHero 2; CurBio 86; FacFETw; HeroCon; IntWW 91; LegTOT; NewYTBS 85; Who 85, 92*

Waits, Tom
American. Musician, Singer, Songwriter
Beatnik revivalist; was opening act for Frank Zappa, 1970s; Grammy award for *Bone Machine,* 1993.
b. Dec 7, 1949 in Pomona, California
Source: *Baker 92; BioIn 14, 15, 16, 17, 19; ConMuA 80A; ConMus 1, 12; ConTFT 6, 13; DcArts; EncFCWM 83; EncPR&S 89; EncRk 88; EncRkSt; HarEnR 86; IlEncRk; IntMPA 92, 94, 96; LegTOT; NewGrDA 86; NewGrDJ 88, 94; PenEncP; RolSEnR 83; WhoAm 90; WhoEnt 92; WhoHol 92; WhoRock 81; WhoRocM 82; WorAlBi*

Waitz, Grete
Norwegian. Track Athlete
Won NY Marathon seven times.
b. Oct 1, 1953 in Oslo, Norway
Source: *BioIn 12, 13, 14, 15, 17, 20; ContDcW 89; CurBio 81; InWom SUP; NewYTBS 79, 84*

Wajda, Andrzej
Polish. Director
Films include *Man of Marble,* 1977; *Man of Iron,* 1981, about Solidarity labor movement.
b. Mar 6, 1926 in Suwalki, Poland
Source: *Benet 87, 96; BiDFilm, 81; BioIn 10, 11, 12, 13, 14, 16, 18, 20; ConAu 102; ConLC 16; ConTFT 2, 8; CurBio 82; DcArts; DcFM; DrEEuF; FilmEn; FilmgC; GrStDi; HalFC 80, 84, 88; IntDcF 2-2; IntMPA 81, 92, 96; IntWW 74, 75, 76, 77, 78, 79, 80, 81, 82, 83, 89, 91, 93; ItaFilm; LegTOT; MiSFD 9; MovMk; NewYTBS 81, 89; OxCFilm; PolBiDi; TheaDir; WhDW; Who 92, 94; WhoSocC 78; WhoSoCE 89; WhoWor 74, 76, 78, 84, 89, 91, 93, 95, 96, 97; WorEFlm; WorFDir 2*

Wakefield, Dan
American. Author
First novel, *Island in the City,* 1959, was an insight into the world of Spanish Harlem.
b. May 21, 1932 in Indianapolis, Indiana
Source: *AmAu&B; AuSpks; BioIn 10, 11, 15, 16; BlueB 76; ConAu 7AS, 21R; ConLC 7; ConNov 86, 91, 96; DcLEL 1940; DrAF 76; DrAPF 80, 91; IndAu 1917; LiJour; WhoAm 74, 76, 78, 80, 82, 84, 86, 88, 90, 92, 94, 95, 96, 97; WhoEnt 92; WhoFI 85; WhoUSWr 88; WhoWrEP 89, 92, 95; WorAu 1985; WrDr 80, 82, 84, 86, 88, 90, 92, 94, 96*

Wakefield, Dick
[Richard Cummings Wakefield]
American. Baseball Player
Baseball's first bonus baby; signed $52,000 contract with Detroit, 1940; had .293 career batting average.
b. May 6, 1921 in Chicago, Illinois
d. Aug 26, 1985 in Detroit, Michigan
Source: *Ballpl 90; BioIn 2, 11, 14; WhoProB 73*

Wakefield, Ruth G
American. Manufacturer
Created tollhouse chocolate chip cookie.
b. 1905?
d. 1977 in Plymouth, Massachusetts
Source: *BioIn 11*

Wakely, Jimmy
American. Actor, Singer, Songwriter
Starred in movie westerns, 1940s; had CBS radio show, 1952-57.
b. Feb 16, 1914 in Mineola, Arkansas
d. Sep 23, 1982 in Los Angeles, California
Source: *ASCAP 66, 80; BgBkCoM; BiDAmM; BioIn 8, 11, 18; CmpEPM; CounME 74, 74A; EncFCWM 69; ForYSC; HarEnCM 87; IlEncCM; IntMPA 75, 76, 77, 78, 79, 80, 81, 82, 84, 86, 88; OxCPMus; PenEncP; WhoHol A*

Wakeman, Frederic
American. Author
Wrote best-seller *The Hucksters,* 1946.
b. Dec 26, 1909 in Scranton, Kansas
Source: *AmAu&B; AmNov; BioIn 1, 2, 4; CurBio 46; LngCTC; REn; REnAL; TwCA SUP; TwCWr; WhoSSW 73*

Wakeman, Rick
English. Musician
Wrote film scores for *The Burning,* 1981; *Journey to the Center of the Earth,* 1974.
b. May 18, 1949 in London, England
Source: *BioIn 10, 11; ConMuA 80A; EncPR&S 89; EncRk 88; HarEnR 86; IlEncRk; LegTOT; OxCPMus; WhoAm 82, 90, 92, 94, 95, 96, 97; WhoEnt 92; WhoRock 81; WhoRocM 82*

Wakoski, Diane
American. Poet
Linked with confessional school; collections include *Cap of Darkness,* 1980.
b. Aug 3, 1937 in Whittier, California
Source: *AmWomWr; ArtclWW 2; BenetAL 91; BioIn 10, 11, 12, 14, 15; CamGLE; CamHAL; ConAu 1AS, 9NR, 13R; ConLC 2, 4, 7, 9, 11, 40; ConPo 70, 75, 80, 85, 91, 96; CroCAP; DcLB 5; DcLEL 1940; DrAP 75; DrAPF 80, 91; FemiCLE; Focus; IntAu&W 86, 89, 91; IntvTCA 2; IntWWP 77; InWom SUP; ModAL S1; ModWoWr; OxCAmL 83, 95; OxCTwCP; OxCWoWr 95; PenC AM; RAdv 1, 13-1; WhoAm 80, 82, 84, 86, 88, 90, 92, 94, 95, 96, 97; WhoUSWr 88; WhoWrEP 89, 92, 95; WorAu 1970; WrDr 76, 80, 82, 84, 86, 88, 90, 92, 94, 96*

Waksman, Selman Abraham
American. Scientist, Physician, Engineer
Main discoverer of streptomycin, 1943; coined term "antibiotic"; won Nobel in medicine, 1952.
b. Jul 22, 1888 in Priluki, Ukraine
d. Aug 16, 1973 in Hyannis, Massachusetts
Source: *AsBiEn; BiESc; BioIn 1, 2, 3, 4, 5, 6, 8, 10, 11, 14, 15, 20; CamDcSc; CurBio 46, 73; DcAmB S9; DcAmMeB 84; DcScB S2; EncAAH; FacFETw; InSci; LarDcSc; McGEWB; McGMS 80; NewCol 75; NewYTBE 73; OxCMed 86; PeoHis; WebAB 74, 79; WhAm 6; WhoAm 74; WhoNob, 90, 95; WhoWor 74; WorAl; WorScD*

Walbrook, Anton
[Adolf Anton Wilhelm Wohlbruck]
British. Actor
Films include *The Red Shoes,* 1948; *Gaslight,* 1940.
b. Nov 19, 1900 in Vienna, Austria
d. Aug 9, 1967 in Munich, Germany (West)
Source: *BiDFilm, 81, 94; BioIn 14; EncWT; Film 2; FilmEn; FilmgC; ForYSC; HalFC 80, 84, 88; IlWWBF; ItaFilm; MotPP; MovMk; NotNAT B; ObitT 1961; OxCFilm; WhoHol B; WhScrn 74, 77, 83; WhThe; WorEFlm*

Walburn, Raymond
American. Actor
Character actor in over 80 films, 1929-55, including *Broadway Bill,* 1934.
b. Sep 9, 1887 in Plymouth, Indiana
d. Jul 26, 1969 in New York, New York
Source: *BiE&WWA; BioIn 8, 21; EncAFC; Film 2; FilmEn; FilmgC; ForYSC; HalFC 80, 84, 88; HolCA; MotPP; MovMk; NotNAT B; OlFamFa; Vers A; WhoHol B; WhScrn 74, 77, 83*

Walcott, Derek (Alton)
West Indian. Poet
Winner of Nobel Prize in Literature, 1992; work includes *In a Green Night,* 1962; *Another Life,* 1973; *Omeros,* 1990.
b. Jan 23, 1930 in Castries, St. Lucia
Source: *Benet 87; BenetAL 91; BioIn 9, 10, 11, 12, 13, 14, 15, 16; BlkAmP; BlkLC; BlkWr 1, 2; BlkWrNE; BlmGEL; CamGEL; CamGLE; CamGWoT; CaribW 1; CasWL; ConAu 26NR, 47NR, 89; ConBlB 5; ConBrDr; ConDr 73, 77, 82, 88, 93; ConLC 2, 4, 9, 14, 25, 42, 67, 76; ConPo 70, 75, 80, 85, 91, 96; ConTFT 6, 13; CrtSuDr; CurBio 84; CyWA 89; DcAfL; DcArts; DcLB 117, Y81B, Y92; DcLEL 1940; DcTwCCu 5; DrAP 75; DrAPF 80, 91; DrBlPA, 90; EncWL 2, 3; FacFETw; FifCWr; GrWrEL DR, P; IntDcT 2; IntLitE; IntWW 91; IntWWP 77; LegTOT; LiExTwC; LngCTC; MagSWL; MajTwCW; ModBlW; ModCmwL; MorBAP; NewYTBS 79, 82, 92; OxCEng 85, 95; OxCTwCP; PenC ENG; PlP&P A; RAdv 14, 13-2; RfGEnL 91; RGTwCWr; SchCGBL; SelBAAf; WebE&AL; WhDW; WhoAm 92, 94, 95, 96, 97; WhoE 95; WhoNob 95; WhoWor 82, 84, 89, 91, 93, 95, 96, 97; WorAu 1950; WrDr 82, 84, 86, 88, 90, 92, 94, 96*

Walcott, Joe
[Arnold Raymond Cream]
"Jersey Joe"
American. Boxer
Heavyweight champion, 1951-52; lost title to Marciano; Hall of Famer.
b. Jan 31, 1914 in Merchantville, New Jersey
d. Feb 25, 1994 in Camden, New Jersey
Source: *BiDAmSp BK; BioIn 1, 2, 3, 5, 6, 7, 8, 9, 10, 11; CurBio 49, 94N; InB&W 80; What 1; WhoAfA 96; WhoBlA 92; WhoBox 74; WorAl; WorAlBi*

Walcott, Mary Morris Vaux
"Audubon of American Wild Flowers"
American. Artist, Naturalist
Illustrated five-volume *North American Wild Flowers,* 1925.
b. Jul 31, 1860 in Philadelphia, Pennsylvania
d. Aug 22, 1940 in Saint Andrew's, New Brunswick, Canada
Source: *AmWomSc; InWom SUP; LibW; NotAW; WomFir*

Wald, George
American. Biologist
Shared Nobel Prize in medicine, 1967, for researching vision.
b. Nov 18, 1906 in New York, New York
d. Apr 12, 1997 in Cambridge, Massachusetts
Source: *AmMWSc 73P, 76P, 79, 86, 89, 92, 95; AsBiEn; BiESc; BioIn 5, 7, 8, 11, 14, 15, 20; BlueB 76; CurBio 68; EncWB; IntWW 74, 75, 76, 77, 78, 79, 80, 81, 82, 83, 89, 91, 93; LarDcSc; McGMS 80; NobelP; NotTwCS; WebAB 74, 79; Who 74, 82, 83, 85, 88, 90, 92, 94; WhoAm 74, 76, 78, 80, 82, 84, 86, 88, 90, 92, 94, 95, 96, 97; WhoE 74, 77, 79, 81, 85, 86, 89, 91, 95, 97; WhoFrS 84; WhoMedH; WhoNob, 90, 95; WhoScEn 94, 96; WhoWor 74, 80, 82, 84, 87, 89, 91, 93, 95, 96, 97; WhoWorJ 72, 78; WorAl; WorAlBi; WorScD*

Wald, Jerry
[Jerome Irving Wald]
American. Producer
Films include *Flamingo Road,* 1949; *Mildred Pierce,* 1945; *Peyton Place,* 1957.
b. Sep 16, 1911 in New York, New York
d. Jul 13, 1962 in Beverly Hills, California
Source: *BiDFilm, 94; BioIn 1, 2, 3, 4, 5, 6, 9; CurBio 62; FilmEn; FilmgC; GangFlm; HalFC 80, 84, 88; IntDcF 1-4, 2-4; LegTOT; ObitOF 79; WhAm 4; WorAl; WorEFlm*

Wald, Lillian D
American. Social Worker
Founded Henry Street Settlement, NYC; founded first public health nursing service, 1902.
b. Mar 10, 1867 in Cincinnati, Ohio
d. Sep 1, 1940 in Westport, Connecticut
Source: *AmAu&B; CurBio 40; DcAmB S2; EncAB-A 2; EncAB-H 1974; HerW; NotAW; OhA&B; WebAB 74; WhAm 1; WhNAA; WomWWA 14*

Walden, Robert
American. Actor
Played Joe Rossi on TV series "Lou Grant."
b. Sep 25, 1943 in New York, New York
Source: *WhoAm 80, 82, 84, 86, 88, 90, 92, 94; WhoHol 92, A*

Waldheim, Kurt
Austrian. Statesman
Elected pres. of Austria, 1986, in spite of Nazi allegations; secretary-general of UN, 1972-81.
b. Dec 21, 1918 in Woerdern, Austria
Source: *BioIn 9, 10, 11, 12, 13, 14, 15, 16; CelR; ConAu 89; CurBio 72, 84, 87; DcPol; DcTwHis; EncCW; EncWB; FacFETw; IntWW 74, 75, 76, 77, 78, 79, 80, 81, 82, 83, 89, 91, 93; IntYB 78, 79, 80, 81, 82; LegTOT; LinLib S; NewYTBE 71; NewYTBS 81, 88; OxCLaw; WhDW; Who 74, 82, 83, 85, 88, 90, 92, 94; WhoAm 74, 76, 78, 80, 82, 86; WhoE 74, 75, 77; WhoGov 72; WhoUN 75; WhoWor 74, 76, 78, 80, 82, 84, 87, 89, 91, 93, 95; WorAlBi*

Waldman, Max
American. Photographer
Known for black and white theater and classical dance subjects, 1947-81.
b. Jun 2, 1920 in New York, New York
d. Mar 1, 1981 in New York, New York
Source: *AnObit 1981; ConAu 103, 105; MacBEP; NewYTBS 81*

Waldock, Humphrey Meredith, Sir
[Claud Humphrey Meredith Waldock]
British. Statesman
An expert in international law; sat on International Court of Justice, 1973-81.
b. Aug 13, 1904 in Colombo, Ceylon
d. Aug 15, 1981 in The Hague, Netherlands
Source: *AnObit 1981; ConAu 108; IntWW 78, 82N; OxCLaw; Who 82N; WhoUN 75; WhoWor 80*

Waldron, Charles D
American. Actor
Specialized in playing stern fathers; films include *The Nurse's Secret,* 1941; *The Gay Sisters,* 1942.
b. Dec 23, 1875 in Waterford, New York
d. Mar 4, 1946 in Hollywood, California
Source: *Film 1; NotNAT B; ObitOF 79; WhoHol B; WhScrn 74, 77; WhThe*

Waldron, Hicks Benjamin
American. Cosmetics Executive, Consultant
President, chairman, Avon Products, 1983-89; currently chairman, Boardroom Consultants Inc.
b. Oct 31, 1923 in Amsterdam, New York
Source: *BioIn 13, 14, 15, 16; ConNews 87-3; CurBio 88; Dun&B 88; InB&W 85; NewYTBS 83, 85; St&PR 84, 87, 91; WhoAm 76, 78, 80, 82, 84, 86, 88, 90; WhoE 83, 85, 86, 89; WhoFI 77, 79, 81, 85, 87, 89, 92; WhoWor 84*

Wales, Salem Howe
American. Journalist
Editor, *Scientific American,* 1848-71.
b. Oct 4, 1825 in Wales, Massachusetts
d. 1902
Source: *ApCAB; NatCAB 3; WhAm 1*

Walesa, Lech
Polish. Political Leader, Labor Union Official
Organized Solidarity, only independent trade union in Communist world, 1980; won Nobel Peace Prize, 1983; pres., Poland, 1990-95.
b. Sep 29, 1943 in Popowo, Poland
Source: *BioIn 12, 13, 14, 15, 16, 17, 18, 19, 20, 21; ColdWar 1, 2; ConAu 128; ConHero 1; CurBio 81, 96; DcTwHis; EncCW; EncRev; EncWB; FacFETw; HeroCon; IntWW 81, 82, 83, 89, 91, 93; LegTOT; News 91, 91-2; NewYTBS 81, 83, 88, 89; NobelP; PolBiDi; RadHan; Who 85, 88, 90, 92, 94; WhoHol 92; WhoNob, 90, 95; WhoSoCE 89; WhoWor 82, 84, 87, 89, 91, 93, 95, 96, 97; WorAlBi*

Waley, Arthur David
English. Author
Scholar, translator of Oriental literature.
b. Aug 19, 1889 in London, England
d. Jun 27, 1966
Source: *CasWL; ChhPo, S1, S2; CnE&AP; CnMWL; ConAu 85; DcLEL; DcNaB 1961; EncJap; EvLB; GrBr; LngCTC; MakMC; NewC; NewCBEL; OxCEng 67, 85, 95; OxCTwCP; PenC ENG; REn; TwCA, SUP; TwCWr; WhDW*

Walford, Roy L(ee, Jr.)
American. Physician, Author
Researcher on aging; wrote *Maximum Life Span,* 1983.
b. Jun 29, 1924 in San Diego, California
Source: *AmMWSc 73P, 92; BioIn 13; ConAu 111*

Walgreen, Charles Rudolph
American. Merchant
Founded Walgreen drugstore chain, 1916.
b. Oct 9, 1873 in Knox County, Illinois
d. Dec 11, 1939 in Chicago, Illinois
Source: *BiDAmBL 83; BioIn 4, 13; DcAmB S2; LegTOT; NatCAB 29; WebAB 74, 79; WhAm 1*

Walgreen, Charles Rudolph, Jr.
American. Businessman
Pres. of Walgreen's, 1939-63; converted stores to self-service after WW II.
b. Mar 4, 1906 in Chicago, Illinois
Source: *BioIn 1, 10; IntWW 74; WhoAm 74, 76, 78; WhoFI 74*

Walgreen, Charles Rudolph, III
American. Business Executive
Chairman and CEO of Walgreen Company, drugstore chain, 1976—.
b. Nov 11, 1935 in Chicago, Illinois
Source: *BiDAmBL 83; BioIn 13, 15, 16; ConNews 87-4; Dun&B 90; St&PR 87, 91; WhoAm 74, 76, 78, 80, 82, 84, 86, 88, 90, 92, 94, 95, 96, 97; WhoFI 74, 75, 77, 79, 87, 89, 92, 94, 96; WhoMW 82, 84, 86, 88, 90, 92, 93, 96; WhoWor 95, 96*

Walinsky, Adam
American. Lawyer
Chm. of NY State Commission of Investigation, 1978-81.
b. Jan 10, 1937 in New York, New York
Source: *BioIn 7, 9, 10; WhoAmL 85, 87, 96; WhoFI 81, 83; WhoWor 91, 93*

Walken, Christopher
American. Actor
Won Oscar for best supporting actor, 1978, for *The Deer Hunter.*
b. Mar 31, 1943 in New York, New York
Source: *BiDFilm 94; BioIn 11, 12, 15; ConTFT 3, 12; CurBio 90; FilmEn; HalFC 80, 84, 88; IntMPA 80, 81, 82, 84, 86, 88, 92, 94, 96; IntWW 91, 93; LegTOT; NewYTBS 78; NotNAT; WhoAm 80, 82, 84, 86, 88, 90, 92, 94, 95, 96, 97; WhoEnt 92; WhoHol 92, A; WhoThe 77, 81; WorAlBi*

Walker, A. Maceo, Sr.
American. Insurance Executive
Pres., CEO, Universal Life Insurance Co., 1952-83, 1985-90; co-founder, pres., Tri-State Bank of Memphis.
b. Jun 7, 1909 in Indianola, Mississippi
Source: *DcWomA; Dun&B 90; WhoBlA 85, 88, 92; WhoIns 92*

Walker, Adam
English. Inventor, Teacher, Author
Taught math at age 15; traveling lecturer on natural philosophy; invented a machine for raising water level.
b. 1766 in Kendal, England
d. 1821
Source: *Alli; BiDLA*

Walker, Albertina
American. Singer
Formed gospel group Caravans, 1952, disbanded, 1967; a force in traditional gosepl music.
b. 1929 in Chicago, Illinois
Source: *ConBlB 10; ConTFT 12; WhoAfA 96; WhoBlA 80, 90, 92, 94*

Walker, Alice
American. Author
Won Pulitzer for novel *The Color Purple,* 1982; filmed, 1985.
b. Feb 9, 1944 in Eatonton, Georgia
Source: *AfrAmAl 6; AfrAmW; AmWomWr, 92; AmWr S3; ArtclWW 2; Au&Arts 3; AuSpks; Benet 87, 96; BenetAL 91; BestSel 89-4; BioIn 11, 13, 14, 15, 16, 17, 18, 19, 20, 21; BlkAuII, 92; BlkAWP; BlkLC; BlkWAm; BlkWr 1; BlkWrNE; BlkWWr; BlmGWL; BroadAu; BroV; CamGLE; CamHAL; CelR 90; ConAu 9NR, 27NR, 37R; ConBlB 1; ConHero 1; ConLC 5, 6, 9, 19, 27, 46, 58; ConNov 86, 91; ContDcW 89; CurBio 84; CyWA 89; DcArts; DcLB 6, 33, 143; DcTwCCu 1, 5; DcVicP 2; DrAF 76; DrAP 75; DrAPF 80, 91; EncAACR; EncSF 93; EncWB; EncWL 3; FacFETw; FemiCLE; GrLiveH; GrWomW; HanAmWH; InB&W 80, 85; IntAu&W 82, 91; IntDcWB; IntWW 91; InWom SUP; LegTOT; LivgBAA; MagSAmL; MajTwCW; ModAL S2; ModAWWr; ModBlW; ModWoWr; NegAl 83, 89; NewYTBS 83; NotBlAW 1; OxCAmL 83; OxCWoWr 95; PeoHis; PostFic; RadHan; RAdv 14; RfGAmL 87; ScF&FL 92; SchCGBL; ShSCr 5; SmATA 31; WhoAm 74, 76, 78, 90; WhoAmW 74, 91; WhoBlA 75, 77, 80, 85, 88, 92; WhoUSWr 88; WhoWrEP 89; WomFir; WorAlBi; WorAu 1975; WrDr 86, 88, 90, 92, 94, 96*

Walker, C. J., Madame
[Sarah Breedlove]
American. Businesswoman
President and owner, Madame C. J. Walker Manufacturing Co., 1906-19, a producer and distributor of a line of hair and beauty preparations for black women.
b. Dec 23, 1867 in Delta, Louisiana
d. May 25, 1919 in Irvington-on-Hudson, New York
Source: *AfrAmAl 6; BioIn 16, 17, 18, 19, 20; DcAmNB; NotBlAW 1; RComAH*

Walker, Chet
[Chester Walker]
American. Basketball Player
Forward, 1962-75, mostly with Philadelphia, Chicago; led NBA in free throw percentage, 1971.
b. Feb 22, 1940 in Benton Harbor, Michigan
Source: *BasBi; BiDAmSp BK; BioIn 6, 15, 21; OfNBA 87; WhoAfA 96; WhoAm 74; WhoBbl 73; WhoBlA 92, 94*

Walker, Clint
American. Actor
Star of TV series "Cheyenne," 1955-63.
b. May 30, 1927 in Hartford, Illinois
Source: *BioIn 4; FilmEn; FilmgC; ForYSC; HalFC 80, 84, 88; IntMPA 75, 76, 77, 78, 79, 80, 81, 82, 84, 86, 88, 92, 94, 96; LegTOT; MotPP; WhoHol 92, A; WorAl*

Walker, Cyril
English. Golfer
Touring pro, 1920s; won US Open, 1924.
b. 1892 in Manchester, England
d. Aug 5, 1948 in Hackensack, New Jersey
Source: *BioIn 1; WhoGolf*

Walker, Daniel
American. Politician
Dem. governor of IL, 1973-77; convicted of fraud, perjury, 1987.
b. Aug 6, 1922 in San Diego, California
Source: *BiDrGov 1789; BioIn 9, 10, 11, 20; BlueB 76; CurBio 76; IntWW 74, 75, 76, 77, 78, 79, 80, 81, 82, 83, 89; PolPar; WhoAm 74, 76, 78; WhoAmL 79; WhoGov 75, 77; WhoMW 74, 76, 78, 80*

Walker, Danton MacIntyre
American. Journalist
Broadway columnist, *NY Daily News;* wrote *Danton's Inferno,* 1955.
b. Jul 26, 1899 in Marietta, Georgia
d. Aug 8, 1960 in Hyannis, Massachusetts
Source: *AmAu&B; BiDAmNC; BioIn 3, 5; ConAu 93; REnAL; WhAm 4*

Walker, David Harry
Canadian. Author
Wrote *Geordie,* 1950; *The Pillar,* 1952.
b. Feb 9, 1911, Scotland
d. Mar 5, 1992
Source: *BenetAL 91; BioIn 6, 10, 11; CanWr; CanWW 70, 79, 80, 81, 83, 89; CasWL; ConAu 1NR, 1R; ConLC 14, 76; ConNov 72, 76; DcLEL 1940; LngCTC; OxCCan, SUP; OxCChiL; REnAL; SmATA 8; Who 74, 82, 83, 85, 88, 90, 92; WhoAm 76, 78, 80, 82, 84, 86, 88, 90; WhoCan 73, 75, 77, 80, 82, 84; WhoCanL 92; WhoWor 80; WorAu 1950; WrDr 76*

Walker, Dixie
[Fred Walker]
"The Peepul's Cherce"
American. Baseball Player
Outfielder, 1931, 1933-49, mostly with Brooklyn; led NL in batting, RBIs; had .306 lifetime batting average.
b. Sep 24, 1910 in Villa Rica, Georgia
d. May 17, 1982 in Birmingham, Alabama
Source: *Ballpl 90; BiDAmSp BB; BioIn 1, 2, 3, 8, 15; FacFETw; LegTOT; NewYTBS 82; WhoProB 73*

Walker, Doak
[Ewell Doak Walker, Jr.]
"Doaker"
American. Football Player
Halfback, won Heisman Trophy, 1948; in NFL with Detroit, 1950-56; led league in scoring twice; Hall of Fame, 1986.
b. Jan 1, 1927 in Dallas, Texas
Source: *BiDAmSp FB; BioIn 1, 2, 3, 5, 8, 9, 10, 14, 16, 17; LegTOT; St&PR 75, 84, 87, 91; WhoFtbl 74; WhoSpor*

Walker, Edyth
American. Opera Singer
Mezzo-soprano, noted for Wagner roles; among first Americans accepted in European opera houses.
b. Mar 27, 1867 in Hopewell, New York
d. Feb 19, 1950 in New York, New York
Source: *Baker 78, 84, 92; CmOp; InWom SUP; MetOEnc; NewEOp 71; NewGrDA 86; NewGrDM 80; NewGrDO; NotAW; PenDiMP*

Walker, Emery, Sir
English. Type Designer, Printer
Influenced William Morris to start Kelmscott Press, 1891; cofounded Doves Press, 1900.
b. Apr 2, 1851 in London, England
d. Jul 22, 1933 in London, England
Source: *BioIn 2, 10, 16; DcNaB 1931; NewCol 75*

Walker, Eric A(rthur)
American. Educator
Pres., PA State U, 1956-70.
b. Apr 29, 1910
d. Feb 17, 1995 in State College, Pennsylvania

Source: *BioIn 4, 5, 9; BlueB 76; CurBio 95N; WhAm 11; WhoAm 74, 76, 78, 80, 82, 84, 86, 88, 90, 92, 94, 95, 96; WhoE 74; WhoFI 74; WhoFrS 84; WhoGov 72, 75, 77*

Walker, Harold Blake
American. Clergy, Author, Journalist
Presbyterian minister; wrote *Prayers to Live By*, 1966.
b. May 7, 1904 in Denver, Colorado
Source: *BlueB 76; ConAu 17R; WhoAm 74, 76, 78, 80, 82, 84, 86, 88, 90, 92, 94, 95, 96, 97; WhoMW 92; WhoRel 92*

Walker, Henry Oliver
American. Artist
Figural, mural painter; did congressional library scenes.
b. May 14, 1843 in Boston, Massachusetts
d. Jan 14, 1929 in Belmont, Massachusetts
Source: *AmBi; DcAmB; NatCAB 9, 13, 22; TwCBDA; WhAm 1*

Walker, Herschel
American. Football Player
Running back, won Heisman Trophy, 1982; in NFL with Dallas, 1986-89, Minnesota, 1989-92, Philadelphia, 1992-95, New York Giants, 1995—.
b. Mar 3, 1962 in Wrightsville, Georgia
Source: *AfrAmSG; BiDAmSp FB; BioIn 12, 13, 14, 15, 16; ConBlB 1; CurBio 85; FootReg 87; InB&W 85; LegTOT; NewYTBS 81, 82, 83, 84, 85, 86, 88; WhoAfA 96; WhoAm 92, 94, 95, 96, 97; WhoBlA 85, 88, 90, 92, 94; WhoE 95; WhoWor 96; WorAlBi*

Walker, Hiram
American. Distiller
Opened Hiram Walker and Sons, Canada; town of Walkerville, ON, named for him.
b. Jul 4, 1816 in East Boston, Massachusetts
d. Jan 12, 1899 in Detroit, Michigan
Source: *DcCanB 12; MacDCB 78*

Walker, Jack
[John Philip Walker]
Canadian. Hockey Player
Left wing. Detroit, 1926-28; Hall of Fame, 1960.
b. Nov 28, 1888 in Silver Mountain, Ontario, Canada
d. Feb 16, 1950
Source: *HocEn; WhoHcky 73*

Walker, Jimmie
[James Carter Walker]
American. Actor, Comedian
Played J J on TV series "Good Times," 1974-78; known for phrase "Dy-no-mite."
b. Jun 25, 1948 in New York, New York
Source: *BioIn 10, 13, 14, 15; BlksAmF; ConTFT 7; DrBlPA 90; EncAFC; InB&W 80, 85; VarWW 85; WhoBlA 80, 85, 92; WhoHol A*

Walker, Jimmy
[James John Walker]
American. Politician, Songwriter
Colorful mayor of NYC, 1925-32; investigation of widespread corruption led to resignation.
b. Jun 19, 1881 in New York, New York
d. Nov 18, 1946 in New York, New York
Source: *ASCAP 66, 80; BiDAmM; BioIn 1, 2, 3, 4, 5, 6, 10; CopCroC; DcAmB S4; DcCathB; NatCAB 34; ObitOF 79; OxCAmH; REn; REnAL; WebAB 74, 79; WhAm 2; WorAl*

Walker, John
American. Curator
Founding chief curator, National Gallery of Art, 1939-56; director, 1956-69.
b. Dec 24, 1906
d. Oct 15, 1995 in Sussex, England
Source: *BioIn 4, 5, 8, 9, 10, 11, 21; BlueB 76; ConAu 5R, 6NR; CurBio 96N; IntWW 74, 75, 76, 77, 78, 79, 80, 81, 82, 83, 89, 91, 93; NewYTBS 95; WhAmArt 85; Who 74, 82, 83, 85, 88, 90, 92, 94; WhoAm 74, 76; WhoGov 72; WhoWor 74; WrDr 80, 82, 84, 86, 88, 90*

Walker, Joseph
American. Photographer, Inventor
Developed first zoom lens, 1922; patented panoramic camera; received special Oscar, 1982.
b. 1892
d. Aug 1, 1985 in Las Vegas, Nevada
Source: *BioIn 14, 15; ConAu 117; FacFETw; FilmEn; FilmgC; GangFlm; HalFC 80, 84, 88; IntMPA 77, 80, 81*

Walker, Joseph Reddeford
American. Explorer, Naturalist
First white man to lead party across Sierra Nevadas; Walker Lake Pass named for him.
b. Dec 13, 1798 in Virginia
d. Oct 27, 1876 in Ignacio Valley, California
Source: *ApCAB; BioIn 2, 7, 13, 15, 18; CmCal; DcAmB; Expl 93; HarEnUS; NatCAB 5; REnAW; WebAB 74, 79; WhAm HS; WhNaAH; WhWE*

Walker, Junior
[Jr. Walker and the All-Stars; Autry DeWalt, Jr.]
American. Musician, Singer
Saxophonist; hits include "Shotgun," 1965; "How Sweet It Is," 1966.
b. Jun 14, 1942 in Blythesville, Arkansas
d. Nov 23, 1995 in Battle Creek, Michigan
Source: *EncRk 88; HarEnR 86; LegTOT; NewGrDA 86; News 96, 96-2; NewYTBS 95; PenEncP; RkOn 84; RolSEnR 83; WorAl*

Walker, Maggie Lena
American.
First US woman bank pres., 1903-32, St. Luke's Penny Thrift Savings Bank, now called the Consolidated Bank and Trust Co.
b. Jul 15, 1867 in Richmond, Virginia
d. Dec 15, 1934 in Richmond, Virginia
Source: *AfrAmAl 6; AmWomM; BiDAmBL 83; BioIn 6, 8, 10, 16, 20, 21; BlkWAm; DcAmNB; EncWB; GrLiveH; InB&W 85; InWom, SUP; LibW; NegAl 76, 83, 89; NotAW; NotBlAW 1; PeoHis; WhoBlA 92*

Walker, Mary Edwards
American. Physician
First woman physician in US, 1855; only woman to receive Medal of Honor, 1865.
b. Nov 26, 1832 in Oswego, New York
d. Feb 21, 1919 in Oswego, New York
Source: *AmBi; AmRef; AmWom; BioAmW; BioIn 2, 5, 6, 8, 11, 12, 15, 21; CivWDc; ContDcW 89; DcAmB; DcAmMeB 84; DcAmSR; DcBiPP; DcNAA; HanAmWH; HerW; InSci; IntDcWB; InWom, SUP; LibW; MedHR, 94; MorMA; NatCAB 13; NotAW; NotWoLS; OhA&B; WebAMB; WhAm 1; WomFir; WorAl*

Walker, Mickey
[Edward Patrick Walker]
"Toy Bulldog"
American. Boxer, Artist
World welterweight champion, 1922-26; middleweight champion, 1926-31.
b. Jul 13, 1901 in Elizabeth, New Jersey
d. Apr 28, 1981 in Freehold, New Jersey
Source: *AnObit 1981; BiDAmSp BK; BioIn 3, 4, 5, 6, 8, 10, 12; BoxReg; ConAu 108; LegTOT; NewYTBS 81; WhoBox 74; WhoSpor; WorAl*

Walker, Mort
[Mortimer Walker Addison]
American. Cartoonist
Created *Beetle Bailey*, 1950; *Hi and Lois*, 1954.
b. Sep 3, 1923 in El Dorado, Kansas
Source: *BioIn 11, 14, 15, 16; ConAu 3NR, 25NR, 49; ConGrA 2; EncACom; EncTwCJ; LegTOT; LinLib L; SmATA 8; WhoAm 74, 76, 78, 80, 82, 84, 86, 88, 90, 92, 94, 95, 96, 97; WhoAmA 73, 76, 78, 80, 82, 84, 86, 89, 91, 93; WhoE 74; WhoWor 74*

Walker, Nancy
[Anna Myrtle Swoyer]
American. Actor
TV shows include "McMillan and Wife," 1971-76, "Rhoda," 1974-76.
b. May 10, 1921 in Philadelphia, Pennsylvania
d. Mar 25, 1992 in Studio City, California
Source: *BiE&WWA; BioNews 74; ConTFT 3; CurBio 65; EncMT; HalFC 80, 84, 88; IntMPA 92; InWom SUP; LegTOT; LesBEnT, 92; MotPP; MovMk; News 92; NewYTBE 73; NewYTBS 76; NotNAT; OxCAmT 84; OxCPMus; WhoAm 74, 78, 80, 82, 86, 88; WhoCom; WhoEnt 92; WhoHol A; WhoThe 77, 81; WorAl; WorAlBi*

Walker, Ralph Thomas
American. Architect
Leading proponent, designer of Art Deco skyscrapers, 1920s.
b. Nov 28, 1889 in Waterbury, Connecticut
d. Jan 17, 1973
Source: *AmArch 70; BioIn 4, 5, 9, 10, 13; CurBio 57, 73; MacEA; WhAm 5; WhoE 74*

Walker, Robert
American. Actor
Starred in Hitchcock's *Strangers on a Train,* 1951.
b. Oct 13, 1918 in Salt Lake City, Utah
d. Aug 28, 1951 in Santa Monica, California
Source: *BiDFilm, 81, 94; EncAFC; FilmEn; FilmgC; IntDcF 1-3, 2-3; MovMk; NotNAT B; OxCFilm; WhScrn 74, 77; WorEFlm*

Walker, Robert James
American. Government Official
Secretary of Treasury under James Polk, 1845-49; helped create dept. of Interior, 1849.
b. Jul 23, 1801 in Northumberland, Pennsylvania
d. Nov 11, 1869 in Washington, District of Columbia
Source: *Alli; BiAUS; BiDrAC; BiDrUSE 71, 89; BiDSA; BioIn 9; Drake; HarEnUS; WhAm HS; WhAmP*

Walker, Sarah Breedlove McWilliams
American. Business Executive, Philanthropist
Made fortune from beauty products designed for black women's hair, 1905.
b. Dec 23, 1867 in Delta, Louisiana
d. May 25, 1919 in New York, New York
Source: *InB&W 80; NotAW; WhoColR*

Walker, Stanley
American. Journalist
Wrote *City Editor,* 1934; city editor of *NY Herald Tribune,* 1928-35.
b. Oct 21, 1898 in Lampasas, Texas
d. Nov 25, 1962 in Lampasas, Texas
Source: *AmAu&B; BioIn 1, 6; ConAu 93; CurBio 44, 63; EncAJ; EncTwCJ; REnAL; TexWr; WhAm 4*

Walker, Stuart Armstrong
American. Producer, Director
Founded experimental mobile Portmanteau Theatre, 1915.
b. Mar 4, 1880 in Augusta, Kentucky
d. Mar 13, 1941 in Beverly Hills, California
Source: *DcAmB S3; NatCAB 38; WhAm 1*

Walker, T-Bone
[Aaron Thibeaux Walker]
"Daddy of the Blues"
American. Singer, Musician, Songwriter
Blues guitarist who popularized the use of the electric guitar.
b. May 28, 1910 in Linden, Texas
d. Mar 16, 1975 in Los Angeles, California
Source: *BiDAfM; BiDAmM; BioIn 15; BluesWW; ConMus 5; DcArts; DcTwCCu 5; EncJzS; EncRk 88; IlEncJ; LegTOT; NewAmDM; NewGrDA 86; NewGrDM 80; OnThGG; OxCPMus; PenEncP; RolSEnR 83; WhoJazz 72; WhoRock 81; WhoRocM 82*

Walker, T. J.
[Thomas Walker]
American. Fashion Designer
Co-founded, with Carl Jones, Cross Colours, 1990.
b. c. 1961 in Toomsuba, Mississippi

Walker, Wesley Darcel
American. Football Player
Wide receiver, NY Jets, 1977-88; led NFL in receiving, 1978.
b. May 26, 1955 in San Bernardino, California
Source: *BioIn 14; FootReg 87; NewYTBS 78; WhoAfA 96; WhoBlA 85, 92, 94*

Walker, William
American. Adventurer
Overthrew Nicaraguan govt., pres., 1856; captured, executed in Honduras.
b. May 8, 1824 in Nashville, Tennessee
d. Sep 12, 1860 in Trujillo, Honduras
Source: *Alli SUP; AmAu&B; AmBi; ApCAB; BenetAL 91; BiD&SB; BiDLAmC; BiDSA; BioIn 1, 2, 3, 4, 6, 8, 9, 11, 12, 16; CmCal; DcAmAu; DcAmB; DcAmDH 80, 89; DcAmSR; DcBiPP; DcNAA; Drake; EncLatA; EncRev; EncSoH; HarEnUS; HisWorL; LinLib S; McGEWB; NatCAB 11; OxCAmH; PeoHis; REnAL; WebAB 74, 79; WhAm HS; WhCiWar*

Walker, Zena
English. Actor
Won Tony for *A Day in the Death of Joe Egg,* 1968.
b. Mar 7, 1934 in Birmingham, England
Source: *ConTFT 5; HalFC 84, 88; VarWW 85; WhoHol 92; WhoThe 72, 77, 81*

Wall, Art(hur Jonathan), Jr.
American. Golfer
Turned pro, 1949; had 19 PGA wins including Masters, 1959; leading money winner, 1959.
b. Nov 25, 1923 in Honesdale, Pennsylvania
Source: *BioIn 2, 5, 10, 21; CurBio 59; WhoGolf*

Wallace, Alfred Russell
English. Engineer, Scientist, Physician
Proposed theory of evolution simultaneously, but independently, of Charles Darwin, 1858.
b. Jan 8, 1823 in Usk, England
d. Nov 7, 1913 in Broadstone, England
Source: *Alli SUP; BbD; BiD&SB; BiDPara; BritAu 19; Chambr 3; DcEnA A; DcEnL; DcEuL; DcLEL; EvLB; Expl 93; McGEWB; NewC; OxCEng 85; REn; WebBD 83*

Wallace, Amy
American. Author
Wrote, with father *The People's Almanac Presents the Book of Lists,* 1977.
b. Jul 3, 1955 in Los Angeles, California
Source: *ArtclWW 2; BiDrAPA 89; BioIn 11, 12, 15; ConAu 27NR, 81; WhAmArt 85; WhoWest 92*

Wallace, Bobby
[Roderick John Wallace]
"Rhody"
American. Baseball Player
Shortstop, 1894-1918, mostly with St. Louis Browns; known for fielding; first AL shortstop elected to Hall of Fame, 1953.
b. Nov 4, 1874 in Pittsburgh, Pennsylvania
d. Nov 3, 1960 in Torrance, California
Source: *WhoProB 73*

Wallace, Chris(topher)
American. Broadcast Journalist
White House correspondent, NBC News, 1982-1989; Prime Time Live 1989—; son of Mike Wallace.
b. Oct 12, 1947 in Chicago, Illinois
Source: *BioIn 12, 14; Dun&B 90; WhoAm 84, 86, 88, 90, 92, 94, 95, 96, 97; WhoE 95; WhoTelC; WhoWor 96*

Wallace, Cornelia Folsom
American.
Second wife of AL governor, George Wallace, 1971-78.
b. Jan 28, 1939 in Elba, Alabama
Source: *BioIn 10, 11, 12*

Wallace, DeWitt
[William Roy DeWitt Wallace]
American. Publisher
With wife, Lila, founded *Reader's Digest,* 1922.
b. Nov 12, 1889 in Saint Paul, Minnesota
d. Mar 30, 1981 in Mount Kisco, New York
Source: *AmAu&B; AnObit 1981; BiDAmJo; BioIn 1, 2, 3, 4, 5, 6, 8, 12, 15, 16, 17, 19, 20; BlueB 76; ConAu 103; CurBio 44, 56, 81, 81N; DcLB 137; EncAB-H 1974, 1996; EncAJ; EncTwCJ; EncWB; IntWW 74, 75, 76, 77, 78, 79, 80; LegTOT; LinLib L, S; NewYTBS 81; RComAH; St&PR 75; WebAB 74, 79; WhAm 7; WhDW; WhoAm 74, 76, 78, 80; WhoWor 74; WorAl; WorAlBi*

Wallace, Ed(ward Tatum)
American. Journalist
Human interest stories were featured in *NY Daily News.*
b. Aug 9, 1906
d. Oct 10, 1976 in New York, New York
Source: *BioIn 11; ConAu 69; NewYTBS 76*

Wallace, Edgar
[Richard Horatio Edgar Wallace]
English. Author
Wrote popular thrillers including *The Terror,* 1930.
b. Dec 1875 in Greenwich, England
d. Feb 10, 1932 in Hollywood, California
Source: *Benet 87, 96; BioIn 2, 7, 8, 10, 14; CamGWoT; CasWL; ConAu 115; CrtSuMy; DcArts; DcLB 70; DcLEL; DcNaB 1931; EncMys; EncSF, 93; EncSoA; EvLB; FilmgC; GrBr; GrWrEL N; HalFC 84, 88; ItaFilm; LngCTC; MnBBF; ModBrL; NewC; NewCBEL; Novels; OxCEng 67, 85; OxCThe 67; PenC ENG; RAdv 14; REn; RfGEnL 91; ScF&FL 1, 92; ScFEYrs; ScFSB; TwCA, SUP; TwCCr&M 80, 85, 91; TwCLC 57; TwCSFW 81, 86, 91; TwCWr; WhoSpyF; WhoTwCL; WorAl; WorAlBi*

Wallace, George Corley
American. Politician
Four-term Dem. governor of AL, 1960s-80s; paralyzed in assassination attempt, 1972; gained renown as strong segregationist, but moderated views, becoming symbol of "New South."
b. Aug 25, 1919 in Clio, Alabama
Source: *AmOrTwC; AmPolLe; BiDrGov 1789, 1978, 1983; BioIn 5, 6, 7, 8, 9, 10, 11, 12, 13, 14, 15, 16, 17, 19, 20, 21; BlueB 76; CivRSt; ConAu 114; CurBio 63; DcAmC; DcTwHis; EncAAH; EncAB-H 1974, 1996; EncSoH; FacFETw; IntWW 74, 75, 76, 77, 78, 79, 80, 81, 82, 83, 89, 91, 93; LinLib S; McGEWB; NewYTBE 72; NewYTBS 74, 86; PolProf J, K, NF; PolsAm 84; PresAR; RComAH; WebAB 74, 79; WhDW; WhoAm 74, 76, 78, 80, 82, 84, 86, 88, 90, 92, 94, 95; WhoAmL 79; WhoAmP 73, 75, 77, 79, 81, 83, 85, 87, 89, 91, 93, 95; WhoGov 72, 75, 77; WhoSSW 73, 75, 76, 78, 84, 86, 88, 91, 95, 97; WhoWor 74, 78, 84, 87; WorAl; WorAlBi*

Wallaçe, Henry Agard
American. US Vice President
VP under FDR, 1941-45; Progressive Party presidential candidate, 1948.
b. Oct 7, 1888 in Adair County, Iowa
d. Nov 18, 1965 in Danbury, Connecticut
Source: *AmAu&B; AmOrTwC; AmPeW; AmPolLe; BiDInt; BiDrAC; BiDrUSC 89; BiDrUSE 71, 89; BioIn 1, 2, 4, 5, 6, 7, 8, 9, 10, 11, 12, 14, 15, 16, 17, 18, 19, 20; ColdWar 2; ConAu 89; CurBio 40, 47, 66; DcAmB S7; DcTwHis; EncAAH; EncAB-A 1, 23; EncAB-H 1974, 1996; LinLib S; McGEWB; MorMA; NatCAB 53; ObitT 1961; OxCAmH; REnAL; REnAW; VicePre; WebAB 74, 79; WhAm 4; WhAmP; WhNAA; WorAl*

Wallace, Horace Binney
American. Author, Critic, Poet
Wrote verse "Hand That Rocks the Cradle."
b. Feb 26, 1817 in Philadelphia, Pennsylvania
d. Dec 16, 1852 in Paris, France
Source: *Alli; AmAu&B; AmBi; ApCAB; BiD&SB; CyAL 2; DcAmAu; DcAmB; DcNAA; Drake; NatCAB 6; OxCAmL 65, 83, 95; WhAm HS*

Wallace, Irving
[Irving Wallechinsky]
American. Author
One of best-read and best-selling 20th-century American authors; wrote *The Chapman Report,* 1960, filmed starring Jane Fonda, Shelley Winters, 1962.
b. Mar 19, 1916 in Chicago, Illinois
d. Jun 29, 1990 in Los Angeles, California
Source: *AmAu&B; AnObit 1990; Au&Wr 71; AuNews 1; AuSpks; BioIn 6, 8, 9, 10, 11, 12, 13, 14, 15, 16, 17; BioNews 74; BkPepl; BlueB 76; CelR, 90; ConAu 1AS, 1NR, 1R, 27NR, 132; ConLC 7, 13; ConPopW; CurBio 79, 90, 90N; DcArts; DcLEL 1940; FacFETw; FilmEn; HalFC 84, 88; IntAu&W 76, 89, 91; IntMPA 75, 76, 77, 78, 79, 80, 81, 82, 84, 86, 88; LegTOT; MajTwCW; News 91, 91-1; NewYTBS 90; Novels; RAdv 14; ScF&FL 92; TwCWr; WhAm 10; Who 74, 82, 83, 85, 88, 90; WhoAm 74, 76, 78, 80, 82, 84, 86, 88; WhoUSWr 88; WhoWrEP 89; WorAl; WorAlBi; WrDr 76, 80, 82, 84, 86, 88, 90*

Wallace, Lew(is)
American. Author, Soldier
Wrote best-sellers *Ben Hur,* 1880; *Prince of India,* 1893.
b. Apr 10, 1827 in Brookville, Indiana
d. Feb 15, 1905 in Crawfordsville, Indiana
Source: *Alli SUP; AmAu; AmAu&B; AmBi; ApCAB, X; ArtsAmW 1; BbD; Benet 87, 96; BenetAL 91; BibAL 8; BiD&SB; BiDrATG; BioIn 1, 2, 3, 5, 6, 7, 12, 14, 16; CamGEL; CamGLE; CamHAL; CarSB; CasWL; Chambr 3; ChhPo, S3; CivWDc; CnDAL; ConAu 120; CyWA 58; DcAmAu; DcAmB; DcAmDH 80, 89; DcAmMiB; DcBiA; DcEnA A; DcLEL; DcNAA; EncAB-H 1974, 1996; EvLB; GayN; GrWrEL N; HalFC 84, 88; HarEnUS; IlBEAAW; JBA 34; LegTOT; LinLib L, S; McGEWB; NatCAB 4; NewYHSD; NotNAT B; Novels; OxCAmL 65, 83, 95; PenC AM; RAdv 1, 14, 13-1; REn; REnAL; RfGAmL 87, 94; TwCBDA; WebAB 74, 79; WebAMB; WhAm 1; WhAmArt 85; WhCiWar; WorAl*

Wallace, Lila Bell Acheson
American. Publisher, Editor
Organizer, YWCA, 1921-22; co-founder, editor *Reader's Digest,* 1921-65.
b. Dec 25, 1889 in Virden, Manitoba, Canada
d. May 8, 1984 in Mount Kisco, New York
Source: *AmAu&B; AnObit 1984; BlueB 76; CanWW 83; ConAu 105, 112; CurBio 56; ForWC 70; InWom, SUP; WebAB 74, 79; WhoAm 74; WhoAmW 81; WhoE 74; WhoWor 74*

Wallace, Lurleen Burns
[Mrs. George Wallace]
American. Politician
Succeeded husband to become first woman governor of AL, 1967.
b. Sep 19, 1926 in Tuscaloosa, Alabama
d. May 7, 1968 in Montgomery, Alabama
Source: *AmPolW 80; BiDrGov 1789; CurBio 67, 68; DcAmB S8; InWom, SUP; LegTOT; WhAm 5; WhoAmW 68*

Wallace, Mike
[Myron Leon Wallace]
American. Broadcast Journalist
CBS correspondent, 1963-76; co-editor, "60 Minutes," 1968—; inducted into Television Academy Hall of Fame 1991.
b. May 9, 1918 in Brookline, Massachusetts
Source: *BioIn 4, 6, 8, 11, 12, 13, 14, 17, 18, 19, 20, 21; BkPepl; BlueB 76; CelR, 90; ConAu 65; ConTFT 10; CurBio 57, 77; EncAJ; EncTwCJ; IntMPA 75, 76, 77, 78, 79, 80, 81, 82, 84, 86, 88, 92, 94, 96; JrnUS; LegTOT; LesBEnT; NewYTET; WhoAm 74, 76, 78, 80, 82, 84, 86, 88, 90, 92, 94, 95, 96, 97; WhoAmJ 80; WhoE 74, 91, 93, 95, 97; WhoWorJ 72, 78; WorAl; WorAlBi*

Wallace, Phyllis A(nn)
American. Economist, Educator
Professor of economics, Massachusetts Institute of Technology, 1975-86; member, Minimum Wage Study Commission, 1978-82.
b. c. 1920 in Baltimore, Maryland
d. Jan 10, 1993
Source: *NotBlAW 1*

Wallace, Richard, Sir
English. Art Collector, Philanthropist
His inherited 19th-c. art collection was bequeathed to British nation, 1897.
b. Jun 21, 1818 in London, England
d. Jul 20, 1890 in Paris, France
Source: *BioIn 2, 12; DcArts; DcBiPP; DcBrWA; DcNaB; OxCArt*

Wallace, Sippie
[Beulah Thomas]
"Texas Nightingale"
American. Singer
Major 1920s blues singer; received Grammy nomination for *Sippie,* 1983.
b. Nov 1, 1898 in Houston, Texas
d. Nov 1, 1986 in Detroit, Michigan
Source: *AnObit 1986; BiDAfM; BiDJaz; BioIn 9, 12, 13, 15, 16, 17, 18, 19, 20; BlkWAm; ConBlB 1; ConMus 6; InWom*

SUP; NewGrDJ 88, 94; NewYTBS 86; NotBlAW 1; PenEncP; WhoJazz 72

Wallach, Eli
American. Actor
Films include *Baby Doll,* 1956; *The Misfits,* 1961.
b. Dec 7, 1915 in New York, New York
Source: *BiE&WWA; BioIn 3, 5, 6, 8, 14, 17, 20; CamGWoT; CelR, 90; CnThe; ConTFT 1, 7; FilmEn; FilmgC; ForYSC; GangFlm; HalFC 80, 84, 88; IntDcF 1-3, 2-3; IntMPA 77, 78, 79, 80, 81, 82, 84, 86, 88, 92, 94, 96; IntWW 76, 77, 78, 79, 80, 81, 82, 83, 89, 91, 93; ItaFilm; LegTOT; MotPP; MovMk; NotNAT; OxCAmT 84; OxCFilm; PlP&P; WhoAm 74, 76, 78, 80, 82, 84, 86, 88, 90, 92, 94, 95, 96, 97; WhoAmJ 80; WhoEnt 92; WhoHol 92, A; WhoThe 72, 77, 81; WhoWor 74, 78, 80, 82, 84; WhoWorJ 72, 78; WorAl; WorAlBi; WorEFlm*

Wallach, Otto
German. Chemist
Won 1910 Nobel Prize for pioneering field of alicyclic compounds, organic chemistry.
b. Mar 27, 1847 in Konigsberg, Prussia
d. Feb 26, 1931 in Gottingen, Germany
Source: *AsBiEn; BiESc; BioIn 1, 3, 5, 6, 15, 19, 20; DcScB; InSci; LarDcSc; NobelP; NotTwCS; WhoNob, 90, 95; WorAl; WorAlBi*

Wallack, James William
American. Actor, Manager
Operated Wallack's Theater in NY, 1852-64.
b. Aug 24, 1795 in London, England
d. Dec 25, 1864 in New York, New York
Source: *AmBi; ApCAB; BioIn 2; CamGWoT; DcAmB; DcNaB; Drake; EncWT; FamA&A; HarEnUS; NatCAB 4; OxCThe 67; TwCBDA; WebAB 74, 79; WhAm HS*

Wallant, Edward Lewis
American. Author
Wrote *The Pawnbroker,* 1961, filmed 1965.
b. Oct 19, 1926 in New Haven, Connecticut
d. Dec 5, 1962 in Norwalk, Connecticut
Source: *AmAu&B; BenetAL 91; BioIn 6, 9, 10, 12, 14, 17, 21; ConAu 1R, 22NR; ConLC 5, 10; ConNov 76; DcLB 2, 28, 143; DcLEL 1940; EncWL 2, 3; GrWrEL N; JeAmFiW; MajTwCW; ModAL; Novels; OxCAmL 65, 83, 95; PenC AM; RfGAmL 87, 94; WebE&AL; WhoTwCL; WorAu 1950*

Wallechinsky, David
American. Author
Co-author: *The People's Almanac,* 1975; *The Book of Lists,* 1977; son of Irving Wallace.
b. Feb 5, 1948 in Los Angeles, California
Source: *BioIn 15; ConAu 27NR, 55NR, 61*

Wallenberg, Marcus
Swedish. Banker
Business empire controlled one-third of all Swedish industry.
b. Oct 5, 1899 in Stockholm, Sweden
d. Sep 13, 1982 in Stockholm, Sweden
Source: *AnObit 1982; BioIn 11, 12, 13, 14; IntWW 74, 75, 76, 77, 78, 79, 80, 81, 82, 83N; IntYB 78, 79, 80, 81, 82; NewYTBS 82; WhAm 8; WhoFI 74; WhoWor 74, 76, 78, 80, 82*

Wallenberg, Raoul Gustav
Swedish. Diplomat
Saved nearly 100,000 Budapest Jews in WW II.
b. Aug 4, 1912 in Stockholm, Sweden
d. Jul 17, 1947 in Moscow, Union of Soviet Socialist Republics
Source: *BioIn 4; HisEWW; NewYTBS 80*

Wallenda, Karl
American. Circus Performer
Patriarch of famed high-wire troupe; killed in 100-foot fall.
b. Jan 21, 1905 in Magdeburg, Germany
d. Mar 22, 1978 in San Juan, Puerto Rico
Source: *BioIn 9, 10, 11, 12; DcAmB S10; LegTOT; NewYTBS 78*

Wallenstein, Alfred Franz
American. Musician, Conductor
Cellist; one of first native American symphonic conductors to gain national status; directed LA Philharmonic, 1943-56.
b. Oct 7, 1898 in Chicago, Illinois
d. Feb 8, 1983 in New York, New York
Source: *AnObit 1983; Baker 78; BiDAmM; BioIn 1, 2, 3, 4, 11, 13; CurBio 40, 52, 83; NewYTBS 83; WhAm 8; WhoAm 74, 76, 78, 80, 82; WorAl*

Waller, Edmund
English. Poet
Served in Parliament under Charles II; lyrics were set to music by Henry Lawes.
b. Mar 3, 1606 in Coleshill, England
d. Oct 21, 1687 in Beaconsfield, England
Source: *Alli; AtlBL; BbD; Benet 87, 96; BiD&SB; BiDRP&D; BioIn 2, 3, 5, 9, 12, 19; BlmGEL; BritAu; BritWr 2; CamGEL; CamGLE; CasWL; Chambr 1; ChhPo, S1; CnE&AP; CroE&S; DcArts; DcEnA; DcEnL; DcLB 126; DcLEL; DcNaB; EvLB; GrWrEL P; LngCEL; MouLC 1; NewC; NewCBEL; OxCEng 67, 85, 95; PenC ENG; REn; RfGEnL 91; WebE&AL; WhDW*

Waller, Fats
[Thomas Wright Waller]
American. Jazz Musician, Songwriter
Stride pianist, famed entertainer, singer; wrote ''Ain't Misbehavin',' ' ''Honeysuckle Rose.''
b. May 21, 1904 in New York, New York
d. Dec 15, 1943 in Kansas City, Missouri
Source: *AllMusG; AmSong; ASCAP 66; Baker 78, 84, 92; BiDAfM; BiDJaz; BioIn 14, 15, 16; CmpEPM; ConMus 7; CurBio 42, 44; DcAmB S3; DcAmNB; DcArts; DcTwCCu 5; DrBlPA, 90; FilmgC; HalFC 80, 84, 88; IlEncJ; InB&W 80, 85; LegTOT; NewAmDM; NewGrDA 86; NewGrDJ 88, 94; NewGrDM 80; NewOxM; NotNAT B; OxCPMus; PenEncP; PopAmC; RAdv 14; WhAm 4; WhoHol B; WhoJazz 72; WhScrn 77; WorAl; WorAlBi*

Waller, Fred(erick)
American. Inventor
Invented Cinerama, 1952; invented, patented first water ski.
b. Mar 10, 1886 in New York, New York
d. May 18, 1954 in Huntington, New York
Source: *BioIn 3; CurBio 53, 54; DcFM; FilmEn; FilmgC; HalFC 80, 84, 88*

Waller, Gordon
[Peter and Gordon]
Scottish. Singer, Musician
Part of Peter and Gordon duo, 1961-68; biggest hit ''World without Love,'' 1964, written by Paul McCartney.
b. Jun 4, 1945 in Braemar, Scotland

Waller, Robert James
American. Author, Educator
Author of *The Bridges of Madison County,* 1991.
b. Aug 1, 1939 in Rockford, Iowa
Source: *BioIn 18, 19, 20, 21; ConAu 147; ConPopW; CurBio 94; WhoAm 95, 96, 97*

Waller, William, Sir
''William the Conqueror''
English. Army Officer, Statesman
Fought in Thirty Years War, 1620-22; served in Parliament as member of Presbyterian party.
b. 1597 in Knole, England
d. Sep 19, 1668 in London, England
Source: *Alli; BioIn 9, 16; DcBiPP; DcEnL; DcNaB; HarEnMi; NewC; WhoMilH 76*

Wallerstein, Jusith S.
American. Psychologist
Studied the effects of divorce on adults and children, proving that many of those affected were feeling poorer one year after the event; wrote *How Children and Parents Cope with Divorce,* 1990.
b. Dec 27, 1921 in New York, New York
Source: *CurBio 96*

Wallerstein, Lothar
Czech. Director
Conducted at La Scala, Milan, 1929; producer at NY Met., 1941.
b. Nov 6, 1882 in Prague, Bohemia
d. Nov 13, 1949 in New Orleans, Louisiana
Source: *Baker 78, 84, 92; BioIn 2; CmOp; IntDcOp; NewEOp 71; NewGrDA 86; ObitOF 79; OxDcOp; PenDiMP*

Walley, Deborah
American. Actor
Played in TV show "Mothers-in-law," 1967-69; starred in film *Gidget Goes Hawaiian,* 1961.
b. Aug 13, 1943 in Bridgeport, Connecticut
Source: *BioIn 16; ForWC 70; ForYSC; MotPP; WhoHol A*

Wallington, Jimmy
[James S Wallington]
American. Actor
Radio announcer on "The Eddie Cantor Show," "The Burns and Allen Show."
b. Sep 15, 1907 in Rochester, New York
d. Dec 22, 1972 in Fairfax, Virginia
Source: *BioIn 9; NewYTBE 72; ObitOF 79; RadStar; WhoHol B; WhScrn 77, 83*

Wallis, Barnes Neville, Sir
English. Engineer, Inventor
Designed "Grand Slam," "Tall Boy bombs, WW II."
b. Sep 26, 1887 in Ripley, England
d. Oct 30, 1979 in Leatherhead, England
Source: *BiESc; BioIn 4, 9, 12, 13, 14; DcNaB 1971; FacFETw; GrBr; IntWW 78; LarDcSc; NewYTBS 79; WhDW; Who 74; WhWW-II*

Wallis, Hal Brent
American. Producer
Produced over 400 films, including *Casablanca,* 1942; *The Maltese Falcon,* 1941; 32 of his films won Oscars.
b. Sep 14, 1899 in Chicago, Illinois
d. Oct 5, 1986 in Rancho Mirage, California
Source: *BiDFilm; BlueB 76; ConNews 87-1; ConTFT 4; FilmgC; HalFC 84; IntMPA 86; OxCFilm; VarWW 85; WebAB 74, 79; WhAm 9; WhoAm 86; WhoWor 82; WorAl; WorEFlm*

Wallis, Samuel
English. Navigator
Around the world voyage, 1766-68; discovered Easter Island, Tahiti.
b. Apr 23, 1728 in Fentonwoon
d. Jan 21, 1795 in London
Source: *ApCAB; BioIn 18, 20; DcNaB; Expl 93; OxCShps; WebBD 83; WhWE*

Wallis, Shani
English. Actor
Films include *Terror in the Wax Museum,* 1973.
b. Apr 16, 1933 in London, England
Source: *FilmgC; HalFC 84, 88; WhoHol A; WhoThe 72, 77A; WhThe*

Wallmann, Margherita
Austrian. Producer
Productions in opera, film, TV, stage known internationally.
b. Jun 22, 1904 in Vienna, Austria
d. May 2, 1992 in Monte Carlo, Monaco
Source: *CmOp; IntDcOp; MetOEnc; NewEOp 71; WhoMus 72*

Wallop, Douglass
[John Douglass, III Wallop]
American. Author
Wrote *The Year the Yankees Lost the Pennant,* 1954, basis for hit musical *Damn Yankees,* 1955.
b. Mar 8, 1920 in Washington, District of Columbia
d. Apr 1, 1985 in Georgetown, Maryland
Source: *AmAu&B; BiE&WWA; BioIn 14; ConAu 13NR, 73, 115; CurBio 85, 85N; DrAPF 80, 83; NotNAT; ScF&FL 1, 92; WhoAm 76*

Wallop, Malcolm
American. Politician
Rep. senator from WY, 1976-94.
b. Feb 27, 1933 in New York, New York
Source: *AlmAP 78, 80, 82, 84, 88, 92; BiDrUSC 89; BioIn 13; CngDr 77, 79, 81, 83, 85, 87, 89, 91, 93; IntWW 89, 91, 93; NewYTBS 82; PolsAm 84; WhoAm 78, 80, 84, 86, 88, 90, 92, 94, 95; WhoAmP 73, 75, 77, 79, 81, 83, 85, 87, 89, 91, 93, 95; WhoGov 77; WhoWest 78, 80, 82, 84, 87, 89, 92, 94; WhoWor 80, 82, 84, 87, 89, 91*

Walls, Everson Collins
American. Football Player
Four-time all-pro cornerback, Dallas, 1981-89; NY Giants 1989-92; Cleveland, 1992—.
b. Dec 28, 1959 in Dallas, Texas
Source: *BioIn 14; FootReg 87; WhoBlA 85, 92*

Walmsley, Jon
American. Actor
Played Jason Walton on TV series "The Waltons," 1972-79.
b. Feb 6, 1956 in Lancashire, England
Source: *BioIn 11, 12; WhoHol 92, A*

Waln, Nora
American. Journalist
Wrote *House of Exile,* 1933.
b. Jun 4, 1895 in Grampian, Pennsylvania
d. Sep 27, 1964 in Madrid, Spain
Source: *AmAu&B; BioIn 4, 7; ConAu 89; CurBio 40, 64; InWom; LngCTC; REnAL; TwCA, SUP; WhAm 4; WhE&EA*

Walpole, Horace
[Fourth Earl of Oxford]
English. Author
His work *The Castle of Otranto,* 1765, began fad for Gothic novels; brilliant prolific letter writer.
b. Sep 24, 1717 in London, England
d. Mar 2, 1797 in London, England
Source: *Alli; AtlBL; BbD; Benet 87, 96; BiD&SB; BioIn 1, 2, 3, 4, 5, 6, 7, 8, 9, 10, 11, 12, 13, 15, 17, 21; BlkwCE; BlmGEL; BritAu; CamGEL; CamGLE; CasWL; Chambr 2; ChhPo, S2; CrtT 2, 4; CyWA 58; DcArts; DcBiA; DcBiPP; DcEnA; DcEnL; DcEuL; DcLB 39, 104; DcLEL; DcNaB; Dis&D; EncAR; EncEnl; EvLB; GrWrEL N; LegTOT; LinLib L, S; LitC 2; LngCEL; MacEA; MouLC 2; NewC; NewCBEL; OxCArt; OxCEng 67, 85, 95; OxDcArt; PenC ENG; PenEncH; RAdv 1, 14, 13-1; REn; RfGEnL 91; ScF&FL 1; SupFW; WebE&AL; WhDW; WhoHr&F; WorAl; WorAlBi*

Walpole, Hugh Seymour, Sir
English. Author
Novels include *The Dark Forest,* 1916.
b. Mar 13, 1884 in Auckland, New Zealand
d. Jun 1, 1941 in Brackenburg, England
Source: *CasWL; Chambr 3; ChhPo S2; CyWA 58; DcBiA; DcLEL; DcNaB 1941; Dis&D; EvLB; FilmgC; GrBr; GrWrEL N; HalFC 80; LinLib L, S; LngCTC; MnBBF; ModBrL; NewC; NewCBEL; NotNAT B; OxCEng 67, 85, 95; PenC ENG; REn; ScF&FL 1; TwCA, SUP; TwCRHW 94; TwCWr; WebE&AL; WhLit; WhoChL; WhoHol B; WhoHr&F; WhoLA; WhoTwCL; WhScrn 74, 77; WhThe; WorEFlm*

Walpole, Robert
[First Earl of Oxford]
English. Statesman
Secretary of war, 1708-1710; treasurer of the navy, 1710-1711; father of Horace Walpole.
b. Aug 26, 1676 in Houghton, England
d. Mar 18, 1745 in Houghton, England
Source: *Alli; Benet 87, 96; BioIn 14, 15, 17, 21; BlmGEL; DcBiPP; DcNaB; EncEnl; HisDBrE; HisWorL; LegTOT; LinLib S; LngCEL; McGEWB; NewC; NewCBEL; OxCEng 85, 95; OxCMus; REn; WhDW; WorAl; WorAlBi*

Walsh, Bill
[William Ernest Walsh]
American. Football Coach
Head coach, San Francisco, 1979-88; won Super Bowl, 1982, 1985, 1989.
b. Nov 30, 1931 in Los Angeles, California
Source: *BiDAmSp FB; BioIn 12, 13, 14, 16, 18, 19, 20; ConNews 87-4; CurBio 89; FootReg 87; LesBEnT 92; NewYTBS 82; WhoAm 86; WhoSpor; WorAlBi*

Walsh, Chad
American. Author, Clergy
Wrote numerous books including *Faith and Behavior,* 1954, *God at Large,* 1971.
b. May 10, 1914 in South Boston, Virginia
d. Jan 17, 1991 in Shelburne, Vermont
Source: *AmAu&B; Au&Wr 71; BioIn 2, 4, 6, 10, 17; ConAu 1R, 6NR, 133; ConPo 70, 75, 80, 85, 91; CurBio 91N; DrAP 75; DrAPF 80, 91; DrAS 74E, 78E, 82E; IntWWP 77; NewYTBS 91; ScF&FL 1, 2, 92; WhoAm 74, 76, 78; WorAu 1950; WrDr 76, 80, 82, 84, 86, 88, 90, 92, 94N*

Walsh, Ed(ward Augustine)
"Big Ed"
American. Baseball Player
Pitcher, 1904-17, mostly with White Sox; won 40 games, 1908; holds ML record for lowest career ERA; Hall of Fame, 1946.
b. May 14, 1881 in Plains, Pennsylvania
d. May 26, 1959 in Pompano Beach, Florida
Source: *Ballpl 90; BiDAmSp BB; BioIn 14, 15; DcAmB S6; LegTOT; WhoProB 73*

Walsh, James Edward
American. Religious Leader
Roman Catholic bishop who spent more than 40 yrs. as missionary to China, 12 yrs. in Shanghai prison.
b. Apr 30, 1891? in Cumberland, Maryland
d. Jul 29, 1981 in Ossining, New York
Source: *AmCath 80; AnObit 1981; BioIn 1, 5, 6, 9, 11, 12; CathA 1930; ConAu 104; NewYTBS 81; WhAm 8; WhoAm 74, 76, 78, 80*

Walsh, Joe
[The Eagles; The James Gang; Joseph Fidler Walsh]
American. Musician, Singer
Joined James Gang, 1971; Eagles, 1976-82; solo albums include *The Confessor,* 1985.
b. Nov 20, 1947 in Wichita, Kansas
Source: *ASCAP 80; BioIn 11, 13; ConMus 5; EncRk 88; EncRkSt; HarEnR 86; LegTOT; OnThGG; PenEncP; RkOn 74; RolSEnR 83; WhoAm 76, 80, 82, 84, 86, 88, 92, 94, 95, 96; WhoEnt 92A*

Walsh, Lawrence E
American. Government Official, Lawyer
Special prosecutor of the Iran-Contra affair.
b. Jan 8, 1912 in Port Maitland, Nova Scotia, Canada
Source: *BioIn 4, 15; CurBio 91; IntWW 91; NewYTBE 71; NewYTBS 75, 86, 87; WhoAm 90; WhoAmL 90; WhoWor 91*

Walsh, Michael Patrick
American. University Administrator
Pres., Boston College, 1958-68; Fordham U, 1969-72.
b. Feb 28, 1912 in Boston, Massachusetts
d. Apr 23, 1982 in Boston, Massachusetts
Source: *AmCath 80; AmMWSc 76P, 79; BioIn 12, 13; LEduc 74; NewYTBS 82; WhAm 8; WhoE 74*

Walsh, Raoul
American. Actor, Director
Directed Hollywood's first outdoor talking movie, *In Old Arizona,* 1929.
b. Mar 11, 1887 in New York, New York
d. Dec 31, 1980 in Los Angeles, California
Source: *AnObit 1980; BiDFilm, 81, 94; BioIn 12, 15, 16; CmMov; ConAu 102; DcAmB S10; DcArts; DcFM; EncAFC; FacFETw; Film 1; FilmEn; FilmgC; GangFlm; HalFC 80, 84, 88; IlWWHD 1; IntDcF 1-2, 2-2; IntMPA 77; ItaFilm; LegTOT; MiSFD 9N; MovMk; NewYTBS 81; OxCFilm; TwYS; WhoHol A; WhScrn 83; WorEFlm; WorFDir 1; WrDr 76, 80*

Walsh, Stella
[Stanislawa Walasiewicz]
Polish. Track Athlete
Sprinter; won gold medal in 100-meter run, 1932 Olympics.
b. Apr 3, 1911 in Wierzchownia, Poland
d. Dec 4, 1980 in Cleveland, Ohio
Source: *AnObit 1980; BiDAmSp OS; BioIn 11, 12; EncWomS; GoodHs; InWom SUP; LegTOT; NewYTBS 80; PolBiDi; WhoSpor; WhoTr&F 73; WorAl*

Walsh, Thomas James
American. Lawyer, Politician
Dem. senator from MT, 1913-33; uncovered Teapot Dome Scandal, 1923.
b. Jun 12, 1859 in Two Rivers, Wisconsin
d. Mar 2, 1933 in Wilson, North Carolina
Source: *AmBi; AmPeW; ApCAB X; BiDInt; BiDrAC; BiDrUSC 89; BioIn 4, 7; DcAmB; EncAAH; EncAB-H 1974; McGEWB; NatCAB 15, 24; WebAB 74, 79; WhAm 1; WhAmP*

Walsh, William B(ertalan)
American. Physician
CEO and medical director, People-to-People Health Foundation, parent organization of Project HOPE, 1958-92.
b. Apr 26, 1920
d. Dec 27, 1996 in Bethesda, Maryland
Source: *BioIn 6; WhoAm 74, 76, 78, 80, 82, 84, 86, 88, 90, 92; WhoWor 76, 78, 80*

Walsingham, Francis, Sir
English. Statesman
Entered service of Elizabeth I, 1563; established spy system that revealed plot of Mary Stuart, led to her execution.
b. 1530? in Footscray, England
d. Apr 6, 1590 in London, England
Source: *Alli; Benet 87, 96; BioIn 3, 4, 7, 8, 9, 10, 11; DcBiPP; DcNaB; REn; SpyCS*

Walston, Ray
American. Actor, Director
Won Tony for *Damn Yankees,* 1955; starred in TV series "My Favorite Martian," 1963-66.
b. Nov 22, 1918 in New Orleans, Louisiana
Source: *BiE&WWA; BioIn 18, 21; ConTFT 3, 10; EncAFC; FilmEn; FilmgC; ForYSC; HalFC 84, 88; IntMPA 75, 76, 77, 78, 79, 80, 81, 82, 84, 86, 88, 92, 94, 96; MovMk; NotNAT; WhoAm 86, 88, 90; WhoEnt 92; WhoHol A; WhoThe 81; WhoWor 89; WorAlBi*

Waltari, Mika
Finnish. Critic, Author, Editor
Popular historical novels include *The Egyptian,* 1945.
b. Sep 19, 1908 in Helsinki, Finland
d. Aug 26, 1979 in Helsinki, Finland
Source: *Au&Wr 71; CasWL; ConAu 9R, 89; CurBio 50, 79N; DcLEL 1940; EncEurC; EncWL; IntAu&W 76, 77; IntWW 74, 75, 76, 77, 78, 79; LinLib L; PenC EUR; REn; ScF&FL 1, 92; TwCA SUP; WhE&EA; Who 74; WhoWor 74, 76*

Walter, Bruno
[Bruno Schlesinger]
American. Conductor, Pianist
An authority on the interpretation of the works of Mahler, Mozart.
b. Sep 15, 1876 in Berlin, Germany
d. Feb 17, 1962 in Beverly Hills, California
Source: *Baker 78, 84, 92; BiDAmM; BioIn 1, 2, 3, 4, 5, 6, 7, 8, 9, 10, 11, 12, 18; BriBkM 80; CmCal; CmOp; ConAmC 76, 82; CurBio 42, 62; DcAmB S7; EncAB-A 33; EncTR, 91; FacFETw; IntDcOp; LegTOT; LinLib S; MetOEnc; MusMk; MusSN; NatCAB 52; NewAmDM; NewEOp 71; NewGrDA 86; NewGrDM 80; NewGrDO; NotNAT B; ObitT 1961; OxCAmH; OxCMus; OxDcOp; PenDiMP; REn; WebAB 74, 79; WhAm 4; WorAl; WorAlBi*

Walter, Cyril
[Cy Walter]
American. Pianist, Songwriter
Played in sophisticated style on radio, TV, nightclubs, 1940s-50s.
b. Sep 16, 1925 in Minneapolis, Minnesota
d. Aug 18, 1968 in New York, New York
Source: *ASCAP 66, 80; BiDAmM; CmpEPM*

Walter, Eugene
American. Dramatist, Screenwriter
Wrote plays *Trail of the Lonesome Pine,* 1911; *Easiest Way,* 1909.
b. Nov 27, 1874 in Cleveland, Ohio
d. Sep 26, 1941 in Hollywood, California

Source: *AmAu&B; BenetAL 91; CamGWoT; CnDAL; CurBio 41; DcAmB S3; DcNAA; LinLib L; McGEWD 72, 84; ModWD; NotNAT B; OhA&B; OxCAmL 65, 83, 95; OxCAmT 84; OxCThe 67, 83; REn; REnAL; WhAm 1; WhThe*

Walter, Jessica
[Mrs. Ron Leibman]
American. Actor
Won Emmy for "Amy Prentiss," 1974-75; films include *Play Misty For Me,* 1971.
b. Jan 31, 1944 in New York, New York
Source: *BioIn 14; ConTFT 1, 7; FilmgC; HalFC 80, 84, 88; IntMPA 77, 86, 92, 94, 96; WhoAm 86, 88, 90, 92; WhoEnt 92; WhoHol A; WorAlBi*

Walter, John, I
English. Newspaper Publisher
Founded *Daily Universal Register,* 1785, which was renamed London *Times,* 1788.
b. 1739 in London
d. Nov 16, 1812 in Teddington
Source: *Alli; DcBiPP; DcEnL; DcEuL; DcNaB; NewCBEL; REn; WebBD 83; WhDW*

Walter, Marie Therese
French. Model
Mistress of Pablo Picasso.
b. 1909?
d. 1977 in Antibes, France
Source: *BioIn 10, 11, 13*

Walter, Thomas Ustick
American. Architect
Built legislative wings, cast iron dome on Capitol, Washington, DC.
b. Sep 4, 1804 in Philadelphia, Pennsylvania
d. Oct 30, 1887 in Philadelphia, Pennsylvania
Source: *Alli; AmBi; ApCAB; BiAUS; BiDAmAr; BioIn 1, 3, 14, 16; BriEAA; DcAmB; DcNAA; Drake; EncAAr 1, 2; HarEnUS; LinLib S; McGDA; NatCAB 9; NewYHSD; OxCAmH; OxCAmL 65; WhAm HS; WhoArch*

Walters, Barbara
American. Broadcast Journalist
First woman to co-anchor the "Today" show, 1963-76; with ABC News since 1976; known for one-on-one interviews, correspondent, "20/20," 1981-84, co-host, 1984—.
b. Sep 25, 1931 in Boston, Massachusetts
Source: *AuNews 2; BioIn 8, 9, 10, 11, 12, 13, 14, 15, 16, 17, 18, 19, 20, 21; BioNews 74; BkPepl; BlueB 76; CelR, 90; ConAu 65; ContDcW 89; ConTFT 6, 13; CurBio 71; EncAJ; EncTwCJ; EncWB; FacFETw; ForWC 70; GoodHs; GrLiveH; HerW 84; IntDcWB; IntMPA 77, 78, 79, 80, 81, 82, 84, 86, 88, 92, 94, 96; IntWW 77, 78, 79, 80, 81, 82, 83, 89, 91, 93; InWom SUP; JrnUS; LegTOT; LesBEnT, 92; LibW; NewYTBE 72; NewYTBS 76; NewYTET; WhoAm 74, 76, 78, 80, 82, 84, 86, 88, 90, 92, 94, 95, 96, 97; WhoAmW 70, 72, 74, 75, 77, 79, 81, 83, 85, 87, 89, 91, 93, 95, 97; WhoEnt 92; WhoWor 78, 80, 82, 84, 87, 89, 91, 93, 95, 96, 97; WomComm; WomFir; WomStre; WorAl*

Walters, Bucky
[William Henry Walters]
American. Baseball Player
Pitcher, 1931-48, 1950; led NL in wins three times, in ERA twice; NL MVP, 1939.
b. Apr 19, 1910 in Philadelphia, Pennsylvania
d. Apr 18, 1991 in Abington, Pennsylvania
Source: *Ballpl 90; BiDAmSp BB; BioIn 2, 10, 15; NewYTBS 91; WhoProB 73*

Walters, Charles
American. Director
Directed musicals *Easter Parade,* 1948; *Unsinkable Molly Brown,* 1964.
b. Nov 17, 1903? in Pasadena, California
d. Aug 13, 1982 in Malibu, California
Source: *AnObit 1983; BiDFilm; CmMov; DcFM; EncMT; FilmgC; IntMPA 82; MovMk; WhoAm 82; WorEFlm*

Walters, David
American. Politician
Dem. governor, OK, 1991—.
b. Nov 20, 1951 in Elk City, Oklahoma
Source: *AlmAP 92; BiDrGov 1988; WhoAm 92, 94, 95; WhoAmP 91, 93, 95; WhoSSW 93*

Walters, Henry
American. Businessman
With father, developed the Atlantic Coast Line Railroad; established Walters Art Gallery in Boston.
b. Sep 26, 1848 in Baltimore, Maryland
d. Nov 30, 1931 in Baltimore, Maryland
Source: *BiDAmBL 83; BioIn 3, 7, 16, 20, 21; DcAmB; DcAmBC; DcLB 140; EncABHB 1; NatCAB 37; WhAm 1; WhAmArt 85*

Walters, Julie
English. Actor
Received Oscar nomination for role of Rita in film *Educating Rita,* 1984.
b. Feb 22, 1950 in Birmingham, England
Source: *ConTFT 7, 15; HalFC 88; IntMPA 92, 94, 96; IntWW 91, 93; VarWW 85; Who 88, 90, 92, 94*

Walters, Lou
American. Business Executive
Operated NYC's famous Latin Quarter nightclub; father of Barbara Walters.
b. 1897
d. 1977 in Miami, Florida
Source: *NewYTBS 77; ObitOF 79*

Walters, Peter Ingram, Sir
English. Business Executive
Chairman of British Petroleum, 1981-90.
b. Mar 11, 1931 in Birmingham, England
Source: *IntWW 89, 91; Who 85, 88, 92; WhoAm 88; WhoE 89; WhoFI 89; WhoWor 87, 91*

Walters, Vernon Anthony
American. Diplomat
US ambassador to UN, replacing Jeanne Kirkpatrick, 1985.
b. Jan 3, 1917 in New York, New York
Source: *BioIn 10, 11, 12, 13, 14, 15, 16; ConAu 122; CurBio 88; DcAmDH 89; IntWW 74, 75, 76, 77, 78, 79, 80, 81, 82, 83, 89, 91, 93; NewYTBS 82, 85; WhoAm 74, 76, 84, 86, 88, 90, 92, 94, 95, 96; WhoAmP 87, 91; WhoGov 75; WhoWor 87, 89, 91; WorDWW*

Walthall, Henry B
American. Actor
First actor to wear motion picture makeup, 1914; starred in film *Birth of a Nation,* 1914.
b. Mar 16, 1878 in Shelby City, Alabama
d. Jun 17, 1936 in Monrovia, California
Source: *DcAmB S2; Film 1; FilmgC; MotPP; MovMk; OxCFilm; TwYS; Vers B; WhScrn 74, 77*

Walton, Bill
[William Theodore Walton]
American. Basketball Player
Center, Portland 1974-79; Los Angeles, 1979-85; Boston 1985-87; led NBA in rebounding, 1977; NBA MVP, 1978; sportscaster NBC Sports, 1993—.
b. Nov 5, 1952 in La Mesa, California
Source: *BasBi; BiDAmSp BK; BioIn 9, 10, 11, 12, 13, 14, 19, 20; BioNews 74; CmCal; CurBio 77; LegTOT; NewYTBS 74, 75, 79, 80, 82; OfNBA 87; WhoAm 78, 80, 82, 84, 86, 88, 92, 94, 95, 96, 97; WhoBbl 73; WhoSpor; WorAl; WorAlBi*

Walton, Ernest Thomas Sinton
Irish. Physicist, Educator
Shared Nobel Prize in physics, 1951, for work on transmutation of atomic nuclei.
b. Oct 6, 1903 in Dungorvan, Ireland
d. Jun 25, 1995 in Belfast, Northern Ireland
Source: *AsBiEn; BiESc; BioIn 1, 2, 3, 14, 15; BlueB 76; CurBio 95N; InSci; IntWW 74, 75, 76, 77, 78, 79, 80, 81, 82, 83, 89, 91, 93; LarDcSc; McGMS 80; NobelP; WhAm 11; Who 74, 82, 83, 85, 88, 90, 92, 94; WhoNob, 90, 95; WhoScEn 94; WhoWor 74, 76, 78, 82, 84, 87, 89, 91, 93, 95; WorAl; WorAlBi; WorScD*

Walton, George
American. Lawyer, Continental Congressman
Signed Declaration of Independence, 1776; active patriot; governor of GA, 1789; US senator.
b. 1741 in Farmville, Virginia
d. Feb 2, 1804 in College Hill, Georgia
Source: *AmBi; ApCAB; BiAUS; BiDrGov 1789; BiDSA; BioIn 1, 7, 8, 9; DcAmB;*

Drake; EncAR; HarEnUS; WhAm HS; WhAmRev

Walton, Izaak
English. Biographer, Author
Wrote *Compleat Angler,* 1676, biographies of John Donne and George Herbert.
b. Aug 9, 1593 in Staffordshire, England
d. Dec 15, 1683 in Winchester, England
Source: *Alli; AtlBL; BbD; Benet 87, 96; BiD&SB; BiDRP&D; BioIn 1, 2, 3, 4, 5, 7, 12, 13, 16, 17, 18, 19, 20, 21; BritAu; BritWr 2; CamGEL; CamGLE; CarSB; Chambr 1; CnDBLB 1; CroE&S; CyWA 58; DcArts; DcEnA; DcEnL; DcEuL; DcLB 151; DcLEL; DcNaB, C; DcScB; EvLB; GrWrEL N; LegTOT; LinLib L, S; LngCEL; McGEWB; NewC; NewCBEL; OxCEng 67, 85, 95; OxCMus; PenC ENG; REn; RfGEnL 91; WebE&AL; WorAl; WorAlBi*

Walton, Jerome O'Terrell
American. Baseball Player
Outfielder, Chicago Cubs, 1989—; NL rookie of year, 1989.
b. Jul 8, 1965 in Newnan, Georgia
Source: *Ballpl 90; WhoAfA 96; WhoBlA 94*

Walton, Joe
[Joseph Frank Walton]
American. Football Coach
Head coach, NY Jets, 1983-89.
b. Dec 15, 1935 in Beaver Falls, Pennsylvania
Source: *BioIn 13, 16; FootReg 87; NewYTBS 83; WhoAm 84, 86, 88; WhoE 85, 86, 89*

Walton, Sam Moore
American. Business Executive
Chm., CEO Wal-Mart; richest man in US, 1991; worth 4.4 billion.
b. Mar 29, 1918 in Kingfisher, Oklahoma
d. Apr 5, 1992 in Little Rock, Arkansas
Source: *BioIn 13, 14, 15, 16; ConAmBL; ConNews 86-2; CurBio 92; Dun&B 90; IntWW 91; News 93-1; WhoAm 86, 90; WhoFI 92; WhoSSW 91; WhoWor 91*

Walton, Tony
English. Designer
Won Tony for set design of *Pippin,* 1973; Oscar for art direction of *All That Jazz,* 1979.
b. Oct 24, 1934 in Walton-on-Thames, England
Source: *BiE&WWA; BioIn 12, 13, 14; ConDes 97; ConTFT 4, 12; HalFC 84, 88; NotNAT; VarWW 85; WhoAm 92; WhoEnt 92; WhoThe 72, 77, 81*

Walton, William Turner, Sir
English. Composer
Composed "Orb and Sceptre" (Coronation March), 1953, for coronation of Elizabeth II.
b. Mar 29, 1902 in Oldham, England
d. Mar 8, 1983 in Ischia, Italy
Source: *Baker 92; BioIn 1, 2, 3, 4, 5, 6, 8, 10, 12, 13; CurBio 40, 83, 83N; DcArts; DcNaB 1981; FilmgC; IntWW 75, 76, 77, 78, 79, 80, 81, 82; McGEWB; NewGrDO; OxCEng 85, 95; OxCFilm; OxCMus; REn; WhAm 8; WhDW; Who 74, 82; WhoAm 74, 76, 78, 80, 82; WhoMus 72; WhoWor 74, 76, 78*

Waltrip, Darrell Lee
American. Auto Racer
Stock car driver; won Daytona 500, 1989; won Winston Cup three times.
b. Feb 5, 1947 in Owensboro, Kentucky
Source: *BiDAmSp OS; BioIn 11, 13, 14; CelR 90; CrtSuMy; HalFC 88; IntAu&W 91; IntvTCA 2; IntWW 91; MajTwCW; NewYTBS 86; TwCCr&M 91; WhoAm 80, 82, 84, 86, 88, 90, 92, 94, 95, 96, 97; WorAlBi; WrDr 92*

Walworth, William, Sir
English. Politician
Lord mayor, London, 1374-1381; money lender to Richard II; defended London Bridge against the Kentish peasants, 1381.
d. 1385
Source: *BioIn 6; DcBiPP; DcCathB; DcNaB, C; WebBD 83*

Walz, Ken
American. Producer
Has produced music videos for Cyndi Lauper, Huey Lewis, Billy Joel; won Billboard, MTV Awards, 1984.
b. Apr 29, 1942 in Holland, Michigan
Source: *BioIn 15; ConTFT 4; WhoAdv 90; WhoEnt 92*

Wambaugh, Joseph Aloysius, Jr.
American. Author
With LA police, 1960-74; wrote police novels *The New Centurions,* 1971; *The Blue Knight,* 1972; *The Choir Boys,* 1975.
b. Jan 22, 1937 in Pittsburgh, Pennsylvania
Source: *AuNews 1; AuSpks; BioIn 10, 11, 12; ConLC 18; CurBio 80; HalFC 84; NewYTBE 73; Novels; TwCCr&M 85; WhoAm 74, 84; WorAl; WrDr 86*

Wambsganss, Bill
[William Adolph Wambsganss]
American. Baseball Player
Second baseman, 1914-26, mostly with Cleveland; best known for only unassisted triple play in World Series history, 1920.
b. Mar 19, 1894 in Garfield Heights, Ohio
d. Dec 8, 1985 in Lakewood, Ohio
Source: *Ballpl 90; BioIn 7, 14; WhoProB 73*

Wanamaker, John
American. Merchant
Started Wanamakers Store in NYC, 1896; US postmaster-general, 1889-93.
b. Jul 11, 1838 in Philadelphia, Pennsylvania
d. Dec 12, 1922 in Philadelphia, Pennsylvania
Source: *AmBi; ApCAB; BiDAmBL 83; BiDrUSE 71, 89; BioIn 1, 2, 3, 6, 7, 8, 9, 10, 12, 18, 20; ChhPo S2; DcAmB; DcNAA; EncAB-H 1974, 1996; HarEnUS; LinLib S; OxCAmH; PeoHis; REnAL; TwCBDA; WebAB 74, 79; WhAm 1; WorAl; WorAlBi*

Wanamaker, Lewis Rodman
American. Merchant
Owner, director of Wanamaker dept. stores, 1922-28; began public concerts in stores; son of John.
b. 1863 in Philadelphia, Pennsylvania
d. Mar 9, 1928 in Atlantic City, New Jersey
Source: *BiDAmBL 83; DcAmB; NatCAB 21; WhAmArt 85*

Wanamaker, Sam
American. Actor, Director
On Hollywood black list, 1950s, for leftist political associations.
b. Jun 14, 1919 in Chicago, Illinois
Source: *BiE&WWA; BioIn 1, 15, 19; BlueB 76; CnThe; ConTFT 3, 12; FilmEn; FilmgC; ForYSC; HalFC 80, 84, 88; IlWWBF; IntMPA 75, 76, 77, 78, 79, 80, 81, 82, 84, 86, 88, 92, 94; IntWW 74, 75, 76, 77, 78, 79, 80, 81, 82, 83, 89, 91, 93; ItaFilm; LegTOT; LesBEnT; MiSFD 9; MotPP; MovMk; NewYTET; NotNAT; OxCThe 83; RadStar; WhAm 11; Who 74, 82, 83, 85, 88, 90, 92, 94; WhoAm 80, 82, 84, 86, 88, 90, 92, 94; WhoEnt 92; WhoHol 92, A; WhoThe 72, 77, 81; WhoWor 74, 78; WorAlBi*

Waner, Lloyd James
"Little Poison"
American. Baseball Player
Outfielder, 1927-42, 1944-45, mostly with Pittsburgh; had .316 lifetime batting average; Hall of Fame, 1967.
b. Mar 16, 1906 in Harrah, Oklahoma
d. Jul 22, 1982 in Oklahoma City, Oklahoma
Source: *BiDAmSp BB; BioIn 10, 11, 13; WhoProB 73*

Waner, Paul Glee
"Big Poison"
American. Baseball Player
Outfielder, 1926-45, mostly with Pittsburgh with brother Lloyd; won NL batting title three times; NL MVP, 1927; Hall of Fame, 1952.
b. Apr 16, 1903 in Harrah, Oklahoma
d. Aug 29, 1965 in Sarasota, Florida
Source: *BiDAmSp BB; BioIn 2, 3, 7, 9, 10; DcAmB S7; WhoProB 73*

Wang, An
American. Business Executive, Engineer
Pioneering giant in computer industry; founded Wang Labs, 1951; developed desktop calculator, 1964; earned more than 40 patents.
b. Feb 7, 1920 in Shanghai, China

d. Mar 24, 1990 in Boston, Massachusetts
Source: *AmMWSc 73P, 79, 82, 86, 89, 92; AnObit 1990; AsAmAlm; BioIn 12, 13, 15; ConAmBL; ConAu 132; ConNews 86-1; CurBio 87, 90, 90N; Dun&B 79, 86, 88, 90; EncWB; Entr; FacFETw; HisDcDP; LElec; News 90, 90-3; NewYTBS 90; NotAsAm; NotTwCS; St&PR 75, 84, 87; WhAm 10; WhoAm 74, 76, 78, 80, 82, 84, 86, 88; WhoE 83, 85, 86, 89; WhoFI 83, 85, 87, 89; WhoTech 84, 89; WhoWor 84; WorInv*

Wang Chang
[Darren Costin; Nick Feldman; Jack Hues]
English. Music Group
Jazz/rock group formed 1981; name is Chinese for ''perfect pitch.''
Source: *RkOn 85*

Wanger, Walter
[Walter Feuchtwanger]
American. Producer
Regarded his films as foremost medium of communication, instrument to promote int'l understanding: *Stagecoach,* 1939.
b. Jul 11, 1894 in San Francisco, California
d. Nov 18, 1968 in New York, New York
Source: *BiDFilm, 81, 94; BioIn 1, 8, 9, 21; CmMov; CurBio 47, 69; DcAmB S8; DcFM; FilmEn; FilmgC; GangFlm; HalFC 80, 84, 88; IntDcF 1-4, 2-4; LegTOT; OxCFilm; WorAl; WorAlBi; WorEFlm*

Wang Hung-Wen
[Wang Hongwen]
Chinese. Political Leader
Sentenced to life imprisonment for being member of ''gang of four,'' 1981.
b. 1937, China
Source: *NewYTBE 73; NewYTBS 76*

Wang Shih-chieh
Chinese. Diplomat
Close adviser of Nationalist China's Chiang Kai-shek.
b. Mar 10, 1891 in Hupeh
d. Apr 1981? in Taipei, Taiwan
Source: *BioIn 1; CurBio 45, 81*

Wank, Roland A
American. Architect
Renowned designer of towns, public buildings; architect, Tennessee Valley Authority, 1933-44.
b. Oct 2, 1898 in Budapest, Austria-Hungary
d. Apr 22, 1970 in New Rochelle, New York
Source: *CurBio 43, 70; NewYTBE 70; WhAm 5*

Wankel, Felix
German. Engineer, Inventor
Developed first viable rotary internal combustion engine, 1934-56.
b. Aug 13, 1902 in Lahr, Germany
d. Oct 9, 1988 in Lindau, Germany (West)
Source: *AnObit 1988; BioIn 12, 16, 20; CamDcSc; DcTwDes; FacFETw; IntWW 74, 75, 76, 77, 78, 79, 80, 81, 82, 83; NewYTBE 72; NewYTBS 88; NotTwCS; WhDW*

Wanzer, Bobby
American. Basketball Player
Guard, Rochester Royals, 1948-57; five-time All-Star; Hall of Fame, 1987.
b. Jun 4, 1921 in New York, New York
Source: *BiDAmSp BK; WhoBbl 73; WhoSpor*

Wapner, Joseph A
American. TV Personality
Arbitrated cases as presiding judge on syndicated TV series ''The People's Court,'' 1981-92; California Superior Court judge, 1961-79.
b. Nov 15, 1919 in Los Angeles, California
Source: *BioIn 13, 14, 15, 16; ConNews 87-1; CurBio 89; WhoAm 90*

War
[Harold Brown; Ron Hammaon; Lonnie Jordan; Charles Miller; Lee Ostar; Luther Rabb; Pat Rizzo; Howard Scott; Tweed Smith]
American. Music Group
Pop hits includes *Me and Baby Brother,* 1974; *Low Rider,* 1975.
Source: *Alli; BiDAfM; BioIn 1, 13, 17; ConMuA 80A; ConMus 14; CurBio 61; EncPR&S 89; EncRk 88; EncRkSt; Film 1; IlEncRk; InB&W 80, 85A; InSci; IntMPA 82, 84, 86, 88; NewGrDA 86; NewYHSD; NewYTBS 76; PenEncP; RkOn 78; RolSEnR 83; SoulM; TwYS A; WhAmArt 85; What 2; WhFla; WhoHol 92; WhoRock 81; WhoRocM 82*

Warburg, Felix Moritz
American. Philanthropist, Banker
Member of Kuhn, Loeb & Co., NYC, 1896-1937; known for philanthropies.
b. Jan 14, 1871 in Hamburg, Germany
d. Oct 20, 1937 in New York, New York
Source: *AmBi; ApCAB X; Baker 78, 84; BioIn 1, 4, 11; DcAmB S2; NatCAB 30; NewGrDA 86; WebBD 83; WhAm 1; WorAl*

Warburg, Frederick Marcus
American. Banker
Son of Felix Moritz Warburg; partner in Kuhn, Loeb & Co., 1931-73.
b. Oct 14, 1897 in New York, New York
d. Jul 10, 1973 in Winchester, Virginia
Source: *BioIn 10, 11; NatCAB 57; NewYTBE 73; WhAm 6; WhoWorJ 72*

Warburg, James Paul
American. Businessman, Philanthropist, Author
Book subjects include US political, economic affairs; member of FDR's ''Brain Trust.''
b. Aug 18, 1896 in Hamburg, Germany
d. Jun 3, 1969 in Greenwich, Connecticut
Source: *AmAu&B; AmPeW; ASCAP 66; BiDInt; BioIn 1, 4, 6, 8, 9, 11, 19; ConAu P-2; CurBio 48, 69; DcAmB S8; NatCAB 56; REnAL; TwCA SUP; WhAm 5; WhE&EA; WhoWorJ 72, 78; WorAl*

Warburg, Otto Heinrich
German. Scientist
Won Nobel Prize in medicine, 1931, for discovery of nature and mode of action of the respiratory enzyme.
b. Oct 8, 1883 in Freiburg, Germany
d. Apr 1, 1970 in Berlin, Germany (West)
Source: *AsBiEn; BiESc; BioIn 3, 5, 9, 12; CamDcSc; DcScB; InSci; LarDcSc; McGMS 80; ObitT 1961; OxCMed 86; WhAm 5, 7; WhoNob, 90, 95; WorAl; WorAlBi; WorScD*

Ward, Artemus
[Charles Farrar Browne]
American. Journalist, Lecturer
Best known as ''moral'' lecturer throughout country; humorous comments influenced Mark Twain.
b. Apr 26, 1834 in Waterford, Maine
d. Mar 6, 1867 in Southampton, England
Source: *Alli, SUP; AmAu; AmAu&B; AmBi; ApCAB; BbD; Benet 87, 96; BenetAL 91; BibAL; BiDAmJo; BiD&SB; BioIn 1, 2, 3, 5, 6, 7, 9, 10, 11, 12, 13, 16; CamGEL; CamGLE; CamHAL; CasWL; CelCen; Chambr 3; ChhPo; CnDAL; DcAmAu; DcAmB; DcArts; DcCathB; DcEnA A; DcEnL; DcLB 11; DcLEL; DcNAA; Dis&D; Drake; EncAAH; EncAJ; EvLB; GrWrEL N; HarEnUS; LegTOT; LinLib L, S; McGEWB; NatCAB 1; NinCLC 37; Novels; OhA&B; OxCAmL 65, 83, 95; OxCEng 67, 85, 95; PenC AM; PeoHis; REn; REnAL; RfGAmL 87, 94; TwCBDA; WebAB 74, 79; WebE&AL; WhAm HS; WhCiWar; WhDW*

Ward, Barbara Mary
English. Author, Economist
Wrote on political, economic affairs: *India and the West,* 1961.
b. May 23, 1914 in York, England
d. May 31, 1981 in Lodsworth, England
Source: *CathA 1930; ConAu 103; CurBio 50, 77, 81; DcNaB 1981; IntAu&W 77; IntWW 78; InWom, SUP; TwCA SUP; WhE&EA; WhoAm 78; WhoAmW 75; WhoEc 86; WhoWor 78; WrDr 80*

Ward, Benjamin
American. Government Official
First black NYC police commissioner, 1984-89.
b. Aug 10, 1926 in New York, New York
Source: *BioIn 13, 16; CopCroC; CurBio 88; NewYTBS 75, 83; WhoAfA 96; WhoAm 86, 88, 90; WhoBlA 75, 77, 80, 85, 88, 90, 92, 94; WhoE 89, 91*

Ward, Burt
[Bert John Gervais, Jr.]
American. Actor
Played Robin on TV series "Batman," 1966-68.
b. Jul 6, 1946 in Los Angeles, California
Source: *BioIn 13, 16; HalFC 88; IntMPA 84, 86, 88, 92; WhoHol A*

Ward, David S
American. Screenwriter
Wrote films *The Sting,* 1973; *The Sting II,* 1983; won Oscar, 1973.
b. Oct 24, 1945 in Providence, Rhode Island
Source: *IntMPA 92; VarWW 85; WhoAm 90; WhoEnt 92*

Ward, Deighton Harcourt Lisle, Sir
West Indian. Political Leader
Governor-General of Barbados, 1976-84.
b. May 16, 1909, Barbados
d. Jan 9, 1984, Barbados
Source: *IntYB 82; Who 83, 85N; WhoWor 78, 80*

Ward, Douglas Turner
American. Director, Dramatist, Actor
Artistic director, co-founder, Negro Ensemble Co., 1967; won Obie for distinguished performance in *River Niger,* 1973.
b. May 5, 1930 in Burnside, Louisiana
Source: *BioIn 9, 10, 11, 12, 14, 20; BlkWr 1; CamGWoT; ConAmD; ConAu 27NR, 81; ConBlAP 88; ConDr 73, 77, 82, 88, 93; ConLC 19; ConTFT 4; CurBio 76; DcLB 7, 38; DcTwCCu 5; DrBlPA, 90; Ent; InB&W 80; IntvTCA 2; LivgBAA; McGEWD 84; MorBAP; NotNAT; PlP&P A; SchCGBL; SelBAAf; TheaDir; WhoAfA 96; WhoAm 74, 76, 78, 80, 82, 84, 86, 88; WhoBlA 75, 77, 80, 88, 90, 92, 94; WhoThe 72, 77, 81; WorAu 1970; WrDr 76, 80, 82, 84, 86, 88, 90, 92, 94*

Ward, Fannie
American. Actor
Films include *The Cheat,* 1915; *Betty to the Rescue,* 1917.
b. Nov 23, 1872 in Saint Louis, Missouri
d. Jan 27, 1952 in New York, New York
Source: *BioIn 2, 3, 9, 15; EncAFC; Film 1, 2; HalFC 80; InWom; MotPP; NotNAT B; ObitT 1951; OxCThe 67, 83; TwYS; WhAm 3; WhoHol B; WhScrn 74, 77, 83; WhThe*

Ward, J(ohn) Q(uincy) A(dams)
American. Sculptor
Famous for portrait busts, equestrian monuments.
b. Jun 29, 1830
d. 1910
Source: *AmBi; ApCAB; BioIn 1, 5, 7, 9, 14; BriEAA; DcAmArt; DcAmB; DcBiPP; Drake; GayN; HarEnUS; IlBEAAW; McGDA; NatCAB 2; NewYHSD; OxCAmH; OxCAmL 65; OxCArt; OxDcArt; PeoHis; TwCBDA; WebAB 74, 79; WebBD 83; WhAm 1; WhAmArt 85*

Ward, Jay
American. Cartoonist
Created cartoon characters Rocky the Flying Squirrel and Bullwinkle Moose with partner Bill Scott, 1959.
b. Sep 21, 1920 in San Francisco, California
d. Oct 12, 1989 in Los Angeles, California
Source: *AnObit 1989; BioIn 16; ConTFT 8; LesBEnT 92; NewYTBS 89; SmATA 63; WhoSSW 84; WhoWest 74, 76*

Ward, Lester Frank
American. Sociologist
Wrote *The Geological Distribution of Fossil Plants,* 1888; professor of sociology, Brown U., 1906-13.
b. Jun 18, 1841 in Joliet, Illinois
d. Apr 18, 1913 in Washington, District of Columbia
Source: *Alli SUP; AmAu; AmBi; AmRef; ApCAB; BiDAmEd; BiDAmS; BiInAmS; BioIn 1, 2, 3, 4, 11, 14, 15, 21; DcAmAu; DcAmB; DcNAA; DcSoc; EncAB-H 1974, 1996; GayN; McGEWB; NatCAB 13; OxCAmH; OxCAmL 65, 83, 95; REnAL; TwCBDA; WebAB 74, 79; WhAm 1, 4A, HSA*

Ward, Lynd
American. Artist
Noted for woodcut illustrations; won 1952 Caldecott for *The Biggest Bear.*
b. Jun 26, 1905 in Chicago, Illinois
d. Jun 28, 1985 in Reston, Virginia
Source: *BiDScF; ChlBkCr; ConAu 116; ConGrA 1; DcLB 22; FourBJA; IlrAm 1880, E; LinLib L; McGDA; PenEncH; ScF&FL 1, 2, 92; SmATA 36, 42N; WhAmArt 85; WhoAm 84; WhoAmA 73, 76, 78, 80, 82, 84, 86N, 89N, 91N; WrDr 84*

Ward, Mary Jane
American. Author
Wrote novel *The Snake Pit,* 1946.
b. Aug 27, 1905 in Fairmount, Indiana
Source: *AmAu&B; AmNov; AmWomWr; BenetAL 91; BioIn 1, 2, 4; CurBio 46; InWom, SUP; LngCTC; REnAL; TwCA SUP; WhNAA; WhoAmW 58, 66, 68*

Ward, Monte
[John Montgomery Ward]
American. Baseball Player
Pitcher-infielder, 1878-94; won 158 games as pitcher; converted to shortstop after arm injury; Hall of Fame, 1964.
b. Mar 3, 1860 in Bellefonte, Pennsylvania
d. Mar 4, 1925 in Augusta, Georgia
Source: *Ballpl 90; BiDAmSp BB; BioIn 3, 7, 14, 15, 16, 17; WhoProB 73; WhoSpor*

Ward, Montgomery
[Aaron Montgomery Ward]
American. Merchant
Founded Montgomery Ward & Co., first mail-order house, 1872.
b. Feb 17, 1843 in Chatham, New Jersey
d. Dec 7, 1913 in Highland Park, Illinois
Source: *BiDAmBL 83; BioIn 3, 4, 15; DcAmB; EncAAH; LegTOT; LinLib S; McGEWB; WebAB 74, 79; WebBD 83; WhAm 4, HSA; WorAlBi*

Ward, Nancy
American. Native American Leader
"Beloved Woman" among the Cherokee people; against land cession; roles included peace neggotiator and General Council voting member.
b. 1738? in Chota, Georgia
d. 1824 in Chota, Georgia
Source: *BioIn 14, 18, 21; EncAmaz 91; EncCRAm; EncNAB; HerW, 84; InWom SUP; LibW; NotAW; NotNaAm; PorAmW; WhNaAH*

Ward, Paul W
American. Journalist
Won 1948 Pulitzer for articles on USSR.
b. Oct 9, 1905 in Lorain, Ohio
d. Nov 24, 1976 in Chevy Chase, Maryland
Source: *BiDInt; BioIn 11, 12, 15; ConAu 69; NatCAB 59; WhAm 7; WhoAm 74, 76*

Ward, Phillip R
[The Hostages]
American. Hostage
One of 52 held by terrorists, Nov 1979 - Jan 1981.
b. Mar 22, 1940
Source: *NewYTBS 81; USBiR 74*

Ward, Rachel
[Mrs. Bryan Brown]
English. Actor, Model
Starred in TV mini-series "The Thorn Birds," 1983; film *Against All Odds,* 1984.
b. 1957 in London, England
Source: *BioIn 12, 13, 16; ConTFT 6; HalFC 84, 88; IntMPA 86, 88, 92, 94, 96; ItaFilm; LegTOT; NewYTBS 82; VarWW 85; WhoAmW 87, 89, 91, 93*

Ward, Robert Eugene
American. Composer, Conductor
Won Pulitzer in music for opera *The Crucible,* 1962.
b. Sep 13, 1917 in Cleveland, Ohio
Source: *Baker 84; BioIn 13, 14, 15; DcCM; DcLP 87B; IntWWM 90; MetOEnc; NewAmDM; NewGrDA 86; WhoAm 86, 90; WhoSSW 73; WhoWor 84*

Ward, Simon
English. Actor
Portrayed Winston Churchill in film *Young Winston,* 1971.
b. Oct 19, 1941 in London, England

Source: *ConTFT 5; FilmgC; HalFC 80, 84, 88; IntMPA 75, 76, 77, 78, 79, 80, 81, 82, 84, 86, 88, 92, 94, 96; IntWW 82, 83, 89, 91, 93; ItaFilm; Who 88; WhoHol 92, A; WhoHrs 80; WhoThe 72, 77, 81; WhoWor 84, 93, 95; WorAl*

Warden, Jack
American. Actor
Oscar nominee for *Shampoo,* 1975; *Heaven Can Wait,* 1978; starred in mid-1980s TV show "Crazy Like a Fox."
b. Sep 18, 1920 in Newark, New Jersey
Source: *BiE&WWA; BioIn 12, 14; ConTFT 1, 8; EncAFC; FilmEn; FilmgC; ForYSC; HalFC 80, 84, 88; HolCA; IntDcF 1-3; IntMPA 84, 86, 88, 92, 94, 96; LegTOT; MotPP; MovMk; NotNAT; WhoAm 78, 80, 82, 84, 86, 88, 90, 92, 94, 95, 96, 97; WhoEnt 92; WhoHol 92, A; WorAl; WorAlBi*

Ware, Andre
American. Football Player
Quarterback, U. of Houston; first black in this position to win Heisman Trophy, 1989; Detroit Lions, 1990-93; Minnesota Vikings, 1994—.
b. Jul 31, 1968 in Dickinson, Texas
Source: *BioIn 21; WhoSpor*

Warfield, David
American. Actor
Starred in Belasco plays including *Return of Peter Grimm,* 1911.
b. Nov 28, 1866 in San Francisco, California
d. Jun 27, 1951 in New York, New York
Source: *ApCAB X; BioIn 1, 2, 3, 4, 10; CamGWoT; CmCal; DcAmB S5; EncWT; FamA&A; NatCAB 14, 38; NotNAT B; ObitOF 79; OxCAmH; OxCAmL 65; OxCAmT 84; OxCThe 67, 83; PlP&P; REn; REnAL; WhAm 3; WhoStg 1906, 1908; WhThe*

Warfield, Marsha
American. Actor, Comedian
Played bailiff Roz Russell on TV series "Night Court," 1986-91.
b. Mar 5, 1955 in Chicago, Illinois
Source: *BioIn 12, 13, 15, 16, 17; ConBlB 2; ConTFT 7; DrBlPA 90; FunnyW; InB&W 85; LegTOT; WhoAfA 96; WhoBlA 92, 94; WhoHol 92*

Warfield, Paul Dryden
American. Football Player
End, 1964-77, with Cleveland, Miami; Hall of Fame, 1983.
b. Nov 28, 1942 in Warren, Ohio
Source: *BiDAmSp FB; NegAl 89; NewYTBE 72; WhoAm 74, 78; WhoBlA 85, 92; WhoFtbl 74*

Warfield, William Caesar
American. Singer
Best known for roles in *Showboat,* 1951; *Porgy & Bess,* 1952; husband of Leontyne Price.
b. Jan 22, 1920 in West Helena, Arkansas
Source: *Baker 84, 92; BiDAfM; BiE&WWA; BioIn 14; DcAfAmP; InB&W 80, 85; NewGrDA 86; NotNAT; WhoAm 74, 76, 78, 80, 82, 84, 86, 88, 90, 92, 94, 95, 96, 97; WhoAmM 83; WhoBlA 75, 80, 88; WhoEnt 92; WhoHol A; WhoWor 74, 76; WorAl*

Warham, William
English. Religious Leader
Archbishop of Canterbury, 1504-15; signed Henry VIII's petition to pope for divorce from Katherine of Aragon, 1527.
b. 1450, England
d. Aug 22, 1532, England
Source: *BioIn 3, 11; DcBiPP; DcCathB; DcNaB, C; NewCol 75; WebBD 83*

Warhol, Andy
[Andrew Warhola, Jr.]
American. Artist, Author
Leader of pop artists since early 1960s; known for paintings of soup cans, celebrities; published *Interview* mag., made several films.
b. Aug 6, 1927 in McKeesport, Pennsylvania
d. Feb 22, 1987 in New York, New York
Source: *AmAu&B; CelR; ConArt 83; ConAu 89, 121; ConNews 87-2; ConPhot 82; CurBio 68, 86, 87; EncAB-H 1974; FacFETw; FilmEn; FilmgC; GayLesB; ItaFilm; MiSFD 9N; OxCArt; OxCFilm; WebAB 79; WhoAm 76, 78, 86; WhoAmA 84; WhoWor 78, 87*

Wariner, Steve
American. Musician, Singer, Songwriter
Country guitarist and vocalist; released first top-ten hit "Your Memory," 1980; released debut album *Steve Wariner,* 1982; recorded first gold record, *I Am Ready,* 1991; won Grammy Award for best country vocal collaboration for single "Restless," 1992; inducted as member of the Grand Ole Opry, 1996.
b. Dec 25, 1954 in Noblesville, Indiana
Source: *BgBkCoM; HarEnCM 87; LegTOT; PenEncP; WhoNeCM*

Waring, Fred Malcolm
"The Man Who Taught America to Sing"
American. Bandleader, Inventor
Music conductor of The Pennsylvanians, 1923-84; invented the Waring blender.
b. Jun 9, 1900 in Tyrone, Pennsylvania
d. Jul 29, 1984 in State College, Pennsylvania
Source: *AnObit 1984; ASCAP 66; Baker 84; BioNews 74; CmpEPM; CurBio 40, 84; IntMPA 84; NewYTBS 80, 84; WhoAm 84; WhoHol A; WorAl*

Warmerdam, Dutch
[Cornelius Warmerdam]
American. Track Athlete
Pole vaulter; first to vault 15 feet, 1940; held world record, 1940-57.
b. Jun 22, 1915 in Long Beach, California
Source: *BiDAmSp OS; BioIn 3, 5, 6, 8, 9, 10; BioNews 74; WhoSpor; WhoTr&F 73*

Warne, William E(lmo)
American. Government Official
Irrigation expert; director, CA Dept. of Water Resources, 1961-67.
b. Sep 2, 1905
d. Mar 9, 1996 in Menlo Park, California
Source: *AmMWSc 73S, 78S; BioIn 3, 21; ConAu 41R, 151; CurBio 96N; IndAu 1917; WhAm 11; WhoAm 74, 76, 78, 80, 82, 84, 86, 88, 90, 92, 94, 95, 96; WhoFI 94; WhoScEn 94, 96; WhoWest 74, 76, 78, 80, 82, 84, 87, 89, 92, 94, 96; WhoWor 76, 78, 80, 82, 84, 87, 89, 91, 93, 95*

Warneke, Lon(nie)
"The Arkansas Humming Bird"
American. Baseball Player, Baseball Umpire
Pitcher, 1930-43, 1945; had 193 career wins, 31 shutouts, one no-hitter; NL umpire, 1949-55.
b. Mar 28, 1909 in Mount Ida, Arkansas
d. Jun 23, 1976 in Hot Springs, Arkansas
Source: *Ballpl 90; BiDAmSp BB; BioIn 3, 10, 15; LegTOT; NewYTBS 76; ObitOF 79; WhoProB 73*

Warner, Albert
[Warner Brothers]
American. Film Executive
Co-founded Warner Brothers Pictures, Inc., 1923.
b. Jul 23, 1884 in Kraznashiltz, Poland
d. Nov 26, 1967 in Miami Beach, Florida
Source: *BiDAmBL 83; BioIn 19; DcFM; NatCAB 54; ObitT 1961; WebAB 74, 79; WhAm 4A; WorAl; WorAlBi*

Warner, Charles Dudley
American. Editor, Author
Best known for collaborating with Mark Twain on *The Gilded Age,* 1873; said, "Everybody talks about the weather but nobody does anything about it."
b. Sep 12, 1829 in Plainfield, Massachusetts
d. Oct 20, 1900 in Hartford, Connecticut
Source: *Alli SUP; AmAu; AmAu&B; AmBi; ApCAB; BbD; Benet 87, 96; BenetAL 91; BibAL 8; BiDAmJo; BiD&SB; BioIn 9, 12, 16, 17; CamGLE; CamHAL; CasWL; CelCen; Chambr 3; ChhPo, S2; CnDAL; CyAL 2; DcAmAu; DcAmB; DcBiA; DcEnA A; DcEnL; DcLB 64; DcLEL; DcNAA; GrWrEL N; HarEnUS; LinLib L, S; NatCAB 2; OxCAmL 65, 83, 95; OxCCan; PenC AM; PeoHis; REn; REnAL; RfGAmL 87, 94; TwCBDA; WebAB 74, 79; WhAm 1*

Warner, Curt
American. Football Player
Running back, Seattle, 1983-89; LA Rams 1989-90.
b. Mar 18, 1961 in Wyoming, West Virginia
Source: *BiDAmSp FB; BioIn 13; FootReg 87; NewYTBS 82; WhoAfA 96; WhoBlA 88, 92, 94*

Warner, David
English. Actor
Starred in *Morgan,* 1965; *Time After Time,* 1979; *Time Bandits,* 1980.
b. Jul 29, 1941 in Manchester, England
Source: *CanWW 31; CnThe; ConTFT 5; Dun&B 90; FilmAG WE; FilmEn; FilmgC; ForYSC; HalFC 80, 84, 88; IlWWBF; IntMPA 78, 79, 80, 81, 82, 84, 86, 88, 92, 94, 96; IntWW 82, 83, 89, 91, 93; NewYTBE 71; OxCFilm; WhoHol 92, A; WhoHrs 80; WhoThe 72, 77, 81; WhoWor 84, 87, 89, 91, 93, 95, 96*

Warner, Denis Ashton
Australian. Author, Journalist
Contributor to leading Australian, US newspapers; specialist on Far Eastern affairs.
b. Dec 12, 1917 in Hobart, Australia
Source: *ConAu 3NR, 5R; IntAu&W 77, 89; IntWW 89, 91, 93; WhoWor 74, 76, 78*

Warner, Emily Howell
American. Pilot
First woman pilot for major US passenger airline (Frontier).
b. 1940 in Denver, Colorado
Source: *BioIn 13*

Warner, Harry Morris
[Warner Brothers]
American. Film Executive
Co-founder, pres., Warner Brothers Pictures, Inc., 1923-56.
b. Dec 12, 1881 in Kraznashiltz, Poland
d. Jul 25, 1958 in Hollywood, California
Source: *BiDAmBL 83; BioIn 5; CurBio 45, 58; DcAmB S6; DcFM; ObitOF 79; WebAB 74; WhAm 3*

Warner, Jack, Jr.
American. Film Executive
Organized Jack M Warner Productions, Inc., 1949.
b. Mar 27, 1916 in San Francisco, California
d. Apr 1, 1995 in Los Angeles, California
Source: *BioIn 20, 21; IntMPA 75, 76, 77, 78, 79, 80, 81, 82, 84, 86, 88, 92, 94; WhoAm 74, 76, 78, 80, 82, 84, 86, 88, 90, 92, 94, 95, 96, 97; WhoEnt 92; WhoWor 78*

Warner, Jack Leonard
[Warner Brothers; Jack Eichelbaum]
American. Film Executive
With brothers, introduced first successful sound film, *The Jazz Singer,* 1927; produced award-winning *My Fair Lady,* 1964.
b. Aug 2, 1892 in London, Ontario, Canada
d. Sep 9, 1978 in Los Angeles, California
Source: *BiDAmBL 83; BioIn 9, 10, 11; ConAu 108; CurBio 45, 78; DcAmB S10; DcFM; FilmgC; IntMPA 77; IntWW 74; WebAB 74; WhAm 7; Who 74; WhoAm 80; WhoHol A; WorAl*

Warner, John William
American. Politician
Rep. senator from VA, 1979—; husband of Elizabeth Taylor, 1976-82.
b. Feb 18, 1927 in Washington, District of Columbia
Source: *AlmAP 88, 92; BiDrUSC 89; BioIn 8, 11, 12, 13, 16; CngDr 79, 81, 83, 85, 87, 89; IntWW 91; IntYB 81, 82; WhoAm 74, 76, 78, 80, 82, 84, 86, 88, 90, 92, 94, 95, 96, 97; WhoAmL 90; WhoAmP 73, 75, 77, 79, 81, 83, 85, 87, 89, 91, 93, 95; WhoSSW 80, 82, 84, 86, 88, 91, 93, 95, 97; WhoWor 78, 80, 82, 84, 87, 89, 91; WorAl; WorAlBi*

Warner, Malcolm-Jamal
American. Actor
Played Theo Huxtable on "The Cosby Show," 1984-92.
b. Aug 18, 1970 in Jersey City, New Jersey
Source: *BioIn 14, 15, 16; ConTFT 5, 10; DrBlPA 90; IntMPA 92, 94, 96; WhoAfA 96; WhoAm 92; WhoBlA 92; WhoEnt 92*

Warner, Pop
[Glenn Scobey Warner]
American. Football Coach
Collegiate coach, 1895-1938; one of game's great innovators, introducing numbering of players, headgear.
b. Apr 5, 1871 in Springville, New York
d. Sep 7, 1954 in Palo Alto, California
Source: *BiDAmSp FB; BioIn 3, 4, 6, 7, 8, 9, 10, 12, 21; CmCal; DcAmB S5; LegTOT; OxCAmH; WebAB 74, 79; WhAm 3; WhoFtbl 74; WhoSpor*

Warner, Rawleigh, Jr.
American. Oilman
Chm. of Mobil Corp., 1976-85.
b. Feb 13, 1921 in Chicago, Illinois
Source: *AmMWSc 92; BioIn 10, 12, 14; BlueB 76; Dun&B 79, 86, 88; IntWW 74, 75, 76, 77, 78, 79, 80, 81, 82, 83, 89, 91, 93; St&PR 75, 84, 87, 91; WhoAm 74, 76, 78, 80, 82, 84, 86, 88, 90, 92, 94, 95, 96, 97; WhoE 74, 77, 79, 81, 83, 85; WhoFI 74, 75, 77, 79, 81, 83, 85; WhoWor 74, 76, 78, 80, 82, 84, 87, 89*

Warner, Roger Sherman, Jr.
American. Engineer
Developed atomic, hydrogen bombs, amphibious equipment for US troops.
b. Jun 12, 1907 in Boston, Massachusetts
d. Aug 3, 1976 in Washington, District of Columbia
Source: *BioIn 6; ObitOF 79; WhAm 7*

Warner, Sam(uel Louis)
[Warner Brothers]
American. Film Executive
Opened studios in CA with brothers, 1918.
b. Aug 10, 1887 in Baltimore, Maryland
d. Oct 5, 1927 in Los Angeles, California
Source: *BioIn 1; NatCAB 21; WebAB 74*

Warner, Susan Bogert
[Elizabeth Wetherell]
American. Author
Wrote sentimental juvenile novels: *Wide, Wide World,* 1851; *Queechy,* 1852.
b. Jul 11, 1819 in New York, New York
d. Mar 17, 1885 in Highland Falls, New York
Source: *Alli, SUP; AmAu; AmAu&B; AmBi; AmWomWr; ApCAB; ArtclWW 2; BbD; BenetAL 91; BibAL 8; BiD&SB; BioIn 1, 4, 8, 12, 15; BlmGWL; CarSB; Chambr 3; ChhPo, S1, S2; CyAL 2; DcAmAu; DcAmB; DcBiA; DcEnL; DcLB 42; DcLEL; DcNAA; EvLB; FemiCLE; InWom, SUP; LibW; NatCAB 5; NotAW; OxCAmL 65, 83, 95; OxCChiL; PenNWW A, B; REnAL; TwCBDA; TwCChW 95A; WhAm HS; WhoChL*

Warner, Sylvia Townsend
English. Author, Poet, Biographer
Best known for short stories in *New Yorker* mag; wrote biography of Jane Austen.
b. Dec 6, 1893 in Harrow, England
d. May 1, 1978 in Maiden Newton, England
Source: *ArtclWW 2; WhoTwCL; WhoWor 74, 76; WrDr 76*

Warnes, Jennifer
American. Singer
Sang Oscar-winning song "Up Where We Belong," 1983, with Joe Cocker.
b. 1947? in Orange County, California
Source: *BioIn 14, 15; ConMus 3; EncFCWM 83; EncRkSt; LegTOT; RkOn 84; WhoRocM 82*

Warnke, Paul Culliton
American. Lawyer, Government Official
Director, ACDA, 1977-78; chief US negotiator for SALT, 1977-78.
b. Jan 31, 1920 in Webster, Massachusetts
Source: *BioIn 8, 10, 11; ColdWar 2; CurBio 77; DcAmDH 80, 89; IntWW 77, 78, 79, 80, 81, 82, 83, 89, 91, 93; NewYTBE 72; NewYTBS 77; PolProf J; WhoAm 74, 76, 78, 80, 82, 84, 86, 88, 90, 92, 94, 95, 96, 97; WhoAmL 83, 92, 96; WhoAmP 77, 79, 81, 83, 85, 87, 89, 91, 93, 95; WhoE 86, 91, 95; WhoGov 77; WorAl; WorAlBi*

Warren, Austin
American. Critic, Author
Texts include *The Theory of Literature,* 1949.
b. Jul 4, 1899 in Waltham, Massachusetts

d. Aug 20, 1986 in Providence, Rhode Island
Source: *AmAu&B; BenetAL 91; BioIn 4, 15, 21; ConAu 17R, 120; ConLCrt 77, 82; REnAL; TwCA SUP; WhAm 9; WhoAm 74, 76, 78, 86; WrDr 80, 82, 84, 86*

Warren, Earl
American. Supreme Court Justice
Chief Justice, 1953-69; wrote many landmark liberal decisions; headed investigation of John F Kennedy assassination.
b. Mar 19, 1891 in Los Angeles, California
d. Jul 9, 1974 in Washington, District of Columbia
Source: *AmDec 1950; AmJust; AmPolLe; AmRef; BiDFedJ; BiDInt; BiDrGov 1789; BioIn 1, 2, 3, 4, 5, 6, 7, 8, 9, 10, 11, 12, 13, 14, 15, 16, 18, 20, 21; BioNews 74; CelR; CmCal; CngDr 74; ConAu 49, 123; CopCroC; CurBio 44, 54, 74, 74N; DcAmB S9; DcAmC; DcPol; DcTwHis; EncAB-H 1974, 1996; EncMcCE; FacFETw; LegTOT; LinLib L, S; McGEWB; NewYTBS 74; ObitT 1971; OxCAmH; OxCLaw; OxCSupC; PolPar; PolProf E, J, K, T; PresAR; RComAH; REn; SupCtJu; WebAB 74, 79; WhAm 6; WhDW; Who 74; WhoAm 74; WhoAmP 73; WhoGov 72; WhoWor 74; WorAl; WorAlBi*

Warren, Gerald Lee
American. Presidential Aide, Editor
Asst. press secretary to Nixon, 1969-74; Ford, 1974-75; editor, *San Diego Union*, 1975-92; editor, *San Diego Union-Tribune* 1992-95.
b. Aug 17, 1930 in Hastings, Nebraska
Source: *WhoAm 74, 76, 78, 80, 84, 92, 94, 95, 96, 97; WhoGov 72, 75; WhoSSW 73; WhoWest 82, 84, 87, 89, 94, 96*

Warren, Harry
[Salvatore Guaragna]
American. Songwriter
Wrote hundreds of popular songs for plays, films; won Oscars for hits "Lullaby of Broadway," 1935; "You'll Never Know," 1940; "On the Atchison, Topeka and the Santa Fe," 1946.
b. Dec 24, 1893 in New York, New York
d. Sep 22, 1981 in Los Angeles, California
Source: *AmCulL; AmPS; AmSong; AnObit 1981; ASCAP 66, 80; Baker 78, 84, 92; BestMus; BiDAmM; BiE&WWA; BioIn 2, 4, 6, 9, 10, 11, 12, 14, 15, 16, 19; CmpEPM; ConAmC 76, 82; ConAu 105; CurBio 43, 81, 81N; FacFETw; FilmEn; HalFC 84, 88; IntMPA 75, 76, 77, 78, 79, 80, 81, 82; LegTOT; NewAmDM; NewGrDA 86; NewGrDM 80; NotNAT; OxCFilm; OxCPMus; PenEncP; PopAmC, SUP; WhAm 9; WhoAm 74, 76; WhScrn 83*

Warren, Joseph
American. Military Leader
Revolutionary general known for sending Paul Revere, William Dawes on their famous ride.
b. Jun 11, 1741 in Roxbury, Massachusetts
d. Jun 17, 1775 in Charlestown, Massachusetts
Source: *Alli; AmBi; AmRev; AmWrBE; ApCAB; BiHiMed; BioIn 6, 8, 9, 19; BlkwEAR; CyAL 1; DcAmB; DcAmMeB, 84; Drake; EncAR; EncCRAm; HarEnUS; NatCAB 1; OxCAmH; TwCBDA; WebAB 74, 79; WebAMB; WhAm HS; WhAmRev; WhoHol A; WorAl; WorAlBi*

Warren, Leonard
American. Opera Singer
Leading baritone from 1940s; noted for Rigoletto role; died on stage at NY Met.
b. Apr 21, 1911 in New York, New York
d. Mar 4, 1960 in New York, New York
Source: *Baker 78, 84, 92; BiDAmM; BioIn 1, 2, 3, 4, 5, 7, 10, 11; BriBkM 80; CmOp; CurBio 53, 60; DcAmB S6; IntDcOp; LegTOT; MetOEnc; MusSN; NatCAB 47; NewAmDM; NewEOp 71; NewGrDA 86; NewGrDM 80; NewGrDO; OxDcOp; PenDiMP; RadStar; WhAm 3; WhScrn 77, 83; WorAl; WorAlBi*

Warren, Lesley Ann
American. Actor, Dancer
Made TV debut in musical "Cinderella," 1964.
b. Aug 16, 1946 in New York, New York
Source: *BioIn 14, 16; ConTFT 1, 2, 6, 13; ForYSC; HalFC 84, 88; IntMPA 86, 88, 92, 96; LegTOT; VarWW 85; WhoAm 88, 90; WhoEnt 92; WhoHol 92, A; WorAlBi*

Warren, Mercy Otis
American. Dramatist, Historian
Wrote political satires attacking Loyalists, history of Revolution, 1805.
b. Sep 14, 1728 in Barnstable, Massachusetts
d. Oct 19, 1814
Source: *Alli; AmAu; AmAu&B; AmBi; AmWomHi; AmWomWr; AmWrBE; ApCAB; ArtclWW 2; Benet 96; BenetAL 91; BiD&SB; BioAmW; BioIn 14, 15, 16, 18, 20, 21; BlkwEAR; BlmGWL; CamGLE; CamGWoT; CamHAL; ChhPo; CnDAL; CyAL 1; DcAmAu; DcAmB; DcBrAmW; DcLB 31; DcNAA; Drake; EncAB-H 1974, 1996; EncCRAm; EncWHA; GoodHs; GrLiveH; GrWrEL DR; InWom, SUP; LibW; McGEWB; NatCAB 7; NinCLC 13; NotAW; NotNAT B; NotWoAT; OxCAmH; OxCAmL 65, 83, 95; OxCAmT 84; OxCWoWr 95; PenNWW A; PeoHis; PorAmW; REn; REnAL; WebAB 74, 79; WhAm HS; WhAmP; WhAmRev; WorAl; WorAlBi*

Warren, Michael
American. Actor
Played Bobby Hill on TV series "Hill Street Blues," 1981-87; former All-American basketball player.
b. Mar 5, 1946 in South Bend, Indiana
Source: *BioIn 13; ConTFT 7; DrBlPA 90; WhoAfA 96; WhoAm 86, 88, 90, 92; WhoBlA 88, 90, 92, 94; WhoHol 92; WhoTelC*

Warren, Robert Penn
American. Author, Poet, Critic
Three-time Pulitzer Prize winner, best known for *All the King's Men*, 1946; first US poet laureate, 1986-87.
b. Apr 24, 1905 in Guthrie, Kentucky
d. Sep 15, 1989 in Stratton, Vermont
Source: *AmAu&B; AmNov; AmWr; AnObit 1989; Au&Wr 71; AuNews 1; Benet 87, 96; BenetAL 91; BioIn 2, 3, 4, 5, 6, 7, 8, 9, 10, 11, 12, 13, 14, 15, 16, 17, 19, 20, 21; BlueB 76; BroV; CamGEL; CamGLE; CamHAL; CasWL; ChhPo S3; CnDAL; CnE&AP; CnMD; ConAmA; ConAu 10NR, 13R, 47NR, 129; ConLC 1, 4, 6, 8, 10, 13, 18, 39, 53, 59; ConLCrt 77, 82; ConNov 72, 76, 82, 86; ConPo 70, 75, 80, 85; Conv 1; CurBio 70, 89, 89N; CyWA 58, 89; DcArts; DcLB 2, 48, 152, Y80A, Y89N; DcLEL; DcTwCCu 1; DrAF 76; DrAP 75; DrAPF 80, 89; EncSoH; EncWL 2, 3; EvLB; FacFETw; FifSWrA; FilmgC; GrWrEL N, P; HalFC 80, 84, 88; IntAu&W 76, 77, 82, 86, 89; IntvTCA 2; IntWW 74, 75, 76, 77, 78, 79, 80, 81, 82, 83, 89; IntWWP 77, 82; LegTOT; LiHiK; LinLib L, S; LngCTC; MagSAmL; MajTwCW; McGEWB; ModAL, S1, S2; ModWD; News 90, 90-1; NewYTBS 89; Novels; OxCAmL 65, 83, 95; OxCEng 85, 95; OxCTwCP; PenC AM; PeoHis; RAdv 1, 14, 13-1; RComWL; REn; REnAL; RfGAmL 87, 94; RfGShF; RGFAP; RGTwCWr; ShSCr 4; SixAP; SmATA 46, 63; SouWr; TwCA, SUP; TwCRHW 90, 94; WebAB 74, 79; WebE&AL; WhAm 10; WhDW; WhE&EA; WhNAA; Who 74, 82, 83, 85, 88, 90N; WhoAm 74, 76, 78, 80, 82, 84, 86, 88; WhoTwCL; WhoUSWr 88; WhoWor 74, 80, 82, 84, 87, 89; WhoWrEP 89; WorAl; WorAlBi; WorLitC; WrDr 76, 80, 82, 84, 86, 88, 90; WrPh*

Warrick, Ruth
American. Actor
In film *Citizen Kane*, 1941; longtime role on TV daytime drama "All My Children."
b. Jun 29, 1915 in Saint Louis, Missouri
Source: *BiE&WWA; BioIn 16; ConTFT 3; FilmEn; FilmgC; ForYSC; HalFC 80, 84, 88; IntMPA 77, 80, 84, 88, 92; InWom SUP; LegTOT; MovMk; NotNAT; RadStar; VarWW 85; WhoAm 90; WhoEnt 92; WhoHol 92, A; WhoThe 77*

Warrington, Lewis
American. Naval Officer
US secretary of navy ad interim, 1844; town in VA named in his honor.

b. Nov 3, 1782 in Williamsburg, Virginia
d. Oct 12, 1851 in Washington, District of Columbia
Source: *ApCAB; BioIn 2; DcAmB; Drake; HarEnUS; NatCAB 6; TwCBDA; WebAMB; WhAm HS*

Warton, Joseph
English. Author, Poet, Critic
Literary critic known for esssays on *Pope*, 1756, 1782.
b. Apr 1722 in Dunsfold, England
d. Feb 23, 1800 in Wickham, England
Source: *Alli; BbD; BiD&SB; BioIn 3, 8, 10, 17; BlmGEL; BritAu; CamGEL; CamGLE; CasWL; Chambr 2; ChhPo; CnE&AP; DcArts; DcBiPP; DcEnL; DcEuL; DcLB 104, 109; DcLEL; DcNaB; EvLB; GrWrEL P; NewC; NewCBEL; OxCEng 67, 85, 95; PenC ENG; RfGEnL 91; WebE&AL*

Warton, Thomas
English. Author
Poet-laureate, 1785-90; wrote *Triumph of Iris*, 1749; brother of Joseph.
b. Jan 9, 1728 in Basingstoke, England
d. May 21, 1790 in Oxford, England
Source: *Alli; BbD; Benet 87, 96; BiD&SB; BioIn 2, 3, 10, 12, 17; BlkwCE; BlmGEL; BritAu; CamGEL; CamGLE; CasWL; ChhPo, S1; CnE&AP; DcBiPP; DcEnA; DcEnL; DcEuL; DcLB 104, 109; DcLEL; DcNaB, C; EvLB; GrWrEL P; LitC 15; MouLC 2; NewC; NewCBEL; OxCEng 67, 85, 95; PenC ENG; PoLE; REn; RfGEnL 91; WebE&AL*

Warwick, Dionne
[Marie Dionne Warwick]
American. Singer
Three-time Grammy winner; hits include "Alfie," 1967; "That's What Friends are For," 1985.
b. Dec 12, 1940 in East Orange, New Jersey
Source: *Baker 84; BiDAfM; BioIn 8, 10, 12, 13, 15, 16; BlkWAm; CelR 90; ConMus 2; CurBio 69; DcTwCCu 5; DrBlPA, 90; EncPR&S 89; EncRkSt; IlEncBM 82; InB&W 80, 85; IntWW 91; InWom SUP; LegTOT; NewAmDM; NotBlAW 1; OxCPMus; PenEncP; RkOn 74; SoulM; WhoAfA 96; WhoAm 86, 88, 95, 96, 97; WhoAmW 70, 72, 77, 91, 95, 97; WhoBlA 75, 92, 94; WhoEnt 92; WhoRock 81; WorAlBi*

Warwick, Robert
[Robert Taylor Bien]
American. Actor
Matinee idol of Broadway, films, 1914-59; in film *Adventures of Robin Hood*, 1938.
b. Oct 9, 1876 in Sacramento, California
d. Jun 4, 1964 in Los Angeles, California
Source: *FilmgC; MotPP; MovMk; NotNAT B; WhScrn 77; WhThe*

Was (Not Was)
[Sweet Pea Atkinson; Harry Bowens; Donald (Don Was) Fagenson; David (David Was) Weis]
American. Music Group
Rhythm-and-blues group formed in early 1980s; albums include *What Up, Dog?*, 1988 and *Are You OK?*, 1990.
Source: *ConMus 6; EncRk 88; PenEncP; WhsNW 85*

Washakie
American. Native American Chief
Chief of Eastern Shoshone tribe; ally of white settlers; signed treaty establishing a Shoshone reservation in Wyoming, 1868.
b. 1804? in Montana
d. 1900 in Flathead Village, Montana
Source: *BioIn 1, 3, 5, 7, 11; DcAmB; EncNoAI; NotNaAm; OxCAmH; REnAW; WebAB 74, 79; WhAm HS; WhNaAH*

Washam, Wisner McCamey
American. Writer
Head writer for soap opera "All My Children," 1971—.
b. Sep 8, 1931 in Mooresville, North Carolina
Source: *VarWW 85*

Washburn, Charles
American. Journalist, Dramatist
Best known as theatrical press agent; clients included Al Jolson, John Barrymore.
b. 1890 in Chicago, Illinois
d. 1972 in Jersey City, New Jersey
Source: *ConAu 104; NewYTBE 72*

Washington, Booker T(aliafero)
American. Educator, Author
Leading black of his time; founded Tuskegee Institute, 1881, turned it into foremost college for blacks; wrote autobiographical *Up From Slavery*, 1901.
b. Apr 5, 1856 in Franklin County, Virginia
d. Nov 14, 1915 in Tuskegee, Alabama
Source: *AmAu&B; AmBi; ApCAB; BiD&SB; BiDSA; BlkAWP; CasWL; Chambr 3; CyAG; DcAmB; DcLEL; OxCAmH; PenC AM; REnAL; WebAB 79; WhAm 1; WorAl*

Washington, Buck
[Buck and Bubbles; Ford Lee Washington]
American. Jazz Musician, Comedian
Part of comedy team with John Sublett, 1919-53.
b. Oct 16, 1903 in Louisville, Kentucky
d. Jan 31, 1955 in New York, New York
Source: *BiDJaz; DrBlPA, 90; NewGrDJ 88, 94; WhoJazz 72*

Washington, Denzel, Jr.
American. Actor
Played Dr. Phillip Chandler on TV series "St. Elsewhere," 1982-84; *Glory*, 1990; *Malcolm X*, 1992.
b. Dec 28, 1954 in Mount Vernon, New York
Source: *AfrAmAl 6; AfrAmBi 2; BiDFilm 94; BioIn 14, 15, 16, 18; ConBlB 1; ConTFT 9; CurBio 92; DcTwCCu 5; DrBlPA 90; InB&W 85; IntMPA 92, 94, 96; IntWW 91, 93; LegTOT; News 93-2; VarWW 85; WhoAfA 96; WhoAm 90, 94, 95, 96, 97; WhoBlA 92, 94; WhoEnt 92; WhoHol 92*

Washington, Dinah
[Ruth Jones]
"Queen of the Blues"
American. Singer
Adapted blues style to pop songs; with Lionel Hampton's band, 1943-49.
b. Aug 29, 1924 in Tuscaloosa, Alabama
d. Dec 14, 1963 in Detroit, Michigan
Source: *AfrAmAl 6; AllMusG; Baker 84, 92; BiDAfM; BiDAmM; BiDJaz; BioAmW; BioIn 6, 12, 13, 15, 16, 18, 19, 20; BlkWAm; BluesWW; CmpEPM; ConMus 5; DcAmB S7; DcTwCCu 5; DrBlPA, 90; EncPR&S 89; EncRk 88; IlEncBM 82; IlEncJ; InB&W 80, 85; InWom, SUP; LegTOT; NegAl 89; NewAmDM; NewGrDA 86; NewGrDJ 88, 94; NotBlAW 1; NotNAT B; ObitOF 79; OxCPMus; PenEncP; RkOn 74; RolSEnR 83; WhoHol B; WhoRock 81; WhScrn 77, 83; WorAl; WorAlBi*

Washington, Fredi
[Fredericka Carolyn Washington]
American. Actor
Stage productions included *Porgy and Bess*, 1943 and *Cry the Beloved Country*, 1952.
b. Dec 23, 1903 in Savannah, Georgia
d. Jun 28, 1994 in Stamford, Connecticut
Source: *BioIn 18, 20; BlksAmF; BlkWAm; ConBlB 10; DcTwCCu 5; DrBlPA, 90; InB&W 85; InWom SUP; NewYTBS 94; NotBlAW 1; ThFT; WhoHol 92*

Washington, George
American. US President
First president, 1789-97; commander-in-chief, Continental Forces, 1775-83; warned against foreign alliances.
b. Feb 22, 1732 in Westmoreland, Virginia
d. Dec 14, 1799 in Mount Vernon, Virginia
Source: *Alli; AmAu&B; AmBi; AmOrN; AmPolLe; AmRev; AmWrBE; ApCAB; BbD; Benet 87, 96; BenetAL 91; BiAUS; BiD&SB; BiDrAC; BiDrUSC 89; BiDrUSE 71, 89; BiDSA; BioIn 1, 2, 3, 4, 5, 6, 7, 8, 9, 10, 11, 12, 13, 14, 15, 16, 17, 18, 19, 20, 21; BlkwCE; BlkwEAR; BlmGEL; Chambr 3; CmdGen 1991; CyAG; CyAL 1; DcAmAu; DcAmB; DcAmC; DcAmMiB; DcBiPP; DcLB 31; DcLEL; DcNAA; Dis&D; Drake; EncAAH; EncAB-H 1974, 1996; EncAI&E; EncAR; EncCRAm; EncRev; EncSoH; FacPr 89, 93; GenMudB; HalFC 80, 84, 88; HarEnMi; HarEnUS; HealPre; HisDBrE; HisWorL; LegTOT; LinLib L; LitC 25; LngCEL; McGEWB; MemAm; NewCBEL; OxCAmH;*

OxCAmL 65, 83, 95; OxCCan; OxCSupC; PeoHis; PolPar; RAdv 13-3; RComAH; REn; REnAL; REnAW; TwCBDA; WebAB 74, 79; WebAMB; WhAm HS; WhAmP; WhAmRev; WhDW; WhNaAH; WhoMilH 76; WorAl; WorAlBi

Washington, Grover, Jr.
American. Musician
Jazz saxophonist; Grammy Award, 1981, for "best jazz fusion performance, vocal or instrumental" for album *Winelight.*
b. Dec 12, 1943 in Buffalo, New York
Source: *AllMusG; ASCAP 80; BiDAfM; BiDJaz; BioIn 13; ConMus 5; DrBlPA 90; EncJzS; EncPR&S 89; IlEncBM 82; InB&W 80, 85; LegTOT; NewGrDJ 88, 94; News 89-1; PenEncP; RkOn 85; RolSEnR 83; SoulM; WhoAfA 96; WhoAm 80, 82, 84, 86, 88, 90, 92, 94, 95, 96, 97; WhoBlA 92, 94; WhoEnt 92; WhoRock 81*

Washington, Harold
American. Politician
First black Dem. mayor of Chicago, 1983-87; suffered massive heart attack in office.
b. Apr 15, 1922 in Chicago, Illinois
d. Nov 25, 1987 in Chicago, Illinois
Source: *AfrAmAl 6; AfrAmBi 1; AlmAP 82; AnObit 1987; BiDrUSC 89; BioIn 12, 13; BlkAmsC; CngDr 81, 83; ConBlB 6; ConNews 88-1; CurBio 84, 88, 88N; Ebony 1; InB&W 80; NegAl 76, 83; NewYTBS 83, 87; PolPar; WhAm 9; WhoAm 76, 84, 86; WhoAmP 73, 75, 77, 79, 81, 83, 85, 87; WhoBlA 75, 77, 80, 85, 88, 90N; WhoMW 82, 84, 86, 88*

Washington, Lawrence
American.
Half-brother of George Washington; George inherited Mount Vernon from him.
b. 1718
d. Jul 1752
Source: *BioIn 11, 18; HarEnUS; PeoHis*

Washington, MaliVai
American. Tennis Player
Winner, U.S. Men's Clay Court Championships, 1992.
b. Jun 20, 1969 in Glen Cove, New York
Source: *ConBlB 8; WhoAfA 96; WhoAm 94, 95, 96, 97; WhoE 95*

Washington, Martha Dandridge Curtis
[Mrs. George Washington]
American. First Lady
Widow who married George Washington, Jan 6, 1759.
b. Jun 2, 1732 in New Kent County, Virginia
d. May 22, 1802 in Mount Vernon, Virginia
Source: *Alli; AmAu&B; AmBi; AmOrN; AmPolLe; AmRev; AmWom; AmWrBE; ApCAB; BbD; Benet 87, 96; BenetAL 91; BiAUS; BiD&SB; BiDrAC; BiDrUSC 89; BiDrUSE 71, 89; BiDSA; BioIn 1, 2, 3, 4, 5, 6, 7, 8, 9, 10, 11, 12, 13, 14, 15, 16, 17, 18, 19, 20, 21; BlkwCE; BlkwEAR; BlmGEL; Chambr 3; CmdGen 1991; CyAG; CyAL 1; DcAmAu; DcAmB; DcAmC; DcAmMiB; DcBiPP; DcLB 31; DcLEL; DcNAA; Dis&D; Drake; EncAAH; EncAB-H 1974, 1996; EncAI&E; EncAR; EncCRAm; EncRev; EncSoH; FacPr 89, 93; GenMudB; GoodHs; HalFC 80, 84, 88; HarEnMi; HarEnUS; HealPre; HerW; HisDBrE; HisWorL; LegTOT; LinLib L; LitC 25; LngCEL; McGEWB; MemAm; NatCAB 1; NewCBEL; NewCol 75; NotAW; OxCAmH; OxCAmL 65, 83, 95; OxCCan; OxCSupC; PeoHis; PolPar; RAdv 13-3; RComAH; REn; REnAL; REnAW; TwCBDA; WebAB 74, 79; WebAMB; WhAm HS; WhAmP; WhAmRev; WhDW; WhNaAH; WhoMilH 76; WorAl; WorAlBi*

Washington, Thomas L.
American. Organization Official
President, National Rifle Association, 1994-95.
d. Dec 5, 1995 in Dearborn, Michigan
Source: *BioIn 21; NewYTBS 95*

Washington, Walter Edward
American. Politician, Lawyer
Mayor of Washington, DC, 1975-79.
b. Apr 15, 1915 in Dawson, Georgia
Source: *AfrAmBi 1; BioIn 8, 9, 10, 11; BioNews 74; BlueB 76; CurBio 68; InB&W 80; IntWW 82, 91; WhoAm 86, 88, 90, 92; WhoBlA 80, 92; WhoE 89, 91; WhoGov 72, 75, 77; WhoWor 82, 87*

Washkansky, Louis
"Washy"
South African. Businessman, Transplant Patient
Received first heart transplant, Dec 3, 1967, performed by Dr. Christiaan Barnard.
b. 1913, Lithuania
d. Dec 21, 1967 in Cape Town, South Africa
Source: *BioIn 8*

Wasserburg, Gerald Joseph
American. Scientist
Known for calculating age of moon rocks; oldest 4.6 billion yrs.
b. Mar 25, 1927 in New Brunswick, New Jersey
Source: *AmMWSc 76P, 79, 82, 86, 89, 92, 95; BioIn 12, 13, 14, 15; BlueB 76; CurBio 86; IntWW 74, 75, 76, 77, 78, 79, 80, 81, 82, 83, 89, 91, 93; McGMS 80; WhoAm 74, 76, 78, 80, 82, 84, 88, 90, 92, 94, 95, 96, 97; WhoScEn 94, 96; WhoWest 94, 96*

Wasserman, Dale
American. Dramatist
Won best musical Tony for *Man of La Mancha,* 1965.
b. Nov 2, 1917 in Rhinelander, Wisconsin
Source: *AmAu&B; BiE&WWA; BlueB 76; ConAu 49; ConDr 73, 77D, 88D; ConTFT 5; EncMT; IntMPA 75, 76, 77, 78, 79, 80, 81, 82, 84, 86, 88, 92, 94, 96; LesBEnT 92; NatPD 81; NewYTET; NotNAT; WhoAm 74, 76, 78, 80, 82, 84, 86, 88, 90, 92, 94, 95, 96, 97; WhoEnt 92; WrDr 76, 80, 82, 84, 86, 88, 90, 92, 94, 96*

Wasserman, Lew(is Robert)
American. Film Executive
Chief exec., MCA, Inc., 1946-90; won special Oscar, 1973.
b. Mar 15, 1913 in Cleveland, Ohio
Source: *BiDAmBL 83; BioIn 10, 11, 14, 16; CelR, 90; CurBio 91; Dun&B 90; IntMPA 77, 80, 84, 92, 94, 96; IntWW 91; NewYTBS 85; St&PR 91; WhoAm 86, 88; WhoEnt 92; WhoFI 92; WhoWest 92*

Wasserman, Lew R
American. Business Executive
Pres. of MCA (Music Corporation of America) 1946-1990, when it was purchased by the Matsushita Corp. of Japan.
b. Mar 15, 1913 in Cleveland, Ohio
Source: *BioIn 14, 16; CurBio 91; Dun&B 90; IntMPA 92; IntWW 91; NewYTBS 74, 83, 85; St&PR 91; WhoAm 88; WhoFI 92; WhoWest 92*

Wassermann, August von
German. Physician
Known for discovering method of detecting syphilis in blood, 1906.
b. Feb 21, 1866 in Bamberg, Bavaria
d. Mar 15, 1925 in Berlin, Germany
Source: *AsBiEn; BioIn 5, 20; CamDcSc; IntMed 80; NewCol 75; WebBD 83; WhDW*

Wassermann, Jakob
German. Author
Novelist best known for strange characters, startling plots: *Doctor Keerkhoven,* 1931.
b. Mar 10, 1873 in Furth, Bavaria
d. Jan 1, 1934 in Altaussee, Austria
Source: *Benet 87, 96; BioIn 1, 3, 5, 16; CasWL; ClDMEL 47, 80; ConAu 104; CyWA 58; DcLB 66; Dis&D; EncWL 2, 3; EvEuW; McGEWB; ModGL; Novels; OxCGer 76, 86; PenC EUR; REn; TwCA, SUP; TwCLC 6; WhE&EA; WhoLA*

Wasserstein, Wendy
American. Dramatist
Playwright's work details changes in modern womens' lives; *The Heidi Chronicles,* 1989.
b. Oct 18, 1950 in New York, New York
Source: *AmWomD; AmWomWr SUP; Benet 96; BioIn 12, 13, 14, 15, 16; BlmGWL; CamGWoT; CelR 90; ConAmD; ConAu 3BS, 53NR, 121, 129; ConDr 88, 93; ConLC 32, 59, 90; ConTFT 1, 8; ConWomD; CrtSuDr; CurBio 89; DcTwCCu 1; DramC 4; FemiCLE; FemiWr; GrWomW; IntAu&W*

91; IntWW 93; InWom SUP; JeAmWW; LegTOT; NatPD 81; News 91, 91-3; NewYTBS 81, 92; NotWoAT; OxCAmL 95; OxCWoWr 95; RAdv 14; WhoAm 90, 92, 94, 95, 96, 97; WhoAmW 85, 87, 91, 93, 95, 97; WhoE 91, 93, 95, 97; WhoEmL 87; WhoEnt 92; WhoWor 95; WorAu 1980

Wasson, R(obert) Gordon
American. Journalist, Scientist
Mushroom expert; wrote *The Wondrous Mushroom,* 1980.
b. Sep 22, 1898 in Great Falls, Montana
d. Dec 23, 1986 in New York, New York
Source: *AmAu&B; AmMWSc 76P, 79, 82, 86; BioIn 15, 16; ConAu 116, 153; EncO&P 1, 2, 3; NewYTBS 86; WhAm 9; WhJnl*

Waterfield, Bob
[Robert Stanton Waterfield]
"Rifle"
American. Football Player
Quarterback, Cleveland-LA Rams, 1945-52; led NFL in passing twice; helped perfect long TD pass—"bomb;" Hall of Fame, 1965.
b. Jul 26, 1920 in Elmira, New York
d. Mar 26, 1983 in Burbank, California
Source: *BioIn 3, 8, 9, 10, 13, 17, 21; CmCal; LegTOT; NewYTBS 83; WhoFtbl 74; WhoSpor*

Waterhouse, Benjamin
American. Physician
First American doctor to use Jenner's smallpox vaccine in general practice, 1800.
b. Mar 4, 1754 in Newport, Rhode Island
d. Oct 2, 1846 in Cambridge, Massachusetts
Source: *Alli; ApCAB; BiDAmS; BiHiMed; BiInAmS; BioIn 2, 3, 4, 6, 9; CyAL 1; DcAmAu; DcAmB; DcAmMeB, 84; DcNAA; Drake; EncAAH; EncAB-H 1974, 1996; InSci; McGEWB; NatCAB 9; NewCol 75; OxCAmH; OxCMed 86; TwCBDA; WebAB 74, 79; WhAm HS*

Waterhouse, Ellis Kirkham, Sir
American. Museum Director, Art Historian
Prominent art historian; wrote *Painting in Britain,* 1953.
b. Feb 16, 1905 in Epsom, England
d. Sep 7, 1985 in Oxford, England
Source: *BioIn 9; BlueB 76; ConAu 65, 117; DcNaB 1981; IntWW 74, 75, 76, 77, 78, 79, 80, 81, 82, 83; Who 74*

Waterhouse, Keith Spencer
English. Author
Best-seller, *Billy Liar,* 1959; successful play, 1960; film, 1963 and a musical, 1974.
b. Feb 6, 1929 in Hunslet, England
Source: *BioIn 10, 13; CamGLE; ConAu 5R; ConDr 88; ConLC 47; ConNov 91; ConTFT 5; CroCD; DcLB 15; DcLP 87A; HalFC 88; IntAu&W 91; IntMPA 92; OxCThe 83; Who 92; WrDr 92*

Waterman, Lewis Edson
American. Inventor
Introduced the first practical fountain pen; operated own co., 1883-1901.
b. Nov 20, 1837 in Decatur, New York
d. May 1, 1901 in New York, New York
Source: *AmBi; BioIn 11; DcAmB; NatCAB 1; WebAB 74, 79; WebBD 83; WhAm HS; WhDW*

Waters, Ethel
American. Singer, Actor
Starred in plays *Cabin in the Sky,* 1940; *The Member of the Wedding,* 1950; Oscar nominee for *Pinky,* 1949; active in Billy Graham's crusades from 1950s.
b. Oct 31, 1896 in Chester, Pennsylvania
d. Sep 1, 1977 in Chatsworth, California
Source: *AllMusG; Baker 78, 84, 92; BiDAfM; BiDJaz; BiE&WWA; BioIn 11, 12, 13, 16, 17, 18, 19, 20; BlksAmF; BlkWAm; BluesWW; CamGWoT; ConAu 73, 81; CurBio 41, 51, 77, 77N; DcAmB S10; DcTwCCu 5; DrBlPA, 90; EncMT; FamA&A; FilmEn; FilmgC; GuBlues; HalFC 84, 88; IntMPA 77; LegTOT; LibW; MotPP; NewAmDM; NewGrDA 86; NewGrDJ 88, 94; NewGrDM 80; NewYTBS 77; NotBlAW 1; NotNAT; OxCPMus; PlP&P; WebAB 79; WhoAm 76; WhoHol A; WhoRel 77; WhoThe 77; WhScrn 83; WorAl*

Waters, Frank (Joseph)
American. Author
Author of more than two dozen books about the Native American culture and the American west.
b. 1902 in Colorado
d. Jun 3, 1995 in Taos, New Mexico
Source: *AmAu&B; AmNov; BioIn 2, 9, 10, 12, 13, 14, 15, 16, 21; CnDAL; ConAu 3NR, 5R, 13AS, 18NR, 149; ConLC 88; CyWA 89; DcLB Y86B; DrAF 76; DrAPF 80; EncFWF; FifWWr; IntAu&W 76, 77, 82; OxCAmL 95; REnAW; RfGAmL 94; TwCWW 82, 91; WhNAA; WhoAm 74, 76, 78; WhoWest 74, 76; WrDr 84, 86, 88, 90, 92, 94, 96*

Waters, John
American. Filmmaker
Off-beat outrageous films include *Pink Flamingos,* 1972; transvestite Divine featured in many films.
b. Apr 22, 1946 in Baltimore, Maryland
Source: *Au&Arts 16; BioIn 16, 17, 19, 20; ConAu 126, 130; ConTFT 5, 10; CurBio 90; DcLP 87A; GayLesB; IntMPA 92, 94, 96; LegTOT; MiSFD 9; News 88-3; WhoAm 92, 94, 95, 96, 97; WhoE 93, 95, 97; WhoEnt 92; WrDr 94*

Waters, Maxine
American. Politician
US Dem. rep from CA, 1991—; founder, Black Women's Forum.
b. Aug 15, 1938 in Saint Louis, Missouri
Source: *AfrAmAl 6; AlmAP 92, 96; BioIn 13, 14, 16; BlkWAm; CngDr 91, 93, 95; ConBlB 3; CurBio 92; InB&W 85; LegTOT; NotBlAW 2; WhoAm 92, 94, 95, 96, 97; WhoAmP 91; WhoAmW 87, 89, 91, 93, 95, 97; WhoBlA 92; WhoWest 87, 89, 92, 94, 96; WomPO 78; WomStre*

Waters, Muddy
[McKinley Morganfield]
American. Singer, Musician
Won five Grammys; hits include "I'm a Man"; "I've Got My Mojo Working."
b. Apr 4, 1915 in Rolling Fork, Mississippi
d. Apr 30, 1983 in Downers Grove, Illinois
Source: *AfrAmAl 6; AnObit 1983; Baker 84, 92; BiDAfM; BiDAmM; BiDJaz; BioIn 8, 9, 11, 12, 13, 14, 15, 16, 17, 19, 20; BluesWW; ConMuA 80A; ConMus 4; CurBio 81, 83N; DrBlPA, 90; EncFCWM 69, 83; EncJzS; EncPR&S 89; EncRk 88; EncRkSt; GuBlues; HarEnR 86; IlEncJ; IlEncRk; InB&W 80, 85; LegTOT; NewGrDM 80; NewYTBS 83; OnThGG; OxCPMus; PenEncP; PeoHis; RkOn 74; RolSEnR 83; WhAm 8; WhoAm 76, 78, 80, 82; WhoBlA 77, 80; WhoRock 81; WhoRocM 82*

Waterston, Sam(uel Atkinson)
American. Actor
Film, TV, stage performer since 1963; Oscar nominee for *The Killing Fields,* 1984.
b. Nov 15, 1940 in Cambridge, Massachusetts
Source: *BioIn 12, 14; CamGWoT; ConTFT 3, 10; CurBio 85; FilmEn; HalFC 80, 84, 88; IntMPA 77, 80, 81, 82, 84, 86, 88, 92, 94, 96; LegTOT; NotNAT; PlP&P A; VarWW 85; WhoAm 80, 84, 86, 88, 92, 94, 95, 96, 97; WhoEnt 92; WhoHol 92, A; WhoThe 81; WorAlBi*

Watie, Stand
American. Military Leader, Native American Leader
Signed the Treaty of New Echota, 1835, which relocated the Cherokee to Oklahoma; Confederate Brigadier General.
b. 1806 in Georgia
d. Sep 9, 1871 in Oklahoma
Source: *AmAu&B; AmBi; BiDConf; BioIn 5, 11, 21; CivWDc; DcAmB; DcAmMiB; EncNAB; EncNoAI; EncSoH; NotNaAm; PeoHis; REnAW; WebAMB; WhAm HS; WhCiWar; WhNaAH*

Watkins, Arthur V(ivian)
American. Politician, Lawyer
Dem. senator from UT, 1947-59; led committee considering charges against Joe McCarthy, 1954.
b. Dec 18, 1886 in Midway, Utah
d. Sep 1, 1973 in Orem, Utah
Source: *BiDrAC; BiDrUSC 89; BioIn 2, 3, 5, 7, 10, 11; ConAu 111; CurBio 50, 73N; DcAmB S9; NewYTBE 73; PolProf E; WhAm 6, 7; WhAmP*

Watkins, James (David)
American. Government Official
Secretary of Energy, 1988-93.
b. Mar 7, 1927 in Alhambra, California
Source: *BiDrUSE 89; BioIn 13, 16; CngDr 89; CurBio 89; IntWW 83, 89, 91, 93; NewYTBS 82, 91; WhoAm 78, 82, 84, 86, 88, 90, 92, 95; WhoAmP 91; WhoE 91, 93; WhoFI 92; WhoScEn 94; WhoWor 91, 93*

Watkins, Levi, Jr.
American. Surgeon
Introduced a procedure that has saved the lives of patients suffering from arrhythmia known as the Automatic Implantable Defibrillator (AID), 1980.
b. Jun 13, 1945 in Parsons, Kansas
Source: *BioIn 12, 20; BlksScM; ConBlB 9; NotTwCS*

Watley, Jody
American. Singer
Won Grammy for best new artist, 1988; hits include "Looking for a New Love," 1987; granddaughter of Jackie Wilson.
b. Jan 30, 1961 in Chicago, Illinois
Source: *BioIn 15, 16; ConMus 9; WhoBlA 92*

Watson, Bryan Joseph
"Bugsy"; "Superpest"
Canadian. Hockey Player
Defenseman, 1963-79, with seven NHL teams; best known for shadowing Bobby Hull, late 1960s; had career 2,212 penalty minutes.
b. Nov 14, 1942 in Bancroft, Ontario, Canada
Source: *HocEn; WhoHcky 73*

Watson, Charles
"Tex"
American. Cultist
Member of Manson cult.
b. Dec 2, 1945 in Coppeville, Texas
Source: *BioIn 8, 10, 11*

Watson, Doc
[Arthel Lane Watson]
American. Musician
Country music entertainer, considered finest interpreter of guitar flat-picking in world; with son, Merle, won two Grammys, 1970s.
b. Mar 2, 1923 in Deep Gap, North Carolina
Source: *BgBkCoM; BioIn 14, 15, 16; ConMus 2; CounME 74, 74A; EncFCWM 69, 83; HarEnCM 87; IlEncCM; LegTOT; NewAmDM; NewGrDA 86; OnThGG; PenEncP; WhoAm 76, 78, 80, 82, 84, 86, 88, 90, 92, 94, 95, 96, 97; WhoEnt 92*

Watson, Elizabeth
American. Police Chief
Chief of Police, Houston, TX, 1990-92.
b. Aug 25, 1949 in Philadelphia, Pennsylvania
Source: *News 91, 91-2*

Watson, Jack Hearn, Jr.
American. Lawyer, Government Official
Appointed chief of the White House staff, assistant to the pres., by Carter, 1980.
b. Oct 24, 1938 in El Paso, Texas
Source: *BioIn 10, 11, 12; CurBio 80; NewYTBS 76, 80; WhoAm 88; WhoE 79, 81*

Watson, James Dewey
American. Biochemist
Shared 1962 Nobel Prize in medicine for DNA studies.
b. Apr 6, 1928 in Chicago, Illinois
Source: *AmAu&B; AmMWSc 73P, 76P, 79, 82, 86, 89, 92, 95; AsBiEn; BiESc; BioIn 5, 6, 7, 8, 9, 12, 13, 14, 15; BlueB 76; CamDcSc; ConAu 25R; CurBio 63; EncAB-H 1974, 1996; FacFETw; IntWW 74, 75, 76, 77, 78, 79, 80, 81, 82, 83, 89, 91, 93; LarDcSc; MakMC; McGEWB; McGMS 80; NewYTBS 80; NobelP; RAdv 14, 13-5; ThTwC 87; WebAB 74, 79; Who 74, 82, 83, 85, 88, 90, 92, 94; WhoAm 74, 76, 78, 80, 82, 84, 86, 88, 90, 92, 94, 95, 96, 97; WhoE 81, 83, 85, 86, 89, 91, 95, 97; WhoFrS 84; WhoMedH; WhoNob, 90, 95; WhoScEn 94, 96; WhoTech 89; WhoWor 74, 76, 78, 80, 82, 84, 87, 89, 91, 93, 95, 96, 97; WorAl; WorScD; WrDr 88*

Watson, John
Irish. Auto Racer
Formula One racer, racing in Grand Prix around world.
b. May 4, 1946 in Belfast, Northern Ireland
Source: *BioIn 11, 13, 14; WhoWor 82*

Watson, John Broadus
American. Psychologist
Founded behaviorist psychology, 1913; denied role of heredity in personality development.
b. Jan 9, 1878 in Greenville, South Carolina
d. Sep 25, 1958 in New York, New York
Source: *ApCAB X; AsBiEn; BiDAmEd; BiDPsy; BioIn 5, 7, 12, 14, 15, 16, 18; CurBio 42, 58; DcAmB S6; EncAB-A 30; EncAB-H 1974, 1996; FacFETw; GaEncPs; InSci; LinLib L, S; LuthC 75; MakMC; McGEWB; NamesHP; NatCAB 48; OxCAmH; OxCPhil; PeoHis; REnAL; WebAB 74, 79; WhAm 3; WorAl*

Watson, Mark Skinner
American. Journalist
Won 1945 Pulitzer for distinguished reporting of international events, WW II.
b. Jun 24, 1887 in Plattsburg, New York
d. Mar 25, 1966 in Baltimore, Maryland
Source: *BioIn 1, 2, 7, 15; ConAu 89; CurBio 46, 66; WhAm 4*

Watson, Moose
[Harry E Watson]
Canadian. Hockey Player
Played amateur hockey, 1920s; Hall of Fame, 1962.
b. Jul 14, 1898 in Saint John's, Newfoundland, Canada
d. Sep 11, 1957 in Toronto, Ontario, Canada
Source: *WhoHcky 73*

Watson, Thomas Edward
American. Politician
Populist; congressman, 1891-93; senator from GA, 1921-27; wrote *Life of Thomas Jefferson,* 1900.
b. Sep 5, 1856 in Thomson, Georgia
d. Sep 26, 1922 in Washington, District of Columbia
Source: *AmAu&B; AmBi; AmPolLe; AmRef; BiDrAC; BiDrUSC 89; BiDSA; BioIn 1, 4, 10, 15, 21; CyAG; DcAmAu; DcAmB; DcAmSR; DcNAA; EncAAH; EncAB-H 1974, 1996; EncSoH; HarEnUS; McGEWB; NatCAB 3; TwCBDA; WebAB 74, 79; WhAm 1*

Watson, Thomas J(ohn), Sr.
American. Business Executive
With IBM, 1914-56, chairman, chief exec., 1949-56; brought company into computer era.
b. Feb 17, 1874 in Campbell, New York
d. Jun 19, 1956 in New York, New York
Source: *BiDAmBL 83; BiDInt; BioIn 1, 2, 3, 4, 5, 6, 7, 8, 9, 10; CurBio 40, 50, 56; DcAmB S6; EncAB-A 27; EncAB-H 1974, 1996; HisDcDP; McGEWB; NatCAB 47; PorSil; WebAB 74, 79; WhAm 3; WorAl*

Watson, Thomas J(ohn), Jr.
American. Business Executive
Chairman, IBM, 1961-71; oversaw growth of company into new fields; ambassador to USSR, 1979-81.
b. Jan 8, 1914 in Dayton, Ohio
d. Dec 31, 1993 in Greenwich, Connecticut
Source: *BiDAmBL 83; BioIn 2, 3, 4, 5, 7, 9, 10, 11, 12, 13, 15; ConAu 138, 143; CurBio 56, 94N; DcAmDH 89; HisDcDP; IntWW 83, 91; IntYB 78, 79, 82; NewYTBS 90; PolProf E, K; St&PR 75; WhoAm 84, 90; WhoAmP 85; WhoFI 74; WhoWor 84; WorAl; WorAlBi*

Watson, Tom
[Thomas Sturges Watson]
American. Golfer
Turned pro, 1971; won British Open five times; Masters twice, US Open once.
b. Sep 4, 1949 in Kansas City, Missouri
Source: *BiDAmSp OS; BioIn 12, 13, 15, 20, 21; CelR 90; CurBio 79; FacFETw; IntWW 81, 82, 83, 89, 91, 93; LegTOT; NewYTBS 79, 80, 82; WhoAm 78, 80, 82, 84, 86, 88, 90, 92, 94, 95, 96, 97; WhoGolf; WhoIntG; WhoSpor; WhoWor 95, 96, 97; WorAl; WorAlBi*

Watson-Watt, Robert Alexander, Sir
Scottish. Scientist, Engineer
Developed the radiolocator (radar), secret weapon of Battle of Britain.
b. Apr 13, 1892 in Brechin, Scotland
d. Dec 5, 1973 in Inverness, Scotland
Source: *AsBiEn; Au&Wr 71; BioIn 1, 2, 3, 4, 5, 6, 7, 9, 10, 12, 14, 20; CamDcSc; ConAu 45, P-1; CurBio 45, 74; DcNaB 1971; DcScB S2; GrBr; InSci; LarDcSc; McGEWB; NewYTBE 73; ObitOF 79; ObitT 1971; WhAm 6; WhDW; Who 74; WorAl*

Watt, Douglas Benjamin
American. Composer, Author
Drama critic for *NY Daily News,* 1937-70; contributor, *New Yorker* mag; wrote *After All These Years.*
b. Jan 20, 1914 in New York, New York
Source: *ASCAP 66; NotNAT; OxCAmT 84; WhoAm 86, 90; WhoE 74, 86*

Watt, George Willard
American. Chemist
Worked with Manhattan Project, U of Chicago, 1943-45; with Exxon Nuclear Co., 1970-80.
b. Jan 8, 1911 in Bellaire, Ohio
d. Mar 29, 1980 in Austin, Texas
Source: *AmMWSc 76P, 79; BioIn 10, 12; NewYTBS 80; WhAm 7; WhoAm 74, 76, 78, 80*

Watt, James
Scottish. Engineer, Inventor
Defined unit of power (horsepower) 1783; the watt was named for him.
b. Jan 19, 1736 in Greenock, Scotland
d. Aug 19, 1819 in Heathfield, England
Source: *Alli; AsBiEn; BiDLA; BiESc; BioIn 1, 2, 3, 4, 5, 6, 7, 8, 9, 10, 11, 12, 13, 14, 17, 20; BlkwCE; BlmGEL; CamDcSc; CelCen; DcBiPP; DcInv; DcNaB; DcScB; Dis&D; EncEnl; InSci; LarDcSc; LegTOT; LngCEL; MacEA; McGEWB; NewC; NewCol 75; WebBD 83; WhDW; WorAl; WorAlBi; WorInv*

Watt, James Gaius
American. Government Official
Outspoken secretary of Interior, 1981-83; known for controversial environmental policies.
b. Jan 31, 1938 in Lusk, Wyoming
Source: *BiDrUSE 89; BioIn 12, 13, 14; CurBio 82; DcAmC; EnvEnc; IntWW 81, 82, 83, 89, 91, 93; IntYB 82; NatCAB 63N; NewYTBS 80; WhoAm 76, 78, 80, 82, 84, 86, 88, 90, 92, 94, 95, 96, 97; WhoAmP 73, 75, 77, 79, 83, 85, 87, 89, 91, 93, 95; WhoE 81, 83; WhoGov 72, 75, 77; WhoWor 82*

Watt, Richard Martin
American. Author
Wrote *Dare Call It Treason,* 1963; *The Kings Depart,* 1969.
b. Nov 10, 1930 in Berwyn, Illinois
Source: *ConAu 5R; St&PR 87, 91; WhoE 75, 77, 79*

Watteau, Jean Antoine
French. Artist
Rococo painter; noted for pastel coloring, courtly fantasies: *Embarkation of Cythera,* 1717.
b. Oct 10, 1684 in Valenciennes, France
d. Jul 18, 1721 in Nogent-sur-Marne, France
Source: *AtlBL; BioIn 1, 2, 3, 4, 6, 8, 9, 11, 12, 13, 14, 15, 19; ClaDrA; DcBiPP; DcCathB; Dis&D; EncEnl; McGDA; McGEWB; OxCArt; OxCFr; REn; WhDW; WorAl*

Wattenberg, Ben J
American. Author
Demographer; book *The Good News Is the Bad News Is Wrong,* 1984, says quality of life in all segments of US society is improving.
b. Aug 26, 1933 in New York, New York
Source: *BioIn 14; ConAu 33NR, 57; CurBio 85; WhoAm 86, 90; WhoE 89; WhoUSWr 88; WhoWrEP 89; WrDr 86, 92*

Watterson, Bill
[William B. Watterson, II]
American. Cartoonist
Drew syndicated comic strip "Calvin and Hobbes," 1985-95.
b. 1958?
Source: *Au&Arts 9; BioIn 15, 16, 18; ConAu 134; EncACom; LegTOT; News 90, 90-3; SmATA 66; WhoAm 90, 92, 94, 95, 96, 97; WrDr 94, 96*

Watterson, Henry
"Marse Henry"
American. Newspaper Editor
Editor, *Courier-Journal,* 1868-1918, Louisville; won Pulitzer, 1917.
b. Feb 16, 1840 in Washington, District of Columbia
d. Dec 22, 1921 in Jacksonville, Florida
Source: *Alli SUP; AmAu&B; AmBi; ApCAB, X; BbD; BenetAL 91; BiDAmJo; BiD&SB; BiDConf; BiDrAC; BiDrUSC 89; BiDSA; BioIn 2, 3, 4, 5, 9, 10, 14, 16; DcAmAu; DcAmB; DcLB 25; DcNAA; EncAAH; EncAJ; EncSoH; HarEnUS; JrnUS; LinLib L, S; MorMA; NatCAB 1; OxCAmH; OxCAmL 65, 83, 95; REnAL; SouWr; TwCBDA; WebAB 74, 79; WhAm 1; WhAmP; WhCiWar*

Wattleton, Faye
[Alice Fay Wattleton]
American. Business Executive, Feminist
Pres., Planned Parenthood Federation of America, 1978-92.
b. Aug 7, 1943 in Saint Louis, Missouri
Source: *AmWomM; BioIn 11, 12, 15, 16; BlksScM; BlkWAm; ConBlB 9; ConNews 85-3; CurBio 90; LegTOT; News 89-1; NewYTBS 89; NotBlAW 1; WhoAm 90, 96, 97; WhoAmW 91, 95, 97; WhoBlA 90, 92, 94*

Watts, Alan Wilson
American. Philosopher
Proponent of Eastern philosophy, Western culture; wrote *The Spirit of Zen,* 1936.
b. Jan 6, 1915 in Chislehurst, England
d. Nov 16, 1973 in Mill Valley, California
Source: *AmAu&B; BiDAmCu; BioIn 5, 6, 7, 9, 10, 11, 12, 15, 17, 19; ConAu 41R, 45; CurBio 62, 74; DcAmB S9; DcAmReB 2; EncARH; EncWB; NewYTBE 73; RAdv 14; RelLAm 91; WebAB 74; WhAm 6; WhoAm 74; WhoWor 74; WomWMM; WorAl; WorAu 1950*

Watts, Andre
American. Musician
Internationally famous pianist; played at Nixon's inaugural concert, 1969.
b. Jun 20, 1946 in Nuremberg
Source: *AfrAmAl 6; Baker 78, 84, 92; BiDAfM; BiDAmM; BioIn 6, 8, 9, 10, 11, 12, 13, 14, 15, 16, 21; BioNews 75; BriBkM 80; CelR, 90; CurBio 68; DcTwCCu 1; DrBlPA, 90; Ebony 1; InB&W 80, 85; IntWWM 77, 80, 90; LegTOT; MusSN; NegAl 89; NewAmDM; NewGrDA 86; NewGrDM 80; NewYTBE 71; NewYTBS 88; NotTwCP; PenDiMP; WhoAfA 96; WhoAm 76, 78, 80, 82, 84, 86, 92, 94, 95, 96, 97; WhoAmM 83; WhoBlA 75, 77, 80, 85, 88, 90, 92, 94; WhoE 74; WhoEnt 92; WhoWor 74, 78, 80, 82, 84; WorAl; WorAlBi*

Watts, Charlie
[The Rolling Stones; Charles Robert Watts]
English. Singer, Musician
Drummer, original member of Rolling Stones, 1964—.
b. Jun 2, 1941 in Islington, England
Source: *AllMusG; BioIn 13, 15; LegTOT; WhoAm 80, 82, 84, 86, 88; WhoAmP 89; WhoRocM 82*

Watts, George Frederic
English. Artist, Sculptor
Best known for 19th-c. British portraiture, busts.
b. 1817 in London, England
d. 1904 in London, England
Source: *BioIn 11; DcNaB S2; DcVicP; McGDA; OxDcArt; VicBrit; WhDW*

Watts, Heather
[Linda Heather Watts]
American. Dancer
Member NYC Ballet, 1970-78; soloist, 1978-79; principle ballerina, 1979-95.
b. Sep 27, 1953 in Los Angeles, California
Source: *BiDD; BioIn 13, 14; CurBio 83; IntDcB; InWom SUP; WhoAm 80, 82, 84, 86, 88, 90, 92, 94, 95, 96, 97; WhoAmW 81, 89, 91, 93, 95*

Watts, Isaac
English. Theologian
Best known for hymns: "O God Our Help in Ages Past"; children's songs: "How Doth the Little Busy Bee."
b. Jul 17, 1674 in Southampton, England
d. Nov 25, 1748 in Stoke Poges, England
Source: *Alli; AnCL; BbD; Benet 87, 96; BiD&SB; BioIn 1, 2, 3, 4, 6, 7, 8, 10, 16, 17; BlkwCE; BlmGEL; BritAu; CamGEL; CamGLE; CarSB; CasWL; ChhPo, S1, S2, S3; CnE&AP; DcBiPP; DcEnA; DcEnL; DcEuL; DcLB 95; DcLEL; DcNaB; EncWM; EvLB; LegTOT; LinLib L, S; LngCEL; LuthC 75; NewC; NewCBEL; OxCChiL; OxCEng 67, 85, 95; OxCMus; PenC ENG; PoChrch; REn; SmATA 52; Str&VC; WebE&AL*

Watts, Pete
[Mott (the Hoople)]
"Overend"
English. Musician
Bassist with hard-rock group, 1969-74.
b. May 13, 1947 in Birmingham, England

Watts, Richard, Jr.
American. Critic
Career spanned 40 yrs. for the *NY Herald Tribune, Post.*
b. Jan 12, 1898 in Parkersburg, West Virginia
d. Jan 2, 1981 in New York, New York
Source: *AmAu&B; BiE&WWA; BioIn 12; CamGWoT; ConAmTC; ConAu 102; IntAu&W 82; NewYTBS 81; NotNAT; OxCAmT 84; OxCThe 67; WhoE 74; WhoThe 72, 77*

Watts, Rolonda
American. TV Personality
Host of "Rolonda," a talk show, 1994—
b. Jul 12, 1959 in Winston-Salem, North Carolina
Source: *ConBlB 9*

Watts-Dunton, Theodore
[Walter Theodore Watts-Dunton]
English. Critic, Poet
Benefactor, companion of Swinburne; wrote *Aylwin,* 1898.
b. Oct 12, 1832 in Saint Ives, England
d. Jun 7, 1914 in London, England
Source: *BiD&SB; BioIn 2, 3, 6, 9, 10; BritAu 19; CamGEL; CamGLE; Chambr 3; ChhPo, S1, S2, S3; DcEnA, A; DcEuL; DcLEL; DcNaB 1912; EvLB; LngCTC; MouLC 4; NewC; NewCBEL; NewCol 75; OxCEng 67, 85; PenC ENG; REn; ScF&FL 1; StaCVF*

Waugh, Alec
[Alexander Raban Waugh]
English. Author
Wrote best-seller *Island in the Sun,* 1955; brother of Evelyn Waugh.
b. Jul 8, 1898 in London, England
d. Sep 3, 1981 in Tampa, Florida
Source: *AnObit 1981; Au&Wr 71; BioIn 4, 5, 6, 7, 8, 10, 11, 12; BlueB 76; CamGLE; ConAu 17R, 22NR, 104, X; ConNov 76, 82; DcLEL; DcNaB 1981; EvLB; FacFETw; IntAu&W 76, 77; IntWW 74, 75, 76, 77, 78, 79, 80, 81; LegTOT; LngCTC; MnBBF; ModBrL; NewC; NewCBEL; NewYTBS 81; Novels; OxCEng 85, 95; PenC ENG; RAdv 1; REn; RGTwCWr; TwCA, SUP; TwCWr; WhAm 8; WhE&EA; WhLit; Who 74; WhoWor 74, 76, 78, 80, 82; WorAl; WorAlBi; WrDr 76, 80, 82*

Waugh, Auberon
English. Critic, Author
Writes novels; contributes articles, book reviews for several newspapers; son of Evelyn Waugh.
b. Nov 17, 1939 in Dulverton, England
Source: *Au&Wr 71; Benet 87; BioIn 6, 9, 11, 13, 14, 16; BlueB 76; ConAu 6NR, 22NR, 45; ConLC 7; ConNov 72, 76, 82; CurBio 90; DcLB 14; DcLEL 1940; DcLP 87A; FacFETw; IntAu&W 77, 91; IntvTCA 2; IntWW 83, 91; LegTOT; Who 85, 92; WhoWor 91; WorAu 1975; WrDr 76, 80, 82, 84, 86, 88, 90, 92*

Waugh, Evelyn Arthur St. John
English. Author, Satirist
Wrote *Decline and Fall,* 1928; *Brideshead Revisited,* 1945.
b. Oct 28, 1903 in London, England
d. Apr 10, 1966 in Taunton, England
Source: *AtlBL; CasWL; CathA 1930; CnMWL; ConAu 85; ConLC 1, 3; CyWA 58; DcArts; DcLEL; DcNaB 1961; EncWL; EvLB; FacFETw; GayLL; GrBr; MakMC; McGEWB; ModBrL S1; NewYTBE 73; OxCEng 85, 95; PenC ENG; RfGShF; TwCA SUP; WhAm 4; WorAl*

Waugh, Frederick Judd
American. Artist
Principally painted marine scenes; designed church of St. Mary's of the Harbor, Provincetown, MA.
b. Sep 13, 1861 in Bordentown, New Jersey
d. Sep 11, 1940 in Provincetown, Massachusetts
Source: *BioIn 1, 2, 4, 7, 8; BriEAA; CurBio 40; DcAmB S2; DcSeaP; WhAm 1*

Wauneka, Annie Dodge
American. Native American Leader, Social Reformer
Won Medal of Freedom, 1963, for efforts to improve health services among Navajos.
b. Apr 10, 1910 in Sawmill, Arizona
Source: *BioIn 21; GrLiveH; HerW, 84; InWom SUP; NotNaAm*

Wavell, Archibald Percival Wavell, Earl
English. Military Leader
Commander in chief for Middle East, 1938-41; Viceroy of India, 1943-47.
b. May 5, 1883 in Colchester, England
d. May 24, 1950 in London, England
Source: *BioIn 1, 2, 5, 6, 7, 8, 10, 11, 13, 14; CurBio 41, 50; DcLEL; WhAm 3*

Waxman, Al
Actor
Played Lt. Samuels in TV series "Cagney and Lacey," 1982-88.
b. Mar 2, 1934 in Toronto, Ontario, Canada
Source: *BioIn 15; ConTFT 3*

Waxman, Franz
German. Conductor, Composer
Only composer to receive consecutive Academy Awards for musical scores of *Sunset Boulevard,* 1950; *A Place in the Sun,* 1951.
b. Dec 24, 1906 in Koenigsbutte, Germany
d. Feb 24, 1967 in Los Angeles, California
Source: *ASCAP 66, 80; Baker 78, 84, 92; BioIn 1, 2, 3, 7, 18; CmMov; CmpEPM; ConAmC 76, 82; DcAmB S8; FilmEn; FilmgC; GangFlm; HalFC 80, 84, 88; IntDcF 1-4, 2-4; LegTOT; NewAmDM; NewGrDA 86; NewGrDM 80; OxCPMus; WhAm 4; WorEFlm*

Waxman, Henry Arnold
American. Politician
US Dem. rep. from CA, 1975—.
b. Sep 12, 1939 in Los Angeles, California
Source: *AlmAP 92; BiDrUSC 89; BioIn 13, 15, 16; CngDr 89; CurBio 92; PolsAm 84; WhoAm 78, 80, 82, 84, 86, 88, 90, 92, 94, 95, 96, 97; WhoAmJ 80; WhoAmP 73, 75, 77, 79, 81, 83, 85, 87, 89, 91, 93, 95; WhoE 95; WhoWest 87, 89, 92, 94, 96*

Wayans, Damon
American. Actor, Comedian
Appeared on TV's "In Living Color," 1990-92.
b. 1961 in New York, New York
Source: *ConBlB 8; ConTFT 10; WhoAfA 96; WhoAm 94, 95, 96, 97*

Wayans, Keenen Ivory
American. Comedian, Filmmaker
Writer, director, and star of *I'm Gonna Get You Sucka!,* 1988; TV series "In Living Color," 1990-92; won Emmy Award, 1990.
b. Jun 8, 1958 in New York, New York
Source: *BioIn 16; BlkWr 2; ConAu 140; ConTFT 10; CurBio 95; DcTwCCu 5; IntMPA 92, 94, 96; LegTOT; MiSFD 9; News 91, 91-1; SchCGBL; WhoAm 94, 95, 96, 97; WhoBlA 92; WhoEnt 92; WhoHol 92*

Waybill, Fee
[The Tubes; John Waldo]
American. Singer
Lead singer for The Tubes since late 1960s.
b. Sep 17, 1950 in Omaha, Nebraska
Source: *LegTOT*

Wayland, Francis
American. Clergy, Educator
Pres. of Brown U., 1827-55.
b. Mar 11, 1796 in New York, New York
d. Sep 30, 1865 in Providence, Rhode Island
Source: *Alli; AmAu&B; AmBi; AmPeW; ApCAB; BbD; BiDAmEd; BiD&SB; BiDMoPL; BioIn 6, 16, 19; CyAL 1; CyEd; DcAmAu; DcAmB; DcAmReB 1, 2; DcAmSR; DcAmTB; DcNAA; Drake; HarEnUS; McGEWB; NatCAB 1, 8; TwCBDA; WebAB 74, 79; WhAm HS*

Waymack, W(illiam) W(esley)
American. Editor
Editor of *Des Moines Register, Tribune;* won Pulitzer for editorial writing, 1938.
b. Oct 18, 1888 in Savanna, Illinois
d. Nov 5, 1960 in Des Moines, Iowa
Source: *BioIn 1, 5, 6; ConAu 93; CurBio 47, 61; DcAmB S6; WhAm 4*

Wayman, Dorothy
[Theodate Geoffrey]
American. Author
Wrote on Quaker history, 1960s.
b. Jan 7, 1893 in San Bernardino, California
d. Oct 27, 1975 in Olean, New York
Source: *AmAu&B; BioIn 1, 3, 10, 11; CathA 1952; ConAu 61; PenNWW B; WhAm 6; WhNAA; WhoAm 74*

Wayne, Anthony
"Mad Anthony"
American. Soldier
American Revolutionary General; helped open the Northwest Territory to settlement, 1794.
b. Jan 1, 1745 in Waynesboro, Pennsylvania
d. Dec 15, 1796 in Erie, Pennsylvania
Source: *Alli; AmBi; AmRev; ApCAB; BiAUS; BiDrAC; BiDrUSC 89; BioIn 1, 3, 5, 6, 7, 8, 9, 10, 14, 16; BlkwEAR; CmdGen 1991; DcAmB; DcAmMiB; Drake; EncAAH; EncAB-H 1974, 1996; EncAR; EncCRAm; GenMudB; HarEnMi; HarEnUS; HisWorL; LinLib S; McGEWB; MorMA; NatCAB 1; OxCAmH; REn; REnAL; REnAW; TwCBDA; WebAB 74, 79; WebAMB; WhAm HS; WhAmP; WhAmRev; WhNaAH; WorAl; WorAlBi*

Wayne, Bernie
American. Composer
Composed the beauty contest theme song, "There She Is, Miss America."
d. Apr 18, 1993 in Marina del Rey, California
Source: *BioIn 18, 19; NewYTBS 93*

Wayne, David
[Wayne David McKeeken; Wayne James McMeekan]
American. Actor
Films include *Three Faces of Eve,* 1957; *Front Page,* 1931.
b. Jan 30, 1914 in Traverse City, Michigan
d. Feb 9, 1995 in Santa Monica, California
Source: *BiDFilm; BiE&WWA; BioIn 4, 20, 21; CmpEPM; ConAu 28NR; ConTFT 7, 14; CurBio 56, 95N; EncAFC; EncMT; FilmEn; FilmgC; ForYSC; HalFC 80, 84, 88; IntMPA 88, 92, 94, 96; LegTOT; MotPP; MovMk; News 95, 95-3; NewYTBS 95; NotNAT; OxCAmT 84; PlP&P; VarWW 85; WhoHol 92, A; WhoThe 72, 77, 81; WorAl; WorAlBi; WorEFlm*

Wayne, John
[Marion Robert Morrison]
"Duke"
American. Actor, Director
Biggest box office attraction in Hollywood history; starred in over 200 westerns; won Oscar, 1968, for *True Grit.*
b. May 26, 1907 in Winterset, Iowa
d. Jun 11, 1979 in Los Angeles, California
Source: *BiDFilm, 78, 79; IntWW 74, 75, 76, 77, 78, 79N; ItaFilm; LegTOT; MiSFD 9N; MotPP; MovMk; NewYTBE 72; NewYTBS 79; OxCFilm; RComAH; WebAB 74, 79; WhAm 7; WhoAm 74, 76, 78; WhoHol A; WhoHrs 80; WhoWor 78; WhScrn 83; WorAl; WorAlBi; WorEFlm*

Wayne, Johnny
[Wayne and Shuster]
Canadian. Comedian
Had documentary-style TV show with Frank Shuster, Wayne and Shuster Take an Affectionate Look at., 1966; got first break in US on Ed Sullivan's show, 1950s.
b. May 28, 1918 in Toronto, Ontario, Canada
d. Jul 18, 1990 in Toronto, Ontario, Canada
Source: *AnObit 1990; BioIn 5; CreCan 2; NewYTBS 90*

Wayne, Patrick
American. Actor
Son of John Wayne, appeared with father in several films: *McClintock!,* 1963; leading man in own right, 1970s.
b. Jul 15, 1939 in Los Angeles, California
Source: *BioIn 10, 11, 15; ConTFT 3; FilmEn; FilmgC; HalFC 80, 84, 88; IntMPA 78, 79, 80, 81, 82, 84, 86, 88, 92, 94, 96; ItaFilm; NewYTBE 71; WhoHol 92, A; WhoHrs 80*

Wayne, Paula
American. Actor
Career in theater, TV, films; dubbed voices for over 50 foreign films.
b. Nov 3, 1937 in Hobart, Oklahoma
Source: *BiE&WWA; NotNAT; WhoAm 74*

Wayne and Shuster
[Frank Shuster; Johnny Wayne]
Canadian. Comedy Team
Ed Sullivan first gave them US exposure, 1950s; popular on Canadian radio, TV, 1940s-60s.
Source: *BioIn 17; LesBEnT; NewYTET*

Weatherford, Teddy
American. Jazz Musician
Pianist, leading exponent of "Chicago-style" jazz, 1920s.
b. Oct 11, 1903 in Bluefield, West Virginia
d. Apr 25, 1945 in Calcutta, India
Source: *Baker 84, 92; BiDAfM; BiDAmM; BiDJaz; InB&W 85; LegTOT; NewGrDJ 88, 94; OxCPMus; PenEncP; WhoJazz 72; WorAl; WorAlBi*

Weather Report
[Alejandro Acuna; Alphonso Johnson; Jaco Pastorius; Wayne Shorter; Chester Thompson; Norada Walden; Josef Zawainul]
American. Music Group
Instrumental hit "Birdland," 1978.
Source: *AllMusG; BiDJaz A; BioIn 12, 14, 15, 16, 21; ConMuA 80A; EncJzS; EncRk 88; FacFETw; HarEnR 86; IlEncBM 82; IlEncJ; IlEncRk; LElec; NewAmDM; NewGrDA 86; NewGrDJ 88, 94; NewYTBS 87; OxCPMus; PenEncP; RolSEnR 83; WhoRock 81; WhoRocM 82*

Weathers, Carl
American. Actor
Played Apollo Creed in *Rocky,* 1976; starred in TV's "Street Justice," 1991-92.
b. Jan 14, 1948 in New Orleans, Louisiana
Source: *ConBlB 10; DrBlPA 90; IntMPA 92, 94, 96; WhoHol 92*

Weathers, Felicia
American. Opera Singer
Soprano with Hamburg State Opera, 1966-70; made NY Met. debut, 1965.
b. Aug 13, 1937 in Saint Louis, Missouri
Source: *Baker 84, 92; BiDAfM; BioIn 7, 8, 16; BlkOpe; CmOp; InB&W 85; IntWWM 90; NewEOp 71; PenDiMP; WhoAm 74, 76, 78; WhoAmW 68, 70, 72, 74; WhoWor 74*

Weatherwax, Rudd B
American. Animal Trainer
Most famous pupils were seven male collies who played Lassie in films, TV.
b. 1908?
d. Feb 25, 1985 in Mission Hills, California

Weaver, Dennis
American. Actor
Starred in TV series "Gunsmoke," 1955-64; "McCloud," 1970-77; "Buck James," 1985-87.
b. Jun 4, 1925 in Joplin, Missouri

Source: *BioIn 9, 10, 11, 12, 15; ConTFT 3; CurBio 77; FilmgC; HalFC 84, 88; IntMPA 75, 76, 77, 78, 79, 80, 81, 82, 84, 86, 88, 92, 94, 96; MotPP; MovMk; NewAgE 90; VarWW 85; WhoAm 86, 90; WhoEnt 92; WhoHol 92, A; WorAlBi*

Weaver, Doodles
[Winstead Sheffield Glendening Dixon Weaver]
American. Actor
Played hayseed comedic roles in over 60 films, 1930s-40s; appeared with Spike Jones band as Professor Feedelbaum, 1948-51.
b. May 11, 1914 in Los Angeles, California
d. Jan 15, 1983 in Burbank, California
Source: *BioIn 10, 13; EncAFC; ForYSC; JoeFr; NewYTBS 83; What 4; WhoHol A*

Weaver, Earl Sidney
American. Baseball Manager
Manager, Baltimore, 1968-82, 1985-86; won four pennants, one World Series; admitted to Baseball Hall of Fame, 1996.
b. Aug 14, 1930 in Saint Louis, Missouri
Source: *Ballpl 90; BiDAmSp BB; BioIn 10, 12, 13, 14, 15, 16; ConAu 116; CurBio 83; WhoAm 74, 76, 78, 80, 82, 84, 86; WhoE 81; WhoProB 73; WorAl; WorAlBi*

Weaver, Fritz William
American. Actor
Won Tony for *Child's Play,* 1970.
b. Jan 19, 1926 in Pittsburgh, Pennsylvania
Source: *BiE&WWA; CamGWoT; ConTFT 8; CurBio 67; FilmgC; HalFC 88; IntMPA 84, 92; NotNAT; OxCAmT 84; WhoAm 74, 76, 78, 80, 82, 84, 86, 88, 92, 94, 95, 96, 97; WhoEnt 92; WhoHol A; WhoThe 81; WorAl; WorAlBi*

Weaver, James Baird
American. Politician
Unsuccessful presidential candidate, 1880, 1892.
b. Jun 12, 1833 in Dayton, Ohio
d. Feb 6, 1913 in Des Moines, Iowa
Source: *AmBi; AmPolLe; ApCAB; BiDrAC; BiDrUSC 89; BioIn 8; CivWDc; DcAmB; DcNAA; EncAAH; EncAB-H 1974, 1996; McGEWB; NatCAB 11, 16; NewCol 75; OhA&B; OxCAmH; REnAL; REnAW; TwCBDA; WebAB 74, 79; WhAm 1; WhAmP*

Weaver, Mike
[Michael Dwayne Weaver]
American. Boxer
Won 1980 WBA heavyweight title.
b. Jun 4, 1952 in Gatesville, Texas
Source: *BioIn 13, 15; InB&W 85; IntWW 91; NewYTBS 79; WhoAm 82*

Weaver, Robert C(lifton)
American. Government Official
First secretary of HUD, 1966-69; first black US cabinet member.
b. Dec 29, 1907 in Washington, District of Columbia
d. Jul 17, 1997 in New York, New York
Source: *AmMWSc 73S; AmPolLe; BiDrUSE 71, 89; BioIn 5, 6, 7, 8, 9, 10, 11, 15, 20; BlkWrNE A; BlueB 76; ConAu 9R; CurBio 61; EncAB-H 1974, 1996; EncSoH; FacFETw; InB&W 80, 85; IntWW 83, 91; IntYB 82; OxCAmH; PeoHis; PolProf J, K; SelBAAf; SelBAAu; WebAB 74, 79; WhoAm 74, 76, 78, 80, 82, 86, 88, 90, 92, 94; WhoAmP 73, 75, 77, 79, 81, 83, 85, 87, 89, 91, 93, 95; WhoBlA 85, 92; WhoE 74; WorAlBi*

Weaver, Sigourney
[Susan Weaver]
American. Actor
Starred in *Alien,* 1979; *Ghostbusters,* 1984; *Working Girl,* 1988.
b. Oct 8, 1949 in New York, New York
Source: *BiDFilm 94; BioIn 14, 15, 16; CelR 90; ConTFT 3, 10; CurBio 89; EncAFC; HalFC 84, 88; HolBB; IntDcF 2-3; IntMPA 86, 88, 92, 94, 96; IntWW 89, 91, 93; JohnWSW; LegTOT; News 88-3; NewYTBS 86; VarWW 85; WhoAm 88, 90, 92, 94, 95, 96, 97; WhoAmW 89, 91, 93, 95, 97; WhoEnt 92; WhoHol 92; WhoHrs 80; WorAlBi*

Weaver, Thomas
American. Anthropologist, Author
Professor of anthropology, U of AZ, 1975—; writings include *Mexican Migration,* 1976.
b. May 1, 1929 in Grenville, New Mexico
Source: *AmMWSc 73S, 76P; ConAu 13NR, 61; FifIDA; WhoAm 80, 82, 84; WhoUSWr 88; WhoWest 74, 76, 78, 80, 82; WhoWrEP 89, 92, 95*

Weaver, William
American. Translator, Journalist
Award-winning translator of Italian prose.
b. Jul 24, 1923 in Washington, District of Columbia
Source: *Au&Wr 71; BioIn 14, 16, 18; ConAu 112, 116; WhoAm 74, 76; WhoWor 74*

Weavers, The
[Erik Darling; Lee Hays; Fred Hellerman; Bernie Krause; Pete Seeger]
American. Music Group
Popular folk group, 1948-63; hits include ''On Top of Old Smoky,'' 1951; ''Good Night Irene,'' 1950; pioneered in making folk music commercially successful.
Source: *AmPS A, B; BiDAmM; BioIn 12, 14, 15, 16, 17, 18, 19, 20, 21; BioNews 74; ConMus 8; CurBio 63; EncFCWM 69, 83; EncRk 88; FacFETw; NewAmDM; NewGrDA 86; NewYTBS 80, 81; OxCPMus; PenEncP; PeoHis; RkOn 74, 78; RolSEnR 83; WhoHol 92*

Webb, Beatrice Potter
[Mrs. Sidney James Webb]
English. Sociologist
Collaborated with husband on many books: *The Truth about Soviet Russia,* 1942.
b. Jan 22, 1858 in Gloucester, England
d. Apr 30, 1943 in Liphook, England
Source: *BioIn 14, 15, 16, 17, 18, 19, 21; BlmGWL; CurBio 43; DcAmSR; DcLEL; EncBrWW; EvLB; InWom SUP; LngCTC; McGEWB; NewC; OxCEng 67, 95; PenNWW A; TwCA SUP; VicBrit; WomFir*

Webb, Chick
[William Webb]
American. Jazz Musician
Drummer, bandleader, 1920s-30s; noted for ''Stompin' at the Savoy''; introduced Ella Fitzgerald.
b. Feb 10, 1902 in Baltimore, Maryland
d. Jun 16, 1939 in Baltimore, Maryland
Source: *BgBands 74; BiDAmM; BiDJaz; BioIn 6, 9, 10, 12; CmpEPM; IlEncJ; NewGrDM 80; WhoJazz 72*

Webb, Clifton
[Webb Parmelee Hollenbeck]
American. Actor
Oscar nominee for *Laura,* 1944; *Razor's Edge,* 1946.
b. Nov 19, 1891 in Indianapolis, Indiana
d. Oct 13, 1966 in Beverly Hills, California
Source: *BiDD; BiDFilm, 94; BiE&WWA; CmpEPM; CurBio 43, 66; EncAFC; EncMT; FacFETw; FilmEn; FilmgC; Funs; HalFC 84; IntDcF 1-3, 2-3; LegTOT; MotPP; MovMk; OxCPMus; WhAm 4; WhScrn 77; WorAl; WorEFlm*

Webb, Jack Randolph
[John Farr; Tex Grady]
American. Director, Author
Played Sgt. Joe Friday on Emmy-winning TV series ''Dragnet,'' 1952-59, 1967-70; also produced ''Adam 12,'' 1968-75.
b. Apr 2, 1920 in Santa Monica, California
d. Dec 23, 1982 in Los Angeles, California
Source: *AnObit 1982; ConAu 108; ConTFT 1; CurBio 55, 83N; FilmgC; HalFC 84; IntMPA 82; LesBEnT; MotPP; NewYTBS 82; OxCFilm; WhAm 8; WhoAm 82; WhoHol A; WhoWest 74; WorEFlm*

Webb, James Edwin
American. Government Official
NASA administrator, 1961-68.
b. Oct 7, 1906 in Granville City, North Carolina
d. Mar 27, 1992 in Washington, District of Columbia
Source: *AmMWSc 73S, 78S; BioIn 1, 2, 3, 5, 6, 7, 8, 11; BlueB 76; FacFETw; IntWW 74, 75, 76, 77, 78, 79, 80, 81, 82, 83; WhAm 10; WhoAm 74, 76, 78, 80, 82; WhoSSW 73; WrDr 90*

Webb, James H(enry), Jr.
American. Government Official
Secretary of Navy, 1987-88; novels on Vietnam War include *Fields of Fire,* 1978; *A Sense of Honor,* 1981.
b. Feb 9, 1946 in Saint Joseph, Missouri
Source: *BioIn 15, 16; ConAu 81; ConLC 22; CurBio 87; IntWW 91; NewYTBS 83, 87; WhoAm 88; WhoAmP 91; WhoWor 89*

Webb, Jim
American. Composer
Wrote songs "Up, Up, and Away," 1967; "MacArthur Park," 1968; "Galveston," 1969.
b. Aug 15, 1946 in Elk City, Oklahoma
Source: *BioIn 8, 13, 14; CelR, 90; EncPR&S 89; EncRk 88; NewAmDM; OxCPMus; PenEncP*

Webb, Sidney James
[Baron Passfield]
English. Political Leader
Among founders of Fabian Society, 1885; wrote many books with wife, Beatrice.
b. Jul 13, 1859 in London, England
d. Oct 13, 1947 in Liphook, England
Source: *BbD; BiD&SB; DcAmSR; DcLEL; DcNaB 1941; DcTwHis; EvLB; GrBr; LngCTC; MakMC; McGEWB; NewC; NewCBEL; OxCEng 67; TwCA, SUP; VicBrit; WebBD 83; WhE&EA; WhoEc 81, 86; WorAl; WorAlBi*

Webb, Spud
[Anthony Jerome Webb]
American. Basketball Player
Guard, Atlanta, 1985—; one of shortest players (5ft. 7in.) in NBA; slam-dunk winner, 1986.
b. Jul 13, 1963 in Dallas, Texas
Source: *BasBi; BioIn 13, 14, 15, 16; NewYTBS 86; OfNBA 87; WhoAfA 96; WhoBlA 92*

Webb, Veronica
American. Model, Actor
Films include *Jungle Fever,* 1991 and *Malcolm X,* 1993; spokesperson for Revlon.
b. Dec 25, 1965 in Detroit, Michigan
Source: *ConBlB 10; WhoAm 95, 96, 97; WhoAmW 95; WhoWor 97*

Webb, Walter Prescott
American. Author
Writings include *More Water for Texas,* 1954.
b. Apr 3, 1888 in Panola County, Texas
d. Mar 8, 1963 in Austin, Texas
Source: *AmAu&B; BenetAL 91; BioIn 3, 4, 5, 6, 7, 8, 9, 10, 11, 13, 14, 16; ConAu 113; DcAmB S7; DcLB 17; EncAB-A 36; NatCAB 51; OxCAmL 65, 83, 95; RAdv 14; REnAL; REnAW; TexWr; WhAm 4; WhE&EA*

Webb, Wellington
American. Politician
Mayor Denver, CO, 1991—.
b. Feb 17, 1941 in Chicago, Illinois
Source: *BioIn 11, 14; ConBlB 3; WhoAmP 91; WhoBlA 92; WhoWest 92*

Webb, William Seward
American. Railroad Executive
Pres. of Mohawk and Malone railroad.
b. Jan 31, 1851 in New York, New York
d. Oct 29, 1926
Source: *ApCAB SUP; DcAmAu; DcNAA; NatCAB 1; TwCBDA; WhAm 1*

Webber, Chris
[Mayce Edward Christopher Webber]
American. Basketball Player
Drafted by Orlando, 1993; forward, Golden State, 1993-94; Washington, 1994—.
b. Mar 1, 1973 in Detroit, Michigan
Source: *News 94, 94-1; WhoAfA 96; WhoAm 97; WhoBlA 94*

Weber, Carl
Director
Has directed for stage, TV, all over the world; won Obie Award, 1973, for *Kaspar.*
b. Aug 7, 1925 in Dortmund, Germany
Source: *ConTFT 3*

Weber, Carl Maria von
German. Composer
Founder, German Romantic school; wrote operas *Der Freischutz,* 1821; *Oberon,* 1826.
b. Nov 18, 1786 in Eutin, Denmark
d. Jun 5, 1826 in London, England
Source: *AtlBL; Baker 84; BioIn 14, 16; BriBkM 80; CmOp; CmpBCM; CnOxB; DancEn 78; DcCom 77; DcCom&M 79; DcPup; GrComp; MetOEnc; MusMk; NewAmDM; NewCol 75; NewEOp 71; NewGrDM 80; NewOxM; OxCEng 67, 85, 95; OxCGer 76; OxDcOp; PenDiMP A; WebBD 83; WorAl; WorAlBi*

Weber, Dick
[Richard Anthony Weber]
American. Bowler
Only pro bowler to win PBA titles in four decades; PBA Hall of Fame; father of Pete Weber.
b. Dec 23, 1929 in Indianapolis, Indiana
Source: *BiDAmSp BK; BioIn 8, 9, 10, 14, 15; CurBio 70; NewYTBS 85; WhoSpor; WhoWor 74*

Weber, Ernst
American. Engineer
Research in microwave technology helped in the production of microwave communications equipment.
b. Sep 6, 1901 in Vienna, Austria
d. Feb 15, 1996 in Columbus, South Carolina
Source: *AmMWSc 73P, 79, 82, 86, 89, 92, 95; BioIn 3, 4, 5, 8, 21; BlueB 76; IntWW 74, 75, 76, 77, 78, 79, 80, 81, 82, 83, 89; LElec; McGMS 80; WhAm 11; WhoAm 74, 76, 88, 90, 92, 94, 95, 96; WhoEng 80, 88*

Weber, Joseph M
[Weber and Fields]
American. Comedian
Formed comedy team with Lewis Fields, 1895-1904; reunited to play in *Roly Poly,* 1912.
b. Aug 11, 1867 in New York, New York
d. May 10, 1942 in Los Angeles, California
Source: *BiDAmM; CurBio 42; DcAmB S3; FamA&A; OxCThe 67; REnAL; WhAm 2; WhoStg 1908*

Weber, Lois
American. Actor, Director, Screenwriter
First woman film director, early 1900s.
b. Jun 13, 1881 in Allegheny, California
d. Nov 13, 1939 in Los Angeles, California
Source: *GrLiveH; IntDcWB; InWom SUP; LibW; NotAW; WhAm 1; WomFir*

Weber, Max
German. Sociologist, Author
Rejected Marx's economic determinism, concentrating on religious roots of modern institutions.
b. Apr 21, 1864 in Erfurt, Prussia
d. Jun 14, 1920 in Munich, Germany
Source: *Benet 87, 96; BiDPsy; BioIn 1, 2, 4, 5, 7, 8, 9, 10, 11, 12, 13, 14, 15, 16, 17, 18; CasWL; ConAu 109; CyWA 89; DcSoc; EncEth; FacFETw; GrEconB; IlEncMy; LegTOT; LuthC 75; MakMC; McGEWB; NamesHP; NewCol 75; NewGrDM 80; OxCGer 76, 86; OxCLaw; RAdv 14, 13-3; REn; ThTwC 87; TwCA SUP; WhDW; WhoEc 81, 86; WorAl; WorAlBi*

Weber, Max
American. Artist, Author
Social themes depicted in *Chinese Restaurant.*
b. Apr 18, 1881 in Bialystok, Russia
d. Oct 4, 1961 in Great Neck, New York
Source: *AmAu&B; AtlBL; Benet 87, 96; BioIn 1, 2, 4, 5, 6, 9, 10, 11, 12, 14, 17; BriEAA; ConArt 83; DcAmArt; DcAmB S7; DcArts; DcCAA 71, 77, 88, 94; McGDA; McGEWB; OxCAmH; OxCArt; OxCTwCA; OxDcArt; PhDcTCA 77; REn; REnAL; WebAB 74, 79; WhAm 4; WhAmArt 85; WhoAmA 78N, 80N, 82N, 84N, 86N, 89N, 91N, 93N; WorArt 1950*

Weber, Pete(r)
American. Bowler
Son of Dick; pro bowler, 1979—; one of tour's money leaders.
b. Aug 21, 1962 in Saint Louis, Missouri
Source: *BioIn 14, 15, 16; ConNews 86-3; NewYTBS 85; St&PR 91; WhoSpor*

Weber, Robert Maxwell
American. Cartoonist
With *New Yorker* mag. since 1962; contributor of cartoons to US newspapers.
b. Apr 22, 1924 in Los Angeles, California

Source: *WhoAm 82, 84, 86, 88, 90, 92, 94, 95, 96, 97*

Weber, Wilhelm Eduard
German. Physicist
Devised an electromagnetic telegraph.
b. Oct 24, 1804 in Wittenberg, Germany
d. Jun 23, 1891 in Gottingen, Germany
Source: *AsBiEn; BiESc; BioIn 8, 12, 14; DcScB; InSci; LarDcSc; LinLib S; NewCol 75; WebBD 83*

Weber and Fields
[Lew Fields; Joseph Weber]
American. Comedy Team
Began theatrical co., 1885; managed Broadway Music Hall, 1895-1904; shows include *Roly Poly,* 1912.
Source: *CamGWoT; CurBio 41; EncAFC; EncVaud; FacFETw; ObitOF 79; OxCPMus; OxCThe 67, 83; REn; WebBD 83; WhoHol 92; WhoTech 82*

Webern, Anton Friedrich Ernst von
Austrian. Composer
Pupil of Schoenberg; works banned by Nazis, 1933, as "cultural Bolshevism."
b. Dec 3, 1883 in Vienna, Austria
d. Sep 15, 1945 in Mittersill, Austria
Source: *AtlBL; CompSN SUP; DcCM; MakMC; NewCol 75; WhAm 4; WhDW; WorAl*

Webster, Ben(jamin)
English. Actor
Movies include *Mrs. Miniver,* 1942; *Lassie Come Home,* 1943; father of Margaret Webster.
b. Jun 2, 1864 in London, England
d. Feb 26, 1947 in Hollywood, California
Source: *BioIn 1, 5, 10; DcNaB 1941; Film 1, 2; HalFC 80, 84, 88; IlWWBF; NotNAT A, B; ObitOF 79; OxCThe 67; WhoHol B; WhScrn 74, 77, 83; WhThe*

Webster, Daniel
American. Orator, Statesman
Senator from MA, 1820s-50s; noted for brilliant constitutional speeches; secretary of state, 1850-52.
b. Jan 18, 1782 in Salisbury, New Hampshire
d. Oct 24, 1852 in Marshfield, Massachusetts
Source: *Alli; AmAu; AmAu&B; AmBi; AmOrN; AmPolLe; ApCAB; BbD; Benet 87, 96; BenetAL 91; BiAUS; BiD&SB; BiDrAC; BiDrUSC 89; BiDrUSE 71, 89; BiDTran; BioIn 1, 2, 3, 4, 5, 7, 8, 9, 10, 11, 12, 13, 14, 15, 16, 17, 20; CelCen; Chambr 3; ChhPo, S1; CyAG; CyAL 1; DcAmAu; DcAmB; DcAmC; DcAmDH 80, 89; DcAmSR; DcBiPP; DcLEL; DcNAA; Dis&D; Drake; EncAAH; EncAB-H 1974, 1996; EvLB; HarEnUS; HisWorL; LegTOT; LinLib L, S; McGEWB; MemAm; NatCAB 3; OxCAmH; OxCAmL 65, 83; OxCEng 85, 95; OxCSupC; PenC AM; PolPar; PresAR; RAdv 13-3; RComAH; REn; REnAL; TwCBDA; WebAB 74, 79; WhAm HS; WhAmP; WhCiWar; WorAl; WorAlBi*

Webster, H(arold) T(ucker)
American. Cartoonist
Newspaper cartoonist known for "The Timid Soul," its character Caspar Milquetoast.
b. Sep 21, 1885 in Parkersburg, West Virginia
d. Sep 22, 1952 in Stamford, Connecticut
Source: *AmAu&B; BioIn 1, 2, 3, 5; CurBio 45, 52; DcAmB S5; ObitOF 79; REnAL; WhAm 3; WhAmArt 85; WorECom*

Webster, Jean
American. Author
Wrote *Daddy Long-Legs,* 1912.
b. Jul 24, 1876 in Fredonia, New York
d. Jun 11, 1916 in New York, New York
Source: *AmAu&B; AmWomPl; AmWomWr; BenetAL 91; BioIn 8, 12, 14; BlmGWL; CarSB; ChhPo, S3; ChlBkCr; CnDAL; DcAmB; DcNAA; EvLB; InWom SUP; JBA 34; LibW; LngCTC; NotAW; NotNAT B; OxCAmL 65, 83, 95; REn; REnAL; TwCA; TwCChW 83, 89, 95; TwCRGW; TwCRHW 90, 94; TwCWr; WhAm 1; WhoChL; WomWWA 14*

Webster, John
English. Dramatist
Wrote *The White Devil,* 1612; *The Duchess of Malfi,* 1613.
b. 1580? in London, England
d. 1634?
Source: *AtlBL; Benet 87, 96; BiD&SB; BioIn 2, 3, 4, 5, 7, 8, 9, 11, 12, 16, 18, 19; BritAu; BritWr 2; CamGEL; CamGLE; CamGWoT; CasWL; ChhPo; CnDBLB 1; CnE&AP; CnThe; CroE&S; CrtT 1, 4; CyWA 58; DcArts; DcEnA; DcEnL; DcEuL; DcLEL; DcNaB; DramC 2; EncWT; Ent; EvLB; GrWrEL DR; LinLib L, S; LitC 33; LngCEL; McGEWB; McGEWD 72, 84; MouLC 1; NewC; NewCBEL; NotNAT A, B; OxCEng 67; OxCThe 67, 83; PenC ENG; PlP&P; RAdv 14, 13-2; REn; REnWD; WebE&AL; WhDW; WorLitC*

Webster, Margaret
American. Actor, Director
Revived Shakespeare on Broadway stage, 1930s-40s; daughter of May Whitty.
b. Mar 15, 1905 in New York, New York
d. Nov 13, 1972 in London, England
Source: *AmAu&B; BiE&WWA; BioIn 1, 2, 8, 9, 10, 12, 16, 17, 19, 20; CamGWoT; CnThe; ConAu 37R; CurBio 40, 50, 73, 73N; DcAmB S9; GrStDi; InWom, SUP; MetOEnc; NewYTBE 72; NotAW MOD; NotNAT A, B; NotWoAT; ObitT 1971; OxCAmT 84; OxCThe 67, 83; REn; TheaDir; WhAm 5; WhoAmW 58, 64, 66, 68, 70, 72, 74; WhoThe 72, 77; WhScrn 77, 83*

Webster, Mike
[Michael Lewis Webster]
American. Football Player
Eight-time all-pro center, Pittsburgh, 1974-88; KC Chiefs, 1989-90; won four Super Bowls.
b. Mar 18, 1952 in Tomahawk, Wisconsin
Source: *BiDAmSp FB; BioIn 12, 14, 15; FootReg 87; NewYTBS 80, 85*

Webster, Noah
American. Lexicographer, Author
Compiled *American Dictionary of the English Language,* 1828; his work helped standardize American pronunciation.
b. Oct 16, 1758 in West Hartford, Connecticut
d. May 28, 1843 in New Haven, Connecticut
Source: *ABCMeAm; Alli; AmAu; AmAu&B; AmBi; AmRef; AmSocL; AmWrBE; ApCAB; BbD; Benet 87, 96; BenetAL 91; BiDAmEd; BiDAmJo; BiD&SB; BiInAmS; BioIn 1, 2, 3, 4, 5, 6, 7, 8, 9, 10, 11, 12, 13, 14, 15, 16, 17, 19, 20; BlkwCE; BlkwEAR; CasWL; CelCen; ChhPo S3; CnDAL; CyAL 1; CyEd; DcAmAu; DcAmB; DcAmMeB, 84; DcBiPP; DcEnL; DcInv; DcLB 1, 37, 42, 43, 73; DcLEL; DcNAA; Dis&D; Drake; EncAB-H 1974, 1996; EncCRAm; EvLB; HarEnUS; JrnUS; LegTOT; LinLib L, S; McGEWB; MemAm; MouLC 3; NatCAB 2; NinCLC 30; OxCAmH; OxCAmL 65, 83, 95; OxCEng 67, 85, 95; PenC AM; REn; REnAL; TwCBDA; WebAB 74, 79; WebE&AL; WhAm HS; WhDW; WorAl; WorAlBi*

Webster, Paul Francois
American. Lyricist
Wrote over 500 songs including Oscar-winning "Shadow of Your Smile," 1965.
b. Dec 20, 1907 in New York, New York
d. Mar 22, 1984 in Beverly Hills, California
Source: *AmPS; BiE&WWA; ConAu 112; VarWW 85; WhoAm 82*

Webster, William Hedgcock
American. Government Official
FBI director, 1978-87; director, CIA, 1987-91.
b. Mar 6, 1924 in Saint Louis, Missouri
Source: *BiDFedJ A; BioIn 11, 12, 14, 15, 16; EncAI&E; IntWW 78, 79, 80, 81, 82, 83, 89, 91, 93; NewYTBS 78, 87, 88; WhoAm 74, 76, 78, 80, 82, 84, 86, 88, 90, 92, 94, 95, 96, 97; WhoAmL 79, 83, 85, 87; WhoAmP 91; WhoE 95; WhoGov 77; WhoMW 74, 76; WorAlBi*

Wechsberg, Joseph
American. Author, Journalist
Wrote for *The New Yorker,* 1938-75.
b. Aug 29, 1907 in Ostrava, Czechoslovakia
d. Apr 10, 1983 in Vienna, Austria

Source: *AmAu&B; Au&Wr 71; BenetAL 91; BiGAW; BioIn 1, 3, 4, 9, 10, 12, 13; BlueB 76; ConAu 34NR, 105, 109; CurBio 55, 83N; EncAJ; EncTwCJ; NewYTBS 83; OxCAmL 65, 83, 95; REnAL; WhAm 8; WhE&EA; WhoAm 74, 76, 78, 80, 82; WhoMus 72; WhoWor 74, 76; WrDr 80, 82, 84*

Wechsler, David
American. Psychologist
Wrote popular intelligence test.
b. Jan 12, 1896 in Lespedi, Romania
d. May 2, 1981 in New York, New York
Source: *AmMWSc 73S; BiDPsy; BioIn 12, 13, 15; ConAu 103; IntEnSS 79; RAdv 14; WhAm 7; WhoAm 74, 76; WhoWorJ 72*

Wechsler, James Arthur
American. Author, Journalist
Columnist, editor, *New York Post.*
b. Oct 31, 1915 in New York, New York
d. Sep 11, 1983 in New York, New York
Source: *AmAu&B; AnObit 1983; BiDAmNC; BioIn 1, 3, 6, 9, 11, 13; ConAu 101; IntWW 74; NewYTBS 83; WhAm 8; WhoAm 82; WhoE 74; WhoWor 74; WhoWorJ 72*

Weddell, James
English. Explorer
Made voyage to S Pole, 1822-24; sea named after him.
b. Aug 24, 1787 in Ostend, Austria
d. Sep 9, 1834 in London, England
Source: *Alli; BioIn 14; DcNaB; NewCol 75; OxCShps; WhDW; WhWE; WorAl; WorAlBi*

Wedekind, Frank
German. Dramatist
Expressionist, social critic; plays on sexual issues include *Pandora's Box,* 1918; play's character, Lulu, subject of Alban Berg's opera, *Lulu,* 1934.
b. Jul 24, 1864 in Hannover, Hannover
d. Mar 9, 1918 in Munich, Germany
Source: *AtlBL; Benet 87, 96; BioIn 1, 2, 5, 7, 8, 10, 15, 18; CamGWoT; CasWL; ClDMEL 47, 80; CnMD; CnThe; ConAu 104; CyWA 58; DcArts; EncWL 2, 3; EncWT; Ent; EuWr 8; EvEuW; GrFLW; LinLib L, S; LngCTC; MajMD 1; McGEWB; McGEWD 72, 84; ModGL; ModWD; NewEOp 71; NotNAT A, B; OxCGer 76, 86; OxCThe 67, 83; PenC EUR; RAdv 14, 13-2; REn; REnWD; TwCA, SUP; TwCLC 7; TwCWr; WhDW; WhoTwCL*

Wedemeyer, Albert Coady
American. Military Leader
Army general, military planner; originated WW II "Victory Program," which eventually led to invasion of Normandy, June 1944.
b. Jul 9, 1897 in Omaha, Nebraska
d. Dec 17, 1989 in Fort Belvoir, Virginia
Source: *BiDWWGF; BioIn 1, 2, 3, 5, 9, 11, 13, 14, 16; ConAu 130; CurBio 45, 90, 90N; DcAmMiB; FacFETw; NewYTBS 89; PeoHis; PolProf T; WebAMB; WhAm 10; WhoAm 76, 78, 80, 82, 84, 86, 88; WhoWor 74, 76, 78; WhWW-II*

Wedgwood, C(icely) V(eronica)
English. Historian
Speicalist in 17th century British history; wrote *The Thirty Years War,* 1938.
b. Jul 20, 1910
d. Mar 9, 1997 in London, England
Source: *Benet 87; BioIn 4, 16, 17; CamGEL; CamGLE; ConAu 21NR, 105; DcLEL; EncWB; IntAu&W 76, 77, 91, 93; IntWW 74, 75, 78, 83, 89; LngCTC; MajTwCW; ModBrL; NewCBEL; REn; WhE&EA; Who 74, 82, 83, 85, 88, 90, 92; WhoAm 74; WhoAmW 68, 70, 72; WhoWor 74, 76, 78; WrDr 76, 80, 82, 84, 86, 88, 90, 92, 94, 96*

Wedgwood, Josiah
English. Artist
Founded firm, 1759; invented translucent, unglazed semiporcelain called jasper ware.
b. Jul 12, 1730 in Burslem, England
d. Jan 3, 1795 in Etruria, England
Source: *Alli; AntBDN M; BioIn 1, 2, 3, 4, 5, 6, 7, 9, 10, 11, 12, 14, 15, 20, 21; BlmGEL; DcArts; DcBiPP; DcD&D; DcInv; DcNaB; DcScB; Dis&D; EncEnl; EncWM; Entr; LegTOT; LinLib S; McGDA; McGEWB; NewC; NewCol 75; OxCDecA; OxCEng 85, 95; OxDcArt; PenDiDA 89; WhDW; WorAl; WorAlBi*

Wedgwood, Thomas
English. Photographer
Credited with inventing several photographic processes; never able to make an image permanent; son of Josiah.
b. May 14, 1771 in Stoke-on-Trent, England
d. Jul 11, 1805
Source: *BioIn 4, 10; BlmGEL; CamDcSc; DcBiPP; DcNaB; ICPEnP; MacBEP*

Weed, Steven Andrew
American. Educator
Fiance of Patty Hearst at time of abduction by SLA; wrote *My Search for Patty Hearst,* 1976.
b. 1947
Source: *BioIn 10*

Weed, Thurlow
American. Journalist, Politician
Influential newspaper owner, head of NY state Whig party; helped elect Rep. presidential candidates, 1840s-50s.
b. Nov 15, 1797 in Cairo, New York
d. Nov 22, 1882 in New York, New York
Source: *ABCMeAm; Alli, SUP; AmAu&B; AmBi; ApCAB; BbD; BenetAL 91; BiDAmJo; BiD&SB; BioIn 1, 8, 9, 14, 16, 17; CyAG; DcAmAu; DcAmB; DcNAA; Drake; EncAB-H 1974, 1996; EncAJ; HarEnUS; JrnUS; LinLib L; McGEWB; NatCAB 3; OxCAmH; PolPar; REnAL; TwCBDA; WebAB 74, 79; WhAm HS; WhCiWar*

Weede, Robert
American. Singer
Baritone with NY Met., San Francisco Opera; starred in Broadway's *Most Happy Fella,* 1956; Tony nominee for *Cry for Us All,* 1970.
b. Feb 22, 1903 in Baltimore, Maryland
d. Jul 10, 1972 in Walnut Creek, California
Source: *BiDAmM; BiE&WWA; BioIn 1, 4, 9; CurBio 57, 72, 72N; DcAmB S9; EncMT; MetOEnc; NewGrDA 86; NewGrDO; NewYTBE 72; NotNAT B*

Weeks, Sinclair
American. Government Official
Secretary of Commerce, 1953-58, under Eisenhower.
b. Jun 15, 1893 in West Newton, Massachusetts
d. Jan 27, 1972 in Concord, Massachusetts
Source: *BiDrAC; BiDrUSC 89; BiDrUSE 71, 89; BioIn 3, 4, 5, 9, 10, 11; CurBio 53, 72, 72N; DcAmB S9; LinLib S; NewYTBE 72; ObitOF 79; PolProf E; WhAm 5; WhAmP*

Weems, Ted
[Wilfred Theodore Weems]
American. Bandleader
Led popular dance style band, late 1920s-40s; wrote "The Martins and the Coys," 1930s.
b. 1900 in Pitcairn, Pennsylvania
d. May 6, 1963 in Tulsa, Oklahoma
Source: *ASCAP 66; BioIn 6, 9; WhoHol B; WhScrn 74, 77*

Wegener, Alfred Lothar
German. Geologist, Explorer
Expert on Greenland who was one of first to propose continental drift theory, 1910.
b. Nov 1, 1880 in Berlin, Germany
d. Nov 1930, Greenland
Source: *AsBiEn; BiESc; BioIn 10, 12, 14, 15, 20; DcScB; FacFETw; InSci; LarDcSc; McGEWB; WhDW; WhWE*

Wegman, William George
American. Artist
Known for work in photography of dogs detailing the dog's innate dignity contrasted with human consumerism.
b. Feb 12, 1942 in Holyoke, Massachusetts
Source: *AmArt; BioIn 13, 16; ConArt 89; ConPhot 88; CurBio 92; ICPEnP A; News 91-1; PrintW 85; WhoAm 90; WhoAmA 91; WhoArt 80*

Wehrwein, Austin Carl
American. Journalist
With *Minneapolis Star,* 1966-82; won 1953 Pulitzer for int'l. reporting.
b. Jan 12, 1916 in Austin, Texas

Source: *ConAu 77; EncTwCJ; WhoAm 74, 76, 78, 80, 82, 84, 86, 88, 90; WhoMW 93, 96*

Weicker, Lowell Palmer, Jr.
American. Politician
Independent governor of CT, 1991—; Republican US senator, 1971-89.
b. May 16, 1931 in Paris, France
Source: *AlmAP 92; BiDrAC; BiDrUSC 89; BioIn 9, 10, 11, 13, 15; BlueB 76; CngDr 87; CurBio 74, 93; IntWW 74, 75, 76, 77, 78, 79, 80, 81, 82, 83, 89, 91, 93; News 93-1; NewYTBS 90, 91; PolsAm 84; WhoAm 74, 76, 78, 80, 82, 84, 86, 88, 92, 94, 95; WhoAmP 73, 75, 77, 79, 81, 83, 85, 87, 89, 91, 93, 95; WhoE 74, 89, 91, 93, 95; WhoGov 72, 75, 77; WhoWor 80, 82, 84, 87, 89, 93, 95; WorAl; WorAlBi*

Weidenbaum, Murray Lew
American. Government Official, Economist
Chm., Council of Economic Advisers, 1981-82; director, Center for Study of American Business, 1975-81, 1982-95.
b. Feb 10, 1927 in New York, New York
Source: *AmEA 74; AmMWSc 73S, 78S; BioIn 9, 12, 13; BlueB 76; ConAu 37R; CurBio 82; IntWW 81, 82, 83, 89, 91, 93; NewYTBS 81; Who 82, 83, 85, 88, 90, 92, 94; WhoAm 74, 76, 78, 80, 82, 84, 86, 88, 90, 92, 94, 95, 96, 97; WhoAmP 73, 75, 77, 79, 81, 83, 85, 87, 89, 91, 93, 95; WhoFI 83, 85, 87, 89, 94, 96; WhoGov 72; WhoMW 92; WrDr 86, 92*

Weidman, Charles Edward, Jr.
American. Dancer
Best known for enhancing the participation of men in dance.
b. Jul 22, 1901 in Lincoln, Nebraska
d. Jul 15, 1975 in New York, New York
Source: *BiE&WWA; CurBio 42; WhAm 6; WhoAm 74*

Weidman, Jerome
American. Author
Won Pulitzer for play, *Fiorello*, 1960.
b. Apr 4, 1913 in New York, New York
Source: *AmAu&B; AmNov; Au&Wr 71; AuNews 2; AuSpks; Benet 87, 96; BenetAL 91; BiE&WWA; BioIn 2, 3, 4, 5, 6, 7, 8, 10, 11, 14, 15; BlueB 76; CnDAL; ConAmD; ConAu 1NR, 1R; ConDr 73, 77, 88D, 93; ConLC 7; ConNov 72, 76, 82, 86, 91; ConTFT 6; CurBio 42; DcLB 28; DcLEL; DrAF 76; DrAPF 80, 87, 91; EncMT; IntAu&W 76, 77, 82; JeAmFiW; LegTOT; LngCTC; NewCBMT; NotNAT; Novels; OxCAmL 65, 83, 95; PenC AM; REn; REnAL; RGTwCWr; TwCA, SUP; WhE&EA; WhNAA; WhoAm 74, 76, 78, 80, 82, 84, 86, 88, 90, 92, 94, 95, 96, 97; WhoAmJ 80; WhoThe 72, 77, 81; WhoTwCL; WhoUSWr 88; WhoWorJ 72, 78; WhoWrEP 89, 92, 95; WrDr 76, 80, 82, 84, 86, 88, 90, 92, 94, 96*

Weil, Andrew (Thomas)
American. Physician
Studied effects of smoking marijuana on patients, proving that the "high" experienced comes from within rather than the drug; wrote *Spontaneous Healing*, 1995.
b. Jun 8, 1942 in Philadelphia, Pennsylvania
Source: *AmMWSc 79, 82, 86, 89, 92, 95; BiDrAPA 89; BioIn 9, 10, 12; ConAu 20NR, 43NR, 73; CurBio 96; NewAgE 90; WhoEmL 89; WhoWest 87*

Weil, Joseph R
"Yellow Kid"
American. Criminal
Made over $8 million as a con man; known for innovative swindles.
b. Jun 30, 1875? in Chicago, Illinois
d. Feb 26, 1976 in Chicago, Illinois
Source: *BioIn 1, 4, 5, 10; EncACr; NewYTBS 76*

Weil, Simone
French. Philosopher
Mystic; activist in French Resistance, WW II; wrote *Gravity and Grace*, published 1952.
b. Feb 3, 1909 in Paris, France
d. Aug 24, 1943 in Ashford, England
Source: *Benet 87, 3; EuWr 12; EvEuW; FacFETw; FrenWW; GuFrLit 1; IlEncMy; InWom SUP; LegTOT; LiExTwC; LngCTC; LuthC 75; MakMC; ModFrL; ModRL; ModWoWr; OxCEng 85, 95; OxCFr; OxCPhil; PenC EUR; RAdv 14, 13-2; REn; ThTwC 87; TwCA SUP; TwCLC 23; TwCWr; WhoTwCL; WorAl; WorAlBi*

Weiland, Cooney
[Ralph Weiland]
Canadian. Hockey Player
Center, 1928-39, mostly with Boston; won Art Ross Trophy, 1930; Hall of Fame, 1971.
b. Nov 5, 1904 in Seaforth, Ontario, Canada
d. Jul 4, 1985 in Boston, Massachusetts
Source: *BioIn 14; HocEn; WhoHcky 73; WhoSpor*

Weill, Claudia
American. Director
Films include *It's My Turn*, 1980; *Girlfriends*, 1977.
b. 1947 in New York, New York
Source: *BioIn 10, 11, 12; ConTFT 1; FilmEn; HalFC 84, 88; IntMPA 92, 94, 96; InWom SUP; MiSFD 9; NewYTBS 78; ReelWom; WhoAm 82, 84, 86, 88; WomWMM A*

Weill, Kurt
American. Composer
Best known work *Threepenny Opera*, 1928; also wrote *One Touch of Venus*, and "September Song."
b. Mar 2, 1900 in Dessau, Germany
d. Apr 3, 1950 in New York, New York
Source: *AmComp; AmPS; AmSong; ASCAP 66, 80; AtlBL; Baker 78, 84; Benet 87, 96; BenetAL 91; BestMus; BiDAmM; BioIn 1, 2, 3, 4, 5, 6, 8, 9, 10, 11, 12, 13, 14, 15, 16, 18, 19, 20, 21; BriBkM 80; CamHAL; CmOp; CmpEPM; CompSN, SUP; ConAmC 76, 82; ConMus 12; CurBio 41, 50; DancEn 78; DcAmB S4; DcCM; DcCom 77; EncMT; EncTR, 91; EncWT; FacFETw; FilmgC; HalFC 80, 84, 88; IntDcOp; LegTOT; MakMC; McGEWB; MetOEnc; MorBAP; MusMk; NewAmDM; NewCBMT; NewEOp 71; NewGrDA 86; NewGrDM 80; NewOxM; NewYTBS 87; NotNAT B; OxCAmT 84; OxCEng 85, 95; OxCFilm; OxCGer 76, 86; OxCMus; OxCPMus; OxDcOp; PenDiMP A; PenEncP; PlP&P; PopAmC, SUP; REn; WebAB 74, 79; WhAm 3; WhDW; WhThe; WorAl; WorAlBi; WorEFlm*

Weill, Sanford I
American. Business Executive
CEO of Shearson/Lehman Bros. Inc. 1960-1984; CEO of Primerica Corp. 1989—; chairman and CEO of Travelers Group, 1996—.
b. Mar 16, 1933 in New York, New York
Source: *BioIn 13, 14, 15, 16; Dun&B 90; IntWW 91; St&PR 84, 87; WhoAm 84, 90; WhoE 83, 91; WhoFI 83, 92; WhoWor 87*

Wein, George Theodore
American. Musician, Producer
Founded Newport Jazz Festival, 1954; produces jazz festivals throughout country.
b. Oct 3, 1925 in Boston, Massachusetts
Source: *BiDAmM; BiDJaz; BioIn 13, 14; CmpEPM; CurBio 85; NewGrDJ 88; WhoAm 84, 86, 88; WhoEnt 92*

Weinberg, Chester
American. Fashion Designer
Director of design/production, Calvin Klein Jeans, 1983-85; won Coty, 1970.
b. Sep 23, 1930 in New York, New York
d. Apr 24, 1985 in New York, New York
Source: *BioIn 14; FairDF US; NewYTBS 85; WhAm 9; WhoAm 78, 80, 82, 84; WhoE 74; WhoFash 88; WorFshn*

Weinberg, Max M
[E Street Band]
"Mighty One"
American. Musician
Drummer with Bruce Springsteen's band since 1974.
b. Apr 13, 1951 in South Orange, New Jersey
Source: *BioIn 15; WhoRocM 82*

Weinberg, Moshe
Israeli. Olympic Athlete, Victim
One of 11 members of Israeli Olympic team kidnapped and killed by Arab terrorists during Summer Olympic Games.
b. 1940?

d. Sep 5, 1972 in Munich, Germany (West)
Source: *BioIn 9*

Weinberg, Steven
American. Physicist
Shared 1979 Nobel Prize in physics with Sheldon Glashow, Abdus Salam.
b. May 3, 1933 in New York, New York
Source: *AmMWSc 73P, 76P, 79, 82, 86, 89, 92, 95; BiESc; BioIn 12, 15; BlueB 76; CamDcSc; ConAu 5NR, 36NR, 53; FacFETw; IntWW 74, 75, 76, 77, 78, 79, 80, 81, 82, 83, 89, 91, 93; LarDcSc; McGMS 80; NobelP; NotTwCS; RAdv 14, 13-5; Who 82, 83, 85, 88, 90, 92, 94; WhoAm 74, 76, 78, 80, 82, 84, 86, 88, 90, 92, 94, 95, 96, 97; WhoE 81, 85, 86; WhoFrS 84; WhoNob, 90, 95; WhoScEn 94, 96; WhoSSW 84, 86, 88, 91, 93, 95, 97; WhoTech 82, 84, 89, 95; WhoWor 80, 82, 84, 87, 89, 91, 93, 95, 96, 97; WorAlBi; WorScD; WrDr 90, 92, 94, 96*

Weinberger, Caspar Willard
"Cap the Knife"
American. Government Official
Secretary of HEW, 1973-75; Secretary of Defense, 1981-87; chairman, Forbes Magazine, 1989—.
b. Aug 18, 1917 in San Francisco, California
Source: *AmPolLe; BiDrUSE 89; BioIn 8, 9, 10, 12, 13, 14, 15, 16; BlueB 76; CngDr 74, 81, 83, 85, 87; ColdWar 2; ConAu 133; CurBio 73; EncWB; IntWW 79, 80, 81, 82, 83, 89, 91, 93; NatCAB 63N; NewYTBE 72; NewYTBS 80, 89; Who 82, 83, 85, 88, 90, 92, 94; WhoAm 74, 76, 78, 80, 82, 84, 86, 88, 90, 92, 94, 95, 96, 97; WhoAmL 79; WhoAmP 73, 75, 77, 79, 81, 83, 85, 87, 89, 91, 93, 95; WhoE 81, 83, 85, 86, 89, 91, 93, 95, 97; WhoFI 74, 92, 94, 96; WhoGov 72, 75, 77; WhoSSW 75; WhoWor 82, 84, 87, 89, 91, 93, 95, 96, 97; WorAlBi*

Weinberger, Edwin B
Writer
Won Emmys for "Mary Tyler Moore Show"; "Taxi."
Source: *VarWW 85*

Weinberger, Jaromir
American. Composer
Wrote immensely popular Bohemian-style opera, *Schwanda the Bagpiper,* 1927.
b. Jan 8, 1896 in Prague, Bohemia
d. Aug 6, 1967 in Saint Petersburg, Florida
Source: *AmComp; ASCAP 66, 80; Baker 78, 84, 92; BiDAmM; BioIn 1, 2, 4, 8, 16; BriBkM 80; CmOp; CompSN; ConAmC 76, 82; DcCom&M 79; IntDcOp; IntWWM 77, 80; MetOEnc; NewEOp 71; NewGrDA 86; NewGrDM 80; NewGrDO; NewOxM; OxCMus; OxDcOp; PenDiMP A*

Weingarten, Violet Brown
American. Journalist, Author
Novels include *Half a Marriage,* 1976; films include *Debbie,* 1964.
b. Feb 23, 1915 in San Francisco, California
d. Jul 17, 1976 in New York, New York
Source: *ConAu 7NR, 9R, 65; ForWC 70; IntAu&W 77; NewYTBS 76; SmATA 3, 27N*

Weingartner, Felix
[Paul Felix Weingartner]
Austrian. Conductor, Composer
Succeeded Gustav Mahler as director of Vienna State Opera, 1908-11, 1930s; wrote operas, seven symphonies.
b. Jun 2, 1863 in Zara, Austria
d. May 7, 1942 in Winterthur, Switzerland
Source: *Baker 78, 84; BioIn 2, 4, 6, 8, 11, 19; BriBkM 80; CmOp; CurBio 42; FacFETw; IntDcOp; MetOEnc; MusMk; MusSN; NewAmDM; NewEOp 71; NewGrDM 80; NewOxM; OxCMus; OxDcOp; PenDiMP; WhE&EA; WhoLA*

Weinman, Adolph A
American. Sculptor
Designed 1916 dime, half dollar.
b. Dec 11, 1870 in Karlsruhe, Germany
d. Aug 8, 1952 in Port Chester, New York
Source: *NatCAB 62; WhAm 3; WhAmArt 85; WhoAmA 84N*

Weinmesiter, Arnie
[Arnold Weinmesiter]
American. Football Player
Tackle, 1948-53, mostly with NY Giants; Hall of Fame, 1984.
b. Mar 23, 1923 in Rhein, Saskatchewan, Canada
Source: *BiDAmSp FB; BioIn 2, 3; WhoFtbl 74*

Weinstein, Bob
American. Film Executive
Co-founder and co-chairman, Miramax Films, 1978—.
b. Oct 18, 1954 in New York, New York

Weinstein, Harvey
American. Film Executive
Co-founder and co-chairman, Miramax Films, 1978—.
b. Mar 19, 1952 in New York, New York

Weintal, Edward
American. Journalist
Award-winning diplomatic correspondent *Newsweek,* 1944-69; special consultant, USIA, 1967-73.
b. Mar 21, 1901 in Warsaw, Poland
d. Jan 24, 1973 in Washington, District of Columbia
Source: *BioIn 9; ConAu 41R; NewYTBE 73; WhAm 5*

Weintraub, Jerry
American. Producer, Agent
Talent agent, clients include Frank Sinatra, Neil Diamond, John Denver.
b. Sep 26, 1937 in New York, New York
Source: *BioIn 11, 12, 15; ConNews 86-1; ConTFT 7, 14; IntMPA 84, 86, 88, 92, 94, 96; WhoAm 84, 86, 95, 96, 97; WhoEnt 92A*

Weir, Benjamin T
American. Hostage
Minister in Lebanon seized by Islamic Jihad May 6, 1984 and released September 14, 1985.
Source: *BioIn 14, 15, 16*

Weir, Bob
[The Grateful Dead; Robert Hall Weir]
American. Singer, Musician
Recorded solo album *Bombs Away,* 1978.
b. Oct 16, 1949 in San Francisco, California
Source: *RkOn 85*

Weir, John F(erguson)
American. Artist
Industrial scenes include *Forging the Shaft;* son of Robert.
b. Aug 28, 1841 in West Point, New York
d. Apr 8, 1926 in Providence, Rhode Island
Source: *AmBi; ApCAB; ArtsNiC; BioIn 4, 12; BriEAA; DcAmArt; DcAmAu; DcAmB; DcNAA; EarABI SUP; HarEnUS; NatCAB 6; OxCAmH; TwCBDA; WhAm 1; WhAmArt 85*

Weir, Julian Alden
American. Artist
Semi-Impressionist works include *The Green Bodice;* son of Robert.
b. Aug 30, 1852 in West Point, New York
d. Dec 8, 1919 in New York, New York
Source: *AmBi; ApCAB; BioIn 5, 9, 20, 21; BriEAA; DcAmArt; DcAmB; LinLib S; NatCAB 11, 22; OxCAmH; OxCAmL 65; TwCBDA; WhAm 1; WhAmArt 85*

Weir, Peter
Australian. Director
Compared with Alfred Hitchcock for ability to combine everyday life with unspeakable terror: *The Year of Living Dangerously,* 1983.
b. Aug 8, 1944 in Sydney, Australia
Source: *BiDFilm 94; BioIn 14, 15, 16; ConAu 113, 123; ConLC 20; ConTFT 1, 6, 13; CurBio 84; FacFETw; HalFC 84, 88; IntDcF 1-2, 2-2; IntMPA 84, 86, 88, 92, 94, 96; IntWW 91; LegTOT; MiSFD 9; Who 92; WhoEnt 92; WhoWor 91; WorFDir 2*

Weir, Robert W
American. Artist, Educator
Noted for *Embarkation of the Pilgrims,* in Capitol rotunda, 1836-40.

b. Jun 18, 1803 in New Rochelle, New York
d. May 1, 1889 in New York, New York
Source: *Alli; AmBi; ApCAB; ArtsNiC; BiAUS; DcAmArt; DcAmB; Drake; EarABI, SUP; TwCBDA; WhAm HS*

Weisgall, Hugo (David)
Czech. Composer, Conductor
Operas include *Night*, 1932; *The Tenor*, 1950; ballets include *Quest*, 1938.
b. Oct 13, 1912 in Ivancice, Czechoslovakia
d. Mar 11, 1997 in Manhasset, New York
Source: *AmComp; ASCAP 66, 80; Baker 78, 84, 92; BiDAmM; BioIn 7, 8, 9, 18; BriBkM 80; CompSN, SUP; ConAmC 76, 82; CpmDNM 79, 81, 82; DcCM; IntWWM 77, 80, 90; MetOEnc; NewAmDM; NewEOp 71; NewGrDA 86; NewGrDM 80; NewGrDO; NewYTBS 76; OxDcOp; WhoAm 74, 76, 78, 80, 82, 84, 86, 88, 90, 92, 94, 95, 96, 97; WhoAmM 83; WhoMus 72; WhoWor 74, 76; WhoWorJ 72*

Weiskopf, Bob
American. Writer, Producer
Won Emmys for "Red Skelton Show," 1971; "All in the Family," 1978.
b. Mar 13, 1914 in Chicago, Illinois
Source: *ConAu 118, 123, X; ConTFT 2; VarWW 85*

Weiskopf, Tom
[Thomas Daniel Weiskopf]
American. Golfer
Turned pro, 1964; won British Open, 1973; has won $2.5 million on PGA tour. Won U.S. Senior Open, 1995.
b. Nov 9, 1942 in Massillon, Ohio
Source: *BiDAmSp OS; BioIn 10, 12, 13; BioNews 74; CurBio 73; NewYTBE 73; NewYTBS 81; WhoAm 74, 76, 78, 80, 82, 84, 86; WhoGolf; WhoIntG*

Weismann, August Friedrich Leopold
German. Biologist
Originator of germ-plasm theory of heredity; wrote *The Germ Plasm*, 1892.
b. Jan 17, 1834 in Frankfurt am Main, Germany
d. Nov 6, 1914 in Freiburg, Germany
Source: *AsBiEn; BbD; BiESc; DcScB; LarDcSc; McGEWB; NewCol 75*

Weiss, George Martin
American. Baseball Executive
With NY Yankees in several capacities, 1932-62, helping to build team in dynasty yrs; first pres., NY Mets, 1962-67; Hall of Fame, 1971.
b. Jun 23, 1894 in New Haven, Connecticut
d. Aug 13, 1972 in Greenwich, Connecticut
Source: *DcAmB S9; NatCAB 57; WhAm 5; WhoProB 73*

Weiss, Peter Ulrich
German. Dramatist
Wrote *Marat/Sade;* won Tony, 1966.
b. Nov 8, 1916 in Nowawes, Germany
d. May 10, 1982 in Stockholm, Sweden
Source: *CasWL; ConAu 3NR, 106; CurBio 68; NotNAT; OxCFilm; OxCGer 76; PenC EUR; PlP&P, A; REnWD; TwCWr; Who 82; WhoThe 81; WhoWor 74; WorAu 1950; WorEFlm*

Weiss, Ted
[Theodore S Weiss]
American. Politician
Dem. congressman from NY, 1976-87; advocated end to arms race.
b. Sep 17, 1927 in Budapest, Hungary
d. Sep 14, 1992 in New York, New York
Source: *AlmAP 88, 92; AnObit 1992; BiDrUSC 89; BiGAW; BioIn 14, 18, 19; CngDr 77, 79, 81, 83, 85, 87, 89, 91; CurBio 85, 92N; DrAPF 91; NewYTBS 92; PolsAm 84; WhoAm 78, 80, 82, 84, 86, 90; WhoAmJ 80; WhoAmP 77, 79, 81, 83, 85, 87, 89, 91; WhoE 79, 85, 91*

Weiss, Theodore (Russell)
American. Poet, Editor
Poem verses include *A Slow Fuse*, 1984; editor, publisher, *Quarterly Review Literature*, 1943—.
b. Dec 16, 1916 in Reading, Pennsylvania
Source: *AmAu&B; BenetAL 91; BioIn 10, 12, 15; BlueB 76; ConAu 2AS, 9R, 46NR; ConLC 3, 8, 14; ConPo 70, 75, 80, 85, 91, 96; CroCAP; DcLB 5; DcLEL 1940; DrAP 75; DrAPF 80; DrAS 74E, 78E, 82E; IntAu&W 77, 82, 86; IntWWP 77, 82; LinLib L; OxCTwCP; PenC AM; WhoAm 74, 76, 78, 80, 82, 84, 86, 88, 90, 94, 95, 96, 97; WhoAmJ 80; WhoE 74; WhoUSWr 88; WhoWorJ 72; WhoWrEP 89, 92, 95; WorAu 1950; WrDr 76, 80, 82, 84, 86, 88, 90, 92, 94, 96*

Weiss, Walt(er William, Jr.)
American. Baseball Player
Shortstop, Oakland, 1987—; AL rookie of year, 1988.
b. Nov 28, 1963 in Tuxedo, New York
Source: *Ballpl 90; BaseReg 88; BioIn 16*

Weissenberg, Alexis Sigismund
American. Pianist
Gives over 85 int'l concerts yearly; has made several records.
b. Jul 26, 1929 in Sofia, Bulgaria
Source: *Baker 84; BiDAmM; BioIn 8, 11, 12, 13, 14; BriBkM 80; CurBio 78; IntWW 91; IntWWM 90; MusSN; NewAmDM; NewGrDA 86; NewGrDM 80; NewYTBE 71; NotTwCP; PenDiMP; WhoAm 86, 88; WhoSoCE 89; WhoWor 91*

Weissmuller, Johnny
[Peter John Weissmuller]
American. Actor, Swimmer
Played Tarzan in 19 movies, 1934-48; won five gold medals in 1924, 1928 Olympics.
b. Jun 2, 1904 in Windber, Pennsylvania
d. Jan 20, 1984 in Acapulco, Mexico
Source: *AnObit 1984; BiDAmSp BK; BiDFilm 94; BioIn 3, 6, 7, 8, 9, 10, 12, 13, 14, 16, 17; CmCal; ConAu 111; FacFETw; Film 2; FilmEn; FilmgC; ForYSC; HalFC 80, 84, 88; IntDcF 1-3, 2-3; IntMPA 75, 76, 77, 78, 79, 80, 81, 82; LegTOT; MGM; MotPP; MovMk; NewYTBE 72; NewYTBS 84; OxCFilm; WebAB 74, 79; What 1; WhoHol A; WhoSpor; WorAl; WorAlBi; WorEFlm*

Weitz, Bruce Peter
American. Actor
Played Mick Belker on TV series "Hill Street Blues," 1981-87; won Emmy award, 1984.
b. May 27, 1943 in Norwalk, Connecticut
Source: *BioIn 13, 15; ConNews 85-4; ConTFT 7; VarWW 85; WhoAm 88, 90; WhoEnt 92; WhoTelC*

Weitz, John
American. Fashion Designer
Founded own fashion house, 1954; won Coty, 1974.
b. May 25, 1923 in Berlin, Germany
Source: *BioIn 8, 12; CelR, 90; ConAu 29R; ConDes 84, 90, 97; ConFash; CurBio 79; FairDF US; NewYTBE 72; WhoAm 76, 78, 80, 82, 84, 86, 88, 90, 92, 94, 95, 96, 97; WhoAmJ 80; WhoFash 88; WhoWor 78, 82, 84, 87, 89, 91, 95; WorFshn*

Weizman, Ezer
Israeli. Politician
Minister of communications, 1984-88; science, 1988-92; elected Pres., 1993.
b. Jun 15, 1924 in Tel Aviv, Palestine
Source: *BioIn 8, 9, 11, 12; ConAu 111; CurBio 79; EncWB; HisEAAC; IntAu&W 86; IntWW 74, 75, 76, 77, 78, 79, 80, 81, 82, 83, 89, 91, 93; IntYB 79, 80, 81, 82; MidE 78, 79, 80, 81, 82; NewYTBS 78; Who 94; WhoWor 80, 82, 95, 96, 97; WhoWorJ 78*

Weizmann, Chaim
Israeli. Political Leader, Religious Leader
Provisional pres. of Israel, 1948-49; first elected pres., 1949-52; first pres., World Zionist Organization, 1923.
b. Nov 27, 1874 in Grodno, Russia
d. Nov 9, 1952 in Rehovot, Israel
Source: *AsBiEn; BioIn 1, 2, 3, 4, 5, 6, 7, 8, 9, 10, 11, 12, 13, 14, 15, 16, 17, 18, 20; CurBio 42, 48, 52; DcNaB 1951; DcPol; DcScB; EncTR 91; FacFETw; GrBr; HisDBrE; HisEAAC; HisWorL; InSci; JeHun; LarDcSc; LegTOT; LinLib L, S; McGEWB; NewYTBS 86; ObitT 1951; PolLCME; WhAm 3, 4; WhWW-II; WorAl; WorAlBi*

Weizsacker, Richard Freiherr von
German. Political Leader
Succeeded Karl Carstens as sixth pres. of W Germany, 1984.
b. Apr 15, 1920 in Stuttgart, Germany
Source: *BioIn 14; CurBio 85; IntWW 91; NewYTBS 84; WhoWor 91*

Welch, Bob
[Fleetwood Mac]
American. Musician
Guitarist with Fleetwood Mac, 1971-75; had solo single "Sentimental Lady," 1977.
b. Jul 31, 1946 in Los Angeles, California
Source: *ConAu X; ConMuA 80A; LegTOT; NewYTBS 80; RkOn 78; WhoRock 81; WhoRocM 82*

Welch, Bob
[Robert Lynn Welch]
American. Baseball Player
Pitcher, LA, 1979-87, Oakland, 1988—; his 27 wins in 1990 was most in AL in 22 years; won AL Cy Young Award, 1990.
b. Nov 3, 1956 in Detroit, Michigan
Source: *Ballpl 90; BaseEn 88; BaseReg 88; BioIn 12, 13, 14, 15, 16, 17, 21; ConAu 112; Dun&B 88; News 91, 91-3; WhoAm 94; WhoSpor; WhoWest 94*

Welch, Herbert
American. Religious Leader
Chm. of Methodist Committee for Overseas Relief, 1940-48; pres., Ohio Wesleyan U, 1905-16.
b. Nov 7, 1862 in New York, New York
d. Apr 4, 1969 in New York, New York
Source: *BioIn 1, 6, 8, 9; ConAu P-1; EncWM; NatCAB 14; OhA&B; WhAm 5; WhE&EA*

Welch, James
American. Author
Themes of novels include Native American acculturation; novels include *Winter in the Blood,* 1975.
b. 1940
Source: *BenetAL 91; BiNAW, B; BioIn 10, 12, 17, 21; CamGLE; CamHAL; ConAu 42NR, 85; ConLC 6, 14, 52; ConNov 91, 96; ConPo 75, 80, 85, 91, 96; ConPopW; DcNAL; DrAP 75; DrAPF 80; EncFWF; EncNAB; NatNAL; NotNaAm; OxCAmL 95; RfGAmL 94; TwCWW 82, 91; WorAu 1980; WrDr 76, 80, 82, 84, 86, 88, 90, 92, 94, 96*

Welch, John Francis, Jr.
American. Business Executive
Chm., CEO of General Electric Co., 1981—.
b. Nov 19, 1935 in Peabody, Massachusetts
Source: *AmMWSc 79, 92; BioIn 12, 13, 14, 15, 16; CurBio 88; Dun&B 90; IntWW 89, 91, 93; St&PR 84, 87, 91, 93, 96, 97; WhoAm 78, 80, 82, 84, 86, 88, 90, 92, 94, 95, 96, 97; WhoE 83, 85, 86, 89, 91, 93, 95, 97; WhoFI 81, 83, 85, 87, 89, 92, 94, 96; WhoWor 84, 87, 89, 91, 95, 96, 97*

Welch, Joseph Nye
American. Lawyer, Actor
Counsel for US Army during McCarthy hearings, 1954; known for civil trials.
b. Oct 22, 1890 in Primghar, Iowa
d. Oct 6, 1960 in Hyannis, Massachusetts
Source: *BioIn 3, 5, 6, 11; CurBio 54, 60; DcAmB S6; EncMcCE; WebAB 74, 79; WebBD 83; WhAm 4; WhScrn 74, 77*

Welch, Ken
American. Writer, Composer, Songwriter
With wife, Mitzie, won Emmys for music for TV specials including "Linda in Wonderland," 1981.
b. Feb 4, 1926 in Kansas City, Missouri
Source: *VarWW 85*

Welch, Larry Dean
American. Military Leader
Vice Chief of Staff of Air Force, 1981-85; commander-in-chief, SAC (Strategic Air Command), 1985-86; chief of staff, USAF, 1986—.
b. Jun 9, 1934 in Guymon, Oklahoma
Source: *BioIn 15; NewYTBS 86; St&PR 91; WhoAm 84, 86, 90; WhoMW 88*

Welch, Mickey
[Michael Francis Welch]
"Smiling Mickey"
American. Baseball Player
Pitcher, 1880-92, mostly with NY Giants; had 311 career wins; thought to be first to throw screwball; Hall of Fame, 1973.
b. Jul 4, 1859 in New York, New York
d. Jul 30, 1941 in Nashua, New Hampshire
Source: *Ballpl 90; BiDAmSp BB; BioIn 14, 15; WhoProB 73; WhoSpor*

Welch, Mitzie
[Marilyn Cottle]
American. Writer, Composer, Songwriter
With husband, Ken, won several Emmys including "Carol Burnett Show," 1976.
b. Jul 25, in McDonald, Pennsylvania
Source: *VarWW 85*

Welch, Raquel
[Raquel Tejada]
American. Actor, Model
Film star known for figure, sexiness: *One Million Years, BC,* 1967; starred on Broadway in *Woman of the Year,* 1982.
b. Sep 5, 1940 in Chicago, Illinois
Source: *BioIn 8, 9, 10, 11, 12, 13, 14, 16, 18, 20; BioNews 74; BkPepl; CelR, 90; ConTFT 3; CurBio 71; DcArts; DcHiB; FilmEn; FilmgC; HalFC 80, 84, 88; HispAmA; IntDcF 1-3, 2-3; IntMPA 82, 92, 94, 96; IntWW 82, 83, 89, 91, 93; InWom SUP; ItaFilm; LegTOT; MotPP; MovMk; NewYTBE 72; NotHsAW 93; VarWW 85; WhoAm 84, 86, 88, 92, 94, 95, 96, 97; WhoAmW 85, 95, 97; WhoEnt 92, 92A; WhoHisp 91, 92, 94; WhoHol 92, A; WhoHrs 80; WorAlBi; WorEFlm*

Welch, Robert Henry Winborne, Jr.
American. Political Activist
Founder of ultraconservative, anti-communist John Birch Society, 1958.
b. Dec 1, 1899 in Chowan County, North Carolina
d. Jan 6, 1985 in Winchester, Massachusetts
Source: *BiDExR; BioIn 5, 6, 7, 10, 11; CurBio 76; PolProf J; St&PR 75; WebAB 74, 79; WhoAm 80, 82; WhoWor 74*

Welch, Thomas B
American. Dentist, Businessman
Prohibitionist, who developed unfermented wine, Welch's Grape Juice, 1872.
b. 1825
d. 1903
Source: *Entr*

Welch, William Henry
American. Pathologist, Bacteriologist
First professor of pathology at Johns Hopkins Hospital & Medical School, 1889; helped establish Rockefeller Institute, NY.
b. Apr 8, 1850 in Norfolk, Connecticut
d. Apr 30, 1934 in Baltimore, Maryland
Source: *AmAu&B; AmBi; AmDec 1910; ApCAB SUP; BiDAmEd; BiESc; BiHiMed; BioIn 1, 2, 3, 5, 7, 8, 9, 10, 11, 13, 15, 19; DcAmAu; DcAmB; DcAmMeB 84; DcNAA; DcScB; EncAB-H 1974, 1996; InSci; LarDcSc; McGEWB; NatCAB 10, 26; OxCAmH; OxCMed 86; REnAL; WebAB 74, 79; WhAm 1*

Welchman, Gordon
American. Mathematician
Solved Nazis' decoding machine; wrote *Hut Six Story: Breaking the Enigma Code,* 1982.
b. 1906, England
d. Oct 8, 1985 in Newburyport, Massachusetts
Source: *AnObit 1985; ConAu 117; DcNaB 1981*

Weld, Tuesday
[Susan Kerr Weld]
American. Actor
Starred in *Return to Peyton Place,* 1961; *Looking for Mr. Goodbar,* 1977.
b. Aug 27, 1943 in New York, New York
Source: *BiDFilm, 81, 94; BioIn 5, 6, 9, 10, 11, 14, 15, 16; CelR; ConTFT 3; CurBio 74; EncAFC; FilmEn; FilmgC; ForYSC; HalFC 80, 84, 88; IntDcF 1-3, 2-3; IntMPA 75, 76, 77, 78, 79, 80, 81, 82, 84, 86, 88, 92, 94, 96; IntWW 91; InWom, SUP; LegTOT; MotPP; MovMk; NewYTBE 71; WhoAm 86, 90; WhoAmW 74, 91; WhoEnt 92; WhoHol 92, A; WorAl; WorAlBi; WorEFlm*

Weld, William F(loyd)
American. Politician
Rep. governor, MA, 1990-97.
b. Jul 31, 1945 in Smithtown, New York
Source: *BioIn 14, 15, 16; CurBio 93; IntWW 91, 93; NewYTBS 88, 90, 91, 92; WhoAm 80, 82, 84, 86, 88, 92, 94, 95, 96, 97; WhoAmL 83, 85, 87, 90, 92, 94, 96; WhoAmP 91; WhoE 93, 95, 97; WhoWor 93, 95, 96, 97*

Weldon, Fay
English. Author
Novels focus on issues in women's lives; *The Life and Loves of a She-Devil,* 1983; *Leader of the Band,* 1988.
b. Sep 22, 1931 in Alvechurch, England
Source: *BioIn 9, 13, 14, 16; BlmGEL; BlmGWL; CnDBLB 8; ConLC 59; ConNov 86, 91, 96; ConPopW; ContDcW 89; CurBio 90; CyWA 89; DcArts; DcLB 14; EncBrWW; EncSF 93; FemiCLE; FemiWr; IntAu&W 86, 89, 91, 93; IntWW 83, 89, 91, 93; InWom SUP; LegTOT; MajTwCW; RfGEnL 91; RGTwCWr; ScF&FL 92; Who 85, 88, 90, 92, 94; WhoWor 97; WrDr 92, 94, 96*

Weldon, Joan
American. Actor
Films include *So This Is Love,* 1953; *Home Before Dark,* 1958.
b. Aug 5, 1933 in San Francisco, California
Source: *ForYSC; IntMPA 75, 76, 77, 78, 79, 80, 81, 82, 84, 86, 88; WhoHol 92, A; WhoHrs 80*

Weldon, John
[Brinsley MacNamara]
Irish. Actor, Dramatist
Plays include *Margaret Gillan,* 1935.
b. Sep 6, 1890? in Hiskenstown, Ireland
d. Feb 4, 1963 in Dublin, Ireland
Source: *BiDIrW; BioIn 13; CasWL; CnMD; ConAu 115; DcIrB 88; DcIrL, 96; DcLB 10; IriPla; LngCTC; McGEWD 72, 84; ModIrL; ModWD; OxCIri; OxCThe 83; RfGEnL 91; WhE&EA*

Welitsch, Ljuba
Austrian. Opera Singer
Soprano, noted for Salome role; with NY Met., 1949-52.
b. Jul 10, 1913 in Borissova, Bulgaria
d. Sep 1, 1996 in Vienna, Austria
Source: *Baker 78, 84, 92; BioIn 1, 2, 3, 4, 7, 9, 11, 13, 14, 15; CmOp; CurBio 49, 96N; IntDcOp; IntWWM 80, 90; InWom, SUP; MetOEnc; MusSN; NewAmDM; NewGrDM 80; NewGrDO; NewYTBE 72; NewYTBS 27; OxDcOp; PenDiMP; WhoMus 72*

Welk, Lawrence
"The King of Champagne Music"
American. Bandleader
Started band, 1927; host of TV's "The Lawrence Welk Show," 1955-71, longest-running show in TV history.
b. Mar 11, 1903 in Strasburg, North Dakota
d. May 17, 1992 in Santa Monica, California
Source: *AnObit 1992; ASCAP 66, 80; Baker 78, 84, 92; BgBands 74; BiDAmM; BiDJaz; BioIn 4, 7, 8, 9, 10, 11, 12, 13, 17, 18, 19; BioNews 74; CelR, 90; CmpEPM; ConAu 105, 134; ConMuA 80B; ConMus 13; ConTFT 12; CurBio 57, 92N; DcTwCCu 1; FacFETw; IntMPA 77, 80, 84, 86, 88, 92; LegTOT; NewAmDM; NewGrDA 86; NewYTBS 92; OxCPMus; PenEncP; RadStar; RkOn 74; WebAB 74, 79; WhoAm 74, 76, 78, 80, 82; WhoMus 72; WorAl; WorAlBi; WrDr 80, 82, 84, 86, 88, 90*

Welland, Colin
English. Screenwriter
Wrote Oscar-winning film *Chariots of Fire,* 1981.
b. Jul 4, 1934, England
Source: *ConDr 77C, 88C; ConTFT 7; FilmgC; HalFC 80, 84, 88; IntAu&W 89, 91, 93; IntWW 89, 91, 93; VarWW 85; Who 82, 83, 85, 88, 90, 92, 94*

Wellcome, Henry Solomon, Sir
American. Manufacturer
Founded pharmaceutical firm, 1880; pioneered the field in US, England; established museums, foundations.
b. Aug 21, 1853 in Wisconsin
d. Jul 25, 1936 in London, England
Source: *BioIn 2, 3, 9, 13; DcNaB 1931; DcTwBBL; OxCMed 86*

Wellek, Rene
American. Author, Educator
Writings include *Confrontations,* 1965; *Chekhov: New Perspectives,* 1984.
b. Aug 22, 1903 in Vienna, Austria
d. Nov 10, 1995 in Hamden, Connecticut
Source: *AmAu&B; Au&Wr 71; BioIn 4, 10, 16; BlueB 76; ConAu 5R, 7AS, 8NR, 150; ConLC 28; ConLCrt 77, 82; DcLB 63; DrAS 74F, 82F; EncWL, 2, 3; IntAu&W 76, 82, 86; IntvTCA 2; IntWW 75, 76, 77, 78, 79, 80, 81, 82, 83, 89, 91, 93; LiExTwC; NewYTBS 74; WhoAm 74, 76, 78, 80, 82, 84, 86, 88; WhoWor 74, 76, 78; WorAu 1950; WrDr 76, 80, 82, 84, 86, 88, 90, 92, 94, 96*

Weller, Michael
American. Dramatist, Screenwriter
Wrote films *Hair,* 1979; *Ragtime,* 1981.
b. Sep 27, 1942 in New York, New York
Source: *BioIn 10, 12, 16; CamGWoT; ConAmD; ConAu 85; ConDr 73, 77, 82, 88, 93; ConLC 10, 53; ConTFT 2; CurBio 89; McGEWD 84; NatPD 81; OxCAmT 84; VarWW 85; WhoAm 90, 92, 94, 95, 96, 97; WhoEnt 92; WhoThe 81; WrDr 76, 80, 82, 84, 86, 88, 90, 92, 94, 96*

Weller, Thomas Huckle
American. Physician
Shared Nobel Prize in medicine, 1954, with Frederick C Robbins.
b. Jun 15, 1915 in Ann Arbor, Michigan
Source: *AmMWSc 76P, 79, 82, 86, 89, 92, 95; AsBiEn; BiESc; BioIn 3, 4, 15, 20; BlueB 76; IntWW 74, 75, 76, 77, 78, 79, 80, 81, 82, 83, 89, 91, 93; LarDcSc; McGMS 80; NobelP; WebAB 74, 79; WebBD 83; Who 74, 82, 83, 85, 88, 90, 92, 94; WhoAm 74, 76, 78, 80, 82, 84, 86, 88, 90, 92, 94, 95, 96, 97; WhoE 77, 79, 81, 83, 85, 86, 89, 91, 93, 95, 97; WhoMedH; WhoNob, 90, 95; WhoScEn 94, 96; WhoWor 74, 82, 84, 87, 89, 91, 93, 95, 96, 97; WorAl; WorAlBi*

Welles, Gideon
American. Politician
Secretary of Navy, 1861-69; credited with building Union Navy, blockading Confederacy; his *Diary of Gideon Welles* was published in 1911.
b. Jul 1, 1802 in Glastonbury, Connecticut
d. Feb 11, 1878 in Hartford, Connecticut
Source: *Alli SUP; AmAu&B; AmBi; ApCAB; BiAUS; BiDrUSE 71, 89; BioIn 4, 5, 7, 10; CivWDc; DcAmAu; DcAmB; DcAmMiB; DcNAA; Drake; EncAB-H 1974, 1996; HarEnUS; McGEWB; NatCAB 2; NewCol 75; OxCAmH; OxCShps; REn; REnAL; TwCBDA; WebAB 74, 79; WebBD 83; WhAm HS; WhCiWar*

Welles, Orson
[George Orson Welles]
American. Actor, Director, Producer, Writer
Considered major film genius; gained reputation with 1938 radio adaptation of *War of the Worlds;* starred in *Citizen Kane,* 1940.
b. May 6, 1915 in Kenosha, Wisconsin
d. Oct 10, 1985 in Los Angeles, California
Source: *AmAu&B; AmCulL; AmDec 1940; AmFD; Benet 87; BenetAL 91; BiDFilm, 81, 94; BiE&WWA; BioIn 1, 2, 3, 4, 5, 6, 7, 8, 9, 10, 11, 12, 13, 14, 15, 16, 17, 18, 19, 20, 21; BkPepl; BlueB 76; CamGWoT; CelR; CmCal; CmMov; CnThe; ConAu 93, 117; ConDr 73, 77A; ConLC 20, 80; ConTFT 3; CurBio 65, 85N; DcAmSR; DcFM; EncAB-H 1974, 1996; EncMT; EncWB; EncWT; Ent; FacFETw; FamA&A; FilmEn; FilmgC; GrStDi; HalFC 80, 84, 88; IlWWHD 1; IntAu&W 76, 77; IntMPA 77, 82, 84, 86; IntWW 74, 75, 76, 77, 78, 79, 80, 81, 82, 83; ItaFilm; LegTOT; LinLib L, S; MakMC; MiSFD 9N; MotPP; MovMk; NewYTBE 72; NewYTBS 85; NotNAT, A; OxCAmH; OxCAmT 84; OxCFilm; OxCThe 67, 83; PlP&P; RadStar; RAdv 13-3; RComAH; REn; REnAL; SaTiSS; ScF&FL 1, 92; VarWW 85; WebAB 74, 79; WhAm 9; WhDW; WhE&EA; Who 74, 82, 83, 85; WhoAm 74, 76, 78, 80, 82, 84; WhoHol A; WhoHrs 80; WhoThe 72, 77A; WhoWor 74; WhThe; WorAl; WorAlBi; WorEFlm; WorFDir 1; WrDr 80, 82, 84*

Welles, Sumner
American. Diplomat, Author
Roosevelt's assistant secretary and undersecretary of state, 1933-43; helped form "good neighbor" policy with Latin America.
b. Oct 14, 1892 in New York, New York
d. Sep 24, 1961 in Bernardsville, New Jersey
Source: *AmAu&B; AmPeW; BiDInt; BioIn 1, 2, 4, 6, 16; CurBio 40, 61; DcAmB S7; EncAB-H 1974; EncLatA; EncTR 91; LegTOT; McGEWB; ObitT 1961; REnAL; TwCA SUP; WhAm 4; WhE&EA; WorAl; WorAlBi*

Wellesley, Dorothy Violet
[Duchess of Wellington]
English. Poet
Wrote collection of poems, *Early Light,* 1956.
b. Jul 30, 1889 in White Waltham, England
d. Jul 11, 1956 in Withyham, England
Source: *Chambr 3; DcLEL; DcNaB 1951; ModBrL; OxCEng 85; REn*

Wellesz, Egon
Austrian. Composer, Musicologist
Expert on Byzantine music; wrote many operas.
b. Oct 21, 1885 in Vienna, Austria
d. Nov 9, 1974 in Oxford, England
Source: *Baker 78, 84; BriBkM 80; CmOp; ConAu 53; DcCM; IntWW 74; NewAmDM; NewEOp 71; NewGrDM 80; NewOxM; NewYTBS 74; ObitT 1971; OxCMus; OxDcOp; WhAm 6; Who 74*

Wellington, Arthur Wellesley, Duke
English. Army Officer, Statesman
Commander, Peninsular War, 1808-14, fighting Napoleon; prime minister, 1828-30.
b. May 1, 1769 in Dublin, Ireland
d. Sep 14, 1852 in Kent, England
Source: *Alli; Benet 87, 96; BioIn 1, 2, 3, 4, 5, 6, 7, 8, 9, 10, 11, 12, 13, 14, 16, 18, 19, 20, 21; BlmGEL; CelCen; DcBiPP; DcInB; HarEnMi; LinLib S; LngCEL; McGEWB; NewC; OxCEng 85, 95; REn; WhDW; WhoMilH 76; WorAl; WorAlBi*

Wellman, Paul Iselin
American. Journalist, Author
Novels include *Bowl of Brass,* 1944; *Magnificent Destiny,* 1962.
b. Oct 14, 1898 in Enid, Oklahoma
d. Sep 17, 1966 in Los Angeles, California
Source: *AmAu&B; AmNov; Au&Wr 71; AuBYP 2, 3; BioIn 1, 2, 4, 7, 8, 9; ConAu 1R, 16NR; CurBio 49; REn; REnAL; REnAW; SmATA 3; TwCA SUP; TwCWW 82; WhAm 4*

Wellman, Walter
American. Journalist
Founded *Cincinnati Post,* 1879; known for travels, record-breaking stunts.
b. Nov 3, 1858 in Mentor, Ohio
d. Jan 31, 1934 in New York, New York
Source: *AmBi; ApCAB X; BioIn 5, 8; DcAmB; DcNAA; EncAB-A 3; InSci; JrnUS; OhA&B; TwCBDA; WebAB 74, 79; WhAm 1*

Wellman, William Augustus
"Wild Bill"
American. Director
Films known for "documentary realism" include *Wings,* 1927; *The High and the Mighty,* 1954.
b. Feb 29, 1896 in Brookline, Massachusetts
d. Dec 9, 1975 in Los Angeles, California
Source: *BiDFilm; BioIn 2, 9, 10, 11, 12, 13, 15, 16, 17, 18; CmMov; ConAu 61; CurBio 50, 76; DcAmB S9; DcFM; Film 1; FilmEn; FilmgC; IntMPA 75; MovMk; ObitOF 79; ObitT 1971; OxCFilm; TwYS; WhAm 6; WhoAm 74, 76; WhoWor 74; WorAl*

Wells, Carolyn
American. Author
Wrote over 170 mysteries, nonsense tales, children's books.
b. Jun 18, 1869 in Rahway, New Jersey
d. Mar 26, 1942 in New York, New York
Source: *AmAu&B; AmLY; AmWomPl; AmWomWr; BenetAL 91; BiD&SB; BioIn 13, 14, 15, 21; CarSB; ChhPo, S1, S2; ConAu 113; CurBio 42; DcAmAu; DcLB 11; DcNAA; DetWom; EncAHmr; EncMys; EvLB; InWom; NatCAB 13; PenNWW A; REn; REnAL; TwCA; TwCCr&M 80, 85, 91; TwCWr; WhAm 2; WhNAA*

Wells, Edward
American. Engineer
Former Boeing Co. chief engineer; held 20 patents for plane parts designs.
b. Aug 26, 1910 in Boise, Idaho
d. Jul 1, 1986 in Bellevue, Washington
Source: *AmMWSc 82; St&PR 84; WhoAm 84; WhoFrS 84*

Wells, George
Screenwriter
Won Oscar for *Designing Woman,* 1957.
b. 1909
Source: *EncAFC; FilmEn; FilmgC; HalFC 80, 84, 88; VarWW 85; WorEFlm*

Wells, H(erbert) G(eorge)
English. Author
Wrote *The Time Machine,* 1895; *The Invisible Man,* 1897; *The War of the Worlds,* 1898.
b. Sep 21, 1866 in Bromley, England
d. Aug 13, 1946 in London, England
Source: *Benet 96; BiDInt; BioIn 1, 2, 3, 4, 5, 6, 7, 8, 9, 10, 11, 12, 13, 14, 15, 16, 17, 18, 19; CasWL; Chambr 3; CurBio 46; DcAmSR; DcArts; DcBiA; DcEnA A; DcLEL; DcNaB 1941; EncSF 93; EncUnb; EncWL 3; EvLB; GrBr; LinLib S; LngCEL; LngCTC; MakMC; McGEWB; MnBBF; NewCBEL; NotNAT B; OxCEng 67, 95; PenC ENG; PlP&P; RAdv 1; RComWL; REn; RfGShF; RGTwCWr; TwCA, SUP; TwCWr; TwCYAW; VicBrit; WebE&AL; WhAm 2; WhDW; WhE&EA; WhoHol B; WhoLA; WhoTwCL; WhScrn 74, 77*

Wells, Henry
American. Businessman
With William Fargo, organized express service, Wells, Fargo, & Co. during California gold rush, 1852.
b. Dec 12, 1805 in Thetford, Vermont
d. Dec 10, 1878 in Glasgow, Scotland
Source: *AmBi; ApCAB; BiDAmBL 83; BioIn 4; DcAmB; EncAAH; EncABHB 6; NatCAB 39; REnAW; TwCBDA; WebAB 74, 79; WhAm HS*

Wells, Horace
American. Dentist
Pioneered in anesthesia for dentistry, 1840s.
b. Jan 21, 1815 in Hartford, Vermont
d. Jan 24, 1848 in New York, New York
Source: *Alli; AmBi; ApCAB; BiESc; BiInAmS; BioIn 1, 2, 3, 4, 6, 7, 14; DcAmB; DcAmMeB, 84; DcNAA; Drake; HarEnUS; InSci; LinLib S; McGEWB; NatCAB 6; OxCAmH; OxCMed 86; TwCBDA; WebAB 74, 79; WhAm HS*

Wells, James Lesesne
American. Artist
Artwork was influenced by African art; art instructor and professor, Howard University, 1929-68.
b. Nov 2, 1902 in Atlanta, Georgia
d. 1993
Source: *AfroAA; AnObit 1993; ConBlB 10; DcTwCCu 5; InB&W 80, 85; WhAmArt 85; WhoAfA 96; WhoAm 78; WhoAmA 73, 76, 78, 80; WhoBlA 75, 77, 80, 85, 90, 92, 94*

Wells, Junior
[Amos Blackmore]
American. Musician
Blues harmonica player; played with the Muddy Waters band, 1952-1953; toured and recorded with Buddy Guy; recorded songs "Little by Little," "Messin' With the Kid," and "Let Me Love You Baby;" released albums *It's My Life,* 1966, *Junior Wells's Southside Blues Jam,* 1970 and *Everybody's Gettin' Some,* 1995.
b. Dec 9, 1934 in Memphis, Tennessee
Source: *BioIn 17; ConMus 17; NewAmDM; NewGrDA 86; PenEncP; RolSEnR 83; WhoRock 81*

Wells, Kitty
[Muriel Deason Wright]
American. Singer
Award-winning Grand Ole Opry star since 1950s; Country Music Hall of Fame, 1976.
b. Aug 30, 1919 in Nashville, Tennessee
Source: *Baker 84, 92; BgBkCoM; BiDAmM; BioIn 14, 15, 17, 19; ConMuA 80A; ConMus 6; CounME 74, 74A; EncFCWM 69, 83; IlEncJ; InWom SUP; NewAmDM; NewGrDA 86; PenEncP;*

WhoAm 76, 78, 80, 82, 84, 86, 88, 94, 95, 96, 97

Wells, Linton
American. Journalist
War correspondent, staff writer for newspapers, mags., 1911-76.
b. Apr 1, 1893 in Louisville, Kentucky
d. Jan 31, 1976 in Washington, District of Columbia
Source: *AmAu&B; BioIn 10, 12; ConAu 61, 97; NatCAB 59; WhAm 6, 7; WhE&EA; WhNAA; WhoAm 74, 76*

Wells, Mary
American. Singer
Sang "Bye, Bye, Baby," 1961; "Two Lovers," 1962; "My Guy," 1964.
b. May 13, 1943 in Detroit, Michigan
d. Jul 26, 1992 in Los Angeles, California
Source: *AfrAmAl 6; AfrAmBi 2; AnObit 1992; BiDEWW; BioIn 15, 18, 19; DcWomA; DrBlPA 90; EncPR&S 74, 89; EncRk 88; FemiCLE; InB&W 85; LegTOT; NewAmDM; NewGrDA 86; News 93-1; NewYTBS 92; PenEncP; RkOn 74, 78; RolSEnR 83; SoulM; WhoRock 81*

Wells-Barnett, Ida Bell
American. Journalist
Regular writer for the black press throughout the country; civil rights activist honored by the US Postal Service with a stamp in 1990.
b. Jul 16, 1862 in Holly Springs, Mississippi
d. Mar 25, 1931 in Chicago, Illinois
Source: *AfrAmOr; AmRef; AmSocL; BiDSocW; BioIn 13, 15; BlkWAm; BriB; ContDcW 89; EncAB-H 1974; EncSoH; EncWHA; HarlReB; HerW 84; InWom SUP; JrnUS; LibW; NotAW; PenNWW A; WomFir*

Wellstone, Paul David
American. Politician
Dem. Senator from MN, 1991—.
b. Jul 21, 1944 in Washington, District of Columbia
Source: *AlmAP 92; BioIn 13; ConAu 107; CurBio 93; NewYTBS 91; WhoAmP 91, 93, 95; WhoMW 92*

Welnick, Vince(nt)
[The Tubes]
American. Musician
Keyboardist with The Tubes since late 1960s.
b. Feb 21, 1951 in Phoenix, Arizona
Source: *WhoRocM 82*

Welsbach, Carl Auer von, Baron
Austrian. Chemist, Inventor
Discovered earth elements neodymium and praseodymium, 1885; lutetium, 1908.
b. Sep 1, 1858
d. Aug 4, 1929
Source: *DcInv; NewCol 75; WebBD 83; WhDW*

Welsh, Matthew E(mpson)
American. Politician
Dem. governor of IN, 1961-65.
b. Sep 15, 1912
d. May 28, 1995 in Indianapolis, Indiana
Source: *BiDrGov 1789; BioIn 6, 7, 9; BlueB 76; CurBio 95N; IntWW 74, 75, 76, 77, 78, 79, 80, 81; WhAm 11; WhoAm 74, 76, 78, 80, 82, 84, 86, 88, 90, 92, 94; WhoAmL 83; WhoAmP 73, 75, 77, 79, 81, 83, 85, 87, 89, 91, 93; WhoWor 78, 82*

Welsing, Frances Cress
American. Psychiatrist
Wrote *The Cress Theory of Color-Confrontation and Racism (White Supremacy),* 1970, proposing that the origin of racism is rooted in skin pigment.
b. Mar 18, 1935 in Chicago, Illinois
Source: *BioIn 19; BlksScM; BlkWr 2; ConAu 142; ConBlB 5; Ebony 1; InB&W 80; NegAl 76; NotBlAW 2; SchCGBL; WhoAfA 96; WhoBlA 77, 80, 85, 90, 92, 94; WrDr 96*

Welty, Eudora
American. Author
Won Pulitzer for *The Optimist's Daughter,* 1972; won National Book Award, 1991, for distinguished contribution to American letters.
b. Apr 13, 1909 in Jackson, Mississippi
Source: *AmAu&B; AmNov; AmWomWr, 92; AmWr; ArtclWW 2; Benet 87, 96; BenetAL 91; BioAmW; BioIn 1, 2, 3, 4, 5, 6, 7, 8, 9, 10, 11, 12, 13, 14, 15, 16, 17, 18, 19, 20, 21; BlmGWL; BlueB 76; CamGLE; CamHAL; CasWL; CelR; ChhPo; CnDAL; ConAu 1BS, 9R, 32NR; ConLC 1, 2, 5, 14, 22, 33; ConNov 72, 76, 82, 86, 91; ContDcW 89; CurBio 42, 75; CyWA 58, 89; DcArts; DcLB 102, 143, DS12, Y87A; DcLEL 1940; DcTwCCu 1; DrAF 76; DrAPF 80, 91; EncAB-H 1996; EncSoH; EncWHA; EncWL, 2, 3; FacFETw; FemiCLE; FifSWrA; GrWomW; GrWrEL N; ICPEnP A; IntAu&W 76, 77, 89, 91; IntDcWB; IntvTCA 2; IntWW 74, 75, 76, 77, 78, 79, 80, 81, 82, 83, 89, 91, 93; InWom, SUP; LegTOT; LibW; LinLib L, S; LiveMA; LngCTC; MacBEP; MagSAmL; MajTwCW; ModAL, S1, S2; ModAWWr; ModWoWr; NewCon; Novels; OxCAmL 65, 83, 95; OxCWoWr 95; PenC AM; PenEncH; RAdv 1, 14, 13-1; REn; REnAL; RfGAmL 87; ShSCr 1; ShSWr; SouWr; TwCA SUP; WebAB 74, 79; WebE&AL; WhDW; Who 85, 92; WhoAm 86, 90; WhoAmW 87, 91; WhoTwCL; WhoUSWr 88; WhoWor 87, 91; WhoWrEP 89; WorAl; WorAlBi; WorLitC; WrDr 76, 80, 82, 84, 86, 88, 90, 92, 94, 96*

Wenders, Wim
[Wilhelm Wenders]
German. Director
Films include *Hammett; American Friend.*
b. Aug 14, 1945 in Dusseldorf, Germany
Source: *BiDFilm 81, 94; BioIn 10, 11, 12, 13, 14, 15, 16; ConAu 93; ConTFT 5, 14; CurBio 84; EncEurC; FilmEn; HalFC 84, 88; IntDcF 1-2, 2-2; IntMPA 79, 80, 81, 82, 84, 86, 88, 92, 94, 96; IntWW 89, 91, 93; LegTOT; MiSFD 9; WhoAm 95, 96, 97; WhoWor 87, 93, 95, 96, 97; WorFDir 2*

Wendt, George
American. Actor
Played Norm Peterson on TV series "Cheers," 1982-93.
b. Oct 17, 1948 in Chicago, Illinois
Source: *BioIn 14; ConTFT 7; IntMPA 92, 94, 96*

Weng, Will
American. Puzzle Maker
Editor, *NY Times* crossword puzzle, 1968-78.
b. 1907? in Terre Haute, Indiana
d. May 2, 1993 in New York, New York
Source: *BioIn 10, 11, 16, 18, 19*

Wengenroth, Stow
American. Lithographer
Called "greatest black-and-white artist in America."
b. Jul 25, 1906 in New York, New York
d. Jan 22, 1978 in Gloucester, Massachusetts
Source: *BioIn 8, 10, 11, 12; ConAu 104; DcAmArt; GrAmP; McGDA; NatCAB 60; WhAm 7; WhAmArt 85; WhoAm 74, 76, 78; WhoAmA 73, 76, 78N, 80N, 82N, 84N, 86, 86N, 89, 89N, 91N, 93N*

Wenner, Jann
American. Journalist, Publisher
Founder, publisher *Rolling Stone* mag, 1967—; also owns *Us* mag.
b. Jan 7, 1946 in New York, New York
Source: *AmDec 1960; BioIn 9, 10, 11, 14, 15; ConAu 101; CurBio 80; EncTwCJ; LegTOT; LiJour; MugS; NewGrDA 86; News 93-1; NewYTBS 87; WhoAm 86, 90; WhoE 86; WhoEnt 92; WhoUSWr 88; WhoWrEP 89*

Wenner-Gren, Axel (Lenard)
Swedish. Industrialist
Founder, chm., Electrolux Co., 1921; manufactured vacuums, refrigerators.
b. Jun 5, 1881 in Uddevalla, Sweden
d. Nov 24, 1961 in Stockholm, Sweden
Source: *BioIn 1, 2, 3, 4, 6; CurBio 42, 62*

Wenrich, Percy
American. Songwriter
Wrote songs "Moonlight Bay," "Put on Your Old Gray Bonnet."
b. Jan 23, 1887 in Joplin, Missouri
d. Mar 17, 1952 in New York, New York
Source: *AmPS; ASCAP 66, 80; BiDAmM; BioIn 4, 6, 9; CmpEPM; NewAmDM; NewGrDA 86; NewGrDM 80; NotNAT B; PopAmC*

Wenzel, Hanni
Liechtenstein. Skier
Won gold medals, women's slalom, giant slalom, 1980 Olympics.
b. 1957
Source: *BioIn 12*

Werblin, Sonny
[David Abraham Werblin]
American. Businessman
Signed Joe Namath to New York Jets 1965; Pres., CEO, Madison Square Garden Corp., 1977-84; chm., MSG Corp., 1984-92; pres., MCA-TV, 1951-65; created $340 million Meadowlands Sports Complex in New Jersey.
b. Mar 17, 1910 in New York, New York
d. Nov 21, 1991 in New York, New York
Source: *BiDAmSp OS; BioIn 6, 7, 11, 12, 17, 18; CurBio 79; NewYTBS 79, 91; WhoAm 74*

Werfel, Franz
Austrian. Author
Noted expressionist; wrote *The Song of Bernadette,* 1942; filmed, 1943.
b. Sep 10, 1890 in Prague, Bohemia
d. Aug 26, 1945 in Beverly Hills, California
Source: *Benet 87, 96; BiDAmM; BiGAW; CamGWoT; CasWL; ClDMEL 47, 80; CmCal; CnMD; CnThe; ConAu 104; CurBio 40, 45; CyWA 58; DcArts; DcLB 81, 124; DcNAA; EncGRNM; EncSF, 93; EncTR, 91; EncWL, 2, 3; Ent; EvEuW; FacFETw; LegTOT; LiExTwC; LinLib L, S; LngCTC; LuthC 75; McGEWB; McGEWD 72, 84; ModGL; ModWD; NewEOp 71; NewGrDM 80; NewGrDO; NotNAT B; Novels; OxCGer 76, 86; OxCThe 67, 83; PenC EUR; PlP&P; RAdv 14, 13-2; REn; REnWD; RfGWoL 95; ScF&FL 1; ScFSB; TwCA, SUP; TwCLC 8; TwCSFW 81A, 86A; TwCWr; WhAm 2*

Werner, Alfred
French. Chemist
Won 1913 Nobel Prize for linking atoms in molecules; noted for inorganic research.
b. Dec 12, 1866 in Mulhouse, France
d. Nov 15, 1919 in Zurich, Switzerland
Source: *AsBiEn; BiESc; BioIn 3, 6, 7, 14, 15, 16, 19, 20; CamDcSc; DcScB; InSci; LarDcSc; LinLib S; NobelP; NotTwCS; WhDW; WhoNob, 90, 95; WorScD*

Werner, Oskar
[Oskar Josef Bschliessmayer]
Austrian. Actor
Starred in *Jules et Jim,* 1961; *Ship of Fools,* 1965; *Fahrenheit 451,* 1966.
b. Nov 13, 1922 in Vienna, Austria
d. Oct 23, 1984 in Marburg, Germany (West)
Source: *AnObit 1984; BiDFilm, 81, 94; BioIn 7, 8, 9, 14; CelR; CurBio 66, 85N; EncEurC; EncWT; FilmAG WE; FilmEn; FilmgC; ForYSC; HalFC 80, 84, 88; IntDcF 1-3, 2-3; IntMPA 75, 76, 77, 78, 79, 80, 81, 82, 84; LegTOT; MotPP; MovMk; NewYTBS 84; OxCFilm; WhoAm 74, 76, 78, 80, 82; WhoHol A; WorAl; WorAlBi; WorEFlm*

Werner, Pierre
Luxembourg. Lawyer, Politician
Prime minister of Luxembourg, 1959-84.
b. Dec 29, 1913 in Saint-Andre, France
Source: *IntWW 74, 75, 76, 77, 78, 79, 80, 81, 82, 83, 89, 91, 93; IntYB 78, 79, 80, 81, 82; WhoEIO 82; WhoGov 72; WhoWor 74, 76, 78, 80, 82, 84*

Werner, Tom
American. Producer
Developed *The Cosby Show* and *Roseanne.*
b. Apr 12, 1950
Source: *ConTFT 12; LegTOT; NewYTBS 90; WhoEnt 92*

Werth, Alexander
English. Journalist, Author
WW II newspaper correspondent in USSR; wrote *Russia at War: 1941-45,* 1964.
b. Feb 4, 1901, Russia
d. Mar 5, 1969 in Paris, France
Source: *BioIn 8, 9; ConAu 25R, P-1; CurBio 43, 69; WhAm 5*

Wertham, Fredric
German. Author
Influential in suggesting violence in films, TV is dangerous to youth; with NYC Dept. of Hospitals, 1932-81.
b. 1895 in Munich, Germany
d. Nov 18, 1981 in Kempton, Pennsylvania
Source: *AmAu&B; Au&Wr 71; BiDrAPA 77; BioIn 1, 2, 4, 12, 13; BlueB 76; ConAu 5R, 105; CurBio 49, 82, 82N; EncACom; InSci; IntAu&W 76, 77, 82; ScF&FL 1, 2, 92; TwCA SUP; WhAm 8; WhoAm 74, 76, 78; WhoWor 74*

Wertheimer, Linda (Cozby)
American. Broadcast Journalist
With NPR since 1971; host of "All Things Considered," 1989—.
b. Mar 19, 1943 in Carlsbad, New Mexico
Source: *CurBio 95*

Wertheimer, Max
American. Psychologist
Co-founder, Gestalt movement, 1912.
b. Apr 15, 1880 in Prague, Bohemia
d. Oct 12, 1943 in New Rochelle, New York
Source: *BiDPsy; BioIn 1, 7, 14, 17; ConAu 123; DcAmB S3; FacFETw; GuPsyc; InSci; McGEWB; NamesHP*

Wertmuller, Lina von Eigg
[Arcangela Felice Assunta Wertmuller von Elgg]
Italian. Director
In popular films: *Seven Beauties,* 1976; *Seduction of Mimi,* 1974.
b. Aug 14, 1928 in Rome, Italy
Source: *Benet 87; BioIn 14; ConAu 97; ConLC 16; ContDcW 89; ConTFT 6; CurBio 76; FilmEn; HalFC 84, 88; IntDcWB; IntMPA 84, 86, 92; MovMk; NewYTBS 75; WomWMM; WorAl*

Wescott, Glenway
American. Author
Novels include *The Grandmothers,* 1927; *The Pilgrim Hawk,* 1940.
b. Apr 11, 1901 in Kewaskum, Wisconsin
d. Feb 22, 1987 in Rosemont, New Jersey
Source: *AmAu&B; AmNov; AnObit 1987; Benet 87; BenetAL 91; BioIn 2, 4, 5, 7, 8, 9, 12, 13, 15, 16, 17; BlueB 76; CamGLE; CamHAL; CasWL; ChhPo S3; CnDAL; ConAmA; ConAmL; ConAu 13R, 23NR, 121; ConLC 13; ConNov 72, 76, 82, 86; CyWA 58; DcLB 4, 9, 102; DcLEL; GrWrEL N; LngCTC; ModAL; NewYTBS 87; Novels; OxCAmL 65, 83, 95; PenC AM; RAdv 1; REn; REnAL; RfGAmL 87, 94; TwCA, SUP; TwCWr; WhAm 9; WhoAm 74, 76, 78, 86; WisWr; WrDr 76, 80, 82, 84, 86*

Wesendonck, Mathilde Luckemeyer
German. Poet
Friend of Richard Wagner; he set five of her poems to music as "The Wesendonck Songs."
b. Dec 23, 1828 in Elberfeld, Austria
d. Aug 31, 1902 in Traunblick, Austria
Source: *Baker 78; OxCGer 76*

Wesker, Arnold
English. Dramatist
Plays include *Their Very Own Golden City,* 1966; *The Merchant,* 1977.
b. May 24, 1932 in London, England
Source: *Au&Wr 71; Benet 87, 96; BiE&WWA; BioIn 6, 7, 8, 9, 10, 11, 12, 13, 14, 17, 18; BlmGEL; BlueB 76; CamGEL; CamGLE; CamGWoT; CasWL; CnDBLB 8; CnMD; CnThe; ConAu 1NR, 1R, 7AS, 33NR; ConBrDr; ConDr 73, 77, 82, 88, 93; ConLC 3, 5, 42; ConTFT 7, 14; CroCD; CrtSuDr; CurBio 62; CyWA 89; DcArts; DcLB 13; DcLEL 1940; EncWL, 2, 3; EncWT; Ent; GrWrEL DR; IntAu&W 76, 77, 82, 86, 89, 91, 93; IntDcT 2; IntvTCA 2; IntWW 74, 75, 76, 77, 78, 79, 80, 81, 82, 83, 89, 91, 93; LinLib L; LngCEL; LngCTC; MajMD 1; MajTwCW; MakMC; McGEWD 72, 84; ModBrL, S1, S2; ModWD; NewC; NotNAT, A; OxCEng 85, 95; OxCThe 67, 83; PenC ENG; PlP&P; RAdv 14, 13-2; REnWD; RfGEnL 91; RGTwCWr; TwCWr; WebE&AL; Who 74, 82, 83, 85, 88, 90, 92, 94; WhoThe 72, 77, 81; WhoTwCL; WhoWor 74, 76, 78, 84, 87, 89, 91, 93,*

95, 96, 97; WorAu 1950; WrDr 76, 80, 82, 84, 86, 88, 90, 92, 94, 96

Wesley, Charles Harris
American. Historian, Educator
Leading figure in modern study of black history; wrote several books, including *Negro Labor in the United States, 1850-1925,* 1927.
b. Dec 2, 1891 in Louisville, Kentucky
d. Aug 16, 1987 in Washington, District of Columbia
Source: *BiDAmEd; BioIn 2, 3, 5, 6, 7, 9, 15; ConAu 101; CurBio 44, 87; EncSoH; InB&W 80; LivgBAA; OhA&B; SelBAAf; WhAm 9; WhoAm 74, 76, 78; WhoBlA 85*

Wesley, John
English. Religious Leader
Founded Methodism at Oxford U, 1729; name derived from methodical devotion to study, religion.
b. Jun 28, 1703 in Lincoln, England
d. Mar 3, 1791 in London, England
Source: *Alli; ApCAB; AtlBL; Baker 78, 84, 92; BbD; Benet 87, 96; BiDAmM; BiD&SB; BioIn 1, 2, 3, 4, 5, 6, 7, 8, 9, 10, 11, 12, 13, 14, 16, 17, 19, 20, 21; BlkwCE; BlmGEL; BritAu; CamGEL; CamGLE; CasWL; Chambr 2; ChhPo, S1; CyEd; DcAfL; DcBiPP; DcEnA; DcEnL; DcEuL; DcLB 104; DcLEL; DcNaB; Dis&D; Drake; EncAAH; EncEnl; EncSoH; EncWM; EvLB; HarEnUS; HisWorL; IlEncMy; LegTOT; LinLib L, S; LngCEL; LuthC 75; McGEWB; NatCAB 5; NewC; NewCBEL; NewCol 75; NewGrDM 80; OxCEng 67, 85, 95; OxCMus; PenC ENG; PoChrch; RAdv 14, 13-4; RComWL; REn; WebE&AL; WhDW; WorAl; WorAlBi*

Wesselmann, Tom
American. Artist
Best known for series of *The Great American Nude* paintings in different set-ups, media.
b. Feb 23, 1931 in Cincinnati, Ohio
Source: *AmArt; BioIn 12, 13, 14, 15; BlueB 76; BriEAA; ConArt 77, 83, 89, 96; ConAu 108; DcAmArt; DcCAA 71, 77, 88, 94; DcCAr 81; IntWW 74, 75, 76, 77, 78, 79, 80, 81, 82, 83, 89, 91, 93; OxCTwCA; OxDcArt; PhDcTCA 77; PrintW 83, 85; WhoAm 74, 76, 78, 80, 82, 84, 86, 88, 90; WhoAmA 73, 76, 78, 80, 82, 84, 86, 89, 91, 93; WhoE 83, 85, 86; WhoWor 74; WorArt 1950*

Wesson, Daniel Baird
[Smith and Wesson]
American. Manufacturer
With Horace Smith, developed repeating action pistol, 1854; open cylinder revolver, 1857.
b. May 25, 1825 in Worcester, Massachusetts
d. 1906
Source: *BioIn 2, 18; DcAmB; NatCAB 10; WhAm 1; WorInv*

Wesson, David
American. Chemist
Discovered refining process for cottonseed oil, 1899, marketed under trade name, Wesson Oil.
b. Jan 14, 1861 in New York, New York
d. May 22, 1934 in Montclair, New Jersey
Source: *EncAB-A 4; Entr; NatCAB 27; WhAm 1*

West, Adam
[William West Anderson]
American. Actor
Played Bruce Wayne/Batman on TV series "Batman," 1966-68.
b. Sep 19, 1938 in Walla Walla, Washington
Source: *BioIn 15, 16; ConTFT 8; FilmgC; HalFC 88; IntMPA 92; WhoHol A*

West, Benjamin
American. Artist
Realistic, historic paintings include *Death of General Wolfe.*
b. Oct 10, 1738 in Springfield, Pennsylvania
d. Mar 11, 1820 in London, England
Source: *Alli; AmBi; AmCulL; ApCAB; AtlBL; Benet 87, 96; BiDLA; BioIn 1, 2, 3, 4, 5, 6, 7, 8, 9, 10, 11, 12, 13, 14, 19; BkIE; BriEAA; CelCen; ClaDrA; DcAmArt; DcAmB; DcArts; DcBiPP; DcBrECP; DcBrWA; DcNaB; Drake; EncAB-H 1974, 1996; EncCRAm; FolkA 87; HarEnUS; IlBEAAW; IntDcAA 90; LegTOT; LinLib S; McGDA; McGEWB; NatCAB 5; NewYHSD; OxCAmH; OxCAmL 65; OxCArt; OxDcArt; REn; TwCBDA; WebAB 74, 79; WhAm HS; WhDW; WorAlBi*

West, Cornel
American. Educator, Author
Professor, Union Theological Seminary, 1977-84, 1987-88; Yale University, 1984-87, Princeton University, 1988-94; Harvard University, 1994—.
b. Jun 2, 1953 in Tulsa, Oklahoma
Source: *ConBlB 5; CurBio 93; DcTwCCu 5; News 94, 94-2; NewYTBS 91; WhoAfA 96; WhoAm 95, 96; WhoBlA 94*

West, Dorothy
American. Author, Editor
Wrote *Living it Easy,* 1948; *The Richer, the Poorer: Stories, Sketches and Reminiscences,* 1995; founded *Challenge* magazine, 1934.
b. Jun 2, 1907 in Boston, Massachusetts
Source: *BlkWAm; BlkWr 2; ConAu 143; ConBlB 12; DcLB 76; DcTwCCu 5; HarlReB; News 96, 96-1; NotBlAW 1; OxCWoWr 95; SchCGBL; WhoAfA 96; WhoBlA 92, 94*

West, Dottie
[Dorothy Marie Marsh; Mrs. Alan Winters]
American. Singer
First woman to win country music Grammy for "Here Comes My Baby," 1964; won Clio for co-writing "Country Sunshine" for commercials, 1973, the first awarded to a country artist.
b. Oct 11, 1932 in McMinnville, Tennessee
d. Sep 4, 1991 in Nashville, Tennessee
Source: *AnObit 1991; Baker 84, 92; BgBkCoM; BioIn 12, 13, 14, 15, 17, 18, 19, 21; ConMus 8; CounME 74, 74A; EncFCWM 69, 83; HarEnCM 87; IlEncCM; LegTOT; News 92, 92-2; NewYTBS 91; OxCPMus; PenEncP; RkOn 85; WhoAm 86, 88; WhoAmW 87, 89; WhoHol 92*

West, James Edward
American. Social Worker
First leader of US Boy Scouts, 1911.
b. May 16, 1876 in Washington, District of Columbia
d. May 15, 1948 in New Rochelle, New York
Source: *AmAu&B; BioIn 1, 2, 3, 7; DcAmB S4; NatCAB 34; WhAm 2*

West, Jerry
[Jerome Alan West]
"Mr. Clutch"
American. Basketball Player
Ten-time all-star guard, LA, 1960-74; led NBA in scoring, 1970, in assists, 1972; Hall of Fame, 1979.
b. May 28, 1938 in Cabin Creek, West Virginia
Source: *BasBi; BiDAmSp BK; BioIn 5, 6, 8, 9, 10, 11, 12, 20, 21; CelR; CmCal; ConAu X; FacFETw; LegTOT; NewYTBS 74; OfNBA 87; WhoAm 74, 78, 80, 86, 90; WhoBbl 73; WhoSpor; WhoWest 92; WorAl; WorAlBi*

West, Jessamyn
American. Author
Wrote stories based on Quaker ancestors; first collection *The Friendly Persuasion,* 1945.
b. Jul 18, 1902 in Indiana
d. Feb 25, 1984 in Napa, California
Source: *AmWomWr; AnObit 1984; BenetAL 91; BioIn 11, 12, 13; CmCal; ConAu 9R, 27NR, 112; ConLC 7, 17; ConNov 76, 82; CurBio 77, 84N; CyWA 89; DcLB 6, Y84N; EncFWF; FemiCLE; InWom SUP; LegTOT; LibW; MajTwCW; NewYTBS 84; REnAL; ScF&FL 92; SmATA 37N; TwCA SUP; TwCRHW 90; TwCWW 91; WhAm 8; WhoAm 76, 78, 80, 82; WhoAmW 79, 81, 83; WrDr 84*

West, Mae
American. Actor
Known for sex appeal, frankness, films with W C Fields, including *My Little Chickadee,* 1940.

b. Aug 17, 1893 in New York, New York
d. Nov 22, 1980 in Hollywood, California
Source: *AmAu&B; AmWomWr; BioAmW; CamGWoT; ConAu 89, 102, 107; CurBio 67, 81, 81N; DcAmB S10; EncWT; Ent; FunnyW; GrLiveH; JoeFr; ModWD; MotPP; MovMk; NewYTBE 70; NewYTBS 80; NotNAT, A; OxCAmH; OxCFilm; ReelWom; REnAL; ThFT; WebAB 74; WhDW; WhoAm 74; WhoCom; WhoHol A; WhoThe 77; WhoWor 74; WomWMM; WorEFlm*

West, Morris Langlo
Australian. Author
Wrote *The Shoes of the Fisherman,* 1963; filmed, 1968.
b. Apr 26, 1916 in Melbourne, Australia
Source: *Au&Wr 71; Benet 87; BioIn 13; ConAu 5R, 24NR; ConLC 6, 33; ConNov 86, 91; CurBio 66; DcLP 87A; HalFC 84, 88; IntAu&W 91; IntWW 83, 91; MajTwCW; ModBrL; OxCAusL; REn; SpyFic; TwCSAPR; TwCWr; Who 85, 92; WhoAm 86, 90; WhoWor 87, 91; WhoWrEP 89; WorAlBi; WorAu 1950; WrDr 86, 92*

West, Nathanael
[Nathan Wallenstein Weinstein]
American. Author
Wrote *Miss Lonelyhearts,* 1933; *The Day of the Locust,* 1939.
b. Oct 17, 1903 in New York, New York
d. Dec 22, 1940 in El Centro, California
Source: *AgeMat; AmAu&B; AmWr; AtlBL; BioIn 14, 15, 17; CamGEL; CamGLE; CamHAL; CasWL; CmCal; CnMWL; ConAu 104, 125; CurBio 41; CyWA 58; DcLB 4, 9, 28; DcLEL; DcNAA; EncWL, 2, 3; FacFETw; FilmgC; LegTOT; LngCTC; MagSAmL; MajTwCW; McGEWB; ModAL, S1, S2; OxCAmL 65, 83, 95; PenC AM; RAdv 1; REn; REnAL; RfGAmL 87, 94; RGTwCWr; ScF&FL 1; ShSCr 16; TwCA, SUP; TwCLC 1, 14, 44; TwCWr; WebAB 74, 79; WebE&AL; WhAm 4; WhDW; WhoTwCL; WorAl; WorAlBi; WrPh*

West, Rebecca, Dame
[Cecily Isobel Fairfield Andrews]
Irish. Author, Journalist
Wrote *The Fountain Overflows,* 1957; nonfiction *The Meaning of Treason,* 1949.
b. Dec 25, 1892 in County Kerry, Ireland
d. Mar 15, 1983 in London, England
Source: *AnObit 1983; ArtclWW 2; Au&Wr 71; Benet 87, 96; BiDBrF 2; BioIn 1, 2, 3, 4, 5, 6, 7, 8, 9, 10, 11, 12, 13, 14, 15, 16, 17, 18, 21; BlmGWL; BlueB 76; CamGEL; CamGLE; CasWL; Chambr 3; ConAu 5R, 19NR, 109; ConLC 7, 9, 31; ConNov 72, 76, 82; ContDcW 89; CurBio 68, 83N; CyWA 58, 89; DcArts; DcLB 36, Y83N; DcLEL; DcNaB 1981; EncBrWW; EncWL, 2, 3; EvLB; FacFETw; FemiCLE; FemiWr; GrWrEL N; IntAu&W 76, 77; IntDcWB; IntWW 74, 75, 76, 77, 78, 79, 80, 81, 82; InWom, SUP; LegTOT; LinLib L, S; LngCTC; MajTwCW; ModBrL, S1, S2; ModWoWr; NewC; NewCBEL; NewYTBS 82, 83; Novels; OxCEng 67, 85, 95; PenC ENG; PenNWW B; RadHan; RAdv 1, 14, 13-1; REn; RfGEnL 91; RGTwCWr; ScF&FL 1, 2, 92; TwCA, SUP; TwCWr; WhAm 8; WhE&EA; Who 74, 82, 83; WhoAmW 66, 68, 70, 72, 74, 75; WhoLA; WhoTwCL; WhoWor 74; WomFir; WorAl; WorAlBi; WrDr 76, 80, 82, 84*

West, Riff
[Molly Hatchet]
American. Musician
Bass player with heavy metal band since 1982.
b. Apr 3, 1950 in Orlando, Florida

West, Togo D., Jr.
American. Government Official
Secretary of the Army, 1993—.
b. Jun 21, 1942

Westall, Robert Atkinson
English. Children's Author
Author of over 30 children's books; won the Carnegie Medal for *The Machine-Gunners,* 1975 and *Scarecrows,* 1980.
b. Oct 7, 1929 in Tynemouth, England
d. Apr 15, 1993 in Cheshire, England
Source: *BioIn 13, 15; ChlLR 13; ConAu 18NR; ConLC 81; DcVicP 2; FifBJA; IntAu&W 91; OxCChiL; SmATA 2AS; TwCChW 89; Who 92; WrDr 92*

Westerman, Floyd
American. Entertainer, Songwriter
Albums include *Custer Died for Your Sins* and *The Land is Your Mother;* played Ten Bears in *Dances with Wolves,.*
b. 1936 in Sissenton-Wahpeton ReservaSouth Dakota
Source: *BioIn 21; NotNaAm*

Westermann, H(orace) C(lifford)
American. Sculptor
Works of metal, wood take on a comic strip flare; known for surrealist displacement.
b. Dec 11, 1922 in Los Angeles, California
d. Nov 3, 1981 in Danbury, Connecticut
Source: *AnObit 1981; BioIn 8, 11, 12, 13, 14, 17; BriEAA; ConArt 77, 83; DcAmArt; DcCAA 71; DcCAr 81; OxCTwCA; PhDcTCA 77; WhAm 8; WhoAm 74, 76, 78, 80, 86, 88, 90, 92, 94, 95, 96, 97; WhoAmA 73, 76, 78, 80, 82N, 84N, 86N, 89N, 91N, 93N; WhoE 83, 85, 86; WhoWor 74*

Westermarck, Edward Alexander
Finnish. Anthropologist, Philosopher
Defender of conservative morality; traced origin of marriage to apes.
b. Nov 20, 1862 in Helsingfors, Finland
d. Sep 3, 1939 in Lapinlahti, Finland
Source: *DcSoc; LinLib S; REn; WhDW; WhE&EA; WhLit*

Westheimer, Irvin Ferdinand
American. Businessman
Credited with the idea for Big Brothers, 1903; started Big Brothers organization, Cincinnati, 1912.
b. Sep 19, 1879 in Newark, New Jersey
d. Dec 29, 1980 in Cincinnati, Ohio
Source: *AnObit 1980; BlueB 76; NewYTBS 81; WhAm 7; WhoAm 74, 76, 78; WhoFI 74, 75*

Westheimer, Ruth
[Karola Ruth Siegel]
"Dr. Ruth"
American. Psychiatrist
Hosts radio, TV shows on sexual relationships.
b. 1929 in Frankfurt am Main, Germany
Source: *BioIn 12, 13, 14, 15, 16; CelR 90; CurBio 87; InWom SUP; NewYTBS 85, 87; WhoAmW 91; WhoTelC; WrDr 92*

Westinghouse, George
American. Inventor, Manufacturer
Invented air brake and automatic railroad signals; held over 400 patents.
b. Oct 6, 1846 in Central Bridge, New York
d. Mar 12, 1914 in New York, New York
Source: *AmBi; ApCAB X; AsBiEn; BiDAmBL 83; BiESc; BiInAmS; BioIn 1, 3, 4, 5, 6, 7, 8, 9, 11, 12, 13, 14, 16, 18, 21; DcAmB; DcInv; DcTwBBL; EncAB-H 1974, 1996; EncABHB 2; Entr; GayN; InSci; LarDcSc; LegTOT; LinLib S; McGEWB; MemAm; NatCAB 11, 15; OxCAmH; TwCBDA; WebAB 74, 79; WhAm 1; WhDW; WorAl; WorAlBi; WorInv*

Westlake, Donald E(dwin) Edmund
American. Author
Subjects include mystery, crime, humor, satire; wrote *Nobody's Perfect,* 1977.
b. Jul 12, 1933 in New York, New York
Source: *AmAu&B; BioIn 14; ConAu 13AS, 16NR, 17R; ConLC 7, 33; CrtSuMy; DcLP 87A; EncMys; HalFC 84, 88; IntAu&W 91; NewYTBS 80; TwCCr&M 85, 91; WhoAm 82, 84, 86, 90; WhoEnt 92; WhoUSWr 88; WhoWrEP 89, 92, 95; WorAu 1975; WrDr 86, 92*

Westley, Helen
[Henrietta Meserole Manney]
American. Actor
Helped found the Theater Guild, 1918-36.
b. Mar 28, 1879 in New York, New York
d. Dec 12, 1942 in Franklin County, New Jersey
Source: *CurBio 43; DcAmB S3; FilmEn; FilmgC; ForYSC; HalFC 80, 84, 88; InWom; MovMk; NotAW; NotNAT B; ObitOF 79; OxCAmT 84; PlP&P; ThFT; Vers B; WhoHol B; WhScrn 74, 77, 83; WhThe*

Westmore, Perc(ival)
American. Cosmetics Executive
Hollywood make-up artist; founded House of Westmore; developed make-up studio at Warner Brothers Studios.
b. Oct 29, 1904 in Canterbury, England
d. Sep 30, 1970
Source: *BioIn 9, 10; CurBio 45, 70; FilmgC; HalFC 84; IntDcF 1-4, 2-4; NewYTBE 70*

Westmoreland, William Childs
American. Military Leader
Commanded US forces in Vietnam, 1964-68; Army chief of staff, 1968-72.
b. Mar 16, 1914 in Spartanburg, South Carolina
Source: *BioIn 5, 6, 7, 8, 9, 10, 11, 12, 13, 14, 15, 16; BioNews 74; BlueB 76; ColdWar 2; ConAu 101; CurBio 61; DcAmMiB; EncAB-H 1974, 1996; EncWB; FacFETw; HarEnMi; IntWW 74, 75, 76, 77, 78, 79, 80, 81, 82, 83, 89, 91, 93; LinLib S; McGEWB; NewYTBS 84; PolProf J, NF; SmATA 63; WebAB 74, 79; WebAMB; WhoAm 74, 76; WhoGov 72; WhoWor 74; WorAl*

Weston, Edward
American. Photographer
One of most influential photographers of 20th c; was subject of film *The Photographer,* 1948.
b. Mar 24, 1886 in Highland Park, Illinois
d. Jan 1, 1958 in Carmel, California
Source: *Benet 87, 96; BioIn 1, 2, 4, 5, 6, 7, 8, 9, 10, 11, 12, 13, 14, 15, 16, 19, 20, 21; BriEAA; CmCal; ConPhot 82, 88; DcAmArt; DcArts; DcTwDes; FacFETw; ICPEnP; LegTOT; MacBEP; ObitOF 79; WebAB 79; WhAm 3; WhAmArt 85; WorAl; WorAlBi*

Weston, Edward F
American. Manufacturer
Joined Western Electric, 1900; pres., 1925; chm., 1944-71.
b. Oct 24, 1879 in Newark, New Jersey
d. Jul 27, 1971
Source: *BioIn 9; NewYTBE 71; WhAm 5*

Weston, Jack
[Morris Weinstein]
American. Actor
Supporting actor in films *The Four Seasons,* 1981; *High Road to China,* 1983.
b. Aug 21, 1925 in Cleveland, Ohio
d. May 3, 1996 in New York, New York
Source: *BioIn 12; ConTFT 8; EncAFC; FilmEn; FilmgC; HalFC 84; IntMPA 86, 88; WhoAm 86; WhoThe 81*

Westover, Russell (Channing)
American. Cartoonist
Created popular working-girl comic strip *Tillie the Toiler,* 1921-50s.
b. Aug 3, 1886 in Los Angeles, California
d. Mar 6, 1966 in San Rafael, California
Source: *BioIn 7; ObitOF 79; WhAm 4, 7; WhAmArt 85; WorECom*

Westphal, Paul Douglas
American. Basketball Player
Three-time all-star guard, 1972-84, with several NBA teams; named comeback player of yr., 1983.
b. Nov 30, 1950 in Torrance, California
Source: *BiDAmSp Sup; BioIn 13; WhoAm 80, 82; WhoBbl 73*

Westrup, J(ack) A(llan), Sir
English. Musician, Lecturer, Educator
Music professor, Oxford U., from 1947; edited *New Oxford History of Music;* knighted, 1960.
b. Jul 26, 1904 in London, England
d. Apr 21, 1975 in Headley, England
Source: *Au&Wr 71; Baker 78, 84, 92; ConAu 115; DcNaB 1971; IntWW 74; NewGrDM 80; NewGrDO; NewOxM; OxCMus; WhoAm 74; WhoMus 72*

Westwick, Harry
"Rat"
Canadian. Hockey Player
Goalie-rover, Ottawa Silver Sevens, 1895-1908; Hall of Fame, 1962.
b. Apr 23, 1876 in Ottawa, Ontario, Canada
d. Apr 3, 1957 in Ottawa, Ontario, Canada
Source: *WhoHcky 73*

Westwood, Jean Miles
American. Politician
Dem. delegate, committeewoman; campaign director for presidential candidates.
b. Nov 22, 1923 in Price, Utah
Source: *BioIn 9, 75, 77, 91; WhoWest 74, 76*

Wettig, Patricia
American. Actor
Played Nancy Weston on TV series *Thirty Something,* 1987-1991.
b. Dec 4, 1951 in Grove City, Pennsylvania
Source: *BioIn 16, 20; ConTFT 9; IntMPA 94, 96; LegTOT; WhoAm 90, 95, 96, 97; WhoAmW 91; WhoEnt 92; WhoHol 92*

Wexler, Haskell
American. Director, Filmmaker
Won Oscars for cinematography for *Who's Afraid of Virginia Woolf?* 1966; *Bound for Glory* 1976.
b. 1926 in Chicago, Illinois
Source: *BioIn 11, 15, 16, 19; ConTFT 7; FilmEn; FilmgC; HalFC 80, 84, 88; IntDcF 1-4, 2-4; IntMPA 75, 76, 77, 78, 79, 80, 81, 82, 84, 86, 88, 92, 94; MiSFD 9; NewYTBE 73; OxCFilm; WhoAm 86, 90; WhoEnt 92; WorEFlm*

Wexler, Nancy Sabin
American. Psychologist
Pres. Hereditary Disease Foundation; research led to development of test which determines whether one will develop Huntington's disease.
b. Jul 19, 1945 in Washington, District of Columbia
Source: *CurBio 94; News 92; WhoAm 96; WhoAmW 95*

Wexler, Norman
American. Screenwriter
Films include *Joe,* 1970; *Saturday Night Fever,* 1977.
b. Aug 16, 1926 in New Bedford, Massachusetts
Source: *ConAu 116, 154; VarWW 85; WhoAm 80, 82, 84; WhoE 91; WhoUSWr 88; WhoWrEP 89, 92, 95*

Wexler, Peter John
American. Designer
Noted for Broadway stage, costume designs: *The Happy Time,* 1968; *On A Clear Day You Can See Forever,* 1966.
b. Oct 31, 1936 in New York, New York
Source: *BioIn 10; BlueB 76; ConTFT 5, 6; MetOEnc; NotNAT; VarWW 85; WhoAm 74, 76, 78, 80, 82, 84, 86, 88, 90, 92, 94, 95, 96, 97; WhoE 95; WhoEnt 92; WhoOp 76; WhoThe 81*

Wexley, John
American. Dramatist
Wrote film *Hangmen Also Die,* 1943; blacklisted by studio.
b. Sep 14, 1907 in New York, New York
d. Feb 4, 1985 in Doylestown, Pennsylvania
Source: *AmAu&B; BenetAL 91; BioIn 14; CnMD; ConAmA; ConAu 115; ModWD; OxCAmL 65, 83, 95; PenC AM; REn; REnAL; WhoThe 77A*

Wexner, Leslie
American. Businessman
Founded The Limited, a women's clothing store, 1963.
b. Sep 8, 1937 in Dayton, Ohio
Source: *ConAmBL; CurBio 94*

Weyden, Rogier van der
[Roger de la Pasture]
Flemish. Artist
Religious, portrait painter; noted for color, emotion, *Descent From the Cross,* 1435.
b. 1399 in Tournai, Belgium
d. Jun 16, 1464 in Brussels, Belgium
Source: *AtlBL; DcArts; McGDA; McGEWB; OxCArt; OxDcArt; REn; WhDW*

Weyerhaeuser, Frederick
"Lumber King"
American. Business Executive
Lumber tycoon; acquired over two million acres of forest land from WI to Pacific NW at time of death.
b. Nov 21, 1834 in Mainz, Germany
d. Apr 4, 1914 in Pasadena, California
Source: *ApCAB X; BiDAmBL 83; BioIn 3, 5, 11, 14, 15; NatCAB 14; WebAB 74, 79; WhAm 1*

Weyerhaeuser, Frederick Edward
American. Business Executive
Son of Frederick Weyerhaeuser, reportedly largest owner of forest land in US.
b. Jan 16, 1895 in Rock Island, Illinois
d. Oct 18, 1945 in Saint Paul, Minnesota
Source: *BiDAmBL 83; CurBio 45; DcAmB S3; EncAB-A 21; NatCAB 37; WhAm 2*

Weygand, Maxime
French. Military Leader
Supreme allied commander, 1939, known for unsuccessful attempt to create new front.
b. Jan 21, 1867 in Brussels, Belgium
d. Jan 28, 1965 in Paris, France
Source: *BiDFrPL; BioIn 1, 3, 7, 17; CurBio 40, 65; DcTwHis; EncTR 91; FacFETw; HarEnMi; HisEWW; WhoMilH 76; WhWW-II*

Whale, James
English. Director
Films include *Frankenstein,* 1931; *Invisible Man,* 1933.
b. Jul 22, 1896 in Dudley, England
d. May 29, 1957 in Hollywood, California
Source: *BiDFilm, 94; BioIn 4, 10, 11; CmMov; DcFM; FacFETw; FanAl; FilmEn; FilmgC; IlWWHD 1; MiSFD 9N; OxCFilm; PenEncH; TwCLC 63; WhThe; WorEFlm*

Whalen, Grover (Michael) A(loysius)
American. Merchant
Pres. of NY World's Fair, 1939-40; NY Police commissioner, 1928-30.
b. Jun 2, 1886 in New York, New York
d. Apr 20, 1962 in New York, New York
Source: *DcAmB S7; WhAm 4*

Whalen, Michael
[Joseph Kenneth Shovlin]
American. Actor
Leading man of B-films, 1936-60, including *Sing, Baby, Sing; Poor Little Rich Girl.*
b. Jun 30, 1902 in Wilkes-Barre, Pennsylvania
d. Apr 14, 1974 in Woodland Hills, California
Source: *FilmEn; FilmgC; MovMk; What 5; WhoHol B; WhScrn 77, 83*

Wham!
[George Michael; Andrew Ridgeley]
English. Music Group
Childhood friends who formed group, 1982-86; had three number one hits, including "Everything She Wants," 1985.
Source: *BioIn 14, 15, 16, 17, 18; EncPR&S 89; EncRk 88; EncRkSt; HarEnR 86; PenEncP; RkOn 85; WhoAm 92; WhoEnt 92*

Wharton, Clifton Reginald, Jr.
American. University Administrator
Pres. of MI State U, 1970-78; chancellor, SUNY System, 1978-87.
b. Sep 13, 1926 in Boston, Massachusetts
Source: *AmMWSc 73S; BioIn 9, 10, 11, 12, 13, 15; BlueB 76; ConAu 41R; CurBio 58, 87; Ebony 1; InB&W 85; IntWW 83, 91; LEduc 74; NewYTBS 77; SelBAAf; SelBAAu; St&PR 91; WhoAm 74, 76, 78, 80, 82, 84, 86, 90, 92, 94, 95, 96, 97; WhoBlA 85, 92; WhoE 79, 81, 83, 85, 86, 93; WhoFI 89, 92, 94; WhoIns 92; WhoMW 74, 76, 78; WhoUSWr 88; WhoWrEP 89, 92, 95*

Wharton, Edith
[Edith Newbold Jones]
American. Author
Won Pulitzer, 1921, for *The Age of Innocence;* noted for *Ethan Frome,* 1911, and novels of NY society.
b. Jan 24, 1862 in New York, New York
d. Aug 11, 1937 in Paris, France
Source: *AmBi; AmCulL; AmDec 1900; AmWomWr 92; ApCAB X; ArtclWW 2; AtlBL; Benet 87; BenetAL 91; BioAmW; BioIn 14, 15, 16, 17, 18, 19, 20, 21; BlmGWL; CamGEL; CamGLE; CamHAL; CasWL; ChhPo S3; ConAu 104, 132; ContDcW 89; CyWA 89; DcAmB S2; DcLB 4, 9, 12, 78, DS13; EncAB-H 1974; EncSF; EncWL 2, 3; FacFETw; FemiCLE; GayN; GoodHs; GrLiveH; GrWomW; HanAmWH; HerW, 84; IntDcWB; LegTOT; LibW; LinLib L; MagSAmL; MajTwCW; MakMC; ModAL S1, S2; ModAWWr; ModWoWr; MorMA; NatCAB 14; NotAW; NotNAT B; Novels; OxCAmL 65, 83; OxCEng 67, 85; OxCWoWr 95; PenC AM; PenEncH; RAdv 1, 13-1; RComAH; RealN; REn; REnAL; RfGAmL 87; RfGShF; ScF&FL 1; ShSCr 6; ShSWr; SupFW; TwCA SUP; TwCBDA; TwCLC 3, 9, 27, 53; TwCRHW 94; TwCWr; WebAB 74, 79; WhAm 1; WhDW; WhE&EA; WhLit; WhoHr&F; WhoTwCL; WomWWA 14; WorAlBi; WorLitC; WrPh*

Wharton, Joseph
American. Manufacturer
First to produce nickel in US, 1873; founded Bethlehem Steel, 1873, Wharton School of Finance, 1881.
b. Mar 3, 1826 in Philadelphia, Pennsylvania
d. Jan 11, 1909
Source: *ApCAB; BiDAmBL 83; BiInAmS; BioIn 4, 15; DcAmB; EncABHB 3; NatCAB 13; TwCBDA; WhAm 1; WorAl; WorAlBi*

Wheat, Zack
[Zachariah Davis Wheat]
"Buck"
American. Baseball Player
Outfielder, 1909-27, mostly with Brooklyn; led NL in batting, 1918; had .317 lifetime batting average; Hall of Fame, 1959.
b. May 23, 1888 in Hamilton, Missouri
d. Mar 11, 1972 in Sedalia, Missouri
Source: *BioIn 14, 15; DcAmB S9; WhoProB 73; WhoSpor*

Wheatley, Phillis
American. Poet
Ex-slave; first black woman to have poetry published, 1770.
b. 1753, Senegal
d. Dec 5, 1784 in Boston, Massachusetts
Source: *AfrA; AfrAmAl 6; AfrAmW; Alli; AmAu; AmAu&B; AmWomWr; ApCAB; ArtclWW 2; Benet 87, 96; BenetAL 91; BioAmW; BioIn 1, 2, 3, 4, 6, 7, 8, 9, 10, 11, 12, 14, 15, 16, 17, 18, 19, 20, 21; BlkAmW 1; BlkAWP; BlkLC; BlkWrNE; BlmGEL; BlmGWL; CamGLE; ChhPo; ColARen; ConAu 1R; ContDcW 89; CyAL 1; DcAmAu; DcAmB; DcAmNB; DcBrAmW; DcLEL; Drake; FemiCLE; GoodHs; GrWomW; GrWrEL P; HanAmWH; HarEnUS; HerW, 84; InB&W 80, 85; IntDcWB; InWom, SUP; LegTOT; LibW; LitC 3; McGEWB; NegAl 76, 83, 89; NotAW; NotBlAW 1; OxCAmL 65, 83, 95; OxCEng 67; OxCWoWr 95; PoeCrit 3; PorAmW; RAdv 13-1; REn; REnAL; RfGAmL 87, 94; SchCGBL; SelBAAf; SelBAAu; WebAB 74, 79; WhAm HS; WhAmRev; WomFir; WorAl; WorAlBi; WorLitC*

Wheatstone, Charles, Sir
English. Scientist, Inventor
Invented the concertina, 1829; electric telegram, 1837; Wheatstone bridge for measuring electrical resistances, 1843.
b. Feb 6, 1802 in Gloucester, England
d. Oct 19, 1875 in Paris, France
Source: *Alli, SUP; AsBiEn; BiDPsy; BiESc; BioIn 2, 7, 8, 9, 10, 14, 15; CamDcSc; CelCen; DcArts; DcBiPP; DcInv; DcNaB; DcScB; ICPEnP; InSci; LarDcSc; MacBEP; NamesHP; NewGrDM 80; OxCMus; WhDW; WorAl; WorAlBi; WorInv*

Wheeler, Bert
[Wheeler and Woolsey; Albert Jerome Wheeler]
American. Comedian
Teamed with Robert Woolsey in over 30 films, including *On Again, Off Again,* 1937.
b. Apr 7, 1895 in Paterson, New Jersey
d. Jan 18, 1968 in New York, New York
Source: *BiE&WWA; BioIn 7, 8, 20; EncVaud; Film 2; FilmEn; FilmgC; ForYSC; HalFC 80, 84, 88; JoeFr; MovMk; NotNAT B; QDrFCA 92; What 1; WhoHol B; WhScrn 74, 77, 83*

Wheeler, Burton Kendall
American. Politician
Dem. politician from MT, 1923-47.
b. Feb 27, 1882 in Hudson, Massachusetts
d. Jan 6, 1975 in Washington, District of Columbia
Source: *AmPolLe; ApCAB X; BiDrAC; BiDrUSC 89; BioIn 1, 6, 7, 10; ConAu 53; CurBio 40, 75; DcAmB S9; EncAAH; WhAm 6; WhAmP; Who 74*

Wheeler, Candace Thurber
American. Designer
Pioneer in textile design; worked with Tiffany, 1879.
b. Mar 24, 1827 in Delaware County, New York
d. Aug 5, 1923 in New York, New York
Source: *BiCAW; InWom SUP; NotAW*

Wheeler, Earle G
American. Government Official
Served as Army chief of staff, 1962-64; confirmed in 1973 that Nixon ordered secret attacks over Cambodia, 1969.
b. Jan 13, 1908 in Washington, District of Columbia
d. Dec 18, 1975 in Frederick, Maryland
Source: *CurBio 65, 76N; IntWW 74, 76N; NewYTBS 75; PolProf J, NF; WebAMB; WhAm 6; WhoAm 74*

Wheeler, Hugh Callingham
English. Writer
Won Tonys for plays based on his books: *A Little Night Music,* 1973; *Candide,* 1974; *Sweeney Todd,* 1979.
b. Mar 19, 1912 in London, England
d. Jul 27, 1987 in Pittsfield, Massachusetts
Source: *BioIn 10, 14, 15; BlueB 76; ConDr 93; ConTFT 5; EncMys; NewGrDO; NewYTBS 87; VarWW 85; WhAm 9; WhE&EA; WhoAm 74, 76, 78, 80, 82, 84, 86; WorAu 1950*

Wheeler, Joseph
American. Military Leader
Resigned from US army to join Confederate army, 1861; tried to reconcile North, South.
b. Sep 10, 1836 in Augusta, Georgia
d. Jan 25, 1906 in New York, New York
Source: *Alli SUP; AmBi; ApCAB; BiDConf; BiDrAC; BiDrUSC 89; BiDSA; BioIn 3, 5, 6, 7, 17; ChhPo S1; CivWDc; DcAmAu; DcAmB; DcAmMiB; DcNAA; EncSoH; GenMudB; HarEnMi; HarEnUS; NatCAB 9; TwCBDA; WebAB 74, 79; WebAMB; WebBD 83; WhAm 1; WhAmP; WhCiWar; WorAl; WorAlBi*

Wheeler, Mortimer
[Robert Eric Mortimer Wheeler]
British. Archaeologist
His book *Alms for Oblivion,* 1966, credited with increased interest in archaeology.
b. Sep 10, 1890 in Edinburgh, Scotland
d. Jul 22, 1976 in Leatherhead, England
Source: *BioIn 1, 3, 4, 5, 6, 8, 11, 12, 13, 14, 21; BlueB 76; ConAu 32NR, 65, 77; CurBio 56, 76N; DcNaB 1971; GrBr; InSci; IntAu&W 77; IntWW 74, 75, 76; LngCTC; NewYTBS 76; ObitOF 79; WhDW; WhE&EA; Who 74; WhoWor 74; WorAl*

Wheeler, Roger Milton
American. Business Executive
Pres., American Magnesium Co., 1968-81; chm., Telex, Inc., 1965-81.
b. Feb 27, 1926 in Boston, Massachusetts
d. May 27, 1981 in Tulsa, Oklahoma
Source: *BioIn 12; BlueB 76; WhAm 8; WhoAm 74, 76, 78, 80, 82; WhoSSW 73*

Wheeler, Schuyler Skaats
American. Inventor
Invented the electric fan.
b. May 17, 1860
d. 1923
Source: *AmBi; BioIn 4; DcAmB; InSci; NatCAB 10, 41; WhAm 1*

Wheeler, William Alrnon
American. US Vice President
Served under Rutherford B Hayes, 1877-81.
b. Jun 30, 1819 in Malone, New York
d. Jun 4, 1887 in Malone, New York
Source: *BiAUS; HarEnUS; WebAB 79*

Wheeler, William Morton
American. Zoologist
A leading expert on ants; books:*Ants: Their Structure, Development, and Behavior,* 1910 and *Social Life among the Insects,* 1923, are classic reference works.
b. Mar 19, 1865 in Milwaukee, Wisconsin
d. Apr 19, 1937 in Cambridge, Massachusetts
Source: *AmBi; AmLY; BioIn 3, 4, 9; DcAmB S2; DcNAA; DcScB; InSci; NamesHP; NatCAB 27; TwCA; WhAm 1*

Wheelock, Eleazar
American. Clergy, Educator
Founded Dartmouth College; served as first pres., 1770-79.
b. Apr 22, 1711 in Windham, Connecticut
d. Apr 24, 1779 in Hanover, New Hampshire
Source: *Alli; AmBi; AmWrBE; ApCAB; BenetAL 91; BiDAmEd; BioIn 1, 3, 9, 17, 19; CyAL 1; CyEd; DcAmB; DcAmReB 1, 2; DcNAA; EncCRAm; EncNAR; HarEnUS; McGEWB; OxCAmH; OxCAmL 65, 83, 95; TwCBDA; WebAB 74, 79; WhAm HS; WhNaAH; WorAl; WorAlBi*

Wheelock, John Hall
American. Poet
First book of poetry was *The Human Fantasy,* 1911.
b. Sep 9, 1886 in Far Rockaway, New York
d. Mar 22, 1978 in New York, New York
Source: *AmAu&B; AmLY; AnMV 1926; Au&Wr 71; BenetAL 91; BioIn 4, 5, 9, 10, 11, 15; BlueB 76; ChhPo, S1, S2, S3; CnDAL; ConAmA; ConAmL; ConAu 13R, 14NR, 77; ConLC 14; ConPo 70, 75; DcAmB S10; DcLB 45; DcLEL; DrAP 75; IntAu&W 77; IntWW 74, 75, 76, 77; ModAL; NewYTBS 78; OxCAmL 65, 83, 95; OxCTwCP; RAdv 1; REn; REnAL; TwCA, SUP; WhAm 7; WhNAA; WhoAm 74, 76, 78; WhoWor 74; WrDr 76*

Whelchel, Lisa
American. Actor
Played Blair on TV series "Facts of Life," 1979-88.
b. May 29, 1963 in Fort Worth, Texas
Source: *BioIn 13; ConTFT 3; LegTOT; VarWW 85; WhoHol 92*

Whicker, Alan Donald
English. Broadcast Journalist
Host of "Whicker's World," 1959-67; winner of numerous awards for his documentaries.
b. Aug 2, 1925 in Cairo, Egypt
Source: *IntAu&W 91; IntWW 91; Who 92*

Whiffen, Marcus
English. Author, Educator
Wrote *American Architecture, 1607-1976,* 1981.
b. Mar 4, 1916 in Weston-under-Penyard, England
Source: *ConAu 12NR, 61, 102; IntAu&W 82*

Whipple, George Hoyt
American. Physician, Educator
Shared 1934 Nobel Prize for discovering treatment for once incurable anemia.
b. Aug 28, 1879 in Ashland, New Hampshire
d. Feb 1, 1976 in Rochester, New York
Source: *AmMWSc 73P; IntWW 74; WebAB 74; WebBD 83; WhAm 6; WhDW; Who 74; WhoAm 82; WhoNob; WhoWor 82*

Whipple, William
American. Continental Congressman, Soldier
Spirited patriot; led militia contingents; signed Declaration of Independence, 1776.
b. Jan 14, 1730 in Kittery, Maine
d. Nov 28, 1785 in Portsmouth, New Hampshire
Source: *AmBi; AmRev; ApCAB; BiAUS; BiDrAC; BiDrUSC 89; BioIn 7, 8, 9; DcAmB; Drake; EncAR; EncCRAm; HarEnUS; NatCAB 4; TwCBDA; WebBD 83; WhAm HS; WhAmP; WhAmRev; WorAl; WorAlBi*

Whistler, Anna Matilda McNeill
"Whistler's Mother"
American.
Best known as subject of son James' painting.
b. 1804
d. 1881
Source: *BioIn 3, 9, 10; InWom, SUP*

Whistler, James Abbott McNeill
American. Artist, Author
Famous for *Arrangement in Gray and Black No.1: The Artist's Mother,* 1872 or, "Whistler's Mother."
b. Jul 10, 1834 in Lowell, Massachusetts
d. Jul 17, 1903 in London, England
Source: *Alli SUP; AmAu; AmAu&B; AmBi; AmCulL; ApCAB; ArtsNiC;*

AtlBL; BiD&SB; BioIn 1, 2, 3, 4, 5, 6, 7, 8, 9, 10, 11, 12, 13; BriEAA; Chambr 3; DcAmArt; DcAmAu; DcAmB; DcArts; DcBrAr 1; DcLEL; DcNAA; DcNaB S2; DcSeaP; DcVicP, 2; EncAB-H 1974, 1996; GayN; LinLib S; McGDA; McGEWB; NatCAB 9; NewCBEL; NewYHSD; OxCAmH; OxCAmL 65; OxCArt; OxCEng 67, 85, 95; OxDcArt; REn; REnAL; ThHEIm; TwCBDA; WebAB 74, 79; WhAm 1; WhAmArt 85; WorAl; WorAlBi

Whistler, Rex
[Reginald John Whistler]
English. Illustrator
Designed posters, prestigious books, stage settings.
b. Jun 24, 1905 in Eltham, England
d. Jul 18, 1944 in Normandy, France
Source: *BioIn 1, 2, 5, 11, 14, 15; ChhPo S3; DancEn 78; DcNaB 1941; McGDA; NotNAT B; OxCArt; OxDcArt; SmATA 30; TwCPaSc; WhThe*

Whitaker, Forest
American. Actor, Director
Films include *Bird,* 1988; *A Rage in Harlem,* 1990; won Cannes Film Festival award best actor for *Bird,* 1988; directed *Waiting to Exhale,* 1995.
b. Jul 15, 1961 in Longview, Texas
Source: *BioIn 16; ConBlB 2; ConTFT 8; DcTwCCu 5; IntMPA 92, 94, 96; LegTOT; News 96, 96-2; WhoAfA 96; WhoAm 94, 95, 96, 97; WhoBlA 92, 94; WhoHol 92; WhoWor 95, 96, 97*

Whitaker, Jack
[John Francis Whitaker]
American. Sportscaster
Covered variety of sports for CBS; commentator, ABC News, Sports since 1982.
b. May 18, 1924 in Philadelphia, Pennsylvania
Source: *LesBEnT 92; WhoAm 76, 78, 80, 82, 84, 86, 88, 90; WhoTelC*

Whitaker, Johnny
American. Actor
Played Jody on TV series ''Family Affair,'' 1966-71.
b. Dec 13, 1959 in Van Nuys, California
Source: *BioIn 20; WhoHol 92, A*

Whitaker, Lou(is Rodman)
''Sweet Lou''
American. Baseball Player
Second baseman, Detroit, 1977-95; AL rookie of year, 1978; with Alan Trammell, formed MLs longest standing double play combination.
b. May 12, 1957 in New York, New York
Source: *Ballpl 90; BaseReg 86, 87; BiDAmSp Sup; BioIn 13, 14, 16; InB&W 80; WhoAfA 96; WhoAm 90, 92; WhoBlA 85, 88, 90, 92, 94; WhoMW 90*

Whitaker, Pernell
American. Boxer
WBC welterweight champion, 1993-96.
b. Jan 2, 1964 in Norfolk, Virginia
Source: *BioIn 14, 19; BlkOlyM; ConBlB 10*

Whitaker, Rogers E(rnest) M(alcolm)
[E M Frimbo]
American. Author, Journalist
With *New Yorker* mag. one yr. after its inception, 1926-81; cowrote *All Aboard With E M Frimbo,* 1974.
b. Jan 15, 1899 in Arlington, Massachusetts
d. May 11, 1981 in New York, New York
Source: *AnObit 1981; BioIn 10; ConAu 103; NewYTBS 81*

Whitcroft, Fred(rick)
Canadian. Hockey Player
Amateur player with several teams, 1907-10; Hall of Fame, 1962.
b. 1880? in Fort Perry, Ontario, Canada
d. 1931 in Vancouver, British Columbia, Canada
Source: *WhoHcky 73*

White, Andrew Dickson
American. Educator, University Administrator
Founded, Cornell U, 1865; author of many books on historical subjects.
b. Nov 7, 1832 in Homer, New York
d. Nov 4, 1918 in Ithaca, New York
Source: *Alli, SUP; AmAu; AmAu&B; AmBi; ApCAB, X; BiDAmEd; BiD&SB; BiDInt; BioIn 1, 2, 3, 5, 6, 7, 12, 14, 15, 16; Chambr 3; CyAL 2; DcAmAu; DcAmB; DcAmBC; DcAmDH 80, 89; DcLB 47; DcNAA; Drake; EncAB-A 1; EncAB-H 1974, 1996; HarEnUS; LinLib L, S; McGEWB; MorMA; NatCAB 4; OxCAmH; OxCAmL 65, 83, 95; REnAL; TwCBDA; WebAB 74, 79; WhAm 1; WorAl; WorAlBi*

White, Antonia
English. Author
Translated over 30 French works; wrote four novels.
b. Mar 31, 1899 in London, England
d. Apr 10, 1980 in London, England
Source: *AnObit 1980; ArtclWW 2; Au&Wr 71; Benet 87, 96; BioIn 3, 4, 7, 10, 12, 13, 14, 15, 16, 18; BkC 5; CamGLE; CathA 1952; ConAu 97, 104; ConNov 72, 76; EncBrWW; FemiCLE; IntAu&W 76, 77; InWom SUP; LegTOT; LngCTC; ModWoWr; NewC; OxCEng 85, 95; REn; RGTwCWr; Who 74; WorAu 1950; WrDr 76, 80*

White, Barry
American. Singer, Songwriter
Hits include ''Never, Never Gonna Give You Up,'' 1973; ''My First, My Last, My Everything,'' 1974.
b. Sep 12, 1944 in Galveston, Texas
Source: *BiDAfM; BioIn 12; BkPepl; ConBlB 13; ConMus 6; DrBlPA, 90; EncRk 88; EncRkSt; IlEncRk; InB&W 85; LegTOT; NewGrDA 86; PenEncP; RkOn 74, 78; RolSEnR 83; SoulM; WhoAfA 96; WhoAm 80, 82; WhoBlA 85, 88, 90, 92, 94; WhoHol 92; WhoRock 81; WorAl; WorAlBi*

White, Betty
American. Actor
Played Sue Ann Nevins on ''The Mary Tyler Moore Show,'' 1970-77; Rose on ''Golden Girls,'' 1985-92; plays same character on CBS' ''Golden Palace,'' 1992-93.
b. Jan 17, 1922 in Oak Park, Illinois
Source: *BioIn 14, 15, 16; CelR 90; ConTFT 3, 13; CurBio 87; IntMPA 92; InWom SUP; LegTOT; LesBEnT 92; WhoAm 82, 86, 88, 90, 92, 94, 95, 96, 97; WhoAmW 89, 93; WhoCom; WhoEnt 92; WhoHol 92, A; WhoWest 96; WorAlBi*

White, Bill
[William Dekova White]
American. Baseball Player, Baseball Executive
All-Star first baseman, 1956-69; succeeded Bart Giamatti as president of NL, 1989-94; first black to head a major US pro sports league.
b. Jan 28, 1934 in Lakewood, Florida
Source: *AfrAmAl 6; AfrAmSG; Ballpl 90; BaseEn 88; BiDAmSp Sup; BioIn 13, 16; ConBlB 1; InB&W 85; NegAl 89; News 89-3; NewYTBS 91; WhoAfA 96; WhoAm 94, 95, 96, 97; WhoBlA 92, 94; WhoWor 96*

White, Byron Raymond
American. Supreme Court Justice
Served on the Supreme Court from 1962-93.
b. Jun 8, 1917 in Fort Collins, Colorado
Source: *AmBench 79; BiDAmSp FB; BioIn 5, 6, 7, 8, 9, 10, 11, 12, 13, 14, 15; BlueB 76; CngDr 74, 77, 79, 81, 83, 85, 87, 89, 91, 93, 95; CurBio 62; DrAS 82P; EncWB; FacFETw; NewYTBE 72; OxCSupC; PeoHis; SupCtJu; WebAB 74, 79; Who 85, 92; WhoAm 86, 90; WhoAmL 85, 92; WhoAmP 85, 91; WhoE 91; WhoGov 77; WorAl; WorAlBi*

White, Charles Raymond
American. Football Player
Running back, won Heisman Trophy, 1979; in NFL with Cleveland, 1980-84, LA Rams, 1985-88.
b. Jan 22, 1958 in Los Angeles, California
Source: *BiDAmSp FB; FootReg 87*

White, Chris(topher Taylor)
[The Zombies]
English. Musician
Bass player with rock group, 1962-67; hits include ''She's Not There,'' 1964.
b. Mar 7, 1943 in Barnet, England
Source: *WhoRocM 82*

White, Dan(iel James)
American. Police Officer
Murdered San Francisco mayor George Moscone, supervisor Harvey Milk, Dec, 1978.
b. 1946?
d. Oct 21, 1985 in San Francisco, California
Source: *BioIn 11, 12, 13*

White, Deacon
[James Laurie White]
American. Baseball Player
Catcher-infielder, 1876-90; won NL batting title, 1877; first catcher to crouch directly behind batter.
b. Dec 7, 1847 in Canton, New York
d. Jul 7, 1939 in Aurora, Illinois
Source: *Ballpl 90; BiDAmSp BB; BioIn 15; WhoProB 73*

White, E(lwyn) B(rooks)
American. Author
Wrote children's classics *Charlotte's Web,* 1952; *Stuart Little,* 1945; awarded Laura Wilder Medal, 1970.
b. Jul 11, 1899 in Mount Vernon, New York
d. Oct 1, 1985 in North Brooklin, Maine
Source: *AmAu&B; AmPeW; AmWr S1; Au&ICB; AuBYP 2, 3; AuNews 2; Benet 96; BioIn 1, 3, 4, 5, 6, 7, 8, 9, 10, 11, 12, 13, 14, 15, 16, 17, 18, 19, 20; BkCL; BlueB 76; CamHAL; CelR; ChhPo, S1, S2, S3; ChlLR 1; CnDAL; ConAu 13R, 16NR, 37NR; ConLC 10; ConPopW; CurBio 60, 85; DcAmChF 1960; DcArts; DcLB 11, 22; DcLEL; EncAB-H 1996; EncAJ; EncWL 3; EvLB; IntAu&W 76, 77; IntWW 74, 75, 76, 77, 78, 79, 80, 81, 82, 83; JrnUS; LinLib L, S; LngCTC; MajAI; ModAL; MorBMP; MorJA; OxCAmH; OxCAmL 65, 83, 95; OxCChiL; PenC AM; PiP; RAdv 1, 14; REn; REnAL; RfGAmL 94; SJGFanW; SmATA 2, 4, 29; TwCA, SUP; TwCChW 78, 83, 95; TwCWr; WebAB 74, 79; WhAm 10; Who 74, 82, 83, 85; WhoAm 74, 76, 78, 80, 82, 84; WhoChL; WhoWor 74, 84; WorAl; WrDr 76, 80, 82, 84*

White, Ed(ward Higgins, III)
American. Astronaut
First American to exit orbiting spacecraft, also first to control movements while in space; died in flash fire during *Apollo* flight simulation.
b. Nov 14, 1930 in San Antonio, Texas
d. Jan 27, 1967 in Cape Canaveral, Florida
Source: *CurBio 65, 67; WhAm 4*

White, Edmund
American. Author
Gay writer and activist; first novel, *Forgetting Elena,* 1973; co-author of *The Joy of Gay Sex,* 1977; Book Critics Circle award, 1994.
b. Jan 13, 1940 in Cincinnati, Ohio
Source: *Au&Arts 7; BenetAL 91; BioIn 13, 15, 16, 17, 18, 19, 20; CamGLE; CamHAL; ConAu 3NR, 19NR, 36NR, 45; ConGAN; ConLC 27; ConNov 91; CurBio 91; DrAPF 80, 91; GayLesB; IntAu&W 91, 93; IntWW 93; MajTwCW; PostFic; ScF&FL 92; WhoUSWr 88; WorAu 1980; WrDr 84, 86, 88, 90, 92, 94, 96*

White, Edward Douglass
American. Supreme Court Justice
Appointed to court by Pres. Cleveland, 1894; served as chief justice, 1910-21; known for "rule of reason" practices.
b. Nov 3, 1845 in Lafourche, Louisiana
d. May 19, 1921 in Washington, District of Columbia
Source: *AmBi; AmJust; AmPolLe; ApCAB; BiDFedJ; BiDrAC; BiDrUSC 89; BioIn 2, 3, 5, 6, 7, 10, 11, 12, 15; DcAmB; DcAmC; EncAB-H 1974, 1996; EncSoH; FacFETw; HarEnUS; McGEWB; OxCAmH; OxCLaw; OxCSupC; SupCtJu; TwCBDA; WebAB 74, 79; WebBD 83; WhAm 1; WhAmP*

White, Ellen Gould Harmon
American. Religious Leader
Co-founder, Seventh-Day Adventists, 1860; claimed 2000 visions.
b. Nov 26, 1827 in Gorham, Maine
d. Jul 16, 1915 in Saint Helena, California
Source: *Alli SUP; AmDec 1900; AmPeW; AmRef; AmWomWr; BiDAmCu; BioIn 15, 18, 19; CmCal; DcAmB; DcAmMeB 84; DcAmReB 1, 2; GoodHs; InWom SUP; LibW; NewCol 75; NotAW; RelLAm 91; WhAm 4, HSA; WorAl*

White, Frank, Jr.
American. Baseball Player
Second baseman, KC, 1973-90; only AL second baseman to win six gold gloves.
b. Sep 4, 1950 in Greenville, Mississippi
Source: *Ballpl 90; BaseReg 86, 87; BiDAmSp Sup; BioIn 12, 14; ConTFT 6; EncAFC; IntMPA 92; LesBEnT 92; WhoAfA 96; WhoBlA 77, 80, 85, 88, 90, 92, 94*

White, George
[George Weitz]
American. Actor, Director, Producer
Produced rival of *Ziegfeld Follies, George White's Scandals,* 1919-31.
b. 1890 in Toronto, Ontario, Canada
d. Oct 11, 1968 in Los Angeles, California
Source: *BiDD; BiE&WWA; BioIn 8; CamGWoT; DcAmB S8; EncMT; EncVaud; Ent; NewCBMT; NotNAT B; OxCAmT 84; OxCPMus; WhoHol B; WhScrn 74, 77, 83; WhThe*

White, Gilbert
English. Naturalist
Wrote classic, *The Natural History and Antiquities of Selborne,* 1789.
b. Jul 18, 1720 in Selborne, England
d. Jun 26, 1793 in Selborne, England
Source: *Alli; Benet 87, 96; BiD&SB; BiESc; BioIn 1, 2, 3, 4, 6, 8, 9, 10, 11, 12, 14, 15, 16, 17; BlmGEL; BritAu; CamDcSc; CamGEL; CamGLE; CasWL; Chambr 2; DcArts; DcBiPP; DcEnA; DcEnL; DcEuL; DcLEL; DcNaB; DcScB; EnvEnc; EvLB; InSci; LarDcSc; LinLib L, S; LngCEL; NewC; NewCBEL; OxCEng 67, 85, 95; PenC ENG; REn; WebE&AL; WhDW*

White, Helen Magill
American. Educator
First American woman to earn Ph.D. degree, 1877.
b. Nov 28, 1853 in Providence, Rhode Island
d. Oct 28, 1944 in Kittery Point, Maine
Source: *BioIn 16; InWom SUP; LibW; NotAW; WomFir; WomWWA 14*

White, Jaleel
American. Actor
Plays Steve Urkel on TV series *Family Matters,* 1989—.
b. Nov 27, 1976 in Los Angeles, California
Source: *LegTOT; News 92, 92-3*

White, Jesse
[Jesse Marc Weidenfeld]
American. Actor, Comedian
TV spokesman for Maytag Co., 1967-89; coined slogan "the loneliest man in the world."
b. Jan 3, 1919 in Buffalo, New York
d. Jan 9, 1997 in Los Angeles, California
Source: *BiE&WWA; ConTFT 6; EncAFC; FilmEn; FilmgC; ForYSC; HalFC 84; IntMPA 75, 76, 77, 78, 79, 80, 81, 82, 84, 86, 88, 92; LegTOT; MovMk; NotNAT; Vers A; WhoAm 82; WorAl*

White, Jo Jo
[Joseph Henry White]
American. Basketball Player
Guard, 1969-81, mostly with Boston; MVP, 1976 playoffs; member, US Olympic team, 1968.
b. Nov 16, 1946 in Saint Louis, Missouri
Source: *BasBi; BiDAmSp BK; BioIn 15; NewYTBS 87; OfNBA 87; WhoAfA 96; WhoBbl 73; WhoBlA 77, 80, 85, 90, 92, 94*

White, Josh(ua Daniel)
American. Singer
Folk singer who recorded, performed internationally, 1930s-60s; known for ballads: "Ballad of John Henry."
b. Feb 11, 1908 in Greenville, South Carolina
d. Sep 5, 1969 in Manhasset, New York
Source: *ASCAP 66; BiDAfM; BiDAmM; BioIn 13, 14, 15; CmpEPM; CurBio 44, 69; DrBlPA, 90; EncFCWM 69, 83; EncJzS; InB&W 85; LegTOT; NotNAT B; PenEncP; WhAm 5; WhoRocM 82*

White, Kevin Hagan
American. Politician
Mayor of Boston. 1967-84.

b. Sep 25, 1929 in Boston, Massachusetts
Source: *AmCath 80; BioIn 8, 9, 10, 11, 12, 13, 14; BlueB 76; CurBio 74; EncWB; PeoHis; WhoAm 74, 76, 78, 80, 82, 84; WhoAmP 73, 75, 77, 79, 81, 83, 85, 87, 89, 91, 93, 95; WhoE 74, 75, 77, 79, 81, 83; WhoGov 72, 75, 77; WhoWor 74, 76*

White, Mark Wells, Jr.
American. Politician
Dem. governor of TX, 1983-87; known for improvements in public education.
b. Mar 17, 1940 in Henderson, Texas
Source: *CurBio 86; IntWW 83, 89, 91, 93; WhoAm 78, 80, 82, 84, 86; WhoAmL 78, 83, 85, 87; WhoAmP 85, 91; WhoEmL 87; WhoGov 77; WhoSSW 84, 86; WhoWor 87*

White, Michael R(eed)
American. Politician
Mayor of Cleveland, 1990—.
b. Aug 13, 1951 in Cleveland, Ohio
Source: *BioIn 19; ConBlB 5; WhoAfA 96; WhoAm 90, 92, 94, 95, 96, 97; WhoAmP 93, 95; WhoBlA 85, 88, 90, 92, 94; WhoMW 88, 90, 92, 93, 96*

White, Michael Simon
Scottish. Producer
Won Tony for *Sleuth,* 1971; films include *The Rocky Horror Picture Show,* 1975.
b. Jan 16, 1936, Scotland
Source: *ConTFT 5; IntWW 89, 91, 93; NotNAT; VarWW 85; Who 85, 88, 90, 92, 94; WhoThe 72, 77, 81*

White, Miles
American. Designer
Won Tonys for costumes in *Bless You All,* 1951; *Hazel Flagg,* 1953.
b. Jul 27, 1914 in Oakland, California
Source: *OxCAmT 84; VarWW 85; WhoThe 72, 77, 81*

White, Minor
American. Photographer
One of the most important photographers of the post-WWII era; founder, with Ansel Adams and others, of *Aperture.*
b. Jul 9, 1908 in Minneapolis, Minnesota
d. Jun 24, 1976 in Cambridge, Massachusetts
Source: *BioIn 9, 10, 11, 12, 13, 14, 18; BriEAA; ConAu 10NR, 17R, 65; ConPhot 82, 88; DcAmArt; DcTwCCu 1; ICPEnP; ModArCr 2; NewYTBS 76; ObitOF 79; WhAmArt 85; WhoAmA 78N, 80N, 82N, 84N, 86N, 89N, 91N, 93N*

White, Neva
American. Basketball Player
Led Nashville based AAU team to ten national championships; one of first two women inducted into Basketball Hall of Fame.
b. Nov 15, 1935 in Macon County, Tennessee
Source: *BiDAmSp BK*

White, Patrick Victor Martindale
Australian. Author
Novels express religious philosophies, isolation themes; and contain complex symbols, myths, and allegories; won Nobel Prize, 1973, for *The Eye of the Storm.*
b. May 28, 1912 in London, England
d. Sep 30, 1990 in Sydney, Australia
Source: *Au&Wr 71; Benet 87, 96; BioIn 13, 14, 15; CamGEL; CamGLE; CamGWoT; CasWL; ConAu 43NR, 81; ConDr 82, 88, 93; ConNov 86; DcArts; DcLEL; EncWL; GayLL; IntAu&W 89; IntDcT 2; IntvTCA 2; IntWW 83; LngCTC; MakMC; McGEWB; NewC; NewYTBE 73; NobelP; OxCAusL; OxCEng 67, 85, 95; PenC ENG; RAdv 1, 13-1; REn; RfGShF; RGTwCWr; TwCA, SUP; TwCRHW 94; WebE&AL; Who 74, 82, 83, 85, 88, 90, 92N; WhoAm 88; WhoNob, 90, 95; WhoWor 87, 89; WorAl; WrDr 86, 88*

White, Paul Dudley
American. Physician
Helped found American Heart Association; personal doctor to FDR.
b. Jun 6, 1886 in Roxbury, Massachusetts
d. Oct 31, 1973 in Boston, Massachusetts
Source: *AmMWSc 73P; BioIn 2, 3, 4, 5, 6, 7, 9, 10, 12, 15; ConAu 45; CurBio 55, 73, 73N; DcAmB S9; DcAmMeB 84; InSci; LinLib S; NatCAB 58; NewYTBE 73; ObitT 1971; OxCAmH; OxCMed 86; WhAm 6; WhoAm 74; WhoE 74; WhoWor 74*

White, Pearl
"Queen of Silent Serials"
American. Actor
Serial star in *The Perils of Pauline,* 1914.
b. Mar 4, 1889 in Green Ridge, Missouri
d. Aug 4, 1938 in Paris, France
Source: *BioAmW; BioIn 4, 8, 9; DcAmB S2; EncAFC; Film 1, 2; FilmEn; FilmgC; HalFC 80, 84, 88; IntDcF 1-3, 2-3; InWom, SUP; LibW; MotPP; MovMk; NotAW; NotNAT B; OxCAmH; OxCFilm; REnAL; SilFlmP; TwYS; WhAm 4, HSA; WhoHol B; WhoHrs 80; WhScrn 74, 77, 83; WorAl; WorAlBi; WorEFlm*

White, Randy Lee
American. Football Player
Eight-time all-pro defensive tackle, Dallas, 1975-88.
b. Jan 15, 1953 in Wilmington, Delaware
Source: *BiDAmSp FB; BioIn 13, 14, 16; FootReg 87; WhoAm 88; WhoSSW 86; WorAlBi*

White, Reggie
[Reginald Howard White]
American. Football Player
Defensive end, Philadelphia, 1985-93; Green Bay, 1993—.
b. Dec 19, 1961 in Chattanooga, Tennessee
Source: *AfrAmSG; ConBlB 6; CurBio 95; News 93; WhoAfA 96; WhoAm 94, 95, 96, 97; WhoBlA 88, 90, 92, 94; WhoMW 93, 96; WhoSpor*

White, Richard Grant
American. Author, Critic
Co-editor of humorous piece *Yankee Doodle,* 1846; with *NY Enquirer,* several other mags.
b. May 23, 1821 in New York, New York
d. Apr 8, 1885 in New York, New York
Source: *Alli, SUP; AmAu; AmAu&B; AmBi; ApCAB; BbD; BenetAL 91; BiD&SB; BioIn 8, 16; Chambr 3; CyAL 2; DcAmAu; DcAmB; DcEnL; DcLB 64; DcNAA; Dis&D; EvLB; OxCAmL 65, 83, 95; REnAL; TwCBDA; WhAm HS*

White, Ryan
American. Victim
Hemophiliac; contracted AIDS from tainted blood transfusion, 1985; waged five-ye ar battle against the disease and influenced public opinion.
b. Dec 6, 1971 in Kokomo, Indiana
d. Apr 8, 1990 in Indianapolis, Indiana
Source: *AmDec 1980; BioIn 15, 16; ConAu 141; ConHero 2; FacFETw; News 90-3; NewYTBS 90*

White, Slappy
[Melvin White]
American. Comedian
Popular on screen, 1970s; films include *Amazing Grace,* 1974.
b. 1921? in Baltimore, Maryland
d. Nov 7, 1995 in Brigantine, New Jersey
Source: *DrBlPA 90; InB&W 80, 85; WhoHol A*

White, Stan(ley Ray)
American. Football Player
Linebacker, 1972-84, mostly with Baltimore; first NFL player to sign with USFL, 1983.
b. Oct 24, 1949 in Dover, Ohio
Source: *BioIn 13; FootReg 81*

White, Stanford
American. Architect
Killed by Harry Thaw over alleged affair with Thaw's wife, showgirl Evelyn Nesbit.
b. Nov 9, 1853 in New York, New York
d. Jun 25, 1906 in New York, New York
Source: *AmBi; AmCulL; ApCAB; AtlBL; BioIn 2, 5, 6, 7, 8, 9, 11, 12, 13, 16, 19; BriEAA; ChhPo; DcAmB; DcArts; DcTwDes; EncAB-H 1974, 1996; GayN; HarEnUS; IntDcAr; LegTOT; LinLib S; LngCTC; MacEA; McGDA; McGEWB; NatCAB 11, 23; OxCAmH; OxCAmL 65; REnAL; TwCBDA; WebAB 74, 79; WhAm 1; WorAl; WorAlBi*

White, Stephen
American. Writer
Wrote report "Public Television: A Program for Action;" helped to start Public TV Network.
b. Nov 22, 1915 in Boston, Massachusetts
d. Mar 27, 1993 in Bethesda, Maryland
Source: *BioIn 18; WhoAm 78, 80, 82, 84, 86, 88, 90, 92*

White, Stewart Edward
American. Author
Wrote on his adventures, spiritualism; books include *African Camp Fires,* 1913.
b. Mar 12, 1873 in Grand Rapids, Michigan
d. Sep 18, 1946 in San Francisco, California
Source: *AmAu&B; ArizL; BenetAL 91; BiDPara; BioIn 1, 4, 17; CarSB; CmCal; CnDAL; ConAmA; ConAmL; CurBio 46; DcAmAu; DcAmB S4; DcLEL; DcNAA; EncFWF; EncO&P 1, 2, 3; EncSF, 93; LinLib L; LngCTC; NatCAB 13; OxCAmL 65, 83, 95; REnAL; REnAW; ScF&FL 1; TwCA, SUP; TwCBDA; TwCWW 82, 91; WhAm 2; WhLit; WhNAA; WhoSpyF*

White, T(erence) H(anbury)
Irish. Author
Fantasy writer, known for Arthurian epics; *The Sword in the Stone,* 1939 was filmed as *Camelot,* 1961.
b. May 29, 1906 in Bombay, India
d. Jan 17, 1964 in Piraeus, Greece
Source: *Benet 96; BioIn 4, 5, 6, 7, 8, 10, 11, 15, 19; CasWL; CnMWL; ConAu 37NR, 73; DcArts; DcIrL 96; DcLEL; DcNaB MP; EncSF 93; EngPo; LngCTC; MajAI; ModBrL; NewCBEL; OxCEng 67, 95; PenC ENG; RAdv 1; REn; RGTwCWr; SJGFanW; SmATA 12; TwCA, SUP; TwCWr; TwCYAW; WhAm 4; WhDW; WhoChL*

White, Theodore Harold
"Teddy"
American. Author
Won Pulitzer for *The Making of the President, 1960,* 1961.
b. May 6, 1915 in Boston, Massachusetts
d. May 15, 1986 in New York, New York
Source: *AmAu&B; Au&Wr 71; BioIn 1, 2, 3, 4, 5, 7, 8, 9, 10, 11, 12, 13; CurBio 86; DcLEL 1940; IntAu&W 77, 82, 86; IntWW 74; LinLib L; OxCAmL 65; REn; REnAL; WhAm 9; WhoAm 74, 76, 78, 80, 82, 84; WhoWor 74, 78, 80, 82, 84; WorAl; WorAu 1950; WrDr 76*

White, Vanna Marie
American. Model, TV Personality
Hostess of TV game show "Wheel of Fortune," 1982—; wrote autobiography: *Vanna Speaks,* 1987.
b. Feb 18, 1957 in Conway, South Carolina
Source: *BioIn 14, 15, 16; CelR 90; CurBio 88; LesBEnT 92; WhoHisp 91, 92, 94*

White, Walter Francis
American. Author, Civil Rights Leader
Active in NAACP, other civil liberties organizations; consultant to UN, 1945, 1948.
b. Jul 1, 1893 in Atlanta, Georgia
d. Mar 21, 1955 in New York, New York
Source: *AmAu&B; AmSocL; BiDSocW; BioIn 11, 12, 14, 15, 17, 19; BlkAWP; CivRSt; CurBio 42, 55; DcAmB S3, S5; DcLB 51; EncAACR; EncAB-H 1974; EncSoH; EncWB; FacFETw; InB&W 80, 85; MorMA; NatCAB 40; ObitOF 79; REn; REnAL; SelBAAf; SelBAAu; SouWr; TwCA, SUP; WebAB 74, 79; WhAm 3; WhLit; WhNAA; WorAl*

White, William Allen
"Sage of Emporia"
American. Journalist
World-famous, small-town newsman; won Pulitzers, 1922, 1946.
b. Feb 10, 1868 in Emporia, Kansas
d. Jan 29, 1944 in Emporia, Kansas
Source: *ABCMeAm; AmAu&B; AmDec 1900; AmLY; AmPeW; AmSocL; ApCAB X; BenetAL 91; BiDAmJo; BiDInt; BioIn 1, 2, 3, 4, 5, 7, 8, 9, 10, 11, 12, 13, 14, 16, 17, 19; ChhPo, S1; CnDAL; ConAu 108; CurBio 40, 44; DcAmAu; DcAmB S3; DcAmSR; DcLB 9, 25; DcLEL; DcNAA; EncAAH; EncAB-H 1974, 1996; EncAJ; EncTwCJ; GayN; JrnUS; LegTOT; LinLib L, S; LngCTC; McGEWB; MemAm; NatCAB 11; OxCAmH; OxCAmL 65, 83, 95; PeoHis; PolPar; REn; REnAL; REnAW; TwCA, SUP; WebAB 74, 79; WhAm 2; WhNAA; WorAl; WorAlBi*

White, William Lindsay
American. Editor, Publisher
Best known for *Journey for Margaret,* 1941.
b. Jun 17, 1900 in Emporia, Kansas
d. Jul 26, 1973 in Emporia, Kansas
Source: *AmAu&B; BiDAmJo; BioIn 1, 4, 10, 12, 16; CnDAL; ConAu 101; EncTwCJ; NatCAB 58; OxCAmL 65; REnAL; TwCA SUP; WhAm 5, 6, 7; WhoAm 74, 76*

White, William S(mith)
American. Journalist
Nationally syndicated columnist, 1958-74; won Pulitzer for *The Taft Story,* 1955.
b. Feb 5, 1907 in De Leon, Texas
d. Apr 30, 1994 in Louisville, Kentucky
Source: *AmAu&B; BioIn 15; ConAu 5R, 145; CurBio 55; IntWW 74, 75, 76, 77, 78, 79, 80, 81, 82, 83, 89, 91; OxCAmL 65, 83; WhoAm 74, 76, 82; WhoSSW 73, 75, 76*

Whitechurch, Victor Lorenzo
English. Clergy, Author
Mystery tales include *Murder at Exbridge,* 1932.
b. Mar 12, 1868 in Norham, England
d. May 1933
Source: *ChhPo, S1; ConAu 116; EncMys; MnBBF; TwCCr&M 80; WhoLA*

Whitefield, George
English. Religious Leader
Joined Methodists, 1732; adapted Calvinist views to Methodism, 1741.
b. Dec 27, 1714 in Gloucester, England
d. Sep 30, 1770 in Newburyport, Massachusetts
Source: *Alli; AmAu&B; AmBi; AmOrN; AmWrBE; ApCAB; BbD; BenetAL 91; BiDAmM; BiD&SB; BiDSA; BioIn 1, 2, 3, 4, 5, 6, 8, 9, 11, 12, 14, 15, 16, 17, 19; BritAu; Chambr 2; DcAmB; DcAmReB 1, 2; DcBiPP; DcEnL; DcNaB; Drake; EncAB-H 1974, 1996; EncAR; EncARH; EncCRAm; EncSoB; EncWM; HarEnUS; LuthC 75; McGEWB; NatCAB 5; NewC; NewCBEL; OxCAmH; OxCAmL 65, 83, 95; OxCEng 67, 85, 95; OxCMus; TwCBDA; WebE&AL; WhDW*

Whitehead, Alfred North
English. Philosopher, Mathematician
Author of popular books on philosophy; also *Principia Mathematica,* with Bertrand Russell, 1910-13.
b. Feb 15, 1861 in Ramsgate, England
d. Dec 30, 1947 in Cambridge, Massachusetts
Source: *AmAu&B; AsBiEn; Benet 87, 96; BenetAL 91; BiDPsy; BiESc; BioIn 1, 2, 3, 4, 5, 6, 8, 9, 10, 12, 13, 14, 15, 17, 20; Chambr 3; ConAu 117; DcAmB S4; DcLB 100; DcLEL; DcNAA; DcNaB 1941; DcScB; EncAB-H 1974, 1996; FacFETw; GrBr; InSci; LarDcSc; LegTOT; LinLib L, S; LngCTC; LuthC 75; MakMC; McGEWB; NamesHP; NatCAB 37; NewC; NewCBEL; NotTwCS; OxCAmH; OxCAmL 65, 83, 95; OxCEng 67; OxCPhil; RAdv 14, 13-4; REn; REnAL; ThTwC 87; TwCA, SUP; WebAB 74, 79; WhAm 2; WorAlBi; WorScD*

Whitehead, Don(ald Ford)
American. Journalist
Won two Pulitzers for international, 1950, domestic reporting, 1952; with Knoxville newspaper, 1957-81.
b. Apr 8, 1908 in Inman, Virginia
d. Jan 12, 1981 in Knoxville, Tennessee
Source: *AmAu&B; AnObit 1981; BioIn 3, 5, 9, 12; ConAu 9R, 102; CurBio 53, 81, 81N; EncTwCJ; NewYTBS 81; SmATA 4; WhAm 7; WhoAm 74, 76, 78, 80*

Whitehead, (Walter) Edward
"Commander Whitehead"
English. Business Executive
Chairman, Schweppes, Ltd., 1967-71; known in US for promoting "Schweppervescence."

b. May 20, 1908 in Aldershot, England
d. Apr 16, 1978 in Petersfield, England
Source: *BioIn 7, 8, 11; BlueB 76; CelR; ConAu 77, 81; CurBio 78, 78N; DcAmB S10; Who 74; WhoWor 76*

Whitehead, Edwin C(arl)
American. Business Executive
Vice chm., Revlon, Inc., 1980-84; founded own research institute.
b. Jun 1, 1919 in New York, New York
d. Feb 2, 1992 in Greenwich, Connecticut
Source: *BioIn 15; St&PR 75, 84, 87; WhoAm 74, 76, 78, 80, 82, 84; WhoE 74; WhoFI 74; WhoWor 74*

Whitehead, Robert
Canadian. Producer
Plays include *Member of the Wedding,* 1950; won Tony for *A Man for All Seasons,* 1962.
b. Mar 3, 1916 in Montreal, Quebec, Canada
Source: *BiE&WWA; BioIn 1, 2, 15; CamGWoT; CanWW 31, 70, 79, 80, 81, 83, 89; ConTFT 2; NotNAT; OxCAmT 84; OxCCanT; PlP&P; WhoAm 74, 76, 78, 80, 82, 84, 86, 88, 90, 92, 94, 95, 96, 97; WhoE 74; WhoThe 72, 77, 81*

Whitehead, William
British. Poet
Wrote play *A Charge to Poets,* 1762, in reply to hostile comments on his appointment as poet laureate, 1757.
b. 1715
d. 1785
Source: *Alli; BiD&SB; BioIn 3, 12, 15, 17; BritAu; CamGLE; ChhPo, S1; DcBiPP; DcEnA; DcEnL; DcEuL; DcLB 84, 109; DcLEL; DcNaB; EvLB; GrWrEL DR; LegTOT; NewC; NewCBEL; OxCEng 67, 85, 95; PoLE; RfGEnL 91*

Whitehill, Clarence Eugene
American. Opera Singer
Bass with NY Met., 1914-32; Wagnerian soloist.
b. Nov 5, 1871 in Marengo, Iowa
d. Dec 19, 1932 in New York, New York
Source: *AmBi; Baker 84; DcAmB; WhAm 1*

Whitelaw, Billie
English. Actor
Films include *Charlie Bubbles,* 1968; *The Omen,* 1976.
b. Jun 6, 1932 in Coventry, England
Source: *BioIn 14; CamGWoT; ConTFT 2; FilmEn; FilmgC; HalFC 80, 84, 88; IlWWBF; IntMPA 77, 80, 84, 92, 94, 96; IntWW 82, 83, 89, 91, 93; NewYTBS 84; OxCThe 83; Who 74, 82, 83, 85, 88, 90, 92, 94; WhoHol 92, A; WhoThe 77, 81*

Whiteman, Paul
"King of Jazz"; "Pops"
American. Bandleader
Popularized jazz music, 1920s-30s; commissioned, introduced George Gershwin's *Rhapsody in Blue,* 1924; had radio show, 1930s-40s.
b. Mar 28, 1891 in Denver, Colorado
d. Dec 29, 1967 in Doylestown, Pennsylvania
Source: *BiE&WWA; BioIn 1, 2, 4, 8, 9, 11, 12; CmpEPM; CurBio 45, 68; FacFETw; FilmgC; OxCAmH; WebAB 74, 79; WhAm 4A; WhoJazz 72; WhScrn 74, 77; WorAlBi*

Whiteman, Roberta Hill
American. Poet
Published *Star Quilt,* 1984.
b. Feb 17, 1947 in Baraboo, Wisconsin
Source: *BioIn 21; DcNAL; NatNAL; NotNaAm*

Whitesnake
[David Coverdale; Aynsley Dunbar; John Sykes; Steve Vai; Adrian Vandenburg]
English. Music Group
British heavy metal band; album *Whitesnake,* 1987 sold over six million copies.
Source: *Alli; BioIn 15; ConMus 5; EncRk 88; EncRkSt; PenEncP; RkOn 85; Who 92, 94; WhoRocM 82*

Whitestone, Heather
American. Beauty Contest Winner
Miss America, 1995; first deaf Miss America.
b. c. 1973 in Dothan, Alabama
Source: *BioIn 20, 21; DeafPAS; News 95, 95-1*

Whitfield, Malvin
American. Track Athlete
Middle distance runner; won gold medals in 880 yds., 1948, 1952 Olympics.
b. Oct 11, 1924 in Bay City, Texas
Source: *BiDAmSp OS; BioIn 2, 3, 4, 6, 8, 11; BlkOlyM; WhoTr&F 73*

Whitfield, Mark
American. Jazz Musician
Jazz guitarist who played with the Blue Note jazz club in NYC, 1987; released debut album, *The Marksman,* 1990; also recorded *True Blue,* 1994 and *7th Ave.,* 1995.
b. Oct 1966 in Long Island, New York

Whiting, Leonard
British. Actor
Film debut as Romeo in *Romeo and Juliet,* 1968.
b. 1950
Source: *BioIn 8, 9; FilmgC; ForYSC; HalFC 80, 84, 88; ItaFilm; MotPP; WhoHol 92, A*

Whiting, Margaret
American. Singer
Popular pop vocalist, 1940s-50s; daughter of Richard.
b. Jul 22, 1924 in Detroit, Michigan
Source: *BioIn 2, 4, 11, 12, 15; CelR 90; CmpEPM; FacFETw; ForYSC; InWom, SUP; LegTOT; NewAmDM; PenEncP; RadStar; RkOn 74; WhoHol 92, A; WomPO 76; WorAl; WorAlBi*

Whiting, Richard Armstrong
American. Composer
Leading composer for 1930s movies; hits include "Sleepy Time Gal," 1925.
b. Nov 12, 1891 in Peoria, Illinois
d. Feb 10, 1938 in Beverly Hills, California
Source: *ASCAP 66; BioIn 4, 5, 6, 10; NatCAB 28*

Whitington, Dick
[Richard Whitington]
English. Politician
Legendary figure who rose from poverty to knighthood, public office; thrice lord mayor of London.
b. 1358
d. 1423
Source: *NewCol 75*

Whitlam, Edward Gough
Australian. Diplomat
Prime minister of Australia, 1972-75; representaive to UNESCO, 1983-86.
b. Jul 11, 1916 in Melbourne, Australia
Source: *BioIn 8, 9, 10, 11, 12; BlueB 76; ConAu 109; CurBio 74; EncWB; FacFETw; FarE&A 81; IntWW 74, 75, 76, 91; IntYB 78, 79, 80, 81, 82; NewYTBE 72; WhDW; Who 85, 92; WhoWor 74, 76, 78; WrDr 86, 92*

Whitley, Keith
American. Singer, Songwriter
Country, bluegrass singer and songwriter; Country Music Association Award for best single "I'm No Stranger to the Rain," 1989.
b. Jul 1, 1956 in Sandy Hook, Kentucky
d. May 9, 1989 in Nashville, Tennessee
Source: *BioIn 16; ConMus 7; WhoNeCM*

Whitlock, Albert
English. Special Effects Technician
Won Oscars for *Earthquake,* 1974; *The Hindenburg,* 1975.
b. 1915 in London, England
Source: *BioIn 11, 12; ConDes 84, 90, 97; ConTFT 10; HalFC 84, 88; IntDcF 1-4, 2-4; VarWW 85; WhAm 8*

Whitlock, Brand
American. Author, Diplomat
Wrote novels *13th District,* 1902; *Uprooted,* 1926; minister to Belgium, 1911-22.
b. Mar 4, 1869 in Urbana, Ohio
d. May 24, 1934 in Cannes, France
Source: *AmAu&B; AmBi; ApCAB X; BenetAL 91; BioIn 8, 9, 13, 16; ConAu 110; DcAmAu; DcAmB; DcAmDH 80,*

89; DcAmSR; DcLB 12; DcLEL; DcNAA; HarEnUS; LinLib L, S; NatCAB 14; OhA&B; OxCAmH; OxCAmL 65, 83, 95; REnAL; TwCA; WebAB 74, 79; WhAm 1

Whitman, Alden
Canadian. Author, Journalist
With *NY Times,* 1951-76; books include *The End of a Presidency,* 19 74.
b. Oct 27, 1913 in New Albany, Nova Scotia, Canada
d. Sep 4, 1990 in Monte Carlo, Monaco
Source: *BioIn 7, 8, 9, 12, 17, 18; ConAu 17R, 29NR, 132; DcLB Y91N; IntAu&W 76, 77; NewYTBS 90; WhoE 74*

Whitman, Charles Joseph
American. Murderer
Shooting spree on Texas U campus left 18 dead, 30 wounded.
b. Jun 24, 1941 in Fort Worth, Texas
d. Jun 24, 1966 in Austin, Texas
Source: *BioIn 7*

Whitman, Christine Todd
American. Politician
Governor of NJ, 1994—.
b. Sep 26, 1946 in New York
Source: *AlmAP 96; BiDrGov 1988; CurBio 95; WhoAm 97; WhoAmW 97; WhoE 97*

Whitman, Marcus
American. Missionary, Physician
Opened part of Oregon Trail; mission taught Indians farming, ranching, c. 1840.
b. Sep 4, 1802 in Rushville, New York
d. Nov 29, 1847 in Fort Walla Walla, Washington
Source: *AmAu&B; AmBi; ApCAB; BioIn 1, 2, 3, 4, 5, 6, 7, 8, 10, 11, 14, 17, 18, 19, 20; DcAmB; DcAmMeB, 84; DcAmReB 1, 2; Dis&D; EncAAH; EncNAR; HarEnUS; LuthC 75; McGEWB; MorMA; NatCAB 11; OxCAmH; OxCAmL 65, 83, 95; REnAW; TwCBDA; WebAB 74, 79; WhAm HS; WhNaAH; WhWE; WorAl; WorAlBi*

Whitman, Marina VonNeumann
American. Economist
VP in charge of economics, GM, 1979-85; group exec. VP for Public Affairs, 1991—.
b. Mar 6, 1935 in New York, New York
Source: *AmMWSc 73S, 78S; AmWomM; BioIn 16; ConAu 17R; CurBio 73; Dun&B 90; IntAu&W 77; IntWW 74, 75, 76, 77, 78, 79, 80, 81, 82, 83, 91; InWom SUP; NewYTBE 72; WhoAm 74, 76, 78, 80, 82, 84, 88; WhoAmW 68, 70, 83, 85, 87, 89, 91; WhoE 74, 75, 77; WhoFI 87; WrDr 76, 86, 90*

Whitman, Sarah Helen Power
American. Poet, Essayist
Once engaged to Edgar Allan Poe, ca. 1848; wrote *Poe and His Critics,* 1860.
b. Jan 19, 1803 in Providence, Rhode Island
d. Jun 27, 1878 in Providence, Rhode Island
Source: *NewCol 75; NotAW*

Whitman, Stephen F
American. Candy Manufacturer
Began candy co. in Philadelphia, 1842; famous for Whitman's Sampler, which is still sold today.
b. 1823
d. 1888
Source: *Entr*

Whitman, Stuart
American. Actor
Oscar nominee for *The Mark,* 1961.
b. Feb 1, 1926 in San Francisco, California
Source: *ConTFT 9; FilmEn; FilmgC; HalFC 80, 84, 88; IntMPA 84, 86, 88, 92; ItaFilm; LegTOT; MotPP; MovMk; WhoHol A; WorAl*

Whitman, Walt(er)
American. Poet
Used free verse style in *Leaves of Grass,* 1855; became inspiration to other poets with his innovative style.
b. May 31, 1819 in West Hills, New York
d. Mar 26, 1892 in Camden, New Jersey
Source: *Alli, SUP; AmAu; AmAu&B; AmBi; AmCulL; AmRef; AmWr; AnCL; ApCAB, X; AtlBL; BbD; Benet 87, 96; BenetAL 91; BiDAmJo; BiDAmM; BiD&SB; BiDTran; BioIn 1, 2, 3, 4, 5, 6, 7, 8, 9, 10, 11, 12, 13, 14, 15, 16, 17, 18, 19, 20, 21; CamGEL; CamGLE; CamHAL; CasWL; CelCen; Chambr 3; ChhPo, S1, S3; CnDAL; CnE&AP; ColARen; CrtT 3, 4; CyWA 58; DcAmAu; DcAmB; DcAmSR; DcArts; DcEnA, A; DcEnL; DcLB 3, 64; DcLEL; DcNAA; Dis&D; Drake; EncAAH; EncAB-H 1974, 1996; EncARH; EncUnb; EvLB; GayLesB; GrWrEL P; HarEnUS; IlEncMy; JrnUS; LegTOT; LinLib L, S; MagSAmL; McGEWB; MemAm; MouLC 4; NatCAB 1; NewGrDA 86; NinCLC 4, 31; OxCAmH; OxCAmL 65, 83, 95; OxCAusL; OxCCan; OxCEng 67, 85, 95; PenC AM; PoeCrit 3; RadHan; RAdv 1, 14, 13-1; RComAH; RComWL; REn; REnAL; RfGAmL 87, 94; RGFAP; SmATA 20; Str&VC; TwCBDA; WebAB 74, 79; WebE&AL; WhAm HS; WhCiWar; WhDW; WorAl; WorAlBi; WorLitC; WrPh*

Whitmire, Kathy
[Kathryn Jean Niederhofer]
American. Politician
First woman mayor of Houston, TX, 1981-91.
b. Aug 15, 1946 in Houston, Texas
Source: *AmWomM; BioIn 14, 15, 16; CurBio 88; News 88-2; NewYTBS 81, 88; WhoAm 86, 90; WhoAmP 87, 91; WhoAmW 87, 91; WhoSSW 86, 91*

Whitmore, James Allen
American. Actor
Famous for one-man shows *Will Rogers, USA,* and *Give 'Em Hell, Harry.*
b. Oct 1, 1921 in White Plains, New York
Source: *BiE&WWA; BioIn 10, 11; ConTFT 7; FilmgC; HalFC 88; IntMPA 84, 92; MotPP; MovMk; WhoAm 74, 76, 78, 80, 82, 84, 86, 88, 90, 92, 94, 95, 96, 97; WhoHol A; WhoThe 81; WorAl; WorAlBi*

Whitney, C(ornelius) V(anderbilt)
American. Businessman, Producer
Founder, board director, Pan Am Airways, 1927-41; co-produced *Gone With the Wind,* 1939.
b. Feb 20, 1899 in New York, New York
d. Dec 13, 1992 in Saratoga Springs, New York
Source: *AnObit 1992; BiDAmBL 83; BioIn 1, 4, 6, 13, 18, 19; CelR, 90; ConAu 85; IntWW 74; LegTOT; NewYTBS 92; St&PR 84, 87; WhAm 10; WhoAm 74, 76, 78, 80, 82, 84, 86, 88, 90, 92; WhoE 74, 75, 77*

Whitney, Eli
American. Inventor
Invented cotton gin, 1793; first to use assembly line in industry, 1801.
b. Dec 8, 1765 in Westboro, Massachusetts
d. Jan 8, 1825 in New Haven, Connecticut
Source: *AmBi; ApCAB; AsBiEn; BiDAmBL 83; BiInAmS; BioIn 1, 2, 3, 4, 5, 6, 7, 8, 9, 10, 11, 12, 13, 14, 15, 17, 18, 20, 21; DcAmB; DcBiPP; DcInv; Drake; EncAAH; EncAB-H 1974, 1996; HarEnUS; InSci; LegTOT; LinLib S; McGEWB; MemAm; NatCAB 4; OxCAmH; RComAH; TwCBDA; WebAB 74, 79; WhAm 1, HS; WhDW; WorAl; WorAlBi; WorInv*

Whitney, Gertrude Vanderbilt
[Mrs. William Collins Whitney]
American. Sculptor, Art Patron
Founded Whitney Museum of American Art, NYC; opened, 1931.
b. Apr 19, 1877 in New York, New York
d. Apr 18, 1942 in New York, New York
Source: *BiCAW; CurBio 42; DcAmB S3; InWom; McGDA; NotAW; ObitOF 79; OxCAmH; WhAm 2; WorAl; WorAlBi*

Whitney, Harry Payne
American. Businessman, Impresario
Active in banking, mining, railroad concerns; organized "Big Four" polo team.
b. Apr 29, 1872 in New York, New York
d. Oct 26, 1930 in New York, New York
Source: *BiDAmBL 83; BioIn 16; DcAmB; NatCAB 21; OxCAmH; WhAm 1*

Whitney, John Hay
"Jock"
American. Diplomat, Publisher
Published *NY Herald Tribune,* 1957-66; ambassador to Great Britain, 1957-66; joined with David O Selznick to form Selznick International Pictures, which made *Gone With the Wind,* 1939.
b. Aug 17, 1904 in Ellsworth, Maine
d. Feb 8, 1982 in Manhasset, New York
Source: *AnObit 1982; WhoWor 74*

Whitney, Josiah Dwight
American. Geologist, Educator
Measured California's highest peak, 1864, later named Mt. Whitney.
b. Nov 23, 1819 in Northampton, Massachusetts
d. Aug 19, 1896 in Lake Sunapee, New Hampshire
Source: *Alli, SUP; AmBi; ApCAB; BiDAmS; BiInAmS; BioIn 7; CmCal; CyAL 1; DcAmAu; DcAmB; DcNAA; DcScB; Drake; LarDcSc; McGEWB; NatCAB 9; OxCAmH; TwCBDA; WebAB 74, 79; WhAm HS*

Whitney, Phyllis Ayame
American. Author
Won Edgar for *Mystery of the Hidden Hand,* 1964; other books include *Flaming Trees,* 1986; Grand Master, 1988.
b. Sep 9, 1903 in Yokohama, Japan
Source: *AmAu&B; AmWomWr; AuBYP 2, 3; AuNews 2; BioIn 1, 2, 7, 9, 11, 12, 14; ConAu 1R, 3NR, 25NR; ConLC 42; CurBio 48; EncMys; ForWC 70; IntAu&W 91; InWom, SUP; JBA 51; LibW; SmATA 1, 30; ThrtnMM; TwCChW 78, 83, 89; TwCCr&M 85, 91; TwCRGW; TwCRHW 90; WhoAm 74, 76, 78, 80, 82, 84, 86, 88, 90, 92, 94, 95; WhoAmW 58, 61, 64, 66, 68, 70, 72, 74, 75, 89, 91, 93, 95, 97; WorAl; WorAlBi; WrDr 76, 80, 86, 92*

Whitney, Richard
American. Business Executive
Pres. of NY Stock Exchange, 1930-35.
b. Aug 1, 1888 in Beverly, Massachusetts
d. Dec 5, 1974 in Far Hills, New Jersey
Source: *BioIn 10, 16, 21; DcAmB S9; NewYTBS 74; ObitOF 79; ObitT 1971; WhAm 6*

Whitney, William Collins
American. Government Official
Secretary of US Navy, 1885-89; noted sportsman, horsebreeder.
b. Jul 5, 1841 in Conway, Massachusetts
d. Feb 2, 1904 in New York, New York
Source: *AmBi; ApCAB; BiDAmBL 83; BiDrUSE 71, 89; BioIn 1, 8, 10, 12; DcAmB; DcNAA; EncAB-H 1974, 1996; HarEnUS; NatCAB 2; OxCAmH; TwCBDA; WebAB 74, 79; WhAm 1; WorAl*

Whitney, William Dwight
American. Linguist
Wrote classic, *Sanskrit Grammar,* 1879; brother of Josiah Dwight.
b. Feb 8, 1827 in Northampton, Massachusetts
d. Jun 7, 1894 in New Haven, Connecticut
Source: *Alli, SUP; AmAu; AmAu&B; AmBi; ApCAB; BbD; BiD&SB; BioIn 7, 12; Chambr 3; CyAL 2; CyEd; DcAmAu; DcAmB; DcInB; DcNAA; Drake; EvLB; HarEnUS; NatCAB 2; OxCAmH; REnAL; TwCBDA; WebAB 74, 79; WhAm HS; WhDW*

Whittemore, Arthur Austin
[Whittemore and Lowe]
"Buck"
American. Pianist
With Jack Lowe, member of two-piano team popular, 1940s-60s.
b. Oct 23, 1916 in Vermillion, South Dakota
d. Oct 23, 1984 in Long Island, New York
Source: *CurBio 54; NewYTBS 84; WhAm 8; WhoAm 74, 76, 78, 80, 82, 84*

Whittier, John Greenleaf
American. Poet, Essayist
Popular rural poet who devoted life to social causes and reform; wrote poem *Snow-Bound,* 1866.
b. Dec 17, 1807 in Haverhill, Massachusetts
d. Sep 7, 1892 in Hampton Falls, New Hampshire
Source: *Alli, SUP; AmAu; AmAu&B; AmBi; AmCulL; AmPeW; AmRef; AmWr S1; AnCL; ApCAB; AtlBL; BbD; Benet 87, 96; BenetAL 91; BiDAmM; BiD&SB; BiDMoPL; BiDTran; BioIn 1, 2, 3, 4, 5, 6, 7, 8, 9, 10, 11, 12, 13, 15, 16, 19; CamGEL; CamGLE; CamHAL; CarSB; CasWL; CelCen; Chambr 3; ChhPo, S1, S2, S3; CnDAL; ColARen; CrtT 3, 4; CyAL 2; CyWA 58; DcAmAu; DcAmB; DcAmSR; DcArts; DcBiPP; DcEnA; DcEnL; DcLB 1; DcLEL; DcNAA; Dis&D; Drake; EncAAH; EncAB-H 1974, 1996; EvLB; GrWrEL P; HarEnUS; LegTOT; LinLib L, S; McGEWB; MouLC 4; NatCAB 1; NewGrDA 86; NinCLC 8; OxCAmH; OxCAmL 65, 83, 95; OxCChiL; OxCEng 67, 85, 95; PenC AM; RAdv 1, 14, 13-1; REn; REnAL; RfGAmL 87, 94; Str&VC; TwCBDA; WebAB 74, 79; WebE&AL; WhAm HS; WhCiWar; WhDW; WorAl; WorAlBi*

Whittingham, Charlie
American. Horse Trainer
Horse trainer, whose horses have won more money than any other thoroughbred trainer's.
b. Apr 13, 1913 in San Diego, California
Source: *BiDAmSp OS; BioIn 15, 16, 21; NewYTBS 86, 89; WhoAm 88; WhoSpor*

Whittington, Dick
[Richard Whittington]
English. Politician
Lord mayor of London, intermittently, 1397-1420; subject of nursery rhyme legends.
b. 1358?
d. 1423?
Source: *Alli SUP; BioIn 2, 6, 9, 10; LngCEL; NewC; OxCChiL; OxCEng 67; WhDW*

Whittle, Christopher
American. Publisher
Maverick entrepreneur founded Whittle Communications; introduced commercial sponsorship of classroom television; originator of Edison Project, national private school system.
b. Aug 23, 1947 in Etowah, Tennessee
Source: *BioIn 14, 16; CurBio 91; News 89-3; NewYTBS 89; WhoAm 92, 94*

Whittle, Frank, Sir
English. Inventor
Invented the jet engine, 1937.
b. Jun 1, 1907 in Coventry, England
d. Aug 8, 1996 in Columbia, Maryland
Source: *AmMWSc 92, 95; BiESc; BioIn 1, 2, 3, 4, 6, 7, 8, 9, 12, 15, 20; BlueB 76; CamDcSc; CurBio 96N; DcInv; HisEWW; InSci; IntWW 74, 75, 76, 77, 78, 79, 80, 81, 82, 83, 89, 91, 93; LarDcSc; McGEWB; McGMS 80; NewYTBS 27; NotTwCS; WhDW; Who 74, 82, 83, 85, 88, 90, 92, 94; WhoAm 92; WhoScEn 94; WhoWor 96; WorInv*

Whittredge, Thomas Worthington
American. Artist
Painted Western scenes, romantic landscapes; posed as Washington in Leutze's *Washington Crossing the Delaware.*
b. May 22, 1820 in Springfield, Ohio
d. Feb 25, 1910 in Summit, New Jersey
Source: *BioIn 15; DcAmArt; DcAmB; EarABI; IlBEAAW; McGDA; NewYHSD; WhAm 1*

Whitty, May, Dame
English. Actor
Oscar nominee for *Night Must Fall,* 1937.
b. Jun 19, 1865 in Liverpool, England
d. May 29, 1948 in Beverly Hills, California
Source: *BioIn 1, 5, 9, 10; CurBio 45, 48; Film 1; FilmAG WE; FilmEn; FilmgC; ForYSC; HalFC 80, 84, 88; HolCA; InWom, SUP; LegTOT; MGM; MotPP; MovMk; NewC; NotNAT A, B; OxCThe 67, 83; ThFT; Vers A; WhoHol B; WhScrn 74, 77, 83; WhThe; WorAl; WorAlBi*

Whitworth, Kathy
[Kathrynne Ann Whitworth]
American. Golfer
Turned pro, 1959; greatest woman golfer in modern times; leading money winner eight times; first woman to win

$1 million on tour; inducted into LPGA Hall of Fame.
b. Sep 27, 1939 in Monahans, Texas
Source: *BiDAmSp OS; BioIn 13, 14, 17; CelR; CurBio 76; EncWomS; GoodHs; HerW, 84; InWom SUP; LegTOT; LibW; NewYTBS 81, 82; WhoAm 76, 78, 80, 82, 84, 86, 88, 90, 92, 94, 95, 96, 97; WhoAmW 75, 77, 79, 81, 83, 85, 87, 89, 91, 93, 95, 97; WhoGolf; WhoSpor; WorAl; WorAlBi*

Who, The
[Roger Daltry; John Entwistle; Kenny Jones; Keith Moon; Peter Towshend]
English. Music Group
Leading rock band, 1960s-70s; hits ranged from hard rock and country to rock opera *Tommy,* 1969.
Source: *BioIn 11; ConMuA 80A, 80B; ConMus 3; DcArts; EncPR&S 74, 89; EncRk 88; EncRkSt; FacFETw; HarEnR 86; IlEncRk; NewAmDM; NewGrDM 80; ObitOF 79; OxCPMus; PenEncP; RkOn 78; RolSEnR 83; WhoHol 92; WhoRock 81; WhoRocM 82*

Whodini
[Ecstacy; Jalil; Grandmaster Dee]
American. Music Group
Brooklyn group with hit singles "Funky Beat," 1986; "Fugitive," 1986.

Whorf, Richard
American. Actor, Director
Films include *Love from a Stranger,* 1947; *The Burning Hills,* 1956.
b. Jun 4, 1906 in Winthrop, Massachusetts
d. Dec 14, 1966 in Santa Monica, California
Source: *BiE&WWA; BioIn 2, 6, 7; FilmEn; FilmgC; ForYSC; HalFC 80, 84, 88; MiSFD 9N; MotPP; MovMk; NotNAT B; ObitOF 79; OxCAmT 84; PlP&P; WhAm 4; WhoHol B; WhScrn 74, 77, 83; WhThe*

Whymper, Edward
English. Artist, Explorer
Wrote, illustrated book on mountain climbing: *Scrambles Amongst the Stars,* 1871.
b. Apr 27, 1840 in London, England
d. Sep 16, 1911 in Chamonix, France
Source: *Alli; BbD; BiD&SB; BioIn 1, 4, 5, 7, 8, 9, 13; BritAu 19; Chambr 3; DcBiPP; DcNaB, S2; EvLB; InSci; NewCBEL; OxCEng 67; WhDW; WhLit*

Whyte, William Hollingsworth
American. Author
Writings include *The Last Landscape,* 1968; active in natural resources conservation.
b. Oct 1, 1917 in West Chester, Pennsylvania
Source: *AmAu&B; Au&Wr 71; BioIn 5, 8, 16; BlueB 76; ConAu 9R; CurBio 59; DcLEL 1940; IntAu&W 76, 77, 82, 89; IntWW 74, 75, 76, 77, 78, 79, 80, 81, 82, 83, 89, 91, 93; NatLAC; REnAL; WhoAm 74, 76, 78, 80, 82, 84, 86, 88, 90, 92, 94, 95; WhoUSWr 88; WhoWor 74, 76, 78; WhoWrEP 89, 92, 95*

Wibberley, Leonard Patrick O'Connor
[Leonard Holton; Christopher Webb]
Irish. Author, Journalist
Author of *The Mouse That Roared,* 1955; filmed, 1959.
b. Apr 9, 1915 in Dublin, Ireland
d. Nov 22, 1983 in Santa Monica, California
Source: *AuBYP 2; ChhPo; ConAu 3NR, 5R, 111, X; CrtSuMy; EncMys; IntAu&W 76, 77, 82; MorJA; NewYTBS 83; REn; SmATA 2; TwCChW 83; TwCCr&M 80, 85, 91; WhoAm 76, 78, 80, 82; WorAu 1950; WrDr 84*

Wick, Charles Z
[Charles Zwick]
American. Government Official
Member Ronald Reagan's "kitchen cabinet"; director, US Information Agency, 1981-89.
b. Oct 12, 1917 in Cleveland, Ohio
Source: *BioIn 13, 14, 15, 16; CurBio 85; IntWW 91; NewYTBS 86, 88; WhoAm 84, 86, 88*

Wickens, Aryness Joy
American. Economist
Research assistant Federal Reserve Board, fundamental in development of consumer price index, 1928.
b. Jan 5, 1901 in Bellingham, Washington
d. Feb 2, 1991 in Jackson, Mississippi
Source: *AmMWSc 73S; BioIn 2, 6, 17; CurBio 91N; InWom; NewYTBS 91; WhAm 10; WhoAm 74, 76, 78, 80, 82, 84, 86, 88, 90; WhoAmW 58, 61, 64, 66, 68, 70, 72, 74, 75, 77; WhoGov 72*

Wicker, Ireene Seaton
"Lady with a Thousand Voices"; "Singing Lady"
American. TV Personality
Children's storyteller on TV, radio, 1931-75; won over 30 awards.
b. Nov 24, 1905 in Quincy, Illinois
d. Nov 17, 1987 in West Palm Beach, Florida
Source: *AuBYP 2S; CmpEPM; ConAu 69; CurBio 43, 88; LegTOT*

Wicker, Tom
[Paul Connelly; Thomas Grey Wicker]
American. Journalist, Author
Washington bureau chief, *NY Times,* 1964-68; author *Kennedy Without Tears: The Man Behind the Myth,* 1964.
b. Jun 18, 1926 in Hamlet, North Carolina
Source: *AmAu&B; AuSpks; BiDAmNC; BioIn 3, 4, 8, 9, 10, 11, 13, 16; BlueB 76; CelR, 90; ConAu 21NR, 46NR, 65, X; ConLC 7; CurBio 73; DcLP 87A; EncTwCJ; IntWW 91, 93; JrnUS; LiJour; WhoAm 74, 76, 78, 80, 82, 84, 86, 88, 90, 92, 94, 95, 96, 97; WhoE 89, 91, 93; WhoSSW 73; WhoWor 74; WorAu 1985; WrDr 76, 80, 82, 84, 86, 88, 90, 92, 94, 96*

Widal, Fernand Isidore
[Georges Fernand Isidore Widal]
French. Bacteriologist, Physician
Work involved many diseases; many contributions; to diagnosis and treatment.
b. Mar 9, 1862 in Dellys, Algeria
d. Jan 14, 1929 in Paris, France
Source: *BioIn 5, 9; InSci; OxCMed 86*

Widdemer, Margaret
American. Author, Poet
Award-winning works include poem, "Lullaby," 1937; book series, "Winona," 1915-23.
b. Sep 30, 1897? in Doylestown, Pennsylvania
d. Jul 31, 1978 in Gloversville, New York
Source: *AmAu&B; AmLY; AmNov; Au&Wr 71; ConAmL; ConAu 4NR, 5R, 77; DcLEL; EvLB; IntWW 74; OxCAmL 65; REn; REnAL; TwCA; TwCWr; WhAm 7*

Widdoes, James
American. Actor
Best known for film debut in *Animal House,* 1977.
b. Nov 15, 1953 in Pittsburgh, Pennsylvania
Source: *ConTFT 3*

Widdoes, Kathleen Effie
American. Actor
TV performances include "Much Ado about Nothing"; "Edith Wharton: Looking Back."
b. Mar 21, 1939 in Wilmington, Delaware
Source: *BiE&WWA; ConTFT 5; FilmgC; HalFC 88; NewYTBE 73; NotNAT; WhoHol A; WhoThe 81*

Wideman, John Edgar
American. Author, Educator
Fiction deals with the struggles of blacks in modern society; novel *Sent For You Yesterday* won PEN/Faulkner Award, 1984.
b. Jun 14, 1941 in Washington, District of Columbia
Source: *AfrAmW; Benet 96; BenetAL 91; BioIn 14, 15; BlkLC; BlkWr 1, 2; ConAu 14NR, 42NR, 85; ConBlB 5; ConLC 5, 34, 36, 67; ConNov 86, 91, 96; CurBio 91; CyWA 89; DcLB 33, 143; DcTwCCu 5; InB&W 85; IntAu&W 91, 93; MagSAmL; NegAl 76, 83, 89; OxCAmL 95; RfGAmL 94; SchCGBL; SelBAAf; WhoAfA 96; WhoAm 86, 90, 92, 94, 95, 96, 97; WhoBlA 92, 94; WorAu 1980; WrDr 88, 90, 92, 94, 96*

Widener, George D
American. Horse Owner
Race horse owner and breeder whose horses won over $25 million, 1915-70.

b. Mar 11, 1889 in Philadelphia, Pennsylvania
d. Dec 8, 1971 in Philadelphia, Pennsylvania
Source: *NatCAB 57; NewYTBE 71; ObitOF 79; WhAm 5*

Widerberg, Bo
Swedish. Director
Films include *Adalen 31*, 1969; *Joe Hill*, 1971.
b. Jun 8, 1930 in Malmo, Sweden
d. May 1, 1997 in Angelholm, Sweden
Source: *BiDFilm, 81, 94; BioIn 11, 12, 16; DcFM; EncEurC; FilmEn; FilmgC; HalFC 80, 84, 88; IntDcF 1-2; IntWW 74, 75, 76, 77, 78, 79, 80, 81, 82, 83, 89, 91, 93; MiSFD 9; MovMk; OxCFilm; WhoWor 89, 95, 96; WorEFlm; WorFDir 2*

Widgery, John Passmore, Baron
English. Judge
Lord Chief Justice, 1971-80, known for 1972 inquiry into killing of 13 Catholic demonstrators by British paratroopers in Londonderry.
b. Jul 24, 1911 in Devonshire, England
d. Jul 25, 1981 in London, England
Source: *AnObit 1981; BioIn 12; DcNaB 1981; IntWW 82N; IntYB 78, 79, 81; NewYTBS 81; Who 82N*

Widmark, Richard
American. Actor
Starred in *Judgment at Nuremberg*, 1961; *Murder on the Orient Express*, 1974.
b. Dec 26, 1914 in Sunrise City, Minnesota
Source: *BiDFilm; BioIn 6, 9, 11, 14, 15, 16, 17, 19; BlueB 76; CmMov; ConTFT 3; CurBio 63; DcArts; FilmEn; FilmgC; ForYSC; GangFlm; HalFC 80, 84, 88; IntDcF 1-3, 2-3; IntMPA 82, 84, 86, 88, 92, 94, 96; IntWW 79, 80, 81, 82, 83, 89, 91, 93; LegTOT; MotPP; MovMk; NewYTBE 71; OxCFilm; RadStar; SaTiSS; VarWW 85; WhoAm 74, 76, 78, 80, 82, 84, 86, 88, 90, 92, 94, 95, 96, 97; WhoEnt 92; WhoHol 92, A; WhoWor 78; WorAl; WorAlBi; WorEFlm*

Widnall, Sheila E.
American. Government Official
Secretary of the Air Force, 1993—.
b. Jul 13, 1938
Source: *NotTwCS; WhoEng 80, 88; WhoTech 89, 95*

Widor, Charles Marie Jean Albert
French. Composer, Organist
Best known for organ ''symphonies''; collaborated with Albert Schweitzer on J S Bach's works.
b. Feb 24, 1844 in Lyons, France
d. Mar 12, 1937 in Paris, France
Source: *Baker 84; BriBkM 80; MusMk; NewGrDM 80; OxCMus*

Wieghorst, Olaf
Danish. Artist
Drew horses, Navajo portraits; a painting sold for $1 million, highest price ever paid to living American artist at the time.
b. Apr 30, 1899 in Jutland, Denmark
d. Apr 27, 1988 in La Mesa, California
Source: *AmArt; ArtsAmW 1; BioIn 4, 8, 9, 15, 16; IlBEAAW; OfPGCP 86; WhAmArt 85; WhoAmA 82, 84, 86*

Wieland, Heinrich Otto
German. Chemist
Won Nobel Prize, 1927; noted for contributions to study of bile acids; set ground for steroid research.
b. Jun 4, 1877 in Pforzheim, Germany
d. Aug 5, 1957 in Starnberg, Germany
Source: *AsBiEn; BiESc; BioIn 3, 4, 5, 6, 14, 15, 19, 20; CamDcSc; DcScB; InSci; LarDcSc; WhAm 3; WhoNob, 90, 95; WorAl; WorAlBi*

Wien, Wilhelm Carl Werner Otto Fritz Franz
German. Scientist
Won 1911 Nobel Prize in physics; researched laws of the radiation of heat.
b. Jan 13, 1864 in Gaffken, Prussia
d. Aug 30, 1928 in Munich, Germany
Source: *DcScB; LarDcSc; WhoNob, 95*

Wiener, Leigh Auston
American. Photographer
Known for photographs of celebrities, historical moments.
b. Aug 28, 1929 in New York, New York
d. May 11, 1993 in Los Angeles, California
Source: *ConAu 47NR, 108, 141; IntAu&W 89*

Wiener, Norbert
American. Mathematician
Professor, MIT, 1932-60; developed science of communication, cybernetics; contributed to development of calculators, computers.
b. Nov 26, 1894 in Columbia, Missouri
d. Mar 18, 1964 in Stockholm, Sweden
Source: *AmAu&B; AmSocL; AsBiEn; BenetAL 91; BiDPsy; BiESc; BioIn 1, 2, 3, 4, 5, 6, 7, 8, 10, 11, 12, 14, 15, 17, 18, 19, 20, 21; CamDcSc; ConAu 107; CurBio 64; DcAmB S7; DcScB; EncAB-H 1974, 1996; EncSF, 93; FacFETw; HisDcDP; InSci; LarDcSc; LinLib L, S; MakMC; McGEWB; McGMS 80; NamesHP; NotTwCS; OxCAmH; RAdv 14; REnAL; ThTwC 87; WebAB 74, 79; WhAm 4; WorAl; WorAlBi; WorScD*

Wieniawski, Henri
[Henryk Wieniawski]
Polish. Violinist, Composer
Virtuoso; toured US with Anton Rubinstein, 1870s; wrote violin classics.
b. Jul 10, 1835 in Lublin, Poland
d. Apr 2, 1880 in Moscow, Russia
Source: *Baker 78, 84, 92; BioIn 1, 2, 7, 14; BriBkM 80; CmpBCM; GrComp; MusMk; NewAmDM; NewGrDM 80; OxCMus; PenDiMP; PolBiDi*

Wierwille, Victor Paul
American. Religious Leader, Clergy
Founder, director of religious group The Way, 1942-82.
b. Dec 31, 1916 in New Knoxville, Ohio
d. May 20, 1985
Source: *BioIn 14; ConAu 2NR, 5R, 116; IntAu&W 76; OhA&B; RelLAm 91; WhoAm 84; WhoMW 76, 78, 80, 82*

Wiese, Kurt
American. Children's Author, Illustrator
Illustrated 300 books by other authors; writings include *Buddy the Bear*, 1936.
b. Apr 22, 1887 in Minden, Germany
d. May 27, 1974 in Idell, New Jersey
Source: *AmAu&B; AuBYP 2, 3; BenetAL 91; BioIn 1, 2, 4, 5, 7, 8, 9, 10, 13, 14, 19; ChhPo; ChlBkCr; ConAu 9R, 49; ConICB; IlsCB 1744, 1946, 1957; JBA 34, 51; LinLib L; MajAI; OxCChiL; REnAL; SmATA 3, 24N, 36; TwCChW 78; WhAmArt 85*

Wiesel, Elie(zer)
American. Journalist, Author
Auschwitz concentration camp survivor whose books deal with Holocaust; won Nobel Peace Prize, 1986.
b. Sep 30, 1928 in Sighet, Transylvania
Source: *AmAu&B; Au&Arts 7; Au&Wr 71; AuNews 1; Benet 87, 96; BenetAL 91; BioIn 8, 9, 10, 11, 12, 13, 14, 15, 16, 17, 18, 19, 20, 21; ConAu 4AS, 5R, 8NR, 40NR; ConHero 1; ConIsC 1; ConLC 3, 5, 11, 37; ConWorW 93; CurBio 86; CyWA 89; DcLB 83, Y87B; DcTwCCu 2; DrAF 76; DrAPF 80, 91; EncWB; EncWL 3; FacFETw; HeroCon; IntAu&W 89, 91, 93; IntWW 89, 91, 93; InWom SUP; JeAmHC; LegTOT; LiExTwC; LinLib L; MagSWL; MajTwCW; NewYTBS 83, 86; NobelP; RAdv 14, 13-2; SmATA 56; TwCYAW; Who 88, 90, 92, 94; WhoAm 74, 76, 78, 80, 82, 84, 86, 88, 90, 92, 94, 95, 96, 97; WhoAmJ 80; WhoE 74, 86, 89, 91, 93, 95, 97; WhoNob 90, 95; WhoRel 92; WhoUSWr 88; WhoWor 89, 91, 93, 95, 96, 97; WhoWorJ 72, 78; WhoWrEP 89, 92, 95; WorAl; WorAlBi; WorAu 1950; WrDr 86, 88, 90, 92, 94, 96*

Wiesel, Torsten Nils
American. Scientist, Educator
Shared 1981 Nobel Prize in medicine for vision research.
b. Jun 3, 1924 in Uppsala, Sweden
Source: *AmMWSc 76P, 79, 82, 86, 89, 92, 95; BioIn 12, 13, 14, 15, 19, 20; LarDcSc; NewYTBS 81; NobelP; Who 83, 85, 88, 90, 92, 94; WhoAm 80, 82, 84, 86, 88, 90, 92, 94, 95, 96, 97; WhoE 83, 85, 86, 89, 91, 93, 95, 97; WhoFrS 84; WhoMedH; WhoNob, 90; WhoScEn 94, 96; WhoWor 84, 87, 89, 91, 93, 95, 96, 97; WorAlBi*

Wiesenthal, Simon
Austrian. Author
Survivor of Nazi death camps who founded Jewish Documentation Center; wrote *The Murderers Among Us,* 1967.
b. Dec 31, 1908 in Buczacz, Poland
Source: *BioIn 6, 7, 9, 10, 11, 12, 13, 15, 16; ConAu 13NR, 21R; ConHero 2; CurBio 75; EncTR, 91; EncWB; FacFETw; IntAu&W 77, 89, 91, 93; IntMPA 84; IntWW 77, 78, 79, 80, 81, 82, 83, 89, 91, 93; LegTOT; SpyCS; WhoWor 74, 76, 78, 80, 82, 84, 87, 89, 91, 93, 95; WhoWorJ 78*

Wiesner, Jerome B(ert)
American. Engineer
Expert on microwave theory; presidential assistant for science and technology, 1961-63.
b. May 30, 1915
d. Oct 21, 1994 in Watertown, Massachusetts
Source: *AmAu&B; BioIn 5, 6, 9, 11, 12; BlueB 76; ConAu 13R, 147; CurBio 95N; InSci; IntWW 74, 75, 76, 77, 78, 79, 80, 81, 82, 83, 89, 91, 93; LElec; PolProf K; WhAm 11; Who 74, 82, 83, 85, 88, 90, 92, 94; WhoAm 74, 76, 78, 80, 82, 84, 86, 88, 90, 92, 94; WhoAmJ 80; WhoE 74, 77, 79, 81, 83, 85, 86, 89, 91, 93, 95; WhoEng 80, 88; WhoFrS 84; WhoScEn 94; WhoWor 87, 89, 91; WhoWorJ 72, 78*

Wiest, Dianne
American. Actor
Won Oscar, best supporting actress, for *Hannah and Her Sisters,* 1986, and for *Bullets Over Broadway,* 1995.
b. Mar 28, 1948 in Kansas City, Missouri
Source: *BioIn 14, 15, 21; ConTFT 5, 12; HalFC 88; IntMPA 86, 92, 94, 96; LegTOT; News 95, 95-2; VarWW 85; WhoAm 88, 90, 92, 94, 95, 96, 97; WhoAmW 91, 93, 95, 97; WhoEnt 92; WhoHol 92; WorAlBi*

Wigg, George (Edward Cecil)
English. Politician, Author
Exposed 1963 Profumo scandal.
b. Nov 28, 1900
d. Aug 11, 1983 in London, England
Source: *AnObit 1983; BioIn 7, 13; BlueB 76; ConAu 115; DcNaB 1981; IntWW 83; NewYTBS 83; Who 74*

Wiggin, Kate Douglas
American. Children's Author
Wrote *Rebecca of Sunnybrook Farm,* 1903.
b. Sep 28, 1856 in Philadelphia, Pennsylvania
d. Aug 24, 1923 in Harrow, England
Source: *Alli SUP; AmAu&B; AmBi; AuBYP 2S, 3; BbD; BenetAL 91; BiDAmEd; BiD&SB; BioAmW; BioIn 1, 2, 3, 4, 6, 8, 10, 11, 12; CamGLE; CarSB; Chambr 3; ChhPo, S1, S2, S3; ChlBkCr; CmCal; CnDAL; ConAmL; ConAu 111; DcAmAu; DcAmB; DcArts; DcLB 42; DcLEL; DcNAA; EvLB; FamAYP; FamSYP; FemiCLE; HerW, 84; JBA 34; LinLib L, S; LngCTC; NatCAB 6; NotAW; OxCAmL 65, 83, 95; OxCChiL; REn; REnAL; TwCA, SUP; TwCChW 78, 83, 89, 95; WebAB 74, 79; WhAm 1; WhoChL; WomWWA 14; WorAl; WorAlBi; WrChl; YABC 1*

Wiggins, Charles Edward
American. Politician
Congressman, 1967-79; defended Nixon during impeachment hearings, 1974.
b. Dec 3, 1927 in El Monte, California
Source: *AlmAP 78; BiDrAC; BiDrUSC 89; BioNews 74; PolProf NF; WhoAm 80, 88, 90, 92, 94, 95, 96, 97; WhoAmL 79, 83, 87, 90, 92, 94, 96; WhoAmP 79; WhoGov 72, 75, 77; WhoWest 74, 76, 78, 89, 94, 96*

Wiggins, J(ames) R(ussell)
American. Journalist, Diplomat
US ambassador to UN, 1968; editor, exec. vp, *Washington Post,* 1961-68.
b. Dec 4, 1903 in Luverne, Minnesota
Source: *AuNews 2; BiDAmNC; BioIn 8, 11, 15, 16; BlueB 76; ConAu 133; CurBio 69; EncTwCJ; IntWW 74, 75, 76, 77, 78, 79, 80, 81, 82, 83, 89, 91, 93; JrnUS; PeoHis; PolProf J; WhoAm 74, 76, 78, 80, 82, 84, 86, 88, 90, 92, 94, 95, 96, 97; WhoE 91; WhoWor 74; WrDr 94, 96*

Wigglesworth, Michael
American. Poet, Clergy, Physician
Known for morally instructive writings; long verse *Day of Doom,* 1662.
b. Oct 18, 1631 in Hedon, England
d. May 27, 1705 in Malden, Massachusetts
Source: *Alli; AmAu; AmAu&B; AmBi; AmWrBE; ApCAB; Benet 87, 96; BenetAL 91; BiD&SB; BioIn 1, 6, 7, 8, 12, 14; CamGEL; CamGLE; CamHAL; CasWL; CnDAL; CyAL 1; DcAmAu; DcAmB; DcLB 24; DcLEL; DcNAA; Drake; EncCRAm; GrWrEL P; HarEnUS; LinLib L; McGEWB; NatCAB 8; NewCBEL; OxCAmH; OxCAmL 65, 83, 95; OxCEng 67, 85, 95; PenC AM; REn; REnAL; RfGAmL 87, 94; WebAB 74, 79; WebE&AL; WhAm HS; WorAl; WorAlBi; WrCNE*

Wightman, Hazel Virginia Hotchkiss
American. Tennis Player
Won 44 nat. tennis titles, beginning 1909; launched volleying technique.
b. Dec 20, 1886 in Healdsburg, California
d. Dec 5, 1974 in Newton, Massachusetts
Source: *BiDAmSp OS; DcAmB S9; InWom SUP; NotAW MOD*

Wigle, Ernest Douglas
Canadian. Physician, Educator
Pres., Canadian Cardiovascular Society, 1984—.
b. Oct 30, 1928 in Windsor, Ontario, Canada
Source: *AmMWSc 73P, 76P, 79, 82, 86, 89, 92, 95; BiDrACP 79; WhoAm 76, 78, 80, 82, 84*

Wigner, Eugene P(aul)
Hungarian. Physicist
Won Nobel Prize, 1963, for extensive work on quantum mechanics.
b. Nov 17, 1902 in Budapest, Hungary
d. Jan 1, 1995 in Princeton, New Jersey
Source: *AmMWSc 76P, 79, 82, 86, 89, 92, 95; AsBiEn; BiESc; BioIn 3, 5, 6, 7, 9, 10, 11, 12, 14, 15, 18; BlueB 76; CamDcSc; ConAu 147, P-2; CurBio 95N; FacFETw; InSci; IntAu&W 77, 82; IntWW 74, 75, 76, 77, 78, 79, 80, 81, 82, 83, 89, 91, 93; LarDcSc; McGEWB; McGMS 80; NobelP; NotTwCS; OxCAmH; RAdv 14; ThTwC 87; WebAB 74, 79; WhAm 11; Who 92, 94; WhoAm 74, 76, 78, 80, 82, 84, 86, 88, 90, 92, 94; WhoE 77, 79, 81, 85, 86, 89, 91, 93, 95; WhoFrS 84; WhoNob, 90, 95; WhoScEn 94; WhoWor 74, 80, 82, 84, 87, 89, 91, 93, 95; WorAl; WorAlBi; WrDr 76, 80, 82, 84, 86, 88*

Wilander, Mats
Swedish. Tennis Player
Winner of three French Open tournaments and three Australian Opens; known for his sense of good sportsmanship.
b. Aug 24, 1964 in Vaxjo, Sweden
Source: *BioIn 13, 15, 16; BuCMET; CelR 90; IntWW 91; NewYTBS 82*

Wilberforce, William
English. Abolitionist
Humanitarian who devoted much of his life to social reform; MP, won abolition of British slave trade, 1807.
b. Aug 24, 1759 in Hull, England
d. Jul 29, 1833 in London, England
Source: *Alli; BiD&SB; BiDLA; BioIn 1, 2, 3, 4, 5, 6, 7, 8, 10, 11, 12, 13, 14, 16, 18; BlkwCE; BlmGEL; BritAu 19; CelCen; Chambr 2; DcAfL; DcAmC; DcAmSR; DcBiPP; DcEnL; DcEuL; DcLB 158; DcLEL; DcNaB, C; EncWM; EvLB; HisDBrE; LegTOT; LinLib S; LngCEL; LuthC 75; McGEWB; NewC; NewCBEL; OxCEng 67, 85, 95; OxCMus; WhDW*

Wilbur, Dwight L(ocke)
American. Physician
Pres., AMA, 1968-69; founded San Francisco Society of Internal Medicine and California Society of Internal Medicine.
b. Sep 18, 1903
d. Mar 9, 1997 in San Francisco, California
Source: *AmMWSc 79, 82, 86, 89, 92, 95; BiDrACP 79; BioIn 8; BlueB 76; WhoAm 74, 76, 78, 97; WhoMedH*

Wilbur, Richard Purdy
American. Author, Poet, Educator
Skilled writer who won 1957 Pulitzer for *Poems;* translated many of Moliere's works to English.

b. Mar 1, 1921 in New York, New York
Source: *AuBYP 3; Benet 87; BenetAL 91; BioIn 13, 14, 15; CamGEL; CamGLE; CamHAL; CasWL; ConAu 2BS, 2NR, 29NR; ConLC 14, 53; ConPo 75, 91; ConTFT 3; CroCAP; CurBio 66; DrAP 75; DrAPF 91; DrAS 82E; EncWB; EncWL; IntAu&W 91; IntvTCA 2; IntWW 74, 91; MajTwCW; ModAL, S2; NewYTBS 87; OxCAmL 65; PenC AM; RAdv 13-1; REn; REnAL; RfGAmL 87; WebE&AL; WhoAm 86, 90; WhoEnt 92; WhoWrEP 89; WorAlBi; WrDr 92*

Wilcock, John
English. Author, Newspaper Editor
One of the founders of *The Village Voice,* NYC; noted for one-dollar-a-day travel books.
b. 1927 in Shackhill, England
Source: *BioIn 10; ConAu 1R, 2NR; IntAu&W 86; MugS; NewYTBE 73; WhoAm 84; WhoUSWr 88; WhoWest 96; WhoWor 89; WhoWrEP 89*

Wilcox, Ella Wheeler
American. Poet
Wrote almost 40 vols. of sentimental verse; most famous lines from "Solitude": "Laugh, and the World laughs with you; weep, and you weep alone."
b. Nov 5, 1850 in Johnstown, Wisconsin
d. Oct 31, 1919 in Short Beach, Connecticut
Source: *Alli SUP; AmAu; AmAu&B; AmBi; AmLY; AmWom; AmWomPl; AmWomWr; ArtclWW 2; BbD; BenetAL 91; BiD&SB; BioAmW; CasWL; Chambr 3; ChhPo, S1, S2; DcAmAu; DcAmB; DcAmTB; DcLEL; DcNAA; EvLB; InWom SUP; LibW; LngCTC; NotAW; OxCAmL 65, 83, 95; OxCEng 67, 85, 95; OxCTwCP; PenC AM; RelLAm 91; REnAL; WebAB 74, 79; WhAm 1; WisWr*

Wilcox, Francis (Orlando)
American. Political Scientist, Government Official
Director general, Atlantic Council, from 1975.
b. Apr 9, 1908 in Columbus Junction, Iowa
d. Feb 20, 1985 in Washington, District of Columbia
Source: *AmMWSc 73S, 78S; BioIn 6, 14; ConAu 37R, 115; CurBio 62, 85; LEduc 74; WhAm 8; WhoAm 74, 76, 78, 80, 82, 84; WhoWor 78*

Wilcox, Herbert
English. Producer
Films include *No, No, Nanette,* 1940; *Heart of a Man,* 1959.
b. Apr 19, 1891 in Cork, Ireland
d. May 15, 1977 in London, England
Source: *BioIn 8, 11; ConAu 57, 118; CurBio 77; DcFM; EncEurC; FilmgC; HalFC 80; IntDcF 1-2, 2-2; IntMPA 77; MovMk; NewYTBS 77; ObitOF 79; OxCFilm; TwYS A; Who 74; WhoThe 81N; WorEFlm*

Wilcox, Larry Dee
American. Actor
Played Officer Jon Baker on TV series "CHIPS," 1977-82.
b. Aug 8, 1947 in San Diego, California
Source: *ConTFT 8; WhoAm 80, 82, 84, 86, 88; WhoWest 82; WhoWor 80, 82, 84*

Wilcoxon, Henry
[Harry Wilcoxon]
British. Actor, Producer
Starred in Cecil B. DeMille films, *Cleopatra,* 1934; *The Crusades,* 1935.
b. Sep 8, 1905, Dominica
d. Mar 6, 1984 in Burbank, California
Source: *BioIn 13, 17; CmMov; FilmEn; FilmgC; ForYSC; HalFC 80, 84, 88; IlWWBF; IntMPA 75, 76, 77, 78, 79, 80, 81, 82, 84; MotPP; MovMk; WhoHol A; WhThe*

Wild, Earl
American. Pianist, Composer
Pianist with NBC Orchestra; performed first piano recital on TV.
b. Nov 26, 1915 in Pittsburgh, Pennsylvania
Source: *Baker 84, 92; BioIn 14, 15, 16, 21; CurBio 88; IntWW 74, 75, 76, 77, 78, 79, 80, 81, 82, 83, 89, 91, 93; IntWWM 77, 80, 90; NewAmDM; NewGrDA 86; NotTwCP; PenDiMP; WhoAmM 83*

Wild, Jack
English. Actor
Oscar nominee for debut in movie *Oliver,* 1968, as the Artful Dodger.
b. Sep 30, 1952 in Manchester, England
Source: *FilmgC; HalFC 80, 84, 88; IntMPA 75, 76, 77, 78, 79, 80, 81, 82, 84, 86; WhoHol 92, A*

Wilde, Cornel
American. Actor, Producer, Director
Oscar nominee for role of Chopin in *A Song to Remember,* 1945.
b. Oct 13, 1915 in New York, New York
d. Oct 16, 1989 in Los Angeles, California
Source: *AnObit 1989; ASCAP 66; BiDFilm, 81, 94; BiE&WWA; BioIn 11, 16, 17; CmMov; ConTFT 8; FilmEn; FilmgC; ForYSC; GangFlm; HalFC 80, 84, 88; IntDcF 2-3; IntMPA 84, 88; ItaFilm; LegTOT; MiSFD 9N; MotPP; NewYTBS 89; WhoAm 84, 90; WhoHol A; WorAl; WorAlBi; WorEFlm*

Wilde, Jimmy
"Mighty Atom"
Welsh. Boxer
Flyweight champion, 1916-23; Hall of Fame, 1959.
b. May 15, 1892 in Pontypridd, Wales
d. Mar 10, 1969 in Cardiff, Wales
Source: *BioIn 7, 8, 14, 15; BoxReg; ObitT 1961; OxCLiW 86; WhoBox 74*

Wilde, Kim
English. Singer
Hit singles include "Kids in America," 1981; "Rage To Love," 1985.
b. Nov 18, 1960 in London, England
Source: *BioIn 15; EncRk 88; EncRkSt; HarEnR 86; LegTOT; NewWmR; RkOn 85*

Wilde, Oscar (Fingal O'Flahertie Wills)
Irish. Poet, Dramatist, Author
Flamboyant wit; wrote *The Importance of Being Earnest,* 1895; imprisoned for sodomy, 1890s.
b. Oct 16, 1856 in Dublin, Ireland
d. Nov 30, 1900 in Paris, France
Source: *AtlBL; BiDIrW; BlmGEL; CasWL; CnOxB; CnThe; CrtT 4; DcAmSR; DcLEL; DcPup; Dis&D; FilmgC; GayLesB; LngCTC; McGEWD 72; ModWD; MouLC 4; NewC; NewEOp 71; OxCEng 67; OxCFilm; OxCFr; OxCThe 67; PenC ENG; PlP&P; REn; REnWD; WebE&AL; WhoChL; WhoHrs 80*

Wilde, Patricia
[Patricia Lorrain-Ann White]
American. Choreographer
Dir. American Ballet Theatre School, 1977-82; artistic director, Pittsburgh Ballet Theatre, 1982—; ballerina, NYC Ballet, 1950-65.
b. Jul 16, 1928 in Ottawa, Ontario, Canada
Source: *BiDD; BioIn 7, 8, 9, 11, 14; CanWW 70; CnOxB; CurBio 68; IntDcB; InWom; WhoAm 74, 76, 78, 80, 82, 84, 86, 88, 92, 94, 95, 96, 97; WhoAmW 87, 91, 93, 95, 97; WhoE 85, 86, 93, 95, 97; WhoEnt 92; WhoWor 74, 95, 96, 97*

Wilder, Alec
[Alexander Lafayette Chew Wilder]
American. Composer
Writer of lyrical pop, jazz, classical works; arranged for Frank Sinatra, Judy Garland, Jimmy Dorsey, others.
b. Feb 17, 1907 in Rochester, New York
d. Dec 24, 1980 in Gainesville, Florida
Source: *AnObit 1980; AuBYP 2, 3; Baker 78, 84, 92; BiE&WWA; BioIn 1, 8, 9, 10, 12, 16, 17, 18, 21; CmpEPM; ConAmC 76, 82; ConAu 102, 104; CpmDNM 80, 81; CurBio 80, 81N; DcAmB S10; DcCM; NewAmDM; NewGrDA 86; NewGrDM 80; NotNAT A; OxCPMus; PenEncP; RAdv 14; WhAm 7, 8; WhoAm 74, 76, 78, 82; WhoHol A; WhoWor 74*

Wilder, Billy (Samuel)
American. Director, Producer
Has over 50 films, six Oscars to credit; films include *Double Indemnity,* 1944; *Some Like It Hot,* 1959; won Lifetime Achievement Award, 1986; Thalberg Award, 1988.
b. Jun 22, 1906 in Sucha, Hungary
Source: *AmCulL; AmFD; BenetAL 91; BiDFilm, 81, 94; BioIn 2, 5, 6, 7, 8, 9,*

10, 11, 12, 13, 14, 15, 16, 17, 18, 19, 20, 21; BlueB 76; CelR, 90; CmMov; ConDr 77A, 82A, 88A; ConLC 20; ConTFT 1, 4; CurBio 51, 84; DcArts; DcFM; DcLB 26; DcTwCCu 1; EncAFC; FacFETw; FilmEn; FilmgC; GangFlm; HalFC 80, 84, 88; IlWWHD 1; IntAu&W 76, 77, 89, 91; IntDcF 1-2, 2-2; IntMPA 75, 76, 77, 78, 79, 80, 81, 82, 84, 86, 88, 92, 94, 96; IntWW 74, 75, 76, 77, 78, 79, 80, 81, 82, 83, 89, 91, 93; ItaFilm; LegTOT; MiSFD 9; MovMk; NewYTBS 86; OxCFilm; WhoAm 74, 76, 78, 80, 82, 84, 86, 88, 90, 92, 94, 95, 96, 97; WhoEnt 92; WhoWest 74; WhoWor 74; WorAl; WorAlBi; WorEFlm; WorFDir 1

Wilder, Clinton
American. Producer
Plays produced include *The Little Foxes, Visit to a Small Planet.*
b. Jul 7, 1921 in Warren, Pennsylvania
d. Feb 14, 1986 in Bedford, New York
Source: *BiE&WWA; NewYTBS 86; NotNAT; WhoThe 81*

Wilder, Douglas
[Lawrence Douglas Wilder]
American. Politician
Democratic governor of VA, 1990-94; first elected black governor in US.
b. Jan 17, 1931 in Richmond, Virginia
Source: *AfrAmAl 6; AfrAmBi 1; AfrAmOr; BiDrGov 1988; CurBio 90; Ebony 1; EncAACR; IntWW 91, 93; NegAl 76, 83, 89A; NewYTBS 85, 91; WhoAfA 96; WhoAm 86, 88, 90, 92, 94, 95; WhoAmP 73, 75, 77, 79, 81, 83, 85, 87, 89, 91, 93, 95; WhoBlA 88, 90, 92, 94; WhoSSW 82, 84, 86, 91, 93, 95; WhoWor 93*

Wilder, Gene
[Jerome Silberman]
American. Actor
Starred in *Blazing Saddles,* 1974; *Young Frankenstein,* 1974; *Stir Crazy,* 1980.
b. Jun 11, 1934 in Milwaukee, Wisconsin
Source: *BiE&WWA; BioIn 10, 11, 12, 16; CelR 90; ConAu X; ConTFT 7; CurBio 78; EncAFC; FilmgC; HalFC 80, 84, 88; IntMPA 86, 92; MovMk; NotNAT; QDrFCA 92; VarWW 85; WhoAm 86, 90; WhoEnt 92; WhoHol A; WorAlBi*

Wilder, Joseph
American. Psychiatrist, Editor
Founder, first pres., Assn. of Advancement of Psychotherapy; originated "Wilder's Law."
b. Feb 13, 1895 in Drohobycz, Austria-Hungary
d. Oct 31, 1976 in West Hartford, Connecticut
Source: *BioIn 11, 12; BlueB 76; ConAu 116; NatCAB 60; WhoWorJ 72, 78*

Wilder, Laura Elizabeth Ingalls
[Mrs. Almanzo James Wilder]
American. Author
Published *Little House in the Big Woods,* 1932; books basis for TV series "Little House on the Prairie," 1974-82.
b. Feb 7, 1867 in Pepin, Wisconsin
d. Feb 10, 1957 in Mansfield, Missouri
Source: *AnCL; AuBYP 2; BkCL; CasWL; ChlLR 2; CurBio 57; DcLB 22; HerW; OxCAmL 83; REnAL; Str&VC; TwCChW 83; WhoChL; WorAl*

Wilder, Robert Ingersoll
American. Author, Journalist
Writings include *Flamingo Road,* 1942; *An Affair of Honor,* 1969.
b. Jan 25, 1901 in Richmond, Virginia
d. Aug 22, 1974 in La Jolla, California
Source: *AmAu&B; AmNov; Au&Wr 71; BioIn 2, 4, 10; ConAu 53, P-2; LngCTC; TwCA SUP; WhAm 6; WhoAm 74*

Wilder, Thornton (Niven)
American. Author, Dramatist
Won Pulitzers for novel, *The Bridge of San Luis Rey,* 1928; plays, *Our Town,* 1938; *Skin of Our Teeth,* 1942.
b. Apr 17, 1897 in Madison, Wisconsin
d. Dec 7, 1975 in Hamden, Connecticut
Source: *AmAu&B; AmCulL; AmNov; AmWr; Au&Wr 71; AuNews 2; Benet 87, 96; BenetAL 91; BiDAmM; BiE&WWA; BioIn 1, 2, 3, 4, 5, 6, 7, 8, 9, 10, 11, 12, 13, 14, 15, 16, 17, 19, 20; BlueB 76; CamGEL; CamGLE; CamGWoT; CamHAL; CasWL; CelR; Chambr 3; CnDAL; CnMD; CnMWL; CnThe; ConAmA; ConAmD; ConAmL; ConAu 13R, 40NR, 61; ConDr 73, 77, 93; ConLC 1, 5, 6, 10, 15, 35, 82; ConNov 72; CroCD; CrtSuDr; CurBio 43, 71, 76N; CyWA 58, 89; DcAmB S9; DcArts; DcLB 4, 7, 9; DcLEL; DramC 1; EncAB-H 1974, 1996; EncWL 2, 3; EncWT; Ent; EvLB; FacFETw; FilmEn; FilmgC; GrWrEL DR, N; HalFC 80, 84, 88; IntAu&W 76; IntDcT 2; IntWW 74, 75; LegTOT; LinLib L, S; LngCTC; MagSAmL; MajMD 1; MajTwCW; McGEWB; McGEWD 84; MemAm; ModAL, S1, S2; ModWD; NewEOp 71; NewYTBS 75; NotNAT A, B; Novels; ObitT 1971; OxCAmL 65, 83, 95; OxCAmT 84; OxCEng 67, 85, 95; OxCThe 67, 83; PenC AM; PiP; PlP&P; RAdv 1, 14, 13-1, 13-2; RComWL; REn; REnAL; REnWD; RfGAmL 87, 94; RGTwCWr; TwCA, SUP; TwCRHW 90, 94; TwCWr; WebAB 74, 79; WebE&AL; WhAm 6; WhDW; WhE&EA; WhLit; WhNAA; Who 74; WhoAm 74; WhoTwCL; WhoWor 74; WhThe; WisWr; WorAl; WorAlBi; WorEFlm; WorLitC; WrDr 76; WrPh*

Wilding, Michael
American. Actor
Son of Elizabeth Taylor, Michael Wilding; stars in TV soap opera "Guiding Light," 1985—.
Source: *IntvTCA 2; WhoHol 92; WhoThe 81N*

Wilding, Michael
English. Actor
Married to Elizabeth Taylor, 1952-57; debonair leading man of British films, 1933-73.
b. Jul 28, 1912 in Westcliff-on-Sea, England
d. Jul 9, 1979 in Chichester, England
Source: *BioIn 10, 78, 79; ItaFilm; LegTOT; MotPP; MovMk; NewYTBS 79; OxCFilm; What 5; Who 74; WhoHol A; WhoThe 81N; WhScrn 83; WhThe; WorAl; WorAlBi*

Wilding, Michael
Australian. Author
Writer of postmodern Australian literature; wrote *Aspects of the Dying Process,* 1972.
b. Jan 5, 1942 in Worcester, England
Source: *CamGLE; ConAu 24NR, 49NR, 104; ConLC 73; ConNov 86, 91, 96; IntAu&W 76, 77, 82, 89, 91, 93; OxCAusL; RfGShF; ScF&FL 92; WhoWor 78, 97; WrDr 76, 80, 82, 84, 86, 88, 90, 92, 94, 96*

Wildmon, Donald Ellis
American. Religious Leader, Social Reformer
Conservative minister, founder of Nat. Federation of Decency; launched crusade to rid media of sexually explicit material.
b. Jan 18, 1938 in Dumas, Mississippi
Source: *BioIn 13, 16; ConAu 61; CurBio 92; LesBEnT 92; News 88; NewYTBS 90; WhoRel 77*

Wildsmith, Brian
English. Illustrator, Children's Author
Self-illustrated works include prize-winning, *Brian Wildsmith's ABC,* 1962.
b. Jan 22, 1930 in Penistone, England
Source: *AuBYP 3; BioIn 6, 8, 9, 11, 12, 14, 16, 18, 19; BritCA; ChlBkCr; ChlLR 2; ConAu 35NR, 85; IntAu&W 91; MajAI; OxCChiL; SmATA 5AS, 16, 18, 69; ThrBJA; Who 92*

Wiles, Andrew J.
English. Mathematician
Professor, Princeton University, 1982—; proved Fermat's Last Theorem, 1993.
b. c. Apr 11, 1953 in Cambridge, England
Source: *CurBio 96; NotTwCS*

Wiley, George A
American. Educator, Civil Rights Leader
Founded National Welfare Rights Organization, 1966; nat. coordinator, Movement for Economic Justice.
b. Feb 26, 1931 in Bayonne, New Jersey
d. Aug 8, 1973 in Maryland
Source: *BioIn 8, 10, 11; InB&W 80, 85; NewYTBE 73*

Wiley, Harvey Washington
American. Chemist, Social Reformer
Wrote books on chemistry including *Foods and Their Adulteration,* 1917.
b. Oct 18, 1844 in Kent, Indiana
d. Jun 30, 1930 in Washington, District of Columbia
Source: *AmBi; AmLY; AmRef; AmRef&R; ApCAB, X; BiDAmS; BioIn 1, 2, 3, 4, 5, 6, 7, 12, 17, 21; CopCroC; DcAmAu; DcAmB; DcAmMeB 84; DcAmSR; DcAmTB; DcNAA; DcScB; EncAAH; EncAB-A 4; EncAB-H 1974, 1996; HarEnUS; IndAu 1816; InSci; LinLib S; McGEWB; NatCAB 9, 21; TwCBDA; WebAB 74, 79; WhAm 1; WhNAA*

Wiley, Ralph
American. Author
Author of *Why Black People Tend to Shout,* 1991.
b. Apr 12, 1952 in Memphis, Tennessee
Source: *ConAu 136; ConBlB 8; WhoAfA 96; WrDr 94, 96*

Wiley, William Bradford
American. Publisher
Chm., John Wiley & Sons, Inc., 1971-92.
b. Nov 17, 1910 in Orange, New Jersey
Source: *AmAu&B; BioIn 4; Dun&B 88; St&PR 87; WhAm 11; WhoAm 74, 76, 78, 80, 82, 84, 86, 88, 90; WhoFI 79, 81, 89*

Wilhelm, Gale
American. Author
Novels include *No Letters for the Dead,* 1936; *The Time Between,* 1942; other novels feature lesbian relationships.
b. Apr 26, 1908 in Eugene, Oregon
d. Jul 11, 1991
Source: *AmAu&B; AmNov; FemiCLE; GayLesB; InWom*

Wilhelm, Hellmut
German. Scholar
Authority on Chinese history, literature; wrote many books on subject.
b. Dec 10, 1905 in Qingdao, China
Source: *ConAu 5R; DrAS 74H, 78H, 82H*

Wilhelm, Hoyt
[James Hoyt Wilhelm]
American. Baseball Player
Pitcher, 1952-72, known for knuckleball; Hall of Fame, 1985.
b. Jul 26, 1923 in Huntersville, North Carolina
Source: *Ballpl 90; BiDAmSp BB; BioIn 5, 7, 9, 10, 13, 14, 15; CurBio 71; LegTOT; NewYTBS 84; WhoProB 73; WhoSpor*

Wilhelm II
[Friedrich Wilhelm Viktor Albert; William II]
German. Ruler
Emperor of Germany, king of Prussia, 1888-1918, whose aggressive colonial policy, expansion of navy contributed to WW I outbreak.
b. Jan 27, 1859 in Berlin, Germany
d. Jun 4, 1941 in Doorn, Netherlands
Source: *CurBio 41; NewCol 75; OxCGer 76; REn*

Wilhelmina
[Wilhelmina Helena Pauline Maria]
Dutch. Ruler
Constitutional monarch, 1890-1948; symbol of Dutch resistance, WW II; established govt. in exile in England; abdicated to daughter Juliana.
b. Aug 31, 1880 in The Hague, Netherlands
d. Nov 28, 1962 in Het Loo, Netherlands
Source: *BioIn 1, 5, 6, 8, 16; ContDcW 89; CurBio 63; DcTwHis; Dis&D; HisWorL; IntDcWB; InWom; LegTOT; LinLib S; McGEWB; ObitT 1961; WhAm 4; WhWW-II; WomFir; WomWR*

Wilkens, Lenny
[Leonard Randolph Wilkens]
American. Basketball Player, Basketball Coach
Guard, 1960-76, mostly with St. Louis; led NBA in assists, 1970; coach, Seattle 1969-72, gen. mgr., 1978-86; Cleveland 1986-93; Atlanta Hawks 1993—; won NBA championship with Seattle, 1979; Hall of Fame, 1989.
b. Oct 28, 1937 in New York, New York
Source: *AfrAmBi 2; AfrAmSG; BasBi; BiDAmSp BK; BioIn 16; BlkWrNE A; ConBlB 11; CurBio 96; InB&W 85; News 95, 95-2; OfNBA 87; WhoAm 82, 84, 86, 88, 90, 92, 94, 95, 96, 97; WhoBbl 73; WhoBlA 85, 92; WhoMW 88, 92; WhoSpor; WhoSSW 95, 97*

Wilkes, Charles
American. Explorer, Naturalist
Circled the globe, 1838-42; explored unknown parts of Antarctica.
b. Apr 3, 1798 in New York, New York
d. Feb 8, 1877 in Washington, District of Columbia
Source: *Alli; AmAu&B; AmBi; ApCAB; BiDAmS; BiD&SB; BiInAmS; BioIn 1, 3, 4, 6, 7, 8, 9, 10, 12, 13, 14, 15, 17, 18, 20; CivWDc; CmCal; DcAmAu; DcAmB; DcAmMiB; DcNAA; EarABI; Expl 93; HarEnMi; HarEnUS; InSci; IntDcAn; LinLib S; McGEWB; NatCAB 2; NewYHSD; OxCAmH; OxCShps; TwCBDA; WebAB 74, 79; WebAMB; WhAm HS; WhCiWar; WhWE; WorAl; WorAlBi*

Wilkes, Jamaal
[Jackson Keith Wilkes]
American. Basketball Player
Forward, 1974-85, mostly with LA; NBA rookie of yr., 1975.
b. May 2, 1953 in Berkeley, California
Source: *BasBi; BiDAmSp Sup; BioIn 12, 14, 15; LegTOT; NewYTBS 85; OfNBA 86; WhoAfA 96; WhoAm 84; WhoBlA 77, 80, 85, 88, 90, 92*

Wilkes, John
English. Social Reformer
Radical critic of govt. policies who became MP, lord mayor of London; helped secure many political rights.
b. Oct 17, 1727 in London, England
d. Dec 26, 1797 in London, England
Source: *Alli; Benet 87, 96; BioIn 2, 3, 4, 6, 7, 8, 9, 10, 12, 14, 17, 19; BlkwCE; BlmGEL; BritAu; CamGEL; CamGLE; CasWL; Chambr 2; DcAmSR; DcBiPP; DcEnA; DcEnL; DcNaB; EncAR; EncCRAm; EvLB; HarEnUS; LngCEL; NewC; NewCBEL; OxCEng 67, 85, 95; OxCLaw; REn; WebE&AL; WhAmRev; WhDW*

Wilkie, David, Sir
Scottish. Artist
Influenced by Spanish art, Flemish realists; pioneered English school of anecdotal or ''subject'' painting.
b. Nov 18, 1785 in Cults, Scotland
d. Jun 1, 1841
Source: *Alli; ArtsNiC; BioIn 1, 2, 5, 8, 9, 10, 13; CelCen; ChhPo, S1; ClaDrA; CmScLit; DcArts; DcBiPP; DcBrBI; DcBrWA; DcNaB; DcVicP, 2; IntDcAA 90; McGDA; OxCArt; OxDcArt; WhDW*

Wilkins, Dominique
[Jacques Dominique Wilkins]
American. Basketball Player
Forward, Atlanta Hawks 1982-94, Boston Celtics 1994—.
b. Jan 12, 1960 in Washington, North Carolina
Source: *AfrAmSG; BiDAmSp Sup; BioIn 12, 15, 16; CurBio 95; OfNBA 87; WhoAfA 96; WhoAm 92, 94, 95, 96, 97; WhoBlA 88, 90, 92; WhoSpor; WhoWor 97; WorAlBi*

Wilkins, Ernest Hatch
American. Educator
Pres., Oberlin College, 1927-46; wrote *The College and Society,* 1932.
b. Sep 14, 1880 in Newton Centre, Massachusetts
d. Jan 2, 1966
Source: *AmAu&B; BioIn 5, 7, 9; NatCAB 53; OhA&B; WhAm 4; WhLit; WhNAA*

Wilkins, George Hubert, Sir
American. Explorer
One of first to use submarines for polar studies; commanded *Nautilus,* 1931, on trip under Arctic Ocean.
b. Oct 31, 1888 in Mount Bryan, Australia
d. Dec 1, 1958 in Framingham, Massachusetts
Source: *InSci; LinLib L, S; McGEWB; OxCShps; REn; WhWE; WorAl; WorAlBi*

Wilkins, Mac
American. Track Athlete
Won gold medal, 1976 Olympics for discus throwing.
b. Nov 15, 1950 in Eugene, Oregon
Source: *BiDAmSp OS; BioIn 11; WhoSpor*

Wilkins, Maurice Hugh Frederick
New Zealander. Scientist
Won Nobel Prize in medicine, 1962, for research on DNA.
b. Dec 15, 1916 in Pongaroa, New Zealand
Source: *AmMWSc 95; AsBiEn; BiESc; BioIn 5, 6, 14, 15, 16, 20; BlueB 76; CurBio 63; IntWW 74, 75, 76, 77, 78, 79, 80, 81, 82, 83, 89, 91, 93; LarDcSc; McGMS 80; NobelP; NotTwCS; RAdv 14; Who 74, 82, 83, 85, 88, 90, 92, 94; WhoMedH; WhoNob, 90, 95; WhoScEn 94, 96; WhoWor 74, 76, 78, 80, 82, 84, 87, 89, 91, 93, 95, 96, 97; WorAl; WorAlBi; WorScD*

Wilkins, Roger (Wood)
American. Author, Educator
Chronicled life as an American black male in book *A Man's Life,* 1982.
b. Mar 25, 1932 in Kansas City, Missouri
Source: *BioIn 12, 13, 16; BlkWr 1; ConAu 109, 117; ConBlB 2; CurBio 94; SchCGBL; SelBAAf; WhoAfA 96; WhoAm 74, 76, 86, 88, 90; WhoBlA 90, 92, 94*

Wilkins, Roy
American. Social Reformer, Civil Rights Leader
Moderate exec. secretary of NAACP, 1955-77.
b. Aug 30, 1901 in Saint Louis, Missouri
d. Sep 8, 1981 in New York, New York
Source: *AfrAmAl 6; AmRef; AmSocL; AnObit 1981; BiDAmNC; BioIn 2, 5, 6, 7, 8, 9, 10, 11, 12, 13, 14, 15, 16, 19, 20; BlkWr 1; BlueB 76; CelR; CivR 74; CivRSt; ConAu 104; ConBlB 4; ConHero 1; CurBio 64, 81N; DcTwHis; Ebony 1; EncAACR; EncAB-H 1974, 1996; EncSoH; FacFETw; HisWorL; InB&W 80, 85; IntWW 74, 75, 76, 77, 78, 79, 80, 81; McGEWB; NegAl 76, 89; NewYTBS 81; PeoHis; PolProf E, J, K, NF; SchCGBL; SelBAAf; WebAB 74, 79; WhAm 8; WhoAm 74, 76, 78, 80; WhoAmP 73, 75, 77, 79; WhoBlA 75, 77, 80; WhoWor 74, 76; WorAl; WorAlBi*

Wilkinson, Bud
[Charles Burnham Wilkinson]
American. Football Coach
Head coach, U of Oklahoma, 1947-63, with 145-29-4 record; won nat. championship three times.
b. Apr 23, 1916 in Minneapolis, Minnesota
Source: *BiDAmSp FB; BioIn 3, 4, 5, 6, 7, 8, 10, 11, 14, 19, 20; ConAu 105; CurBio 62, 94N; WhoAmP 73, 75, 77, 79; WhoFtbl 74; WhoGov 72; WhoSSW 73; WhoTelC*

Wilkinson, Charles (Burnham)
American. Football Coach
Head coach, Univ. of Oklahoma, 1947-63; team won 47 consecutive games, 1953-57, an NCAA record.
b. Apr 23, 1916
d. Feb 9, 1994 in Saint Louis, Missouri
Source: *BioIn 2, 3, 4, 5, 6, 7, 8, 10, 11, 19, 20; CurBio 94N; WhoAmP 73, 75, 77, 79; WhoGov 72; WhoSSW 73*

Wilkinson, Geoffrey
English. Educator
Won Nobel Prize in chemistry, 1973.
b. Jul 14, 1921 in Todmorden, England
Source: *AmMWSc 89, 92, 95; BiESc; BioIn 4, 7, 9, 10, 14, 15, 19, 20; BlueB 76; CamDcSc; IntWW 74, 75, 76, 77, 78, 79, 80, 81, 82, 83, 89, 91, 93; LarDcSc; McGMS 80; NobelP; NotTwCS; Who 74, 82, 83, 85, 88, 90, 92, 94; WhoAm 76, 78, 88, 90, 92, 94, 95; WhoNob, 90, 95; WhoScEn 94, 96; WhoWor 74, 76, 78, 80, 82, 84, 87, 89, 91, 93, 95, 96, 97; WorAl; WorAlBi*

Wilkinson, J(ohn) Burke
American. Author
Books include *By Sea and by Stealth,* 1956; *Night of the Short Knives,* 1964.
b. Aug 24, 1913 in New York, New York
Source: *AmAu&B; Au&Wr 71; BioIn 9; BlueB 76; ConAu 9R; IntAu&W 76, 77, 82; SmATA 4; WhoAm 74, 76, 78, 80, 82, 84, 86, 88, 90, 92, 94, 95, 96, 97; WhoAmA 91N; WhoWor 74, 76, 78, 80, 82; WrDr 76, 80*

Will, George F(rederick)
American. Journalist, TV Personality
Conservative political syndicated columnist; won Pulitzer, 1977; commentator, ABC News; syndicated columnist, *Washington Post,* 1974—; contributing editor, *Newsweek* magazine, 1976—.
b. May 4, 1941 in Champaign, Illinois
Source: *BiDAmNC; BioIn 10, 12, 13, 14, 15, 16; CelR 90; ConAu 32NR, 77; ConPopW; CurBio 81; EncTwCJ; FacFETw; IntAu&W 91, 93; WhoAm 86, 90, 92, 94, 95, 96, 97; WhoAmP 91; WhoE 91; WhoUSWr 88; WhoWrEP 89; WorAu 1985; WrDr 92*

Willard, Archibald MacNeal
American. Artist
Painted *The Spirit of '76.*
b. Aug 22, 1836 in Bedford, Ohio
d. Oct 11, 1918 in Cleveland, Ohio
Source: *BioIn 4, 5, 6, 11; NatCAB 24; NewYHSD; WhAm 4, HSA*

Willard, Daniel
American. Railroad Executive
Pres., chm., Baltimore and Ohio Railroad, from 1910.
b. Jan 28, 1861 in North Hartland, Vermont
d. Jul 6, 1942 in Baltimore, Maryland
Source: *BiDAmBL 83; BioIn 1; DcAmB S3; EncABHB 1; NatCAB 18, 30; WhAm 2; WorAl; WorAlBi*

Willard, Emma Hart
American. Educator
Pioneer in women's education; founded Troy (NY) Female Seminary, 1821, forerunner of Emma Willard School.
b. Feb 23, 1787 in Berlin, Connecticut
d. Apr 15, 1870 in Troy, New York
Source: *Alli; AmAu; AmAu&B; AmBi; BiD&SB; CyAL 2; DcAmB; EncAB-H 1974, 1996; EncWHA; FemiWr; McGEWB; NatCAB 1; NotAW; OxCAmL 83; REn; REnAL; WebAB 79; WhAm HS; WomFir*

Willard, Frances Elizabeth Caroline
American. Social Reformer
President, Women's Christian Temperance Union, 1879-98; toured US, speaking on temperance, women's suffrage.
b. Sep 28, 1839 in Churchville, New York
d. Feb 18, 1898 in New York, New York
Source: *Alli SUP; AmAu; AmAu&B; AmBi; AmRef; AmSocL; AmWom; AmWomWr; ApCAB; BbD; BiDAmEd; BiD&SB; ChhPo, S1; DcAmAu; DcAmB; DcAmReB 1, 2; DcAmTB; DcNAA; Drake; EncAB-H 1974, 1996; EncARH; EncWHA; GayN; InWom, SUP; LibW; LuthC 75; McGEWB; NatCAB 1; NotAW; OhA&B; OxCAmL 65; REn; REnAL; TwCBDA; WebAB 74, 79; WhAm HS; WhAmP; WorAl*

Willard, Frank Henry
American. Cartoonist
Created "Moon Mullins," "Kitty Higgins" cartoons.
b. Sep 21, 1893 in Chicago, Illinois
d. Jan 12, 1958 in Los Angeles, California
Source: *ArtsAmW 2; BioIn 1, 3, 4, 5, 6; DcAmB S6; LegTOT; NatCAB 46; WhAm 3, 4; WhAmArt 85; WorECom*

Willard, Jess
"Pottawatomie Giant"
American. Boxer, Actor
World heavyweight champ, 1915-16, lost to Jack Dempsey; starred in film *The Heart Punch,* 1919.
b. Dec 29, 1881 in Pottawatomie County, Kansas
d. Dec 15, 1968 in Los Angeles, California
Source: *BiDAmSp BK; BioIn 10, 11; Film 1; WhoBox 74; WhScrn 77, 83*

Wille, Frank
American. Government Official, Banker
Chm., Federal Deposit Insurance Corp., 1970-76.
b. Feb 27, 1931 in New York, New York
Source: *BioIn 9, 16; NewYTBS 88; St&PR 84, 87; WhAm 9; WhoAm 74, 76, 78, 80, 82, 84, 86, 88; WhoAmP 75, 77; WhoE 83, 85, 86; WhoGov 72, 75; WhoSSW 73, 75, 76*

Wille, Lois Jean
American. Journalist
Associate editor, *Chicago Sun-Times,* 1978-83; associate editorial page editor, *Chicago Tribune,* 1984-87; editor, 1987-91.
b. Sep 19, 1932 in Arlington Heights, Illinois
Source: *InWom SUP; WhoAm 82, 84, 86, 88, 90, 92, 94; WhoAmW 91, 93; WhoMW 84, 86, 90, 92*

Willeford, Charles Ray, II
[Will Charles]
American. Author
Noted for series of works on Miami detective, Hoke Moseley: *Miami Blues,* 1984.
b. Jan 2, 1919 in Little Rock, Arkansas
d. Mar 27, 1988 in Miami, Florida
Source: *BioIn 9; ConAu 15NR; WrDr 86*

William
[William the Lion]
Scottish. Ruler
Founded Arbroath Abbey, 1178, during reign, 1165-1214.
b. 1143
d. 1214
Source: *BioIn 6, 9; DcCathB; NewCol 75; WebBD 83*

William, Warren
[Warren Krech]
American. Actor
Played sleuths in 1930s thrillers.
b. Dec 2, 1895 in Aitkin, Minnesota
d. Sep 24, 1948 in Encino, California
Source: *BioIn 21; Film 2; FilmEn; FilmgC; ForYSC; GangFlm; HalFC 80, 84, 88; MotPP; MovMk; NotNAT B; WhScrn 74, 77, 83; WhThe*

William II
English. Ruler
King of England, 1087-1100, succeeding father William the Conqueror; died in hunting accident possibly arranged by brother, Henry I, who succeeded him to throne.
b. 1056?
d. Aug 2, 1100

William III
Dutch. Ruler
Stadtholder, 1672-1702; ruled England, 1689-1702; signed many treaties, passed Act of Settlement, 1701.
b. Nov 4, 1650 in The Hague, Netherlands
d. Mar 8, 1702 in London, England
Source: *NewCol 75; WebBD 83; WhAm HS; WhDW*

William of Ockham
"Doctor Invincibilis"; "Venerabilis Inceptor"
English. Philosopher
Joined the Franciscans, later became general of the order, 1342; wrote *Dialogus,* 1343.
b. 1290? in Surrey, England
d. 1349? in Munich, Bavaria
Source: *Alli; BiD&SB; BritAu; CasWL; DcEnL; EvLB; NewC; NewCol 75; OxCEng 67; REn; WebBD 83*

William of Wales
[William Arthur Philip Louis]
"Wills"
English. Prince
First son of Prince Charles and Princess Diana; second in line to British throne.
b. Jun 21, 1982 in London, England
Source: *BioIn 13, 16*

William of Waynflete
[William Patyn]
English. Religious Leader
Bishop of Winchester, 1447-86; founded Magdalen College, Oxford, 1448.
b. 1395
d. Aug 11, 1486
Source: *Alli; NewCol 75; WebBD 83*

Williams, Andy
[Howard Andrew Williams]
American. Singer
Award-winning crooner known for easygoing style; hits include "Where Do I Begin?", 1971; "Lonely Street," 1959.
b. Dec 3, 1930 in Wall Lake, Iowa
Source: *Baker 84, 92; BioIn 5, 6, 7, 8, 9, 10, 11, 12, 15; BioNews 74; BkPepl; BlueB 76; ConMus 2; CurBio 60; NewGrDA 86; OxCPMus; PenEncP; WhoAm 74, 76, 78, 80, 82, 84, 86, 88, 92, 94, 95, 96, 97; WhoEnt 92; WhoHol 92, A; WorAl; WorAlBi*

Williams, Anson
[Anson William Heimlick]
American. Actor, Singer
Played Potsie on TV series "Happy Days," 1974-83.
b. Sep 25, 1949 in Los Angeles, California
Source: *BioIn 11; ConTFT 9; LegTOT; VarWW 85; WhoHol 92*

Williams, Barry
American. Actor
Played Greg on TV series "The Brady Bunch," 1969-74.
b. Sep 30, 1954 in Santa Monica, California
Source: *ConTFT 8; WhoAm 74, 76, 78, 80; WhoHol 92, A*

Williams, Ben Ames
American. Journalist, Author
Writings include *Crucible,* 1937; *The Unconquered,* 1953.
b. Mar 7, 1889 in Macon, Mississippi
d. Feb 4, 1953 in Brookline, Massachusetts
Source: *AmAu&B; AmNov; BenetAL 91; BioIn 1, 2, 3, 4, 17; CnDAL; DcAmB S5; DcLB 102; LiveMA; OhA&B; OxCAmL 65, 83, 95; SouWr; TwCA, SUP; WhAm 3; WhE&EA; WhLit; WhNAA*

Williams, Bert
[Egbert Austin Williams]
American. Actor, Comedian
Best known as star comedian of Ziegfeld Follies, 1909-19, where his most famous song was "Nobody."
b. Nov 12, 1874 in New Providence Island, Bahamas
d. Mar 4, 1922 in New York, New York
Source: *AmAu&B; AmDec 1900; BiDAfM; BioIn 18, 20; BlkAWP; CamGWoT; CmCal; CmpEPM; DcAmB; DrBlPA, 90; EncMT; EncVaud; Ent; FamA&A; Film 1; JoeFr; NewAmDM; NewGrDA 86; OxCPMus; OxCThe 67; REnAL; WebAB 74; WhAm 4; WhoHol B; WhScrn 74, 77*

Williams, Betty Smith
Irish. Social Reformer
With Mairead Corrigan, won Nobel Peace Prize for forming N Ireland Peace Movement, 1976.
b. May 22, 1943 in Andersontown, Northern Ireland
Source: *BioIn 14, 15, 16; ConHero 1; ContDcW 89; CurBio 79; FacFETw; InB&W 80; IntWW 91; InWom SUP; LadLa 86; NobelP; Who 88, 92; WhoBlA 80, 92; WhoWor 91*

Williams, Billy
English. Filmmaker
Won Oscar for cinematography of *Gandhi,* 1982.
b. Jun 3, 1929 in Walthamstow, England
Source: *BioIn 15; ConTFT 12; HalFC 80, 84, 88; VarWW 85*

Williams, Billy Dee
American. Actor
Best known for playing Gale Sayers in TV movie "Brian's Song," 1971, Louis McKay in film *Lady Sings the Blues,* 1972.
b. Apr 6, 1937 in New York, New York
Source: *AfrAmAl 6; AfrAmBi 1; BiE&WWA; BioIn 13, 14, 16; BlksAmF; CelR 90; ConBlB 8; ConTFT 2, 8; CurBio 84; DcTwCCu 5; DrBlPA, 90; FilmEn; HalFC 80, 84, 88; IntMPA 75, 76, 77, 78, 79, 80, 81, 82, 84, 86, 88, 92, 94, 96; LegTOT; NegAl 89; NewYTBS 76; WhoAfA 96; WhoAm 78, 80, 82, 84, 86, 88, 90, 92, 94, 95, 96, 97; WhoBlA 77, 85, 88, 90, 92, 94; WhoEnt 92; WhoHol 92, A; WhoThe 77, 81; WorAlBi*

Williams, Billy Leo
American. Baseball Player
Outfielder, Chicago Cubs, 1959-76; set record for most consecutive games played in NL, 1963-70; Hall of Fame, 1987.
b. Jun 15, 1938 in Whistler, Alabama
Source: *BaseReg 87; BiDAmSp BB; BioIn 8, 9, 10, 11; InB&W 80; WhoAfA 96; WhoAm 74, 88, 90, 92, 94, 95, 96, 97; WhoBlA 80, 85, 88, 90, 92, 94; WhoProB 73*

Williams, Carroll Milton
American. Biologist
Harvard biologist; worked out fundamental principles of insect development.
b. Dec 2, 1916 in Richmond, Virginia
d. Oct 11, 1991 in Watertown, Massachusetts
Source: *AmMWSc 76P, 79, 82, 86, 89, 92; BioIn 2; BlueB 76; ConAu 65; IntWW 74, 75, 76, 77, 78, 79, 80, 81, 82, 83, 89, 91; McGMS 80; NewYTBS 91; WhAm 10; WhoAm 74, 76, 78, 80, 82, 84, 86, 88, 90; WhoFrS 84*

Williams, Charles
[K C and the Sunshine Band]
American. Musician
Trombone player with Sunshine Band since 1973.
b. Nov 18, 1954 in Rockingham, North Carolina

Williams, Charles Linwood
"Buck"
American. Basketball Player
Forward, NJ, 1981-89; Portland, 1989—.
b. Mar 8, 1960 in Rocky Mount, North Carolina
Source: *OfNBA 87; WhoAm 84, 86, 88, 90, 92, 96, 97; WhoWest 96*

Williams, Cindy
American. Actor
Starred in TV series "Laverne and Shirley," 1976-82.
b. Aug 22, 1948 in Van Nuys, California
Source: *BioIn 13, 16; BkPepl; ConTFT 3; HalFC 80, 84, 88; IntMPA 77, 86, 92; InWom SUP; MovMk; WhoAm 82; WhoEmL 91; WhoEnt 92; WhoHol A; WorAl; WorAlBi*

Williams, Clarence, III
American. Actor
Starred in TV series "The Mod Squad," 1968-73.
b. Aug 21, 1939 in New York, New York
Source: *ConTFT 7, 15; DrBlPA, 90; InB&W 80; IntMPA 96; NotNAT; WhoHol 92, A; WhoThe 72, 77, 81*

Williams, Cliff
English. Musician
Bass guitarist with rock band AC-DC, replacing Mark Evans, 1977.
b. Dec 14, 1949 in Rumford, England

Williams, Cootie
[Charles Melvin Williams]
American. Jazz Musician
Last surviving member of Duke Ellington Orchestra of 1920s; known for growling, muted trumpet.
b. Jul 24, 1908? in Mobile, Alabama
d. Sep 15, 1985 in Long Island, New York
Source: *ASCAP 66, 80; BiDAfM; BiDAmM; BiDJaz; BioIn 6, 14, 15, 16, 20; CmpEPM; DrBlPA, 90; EncJzS; InB&W 80, 85; LegTOT; NewGrDM 80; OxCPMus; PenEncP; WhoJazz 72; WorAl*

Williams, Curtis
[Kool and the Gang]
American. Musician
Keyboardist with Kool and the Gang since 1980.
b. Dec 11, 1962 in Buffalo, New York

Williams, Daniel Hale
American. Surgeon, Educator
Performed first successful surgical closure of heart wound; successful in stopping hemorrhage from spleen.
b. Jan 18, 1858 in Hollidaysburg, Pennsylvania
d. Aug 4, 1931 in Idlewild, Michigan
Source: *BioIn 2, 3, 5, 6, 7, 8, 9, 10, 11, 12, 13; DcAmB; DcAmMeB 84; InSci; NegAl 83; NotTwCS; WebAB 74, 79; WhAm 1; WhoColR; WorInv*

Williams, Darnell
American. Actor
Won Emmy for role as Jesse Hubbard on soap opera "All My Children," 1983.
b. Mar 3, in London, England
Source: *BioIn 13; DrBlPA 90; InB&W 85; VarWW 85; WhoMW 86*

Williams, Deniece
[June Deniece Williams]
American. Singer
Number one hits "Too Much, Too Little, Too Late," with Johnny Mathis, 1978; "Let's Hear It for the Boy," 1984.
b. Jun 3, 1951 in Gary, Indiana
Source: *BioIn 14, 15, 16; ConMus 1; DrBlPA 90; EncRk 88; EncRkSt; InB&W 80, 85; LegTOT; RkOn 85; SoulM; WhoAfA 96; WhoAmW 91; WhoBlA 94*

Williams, Dick
[Richard Hirshfield Williams]
American. Baseball Player, Baseball Manager
Infielder-outfielder, 1951-64; has managed six different teams, won four pennants, two World Series.
b. May 7, 1928 in Saint Louis, Missouri
Source: *Ballpl 90; BaseEn 88; BaseReg 88; BiDAmSp BB; BioIn 13, 14, 15, 17, 18, 19; CurBio 73; WhoAm 84, 88; WhoE 81; WhoProB 73; WhoSSW 84; WhoWest 84, 92*

Williams, Don
American. Musician, Singer
Guitarist; laid-back style in hits *Cafe Carolina,* 1984.
b. May 27, 1939 in Floydada, Texas
Source: *ASCAP 80; BgBkCoM; BioIn 14, 15; ConMus 4; EncFCWM 83; HarEnCM 87; HarEnR 86; IlEncCM; LegTOT; PenEncP; RkOn 85*

Williams, Doug(las Lee)
American. Football Player
Quarterback, Tampa Bay, 1978-82, USFL, 1984-85, Washington, 1986-89; first black quarterback in Super Bowl, 1988; MVP Super Bowl, 1988.
b. Aug 9, 1955 in Zachary, Louisiana
Source: *AfrAmBi 1; BioIn 11, 12, 13, 14, 15; FootReg 87; InB&W 80; News 88, 88-2; NewYTBS 88; WhoBlA 80, 85, 88, 90, 92; WorAlBi*

Williams, Edward Bennett
American. Lawyer, Baseball Executive
Trial lawyer with many well-known clients; owner, president, Baltimore Orioles.
b. May 31, 1920 in Hartford, Connecticut
d. Aug 13, 1988 in Washington, District of Columbia
Source: *BioIn 4, 5, 6, 7, 10, 11, 13; CelR; ConAu 1R, 126; CopCroC; CurBio 65, 88, 88N; EncMcCE; FacFETw; News 88; NewYTBS 83, 88; WebAB 74, 79; WhAm 9; WhoAm 74, 76, 78, 80, 82, 84, 86, 88; WhoAmL 78, 79, 87; WhoAmP 75, 77, 79; WhoE 79, 81, 83, 85, 86; WhoFI 74; WhoSSW 73, 75, 76; WorAl; WorAlBi*

Williams, Edward Porter
American. Manufacturer
Cofounded Sherwin-Williams paint co., first to offer money-back guarantee.
b. May 10, 1843 in Cleveland, Ohio
d. May 4, 1903 in Glenville, Ohio
Source: *Entr; NatCAB 21*

Williams, Elizabeth Betty Smyth
[Mrs. J T Perkins]
Irish. Civil Rights Leader
Shared 1976 Nobel Peace Prize with Mairead Corrigan; co-founded Peace People to end fighting in N Ireland.
b. May 22, 1943 in Belfast, Northern Ireland
Source: *CurBio 79; IntWW 81, 91; Who 85, 92; WhoAm 88; WhoAmW 91; WhoNob, 90*

Williams, Emlyn
[George Emlyn Williams]
Welsh. Dramatist, Actor
Wrote, starred in *The Corn Is Green,* 1930s; best known for one-man show on Charles Dickens.
b. Nov 26, 1905 in Mostyn, Wales
d. Sep 25, 1987 in London, England
Source: *AnObit 1987; Au&Wr 71; Benet 87; BiE&WWA; BioIn 1, 2, 3, 4, 5, 6, 8, 10, 12, 13, 15, 17; BlueB 76; CamGWoT; CasWL; CnMD; CnThe; ConAu 36NR, 93, 104, 123; ConDr 73, 77, 82; ConLC 15; ConTFT 5; CroCD; CrtSuDr; CurBio 41, 52, 87, 87N; DcLB 10, 77; DcLEL; EncMys; EncWT; Ent; EvLB; FamA&A; FilmAG WE; FilmEn; FilmgC; ForYSC; GrWrEL DR; HalFC 80, 84, 88; IlWWBF, A; IntAu&W 76, 77; IntMPA 75, 76, 77, 78, 79, 80, 81, 82, 84, 86; IntWW 74, 75, 76, 77, 78, 79, 80, 81, 82, 83; LegTOT; LngCTC; MajTwCW; McGEWD 72, 84; ModBrL; ModWD; MotPP; MovMk; NewC; NewCBEL; NewYTBS 81, 87; NotNAT, A; OxCAmT 84; OxCLiW 86; OxCThe*

67, 83; PenC ENG; PlP&P; REn; TwCA, SUP; TwCWr; WhAm 9; WhE&EA; Who 74, 82, 83, 85; WhoAm 74, 76, 78, 80, 82, 84, 86; WhoHol A; WhoThe 72, 77, 81; WhoWor 74, 76, 78; WorAl; WorAlBi; WorEFlm; WrDr 76, 80, 82, 84, 86

Williams, Eric Eustace
Trinidadian. Politician, Educator, Historian, Author
First prime minister of Trinidad and Tobago, 1962-80; widely recognized authority on Caribbean.
b. Sep 25, 1911 in Port of Spain, Trinidad and Tobago
d. Mar 29, 1981 in Port of Spain, Trinidad and Tobago
Source: *AnObit 1981; BioIn 4, 7, 8, 9, 10; ConAu 103; CurBio 66, 81; DcPol; InB&W 80; IntWW 74, 75, 76, 77, 78, 79, 80; WhoGov 72; WhoWor 74, 76, 78, 80*

Williams, Esther
[Mrs. Fernando Lamas]
American. Actor, Swimmer
Olympic swimmer who starred in MGM aquatic musicals *Neptune's Daughter,* 1949; *Dangerous When Wet,* 1953.
b. Aug 8, 1923 in Los Angeles, California
Source: *BiDFilm, 81, 94; BiE&WWA; BioIn 3, 4, 8, 11, 14; CmMov; CurBio 55; EncAFC; FilmEn; FilmgC; ForYSC; HalFC 80, 84, 88; IntDcF 1-3, 2-3; IntMPA 75, 76, 77, 78, 79, 80, 81, 82, 84, 86, 88, 92, 94, 96; InWom, SUP; LegTOT; McGEWD 84; MotPP; MovMk; OxCFilm; What 2; WhoAmW 58; WhoHol A; WorAl; WorAlBi; WorEFlm*

Williams, Evelyn
American. Lawyer
Defense attorney for members of the Black Liberation Army, 1973-79; wrote autobiography, *Inadmissible Evidence,* 1993.
b. c. 1922 in North Carolina
Source: *ConBlB 10*

Williams, G(erhard) Mennen
"Soapy"
American. Politician, Diplomat, Judge
Six-term Dem. governor of MI, 1949-60; ambassador to Africa, 1961-66.
b. Feb 23, 1911 in Detroit, Michigan
d. Feb 2, 1988 in Detroit, Michigan
Source: *AmBench 79; BiDrGov 1789; BioIn 1, 2, 3, 4, 5, 6, 7, 8, 11, 15, 16; BlueB 76; ConAu 124; CurBio 63, 88, 88N; IntWW 74, 75, 76, 77, 78, 79, 80, 81, 82, 83; News 88-2; NewYTBS 86, 88; PolProf E, K, T; St&PR 87; WhAm 9; WhoAm 74, 76, 78, 80, 82, 84, 86; WhoAmL 83, 85; WhoAmP 73, 75, 77, 79, 81, 83, 85, 87; WhoGov 72, 75, 77; WhoMW 74, 76, 78, 80, 82, 84, 86, 88*

Williams, Garth Montgomery
American. Illustrator
Illustrator of children's books: "Little House" series, *Stuart Little,* 1945, *Charlotte's Web,* 1952.
b. Apr 16, 1912 in New York, New York
d. May 8, 1996 in Guanajuato, Mexico
Source: *AmAu&B; AuBYP 2, 3; BenetAL 91; BioIn 14, 16; ConAu 134; FacFETw; IlsCB 1744, 1946, 1957; MorJA; REnAL; SmATA 18, 66; Str&VC; WhAmArt 85; WhoAm 86, 90*

Williams, Gluyas
American. Cartoonist
Satirized middle-class America in *The New Yorker,* 1928-53.
b. Jul 23, 1888 in San Francisco, California
d. Feb 13, 1982 in Boston, Massachusetts
Source: *AmAu&B; AuNews 2; BioIn 1, 2, 3, 5, 11, 13, 14; ChhPo, S1; ConAu 108; CurBio 46, 82, 82N; REnAL; WhAm 9; WhAmArt 85; WhoAmA 73, 76; WorECar*

Williams, Gregory (Howard)
American. Educator, University Administrator
Dean and professor, Ohio State University College of Law, 1993—.
b. Nov 12, 1943 in Muncie, Indiana
Source: *ConBlB 11; WhoAfA 96; WhoAm 86, 88, 90, 92, 94, 95, 96, 97; WhoAmL 96; WhoBlA 80, 85, 88, 90, 92, 94*

Williams, Gus
American. Actor
Comedian at Tony Pastor's theatre, 1868-79, starred in *Our German Senator.*
b. Jul 19, 1847 in New York, New York
d. Jan 16, 1915 in Yonkers, New York
Source: *NewGrDA 86; NotNAT B; WhoStg 1906*

Williams, Gus
American. Basketball Player
Guard, 1975-87, mostly with Seattle; set NBA record for steals in career; named comeback player of yr., 1982.
b. Oct 10, 1953 in Mount Vernon, New York
Source: *BasBi; BioIn 12; LegTOT; OfNBA 87; WhoAfA 96; WhoAm 84; WhoBlA 85, 88, 90, 92, 94*

Williams, Hank
[Hiram King Williams]
"The Drifting Cowboy"; "The Hillbilly Shakespeare"
American. Singer, Songwriter
Instrumental in popularizing country-western music; hits include "Your Cheatin' Heart" and "Jambalaya."
b. Sep 15, 1923 in Georgiana, Alabama
d. Jan 1, 1953 in Oak Hill, West Virginia
Source: *AmSong; Baker 84, 92; BgBkCoM; BiDAmM; BioIn 3, 4, 6, 8, 9, 10, 12, 13, 14, 15, 17, 19, 20, 21; CmpEPM; ConMus 4; CounME 74, 74A; DcAmB S3, S5; EncFCWM 69, 83; EncRk 88; EncRkSt; FacFETw; HarEnCM 87; HarEnR 86; IlEncCM; IlEncRk; LegTOT; NewAmDM; NewGrDA 86; NewGrDM 80; OxCPMus; PenEncP; PopAmC SUP; RolSEnR 83; WhoRock 81; WhScrn 77; WorAl; WorAlBi*

Williams, Hank, Jr.
American. Singer
Country-western star since 1960s; hits include "Texas Women," 1981; Country Music Entertainer of the Year, 1987, 1988.
b. May 26, 1949 in Shreveport, Louisiana
Source: *BgBkCoM; BioIn 11, 12, 14, 16; ConAu 117; ConMus 1; CounME 74, 74A; EncFCWM 69, 83; HarEnCM 87; IlEncCM; LegTOT; NewAmDM; NewGrDA 86; OxCPMus; PenEncP; RolSEnR 83; WhoAm 82, 84, 86, 88, 90, 92, 94, 95, 96, 97; WhoEnt 92; WhoHol 92, A; WhoNeCM; WhoRock 81; WorAlBi*

Williams, Harrison Arlington, Jr.
American. Lawyer, Politician
Dem. senator from NJ, 1959-82; convicted in Abscam bribery scandal, 1981.
b. Dec 10, 1919 in Plainfield, New Jersey
Source: *AlmAP 80; BiDrAC; BiDrUSC 89; BioIn 3, 5, 6, 7, 9, 10, 11, 12, 13, 14; BlueB 76; CngDr 74, 77, 79, 81; CurBio 60; IntWW 74, 75, 76, 77, 78, 79, 80, 81, 82, 83, 89, 91, 93; IntYB 78, 79, 80, 81, 82; NewYTBE 73; NewYTBS 80, 82, 86; PolProf E, NF; WhoAm 74, 76, 78, 80, 82; WhoAmP 73, 75, 77, 79, 81, 83; WhoE 74, 75, 77, 79, 81; WhoGov 72, 75, 77; WhoWor 80, 82*

Williams, Hosea Lorenzo
American. Civil Rights Leader, Clergy, Author
Nat. program director, SCLC, 1971.
b. Jan 5, 1926 in Attapulgis, Georgia
Source: *AfrAmBi 2; BioIn 11; BlueB 76; ConAu 49; EncAACR; InB&W 85; WhoAmP 75, 77, 79, 81, 83, 85, 87, 89, 91, 93, 95; WhoBlA 92; WhoSSW 73, 84*

Williams, J(ames) R(obert)
American. Cartoonist
Created comic strip "Out Our Way, With the Willits."
b. Aug 18, 1888 in Halifax, Nova Scotia, Canada
d. Jun 18, 1957 in Pasadena, California
Source: *ArtsAmW 1; BioIn 1, 2, 3, 4, 7, 8, 11; IlBEAAW; NatCAB 47; WhAm 3; WhAmArt 85; WorECom*

Williams, Jay
[Michael Delving]
American. Children's Author
Wrote *Danny Dunn* series of books for children.
b. May 31, 1914 in Buffalo, New York

d. Jul 12, 1978 in London, England
Source: *AuBYP 2S, 3; BioIn 4, 7, 9, 10, 11, 13, 14, 15, 19; ChlLR 8; ConAu 1R, 2NR, 39NR, 81; CurBio 55, 78N; FourBJA; IntAu&W 76, 77; MajAI; NatCAB 61; ObitOF 79; ScF&FL 1, 2, 92; SmATA 3, 24N, 41; TwCChW 78, 83, 89, 95; TwCCr&M 80, 85; WhScrn 83; WorAu 1950; WrDr 76*

Williams, Jimy
[James Francis Williams]
American. Baseball Manager
Toronto, coach, 1980-85, manager, 1986-89; Boston Red Sox, manager, 1997—.
b. Oct 14, 1943 in Santa Maria, California
Source: *Ballpl 90; BaseReg 86, 87; BioIn 16; WhoAm 86, 88; WhoE 89; WhoMW 88; WhoWor 89*

Williams, JoBeth
[Margaret JoBeth Williams]
American. Actor
Films include *The Big Chill,* 1983; *Murder Ordained,* 1987.
b. 1953 in Houston, Texas
Source: *BioIn 13, 14, 15; ConTFT 6; HalFC 84, 88; IntMPA 92; LegTOT; WhoAm 95, 96, 97; WhoAmW 95*

Williams, Joe
[Joseph Goreed]
American. Singer
Blues, jazz, ballads singer, known for hits with Count Basie, including "Everyday I Have the Blues," 1955.
b. Dec 12, 1918 in Cordele, Georgia
Source: *AllMusG; BiDAfM; BiDAmM; BiDJaz; BioIn 4, 11, 12, 14, 15, 16; BluesWW; CmpEPM; ConBlB 5; ConMus 11; CurBio 85; DcTwCCu 5; DrBlPA, 90; EncJzS; GuBlues; LegTOT; NewAmDM; NewGrDJ 88, 94; NewYTBS 89; PenEncP; WhoAfA 96; WhoAm 82, 84, 86, 88, 90, 92, 94, 95, 96, 97; WhoBlA 85, 88, 90, 92, 94; WhoHol 92; WorAlBi*

Williams, John
Australian. Musician
Classical guitarist; solo album *Echoes of London,* 1986.
b. Apr 24, 1941 in Melbourne, Australia
Source: *Baker 84; BiDJaz; BioIn 11, 12, 13, 14; BlueB 76; BriBkM 80; ConMus 9; CurBio 83; IntWW 74, 75, 76, 77, 78, 79, 80, 81, 82, 83, 89, 91, 93; IntWWM 77, 90; MusSN; NewGrDJ 88; NewYTBS 86; OnThGG; PenDiMP; PenEncP; Who 74, 82, 83, 85, 88, 90, 92, 94; WhoAm 80, 82; WhoMus 72; WhoWor 84, 87, 89, 91, 93, 95*

Williams, John A(lfred)
American. Writer
Wrote *One for New York,* 1960; *The Man Who Cried I Am,* 1967.
b. Dec 5, 1925 in Jackson, Mississippi
Source: *AmAu&B; Au&Wr 71; Benet 96; BioIn 8, 9, 10, 11, 12, 14, 15, 17, 20; BlkAmP; BlkAWP; BlkWr 2; ConAu 51NR, 53; ConLC 5; ConNov 72, 76, 96; CurBio 94; DcLB 2; DrAF 76; DrAPF 80; EncSF 93; InB&W 80, 85; IntAu&W 93; LiveMA; LivgBAA; OxCAmL 95; PenC AM; RAdv 1; RfGAmL 94; SelBAAf; SelBAAu; SouWr; TwCSFW 81; WhoAfA 96; WhoAm 97; WhoBlA 80, 85, 88, 90, 92, 94; WorAu 1950; WrDr 76, 94, 96*

Williams, John James
"Conscience of the Senate"
American. Politician
Rep. senator from DE, 1947-71; led investigation to expose fraud in IRS, early 1950s.
b. May 17, 1904 in Frankford, Delaware
d. Jan 11, 1988 in Lewes, Delaware
Source: *BiDrAC; BiDrUSC 89; BioIn 2, 3, 4, 6, 7, 8, 11, 12; BlueB 76; CurBio 88; PolProf E, J, K, NF, T; WhoAmP 73, 75, 77, 79, 81, 83, 85, 87*

Williams, John Towner
American. Composer, Conductor
Conductor, Boston Pops, 1980—; won Oscars for scores of *Jaws,* 1975; *Star Wars,* 1977.
b. Feb 8, 1932 in Flushing, New York
Source: *Baker 92; BioIn 12; CelR 90; ConTFT 3; FacFETw; HalFC 88; IntMPA 92; OxCPMus; PenDiMP; PenEncP; VarWW 85; Who 82, 83, 85, 88, 90, 92, 94; WhoAm 86, 88, 92, 94, 95, 96, 97; WhoAmM 83; WhoE 89, 91, 97; WhoEnt 92; WhoWor 87, 89, 91, 93, 95; WorAlBi*

Williams, Kit
English. Author, Artist
Wrote *Masquerade,* 1979, which sparked one of most exciting treasure hunts ever held on British soil.
b. 1947 in Romney Marshes, England
Source: *BioIn 13, 15; ConAu 107; NewYTBS 80, 81; SmATA 44; TwCPaSc; WrDr 84*

Williams, Lucinda
American. Singer, Songwriter
Sings short-story like songs marked with a country and blues music influence; recorded debut album, *Rambling on My Mind,* 1979; later released *Lucinda Williams,* 1988 and *Passionate Kisses,* 1992.
b. 1953 in Lake Charles, Louisiana
Source: *BgBkCoM; ConMus 10; WhoAm 95, 96, 97*

Williams, Lynn Russell
Canadian. Labor Union Official
President of United Steelworkers of America, 1983—.
b. Jul 21, 1924 in Springfield, Ontario, Canada
Source: *ConNews 86-4; IntWW 89, 91, 93; NewYTBS 84; WhoAm 86, 88, 92, 94, 95, 96, 97; WhoFI 94, 96*

Williams, Maggie
[Margaret Ann Williams]
American. Government Official
Assistant to the President and Chief of Staff to the First Lady, Clinton Administration, 1993—.
b. Dec 25, 1954 in Kansas City, Missouri
Source: *BioIn 19, 20, 21; ConBlB 7; NewYTBS 93; WhoAfA 96; WhoAmP 95*

Williams, Mary Lou
"Queen of Jazz"
American. Composer, Musician
Contributed to growth of bebop style, 1940s; wrote for Benny Goodman, Duke Ellington.
b. May 8, 1910 in Pittsburgh, Pennsylvania
d. May 28, 1981 in Durham, North Carolina
Source: *AfrAmAl 6; AllMusG; AnObit 1981; ASCAP 66, 80; Baker 84, 92; BiDAfM; BiDAmM; BiDJaz; BioIn 2, 4, 6, 7, 9, 10, 11, 12, 13, 14, 16, 17, 18, 19, 20; BlkWAB; BlkWAm; CmpEPM; ConAmC 76, 82; ContDcW 89; CurBio 81N; DcTwCCu 5; DrBlPA, 90; EncJzS; FacFETw; GrLiveH; IlEncJ; InB&W 85; IntDcWB; InWom, SUP; NegAl 89; NewGrDA 86; NewGrDJ 88, 94; NewGrDM 80; NewYTBS 81; NotBlAW 1; OxCPMus; PenEncP; WhoBlA 80; WhoJazz 72; WomFir*

Williams, Mason
American. Composer, Musician, Author
Won Grammy, 1969, for "Classical Gas."
b. Aug 24, 1938 in Abilene, Texas
Source: *BiDAmM; BioIn 8; ConAu 25R; RkOn 74, 78; WhoAm 74, 76, 78, 80, 82; WhoRock 81*

Williams, Matt
American. Writer
Created television show *Roseanne,* co-created *Home Improvement.*
Source: *BioIn 18, 20, 21; LesBEnT 92*

Williams, Milan
[The Commodores]
American. Musician, Singer
Drummer since group's founding, 1971; wrote hit instrumental "Machine Gun," 1974.
b. 1947 in Mississippi
Source: *BkPepl*

Williams, Montel B
American. TV Personality
Known as talk show host on TV's "Montel Williams Show," 1991—.
b. Jul 3, 1956 in Baltimore, Maryland

Williams, Patricia J(oyce)
American. Educator, Lawyer
Professor of law, Columbia University, 1992—; wrote *The Alchemy of Race and Rights: Diary of a Law Professor,* 1991.

b. Aug 28, 1951 in Boston, Massachusetts
Source: *ConAu 154*

Williams, Patrick
American. Composer
Won Emmys for theme songs for TV shows ''Lou Grant,'' 1980; ''The Princess and the Cabbie,'' 1982.
b. Apr 23, 1939 in Bonne Terre, Missouri
Source: *ConTFT 12; IntWWM 85; VarWW 85; WhoAm 86, 90; WhoE 85; WhoEnt 92*

Williams, Paul Hamiltón
American. Singer, Songwriter
Won 1976 Oscar for best song: ''Evergreen.''
b. Sep 19, 1940 in Omaha, Nebraska
Source: *BioIn 16; BkPepl; ConMus 5; ConTFT 4; CurBio 83; EncFCWM 83; HalFC 84, 88; IntMPA 92; RkOn 74; Who 88; WhoAm 74, 76, 78, 80, 82, 84, 86, 88, 90, 92, 94, 95, 96, 97; WhoEnt 92; WhoHol A; WorAlBi*

Williams, Paul R(evere)
American. Architect
One of America's first black architects; designed thousands of homes, commercial, public buildings.
b. Feb 18, 1894 in Los Angeles, California
d. Jan 23, 1980 in Los Angeles, California
Source: *AfrAmAl 6; AfroAA; AnObit 1980; BioIn 1, 8, 9, 12, 15; CurBio 41, 80N; Ebony 1; InB&W 80; IntWW 78; NewYTBS 80; WhoAm 76; WhoBlA 77*

Williams, Randy
American. Track Athlete
Long jumper; won gold medal, 1972 Olympics.
b. Aug 23, 1953 in Fresno, California
Source: *BlkOlyM; WhoTr&F 73*

Williams, Robert F(ranklin)
American. Civil Rights Activist
Advocated ''meeting (racist) violence with violence,'' 1959; founder and publisher *Crusader* magazine, 1959-66.
b. Feb 26, 1925 in Monroe, North Carolina
Source: *InB&W 80, 85; WhoAfA 96*

Williams, Robin
American. Comedian, Actor
Starred in TV's ''Mork and Mindy,'' 1978-82; won Grammy, 1979, for album, *Reality, What a Concept;* films include *Good Morning, Vietnam,* 1987 and *The Birdcage,* 1996.
b. Jul 21, 1951 in Chicago, Illinois
Source: *BioIn 13, 14, 15, 16; BkPepl; CelR 90; ConTFT 3, 10; CurBio 79; EncAFC; HalFC 84, 88; IntMPA 86, 92, 94, 96; IntWW 91, 93; LesBEnT 92; News 88; NewYTBS 78, 84, 89, 90; Who 92; WhoAm 86, 90, 92, 94, 95, 96, 97; WhoEnt 92; WhoTech 89; WorAlBi*

Williams, Roger
American. Clergy
Founded RI colony and Providence, RI, 1636; first to advocate complete religious tolerance in America.
b. 1603? in London, England
d. 1683 in Providence, Rhode Island
Source: *Alli; AmAu; AmAu&B; AmBi; AmPolLe; AmRef; AmSocL; AmWrBE; BbD; Benet 87, 96; BenetAL 91; BiD&SB; BiDrACR; BioIn 1; CamGLE; CamHAL; CasWL; CnDAL; CyAG; CyAL 1; DcAmAu; DcAmB; DcAmReB 1, 2; DcLB 24; DcLEL; DcNAA; EncAAH; EncAB-H 1974, 1996; EncARH; EncCRAm; EncNAB; EncNAR; EncSoB; HisWorL; LuthC 75; McGEWB; OxCAmH; OxCAmL 65, 83, 95; PenC AM; RComAH; REn; REnAL; WebAB 74, 79; WebE&AL; WhAm HS; WhAmP; WhDW; WhNaAH; WorAl; WorAlBi*

Williams, Roger
American. Pianist
Popular hits include ''Autumn Leaves,'' 1955; ''Born Free,'' 1966.
b. Oct 1, 1926 in Omaha, Nebraska
Source: *ASCAP 66, 80; BiDAmM; BioIn 5, 8; ForYSC; IntMPA 80, 84, 86, 88, 92, 94, 96; LegTOT; PenEncP; WhoAm 90; WorAl*

Williams, Roger J
American. Biochemist
Discovered growth promoting vitamin, pantothenic acid (B Complex); wrote *Introduction to Organic Chemistry,* 1928.
b. Aug 14, 1893 in Ootacamund, India
d. Feb 20, 1988 in Austin, Texas
Source: *AmMWSc 73P, 82; BioIn 15, 16; ConAu 7NR; CurBio 88, 88N; FacFETw; IntAu&W 77, 82; IntWW 74, 75, 76, 77, 78, 80, 81, 82, 83; NewYTBS 88; WhoAm 86; WrDr 86*

Williams, Roy Lee
American. Labor Union Official
Pres. of Teamsters, 1981-83; resigned following attempted bribery conviction.
b. Mar 22, 1915 in Ottumwa, Iowa
d. Apr 28, 1989 in Leeton, Missouri
Source: *BiDAmL; BioIn 12, 13, 15, 16; NewYTBS 81, 89; WhoAm 82*

Williams, Samm-Art
American. Actor, Dramatist
Plays include *Home,* 1979; *The Sixteenth Round,* 1980.
b. Jan 20, 1946 in Burgaw, North Carolina
Source: *BioIn 14, 15; BlkWr 1; ConAu X; ConBlAP 88; ConTFT 8; DcLB 38; DrBlPA 90; McGEWD 84; NatPD 81; SchCGBL; WhoAfA 96; WhoBlA 90, 92, 94*

Williams, Sherley Anne
American. Author
Author of *Dessa Rose,* 1986, about the life of an escaped slave.
b. Aug 25, 1944 in Bakersfield, California
Source: *AmWomWr SUP; BioIn 13, 15, 19, 20, 21; BlkLC; BlkWAm; BlkWr 1, 2; ConAu 25NR, 73; ConLC 89; DcLB 41; DcTwCCu 5; FemiCLE; InB&W 85; ModWoWr; OxCWoWr 95; SchCGBL; SelBAAf; SmATA 78; WhoAfA 96; WhoAmW 79; WhoBlA 90, 92, 94*

Williams, Shirley
English. Politician
Paymaster-General, 1976-79; member of Labour Party National Exec. Com., 1970.
b. Jul 27, 1930 in London, England
Source: *BioIn 20, 21; BlkWr 1; BlueB 76; ConAu X; ContDcW 89; CurBio 76; DcWomA; FacFETw; IntAu&W 89; IntDcWB; IntWW 74, 75, 76, 77, 78, 79, 80, 81, 82, 83, 89, 91; InWom SUP; Who 92; WhoWor 91*

Williams, Simon
English. Actor
Played James Bellamy in PBS series ''Upstairs, Downstairs.''
b. Jun 16, 1946 in Windsor, England
Source: *ConAu 133; HalFC 84, 88; WhoHol 92, A*

Williams, Ted
[Theodore Samuel Williams]
''The Splendid Sprinter''; ''The Thumper''
American. Baseball Player
Outfielder, Boston, 1939-42, 1946-60; won Triple Crown twice; last player to bat over .400; had .344 lifetime batting average; Hall of Fame, 1966.
b. Aug 30, 1918 in San Diego, California
Source: *Ballpl 90; BiDAmSp BB; BioIn 1, 2, 3, 4, 5, 6, 7, 8, 9, 10, 11, 12, 13, 14, 15, 16, 17, 18, 19, 20, 21; CelR; CmCal; CurBio 47; FacFETw; LegTOT; NewYTBS 88; WebAB 74, 79; WhoAm 76, 78, 80, 82, 84, 86, 88, 90, 92, 94, 95, 96, 97; WhoHol A; WhoProB 73; WhoSpor; WorAl; WorAlBi*

Williams, Tennessee
[Thomas Lanier Williams]
American. Dramatist, Author
Won Pulitzers for classic plays *A Streetcar Named Desire,* 1947; *Cat on a Hot Tin Roof,* 1955.
b. Mar 26, 1911 in Columbus, Mississippi
d. Feb 25, 1983 in New York, New York
Source: *AmAu&B; AmCulL; AmWr; AnObit 1983; Au&Wr 71; AuNews 2; Benet 87, 96; BenetAL 91; BiDConC; BiE&WWA; BioIn 9, 10, 11, 12, 13, 14, 15, 16, 17, 18, 19, 20, 21; BioNews 74; BlueB 76; CamGEL; CamGLE; CamGWoT; CamHAL; CasWL; CelR; CnMWL; CnThe; ConAmD; ConAu 3BS, 31NR, 108; ConDr 73, 77, 82, 93;*

ConLC 1, 2, 5, 7, 8, 11, 15, 19, 30, 39, 45, 71; ConNov 72, 76, 82; ConTFT 1; CroCD; CrtSuDr; CurBio 72, 83N; CyWA 89; DcArts; DcLB 7, DS4, Y83N; DcTwCCu 1; DrAF 76; DramC 4; EncAB-H 1974, 1996; EncSoH; EncWL, 2, 3; EncWT; Ent; FacFETw; FifSWrA; GayLesB; GayLL; GrWrEL DR; HalFC 84, 88; IntAu&W 76, 77, 82; IntDcT 2; IntWW 76, 77, 78, 79, 80, 81, 82; LegTOT; LinLib L, S; LiveMA; LngCTC; MagSAmL; MajMD 1; MajTwCW; McGEWB; McGEWD 72, 84; ModAL S1, S2; ModWD; NatPD 77, 81; NewCon; NewYTBS 83; NotNAT; Novels; OxCAmL 83, 95; OxCAmT 84; OxCEng 85, 95; OxCThe 83; OxCTwCP; RAdv 14, 13-2; RComAH; REnWD; RfGAmL 87, 94; RGTwCWr; ScF&FL 92; SouWr; TwCA SUP; WebAB 74, 79; WebE&AL; Who 74, 82, 83; WhoThe 72, 77, 81; WhoTwCL; WorAl; WorAlBi; WorLitC; WrDr 76, 80, 82; WrPh

Williams, Tex
American. Musician, Actor
Country-western singer popular in films, 1930s-50s; best-selling hit singles include "Smoke! Smoke! Smoke!"
b. Aug 23, 1917 in Ramsey, Illinois
d. Oct 11, 1985 in Newhall, California
Source: *BgBkCoM; BioIn 14; CounME 74, 74A; EncFCWM 69, 83; HarEnCM 87; IlEncCM; NewYTBS 85; PenEncP*

Williams, Tiger
[David James Williams]
Canadian. Hockey Player
Left wing, 1974-88; holds NHL record for career penalty minutes (over 3,800); wrote autobiography *Tiger: A Hockey Story,* 1986.
b. Feb 3, 1954 in Weyburn, Saskatchewan, Canada
Source: *HocEn; HocReg 87*

Williams, Tommy
[Thomas Mark Williams]
American. Hockey Player
Center, 1961-76, mostly with Boston; held all NHL scoring records by American-born player until broken by Reed Larson; youngest gold medalist US Olympic hockey team, 1960.
b. Apr 17, 1940 in Duluth, Minnesota
d. Feb 8, 1992 in Hudson, Massachusetts
Source: *BiDAmSp BK; HocEn; WhoAdv 90; WhoE 89; WhoHcky 73*

Williams, Tony
[Anthony Williams]
American. Composer, Musician
Drummer; prime influence on jazz styles of the 1970s.
b. Dec 12, 1945 in Chicago, Illinois
d. Feb 23, 1997 in Daly City, California
Source: *AllMusG; BiDJaz; BioIn 12, 13, 16; ConMus 6; DcTwCCu 5; EncJzS; InB&W 80, 85; NewGrDA 86; NewGrDJ 88, 94; PenEncP; WhoAm 82, 84, 86, 88, 92, 94, 95, 96, 97; WhoEnt 92*

Williams, Treat
[Richard Treat Williams]
American. Actor
Starred in films *Hair,* 1979, *Prince of the City,* 1981, *Dead Heat,* 1988.
b. Dec 1, 1951 in Stamford, Connecticut
Source: *BioIn 13; CelR 90; ConTFT 8; HalFC 84, 88; HolBB; IntMPA 88, 92; LegTOT; NewYTBS 79, 80, 81; WhoAm 86, 88, 90, 92, 94, 95, 96, 97; WhoEnt 92*

Williams, Ursula Moray
English. Children's Author
Writings include *The Noble Hawks,* 1959; *The Three Toymakers,* 1946.
b. Apr 19, 1911 in Petersfield, England
Source: *Au&Wr 71; AuBYP 2S; BioIn 8, 9, 14, 19; ConAu 10NR, 13R, X; DcLB 160; FourBJA; IntAu&W 76, 77, 82, 86; IntWWP 77; NewCBEL; OxCChiL; ScF&FL 1, 2, 92; SmATA 3; TwCChW 78, 83, 89; WhoChL; WhoWor 76; WrDr 86, 92*

Williams, Vanessa
American. Actor, Beauty Contest Winner, Singer
First black crowned Miss America, 1983; first to give up title for violating pageant's morals code; was in film *The Pick-Up Artist,* 1987; *Eraser,* 1996.
b. Mar 18, 1963 in New York, New York
Source: *AfrAmBi 1; AmDec 1980; BioIn 13, 14, 15, 16; CelR 90; ConBlB 4; ConMus 10; ConTFT 14; CurBio 84; DcTwCCu 5; DrBlPA 90; InB&W 85; InWom SUP; LegTOT; NewYTBS 84; WhoAfA 96; WhoAm 94, 95, 96, 97; WhoAmW 95, 97; WhoBlA 92; WhoHol 92*

Williams, Victoria
American. Singer, Songwriter
Released album *Happy Come Home,* which includes songs "Frying Pan" and "Opelousas," 1987; later recorded *Loose,* 1994 and *This Moment: Live in Toronto,* 1995.
b. 1959 in Forbing, Louisiana
Source: *ConMus 17*

Williams, Walter Edward
American. Economist
Conservative author of numerous books and articles; blames government programs for many social ills.
b. Mar 31, 1936 in Philadelphia, Pennsylvania
Source: *AfrAmOr; AmMWSc 78S; BiDAmNC; ConAu 123; WhoBlA 77, 80, 85, 88; WrDr 92*

Williams, Wayne Bertram
American. Murderer
Freelance photographer convicted of Atlanta's child killings, 1982.
b. May 27, 1958 in Atlanta, Georgia
Source: *BioIn 12, 13, 15; InB&W 85; MurCaTw; NewYTBS 81*

Williams, Wendy O(rlean)
[The Plasmatics]
American. Entertainer
Lead singer known for outrageous appearance and stage antics.
b. 1946? in Rochester, New York
Source: *BioIn 12, 13; NewWmR; WhoRocM 82*

Williams, William
American. Merchant, Judge
Signed Declaration of Independence, 1776; member, Continental Congress, 1776-78, 1783-84.
b. Apr 23, 1731 in Lebanon, Connecticut
d. Aug 2, 1811 in Lebanon, Connecticut
Source: *AmBi; ApCAB; BiAUS; BiDrAC; BiDrUSC 89; BioIn 7, 8, 9, 10; DcAmB; Drake; EncAR; EncCRAm; HarEnUS; NatCAB 10; TwCBDA; WhAm HS; WhAmP; WhAmRev*

Williams, William Carlos
American. Author, Poet
Revolutionized American poetry; won 1963 Pulitzer for *Pictures From Brueghel.*
b. Sep 17, 1883 in Rutherford, New Jersey
d. Mar 4, 1963 in Rutherford, New Jersey
Source: *AmAu&B; AmCulL; AmWr; AtlBL; Benet 87, 96; BenetAL 91; BiDAmM; BioIn 1, 2, 4, 5, 6, 7, 8, 9, 10, 11, 12, 13, 14, 15, 16, 17, 19, 20; CamGEL; CamGLE; CamHAL; CasWL; ChhPo; CnDAL; CnE&AP; CnMD; CnMWL; ConAmA; ConAmL; ConAu 34NR, 89; ConLC 1, 2, 5, 9, 13, 22, 42, 67; CyWA 58, 89; DcAmB S7; DcAmMeB 84; DcArts; DcLB 4, 16, 54, 86; DcLEL; DcTwCCu 1; EncAB-H 1996; EncWL, 2, 3; EvLB; FacFETw; GrWrEL P; InSci; LinLib L, S; LngCTC; MagSAmL; MajTwCW; MakMC; McGEWB; ModAL, S1, S2; ModWD; NewGrDA 86; Novels; OxCAmL 65, 83, 95; OxCEng 67, 85, 95; OxCTwCP; PenC AM; PlP&P; PoeCrit 7; RAdv 1, 14, 13-1; RComAH; REn; REnAL; RfGAmL 87, 94; RfGShF; RGFAP; RGTwCWr; SixAP; Tw; TwCA, SUP; TwCWr; WebAB 74, 79; WebE&AL; WhAm 4; WhDW; WhLit; WhNAA; WhoTwCL; WorAl; WorAlBi; WorLitC*

Williams, William T(homas)
American. Painter
First black artist to be included in *History of Art,* H. W. Janson's widely used art textbook; professor of art, Brooklyn College, 1971—.
b. Jul 17, 1942 in Cross Creek, North Carolina
Source: *WhoAfA 96; WhoAm 82, 84, 86, 88, 90, 92, 94, 95, 96, 97; WhoAmA 80, 82, 84, 86, 89, 91, 93; WhoBlA 77, 80, 85, 88, 90, 92, 94*

Williams, Willie Lawrence
American. Police Chief
Succeeded Daryl Gates as chief of police, Los Angeles, CA, 1992-97.

b. Oct 1, 1943 in Philadelphia, Pennsylvania
Source: *News 93-1*

Williamson, Cris
[Mary Cristine Williamson]
American. Musician
Recorded album *The Changer and the Changed,* 1974, the best-selling women's music album of all time.
b. 1947 in Deadwood, South Dakota
Source: *Baker 92; GayLesB*

Williamson, David
Australian. Screenwriter
Films include *The Year of Living Dangerously,* 1983.
b. Feb 24, 1942 in Melbourne, Australia
Source: *AuLitCr; CamGLE; ConDr 77, 82, 88; ConLC 56; CrtSuDr; IntLitE; IntvTCA 2; McGEWD 84; OxCAusL; OxCThe 83; RAdv 14; VarWW 85; WhoThe 77, 81; WrDr 82, 84, 86, 88, 90, 92*

Williamson, Marianne
American. Lecturer, Author
Founder of spiritual organizations Los Angeles Center for Living and Manhattan Center for Living, 1987; author of spiritual guide *Return to Love,* 1992.
b. Jul 8, 1952 in Houston, Texas
Source: *ConAu 141; CurBio 93; News 91*

Williamson, Nicol
Scottish. Actor
Films include *The Seven-Percent Solution,* 1976; *Excaliber,* 1980.
b. Sep 14, 1938 in Hamilton, Scotland
Source: *BioIn 7, 8, 9, 13; CamGWoT; CelR, 90; CnThe; ConTFT 2, 8; CurBio 70; Ent; FilmEn; FilmgC; HalFC 84, 88; IntDcF 1-3; IntDcT 3; IntMPA 86, 88, 92, 94, 96; IntWW 79, 80, 81, 82, 83, 89, 91, 93; ItaFilm; LegTOT; MovMk; NewYTBE 73; NotNAT; Who 82, 83, 85, 88, 90, 92, 94; WhoAm 80, 82, 84, 86, 88, 90, 92; WhoEnt 92; WhoHol A; WhoThe 72, 77, 81; WhoWor 84, 87, 89, 91, 93, 95, 96, 97; WorAl; WorAlBi*

Williamson, Robin
[Incredible String Band]
Scottish. Musician
Sang, played many instruments for rock band, 1967, then began solo career; albums include *Journey's Edge,* 1977.
b. Nov 24, 1943 in Glasgow, Scotland
Source: *ConAu 102; IntAu&W 91, 93; IntWWP 77, 82; WhoRocM 82; WrDr 84, 86, 88, 90, 92*

Williamson, Sonny Boy
"Little Boy Blue"; "The One Man Band"
American. Singer, Musician
Singer and harmonica player; an early contributor in the formation of electric blues and rock and roll.
b. Dec 5, 1899 in Glendora, Mississippi
d. Mar 25, 1965 in Helena, Arkansas
Source: *BluesWW; ConMuA 80A; ConMus 9; EncRk 88; GuBlues; NewAmDM; NewGrDA 86; PenEncP; RolSEnR 83*

William the Conqueror
[William the Norman]
English. Ruler
Conquered England, 1066, replacing English nobility with Norman followers; King of England, 1066-87, succeeded by son, William II.
b. 1027 in Falaise, France
d. 1087 in Rouen, France
Source: *Benet 87, 96; DcNaB; HisWorL; NewC; REn; WorAl*

Willig, George
American. Actor, Stunt Performer
Became instant celebrity when he climbed World Trade Center, NYC, 1977; wrote *Going It Alone,* 1979.
b. Jun 11, 1949 in New York, New York
Source: *BioIn 11, 17, 18; ConAu 102; NewYTBS 77*

Willingham, Calder Baynard, Jr.
American. Writer
His first novel, *End As a Man,* 1947, became film, play; wrote screenplay for *The Graduate,* 1967.
b. Dec 23, 1922 in Atlanta, Georgia
d. Feb 19, 1995 in Laconia, New Hampshire
Source: *Benet 87; BenetAL 91; BiE&WWA; BioIn 15; CnMD; ConAu 3NR, 5R; ConLC 5, 51; ConNov 86, 91; DcLB 2, 44; DcLEL 1940; DrAPF 91; EncWL; NotNAT; OxCAmL 83; OxCAmT 84; REnAL; TwCA SUP; TwCWr; WhAm 11; WhoAm 74, 76, 78, 80, 82, 84, 86, 88, 95; WhoUSWr 88; WhoWrEP 89, 92, 95; WrDr 86, 92*

Willis, Bill
[William Willis]
American. Football Player
Guard, Cleveland, 1946-53; first black player in pro football after WW II; Hall of Fame, 1977.
Source: *BiDAmSp FB; BioIn 9, 16; CabMA; ProFbHF; WhoFtbl 74*

Willis, Bruce
[Walter Bruce Willis]
"Bruno"
American. Actor
Played David Addison on TV series "Moonlighting," 1985-89; won 1987 Emmy; starred in film *Die Hard,* 1988, *Die Harder,* 1990.
b. Mar 19, 1955 in Idar-Oberstein, Germany
Source: *BiDFilm 94; BioIn 14, 15, 16; CelR 90; ConNews 86-4; ConTFT 3, 9; CurBio 87; HalFC 88; HolBB; IntMPA 92, 94, 96; IntWW 91; LegTOT; WhoAm 90; WhoEnt 92; WhoHol 92*

Willis, Gordon
American. Filmmaker
Cinematographer whose major films include *Klute,* 1971; *Annie Hall,* 1983.
Source: *BioIn 11, 12, 15; ConTFT 7; FilmEn; FilmgC; HalFC 80, 84, 88; IntMPA 76, 77, 78, 79, 80, 81, 82, 84, 86, 88, 92, 94, 96; MiSFD 9; VarWW 85; WhoAm 82, 84, 86, 88, 90, 92, 94, 95, 96, 97; WhoEnt 92*

Willis, Mary
American. Designer
Won Oscar for costumes in *The Wonderful World of the Brothers Grimm,* 1963.
b. Jul 4, 1919 in Prescott, Arizona
Source: *InWom SUP; VarWW 85*

Willis, Nathaniel Parker
American. Journalist
Foreign correspondent for *NY Mirror,* 1832-36; cofounded weekly *Corsair,* 1839-40.
b. Jan 20, 1806 in Portland, Maine
d. Jan 20, 1867 in Tarrytown, New York
Source: *Alli; AmAu; AmAu&B; AmBi; ApCAB; BbD; BenetAL 91; BiD&SB; BiDTran; BioIn 1, 3, 4, 6, 7, 8, 9, 12, 16; CamGWoT; CasWL; Chambr 3; ChhPo, S1, S2; CnDAL; CyAL 2; DcAmAu; DcAmB; DcEnL; DcLB 3, 59, 73, 74; DcLEL; DcNAA; EncAJ; EvLB; GrWrEL N; HarEnUS; JrnUS; LinLib L; McGEWD 72, 84; NatCAB 3; NotNAT B; OxCAmL 65; OxCCan; OxCEng 67; OxCThe 67; REn; REnAL; RfGAmL 87, 94; TwCBDA; WebAB 74, 79; WhAm HS*

Willis, Paul S
American. Business Executive
President, Grocery Manufacturers of America, 1932-65; coordinated food supplies sent to US troops, WW II.
b. Nov 8, 1890 in Hallettsville, Texas
d. Jun 5, 1987 in New Rochelle, New York
Source: *BioIn 2; CurBio 51, 87*

Willkie, Wendell Lewis
[Lewis Wendell Willkie]
American. Politician, Business Executive
Critic of New Deal programs; Rep. nominee for pres., 1940, defeated by FDR.
b. Feb 18, 1892 in Elwood, Indiana
d. Oct 8, 1944 in New York, New York
Source: *AmAu&B; AmPolLe; BioIn 1, 2, 3, 4, 5, 6, 7, 8, 9, 13, 14, 17, 18; ChhPo S1; CurBio 40, 44; DcAmB S3; DcNAA; EncAB-A 19; EncAB-H 1974, 1996; IndAu 1917; LinLib S; NatCAB 32; OhA&B; OxCAmH; OxCAmL 65; REnAL; WebAB 74, 79; WhAm 2; WhAmP; WhWW-II; WorAl*

Willmar 8
[Glennis Andresen; Doris Boshart; Sylvia Erickson; Jane Harguth; Teren Novotny; Shirley Solyntjes; Sandi Treml; Irene Wallin]
American. Social Reformers
Women employees of Citizens National Bank, Willmar, MN; staged strike, 1976, over sexual discrimination.

Willners, Hal
American. Producer
Music director of NBC's "Saturday Night Live," 1980—; produced compilations *Stay Awake: Various Interpretations of Music From Vintage Disney Films,* 1988 and *Weird Nightmare: Meditations on Mingus,* 1992.
b. 1948 in Philadelphia, Pennsylvania

Wills, Bob
[James Robert Wills]
American. Musician, Songwriter
Pioneered Western swing music; best known for song "San Antonio Rose," 1940.
b. Mar 6, 1905 in Limestone County, Texas
d. May 13, 1975 in Fort Worth, Texas
Source: *ASCAP 80; Baker 84, 92; BgBands 74; BgBkCoM; BioIn 1, 10, 11, 12, 14, 15, 16, 20, 21; CmpEPM; ConMus 6; DcAmB S9; DcArts; EncFCWM 69, 83; HarEnCM 87; IlEncCM; LegTOT; NewAmDM; NewGrDA 86; NewGrDJ 88, 94; NewYTBS 75; OxCPMus; PenEncP; WhAm 6; WhoAm 74; WhoHol C; WhoRock 81; WhScrn 77, 83*

Wills, Chill
American. Actor
Voice of Francis the Talking Mule in film series, 1940s-50s.
b. Jul 18, 1903 in Seagoville, Texas
d. Dec 15, 1978 in Encino, California
Source: *BioNews 74; LegTOT; MotPP; MovMk; Vers A; WhoHol A; WhScrn 83; WorAl*

Wills, Frank
American. Guard
Security guard at Watergate Hotel who reported burglary of Dem. headquarters, Jun 17, 1972.
b. 1948?
Source: *BioIn 9, 10, 12, 14; InB&W 80; NewYTBS 74*

Wills, Garry
American. Author, Journalist
Syndicated political columnist since 1970; books include *Bare Ruined Choirs,* 1972; *The Kennedy Imprisonment,* 1982.
b. May 22, 1934 in Atlanta, Georgia
Source: *AmAu&B; AmCath 80; AmSocL; BiDAmNC; BioIn 8, 9, 11, 12, 13, 19; ConAu 1NR, 1R; CurBio 82; DcAmC; DrAS 74F, 78F, 82H; EncAJ; EncTwCJ; FacFETw; LiJour; PeoHis; WhoAm 78, 80, 82, 84, 86, 88, 90, 92, 94, 95, 96, 97; WhoE 74; WhoMW 92, 93, 96; WhoRel 92; WhoUSWr 88; WhoWrEP 89, 92, 95; WorAu 1975; WrDr 76, 80, 82, 84, 86, 88, 90, 92, 94, 96*

Wills, Harry
"Black Panther"
American. Boxer
Heavyweight champion, 1919-22; Hall of Fame, 1970.
b. May 15, 1892 in New Orleans, Louisiana
d. Dec 21, 1958 in New York, New York
Source: *BioIn 1, 5; InB&W 80; WhoBox 74*

Wills, Maury
[Maurice Morning Wills]
American. Baseball Player
Shortstop, 1959-72, mostly with Dodgers; NL MVP, 1962; had 586 career stolen bases.
b. Oct 2, 1932 in Washington, District of Columbia
Source: *Ballpl 90; BiDAmSp BB; BioIn 6, 7, 8, 9, 10, 11, 12, 15; CmCal; ConAu 105; CurBio 66; InB&W 85; LegTOT; NewYTBE 72; WhoHol A; WhoProB 73; WhoSpor*

Willson, Meredith
American. Composer
Best known for Broadway hits *The Music Man,* 1957; *The Unsinkable Molly Brown,* 1960.
b. May 18, 1902 in Mason City, Iowa
d. Jun 15, 1984 in Santa Monica, California
Source: *AmAu&B; AmSong; ASCAP 66, 80; Baker 78, 84; BestMus; BiDAmM; BiE&WWA; BioIn 1, 2, 3, 4, 5, 6, 7, 10, 11, 12, 14, 15; CmpEPM; ConAmC 76, 82; ConAu 49, 113; ConDr 73, 77D; CurBio 58, 84, 84N; EncMT; HalFC 80, 84, 88; IntWWM 77, 80; LegTOT; LinLib L, S; NewAmDM; NewCBMT; NewGrDA 86; NewGrDM 80; NewYTBS 80, 84; NotNAT, A; OxCAmT 84; OxCPMus; PenEncP; PopAmC, SUP; RadStar; SaTiSS; WhAm 9; WhoAm 74, 76, 78, 80, 82, 84, 86; WhoMus 72; WorAl; WorAlBi*

Willson, S. Brian
American. Political Activist, Veterans' Leader
Head of Veterans Peace Action Team; lost legs when struck by a train during demonstration opposing government aid to Nicaraquan contras, 1988.
b. 1942

Willstater, Richard Martin
German. Chemist
Won Nobel Prize, 1915, for research on chlorophyll; developed techniques of partition chromatography.
b. Aug 13, 1872 in Karlsruhe, Germany
d. Aug 3, 1942 in Locarno, Switzerland
Source: *AsBiEn; BiESc; CurBio 42; DcScB; Dis&D; ObitOF 79; WhDW; WhoNob, 90, 95*

Willys, John North
American. Industrialist
Bought automobile plant, 1907; manufactured Willys-Overland cars; pres., 1907-29, 1935; chm., 1929-35.
b. Oct 25, 1873 in Canandaigua, New York
d. Aug 26, 1935 in Riverdale, New York
Source: *ApCAB X; DcAmB S1; EncABHB 4; NatCAB 28; WebAB 74, 79; WebBD 83; WhAm 1; WorAl*

Wilmerding, John
American. Author
American art expert who wrote *Genius of American Painting,* 1973.
b. Apr 28, 1938 in Boston, Massachusetts
Source: *ConAu 111; DrAS 78H, 82H; WhoAm 74, 76, 78, 80, 82, 84, 86, 88, 90, 92, 94, 95, 96, 97; WhoAmA 78, 80, 82, 84, 86, 89, 91, 93; WrDr 90, 92, 94*

Wilmot, David
American. Politician
Wrote *Wilmot Proviso,* 1846, prohibiting slavery in territory purchased from Mexico.
b. Jan 20, 1814 in Bethany, Pennsylvania
d. 1868
Source: *AmBi; AmPolLe; ApCAB; BiAUS; BiDFedJ; BiDrAC; BiDrUSC 89; BioIn 7; DcAmB; Drake; EncAAH; EncAB-H 1974, 1996; HarEnUS; McGEWB; NatCAB 3; NewCol 75; PolPar; TwCBDA; WebAB 74, 79; WhAm HS; WhAmP; WhCiWar*

Wilmut, Ian
English. Scientist
Cloned a lamb at Scotland's Roslin Institute, 1996.
b. Jul 7, 1944 in Hampton Lucey, England

Wilson, A(ndrew) N(orman)
English. Critic, Writer
Wrote *The Life of John Milton,* 1983; *C. S. Lewis: A Biography,* 1990; won the Whitbread Award for *Tolstoy,* 1988.
b. Oct 27, 1950 in Stone, England
Source: *Benet 96; BioIn 16, 17, 18, 19; ConNov 96; CurBio 93; IntAu&W 86, 93; OxCEng 95; RGTwCWr*

Wilson, Alexander
American. Explorer, Naturalist, Poet
Wrote *American Ornithology,* 1808-14; preceded Audubon's work by 20 yrs.
b. Jul 6, 1766 in Paisley, Scotland
d. Aug 23, 1813 in Philadelphia, Pennsylvania
Source: *Alli; AmAu; AmAu&B; AmBi; ApCAB; BenetAL 91; BiDAmS; BiD&SB; BiESc; BiInAmS; BioIn 2, 3, 4, 5, 6, 7, 8, 9, 10, 11, 13; CelCen; ChhPo, S1; CyAL 1; DcAmAu; DcAmB; DcBiPP; DcBrBI; DcEnL; DcNAA; DcNaB; DcScB; Drake; EvLB; GrBIl; HarEnUS; InSci; LinLib L, S; McGEWB; NatCAB 7; NewCBEL; NewYHSD; OxCAmH; OxCAmL 65, 83, 95; REnAL; TwCBDA; WebAB 74, 79; WhAm HS*

Wilson, Allan C
American. Biochemist
Responsible for African Eve theory of evolution in which all humans descended from a single woman who lived in Africa 200,000 years ago.
b. Oct 18, 1934 in Ngaruawahia, New Zealand
d. Jul 21, 1991 in Seattle, Washington
Source: *AmMWSc 92; NewYTBS 91; Who 92N; WhoAm 90; WhoTech 89; WhoWest 89*

Wilson, Angus
[Sir Frank Johnstone]
English. Author
Writings include *As If By Magic,* 1973; *Setting the World on Fire,* 1980.
b. Aug 11, 1913 in Bexhill, England
d. May 31, 1991 in Bury Saint Edmunds, England
Source: *AnObit 1991; Au&Wr 71; Benet 87, 96; BioIn 4, 5, 8, 11, 12, 13, 14, 15, 16; BlmGEL; BlueB 76; BritWr S1; CamGEL; CamGLE; CasWL; ConAu 5R, 21NR, 134; ConLC 2, 3, 5, 25; ConNov 72, 76, 82, 86; CurBio 59, 91N; CyWA 89; DcLB 15, 139, 155; EncSF; EncWL 2, 3; GrWrEL N; IntAu&W 76, 77, 82, 89, 91; IntvTCA 2; IntWW 74, 75, 76, 77, 78, 79, 80, 81, 82, 83, 89, 91; LegTOT; LngCEL; LngCTC; MajTwCW; ModBrL, S1, S2; NewC; NewCBEL; NewYTBS 80, 91; Novels; OxCEng 85; PenC ENG; RAdv 1, 14, 13-1; REn; RfGEnL 91; ScF&FL 1, 2, 92; ScFSB; ShSCr 21; TwCA SUP; TwCWr; WebE&AL; WhAm 10; WhDW; Who 82, 83, 85, 88, 90, 92N; WhoTwCL; WhoWor 89, 91; WrDr 76, 80, 82, 84, 86, 88, 90*

Wilson, Ann
American. Singer, Musician
Lead singer of Heart since 1972.
b. Jun 19, 1951 in San Diego, California
Source: *LegTOT; WhoRocM 82; WhoWest 82*

Wilson, August
[Frederick August Kittel]
American. Dramatist
Won 1987 Pulitzer, Tony for drama: *Fences,* about a 1950s black American family.
b. Apr 27, 1945 in Pittsburgh, Pennsylvania
Source: *AfrAmAl 6; AmDec 1980; Au&Arts 16; Benet 96; BenetAL 91; BioIn 14, 15, 16; BlkAWP; BlkLC; BlkWr 1, 2; CamGWoT; ConAmD; ConAu 42NR, 54NR, 115, 122; ConBlAP 88; ConBlB 7; ConDr 88, 93; ConLC 39, 50, 63; ConTFT 5, 10; CrtSuDr; CurBio 87; CyWA 89; DcTwCCu 1, 5; DramC 2; DrBlPA 90; EncWL 3; IntAu&W 91; IntDcT 2; IntWW 91, 93; LegTOT; MajTwCW; NegAl 89; NewYTBS 84, 87, 90; OxCAmL 95; RAdv 14; RfGAmL 94; SchCGBL; WhoAfA 96; WhoAm 90, 92, 94, 95, 96, 97; WhoBlA 92, 94; WhoE 95, 97; WhoMW 90, 92; WorAlBi; WorAu 1980; WrDr 88, 90, 92, 94, 96*

Wilson, Bertha
Canadian. Supreme Court Justice
First woman named to Supreme Court of Canada, 1982.
b. Sep 18, 1923 in Kirkcaldy, Scotland
Source: *BioIn 12, 15; CanWW 31, 89; ConNews 86-1; WhoAm 84, 86, 88, 90, 92, 94, 95, 96; WhoAmW 87, 89, 91, 93; WhoE 86, 91; WomLaw*

Wilson, Brian Douglas
[The Beach Boys]
American. Singer, Songwriter
Vocalist, bassist, pianist with CA rock group; hits include "Help Me, Rhonda," 1965; wrote *Wouldn't It Be Nice: My Own Story,* 1991.
b. Jun 20, 1942 in Hawthorne, California
Source: *Baker 84; BioIn 15; BkPepl; BlueB 76; ConLC 12; CurBio 88; EncPR&S 74; IlEncRk; NewYTBS 88; WhoAm 78, 80, 82, 84, 86, 90, 92, 94, 95, 96, 97; WhoEnt 92*

Wilson, Carl Dean
[The Beach Boys]
American. Singer
Vocalist, guitarist with the Beach Boys since 1961; famous CA rock hits include "Surfin USA," 1963.
b. Dec 21, 1946 in Hawthorne, California
Source: *BkPepl; EncPR&S 74; RkOn 85; WhoAm 76, 78, 80, 82, 84*

Wilson, Cassandra
American. Singer
Recorded first solo album,*Point of View,* 1986; *New Moon Daughter,* 1996.
b. 1955 in Jackson, Mississippi
Source: *AllMusG; ConMus 12; DcTwCCu 5; News 96, 96-3; WhoAmW 97*

Wilson, Charles Edward
American. Business Executive
Pres., General Electric Co., 1940-42, 1944-50; board of governors, NY Stock Exchange, 1955-72.
b. Nov 18, 1886 in New York, New York
d. Jan 3, 1972 in Scarsdale, New York
Source: *BiDAmBL 83; BioIn 1, 2, 3, 4, 5, 9, 11; CurBio 43, 51, 72; DcAmB S9; InSci; NatCAB 56; NewYTBE 72; WhAm 5*

Wilson, Charles Erwin
American. Government Official, Business Executive
Secretary of Defense, 1953-57; pres., General Motors, 1941-53.
b. Jul 18, 1890 in Minerva, Ohio
d. Sep 26, 1961 in Norwood, Louisiana
Source: *AmPolLe; BiDAmBL 83; BiDrUSE 71, 89; BioIn 1, 2, 3, 4, 6, 7, 10, 11, 12; CurBio 41, 50, 61; DcAmB S7; EncABHB 5; EncWB; InSci; NatCAB 57; WebAB 74, 79; WhAm 4; WorAl*

Wilson, Charles Thomson Rees
Scottish. Scientist
Won 1927 Nobel Prize for work on condensation of vapour.
b. Feb 14, 1869 in Glencorse, Scotland
d. Nov 15, 1959 in Carlops, Scotland
Source: *AsBiEn; BiESc; BioIn 3, 5, 6, 8, 14, 15, 20; CamDcSc; DcNaB 1951; DcScB; FacFETw; GrBr; InSci; LarDcSc; McGEWB; ObitOF 79; WhoNob, 90, 95; WorAl*

Wilson, Colin Henry
English. Author
Books include *Ritual in the Dark,* 1960; *The Space Vampires,* 1975.
b. Jun 26, 1931 in Leicester, England
Source: *Au&Wr 71; Benet 87; BioIn 13, 14, 15, 16; CamGLE; CasWL; ConAu 1NR, 1R, 5AS, 22NR, 33NR; ConLC 14; ConNov 86, 91; EncO&P 2, 3; FacFETw; IntAu&W 91; IntWW 83, 91; LngCTC; ModBrL S1; NewC; NewEScF; OxCEng 85; PenEncH; RAdv 1, 13-1; ScFSB; TwCCr&M 91; TwCSFW 91; TwCWr; Who 85, 92; WhoAm 86, 90; WhoWor 91; WorAu 1950; WrDr 86, 92*

Wilson, Demond
American. Actor
Starred in "Sanford and Son," 1972-77; "The New Odd Couple," 1982-83.
b. Oct 13, 1946 in Valdosta, Georgia
Source: *BioIn 14; BlksAmF; DrBlPA, 90; LegTOT; NegAl 89; WhoBlA 85, 92; WhoHol 92, A*

Wilson, Dennis
[The Beach Boys]
American. Musician, Singer
Drummer, keyboardist, singer; only member to release solo album, *Pacific Ocean Blue.*
b. Dec 4, 1944 in Hawthorne, California
d. Dec 28, 1983 in Marina del Rey, California
Source: *AnObit 1983; BioIn 11, 12, 13; BkPepl; EncPR&S 74; IlEncRk; LegTOT; NewYTBS 83; WhoHol A; WhoRock 81; WhoRocM 82*

Wilson, Don(ald Harlow)
American. Radio Performer, TV Personality
Jack Benny's announcer, foil on TV, radio shows over 40 yrs.
b. Sep 1, 1900 in Lincoln, Nebraska
d. Apr 25, 1982 in Palm Springs, California
Source: *BioIn 12, 13, 17; CurBio 44, 91N; LegTOT; NewYTBS 82; RadStar; WhAm 8; WhoHol A; WorAl*

Wilson, Dooley
[Arthur Wilson]
American. Actor, Musician
Played Sam, the piano player, in *Casablanca,* 1943.
b. Apr 3, 1894 in Tyler, Texas
d. May 30, 1953 in Los Angeles, California
Source: *BioIn 10; BlksAmF; DrBlPA, 90; EncAFC; FilmEn; FilmgC; HalFC 80,*

84, 88; HolP 40; LegTOT; WhE&EA; WhoHol B; WhScrn 74, 77, 83

Wilson, Dorothy Clarke
American. Author
Religious writings include over 70 plays; books include *Climb Every Mountain,* 1976.
b. May 9, 1904 in Gardiner, Maine
Source: *AmAu&B; AmNov; AmWomPl; Au&Wr 71; BioIn 2; ConAu 1R, 6NR; CurBio 51; ForWC 70; IntAu&W 76, 77, 82, 86, 89, 91; InWom; SmATA 16; WhoAm 74, 76, 78, 80, 82, 84, 86, 88, 90, 92, 94, 95, 96, 97; WhoAmW 58, 70, 72, 74; WrDr 76, 80, 82, 84, 86, 88, 90, 92, 94, 96*

Wilson, Earl
[Harvey Earl Wilson]
American. Journalist
Best known for syndicated gossip column, "It Happened Last Night," 1943-83.
b. May 3, 1907 in Rockford, Ohio
d. Jan 16, 1987 in Yonkers, New York
Source: *AmAu&B; AnObit 1987; ASCAP 66, 80; BiDAmJo; BiDAmNC; BioIn 1, 2, 4, 10, 13; CelR; ConAu 69, 121; EncTwCJ; IntAu&W 91; LegTOT; NewYTBS 87; OhA&B; REnAL; WhAm 9; WhAmP; WhE&EA; WhoAm 74, 76, 78, 80, 82, 84, 86; WhoE 74; WhoHol A; WorAl; WrDr 80, 82, 84, 86, 88*

Wilson, Edith Bolling Galt
[Mrs. Woodrow Wilson]
American. First Lady
Married pres., 1915; nursed him after his 1919 stroke, virtually running country until his term expired.
b. Oct 15, 1872 in Wytheville, Virginia
d. Dec 28, 1961 in Washington, District of Columbia
Source: *BioIn 16, 17, 18, 19, 21; DcAmB S7; FacPr 89; InWom, SUP; NotAW MOD; ObitT 1961*

Wilson, Edmund
American. Author, Critic
Considered among this century's finest literary critics; wrote *Axel's Castle,* 1931.
b. May 8, 1895 in Red Bank, New Jersey
d. Jun 12, 1972 in Talcottville, New York
Source: *AmAu&B; AmCulL; AmWr; Au&Wr 71; Benet 87, 96; BenetAL 91; BiE&WWA; BioIn 1, 3, 4, 5, 6, 7, 8, 9, 10, 11, 12, 13, 14, 15, 16, 17, 18, 19, 20, 21; CamGEL; CamGLE; CamHAL; CasWL; ChhPo S1; CnDAL; CnMD; ConAmA; ConAu 1NR, 1R, 37R, 46NR; ConLC 1, 2, 3, 8, 24; ConLCrt 77, 82; ConNov 72; CurBio 72N; CyWA 89; DcAmB S9; DcArts; DcLB 63; DcLEL; EncAB-H 1974, 1996; EncAJ; EncWL 2, 3; EvLB; FacFETw; GrWrEL N; JrnUS; LegTOT; LiJour; LinLib L, S; LngCTC; MajTwCW; MakMC; McGEWB; ModAL, S1, S2; ModWD; NotNAT A; Novels; ObitT 1971; OxCAmL 65, 83, 95; OxCCan; OxCEng 67, 85, 95; OxCTwCP; PenC AM; PolProf T; RAdv 1, 14, 13-1; REn; REnAL; RfGAmL 87, 94; RGTwCWr; ScF&FL 1, 2; ThTwC 87; TwCA, SUP; TwCWr; WebAB 74, 79; WebE&AL; WhAm 5; WhoTwCL; WorAl; WorAlBi*

Wilson, Edward Arthur
American. Artist, Illustrator
Noted woodcut illustrator of sea adventures: *The Pirate's Treasure,* 1926.
b. Mar 4, 1886 in Glasgow, Scotland
d. Oct 2, 1970 in Dobbs Ferry, New York
Source: *BioIn 1, 3, 4, 5, 9; ChhPo, S1, S2; ConAu 116; IlrAm 1880, B; IlsBYP; IlsCB 1744, 1946; WhAm 5, 7*

Wilson, Edward Foss
American. Business Executive
President, Wilson & Co., 1934-56, the third-largest meatpacker in the US.
b. Jan 6, 1905
d. Mar 19, 1994 in Washington, District of Columbia
Source: *BioIn 4, 5, 19, 20; CurBio 94N; St&PR 75; WhoAm 74, 76*

Wilson, Edward Osborne
American. Biologist
His book, *On Human Nature,* won the 1979 Pulitzer Prize; one of the world's authorities on ants.
b. Jun 10, 1929 in Birmingham, Alabama
Source: *AmMWSc 76P, 79, 82, 86, 89, 92, 95; BiESc; BioIn 9, 11, 12, 13, 14, 16; CamDcSc; ConAu 16NR, 61; CurBio 79; EncWB; EnvEnc; FacFETw; IntAu&W 91, 93; IntWW 81, 82, 83, 89, 91, 93; LarDcSc; MajTwCW; McGMS 80; ThTwC 87; WhoAm 74, 76, 78, 80, 82, 84, 86, 88, 90, 92, 94, 95, 96, 97; WhoE 86, 89, 93, 95, 97; WhoFrS 84; WhoScEn 94, 96; WhoTech 89; WhoThSc 1996; WhoWor 95, 96, 97; WrDr 88, 92*

Wilson, Ellen Axson
[Mrs. Woodrow Wilson]
American. First Lady
Prodded Congress to improve Washington, DC slums; first wife of Woodrow Wilson.
b. May 15, 1860 in Savannah, Georgia
d. Aug 6, 1914 in Washington, District of Columbia
Source: *BioAmW; FacPr 89; NatCAB 19; NotAW; WhAm 1; WomWWA 14*

Wilson, Erica
English. Author
Owner, Erica Wilson Needle Works retail stores; wrote *Erica Wilson's Embroidery,* 1979.
b. 1929? in Shropshire, England
Source: *BioIn 14, 16; ConAu 7NR, 23NR, 53; InWom SUP; NewYTBE 71; SmATA 51*

Wilson, Flip
[Clerow Wilson]
American. Actor, Comedian
Star of TV series "The Flip Wilson Show," 1970-74; best known character, Geraldine.
b. Dec 8, 1933 in Jersey City, New Jersey
Source: *AfrAmAl 6; BioIn 8, 9, 10, 16; BkPepl; BlksAmF; BlueB 76; CelR; ConTFT 3; CurBio 69; DcTwCCu 5; DrBlPA, 90; Ebony 1; EncAFC; HalFC 80, 84, 88; InB&W 80, 85; IntMPA 77, 80, 84, 86, 88, 92, 94, 96; JoeFr; LegTOT; NegAl 76, 83, 89; NewYTBE 71; VarWW 85; WhoAfA 96; WhoAm 74, 76, 78, 80, 82, 84, 86, 88, 92, 94; WhoBlA 75, 77, 80, 85, 88, 90, 92; WhoCom; WhoEnt 92; WhoHol 92, A; WorAl; WorAlBi*

Wilson, Gahan
American. Author, Cartoonist
Known for macabre cartoons in magazines, books; collections include *Is Nothing Sacred?,* 1982; *Gahan Wilson's America,* 1985.
b. Feb 18, 1930 in Evanston, Illinois
Source: *BiDScF; BioIn 12, 13, 14, 15; ConAu 19NR, 25R; ConGrA 2; IlsBYP; IntvTCA 2; LegTOT; PenEncH; PrintW 85; ScF&FL 92; SmATA 27, 35; WhoAm 78, 80, 82, 84, 86, 88, 92, 94, 95, 96, 97; WorECar*

Wilson, Hack
[Lewis Robert Wilson]
American. Baseball Player
Outfielder, 1923-34; holds ML record for RBIs in season, 190, 1930; had .307 lifetime batting average; Hall of Fame, 1979.
b. Apr 26, 1900 in Ellwood City, Pennsylvania
d. Nov 23, 1948 in Baltimore, Maryland
Source: *Ballpl 90; BiDAmSp BB; BioIn 1, 3, 11, 14, 15, 17; LegTOT; WhoProB 73; WhoSpor*

Wilson, (James) Harold, Sir
English. Statesman
British Prime Minister, 1964-70, 1974-76.
b. Mar 11, 1916 in Huddersfield, England
d. May 24, 1995 in London, England
Source: *BioIn 1, 2, 5, 6, 7, 8, 9, 10, 11, 12, 14, 15, 16, 18, 19, 20, 21; BlueB 76; ColdWar 1, 2; ConAu 16NR, 53, 148; CopCroC; CurBio 63, 78, 95N; DcPol; DcTwHis; EncCW; FacFETw; HisDBrE; HisWorL; IntAu&W 91, 93; IntWW 74, 75, 76, 77, 78, 79, 80, 81, 82, 83, 91; IntYB 78, 79, 80, 81, 82; LinLib L, S; McGEWB; NewYTBE 70, 72; NewYTBS 74, 76, 95; PolLCWE; WhDW; Who 74, 83, 90; WhoAm 74; WhoWor 74, 76, 78; WorAl; WorAlBi; WrDr 80, 82, 84, 86, 88, 90, 92, 94, 96*

Wilson, Hazel Hutchins
American. Children's Author
Series on Herbert character includes *Herbert's Space Trip,* 1965; *Herbert's Stilts,* 1972.
b. Apr 8, 1898 in Portland, Maine
d. Aug 20, 1992 in Bethesda, Maryland
Source: *ArtsAmW 2; AuBYP 2; BioIn 19; ConAu 1R, 6NR, 139; DcWomA; SmATA 3, 73; WrDr 86, 88*

Wilson, Henry
American. US Vice President
VP under U S Grant, 1873-77.
b. Feb 16, 1812 in Farmington, New Hampshire
d. Nov 10, 1875 in Washington, District of Columbia
Source: *Alli, SUP; AmAu&B; AmBi; AmPolLe; ApCAB; BiAUS; BiD&SB; BiDrAC; BiDrUSC 89; BiDrUSE 71, 89; BioIn 1, 4, 7, 8, 9, 10, 14, 16; CyAL 2; DcAmAu; DcAmB; DcAmSR; DcAmTB; DcBiPP; DcNAA; Dis&D; Drake; EncAAH; HarEnUS; LegTOT; McGEWB; NatCAB 4; PolPar; TwCBDA; VicePre; WebAB 74, 79; WhAm HS; WhAmP; WhCiWar*

Wilson, Henry Braid
American. Naval Officer
Led patrol force of Atlantic fleet, 1917-18; commander in chief, 1919-21.
b. Feb 23, 1861 in Camden, New Jersey
d. Jan 30, 1954 in New York, New York
Source: *BioIn 3; WebAMB; WebBD 83; WhAm 3*

Wilson, Jackie
"Mr. Excitement"
American. Singer
Hits include "Lonely Teardrops," 1959; "Higher and Higher," 1967.
b. Jun 9, 1932 in Detroit, Michigan
d. Jan 21, 1984 in Mount Holly, New Jersey
Source: *BiDAmM; BioIn 12; EncPR&S 74; InB&W 80; LegTOT; NewYTBS 84; WhoRock 81*

Wilson, James
American. Supreme Court Justice, Continental Congressman
Served 1789-98; appointed by Washington; signed Declaration of Independence, 1776.
b. Sep 14, 1742 in Fifeshire, Scotland
d. Aug 21, 1798 in Edenton, North Carolina
Source: *Alli; AmAu&B; AmBi; AmJust; AmWrBE; ApCAB, X; BenetAL 91; BiAUS; BiDFedJ; BiDrAC; BiDrUSC 89; BioIn 2, 3, 4, 5, 7, 8, 9, 10, 11, 12, 15, 16; BlkwCE; BlkwEAR; CyAG; DcAmB; DcNAA; Drake; EncAB-H 1974, 1996; EncAR; EncCRAm; HarEnUS; McGEWB; NatCAB 1; OxCAmH; OxCAmL 65, 83, 95; OxCLaw; OxCSupC; REnAL; SupCtJu; TwCBDA; WebAB 74, 79; WhAm HS; WhAmP; WhAmRev*

Wilson, Jerry
American. Inventor
Took over open market area of home exercise equipment with Soloflex, Inc., 1978.
b. 1944?
Source: *BioIn 15; ConNews 86-2*

Wilson, John Johnston
American. Lawyer
Represented Haldeman, Ehrlichman in Watergate hearings, 1973.
b. Jul 25, 1901 in Washington, District of Columbia
d. May 18, 1986 in Washington, District of Columbia
Source: *BioIn 9, 10, 14, 15; WhoAm 74, 76, 78, 80, 82, 84; WhoAmL 78, 79*

Wilson, Julie
American. Singer, Actor
NYC cabaret performer.
b. Oct 21, 1924 in Omaha, Nebraska
Source: *BioIn 15; CelR 90; ConTFT 9; WhoHol 92*

Wilson, Kemmons
American. Hotel Executive
Opened first Holiday Inn, 1952; formed Holiday Inns of America, 1953; chm., CEO until 1979.
b. Jan 5, 1913 in Osceola, Arkansas
Source: *BiDAmBL 83; BioIn 7, 9, 10, 12, 14, 16; BlueB 76; CelR; CurBio 73; Dun&B 79, 86, 88, 90; St&PR 75, 84, 87, 91, 93, 96, 97; WhoAm 74, 76, 78, 80, 82, 84; WhoFI 74, 79; WhoSSW 73; WorAl; WorAlBi*

Wilson, Kenneth Geddes
American. Physicist
Developed renormalization method for physical systems; won Nobel Prize, 1982.
b. Jun 8, 1936 in Waltham, Massachusetts
Source: *AmMWSc 73P, 76P, 79, 82, 86, 89, 92, 95; BioIn 10, 12, 13, 15, 20; CamDcSc; CurBio 83; IntWW 93; LarDcSc; NewYTBS 82; NobelP; Who 85, 88, 90, 92, 94; WhoAm 84, 86, 88, 90, 92, 94, 95, 96, 97; WhoCanF 86; WhoE 83, 85, 89; WhoFrS 84; WhoMW 90, 92, 93, 96; WhoNob, 90, 95; WhoScEn 94, 96; WhoTech 89; WhoWor 84, 87, 89, 91, 93, 95, 96, 97; WorAlBi*

Wilson, Lanford
American. Dramatist
Won Pulitzer Prize, 1980, for *Talley's Folly.*
b. Apr 13, 1937 in Lebanon, Missouri
Source: *Benet 87, 96; BenetAL 91; BioIn 10, 11, 12, 13, 15, 16, 18; CamGWoT; CelR 90; ConAu 3BS, 17R, 45NR; ConDr 73, 77, 82, 88; ConLC 7, 14, 36; ConTFT 1, 3; CrtSuDr; CurBio 79; CyWA 89; DcLB 7; DcTwCCu 1; EncWL 3; IntAu&W 91, 93; LegTOT; McGEWD 84; ModAL S2; NatPD 77, 81; NotNAT; OxCAmL 83, 95; OxCAmT 84; RAdv 14, 13-2; WhoAm 74, 76, 78, 80, 82, 84, 86, 88, 90, 92, 94, 95, 96, 97; WhoEnt 92; WhoThe 72, 77, 81; WorAlBi; WorAu 1975; WrDr 76, 80, 82, 84, 86, 88, 90, 92, 94, 96*

Wilson, Larry
[Lawrence Frank Wilson]
American. Football Player
Defensive back, St. Louis Cardinals, 1960-72; known for safety blitz; Hall of Fame, 1978.
b. Mar 24, 1938 in Rigby, Idaho
Source: *BiDAmSp FB; BioIn 16, 17; Law&B 89B; LegTOT; WhoAm 84, 86, 88, 92, 94, 95, 96, 97; WhoFtbl 74; WhoSpor; WhoWest 92*

Wilson, Logan
American. Educator, Sociologist
Educational innovator; introduced first racial integration in higher learning systems as pres. of the U of Texas, 1954-61.
b. Mar 6, 1907 in Huntsville, Texas
d. Nov 7, 1990 in Austin, Texas
Source: *AmMWSc 73S; BioIn 4, 5, 6, 12, 17; ConAu 45; CurBio 91N; LEduc 74; NewYTBS 90; WhAm 10; WhE&EA; WhoAm 74, 76; WhoSSW 80, 82, 84; WhoWor 78*

Wilson, Louis Hugh
American. Army Officer
Marine Corps commandant, 1975-79.
b. Feb 11, 1920 in Brandon, Mississippi
Source: *BioIn 10, 17, 19; IntWW 76, 77, 78, 79, 80, 81, 82, 83, 91, 93; MedHR, 94; NewYTBS 75; St&PR 91; WebAMB; WhoAm 74, 76, 78, 80, 82; WhoGov 77; WhoWor 78; WorDWW*

Wilson, Lyle Campbell
American. Journalist
Washington general mgr., UPI, 1943-64.
b. Aug 2, 1899 in Topeka, Kansas
d. May 23, 1967 in Stuart, Florida
Source: *BiDAmNC; BioIn 6, 7; EncAB-A 40; EncTwCJ; WhAm 4*

Wilson, Malcolm
[Charles Malcolm Wilson]
American. Politician
Rep. lt. governor of NY, 1959-73; assumed governorship after Nelson Rockefeller's resignation, 1973; defeated by Hugh Carey, 1974.
b. Feb 26, 1914 in New York, New York
Source: *AmCath 80; BiDrGov 1789; BioIn 5, 10; BlueB 76; CurBio 74; NewYTBE 72, 73; NewYTBS 76; St&PR 84, 87, 91, 93; WhoAm 74, 76, 80, 82, 84, 86, 88, 90, 92, 94, 95; WhoAmP 73, 75, 77, 79; WhoE 74, 75, 77, 79, 89; WhoFI 85, 87, 89; WhoGov 72, 75*

Wilson, Margaret
American. Author, Missionary
Novels from women's perspective include 1924 Pulitzer winner, *The Able McLaughlins.*
b. Jan 16, 1882 in Traer, Iowa
d. Oct 6, 1973 in Droitwich, England

Source: *AmAu&B; BenetAL 91; BioIn 12; ConAu 113; DcLB 9; FacFETw; FemiCLE; InWom SUP; LegTOT; OxCAmL 65, 83; REnAL; TwCA*

Wilson, Marie (Katherine Elizabeth)
American. Actor
Starred on film, radio, TV, as "My Friend Irma."
b. Aug 19, 1916 in Anaheim, California
d. Nov 23, 1972 in Hollywood Hills, California
Source: *BioIn 1, 2, 9, 15; DcAmB S9; EncAFC; FilmEn; FilmgC; FunnyW; HalFC 80, 84, 88; InWom, SUP; LegTOT; MotPP; MovMk; NewYTBE 72; SaTiSS; ThFT; What 3; WhoHol B; WhScrn 77, 83; WorAl*

Wilson, Mary
[The Supremes]
American. Singer
Original member of 1960s-70s pop group; hits include "Where Did Our Love Go?," 1964.
b. Mar 6, 1944 in Greenville, Mississippi
Source: *AfrAmAl 6; BioIn 13, 15, 17, 20; ConTFT 4; DcLP 87B; DcWomA; DrBlPA, 90; Ebony 1; InB&W 80, 85; InWom SUP; LegTOT; PenNWW A; WhoBlA 75, 77, 80, 85, 88, 90, 92; WhoRocM 82; WrDr 86, 92*

Wilson, Michael (Holcombe)
Canadian. Politician, Businessman
Canadian finance minister 1984-91.
b. Nov 4, 1937 in Toronto, Ontario, Canada
Source: *BioIn 15; CanWW 31, 89; CurBio 90; IntWW 89, 91, 93; NewYTBS 86; WhoAm 80, 82, 84, 86, 88, 92; WhoCan 77, 82, 84; WhoCanF 86; WhoE 86, 89, 91, 93; WhoFI 85, 96; WhoWor 87, 89, 91, 93, 95, 96, 97*

Wilson, Mitchell A
American. Author
Novels about scientists were popular in USSR: *Live with Lightning,* 1949.
b. Jul 17, 1913 in New York, New York
d. Feb 26, 1973 in New York, New York
Source: *AmAu&B; AmNov; BioIn 2, 5, 6, 9; ConAu 1R, 3NR; ConNov 72; NewYTBE 72, 73; OxCAmL 83*

Wilson, Nancy
American. Singer
Hit singles since 1963 include "Tell Me the Truth," 1963; "Face It Girl, It's Over," 1968.
b. Feb 20, 1937 in Chillicothe, Ohio
Source: *AllMusG; Baker 84; BiDAfM; BiDAmM; BiDJaz; BioIn 9, 10, 12, 15; BlkWAm; CelR; ConBlB 10; ConMus 14; DcTwCCu 5; DrBlPA, 90; EncJzS; IlEncBM 82; InWom, SUP; LegTOT; NewGrDA 86; NewGrDJ 88; NotBlAW 1; PenEncP; RkOn 82; WhoAfA 96; WhoAm 74, 76, 78, 80, 82, 84, 86, 88, 90, 92, 94, 95, 96, 97; WhoAmW 68, 70, 72, 74, 81, 83; WhoBlA 75, 77, 80, 85, 88, 90, 92, 94; WhoEnt 92*

Wilson, Nancy
American. Singer, Musician
Featured guitarist with Heart since 1972.
b. Mar 16, 1954 in San Francisco, California
Source: *BioIn 13; LegTOT; OnThGG; WhoRocM 82*

Wilson, Pete Barton
American. Politician
Rep governor, CA, 1991—; senator, 1983-91, mayor of San Diego, 1971-83.
b. Aug 23, 1933 in Lake Forest, Illinois
Source: *AlmAP 88, 92; BiDrUSC 89; BioIn 13, 16; CngDr 87, 89; CurBio 91; IntWW 91; News 92; PolsAm 84; WhoAm 86, 90; WhoAmL 87; WhoAmP 87, 91; WhoWest 92; WhoWor 91; WorAlBi*

Wilson, Peter Cecil
English. Business Executive
Chm., Sotheby auction house, 1958-80.
b. Mar 8, 1913 in Yorkshire, England
d. Jun 3, 1984 in Paris, France
Source: *BioIn 6, 7, 8, 12; BlueB 76; ConAu 113; ConNews 85-2; CurBio 68, 84; DcNaB 1981; IntWW 74, 75, 76, 77, 78, 79, 80, 81, 82, 83; NewYTBS 79; WhAm 9; Who 74, 82, 83; WhoAm 78, 80, 82, 84; WhoWor 74*

Wilson, Phill
American. AIDS Activist
Director of public policy, AIDS Project Los Angeles, 1992—.
b. Apr 22, 1956 in Chicago, Illinois
Source: *ConBlB 9*

Wilson, Ransom
American. Musician
Flutist; founder of Solisti New York, 1981; performs as a soloist with world's leading chamber orchestras.
b. Oct 25, 1951 in Tuscaloosa, Alabama
Source: *Baker 84, 92; BioIn 12, 13, 15; ConMus 5; WhoAmM 83*

Wilson, Richard
American. Producer, Director
Founded Mercury Theater in 1930s with Orson Welles and John Houseman; worked on Welles' films, radio shows until 1951; directed film *Three in the Attic,* 1968.
b. Dec 25, 1915 in McKeesport, Pennsylvania
d. Aug 21, 1991 in Santa Monica, California
Source: *BioIn 17, 19; FilmEn; FilmgC; GangFlm; HalFC 80, 84, 88; IntMPA 75, 76, 77, 78, 79, 80, 81, 82, 84, 86, 88; MiSFD 9N; NewYTBS 91; WorEFlm*

Wilson, Robert M
American. Dramatist, Producer
Won special Obie for *The Life and Times of Joseph Stalin,* 1974; has won many awards for contributions to theater.
b. Oct 4, 1944 in Waco, Texas
Source: *BenetAL 91; ConArt 83, 89; ConAu 2NR, 49; ConDr 82, 88; ConTFT 5; CurBio 79; IntvTCA 2; MajTwCW; NotNAT; WhoAm 86, 90; WhoE 86; WhoEnt 92; WrDr 82*

Wilson, Robert R
American. Physicist, Sculptor
Designer of Fermi National Accelerator Laboratory.
b. Mar 4, 1914 in Frontier, Wyoming
Source: *AmMWSc 92; BioIn 9, 10, 11, 13, 14, 16; CurBio 89; IntWW 89; WhoAm 86; WhoTech 89*

Wilson, Robert Woodrow
American. Physicist
With Arno Penzias, shared 1978 Nobel Prize in physics for researching "big bang" theory of creation.
b. Jan 10, 1936 in Houston, Texas
Source: *AmMWSc 73P, 76P, 79, 82, 86, 89, 92, 95; BiESc; BioIn 11, 12, 14, 15, 20; CamDcSc; IntWW 79, 80, 81, 82, 83, 89, 91, 93; LarDcSc; McGMS 80; NotTwCS; Who 82, 83, 85, 88, 90, 92, 94; WhoAm 78, 80, 82, 84, 86, 88, 90, 92, 94, 95, 96, 97; WhoE 79, 81, 83, 85, 86, 89, 91, 93, 95, 97; WhoFrS 84; WhoNob, 90, 95; WhoScEn 94, 96; WhoWor 80, 82, 84, 87, 89, 91, 93, 95, 96, 97; WorAlBi*

Wilson, Samuel
"Uncle Sam"
American. Merchant
Meat packer whose nickname became synonymous with US during War of 1812; inspected, stamped meat barrels for govt.
b. Sep 16, 1766 in Arlington, Massachusetts
d. Jul 31, 1854 in Troy, New York
Source: *BioIn 2, 4, 5, 6, 11, 12; DcAmB; WebAB 74, 79; WebBD 83; WhAm HS; WhAmRev*

Wilson, Sandy
[Alexander Galbraith Wilson]
American. Dramatist, Composer
Wrote play *The Boy Friend,* 1953.
b. May 19, 1924 in Sale, England
Source: *Au&Wr 71; BestMus; BiE&WWA; BioIn 3, 10, 12; BlueB 76; ConDr 73, 77D, 82D, 88D; DcLEL 1940; EncMT; EncWT; HalFC 80, 84, 88; IntAu&W 76, 77, 82, 89, 91, 93; IntWW 74, 75, 76, 77, 78, 79, 80, 81, 82, 83, 89, 91, 93; IntWWM 90; NewGrDM 80; NewOxM; NotNAT, A; OxCPMus; ScF&FL 1; Who 74, 82, 83, 85, 88, 90, 92, 94; WhoThe 72, 77, 81; WhoWor 74, 76, 78; WrDr 76, 80, 82, 84, 86, 88, 90, 92, 94, 96*

Wilson, Sarah
[Marchioness de Waldegrave]
English. Imposter
Escaped US indentured servitude to pose as sister of Queen Charlotte of England.
b. 1750 in Staffordshire, England
Source: *CarSB; DcCanB 6; FolkA 87; InWom SUP; NotAW*

Wilson, Sloan
American. Author
Best known for novels *The Man in the Gray Flannel Suit,* I and II, 1955, 1983.
b. May 8, 1920 in Norwalk, Connecticut
Source: *AmAu&B; Benet 87; BenetAL 91; BioIn 4, 5, 7, 10, 11; ConAu 1NR, 1R, 44NR; ConLC 32; ConNov 72, 76, 82, 86, 91, 96; CurBio 59; DcLEL 1940; IntAu&W 76, 77; LegTOT; Novels; PenC AM; PolProf E; REnAL; WhoAm 74, 76, 78, 80, 82, 84, 86, 88, 90, 92, 94, 95, 96, 97; WorAl; WorAu 1950; WrDr 76, 80, 82, 84, 86, 88, 90, 92, 94, 96*

Wilson, Sunnie
[William Nathaniel Wilson]
American. Entertainer, Entrepreneur, Impresario
Promoter of stage shows and boxing matches, 1950s; political consultant for the mayoral campaigns of Detroit Mayor Coleman A. Young, 1972-88.
b. Oct 7, 1908 in Columbia, South Carolina
Source: *BioIn 20; ConBlB 7*

Wilson, Teddy
[Theodore Wilson]
American. Jazz Musician
Pianist who played with Benny Goodman, 1935-39; one of first blacks to be accepted playing with white musicians.
b. Nov 24, 1912 in Austin, Texas
d. Jul 31, 1986 in New Britain, Connecticut
Source: *AfrAmAl 6; AllMusG; AnObit 1986; ASCAP 66, 80; Baker 84, 92; BgBands 74; BiDAfM; BiDAmM; BiDJaz; BioIn 4, 10, 11, 12, 13, 14, 15, 16; CmpEPM; DcArts; DcTwCCu 5; DrBlPA, 90; EncJzS; FacFETw; IlEncJ; NegAl 89; NewAmDM; NewGrDA 86; NewGrDJ 88, 94; NewGrDM 80; NewYTBS 74, 86; OxCPMus; PenEncP; WhoBlA 75, 77, 80, 85; WhoHol A; WhoJazz 72*

Wilson, Theodore Roosevelt
American. Actor
Has had supporting roles in films: *The River Niger,* 1976; TV shows include *That's My Mama,* 1974-75.
b. Dec 10, 1943 in New York, New York
d. Jul 21, 1991 in Los Angeles, California
Source: *VarWW 85; WhoBlA 80, 85*

Wilson, Tom
American. Cartoonist
Created "Ziggy" comic strip; syndicated since 1971.
b. Aug 1, 1931 in Grant Town, West Virginia
Source: *BioIn 14; ConAu 106; SmATA 30, 33; WhoAm 74, 76, 78, 80, 82, 84, 86, 88, 92, 94, 95, 96, 97; WhoAmA 86, 89, 91, 93*

Wilson, William Griffith
American. Social Reformer
Co-founder with Dr. Robert H. Smith (Dr. Bob) of Alcoholics Anonymous (AA).
b. Nov 26, 1895 in East Dorset, Vermont
d. Jan 24, 1971 in Miami Beach, Florida
Source: *AmSocL; BioIn 9, 15, 16, 17, 18, 19, 20; ConHero 2; DcAmB S9; DcAmTB; WorAl; WorAlBi*

Wilson, William Julius
American. Sociologist
Author of *Power, Racism, and Privilege,* 1973; *When Work Disappears,* 1987.
b. Dec 20, 1935 in Derry Township, Pennsylvania
Source: *AmMWSc 73S; News 97-1; RAdv 14; SelBAAf; WhoAfA 96; WhoAm 80, 82, 84, 86, 88, 90, 92, 94, 95, 96, 97; WhoBlA 80, 85, 88, 90, 92, 94; WrDr 92, 94, 96*

Wilson, Willie James
American. Baseball Player
Outfielder, KC, 1976-90; Oakland, 1991-92; Chicago Cubs, 1992—; led AL in runs scored, 1980, in batting, 1982; jailed three mos. on cocaine charges.
b. Jul 9, 1955 in Montgomery, Alabama
Source: *Ballpl 90; BaseReg 86, 87; BiDAmSp BB; BioIn 13, 14, 15; InB&W 85; WhoAfA 96; WhoBlA 85, 94*

Wilson, Woodrow
[Thomas Woodrow Wilson]
American. US President
Dem., 28th pres., 1913-21; WW I leader awarded Nobel Peace Prize for Versailles Treaty, 1919; domestic reforms included 1914 creation of Federal Researve.
b. Dec 28, 1856 in Staunton, Virginia
d. Feb 3, 1924 in Washington, District of Columbia
Source: *Alli SUP; AmAu&B; AmBi; AmDec 1910; AmJust; AmLY; AmOrTwC; AmPeW; AmPolLe; ApCAB, X; BbD; Benet 87; BenetAL 91; BiDAmEd; BiD&SB; BiDInt; BiDrAC; BiDrGov 1789; BiDrUSE 71, 89; BiDSA; BioIn 1, 2, 3, 4, 5, 6, 7, 8, 9, 10, 11, 12, 13, 14, 15, 16, 17, 18, 19, 20, 21; Chambr 3; CopCroC; CyAG; DcAmAu; DcAmB; DcAmC; DcAmSR; DcLB 47; DcLEL; DcNAA; DcTwHis; Dis&D; EncAAH; EncAB-H 1974, 1996; EncSoH; EvLB; FacFETw; FacPr 89, 93; HarEnUS; HealPre; HisEAAC; HisWorL; LegTOT; LinLib L, S; LngCTC; McGEWB; MemAm; NatCAB 19; NobelP; OxCAmH; OxCAmL 65, 83; OxCLaw; PolPar; RAdv 13-3; RComAH; REn; REnAL; TwCBDA; WebAB 74, 79; WebBD 83; WhAm 1, 4A, HSA; WhAmP; WhDW; WhoNob, 90, 95; WorAl; WorAlBi*

Wilson Phillips
[Chynna Phillips; Carnie Wilson; Wendy Wilson]
American. Music Group
Pop singing trio, first album *Wilson Phillips,* 1990 contains *Hold On, a Reason to Believe,* and *Eyes Like Twins.*
Source: *BioIn 15, 16, 17, 18, 20, 21; ConMus 5; EncRkSt*

Wilt, Fred(erick Loren)
American. Track Athlete
Won several NCAA titles and set many American records; National Track and Field Hall of Fame, 1981.
b. Dec 14, 1920
d. Aug 31, 1994 in Anderson, Indiana
Source: *BiDAmSp Sup; BioIn 2, 3, 20; ConAu 9NR, 57; CurBio 94N; IndAu 1967*

Wimsatt, William Kurtz, Jr.
American. Author, Critic, Educator
Yale U English professor, 1955-75; wrote *Literary Criticism, Idea and Act,* 1974.
b. Nov 17, 1907 in Washington, District of Columbia
d. Dec 17, 1975 in New Haven, Connecticut
Source: *AmAu&B; BioIn 1, 5, 10, 11; BlueB 76; CasWL; CathA 1930; ConAu 1R, 3NR, 61; DcAmB S9; DrAS 74E; NewYTBS 75; PenC AM; RAdv 14; WhAm 6, 7; WhoAm 74, 76; WhoTwCL; WorAu 1950; WrDr 76*

Wincelberg, Shimon
German. Writer
TV shows include "Gunsmoke"; "Star Trek"; "Police Woman."
b. Sep 26, 1924 in Kiel, Germany
Source: *BiE&WWA; ConAu 45, 46NR; NatPD 77, 81; NotNAT; VarWW 85; WhoWorJ 72, 78*

Winchell, Paul
American. Ventriloquist, Actor
Had TV show with dummy, "The Paul Winchell-Jerry Mahoney Show," 1950-54; voice of "Smurfs" cartoon show.
b. Dec 21, 1922 in New York, New York
Source: *BioIn 1; ConTFT 9; IntMPA 92, 96; LegTOT; VarWW 85; WhoAm 74, 76, 78, 80, 82, 84, 86, 88, 92; WhoEnt 92; WhoHol 92, A; WorAl*

Winchell, Walter
American. Journalist
First of modern gossip columnists; had popular syndicated column, radio show, 1930s-50s; known for aggressive style, use of slang.

b. Apr 7, 1897 in New York, New York
d. Feb 20, 1972 in Los Angeles, California
Source: *AmAu&B; AmDec 1920, 1930; ASCAP 66; BiDAmJo; BiDAmNC; BiDD; BioIn 1, 2, 3, 4, 5, 8, 9, 10, 11, 12, 16, 17, 18, 20, 21; ConAu 33R, 101; CopCroC; CurBio 43, 72N; DcAmB S9; DcLB 29; EncAJ; EncTwCJ; FacFETw; FilmgC; HalFC 80, 84, 88; JrnUS; LegTOT; LinLib L, S; NewYTET; NotNAT, A, B; ObitT 1971; OxCAmT 84; PlP&P; PolProf T; RadStar; REnAL; WebAB 74, 79; WhAm 5; WhJnl; WhoHol B; WhScrn 77, 83; WhThe; WorAl; WorAlBi*

Winchester, Jesse (James Ridout)
Canadian. Singer, Songwriter
Wrote pop songs, 1970s, that became hits for others: "Brand New Tennessee Waltz," "Isn't That So"; moved to Canada to avoid draft, 1967.
b. May 17, 1944 in Bossier City, Louisiana
Source: *BioIn 11, 14; EncFCWM 83; IlEncRk; PenEncP; RkOn 85; RolSEnR 83; WhoAm 82*

Winchester, Oliver Fisher
American. Industrialist
Bought arms manufacturing co., 1857; name associated with co.'s repeating rifle, Winchester 73.
b. Nov 30, 1810 in Boston, Massachusetts
d. Dec 11, 1880 in New Haven, Connecticut
Source: *AmBi; ApCAB; BioIn 18; DcAmB; EncAAH; HarEnUS; LegTOT; NatCAB 11; WebAB 74, 79; WebBD 83; WhAm HS; WhCiWar*

Wind, Herbert Warren
American. Journalist, Author
On staff of *New Yorker* mag., 1947-54, 1962-90; has written numerous books on golf.
b. Aug 11, 1916 in Brockton, Massachusetts
Source: *ConAu 1R, 6NR; DcLB 171; WhoAm 80, 82, 90, 92, 94, 95, 96, 97; WhoGolf*

Windaus, Adolf Otto Reinhold
German. Chemist
Won Nobel Prize in chemistry, 1928, for research of sterols; discovered histamine; worked in chemotherapy.
b. Dec 25, 1876 in Berlin, Germany
d. Jun 9, 1959 in Gottingen, Germany (West)
Source: *AsBiEn; BiESc; DcScB; Dis&D; WhoNob, 90, 95*

Windgassen, Wolfgang Friedrich Hermann
German. Opera Singer
Leading post-War Heldentenor; at Bayreuth Festival, 1951-70.
b. Jun 26, 1914 in Annemasse, Germany
d. Sep 8, 1974 in Stuttgart, Germany (West)
Source: *Baker 84; IntWW 74; MusSN; NewYTBS 74; WhAm 6; WhoWor 74*

Winding, Kai Chresten
American. Jazz Musician
Instrumental in creating Be-Bop style of jazz; leading trombonist, 1940s-50s'; with World's Greatest Jazz Band, 1960s.
b. May 18, 1922 in Aarhus, Denmark
d. May 6, 1983 in Yonkers, New York
Source: *ASCAP 80; BiDAmM; BiDJaz; EncJzS; NewYTBS 83; RkOn 78; WhoAm 74*

Windom, William
American. Actor
Starred in "The Farmer's Daughter," 1962-65; "My World and Welcome to It," 1969-70.
b. Sep 28, 1923 in New York, New York
Source: *BiDrUSC 89; BiDrUSE 89; BiE&WWA; ConTFT 2, 7; FilmgC; ForYSC; HalFC 80, 84, 88; IntMPA 92, 94, 96; LegTOT; NotNAT; PeoHis; WhoAm 74, 76, 78, 80, 82, 84, 86, 88, 92, 94; WhoEnt 92; WhoHol 92, A; WorAl; WorAlBi*

Windsor, Claire
[Claire Viola Cronk]
American. Actor
Starred in 45 silent films, 1920-29.
b. Apr 14, 1897 in Coffee City, Kansas
d. Oct 24, 1972 in Los Angeles, California
Source: *BioIn 8, 9, 10; Film 1, 2; FilmEn; ForYSC; HalFC 84; InWom SUP; MovMk; NewYTBE 72; SilFlmP; SmATA X; TwYS; What 2; WhScrn 77, 83*

Windsor, Marie
[Emily Marie Bertelson]
American. Actor
Known for supporting roles in films: *Outpost in Morocco,* 1949; *Support Your Local Gunfighter,* 1971.
b. Dec 11, 1924 in Marysvale, Utah
Source: *FilmgC; HalFC 84, 88; IntMPA 75, 76, 77, 78, 79, 80, 81, 82, 84, 86, 88; MotPP; MovMk; WhoHol 92, A*

Wine, Sherwin T(heodore)
American. Clergy
Founded Humanistic Judaism, 1963; rabbi, Birmingham (MI) Temple, 1964—.
b. Jan 25, 1928 in Detroit, Michigan
Source: *ConAu 93; WhoAm 74, 76, 78, 80, 82, 84, 86, 88, 90, 92, 94, 95, 96, 97; WhoAmJ 80; WhoMW 88; WhoRel 85, 92*

Winebrenner, John
American. Clergy
Organized church, 1830; published *Church Advocate,* 1846-47; wrote religious books.
b. Mar 25, 1797 in Walkerville, Maryland
d. Sep 12, 1860 in Harrisburg, Pennsylvania
Source: *AmBi; ApCAB; BiDAmCu; BiDSA; BioIn 10; DcAmAu; DcAmB; DcNAA; Drake; LuthC 75; NatCAB 1; WhAm HS*

Winfield, Dave
[David Mark Winfield]
American. Baseball Player
Outfielder, 1973—; led NL in RBIs, 1979; also drafted by pro basketball, football teams; commentator, Fox Broadcasting Co., 1996—.
b. Oct 3, 1951 in Saint Paul, Minnesota
Source: *AfrAmSG; Ballpl 90; BaseReg 86, 87; BiDAmSp BB; BioIn 12, 13, 14, 15, 16, 17, 18, 19, 20, 21; CelR 90; ConBlB 5; CurBio 84; InB&W 85; LegTOT; NegAl 89; NewYTBS 80, 81, 85, 90; WhoAfA 96; WhoAm 82, 84, 86, 88, 90, 92, 94, 95, 96, 97; WhoBlA 88, 92, 94; WhoE 86, 89; WhoMW 93, 96; WhoSpor; WhoWest 92*

Winfield, Paul Edward
American. Actor
Oscar nominee for *Sounder,* 1973; Emmy nominee for *King,* 1978; *Roots II,* 1980.
b. May 22, 1941 in Los Angeles, California
Source: *BioIn 16; BlksAmF; ConBlB 2; ConTFT 6; DrBlPA 90; HalFC 84, 88; InB&W 80, 85; IntMPA 92; MovMk; WhoAfA 96; WhoAm 78, 80, 82, 84, 86, 88, 92, 94, 95, 96, 97; WhoBlA 92, 94; WhoEnt 92; WhoHol A; WorAl; WorAlBi*

Winfrey, Oprah Gail
American. TV Personality, Actor
Nationally syndicated talk show has won three daytime Emmy Awards; received Oscar nomination for role of Sophia in *The Color Purple,* 1985.
b. Jan 29, 1954 in Kosciusko, Mississippi
Source: *AfrAmBi 1; BioIn 14, 15, 16; ConBlB 2; ConNews 86-4; ConTFT 3, 9; CurBio 87; DrBlPA 90; HalFC 88; IntMPA 92; IntWW 91; LesBEnT; NewYTBS 86, 89; NotBlAW 1; WhoAmW 89; WhoBlA 88, 92; WhoEnt 92; WhoMW 92*

Wingate, Orde Charles
English. Army Officer
Expert on mobile tactics; active in China, Burma campaigns, WW II.
b. Feb 26, 1903 in Naini Tal, India
d. Mar 24, 1944 in Assam, Burma
Source: *BioIn 1, 2, 4, 5, 6, 8, 9, 12, 13, 14, 21; CurBio 44; DcNaB 1941; DcTwHis; GrBr; HarEnMi; HisDBrE; HisEAAC; HisEWW; ObitOF 79; WhoMilH 76; WhThe; WhWW-II; WorAl; WorAlBi*

Winger, Debra
[Mary Debra Winger]
American. Actor
Oscar nominee for *Terms of Endearment,* 1983; also starred in *Urban Cowboy,*

1980; *An Officer and a Gentleman,* 1982; *Shadowlands,* 1994.
b. May 17, 1955 in Cleveland, Ohio
Source: *BiDFilm 94; BioIn 12, 13, 14, 15, 16; CelR 90; ConTFT 2, 6, 13; CurBio 84; HalFC 84, 88; HolBB; IntMPA 88, 92, 94, 96; IntWW 91, 93; InWom SUP; LegTOT; News 94, 94-3; NewYTBS 86; VarWW 85; WhoAm 88, 90, 92, 94, 95, 96, 97; WhoAmW 87, 89, 91, 93, 95; WhoEnt 92; WhoHol 92; WorAlBi*

Wingler, Hans Maria
German. Author
Expert in field of graphic design, architecture; wrote, edited many books on subject.
b. Jan 5, 1920 in Constance, Germany
Source: *BioIn 14; ConAu 14NR; WhoWor 78*

Winkelmann, Hermann
German. Opera Singer
Brilliant tenor of Vienna Opera, 1880-1900; excelled in Wagnerian roles.
b. Mar 8, 1849 in Brunswick, Germany
d. Jan 18, 1912 in Vienna, Austria
Source: *Baker 78, 84, 92; CmOp; MetOEnc; NewEOp 71; NewGrDM 80; NewGrDO; OxDcOp*

Winkler, Henry Franklin
American. Actor
Played Fonzie on TV series "Happy Days," 1974-84.
b. Oct 30, 1945 in New York, New York
Source: *BkPepl; CelR 90; ConTFT 2; CurBio 76; EncAFC; HalFC 88; IntMPA 86, 92; NewYTBS 77; VarWW 85; WhoAm 78, 80, 82, 84, 86, 88, 90, 92, 94, 95, 96, 97; WhoEnt 92; WhoHol A; WhoWor 80; WorAl; WorAlBi*

Winkler, Irwin
American. Producer
Films include *They Shoot Horses Don't They?,* 1969; *Raging Bull,* 1980; *The Right Stuff,* 1983.
b. May 28, 1931 in New York, New York
Source: *BioIn 16; ConTFT 3, 10; HalFC 84, 88; IntDcF 2-4; IntMPA 92, 94, 96; MiSFD 9; WhoAm 78, 80, 82, 84, 86, 88, 90, 92, 94, 95, 96, 97; WhoEnt 92; WhoWest 82, 84, 87, 89, 92*

Winnemucca, Sarah
American. Translator
Served as an interpreter for her father, Chief Winnemucca, during meetings with Native American agents, army officers, and inter-tribal councils.
b. 1844? in Nevada
d. Oct 16, 1891 in Henry's Lake, Idaho
Source: *BioAmW; BioIn 4, 7, 10, 11, 12, 13, 16, 17, 18, 19, 20; ContDcW 89; DcAmB; DcNAL; EncNoAI; EncWHA; GayN; GoodHs; GrLiveH; HerW 84; HisWorL; IntDcWB; InWom SUP; LibW; NatNAL; NotAW; NotNaAm; OxCWoWr 95; RfGAmL 94; WhAm HS; WhNaAH; WomFir; WorAl; WorAlBi*

Winninger, Charles
American. Actor
Played Cap'n Andy in original Broadway production of *Show Boat,* 1927-30.
b. May 26, 1884 in Athens, Wisconsin
d. Jan 1969 in Palm Springs, California
Source: *BiE&WWA; BioIn 8; CmpEPM; EncAFC; EncMT; Film 1, 2; FilmEn; FilmgC; ForYSC; HalFC 80, 84, 88; HolCA; LegTOT; MotPP; MovMk; NotNAT B; OxCAmT 84; OxCPMus; PlP&P; RadStar; Vers A; WhoHol B; WhScrn 74, 77, 83; WhThe; WorAl; WorAlBi*

Winograd, Arthur
American. Conductor
Founder, member, Julliard String Quartet, 1946-55; staff conductor, MGM Records, 1954-58.
b. Apr 22, 1920 in New York, New York
Source: *Baker 78, 84, 92; NewAmDM; NewGrDA 86; PenDiMP; WhoAm 74, 76, 78, 80, 82, 84, 86, 88; WhoAmM 83; WhoE 74, 83, 85, 86*

Winpisinger, William Wayne
"Wimp"; "Wimpy"
American. Labor Union Official
Joined International Assn. of Machinists and Aerospace Workers, 1947; president, 1968-89.
b. Dec 10, 1924 in Cleveland, Ohio
Source: *BioIn 14; CurBio 80; WhoAm 86, 88; WhoE 81, 83; WhoFI 87*

Winship, Elizabeth
American. Author
Books on sex education for adolescents include *Masculinity and Femininity,* 1978.
b. May 17, 1921 in Pittsfield, Massachusetts
Source: *ConAu 41R; PenNWW A; WhoAmW 77*

Winslow, Edward
English. Colonial Figure
Mayflower passenger who governed Plymouth Colony, 1633, 1636, 1644.
b. Oct 18, 1595 in Droitwich, England
d. May 8, 1655
Source: *Alli; AmAu; AmAu&B; AmBi; AmWrBE; ApCAB; BenetAL 91; BiD&SB; BiDrACR; BioIn 2, 3; DcAmAu; DcAmB; DcNaB; Drake; EncCRAm; HarEnUS; LinLib L; McGEWB; NatCAB 1, 7; NewCBEL; OxCAmH; OxCAmL 65, 83, 95; REnAL; TwCBDA; WebAB 74, 79; WhAm HS; WhNaAH; WhWE; WrCNE*

Winslow, Kellen Boswell
American. Football Player
Tight end, San Diego, 1979-87; led NFL in pass receptions, 1980, 1981.
b. Nov 5, 1957 in Saint Louis, Missouri
Source: *BiDAmSp FB; BioIn 13, 15; FootReg 87; NewYTBS 82; WhoAfA 96; WhoAm 84, 86, 88; WhoBlA 85, 88, 90, 92, 94*

Winslow, Ola Elizabeth
American. Author, Educator
Colonial history expert who won Pulitzer for *Johnathan Edwards, 1703-1758,* 1940.
b. 1885 in Grant City, Missouri
d. Sep 27, 1977 in Damariscotta, Maine
Source: *AmWomHi; AmWomWr; BioIn 11; ConAu 1R, 3NR, 73; DcAmB S10; DrAS 74H; InWom SUP; OxCAmL 65, 83; REnAL; TwCA, SUP; WhoAm 74*

Winsor, Justin
American. Historian, Librarian
Founder, first president of American Library Assn., 1876-88; edited eight-vol. *Narrative and Critical History of America,* 1884-89.
b. Jan 22, 1831 in Boston, Massachusetts
d. Oct 22, 1897 in Cambridge, Massachusetts
Source: *Alli, SUP; AmAu; AmAu&B; AmBi; ApCAB; BenetAL 91; BiD&SB; BioIn 1, 2, 3, 6, 10, 11, 12, 13, 15; DcAmAu; DcAmB; DcAmLiB; DcLB 47; DcNAA; Drake; HarEnUS; NatCAB 1; OxCAmH; OxCAmL 65, 83, 95; REnAL; TwCBDA; WebAB 74, 79; WhAm HS*

Winsor, Kathleen
American. Author
Writings include historical novel that took five years, *Forever Amber,* 1944; *Calais,* 1979.
b. Oct 16, 1916 in Olivia, Minnesota
Source: *AmAu&B; AmNov; BenetAL 91; BioIn 14; ConAu 97; CurBio 46; InWom, SUP; LngCTC; REn; REnAL; TwCRHW 90; TwCWr; WhoAm 86, 88, 90; WhoUSWr 88; WhoWrEP 89; WrDr 88, 92*

Winsten, Archer
American. Critic
Movie critic, *NY Post,* 1936-86; documentary script writer, 1944-48.
b. Sep 18, 1904 in Seattle, Washington
d. Feb 21, 1997 in Moreau, New York
Source: *BlueB 76; IntMPA 75, 76, 77, 78, 79, 80, 81, 82; WhoAm 74, 76, 78, 80, 82, 84, 86, 88, 90, 92, 94, 95, 96, 97*

Winston, George
American. Composer, Pianist
Known for acoustic solo piano music; albums include *Autumn,* 1980.
b. 1949 in Hart, Michigan
Source: *BioIn 13, 15, 16; ConMus 9; ConNews 87-1; NewAgMG; WhoAm 94, 95, 96, 97*

Winston, Harry
American. Jeweler
Known for stunning purchases of estate jewelry.
b. Mar 1, 1896 in New York, New York
d. Dec 1978 in New York, New York
Source: *BioIn 5, 7, 11, 12, 14; BlkAWP; CurBio 65, 79N; DcAmB S10; NatCAB 60; NewYTBS 78; WhoAm 74, 76; WhoWor 74; WorAl; WorAlBi*

Winter, Alice Vivian Ames
American. Writer
Pres., General Federation of Women's Clubs, 1920-24; contributing editor, *Ladies Home Journal,* 1924-28.
b. Nov 28, 1865 in Albany, New York
d. Apr 5, 1944 in Pasadena, California
Source: *BiCAW; InWom SUP; NotAW; WhAm 2; WomWWA 14*

Winter, Edgar Holand
[Edgar Winter Group; White Trash]
American. Singer, Musician
Album *They Only Come Out at Night,* 1973, had hit "Frankenstein."
b. Dec 28, 1946 in Beaumont, Texas
Source: *BkPepl; EncPR&S 89; EncRk 88; HarEnR 86; IlEncRk; NewGrDA 86; PenEncP; RkOn 74, 84; WhoAm 82, 84; WhoRocM 82*

Winter, Johnny
[John Dawson Winter, III]
American. Singer, Musician
Noted blues guitarist; produced albums for Muddy Waters.
b. Feb 23, 1944 in Beaumont, Texas
Source: *BioIn 11, 14; BluesWW; ConMuA 80A; ConMus 5; EncPR&S 74, 89; EncRk 88; GuBlues; HarEnR 86; IlEncRk; LegTOT; NewGrDA 86; OnThGG; PenEncP; RkOn 74, 78; RolSEnR 83; WhoAm 76, 78, 80, 82, 84, 86, 88, 90, 92, 94, 95, 96, 97; WhoEnt 92A; WhoRock 81; WhoRocM 82*

Winter, Paul Theodore
American. Musician
Leader of Paul Winter Sextet, 1961-65; first jazz group to perform at White House, 1962.
b. Aug 31, 1939 in Altoona, Pennsylvania
Source: *BiDJaz; BioIn 15; CurBio 87; EncJzS; NewAgE 90; NewAgMG; NewGrDJ 88; News 90-2; WhoAm 78, 80, 82, 84, 86, 88, 90, 92, 94, 95, 96, 97; WhoEnt 92; WhoMus 72*

Winter, William Forrest
American. Politician
Dem. governor of MS, 1980-84.
b. Feb 21, 1923 in Grenada, Mississippi
Source: *BiDrGov 1978, 1983; BioIn 12; WhoAm 74, 76, 78, 80, 82, 84, 86, 88, 90, 92, 94, 95, 96, 97; WhoAmL 78, 79; WhoAmP 73, 75, 77, 83, 85, 87, 89, 91, 93, 95; WhoGov 75, 77; WhoSSW 76, 80, 82, 84, 95; WhoWor 82*

Winterhalter, Hugo
American. Bandleader
Arranger of 11 gold records, 1950s; songs performed by Perry Como, Doris Day.
b. Aug 15, 1909 in Wilkes-Barre, Pennsylvania
d. Sep 17, 1973 in Greenwich, Connecticut
Source: *ASCAP 66, 80; BiDAmM; BioIn 10; CmpEPM; DcAmB S9; NewYTBE 73; OxCPMus; PenEncP*

Winterich, John Tracy
American. Author, Editor
Wrote on book collecting, literary history: *American Books and Printing,* 1935.
b. May 25, 1891 in Middletown, Connecticut
d. Aug 15, 1970 in Springfield, Massachusetts
Source: *AmAu&B; BioIn 1, 4, 8, 9, 10; ChhPo, S1, S2, S3; NatCAB 55; NewYTBE 70; OxCAmL 65; REnAL; TwCA, SUP*

Winters, Jonathan (Harshman, III)
American. Comedian, Actor
Known for characterizations, improvisations; films since 1963 include *The Loved One,* 1965.
b. Nov 11, 1925 in Dayton, Ohio
Source: *BioIn 4, 5, 6, 7, 8, 9, 12, 15, 16, 17, 21; BkPepl; CelR, 90; ConTFT 5, 12; CurBio 65; EncAFC; FilmEn; FilmgC; ForYSC; HalFC 80, 84, 88; IntMPA 75, 76, 77, 78, 79, 80, 81, 82, 84, 86, 88, 92, 94, 96; JoeFr; LegTOT; MotPP; MovMk; VarWW 85; WhoAm 74, 76, 78, 80, 82, 84, 86, 88, 90, 92, 94, 95, 96, 97; WhoCom; WhoEnt 92; WhoHol 92, A; WhoWest 74, 76; WhoWor 74; WorAl; WorAlBi*

Winters, Shelley
[Shirley Schrift]
American. Actor
Won Oscars for *The Diary of Anne Frank,* 1959; *A Patch of Blue,* 1966.
b. Aug 18, 1922 in Saint Louis, Missouri
Source: *BiDFilm, 81, 94; BiE&WWA; BioIn 1, 2, 3, 6, 7, 8, 9, 10, 11, 12, 16; BkPepl; CelR, 90; ConAu 110, 113, X; ConTFT 4, 13; CurBio 52; EncAFC; FilmEn; FilmgC; ForYSC; GangFlm; GoodHs; HalFC 80, 84, 88; IntDcF 1-3, 2-3; IntMPA 75, 76, 77, 78, 79, 80, 81, 82, 84, 86, 88, 92, 94, 96; IntWW 74, 75, 76, 77, 78, 79, 80, 81, 82, 83, 89, 91, 93; InWom, SUP; LegTOT; MotPP; MovMk; NewYTBE 71; NewYTBS 80; NotNAT; OxCFilm; VarWW 85; WhoAm 74, 76, 78, 80, 82, 84, 86, 88, 90, 92, 94, 95, 96, 97; WhoAmW 58, 61, 64, 66, 68, 70, 72, 74, 91, 95; WhoEnt 92; WhoHol 92, A; WhoHrs 80; WhoThe 72, 77, 81; WhoWor 74; WorAl; WorAlBi; WorEFlm*

Winterson, Jeanette
English. Author
Oranges Are Not the Only Fruit, won the Whitbread Prize for best first novel, 1985.
b. 1959 in Lancashire, England
Source: *BioIn 16, 18, 19, 20, 21; BlmGWL; ConAu 136; ConLC 64; ConNov 91, 96; ConPopW; DcArts; FemiCLE; FemiWr; GayLesB; GayLL; IntWW 91, 93; OxCEng 95; RGTwCWr; ScF&FL 92; SJGFanW; TwCRHW 94; Who 94; WorAu 1985; WrDr 94*

Winthrop, John
English. Politician
Governor, Massachusetts Bay Colony, 12 times, 1629-48; helped banish Ann Hutchinson.
b. Jan 12, 1588 in Suffolk, England
d. Mar 26, 1649 in Boston, Massachusetts
Source: *Alli; AmAu; AmAu&B; AmBi; AmPolLe; AmWrBE; ApCAB; Benet 87, 96; BenetAL 91; BiD&SB; BiDrACR; BioIn 1, 2, 3, 4, 6, 7, 8, 10, 11, 14, 15, 17, 19; CamGEL; CamGLE; CamHAL; CasWL; CyAL 1; DcAmAu; DcAmB; DcAmReB 1, 2; DcLB 24, 30; DcNAA; DcNaB; Drake; EncAB-A 31; EncAB-H 1974, 1996; EncARH; EncCRAm; EvLB; HarEnUS; HisWorL; LegTOT; LinLib L, S; LitC 31; McGEWB; NatCAB 6; NewCBEL; OxCAmH; OxCAmL 65, 83, 95; PenC AM; RComAH; REn; REnAL; TwCBDA; WebAB 74, 79; WebE&AL; WhAm HS; WhDW; WorAl; WorAlBi; WrCNE*

Wintle, Justin Beecham
[Justin Beecham]
English. Author
Non-fiction writings include *Makers of Modern Culture,* 1981.
b. May 24, 1949 in London, England
Source: *ConAu 13NR, 77*

Winton, Alexander
American. Auto Manufacturer
Formed the Winton Motor Carriage Co., 1897.
b. Jun 20, 1860 in Grangemouth, Scotland
d. Jun 21, 1932 in Cleveland, Ohio
Source: *BiDAmBL 83; BioIn 1; DcAmB; EncABHB 4; NatCAB 12; WebAB 74, 79; WhAm 1*

Wintour, Anna
English. Editor
Editor American Vogue 1988—.
b. Nov 3, 1949 in London, England
Source: *BioIn 15; CurBio 90; IntWW 91, 93; LegTOT; News 90; Who 88, 90, 92, 94; WhoAm 90, 92, 94, 95, 96, 97; WhoAmW 89, 91, 93, 95, 97; WhoE 95*

Winwar, Frances
[Francesca Vinciguerra Winwar]
American. Author, Critic
Writes romantic novels, biographies; won Edgar for *The Haunted Palace,* 1959.
b. May 3, 1900 in Taormina, Sicily, Italy
d. Jul 24, 1985
Source: *AmAu&B; AmWomWr; Au&Wr 71; AuBYP 2, 3; BioIn 2, 4, 7; ConAu 89; DcLP 87B; InWom SUP; LinLib L; OxCAmL 65, 83, 95; PenNWW B; REn; REnAL; TwCA, SUP; WhAm 9; WhE&EA; WhoAm 74, 76, 78, 80, 82, 84; WhoAmW 58, 61, 64, 66, 72, 74*

Winwood, Estelle
[Estelle Goodwin]
"Cow Eyes"
English. Actor
Character actress whose career spanned 90 years; played the fairy godmother in *The Glass Slipper*, 1955.
b. Jan 24, 1883 in Leeds, England
d. Jun 20, 1984 in Los Angeles, California
Source: *AnObit 1984; BiE&WWA; BioIn 7, 10, 11, 13, 14; FamA&A; FilmEn; FilmgC; ForYSC; HalFC 80; InWom, SUP; LegTOT; MovMk; NewYTBS 83, 84; NotNAT; OxCAmT 84; Vers A; WhoHol A; WhoThe 72, 77A; WhThe; WorAl*

Winwood, Steve
[Blind Faith; The Spencer Davis Group; Traffic; Stephen Lawrence Winwood]
English. Musician, Singer
R&B vocalist; performed with several groups before solo career; hit songs include "While You See a Chance," 1982.
b. May 12, 1948 in Birmingham, England
Source: *Baker 84; BioIn 8, 12, 13, 15, 16; CelR 90; ConMuA 80A; ConMus 2; EncPR&S 89; EncRk 88; EncRkSt; HarEnR 86; IlEncRk; LegTOT; NewYTBS 81; OnThGG; PenEncP; RkOn 85; RolSEnR 83; WhoAm 84, 86, 88, 90, 92, 94, 95, 96, 97; WhoEnt 92; WhoRock 81; WhoRocM 82; WorAlBi*

Wirth, Timothy E
American. Politician
Dem. senator from Colorado 1987-93; counselor, US State Dept., 1993-94.
b. Sep 22, 1939 in Santa Fe, New Mexico
Source: *AlmAP 78, 80, 82, 84, 88, 92; BiDrUSC 89; CngDr 77, 79, 81, 83, 85, 87, 89, 91; CurBio 91; IntWW 91; NewYTBS 84, 93; PolsAm 84; St&PR 75; WhoAm 90; WhoAmP 75, 77, 79, 81, 83, 85, 87, 89, 91, 93, 95; WhoWest 92; WhoWor 91*

Wirtz, Arthur Michael
American. Businessman, Hockey Executive
Owner, Detroit Red Wings, 1931-54, Chicago Blackhawks, 1954-83; owned several NHL arenas, including Madison Square Garden; Hall of Fame, 1971.
b. Jan 23, 1901 in Chicago, Illinois
d. Jul 21, 1983 in Chicago, Illinois
Source: *AnObit 1983; NewYTBS 83; St&PR 84; WhAm 8; WhoAm 74, 76, 78, 80, 82; WhoFI 83; WhoHcky 73; WhoMW 82; WhoWor 82*

Wirtz, William Willard
American. Government Official
Secretary of Labor, 1962-69.
b. Mar 14, 1912 in De Kalb, Illinois
Source: *BiDrUSE 71, 89; BioIn 1, 2, 5, 6, 7, 8, 10, 11; ConAu 101; IntWW 74, 75, 76, 77, 78, 79, 80, 81, 82, 83, 89; WhoAm 74, 76, 78, 80, 82, 84, 86, 88, 90, 92, 94, 95, 96, 97; WhoMW 90*

Wisdom, Norman
English. Actor, Comedian
Starred in plays *Where's Charley*, 1960; *Walking Happy*, 1970.
b. Feb 4, 1925 in London, England
Source: *BlueB 76; EncMT; FilmgC; HalFC 84, 88; IntMPA 84, 86, 92; NotNAT; Who 74, 85, 92; WhoHol A; WhoThe 81*

Wise, Isaac Mayer
American. Religious Leader
Founded Reform Judaism in US; pres., Hebrew Union College, Cincinnati, 1875-1900.
b. Mar 29, 1819 in Steingrub, Bohemia
d. Mar 26, 1900 in Cincinnati, Ohio
Source: *Alli, SUP; AmAu&B; AmBi; AmRef; AmSocL; ApCAB; BenetAL 91; BiDAmEd; BiDAmJo; BiD&SB; BioIn 1, 2, 3, 4, 5, 7, 8, 10, 11, 14, 15, 16, 17, 18, 19; DcAmAu; DcAmB; DcAmReB 1, 2; DcNAA; EncAB-H 1974, 1996; EncARH; JeAmHC; McGEWB; NatCAB 10; OhA&B; OxCAmH; RelLAm 91; REnAL; WebAB 74, 79; WhAm HS; WorAl; WorAlBi*

Wise, Robert
American. Director, Producer
Won Oscars for direction of *West Side Story*, 1961; *Sound of Music*, 1965.
b. Sep 10, 1914 in Winchester, Indiana
Source: *BiDFilm, 81, 94; BioIn 15, 16, 17, 18, 20; CmMov; CurBio 89; DcArts; DcFM; EncSF, 93; FilmEn; FilmgC; GangFlm; HalFC 80, 84, 88; HorFD; IlWWHD 1; IntDcF 1-2, 2-2; IntMPA 75, 76, 77, 78, 79, 80, 81, 82, 84, 86, 88, 92, 94, 96; ItaFilm; LegTOT; MiSFD 9; MovMk; NewEScF; OxCFilm; PenEncH; WhoAm 74, 76, 78, 80, 82, 84, 86, 88, 90, 92, 94, 95, 96, 97; WhoEnt 92; WhoHrs 80; WhoWest 74, 76, 78; WhoWor 78, 80, 82, 84, 87, 89, 91, 93, 95, 96, 97; WorAl; WorAlBi; WorEFlm; WorFDir 1*

Wise, Stephen Samuel
American. Religious Leader
Zionist spokesman; founded Federation of American Zionists, 1898, Jewish Institute of Religion, 1922; worked to establish Palestine as national home for Jews.
b. Mar 17, 1874 in Budapest, Austria-Hungary
d. Apr 19, 1949 in New York, New York
Source: *AmAu&B; AmDec 1930; BiDMoPL; BiDSocW; BioIn 1, 2, 4, 5, 6, 7, 8, 9, 11, 12, 14, 16, 17, 19; CurBio 41, 49; DcAmB S4; DcAmReB 1, 2; EncAB-A 2; EncAB-H 1974, 1996; McGEWB; NatCAB 41; OxCAmH; RelLAm 91; REnAL; WebAB 74, 79; WhAm 2; WhNAA*

Wise, Thomas J
English. Bibliographer
Highly esteemed bookman, collector who was later exposed as forger.
b. Oct 7, 1859 in Gravesend, England
d. May 13, 1937 in London, England
Source: *CasWL; DcLEL; DcNaB 1931; EvLB; LngCTC; NewC; OxCEng 67; TwCA, SUP; WhE&EA*

Wise, William H
American. Author
Writings for juveniles include *The Cowboy Surprise*, 1961; *The Terrible Trumpet*, 1969.
b. Jul 21, 1923 in New York, New York
Source: *AuBYP 2; ConAu 13R; Dun&B 90; SmATA 4; WhoEng 88*

Wise, Winifred E
American. Children's Author
Biographies for juveniles include *Lincoln's Secret Weapon*, 1962; *Fanny Kemble*, 1966.
Source: *AuBYP 2, 3; ForWC 70; SmATA 2; WrDr 86, 88*

Wiseman, Frederick
American. Filmmaker
Known for "cinema verite" documentaries; specializes in examining US institutions for public TV.
b. Jan 1, 1930 in Boston, Massachusetts
Source: *BiDFilm 81, 94; BioIn 9, 10, 11, 12, 13, 16; ConLC 20; ConTFT 8; CurBio 74; EncAJ; EncWB; HalFC 80, 84, 88; IntDcF 1-2, 2-2; IntMPA 92, 94, 96; LesBEnT, 92; MiSFD 9; OxCFilm; WhoAm 82, 84, 86, 88, 90, 92, 94, 95, 96, 97; WhoEnt 92; WorFDir 2*

Wiseman, Joseph
Canadian. Actor
Played villainous title role in first James Bond film *Dr. No*, 1962.
b. May 15, 1918 in Montreal, Quebec, Canada
Source: *BiE&WWA; BioIn 5; ConTFT 9; FilmEn; FilmgC; ForYSC; HalFC 88; IntMPA 80, 81, 82, 84, 86, 88, 92, 94, 96; ItaFilm; MotPP; NotNAT; WhoHol 92, A; WhoThe 72, 77, 81; WhoWorJ 72, 78*

Wiseman, Nicholas Patrick Stephen
English. Religious Leader
First archbishop of Westminister, 1850.
b. Aug 2, 1802 in Seville, Spain
d. Feb 15, 1865 in London, England
Source: *Alli; BbD; BiD&SB; BioIn 2; BritAu 19; DcBiPP; DcCathB; DcEnL; DcEuL; DcNaB; LuthC 75; NewC; NewCBEL; PoIre; VicBrit; WebBD 83*

Wister, Owen
American. Author
Novel, *The Virginian*, 1902, has been the basis for long-running stage play, three movies.

b. Jul 14, 1860 in Germantown, Pennsylvania
d. Jul 21, 1938 in North Kingstown, Rhode Island
Source: *Alli SUP; AmAu&B; AmBi; AmLY; ApCAB SUP; ArizL; BenetAL 91; BiD&SB; BioIn 1, 3, 4, 5, 7, 9, 10, 12, 13, 14, 16, 17, 21; CamGEL; CamGLE; CamHAL; CarSB; CasWL; Chambr 3; ChhPo, S2; CnDAL; ConAmA; ConAmL; ConAu 108; CyWA 58; DcAmAu; DcAmB; DcArts; DcLB 9, 78; DcLEL; DcNAA; EncAAH; EncAB-H 1974, 1996; EncFWF; FifWWr; GayN; GrWrEL N; HalFC 84, 88; HarEnUS; LegTOT; LinLib L, S; LngCTC; MemAm; NatCAB 13; Novels; OxCAmL 65, 83, 95; PenC AM; PeoHis; RAdv 1, 14, 13-1; REn; REnAL; REnAW; RfGAmL 87, 94; ScF&FL 1; SmATA 62; TwCA, SUP; TwCLC 21; TwCWW 82, 91; WebAB 74, 79; WebE&AL; WhAm 1; WhE&EA; WhLit; WhNAA; WorAlBi*

Witcover, Walt
[Walter Witcover Scheinman]
American. Director, Actor
Won best actor Obies for *Maedchen in Uniform,* 1955; *Exiles,* 1957.
b. Aug 24, 1924 in New York, New York
Source: *BiE&WWA; ConTFT 4; NotNAT; WhoEnt 92*

Withers, Bill
American. Singer, Songwriter
Hits include "Ain't No Sunshine," 1971; "Lean On Me," 1972; "Lovely Day," 1978.
b. Jul 4, 1938 in Slab Fork, West Virginia
Source: *DrBlPA, 90; EncJzS; EncPR&S 89; EncRk 88; EncRkSt; HarEnR 86; IlEncBM 82; IlEncRk; InB&W 80; LegTOT; NewGrDA 86; NewYTBE 72; PenEncP; RkOn 78; RolSEnR 83; SoulM; WhoRock 81; WhoRocM 82*

Withers, Googie
[Georgina McCallum]
English. Actor
British films include *Miranda; Lady Vanishes.*
b. Mar 12, 1917 in Karachi, Pakistan
Source: *BioIn 12, 14, 19; ConTFT 9; EncEurC; FilmAG WE; FilmEn; FilmgC; HalFC 80, 84, 88; IlWWBF; IntDcF 2-3; IntMPA 75, 76, 77, 78, 79, 80, 81, 82, 84, 86, 88, 92, 94, 96; MovMk; OxCFilm; OxCThe 83; Who 74, 82, 83, 85, 88, 90, 92, 94; WhoHol 92, A; WhoThe 72, 77, 81; WhoWor 74, 76*

Withers, Jane
American. Actor
Child star of 1930s films; TV commercials as Josephine the Plumber.
b. Apr 12, 1926 in Atlanta, Georgia
Source: *BioIn 7, 8, 9, 11, 15, 17; EncAFC; FilmEn; FilmgC; HalFC 80, 84, 88; HolP 30; IntMPA 77, 86, 92; InWom, SUP; LegTOT; MotPP; MovMk; ThFT; WhoHol 92, A; WorAlBi*

Witherspoon, Herbert
American. Opera Singer
First basso; NY Met., 1908-16; director of Met., 1935.
b. Jul 21, 1873 in Buffalo, New York
d. May 10, 1935 in New York, New York
Source: *AmBi; Baker 78, 84, 92; BiDAmM; BioIn 1, 11; DcAmB S1; MetOEnc; MusSN; NatCAB 29; NewAmDM; NewEOp 71; NewGrDA 86; NewGrDO; NotNAT B; WhAm 1*

Witherspoon, John
American. Educator, Religious Leader, Continental Congressman
Only clergyman in first Continental Congress; signed Declaration of Independence; president, Princeton College; coined term "Americanism."
b. Feb 5, 1723? in Gifford, Scotland
d. Nov 15, 1794 in Princeton, New Jersey
Source: *Alli; AmAu; AmAu&B; AmBi; AmSocL; AmWrBE; ApCAB; BenetAL 91; BiAUS; BiD&SB; BiDrAC; BiDrUSC 89; BioIn 1, 3, 7, 8, 9, 10, 11, 14, 15, 16, 18, 19; BlkwEAR; CyAL 1; DcAmB; DcAmReB 1, 2; DcEnL; DcLB 31, 31B; DcNaB; Drake; EncAR; EncCRAm; HisWorL; LuthC 75; McGEWB; NewCBEL; OxCAmH; OxCAmL 83, 95; REnAL; TwCBDA; WebAB 74, 79; WhAm HS; WhAmP; WhAmRev; WorAl; WorAlBi*

Witkin, Joel-Peter
American. Photographer
Photographer since the 1950s; works collected in *Forty Photographs,* 1985; *Gods of Earth and Heaven,* 1989.
b. Sep 13, 1939 in New York, New York
Source: *BioIn 15, 19; ConPhot 88, 95; ICPEnP A; MacBEP; News 96, 96-1; WhoAm 82, 84, 86, 88, 90, 92, 94, 95, 96, 97; WhoAmA 80, 82, 84, 86, 89, 91, 93; WhoWest 84, 94, 96*

Witmark, Isidore
American. Music Executive, Publisher
Internationally known music publisher, 1880s-1920s; big promoter of ragtime music.
b. Jun 15, 1869 in New York, New York
d. Apr 9, 1941 in New York, New York
Source: *BioIn 16; DcAmB S3*

Witt, Katarina
German. Skater
Three-time world champion figure skater; won gold medals, 1984, 1988 Olympics; first woman to win two gold medals in sport since Sonja Henie.
b. Dec 1965 in Karl-Marx-Stadt, German Democratic Republic
Source: *BioIn 14, 15, 16; CurBio 88; LegTOT; News 91-3; NewYTBS 91; WorAlBi*

Witt, Mike
[Michael Atwater Witt]
American. Baseball Player
Pitcher, California, 1981-90; NY Yankees 1990—; threw first perfect game in MLs since Len Barker in 1981, 1984.
b. Jul 20, 1960 in Fullerton, California
Source: *Ballpl 90; BaseReg 86, 87; BioIn 14*

Witt, Paul Junger
American. Producer, Director
TV shows include "The Rookies," 1972-76; won Emmy for "Brian's Song," 1972.
b. Mar 20, 1943 in New York, New York
Source: *BioIn 16; ConTFT 3; IntMPA 94; LesBEnT, 92; VarWW 85; WhoAm 86, 88; WhoEnt 92*

Witte, Edwin Emil
American. Economist
Exec. director of FDR's Committee on Economic Security which resulted in Social Security Act, 1934-35.
b. Jan 4, 1887 in Jefferson County, Wisconsin
d. May 20, 1960
Source: *BioIn 1, 4, 5, 6, 8; DcAmB S6; NatCAB 45; WhAm 4; WorAl*

Witte, Erich
German. Opera Singer, Producer
Berlin Opera dramatic tenor, originally Spieltenor, 1945-60.
b. Mar 19, 1911 in Bremen, Germany
Source: *CmOp; IntWWM 90; NewEOp 71; NewGrDM 80; NewGrDO; PenDiMP*

Witte, Sergey Yulyevich
Russian. Statesman
Negotiated treaty ending Russo-Japanese War, 1905; first constitutional Russian premier, 1905.
b. 1849 in Tiflis, Russia
d. Mar 12, 1915 in Saint Petersburg, Russia
Source: *McGEWB; REn; WebBD 83*

Witten, Edward
American. Physicist
Works on "string theory," searching for a set of equations that would explain all of the universe's matter and energy.
b. Aug 26, 1951 in Baltimore, Maryland
Source: *AmMWSc 92, 95; IntWW 93; NotTwCS; WhoAm 96; WhoScEn 96*

Wittenmyer, Annie Turner
American. Social Reformer
First president, Woman's Christian Temperance Union; known for church, charity work.
b. Aug 26, 1827 in Sandy Springs, Ohio
d. Feb 2, 1900 in Sanatoga, Pennsylvania
Source: *AmWom; DcAmTB; InWom SUP; LibW; NatCAB 12; NotAW; RelLAm 91; WomFir; WorAl; WorAlBi*

Wittgenstein, Ludwig
Austrian. Philosopher, Educator
Wrote *Tractatus Logico-Philosophicus,* 1922, which attempted to prove all metaphysical propositions to be nonsense.
b. Apr 26, 1889 in Vienna, Austria
d. Apr 29, 1951 in Cambridge, England
Source: *Benet 87, 96; BioIn 2, 3, 4, 5, 7, 8, 9, 10, 11, 12, 13, 14, 15, 16, 17, 20, 21; ConAu 113; CyWA 89; DcNaB 1951; LegTOT; LngCTC; LuthC 75; ObitT 1951; OxCEng 67; OxCGer 76, 86; REn; ThTwC 87; TwCLC 59; WhAm 4; WorAl; WorAu 1950*

Wittgenstein, Paul
American. Pianist
One-armed virtuoso who played left-hand concertos; brother of Ludwig.
b. Nov 5, 1887 in Vienna, Austria
d. Mar 3, 1961 in Long Island, New York
Source: *Baker 78, 84, 92; BioIn 1, 5, 6, 21; DcArts; MusMk; NewAmDM; NewGrDA 86; NewGrDM 80; OxCMus; PenDiMP*

Wittig, Georg Friedrich Karl
German. Educator
Won Nobel Prize in chemistry, 1979; discovered Wittig reaction.
b. Jun 16, 1897 in Berlin, Germany
d. Aug 26, 1987 in Heidelberg, Germany (West)
Source: *AmMWSc 89, 92; BiESc; WhAm 9; Who 85; WhoNob, 90, 95; WhoWor 74, 76, 78, 80, 82, 84, 87*

Wittig, Monique
French. Writer
One of her many feminist theories is that lesbians are not women because the latter is a term meaningful only in the heterosexual community; wrote *The Straight Mind,* 1992.
b. 1935, France
Source: *BioIn 17; ConAu 116, 135; ConLC 22; ContDcW 89; ConWorW 93; DcLB 83; DcTwCCu 2; EncSF, 93; EncWL 3; FemiCLE; FemiWr; FrenWW; GayLesB; GayLL; ModWoWr; PostFic; ScF&FL 92; WomFir; WorAu 1970*

Wittop, Freddy
Dutch. Designer
Won Tony for costumes in *Hello Dolly!* 1964.
b. Jul 26, 1921 in Bussum, Netherlands
Source: *BiE&WWA; NotNAT; VarWW 85; WhoThe 77, 81*

Witz, Konrad
Swiss. Artist
Among first to use realistic landscapes in religious scenes: *Christ Walking on the Waters.*
b. 1400 in Rottweil, Germany
d. 1447 in Basel, Switzerland
Source: *AtlBL; DcArts; IntDcAA 90; McGDA; McGEWB; NewCol 75; OxCArt; OxDcArt*

Wodehouse, P(elham) G(renville)
English. Author
Created characters Bertie Wooster and Jeeves; *The Inimitable Jeeves,* 1924.
b. Oct 15, 1881 in Guildford, England
d. Feb 14, 1975 in Long Island, New York
Source: *AmPS; ASCAP 66, 80; Au&Wr 71; AuNews 2; Benet 96; BestMus; BiDAmM; BioIn 1, 2, 3, 4, 5, 6, 7, 8, 9, 10, 11, 12, 13, 14, 16, 17, 18, 19; CasWL; Chambr 3; CmpEPM; ConAu 57; ConLC 22; ConPopW; CurBio 71; DcAmB S9; DcArts; DcLEL; DcNaB 1971; EncSF 93; EncWL 3; Ent; EvLB; GrBr; IntWW 74; LinLib S; MakMC; McGEWD 72; MnBBF; ModBrL S1; NewC; NewCBEL; NewCBMT; NotNAT A; Novels; OxCEng 67, 95; PenC ENG; PlP&P; RAdv 1; REn; RfGShF; RGTwCWr; SmATA 22; TwCA, SUP; WebE&AL; WhAm 6; WhDW; WhLit; Who 74; WhoAm 74; WhoChL; WhoWor 74*

Woffington, Margaret
"Peg"
Irish. Actor
Best role as male in *Constant Couple.*
b. Oct 18, 1714 in Dublin, Ireland
d. Mar 28, 1760 in London, England
Source: *BioIn 2, 3, 5, 8, 9, 11, 17; BlmGEL; CamGWoT; DcBiPP; DcIrB 78, 88; DcNaB, C; EncWT; InWom SUP; NewC; NewGrDM 80; WhDW*

Wohler, Friedrich
German. Chemist
First to synthesize an organic compound, urea, 1828; isolated aluminum; devised process of manufacturing nickel.
b. Jul 31, 1800 in Eschershelm, Germany
d. Sep 23, 1882 in Gottingen, Germany
Source: *AsBiEn; BiESc; BioIn 2, 3, 5, 6, 11, 12, 14; CamDcSc; CelCen; DcBiPP; DcInv; DcScB; InSci; LarDcSc; LinLib S; RAdv 14; WebBD 83; WhDW; WorScD*

Woiwode, Larry
American. Author
Work includes *What I'm Going to Do, I Think,* 1969; *Beyond the Bedroom Wall,* 1975; *Born Brothers,* 1988.
b. Oct 30, 1941 in Carrington, North Dakota
Source: *BenetAL 91; BioIn 8, 10, 16; ConAu 16NR, 73; ConLC 6, 10; ConNov 82, 86, 91; CurBio 89; CyWA 89; DcLB 6; DrAF 76; DrAP 75; DrAPF 80, 91; IntvTCA 2; MagSAmL; OxCAmL 83; WhoAm 97; WorAu 1975; WrDr 80, 82, 84, 86, 88, 90, 92*

Wojciechowicz, Alex(ander)
"Wojie"
American. Football Player
Center-linebacker, Detroit, 1938-45, Philadelphia, 1946-50; Hall of Fame, 1968.
b. Aug 12, 1915 in South River, New Jersey
d. Jul 13, 1993 in South River, New Jersey
Source: *BiDAmSp FB; BioIn 8, 9, 17, 18; LegTOT; WhoFtbl 74*

Wojnilower, Albert Martin
American. Economist
Chief economist, First Boston Corp., NYC, 1964-86; wrote *The Quality of Business Loans,* 1960.
b. Feb 3, 1930 in Vienna, Austria
Source: *BioIn 13; St&PR 75, 84, 87; WhoAm 84, 86, 88, 90, 92, 94, 95, 96, 97; WhoFI 83; WhoSecI 86*

Wolcott, Oliver, Sr.
American. Judge, Military Leader, Continental Congressman
Signed Declaration of Independence, 1776; governor of CT, 1796.
b. Nov 26, 1726 in Windsor, Connecticut
d. Dec 1, 1797 in Litchfield, Connecticut
Source: *AmBi; ApCAB; BiAUS; BiDrAC; BiDrGov 1789; BiDrUSC 89; BioIn 3, 5, 7, 8, 9; DcAmB; DcAmMeB; Dis&D; Drake; EncAR; EncCRAm; HarEnUS; NatCAB 10; TwCBDA; WebAB 74, 79; WhAmP; WhAmRev; WorAlBi*

Wolcott, Roger
American. Colonial Figure
Governor of CT, 1750-54; wrote epic poem about John Winthrop.
b. Jan 4, 1679 in Windsor, Connecticut
d. May 17, 1767 in East Windsor, Connecticut
Source: *Alli; AmAu&B; AmBi; AmWrBE; ApCAB; BenetAL 91; BiDrACR; BioIn 14; CyAL 1; DcAmAu; DcAmB; DcLB 24; DcLEL; DcNAA; Drake; HarEnUS; NatCAB 10; OxCAmL 65, 83, 95; REnAL; TwCBDA; WebAB 74, 79; WhAm HS; WhAmP; WrCNE*

Wolf, Hugo
Austrian. Composer
Wrote *Italienische Serenade,* 1893; died in an asylum for the insane.
b. Mar 13, 1860 in Windischgraez, Austria
d. Feb 22, 1903 in Vienna, Austria
Source: *AtlBL; Baker 78, 84; BioIn 1, 2, 3, 4, 5, 6, 7, 8, 9, 11, 12, 14, 15, 16, 20; BriBkM 80; CmOp; CmpBCM; DcCom 77; DcCom&M 79; Dis&D; GrComp; IntDcOp; MetOEnc; MusMk; NewAmDM; NewEOp 71; NewGrDM 80; NewOxM; OxCEng 85, 95; OxCGer 76, 86; OxCMus; OxDcOp; WhDW; WorAlBi*

Wolf, Naomi
American. Author
Author of *The Beauty Myth,* 1991; *Fire With Fire,* 1993.
b. 1963 in San Francisco, California
Source: *CurBio 93; LegTOT; News 94, 94-3*

Wolf, Peter
[J. Geils Band]
American. Singer
Lead vocalist, J Geils Band until 1984; solo single "I Need You Tonight," 1984.
b. Mar 7, 1946 in Boston, Massachusetts
Source: *BioIn 12; LegTOT; RkOn 85; WhoRocM 82*

Wolf, Stephen M
American. Airline Executive
Revived two finacially troubled airlines; pres. and CEO Allegis Corp. 1987-92; chm., CEO, UAL Corp. and United Airlines, 1992-94; adviser, air France, 1994-96; chm., CEO, USAIR Inc., 1996—.
b. Aug 7, 1941 in Oakland, California
Source: *BioIn 15, 16; Dun&B 90; IntWW 91; News 89-3; St&PR 87; WhoAm 88; WhoFI 92; WhoMW 92*

Wolfe, Digby
English. Writer
Emmy winner for writing TV specials, shows including "Laugh-In," 1968.
b. Jun 4, 1932, England
Source: *ASCAP 80; VarWW 85; WhoUSWr 88*

Wolfe, George C.
American. Director, Dramatist, Producer
Head of New York Shakespeare Festival, 1993—.
b. Sep 23, 1954 in Frankfort, Kentucky
Source: *ConAmD; ConAu 149; ConBlB 6; ConDr 93; ConLC 49; CurBio 94; WhoAm 95, 96, 97; WhoE 95*

Wolfe, James
English. Military Leader
British commander who captured Quebec from French on Plains of Abraham, 1759; killed in battle.
b. Jan 2, 1727 in Westerham, England
d. Sep 13, 1759 in Quebec, Canada
Source: *Alli; ApCAB; BbtC; Benet 87, 96; BioIn 1, 2, 3, 4, 5, 6, 7, 8, 9, 10, 16, 17; DcAmMiB; DcCanB 3; DcNaB; Dis&D; Drake; EncAR; EncCRAm; GenMudB; HarEnMi; HarEnUS; HisDBrE; LinLib S; MacDCB 78; McGEWB; NatCAB 1; OxCAmH; OxCCan; REn; WebBD 83; WhAm HS; WhDW; WhNaAH; WhoMilH 76; WorAl; WorAlBi*

Wolfe, Thomas (Clayton)
American. Author
Wrote *Look Homeward, Angel,* 1929; *You Can't Go Home Again,* 1940.
b. Oct 3, 1900 in Asheville, North Carolina
d. Sep 15, 1938 in Baltimore, Maryland
Source: *AgeMat; AmAu&B; AmBi; AmCulL; AmWr; ASCAP 66, 80; AtlBL; Benet 87, 96; BenetAL 91; BioIn 1, 2, 3, 4, 5, 6, 7, 8, 9, 10, 11, 12, 13, 14, 15, 16, 17, 19; CamGEL; CamGLE; CamHAL; CasWL; CnDAL; CnMD; CnMWL; ConAmA; ConAu 104, 132; CyWA 58; DcAmB S2; DcArts; DcLB 9, 102, DS2, Y85A; DcLEL; DcNAA; EncAB-H 1974, 1996; EncSoH; EncWL 2, 3; EncWT; EvLB; FacFETw; FifSWrA; GrWrEL N; LegTOT; LinLib L, S; LngCTC; MagSAmL; MajTwCW; MakMC; McGEWB; ModAL, S2; ModWD; Novels; OxCAmH; OxCAmL 65, 83, 95; OxCEng 67, 85, 95; PenC AM; PeoHis; PlP&P; RAdv 1, 14, 13-1; REn; REnAL; RfGAmL 87, 94; RGTwCWr; SouWr; TwCA, SUP; TwCLC 4, 13, 29; TwCWr; WebAB 74, 79; WebBD 83; WebE&AL; WhAm 1; WhDW; WhoTwCL; WorAl; WorAlBi; WorLitC; WrPh*

Wolfe, Tom
[Thomas Kennerly Wolfe, Jr.]
American. Author
Wrote *The Electric Kool-Aid Acid Test,* 1968; *The Right Stuff,* 1979.
b. Mar 2, 1931 in Richmond, Virginia
Source: *AmAu&B; AmSocL; AmWr S3; Au&Arts 8; AuNews 2; Benet 87, 96; BenetAL 91; BestSel 89-1; BioIn 7, 8, 9, 10, 11, 12, 13, 16, 20; BlueB 76; CelR, 90; CmCal; ConAu 9NR, 13R, 33NR; ConLC 1, 2, 9, 15, 35, 51; ConNov 91; CurBio 71; CyWA 89; DcAmC; DcArts; DcLB 152; DcLEL 1940; EncAJ; EncTwCJ; FacFETw; IntAu&W 91; IntWW 89, 91, 93; JrnUS; LegTOT; LiJour; MagSAmL; MajTwCW; MakMC; NewYTBS 81; OxCAmL 83, 95; PenC AM; PostFic; RGTwCWr; SourALJ; SouWr; WebE&AL; Who 94; WhoAm 74, 76, 78, 80, 82, 84, 86, 88, 90, 92, 94, 95, 96, 97; WhoE 91, 93, 95, 97; WhoTwCL; WhoUSWr 88; WhoWor 74, 95, 96, 97; WhoWrEP 89, 92, 95; WorAl; WorAlBi; WorAu 1970; WrDr 86, 92*

Wolfe, Willie
[S(ymbionese) L(iberation) A(rmy); William Lawton Wolfe]
American. Revolutionary
Member of terrorist group that kidnapped Patricia Hearst, 1974.
b. 1952?
d. May 24, 1974 in Los Angeles, California
Source: *BioIn 10*

Wolfenden, John Frederick, Sir
English. Museum Director
Director, British Museum, 1969-73; led com. which recommended liberalizing nation's homosexuality laws, 1967.
b. Jun 26, 1906 in Swindon, England
d. Jan 18, 1985 in London, England
Source: *ConAu 106, 114; CurBio 70, 85; DcNaB 1981; IntWW 83; IntYB 79; NewYTBS 85; Who 85*

Wolfensohn, James David
American. Business Executive
Chm. of John F. Kennedy Center for the Performing Arts, 1990-95; pres., World Bank, 1995—.
b. Dec 1, 1933 in Sydney, Australia
Source: *BioIn 12, 16, 17, 18, 19, 20, 21; IntWW 82, 83, 89, 91; NewYTBS 93; St&PR 75, 84, 87, 91, 93, 96, 97; WhoAm 74, 76, 78, 80, 82, 88, 92, 94, 95, 96, 97; WhoE 93, 95; WhoEnt 92; WhoFI 83; WhoWor 97*

Wolfert, Ira
American. Journalist
War correspondent; won Pulitzer, 1943; writings collected in *Battle for the Solomons,* 1943.
b. Nov 1, 1908 in New York, New York
Source: *AmAu&B; AmNov; BioIn 1, 2, 3, 4; CurBio 43; EncAJ; OxCAmL 65, 83; TwCA SUP; WhoWorJ 72*

Wolff, Albert Louis
French. Conductor
Led Opera-Comique, 1920s; wrote opera *Oiseau Bleu,* 1919.
b. Jan 19, 1884 in Paris, France
d. Feb 1970 in Paris, France
Source: *Baker 84; NewEOp 71*

Wolff, Fritz
German. Opera Singer
Tenor, admired for Wagner roles; Bayreuth, 1925-41.
b. Oct 28, 1894 in Munich, Germany
d. Jan 18, 1957 in Munich, Germany (West)
Source: *Baker 84, 92; NewEOp 71; NewGrDM 80; NewGrDO*

Wolff, Geoffrey (Ansell)
American. Author
Wrote memoir *The Duke of Deception,* 1979; novel *The Age on Consent,* 1995.
b. Nov 5, 1937 in Los Angeles, California
Source: *BenetAL 91; BioIn 15, 16, 17, 19; ConAu 29NR, 29R, 43NR; ConLC 41; DcLEL 1940; DrAPF 80; IntAu&W 76, 93; OxCAmL 95; WhoAm 74, 76, 78, 80, 82, 84, 90, 92, 94, 96, 97; WhoUSWr 88; WhoWrEP 89, 92, 95; WorAu 1975; WrDr 80, 82, 84, 86, 88, 90, 92, 94, 96*

Wolff, Helen
[Mrs. Kurt Wolff]
American. Publisher
Founded Pantheon Books, 1942-61; introduced European writer to US.
b. Jul 27, 1906 in Veskueb, Yugoslavia
Source: *ArtclWW 2; BioIn 9, 13, 19, 21; ConAu 113, 117, 144; DcLB Y94N; NewYTBS 94*

Wolff, Mary Evaline
[Sister Mary Madalena]
American. Religious Figure, Educator
Pres., St. Mary's College, Notre Dame, 1934-61; wrote *Chaucer's Nuns.*
b. May 24, 1887 in Cumberland, Wisconsin
d. Jul 25, 1964 in Boston, Massachusetts
Source: *AmAu&B; BenetAL 91; BioIn 1, 2, 4, 5, 7, 8, 12; ConAu 116; CurBio 42, 64; IndAu 1917; PenNWW A; REnAL; TwCA, SUP*

Wolff, Tobias (Jonathan Ansell)
American. Writer
Writer of short stories and memoirs; wrote *Garden of the North American Martyrs,* 1981; *In Pharaoh's Army: Memoirs of the Lost War,* 1994.
b. Jun 19, 1945 in Birmingham, Alabama
Source: *Au&Arts 16; BenetAL 91; BestSel 90-2; BioIn 16, 17, 18, 19, 20, 21; ConAu 22AS, 54NR, 114, 117; ConLC 39, 64; ConNov 91, 96; CurBio 96; CyWA 89; DcLB 130; IntAu&W 89, 91, 93; IntWW 91; LegTOT; OxCAmL 95; RGTwCWr; WhoAm 94, 95, 96, 97; WhoUSWr 88; WhoWrEP 89, 92, 95; WrDr 90, 92, 94, 96*

Wolf-Ferrari, Ermanno
German. Composer
Comic operas include *L'Amore Medico,* 1913.
b. Jan 12, 1876 in Venice, Italy
d. Jan 21, 1948 in Venice, Italy
Source: *Baker 78, 84, 92; BioIn 1, 3, 4, 7, 8, 11; BriBkM 80; CmOp; CompSN; DcArts; DcCom&M 79; IntDcOp; MetOEnc; MusMk; NewAmDM; NewEOp 71; NewGrDM 80; NewGrDO; NewOxM; NotNAT B; OxCMus; OxDcOp; PenDiMP A*

Wolfgang, Myra K
American. Labor Union Official
Helped organize Coalition of Labor Union Women, 1974.
b. 1914?
d. Apr 12, 1976 in Detroit, Michigan
Source: *BioIn 10, 12; ObitOF 79; WhoAmW 74; WomPO 76*

Wolfington, Iggie
American. Actor
Tony nominee for *The Music Man,* 1958.
b. Oct 14, 1920 in Philadelphia, Pennsylvania
Source: *BiE&WWA; NotNAT; WhoHol 92, A*

Wolfit, Donald, Sir
English. Actor
Knighted, 1957, for achievements in presenting plays in England.
b. Apr 20, 1902 in Newark, England
d. Feb 17, 1968 in London, England
Source: *BioIn 3, 7, 8, 9, 10, 11; CamGWoT; CnThe; CurBio 65, 68; DcArts; DcNaB 1961; EncWT; Ent; FilmEn; FilmgC; ForYSC; HalFC 80, 84, 88; IlWWBF, A; IntDcT 3; MotPP; MovMk; NotNAT A, B; ObitOF 79; ObitT 1961; OxCFilm; OxCThe 67, 83; WhAm 4, 4A, 5; WhoHol B; WhoHrs 80; WhScrn 74, 77, 83; WhThe; WorEFlm*

Wolfman Jack
[Robert Smith]
American. Radio Performer
Best known for wild, jive-talking radio program, 1970s; in film *American Graffiti,* 1973.
b. Jan 21, 1938 in New York, New York
d. Jul 1, 1995 in Belvidere, North Carolina
Source: *BioIn 10, 16, 21; BkPepl; CanWW 79, 80, 81, 83, 89; CmCal; LegTOT; News 96, 96-1; NewYTBS 95; RadMoSP; VarWW 85; WhAm 11; WhoAm 80, 90, 92, 94, 95, 96, 97; WhoCan 73, 75, 77, 80, 82, 84; WhoCanB 86; WhoEnt 92; WhoHol 92*

Wolfson, Erwin Service
American. Businessman
NYC leading builder; constructed Pan Am Building, completed 1963.
b. Mar 27, 1902
d. Jun 26, 1962
Source: *BioIn 5, 6, 7; DcAmB S7; NatCAB 48; WhAm 4*

Wolfson, Louis Elwood
American. Industrialist
Known for financial manipulations, attempted takeovers of Montgomery Ward, AMC, 1950s-60s; jailed for conspiracy, 1969.
b. Jan 28, 1912 in Saint Louis, Missouri
Source: *BioIn 3, 4, 5, 6, 8, 11; IntWW 74, 75, 76, 77, 78, 79, 80, 81, 82, 83; PolProf E; WhoFI 83, 85, 87*

Wolheim, Louis
American. Actor
Character actor, 1917-31, in films *Dr. Jekyll and Mr. Hyde; America.*
b. Mar 23, 1880 in New York, New York
d. Feb 18, 1931 in Los Angeles, California
Source: *DcAmB S1; Film 1, 2; FilmEn; FilmgC; HalFC 80, 84, 88; MotPP; MovMk; OxCThe 67; SilFlmP; TwYS; WhoHol B; WhScrn 74, 77, 83*

Wolper, David Lloyd
"Mr. Documentary"
American. Producer, Business Executive
Produces documentaries, TV shows, including "Roots," 1976; won 11 Emmys, one special Oscar.
b. Jan 11, 1928 in New York, New York
Source: *BioIn 14, 15, 16; ConTFT 1, 2, 4; CurBio 86; FilmgC; HalFC 88; IntMPA 92; IntWW 89, 91, 93; LesBEnT, 92; VarWW 85; WhoAm 74, 76, 78, 80, 82, 84, 86, 88, 90, 92, 94, 95, 96, 97; WhoEnt 92; WhoWest 74; WhoWor 74, 76, 78, 91, 93*

Wolsey, Thomas, Cardinal
English. Religious Figure
Cardinal and lord chancellor with papal ambitions; Henry VIII's ally in attempt to secure divorce from Catherine of Aragon.
b. 1475 in Ipswich, England
d. Nov 29, 1530 in Leicester, England
Source: *Alli; Benet 87, 96; BioIn 1, 2, 3, 4, 5, 6, 7, 9, 10, 11, 12, 13, 14, 15, 17, 20; BlmGEL; DcCathB; DcNaB; Dis&D; LegTOT; LinLib S; LngCEL; LuthC 75; McGEWB; NewC; REn; WhDW; WorAlBi*

Wolsky, Albert
French. Designer
Won Oscar for costumes in *All That Jazz,* 1979; *Bugsy,* 1992; designed for *Sophie's Choice,* 1982; *Moscow on the Hudson,* 1984.
b. Nov 24, 1930 in Paris, France
Source: *BioIn 13; VarWW 85*

Woltman, Frederick Enos
American. Journalist
Reporter, staff writer, *NY World-Telegram,* 1927-70; won Pulitzers, 1946, 1947.
b. Mar 16, 1905 in York, Pennsylvania
d. Mar 5, 1970 in Sarasota, Florida
Source: *ConAu 89; CurBio 47, 70; NewYTBE 70; WhAm 5*

Womack, Bobby
American. Singer, Songwriter
Prolific songwriter; protege of Sam Cooke; no. 1 soul album *The Poet,* 1982.
b. Mar 4, 1944 in Cleveland, Ohio
Source: *BioIn 12, 16; ConMuA 80A; ConMus 5; DrBlPA, 90; EncPR&S 89; EncRk 88; EncRkSt; IlEncRk; LegTOT; OnThGG; PenEncP; RkOn 78; RolSEnR 83; SoulM; WhoBlA 88; WhoRock 81; WhoRocM 82*

Wonder, Stevie
[Steveland Morris Hardaway]
American. Singer, Musician, Songwriter
Hits include "My Cherie Amour," "You Are the Sunshine of My Life;" album *Innervisions,* won 1974 Grammy; inducted into Rock and Roll Hall of Fame, 1989.
b. May 13, 1950 in Saginaw, Michigan
Source: *AfrAmAl 6; AfrAmBi 1; AmDec 1970; AmSong; Baker 78, 84, 92; BiDAfM; BiDJaz; BioIn 9, 10, 11, 12, 13, 14, 15, 16; BioNews 74; BkPepl; CelR 90; ConAu X; ConBlB 11; ConHero 2; ConLC 12; ConMus 2, 17; CurBio 75; DcArts; DcTwCCu 5; DrBlPA, 90; Ebony 1; EncPR&S 89; EncRk 88; EncRkSt; FacFETw; HarEnR 86; IlEncRk; InB&W 80, 85; IntWW 78, 79, 80, 81, 82, 83, 89, 91, 93; LegTOT; NegAl 83, 89; NewAmDM; NewGrDA 86; NewYTBE 71; NewYTBS 75, 85; OxCPMus; PenEncP; RkOn 74, 78; RolSEnR 83; SoulM; WhoAfA 96; WhoAm 76, 78, 80, 82, 84, 86, 88, 90, 92, 94, 95, 96, 97; WhoBlA 75, 77, 80, 85, 88, 90, 92, 94; WhoEnt 92; WhoRock 81; WhoRocM 82; WhoWor 84, 87, 89, 91, 93, 95, 96, 97; WorAl; WorAlBi*

Wong, Anna May (Lu Tsong)
American. Actor
Star in 1920s-30s as mysterious Oriental in *Shanghai Express; Thief of Bagdad.*
b. Jan 3, 1907 in Los Angeles, California
d. Feb 3, 1961 in Santa Monica, California
Source: *AsAmAlm; BioIn 7, 11, 16, 20; DcAmB S7; DcAmNB; Film 1, 2; FilmEn; FilmgC; ForYSC; GangFlm; HalFC 80, 84, 88; HolP 30; IntDcF 1-3,*

2-3; InWom, SUP; ItaFilm; LegTOT; MotPP; MovMk; NotAsAm; NotNAT B; ObitOF 79; ThFT; TwYS; WhoHol B; WhScrn 74, 77, 83; WhThe; WorAl; WorAlBi

Wong, B. D
American. Actor
Films include *The Karate Kid.*
b. Oct 24, 1962 in San Francisco, California
Source: *CelR 90; ConTFT 7; WhoEnt 92*

Woo, John
Chinese. Director
Directed *From Rags to Riches,* 1979; *Hard Target,* 1993.
b. c. 1945 in Guangchou, China
Source: *News 94, 94-2*

Woo, Merle
American. Writer
Work has been published in many different kinds of periodicals and anthologies; wrote "Letter to Ma," 1981.
b. Oct 24, 1941 in San Francisco, California
Source: *GayLesB*

Wood, Anthony
English. Antiquarian
Noted for *Athenae Oxonienses,* 1692, containing biographies of famous Oxford graduates.
b. Dec 17, 1632 in Oxford, England
d. Nov 28, 1695 in Oxford, England
Source: *Alli; BbD; BiD&SB; BritAu; CasWL; Chambr 1; DcEnA; DcNaB; EvLB; NewC; NewGrDM 80; NewOxM; OxCEng 67, 85, 95; OxCMus; PenC ENG; REn; WebE&AL*

Wood, Chris
English. Musician
Hit LP's include *When the Eagle Flies,* 1974; *Traffic,* 1968.
b. Jun 24, 1944 in Birmingham, England
d. Jul 12, 1983 in Birmingham, England
Source: *WhoRocM 82*

Wood, Craig Ralph
American. Golfer
Touring pro, 1930s-40s; won US Open, Masters, 1941.
b. Nov 18, 1901 in Lake Placid, New York
d. May 8, 1968 in Palm Beach, Florida
Source: *BiDAmSp OS; BioIn 6, 8, 13; DcAmB S8; ObitOF 79; WhoGolf*

Wood, Edward D., Jr.
American. Filmmaker
B-movie producer; received the "Worst Director of All Time" award from the Golden Turkey awards, 1980.
b. Oct 10, 1924 in Poughkeepsie, New York
d. Dec 10, 1978 in Los Angeles, California
Source: *HalFC 84; HorFD; MiSFD 9N; ScF&FL 92*

Wood, Elijah
American. Actor
Appeared in *Back to the Future II,* 1989.
b. Jan 28, 1981 in Cedar Rapids, Iowa
Source: *IntMPA 94, 96; WhoAm 95, 96, 97*

Wood, Evelyn
American. Educator
Founded the Evelyn Wood Reading Dynamics Institute, 1959, to teach high-speed reading.
b. Jan 9, 1909 in Ogden, Utah
d. Aug 26, 1995 in Tucson, Arizona
Source: *BioIn 14, 21; NatCAB 63N; NewYTBS 95; WhoAm 90; WhoAmW 91*

Wood, Fernando
American. Politician
Dem. congressman, NY, 1863-71; NYC mayor, 1854-56 and 59.
b. Jun 14, 1812 in Philadelphia, Pennsylvania
d. Feb 14, 1881 in Hot Springs, Arkansas
Source: *AmBi; ApCAB; BiAUS; BiDrAC; BiDrUSC 89; BioIn 1, 2, 7, 17; CopCroC; DcAmB; Drake; HarEnUS; McGEWB; NatCAB 3; PolPar; WebAB 74, 79; WhAm HS; WhAmP; WhCiWar*

Wood, Gar(field A)
American. Boat Racer
Powerboat champion of 1920s-30s with boat *Miss America.*
b. Dec 4, 1880 in Mapleton, Iowa
d. Jun 19, 1971 in Miami, Florida
Source: *BioIn 3, 5, 6, 7, 9, 10; BioNews 74; NewYTBE 71*

Wood, Grant
American. Artist
Depicted rural life in Midwest: *American Gothic,* 1930.
b. Feb 13, 1892 in Anamosa, Iowa
d. Feb 12, 1942 in Iowa City, Iowa
Source: *ArtsAmW 3; AtlBL; Benet 87, 96; BioIn 1, 2, 4, 6, 7, 9, 10, 12, 13, 14, 15, 17, 19, 21; BriEAA; CurBio 40, 42; DcAmArt; DcAmB S3; DcArts; DcCAA 71; EncAAH; LegTOT; LinLib S; McGDA; NatCAB 35; OxCAmH; OxCAmL 65; OxCArt; OxCTwCA; OxDcArt; PhDcTCA 77; REn; WebAB 74, 79; WhAm 1; WhAmArt 85; WorAl; WorAlBi*

Wood, Henry, Mrs.
[Ellen Price]
English. Author
Wrote successful melodrama *East Lynne,* 1861.
b. Jan 17, 1814 in Worcester, England
d. Feb 10, 1887 in London, England
Source: *Alli; ArtclWW 2; Benet 87; BiD&SB; BioIn 16; BlmGWL; CamGEL; CamGLE; Chambr 3; ContDcW 89; DcArts; DcEnA; DcEnL; DcLB 18; DcLEL; DcNaB; HalFC 84, 88; HsB&A; NewC; NewCBEL; Novels; OxCEng 67; PenC ENG; REn; StaCVF; SupFW; TwCCr&M 80A, 85A, 91A*

Wood, Henry Joseph, Sir
English. Conductor, Composer
Led London's popular promenade concerts, 1897-1944; introduced unknown composers.
b. Mar 3, 1869 in London, England
d. Aug 19, 1944 in London, England
Source: *Baker 84; BioIn 1, 3, 5, 8, 9, 11, 14; CurBio 44; DcNaB 1941; GrBr; OxCMus; WhDW*

Wood, James Rushmore
American. Surgeon
A founder, Bellevue Hospital, NYC, 1847; began first hospital ambulance service in US, 1869; developed first training school for nurses in US, 1873.
b. Sep 14, 1816 in Mamaroneck, New York
d. May 4, 1882 in New York, New York
Source: *AmBi; ApCAB; BioIn 1; DcAmB; NatCAB 9; WebAB 74; WhAm HS*

Wood, Joe
[Joseph Wood]
"Smokey Joe"
American. Baseball Player
Pitcher-outfielder, 1908-15, 1917, 1919-20, mostly with Red Sox; led AL in wins, 1912, in ERA, 1915.
b. Oct 25, 1889 in Kansas City, Missouri
Source: *Ballpl 90; BiDAmSp BB; BioIn 7, 11, 14, 15; NewYTBS 85; WhoProB 73*

Wood, John
English. Actor
Won 1976 Tony for *Travesties.*
b. 1930? in Derbyshire, England
Source: *BioIn 10, 11, 13; ConTFT 5; CurBio 83; VarWW 85; Who 88; WhoHol 92*

Wood, John Howland, Jr.
"Maximum John"
American. Judge
Appointed 1970-79; only federal judge assassinated in this century.
b. Mar 31, 1916 in Rockport, Texas
d. May 29, 1979 in San Antonio, Texas
Source: *BiDFedJ A*

Wood, John the Elder
English. Architect
England's first great town planner; creator of Bath.
b. 1705?
d. May 23, 1754?
Source: *Alli; McGDA; WhoArch*

Wood, Leonard
American. Physician, Army Officer
Governor general, Philippines, 1921-27; ran for US Rep. presidential nomination, 1920.
b. Oct 9, 1860 in Winchester, New Hampshire

d. Aug 7, 1927 in Boston, Massachusetts
Source: *AmBi; AmLY; ApCAB SUP, X; BioIn 2, 5, 7, 9, 11, 16; CmdGen 1991; CyAG; DcAmB; DcAmDH 80, 89; DcAmMiB; DcNAA; EncAB-H 1974, 1996; EncLatA; GayN; HarEnMi; HarEnUS; LinLib S; McGEWB; MedHR 94; NatCAB 9, 28; OxCAmH; PolPar; REnAW; TwCBDA; WebAB 74, 79; WebAMB; WhAm 1; WorAl; WorAlBi*

Wood, Louise Aletha
American. Social Reformer
Nat. exec. director, Girl Scouts of the USA, 1961-72; recreational supervisor, Federal Works Agency, 1934-42; won Medal of Freedom, 1947.
b. Feb 19, 1910 in Mankato, Minnesota
d. May 16, 1988 in Aurora, California
Source: *BioIn 5, 6, 15, 16; CurBio 61, 88; InWom; WhoAm 74, 76; WhoAmW 64, 66, 68, 70, 72, 74*

Wood, Natalie
[Natasha Gurdin; Mrs. Robert Wagner]
American. Actor
Starred in *Miracle on 34th Street,* 1946; *Rebel Without a Cause,* 1955; *West Side Story,* 1961.
b. Jul 20, 1939 in San Francisco, California
d. Nov 29, 1981 in Catalina Island, California
Source: *BiDFilm; BioAmW; CurBio 82; FilmgC; ForWC 70; GoodHs; IntMPA 82; MotPP; MovMk; OxCFilm; WhoAm 80; WhoAmW 72, 74; WhoHol A; WorEFlm*

Wood, Peggy
American. Actor, Author
Played in TV show "Mama," 1949-57; Oscar nominee for *Sound of Music,* 1965.
b. Feb 9, 1892 in New York, New York
d. Mar 18, 1978 in Stamford, Connecticut
Source: *AmWomPl; BiE&WWA; BioIn 3, 5, 6, 10, 11, 16; CmpEPM; ConAu 77; CurBio 42, 53, 78, 78N; DcAmB S10; EncAFC; EncMT; FamA&A; Film 1, 2; FilmEn; FilmgC; ForYSC; HalFC 80, 84; IntMPA 77; InWom, SUP; LegTOT; MotPP; NewYTBS 78; NotNAT; NotWoAT; OxCAmT 84; OxCPMus; WhAm 9; What 4; WhoAmW 58, 61, 64, 66, 68, 70, 72, 74; WhoE 74; WhoHol A; WhoThe 72, 77; WhScrn 83; WorAl*

Wood, Robert Dennis
American. TV Executive
Pres., CBS, 1969-76; introduced comedies "The Mary Tyler Moore Show"; "All in the Family"; "M*A*S*H."
b. Apr 17, 1925 in Boise, Idaho
d. May 20, 1986 in Santa Monica, California
Source: *BioIn 10, 14, 15; BlueB 76; CurBio 86; LesBEnT; WhoAm 82*

Wood, Robert Elkington
American. Business Executive
Pres., Sears Roebuck and Co., 1928-39; chm., 1939-54.
b. Jun 13, 1879 in Kansas City, Missouri
d. Nov 6, 1969 in Lake Forest, Illinois
Source: *BiDAmBL 83; BioIn 1, 2, 3, 4, 6, 7, 8, 9, 10, 11, 14; CurBio 41, 69; DcAmB S8; McGEWB; NatCAB 55; WebAB 74, 79; WhAm 5; WorAl*

Wood, Robert Williams
American. Physicist
Known for work in atomic, molecular radiation, diffraction method in color photography.
b. May 2, 1868 in Concord, Massachusetts
d. Aug 11, 1955 in Amityville, New York
Source: *BiESc; BioIn 2, 4, 6, 8, 12; DcScB; InSci; LarDcSc; NatCAB 14, 46; NewCol 75; OxCAmH; ScF&FL 1; WhAm 3; WhLit*

Wood, Ron(ald)
[The Rolling Stones]
English. Musician
Guitarist with rock band since 1975; hits include "Going to a Go-Go," 1982.
b. Jun 1, 1947 in London, England
Source: *BioIn 13, 14, 15; ConMuA 80A; OnThGG; WhoAm 80, 82, 84, 86, 88, 90, 92, 94, 95, 96, 97; WhoEnt 92; WhoRock 81; WhoRocM 82*

Wood, Samuel Grosvenor
American. Director
Directed Marx Brothers film *A Night at the Opera,* 1935.
b. Jul 10, 1884 in Philadelphia, Pennsylvania
d. Sep 22, 1949 in Hollywood, California
Source: *BiDFilm; BioIn 2; CurBio 49; DcFM; Film 1; FilmgC; MovMk; OxCFilm; TwYS; WhAm 2; WhoHol B; WhScrn 74, 77; WorEFlm*

Wood, Sarah Sayward Barrell Keating
American. Author
Published anonymous gothic romances: *Amelia, or Influence of Virtue,* 1802.
b. Oct 1, 1759 in York, Maine
d. Jan 6, 1855 in Kennebunk, Maine
Source: *AmAu; AmAu&B; BiD&SB; BlmGWL; DcAmAu; DcAmB; NotAW; OxCAmL 65, 83, 95; REnAL; WhAm HS*

Wood, Sharon
Canadian. Mountaineer
First North American woman to reach the top of Mt. Everest, 1986.
b. May 18, 1957 in Halifax, Nova Scotia, Canada
Source: *BioIn 15; ConNews 88-1; WhoAm 94, 95, 96, 97; WhoAmW 89, 91, 93, 95, 97*

Wood, Stuart
[Bay City Rollers]
"Woody"
Scottish. Musician, Singer
Guitarist with rock group; albums include *Strangers in the Wild,* 1978.
b. Feb 25, 1957 in Edinburgh, Scotland
Source: *BkPepl*

Wood, Tim
American. Skater
Three-time US champion, 1968-70, two-time world champion, 1969-70, figure skater.
b. 1949?
Source: *BiDAmSp BK; BioIn 9*

Wood, Wilbur Forrester
American. Baseball Player
Knuckleball pitcher, 1961-78; led AL in wins, 1972, 1973, in losses, 1975.
b. Oct 22, 1941 in Cambridge, Massachusetts
Source: *Ballpl 90; BiDAmSp Sup; BioIn 9; WhoProB 73*

Woodall, Mary
English. Museum Director
First female director of major British provincial museum, Birmingham Museum and Art Gallery, 1956-64.
b. Mar 6, 1901
d. Mar 1, 1988
Source: *ConAu 125; Who 74, 82, 83, 85, 88; WhoArt 80, 82, 84; WhoWor 74*

Woodard, Alfre
American. Actor
Award-winning TV roles include "St. Elsewhere," "L.A. Law," "Hill Street Blues"; cable TV film *Mandela,* 1987.
b. Nov 8, 1953 in Tulsa, Oklahoma
Source: *BiDFilm 94; BioIn 14, 15, 16; BlksAmF; ConBlB 9; ConTFT 5, 9; CurBio 95; DrBlPA 90; HalFC 88; InB&W 85; IntMPA 92, 94, 96; LegTOT; VarWW 85; WhoAm 92, 94, 95, 96, 97; WhoAmW 91, 95; WhoBlA 85, 92; WhoEnt 92; WhoHol 92*

Woodard, Lynette
American. Basketball Player
Won gold medal, 1984 Olympics; first female member, Harlem Globetrotters, 1985-87; 1993 Flo Hyman award winner.
b. 1959? in Wichita, Kansas
Source: *BasBi; BiDAmSp BK; BioIn 14, 15; BlkOlyM; BlkWAm; ConNews 86-2; EncWomS; InB&W 85; NewYTBS 86; WhoSpor; WomFir*

Woodbridge, Frederick James Eugene
American. Educator
U. professor who wrote *The Purpose of History,* 1916; *Nature and Mind,* 1937.
b. Mar 26, 1867 in Windsor, Ontario, Canada
d. Jun 1, 1940 in New York, New York

Source: *AmAu&B; BiDAmEd; BioIn 2, 4; CurBio 40; DcAmB S2; DcNAA; REnAL; WebAB 74, 79; WhAm 1*

Woodbury, Levi
American. Supreme Court Justice, Politician
Supreme Court Justice 1846-51; advocate of states' rights; held various positions of power at both the state and national level.
b. Dec 22, 1789 in Francestown, New Hampshire
d. Sep 4, 1851 in Portsmouth, New Hampshire
Source: *Alli; AmBi; ApCAB; BiAUS; BiDFedJ; BiDrAC; BiDrGov 1789; BiDrUSC 89; BiDrUSE 71, 89; BioIn 2, 5, 10, 15; CyAL 1; DcAmB; DcNAA; Drake; EncABHB 6; HarEnUS; NatCAB 2; OxCSupC; SupCtJu; TwCBDA; WebAB 74, 79; WhAm HS; WhAmP*

Woodcock, Amos Walter Wright
American. Government Official, Lawyer
Dist. attorney, MD, 1922-30; prosecuted Japanese war criminals for US, 1945-46.
b. Oct 29, 1883 in Salisbury, Maryland
d. Jan 17, 1964 in Salisbury, Maryland
Source: *BiDWWGF; BioIn 6; EncAB-A 22; ObitOF 79; WhAm 4*

Woodcock, Leonard Freel
American. Labor Union Official, Diplomat
Pres., UAW, 1970-77; ambassador to China, 1979-81.
b. Feb 15, 1911 in Providence, Rhode Island
Source: *BiDAmL; BiDAmLL; CurBio 70; EncABHB 5; FacFETw; IntWW 83, 91; NewYTBE 70; NewYTBS 79; PolProf NF; Ward 77C; WhoAm 84, 90; WhoAmP 85, 91; WhoGov 77; WhoMW 74; WhoWor 80; WorAl; WorAlBi*

Wooden, John Robert
American. Basketball Coach
Head coach, UCLA, 1949-75; won 10 NCAA championships; Hall of Fame, 1970.
b. Oct 14, 1910 in Martinsville, Indiana
Source: *BiDAmSp BK; BioIn 6, 9, 10, 11, 12, 14, 15, 16; CmCal; CurBio 76; IndAu 1917; NewYTBE 72, 73; NewYTBS 75; WhoAm 76, 78, 80, 82, 84, 86, 88, 90, 92, 94, 95, 96, 97; WhoWest 94, 96; WorAl; WorAlBi*

Woodhouse, Barbara Blackburn
English. TV Personality
Hosted popular dog training show on BBC, 1980; wrote *Dog Training My Way,* 1981; *No Bad Dogs: The Woodhouse Way,* 1982.
b. May 9, 1910 in Rathfarnham, Ireland
d. Jul 9, 1988 in Buckinghamshire, England
Source: *Au&Wr 71; ConAu 13NR; CurBio 85, 88; NewYTBS 88*

Woodhull, Victoria Claflin
American. Social Reformer
With sister, Tennessee Claflin, founded *Woodhull and Claflin's Weekly,* 1870, which advocated equal rights for women; Equal Rights Party presidential candidate, 1872.
b. Sep 23, 1838 in Homer, Ohio
d. Jun 10, 1927 in Norton Park, England
Source: *Alli SUP; AmAu; AmAu&B; AmBi; Benet 96; DcAmB; EncAB-H 1996; EncWHA; NotAW; OhA&B; OxCAmL 65; REn; REnAL; WebAB 74; WhAm 4; WhAmP; WomFir*

Woodiwiss, Kathleen (Erin)
American. Author
Best-selling novels include *Shanna,* 1977; *Ashes in the Wind,* 1979.
b. Jun 3, 1939 in Alexandria, Louisiana
Source: *ArtclWW 2; BioIn 12, 13, 14; ConAu 23NR, 89; MajTwCW; NewYTBS 79; RAdv 14; TwCRHW 90; WhoAm 78, 80, 82, 84, 86, 88; WhoAmW 81; WhoUSWr 88; WhoWrEP 89, 92, 95; WrDr 86, 92*

Woodruff, Hale (Aspacio)
American. Artist
Created mural series for the Atlanta University library, *The Art of the Negro,* tracing the history of African art and showed its influence on modern art.
b. Aug 26, 1900 in Cairo, Illinois
d. Sep 1980 in New York, New York
Source: *AfrAmAl 6; BioIn 9, 11, 12, 16, 19; ConBlB 9; DcAmArt; DcTwCCu 5; InB&W 80, 85; NegAl 76, 83, 89; NewYTBS 80; WhAm 7; WhAmArt 85; WhoAm 76, 78, 80*

Woodruff, John
American. Track Athlete
Middle-distance runner; won gold medal in 800-meters, 1936 Olympics.
b. Jul 5, 1915 in Connellsville, Pennsylvania
Source: *BiDAmSp OS; BlkOlyM; WhoTr&F 73*

Woodruff, Judy Carline
American. Broadcast Journalist, Author
White House correspondent, NBC News, 1977-82.
b. Nov 20, 1946 in Tulsa, Oklahoma
Source: *BioIn 13; ConAu 13NR, 73; CurBio 86; EncTwCJ; IntWW 89, 91, 93; InWom SUP; WhoAm 80, 82, 84, 86, 88, 90, 92, 94, 95, 96, 97; WhoAmW 74, 75, 81, 85, 95, 97; WhoE 89, 91*

Woodruff, Robert Winship
American. Business Executive
Pres., Coca-Cola, 1923-39; innovations included vending machines, six-pack cartons, large bottles.
b. Dec 6, 1889 in Columbus, Georgia
d. Mar 7, 1985 in Atlanta, Georgia
Source: *BiDAmBL 83; BioIn 1, 2, 4, 7, 8, 11, 12, 13; ConNews 85-1; FacFETw; IntYB 78, 79, 80, 81, 82; WhAm 8*

Woods, Donald
[Ralph L Zink]
American. Actor, Real Estate Executive
Appeared in over 40 films, including *True Grit,* 1969.
b. Dec 2, 1904 in Brandon, Manitoba, Canada
Source: *BiE&WWA; FilmEn; FilmgC; ForYSC; HalFC 84, 88; IntMPA 84, 86, 92; MotPP; MovMk; NotNAT; SaTiSS; WhoHol A*

Woods, Donald
South African. Journalist, Author
Active against apartheid; relationship with Steven Biko is subject of first major anti-apartheid film, *Cry Freedom,* 1987.
b. Dec 15, 1933 in Elliotdale, South Africa
Source: *BioIn 11, 12, 13, 15, 16, 17; ConAu 114, 121; CurBio 82; WhoEng 88*

Woods, Granville T
American. Inventor
Invented electric incubator, railroad telegraph system.
b. Apr 23, 1856 in Columbus, Ohio
d. Jan 30, 1910 in New York, New York
Source: *BioIn 6, 8, 9, 10*

Woods, James
American. Actor
Films include *Against All Odds,* 1984; *Salvador,* 1986; won Emmy, 1987.
b. Apr 18, 1947 in Vernal, Utah
Source: *BiDFilm 94; BioIn 12, 13, 15; ConTFT 5, 12; CurBio 89; GangFlm; HalFC 88; HolBB; IntMPA 86, 88, 92, 94, 96; IntWW 91, 93; LegTOT; News 88-3; VarWW 85; WhoAm 86, 88; WhoHol 92, A; WorAlBi*

Woods, Rose Mary
American. Secretary
Exec. secretary to Nixon, 1969-75; erased portions of Watergate tapes.
b. Dec 26, 1917 in Sebring, Ohio
Source: *BioIn 5, 8, 10, 12, 13; InWom SUP; NewYTBE 73; PolProf NF; WhoAm 74, 76, 78, 80, 82, 84, 86, 88, 90, 92, 94, 95, 96, 97; WhoAmW 74, 95, 97; WhoGov 72; WhoSSW 73*

Woods, Tiger
[Eldrick Woods]
American. Golfer
Golfweek/Titleist, Jr. Golfer of the Year, 1991; youngest player to compete in the Masters, 1995; won Las Vegas Invitational at age 20, 1996; youngest player to win Masters, 1997.
b. Dec 30, 1975 in Cypress, California
Source: *News 95; NewYTBS 95; WhoAfA 96; WhoBlA 94*

Woodson, Carter Godwin
American. Editor, Author
Wrote *The African Background Outlined,* 1936; *The Rural Negro,* 1930; won Spingarn, 1926.
b. Dec 19, 1875 in New Canton, Virginia

d. Apr 3, 1950 in Washington, District of Columbia
Source: *AmAu&B; AmDec 1910, 1920; AmSocL; BenetAL 91; BiDAmEd; BiDAmNC; BioIn 1, 2, 3, 4, 5, 6, 7, 8, 9, 10, 11, 12, 13, 14, 15, 16, 17, 18, 19; CurBio 44; DcAmB S4; DcAmNB; EncAACR; EncAB-H 1974, 1996; EncSoH; FacFETw; InB&W 80, 85; NatCAB 38; REnAL; SelBAAf; SelBAAu; WebAB 74, 79; WhAm 3; WorAl*

Woodson, Robert L.
American. Sociologist
Founder and president, National Center for Neighborhood Enterprise, 1981—.
b. Apr 8, 1937 in Philadelphia, Pennsylvania
Source: *ConAu 127; ConBlB 10; WhoAfA 96; WhoBlA 80, 85, 88, 90, 92, 94*

Woodson, Rod(erick Kevin)
American. Football Player
Cornerback, Pittsburgh Steelers, 1987—.
b. Mar 10, 1965 in Fort Wayne, Indiana
Source: *News 96; WhoAfA 96; WhoAm 94, 95, 96, 97; WhoBlA 94*

Woodsworth, James Shaver
Canadian. Clergy, Politician
Leader, Cooperative Commonwealth Federation Party, 1932 until WW II; member, House of Commons.
b. Jul 29, 1874 in Toronto, Ontario, Canada
d. Mar 21, 1942 in Vancouver, British Columbia, Canada
Source: *BiDMoPL; BioIn 2, 3, 5, 10, 11, 13; DcNAA; DcTwHis; EncWM; MacDCB 78; McGEWB; ObitOF 79; OxCCan*

Woodville, Richard Caton
American. Artist
Painted genre themes of life in Baltimore, MD; known for humorous manner in technique.
b. 1825 in Baltimore, Maryland
d. 1855 in London, England
Source: *ApCAB; BioIn 7, 11; BriEAA; DcAmArt; DcBrBI; Drake; McGDA; NewYHSD; PeoHis*

Woodward, Bob
[Robert Upshur Woodward]
American. Journalist
With Carl Bernstein uncovered Watergate scandal; wrote *All the President's Men,* 1974.
b. Mar 26, 1943 in Geneva, Illinois
Source: *AmDec 1970; AuNews 1; BioIn 10, 11, 12, 13, 14, 15, 16, 17, 18, 19, 20, 21; BioNews 74; BkPepl; ConAu 31NR, 69; CurBio 76; EncAJ; EncTwCJ; IntAu&W 89, 91, 93; JrnUS; LegTOT; LiJour; MajTwCW; NewYTBS 82, 92; PolProf NF; WhoAm 74, 76, 78, 80, 82, 84, 86, 88, 90, 92, 94, 95, 96, 97; WhoE 93, 95, 97; WhoUSWr 88; WhoWrEP 89, 92, 95; WorAl; WrDr 80, 82, 84, 86, 88, 90, 92, 94, 96*

Woodward, C(omer) Vann
American. Historian
Known for studies of history of American South.
b. Nov 13, 1908 in Vanndale, Arkansas
Source: *AmAu&B; AmSocL; Au&Wr 71; BioIn 9, 11, 13, 14, 15, 16, 17, 19; BlueB 76; ConAu 2NR, 5R, 17NR, 44NR; CurBio 86; DrAS 74H, 78H, 82H; EncAAH; EncSoH; IntAu&W 82; IntWW 83, 91, 93; McGEWB; OxCAmL 95; PeoHis; RAdv 14, 13-3; ThTwC 87; WebAB 74, 79; WhNAA; Who 92; WhoAm 74, 78, 84, 86, 88, 90; WhoE 89; WhoUSWr 88; WhoWor 84, 87; WhoWrEP 89, 92, 95; WorAu 1970; WrDr 84, 92, 94, 96*

Woodward, Edward
English. Actor
Starred in Shakespearean roles, British TV, films; featured in US TV series "The Equalizer."
b. Jun 1, 1930 in Croydon, England
Source: *BiE&WWA; BioIn 15; CelR 90; ConTFT 6; FilmgC; HalFC 80, 84; IlWWBF; IntMPA 75, 76, 77, 80, 88, 92, 94, 96; IntWW 82, 83, 89, 91, 93; LegTOT; NotNAT; Who 82, 83, 85, 88, 90, 92, 94; WhoAm 90, 92; WhoHol 92, A; WhoThe 72, 77, 81*

Woodward, Joanne Gignilliat
[Mrs. Paul Newman]
American. Actor
Won Oscar, 1957, for *The Three Faces of Eve.*
b. Feb 27, 1930 in Thomasville, Georgia
Source: *BiDFilm; BioIn 13, 15, 16; BkPepl; CelR 90; ConTFT 3; CurBio 58; FilmgC; HalFC 84, 88; IntMPA 86, 92; IntWW 77, 78, 79, 80, 81, 82, 83, 89, 91, 93; InWom SUP; MotPP; MovMk; OxCFilm; WhoAm 74, 76, 78, 80, 82, 84, 86, 88, 90, 92, 94, 95, 96, 97; WhoAmW 61, 64, 66, 68, 70, 72, 83, 85, 89, 91, 93, 95; WhoEnt 92; WhoHol A; WhoWor 74, 78, 95, 96, 97; WorAl; WorAlBi; WorEFlm*

Woodward, Robert Burns
American. Educator
Won Nobel Prize in chemistry, 1965, for contributing to art of chemical synthesis.
b. Apr 10, 1917 in Boston, Massachusetts
d. Jul 8, 1979 in Cambridge, Massachusetts
Source: *AmMWSc 76P, 79; AsBiEn; BiESc; BioIn 1, 2, 3, 4, 5, 6, 7, 8, 12, 13, 14, 15, 18, 19, 20; CamDcSc; CurBio 52; DcAmB S10; InSci; IntWW 74, 75, 76, 77, 78; LarDcSc; McGMS 80; NewYTBS 79; OxCAmH; RAdv 14; WebAB 74, 79; WhAm 7; WhDW; WhoAm 74, 76, 78; WhoE 74, 77, 79; WhoNob, 90, 95; WhoWor 74, 76, 78; WorAl; WorScD*

Woodward, William E
American. Author
Wrote *Lottery,* 1924; *A New American History,* 1936.
b. Oct 2, 1874 in Ridge Spring, South Carolina
d. Sep 27, 1950 in Augusta, Georgia
Source: *AmAu&B; ConAmL; OxCAmL 65; REn; REnAL; TwCA, SUP; WhAm 3; WhE&EA; WhNAA*

Woodwell, George M(asters)
American. Biologist
Outspoken ecologist known for comments on carbon dioxide and the "greenhouse effect"; founded Woods Hole Research Center, 1985.
b. Oct 23, 1928 in Cambridge, Massachusetts
Source: *AmMWSc 76P, 79, 82, 86, 89, 92, 95; BioIn 7, 13; ConNews 87-2; NatLAC; WhoAm 74, 76, 78, 80, 82, 84, 86, 88, 90, 92, 94, 95, 96, 97; WhoE 95; WhoOcn 78; WhoScEn 94, 96*

Woodworth, Samuel
American. Journalist, Author
Editor, *NY Mirror,* 1823-24; best known novel *The Forest Rose,* 1825.
b. Jan 13, 1784 in Scituate, Massachusetts
d. Dec 9, 1842 in New York, New York
Source: *Alli; AmAu; AmAu&B; AmBi; ApCAB; BenetAL 91; BiDAmM; BiD&SB; BioIn 1, 5; DcAmB; DcLEL; Drake; EvLB; JrnUS; McGEWD 72, 84; OxCAmL 65; OxCThe 67; PenC AM; REnAL; TwCBDA; WhAm HS*

Woody, Elizabeth
American. Poet
Published poetry collection *Hand into Stone,* 1988; co-founder of the Northwest Native American Writers Association.
b. 1959 in Ganado, Arizona
Source: *BioIn 21; ConAu 152; NotNaAm*

Woody, Regina Llewellyn Jones
American. Children's Author
Writings include *Starlight,* 1946; *One Day at a Time,* 1968.
b. Jan 4, 1894 in Boston, Massachusetts
Source: *AuBYP 2, 3; ConAu 3NR, 5R; ForWC 70; MorJA; SmATA 3; WhoE 74; WrDr 76*

Wooley, Sheb
American. Singer, Musician, Actor
Films include *Giant,* 1956; *High Noon,* 1952.
b. Apr 10, 1921 in Erick, Oklahoma
Source: *ASCAP 66, 80; BgBkCoM; BioIn 12, 14, 15; CounME 74, 74A; EncFCWM 69, 83; EncFWF; HarEnCM 87; IlEncCM; LegTOT; PenEncP; RkOn 74; WhoHol 92, A; WhoRock 81; WhoRocM 82*

Woolf, Leonard Sidney
English. Author, Publisher
Wrote novel *The Village in the Jungle,* 1913; play *Hotel,* 1939; founded Hogarth Press, 1917, with wife Virginia.
b. Nov 25, 1880 in London, England
d. Aug 14, 1969 in Rodmell, England
Source: *BiDInt; BioIn 4, 5, 6, 7, 8, 9, 10, 11, 12, 13; CamGEL; ConAu 5R; CurBio 65, 69; DcLEL; DcNaB 1961; EvLB; GrBr; LngCTC; ModBrL, S1; NewC; NewCBEL; OxCEng 85, 95; PenC ENG; RAdv 1; REn; TwCA, SUP; TwCWr; WhE&EA; WhLit; WhoLA*

Woolf, Virginia
[Adeline Virginia Stephen Woolf]
English. Author, Critic
Wrote *To the Lighthouse,* 1927; member, the "Bloomsburys."
b. Jan 25, 1882 in London, England
d. Mar 28, 1941 in Lewes, England
Source: *ArtclWW 2; AtlBL; Benet 87; BiDBrF 2; BioIn 1, 2, 3, 4, 5, 6, 7, 8, 9, 10, 11, 12, 13, 14, 15, 16, 17, 18, 19, 20, 21; BlmGEL; BlmGWL; BritWr 7; CamGEL; CasWL; Chambr 3; CnDBLB 6; CnMWL; ConAu 104, 130; ConLCrt 77, 82; ContDcW 89; CurBio 41; CyWA 58, 89; DcArts; DcLB 36, 100, 162, DS10; DcLEL; DcNaB 1941; EncBrWW; EncSF, 93; EncWL, 2, 3; EvLB; FacFETw; FemiCLE; GayLesB; GoodHs; GrWomW; GrWrEL N; HalFC 84, 88; IntDcWB; InWom, SUP; LegTOT; LinLib L, S; LngCEL; LngCTC; MagSWL; MajTwCW; ModBrL, S1, S2; ModWoWr; NewC; Novels; OxCEng 67, 85; OxCWoWr 95; PenC ENG; RadHan; RAdv 1, 14, 13-1; RComWL; REn; RfGEnL 91; ScF&FL 1; ScFSB; ShSCr 7; TwCA, SUP; TwCLC 1, 5, 20, 43; TwCWr; WebE&AL; WhDW; WhoTwCL; WomFir; WorAl; WorAlBi; WorLitC; WrPh*

Woollcott, Alexander Humphreys
"Town Crier"
American. Author, Critic
Model for egotist in Kaufman and Hart's *The Man Who Came to Dinner.*
b. Jan 19, 1887 in Phalanx, New Jersey
d. Jan 23, 1943 in New York, New York
Source: *CasWL; DcAmB S3; EvLB; LngCTC; ModWD; OxCAmL 65; OxCThe 67; PlP&P; REn; REnAL; TwCA, SUP; WebAB 74; WhAm 2; WhoHol B; WhScrn 74, 77*

Woolley, Catherine
[Jane Thayer]
American. Author
Juvenile books include *Gus Was a Real Dumb Ghost,* 1982.
b. Aug 11, 1904 in Chicago, Illinois
Source: *Au&Wr 71; AuBYP 2, 3; BioIn 6, 7, 9; ConAu 1R, 6NR; DcLP 87A; ForWC 70; MorJA; PenNWW A, B; SmATA 3; WhoAm 78, 80, 82, 84, 86, 88, 90, 92, 94, 95, 96, 97; WhoAmW 64, 66, 68, 70, 72, 74, 75, 77, 79, 81, 83, 85, 87, 89, 91, 93, 95, 97; WhoE 75, 77, 95; WhoWor 93, 95*

Woolley, Charles Leonard, Sir
English. Archaeologist
Best known for discovery of Royal Graves of Ur in ancient land of Sumer.
b. Apr 17, 1880 in London, England
d. Feb 20, 1960 in London, England
Source: *BioIn 3, 21; CurBio 54, 60; DcLEL; DcScB; LngCTC; LuthC 75; NewCBEL; REn; WhE&EA; Who 74*

Woolley, Monty
[Edgar Montillion Woolley]
"Mr. Beard"
American. Actor
Best known for stage, screen title role in *The Man Who Came to Dinner.*
b. Aug 17, 1888 in New York, New York
d. May 6, 1962 in Albany, New York
Source: *BioIn 6, 13; CurBio 63; DcAmB S7; EncAFC; EncMT; FilmEn; FilmgC; HalFC 80, 84, 88; LegTOT; MotPP; MovMk; NatCAB 62; NotNAT B; ObitOF 79; OxCAmT 84; RadStar; WhAm 4; WhoHol B; WhScrn 74, 77, 83; WhThe; WorAl*

Woolman, John
American. Religious Leader
Quaker preacher, 1743-72; best known for his journal, first published in 1774.
b. Oct 19, 1720 in Ancochs, New Jersey
d. Oct 7, 1772 in New York, New York
Source: *Alli; AmAu; AmAu&B; AmBi; AmRef; AmWrBE; ApCAB; BenetAL 91; BiD&SB; BiDSocW; BioIn 1, 2, 3, 4, 5, 6, 7, 8, 9, 14, 15, 19; CasWL; CnDAL; CyAL 1; DcAmAu; DcAmB; DcAmReB 1, 2; DcAmSR; DcBiPP; DcLB 31; DcNaB; Drake; EncAB-H 1974; EncARH; EncCRAm; EvLB; IlEncMy; LinLib L; LuthC 75; McGEWB; NatCAB 1; NewCBEL; OxCAmH; OxCAmL 65, 83, 95; OxCEng 67, 85, 95; PenC AM; RAdv 13-3; RComAH; REn; REnAL; WebAB 74, 79; WebBD 83; WebE&AL; WhAm HS; WhNaAH*

Woolpert, Phil
American. Basketball Coach
Inducted into Basketball Hall of Fame, 1992.
b. Dec 19, 1915 in Los Angeles, California
Source: *BioIn 8, 12, 21; NewYTBS 81; WhoBbl 73*

Woolrich, Cornell
[George Hopley; Cornell George Hopley-Woolrich; William Irish]
American. Author
Wrote novels *Cover Charge,* 1926; *The Bride Wore Black,* 1940.
b. Dec 4, 1903 in New York, New York
d. Sep 25, 1968 in New York, New York
Source: *AmAu&B; Benet 96; BenetAL 91; BioIn 8, 14, 16, 18; ConAu P-1, X; ConLC 77; CrtSuMy; DcArts; EncMys; HalFC 80, 84, 88; LegTOT; Novels; REnAL; ScF&FL 1, 2, 92; TwCA SUP; TwCCr&M 80, 85, 91*

Woolsey, Janette
American. Author
Wrote *It's Time for Thanksgiving,* 1957; *It's Time For Easter,* 1961, with Elizabeth Hough Sechrist.
b. Dec 11, 1904 in Livingston, New York
Source: *AuBYP 2, 3; BioIn 7, 9; ConAu 1R, 2NR; ForWC 70; ScF&FL 1, 2, 92; SmATA 3; WhoAmW 68*

Woolsey, R. James
American. Government Official
Director, CIA, 1995-95.
b. Sep 21, 1941 in Tulsa, Oklahoma
Source: *WhoAm 84; WhoAmP 91; WhoGov 77*

Woolsey, Robert
[Wheeler and Woolsey]
American. Actor, Comedian
Teamed with Bert Wheeler in Broadway musical, film *Rio Rita,* 1929; vaudeville and comedy film stars, 1927-38.
b. Aug 14, 1889 in Oakland, California
d. Oct 31, 1938 in Malibu Beach, California
Source: *BioIn 20; Film 2; FilmEn; FilmgC; HalFC 80, 84, 88; JoeFr; MovMk; NotNAT B; WhoHol B; WhScrn 74, 77; WhThe*

Woolsey, Sarah Chauncey
[Susan Coolidge]
American. Author
Best known for Katy Did series for children: *What Katy Did,* 1872.
b. Jan 29, 1835 in Cleveland, Ohio
d. Apr 9, 1905 in Newport, Rhode Island
Source: *Alli SUP; AmAu; AmAu&B; AmBi; AmWom; AmWomPl; AmWomWr; ApCAB; BbD; BenetAL 91; BiD&SB; BioIn 15; CarSB; Chambr 3; ChhPo, S2; ConAu 115; DcAmAu; DcAmB; DcLB 42; DcLEL; DcNAA; EvLB; InWom SUP; JBA 34; LibW; LinLib L; NatCAB 11; NotAW; OhA&B; OxCChiL; PenNWW A, B; REnAL; TwCBDA; TwCChW 78A, 83A, 89A, 95A; WhAm 1; WhoChL; WomNov*

Woolworth, Frank Winfield
American. Merchant
Founded F W Woolworth Co., 1879; sold only five and ten cent items.
b. Apr 13, 1852 in Rodman, New York
d. Apr 8, 1919 in Glen Cove, New York
Source: *AmBi; BiDAmBL 83; BioIn 3, 5, 6, 7, 9, 11, 12, 16, 18, 21; DcAmB; EncAB-H 1974, 1996; LinLib S; McGEWB; NatCAB 11, 23; OxCAmH; WebAB 74, 79; WhAm 1; WhDW; WorAl*

Wopat, Tom
American. Actor
Co-star of TV series "The Dukes of Hazzard," 1979-85.
b. Sep 9, 1951 in Lodi, Wisconsin
Source: *BioIn 12, 13, 15; ConTFT 7; IntMPA 86, 88, 92, 94, 96; LegTOT*

Worcester, Joseph Emerson
American. Lexicographer
His *Comprehensive Pronouncing Dictionary of the English Language,* 1830 caused plagiarism charge from Noah Webster, resulting in "War of the Dictionaries."
b. Aug 24, 1784 in Bedford, New Hampshire
d. Oct 27, 1865
Source: *Alli; AmAu; AmAu&B; AmBi; ApCAB; BbD; BenetAL 91; BiDAmEd; BiD&SB; BilnAmS; BioIn 3, 6, 11, 13; CyEd; DcAmAu; DcAmB; DcBiPP; DcLB 1; DcNAA; Drake; HarEnUS; NatCAB 6; OxCAmH; OxCAmL 65, 83, 95; REnAL; TwCBDA; WebAB 74, 79; WebBD 83; WhAm HS*

Worden, Alfred Merrill
American. Astronaut
With NASA, 1966-72; command module pilot of *Apollo 15,* 1971.
b. Feb 7, 1932 in Jackson, Michigan
Source: *BlueB 76; ConAu 101; IntWW 74; NewYTBE 71; WhoAm 74, 76, 78, 80, 82, 84, 86, 88, 90, 92, 94, 95, 96, 97; WhoSpc; WhoSSW 73; WhoWest 76, 78; WorDWW*

Worden, John Lorimer
American. Naval Officer
Union commander of the *Monitor* in its fight against the *Virginia,* the first such battle of ironclads, 1862.
b. Mar 12, 1818 in Westchester County, New York
d. Oct 18, 1897 in Washington, District of Columbia
Source: *AmBi; ApCAB; BioIn 4; CivWDc; DcAmB; DcAmMiB; Drake; HarEnUS; OxCShps; TwCBDA; WebAMB; WhAm HS; WhCiWar*

Wordsworth, William
English. Poet
Wrote *Lyrical Ballads,* 1798, with Coleridge; poet laureate, 1843-50.
b. Apr 7, 1770 in Cockermouth, England
d. Apr 23, 1850 in Grasmere, England
Source: *Alli; AnCL; AtlBL; BbD; Benet 87, 96; BiD&SB; BiDLA; BiDTran; BioIn 1, 2, 3, 4, 5, 6, 7, 8, 9, 10, 11, 12, 13, 14, 15, 16, 17, 18, 19, 20, 21; BlkwCE; BlmGEL; BritAu 19; BritWr 4; CamGEL; CamGLE; CasWL; CelCen; Chambr 3; ChhPo, S1, S2, S3; CnDBLB 3; CnE&AP; CrtT 2, 4; CyEd; CyWA 58; DcArts; DcBiPP; DcEnA; DcEnL; DcEuL; DcLB 93, 107; DcLEL; DcNaB; DcPup; Dis&D; EvLB; GrWrEL P; IlEncMy; LegTOT; LinLib L, S; LngCEL; LuthC 75; MagSWL; McGEWB; MouLC 3; NewC; NewCBEL; NinCLC 12, 38; OxCEng 67, 85, 95; OxCMus; PenC ENG; PoeCrit 4; PoLE; RAdv 1, 14, 13-1; RComWL; REn; RfGEnL 91; RGFBP; Str&VC; WebE&AL; WhDW; WorAl; WorAlBi; WorLitC; WrPh*

Workman, Fanny Bullock
American. Explorer
Pioneer Himalayan explorer.
b. 1859 in Worcester, Massachusetts
d. Jan 22, 1925 in Cannes, France
Source: *AmAu&B; AmBi; BenetAL 91; BiD&SB; BioIn 3, 7, 11, 12, 14, 18, 20; DcAmAu; DcAmB; DcNAA; Expl 93; GrLiveH; IntDcWB; InWom, SUP; LibW; NotAW; REnAL; WhAm 1; WhWE; WomFir; WomWWA 14*

Worl, Rosita
American. Anthropologist
Publisher, editor, and founder, *Alaska Native News,* 1982-87; special staff assistant for Native affairs to Alaska governor Steve Cowper, 1987-89; won Gloria Steinem Award for Empowerment, 1989.
Source: *BioIn 21; NotNaAm*

Worley, Jo Anne
American. Comedian, Actor, Singer
Starred on TV series "Laugh-In," 1968-73.
b. Sep 6, 1937 in Lowell, Indiana
Source: *BiE&WWA; IntMPA 96; LegTOT; NotNAT; WhoEnt 92; WhoHol 92*

Worner, Manfred
German. Statesman
First German secretary-general of NATO, 1988-94; W German defense minister, 1982-88.
b. Sep 24, 1934 in Stuttgart, Germany
d. Aug 13, 1994 in Brussels, Belgium
Source: *BioIn 13, 15, 16; CurBio 88, 94N; IntWW 83, 89, 91, 93; NewYTBS 87, 94; WhAm 11; Who 90, 92, 94; WhoWor 84, 87, 89, 91, 93*

Worrell, Todd Roland
American. Baseball Player
Pitcher, St. Louis, 1985-92; LA Dodgers, 1992—; led NFL in saves, 1986; rookie of year, 1986.
b. Sep 28, 1959 in Arcadia, California
Source: *Ballpl 90; BaseEn 88; BaseReg 87, 88; BioIn 15; NewYTBS 87*

Worsham, Lew(is Elmer)
American. Golfer
National Open champion, 1947; leading money winner in 1952 tournaments.
b. Oct 5, 1917 in Altavista, Virginia
d. Oct 19, 1990 in Poquoson, Virginia
Source: *BiDAmSp Sup; BioIn 3, 7, 10, 17; CurBio 54, 91N; WhoGolf*

Worsley, Gump
[Lorne John Worsley]
Canadian. Hockey Player
Goalie, 1952-74, with three NHL teams; won Vezina Trophy twice; Hall of Fame, 1980.
b. May 14, 1929 in Montreal, Quebec, Canada
Source: *BioIn 10, 12; ConAu 111; HocEn; LegTOT; NewYTBE 72; WhoHcky 73; WhoSpor*

Worters, Roy
"Shrimp"
Canadian. Hockey Player
Goalie, 1925-37, mostly with NY Americans; won Hart Trophy, 1929, Vezina Trophy, 1931; Hall of Fame, 1969.
b. Oct 19, 1900 in Toronto, Ontario, Canada
d. Nov 7, 1957 in Toronto, Ontario, Canada
Source: *HocEn; WhoHcky 73*

Worth, Charles Frederick
English. Fashion Designer
Founded House of Worth, Paris, 1858; began Parisian haute couture.
b. Oct 13, 1825 in Bourne, England
d. Mar 10, 1895 in Paris, France
Source: *BioIn 2, 3, 5, 6, 12, 13; DcArts; DcNaB; EncFash; WhoFash, 88; WorAl; WorAlBi; WorFshn*

Worth, Irene
American. Actor
Won Tony for *Sweet Bird of Youth,* 1976.
b. Jun 23, 1916 in Nebraska
Source: *BiE&WWA; BioIn 8, 16; BlueB 76; CamGWoT; CnThe; ConTFT 3, 10; CurBio 68; EncWT; Ent; FacFETw; FilmgC; HalFC 80, 84, 88; IntDcT 3; IntMPA 81, 82, 84, 86, 88, 92, 94, 96; IntWW 74, 75, 76, 77, 78, 79, 80, 81, 82, 83, 89, 91, 93; InWom, SUP; ItaFilm; LegTOT; NotNAT; NotWoAT; OxCAmT 84; OxCThe 83; PlP&P; Who 74, 82, 83, 85, 88, 90, 92, 94; WhoAm 74, 76, 78, 80, 82, 84, 86, 88, 90, 92, 94, 95, 96, 97; WhoAmW 74, 81, 83, 93, 95, 97; WhoE 93, 95, 97; WhoEnt 92; WhoHol 92, A; WhoThe 72, 77, 81; WhoWor 74; WorAl; WorAlBi*

Worthy, James Ager
American. Basketball Player
Forward, LA Lakers, 1982-94; won three NBA championships; MVP, 1988 playoffs.
b. Feb 27, 1961 in Gastonia, New York
Source: *BiDAmSp Sup; BioIn 13, 15; News 91; NewYTBS 83; OfNBA 87; WhoAm 90, 96, 97; WhoBlA 85, 92; WhoWest 92, 96; WorAlBi*

Wortman, Denys
American. Cartoonist
Worked for *NY World,* 1924-30; *NY World-Telegram; Sun,* 1930-54; proofs collected in Metropolitan Museum of Art, NYC.
b. May 1, 1887 in Saugerties, New York
d. Sep 20, 1958 in Massachusetts
Source: *BioIn 1, 3, 5; EncACom; IlrAm 1880, D; ObitOF 79; WhAm 3; WhAmArt 85; WhoAmA 84N; WorECar*

Wortman, Sterling
American. Geneticist
Work at Rockefeller Foundation included "miracle grains."
b. Apr 3, 1923 in Quinlan, Oklahoma

d. May 26, 1981 in Greenwich, Connecticut
Source: *AmMWSc 82; AnObit 1981; ConAu 108; FacFETw; NewYTBS 81; WhAm 7, 8; WhoAm 74, 76, 78, 80, 82; WhoWor 74, 80*

Woss, Kurt
Austrian. Conductor
Directed Tokyo's Fumiwara Opera, 1970s.
b. May 2, 1914 in Linz, Austria
Source: *Baker 78, 84, 92; PenDiMP*

Wottle, Dave
[David J. Wottle]
American. Track Athlete
Middle-distance runner; won gold medal in 800-meters, 1972 Olympics; known for running in golf cap.
b. Aug 7, 1950 in Canton, Ohio
Source: *BiDAmSp OS; BioIn 10; NewYTBS 74; WhoSpor; WhoTr&F 73*

Wouk, Herman
American. Author, Dramatist
Wrote *The Caine Mutiny; The Winds of War,* 1971; *War and Remembrance,* 1978; won Pulitzer for *The Caine Mutiny.*
b. May 27, 1915 in New York, New York
Source: *AmAu&B; AmNov; Au&Wr 71; Benet 87, 96; BenetAL 91; BiE&WWA; BioIn 1, 2, 3, 4, 5, 8, 9, 13, 17; BlueB 76; CelR 90; CnMD; ConAu 5R, 6NR, 33NR; ConLC 1, 9, 38; ConNov 72, 76, 82, 86, 91, 96; ConPopW; ConTFT 1; CroCD; CurBio 52; CyWA 89; DcLB Y82B; DcLEL 1940; EncSF, 93; EncWL; EncWT; FilmgC; HalFC 80, 84, 88; IntAu&W 76, 77, 82, 89, 91, 93; IntWW 74, 75, 76, 77, 78, 79, 80, 81, 82, 83, 89, 91, 93; JeAmFiW; JeAmHC; LegTOT; LinLib L; LngCTC; MajTwCW; ModAL; ModWD; NatPD 81; NotNAT; Novels; OxCAmL 65, 83, 95; PenC AM; REn; REnAL; ScF&FL 1; ScFSB; TwCA SUP; TwCWr; WebAB 74, 79; Who 74, 82, 83, 85, 88, 90, 92, 94; WhoAm 74, 76, 78, 80, 82, 84, 86, 88, 90, 92, 94, 95, 96, 97; WhoAmJ 80; WhoE 83; WhoRel 92; WhoUSWr 88; WhoWor 74, 76, 78, 80, 82, 84, 87, 89, 91, 93, 95, 96, 97; WhoWorJ 72, 78; WhoWrEP 89, 92, 95; WorAl; WorAlBi; WrDr 76, 80, 82, 84, 86, 88, 90, 92, 94, 96*

Wovoka
[Jack Wilson]
American. Religious Leader, Mystic
Originator of "Ghost Dance," 1890-91 regarded as messiah by followers.
b. 1856 in Esmeralda County, Nevada
d. Sep 29, 1932 in Schurz, Nevada
Source: *BioIn 7, 11, 12; DcAmB; DcAmReB 1, 2; EncARH; EncNAB; EncNAR; NotNaAm; OxCAmH; RelLAm 91; TwCSAPR; WebAB 74, 79; WhAm 4, HSA; WhNaAH*

Wozniak, Steven
"Rocky Raccoon Clark"
American. Computer Executive
Co-founder, Apple Computers, Inc; had sales of $583 million in 1982.
b. 1950? in Sunnyvale, California
Source: *BioIn 12, 13; LElec*

Wragge, Sidney
American. Designer
Uniform, understated sportswear for men, women sold under B H Wragge label since 1935.
b. Mar 10, 1908 in New York, New York
d. Mar 28, 1978 in Boca Raton, Florida
Source: *WorFshn*

Wrangel, Ferdinand Petrovich, Baron
Russian. Explorer
Governor of Russian America (Alaska); promoted civilization of area, 1827-34.
b. Jan 9, 1797 in Pskov, Russia
d. Jun 6, 1870 in Tartu, Estonia
Source: *Drake*

Wrangel, Pietr Nikolayevich
Russian. Army Officer
General; served in Russo-Japanese War, 1904-05, WW I, 1914-17; commanded volunteer army, 1920.
b. Aug 27, 1878 in Novo-Aleksandrovsk, Lithuania
d. Apr 25, 1928 in Brussels, Belgium
Source: *REn; WebBD 83*

Wrather, William Embry
American. Geologist, Government Official
Petroleum expert; director, US Geological Survey, 1943-56.
b. Jan 20, 1883 in Meade County, Kentucky
d. Nov 28, 1963 in Washington, District of Columbia
Source: *BioIn 1, 3, 6, 7, 9; DcAmB S7; EncAB-A 36; NatCAB 52; WhAm 4*

Wray, Fay
Canadian. Actor
Starred in *King Kong,* 1933.
b. Sep 10, 1907 in Cardston, Alberta, Canada
Source: *BiDFilm 94; BioIn 8, 11, 12, 14, 16, 17, 18, 20; CmMov; ConTFT 8; DcArts; Film 2; FilmEn; FilmgC; ForYSC; GangFlm; HalFC 80, 84, 88; HolP 30; IntDcF 1-3, 2-3; IntMPA 75, 76, 77, 78, 79, 80, 81, 82, 84, 86, 88, 92, 94, 96; InWom SUP; LegTOT; MotPP; MovMk; NewYTBS 89; OxCFilm; ThFT; TwYS; What 2; WhoHol 92, A; WhoHrs 80; WorAl; WorAlBi*

Wray, Link
[Lincoln Wray]
American. Musician, Singer, Songwriter
Recorded instrumental hit single "Rumble," 1958; released debut album *Link Wray and the Wraymen,* 1960; later recorded *Beans and Fatback,* 1973 and *Indian Child,* 1993.
b. May 2, 1935 in Dunn, North Carolina
Source: *ConMus 17; PenEncP; WhoRock 81*

Wren, Christopher, Sir
English. Architect
Built 52 London churches; helped rebuild London after 1666 fire.
b. Oct 20, 1632 in East Knoyle, England
d. Feb 25, 1723 in London, England
Source: *Alli; AsBiEn; AtlBL; Benet 87, 96; BiDBrA; BiHiMed; BioIn 1, 2, 3, 4, 5, 6, 7, 8, 9, 10, 11, 12, 13, 14, 17, 20; BlmGEL; DcArts; DcBiPP; DcD&D; DcNaB, C; DcScB; Dis&D; EncEnl; EncUrb; InSci; IntDcAr; LegTOT; LinLib S; LngCEL; MacEA; McGDA; McGEWB; NewC; NewCBEL; NotNAT B; OxCArt; OxCEng 95; OxCMed 86; OxCThe 67; RAdv 14, 13-3; REn; WhDW; WhoArch; WorAl; WorAlBi*

Wright, Almroth Edward, Sir
English. Physician, Bacteriologist
One of founders of modern immunology; caricatured in Shaw's *The Doctor's Dilemma.*
b. Aug 10, 1861 in Richmond, England
d. Apr 30, 1947 in Cliveden, England
Source: *BiESc; BioIn 7, 14, 20; DcNaB 1941; DcScB; GrBr; InSci; LarDcSc; LinLib S; NewCol 75; NotTwCS; ObitOF 79; OxCMed 86; WhLit; WorScD*

Wright, Bruce McMarion
American. Government Official
NY State Supreme Court justice, 1983— ; book *Black Robes, White Justice,* addressed the issue of racism in law, 1987.
b. Dec 19, 1918 in Princeton, New Jersey
Source: *BlkAWP; ConBlB 3; InB&W 80, 85; NewYTBS 79; WhoBlA 92*

Wright, Cobina
American. Journalist, Singer
Had leading roles in several operas; columnist for Hearst Newspapers.
b. Aug 14, 1921 in Lakeview, Oregon
d. Apr 9, 1970 in Hollywood, California
Source: *BioIn 15; InWom SUP; NewYTBE 70; WhAm 5; WhoHol 92, A*

Wright, Frances
[Fanny Wright]
American. Social Reformer, Author
Scandalized America by lecturing on birth control, woman's rights; co-founded colony for freed slaves, 1827.
b. Sep 6, 1795 in Dundee, Scotland
d. Dec 13, 1852 in Cincinnati, Ohio
Source: *Alli; AmAu; AmAu&B; AmBi; AmPeW; AmRef; AmSocL; ApCAB; ArtclWW 2; BenetAL 91; BiDAmJo; BiDAmLf; BiD&SB; BiDBrF 1; BioIn 3, 4, 6, 7, 9, 10, 11, 12, 13, 14, 15, 16, 18, 19, 20, 21; ContDcW 89; DcAmAu; DcAmB; DcAmSR; DcLB 73; DcNaB; Drake; EncAB-H 1974, 1996; EncBrWW; EncUnb; FemiCLE; GoodHs;*

HarEnUS; HerW, 84; IntDcWB; InWom SUP; LibW; McGEWB; NatCAB 2; NotAW; OhA&B; OxCAmH; OxCAmL 65, 83, 95; PenNWW A; PeoHis; RadHan; RComAH; REnAL; WebAB 74, 79; WhAm HS; WhAmP; WorAl; WorAlBi

Wright, Frank Lloyd
American. Architect
Designer of homes of functional, dramatic simplicity who helped develop skyscrapers, 1912-36.
b. Jun 8, 1869 in Richland Center, Wisconsin
d. Apr 9, 1959 in Phoenix, Arizona
Source: *AmAu&B; AmDec 1950; AtlBL; Benet 87, 96; BenetAL 91; BioIn 1, 2, 3, 4, 5, 6, 7, 8, 9, 10, 11, 12, 13; BriEAA; CmCal; ConHero 1; CurBio 59; DcArts; DcD&D; DcLEL; EncAAH; EncAB-H 1974, 1996; EncUrb; GayN; LinLib L, S; LngCTC; MakMC; McGDA; McGEWB; MemAm; ModArCr 1; ObitT 1951; OxCAmH; OxCAmL 65, 83, 95; OxCArt; OxCDecA; PlP&P; REn; REnAL; TwCA SUP; WebAB 74, 79; WhAm 3; WhAmArt 85; WhDW; WhFla; WhLit; WorAl*

Wright, Gary
[Spooky Tooth]
American. Musician
Left rock band Spooky Tooth, 1970, for solo career; hit albums include *Dream Weaver,* 1976; *Really Wanna Know You,* 1981.
b. Apr 26, 1943 in Englewood, New Jersey
Source: *ASCAP 80; ConMuA 80A; IlEncRk; LegTOT; RkOn 78; RolSEnR 83; WhoRock 81*

Wright, George
American. Baseball Player
Shortstop, 1876-82; first batter in NL history; Hall of Fame, 1937.
b. Jan 28, 1847 in New York, New York
d. Aug 31, 1937 in Boston, Massachusetts
Source: *Ballpl 90; BiDAmSp BB; BioIn 3, 4, 7, 14, 15; DcAmB S2; WhoProB 73; WhoSpor*

Wright, Harold Bell
American. Author
Best known novels *The Shepherd of the Hills,* 1907; *The Winning of Barbara Worth,* 1911; works popular for moral lessons.
b. May 4, 1872 in Rome, New York
d. May 24, 1944 in La Jolla, California
Source: *AmAu&B; AmLY; ArizL; BenetAL 91; BioIn 1, 2, 4, 10, 12, 15, 20; CmCal; ConAu 110; CurBio 44; DcAmB S3; DcLB 9; DcLEL; DcNAA; Dis&D; EncFWF; EncSF 93; EvLB; LinLib L; LngCTC; NatCAB 34; OxCAmL 65, 83, 95; PeoHis; REnAL; ScF&FL 1; TwCA, SUP; TwCSFW 81; TwCWW 91; WebAB 74, 79; WhAm 2; WhE&EA; WhNAA*

Wright, Harry
[William Henry Wright]
American. Baseball Manager
Organized, managed baseball's first pro team, Cincinnati Red Stockings, 1866; Hall of Fame, 1953.
b. Jan 10, 1835 in Sheffield, England
d. Oct 3, 1895 in Atlantic City, New Jersey
Source: *Ballpl 90; BiDAmSp BB; BioIn 3, 7, 14, 15, 21; LegTOT; WhoProB 73; WhoSpor*

Wright, Henry
American. Architect
Landscape designer, town planner; wrote *Rehousing Urban America,* 1935.
b. Jul 2, 1878 in Lawrence, Kansas
d. Jul 9, 1936 in Newton, New Jersey
Source: *BiDAmAr; BioIn 3, 4, 5; DcAmB S2; EncUrb; MacEA; NatCAB 27; WebAB 74, 79*

Wright, Horatio Gouverneur
American. Army Officer, Engineer
Civil War Union general who led defense of Washington, DC, 1864.
b. May 5, 1820 in Clinton, Connecticut
d. Jul 2, 1899 in Washington, District of Columbia
Source: *AmBi; ApCAB; Baker 84; BioIn 7; CivWDc; DcAmB; HarEnMi; HarEnUS; TwCBDA; WebAMB; WhAm HS; WhCiWar*

Wright, James Arlington
American. Poet
Writings include *The Green Wall,* 1957; *Shall We Gather at the River,* 1968.
b. Dec 13, 1927 in Martins Ferry, Ohio
d. Mar 25, 1980 in New York, New York
Source: *AmAu&B; AuNews 2; BioIn 10, 11; ChhPo, S1; CnE&AP; ConAu 4NR, 49, 97; ConLC 3, 5, 10; ConPo 70, 75; CroCAP; DcLEL 1940; DrAP 75; IntWWP 77; ModAL, S1; PenC AM; RAdv 1; WebE&AL; WhoAm 74, 76, 78, 80; WhoTwCL; WorAu 1950; WrDr 76*

Wright, Jane Cooke
American. Physician
Pioneered in cancer chemotherapy research.
b. Nov 30, 1919 in New York, New York
Source: *AmMWSc 76P, 79, 82, 86, 89; BioIn 8, 11, 20; BlksScM; CurBio 68; InB&W 80, 85; InWom, SUP; NegAl 83, 89; NotBlAW 1; NotTwCS; NotWoLS; WhoAm 74, 76, 78, 80, 82, 84, 86, 88, 90, 92, 94, 95, 96, 97; WhoAmW 58, 61, 64, 66, 68, 70, 72, 74, 75, 77; WhoBlA 85, 92*

Wright, Jerauld
American. Naval Officer, Diplomat
Commanded US naval forces in the eastern Atlantic and Mediterranean, 1952-54; ambassador to Taiwan, 1963-65.
b. Jun 4, 1898
d. Apr 27, 1995 in Washington, District of Columbia
Source: *BioIn 3, 4, 5, 20, 21; CurBio 95N; WhAm 10; Who 74, 82, 83, 85, 88, 90, 92, 94; WhoAmP 73, 75, 77, 79*

Wright, Jim
[James Claud Wright, Jr.]
American. Politician
Dem. con. from TX, 1955-87; succeeded Tip O'Neill as Speaker of House, 1987.
b. Dec 22, 1922 in Fort Worth, Texas
Source: *AlmAP 78, 80, 82, 84, 88; AmPolLe; BiDAmNC; BiDrUSC 89; BioIn 12, 14, 15, 16, 19; CngDr 87, 89; ConAu 49, 127; CurBio 79; IntWW 91; NewYTBS 87; PolsAm 84; Who 92; WhoAm 86, 90; WhoAmP 87, 91; WhoSSW 91; WhoWor 91; WorAlBi*

Wright, John Joseph
American. Religious Leader
Cardinal who was highest ranking American in Vatican, 1967-79; author, *The Christian and the Law,* 1962.
b. Jul 18, 1909 in Boston, Massachusetts
d. Aug 10, 1979 in Cambridge, Massachusetts
Source: *AmCath 80; BioIn 6, 11, 12; ConAu 2NR; CurBio 79; DcAmB S10; IntWW 74, 75, 76, 77, 78, 79; NewYTBS 79; RelLAm 91; WhoAm 78; WhoWor 74, 78*

Wright, John Lloyd
American. Architect, Engineer
Son of Frank Lloyd Wright; established own practice, 1926.
b. Dec 12, 1892 in Oak Park, Illinois
d. Dec 20, 1972
Source: *BioIn 3, 4, 10, 12, 13; McGDA; WhAm 5*

Wright, Lloyd
[Frank Lloyd Wright, Jr.]
American. Architect
Best known for cleaning up slum areas; designed Wayfarer's Chapel in LA, CA.
b. Mar 31, 1890 in Oak Park, Illinois
d. May 31, 1978 in Santa Monica, California
Source: *BioIn 10, 11; ConArch 80, 87; MacEA; NewYTBS 78; ObitOF 79; WhoAmA 80N, 82N, 84N, 86N, 89N, 91N, 93N; WhoArch*

Wright, Louis Booker
American. Educator, Library Administrator
Director, Folger Shakespeare Library, 1948-68.
b. Mar 1, 1899 in Greenwood, South Carolina
d. Feb 26, 1984 in Chevy Chase, Maryland
Source: *AmAu&B; AnObit 1984; Au&Wr 71; BioIn 1, 2, 3, 8, 13; BlueB 76; ChhPo S1, S3; ConAu 1NR, 1R, 112; CurBio 50, 84; DrAS 74H, 78H, 82H; IntAu&W 77, 82; IntWW 74, 75, 76, 77, 78, 79, 80, 81, 82, 83; REnAL; WhAm 8;*

WhE&EA; Who 74, 82, 83; WhoAm 74, 76, 78, 80, 82, 84; WrDr 76, 80, 82, 84

Wright, Louis Tompkins
American. Surgeon
One of the first US African-American surgeons; many accomplishments as a doctor and researcher.
b. Jul 23, 1891 in La Grange, Georgia
d. Oct 8, 1952 in New York, New York
Source: *BioIn 3, 6, 8, 9, 11, 19, 20; BlksScM; ConBlB 4; DcAmMeB 84; DcAmNB; InB&W 80, 85; InSci; NatCAB 43; NegAl 83, 89; NotTwCS; WhAm 3; WorScD*

Wright, Martha
American. Singer, Actor
Replaced Mary Martin in *South Pacific*, 1951; played Nellie Forbush role 1,080 times.
b. Mar 23, 1926 in Seattle, Washington
Source: *BiE&WWA; BioIn 3, 4; CurBio 55; InWom; NotNAT; WhoE 89; WhoEnt 92*

Wright, Mickey
[Mary Kathryn Wright]
American. Golfer
Turned pro, 1954; has 82 career wins, including record 14, 1963; LPGA leading money winner, 1961-64.
b. Feb 14, 1935 in San Diego, California
Source: *BiDAmSp OS; BioIn 5, 6, 7, 9, 12, 14, 17; CmCal; CurBio 65; EncWomS; GoodHs; InWom, SUP; LegTOT; LibW; NewYTBS 76; WhoGolf; WhoSpor; WorAl; WorAlBi*

Wright, Orville
[The Wright Brothers]
American. Inventor, Aviator
Designed engine and flew first flight in power-driven airplane, 1903.
b. Aug 19, 1871 in Dayton, Ohio
d. Jan 30, 1948 in Dayton, Ohio
Source: *AmDec 1900; AsBiEn; BenetAL 91; BioIn 1, 2, 3, 4, 5, 6, 7, 8, 9, 10, 11, 12, 13, 14, 15, 16, 17, 18, 20, 21; CurBio 46, 48; DcAmB S4; DcScB; DcTwDes; EncAB-H 1974, 1996; FacFETw; InSci; LarDcSc; LegTOT; McGEWB; MemAm; NatCAB 14; OxCAmH; RComAH; REn; REnAL; WebAB 74, 79; WhAm 2; WhDW; WorAl; WorAlBi; WorInv*

Wright, Peter (Maurice)
English. Author, Spy
Memoirs of his yrs. as British counterintelligence officer, *Spycatcher*, became int'l. best seller, 1987.
b. 1916 in Chesterfield, England
d. Apr 27, 1995 in Sydney, Australia
Source: *ConAu 128, 148; CurBio 88, 95N; FacFETw*

Wright, Richard (Nathaniel)
American. Author
Became country's leading black author with publication of *Native Son*, 1940.
b. Sep 4, 1908 in Natchez, Mississippi
d. Nov 28, 1960 in Paris, France
Source: *AfrAmAl 6; AfrAmW; AgeMat; AmAu&B; AmCulL; AmDec 1940; AmNov; AmWr; Au&Arts 5; Benet 87, 96; BenetAL 91; BioIn 1, 2, 3, 4, 5, 6, 7, 8, 9, 10, 11, 12, 13, 14, 15, 16, 17, 18, 19, 20, 21; BlkAmP; BlkAmW 2; BlkAWP; BlkLC; BlkWr 1; CamGEL; CamGLE; CamHAL; CasWL; CnDAL; ConAu 108; ConBlB 5; ConLC 1, 3, 4, 9, 14, 21, 48, 74; ConNov 76; CyWA 58, 89; DcAmB S6; DcAmNB; DcAmSR; DcArts; DcLB 76, 102, DS2; DcLEL; DcTwCCu 5; Dis&D; DrBlPA, 90; EncAACR; EncAB-H 1974, 1996; EncAL; EncSoH; EncWL, 2, 3; EvLB; FacFETw; FifSWrA; GrWrEL N; InB&W 80, 85; LegTOT; LiExTwC; LinLib L; LiveMA; LngCTC; MagSAmL; MajTwCW; McGEWB; ModAL, S1, S2; ModBlW; NegAl 76, 83, 89; NotNAT A, B; Novels; ObitT 1951; OxCAmL 65, 83, 95; OxCEng 85, 95; PenC AM; PeoHis; PlP&P; RAdv 1, 14, 13-1; RComAH; REn; REnAL; RfGAmL 87, 94; RfGShF; RGTwCWr; SchCGBL; SelBAAf; SelBAAu; ShSCr 2; SouBlCW; SouWr; TwCA, SUP; TwCWr; TwCYAW; WebAB 74, 79; WebE&AL; WhAm 4; WhDW; WhoTwCL; WorAl; WorAlBi; WorLitC; WrPh*

Wright, Rick
[Pink Floyd; Richard Wright]
English. Singer, Musician
Keyboard player with band on and off since its formation.
b. Jul 28, 1945 in London, England
Source: *WhoRocM 82*

Wright, Robert C
American. TV Executive
Chm., CEO, NBC, 1986—.
b. Apr 23, 1943 in Hempstead, New York
Source: *BioIn 15; CurBio 89; Dun&B 90; IntMPA 92; LesBEnT 92; WhoAm 90; WhoE 91; WhoEmL 87; WhoEnt 92; WhoFI 87*

Wright, Russel
American. Designer
Industrial designer who combined functional efficiency with ease, integrity of design; designed chair, 1933, now in Museum of Modern Art.
b. Apr 3, 1904 in Lebanon, Ohio
d. Dec 22, 1976 in New York, New York
Source: *BioIn 11, 13; ConAu 69; ConDes 84, 90, 97; CurBio 77; DcTwDes; McGDA; PenDiDA 89; WhAm 7; WhoAm 74, 76, 78; WhoAmA 73, 76, 78N, 80N, 82N, 84N, 86N, 89N, 91N, 93N*

Wright, Steven
American. Comedian
Stand-up comic since 1979; films include *Desperately Seeking Susan*, 1985.
b. Dec 6, 1955 in New York, New York
Source: *BioIn 14, 15, 16; ConNews 86-3; ConTFT 9; LegTOT; NewYTBS 85; WhoCom*

Wright, Syretta
American. Singer, Songwriter
Ex-wife of Stevie Wonder; had hit "With You I'm Born Again," 1980 with Billy Preston.
b. 1946 in Pittsburgh, Pennsylvania
Source: *BioIn 10; InB&W 85; RolSEnR 83*

Wright, Teresa
American. Actor
Won 1941 Oscar for *Mrs. Miniver;* nominated in same year for *Pride of the Yankees.*
b. Oct 27, 1918 in New York, New York
Source: *BiDFilm, 94; BiE&WWA; BioIn 10, 17; ConTFT 3, 10; CurBio 43; FilmEn; FilmgC; ForYSC; HalFC 80, 84, 88; HolP 40; IntDcF 1-3, 2-3; IntMPA 79, 80, 81, 82, 84, 86, 88, 92, 94, 96; InWom, SUP; LegTOT; MotPP; MovMk; NotNAT; PlP&P; WhoHol 92, A; WhoThe 72, 77, 81; WorAl; WorAlBi; WorEFlm*

Wright, Wilbur
[The Wright Brothers]
American. Inventor, Aviator
With brother, Orville, made first sustained, controlled flight in power-driven airplane, 1903.
b. Apr 16, 1867 in Millville, Indiana
d. May 30, 1912 in Dayton, Ohio
Source: *AmBi; AmDec 1900; ApCAB X; AsBiEn; BenetAL 91; BiInAmS; BioIn 1, 2, 3, 4, 5, 6, 7, 8, 9, 10, 11, 12, 13, 14, 15, 16, 17, 18, 20, 21; CamDcSc; DcAmB; DcScB; DcTwDes; EncAB-H 1996; FacFETw; HarEnUS; IndAu 1967; InSci; LarDcSc; LegTOT; McGEWB; MemAm; NatCAB 14; NotTwCS; OxCAmH; RComAH; REn; REnAL; WebAB 74, 79; WhAm 1; WhDW; WorAl; WorAlBi; WorInv*

Wrightsman, Charles Bierer
American. Business Executive, Philanthropist
Pres., Standard Oil Co., 1932-53; donated to NYC art museums.
b. Jun 13, 1895 in Pawnee, Oklahoma
d. May 27, 1986 in New York, New York
Source: *AnObit 1986; BioIn 7, 14, 15; CelR; NewYTBS 86; WhAm 9; WhoAm 74, 76, 78, 80; WhoAmA 73, 76, 78, 80, 82*

Wrightson, Earl
American. Singer
Popular baritone; specialized in show tunes, 1940s-50s.
b. Jan 1, 1916 in Baltimore, Maryland
d. Mar 7, 1993 in New York, New York
Source: *AnObit 1993; BiDAmM; BioIn 18; CmpEPM; RadStar*

Wrightson, Patricia
Australian. Author
Wrote *The Crooked Snake,* 1955; *The Ice is Coming,* 1977.
b. Jun 19, 1921 in Lismore, Australia
Source: *Au&Arts 5; AuBYP 2, 3; AuWomWr; BioIn 8, 11, 15, 17, 19; BlmGWL; CamGLE; ChlBkCr; ChlLR 4, 14; ConAu 3NR, 19NR, 36NR, 45; FourBJA; OnHuMoP; OxCAusL; OxCChiL; ScF&FL 1, 2, 92; SenS; SmATA 4AS, 8, 66; TwCChW 78, 83, 89; WrDr 80, 82, 84, 86, 88, 90, 92*

Wrigley, Philip Knight
American. Business Executive, Baseball Executive
Son of William Jr; president, Wm Wrigley chewing gum co., 1925-61; owner, Chicago Cubs, 1932-77.
b. Dec 5, 1894 in Chicago, Illinois
d. Apr 12, 1977 in Elkhorn, Wisconsin
Source: *BiDAmBL 83; BiDAmSp BB; BioIn 10, 11, 15; CurBio 75, 77; DcAmB S10; ObitOF 79; St&PR 75; WhAm 7; WhoAm 74, 76; WhoFI 74; WhoMW 74*

Wrigley, William, Jr.
American. Business Executive, Baseball Executive
Founded Wm Wrigley chewing gum co., 1891; developed Catalina Island into major resort; bought Chicago Cubs, 1916.
b. Sep 30, 1861 in Philadelphia, Pennsylvania
d. Jan 26, 1932 in Phoenix, Arizona
Source: *BiDAmBL 83; BioIn 1, 15, 18; DcAmB S1; Entr; GayN; LegTOT; NatCAB 23; WebAB 74, 79; WhAm 1; WorAl; WorAlBi*

Wrigley, William, III
American. Business Executive
Son of Philip Knight; pres., CEO, Wm Wrigley chewing gum co., 1961—.
b. Jan 21, 1933 in Chicago, Illinois
Source: *BiDAmBL 83; BioIn 12, 15; Dun&B 79, 86, 88, 90; IntYB 78, 79, 80, 81, 82; St&PR 75, 84, 87, 91, 93, 96, 97; WhoAm 74, 76, 78, 80, 82, 84, 86, 88, 90, 92, 94, 95, 96, 97; WhoFI 74, 75, 77, 79, 81, 83, 85, 87, 89, 92, 94; WhoMW 74, 76, 78, 80, 82, 84, 86, 88, 90, 92, 93; WhoWest 96; WhoWor 74*

Wriston, Walter Bigelow
American. Banker
With Citibank since 1946; pres., 1967-70, chm., 1970-84; director, Citicorp until 1984.
b. Aug 3, 1919 in Middleton, Colorado
Source: *BioIn 7, 9, 10, 11, 12, 13, 14, 15; BlueB 76; CurBio 77; Dun&B 79, 86; EncABHB 7; IntWW 83, 91; IntYB 78; NewYTBS 85; PolProf NF; St&PR 87, 91; WhoAm 74, 76, 78, 80, 82, 84, 86, 88, 90, 92, 94, 95, 96, 97; WhoE 74, 77, 79, 81, 83, 85, 86; WhoFI 74, 75, 79, 81, 83, 85; WhoWor 74, 87; WorAl*

Wroth, Lawrence Counselman
American. Librarian, Historian
With John Carter Brown Library, 1923-57; wrote historical, biographical books.
b. Jan 14, 1884
d. Dec 25, 1970
Source: *AmAu&B; BioIn 1, 9, 10; ChhPo S3; ConAu 29R; DcAmLiB; NewYTBE 70; OxCAmL 65, 83; REnAL; WhNAA*

Wroth, Mary, Lady
[Mary Sidney]
English. Author, Poet
Considered to be the first woman writer of English original prose fiction; wrote *The Countesse of Mountgomeries Urania,* 1621.
b. 1587, England
d. 1653?
Source: *BlmGWL; DcLB 121; FemiCLE; LitC 30*

Wu, Chien Shiung
American. Physicist
Proved that the principle of left/right parity conservation does not apply to weak interactions of subatomic particles, 1957.
b. May 29, 1912, China
d. Feb 16, 1997 in New York, New York
Source: *BioIn 5, 20; InSci; InWom; WhoAm 96; WhoScEn 96; WomFir*

Wu, Gordon (Ying Sheung)
Chinese. Entrepreneur
Founder, Hopewell Holdings Ltd., 1972; real estate developer in Hong Kong and China.
b. Dec 3, 1935, Hong Kong
Source: *BioIn 13; CurBio 96; IntWW 91, 93*

Wu, Harry
[Wu Hongda]
Chinese. Political Activist
Political prisoner in China, 1957-79; founder and executive director, Laoghai Research Foundation, 1992—; exposed human rights abuses in China.
b. Feb 8, 1937 in Shanghai, China
Source: *ConAu 145; CurBio 96; HeroCon; News 96, 96-1*

Wulff, Lee
American. Sports Fisherman
Sports fisherman; popularized dry fly fishing for salmon; designed Short Wading vest for fly fishermen in early 1930s.
b. Feb 10, 1905 in Valdez, Alaska
d. Apr 28, 1991 in Hancock, New York
Source: *AnObit 1991; BioIn 13, 14, 17, 18; ConAu 61, 134; IntAu&W 89; NewYTBS 83, 91*

Wummer, John
American. Musician
First flutist, NY Philharmonic Orchestra, 1942-65; original member of NBC Orchestra under Arturo Toscanini, 1937.
b. Dec 31, 1899 in Philadelphia, Pennsylvania
d. Sep 6, 1977 in San Francisco, California
Source: *BioIn 2, 11; NewGrDA 86; NewGrDM 80; NewYTBS 77*

Wunder, George S
American. Cartoonist
Succeeded Caniff as artist for comic strip "Terry and the Pirates," 1947-73.
b. Apr 24, 1912 in New York, New York
d. Dec 13, 1987 in New Milford, Connecticut
Source: *BioIn 15; WorECom*

Wunderlich, Fritz
German. Opera Singer
Tenor who appeared in *The Silent Woman,* 1959; died before scheduled US debut at Metropolitan Opera.
b. Sep 26, 1930 in Kassel, Germany
d. Sep 17, 1966 in Heidelberg, Germany (West)
Source: *Baker 84, 92; BioIn 7, 21; FacFETw; IntDcOp; MetOEnc; NewAmDM; NewGrDM 80; NewGrDO; ObitT 1961; OxDcOp; PenDiMP; WhAm 4; WhoMus 72*

Wurdemann, Audrey May
American. Poet
Won 1935 Pulitzer for verse *Bright Ambush.*
b. Jan 1, 1911 in Seattle, Washington
d. May 18, 1960 in Miami, Florida
Source: *AmAu&B; ChhPo; ConAmA; ConAu 116; DcLEL; InWom; OxCAmL 65; REn; REnAL; TwCA, SUP; WhAm 4; WhNAA*

Wurf, Jerry
[Jerome Wurf]
American. Labor Union Official
Pres., AFSCME, 1964-81.
b. May 18, 1919 in New York, New York
d. Dec 10, 1981 in Washington, District of Columbia
Source: *AmDec 1960; AnObit 1981; BiDAmL; BiDAmLL; BioIn 5, 9, 10, 11, 12, 13; CurBio 79, 82, 82N; NewYTBS 74, 76, 78, 79, 81; PolProf J, NF; WhAm 8; WhoAm 74, 76, 78, 80; WhoAmP 73, 75, 77, 79, 81, 83; WhoE 79, 81; WhoLab 76; WhoSSW 73, 75, 76; WorAl*

Wurlitzer, Rudolph
American. Manufacturer
Introduced first automatically played, electric instruments, 1892.
b. Jan 31, 1831 in Schoneck, Germany
d. Jan 14, 1914 in Cincinnati, Ohio
Source: *Baker 92; Entr; NatCAB 16; NewAmDM; WorAl; WorAlBi*

Wurster, William
American. Architect
Designs include Ghirardelli Square, San Francisco; Cowell College, U of CA, Berkeley.
b. Oct 20, 1895 in Stockton, California
d. Sep 19, 1973
Source: *AmArch 70; CmCal; CurBio 46, 73; WhAm 6; WhoAm 74; WhoGov 72; WhoWor 74*

Wyatt, Jane
American. Actor
Starred in TV series "Father Knows Best," 1954-62.
b. Aug 13, 1912 in Campgaw, New York
Source: *BiE&WWA; BioIn 4, 9, 11, 18, 21; ConTFT 3; CurBio 57; FilmgC; HalFC 80, 84, 88; HolP 30; IntMPA 86, 92; InWom SUP; MotPP; MovMk; NotNAT; SmATA X; ThFT; WhoAm 74, 76, 78, 80, 82; WhoAmW 58, 61, 64, 66, 68, 70, 72, 74; WhoHol A; WhoThe 72, 77A; WhThe; WorAl; WorAlBi*

Wyatt, Thomas, Sir
English. Poet
Introduced sonnet ending with a rhymed couplet; wrote three satire couplets.
b. 1503 in Kent, England
d. Oct 11, 1542 in Sherbourne, England
Source: *AtlBL; BbD; Benet 87, 96; BiD&SB; BiDRP&D; BioIn 1, 3, 5, 6, 7, 8, 9, 10, 11, 12, 13, 19, 20; BlmGEL; BritAu; CamGEL; CamGLE; CasWL; Chambr 1; ChhPo; CnE&AP; CroE&S; CrtT 1, 4; DcArts; DcBiPP; DcEnA; DcEnL; DcEuL; DcLB 132; DcLEL; DcNaB, C; EvLB; GrWrEL P; LinLib L; LngCEL; McGEWB; MouLC 1; NewC; NewCBEL; OxCEng 67, 85, 95; PenC ENG; RAdv 1, 13-1; REn; RfGEnL 91; RGFBP; WebBD 83; WebE&AL; WhDW*

Wyatt, Wilson W(atkins)
American. Politician
Mayor, Louisville, KY, 1941-45.
b. Nov 21, 1905
d. Jun 11, 1996 in Louisville, Kentucky
Source: *BioIn 1, 3, 5, 11, 14; CurBio 96N; WhAm 11; WhoAm 74, 76, 78, 80, 82, 84, 86, 88, 90, 92, 94, 95, 96; WhoAmP 73, 75, 77, 79, 81, 83, 85, 87, 89, 91, 93, 95; WhoFI 81, 83; WhoSSW 73, 75, 76, 78, 80, 82, 95*

Wycherley, Margaret
American. Actor
1941 Oscar nominee for *Sergeant York.*
b. 1881 in London, England
d. Jun 6, 1966 in New York, New York
Source: *ObitOF 79; PlP&P*

Wycliffe, John
English. Social Reformer, Theologian
Involved in rejection of formalism; major force behind Protestant Reformation; compiled English translation of Bible.
b. Dec 31, 1320 in Richmond, England
d. Dec 31, 1384 in Lutterworth, England
Source: *Alli; AmAu&B; BiD&SB; BioIn 1, 2, 3, 4, 5, 6, 7, 8, 9, 10, 11, 12, 13; BlmGEL; BritAu; CamGLE; CasWL; Chambr 1; CrtT 1; DcEnA; DcEnL; DcLEL; EvLB; HisWorL; LngCEL; LuthC 75; NewC; OxCEng 67; PenC ENG; REn; WebBD 83; WebE&AL; WorAl; WorAlBi*

Wyden, Ron
American. Politician
Dem. senator, OR, 1996—.
b. May 3, 1949
Source: *AlmAP 82, 84, 88, 92, 96; CngDr 89, 91, 93, 95; PolsAm 84*

Wyeth, Andrew
American. Artist
Son of Newell Convers Wyeth; subjects are people, places of northeastern states; best-known painting: *Christina's World.*
b. Jul 12, 1917 in Chadds Ford, Pennsylvania
Source: *AmArt; Benet 87; BenetAL 91; BioIn 1, 2, 3, 4, 5, 6, 7, 8, 9, 10, 11, 12, 13, 14, 15, 16, 17, 19; BkPepl; BlueB 76; BriEAA; CelR, 90; ConArt 77, 83, 89; CurBio 81; DcAmArt; DcCAA 71, 77, 88, 94; DcCAr 81; DcTwCCu 1; EncAB-H 1974; FacFETw; IntWW 83, 91; LegTOT; McGEWB; OxCAmH; OxCAmL 65; OxCTwCA; OxDcArt; PhDcTCA 77; REn; WebAB 79; WhAmArt 85; Who 83, 92; WhoAm 74, 76, 78, 80, 82, 84, 86, 88, 90, 92, 94, 95, 96, 97; WhoAmA 84, 91; WhoE 74; WhoWor 74, 78, 80, 82, 84; WorAlBi; WorArt 1950*

Wyeth, Henriette (Zirngiebel)
[Mrs. Peter Hurd]
American. Artist
Specialized in portraits, murals; sister of Andrew.
b. Oct 22, 1907 in Wilmington, Delaware
d. Apr 3, 1997 in Roswell, New Mexico
Source: *BioIn 17; GrLiveH; IlBEAAW; PrintW 83, 85; WhAmArt 85; WhoAmA 73, 76, 78, 80, 82, 84, 86, 89, 91, 93; WhoAmW 58, 61, 85; WhoWest 84, 87, 89, 92*

Wyeth, Jamie
[James Browning Wyeth]
American. Artist
Called most commercially successful artist of his generation; son of Andrew, grandson of N.C.
b. Jul 6, 1946 in Wilmington, Delaware
Source: *AmArt; BioIn 14, 15; BioNews 75; BkPepl; CelR 90; CurBio 77; LegTOT; PrintW 83, 85; WhoAm 74, 76, 78, 80, 82, 84, 86, 88, 90, 92, 94, 95, 96, 97; WhoAmA 73, 76, 78, 80, 82, 84, 86, 89, 91, 93; WhoWor 78; WorAlBi*

Wyeth, N(ewell) C(onvers)
American. Illustrator, Artist
Illustrated popular children's novels; father of Andrew, grandfather of Jamie.
b. Oct 22, 1882 in Needham, Massachusetts
d. Oct 19, 1945 in Chadds Ford, Pennsylvania
Source: *AmAu&B; AntBDN B; ArtsAmW 3; BioIn 1, 2, 4, 5, 7, 8, 9, 10, 12, 13, 15, 17, 19; ChhPo, S2, S3; ConICB; CurBio 45; DcAmB S3; FacFETw; IlBEAAW; IlrAm 1880, B, G; IlsBYP; JBA 34, 51; MajAI; OxCAmH; OxDcArt; REnAL; SmATA 17; WebAB 74, 79; WhAm 2; WhAmArt 85*

Wyle, Noah
American. Actor
Plays Dr. John Carter on TV's "ER," 1994—.
b. Jun 2, 1971 in Los Angeles, California

Wyler, Gretchen
[Gretchen Wienecke]
American. Actor
Stage performances include *Silk Stockings,* 1955; *Damn Yankees,* 1956.
b. Feb 16, 1932 in Oklahoma City, Oklahoma
Source: *BiE&WWA; ConTFT 1, 6; ForWC 70; LegTOT; NotNAT; VarWW 85; WhoEnt 92; WhoHol A*

Wyler, William
American. Director, Producer
Won Oscars for *Mrs. Miniver,* 1942; *The Best Years of Our Lives,* 1946; *Ben Hur,* 1959.
b. Jul 1, 1902 in Muhlhausen, Germany
d. Jul 27, 1981 in Beverly Hills, California
Source: *AmFD; AnObit 1981; BiDFilm, 81, 94; BioIn 2, 5, 7, 10, 11, 12, 15, 16, 18, 21; BioNews 74; BlueB 76; CelR; CmMov; ConAu 108; CurBio 81, 81N; DcArts; DcFM; FacFETw; FilmEn; FilmgC; GangFlm; HalFC 80, 84, 88; IlWWHD 1; IntDcF 1-2, 2-2; IntMPA 75, 76, 77, 78, 79, 80, 81; IntWW 74, 75, 76, 77, 78, 79, 80, 81, 82N; ItaFilm; LegTOT; MiSFD 9N; MovMk; OxCFilm; TwYS A; WhAm 8; Who 74, 82N; WhoAm 74, 76, 78, 80; WhoWor 74, 78; WorAl; WorAlBi; WorEFlm; WorFDir 1*

Wylie, Elinor Hoyt
American. Author
Wrote *The Orphan Angel,* 1927; *Mr. Hodge and Mr. Hazard,* 1928.
b. Sep 5, 1885 in Somerville, New Jersey
d. Dec 16, 1928 in New York, New York
Source: *AtlBL; CasWL; DcAmB; NotAW; OxCAmL 65; OxCEng 67; PenC AM; RAdv 1; REn; REnAL; SixAP; Str&VC; TwCA, SUP; TwCWr; WebAB 74; WhAm 1*

Wylie, Paul
American. Skater
Source: *BioIn 15, 18; WhoAm 94*

Wylie, Philip Gordon
American. Author
Critic of US society known for attack on "momism" in *Generation of Vipers,* 1942.
b. May 12, 1902 in Beverly, Massachusetts
d. Oct 25, 1971 in Miami, Florida
Source: *AmAu&B; AmNov; ChhPo S2; CnDAL; ConAu P-2; ConNov 72; DcAmB S9; EncMys; EncSF 93; EvLB; LinLib S; NewYTBE 71; REn; REnAL; RGSF; SpyFic; TwCA, SUP; TwCCr&M 85; TwCSFW 81, 86; TwCWr; WebAB 74, 79; WhAm 5; WhFla*

Wyman, Bill
[The Rolling Stones; William George Wyman]
English. Musician
Bass player with The Rolling Stones; hits include *Paint It Black,* 1966; *Hang Fire,* 1982.
b. Oct 24, 1941 in London, England
Source: *BioIn 12, 13, 16; IntWW 91, 93; LegTOT; WhoAm 80, 82, 84, 86, 88, 90, 92, 94, 95, 96; WhoEnt 92; WhoRocM 82*

Wyman, Jane
[Sarah Jane Fulks]
American. Actor
Won Oscar, 1948, for *Johnny Belinda;* starred in TV series "Falcon Crest," 1982-90; first wife of Ronald Reagan.
b. Jan 4, 1914 in Saint Joseph, Missouri
Source: *BiDFilm, 81, 94; BioAmW; BioIn 1, 2, 3, 4, 7, 8, 11, 12, 13, 14, 15, 16; CelR 90; CmMov; ConTFT 3; CurBio 49; EncAFC; FilmEn; FilmgC; ForYSC; GangFlm; GoodHs; HalFC 80, 84, 88; IntMPA 75, 76, 77, 78, 80, 81, 82, 84, 86, 88, 92; IntWW 91, 93; InWom, SUP; LegTOT; MotPP; MovMk; NewYTBS 81; ThFT; WhoAm 74, 76, 84, 86, 88, 90, 92, 94, 95, 96, 97; WhoAmW 74, 91, 93, 95; WhoEnt 92; WhoHol 92, A; WhoTelC; WorAl; WorAlBi; WorEFlm*

Wyman, Thomas Hunt
American. TV Executive
President, CEO of CBS, 1980-86.
b. Nov 30, 1929 in Saint Louis, Missouri
Source: *BioIn 10, 11, 12, 13; BlueB 76; CurBio 83; Dun&B 79, 88; IntMPA 92; IntWW 82, 83, 89; LesBEnT, 92; St&PR 84, 87, 91; WhoAm 74, 76, 78, 80, 82, 84, 86; WhoE 83, 85, 86; WhoFI 74, 77, 79, 81, 83, 85; WhoWor 82, 84, 87*

Wyman, Willard Gordon
American. Military Leader
First chief of staff for US Army, 1947-50; honored with many medals including Bronze Star.
b. Mar 21, 1898 in Augusta, Maine
d. Mar 29, 1969 in Bethesda, Maryland
Source: *BiDWWGF; BioIn 3, 4, 8, 9; EncAI&E; ObitOF 79; WhAm 5*

Wynette, Tammy
[Virginia Wynette Pugh]
American. Singer
CMA female vocalist of year, 1968, 1969, 1970; autobiography *Stand by Your Man,* 1979.
b. May 5, 1942 in Itawamba County, Mississippi
Source: *Baker 84, 92; BgBkCoM; BiDAmM; BioIn 9, 10, 11, 12, 13, 14, 15, 16; BioNews 74; BkPepl; CelR 90; ConAu X; ConMus 2; ContDcW 89; CounME 74, 74A; CurBio 95; EncFCWM 69, 83; EncRk 88; GoodHs; HarEnCM 87; HarEnR 86; IlEncCM; IlEncRk; IntDcWB; IntWW 93; InWom SUP; LegTOT; NewGrDA 86; OxCPMus; PenEncP; PeoHis; RkOn 78; WhoAm 74, 76, 78, 80, 82, 84, 86, 88, 90, 92, 94, 95, 96, 97; WhoAmW 81, 83, 95, 97; WhoEnt 92; WhoHol 92; WhoRock 81; WorAl; WorAlBi*

Wynn, Early
"Gus"
American. Baseball Player
Pitcher, 1939, 1941-44, 1946-63; had 300 career wins; won Cy Young Award, 1959; Hall of Fame, 1971.
b. Jan 6, 1920 in Hartford, Alabama
Source: *Ballpl 90; BiDAmSp BB; BioIn 3, 5, 6, 10, 11, 14, 15, 17; FacFETw; LegTOT; WhoProB 73; WhoSpor; WorAl; WorAlBi*

Wynn, Ed
[Isiah Edwin Leopold]
American. Comedian
Ziegfeld Follies star; won Emmy for "Requiem for a Heavyweight," 1956; films include *Mary Poppins,* 1964.
b. Nov 9, 1886 in Philadelphia, Pennsylvania
d. Jun 19, 1966 in Beverly Hills, California
Source: *ASCAP 66, 80; BiE&WWA; BioIn 1, 2, 3, 4, 5, 7, 8, 11, 15, 16; CamGWoT; CurBio 45, 66; DcAmB S8; EncAFC; EncMT; EncVaud; Ent; FamA&A; Film 2; FilmEn; FilmgC; Funs; HalFC 80, 84, 88; JoeFr; LegTOT; MotPP; MovMk; NewYTET; NotNAT B; OxCAmH; OxCAmT 84; OxCPMus; QDrFCA 92; RadStar; WebAB 74, 79; WebBD 83; WhAm 4; WhoCom; WhoHol B; WhScrn 74, 77, 83; WhThe; WorAl; WorAlBi*

Wynn, Keenan
[Francis Xavier Aloysius Wynn]
American. Actor
Mustachioed character actor best remembered for film roles in *Dr. Strangelove,* 1963; *Kiss Me Kate,* 1953; son of comedian Ed.
b. Jul 27, 1916 in New York, New York
d. Oct 14, 1986 in Brentwood, California
Source: *AnObit 1986; BiE&WWA; BioIn 1, 2, 4, 5, 10, 15, 16, 17; BioNews 75; ConAu 120; ConNews 87-1; ConTFT 4; EncAFC; FilmEn; FilmgC; ForYSC; HalFC 80, 84, 88; IntDcF 1-3; IntMPA 75, 76, 77, 78, 79, 80, 81, 82, 84, 86; ItaFilm; LegTOT; MGM; MotPP; MovMk; NotNAT A; SaTiSS; WhAm 9; WhoAm 74, 76, 78, 80, 82, 84, 86; WhoHol A; WorAl; WorAlBi*

Wynn, Stephen A.
American. Businessman
Chairman and president of Mirage Resorts Inc. (formerly Golden Nugget, Inc.),. 1973—.
b. Jan 27, 1942 in New Haven, Connecticut
Source: *News 94, 94-3; St&PR 93, 96, 97*

Wynn, Tracy Keenan
American. Writer
Won Emmys for "Tribes," 1971; "The Autobiography of Miss Jane Pittman," 1974.
b. Feb 28, 1945 in Los Angeles, California
Source: *ConTFT 1, 8; HalFC 84, 88; IntMPA 86, 88, 92, 94, 96; LesBEnT, 92; MiSFD 9; VarWW 85; WhoEnt 92; WhoHol 92; WrDr 96*

Wynonna
[The Judds; Christina Ciminella; Wynonna Judd; Mrs. Arch Kelley, III]
American. Singer, Musician
The daughter in the mother-daughter country duo 1984-91; first solo album, *Wynonna,* 1992; album *Revelations,* 1996.
b. May 30, 1964 in Ashland, Kentucky
Source: *CelR 90; ConMus 2, 11; CurBio 96; LegTOT; News 93-3; NewYTBS 84; WhoAm 90, 92, 94, 95, 96, 97; WhoAmW 91, 93, 95, 97; WhoEnt 92*

Wynter, Dana
[Dagmar Spencer-Marcus]
English. Actor
Appeared in many TV shows including "Gunsmoke," 1969; films include *Airport,* 1970.
b. Jun 8, 1932 in London, England
Source: *BioIn 3, 4; ConTFT 7; FilmEn; FilmgC; HalFC 84, 88; IntMPA 86, 92; InWom; MotPP; MovMk; WhoAm 86, 90; WhoHol A*

Wynyard, Diana
[Dorothy Isobel Cox]
English. Actor
Oscar nominee for *Cavalcade,* 1933.
b. Jan 16, 1906 in London, England
d. May 13, 1964 in London, England
Source: *BioIn 5, 6, 9; DcNaB 1961; EncWT; FilmAG WE; FilmEn; FilmgC; ForYSC; HalFC 80, 84, 88; InWom, SUP; MotPP; MovMk; NotNAT B; ObitT 1961; OxCFilm; OxCThe 67, 83; ThFT; WhoHol B; WhScrn 83; WhThe*

Wyss, Johann David
Swiss. Author
Wrote classic shipwreck, adventure novel, *Swiss Family Robinson* 1812-27; translated by son Johann Rudolf.
b. 1743 in Bern, Switzerland
d. 1818 in Bern, Switzerland

Source: *AuBYP 2S; BioIn 1, 3, 8, 13, 19; CarSB; CasWL; ChlBkCr; DcArts; NinCLC 10; OxCGer 76, 86; Str&VC; WhoChL*

Wyss, Johann Rudolf
Swiss. Author
Wrote Swiss national anthem, 1811; translated father's novel *Swiss Family Robinson* to English, making it adventure classic.
b. Mar 13, 1782 in Bern, Switzerland
d. Mar 21, 1830 in Bern, Switzerland
Source: *BioIn 5, 8; NewCBEL; WebBD 83*

Wyszynski, Stefan
Polish. Religious Leader
Responsible for peaceful co-existence of Roman Catholic church and socialist state in Poland.
b. Aug 3, 1901 in Zuzela, Russia
d. May 28, 1981 in Warsaw, Poland
Source: *AnObit 1981; BioIn 3, 4, 5, 6, 7, 11, 12, 13, 18; ColdWar 1, 2; ConAu 108; CurBio 81N; DcPol; EncCW; FacFETw; IntWW 74, 75, 76, 77, 78, 79, 80, 81, 81N; NewYTBS 81; PolBiDi; WhAm 7; WhoSocC 78; WhoWor 74, 78, 80*

Wythe, George
American. Judge, Lawyer, Continental Congressman
Singed Declaration of Independence, 1776; first law professor, William and Mary College, 1779-89; poisoned by grandnephew.
b. 1726 in Elizabeth City, Virginia
d. Jun 8, 1806 in Richmond, Virginia
Source: *Alli; AmBi; ApCAB; BiDAmEd; BiDrAC; BiDrUSC 89; BiDSA; BioIn 3, 4, 6, 7, 8, 9, 10, 11, 15, 16; BlkwEAR; CyAL 1; DcAmAu; DcAmB; Drake; EncAB-H 1974; EncAR; EncCRAm; EncSoH; HarEnUS; McGEWB; NatCAB 3; OxCAmH; OxCLaw; TwCBDA; WebAB 74, 79; WhAm HS; WhAmP; WhAmRev; WorAl; WorAlBi*

X

X

[D(on) J Bonebrake; Christine ''Exene'' Cervenka; John Doe; Billy Zoom]
American. Music Group
Group formed 1977; influenced by punk, heavy metal, rockabilly, country music.
Source: *ConMus 11; DcLP 87B; DcNAA; EncCoWW; EncPR&S 89; EvLB; NewAmDM; NewGrDA 86; NewYHSD; OnThGG; PenEncP; RolSEnR 83; ScF&FL 1; TwCCr&M 91; WhCiWar; WhLit; WhNAA; WhoMus 72; WhoRocM 82; WhsNW 85; WomNov*

Xenakis, Iannis

French. Composer
Avant-garde musical theorist who developed computerized music; wrote compositions for all media including ''Kottos,'' 1977.
b. May 29, 1922 in Braila, Romania
Source: *Baker 78, 84, 92; BioIn 7, 8, 9, 15; BriBkM 80; CnOxB; CompSN SUP; ConCom 92; CurBio 94; DcArts; DcCM; IntWW 74, 75, 76, 77, 78, 79, 80, 81, 82, 83, 89, 91, 93; IntWWM 77, 80, 90; McGEWB; MusMk; NewAmDM; NewGrDM 80; NewOxM; NewYTBS 76; OxCTwCA; PenDiMP A; PenEncH; RAdv 14, 13-3; Who 90, 92, 94; WhoMus 72; WhoWor 74, 78, 82, 84, 89, 91*

Xenophanes

Greek. Philosopher
Founder of Eleatic philosophy who rejected anthropomorphic gods.
b. 570BC in Colophon, Asia Minor
d. 480BC
Source: *AsBiEn; BbD; BiD&SB; CasWL; Grk&L; InSci; LinLib L, S; LuthC 75; NewC; OxCEng 67; PenC CL*

Xenophon

Greek. Historian, Essayist
Wrote *Memorabilia,* recollections of his teacher Socrates; *Hellenica,* which continued the history begun in Herodotus's *History of the Peloponnesian War.*
b. c. 430BC in Athens, Greece
d. c. 354BC in Corinth, Greece
Source: *AtlBL; BbD; Benet 87, 96; BiD&SB; BlmGEL; CasWL; ClMLC 17; CyEd; CyWA 58; DcEnL; GenMudB; HarEnMi; McGEWB; NewC; OxCClL; OxCEng 67; PenC CL; RAdv 14, 13-4; RComWL; REn; WhDW; WhWE; WorAl*

Xerxes I

Persian. Ruler
Son, successor of Darius I, 486-465 BC.
b. 519BC
d. 465BC
Source: *DcBiPP; LngCEL; McGEWB; REn*

Xuan Thuy

Vietnamese. Politician
Secretary, Central Committee, 1976; Vice-chm., Socialist Republic of Vietnam, 1976—; minister of foreign affairs, 1963-65.
b. Sep 2, 1912 in Hanoi, Vietnam
d. Jun 18, 1985 in Hanoi, Vietnam (North)
Source: *AnObit 1985; BioIn 8; FarE&A 78, 79, 80, 81; IntWW 74, 76, 77, 78, 79, 80, 81, 82, 83; WhoSocC 78*

Xuxa

[Maria da Graca Meneghel]
Brazilian. Entertainer
Host of children's program in Brazil; syndicated to South America and the United States.
b. c. 1963, Brazil
Source: *News 94, 94-2*

Y

Yablans, Frank
American. Producer
Films include *The Other Side of Midnight,* 1977; *Mommie Dearest,* 1982.
b. Aug 27, 1935 in New York, New York
Source: *BioIn 13; ConTFT 1, 8; HalFC 84, 88; IntMPA 75, 76, 77, 78, 79, 80, 81, 82, 84, 86, 88, 92, 94, 96; VarWW 85; WhoAm 74, 76, 78, 80, 82, 84, 86, 88, 92, 94, 95, 96, 97; WhoEnt 92A*

Yablonski, Joseph
"Jock"
American. Labor Union Official
Lost UMW presidency to Tony Boyle, 1969; Boyle convicted of his murder.
b. 1910 in Pittsburgh, Pennsylvania
d. Jan 5, 1969 in Clarksville, Pennsylvania
Source: *FacFETw; PolProf NF; WorAl*

Yadin, Yigael
Israeli. Archaeologist
Organized digs at Masada, Dead Sea caves, published many scholarly works.
b. Mar 21, 1917
d. Jun 28, 1984 in Hadera, Israel
Source: *AnObit 1984; BioIn 6, 7, 8, 9, 10, 11, 14, 16, 19, 21; ConAu 6NR, 9R, 113; CurBio 66, 84N; FacFETw; HisEAAC; IntAu&W 77, 82; IntWW 74, 75, 76, 77, 78, 79, 80, 81, 82, 83; MidE 78, 79, 80, 81, 82; NewYTBS 84; SmATA 55; WhoAm 74, 76, 78; WhoWor 74, 76, 78, 80, 82; WhoWorJ 72, 78*

Yahya Khan, Agha Muhammad
Pakistani. Political Leader
Pres., Pakistan, 1969-71; sentenced to five yrs. house arrest after forced resignation.
b. Feb 4, 1917 in Peshawar, Pakistan
d. Aug 8, 1980 in Rawalpindi, India
Source: *FacFETw; FarE&A 78, 79; IntWW 74, 75, 76, 77, 78, 79, 80; NewYTBE 71; Who 74*

Yakovlev, Aleksandr Sergeyevich
Russian. Aircraft Designer
Well-known for designing Soviet fighter aircraft used during WWII.
b. Apr 1, 1906 in Moscow, Russia
d. Aug 22, 1989 in Moscow, Union of Soviet Socialist Republics
Source: *BioIn 2, 14, 15, 16; DcRusLS; FacFETw; IntWW 77, 78, 79, 80, 81, 82, 83, 89; NewYTBS 89; WhoWor 89*

Yale, Elihu
American. Colonial Figure, Philanthropist
Yale U named in his honor, 1718; governor, Fort St. George at Madras, 1687-92.
b. Apr 5, 1649 in Boston, Massachusetts
d. Jul 8, 1721, England
Source: *Alli; AmAu&B; AmBi; ApCAB; BioIn 8, 11; CyAL 1; CyEd; DcAmB; Drake; EncCRAm; LinLib S; NatCAB 1; TwCBDA; WhAm HS; WhDW; WorAl; WorAlBi*

Yale, Linus
American. Manufacturer
Developed lock for banker's safes, 1865; basic principle still used today.
b. Apr 4, 1821 in Salisbury, New York
d. Dec 25, 1868 in New York, New York
Source: *AmBi; ApCAB; BioIn 21; DcAmB; Entr; NatCAB 9; OxCDecA; WebAB 74, 79; WhAm HS*

Yalow, Rosalyn Sussman
American. Physicist
Developed technique for measuring amounts of biological substances in body, radioimmunoassay (RIA); second woman to win Nobel Prize in medicine, 1977.
b. Jul 19, 1921 in New York, New York
Source: *AmDec 1970; AmMWSc 76P, 79, 82, 86, 89, 92, 95; AmWomSc; BiESc; BioIn 13, 14, 15; CurBio 78; EncWB; EncWHA; FacFETw; IntWW 78, 79, 80, 81, 82, 83, 89, 91, 93; InWom SUP; LadLa 86; LibW; McGMS 80; NewYTBS 77; NobelP; NotTwCS; NotWoLS; Who 82, 83, 85, 88, 90, 92, 94; WhoAm 74, 76, 78, 80, 82, 84, 86, 88, 90, 92, 94, 95, 96, 97; WhoAmJ 80; WhoAmW 64, 66, 68, 70, 72, 74, 75, 79, 81, 83, 85, 87, 89, 91, 93, 95, 97; WhoE 79, 81, 83, 85, 86, 89, 91, 95, 97; WhoFrS 84; WhoMedH; WhoNob, 90, 95; WhoScEn 94, 96; WhoTech 89; WhoWor 78, 80, 82, 84, 87, 89, 91, 93, 95, 96, 97; WorAlBi*

Yamaguchi, Kristi Tsuya
American. Skater
Winner of gold medal in the 1992 Olympics.
b. Jul 12, 1971 in Hayward, California
Source: *CurBio 92; News 92; WhoAm 94, 95, 96, 97; WhoAmW 93, 95, 97*

Yamamoto, Isoroku
Japanese. Military Leader
Admiral who planned attack on Pearl Harbor, 1941.
b. Apr 4, 1884 in Nagaoka, Japan
d. Apr 18, 1943, Solomon Islands
Source: *BioIn 1, 2, 7, 8, 11, 12, 17; GenMudB; HarEnMi; HisEWW; HisWorL; OxCShps; WhDW; WhWW-II; WorAl; WorAlBi*

Yamamoto, Kenichi
Japanese. Auto Executive
Automotive Industries Man of the Year, 1986; Chairman Mazda Motoe Corp., 1987-92; exec. advisor, 1992—.
b. Sep 16, 1922 in Hiroshima, Japan
Source: *BioIn 12, 14, 16; IntWW 89, 91, 93; News 89-1; WhoFI 96; WhoWor 89, 93, 95, 96*

Yamani, Ahmad Zaki, Sheik
Saudi. Government Official
Minister of state, 1960-62; minister of Petroleum and Mineral Resources 1962-86; influential OPEC spokesman, Western ally.
b. 1930 in Mecca, Saudi Arabia
Source: *BioIn 13, 14, 15, 16; CurBio 75; DcMidEa; EncWB; IntWW 83, 91; MidE 82; NewYTBS 86; WhoWor 87*

Yamasaki, Minoru
American. Architect
His more than 300 designs include World Trade Center, NYC; Westin Century Plaza Hotel, LA.
b. Dec 1, 1912 in Seattle, Washington
d. Feb 6, 1986 in Detroit, Michigan
Source: *AmArch 70; AmDec 1970; AnObit 1986; AsAmAlm; BioIn 4, 5, 6, 7, 8, 9, 12, 14, 15, 20, 21; BriEAA; CelR; ConArch 80, 87, 94; ConAu 118; ConNews 86-2; CurBio 86N; DcD&D; EncAAr 1, 2; EncMA; FacFETw; IntDcAr; IntWW 74, 75, 76, 77, 78, 79, 80, 81, 82, 83; MacEA; McGDA; NotAsAm; WebAB 74, 79; WhAm 9; WhoAm 74, 76, 78, 80, 82, 84; WhoWor 74*

Yamashita, Kazuhito
Japanese. Musician
Clasical guitarist; as a teenager won three international competitions.
b. 1961, Japan
Source: *BioIn 11; ConMus 4*

Yamashita, Tomoyuki
Japanese. Army Officer
Led Japanese troops in Philippines, 1944; executed for war atrocities.
b. Nov 8, 1885 in Kochi, Japan
d. Feb 23, 1946 in Luzon, Philippines
Source: *BioIn 1, 2, 3, 8, 9, 10, 12, 15, 18; GenMudB; McGEWB; WebBD 83; WhDW; WhWW-II; WorAl; WorAlBi*

Yancey, Jimmy
[James Edward Yancey]
American. Jazz Musician
Pianist who helped develop boogie woogie, 1930s-40s.
b. Feb 20, 1898 in Chicago, Illinois
d. Sep 17, 1951 in Chicago, Illinois
Source: *BiDAfM; BiDAmM; BioIn 1, 2; BluesWW; CmpEPM; GuBlues; IlEncJ; InB&W 85; NewGrDM 80; OxCPMus; PenEncP; WhoJazz 72*

Yang, Chen Ning
American. Physicist
Won Nobel Prize, 1957, with Lee for disproving principle of parity.
b. Sep 22, 1922 in Hefei, China
Source: *AmMWSc 76P, 79, 82, 86, 89, 92, 95; AsBiEn; BiESc; BioIn 4, 5, 6, 13, 14; CamDcSc; CurBio 58; InSci; IntWW 74, 75, 76, 77, 78, 79, 80, 81, 82, 83, 91; McGEWB; McGMS 80; NobelP; NotAsAm; NotTwCS; RAdv 14; WebAB 74, 79; Who 74, 82, 83, 85, 88, 90, 92, 94; WhoAm 74, 76, 78, 80, 82, 84, 86, 88, 90, 92, 94, 95, 97; WhoAsA 94; WhoE 77, 79, 81, 83, 85, 89, 91, 93, 95; WhoNob, 90, 95; WhoPRCh 87; WhoScEn 94, 96; WhoWor 74, 76, 78, 80, 82, 84, 87, 89, 91, 93, 95; WorAl; WorAlBi*

Yankelovich, Daniel
American. Sociologist
Pres., Public Agenda Foundation; wrote *The Changing Values on Campus* 1972.
b. Dec 29, 1924 in Boston, Massachusetts
Source: *BioIn 12, 13, 14; ConAu 105; CurBio 82; Dun&B 79; Future; PolPar; St&PR 75, 84; WhoAm 74, 76, 78, 80, 82, 84, 86, 88, 90, 92, 94, 95, 96*

Yankovic, Weird Al
[Alfred Matthew Yankovic]
American. Singer, Comedian
Best known for satirizing rock hits: "Like a Surgeon," 1985; "I'm Fat," 1988.
b. Oct 23, 1959 in Los Angeles, California
Source: *BioIn 15; ConMus 7; ConNews 85-4; PenEncP; RkOn 85; WhoCom; WhoEnt 92; WorAlBi*

Yanni
[Yanni Chryssomallis]
Greek. Musician
Debut album *Optimystique,* 1986.
b. Nov 4, 1954 in Kalamata, Greece
Source: *ConMus 11; LegTOT*

Yarborough, Cale
[William Caleb Yarborough]
American. Auto Racer
Stock car racer; has won Daytona 500 four times, second only to Richard Petty.
b. Mar 27, 1939 in Timminsville, South Carolina
Source: *BiDAmSp OS; BioIn 8, 10, 11, 13, 15, 21; BioNews 74; CelR 90; CurBio 87; LegTOT; WhoAm 78, 80, 82, 84, 86, 88, 92, 94, 95, 96, 97; WhoSpor; WhoSSW 95; WorAlBi*

Yarborough, Ralph W(ebster)
American. Politician, Lawyer
Dem. senator from TX, 1957-71.
b. Jun 8, 1903 in Chandler, Texas
d. Jan 27, 1996 in Austin, Texas
Source: *BiDrAC; BiDrUSC 89; BioIn 4, 5, 6, 8, 9, 11, 13; BlueB 76; CurBio 60, 96N; DcAmImH; IntWW 74, 75, 76, 77, 78, 79, 80, 81; IntYB 78, 79, 80, 81; PolProf E, J, K; WhAm 11; WhoAm 74, 76, 78, 80, 82, 84, 86, 88, 92; WhoAmL 85; WhoAmP 73, 75, 77, 79, 81, 83, 85, 87, 89, 91, 93, 95; WhoSSW 73; WhoWor 87*

Yarbrough, Glenn
American. Singer, Musician
Best known for top-ten hit "Baby, the Rain Must Fall," from 1965 film.
b. Jan 12, 1930 in Milwaukee, Wisconsin
Source: *ASCAP 66, 80; BiDAmM; BioIn 6, 8; EncFCWM 69; LegTOT; RkOn 78, 84; WhoRock 81; WorAlBi*

Yarbrough, Lee Roy
American. Auto Racer
Stock car racer who was top driver, 1969; won $188,609, then a record, for Grand National stock race, 1969.
b. Sep 17, 1938
d. Dec 7, 1984 in Jacksonville, Florida
Source: *BioIn 8, 10; NewYTBS 84*

Yard, Molly
[Mary Alexander Yard]
American. Political Activist
President of NOW, 1987-91.
b. 1910? in Shanghai, China
Source: *BioIn 15, 16; CurBio 88; News 91; NewYTBS 87; WhoAmW 91*

Yardbirds
[Jeff Beck; Eric Clapton; Chris Dreja; James McCarty; Jimmy Page; Keith Relf; Paul Samwell-Smith; Anthony Sopham]
English. Music Group
Blues-based rock band, formed 1963; albums include *Little Games,* 1967.
Source: *BioIn 14, 15, 16, 17, 18, 19, 20, 21; ConMuA 80A, 80B; ConMus 10; EncPR&S 74, 89; EncRk 88; EncRkSt; HarEnR 86; IlEncRk; NewAgMG; NewAmDM; PenEncP; RkOn 78, 84; RolSEnR 83; WhoAm 74, 76, 78; WhoRock 81; WhoRocM 82; WhoWor 78*

Yardley, George Harry
American. Basketball Player
Forward, 1953-60, mostly with Ft. Wayne-Detroit; first NBA player to score over 2,000 pts. in season, led league in scoring, 1958.
b. Nov 23, 1928 in Hollywood, California
Source: *BiDAmSp BK; BioIn 5, 14; NewYTBS 75, 85; OfNBA 87*

Yardley, Jonathan
American. Journalist
Book critic, *Washington Post,* 1981—.
b. Oct 27, 1939 in Pittsburgh, Pennsylvania
Source: *BiDAmNC; BioIn 13, 16; ConAu 73; IntAu&W 89, 91, 93; WhoAm 80, 82, 84, 86, 88, 90, 92, 94, 95, 96, 97; WhoE 93, 95; WhoSSW 73*

Yarmon, Betty
American. Journalist, Author
Contributing editor, *Good Housekeeping;* books include *Getting the Most for Your Money When You Buy a Home.*
b. Nov 14, in Plainfield, New Jersey
Source: *ForWC 70; WhoAdv 90; WhoAm 80, 82, 84, 86, 88, 90, 92, 94; WhoAmW 81; WhoE 89*

Yarnell, Bruce
American. Actor
Appeared on stage with Ethel Merman in revival of *Annie Get Your Gun.*
b. Dec 28, 1938 in Los Angeles, California
d. Nov 30, 1973 in California
Source: *NewYTBE 73; ObitOF 79; WhoHol B; WhScrn 77, 83*

Yarnell, Harry Ervin
American. Naval Officer
Commander, Pearl Harbor Naval Station, 1933-36; commander-in-chief of Asiatic fleet, 1936-39.
b. Oct 18, 1875 in Independence, Iowa
d. Jul 7, 1959 in Newport, Rhode Island

Source: *BiDWWGF; BioIn 1, 5, 7; NatCAB 48; OxCShps; WhAm 3*

Yarrow, Peter
[Peter, Paul, and Mary]
American. Composer, Author, Singer
With group Peter, Paul and Mary, 1962-70, 1978—; won Grammy 1963; solo albums include *That's Enough for Me.*
b. May 31, 1938 in New York, New York
Source: *ASCAP 66, 80; Baker 84, 92; BiDAmM; BioIn 12, 14, 21; EncFCWM 69; LegTOT; NewAmDM; WhoAm 74, 76, 78, 80, 82, 84, 86, 88, 90, 92, 94, 95, 96, 97; WhoHol 92, A; WorAl; WorAlBi*

Yastrzemski, Carl Michael
"Yaz"
American. Baseball Player
Outfielder, Boston, 1961-83; only player in AL with 400 home runs, 3,000 hits; won Triple Crown, 1967; Hall of Fame, 1989.
b. Aug 22, 1939 in Southampton, New York
Source: *Ballpl 90; BiDAmSp BB; BioIn 5, 6, 8, 9, 10, 11, 12, 13, 14, 15, 16; CelR 90; ConAu 104; CurBio 68; NewYTBS 83, 86; PeoHis; WhoAm 74, 76, 78, 80, 82, 84, 86, 88, 90, 92, 94, 95, 96, 97; WhoE 95; WhoProB 73; WorAl; WorAlBi*

Yates, Bill
[Floyd Buford Yates]
American. Cartoonist
Drew comic strip "Professor Phumble," 1960-78; comics feature editor of King Features Syndicate, 1978-88.
b. Jul 5, 1921? in Samson, Alabama
Source: *BioIn 5, 12; EncACom; WorECar*

Yates, Elizabeth
[Mrs. William McGreal]
American. Children's Author
Won 1951 Newbery for *Amos Fortune, Free Man.*
b. Dec 6, 1905 in Buffalo, New York
Source: *AmAu&B; AmNov; AmWomWr; Au&ICB; Au&Wr 71; AuBYP 2, 3; BenetAL 91; BioIn 1, 2, 3, 4, 5, 7, 9, 10, 12, 14, 17, 19; ChhPo; ChlBkCr; ConAu 1R, 6NR, 13R, 21NR; CurBio 48; HerW 84; IntAu&W 77, 91; InWom, SUP; JBA 51; MajAI; MorBMP; NewbMB 1922; OxCChiL; REnAL; SmATA 4, 6AS, 68; TwCA SUP; TwCChW 78, 83, 89; TwCYAW; WhoAm 74, 76, 78, 80, 82, 84, 86, 88, 90; WhoAmW 58, 61, 64, 66, 68, 70, 72, 74, 97; WhoProB 73; WrDr 80, 82, 84, 86, 88, 90, 92, 94, 96*

Yates, Peter
English. Director
Oscar nominee for *Breaking Away,* 1979; other films include *The Deep,* 1977.
b. Jul 24, 1929 in Aldershot, England
Source: *BiDFilm, 81, 94; BioIn 12; ConTFT 6; FilmEn; FilmgC; GangFlm; HalFC 80, 84, 88; IlWWBF; IntDcF 1-2, 2-2; IntMPA 75, 76, 77, 78, 79, 80, 81, 82, 84, 86, 88, 92, 94, 96; IntWW 89, 91, 93; MiSFD 9; MovMk; OxCFilm; Who 85, 88, 90, 92; WhoAm 86, 88, 90, 92, 94, 95, 96, 97; WhoEnt 92; WhoWor 89, 91, 93, 95, 96; WorEFlm; WorFDir 2*

Yates, Richard
American. Author
Writings include *Revolutionary Road,* 1961; *Liars in Love,* 1981.
b. Feb 3, 1926 in Yonkers, New York
d. Nov 7, 1992 in Birmingham, Alabama
Source: *AmAu&B; BenetAL 91; BioIn 10, 13, 18, 19; ConAu 5R, 10NR, 43NR, 139; ConLC 7, 8, 23, 76; ConNov 72, 76, 82, 86, 91; DcLB 2, Y81A, Y92N; DcLEL 1940; DrAF 76; DrAPF 80; IntAu&W 76, 77; LinLib L; WorAu 1950; WrDr 76, 80, 82, 84*

Yates, Sidney R(ichard)
American. Politician
Dem. congressman from IL, 1949—.
b. Aug 27, 1909 in Chicago, Illinois
Source: *BiDrAC; BiDrUSC 89; BioIn 11, 13; CurBio 93; WhoAm 74, 76, 78, 80, 82, 84, 86, 88, 90, 92, 94, 95, 96, 97; WhoAmJ 80; WhoMW 88, 90, 92, 93, 96; WhoScEn 96*

Yawkey, Thomas Austin
American. Baseball Executive
Owner, Boston Red Sox, 1933-76.
b. Feb 21, 1903 in Detroit, Michigan
d. Jul 9, 1976 in Boston, Massachusetts
Source: *BiDAmSp BB; BioIn 2, 11; DcAmB S10; WhoAm 76*

Ydigoras Fuentes Miguel
Guatemalan. Political Leader
President of Guatemala, 1958-63; overthrown in coup.
b. Oct 17, 1895
d. Oct 6, 1982 in Guatemala City, Guatemala
Source: *BioIn 4, 13; CurBio 58; IntWW 83N; NewYTBS 82*

Yeager, Chuck
[Charles Elwood Yeager]
American. Pilot
First man to break sound barrier; featured in Tom Wolfe's book, movie *The Right Stuff.*
b. Feb 13, 1923 in Myra, West Virginia
Source: *AmMWSc 95; BioIn 13, 14, 15, 16, 18, 20; ConAu 154; ConHero 1; CurBio 54; FacFETw; InSci; LegTOT; NewYTBS 85; PeoHis; WebAMB; WhoAm 76, 86, 88, 90, 94, 95, 96; WhoHol 92; WhoScEn 94; WhoWest 94; WorAlBi*

Yeager, Jeana
American. Pilot
With Dick Rutan, made longest flight without refueling, flying *Voyager* around the world, Dec 1986.
b. 1952 in Texas
Source: *BioIn 14, 15, 16; ConHero 1; ContDcW 89; CurBio 87; WomStre*

Yearwood, Trisha
American. Singer, Songwriter
Country music singer; released *Trisha Yearwood,* 1991 and *Hearts in Armor,* 1992, both became platinum records; received best new artist award from Academy of Country Music; recorded *The Song Remembers When* in 1993.
b. 1964 in Monticello, Georgia
Source: *BgBkCoM; ConMus 10; LegTOT; WhoAm 94, 95, 96, 97; WhoAmW 95*

Yeats, William Butler
Irish. Poet, Dramatist
Leader, Irish literary renaissance; founded Abbey Theater, Dublin; won Nobel Prize for literature, 1923.
b. Jun 13, 1865 in Dublin, Ireland
d. Jan 28, 1939 in Menton, France
Source: *Alli SUP; AnCL; ArizL; BbD; Benet 87, 96; BiD&SB; BiDIrW; BioIn 1, 2, 3, 4, 5, 6, 7, 8, 9, 10, 11, 12, 13, 14, 15, 16, 17, 18, 19, 20; BritWr 6; CamGEL; CamGLE; CamGWoT; CasWL; Chambr 3; ChhPo, S1, S2, S3; CnDBLB 5; CnE&AP; CnMD; CnMWL; CnThe; ConAu 45NR, 104, 127; CrtSuDr; CyWA 58; DcEnA, A; DcIrB 78, 88; DcIrL, 96; DcIrW 1; DcLB 10, 19, 98, 156; DcLEL; DcNaB 1931; Dis&D; EncPaPR 91; EncWL, 2, 3; EncWT; Ent; EvLB; FacFETw; GrBr; GrWrEL DR, P; IriPla; LegTOT; LinLib L, S; LngCTC; MagSWL; MajMD 1; MajTwCW; MakMC; McGEWB; McGEWD 72, 84; ModBrL, S1, S2; ModIrL; ModWD; NewC; NewCBEL; NewEOp 71; NobelP; NotNAT A, B; OxCEng 67, 85, 95; OxCThe 67, 83; OxDcOp; PenC ENG; PenEncH; PlP&P; PoIre; RAdv 1, 14, 13-1, 13-2; RComWL; REn; REnWD; RfGEnL 91; TwCA, SUP; TwCLC 1, 11, 18, 31; TwCWr; VicBrit; WebE&AL; WhDW; WhE&EA; WhoNob, 90, 95; WhoTwCL; WhThe; WorAl; WorAlBi; WorLitC; WrPh*

Yeats-Brown, F(rancis Charles Claypon)
English. Author, Army Officer
Best known for autobiographical *Lives of a Bengal Lancer,* 1930.
b. Aug 15, 1886 in Genoa, Italy
d. Dec 19, 1944 in London, England
Source: *ConAu 119; CurBio 45; DcLEL; EvLB; LngCTC; REn; TwCA, SUP; TwCWr; WhE&EA*

Yegorov, Boris (Borisovitch)
Russian. Cosmonaut, Physician
Made 16 orbits of Earth in Voshkod I, the first multi-passenger spacecraft, becoming the first physician to practice medicine in outer space, 1964.
b. Nov 26, 1937
d. Sep 12, 1994 in Moscow, Russia
Source: *BioIn 8, 15, 20; CurBio 94N; FacFETw; WhoSpc*

Ye Jianying
Chinese. Political Leader
A founder, People's Liberation Army; one of leaders of the "Long March," 1934-35.
b. May 14, 1897 in Meixien, China
d. Oct 22, 1986 in Beijing, China
Source: *AnObit 1986; ConNews 87-1; EncRev; FacFETw*

Yellen, Jack
American. Author, Songwriter
Wrote "Happy Days Are Here Again," 1929, which became campagin theme song for Franklin Delano Roosevelt, 1932.
b. Jul 6, 1892 in Razcki, Poland
d. Apr 17, 1991 in Springville, New York
Source: *AmPS; AmSong; ASCAP 66, 80; BiDAmM; BiE&WWA; BioIn 4, 15, 17; CmpEPM; NewCBMT; NotNAT; OxCPMus; Sw&Ld C; WhAm 10; WhoEnt 92; WorAl; WorAlBi*

Yellow Robe, Rosebud
American. Author
Published stories she learned from her father in *Tonweya and the Eagles, and Other Lakota Indian Tales,* 1979.
b. Feb 26, 1907
d. Oct 5, 1992
Source: *BioIn 21; NotNaAm*

Yeltsin, Boris (Nikolayevich)
Russian. Political Leader
First popularly elected pres. in Russia's history, 1991—.
b. Feb 1, 1931 in Sverdlovsk, Union of Soviet Socialist Republics
Source: *BioIn 15, 16, 18; ConAu 140; CurBio 89; EncCW; FacFETw; IntWW 89, 91, 93; News 91, 91-1; NewYTBS 90, 91; Who 94; WhoRus; WhoWor 91, 93, 95, 96, 97; WorAlBi; WrDr 96*

Yen, Samuel
Chinese. Endocrinologist
Known for studies on growth hormone Dehydroepiandrosterone.
b. Feb 22, 1927 in Beijing, China
Source: *News 96*

Yeon, John B
American. Architect
Mostly self-taught; noted for manipulation of landscape in designs: Visitors Information Center, Portland, 1948.
b. 1910 in Portland, Oregon
Source: *MacEA; McGDA*

Yepremian, Garo
[Garabed Sarkis Yepremian]
American. Football Player
Kicker, 1966-67, 1970-81, mostly with Miami; led NFL in scoring, 1971.
b. Jun 2, 1944 in Larnaca, Cyprus
Source: *BioIn 13, 14; NewYTBE 72; NewYTBS 80; WhoAm 82; WhoFtbl 74*

Yerby, Frank (Garvin)
American. Author
Popular historical romances include *Foxes of Harrow,* 1946; *McKenzie's Hundred,* 1986.
b. Sep 5, 1916 in Augusta, Georgia
d. Nov 29, 1991 in Madrid, Spain
Source: *AmAu&B; AmNov; AnObit 1992; Au&Wr 71; Benet 87, 96; BenetAL 91; BioIn 1, 2, 3, 4, 5, 7, 9, 12, 14, 17, 18, 19; BlkAWP; BlkLC; BlkWr 1; BlueB 76; CamGLE; CamHAL; CivR 74; ConAu 9R, 16NR; ConLC 1, 7, 70; ConNov 72, 82, 86, 91; CurBio 46, 92N; DcEnL; DcLB 76; DcLEL 1940; DcTwCCu 5; EarBlAP; EncSoH; GrWrEL N; InB&W 80, 85; IntAu&W 76, 77, 82, 89, 91, 93; IntWW 74, 75, 76, 77, 78, 79, 80, 81, 82, 83, 89, 91; LegTOT; LinLib L; LivgBAA; LngCTC; MajTwCW; NegAl 76, 89; Novels; OxCAmL 65, 83, 95; PenC AM; RAdv 14; RfGAmL 87, 94; ScF&FL 92; SchCGBL; SelBAAf; SelBAAu; SouBlCW; SouWr; TwCA SUP; TwCRGW; TwCRHW 90, 94; WebAB 74, 79; WhAm 10; Who 74, 82, 83, 85, 88, 90, 92; WhoAm 74, 76, 78, 80, 82, 84, 86, 88, 90; WhoBlA 75, 77, 80, 85, 90, 92, 94N; WhoUSWr 88; WhoWrEP 89, 92; WorAl; WrDr 76, 80, 82, 84, 86, 88, 90, 92, 94N*

Yergin, Daniel
American. Author
Winner of Pulitzer Prize for general non fiction, *The Prize: The Epic Quest for Oil, Money and Power,* 1992.
b. Feb 6, 1947 in Los Angeles, California
Source: *ConAu 103; RAdv 14; WhoAm 90*

Yermolova, Maria Nikolayevna
Russian. Actor
Dramatic actress; career spanned 50 years; first person in Soviet Union to be named People's Artist of the Republic, 1920.
b. Jul 3, 1853 in Moscow, Russia
d. Mar 12, 1928 in Moscow, Union of Soviet Socialist Republics
Source: *ContDcW 89; EncWT; IntDcWB; NotNAT B*

Yes
[Jon Anderson; Peter Banks; Bill Bruford; Geoff Downes; Trevor Horn; Steve Howe; Tony Kaye; Patrick Moraz; Trevor Rabin; Chris Squire; Rick Wakeman; Alan White]
English. Music Group
Biggest hit single "Owner of a Lonely Heart," 1983.
Source: *Au&Wr 71; BioIn 11, 14, 15, 16, 17, 18; ConAu 3NR, 45; ConMuA 80A; ConMus 8; DcLEL 1940; DcLP 87A; DrAPF 80, 83, 85, 87, 89, 91, 93, 97; EncPR&S 74, 89; EncRk 88; EncRkSt; HarEnR 86; IlEncRk; MotPP; NewAgMG; NewAmDM; NewYTBS 85; OxCPMus; PenEncP; RkOn 78; RolSEnR 83; St&PR 96, 97; WhoAm 76, 78, 80, 82, 84, 86, 88, 90; WhoEnt 92; WhoHol 92; WhoRock 81; WhoRocM 82; WhoScEu 91-1; WrDr 76, 80, 82, 84, 86, 88*

Yeshurun, Avot
[Yehiel Perlmutter]
Israeli. Poet
Poetry collections include *The Wisdom of the Road,* 1942 (*Al Hahmot Derahim*); one of the first Israeli poets to discuss the establishment of a Palestinian homeland.
b. Sep 1904 in Niskish, Poland
d. Feb 22, 1992 in Jerusalem, Israel
Source: *ConAu 132, 136; ConLC 76; WhoWorJ 72, 78*

Yetnikoff, Walter
American. Music Executive
Pres. CBS/Records Group, 1975—; vp, director, CBS Inc.
b. Aug 11, 1933 in New York, New York
Source: *BioIn 15, 16; ConNews 88-1; Dun&B 88; WhoAm 90; WhoEnt 92*

Yeutter, Clayton Keith
American. Government Official
US trade representative, 1985-1989; US Secretary of Agriculture, 1989-1993.
b. Dec 10, 1930 in Eustis, Nebraska
Source: *BiDrUSE 89; BioIn 14, 15, 16; CngDr 89; CurBio 88; IntWW 91; NewYTBS 85, 86; WhoAm 74, 76, 82, 86, 88, 90, 92, 95, 96; WhoAmL 79; WhoAmP 73, 75, 77, 79, 81, 83, 85, 87, 89, 91, 93, 95; WhoE 91, 93, 95; WhoFI 81, 85, 87, 89, 92; WhoGov 72, 75, 77; WhoWor 91, 93, 95*

Yevtushenko, Yevgeny
Russian. Poet
Wrote poems critical of Stalin's legacy; wrote "Babiy Yar," 1961, attacking anti-Semitism, and "Stalin's Heirs," 1962.
b. Jul 18, 1933 in Zima Junction, Union of Soviet Socialist Republics
Source: *ConAu 33NR, 81; ConLC 26, 51; CurBio 94; LegTOT; LinLib L; MagSWL; MajTwCW; MakMC; RAdv 14, 13-2; WhoHol 92; WorAlBi*

Yezierska, Anzia
American. Author
Wrote of NY's Jewish immigrants: *Hungry Hearts,* 1920.
b. 1885 in Sukovoly, Russia
d. Nov 21, 1970 in Ontario, California
Source: *AmAu&B; ArtclWW 2; BenetAL 91; BioIn 2, 4, 7, 9, 12, 14, 15, 17, 19, 20, 21; BlmGWL; CamGLE; CamHAL; ConAu 89, 126; ConLC 46; DcAmImH; DcLB 28; InWom, SUP; JeAmFiW; LinLib L; MajTwCW; NotAW MOD; OxCAmL 65, 83, 95; REnAL; TwCA, SUP; WhAm 7; WomNov*

Yoakam, Dwight
American. Singer
Country singer's hits include *Honky Tonk Man,* 1987; named best new male

vocalist 1987 by the American Academy of Country Music.
b. Oct 23, 1956 in Pikeville, Kentucky
Source: *BgBkCoM; BioIn 16; CelR 90; ConMus 1; EncRkSt; LegTOT; News 92; WhoAm 92, 94, 95, 96, 97; WhoEnt 92; WhoNeCM*

Yoba, Malik
[Abdul-Malik Kashie Yoba]
American. Actor
Appeared in films *Cool Runnings,* 1992; *Smoke,* 1995.
b. Sep 17, 1967 in New York, New York
Source: *ConBlB 11; WhoAfA 96*

Yogananda, Paramahansa, Swami
[Mukunda Lal Ghosh]
Indian. Mystic
Founder, Self-Realization Fellowship, 1950; taught Kriya yoga.
b. Jan 5, 1893 in Gorakhpur, India
d. Mar 7, 1952 in Los Angeles, California
Source: *BiDAmCu; EncO&P 1, 2, 3; NewAgE 90; ObitOF 79*

Yokich, Stephen P.
American. Labor Union Official
President of the International Union of United Automobile, Aerospace, and Agricultural Implement Workers of America (UAW), 1995—.
b. Aug 20, 1935 in Detroit, Michigan
Source: *BioIn 13; News 95*

Yon, Pietro Alessandro
American. Organist, Composer
Organist, musical director, NY's St. Patrick's Cathedral since 1926.
b. Aug 8, 1886 in Turin, Italy
d. Nov 22, 1943 in Long Island, New York
Source: *ASCAP 66, 80; Baker 78, 84, 92; BioIn 1, 4, 6; ConAmC 76, 82; CurBio 44; DcAmB S3; DcCathB; NewGrDA 86; WhAm 2*

Yonge, Charlotte Mary
English. Author
Writings include *The Heir of Redclyffe,* 1853; *The Daisy Chain,* 1856.
b. Aug 11, 1823 in Otterbourne, England
d. Mar 24, 1901 in Elderfield, England
Source: *Alli; BiD&SB; CasWL; DcBiA; DcBiPP; DcEnA, A; DcEnL; DcEuL; DcLB 163; DcLEL; EvLB; FamSYP; JBA 34; NewC; OxCEng 67; PenC ENG; REn; WhoChL*

Yonger Brothers, The
[Bob Younger; Cole Younger; Jim Younger]
American. Criminals
Famous gang of robbers, murderers; rode with James brothers.
Source: *BioIn 2, 4, 7, 8, 9, 10; DrInf; REnAW*

Yordan, Philip
American. Screenwriter
Won Oscar for *Broken Lance,* 1954; films include *God's Little Acre,* 1958.
b. 1913 in Chicago, Illinois
Source: *BiDFilm 94; CmMov; ConAu 116, 129; FilmEn; FilmgC; GangFlm; HalFC 80, 84, 88; IntMPA 77, 86, 92, 94; ItaFilm; NotNAT; OxCAmT 84; OxCFilm; VarWW 85; WorEFlm*

York, David
American. Social Worker
Founded Toughlove to help parents solve problems with children through strict discipline.
b. 1929? in Long Island, New York
Source: *BioIn 12*

York, Dick
[Richard Allen York]
American. Actor
Played the first Darrin in TV series "Bewitched," 1964-69.
b. Sep 4, 1928 in Fort Wayne, Indiana
d. Feb 20, 1992 in Grand Rapids, Michigan
Source: *AnObit 1992; BioIn 16, 19; EncAFC; FilmgC; ForYSC; HalFC 80, 84, 88; IntMPA 75, 76, 77, 78, 79, 80, 81, 82, 84, 86, 88, 92; LegTOT; MotPP; News 92; NewYTBS 92; RadStar; WhoHol 92, A*

York, Edward Palmer
American. Architect
Designs include post office, customs house, courts bldg., Honolulu, HI.
b. 1865 in Wellsville, New York
d. Dec 30, 1928
Source: *BiDAmAr; BioIn 2; BriEAA; MacEA; WhAm 1*

York, Michael
[Michael York-Johnson]
English. Actor
Starred in *The Island of Dr. Moreau,* 1977; on tour in *Cyrano de Bergerac,* 1981.
b. Mar 27, 1942 in Fulmer, England
Source: *BioIn 8, 10, 11, 18; BkPepl; CelR, 90; ConTFT 1, 6, 13; CurBio 76; FilmAG WE; FilmEn; FilmgC; HalFC 80, 84, 88; IlWWBF; IntDcF 1-3; IntMPA 75, 76, 77, 78, 79, 80, 81, 82, 84, 86, 88, 92, 94, 96; IntWW 82, 83, 89, 91, 93; ItaFilm; LegTOT; MotPP; MovMk; OxCFilm; Who 85, 88, 90, 92, 94; WhoAm 76, 78, 80, 82, 84, 86, 88, 90, 92, 94, 95, 96, 97; WhoEnt 92; WhoHol 92, A; WhoHrs 80; WorAl; WorAlBi*

York, Rudy
[Rudolph Preston York]
American. Baseball Player
First baseman, 1934, 1937-48, mostly with Detroit; led AL in home runs, RBIs, 1943.
b. Aug 17, 1913 in Ragland, Alabama
d. Feb 5, 1970 in Rome, Georgia
Source: *Ballpl 90; BioIn 1, 4, 6, 8; WhoProB 73; WhoSpor*

York, Sergeant
[Alvin Cullum York]
American. Soldier
WW I hero; autobiography *Sergeant York* was filmed, 1941; won 50 medals including Congressional Medal of Honor.
b. Dec 13, 1887 in Pall Mall, Tennessee
d. Dec 2, 1964 in Nashville, Tennessee
Source: *BioIn 1, 2, 4, 5, 6, 7, 8, 9, 12, 14, 15; DcAmB S7; DcAmMiB; NewCol 75; WebAB 74, 79; WebAMB; WorAl*

York, Susannah
[Susannah Yolande Fletcher]
English. Actor
1969 Oscar nominee for *They Shoot Horses, Don't They?*
b. Jan 9, 1941 in London, England
Source: *BiDFilm, 81, 94; BioIn 5, 6, 9, 10, 11, 16; CelR; ConAu 130; ConTFT 5; FilmEn; FilmgC; HalFC 84, 88; IlWWBF; IntMPA 86, 88, 92, 94, 96; IntWW 77, 78, 79, 80, 81, 82, 83, 89, 91, 93; InWom SUP; LegTOT; MotPP; MovMk; OxCFilm; Who 85, 92; WhoAm 76, 86, 90; WhoEnt 92; WhoHol A; WhoWor 87, 91; WorAlBi; WrDr 94, 96*

Yorty, Sam(uel William)
American. Politician
Mayor of Los Angeles, 1961-73.
b. Oct 1, 1909 in Lincoln, Nebraska
Source: *BiDrAC; BiDrUSC 89; BioIn 5, 7, 8, 9, 10, 11, 12; BlueB 76; CmCal; IntWW 74, 75, 76, 77, 78, 79, 80, 81, 82, 83; PolProf J, K, NF; WhoAm 74, 76, 78, 80, 82, 84, 86, 90; WhoAmP 73, 75, 77, 79, 81, 83, 85, 87, 89, 91, 93, 95; WhoGov 72; WhoWor 74*

Yoshida, Shigeru
Japanese. Political Leader
Prime minister of Japan, 1946-47, 1948-49; signed peace treaty with Allied Nations, 1951.
b. Sep 22, 1878 in Tokyo, Japan
d. Oct 20, 1967 in Oisi, Japan
Source: *Au&Wr 71; BioIn 1, 2, 3, 8, 12, 13, 14, 16; ConAu 113; CurBio 46, 68; FacFETw; HisEWW; McGEWB; ObitT 1961; REn; WhAm 4A; WhDW*

Yoshihito
Japanese. Ruler
Father of Hirohito; reigned as emperor, 1912-26.
b. Aug 31, 1879 in Tokyo, Japan
d. Dec 25, 1926 in Hayama, Japan

Yoshimoto, Banana
[Mahoko Yoshimoto]
Japanese. Author
Wrote novels *Tugumi,* 1989; *NP,* 1991.
b. 1964 in Tokyo, Japan
Source: *BioIn 21; ConAu 144; ConLC 84; WrDr 96*

Yost, Charles Woodruff
"The Gray Ghost"
American. Diplomat
One of founders of UN; chief American delegate, 1969-71.
b. Nov 6, 1907 in Watertown, New York
d. May 21, 1981 in Washington, District of Columbia
Source: *BioIn 4, 5, 8, 10, 11, 12, 16; BlueB 76; ConAu 3NR, 9R, 104; CurBio 59, 81; DcAmDH 80, 89; IntWW 74, 75, 76, 77, 78, 79, 80, 81, 81N; PolProf K; WhAm 8, 10; Who 74; WhoAm 74, 76, 78, 80, 82; WhoGov 72, 75; WhoWor 74*

Yost, Fielding Harris
"Hurry Up"
American. Football Coach
Head coach, U of MI, 1901-25; won first Rose Bowl, 1902.
b. Apr 30, 1871 in Fairview, West Virginia
d. Aug 20, 1946 in Ann Arbor, Michigan
Source: *BiDAmSp FB; BioIn 1, 4, 10; CurBio 46; DcAmB S4; WhAm 2; WhoFtbl 74*

Yothers, Tina
American. Actor
Played Jennifer Keaton on TV comedy "Family Ties," 1982-89.
b. May 5, 1973 in Whittier, California
Source: *BioIn 14, 15; LegTOT; WhoHisp 91, 92, 94; WhoHol 92*

Youmans, Vincent
American. Composer
Wrote song "Tea for Two," 1926; Broadway scores include *No, No, Nanette,* 1925.
b. Sep 27, 1898 in New York, New York
d. Apr 5, 1946 in Denver, Colorado
Source: *AmPS; AmSong; ASCAP 66, 80; Baker 78, 84; BestMus; BioIn 1, 3, 4, 5, 6, 9, 10, 12, 14, 15, 16; CmpEPM; ConAmC 76, 82; CurBio 44, 46; DcAmB S4; EncMT; EncWT; FacFETw; HalFC 80, 84, 88; LegTOT; NewAmDM; NewCBMT; NewGrDA 86; NewGrDM 80; NotNAT B; OxCAmT 84; OxCPMus; PenEncP; PlP&P; PopAmC, SUP; Sw&Ld C; WorAlBi*

Young, Alan (Angus)
American. Comedian, Actor
Starred in TV series "Mister Ed," 1961-65.
b. Nov 19, 1919 in North Shields, England
Source: *BioIn 2, 3, 18, 21; CurBio 53; EncAFC; FilmEn; FilmgC; ForYSC; HalFC 80, 84, 88; IntMPA 75, 76, 77, 78, 79, 80, 81, 82, 84, 86, 88, 92, 94, 96; JoeFr; LegTOT; RadStar; VarWW 83; Who 92; WhoHol 92, A; WhoHrs 80; WorAl; WorAlBi*

Young, Andrew
Scottish. Author
Writings include *Burning as Light,* 1967.
b. Apr 29, 1885 in Elgin, Scotland
d. Nov 26, 1971 in Bognor Regis, England
Source: *Au&Wr 71; BioIn 3, 4, 5, 6, 10; CamGLE; CmScLit; CnE&AP; CnMWL; ConAu 5R, 7NR, 29NR; ConBlB 3; ConLC 5; ConPo 70; DcLEL; EngPo; EvLB; LngCTC; NewC; OxCEng 67; PenC ENG; RfGEnL 91; TwCWr; WebE&AL; WhE&EA; WhoTwCL; WorAu 1950*

Young, Andrew Jackson, Jr.
American. Politician
Ambassador to UN, 1977-79; mayor of Atlanta, 1982-90; awarded Spingarn Medal, 1980; French Legion of Honor, 1982-89; chm., Law Cos. International Group Inc., 1990—.
b. Mar 12, 1932 in New Orleans, Louisiana
Source: *AfrAmBi 1; AfrAmOr; AmDec 1970; AmPolLe; BiDrUSC 89; BioNews 74; BkPepl; BlkAmsC; DcAmDH 80, 89; Ebony 1; EncWB; InB&W 80, 85; NewYTBS 76, 77, 79; PolProf NF; Who 85; WhoAm 86; WhoAmP 87; WhoBlA 85; WhoSSW 97; WhoWor 84*

Young, Angus
Scottish. Musician
Knickers-clad guitarist with AC-DC since 1973.
b. Mar 31, 1959 in Glasgow, Scotland
Source: *AmPolLe; BiDrUSC 89; BioIn 14, 15; BlkAmsC; DcAmDH 89; LegTOT; OnThGG; Who 88; WhoAm 88; WhoAmP 87; WhoBlA 92; WhoSSW 88*

Young, Ann Eliza Webb
American. Author, Lecturer
An ex-wife of Brigham Young, 1869; exposed Mormon polygamy: *Life in Mormon Bondage,* 1876.
b. Sep 13, 1844 in Nauvoo, Illinois
d. 1908?
Source: *AmWomWr; InWom, SUP; LibW; NotAW*

Young, Art(hur Henry)
American. Cartoonist, Author
Contributed cartoons to *Life; Puck; Colliers* magazines.
b. Jan 14, 1866 in Orangeville, Illinois
d. Dec 29, 1943 in Bethel, Connecticut
Source: *AmAu&B; BenetAL 91; BiDAmJo; BioIn 11, 12, 16; BriEAA; ChhPo S3; CurBio 40, 44; DcAmB S3; DcAmSR; DcNAA; EncAJ; EncAL; OxCAmL 65, 83; REnAL; WhAm 2; WhNAA*

Young, Brigham
American. Religious Leader
Baptized into Mormon faith, 1832; emigrated church to Utah, 1848, governor, 1850-58; had 27 wives, 47 children.
b. Jun 1, 1801 in Whitingham, Vermont
d. Aug 29, 1877 in Salt Lake City, Utah
Source: *AmAu&B; AmBi; AmSocL; ApCAB; BenetAL 91; BiAUS; BiDAmCu; BiDrATG; BioIn 1, 2, 3, 4, 5, 6, 7, 8, 9, 10, 11, 12, 13, 14, 15, 17, 18, 19, 20, 21; CelCen; CyAG; DcAmB; DcAmReB 1, 2; DcBiPP; Drake; EncAAH; EncAB-H 1974, 1996; EncARH; HarEnUS; HisWorL; LegTOT; LinLib L, S; LuthC 75; McGEWB; MemAm; NatCAB 7, 16; OxCAmH; OxCAmL 65, 83, 95; PeoHis; RComAH; REn; REnAL; REnAW; TwCBDA; WebAB 74, 79; WhAm HS; WhNaAH; WhWE; WorAl; WorAlBi*

Young, Burt
American. Actor, Screenwriter
Oscar nominee for *Rocky,* 1976.
b. Apr 30, 1940 in New York, New York
Source: *BioIn 15; ConTFT 5; EncAFC; HalFC 84, 88; IntMPA 84, 86, 88, 92, 94, 96; ItaFilm; LegTOT; WhoAm 80, 82, 84, 86, 88, 90, 92, 94; WhoEnt 92A; WhoHol 92, A*

Young, Candy
[Canzetta Young]
American. Track Athlete
b. 1963?
Source: *BioIn 12; InB&W 80*

Young, Charles Augustus
American. Astronomer
Discovered solar reversing layer, 1870.
b. Dec 15, 1834 in Hanover, New Hampshire
d. Jan 4, 1908 in Hanover, New Hampshire
Source: *Alli SUP; AmBi; ApCAB; BbD; BiDAmEd; BiDAmS; BiD&SB; BilnAmS; BioIn 1, 11, 14; DcAmAu; DcAmB; DcNAA; DcScB; InSci; NatCAB 6; TwCBDA; WhAm 1*

Young, Chic
[Murat Bernard Young]
American. Cartoonist
Created comic strip "Blondie," 1930.
b. Jan 9, 1901 in Chicago, Illinois
d. Mar 14, 1973 in Saint Petersburg, Florida
Source: *BioIn 1, 3, 9; ConAu 41R; EncACom; EncTwCJ; LegTOT; LinLib L; NewYTBE 73; WebAB 74, 79; WhAm 5, 6; WhoAm 74; WhoAmA 76, 78N, 80N, 82N, 84N, 86N, 89N, 91N, 93N*

Young, Clara Kimball
American. Actor
Starred in Vitagraph films, 1909-15.
b. Sep 1890 in Chicago, Illinois
d. Oct 15, 1960 in Woodland Hills, California
Source: *EncAFC; Film 1, 2; FilmEn; FilmgC; HalFC 80, 84, 88; InWom SUP; LegTOT; MotPP; MovMk; NotNAT B; ObitOF 79; OxCFilm; SilFlmP; TwYS; WhAm 4; WhoHol B; WhScrn 74, 77, 83; WomWMM; WorAl*

Young, Coleman A(lexander)
American. Politician
First black mayor of Detroit, 1974-93; served longer than any other mayor in city's history; won Spingarn, 1980.
b. May 24, 1918 in Tuscaloosa, Alabama

Source: *BiDAmL; BioIn 10, 11, 12, 13, 14, 16; BioNews 74; BlueB 76; ConBlB 1; CurBio 77; EncWB; InB&W 80, 85; NegAl 89A; WhoAm 76, 78, 80, 82, 84, 86, 88, 90, 92, 94; WhoAmP 85, 87, 91; WhoBlA 85, 92; WhoGov 75, 77; WhoMW 80, 82, 84, 86, 88, 90, 92, 93; WorAl; WorAlBi*

Young, Cy
[Denton True Young]
American. Baseball Player
Pitcher, 1890-1911; holds many ML records, including most wins, 511, most losses, 313; Hall of Fame, 1937.
b. Mar 29, 1867 in Gilmore, Ohio
d. Nov 4, 1955 in Peoli, Ohio
Source: *Ballpl 90; BiDAmSp BB; BioIn 2, 3, 4, 5, 6, 7, 8, 9, 10, 14, 15, 17; DcAmB S5; FacFETw; LegTOT; WebAB 74, 79; WhAm 4, HSA; WhoProB 73; WhoSpor; WorAl; WorAlBi*

Young, Edward
English. Author
"Graveyard School" poet; wrote blank verse *Complaint, or Night Thoughts,* 1742-44.
b. Jun 1683 in Upham, England
d. Apr 5, 1765 in Welwyn Garden City, England
Source: *Alli; AtlBL; BbD; Benet 87, 96; BiD&SB; BioIn 1, 2, 3, 6, 8, 9, 10, 16, 17; BlkwCE; BlmGEL; BritAu; CamGEL; CamGLE; CasWL; ChhPo, S2, S3; CnE&AP; CrtT 2, 4; DcArts; DcEnA; DcEnL; DcEuL; DcLB 95; DcLEL; DcNaB; EvLB; GrWrEL P; LinLib L; LitC 3; LngCEL; MouLC 2; NewC; NewCBEL; OxCEng 67, 85, 95; OxCFr; OxCGer 76; PenC ENG; REn; RfGEnL 91; WebE&AL*

Young, Faron
"The Sheriff"
American. Singer, Musician
Recorded over 60 albums, 105 singles, including 32 number-one hits; wrote "I Miss You Already," 1957.
b. Feb 25, 1932 in Shreveport, Louisiana
d. Dec 10, 1996 in Nashville, Tennessee
Source: *Baker 84, 92; BgBkCoM; BiDAmM; BioIn 14; ConMus 7; CounME 74; EncFCWM 69, 83; HarEnCM 87; IlEncCM; LegTOT; OxCPMus; PenEncP; RkOn 74; WhoAm 82, 84, 86, 88; WhoHol 92, A*

Young, George
American. Track Athlete
Long-distance runner; first American runner on four Olympic teams, 1960-72; won bronze medal in steeplechase, 1968 Olympics.
b. Jul 24, 1937 in Roswell, New Mexico
Source: *WhoTr&F 73*

Young, Gig
[Bryon Ellsworth Barr; Roland Reed]
American. Actor
Won Oscar for *They Shoot Horses, Don't They?,* 1969.
b. Nov 4, 1913 in Saint Cloud, Minnesota
d. Oct 19, 1978 in New York, New York
Source: *BiE&WWA; BioIn 9, 10, 11; CelR; EncAFC; FilmEn; FilmgC; HalFC 80, 84, 88; HolP 40; IntDcF 1-3; IntMPA 77; ItaFilm; MotPP; MovMk; ObitOF 79; WhAm 7; WhoAm 74; WhoHol A; WhoThe 81N; WhScrn 83*

Young, John Alan
American. Business Executive
President, Hewlett-Packard Co., electronics and computer firm, 1977-92.
b. Apr 24, 1932 in Nampa, Idaho
Source: *BioIn 13; CurBio 86; Dun&B 90; WhoAm 76, 78, 80, 82, 84, 86, 88, 90, 92, 94, 95, 96, 97; WhoFI 75, 77, 79, 81, 83, 85, 87, 89, 92, 94, 96; WhoScEn 94, 96; WhoWest 82, 84, 87, 89, 92, 94, 96; WhoWor 84, 87, 89*

Young, John Watts
American. Astronaut
On maiden voyage of space shuttle *Columbia,* 1981.
b. Sep 24, 1930 in San Francisco, California
Source: *AmMWSc 92; BioIn 7, 8, 9, 10, 12, 13; IntWW 74; WhoAm 80, 82, 84, 86, 88, 90, 92, 94, 95, 96, 97; WhoScEn 94; WhoSSW 73, 95, 97; WhoWor 74; WorAl*

Young, Kevin
American. Track Athlete
Won gold medal, 400-meter hurdle, 1992; first person to break 47 seconds in the 400-meter hurdle.
b. Sep 16, 1966 in Los Angeles, California
Source: *AfrAmSG; BioIn 15; Law&B 89A; WhoEmL 89; WhoMW 90*

Young, Lester Willis
"Prez"
American. Jazz Musician
Leading tenor saxist, prominent 1930s-40s; pioneered modern "cool" style.
b. Aug 27, 1909 in Woodville, Mississippi
d. Mar 15, 1959 in New York, New York
Source: *ASCAP 66; BiDAmM; CmpEPM; IlEncJ; MusMk; NewGrDM 80; WhAm 5; WhoJazz 72*

Young, Loretta Gretchen
American. Actor
Won Oscar for *The Farmer's Daughter,* 1947; star of TV series "The Loretta Young Show," 1953-61.
b. Jan 6, 1913 in Salt Lake City, Utah
Source: *BiDFilm; BioIn 14, 15; CurBio 48; EncAFC; Film 1; FilmgC; HalFC 84; IntMPA 86, 88; MotPP; MovMk; OxCFilm; ThFT; TwYS; WhoAm 82, 88; WhoAmW 89; WhoHol A; WorEFlm*

Young, Lyman
American. Cartoonist
Best known for comic strip "Tim Tyler," 1940s-50s.
Source: *EncACom; WorECom*

Young, Mahonri Mackintosh
American. Sculptor
Executed Mormon statues, Indian groups; first prize for sculpture, 1932 Olympic Games.
b. Aug 9, 1877 in Salt Lake City, Utah
d. Nov 2, 1957 in New York, New York
Source: *BioIn 4, 7; DcAmArt; DcAmB S6; GrAmP; IlBEAAW; McGDA; WhAm 3; WhAmArt 85*

Young, Malcolm
Scottish. Musician
Guitarist, who helped form AC-DC, 1973.
b. Jan 6, 1953 in Glasgow, Scotland

Young, Margaret Ann Buckner
American. Children's Author
Writings include *Black American Leaders,* 1969; *The Picture Life of Thurgood Marshall,* 1970.
b. Mar 20, 1922 in Campbellsville, Kentucky
Source: *BioIn 16; BkP; BlkAuII; InB&W 85; SelBAAf; SmATA 2; WhoAmW 91; WhoBlA 85, 92; WhoE 91; WhoWor 87, 91*

Young, Marguerite (Vivian)
American. Author
Wrote epic novel *Miss MacIntosh, My Darling,* 1965.
b. 1909 in Indianapolis, Indiana
Source: *AmAu&B; AmWomWr; ArtclWW 2; BenetAL 91; BioIn 7, 10, 11, 14; ChhPo, S2; ConAu 150, P-1; ConLC 82; ConNov 72, 76, 82, 86, 91, 96; DrAF 76; DrAPF 80; FemiCLE; Focus; IndAu 1917; IntAu&W 76, 77; ModWoWr; WorAu 1950; WrDr 76, 80, 82, 84, 86, 88, 90, 92, 94, 96*

Young, Marian
[Martha Deane]
American. Radio Performer
Noted for hosting daily radio program, 1941-73; editor of daily newspapers.
b. Nov 21, 1908 in Star Lake, New York
d. Dec 9, 1973 in New York
Source: *BiDrLUS 70; BioIn 10, 11; CurBio 52, 74; ForWC 70; InWom SUP; NewYTBE 73; RadStar; WhoAm 74*

Young, Neil
[Buffalo Springfield; Crosby, Stills, Nash, and Young]
Canadian. Musician
Albums include *Rust Never Sleeps,* 1979; *Freedom,* 1989; *Ragged Glory,* 1990.
b. Nov 12, 1945 in Toronto, Ontario, Canada
Source: *Baker 84, 92; BgBkCoM; BioIn 12, 13, 14, 16; CanWW 31, 89; ConAu 110; ConCaAu 1; ConLC 17; ConMuA 80A; ConMus 2, 15; CurBio 80; DcArts;*

EncFCWM 83; EncPR&S 89; EncRk 88; EncRkSt; HarEnCM 87; HarEnR 86; IlEncRk; LegTOT; NewAmDM; NewGrDA 86; News 91, 91-2; NewYTBS 92; OnThGG; PenEncP; RolSEnR 83; Who 92; WhoAm 78, 80, 82, 84, 86, 88, 90, 92, 94, 95, 96, 97; WhoEnt 92; WhoHol 92, A; WhoRock 81; WhoRocM 82; WorAl; WorAlBi

Young, Owen D
American. Lawyer, Diplomat
Founded RCA, 1919; chm., German Reparations Commission, 1929.
b. Oct 27, 1874 in Van Hornesville, New York
d. Jul 11, 1962 in Saint Augustine, Florida
Source: *BiDInt; BioIn 13, 16; DcAmBC; DcAmB S7; DcAmDH 89; EncABHB 7; PeoHis*

Young, Paul
[Q-Tips; Streetband]
English. Singer
Lead singer turned soloist who had hit single "Everytime You Go Away," 1985.
b. Jan 17, 1956 in Bedfordshire, England
Source: *BioIn 14, 15; EncPR&S 89; EncRk 88; EncRkSt; HarEnR 86; LegTOT; PenEncP; RkOn 85; WhoHisp 92*

Young, Philip
American. Government Official
Ambassador to Netherlands, 1957-60; director of International Chamber of Commerce, 1960-65.
b. May 9, 1910 in Lexington, Massachusetts
d. Jan 15, 1987 in Arlington, Virginia
Source: *AnObit 1987; BioIn 2, 3, 15; CurBio 51, 87, 87N; NewYTBS 87; WhAm 9; WhoAm 74, 76, 78, 80*

Young, Ralph
[Sandler and Young]
American. Singer
Partner with Tony Sandler, 1960s-70s; albums include *More and More.*
Source: *CmpEPM*

Young, Robert George
American. Actor
Starred in TV series "Father Knows Best," 1954-62; "Marcus Welby, MD," 1969-76.
b. Feb 22, 1907 in Chicago, Illinois
Source: *BiDFilm; CmMov; FilmgC; HalFC 84; IntMPA 86; MovMk; OxCFilm; WhoAm 74, 78, 86; WorEFlm*

Young, Roland
English. Actor
Oscar nominee for *Topper,* 1937.
b. Nov 11, 1887 in London, England
d. Jun 5, 1953 in New York, New York
Source: *BioIn 2, 3, 4, 7, 9, 21; ChhPo; EncAFC; Film 2; FilmEn; FilmgC; ForYSC; HalFC 80, 84, 88; HolCA; LegTOT; MotPP; MovMk; NatCAB 40; NotNAT B; OlFamFa; OxCAmT 84; OxCFilm; PlP&P; QDrFCA 92; Vers A; WhAm 3; WhoHol B; WhoHrs 80; WhScrn 74, 77, 83; WhThe; WorAlBi*

Young, Sean
American. Actor
Films include, *Bladerunner,* 1982; *No Way Out,* 1987.
b. Nov 20, 1959 in Louisville, Kentucky
Source: *BioIn 14, 15, 16; ConTFT 7, 14; HalFC 88; IntMPA 92, 94, 96; LegTOT; NewYTBS 87; WhoEnt 92*

Young, Sheila
[Mrs. Jim Ochowicz]
American. Skater
Speed skater; first American to win three medals in single Olympics, 1976; is also champion cyclist.
b. Oct 14, 1950 in Birmingham, Michigan
Source: *BiDAmSp OS; BioIn 10, 11, 12, 17; CurBio 77; EncWomS; InWom SUP; LegTOT; NewYTBS 74, 76; WorAl*

Young, Stark
American. Author
Best known for *So Red the Rose.*
b. Oct 11, 1881 in Como, Mississippi
d. Jan 6, 1963 in New York, New York
Source: *AmAu&B; BenetAL 91; BioIn 1, 2, 4, 5, 6, 8, 9, 11, 12, 17; CamGWoT; CasWL; CnDAL; ConAmA; ConAmL; ConAu 89, 105; CyWA 58; DcAmB S7; DcLB 9, 102; EncAJ; EncSoH; EncWB; EncWT; FifSWrA; JrnUS; LiveMA; LngCTC; ModAL; NatCAB 52; NotNAT B; OxCAmL 65, 83, 95; OxCAmT 84; OxCThe 67; PenC AM; REnAL; SouWr; TexWr; TwCA, SUP; TwCRHW 90, 94; WhAm 4; WhE&EA; WhNAA; WhThe*

Young, Stephen
Canadian. Actor
Starred in TV series "Judd for the Defense," 1967-69.
b. May 19, 1939 in Toronto, Ontario, Canada
Source: *FilmgC; HalFC 88; ItaFilm; WhoHol 92, A*

Young, Steve
[Jon Steven Young]
American. Football Player
Quarterback, signed biggest contract in pro sports history, $36 million with USFL LA Express, 1984; with Tampa Bay Buccaneers, 1985-87; quarterback for San Francisco 49ers, 1987—; Superbowl MVP, 1994.
b. Oct 11, 1961 in Salt Lake City, Utah
Source: *BioIn 13, 14; CurBio 93; FootReg 87; News 95, 95-2; WhoSpor*

Young, Terence
American. Director
Noted for James Bond films *Dr. No,* 1963; *From Russia With Love,* 1965; *Thunderball,* 1967.
b. Jun 20, 1915 in Shanghai, China
Source: *BiDFilm, 81; BioIn 20; CmMov; ConTFT 7, 13; FilmEn; FilmgC; HalFC 80, 84, 88; IlWWBF; IntMPA 75, 76, 77, 78, 79, 80, 81, 82, 84, 86, 88, 92, 94; ItaFilm; LegTOT; MiSFD 9; MovMk; OxCFilm; WhAm 11; WhoAm 74, 76, 78, 80, 82, 84, 86, 88, 90, 92, 94, 95; WhoHrs 80; WorEFlm*

Young, Trummy
[James Osborne Young]
American. Jazz Musician
Brash trumpeter; prominent, 1930s-50s.
b. Jan 12, 1912 in Savannah, Georgia
Source: *AllMusG; AnObit 1984; BioIn 16; CmpEPM; EncJzS; InB&W 85; NewGrDJ 88, 94; OxCPMus; WhoJazz 72*

Young, Victor
American. Songwriter, Conductor
Won Oscar for scoring *Around the World in Eighty Days,* 1956; wrote words for "Sweet Sue—Just You," 1928.
b. Aug 8, 1900 in Chicago, Illinois
d. Nov 11, 1956 in Palm Springs, California
Source: *AmPS; ASCAP 66, 80; Baker 78, 84, 92; BiDAmM; BioIn 1, 4, 6, 14; CmMov; CmpEPM; ConAmC 76, 82; FacFETw; FilmEn; FilmgC; HalFC 80, 84, 88; IntDcF 1-4, 2-4; LegTOT; NewAmDM; NewGrDA 86; NewGrDM 80; NotNAT B; OxCFilm; OxCPMus; PenEncP; PopAmC; RadStar; RkOn 74; WhAm 3; WorEFlm*

Young, Whitney Moore, Jr.
American. Civil Rights Leader
Director, National Urban League, 1961-71; wrote *Beyond Racism,* 1969.
b. Jul 31, 1921 in Lincoln Ridge, Kentucky
d. Mar 11, 1971 in Lagos, Nigeria
Source: *AmRef; AmSocL; BiDSocW; BioIn 6, 7, 8, 9, 10, 11, 12, 15, 16, 19; ConAu P-1; CurBio 65, 71; DcAmB S9; EncAACR; EncAB-H 1974, 1996; EncSoH; InB&W 80, 85; McGEWB; NatCAB 57; NewYTBE 70, 71; SelBAAf; SelBAAu; WebAB 74, 79; WhAm 5; WorAl*

Youngblood, Jack
[Herbert Jackson Youngblood, III]
American. Football Player
Seven-time all-pro defensive end, LA Rams, 1971-84.
b. Jan 26, 1950 in Jacksonville, Florida
Source: *BiDAmSp Sup; BioIn 13, 14, 16; FootReg 85; LegTOT; NewYTBS 84; WhoAm 78, 80, 82; WhoFtbl 74; WorAl*

Youngblood, Johnny Ray
American. Clergy
Senior pastor, St. Paul Community Baptist Church, Brooklyn, NY; played a leading role in developing the Nehemiah Housing Project in Brooklyn.
b. Jun 23, 1948 in New Orleans, Louisiana

Source: *BioIn 20; ConBlB 8; News 94, 94-1*

Youngdahl, Luther Wallace
American. Politician, Judge
District of Columbia Federal judge, 1951-66; dismissed indictments against Owen Lattimore in McCarthy witch-hunt; three-term Rep. governor of MN.
b. May 29, 1896 in Minneapolis, Minnesota
d. Jun 21, 1978 in Washington, District of Columbia
Source: *AmAu&B; WhoSSW 73*

Younger, Bob
[Younger Brothers; Robert Younger]
American. Outlaw
Started life of crime with brothers at age 12; died in jail.
b. 1853 in Lee's Summit, Missouri
d. 1889 in Minnesota
Source: *BioIn 17; REnAW; WhCiWar*

Younger, Cole
[Younger Brothers; Thomas Coleman Younger]
American. Outlaw
Known for famous Northfield, MN, bank raid, 1876; wrote *The Story of Cole Younger,* 1903.
b. Jan 15, 1844 in Jackson County, Missouri
d. Mar 21, 1916 in Jackson County, Missouri
Source: *BioIn 2, 4, 7, 8, 9, 10, 17, 18, 20; DcAmB; DcNAA; NewCol 75; REnAW; WebAB 74, 79; WhAm 4, HS, HSA; WhCiWar*

Younger, Jim
[Younger Brothers; James Younger]
American. Outlaw
Famous for raids with brothers; committed suicide after release from jail.
b. Jan 15, 1850 in Lee's Summit, Missouri
d. Oct 19, 1902 in Saint Paul, Minnesota
Source: *REnAW*

Youngerman, Jack
American. Artist
Abstract paintings include "Dive," 1980; "Ohio," 1977.
b. Mar 25, 1926 in Webster Groves, Missouri
Source: *BioIn 6, 7, 8, 15; BlueB 76; BriEAA; ConArt 77, 83, 89, 96; CurBio 86; DcCAA 71, 77, 88, 94; DcCAr 81; OxCTwCA; PhDcTCA 77; PrintW 83, 85; WhoAm 74, 76, 78, 80, 84, 86, 88, 90, 92, 94, 95, 96, 97; WhoAmA 73, 76, 78, 82, 84, 86, 89, 91, 93; WhoWor 74, 76; WorArt 1950*

Youngman, Henny
American. Comedian
Best known for line "Take my wife, please!"
b. Jan 12, 1906 in Liverpool, England
Source: *BioIn 15; CelR; ConAu 107, 134; CurBio 86; EncAFC; EncVaud; JoeFr; LegTOT; NotNAT A; WhoAm 86, 88; WhoCom; WhoHol 92, A; WorAl; WorAlBi; WrDr 94, 96*

Young Man Afraid of His Horses
[Tasunka Kokipapi]
American. Native American Chief
Chief of the Ogala Sioux of the great plains; signed the Fort Laramie Treaty, 1868.
b. 1830
d. 1900
Source: *BioIn 11; NotNaAm*

Young MC
American. Rapper
Rap artist; album *Stone Cold Rhymin',* 1989 went platinum; won rap Grammy, 1990.
b. 1968 in London, England
Source: *ConMus 4*

Youngs, Ross Middlebrook
"Pep"
American. Baseball Player
Outfielder, NY Giants, 1917-26, known for fielding; had .322 lifetime batting average; Hall of Fame, 1972.
b. Apr 10, 1897 in Shiner, Texas
d. Oct 22, 1927 in San Antonio, Texas
Source: *BiDAmSp BB; WhoProB 73*

Yount, Robin (R.)
American. Baseball Player
Shortstop-outfielder, Milwaukee, 1974-93; led AL in hits, 1982; 17th player in history to reach 3,000 hits.
b. Sep 16, 1955 in Woodland Hills, California
Source: *Ballpl 90; BaseReg 86, 87; BiDAmSp BB; BioIn 12, 13, 14, 15, 16; CurBio 93; LegTOT; WhoSpor; WorAlBi*

Yourcenar, Marguerite
[Marguerite Antoinette Jeanne Marie Ghislaine C. de Crayencour]
French. Author
First woman ever admitted to Academie Francaise, 1980; masterpiece novel: *Memoires d'Hadrien,* 1951.
b. Jun 8, 1903 in Brussels, Belgium
d. Dec 17, 1987 in Bar Harbor, Maine
Source: *AnObit 1987, 3; EuWr 12; ForWC 70; FrenWW; GayLesB; GayLL; GrWomW; GuFrLit 1; IntAu&W 76, 77, 82, 89; IntDcWB; IntWW 74, 75, 76, 77, 78, 79, 80, 81, 82, 83; InWom SUP; LegTOT; LiExTwC; LinLib L; MajTwCW; ModFrL; ModWoWr; NewYTBS 79, 81, 87; RAdv 14, 13-2; REn; RfGWoL 95; ScF&FL 92; WhAm 9; WhoAm 74, 76, 78, 82, 84, 86; WhoAmW 61, 68, 70, 72, 74, 75, 81; WhoFr 79; WhoWor 74, 82, 84, 87; WomFir; WorAu 1950*

Youskevitch, Igor
Russian. Dancer
Debuted in US at NY Met., 1938; starred in film *Invitation to the Dance,* 1956.
b. Mar 13, 1912 in Kiev, Russia
d. Jun 13, 1994 in New York, New York
Source: *BiDD; BioIn 3, 4, 5, 12, 13, 20, 21; BlueB 76; CnOxB; CurBio 56, 94N; DancEn 78; IntDcB; NewYTBS 94; WhAm 11; WhoAm 94; WhoHol 92, A; WhoWor 74*

Ysaye, Eugene
Belgian. Conductor, Violinist
Violin virtuoso, 1880s-90s; led Cincinnati Symphony, 1920s; formed own orchestra in Brussels.
b. Jul 16, 1858 in Liege, Belgium
d. May 13, 1931 in Brussels, Belgium
Source: *Baker 78, 84; BioIn 1, 2, 5, 11, 12, 14; BriBkM 80; MusSN; NewAmDM; NewGrDA 86; NewGrDM 80; NewGrDO; NewOxM; OxCMus; OxDcOp; PenDiMP; WhAm 1*

Yuan, Shih-Kai
Chinese. Political Leader
Pres. of China, 1913-16; sought to be dictator, suppressing Sun Yat-sen, 1914.
b. 1859 in Henan Province, China
d. Jun 6, 1916
Source: *BioIn 1, 6, 9, 10, 11; McGEWB; NewCol 75*

Yukawa, Hideki
Japanese. Physicist, Educator
Won Nobel Prize in physics, 1949; discovered meson particles.
b. Jan 23, 1907 in Tokyo, Japan
d. Sep 8, 1981 in Kyoto, Japan
Source: *AnObit 1981; AsBiEn; BiESc; BioIn 1, 2, 3, 12, 13, 20; CamDcSc; ConAu 108; CurBio 81, 81N; DcScB S2; FacFETw; FarE&A 78, 79, 80, 81; InSci; IntWW 74, 75, 76, 77, 78, 79, 80, 81, 82N; LarDcSc; McGEWB; McGMS 80; NewCol 75; NewYTBS 81; NobelP; NotTwCS; RAdv 14, 13-5; WhDW; Who 74, 82N; WhoNob, 90, 95; WhoWor 74, 80; WorAl; WorAlBi; WorScD*

Yung, Victor Sen
American. Actor
Played Hop Sing on TV series "Bonanza," 1959-73.
b. Oct 18, 1915 in San Francisco, California
d. Nov 9, 1980 in North Hollywood, California
Source: *HalFC 84; WhAm 7; WhoAm 80; WhoHol A*

Yunich, David Lawrence
American. Merchant, Businessman
Pres., Macy's, NY, 1962-71.
b. May 21, 1917 in Albany, New York
Source: *Dun&B 90; IntWW 74, 75, 76, 77, 78, 79, 80, 81, 82, 83, 89, 91, 93; NewYTBE 73; St&PR 87, 91; WhoAm 74, 76, 78, 80, 82, 84, 86, 88, 90, 92, 94, 95, 96; WhoE 75, 77, 79, 81, 83, 85, 86, 89; WhoFI 74, 75, 77, 79, 81, 83, 85, 87; WhoWor 78, 82, 84, 87, 89, 95*

Yurka, Blanche
American. Actor
Numerous classical roles included 130 performances of *Hamlet* with John Barrymore, 1922.
b. Jun 19, 1887 in Saint Paul, Minnesota
d. Jun 6, 1974 in New York, New York
Source: *BiE&WWA; BioIn 12, 16; ConAu 9R, 120; FamA&A; FilmEn; FilmgC; GangFlm; HalFC 80, 84, 88; HolCA; MotPP; MovMk; NewYTBS 74; NotAW MOD; NotNAT A, B; NotWoAT; OxCThe 83; ThFT; Vers A; WhAm 6; What 4; WhoHol B; WhoThe 72; WhScrn 77, 83; WhThe*

Yust, Walter
American. Editor
Editor-in-chief of the *Encyclopedia Britannica,* 1938-1960.
b. May 16, 1894 in Philadelphia, Pennsylvania
d. Feb 29, 1960 in Evanston, Illinois
Source: *AmAu&B; BioIn 5; CurBio 60; ObitOF 79; WhAm 3*

Yzerman, Steve
Canadian. Hockey Player
Center, Detroit, 1983—; youngest player ever to play in NHL All-Star game, 1984; Stanley Cup, 1997.
b. May 9, 1965 in Cranbrook, British Columbia, Canada
Source: *BioIn 16; HocReg 87; News 91, 91-2; WhoAm 92, 94, 95, 96, 97; WhoMW 93, 96; WorAlBi*

Z

Zabach, Florian
American. Violinist
Noted for sometimes whistling while performing in concert; mastered classic music then turned to pop.
b. Aug 15, 1921 in Chicago, Illinois
Source: *ASCAP 66, 80; BioIn 4; CmpEPM; CurBio 55; PenEncP*

Zabaleta, Nicanor
Spanish. Musician
Known as king of the harpists; harp works written for him include *Aria and Passepied,* 1965.
b. Jan 7, 1907 in San Sebastian, Spain
Source: *Baker 78, 84, 92; BioIn 3, 9, 11; BriBkM 80; CurBio 71; IntWW 89, 91; IntWWM 77, 80, 90; MusSN; NewAmDM; NewGrDM 80; PenDiMP; WhoMus 72; WhoSSW 73, 75; WhoWor 76, 89*

Zablocki, Clement John
American. Politician
Congressman from WI, 1949-83; chm., House Foreign Affairs Committee, 1977-83.
b. Nov 18, 1912 in Milwaukee, Wisconsin
d. Dec 3, 1983 in Washington, District of Columbia
Source: *AlmAP 84; AmCath 80; BiDrAC; BiDrUSC 89; BioIn 4, 5, 11, 12; CngDr 83; CurBio 84; IntWW 83; PolProf J, NF; WhAm 8; WhoAm 74, 76, 78, 80, 82; WhoAmP 73, 75, 77, 79, 81, 83; WhoGov 72, 75, 77; WhoMW 74, 76, 78, 80, 82*

Zabolotskii, Nikolai Alekseevich
Russian. Poet
Now regarded as one of Soviet's finest poets; wrote verse *Stolbtsy,* 1929.
b. May 7, 1903 in Kazan, Russia
d. Oct 14, 1958 in Moscow, Union of Soviet Socialist Republics
Source: *BiDSovU; BioIn 5, 8, 9, 10; ConAu 116; PenC ENG; WorAu 1950*

Zacharias, Jerrold R(einarch)
American. Engineer, Physicist
Director of engineering, Manhattan Project, which developed first atomic bomb.
b. Jan 23, 1905 in Jacksonville, Florida
d. Jul 16, 1986 in Belmont, Massachusetts
Source: *AmMWSc 73P, 82; CurBio 64, 86; IntWW 83; NewYTBS 86; WhoAtom 77*

Zadkine, Ossip
Russian. Artist
Sculptures include *The Destroyed City; Musicians.*
b. Jul 14, 1890 in Smolensk, Russia
d. Nov 25, 1967 in Paris, France
Source: *BioIn 2, 4, 5, 7, 8, 9, 12, 14, 17; ConArt 77, 83; CurBio 57, 68; DcArts; DcTwCCu 2; IntDcAA 90; McGDA; ObitT 1961; OxCArt; OxCTwCA; OxDcArt; PhDcTCA 77; WhAm 4A; WorArt 1950*

Zadora, Pia
[Mrs. Jonathan Kaufer]
American. Actor, Singer
Had successful first album *Pia and Phil,* 1985.
b. May 4, 1955 in New York, New York
Source: *BioIn 12, 14, 16; ConTFT 9; HalFC 84, 88; IntMPA 88; LegTOT; RkOn 85*

Zaentz, Saul
American. Producer
Won Oscars for *Amadeus,* 1984; *One Flew Over the Cuckoo's Nest,* 1975.
b. Feb 28, 1921 in Passaic, New Jersey
Source: *BioIn 14; ConTFT 9; IntMPA 84, 86, 92; VarWW 85; WhoAm 90; WhoEnt 92*

Zafrulla Khan, Muhammad, Sir
Pakistani. Diplomat
Long time diplomat; positions included: Pakistani UN delegate, 1947-54, 1961-64; pres. UN General Assembly 1962-63.
b. Feb 6, 1893 in Sialkot, India
d. Sep 1, 1985 in Lahore, Pakistan
Source: *BioIn 1, 6; CurBio 47; FarE&A 78, 79, 80, 81; IntWW 74, 75, 76, 77, 78, 79, 80, 81, 82, 83; IntYB 80, 82; Who 83, 85; WhoUN 75; WhoWor 74, 76*

Zah, Peterson
American. Native American Leader
First president of the Navajo Nation, 1990-94.
b. Dec 2, 1937 in Low Mountain, Arizona
Source: *BioIn 13, 21; NewYTBS 83; NotNaAm; WhoAm 86, 92, 94, 95, 96; WhoWest 84, 92*

Zaharias, Babe Didrikson
[Mildred Ella Didrickson; Mildred Ella Didrickson Zaharias; Mrs. George Zaharias]
American. Golfer
Outstanding female athlete, especially in track, golf; won two gold medals, 1932 Olympics; won US Women's Open three times.
b. Jun 26, 1914 in Port Arthur, Texas
d. Sep 27, 1956 in Galveston, Texas
Source: *ConAu 117; CurBio 47, 56; DcAmB S6; GayLesB; GrLiveH; NotAW MOD; OxCAmH; WebAB 79; WhAm 4; WhoGolf; WhoTr&F 73*

Zaharias, George
"The Crying Greek from Cripple Creek"
American. Wrestler
World-class wrestler; husband, manager of Babe Didrickson.
b. 1908?
d. May 22, 1984 in Tampa, Florida
Source: *BioIn 13*

Zaharoff, Basil, Sir
[Basileios Zacharias]
"Mystery Man of Europe"
English. Financier
Considered world's greatest armament salesman; allied intelligence agent, WW I.
b. Oct 6, 1849 in Mugla, Turkey

d. Nov 27, 1936 in Monte Carlo, Monaco
Source: *BioIn 7; DcNaB MP; WebBD 83*

Zahir Shah, Mohammad
Afghan. Ruler
Afghan king, 1933-73; deposed by his brother-in-law, General Mohammad Daud Khan; abdicated on Aug. 24, 1973.
b. Oct 15, 1914 in Kabul, Afghanistan
Source: *BioIn 15, 16; CurBio 56; IntWW 91; NewYTBE 73; NewYTBS 79, 88*

Zahn, Paula
American. Broadcast Journalist
Co-anchor "CBS This Morning," 1990-95.
b. Feb 24, 1956 in Naperville, Illinois
Source: *BioIn 16; LegTOT; News 92, 92-3; WhoAm 96, 97; WhoAmW 95, 97*

Zaitsev, Aleksandr
[Rodnina and Zaitsev]
Russian. Skater
With Irina Rodnina, won gold medals in pairs figure skating, 1976, 1980 Olympics.
b. 1952, Union of Soviet Socialist Republics
Source: *BiDSovU; BioIn 11, 12*

Zal, Roxana
American. Actor
Won Emmy for title role in *Something About Amelia,* 1984.
b. Nov 8, 1969 in Los Angeles, California
Source: *BioIn 13, 14, 16; ConTFT 4*

Zale, Tony
[Anthony Florian Zaleski]
"Man of Steel"
American. Boxer
Middleweight champion; known for fight to defend title against Rocky Graziano, 1946; lost, 1947, regained 11 months later.
b. May 29, 1913 in Gary, Indiana
d. Mar 20, 1997 in Portage, Indiana
Source: *BiDAmSp BK; BioIn 13; BoxReg; NewYTBS 82; WhoBox 74; WhoMW 92; WhoSpor*

Zaleski, August
Polish. Statesman
Pres., Polish Democratic Committee, 1914-18; minister of foreign affairs, 1926-32.
b. 1883
d. Apr 7, 1972 in London, England
Source: *BioIn 9, 17; FacFETw; PolBiDi*

Zambelli, Joseph
"The Grandfather of Fireworks"
American. Special Effects Technician
Pyrotechnics were used in six presidential inaugurations and at Statue of Liberty centennial, 1986.
d. May 4, 1988 in Castle, California
Source: *BioIn 12, 15*

Zamboni, Frank J
American. Inventor
Invented ice resurfacing machine that bears his name, 1947.
b. 1901? in Eureka, Utah
d. Jul 27, 1988 in Long Beach, California
Source: *ConNews 86-4*

Zamenhof, Ludwik Lazar
Polish. Linguist
Developed artificial language, Esperanto, 1887.
b. Dec 15, 1859 in Bialystok, Poland
d. Apr 14, 1917 in Warsaw, Poland
Source: *BiDInt; BioIn 5; Dis&D; LinLib L, S; WorAl*

Zamora, Bernice
American. Poet
Published poetry collection *Restless Serpents,* 1976.
b. 1938 in Aguilar, Colorado
Source: *ConLC 89; DcHiB; DcLB 82; HispLC; HispWr; NotHsAW 93; OxCTwCP*

Zamora, Pedro
Cuban. AIDS Activist
Educated teenagers about AIDS after contracting it at age 17.
b. 1972, Cuba
d. Nov 11, 1994 in Miami, Florida
Source: *BioIn 20, 21; News 95, 95-2*

Zamora, Ruben
Salvadoran. Politician
Member of El Salvador's democratic left; after an exile of nearly 8 years, his return was considered the most important development in the country since civil war erupted in 1980.
b. 1942, El Salvador
Source: *CurBio 91*

Zampa, Luigi
Italian. Director
Films include *A Yank in Rome,* 1945; *Difficult Years,* 1948; *Anyone Can Play,* 1967.
b. Jan 2, 1905 in Rome, Italy
d. Aug 15, 1991 in Rome, Italy
Source: *AnObit 1991; BioIn 5, 14, 15, 16, 17, 18; CelR 90; ConTFT 7; DcFM; EncEurC; FilmEn; FilmgC; HalFC 80, 84, 88; IntDcF 1-2; IntMPA 75, 76, 77, 78, 79, 80, 81, 82, 84, 86, 88, 92; IntWW 91; ItaFilm; OxCFilm; St&PR 91; WhoAm 90; WhoEnt 92; WorEFlm*

Zander, Robin
[Cheap Trick]
American. Singer, Musician
b. Jan 23, 1953
Source: *WhoRocM 82*

Zandonai, Riccardo
Italian. Composer
Wrote operas *Francesca da Rimini,* 1914; *Giuliette e Romeo,* 1922; *I Cavalieri di Ekebu,* 1925.
b. May 28, 1883 in Sacco, Italy
d. Jun 5, 1944 in Pesaro, Italy
Source: *Baker 78, 84, 92; BioIn 13, 14; CmOp; CurBio 44; IntDcOp; ItaFilm; MetOEnc; NewAmDM; NewEOp 71; NewGrDM 80; NewGrDO; NewOxM; OxCMus; OxDcOp; WebBD 83*

Zane, Ebenezer
American. Pioneer
Established first permanent site on Ohio river, 1770, known as Wheeling, VA.
b. Oct 7, 1747 in Berkeley County, Virginia
d. 1811 in Wheeling, Virginia
Source: *AmBi; ApCAB; DcAmB; Drake; EncAAH; EncAR; EncSoH; HarEnUS; LinLib S; NatCAB 11; WhAm HS; WhAmRev*

Zanelli, Renato
[Renato Morales]
Chilean. Opera Singer
Tenor, originally baritone; noted for Othello role; NY Met., 1919-23.
b. Apr 1, 1892 in Valparaiso, Chile
d. Mar 25, 1935 in Santiago, Chile
Source: *Baker 84; BioIn 10, 12, 14; CmOp; MetOEnc; NewEOp 71; NewGrDM 80; OxDcOp; PenDiMP*

Zangara, Joseph
[Guiseppe Zangara]
American. Assassin
Shot mayor of Chicago, in attempt to kill FDR, Feb 15, 1933.
b. 1900, Italy
d. Mar 21, 1933
Source: *BioIn 9; EncACr*

Zangwill, Israel
English. Dramatist, Author
Popularized term "melting pot" in play of same name, 1908; wrote novels on Jewish themes.
b. Feb 14, 1864 in London, England
d. Aug 1, 1926 in London, England
Source: *BbD; BiD&SB; BiDBrF 2; BioIn 4, 5, 6, 7, 8, 9, 12, 13, 14, 16, 17, 20; CamGLE; Chambr 3; ChhPo S2; ConAu 109; CrtSuMy; CyWA 58; DcAmImH; DcAmSR; DcBiA; DcEnA A; DcEuL; DcLB 10, 135; DcLEL; DcNaB 1922; EncMys; EncWL; EvLB; GrWrEL N; LegTOT; LinLib L; LngCTC; McGEWB; ModWD; NewC; NewCBEL; NotNAT A; OxCEng 67, 85, 95; OxCThe 67, 83; PenC ENG; RfGEnL 91; ScFEYrs; StaCVF; TwCA; TwCCr&M 80, 85, 91A; TwCLC 16; TwCWr; VicBrit; WhLit; WhoStg 1906; WhThe*

Zanuck, Darryl Francis
American. Film Executive, Producer
Produced first sound film, 1927; co-founded 20th Century Pictures, 1933; won three special Oscars.
b. Sep 5, 1902 in Wahoo, Nebraska
d. Dec 22, 1979 in Palm Springs, California
Source: *BiDFilm; BioIn 2, 3, 6, 7, 8, 9, 10, 12, 13; BlueB 76; CmMov; ConAu 93; CurBio 80N; DcAmB S10; DcFM;*

FilmgC; IntMPA 77; IntWW 74, 75, 76, 77, 78, 79; OxCFilm; WebAB 74, 79; WhAm 7; Who 74; WhoAm 74, 76, 78; WhoWor 74, 78; WorAl; WorEFlm

Zanuck, Lili Fini
American. Director, Producer
Co-produced *Driving Miss Daisy,* 1989.
b. 1954 in Massachusetts
Source: *IntMPA 94, 96; News 94, 94-2; WhoAmW 97*

Zanuck, Richard Darryl
American. Film Executive, Producer
Produced two of the biggest box office draws in film history: *The Sting,* 1973, *Jaws,* 1975; won Oscar for *Driving Miss Daisy,* 1990; son of Darryl.
b. Dec 13, 1934 in Los Angeles, California
Source: *BioIn 8, 9; BkPepl; FilmEn; FilmgC; HalFC 80, 84; IntMPA 75, 76, 78, 79, 80, 81, 82, 84, 86, 88, 92, 94, 96; IntWW 89, 91, 93; OxCFilm; St&PR 84, 87; WhoAm 74, 76, 78, 80, 82, 84, 86, 88, 90, 92, 94, 95, 96, 97; WhoEnt 92*

Zao-Wou-Ki
French. Artist
Known for imaginative landscapes, animals; brushstrokes resemble a type of calligraphy.
b. Feb 13, 1921 in Beijing, China
Source: *BioIn 16; McGDA; WhoArt 84*

Zapata, Emiliano
Mexican. Revolutionary
Guerilla leader of Mexican Aqarian Movement; helped Madero overthrow Porfiro Diaz, 1911; assassinated.
b. Aug 8, 1879? in Anenecuilco, Mexico
d. Apr 10, 1919 in Chinameca, Mexico
Source: *BiDLAmC; BioIn 9, 10, 16, 17, 19, 20; DcHiB; DcTwHis; EncLatA; FacFETw; HarEnUS; HisWorL; LegTOT; McGEWB; RadHan; REn; WorAl*

Zapf, Hermann
German. Type Designer
Expert on printing, book design; designed numerous type faces.
b. Nov 8, 1918 in Nuremberg, Germany
Source: *BioIn 6, 7, 15; ConDes 84, 90, 97; CurBio 65; DcTwDes; WhoAm 78, 80, 82, 84, 86, 88, 90, 92, 94, 95, 96, 97; WhoGrA 62, 82; WhoWor 78, 80, 82, 87, 93, 95, 96, 97*

Zappa, Dweezil
American. Musician, Actor
Solo albums *Havin' a Bad Day,* 1987; film *Running Man,* 1987; son of Frank.
b. Sep 5, 1969 in Los Angeles, California
Source: *BioIn 15, 16; LegTOT; WhoHol 92*

Zappa, Frank
[The Mothers of Invention; Francis Vincent Zappa, Jr.]
American. Musician, Singer
Early leader of hard-rock style; founded Mothers of Invention, 1964.
b. Dec 21, 1940 in Baltimore, Maryland
d. Dec 4, 1993 in Los Angeles, California
Source: *AmCulL; AnObit 1993; ASCAP 80; Baker 78, 84, 92; BiDAmM; BiDJaz; BioIn 8, 9, 10, 11, 12, 13, 14, 15, 16; BioNews 74; CmCal; ConAu 108, 143; ConLC 17; ConMuA 80A; ConMus 1, 17; CurBio 90, 94N; DcArts; DcTwCCu 1; EncJzS; EncPR&S 89; EncRk 88; EncRkSt; FacFETw; HarEnR 86; IlEncRk; IntWW 89, 91, 93; LegTOT; MiSFD 9; NewAmDM; NewGrDA 86; NewGrDJ 88, 94; News 94, 94-2; NewYTBS 93; OnThGG; OxCPMus; PenEncP; RkOn 78; RolSEnR 83; WhAm 11; WhoAm 78, 80, 82, 84, 90, 92, 94; WhoEnt 92; WhoHol 92, A; WhoRocM 82; WorAl; WorAlBi*

Zappa, Moon Unit
American. Singer
Daughter of Frank Zappa; had hit song "Valley Girl," 1982.
b. Sep 28, 1968? in Hollywood, California
Source: *BioIn 16*

Zaslofsky, Max
American. Basketball Player
Guard, 1946-56, with five NBA teams; led league in scoring, 1948.
b. Dec 7, 1925 in New York, New York
d. Oct 15, 1985
Source: *AnObit 1985; BiDAmSp BK; BioIn 8, 14; OfNBA 87; WhoBbl 73*

Zaslow, Jeff
American. Journalist
Co-winner of nationwide search for Ann Landers' advice column replacement, 1986.
b. 1959?
Source: *BioIn 15, 16; NewYTBS 89; WhoAm 90*

Zatopek, Emil
Czech. Track Athlete
Long distance runner; won one gold medal, 1948 Olympics, three gold medals, 1952 Olympics.
b. Sep 19, 1922 in Koprivnice, Moravia
Source: *BioIn 2, 3, 5, 8, 9, 10, 12, 13; CurBio 53; IntWW 81, 82, 83, 89, 91, 93; LegTOT; WhoSoCE 89; WhoTr&F 73; WhoWor 91; WorAl*

Zaturenska, Marya
[Mrs. Horace Gregory]
American. Poet
Won Pulitzer, 1938, for *Cold Morning Sky.*
b. Sep 12, 1902 in Kiev, Russia
d. Jan 19, 1982 in Shelburne Falls, Massachusetts
Source: *AmWomWr; AnObit 1982; ArtclWW 2; BenetAL 91; BioIn 4, 11, 12, 17; CamGLE; CamHAL; ChhPo, S3; CnDAL; ConAu 13R, 22NR, 105; ConLC 6, 11; ConPo 70, 75, 80; DrAP 75; DrAPF 80; FemiCLE; ForWC 70; InWom SUP; OxCAmL 65, 83, 95; PenC AM; REn; REnAL; SixAP; TwCA, SUP; WhAm 8; WhoAm 74, 76, 78, 80; WhoAmW 68, 70, 72, 74, 75, 77; WhoPolA; WrDr 76, 80, 82*

Zayak, Elaine
American. Skater
World champion figure skater, 1982.
b. Apr 12, 1965 in Paramus, New Jersey
Source: *BiDAmSp Sup; BioIn 12, 13, 14; NewYTBS 83, 84; WhoSpor*

Zech, Lando William, Jr.
American. Government Official
Chairman of Nuclear Regulatory Commission, 1984-89.
b. Jun 29, 1923 in Astoria, Oregon
Source: *BioIn 16; ConNews 87-4; WhoAm 78, 80; WhoAmP 91*

Zedillo Ponce de Leon, Ernesto
Mexican. Political Leader
Pres., of Mexico, 1994—.
b. Dec 27, 1951 in Mexico City, Mexico
Source: *CurBio 96; WhoAm 96, 97; WhoWor 95, 96, 97*

Zeeman, Pieter
Dutch. Scientist
Shared Nobel Prize in physics, 1902; researched effect of magnetism on radiation.
b. May 25, 1865 in Zonnemaire, Netherlands
d. Oct 9, 1943 in Amsterdam, Netherlands
Source: *AsBiEn; BiESc; BioIn 3, 7, 14, 15, 20; CamDcSc; CurBio 43; DcInv; DcScB; InSci; LarDcSc; NobelP; NotTwCS; ObitOF 79; WhDW; WhoNob, 90, 95; WorAl; WorAlBi*

Zeffirelli, Franco
Italian. Director
Films include *Taming of the Shrew,* 1967; *Romeo and Juliet,* 1968; TV work includes mini-series *Jesus of Nazareth,* 1977.
b. Feb 12, 1923 in Florence, Italy
Source: *Baker 92; BiE&WWA; BioIn 6, 7, 8, 9, 12, 13, 15, 16; CamGWoT; CelR, 90; CmOp; ConDes 84, 90; ConTFT 4; CurBio 64; DcArts; EncWT; Ent; FacFETw; FilmEn; FilmgC; GayLesB; HalFC 84, 88; IntDcF 1-2, 2-2; IntDcOp; IntMPA 86, 88, 92, 94, 96; IntWW 74, 75, 76, 77, 78, 79, 80, 81, 82, 83, 91; IntWWM 90; ItaFilm; LegTOT; MetOEnc; MiSFD 9; MovMk; NewEOp 71; NewGrDA 86; NewGrDM 80; NewGrDO; News 91, 91-3; NewYTBE 72; OxCFilm; OxCThe 67, 83; OxDcOp; TheaDir; Who 92; WhoAm 80, 82, 84, 86, 88, 90, 92, 94, 95, 96, 97; WhoEnt 92; WhoHol 92, A; WhoWor 80, 82, 84, 87, 89, 91, 93, 95; WorAl; WorAlBi; WorEFlm*

Zeiss, Carl
German. Manufacturer
Founded optical instruments co., 1846.
b. Sep 11, 1816 in Weimar, Germany
d. Dec 3, 1888 in Jena, Germany
Source: *BioIn 2, 12; DcInv; DcTwDes; ICPEnP; InSci; LinLib S; MacBEP; OxCMed 86; WebBD 83*

Zeitlin, Zvi
American. Musician
Toured with major symphonies; known for furthering relations between Israel, US.
b. Feb 21, 1923 in Dubrowna, Union of Soviet Socialist Republics
Source: *Baker 84, 92; IntWWM 77, 80, 85, 90; NewAmDM; NewGrDA 86; NewGrDM 80; PenDiMP; WhoAm 76, 78, 80, 82, 84, 86, 88, 90; WhoAmJ 80; WhoAmM 83; WhoEnt 92; WhoMus 72; WhoWorJ 72, 78*

Zelazny, Roger
American. Author
Science fiction writer of the New Wave school.
d. Jun 14, 1995 in Santa Fe, New Mexico
Source: *BioIn 15, 16, 17, 21; ConSFF; DcLP 87A; DrAPF 83, 85, 87, 89, 91, 93, 97; IntvTCA 2; NewYTBS 95; WhoSciF*

Zellerbach, William Joseph
American. Manufacturer
Pres., Crown Zellerbach Corp., 1946-85.
b. Sep 15, 1920 in San Francisco, California
Source: *BioIn 11; Dun&B 90; IntMPA 82; IntWW 74, 75, 76, 77, 78, 79, 80, 81, 82, 83, 89, 91, 93; IntYB 78, 79, 80, 81, 82; St&PR 84; WhoAm 74, 76, 78, 80, 82, 84, 86, 88, 90, 92, 94, 95, 96, 97; WhoFI 74*

Zemeckis, Robert
American. Director
Films include *Back to the Future*, 1985, *Who Framed Roger Rabbit*, 1988.
b. May 14, 1951 in Chicago, Illinois
Source: *BioIn 14, 16; ConTFT 7; HalFC 88; IntDcF 2-2; IntMPA 92; WhoAm 90; WhoEnt 92*

Zemlinsky, Alexander von
Austrian. Composer, Conductor
Led Berlin State Opera, 1927-32; fled to US, 1938; taught Arthur Schoenberg.
b. Oct 4, 1872 in Vienna, Austria
d. Mar 16, 1942 in New York, New York
Source: *BioIn 2, 11, 18; CurBio 42; DcCM; WhAm 4A*

Zenatello, Giovanni
Italian. Opera Singer
Sang with Manhattan Opera Company, NYC, 1907-09; Boston Opera, 1909-14.
b. Feb 22, 1876 in Verona, Italy
d. Feb 11, 1949 in New York, New York
Source: *Baker 78, 84, 92; BiDAmM; BioIn 1, 14; CmOp; IntDcOp; MetOEnc; NewEOp 71; NewGrDM 80; NewGrDO; OxDcOp; PenDiMP*

Zenger, John Peter
German. Printer, Publisher, Journalist
His acquittal in famous libel trial, 1735, helped establish freedom of press in US.
b. 1697, Germany
d. Jul 28, 1746 in New York, New York
Source: *Alli; AmAu; AmAu&B; AmBi; AmRef; AmSocL; AmWrBE; Benet 87, 96; BiDAmJo; BioIn 2, 3, 4, 5, 6, 7, 8, 9, 10, 11, 14, 15, 16, 19, 20; DcAmB; DcAmSR; DcLB 24, 43; Drake; EncAJ; EncCRAm; JrnUS; LegTOT; McGEWB; NatCAB 23; OxCAmH; OxCAmL 65, 83, 95; REn; REnAL; TwCBDA; WebAB 74, 79; WhAm HS; WorAl; WorAlBi*

Zeno, Apostolo
Italian. Poet, Librettist
Wrote libretti for melodrama, with subjects taken from classical history, mythology, 1600s-1700s.
b. Dec 11, 1668 in Venice, Italy
d. Nov 11, 1750 in Venice, Italy
Source: *Baker 78, 84, 92; BiD&SB; BlkwCE; BriBkM 80; CasWL; DcBiPP; DcEuL; EvEuW; IntDcOp; MetOEnc; NewEOp 71; NewGrDM 80; NewGrDO; NotNAT B; OxCThe 67; OxDcOp*

Zeno of Citium
Greek. Philosopher
Founded Stoicism, which emphasized practical ethics.
b. 334BC, Cyprus
d. 262BC
Source: *BiD&SB; CasWL; DcScB; LuthC 75; McGEWB; OxCPhil; PenC CL; REn*

Zeno of Elea
Greek. Philosopher
Student of Parmenides, known as an inventor of paradoxes.
b. 490BC
d. 430BC
Source: *BiESc; DcScB; InSci; LarDcSc; McGEWB; NewCol 75; OxCClL 89; REn*

Zepeda, Ofelia
American. Linguist
Became co-director of the American Indian Language Development Institute, 1989.
b. Mar 24, 1954 in Stanfield, Arizona
Source: *ConAu 114; NotNaAm*

Zeppelin, Ferdinand Adolf August Heinrich von, Count
German. Soldier, Aircraft Designer
Built first rigid airship, 1900.
b. Jul 8, 1838 in Konstanz, Germany
d. Mar 8, 1917 in Charlottenburg, Germany
Source: *AsBiEn; InSci; LinLib S; NewCol 75; REn; WorAl*

Zerbe, Anthony
American. Actor
Won Emmy, 1976, for "Harry-O."
b. May 20, 1936 in Long Beach, California
Source: *ConTFT 6; FilmgC; HalFC 88; IntMPA 92, 94, 96; WhoAm 84, 86, 90; WhoEnt 92; WhoHol A*

Zernial, Gus Edward
"Ozark Ike"
American. Baseball Player
Outfielder, 1949-59; led AL in home runs, RBIs, 1951.
b. Jun 27, 1923 in Beaumont, Texas
Source: *Ballpl 90; BiDAmSp Sup; BioIn 3; WhoProB 73*

Zernike, Frits
Dutch. Physicist, Educator
Won Nobel Prize, 1953, for invention of phase-control microscope.
b. Jul 16, 1888 in Amsterdam, Netherlands
d. Mar 10, 1966 in Naarden, Netherlands
Source: *BiESc; BioIn 3, 4, 7, 8, 15, 20; DcScB; LarDcSc; McGMS 80; NobelP; NotTwCS; ObitT 1961; WhAm 4; WhoNob, 90, 95*

Zeroual, Liamine
Algerian. Political Leader
President of Algeria, 1994—.
b. 1951
Source: *News 96, 96-2*

Zetterling, Mai (Elisabeth)
Swedish. Actor, Director
Pursued successful careers on both stage, screen; directed several feature films in Sweden including *Night Games*, 1966.
b. May 24, 1925 in Vasteras, Sweden
d. Mar 15, 1994
Source: *Au&Wr 71; BiDFilm, 81, 94; BioIn 7, 10, 15, 16, 19; ConAu 111, 126, 144; ConLC 86; ContDcW 89; ConTFT 13; EncEurC; FilmEn; FilmgC; ForYSC; HalFC 80, 84, 88; IlWWBF; IntAu&W 91, 93; IntDcF 1-2, 2-2; IntDcWB; IntMPA 75, 76, 77, 78, 79, 80, 81, 82, 84, 86, 88, 92, 94; IntWW 74, 75, 76, 77, 78, 79, 80, 81, 82, 83, 89, 91, 93; InWom SUP; LegTOT; MiSFD 9; MotPP; MovMk; OxCFilm; ReelWom; WhAm 11; Who 83, 92; WhoHol 92, A; WhoWor 84, 87, 89, 91, 93; WhThe; WomWMM; WorAl; WorEFlm; WorFDir 2; WrDr 80, 82, 84, 86, 88, 90, 92, 94, 96*

Zevin, B(enjamin) D(avid)
American. Publisher
Pres., World Publishing Co., 1945-62; founded Tower Books, 1939.
b. May 16, 1901? in New York, New York
d. Dec 27, 1984 in Miami Beach, Florida
Source: *BioIn 3; CurBio 43, 85, 85N*

Zevon, Warren
American. Singer, Songwriter
Known for his hit song "Werewolves of London," 1978.
b. Jan 24, 1947 in Chicago, Illinois
Source: *BioIn 11, 12, 13, 16; ConMus 9; EncPR&S 89; LegTOT; NewGrDA 86; PenEncP; RkOn 85; RolSEnR 83; WhoAm 80, 82, 84, 86, 88, 90, 92, 95, 96, 97; WhoEnt 92; WhoRocM 82*

Zhang Yimou
Chinese. Filmmaker
Most celebrated filmmaker in China; films include *Red Sorghum,* 1987 and *Operation Cougar,* 1989.
b. 1951 in Xi'an, China
Source: *BioIn 16; CurBio 92; IntWW 89, 91, 93*

Zhao Ziyang
Chinese. Political Leader
Premier, 1980-87; replaced Deng Ziaoping as chief of Chinese Communist Party, 1987-89.
b. Oct 17, 1919 in Hunan, China
Source: *BioIn 13, 14, 15; ColdWar 2; CurBio 84; FarE&A 79, 80, 81; IntWW 80, 81, 82, 83, 89, 91, 93; LegTOT; News 89-1; NewYTBS 80, 84, 87; Who 88, 90, 92, 94; WhoAsAP 91; WhoPRCh 81, 87, 91; WhoWor 91, 93*

Zhdanov, Andrei Alexandrovich
Russian. Political Leader, Army Officer
Pres., foreign affairs com., 1943; received Order of Lenin, 1945; Order of Suvorov, 1944.
b. Feb 26, 1896 in Mariupol, Ukraine
d. Aug 31, 1948 in Moscow, Union of Soviet Socialist Republics
Source: *ColdWar 1; FacFETw; REn; WhAm 2; WorAl*

Zhirinovsky, Vladimir
Russian. Politician
Founded Liberal Democratic Party of Russia, 1990.
b. Apr 25, 1946 in Alma-Ata, Union of Soviet Socialist Republics
Source: *CurBio 95; News 94, 94-2*

Zhivkov, Todor Khristov
Bulgarian. Politician
Prime minister, 1962-71; pres., 1971-89.
b. Sep 7, 1911 in Pravets, Bulgaria
Source: *ColdWar 1; CurBio 76; EncRev; FacFETw; IntWW 83, 91; WhoWor 87, 89, 91*

Zhukov, Georgi Alexandrovich
Russian. Journalist, Politician
Pres., USSR-France Society who wrote *Three Months in Geneva,* 1954.
b. Apr 23, 1908 in Almazny, Russia
Source: *CurBio 60; IntWW 74, 75; Who 74, 82, 83, 85, 88, 90, 92, 94; WhoWor 74*

Zhukov, Georgi Konstantinovich
"The Eisenhower of Russia"
Russian. Military Leader
WW II hero; led defense of Moscow, Leningrad, capture of Berlin; minister of Defense, 1955-57.
b. Dec 2, 1896 in Stelkovka, Russia
d. Jun 18, 1974 in Moscow, Union of Soviet Socialist Republics
Source: *ColdWar 1; CurBio 42, 55, 74; DcTwHis; EncCW; EncTR 91; FacFETw; HarEnMi; HisEWW; LinLib S; McGEWB; NewYTBS 74; WhAm 6; Who 74; WhoWor 74; WorAl*

Zia-ul-Haq, Mohammad
[Mohammad Zia Al-Haq]
Pakistani. Political Leader
Overthrew Bhutto government, pres., 1978-88; died in plane crash.
b. Aug 12, 1924 in Jullunder, British India
d. Aug 17, 1988 in Bahawalpur, Pakistan
Source: *BioIn 11; ColdWar 1; CurBio 80, 88; FarE&A 78, 79; IntWW 83; IntYB 79; NewYTBS 77; WhoWor 87*

Zieff, Howard
American. Director
Films include *Private Benjamin,* 1980; *Unfaithfully Yours,* 1984.
b. 1943 in Los Angeles, California
Source: *ConTFT 10; HalFC 84, 88; IntMPA 84, 86, 88, 92, 94, 96; MiSFD 9; NewYTBE 73*

Ziegfeld, Flo(renz)
American. Producer
Produced lavish, musical revues, "Ziegfeld Follies," 1907-30.
b. Mar 21, 1867 in Chicago, Illinois
d. Jul 22, 1932 in Hollywood, California
Source: *AmBi; AmDec 1910; BiDD; DcAmB; EncAB-H 1974; EncMT; EncVaud; FilmgC; HalFC 80, 84, 88; NewAmDM; NewGrDA 86; NotNAT B; OxCAmL 65; OxCAmT 84; OxCPMus; OxCThe 67, 83; PlP&P; RComAH; REn; WebAB 74; WhAm 1; WhDW; WhThe*

Ziegler, Edward
American. Critic, Manager
Music, drama critic for *NY Herald,* 1908-16; GM, consultant for Met. Opera House, 1920-47.
b. Mar 25, 1870 in Baltimore, Maryland
d. Oct 25, 1947 in New York, New York
Source: *AmAu&B; BiDAmM; BioIn 1, 13; MetOEnc; NewEOp 71; NotNAT B; WhAm 2*

Ziegler, John Augustus, Jr.
American. Hockey Executive
Succeeded Clarence Campbell as president of NHL, 1977-92.
b. Feb 9, 1934 in Grosse Pointe, Michigan
Source: *St&PR 75, 84, 87; WhoAm 76, 78, 80, 82, 84, 86, 88, 90, 92, 94, 95, 96, 97; WhoE 81, 83, 85, 86, 89*

Ziegler, Karl
German. Scientist
Won 1963 Nobel Prize in chemistry with Giulio Natta; studied polymerization.
b. Nov 26, 1898 in Helsa, Germany
d. Aug 12, 1973 in Mulheim, Germany (West)
Source: *AsBiEn; BiESc; BioIn 4, 5, 6, 10, 14, 15, 19, 20; LarDcSc; McGMS 80; NobelP; NotTwCS; WhAm 6; WhoNob, 90, 95; WhoWor 74; WorInv*

Ziegler, Ron(ald Louis)
American. Government Official
Press secretary to Richard Nixon, 1969-74.
b. May 12, 1939 in Covington, Kentucky
Source: *BioIn 13, 16; BioNews 74; CurBio 71; Dun&B 90; IntWW 74, 75, 76; NewYTBE 71, 73; WhoAm 74, 76, 78, 80, 82, 84, 86, 88, 90, 92, 94, 95, 96, 97; WhoAmP 73, 75, 77, 79, 81, 83, 85, 87, 89, 91, 93, 95; WhoFI 85, 87; WhoGov 72; WhoSSW 73, 95, 97; WhoWor 91, 93, 95, 96, 97*

Ziff, William Bernard
American. Publisher
Publications include *Photography, Modern Bride* mags.
b. Aug 1, 1898 in Chicago, Illinois
d. Dec 20, 1953 in New York, New York
Source: *AmAu&B; BioIn 1, 3; CurBio 46, 54; DcAmB S5; WhAm 3*

Zigler, Edward
American. Psychologist
Co-founder of Project Head Start, 1965.
b. Mar 1, 1930 in Kansas City, Missouri
Source: *AmMWSc 92, 95; News 94, 94-1*

Zim, Herbert S(pencer)
American. Author
Science books include *Life and Death,* 1970; *The Universe,* 1973.
b. Jul 12, 1909 in New York, New York
d. Dec 5, 1994 in Plantation Key, Florida
Source: *AmAu&B; Au&Wr 71; AuBYP 2, 3; BioIn 2, 3, 4, 7, 9, 14, 15; BkP; ChhPo S3; ChlLR 2; ConAu 13R, 17NR, 147; CurBio 56, 95N; JBA 51; LinLib L; MajAI; SmATA 1, 2AS, 30, 85; WhAm 11; WhoAm 74, 76, 78, 80, 82, 84, 86, 88, 90, 92, 94, 95, 96; WrDr 86, 92, 94*

Zimbalist, Efrem
American. Violinist, Composer
Performances contained high technical polish, emotional understatement; composer of chamber music, opera *Landara.*
b. Apr 1890 in Rostov-on-Don, Russia
d. Feb 22, 1985 in Reno, Nevada
Source: *ASCAP 80; Baker 84; BiDAmM; BioIn 14; CurBio 85; FacFETw; IntWW 83; LegTOT; NewAmDM; NewGrDM 80; NewYTBS 85; Who 85*

Zimbalist, Efrem, Jr.
American. Actor, Composer
Played Lewis Erskine on TV series "The FBI," 1965-74.
b. Nov 30, 1923 in New York, New York
Source: *BiE&WWA; BioIn 5, 6, 14; ConTFT 3; CurBio 60; FilmEn; FilmgC; ForYSC; HalFC 84, 88; IntMPA 75, 76, 77, 78, 79, 80, 81, 82, 84, 86, 88, 92, 94, 96; MovMk; NotNAT; VarWW 85; WhoAm 74, 76, 78, 80, 82; WorAl; WorAlBi*

Zimbalist, Stephanie
American. Actor
Daughter of Efrem Zimbalist, Jr; starred in TV series "Remington Steele," 1982-87.
b. Oct 8, 1956 in Encino, California
Source: *BioIn 13, 14; CelR 90; ConTFT 6; IntMPA 92, 94, 96; InWom SUP; LegTOT; VarWW 85; WhoHol 92; WhoTelC*

Zimmer, Don(ald William)
American. Baseball Player, Baseball Manager
Infielder, 1954-65; manager of four different teams including Chicago Cubs, 1988 -1991.
b. Jan 17, 1931 in Cincinnati, Ohio
Source: *Ballpl 90; BioIn 5, 15, 16, 17, 19; LegTOT; WhoAm 78, 80, 82, 84, 86, 88, 90, 92, 94, 95; WhoE 79; WhoMW 90, 92, 93, 96; WhoSSW 82, 84, 95, 97; WhoWest 94, 96; WhoWor 80*

Zimmerman, Paul L
American. Author
Senior writer *Sports Illustrated,* 1979-83; wrote *The Last Season of Weeb Ewbank,* 1974.
b. Oct 23, 1932 in Philadelphia, Pennsylvania
Source: *ConAu 10NR, 25R*

Zimmerman, Udo
German. Composer
Composer of opera *Die Weisse Rose* which has enjoyed tremendous international acclaim since its premier in 1986.
b. Oct 6, 1943 in Dresden, Germany
Source: *ConMus 5*

Zindel, Paul
American. Author, Dramatist
Won 1971 Pulitzer for *The Effects of Gamma Rays on Man-in-the-Moon Marigolds.*
b. May 15, 1936 in New York, New York
Source: *Au&Arts 2; AuBYP 2, 3; BenetAL 91; BioIn 9, 10, 11, 12, 15; CamGWoT; CelR; ChlBkCr; ChlLR 3; CnThe; ConAmD; ConAu 31NR, 73; ConDr 73, 77, 82, 88, 93; ConLC 6, 26; ConTFT 3; CrtSuDr; CurBio 73; DcAmChF 1960; DcLB 7, 52; DcLEL 1940; DramC 5; FifBJA; IntAu&W 91, 93; LegTOT; MagSAmL; MajAI; MajTwCW; McGEWD 72, 84; NatPD 77, 81; NotNAT; OnHuMoP; OxCAmL 83, 95; OxCAmT 84; OxCChiL; RAdv 14; SmATA 16, 58; TwCChW 78, 83, 89; TwCYAW; WhoAm 74, 76, 78, 80, 82, 84, 86, 88, 90, 92, 94, 95, 96; WhoThe 72, 77, 81; WhoUSWr 88; WhoWrEP 89, 92, 95; WorAl; WorAlBi; WorAu 1970; WrDr 76, 80, 82, 84, 86, 88, 90, 92, 94, 96*

Zingarelli, Nicola Antonio
Italian. Composer, Musician
Wrote 34 operas including comic opera, *Berenice,* 1811.
b. Apr 4, 1752 in Naples, Italy
d. May 5, 1837 in Torre del Greco, Italy
Source: *Baker 78, 84, 92; NewAmDM; OxCMus*

Zinn, Howard
American. Historian
Historical, political writings include *A People's History of the United States,* 1980.
b. Aug 24, 1922 in New York, New York
Source: *AmAu&B; AmMWSc 73S, 78S; BioIn 10, 11, 20; ConAu 1R, 2NR, 33NR; DrAS 74H, 78H, 82H; EncWB; MugS; PolProf J; WhoAm 74, 76, 78, 80, 82, 84, 86, 88, 90; WhoWor 74; WrDr 76, 80, 82, 84, 86, 88, 90, 92, 94, 96*

Zinn, Walter Henry
American. Physicist
Member of the Manhattan Project; built first breeder reactor, 1951.
b. Dec 10, 1906 in Kitchener, Ontario, Canada
Source: *AmMWSc 76P, 79, 82, 86, 89, 92, 95; BiESc; BioIn 4, 5; BlueB 76; CanWW 70, 79, 80; FacFETw; IntWW 74; WorAlBi*

Zinnemann, Fred
American. Director
Won Oscars for *From Here to Eternity,* 1953; *A Man for All Seasons,* 1966.
b. Apr 25, 1907 in Vienna, Austria
d. Mar 14, 1997 in London, England
Source: *AmFD; BiDFilm, 81, 94; BioIn 2, 3, 4, 5, 7, 8, 11, 12, 13, 14, 15, 17, 21; BlueB 76; CmMov; ConTFT 1, 7; CurBio 53; DcFM; FilmEn; FilmgC; HalFC 80, 84, 88; IlWWHD 1; IntDcF 1-2, 2-2; IntMPA 75, 76, 77, 78, 79, 84, 86, 88, 92, 94, 96; IntWW 74, 75, 76, 77, 78, 79, 80, 81, 82, 83, 89, 91, 93; LegTOT; MiSFD 9; MovMk; OxCFilm; Who 74, 82, 83, 85, 88, 90, 92, 94; WhoAm 74, 76, 78, 80, 82, 84, 86, 88, 90, 92, 94, 95, 96, 97; WhoEnt 92; WhoWest 74, 76; WhoWor 74, 82, 84, 96; WorAl; WorAlBi; WorEFlm; WorFDir 1*

Zinoviev, Grigori Evseevich
[Hirsch Apfelbaum]
Russian. Political Leader
Associate of Lenin accused of conspiring with Trotsky, 1927; expelled from party.
b. Sep 1883 in Elisavetgrad, Russia
d. Aug 25, 1936 in Moscow, Union of Soviet Socialist Republics
Source: *BlkwERR; DcPol; McGEWB; NewCol 75; REn; WhDW; WorAl*

Ziolkowski, Korczak
American. Sculptor
Spent 35 years blasting Thunderhead Mt. creating monument to Crazy Horse.
b. Sep 6, 1908 in Boston, Massachusetts
d. Oct 20, 1982 in Sturgis, South Dakota
Source: *AnObit 1982; BioIn 1, 2, 4, 7, 8, 9, 11, 12, 13, 14, 16; CelR; NewYTBS 82; WhAm 8; WhAmArt 85; WhoAm 76, 78, 80, 82; WhoAmA 73, 76, 78, 80, 82, 84N, 86N, 89N, 91N, 93N; WhoPolA*

Zipprodt, Patricia
American. Designer
Won Tony for costume designs in *Fiddler on the Roof,* 1965; films include *The Graduate,* 1967.
b. Feb 25, 1925 in Evanston, Illinois
Source: *BioIn 16; CamGWoT; ConDes 84, 90, 97; ConTFT 2, 7; MetOEnc; NotNAT; NotWoAT; VarWW 85; WhoAm 74, 76, 86, 88; WhoAmW 72, 74, 91; WhoEnt 92; WhoThe 77, 81*

Zirato, Bruno
American. Secretary, Manager
Private secretary to Enrico Caruso, 1915-21; director, NY Philharmonic, 1956-59.
b. Sep 27, 1884 in Calabria, Italy
d. Nov 28, 1972 in New York, New York
Source: *BioIn 4, 5, 8, 9, 10; CurBio 73, 73N; NewYTBE 72; WhAm 5; WhoMus 72*

Zita of Bourbon-Parma
Italian. Consort
Wife of Karl I; last empress of Austria and queen of Hungary; crowned on death of Franz Josef, 1916, reigned two years.
b. Mar 9, 1892 in Viareggio, Italy
d. Mar 14, 1989 in Zizers, Switzerland
Source: *NewCol 75*

Zmed, Adrian
American. Actor
Made Broadway debut as Danny Zuko in *Grease,* 1977; played Johnny Nogerilli in film *Grease 2,* 1982, Vince Romano on TV series "T J Hooker," 1982-85.
b. Mar 14, 1954 in Chicago, Illinois
Source: *BioIn 13, 14; ConTFT 8; LegTOT; VarWW 85; WhoHol 92*

Zodiac Killer
American. Murderer
Killed at least six in CA beginning 1966; letters, cryptograms sent to papers; nothing heard since mid-1970s; never caught.
Source: *EncACr*

Zoeller, Fuzzy
[Frank Urban Zoeller]
American. Golfer
Touring pro, beginning 1970s; won Masters, 1979, US Open, 1984.
b. Nov 11, 1951 in New Albany, Indiana
Source: *BiDAmSp Sup; BioIn 11, 12; LegTOT; NewYTBS 79, 85*

Zog I
[Ahmed Bey Zogu]
Albanian. Ruler
King of Albania, 1928-39; formally deposed, 1946.
b. Oct 8, 1895 in Burgayeti, Albania
d. Apr 9, 1961 in Suresnes, France
Source: *CurBio 44, 61; WebBD 83*

Zola, Emile (Edouard Charles)
French. Author, Journalist
Leader of French naturalism; defended Dreyfus, 1898; wrote novel, *Nana,* 1880.
b. Apr 2, 1840 in Paris, France
d. Sep 29, 1902 in Paris, France
Source: *AtlBL; BbD; Benet 87, 96; BiD&SB; BiDFrPL; BioIn 1, 2, 3, 4, 5, 6, 7, 8, 9, 10, 11, 12, 13, 14, 15, 16, 17, 18, 19, 20, 21; CamGWoT; CasWL; CelCen; ClDMEL 47, 80; CnThe; ConAu 104; CyWA 58; DcAmSR; DcBiA; DcEuL; DcLB 123; Dis&D; EncWL; EncWT; EuAu; EuWr 7; EvEuW; FilmgC; GrFLW; GuFrLit 1; HalFC 80, 84, 88; IntDcT 2; LegTOT; LinLib L, S; MagSWL; McGEWB; McGEWD 72, 84; ModWD; NewC; NewCBEL; NewEOp 71; NewGrDO; NotNAT A, B; Novels; OxCEng 67, 85, 95; OxCFr; OxCThe 67; OxDcOp; PenC EUR; RAdv 14, 13-2; RComWL; REn; REnWD; RfGWoL 95; ScF&FL 92; ThHEIm; TwCLC 1, 6, 21, 41; WhDW; WhoTwCL; WorAl; WorAlBi; WorLitC*

Zolotow, Charlotte Shapiro
American. Children's Author
Writings include *Big Brother,* 1960; *Say It!* 1980.
b. Jun 26, 1915 in Norfolk, Virginia
Source: *AmWomWr; ArtclWW 2; AuBYP 2, 3; BioIn 13, 14, 15; BkP; ChlLR 2; ConAu 3NR, 5R, 18NR; DcLB 52; ForWC 70; IntAu&W 91; MorJA; OxCChiL; PenNWW A; PiP; SmATA 1, 35; St&PR 91; TwCChW 83, 89; WhoAm 76, 78, 80, 82, 84, 86, 88, 90, 92, 94, 95, 96, 97; WhoAmW 66, 68, 70, 72, 74, 75, 77, 79, 81, 83, 85, 87, 89, 91, 93, 95, 97; WhoUSWr 88; WhoWrEP 89, 92, 95; WrDr 76, 86, 88, 92*

Zolotow, Maurice
"The Boswell of Broadway"
American. Author
Writings include *Never Whistle in a Dressing Room,* 1944; *A Gift of Laughter,* 1965.
b. Nov 23, 1913 in New York, New York
d. Mar 14, 1991 in Los Angeles, California
Source: *AmAu&B; Au&Wr 71; BenetAL 91; BioIn 2, 4, 15, 17; ConAu 1NR, 1R, 133; CurBio 57, 91N; NewYTBS 91; REnAL; WhAm 10; WhoAm 74, 76, 78, 80, 82, 84, 86, 88, 90, 92; WhoWorJ 72, 78; WrDr 76, 80, 82, 84, 86, 88, 90, 92, 94, 96*

Zombies, The
[Rod Argent; Paul Atkinson; Colin Blunstone; Hugh Grundy; Chris Taylor White]
English. Music Group
Formed, 1963; hits include "Tell Her No," 1964; "Time of the Season," 1968.
Source: *BioIn 9, 15; ConMuA 80A; EncPR&S 74, 89; EncRk 88; EncRkSt; HarEnR 86; IlEncRk; PenEncP; RkOn 78; RolSEnR 83; WhoRock 81; WhoRocM 82*

Zondervan, Peter
American. Publishing Executive
Founder of Zondervan Publishing, 1931, one of the world's largest publishers of religious material.
b. Apr 2, 1909 in Paterson, New Jersey
d. May 10, 1993 in Boca Raton, Florida
Source: *Dun&B 86; St&PR 91; WhoAm 90; WhoFI 92; WhoMW 92; WhoWor 89*

Zorach, William
American. Artist, Sculptor
Sculptures include post office in Washington, DC; facade for Mayo Clinic Building.
b. Feb 28, 1887 in Eurburg, Lithuania
d. Nov 15, 1967 in Bath, Maine
Source: *ArtsAmW 3; CurBio 43, 63, 67; DcAmArt; DcCAA 71, 77, 88, 94; FacFETw; IlBEAAW; McGDA; McGEWB; OxCAmH; OxCTwCA; OxDcArt; PhDcTCA 77; WebAB 74, 79; WhAm 4; WhAmArt 85; WhoAmA 78N, 80N, 82N, 84N, 86N, 89N, 91N, 93N; WorArt 1950*

Zorbaugh, Geraldine B(one)
American. Broadcasting Executive, Lawyer
Attorney, ABC, 1943-57; CBS, 1957-68.
b. May 1, 1905
d. Jun 29, 1996 in Pinehurst, North Carolina
Source: *CurBio 96N; InWom; WhoAmW 58, 64, 66*

Zorina, Vera
[Eva Brigitta Hartwig]
German. Dancer, Actor
Appeared on Broadway in *On Your Toes,* 1954; films include *The Goldwyn Follies,* 1938.
b. Jan 2, 1917 in Berlin, Germany
Source: *BiDD; BiE&WWA; BioIn 6, 8, 9, 11, 12, 15, 21; CnOxB; CurBio 41; DancEn 78; EncAFC; EncMT; FilmEn; FilmgC; ForYSC; HalFC 80, 84, 88; IntDcB; InWom, SUP; LegTOT; MotPP; MovMk; NotNAT; ThFT; What 3; WhoAm 74, 76, 78; WhoAmW 58, 70, 72, 74; WhoHol 92, A; WhoThe 72, 77, 81*

Zorinsky, Edward
American. Politician
Dem. senator from NE, 1977-87.
b. Nov 11, 1928 in Omaha, Nebraska
d. Mar 6, 1987 in Omaha, Nebraska
Source: *AlmAP 78, 80, 82, 84; BiDrUSC 89; BioIn 11; CngDr 77, 79, 81, 83, 85; PolsAm 84; WhAm 9; WhoAm 78, 80, 82, 84, 86; WhoAmJ 80; WhoAmP 77, 79, 81, 83, 85; WhoGov 77; WhoMW 80, 82, 84, 86; WhoWor 80, 82, 87*

Zorn, Anders Leonard
Swedish. Artist
Paintings are usually Swedish subjects, nudes, portraits including *Portrait of the Artist and His Wife.*
b. Feb 18, 1860 in Mora, Sweden
d. Aug 22, 1920 in Mora, Sweden
Source: *BioIn 1, 2, 5, 6; ClaDrA; McGDA; NewCol 75; OxCArt*

Zoroaster
Persian. Religious Leader, Prophet
Founded Zoroastrianism, circa 575 BC, which replaced Persian polytheism.
b. 628BC, Persia
d. 551BC
Source: *BbD; CasWL; DcOrL 3; LegTOT; NewC; PenC CL; RComWL; REn; WhDW; WorAl*

Zsigmond, Vilmos
Hungarian. Filmmaker
Won Oscar for cinematography for *Close Encounters of the Third Kind,* 1977.
b. Jun 16, 1930 in Czeged, Hungary
Source: *BioIn 12, 13, 14, 15, 17; ConTFT 2, 8; FilmEn; HalFC 80, 84, 88; IntDcF 1-4, 2-4; IntMPA 80, 86, 92, 94, 96; MiSFD 9; VarWW 85; WhoAm 80, 82, 84, 86, 88, 90, 92, 94, 95, 96, 97; WhoEnt 92*

Zsigmondy, Richard Adolf
Austrian. Chemist
Co-invented ultramicroscope; studied colloidal soultions; won Nobel Prize, 1925.
b. Apr 1, 1865 in Vienna, Austria
d. Sep 24, 1929 in Gottingen, Germany
Source: *AsBiEn; BiESc; BioIn 3, 6, 14, 15, 19, 20; CamDcSc; DcInv; DcScB; Dis&D; InSci; LarDcSc; WhDW; WhoNob, 90, 95; WorAl*

Zucco, George
English. Actor
Had villainous supporting roles in over 100 films, 1931-51.
b. Jan 11, 1886 in Manchester, England
d. May 28, 1960 in Hollywood, California
Source: *BioIn 17, 21; FilmEn; FilmgC; ForYSC; HalFC 80, 84, 88; HolCA; MovMk; NotNAT B; ObitOF 79; ObitT 1951; OlFamFa; Vers A; WhoHol B; WhoHrs 80; WhScrn 74, 77, 83; WhThe*

Zuckerman, Ben
American. Fashion Designer, Manufacturer
Zuckerman suit was considered status symbol, 1950s-60s; won three Cotys; Hall of Fame, 1961.
b. Jul 29, 1890, Romania
d. Aug 9, 1979 in New York, New York
Source: *BioIn 12; NewYTBS 79; WhAm 7; WorFshn*

Zuckerman, Mortimer Benjamin
American. Publisher
Owner, editor-in-chief, *US News & World Report,* 1984—.
b. Jun 4, 1937 in Montreal, Quebec, Canada
Source: *BioIn 14, 15, 16; ConNews 86-3; CurBio 90; EncTwCJ; NewYTBS 85; WhoAm 82, 84, 86, 88, 90, 92, 94, 95, 96, 97; WhoE 95; WhoWor 96*

Zuckerman, Solly, Lord
English. Scientist, Author
Chief scientific adviser to British Govt., 1964-71; wrote *The Social Life of Monkeys and Apes,* 1931.
b. May 30, 1904 in Cape Town, South Africa
d. Apr 1, 1993 in London, England
Source: *AnObit 1993; Au&Wr 71; BioIn 14, 15, 16, 18, 19; ConAu 28NR, 65; IntAu&W 82, 89; LarDcSc; WhE&EA; WhoWor 74, 78, 80, 82, 84, 87; WrDr 76, 80, 82, 84, 86, 88, 90, 92, 94N*

Zuckmayer, Carl
German. Dramatist
Best known for satire *The Captain of Kopenick;* wrote film *The Blue Angel,* 1930.
b. Dec 27, 1896 in Nackenheim, Germany
d. Jan 18, 1977 in Visp, Switzerland
Source: *Au&Wr 71; Benet 87, 96; BiGAW; BioIn 9, 10, 11, 13, 16, 17, 19; CamGWoT; CasWL; ClDMEL 47, 80; CnMD; ConAu 69; ConLC 18; CroCD; DcLB 56, 124; EncGRNM; EncTR, 91; EncWL, 2, 3; EncWT; Ent; EvEuW; FilmEn; HalFC 84, 88; IntAu&W 76; IntDcT 2; IntWW 74, 75, 76; LegTOT; LiExTwC; MajMD 1; McGEWD 72, 84; ModGL; ModWD; OxCGer 76, 86; OxCThe 67, 83; PenC EUR; REn; REnWD; RfGWoL 95; TwCWr; WhAm 7; WhDW; WhoThe 72, 77; WhoTwCL; WhoWor 74; WorEFlm*

Zukerman, Pinchas
Israeli. Violinist
International concertist, 1968—; known for playing late-German romantics.
b. Jul 16, 1948 in Tel Aviv, Israel
Source: *Baker 78, 84, 92; BioIn 12, 14, 21; BriBkM 80; CelR 90; ConMus 4; CurBio 78; IntWW 74, 75, 76, 77, 78, 79, 80, 81, 82, 83, 89, 91, 93; IntWWM 90; MidE 78, 79, 80, 81, 82; MusSN; NewAmDM; NewGrDA 86; NewGrDM 80; NewYTBE 72; NewYTBS 79, 81; PenDiMP; Who 82, 83, 88, 90, 92, 94; WhoAm 78, 80, 82, 84, 86, 88, 90, 92, 94, 95, 96, 97; WhoAmM 83; WhoEnt 92; WhoMW 86, 88; WhoWor 74, 82, 87, 89, 91, 93, 95*

Zukofsky, Louis
American. Author
Translated works of poet Catullus, 1971; wrote ''A-24.''
b. Jan 23, 1904 in New York, New York
d. May 12, 1978 in Port Jefferson, New York
Source: *AmAu&B; AmWr S3; Benet 87, 96; BenetAL 91; BioIn 8, 10, 11, 12, 16, 17; CamGLE; CamHAL; ConAu 9R, 39NR, 77; ConLC 1, 2, 4, 7, 11, 18; ConPo 70, 75, 80A, 85A; DcAmB S10; DcArts; DcLB 5, 165; DcLEL 1940; DrAF 76; DrAP 75; EncWL 2, 3; GrWrEL P; IntWWP 77; MajTwCW; ModAL S1, S2; OxCAmL 83, 95; OxCTwCP; PenC AM; PoeCrit 11; RAdv 1, 14, 13-1; RfGAmL 87, 94; RGFAP; RGTwCWr; WebE&AL; WhAm 7; WhLit; WhoAm 76, 78; WhoTwCL; WorAu 1950; WrDr 76*

Zukor, Adolph
American. Film Executive, Producer
Founded Famous Players Lasky Corp., 1916; Paramount Pictures, 1927.
b. Jan 7, 1873 in Riese, Austria-Hungary
d. Jun 10, 1976 in Los Angeles, California
Source: *AmCulL; ApCAB X; BiDAmBL 83; BiDFilm 81, 94; BioIn 2, 3, 4, 5, 9, 10, 11, 15, 19; BlueB 76; BusPN; CelR; CmCal; CurBio 50, 76N; DcAmB S10; DcFM; FacFETw; FilmEn; FilmgC; HalFC 80, 84, 88; IntDcF 2-4; IntMPA 75, 76; IntWW 74, 75, 76; LegTOT; NatCAB 15; NewYTBE 73; NewYTBS 76; OxCFilm; WhAm 6, 7; Who 74; WhoAm 74; WorAl; WorAlBi; WorEFlm*

Zumwalt, Elmo Russell, Jr.
American. Naval Officer
Youngest four-star admiral in US naval history; commanded US forces in Vietnam, 1968-70; ordered use of Agent Orange, now believed to cause cancer; wrote of son's illness in *My Father, My Son,* 1986.
b. Nov 24, 1920 in San Francisco, California
Source: *BioIn 8, 9, 10, 11, 12, 16; ColdWar 2; ConAu 85; DcAmMiB; EncWB; HarEnMi; IntWW 74, 75, 76, 77, 78, 79, 80, 81, 82, 83, 89, 91, 93; IntYB 78, 79, 80, 81, 82; LinLib S; NewYTBE 70; NewYTBS 86; St&PR 84, 87, 91, 93, 96, 97; WebAMB; WhoAm 74, 76, 78, 80, 82, 84, 86, 88, 90, 92, 94, 95, 96, 97; WhoFI 85; WhoGov 72; WhoSSW 73; WhoWor 78; WorAl; WorAlBi; WorDWW*

Zumwalt, Elmo Russell, III
American. Author, Soldier, Victim
Believed to have contracted cancer from exposure to chemical Agent Orange, ordered used in Vietnam by father; with father, wrote *My Father, My Son,* 1986.
b. Jul 30, 1946? in Tulare, California
d. Aug 13, 1988 in Fayetteville, North Carolina
Source: *ConAu 126*

Zuniga, Daphne
American. Actor
Appreared in *The Sure Thing,* 1985.
b. 1962 in Berkeley, California
Source: *IntMPA 94, 96; WhoHol 92*

Zuppke, Robert Carl
''Rembrandt of the Prairies''; ''Zupp''
American. Football Coach
Head coach, U of IL, 1913-41, compiling 131-81-12 record; introduced onside kick, screen pass, among others.
b. Jul 12, 1879 in Berlin, Germany
d. Dec 22, 1957 in Champaign, Illinois
Source: *BiDAmSp FB; BioIn 4, 5, 6, 10; DcAmB S6; WhAm 3; WhoFtbl 74*

Zurbaran, Francisco
Spanish. Artist
Baroque painter known for religious, monastic work: *Immaculate Conception,* 1616.
b. Nov 7, 1598 in Fuentes de Cantos, Spain
d. Aug 27, 1664 in Madrid, Spain
Source: *AtlBL; DcBiPP; DcCathB; LinLib S; McGEWB; OxCArt; OxDcArt; WhDW; WorAl*

Zurbriggen, Pirmin
Swiss. Skier
Won gold medal in downhill, 1988 Olympics.
b. 1964? in Saas-Almagell, Switzerland
Source: *BioIn 15, 16; NewYTBS 87*

Zweig, Arnold
German. Author, Dramatist
Best known for novel *Case of Sergeant Grischa,* 1927.
b. Nov 10, 1887, Prussia
d. Nov 26, 1968 in Berlin, German Democratic Republic
Source: *Benet 87, 96; BioIn 1, 4, 5, 7, 8, 9, 10, 11, 15, 16; CasWL; ClDMEL 47, 80; CnMD; ConAu 115; CyWA 58; DcArts; DcLB 66; EncGRNM; EncTR, 91; EncWL, 2, 3; EvEuW; LiExTwC; LinLib L, S; LngCTC; ModGL; ModWD; ObitT 1961; OxCEng 67; OxCGer 76, 86; PenC EUR; REn; TwCA, SUP; TwCWr*

Zweig, Stefan
Austrian. Author
Wrote psychological biographies of literary, historical figures: *Paul Verlaine,* 1913.
b. Nov 28, 1881 in Vienna, Austria
d. Feb 22, 1942 in Petropolis, Brazil
Source: *Benet 87, 96; BiDMoPL; BioIn 1, 2, 3, 6, 7, 9, 10, 11, 12, 13, 14, 17, 18, 21; CasWL; ClDMEL 47, 80; CnMD; CnMWL; ConAu 112; CurBio 42; DcArts; DcLB 81, 118; Dis&D; EncTR, 91; EncWL, 2, 3; Ent; EvEuW; FacFETw; LegTOT; LiExTwC; LinLib L,*

S; LngCTC; MakMC; McGEWD 72, 84; ModGL; ModWD; NewGrDM 80; NewGrDO; NotNAT A, B; Novels; OxCGer 76, 86; OxCThe 83; OxDcOp; PenC EUR; PlP&P; RAdv 14, 13-2; REn; REnWD; TwCA, SUP; TwCLC 17; TwCWr; WhAm 2; WhDW

Zwicky, Fritz
Swiss. Astronomer, Inventor
Expert on jet propulsion whose inventions included the aeropulse, hydroturbojet, monopropellants.
b. Feb 14, 1898 in Varna, Bulgaria
d. Feb 8, 1974 in Pasadena, California
Source: *AmMWSc 73P; AsBiEn; BiESc; BioIn 3, 4, 10, 14; BlueB 76; ConAu 49; CurBio 74, 74N; DcAmB S9; DcScB S2; InSci; LarDcSc; LinLib L, S; ObitOF 79; WhAm 6; WhoWor 74; WorAl; WorAlBi; WorScD*

Zwilich, Ellen Taaffe
American. Composer
First woman to win Pulitzer for music, 1983, for *Three Movements for Orchest ra.*
b. Apr 30, 1939 in Miami, Florida
Source: *Baker 78, 84, 92; BioIn 13, 14, 15, 16, 17, 18; ConAmC 76, 82; ConCom 92; CpmDNM 80, 81, 82; CurBio 86; DcTwCCu 1; EncWB; GrLiveH; IntWWM 85, 90; InWom SUP; NewAmDM; NewGrDA 86; News 90; NewYTBS 85; WhoAm 86, 88, 90, 92, 94, 95, 96, 97; WhoAmM 83; WhoAmW 85, 87, 89, 91, 93, 95, 97; WhoE 85, 86, 89; WhoEnt 92; WomFir*

Zwingli, Huldreich
Swiss. Social Reformer
Sermons criticizing the Mass started Reformation in Switzerland.
b. Jan 1, 1484 in Wildhause, Germany
d. Oct 10, 1531 in Kappel, Switzerland
Source: *CasWL; CyEd; DcBiPP; Dis&D; LuthC 75; McGEWB; NewGrDM 80; REn; WhDW*

Zworykin, Vladimir K(osma)
''Father of Television''
American. Engineer, Physicist
Invented the iconoscope, a television camera tube; later developed first all-electronic television system.
b. Jul 30, 1889 in Mourom, Russia
d. Jul 29, 1982 in Princeton, New Jersey
Source: *AmMWSc 76P, 79, 82; AsBiEn; BiESc; BioIn 2, 3, 4, 6, 8, 9, 10, 12, 13; ConAu 107; CurBio 82; FacFETw; ICPEnP; IntWW 74, 75, 76, 77, 78, 79, 80, 81, 82; LarDcSc; LElec; LesBEnT; McGEWB; McGMS 80; NewYTBS 82; OxCAmH; WebAB 74, 79; WhAm 8; WhoAm 74, 76, 78, 80; WhoEng 80, 88; WhoWor 74, 78; WorAl; WorInv*

Zylis-Gara, Teresa
Polish. Opera Singer
Soprano with NY Met. since 1969.
b. Jan 23, 1937 in Vilna, Poland
Source: *Baker 84; BioIn 13; IntWW 91; IntWWM 90; MetOEnc; MusSN; NewAmDM; NewEOp 71; NewGrDM 80; NewYTBS 74; PenDiMP; WhoAm 86, 90; WhoAmW 83; WhoSoCE 89*

Zyuganov, Gennadi A(ndreyevich)
Russian. Political Leader
Leader of the Russian Communist Party, 1991—.
b. 1944 in Mymrino, Union of Soviet Socialist Republics
Source: *CurBio 96; WhoRus*

ZZ Top
[Frank Beard; Billy Gibbons; Dusty Hill]
American. Music Group
Texan group, formed 1970; frequent tours have made all albums gold or platinum.
Source: *Alli SUP; ApCAB; BioIn 11; ChhPo; ConMuA 80A; ConMus 2; CurBio 70; DcNAA; EncPR&S 89; EncRk 88; HarEnR 86; IlEncRk; LinLib LP; OhA&B; PenEncP; RkOn 78; RolSEnR 83; WhoRock 81; WhoRocM 82*